D0787285

FACLAIR = = Gàidhlig

air son nan sgoiltean.

Le Dealbhan,

AGUS
A H-UILE FACAL ANNS NA FACLAIREAN GÀIDHLIG EILE,
LE IOMADH CEUD NACH FHAIGHEAR AN GIN DHIUBH,
ACH A CHAIDH A THIONAL BHO LUCHD-BRUIDHINN AGUS
SGOILEARAN NA GÀIDHLIG ANNS GACH CEARN.

Camus-a'-Chorra:
AIR A CHUR A MACH LE E. DOMHNULLACH 'S A CHD.,
AIG A' CHLÒDH-CHLÀR GHÀIDHLIG.

A

GAELIC DICTIONARY

SPECIALLY DESIGNED

FOR BEGINNERS AND FOR USE IN SCHOOLS.

Profusely illustrated,

and contains every Gaelic word in all the Dictionaries hitherto published, besides many hundreds collected from Gaelic-speakers and scholars all over the world.

This edition published in 2001 by
Birlinn Limited
8 Canongate Venture
5 New Street
Edinburgh
EH8 8BH

www.birlinn.co.uk

First published in parts between 1902 and 1912 by E. MacDonald & Co.
(The Gaelic Press), Herne Bay

ISBN 1 84158 109 7

British Library Cataloguing-in-Publication Data
A catalogue record for this book is available from the British Library

Facsimile origination by Brinnoven, Livingston
Printed and bound by MacKays of Chatham PLC, Kent

CONTENTS

THE WORDSMITH – EDWARD DWELLY

by
Peter Berresford Ellis

Edward Dwelly's dictionary, originally entitled simply *Faclair Gàidhlig le dealbhan*, is the most famous of the dictionaries of the Scottish Gaelic language. Dwelly was acclaimed by the scholar Girvan McKay as 'the man who has done most for Gaelic lexicography'.[1] McKay, who called the dictionary 'monumental', observed: 'Had he been the lexicographer of almost any other language, his name would have been familiar to every schoolchild in the country whose tongue it was, and statues would have been erected in his memory. But no such fame came to Edward Dwelly.'[2] In fact, while the *Faclair Gàidhlig* is now in its twelfth edition, and well-known among all students of the language, Dwelly, the man, has remained something of a mystery. The facts of his life have been obscured and legend has often been substituted in their place.

Just before his death, the Scottish journalist and author, Seumas Mac a' Ghobhainn (1930–1987), began to gather the fragmentary facts of biography in an attempt to make a study which would clear up the mystery of Dwelly once and for all. He had placed an advertisement in the January 1987 edition of the *Scots Magazine*, seeking information. Seumas was taken ill and died on 21 January 1987, at the age of fifty-seven. A few days later a letter arrived from Flora Dwelly, Edward Dwelly's daughter, with an offer of help with his project.

Realising that Flora must be about ninety years old and that it was imperative that her knowledge of her father should not be lost, I took over the project and found that one of Dwelly's sons, Ewen, was also still living. Thanks to the initial work of Seumas Mac a' Ghobhainn, the mysteries surrounding Edward Dwelly's life were to be resolved. Although this biographical essay was ready by October 1988, at that time I could find no Scottish editor interested in Dwelly's life. It was claimed there was little interest in the subject. Thankfully, there now seems new attitudes permeating Scotland and a new generation has become more interested in Dwelly's monument to Gaelic culture.

Edward Dwelly was, in fact, an Englishman. He was born in Twickenham, Middlesex, on 2 February 1864, and was the scion of an old English military family. The family, which had no Scottish connections whatsoever, was originally of Somerset extraction, and the name Dwelly is an old Anglo-Saxon one – *dweollic*, meaning 'foolish' or 'erring'. Dwelly wrote his own study of his family origins and says: 'The first undisputed use of Dwelly as a surname I have come across is John Duelye, mentioned in the Close Roll, 1229.'[3]

Dwelly's great-grandfather, Thomas (1775–1850), served as an officer in the Coldstream Guards under Wellington, then Sir Arthur Wellesley, at Copenhagen in 1807. He became Wellington's Quartermaster during the Peninsular Wars. Curiously enough, there is a tenuous connection with Thomas Dwelly and my own family for my 3 x great-grandfather served under Thomas Dwelly's command during the Peninsular Campaign between 1811 and 1814. Our family still retain the letters my ancestor wrote home to his wife during this period.

Thomas' son was named Thomas Edward (1808–1873). He was employed by the Army Agents, Cox & Company's Bank, London, where he worked until his death. He had two sons: Thomas Edward and Henry James. The elder, Thomas Edward Dwelly (1831–1893), was educated at Christ's Hospital and followed his father into Cox & Company's Bank. He had a passion for music, was an accomplished flautist and a fine watercolour artist to the extent that he exhibited at the Royal Academy. He was described as 'a man of refined tastes, a lover of nature and a perfect gentleman'.[4] His brother, Henry James Dwelly, became a Member of the Royal College of Surgeons and a Licentiate of the Royal College of Physicians, working at Guy's Hospital. The military tradition died hard, for Henry James also found time to serve in a reserve army unit, the 1st City of London Artillery Regiment, achieving the rank of major.

Thomas Edward Dwelly became engaged to Clara Isabella Hill, the daughter of a military family, who was born in London on 20 December 1828. They were married in the military chapel of St Mary-in-the-Castle, Hastings, Sussex, on 16 September 1862. Eighteen months later, their only son, Edward, was born.

Edward Dwelly was educated in schools at Twickenham between 1872 and 1876 before finishing his schooling in Wandsworth from 1876 to 1878. From 1879 to 1881 he was sent to King's College, in the Strand, London, and excelled in engineering. His father encouraged him in this speciality and they worked together on various joint engineering projects. They both obtained a prize for metal and machine work from King's College, awarded for producing a five-inch centre lathe and set of metal turning tools with a half-horsepower steam engine.[5] But young Edward soon abandoned engineering to join his father, working as a clerk in Cox & Company's Bank in Charing Cross, London. The position was apparently achieved through his father's influence. Edward was now the third generation to join the famous bank.

With his family's military background, and Cox & Company's role as army agents, it was inevitable that Edward should become interested in the army. The Territorial Army was not introduced in the United Kingdom until 1907, but there existed volunteer units which, like the later Territorials, comprised men willing to give up evenings, weekends and holidays to drill and train as an emergency army reserve. These were militia units which had come into being with the Army Reserve Act of 1867.

In July 1881, aged seventeen years and five months, Edward joined the Queen's Westminster Rifle Volunteers as a part-time soldier. But a few months later, significantly perhaps, on St Andrew's Day (30 November), he transferred to the London Scottish Rifle Volunteers and was posted to 'G' Company as a piper.

In this decision lays the biggest mystery of Dwelly's career. Why had he made the change to a Scottish unit when he had no Scottish connections? And why had he volunteered to become a piper? His two children, Flora and Ewen Dwelly, were unable to shed light upon the mystery. Whatever the reason, from this point onwards, young Edward threw himself wholeheartedly into a lifelong interest in Scottish culture. He was determined not only to master the pipes but the Scottish Gaelic language as well.

Piper Dwelly fulfilled his military duties by attending all the unit's camps between 1882 and 1886 and competing as a marksman with a Martini rifle at the Wimbledon Ranges in the days before the National Rifle Association Ranges were established at Bisley.[6] Flora recalled that her father recounted to his children how he used to rise early and go to Hyde Park in order to practise his pipes in the dawn light.[7] It was the only place where his playing did not arouse protest from his neighbours.

A young Scotsman who joined the London Scottish Rifle Volunteers in January 1883 was William Gillies, the grandfather of Anne Lorne Gillies. He became a lifelong friend of Dwelly. According to his son, Iain Gillies (Anne's father): 'they were both learners of Gaelic . . . members of the Gaelic Society of London intermittently with "fringe" groups started by my father because the venerable society did not concern itself with the needs of learners or of the *illiterati* among the "native speaking" members.'[8]

Comunn Gàidhealeach an Lunainn, the Gaelic Society of London, had been formed in 1777, mainly to secure the repeal of the Disarming Acts which, after the suppression of the 1745 uprising, forbade the wearing of the kilt, tartan and playing of bagpipes and the speaking of the Gaelic language. It secured some success in the repeal measures of 1782 and 1784 and thereafter provided a translation service for Government, putting into

Gaelic the text of proclamations, Acts of Parliament and other notices for distribution and display in Gaelic-speaking areas of Scotland. It could be argued that because of this, Gaelic enjoyed some measure of governmental recognition during that period.

Today, after over 200 years, the society continues to flourish, organising cultural and social events throughout the year and is represented in the London Association for Celtic Education.

Edward Dwelly apparently joined the Gaelic Society of London in 1882 and remained an active member until 1891, when he left London.

His friend William Gillies, who was to become a teacher of the language, was a radical in politics and committed to Scottish self-government. It was Gillies who suggested that Dwelly adopt the name of 'Ewen MacDonald', for Dwelly was conscious of his English background when among his Scottish comrades. Gillies dubbed Dwelly with the name in a mock christening ceremony in Epping Forest.[9]

Dwelly, being English, was not committed to Gillies' political nationalism, but he seemed sympathetic to the cultural plight of Scotland. In 1886 the passing of the Crofters' Act gave crofters in Scotland the right of perpetual tenancy, whereas before they were subjected to the whims of a feudal landlord system which had been responsible for the genocidal 'Clearances'. Scots could be evicted by landlords, turned out in the glen and mountains, without shelter, food, or any protection at all. The Act of 1886 also set up a Crofters' Commission with power to enlarge buildings and erect new ones. However, the Act also created several problems which subsequent Acts of 1897, 1911 and 1955 sought to remedy. It was the problems created by this Act which caused Dwelly's friend, William Gillies, to resign from the London Scottish Volunteer Rifles as a personal protest. Gillies now became an enthusiastic member of the Scottish Home Rule Association, which was formed in that year.[10]

The Scottish Home Rule Association's first chairman was Professor John Stuart Blackie (1809–1895), who had championed the rights of crofters and was equally devoted to the rights of the Gaelic language and culture. He had founded and endowed the chair of Celtic Studies at Edinburgh in 1882. Although there had been a national movement in Scotland seeking to re-establish Scottish self-government ever since the Union of 1707, this cause became particularly popular, coinciding with Gladstone's conversion to the 'Home Rule' cause. There is no evidence that such political events influenced or interested Dwelly.

Iain Gillies recalled: 'Dwelly was, and remained, non-political . . . Though sociable, he appears to have been somewhat of a private man – perhaps that is relatively in comparison with my father, a born extrovert! Certainly my father was already a nationalist.' The two men remained friends and active members of the Gaelic Society of London even after Gillies had left the London Scottish Volunteer Rifles for political reasons.

Dwelly was still only twenty-two years old in 1886. He now found himself unhappy at his progress in Gaelic due to the lack of regular conversations with native speakers. On 30 July 1887, he joined another militia unit, the Argyll Volunteer Rifles, and trained with them in Scotland during a month's extended leave from Cox Company's Bank. It was the first time he had ever been to Scotland.[11] He found his Gaelic was progressing well and he made such progress within the Argyll Volunteer Rifles that he was offered a commission. He turned it down, 'finding that he could learn more Gaelic from pipers than in the officer's mess'.[12]

By 1891 Dwelly was living at 43 Chandos Street, Charing Cross, in central London. He was not only a member of the Gaelic Society of London but the Gaelic Society of Islington. This was the year that he won a Gaelic Society of London prize for translation and the same year that his friend William Gillies won a prize for an original essay in Gaelic. Dwelly was now using the name 'Ewen MacDonald'.

It was in this same year that he told William Gillies that he was moving permanently to Scotland.[13] He found life as a clerk in a bank dull and unattractive. He also thought his health was being affected by the foggy atmosphere of London. He therefore relinquished his job at Cox & Company and resigned from the Argyll Volunteer Rifles.

Iain Gillies said that his father believed that Dwelly moved to Scotland and worked in forestry in the Gàedhealtachd, the Gaelic speaking area.[14] *The Celtic Review* believed that his early training in engineering and mechanics was put to good use in an engineering job in Scotland.[15] Flora Dwelly, however, flatly rejects that her father pursued any such occupations and says that he had enough money to buy some property in Scotland and devote himself to his language studies.[16] Certainly, it was about this time that Dwelly began a writing career and was contributing articles to various publications as Ewen MacDonald, together with a Gaelic form of the name 'Eoghan Domhnullach'. He also contributed pieces under the pen-names of 'Lamh-Dearg' ('Red Hand') and 'Creag-an-Fhithich' ('Raven's Rock'). These articles have never been entirely collected, but they appeared in a variety of newspapers and journals, particularly in the *Oban Times*.

One mystery is resolved by the fact that on 3 June 1891, 'Ewen MacDonald' joined the 1st Volunteer Battalion of the Seaforth Highlanders in Gairloch. But another mystery raises itself for, on a surviving manuscript, Dwelly observed that he had served in the 5th Volunteer Battalion of the Argyll and Sutherland Highlanders in Gairloch from 1891. There is no official record of his service in that unit and in 1891 he was actually serving in the 1st Volunteer Battalion of the Seaforths. Perhaps Dwelly had become confused with his service in the Argyll Volunteer Rifles.

'He was accepted by his comrades as one of themselves, able to speak their own Gaelic and play the pipes better than most.'[17] Dwelly, in fact, had become a virtuoso on the pipes and, as early as 1882, had started a collection of pipe music in manuscript. This manuscript collection is now believed to be in possession of the estate of M.R. MacCrimmon of Canada, having been presented to him by Edward Dwelly's widow, Mary, in September 1940. A recent attempt to find this estate has proved unproductive.

Living in the Gàedhealtachd, Dwelly was now able to reach a fluency in the language which had previously eluded him in London. He was, according to all reports, able to pass as a native speaker in spite of the barriers. 'It is well known how very difficult it is to get a native Gaelic speaker to engage in a Gaelic conversation in the presence of any one they suppose to know English better than Gaelic.'[18]

Dwelly wrote:

> No one who has always spoken a language like Gaelic from the cradle can ever realise the extraordinary difficulties presented to a stranger who wishes to acquire it. First, the majority of Gaelic speakers only a very few years ago could neither read nor write it, so when one heard an unfamiliar word or phrase and the first instinct was of course to write it down lest it should be forgotten, the question was how to spell it – of course, the speaker could not tell! I was balked in this way many times without number, and my progress with the language immensely retarded in consequence. Next, the great difficulty of inducing a Gael to engage in a Gaelic conversation if he thinks he can make himself understood at all by means of indifferent English, or even if there is anyone present who cannot understand Gaelic, makes the acquisition of knowledge of colloquial Gaelic much more difficult than is the case with other modern tongues, for it is only by posing as a Highlander and one who knows Gaelic that one can ever hope to hear it spoken habitually and without restraint.[19]

'Ewen MacDonald' passed as a native Gael for many years. He was also in demand as a piper at local weddings and *ceilidhs*.

It was at this time that he started serious work on compiling a reliable up-to-date dictionary of the language. The work arose out of his own frustrations in learning the language. He had found from the outset that the absence of a dictionary covering colloquialisms and provincial idioms was a great handicap. It is true that there were existing dictionaries, but these were hard to come by and were generally outdated. According to the *Oban Times* Dwelly started the work in 1891, the date of his removal from London to Scotland.

In the second edition of his dictionary, published in 1920, Dwelly appears to confirm this: 'The work was originally undertaken solely for my own private use, but after continued urging by other Gaelic students who had seen it, and proved its utility by experience, I at last consented to print it and so make the result of my labours accessible to all.'

Legends have sprung up about this period. Dwelly is said to have worked for the Ordnance Survey, and tales proliferate of him riding the Highlands on horseback with his dictionary manuscript in his saddlebag, descending on crofting and fishing communities and demanding to know the meanings of various words. Douglas Clyne, in an article 'You'll Find it in Dwelly', believed Dwelly had been 'posted to the Highlands with the Ordnance Survey'.[20] Both Flora and Ewen Dwelly strenuously denied that their father was ever connected with the Ordnance Survey and there is certainly no official records of any connection.

In 1894 Dwelly was promoted to Corporal Piper 'Ewen MacDonald' and transferred to the 4th Battalion of the Seaforth Highlanders. He remained in the regiment until 1896. The army career of Corporal Piper Ewen MacDonald closed with his resignation from the 4th Battalion, significantly, shortly before he married.

Edward Dwelly married on 30 November 1896 Mary MacDougall, a native Gaelic speaker who had been born on 19 May 1869 at Ardchatten, Argyll. The wedding ceremony took place in the Woodside Hotel, Doune, Perthshire. Dwelly described himself as a landowner on his marriage certificate.

He and his wife bought a house in Gartmore, Perthshire, which they called 'Criopach Ard'. Their close neighbour and friend was the famous traveller, writer and politician, Robert Bontine Cunninghame Graham (1852–1936), a radical Liberal Member of Parliament and friend of Keir Hardie. Cunninghame Graham was the leader of the Scottish Home Rule Association and was elected first President of the National Party of Scotland in 1928, and in 1934 became President of the new Scottish National Party. The writer Andrew Lang hailed him as 'the uncrowned king of the Scots'.

It was at Gartmore that Edward Dwelly's first child, Flora Isabella Mary, was born on 27 September 1897. The following year the family moved to Lentran, overlooking Beauly Firth, where they took a house named 'Blar nan Craobh'.

However, there were pressures pulling Dwelly back to London. His father had died on 13 May 1893, leaving his mother living alone at the family home in King's Road, Kingston-on-Thames. Towards the end of 1899 Clara Dwelly's health began to suffer. She was seventy-one years old. She was too frail and set in her ways to move to Scotland and so Dwelly decided to move his family back to England. He took a house in Stone

Street in Lyminge, Kent. Dwelly remained there until late in 1903. It was here that his two sons were born. Thomas William was born on 18 September 1901, and Ewen John George was born on 8 June 1903.

Dwelly now acquired some land on Margate Road, Herne Bay, on the north Kent coast, and began to build a house there which he was to call 'Ardmore'. While the house was being built he moved the family to 2 Kingsbury Villas, Herne Bay. The plan was for his mother to move into 'Ardmore' with them so that they could look after her. But Clara Dwelly died in 1906 just before 'Ardmore' was completed.

Dwelly moved the family into 'Ardmore' soon afterwards. He was now in his early forties. He had a small income from his savings and had a young family to support. His talent as a virtuoso on the pipes and fluency as a Gaelic speaker were hardly assets for one seeking to earn a living in south-east England.

However, Dwelly decided to turn his knowledge into something practical. He had bought a cheap, wooden block printing press and established his own publishing company, which he called E. MacDonald & Company – The Gaelic Press, before moving into 'Ardmore'. His first attempt at publishing was in the form of an almanac, *Am Feillire agus Leabhar Poca Gàidhealach* (*Almanac and Gaelic Pocket Book*). He was to print this almanac yearly from 1900 until 1908. In 1902 Dwelly had rejoined the Gaelic Society of London and renewed his friendship with William (now Dr) Gillies, now a teacher of Gaelic in London.

It was also in 1900 that Dwelly turned his thoughts to the idea of publishing the lexicographical Gaelic material which he had spent the previous ten years collecting. He decided to produce a dictionary. Dwelly threw himself into the project with an intense enthusiasm, sometimes working on it as much as ten hours a day and six days a week. He decided that it was to be an illustrated work with himself as the compiler, editor, compositor, proof-reader, as well as publisher. At that stage he did not see himself as its printer. He also decided that it should be published in parts, on subscription at 6½d per part. His project was to grow into a volume of over 1,000 pages with 675 illustrations.

In compiling his *Faclair Gàidhlig*, Dwelly had gathered copies of all the available dictionaries which had hitherto been published. He decided that he would use MacLeod and Dewar's *Dictionary of the Gaelic Language* (Norman MacLeod and Daniel Dewar, London, 1845, 2 volumes) as a basic text on which to expand. According to *The Celtic Review*:

> He then began to go through the Gaelic/English part of each of the other dictionaries, and afterwards the English/Gaelic part where one existed, because it was found the two parts did not correspond with one another in any of the

> dictionaries which had both. The plan followed was, when comparing another dictionary with that used as a basis, to write down on slips every Gaelic word or meaning of such met with and not to be found in the latter, with a reference mark showing where the addition had been followed. This plan was followed steadily on to the end of the last dictionary published. This part of the work, included searching of all modern Scottish Gaelic books for words not in any dictionary took about twelve years to accomplish, counting ten hours daily, and when all the slips, amounting to many thousand were finished, the next step was to sort them into alphabetical order – no mean job.[21]

Dwelly's difficulty was to get his manuscript efficiently revised because, although the contents of all the dictionaries were now arranged in one alphabetical vocabulary, there were many varieties of spelling certain words, of which the best had to be selected and used consistently throughout the work. It was also inevitable that many small errors in grammar, idiom and so forth would occur, owing to the work being done by someone who was not a native Gaelic-speaker and only, as Dwelly himself admitted, an indifferent linguistic scholar when he commenced the dictionary.[22] He obtained promises of help from several prominent Gaelic scholars, such as William J. Watson (1865–1948), who was Professor of Celtic at Edinburgh University from 1914 to 1938. Watson's seminal work remains *A History of the Celtic Place-Names of Scotland* (Blackwoods, Edinburgh, 1926). These contributing scholars agreed that they would revise the proofs and they all eagerly welcomed the idea of a new Gaelic dictionary. Dwelly decided to issue about ten sheets of proofs to each of these revisers at the same time and then combined all their notes on one final proof before altering the type.

Dwelly received invaluable aid from these scholars and made a full acknowledgment to them all by name in the preface to his work. His wife, Mary, being a native Gaelic speaker, was also of fundamental assistance in the work, proof-reading as well as even folding pages. He also paid tribute to her in his preface:

> I am also indebted to my wife for revising proofs, assisting in folding sheets, and preparing parts for post, as well as for advising many translations. The success of the work is in no small measure due to her assistance in household matters, and by keeping down domestic expenses making money available for its production that would otherwise have been spent in an unproductive way.

Having arrived at a system by which the proofs were satisfactorily revised, the next step was to find a general printer and distributor who would produce the work at a price which Dwelly was able to afford. Such a printer was not to be found because there was not a sufficient financial inducement. Dwelly's experience with printing and distributing *Am Feillire* was only limited. He produced this almanac on a rough, wooden printing press at a profit of only a few shillings. Now Dwelly began to look for a second-hand iron press. He found one, purchased it, and for some weeks studied a book entitled *Practical Printing*. He then set up a specimen page and an order form which he then sent off to hundreds of possible subscribers to the work. Incredibly, Dwelly learnt the art of printing entirely from the production of his dictionary with no assistance from any professional printer. By 1902 Dwelly was ready to issue the first of his partwork dictionary.

The first major drawback was that the response to his circular inviting subscriptions was bitterly disappointing. Only his friends and those Gaelic scholars helping him placed orders, while many others replied that the old dictionaries were good enough. Dwelly placed advertisements in *Am Bard*, an Aberdeenshire monthly; *Celtia*, published from Dublin, and *Guth na Bliadhna*. He persuaded newspapers such as the *Oban Times* and *Stornoway Gazette* to publish pieces about the projected work. They gave it unqualified praise and urged their readers to subscribe.

Curiously, some newspapers, picking up on the story, claimed that 'Ewen MacDonald', under which name Dwelly was still working, was the brother of Sir Hector MacDonald (1853–1903). Sir Hector was the son of a Dingwall crofter, who had risen to become a Major-General in the British Army. At this time, while commanding in Ceylon (Sri Lanka), 'an opprobrious accusation' was made against him. He was granted home leave but shot himself in a Paris hotel room, causing a great scandal of the day. Dwelly resented the sensationalism of the press and was forced to issue a denial of any such relationship.

The Celtic Review, in its retrospect, pointed out that when the dictionary was issued, no newspaper ever published an unfavourable review.

The work was hard. However, many of Dwelly's old friends came to visit him in Herne Bay to encourage him. One of these was Dr William Gillies, who brought his young son Iain along. They found that Dwelly, in spite of the poor subscription response, was pressing determinedly ahead. 'We are very glad he did so,' observed *The Celtic Review*, 'otherwise the work would no doubt be still packed away gathering dust in some forgotten corner.'[23]

Dwelly obtained the necessary type to keep ten or twelve pages standing at the same time. The next thing was to get the pages stereotyped – that is made into a solid metal plate cast from the mould of the movable type. There were no printers in the area who could do this job. A newspaper in Maidstone, halfway between his home and London, undertook to do this work. The problem was not only the cost of transportation but the physical handling of the metal from 'Ardmore' to the local railway station and then from Maidstone station to the printers and then back again. This involved a journey of over a mile-and-a-half with a wheelbarrow containing 150 lbs of metal type up and down some of the steepest hills in Kent. The expense of transportation also became a serious problem. After the sixth part of the dictionary was produced, Dwelly decided to scrape together enough money to buy his own foundry in order to caste the stereotype plates himself.

As the aim was to produce an illustrated dictionary, illustrators had to be found. Of course Dwelly, the polymath, produced many drawings himself, but the line drawings and sketches were mostly executed by Malcolm MacDonald of Stornoway. Born in 1880, MacDonald had been educated at the Nicolson Institute and went to study at the Glasgow School of Fine Arts. He continued his education at the Ecole des Beaux Arts in Paris. He was known as 'Mara' (sea/wave) to his friends on the Isle of Lewis and was responsible for designing and executing the Guild and Craft shields which are still on display on the walls of Stornoway Town Hall. He emigrated to Canada in 1928 and died in 1966.

MacDonald produced illustrations of tools and various implements used in the Highlands for which no models could be found in London. Many of these implements have now disappeared from use, and, were it not for the dictionary with its illustrations, we might never have known of their existence or what they looked like.

The project was drawing heavily on Dwelly's own income and savings. The work was becoming more arduous and, as time went on, the problems seemed almost insurmountable. The number of subscribers did not increase in proportion to the increase in expense and effort. According to *The Celtic Review*: 'This obliged him to realise part of his capital from time to time to keep the dictionary going. Over one-third of the whole (capital) had been invested in a house and land which was much larger than he now required or could afford. Expenses increased both in the family and in the business, as he now regarded the work of the *Faclair*.'[24]

Dwelly turned to other projects in an attempt to create additional capital. A friend suggested the idea of producing Christmas and New Year greetings cards in Gaelic. Dwelly did so and found a ready market for them. In addition, he went into the bookselling business. Additional labour was needed for his new business ventures for Dwelly and his wife, Mary, had been doing all the work between them. Sometimes the two of them would work until midnight, folding and packing. Even Flora remembered being enlisted to help pack greetings cards at the age of five. Eventually, as Dwelly's expertise in printing grew, he took on jobbing printing to help with the income.

Another mystery occurs in Dwelly's career and it is one that he himself contributed to. In the preface to the first bound volume of his dictionary, which has been maintained in all subsequent editions, Dwelly spoke of the financial problems involved in producing the work. He then stated:

> My thanks are chiefly due to His Most Gracious Majesty, the late King Edward, for graciously awarding me a Civil List Pension when only about one half of the Dictionary had been issued to the public, and His Majesty's lamentable death is one of the dark shadows that mars my pleasure at the completion of my life-work, by preventing the possibility of my offering a copy for his acceptance. The great expense entailed by the publication of a book of this magnitude single handed, is a constant and heavy drain on the income of anyone of small means, and were it not for the receipt of this pension when it was awarded, the continuation of the publication beyond page 600 would have been, at least for many years, an absolute impossibility. Before proceeding any further, I should have had to execute enough remunerative work to enable me to purchase the necessary materials to continue the Dictionary as well as to live upon, an exceedingly hard task after the struggles I had already gone though, and one which would have no doubt eventually ended in the abandonment of the publication in an unfinished state. Owing to unfortunate investments, I had already had to earn all the money to purchase the necessary materials to produce this book as well as much of my living for some years by doing any printing I could get; but the strain on brain and eyesight entailed by this always working at the highest pressure and for exceptionally long hours, so that the Dictionary might be completed as quickly as possible, could not have been continued much longer.[25]

The mystery that arises from this is that Dwelly was granted his Civil List Pension in 1912, and King Edward VII had died on 6 May 1910.[26] The sum granted in 1912 was £50 per annum. For a comparison, a Member of Parliament's salary was £400 per annum. The award was also made after the first three-volume edition of the Dictionary had been sent to King George V and Prime Minister Herbert Henry Asquith (later first Earl of Oxford and Asquith) in August 1911. Both official records and Flora Dwelly confirm this date.[27] Why, then, in his introduction does Dwelly claim that the Civil List Pension was awarded five or six years *before* official records show that it was? Halfway through the project would have placed the award in 1905/06. But there is no record of such an award at that time. Did an unrecorded royal patronage help produce the dictionary, as Dwelly maintained, or was the award made only after he had completed and published it in 1912, as records show? If the official record is correct, Flora Dwelly wondered why her father enthused so glowingly in public about the alleged patronage of King Edward VII? It has been suggested that the answer might be that while it was King Edward who approved the Civil List Pension, its payment was actually deferred. But if so, is it reasonable to suggest a delay of six years before paying the pension? Such a delay seems unreasonable. Perhaps we shall never know the truth.

One thing is certain: Dwelly had completed his monumental task in 1911. The partworks were issued between 1902 and 1911 and then, in 1911, the three-volume bound dictionary was issued as *Faclair Gàidhlig – The Illustrated Gaelic Dictionary.* A further three-volume edition was printed in 1918, not 1920 as the printing history on later editions claim. The first single volume issue came out in 1930. The dictionary was not reprinted again in Dwelly's lifetime. Sales were a very slow business. When, during the course of production, Dwelly complained to *The Celtic Review* that lack of financial return for his efforts 'is now compelling him to offer for sale his library of Gaelic books which he has been collecting for about thirty years',[28] the magazine chided its readers for the neglect of Dwelly and his work.

> This should not be necessary, and is not creditable to the many persons now professing an interest in Gaelic study nor to the many Highland societies among whose 'objectives' and 'promotion of the Gaelic language' occupies a foremost place. The 'Kent' Dictionary, as it is often called, deserves, and we trust will forthwith get, the hearty support of all such persons and societies. Six or seven pence a number is surely within the means of all such.[29]

It was not until after his death that the dictionary became eagerly sought after. A fourth edition was issued by the commercial publishers Maclaren of Glasgow in 1941; a fifth came out in 1949; a sixth in 1967; a seventh in 1971; an eighth in 1973 and a ninth in 1977. By 1989 Gairm Publications of Glasgow were publishing it and by 1999 Birlinn of Edinburgh had acquired rights to issue a new edition with enhanced and enlarged reproduction in 1034 pages. The *Faclair Gàidhlig* had secured a place in history as the most popular, as well as influential, of the Gaelic Dictionaries.

This is not to say that Dwelly received no recognition during his lifetime. He was made honorary life member of both the Gaelic Society of London and of An Comunn Gàidhealach. Dwelly had been one of the founder members of An Comunn in 1891. It was, in fact, a young Edward Dwelly who called for the foundation of an annual festival on the lines of the Welsh Eisteddfod to celebrate Gaelic music, poetry and literary endeavour.[30] An Comunn took up his suggestion to form the National Mòd, launched in Oban in 1892 with a subsequent network of local and provincial Mòds. His work was also recognised by academic circles and he was honoured by becoming a Fellow of the Society of Antiquaries of Scotland.

In its obituary of Dwelly, the *Oban Times* said:

To have compiled and printed, in Gaelic, a dictionary was a remarkable feat. And the more so, that it was undertaken while engaged in other pursuits. Perhaps the dictionary did not gain the acceptance it deserved for the reason that it was in parts, and was in rather small print. But there was a thoroughness about it which is exhibited in the illustrations and conjoined references.[31]

John Lorne Campbell, author of *Gaelic in Scottish Education and Life* (1945), wrote this tribute:

I would like to take this opportunity of paying tribute to the memory of Edward Dwelly, who compiled and printed with his own hands what is by far the most exhaustive Gaelic–English Dictionary that we possess, making this to a great extent his life work under conditions that were frequently both difficult and discouraging. It is much regretted that owing apparently to the low prestige of Gaelic studies in Scotland no academic recognition was ever paid to Mr Dwelly by any of our universities.[32]

For a work of such importance to the national culture of Scotland, one might have expected an honorary doctorate as acknowledgment to be bestowed by one of the Scottish universities. *An Gàidheal* felt that the Civil List Pension had gone some way to acknowledging the work as it 'gave much satisfaction to all who value Gaelic literature and esteem noble work well done'.[33] However, there seemed a poignant truth in Reverend McKay's remark that had Dwelly chosen some other language to spend his lifetime working on, he might have had statues raised in his honour.

After the dictionary was published, Dwelly continued to work on revisions and produced a lengthy supplement.

John Lorne Campbell announced:

It is much to be hoped that means will be found to publish the Supplement to the Dictionary which Mr Dwelly had prepared but which he was not able to publish. The publication of this Supplement would be the most practical way of honouring the memory of a man to whom all serious students of Scottish Gaelic must be greatly indebted.[34]

This supplement, however, went astray after Dwelly's death. Its 530 sides of closely written text was finally identified in the National Library of Scotland as MS 14957. It was eventually published in 1991 and is an essential part of his work.

During the long years of work on his dictionary, Dwelly was producing other publications. In 1905, for example, he published *Coinneamh Ghàidhlig* (*A Gaelic Meeting*) under the imprint of E. MacDonald & Co. of 2 Kingsbury Villas, Herne Bay.

From 1906 until 1912 the family lived at 'Ardmore' and then moved into a house called 'Holly Bush' nearby. Here the family remained until 1915, when German bombing of coastal towns caused Dwelly to decide to move his family inland to St Andrew's Fleet, in Hampshire. It was here in 1915, his lack of finances forced him to go back to work at Cox & Company's Bank in London. He remained there until 1919, working at his other interests in the evenings and at weekends. In 1918 another move was made to a house called 'The Oaks', Pinewood Hill, Fleet.

Throughout this period Dwelly continued to work on new projects. He was particularly interested in genealogy and amassed a card index of nearly one million names. His files became one of the largest genealogical collections in existence. He commenced with his own family, producing *Compendium of Notes on the Dwelly Family* (1912), *The Dwelly Pedigree* (1915) and, more ambitiously, *Dwelly's National Records* (1916–1932) and *Dwelly's Parish Records* (1913–1926).

In 1921 he moved his family yet again. This time to Topsham, Devon, where he became an active member of the Devon Archaeological Society. In Devon he took up fishing as a means of enforced relaxation and became a keen fisherman.

In 1924 he made another move. He took a house in Ewell, Surrey. Four years later he was back in Fleet once again. The publications continued. *A Muster Roll of the British Non-Commissioned Officers and Men Present at the Battle of Waterloo* (1934) received some acclaim from historians. Other works such as *Hearth Tax for Somerset 1664–5* (1929) and *A Directory of Somerset in the Seventeenth Century* (1929–32), with 38,000 references, won him recognition among genealogists. He was made a Fellow of the Society of Genealogists and an Honorary Life Member of the American Institute of Genealogy and the Society of Australian Genealogists.

Despite his work in other fields, Dwelly always remained devoted to the cause of Scottish Gaelic. A year before his death the BBC asked him to take part in a series of 'Gaelic Talks', which they were going to broadcast. Unfortunately, ill-health prevented him from doing so.[35]

Edward Dwelly died at his home in Kenilworth Road, Fleet, on 25 January 1939, at the age of seventy-four. His death was sudden and he died without making a will. There was little money to leave and, according to Flora, the sale of her father's books and manuscripts raised about £1,000. In 1987 both the surviving Dwelly children, Flora and Ewen, recalled that the family had nothing to do with the clearing out of his invaluable library, manuscripts and papers. Ewen Dwelly remembered that Alexander Maclaren, the Glasgow publisher, visited his mother in Fleet and purchased all his father's papers, the plates of the famous dictionary and the copyrights and all other materials. 'As there seemed no longer any demand for the Dictionary, she [Dwelly's widow] thought Mr Maclaren of Glasgow was the most suitable buyer of the plates and did the vital deal in my absence,' wrote Ewen. 'The copyright would have been assumed to go with the plates.'[36] Dwelly's pipe-music manuscript collection, however, went to M.R. MacCrimmon of Canada, as mentioned earlier.

The dispersal of Edward Dwelly's library left many unanswered questions about his life and work, which his surviving offspring were no longer able to clarify in 1987. Lost was his collection of press cuttings, consisting of several volumes which had been known to Flora and Ewen, containing all his published articles and papers. Of particular loss were those he had written on matters of Gaelic culture, history and music, which he was known to have published not only under his own name, but also as 'Ewen MacDonald' and several Gaelic 'noms de plume'.

On Dwelly's many interests, his daughter, Flora, observed: 'How he found time to fulfil them all is amazing.' Yet in spite of his many work commitments and financial worries, he found time to devote himself to his children. 'I remember in my own childhood how he never failed to fill the flower beds with lovely flowers, how he spared time to teach my brothers cricket in our garden. Our house in Scotland, by the Beauly Firth, when it was purchased, was well established, having been planted by my father with fruit trees, fruit bushes and strawberries . . .'[37]

An Gàidheal called Dwelly 'a remarkable man'. His name has been blessed by generations of Gaelic speakers and learners. 'C.McL.', writing in *An Gàidheal* summed up: 'As one of his correspondents while a student in Edinburgh we can testify to his painstaking labour of love, his enthusiasm, his courtesy, and his high ideals. He was a great Celt.

'We regret his passing but he has left us an enduring monument – "more lasting than brass".'[38]

Peter Berresford Ellis
FRSAI, FRHistS

Acknowledgment and Source Notes

This article was first written in October, 1988. It was inspired by some initial notes left by the late Seumas Mac a' Ghobhainn which brought me into contact with Edward Dwelly's daughter, Flora Isabella Dwelly, of Oxford, and her brother, Ewen John George Dwelly, of Fleet, Hampshire. Both are now deceased. Without their assistance and helpful correspondence, this biographical sketch would not have been possible.

1 Girvan McKay, *English–Gaelic Key to Dwelly's Gaelic–English Dictionary*, Gairm Publications (No. 38), Glasgow 1974, p. 5

2 Ibid.

3 *The Dwelly Pedigree*, Edward Dwelly, West Ewell 1925

4 Ewen Dwelly to author, 25 July 1988

5 Ibid.

6 *London Scottish Regimental Gazette*, March 1939

7 Flora Dwelly to author, 21 February 1987

8 Iain Gillies to author, 21 February 1987

9 Ibid.

10 Ibid.

11 *London Scottish Regimental Gazette* (above)

12 Ibid.

13 *The Celtic Review*, 15 January 1909 ('Some Notes on a Well-Known Work by its Little-Known Author')

14 Iain Gillies to author, 21 February 1987

15 *The Celtic Review* (above)

16 Flora Dwelly to author, 23 May 1988

17 *London Scottish Regimental Gazette* (above)

18 *The Celtic Review* (above)

19 *Faclair Gàidhlig – The Illustrated Gaelic Dictionary* (see preface by Edward Dwelly, 1977 edition, p. iv)

20 *The Scots Magazine*, January 1989

21 *The Celtic Review* (above)

22 Ibid.

23 Ibid.

24 Ibid.

25 *Faclair Gàidhlig* – (above – see preface p. ii)

26 Flora Dwelly to author, May 23 1988. See also London *Daily Express*, 25 August 1911.

27 Ibid.

28 *The Celtic Review* (above)

29 Ibid.

30 *Aldershot News & Farnborough Chronicle & Fleet Times*, 3 February 1939. See also *The Times*, London, 28 January 1939.

31 *Oban Times*, 3 February 1939

32 John Lorne Campbell, also published in *Oban Times*, 3 February 1939

33 *An Gàidheal.* March 1939

34 John Lorne Campbell in *Oban Times*, 3 February 1939

35 *Aldershot News* & etc. (above)

36 Ewen Dwelly to author, 25 July 1988

37 Flora Dwelly to author, 29 May 1988

38 *An Gàidheal*, March 1939

ROIMH-RADH.

(PREFACE.)

THE vocabulary of this Dictionary is based on that of MacLeod and Dewar, so much appreciated by Gaelic students. All the words not appearing in that work, but to be found in any of our other Gaelic Dictionaries, are also included here, besides many hundreds of words which now appear in print for the first time. All the names of Plants, Diseases, Birds, &c., collected from various special works on those subjects, together with all the examples of proverbs, idiomatic phrases, &c., given by MacAlpine, have been included, and many additional examples have been added from *Carmina Gadelica*, and other sources.

MacLeod & Dewar's and Armstrong's are, without doubt, the best all-round dictionaries hitherto available for students, especially when requiring to translate English into Gaelic. There are various small defects in these works, however, which we have attempted to rectify. In the former work, many words are out of alphabetical order, a word is often spelt differently in the two parts and even in the same part, and in many cases words occuring in the English-Gaelic part are not to be found in the Gaelic-English and *vice versa*. The last remark also applies in a peculiar degree to MacAlpine's work. The word *clarsach* does not appear at all in the Gaelic part of MacLeod & Dewar's, nor *kilt* in the English part ! The large size of Armstrong's Dictionary makes it unportable and awkward to handle, and its high price, like that of the Highland Society's, has always kept it out of the reach of the bulk of Gaelic students. It has now been out of print for many years.

Should any word required not be found in its proper alphabetical order, reference should be made to the appendix, as great numbers of words were received, especially after the issue of Part II., from sources not available before that part was published.

This is the first Dictionary of the Gaelic language in which an attempt has been made to explain words by means of diagrams, and the first in which especial care has been taken in collecting localisms, the names of old Highland implements, &c., and their parts, many of which are now only to be found in one or two remote parishes of the Western Isles, from which they are fast disappearing. The lists of technical terms here given have never been published before, and the whole of the illustrations, with one or two exceptions, have been specially drawn for the work.

This Dictionary is of especial value to the beginner. Many who did not learn the language in infancy, but acquired it in later life through the medium of books, have notified us of the difficulties of grammar and idiom they met with. Such difficulties are likely to puzzle other novices, and have therefore been explained under their appropriate headings. Grammatical difficulties have been elucidated by good Gaelic scholars, and no labour has been spared to make the work as complete and reliable as possible.

Some scholars object to some of the words given in other Dictionaries as being Irish and not Scottish Gaelic, but the difference between the Irish and the Scots is geographical only and not racial, as the records of both amply and abundantly prove. Both call themelves "Gàidheal" in their own language, and fraternize instantly, as soon as English, the language of disunion is dropped. Any difference between them is more imaginary than real, and has been invented and assiduously accentuated for political reasons only, on the old and barbarous plan of "Divide and rule." Many of these so-called Irish words are in use in Cantyre and appear in the Bible, and the close similarity the Gaelic speech of the West of

Scotland has to that of the North of Ireland (much closer than the native English of places not farther removed from each other and with no sea between them) makes the interchange of words easy and often convenient. Many of those who condemn the use of what they call "Irish" words, have no scruple in introducing English and Broad Scots words, which they try to pronounce and write according to Gaelic rules, apparently to make their identity somewhat obscure, when there are already two or three native Gaelic words much more to the point. What would a Frenchman say if addressed "How vous portez yourself?" Yet that is no more absurd than "an do ring thu am bell?" which may be heard in most parts of Gaeldom at any time!

A few correspondents have found fault with this work as being too crowded, in places, with obsolete or English words, but only those given in other Dictionaries figure here, although more prominence has been given to the character of Anglicisms. Words marked obsolete by some, may have often been obsolete for a long period in the districts to which the compilers of those particular Dictionaries belonged, while still used in other parts! Further, the usual rule hitherto adopted in Gaelic Dictionaries with regard to English words in Gaelic dress has been thus—

clàrc, *s.m.* A clerk.

Sometimes *Eng.* or *Eng. word* is added, but not often. A new system has been adopted here, and all such words have been inserted thus—

clàrc, *s.m.* Gaelic spelling of *clerk*.

We hope this will be the means of expelling many Anglicisms from the language, for if anyone is in doubt whether a word is Gaelic or not, he should refer to the Dictionary. If he finds it is not a Gaelic word, HE MUST ON NO ACCOUNT USE IT. Such words are only inserted in the Gaelic-English part as warnings or danger-signals, and they will not be found in the English-Gaelic part. It cannot be impressed too strongly on all who read this, never to introduce a single English word when speaking or writing Gaelic.

We have much pleasure in acknowledging the great

kindness shown and the immense assistance given by our correspondents in all parts of the world, not only by sending lists of words not otherwise obtainable, but also by materially increasing the sales and so lightening the burden of expense that the issue of such a publication lays upon our shoulders. We are especially indebted to the following gentlemen for the unremitting care with which they have perused each page of the Dictionary during its progress through the press, for it has only been through their labours that the compilation of such a correct vocabulary of modern Gaelic has been made possible—William Cameron, Poolewe; D. Campbell, M.A., PH.D., Grimsay; Rev. A. Gunn, Durness; A. Henderson, Kilchoan; Mal. MacDonald, Stornoway; M. Macfarlane, Elderslie; Dun. MacIsaac, Oban; J. G. MacKay, London; M. MacLeod, M.A., Edinburgh; Rev. J. MacRury, Snizort; Rev. Charles Robertson, Inverness; D. Urquhart, M.A., Kyle, Lochalsh; and H. Whyte, ("Fionn,") Glasgow.

We must not omit our great obligation to the Press both at home and abroad, for the detailed reviews they have given of the parts as they appeared, and for their hearty appreciation of our labours.

It is a cause of regret that type of a larger size could not have been used, but, owing to the inconvenience that would have been caused by increasing the bulk of the book, this was found to be impossible.

The greatest care has been taken to prevent misprints, or omissions, but if readers will kindly notify any they may find, the plates will be corrected in every case before further copies are printed.

No attempt has been made to give a so-called phonetic spelling of each word according to English rules as MacAlpine does. The Gaelic language being itself practically phonetic on its own lines, by far the simplest way is to learn the correct sounds of the various Gaelic combinations from some good text-book, of which there are many, and if possible with the aid of a Gaelic-speaker. The phonetic range of English is so meagre compared with that of Gaelic, as to make an explanation of the exact sounds of the latter by means of known combinations of the former almost an impossibility.

This Preface is being issued with Part X, to enable those subscribers who so desire to bind together the parts already published.

THE COMMERCIAL VALUE OF GAELIC.

As we see and hear so frequently such foolish remarks as "it does not pay to learn Gaelic," "Gaelic is a hinderance in a commercial career," and what is only a little less apathetic, "it is a burden which is easily borne," &c., we have decided to treat the matter at some length, although some may object that a Dictionary is hardly the place in which to discuss the merits of a language.

And first, it cannot be too widely known that the speakers of English only, are always baulked by a peculiar disability from acquiring foreign tongues, and that this peculiar disability has disastrous results for British commerce. Before Continental rivals appeared to dispute with Britain the right to supply the best markets of the world, very little attention was paid to languages, but to-day the ready ability to acquire any language in a short time, gives Continental students such a great advantage, that many British industries can only be continued at all by employing such Continental rivals as clerks. These foreigners having learnt the trade secrets of the English, soon afterwards set np a counter trade, and beat the English at their own game.

To give our countrymen technical education and the faculty of easily mastering foreign tongues is the most urgent and crying need of our day.

There are four main reasons that disable those who know no language but English in acquiring foreign tongues :—

1. British insularity.
2. Phonetic poverty of the English language.
3. The prominence given in Britain to the study of dead languages.
4. The Englishman is accustomed to fail with languages, and is proud of his failure. Other languages are mere mockery to him. But the mastery of tongues comes as a matter of course to Germans, Swiss, Russians, &c. Englishmen have not the opportunity to become a bi-lingual people : no but Scotsmen have, for one can obtain constant practice in speaking Gaelic without going outside the country, there being hardly a village, even in the Lowlands where at least one Gaelic speaker can not be found.

The only speech that those who are restricted to English ever hear, is one that has a very small phonetic range, besides being distinctly poor in grammatical development. English people pronounce their vowels as if they were diphthongs, and cannot easily see how the pure open vowel sound differs from a diphthong. Their language has no inflections, no genders or declension of adjectives, &c. This linguistic poverty goes far to deprive an Englishman of the capacity to take the very first step necessary in language learning. The first stage, the mechanical, begins with a thorough mastery of the pronunciation of the language which is being learnt, which, of course, pre-supposes a practical knowledge of phonetics based on the learner's native language. When the main part of the language to be learnt consists firstly, of sounds never before heard by the learner, and secondly, what is infinitely more subtle and more difficult to grasp, when its system of word-arrangement has never before been dreamt of by the learner, how can such learner ever succeed? The phonetic range of Gaelic is, if we except Russian, about the richest of any language in the world, and includes all the sounds used in the other European tongues. Thus, while one who can only speak English is handicapped by the difficulty of having to master numbers of new sounds in whatever tongue he elects to study, the speaker of Gaelic and English is already acquainted with all these sounds.

Our difficulty with languages is more imaginary than real. Germans, in their own country, devote years of dogged, persistent labour to the grammatical and oral study of foreign tongues, and the methods of instruction in German schools are so superior, that there is an incomparable difference in the result of study.

The art of learning a living language has been brought to perfection on the Continent by acquiring the details in the following order—sounds, speech, language. Speech cannot be articulated until the vocal organs have learned to form its component sounds, language cannot be studied to any practical purpose until a certain degree of familiarity has been acquired with it as a living tongue. In English schools, the first strange tongue that is introduced to the student is Latin. This, being a dead language, necessarily reverses the proper order for learning the component parts of a language, and makes the student begin at the end instead of the beginning. In Germany, all boys must first learn French for three years, before they begin Latin, that is, they must acquire the sense of mastery over French as a conversational language, before they take up the study of a dead language by the eyes, with texts, dictionaries, &c. It is chiefly this reform that has endowed Germans with their linguistic abilities.

It is no business of educational authorities to decide whether this or that language shall be studied or not, but it is their duty strictly to prohibit the study of any strange tongue under unnatural conditions, as is now the rule. The point to be enforced is, the vital importance of making certain that the first time a student attempts to learn any language other than his own, he shall learn it by the right method. If he have acquired any language by the right method, he has not only acquired that language, but the faculty of learning any other language, and the sense of mastery with which the knowledge of having conquered inspires him. The average English-speaker is accustomed to fail with languages, for unlike other nations, he has not acquired from infancy the sense of mastery which the successful acquirement of a second spoken language gives.

These are some reasons why instruction in the Gaelic language must, yes, must be encouraged in every possible way, especially where still spoken, for to neglect it is to deprive the children of a priceless heritage for which they pay nothing, (and very little is obtainable free now-a-days.) Consider a moment,—did the ordinary Gaelic-and-English speaking child ever have any trouble or expense in attaining these two languages? Of course not. Well then, he got his advantage free, and that this is an overwhelming advantage may be proved thus: Take little ten-year-old bi-lingual Donald MacDonald from the Gaeldom, and little ten-year-old Jamie Steenson, a uni-lingual from the Galltachd. Which of them will learn French in no time, and which of them will never do anything but boggle at French?

The effect of the study of Gaelic upon the general intelligence of school children is very marked, and a well-known inspector of schools, who has examined bi-lingual children for thirty years, declares that Gaelic-speaking children are much more intelligent and brighter, and possess a better knowledge of English than the uni-lingual Lowland child.

The late Dowager Lady Mackenzie, who had charge of the Gairloch estate from 1843 to 1853, started some ten schools there during that period, and it was the rule in all those schools that no child was to learn any English till he or she could read the Gaelic Bible fluently. Men and women broughtup under that system were naturally far superior in intelligence and every other good quality to those crammed by modern Educational Act regulations. The effect of their having learnt both languages intelligently and thoroughly is noticeable even in their descendants, for it would not be easy to find a more correct speaker of Gaelic and English than a person brought up in Gairloch.

The despotic way in which children who could only speak Gaelic have been crammed with a mass of English by non Gaelic-speaking teachers, to be forgotten as soon as they left school, and their minds so starved instead of nourished, is simply astounding. The manner in which persons in authority in the various districts have done their utmost to poison the minds of the people against the value of their native language and bring it into contempt with them, is what one would expect in Russia instead of Scotland, or in a record of the darkest ignorance of the Middle ages. It has, of course, been done to serve their own ends, by making it unnecessary for them to learn the language, which they could not dispense with in a Gaelic-speaking place, so long as it held the first place in the esteem of the natives. The absurdity of the teachings of such people has now been fully exposed, and no Gael who has reached years of discretion would look with anything but contempt and ridicule an anyone who would presume to underrate the Gaelic language.

Any adult who has a desire to learn foreign tongues will find it immensely to his advantage to learn Gaelic in the first place. He can do this colloquially without any difficulty in most parts of Britain, and very few are so situated as not to be able to meet with a Gaelic-speaker at least two or three times a week.

The Gaelic Language.

PRONUNCIATION.

THE Gaelic Alphabet contains eighteen letters—a, b, c, d, e, f, g, h, i, l, m, n, o, p, r, s, t, u.

The vowels are divided into broad and small. The broad are a, o, and u ; the small e, and i.

The Consonants are classed as—dentals d, t, s ; labials b, f, m, p ; linguals l, n, r ; palatals c, g.

H is the mark of aspiration and is never found alone in a word, but always after the letters b, c, d, f, g, m, p, s, t.

There are two accents—the grave and acute. Either of these placed over a vowel indicates that it is long, and that it has a specific sound according to which is used. The accents also serve to distinguish between words that are the same in spelling but different in meaning.

In almost all polysyllables, excepting some words compounded with a preposition, the accent falls on the first syllable. The others are short and unaccented, and the vowels in that situation have in general short obscure sounds. Hence it happens that the vowels in these syllables are so often used indiscriminately.

There are no quiescent final vowels.

There are some sounds in Gaelic to which there are none perfectly similar in English, and the same combination does not invariably represent the same sound in different parts of the Highlands. The powers of the different letters may be explained with a certain degree of accuracy, yet much will still remain to be learned by the ear alone. As this subject is fully discussed and explained in "Gaelic as a Specific Subject" we must refer the reader to that work for fuller information on account of our limited space here. The following remarks are, however, reproduced, chiefly from "Còmhraidhean an Gàidhlig is am Beurla," by Rev. D. MacInnes, as giving a good general idea of Gaelic pronunciation to those quite unacquainted with the language.

Further remarks on pronunciation will be found in the body of this work under the respective letters.

SOUNDS OF THE VOWELS.

à long like *a* in *far*, as dàn, *a poem* ; bàn, *white*.
ă short like *a* in *that*, as pronounced by a Lowlander, not as by an Englishman, as fad, *length*; gad, *withe*.
ā long before *dh* like *u* drawled in *burn*, as ladhran, *hoofs*.
ă short sound of foregoing, as lagh, *law*.
â before nn and ll, like à above and *u* in *fully*, as clann, *children* ; call, *loss*.
a in unaccented syllables has the obscure broad sound mentioned above.
è long like *e* in *there*, as gnè, *kind*.
é long like *a* in *fame*, as dé, *yesterday*; cé, *earth*.
ĕ short like *e* in *jet*, as dheth, *of him* or *it*.
ĕ short like *a* in *rate*, as teth, *hot*; leth, *half*.
e in unaccented syllables, has generally the short obscure sound, as coille, *a wood*.
ì long like *e* in *me*, as sìd, *weather*; dìth, *want*.
ĭ short like *i* in *king*, as fir, *men*; min, *meal*.
ĭ short like *i* in *tight*, as tigh, *house* ; a stigh, *within*; used only in these two words.
ò long like *aw* in *fawn* as còrr *heron*; òl, *drink*.
ò2 long like *o* in *bold*, as lòn, *meadow*; bò, *cow*.
ŏ short like *o* in *modest*, as cor, *condition* ; orra, *on them*.
ŏ short like *o* in *bowl*, as dol, *going*; crodh, *cattle*.
o3 long like *ow* in *down*, as fonn, *land*; toll, *hole*.
ù long like *oo* in *poor*, as ùr, *new*; ùprait, *bustle*.
ŭ short like *u* in *fully*, as cur, *sending* ; guth, *voice*.

SOUNDS OF THE DIPHTHONGS.

ai 1 like à & ì, as daimh, *kinship*.
ai 2 ,, ă & ĭ, as daimh, *of an ox*.
ai 3 ,, à, the *i* being silent, as fàilte, *welcome*.
ai 4 ,, ă, the *i* being silent, as tais, *soft*.
ai 5 ,, ă, short, the *i* being silent, as tairbhe, *profit* ; airm, *arms*.
ao 1 ,, ā, the *o* being silent, as aog, *death* ; caol, *slender*.
ea 1 ,, ĕ short, & à, as geall, *wager*.
ea 2 ,, ĕ, short, & ă, as geal, *white*.
èa 3 ,, è, a being silent, as dèan, *do*.
ea 4 ,, ĕ, a being silent, as lean, *follow*.
éi 1 ,, é, *i* being silent & *dh* sounded, as déidh, *wish*.
ei 2 ,, ĕ, *i* is silent & *ch* sounded, as deich, *ten*.
éi 3 ,, é, the *i* being silent, as céile, *spouse*.
ei 4 ,, ĕ, the *i* being silent, as ceist, *question*.
eò 1 ,, ĕ slightly sounded & ò, as ceòl, *music*.
eo 2 ,, ĕ slightly sounded and ŏ, as beothail, *lively*.
eu 1 ,, é, the *u* being silent, as ceum, *a step*.
ia 1 ,, ì & a obscure, as ciall, *sense* ; iar, *west*.
ìo 1 ,, ì the *o* being silent, as lìon, *fill*.
io 2 ,, ĭ obscure & *o* silent, as ciont, *guilt*.
io 3 ,, ĭ, the *o* being silent, as iomlan, *complete*.
io 4 ,, *u* in *up*, as ciod? *what?*
iù 1 ,, ì & ù, as fiù, *worthy*.
iu 2 ,, ĭ & ŭ, as iubhar, *a yew-tree*.
iù 3 ,, ù, the *i* being silent, as diùlt, *refuse*.
iu 4 ,, ŭ, the *i* being silent, as diugh, *to-day*.
òi 1 ,, ò & ì, as clòimh, *wool*.
oi 2 ,, ŏ & ĭ, as cloimh, *mange*.
oi 3 ,, ŏ, the *i* being silent, as toiseach, *beginning*.
ua 1 ,, ŭ & a obscure, as cluas, *ear*.
ùi 1 ,, ù & *i* silent, as dùil, *hope*.
ui 2 ,, ŭ & *i* silent as sluig, *swallow* ; duine, *man*.

SOUNDS OF THE TRIPHTHONGS.

The Triphthongs are aoi, eai, eoi, iai, iui, uai.

As the sounds of the diphthongs depend on those of the dual vowels, so the sounds of the triphthongs depend on those of the diphthongs. The rule that the vowel immediately before or immediately after a plain palatal or lingual often loses its sound holds good in regard to the triphthongs. The vowel in the triphthong that loses its sound is the last *i*.

SOUNDS OF THE CONSONANTS.

b, like *b* in *boat*, as bàrd, *a poet*.
bh, at the beginning and end of a word is like *v*, as bha, *was*. In the middle of a word it is sometimes like *v*, and sometimes like *w*, as leabhar, *book* ; but often silent, as dubhar, *shade*.

c, before a broad vowel, like *c* in *can*, as càrn, *a heap of stones*.
before a small vowel, like *k* in *keen*, as cinn, *heads*.

ch, before or after a broad vowel, is like *ch* in *loch*, as chuir, *put*; deoch, *a drink*.

ch, before or after a small vowel is like the Greek *chi* as pronounced in Scotland, as chi, *shall see*; deich, *ten*.

c, at the end of a syllable is like *chk*, as mac, *son*.—Exceptions, chunnaic, ionraic, òirdheirc, éiric.

chd, is like *ch* in *loch* with *k* added.

d, before a broad vowel is like *d* in *door*, as dorus, *door*.

d, before a small vowel is like *d* in *dew*, as dèan, *do*.

dh, before or after a broad vowel has no sound in English exactly like it.

dh, before or after a small vowel is like *y* in *yield*, as dhibh, *of you*; féidh, *deer* (pl.)

f, is like *f* in English.

fh, at the beginning of a word is silent, except in the words *fhuair*, *fhathast*, when it is like *h* in *hat*.

g, before a broad vowel is like *g* in *go*, as gabh, take.

g, before a small vowel is like *g* in *give*, as géill, *yield*.

gh, before or after a small vowel is like *y* in *yield*, as ghéill, *yielded*; faigh, *get*.

gh, before or after a broad vowel, has no sound in English exactly like it.

l, before a broad vowel has no sound in English exactly like it.

l, before a small vowel is like *l* in *lure*, as liadh, *a ladle*, or *blade of an oar*.

ll, at the end of a syllable or word preceded by *i*, is like *ll* in *million*, as pill, *return*; pilltinn, *returning*; when preceded by a broad vowel it has no sound like it in English.

m, is like *m* in English.

mh, at the beginning and end of a word or flanked by vowels, is like *v*, as mharbh (pro. varv) *killed*; nàmh, *an enemy*.

mh, after a vowel and followed by a consonant, is generally silent, but it imparts a nasal sound to the vowel preceding it, as còmhradh, *dialogue*; and is sometimes sounded *u* or *w*, as in samhradh, summer.

n, before a broad vowel has no sound in English exactly like it.

n, before a small vowel is like *n* in *new*, as neach, *a person*.

nn, after a broad vowel has no sound exactly like it in English.

nn, after *i* is like *n* in *pinion*.

n, after c, g, m, t, is usually like *r*, as cnàmh, *decay*, *digest*; gnìomh, *deed*, *action*; mnathan, *women*; tnù, *envy*; but correct speakers pronounce it *n*.

p, like *p* in English.

ph, at the beginning of a word is like *f* as phill, *returned*.

s, before or after a broad vowel is like *s* in English.

s, before or after a small vowel is like *sh*, as sìn, *stretch*; tais, *soft*.

sh, at the beginning of a word is like *h*, as shìn (pro. heen,) *stretched*.

t, before or after a broad vowel is like *t* in *tone*, as tog, *raise*; lot, *a wound*.

t, before or after a small vowel is like the first element of *ch* in *chin*, as teine, *fire*.

th, at the beginning of a word is like *h*, as thig, *come*.

th, in the middle and end of a word is silent, as bathar, (pro. ba-ar,) *goods*; bàth (pro. bà) *drown*.

l, n, r, are the only letters that are doubled in the middle of a word. No letter is doubled at the beginning of a word.

ORTHOGRAPHY.

The chief exceptions to the above rules frequently met with in writing are :—
is, *is*; so, *this*; sud, *yonder*; ged, *although*; and tigh, *a house*.
We have continued the usual way of spelling *is* and *ged* throughout this work, but there is an increasing tendency to spell "so" *seo*, "sud" *siod*, and "tigh" *taigh*, so we have adopted these forms as being more in uniformity with the spelling of the rest of the language. *Seo* and *siod* are also the more correct as representing the Old Gaelic forms *seo* and *siut*.
The Orthography generally adopted in this Dictionary is that used by the best scholars of the present day.

INFLECTIONS.

OF THE ARTICLE.

The following statement from Dr. Gillies' Gaelic Grammar, shows the Article in position before Nouns of both genders beginning with every letter of the Alphabet, and in such relation with Prepositions as to bring out all the possible forms.

Masculine Nouns.

Singular.

Nom.	Gen.	Dat.	
an t-athair, *the father*,	an athar,	aig an athair,	do'n athair.
am bràthair, *the brother*,	a' bhràthar,	a' bhràthair,	'n bhràthair.
an caraid, *the friend*,	a' charaid,	a' charaid,	'n charaid.
an duine, *the man*,	an duine,	an duine,	'n duine.
an t-each, *the horse*,	an eich,	an each,	'n each.
am fear, *the man*,	an fhir,	an fhear	'n fhear.
an gàradh, *the garden*,	a' ghàraidh,	a' ghàradh,	'n ghàradh.
an t-isean, *the gosling*,	an isein,	an isean,	'n isean.
an laoch, *the hero*,	an laoich,	an laoch,	'n laoch.
am mac, *the son*,	a' mhic,	a' mhac,	'n mhac.
an neul, *the cloud*,	an neòil,	an neul,	'n neul.
an t-òglach, *the youth*,	an òglaich,	an òglach,	'n òglach.
am port, *the harbour*,	a' phuirt,	a' phort,	'n phort
an rìgh, *the king*,	an rìgh,	an rìgh,	'n rìgh.
an sgadan, *the herring*,	an sgadain,	an sgadan,	'n sgadan.
an taigh, *the house*,	an taighe,	an taigh,	'n taigh.
an t-uircean, *the y'ng pig*,	an uircein,	an uircean,	'n uircean.

Plural.

na h-athraichean,	nan athraichean,	na h-athraichean,	na h-athraichean.
na bràithrean,	nam bràithrean,	na bràithrean (or -aibh.)	
na càirdean,	nan càirdean,	na càirdean.	

Feminine Nouns,

Nom.	Gen.	Dat.	
	Singular.		
an abhainn, *the river,*	na h-aibhne,	aig an abhainn,	do'n abhainn.
a' bhreug, *the lie,*	na bréige,	a' bhréig,	'n bhréig.
a' chearc, *the hen,*	na circe,	a' chirc,	'n chirc.
an dùthaich, *the country,*	na dùthcha,	an dùthaich,	'n dùthaich.
an eala, *the swan,*	na h-eala,	an eala,	'n eala.
an fhìrinn, *the truth,*	na fìrinn,	an fhìrinn,	'n fhìrinn.
a' ghòraich, *the folly,*	na gòraich	a' ghòraich,	'n ghòraich.
an iteag, *the feather,*	na h-iteig,	an iteig,	'n iteig.
an lach, *the wild duck,*	na lacha,	an lach,	'n lach.
a' mhàthair, *the mother,*	na màthar,	a' mhàthair,	'n mhàthair.
an nighean, *the daughter,*	na h-inghne,	an nighinn,	'n nighinn.
an òrdag, *the thumb,*	na h-òrdaig,	an òrdaig,	'n òrdaig.
a' phiseag, *the kitten,*	na piseig,	a' phiseig,	'n phiseig.
an ròineag, *the hair,*	na ròineig,	an ròineig,	'n ròineig.
an sguab, *the sheaf,*	na sguaibe,	an sguaib,	'n sguaib.
an t-sùil, *the eye,*	na sùla,	an t-sùil,	'n t-sùil.
an tunnag, *the duck,*	na tunnaig,	an tunnaig,	'n tunnaig.
an uaigh, *the grave,*	na h-uaighe,	an uaigh,	'n uaigh.
	Plural		
na h-aibhnichean,	nan aibhnichean,	na h-aibhnichean.	
na breugan,	nam breug,	na breugan.	
na cearcan,	nan cearc,	na cearcan.	

OF VERBS.

In this Dictionary the root of the verb is always given first, immediately followed by the Pres. Part. Irregular inflections of all Verbs are also given.

The 2nd. Pers. singular *Imperative* Mood is the ROOT or THEME of every Gaelic Verb.

Indicative Mood, Active Voice—

The Past Tense of a Verb is formed by aspirating the initial consonant of its root, as—Paisg, *fold thou* ; phaisg e, *he folded.* Verbs beginning with l, n, r, sc, sg, sm, sp, st, do not take the aspirated form, and when a Verb commences with a vowel the past tense is formed by prefixing *dh'* to the root, as—òl, *drink thou*; dh'òl e, *he drank.*

The Future Tense is formed by adding *idh* to the root of all Verbs, as—Buail, *strike thou* ; buailidh mi, *I shall strike.* When the last vowel of the root is broad *aidh* is added instead of *idh.*

The *Infinitive Mood* and *Pres. Part.* are generally formed by adding *adh* to the root, as—Buail, *strike,* a bhualadh *to strike*; a' bualadh, *striking.*

OF SUBSTANTIVES.

In this Dictionary the noun is given in the Nom. Sing., immediately followed by the terminations of the Gen. Sing. and Nom. Plur. All irregular inflections of other cases are also given. When only one termination, *a* or *an*, is given, it is that of the Nom. Plur., and the Gen. Sing. is in such cases the same as the Nom. Sing. When the only termination given is not *a* or *an*, it is that of the Gen. Sing. and Nom. Plur., which in such cases are alike.

General Rules.—The Nom. and Dat. Sing. of Masc. Nouns are alike.

The Gen. and Dat. Sing. of Fem. Nouns are alike.

The Gen. and Voc. Sing. of Masc. Nouns are alike.

The Nom. and Voc. Sing. of Fem. Nouns are alike.

Plural.—The Nom. Plur. is often like the Gen. Sing., or it is formed by adding *a, an,* or *ean* to the Nom. Sing.

The Gen. Pl. is either like the Nom. Sing. or Nom. Plur.

The Dat. Pl. is like the Nom. Pl., the older form in *ibh* or *aibh* being practically obsolete.

The Voc. Pl. is the same as the Nom., aspirated and ending in *a* or *an.*

A noun with the article before it is *definite,* and without the article, *indefinite.*

A definite masc. noun aspirates the Gen. and Dat. Sing; but a definite fem. noun aspirates the Nom. and Dat. Sing.

A definite noun beginning with d, l, n, r, s, or t, does not aspirate any case.

Nouns beginning with a consonant, and whose last vowel is broad.

The Gen. Sing. is usually formed by inserting *i* after the last vowel of the Nom. Sing.

Nouns beginning with a consonant, and whose last vowel is small.

The Gen. Sing. masc. and fem. is generally formed by adding *e* to the Nom.; but Nouns of more than one syllable generally terminate alike in all cases in the Singular.

Nouns commencing with a vowel.

A definite masc. Noun requires *t-* before it in the Nom. Sing., and *h-* in the Nom. and Dat. Pl.

A definite fem. Noun requires *h-* before it in the Gen. Sing., and in the Nom. and Dat. Plur.

A definite masc. Noun beginning with *s* followed by a vowel, or a liquid requires *t-* before it in the Gen. and Dat. Sing., and a definite fem. Noun in the Nom. and Dat. Sing.

OF ADJECTIVES.

In this Dictionary Adjectives are given in the Positive form, followed by the termination of the first Comparative.

Adjectives are declined by number, gender, case, and form, and their oblique cases are formed from the Nom., according to the rules already given for the formation of the cases of nouns.

The Nom. Sing. Masc. and Fem. end alike, but the feminine is aspirated.

The Gen. Sing. Fem. is formed from the Gen. Sing. Masc., by dropping the aspirated form, and, if a monosyllable, it generally ends in *e* or *a.*

The Plural of all adjectives of one syllable ends in *a* (*e* if the preceding vowel is small) and of those of more than one syllable, like the Nom. Sing.

The Nom. Dat. and Voc. Fem., and the Gen. and Voc. Masc. are aspirated in the Sing. either with or without the article.

The Dat. of an adjective combined with a definite noun is aspirated in both genders.

Adjectives of two or more syllables seldom add *e* to the Gen. Sing.

An adjective beginning with a vowel admits of no initial change, and one ending in a vowel admits of no final change.

COMPARISON.—There are only two degrees of comparison in Gaelic, the *Positive*, and *Comparative*, and a Superlative of extent.

The Comparative has three forms of Comparison, the *first*, *second*, and *third*.

The first form is like the Gen. Sing, Fem., the second is formed from the first by changing *e* into *id*, and the third from the second by changing *id* into *ead*; as—

Bàn, *fair*, 1stC.bàine, 2ndC.bainid, 3rdC. and Abst. Noun, bàinead, *whiteness*

Crìon, *little*, 1stC.crìne, 2ndC.crìnid, 3rdC.crìnead, *littleness*.

The three forms of comparison take the aspirated form, but no final change whatever.

EXAMPLES.

NOUNS WITH AND WITHOUT ARTICLE.

A REGULAR BROAD VOWEL NOUN.

Bàrd, *masc.* a poet.

	Sing.	Plur.
Nom.	bàrd, *a poet.*	bàird, *poets.*
Gen.	bàird, *of a poet.*	bhàrd, *of poets.*
Dat.	air bàrd, *on a poet.*	air bàird, (bàrdaibh) *on poets*
Voc.	a bhàird ! *O poet !*	a bhàrda ! *O poets !*

☞ The Dative case of an indefinite Noun is plain, unless preceded by a preposition which aspirates the noun following, as—*de, do, fo,* &c.

Am Bàrd, *the poet.*

Nom. am bàrd, *the poet.* na bàird, *the poets.*
Gen. a' bhàird, *of the poet.* nam bàrd, *of the poets*
D. { air a' bhàrd, *on the poet.* do na bàird [bàrd-
{ do'n bhàrd, *to the poet.* [aibh] *to the poets.*

Sing.	*Plur.*	*Sing.*	*Plur.*
Bròg, *fem.* a shoe.		A' bhròg, *the shoe.*	
Nom. bròg,	brògan.	a' bhròg,	na brògan.
Gen. bròige,	bhròg.	na bròige,	nam bròg.
Dat. bròig,	brògan.	{a' / 'n} bhròig	na brògan.
Voc. a bhròg !	a bhrògan !		

A REGULAR SMALL VOWEL NOUN.

Mìr, *masc.*, a piece		Am mìr, *the piece.*	
Nom. mìr,	mìrean.	am mìr	na mìrean.
Gen. mìre,	mhìrean.	a' mhìre,	nam mìrean.
Dat. mìr,	mìrean,-ibh.	do'n mhìr,	do na mìr-
Voc. a mhìr !	a mhìrean !		[ean, or mìribh.

Poit, *fem.*, a pot.		A' phoit, *the pot.*	
Nom. poit,	poitean.	a' phoit,	na poitean
Gen. poite,	phoit.	na poite,	nam poit.
Dat. poit,	poitean, -ibh.	do'n phoit,	do na
Voc. a phoit !	a phoitean !		[poitean, -ibh.

A FEMININE NOUN DECLINED WITH AN ADJ.

Cluas mhór, *a large ear.*

	Sing.	Plur.
Nom.	cluas mhór,	cluasan móra.
Gen.	cluaise móire,	chluasan móra.
Dat.	cluais mhóir,	cluasan [or-aibh] móra.
Voc.	a chluas mhór !	a chluasa móra !

A' chluas mhór, *the large ear.*

Nom. a' chluas mhór na cluasan móra.
Gen. na cluaise móire, nan cluasan móra.
Dat. do'n chluais mhóir, do na cluasan [-aibh] [móra.

A MASCULINE NOUN DECLINED WITH AN ADJ.

Uan beag, *a little lamb.*

Nom.	uan beag,	uain bheaga.
Gen.	uain bhig,	uan beaga.
Dat.	uan beag,	uain bheaga *or* uan-[aibh beaga.
Voc.	uain bhig !	uana beaga !

An t-uan beag, *the little lamb.*

Nom.	an t-uan beag,	na h-uain bheaga.
Gen.	an uain bhig,	nan uan beaga.
Dat.	do'n uan bheag,	na h-uain bheaga, *or* [uanaibh beaga.

COMPOUND NOUNS.

When two Nouns combine to form a compound Noun the first is declined regularly. The second has the Genitive form always and in all the cases. It may be Singular or Plural. If it is Singular, it takes the Aspiration of an Adjective in agreement with the first Noun, if Plural it takes the Aspirate throughout.

Singular.

	a full tide	*a hen-house*	*a nut-wood*
Nom.	làn-mara	taigh-chearc	coille-chnò
Gen.	làin-mhara	taigh-chearc	coille-chnò
Dat.	làn-mara	taigh-chearc	coille-chnò
Voc.	a làin-mhara,	a thaigh-chearc,	a choille-chnò

When a Noun and Adjective combine to form a Compound Noun both parts are regularly declined as if they stood apart.

Coileach-dubh, *a black-cock.*

	Singular.	Plural.
Nom.	coileach-dubh	coilich-dhubha
Gen.	coilich-dhuibh	coileach-dubha
Dat.	coileach-dubh	coilich-dhubha
Voc.	a choilich-dhuibh	a choileacha-dubha

Final *n* and *l* of the first element prevents aspiration of initial dental of the second—aig sgoil-dannsaidh, *at a dancing-school.*

When an Adjective and Noun combine, the Adjective retains the Nominative form throughout, and the Noun is regularly declined and has the aspiration throughout.

Dubh-fhacal, *a dark saying*

	Singular.	Plural.
Nom.	dubh-fhacal	dubh-fhacail
Gen.	dubh-fhacail	dubh-fhacal
Dat.	dubh-fhacal	dubh-fhacail
Voc.	a dhubh-fhacail	a dhubh-fhacla

VERBS.

There are two Conjugations in Gaelic,—the First and the Second. Verbs beginning with a consonant, except *f* pure, are of the First conjugation, and those beginning with a vowel or *f* pure are of the Second,

A REGULAR VERB OF THE FIRST CONJUGATION

Paisg, Fold or wrap.

—*Active Voice*—

Simple Tenses.

Indicative or Affirmative Mood

Past Tense,

Sing. 1. Phaisg mi, *or* do phaisg mi, I folded
2. Phaisg thu, thou foldedst
3. Phaisg e, he folded
Plur. 1. Phaisg sinn, we folded
2. Phaisg sibh, ye folded
3. Phaisg iad, they folded

Future Tense.

Sing. 1. Paisgidh mi. I shall *or* will fold
2. Paisgidh tu, thou shalt *or* wilt fold
3. Paisgidh e, he shall *or* will fold
Plur. 1. Paisgidh sinn, we shall fold
2. Paisgidh sibh. ye shall fold
3. Paisgidh iad, they shall fold

Negative or Interrogative Mood

Past Tense.

(an.., cha.., nach.., mur.., &c.)

Sing. 1. An do phaisg mi ? did I fold ?
Sing. 1. Cha do phaisg mi, I did not fold
Sing. 1. Nach do phaisg mi ? did I not fold ?
Sing. 1. Mur do phaisg mi, if I did not fold

Future Tense.

(am.., cha ph—, nach.., mur..)

Sing. 1. ....paisg mi, (shall &c.) I fold

Subjunctive Mood.

Past Tense.

Sing. 1. Phaisginn, I would fold
2. Phaisgeadh tu, thou wouldst fold
3. Phaisgeadh e, he would fold
Plur. 1. Phaisgeamaid, we would fold
2. Phaisgeadh sibh, ye would fold
3. Phaisgeadh iad, they would fold

Future Tense

Sing. 1. (Ma) phaisgeas mi, (if) I shall fold
2. ,, phaisgeas tu, (if) thou shalt fold
3. ,, phaisgeas e, (if) he shall fold
Plur. 1. ,, phaisgeas sinn, (if) we shall fold
2. ,, phaisgeas sibh, (if) ye shall fold
3. ,, phaisgeas iad, (if) they shall fold

Imperative Mood.

Sing. 1. Paisgeam, let me fold
2. Paisg, fold thou
3. Paisgeadh e, let him fold
Plur. 1. Paisgeamaid, let us fold
2. Paisgibh, fold ye
3. Paisgeadh iad, let them fold

Infinitive Mood.

A phasgadh, to fold.
A' pasgadh, folding. (pres. part.)
Air pasgadh, folded

Compound Tenses.

Affirmative Mood

Present Tense,

Sing. 1. Tha mi a' pasgadh, I am folding.
2. Tha thu a' pasgadh, thou art folding.
3. Tha e a' pasgadh, he is folding
Plu. 1. Tha sinn a' pasgadh, we are folding
2. Tha sibh a' pasgadh, ye are folding
3. Tha iad a' pasgadh, they are folding

Present Tense, No. 2 Form.

Sing. 1. Tha mi air pasgadh, I have folded
2. Tha thu air pasgadh, thou hast folded
3. Tha e air pasgadh, he has folded
Plur. 1. Tha sinn air pasgadh, we have folded
2. Tha sibh air pasgadh, ye have folded
3. Tha iad air pasgadh, they have folded

Past Tense.

Sing. 1. Bha mi a' pasgadh, I was folding
2. Bha thu a' pasgadh, thou wast folding
3. Bha e a' pasgadh, he was folding
Plur. 1. Bha sinn a' pasgadh, we were folding
2. Bha sibh a' pasgadh, ye were folding
3. Bha iad a' pasgadh, they were folding

Past Tense, No. 2 Form.

Sing. 1. Bha mi air pasgadh, I had folded
2. Bha thu air pasgadh, thou hadst folded
3. Bha e air pasgadh, he had folded
Plur. 1. Bha sinn air pasgadh, we had folded
2. Bha sibh air pasgadh, ye had folded
3. Bha iad air pasgadh, they had folded

Future Tense.

Sing. 1. Bithidh mi a' pasgadh, I shall *or* will be folding [folding
2. Bithidh tu a' pasgadh, thou shalt be
3. Bithidh e a' pasgadh, he shall be folding
Plur. 1. Bithidh sinn a' pasgadh, we shall be folding [folding
2. Bithidh sibh a' pasgadh, ye shall be,
3. Bithidh iad a' pasgadh, they shall be folding

Future Tense, No. 2 Form.

Sing. 1. Bithidh mi air pasgadh, I shall have folded
2. Bithidh tu air pasgadh, thou shalt have folded [folded
3. Bithidh e air pasgadh, he shall have
Plur. 1. Bithidh sinn air pasgadh, we shall have folded
2. Bithidh sibh air pasgadh, ye shall have folded [folded
3. Bithidh iad air pasgadh, they shall have

Negative Mood

(am bheil ? cha'n 'eil, nach 'eil, mur 'eil)

Present Tense.

Sing. 1. Cha'n 'eil mi a' pasgadh. &c., I am not folding, &c.,

Present Tense, No. 2 Form.

Sing. 1. Cha'n 'eil mi air pasgadh, &c., I have not folded, &c.,

Past Tense.

Sing. 1. Cha robh mi a' pasgadh, &c., I was not folding, &c.,

Past Tense, No. 2 Form.

Sing. 1. Cha robh mi air pasgadh, &c., I had not folded

Future Tense.

Sing. 1. Cha bhi mi a' pasgadh, &c., I shall not be folding, &c.,

Future Tense, No. 2 Form.

Sing. 1. Cha bhi mi air pasgadh, &c., I shall not have folded, &c.,

Subjunctive Mood.

Past Tense.

Sing. 1. Bhithinn a' pasgadh, &c., I would be folding, &c.,

Past Tense, No. 2 Form.

Sing. 1. Bhithinn air pasgadh, &c., I would have folded, &c.,

Future Tense.

Sing. 1. Ma bhitheas mi a' pasgadh, &c., If I shall be folding, &c.,

Future Tense, No. 2 Form.

Sing. 1. Ma bhitheas mi air pasgadh, &c., If I shall have folded, &c.,

Imperative Mood.

Sing. 1. Bitheam a' pasgadh, let me be folding

No. 2 Form

Sing. 1. Bitheam air pasgadh, let me have folded

Infinitive Mood

A (or do) bhith a' pasgadh, to be folding.
Air bhith a' pasgadh, been folding.
Do bhith air pasgadh, to have been folding.

—Passive Voice—

Simple Tenses.

Affirmative Mood

Past.

Sing. 1. Do phaisgeadh mi, *or* Phaisgeadh mi, I was folded, &c.,

Future.

Sing. 1. Paisgear mi, I shall be folded, &c..

Negative Mood.

(an .., cha.., nach.., mur..)

Past.

Sing. 1. Cha do phaisgeadh mi, I was not folded.

Future.

Sing. 1. Cha phaisgear mi, I shall not be folded.

Subjunctive Mood.

Past.

Sing. 1. Phaisgteadh mi, I would be folded, &c.,

Future.

Sing. 1. Ma phaisgear mi, If I shall be folded.

Imperative Mood.

Sing.1. Paisgtear mi, let me be folded, &c.

Participle.

Paisgte, Folded.

Compound Tenses.

Affirmitive Mood.

Present.

Sing.1. Tha mi paisgte, I am folded, &c.

Present, No. 2.

Sing.1. Tha mi air mo phasgadh, I have been folded

Past.

Sing.1. Bha mi paisgte, I was folded.

Past, No. 2.

Sing.1. Bha mi air mo phasgadh, I had been folded

Future.

Sing.1. Bithidh mi paisgte, I shall be folded.

Future, No. 2.

Sing.1. Bithidh mi air mo phasgadh, I shall have been folded

Negative Mood.

Present.

Sing.1. Cha'n 'eil mi paisgte, I am not folded.

Present, No. 2.

Sing. Cha'n 'eil mi air mo phasgadh, I have not been folded.

Past.

Sing.1. Cha robh mi paisgte, I was not folded.

Past, No. 2.

Sing.1. Cha robh mi air mo phasgadh, I had not been folded.

Future.

Sing.1. Cha bhi mi paisgte, I shall not be folded

Future, No. 2.

Sing.1. Cha bhi mi air mo phasgadh, I shall not have been folded.

Subjunctive Mood.

Past.

Sing.1. Bhithinn paisgte, I would be folded.

Past, No. 2.

Sing.1. Bhithinn air mo phasgadh, I would have been folded.

Future.

Sing.1. Ma bhitheas mi paisgte, If I shall be folded.

Future, No. 2.

Sing.1. Ma bhitheas mi air mo phasgadh, If I shall have been folded.

Imperative Mood.

Bitheam paisgte, Let me be folded

Bitheam air mo phasgadh, Let me have been folded.

Infinitive Mood.

Air (*or* do) bhith paisgte, to be folded.

Do bhith air mo phasgadh, to have been folded

A Regular Verb of the Second Conjugation.

Orduich, appoint.

—Active Voice—

Simple Tenses.

Mood.	Past.	Future.
Affirmative,	Dh'orduich,	Orduichidh.
Negative.	D'orduich,	Orduich.
Subjunctive,	Dh'orduichinn,	Dh'orduicheas
„ 1p *pl*	Dh'orduicheamaid	
„	Dh'orduicheadh tu, e, sibh, & iad.	

Imperative, Orduicheam ; Infinitive, Orduchadh.

—Passive Voice—

Affirmative,	Dh'orduicheadh,	Orduichear
Negative,	D'orduicheadh,	Orduichear
Subjunctive,	Dh'orduichteadh,	Dh'orduichear

Imperative, Orduichtear ; Participle, Orduichte

A Verb beginning with *F*.

Falaich, hide.

—Active Voice—

Mood.	Past.	Future.
Affirmative,	Dh'fhalaich,	Falaichidh
Negative,	D'fhalaich,	Falaich
Subjunctive,	Dh'fhalaichinn,	Dh'fhalaicheas
„ 1p *pl*	Dh'fhalaicheamaid	
„	Dh'fhalaicheadh tu, e, sibh, & iad.	

Imperative, Falaicheam ; Infin. Dh'fhalachadh

—Passive Voice—

Affirmative,	Dh'fhalaicheadh,	Falaichear
Negative,	D'fhalaicheadh,	Falaichear
Subjunctive,	Dh'fhalaichteadh,	Dh'fhalaichear

Imperative, Falaichtear ; Part. Falaichte.

The Compound Tenses of Verbs of the Second Conjugation are formed in exactly the same manner as those of the First.

PREPOSITIONAL PRONOUNS.

	Singular.				Plural.		
	1	2	3 *m.*	3 *f.*	1	2	3
	mi *me*	tu *thee*	e *him*	i *her*	sinn *us*	sibh *you*	iad *them*
aig, *at*,	agam	agad	aige	aice	againn	agaibh	aca
air, *on*,	orm	ort	air	oirre	oirnn	oirbh	orra
ann, *in*,	annam	annad	ann	innte	annainn	annaibh	annta
as, *out of*,	asam	asad	as	aiste	asainn	asaibh	asta
de, *of*,	diom	diot	deth	dith	dinn	dibh	diubh
do, *to*,	domh	duit	da	di	duinn	duibh	doibh
eadar, *between*,					eadarainn	eadaraibh	eatorra
fo, *under*,	fodham	fodhad	fodha	foipe	fodhainn	fodhaibh	fopa
gu, *towards*,	chugam	chugad	chuige	chuice	chugainn	chugaibh	chuca
le, *with*,	leam	leat	leis	leatha	leinn	leibh	leo
mu, *about*,	umam	umad	uime	uimpe	umainn	umaibh	umpa
o, *from*,	uam	uait	uaidh	uaipe	uainn	uaibh	uapa
ri, *to*,	rium	riut	ris	rithe	rinn	ribh	riu
roimh, *before*,	romham	romhad	roimhe	roimpe	romhainn	romhaibh	rompa
thar, *over*,	tharam	tharad	thairis air	thairis oirre	tharainn	tharaibh	tharta
troimh, *through*,	tromham	tromhad	troimhe	troimpe	tromhainn	tromhaibh	trompa

The above abbreviated remarks, with the exception of those on pronunciation, are inserted here for the use of those already acquainted with the rudiments of the Gaelic language. Those wishing to study the language *thoroughly* from the very commencement should, if possible, obtain a copy of John Forbes' Double Grammar of English and Gaelic, which may sometimes be purchased secondhand although long out of print. Stewart's Gaelic Grammar is a classical work, a number of other good grammars being based on it. "Scottish Gaelic as a Specific subject," by Malcolm MacFarlane, is a mertiorious little book, noted for its correctness.

Some readers may consider the vocabulary given in the following pages too detailed and much of it superfluous, but one of the chief objects kept in view during compilation has been to include all words or forms of words likely to present difficulties to those commencing to study the Gaelic Language.

AUTHORITIES.

Most of the words not marked are from Mac Leod & Dewar's Gaelic Dictionary, but the sources of all the important additions have been marked as follows,

* Words or meanings from MacAlpine's G. D.
† Obsolete words or meanings,
‡ " " MacBain's Ety'lG.D.
§ " " Cameron's G. names of Plants, 1900.
¶ " " Ferguson's G. names of Birds; Trans. G. Society of Inverness, vols. xi and xii.
** " " Armstrong's G D.
†† " " MacEachan's G. D. (new edition.)
‡‡ " " Highland Soc'y's GD
A.C.—Alex. Carmichael author of "Carmina Gadelica."
A.G.—Rev. A. Gunn, Durness.
C.R.—Rev. Chas. M. Robertson, Torridon.
D.M.—Duncan MacIsaac, Oban,
I.M.—Ian MacKenzie, London.
J.M.—Rev. John MacRury, Snizort,
M.M.—Malcolm MacFarlane, Elderslie.
N.G.P.—Nicolson's Gaelic Proverbs.
A. F.—Alex. Forbes, Edinburgh.
A. H.—Angus Henderson, Ardnamurchan.

ABBREVIATIONS USED IN THIS WORK.

a.	active voice.
a.	adjective.
art.	article.
adv.	adverb.
aff.	affirmative.
col.	colloquial.
comp.	comparative.
conj.	conjunction.
conj. interr.	interrogative conjunction.
contr.	contraction.
dat.	dative case.
def. v.	defective verb.
dim.	diminutive.
f.	feminine.
fut.	future tense.
gen.	genitive case.
i. e.	that is.
impers.	impersonal.
impr.	improper.
ind.	indeclinable.
indic.	indicative.
infin.	infinitive.
int.	interjection.
interr.	interrogative.
m.	masculine.
n., nom.	nominative case.
neg.	negative.
pass.	passive.
pl.	plural.
poss.	possessive.
poss pron.	possessive pronoun.
pref.	prefix.
prep.	preposition.
prep. pron.	prepositional pronoun.
part.	participle.
pr. part.	present participle.
pt. part.	past participle.
pron.	pronoun.
p., prov.	provincial.
rel.	relative.
rel. pron.	relative pronoun.
s.	substantive.
s. f.	feminine substantive.
sing.	singular number.
s.m.	masculine substantive.
sup.	superlative degree.
v.	verb.
v.a.	active verb.
v.n.	neuter verb.
v.irr.	irregular verb.

GÀIDHLIG-BEURLA.

[Mur faigh thu am facal a tha thu ag iarraidh 'na àite fèin a rèir ordugh na h-aibidil, seall air a shon 's an Leasachadh.]

[If you cannot find the word you want in the body of the work, look for it in the Appendix.]

A a

A, ailm, the Elm-tree. The 1st. letter of the Gaelic alphabet, now in use.

It has three sounds; (1) both long and short. Long, like *a* in father as—àl, *brood*, àr, *slaughter*. Short, like *a* in fat, cat, as pronounced by a Lowlander, but not as pronounced by an Englishman, as—falt, *hair*; cas, *foot*. (2) both long and short, when immediately preceding *dh* and *gh*; in which state it has no corresponding sound in English. Long as adhradh, *worship*, teaghlach, *family*. Short, as lagh, *law*; cladh, *trench*. (3) short and obscure, like *e* in hinder, as—an, am, a', *the*; ma, *if*; na'm, na'n, *if that*; and the plural terminations -a, -an, as laghanna, *laws*: beanntan, *mountains*.

a', *gen. & dat. masc.*, and *nom. & dat. fem.*, of the *art*. The.

Used before the three labials B M P, and the two palatals C and G, when aspirated. A' mhàthair, *the mother*; a' choin, *of the dog*; a' phàisde, *of the child*; a' ghruagach, *the damsel*. Aspirated F is preceded by *an*, as—*an fhir*, of the man; *an fhreagairt*, the answer.

A, the sign of the Vocative case of substantives, as—A dhuine dhìomhain! *O vain man!*

a, *poss. pron.* His, her, its. After a, *his*, the substantive is always aspirated, but after a, *her*, it is plain.

A mhac, *his son*; a nighean, *her daughter*. *A*, his, is omitted and an apostrophe inserted in its place before a word commencing with a vowel or fh, and before a consonant when preceded by a prep, ending in a vowel; as—gu 'mhac, *to his son*; 'fhalt, *his hair*; 'aghaidh, his countenance. In the *fem*, an *h-* is interposed between *a*, her, and the noun, as—a h-each *her horse*; a h-eun, *her bird*. When the *fh* is followed by a consonant, the pronoun is retained in the *masc.*, as—a fhliuiche, *his wetness*. Cha b'urrainn iad a thogail no 'fhagail, *they could neither lift nor leave him* (lit.—his lifting or leaving); theab iad a mharbhadh, *they had almost killed him*, (lit.—his killing.) In *a nighean*, his daughter, *n* is aspirated in pronunciation, but the letter *h* is not written after *l, n, r*, in Scottish Gaelic. In some instances the difference between the plain and aspirated sound of these letters is only to be detected by a keen ear, while in others it is easily distinguishable.

a, *rel. pron., gen. & dat.* Who, which, whom, that, what.

Gach gaisgeach a b'aosda, dàn; *each hero that was aged and bold*; a' bhean a bha tinn, *the woman that was sick*; an cù a bha caillte, *the dog that was lost*; na daoine a chaidh seachad, *the men that went by*.

**Sometimes a sign of the *past tense*, 'Nuair a thubhairt e rium, *when he said to me*.

a, *prep.* 1 At, to, into. 2 About, in the act of.

á, *prep.* Out of.

á taigh na daorsa, *out of the house of bondage*; á tìr na h-Eiphit, *out of the land of Egypt*; á baile, *out of town, from home*.

a', *prep.* for ann, *in*. Ciod a chuir sin a' d' cheann? *what put that into your head?*

a, *particle* used in adverbs, phrases, or before numerals when not followed by nouns, as—a bhos, *on this side*; a dhà, *two*.

a', sign of the *pres, part.* (for ag.) Used before consonants, as—a' fàs, *growing*; a' dùnadh, *shutting*; a' dol, *going*.

a, sign of the *infin.* mood, as—a bhualadh, *to strike*; a cheangal an duine, *to bind the man*. [Always aspirates word following.]

†a,** Chariot, car, waggon. 2 Ascent, hill, promontory.

aaid,¶ *s.f.* Magpie, see pigheid.

†ab-,** negative particle.

†ab,** *s.m.* Water.

ab, -a, -achan, *s. m.* †Father, title of respect, 2 lord, abbot.

†ab, *past. def. v.* Is, for a b',—see *bu*.

ab ! *int.* Fie ! for shame !
†aba, *s.m.* Cause, matter, business.
aba, *s.m.* Abbot. An ni a ni an dara h-aba subhach, ni e dubhach an t-aba eile, *what makes one abbot glad makes the other abbot sad.* 2 *gen sing.* of ab.
abab! *int.* Fie ! Oh, for shame ! pshaw !
abab,* *s.m.* Filth, dirt.
ababach,* *a.* Filthy, dirty.
ababachd,* *s.f.* Filthiness, dirt.
ababardaich*, *s.f.* repetition of *abab.*
†abac,** -aic, see abhag.
†abach, *s.m.* Entrails, pluck. 2 Proclamation.
abachadh, -aidh, *s. m.* Ripening, state of ripening. 2 Progress toward maturity. Ag a—, *pr. part. v.* abaich
abachd, -an, *s. f.* Abbey, see abaid. 2 Priorship
abachd, *s. f. ind.* see abaichead.
†abachd, *s. f. ind.* Exploits. 2 Gain, lucre.
†abact, *s. f.* Taunting, ironical joking.
abadh, -aidh, -ean, *s. m.* Syllable, utterance. 2† Satirical poem.
abag,** -aig, *s.f.* Voice.
abaich, *a.* Ripe, mellow, mature. 2**Ready, prepared, expert.
abaich, *v.a. & n.* Ripen, mellow, maturate, become ripe. 2 Bring to maturity.
abaichead, -eid, *s. m.* Ripeness, maturity. 2 Pertness. Tha e dol an abaichead, *it is growing riper and riper.*
abaichear, *fut. pass.* of *v.* abaich. Shall or will be ripened.
abaicheas, *fut. sub. act. v.* abaich. Ma dh'abaicheas e, *if it shall ripen.*
abaid, -ean, *s.f.* (aba) Abbey. 2 Cowl or hood of a monk. A' triall chum na h-abaid, *strolling to the abbey.*
abaid,** *s.m.* Abbot. Lios an abaid, *the abbot's court.*
abaideachd, *s. f. ind.* Abbacy.
abaideal,* *s.f.* Colic.
abaidealach*, *a.* Griping.
abaidh*, *a.* (for abaich) Pert. Duine abaidh, *a pert person.*
†abaidh,** *s.f.* Bud, blossom.
†abail,** *s. f.* Death.
abailt, -e, -ean, *s.f.* Abbey. †2 Death.
abair, *v.a. & n. irr.* Say, utter, affirm, express.
Active Voice—
IND. *past* thubhairt mi &c., *I said,* Also dubhairt—*Stewart.*
,, *fut.*, their mi, &c., *I shall* or *will say,*
INTERR. *past* (an ? nach ? cha) dubhairt mi, &c.,
,, *fut.* (an ? nach ? cha'n) abair mi, &c.,
SUBJUNC. *past* (ged) theirinn, (though) *I would say* ; ged theireadh tu, &c. *though thou wouldst say* ; ged theireamaid, *though we would say* ; ged theireadh sibh, &c., *though you would say,*
,, *fut.* (ma) their mi, &c., (if) *I shall say,*
IMPER. Abaiream, *let me say,*
INFIN. A radh, *to say,*
PRES. PART. Ag radh, *saying,*
Passive Voice—
IND. *past* thuirteadh e, *it was said,*
,, *fut.* theirear e, *it shall be said,*
INTER. *past* (an ? nach ? cha) dubhairteadh
,, *fut.* (an ? nach ? cha'n) abairear,
SUBJ. *past* (ged) theirteadh,
,, *fut.* (ma) theirear.
☞Abair has another form of the Past Subj. used after interr. and neg. particles , as (ma) theirinn, *if I would say* ; but (nan) abarainn. The Passive has also a parallel impers. form —(ma) theirteadh, *if it would be said* ; but (nan) abairteadh e.

Na abair ach beagan, agus abair gu math e, *say but little and say it well.*
abaiream, 1 *per. sing. imp. act. of* abair.
abairear, *imp.*, & *fut. ind. pass. v.* abair. Sometimes contracted "abrar," as—Abrar e, *let it be said,* or *it will be said.*
abairinn, *irr. pt. subj. v* abair.
†abairt, *s.f.* Accoutrements, apparatus. 2 Custom, usage, habit.
abairt,* *s.f.* Babbling 2 Recrimination, scolding. 3 Politeness in idiom. 4 Education. 5 Speech, articulation.
abaist, -ean, *s.m.* Brat, impudent person.
abait, *s.f.* 1 see abaid. 2 speech.
†abalta,* *a.* Expert, proficient, masterly, able. 2 Strong, active, powerful.
†abaltachd, *s.f.* Ability, proficiency, dexterity. 2 Strength.
†abaltaiche,* *s.m.* Proficient, adept.
†abaoi, *s.f.* Descent, sun-setting.
†abar, -air, -ean, *s.m.* 1 Confluence, place where two or more streams meet. 2 Marsh, bog, fen, fenny ground. 3 see abairt.
abarach, *a.* (abair) Bold, courageous. 2 (abar) Fenny, boggy, marshy, of, or pertaining to a marsh.
abarachd, *s.f.* Marshiness, bogginess.
abarainn, see abairinn.
abardair, *s.m.* (abair) Dictionary.
abardairiche, *s.m.* Lexicographer.
abarrach,* *s.f.* Bold masculine female.
———* *a.* Indelicate, as a female. see [abartach.
abarrachd,* *s.f.* see abartachd.
abarsgaic,* -ean, see aparsaig.
abarta, for abartach. Tha e ro abarta, *he is too pert*—Isles.
abartach, *a.* (abair) Bold, daring, impudent, talkative.
abartachd, *s.f.* Mode of speech, idiom. 2 Loquacity. 3* Indelicacy, as of a female, impudence, turbulence.
abartair,* *s.m.* Babbler. 2**see abardair.
abartairiche, see abardairiche.
àbh, -a, -an, *s.m.* Hand-net, hose-net, sock-net, landing-net. 2 Skill, dexterity. 3** Instrument. †4 Water.
abh, *s.m.ind.* Barking of a dog.
abhac, -aic, -an, *s.m.* see abhag.
abhacan, see abhagan.
àbhacas, -ais, *s.m.* Diversion, sport, merriment, 2 Ridicule. 3** Boisterous day. Ball àbhacais, *a laughing-stock*, fear an àbhacais, *a merry fellow*, ri àbhacais ann an teaghlach a mhoirfeir, *making diversion in his lordship's family.*
†àbhach, -aiche, *a.* see àbhachdach.
àbhachd,* *s.f. ind.* Sport, diversion, joy, humour, hilarity. 2** Gibe, irony. 'N a aobhar spòrs agus àbhachd, *a cause of sport and diversion.*
àbhachdach,-aiche, *a.* Humorous, merry, joyful, joyous, jolly. 2** Corpulent. 3** Inclined to gibe, jesting or raillery. Gach creutair a' togail an cinn gu h-àbhachdach, *each creature lifting their heads joyfully.*
àbhachdaiche, *s.m.* Humorous person 2**Railer.
———, comp. of *a.* àbhachdach.
àbhachdail,** *a.* Joyful, humorous, jocose.
àbhachdas, -ais, see àbhacas.
àbhadh,** -aidh, *s.m.* see àbh. 2 Fold, hollow. 3 Instrument. 4 Flying camp. 5 Abode. 6 Lampoon.
àbhadh-ciùil*, *s.f.* Musical instrument.
abhag, -aig, -an, (abh) *s.f.* Terrier 2** Dwarf, spectre 3** in derision, petulant person. An abhag a bh'aig Fionn, *the terrier F. had.*
abhagach, -aiche, (abhag) *a.* Like a terrier, of, or relating to a terrier, 2 Petulant, snappish,

waspish, carping, yelping.
abhagail, *a.* see abhagach.
abhagan, n. pl. of abhag.
abhagas, -ais, -an, *s.f.* Flying rumour, surmise. Gheibh duine duais na h-abhagais, *a man will receive the reward of false suspicion.*
abhaic, gen.sing. of abhac.
†abhaiche, comp. of *a.* abhach.
abhaig, gen. sing. of abhag.
abhail, *s.m.* †Death. 2 gen. sing. of abhal.
abhaill, gen. sing. of abhall.
a bhàin, see a bhàn.
abhainn, *gen.s.* aibhne, *n.* & *gen. pl.* aibhnichean, *s.f.* River, stream. Bruach na h-aibhne, *the bank of the river*; far an taine an abhainn 's ann a's mó a fuaim, *where the river is shallowest it makes most noise.*
abhainneach, -eiche *a.* Fluvial, abounding in rivers, of, or pertaining to, a river.
àbhair, gen. sing. of àbhar.
àbhais, *s.f.* see àbhaist. 2† Bird.
àbhaiseach, see àbhaisteach.
àbhaiseachd, see àbhaisteachd.
àbhaist, *s.f.* Habit, usage, custom, manner, consuetude. A' leanachd na h-àbhaist a b' aoibhinn, *following the habit that once was pleasant*; cha b'e siod àbhaist Theadhaich, *that was not Tedaco's custom*; tha thus' an sin mar a b' àbhaist, *or* mar a b'abhaist dhuit, *you are there as usual.*
àbhaisteach, -tiche, *a.* Usual, habitual, customary, adhering to custom, according to custom.
àbhaisteachd, *s.f.* Customariness, frequency, habit.
Abhaisteir, see Abharsair.
abhaistiche, comp. of *a.* àbhaisteach.
abhal, -ail, abhlan, see ubhal.
abhall, -aill, *s.m.* Apple-tree. 2 Orchard.
abhallach, see ubhalach.
abhall-fiadhaich, see ubhal-fiadhaich.
abhall-ghort, see ubhal-ghort.
abhall-ghortach, see ubhal-ghortach.
a bhàn, *adv.* Down, downwards.
àbhar, -air, -an, see aobhar.
àbharach, -aiche, see aobharach.
†abharach,** -aich, *s.m.* Youth under age, who acts as a man.
àbharachd, *s.f. ind.* see aobharachd.
abharr,* *s.f.* Silly jest or joke.
a bhàrr, *prep,* Above. 2 Down, down from.
abharrach,* *a.* Given to silly jests or jesting.
a bharrachd, *prep.* Besides, over and above. A bharrachd air a' cheud ghorta, *besides the first famine.*
Abharsair, -ean, *s.m.* The Devil, Satan.
abharta, abhartach, abhartadh, } A.C. *s.* Feast, festival, rich entertainment.
abhastrach, -aich, *s.m.* Barking of a dog.
abhcaid, -ean, *s.f.* (àbhachd) Jest, anything ludicrous. 2 Pleasantry.
abhcaideach, -eiche, *a.* Humorous, sportive, to make merry.
abhcaideachd, *s.f. ind.* Pleasantry, gaiety, merriment, cheerfulness.
†àbh-ciùil, see àbhadh-ciùil.
a bheil ? (for am bheil ?) *v. irr.* see bi.
†abh-labhrach, -aiche, Mute, dumb, speechless, silent.
abhlach, see ablach.
abhlain, gen. sing. and n. pl. of abhlan.
abhlan, -ain, -an, *s m.* Wafer, round cake. 2** see annlan. 3** *n.pl.* of abhal & abhall. Abhlan coisrigte, *consecrated wafers.*
abhlanach,** *a.* Wafery, like a wafer.
ab hlar, air,-airean, see amhlair.
abh-mh àthair -ar, *s.f.* Mother abbess.

abh a, (for aibhne) gen. & dat. sing. of abhainn.
abhnag, -aig, *s.f.* A little river.
a bhobuig ! see boban.
a bhos, *adv.* On this side, here. An taobh a bhos, *on this side*; thall 's a bhos, *hither and thither.*
†abhra,** *a.* Dark.
abhra, -an, abhrad, -aid, -aidean, abhradh, -aidh, -aidhean } see fabhra.
abhrais, gen. sing. of abhras.
abhran, -ain, see òran. 2 n. pl. of abhra.
abhras, -ais, *s.m.* **Yarn. 2 Spinning. 3 Flax, wool. 4 Worsted, any materials of woollen manufacture. 5 Manual produce. 6**Ready answer. Ag abhras, *spinning*; clòimh abhrais, *oiled wool, wool prepared for spinning.* AC
abhrasach, -aiche, *a.* Of, or belonging to yarn, or spinning of wool. 2 Well supplied with materials of woollen manufacture. 3 Engaged in house or home thrift.
abhrasaiche, -ean, *s.m.* Carder of wool or flax.
†abhron, *s.m.* Cauldron.
abhsadh, -aidh, -ean, *s.m.* Down-haul or slackening of a sail.
†abhsan,** -ain, *s.m.* Hollow. 2 Furrow.
abhsporag, -aig, -an, *s.f.* Paunch. 2 Tripe. 3 Stomach of a cow.
abhuinn, *s.f.* see abhainn.
abhuinneach, *a.* see abhainneach.
àbhuist, *s.f.* see àbhaist.
abhull,‡‡ *s.m.* see abhall. "Bu tu m'abhull a's m'ùbhlan"—Filidh nam beann, p. 75.
abhus, -uis, -an, *s.m.* see amhas.
†abile, *s.m.* Wooded hill.
ablach, -aich, *pl.* -aich, & -aichean, *s.m.* Mangled carcase. 2 Carrion. 3 Remains of a creature destroyed by wild beasts. 4 Brat, term of personal contempt. Ablach gun deo, *a breathless carcase.*
ablaich, *gen. and voc. sing.*, and *nom. pl.* of ablach. Ablaich tha thu ann ! *brat that you are!*
———,* *v.a.* Mangle, spoil.
ablaoch, -aoich, *s.m.* (ab *neg.*+laoch) Brat, pithless person. see ablach 4.
ablaoich. *gen. and voc. sing.*, and *nom. pl.* of ablaoch.
†abrad, *a.* Exalted. 2 Far removed.
abram, *contr.* of abaiream.
abran, -ain, -an, *s.m.* (aparan) Oar-patch or sheath on a boat's gunwale, to prevent the oars wearing it down 2**see abhran.
†abrann,** *s.m.* Bad news.
† ———,** *a.* Lustful, lecherous, lascivious.
Abraon, -aoin, *s.m.* April.
abrar, *fut. ind. pass.* of *v.* abair.
absaloid,** *s.f.* Absolution.
abstoil, see abstol.
abstol, -oil, [& -olan] *s.m.* Apostle. Litir an abstoil, *the letter of the apostle;* litrichean nan abstol, *the letters of the apostles.*
abstolach, -aiche, *a.* Apostolical, of, or belonging to an apostle.
abstolachd, *s.f. ind.* Apostleship. Gràs agus a., *grace and apostleship.*
abù ! *int.* An ancient war-cry of the Gaidheal.
abuchadh, -aidh, *s.m.* abuich, *a.* and *v.* abuicheachd, *s.* abuichead, *s.* abuichear, *v.* abuicheas, *v.* abuidh,* *a.* } see aba———
abuidheachd,* *s.f. ind.* see abaichead.
†abuirt, *s.f.* Speech, conversation.
†abulta, *a.* see abalta.
†abultachd, *s.f. ind.* see abaltachd.

ac, -a, -an & -annan, *s.f.* see achd.

†ac, -a, *s.m.* Denial, refusal. 2 Son. 3 Speech, tongue.

aca, *or* ac', *prep. pron.* (aig+iad) Of them, on their side, with them, at them, on them, in their possession, their. Tha móran ac' ag radh, *many of them say;* tha e aca 'na sheirbhiseach, *he is with them as a servant;* aca siod, *in the possession of those people;* an taigh aca, *their house,* that is, an taigh a th'aca, lit. *the house which is to them;* chaidh ac' air a cheannsachadh, *they conquered him;* théid ac' orm, *they shall conquer,* or *get the better of me.*

†acadamh, -aimh, *s.m.* Academy.

acaid, -e, -ean, *s.f.* Pain, hurt, a transient lancinating pain, stitch. Is trom an acaid a tha 'm lot, *intense is the pain that is in my wound.*

acaideach, -diche, *a.* Uneasy. 2 Painful. 3 Sickly. 4 Groaning.

†acaideadh, -didh, *s.m.* Inhabitant, tenant.

acaidiche, *comp.* of *a.* acaideach.

acain, -e, -in, *s.f.* Moan, sob, sigh. 2 Complaint. 3 Wailing, weeping, murmur. 4** for acfhuinn. Gun och gun acain, *without alas or moan ;* crathaidh e a cheann 's e ag acain, *he shall shake his head moaning,*—lit. *and he moaning.*

acain, *pr. part.* acain, *v.n.* Sigh, moan.

acaineach, -niche, *a.* Plaintive. 2 Distressful. 3 Sickly. 4 Sobbing. 5 Causing sorrow or wailing. Guth *a.*, *a sobbing voice.*

acainear, -ir, *s.m.* (acain+fear) Complainer. 2 Mourner, sobber, wailer. 3**One who ails.

acainich,* *s.f.* Grief. 2 Sobbing, plaintive moaning. Iadsan a b'aille m'acainich, *they who would desire to partake of my grief.*

acainiche, *comp.* of acaineach.

————,** *s.m* Wailer, mourner, sobber, weeper, complainer.

acair, acrach, acraichean, *s.f.* Anchor. 2 A.C. Stone, originally one used as an anchor. 3 Acre of land. 4(AG) Small stack of corn on field. 5(AG) Hand-screw. Acair an anama, *the anchor of the soul;* ceithir acraichean, *four anchors.*

acair-pholl, -phuill, *s.m.* Anchorage, road for ships. 2 Harbour.

acairseid, -ean, *s.f.* Port, harbour, haven. 2 Anchorage.

†acais,** *s.f.* Poison.

†acalla,** *s.* Conversation. see agalladh.

acan, *s.* & *v.* see acain.

acanaich, see acainich

†acar,** *a.* Sharp, sour, bitter.

acarach, -aiche, *a.* Gentle, mild. 2 Obliging. 3 Moderate. 4 Kind, merciful. 5**Respectful.

acarachd, *s.f. ind.* Gentleness, mildness. 2 Moderation. 3 Kindness, mercifulness. 4 Respectfulness. Gun acarachd, *without mercy;* ghlac e sinn le h-acarachd, *he grasped us (our hands) with kindness.*

†acaradh, -aidh, *s.m.* see ocar.

acaraiche, *comp.* of *a.* acarach.

†acaran, -ain. *s.m* Lumber.

acarra,* *a.* see acarach. 2 (JM) *W. Isles*—Handy, useful. Seo agad spaid cho acarra 's a laimhsich mi riamh, *here's as handy a spade as I ever used.*

acarrachd,* see acarachd.

acarsaid,* see acairseid.

acartha,‡ *s.* Profit.

————,** *a.* see acarach.

aca-sa, Emphatic form of *prep. pron.* aca.

aca-san, ,, ,, ,, ,,

acasdair, see acastair.

acastair, -ean, *s.f.* Axle-tree.

†acastaran, -ain, *pl.* -ain. [& -ana], see acastair.

acduinn, see acfhuinn

acduinneach, ,, acfhuinneach.

acduinniche, ,, acfhuinniche.

acfhuinn, -e, -ean, *s.f.* Apparatus, implements, utensils, tackle, tools, appendages of any kind. 2 Salve, ointment. 3 Harness, equipage. 4 Rigging. Acfhuinn an t-saoir, *the carpenter's tools;* *a.* airson na coise, *a salve for the (sore) foot;* *a.* gunna, *the lock of a gun;* *a.* thogallach *distilling implements;* *a.* an eich, *the horse's harness;* *a.* na slaite, *the tackling of the fishing rod;* *a.* na luinge, *the rigging of the ship;* *a.* sgriobhaidh, *writing utensils;* *a.* is inneil ciùil, *instruments of music;* *a.* shaoirsneachd, *joiner's* or *carpenter's tools;* *a.* na cartach, *cart harness;* *a.* threabhaidh, *ploughing harness* *a.* chliathaidh, *harrowing harness.*

PARTS OF A HORSE'S HARNESS—(see illustration.

1 Sréinean dùbailt, *double reins.* "Srian" in W. Isles generally means the head gear and the lines together; "claigionn" the part of the reins about the head.—J.M.

2 Strap *no* Iall na h-iasgaid, *haunch-strap.*

3 Bràid,‡ *collar.* Bràighde,—*W. Isles*, J.M.

4 Bràid chluaisean, *hames.* Siollachan, —*W. Isles*, J.M.

5 Srathair, *saddle.*

A riding-saddle is Diollaid.

6 Briogais, *breeching.*

6A ,, *breech-chains.*—J.M. (not seen in illust.)

7 Dromanach, *back-chain,* in *groove* of saddle.

8 Cromagan na briogais, *breeching-hooks.*

9 Giort na cartach, *cart belly-band.*

10 Guailleachain, *shoulder-slings, draught-chains, shoulder-chains.* An tarruinn, —*W. Isles*, J.M.

11 Sparrag. aill-bheul, cabstar, ***bit.* Sparrag, *bridle-bit.*—D.M. Mirionnach Part of *bit* in horse's mouth.—*W. Isles*, J.M.

12 Gogalaich, *blinders.*

13 Arannach sréine, *bridle-rein.*

14 Iall na leasraidh, *loin-strap.*

15 Bann-droma, *back-band.* Draim (druimeal—*Tiree*)—J.M.

16 Sìneachain-tarruing, *trace-chains.* An tarruinn—*W. Isles*, J.M.

17 Cromag-tharruing, *draught-hook.*

18 Greallag, *stretcher,*—*W. Isles*, J.M.

19 Giort, *belly-band.* (not seen in illust. of shaft-horse.) Tarrach (from "tarr" *belly*)—*W. Isles*, J.M.

20 Bonn dronnain, *rump-band.*

21 Sròinein, *Strap across the nose.*—*W. Isles.*

22 Smeachan, *Strap below the jaws*—*W. Isles*, J.M.

23 Cruipean, eislean, braman, ***crupper.* (Strap through which the tail passes, not in illust.) Gurpan, bod-chrann—D.M.

24 Bann-bhràid, Truis-bhràid, } ***Band* (strap joining the hames.)

PLOUGHING HARNESS.—*W Isles*, J.M.

Drumannach, *back-band,* used to keep the traces (sintean) in position. The other parts are Srian, braighde, and siollachan, as above.

RIGGING OF A SHIP, see long.

PARTS OF A BOAT, see bàta.

TOOLS or IMPLEMENTS used in trades, see under respective trades.

acfhuinneach, -niche, *a.* Equipped. 2 harnessed. 3 Expert. 4 Potent. 5**Of, or per-

taining to tools, tackling, harness, or furniture.
acfhuinnean, *n. pl.* of acfhuinn.
acfhuinniche, *comp.* of *a.* acfhuinneach.
acfuinn, see acfhuinn.
acfuinneach, see acfhuinneach.
ach ! *int.* Ah ! ah ! expression of disgust.
ach, *conj.* But, except, besides. Ach mise, *but me ;* cha d'rinn neach ach thus' e, *none but you did it;* ach co siod air a' charraig mar cheo *but who is yonder on the hill like mist ?* dh' fhalbh iad uile ach a h-aon, *they all departed but one;* ach beag, *almost, nearly;* gabhaidh mi faclair mur bi an clòdh-bhualadh ach air an dara taobh a mhàin, *I will take a Dictionary if the printing be on one side (of the paper) only.* The literal Eng. trans. of this sentence—" if the printing be not but on one side" &c., conveys an exactly opposite meaning. Bheirinn dhuit e ach gu bheil thu gun chiall, *I would give it to you were it not that you are without understanding ;* b'e mo chomhairle dha a' cheud obair a ghabhail ach i a bhith onorach, *I would advise him to take the first work if honest.* See also "ach am."
†ach, -a, *s.f.* Skirmish.
†——, -a, -an, *s.m.* Mound, bank.
——, see achadh.
achadh, -aidh, *pl.* -aidhean, -aidhnean, & achanna, *s.m.* Field, plain, meadow. Cornfield newly cut or ready for reaping. Bha sinn a' ceangal sguab 's an achadh, *we were binding sheaves in the field;* an t-achadh a cheannaich Abraham, *the field that A. bought.*
achaidh, *gen. sing.* of achadh.
†——, -ean, *s.f.* Given in some dictionaries with the meaning "home" as the derivation of "dachaidh," which should be do+thaighf.
achain, -e, -ean, *s.f.* *Prov.* for athchuinge.
achaineach, see athchuingeach.
achainiche, see athchuingiche.
ach am, ach an, *adv.* Till. Fuirich thus' an sin ach gus an téid mise far a bheil thu, 's bheir mise ort e ! *wait you but till I come where you are, and I'll give it to you !*
†achamair, -e, *a.* Short, abridged. 2 Timely, soon.
†achamaireachd, *s.f. ind.* Abridging, abridgment.
achanaich, -e, -ean, *s.f.* see athchuinge.
————,* *v.n.* see athchuingich.
a chaoidh, *adv.* For ever. Cha till e a chaoidh, *he shall never return;* a seo suas a chaoidh, *henceforth and for ever.*
†achar, -air, *s.m.* Distance.
†acharadh, -aidh, -aidhean, *s.m.* Sprite. 2 Dwarf, diminutive person.
achasan, -ain, -an, see achmhasan.
achasanaich, see achmhasanaich.
ach beag, *adv.* Almost, well nigh.
achd, *pl.* -anna, *s.f.* Act, statute, decree. 2 Deed. 3 Case. 4 Account. 5 State, condition. 6 manner, way. 7* Objection. Is mór na h-achdanna a th'agad, *you have many objections;* air aon achd, *on any account;* air na h-uile achd, *at all events;* Achd Pàrlamaid, *an Act of Parliament;* air an achd seo, *in this way.*
——,* *v.a.* see achdaich.
†——, *s.f.* Body. 2 Peril. 3 Nail. 4 Claw.
achdaich, *v.a.* Enact, decree.
————, *s.* Law, established rule.
achdaidh,(AG) *adv.* Certainly. Gu h-achdaidh, *according to rule.*
achdair, -drach, -draichean, *s.f.* see acair.
achdair-pholl, see acair-pholl.
achdairseid, see acairseid.
achdarra, *a.* Methodical. 2 Expert, skilful.

achdartha, see achdarra.
†achdra,** *s.f.* Naval expedition.
†achdran, -ain, *s.m.* Foreigner, adventurer.
†achdrannach, *a.* Foreign, adventurous.
† ———, *s.m.* see achdran.
achduinn, see acfhuinn.
achduinneach, see acfhuinneach.
a cheana, *adv.* Already.
a chéile, Each other.
a chianamh, *adv.* A little while ago.—*Forbes' G.*
†achiar, *a.* Sharp, sour, bitter.
a chionn, *adv.* Because, as.
achladh, -aidh, *s.m.* Fishery, art of fishing.
achlaid, -e, -ean, *s.f.* Chase, pursuit.
†achlaidh, *a.* Smooth, fine, soft.
achlais, -e, -ean, *s.f.* Arm-pit, "oxter," 2 **Arm. 3 Bosom, breast. Fo 'achlais, *under his arm;* ràimh 'g an sniomh ann an achlais nan àrd-thonn, *oars twisting in the bosom of lofty waves;* lag na h-achlaise, *the arm-pit*
achlais-dheireadh, -aise-deiridh, -ean-deiridh, *s.f.* Stern-collar (of a boat.)
achlaise, *gen. sing.* of achlais.
achlaisean, *s.f. pl.* Knees to rowers' benches (in a boat.)
achlaisich, *v.a.* Put under the arm. 2 Cherish.
achlais-thoiseach, -aise-toisich, -ean-toisich, *s.f.* Bow-collar of a boat.
achlan, -ain, *s.m.* Lamentation.
achlas,** -ais, *s.f.* Bundle, little truss. 2 see achlais.
achlasan, -ain, *s.m.* Armful. 2 Anything carried under the arm. 3 Parcel.
achlasan Chaluim Chille§, *. f.* (*lit.* armpit package of St Columba.) Perforated St. John's wort, see eala bhuidhe.
a chlisge, *adv.* Soon, in a short time, instantly.
†achmhaing, *a.* Powerful.
achmhaingidh, *a.* see acfhuinneach.
achmhas, *v.a.* see achmhasanaich.
achmhasaich, ,, ,,
achmhasain, *gen. sing. & nom. pl.* of achmhasan.
achmhasan, -ain, *s. m.* Reproof, reprimand, rebuke, scold. 2 Reproach. Thug 'athair achmhasan da, *his father rebuked him;* achmhasain teagaisg, *the reproofs of instruction;* fuath no eud no achmhasan, *nor hate nor jealousy nor reproach.*
achmhasanach, -aiche, *a.* Causing a rebuke, liable to rebuke, of, or pertaining to rebuke, reprehensible.
achmhasanaich, *v.a.* Rebuke, reprove, chide, censure, reprehend.
achmhasanaiche, *s. m.* One who rebukes or censures, animadverter.
———, *comp.* of *a.* achmhasanach.
acnamhach,** -aich, *s.m.* Food of a labourer.
a chòir, *prep.* Near to.
†achran, -ain, *s.m.* Intricacy, entanglement, perplexity.
achrannach, -aiche, *a.* Intricate, entangled. 2 what retards progress, or confounds.
achrannaich, *v.a.* Entangle.
†achsal, *s.m.* Angel.
†acht, see ach, *conj.*, and achd. *s.f.*
†achta, *s.* see achd.
†achtain, *v.* see achdaich.
achuinge, see athchuinge.
achuingeach, see athchuingeach.
a chum, *prep.* For, in order that, for the purpose of. 2 Therefore. 3 To, towards.
†acmhaing see acfhuinn.
†acmhaingeach, see acfhuinneach.
†acmhuing, *s.f.* Address, ability, power, strength, influence.
†———, *v.a.* Subdue, vanquish, conquer, overcome.
†acobhar, *s.m.* Avarice, covetousness.
†acobhrach, *a.* Inordinately desirous, covetous.
†acomail, *v. a.* Heap together, congregate, increase.—*s.f.* Assembly, meeting, gathering.
†acon, -oin, -ean, *s.m.* Refusal, negation, denial.
†acor, -oir, *s.m.* see ocar.
†acorach, see acrach.
†acra, see acair.
acrach, -aiche, *a.* Hungry.
———,** -aich, *s.m.* Hungry person. Biadh do'n acrach, *food to the hungry.*
acraich, *v.a.* Anchor, moor.
acraiche, *comp.* of *a.* acrach.
acraichean, *n.pl.* of acair.
acraichte, *pt. part.* of acraich.
acrais, *gen. sing.* of acras.
†acrann, -ainn, *s.m.* see achran.
†acrannach, *a.* see achrannach.
acras, -ais, *s.m.* Hunger. 2 Famine. Tha acras orm, *I am hungry;* tha mi air acras, *I am hungry;* am bheil acras ort? (oirre, air, oirbh, orra) *art thou (is she, he, are you, they) hungry?* mar mhial-choin air acras, *like hungry hounds.*
acrasach, -aiche, *a.* Hungry.
acsa, acsan, see aca-san.
acsal,** -ail, *s.m.* Angel.
———** -aile, *a.* Generous, noble.
†acuil, *s.f.* Eagle.
acuinn, see acfhuinn.
acuinneach, see acfhuinneach.
acus, see agus.
†ad, *pers. pron. 2nd. pers. sing.* Thou. 2 *s. m.* Water. 3 Old sign of past ind. act. of verbs, now *do.* Ad chualaim, *I have heard;* ad chualamar, *we have heard.*
a' d', (ann ad *for* ann do) Na bi a' d' uamhas dhomh, *be not (as) a terror to me.*
ad, *poss. pron.* Thy, thine. Ann ad ghialaibh, *in thy jaws;* 'n ad chluais, *in thine ear.* [Aspirates noun following.]
àd, *Prov.* for iad. [Emphatic, àdsan.]
ad, aide, *pl.* adan, adachan, *s.f.* Hat. Ad a' bhile òir, *the gold-rimmed hat;* bile na h-aide, *the rim of the hat.*
ad-,‡ *insep. prefix,* in force and origin same as Latin *ad.* It is to be separated, though with difficulty, from the *ad-* arising from *aith-* or *ath-.*
†ada,** adai, *s.f.* Victory.
adad! *int.* Hah! ahah! atat!
adag, -aig, *s.f.* Shock of corn, consisting of 12 sheaves, "stook." 2 Haddock (fish.) An dà chuid na h-adagan agus an t-arbhar, *both the shocks and the standing corn;* is cho math sguab ri adaig deth, *a sheaf is as good as a shock of it*—i.e. *I have had enough of it.*
adagach, *a.* Abounding in shocks of corn, of, or pertaining to shocks of corn.
adagachadh, -aidh, *s.m.* Employment of making shocks of corn, "stooking." ag a—, *pr. part.* of *v.* adagaich. Gathering corn into shocks.
adagaich, *v.a.* Gather corn into shocks.
adagaichte, *pt. part.* Gathered into shocks.
adagan, -ain, *s.m.* Little hat or cap. 2 *n.pl.* of adag.
adamant, -aint, *s.* Adamant.
†adamhair, *s.f.* Play, sport, diversion. 2 *v.* Play, sport, divert.
†adamhradh, -aidh, *s.m.* Admiration, wonder.
†adbheart, for a thubhairt.
†adchuas, adchualas, *pt. pass.* of cluinn. Was heard.
†adh, adha, *s.m.* Law.
àdh, àdha, see àgh.
adh-‡, see ad-‡.
adh, *s.f.* Heifer. 2 Hind.
àdha, *pl.* àinean, *s.m.* The liver. àinean nam piocach, *livers of the coal fish.*

àdhach. see àghach.
adhach,**] a. Bashful.
——d,** s.f. Bashfulness.
àdhachd, see àgh.
àdha-geir, -e, s.f. The fat of liver. 2 Fish- or train-oil.
adhail, gen.sing. of adhal.
†adhailg, s.f. Desire. 2 Will, inclination.
adhaill,** s.f. Precipice.
a dh'aindeòin, adv. In spite of. A dh'aindeòin co theireadh e! *in spite of all opposition*—motto of MacDonald of Clanranald; a dheòin no a dh'aindeòin, *with or without one's consent*.
adhainn, see aghann.
†adhair, gen. sing. of adhradh (aoradh.) Bile magh adhair, *a tree in the plain of adoration*.
adhair,** s.f. Fire.
adhairc, gen. sing. of adharc.
adhairceach, -eiche, a. Horned. 2 having large horns. Bò adhairceach, *a horned cow*.
adhaircean, n.pl. of adharc.
————, see adharcan.
adhairt, see aghairt. 2 gen.sing. of adhart.
adhais, see athais.
adhaiseach, see athaiseach.
adhaiseachd, see athaiseachd.
adhal, -ail, -ean, s.m. Flesh-hook.
adhalach, a. Like a flesh-hook, of, or pertaining to a flesh-hook.
†adhall, a. Dull, deaf, stupid, senseless.
†——**, -aill, s.m. Sin, corruption.
†adhallach, -aiche, a. Sinful, corrupt, perverse.
†adhalrach, s.m. Nourisher.
adhaltan, -ain, s.m. Simpleton, dull stupid fellow.
adhaltrach, -aiche, a. Adulterous, guilty of adultery.
adhaltrachd, s.f. Adultery.
adhaltraiche, s.m. Adulterer.
adhaltranach, -aiche, a. Adulterous. Urra a., leanabh a., *an adulterous child*, ginealach a., *an adulterous generation*.
————, -aich, s.m. Adulterer.
adhaltranachd, s.f. Adultery.
adhaltranaich, gen.sing. of adhaltranach.
————ean, n.pl. of ,,
adhaltranais, gen.sing. of adhaltranas. Fear adhaltranais, *an adulterer*.
adhaltranas, -ais, s.m. Adultery, cuckoldom. A' deanamh adhaltranais, *committing a.*; làn de dh'adhaltranas, *full of adultery*.
adhaltras, -ais, s.m. Adultery. Urra adhaltrais, *an adulterous child*.
adhaltrasach, see adhaltranach.
adhaltrasachd, see adhaltranachd.
adhaltrus, see adhaltranas.
————ach, see adhaltranach.
————achd, see adhaltranachd.
†adhamhra, a. Glorious, noble, illustrious, excellent.
†adhamhrach, -aiche, a. Blessed, happy.
adhan,* -ain, s.m. see aghan.
adhann, -ainn & aidhne, s.f. see aghann.
†——, -ainne, s.f. Colt's foot (plant.) for athan—see cluas liath.
†adhannadh, s.f. Kindling. inflaming.
†adhannta, a. Kindled, inflamed. 2 Exasperated
†adhanntach, -aiche, a. Bashful, modest.
†adhanntachd, s.f. Blush, bashfulness.
a dh'aon obair, adv. Purposely.
adhar, -air, s.m. see athar 1.
†——, gen. aidhre, s.m. Snow, 2 Frost.
adharach, -aiche, see atharail.
adharachd, see atharachd.
adharadh, see aoradh.
adharag, -aig, -an, see atharag.
adharail, see atharail.
adharc, -airc, -ean, s.f. Horn, sounding horn.
adharcach. a. Horned. 2 Horny. 3 Attired, *in heraldry*.
adharcag, -aig, s.f. Little horn. 2 (AG) Lapwing.—*Reay country*.
adharcail, a. Horny, full of horns.
adharcan, -ain, s.m. Lapwing. see a.-luachrach
adharc an diabhoil,§ s.f. Bird's foot trefoil. see barra-mhislean.

Adharcan-luachrach.

adharcan-luachrach, -ain-aich, s.m. Lapwing or peewit.—*vanellus cristatus*.
adharc-fhaghaid, -airc, -ean, s.f. Bugle-horn.
adharc-fhùdair, -airc, -ean, s.f. Powder-horn.
adhar-mheidh, s.f. see athar-m—.
adhar-sheòladair, -air, -ean, s.f. see athar-s—.
adhart, -airt, s.m. Pillow, bolster. 2 Head of a bed. 3**Linen. 4**Bed-linen.
——, -airt, s. m. Progress, forwardness. 2 Front, van, advance. **Seldom used except in connection with prep. air, as,—thig air t' adhart, *come forward;* tha i 'teachd air a h-adhart, *she is very forward, she is coming on*.
adhartach, -aiche, a. Forward, progressive. 2 Diligent, assiduous, having a wish or tendency to be forwards or onwards. 3**Like linen, of, or belonging to linen.
adhartachd. s.f. Advancement.
adhartaich, v.a. Bolster. 2 Forward.
adhartan, -ain, s. m. dim. of adhart. Little bolster or pillow. 2**n.pl. of adhart, Linens, bed-linens.
†adhartar, -air, s.m. Dream. 2 Dreamer.
†adhartha, a. Aërial.
adhar-thomhas, -ais, -sean, s.m. see athar-t—.
†adhas, -ais, s. m. Prosperity, success, good fortune.
†——,** a. Good, proper.
adhastar, -air, -ean, s.m. see aghastar.
†adhbha, gen. aidhbh, & aidhbhe, s.f see abhadh. 2 see adhbhadh.
†adhbhachtach, -aiche, a. Gross, fat.
†adhbhadh, -aidh, -a, s.m. Fortress, garrison. 2 Palace. 3 Habitation, house.
†adhbhagan,** -ain, dim. of abhadh.
àdhbhal, -aile, a. Vast, huge. 2 Terrible, awful, wonderful, fearful.
†adhbhal-thròcaireach, a. Abounding in mercy.
†adhbhan-trireach, s'm. Kind of music in three parts, or sung by three voices.
†adhbhan-triùireach, see a—trireach.
adhbhar, -air, see aobhar.
————ach, see aobharach.
————achd, see aobharachd.
†adhbharas, -ais, see abharas.
†adhbharrach, see aobharrach.
†adhbharsach, s.m. Comber or carder of wool. 2 Dresser of flax.
adhbhas,** -ais, s.m. Garrison.
†adhbhuidh,** s.f. Joy, merriment.
adhbronn,' see aobrann.
a dh'easbhuidh, prep. Without, in want of.
a dheòin, adv. Willingly.
a dh'fhios, prep. To the knowledge of. 2MMI Towards. 3CR In case. Thoir leat e (a) dh' fhios am bi feum air, *take it in case there be need of it*.
†adhfhlath, -aith, s.m. Lawful sovereign.

†adh-fhuar, -uaire, *a.* Excessively cold.
†adh-fhuathmhaireachd, *s. f.* Abomination, hatred, detestation.
†adh-fhuathmhar, *a.* Frightful, terrible, dreadful, dismal, hideous, horrible.
a dh'ionnsuidh, *prep.* Towards, unto, to.
a dhìth, *adv.* Wanting, without. Chaidh e a dhìth, *he went to nothingness.*
adhlac, -aic, *s.f.* Burial, interment, funeral. àit' adhlaic, *a burying-place.*
adhlacadh, -aidh, *s.m.* Burial, ceremony of interring. àit' adhlacaidh, *a burying-place.* ag a—, *pr.part.* of *v.* adhlaic. Burying, interring.
adhlacair, -ean, *s. m.* Burier, undertaker. 2 Grave-digger.
adhlacanach, see adhlacair.
adhlaic, *v.a.* Bury, inter. M'anam adhlacadh an sgleò, *to bury my spirit in the mist.*
†——,** *s.f.* Longing desire for what is good,
adhlaicear,** *fut.pass.* of *v.* adhlaic.
adhlaichte, *a.* & *pt.part.* Buried, interred.
†adhlan,** -ain, *s.m.* Hero, champion.
†adhloighe, *s.f.* (adhall) Dullness, heaviness.
†adhm, *s.m.* Knowledge, intelligence. 2 Exercise, continual practice.
†adhma. *a.* see teòma.
†adhmad, -aid, *s.f.* see maide.
†adhmall, *a.* Unsteady, weak, debilitated, sickly, feeble.
àdhmhoire, *comp.* of *a.* àghmhor.
adhmhol, see àrd-mhol.
adhmholadh, see àrd-mholadh.
adhmholta, see àrd-mholta.
àdhmhor, -oire, *a.* see àghmhor.
àdhmhorachd, see àghmhorachd.
adhna, aidhne, *s.m.* Advocate.
†adhnac, *s.m.*, †adhnacal, *s.m.*, †adhnach, *s.m.* — see adhlac.
†adhnadh, -aidh, *s.m.* Advocate. 2 Encouraging. 3 Recruiting. 4 Kindling of fire.
†adhnair, *s.f.* Wickedness, baseness, depravity, villany.
†adhnàire, *s. f.* (ad, *insep. intens. prefix,* + nàire) Shame, disgrace, ignominy, reproach. 2 Blushing face.
adhnàireach, -eiche, *a.* Modest, shamefaced, bashful.
adhnaireachd, *s.f.* (adhna) Pleading, defence. 2 Discussion.
adhnàrach, -aiche, *a.* (adh + nàrach) Causing shame.
adh'or, see àghmhor.
adhrach, adhrachail — see aoradh.
adhradair, *s. m.* (adhradh + fear) see aoradair.
adhradh, -aidh, *s.m.* see aoradh.
†adhram, *v. pres. ind.* I venerate, worship.
†adhuatharra, *a.* Abominable.
†————chd, *s. f.* Abomination, horror. abominableness.
†adhudh, (teine Chriosda) *s.m.* Circle-fire.
†adhuigh, *s.f.* Night.
†adhmhall, -aille, *a.* see adhmall.
ad-olaiun, *s.f.* Felt.
†adrai, †adraigh, — *v.n.* He arose.
†adrime, *a.* Aforesaid. as I have said.
†aduadh, -aidh, *s.m.* Horror, detestation.
†aduan, -ain, *s.m.* Stranger.
†aduarra, *a.* Horrible. detestable.
†aduath, *s.m.* (àdh + fuath) Horror.
adubhairt, see thubhairt.
†adubhram, -air, -amar, -adar, *v.* I, thou, we, they said.
ae, *n.pl.* àinean, *s.m.* The liver. see adha.

†ae, *a.* see aon.
†aedach. see aodach.
†aedhar, see athar 1.
aeir, *gen.sing.* of aer.
†aen, see aon.
†aenachd. see aonachd.
†aenosd, *s.f.* Church.
†aenta, *s. f.* Unity, harmony of sentiment brotherly harmony.
†aer, see athar 1.
†aerdha, *a.* Airy.
†aerdhaite, *a.* Sky-coloured.
†aes, see aos, aois.
afraighe, *s. f.* Rising or preparing for battle.
ag, *v.a.* Hesitate, refuse, doubt, contradict, scruple.
ag, aig, *s.m.* Doubt, hesitation, contradiction, scruple. 2**Hesitation or lisp in speech.
ag. *prep.*, (aig) sign of *pr.part.* as— ag èirigh, *rising;* ag iasgachd, *fishing.* [Used before words beginning with a vowel, also *ràdh,* and sometimes before other words beginning with a consonant.]
ag, *dim.termination, fem.,* as— nighean, *a girl;* nighneag (or nionag) a little girl.
†aga, *s f.* Bottom of any depth.
agach, *a.* Inclined to doubt or refuse, scrupulous, sceptical. 2**Stammering, lisping.
agad, *prep. pron.* (aig + tu) At thee, on thee, with thee, in thy possession. *Agad* is also used in the sense of a possessive pronoun, as an taigh agad, *thy house;* a' bhean agad, *thy wife.* **This use of *agad* is not often met with in our classical writers, but in common language it is very frequent. Tha *is,* or *are,* is understood, as— a' bhean (a th')agad, *your wife.* Fan mar a th'agad, *stay as you are.* [Emphatic form—agad-sa, agad-fhéin.]
agadh, -aidh, *s.m.* Doubt, hesitation. 2 Contradiction. 3‡ Hesitancy in speech.
àgadh, -aidh, *s.m.* Ox.
agad-sa, emphatic form of agad.
†agag,** -aig, *s.f.* Habitation, settlement.
agaibh, *prep. pron.* (aig + sibh) At you, on you, with you, in your possession. 2**Of you, from among you. Co agaibh do'n iarrar i? *whom of you is she sought for?* ; chaidh agaibh orra, *you got the better of them.* Also used as a possessive pronoun, as—an taigh agaibh, *your house.* [Emphatic form—agaibh-se, agaibh-fhéin.]
agaibh-se, emphatic form of agaibh.
agaid, (AG) *s.f.* Giddy female.
agaidh, *gen.sing.* of agadh.
agail, *a.* Doubtful. 2 Sceptical. 3 Suspicious. 4 Lisping. 5**In jeopardy.
agaileachd, *s.f.* Doubtfulness, suspiciousness, 2 scepticism. 3 Tenderness. 4 Tendency to lisp, habit of lisping.
againn, *prep.pron.* At us, with us, in our possession. 2 Of us from amongst us. Faoileagan a' chladaich againn fhéin, *The seagulls of our own shore.* In other words, we prefer our own country, our own people, even our own seagulls. [Emphatic form—againne, againn-fhéin.]
agair, *pr.part.* ag agairt, *v.a.* Plead, claim. 2 accuse. 3 Crave, require, demand. Na agrar orra e, *let it not be laid to their charge.*
agairg,§ *s.f.* Mushroom—*agoricus.*
agairt, *s.m.* Claiming. 2 Pleading, craving. 3 Accusing, blaming. 4 Pursuing. Ag a—, *pr.part.* of *v.* agair. Tha a chogais 'g a agairt, *his conscience accuses him;* tha e ag *a.* orm, *he craves me;* tha e 'g agairt, *he prosecutes.*
agait,** *s.f.* Agate.
agaiteach,** *a.* Like an agate, of, or pertain-

ing to an agate, full of agates.
agalachd,* *s.f.* see agaileachd.
agall,** -aill, *s.m.* Speech, dialogue.
agallach, *a.* Conversational, of, or pertaining to speech or dialect.
agalladh, -aidh, *s. m.* Conferring, arguing, speaking, speech.
agallaich,(AC) *s.* Eloquence.
agallamh, -aimh, *s.m.* see agalladh.
agam, *prep. pron.* (aig+mi) At me, with me, in my possession. It is also used as a possessive pronoun, as, an claidheamh agam, *my sword.* [Emphatic form—agam-sa, agamfhéin (pronounced "agam-fhin" in Skye over W. Isles and in N. Counties, "agam-fhian" in some places.)]
agamh,** -aimh, *s.m.* Doubt, suspicion.
†agan,** *a.* Precious, dear.
agarach, -aich, *s.m.* (agair) Pretender, claimant.
———, -aidhe, *a.* Prone to plead, crave, or accuse. 2 Litigious. 3 Vindictive, quarrelsome.
agart,** -airt, *s.m.* Revenge, quarrel.
agartach, -aiche, see agarach.
agartachd,* *s.f.* Litigation, litigiousness.
agartaiche, *comp.* of *a.* agartach.
agartas, -ais, *s.m.* Plea, suit-at-law, prosecution. 2 Claim. Agartas coguis, *remorse;* féin-agartas, *self-reproach, compunction;* inntinn saor o fhéin-agartas, *a mind free from self-reproach*
†agh, aigh, *s.m.* Battle, conflict.
àgh, aigh, *s.m.* Joy, happiness, felicity. 2 Success, prosperity, luck. Is fhearr àgh na ealdhain, *good luck is better than a trade;* bithidh àgh aig na naoimh, *the holy shall have joy;* A thréin a b'fhearr àgh! *thou hero who excellest in success.*
àgh, *a.* Joyful. happy.
agh, aighe, -ean, *s.f.* Heifer, young cow. 2 Hind, fawn. 3** *rarely* Ox, bull, cow. Agh thri bliadhna dh'aois, *a heifer three years old;* reamhar mar agh, *fat as a heifer;* air tòir nan agha ciar, *in pursuit of the dusky fawns;* luaithre aighe, *the ashes of a heifer;* oidhche Fhéill Eoin theirear "aighean" ris na gamhna, *on St. John's eve the stirk is called a heifer.*
àgh,** aigh, *s.m.* Fear, astonishment, awe.
aghach, *a.* Abounding in hinds, heifers, &c.
àghach, -aiche, *a.* Warlike. 2 Brave. 3 Prosperous, fortunate, successful. 4 Conquering. 5 Happy, joyous.
aghaib,* *s.f.* (oidheirp) Attempt, essay, trial.
aghaibeach,* *a.* Persevering, industrious,
aghaibeachd,* *s.f.* Industry, perseverance.
aghaidh, -nean, *s.f.* Face, visage, countenance. 2 Brow. 3 Surface. 4 Reproach. Thug e an aghaidh orra, *he reproached them, withstood them to the face, "faced" them;* theirig (or gabh) air t' aghaidh, *pass on, go forward;* aghaidh ri aghaidh *face to face;* cuir an aghaidh a's fhearr a dh'fhaodas tu air, *put the best face on it you can;* as an aghaidh, *outright;* aghaidh na talmhainn, *the face of the earth;* 'S ann agad tha'n aghaidh 'g a iarraidh! *what a face you have to ask it!*
aghaidh, (an aghaidh) *prep.* Against, in opposition. An aghaidh na gaoithe, *against the wind;* an aghaidh mic an righ, *against the king's sons;* am aghaidh, *against me;* cuir 'n a aghaidh, *oppose* or *thwart him;* cuir 'n a h-*a.*, *oppose her;* cuir 'n an *a.*, *oppose them;* an *a.* a chéile, *against each other, at war.* [Governs the Genitive case.]
aghaidhich, *v.a.* Affront.
aghaidhichte, *a.* Opposed, opposing. 2 Fronting, facing. 3 Confronted.
aghaidh riut, *adv.* Affronté, *in heraldry.*
aghaidh-sneachda, *s.f.* Face of snow.
aghais, *s.f.* see athais.
aghaiseach, *a.* see athaiseach.
aghan, -ain, *s.m.* Proverb. Mar a tha an t-aghan ag radh, *as the proverb says.*
†aghanaich,** *s.m.* Advocate, pleader.
aghann, aighne, *n.pl.* aigheannan, & aghannau, *s.f.* Large shallow iron pan, generally with three small legs and iron lid, used for boiling potatoes, &c. 2**Goblet, skillet, small kettle or boiler.
——— -shilidh, *s.f.* Dripping-pan.
——— -uisgiche, *s.f.* Watering-can.
aghar, AC *s.m.* Progeny.
aghart, see adhart.
aghartach, see adhartach.
aghastar, -air, *s.m.* Horse's halter.
àghmhaireachd, see àghmhorachd.
àghmhor, -oire, *a.* Glorious, awful, magnificent. 2 Pleasant. 3 Prosperous, fortunate, blessed. 4 Auspicious. 5 Joyful, happy. 6 Bold, brave. 7 Renowned. Gu h-àghmhor, abarach, *in a bold and brave manner;* mu'n do bhoillsg an solus gu h-àghmhor, *ere the light shone joyfully.*
àghmhorachd, *s.f.ind.* Prosperity, auspiciousness.
a ghnàth, *adv.* Always.
aghnas,** -ais, *s.m.* Pleading, argumentation.
àgh'or, -oire, see àghmhor.
aghradhaidh,** *s.m.* Expostulation, challenging.
agrach,** *a.* Accusatory. 2 Pleading, craving. 3 Inclined to accuse, plead, or crave.
agradh, -aidh, *s. m.* Accusation. 2 Pleading, craving.
———, *3rd. sing. & pl. imp.* of *v.* agair.
agraidh, *gen. sing.* of agradh.
agrar, *fut. pass.* of *v.* agair.
aguinn, aguinne, see againn.
†agsal,** *a.* Generous, noble.
agus, *conj.* And. 2 as. Thus' a's mise, *thou and I;* tha e cheart cho math agus a bha e, *it is just as good as it was.* "'Us" has generally been supposed, of late years, to be a contraction of *agus*, but the late Dr. Cameron of Brodick, always maintained that "is" and not "'us" should be used as a mere copulative conjunction. *Is* couples words and phrases only, and should never be preceded by a comma. *Agus* is not only a mere copulatve conjunction, but also an emphatic copulative conj., and should always be used after a comma. Nach truagh leat mi, agus mi am priosan? *do you not pity me, and I in prison?;* cho luath 's is urrainn domh, *as soon as I can;* am bi thu cho math agus mo fhreagairt? *will you be so good as to answer me?* *Is* according to Windisch, is not an abbreviation of *agus*. See "Is."
aha! aha! *int.* Ahah!
a h-uile, *a.* Every, all.
†ai, *s.f.* Controversy. 2 Cause. 3 Region, territory. 4 Inheritance of land, possession. 5 Herd. 6 Cow.
— *s.f.* Whiteness.(AC) 2 Sheep. 3 Swan. Cuir a staigh an ai, *put in the sheep;* chi mi ai air loch a' mhuilinn, *I see a swan on the mill loch.*
aibeal,(CR) *a.* Impertinent.—*Arran.*
†aibghitir, *s.f.* Alphabet.
-aibh, termination of Dative Pl. of nouns, is still used for monosyllabic and some dissyllabic words with good taste, and it comes in well in poetry.
†aibh, *s.f.* Likeness. similitude, resemblance.
†aibhe! *int.* Hail! all hail!

aibheall, -ill, -an, see eibheall.
aibhearsair, see aibhistear.
aibheis, *s.f.* The sea, ocean. 2 Gulf. 3 Boasting. 4 Emptiness. 5 Place full of fairies. 6 the air, atmosphere. 7AC Abyss. 8AC Place or person in ruins or unkempt. An aibheis uile làn bhòcain, *the whole atmosphere full of goblins;* ged a tha thu an diugh a'd aibheis fhuair, *though thou art to-day a cold ruin;* ri aodann aibheis, *on the surface of the sea.*
aibheiseach, *a.* Vast, void, immense, ethereal, atmospherical. 2 Full of ruins, like a ruin.
aibheiseachadh, -aidh, *s. m.* Exaggeration, exaggerating, enormity, incredibility.
aibheiseachd,* see aibheiseachadh.
aibheisear, see aibhistear.
aibheisich* *v.a.* Exaggerate from various motives.
aibhghitir, see aibghitir.
aibhideach,** *a.* Great, monstrous, enormous.
aibhist,* *s.f.* Old ruin. 2 Ruin, destruction. see aibheis.
aibhistear, -ir, *s.m.* The Devil. 2 Destroyer.
aibhistearachd, *s.f.* Demonism, conduct of a devil. 2 Conduct of a destroyer, destructiveness.
aibhle,** see eibheall.
aibhleag, see eibhleag.
aibhlitir, -ean, *s.f.* Alphabet.
aibhlitreach, *a.* Alphabetical. Ordugh aibhlitreach, *alphabetical order.*
aibhne, *gen.sing.* of abhainn.
aibhneach, *a.* Fluvial, full of rivers.
aibhnean, } *n.pl.* of abhainn. Ri taobh nan
aibhnichean, } aibhnichean, *beside the streams*
†aibhreann, *s.m.* Castrated goat. (eirionnach in Lochaber.)
aibhse, *s. f.* Spectre. 2 Sprite, diminutive creature. also taibhse.
aibhseach, -iche, *a.* see aibheiseach. 2**Like a spectre or sprite.
aibhseachadh, see aibheiseachadh.
aibhsich, see aibheisich.
†aibid,** *s.f.* Habit.
aibidil, -ean, *s.f.* Alphabet.
aibidealach,* *a.* Alphabetical. Ordugh a. *alphabetical order.*
aibirsidh, (from the old learning system, beginning "A per se," *A by itself.*‡) see aibidil.
aibisidh, (from A, B, C, the first three letters of the Alphabet.) see aibidil.
†Aibreann, see Abraon.
aice, *s.f.* Proximity. 2 (faice) Lobster's hole, crab hole. †3‖ Band, tying.
aice, *prep.pron.* With her, at her, on her, in her possession. 2 In her remembrance. Tha duslach òir aice, *she hath gold dust.* *Aice* is often used as a possessive pronoun, as, an taigh aice,—an taigh a th'aice—*her house, the house she has.*
[Emphatic form—aice-se, aice-fhéin.]
†aice, *adv.* Near, close at hand. also taice.
aicear, *a.* Angry, severe, cruel.
aiceid, see acaid.
aiceideach, see acaideach.
aichbheil, *s.f.* Revenge, vengeance. Thoir dhomh aichbheil, *revenge me.*
aichbheileach, -liche, *a.* Revengeful, vindictive, full of vengeance.
aichbheileachd,** *s.f.* Revengefulness, vindictiveness.
aichbheiliche,** *s.m.* Avenger.
àicheadh, *pr. part.* àicheadh, *v.a.* Deny, refuse, disavow, recant, renounce. Dh'àicheadh e a chreideamh, *he renounced his religion;* àicheadhaidh mise esan, *I will deny him.*
àicheadh, -eidh, *s. m.* Denial, refusal, recantation. 'S e an t-àicheadh math an dara punc a's fhearr 's an lagh, *a stout denial is the second best point in law;* cuir as àicheadh, *deny, disavow.*
àicheadhaidh, *fut. aff. act.* of *v.* àicheadh.
àicheadh-chreidimh, *s.m.* Apostacy.
aicheallach, *a.* Able, potent, mighty, fierce.
aicheamhail,‡ *s.* (ath+gabhail) Reprisal.
àicheidh, } see àicheadh.
àicheun, }
†aichill, *a.* Able, powerful. 2 Dexterous, handy.
†aichilleachd, *s.f.* Strength. 2 Dexterity.
aichmheil, see aichbheil.
aichmheileach, see aichbheileach.
aicil, see faicill.
†aicme,‡ *s.f.* Race.
†aicne,** *s f.* Nature.
aicre,** *s f.* Inheritance, patrimony.
†aid,** *s.m.* Piece, portion, morsel.
†aidbheil,** *a.* Huge, enormous, vast.
aideachadh, -aidh, *s. m.* Confession, acknowledgement, avowal. Registration, as of a letter. Luchd-aideachaidh, *communicants, professors.*
aideachaidh, *gen.sing.* of aideachadh.
aideachail, *a.* Affirmatory, confessing.
aideachair,** *s.m.* Avoucher.
†aidhbhean,** *s.m.* Stranger, foreigner.
†aidhbheil, *s.* Wonder. 2 Boasting.
†———-,** *a.* Huge, enormous, vast.
aidhbheileachd, *s. f.* Vastness, terribleness, hugeness.
aidhbheis, see aibheis.
————each, see aibheiseach.
†aidhblich, *v.a.* Aggrandize.
†aidh-bhrugh, *a.* Bewitching, fascinating.
†aidhbhseach, *a.* Vast,*capacious.
†aidhbhsean,** -ain, *s.f.* Spectre, phantom, sprite.
aidhe,** *s.f.* Monition. 2 House. 3 Fortress.
†aidheach,** -ich, Milch cow.
————d,* see aoidheachd.
aidheam, *s.f.* Joyous carol.
aidhean, For aighean, *n.pl.* of agh.
aidheann, -inn, see aghann.
aidhear, -ir, see aighear. 2**Cracking of the skin from exposure to the weather.
————ach, see aighearach.
————achd, see aighearachd.
aidhle,** *s.f.* Cooper's adze.
aidhlinn, *dat.* of adhal.
†aidhme, *s.f.* see uidheam.
†aidhmhill, *v.a.* Spoil, destroy.
†aidhmhilleadh, *s.m. & pr. part.* Consuming. 2 Confusion.
aidhmhillte, *pt. part.* Consumed.
†aidhmhillteach, -eich, *s.m.* Destroyer. 2 Spendthrift. 3 Beast that steals from the pastures to feed on the growing corn.
aidhne,** *s.f.* Advocate. 2†Age.
aidhseachadh, *pr. part.* of *v.* aidhsich. Envying. Is iomadh neach a tha 'g am aidhseachadh an diugh nach do chuir dad riamh g' am leasachadh, mar a thubhairt am famhair ris an troich, *many a man envies me to-day who never helped me one bit to grow, as the giant said to the dwarf.*
aidhsich, *pr. part.* ag aidhseachadh, *v.a.* Envy.
aidich, *pr.part.* ag aideachadh, *v.a.* Confess, own, acknowledge. 2 Affirm, avow. Ag aideachadh a chionta, *confessing his sin;* dh' aidich e, *he confessed;* cha'n aidich mi, *I will not confess.*
aidicheam, *1p. sing. imp.* of *v.* aidich. 2** For aidichidh mi, *1 p. sing. fut. aff.* of *v.* aidich.
aidichear, *fut. pass.* of *v.* aidich.
aidichte, *pt. part. v.* aidich. Confessed, owned

acknowledged, affirmed.
aidmeach, *s.m.* } see aideachadh.
aidmeachadh, *s.m.* }
aidmheil, -e, -ean, *s.f.* Confession, profession, persuasion. 2 Declaration, acknowledgement, Dè an aidmheil a tha e a' leantuinn? *what persuasion does he follow?* ; a réir bhur n-aidmheil, *according to your profession* ; aidmheil na fìrinn, *the acknowledgement of the truth.*
——— *v.n.* see aidich.
aidmheileach, *a.* Of, or belonging to a confession, or profession. 2 Declaratory. 3 Acquiescent. 4 Forthcoming. Bithidh mise aidmheileach dhuit-se, *I will be responsible to you.*
aidmheileach,** *s.m.* Avoucher.
—————d,* *s.f.* Acquiescence, 2 Responsibility. 3 Acknowledgement.
aidmheilear, -eir, *s.m.* Confessor. 2 Professor. 3 Declarer.
aidmheiliche,* see aidmheileach.
aidmheint,** *s.f.* The Advent.
aidmhich, see aidich.
————te, see aidichte.
†aifir,** *s.f.* Blame, fault.
aifrionn, -rinn *or* -rinne, *s. m.* Mass in the Church of Rome. 2 Chapel.
aig, *prep.* At, near, close by. 2 In possession. 3 On account of. 4 For. 5 On. Is mór agam sin, *I value that greatly* ; tha déidh agam air, *I desire it* or *him* ; tha cuimhn' agam air, *I remember him* ; tha tasdan agam air, *he owes me a shilling* ; tha tasdan aig' orm, *I owe him a shilling* ; cha'n 'eil agam air, *I dislike him, I cannot help it* ; chaidh agam air, *I have overcome him* ; tha dòchas agam dheth *I have hope in him* or *it* ; tha gràdh agam dha, *I love him* ; tha truas agam ris, *I pity him* ; cha'n 'eil omhail agam dha, *he is no concern to me* ; tha bàigh agam ris, *I feel kindly towards him;* tha fiughair agam ris, *I expect him* ; aig an taigh, *at home* ; aig baile, *at home* ; aig na dorsaibh, *at the doors* ; aig meud 'aighe, *on account of his excessive joy* ; bha aig duine àraidh dithis mhac, *a certain man had two sons* ; tha dithis aige, *he has two* ; cha'n 'eil mìr aige, *he has not a particle*; tha'n t-àm againn falbh, *it is time for us to go* ; bha mios aige a mach, *he had spent a month* (a month had gone past him) ; bithidh mi agad a thiotadh, *I will be with you in a minute;* cha'n 'eil thu agad fhéin, *you are not yourself* ; cha ghabh mi agad, *I will not engage with you;* cum agad fhéin e, *keep it yourself*; [cha'n fhaic mi dad] mur faic biodh agad, *well then, be it so, I don't care if you don't.* Combined with the pers. pronouns thus :—

1 *Sing.*	agam	*Plur.*	againn,
2	agad		agaibh
3	aige, *m.* / aice, *f.*		aca, *m. & f.*

Emphatic Forms.

1 *Sing.* agam-sa, agam-fhéin, *pl.* againne, againn-fhéin.
2 agad-sa, agad-fhéin, *pl.* agaibh-se, agaibh-fhéin.
3 aige-san, aige-fhéin *m.* ; aice-se, aice-fhéin *f.* ; *pl.* aca-san, aca-fhéin, *m. & f.*

Aig enters into composition with the possessive pronouns thus, 'g am, 'g ad, 'g ar, 'g ur, &c., before the Infin. Mood or a verbal Noun, as, 'G am bhualadh (*lit.* at my striking) *striking me* ; bha mi 'g am fhalach féin. *I was hiding myself.* It is often used to give the signification of a genitive case to the noun it governs, as, An stoc aig Fionn, *Fingal's horn.*
†aigbheil,** see eagal.
†————each,** see eagalach.
aige, *prep. pron.* (aig+e) At him *or* it, with him *or* it, in his possession. 2 His, its. [Emphatic forms—aige-san, aige-fhéin.]
†aige, *a.* Brave, valiant.
àigeach, *s.m.* see òigeach.
aigeachd, (CR) *s.f.* Frolicsomeness.—*Arran.*
aigeal, -eil, -an, *s.m.* (W. Isles) see aigeann. Do bhreacan air uachdar an aigeil, *thy plaid (floats) on the pool* ; faochagan croma, ciar' an aigeil, a' glagadaich air a h-ùrlar—*i.e.* air ùrlar a' bhàta. (*from a description of the raging of the sea in a gale.*)
aigealach, -aich, *s.m.* see aigeannach.
aigealan, *n.pl.* of aigeal.
aigeallach, -aiche, *a.* see aigeannach.
aigealladh,** -aidh, *s.m.* Speech, conversation, language. 2 Dialogue. Ag éisdeachd aigeallaidh do bheòil, *listening to thy speech.*
aigeallaiche, *comp.* of aigeallach. Is tu a's aigeallaiche dhe'n triùir, *thou art the most spirited of the three.*
aigeallan,** *s.m.* Breast-pin. 2 Jewel. 3 Earring. 4 Tassel. 5 Toy.
aigeann, -einn, *s. m.* Abyss. 2 Deep pool. 3 Sea, ocean. 4 Bottom of an abyss. Thuit m' aigne 's an aigeann, *my mind sank into the abyss* ; 'n a shuidhe air an aigeann dhorch thiugh, *sitting on the dark misty deep* ; grunnd an aigeinn, *the bottom of the abyss.*
aigeannach, -aich, *s.m.* Sounder of the deep. 2 ‡see aigneach.
—————,* *s. f.* Self-willed, boisterous female.
—————,-aiche, *a.* Of, or belonging to an abyss. 2 Full of abysses. 3 see aigneach. 4* Self-willed, stubborn, mulish, uncontrollable.
aigeannachd, *s. f.* see aigneachd. 2 Stubbornness, turbulent disposition. 3‡‡Courage.
aigeanta,* *a.* Self-willed.
aigeantach, -aiche, *a.* see aigeannach.
——————,* *s. f.* Turbulent female.
——————d, *s. f.* see aigeannachd, and aigeantas.
aigeantas, * ais, *s. m.* Gaiety. 2**Alacrity.
àigeich, *gen. sing.* of àigeach, for òigeach.
aigeil, *gen. sing.* of aigeal.
aigeinn, see aigeann.
àigh, *gen. sing.* of àgh.
àigh, *s. m.* Happiness. 2 Prosperity. 3 Joy. 4 Mettlesomeness. 5 Liberality 6**Gloriousness, glory. 7**Auspiciousness. An do thréig thu mi, a sholuis m'àigh? *hast thou left me thou light of my joy?* meirghe rìgh Lochlainn an àigh, *the standard of the king of Lochlinn the fortunate* ; sonas is àigh ort! *may success and happiness attend you!*
àigh,** *a.* Happy. 2 Prosperous. 3 Liberal. 4 Auspicious. 5 Proud. 6 Mettlesome. 7 Glorious.

3. Aigh-ban.

aigh,** *s.m.* Deer. Aigh do choillte féin, *the deer of thine own woods.*
aigh-ban,‡ -ain, *s.m.* Box (plant)—*buxus sempervirens.* Badge of many branches of Clan Chattan.
aighe, *gen. sing.* of agh.
aigheach, *a.* Happy, joyous.
aigheal, see aingeal.
aighean, *n. pl. & dim.* of agh. 2**alacrity.
aighean, *n. pl.* of agh.

Aighean siùbhlach, *the wandering deer.*
aigheann, -ne, *pl.* aighnean, & aigheannan, *s.f* see aghann.

4. *Aigheannach.*

aigheannach, -aich, *s.m.* Corn thistle (plant)—*carduus arvensis.* 2 Place where thistles grow.
aigheannaich, *gen. sing.* of aigheannach.
aighear, -ir, *s.m.* Gladness, mirth, joy. gaiety, happiness, felicity, festivity. Tha aighear a' bruchdadh 'n a shùil, *gladness bursts from his eyes* ; ceòl is aighear, *music and mirth* ; aighear t'òige, *the joy of thy youth.*
àighearach, *a.* Glad, mirthful, joyful, gay, festive. 2 Odd. òglach aighearach, *an odd fellow.*
——————d, *s. f. ind.* Gladness, merriment, mirthfulness, joyfulness, festivity. 2 Oddness. 3**Alacrity.
aighne, *gen. sing.* of aghann. 2**Prophet. 3** Pleader,
†aighneach, -niche, *a.* Liberal, generous.
†aighnios, *s.m.* Pleading, reasoning, arguing.
aigh-rìomhach,** *s.m.* Belle.
aigilean, -ein, -an, *s.m.* Tassel. 2 Ear-ring. 3 Toy.
aigileanach, *a.* Hung with tassels. 2 Gaudy, beauish.
aiginneach, } aigionnach, } aigiontach, } *a.* see aigeannach.
aiglean, -ein, see aigilean.
aigleanach, see aigileanach.
aigne, *s. f.* Mind, temper, disposition. 2 Spirit, affection, thought. 3 (AC) The bird swift. 4 (AC) Anything of unusually quick motion. Cho luath ri aigne nam ban baoth, *as swift as the thoughts of the foolish women.* Is cianail m'aigne, *sad is my mind* ; lean mi le aigne neo-ghlic, *I followed with unwise affection.*
aigneach, -eiche, *a.* (aigne) Liberal. 2 Spirited, lively, brisk. 3 Affectioned. 4 Of, or belonging to mind, temper, affection, or thought. 5**Gallant.
————d, *s. f. ind.* Mettlesomeness, sprightliness, magnanimity, cheerfulness, courage.
aigneadh, -idh, -idhean, *s.m.* see aigne.
aignidh, *gen. sing.* of aigneadh.
-ail, *termination* of adjs., changes into -eil -oil, -uil, as preceded by kindred vowels.
àil, *gen. sing.* of àl. 2‡see àill.
ail,‡ *s. m.* Mark, impression, trace. 2* Scar. 3*Postage-stamp. Ail do choise, *the trace of thy foot.*
†ail, *s.m.* Mouth. 2 Rebuke. 3 Stone. 4 Request. 5 Weapon. 6‡Rock.
ailbh,** -e, -ean, *s. f.* Rock, foundation, anything hard, solid, rigid, or immoveable. (Also ailbhinn.)
ailbheach, -bhiche, see ailbhinneach.
ailbheag, eig, -an, *s. f.* Ring. 2 Ring of any coarse metal. Ailbheagan airgid, *silver rings* ; ailbheag cluais, *an ear-ring.*
————ach, *a.* Full of rings, like a ring, of or belonging to a ring.
ailbheinn, *s. f.* see ailbhinn.
ailbhinn, *s.f.* Flint, stone. 2 Rock, flinty rock. 3 Projection. 4 Precipice. An deòir a' sileadh mar bhoinne na h-ailbhinn, *their tears dropping as water from a projecting rock*; Ag imeachd air an ailbhinn oillteil, *walking on the dreadful precipice* ; do sgiath mar ailbhinn, *thy shield like a rock.*
ailbhinneach, -eiche, *a* Flinty, stony. 2 Rocky.
†ailcne,** *s. pl.* Paving stones.
†ailcneach,** -ich, *s.m.* Pavier.
àilde, *s. f.* see àilleachd.
àildeachd, see àilleachd.
aildiche, see àlainn.
†aile,** *s. f.* Stone. 2 Behaviour, manners.
àile, *s. m.* The air. 2 Scent, smell. 3 Wind, breeze, strength of the breeze. àile deagh bholaidh, *an odour of sweet smell* ; trath chaidleas 's a' ghleann an t-àile, *when the air sleeps* [*is still*] *in the valley* ; sròinean gun àile, *noses without the sense of smell* ; droch àile, *a bad smell* ; tha'n t-àile fuar, *the air is cold.*
aile,* *s.m.* see ail.
——, *a.* see àilleach.
ail-each,** -eich, *s. m.* (*lit.* a stone horse) Stallion.
àileach,* *a.* (àile) Airy, well-aired. 2**Atmospheric, of, or belonging to the atmosphere, air, breath, or smell. 3**Savoury. Iongantas àileach, *an atmospheric phenomenon.*
aileach,** *a.* Causing marks or impressions.
àileachd, *s.f. ind.* see àileadh.
aileadh, -eidh. *s. m.* see ail. Aileadh coise, *a footstep.*
àileadh, -eidh, *s.m.* see àile.
àileadhach, *a.* Pneumatic.
àile-bheathail,** (*lit.* vital air) Oxygen.
àile-churach, **s.m. see curach-àile.
àil-eathar, ,, ,, eathar-àile.
àile-ghuail *s, .m.* Gas.
àile-mheidh,** *s. f.* see meidh-àile.
——————each,** *a.* Barometrical.
aileag, -eig, -an, *s.f.* Hiccup. [Always preceded by art. *an.*] Tha'n aileag orm, *I have the hiccup.*
————ach, *a.* Causing the hiccup, hiccuppy, relating to the hiccup.
————ail, *s.f.* Hiccupping. 2**Vexing.
ailean, *n.pl.* of ail.
àilean, -ein, *s.m.* Green, plain, meadow. 2 Esplanade. 3 Oasis. Cath air an àilean réidh, *a battle on the level plain.*
àileanta, *a.* (àileadh) Fragrant, odorous. 2 Keen-scented. 3**Bodiless. †4**Atmospheric, aërial.
àilear, -eir, *s.m.* Porch.
aileas,** *a.* Akin.
————,** -eis, *s.m.* Pleasant country.
ailebeart,** -beairt, *Gaelic spelling of* halbert.
ai'leathan, see aimh-leathan.
àil-eòlas, -ais, *s.m.* Pneumatics.
àilgheas, -is, *s.m.* (àil+gheas) Pleasure, will. 2 Power. 3 Pride, imperiousness. 4** Desire, longing. àilgheas dhaoine, *the pride of men* ; nach lùb air àilgheas na garbh ghaoith, *that will not bend at the pleasure of the rough wind* ; fearann gu'r n-àilgheas, *land to your will.*
——————ach, -aiche, *a.* Fastidious. 2 Proud, haughty, imperious, arrogant. 3** Wilful, headstrong.
——————achd,** see àilleasachd.
——————aiche, *comp.* of àilgheasach.
àilghios, -is, *s.m,* }
——————ach, *a.* }
——————achd, *s.f.* } see àilgheas——.
——————aiche, }
àilinde, (AC) *comp* of àlainn.
àilindeach, see àlainn.
àilineachd, see àlainneachd. àilineachd mna na Gréige, *the beauteousness of the woman of Greece* (*Helen.*)—A.C.
ail-innisean,** -ein, *s.m.* Anemoscope.

aillionta, see àilleanta.
ailis, -e, -ean, *s.f.* Defect, fault, blemish. 2 Reproach.
àill', *s.f.* see àille.
àill, *s.f.* Desire, will, pleasure. Dè is àill leibh? *what is your will?*; an ni a b'àill leam, *the thing that I would wish*; ma's àill leibh seo, *if you desire or wish this*; an àill leat? *do you wish*; dean àille de'n éiginn, *make a virtue of necessity.*
†aill,** *s.f.* Rugged bank, rough steep. 2 Steep river bank. 3 Bridle. 4 Course. 5 Place, stead. 6 Praise.
aill air n-àill, *adv.* Willing or unwilling, *nolens volens.*
àill-bhruach, -aich, *s.f.* Rock, rugged bank, rocky steep.
àill-bhruachach, *a.* Having steep or rocky banks.
àill-bhil, *s.f.* Bridle-bit.
àille, *s.f.* see àilleachd.
——, *comp.* of *a.* àlainn. Is àille leam seo na sin, *I prefer this to that.*
àilleach, *a.* Beautiful, handsome, comely, fair.
àilleachd, *s.f.ind.* Beauty, beautifulness, handsomeness, comeliness. 2 Sublimity. 3 Dignity. àilleachd thalmhaidh air cha bhi, *no earthly beauty shall be found in him*; thàinig i 'n a h-àilleachd, *she came in her beauty*; bha a h-àilleachd gun choimeas, *her beauty was unequalled.*
àillead, -eid, *s.m.* Degree of beauty.
àilleag, -eig, -an, *s.m.* Jewel. 2 Gewgaw. 3 Pretty young maid. Nach cuimhne leat an àilleag? *dost thou not remember the beauteous maid?*
àilleagan, -ain. *pl.* -ain & -ana, *s.m.* Little jewel. 2 Term of affection for a young person. 3 Pretty maid. 4 Toy. Soraidh slàn do'n àilleagan! *farewell to the pretty maid!*
——, ——a, } *n. pl.* of àilleag.
ailleagan, -ain, see faillean.
àillealachd, *s.f.ind.* Bashfulness, modesty.
aillean,** -ein, *s.m.* Causeway.
ailleann,§ -einn, *s.f.* Elecampane,—*inula Helenium.* 2 Young beau. 3 Minion.
àilleanta, *a.* Beautiful, handsome, comely, delicate, bashful. 2 Having an imposing appearance. 3 Reserved, shy, distant.
——chd, *s.f. ind.* Personal beauty. 2 Delicacy, bashfulness, modest reserve. Is i àilleantachd maise nam ban, *delicacy is the ornament of females*

5. Ailleann.

àilleas, *s f.* see àilgheas. 2 Jewellery.
——ach, -aiche, *a.* Wilful, head-strong, proud.
——achd, *s.f. ind.* Wilfulness, pride.
ailleig, *gen. sing* of ailleag.
aillein, *s.m.* Favourite. 2***gen.sing.* of aillean.
ailleinn, *gen. sing.* of ailleann.
ailleort, *a.* (†ail 6) High-rocked.
àillghios, *s m.* see àilgheas.
àillidh, *a.* Bright, resplendent. 2 Beautiful, exquisite, fair. Lasair nan lochran àillidh, *the flame of the resplendent lamps*; do'n òg-mhnaoi a b'àillidh leac, *to the virgin of the fairest cheek.*
†aillin,** *a.* Another.
aillionair, *s.m.* Caterer.

aillis,** see aillse 3.
àillne, *s.f. ind.* see àilleachd.
àillneachd, see àilleachd.
aillse, *s.f.* Fairy. 2 Ghost. 3 Diminutive creature. 4‖ *rarely* Cancer, canker. 5 Delay.
——ach,** *a.* Like a fairy, of, or pertaining to a fairy. 2 Spectral. 3**Negligent.
aillseachadh, -aidh, *s.m.* see aibheiseachadh.
aillseag, -eig, -an, *s.f.* (aillse 3) Caterpillar.
aillsich, *v.a.* see aibheisich.
àillte,* *s.f.* see àilleachd.
aillte, *s.f.* High precipitous rock.
àillteachd, *s.f. ind.* see àilleachd.
ailltei1, *a.* see oillteil.
ailm, -e, -ean, *s.f.* †Elm-tree, *now* **leamhan.** 2 Letter "A." 3 Fir-tree. 4 Helm. 5 Science.
†ailmeadh, -eidh, *s.m.* Prayer.
ailmeag, -eig, -an, *s.f.* Elm. 2 Young or little elm-tree.
——an, *n.pl.* of ailmeag.
ailmean, *n.pl.* of ailm.
ailmeig, *gen. sing.* of ailmeag.
ailmh, -e, -ean, *s.f.* Flint stone. 2 Boundary-stone.
àil-mheidh,** -e, -ean, *s.f.* Anemometer.
ailmse, -ean, *s.f.* Mistake, error. 2**Spectre. 3**Spectral-looking person.
ailmseach, -eiche, *a.* Spectral, ghastly.
ailn, *s.f.* (AC) Loch. Chi mi ai air ailn an eilein, *I see a swan on the loch of the island.*
àilne, *comp.* of *a.* àlainn.
àilne, àilneachd, } *s.f.* see àilleachd.
àilnich, *v.a.* Beautify, adorn. 2 Accomplish.
àilnichte, *pt.part.* Adorned.
ailp, *gen.* of alp.
†—,** *s.m.* Protuberance. 2 Any gross lump. 3 Mountain.
†—,** *a.* White.
ailpeach,** *a.* Alpine.
ailse,** **†ailsin,**‖ } *s.f.* Cancer.
ailseach,** *a.* Cancerous.
ailseag,** *s.f.* Caterpillar.
ailt, *s.f.* see athailt. †2**House. 3‡ see ail.
àilt, -e, *a.* Noble, stately, grand, high. 2 Charming, beautiful. Aghaidh is àilte lìth, *a face of the most beautiful colour.*
àilte, *comp.* of àilt.
àilteach, see fàilteach.
àilteachadh, (*Suth'd*) see fàilteachadh.
àilteachd, *s.f. ind.* see àilleachd. Barrachd air t'àilteachd, *superiority over thy handsomeness.*
†ailtear,** *s.m.* Carpenter.
aim-, *privative particle* or prefix, see am, an, *priv.*
aimbeairt, (for aimbeirt) *gen. sing.* of aimbeart.
aimbeart, -eirt, *s.f.* Poverty, want, indigence. 2 Calamity. 3 Mischief. Cridhe fial an aimbeirt, *a generous heart in poverty.*
——ach, *a.* Poor, needy, indigent, necessitous. 2 Calamitous. 3 Mischievous. Tha mi aimbeartach, *I am indigent.*
——as, -ais, *s.m.* Same meanings as aimbeart.
aimcheist, see imcheist.
——each, see imcheisteach.
aimeas, -eis, see amas.
aimeasguidh, see aimsgith.
aimhdheòin, see aindeòin.
aimheagan,** see aigeann.
aimheal, -eil, *s.m.* Vexation, grief. 2 Dismay. 3 Uneasiness, trouble, sorrow. 4** Repentance, compunction, fear. Fo aimheal is fo sgios, *vexed and wearied.*
——ach, -aiche, *a.* Vexing, uneasy, vexa-

tious. 2**Repentant.
———achd,* s.f.ind. The greatest mortification.
aimhealaich,* v.n. Gall, pique, vex. Air 'aimhleachadh, galled, vexed.
aimhealtach, see aimhealach.
†aimhean,** a. Pleasant, agreeable, smooth.
aimhfheòil, see ainfheòil.
aimhgheur, a. Edgeless, blunt.
aimhghlic, a. Foolish, unwise.
aimhghliocas, -ais, s.m. Folly.
aimhi, see amaidh.
àimhinn,* s.f. see àmhuinn.
àimhinnich,* see àmhuinnich.
aimhleas, -eis, s.m. Hurt, harm, mischief, disaster. 2 Danger. 3 Injury. 5 Ruin, misfortune. 5 Perverseness. 6 Folly. 7 Destruction. B'e sin car t'aimhleis, that would be your ruination; ag iarraidh m'aimhleis, bent on my destruction; a' labhairt aimhleis, uttering perverseness; luchd aimhleis, unfortunate people; ni thu t'aimhleas, thou wilt harm thyself.
aimhleasach, -aiche, a. Hurtful. 2 Unfortunate. 3 Mischievous. 4 Ruinous. 5 Foolish. 6 Imprudent. 7 Destructive. Nithe aimhleasach, mischievous things.
aimhleasachd, s. f. ind. Condition or state of being unfortunate. 2 Mischievousness. 3 Ruinousness. 4 Imprudence. 5 Foolishness.
aimhleasaiche, comp. of a. aimhleasach.
aimhleasg, a. Lazy, indolent, inactive, drowsy, sluggish.
aimhleathan, -aine, a. Narrow, straight, tight. Is aimhleathan an t-slighe, narrow is the way.
aimhleathanachd,* s.f.ind. Narrowness, straitness, tightness
aimhleisge,** s. f. Laziness, indolence, inactivity, drowsiness, sluggishness.
aimhne, (for aibhne) gen.sing. of abhainn.
aimhneach, -eiche, see aibhneach.
aimhneart, -eirt, see ainneart.
————ach, see ainneartach.
————aiche, see ainneartaiche.
————mhor, see ainneartmhor.
aimhneirt, see ainneirt.
aimhnichean (for aibhnichean) pl. of abhainn.
aimhreadh, -eidh, s. m. (‡am+réidh) Disturbance, disagreement, confusion.
————, a. Wrong, disturbed, disagreeing. Tha seo air aimhreadh, this is wrong; tha thu 'g am chur air aimhreadh, you are putting me wrong; cuireamaid an cainnt air aimhreadh, let us confound their language.
aimhreidh, gen.sing. of aimhreadh.
†aimhreidhe, s. pl. Defiles, passes, straits. fastnesses. 2 Forests.
†aimhreis, a. Difficult, arduous.
aimhreit, -e, -ean, s. f. Confusion, disorder, disagreement, contention, disturbance.
————each, -eiche, a. Quarrelsome, litigious, contentious. 2 Of, or belonging to a quarrel or disturbance. 3 Entangled. Maille ri mnaoi aimhreitich, along with a quarrelsome woman.
aimhreiteachd,* s. f. ind. Degree of disorder, confusion, or quarrelsomeness.
aimhreith, see aimhreit.
aimhreitich, v.a. Confound, entangle, put through other. Entwine as thread.
†aimhriar, s.m. Mismanagement.
aimhriochd, s.m. Disguise, concealment.
————ach, a. Assuming a false figure.
aimid, s.f. see amaid.
———each, see amaideach.
———eachd, s.f. see amaideachd.
aimideag, see amaideag.
aimisichte, see aimsichte.
†aiminn,** a. Pleasant, agreeable, smooth.
aimlisg, -e, -ean, s. f. Confusion, disorder, calamity. Is a. e, it is confusion.
————each, a. Confusion. 2 Causing confusion. 3 Of, or pertaining to confusion, 4 Mischievous. 5 Quarrelsome.
aimrid, a. Barren, unproductive.
———each,* s. f. Barren woman.
———eachd,* s. f. ind. Barrenness.
aimrios,** s.m. Error.
aimseach, see amaiseach.
aimsgith, a. Mischievous. 2 Impure, bawdy. 3 Impious, profane.
————eachd, s.f.ind. Mischievousness. 2 Impurity. 3 Profanity, impiety. Le tuairisgeul 's le a., with slander and impurity.
aimsichte, a. Bold, daring, resolute.
aimsidh, (for amaisidh) fut.ind. of v. amais.
aimsir, -e & -each, pl.-ean, s.f. Time. 2 Season. 3 Weather. A réir na h-aimsire a bhitheas ann, according to the weather we may have; a. ghaillionnach, stormy weather; a. bhrèagh, fine weather; a. a' gheamhraidh, the winter season; a. an earraich, the spring season; a. an t-samhraidh, the summer season; a. an fhogharaidh, the harvest season; a. foghARAIDH, harvest weather; an a. seo, this weather.
———eil, a. Temporal, worldly. 2 Seasonable. Tha na nithe a chithear aimsireil, the things which are seen are temporal.
aimsiorrtha, see aimsireil.
aimsith, -e, -ean, s.m. (‡am + -mis, of eirmis+ ith) Mischance. 2 The missing of an aim, being unfortunate.
ain-, intens. & priv. particle, prefixed to words and corresponding with English -un, or -in.
àin, -e, s.f. Heat, heat of noon. 2 Light. Ain an là, broad day-light.
†ain, s. f. Water.
†àin, a. Honourable, praiseworthy, respectable. 2**Respectful. T'uirghiol àin, thy respectful speech.
†ainbheach, a. Manifold, abundant.
————,** s.m. Drone bee. 2 Much rain. 3* see ainfhiach.
ainbheart,** -bheirt, s. f. Misdeed.
†ainbheil, s. f. Impudence, rudeness, impertinent language. 2 Stinginess.
†————each, a. Impudent, rude. 2 Stingy.
ainbheus, -a, -an, s.m. Immorality, dishonesty, want of virtue.
————ach, -aiche, a. Immoral, dishonest, vicious.
†ainbhfeile, see ainbheil.
ainbhfheas, see ainfhios.
†ainbhfheileach, a. see ainbheileach.
ainbhfheòil, see ainfheòil.
ainbhfhiach, -eich, -an, see ainfhiach.
†ainbhfhiosach, a. Rude, ignorant, headstrong, resentful.
†ainbhidh,** s. f. Rainy weather.
ainbhios,* see ainfhios.
ainbhith, see ainmhidh.
————each, -eiche, a. Stormy, tempestuous. 2 Violent, passionate. see onfhadhach.
ainbith, a. (‡an+bith, un-world-like) Odd, extraordinary.
†aincheard, -cheirde, s.m. Buffoon, ingenious fellow, imposter. 2 Buffoonery, low jesting.
————ach, -aiche, a. Jocose, humorous, jesting, buffoon-like, merry.
†————, see aincheard.
ainceardach. a. **Like a buffoon, of, or belonging to a buffoon. or buffoonery. 2 Ingenious.
aincheart,** a. Unjust, iniquitous.
————,** -cheirt, s.m. Prank, trick. 2 In-

justice.
aincheas, -eis, see aincheist.
ainchéirde, *gen.sing.* of aincheard.
aincheist, *s.m.* Danger, jeopardy, dilemma. 2 Perplexity, doubt. 3 Puzzle, riddle.
———each, *a.* Doubtful, puzzling. 2 Of, or pertaining to doubt or perplexity. 3 In jeopardy, doubt, or danger.
ainchiall,** -chéill, *s.f.* Peevishness. 2 Forwardness. 3 Testiness. 4 Madness.
†———ach, -aiche, *a.* Peevish. 2 Forward. 3 Testy. 4 Mad.
ainchis, -e, *s.f.* Curse, rage, fury.
ainchliste, *a.* Slow, tedious.
†ainchliù, *s.m.* Peevish person.
ainchrionailt, *s.f.* Acuteness, discernment, sagacity.
ainchrionna, *a.* Acute, sagacious.
†aincidh,** *s.f.* Doubt.
†aincis,** *s.f.* Skin, hide.
aindealbh, *s.m.* Unseemly figure, 2 Distorted picture.
———ach, -aiche, *a.* Unseemly, deformed
†aindear, see ainnir.
aindeas, -eise, *a.* Unprepared. 2 Awkward, not clever, not ready-handed.
aindeas,** *s.m.* Adversity.
†aindeise, *s.f.* Affliction, calamity, awkwardness.
aindeòin, *s.f.* Reluctance. 2 Compulsion, force. 3 Defiance. Co dhiùbh is deòin leat no 's aindeòin, *whether it be your will or not;* g' ad' aindeòin *in spite of you.*
aindeònach, *a.* Reluctant, unwilling. Chaidh e dhachaidh gu h-aindeònach, *he went home unwillingly.*
———d, *s.f.* Unwillingness, reluctance, obstinacy. 2 Compulsion.
aindeiseil, -seala, *a.* Unpropitious, unprepared.
aindeisealachd, *s.f.* Want of preparation. 2 Want of luck.
†aindhiarraidh,** *a.* Angry.
ain-diadhach, -aich, *s.m.* Atheist. 2 Ungodly person.
ain-diadhachd, *s.f. ind.* Ungodliness, profaneness, iniquity, impiety.
ain-diadhaidh, *a.* Profane, ungodly, wicked, impious, irreligious.
ain-diadhaidheachd, see ain-diadhachd.
ain-diadhail, *a.* see ain-diadhaidh.
ain-diadhalachd, see ain-diadhachd.
ain-dìleas, *a.* False, unfaithful, faithless.
ain-dìlseachd, *s.f. ind.* Faithlessness. 2 Unfriendliness.
ain-dìsleachd, see ain-dìlseachd.
aindìth,** *s.f. ind.* Extreme poverty.
ain-diùid, -e, *s.f.* Boldness, obstinacy, impertinence.
———each, -eiche, *a.* Obdurate, obstinate, petulant.
ain-dlighe, *s.m.* Injustice, unlawfulness, unjust law. 2 Trespass. 3 Usury.
ain-dligheach, -eiche, *a.* Lawless, unlawful, illegal, transgressing, unjust, undutiful.
———, -ich, *s.m.* Transgressor.
———d, *s.f. ind.* Unlawfulness, practice of injustice.
ain-dreann,* *s.m.* Fretfulness.
———ach, -aiche, *a.* Fretful, peevish.
———achd, *s.f. ind.* Fretfulness, peevishness.
aine,** *s.f. ind.* Delight, joy, pleasure. 2 Music, harmony.
†aine, *s.f.* Experience. 2 Good-will. 3 Agility, expedition. 4 Platter.
àine, (AC) *s.f.* Fire. Bhruich mi e ri àine caoire, *I toasted it to a fire of red-hot embers.* Also see àin.
aine,*' see adha *and* ae.
aineach, *a.* Imperative (*i.* mood in Grammar) —*Forbes' G. Gram.*
aineadach, -eiche, *a.* Vexing, galling.
aineadas, -ais, *s.m.* Vexation.
aineal, see aineòl.
ainealach, see aineolach.
aineamh, -eimh, *s.m.* Flaw, blemish, fault, injury, defect. Ceilidh seirc aineimh, *charity conceals faults;* dà reithe gun aineamh, *two rams without blemish.*
aineamhach, -aiche, *a.* Faulty, blemished, maimed, having defects or injuries. 2 Causing defects or injuries.
aineamhag, -aig, see ainneamhag.
aineamhaig, *gen.sing.* of aineamhag.
àinean, *pl.* of adha *or* ae. Os cionn nan àinean, *above the livers.*
aineart, *s.m.* see ainneart.
àineartaich, -e, *s.f.* (àinich) Yawning.
ain'eas, -eis, *s.m.* see ainteas.
aineas, -eis, *s.f.* (an+theas) Passion, joy. 2 Fury, frenzy. 3 Cruelty. 4 Bravery. Dùthaich gun aineas, *a friendly country.*
———ach, -aiche, *a.* Passionate, furious, enraged, raging, frantic. 2 Cruel. 3 Brave. 4 Hardy. Mar stuadhan aineasach, *like furious billows.*
———achd, *s.f. ind.* Furiousness, passionateness, frenzy, fury.
†aineasgair, *a.* see ainsheasgair.
ainéifeachd, *s.f. ind.* Insufficiency.
aineil, *gen.sing.* of aineal.
aineimh, *gen. sing.* of aineamh.
aineis, ,, ,, aineas.
†aineogail, *s.f.* Astonishment. 2 Stupor, torpor.
aineol, -oil, *s.m.* Stranger, foreigner. 2 Guest. 3 Unacquaintance. Ann an tìr m'aineoil, *in the country where I am unacquainted;* a' dol air aineol, *going where not known, wandering abroad;* cha'n fhaic aineol c'n lear no o'n fhasach, *a stranger from sea or wilderness will not behold;* is tròm geum bà air a h-aineol, *deep is the low of a cow on a strange pasture.*
———,** *a.* Strange, foreign, ignorant.
———ach, -aiche, *a.* Ignorant, unintelligent, rude, unlearned. Aineolach air seo, *ignorant of this.*
———aiche, *comp.* of aineolach.
aineolas, -ais, *s.f.* Ignorance, want of knowledge, nescience, illiterateness. Is tròm an t-eallach an t-aineolas, *ignorance is a heavy burden;* àm bhur n-aineolais, *the time of your ignorance.*
†ainer,** *a.* Proud. 2 Great. 3 Cruel.
ain-fheasach, *a.* Sensuous, lewd, lustful.
ainfheich, *gen. sing.* of ainfhiach.
ainfheòil, -fheòla, *s.f.* (aimh+feòil) Proud flesh, corrupt flesh.
ainfheòla, *gen. sing.* of ainfheòil.
ainfhiach, -fheich, -fhiachan, *s.m.* Debt, obligation. Fo ainfhiach dhuit-sa, *under obligation to you.*
ain-fhìor, -a, *a.* Untrue.
ainfhios, -a, *s.m.* Ignorance. Air ainfhios dhuit, *unknown to you.*
———ach, -aiche, *a.* Ignorant, illiterate. 2 unintelligent.
ainfhiosrach, -aiche, *a.* Ignorant, illiterate, unintelligent.
ainfhiosrachd, *s.f.* Ignorance, illiterateness.
ain-fhìrinn, -ean, *s.f.* Untruth.
ain-fhiùgh, *a.* see ain-fhiùghach.
———ach, -aiche, *a.* Worthless. 2 Insignificant, contemptible.

——achd, *s. f.* Unworthiness.
†ain-fhuail, *s. f.* Chamber-pot.
aing'eachd, see aingidheachd.
aingeal, -il, *pl.* -il, -gle, -glean, -glich,(AC) *s.m.* Angel. 2 Messenger. 3 Fire. 4 Light. 5 Sunshine.
——ach, *a.* Angelic, of, or pertaining to an angel. 2 Of, or pertaining to fire.
——ach, *s.m.* see aingealachd.
——achd, ‖ *s. f. ind.* Numbness, torpidness, chillness.
aingealag,? -eig, *s. f.* Wood angelica. see lus nam buadha.
aingealail,** see aingealach.
aingealta, *a.* Malicious, vindictive. 2 Perverse, wicked, headstrong, froward.
——chd, *s. f. ind.* (aingidh) Frowardness, malignity, perverseness, wickedness. A gabhail tlachd an aingealtachd, *taking pleasure in wickedness* : aingealtachd 'n a chridhe, *frowardness in his heart.*
aingealtas, -ais, see aingealtachd.
†aingeis, *s. f.* Curse.
ainghean, -ein, *s.m.* Excessive love. 2 Excessive greed or avarice.
——ach, *a.* Exceedingly attached. 2 Excessively greedy or avaricious.
ainghearradh, -aidh, *s.m.* Short cut.
ain-ghniomh, *s.m.* Bad deed.
ain-ghniomhach, *a.* Facinorous. 2 Wicked, atrocious, detestably bad.
aingidh, -e, *a.* Wicked, impious, vicious, bad. 2 Perverse, mischievous. 3 Cross, ill-natured.
aingidheachd, *s. f. ind.* Iniquity, sin, evil, wickedness, viciousness. 2 Perverseness. 3 Wrath. *A.* a' bhaile, *the wickedness of the city*; *a.* ur deanadais, *the evil of your doings*.
aingil, *s.m.*, *pl.* of aingeal.
aingle, -an, see aingeal.
ainglich,(AC) *pl.* of aingeal.
ainglidh, *a.* Angelic.
——each, *a.* see ainglidh.
——eachd,** *s. f.* Angelicalness.
ainglionta, *a.* see ainglidh.
ain-iarmartach, -aiche, *a.* Most furious.
ainich, -e, *s. f.* Panting, breathing hard.
ainich, see aithnich.
ainid, *a.* Vexing, galling.
——each, -eiche, *a.* see ainid.
ain-iochd, see an-iochd.
——mhoireachd, see an-iochdmhoireachd.
——mhor, see an-iochdmhor.
ain-iomad, -aid, *s. f.* Too much.
——achd, *s. f.* Superfluity, superabundance
ain-iomadaidh, *a.* Superfluous, unnecessary. 2 Exuberant.
ain-iosal, *a.* Haughty, imperious.
ainirich, see eanraich.
ainis, *s. f.* Anise.
ain-iùl, see an-iùl.
†ainle,** *a.* Fair, comely, well-featured.
ainle, *s. f.* Wild cat. (?)2 Green-fly.
†ainleachd, *s. f.* Comeliness.
†ainleag, -eig, *s. f.* Snare. 2 Sting.
——, -eig, (for faineag) Swallow, see gobhlan-gaoithe.
—— dhubh, *s. f.* Swift (bird) see gobhlan mór.
—— -mhara, *s. f.* Swift (bird) see gobhlan mór. 2**Black martin.
—— -mhonaidh, *s. f.* Alpine swift (bird) see gobhlan-monaidh.
—— mhór, *s. f.* Swift (bird) see gobhlan mór.
†ainlean, *v.a.* Persecute, pursue.
ainleanmhuinn, *s. f.* Persecution.

ain-leas, -eis, *s.m.* Slander. 2**Difference. 3 **Mischief. 4**Theft.
ain-leatrom, -uim, *s. m.* Oppression, injustice.
——ach, -aiche, *a.* Highly injurious.
ainm, -e, *pl.* -ean, -eannan, *s.m.* Name. 2 Substantive noun. 3 Character. An t-ainm gun an tairbhe, *the name without the profit*; is fhasa deagh ainm a chall na 'chosnadh, *a good name is easier lost than won*; c'ainm a th'ort? *what is your name?* ciod is ainm do seo, *or* c' ainm th'air seo? *what is the name of this?*; duine d'am b'ainm Aonghas, *a man named Angus*; Maighistir——c'ainm a th'air? *Mr. ——what's his name?*
ainm-chlàr, -àir, -an, *s.m.* Catalogue. 2 Index.
ainmeachadh, -aidh, *s.m.* Naming, appointing. 2 Mentioning. 3 Nominating. 4 Nomination. Ag a—, *pr. part.* of ainmich.
ainmeachail,** *a.* Appellative.
ainmeachair,** *s.m.* Assigner.
ainmeachas, -ais, *s.m.* Mere naming, nothing but the name.
ainmealachd, *s. f. ind.* Celebrity, fame, renown, notoriety.
ainmeanach, -aich, *s.m.* Nominative (case in grammar.) 2 Nominator. 3 see ainmeanaiche.
ainmeanaiche, *s.m.* Denominator.
ainmear, *s.m.* Substantive *or* noun in grammar.
ain-measarrach,** -aiche, *a.* see ana-m—.
ain-measarrachd,** *s. f. ind.* see ana-m—.
ain-measarradh, see ana-measarradh.
ainmeic, ainmeig, } *adv.* see ainmig.
ainmeil, -e, *a.* Celebrated, renowned, famed, famous. 2**Namely. Dh'fhàs iad sin 'n an daoine ainmeil, *those became men of renown*; gu h-ainmeil, *especially*, *famously*.
——eachd,** *s. f. ind.* see ainmealachd.
ain-mèin, -e, *s. f.* Pride, haughtiness, arrogance, frowardness.
——each, -iche, *a.* Perverse, froward. 2 Illiberal, churlish.
——eachd, *s. f. ind.* Perverseness, frowardness. 2 Illiberality, churlishness.
ain-mèinn, -e. see ain-mèin.
ain-mheas, -eis, *s.m.* Reward, recompense, remuneration.
——ach, -aiche, *a.* Proud-spirited, 2 Immeasurable, huge.
ain-mheasardha, ain-measarra, } *a.* see ana-measarrach.
ain-mheasardhachd, *s. f. ind.*, ain-mheasardhas, -ais, *s.m.*, ain-mheasarrachd, *s. f. ind.*, ain-mheasarras, -ais, *s.m.* } see ana-measarrachd.
ain-mheid,** *s. f.* Wonder, rarity.
ain-mhèin, see ain-mèin.
——neach, see ain-mèineach.
ain-mhiann, see ana-miann.
——ach, see ana-miannach.
ainmhide, -ean, *s.m.* Rash fool, loquacious fool, babbler.
——achd, *s. f. ind.* Rash folly.
ainmhidh, -e, -ean, *s.m.* Brute, animal, beast. An ainmhidhean uile, *all their beasts.*
——each,** -eiche, *a.* Brutal, brutish. 2 Of, or belonging to a brute.
——eachd, *s. f. ind.* Brutality. brutishness.
ain-mhireach, -ich, see ana-bhiorach.
ain-mhisneachd, *s. f. ind.* Pusillanimity.
ain-miann, *pl.* -mianna, see ana-miann.
anmic, see ainmig.
ainmich, *pr.part.* ag ainmeachadh, *v.a.* Name, appoint, mention, fix upon, nominate. Ainmich do thuarasdal, *appoint your wages*; ainmich co e siod, *mention who yonder man is.*

ainmichte, *pt.part. v.* ainmich, Named.
ainmig, *adv* (an+minig) Seldom, rarely, scarcely. Is ainmig a thig e, *he seldom comes ;* b'ainmig a leithid, *his like (equal) was rare ;* b'ainmig bha mo bhuillean fann, *seldom were my blows weak.*
ainmigead,** -eid, *s.m.* Rareness, scarceness. 2 Increase in scarceness. A' dol an ainmigead, *getting scarcer and scarcer.*
ainm-lite,** *s. f.* Catalogue, index.
ainm'nic, see ainmig.
ainmnichte, see ainmichte.
ainmnichthe, -ean, *s.m.* Assignee.
†ainn,** ainne, *s.* Circle. 2 Ring.
ainndeònachadh, see aindeònachd.
†ainneadh,** -eidh, *s.m.* Patience.
ainneal, -eil, *s.m* see aingeal.
———ta, see aingealta.
ainneamh, -eimhe, *a.* Rare, scarce, curious. 2 Curiously formed 3**Valuable. Orios ainneamh, *a curious girdle ;* is ainneamh a leithid, *his match is seldom met with.*
———,* *adv.* Seldom. Is ainneamh a thig thu, *you seldom come.*
———ach, see ainneamh.
———achd, *s. f. ind.* Rareness, scarceness.

6. Ainneamhag.

ainneamhag, -aig, *s.f.* Phœnix.
ainneanta,** *a.* Dogmatic.
ainneart, -eirt, *s.m.* (ain, *excess*+neart) Violence, force, oppression. Ainneart air a' choigreach, *violence on the stranger ;* luchd ainneirt, *oppressors.*
———ach, -aiche, *a.* Oppressive, violent, tyrannical, overbearing.
———achd, *s. f. ind.* Practice of oppression. 2 Force, violence.
———mhor, *a.* Feeble.
ainneoin, see aindeòin.
ainngealta, see aingealta.
ainnichte, *a* Made patient. 2 Tamed.
àinnighte,* (ainneadh) see ainnichte.
ainnir, -e, -ean, *s. f.* Virgin, maid. 2** Marriageable woman 3**Young woman. Ainnir fo bhròn, *a maiden mourning;* ainnir a cheud ghràidh, *the maid of his first love.*
———each, *a.* Like a beauty.
ainnis, } ainniseach, } *a.* Poor, destitute, needy, abject. Tha mi ainnis lom, *I am poor and naked.*
ainnis, } ainniseachd, } *s.f.* Poverty. 2 Abjectness. 3 Poor or needy person. 4** Desperateness. A' slugadh an ainnis, *swallowing up the needy.*
àinniuigh, -ean, *s. m.* Sigh, sob.
ainnsteil, *s. f.* Disturbance, commotion. 2 Disorder.
ainreite, see aimhreit.
ainriochd, *s m.* Miserable plight. 2 Pitiful condition. 3 Frightful bodily appearance.
———ail *a.* Shapeless, ill-formed. 2 Disguised.
ainsearc, -eirc, *s. f.* Hatred.
ainseirceach, -aiche, *a.* Malignant, unfeeling, uncharitable, cruel.
ainseircealachd, *s. f. ind.* Uncharitableness, want of affection.
ainseirceil, -e, *a.* see ainseirceach.
ainsgean, -ein, *s.m.* Fury. 2 Fright, terror. 3 Bad temper. Chaidh an t-each air ainsgean, *the horse ran off in a fright.*
ainsgein, -e, *s.f.* Sudden movement, starting fit. 2 see ainsgean.
———ach, -aiche, *a.* Ill-tempered. 2 Furious, wild. 3 Apt to take fright, as a horse.
ainsgian, *s.m.* see ainsgean.
ain-sheasgair, *a.* Without favour or protection, destitute.
———eachd, *s.f.* Rudeness, violence.
ain-sheirc,** *s.f.* Excessive hatred. 2 Cruelty.
———eil, *a.* Hating, abominating. 2 Cruel.
ain-spiorad, *s.m.* Evil spirit.
ain-srianta, *a.* Unbridled, untamed. 2 Debauched. 3 Obstinate.
ain-sriantach,-aich, *s.m.* Libertine. 2 Debauchee.
ain-sriantas,-ais, *s. m.* Libertinism. 2 State of being untamed, as a horse.
ainteach,** *s.m.* Religious abstainment from eating flesh.
†———,** *a.* Boastful, vain-glorious.
ainteann, *a.* Bound, 2 Very stout. 3 Bold.
ain-teas, -eis, *s.m.* Excessive heat. 2 Inflamation. 3 Impetuosity, keenness, violence of manner. 4 Ardour, fervour, zeal, enthusiasm.
———ach, -aiche, *a.* Violently hot. 2 Fiery, impetuous.
———achail, see ain-teasach.
———achd, *s.f.ind.* Feverishness.
ain-teasaigheachd, see ain-teasachd.
ainteil, *a.* Preceptive, mandatory.
ain-teist, -ean, *s.m.* False-witness. 2 Bad character.
———eanas, -ais, *s.m.* False testimonial, false certificate, unjust certificate.
———eas, -eis, *s.m.* False testimony.
———eil, -e, *a.* Ill-famed, uncreditable.
ain-teth, *a.* Scorching, exceedingly hot. 2 Ardent, vehement, eager. 2 Inflamed. Ain-teth chum àir, *ardent for battle.*
aintheasachd, see ain-teasachd.
†ainthinne, see athainte.
aintighearn, -a, *s.m.* Tyrant. 2 Oppressor, overbearing ruler.
———achd, see aintighearnas.
———ail, -e, *a.* Tyrannical. 2 Oppressive.
———as, -ais, *s.m.* Tyranny. 2 Oppression. 3 Domineering. 4 Despotism. 5**Absoluteness. Am fuath a th'againn air *a.*, *the hatred we have of despotism.*
ain-tioma, *s. f. ind.* Intrepidity, valour.
ain-tiomail, -e, *a.* Intrepid, valiant.
ain-tiomalachd, *s. f. ind.* Fearlessness, courage, boldness, bravery.
ain-treun, -tréine, *a.* Ungovernable. 2 Very powerful.
———as,** -ais, *s.m.* Great strength.
-air, *termination* of nouns, appearing also as -eir, -ir, -oir, and -uir, and signifying *agent* or *doer.*
air, *prep.* On, upon. 2 Of, concerning. 3 For, on account of. 4 By. 5 With. 6 Also signifying the same as if joined in its first sense with the pers. pronoun *e.* 7 On, an oath or assertion. 8 On, upon, denoting time. 9 With, accompanied by. 10 Claim of debt.

The above are the meanings of *air* used as a simple preposition, but it has idiomatic uses almost without number in various combination with verbs and other parts of speech.

air (*cont.*)—
Na'm faighinn am fear a tha air chall oirbh, *if I should find the man that is lost* FROM *you*, [if translated here BY *you*, it implies that "you" lost the man, which may not be true] theich e orm, *he fled* AWAY FROM *me*; chluich e an cleas orm, *he played the trick* ON *me;* cheil e an gnothach orm, *he hid the matter* FROM *me;* ghàir e orm, *he laughed* AT *me*; ni mi sgeul ort, *I will make a tale (inform)* AGAINST *you*; dh'ith e ar n-iasg oirnn, *he ate our fish* FOR (ON) *us*, [i.e. in spite of us, *not* to oblige us.]

In these examples *air* translates differently into English in every case, but the differences are caused by the English verbs, each of which requires its own preposition as a complement. Classing these under the various meanings would hide from the learner the fact that the Gaelic prep. has the same meaning in each case—adversity, adverse circumstances, mishap, disaster, trickery suffered, &c.

Examples given by MacAlpine:—
Iomradh air do ghliocas, *a report of thy wisdom*; air beinn, *on a mountain*; air sgàth, *for the sake of*; air ainm, *by name*; air bheagan, *possessing little*; air an aobhar sin, *for that reason*; air mo shon-sa dheth, *for my part, as far as I am concerned*; air éigin, *with much ado*, [*with much difficulty, scarcely, hardly*]; air a h-aon, *for one*, [thuit tri le Bran air a h-aon, *Bran, for one, killed three*]; air seachran, *astray*; air falbh, *away, from home*; air uairibh, *sometimes;* tha eagal air, *he is afraid*; tha acras air, *he is hungry;* air chor, *so that*; air chor éigin, *somehow or other*; duine air chor éigin, *some person or other*; air meud 's gu bheil e, *let it be ever so great*; [air a mheud 's gu'n tig dhiubh, *however many of them come*]; cha d'fhuair mi ni air, *I got nothing for it*; dè tha a' cur air? *what is the matter with him?*

Examples from Stewart's Gaelic Grammar‡*:*
ON, UPON—air an làr, *on the ground*; air an là sin, *on that day.* CLAIM OF DEBT—ioc dhomh na bheil agam ort! *pay me what thou owest!* cia meud a th'aig mo thighearn ort-sa? *how much owest thou unto my lord?* OATH—air m'fhacal, *upon my word*; air làimh t'athair 's do sheanair. *by the hand of your father and grandfather;* [air na chunnaic thu riamh na fosgail e, *for the sake of all you ever saw do not open it.*] (Thig air) SPEAK OR TREAT OF—thig mo bheul air do cheartas is air do chliù, *my mouth shall speak of thy justice and thy praise*; sin cùis air a bheil mi nis a' teachd, *that is a matter of which I am now to treat*‡; tog ort! *rouse thyself!* chaidh agam air, *I prevailed over him;* 's ann orms' a chaidh, *it is I that was worsted.* Thug e am monadh air, *he betook himself to the mountain.* IN RESPECT OF—cha'n fhaca mi an samhuil air olcas, *I never saw their like for badness*; air a lughad, *however small it be.* JOINED WITH, ACCOMPANIED BY—móran iaruinn air bheag faobhar, *much iron with little edge*; oidhche bha mi 'n a theach air mhóran bidh 's air bheagan aodaich, *I was a night in his house with plenty of food but scanty clothing*; air leth làimh, *having but one hand.* MEASURE, DIMENSION—dà throidh air àirde, *two feet in height.* ALTERNATION—Olc air mhath leat e, *whether you take it well or ill.*

Examples from Armstrong:—
Air chòir, *nobly, properly, as usual* [*truthfully*]; air seo, *upon this, then*; air iomrall, *astray*; air chuthach, *mad*; air neo, *else, or else*; air muin, *on, upon, above*; chaidh e air a muin, *he had carnal connection with her*; bithidh sin air bhuil, *that will come to pass.*

Additional:—
'Nuair a thig air duine thig air uile, this means that fortunes and misfortunes do not come singly, and is a Gaelic equivalent of *it never rains but it pours*; tha a' mhisg air, *he is drunk*; cha'n 'eil air ach—, *there is nothing for it but—.* Chaidh e air chéilidh orra, *he went to visit them;* air tòrradh, *at a funeral;* air banais, *at a wedding*; air a lughad is fheàirrd, *the smaller the better*; bha e air mo mhuin gu'n &c., *or* bha e air m'aodann gu'n &c., *he was always worrying me to &c.*, gabh air, *thrash him*; éirich air, *belabour him*; éirich air an òran, *sing the song well*; mór orm agus beag agam, *very patronizing to me and little thought of by me.*

☞ *Air*, it may be stated, always signifies something of a very temporary duration.

[*Air* governs the Dative case of nouns following it. Though it is said not to cause aspiration by rule, there are many instances in set phrases in which it does, as, air dheireadh, *behind*; air thoiseach, *before*; air chionn, *in readiness for*, [air chionn dhomh bhi deas, *by the time I was ready.*] It may be observed that where it causes aspiration it cannot be translated *upon*,—tha i air chall, *she is lost.* The reason for this difference seems to be that *air* in Modern Gaelic misrepresents the old prepositions *ar* and *for*. *Ar* meant *before, against, beside*, and it caused aspiration of the word following, because it formerly ended in a vowel (*are* or *ari*.) *For* meant *upon*, and did not cause aspiration. This *for* is the *air* proper of Modern Gaelic grammar.‡]

Examples given above in brackets, thus [ ] are additions to those given by the authors mentioned.

Combined with the personal pronouns thus:

1 Sing.	orm,	*Plur.*	oirnn,
2	ort,		oirbh,
3	air, *m.* / oirre *f.*		orra, *m. & f.*

Emphatic forms.

1 Sing. orm-sa, orm-fhéin, *pl.* oirnne, oirnn-fhéin.
2 Sing. ort-sa, ort-fhéin, *pl.* oirbh-se, oirbh-fhéin.
3 Sing. (*m.*) air-san, air-fhéin; (*f.*) oirre-se, oirre-fhéin, *pl., m. & f.* orra-san orra-fhéin.

air, *prep. pron.* On him, on it. 2 Upon him, upon it. 3 In his possession. 4 On him as a duty. Tha 'aodach air, *his clothes are on him*; cha d'fhuair mi ni air, *I got nothing in his possession*; tha e air ri phàigheadh, *he is bound to pay*; chaidh agam air, *I got the better of him, I managed to do it.*

àir, *gen. sing.* of àr.

àir, *v.a.* Plough, till, cultivate. 2 Number, count. Iadsan a dh'àireas euceart, *they who plough iniquity.*

air achd, *adv.* So that.

air a chor sin, *adv.* In that state, in that manner.

air adhart, *adv.* Forward.

air a h-uile cor, *adv.* At all events.

air àird, *adv.* In order, in train.

air alt's, *adv.* So that.

air a' mhionaid, *adv.* This moment, immediately.

air an aobhar sin, *adv.* Therefore.

air an uair, *adv.* Presently, instantly.

air athais, *adv.* Slowly.

air ball, *adv.* Immediately, on the spot.

air bàrr, *adv.* Atop.
air beulaobh, *prep.* (‡beulaibh, *dat. pl* of beul) Before, in front of.
†àirbhe, *s.f.*, Ribs. 2 Story. 3 Emolument, profit. 4 Produce.
†àirbheach, *a.* Ribbed, furrowed.
àirbheart, -eirt, *s.m.* Meaning. 2 Leading idea. 3 Leading. 4 Practising.
———ach, -aiche, *a.* Sagacious.
air bhoil, *adv.* Mad, crazy.
air bhò'n dé, *adv.* The day before yesterday.
air bhò'n raoir, *adv.* The night before last.
air bhò'n uiridh, *adv.* The year before last.
air bhòrd, *adv.* Boarded, as a boarder.
air bhraise, *adv.* Agog.
airbhinneach, -eiche, *a.* Honourable. 2 Venerable.
airbhre, *s. f.* Multitude, host. 2 Army, legion.
air bòrd, *adv.* On board, as of a ship.
àirc, -e, -ean, *s. f.* Ark. 2 Large chest. 3 Granary. Stad an àirc, *the ark rested.*
airc, -e, *s.f.* Distress, affliction, difficulty, trouble, poverty, strait, hardship. Saoi 'n a airc, *a hero in distress* ; 's mairg a shìneadh làmh na h-airce do chridhe na circe, *woe to him who stretches poverty's hand to the hen-hearted (cowardly)*; aran na h-airce, *bread of affliction; tha mi an airc, I am in a strait.*
†airc,** -e, *s. f.* Cork-tree. 2 Sow. 3 Lizard. Airc luachrach, *a lizard.*
†——each,** *a.* Ingenious. 2 Shifty.
airceach, -eiche, *a.* Indigent, poor.
———, -eich, *s. f.* Indigent person.
†airceadh,** -eidh, *s. m.* Earnest penny.
airceann, *a.* Certain, positive.
———as, -ais, *s.m.* Certainty, positiveness.
airceas, -ais, *s.m.* Scarcity. 2 Poverty, indigence. 3 Straitness. 4 Sorrow, distress, trouble. 5 Pain. 6 Difficulty. 7 Restraint. 8**Maturity. Gun airceas mealaidh sibh, *ye shall enjoy without restraint* or *without trouble.*
———ach, *a.* Sorrowful. 2 Troublous. 3 Causing sorrow or pain.
airceil, -e, *a.* see airceach.
air chall, *adv.* Astray, lost.
air chàrn, *adv.* Outlawed.
airchealla, see airchealladh.
airchealladh, -aidh, *s.m.* Sacrilege, theft.
airchill, *s.f.* Keeping.
air chionn, *adv.* To the end that. 2 For the use or purpose of. Air chionn daibh a bhi deas, *by the time they were ready.*
airchiosach, -aiche, *a.* Greedy, gluttonous.
airchis, *s. f.* Complaint. 2**Pledge. 3**Meeting.
air chòir, *adv.* Right, well. Cha d'fhuair e oibreachadh air chòir, *he did not get a proper chance of working.*
air chor éigin, *adv.* Somehow or other.
air chruaidh, (AC) *adv.* (cruaidh, *stone used as an anchor*) At anchor.
air chuairt, *adv.* Sojourning.
air chùl *adv.* Behind.
air chuthach, *adv.* Mad, crazy.
aircill, *v.a.* Lie in wait. 2 Listen secretly.
airciseach, -eiche, *a.* Difficult. 2 Strait. 3 Hungry.
airclеach, -eich, *s.m.* Cripple, any disabled or slovenly person. An dall air muin an aircleich, *the blind on the back of the cripple.*
airc luachrach, see dearc-luachrach.
air cùlaobh, *adv.* (‡cùlaibh, *dat. pl.* of cùl) Behind, at the back of.
àird, *gen. sing.* of àrd.
àird-, *a.* Often prefixed to words whose first vowel is small, but "àrd-" when the first vowel is broad, having the effect of an intensitive particle, as English *arch-* in arch-enemy.
àird, -e, -ean, *s.f.* Quarter of the heavens, "airt," or point of the compass, cardinal point. 2 Heaven. 3 Condition, state. 4 Preparation. 5 Improvement. 6 Order. 7‡‡ Happiness, comfort. 8‡‡Device, Expedient. Dè an àird a dh'fhàg thu air ? *in what condition did you leave him ?*; cuir àird air, *prepare*; o gach àird, *from every quarter* ; gu'n deanadh e àird air a chur 'am charaibh, *that he would devise a plan to put me in possession of it*; thàinig iad as gach àird, *they came from every quarter*; dheanadh e àird, *he would make preparation*; an àird, *aloft, upwards*; anns na h-àirdibh, *on high, in heaven*; an àird mhóir, *in high condition.*
àird-deas, -e-deas, *s. f.* The South, the south point. Gaoth na h-àirde-deas, *the south wind*; a dh'ionnsuidh na h-àirde-deas, *to the South.* [Always preceded by the article.]
àird-an-ear, -d'-an-ear, *s.f.* The East, the east point. Gaoth na h-aird'-an-ear, *the east wind*, a dh'ionnsuidh na h-aird'-an-ear, *to the East.* [Always preceded by the article.]
àird-an-iar, -d'-an-iar, *s. f.* The West, the west point. Gaoth na h-àird'-an-iar, *the west wind*; a dh'ionnsuidh na h-aird'-an-iar, *to the West.* [Always preceded by the article.]
àirde, *s. f. ind.* Height, altitude, eminence, high place, highness, excellence. 2 Promontory. Dè an àird' a tha e ? *what is his stature ?* ; àirde nam beann, *the height of the mountains*; bha a' ghrian 'n a h-àirde, *the sun was at its height*; ged éirich 'àirde, *though his excellence should mount.*
àirde, *comp.* of *a.* àrd.
àirdeachd, *s. f. ind.* Highness, greatness, quality, excellency.
àirdead, -eid, *s.m.* Degree of highness or greatness.
àirdealachd, *s. f. ind.* Ingenious contrivance.
àirdeanna, *s. pl.* Constellations.
àirdeil, -e, *a.* Inventive, contriving, ingenious.
air deireadh, *adv.* Last
†airden,‖ *s.* Symptom.
àirde 'n làin, *s. f.* High-water, full tide.
àirdhe, *s. f.* Wave. 2 Sign.
air dheadh, *conj.* Otherwise, or else.
air dheireadh, *adv.* Behind.
àird inbhe, *s. f. ind.* see àrd inbhe.
airdleag,** See airleag.
air do, *conj.* As. Air dhomh bhi teàrnadh, *as I was coming down*; air dhomh a thogail (in the past sense) *after I had lifted it.*
air dòigh, *adv.* In order.
àird-reachd, *s. m.* Supreme law. 2 Synod.
†àirdreim, *s. f.* High style, magnificence. 2 Flights in poetry.
àird-rìgh, see àrd-rìgh.
àird-thoir, see àird-an-ear.
àird-tuath, -e-tuath, *s.f.* The North, the north point. Gaoth na h-àirde-tuath, *the north wind*; a dh'ionnsuidh na h-àirde-tuath, *to the North.* [Always preceded by the article.]
aire, *s.f. ind.* Notice, heed, attention. 2 Regard. 3 Caution, watching, watchfulness, observation. 4 Mind, intention, thoughts, design. Thug iad aire dhomh, *they gave me their attention*; fo aire, *under observation, in custody*; gun aire dhomh, *unknown to me* ; *without my notice*; thoir an aire, *take care*; àit' aire, *observatory*; taigh aire, (also taigh faire) *observatory, a house where a corpse is or where vigils are held over a corpse, (late-wake)*; 'aire leagta air saoghail dhorcha, *his thoughts fixed on worlds unknown*; thoir an aire dhomh, *attend to me.*
aireach, -eiche, *a.* Attentive. 2 Cautious, circumspect. 3 Subtle. 4 *rarely* violent, hostile. 5** see aireachail.

àireach, -ich, *s.m.* Cattleman. 2 Grazier. 3 Dairyman. 4** Shepherd.
There is confusion in Gaelic between "àireach" and Old Irish "aire(ch)"—from which "airidh", *worthy*. The bó-aire, *cow-lord*, was the free tenant of ancient Ireland. "àireach" owes its long vowel to a confusion with àraich, *rear*.‡

aireach, (W. Isles) *a.* see aithreach.

aireach, *s.m.* †Shield. 2† Watch, guard. 3** Watchman.

——adh, -aidh, *s.m.* Attention, on one's guard.

——ail, -e, *a.* Attentive, watchful, observant, circumspect, applicative, aware. 2** Sober. 3***rarely* hostile, violent.

àireachas, -ais, *s.m.* Pastoral life. 2 Tending cattle. 3 Office of a herdsman. 4 Summer pasture for black cattle. 5** Watchfulness.

air eagal gu, *conj.* Lest.

‡aireal,‡ *s.* Bed.

†airealach,** *a.* Feeble.

àireamh, -eimh, *s.f.* Number, quantity. 2 Numbering, numeration, account. Gann an àireamh, *few in number*.

àireamh, *pr.pt.* àireamh, *v.a.* Number, count, compute. Có a dh'àirmheas duslach Iacoib ? *who can count the dust of Jacob ?*

——ach, -aich, *s.m.* Accountant. 2 Numerator. 3 Numeral.

——ach, *a.* Numerical.

——achail,** *a.* Arithmetical.

——achd, *s.f.ind.* Numbering, numeration, computation. 2 Arithmetic.

——aich, *v.a.* see àireamh.

——air,** *s.m.* Arithmetician. 2 Accountant.

——ar,** *fut. pass.* of *v.* àireamh.

——daireachd, *s.f.* see àireamhachd.

——fhear, -fhir, see àireamhair.

—— -tomhais,‡‡ *s.f.* Mensuration, mathematics.

airean, -ein, -eanan, *s. m.* Ploughman. 2 Goadsman.

——ach,* *a.* Agricultural.

——achd,* *s.f. ind.* Agriculture.

†aireannach,** -aich, *s.m.* Beginning.

†airear,** -ir, *s.m.* Food. 2 Satisfaction, choice. 3 Harbour, bay.

†airearra,** *a.* Pleasant, satisfactory.

aireasg,** -eisg, *s. f.* Apple of the eye. 2 Vision, sight.

air éiginn, *adv.* With difficulty.

aire-ionad,** *s.m.* Observatory.

air fad, *prep.* Through, throughout. 2 Among. 3 During. Mharbhadh iad air fad, *they were all killed.*

air falbh, *adv.* Away, gone.

air falbh ! *int.* Avaunt !

air falbhan,** *adv.* A-foot.

air fasgadh, *adv.* A-leeward.

air feadh, *adv.* Throughout. 2 Among. 3 During. [Governs the Genitive case.]

air 'fhad, *adv.* (*lit.* on its length) Lengthwise.

†airfid, see oirfeid.

†——each, -eiche, *a.* see oirfeideach, *a.*

†——each, -ich, *s.m.* ,, ,, *s.*

†——eachd, } see oirfeideachd.
†——eadh,** }

air fògradh, *adv.* In exile.

air fuaradh, *adv.* A-head, a-windward, a-hold.

†airg,** *s.m.* Prince.

airgead, (MM) see airgiod.

air ghaol, *prep.* For the love of, on account of.

airghealladh, -aidh, *s.m.* Cause of woe.

airghean, -ein, -eanna, *s.m.* Bridle-rein. 2 Symptom. Airgheanna bàis, *the symptoms of death.*

airghir,** *s. f.* Cow-calf.

air ghleus, *adv.* Ready. 2 In tune.

air ghràdh, *adv.* For the love of, on account of.

air ghràn, *adv.* On ball bearings, as a cycle.

airgiod, -id, *s.m.* Silver. 2 Money. 3 Riches, money in general of whatever kind. 'S e gaol an airgid freamh gach uilc, *the love of money is the root of all evil;* uaireadair airgid, *a silver watch*; cha robh mi gun airgiod, *I was not without money.* For compound words see below.

——ach, -aiche, *a.* Abounding in silver or money, rich, silvery.

—— -aiseig, -id-, *s.m.* Ferry-money.

—— -beò, -id-, *s.m.* Quicksilver, mercury.

—— -cagailte, -id-, *s.m.* Hearth-money.

—— -caorach, (CR) -id-, *s.m.* Slate diamond.

—— -ceann, (JM) -id-, *s.m.* Reward offered for the head of a rebel or outlaw.

—— -cinn, -id-, *s.m.* Poll-tax.

—— -geal, -id-ghil, *s.m.* Silver money.

—— -iasaid, -id-, *s.m.* Lent money, money given on loan.

—— -làimhe, -id-, *s.m.* Ready-money.

—— -luachra,§ -id-, *s.m.* (*lit.* silver rush) Meadow-sweet. see crios Chuchulainn.

—— -réidh,** -id-, *s.m.* Interest of money.

—— -ruadh, -id-, *s.m.* Copper money.

—— -teintein, -id-, *s.m.* Hearth-money.

—— -toite, -id-, *s.m.* ,, ,,

—— -ullamh, -id-, *s.m.* Ready money.

†airgne, } *s.m.* Robbery, pillage, plunder.
†airgneadh, }

àirid, see àraidh.

airidh, *s. f. ind.* Merit, desert, worth. Is math an *a.* e, *he richly deserves it;* is olc an *a.* e, *it is a pity.*

airidh, *a.* Worthy, deserving, excellent. 2 Famous. 3 Fit, meet, suitable. Cha'n airidh mi air, *I am not worthy of it;* is ro airidh thu air moladh, *thou art very worthy of praise; a.* air aithreachas, *meet for repentance.*

àiridh, -e, *pl.* -ean, & -nean, *s. f.* Summer residence for herdsmen and cattle. 2 Hill pasture. 3 Level green among hills. 4§ Wild plum, see plumbais fiadhain.
Bothan àiridhe, *or* taigh àiridhe, *the sheiling;* àiridh dhamh, *a pasture for oxen.*

airidh,** *s.m.* Green grove. 2 Place where osiers grow.

airidh-ghaoil, *a.* Lovely. 2 Deserving. 3 Amiable.

airidh-mhagaidh, *a.* Ridiculous, worthy of derision.

†airigh, see àraidh. 2***s.m.* Prince, ruler.

airilleach, -eich, *s.m.* (†aireal) Sleepy person.

†airillean,** -ein, *s.m.* Party, faction.

air iomadan, *adv.* Adrift.

air iomrall, } *adv.* Astray.
air ionndrainn, }

†airis,** *s. f.* Firebrand. 2 Charcoal. 3 Knowledge.

——, *s. f. & v. a.* see aithris.

——each, -ich, -ichean, see aithriseach.

†airisean,** -ein, *s.m.* Appointment, order.

air lagh, *adv.* Ready. 2 Cocked up. 3 Strung, as a bow.

†airle,** *s. f.* Advice.

†airleac,** *v.* Borrow. 2 Lend. see airleag.

airleacach,** *a.* Ready or willing to lend. 2 Ready to borrow. 3 Of, or pertaining to a loan. see airleagach.

†airleacadh,** -aidh, *s.m.* Borrowing. 2 Lending. see airleagadh.

†airleach,** -ich, *s.m.* Skirmish, rencontre.

àirleag, -eig, *s. f.* High flight. 2 Project. 3 Fancy, whim.

airleag, -eig, *s. f.* Jerk, sudden pull, shove, toss, fling, jostle. 2 Strait, want.

——, *v.a.* Borrow. 2 Lend.

airleagach, *a.* Ready or willing to lend, 2 Ready to borrow. 3 Of, or pertaining to a loan.
àirleagach, *a.* Flighty, fanciful, whimsical.
airleagadh, -aidh, -aidhean, *s.m.* Borrowing. 2 Lending.
airleas, -eis, *s.m.* Earnest, pledge.
airleig, -e, *s.f.* Strait. Tha mi 'n airleig, *I am in a strait.*
airleigeach,* *a.* Urgent.
air leth, *adv.* Separately, apart.
airlich, see fairtlich.
——, -ichean, *s.m.* Lender.
airlig, see airlich.
airlis, see airleas.
air los, *prep.* For the purpose of.
airm, *n.pl.* of arm. (*gen. pl.* arm) Arms, weapons. 2 Armour. 3 Place. Gun airm, *without arms*; airm àlainn, *beauteous armour;* ball airm, *a weapon.*
—— -chrios, -is, *s.m.* Military shoulder-belt.
—— -cheard, *s.m.* Armourer.
—— -cheardach, -aich, *s.m.* Armourer's smithy.
†airmeart,** -eirt, *s.m.* Order. 2 Custom.
air mhàgaran, *adv.* On all fours.
àirmheadh, *3p. sing. & pl. imper.* of *v.* àireamh.
àirmhear, *fut. pass.* of *v.* àireamh.
air mhearaichinn,** *adv.* Insane.
àirmhich, *v.a.* see àireamh.
àirmhidh, *fut. aff. act.* of *v.* àireamh.
†airmhidh,** *s.m.* Vow, promise.
air mhodh, *adv.* So that, in such a manner that.
†airmid.** *s.f.* Honour, worship, reverence. 2 Custom. 3 Swan.
airmis, see eirmis.
——each, see eirmiseach.
——eachd, see eirmiseachd.
airm-lann, -lainn, *s.m.* see arm-lann.
airm-mhuir,** *s.m.* Naval arms, navy.
airm-neimhneach, *s.pl.* Poisoned arms.
airmseach, see eirmiseach.
——d, see eirmiseachd.
airm-theine, *s.pl.* Fire-arms.
airm-thilgidh, *s.pl.* Missive weapons.
air muin, *prep.* On the back, mounted on. 2 On the top or summit. 3** On, upon, above. Air a mhuin, *on his back, upon him;* air a muin, *on her.*
air mullach, *adv.* A-top.
airndeal, (AF) *s.m.* Stag.
àirne, *s.f.* Sloe, wild plum, damascene—*prunus spinosa.*
airne (for àirnean) see àra.
àirneach, *a.* Kidneyed. 2 Valiant. 3 Full of sloes.
àirneach, -ich, *s.m.* Murrain in cattle. †2** Seed of shrubs.
àirneag, -eig, -an, *s.f., dim.* of àirne. Preas àirneag, *a sloe bush.*
——ach, -aiche, *a.* Full of sloes. 2 Like a sloe. 3 Of, or belonging to a sloe. Preas *a.*, *a bush loaded with sloes,* also *a sloe bush.*
àirneagaibh, *dat. pl.* of àirneag.
†airneamh,** -eimh, *s.m.* Grinding stone. 2 Hone.
airnean,** -ein, *s.m.* Watching at night.
àirnean, *s., pl.* of àra. Tha m'àirnean 'g am theagasg, *my reins teach me.*
airneas,** -eis, *s.m.* Watchfulness.
——ach,** *a.* Watchful. 2 Nephritic.
àirneig, *gen. sing.* of àirneag.
àirneis, *s.f. ind.* Household furniture or stuff. 2 Cattle, stock. 3 Moveables. 4 Accoutrements. 5**Assortment. Am measg an airneis féin, *in the midst of their own stuff*; àirneis taighe, *household furniture.*
——each, -eiche, *a.* Belonging to furniture.
—— -iarruinn, *s.f.* Implements, tools.

7. *Àirne.*

àirneisich, *v.a.* Furnish. 2 Equip.
air neo, *adv.* Else, otherwise. Air neo an t-sleagh mu bheil do làmh, *otherwise the spear your hand grasps.*
àirnibh, *dat. pl.* of àirne.
airnmheadh, (AF) *s.m.* Herd of cattle.
airn-sgrùdach,** *a.* Antinephritic.
air-san, *Emphat. form* of *prep. pron.* air.
airse,** *s.f.* Arch, vault.
air seachran, *adv.* Astray.
air sgàth, *prep.* For the sake of.
†airsge,** *s.f.* Contemplation, musing.
air sgeul, *adv.* Found. not lost.
air sheòl, *adv.* So that, in such manner.
airsid,* *s.f.* Unanimity.
——each, -diche, *a.* Unanimous, harmonious, agreeing.
——eachd, *s.f.* Unanimity, harmony, agreement, concord.
air siùdan, *adv.* Adrift.
airsneag, ** -eig, *s.f.* Arsenic.
airsneal, -eil, *s.m.* see airtneal.
——ach, see airtnealach.
——achd,* see airtnealachd.
air son, *prep.* For, on account of. 2 By reason of. 3 Instead of. [Governs the Genitive case.] Air a son, *for her*; air an son, *for them;* air son an fhuachd, *by reason of the cold*; tha iad ag ullachadh air son na seilge, *they are preparing for the hunting*; tha mi fada 'n ad chomain air son mar a ghabh thu ris na thubhairt mi, *I am much obliged to you for (in respect of) the attention you paid to what I said;* air son nam fìrean, *for the sake of the righteous.*
air son gu, *adv.* Because that.
air son sin, *adv.* Because of that, notwithstanding.
airsteal, see airtneal.
——ach, see airtnealach.
airt, *gen. sing.* of art.
airteagal, -ail, *s.m.* Article.
airteal, see airtneal.
——ach, see airtnealach.
airtean, } see artan.
airtein, }
air thoiseach, *adv.* Foremost, in the van. 2 **A-head.
airtine, see artan.

airtneal, -eil, *s.m.* Weariness, fatigue. 2 Sadness, langour, depression of spirits, distress, sorrow. 3 Strait, difficulty. Spiorad airtneil, *the spirit of heaviness;* co a dh'innseas *a.* na Féinne? *who can tell the sorrows of the Fingalians?*
———ach, -aiche, *a.* Weary. 2 Depressed, sad, melancholy, troubled. 3 Vexing. 4 Causing sadness. Tìr *a.*, *a weary land.*
air tìr, *adv.* On land.
air tòir air, *prep.* After, in pursuit of.
air traigh. *adv.* Ashore.
air tùs, *adv.* First, foremost.
air uairibh, *adv.* Occasionally, sometimes.
air uamhann,** *adv.* Aghast.
ais, *adv.* Back, backwards This word is only used in composition. Air t'ais! *stand back!* thàinig e air 'ais, *he returned;* thàinig i air a h-ais, *she returned;* bheir mi iad air an ais, *I will bring them back.* Air is 's air ais, *forwards and backwards—Reay country.*—A.G.
†ais, *s.m.* Hill. 2 Stronghold. 3 Covert. 4 Shingles to cover houses. 5 Dependence. 6 Loan. 6 Cart, waggon. 7** Money.
àis,(AC) *s.m.* Milk. 2 Milk preparation. 3 Dainty, delicacy, nectar, ambrosia. 4 Wisdom. àis na mnà sìthe, *the wisdom of the fairy woman.*
ais-adhlaic,** *v.a.* Disinter.
†aisc,** -e, *s.f.* Request, petition. 2 Damage. 3 Trespass. 4 Reproach.
ais-cheumnaich, *v.n.* Retire, withdraw.
aisde, *prep. pron.* Out of her, out of it. [Emphatic forms, aisde-se, aisde-fhéin.] Earbaidh e aisde, *he will trust in her.*
†aisde,** *s.f.* Poem. 2 Ingenuity.
aisdeach,** -ich, *s.m.* Gay diverting fellow.
———,** -iche, *a.* Mimic.
———an,** *s.pl.* Sports, diversions, pastimes.
ais-dhealradh, -aidh, *s.m.* Catoptrics.
aisdigheachd,** *s.f.* Jest.
†ais-dreoir, *s.m.* Traveller.
†aisdridh, *s.f.* Translation, digression.
aisead, -eid, *s.f.* Delivery, child-birth. 2** see aiseid. Ag a—, *pr.pt.* of aiseid.
aiseadadh, -aidh, *s.m. & pr part.*, see aisead.
aiseag, -eig, -an, *s.m.* Ferry. 2**Deliverance. 3**Return. 4**Vomit. Fear aiseig, *a ferryman;* fear an aiseig, *the ferryman;* fhuair e an t-aiseag a nasgaidh, *he got over the ferry free;* tha 'n droch dhuine a' gabhail an aiseig air oidhche dhorcha gheamhraidh agus a bhàta briste, *the wicked man crosses the ferry on a dark winter night and his boat broken*—a saying only fully appreciated by such as have had experience of Hebridean ferries in winter time. Ag a—, *pr. part.* of *v.* aisig.
aiseal, -eil & aisle, *n.pl.* aislean, *s.f.* see aisil.
aiseal, -eil, *s.m.* Jollity, fun, merriment. 2 (AG) Ass,—*Suth'd.* see asal. Ri h-aiseal, *merry-making.*
———ach, -aiche, *a.* Jolly, funny, merry. 2 Of, or pertaining to fun.
aisean, aisne, *pl.* aisnean [& aisnichean] *s.f.* Rib. Aon d'a aisnibh, *one of his ribs;* an aisean a thug e o'n duine, *the rib he took from the man.*
aisearan, -ain, *s.m.* Weanling.
aiseid, *pr. part.* ag aisead, & aiseadadh, *v. n.* Be delivered. *v.a.* Bear. Tha i air a h-aisead, *she is delivered.*
aiseid, *s.f.* Salver, plate.
aiseil, *gen. sing.* of aiseal.
aiseirich, *pr.pt.* ais-eirigh, *v.n.* Rise again, as in the resurrection.
aiseirigh, *s.f.* Resurrection, second rising. *A.* nam marbh, *the resurrection of the dead;* là na h-aiseirigh, *the day of resurrection.*
aisg, -e, -ean, *s.f.* Request. 2 Spot, blemish. 3 Gift, love token or pledge. 4 (AG) Leanness in cattle. Tha 'bhó air an aisg, *the cow is but skin and bone;* gu dè tha sin ach an aisg? *what is there but the frame?*
aisgeir, -e, *s.f.* Rocky mountain. 2 Ridge of high mountains.
†aisgidh, *s.f.* Present, gift. Hence "a nasgaidh," *free, gratis.*
aisig, *pr. part.* aiseag, *v.a.* Restore, deliver, give back, 2 Ferry over. Aisigidh e, *he will restore;* aisig dhomh gairdeachas do shlàinte, *restore unto me the joy of thy salvation.*
aisig, *s.f.* see aiseag.
aisigear, *fut. pass.* of *v.* aisig.
aisigidh, *fut. aff. a.* of *v.* aisig.
aisigte, *pt. part.* of *v.* aisig. Restored, delivered. 2 Ferried over.
aisil, -sle, -slean, *s.f.* Axle-tree. 2 Axis. Tarrang aisle, *a lynch-pin;* aisil na carbaid, *the axle-tree of the chariot;* aislean nan roth, *the axle-trees of the wheels.*
aisinn, *s.f.* see aisne. 2 see aisling.
aisinneach, -aiche, *a.* Costal.
ais-innis,** *v. a. & n.* Rehearse, narrate. 2 Say or tell over again, repeat.
ais-innleachd, *pl.* -dan, *s.f.* Wicked contrivance or invention. 2 Destructive artifice.
——————ach, -aiche, *a.* Cunning, crafty, plotting, mischievous. An comhairlibh aisinnleachdach, *in crafty counsels.*
ais-innseadh, -sidh, *s.m.* Telling, rehearsing, repeating. Ag a—, *pr. part.* of *v.* ais-innis.
ais-innsear, *fut.pass.* of *v.* ais-innis.
ais-innsidh, *fut. aff. a.* ,, ,,
aisiol, *s.f.* see aisil.
†aision,** *s.m.* Relic. 2 Diadem.
aisir, -sre, -srean, *s.f.* Passage, pass, path, defile.
aisith, *s.f. ind.* Strife, contention, discord, wrangling, disturbance. Sìol-chuiridh e aisith, *he will sow discord.*
aislear, -eir, *s.m.* Spring-tide.
ais-léine, *pl.* -léintean, *s.f.* Death-shroud.
aisleir, *gen. sing.* of aislear.
aisleth, see as leth.
aisling, -e, *pl.* -e & -ean, *s.f.* Dream, reverie, vision. Mhosgail e o aisling an laoch, *he awoke the hero from his dream;* chunnaic e aisling, *he saw a vision; a.* chonnain, *a lascivious dream; a.* fhaoin, *an empty dream.*
———each, *a.* Dreamy, visionary, of, or relating to a dream.
———, *s.m.* see aislingiche.
aislingean, *n. pl.* of aisling.
aislingiche, -ean, *s.m.* Dreamer, visionary. Tha'n t-aislingiche seo a' teachd, *this dreamer is coming.*
aisling-chonnain, *s.f.* Lascivious dream.
aislinn, see aisling.
———each, -aiche, *a.* see aislingeach.
aislinniche, see aislingiche.
aisne, *gen. sing.* of aisean.
aisneach, *a.* Ribbed. 2 Having large or strong ribs. 3 Of, or belonging to a rib.
aisneas, see aisneis.
aisneis, -e, -ean, *s.f.* ‡Rehearsing, tattle. 2 (JM) Very exaggerated account of any incident.
aisnichean, *n.pl.* of aisean.
ais-òrdugh, *s.m.* Countermand.
ais-òrduich, *v.a.* Countermand.
aisre, see aisridh.
aisreamnach,**, *a.* Mutual.
aisridh, *s.f.* Abode. 2 Receptacle. 3 Hill. 4 Path. *A.* nam ban, *the abode of women, a*

seraglio; an ruadh *a.*, *the red path.*
ais-sith, see aisith.
aiste, see aisde.
aisteach, -ich, -ichean, *s. m.* Gay diverting fellow.
†aisteidh, *s. f.* Hatches of a ship.
ait, -e, *a.* Glad, joyful, cheerful. 2*Odd, funny. òlach ait, *an odd fellow.*
àit, see àite.
àit'-adhlaic, *s.m.* Burying-place.
àit'-aire, *s.m.* Observatory.
†ait-cheas, *s. f.* Warrior's concubine.
ait-chiomach, -aich, -aichean, *s.m.* Petitioner.
———, -aiche, *a.* Causing laughter or merriment.
aite, *comp.* of ait.
àite, [*n.pl.*[-ean &] -eachan, *dat. pl.* -tibh & -achaibh] *s.m.* Place, spot. 2 Part, region. *A.*-suidhe, *a seat;* c'àite? *where?*
—— -còmhnuidh, *s. m.* Dwelling-place. 2 Dwelling, abode. Thog sinn àite-còmhnuidh do'n mhnaoi, *we built a house for the dame.*
àiteach, -ich, *pl.* -eacha & -eachan, *s.m.* Agriculture. 2 Inhabitant. 3 Habitation, dwelling. Tha àitich Innse-torrain fo ghéilt, *the inhabitants of Innistore are in terror;* air neul am bheil an àiteach fuar, *on a cloud is their cold habitation.* Ag a—, *pr. part.* of *v.* àitich. Inhabiting. 2 Cultivating. 3** Placing. Ag àiteach an fhearainn, *cultivating the land.*
†aiteach,** *a.* Anxious, careful.
àiteachadh, -aidh, *s.m. & pr. part.* of *v.* àitich, see àiteach.
aiteachadh, see aideachadh.
àiteachail,* *a.* Agricultural.
àiteachan, -ain, *s.m. dim.* of àite. Little place.
àiteachas, -ais, *s.m.* Colony. 2 Inhabiting, dwelling. 3 Cultivation.
àiteachd, *s. f. ind.* Agriculture. 2 Accommodation.
àiteag, -eig, -an, *s. f.* Shy girl. 2 Coquette.
———ach, -aiche, *a.* Indifferent, scornful. 2 Coquettish, shy. Ainnir *à. a shy maid.*
aiteal, -eil, *s.m.* Juniper, see aitionn. 2 Colour, gloss. 3 Glimpse, transient view. 4 Breeze. 5 Very small portion or quantity of anything. 6**Music. 7**Light, gleam of light. Fhuair mi aiteal dheth, *I got a glimpse of him;* aiteal mine, *a sprinkling of meal; a.* an Earraich, *the fanning breeze of Spring; a.* an òir, *the tinge of gold;* gun aiteal o reul air sàil, *on the deep without starlight.*
———ach, -aiche, *a.* see aitionnach. 2 Bright, shining, luminous. 3 Breezy, in slight breezes. 4 In glimpses.
———achd,** *s. f.* Breeziness.
aiteam, -eim, *s.m. & f.* People, folks, persons. 2 Tribe. 3* Wicked people—*Hebrides.* 4 Generation. Is beannaichte an *a.*, *blessed are the people; a.* chathach, *a warlike people.*
aiteamh, *pr. part.* ag aiteamh, *v.n.* Thaw. Tha e ag aiteamh, *it is thawing.*
———, -eimh, *s.m.* Thaw, fresh weather. Tha an là ris an aiteamh, *it is thawing; a.* na gaoithe tuath air an t-sneachda—tuilleadh a chur 'n a cheann, *the north wind's way of thawing the snow is to add more to it* (often used in the sense of people trying to make a thing better and invariably making it worse.)
†———, -eimh, *s.m.* Convincing proof, demonstration. 2 Argument.
aiteann, *s.m.* Juniper, see aitionn. 2**Furze(?)
———ach, *s.m. & a.* see aitionnach.
àitear, -eir, -an, *s.m.* Husbandman.
———achd, *s. f.* see àiteachd.
aiteas, -eis, *s.m.* Joy, gladness, blythesomeness. 2 Laughter. 3 Fun. 4 Comfort. 5* Oddness. T'aiteas, *your oddness; a.* an sùil Ghorm-àlainn, *gladness in the eye of Gormaline;* a chuireas aiteas orm, *that will make me glad; a.* air na sléibhtibh uaine, *joy on the green mountains;* cuirm chum aiteis, *a feast for laughter.*
àiteas, -eis, *s.m.* Dwelling-place.
aiteasach,** -aiche, *a.* Glad, joyful.
àite-coinnimh, *s.m.* Focus.
aiteig, *gen. sing.* of aiteag.
aiteil, „ „ aiteal.
aitgheal, -ghile, *a.* Bright, joyous.
aith,* (*for* àth) Kiln. Aith aoil, *a lime-kiln.*
†aith,** *s.m.* Hill. 2 Skirmish.——*a.* Keen, sharp. 2 Anxious.
aith-, *iterative particle* and *prefix.* Eqivalent to Latin and English *re-*. Thus generally written when used before a small vowel, but *ath-* before a broad vowel.
aith-cheas, -chise, *s.f.* Whore, bawd.
aith-chreideamh,** *s.m.* Apostacy.
aith-chuimir, see ath-chuimir.
†aithe, *s.f.* Revenge. *a.*** Keen.
aitheach, -ich, *s.m.* False assertion, lie. 2 Sow, boar. 3 see athach.
———, *a.* Swinish. 2 see athach.
aitheadh,** -hidh, *s.m.* Elf-shot. 2 Stealing away or retiring privately.
aitheal, see aingeal.
aitheamh, -eimh, *pl.* -eamhan [*contr.* aithean**] Fathom. Fichead aitheamh, *twenty fathoms.*
———aich,* *v.a.* Fathom.
àithean, *n.pl.* of àine.
aithearnach, -aich, *s. f.* see aitheornach.
aitheas, -eis, see aithis.
†aitheasg,** -eisg, *s. f.* Admonition, advice.
aitheimh, *gen. sing.* of aitheamh.
aith-éisdeachd, *s. f.* Appeal.
aitheornach, -aich, *s. f.* Land ploughed for a second crop. 2 Land where barley has been the last crop.
aithghearr, -a & -ghiorra, *a.* Short, concise, brief. 2 Quick, instantaneous. 3*Short-tempered. Tha e aithghearr, *he is short-tempered;* sgaoil sinn cho aithghearr, *we dispersed so soon;* an aithghearr, *in a short time;* gu h-aithghearr, *soon.*
aithghearr, *s.m.* see aithghearradh.
aith-ghearr, *pr.pt.* -ghearradh, *v.a.* Cut again. 2 Subdivide. 3 Shorten, curtail, abridge.
aithghearrachadh, -aidh, *s.m.* Abbreviation, abridgement, abstract.
———achd, *s. f.* Briefness, shortness.
———ad,** -aid, *s.m.* Contraction.
———adh, -aidh, *s.m.* Abbreviation, contraction. 2 Short way. 3 Short time.
aith-ghearradh, *pr. pt.* of aith-ghearr. Shortening. 2 Cutting again.
———aichte, *pt. part.* Abridged, shortened, abbreviated.
aithghin, see ath-ghin.
———eamhuinn, *s.m.* see ath-gh—.
———te, see athghinte.
†aithid,** *s.m.* Viper, snake.
†———ean,** -ein, *s.m.* Any venomous reptile. 2 Little beast.
aithine, see aithinne.
aithinne, -ean, & -nntean *s.m.* Fire-brand. 2 Charcoal. Mar *a.* as an losgadh, *like a firebrand from the burning.*
aithir, see nathair.
aithis, -e, -ean, *s. f.* Check. 2 Affront, abuse. 3 Fit means to do evil—*Islay.* 4 Scandal, reproach. 5 Blaming, upbraiding. 6 Rebuke. 7 Blemish, fault. 8 see athais. Na gabh té air bith mar mhnaoi, ach té air am bi aithis agad, *take no woman for a wife in whom you*

cannot find a flaw—N.G.P.
†aithis,** Reproach, rebuke, abuse, affront.
——each, -ich, -ichean, *s.m.* Abuser, reviler, abusive person. 2** see athaiseach.
——each, -eiche, *a.* Reproachful, reviling, rebutting, scandalous. 2 see athaiseach.
——eachadh, -aidh, *s.m.* Defamation, abuse.
aithisg, -e, -ean, *s.f.* Report, intelligence.
aithisich, see athaisich.
aithlis,* *v.a.* Imitate, mimic.
——, -e, -ean, *s.f.* Disgrace, reproach. 2 Mimicry.
——each, -siche, *a.* Reproachful, disgraceful. 2 Imitative.
aithmheal, -eil, see aimheal.
——ach, *a.* see aimhealach.
†aithmheas,** *s.m.* Ebbing of the sea.
àithn, *pr.pt.* ag àithne & àithneadh, *v.a.* Command, charge, order, bid, direct, enjoin. Cha 'n àithn iad, *they shall not order*; dh'àithn an Tighearn, *the Lord commanded.*
àithn,* *s.f.* Circle. àithn an là, *broad day-light.*
aithnchear, see aithnichear.
àithne, *pl.* àithnte, àitheanta, & -tan, *s.f.* Command, commandment, order, injunction, mandate, direction, charge. 2 *rarely* store. 3**Aphorism. Thug mi àithne dhuit, *I ordered you;* m'àitheanta, *my commandments.*
aithne, *s.f.* Knowledge, discernment, acquaintance. Cha'n 'eil aithn' agam air, *I have no knowledge of him.*
——ach,* *a.* Discerning, 2 Considerate, attentive. Tha i glé *a.*, *she is very considerate.*
——ach, -ich, *pl.* -ichean, & -ichinn, *s.m.* Stranger. Guest, visitor. Leis nach dragh aithn chean, *by whom guests were not counted a trouble.*
——ach,* *s.m.* Wood-rush, wild leek.
——achadh, -aidh, *s.m.* Knowing, recognition, discerning. 2 What is discernible. 3 Slight degree. Cuir *a.* an taobh seo e, *put it a slight degree ("kenning") this way.* Ag a—, *pr. part.* of *v.* aithnich. Ag *a.* gliocais, *knowing wisdom*
——achail, *a.* Intelligent, discerning.
aithneachd, *s.f. ind.* Knowledge, discernment. 2 Recognition. 3*Humanity.
——ail, -e, *a.* Recognising, knowing. 2 Familiar. 3 Kind.
aithneadail,‡‡ -e, *a.* see aithneachdail.
aithneanas,** -ais, *s.m.* Knowledge, perception.
aithne-chuiseach, *a.* Casuistical.
————d, *s.f.* Casuistry.
aithne-chuisiche, *s.m.* Casuist.
aithneadail, see aithneachdail.
aithneadair, -e, -ean, *s.m.* One who knows, or is conversant with, learned man.
àithneadh, -eidh, *s.m.* Commanding, ordering, enjoining, charging. Ag à—, *pr. part.* of *v.* àithn.
†aithneamsa, (*for* †aithnicheamsa) I know.
aithneil, -e, *a.* Knowing. 2 (AG)Polite.
aithn'ghinn, (*for* [dh']aithnichinn) *v.* I would know.
aithnich, *pr.part.* ag aithneachadh, *v.a.* Know, recognise. 2 Feel. 3 Discern, perceive. 4** Have sexual intercourse. Cha d'aithnich mi orm e, *I did not feel its effect on me.*
aithnichean,** -ein, *s.m.* Stranger, visitor, acquaintance.
aithnichear, *fut.pass.* of *v.* aithnich.
aithnichidh, *fut. aff. act.* of *v.* aithnich.
àithnichte, *a.* & *pt. part.* of *v.* aithnich. Known, recognised. 2 Plain, manifest. 3(AG) Exceedingly. Dean aithnichte, *make known*; *a.* fuar, *very cold.*

aithninn (*for* aithnichinn) *1 per. sing. past subj* of aithnich. Dh'*a.* *I would know.*
aithnisg,* *s.f.* Nickname.
àithnte, see àithne.
aithre, *s.m.ind.* Repentance.
——,‡ -ean, *s.m.* [& *f.*] Ox. 2 Bull. 3 Cow.
——ach, -eiche, *a.* Penitent, sorry. 2 Giving cause for regret. †3** see aighearach. Is *a.* (aighearach) leinn do bhuaidh, *we are surprised at your prowess;* is *a.* (aighearach) an t-òglach thu, *you are a droll fellow;* cha'n *a.* leam, *I have no cause to regret;* b'*a.* leis an Tighearn, *it repented the Lord.*
——,** -ich, *s.m.* Farmer. see àireach.
——a, see aithriche.
——achag, -aig, -an, *s.f.* Female penitent.
——ail, *a.* Penitent, repentant.
aithreachais, *gen. sing.* of aithreachas.
aithreachan, -ain, -an, *s.m.* Penitent.
aithreachas, -ais, *s.m.* Repentance, penitence, regret. Dean (*or* gabh) *a.*, *repent;* ni (*or* gabhaidh) mi *a.*, *I will repent;* gun *a.* cha bhi mathanas, *without repentance there shall not be forgiveness.*
aithreachd,** *s.f. ind.* Ancestry. A chaoidh cumaibh an cuimhne ur n-*a.*, *ever keep your ancestry in mind.*
aithreas, } see aithreachas.
aithri, }
aithriche, } *n. pl.* of athair. Fathers., ancestors.
aithrichean }
aithrichibh, *dat.pl.* of athair.
†aithridh,* *s.f.* Repentance, sadness, tears, sorrow.
——each,** *a.* Repentant, sad, sorrowful.
aithrin, *s.f.* Sharp point. 2 Conflict. 3**Satirizing tongue.
†aithrine,** *s.f.* Calf.
aithris, -e, -ean, *s.f.* Recital, rehearsal, report, narration. 2 see atharrais. 3 Tradition, tale. Ag a—, *pr.part.* of *v.* aithris.
——, *pr. pt.* ag aithris & -eadh, *v.a.* Rehearse, declare, report, narrate, tell, repeat. 2 see atharrais. Agus dh'aithris e na nithe sin uile 'n an éisdeachd, *and he told all those things in their hearing*; sgeul ri aithris, *a tale to tell*; aithrisibh-se agus aithrisidh sinne, *report you, and we will report.*
—— -bheulain, *s.f.* Mimicry, mockery, ludicrous gesticulation.
——each, -ich, -ichean, *s.m.* Relater, narrator, reciter. 2 Talebearer. 3 Tautologist. 4 Imitator.
——each, -eiche, *a.* Widely celebrated. 2 Repeating. 3 Tautological. 4 Traditionary. 5 Imitative.
——eachd, ** *s.f.* Frequent repetition, tautology.
——eadh, -eidh, *s.m.* Tautology, act of repeating, repetition. Ag a—, *pr.pt.* of aithris.
——ear, -eir, *s.m.* } Same meanings as aith-
——iche, *s.m.* } riseach.
aithris-leabhar,** *s.m.* Common-place book, note-book, day-book.
àitich, *pr.pt.* ag àiteachadh, *v.a.* & *n.* Inhabit, dwell, settle. 2 Cultivate, till, improve. 3 **Place. 4 Anchor, as a ship. 5**Give place to. 6**Accommodate. Gach neach a dh'àitich colann riamh, *every one that ever dwelt in a body;* dh'àitich an long, *the ship anchored;* ag àiteachadh an fhearainn, *cultivating the land.*
aitich, see aidich.
àitichte, *pt. part.* of àitich. Inhabited, settled. 2 Placed. Tir *a.*, *an inhabited land.*
aitidh, -e, *a.* Moist, damp, wet. Tha t'aodach

aitidh, *your clothes are damp.*
——eachd, *s. f. ind.* Moistness, dampness, wetness.
aitim, *s. f. ind.* see aiteam.
people.
aitiol, -il, see aitionn.
aitinn, *gen. sing.* of aitionn.
aitionn, -inn, *s.m.* Juniper (plant)—*juniperus communis.* Badge of Clan Gunn—(AG); of the Murrays, Rosses, MacLeods, & Athole Highlanders.§
——ach, *a.* Abounding in, or pertaining to juniper.
——,** *s. m.* Place where junipers grow. 2 Quantity of juniper bushes.

S. Aitionn.

aitreabh, -eibh, -an, *s.m.* Abode, building, dwelling. 2 Steading. 3†† Houses. Generally understood in W. Isles to mean large buildings. Thog e *a.* mhór. *he built large buildings*; aitreabh thaighean, *a number of attached houses,* as an exhibition. Taigh agus *a., mansion-house and premises;* théid an *a.* sios, *their building will decay.*
†aitreabh, *v.n.* Dwell.
——ach, -aiche, *a.* Habitable. 2 Of, or pertaining to an abode. 3 Domestic.
——ach, -aich, *n. pl.* -aichean, *s.m.* Inhabitant. 2 Tenant. 3 Lodger. 4 Farmer.
——ail, -aile, *a.* Full of policy. 2 Domestic.
aitreabhan, *n. pl.* of aitreabh.
aitreabh-nochdaidh, -eibh, *s.m.* Exhibition.
aitreabhta, *pt. part.* Inhabited.
aitreach, -eich, see aitreabhach.
aitreamh, see aitreabh.
——ach, see aitreabhach.
àl, àil, *s.m.* Brood, young of any kind. 2 Generation. A' solar dhearc d'a cuid àil, *gathering berries for her young*; àl stiallach, *speckled offspring*; an t-àl a ta ri teachd, *the generation to come;* tràth thig an sealgair gun fhios air àl, *when the hunter comes unexpectedly on a covey*; a' mhuc agus a h-àl, *the sow and her litter.*
†àl, *s.m.* (& *f.*) Rock. 2 Stone. 3 Fear. 4(AC) Anything hard, solid, rigid, or immoveable. see †ail 1, *s.*
àl,** àil, *s.m.* Nurture. 2 Food.
†—,** *v.a.* Nurse. 2 Praise.
a là, *adv.* By day.
†ala,** -ai, *s.m.* Trout. 2 Wound.
àlach, -aich, -ean, *s.m.* Levy, set, tribe, crew. 2 Set, or bank of oars. 3 Set of nails. 4 Activity. 5 Alacrity. 6**Request. 7 see àl. àlach ràmh, *a bank of oars.*
——, *a.* Of, or belonging to a brood. 2 Prolific.
alachag, } see ealachainn
alachain, }
alachagach, see ealachagach.
†àlacht,‖ *s.* Pregnancy.
alachuin, see ealachainn.
†alad,‖ *s.* Wound.
àladh, -aidh, *s.m.* Nursing. †2 Wisdom, skill, craft. †3**Malice. †4**Lie.
——, -aidhe, *a.* Speckled, variegated.
alag, -aige, *s. f.* *Hard task. 2 see aileag.
àlaich, *v.a.* Bear, produce, bring forth. 2 Multiply. 3 Nourish, nurse. 4 Commence, fall to. 5 Attack. 6 Adopt. Dh'àlaich iad air, *they attacked him;* is luath a 'dh'àlaich iad, *how soon they have multiplied.*
àlainn, -e & ailne [AC—aluinnde, ailindeach, aildiche, & ailinde] *a.* Beautiful, exceedingly fair. 2 Handsome, elegant. 3 Glorious, 4**White. 5**Bright, clear. 6**Amiable.
——eachd, *s. f.* Beauty. 2 Whiteness. 3 Brightness, clearness. 4**Amiableness.
alaire, *s.f.* ‡Brood mare. 2 see falair.
a làthair, *adv.* Present, at hand. 2 In existence, alive. Tha e 'làthair,*he is present, he is alive;* thoir a làthair a chéil' iad, *bring them face to face ;* ma bhitheas mi a làthair, *if I live.*
†alb,** ailb, *s.m.* Eminence, height.—*a.*White.
ald, uild, see allt.
aldan, -ain, see alltan.
——ach, see alltanach.
a leas, *adv.* Need. Cha ruigear leas, *there is no need;* cha ruig thu leas, *you need not.*
a leth taobh, *dv.* Apart, aside.
†alfad,** -aid, *s.m.* Cause, reason.
†alga,** *a.* Noble, great.
†——chd,** *s. f.* Nobleness, greatness, nobility.
all-, *prefix,* Over.
†all,** aill, *s.m.* Horse. 2 Rock, cliff. 3 Great hall. 4 Generation. 5 Race.
†all,** *a* White. 2 Foreign. 3 Great, prodigious.
alla, see alladh.
——, *a.* Wild, fierce. see allaidh.
allaban, -ain, *s.m.* Wandering. 2 Deviation. 3 Aberration. 4 Fatigue.
——ach, -aiche, *a.* Wandering.
†allabhair, *s.m.* Echo.
†àllabhar, *a.* Strange, wild, savage.
allabharrach, -aiche, *a.* Wild, savage, untameable.
——, -aich, *s.m.* Savage, barbarian.
——d, *s.f.* Barbarity, cruelty.
allabhuadhach, -aiche, *a.* see allbhuadhach.
alla-cheò, *s.m.ind.* Troubled mist.
alladh, -aidh, *s.m.* Excellence, fame, greatness. 2 Renown, applause. 3 Report. 4 Defamation, libel. Droch *a., a bad report*; deagh *a., a good report; a.* Dhaibhidh, *the fame of David;* thug e a bhriathrau gu'n robh i a' togail allaidh air, *he declared that she was laughing at him.*
alla-ghlòir, *s.f.* Gibberish, jargon, vain-glory, gasconading.
alla-ghlòrach, *a.* Inclined to utter jargon. 2 Vain-glorious, boastful.
allaidh, -e *pl.* allda, & allaidh *a.* Savage, wild, ferocious, terrible. 2 Proud, haughty. 3 **Boisterous. 4**Beauteous. Beathaichean allaidh, *wild beasts.*
allaidh, (AF) see madadh-allaidh.
allail, *a.* Noble, illustrious, excellent. celebrated. 2 Glorious. 3 Defamatory, detracting. Daoine *a., illustrious men.*
——eachd, *s.f.* Nobleness, excellency, illustriousness. 2 Gloriousness. 3 Renown.
allamaireach, see allmharach.
alla-mhadadh, -aidh, see madadh-allaidh. Chual' an t-a. an fhuaim, *the wolf heard the sound.*
allamharach, -aich, see allmharach.
——d, see allmharachd.
alla Mhoire,(AC) for allas Mhoire.
allanta, *a.* Ferocious. see allaidh.
†allas,‡‡ *s.m.* see fallus.
allas Chaluim Chille, (AC) (lit. St. Columba's glory) St. John's wort, see eala bhuidhe.
allas Mhoire,§ *s.m.* St. John's wort, see eala bhuidhe.
allbhuadhach, -aiche, *a.* Triumphant, conquering, victorious.
†——,** -aich, *s.m.* Prince's hall.
†allchur, *s.m.* Transposition.
allda, see allaidh.

†all-ghort, see ubhal-ghort.
allmhadadh, see madadh-allaidh.
allmhaidh, see allaidh. Armailt *a.*, *a terrible army.*
allmhara, see allmharach.
allmharach, -aiche, *a.* (all-, *beyond*+muir, *sea.*) Foreign, strange, transmarine, exotic. 2 see allabharrach.
————, -aich, *s.m.* Stranger, foreigner, alien, 2 One from beyond the seas. 3 Foreign foe. 4 see allabharrach. Iarmad nan allmharach, *the remnant of the strangers*; luingeas nan allmharach. *the fleet of the sea-borne foe.*
————achd, *s.f.* State of being foreign. 2 see allabharrachd.
allmharrach, see allmharach.
†allod,** *adv.* Formerly, of old.
alloil, see allail.
——eachd, see allaileachd.
allonta, Same meanings as allail.
————chd, „ „ allaileachd.
†allraon,** -raoin, *s.m.* Foreign expedition.
allsachail, *a.* Prone to respite, worthy of respite.
allsachd, *s.f.* Respite, reprieve, suspension.
allsadh, see abhsadh.
allsaich, *v.a.* Suspend, respite, reprieve. 2 Jerk. 2 Lean to one side.
allsga, *s.* Shudder.
allsgach, *a.* Terrible.
allsmuain, *s.f.* Great buoy, float.
allsporag, see abhsporag.
allt, uillt, *s.m.* Mountain stream, rill, brook. 2 *River with precipitous banks. Bruach an uillt, *the bank of the brook*; thréig torman nan allt, *the murmur of the brooks has subsided;* ag aomadh thar an uillt, *bending over the stream.*
allta, *a.* Fierce, savage, wild. 2 Strange, foreign. Beathaich *a.* na machrach, *the wild beasts of the field;* mar leòghann *a.*, *like a fierce lion.*
——chd, *s.f.ind.* Savageness.
alltadh,** see allta.
alltan, *n. pl.* of allt.
——, -ain, -an, (*dim.* of allt) *s.m.* Little brook, streamlet. Drochaid air gach alltan, *a bridge over every streamlet.*
——ach,** *a.* Abounding in rivulets. 3 Of, or belonging to a rivulet.
all-tapadh,†† -aidh, *s.m.* Mishap.
alltas,** -ais, *s.m.* Wildness, savageness.
alluidh, see allaidh. B'*a.* do shùil, *fierce was thine eye ;* dh'aom e air a sgéith umha *a.*, *he bowed over his beauteous brazen shield.*
alluigh, see allaidh.
†alluin,** *a.* Fair, handsome.
allum, (AF) *s.m.* Hind.
alm, ailm, *s.m.* Alum.
†almachadh,** *a.* Charitable.
almadh, -aidh, *s.m.* Tincture of alum.
almon,§ -oin, *s.m.* Almond—*amydalis communis*
àloe,§ *s.m.* Aloe (plant)—*aloe.*
a los, *adv. & prep.* About, intending, in order to. A los dol dhachaidh, *about going home* ; a los falbh, *with the intention of going.*
àlos, -ois, *s.m.* Aloe, see àloe.
alp, ailp, & -a, *s.f.* Height, eminence. †2 Mountain. also †alb
——, *v.a.* Ingraft, join closely together. 2*Indent. 3*Dovetail, *in joinery.*
alpadh, -aidh, *s.m.* Ingrafting, joining closely together. 2 Dovetailing. Ag a—, *pr.pt.* of *v* alp.
alt, uilt, altan, *s.m.* Joint, joining. 2 Condition, state, order, method. 2** Articulation. As an alt, *out of joint;* ni sinn alt eile air, *we will try another method for it*; air na h-uile alt, *at all events*; eadar altaibh na lùirich, *between the joints of the harness.*

9. *Aimon.*

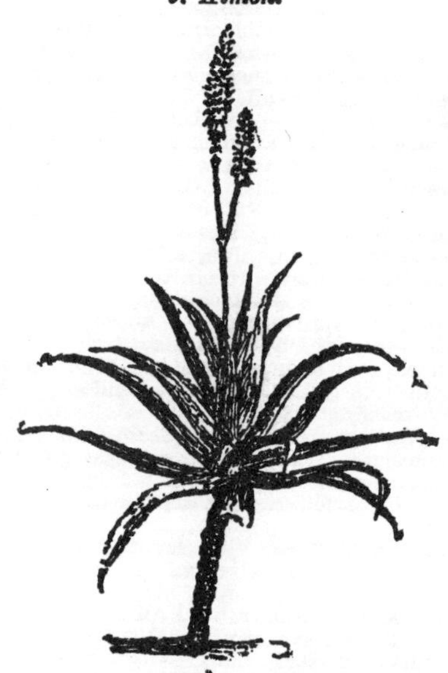

10. *Aloe.*

†alt,** uilt, *s.m.* Nursing, rearing, feeding.
†alt, uilt, *s.m.* Section of a book. 2 Time.
†—,** uilt, *s.m.* Leap. 2 Valley. 3 High place, eminence, hill. 4 Exaltation.
altach, *a.* Articular, jointed.
————,** -aich, -aichean, *s.m.* see altachadh 2.
altachadh, -aidh, -ean, *s.m.* Articulation of the joints. 2 Grace before or after meat. 3 **Salute, act of saluting. 4**Bracing, as of the joints. 5**Moving, budging. *A.* beatha, *welcoming, saluting ;* 's ann do'n làimh ghlain bu chòir *a.*, *it is the clean hand that should salute* (*one rogue should not accuse another.*) Ag a—, *pr. pt.* of *v.* altaich. Saluting, thanking. 2 Bracing, as of the joints. 3 Moving, budging.
———— -beatha, *s.m.* Salutation, greeting, welcome.
———— -cadail, (AC) *s.m.* Sleeping prayer —prayer before retiring at night.
altaich, *pr. pt.* ag altachadh, *v.a.* Salute. 2

Thank. 3 Relax the joints. 4 Brace. 5 Move, budge. 6 Join, knot. 7**Ask after one's welfare. 8(AC) Nurture, nourish, bring up. Dh' altaich iad beath' a chéile, *they asked for each other's welfare.*

altaich, *gen. sing.* of altach.

———e, see altachadh.

———ean, *n.pl.* of altach.

———ear, *fut.pass.* of altaich.

———idh, *fut.aff.act.* „ „

———te, *pt.part.* of altaich. Knotted.

altail,** *a.* Arthritic, articular.

altair, -air & altarach, *n.pl.* -raichean, & -raiche, *s.f.* Altar. Fa chomhair na h-altarach, *opposite the altar*; adhaircean na h-altarach, *the horns of the altar.*

altan, *n. pl.* of alt.

——, -ain, *dim.* of alt.

altanach,‡ *s.m.* Knot grass, see glùineach bheag.

alt-cheangal, -ail, *s.m.* Articulation, inosculation, juncture of the bones.

alt-eucail, *s.f.* } **Arthrisis.
alt-ghalar, *s.m.* }

alt-labhairt, *s.m.* Articulation.

alt-lùthaidh, *s.m.* Pith-joint. Sud mar a thaghadh Fionn a chù, —an t-*a.-l.* fad' o'n cheann, *thus would Fingal choose his hound—the pith-joint far from head.*—N.G.P.

altmhorachd, *s.f.ind.* Articulation.

altrach, (*for* altarach) *gen. sing.* of altair.

——, -aich, -aichean, *s.m.* Fosterer, one who fosters. 2 Nurse. Ban-altrach, *a female nurse.*

altradh,**-aidh, *s.m.* Fosterer.

altraiche,**-ean, *s.m.* see altrach.

altram, see altruim.

altranas,** see altrum.

altrap, -aip, *s.m.* Accident, mishap.

altruim, *pr.part.* ag altrumadh, *v.a.* Nurse, nourish, maintain, educate, foster, cherish.

altrum, -uim, *s.m.* Fostering, nourishing, nursing, rearing.

———ach,** *a.* Fostering, rearing, educating.

altrumachadh, -aidh, *s.m.* Same meanings as altrum. Ag a—, *pr.part.* of altrumaich.

altrumadh, -aidh, *s.m.* Same meanings as altrum.

altrumaich, *pr. part.* ag altrumachadh, *v.a.* Same meanings as altruim.

altrumaidh, *fut. aff. act.* of altruim.

altrumain, *gen. sing. & n. pl.* of altruman.

altruman, -ain, Nursling. 2**Chief. Seachd altrumain aig loch Làin, *seven chiefs at the lake of Lanno.*

altrumas, -ais, *s.m.* Nursing. Leanabh air a chur air *a.*, *a child sent a-nursing.*

alt-shligeach, -eiche, *a.* Crustaceous, like shells.

———d *s.f.ind.* Crustaceousness.

alt-thinneas,** *s.m.* Arthrisis.

altuchadh, see altachadh.

altuich, see altaich.

†alughain,** *s.f.* Potter's clay.

àluinn, -e, & àilne, *a.* see àlainn.

———de, see àlainn.

———eachd, *s.f. ind.* see àlainneachd.

am, *poss.pron.* Their. Am fearg, *their wrath;* am màthair, *their mother;* am bainne, *their milk;* am pàisd, *their child.* [Used before words words beginning with B, F, M, or P, which are not aspirated. The other letters are preceded by *an.*]

am, *def. art.* (*Nom. sing. masc.*) The. [Used before words beginning with B,F,M, or P.] Am baile, *the town;* am fear, *the man;* am moirear, *the lord* or *laird;* am pàisd, *the child.*

am, *interr. particle.* [Used instead of *an* before B,F,M,or P.] Am buail thu? *will you strike?*

am, (*for* mo) *poss.pron.* My. Ann am thaigh, (often written "am thaigh") *in my house.*

am-, *privative prefix.* Labialised form of *an-*.

am, (*equivalent* to anns am) Lagain am bi na neòinein, *dells where daisies are.*

am, *prep.* In. [Used for *an* before a word beginning with B, F, M, or P.] Am baile, *in a town;* am buthaibh, *in tents*; am meadhon, *in the middle;* am mearachd, *in error.* [see ann an.]

àm, ama, amannan, *s.m.* Time in general, past or present. 2 Season. 3 Convenience. 'S e seo an t-àm, *this is the time;* am fear a ni 'obair 'n a h-àm bithidh e 'na leth thàmh, *he that executes his task in due time shall be half at rest;* gabh àm air sin, *watch an opportunity to do that;* àm 'sam bith, *any time;* tha 'n t-àm ann, *it is full time;* àm iomchuidh, *fit time;* an àm na h-oidhche, *in the night-time;* an àm is an an-àm, *in season and out of season*; àm na cuireachd, ceithir-là-deug roimh Bhealltuinn is ceithir-là-deug 'n a déidh *sowing-time, a fortnight before May-day and a fortnight after;* na h-àmanna seo, *these times*; àm o aois, *olden times;* 's an àm, *at the time, in the meantime;* àm a' gheamhraidh, *the winter season;* àm an t-samhraidh, *the summer season.*

†am, *a.* Soft, moist, damp.

†ama,** -ai, *s.m.* Hame of horse's collar.

amach,** -aich, -aichean, *s.f.* Vulture. 3 Any ravenous bird.

a mach, *adv.* Out. 2 Out of. Thig a mach, *come out;* a mach air a chéile, *at variance.* [*A mach* includes the idea of motion to or from, but *a muigh* signifies resting outside. 'Mach 's a steach, *out and in,* implies motion to and from a place.]

amad, -aid, see amadan.

amadain, *gen. sing. & n. pl.* of amadan.

amadan, -ain, *n. pl.* -ain, & -ana, *s.m.* Fool. Cha tuig an t-amadan seo, *the fool shall not understand this;* ni e amadain, *he will make fools.*

amadanach, -aiche, *a.* Foolish, like a fool. Aodann *a.*, *a foolish expression of countenance.*

———d, *s.f. ind.* Foolishness, conduct of a fool.

amadan-Dé,(AC) *s.m.* Butterfly, see dearbadan-dé. 2 Also applied to foolish children.

amadan-léigh, see dearbadan-dé.

11. *Amadan-mòintich.*

amadan-mòintich, *s.m.* Dotterel (bird)—*charadrius morinellus.*¶

amadanta,** *a.* Foolish.

amaid,** *a.* Foolish, silly.

——, *s.f.* Folly, silliness. 2 Foolish woman.

———each, -eiche, *a.* Foolish. Aodann *a.*, *a foolish expression of countenance.* Gu h-amaideach, *foolishly.*

———eachd, *s.f.ind.* Foolishness, folly, silliness.

amaideag, -eig, -an, *s.f.* Foolish woman.
àmail, -e, *a.* Seasonable, timely, in time. 2 Temporal.
amail, -e, -ean, *s.f.* Evil, mischief. 2 Hinderance. A' cur *a.* orm, *hindering me.*
†amail, *adv.* see amhuil.
amail, *pr.pt.* ag amal & amaladh, *v a.* Hinder, prevent, stop, interrupt. 2 Entangle, clog. Dh'amail thu an lion, *you have entangled the net.*
——each, -eiche, *a.* Impedimental, obstructive, cloggy.
——idh, *fut. aff. a.* of amail.
amailist, see aimlisg.
amaill, *gen. sing.* of amall. 2 *v.a.& s.* see amail.
amain-fheithe, (AF) *s.* Amphibious animal.
amair, *gen. sing.* of amar.
amais, *pr.pt.* amas & amasadh, *v.n.* Hit, mark, aim, chance. 2 Find. Amais seo, *hit this;* an d'*a.* thu air? *did you find it?* is sona an duine a dh'amaiseas air gliocas, *happy is the man that finds wisdom.* [Should be used in reference to things and the lower animals only though sometimes met with otherwise. Use *coinnich* in reference to persons.]
——ceach,** -eiche, *a.* Wanton, lewd, lustful. Gu h-*a*, *wantonly.*
——ceachd,** *s.f.* Wantonness. lewdness.
——each, -eiche, *a.* Hitting well, taking a sure aim.
——idh, *fut.aff. act.* of amais.
amal, -ail, *s.m.* see amail. Ag a—, *pr. part.* of amail. 2 see amall.
amalach, *a.* see amaileach. 2**Curled.
àmalachd,* *s.f.* Seasonableness, timeousness.
amaladh, -aidh, -aidhean, *s.m.* Stop, impediment, hinderance, interruption, 2 Dovetail. 3 Balk. 4 Entangling, entwining. Ag a—, *pr.pt.* of amail. Hindering, impeding, stopping. Tha thu 'g am *a.*, *you are hindering me.*
àm-àireamh, -eimh, *s.m.* Chronology.
amall, -aill, *s.m.* Swingle-tree 2 Muzzle-bar. 3**Curb. 4**Yoke.

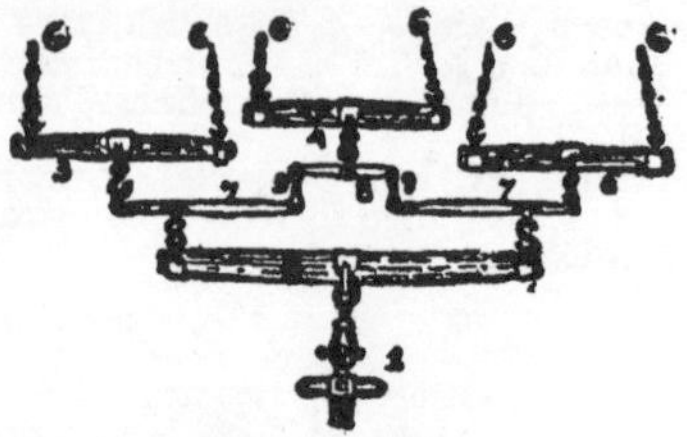

12. *Amall.*

Parts of a Swingle-tree :—

1 Muiseal, *bridle of plough.*
2 An t-amall, *swingle-tree.*
3 An greallag ceannarach, *land or nigh side small swingle-tree.*
4 An greallag meadhonach, *middle swingle-tree.*
5 An greallag clais, an greallag sgriob, *furrow small swingle-tree.*
6 Beairt-tharruing, *trace-chains.*
7 Liùdain, *levers.*
8 An liùdan ceangail, *connecting lever.*
9 Na tinneachan dùbailte, *double short links.*

Only two horses are generally used in the plough in the Highlands, but as three are sometimes employed for subsoiling, &c., it has been thought advisable to give an illustration of a swingle-tree for 3 horses, so that that the name of any part may be found if required. When swingle-tree for 2 horses is used, "the middle swingle-tree" (No. 4) is wanting, and the compensating lever apparatus (Nos. 7, 8, and 9) is dispensed with. In such cases the other parts retain the names given above.
†aman,** -ain, see abhainn.
àmanna, àmannan, } *n. pl.* of àm.
àmanta, *a.* see àmail.
——chd, *s.f. ind.* Seasonableness.
amar, -air, *n.pl.*-an & amraichean, *s.m.* Trough. 2 Channel. 3**Ditch. 4 Mill-dam. 5 Hod. 6**Manger. Amar na h-aibhne, *the bed of the river*, *a.* caol, *a narrow channel*; dh'fhalmhaich i a soitheach 's an amar, *she emptied her vessel in the trough.*
†amar,** -air, *s.m.* Chain, cable.
amarach, -aiche, *a.* Channelled.
amaraich,** *s.f.* Scurvy-grass.
amaran,** -ain, *s.m.* Distress. 2 Bungler.
amar-aoil, -ain-, -an-, *s.m.* Hod.
—— -baistidh, *s.m.* Baptismal font.
—— -brùthaidh, *s.m.* Wine-press, pressing vat.
amarcach,** *a.* Fond of.
amar-fuail, *s.m.* Chamber-pot, urinal.
amar-fuinidh, *s.m.* Baking-trough.
amar-mùin, -air-m-, air-mh-, *s.m.* Chamber-pot. 'S tric a bha na loingeis mhór a' crìonadh is na h-amair-mhùin a' seòladh, *often have large ships been rotting while the little pots are floating.*—N.G.P.
amarlaich, *a.* Blustering, careless.
amarlaid,* *s.f.* Blustering female, careless woman.
————each,* -aiche, *a.* see amarlaich.

13. *Amar-uisge.*

amar-uisge, -air-, -an-, *s.m.* Aqueduct.
amas, -ais, *s.m.* Hitting, aiming, marking. 2 Finding. 3 Chance. Chaill thu t'amas, *you have lost your power of hitting.* Ag a—, *pr.pt.* of amais. Is tearc iadsan a tha ag amas oirre, *few there be that find it.*
amasadh, -aidh, *s.m.* Same meanings as amas. Ag a—, *pr.pt.* of amais.
amasgaidh, See amasguidh.
amasguidh, -e, *a.* Profane. 2 Helter-skelter. 3 Mischievous. 4 Impure, obscene. Each *a.*, *a horse inclined to shy.*
————eachd, *s.f.* Profaneness. 2 Impurity.
am bheil? *v.* Is? are? Used also subjunctively—*is, are.* see bi.
am bitheantas, *adv.* Habitually.
am bun, *prep.* Waiting on, near to.
a measg, see am measg.
ametist, *s.f.* Amethist.
am fad, *adv.* Afar.
am fagus, *adv.* Near, at hand.
am feadh, *adv.* While.
am feasd, *adv.* For ever. Cha tig e am feasd, *he shall never come*; an do sguir a ghràs am feasd? *has his grace ceased for ever?*
am fochair, *adv.* Alongside.
am follais, *adv.* Above-board, publicly, openly.
amh, aimhe, *a.* Raw, crude. 2 Unsodden. un-

boiled, unroasted. 3 Unskilful. 4 Bad, naughty. 5 Dull, lifeless. 6 Unripe. 7 Bitter, sour. 7 Chilly. Feòil amh, *raw flesh*; na ithibh dheth amh, *eat not of it raw.*

amh,** *s.m.* Fool, simpleton. 2 Dwarf. †3 Water, †4 Ocean. see †àbh. †5 Denial.

——, aimh, see tabh.

àmh, àimh, see àbh.

†amh,** see amhuil.

†amhach,** -aich, *s.m.* Vulture. 2 (AF) see abhag.

amhach, -aich, -aichean, *s. f.* Neck. G' ar n-amhach, *up to our necks*; brisidh tu 'amhach, *thou shalt break its neck*; tha rud eiginn 'n am amhaich, *something has stuck in my throat.*

————,** *a.* Like a dwarf. 2 Like a fool.

————d, *s. f. ind.* Rawness. 2, Gloominess, sulkiness. 3 Insipidity. 4 Conduct of a fool or simpleton.

amhad,** -aid, *s.m.* Rawness, crudeness. Air *a.*, *however raw.*

amhadh. -aidh, *s.m.* Turn. Thug e *a.* air a cheann a dh'amharc air, *he turned his head to look at it.*

amhaidh, -e, *a.* Sour, sulky, surly. 2 Gloomy, as weather.

————eachd, see amhachd.

amhail, *adv.* see amhuil.

————,** *s.* Evil, mischief.

†amhailt,** *s. f.* Death.

àmhailteach, see amhuilteach.

amhain,* *s.m.* Entanglement by the neck. 2 Lying on the back without power of motion, as a horse.

————,* *a.* Entangled by the neck. 2 Un able to rise after falling, as a horse.

a mhàin, *adv.* Only, alone. Cha'n e a mhàin, *not only.*

amhainn, *gen. sing.* aimhne, amhna & amhann, *n. pl.* aimhne & aimhnichean, see abhainn.

————each, see abhainneach.

amhairc, *pr.pt.* ag amharc, *v.n.* Look. 2 See, behold. 3 Observe, regard. *A.* thairis, *overlook, take no notice of*; am fear nach amhairc roimhe amhaircidh e 'n a dhéidh, *he that will not look before him must look after him*—i.e. look before you leap; amhaircidh mi oirbh, *I will have respect unto you.*

a mhairg! *int.* Woe!

amhall,** -aill, *s.m.* Visit.

amhaltach, -aiche, see aimhealach.

amhaltas, -ais, see aimheal.

a mhàn, see a bhàn.

†amhantas,** -ais, *s.m.* Royal privilege. 2 Good luck.

†amhaon,** *s.* Twins. 2 Plurality.

amhar, see amar. †2**Music.

amharag,‡ -aig, *s. f.* Cherlock, wild mustard. see marag bhuidhe. 2** Sweet marjoram. see oragan.

amharc, -airc, *s.m.* Seeing, viewing. 2 Vizzy or sight on a gun. 3 View, sight, observation. 4 Beholding. 5 Inspecting. 6 Look, appearance. †7** Fault. Is bochd an t-amharc a th'air! *what a miserable appearance he has!* 's an *a.*, *in view*; a' dol as an *a.*, *getting out of sight.* Ag a—, *pr.pt.* of amhairc. Looking, viewing, observing, inspecting, beholding.

————ach, -aiche, *a.* Perceptive. 2 Watchful, vigilant. 3 Considerate, humane. Bha sin *a.* uaith, *that was very considerate of him.*

————aiche, -ean, *s.m.* Spectator.

amharcholl,** *s.* Apthongs.

amharra, *a.* Sour-tempered.

amhartan, -ain, *s.m.* Fortune, luck, prosperous. 2** Lucky person.

————ach, -aiche, *a.* Lucky, fortunate, prosperous.

amhartanachd, *s.f.* Good fortune, course of good fortune, prosperity.

amharus, -uis, *s.m.* Suspicion, doubt, distrust. Is mór m'*a.*, *I very much suspect*; tha, gun *a.*, *yes, most undoubtedly*; fo *a.* umaibh, *in doubt about you*; am bi thusa gun *a.* ad rìgh? *wilt thou indeed be a king?*

————ach, -aiche, *a.* Distrustful, doubtful, suspicious. 2 Ambiguous. Deasboireachd *a.*, *doubtful disputation.*

————achadh, -aidh, *s.m.* Mistrusting, doubting. Ag a—, *pr.pt.* of amharusaich.

————achd, *s.f.ind.* Distrustfulness, suspiciousness, doubtfulness, apprehensiveness. 2 **Ambiguity.

————aich, *pr.pt.* ag amharusachadh, *v.a.& n.* Doubt, suspect, mistrust.

amhas, -ais, -an, *s.m.* Wild ungovernable man. 2 Madman. 3 Wild beast. 4 Stall for cattle. 5 **Dull, stupid person.

————ach, -aiche, *a.* Wild, ungovernable. 2 Like a madman. 3 Dull, stupid.

————ag, -aig, -an, *s.f.* Silly woman.

†amhasan,** -ain, *s.m.* Sentry.

amhasan, *n. pl.* of amhas.

amhcha, *s.f.* Cravat.

amhdadh,** -aidh *s.m.* Permission, permit.

a mheud, *adv.* Inasmuch.

amhfhortan, -ain, *s.m.* Luck. 2 Misfortune.

àmhghair, *gen.sing.* of àmhghar.

àmhghar, -air, -an, *s.m.* Affliction, tribulation, anguish, trouble, sorrow, distress, adversity, calamity. Dh'amhairc e air m'*à.*, *he looked on my affliction*; àm tharruingeas ar n-*à.* gu ceann, *a time which shall draw our troubles to a close.*

————ach, -aiche, *a.* Afflicted, sorely troubled, distressed. 2 Calamitous.

————aiche,** *s.m.* Distressed person, one who has long been in distress.

————, *comp.* of àmhgharach.

†amhlabhair,** *a.* Mute, dumb, speechless.

amhlach, *a.* see amlach 2**Voracious.

amhladh, -aidh,‡ *s.m.* Duplicate, copy, transcript. 2**Voracity.

amhlag-mhara, -aig-,-an, *s.f.* Storm-petrel(bird) see luaireag.

amhlaich, *v.a.* Tangle.

amhlaidh, *adv.* see amhluidh.

amhlair, -e, -ean, *s. m.* Dull, stupid or ignorant person. 2 Fool, idiot. 3**Changling. 4 Driveller. 5**Brutish man.

————each, -reiche, *a.* Foolish, like an idiot. 2 Brutal. 3 Boorish.

————eachd, *s.f.ind.* Foolishness, trifling conduct, fooling away one's time. 2 Brutality, 3 Boorishness.

amhlaisg, *s.f.* Bad beer, taplash.

————each, -geich, *s.m.* Brewer of bad beer.

————, -geiche, *a.* Insipid or weak, as bad beer.

amhlar, -air, -an, see amhlair.

amhluadh, -aidh, -aidhean, *s.m.* Confusion. 2 Trouble. 3 Dismay, astonishment. Is amhluadh e, *it is confusion*; air an *a.* cheudna, *in like manner.*

amhluaidh, *gen. sing.* of amhluadh.

amhluidh, *adv.* As, like as, in like manner, resembling, so. *A.* mar shruth a ruitheas bras, *like as a stream that runs amain*; ni h-*a.* sin a bhios na daoine peacach, *not so shall be the wicked.*

amhnag, see abhnag.

amhnarach, -aiche, *a.* Shameless, impudent.

†amhnas, -ais, *s.m.* Shamelessness, impudence.

†amhra, -ai, *s.m.* Dream. 2 Poem. 3 Sword-hilt.
†amhra,** *a.* Great, noble, good. 2 Dark.
†amhradh,** -aidh, *s.m.* Mourning, wailing, lamentation.
amhran, (*for* fabhran) *n.pl.* of fabhra.
———, -ain, -an, see òran.
amhrath, -aith, *s.m.* Misfortune.
amhsainn, see amhsan.
amhsan, -ain, *s.m.* Gannet, solan goose, see sùlaire.
amhsgaoileadh, -lidh, *s.m.* Flux, diarrhœa, looseness.
àmhtha, see àth.
amhuil, *adv.* As, like as, even as, such as, in like manner, resembling. *A.* mar Nimrod an sealgair, *even as Nimrod the hunter*; is *a.* mar sin a bhitheas na peacaich, *even so shall sinners be*; *a.* tonn air tràigh, *like a wave on the shore*; *a.* mar seo, *even like this, just like this*; *a.* sin, *in like manner*; *a.* mar an duine seo, *just like this man.*
amhuil,* *s.f.* Attention, regard. see umhail. Na biodh *a.* agad dha, *never mind him* air an *a.* cheudna, *in like manner.*
†———,** *v.* Spoil, plunder.
amhuil sin,** *adv.* So, in like manner.
amhuilt,‡ -e, -ean, *s.f.* Antic, odd, fanciful, or wild gesticulation, buffoonery. 2 Odd appearance. 3 Stratagem, deceit, trick.
———each, -eich, *s.m.* Antic, buffoon, harlequin. 2 Strategist, cunning fellow.
———each, -eiche, *a.* Ludicrous, odd. 2 Deceitful, stratagetical. 3 (JM) Pretending, tricky. 4 Wicked.
———eachd, see amhuilt.
———ear, see amhuilteach.
———earachd, see amhuilt.
amhuinn, aimhne, aimhnaichean, see abhainn.
àmhuinn, -e, -ean, *s.f.* Oven. 2 Furnace. *A.* dheataich, *a furnace of smoke.*
———ich, *v.a.* Stew, seethe.
amhultas, -ais, see aimheal.
amhusg, see amhas.
†amlabar,‖ *a.* Dumb.
amlach, -aiche, *a.* Curled, having ringlets. 2 Flowing, as hair.
amladh, -aidh, *s.m.* see amaladh.
amlag, -aig, -an, *s.f.* Curl, ringlet.
———ach, -aiche, *a.* Forming ringlets. 2 Curled, tressy, full of ringlets. *a.*, cleachdach, *curled and tressy.*
———aich, *v.a.* Curl, make into ringlets.
amlubach, -aiche, *a.* Curling.
am màireach, *adv.* To-morrow.
am measg, *prep.* Among, amongst.
àmon, -oin, *s.m.* Almond, see almon.
†ampal, *s.m.* Hunger.
amraiche, -ean, *s.m.* [*& f.*] One that works about troughs. 2 Trull.
———an, *pl.* of amar.
àmraidh, *s.f.* Cupboard, "press." 2**Almonry.
a muigh, *adv.* Out, without, the outside. Air an taobh a muigh, *on the outside*; tha e a muigh, *he is outside*; tha 'm fuachd a muigh 's a staigh an diugh, *the cold is outside and inside to-day.* see note on "a mach."
amuis, see amais.
†amus,**-uis, *s.m.* Ambush, surprise. 2 Sudden onset. 3 Leisure.
amusach, -aich, *s.m.* One who keeps his appointment.
†———, *a.* Of, or pertaining to an ambush.
amusadh, -aidh, see amasadh.
an, *prep.* In.
an-, *negative prefix,* Not, un-. An-aoibhinn, *joyless, distressful.*

-an, *dim.* termination of singular nouns. Balg, *a bag,* balgan, *a little bag*; cnoc, *a hill,* cnocan, *a little hill.*
-an, *plural* termination of nouns.
an, *def. art. m.* The. [Used 1 Before palatals in the nominative singular. 2 Before linguals in nom., gen., and dat. sing. 3 Before a vowel in the gen., and dat. sing. 4 Before *fh* in the gen., and dat. sing. It takes "t-" before vowels in the nom. sing., and before *s*, followed by a vowel or *l*, *n*, *r*, in the gen. and dat. sing.] An cù, *the dog*; an gnìomh, *the deed*; an t-each, *the horse*; an t-eun, *the bird*; an lìon, *the net*; an t-sluaigh, *of the people*; toil an athar, *the father's will*; anns an t-saoghal, *in the world.*
—, *def. art. fem.* The. [Used 1 Before a lingual in the nom., and dative singular. 2 Before a vowel, or *fh* in the nom. and dat. sing. It takes "t-" in the nom. and dative sing. of nouns beginning with *s*, followed by a vowel or *l*, *n*, *r*.] An doimhne mhór, *the great deep.*
The article is often used in Gaelic in cases where it is absent in English, as—1 When a noun is followed by *seo*, *siod*, or *sin*, as An cù seo, *this dog*; am bealach sin, *that breach.* 2 Before the names of some countries, as Anns an Eadailt, *in Italy*; anns an Fhraing, *in France.*
an ? *interr. particle,* An tu esan? *art thou he?* an cù do sheirbhiseach? *is thy servant a dog?*
an, *poss. pron.* Their. An cuid, *their property.* [Changes into *am* before B, F, M, or P.]
an, *rel.pron.* Whom, which, that. Leis an d' fhàg mi e, *with whom I left it*; leis an d' fhalbh e, *with whom he went.* Contracted 'n after a vowel, as, o'n d'thàinig e, *from whom he came.* [Changes into *am* before B, F, M, or P.]
an, *expletive particle,* placed before all verbs, excepting those beginning with B, F, M, or P which take *am.* Gus an abair iad, *till they say.*
an-, *intensitive particle* as in an-bhruid, *tyranny.*
†an,** *s.m.* Element. 2 Principle. 3 Water. 4 Falsehood. 5 Planet.
†an, *a.* see aon.
†an,** *a.* Still. 2 Pleasant. 3 Pure. 4 Noble. 5 True. 6 Swift.
†ana,** *s.* Riches. 2 Fair weather. 3 Silver cup.
ana-, *neg. pref.* Not, un-.
an-abaich, -e, *a.* Unripe. 2 Premature, abortive. 3 Raw. Torrachas anabaich, *an untimely birth.*
———eachd, *s.f.* } Unripeness, crudity, im-
———ead,-eid, *s.f.* } maturity, abortiveness.
an-abaidh, see an-abaich.
ana-baisteach, -aich, *n.pl.* -aiche, *s.m.* Anabaptist.
——— ———, *a.* Anabaptist.
anaban, see anabarr.
anabarr, -a, *s.m.* Excess, superfluity. 2** Rioting. 3**Atrocity.
———ach, -aiche, *a.* Exceeding, excessive. 2 Redundant, superfluous. 3 Desperate, indispensable. 4** Shocking, terrible. Meudaichidh mi thu gu h-anabarrach, *I will increase you exceedingly.* [Sometimes used as an adverb] *a.* fireanta, *over much righteous*; *a.* aingidh, *desperately wicked.*
———chd, *s.f.ind.* see anabarr.
———as, see anabarr.
anabas, -ais, *s.m.* Unripeness. 2 Refuse, dregs, off-scouring.
———ach, -aiche, *a.* Unripe. 2 Dreggy. 3

Muddy.
——-achd, *s.f.ind.* State of being full of dregs. 2 Muddiness.
ana-beachd,** *s.f.* Strange fancy. 2 Wild idea. 3 Ambition.
———-ail, -e, *a.* Haughty. 2 Inattentive. 3 Not recollecting. 4 Unpunctual. 5** Fanciful, wild, chimerical. 6 Ambitious.
ana-beachdalachd, *s.f.ind.* Dignity, grandeur of mind, haughtiness. 2 Fancifulness, wildness. 3 Ambition.
anabharr, see anabarr.
ana-bheus, -a, -an, *s.m.* Immorality.
———-ach, *a.* Immoral.
ana-bhàthadh, -aidh, *s.m.* Deluge, inundation. 2 Melancholy drowning.
ana-bhiorach, -aich, *s.m.* Centipede. 2‖ Whitlow, [preceded by article *an.*]
————,** *a.* Very sharp, very pointed.
anabhuil,* *s.f.* see an-bhuil.
ana-bith,†† *a.* Huge. 2 Extraordinary.
anablach, -aich, *s.m.* Offal. 2 Coarse flesh.
anablas, -ais, *s.m.* Insipidity, tastelessness. 2 Bad taste. *A.* t'uirighioll, *the insipidity of your eloquence.*
ana-blasda, *a.* Insipid, tasteless. 2 Of bad taste. Deoch *a.*, *an insipid drink.*
ana-blasdachd, *s.f.ind.* Same meanings as anablas.
ana-brais, *s.f.* Lust.
an-abuich, see an-abaich.
———-eachd, see an-abaicheachd.
an-abuichead, see an-abaichead.
an-abuidh, see an-abaich.
———-eachd, see an-abaichead.
ana-bùirt, -e, *s.f.* Madness, fury.
†anac,** -aic, *s.m.* Wound.
anacail, -e, *s.f.* Quietness, tranquility. 2 Preservation, safety.
——, *pr.pt.* anacladh, *v.a.* Defend, protect. 2 Deliver, save, preserve. 3 Secure. 4 Manage.
ana-cainnt, -e, *s.f.* Abuse. 2 Ribaldry. 3 Blasphemy.
———-each, -eiche, *a.* Reproachful. 2 Abusive. 3 Prone to ribaldry. 4 Blasphemous. Gu h-ana-cainnteach, *abusively.*
anacair, see anshocair.
anacrach, (AG) *a.* (an-shocair) Painful.
ana-caith,* *v.a.* Squander, waste, be profuse or prodigal.
———-each, -eiche, -ichean, *s.m.* Spendthrift, prodigal, squanderer.
———-eadh, -eidh, see ana-caitheamh.
———-eamh, -eimh, *s.m.* Extravagance, prodigality, waste. 2 see ana-caitheach. 3††Profusion. 4 Riot. 'S thaobh *a.*, *on account of riot.*
———-teach, -tiche, *a.* Extravagant, wasteful, prodigal.
————, -iche, -an, see ana-caitheach.
———-tiche, see ana-caitheach. 2 *comp.* of ana-caithteach.
anacal, -ail, *s.m.* Quiet person. 2 Healthfulness.
anacaladh, see anacladh.
anaceart, -eirte, *a.* Unjust, partial, iniquitous, unfair. Gnìomh *a.*, *an unjust deed.*
————, *s.* see ana-ceartas.
———-as, -ais, *s.m.* Injustice, iniquity, unfairness, partiality, injury.
ana-ceist, -e, *s.f.* Difficulty, dilemma. 2 Puzzle, riddle.
†anach,** -aich, *s.m.* Path. 2 Washing, cleansing. 3 Anger.
†——-ain,** *s.f.* Danger, peril, hazard, crisis. 2 Misfortune.
†anachan,** -ain, *s.m.* One who keeps in the way. 2 Intruder.
ana-chaoin, *v.n.* Lament, deplore to excess.
————-eadh, -nidh, *s.m.* Excessive weeping, wailing.
†anachrach,** *a.* Full of pity, compassionate.
†anachdrach, see anshocrach.
†anachradh, -aidh, *s.m.* Wretch, object of pity.
†anachras, -ais, *s.m.* Pity, compassion.
ana-chruas,** -ais, *s.m.* Extreme avarice.
ana-chùirtear,** *s.m.* Anti-courtier.
ana-chùram,** -aim, *s.m.* Care, anxiety.
————-ach,** -aiche, *a.* Anxious, solicitous. Gu h-*a.*, *over-anxiously.*
ana-cinnte, *s.f.* Uncertainty.
————-ach, -eiche, *a.* Uncertain, unsure.
anacladh,** -aidh, *s.m.* Preserving, preservation. 2 Delivering, deliverance. Ag a—, *pr.pt.* of anacail, Preserving, saving, securing, protecting.
ana-cleachd,* *v.a.* Discontinue the practice of.
————,** *s.f.* Inexperience. Is mór t'ana-cleachd, *great is your inexperience.*
————-adh, -aidh, -aidhean, *s.m.* Inexperience. 2 Want of practice. 3 Bad custom or habit. 4**Desuetude.
ana-cleachdainn, see ana-cleachdadh.
ana-cleas, -eis, -easan, *s.m.* Bad or wicked deed.
ana-cnàmhadh,** *s.m.* Indigestion.
ana-cneasda, *a.* Uncharitable, unfeeling. 2 Dishonest. 3 Inhuman, cruel. 4 Dangerous. 5 Froward, perverse. 6 Barbarous, savage. Le beul *a.*, *with a perverse mouth.*
————-chd, *s.f.ind.* Unfeelingness. 2 Inhumanity, cruelty. 3 Perverseness.
ana-coireach, see neo-choireach.
ana-cothrom, -oim, *s.f.* Injustice, unfairness, hardship. 2 Violence, oppression. 3 Disadvantage. Luchd ana-cothroim, *oppressors.* "Ana-cothrom" is always used in the W. Isles as applicable to people who are receiving injustice, not to those who are doing injustice. It is generally used to signify some natural disadvantage.—J.M.
————-ach, -aiche, *a.* Unjust, unfair. 2 Violent, oppressive. Gu h-*a.*, *oppressively.*
anacrach,* *a.* Sick, unwell.
ana-creideach, -ich *s.* & -eiche, *a.* see ana-creidmheach.
ana-creideamh, -eimh, *s.m.* Infidelity, unbelief, scepticism, atheism.
ana-creidmheach, -mhich, *s.m.* Sceptic, infidel, unbeliever.
—————, -eiche, *a.* Sceptical, unbelieving, atheistical, irreligious. Bean *a.*, *an unbelieving wife.*
ana-criosd, -a, *s.m.* Antichrist. Thig an t-*a.*, *Antichrist will come.*
————-achd, *s.f.ind.* Paganism, heathenism, infidelity, irreligion.
————-ail, -aile, *a.* Unchristian, anti-christian. 2 Inhuman, cruel, barbarous.
————-alachd, see ana-criosdachd.
————-uidh, -ean, *s.m.* Infidel, pagan, heathen, one not a christian.
————-uidheachd, see ana-criosdachd.
ana-cruas, -ais, *s.m.* Avarice, covetousness.
ana-cruinn, -e *a.* Not round.
ana-cuibheas, -eis, *s.m.* Immensity, infinity. 2 Excess. 3 Incredible thing.
ana-cuibheasach, -eiche, *a.* Immoderate, excessive. Used also adverbially as—*a.* aingidh, *desperately wicked.*
—————-d,* see ana-cuibheas.
ana-cuimhne, *s. f. ind.* Forgetfulness, negligence.
————-ach, -aiche, *a.* Forgetful, inattentive, negligent.
ana-cuimhnich,* *v. a.* Forget, neglect.
ana-cuimse, *s.f.* Vastness, immensity. 2 Im-

moderateness, intemperance. Fear na h-ana-cuimse, *an intemperate man.*
————ach, -siche, *a.* Vast, immense. 2 Immoderate, intemperate. Gu h-*a.*, *immoderately.*
————achd, *s.f.ind.* Immenseness. 2 Immoderateness, intemperance.
ana-cuimsich,* *v.a.* Exaggerate, make exorbitant.
ana-cul,** *s.f.* Lean condition of body. Is buileach a chaith thu gu n-*a.*, *how very lean you have become!*
———ach, -aiche, *a.* Lean, thin, slender. 2 Ill-looking. 3 Ill-clothed.
ana-cùram, aim, *s.m.* Negligence, carelessness.
————ach, -aiche, *a.* Negligent, careless.
ana-gairios, see ana-goireas.
————ach, see ana-goireasach.
————d, see ana-goireasachd.
ana-gealtach, -aiche, *a.* Fearless, intrepid.
ana-géillidh, -e, *a.* Huge, monstrous.
ana-géilt, *s.f.* Courage, bravery.
an-àgh, -àigh, *s.m.* Misfortune.
an-aghaidh, *s.f.ind.* Confusion of countenance. An-aghaidh ort! *may shame befall you!*
an aghaidh, *prep.* Against, in opposition. An aghaidh na gaoithe, *against the wind.* [Governs the Genitive case.]
ana-gheur,‡‡ -eòire, *a.* Blunt.
ana-ghlais,** *s.f.* Hog wash.
ana-ghlas, -ais, see eanghlas.
ana-gheur, -éire, *a.* Blunt, obtuse.
ana-ghleus, *s.m.* ††State of being unprepared. 2 Disorder. 3 Mischief.
————ta, *a.* Unprepared. 2 Discordant. 3 Spiritless.
ana-ghlic, see neo-ghlic.
ana-ghliocas, -ais, *s.m.* Imprudence, indiscretion, foolishness.
ana-ghlòir, -e, *s.f.* Bad language.
————each, -eiche, *a.* Reproachful, scurrilous, shameful.
ana-ghlonnach, -aiche, *a.* Renowned for valour. 2 Famous, celebrated.
anaghnàth, -thanna, *s.m.* Bad custom, irregular habit, innovation.
————ach, -aiche, *a.* Unusual, not customary, irregular.
————aich, *v.a.* see mi-ghnàthaich.
————anna, *n.pl.* of ana-ghnàth. Bad customs.
————s, -aiths, *s.m.* Bad customs, irregularity, innovation.
ana-ghrinn, -e, *a.* Incompact, inelegant, 2 Unkind.
anagladh, see anacladh.
ana-glaodh, -aoidh, *s.m.* Loud shout.
ana-gleusta, *a.* see ana-ghleusda.
ana-glic, see ana-ghlic.
ana-gliocas, see ana-ghliocas.
ana-gnàth, -a, see ana-ghnàth.
————ach, see ana-ghnàthach.
ana-gnèitheil, -e, *a*, Pernicious, mischievous. 2 Destructive.
ana-goireas, *s.m* Inconvenience. 2 Excess, want of moderation. Chaidh e gu h-*a.*, *he went to excess.*
————ach, -aiche, *a.* Inconvenient, incommodious. 2*Very needful, requisite. 3**Excessive, immoderate.
————achd, *s.f.ind.* Incommodiousness. 2 Excessiveness, immoderateness.
an-agrach, -aiche, *a.* Quarrelsome. 2 Petulant.
ana-gràdh, -àidh, *s.m.* Doting love.
————ach, -aiche, *a.* Loving excessively.
anail, *gen.* analach & anaile, *n. pl.* anailean, *s.f.* Breath. 2 Breeze, air. 3 Rest. A. a shròin, *the breath of his nostrils; a.* na beatha, *the breath of life; a.* na gaoithe, *the breath of the wind; a.* nan speur, *the breath of the skies (wind)*; leig t'anail, gabh t'*a.*, *rest, take your breath*; leigibh ur n-*a.*, *rest yourselves*; is blàth *a.* na màthar, *warm is the mother's breath*; is *a.* atharrachadh ceàird, *change of work is a rest.*
anaim, *gen.sing.* of anam.
an-aimsir, -e, -ean, *s.f.* Unmeet time. 2 Unfavourable weather. 3 Tempest.
————eil, -e, *a.* Untimely. 2 Unseasonable.
anainn, -e, -ean, *s.f.* Top of a house or wall. 2 Eaves.
anaisg, *s.f.* Fling, reproach.
an àite, *prep.* In place of, instead. An àite droighne fàsaidh an giuthas, *instead of the thorn shall grow the fir-tree.*
an-airc, -e, *s.f.* Necessity, compulsion.
an àird, *adv.* Upwards, from below. Gun éirigh an àird a chaoidh, *never more to rise.*
an-àireamhta, *a.* Innumerable.
anairt,** *a.* Soft, tender. 2 Mild, gentle, humane.
†an-aithne,** *s.m.* Private man, obscure man.
†an-aithnichte,** *a.* Unknown, obscure, unnoticed.
anal, see anail.
——ach, *gen.sing.* of anail.
analaich, *v.n.* Breathe.
a nall, *adv.* Hither, to this side, over, from the other side.
an-àm, *s.m.* Unseasonableness.
anam, anma, *pl.* anman, anmanna, *s.m.* Soul, spirit. 2 Mind. 3 Life, breath. 4 Term of affection, love. 5 Courage. Teich air son t'anam, *escape for thy life*; air m'anam, *on my soul*; is aoibhinn t'*a.* 'ad neòil, *joyous is thy soul in thy clouds.*
an-àmach,** *a.* Late, unseasonable. Gu h-an-àmach, *unseasonably.*
anama-chara, (AC) *s.m.* see anam-chara.
anamadach, -aiche, *a.* Lively, sprightly, active, having soul, life, or animal spirits.
anamadaich, -e, -ean, *s.f.* Dying convulsions.
anamadail, -e, *a.* see anamadach.
anamain, *gen. & voc. sing.* of anaman.
anaman, -ain, -annan, *s.m.* Little soul. 2 Darling, dear soul. An t-anam truagh, *the poor soul.*
anaman-dé, see dearbadan-dé.
anamanta, *a.* see anamadach. 2 Courageous, bold.
anamantachd,** *s.f.* Liveliness.
†anam-chaidh, *a.* Brave.
anam-chara, see anam-charaid. } *s.m.* Bosom
anam-charaid, -chairdean, } friend. 2AC Soul-friend. A man or woman who says the death-blessing over a dying person.
ana-measarra, *a.* Intemperate, immoderate. 2 Lewd. 3** Vast, huge. Caitheamh *a.*, *immoderate expense.*
————chd, *s. f. ind.* Intemperance, immoderateness. 2 Vastness, prodigiousness. 3 Licentiousness, excess.
ana-measarradh, see ana-measarra.
ana-meidhidh,* *a.* Premature, abortive.
ana-meidheachd,* *s.f.* Prematurity, abortiveness.
ana-mèin, see ain-mèin.
————each, see ain-mèineach.
————eachd, see ain-mèin.
anam fàis,** *s.m.* Vegetative soul.
—— fàsmhor,** *s.m.* ,, ,,
†anamhach,** *a.* Lively, sprightly.
†anamhain,** *s.m.* Panegyrist.
an-amharus, -uis, -an, *s.m.* Extreme distrust

or suspicion. **Builteach dh'a.**, *liable to suspicion.*
———ach, -aiche, *a.* Suspicious, mistrustful 2 Jealous.
ana-mhiann, see ana-miann.
———ach, see ana-miannach.
ana-mhór, see an-mhór.
an-amhrus, see an-amharus.
an-amhrusach, see an-amharusach.
ana-miann, -nnan, *s. m.* Sensuality, lust. Fear *a.*. *sensualist*; ana-miannan na feòla, *the lusts of the flesh.*
———ach, *a.* Sensual, lustful, carnal.
ana-miosarra, see ana-measarra.
anamoch, see anmoch.
anam mothachail,** *s.m.* Sensitive soul.
——— reusonta,** *s.m.* Reasonable soul.
an-aobhach, -aiche,*a.* Cheerless,joyless,gloomy, unamiable. *A.* gun solus do chiùil-sa, *joyless without the light of thy song.*
an-aoibhinn, *a.* Mournful, unhappy. Is *a.* dhà-san ! *woe unto him !*
an-aoibhinneach, see an-aoibhneach.
an-aoibhneach, -eiche, *a.* Joyless, mournful, unhappy.
an-aoibhneas, -eis, *s.m.* Woe, sadness, sorrow, grief, misery, discomfort.
an-aois, -e, *s.f.* Non-age, minority.
an aonar,* *adv.* Four days hence. (?)
an-àrd, *a.* Very high.
an-àrdach, *a.* Superlative *in grammar.*
anart, -airt, -an, *s.m.* Linen. *A.* grinn, *fine linen*; *a.* bùird, *table linen* ; *a.* gealaichte, *bleached linen* ; *a.* glas, *dowlass* ; *a.* canaich, *fustian* ; *a.* bàis, *shroud.*
———, -airt,** *s.f.* Draught causing death.
ànart, -airt, *s.m.* Pride, disdain. 2 Contempt.
———ach, -aiche, *a.* Disdainful, contemptuous. 2 Indignant.
anasdolach, *a.* Intransitive *in grammar.*
anasgar, *a.* †**Restless. †2**Irksome. 3††Excessive.
anasgrachd, *s.f.* †**Restlessness. †2**Irksomeness. 3††Excess.
an asguidh, *adv.* Gratis, freely, as a present.
anasta, *a.* Stormy.
———chd, *s.f.ind.* Shattering or ill-guiding of anything. 2 Tempestuous weather. 3 Exposure to the blast. 4††Trouble, hardship.
an-athach, -aiche, *a.* Bold, courageous, fearless. 2 Fierce. Gu h-aighannach, an-athach, *in a joyous and fearless manner.*
an ath-oidhche, *adv.* To-morrow's night. (*lit.* the next night.)
anbarrach, see anabarrach.
†anbhail,** *a.* Shameless, haughty.
†anbhal,** *a.* Prodigious.
anbhann, see anfhann.
anbhar, }
anbharr, } *s.m.* see anabarr.
anbharra, }
anbharrach, -aiche, see anabarrach.
an-bhàs, -àis, *s.m.* Sudden death. 2 Shocking death. 3 Catastrophe.
an-bhàthadh, see ana-bhàthadh.
an-bheus, see ain-bheus & ana-bheus.
ana-bhiorach, *a.* Very pointed or cone-shaped.
an-bhlas, see ana-blas.
an-bhochd, *a.* Extremely poor.
———ainn, *s.m.* Extreme poverty. 2 Extreme misfortune.
†anbhrod,** -oid, *s.m.* Tyrant.
an-bhroid, see an-bhruid.
an-bhruid, -e, *s.f.* Tyranny.
———each, -ich, *s.m.* Tyrant.
———ich, *v.a.* Tyrannize.
an-bhuil, -e, *s.f.* Confusion, dismay. 2 Misapplication. 3††Damage, abuse.

†anbhuinne, see anfhainne.
†———achd, see anfhannachd.
†anbracnt,‖ *s.* Consumption.
an-braise, see anabrais.
an-buirte, see anabuirt.
an-cainnt, see anacainnt.
an cais,** *adv.* By and by.
an caraibh, *adv.* Beside, near.
an càs air,** *adv.* Desirous. Tha e an càs air, *he is very desirous to have it.*
an ceann, *prep.* In the end,at the expiration of.
———, *adv.* A-head.
an ceann a chéile, *adv.* Together.
an ceartair, *adv.* Just now.
an céin, *dv.* Afar.
†ances,‖ *s.* Ailment. (old spelling.)
an ceud, *a.* The first. see ceud.
an-chaith, see ana-caith.
an-chinnteach, see ana-cinnteach.
ana-chleachdadh, see ana-cleachdadh.
an-chleas, see ana-cleas.
an-chreideamh, see ana-creideamh.
an-chruas, -ais, see ana-cruas.
an-chù, (AF) Fox.
an-chùram, see ana-cùram.
an còdhail, see an còmhail.
an coinneamh, *adv.* Well nigh. 2 To meet.
an coinneamh a' chùil, *adv.* Backwards.
an còmhnaidh, *adv.* Always.
an cuairt, *adv.* About.
†andach,** -aich, *s.m.* Wrath, anger. 2 Evil.
†andadh,** *a.* Just.
†andagh,** *s.m.* Sin.
an dàil, *prep.* Against, as a foe. 2 Searching for, in the track of. 3‡‡To meet.
an dàil,‡‡ *adv.* Near to.
an-dàna, -dàine, *a.* Presumptuous, fool-hardy. 2**Impudent.
———chd, see andànadas.
———das, -ais, *s.m.* Presumption, fool-hardiness. 2**Arrogance, impudence.
an-daoine, *s.*, *pl.* of an-duine.
an dara cuid....no..... *conj.* Either....or..
an dé, *adv.* Yesterday. Air bhò'n dé, *the day before yesterday* ; an diugh is an dé, *to-day and yesterday.*
an deaghaidh, see an déidh.
an-dealbh, -a, -an, *s.m.* see aindealbh.
an déidh, *prep.* After, behind. Fond of, wishing for. An déidh seo, *after this, afterwards;* tha e 'n déidh oirre, *he is fond of her.*
an déidh làimhe,** *adv.* Afterwards. 2**Behindhand.
an déign, see an déidh.
an déis, *prep.* see an déidh.
an déis,‡‡ *adv.* Afterwards.
an-deisealachd,†† *s.f.* see ain-deisealachd.
an-deiseil,†† -e, *a.* see ain-deiseil.
an-déistinn, -e, *s.f.* Squeamishness, fastidiousness. 2 Loathsomeness.
———each, *a.* Squeamish. 2 Loathsome.
an-deurach,** *a.* Mournful, tearful, weeping excessively. 4 Causing excessive grief.
an-diadhach, -aich, see ain-diadhaidh.
an-diadhachd, see ain-diadhachd.
an-diadhalachd, see ain-diadhachd.
an-diadhaidh, -e, see ain-diadhaidh.
———eachd, see ain-diadhachd.
an diugh, *adv.* To-day. Thig e an diugh, *he will come to-day.*
an-dlighe, *s.f.* Undutifulness. 2**see ain-dlighe.
———ach, -eiche, *a.* Undutiful. 2** see ain-dligheach.
an-dòchas, -ais, *s.m.* Despair, despondency. 2 **Presumption. 3**Sanguine expectation.
———ach, -aiche, *a.* Without hope. 2 Distrustful. 2**Presumptuous. 3**Sanguine.
an-dòigh, -e, -ean, *s.f.* Bad condition, bad state

andòighe 1,†† *a.* Unsystematic, badly appointed. 2 Bad-tempered.
an-dòlas, *s.m.* Excessive sadness, distress, unhappiness. 2 Discomfort.
———ach, *a.* Sad, sorrowful. 2 Comfortless. 3 Irksome.
†andras,** -ais, *s.m.* Fury, infernal divinity.
an dràsd, *adv.* Now, at present. An dràsd 's a rithist, *now and then.*
an dràsdaich, *prov.* for an dràsd.
an dràsta, see an dràsd.
†an-drobhlasach,** -aich, *s.m.* Spendthrift.
†—————d,** *s.f.* Extravagance, prodigality.
an-dualach, *a.* Degenerate.
an-dualachas, -ais, } an-dùchas.
an-dualchas, -ais, }
†andualarasc,** *s.* Catachresis.
an-dùchas, -ais, *s.m.* Degeneracy. 2 Meanness.
————ach, -aich, *a.* Degenerate. 2 Unworthy, base. 3 Not hereditary.
an-duine, *pl.* an-daoine, *s.m.* Wicked man. 2 Insignificant person. 3 Decrepid person.
†an-dul,** -uil, *s.m.* Avidity. 2 Inordinate desire.
an e? Is it? is it he? An i? *is it she?* see *v.*is.
an-eadargnaidh,** *s.m.* Stranger.
an-eagal, -ail, *s.m.* Fearlessness, boldness. 2 **Astonishment, terror.
————ach,* *a.* Fearless. 2 Timid. 3 Formidable, causing terror.
an-ealamh, -aimhe, *a.* Indolent, inactive. 2 Inexpert.
an-ealanta, *a.* Inexpert, unskilful.
————chd, see an-ealantas.
————s, -ais, *s.m.* Inexpertness, unskilfulness.
an-eanraisd, -e, *s.f.* Storm.
an earar, *adv.* Two days hence, day after tomorrow.
an eararais, *adv.* Three days hence.
an-earb,* *v.a.* Distrust, despair, mistrust, doubt, suspect.
an-earbsa, *s.f.ind.* Distrust, suspicion, jealousy, non-reliance.
an-earbsach, -aiche, *a.* Distrustful, suspicious. 2 Diffident. 3 Timorous. 4 Causing suspicion or distrust.
—————d, *s.f.* Distrustfulness, suspiciousness.
an ear-thràth, see an earar.
an-èasguidh, -e, *a.* Lazy, idle. 2 Sluggish, slow.
an-éibheinn, see an-éibhinn.
an-éibhinn, -e, *a.* Woeful, sorrowful, wretched. 2 Afflicted. 3†† Uncomfortable.
————each, see an-éibhinn.
an-éibhneach, -eiche, *a.* see an-aoibhneach, & an-éibhinn.
an-éibhneas, -eis, see an-aoibhneas.
an-éifeachd, *s.f.* Inefficacy, want of power.
————ach, -aiche, *a.* Ineffectual, weak.
an-eireachdail, -e, *a.* Unhandsome, ungraceful. 2 Ungenteel, unseemly.
an-eireachdas, -ais, *s.m.* Uncomeliness. 2 Unseemliness, indecency.
an éirig, *prep.* In return for, in ransom for.
anfach, -aiche, *a.* Overflowing.
anfadh, -aidh, see onfhadh.
anfadhach, -aiche, see onfhadhach.
†anfas,** -ais, *s.m.* Fear, terror.
an-fhacal, -ail, *s.m.* Reproach, taunt. 2 Bad word, improper expression.
an-fhad, *a.* Too long.
anfhadh, see onfhadh.
an-fhaidhidinn, *s.m.* Impatience, restlessness.
an-fhaidhidneach, *a.* Impatient, restless.
an-fhaighidinn, see an-fhaidhidinn.

anfhainne, *comp.* of anfhann.
anfhainne } *s.f.ind.* Feebleness, weak-
anfhainneachd, } ness, debility, decrepitude, unhealthiness, infirmity.
anfhann, -ainne, *a.* Weak, feeble, tender. 2 Infirm, debilitated, decrepit, sickly. 3 Slender. 4 Pliant, not stiff. Suilean *a.*, *weak eyes.*
anfhannachadh, -aidh, *s.m.* Weakening, debilitating, enfeebling. Ag a—, *pr. pt.* of *v.* anfhannaich.
anfhannachd, *s.f.ind.* Weakness, infirmity, debility.
anfhannaich, *v.a.* Enfeeble, weaken, debilitate, enervate. 2 Make infirm.
anfhannaichidh, *fut. aff. act.* of anfhannaich.
an-fharsning, -e, *a.* Narrow, tight, circumscribed.
an-fharsuingeachd, *s.f.* Narrowness, tightness.
an-fhéilidh, -e, *a.* Inhospitable. 2 Loud, boisterous. 3 Fierce. Le toirm *a.*, *with a boisterous noise.*
an-fheòil, see ain-fheòil.
an-fhiachail, -e, *a.* Mean, low, base. 2 Ungenerous. 3††Worthless.
an-fhialaidh, see an-fhéilidh.
an-fhios, *s.m.* see ain-fhios.
an-fhiosach, see ain-fhiosrach.
an-fhiosrach, -aiche, *a.* see ain-fhiosrach.
an-fhiosrachd, *s.f.ind.* see ain-fhiosrachd.
an-fhìrinn, see ain-fhìrinn.
†anfhocain,** *s.f.* Danger, hazard.
an-fhoighidinn, see an-fhaidhinn.
†an-fhoralamh,** -aimh, *s.m.* Constraint. 2 Danger.
†an-fhorlan,** -ain, *s.m.* Power. 2 Plundering. 3 Oppression. 4 Storm.
an-fhosgladh, -aidh, -ean, *s.m.* Chasm. 2 Cleft, opening.
an-fhuachd, -a, *s.m.* Excessive cold.
an-fhulangach, -aiche, *a.* Impatient, restless. 2 Uneasy.
an-fhurachail, -e, *a.* Unobservant, inattentive.
an-fhurachar, *a.* see an-fhurachail.
an-fhurachas, -ais, *s.m.* Inattention, disregard, negligence.
an-fhurachras, see an-fhurachas.
an-fhuras, -ais, *s.m.* Impatience.
————,** *a.* see an-fhurasda.
————ach, -aiche, *a.* Impatient, fretful. 2 Hasty, eager.
an-fhurasda, *a.* Difficult.
†an-fhusgais, *s.f.* Impatience, restlessness.
†ang,** aing, *s.m.* Renown. 2 Rank. 3 String. 4 Twist.
†angach,** *a.* Full of nails.
angadh,** *s.m.* Gusset of a shirt.
anganach,** -aich, *s.m.* Snare.
angar,** -air, *s.m.* Stall for cattle.
an gar,‡‡ *adv.* Near, close by.
an geall, *adv.* Wishing for, desirous.
an-gathlannach, -aiche, *a.* Glittering, bright.
an-ghlaodh,** *s.m.* Loud shout, piercing cry.
————aich,** *s.m.* Continued loud shouting.
an-ghràdh, -aidh, *s.m.* Great attachment, ardent love.
————ach, -aiche, *a.* Very fond, ardently loved.
————aiche,** *s.m.* Dotard.
anglonn, *a.* Very powerful. 2 Brave.
————, -oinn, *s.m.* Adversity, distress. 2 Danger. 3 Strength.
————ach, *a.* Very powerful. 2 Brave. 3 Adverse. 4 Dangerous.
an-gnàth, see ana-ghnàth.
————ach, see ana-ghnàthach.
angrach, Gaelicized form of "angry."

an gradaig, *adv.* Anon.
†angraidh,** *s.m.* Man of rank. 2 Ruler. 3 Nobility.
†angrais,** *s.m.* Engine, machine.
an-iarrtas, -ais, *s.m.* Unreasonable demand. 2 Mandate.
an-iochd, *s.f.* Cruelty, want of feeling, rigour, oppression. Le h-an-iochd, *with rigour.*
———air,* -e, -ean, *s.m.* Tyrant.
———ar, see an-iochdmhor.
———mhoire, *comp.* of an-iochdmhor.
———mhoireachd,* *s.f.ind.* Mercilessness, oppression.
———mhor, -oire, *a.* Cruel, unkind, merciless. 2**Imperious. Bha i *a.*, *she was cruel;* creachadairean *a.*, *merciless plunderers.*
a nìos, *adv.* Up, from below (towards one.) 2 **From the East. Thig a nìos an seo, *come up here.*
a nìos, see a nis.
an-ìosal, -ìsle, *a.* see ain-ìosal.
anis, -e, *s.f.* Anise.
a nis, *adv.* Now, at this time. Dean a nis e, *do it now;* a nis ma ta, *now then.*
a nise, see a nis.
†aniudadh,** *a.* Depraved.
†aniuid,** *s.f.* Error. 2 Depravity.
an-iùl, -ùil, *s.m.* Want of guidance or command. 2 Bad instruction or guidance. 3 Error of judgment. 4††Misrule.
an-iùlmhor, -oire, *a.* Void of conduct.
an làimh, *adv.* In custody.
anlamh, -aimh, -ean, see amhluadh.
an-làn, ———aichte, } *a.* Incomplete.
an-laoch, -aoich, *s.m.* Exasperated hero or warrior. 2**Bloody warrior. 3††Weak or inferior hero. Fo chasaibh nan anlaoch, *under the feet of the bloody warriors.*
an-laoich, *gen. & voc. sing. & n. pl.* of an-laoch.
an lorg, *prep.* In consequence of. 2 In track of.
an-luchd, *s.m.* Grevious weight. 3 Overweight. 3 Oppressive burden. Fo an-luchd, *oppressed.*
———aich, *v.a.* Overload. 2 Surcharge.
an'madaich, see anamadaich.
an'madail, see anamadail.
an'man, see anaman.
anmanach, see anamanta.
an'manta, see anamanta.
anmaoin, *s.f.* Strife. 2 Great riches.
an'measarra, see anameasarra.
an'mèin, *s.f.* see ainmèin.
ainmèinneach, -eiche, see ainmèineach.
anmhainn, -e see anfhann.
———eachd, see anfhannachd.
———ich, see anfhannaich.
an-mhaoin, see anmaoin.
an'mhiann, see anamiann.
———ach, see anamiannach.
an-mhodh, *s.m.* Disrespect, incivility. 2 Rudeness. 3 Bad breeding. 4 Bad habit. (Mimhodh *is a more usual form.*)
———ail, see mi-mhodhail.
an-mhór, *a.* Very great, exorbitant, exceeding, excessive. Sonas an-mhór, *excessive joy.*
———ach, *a.* Valiant, stout, brave.
anmhuinne, see anfhainne.
———achd, see anfhannachd.
anmhunn, -uinne, *a.* see anfhann.
———achadh, see anfhannachadh.
———achd, see anfhannachd.
———aich, see anfhannaich.
anmhurrach, -aiche, *a.* Valiant, brave, intrepid. 2 Powerful.
anmoch, -oiche, *a.* Late. 2 Unseasonable. Tha e anmoch, *he* or *it is late.*
———, -oich, *s.m.* Evening, night. 'S an anmoch, *in the evening.* Madadh-alluidh an anmoich, *the evening wolf.*
anmoiche,** *s.f.* Lateness.
anmoichead,** *s.m.* ,,
anmuinneach, -eiche, see ainmèineach.
anmunnach, -aich, *a.* Lively, brisk, vigorous, vivacious.
†ann,** *s.m.* Circle. 2 Revolution.
ann, *prep.* In, within. 2 Therein, there. 3 In existence, alive. *Ann* also expresses emphasis, as, Is ann a thachair e gu math dha, *it has happened well to him.* An linn a bh' ann, *the former race;* ann o shean, *in existence of old;* a th'ann, *that exists, that is;* am bheil thu ann? *are you there?* an tu a th' ann, ? *is it you that is there?* is mi, *(yes) it is I*; ann mo bheachd-sa, *in my opinion*; a chrochair tha thu ann! *rascal that you are!* Combined with the personal pronouns thus:

1 Sing.	annam,	*Plur.*	annainn,
2	annad,		annaibh.
3	ann, *m.* / innte, *f.*	}	annta, *m. & f.*

Emphatic forms.

1 Sing. annam-sa, annam-fhéin, *pl.* annainne, annainn-fhéin.
2 Sing. annad-sa, annad-fhéin, *pl.* annaibhse, annaibh-fhéin.
3 Sing. (*m.*) ann-san, ann-fhéin, (*f.*) inntese, innte-fhéin, *pl.* (*m. & f.*) anntasan, annta-fhéin.

ann, *prep. pron.* In him, in it. Cha'n 'eil coire 'sam bith ann, *there is no fault in him at all;* cha'n 'eil ann ach crochair, *he is but a rascal.* *Emphatic:* ann-san, ann-fhéin.
†annach,** *a.* Clean.
annad, *prep. pron.* (ann+tu) In thee.
†annadh,** -aidh, *s.m.* Delay.
annag,** -aig, *s.m.* Evil. 3 Anger, displeasure.
annaibh, *prep.pron.* (ann+sibh) In you. Cha 'n 'eil ciall *a.*, *you have no judgment.*
†annaid, *s.* Church.
annainn, *prep. pron.* (ann+sinn) In us. 2**In our power. *Emphatic:* annainne, annainn-fhéin.
annaladh, -aidh, *s.m.* Age, era. 2 Calendar.
annam, *prep. pron.* (ann+mi) In me. 2**In my power.
annamh, see ainneamh.
annamh,** -aimh, *s.m.* Wilderness.
———achd, see ainneamhachd.
ann am, *prep.* Reduplication of *ann*, used before a word beginning with B, F, M, or P, (only when not preceded by the article.) Ann am monadh, *in a hill;* ann am botuil, *in bottles.*
ann an, *prep.* Reduplication of *ann*, used before a word beginning with a lingual or dental, (only when not preceded by the article.) Ann an toll, *in a hole*; ann an creagan, *in rocks.*
annas, -ais, -an, *s.m.* Rarity. 2 Novelty. 3 Change for the better.
———ach, -aiche, *a.* Rare, unusual, strange. 2 Dainty. 3 Desirable, delightful. Nithe *a.*, *dainties, rarities.*
———achd,* *s.f.* Rareness. 2 Novelty.
annas-na-làimhe, -ais-, -an-, *s.m.* Masterpiece. Annas do làimhe, *your masterpiece.*
ann-athach, see an-athach.
ann-dòchas, see an-dòchas.
———ach, see an-dòchasach.
ann-dòigh, see an-dòigh.
ann-dùchas, see an-dùchas.
ann-fhacal, -ail, *s.m.* Word of course.
anniseachd, see ainniseachd.

annlamh, see amhluadh.
annlan, -ain, *s.m.* Condiment. 2 Whatever is eaten with bread, particularly dairy produce. 3**Whatever food, as butcher's meat, butter, cheese, eggs,&c. is taken at dinner after broth, which forms the first course of a Scottish dinner.
ann-laoch, see an-laoch.
ann-luchd, see an-luchd.
an nochd, *adv.* To-night, this night. Cha tig e 'n nochd, *he will not come to-night*; an nochd is an raoir, *to-night and last night.*
†annoid, see annaid.
annos, -ois, see annas.
annrach, see ànrach.
———d, see annradh 2.
———dach, -aich, see ànrachdach.
annradh, -aidh, *s.m.* see ànradh. 2 The highest degree in poetry next to an *ollamh.* 3 Boon. 4 **Petition.
†annradh, *v.* Grieve, afflict, harass.
annraidh,** *s.m.* Champion.
annranach, see ànradhach.
annrath, see ànradh.
annriadh, -reidh, see an-riadh.
ann-righ, *s.m.* Tyrant.
anns, *prep.* In, in the. Anns gach beul, *in every mouth.* [Used before the article *an,* and adj. *gach.*] Anns a' bhaile, *in the town*; *a.* na miosan, *in the months*; *a.* an arm, *in the army*; tha fad math a' tighinn anns an là, *the day is growing pretty long.* Often abbreviated *'s,* as 'san toiseach, *in the beginning.*
annsa,** *a.* Dear, attached, beloved. 2 Desirable, acceptable, 3 Glad. B'annsa leo sgur, *they were glad to desist*; ged nach b'*a.* dhi an t-òganach, *though the youth was not dear to her*; an caladh aigh *a.*, *the joyous wished for harbour.*
annsa, *comp.* of *a.* toigh. More dear, more beloved. Is toigh leam thusa, ach is *a.* leam esan, I *love you, but he is more dear to me*; cò is *a.* leat? *whom do you like best?* b'*a.* thusa na deàrrsadh na gréine, *more acceptable wert thou than the sunbeam.*
annsa, see annsachd.
———chd, *s.f.ind.* Love, affection, attachment, 2 Person beloved. A thug rùn agus *a.*, *that bestowed great love and affection*; is tu m'*a.*, *thou art my beloved*; *a.* Dhé, *the beloved one of God.*
———dh, -aidh, see annsachd.
ann-san, *Emphat. form* of *prep pron.* ann.
annsgairt,** -e, -ean, *s.f.* Shriek, loud cry.
———each, *a.* Shrieking.
ann-spiorad, -aid, -an, *s.m.* Devil, demon.
annta, *prep.pron.* (ann+iad) In them. *Emphatic*: annta-san, annta-fhéin.
ann-tighearnas, see aintighearnas.
ann-tlachd, see an-tlachd.
———mhoireachd, see an-tlachdmhoireachd.
———mhor,* see an-tlachdmhor.
anntoil, see antoil.
anntrom, see antrom.
———achadh, see antromachadh.
———aich, see antromaich.
ann-truas, see antruas.
an-obair, -oibre, *s.f.* Idle work. 2 Trifle.
an-oircheas, -is, *s.m.* Want of pity.
———ach, -aiche, *a.* Pitiless, merciles s.
a nois, see a nis.
ànrach, -aich*, *s.m.* Wanderer, stranger. 2 Weather-beaten person. 3 Distressed person. Tha dorus Fhinn do'n ànrach fial, *Fionn's door is open (liberal) to the wanderer*; is i do ghnùis do'n ànrach a ghrian, *your countenance is as the sun to the weather-beaten stranger.*
———,* *a.* see ànradhach.
———d, *s.f.ind.* Violent weeping.
———dach, -aich, *s.m.* Miserable wanderer.
ànradh, -aidh, *s.m.* Storm, tempest. 2 Distress, misfortune, disorder. Mac Morna 's e 'm meadhon ànraidh, *the son of Morni in the midst of a tempest*; theirgeadh mo dheòir na'n teirgeadh gach *a.*, *my tears would cease if every trouble were to vanish.*
———ach, -aiche, *a.* Stormy. 2 Distressed. 3 Wandering. 4 Disordered. 5**Floating, streaming, as hair on the wind. T'fhalt *à.*, *thy disordered hair.*
———ach, -aich, *s.m.* Distressed person.
ànraidh, *gen.sing.* of ànradh.
———,** *a.* Distressful, sorrowful, sad.
an raoir, *adv.* Last night, last evening.
an-rath,** -aith, *s.m.* see ànradh.
———ach, see ànradhach.
an reidhir, see an raoir.
an-riadh, -reidh, *s.m.* Usury, extortion.
an-riadhair,‡‡ -e, -ean, *s.m.* Usurer.
an-riaghailt, *s.f.* Disorder, confusion. 2 Tumult, uproar, riot. 3 Misrule, mismanagement.
———each, -tiche, *a.* Confused, disordered. 2 Riotous, tumultuous.
an-riar,‡‡ -reir, *s.m.* Wrong gratification.
†anrodhach, see ànradhach.
†anrodhaidh, see ànradh.
an roir, see an raoir.
an-sacaich, *v.a.* Overload.
ansamhlachd, ‡‡ *s.f.ind.* Incomparability.
ansan, (for amhsan) see sùlaire.
an sàs, *adv.* In custody. 2 Embedded, as a thorn in one's flesh or a needle in cloth. 3 **Hooked.
an seo, *adv.* Here.
an-sgàineadh, -eidh, *s.m.* Violent bursting. 2 Chasm.
an-sgàinteach, -tiche, *a.* Apt to open in chasms, causing chasms. 2 Apt to burst.
ansgairt, *s.f.* Loud shout, piercing shriek or cry. 3**Thicket of brambles. Phill sibh le'r n-ansgairt, *you returned with your piercing shrieks.*
†———,** *v.n.* Shriek aloud, cry.
———each, -tiche, *a.* Uttering a loud shriek, shouting, shrieking. 2 Loud, piercing.
an-sgeulach, see aon-sgeulach.
an-shamhlachd, *s.f.* Incomparability.
an-shamhluichte, *pt.part.* Incomparable, unmatched.
an-shannt, *s.m.* Greed, covetousness.
———ach, -aiche, *a.* Greedy, covetous.
———ach,** -aich, *s.m.* Greedy person.
an-shaoghalta, *a.* Worldly-minded, covetous.
———chd, *s.f.* Worldliness, covetousness.
an-sheirc, *s.f.* Dislike, hatred. 2 Cruelty, unkindness. *better* mi-sheirc.
———eil, *a.* Hating. 2 Cruel. *better* mi-sheirceil.
an-sheasgair,* *a.* Restless.
———eachd,* *s.f.* Restlessness. 2 Rudeness. 3 Violence.
an-shocair, *pl.* -cran, *s.f.* Pain, distress, trouble. 2 Uneasiness, restlessness. 3 Affliction, sickness.
———,* *a.* see an-shocrach.
an-shocrach, -aiche, *a.* Painful. 2 Distressing, difficult. 3 Uneasy, disquieted. 4**Afflicted. Uair *a.*, *unsettled weather*; sluagh *a.*, *an afflicted people.*
———d, see an-shocair.
an-shocraiche, *comp.* of an-shocrach.

an-shògh,* *s.m.* Discomfort, misery. 2 Adversity. 3 Mischance.
———ail, *a.* Miserable. 2 Adverse. 3 Unfortunate.
an-smachdail,** *a.* Arbitrable.
an so, see an seo.
an-sriantachd,** *s.f.* see ain-sriantas.
an-stròdh, -tròdha, *s.f.* Prodigality, extravagance.
———ail, *a.* Prodigal, extravagant. Duine *a,, a prodigal.*
an-struidh, *s.f.* Prodigality, wastefulness.
———,* *v.a.* Waste, squander, spend.
———eachadh,** -aidh, *s.m.* Act of wasting or spending extravagantly.
———eachd,** same meaning as an-struidh
———ear, -eir, -ean, *s.m.* Waster, prodigal, spendthrift.
an-struidheas,* -eis, *s.m.* see an-struidheachd.
———ach, -aiche, *a.* Prodigal, wasteful.
———achd,* see an-struidheachd.
an t-, *def. art.* For examples see *an.* The *t-* originally formed a part of the article itself, but is now generally written separately.
an taice, *adv.* In support of, in contact.
an-thapaidh, -e, *a.* Slow, inactive. 2 Effeminate.
an-thrianaidiche,** *s.m.* Unitarian.
an-tighearn, see ain-tighearn.
———ach, see ain-tighearnail.
———ail, ,, ,,
———as, see ain-tighearnas.
an-tìorail, -e, *a.* Tempestuous. 2 Uncomfortable.
ain-tìoralachd, *s.f.* Badness of climate. 2 Discomfort.
an-tlachd, *s m.* Dislike, displeasure, disgust, dissatisfaction. 2 Rudeness, indecency. 3 Nuisance. Saor o bhraid 's o *a., free from theft and discontent.*
———mhoire, *comp.* of an-tlachdmhor.
———mhoireachd, *s.f.* Disgustfulness, unpleasantness.
———mhor, -oire, *a.* Disgusting, unpleasant. 2 Causing discontent. 3 Unhandsome.
antlas, -ais, *s.m.* Ludicrous trick, frolic. 2 Cattle market.
———ach, -aiche, *a.* Frolicsome.
———ach, -aich, *s.m.* Frolicsome fellow.
an-togair,* *v.a.* Lust after.
an-togar,** -air, *s.m.* Inordinate wish, unreasonable desire. 2 Ambition.
an-togarrach,** -aiche, *a.* Lustful, immoderately desirous. 2 Covetous.
an-togradh, -aidh, -aidhean, *s.m.* Criminal propensity, concupiscence. 2 Ambition.
an-toil, -e, *s.f.* Self-will, unwillingness. 2 Lust. 3**Ambition. Fear na h-antoile, *the ambitious man;* iomadh gnè de dh'an-toilibh, *many sorts of lusts.*
———each, -liche, *a.* Perverse, unwilling. 2 **Lustful, inordinately desirous. 2**Ambitious.
———eachd, *s.f.ind.* Wilfulness, obstinacy.
———eil, -e, *a.* Wilful, obstinate, perverse. Gu h-*a., perversely.*
———ich, *v.n.* Lust after.
an tòir, *adv.* In pursuit.
†antomhail,** *s.f.* Gluttony.
†———tear,** -teir, -tearan, *s.m.* Glutton.
an-torras,** -ais, *s.m.* Abortion.
an-torrach,** -oiche, *a.* Abortive.
an tràth, *adv.* When, the time when.
an-tràth, -a, *s. m.* Unfavourable weather, stormy weather, storm. 2 Wrong season.
———,* *a.* see an-tràthach.
———ach, -aiche, *a.* Unseasonable, untimely. 2 Abortive.
an-tréibhdhireach, -eiche, *a.* Insincere.
an-tréibhdhireas, -eis, *s.m.* Insincerity.
an-tròcair, *s.f.* Mercilessness, cruelty.
———each, -riche, *a.* Merciless, cruel. Fear *a., a merciless man.*
———eachd, *s, f. ind.* Unmercifulness, cruelty.
an-trom, -uime, *a.* Grievous, burdensome. 2 Oppressive. 3 Intolerable. 4**Atrocious.
———ach, see an-trom.
———achadh, -aidh, *s.m.* Act or circumstance of aggrieving, aggravating, or making heavy or burdensome. Ag a—, *pr.part.* of antromaich.
———aich, -achadh *v.a.* Aggravate. 2 Aggrieve. 3 Oppress. 4 Overload. Ag an-tromachadh do chionta, *aggravating your guilt.*
———aichear, *fut.pass.* of an-tromaich.
———aichidh, *fut. aff. a.* of ,, ,,
antruacanta, *a.* (an-, *neg.*) Pitiless, merciless. 2**(an-, *intens.*) Compassionate, merciful.
———chd, *s.f.* Want of compassion.
antruas, -ais, *s.m.* (an-, *neg.*) Want of pity or sympathy. 2** (an-, *intens.*) Great pity, or sympathy.
an-truime, *comp.* of an-trom.
———,* *s.f.* Oppression, tyranny. Luchd na h-an-truime, *oppressors.*
an tùs, *adv.* At first.
an-uabhar, -air, *s.m.* (an-, *neg.*) Affability, want of pride. 2** (an-, *intens.*) Excessive pride. Luchd an *a., the excessively proud.*
an uachdar, (AH) *adv.* Above-water.
an-uachdaran, -ain, *s.m.* Despot.
———achd, *s.f.* Despotism.
an-uaibhreach, -eiche, *a.* (an-, *neg.*) Gentle, humble, kind. 2**(an-, *intens.*) Excessively proud.
an-uaill, *s.f.* (an-, *neg.*) Humility. 2 Affability. 3*(an-, *intens.*) Excessive pride. Air mhór *a.* is air bheag céille, *excessively proud and senseless.*
an-uair, -e, *s.f.* Storm, unfavourable weather. 2**Mischief.
an uair, *adv.* When. *Often written and generally pronounced* 'nuair.
†anuais,** *a.* Fierce, barbarous.
an-uaisle, *s.f.ind.* Meanness, baseness.
———, *comp.* of an-uasal.
an-uallach, -aiche, *a.* (an-, *neg.*) Not haughty, humble-minded. 2**(an-, *intens.*) Indifferent, airy, supercilious. 3**Haughty, proud.
———, -aich, *s.m.* Oppressive burden. 2** Oppression. 3**Hardship.
a nuas, *adv.* Down, downwards, from above, (towards one.) Thig a nuas an seo, *come down here.*
an-uasal, *a.* Mean, ignoble, low. 2 Not proud, not dignified.
anuinn, see anainn.
an uiridh, *adv.* Last year.
a null, *adv.* To the other side. A null 's a nall, *thither and hither.*
an-ùmhlachd,‡‡ *s.f.ind.* Disobedience.
a nunn, see a null.
anur,** *s.m.* Mean sorry person. 2 Miscreant.
an uraidh, see an uiridh.
ao-, *privative prefix,* Not. *Eqvivalent to English in-, un-, dis-.*
†aobh, aoibh, *s.m.* Similitude.
aobhach, -aiche, *a.* Joyous, glad, cheerful. 2 Beautiful, pleasant, lovely. Ceud òganach *a., a hundred joyous youths;* b'a. mise, *I was glad.*
aobhachd, *s.f.ind.* Joyfulness, cheerfulness 2 Beauty.

aobhaiche, *comp.* of aobhach.
aobhair, *gen. sing.* of aobhar.
aobhar, -air, -airean, *s.m.* Cause, reason. 2 Subject, matter. *A.* bròin, *a cause of grief* ; cha'n 'eil *a.* gearain ann, *there is no reason to complain*; air an *a.* sin, *for that reason, therefore*; *a.* còta, *materials for making a coat*; *a.* bhròg, *materials for making shoes;* gun *a.*, *without reason;* is mór m'*a.*, *great is my reason;* thuit iad ann an deagh *a.*, *they fell in a good cause; a.* eagail, *cause of terror; a.* gàire, *a laughing-stock*; *a.* guil, *a cause for weeping.*
———ach, -aiche, *a.* Casual. 2 Reasonable. 3*Giving rise to.
———achd, *s.f.ind.* Causality.
aobharrach, -aich, *s.m.* Elements. 2 Materials. 3 Young person. 4 Young beast of good or bad promise. Is math an t-*a.* an gamhainn sin, *that stirk promises well;* is tu an t-*a.* ciatach, *you are a youth that promises well indeed.*
aobrainn, *gen.sing.* of aobrann.
aobrainnean, *n.pl.* of „ „
aobran, see aobrann.
aobrann, -ainn, *pl.* -ainnean, [** -anna & -annan,] *s.m.* Ankle. 2**Ankle-bone,ankle-joint. Gu ruig na h-aobranna, *to the ankles;* as an *a.*, *out of the ankle-joint.*
aobranna, aobrannan, } *n.pl.* of aobrann.
aobrunn, -uinn, see aobrann.
aoc, (AF) *s.m.* Flock of sheep.
ao-coltach, see eu-coltach.
————d, see eu-coltachd.
ao-cosail, see eu-coltach.
ao-cosalachd, see eu-coltas.
ao-coslach, see eu-coltach.
aodach, -aich, -aichean, *s.m.* Cloth. 2 Clothes, dress. 3(AH)Sails of a boat. Aodach 'sa' bheairt, *cloth in the loom;* cuir ort t'aodach, *put on your clothes; a.* canaich, *cotton cloth, calico*; *a.* leapach, *bed-clothes ; a.* lìn, *linen cloth*; *a.* olla, *woollen cloth.*
———adh, -aidh, *s.m.* Clothing, dressing, covering.
aodaich, *pr.pt.* ag aodachadh, *v.a.* Clothe, dress, cover.
———, *gen.sing.* of aodach.
———ear, *fut.pass.* of aodaich.
———idh, *fut aff. a.* of aodaich.
———te, *pt.pt.* of aodaich.
aodainn, *gen.sing.* of aodann.
aodann, -ainn, *n.pl.* -ainnean, *s.f.* Face, forehead, visage. 2 Surface. 3 **Impudence. As an *a.*, *expressly, to the face, outright, in defiance ;* an cron a bhitheas 'san aodann cha'n fhaodar a chleith, *the blemish in the face cannot be hidden ;* nach ann aige tha'n aodann ! *what impudence the fellow has !* ri *a.* sléibh a' leumnaich, *bounding on the face of the hill ;* clàr an aodainn, *the brow, forehead.*
aodannach, -aiche, *a.* Aspected.
———— -sréine, *s.f.* Front-stall of a bridle.
aodannan, -ain, *s.m.* Little face. 2 Frontlet. 3 Frontispiece.
aodarman, see eutroman.
†aodh,** *s.m.* Liver. 2 Eye. 3 Sheep.
†aodh,** *s.f.* Fire.
aodhair, -ean, *s.m.* see aoghair. †2**Fiery desolation, conflagration.
———eachd, see aoghaireachd.
aodhairean, see aoghairean.
†aodhar,** -air, *s.m.* Worship. Bheir sinn *a.* dhà, *we will worship him.* see aoradh.
aodhlamaid, -e, -ean, see foghlumaiche.
aodhuair,** -ean, *s.m.* Gaelicized form of *owner.* 2 Author.
aodhnaireachd,** *s.f.ind.* Ownership. 2 Authorship.
ao-dìon, *s. m. ind.*
ao-dìonach, -aiche, *a.*
ao-dìonachd,* *s.f.*
ao-dòcha, *a.*, *comp.*
ao-dòchas, -ais, *s.m.*
ao-dòchasach, -aiche, *a.*
ao-dòchasachd, *s.f.* } see eu-d—.
aodramain, *gen.sing.* of aotraman.
aodroman, -ain, see aotroman.
aodunn, see aodann.
aog, aoig, *s.m.* Death. 2 Ghost. 3 Spectre. 4 Skeleton. Is tu an t-aog duaichnidh, *you are a miserable-looking skeleton;* neul an aoig, *the colour of death*; a' dol aog, *dying, getting useless, becoming vapid as liquor.* see eug.
aogachadh, see aognachadh.
aogaidh, see aogail.
aogail, -e, *a.* Ghastly, death-like. 2 Deadly.
aogaileachd,** *s.f.* Ghastliness. 2 Ghostliness.
aogais, see eugmhais.
aogas, -ais, -ean, *s.m.* Countenance. 2 Image, likeness, resemblance. 3 Appearance. Is cosmhuil 'aogas ri Diarmad, *his form is like Dermot's;* t'*a.* maiseach, *thy lovely countenance a.* do bharca, *the likeness of thy bark.*
aogasach, -aiche, *a.* Seemly, decent, becoming. 2 Pretty, comely, of good appearance.
aogasachd, *s.f.* Seemliness,comeliness,decency.
aogasaiche, *comp.* of aogasach.
aogasail,** -e, *a.* Seemly, comely, becoming. 2 Of an imposing exterior.
aogasg, -aisg, see aogas.
aoghair, -e, -ean, *s.m.* Shepherd, herdsman, pastor. 3**Protector. The *aoghairean* of the Hebrides, according to Pennant, are farm servants who have the charge of cultivating a certain portion of land and of overseeing the cattle it supports. They have grass for 2 milch cows and 6 sheep, and also one tenth sheaf of the produce of the said ground, and as many potatoes as they choose to plant.
aoghaireachd, *s.f.ind.* Shepherding.
aoghairean, *n.pl.* of aoghair.
aognachadh, -aidh, *s.m.* Becoming lean or death-like. 2 Withering, fading. Ag a—, *pr.part.* of aognaich.
aognaich, *pr.part.* ag aognachadh, *v.n.* Become lean or pale, as death. 2 Wither, fade. 3 **Disfigure. Aognaichidh aogas nan aonach, *the face of the hills shall grow pale.*
aognaich, *v.a.* Emaciate, make lean or pale.
aognuidh, -e, *a.* Emaciated, frightful.
aogus, -uis, see aogas.
†aoi, *s.m. & f.* Age 2 see aoigh, *s.m.* 3 Trade, handicraft. 4 Law, rule. 5 Cause. 6 Controversy. 7 Confederacy. 8 Compact. 9 Flock of sheep. 10 Sheep. 11 Swan. 12 The liver. 13 Possession. 14 Hill. 15 Place, region. 16 Island. 17 Honour. [For the meanings nos. 5, 6, 10, 11, 13, and 15 see also †ai.]
aoibh, -e, *s.f.* Courteous civil look. 2*Cheerful countenance. 3** Patrimony. Is fuar taigh mur bi *a.* air bean-an-taighe, *cold is the house if the goodwife be not cheerful.*
aoibh, *a.* Pleasant, comely, joyous, courteous, cheerful.
aoibh ! *int.* Huzza !
aoibhe,** *s.f.* Neatness, elegance.
aoibheachd, *s.f.ind.* Cheerfulness 2 Politeness.
aoibheal, -eil, see eibhle.
aoibhealachd,* see aoibheachd.
aoibheil,* *a.* Kind, courteous, affable. 2 Handsome, comely, beautiful.
aoibhinn, -e, *a.* Pleasant, comely. 2 Joyful,

glad, Oigridh *a.*, *pleasant or joyous youth*; mo ghàir *a.*, *my joyful laugh.*
aoibhinn,** *s.f.* Joy. *A.* dhuit, *joy be with you.*
aoibhinneach, see aoibhneach.
†aoibhle,** *s.f.* Sign, mark, omen, token.
†aoibhlich,** *v.* Explain an omen.
aoibhneach, -eiche *a.* Pleasant, cheerful, glad, joyful, happy, agreeable. A' toirt sgéil aoibhnich, *giving glad tidings.*
aoibhneas, -eis, *s.m.* Gladness joy, pleasure. *A.* a shlighe, *the joy of his way;* ni t'athair *a.*, *thy father will rejoice.*
aoibhneasach,** -aiche, *a.* Joyful, glad 2 causing joy.
aoibhneich, *gen. sing.* of aoibhneach.
aoibhneiche, *comp.* of „
†aoide,** *s.f.* Web. 2 Youth.
aoideach, -aiche, *a.* Youthful.
aoideag, -eig, *s.f.* Hair lace, fillet.
†aoidean, -ein, *s.m.* Leak.
†aoideanach, -eiche, *a.* Leaky. 2 Yonthful.
aoidh, -e, *s.f.* see aoibh.
aoidh, -e, *pl.* -ean & -eanna, *s.m.* see aoigh.
aoidheach, -eiche, *a.* } see aoigheach.
aoidheach, -eich, *s.m.* } see aoigheach.
aoidheachd, } see aoigh—.
aoidheachdach, } see aoigh—.
aoidheil, } see aoigh—.
aoidhealachd. } see aoigh—.
aoi-dìon, } see ao-d—.
aoi-dìonach, } see ao-d—.
aoi-dìonachd, } see ao-d—.
aoig, *gen.sing.* of aog.
aoigh, -e, -ean & -eanna, *s.m.* Stranger, guest, traveller. 2**Skilful person. †3**Hero.
aoigh,†† -e, -ean, *s.f.* see aoibh.
aoigheach,** -eich, *s.m.* Guest, stranger. 2 Hospitable person.
aoigheach, see aoigheil. 2††Beggary.
aoigheachd, *s.f.ind.* Entertainment, lodging, hospitality. 2 see aoibheachd. Air aoigheachd, *enjoying hospitality;* thug iad *a.* dhuinn, *they lodged* or *entertained us; a.* Mhuisein, siùthad, siùthad, a bhean-an-taighe, cha'n 'eil thu a' gabhail sìon, *the churl's hospitality, help yourself goodwife, you're not taking anything* (the churlish host instead of attending to the guest is attending to his own wife); *a.* Thormaid mhóir, fuirich, fuirich, tha a' chearc 'sa' chliabh agus a' bhean 'sa' chladach, *big Norman's hospitality the hen 's in the creel and the wife 's at the shore,* (this meant a wholesome diet of eggs and shell-fish, and illustrates well that true Highland hospitality which gladly shares its all, however little that may be, with a stranger.)
aoigheachdach, -aich, *s.m.* Sorner, one who taxes the hospitality of his friends too much.
aoighealachd, see aoigheachd.
aoigheil, -eala, *a.* see aoibheil. 2 Hospitable, cheerful. An gasan *a.*, *the hospitable stripling.*
aoighean, *n.pl.* of aoigh.
aoil, *gen.sing.* of aol.
†aoil,** *s.f.* The mouth.
†aoilbhinn,** *s.f.* Small flock.
†aoilbhreo,** *s.m.* Lime kiln.
†aoileach,** -eich, *s.m.* Gazing-stock. 2 see aolach.
aoileanach,** see oileanach.
aoileann, -inn, *s.f.* see faoileann.
aoileann,** *a.* Fine, excellent, charming.
aoileannachd,** *s.f.* Beauty.
aoileanta,** *a.* Beautiful, charming. Oigh aoibhinn *a.*, *a cheerful beauteous maid.*
aoilinn, *gen. sing.* of aoileann.
aoilinneach, *a.* see faoilinneach.
aoilseag, -eig, -an, *s.f.* Caterpillar.
aoilseagach,** *a.* Abounding in caterpillars. 2 Like a caterpillar.
aointe, see aonta.
aoin, *pr.pt.* ag aonadh, *v.a.* Unite, join. Air aonadh ris, *joined to him.*
aoin, *gen.sing.* of aon. Làmh gach aoin, *the hand of every one.*
†aoin, *s.f.* Rush. 2 Honour. 3 see Aoine.
aoine, *s.f.* Skill.
†Aoine, *s.f.* Friday,—*now* Di-haoine. 2 Fast. Aoine-na-Ceusda, *Good Friday.*
aoineach,** *a.* Fasting.
aoineadh, -nidh, *s.m.* Steep promontory.
aoineagan, -ain, -an, see aonagail.
aoin-fhillte, *a.* see aon-fhillte.
— ———achd, *s.f.ind.* Singleness.
aoin-inntinn, see aon-inntinn.
————each, *a.* see aon-inntinneach.
aoin-sgeulach, see aon-sgeulach.
aoir, *v.a.* Satirize, lampoon. 2††Curse.
aoir, -e, -ean, *s.f.* Satire, lampoon, ribaldry, raillery. 2††Curse.
aoir, -e, -ean, *s.m.* Sheet *or* bolt-rope of a sail. Fear gealtach 'san *a.*, *a timorous person holding the sheet* (*i.e.* a cause of danger.)
aoir,** Contraction of aoghair.
aoireachas, -ais, see aoireadh.
aoireachd, *s.f.ind.* Lampooning, satirizing. 2*Libel.
aoireadh, -ridh, -ridhean, *s.m.* Lampooning, satirizing. 2**Corner of a sail. 3††Cursing.
aoireannan, (*for* aoghairean) *pl.* of aoghair.
aoiridh, *fut.aff.a.* of *v.* aoir.
aoirneagaich, see aonagaich.
aoirneagan,* see aonagail. 'G *a.* 'na fhuil, *weltering in his blood.*
aoirneagain,* see aonagail.
aois, -e, *s.f.* Age. 2 Old age. 3 Antiquity. Dè 'n aois a tha thu? *what is your age?* is mairg a dh'iarradh an aoise! *pity him that wishes extreme old age!* air son 'aoise, *for its antiquity;* iarguinn na h-aoise, *the evil effects of old age;* bha Noah còig ceud bliadhna dh' aois, *N. was 500 years old;* ann an làn aois, *in full age;* 'n uair a thig thu gu h-aois; *when you come to age;* tha m'aois fo dhòruinn, *my old age is sorrowful;* aois leisgein, ceithir fichead ri muir-tràigh, is tri fichead ri muir-làn, is gann fichead 'n uair bhios a' ghealach làn, *the sluggard's age, eighty at low-water, sixty at high-water, and scarcely twenty when there's a full moon.* (At low-water, while the sea-ware is being gathered for manure, the sluggard is as feeble as a man of eighty, at high-water, when less difficult work is engaged in, he is a little livelier, but still incapable of much exertion, but when night comes, especially if there should be moonlight, he is as lively as a young fellow of twenty, and probably walks many miles on courting errands.)
aois, *s.f.pl.* People, community of any particular kind, designated by its adjacent. Aois-ciùil, *musicians.*
aois-dàna,** *s. pl.* Bards, poets. 2 Rehearsers of ancient poetry. 3 Genealogists. 4 Soothsayers. The *aois-dàna* were in high esteem throughout the Highlands. So late as the end of the 17th. century they sat in the *sreath* or circle among the nobles and chiefs of families. They took the preference of the *ollamh* or doctor in medicine. After the extinction of the Druids, they were brought in to preserve the genealogy of families, and to repeat genealogical traditions at the success-

ion of every chieftain. They had great influence over all the powerful men of their time. Their persons, their houses, their villages, were sacred. Whatever they asked was given them; not always, however, out of respect, but from fear of their satire, which frequently followed a denial of their requests. They lost by degrees, through their own insolence and importunity, all the respect which their order had so long enjoyed, and consequently all their wonted profits and privileges. Martin says "They shut their door and windows for a day's time, and lay on their backs in darkness with a stone upon their belly, and plaids about their heads and eyes, and thus they pumped their brains for rhetorical encomiums."

aois-dànachd,** *s.f.* Employment of rehearsing ancient poetry. 2 Bardism. 3 Genealogical tradition.

aois-dhlighe,‡‡ *s.f.* Primogenitureship.

aoisid, see faoisid.

aois-liath, *a.* Hoary, aged.

aol, aoil, *s.m.* Lime. Aol gun bhàthadh, *quick-lime*; àth-aoil, *a lime-kiln.*

aol, *pr.pt.* ag aoladh, *v.a.* Lime, plaster or cover with lime. 2** Manure land with lime.

aolach, -aich, *s.m.* Dung, manure. 2 Mire. 3 **Dross, rubbish. Bithidh iad 'nan aolach, *they shall be as dung.*

aolachadh,** -aidh, *s.m.* Process of manuring with lime. Ag a—, *pr.pt.* of aolaich.

aoladair, -e, -ean, *s.m.* Plasterer, one who works among lime, lime burner.

aoladaireachd, *s.f.* Occupation of a plasterer, plastering, working among lime.

aoladh, -aidh, *s.m.* Liming, plastering.

aolaich, *v.a.* Lime, manure with lime, cover with lime. 2‡‡Compost.

†aolain,‡‡ see oilean.

†——aich, see oileanaich.

†——aiche, see oileanaiche.

aolais, -e, *s.f.* Indolence, slothfulness, sluggishness.

——deach, -diche, *a.* Lazy, indolent. 2 Sluggish.

aolam, see foghlum.

aolar, *a.* (aolmhor) Abounding in lime, limy.

aol beò, *s.m.* Quicklime.

aol-chlach, -oiche, *s.f.* see clach-aoil.

aolmann, -ainn, *s.m.* Ointment.

aol-phlàsda, *s.m.* Lime-plaster.

aol-shùirn, -ùirne, *s.m.* Lime-kiln.

aol-tàthaidh, aoil-, *s.m.* Mortar.

aol-thaigh, see oil-thaigh.

aol-uisge, *s.m.ind.* Lime-water. 2 Whitewash.

aom, *pr.pt.* ag aomadh, *v.a. & n.* Incline, bow, bend, droop. 2 Yield. 3 Lean. 4 Persuade. 5 Dispose. 6 Fall. 7*Bulge, project'. 8*Be seduced by. 9**Descend. 10**Pass by. 11**Decay. Dh'aom i leis, *she was seduced by him*; aomaibh ur cluas, *incline your ear*; tha'm balla ag aomadh, *the wall is bulging*; dh'*a.* e a thriall, *he bent his way*; aomaidh an aitreabh, *their buildings shall decay*; an t-àm a dh'aom, *the time that has passed, the past.*

aoma, see aomadh.

aomach,* *a.* Inclining, tending, bending.

aomachadh, see aomadh.

aomachd,* see aomadh.

aomachdail, -e, *a.* Tending to incline or bend.

aomadh, *3rd. sing. & pl.* of aom. *A.* e, *let him bend.*

aomadh, -aidh, *s.m.* Inclination, act of inclining, bending, or drooping. 2 Yielding. 3 Leaning. 4 Persuading. 5 Disposing. 6 Falling. 7 Bulging. 8*Tendency, aptitude. 9 Declivity. 10**Descending, passing by. 11** Surface of the sea. Ag a—, *pr. pt.* of aom. A cheann air aomadh, *his head drooping*; dubhach air aomadh na créige, *sorrowful on the slope of the rock*; ag aomadh air a ghlùn, *bending on his knee*; an t-*a.*, *the downfall.*

aomaich, *v.a.* Incline, &c. see aom.

aomaidh, *gen, sing.* of aomadh. 2 *fut. aff. a.* of aom.

aomar, *fut. pass.* of aom.

†aomilleadh, see †aidhmbilleadh.

aomta, *pt.pt.* Inclined, bent, bulged.

aon, aoin, *a.* One. 2 Alone. 3 Same. 4 Only. 5 Ace. [Aspirates noun following except one beginning with D, T, or S.] Aon bhean, *one woman*; aon eile, *one other*; aon 'sam bith, *anyone*; gun aon eile, *without any other*; bithidh sibhse mar mise aon là, *you shall be as I am (one day) some day or other*; aon seach aon, *neither one nor the other*—cha toigh leam aon seach aon dhiubh, *I like neither one nor the other*, used in a negative sense only—AH; aon seach aon, *one from another*—aithnichidh e aon seach aon dhiubh, *he will know one from another of them*; m'aon chearc, *my only hen*; is aon ni e, *it is all the same*; is esan an t-aon duine air son sin, *he is the best man in the world for that*; 's e fhèin an t-aon duine, *it is he himself that rules the roast*, i.e. *he is cook, mate, and steward*; trì laithean bha e'na aon (aonar), *three days he was all alone*; gach aon, *every one*; a lìon aon is aon, *one by one*; mar aon, *united, hand in hand*; gun aon duine, *without a single individual*; anns an aon taigh rinne, *in the same house with us*; 'san aon luing, *in the same ship*; do dh'aon seach a chéile, *to one more than the other*; aon a thàinig a steach, *an individual that came in*; tha mac an t-aon aca, *they have a son each.*

†aon, aoin, *s.m.* Country.

†aon, *a.* Excellent. 2 Noble. 3 Illustrious.

aona, *a.* *An t-aona* is used with *deug* in compound numbers, but does not aspirate its noun. *An aona* is used before a feminine noun. An t-aona bòrd deug, *the 11th. table.*

†aonac,‡‡ *s.m.* Tin, lead.

aonach, -aich, -aichean, *s.m.* Hill, steep, height. 2 Heath, moor. 3 Desert place. 4 *Meeting. 5‡‡ Fair, great assembly. 6* *provincial* Green plain near the shore on a stony bottom (a *machair* has a sandy bottom.) 7***rarely* Fir. 8**Prince. 9**Market. †10** Galloping. 11‡‡ Panting for breath. Ceum do theachd air an *a.*, *thy coming (the step of thine approach) on the heath*; a' siubhal nan aonach ciar, *travelling the dusky plains*; *a.* na Samhna, *the Martinmas fair.*

aonachadh, -aidh, *s.m.* Uniting, reconciling. 2 Assenting. 3 Galloping, hand-gallop. 5 Swift running. Ag a—, *pr.pt.* of aonaich.

aonachail,‡‡ -e, Mountainous.

aonachd, *s.f.* Unity. 2 Concord. 3 Sameness. 4 Unanimity. *A.* an Spioraid, *the unity of the Spirit*; còmhnaidh a ghabhail cuideachd ann an *a.*, *to dwell together in unity.*

aonadh, -aidh, Ag a—, *pr.pt.* of aoin.

aon-adharcach, -aich, *s.m.* Unicorn.

————, *a.* Unicorned, having one horn.

aonagaich, *pr.pt.* ag aonagail, *v.n.* Wallow, welter. *A.* thu fhéin, *wallow thyself*; aonagaichibh sibh fhein, *wallow yourselves.*

aonagail, *s.f.ind.* Wallowing, weltering, rolling on the ground. Ag a—, *pr.pt.* of aonagaich.

aonagan, see aonagail.

aonaich, *pr.pt.* ag aonachadh, *v.a.* Unite, reconcile. 2 Assent. 3 Side with. Aonaich mo chridhe. *unite my heart*

aonaichear, *fut. pass.* of aonaich.
aonaichidh, *fut. aff. a.* of aonaich.
aonaichte, *pt.pt.* United reconciled. Gàidheil aonaichte cruadhaichte, *united hardy Highlandmen.*
aonairt, see aonagail.
aonais, see iùnais.
aonar, -air, *s.m.* One person 2††Unity, aloneness.
aonar, *a.* Alone, solitary. 2 Singular *in grammar.* Duine 'na aonar, *a man all alone, a singular man*; 'na aonar 'sa mhonadh, *alone on the hill;* cha'n 'eil thu 'ad aonar mar sin, *you are not alone like that* ; rinn e seo 'na aonar, *he did this alone.*
aonarach, -aiche, *a.* Desolate, solitary, forsaken.
aonarachd. *s.f.ind.* Desolation, solitariness. 2 Singularity.
aonaran, -ain, -ranan, *s.m.* Recluse, hermit, solitary person. 2 Forsaken person, ascetic. Aonaran liath nan creag, *the grey-headed hermit of the rocks.*
aonaranach, see aonarach.
———d, see aonarachd.
†aonardha, see aonar, *a.*
aon-bharail * *s.f.* Unanimity.
†aon-bheannach, -aich, *s.f.* Unicorn. *a.* Unicorned.
aon-bheachd, *s.f.* Unanimity, agreeing in design or opinion.
aon-bhith, *s.f.ind.* Co-essentiality. 2 Co-substantiality.
———each, *a.* Co-essential. 2 Co-substantial.
aon-chasach, *a.* One-footed. 2 Single-stemmed, as an herb.
———,ʒ -aich, *s.m.* Serrated seaweed, see feamainn dubh.
aon-chathaireach, -eich, -chan, *s.m.* Fellow-citizen.
———, *a,* Of, or pertaining to, the same city. 2** Having one city. Luchd *a.*, *fellow-citizens.*
aon-choltach‡‡ -aiche, *a.* Consonous.
aon-chridhe, *s.m.* Unanimity.
———ach, *a.* Unanimous. 2 One-hearted. Gu h-aon-ghuthach aon-chridheach, *with one voice and one heart.*
†aon-chu, (AF) *s.m.* see onchu.
aonda, *a.* Singular, particular.
———, *s.m.* see aonta.
aondachd, *s.f.* see aontachd.
aondadh, -aidh, see aonta.
aon-dathach, *a.* Of one colour.
aon-dealbhach, *a.* Uniform. 2 Similar, 3 Consistent.
aon-deug, *a.* Eleven. Bha aon-deug ann, *there were eleven ;* aon fhear deug, *11 men* ; aon chlach dheug, *11 stones*, a h-aon-deug, *eleven.*
aon-dhearc,ʒ *s.f.* The herb Paris—*paris quadrifolia.*
aon-fneachd, *adv.* Together, at once.
aon-fhillte, *a.* Single, consisting of one fold or plait. 2 Simple, innocent. 3 Foolish. 4 Candid, honest, sincere. A' deanamh an duine *a.* glic, *making the simple wise*; na daoine *a.*, *the innocent.*
———achd, *s.f.* Singleness of mind. 2 Simplicity, sincerity, candour. 3**Foolishness. Le *a.*, *with simplicity.*
aon-fhlath, -aith, -aithean, *s.m.* Monarch.
aon-fhlathach, *a.* Monarchial.
aon-fhlathachd, *s.f.ind.* Monarchy.
aon-fhlathachdail, see aon-fhlathach.
aon-fhuaimneach,‡‡ *a.* Consonous.
———d, *s.f.* Consonantness.

14. Aon-dhearc.

aon-fhuirm, Gaelicized form of "one form."
aon-ghin, *s.m.* Only begotten one. Mar *a.* mic, *like an only begotten son* ; m'*a.* cloinne, *my only begotten child.*
aon-ghnèitheach, *a.* Homogeneous.
———d, *s.f.ind.* Homogeneousness.
aon-ghràdh, *s.m.* (*& f.*) Beloved object. M'*a.*, *my best beloved.*
aon-ghuthach, -aiche, *a.* Having one voice or vote. 2 Consonous. 3 Symphonious.
aon-inntinn, *s.f.* One mind, one accord. Le h-*a.*, *with one accord.*
aon-inntinneach, *a.* Unanimous, consentient. Gu h-*a.*, *unanimously.*
———d, *s.f.ind.* Unanimousness.
aon-mhac, -mhic, *s.m.* Only son. Thuit e air aodann 'aoin-mhic, *he fell on the face of his only son.*
†aonmhadh, *a.* see aona.
aon-mhaide, *s.m.ind.* Simultaneous pull in rowing, *fuaim an aon-mhaide.*
aon-mhargadh, -aidh, *s.m.* Monopoly.
aon-mharsanta,* *s.m.* Monopolizer.
———chd,* see aon-mhargadh.
aon-mhéinn,‡‡ *s.f.* One mind.
aonracan, see aonragan.
———ach, see aonraganach.
aonrachd, see aonarachd.
aonrachdach, see aonarach.
aonrachdan, see aonragan.
aonragan, -ain, *s.m.* Solitary person, recluse. 2 Widower. 3**Orphan. 4**Deserted person.
aonraganach, -aiche, *a.* Solitary. 2 Of, or belonging to, a recluse.
aonraganachd, *s.f.ind.* Solitariness. 2 Condition of a recluse or deserted person.
†aonrais, *s.f.* Tempest.
aonranach, *a.* see aonarach.
aonranachd, see aonrachd.
aon-reiceadair,‡‡ *s.m.* Monopolizer.
aon-righ, *pl.* -re, & -rean, *s.m.* Monarch.
aon-seadhach,‡‡ *a.* Co-significative.
aon-sgeulach, -aiche, *a.* Harmonious, unanimous.
aonsgoch,ʒ *s.m.* Swallow-wort or celandine, see an ceann ruadh.
aon-sloinneadh, -eidh, *s.m.* One surname.
†aonsuirt,** *s.f.* Wallowing, weltering.

aonta, *s.m.* Lease. 2 License. 3 Vote. 4 Admission. 5 Assent, acquiescence, consent. 6**Bachelor. Tha mi 'toirt *a.* do na tha thu ag ràdh, *I agree with what you say.*
aontach, -eiche, *a.* Acceding to, conniving at. 2 Ready to yield.
aontachadh, -aidh, *s.m.* Consenting, yielding, acceding, reconciliation, acquiescence, admission, unanimity, agreement, abetting. Ag a—, *pr.pt.* of aontaich.
aontachair, -eir, *s.m.* Subscriber. 2*Accessory.
aontachd, *s.f.* Consent, unanimity, agreement, admission. 2**State of being particular or singular.
aontaidh, see aonta.
aontaich, *pr. part.* ag aontachadh, *v.n.* Consent, agree, accede, acquiesce, admit, yield. 2**Abet, take part or side with. Dh'aontaich i leis, *she yielded to him*; *a.* leis, *take his part*; tha mi ag aontachadh gu'm bheil, *I admit that it is*; thug i air aontachadh, *she constrained him to yield*; na aontaich thusa leo, *consent not thou to them*; aontaichidh sinn leibh, *we will consent unto you*; ma dh'aontaicheas tu aon uair, *if you consent once.*
aontaiche,** -ean, *s.m.* Abettor, conniver.
aontaichear, *fut.pass.* of aontaich.
aontaichidh, *fut. aff. a.* of aontaich.
aontaichte, *pt.part.* of aontaich.
aon-taigheachd, see aon-taigheadas.
aon-taigheadas, -ais, *s.m.* Co-habiting, living under one roof.
aon-taigheas, see aon-taigheadas.
aontainn, see aonta.
†aontanach, see aonarach.
aon-tlachd, *s.m.* Sole source of joy, only beloved. 2 Favourite.
aon-toil, -e, *s.f.* Unanimity, agreement.
aor, *pr. part.* ag aoradh, *v.a.* Worship, adore. 2**Join. 3**Adhere. Aoraibhse gu ceart, *worship in sincerity.*
†—, *s.m.* Curse.
aorabh, -aibh, *s.m.* Constitution, mental or bodily. Tha galar 'na aorabh, *there is a disease in his constitution.*
aorach, -aiche, *a.* Devout, religious, reverent, worshipping, pious.
aorachail, *a.* Devotional. Dleasnasan *a.*, *devotional duties.*
aoradair, -ean, *s.m.* Worshipper, adorer. 2‡‡ Foul-mouthed bard.
aoradh, -aidh, *s.m.* Worship, adoration, devotion. 2 Joining. 3 Adhering. Ag *a.* dha, *worshipping him*; *a.* féin-thoileil, *will-worship*; thoir *a.*, *worship.* Ag a—, *pr. part.* of aor.
aoradhail,** *a.* Adorable.
aoradhalachd, *s.f.ind.* Adorableness.
aoraidh, *gen.sing.* of aoradh.
†aoram, *fut. aff. a.* of aor. I will worship.
aornagaich, see aonagaich.
aornagail, see aonagail.
aornagan, *s. & v.* see aonagail.
aoruibh, see aorabh.
†aos,** *s.m.* Community, set of people. 2 Fire. 3 Sun. 4 God.
†aos, -ois, *s.f.* Age.
aosail, ,, ,, ,,
aosalachd, see aosmhoireachd.
aosar, see aosmhor.
aos-chiabh, -an, *s.f.* Aged locks, hoary hair. C'uim' am bheil t'*a.* snitheach? *why are thine aged locks moist?*
aos-chrann, -ainn, *s.f.* Aged tree, trunk. *A.* briste, *an aged broken trunk.*
aos-chrith, *s.m.* Tremor of age. *A.* air mo cheann, *the tremor of age on my head.*
aos-chritheach, *a.* Trembling with age.
aosda, *a.* Old, aged, ancient. An déidh dhomh fàs *a.*, *after I have become old*; a bhàrda *a.* nan linn a thréig! *ye aged bards of by-gone ages!* anns na h-*a.* tha gliocas, *in the aged there is wisdom.*
aosdachd, *s.f.* Agedness, antiquity.
aos-dàna, *s.m.* see aois-dàna.
aos-dànachd, see aois-dànachd.
aos-deanta, *s.m.* Mechanic.
aosd-shùil, *s.f.* Aged eye.
aos-làrach,** -aich, *s.m.* Aged site. 2 Aged ruin. An e an torr seo t'*a.*? *is this hillock thine aged seat?*
aos-liath, *a.* Grey-headed, old. Aos-liath, lag, *aged and weak.*
aosmhoire, *comp.* of aosmhor.
aosmhoireachd, *s.f.ind.* Properties of old age. 2 Great age, antiquity, agedness.
aosmhor, -oire, *a.* Aged, old, ancient.
———, -oir, *s.m.* Aged person. Tuigse nan *a.*, *the understanding of the aged.*
†aos-teas, *s.* Summer.
†aoth, *s.m.* Bell. 2 Crown.
†——, *a.* Small.
†——achd, *s.f.* Ringing of bells, chime of bells.
†——adh, *a.* Clean, pure.
aotrom, -uime, *a.* Light, not heavy. 2 Giddy, agog. Creutair *a.*, *a giddy creature.*
———achadh, -aidh, *s.m.* Alleviation, lightening. 2 Respite, as of fever. 3 Abatement, as of rain. Ag a—, *pr.pt.* of aotromaich. Tha 'n t-uisg' ag *a.*, *the rain is abating*; fhuair e *a.* o'n fhiabhrus, *he got a slight respite from the fever.*
———achd, *s.f.ind.* Lightness.
———aich, *pr. pt.* ag aotromachadh, *v.a.* Lighten. 2 Alleviate. 3 Abate.
aotromaichear, *fut. pass.* of aotromaich.
aotromaichidh, *fut. aff. a.* of aotromaich.
aotromaichte, *pt.pt.* of aotromaich.
aotroman, -ain, *s.m.* Bladder. 2 Any light thing.
aotromas, -ais, *s.m.* Lightness. 2 Delirium.
aotruime, *comp.* of aotrom.
aotruimid, *s.f.* Lightness.
———, *comp.* of aotrom. Is *a.* thu e, *you are the lighter of it.*
†ap,** *a.* Fit, proper, ripe.
ap, -a, *s.m.* Ape. 2 Mimic. 3 Shameless woman. †4** Any little creature. A' giùlan apa, *carrying apes.*
apach, *a.* Like an ape, abounding in apes.
apag, -aig, -an, *s.f.* Little ape. 2 Prating woman.
†apaich, see abuich.
apainn,** *s. f.* Abbey lands.
aparan, -ain, *s.m.* Apron. 2(AH)Inner stem and stern posts of a boat.
———aich, *v.a.* Cover with an apron.
———aichte, *a. & pt. part.* of aparain. Aproned.
aparr,* -a, *a.* Expert. 2‡‡Quick, nimble.
aparran, see aparan.
aparsaig, *s.f.* Transposed form of *knapsack.*
app, see ap.
apricoc,§ *s.m.* Apricot—*prunus armeniaca.*
ar, *poss. pron.* Our. Ar fearann, *our land*; ar còmhstri ri daimh†, *our battle with strangers.* [Takes *n-* before a word beginning with a vowel, as, ar n-each, *our horse*; ar n-athair, *our father.*]
ar, *prep.* see air.
-ar, *termination* of verbs used impersonally, as Gluaisear leam, *I will move.*
ar, see ar leam.
àr,(AH) *s.m.* Deadwood in stern of boat. Pre

ceded by the article *an t-*.]
†ar, *a.* Slow.
†ar. *s.m.* Bond, tie, chain. 2 Guiding, conducting. 3 *s.f.* Land, earth.
†ar, *v.* see arsa.
†—, see àra.
àr, *s.m.ind.* Ploughing, tillage, agriculture, Ag à—, *pr.pt.* of àr. Tha e rìs àr, *he is ploughing.*
àr, *pr. part.* ag àr, *v.a.* Plough, till, cultivate. Bha na daimh ag àr, *the oxen were ploughing;* àr meadhonach, *second ploughing;* iadsan a dh'àras euceart, *they that plough iniquity.*
àr, àir, *s.m.* Battle, slaughter. 2 Field of battle. Dàn an àir, *the song of battle*; na fulaing àr nan Criosdaidh, *permit not the slaughter of the Christians*; tuagh chum àir, *a battle-axe*; dithis 'nan cadal 'san àr seo, *two asleep on this field of battle.*
ar,(AC) [? seachd car—CR]—Théid e seachd ar air bean-an-taighe, *he will go seven times round the housewife.*
†ara,** arai, *s.m.* Conference. 2 Bier. 3 Page 4 Charioteer.
†àra, *n.pl.* of àr, *slaughter.*
àra, -ann, & -ainn *pl.* àirnean [& àran] *s.f.* Kidney. 2 Rein. An dà àra, *the two kidneys*; geir nan àra, *kidney suet.*
†araba, *prep.* For the sake of.
àrabhaig, -e, -an, see arrabhaig.
àrach, *a.* Slaughtering.
àrach, -aich, -aichean, *s.f.* Field of battle, plain. 'Na laidhe 'san àraich, *outstretched on the battlefield*; nach seachnadh le 'dheòin an àrach, *who would not willingly shun the battlefield.*
àrach, -aich, *s.m.* Tie, bond, or collar on a beast, stall-tie for a cow. 2 Restraint. 3 see atharrach. 4** Authority. 5**Strength. 6** Fishing ware. 7** Bier. 8** Gallows. 9 Milkman.
†àrach, -aich, *s.m.* Ploughshare. 2‡‡Utensils for ploughing.
àrach, -aich, *s.m.* Nursing, rearing, training. 2 Maintenance. 3 Strength, power. 4 Authority. 5 See àireach.
àrachail,‡‡ -e, *a.* Nutrimental.
arachair,** *s.m.* Insurer.
àrachas, -ais, *s.m.* Insurance. 2 Mansion, dwelling. Fear àrachais, *an insurer*; buth àrachais, *an insurance office*; taigh fo àrachas, *a house insured.*
arachas,** *s.m.* Strength, might.
arachd, see arrachd. 2† see àros.
———ach, see arrachdach.
arachdas, see àrachas.
†aracul, -uil, *s.m.* Cell, grotto.
†arad,** *a.* Strong, brave.
†àrad, -aid, *s.m.* see fàradh.
†aradain, *s.m.* Desk. 2 Pulpit.
aradair, *s.m.* Agriculturist. 2 Ploughman. 3 Tiller of the ground.
†àradh,** -aidh, -aidhean, *s.m.* see àra. 2 see fàradh.
†ara-fhlusga, *s.m.* Running of the reins.
aragarradh,** -aidh, *s.m.* Abandonment. 2 Prescience, secret anticipation.
aragarraich,** *v.a.* Forebode.
aragradh, -aidh, see aragarradh.
araiceil, -e, *a.* Valiant. 2 Precious. Gnothach *a.*, *a precious* or *an important affair.*
àraich, *pr.part.* ag àrach, *v.a.* Rear, bring up, educate. 2 Maintain, support. Is mairg a dh'àraich thu! *pity him that reared you!*
àraich, *gen. sing.* of àrach. 2 see làraich.
araichd, -e, -ean, *s.m.* Present, gift, donation. 2(AH) Boon, godsend. (* says "a lady's or gentleman's clothes given as a perquisite to servants. 2 Wealth in clothing.")
àraichd, *s. m.* Fit or deserving object.
araichdeil,* see araiceil.
araichdin, -e, -ean *s.m.* *Dim.* of araichd.
àraid, see àraidh.
araideach, -eiche, *a.* Joyous, glad, elated, elevated.
àraidh, *a.* Certain. 2 Particular, peculiar, special. 3 Proper, expedient. 4 Worthy, generous. 5 Liberal, hospitable. Duine àraidh, *a certain man*; gu h-àraidh (*adv.*) *especially, particularly*; gnothach *à.*, *an important affair.*
———,‡‡ -ean, *s.m.* Hero. 2 Cautioner.
———eachd,* *s.f.* Importance. Particularity, peculiarity, singularity.
àraig,‡‡ -e, -ean, *s.* Present.
†araigh,** *s.pl.* Reins of a bridle.
†araill, *a.* The other.
arain, *gen. sing.* of aran.
àrainn, see àra.
àrair,** -e, -ean, Slaughterer, warrior. see àradair.
aralach,* -aiche, *a.* Finical.
————d,* *s.f.* Niceness.
ar-a-mach, *s.m.* Rebellion, insurrection, mutiny. 2 Treason. Rinn iad *a.*, *they have rebelled.*
àran, *n.pl.* of àra. 2 *for* fàraidhean, (ladders)
†aran, -ain, *s.m.* Familiar conversation, discourse, dialogue.
aran, -ain, *s.m.* Bread, loaf. 2 Livelihood, sustenance. A tha 'cumail t'arain riut, *who gives you your livelihood*; cha bhi thu gun aran, *you shall not want a livelihood*; greim arain, *a piece of bread.*
aranach,** -aich, *s.m.* Pantry.
————, see arannach-sréine.
————, *a.* Full of bread. 2**Alimental.
aranaid,* see aranailt.
aranailt, *s.f.* Bread basket. 2 Pannier.
aran-coirce, Oat-bread, oat-cake.
aran-cruithneachd, Wheaten bread.
aran-donn, Brown bread. 2††Ginger-bread.
aran-eòrna, Barley-bread.
aran-lann,‡‡ -ainn, -an, *s.m.* Bread-room.
aran lathail, Daily bread.
aran-milis, Sweetbread. 2 Ginger-bread.
arannach-sréine, *s.m.* Bridle-rein.
aran-peasrach, Pease bread.
aran-seagaill, Rye-bread.
aran taisbeanta, Shewbread.
àrann, see àra.
†aroid,** *s.f.* Cover, table-cloth.
araon, *adv.* Together. 2 Both. 3 As one. Bheir an Tighearna solus d' an sùilibh *a.*, *the Lord will enlighten the eyes of both*; *a.* thus' agus esan, *both of you.*
ar'ar, see arbhar.
——ach, see arbharach.
àras, see àros.
——ach, see àrosach.
†arasg, -aisg, -an *s.m.* Word.
†arba, *conj.* Nevertheless.
†——, *s.m.* Chariot.
arbhach, -aiche, *a.* Destructive, slaughtering.
arbhadh, -aidh, Destruction, slaughtering.
arbhaitichte, *a.* Arable, producing corn.
arbhar, -air, *s.m.* Corn, growing or in sheaf. 2 ***rarely* host, army. Pailteas arbhair, *plenty of corn*; deasaichidh tu *a.*, *thou shalt prepare corn.*
————ach,** -aiche, *a.* Abounding in corn, of, or belonging to, corn crops. 2 Fertile.
————achd,** *s.f.* Embattling, as an army, forming into line.
arbharrachd,* see arbharachd.

arbhartachadh, -aidh, *s.m.* Dispossessing, act of ejecting from lands.
arbhartaich, *pr. part.* ag arbhartachadh, *v. a.* Dispossess, confiscate, disinherit. 2 Forfeit.
————te, *a. & pt. part.* of arbhartaich. Expelled, ejected from lands. 2 Confiscated. Am fearann *a.*, *the confiscated estates.*
arbhraigneach, -nich, *s.m.* Snare.
àrbhuidhe, see òrbhuidh.
†arc, *s.m.* Sow. 2 Sucking pig. 3 Lizard. 4 Body. 5 Dwarf. 6 (AF) Bear. 7 (AF) Stag, hind. 8 Collection. 9 Hero.
†arc, *s.f.* Bee. 2 Wasp. 3 Impost, tax. 4 Femen.
àrc,‡‡ -a, -ainn, *s.f.* Vulva vaccinea.
àrc, àirc, see àirc.
àrc, -an, *s.m.* Species of fungus on decayed timber.
àrc, àirce, *s.f.* Cork. Crann àirce, *cork tree.*
àrca, *s.m.* Buoy. 2 see àrc.
àrcain, *gen. sing.* of àrcan.
àrcan, -ain, *s. m.* Cork, stopple. Arcan buideil, *a bottle cork or stopple*; àrcan baraille, *a bung;* crann àrcain, *a cork-tree.*
arcan, *s.m.* see uircein. 2 see arc.
àrcanach, -eiche, *a.* Full of corks.
arcan-luachrach, -ain-, see dearc-luachrach.
arc-aoghair, *s.m.* Bear's guard or herdsman.
†ar-cheana, *adv.* Henceforth.
†àr-choin, *s.m.* see àr-chù.
†àr-chù, -choin, *n. pl.* -coin, *dat. pl.* -conaibh, *s.m.* Chained dog, fierce dog. 2 Mastiff. 3 Bloodhound.
†archuisg, -e, -ean, *s.f.* Experiment.
†arciseach, *a.* Ravenous.
arc-luachrach, see dearc-luachrach.
†arcmhuc, -muice, *s.m.* Male pig.
arcuinn, -e, *s.f.* Cow's udder.
†ar-cùl, *adv.* Behind. [air cùl]
†Ard,** Aird, see Art.
àrd, àirde, *n.pl.*-a, *a.* High, lofty, 2 Mighty, great, noble, eminent, excellent, supreme. 3 Proud. 4** Loud. Is esan a's àirde, *he is the tallest;* beinn àrd, *a lofty hill*; fuil àrd nan saoi, *the noble blood of heroes*; sealladh àrd, *a proud look*; fear a b'àirde guth, *the man of loudest voice.* *Ard-* answers to *arch-* as a prefix in English. Before an adj. as a prefix it supplies the place of an adv., as àrd-shona, *supremely happy*; àrd-éibhneach, *ecstatic.*
àrd, àird, *n.pl.* àird [& àrda] *dat. pl.* -aibh, *s.m.* see àirde. 2 Chief, eminent person. Uaigh an àird, *the chief's grave.*
àrda, *n. pl.* of àrd, *a. & s.* Choimh-fhreagair na creagan àrda, *the lofty rocks re-echoed.*
àrd-abhcaid,‡‡ -e, -ean *s.f.* Master jest.
àrdachadh, -aidh, *s.m.* Act of raising, exalting, or heightening. 2 Advancement, promotion, honour, preferment. 3* Augmentation, increase. 4 Praise. Ag a—, *pr. pt.* of àrdaich. *A.* tuarasdail, *increase of salary*; à. nan amadan, *the promotion of fools;* 'g a à. féin, *exalting himself.* When a person is delirious in sickness, it is said "tha àrdachadh air"—JM
àrdachair,** *s.m.* Aggrandizer.
àrdaich, *pr. part.* ag àrdachadh, *v.a.* Exalt, extol, elevate, raise aloft, heighten, promote. 2*Increase. *A.* i, *exalt her;* ardaich a thuarasdal, *increase his salary.*
àrdaichear, *fut. pass.* of àrdaich.
àrdaichidh, *fut. aff. a.* of àrdaich.
àrd-aigne, *s.m.* Magnanimity, greatness of mind. 2 Bravery. 3**Ambition.
————ach, -eiche, *a.* Magnanimous, high-minded. 2 Brave. 3**Ambitious. 4*Nettlesome.
àrdail, *a.* Cardinal (numbers in *gram.*)
àrdain, *gen. sing.* of àrdan.
àrd-aingeal, -gil, *pl.* -gil, -gle, -glean, *s.m.* Archangel.
àrd-aingealach,‡‡ -aiche, *a.* Archangelic.
àrd-aithrichean, *n.pl.* of àrd-athair.
†àrd-allata, *a.* High-famed.
àrd-amas, -ais, *s.m.* High aim or mark, ambition.
àrd-amhailt, see àrd-abhcaid.
àrdan, -ain, *s.m.* Pride, haughtiness. 2 Anger, wrath. 3 Height, eminence, hillock. 4 *n. pl.* of àrd, *s.* 'Na shuidhe air àrdan, *sitting on an eminence;* uabhar is àrdan, *pride and arrogance;* an droch dhuine 'na àrdan borb, *the wicked man in his fierce pride;* àrdan gruaidh, *pride of face*; tha m'àrdan 'nad chliù, *my pride is in thy fame*; dh'at àrdan 'na chridhe, *proud wrath swelled in his heart.*
———ach, -aiche, *a.* Proud, haughty. 2 Prone to take offence. 3 Arrogant. 4 Elated. Spiorad à., *a haughty spirit.*
———achd, *s.f.* Haughtiness, proudness, arrogance. Uaill is à., *pride and haughtiness.*
†àrdanair *s.f.* (àrd+onoir) High honour.
†àrdarc, -airc, *s.m.* Blazon. 2 Armorial bearings.
àrd-aoibhneach, *a.* Very joyful, exulting.
àrd-athair, -ar, -thraichean, *s.m.* Patriarch.
àrd-bhaile, *pl.* -ltean, *dat. pl.* -tibh, *s.m.* City, metropolis. Esan a ghlacas à., *he that takes a city.*
àrd-bhailtean, *n. pl.* of àrd-bhaile.
àrd-bhan-diuc, *s.f.* Archduchess.
àrd-bheachd,‡‡ *s.f.ind.* Elevation of sentiment.
àrd-bheann, *gen. pl.* of ard-bheinn.
àrd-bheinn, -e, *pl.n.* -bheanntan, *gen.* -bheann, *dat.* -bheanntaibh, *s.f.* Pinnacle. 2 Mountain. Ait mar iolair nan àrd-bheann, *joyous as the mountain eagle.*
àrd-bhlàth, *s.m.* Height of flourish, prime. 2 Flower, blossom. Tha i 'n à. a h-aimsir, *she is in the prime of life.*
àrd-bhreitheamh, -eimh, -na, *s.m.* Supreme judge. 2 Chief justice, chancellor.
àrd-bhuachaill, -e, -ean, *s.m.* Head shepherd.
àrd-bhùirdeasach,** *s.m.* Burgomaster.
àrd-bhurgair, (àrd+*Eng.* burgher.)
àrd-chabrach, -aiche, *a.* High-branched.
àrd-chantair, -e, -ean, *s.m.* Arch-chanter.
àrd-chath,** *s.m.* General engagement, pitched battle. 2 Thick of the battle. Gaoir an àrd-chath, *the din of the pitched battle.*
————air, -thrach, -thraichean, *s.f.* Metropolis, chief city, archbishop's see. 2 Throne.
àrd-cheann, *s.m.* Superior, ruler, head. Ard-cheann na h-eaglais, *the head of the church.*
àrd-cheann } -chinn-, *s.m.* Chief general.
———— -airm, }
————abhard, see àrd-cheannard.
————ach, -aiche, *a.* Proud, haughty. lofty. 2 Insolent, arrogant.
————ard, -aird, -ardan, *s.m.* Supreme head, chief, superior.
àrd-cheannas, -ais, *s.m.* Superiority, pre-eminence, supremacy. 2 Dominion, command. *A.* anns gach uile, *pre-eminence in all things.*
àrd-cheann-fheachd‡‡ *s.m.* Generalissimo.
àrd-cheannsal, see àrd-cheannas.
àrd-cheum, -chéim, *s.m.* Strut. 2 Bound. 3 Lofty gait. 4**Prancing.
————ach, -aiche, *a.* High-bounding.
àrd-cheumnachadh, -aidh, *s.m.* Strutting. 2 Bounding. 3 Walking proudly. 4**Prancing. Ag à—, *pr. pt.* of àrd-cheumnaich.
àrd-cheumnaich,** *v.a.* Strut. 2 Bound. 3 Walk proudly. 4 Prance.
àrd-chìs,‡‡ *s.f.* Tribute.

àrd-chlachair, -e, -ean, *s.m.* Architect. 3 Master mason.
————eachd, *s.f.* Architecture. 2 Business of a master mason.
àrd-chliu, *s.m.* High fame.
àrd-chnoc-faire, -chnuic-faire, *s.m.* Great beacon. 2 Sconce.
àrd-cholaisde, -ean, *s.m.* University, college.
àrd-chomas, -ais, *s.m.* Discretionary or despotic power. Thug e à. dhomh, *he gave me discretionary power.*
————ach, *a.* Having discretionary or despotic power. 2 Supreme, unlimited.
àrd-chomhairle, *s.f.* Parliament. 2 Supreme council. 3 Synod. *A.* Bhreatuinn, *the British Parliament*; ball na h-A., *a member of Parliament.*
————ach, -eiche, *s.m.* Chief counsellor. 2 Consul. 3**Chancellor.
àrd-chomhairliche, see àrd-chomhairleach.
àrd-chrann, (AH) *s.m.* Topmast.
àrd-chreagach, -aiche, *a.* High rocked, rugged.
àrd-chuan, -chuain, -chuantan, *s.m.* The high sea.
àrd-chùiseach, -eiche, *a.* Sublime, noble, lofty.
àrd-chumhachd, -an, *s.f.* Supreme power. 2 High power, 3 State, office. 4 Authority. 5 Absoluteness.
————ach, -aiche, *a.* High in dignity and authority.
àr-dhamh, -dhaimh, *s.m.* Ploughing ox.
àrd-dhruidh, *s.m.* Arch-druid. He was chosen by a plurality of voices from the worthiest and most learned of the order. He was deemed infallible. He was referred to in all cases of controversy, and from his judgment there was no appeal. He was the president of the general assemblies of the Druids, and had the casting vote. His aid and friendship were much valued and confided in. [see note on "Coimhdhe."]
àrd-dorus, -uis, -orsan, *s.m.* Lintel.
àrd-eaglais,** *s.f.* Cathedral.
àrd-ealantachd,‡‡ *s.f.ind.* Masterliness.
àrd-easbuidheachd, see àrd-easbuigeachd.
àrd-easbuig, -e, -ean, *s.m.* Archbishop.
————each, *a.* Archepiscopal, like, or pertaining to an archbishop.
————eachd, *s.f.* Archbishopric.
àrd-fhaclach, -aiche, *a.* Lofty in speech.
àrd-fhàidh, -e, -ean, *s.m.* Chief prophet.
àrd-fheamanach,** -aich, *s.m.* High steward.
————d, *s.f.* High stewardship.
àrd fhear-gionach,(AF) *s.m.* Asp.
———— -gnothaich,‡‡ *s.m.* Attorney.
———— -nimh,(AF) Asp.
àrd-fheasgar, -air, *s.m.* Late at even, towards night.
àrd-fhéill, *s.f.* Great festival or solemnity. *A.* na h-Eadailt, *the Carnival.*
àrd-fhiosachd, *s.f.ind.* Prophesying, predicting.
àrd-fhlaitheachd, see àrd-fhlaitheas.
àrd-fhlaitheas, -ais, *s.m.* Supreme dominion.
àrd-fhlath, -aith, -an, *s.m.* Monarch, prince, chief, archduke.
àrd-fhoclach, see àrd-fhaclach.
àrd-fhoghlum, -uim, *s.m.* High learning.
àrd-fhrithealachadh,** *s.m.* Archdeaconry.
àrd-fhrithealachd, see àrd-fhrithealachadh.
àrd-fhrithealachair, see àrd-fhrithealaiche.
àrd-fhrithealaiche,** *s.m.* Archdeacon.
àrd-fhuaim, *s.f.* Loud noise, murmur.
————neach, -eiche, *a.* Sounding, murmuring, making a loud noise.
àrd-fhuaimnich, *s.f.* Any loud noise, continued loud noise.
àrd-ghairm, -ghairme, *s.f.* Loud shout. 2 High calling. Duais na h-àrd-ghairme, *the reward of the high calling.*
àrd-ghaisgealachd,‡‡ *s.f.* Chivalry.
àrd-ghaoir, -e, *s.f* Loud noise or cry.
†**àrd-ghaois**, -ean, *s.f.* Liberal art.
†————ear, *s.m.* Master of arts.
àrd-ghaoth, -ghaoithe, *s.f.* High wind.
————ach, -aiche, *a.* Windy, stormy, blowing loudly. A bhuilg-shéididh à., *his loudly blowing bellows.*
àrd-ghlan, -aine, *a.* Illustrious, conspicuous.
àrd-ghlaodh, -aoidh, *s.m.* Loud cry, scream.
†**àrd-ghleadhraich**, *s.f.* Any loud noise, a rattling noise.
†**àrd-ghliaidh**, *s.m.pl.* Famous deeds.
àrd-ghlòir, -e, *s.m.* Bombast, loud speaking, lofty style, boasting, vain-glory.
————each -eiche, *a.* Bombastic, inclined to speak loud, boasting, vain-glorious.
àrd-ghlonn, -an, *s.m.* Noble exploit.
————ach, -aiche, *a.* Renowned for bravery, celebrated, famed.
àrd-ghniomh, *pl.* -arra, -artha, & -arran, *s.m.* Lofty deed, feat, achievement. *A.* an rìgh, *the exploit of the king.*
————aran, *n. pl.* of àrd-ghniomh.
àrd-ghul, -ghuil, *s.m.* Loud weeping, howling. Tha e ri àrd-ghul, *he is weeping aloud.*
àrd-ghuth, *s.m.* Loud voice, 2 Loud cry, shout.
————ach, -aiche, *a.* Clamorous, loud. 2 Shouting loudly.
àr-dhamh, see àr-damh.
àr-dhìth, -e, *s.m.* War havoc.
àrd-iarla, *s.m.* First earl.
àrd-inbhe, -ean, *s.f.* Dignity, eminence, high rank. Oirdheirceas àrd-inbhe, *the excellence of dignity.*
————ach, -eiche, *a.* Eminent. 2 High in office.
————achd, *s.f.* Eminence, dignity, rank.
àrd-inntinn, *s.f.ind.* Haughtiness, arrogance, pride. 2 High spirit.
————each, -eiche, *a.* Haughty, arrogant, proud, vain. Na bi à., *be not high-minded.*
————eachd, *s.f.ind.* Haughtiness, pride, conceit, vanity. *A.* 'nur measg, *pride among you.*
àrd-iolach, -aich, *s.f.* Loud shout, acclamation. Le h-àrd-iolach, *with a loud shout.*
àrd-iuchar,‡‡ -air, -chraichean, *s.f.* Master-key.
àrd-labhar, see àrd-labhrach.
àrd-labhrach, -aiche, *a.* Loud voiced. 2 Eloquent, sublime (in speaking.) à. a' chinn, *the tongue.*
àrd-leumach, -aiche, *a.* High bounding.
àrd-leumannach, see àrd-leumach.
àrd-losgadh, -aidh, *s.m.* Extreme burning. 2 Extreme heat. 3 Inflammation. Le h-àrd-losgadh, *with extreme burning.*
àrd-luathghair, *s.f.* Triumphant exclamation.
àrd-mhailgheach, *a.* Beetle-browed.
àrd-mhaighstireachd, *s.f.* Supreme authority.
ard-mhalaideach,‡‡ -eiche, *a.* Beetle-browed.
àrd-mhaor-righ, *s.m.* Herald, pursuivant.
àrd-mharaiche, *s.m.* Admiral. Prìomh à., *lord high admiral.*
àrd-mhath, -aith, *s.m.* Supreme good.
àrd-mheanmnach, -aiche, *a.* Magnanimous, high mettled.
àrd-mhiann,** *s.m.* & *f.* Aspiration.
àrd-mhilidh, -ean, *s.m.* Heroic chief.
àrd-mhol, *v.a.* Extol highly, magnify, praise, laud, celebrate.
àrd-mholadh, -aidh, *s.m.* Praise. Ag à—, *pr. pt.* of àrd-mhol.
àrd-mholta, *a.* & *pl. part.* Highly extolled, magnified. 2 Celebrated.
àrd-mhorair, -ean, *s.m.* Admiral. 2 Lord Pre-

sident. *A.* an t-seisein, *Lord President of the Court of Session.*
àrd-mhorfhear, àrd-mhormhaor, } see àrd-mhorair.
àrd-mhuingeach, -eiche, *a.* High-maned.
àrdoch, -oich, see fàrdoch.
†àrdog, see òrdag.
àrd-ollamh, -aimh, *s.m.* Chief professor or doctor. 2 Principal of a university. 3 historiographer royal.
àrdorus, see àrd-dorus.
àrdrach, -aich, *s.f.* Eight-oared galley.
àrd-ramhach, see àrdrach.
àrd-rath, -a, *s.m.* Sunshine of prosperity.
àrd-reachdas, -ais, *s.m.* General assembly. 2 Synod. 3 Convention.
àrd-reim,** *s.* Rant.
àrd-riaghladh, -aidh, *s m.* Supreme rule.
àrd-riaghailt, -e, *s.f.* Supreme rule.
àrd-righ, *pl.* -re, & -rean, *s.m.* Supreme king, God. 2 Monarch. 3 Emperor.
àrdroch, see àrdrach.
àrd-sgeimhleir,** -ean, *s.m.* Curious person.
àrd-sgoil, -e, -ean, *s.f.* Academy, college, high school. 2* see àrd-sgoilearachd. à. Dhunéideann, *Edinburgh University.*
———ear, -ir, -ean, *s.m.* Student at a university or academy. 2 High-school boy. 3 *Philosopher. 4 Excellent scholar.
———achd,* *s.f.ind.* Philosophy. 2 Choice education.
àrd-sgoil mhaighstir, -irean, *s.m.* Master at an academy or high-school. 2 Professor.
àrd-shagart, -airt, -ean, *s.m.* High priest.
———ach,‡‡ *a.* Pontifical.
———achd, *s.f.ind.* High priesthood, primateship.
àrd-sheanadh, -aidh, *s.m.* General assembly. 2 Supreme council. 3 Parliament, Ard-sheanadh Eaglais na h-Alba, *The General Assembly of the Church of Scotland.*
àrd-sheanair, -ean, *s.m.* Member of a general assembly, 2 of a senate, or 3 of any supreme council.
àrd-sheanalair, -e, -ean, *s.m.* Generalissimo. 2 Supreme commander.
àrd-sheòl, *s m.* Topsail.
àrd-shodan,** -ain, *s.m.* Ecstasy.
àrd-shona, *a.* Supremely blest, or 2 happy.
———s, -ais, *s.m.* Supreme bliss. 2 Perfect happiness. *A.* mo chridhe, *the supreme bliss of my heart.*
àrd-shubhas, see àrd-shonas.
àrd-shuidhear, -ir, -ean, *s.m.* President.
àrd-shunntach, -aiche, *a.* Highly cheerful, in high spirits, mirthful, gay.
àrd-theud,‡‡ *s.f.* Master-string.
àrd-thighearna, -an, *s.m.* Supreme lord.
———s, -ais, *s.m.* Supreme rule or power.
———il, *a.* Lordly, proud, haughty.
àrd-thonnach, -aiche, *a.* High-waved.
àrd-threith, *gen. sing.* of àrd-thriath.
àrd-thriath, -threith, *s.m.* Supreme chief or ruler. 2 Hero. *A.* na cruinne-cé, *Supreme Ruler of the universe.*
àrd-uachdaran, -ain, *s.m.* Chief ruler, sovereign.
———achd, *s. f. ind.* Chief rule, supreme authority.
àrd-uaislean, *s.pl.* Nobles, nobility. 2 Princes. 3 Gentry. Tàir air àrd-uaislibh, *contempt on princes.*
àrd-uaislich,‡‡ *v.a.* Nobilitate.
àrduchadh, see àrdachadh.
àrd-ùghdarras, -ais, *s m.* Chief authority, discretionary power. Fhuair mi à., *I received full authority.*

àrduich, see àrdaich.
arduichear, àrduichidh, àrduichte, } see àrdaich——.
ar-ear, -ir, *s.m.* *better* àradair.
àr-ear, -ir, *s.m.* (àr+fear) Hero.
†àreile, *adv.* Other.
a réir, *prep.* According to.
a réir sin, *adv.* According to that.
ar feadh, *prep.* see feadh.
ar-fhaich, -e, -ean, *s.f.* Field of battle.
†arfud, see air feadh.
arfuntaich, *pr.pt.* ag arfuntachadh, *v.a.* Disinherit, dispossess. 2 Forfeit.
arfuntachadh, -aidh, *s.m.* Disinheriting. 2 Forfeiting
arfuntaichte, *pt.part.* Forfeited. Na h-oighreachdan *a.*, *the forfeited estates.*
†arg, *s.m.* Champion. 2 Chief, commander. 3 Learning. 4 Ark, ship. †*a.***White.
argair,** *s.m.* Plunderer. 2 Destroyer.
†———, *v.a.* Keep, herd.
†argam, see airg, *v.*
argarrach, -aich, see agarach.
†àrglorach, see àrd-ghlorach.
†argnach, -aich, *s.m.* Robber—.*a.* Loud, mighty.
†argnadh, -aidh, *s.m.* Robbery. 2**Prey. 3 Ingenuity.
†argnoir, see argnach.
†argthoir, -e, -ean, *s.m.* Destroyer. 2 Plunderer.
†arguin, *v.* Lay waste. *s.f.* Argument.
†———te, *a.* Argumentative.
arguinn, *v.a.* Argue, dispute, wrangle.
———, *s.f.* Argument.
†——— -iomlan, *s.f.* Syllogism.
———each, *a.* Dialectical.
———eachd,** *s.f.* Argumentation.
———ear,** *s.m.* Discusser.
———iche,** *s.m.* Arguer.
argumaid,** *s. f. ind.* Argument, motive, reason. Le h-argumaidibh, *with arguments.*
———each,** *a.* Argumentative.
———ich,* *v.n.* Argue, reason. 2 Foil.
——— -ribidh, *s.f.* Dilemma.
†arigh,** *s.pl.* Chiefs.
†arinn,** *s.f.* Friendship.
a rìs, *adv.* see a rithist.
a rithis, *adv.* Again. 2 Second time, another time. (In some parts of the Southern Highlands they say *a rithistich.*)
†arladh, *s.m.* Kindling.
arlain, see earlain.
arlas, -ais, see airleas.
àrlas, -ais, -an, see fàrlus.
†àrleag, -eig, see àirleag.
———ach, see àirleagach.
ar leam, *v.defect.* Methinks, methought.
ar leom, see ar leam.
arlogh, -oigh, Cartage of corn. Féisd an arloigh, *the harvest feast, harvest home.*
arm, *v.a.* Oil or grease wool. 2 see armaich.
arm, airm, *dat.pl.* armaibh, *s.m.* Weapon. 2 Army. 3 *pl.* Arms, armour. Sgian, arm a bu mhiann leis, *the knife, a weapon he was fond of*; tha e 'san arm, *he is in the army*; chaidh e do'n arm, *he joined the army*; fo armaibh, *armed, under arms.*
†——, *s.m.* Origin, root, stock. 2 Father, God.
arma, *for* airm.
armach, -aiche, *a.* Armed. 2 Covered with armour, mailed. 3 Warlike. Gach gaisgeach *a.*, *every armed hero.*
armach,* -aich, *s.m.* Armed person. 2 Warrior. Labhair an dubh *a.*, *the dark warrior spoke.*
armachd, *s.f.ind.* Armour. 2 Arms. 3 Feats of arms. Nigh iad an *a.*, *they washed their*

armour ; *a.* an t-soluis, *the armour of light.*
armadair,** *s.m.* Armourer.
armadh, -aidh, *s.m.* Oil or butter for anointing wool. 2 Act of anointing wool. Ag *a.* na h-olainn, *anointing the wool.*
armaich, *v.a.* Arm, gird on arms, clothe with armour. Armaichibh sibh féin,*arm yourselves.*
———e, *s.m.* Armourer.
———idh, *fut.aff.a.* of armaich.
———te, *pt.part.* of armaich.
armail,** *s.f.* Arms, weapons, armour. 2 Armoury. —*a.* Armed.
———t, -ailte, *s.m.* Army. Ann an *a.*, *in an army*; *a.* nam breacan, *the Highland Army.*
———teach, -eiche, *a.* Trained to arms. 2 Of, or belonging to, an army. 3 Having great armies.
†armain, see àrmunn.
†armair, -e, *s.f.* Reproof.
———,** *s.m.* Armiger.
———e, see àmraidh.
†armalta, see armaichte.
armaradh, -aidh, *s.m.* Reproof, scold, check.
arm-chaismeachd, *s.f.ind.* Alarm of battle.
arm-cheard,** *s.m.* Armourer.
arm-chleasach, -aiche, *a.* Exercised in martial feats.
arm-chliseach, -eiche, *a.* Expert in battle. 2 Alert, active.
†Arm-chosal, *s.m.* Satan, the Devil.¶
arm-chreuchdach, -aiche, *a.* Inflicting wounds.
arm-coise, *s.m.* Infantry.
†armed, *s.m.* Primitive ancestor.
†arm-eineach, *a.* Destructive in war. 2 Warlike. 3 Sanguinary.
arm-ghille, *s.m.* Armour-bearer.
àrmhach, -aiche, *a.* Destructive.
†———, *s.f.* Slaughter.
àr-mhagh, -aighe, *s.m.* Field of slaughter or battle.
†armhaigh, *s.m.* Buzzard.
†àr-mhiannach ** *a.* Sanguinary. 2 Warlike.
†armhind, *s.f.* Respect, reverence.
arm-lann, -na, -ainn, *s.m.* Armoury, magazine, military depôt, citadel.
arm-leònach, -aiche, *a.* see arm-chreuchdach.
arm-oilean, -ein, *s.m.* Military discipline, drilling.
†armoraich, *s.m.pl.* Maritime people. (*lit.* Armoricans—natives of Brittany.)
arm-righ, *s.m.* King-at-arms.
armta, *a.* Armed, oiled as wool.
arm-thaigh, *s.m.* see arm-thaisg.
arm-thaisg, *s.f.* Armoury, military magazine.
arm-thasgaidh, see arm-thaisg.
†arm-thor, *s.m.* Armoury.
†arm-thur, see arm-thor.
†armuinn, *v.a.* Bless, revere.
———, *gen. sing.* of àrmunn.
†armuint, see armuinn.
armuinte, *pt. part.* of armuinn.
àrmunn, -uinn, *s.m.* Hero, warrior. 2 Chief, brave man, chieftain, chief of a clan. 3 Officer. Air slios an àrmuinn, *on the warrior's side* ; sùil mheallach an àrmuinn, *the winning eye of the hero.*
†arn, airn, *s.m.* Judge.
†àrn, *s.f.* see àra.
†arna, *prep.* (*for* air na) After his or its.
arnach, see eàrnach.
†arnaidh, *s.f.* Bond, surety. 2 Band.
àrna Moire (AC)—*for* àra, *lit.* kidneys of Mary. A square thick Atlantic nut sometimes found indented in the form of a cross.
†arnuidh, *a.* Fierce, impetuous.
àroch, *a.* Straight, upright.
———, -oich, *s.f.* Little hamlet, village. 2 Summer grazing. 3 Residence, dwelling. 4 see ar-fhaich.
àrois, *gen. sing.* of àros.
†aroll,** -oill, *s.m.* Great slaughter. 2 Great many, great deal.
àros, -ois, -an, *s.m.* House, abode, palace, habitation. 2** Settlement, apartment. An loisgear à. nam Fiann? *shall the habitation of the Fingalians be burnt?* àros nan long, *the abode of ships.*
——ach, -aiche, *a.* Habitable. 2 Abounding in houses or dwellings, of or belonging to a house. 3**Having many apartments.
——ach, -aich, -aichean, *s.m.* Inhabitant. 2 Lodger. 3 Resident householder.
arpag, -aig, -an, *s.f.* Harpy, any ravenous creature. 2 Great black-beaked gull, see farspach. 3(AF) Snake, adder. 4* Triangular cake.—*Islay.*
———ach, -aiche, *a.* Ravenous, grasping.
arphuntachadh, see arfuntachadh.
arphuntaich, see arfuntaich.
†arr, *s.m.* Stag, hind.
†arra, -ai, *s.m.* Treachery. 2 Pledge.
arraban, -ain, *s.m.* Distress, perplexity, anxiety.
———ach,†† *a.* Sorrowful.
arrabhaig, -e, -ean, *s.f.* Strife, quarrel, discord.
arra-bhalach, -aich, *s.m.* Traitor, treacherous fellow. 2*Eavesdropper. *A.* garg, *a fierce traitor.*
arrach, -aich, *s.m.* Runt. 2**Minim. 3 see arrachd.
arrachar, -air, *s.m.* Rowing. 2 Steering.
arrachd, -an, *s.m.* Spectre, apparition. 2 Pigmy, dwarf, mannikin. 3**Centaur. Uaill 'san *a.*, *pride in the dwarf.*
———a, see arrachdach.
———ach, -aiche, *a.* Spectral, unworldly. 2 Dwarfish, diminutive. 3 see arraiceach.
———ail, -aile, *a.* see arrachdach.
———an, -ain, *dim.* of arrachd. 2 Fairy.
———as,** -ais, *s.m.* †Dignity. 2 Dwarfishness. 3‡‡ Strength, manliness.
arra-cholas, -ais, *s.m.* Power.
arra-chogaidh, *s.m.* *s.m.* The hound that first winds or comes up with the deer.
†arradh, -aidh, *s.m.* Armament. 2 Merchandise. 3 Ornament.
arraghaideach, -aiche, *a.* Negligent, careless. 2 Idle.
arra-ghlòir, -e. *s.f* Prattle, garrulity, idle talk.
———each, -eiche, *a.* Garrulous, given to prattle, nonsensical.
arraiceach, -iche, *a.* Large, ample, able-bodied. 2 Manly. 3 Magnanimous. 4 Courageous. 5† Effectual. Each *a.* treasdach, *a large thorough-pacing horse.*
arraiceas, -eis, *s.m.* 3 Power, strength, manliness.
arraiceil, -eile, *a.* see arraiceach.
arraichdeach, see arraiceach.
arraichdean, *s.m.pl.* Jewels, precious things.
arraichdeil, -eile, *a.* see arraiceach.
arraid, *s.f.* Wandering, error. 2 Vice. 3 Man sunk in vice. 4*Toiling in vain.
———,** *v.a.* Corrupt, deprave, make vicious.
àrraid, *a.* see àraidh.
arraideach, -eiche, *a.* Erratic, irregular, wandering. 2*Willing to no purpose.
àrraidh, *a.* see àraidh.
†———, *s.m.pl.* Evil actions, misconduct.
arraidh,** *a.* Generous, liberal. 2 Hospitable.
arraing, -ean, *s.m.* Stitch, convulsions.
†arrais,** *v.n.* Arrive at, reach.
arrais,(AC) *a.* Evil, wicked. *s.* Demon.
———,** *s.f.* Joy, pleasure. 2 Streaming, running.

arral, -ail, *s.m.* Foolish pride, fastidiousness. 2 ††Insolence.
——ach, -aiche, *a.* Disdainful, squeamish, insolently nice, fastidious.
†arroch, *v.a.* Govern, command.
arronach, -aiche, *a.* Becoming, fit, suitable. 2 Decent.
————d, *s.f.* Fitness, suitableness. 2 Decentness.
†arronaich, *v.n.* Fit, suit.
————e, *comp.* of arronach.
arronta, *a.* Bold, brave, daring. 2 Confident. 3 High-spirited. 4 Suitable. 6 Competent. 7††Intrepid. 8††Stout. Fìor-dheas *a.*, *truly active and bold.*
————chd, *s.f.* Boldness, bravery. 2 Confidence.
†arruig, see àraichd.
†arruiseach, *a* Obvious.
àrrusg, -uisg, *s.m.* Awkwardness. 2 Indecency.
ars', see arsa.
arsa, *v.defect.* Said, quoth. [The *s* of the Gaelic really belongs to the pronoun, "sé" or "sì"—ar sé, *said he*; ar sì, *said she.*‡] This verb is never used with propriety, except in expressions corresponding to *said I, said he,* &c. In the order of syntax, the nom. case never precedes this verb, not even by poetical license; this forms the distinction between it and the corresponding *thubhairt.* It is right to say "duine a thubhairt sin," wrong to say "duine arsa sin," *a man who said that.* Ars' an ceannaiche, *saith the buyer*: ars' òighean nan aodann gràdhach, *said the maids of the lovely visages.*
àrsachd, *better* àrsaidheachd.
àrsadair,* see àrsair.
àrsadh, -aidh, *s.m.* Antiquity, age.
àrsaich,** *v.a.* Antiquate.
àrsaidh, *a.* Old, superannuated, old-fashioned, ancient, antique.
———,** -ean, *s.m.* One who relates traditions.
àrsaidheachd, *s.f.* Antiquity. 2 Antiquarianism.
àrsaidhear, -eir, -an, *s.m.* see àrsair.
————achd, see àrsaireachd.
àrsair, *s.m.* Antiquary.
———eachd, *s.f.* Antiquarianism.
àr-samhraidh,** *s.m.* Fallow ground.
arsannach,‡‡ -aich, *s.m.* Guest.
àrsantach, *a* Old, antique, ancient. 2 Old-fashioned. 3 Fond of the study of antiquities.
arseap,* see artreud.
arsfhear, see àrsair.
arsnaig, -e, *s.f.* Arsenic.
arsneal, see airtneal.
———ach, -aiche, see airtnealach.
arson, see air son.
arspag,¶ *s.f.* Great black-beaked gull. see farspach.
†àrsuidh, †àrsuigh, } see àrsaidh.
†Art, airt, *s.m.* God.
†art, airt, *s m.* Bear. 2 Flesh. 3 Limb, joint.
†——, *a.* see †artach.
art, airt, *s.m.* Stone. 2 House. 3 Tent. Tarruing art, *a loadstone*; gach réile-art, *every shining pebble.*
†artach, -aich *s.m.* Quarry. 2 Stony gronnd.
———, -aiche, *a.* †Noble, great, worthy, illustrious, exalted. 2 Stony.
artan,** -ain, *s.m.* Little stone, pebble.
artarach,** -aich, *s.m.* Ship's boat.
†art-chaileir, *s.f.* Quarry.
†arthrach, -aich, *s.m.* Boat, wherry. 2 Ship.
†arthraich, *v.a.* Navigate. 2 Enlarge.
artlaich, artluich, } see fairtlich.

†artragham, *v.a.* I do make.
artreud, *s.m.* Transposed form of Eng *retreat.*
art-theine, *s.m.* (*lit.* fire stone) Flint.
àruinn, -e, -ean, *s.f.* see àra. 2 Forest, *properly* a deer-forest. 3††Bounds.
àrus, see àros.
†arusg, -uisg, *s.m.* Neck.
àrusg, see àrrusg.
as, *prep.* Out of, from out. [*As* drops the *s* when followed by a consonant.] á taigh na daorsa, *out of the house of bondage*; as a chéile, *loosened, asunder*; as a' mhachair, *out of the field*; an ann á Tuath a tha sibh? *are you from the North?* thug i sgreuch aisde, *she gave a shriek*; tha sinn as na geasan aice, *we are free from her spells*; spìon as a bhun e, *eradicate it*; thug iad an car asam, *they cheated me*; tha iad as mo dhéidh, *they are after me*; as an Eadailt, *from Italy*; tha iad ag iomairt á làmhan a chéile, *they understand one another, there is collusion between them (lit. they are each playing out of the other's hand)*; thubhairt iad e á beul a chéile, *they said it simultaneously.*
Combined with the personal pronouns thus:

1 Sing.	asam,	*Plur.*	asainn,
2	asad,		asaibh,
3	as, *m.* } aiste, *f.* }		asta, *m. & f.*

Emphatic forms.
1 Sing. asam-sa. asam-fhéin; *pl.* asainne, asainn-fhéin.
2 Sing. asad-sa, asad-fhéin; *pl.* asaibh-se, asaibh-fhéin.
3 Sing. (*m.*) as-san, as-fhéin; (*f.*) aiste-se, aiste-fhéin; *pl.* asta-san, asta-fhéin.
as, *prep. pron.* (as+e) Out of him *or* it. 2 From him *or* it. [Emphatic—as-san, as-fhéin.] Tha mi mór as, *I am proud of him*; cha d'thug mi ni sam bith as, *I took nothing out*; dubh as, *blot out*; tha 'n solus air dol as, *the light has gone out*; cuir as da, *destroy him or it*; chaidh as da, *he perished*; chaidh e as, *he escaped*; leig as, *let go*; leig as e, *let him* or *it go*; cia as? (*adv.*) *whence?* cia as a thàinig sibh? cia as duibh? *where did you come from?* chuir an t-eagal as da, *fear deprived him of his senses,* or *killed him.*
†as, *s.f.* see asal.
†as, ais, *s.m.* Milk. 2 Beer, ale.
†as, *v.a.* Kindle, as a fire. 2**Do. 3**Make.
†as, *v. defect.* see is.
as,‡ *priv. part.* Not, un-.
a's, *prep.* (anns) In. [Generally used when speaking of the seasons as—a's t-Earrach, *in the Spring*; a's t-samhraidh, a's t-fhoghar, *in the summer, in the autumn.* "A's geamhradh" is not used for *in the winter.*]
a's, *conj.* see agus.
a's, *sign* of the 1st. comparative in Gaelic when translated by the superlative in Eng. (a, *rel. pron.*+*v.* is.) Oigh a's gile làmh, *maid of the fairest hands*; fear a's léithe colg, *a man of the greyest hair.*
†asa, see fasa.
†——ch, -aich, *s.m.* Shoemaker.
†asach, *a.* Shod. 2 Milky, watery. 3 Like beer or ale.
as a chéile, *adv.* Asunder.
as a chiall,‖ *adv.* Mad. (Out of his senses.)
asad, *prep. pron.* (as+tu) Out of thee, from thee, in thee, on thee. [*Emphatic*: asad-sa, asad-fhéin.] Tha mi ag earbsadh asad, *I trust in you.*
†asadh, -aidh, *s.m.* Anchoring, resting, settling.
asad-sa, *Emphatic of* asad.
asaibh, *prep. pron.* (as+sibh) Out of you, from

you, in you, on you. [*Emphatic:* asaibh-se, asaibh-fhéin.]
asaichte,** *a. & pt. part.* Shod.
asaid, *v. & s.* see aisead.
asaidh, *gen. sing.* of asadh.
†——, see †asadh.
†——, *v.n.* Rebel, revolt.
asaig, *s.f.* see àsuing.
asail, *gen.sing.* of asal.
——eag, (AF) *s.f.* Stormy petrel, storm-finch, alamonti.
asain,(AF) see asal.
àsainn, *s.f.* see àsuing.
asainn, *prep. pron.* Out of us, from amongst us. [*Emphatic:* asainne, asainn-fhéin.]
àsainneach, *a.* Well furnished.
asair,§ -ean, *s.m.* Common asarum—*asarum europæum.*
——, *v.a.* see asairich.
——, -e, -ean, *s.m.* Shoemaker. 2 Harness of a horse, equipage.
àsaireadh, *s.m.* Decline, disease of sheep.
asairich, *v.a.* Harness.
†asait,‖ *s.f.* Parturition.
†as-àitich,** Abandon, quit, evacuate. 2 Put out of place. 3 Eject.
asal, -ail, *s.f.* Ass. A' marcachd air asail, *riding on an ass;* mac na h-asail, *a donkey colt.*

15. Asair.

asalach,** -aiche, *a.* Asinine.
asam, *prep. pron.* (as+mi) Out of me, from me, on me, in me. [*Emphatic:* asam-sa, asam-fhéin.]
†asan, -ain, *s.m.* Staff. 2 see osan. 3 see ansa. —*adv.* There, then.
as an aghaidh, *adv.* To the face.
†asantadh, -aidh, *s.m.* Mutiny, sedition, rebellion.
as aonais, see as eugmhais.
†asard, -aird, *s.m.* Debate. 2 Assertion.
†——ach, *a.* Litigious, quarrelsome.
†——air, *s.m.* Litigious person, disputant.
asarlachd,** *s.f.ind.* Conjuration, magic. 2 Intoxication.
asarlaigheachd, see asarlachd.
as a seo, *adv.* Hence, out of this.
†as-bheanailt, *s.f.* Exception.
asbhuain, *s.f.ind.* Stubble. *A.* an àite cònlach, *stubble instead of straw.* [In some places "cònlach" means *stubble* too.]
asbhuaineach,** *a.* Having stubble, stubbly.
asbhuainiche,** *s.m.* Stubbler, creature that grazes among stubble. 2 Starveling. 3 *in ridicule,* a probationer of the Church.
†asc, aisc, -an, *s.m.* Snake, adder. 2 Newt.
†ascach, -aich, *s.m.* Escape.
†ascaich, *v.n.* Escape.
ascaill, *gen.sing.* of ascall.
†ascaim, *v.* I enquire, ask, beg.
ascain, see asgain.
ascair, *s.m.* Apostrophe (') in *gram.*
ascaird, *gen.sing.* of ascard *for* ascart.
ascairt, *s.f.* Budding, sprouting. 2 *gen.sing.* of ascart.
ascall, -aill, *s.m.* Loss. 2 Onset, attack. 3 Conference. 4 Flowing of the tide. 5 Mangling. 6 Personal contempt. 7 Miscreant. 8 Mangled carcase, carrion. *A.* earraich, *loss of cattle in spring;* an t-*a.* a rinn tàir oirnn, *the miscreant who has reviled us.*
——, *s.f.* see asgall.
——, *a.* Mangled.

ascaoin, -e, *a.* Harsh. 2 Inclement. 3 Unkind. 4 Stubborn. Caoin air ascaoin, *inside out.*
——, -e, *s f.* Harshness. 2 Unkindness. 3 Enmity. 4 Curse. 5 Excommunication. 6 Inclemency. Tionndadh *a.* na sìne gu tlàths, *turn to mildness the inclemency of the blast.*
——, *v.a.* Curse. 2 Excommunicate.
——each, -eiche, *a.* Fierce. 2 Of, or belonging to a curse. 3 Harsh. 4 Inclement.
——eachd, *s. f. ind.* Brutality, ferocity, savageness, churlishness.
——eadh,** -nidh, *s.m.* Act of cursing, or 2 excommunicating.
—— -eaglais,** *s.f.* Excommunication. 2 Cursing, commination.
——tich, *v.a.* Curse. 2 Excommunicate.
ascart, -airt, *s.m.* Tow, coarse lint. Snathainn ascairt, *a thread of tow.*
†ascath, *s.m.* Soldier, combatant.
as-chrodh, (AF) *s.m.* Dry cow.
ascnadh, -aidh, see asgnadh.
†ascnaim, *v.n.* I go, enter.
†as-chu, -choin, *s m.* Water dog, eel, conger eel.
ascull, see asgall.
asda, see asta.
asdail, *s.* Binding.
asdar, -air, see astar.
——ach, see astarach.
asdolach, *a.* Transitive in *gram.*
a seadh, see seadh.
a seo suas, *adv.* Henceforth.
as eugmhais, *prep.* Without.
asgach, -aich, -aichean, *s m.* Winnower.
asgaidh, *s.f.* Boon, present,
asgaill, *gen. sing.* of asgall.
——each, -aiche, *a.* Axillar, axillary.
asgailt, -e, -ean, *s.f.* Retreat, shelter. [Sometimes confused with asgall.]
asgain, *pr.part,* ag asgnadh, *v.n.* Ascend, mount, climb.
asgair, -e, -ean, *s.f.* Chronicle, record.
asgairt, see ascart.
asgal, -ail, see ascall.
asgall, -aill, -ean, *s.m.* Bosom, breast, armpit. 2 Embrace. [Sometimes confused with asgailt.] Thug mi do d' *a.*, *I gave to thy bosom.*
asgan, -ain, Grig, merry creature. 2 Dwarf. 3 Anything below the natural size.
†asgath,** see †ascath.
asgnadh, -aidh, *s.m.* Climax in *gram.* 2‡ Mounting, climbing, ascending.
asgnag, see fasgnag.
asgnail, *s.f.* } see asgall.
asguill, }
asgul, }
†asguidh, see an asguidh.
†asion, *s.f.* Crown, coronet.
as-innleachd, *pl.* -an, Destructive artifice.
————ach, -aiche, *a.* Plotting mischief, conspiring, contriving, mischievous.
a sìos, see sìos.
as is as, *adv.* Altogether, out and out.
aslach, -aich, -aichean, see aslachadh.
aslachadh, -aidh, *s.m.* Entreating, earnest supplication. 2 Conjurement. Ag a—, *pr. part.* of aslaich.
aslachair,** *s.m.* Asker, entreater.
aslachan, see achlasan.
asladh,** -aidh, *s.m.* Supplication, entreaty.
aslaich, *v.a.* Supplicate, beseech, request, entreat. Na'n aslaicheadh tu, *if thou wouldst entreat.*
aslaich, *s.f.* Bosom, breast, armpit. Sgian aslaich, *dirk;* 'na aslaich, *in his bosom.*
aslonnach, -aiche, *a.* Prone to tell, tattling.
aslonnadh, -aidh, *s.m.* Discovery, telling.

as leth, *prep.* On behalf of, for the sake of.
asluchadh, } see asla—.
asluich,
asna, see aisne.
†asnach, *for* aisnean, *n. pl.* of aisean.
———adh, see aslachadh.
asnadh, see aisne. 2 see asgnadh.
asnag, see fasgnag.
———ach,** see fasgnagach.
asnaich, *v.* see aslaich.
as-onoir, see eas-onoir.
asp, -a, -an, *s.m.* Asp. 2 Adder.
aspaic, see asp.
aspainn, see asbhuain. 'S cinnteach gu'n robh ise làn iospainn is aspuinn, *it is certain that she was stuffed full of sausages and tow.—Duanaire* p. 38.
aspàrag,‡ -aig, *s.f.* Asparagus. see creamh na muice fiadhaich.
asradh, -aidh, *s.m.* Harnessing.
àsran, -ain, -an, *s.m.* Forlorn object. 2 Destitute wanderer.
———ach, -aich, *s.m.* Stranger, guest, traveller, wayfaring man, rover, rambler.
†asrus, *s.f.* (aisir) Path, way, foot-path.
†assain, *s.m.pl.* Plates, greaves.
†as seadh, *adv.* It is so, yes.
†assuan, see asbhuain.
asta, *prep.pron.* (as+iad) Out of them, from them, in them, on them. [*Emphatic:* astasan, asta-fhéin.]
a staigh, *adv.* In, within. (*lit.* in the house.) *See note on* a mach.
astail, -e, -ean, *s.f.* see fasdail. 2 *s.m.* Contemptible fellow.
astair, see astaraich.
astal,** -ail, *s.m.* Javelin, spear, pike. 2 Pike-staff. 3 Chip, lath.
astar, -air, -an, *s.m.* Journey. 2 Space, distance. 3 Way, path. *A.* mór, *a great distance; a.* thrì làithean, *a three days' journey; a.* math air falbh, *a good distance away;* fad air *a.*, *far away, as a ship;* a' dol fo *a.*, *going under way,* a' gearradh a h-*a.*, *cutting her way;* thug e gu *a.*, *he sped;* air *a.* gu dian, *journeying with speed; a* nam faobh, *the path of spoils* or *conquest;* chluinnteadh an saltraich *a.* cian, *their tread was heard at a great distance;* ag *a.* o'n ear, *travelling from the East.*
———ach, -aiche, *a.* Journeying, travelling. 2 Speedy, expeditious.
———aich, *v.n.* Travel, journey, go. 2††March.
———aiche, -traichean, *s.m.* Pedestrian, traveller.
———air, *s.m.* Porter.
———an, *n.pl.* of astar.
———anaiche,** *s.m.* see astaraiche.
†astas, *s.m.* Spear, javelin. 2 Missile weapon.
asta-san, *emphat.* form of asta.
a steach, *adv.* In, into. Chaidh iad a steach, *they went in.* *See note on* a mach.
as-tharruing, -e, -ean, *s.f.* Abstract. 2 Extraction, drawing out.
————,** *v.a.* Abstract. 2 Extract.
————eadh, *s.m.* Abstracting. 2 Extracting.
a stigh, see a staigh.
astrachadh,** -aidh, *s.m.* Travelling, journeying. Ag a—, *pr. part.* of astaraich.
astradh, -aidh, (AC) Fastness. Air *a.* a' ghlinne, *in the fastness of the glen.*
astraichean,** *n.pl.* of astaraiche.
astranach,** -aich, see astaraiche.
a suas, see suas.
asuibh, see asaibh.
àsuig, see àsuing.
———each, see àsuingeach. 'S crith gu h-obair air gach crois alt tha na collainn àsuigeach, *with a shaking to work upon each cross-joint that is in her well-furnished (with tools, machinery &c.) body.*—Filidh nam Beann. Duine *à.*, *a man who has a great variety of tools or implements ready to hand.*
àsuing, -e, -ean, *s.f.* Apparatus, tools, implements, instruments, utensils.
———each, -eiche, *a.* Well furnished with implements, tools, tackle, &c.
asuinn, see asainn.
àsuinn, see àsuing.
as ùr, *adv.* Anew, afresh. 2 Recently, lately.
at, *s.m.ind.* Swelling, tumour. 2 Protuberance, prominence. At bàn, *a white swelling.*
at, *pr.part.* ag at, [& atadh] *v.n.* Swell, puff up, become tumid. Tha m'aodann air at, *my face is swollen.*
†atà, *simple pres.* of Bì.
ata, see ad.
atach, -aich, *s.m.* Request. 2 Fermentation. 3 see ath-aodach.
†atà 'd, *v.* (*for* tha iad) They are. Ni's millse na mil atà 'd, *sweeter are they than honey.*
atadh, -aidh, *s.m.* Swelling, tumour. Ag a—, *pr.part.* of at
ataich, *v.n.* Entreat, request.
atàid, see atà'd.
ataig, -e, -ean, *s.f.* Palisade, stake, pale. 2 (CR) Hurdle, "flake"—*W. coast of Ross.*
†ataii,** *a.* Deaf.
†atàim, *v.* (*for* tha mi) I am.
†Atàim, [I am] The name of God.
†ataimheachd, *s.f.* Redemption.
atàim-se, *emphatic* form of atàim.
atain,‡ *s. m.* Furze, gorse, see conasg. [‡attin]
ataireachd, see atmhoireachd.
†atais,* *s.f.* Woe, grief, lamentation.
†ataiseach, *a.* Blasphemous.
atamach,* *a.* Fondling, indulgent, caressing, lenient, partial.
————d.* *s.f.* Fondling, lenience, partiality. Gun *a.* do dhuine seach duine, *without partiality to anyone.*
atamaich,* *v.a.* Fondle, caress, indulge.
†atàmaid, *v.* (*for* tha sinn) We are.
atan, -ain, *s.m., dim.* of at. Cap. 2 Garland.
†ataoir, (*for* tha thu) Thou art.
atar, (AC) see atmhor.
†atathaoi, (*for* tha sibh) You are.
at-bàn,‖ *s.m.* The white swelling. [Preceded by the article *an t-.*]
at-bràghad,‖ *s.m.* Quinsy.
†atchiu, (*for* chi mi) I see, *or* shall see.
at-chuisle, *s.m.* Aneurism, disease of the arteries.
at-fhuachd, *s.m.* Chilblain.
ath, *a.* Next, again. An ath uair, *the next time,* or *next hour;* 'san *a.* dhorus, *in the next door;* taghlaidh bó a h-ath-bhuaile, *a cow will resort to her fold again* (*if the pasture be good*); dàna, ath-bhuailte, *bold, twice beaten,* (and trying again); obair is ath obair, *work and work again,* (*work badly done at first*); dheanadh Fionn an ath chadal, *F. would take another sleep;* gaoth an ath thionndaidh, *the eddy-wind.*
ath-, *prefix,* Repetition, corresponding with English re-.
àth. *s.m.ind.* Ford, any part of a river that is fordable. àth nan sùl, *the corner of the eyes;* aig àthaibh Arnoin, *at the fords of Arnon;* is fheàrr tilleadh am meadhon an àth na bàthadh uile, *better turn in the middle of the ford than drown yourself completely.*
àth, àtha, *pl.* -an, & -annan, *s.f.* Kiln. 'N uair bha sinn 'san àth le chéile, *when we were*

in the kiln together; air son mo chuid-sa dhe'n ghràn gabhadh an àth teine, *for my part of the grain let the kiln take fire.*
ath, *v.n.* Flinch, shrink, hesitate. 2 Refuse. 3 Blush. Na seòid nach athadh an cruadal, *the heroes that would not flinch in time of hardship.*
†àtha, see aimsir.
athach, -aich, *s.m.* Giant, champion. 2 Monster. 3 Yeoman, husbandman. Chunnaic sinn athaich, *we saw giants.*
——, -aiche, *a.* Bashful, modest, timid. 2 Monstrous, gigantic. 3 Clownish. 4 Sparing, pitying. Oganach *a.*, a bashful youth ; b' *a.* an torc a mhill e, *monstrous was the boar that destroyed him.*
†——, -aich, *s.m.* Space. 2 Waves. 3 Blast. breeze. 4 Fermentation. 5 Desire, request.
athadh, -aidh, *s.m.* Fear, cowardice, timidity. 2 Modesty, bashfulness. 3 Reverence, homage. 4 Shame. 5 Blush. 6 Daunt. 7** Gust or blast of wind. Duine gun nàire gun *a.*, *a man without shame or reverence of face ;* beul an athaidh agus an anmoich, *at the fall of fear and lateness.*
athaich, *gen. sing. & n. pl.* of athach.
——, *v.n.* Abash.
†athaile, *s. f.* Inattention, neglect.
athailt, -e, -ean, *s.m.* Mark, scar, impression. 2 Vestige, trace. see ail.
——each, -eiche, *a.* Full of scars or marks, causing a scar or mark, of or pertaining to a scar.
athain, *gen. sing.* of athan.
ath-ainm, -e, *pl.* -ean, & -meannan, *s.m.* Nickname.
athainne, see aithinne.
athaintean, *pl.* of athainne. (*for* aithinntean.)
athair, athar, *pl.* aithriche & -ean, *s.m.* Father, ancestor.
—— -ainmeach, *a.* Patronymical.
—— -baistidh, *s.m.* Godfather.
—— -céile, *s.m.* Father-in-law.
——e, *for* aithrichean, *n.pl.* of athair.
†——eag,** -eig, *s. f.* Paternal aunt.
——ealachd, *s. f.* Fatherliness. 2 Affectionateness, kindness.
——eil, -e, *a.* Fatherly, paternal.
—— -faosaid, *s.m.* Father confessor.
——ich, *v.a.* Adopt, father.
—— -liath,§ athar-, &c., *s.m.* Garden sage, *salvia officinalis.* **Mountain sage.
—— -lus, -uis, *s.m.* Ground ivy. see iadhshlat thalmhainn.
—— -mhaoin *s.m.* Patrimony.
—— -mhort, *s.m.* see *a.*-mhortadh & *a.*-mhortair.
—— -mhortach, -aiche, *a.* Parricidal.
—— -mhortadh, -aidh, *s.m.* Parricide (act.)
—— -mhortair, *s.m.* Parricide (person.)
—— -neimh, see nathair-nimhe.
—— -thalmhainn,§ *s.m.* Yarrow. see lus chosgadh na fola.
athais, *s. f.* Leisure, ease. 2 Personalty. 3 see aithis. A' cheud *a.* a bhitheas orm, *the first opportunity I get* ; gun dad *a.*, *without any leisure ;* am bheil thu air t'*a.* ? *are you at leisure ?* air t'*a.*, *avast ! hold on !*
†——, *v.a.* see †aithis.
——each, -eiche, *a.* Slow, tardy. 2 see aithiseach.
——each, -eich, -an, *s.m.* Dilatory person. 2 see aithiseach.
——eachd, *s. f. ind.* Slowness, laziness. 2** Easiness.
——eil,** *a.* Anodyne.
——ich,* *v.n.* Get calmer, abate, as rain. 2 ease. 3 see aithis.
ath-aithris, *v.a.* Repeat, imitate.
athal, -ail, *s.m.* see adhal & aingeal.
†——, *a.* Deaf.
athamanachd, see anmoch.
àthan, -ain, *s.m.* Little ford, shallow part of river reaching from bank to bank.
——na, *pl.* of àthan. à. Iordain, *the fords of Jordan.*
athan,§ -ain, *s.m.* Colt's-foot, see cluas-liath.
a thaobh, *prep.* Regarding, according.
ath-aodach,(AC) *s.m.* Cast-off clothes. 2 New cloth.
àth-aoil, *s. f.* Lime-kiln.
athar, -air, *s.m.* Sky, firmament. 2 Atmosphere, air, cloud. 3 Dregs of a disease. 4* Evil effects of anything. Agus rinn Dia an t-*a.*, *and God made the firmament* ; tha 'n t-*a.* dorch, *the atmosphere is dark* or *hazy ; a.* na griuthaich, *the evil effects of the measles; a.* òil, *the dregs of a debauch;* bithidh thu an athar sin ri d' bheò, *you will feel the effects of that as long as you live.*
——, *gen. sing.* of athair.
——,** } *a.* see atharail.
——ach, }
——achd, *s. f. ind.* Airiness.
——ag, -aig, -an, *s. f.* Aërial being.
——ail, -e, *a.* Ethereal, atmospheric, airy, aërial. 2 Glorious.
†——ais,** *s. f.* Mimicry, mocking. 2 Ludicrous gesticulation.
—— -amharc, *s.m.* Aëroscopy, observation of the air.
†——dha, *s.m.* One's Native country.
†——dha, *a.* Fatherly.
——eòlas, *s.m.* Aëromancy, aërology, art of divining by the air.
†——gadh, -aidh, *s.m.* Sharp engagement. 2 Adoption.
†——gaibh, *s. f.* Importunity, solicitation.
athar-gheasachd,‡‡ *s. f.* Aëromancy.
athar-iùl, -iùil, *s. f.* aërology, aëromancy.
——la, -an, *s. f.* Quey, heifer.
†——mhactadh, *s.m.* Parricide.
athar-mhéidh, -ean, *s. f.* Barometer, aërometer.
atharnach, -aich, *s. f.* Second crop. 2 (AH) Ground from which potatoes or turnips have been lifted.
†atharrach, *a.* Strange, curious, droll. 2†† Foreign.
——, -aich, *s.m.* Stranger, alien. 2 Alteration, change. Nach faiceadh call an atharraich, *who would not see a stranger lose ;* cha d' thàinig *a.* riamh, *another never came ;* cha 'n e math an *a.* a th' air 'aire, *it is not the interest of another he has in view.* Cha'n 'eil atharrach agad r'a dheanamh, *you have no alternative* ; cha'n 'eil math 'na *a.*, *there is no good in a change ;* cha robh thu riamh air *a.*, *you were never otherwise ;* cha'n 'eil *a.* air, *there is no help for it.*
——adh, -aidh, *s.m.* Change, alteration. 2 Removal, flitting. 3 Version. 4 Another. Ag a—, *pr. part.* of atharraich. Changing, altering, removing, flitting. *A.* giùlain, *an opposite line of conduct ;* is mór an t-*a.* a thàinig air, *there is a great change in him.*
——ail, *a.* Changing. 2 Changeable, unsteady. 3 Alternative.
atharraich, *pr.pt.* ag atharrachadh,*v.a.* Change, alter. 2 Remove, flit. 3 Turn. 4 Budge. 5 Translate. Dh'*a.* iad an aodach, *they changed their clothes*; a shaor agus a dh'*a.* sinn, *that delivered and translated us.*
——te, *pr.part.* of atharraich.
atharrais, *pr.pt.* ag atharrais, *v.a.* Mimic, imi-

tate. Ag *a.* ormsa, *mimicking me.*
———,** *s. f.* Mimicry, foolish repetition. Ag a—, *pr. pt.* of atharrais.
——— -beulain, *s. f.* see aithris-bheulain.
atharraiseach, -eiche, } ‡‡ *a.* Mimical.
atharraiseil, -e,
atharraisich, *v.a.* see atharrais.
athar-sheòladair, *s.m.* Aëronaut.
athar-sheòladaireachd, *s. f. ind.* Aërostation.
athar-thomhas, -ais, *s.m.* Aërometry.
——— -thìr, -e, *s.f.* One's native country.
athas,** -ais, *s.m.* Victory.
athbhach, -aich, *s.m.* Strength.
ath-bhàrr, -a, -an, *s.m.* Second crop, after crop.
athbhàs, -àis, *s.m.* Second death.
ath-bheachd, -an, *s.m.* Retrospect. 2 Second thought, after-thought, consideration, reconsideration.
———aich, *v.n.* Look steadfastly or a second time. 2 Reconsider.
ath-bheothachadh, -aidh, *s.m.* Reviving, rekindling, refreshing, reanimating, quickening. Rinn do bhriathran m'*a.*, *your words have revived me.* Ag a—, *pr.pt.* of ath-bheothaich.
ath-bheothachail, *a.* Reviving, quickening, rekindling.
ath-bheothaich, *pr.pt.* -achadh, *v.a.* Revive, rerefresh, rekindle, reanimate, quicken, sharpen, excite. *A.* an gealbhan, *rekindle the fire.*
———idh, *fut.aff.a.* of ath-bheothaich.
———te, *past pt.* of ,,
ath-bheum, -an, *s.m.* Second wound or hurt.
ath-bhlas,** *s.m.* After-taste.
ath-bhliadhna, *s.f.* Next year. 2 Second year. Mu'n tràth seo an ath-bhliadhna, *about this time next year.*
ath-bhliochd, *s.f.* Second milking, after-milking. 2*Second month after calving. Dhaireadh as a h-*a.* a' bhò, *the cow was lined the second month after calving.*
àth-bhrachaidh,** *s.f.* Malt-kiln.
ath-bhreith, *s. f.* After-birth. 2 Second birth, regeneration. 3‡‡Second judgment.
ath-bhriathar, -air, *s.m.* Tautology, repetition. 2**Secondhand saying.
ath-bhriathrach, -aiche, *a.* Tautological.
———as, -ais, *s.m.* Tautology.
ath-bhriathraiche, *s.m.* Tautologist. 2**One who uses secondhand expressions. 3 One who repeats tediously.
†ath-bhrod, *v.a.* Resuscitate, reawaken.
ath-bhrosnachadh, -aidh, *s.m.* Rallying, reinspiring with courage. 2 Resuming of courage. Ag a—, *pr.part.* of ath-bhrosnaich. Ag ar n-*a.*, *rallying us.*
ath-bhrosnaich, *pr.pt.*ag ath-bhrosnachadh,*v.a.* Rally, re-encourage. 2 Resume courage.
———te, *past pt.* of ath-bhrosnaich.
ath-bhuail, *pr.pt.* ag ath-bhualadh, *v.a.* Strike or beat again. 2 Re-thrash. C'uime nach d' *a.* thu do shleagh? *why did you not restrike your spear?*
ath-bhuaile, see note under ath.
ath-bhuaillidh, *fut.aff.a.* of ath-bhuail.
†ath-bhuailt, *adv.* Again.
ath-bhuailte, *past pt.* of ath-bhuail. Sgrios *a.*, *double destruction*; gu bràth na pillibh *a.*, *never come back reconquered;* dàna, ath-bhuailte, *bold, twice beaten.*
———ach, *a.* Restriking. 2 Reconquering.
ath-bhuain, *v.a.* Cut down or shear again.
ath-bhualadh, -aidh, *s.m.* Second striking. 2 Reconquering. 3 Repercussion. 4‡‡Reaction.
ath-bhuannaich, *v.a.* Regain, recover.
———te, *pt.pt.* & *a.* Regained, recovered. 2 Restored.
ath-bhuidhinn, *v.a.* Regain, recover, repossess, retrieve.
———eadh, -idh, *s.m.* Regaining, recovering, repossessing.
ath-bhuille,** *s.m.* After-clap.
†athcaoid, see acaid.
†———each, see acaideach.
ath-chadal, Second sleep. Rudhadh shuas 'sa mhoch mhaduinn, dheanadh Fionn an ath-chadal, *when there was a rosy sky at dawn* (sign of bad weather) *F. would take another sleep.*
ath-chagainn, *pr. pt.* ag ath-chagnadh, *v.n.* Chew again, ruminate. 5 Chew the cud.
ath-chagnach, *a.* Cud-chewing. 2 Ruminating. Ainmhidh *a.*, *an animal that chews the cud.*
ath-chagnadh, -aidh, *s.m.* Chewing of the cud. 2 Rumination.
ath-chàirich, *v.a.* Repair, remend.
ath-chairt, *s.f.* Granting of a charter. 2 Renewal of a lease.
ath-chaithte, *a.* Worn out, cast off.
ath-chanaich, see ath-chuingich.
ath-channtaireachd, *s. f.* Singing again.
†athchaoin, -e, *s.f.* Complaint.
ath-chàramh, *s.m.* Repairing, second mending.
ath-chas, *v.a.* Retwist.
ath-chasadaich, -e, *s.f.* Second coughing.
ath-chasaid, *s.f.* Second charge, second complaint or accusation.
ath-chasta, *a.* Retwisted. 2 Strongly twisted.
ath-cheangal, -ail, *s.m.* Rebinding. 2 Renewal of an agreement.
ath-cheannach, -aich, *s.m.* Repurchasing, redemption. Ag a—, *pr.pt.* of ath-cheannaich. Ag *a.* na h-aimsir, *redeeming the time.*
———adh, -aidh, *s.m.* see ath-cheannach.
ath-cheannaich, *pr .pt.* ag ath-cheannach [& -cheannachadh**] *v.a.* Redeem, repurchase.
———te, *pt.pt.* of ath-cheannaich.
ath-cheannsaich,* *v.a.* Reconquer, subdue a second time. 2 Retrieve.
ath-cheasnachadh, -aidh, *s.m.* Re-examination.
ath-cheasnaich, *pr.pt.*ag ath-cheasnachadh,*v.a.* Re-examine.
†ath-cheileabhras, *s.m.* Second farewell.
ath-cheumnachadh, -aidh, *s.m.* Repacing. 2 Recapitulation.
ath-cheumnaich, *v.a.* Repace. 2 Recapitulate.
ath-chlaon,* *v.a.* Relapse into error. 2 Deviate a second time.
———adh, -aidh, -aidhean, *s.m.* Further error or offence. 2 Second deviation.
ath-chleamhnas, -ais, *s.m.* Connection by a second marriage. Is fuar comunn an ath-chleamhnais, *cold are the connections of a first marriage after a second.* [see note under "ath-chneadh."]
ath-chluich,** -e, *s.f.* After-game.
ath-chnàmh, -a, *s.m.* Second digestion. 2 Second concoction.
ath-chneadh, -eidh, -neidhean, *s.f.* Second wound. Is léigh fear an ath-chneidh, *the man of the first wound is surgeon (for a second*—ath *signifying a second to come.)* This sentence and the one given under "ath-chleamhnas" show that "ath-" does not always signify *again*, but sometimes *first* implying a *second* to come.
ath-chog, *v.n.* Rebel.
———adh, -aidh, *s.m.* Insurrection,rebellion.
ath-choimhearan, -ain, *s.m.* Register.
ath-choimhre, *s.f.* Abridgment.
ath-choisich, *v.n.* Repass, travel again,retrace.
———te, *pt. pc* Repassed, retravelled, retraced.
ath-chomain, -e, -ean, *s.f.* Second obligation. 2 Recompense, requital, retaliation.

ath-chomair, -e, *a.* see ath-chuimir.
†ath-chomhairc, *v.a.* Shout again.
ath-chomhairle, -an, *s.m.* Second thought. 2 Second advice.
————achadh, -aidh, *s.m.* Re-advising, re-admonishing.
ath-chomhairlich, *v.a.* Re-advise, re-admonish.
————te, *pt. pt.* Re-advised, re-admonished.
†ath-chomharaich, *v.a.* Ask.
ath-chomharraich,** *v.a.* Countermark.
ath-chosdas, -ais, *s.m.* After-cost.
ath-chràdh, -àidh, *s.m.* Second pain or torment.
àth-chrè, *s.m.* Brick-kiln.
àth-chriadh, see àth-chrè.
ath-chronaich, *v.a.* Rebuke a second time.
àth-chruachaidh,** -a-, -an-, -annan-, *s.f.* Drying kiln.
ath-chruinneachadh, -aidh, *s.m.* Regathering, reassembling. 2 Rallying. 3 Reuniting.
ath-chruinnich, *v.a.* Regather, reassemble. 2 Reunite. 3 Rally, as an army.
————ear, *fut. pass.* of ath-chruinnich.
————te, *pt. pt.* Gathered again, reassembled. 2 Reunited. 3 Rallied.
ath-chruth, *s.m.* Change of form. 2†† Second form or appearance.
ath-chruthachadh, *s.m.* Recreating. 2 Regeneration. 3 Reformation. Ag a—, *pr.pt.* of ath-chruthaich.
ath-chruthaich, *v.a.* Recreate. 2 Regenerate. 3 Reform. 4 Reconstruct.
————ear, *fut.pass.* of ath-chruthaich.
————te, *pt.pt.* of ath-chruthaich.
ath-chuibhlich, *v.a.* Wheel back. 2 Revolve.
ath-chuimhne, *s.f.* Recollection, remembrance.
————achadh, -aidh, Remembrance, recollection. Ag a—, *pr.pt.* of ath-chuimhnich.
ath-chuimhnich, *v.n.* Recollect, remember, put in mind a second time, recall.
ath-chuimir, -e, *a.* Brief. 2 Compendious.
† ————ic, *s. f.* Rehearsal of a cause.
ath-chuimrich,* *v.a.* Pare a second time, or minutely.
athchuinge, -ean, *s. f.* (ath+cuinge) Prayer, petition, request, entreaty.
————ach, *a.* Supplicatory, entreating, of or belonging to, a prayer or petition.
————an, *n. pl.* of athchuinge.
————ar, see athchuingiche.
athchuingich, *v.a.* Petition, supplicate, entreat.
————e, *s.m.* Petitioner, supplicant.
†ath-chuir, *v.a.* Banish. 2 Surrender.
ath-chùiteachadh, -aidh, *s.m.* Recompense.
ath-chum, *v.a.* Form or shape anew. 2 Deform, disfigure. 3†† Reform.
ath-chumadh, -aidh, *s.m.* Shaping or forming anew. 2 Deforming, disfiguring.
†ath-chumain, *v.a.* Deform. 2 Transform.
ath-chumta, *a.* Formed or shaped anew. 2 Deformed, mangled.
ath-chunn,* *v.a.* Reshape, transform.
†ath-chur, *s.m.* Banishment, exile. 2 (AH) Lastingness, wear-resisting property.
ath-dhàn, -àin, *s.m.* Byeword, byename, nickname. 2 See aghan. Bithidh tu a d' *a.*, *thou shalt be a byeword.*
ath-dhealbh,* *v.a.* Transform.
————adh, -aidh, *s.m.* Transformation, change of shape, metamorphosis.
ath-dheanadach, *a.* Itinerant, circumlocutory.
ath-dheanamh, -aimh, *s.m.* Doing over again.
ath-dhìoghail, see ath-dhìol.
ath-dhìoghaltach, see ath-dhìoltach.
ath-dhìoghladh, see ath-dhìoladh.
ath-dhìol, -a, *s.m.* see ath-dhìoladh.
ath-dhìol, *v.a.* Requite, refund, recompense, repay.
ath-dhìoladh, -aidh, *s.m.* Requital, repayment, refunding, restitution. 2 Retaliation. Ag a—, *pr.pt.* of ath-dhìol.
ath-dhìolta, *a.* Requited, repaid, recompensed.
————ch, *a.* Revengeful, vindictive.
ath-dhreachadh, -aidh, *s.m.* Shaping again, remodelling.
ath-dhruid, *v.a.* Reshut, close again.
————te, *pt. pt.* of ath-dhruid.
ath-dhùblachadh, -aidh, *s.m.* Redoubling, reduplication. Ag a—, *pr.pt.* of ath-dhùblaich.
ath-dhùblaich, *v.a.* Redouble.
————te, *pt.pt.* of ath-dhùblaich.
ath-dhùin,* *v a.* Reshut.
ath-dhurmanaich,** *v.a.* Remurmur.
ath-éisdeachd, see aith-éisdeachd.
ath-fhàs, *v.n.* Grow again.
————,**-àis, *s.m.* After growth, second crop.
ath-fhear, -fhir, *s.m.* An ath-fhear, *the next or second man.* 2 *The next or second thing.*
ath-fheuchainn, -e, *s. f.* Second trial, revisal.
ath-fhuarachadh, -aidh, *s.m.* Recooling, act of cooling a second time. Ag a— *pr. pt.* of ath-fhuaraich.
ath-fhuaraich, *v.n.* Cool again, recool.
————te, *pt.pt.* Recooled.
ath-fhuasgladh, -aidh, *s.m.* Redemption. 2 Ransom. 3 Release.
ath-ghabh, *v.a.* Retake, recover, regain, resume.
————ail, *s.m.* Resuming, recovering, retaking, as of spoil.
————ta, *pt. pt.* Retaken, recovered, regained, resumed.
ath-ghairm, *v.n.* Call again. 2 Repeat, echo, re-echo.
————, *s. f.* Echo.
ath-ghamhnach, -aich, -aichean, *s. f.* Cow that has been two years without a calf.

ath-ghearr, -a, -iorra, *a.*	see aith—.
————, -iorra, *s.m.*	
————, *v.a.*	
————achadh, -aidh, *sm*	
————ad, -aid, *s.m.*	
————adh, -aidh, *s.m.*	
————aich, *v.a.*	

————aichte, see aith-ghearraichte.
ath-ghin, *v.a.* Regenerate, renew, produce a second time. 2 Recreate, renovate.
ath-ghineamhuinn, *s. f.* Regeneration. 2 Reproduction.
ath-ghintinn, see ath-ghineamhuinn.
ath-ghinte, *pt. pt.* of ath-ghin. Regenerated. 2 Reproduced.
ath-ghiorra, *a.*(for aith-ghiorra)see aith-ghearr.
————ich, see aith-ghearr.
ath-ghlac, *v.a.* Retake, resume. 2 Apprehend a second time. 3 Catch again.
————te,[1] *pt.pt.* Retaken. 2 Re-apprehended. 3 Recaught.
ath-ghlan, *v.a.* Repolish, refine, recleanse. 2 Purify, strain.
————adh, -aidh, *s.m.* Recleansing. 2 Refining, purifying. Ag a—, *pr. pt.* of ath-ghlan.
————te,[1] *a. & pt. part.* Recleansed, repol-

1. In adding the suffix *te*, the rule that consonants must come between vowels of the same class is not in every case regarded, because in speech it is not conformed to. In the case of Verbs of one syllable ending in *l*, *n*, *r*, or *s*, and all those of more than one syllable, the letter *i* is introduced before the final consonant to make the spelling accord with the pronunciation. It is left out in other cases for the same reason. —M.M

ished, refined, purified, scoured, burnished.
ath-ghlaodh, -aoidh, *s.m.* Second call.
——————aich, *v.n.* Cry again, re-echo.
ath-ghnàthach, *a.* Secondhand.
ath-ghnìomh, *s.f.* After doing, after act.
ath-ghointe, *a.* Wounded again.
ath-ghoirid, *a.* see aithghearr.
——————,* *s.f.* Short road, way, or method. 2** Short time, moment.
ath-ghràdh,** *s.m.* After love.
ath-iarr, *v.a.* Seek or search again. 2 Request.
————aidh, *s.f.* Seeking again. 2 Requesting. Ag a—, *pr.pt.* of ath-iarr.
————tas, -ais, *s.m.* Request. 2 Second asking or seeking. 3 Second order. 4 Repetition as in prayer.
ath-ith,(AG) Second eating. 2 (†ith *or* †ioth) Corn damaged by cattle on a field before it is cut. Crodh air an *a.*, *cattle on ground bearing a second crop*; cha'n 'eil ni an seo ach *a.*, *there is nothing here but damaged corn.*
ath-ionnsuidh, *s.m.* After-attempt, second or repeated attempt.
a thiota,‡‡ *adv.* Quickly, immediately.
ath-là, *s.m.* Next day.
†ath-laghadh, *s.m.* Procrastination.
ath-laimhsich, *v.a.* Handle again.
ath-làmh, -àimh, *s.f.* Second hand.
athlamh, see ealamh.
ath-làn, *s.m.* Refilling. 2 Second full of a measure.
ath làn-mara, *s.m.* Next high-tide, reflux of the sea.
ath-laoch, -aoich, *s.m.* Champion. 2 Youth fit for battle.
ath-lath, see ath-laoch.
ath-lathachadh, -aidh, *s.m.* Procrastination.
ath-lathaich, *v.n.* Procrastinate, delay.
ath-leagh, *v.a.* Remelt.
————te,[1] *pt.pt.* Remelted.
ath-leasachadh, -aidh, -ean, *s.m.* Reforming, mending, reformation, amendment, correction, amelioration, improvement. 2 Second dunging of land. Ag a—, *pr.pt.* of ath-leasaich.
ath-leasachair, -ean, *s.m.* Reformer, correcter. 2**Amender.
ath-leasaich, *v.a.* Reform, amend, ameliorate, correct, improve. 2 Dung land again. *A.* do chòmhradh agus do bheusan, *amend your conversation and manners.*
ath-leasaiche, see ath-leasachair.
ath-leasaichte, *pt.pt.* Reformed, amended, corrected, improved.
ath-leithid, -e, *s.f.* Requital.
ath-leum, *v.n.* Rebound, spring or leap again.
—————, -eim, -an, -annan, *s.m.* Second leap.
—————artaich, *s.f.* Rebounding. 2 Continual jumping or bounding.
ath-lìon, *v.a.* Refill, replenish, recruit, reflow.
————adh, -aidh, *s.m.* Refilling, replenishing, recruiting, reflowing. Ag a—, *pr.pt.* of ath-lìon.
†athlo, see ath-là.
†athloimhe, *s.f.* Dexterity.
ath-loisg, *v.a.* Reburn, burn thoroughly.
†athlomh, see ealamh.
ath-lorg, -uirg, *s.f.* Retracking.
————aich, *v.a.* Retrace, trace over again.
ath-losgadh, -aidh, *s.m.* Second burning, thorough burning.
ath-luasganachd, *s.f.* Alternateness.
ath-mhalairt, *s.f.* Re-exchange. 2 Second bargain.
——————, *v.* see ath-mhalairtich.

1. See note on page 53.

ath-mhalairtich, *v.a.* Re-exchange. 2 Make a second agreement.
——————te, *pt.pt.* of ath-mhalairtich.
ath-mhaoin, *s.f.* Second advantage.
ath-mhaoltas, -ais, *s.m.* Shame.
ath-mheal, *v.a.* Re-enjoy.
————tuinn, *s.f.* Re-enjoyment. Ag a—, *pr.pt.* of ath-mheal, Re-enjoying.
ath-mhògach, *s.f. for* fath-mhùgach.
ath-mhuinntireas, -ris, *s.m.* Second engagement with a master.
†ath-mhunadh, *s.m.* Admonition.
†athnnachd, *s.f.* Burial, interment.
ath-neartachadh, -aidh, *s.m.* Restrengthening, recruiting, reinforcing, reinforcement. Ag a—, *pr.pt.* of ath-neartaich.
ath-neartachail, *a.* Strengthening, recruiting. Leigheas *a.*, *a strengthening medicine.*
ath-neartaich, *v.a.* Reinforce, recruit, refresh, restrengthen, renew.
ath-nuadhachadh, -aidh, *s.m.* Renovation, renovating, renewing. Ag a—, *pr.pt.* of ath-nuadhaich. *A.* bhur n-inntinn, *the renewal of your minds.*
ath-nuadhaich, *v.a.* Renew, renovate, Ath-nuadhaichear a' bhliadhna, *the year shall be renewed.*
——————te, *pt.pt.* of ath-nuadhaich.
ath-obair, *s.f.* Work done again. [ex. under ath.]
ath-oidhch', *adv.* i.e. an ath-oidhche, *to-morrow night.*
ath-oidheirp,** *s.* After-endeavour.
ath-phill, *v.n.* Return. 2 Turn again.
————eadh, -lidh, *s.m.* Return, returning, coming back. 2 Circulation. 3(AH) Return of a disease after convalescence. Bhitheadh *'a.* mar a' ghrian, *his return would be like the sun.*
ath-philltinn, see ath-philleadh.
athraiche, athraichean, } *pl.* of athair.
ath-réiteachadh, -aidh, *s.m.* Reconciliation, reconcilement. 2 Atonement, expiation. 3** Second disentangling. 4**Second clearing or arranging. Ag a—, *pr. pt.* of ath-réitich.
ath-réiteachail, *a.* Reconciliatory, pacificatory.
ath-réitich, *v.a.* Reconcile. 2 Re-expiate, reatone. 3 Disentangle again. 4 Clear again. 5 Rearrange.
——————te, *past pt.* of ath-réitich.
ath-roinn, *v.a.* Subdivide, divide again.
——————,** *s.f.* Subdivision, second division.
——————te, *past pt.* Subdivided.
ath-ruamhar, *v.a.* Redelve, dig again.
ath-ruamhradh, -aidh, *s.m.* Second digging or delving. Ag a—, *pr. pt.* of ath-ruamhar.
†ath-rughadh, †ath-ruigheadh, } see atharrachadh.
ath-sdiùir, see ath-stiùir.
ath-sgal, *s.m.* Second squall. 2 Echo. 3 Skirl of the bagpipes. 4 Any loud and shrill sound.
ath-sgath, *v.a.* Reprune, lop again, cut down again.
ath-sgeul, -eòil, *s.m.* Tale at second hand, second telling. 2 Repetition. Is tric nach tig ath-sgeul air an droch sgeul, *bad news is seldom (not often) refuted.*
ath-sgìos, -a, *s.m.* Second fatigue.
ath-sgrìobh, *v.a.* Transcribe, copy. 2 Write again. A dh'*a.* daoine Heseciah, *which the men of H. copied.*
——————adh, -aidh, *s.m.* Transcript, transcribing, copy. Ag a—, *pr. part.* of ath-sgrìobh
——————air, -e, -ean, *s.m.* Transcriber.
——————ar, *fut. pass.* of ath-sgrìobh.
——————te,[1] *past pt.* „ „

ath-shaor, *v.a.* Redeliver.
————adh, -aidh, *s.m.* Redelivering, redeliverance, second redeeming. Ag a—, *pr.pt.* of ath-shaor.
————te,[1] *past pt.* of ath-shaor.
ath shaothrachail, *a.* Assiduous, diligent, constant in application.
ath-shealbhachadh, -aidh, *s.m.* Re-inheriting, repossessing. 2 Reversion, re-investment. Ag a—, *pr. pt.* of ath-shealbhaich.
ath-shealbhaich, *v.a.* Reposses, re-inherit.
————te, *pt. pt.* of ath-shealbhaich.
ath-sheall, *v.n.* Reconsider. 2 Look again.
————ach, *a.* Looking back, retrospective.
————adh, -aidh, -aidhean, *s.m.* Second look. 2 Retrospect. 3 Second sight, or view.
————tuinn, *s. f.* Second looking or viewing. Ag a—, *pr. pt.* of ath-sheall.
ath-sheinn, *v.a.* Sing again.
ath-shlàinte, *s. f.* Convalescence.
————ach, -eiche, *a.* Convalescent.
ath-shnàmh, *v.n.* Reswim, swim again.
————adh, -aidh, *s.m.* Reswimming, swimming back again.
————ta, *pt. pt.* of ath-shnàmh.
†ath-shuidheachadh, -aidh, *s.m.* Replanting, second settlement.
ath-shuidhichte, *pt.pt.* Replanted, resettled.
ath-smaoin, see ath-smuain.
ath-smaoineachadh, ath-smaoinich, ath-smaointeachadh, ath-smaointich, } see ath-smuaint—.
ath-smuain, -e, -tean, *s. f.* Second thought, after-thought.
————teachadh, -aidh, *s.m.* Consideration, pondering, reflecting, reconsidering. Ag a—, *pr. pt.* of ath-smuaintich.
————teachail,** *a.* Apt to reflect or considerate.
————tean, *n. pl.* of ath-smuain.
————tich, *v.a.* Reconsider, ponder, meditate, reflect.
ath-stiùir, *v.a.* Steer again. 2 Reconduct.
athte,[1] *a.* & *pt.pt.* of at. Swelled, swollen.
ath-thagh, *v.a.* Rechoose, make a second choice. 2**Reflect.
————adh, -aidh, *s.m.* Re-electing, rechoosing.
————ta, *past pt.* Re-elected, rechosen.
ath-thalmhainn,(AF) see famh-thalmhainn.
ath-theachd, *s.m.* Second coming. 2 Next arrival. 3 Second growth.
ath-theine, *s.m.* Second firing, or volley. ††see aithinne.
ath-theist, -e, -ean, *s. f.* Second testimony.
ath-theòdh, *v.a.* Rewarm, warm again.
ath-theòdhadh, -aidh, *s.m.* Warming a second time. Ag a—, *pr.pt.* of ath-theòdh.
ath-thighinn, *s.f.* Second coming.
ath-thill, *v.a.* see ath-phill.
ath-thilleadh, -eidh, see ath-philleadh.
ath-thinneas-cloinne, *s.m.* After-pains.
ath-thionndadh, -aidh, *s.m.* Second turning. 2 Returning a second time. 3 Causing to turn a second time, 4**Eddy. Gaoth an *a.*, *the wind of the eddy.*
————, *v.a.* Return a second time.
ath-thionnsgain, *v.a.* Recommence, resume, redevise.
ath-thionnsgnadh, -aidh, *s.m.* Recommencing, recommencement, resuming, redevising.
ath-thodhar, -air, *s.m.* Second crop after a field has been manured by the folding of cattle or sheep. 2‡‡Remanuring. 3‡‡ Second bleaching. 4‡‡Lea land remaining two years untilled.
ath-thog, *v.a.* Rebuild, rear again, lift or take up again.
ath-thogail, -thogalach, -thoglaichean, *s.f.* Rebuilding, second raising, rearing or lifting.
ath-thogte,[1] *pt. pt.* Rebuilt.
ath-thòiseachadh, -aidh, *s.m.* Recommencing, resuming.
ath-thòisich, *v.a.* Recommence, resume.
ath-threòrachadh, -aidh, *s.m.* Reconducting, reguiding. Ag a—, *pr. pt.* of ath-threòraich.
ath-threòraich, *v.a.* Reconduct, reguide.
ath-threòraichte, *pt.pt.* of ath-threòraich.
ath-thruas, -ais, *s.m.* Compassion.
————ach,‡‡ -aiche, *a.* Compassionate.
ath-thugh, *s.m.* Second thatching. 2 Second cover.
————, *v.a.* Thatch again. 2 Recover.
ath-thughta, *pt.pt.* Thatched again.
ath-thuisle, *s. f.* Second fall or stumble.
ath-thuisleachadh, -aidh, *s.m.* Second stumbling or slipping. 2 Relapse. Ag a—, *pr. pt.* of ath-thuislich.
ath-thuislich, *v.n.* Fall or stumble again. 2 Relapse.
ath-thuit, *v.n.* Fall again. 2 Relapse.
ath-thuiteam,-eim, *s.m.* Second fall. 2 Relapse.
ath-thulgadh,** *s.m.* After-tossing (of waves)
ath-uair, -e, -ean, *s.f.* Next time. 2 Second time.
ath-uamharra, *a.* Terrible, direful, abominable, odious, execrable, detestable, horrible.
ath-uamharrachd, *s. f.* Abomination, detestation, hatefulness, atrociousness.
†ath-uamharrtha, see ath-uamharra.
†ath-uasgladh, see ath-fhuasgladh.
a thubhradh, *a.* Above-cited.
a thuilleadh, *adv.* More, moreover.
†athuis, see athais.
ath-ùrachadh, -aidh, *s.m.* Renewing, reviving, refreshing, reanimating, refreshment, renewal, reanimation. 2 Regeneration. Ag a—, *pr.pt.* of ath-ùraich.
ath-ùraich, *v.a.* Revive, refresh, renew, renovate. 2 Regenerate.
ath-ùraichte, *pt.pt.* of ath-ùraich.
†atlaige, *s.f.pl.* Repeated praise.
atmhoire, *comp.* of atmhor.
atmhoireachd, *s. f.* Tendency to swell. 2 Turgidness. 3 Pride, vanity. 4 Bombast. 5 Boisterousness. 6 Fermentation. *A.* Iordain, *the swelling of Jordan.*
atmhor, -oire, *a.* Swelling. 2 Turgid. 3 Raging. 4 Boisterous. 5 Bombastic.
†atrach, see àrdrach.
atruas, see ath-thruas.
atruasach, see ath-thruasach.
†attaca, *adv.* (an taic) Hard by.
atuigean, (for ataigean) *n.pl.* of ataig.
atuingean, *n. pl.* of atuinn.
atuinn, -e, *pl.* -ean [‡‡&-nngean] *s. f.* Gate wicket. 2 Palisade. 3 Rafter.
atuinnean, *pl.* of atuinn.
†auer-coille, *s.m.* Capercailzie, see capull-coille.

au-, For words beginning with *au*, *abh-* or *amh-* may be consulted, the diphthong *au* not being admissible in modern Gaelic orthography. It frequently occurs in old manuscripts, as well as in several writings of later date.
†audhacht. (for bàs) Death.
†aur *s.m.* See òr.

1. See note on page 53.

B b

b, Beith, *birch-tree*, the second letter of the Gaelic alphabet now in use. It sounds somewhat harder than *b*, and softer than *p* in English. When immediately followed by *h*, it has an aspirated sound like *v* in English, as bhuail, *struck*. At the end of a word or syllable, however, the aspiration sometimes passes, in certain dialects, into the sound of the vowel *u*, as searbh, *bitter*; fiabhrus, *fever*; and before consonants it is frequently silent.

b',** (for a bu) Who was, who were, which was, which were.

b', (bu) *past aff.* of is. Used before an initial vowel or *fh*. B'uamhasach an là, *terrible was the day*; b'fhearr t'ainm na do ghniomh, *your name was better than your deed*; b'fhearr leam, *I would prefer*; b'eòlach mis' air, *I knew him well.*

†bà, *a.* Good, honest. 2**Simple-minded, easy, foolish.

bà,(NGP) *s.m.* Simpleton. Is furasd' am bà a mhealladh gun a làmh a lòmadh, *the simpleton may be deceived without being robbed.*

bà bà! *int.* A lullaby. Bà bà mo leanabh! *sleep sleep my child!*

†ba,** *v.* now bàth.

†ba, *s.m.* see bàs.

bà, *gen. sing.* and *n. & dat. pl.* of bó. An àite guth mànaich bithidh geum bà, *instead of the voice of a monk there shall be the lowing of cows.*

†ba'an, *v.* see buain.

†ba'ain, *s.f.* The cleansing of a cow after calving. 2‡‡Matrix of a cow.

bàb,** *s.m.* Babe.

bab,‡‡ -a, *pl* -an, & annan, *s.m.* Tuft, tassel. 2* Child's excrement. 3(AG)Stain. Bithidh sin 'n a bhab air fhad 's is beò e, *that will be a stain on him as long as he lives*; bab air a chliù, *a stain on his fame.*

babach,* *a.* Filthy, abominable. 2‡‡Tufted, tasselled.

†bàbach, *a.* Sweet, innocent.

†———d, *s.f.* Sweetness, innocence.

babachd, *s.f.* Filthiness, abomination.

babag, -aig, -an, *s f.* Tassel. 2 Fringe. 3 Cluster. 4**Short pieces of yarn. 5*Filthy female. 6††Broom, besom. Babagan an òir, *golden tassels.*

babagach, -aiche, *a.* Tasselled, fringed.

babaid,‡‡ -e, -ean, see babag.

———each, see babagach.

babaig, *gen. sing.* of babag.

†bàban, -ain, -an, *s.m.* Baby.

baban, -ain, *s. f.* see babag. 2 *n. pl.* of bab.

baban,* -ain, *s.m.* Bobbin.

———ach, *a.* see babagach.

†babhachd, *s. f. ind.* Innocence, childishness, sweetness.

babhaid, *s.f.* Tassel.

———each, *a.* Hung with tassels, like a tassel.

†babhair, (*for* bha) see bi.

babhd,* *s.m.* Surmise, rumour. 2††Quirk.

———ach,* *a.* Spreading a surmise or rumour.

———air,* *s.m.* Surmiser.—*Islay.*

———aireachd, *s.f.* *Spreading rumours. 2 Puzzlement of mind. Dh'fhalbh mi 's a' bh. feadh a' bhaile, *I wandered round the town in great puzzlement of mind.*

babhsgach, see babhsganta.

babhsgaire, see ballsgaire.

babhsganta, *a.* Cowardly, apt to be frightened. 2 Blustering.

———chd, *s. f.* Cowardice, fright from false alarm.

bàbhuin, *gen. sing.* of bàbhun.

———each, see bàbhunach.

bàbhun, -uin, *pl.* -uin & -uinean, *s.m.* Bulwark, rampart. 2 Tower. 3 Enclosure. 4 Fold where cattle are milked. Brisidh iad a bàbhuin, *they shall break her bulwarks*; thugaibh fainear a bàbhuin bhrèagha, *mark ye her beautiful bulwarks.*

———ach, *a.* Having bulwarks, ramparts, &c., of, or pertaining to, bulwarks, &c.

——— -cabhaig, *s.m.* Fortification hastily constructed.

†bablair, Gaelic spelling of *babbler.*

†bac,** *s.m.* Boat.

bac, *pr.part,* a' bacadh. & bacail, *v.a.* Interrupt, hinder, obstruct, oppose, stop, prevent. 2 Lame. Bac an aoibhneas, *interrupt their joy.*

bac, -a & -aic, *pl.* -an, *s.m.* Stop, hinderance, restraint, delay, interruption, impediment. 2 Hollow, pit, bend in the ground. 3 Thowl or pin in a boat's gunwale, ‡‡fulcrum of an oar. 4‡‡Piece of timber on boat's gunwale to protect it from the friction of the oars. 5 Notch of a spindle. 6 Crook. 7 Hook. 8 Hinge of a door. 9 (AF)Hog, pig. 10‡‡Bog, marsh. 11‡‡Prop, support. 12‡‡Spade, shovel. 13**Barricade. 14 Sandbank.—*Coll.* 15 Hollow. Cuir bac air, *hinder him*; cogull ràmh air na bacaibh, *the rattle of oars on the thowls*; bac na h-achlaise, *the arm-pit*; bac na righe, *the bend of the arm*; bac na h-iosgaid, *the hough*; bac na cruachainn, *the haunch.*

bacach, -aiche, *a.* Lame, crippled, maimed. 2 Rugged. 3**Causing hinderance or delay. 4 Hilly. Duine *b.*, *a lame man*; *b.* air aon chois, *lame on one leg*; *b.* air a dhà chois, *lame on both his legs*; àite *b.*, *a rugged place.*

———, -aich, *s.m.* Lame person.

bacadh, -aidh, -aidhean *s.m.* Hinderance, obstruction, delay, act of hindering or preventing. 2**Cow dung. A' b—. *pr.pt.* of bac.

bacag, -aig, -an, *s. f.* Little hollow. 2 Trip, fall, stumble. Cuir cas bacaig air, *trip him.*

bacaich, *v.a.* Lame. 2 Stop, obstruct, oppose.

———e, *s. f.* Lameness. 2 Imperfection.

———e, *comp.* of bacach.

———ead, -eid, *s.m.* Degree of lameness. Tha e dol am *b.*, *he is getting lamer and lamer.*

———idh, *fut. aff. a.* of bacaich.

bacaid, *s.f.* see bucaid. 2‡‡Ash holder.

bacaideach, *a.* Resisting.

bacaidh, *fut. aff. a.* of bac.

bacail, -e, *a.* Obstructive, preclusive.

bacail,†† *pr. pt.* of bac.

†bacaiseach, *a.* Hindering, obstructive.

bacal, -ail, -alan, *s.m.* Obstacle, stop, hinderance, interruption. 2** Thowl. †3 *rarely* slave, prisoner.

bacaladh, -aidh, *s.m.* Oven, bakehouse.

†bacalta, *a.* Baked.

bac-amail, *v.a.* Counteract.

bacan, -ain, *s.m.* ‡‡Hinderance. 2 Spindle notch. 3 Crook, crooked staff. 4 Hook. 5 Door-hinge. 6 Stake of any kind, *especially* a tether-stake. 7 Knoll. 8 Covering. 9 Cottage. 13 Balcony. An smeòrach air *b.*, *the mavis (perched) on a stake.*

bàcan,(AG) *pr. pt.* Mocking. Tha e a' *b.* air, *he is mocking him.—Reay country.*
bacanach, *a.* Full of stakes. 2** Like a palisade. 3 Knotty. 4 Knolly, uneven.
bacan-doruis, *s.m.* Door-hinge.
bacar, *fut. aff. pass.* of bac.
bacas,** -ais, *s.m.* Captive, hostage.
†**bacastair**, Gaelic spelling of *baxter*, an old form of *baker*.
†———eachd, *s.f.ind.* Baking.
†**bacat**, *s.m.* Captive.
bac-bhòrd, -ùird, *s.m.* Windward or weather side of a ship.
†**bacclam**,‖ "Lame-handed" person.
bach, -a, *s.m.* Drunkenness, revelling, rioting.
†**bach**, *v.a.* Make drunk, revel.
†**bàch**, *a.* see bàidheach.
†**bach**, *s.m.* Breach. 2 Violent attack. 3 Surprise. 4**Loving.
†**bachaid**, *s.f.* Boss of a shield.
bachaill,** *v.a.* Clip round, trim.
bachair, -ean, *s.m.* Drunkard, reveller, rioter.
bachaireachd, *s.f. ind.* Drinking, revelling, rioting.
bachal,‡‡ -ail, *s.m.* Curl.
bachall, -aill, *s.m.* Shepherd's crook. 2 Staff. 3 Crozier. 4* Old shoe *or* slipper. 5 Rim of a cart. 6 Tennis-racket. *B.* aoghaire, *a shepherd's staff* ; *b.* sealgair, *a hunter's staff*. By virtue of an ancient grant from an Earl of Argyll, a piece of land in the island of Lismore was held on condition that the holder kept and took care of the crozier of St. Maluag, from whom its church is named. Hence the holder is known as Baran a' Bhachaill.
bachallach,** *a.* Like a staff, crook, or crozier. 2 Relating to a staff, crook, or crozier. 3 Provided with a rim, as a cart. 4 Curled, as hair. 5 Having ringlets.
bachanta, *a.* Clamorous, prating, garrulous.
bachantachd, *s.f.* Clamorousness, garrulity.
bàchar, *s.m.* Beech mast. 2 Acorn.
bachar, *s.m.* Celtic nard *or* lady's glove (plant) —*valeriana celtica.*
bàcharan, -ain, see buacharan.
bachd, see bac.
bachdach, see bacach.
bachdaiche, see bacaiche.
bachdan, see bacan.
bàchdanach,** *a.* Noisy, tumultuous, contentious.
bachlach, -aiche, *a.* Curled, having ringlets, full of curls. 2**Bushy, as hair, crispy. 3 Throwing out twigs or shoots.
bachlach,** -aich, *s.m.* Cudgeller.
bachlachadh, -aidh, *s.m.* Crisping, curling, act of forming ringlets or curls.
†**bachladh**, *s.m.* Armful. 2 Cup, chalice. 3 Head of a stick.
bachlag, -aig, -an, *s.f.* Shoot, as of a plant, especially potato. 2 Tender root. 3 Little curl. 4 Head of a staff. †5 Lisp or halt in speech.
bachlagach, -aiche, *a.* Curled, having curls or ringlets, full of curls or ringlets. 2 Like a curl or ringlet. 3 Bushy, as hair. 4 Crisp. 5††Having shoots, as a plant. Falt *b.*, dualach, *curled luxuriant hair.*
bachlaich, *v.a.* Curl, form into curls or ringlets.
†**bach-lobhra**,‡‡ *s.f.pl.* Pimples on the face.
bachoid, see bucaid.
bachoil, -e, *a.* Bacchanalian.
bach-thinneas,‖ *s.m.* Sickness after drunkenness. 2**Surfeit.
bach-thoirm, *s.f.* } Noise of revelry or of
bach-thorman, *s.m.* } drunkenness.
bachull, see bachall.
bachullach, see bachallach.
bac-lamh, *s.m.* Manacle, hand-cuff.
bac-làmhach, *a.* Disabled in hand or arm. 2 Preventing the free use of one's hand or arm.
bac-mòine,‡ *s.m.* Peat-bank, turf-pit or bank.
b'àd, (*for* b'iad) It was they.
bad, *v.a.* Make into tufts or bunches. 2 Separate, divide into small heaps. 3 Prune.
bàd,** -àid, see bàt.
bad, -aid, -a, *s.m.* Tuft, cluster, bunch. 2 Top cluster, hair on the upper part of the head. 3 Tuft of wool. 4 Thicket, clump of trees or shrubs. 5 Grove. 6 Flock. 7 Ragged garment. 8 Plain. 9 Spot. 10**Wish. 11 Piece, portion. Bad fuilt, *a tuft of hair* ; *b.* chaorach, *a flock of sheep* ; ann am badaibh nam bonn, *immediately* (*lit.* in the impression of the soles of the feet) ; ann am badaibh a chéile, *seizing each other's scalp-locks (probably a survival of ancient war customs.)*
†**bàd**, *s. f.* Wind.
badach, -aiche, *a.* Same meanings as badanach.
badag, -aig, -an, *s.f.* Small bunch, cluster or tuft. 2 Grove, &c. 3(AH) Besom, generally of heather. *B.* fhraoich, *a heather brush.*
badag lus,* *s.f.* Anthology.
bad-alan, (AC) *s.* Water-vole.
badan, *n. pl.* of bad.
badan, -ain, *s.m.* (*dim.* of bad) Small cluster or tuft. 2 Little grove, &c. *B.* coille, *a thicket of wood, clump or grove* ; ghearr e na badain, *he cut down the thickets.*
badanach, -aiche, *a.* Abounding in groves. 2 Tufty, tufted. 3 Bushy, clustered. 4 Shaggy. 5 Like, or pertaining to, thickets, groves, &c. An sòbhrach a chinneas *b.*, *the primrose that grows in tufts.*
badan-dlùth, -ain-, *s.m.* Covert.
badan-measgain,§ *s.m.* Bog violet. [see mòthan.]
†**bàdar**, *v.* They were.
badh(AF) *s.m.* Vulture. 2 Royston crow. 3 Any ravenous bird.
bàdh, -àidh, -annan, *s.m.* see bàgh.
bàdh, *s. f.* see bàidh.
bàdhach, -aiche, *a.* Kind, friendly, loving.
bàdhachd, *s. f.* Kindness, friendliness. 2 Obligatoriness.
badhal, -ail, -an, *s.m.* Wandering. Cù badhail, *a strange dog*; aithneachadh bó badhail, no fàilt' a' chruidh, *the wandering cow's welcome, or the kine's salute.*
badhalach, -aiche, *a.* Wandering, given to wander.
bàdhan, see bàbhun. 2 see bàghan.
bàdhar, see bàthar.
bàdhar, -air, *s.f.* After-birth of a cow at calving, placenta of a cow.
bàdharan, -ain, -an, Helpless wanderer. 2 Unimportant, puny person. 3‡‡ Helpless wandering.
bàdharanaich, *s. f.* Creeping or moving slowly.
badhsgach, -aiche, *a.* Easily frightened, foolish.
badhsgaire, -an, *s.m.* Foolish inconsistent fellow. 2 Blusterer. 3‡‡Coward.
badhsgaireachd, *s. f.* Inconsistency. 2 Folly. 3 Nonsensical talking, blustering. 4‡‡Cowardice.
badsadh,** -aidh, *s.m.* Provision for a journey.
bag, (Eng. bag.)
bagach, -aiche, *a.* Corpulent, bulky, bellying, unwieldy. 2**Warlike. 3‡‡Tight, neat.
bagaich, *v.a.* & *n.* Make bellied or corpulent. 2 Become corpulent.
bagaiche, *comp.* of bagach.
bagaichean, *n. pl.* of bag.
bagaid, -e, -ean, *s. f*, Cluster, bunch, as of nuts

or grapes. 2‡‡Cod, husk. 3‡‡Crowd. 4* Corpulent female. Bagaidean searbha, *sour clusters.*
bagaideach, *a.* Full of clusters. 2 In bunches. 3 Corpulent, overgrown, unshapely. 4‡‡ Husky.
bagaideachd,‡‡ *s. f.* Bunchiness.
bagaidean, *n. pl.* of bagaid.
bagailt, see bagaid. Bagailt chnò bu taine plaosg, *a cluster of thinnest shelled nuts.*
bagailteach, *a.* see bagaideach.
bagair, *pr. pt.* a' bagairt & bagradh, *v.a.* Threaten, denounce evil, terrify. [This verb is generally followed by the prep. *air*, as, bagramaid orra, *let us threaten them.*
bagair, -ean, *s. m.* Glutton, epicure. 2* Corpulent man.
bagaireachd, *s. f.* Gluttony. 2 Threatening.
bagairt, *s. f.* Threat, threatening. 2 Denouncing. Cha téid plàsd air *b.*, *no plaster is applied to a threat.* A' b—, *pr. pt.* of bagair. Tha e 'bagairt an uisge, *it threatens rain*; a' *b.* oirnn, *threatening us*; a' bagairt sgàinidh, *threatening to burst.*
bagairteachd,** *s. f.* Menace.
†bagaist, *s. f.* Gaelic form of *baggage.* 2** see bagaid.
bagaisteach, *a.* Deriv. of Eng. *baggage.* 2 ** see bagaideach.
bagan, see baigean.
baganta, *a.* Warlike. 2 Plump, corpulent. 3 Neat, tidy. 4 Lively. An dreathan *b.*, *the plump wren.*
bagantachd,* *s. f.* Corpulency.
bagar, -air, -ain. *s.m.* Threat.
bagaradh, see bagradh.
bagarrach, see bagrach.
bagarrach, -aich, *s.m.* Threatener.
bagarrachd, *s. f.* Threatening, habit of threatening.
bàgh, -àigh, -an, *s.m.* Bay. 2 Harbour. 3 Creek. 4 Estuary.
bàgh, *s. f.* see bàidh.
†bagh,‡‡ *s.m.* Promise, bond, tie. 2 Strength, power, virtue. 3 Word. 4 Battle.
bàghach, *a.* Abounding in, or pertaining to, bays, harbours, creeks, or estuaries. 2 see bàdhach. 3 Binding, obligatory.
bàghachd, see bàdhachd.
†baghadh,** -aidh, *s.m.* Fighting, quarrelling.
baghair, -ean, *s.m.* see baoghaire & baodhaire.
bà-ghamhna, see bo-g—.
bàghan, -ain, *s.m.* Little harbour. 2 Creek. 3 Road for ships.
bàghan, -ain, *s.m.* see bàbhun. 2 Church-yard.
baghan,‡ -ain, *s.m.* Stomach.
baghlach, see †baoghalach.
baghlachd, see baoghalachd.
baghte,** *s.* Bait.
bagrach, *a.* Threatening, menacious, prone to threaten. 2**Imminent. Is i an Aoine bhagrach a ni 'n Sathurna deurach, *the gloomy Friday makes the rainy Saturday.*
bagradh, aidh, *s. m.* Threatening, menacing, denouncing. A' b—, *pr. pt.* of bagair.
baguid, see bagaid.
baguideach, *a.* see bagaideach.
baguilte, -an, *s.m.* see bagaid.
baibeil, -e, *a.* Addicted to fables, lying. 2‡‡ Stammering. 3* see baibheil.
baibeulachd, *s. f.* Habit of lying. 2‡‡Silly talk.
baibh,* *s.m.* Terrible sight. 2 Incredible thing. 3 Fairy. 4 Goblin.
baibhealachd,* *s. f.* Enormity, exaggeration, terribleness.
baibheil,* -e, *a.* Incredible, enormous, exaggerated, terrible. Pris *bh.*, *an exorbitant price.*
baibheist, (AF) *s. f.* Toad.
baibleach,** *a.* Profuse.
baibleachd,** *s. f.* Profuseness.
†baic, -e, *s. f.* Turn, twist.
baic, *gen. sing.* of bac.
†——each, *a.* Twisted, having turns.
†baic-bheurla, *s. f.* Solecism, impropriety in language.
bàich, see bàthaich.
baic-labhradh, see baic-bheurla.
†baid, *s.m.* Sage, prophet, philosopher.
baideal, -eil, -an, *s.m.* Pillar. 2 Fortress. 3 Tower. 4 Cloud. 5 Ensign, standard. *B.* neóil, *a pillar of cloud*; mo *bh.* àrd, *my high tower.*
baidealach, -aiche, *a.* Abounding in, or pertaining to, pillars, towers, or fortresses. 2‡‡ Cloudy. 3‡‡Sheeted, like clouds or sails. 4 Bannered. Na siùil *bh.*, *the expansive sails.*
baidean, -ein, -anan, *s.m.* Group. 2 Handful. 3 Small flock of sheep or goats. 4** Little boat, yawl, pinnace.
baideanach,†† *a.* Abounding in small flocks of goats or sheep.
baideil, *gen. sing.* of baideal.
bàidh, -e, *s. f.* Kindness, benignity, humanity, mercy. 2 Hospitality. 3 Affection, love, attachment, fondness. †2 Wave. Dh'fheòraich i le *b.*, *she enquired affectionately;* is mór a *bh.* ris, *great is his partiality for him*; shéid osnadh gun *bh.*, *a wind blew without mercy*; ceann-uidhe nam mìle *b.*, *the abiding-place of boundless hospitality.*
†bàidhe, *s. f.* Amity, alliance, gratitude. 2 Compassion. 3 Predicting, prophesying.
bàidheach, *s.m.* Companion, co-adjutor. 2 Favourite. 3 Champion.
bàidheach, -eiche, *a.* Friendly, kind, merciful, loving, attached. 2 Humane, hospitable, noble.
bàidheachas, -ais, *s.m.* Grace, friendship, favour, kindness. 2 Humanity.
†bàidheal,** -eil, *s.m.* Cow-stall.
bàidheachd, } *s. f.* Friendliness, kindness,
bàidhealachd, } humanity, mercy. 2 Fondness, affection. 3**Hospitality. 4**Companionship.
bàidheil, *a.* Merciful, kind, humane. 2 Friendly, affectionate, loving, attached. 3 Favourable. †4 Binding, obligatory. Cha bhi thu *b.*, *thou shalt not be favourable.*
baidne, *gen. sing.* of baidein.
baidein, -dne, -dnean, *s.m.* Small group, cluster or flock. [see baidean.]
baidreach,* *a.* see baidreagach.
baidreach,* -ich, *s.m.* see baidreag.
baidreag, -eig, -an, *s. f.* Patched ragged garment, rag.
baidreagach, *a.* Ragged, patched.
bàidse, *s.m.* Musician's fee, especially at a country wedding. 2 Voyage. 3 Enormous load or cargo.—*West Highlands.*
baidsear,** *s.m.* Day-labourer.
bàidsire,* *s.m.* Voyager, adventurer.
bàidsireachd,* *s. f. ind.* Adventuring, cruising, sea-faring life.
baigean, -ein, *s.m.* Little bag. 2 Little glutton. 3 Little corpulent person. *B.* lèasaiche, *a rennet bag.*
baigeanach, *a.* Corpulent, bagged, bellied.
baigeir, -ean, Gaelic spelling of *beggar.* Peilear nam baigearan, *a pebble*, (*lit.* the beggar's bullet.)
baigeireach, *a.* (*beggar*) Inclined to beg, needy, beggarly.
baigeireachd, (*beggar*) *s. f.* Beggary. Air *b.*,

engaged in beggary.
†bàigh,** *v.a.* Endear.
bàigh, *s.f.* see bàidh.
bàigheach, *a.* & *s.* see bàidheach, *a.* & *s.*
bàigheil, *a.* see bàidheil.
†baighein, *s.f.* Chariot, waggon, dray.
†baighle, *s.f.* Fawn.
bail, -e, *s.f.* Economy, thrift, management, carefulness. †2 Place, residence. †3 Luck, prosperity. †4 Allowance from a mill to the poor. 5‡‡Sling. Cha bhi bail air aran fuinte, *baked bread is not spared*; am fear nach dean *b.* air beul a' bhuilg, ni an t-iochdar *b.* air féin, *if you don't spare the mouth of the bag, the bottom will spare itself.*—N.G.P.
†bàil, see b'àill.
bailbh, *gen sing.* of balbh.
bailbhe, *s.f.* Dumbness, muteness.
bailbheachd, see bailbhe & balbhachd.
bailbheag, -eig, -an, see meilbheag.
———ach, *a.* see meilbheagach.
†bailc, *a.* Strong, bold, daring.
bailc, -e, -ean, *s.f.* Balk, ridge of earth between two furrows. 2 Land-mark. 3 Strip of corn-land left fallow (see under "leum-iochd) 4‡‡Crust or hardness formed on the earth by the weather. 5 Flood, mountain torrent, "spate." 6 Seasonable rain, genial showers. 7 Shower that comes suddenly, ††plump of rain. 8**Loud noise. 9**Ligature. 10‡‡Defiance. 11‡‡ Strait, hardship. 12†† Calf of the leg. 13(AH) Twisted or mis-shapen foot or ankle. *B.* nan sgiath, *the noise of the shields.*
bailceach, -eich, *s.m.* Tall, erect man, stout man. 2‡‡ *s. f.* Storm.
bailceach, *a.* Rainy, inundating, causing a flood. 2 In seasonable showers. 3 Balked, like a balk. 4††Stout, strong. 5‡‡Ridgy. A' Bhealltainn *bh.*, *rainy May.*
bailceanta, *a.* Defying, boastful. 2††Stout, strong.
bailcire,(AH) *s.m.* Man with a mis-shapen foot or ankle.
baile, -tean, *s.m.* Village, hamlet, town. 2 Home. 3 Farm. †5‡‡Clan, tribe. Am bheil t' athair aig baile? *is your father at home?* am bail' ud thall, *yonder town*; fear a' bhaile, *the proprietor* or *tenant of the farm*; tha bail' aige, *he has a whole farm.*
baileach, -eiche, *a.* Thrifty, economical, frugal, careful. 2 Excessive. 3 Thorough, complete. Gu *b.*, *wholly, completely, thoroughly.* [see buileach.
———adh, *s.m.* see buileachadh.
bàileag,(AG) *s.f.* Ball, as of yarn. *B.* snàtha, *a ball of worsted.*
baile-daingnichte,‡‡ *s.m.* Fortified town.
—— -dùthcha,‡‡ *s.m.* Country town.
—— fearainn,‡‡ *s.m.* Farm.
—— -geamhraidh, *s.m.* Infield, the low grounds of a Highland farm. 2‡‡ Strath residence.
—— -malairt, *s.m.* Exchange.
—— -margaidh, *s.m.* Market town. 2 Burgh.
—— mór, *pl.* bailtean móra, *s.m.* City, large town. 2 Metropolis.
†baileog, -oig, -an, see bailleag.
—— puirt, -tean-, *s.m.* Seaport town.
bailgeann, see bailg-fhionn.
bailg-fhionn, *a.* Spotted, speckled, piebald. 2 White-bellied. Na gabhair *bh.*, *the speckled goats.*
bailgneach, (AC) *a.* White-bellied. Le laoigh bhreaca bhailgneach, *with speckled white-bellied calves.*
bailich, *v.a.* see builich. 2 Use badly.—*Suth'd.*
†bàilich, see boilich.
bàilidh, see bàillidh.
———eachd, see bàillidheachd.
†bailire, *s.m.* Slinger.
bàilisdeir, -e, -ean, *s.m.* Vain-glorious fellow. 2 Man who talks idly, blusterer, babbler.
———each, *a.* Vaunting. 2 Inclined to talk idly, blustering, babbling.
———eachd, *s.f.* Habit of talking idly, foolishly or blusteringly.
b'àill, (*for* bu àill) Would. B'àill leam, leat, leis, &c., *I, thou, he, &c. would*; am b'àill leat mo mharbhadh? *wouldst thou kill me?* ciod a b'àill leibh? *what would you have?* "B'àill leibh?" (*a slovenly pronunciation of the last*) is often used as an equivalent of *I beg your pardon?* when one speaker has not understood a remark made by another and wishes it repeated.
bailleag, -eig, -an, *s. f.* Twig, sprout. 2 Sucker.
———ach, -aiche, *a.* Full of, or like, sprouts, twigs, or suckers. 5 Slender. 3 Pliable. 4‡‡ Cheerful, lively.
†baillean, -ein, *s.m.* Boss, stud. 2 Little bubble. 3 Anything round.
†———ach, *a.* Bossy, studded.
bailleartach, -aiche, *a.* see pailleartach.
bàillidh, *s.m.* Magistrate, "baillie," bailiff.
———neachd, *s. f.* Office of a town or country magistrate. 2 Bailiwick, province, district.
baillsgeach, see boillsgeach.
bailm,** *s.f.* Balm, balsam.
bailmeach,** *a.* Balmy, abounding in, or made of balm, balsamic.
bailmeanta,** *a.* see bailmeach.
bailt,** Gaelic spelling of *belt.* 2 *gen.* of balt.
bailte, *n. pl.* of bailtean.
bailteach,** *a.* Abounding in, or belonging to, towns or villages, civic.
———as, -ais, *s.m.* Planting or founding towns. 2 Colonization. 3 Country township.
bailteachas mór,‡‡ *s.m.* Affected state, pride, haughtiness.
bailtean, *n. pl.* of baile.
bàin, *gen. sing.* of bàn.
bainbh, *s.m.* Young pig.
bainbh, *pr. part.* a' bainbheachd, *v.a.* Pig.
———idheachd,** (*contr.* bainbheachd) *s. f.* Piggishness. 2 Pigging, furrowing. A' b—, *pr. pt.* of bainbh. Tha a' mhuc a' teannadh ri *b.*, *the sow is about pigging.*
bainbhinn,** *s, f.* Suckling pig.
†bàinchead, *v.a.* Authorize.
†———,** *s. f.* Authority, license.
†———ach,** *a.* Authorizing, licensing.
†———aichte,** *pt. part.* Authorized, licensed.
baindeachd, *s.f.* Female modesty, bashfulness, reserve, delicacy. Effeminacy.
baindealach,** *a.* Drizzly.
bàin-dearg,‡‡ *a.* Flesh-coloured.
bain-dia, see ban-dia.
baindidh, -e, *a.* Modest, feminine. 2 Effeminate. 3 Unassuming.
———eachd, see baindeachd.
bàine, *s.f.* Paleness, whiteness, fairness. A' sioladh a *bh.*, *concealing his whiteness.*
bàine, *comp.* of bàn.
baineach, (AF) *s.f.* Mare.
†baineachd, *s.f.* Woman slaughter.
bàinead, *s.* Degree of whiteness or fairness.
†baineamhuil, *a.* see banail.
baineasag, see baineasg.
baineasg, -eisg, *s. f.* (‡bàn+neas, *white weasel*) She-ferret.
———ach, *a.* Like a ferret, abounding in, or pertaining to, ferrets.
bainfheis, see banais.

†bainfhirinsge, *s.f.* (ban+firionn) Common gender.
†bainfhreagradh, *s.m.* see bainn-fhreagradh.
†bainfid, (buinidh iad) They shall take.
†baing, *adv.* On a sudden.
†——, -ean, *s.f.* Surprise, sudden attack.
†——hearachd, *s.f.* Goddess.
bàinidh, *s.f.* Fury, madness, rage. Tha e air *b., he is raging, quite furious.*
bainionn, *a.* see boirionn. Na gabhair *b., the she-goats.*
————ach, see boirionnach.
————achd, see boirionnachd.
————as, see boirionnas.
bainionta, *a.* see boireanta.
bainis, -e, *pl.* bainnsean, see banais.
bainisg, -ean, *s.f.* Little old woman. 2 Female satirist. 3(AC) Singing naiad.
————eag, -eig, -eagan, *dimin.* of bainisg.
————eil, *a.* Like an old woman.
bàin-leus, see bàn-leus.
bain-lighiche, -ean. *s.f.* see ban-lighiche.
bainndidh, see baindidh.
bainne, *s.m.* Milk, milky juice. †2 see boinne. Bò-*bh., a milch-cow*; crodh-*b. milch-cattle*; camhail-*bh., milch-camels.*
bainne asal, *asses' milk.*
—— blàth, *warm* or *fresh milk.*
—— binntichte, *curdled milk.*
—— briste, „ „
—— buaile, *fold-milk.*
—— buidhe, *milk yielded by a cow during first two days after calving.*
—— chapull, *mare's milk, kumiss.*
—— cnàmha, *fermentation of fresh and butter-milk, frothed with the* loinid *or frothing-stick.*
—— chaorach, *sheep's milk.*
—— gamhnaich, *milk of a farrow cow(one with a year-old calf and still being milked.)* see also below.
—— ghobhar, *goat's milk.*
—— goirt, *sour milk 2 Butter-milk—Argyll &c.,* (*better* blàthaich.)
—— lom, *skimmed milk.*
—— maistridh, *whipped cream or milk, frothed with the* loinid.
—— milis, *sweet milk.*
—— muidhe,** *butter-milk.*
—— na ciche, *milk of the breast.*
—— na cìpe, *the milky juice of the mountain herb.*
—— nòis, *beastings.*
—— reamhar,‡‡ *sheep's milk boiled and curdled.*
—— tàig, (*for* boinne t—)' *rain-drop.*
—— ùr, *fresh milk.*
bainneach, -eiche, *a.* Milky, lacteal, like milk. 2 Milk-producing, abounding in milk. A' Bhealltuinn *bh., milk-producing May.*
————as, *s.f.* Milkiness.
†bainnealach, -aich, see boinnealach.
bainnear, *a.* Milky, abounding in milk.
————,* *s.f.* Fold for milking sheep &c. *Lewis*
————achd,** *s.f.* Milkiness.
————daich,* see boinnealaich.
bainneasag,** see baineasg.
bainne-gamhnaich,§ *s.m.* (*lit.* the yearling's milk—signifying the scanty results yielded by sucking it) Red rattle in the Highlands, honeysuckle in Ireland. see uilleann *and* lus riabhach.
bainne-ghabhair,§ *s.m.* Lousewort, red rattle. see lus riabhach.
bainn-fhreagradh, -aidh, *s.m.* Bond. 2 Stipulation.
bainnse, *gen. sing.* of banais.
bainnseach,‡‡ *a.* Full of weddings. 2 Retired, desolate.
†————,** *s.f.* Field, sheep-walk, plain, solitary place.
————d, *s.f.* Feasting, banquetting.
†bainnseaghadh, *s.m.* Desolation, destruction.
bainnsean, *n. pl.* of banais.
bainnsich, *v.a.* Waste, consume.
bain-speireag, -eig, -an, *s.f.* Female sparrow-hawk.
————————ach, *a.* Like, or pertaining to sparrow-hawks.
bain-stiùbhard, -aird, *s.f.* see ban-s—.
————————achd, *s.f. ind.* see ban-s—.
bainteag,(AF) *s.f.* Small clam (fish.)
†bain-teoladh,‡‡ *s.f.* Female thief or secret criminal.
baintighearna, -an, *s.f.* Lady. 2 Wife of a baronet or knight. 3 Gentlewoman.
baintighearnachd, *s.f.* Ladyship.
baintighearnas, -ais, *s.m.* Ladyship. 2 Rule or sway of a lady. Tha e fo *bh., he is under petticoat government.*
bain-treabhach, see bantrach.
bain-treabhachas, -ais, *s.m.* see bantrachas.
baintreach, see bantrach.
baintreachas, see bantrachas.
bàir, -e, *s.f.* †Battle, strife. 2 Game, goal. 3 Path, road. Beaten path, commonly applied to one opened through deep snow, hence, fear brisidh bàire, applied to a chieftain or leader in an arduous enterprise.‡‡ 4(AC) Rutting. 5‡‡Wheat. Chuir iad leth-bhàire shuas agus leth-bhàire shios a staigh orra, *they beat them first before changing goals and then after.—Campbell's Tales.* Air màgh na bàire, *on the plain of battle*; ràinig iad a' *bh., they reached the goal*; bhuidhinn iad *b., they won a game.*
†bair, *s.f.* Wave. 2 The sea.
bairceàn, -ein, *s.m.* Ferret.
bairceàn, *s. pl.* Cross-sticks or side timbers in a house, between the rafters.
†bairche, *a.* Strong, brave.—*s.m.* Battle.
†bairchne, *s.m.* Fight by women.
†bairein, *s.f.* see bairceàn.
baircinn, *s.pl.* see bairceàn.
bairene,(AF) *s.f.* Female cat. 2 White cat.
bàird, *gen. sing.* & *n. pl.* of bàrd.
†bairdheis,** *s.f.* Point, tip, or end of any sharp instrument.
————, *v.n.* Sharpen to a point.
baireachd,(AC) *s.f.* Quarrelling, wrangling.
†bairead, now biorraid.
bàireadh, -eidh, see bàir.
†bair-eatrom, *a.* Light-headed. 2 Quick, nimble, swift.
†baireise, *s.m.* Froth of water.
bairgeanta, *a.* Strong, stout, sturdy. 2 Swift.
†bairghean,** -ein, *s.m.* Cake. 2 Floor. 3 Plot of ground.
†bair-ghin,** *s.m.* Begotten son.
†————teach, *a.* Begetting sons. —*s.f.* Woman that begets sons.
†bairicean,** -ein, *s.m.* see bairceàn.
bàirich,** *pr. part.* a' bàirich, & a' bàirich-eadh, *v. a.* Low, bellow, roar.
————, *s.f. ind.* Lowing, bellowing, roaring of cattle. Ciod a' *bh.* a th'ort ? *what are you bellowing at ?*
————eadh,** -eidh, *s.m.* Lowing, bellowing, continued lowing or bellowing.
————idh, *fut. aff. a.* of bàirich.
bàirig, *pr. part.* -eadh, *v.a.* Bestow, confer, grant, present, endow.
————eadh, -eidh, *s.m.* Bestowing, conferring. A' b—, *pr. part.* of bàirig.

†bairighean, *s.m.* Floor, flat of ground.
†bairile, *s. f.* Helmet.
bairill, see baraill.
†bairin breac,‡‡ *s.m.* Small cake offered to the moon at the autumnal equinox.
†bairinn, *s.f.* Firebrand.
bàirisg, *s.* Fool.
bàirleigeadh, -eidh, -leigean, see bàrnaigeadh.
bàirlinn, *s. f.* Warning, summons of removal. 2 Rolling wave or sea, high sea, surge, billow. 3(AH) Water flung back from an oar in hard rowing.
———each, *a.* Summoning, warning to quit. 2 Rolling, as a high sea. 3 Billowy.
———ich, *v.a.* Serve with summons of removal.
†bàirn, *v.a.* Judge. 2**Assure, warrant.
bàirneach, -ich, *s. f.* Limpet. Cha'n fhaighinn òrd air bàirnich air, *he was too many for me* ; b'e sin cead 'iarraidh òrd a bhualadh air bàirnich, *requesting permission to do something that no man can prevent, such as eating, breathing, &c.*
†bàirneach, *a.* Perverse. 2 Obstinate. 3 Filial.
bàirneachd, *s. f.* Judging. 2 Judgment, decision at law. 3 Perverseness. 4 Fretfulness.
bàirneag-cathan,(AF) *s.f.* Barnacle, limpet.—*Arran.*
†bàirnich, *v.a.* Fret. 2 Judge.
†bairridh-bhuaghbhail, *s. f.* Sounding horn.
†bairrin, *s.m.* Mitre.
bàirseach, -sich, -sichean, *s.f.* Scold, shrew.

16. Bàirneach.

———d, *s. f.* Scolding, raillery. 2 Satire.
bàirseag, -eig, -an, *s.f.* (*dim.* of bàirseach.) Young scold. 2 Young shrew. 3**Top of the windpipe.
bàirsich, *v.a.* Scold, rail. 2 Satirize, lampoon
†bais, *s. f.* Water.
bais, *gen. sing.* of bas.
bàis, *gen. sing.* of bàs. 2 see bathais.
†baisc, *a.* Round.
baisceall, -ill, *s.m.* Wild, ungovernable person. 2**Mad person. 3**Attempter.
baisceanta, see basganta.
baischailc, *s.f.* Ruddle, red earth.
baischriadh, " " "
baiscmheall, -eill, *s.m.* Ball. 2 Round mass.
baisd, see baist.
baisdeadh, see baisteadh.
baiseach, *a.* Having a large palm. 2 Smooth. 3 see baoiseach.
baiseach, -aich, *s.m.* Heavy shower.
———d, *s. f. ind.* Palmistry.
†baiseal, -eil, *s.m.* Pride, arrogance, haughtiness.
baisealach, -aiche, *a.* Proud, arrogant.
†baisfhionn, *a.* Flesh-coloured, reddish.
baisgeanta, *a.* see boillsgeanta.
baisgeil, -e, *a.* see boillsgeil.
baisin, see basaidh.
†baisleach, *s.m.* Ox. 2 Plash of water, heavy rain. 3 Handful of anything. 4 Stone where women were wont to wash.
baist, *v.a.* Baptize, perform the ceremony of baptism. 2‡‡Immerse, plunge in water. 3‡‡ Dilute as strong liquors.
baiste, *pt. pt.* of baist.
———ach, -ich, -ichean, *s.m.* Baptist. †2 *s. f.* Rain. Na Baistich, *the Baptists.*
———ach, *a.* Baptismal, of, or pertaining to, baptism.
———achail, *a.* see baisteach, *a.*
———adh, -idh, *s.m.* Baptism, act of baptizing. 'G a *bh.*, *baptizing him* ; tha e air a *bh.*, *he is baptized* ; uisge beatha gun *bh.*, *whisky unreduced* ; mullach do bhaistidh, *your forehead* ; òltar fìon os cionn do bhaistidh, *wine will be drunk on the occasion of your baptism—said when the chief had an heir born to him.*
baisteir, -ean, *s.m.* Baptizer, baptist.
baistiche,** see baisteach, *s.*
baistidh, *fut. aff. a.* of baist.
———, *a.* Baptismal. Amar *b.*, *a baptismal font.*
†baistidhe, *s.m. pl.* Drops from the eaves of a house, rain drops.
bàite, *pt. pt.* of bàth. Drowned. 2 Quenched, extinguished, (*fig.* overwhelmed.) Tha m' anam *b.* gu cràiteach ann am chom, *my soul is overwhelmed grievously within me.*
bàiteach, -ich, *s. f.* Soft marshy ground.
baiteach, -eich, *s.m.* Farmer. 2 Cup. 3 Jug.
baiteal, -eil, *s.m.* Battle. 2 see baideal.
———ach, -aiche, *a.* Battalious. 2 see baidealach.
bàith, -e, *s.f.* Folly. 2 Lure, decoy.
baitheach, see bàthaich.
baithis, see bathais.
bàithte, see bàite.
†bàitin, *s.m. pl.* (*for* bàtaichean) *pl.* of bàta.
†baitin, -e, -ean, *s.m,dim.* of bata, Small stick.
———eachd, *s. f.* Beating with a stick.
baitsear,** *s.m.* Charman.
bàl,** -àil, see ball.
†bal, *s.m.* Lord. 2 The sun. see Beal.
balach, -aich, *s. m.* Clown, peasant of the lower class. 2 Young man, fellow. 3 Sturdy fellow. 4 "Pam" or jack in cards. *B.* na h-aimhreit, *a quarrelsome disorderly fellow.*
balachail, *a.* Clownish, vulgar, clumsy, ungainly. 2 Boyish, puerile.
balachain, *gen. sing.* of balachan.
balachan, -ain, -an, *s.m.* Boy. 2 Young boy. 3 Little boy. 4†† Little clown. Maide balachain, *a boy's stick.*
———as, -ais, *s.m.* Boyhood, adolescence, age succeeding childhood.
†baladh, *s.m.* Fighting. 2 Smell (boladh.)
balagam, see balgam.
†balaighe, *s. f.* Advantage, profit, thrift.
†balaist, *s. f.* Gaelic spelling of *ballast* and *balance.*
balaistich,** *v.a.* (Eng. *ballast*) Ballast.
balanta,** *s.m.* Gaelic spelling of *ballant*, the Scotch form of *ballad.*
balantaiche,** *s.m.* Ballad-singer.
balaoch, see balach.
balardach,** *a.* Gorgeous.
balbh, -ailbhe, *a.* Dumb, mute. 2 Silent, quiet, at peace. Mar uisge *b.* a' ghlinne, *like the silent water of the valley* ; mar *bh.* dhriùchd, *like silent dew* ; air son an duine *bh.*, *for the dumb man* ; éiridh tonn air uisge balbh, *wave will rise on silent water—calm people when stirred may astonish.*
balbhachd, *s. f. ind.* Dumbness, muteness. 2 Silence. Marbh *bh.* na h-oidhche, *the dead silence of night.*
†balbhadh, -aidh, *s.m.* Becoming mute.
balbhag, -aig, -an, *s. f.* Pebble, small stone.
———ach, *a.* Pebbly.
balbhan, -ain, -an, *s.m.* Dumb person. Labhair am *b.*, *the dumb spoke.*
———achd, *s. f.* Dumbness, muteness. 2 Dumb show, communication by mute signs. Ri *b.*, *communicating ideas by mute signs.*
balbh-thinneas, *s.m.* Apoplexy.
balc, -ailc, *s.m.* see bailc.
†——, *a.* see †bailc.
balcach -aiche, *a.* Splay-footed. 2 see bailceach.

balcaiche, *s. f.* Splay-foot. 2 Splay-footedness.
balcanta, *a.* Stout, firm, strong, muscular., Gu *b., firmly, stoutly.*
balc-chasach, *a.* see balcach.
balcmhor, -oire, *a.* Great, corpulent.
balg, builg, *s.m.* Leather bag, budget, wallet, scrip, satchel. 2 Seed of an herb. 3 Boss of a shield. 4 Belly. 5 Womb. 6 Blister on the skin. 7 Air-tube of a cycle. 8 Quiver. 9 Pair of bellows. Séid am balg, *blow the bellows* ; á balg na maidne, *from the womb of the morning* ; balg ri gréine, *basking* ; is labhar na builg fhàs, *noisy are the empty bags,* NGP; arra-bhalg, *an eyelid*—J.M.
†**balg,**** *s.m.* Man of learning.
balg, *v.a.* see balgaich.
balg-abhrais, *s.m.* Wool-bag. 2 Batch of wool.
balgach, -aiche, *a.* Full of bags or blisters. 2 Like a bag or wallet. 3 Bellied, bulging, jutting. 4 Knobby, massy.
balgach,* *s. f.* Corpulent female. 2 The small pox. 3‖ Boil, bubo. [When having either of meanings 2 or 3, it is preceded by the article *a'*] A' bhalgach Fhrangach, *the French-pox.*
balgaich, *v.a.* Belly out, as a sail. 2 Stow in a bag or satchel. 3 Puff, blister, swell.
balgair, -e, -ean, *s.m.* Fox. 2 *in contempt* Cunning fellow. 3 Dog. 4 Impudent person. 5 Glutton. 6 Big-bellied man. 7(AC) Thief, rogue, robber. 8(AF) Otter. A bhalgair tha thu ann ! *fox that thou art !* buail am balach air a charbad is buail am balgair air an t-sròin, *hit the flunkey on the cheek and the dog on the nose* ; balgair balaich, *a worthless fellow.*
——**each,** -eiche, *a.* Currish.
——**eachd,** *s. f. ind.* Slyness, craftiness. 2 Currishness.
balgairean, *n. pl.* of balgair.
balgam, -aim, *s.m.* Mouthful of any liquid, sip, gulp. *B.* bainne, *a mouthful of milk.*
balgan, -ain, *s.m.* (*dim.* of balg) Little bag, satchel, wallet. 2 Little sack. 3 Little blister. 4 Belly. 5 Calf of the leg. 6 Tubercle. 7 Middle part of the body, waist.
balganach,†† *a.* Belonging to a small bag, blister, calf of the leg, &c.
balgan-beice
——**-beiceach,**‡ } see caochag.
——**-beucan,***
——**-iongrach,** *s.m.* Cyst.
——**-losgainn,**‡ *s. m.* Truffle, *tuber cibarium* 2 Subterraneous ball-like bodies, something like potatoes, found in Glenlyon.

17. *Balgan-losgainn.*

——**-péiteach,** *s.m.* see caochag.
——**-séididh,** *s. m.* Small pair of bellows. 2 see caochag.
——**-snàmha,** *s.m.* Air-bladder in fishes.
——**-suain,** ** *s.m.* Sleeping-bag. Chuir iad am balgan-suain fo'n ceann, *they have put the sleepy-bag under their heads* (applied to a person who sleeps too much.)
——**-uisge,** *s.m.* Water-bubble. 2** Blister full of watery humour.
balg-bannaig,(AC) *s.m.* Bannock-bag. 2 The sacred shrine in which the Host was carried. 3 The bag in which the gifts of Christmas, Easter, and other sacred seasons were placed. It is now used to carry the various kinds of food-stuffs given to carollers at Christmas and the New Year.
balg-beice,†† *s.m.* Fuzzball, sponge mushroom.
——**-bhonn,** *s.m.* Pneumatic tyre of a cycle.
——**-bhronnach,** *a.* Swag-bellied. Balach beag *b., a swag-bellied little churl.*

18. *Balg-bhuachair.*

balg-bhuachaill, *s.m.* see balg-bhuachair.
balg-bhuachair,‡ builg-, *s.m.* Mushroom—*agaricus campestris.* 2**Toad-stool, "puddock-" stool.
balg-chasach, *a.* Bow-legged, bandy-legged.
balg-dhubh, -uibhe, *a.* Cloudy, dark, gloomy.
balg dubh,§ *s.m.* Large fuzzball. see beach.
balg-iongrach, *s.m.* Abscess.
balg-losgainn, builg-, see balgan-losgainn.
balg-meadhoin,‡‡ *s.m.* Waist, belly.
balg-péiteach, *s.m.* Puffball. see caochag.
balg-saighead, see balg-shaighde.
balg-séididh, *s.m.* Pair of bellows. 2 Puffball, see caochag.
balg-shaighde, *s.m.* Quiver.
balg-shuil, *s. f.* Large prominent eye.
——**each,** *a.* Having large, round, prominent eyes,
balg-smùid, *s.m.* Puffball, see caochag.
balg-snàmha,†† see balgan-snàmha.
balg-solair, -e, *s.m.* Magazine.
balg-thional, *s.m.* Wallet.
balgum, -uim, -an, see balgam.
†**ball,** *s.m.* Skull.
ball, buill, *s.m.* Member, limb. 2 Member of a society. 3 Male instrument of generation. 4 Any part of male or female dress. 5 Instrument, tool, implement. 6 Ball, globe. 7 Football. 8 Dance. 8 Spot or plot of ground. 10**Boss. 11‡‡ Stud, nail. 12**Bowl. 13 Cable, rope. Tha 'n deagh bhall aodaich agad an sin, *you have an excellent piece of dress there*; do 'n bhacach lùth nam ball, *strength of limbs to the lame* ; buill a' Chomuinn Ghàidhlig, *members of the Gaelic Society* ; aghaidh gach buill ceangailt' is fuasgailte, *the end of each rope bound and running loose—as the ship's tackling required* ; thug iad aghaidh am buill is an caman air, *they turned all their force against him*—lit. *turned their balls and shinty clubs on him.*
ball, (air ball) *adv.* Immediately, on the spot.
balla, *pl.* -achan, *s.m.* Wall. 2 Bulwark. 3** Boss of a shield.
balla-bacaidh, *s.m.* Wall of defence, bulwark.
ball-àbhachais, *s.m.* } Gazing stock. 2 Laugh-
ball-àbhachd, *s. f.* } ing stock. 3 Object of mockery.
ball-acfhuinn, *s.m.* Tool, instrument, tackling.
ballach, -aiche, *a.* Spotted, speckled. 2 Striped. 3**Tartan. 4 Walled, mural. 5 Having lofty walls. 6 Bossy, studded. An sgiath bhallach, *the bossy shield* ; bonaid bhallach, *a spotted or tartan bonnet.*

ballachd, *s. f.* Piedness. 2(JM) Dirty trick. **Rinn iad ballachd air**, *they played a dirty trick on him.*
ballach-muir,(AF) *s.m.* Rock-fish.
ball-acrach,* *s.m.* Cable.
balla-dealachaidh,** *s.m.* Partition-wall.
balladh, see balla.
ballag, -aig, -an, *s. f.* The cranium, skull. 2 Egg-shell. 3 Neat little woman. 4 *f. dimin.* of ball.
ballag-losgainn, see balgan-losgainn.
ballaich, *v.a.* Spot, speckle. 2 Stain, discolour.
——te, *pt. part.* Spotted.
ballail, *a.* Parietal.
ball-aimhleis, *s.m.* Unruly member, instrument of mischief.
ball-aimlisge, see ball-aimhleis.
ballaire, } Common cormorant. see
ballaire-bòthain, } sgarbh.
ball-airm, *s.m.* Weapon.
ball-airneis, *s.m.* Piece of furniture.
ballairt, *gen. sing.* of ballart.
ball-amharc, *s.m.* Spy-glass. **Buill-amharc**, *a pair of spectacles.*
ballan, -ain, -an, *s.m.* Shell. 2 Covering. 3 Bucket. 4 Tub. 5 Any wooden vessel. 6 Teat. 7 Cupping-glass. 8**Churn. 9 Broom. 10 Balsam. 11 Tub, trough. ††vat. 12(CM) Udder—*Arran.* **A' cur nam ballan**, *applying the cups* ; **ballan basmuinn**, *reviving balsam.*
ballan-bainne, *s.m.* Milk-tub.
——-binnteachaidh, *s.m.* Cheese-vat.
——-binntiche, *s.m.* see b—binnteachaidh. 2(AC) Cheese-press.
——-blàthaich, *s.m.* Butter-milk tub.
——-bùirn, *s.m.* Water-tub.
——-iocshlaint, (AC) *s.m.* Vessel of healing in which, according to the old Gaelic tales, was kept the balsam for restoring to health and life those wounded or killed in battle.
——-losgainn, see balg-losgainn.
——-nigheachain, } *s.m.* Washing-tub.
——-nigheadaireachd, }
——-òir, (AF) *s.m.* (*lit.* gold spot) Wren.
——-seilcheig, *s.m.* Snail-shell.
——-stiallach *s.m.* A kind of pillory, used of old in the Highlands, for punishing liars and petty offenders. It was a sort of frame erected on a pillar, to which the culprit was tightly bound with a rope about the shoulders, by which he hung, exposed to the ridicule and maltreatment of passers by.
†**ballard**, see ballart.
ballart, -airt, *s.m.* Noisy boasting, fuss about one's family. 2 Clamour, turbulence. **Gun bhallart gun mhórchuis**, *without noise or boasting.*
——ach, -aiche, *s.* Noisy, turbulent, clamorous, troublesome. 2 Boastful. 3**Conspicuous.
——achd, *s. f. ind.* Proclamation. 2 Noise, clamour.
——achadh,** -aidh, *s.m.* Proclamation. 2 Act of proclaiming, bawling, or making a noise.
——adh,** -aidh, *s.m.* Proclamation.
——aich, *s. f.* Loud noise. 2 Howling, shouting, hooting. **Ciod a' *bh.* a th'ort?** *what are you howling at?*
——aich, *v.n.* Proclaim. 2 Howl, shout, hoot.
ball-bhreac, *a.* Variegated, chequered, spotted, grizzled. **A' bheatha bhall-bhreac**, *variegated life* ; **mar neulaibh *b.***, *like spotted clouds.* (cirro-cumulus.)
ball-bhreachd, see ball-bhreac.
ball-bùird, *s.m.* Butt, object of derision.
ball-bùirte, see ball-bùird.
ball-cainb,* *s.m.* Hempen rope.
ball-chrith, *s. f. ind.* Trembling. 2 Terror. 3 Tremor of the limbs. 4 Trembling with terror. 5**Chilliness.
——each, *a.* Trembling.
ball-chruinn, *a.* Round-limbed. 2 Round-spotted.
ball-cluaise, *s.m.* Sheet (rope) of a sail.
ball-cogaidh, *s.m.* Warlike instrument.
ball-coise, *s. f.* Football.
ball-deise, *s.m.* Instrument to which two persons have a right. 2 Tool 3 Any useful instrument or weapon. 4 see ball-fearais.
ball-dhearg, *a.* Grizzled. 2 Bay-coloured. **Eich bhall-dhearg**, *bay horses.*
ball-dìmeis, *s.m.* Object of contempt.
ball-dìomhair, *s.m.* Private member. 2‡‡Useful instrument. **Na buill-dhìomhair**, *the private members.*
ball-dòbhrain,‖ *s.m.* Mole on the skin.
ball-donais, *s.m.* Pettifogger.
ball-dubh,* *s.m.* Black spot. 2**Blot, blemish.
ball-fanaid, see ball-fanoid.
ball-fanoid, *s.m.* Laughing-stock, object of derision.
ball-fàitheam,(AH) *s.m.* Bolt-rope.
ball-faobhrach,** -aich, *s.m.* Sharp-edged instrument.
ball-fearais, *s.m.* Membrum virile.
ball-fochaid,** *s.m.* Laughing-stock, object of derision.
ball-gaoir,(AH) *s.m.* Object of disdain, object of universal remark and gossip.
ball-ghalar, -air, *s.m.* Plague. 2 Gonorrhœa.
ball-gobhfa, *s.m.* Golf-ball.
ball-iomachair,** *s.m.* Support, prop. 2 Undersetter.
ball-iomair, *s.m.* Foot-ball.
ball-làimhe,‡‡ *s.m.* Hand-ball.
ball-langais,(AH) *s.m.* Towing-rope.
ball-langastaiche, *s.m.* " "
ball-leithir,‡‡ *s.m.* Leather ball.
†**ball-loisgteach**, *s.m.* Lobster.
ball-magaidh, *s.m.* Laughing-stock, bject of derision.
ball-maise, *s.m.* Ornament.
ball-maslaidh,‡‡ *s.m.* Object of derision.
ball-mosglaidh,** *s.m.* Instrument for sounding an alarm.
ball-nasg,‡‡ *s.m.* Joint. 2**Ligament connecting the bones at the joints to prevent dislocation.
ball-oibre,** *s.m.* Tool to work with.
ball-òir, see ballan-òir.
ball-òtraiche,** *s.m.* Puddle, slough. 2 Miry place.
ball-roghnachaidh, ** *s.m.* Ballot.
ball-sampuill,* *s.m.* Example, specimen. 2‡‡ Spectacle of shame.
ball-seirce, *s.m.* Beauty-spot.
†**ballsg**, *s.m.* Blot, spot, freckle.
ballsgach,***a.* Burlesque. **Cainnt *b.***, *burlesque.*
ballsgair, -ean, *s.m.* Giddy, foolish person.
——eachd, *s. f. ind.* Sallies of folly, any kind of silly ridiculous folly.
ball-sgeig,** *s.m.* Laughing stock, object of derision.
ball-sgéimhe, *s.m.* Beauty-spot.
ball-sgiath, -eithe, *s. f.* Bossy shield. **Fionn nam *b.***, *F. of bossy shields.*
ball-sgiorradh, -aidh, *s.m.* Deed done unexpectedly. 2**Feat.
ball-sgiorrail, *a.* Performing unexpected deeds.
ball-sgòid, *s.m.* Rope. 2**Spot, blemish. 3‡‡ Blister.
ball-sgot, see ball-sgòid.

ball-sinnsearachd, *s.m.* Old article of family furniture. 2 Heir-loom.
ball-spéil,* *s.m.* Hand-ball.
ball-spòrs,* *s.m.* Laughing-stock.
ball-taghaidh,** *s.m.* Ballot.
ball-tairgne, -uill-, *s.m.* Tackle. 2 Halliard.
ball-tàmailt, *s.m.* Object of disgrace or reproach Tha thu ad' bhall-tàmailt, *thou art an object of disgrace.*
ball-tarruing,‡‡ *pl.* buill-, *s.m.* Tackle.
ball-toirmisg, *s.m.* Forbidden tool or weapon. 2 Obstruction. 3‡‡Detestable object. 4(JM) Man to be avoided.
balluich, *v.a.* see ballaich.
†**balma**, *s.m.* Balm.
†——ich, *v.a.* Embalm.
†**bal-seirc**, *s.m.* Carver at a prince's table. 2 Master of ceremonies at high feasts. 3 Herald.
balt, -uilt, -an, *s.m.* Welt of a shoe. 2 Border, belt. 3 Selvidge of cloth. Balt nan sùl, *the eyelids.*
baltach, *a.* Belted, welted, bordered.
——adh,** -aidh, *s.m.* Skirting.
†**baltadh**, *pl.* -aidhe, *s.m.* Welts, fetters, borders.
baltaich. *v.a.* Welt, belt, border.
bamhsgach,(AH) *a.* Restless. 2 Erratic.
bamhsgaire(AH) *s.m.* Restless, unreliable fellow.
——achd,(AH) *s. f. ind.* Restlessness. 2 Unreliability.
†**ban**, -ain, *s.m.* Copper. 2 Copper mine. 3 Brass. 4‡‡Foot, pedestal.
bàn, -âine, *a.* White, pale, light in colour, wan, fair, fair-haired. 2 Vacant, waste. 3‡‡True. Eich bhàna, *white horses ;* talamh b., *waste ground.*
bàn, -àin, *s.m.* Left-hand side of furrow in ploughing, as distinguished from the "dearg" (red) right-hand side. 2** Matrix of a cow. 3(JM) Fallow ground.
ban, *gen. pl.* of bean.
ban- (female, she-.) A prepositive in compounds usually pronounced *bana* before labials (B, M,P) and palatals (C,G) ; but *ban* before linguals (L, N, R) dentals (D, T, S) and labial F. Fàidh, *a prophet ;* ban-fhàidh, *a prophetess ;* gaisgeach, *a hero,* bana-ghaisgeach, *a heroine ;* caraid, *a relation,* bana-charaid, *a female relation.* *Ban* must be prefixed in speaking of a female's country, as, Bana-Ghàidheal, *a Highland woman;* Ban-Albannach, *a Scotswoman ;* Ban-Fhrangach, *a Frenchwoman ;* Ban-Duitseach, *a Dutchwoman.*
ban-aba, -achan, *s. f.* Abbess.
bana-bharan, -ain, *s. f.* Baroness.
bana-bhàrd, -àird, *s. f.* Poetess.
——achd, *s. f.* Verses of a bardess.
†**bana-bhiocais**, *s. f.* Viscountess.
bana-bhuachaille, -an, *s. f.* Shepherdess. 2 Female who tends sheep or cattle.
bana-bhuachailleachd, *s. f.* Business or condition of a shepherdess.
bana-bhuidseach, -sich, -sichean, *s. f.* Witch, sorceress.
bana-bhusdraich,** Witch, sorceress.
bànachadh, -aidh, *s.m.* Whitening, bleaching. 2 Growing pale. 3 Laying waste. A' b—, *pr. part.* of bànaich.
bàn-achadh,‡‡ -aidh, -nean, *s.m.* Waste field.
banachag, -aig, -ean, *s. f.* Dairymaid. 2‡‡ Milker.
banachaigeachd, *s. f. ind.* Business of a dairymaid, the making or preparing of dairy produce. 2 Office of a dairymaid.
bana-channtair,** *s.m.* Chantress.
bana-chara, see bana-charaid.
bana-charaid, -chàirdean, *s.f.* Female relative, kinswoman.
bànachd, *s.f.* Whiteness, paleness, fairness.
banachdach, *s. f.* Vaccination. [Preceded by the article *a'*.]
bana-cheard, *s. f.* Female gipsy or tinker. 2 *in contempt,* Mannerless female.
bana-chéile, see bean-chéile.
bana-chéileadair, -ean, *s. f.* Executrix. 2 Female guardian.
bana-chleasaiche, *s. f.* Actress.
bana-chle'in, see bana-chliamhuinn.
bana-chliamhuinn, *s. f.* Daughter-in-law. 2** sister-in-law, brother's wife or a wife's sister. 3‡‡Any female relation by marriage.
†**bana-chliaraiche**, -ean, *s. f.* Songstress.
bana-chòcaire, -ean, *s. f.* Female cook, cook maid.
bana-chòcaireachd, *s. f.* Business of a female cook. 2 Handiwork of a female cook. Tha i ag ionnsachadh na *b.*, *she is learning cookery.*
bana-choigle, *s. f.* Female gossip or companion.
bana-choigreach, -rich, *s. f.* Female stranger, strange woman.
†**bana-chointeach**, *s. f.* Waiting maid.
bana-chòmhdhalta, *s.f.* Foster-sister.
bana-chompanach, -aich, *s. f.* Female companion.
bana-chompanas, -ais, *s.m.* Female companionship. Na dean *b.* rithe, *do not associate with her.*
†**bana-chonganta**, (bean-chòmhnuidh) Midwife.
banachrach,‖ *s. f.* Small-pox. [Preceded by the article a'.]
bàn-chraicneach,‡‡ -eiche, *a.* White or fair-skinned.
bana-chrìosdaidh, *s. f.* Female Christian.
bana-chruitear, -e, -ean, *s. f.* Female harper, female minstrel.
bana-chuisleanaiche *s. f.* Female performer on a wind-instrument, female piper.
bana-churadair,* *s. f.* Executrix. 2 Female guardian.
bana-churaidh, *s. f.* Amazon.
†**bànadh**, *s.m.* Wasting,
ban-adhaltraiche, see ban-adhaltranach.
ban-adhaltranach, -aiche, *s. f.* Adultress.
bànag, -aig, -an, *s. f.* Grilse. 2 Anything white. 3 White-faced girl. 4** Cant term for a shilling.
banag, -aig, -an, *s. f.* Smart little woman.
bana-ghaisge, *s. f.* Surprising feats of a female.
bana-ghaisgeach, -eich, *s. f.* Heroine. 2 Female warrior.
bana-ghoistidh, -ean, *s. f.* God-mother.
bana-ghrùdair, *s. f.* Landlady of an ale-house or inn. 2 Female brewer. 3 Hostess. Cagar na *b.*, *the ale-wife's whisper* (soon turns loud.)
ban-aibhistear, -ir, -ean, *s. f.* She-devil.
bànaich, *v. a.* & *n.* Whiten, make pale, bleach. 2 Grow pale. 3**Make waste or vacant.
bànaiche, -ean, *s.m.* The outer of two ploughing horses.
bànaidh, *a.* Sallow, pale.
banail, -e, *a.* Modest, womanly, feminine, delicate. 2 Comely, elegant. A bhean bhanail, *his modest wife.*
†**banailt**, *s. f.* Nurse.
banair, -e, -ean, see mainnir.
ban-àireach, see banarach.
banais, bainnse, *pl.* bainnsean, *s. f.* Wedding-feast. Fear na bainnse, *the bridegroom ;* bean na bainnse, *the bride ;* culaidh bainnse, *a wedding dress.*
banais-mhagaidh,(JM) *s. f.* Mock wedding. [At one time common in Uist.]

banais-pheighinn,‡‡ *s.f.* Penny wedding.
†**banaiteach**,** *a.* Serious. grave, sedate.
banal, see banail.
banalachd, *s. f.* Female modesty, behaviour becoming a female.
banalas, see banalachd.
banaltrachd, *s. f.* Nursing. 2 Business of a nurse. Mach air *bh.*, *out at nursing.*
banaltradh, -aidh, *s. f.* see banaltrum.
banaltraich,* *v.a.* Nurse.
banaltruim,* *v.a.* Nurse.
banaltrum, -uim, *s f.* Nurse.
banaltrumachd, see banaltrachd.
banaltrumas, „ „ „
bana-mhaighstir, -ean, *s. f.* Mistress. 2 Female who employs one or more servants. 3 School-mistress.
bana-mhaighstireas, -eis, *s.m.* Rule of a mistress.
bana-mhàlta, *a.* Shamefaced, modest, bashful.
bana-mhàltachd, *s. f.* Shamefacedness, bashfulness, modesty.
bana-mharcaiche, *s. f.* Female rider.
bana-mharcair,** see bana-mharcaiche.
bana-mharcus, -uis, -uisean, *s. f.* Marchioness.
bana-mharsanta.* *s. f.* Female merchant.
bana-mheirleach, *s. f.* Female thief.
bana-mhisgear, *s.f.* Female drunkard.
bana-mhorair, -ean, *s. f.* Lady. 2 Wife of a lord or baronet. 3 Countess.
bana-mhormhair, see bana-mhorair.
bana-mhortair, *s. f.* Murderess.
bana-phrionnsa, *s. f.* Princess.
†**ban-ara**, *s. f.* Maid-servant.
banarach, -aich, *s. f.* Dairymaid, milkmaid.
banarachas, -ais, *s.m.* Office of a dairymaid or milkmaid.
ban-asal, -ail, *s.f.* She-ass. (*asal boirionn.*)
banasgal, see †bansgal.
banas-taighe, *s. f.* Female occupations, housewifery.
banbh, bainbh, *s.m.* Land unploughed for a year. †2 Pig.
banbhan, see banbh.
bàn-bhroilleach, *a.* White-bosomed. Còmhnuidh nam bàn-bhroilleach òigh, *the dwelling of the white-bosomed maids.*
ban-bhusdraich, see bana-bhusdraich.
banc, -ainc, -an, *s.m.* see bailc.
banc, -a, *pl.* -an, & -annan, *s.m.* Gaelic spelling of *bank*, (*taigh-réidh. bailc.*)
bancach, see bailceach.
bancaid, see bangaid.
bancair, *s.m.* Gaelic spelling of *banker.*
ban-chag,
ban-charaid, } see bana-ch—.
ban-chèard,
ban-chéile, see bean-chéile.
ban-cheileadair,
ban-chliamhuinn,
†**ban-chliaraiche**,
ban-chòcaire,
ban-chocaireachd
ban-choigle,
ban-choigreach, } see bana-ch—.
†**ban-chointeach**,
ban-chòmhdhalta,
ban-chompanach,
ban-chompanas,
†**ban-chonganta**,
bàn-chraicneach, -eiche, *a.* White-skinned, fair-skinned.
ban-chruitear, see bana-chruitear.
bàn-chruthach, *a.* Pale-complexioned, pale, wan.
bàn-chu, -choin, *s.m.* White dog. 2‡‡Illustrious hero.

†**bàn-chuir**, *s. f. ind.* Sea-sickness where no eructation is produced.
ban-chuisleanaiche, see bana-ch—.
ban-churadair, } see bana-ch—.
ban-churaidh,
†**banda**, *a.* Female, feminine, modest.
bandachd, *s. f. contr.* for baindeachd.
bandaidh, *a.* see baindidh.
———eachd, see baindeachd.
ban-dalta, -achan, *s. f.* Foster-daughter.
ban-dalta-baistidh, *s. f.* God-daughter.
bàn-dhearg, *a.* Pink.
ban-dia, *gen.s.* bain-dé, *pl.* -dée & -diathan, *s.f.* Goddess. A' bhan-dia a ni am bogha-frois, *the goddess that forms the rainbow* ; ach mar an ceudna gu'n cuirear teampull na ban-dé móire Diana an neo-phrìs, *but also that the temple of the great goddess Diana should be despised.*
ban-diabhol, -oil, *s.f.* Female devil, or fury.
ban-diùc, -an, *s.f.* Duchess.
ban-draoidh, see ban-druidh.
ban-druidh, *s.f.* Enchantress. sorceress.
ban-drùncair, see bana-mhisgear.
ban-dubhairiche, *s.f.* Dowager.
†**ban-duileamhuin**,‡‡ *s.f.* Goddess.
ban-éigneachadh, -aidh,** *s.m.* Rape.
ban-fhàidh, -e, -ean, *s.f.* Prophetess. Agus ghlac Miriam, a' bhan-fhàidh, tiompan 'na làimh, *and Miriam the prophetess took a timbrel in her hand.*
†**ban-fheadanach**, -aiche, *s.f.* Female piper. 2 Female who plays any wind instrument.
ban-fhigheach, -iche, -ichean, *s.f.* Female weaver. 2 Female who knits. [Pronounced *baineach.*]
ban-fhigheadair, see ban-fhigheach.
ban-fhigheadaireachd, *s.f.ind.* Work or occupation of a female weaver.
ban-fhiosaiche, -chean, *s.f.* Fortune-teller. 2 Prophetess. 3 Gipsy.
ban-fhlath, -aith, -ean, *s.f.* Chief's wife. 2 Heroine. 3***pl.* Ladies.
ban-fhluasg, *s.m.ind.* see ban-fhluasgadh.
ban-fhluasgach, *a.* Menstrual.
ban-fhluasgadh, -aidh, *s.m.* Menstrual courses.
ban-fhuadach, -aich, *s.m.* Fornication.
————d, *s. f. ind.* Rape. 2 Forcibly carrying off a woman.
ban-fhuaighealachd, *s. f.* Sewing, business of a sempstress or milliner, millinery. [Pronounced *banalachd.*]
ban-fhuaighealaiche, -ean, *s. f.* Sempstress, milliner. [Pronounced *banalaiche.*]
ban-fhuineadair, *s.f.* Female baker. 2 Female cook.
bang,* *s. f. ind.* Drum. A' toirt fuaim á *b.*, *making a drum-beat masterly.*
†**bang**,‡‡ *s.m.* Nut. 2 The touch. 3 Hinderance. 4 Reaping.
†———, *v.a.* Bind, obtain a promise.
bangadh, -aidh, *s.m.* Binding, promise.
bangaid, Gaelic spelling of *banquet.*
———each,** *a.* Banqueting. 2 Fond of banqueting.
———eachd, *s.f.ind.* Continued banqueting.
ban-ghaisgeach, see bana-ghaisgeach.
†**banghal**, *s.m.* Female heroism.
bàn-gheal,‡‡ -ile, *a.* Milk-white, dead white.
bàn-ghlas, *comp.* bàin-ghlaise, *a.* Pale, wan, ashy (colour.)
ban-ghoistidh, see bana-ghoistidh.
ban-ghrùdair, see bana-ghrùdair.
bàn-ghucach, -aich, *s. f.* The small-pox.
ban-iarla, -iarlan, *s. f.* Countess.
ban-iasg, (AF) *s. f.* Female or spawning fish.
———air, -e, -ean, *s. f.* Fisherwoman.

ban-ifrinneach, *s. f.* Fury, turbulent, raging woman.
ban-iofarnach, see ban-ifrinneach.
ban-iompair,‡‡ *s. f.* Empress.
ban-iutharnach, *s. f.* see ban-ifrinneach.
ban-laoch, -laoich, *s. f.* Heroine. 2 Amazon. 3 Virago.
ban-léigh, -e, -ean, *s. f.* Female physician.
ban-leòghann, *s. f.* Lioness.
ban-leòmhann, see ban-leòghann.
bàn-leus, -leois, *s.m.* Thin white cloud.
ban-lighich, -e, -ean, *s, f.* Female doctor.
†bàn-mhac, *s.m.* Son-in-law.
ban-mhaighstir, ———eachd, ———eas, ban-mharcaiche, ban-mharcus, } see bana-mh——.
†bàn-mhathair, *s. f.* Mother-in-law.
ban-mhorair, see bana-mhorair.
ban-mhortair, see bana-mhortair.
bann, bainne [& boinne] *pl.* bannan, banntan [& boinn,] *dat.pl.* bannaibh&-taibh,*s.m.* Belt, girth, sash. 2 Bond, bill. 3 Tie, key-stone. 4 Hinge. 5 Band, as of a shirt or any article of clothing. 5**Band of men. 6 Band of music. 7 Chain, fetter,cord. 8 Bann. 9**Interdict. 10 Proclamation. 11 Sling. 12** Death. 13‡‡ Ball. 14**Marching, journeying. 15 Brace in writing (⏜) Bann an doruis, *the door-hinge* ; théid mis' am bannaibh dhuit, *I can assure you* ; na boinn a b'àill leo iadhadh oirnn, *the cords with which they would wish to surround us* ; cuir boinn anns a' bhalla, *put key-stones in the wall ;* a' ceangal bhann mu sguaban, *binding sheaves*; a' fuaigheal bhann, *sewing bands* ; le banntaibh daingeann, *with firm bands ;* bannan bhur cuinge, *the bonds of your yoke.*
bann,* *v.a.* Bind, tie, band. 2 Fix with key-stones, Balla air a dheagh bhannadh, *a wall well secured with key-stones.*
bann,** *a.* High.
†banna, *s.m.pl.* Band, troop.
†bannach, *a.* Active. 2 Expert. 3 Crafty. 4‡‡ Actual.
†———, *s.m.* Crafty person. 2 *in ridicule* Fox. 3 see bonnach.
†———d, *s. f.* Craftiness, deceit.
bannag, -aig, *s. f.* New-year's gift. 2 Treat given to one on his first visit on New-year's day. 3 New-year's cake. 4‡‡ Yule cake. 5 Corn-fan. 5(AH) Ball used in shinty. Là nam bannag, *the day before Christmas Day* ; oidhche nam bannag, *the night before Christmas* ; Mo *bh.* ort ! *a method of asking a New-year's cake ;* is mairg a rachadh air a *bh.*, agus a theann-shàth aige-fhéin, *'twere pitiful to go begging bannocks, with plenty of one's own.*
Bannag,(AC) *s.f.ind.* The Eucharist.
†bannair,‡‡ *s.m.* Ingrafter.
bannal, -ail, -an, *s.m.* Assemblage. 2 Bad company. 3 Troop, band, covey. 4 Crowd of women. 5 Gathering, collection. Am *b.* uchd-ruadh, *the red-breasted covey.*
———ach, *a.* In companies, troops or crowds.
———as,** -ais, *s.m.* Association.
——— dannsaidh,** *s.m.* Ball.
bann-amh'cha,(AH) *s.f.* Neck-band of a shirt.
ban-naomh, -naoimh,§ *s. f.* Female saint. 2 Nun. 3 Saintly female.
bannas, -ais, *s.m.* Roof of the mouth.
bann-bhràghad, -aid,-ean,§*s.m.* Cravat, neck-tie. 2 (AH) Front band of a woollen or cotton shirt, extending from the neck downwards and containing the front button-holes.
bann-bhràighe,** *s.m.* Cape.
bann-cèirde, -an-, *s.m.* Deed of Indenture.
bann-cheangail, *v.a.* Bind by bond, article.
———, bannan-, *s. m.* Obligatory bond, cautionary bond.
banndair, see banntair.
banndalach, *a.* Foppish.
bann-dùirn, bannan-, *s. m.* Wrist-band. *B.* léine, *the wrist-band of a shirt.*
ban-nigh,(AC) *s. f.* Water-wraith.
bann-iomlaid, *s.m.* Bill.
bann-làmh, *s. m.* Cubit. 2 Handcuff. 3‡‡ Fathom. Aon *bh.*, *one cubit.*
bann-muineal,** *s.m.* Collar.
†bannrach, *s.m.* see banrach.
†bannsach, -aich, -aichean, *s.m.* Arrow. 2 Any sharp-pointed missile weapon.
bann-sgrìobhadh, *s.m.* Indenture.
†bann-shampla, *s.m.* Example.
bann-saoirseach, see bann-saor.
bann-saor, *a.* Free by law, licensed, authorized.
———sachd, *s. f.* Condition of being free by law or bond, freedom from obligation.
———sadh, -aidh, *s.m.* Freedom or liberty sanctioned by law or bond, manumission.
———saich, *v.a.* License, make free.
bann-seilbhe, *s. f.* Deed of infeftment.
bann-sorn, -oirn, *s. m.* Kind of griddle or baking stove.
banntach, -aich, -aichean, *s. f.* Hinge. 2 Bond, obligation.
banntaich,** *v.a.* Article, bind.
banntair,** -ean, *s.m.* Covenanter, drawer up of bills or bonds, contractor.
———eachd,** *s. f.* Covenant-making, confederacy.
bann-taisbeanaidh, *s.m.* Bond of appearance, bail-bond.
bann-tarsuing, *s.m.* Bend *in heraldry* (representing a shoulder-belt.)
19. Bann-tarsuing.
banntrach, see bantrach.
———as, see bantrachas.
ban-ogha, *s. f.* Grand-daughter. Ban-ogha 'n ogha, *the grand-son's grand-daughter* ; ban-ogha 'n iar ogha, (nighinn mhic, [*or* nighinn nighinn]an iar ogha), *the great-grand-son's grand-daughter.*
ban-òglach, -aich,*s. f.* Female servant, maid-servant, hand-maiden. 2 Maiden. 3 Female slave. Do bhan-òglaich, *thy maidens.*
banoglach, see ban-òglach.
ban-oidhre, see ban-oighre.
ban-oighre, -oighrean, *s. f.* Heiress.
———achd, *s. f.* Estate that goes to heirs female.
ban-oirchisiche,** *s.f.* Benefactress.
ban-òranaiche,** *s. f.* Chantress.
ban-phrionnsa, see bana-phrionnsa.
†banrach, -aich, *s.m.* Fold for sheep, pen. 2 Cow-house. 3‡‡Shift, smock.
†banraich, *v.a.* Pen, shut up.
ban-ridir, -e, -ean, *s. f.* Baroness, wife of a knight or baronet.
ban-rìgh, *s. f.* Queen. Màiri, ban-rìgh na h-Alba, *Mary, Queen of Scotland* ; *b.* Bhreatuinn, *the Queen of Great Britain.*
ban-righinn, -righinnean, *s. f.* Queen. Port na ban-righinn, *Queensferry, in the Firth of Forth.*
bànrinn, see ban-righinn.
banscar, see bansear.
ban-sealgair, -e, -ean, *s. f.* Huntress.
ban-sear, ban-searrach, } (AF) *s. f.* Filly.
ban-seirbhiseach, *s. f.* Female servant.

†bansgal, -ail, -alan, *s. f.* Aged female, often applied as a term of reproach. 2(AC) Unmarried woman. 3(AC) Masculine woman, amazon. 4(AC) Whale, leviathan.

†———, *a.* Effeminate, womanish.

bansglach, see ban-òglach.

bàn-sgoth,** *s.m.* Son-in-law.

ban-searrach, -aich, *s. f.* Mare-foal.

ban-sith, *s. f.* Female fairy. It was believed by the Highlanders of old that the wailings of this being were frequently heard before the death of a chieftain. She seldom made her appearance, but when she did, it was in a green mantle with dishevelled hair.

ban-sniomhaiche, -ean, *s. f.* Spinster.

ban-solaraiche, -ean, *s. f.* Cateress.

†ban-spiorag, -aig, -agan, *s. f.* Sparrow-hawk.

ban-stiùbhart, -airt, -an, *s. f.* Housekeeper.

——— ———achd, *s. f.* Office or business of a housekeeper.

†banta, *s. f.* Niece.

bàn-talamh,‡‡ -mhainn, *s.m.* Lea ground.

ban-tighearn, *s. f.* see baintighearna.

———ail, *a.* see baintighearnail (in appendix.)

bantrach, -aich, -aichean, *s. f.* Widow. 2 *s.m.* Widower. Do *bh.* mar eun tiamhaidh, *thy widow like a lonely bird;* is olc a' bhantrach a' phìob, *the bagpipe is a poor widow* (suggestive of the improvidence of pipers) ; is *b.* i, *she is a widow ;* is *b.* e, *he is a widower.*

———as, -ais, *s.m.* Widowhood. 2 Living in widowhood.

†———d, *s. f. ind.* Company of women.

ban-traill, -e, -ean, *s. f.* Female slave, bondmaid. 2 Maid-servant. Ceud-ghin na bantràille, *the first-born of the bond-maid.*

ban-treabhach, see bantrach.

ban-tuathanach, -aich, -aichean, *s. f.* Female who farms. 2 Farmer's wife. 3 Peasant's wife.

——— ———as, -ais, *s.m.* Agriculture done by, or under the direction of, a female.

ban-tuathanaich, *gen. sing.* of ban-tuathanach.

——— ———ean, *n. pl.* of „ „

†bànughadh, *s.m.* Waxing pale.

bao', see baobh & baoth.

baobach,* *s. f.* Panic, terrible fright. 2 Female easily frightened.

———,* *a.* Panic-struck, terribly afraid.

baobair,* -e, -ean, *s.m.* Panic-struck man. 2 Man easily frightened.

baobh, -aoibh, baobhan, *s. f.* Wizard. 2 Wicked mischievous female, who invokes a curse or some evil on others. 3 Foolish, disagreeable female. 4 She-spirit supposed to haunt rivers. Càineam agus aoiream a' *bh.* a rinn an t-óran, *let me satirize and lampoon the furious woman that made the song* ; eadar a' bhaobh is a' bhuarach, *a dilemma—referring to the superstition that a blow from a "buarach" renders childless ;* gheibh baobh a guidhe ged nach fhaigh a h-anam tròcair, *a wicked woman will get her wish though her soul get no mercy.*

———achd, *s. f.* Conduct of a mischievous, foolish or wicked woman. 2**Croaking of a raven.

———ag, *dimin.* of baobh.

———aidh, see baobhail.

———ail, -e, *a.* Wicked. 2 Savage, fierce, mad, wild, furious. 3 Foolish. 4 Destructive. 5**Fearful. 6††Pertaining to a wizard or hag. Dearg nam feachd *b.*, *Dargo of destructive hosts* ; buillean trom, *b.*, *heavy fearful blows.*

———aileachd, *s. f. ind.* Madness, wildness, furiousness. 2 Destructiveness, direfulness. 3**Fearfulness.

———alachd, see baobhaileachd.

———anta, *a.* Elfish.

baodh, see baoth.

baodhail, *a.* see baoghalta.

baodhaire, see baothaire.

———achd, see baothaireachd.

baodhaiste,†† *s.m.* Hardship, trouble. 2 Rough usage or fatigue through bad weather.

———achadh, see baodhaiste.

baodhaistich,* *v.a.* Drench, give a miserable appearance. 2 Spoil one's clothes in bad weather.—*Isles.*

baodhan, *s.m.* see baoghan, & baothan.

———ach, see baoghanach & baothanach.

baodhannach,(AF) *s.m.* Elk, moose deer.

†baodrod, *s.m.* Scolding.

baogadh, -aidh, *s.m.* Sudden start.

baogaid,* *s. f.* Whim, caprice.

———each,* *a.* Whimsical, capricious, odd, fanciful.

———each,* *s. f.* Fanciful, whimsical female.

———eachd,* *s. f.* Whimsicality, fancifulness, oddity, capriciousness.

baogh, -aoigh, see baobh.

———air, see baothair.

baoghal, -ail, *s.m.* Peril, danger. 2 Crisis. 3 Matter of consequence from its bad effects. 4(AH) Lull in a storm. 5(AH) Favourable opportunity. Uisge-beatha baoghal, *whiskey four times distilled* ; fear an t-saoghail fhada, cha bhi *b.* chuige, *nothing will cut short the life of the long liver.*

———ach, -aiche, *a.* Wild, furious, destructive. 2 Perilous, dangerous. 3**Adventurous. Roimh na gaothaibh *b.*, *before the perilous winds ;* lag ri uair *bh.*, *weak in the hour of danger* ; is *b.* am buille, *perilous is the blow.*

———achd, *s. f.* Danger, hazard.

———lan, -ain, *s.m.* Foolish fellow, cuddy, silly blockhead.

———lanachd, *s. f.* Behaviour of a stupid fellow, foolishness, stupidity.

———ta, *a.* Foolish, credulous, silly, idiotical, simple. Creididh an duine baoghalta, *the simple shall believe.*

———tachd, *s. f. ind.* Foolishness, credulousness, silliness, simpleness, idiocy.

baoghan, -ain, *s.m.* Anything bulky, or 2 Jolly. 3 Calf. 4 Young fool. Baoghan an cois gach bò, *each cow followed by a calf.*

———ach,** -aiche, *a.* Like a calf, of, or belonging to, a calf.

baoghlach, *a.* see baoghalach.

baoghlair,** *s.m.* Adventurer.

baoghlan, -ain, see baoghallan.

———achd, see baoghallanachd.

baogram,‡ -aim, *s.m.* Flighty emotion.

†baoil, *s. f.* Water. 2‡‡Madness.

———eag, *s. f.* Blaeberry.

baoireadh, -aidh, *s.m.* Foolish talk.

baois, *s. f.* Concupiscence, lust. 2 Levity, idle talk. 3 Madness.

———each, -siche, *a.* Lewd, lascivious, lustful. 2 Giddy.

———eachd, *s. f. ind.* Concupiscence, lust, lasciviousness,. 2 Levity. 3 Madness. Luchd baoiseachd, *lewd people.*

———eid, see boiseid.

baoisealachd, see baoiseachd.

baoiseil, *a.* see baoiseach.

baoisg, *v.n.* see boillsg.

baoisge, see boillsge.

baoisgeach, see boillsgeach.

baoisgeadh, see boillsgeadh.

baoisgeil, *a.* see boillsgeil.

baoisleach, -eich, *s.m.* House of revelry or riot. 2 Brothel. 3 Frequenter of brothels.

———d, see baoiseachd.

baoisteach, see baoisleach.
baoisteadh, see baoisleachd.
baoit,* *s. f.* Giddy, foolish female. 2 (JM) Bait.—*Lewis.*
baoite, see baghte.
baoiteadh, (AH) *s.m.* Spell of activity. 2 Act of making progress with a task or work.
baoiteag, -eige, *s. f.* see boiteag. 2 Bait for fishing.
——— -dhrùchda, *s.f.* Brandling.
baoith, *a.* see baoth.
baoithe, *s.f.* Airiness, foolishness, giddiness, lightness, levity. 2 Youthfulness.
———, *comp.* of baoth.
baol,* *s.m.* Approximation, nearness in doing anything.
baol,* *v.n.* Approach, or come near doing anything. Cha bhaol e air, *it will not come near it.*
baolach, see baoghalach.
baolum, -uim, *s. m.* Nearness. Théid mi 'shealg, is gheibh mi baolum ort, gar (ged) am marbh, *I shall go a-hunting, and will get near enough to master you although dead—Duanaire, p. 101.*
baor,(AC) *s.m.* (?beur) Sharp. Thig na baor, *the sharp will come.*
†**baos**, *s.m.* Fornication, lewdness. 2 Caprice. 3 Frenzy.
†——, *a.* Capricious, giddy.
——ach,** *a.* Wanton, capricious.
baosganta, -ainte, *a.* see babhsganta.
baosrach, -aich, *s.m.* Madness, fury.
———, -aiche, *a.* Mad, frantic.
baosradh,** -aidh, *s.m.* Vanity.
baoth, -aoithe, *a.* Foolish, simple, unwise, stupid. 2 Profane, wicked. 3 Wild, fierce. 4 Careless, giddy, regardless, unsteady. 5** Dreadful, horrid. 6**Youthful. 7**Vast. 8 **Soft. 9 **Useless. 10**Deaf. 11‡‡Mad. Baoth bheus, *immorality, folly;* baoth chreideamh, *superstition*; baoth shùgradh, *foolish and profane jesting*; baoth smuain, *a foolish thought*; fuaim bhaoth, *a horrid sound*; cho baoth ri t'airm, *as useless as thine arms*; an cunnart baoth, *in dreadful danger*; tional baoth an t-sluaigh, *the vast concourse of the people*; le sòlas baoth, *with giddy joy*; gheibh bean bhaoth dlùth gun cheannach, ach cha'n fhaigh i inneach, *a silly woman will get the warp without paying, but will not get the woof.* N.G.P.
baothachd, see baothaireachd.
baothail, -e, *a.* see baoth.
baothair, -ean, *s.m.* Simpleton, foolish fellow, idiot. 2**Calf. 3 (AF) Snipe. 4(JM) Foolish *or* immoral talker. Cha leannan *b.* thu, *said of one whose charms are more substantial than personal beauty*; is tu am baothair! *what a fool you are!*
baothaireach,‡‡ -aiche, Cullionly.
———d, *s. f.* Talk or conduct of a fool, stupidity, absurdity, foolishness.
baothairean, *n. pl.* of baothair.
baothan, -ain, *s.m.* Young fellow. 2 Blockhead.
———ach, *a.* Foolish, simple, silly. Gu baothanach, *foolishly.*
———achd, *s. f.* Foolishness, simpleness, silliness.
———tas, -ais, *s.m.* Same meanings as baothantachd.
baoth-bhallan, -ain, *s.m.* Fool.
baoth-bharaileach,‡‡ -aiche, *a.* Paradoxical.
baoth-bheus, -an, *s.m.* Immorality, improper conduct, misbehaviour.
———ach, *a.* Immoral. 2 Dishonest. Gu baoth-bheusach, *immorally.*
———an, *n.pl.* of baoth-bheus.
baoth-bhrìathar,** *s.m.* Blasphemy.
†**baoth-chaisgidh**, *a.* Riotous.
baoth-cheannach,‡‡ -aiche, *a.* Paradoxical.
baoth-chleasach,‡‡ -aiche, *a.* Pantomime.
baoth-chleasachd, *s. f.* Buffoonery, farce. 2 ††Immodest play.
baoth-chleasaidheachd, see baoth-chleasachd.
baoth-chluich,‡‡ -e, -ean, *s.m.* Farce.
baoth-choltas, -ais, *s.m.* Affectation.
baoth-chreideamh, *s.m.* Superstition. 2 Erroneous opinions in regard to religious matters. 3**Wild creed.
baoth-chreidmheach, *a.* Credulous. 2 Superstitious. 3**Professing a wild creed.
baoth-chreidmhiche, *s.m.* One who professes an extravagant or erroneous creed.
baoth-dhòchas,** *s.m.* Chimera.
baoth-ghlòir, -e, *s. f.* Foolish talk, rant, bombast.
baoth-leum, *s.m.* Fearful or dangerous leap. 2 Prancing, vaulting. 3**Bound.
———nach, *a.* Wildly leaping, proudly prancing. Each baoth-leumnach, *a proudly prancing horse.*
baoth-ràdh, *s.m.* Foolish or profane expression. 2**Idiotism.
———ach, *a.* Profane, impious, blasphemous. 2 Given to idle or foolish talking. An teanga baoth-ràdhach, *the profane tongue.*
baoth-shùgrach, *a.* Inclined to profane jesting. 2 Of, or pertaining to, a profane jest.
baoth-shùgradh, -aidh, *s.m.* Profane jesting. 2 Lascivious talk.
baoth-smuain, *s.f.* Foolish thought. 2 Maggot.
†**bar**, *a.* Expert, excelling.
†**bàr**, *s.m.* Son.
†**bàr**, -àir, *s.m.* Learned man. 2 Man. 3 Dart. 4 Bread. 5‡‡Crop, corn. 6‡‡Hero. 7 see bàrr.
†**bàr**, -àir & bàrach, *s.m.* The sea.
†**bara**, *v.n.* Go, march.
bara, (? barail) *s.* Thoughts, mind. Is misde baile fear is a' bhara ri falbh, *a township is the worse of a man who intends to leave.* [J.M. gives "bharra," and D.M. "bhrath" for *bhara.*]
bara, *pl.* -achan, *s.m.* Barrow. 2 Bier. †3‡‡Act of going or marching. Bara-rotha, *a wheelbarrow*; bara-làimhe, *a hand-barrow*; bara-bocsa, *a box-barrow*; chuir e bara dheth fhéin, *he tumbled himself.*
bàrach, *a.* see barrach.
†**bàrach**, *gen. sing.* of bàir, *the sea.*
barachdail,** *a.* Rife.
barag, see barrag.
baragan, see bargan.
baraig, see bairig.
barail, -e [& baralach], *pl.* baralaichean, *s.f.* Opinion, conceit. 2 Conjecture, guess. 3 Supposition. 4 Expectation. Tha mi 'm barail, *I suppose*; ma's math mo bharail-sa, *if I judge aright*; a réir mo bharaile, *to the best of my belief*; ciod e do bharail? *what do you think?* thoir dhomh do bharail, *give me your opinion*; is faoin do bharail, *vain is thy expectation*; thoir barail, *guess.*
———each, *a.* see baralach.
baraill, -e, -ean, *s.m.* Barrel, cask. 2 Barrel of a gun.
baraille, see baraill.
barailte, see baraille.
baraisd, -e, *s.m.* see barraisd.
———each, *a.* see barraisdeach.
baralach, *gen. sing.* of barail.
———, -aiche, *a.* Conjectural. 2 Hypothetical. 3 Opinionative, notional. Ro *bh.* 'na ghnìomh, *very conceited of his own doings.*—

Uist Bards.
——adh, -aidh, *s.m.* Conjecturing, guessing, supposing. A' b—, *pr.pt.* of baralaich.
baralaich, *pr.pt.* a' baralachadh. *v.a.* Guess, conjecture, think, suppose.
†baramhlach, *a.* Censorious.
baramhluich, *v.a.* see baralaich.
†baramhuil, *a.* (see barrail) Excellent.
baran, -ain, *s.m.* Baron.
——ach, *a.* Baronical.
——achd, *s.f.* Barony.
barandach, barandachadh, barandaich, barandail, } see barant—.
barandas, -ais, *s.m.* see barantas.
†barann, -ainn, *s.m.* Degree, step.
——aich, *v.a.* see barantaich.
barant, -an, *s.m.* Support, surety, safeguard. Is tu bu bharant dòchais dhomh, *thou wast the surety of my hope.*
——ach, -aiche, *a.* Warranting, warranted, warrantable. 2 Sure, certain, confident, assured.
barantachadh, -aidh, *s.m.* Warranting. 2 Warrant. A' b—, *pr.pt.* of barantaich.
barantadh,** -aidh, *s.m.* Warrant, commission.
barantaich, *pr.pt.* a' barantachadh, *v.a.* Warrant, give privilege. 2 Assure, confirm, make certain.
barantail, -e, *a.* Warrantable, lawful. 2 Reasonable.
barantas, -ais, *s.m.* Commission, warrant. 2 Confidence, security. 3 Authority. 4 Pledge, in pawning. 5** Docket. Barantas-glacaidh, *a warrant to apprehend.*
barasach, see barrasach.
†barath, *s.m.* Lying in wait.
†barba, -uirbe, *s.f.* Severity, passionateness, fierceness.
†bar-baile, see barr-bhalla.
barbair, Gaelic spelling of *barber.*
——eachd (*barber*) *s. f.* Business of a barber or hair-dresser.
barbarra, see borbarra.
bar-bhrigein,‡ see brisgean.
bar-brag,‡‡ -aig *s.m.* Tangle-tops cast ashore in May.
barbrag,§ -aig, *s. f.* Barberry—*berberis vulgaris.*
bar-brisgein, *s.m.* see brisgean.
bàrc, -àirc & bàrca, -annan, *s. f.* Bark, boat, skiff. 4 Barque. 3 Billow. 4 †Book. Chunnacas bàrc, *a skiff was seen ;* bàrc bréid-gheal, *a white-sailed boat.*
bàrc, *v.a.* Rush. 2 Burst forth, burst out. 3**Embark.
——ach, -aiche, *a.* Rushing in torrents.

20. *Barbrag.*

——achadh, see barcachd.
——achd, *s. f.* Embarkation.
——adh, -aidh, s.m. Rushing or pouring impetuously, as waves. A' b—, *pr.pt.* of bàrc. Muir mhòr a' bàrcadh mu'm cheann, *a huge wave rushing on my head.*
†——aidh,‡‡ *v.n.* Embark.
†bàrc-lann, *s.m.* Library.
bàrd, -àird, *pl.* -àird [bàrda & bàrdan,] *s.m.* Bard, rhymer, poet. Sheinn am bàrd, *the bard sang.* [**Poetry being, in the opinion of the warlike Celts, the likeliest method of perpetuating their bravery, the bards were held by them in the highest veneration. Princes and warriors did not disdain to claim affinity with them. The Celts, being passionately fond of poetry, would listen to no instruction, whether from priest or philosopher, unless it were conveyed in rhymes. Hence the word *bàrd* meant also a priest, philosopher, or teacher of any kind. We often find a bard entrusted with the education of a prince, and about three hundred years ago, a Highland chief had seldom any other instructor. Such was the respect paid to the ancient bards, that, according to Diodorus, the Sicilian. they could put a stop to armies in the heat of battle. After an engagement they raised the song over the deceased, and extolled the heroes who survived.

When a bard appeared in an army, it was either as a herald or ambassador, hence his person and property were sacred in the midst of his enemies and amid their wildest ravages. In earlier times he never bore arms, and Owen asserts that it was unlawful to unsheathe a weapon in his presence. Among the ancient British there were, according to Jones, three orders of bards—the Privardd, (Prìomh-bhàrd) or chief bard; the Poswardd, who taught what was set forth by the privardd ; and the Arwyddwardd, *i.e.* the ensign bard, or herald-at-arms, who employed himself in genealogy, and in blazoning the arms of princes and nobles, as well as altering them according to their dignity or deserts. Owen observes that their dress was sky-blue, an emblem of peace.

Among the Irish Celts the bards enjoyed many extraordinary privileges. The chief bard was called Filidh, or Ollamh ri dàn, a graduate or doctor in poetry, and had thirty inferior bards as attendants, whilst a bard of the second order had fifteen. The Gael of Scotland was not behind his brother Celts in his veneration for the bards, for they had lands bestowed on them, which became hereditary in their families. A Highland chief retained two bards, who, like those of the Irish, had their retinue of disciples ; and though the office did by no means procure the same deep respect as in times of old, yet it was always filled to the utmost. The reasons for the decline of their power will be found under "aois-dàna."]
†bàrd, -àird, -àird & -an, *s.m.* Dyke, fence. 2 Park. 3 Garrison. 4 Corporation.
bàrda, *n. pl.* of bàrd.
bàrdach, *a.* see bàrdail.
bàrdachd, *s. f.* Poetry, rhyming. 2 Satire, lampooning, sarcasm. 3 *rarely* Corporation town. Ged theirinn e cha bhàrdachd e, *though I were to say it, it would be no satire.*
†bardag,**-aig, -an, *s. f.*Box, pannier, hamper.
bàrdail, *a.* Poetical. 2 Satirical.
bàrdainn,—*Islay,* see bàirlinn.
†bàrdal, -ail, *s.m.* Drake.
bàrdalachd, *s. f.* Quantity of poetry. 2 Satire. 3 Unseemly language.
bàrdan, (*dim.* of bàrd) *s.m.* Poetaster.
bàrdas, -ais, *s.m.* Satire, lampoon. 2††Poetry.
bàrd-cluiche, -chluiche, *s.m.* Dramatist.
bàrd-dealbh-cluiche, see bàrd-cluiche.
bàrd-dhàn, *s.m.* Poetry, rhyme.
†barg, *a.* Red-hot.
bargan, -ain, -an, *s.m.* Gaelic spelling of *bargain.* (còrdadh *or* cùmhnant.)
——aich, *v.a.* Make a bargain.
——aiche,** *s.m.* Bargainer.
†barghal, *s.m.* Branches.

bàr-gheal, *a.* see bàrr-gheal.
bàrlag, -aig, -an, *s. f.* Rag, tatter. 2 Person in rags.
———ach, -aiche, *a.* Ragged, tattered, clouted.
bàrlaid,(AC) -e, -ean, *s. f.* see barrlait.
bar-linn, see bàirlinn.
bàrluath, *s.m.* Portion of pipe-music in "ceòl mór" which precedes the *taorluath.* It does not occur in all tunes, but only in those of the "Moladh Màiri" type.
bàr-mhór, see bàrr-mhór.
†**barn,** -airn, *s.m.* Nobleman. 2 Judge. 3 Battle.
bàrnach, see báirneach.
bàrnag,** -aig, *s. f.* Summons of removal.
bàrnaig, *pr. pt.* a' bàrnaigeadh, *v.a.* Summon. 2 Warn, give summons of removal.
———eadh, -eidh, *s.m.* Summoning. 2 Warning, summons of removal. A' b—, *pr. pt.* of bàrnaig.
bàrnuigh, (AF) see bàirneag.—*Arran.*
†**baroil,** see barail.
barpa, -annan, *s.m.* Cairn, supposed to be a memorial of the dead, barrow.
barpail, a. *Monumental. 2**Arrogant.
bàrr, -a, *s.m.* Top, uppermost part of anything. 2 Point, as of a weapon or shoe. 3 Crop of grain, grass, or vegetables. 4 Harvest. 5 Superiority. 6 Suet. 7 Cream, ‡‡fat floating on the surface. 8 Scum. 9**Bread, food. 10 **Acme. 11**Branch. 12**Height, hill. 13 **Head, helmet. 14‡‡Battlement. 15***rarely* son, (see †bàr.) Tha 'n deagh bhàrr aca, *they have an excellent crop ;* bàrr na snàthaid, *the point of the needle;* bàrr a bhata, *the end of his staff* ; thug sin bàrr air na chuala mi riamh, *that excels everything I ever heard ;* a bhàrr air sin, *besides, moreover* ; bàrr maise, *superiority in beauty* ; mar cheò air bàrraibh nam beann, *like a mist on the tops of the hills ;* buntàta a' crathadh o'n bhàrr, *potatoes shaking from the haulms* ;cha'n fhàg e bun no bàrr, *he will leave neither root nor branch*; a' chuach leis fo bhàrr, *his cup brimming over* ; lìon a mach le bàrr is le gucaig e, *pour it out up to the brim,* or *with a head on it* , Dia air bàrr, *God above all,—an invocation used when in great danger or distress.*
barr', see barradh.
bàrr, *v.a.* See bearr.
barra, *s.m. ind.* Spike. 2 Bar. 3 Court of justice.
barra,(JM) see bara.
barra-bhailc, see barr-bhailc.
barra-bhalla, see barr-bhalla.
———dh, see barr-bhalla.
barra-buidhe, *a.* see barr-bhuidhe.
barracaid,†† *s. f.* Pride. 2 Loud talk.
———each, -diche, *a.* Proud, saucy. Gu barracaideach, *proudly.*
———eachd, *s. f.* Pride, sauciness.
barrach, -aich, *s.m.*Top branches of trees,brushwood. 2 Birch. 3 Fine tow ("firsts"—"seconds" are bunnach, "thirds" sgath.) Fo sgàil a' bharraich, *beneath the shade of the branches*; snàthainn barraich, *a thread of tow.*
barrach, -aiche, *a.* High-topped. 2 Pinnacled. 3 Heaped up, as a measure. 4 Heaped over the brim of any dish. 5 Beetling, overtopping. 6 Excessive. Cairt bharrach, *a cart loaded over the brim.*
†**barrachad,** -aid, *s.m.* Cottage, hut, booth.
barrachadh, (a') *pr. part.* of barraich.
barrachaol, see barrchaol.
barrachas, -ais, *s.m.* see barrachd. 2 see barrchas.
barrachd, *s.f.* Superiority, pre-eminence. 2 Advantage, mastery. 3 Overplus. B'iongantach do ghràdh dhomh-sa, a' toirt barrachd air gràdh nam ban, *thy love for me was wonderful, surpassing the love of women* ; barrachd ort-sa, *more than you have* ; ma bhitheas barrachd agad, *if you have any surplus*; a bharrachd air sin, *besides that* ; chi dithis barrachd air aon fhear, *two will see more than one.*
———ail, -e, *a.* Surpassing, superior. 2 Bold, brave.
———as,‡‡ -ais, *s.m.* see barrachd.
†**barra-chust,** *s.m.* Pericranium.
barradh, -aidh, *s.m.* Hinderance, obstacle. 2 see bara. A' b—, see bearradh.
barradh, see bàrr. A' suidh air a' bharradh (bhàrr) ud, *sitting on the brow of yonder hill.*
barradh-dhias, -dheis, see barr-dhias.
barradhriopair, see barr-dhriopair.
barrag, -aig, -an, *s. f.* Posset. 2 Scum, cream. 3 Sudden pain. 4 Grappling, wrestling. 5 Young girl. 6 ‡‡Knot. 7‡‡Rod, switch. †8** Weeds that float on the water. Cha chinn barrag air cuid cait, *cream does not come on a cat's milk.*
barragach, -aiche, *a.* Creamy, frothy.
barraghlach, *s.m.* Tops or branches of trees, brushwood.
barrag-ruadh, -ruaidh, *s. f.* Yellow-horned poppy—*glaucium luteum.* The flower is yellow and not red, although called *ruadh.*

21. Barrag-ruadh.

barrag-uaine, *s. f.* see barraig-uaine.
barra-gùg, see barr-gùg.
barraibh, *dat. pl.* of bàrr.
barraich, *v.a.* Top up, heap, as a measure of grain. 2 Excel, surpass.
barraich,** *a.* Matchless, surpassing, pre-eminent, transcendent.
———te, *a.* Surpassing, excelling. 2 Superior, pre-eminent, matchless. ††3Lofty. *Pt. part.* of barraich, Tipped, topped. 2 Excelled, surpassed. Barraichte mar na seudair, *excellent as the cedars.*
barraidheachd, see barrachd.
bàrraig, *v.a.* see bàirig.
†**barraighin,** *s. f.* Mitre.
barraig-uaine,§ *s. f.* Green scum on stagnant water.—*confervae.*
barrail, -ala, *a.* Excellent, eminent, surpassing. 2 Generous. 2 Gay, sprightly. 4 Transcendant. 5 Genteel. A' mhaighdean bharrail, *the sprightly maiden.*

barrain, *gen. sing.* of barran.
barraisd, -e, *s.m.* Borage,—*borago officinalis.* 2** Green kale.

22. *Barraisd.*

barraisdeach, *a.* Full of borage. 2 Like borage. 3 Of borage.
bàrraisg,†† -e, -ean, *s.m.* Boaster, braggadocio.
barrall,* see barr-iall.
barramhais, see barr-mhais.
barra-mhanadh, see barr-mhanadh.
bàrr-a'-mhilltich,§ *s.m.* Arrow grass,—*triglochin palustre.*
barra-mhislein,§ *s. m.* Bird's foot trefoil,—*lotus corniculata.*
†**barramhuil**, *a.* see barrail.
barran, -ain, -an, *s.m.* Any kind of coping on the top of a wall, as nails, glass, &c. to serve as a fence. 2 Hedge, fence. 3 Top of a rock or mountain. 4**Tip. 5**Crest. 6** Elder tree. 7‡‡ Ragged covering. 8 (J.M.) Bandage tied round the head, i. e. covering the whole head, when sick, especially when suffering from headache. Anns na barranaibh, *in the fences*; fraoch sléibhe mar bharran air, *tipped with mountain heath.*

23. *Barr-a'-mhilltich.*

———dach, see barantach.

24. *Barra-mhislein.*

barrant, see barant.
———ach, see barantach.
———adh, see barantadh.
———as, see barantas.
barr-aotrom,‡‡ -uime, *a.* Nimble, quick.
barra-roc, see barr-roc & barr-staimh.
barras, -ais, *s.m.* Superiority. 2 Residue, surplus. A bharras air sin, *over and above that, moreover.* (see barrachd.)
———ach, -aiche, *a.* Distinguished, excellent, superior. 2 Lofty. 3 Ambitious. 4** Residual. 6††Topped.
barra-sgaoilteach, see barr-sgaoilteach.
barra-thonn, see barr-thonn.
barr-bhailc, -ean, *s.m.* Cornice. 2 Entablature. 3 Constellation.
barr-bhalla, *s.m.* Parapet. 2 Battlement, embrazure, bartizan.
barr-bhàrd, -àird, *s.m.* Chief poet. 2 Poet laureate. 3 Graduate in poetry, also *filidh*, see note under *bàrd.*
———achd, *s.f.* Condition of a poet laureate. 2 Compositions of a poet laureate.
barr-bhile, *s.m.* Cornice.
barr-bhòrd,* *s.m.* Deck of a ship.
barr-brisgein, see brisgean.
barr-buidhe, *a.* Yellow-tipped, yellow-topped. 2 Yellow-haired.
barr-biorach, *s.m.* Cusp.
barr braonan-nan-con,§ *s.m.* Common tormentil *or* septfoil, see leamhnach.
barrbrog, -oig, see barbrag.
barr-caideach, -aiche, *a.* see barra-caideach.
barrchaol, -aoil, *s.m.* Pyramid.
———, *a.* Pyramidical, conical, tapering.
barrchaoin, *a.* Very mild, very gentle. Triùir bhràithre bharrchaoin, *three gentle brothers.*
bàrr-chas, -aise, *a.* Curly-haired.
———, *s.f.* Curly locks.
bàrr-cinn,‡‡ *s.m.* The hair.
barr-cluigeanach, *s.m.* The order *campanulaceæ* of plants.
barr-dearg,§ -eirge, *s.f.* Thrift (plant) see tonn-a'-chladaich. 2(JM) Sea-weed, tangles.
barr-deubhaidh, *s.m.* Battlement.
bàrr-dhealg, -eilg, an, *s.f.* Hair bodkin.
bàrr-dhias, -dhéis, *s. f,* Top of a blade of corn. 2 Blade or point of a sword.
bàrr-dhuine,‡‡ *s.m.* Growing youth.
†**barr-dog**, *s.m.* Box, pannier, hamper.
barr-dhriopair, *pl.* ean, *s.m.* Butler,
———eachd, *s. f.* Employment of a butler.
bàrr-fhionn, *a.* White-headed, white-topped. 2 Fair-headed. Canach barr-fhionn, *white-topped cotton-sedge.*
bàrr-gheal, -ghile, *a.* White-topped.
bàrr-gheug.(AH) *s. f.* Highest and most flourishing branch of a tree. 2 Tall, handsome woman.
bàrr-ghniomh, *s.m.* Work of supererogation. 2 Transcendent exploit.
bàrr-ghniomhach, -aiche, *a.* Superfluous.
bàrr-gruaig,‡‡ *s. f.* The hair.
barr-gùc, -an, *s. f.* Blossom, bloom, most frequently applied to those of leguminous vegetables, as pease, potatoes, &c. see luis meiligeagach. Barr-gùc air a mheuraibh, *a bloom on its branches.*
barr-gùg, see barr-gùc.
barr-iall, -éill, *s. f.* Latchet, shoe-tie, thong. 2‡‡Manacles.
bàrrlait, -e, -ean, *s. f.* Check, hinderance, prevention, suppression.
bàrr-madaidh, (AH) *s.m.* Act of scolding with asperity, as one would scold a dog. Thug e bàrr-madaidh orm, *he scolded me as he would*

a dog.
barr-mhais, -e, -ean, s. f. Cornice.
——————each, a. Having cornices, of, or pertaining to, a cornice.
——————ich, v.a. Ornament.
barr-mhanadh, -aidh, s.m. Destiny. Am fear a bhitheas a bharr-mhanadh a mach, *he whose destiny is cast.*—NGP.
barr-mhór, -oire, a. Large-topped. 2 Branchy.
barr-roc,** s. f. Sea-weed, tangles.
barr-sgaoil,‡‡ v.a. Lavish.
barr-sgaoilteach,** a. Capacious.
barr-staimh, s.m. Broad leaves on top of sea-girdles. see stamh.
barr-tachair, s.m. Crop sprung from seed left on the ground from former harvest.
barr-thonn, s.m. High surge. 2 Top of the waves. 3** Surface of the deep. A' siubhal nam barr-thonn, *bounding o'er the surges.*
†barrugal chrann,‡‡ s.m. Branches of trees.
bàruig, see bàirig.
baruille, see baraill.
bas, boise [& baise] -an & -a, s. f. The palm of the hand. Buailibh 'ur basan uil', a shluaigh! *clap your hands O all ye people!* bas réidh, *a smooth palm*; leòis air a basaibh, *blisters on her hands*; bonnach air bois, cha bhruich e is cha loisg, *a cake in the hand will neither cook nor burn—said of the shilly-shally*; sgailc air bois, *shaking hand upon a bargain.*
bas, -ais, s. f. Spoke of a wheel.
bas, -ais, s.m. Hollow or concave part of a club.
bàs, -àis, s. m. Death. 2**Destruction. Is e rìgh nan uamhas am bàs, *death is the king of terrors*; cha'n 'eil bàs ach ruaig, *there is no death but defeat*; faigh bàs, *die, starve*; gheibh gach ni bàs, *everything shall die*; droch bhàs ort! *bad death to you!* (a common form of imprecation); guin bàis, *the agony of death*; dealan bàis, *the lightning of death*; ma shaltraicheas sluagh air mo bhàs, *if people tread on my death—a poetical substitution of* death *for the* dead body, *which is not apparent to those who blindly infer that* bàs *means* a dead body.
†basa s.m. Fate, fortune.
basach, -aiche, a. Streaked, variegated.
bàsachadh, -aidh, s.m. Expiring, dying, perishing (of animals.) 2 Withering. A b—, *pr. pt.* of bàsaich. A' bàsachadh leis an fhuachd, *dying, withering or starving with cold*; tha e air bàsachadh, *it has died or withered.*
basadh,** -aidh, s.m. The rubbing of the thread ends of tape-work, to prevent their running into threads. ("basing".)
bàsaich, *pr. pt.* a' bàsachadh, v.n. Die (as an animal), perish. 2 Starve. 3 Wither, as a plant. 4 Grow vapid, as beer. An ni sin a bhàsaicheas leis fhéin, *that which dies of itself.* [Note that "bàsaich" is only used in relation to animals. "Siubhail," "eug," "caochail," or "teasd" is always used when speaking of persons, as, bhàsaich an cù, *the dog died*; shiubhail an duine, *the man died.* The expression "fhuair an duine bàs" is always used in Scripture for *the man died,* but "fhuair an duine am bàs" would be better Gaelic.]
basaidh, -ean, s.m. (bas, *palm*) Gaelic spelling of "bassie"—basin.
bàsail, -e, a. Deadly, fatal. 2**Death-like. 3 Mortal. 4 Destructive.
bàs-airm, *gen. sing.* of bàs-arm.
†basal, -ail, s.m. Judgment. 2 Judge. 3**Pride, arrogance.
bàsalachd, s. f. ind. Mortality. 2 Deadliness.
bàs'ar, see bàsmhor.
basardaich,* s.m. Clapping of the hands for joy, acclamation, rejoicing.
bàs-arm, -airm, s.m. Deadly weapon.
basart,**-airt,-artan, Gaelic spelling of *bastard.*
†bas-ascanas, s.m. Bass in *music.*
basbair, -ean, s.m. Fencer, swordsman. Bha thu 'n ad bhasbair còir, *thou wert a noble swordsman.*
basbaireachd, s. f. Swordsmanship, fencing.
basbairean, *n.pl.* of basbair.
basbairich,** v.n. Parry.
basbhaidh, a. Haggish.
bas-bhuail, v.a. Applaud by clapping the hands.
bas-bhualadh, -aidh, s.m. Clapping or rubbing of hands, from grief or joy.
bàs-bhuille, s.m. Death-blow. Fhuair e a bhàs-bhuille, *he received his death-blow.*
†basbruidheach, a. Lecherous.
†——————d, s. f. Lechery, lecherousness.
†basc, a. Round. 2 Red, scarlet.
†——ach, -aich, -aichean, s.m. Catch-pole, bailiff.
bascaid, -e, -ean, s. f. Gaelic spelling of *basket.*
————each,†† a. Belonging to baskets.
†basc-airm, s.m. Circle.
†bascall, -aill, s.m, Wild man, savage.
†bascarnach, -aich, s.m. Lamentation. 2 ‡‡ Stammering.
†bascart, -airt, s.m. Cinnamon. 2**Cinnabar.
†bas-chailc, s.m. Ruddle.
bas-charnta,** a. Globy, globular.
bàs-chlar, -air, s.m. Obituary.
†bas-chriadh, s.m. Ruddle.
basdal, -ail, s.m. Noise, glitter, gaiety of appearance, show.
———ach, -aiche, a. Gay, showy, flashy. 2 Cheering. 'Nuair a thig an gloine basdalach, *when the cheering glass comes round*, òg basdalach, *a gay youth*; a ribhinn bhuidhe bhasdalaich, *thou yellow-haired showy maid.*
———achd, s. f. ind. Showiness, gaiety. Cha 'n fhaca mi a leithid air basdalachd, *I have not seen his equal for showiness.*
basdard, s.m. Gaelic spelling of *bastard.*
†basg, v.a. Stop, stay.
basgair, v.n. Applaud.
basgaird, v.n. Applaud.
basgairdeachas, -ais, s.m. see basgaireachd.
basgairdeadh, -eidh, s.m. Applause. A' b—, *pr. pt.* of basgaird.
basgaire, s. f. ind. Applause. 2‡Mourning.
————ach,** a. Clapping the hands in the agitation of grief.
————achd, s. f. Mournful clapping or wringing of hands. 2 Applause.
basganta, a. Warbling, melodious.
basgart,** see bas-cart.
basg-chriadh, s. f. Red-lead.
basg-luaidh, s. f. Vermillion. 2 Red-lead.
basg-luath, see basg-luaidh.
bàs-guineach,‡‡ -eiche, a. Death-darting.
basguir, see basg-luaidh.
bà-shruth,†† s.m. Calm stream.
baslach, -aich, -ean, s.m. Handful, the full of the two palms placed together. 2 Bunch, cluster.
bàs-lag, s.m. Place of execution. [Usually a pit in which the culprit stood. One is to be seen at Finlarig,—M.M.]
bas-luaidh, s.m. Applause, approbation expressed by clapping of hands.
bas-luath, a. Ready- or nimble-handed.
bas-mhìn, -e, a. Soft-palmed, smooth-handed.
bàsmhoire, *comp.* of bàsmhor.
————achd, s. f. *ind.* see bàsmhorachd.
bàsmhor, -oire, a. Mortal, liable to death. 2

Deadly, fatal. An corp bàsmhor, *the mortal body.*

———ach,** *a.* Mortal, liable to death. Tha gach crè bàsmhorach, *every body is liable to death.*

———achd, *s.f.* Mortality, deadliness. 2 **Fatality.

bas-mhol,** *v.n.* Applaud.

———adair,** *s.m.* Applauder.

†basoille, *s.m.* Vassal. 2 Tenant.

basraich, *s.f.* Clapping or wringing of hands in mourning. 2** Shouting, roaring, calling aloud. Is i a' basraich, a' taomadh a h-osnaich air ceò, *and she wailing, pouring her complaint on the mist.*

bàs-shleagh, *s.m.* Deadly spear. Bàs-shleagh nan triath, *the deadly spear of the chiefs.*

bastalach, see basdalach.

bastul, see basdal.

bat, *s.m.* Bath. Bat fìona, *a wine bath* ; bat olaidh, *an oil bath.*

bat, *v.a.* Beat, cudgel.

bat, bata, } *s.m.* Stick, staff, baton, cudgel, bludgeon. Gabh mo bhata, *take my stick ;* ni thu bataichean, *thou shalt make staves.*

bata, *gen. sing.* of bat.

bàta, -aichean, *s., m.* on land, *f.* on sea. Boat, pinnace, barge. Fear bàta, *a boatman* ; bàt' aiseig, *a ferry-boat*; stiùireadair a' bhàta, *the steersman of the boat* ; bàt' iasgaich, *a fishing-boat* ; chuir e a bhàt' air adair, *he brought his boat to anchor.*

Names of Parts of a Boat;— (see illust.) [Roinnean bàta]

A 1 Ceann ùrlair, ceann nan ùrlar,—*Lewis*, Head.
2 Fliuch-bhòrd, Garb.
3 Sgar an droma, sgar an leigeill,—*Lewis*, Rebat.
4 Forra-dhruim, Slip-keel.—*Lewis.* 2 False keel—a second stick nailed to the original keel to restore it to its former thickness, when worn down by continually dragging the boat up and down the beach.

B Sùdh, Clincher, overlap in planks.

C Reang, aisean, Joggled frame.—*Gairloch.*

D Doire, an t-slige, Bent timber.—*Lewis.*

E 1 Claigeann, Stem.
2 Aparan, Apron.
3 Aiseann, reang, rong, rongas, rungas. Reangan—*Sutherland.* Rib.
4 An t-slige, Sk'n.
5 Tarsann, Breast-hook.
6 Maide sreinge—*Lewis.* Rubbing-piece.
7 Beul mór, ‡‡slat beòil, ‡‡taobh-shlat. Beul stoc—*Islay.* Gunwale.
8 Beul beag ; a' chuairt bheòil,—*Lewis*, Saxboard *or* gunwale strake.
9 Am beul a staigh—*Lewis.* Inside wale.

F 1 As E7 Gunwale.
2 As E6 Rubbing-piece.
3 As E8 Saxboard.
4 Cìrean tarsuing, na cìrean,—*Lewis*, Coaming.
5 Maide reang,—*Gairloch &c*, ‡‡maide rongais, Taobhan, reangas,—*Lewis*, Stringer.
6 ùrlar, Flat floor.
7 Limber.
8 Leud iochdair, bulg, na sgiathan, slat-an-builg; maide builg—*Lewis*, Bilge-piece *or* bilge-keel.
9 Druim, eàirlin, Kelson.
10 As A4 Keel.

G 1 Saidh-thoisich. Bior dubh, claigionn toisich,—*Gairloch, Lewis, &c.* Stem-post.
2 Coileir, tarsann. Cuairt thoisich.—*Gairloch, &c.*, a' chuairt bheag—*Lewis* Breasthook, brace-stick.
3 As F5 Stringer.
4 As F6 Flat floor.
5 Fiodhraich tharsuing, Cross timbers.
6 As F9 Kelson.
7 As A4 Keel.
8 Fliuch-bhòrd, gearr-bhòrd, Keelboard *or* garboard.
9 Lunn chas—*Lewis*, Foot-waling.
10 As F5 Stringer.
11 As F8 Bilge-piece *or* bilge-keel.
12 Cuairtean—*Gairloch.* bòrd (*pl.* bùird), stràc, (*pl.* stràcan)—(AH.) Strakes.
13 As E8 Saxboard.
14 As E6 Rubbing-piece.
15 As E7 Gunwale.
16 Ceann roinge ; ceanna chnàmhan—*Lewis*, Head *or* rib.

H Slat an t-siùil mhóir, slat-shiùil, an t-slat ladhrach, Gaff.
1 Gobhlag.—*Lewis.* Clipt.
2 Giall, Cheek *or* jaw.
3 Na roithleanan, Trucks.
4 Na buill mhóra, Main halyards.
5 Na bàrran, na bideinean, Peaks.
6 Ceann an còpa* ghleididh, Guy end.
7 Ball an t-siùil àird, ball sgòid an t-siùil mhullaich, Top-sail sheet.
8 Cùird nam bàrra, Peak-lines.

I Geamann, Gammoning-iron.

K 1 Stoc, Stock of bowsprit.
2 Geamann, Knighthead.
3 As G1 Stem-post.
4 Leabaidh a' chroinn-spreòid, Bed of bowsprit.
5 Maid' a' chroinn spreòid, Bitt.
6 Maide tarsuinn, Cross-bitt.

L Slatag sgòid, Bumkin.

M 1 Crann spreòid, crann dall‡‡, crann uisge, Bowsprit.
2 ? Bobstay purchase.
3 ? Bobstay.
4 ? Triangline.
5 Beart a' chroinn spreòid, Bowsprit shroud.
6 Maidean a' chroinn-spreòid, Bitts.
7 Stàdh an àrd-chroinn, Top-mast stay.

N 1 Saidh-thoisich, bior dubh, Stem-post.
2 Aparan-thoisich, Inner stem-post.
3 As A4
4 Lionadh-toisich, Deadwood in bow.

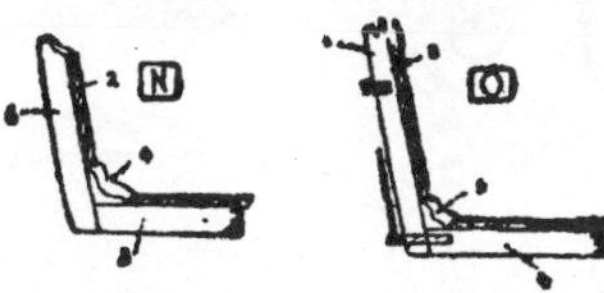

25. Saidh thoisich. 26. Saidh dheiridh.

O 1 Saidh-dheiridh, bior dubh, Claigionn deiridh,—*Gairloch, Lewis, &c.* Stern-post.
2 Aparan-deiridh, Inner stern-post.
3 Lionadh-deiridh, an t-àr, earr, Deadwood in stern.
4 Druim, Keel.
6 Toll na stiùireach. Rudder-band.
7 Iarunn na stiùireach, am brod ìosal, *and when in the position of* O 6, am brod àrd, Pintle. (6 & 7 together are called in Eng., "rudder-irons" or "rudder-bands," in Gaelic "ceanglaichean na

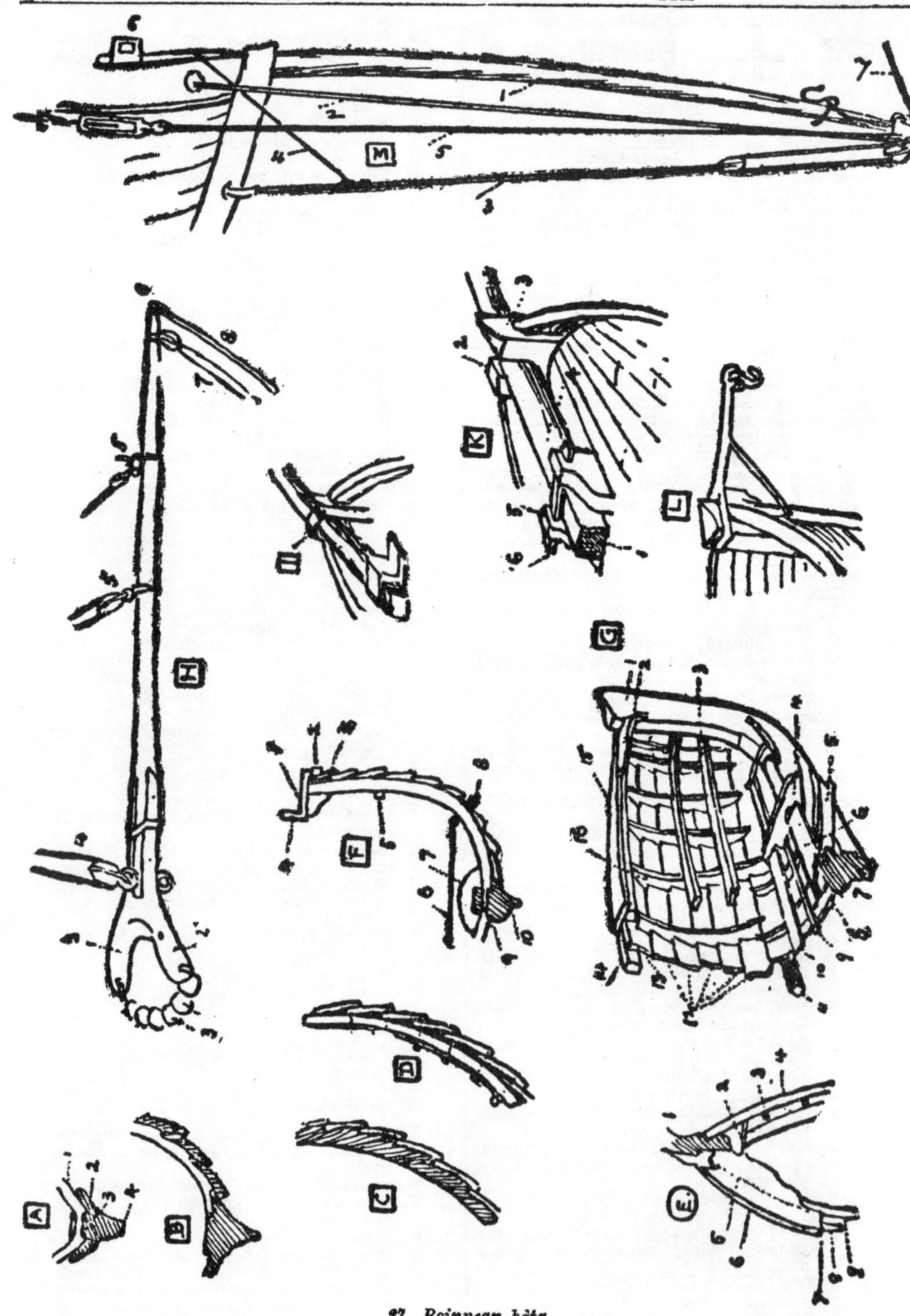

27. *Roinnean bàta.*

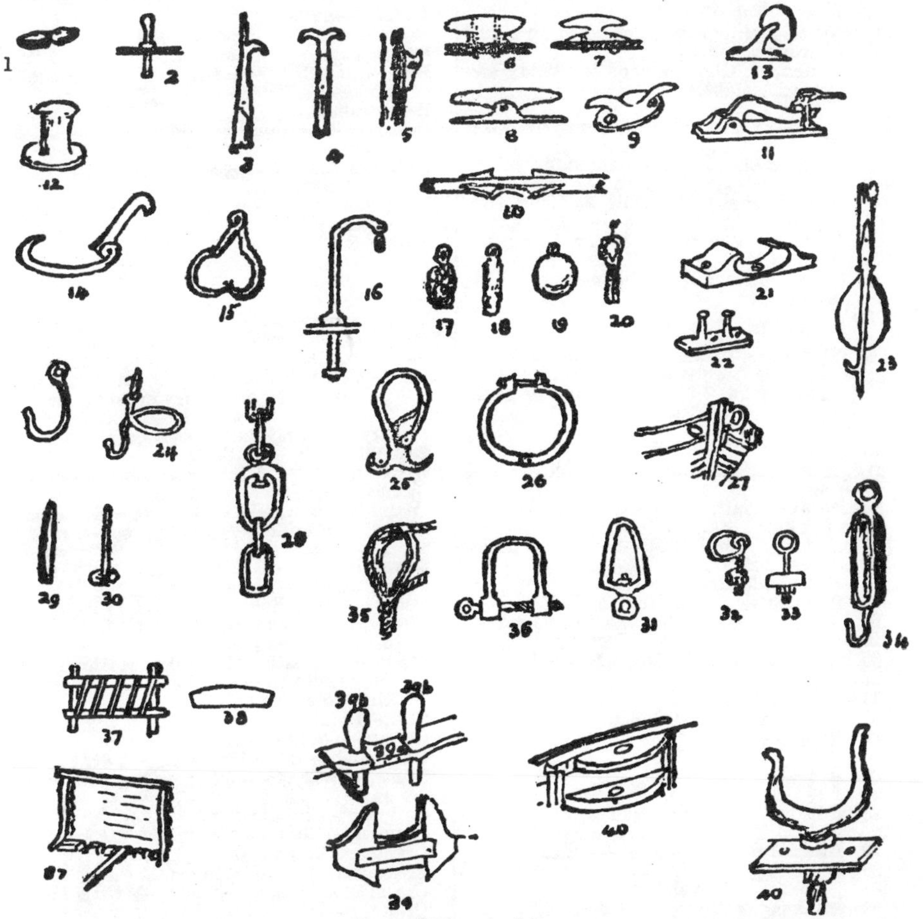

28. Acfhuinnean bàta.

stiùireach," or "bannan na stiùireach.") The Ness (Lewis) boats have the "brods" on the rudder and the bands on the stern-post, but the herring-boats have the "brods" on the stern-post and the bands on the rudder.

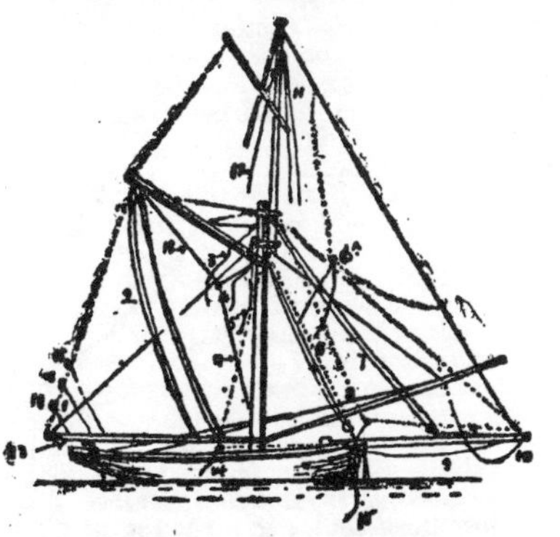

29. Cùird agus tarruingean.

NAMES OF SHEETS (Cùird *no* buill nan seòl) AND HALYARDS (Tarruingean.)

1 ? Topping-lift.
2 Tarruingean bhratach, Peakline *or* signal halyards.
3 ? Peaks.
4 ? Throats.
5 ? Tricing-line.
6 Tarruingean an t-siùil thoisich, Fore-sail halyards.
7 Tarruingean an t-siùil spreòid, Jib halyards.
8 ? Spinnaker after-guy *or* spinnaker boom.
9 ? Jibstay *or* jib outhaul.
10 ? Fore spinnaker guy.
11 ? Spinnaker and top-mast fore-sail halyards.
12 Tarruing an àrd-shiùil. Top-sail halyard.
13 Sgòd an t-siùil mheadhoin, ball, sgòd, sgòid. Main sheet.
14 Sgòd an t-siùil-thoisich, Fore sheet.
15 Sgòd an t-siùil spreòid, sgód an t-siùil chinn, Jib sheet.
16 Crochadair na cearb, Reef pendant.
16a ? Top-mast staysail sheets.
17 Cluas an t-siùil mhullaich, cluas an t-

siùil àird, Topsail tack.
18 Sgòd an t-siùil mhullaich, sgòd an t-siùil àird, Top-sail sheet.
Ball stadha, Guy (a rope to steady any suspended weight.)

NAMES OF FITTINGS (acfhuinnean) OF BOAT.
—see illustrations.—

1 Cnag-grabaidh, dealg-bhacaidh, putan, —Sny *or* toggle (a short bar of wood tapering from the middle to each end, placed in an eye at the end of a rope, to keep the end from passing through a loop or knot, especially in a flag.)
2 Dealg cheangail, dealg snaime, Belaying pin.
3, 4 Geadha,—Boat-hook.
5 (?) Spor Thumb-cleat *or* spurs.
6, 7, 8 Greimiche, {Wooden- / Metal- / Patent-} cavil *or* cleat.
9, 10 Greimiche, Cleat.
11 Cromag sgòid, dubhan na sgòid, Sheet clip.
12 Post ceangail, Bollard.
13 Cromag, Clip.
14 Cromag chumail, } Clip-hook, sail-hook.
15 Bacan dùinidh, } Cliphook.
16 Slachdan bàta, Davits.
17 Dìonadair, Pudding fend-off.
18 „ chas-saibh, Sawdust fend-off.
19 „ leathrach, Leather „
20 „ ròpa, Rope fend-off.
21, 22 ? Fairleads.
23 ? Paddle boat-hook.
24 Ràc, Traveller.
25 ? Springhank.
26 Iarna, Hank.
27 ? Hawse-pipe.
28 Udalan, udlan; carrachan—*Lewis*, Swivel.
29 Bior iaruinn, Marline-spike.
30 Biordainge, Pricker.
31 As 28 Swivel.
32 Ailbheag, failbhe, Ring-bolt.
33 ? Eye-bolt.
34 (?)Sgrobha sìnidh. Wire stretcher *or* sett-screw.
35 ? Thimble.
36 (?)Geimhle, Shackle.
37 ? Stretcher guides.
38 Sìneadair, Stretcher.
39 Bac, Thole, (oar-cleats.)
Baca bhràghad, the fore cleats.
Baca meadhon, the middle cleats.
Baca h-amar, the quarter cleats.
39a Apran, bac, Sheath on gunwale to prevent wearing by the oars.
39b Putagan, bac, bacal, urcag, uracagan. Cnagan, (cnag thoisich & cnag dheiridh)—*Lewis*. Thole-pins.
40 Buthal ràimh, Rowlock.

NAMES OF OTHER PARTS REQUIRING NO DIAGRAM TO EXPLAIN THEM.

Acfhuinn (an),—The sails.
Acfhuinnean (na h-),—The fittings.
Achlaisean, glùinean,—Beam knees, used to fix the thwarts to the side or planks of the boat, as the "cinn-tobhta" fix them to the gunwale. The "achlasan" lies horizontally in the angle which the thwart makes with the side, but the "ceann-tobhta" is upright.
Aodach,—Sails.
Aoir,—Sheet, bolt-rope of a sail.
àrd-chrann,—see crann àrd.
Bac,—Space between the rowlocks or thole-pins,—*Skye*.
Ball—Rope.
Ball cluaise,—Rope by which the tack is fastened.
Ball langais—Towing rope.
Bann,—Boom.
Bior snaois,‡‡—Top of stem, (*also* ceann saidhe.)
Bìdh,—Caulking.
Boitig,—Carriage.—*Lewis*.
Bòrd,—Plank.
Bratach,—Flag.
Bròg a' chroinn,—Mast step, (square hole in which the lower end of mast rests.
Broilleach bàta,—The bows or stem. "A broilleach" (*her bows*) is said when looking in front from the outside, but "a bràigh" is used when looking inside from "tobhta bràghad" to the bow.
Calcadh, bìdh,—Caulking.
Calpannan, see tairngnean calpa,—*Lewis*.
Camus, (an,)—Stern seat.
Ceann a' chnac,—Thwart brace,—*L. Broom*.
Ceann a' chraidh,—Thwart brace,—*Gairloch*, *Lewis, &c.*
Ceann deiridh,—Quarter-deck.
Ceann tobhta,—Thwart brace.
Ceàrn,—Ship's hold.
Cheall, (a'),—Mast-step,—*Gairloch*.
Chrois, (a'),—see glac.
Clàdain,—Sheaths of wood or leather placed on oars to prevent their being worn by the thole-pins.
Clàr,—Plank.
Cl.:ag,—Square stern.
Cliathaich,—Bilge.
Cluas,—Tack, (foremost lower corner of any sail.
Coilpean,—Rope *or* tow.
Crannag,—Round top of mast. 2 Cross-trees.
Crann àrd,—Top-mast.
Crann deiridh,—Mizzen mast.
Crann meadhon, crann mór,—Main mast.
Crann mullaich,—Topmast.
Crann sgòide,—Boom.
Croinn-grith,—Mast rigging.
Crotan,—*Lewis*. see clàdain.
Cuairt bheòil,—Top stroke.
Cudthrom socrachaidh,—Ballast.
Cupuill, *or* cuplaichean, (na),—Shrouds.
Déile,—Plank.
Deireadh,—Stern.
Deireadh cuaich,—Round stern.
Dòirneag, an,—the oar-handle.
Dòrn chur,—Oar-handle,—*Lewis*.
Eadar-bhacain,—Space between the rowlocks
Fàradh,—Shrouds.
Fàsag,—Plug-hole.
Fiodhannan,—Timbers in general.
Fuaigh-shlat,—Stock of a ship while building.
Glac,—Fork. An upright piece of timber near the stern in fishing boats, used for resting the upper part of the mast on when not up.
Glas a' chroinn,—Mast-lock.
Glùinean,—Beam knees. (see achlaisean.)
Greimiche,—Anchor. *prov.*
Gualainn,—Shoulder, (curved part of the hull extending from the foremost stays, or foremost tholes in a rowing-boat, to the stem.)
Iall-theannaidh,—Brace.

Iarunn comhalach,—*Lewis.* **Clip for striking into the head of a fish when it comes to the boat's side.**
Iomram,—Rowing.
Ite,—Oar-blade.
"**Làmh ud thall**" (yonder hand) is only said when hauling or shooting lines with oars. The shooting and hauling is done on the right side, so this applies to the port oars. "An làmh seo fhéin" or "an làmh a bhos" is applied to the starboard or right side oars.
Lannan,—Scales, roves (round pieces of metal on which the nails are clinched inside.
Leabaidh na taoma, leabaidh na taoime,—*Skye*; leabaidh-taomaidh,—Vacant space for baling.
Liagh, an,—Oar-blade.
Leagail, (an)—That part of a boat which is flattened out before building up the sides. —*Lewis.*
Luitig,—Bilge-water.—*Lewis.*
Lunn, (an,) *pl.* -an, —the midpart of boat or oar. 2 Piece of wood placed under the keel when hauling a boat on the beach. 3 Oar. 4(MM) Lever.
Puc-tholl,—Plug hole.
Racas,—Sail-hoop.
Ràmh-bràghad, *or* ràmh-gualainn,—Stroke-oar.
Ruadh-bhòrd—Next board to "fliuch-bhord."
Sàil,—Heel, (between keel and stern-post.)
Sailtichean,††—Hatches.
Seas-aothar,**—Seat a-thwart.
Sgairean,—Nails. (see tairngnean sgair.)
Sgar, sgairean.—*Gairloch.* see sùidhean.
Sgiathan,—Side wings. Flat pieces put on each side under water to keep boat steady and from rolling. They are much shorter and broader than the bilge-piece, and are used for "crank" boats.
Sgruig thoisich *and* **sgruig dheiridh,**—the parts of the stem- and stern-posts about the gunwale.—*Skye.*
Sgnit, (an)—Stern-seat,—*Lewis.*
Sguit thoisich, sguit dheiridh,—Board on the bottom of an open boat fore and aft on which passengers place their feet.
Sguman,—Baling-dish.—*Lewis.*
Slatan,—Yards.
Slat sgòid,—Boom.
Slat shiùil,—Sail-yard.
Sliasaid,—Quarter.
Slige,—Hull.
Snaois,††—Prow.
Spùidsear,—Baling-dish.
Sròl,—Flag.
Stàdhannan,(*sing.* stàdh,)—Stays.
Strac beòil,—Top stroke.
Suaicheantas,—Flag having a crest or badge as of a yacht club.
Sùdh,—Overlap in planks.
Suidheachan, an,—the stern seat.
Sùidhean,—Scarf-joint. When in building a boat a plank is too short to extend from stem to stern, it is supplemented by another, the two being united by a scarf-joint. The nails used in such joints are called "tairngnean-sgair."
Tairngnean barraidh,—*Skye.* Rivet nails.
Tairngnean calpa,—Nails for joining the skin to the stem, keel, and cross timbers. They are not clinched.
Tairngnean daraich,—Nails of various sizes, the larger ones to fix planks to timbers, the smaller to fix keel-board to keel, and ends of planks to stem- and stern-posts.
Tairngnean fruillichd,—Roves (nails.)
,, fuaigheil, see t.— daraich.
Tairngnean rang,—*Skye.* see t— daraich.
Tairngnean sgair, see note under sùidhean.
Taoim,—Bilge-water.
Taoman,—Baling-dish.
Tarsnan,—Transom.
Teannadan,—Brace.
Tiolpadair,—Check.
Tiolpadh,— ,,
Tobhta, *pl.* -aichean,—Seat *or* thwart. There are generally five thwarts in a boat, named as follows :—
1. An tobhta chroinn *or* t— thoisich, (to which the mast is fixed.) 2. An tobhta bhràghad. 3. An tobhta mheadhon. It is called "an tobhta thogalaich" when in a moveable condition, and it can then be taken up and laid down in the bottom of the boat when desired. 4. An tobhta amar. 5. An tobhta dheiridh, an sguit, an camus, *or* an suidheachan. There is no seat a-stem "tobhta chroinn."
Togail—*Lewis,* Carriage.
Toiseach,—Stem or bow.
Toll an tùc,—Plug-hole,—*Lewis.*
Toll-cnaig,—Plug-hole.
Toll sìolaidh, *or* t— silidh,—Plug-hole.
Treobhair (an),—That part of boat below the "leagail."
Trotha,—*Lewis.* Mast-step.
Uidheam,—Set of sails.
Urluinn,‡‡—Fore part of a ship.

30. Roinnean Acrach.

Names of parts of an Anchor (Roinnean acrach.)
1 **Fàinne,**—Ring.
2 **Ciabhag,**—Forelock.
3 **Gualann,**—Shoulder.
4 **Stoc,**—Stock.
5 **Dealg na ciabhaig,**—Forelock pin.
6 **Calpa,**—Shank.—*Lewis.*
7 **Fiacal, Spòg ; spàg [Fliùc,]**—Fluke. Dà spàg na h-aerach, *the two flukes of the anchor.*—*Lewis.*
8 **Bas,**—Palm.
9 **Gob, bàrr**—Bill *or* pee.
10 **Gàirdean,**—Arm.
11 **Crùn,**—Crown.
12 **Amhach,**—Throat.
Còrd failbheig,—Part of a cable which is fastened to the ring of the anchor.

Names of parts of a Block or Pulley, (Ulag)
1 **Ceann,**—Head.
2 **Eag,**—Score.
3 **Cochull,**—Block *or* shell.

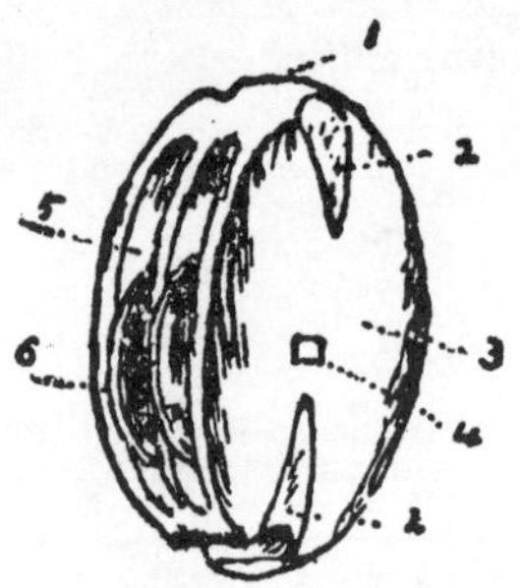

31. Ulag.

4 Dealg,—Pin.
5 Slugan—Sheafswallow.
6 Ruidhlean, reidhlean, roithlein,—Wheel *or* sheave.

Names of parts of a Rudder, (Failm, stiùir.)
1 Cuing,—Yoke.
2 Iarunn na stiùireach, brod,—Pintle. see 07
3 Stoc,—Stock.
4 Toll na stiùireach—Rudder-band.
5 Falmadair,failm, maide stiùraidh,**—Tiller.
2 & 4 Ceanglaichean na stiùireach, — Rudder-bands.
Claigeann,—Head, where yoke or tiller goes on the rudder.
Ghlas (a')—Key on stern-post.

32. Failm.

Different kinds of boats.
Bàidean, — Little boat, yawl, pinnace.
Bàrca,—Barque.
Bàta dà chroinn,—Wherry.
Birlinn,—Galley,12- or 16-oared boat. "Birlinn Tighearna Chloinn Raonuill" had 16 oars.
Ceithir-ràmhach, — Double-banked boat seating two men on each thwart with an oar each, one on each side.
Clàrach,(AC)—Small boat.
Clàrag,—Square stern boat.
Coite,—Skiff, light pleasure boat for sculling on lakes and rivers (called *skiff* in England.) 2 Small fishing-boat, coracle.
Culaidh, eathar,—Coble, boat with cutwater head, flat-bottomed stern and transom set up obliquely. [*Culaidh* is a general term for a boat in the Reay country.—AG]
Curach, curachan,—Coracle, canoe.
Curaidh, iùbhrach, †atrach,*—Wherry, boat to row 2 oars, for landing passengers.
Dà-ràmhach,—Single-banked boat having one rowlock (rowing one on a seat.)
Deich-ràmhach—Launch, boat using 8 or 10 oars.
Gàbart,—Lighter, one-masted, round-sterned vessel, with a long hatchway, cutter-rigged.
Geòla,—Yawl.
Iùbhrach,—Cutter, good sailing vessel of tidy build.—*Barra.*
Long—Square-rigged vessel with 3 and sometimes 4 masts.
Long-ràmhach,—Pinnace, large boat used by war-ships.
Luath bhàta, } Luath long, } —Cutter, small vessel with 1 mast, mainsail, forestaysail and jib set to bowsprit-end. 2 Any sloop of narrow beam and deep draught.
Naomhag,**—Coble.
Pacaid,—Mail-boat.
Plodan,(CM)—Small boat of a smack, fishing or otherwise.
Ràmh-long,‡‡—Galley.
Sgollag,—(?) Dinghey, small rowing-boat for use in a harbour.
Sgoth,—Skiff, (sailing-boat, sharp at stem & stern, carrying lugsail, or lugsail and jib, and measuring from about 14ft. to 30ft. keel. The mast is lowered a-stem, not a-stern as in other boats.
Sgoth long,—Yacht. 2‡‡Ship's fly-boat.
Sgoth luath, geàrradair,—Cutter, row-boat attached to war-ship.
Sia-ràmbach,—Gig, boat with straight gunwale for 2, 4, or 6 oars.
Slaod uisge; ràth—*Lewis, W. Ross, &c.*,—Raft.
Smag, Gaelic spelling of *smack.*
Treachaill-mhara, (an)—Fingal's boat.

☞ *When the name of a particular district is given for any term above, it does not follow that such term is peculiar to that district, but only that it is in use there. Many of the terms are common to the whole of the Highlands.*
A number of additional boating terms were, unfortunately, received too late to be stereotyped here ; but they will be found in the Appendix.
In addition to the authorities mentioned on p. xv, *considerable assistance has been obtained in compiling these boating terms from :—*
Trans. Gaelic Soc. Inverness, xix, 213.
"Fionn's" letter to Highland News, 2/10/97.
Donald MacLachlan, Connel.
Michael MacNeill, Castlebay.
M. MacLeod, Uig, and Donald Murray, Aberdeen (chiefly for Lewis.)
Farquhar Mackenzie, Paris, and A. R. MacLeod, Glasgow, (chiefly for Gairloch, Loch Broom, &c.)
Miss Carmichael, Edinburgh, (for Western Isles.)

For names of sails and parts of a sail, see seòl.

bàtachan, -ain, *s.m.* (*dim.* of bàta) Little boat.
batachan, -ain, *s.m.* (*dim.* of bata) Little staff.
bata cuilce,‡‡ -aichean-, *s.m.* Cane.
bataichean, *n. pl.* of bata.
bàtaichean, *n. pl.* of bàta.
batadh (a'), *pr.pt.* of bat.
batail, Gaelic spelling of *battle.* 2‡‡Threat.
batailte, see batail.
batailteach,‡‡ -eiche, *a.* Battalious.
batair, -ean, *s.m.* Cudgeller. 2 Noisy fellow. 3**Lounger, idler.
bataireachd, *s. f. ind.* Cudgelling. 2 Idleness. 3 Lounging. 4 Making a rattling noise. Is ann ort tha a' bhataireachd ! *what a noise you are making !*
bàta-speur, -aichean-, *s. m.* Balloon.
bàt'-athair,** see bàta-speur.
bàt-bhùth,** *s.m.* Awning.
†bàth, *s.* The sea. 2 Slaughter, massacre, murder. 3 Death. 3 Thirst.
bàth, *v.a.* Drown, immerse. 2 Quench, slake. 3 Extinguish, smother. 4***rarely* faint. 5‡‡Die, perish. Bhàthadh e, *or* chaidh a bhàthadh, *he was drowned* ; bhàth i an gealbhan, *she extinguished the fire* (by pouring water on it);

bhàth e a phathadh, *he quenched his thirst*; bàthamaid gach smalan, *let us drown all care.*
bàth, *a.* see baoth.
——, *s.m.* see baothair.
bàthach,-aich,-aichean, see bàthaich. 2††Sloth.
bàthachd, see baothaireachd. Thig *b.* ort, *foolishness shall come upon thee.*
bàthadh, -aidh, *s.m.* Drowning. 2 Quenching, slaking. 3 Smothering. 4‡‡ Faint, swoon. A' b—, *pr. pt.* of bàth. Bàthadh mór aig oirthir, *a great drowning near the land* (applied to persons who die as soon as they get their luck); is e barrachd de'n aodach a ni na longannan caola 'bhàthadh, *'tis too much sail that capsizes the narrow ships*, (applied to persons with more ambition than grit.)

33. Bàthaich.

bàthaich, -ean, *s.m.* Byre, cowhouse.
Parts of a byre—
1 Balla,—Wall.
3 Amar,—Trough.
4 Post deiridh,—Hind-post.
5 Maide mullaich,—Top rail.
6 Clach amail,—Curb-stone.
7 Bùird tharsuinn,—Travis boards.
8 Bacan,—Stake.
12 Inne, carcair, gruip,(MM)—Gutter.
13 Urlar,—Paved floor.
Buall, buist,—Stall.
Prasach,—Manger. (not in illust.)
bà-thaigh, see bàthaich.
†bathainte, *pl.* Cattle spoil.
bathaire, see baothair.
bathais, -ean, *s.f.* Forehead, front. 2 Crown of the head. 3 Impudence. Nach ann aige a bha a' bhathais! *what impudence the fellow had!* cuiridh mi aghaidh bhur bonn ri bhur bathais, *I will make you set about the work in earnest* (*lit.* put the face of your soles to your forehead); chaidh mi thar bathais an ùrlair de leum, *I went right across the floor at one jump*; bathais gun fhallus, *a brow without sweat*, (said of one void of shame or common sense.
———each, *a.* Of, or belonging to, the forehead. 2 Assuming in manner, impudent, bold.
———eachd,‡‡ *s.f.* Effrontery.
bathal, see badhal.
bathalaich, *s.m.* Vagabond.
bathar, -air, *s.m.* Wares, goods, merchandise. 2**Bale. 3**see bàrr. Bathar òir agus airgid, agus chlach luachmhor, *the merchandise of gold, silver and precious stones*; am *b.* a bha 'san luinge, *the wares that were in the ship.*
bathar-bhòrd,* -bhùird, *s.m.* Counter.
batharnach,* *s.m.* Warehouse, shop, storehouse.
†bathghorm, see liath-ghorm.
bathlach, see balach.
†bathlan, *s.m.* Flux of the sea. 2 Tide. 3 Calm.

†bath-laodh, *s.m.* Helmet.
†bathroid,** -ean, *s.f.* Token.
bàth-ròs, -rois, *s.m.* Rosemary. see ròs Màiri.
bàth-shruth, *s.m.* Calm or smooth stream.
†bath-throid, *s. f.* Helmet, head-piece.
bàt-phubull,** *s.m.* Awning.
†batròs, see ròs Màiri.
b'e, (*for* bu e), *3rd. pers.sing.. past ind., irr. v.* is. It was he, *or* it. B'e sin iarrtas do chridhe, *that was the desire of thine heart.*
†bè, *s. f.* Life. 2 Wife, woman, female. 3 Night.
†beabh, *s. f.* Tomb, grave.
beabhar, Gaelic spelling of *beaver.*
†beacan, -ain, *s.m.* Large fuzzball, see beach. 2 Mushroom, see balg-bhuachair.
†-———ach, *a.* Abounding in mushrooms, of mushrooms, like a mushroom.
†beacarna, *s. f.* Common prostitute.
beach, -a, -an, *s.m.* Bee. 2 Bee-hive. 3 Wasp. 4**Beast. 5**Bird. Mar bheachaibh, *as bees*; dranndan bheachan an aonaich, *the murmur of the mountain bees.*
———,§ -a, -an, *s.m.* Devil's snuffbox or fuzzball—*lycoperdon gigantum.*
———ach, -aiche, *a.* Abounding in bees or wasps. 2 Waspish. 3 Of, or belonging to, a bee or wasp. Mios *b.* seilleanach, *the month that produces wasps and bees.*
beachaid,* see beachair.
beachair, -ean, *s.m.* Bee-hive.
beachan, *s.m.* *see beach. 2**Little bee.
beachan-chapuill, } *s.m.* Wasp. 2 Horse-fly.
——— -each, }
beachanta,** -ainte, *a.* Waspish, cross. Gu *b.*, *waspishly.*
beacharn,** -airn, -airnean, *s. f.* Prostitute.
beachd, -a, -an, *s.m.* Notice, attention, observation, perception. 2 Feeling. 3 Ambition. 4 Idea, conception. 5 Distinct recollection. 6 Opinion. 7 Behaviour. 8 Sense, judgment. 9 Conceit. 10 Aim, intention. 11 Carriage. 12**Vision, eyesight. 13 Surety. Gu beachd, *surely, clearly*; as a bheachd, *out of his senses*; ma's math mo bheachd-sa, *if I have a distinct recollection*; mór 'na beachd, *conceited in her ideas*; tha mi 'san aon bheachd, *I am of the same opinion*; geur shaighdean laoich a's cinntiche beachd, *the arrows of the hero of surest aim*; am bheil beachd agad far an d'fhàg thu e? *have you any recollection where you left it?* gabh beachd air, *pay particular attention to it*; cha robh mi dorch gun bheachd, *I was not so ignorant and void of perception*; a réir mo bheachd-sa, *to the best of my recollection* or *opinion*; cum sin 'nad bheachd, *keep that steadily in view*; 's e sin a bha 'm bheachd-sa 'san àm, *that is what I had in view at the time*; an do chaill thu, mar mise, do bheachd? *hast thou, like me, lost thy memory?* chuir na bàird am beachd air na triath, *the bards fixed their notice on the chiefs*; ma's còmhrag do bheachd, *if battle be thine intention*; o bheachd, *out of sight.*
†———, *s.m.* Covenant, surety. 2 Circle, ring, 3 Multitude.
†———, *v.n.* see beachdaich. 2**Embrace, compass.
-———ach,‡‡ -aiche, *a.* Notional. 2 Perceptive.
-———achadh, -aidh, *s. m.* Considering, meditating, contemplating. 2 Viewing, watching. 3 Consideration, meditation. 4*Minutely observing. A' b—, *pr.pt. v.* beachdaich.
-———achail,‡‡ -e, *a.* Imaginative.
-———adair,** *s.m.* see beachdair.
-———aich, *pr.pt.* a' beachdachadh, *v.n.* O

serve, perceive. 2 Attend to. 3 Mark. 4 Consider, meditate. 5 Stare, eye. 6 Review, criticise. Cha *bh.* sùil a h-àite, *no eye shall discern her place*, bheachdaich mi gu dùr. *I observed attentively;* bheachdaich iad am fear mór, *they eyed the mighty man.*
———aichte, *a., & pt.pt.* of beachdaich. Considered. 2 Observed, watched. 3 Ascertained, certain.
———aid,* see beachd-àite.
———aidh, *a.* Certain, authoritative, sure. 2 Observant, watchful, meditative. 3 Judicious. 4 Exact, sure in aim. 5‡‡High-minded. 6**Considerate. 7‡‡Notable. Gu beachdaidh, *considerately*, also *most decidedly, most assuredly;* tha thu beachdaidh gu'm bi, *you are quite certain it shall be so.*
———aidheachd,‡‡ *s.f.* Notableness.
———ail, *a.* see beachdaidh. 2** *rarely* circular. Nach beachdail an t-sùil a th'aige! *how keenly observant his eye is!*
beachdair, -ean, *s.m.* Observer, spy, scout. 2 Critic, reviewer. 3** Apprehender.
———eachd, *s.f.* Spying, informing, espionage. 2 Criticism, reviewing, (as of a book.)
beachd-àite, *pl.* [-àitean &] -àiteachan, *s.m.* Observatory. 2 Watch-tower,
beachdalachd, *s. f. ind.* Circumspection, caution, attention. 2 Self-conceit. 3 Sureness of aim. 4 Great punctuality in observing. 5 ambition.
beachd-bhorb, *a.* Haughty, imperious, insolent.
——— -eòlas,‡‡ *s.m.* Intuition.
——— -ionad, -an, *s.m.* see beachd-àite.
——— -maraiche, *s.m.* Mariner's compass.
——— -sgeul, -sgeòil, *s.m.* Information.
——— -shùil, a, *s.m.* Observation, vision.
——— -shùileach, -eiche, *a.* Minutely observant, keen-eyed.
——— -smaointeachadh, see beachd-smuainteachadh.
——— -smaointich, see beachd-smuaintich.
——— -smuaineachadh, see b—smuainteachadh.
——— -smuainich, see b—smuaintich.
——— -smuainteach, *a.* see b—smuainteachail.
———————adh, -aidh, *s.m.* Meditating, contemplating, musing. A' b—, *pr.pt.* of beachd-smuaintich.
———————ail,** *a.* Contemplative, meditative.
——— -smuaintich, *v.n.* Muse, meditate, contemplate. 2**Talk. A bheachd-smuainteachadh 'san fhaiche, *to meditate in the field.*
beachdta, *a.* Certain, sure, accurate.
beach-each, (DM) *s.m.* Wasp. 2 Horse-fly.
—— -lann, *s.m.* Bee-hive.
†beachlannach, *s. f.* Place suitable for bee-hives.
†———————, *a.* Abounding in bee-hives.
beach mór, (AF) *s.m.* Hornet.
beachnuadh firionn,} *s. m.* Square-stemmed St. John's wort,—*hypericum quadrangulum.* (*lit.* male St. John's wort)[ordinary St. John's wort is called *beachnuadh boirinn* by O' Reilly.]
†beachran, *v.a.* Grieve, molest, trouble, annoy.
†beachran, -ain, *s.m.* Wandering, straying.
beach-thaigh, see beach-lann.
†bead, *s.m.* Flattery. 2 Cunning. 3 Trick. 4‡‡ Pity. 5‡‡Book.

34. Beachnuadh firionn.

beadach, -aiche, *a.* Forward, impudent. 2 Prone to flatter. 3 Pettish.
———d, *s. f. ind.* Forwardness, impudence. 2 Flattery.
beadag, -aig, -an, *s. f.* Lying enticing young woman. 2 Impudent, impertinent young woman. 3 Gossip.
———ach,** *a.* Like a lying female. 2 Like a gossip.
———ag, see beadag.
———an, -ain, *s.m.* Impertinent, impudent, petulant, *or* trifling fellow, 2** Tale-teller. [Originally a tup lamb about six months old, as it was very keen at that age to cover the sheep. Lads in their teens inclined to have carnal connection with women are called *beadagan* in the W. Isles.—J.M.]
———an, *n. pl.* of beadag.
———anach,‡‡ -aiche, *a.* Pedantic.
—————d,‡‡ *s.f.* Pedagogy.
beadaiche, *comp.* of beadach.
————,** *s.m.* Flatterer, cajoler. 2 Enticing fellow.
beadaidh, -e, *a.* Impudent, petulant, forward, pert. 2 Fastidious, nice, luxurious. 3 Pettish. 4** Mannerless. 5** Sweet-mouthed, flattering. 6**Alert. An Inid bheadaidh thig an là roimh 'n oidhche, *the forward Shrove-tide the day comes before the night* (the feast before the vigil); beadaidh ri linn socair, *luxurious in time of peace;* cho *b.*, *so forward;* òran na circe beadaidh, *a song from the pert hen;* breac beadaidh, *a trout.*
————eachd, *s. f. ind.* Impudence, petulance, impertinence, incivility, forwardness. 2 Luxuriousness. 3 Capriciousness. 4 Pettishness. 5** Flattery. 6** Alertness. 7 Assurance.
†————ean, *s.m.* Scoffer. 2‡‡ Parasite.
†beadaighe, see beadaiche.
beadair,* *v.a.* see beadraich.
beadal,** Gaelic spelling of *beadle.*
beadamanachd,** *s.f.* Procacity, presumption.
beadan, -ain, *s.m.* Calumny. 2**Forward, petulant person.
———ach, -aiche, *a.* Calumnious 2 Forward. 3 Petulant. Gu beadanach, calumniously.
———achd, *s.f.* Scurrility, calumny. 2** Habit of calumniating. 3** Forwardness, pertness.
beadarach, -aiche, *a* Beloved, lovely. 2 Flattering, cajoling, coaxing. 3 Pampered, delicate, indulged. 4 Fond. 5 Sportive, playful. Is beadarach an ni an onoir, *honour is delicate;* Albainn bheadarrach! *beloved Scotland!*
————d, *s. f. ind.* Buxomness, playfulness
beadaradh, see beadradh.
bead-fhaclach, -aiche, *a.* Impudently loquacious.
†bead-fhoraobhadh,‡‡ *s.m.* Register, commentary.
†beadrach, -aich, *s. f.* Playful girl.
————, *a.* see beadarach.
beadradh, -aidh, *s.m.* Fondling, flirting. 2 Flattering. 2 Caressing. 4 Toying. 5** Fondness, endearment. 6††Fun, sport, play. A' b—, *pr. pt.* of beadraich. Beadradh gu leòir, *enough of flirting;* chuireadh tu bodaich gu beadradh, *you would set old men a-fondling.*
beadragan, see beadradh.
beadraich, *pr. pt.* a' beadradh, *v. a.* Fondle, caress, indulge, cajole, coax.
beaduidh, see beadaidh.
————eachd, see beadaidheachd.
beag, *a.* Little, short, diminutive. 2 Dis-

agreeable, often used to express disapprobation. 3 Light, trifling, insignificant. 4** Young. 5**Few. 6(AH) Sordid, miserly, niggardly. Declined thus in connection with a noun :

	Sing.		Plur.
Nom. *(m.)* beag,	*(f.)* bheag,		*(m. & f.)* beaga.
Gen.	bhig,	bige,	beaga.
Dat.	beag,[1]	bhig,	beaga.
Voc.	bhig,	bheag,	beaga.

[1] When the noun preceding *beag* has the article before it, the dat. sing. masc. is aspirated (bheag.) *Beag* is compared thus : *1st. Comp.* bige, *or* lugha. *2nd. Comp.*, bigid, *or* lughaid. *3rd. Comp.* bigead, *or* lughad. Ach beag, air bheag, *almost* ; is beag nach, *almost ;* rud beag, *a little thing* ; duine beag, *a diminutive man ;* ùine bheag, *a short time ;* is beag orm thu, *I hate you;* iad-san air am beag sibh, *they who hate you* ; is beag seo, *this is a trifling (light) thing ;* is beag an dolaidh, *it is a small loss* (he or she richly deserves it); na sionnaich bheaga, *the young foxes* ; na coin bheaga, *the little dogs* ; na fir bheaga [na daoine beaga,] *the little men* ; leanabh beag, *a babe* ; air bheag de làithibh, *in a few* days ; air glé bheag de'n oidhche, *very early in the night* ; is beag sin de Ghàidhlig, *that is a poor sort of Gaelic* ; tha e fìor bheag 'n a nàdur, *he has a very niggardly disposition* ; cha'n fheairrd duine a bhi cho beag siod, *a person is not any better of being so niggardly as that.*

——,* *v.a.* see beagaich.

——, *s.m. & f.* (*n. pl.* big, declined in sing. as *a.* beag.) Little one. 2 Nothing. 3 Any, the least. 4 *pl.* The young. Am bheil a bheag de mhath air ? *is it worth anything ?* am beag agus am mór, *both great and small* ; an ni a chì na big, is e a nì na big ; *what the young see, they do;* a bheag a dh'aon ni is leatsa, *the least particle of what is thine* ; cha'n fhaigh a bheag [am] bàs ; *nothing shall die* ; beag is beag, *little and little, by degrees.*

beagachadh, -aidh, *s.m.* Diminishing, lessening, diminution. A' b—, *pr.pt.* of beagaich.

beagachd,‡‡ *s. f. ind.* Littleness.

beagaich, *pr.pt.* a' beagachadh, *v.a.* Diminish, lessen, abate. 2 Destroy.

beagaiche, *s.m.* Abater, diminisher.

beagaichear, *fut. pass.* of beagaich.

beagaichidh, *fut. aff. a.* of beagaich.

beagaichte, *past. part.* of beagaich.

beagan, -ain, *s.m.*, *& a.* Little. 2 Few, small number, small quantity. Air bheagan chéille, *with little wisdom, witless* ; beagan uisge, *a little water* ; fuirich beagan, *stop a little* ; beagan crìon, *a very little* ; a' dol am beaganaibh, *growing into small portions, crumbling* ; a lìon beagan is beagan, mar a dh'ith an cat an sgadan, *by degrees (little and little) as the cat ate the herring* ; beagan eile, *a little more*; air bheagan maith, *worth little, of no value ;* air bheagan tuireim, *having little sense.*

beag-chionta, -an, *s.m.* Petty crime, foible, slight fault.

beag-chreidmheach, -eiche, *a.* Of little faith, sceptical, incredulous.

†**beagdhata**, *s.m.* Stingy fellow.

beag-eagalach, -aiche, *a.* Bold, fearless.

beag-ghaduidheachd,‡‡ *s.f.* Larceny.

beag-luach, see beag-luachach.

beag-luachach, -aiche, *a.* Valueless, useless.

beag-nàire, -e, *s.f.* Impudence, indelicacy.

beag-nàrach, -aiche, *a.* Impudent, shameless. Gu *b.*, *shamelessly.*

——————d, *s. f. ind.* Shamelessness, impudence.

beag-seadhach, -aiche, *a.* Inconsiderate. Is fhearr am beag-seadhach na'n draghaiche mòr, mi-ghnìomhach, *the little sensible man is better than the great inactive burdensome man.*

beag-shuileach, -eiche, *a.* Pink-eyed.

beairdean, see boitean.

beairt, see beart.

——each, see beartach.

——ean, *pl.* of beairt (*for* beart.)

——eas, see beartas.

——ich, see beartaich.

†**beal**, see beul.

bealach, -aich, -aichean, *s.m.* Defile, passage, pass or gorge of a mountain, glen. 2 Gap, breach in a wall or fence. 3 Gateway. 4 Gate. Tog am bealach, *build the breach;* mar eibhle 'sa bhealach, *like a fire in the mountain gorge ;* ciod am bealach am buail sinn ? *through which pass shall we strike our way* ; air bealach ceart, *on a right way* ; druid am bealach, *shut the way.*

bealach—*Arg.* Erroneously used for *bealaidh.*

†**bealadh**,‡‡ *s.m.* Anointing.

bealag,** see mealg.

bealaidh, *s.m.ind.* Broom, —*sarothamnus scoparius.* [§Badge of Clan Forbes.]

bealaidh Chattach,§ *s. m.* Butcher's broom. see calg-bhealaidh.

bealaidheach,‡‡ -eiche, *a.* Broomy.

bealaidh Frangach,§ *s.m.* Laburnum—*cytisus laburnum.*

bealaidh Sasunnach, *s.m.* Laburnum. see bealaidh Frangach.

35. *Bealaidh.*

bealamas,* -ais, *s.m.* Refuse of a feast, crumbs that fall from the table or from the mouth.

36. *Bealaidh Frangach.*

bealbhach,‡‡ *s.m.* Horse's bit.

bealbhan-ruadh, -ain-ruaidh, -ain-ruadha, *s.m.* Species of hawk, buzzard or 2 Frog.

†**bealchaithteach**, *a.* Talkative.

†**bealgach**, *a.* Garrulous, prattling.

——————,** *s.m.* Interpreter.

beall, see beoll.

Bealltainn, see Bealltuinn.

Bealltuinn, -e, *s.f.* May-day, first day of May. On the first of May was held a great Druidical festival in favour of the god Belus. On this day fires were kindled on the mountain tops for the purposes of sacrifice ; and between these fires the cattle were driven, to preserve them from contagion till next May-day. On this day it was usual to extinguish all the hearth fires, in order that they should be re-kindled from this purifying flame. In many parts of the Highlands the young folks of the district used to meet on the moors on 1st. May. They cut a table in the green sod, of a round figure, by cutting a trench in the ground of sufficient circumference to hold the whole company. They then kindled a fire, and dressed a repast of eggs and milk of the consistency of custard. They kneaded a cake of oatmeal, which was toasted at the embers against a stone. After the custard was eaten, they divided the cake into as many portions as there were persons in the company, as much alike as possible in size and shape. They daubed one of the pieces with charcoal till it was black all over, and they were then all put into a bonnet together, and each one, blindfolded, drew out a portion. The bonnet holder was entitled to the last bit, and whoever drew the black bit was the devoted person who was to be sacrificed to Baal, whose favour they meant to implore in rendering the year productive. The devoted person was compelled to leap three times over the flames.**

Là buidhe Bealltuinn, *a common name for May-day.*

†bealràidheach, *a.* Famous.

†bealràidhteach, *a.* Prattling, babbling, talkative. 2 see bealràidheach.

†bealtaine, *s.f.* Agreement, compact, bargain.

bealtair,** *s.m.* Compact.

†bealtuidh, *a.* Nasty, dirty.

†————eachd, *s.f.* Uncleanness, filthiness.

bealuidh, see bealaidh.

†beam, *s.m.* see beum.

bean, *pr.part.* a' beantainn [beanail, beantail, & beanailt,] *v. a. & n.* Touch. 2 Handle. 3 Meddle with. Cha bhean sibh ris, *ye shall not touch it* ; an ti a bheanas ribh, *he who touches you.*

bean, *s.f.* Woman, female. 2 Wife.

Thus declined :—

		Sing.	Plur.
Indef.	*Nom.*	bean,	mnathan, *and* mnai,
	Gen.	mnà,	bhan,
	Dat.	mnaoi,	mnathaibh,
	Voc.	a bhean !	a mhnathan !
Def.	*Nom.*	a' bhean,	na mnathan,
	Gen.	na mnà,	nam ban,
	Dat.	(do)'n mhnaoi,	(do)na mnathaibh
	,,	ris a' mhnaoi,	ris na mnathaibh

Bean a ghaoil, *the wife of his affections* ; goirear bean dith, *she shall be called woman*; bean nan deagh bheus, *a virtuous woman ;* air a bhreith le mnaoi, *born of a woman* ; mar mhnaoi, *as a wife ;* bean a' bhaile, *the tenant or proprietrix of a place* ; bean an taighe, *the landlady* or *goodwife ;* bithidh taobh an teine aig caraid bean an taighe, *the goodwife's friend will be near the fire;* bithidh caraid bean an taighe an uachdar an taighe, *the goodwife's friend will be over the house.* The last two sayings do not necessarily mean that the goodwife will be nasty to her husband's friends, but merely that her own friends will naturally feel more at home in the house. When addressing one's mother in Gaelic, the expression " a bhean " (woman) is used and not "a mhàthair."

bean,(AF) *s.f.* She-goat. 2‡‡Step, degree.

†——, *a.* Active, quick, nimble.

beanachas-taighe, see banas-taighe.

†beanadh, -aidh, *s.m.* Dullness, bluntness.

†————, *v.a.* Take. 2 Belong. 3 Reap, shear.

beanag, -aig, -an, *s. f.* Little woman or wife. 2 Term of endearment for a female. 3** Pundle.(?) Mo bheanag ghaolach, *my dear little woman.*

beanail, see banail.

beanailt, *s.m.* Touching. A' b—, *pr. pt.* of bean.

————each, -eiche, *a.* Touching. 2 Meddling. 3 Tangent.

†beanamhuil, *a.* see banail.

†beanann,‡‡ *s.pl.* Appurtenances, furniture.

†beanas-taighe, see banas-taighe.

bean-baile, *s. f.* Proprietrix of a village. 2 Wife of a farm tenant.

bean-bainnse, *s.f.* (*lit.* the woman of the wedding) Bride.

bean-bharain, *s.f.* Baron's wife.

bean-bhochd, *s.f.* Female mendicant. 2 Poor woman. Mnathan bochda, *poor women ;* an t-sean bhean bhochd, *a poetical name for Ireland, used there.*

bean-bhràthair-athar, *s.f.* Uncle's wife, wife of a father's brother. Bean-bràthair-m'athar, *my paternal uncle's wife.*

bean-bràthair-màthar, *s.f.* Uncle's wife, wife of a mother's brother. Bean-bràthair mo mhàthar, *my maternal uncle's wife.*

bean-bhràthair-seanair, *s. f.* Grand-uncle's wife, wife of a grandfather's brother.

bean-bhràthar, *s.f.* Sister-in-law.

bean-charaid, see bana-charaid.

bean-chéile, *s.f.* Spouse, wife.

bean-chìche, *s.f.* Wet-nurse.

bean-chinnidh, *s.f.* Kinswoman. 2 Clanswoman, female namesake.

bean-chliamhuinn, see bana-chliamhuinn.

†beanchobhar, *s.m.* Horn.

†beanchobhrach, *a.* Horny, horned.

bean-choimheadachd, *s.f.* Waiting-maid. 2 Bride's-maid.

bean-chomharbadh,** *s.f.* Dowager.

†beanchuir, see beanchobhar.

bean chumanta,‡‡ *s.f.* Harlot.

bean-dalta, see ban-dalta.

bean-éigin, see b— éigneachadh.

bean-éigneachadh, -aidh, *s.m.* Rape.

†beangan, see meangan.

bean-ghlùin, *s.f.* Midwife. Thubhairt a' bhean-ghlùin rithe, *the midwife said to her.*

bean-iasg, *s.f.* Spawner, female fish.

bean-léigh, mna-l—, mnathan-l—, *s.f.* Female physician.

bean-mhath,* *s.f.* Small-pox. [Always preceded by the article *a'*.]

bean-mhic,* *s. f.* Daughter-in-law.

beann, beinn, *s.f.* Degree. 2 Step. 3 Beam. 4 Corner. 5 Skirt. 3 Attention. 7 Regard. 8 Horn (*Islay.*) 9 Top, peak. 19** Drinking cup. 11‡‡Rock. 12 Arm of a cross. 13 Prong of a cycle-fork. 14***rarely* Bone. A bheann iùbhraidh, *its beam of yew ;* bràigh lìn air a ceithir beannaibh, *a sheet by the four corners*; na toir beann air ciod a their e, *pay no attention to what he says.*

beann, *gen.pl.* of beinn.

————ach,** -aich, *s.m.* Fork.

————, -aiche, *a.* Skirted. 2 Corner-wise. 3 Horned. 4 Pointed. 5 Forked. 6** Chequered. 7**Mosaic. 8 see beanntach.

beannachadh, -aidh, *s.m.* Blessing, benediction. 2 Act or circumstance of blessing. 3 Compliment. 4 Grace before or after food. A' b—, *pr.part.* of beannaich. Iarr *b.*, *ask a blessing*; sruth-bheannachadh nan ceatharn, *the smooth address of the robbers.*

beannachadh-bàird, *s.m.* Poet's congratulation. It was the custom in the Highlands, of old, to meet the bride coming forth from her chamber with her maidens on the morning after her marriage, and to salute her with a poetical blessing called *beannachadh-bàird.—An Gàidheal*, ii, 63. If, at any jovial meeting, any man retired, for however short a time, he was obliged, before he was permitted to resume his seat, to make an apology for his absence in rhyme. If he had no talent for poetry, or if, from humour, he did not choose to comply, which was seldom the case, he was obliged to pay such a proportion of the reckoning as the company thought proper to propose. This, according to Martin, was *beannachadh-bàird*.**

——— -beinge, *bench-blessing*.
——— bobhstair, *bolster-blessing*.
——— -cluasaig, *pillow-blessing*.
——— -cuaiche, *couch-blessing*.
} Forms of blessing said or sung on various occasions, now only in the Western Isles.—(A.C.)

beannachan,** -ain, *s.m.* Cuckold.

beannachd, -an, *s.f.* Blessing. 2 Farewell expression. 3 Compliments, salutation. (see beannachadh. Cuir mo *bh.*, *send my compliments* ; thoir mo bheannachd, *give my compliments* ; beannachd Dhé leat, *may the blessing of God attend you* ; tha mo bheannachd-sa agad, *you have my blessing* ; beannachd leat ! *farewell, adieu !* fàg beannachd aige, *bid him adieu, say good-bye to him;* beannachd do t' anam is buaidh, *a blessing to thy soul and victory* ; beannachd a shaoid is a shiubhail leis, *may he fare as he deserves* ; beannachd le cleachdadh na h-òige, *farewell to the pursuits of youth* ; mo bheannachd 'na chuid is 'na chuideachd, *I wish increase of prosperity to his gear and relations*.

beannachdach, *a.* Prone to bless. 2 Ready to salute.

beannachdail,* *a.* see beannachdach.

beannachdan,* -ain, *s.m.* Insect that strikes one's finger when holding it.

beannag,‡ -aig, *s.f.* Kerchief, head-band. 2 Corner of a plaid or shawl. 3 Skirt. 4 Coif, linen cap. 5 see bannag. [Seems to be the true Gaelic equivalent of *shawl*. In Lewis it is a square piece of home-made tweed worn by women about their shoulders when at any work outside on a cold day. It is essentially quite square, so that when doubled the upper corner exactly covers the lower.—J.M.]

———ach, -aiche, *a.* Having corners. 2 Skirted. 3 Plaited. 4**Having a coif, like a coif.

beannaich, *pr. part.* a' beannachadh, *v. a.* Bless, invoke a blessing. 2 Salute, hail. Na beannaich dha, *do not salute him* ; Dhia beannaich sinn ! *God bless us !*

———idh, *fut. aff. act.* of beannaich.

———te, *a. & pt. part.* of beannaich. Blessed. 2 Saluted. 3 Holy. 4 Happy. Is beannaicht' an duine, *blessed is the man* ; tha thu a' fàs beannaichte, *you are getting holy* (a remark frequently made in derision when the person addressed refuses to join in such as a Highland reel or a game of shinty, because he pretends that it is wicked to do so !).

†**beannam**, *v.a.* I steal, or thieve.

beannan, -ain, *s.m.* Little hill.

bean-nighe, see bean-nigheadaireachd. 2 (JM) Female wraith of very small stature believed to be seen or heard at a loch or burn washing clothes when some person in the neighbourhood was about to die.

bean-nigheachain, see bean-nigheadaireachd.

bean-nigheadaireachd, *s. f.* Washerwoman, laundry-maid.

bean-nighidh, see bean-nigheadaireachd.

beannta, *n.pl.* of beinn. A bheannta ! *voc.pl.* of beinn.

beanntach, -aiche, *a.* Hilly, mountainous. 2 Rocky. 3 Pinnacled.

———d, *s. f. ind.* Hilliness, mountainousness. 2 Steepness.

beanntainn,†† *s.m.* Mint. see meannt.

——— -dìge,†† -e-, *s.m.* Wild mint.

beanntair,* *s.m.* Mountaineer.

beanntan, *n. & dat.pl.* of beinn.

bean nuadh-phòsda,‡‡ *s.f.* Bride.

beannuchadh, see beannachadh.

beannuich, see beannaich.

———te, see beannaichte.

bean-òsda, *s.f.* Hostess.

bean-ridir, see ban-ridir.

bean-shìth, see ban-sìth.

bean-shiùbhlaidh, *s.f.* Woman in child-bed.

bean-shnìomhaich,‡‡ *s.f.* Spinster, (i.e. female spinner, not necessarily an unmarried woman.)

bean-sìthe, *s.f.* see ban-sìth.

bean-striopachais, *s. f.* Fornicatress. 2 Adultress.

beantag,‡‡ -aig, -an, *s.f.* Corn-fan.

bean-taighe, *s.f.* House-wife.

beantainn, *s.m.* Touching, act of touching. A' b—, *pr.pt.* of bean.

bean-tuath, see ban-tuathanach.

bean-uasal, *s.f.* Lady, gentlewoman.

†**beanughadh**, *s.m.* Recovering.

bean-uibe, (AC) *s.f.* Witch.

†**bear**, bir, see bior.

†**bear**,** see beithir.

†**beara**, *s.m.* Judge.

———ch,* *s.f.* Dog-fish. see gobag.

———chd, *s. f.* Judgment.

bearaideach, -eiche, *a.* Having means—J.M. 2(AH) Rude, derisive, sarcastic, ready to apply nicknames to other people. 3 (D.M.) see biorraideach, & bearraideach. Cha'n 'eil e bearaideach, *he is without means* ; a mhilidhibh bearaideach ; *ye agile warriors !—Filidh nam beann, p. 67.*

†**bearam**, *v.a.* see beir.

†**bearan**, -ain, *s.m.* Young man. 2 Pin. 3 see bioran.

bearbh,** *v.a. & n.* Seethe. 2‡‡Melt.

———adh,‡‡ -aidh, *s.m.* Seething, boiling. 2 melting. A' b—, *pr.part.* of bearbh.

———ain, *s.f.* Vervain.

† ———air, *s.m.* Refiner of metals.

†**bearg**, *s.m.* Anger. 2 Champion.

†———achd, *s.f.* Diligence.

†**beargnadh**, *s.f.* Vernacular language of a country.

bearla, see beurla.

beàrn, -eirn & -eàirn, *pl.* bearnan, *s.f.* Breach, fissure, gap, aperture. 2 Cranny, crevice. 3 Ellipsis in *gram.* (written thus, * * * or ———) 5**Separation. Troimh bheàrnan nan neul, *through the fissures of the clouds*; le beàrnaibh, *with breaches.*

———, *v.a.* Notch. 2 Hack. 3 Make a gap or breach.

———ach, -aiche, *a.* Abounding in gaps or breaches. 2 Notched. 3 Hacked. 4 Having or causing, fissures, apertures, clefts, or openings. 5 Having broken teeth. 6**Chopped. An sgiath mheallach bheàrnach, *the bossy scalloped shield.*

———ag, -aig, -an, *dimin.* of beàrn.

——an, *n.pl.* of beàrn. 2 *dimin.* of beàrn. 3 ‡‡Person with broken or uneven teeth.
beàrnan-Bealltuinn,§ Marsh-marigold. see a' chorrach shod.
——— -beàrnach, Dandelion. see beàrnan-Brìde.
——— breac,§ Milk-thistle. see fothannan breac.
——— -Brìde, *s.m.* Dandelion — *taraxacum dens leonis.*
beàrn-mhìol, *s.m.* Hare-lip.
†beàrr, *a.* Short, brief.
beàrr, *v.a.* Shave. 2 Shear, clip, crop, curtail, prune. 3 Taunt, gibe.
——a, -an, see bearradh.
——adair, -ean, *s.m.* Barber, hairdresser. 2 Critic. 3 Shearer. 4 Giber. Ealtain bearradair, *a barber's razor.*

37. Bearnan-Brìde.

——adaireachd, *s.f.* Occupation of a barber. 2 Shearing, clipping, cropping. 3 Carping, criticizing. 4 Satirizing, gibing.
bearradairean, *pl.* of bearradair.
bearradan,‡‡ -ain, *s.m.* Scissors. 2 Snuffers.
——dh, -aidh, -aidhean, *s.m.* Cutting, as of hair or any other crop. 2 Shearing, clipping, lopping, pruning. 3 Shaving. 4 Spear, dart. 5 Short hair. 6 Cut, slice, shred, segment, fragment. 7**Sharp-pointed instrument. 8 ††Mountain ridge. 8‡‡Precipice. 9‡‡ Tripping along. A' bearradh, *pr.pt.* of bearr. Dean do bhearradh, *shave thyself* a' bearradh na mòine, *paring the peat-moss* ; a' bearradh a' bhuntata, *cropping the potatoes* ; a' bearradh nan craobh, *pruning the trees ;* a' cromadh le bearradh a' chnuic, *stooping* (as a hawk at full speed) *down the slope of the hill.*
bearrag, -aig, *s.f.* Razor.
bearraiche, -an, *s.m.* see bearradair.
bearraideach, -eiche, *a.* Light, nimble, active. 2 Flighty, giddy. Gu bearraideach, *lightly.*
————d,* *s.f.* Flightiness, giddiness, lightheadedness.
bearranach,** *a.* Miserable, mournful.
bearra-phlub,** *s.m.* Roundhead.
bearrchasach, -aiche, *a.* High-mettled, of ardent spirit.
bearr-sgian, -éine, -sgéinean, *s.f.* Pruning-knife. 2 Razor.
bearrta, *pt. part.* of bearr. Shaved. 2 Cropped, clipped, pruned, shorn. An treud bhearrta, *the shorn flock.*
bearrtach,** *a.* Shaving. 2 Cropping, clipping, pruning. 3 Carping. 4 Fond of cropping, clipping, or pruning.
bearrthach, see bearradair.
bearrthag,‡‡ -aig, -an, *s.f.* Razor.
beart, beairt, *pl.* beairt [& bearta] *s. f.* Machine, engine. 2 ¦Loom, frame. 3 Deed, work, exploit. 4 Harness, yoke. 5 Burden. 6 Shrouds, tackling of a ship. 7 Sheath, scabbard. 8 Bundle, truss. 9 Clothes. 10 ‡‡Appendages of any kind. 11‡‡Threatening. †12 Game at tables. †13 Judgment. †14 Covenant, agreement. A bhearta iongantach, *his wonderful works* ; bearta treubhantais, *feats of valour* ; cóig luingis fo'm beart, *five ships in full equipment* ; a lann fo bheart, *his sword in the scabbard*; ar siùil is ar bearta, *our sails and our shrouds* ; eige anns a' bheart, *a web in the loom ;* dà steud fo bheart, *two steeds in harness*; beart-dheiridh-dialta, *a crupper* ; cuiridh aon bheart as gu lòm gu duine is gun a chonn fo chéill, is cuiridh beart eil' e ann, ach a gabhail 'na h-àm, *one deed may a man undo when his reason ruleth not, and a step may set him up, if taken in due time.*
——ach, -aiche, *a.* Rich, wealthy. 2 Of, or belonging to, a machine. 3**Sheathed. 4** Like a sheath or scabbard. 5††Too much. Duine *b., a man of deeds, one rich in works,* also *a rich man.*
beartachadh, -aidh, *s.m.* Beaming, putting warp in the loom. A' b—, *pr. part.* of beartaich.
——aich, *v.a.* Equip, adjust. 2 Yoke, harness. 3 Prepare, make ready. 4 Brandish, flourish. 5**Begin. 6**Enrich. 7**Meditate. 8 Put a web in the loom. 9 Provide with tackling. Bheartaich e a charbad, *he yoked his chariot.*
beartail, -e, *a.* Well-furnished.
beartair, *s.m.* Brandisher. 2** Achiever.
beartar,** -air, *s.m.* Stroke, shot, cast.
beartas, -ais, *s.m.* Riches. 2 Honour. 3 Abundance. Beartas is urram, *riches and honour.*
beart-chogaidh, -airt-, *s.f.* Arms.
beart-deilbh, *s. f.* Warping sticks. see crann deilbh.
beart-éididh, *s.f.* see b— -fhigheadaireachd.
beart féin-ghluasad, -airt-, *s.f.* Automaton.
beart-fhighe, see beart-fhigheadaireachd.
beart-fhigheadaireachd, -airt-, *s. f.* Weaver's loom, (see illustration 38.) The parts of a weaver's loom are named as follows :

1 Beart—*Barra.* Frame.
2 Crann snàth, garman shnàth—Yarn beam.
3 Crann aodaich, garman aodaich—Cloth beam.
4 Maide teannaidh.—*Barra.* Beam (or weights) to keep threads of warp tight.
5 [1]Acfhuinn, iomallan,—Heddles.
6 Ullagan,—*Barra.* Batten.
7 Croinn chas, greallagan, cranna cas, cliath, casan, casaichean(*Barra, Skye, &c.,*)—Treadles.
8 Spàl, [**smol]—Shuttle.
9 Iteachan, boban—Bobbin.
10 Bàrran,—Points.
11 Snàth,—Thread.
12 [1]Slinn,—Sleay.—Reed.
The "slinn" is formed of 4 frames of reeds placed close to each other, the degree of closeness being in proportion to the texture of cloth to be woven. It is surmounted by a moveable smooth board called
13 Slinn-chlàr,—Sleay-board.
14 Sliasd, sliasdan,**—Ledge.
15 Dlùth—Warp.
16 Inneach. Inneadh. Cuirreadh—*Lewis.* Uachdar—*Barra.* Woof.
17 Sméideagan,—Heddle-bar.
18 Eige, Clò—*Barra.* Web.
19 Garman-uchd—*Argyll.* Sliseag-uchd—*Hebrides.* Breast-beam, (square beam at weaver's' breast when sitting at the loom.)
20 Mogul,—Heddle-eye, mesh.
21 Sliosan,—Plates.
22 Uchd suidhichte,—Standing back.
23 Uchd crochta,—Hanging back.

OTHER WEAVING TERMS.

Ceithir-chuairt, 4-ply.
Cuidheall-iteachan, Wheel on which bobbins are filled.
Cuibean, Knots of the warp, tied to a

[1] Nos. 5 & 12 together, *acfhuinn meadhon.*

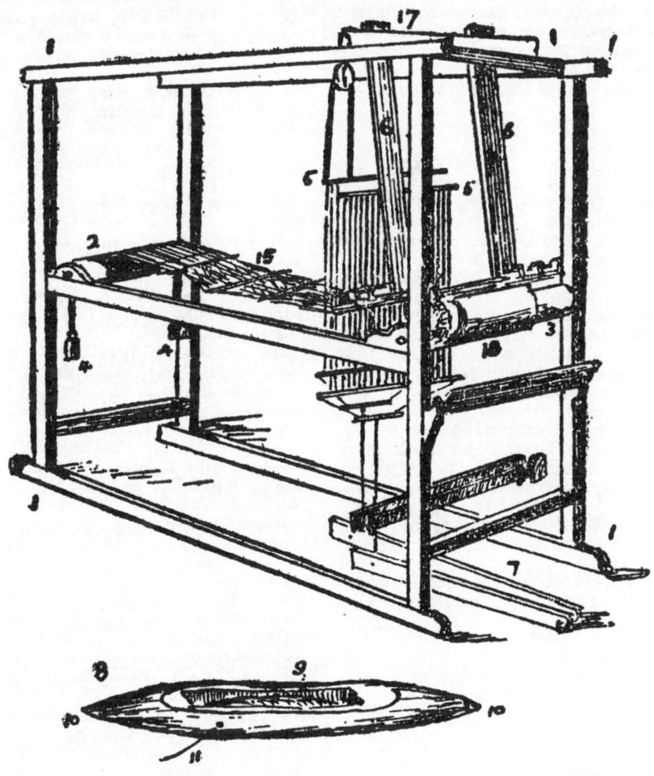

38. Beart-fhigheadaireachd.

small rod before beginning to weave.

Dà-fhillt, Twill, double ply.

Dealg, Thin piece of wood or reed, put through the reed (iteachan.)

Eàrrach (an), Stick with a nail in each end for keeping the cloth stretched broadways as it is woven.

Faochagan,** see fuigheagan.

Fuigheagan, Thrums (threads that fasten the last end of web.)

Iteachan, Reed.

Luigheagan, Thrums (the threads that fasten first end of web.)

Maide-leigidh, Turning-stick.

Riaghailt, is for spreading the thread before putting it in the loom.

Rolagan, Rowans, rolls of wool after leaving the cards.

Teannadh, is a 2-pointed piece of wood put at the edge of the cloth as it proceeds (the sleay is brought against it) to make the cloth firm.

†beartha, *a.* Clean, fine, nice, genteel. 2‡‡ Sharp, piercing. 3‡‡Boiled.

†beartrach, *s.f.* Pair of tables. 2 Chess-board.

beart-thuairneir, *s.f.* Turner's lathe.

——— -treabhaidh, *s.f.* Plough.

——— -uchd, *s.f.* Poitrel.

†beas, *a.* Certain, correct.

†——, *s.m.* see beus. 2 *s.f.* Speech, dialect.

beasan,‽ -ain, *s.m.* Adder's tongue fern. see lus na nathrach. 2**Gaelic spelling of *basin*.

†beas-chon, *s.m.* Syllogism.

†beascnaghadh, *s.m.* Agreement, accommodation.

†beascnaich, *v.n.* Confederate, agree, accommodate.

†beascnaidh, *v.n.* Agree, accommodate.

†beasg, *s.f.* Prostitute.

†——nadh,** -aidh, *s.m.* Speech, dialect. 2 Peace.

†beastan, *s.m.* Grievance.

beath, *s.f.* see beith. 2**Blood.

beatha, -annan, *s.f.* Life. 2 Victuals, food. 3 Livelihood. 4 Welcome, salutation. 5 see beithir. Is amhuil aisling ar beatha, *our life is like a dream*; gheibh e a bheatha, *he will get his livelihood*; do bheatha-sa, a ghaisgich! *you are welcome, O hero!* dean a bheatha, *welcome him*; is e slàinte do bheatha e, *you are quite welcome to it;* fad làithean a bheatha, *all the days of his life*; bhur beatha an dùthaich, *your welcome to the country*; an e mo bheatha? *am I welcome?* bheir duine beatha air éigin, ach cha toir e rath air éigin, *a man may force a livelihood, but he cannot force success.*

beathach, -aich, *s. m.* Beast, animal. 2** *strictly speaking* any living animal. 3 Never applied, but by way of reproach or pity, to a human being. A bheathaich bhochd! *poor creature!* a bheathaich mhi-mhodhail! *you impertinent brute!* [McL & D. says "sometimes applied to persons as a term of affection.]

beathachadh, -aidh, *s.m.* Living, benefice,

maintenance, livelihood. 2 Food, nourishment, sustenance. Air son beathachaidh, *for food*; fhuair am ministear òg *b.*, *the young minister obtained a benefice (living.)* A' b—, *pr. part.* of beathaich. Supporting, maintaining, feeding.
beathachail,** *a.* Alimental.
beathachair,** *s.m.* Animator.
beathachan, -ain, -an, *s.m.* Little animal. Mo *bh.* gaolach, *my dear little creature.*
beathachan-feòir, (AF) *s.m.* Lesser shrew.
beathadach,** -aich, *s.m.* Beaver.
beathag, -aig, *s.m.* see beach. 2 see beith. 3(AC) *s.f.* ? Breath. 4(AF) *prov.* Bird.
beathaich, *pr.part.* a' beathachadh, *v.a.* Feed, cherish, nourish, maintain, support. 2 Welcome, salute. Bheathaich e a' chuid eile, *he fed the rest*; *b.* mo chaoraich, *feed my sheep*; *b.* thusa mis' an diugh, agus beathaichidh mise thus' am màireach, *you feed me to-day, and I will feed you to-morrow.*
————ean, *n.pl.* of beathach.
————idh, *fut. aff. a.* of beathaich.
————te, *pt.part.* of beathaich. Fed, nourished, maintained, supported. 2 Welcomed.
beathail, *a.* Lively, vigorous, vital, pertaining to life.
beath'-aile,** *s.f.* Vital air, oxygen.
beathain,** *s.* Income.
beathair, see beithir.
beathalach, *a.* Lively, sprightly. Gu *b.*, *lively.*
————d, *s.f.* Liveliness, sprightliness. 2 *Vitality.
beathan,** -ain, *s.m.* Diet.
————an, *for* beathannan.
————nan, *pl.* of beatha. Victuals.
beath'-eachdraiche,** *s.m.* Biographer.
beath'-eachdraidh, *s.f.* Biography.
†beathmhan,(AF) -ain, *s.m.* Bee.
†beathodach, *s.m.* Beaver.
†beathra, *s.m.* Water.
†————ch, *gen.sing.* of beithir.
†————cha, Pertaining to a serpent or (2) a skate.
beathraichean, *pl.* of beithir.
†bec, *s.m.* Beak, bill of a bird. 2 Point.
becora-leacra, *s.m.* Juniper. see aitionn.
beic, -e, -eannan, *s.f.* Courtesy. Dean *b.*, *make a courtesy.*
——,‡‡ *pr.part.* a' beiceil, *v.n.* Courtesy.
——, *s.f.* Point, nib. 2 Bill of a bird.
béic, *s.f.* see beuc.
beiceadaich, (AG) *s.f.* Courtesying.
——eadh, see beucaich.
beiceil, *s.f.* Making obeisance, courtesying, bobbing. 2 Frisking. Ciod a' bheiceil a th'ort ? *why do you bob so ?* A' b—, *pr.part.* of beic.
béiceil, -il, see beucail.
beiceis,* *s.f.* see beiceil.
————each, -eiche, *a.* Bobbing, courtesying. 2 Skipping, hopping. 3 Frisky.
†beich-airc, *s.f.* Bee-hive.
beichd, see beic.
†beichneal, *s.m.* Gavel kind, (a form of law still observed in Kent.)
beicil,‡‡ *gen.sing.* of beiceil.
beic-leumnach, *a.* Prancing, skipping, hopping, curvetting.
————————d, *s.f.* Dancing, skipping, hopping.
†beid, *for* bithidh iad.
†——eadh, *s.m.* Patching.
beideal,** Gaelic spelling of *beadle.*
béidh, *gen. sing.* of biadh.
beididh, (AF) Lamprey (fish.)
†beidse, *s.f.* see turus.
beigleid, see beigneid.
beigneid, -ean, *s.f.* Gaelic spelling of *bayonet.*
beil ? *for* am bheil ? see bi.
——, *v.a.* see meil. 2††see bleith.
béil, incorrect form of beòil.
†beil, *s.f.* Diet, meal of meat.
beilbheag, -aig, see meilbheag.
————ach, see meilbheagach.
beilbhean-ruadh, -ein-ruaidhe, *s.m.* Frog. 2 see bealbhan-ruadh.
beile,* *s.m.* Bridle-bit.
beileach,* *s.f.* Muzzle for a horse, or other animal.
beileag,* *s.f.* —*Lewis*, for beileach. 2*Outer coating of a birch-tree.
†beileam, *s.m.* Taunt, reproach.
beileaman-ruadh, see bealbhan-ruadh.
béilean, -ein, *s.m.* Mouth, prattling mouth, little mouth. 2**Prattling. 3 Prattling person. 4 Futility. 5‡‡Quick scolding. Ciod a' *bh.* a th' ort ? *why do you prattle so ?*
————ach, *a.* Garrulous, prattling, loquacious, talkative, petulant.
————,* *s.f.* Prating, garrulous female.
————achd, *s.f. ind.* Garrulity, talkativeness, loquacity, petulance. Is ann ort tha a' bhéileanachd ! *how you do prate !*
beileich,* *v.a.* Muzzle, stop impertinent talk.
beilgeag, (AF) *s.f.* Small trout.
†beille,** -achan, *s.f.* Kettle, caldron.
béilleach, *a.* Blubber-lipped, having thick lips.
————achas, -ais, see beilleachd.
————achd, *s.f.* Deformity of blubber-lips.
beilleag, -eig, -an, *s.f.* Rhind, outer covering, especially of a birch-tree.
beillean,** *s.m.* Contumely, reproach.
beilt,** -e, Gaelic spelling of *belt.*
†beim,‡‡ *s.m.* Tribe, stock, generation. 2 Help. 3 Blemish, spot. 4 Oppression, reproach. 5 Gaelic spelling of *beam.* 6 *gen. sing.* of beum.
béim-cheap, -chip, *s.m.* Whipping-post.
béime, *gen.sing.* of beum.
béimeach, -eiche, *a.* see beumach.
†beimis, *for* bitheamaid (let us be.)
béimneach, -eiche, *a.* Talkative, loquacious.
†beimnead,‡‡ -eid, *s.m.* Furious smiter.
béin, *gen.sing.* of bian. Clogaid béin an ruadhbhuic, *a helmet of roe-buck's skin.*
beinc, see being.
†beinc, *s.f.* Separation, partition, disjunction.
†beine, *s.m.* Champion. 2 Evening.
beinean, -ein, *s.f.* Little woman.
being, -e, -eannan, *s.f.* Bench. 2 Side bench or plank of a bed. 3**Bank.—*Islay.*
——-bhreith,‡‡ -e- -ean-breith, *s.f.* Bar of judgment.
beinge, *Uist* for being.
beingich,** *v.a.* Bench.
beingidh,* *s.f.* see being.
beinn, *s.f. irreg.* Mountain, hill. 2 Pinnacle. 3**Bin. 4‡‡Head, top, high place. Declined thus :—

Nom.Sing.	beinn,	*Plur.*	beanntan,
Gen.	beinne,		beann,
Dat.	beinn,		beanntan,
Voc.	a bheinn !		a bheannta !

Mar an ceò thall air a' bheinn, *as the distant mist on the hill.*
beinne, *gen.sing.* of beinn.
beinneach, *a.* Full of mountains or hills.
beinneagaich,** *v.n.* Carol.
beinneal,* -eil, *s.m.* Binding of a sheaf of corn.
beinnean, -ein, *s.m.* Little hill. 2 see binnein.
beinnse,** Gaelic spelling of bench.
beir, *v.irr.* Take hold. 2 Bring forth, bear, produce. 3 Get out of sight with. 4*†Give. 5**

Overtake. 6**Carry. Conjugated thus—
Active Voice—
IND.*past*. rug mi, &c., *I, &c. bore* or *bare*.
„ *fut*. beiridh mi, &c., *I, &c. shall bear*.
INTERR.*past*, (an ? nach ? cha) d'rug mi,&c.
„ *fut*. (am b— ? nach b—, cha bh—) beir mi, &c.
SUBJUNC. *past*, (ged) bheirinn, *(though) I would bear*; (ged) bheireadh tu, *(though) thou wouldst bear*;(ged)bheireadh e,*(though) he would bear*; (ged) bheireamaid, *(though) we would bear*; (ged) bheireadh sibh, iad, *(though) you, they would bear*.
„ *fut*. (ma) bheireas mi, &c., *(if) I,&c. shall bear*.
IMPER. *1st. per. sing*. beiream, *let me bear*.
INFIN. A bhreith, [a bheirsinn,] *to bear*.
PRES.PART. a' breith, [a' beirsinn] *bearing*.
Passive Voice—
IND.*past*, rugadh mi, &c., *I, &c. was born*.
„ *fut*. beirear mi, &c.. *I, &c. shall be born*.
INTERR.*past*, (an ? nach ? cha) d'rugadh mi, &c., *was I, &c. (not) born ?*
„ *fut*. (am b—? nach b—? cha bh—)beirear mi, &c., *shall I, &c. (not) be born ?*
SUBJ.*past*, (ged) bheirteadh mi, &c., *(though) I, &c. should be born*.
„ *fut*. (ma) bheirear mi, &c., *(if) I, &c. shall be borne, &c.*
PAST PART. beirte, *born*.
Agus beiridh tu mac, *and thou shalt bear a son*; agus beiridh i mac, agus bheir thu Iosa mar ainm air, *and she shall bring forth a son, and thou shalt call his name Jesus*; agus rug e air, *and he overtook him*; beir uam e ! beir uam e ! *away with him* ! *away with him* ! mur beirear duine a rithist, *unless a man be born again*; beir air an uan, *catch (lay hold of) the lamb*; 'nuair a chi thu bean oileanach beir oirre, mur beir thus' oirre, beiridh fear eile oirre, *when you see an accomplished lady (female) take her, if you do not wed her another will*; fhuair mi fios bho phiuthar dhomh nach beirinn beò oirre, *I heard from my sister that I shall scarce find her alive*. Beir in combination with the prep. *air*, means "overtake, take hold of." [For additional uses of *beir* see under *breith*.]
†beirbheis, *s.f.* Anniversary, feast, vigil.
béire, *s.f.* Bitterness.
beiream, *1st. p. sing. imp.* of beir.
beiridh, *fut. aff. act.* of beir.
beirm, -e, *s.f.* Barm, yeast, ferment.
——each,** *a.* Barmy.
beirn, see bearn.
——each, see bearnach.
†beirr-sgian, *s.f.* Razor.
beirsinn, *s.m.* Bringing forth, producing, 2 (combined with *air*) Catching. A' b—, *pres. part.* of beir.
beirt, see beart.
†——,*s.f.* Burden. 2 Two persons. 3 Help, assistance.
beirte, *past part.* of beir. Born, borne, brought forth.
beirteach,‖ see beartach.
†beirtean, -ein, *s.m.* Little burden.
beirteas, see beartas.
beirtich, see beartaich.
†beis, *s.f.* Marshy ground.
——eil,** *s.f.* Shelf.
†——gne, *s.f.* Peace, quiet.
béist, -e, -ean, *s.f.* Beast, monster. 2 Beast of prey. 3**Wretch. A' tuiteam an strì na béiste, *falling in contest with the monster*; chuir droch bhéist as da, *an evil beast hath devoured him*; béistean doirbh, *oppressive wretches*.
—— -dà-liunn,‖ *s.f.* Tapeworm.
—— -donn,* see béist-dubh.
—— -dubh, -uibhe, *s.f.* Otter.
——eag,* *s.f.* Earthworm.
——ealachd, *s.f.* Brutality, beastliness.
——ean, -ein, *s.m. Dim.* of béist. Little beast. 2 *n.pl.* of béist.
——eil, -e, *a.* Beastly, bestial, like a beast.
—— -mhaol, -mhaoil, *s.f.* Seal, sea-calf.

39. Beitein.

40. Beith bheag.

beitein,§ *s.m.* Mat-grass *or* moor-grass—*nardus stricta*.

41. Beith.

beith, -e, *s.f.* First letter of the old Gaelic alphabet. 2 Birch tree—*betula alba*. 'Sa bheith chùbhraidh, *in the fragrant birch*. §Badge of Clan Buchanan.
—— bheag,§ *s.f.* Dwarf birch—*betula nana*.
—— charraigeach,§ *s.f.* Knotty birch—*betula verrucosa*.
—— chluasach,§ *s.f.* see beith dubhach. *Rannoch, Breadalbane, &c.*
—— dubhach,§ *s.f.* Weeping birch—*betula pendula*.
—— dubh-chasach, Knotty birch. see beith charraigeach.
——each, *a.* Of, or belonging to birch trees.
beitheach, see beathach.
†beitheamhain, *pl.* of beach.
†beith-éigneachadh,‡‡ -aidh, *s.m.* Rape.
beithir, beathrach, beithrichean[& beathraichean,] *s.m.* Bear, *prov.* 2 Serpent. 3 Any wild beast. 4 Thunder-bolt 5 Large skate. 6(AC) Lightning.
————,** *a.* Wild, destructive, savage.
†beith, luis, nuin, The Ogham Chraobh or old Gaelic alphabet. This is the Gaelic equivalent of the English expression "A,B,C" for alphabet, the words *beith,luis,nuin*,being the names of what were formerly the first three letters of the Gaelic alphabet.
beith-na-measa,§ *s.f.* (*lit.* the fruiting birch) Beech-tree. see craobh fhaidhbhile.
†beitin, see beitean.
beitir, -e, *a.* Tidy, neat, clean.
bel-ain, ? The circle of Bel or of the sun.
†bemis, *for* bhitheamaid(we should have been.)
†ben,** *s.f.* Wain, chariot.
benedin,§ Common avens. see machall coille.
beò, *a.* Alive, living. 2 Quick, lively, sprightly. Am beò e ? *is he alive* ? tha e gu math

beò, *he is pretty lively*; air gaoith chithear suinn nach beò, *on the wind are seen heroes that are dead*; ma bhitheas mi beò, *if I live*; mar is beò mise, deir an Tighearna, *as I live, saith the Lord*; am bheil e beò? *is he alive?* am beò dhuit, a Dheirg? *are you alive, Dargo?* thoir beò, *bring alive*; gu ma fada beò an righ! *long live the king!* am feadh is beò mi, *while I live*; cho cinnteach 's a tha thu beò, *as sure as you are alive*; chuir e a' chlach mhuilinn a bheò bheum bhàrr na sorchain, *he put the millstone with one tremendous effort off the support*; thilg i i féin beò slàn air a bhroilleach, *she threw herself in one tremendous leap on his breast*; is beò na h-eoin ged nach seabhagan uil' iad, *the birds manage to live, though they be not all hawks*.
beò,* *s.m.* Life-time. 2 The living. 3†Cattle. 4 Living flesh. B'àluinn thu ri d' bheò, *thou wert handsome when alive*; chaidh an tarrang 'sa bheò, *the nail penetrated the living flesh*; cha'n fhaic thu ri d' bheò e, *you shall never see him*; am beò is am marbh, *the living and the dead*; an tìr nam b., *in the land of the living*.
beò-airgideach,‡‡ *a.* Mercurial.
beò-airgiod, *s.m.* see airgiod beò.
beòchan, -ain, *s. m.* Small fire. *B.* teine, *a small flickering fire.*
———ta, -ainte, a. Vigorous, lively, sprightly.
———tachd, *s.f.ind.* Vigorousness, liveliness, sprightliness.
†beochomhan, *s.m.* Warren.
beodha, see beòthail.
———ch, }
———chadh, } see beòthachadh.
———chain, }
———ich, see beòthaich.
———il, see beòthail.
beodhalachd, see beòthalachd.
beodhanta, see beòthail & beòchanta.
———chd, see beòthalachd.
beò-dhealachadh, -aidh, *s.m.* Separation with life.
— -dhùil, -e, -ean, *s.f.* Living creature.
— -eachdaireachd,** *s.f.* Biography.
— -eachdraiche, -ean, *s.m.* Biographer.
— -eachdraidh. *s.f.* Biography.
————iche, see beò-eachdraiche.
— fhàl, -àil, -àilean, *s.m.* Enclosure.
beò-fhradharc, -airc, *s.m.* Quick sight, clear sight, lively view.
————ach, -aiche, *a.* Quick-sighted, clear-sighted.
— ghaineamh, -eimh, *s.f.* Quicksand.
— ghlac, *v.a.* Take alive. 2 Take prisoner alive. Bheò-ghlac iad e, *they took him alive.*
— ghrìosach, -aich, *s.f.* Hot embers.
— iarraidh, *s.m.* Inspection. 2 Aspiration.
beòil, *gen. sing.* of beul. Làn *b.* de bhiadh is làn baile de nàire, *a mouthful of meat and a townful of shame.*
†beoilean, see béilean.
†beoill,** *s.f.* Fatness.
beò-ìobairt, -e, -ean, *s.f.* Living sacrifice.
beòir, -e & beòrach, *s.f.* Beer, ale. 2(AC) Spruce, spruce beer. 3(AG) Black beer as distinguished from ale—*Reay Country.* *B.* chaol, *small beer*; *b.* làidir, *strong beer*; gloine beòrach, *a glass of beer*; beòir dhubh, *black beer.*
beol, -oil, *s.m.* see beul. †2 Robber.
——ach, *a.* Talkative, loquacious.
——ach,* *s.f.* (‡beò+luathach) Ashes with living embers, hot ashes.
——ach, -aich, ‡*s. m.* (‡beò+ -lach of òglach) Livelyyouth. 2 Hero.
——adas, see beòlaideas.
——aiche, *s.m.* Chronicler. 2 Talkative person.
beòlaideas, -eis, *s.m.* Oral tradition.
beò-laoch, see beolach.
beò-leatromach, *a.* Quick with child.
beoll,(AC) *s.m.* Fire, glowing fire, embers.
——ag, (AC) *s.f.* Bright little flame.
beò-luath, -luaithre, *s.f.* Hot ashes or embers
beolum, -uim, *s.m.* Scold. 2 Ridicule. 3 ‡‡Censoriousness.
†beòsach, -aiche, *a.* Bright, luminous, glittering. 2 Brisk. 3 Trim, spruce, dapper.
†beòsaich, *v.a.* Beautify, adorn, deck out. 2 Make spruce or tidy.
beò-sgar,** *v.a.* Divorce.
———adh, -aidh, *s.m.* Divorce. 2 Separation during life.
beò-shlàinte, *s.f.* Life-rent, livelihood. 2††Lifetime. Tha a *b.* aice dheth, *she has a life-rent of it*; ridir *b.*, *a knight bachelor.*
————ach, *a.* Of, or pertaining to a life-rent. 2‡‡Fabulous.
beothach, -aich, see beathach.
beòthachadh, -aidh, *s.m.* Re-animating, quickening, refreshment. 2 Kindling. 3 Enlivening. 4‡‡ Sparks or coals by which a fire is kindled. A' b—, *pr.pt.* of beòthaich.
———ail, *a.* see beòthail. 2*Having a livening or quickening influence.
———air,** *s.m.* Reviver. 2 Kindler.
———an,* *s.m.* see beòchan.
beothachan-feòir, see beathachan-feòir.
beòthachan-teine,‡‡ *s.m.* Little fire.
———d, *s.f.* Courage, vigour.
†beòthadh, -aidh, *s.m.* Stimulating, urging on.
beòthaibh, *dat.pl.* of beò, *s.*
beòthaich, *gen.sing.* of beòthach.
———, *v.a.* Kindle, light. 2 Re-animate, arouse, revive, quicken. Is tric a *bh.* srad bheag teine mór, *a little spark has often kindled a conflagration.*
———idh, *fut.aff.act.* of beòthaich.
——— te, *past part.* of beòthaich. Quickened, animated, enlivened. 2 Kindled.
beòthail, -e, *a.* Vigorous, active, lively. 2 Vital. 3 Courageous, intrepid. 4** Fervent, zealous. Tha iad beòthail, *they are lively*; beòthail 'n ur spioraid, *fervent in your spirit.*
beòthalachd, *s.f.* Liveliness, smartness, agility. 2 Vigour, vitality. 3**Acuteness.
beòthalas, see beòthalachd.
beòthan-teine, see beòthachan-teine.
beò-thorrach, *a.* Quick with child, ready to conceive.
beò-thuisleach, *a.* Viviparous.
†bes, *conj.* And.
†betearlagh, *s.m.* Ancient law.
beth, see beith.
betis, see biatas.
beuban, -ain, -anan, *s.m.* Anything mangled or spoiled.
———achadh, -aidh, *s.m.* Mangling, bruising, maltreating, spoiling. Fhuair e a bheubanachadh, *he got maltreated.* A' b—, *pr.part.* beubanaich.
beubanachd, *s.f.* Mangling, bruising, tearing, maltreatment. 2**Carnage.
beubanaich, *pr. part.* a' beubanachadh, *v. a.* Mangle, bruise, maltreat, tear. 5**Bedaub. 8‡‡Destroy.
————te, *past part.* Torn, mangled, bruised, maltreated, spoiled.
beuc, *s.m.* Roar, bellow, yell, outcry. 2 Noise, clamour.
——, *pr. part.* a' beucaich & a' beucail, *v.n.* Roar, bellow, make a noise. as the sea.

beucach, -aiche, *a.* Roaring, bellowing. 2 Noisy, clamorous. 3 Apt to roar or bellow. *B.* dubhlaidh, *roaring and dark*; muir *bh.* fo ghaoith a' stri; *the roaring main contending with the winds.*
beucaich, *s.f.* Roaring, loud noise, roar. 2 Yelling, bellowing A' b—, *pr.part.* of beuc. Beacaich do thonn, *the roaring of thy waves*; ciod a' bheucaich a th' ort? *what are you roaring at?*
beucaidh, *fut. aff. a.* of beuc.
beucail, *s.f.* Roaring, yelling, dismal crying.
beucair, -ean, *s.m.* Roarer.
beuchd, see beuc.
beuchdaich, see beucaich.
beuchdail, see beucail.
beuchdair, see beucair.
beuc-shruth, *s.m.* Roaring stream. 2 Cataract.
beud, -an, *s.m.* Loss, injury, harm, pity. 2 Defect, blemish. 3 Distress. 4 Fate. 5 Blow. 6 Action, evil deed, infamy. 7 Vice. 8 Mischief. 9 Nothing. 10** Gloom. 11‡‡ Fruit. Cha'n 'eil beud air, *there is nothing the matter with him*; is mòr am beud e, *it is a great pity*; cha d'éirich beud dha, *no harm has happened to him*; duan gun bheud, *a poem without blemish*; cha d'fhulaing e beud, *he sustained no loss*; druidear beul nam beud, *the mouth of iniquity shall be stopped*; cha bhi beud ort, *nothing shall be wrong with you*; 'aodann fo bheud, *his visage under a gloom*; faiceam mo bheud, *let me see my fate.*
——ach, -aiche, *a.* Hurtful, iniquitous. 2 Blemished. 3 Mournful, dismal. 4**Guilty. 5**Fatal, 6**Gloomy. Is beudach borb am buille, *fatal and fierce is the blow*; am fear a bhitheas beudach e fhéin, cha sguir e dh'éigneacnadh chàich, *he that is guilty himself tries to involve others.*
——achd, *s.f.ind.* Hurtfulness, iniquity, harm. 2 Mournfulness, dismalness.
——ag, -aig, -an, *s.f.* Trifling, idling, tattling little woman, gossip. 2**Lying woman.
——agach, *a.* Gossipping, trifling. 2 Lying.
——agan, *n.pl.* of beudag.
beudaich, *pr.part.* a' beudachadh, *v.a.* Harm. injure, hurt, wrong.
beud-fhacal, -ail, *s.m.* Taunting word or expression.
beud-fhaclach, *a.* Foul-mouthed, opprobrious, taunting. 2 Contumelious. 3 Scornful.
†**beud-fhoireobhadh**, *s.m.* Commentary,
beugadh, see biogadh. A dh'fhàg mo ghrua'ch air beugadh, *that left my cheeks smarting*—*Oran an t-saighdeir*, p. 66 in *an Duanaire.*
beul, *gen. sing. & n.pl.* beòil, *s.m.* Mouth. 2 Opening, aperture, orifice. 3 Approach, nearness. Is tobar beatha beul an fhìrein, *the mouth of a righteous man is a well of life*; beul an là, *the dawn of day*; beul na h-oidhche, *dusk of the evening*; an taobh beòil, *the fore part, front*; beul ri, *near, about*; beul ri trì miosan, *about three months*; beul an làin, *high-water mark*; beul a bhi deas, *nearly ready*, *nearly done*; boinne am beul na gaoithe, *a sign of rain* (lit. a drop in the wind's mouth); is mairg do'n bheul-iochd sùil a' choimhich, *one must be in a bad way if a stranger's eye is full of pity for him*; cha b' urrainn mi beul thoirt dha, *I cannot touch (taste) it*; o bheul na tuinne gu feur gorm, *from the margin of the sea to green crops*; leaghaidh a' chòir am beul an anfhainn, *a good cause suffers in the mouth of the incompetent.*
beulach, -aiche, *a.* Fair-spoken. 2 Plausible. 3 Prating. 4 Flattering. 5 Fawning. 6** Large-mouthed. 7** Mouthed.
————as, -ais, *s.f.* Artful speaking. 2 Prating, babbling.
beulag, -aig, -an, *s.f.* Fore-tooth (—back tooth or grinder is *cùlrag* or *cùlag*.) 2 Gap, fissure. 3(AC) Person in front of another on horseback.
beulaibh,†† *s.m.* Front, foreside. 2 Presence. Beulaibh an taighe, *the front of the house*; air mo bheulaibh, *in my presence*; cuir air a bheulaibh e, *put it before him*; ma tha dad agad air mo bheulaibh, *if you have anything you wish me to do*; cha b' uan sin air beulaibh òisge, *that is no lamb in comparison with a yearling*—N.G.P. [if applied to a woman, this apparently means that that was not her first production, or that she was far advanced in years before she produced anything.—JM] tha siod air mo bheulaibh, *I have yet to do that.*
beulais,** *s.f.* Prating, babbling.
————each,** *a.* Argute.
beul-aithris, *s.f.* Oral representation or tradition. *B.* nan seanair, *the tradition of the elders.*
beulan, -ain, *s.m.* Little mouth. 2 Orifice.
beulan, *s.f.* see beulanach.
————ach, -aiche, *a.* Fair-spoken, inclined to flatter.
————ach, -aich, *s.f.* Of two waves on the sea this is the nearer to the speaker. 2 Bridle-bit.
beulanaich,†† *pr. part.* a' beulanachadh, *v. a.* Allure with words.
beulannach,‡‡ -aich, see beulanach.
beulaobh, *s.m.* Front, foreside. 2 Presence. "beulaibh" is the more correct form.
beulas, -ais, *s.f.* Prattling, babbling. 2 Quibble.
beul-a-staigh, *s.m.* Inside wale of a boat. see bàta, E9 p. 73 and illust.
beul-àtha, -ain, *s.m.* Ford, shallow part of a river.
beul-a-theach, *s.m.* Band of a pair of trousers, —N.G.P.
beul beag,‡ *s.m.* Saxboard of a boat, see bàta, E8, p. 73.
beul-bhac,** -aic, *s.m.* Bridle-bit.
beul-binn, *s.m.* Nightingale, see spideag. 2AC Long-tailed duck.
beul-bochd, *s.m.* Pleading of poverty.
beul-bòidheach,(AH) *s.m.* Flattering mouth blandishment, fawning. wheedling, sycophancy.
beul brèagh, *s.m.* Flattering mouth. 2 Flattery.
beul-chainnt, -e, *s.f.* Oral speech.
————————each, -eiche, *a.* Talkative, loquacious, garrulous.
beulchair, -e, *a.* Fair-spoken, flattering, smooth worded. 2 **Communicative.
————eachd, *s.f.* Pleasing loquacity.
beul-chòmhrag,‡‡ -aig, -an, *s.m.* Daggers-drawing.
beul-chràbhach, -aiche, *a.* Lip-religious, hypocritical, canting.
beul-chràbhadh, -aidh, *s.m.* Lip-religion, cant, hypocrisy.
beul-dearg, -eirge, *a.* Red-lipped.
beul-dhraoidheachd, *s. f.* Incantation, enchantment.
beul-dhruid, *v.a.* Silence, shut the mouth.
†**beul-fharagadh**, see beul-fhothraghadh.
beul-fharsuing, -e, *a.* Wide-mouthed.
†**beul-fhothraghadh**, *s.m.* Gargarism.
beul-ghràdh, -àidh, *s.m.* Lip-love, flattery, dissimulation.
beul-maothain, *s.m.* The sloat of the throat.

2‡‡Pit of the stomach.
†beulmhach, see beulanach.
beul-mheillireadh, -eidh, *s.m.* Officiousness, flattery, fawning, soothing.
beul-mór, -óir, *s.m.* Wide mouth. 2 Bung-hole. 3 Gunwale of a boat or ship, see bàta E7 p.74 for illust.
beul-oideas, -eis, *s.m.* Tradition, oral tradition.
beul-oilean, -ein, *s.m.* Oral teaching, tradition.
beul-phurgaid, -eau, *s. f.* Gargle.
————each, *a.* Gargling. 2 Of, or belonging to, a gargle.
————eachd, *s. f.* Gargarization.
beul-ràdh, -aidh, *s.m.* Proverb, phrase, by-word. 2 Dialect. 3 Speech.
beul-ràidhteach, -eiche, *a.* Renowned, celebrated, famous. 2 ‡‡Talkative.
beul sios ort! *int.* A form of malediction. (*lit* may you be down in the mouth.)
beul-snaipe,-*s.m.* Flint socket of a gun-lock, dog-head.
beul-stoc,* *s.m.* Gunwale of a boat—*Islay*, see bàta E7. p. 74 for illust.
beul-thaobh, see beulaibh.
beum, *gen.* beuma [& béime] *pl.* -an, -annan, *s.m.* Stroke, blow. 2 Wound. 3 Gash, cut. 4(AC) Handful of corn cut at one stroke of the reaping-hook. 5 Taunt, sarcasm, insult, reproach. 6 Stream. 7 Torrent. 8 Knell. 9 Misfortune. 10**Gap. Gach cath 's na bhuail mi beum, *every battle in which I struck a blow*; cha ruig thu leas beum a thoirt dhomh, *you need not taunt or gibe me*; chuir e beum air an stiùir, *he gave the rudder a vigorous turn*; mo chuislean mar bheum, *my veins like a torrent*; bhrùchd iad a mach a dh' aon bheum, *they poured forward in one body.*
beum, *pr. part.* a' beumadh, *v. a.* Smite. 2 Cleave. 3 Strike, as a bell. 4 Toll. 5 Taunt, reproach, vilify, cut, make a cutting remark, utter a sarcasm or criticism. 6‡‡Sound, resound. O'n bheum na cluig, *since the bells have tolled.*
beumach, -aiche, *a.* Full of gaps. 2 Destructive. 3 Taunting, sarcastic,cutting. 4 Wounding. 5 Tart. 6**Reproachful, depraved. 7 ‡‡Resounding. Mar theine bheumach, *like a destructive fire*; aineolach, beumach, *ignorant and sarcastic*; bilean beumach, *reproachful lips*; buillean cothromach, beumach, *well aimed, destructive blows.*
beumadh, -aidh, *s.m.* Striking. 2 Resounding, tolling. 3 Cleaving, cutting. 4 Reproaching, vilifying. A' b—, *pr.part.* of beum. Beumadh sheòl, *furling of sails*; beumadh chlag, *the tolling of bells*; an dubh-bhàs 'g am beumadh 'n an ruaig, *gloomy death smiting them in their flight*; teine-athair a' beumadh nan neòil, *lightning cleaving the clouds.*
beumair,** *s.m.* Biter.
beumannach, *a.* see beumach.
beum-cheap,** -chip, *s.f.* Whipping-stock.
beum-cluig,** -an-cluig, *s.m.* Knell.
beum-gréine,** *s.m.* Coup-de-soleil.
beumnach, *a.* see beumach.
————d,‡‡ *s.f.ind.* Invection.
beum-sgéithe, *s.m.* Striking the shield the old method of sounding an alarm or challenge. 2* Severe sarcasm, sly insinuation.—*Islay.* Le *b.* ghlaodh iad còmhrag, *with a blow on the shield they called to battle*; bhuail Treunmor *b.*, *T. sounded an alarm.*
beum-sice, *s.m.* Rupture. 2‡‡Disorder in the coating of the viscera.
beum-sléibhe, *s.m.* Mountain torrent, violent sudden stream caused by rain, or the bursting of a thunder-cloud, "spate."

beum-soluis, *s.m.* Beam of light. 2**Sunbeam. Feuch am beum-soluis caol ud, *behold yon small beam of light.*
beum-sùl, *s.m.* Influence of the evil-eye. Optical delusion. 3 Coup d'œil. 4‡‡Disease in the eyes.
beum-taire, *s.m.* Fling.
beum-tuathal,‡‡ *s.m.* Blow or thrust in the wrong direction.
†beur, *v.a.* see beir.
beur, -éire, *s.m.* Point, pinnacle. Beur àrd, *a lofty pinnacle.*
beur, béire, *a.* Shrill, sonorous. 2 Loud-lunged, giving a loud or shrill laugh. 3 Genteel. 4 Well spoken, eloquent. 5 Clean, sharp. 6‡‡ Prickled. 7‡‡Indented. 8 *fig.* Witty, sarcastic. 9‡Sharp, pointed. Fir bheur, *genteel men*; troimh bhearna beur nan neul, *through the fissures of the clouds.*
beura,(AC) *a.* see beur.
———chd, *s.f.ind.* Shrillness, sharpness.
beuradair,‡‡ see beurradair.
beurau, -ain, *s.m.* Witty, prating, garrulous little fellow.
beurla, *s.f.ind.* Speech,language. 2 The English language. Gnàth-bheurla na h-Eireann, *the vernacular dialect of the Anglo-Irish.*
Beurla Albannach, *s.f.* Anglo-Scottish.
Beurlach, *a.* Of, or belonging to, the English language. 2*Well versed in the English language.
Beurlachd,‡‡ *s.f.ind.* Anglicism.
Beurla leathann, *s.f.* Broad Scots.
beurla na Féinne, *s.f.* Fingalian or military Gaelic. 2 Lawyers' Gaelic.
beurla nam filidh,‡‡ *s.f.* Poetical language.
beurla nan deagharsan,‡‡ *s.m.* Historical dialect.
Beurl' an Taoibh dheis,‡‡ *s.f.* Broad Scots.
Beurla Shasunnach, *s.f.* English as spoken in England.
beurla theibide,‡‡ *s.f.* Medical dialect.
beurl' eagair,‡‡ *s.f.* Technical language.
beurra, *a.* see beur.
———ch,* *s.f.* Prating female.
———ch, *a.* Witty, eloquent.
———chd,* *s.f.ind.* Eloquence, wit, waggery.
———dair, -ean, *s.m.* Satirist, wit, wag.
———daireachd,†† *s.f.ind.* Satire.
———dh-theine, *s.f.* see beur-theine.
beurtha, *a.* see beur.
beur-theine, *s.f.* Bright fire. 2 Falling star, meteor. 3 Name of a star on the boss of a warrior's shield—*Ossian.*
beus, -a, -an, *s.f.* Moral qualities or manners, whether good or bad, virtue. 2 Behaviour, deeds, custom, conduct. 3 Amiability. 4 Bass viol. Bean nan deagh bheus, *a virtuous woman*; fo bheus, *quiet, on one's good behaviour*; fo dheagh bheus, *under a good character*; fo dhroch bheus, *under a bad character*; aithnichear leanabh air 'bheus, *a child is known by his manners*; rìgh nam beusa mòra, *the king of lofty manners*; gheibh thu beus is gnàth na dùthcha, *you shall get what the use and wont of the country sanction—Islay*; beus na tuath air am bithear is e a nithear, *the customs of your associates you will follow*; beus an àite far am bithear is e a nithear, *the use and wont of the place you dwell in you will conform with*; tonnan fo bheus, *waves at peace*; deagh bheusan, *good morals*; droch bheusan, *bad morals*; beus na dh'fhalbh, *the deeds (conduct) of the departed.*
†beus, *s.m.* Trade. 2 Art. 3 Rent, revenue, tax. 4 Fornication. 5 Bottle. 6††Belly.
———ach, -aiche, *a.* Well-behaved, well-bred

2 Modest, bashful. 3 Virtuous, chaste, moral, opposite of vicious. 4**Gentle. Mar aiteal beusach, *like a gentle breeze.*
beusachd, *s.f.* Good behaviour, moral rectitude, inoffensive conduct. 2 Manners, morals. 3 **Bashfulness.
beusaichead, -eid, *s.m.* Degree of moral purity or modesty.
beusail, see beusach.
beusalachd, see beusachd.
beusan, *n.pl.* of beus.
beus-ghrinn,‡‡ -e, *s.m.* Good behaviour.
beusmhor,** *a.* Bashful.
————achd,** *s.f.ind.* Bashfulness.
beus-oide,‡‡ *s.m.* Moralist.
beutail, *s.f.* Cattle, herds. 2 Cow.
b'fhearr, (*for* bu fhearr) Were better, was better. B'fhearr leam, *I wish, I would prefer*; b'fhearr dhomh, dhuit, dha, &c., *it were better for me, you, him, &c.*
bh, For words beginning with *bh* not appearing below, see under *b.*
bh', (*for* bha) Used before a word beginning with a vowel, as, an duine a bh'ann, *whoever it was, the man that was,* (in composition); is e Beurla a bh'aice féin air an fhuaim a bh' ann, *whatever the queer noise was that she made, she herself called it English* (*sarcastic.*)
bha, *past ind.* of bì. Was, wert, were.
†bhàbhair, *v.* Ye were.
†bhàdar, *v.* They were.
bhàirnis,‡‡ Gaelic spelling of *varnish.*
†bhàmar, *v.* We were.
bhàn, *adv.* see a bhàn.
bhaoth, see baoth.
†bhaoi, see bha.
†bhar, *poss.pron.* see bhur.
bhàrr, *prep.* (formerly de bhàrr) From, from off. 2 Down from. Bhàrr aghaidh na talmhuinn, *from the surface of the earth*; theirinn i bhàrr a' chamhuil, *she alighted from the camel;* bhàrr do chos, *from off thy feet*; 2. *come to grief as regards worldly matters*; a bhàrr air sin, *besides that;* bhàrr an rathaid, *off the way*; bhàrr a leapach, *off his bed, from his bed;* bhàrr na cìche, *weaned*; 'n uair a bha teine ris an taigh, chunnaic e toit bhàrr a taighe, *when the house was on fire, he saw smoke coming from her house*; thig uair bhàrr fad' an là (air a' mhìos seo), *the day will be an hour shorter* (*this month*) [gaining is *tighinn ann*]; fhuair iad bhàrr an turuis, *they reached the end of their journey;* chuir na breacain sealladh brèagh bhàrr na cuideachd, *the tartans gave the company a grand appearance* (*lit.* put a beautiful appearance from off the company. [Always followed by the Genitive case.]
bhàrr, s. see bàrr.
bhàrr,†† (a bhàrr) *adv.* Moreover.
bharrachd, *prep.* see a bharrachd.
bhatas, *v.* see bì.
bheairt, see beart.
bheil? see am bheil? *and* bì.
†bheileam? (*for* am bheil mi?) Am I? Am bheileam féin am aonar? *am I left alone?*
bheir, *fut.aff.* of tabhair *or* thoir. Cò e a bheir còmhrag? *who will give battle?* bheir mise ort sin a dheanamh, *I will make you do that*; bheir mi ort gu'm faithnich thu e, *I will let you know it*—make you smart for it; is math an long a bheir a mach an caladh as an d'fhalbh i, *a good ship—that which gains the port whence she sailed* (a remark sometimes made by ministers of the "Auld Kirk" when they see or hear of seceders returning to their own communion. An Aulder Kirk might use the saying with even greater effect.)
bheireamaid, *1st. per. pl. past subj.* of beir. We would bear.
bheireamaid, *1st. per. pl. past subj.* of tabhair. We would give.
bheirear, *fut. pass.* of beir. Shall be born.
————, *fut. pass.* of tabhair. Shall be given.
bheirinn, *1st. per. sing. past subj.* of beir. I would bear.
————, *1st. per. sing. past subj.* of tabhair. I would give.
bheirteadh, *past subj. pass.* of beir. (Ged) bheirteadh e, (*though*) *he were born.*
bheirteadh, *past subj. pass.* of tabhair. Is impersonal and requires a prepositional pronoun after it thus, (ged) bheirteadh dhomh (e), (*though*) (*it*) *were given to me.*
bhi, *neg.fut.* of bì. Cha bhi mi, *I shall not be.*
†bhias, see bhitheas.
†bhid, (*for* bha iad) They were.
†bhìm, (*for* bha mi) I was.
bhiocar, -air, *s.m.* Gaelic spelling of *vicar.*
bhiodh, see bhitheadh.
†bhiom, (*for* bha mi) I was.
bhios, see bhitheas.
bhiotailt, *s.f.* see biotailt.
bhiotar, see bhithear.
bhith, (a) *infin.* of bì. To be.
bhitheadh, *2nd. & 3rd. per. sing. and pl.* of bì. Should be, would be.
†bhitheam, (*for* bha mi) I was.
bhithear, *fut. subj. impers.* of bì. (If) (it) shall be. [Preceded by a subj. particle as ma.]
bhitheas, *fut.subj.* of bì. (If) shall or will be. [Preceded by a subj. particle as ma.]
bhithinn, *1st. per. sing. past subj.* of bì. (If) I should be, (if) I would be. [Preceded by a subj. particle, as, ma. (ma bhithinn *but* na'm bithinn.)]
bho, *prep.* Another form of "o" which is the better of the two. Often written in conjunction with the personal pronouns thus:—
1st.sing. bhuam, *from me*, *pl.* bhuainn, *from us.*
2nd. bhuat, *from thee*, bhuaibh, *from you.*
3rd.m. bhuaith, *from him*, bhuapa, (*m. & f.*)
f. bhuaipe, *from her*, *from them.*
The forms under *o* are preferable to these. [Dr. Gillies says— "The *p* of (bhuaipe or) uaipe, now used for the fem. form of the 3rd per. sing. is both phonetically and historically wrong. The form "uaithe" is fem. in structure, and analogous to *leithe* and *rithe*, and its use as a masculine prep. pronoun is grossly incorrect. Uaidh (or bhuaidh) is the correct modern form of Old Gaelic *uad*, from him." Dr. G. is literally right, although custom is against him, and "bhuaipe" *from her*, being a firmly established form, both in speaking and writing, it is never likely to be altered in the Highlands. To substitute *bhuaithe* for *bhuaipe* now would cause unnecessary confusion, but *bhuaidh* for him, could be used as easily as *bhuaith* or *bhuaithe.* Were the Gaelic language taught in all the schools in the Highlands, popular mistakes like this would never get a hold.] "Bho" is used after a vowel or vowel sound, also when it begins a sentence; "o" is used after a pronounced consonant according to choice. —D.M. ‡‡ says "bho" in the best dialects. * says "bho" is used in all the Isles.
bhobagan, see boban.
bhòbh! *int.* O dear! strange!
†bholam, Gaelic spelling of *volume.*
bhò'n dé, *adv.* see air bhò'n dé.
bhos, see a bhos.
bhuaibh, see uaibh.
bhuaidh, see uaith.
bhuainn, see uainn.

bhuaipe, *prep.pron.* (bho) From her.

bhuaith, see bho. Tha e 'tighinn bhuaith, *he is recovering*; tha e 'dol bhuaith, *he is getting worse*.

bhuam, see uam.

bhuapa, see uapa.

bhuat, see uat.

†bhui, see bha.

†bhuil, see bheil.

bhur, *poss. pron.* Your. Gu'm fosglar bhur sùilean, *that your eyes shall be opened;* spiorad bhur n-inntinn, *the spirit of your minds.* Often contracted *'ur,* [Takes *n-* after it when followed by a word beginning with a vowel.]

bì, *irreg. v.* Be, exist. Conjugated thus :—

IND. *pres.* tha mi, &c., *I am, &c.*
,, *past,* bha mi, &c., *I was, &c.*
,, *fut.* bithidh mi, &c., *I shall be, &c.*

INTERR. *pres.*, am bheil mi ? &c., *am I ? &c.*
(mur) 'eil mi, &c., *(if) I am (not) &c.*
nach 'eil mi ? &c., *am I not ? &c.*
cha'n 'eil mi, &c., *I am not, &c.*
,, *past*(an ? nach ? cha, mur) robh mi, &c., *was I (not) &c.*
,, (am ? nach ? cha bh—, mur) bi mi, &c., *(shall ?) I (not) be, &c.*

SUBJUNC. *pres.*,(ma) bhitheas mi,&c.,*(if) I be.*
,, *past,* (na'n) robh mi *or* (na'm) bithinn, *(if) I were*; (na'n) robh thu, e, sibh, iad, *or* (na'm) bitheadh tu, e, sibh, iad, *(if) thou wert, (if) he, you, they were*; (na'n) robh sinn, *or* (na'm) bitheamaid, *(if) we were.*

IMPER. *1 sing.* bitheam, *let me be, pl.* bitheamaid, *let us be ; 2 sing.* bi, *be thou, pl.* bithibh, *be ye*; *3 sing.* bitheadh e, *let him be* ; *pl.* bitheadh iad, *let them be.*

INFIN. a bhith, *to be.*

PRES. PART. bith, *being.*

☞BHEIL is often used subjunctively as, Tha iad ag ràdh gu'm bheil, *they say it is so.*

IMPERSONAL forms of verb Bì.

	Pres.	*Past.*	*Future.*
Ind.	thatar.	bhatar.	bitear.
,,	thathar.	bha'har.	bithear.
,,	thathas.	bhathas.	bitheas.
Interr.	(am)beilear?	(an)robhar?	(am)bitear?
,,	(am)beileas?	(an)robhas?	(am)biteas?
,,	nach'eilear?	nach robhar?	nach bitear?
,,	nach'eileas?	nach robhas?	nach biteas?
Subj.	(ma) thatar.	bhatar.	bhithear.

The past subjunctive form *biteadh* is used impersonally, as, n'am biteadh a' togail an taighe, *if the people had been building the the house* ; thatar ag radh gu'm bheil a' bhanrìghinn a' tighinn do dh'Alba, *it is said that the Queen is coming to Scotland.* Tha, gu dearbh, *yes, indeed* ; bithidh iad an sin, *they shall be there* ; is dubh na mnathan ris nach bitear, *dark are the dames that none will flirt with*—N.G.P.; tha 'n t-àm agam a bhith tarruing, *it is time for me to be moving.*

[Bì, when used in expressing the name or profession pertaining to objects, must be followed by the prep. *ann,* joined with a possessive pronoun of the same number and person, as the person or thing whose name, trade, or condition is mentioned ; as, tha mi 'nam (ann mo) shaor, *I am a carpenter* (*lit.* in my [state of being a] carpenter) ; bha sinn 'nar (ann ar) coigrich 'san tìr, *we were strangers in the land* ; tha Ceit 'na (ann a) banaltrum, *Kate is a nurse ;* bithidh Seumas 'na dheagh sgoilear, *James will be a good scholar.*

†bì, *gen.* of beò.

b'i, (*for* bu i) It was she. 2 It was. Am b'i a bha siod ? *was it she that was yonder ?*

biacaich, see beucaich.

biacail, see beucail.

biacair, see beucair.

biachar, see biadhchar.

b'iad, (*for* bu iad) They were. B'iad am feasgar agus a' mhaduinn an ceud là, *the evening and the morning were the first day.*

biadh, *pr. part.* a' biadhadh, *v.a.* Feed, nourish, maintain. 2 Fatten. Gu'm biadhar e ann am fearann duin' eile, *that it shall be fed in another man's field (land)*; biadh orra e, *dole it out in small equal quantities* (as short provisions.)

biadh, *gen.* bìdh [béidh & bithidh] *pl.* biadhan [& bidheanna,] *s.m.* Meat, food victuals, diet, provision. 2** Fodder, provender. B., is aodach, *food and clothing*; dhuibh-se bithidh e mar bhiadh, *to you it shall be for food.*

biadhach,** *a.* Alimental.

———adh,** -aidh, *s.m.* Alimentation.

biadhadh, -aidh, *s.m.* Feeding, nourishing. 2 Fattening. 3 Doling out piecemeal. 4 Feed, victuals, meat, provender. A' b—, (†† gives bia*th*adh) *pr. part.* of biadh.

biadhaid,* *s.m.* see biadh-lann.

biadhar, *a.* Alimentary.

biadh-briste,** *s.m.* Fragments. 2 Crumbled food.

biadh an t-sionaidh, *s. m.* White or pink sedum—*sedum anglicum.*

42. Biadh an t-sionaidh.

biadhchar, -aire, *a.* Fruitful, 2 Substantial. 3 Affording substance. 4 Esculent. Sìol biadhchar, *productive corn, corn that produces a large quantity of meal.*

———achd, *s. f.* Abundance of provision, substance. 2 *Productiveness.

biadh-chluan, -ain, *s.m.* Kitchen. (place to cook in, not condiment.)

biadhchor, see biadhchar.

biadh eòinein, *s.m.* Woodsorrel, see seamrag.

biadh eun,‡‡ see b— eòinein.

biadh feasgair,** *s.m.* Supper, evening meal.

biadh-lann, -lainn, *s.m.* Pantry.

biadh luibh,** *s.m.* Salad.

biadh lus, -luis, *s.m.* Salad.

biadh maduinn,** *s.m.* Breakfast.

biadh-nan-eòinein, see b— -eòinein.

biadh-nòin,** *s.m.* Luncheon, mid-day meal.

biadh-sholar, -air, *s.m.* Pabulation.

biadh-siubhail, (AG) *s.m.* Provisions for the way.

biadhta, *past part.* of biadh. Fed, nourished. Damh biadhta, *a stalled or fed ox.*

biadhtach, -aich, -aichean, *s.m.* Grazier. 2 Farmer. 3 Hospitable farmer, hospitable person. 4 Host, hostess—*Islay.* 5 Kitchen. 6(AC) Raven. 7(AF) Glutton. 8**Order of Irish tenants who procured provisions for the nobles. Tha e 'na dheagh bhiadhtach, *he is a liberal host.*

———d,** *s. f. ind.* Hospitality. Is bochd a' bhiadhtachd seo, *this is a poor entertainment.*

biadhtaich, *v.a.* Share, impart, divide food.

———e, *s.m.* see biadhtach.

biadh-thaigh,** *s.m.* Eating-house.

biagais, (AF) *s. f.* Dogfish.

†biaidh, *for* bithidh.

†biail, *s. f.* Axe, hatchet.

†bial, -ail, *s.m.* Water.

bial, see beul.

——ag, see beulag.

bialanaich, see beulanaich.

bian, *gen.sing.* & *n. pl.* béin, *s.m.* Hide, skin, pelt. 2**Abode. [Generally applied to the skins of wild animals only.] Bian an tuirc, *the boar's hide;* bu ghile a bian na canach sléibhe, *whiter was her skin than mountain sedge;* bian ròin, *a seal's skin;* bian béiste duibhe, *an otter's skin;* bian coinein, *a rabbit's skin.*

——adair,* *s.m.* Currier.

—— deasaiche,‡‡ *s.m.* Currier.

—— -dhubh, *a.* Swarthy. 2 Black-skinned.

—— -gheal, *a.* Fair-skinned, white-skinned.

—— leasaiche, -an, *s.m.* Currier, tanner.

†bias, see bitheas.

biasgach, -aiche, (‡biadh+sgathach, *catching at morsels*) *a.* Niggardly, miserly. 2 Catching at trifles.

biasgaire, -ean, *s.m.* Sordid, mean person. 2 ‡‡Glutton.

————achd, *s.f.* Niggardliness. 2‡‡Gluttony.

biast, béiste, -an, *s.f.* See béist. 2 Wretch. 3 Unmannerly child. 4‡‡Worm or screw of a ramrod. 5‡Niggardly person. [*Biast* is not such a strong expression as *béist.* The former might be used in correcting vulgarity or mischief in a child, while the latter would be applied to a drunkard or other disreputable person.—*Argyll.*] Mìr á beul bhiastan, *receiving anything from parties who do not wish to part with it* (*lit.* getting a morsel out of the mouth of brats.)

biast, *pr.part.* a' biastadh, *v.a.* Abuse, revile.

———adh, *s.m.* Abusing, reviling. A' b—, *pr. part.* of biast.

biastag, -aig, -an, see béisteag.

biastail, -e, *a.* see béisteal. 2‡‡Churlish, niggardly.

biastalachd, see béistealachd.

biast-donn, see béist-donn.

biast-dubh, see béist-dubh.

biata, see biadhta.

biatach, see biadhtach.

————as,** -ais, *s.m.* Food, victuals, nourishment.

————d, see biadhtachd.

biataiche, see biadhtach.

biatas, -ais, *s.m.* Betony.—*beta maritima.* 2 Beetroot. 3 Mangold wurzel.

biath, see biadh.

———achail, see biadhchar.

———achadh, see biadhachadh.

———achd, see biadhtachd.

———adh see biadhadh. 2‡Entice.

———aidh, ‡ see biathainne.

biathainne, *s. f.* Earthworm. 2 Bait.

43. Biatas.

biathmhor, see biadh-char.

biathsadh, *s.m.* Provision for a journey, viaticum.

bibh, see bithibh.

bibhidh,* *s.m.* Very large fire.—*Islay.*

bicas, -ais, *s.m.* see biocas.

bicein,†† -ean, *s.m.* One single grain.

biceir, -ean, *s.m.* Small wooden dish. 2 Drinking-cup. 3 Bottle. 4 Beaker ("bicker".) 5†† "Luggie."

bicheanta, see bitheanta.

————chd, *s.f.* see bitheantas.

†bichearb, -chirb, *s.m.* Mercury, quicksilver.

†bi-cheardach, -aich, *s.m.* Victualling house, tavern.

†bichim, see bichearb.

bichionta, *a.* & *adv.* see bitheanta.

bichiontas, -ais, *s.m.* see bitheantas.

bi-chùram, -aim, *s.m.* see bith-chùram.

†bid, *s.f.* Hedge, fence.

†bid, (*for* bithidh iad,) They shall be.

bìd, -e, -ean, *s.m.* Shrill chirping sound. 2 Chirping of birds. 3 Very small portion. 4‡‡Nipping, pinching.

†bìd, *v.a.* Nip, pinch. 2‡‡Nibble.

bìd, *pr.part.* a' bìdil, *v.a.* Chirp.

bìdeach, -eiche, *a.* Very little. 2 Trifling. 3 Diminutive.

bìdeachas,‡‡ -ais, *s.m.* Mordacity.

bìdeachd,* *s.f.* Littleness, smallness.

bìdeadh, *s.m.* Nipping, pinching. A' b—, *pr. part.* of †bìd.

bìdeag, -eig, -an, *s. f.* Very small portion of anything, bit, fraction. 2 Crumb. 3 Morsel. 4‡‡ Pinching. Bìdeag chrìon, *a little piece.* Chaidh e 'na bhìdeagan, *it went into fragments.*

———ach,- aiche, *a.* Nipping, pinching.

bidean, -ein, *s.m.* Hedge, fence. 2 see bìdein.

bìdean, see bìdein.

bìdear,‡‡ -eir, -ean, *s.m.* see bìdein.

bideil, see bìdil.

bidein, -ean, *s.m.* Point, summit, pinnacle.

bìdein, -ean,** *s.m.* Chirper, peeper, young bird or fowl. 3 Diminutive person or animal.

———each, -eiche, *a.* Sharp-topped as a hill or rock. 2‡‡ *fig.* Light-headed.

bìdh, *gen. sing.* of biadh.

——, *a.* see bìth.

quiet as a lamb; cho bìdh ri luchaig, *as quiet as a mouse.*

bidh, *for* bithidh, see *v.* bi.

†bìdh-cheartach, *s.f.* Tavern.

bìdh, *s. f.* see bìth.

bìdheag,** *s.f.* Bait (on a hook.)

bidheanta, see bitheanta.

————chd, see bitheantachd.

————s, see bitheantas.

bi-dheantas,** *s.m.* Endlessness.

†bidhearg, *a.* Red, unctuous, as fir or pine.

bidhis, -ean, *s. f.* Screw. 2 Vice. (††bithis)

———each, *a.* Like a screw. 2 Spiral.

bìdil, *s. f.* Continual chirping. 2 Shrill sound. 3 Squeak, as of rats, mice, or birds. A' b—, *pr.part.* of bìd.

†bidis, *v.* Were. 2 Let them be.

bidse, *s.f.* Gaelic spelling of *bitch.* 2 Whore.

———ach, *a.* Addicted to whoredom.

———achd, *s.f.* Whoremongering, conduct of a prostitute.

bidsich, *v.n.* Play the whore.

big, *s.m.* & *pr.part.* see bìd.

big, *pr.part.* a' bìgil, *v.n.* see bìd.

†big, *a.* Tender.

big! big! *int.* Mode of calling to chickens.

big, *n.pl.* of *s.* beag. 2 *gen.sing.m.* of *a.* beag.

bigeach,(AG) *a. dim.* of beag. Very small.

bigeal, see bìdil.

bigean,** *s.m.* Cap, hair lace.

bigeil, see bìdil.

bigein,¶ *s.m.* Rock-pipit. see gabhagan. 2 Golden-crested wren, see dreathan a' chinn bhuidhe. 3(AF) Meadow pipit. 4 Any little bird. 5‡ see biceir.

bigein-baintighearna,¶ *s. m.* Mountain linnet or twite.—*Uist.* see riabhag mhonaidh.

bigein Brìghde, (AC) (*lit.* St. Bridget's little bird) *s.m.* Linnet.

bigein mór, (AF) *s.m.* Black shore-lark.

bigein-sneachda, (AF) *s.m.* Little snow-bunting.

bigeir, *s.m.* see biceir.

bìg-eun, -eòin, *s.m.* Any small bird.
bìgh, e, *s.f.* see bìth. 2 Pillar, post. Eadar dà bhìgh an doruis, *between the two door-posts.*
bìgh-chraoibh, -e-e, *s. f.* } see bìth.
bìgheach, -eiche, *a.* }
bìgheanta, see bìtheanta.
bìgh-eòin, *s. f.* see bìth-eòin.
bìgh-thalmhuinn, *s. f.* see bìth-thalmhuinn.
†bigil, see bìdil.
bigirein, see biceir.
†bil, *s. f.* see bile.
†bil, *a.* Good.
bilbheag, -eig, see meilbheag.
bile, -an, *s. f.* Lip. 2 Rim, brim, edge, margin of anything. 3‡‡Cluster of trees. 4‡Leaf, blade, Bheir mo bhilean cliù dhuit, *my lips shall praise thee*; bilean nan sruthan uaigneach, *the margin of the lonely brooks ;* bile na h-aide, *the brim of the hat ;* air a bhil' uachdaraich, *on his upper lip*; ag imeachd air bile na tràighe, *walking on the sea-shore.*
†bile, *s. f.* Mouth. 2 Bird's bill. 3 Blossom. 4 Beard.
bileach, -eiche, *a.* Lipped. 2 Bladed, as grass. 3 Fringed, bordered, edged, welted. 4 Billed, as a bird. 5‡‡ Full of leaflets. Bròg bhileach, *a welted shoe.*
———, -lich, -lichean, *s.m.* Leaf of a tree or herb. 2 Quantity of leaves. 3**Young leafy tree. Bàrr nam bilichean blàthmhor, *the tops of the flourishing green trees.*
bileach-choigeach, -eich, *s.m.* Corn-marigold. see bile-bhuidhe.

44. Bileach-losgainn.

bileach-losgainn, (a' bh—) *s.f.* Burnet—*sanguis orba*
bileag, -eig, -an, *s.f.* Leaflet. 2 Little blade. 3 bag. 4 Leaf of a tree or herb. 5†† Tongue. *B.* fheòir, *a blade of grass* ; bileag chàile, *a blade of colewort.*
bileagach, *a.* see bileach.
————adh, -aidh, *s.m.* Continual licking or sipping in small quantities. A' b—, *pr. part.* of bileagaich.
bileagaich, *pr.part.* a' bileagachadh, *v.a. & n.* Lick up continually or in small drops. 2**Browse.
bileag-an-spuing,§ *s.f.* Colt's foot. see cluas liath.
bileagan-nan-eun,‡‡ *s.f.* Bird leaflets, a sort of acrid plant—*avium foliola.* **Species of wood-sorrel.
bileag-bhàite, *s.f.* Water-lily. see duilleag-bhàite.
bileag-chapuill,§ *s. f.* Red clover, see seamrag-chapuill.
bilean, *n.pl.* of bile.

45. Bilearach.

bileanach,§ *s.m.* Sweetsea-grass. see bilearach.
bilearach,§ *s.m.* Sweet sea-grass—*zostera marina.*
bile-bhuidhe, *s. f.* Corn-marigold — *chrysanthemum segetum.*
†bileid, Gaelic spelling of *billet.*
bileil, *a.* Labial. 2 Talkative.
bileineach,†† *s. f.* see bilearach.
bil-fhaclach, *a.* Labial.
bilidh,** (*for* bile.) A bilidh a' cur fàilt' ort, *her lips saluting thee.*
bilisteir,-e, -ean, *s. m.* Mean beggarly fellow. 2‡Glutton, 3 (*Isles*) Rancid butter or tallow.
bilisteireachd, *s. f.* Mean hankering or searching after food.
†bill, *s.m.* ||Leper. 2‡‡Fool.
†bille, *s. f.* Rag.
†bille, *a.* Mean, weak.
billeachd, *s. f.* Poverty. 2 Raggedness. 3 Weakness.
†billeog, see bileag.
†billian, *s.m.* Little dish.
bi'm, (*for* bithidh mi) I shall be. 2 (*for* bitheam) Let me be.
bi'mid, (*for* bitheamaid) Let us be.
†binbhrianachd, see binn-bhriathrachd.

46. Bile-bhuidhe.

47. Bile bhuidhe.

bineach, see binneach.
binealta, see finealta.
binid, binnde [& binide] binndean, *s. f.* Cheese-rennet. 2 Stomach of a calf, lamb, or hare.
———each, *a.* Like rennet, of, or belonging to, rennet.
†binigear, *s. f.* Gaelic spelling of *vinegar.* 2 Pickle.
binn, -e, *a.* Melodious, musical; sweet. 2 Shrill. 3 Harmonious. 4‡‡True. An ni nach binn le duine cha chluinn duine, *what a man likes not he hears not* ; is balbh do bheul a bha binn, *mute is thy mouth that was musical* ; is binn leam do cheum, *musical to me is the sound of thy footstep*; bu mhór am beud gu'n rachadh do bheul binn gu bràth fo thalamh, *'twere a pity thy sweet mouth should ever go underground* (said ironically of bad singers. N.G.P. It is not the *i* but the *nn* that is long, except in the far north.
binn, -e, *s. f.* Sentence, judgment, decision, condemnation. 2 Fate. 3**Melody. 4**Hopper of a mill. Thoir binn a mach, *give a decision, pronounce judgment* ; binn an aghaidh droch oibre, *sentence against an evil work* ; faigh binn, *receive sentence.*
†binn, (*for* bha mi.)
binn-bheul, -eòil, *s.m.* Musical, sweet, melodious voice.
—————ach, -aiche, *a.* Sweet-voiced, eloqu-

ent.
binn-bhriathrach, -aiche, *a.* Melodious. 2 Eloquent.
——————d, *s.f.* Melodiousness. 2 Eloquence.
binn-cheòl, -iùil, *s.m.* Sweet music.
————ach, -aiche, *a.* Melodious, harmonious.
binndeach, *a.* Coagulative, curdling. 2 Apt to coagulate.
————adh, -aidh, *s.m.* Curdling, coagulating. 2*Making cheese. Ballan binndeachaidh, *a cheese-vat.* A' b—, *pr. part.* of binndich.
binndeal, -eil, -an, *s.m.* Head-dress. 2(DM) Forehead cloth.
†binndean, -ein, see binid.
binndich, *pr. pt.* a' binndeachadh, *v.a.* Coagulate, curdle. 2*Make cheese.
————te, *past part.* Curdled, coagulated.
binne,* *s. f.* see binneas.
binne, *comp.* of binn. Is binne do ghuth na'n smeòrach, *sweeter is thy voice than the thrush.*
binneach, -eiche, *a.* Light, light-headed, fanciful. 2 Hilly, pinnacled, mountainous. 3 Pointed. 4**Horned, antlered. 5*High-topped. Eilid bhinneach, *the antlered deer.*
binnead, -eid, *s.m.* Degree of melody, sweetness, or harmoniousness. Is fhearr leam do ghuth na'n smeòrach air binnead, *I prefer thy voice to the thrush for melody.*
binneag, -eig, -an, *s. f.* Chimney-top, chimney-stalk. [In Benbecula and the Uists, a gable without a vent in it, especially one made of turf. One built of stone and lime is generally called *stuadh.*—J.M.]
————ach, -aiche, *a.* Towered, turreted. Ro shuuagh'or, fineant, binneagach, *very good-looking, maidenly, towering.—Oran Chlann Domhnuill nan Eilean,*in *Filidh nam Beann. p. 22.*
binnealach, -aiche, *a.* Melodious, harmonious, chirping.
binnealaich, *s. f.* Chirping of birds.
binnealta, *a.* see finealta. 2‡‡Melodious.
————ch, -aiche, *a.* see finealta.
binnean, -ein, *s.m.* see binnein.
————ach,* *a.* see binneineach.
binnear,** -eir, *s.m.* Hill, pinnacle. 2 Pin, bodkin, hair-pin.
binneas, -eis, *s.m.* Music, harmony, melody. 2 Euphony in *grammar.* A' togail a guth le binneas, *raising her voice with melody.*
binne-bheathach,(AF) *s.m.* Horned beast or animal.
binnein, *s.m.* Pinnacle, apex of a hill. 2 High conical hill. 3 Turret. 4**Bell. Binnein na carraige, *the pinnacle of the rock.*
————each, -eiche, *a.* Acuminated, pinnacled.
†binneochaidh, see beannaichidh.
binn-fhaclach, -aiche, *a.* Melodious, having a sweet-toned voice. 2 Sweet-worded. Eunlaith binn-fhaclach, *melodious birds.*
binn-fhuaim, -e, *s.m.* Sweet sonorous sound.
——————each,‡‡ -eiche, *a.* Euphonical.
binn-ghuth, *s.m.* Melodious voice. 2 Sweet tone or note. Mar bhinn-ghuth ealaidh, *like the sweet note of a swan.*
binnid, see binid.
————each, *a.* see binideach.
†binnse, -achan, Gaelic spelling of *bench.*
binnseach,** *a.* Having benches. 2 Like a bench.
binnteach, see binndeach.
————adh, see binndeachadh.
binntean, see binid.
————ach, see binideach.
binntich, see binndich.
biob, *s.m.* *for* bab—*Perthshire.*
Bi-ball, see Bìobull.
bioban, -ain, *s.m.* Disease in poultry, "pip."
biobhuan, see bith-bhuan.
————tachd, see bith-bhuantachd.
Bìobull, -uill, *s.m.* Bible.
————ach, *a.* Biblical.
biocas, -ais, *s.m.* Viscount.
biochar,(AC) *a.* see biadhchar.
bioda, -an, *s.m.* Pointed top. 2 Hill-top. Air chorra bioda, *on tiptoes.*
biod,* *v.a. & n.* Pique, gall, vex. 2 Bicker, canker.
biodach, -aiche, *a.* Sharp-topped, pyramidical.
bìodach, see bìdeach.
biodaich, *v.a.* Bud.

48. Biodag.

biodag, -aig, -an, *s. f.* Dirk. 2 Dagger. Cha mhisd' a thig dhuit am biodag, *no worse does the dirk become thee;* cha do chleachd am bodach biodag, *the fellow was not used to a dirk.*
————ach, *a.* Like a dirk or dagger. 2 Having a dirk or dagger.
————aich, *v.a.* Poniard, wound with a dirk or dagger.
————an, *n.pl.* of biodag.
biodagraich,* *s.* Snick and snee. (fight with knives.)
biodaich,‡‡ *v.a. & n.* Bud.
biodailt, Gaelic form of *victuals.* 2 Spirits—J.G.M.
biodan,* -ain, *s.m.* see biodanach.
————ach, -aiche, *a.* Sharp-topped. 2 Bickering. 3 Cankering. 4**Tattling, prating.
†————ach, -aich, *s.m.* Tattler, prater. 2* Bickering fellow. 3**s.f.* Bickering female.
†biodarnach, -aiche, *a.* Chirping.
biod-chas, *s. f.* Splay-foot.
biod-cheann, -inn, *s.m.* Pointed head.
——————ach, -aiche, *a.* Sharp-headed.
biodh, *3rd. pers. sing. imper.* of bi. (Contraction of bitheadh.)
†biodh,** *s.m.* The World.
†biodhanas, -ais, *s.m.* Discord.
†biodhbha, see biùthaidh.
‡————nas, -ais, *s.m.* see biodhanas.
biog, -a, -an, *s.m.* see bìd, *s.m.* 2***s.f.* Start.
——, *v.a.* Gripe, start.
——ach, -aiche, *a.* Apt to start, causing to start. 2 Small, very little.
——adh, -aidh, *s.m.* Starting, palpitation, strong or sudden emotion. 2 Griping. 3 Whim.
biogail, *s. f.* see bìdil.
biogail, -e, *a.* Active, lively, frisky. 2 Apt to start. 3 Neat. 4 Small.
bioganta, *a.* Thrilling, sharp tingling sensation.
biogaran,(AG) *s.f.* Small wooden dish.
biogarra, *a.* Mean, churlish, surly. 2 Censorious. 3‡"Cheepish."
————chd, *s. f.* Meanness, churlishness, inhospitableness.
biog-ghairm, *s. f.* The death-watch.
†biol, *s. f.* Little musical instrument. 2 Violin, fiddle.
biolag,** -aig, *s. f.* Little musical instrument, 2 *in derision,* a person who is fond of singing

or whistling.
———ach, -aiche, *a.* Musical, melodious. 2 Fond of singing or whistling. 3**Blythe.
biolair, -e, -ean, *s. f.* Water-cress—*nasturtium officinalis.* [*Biolair* is applied to all kinds of cresses.]
biolair-an-fhuarain, *s. f.* Fountain cresses.
biolaireach, -eiche, *a.* Abounding in cresses. 2 Of, or belonging to, cresses. Glacag bhiolaireach, *a dell abounding in cresses.*
biolair-Fraing,§ *s. f.* French or garden cress.
biolair-ghriagain,§ *s. f.* Ladies' smock or cuckoo flower. see plùr-na-cubhaig.
biolair-uaine, *s. f.* Green water-cress.
†biolar, -aire, *a.* Neat, fine, dainty, spruce.
biolarach, see biolaireach.
biolasg, -aisg, *s.m.* Prattle, gabble, loquacity.
———ach, -aiche, *a.* Loquacious, prattling.
———adh, -aidh, *s.m.* Loquacity, prattling.
biolur, -uir, *s.m.* Bistort or snake-weed—*polygonum bistorta.*

49. Biolur.

bìom, (contraction of bitheam.
†bion, *adv.* Readily, easily, usually.
bionn,(AC) *a.* Symmetrical, well-featured, beauteous. Is i mo leannan an té bhionn, *my love is the beauteous maid.*
bior, -a, -an, *s.m.* Thorn. 2 Prickle. 3 Small or sharp-pointed stick. 4 Any sharp-pointed thing. 5 Spit. 6 Pin. 7**Goad. 8 **Bodkin. Bior 'nad dhòrn na paisg; *do not squeeze a thorn in thy fist*; a' geurachadh nam bior, *sharpening the goads*; 'nam bioraibh 'n 'ur sùilibh, *as thorns in your eyes* is bior gach sràbh 'san oidhche, *every straw is a thorn at night.*—N.G.P.
bior, *pr.pt.* a' bioradh, *v.a.* Prick. 2 Sting. 3 Gall, vex. 4 Goad, spur on.
†bior.*s.m.* Well, fountain. 2 Water.—*a.*‡‡Short.
bìor.(AH) *s.f.* Sour or angry look. Tha droch bhìor air, *he looks very displeased.*
biorach, -aiche, *a.* Sharp-pointed. 2 Piercing. 3 Horned, having branching antlers. 4 Sharp-sighted. †5**Watery. Sùil bhiorach, *a sharp or quick eye*; le d' lannaibh biorach, *with thy pointed swords*; a' gnréigh bhiorach 'na dhéidh, *the branching-antlered herd behind him.*
———, -aich, -aichean, *s. f.* Two-year old heifer. 2 Year old horse or colt. 3(AF)Cow-calf, steer, filly. 4 Ox, bullock. 5 Dog-fish, see gobag. 6 Instrument to prevent calves from sucking, [bùthach in Uist.—JM] 7** Boat ‡ see birlinn.
biorachas, -ais, *s.m.* Pointedness, sharpness, epigrammatical sharpness.
bioradh, -aidh, *s.m.* Stinging, pricking, piercing. A' b—, *pr. part.* of bior.
biorag, -aig, -an, *s. f.* Tusk or side tooth in the mouth of a horse.
biorag,§ -aig, -an, *s.m.* Dutch rushes or shave grass—*equisetum hyemale.*
biorag-lodain, *s. f.* Bandstickle.
bioragach,** *a.* Aculeated.
bioraich, *v. a.* Sharpen at the point, make pointed. 2 Stare, look steadfastly.

50. Biorag.

bioraiche, *comp.* of biorach. Sharper, sharpest.

51. Biorag-lodain.

bioraiche, -ean, *s. f.* see bioraich-ead. 2 see biorach, *s.* 3 Sharp, angular person. Bioraiche, mac na h-asail, *a colt the foal of an ass*
bioraichead, *s. m. & f.* Conicalness, pointedness, sharpness, epigrammatical sharpness.
bioraid, see biorraid.
———each, see biorraideach.
†bioraidh,** *s.m.* Bullock. 2(AF) Steer.
biorain, *gen. sing.* of bioran.
bioran, -ain, *s.m.* Stick, staff, little stick. 2 3**Any sharp-pointed thing. †3**Strife. 4** Anguish, vexation. Bioran 'na làimh, *a stick in his hand*; bioran de sgithich, *a twig of white-thorn*; is math cobhair nam bioran le 'chéile, *the union of sticks is helpful.*—N.G.P.
bioranach, -aiche, *a.* Abounding in sticks. 2 Like a stick. 3 Full of prickles.
———, -aich, *s.m.* Pin-cushion. 2‡‡Needle 3 Troublesome or contentious person.
———an, -ain, *s.m.* Pinmaker.
bioranaich,** *v.a.* Vex.
———e, -chean, see bioranachan.
———te, *a.* Vexed, grieved.

52. Bior an-deamhnaidh.

bioran-deamhnaidh, *s.m.* Minnow, pink.
bioran-donais,(AH) *s.m.* Minnow, pink.
bioran-druma,* *s.m.* Drum-stick.
bior-an-iasgair, (AC) } Kingfisher, see
bior-an-uisge,(AC) } biorra-cruidein.
biorar, *s. f.* Cress, see biolair.
bioras, -ais, -an, *s.m.* Water-lily, see duilleag-bhàite.
biorasg, see bior-iasg.
†bior-bhogha, *s.m.* Rain-bow.
bior-bhogha,§ *s.m.* Yellow flag, see bog-uisge.
†bior-bhualan,(AF) *s.m.* Toad. 2 Water serpent.
†bior-bhuasach, -aich, *s.m.* Water serpent. 2 Conger-eel.
bior-chluaiseanach, see bior-chluasach.
bior-chluas, -ais, -an, *s. f.* Sharp-pointed ear, as of a dog when listening eagerly.
bior-chluasach, *a.* Sharp-eared, quick of hearing. 2**Having sharp or pointed ears.
†biorchoil, *s.m.* Instrument for beheading.
bior-chòmhladh, -aidh, *s. f.* Flood-gates,sluice.
biordainge, *s. f.* Pricker, see bàta G1 p. 73.
bior-deighe, *s. f.* Icicle.
†biordhach, *a.* Watery.
bior-dhorus, -dhorsan, *s. f.* Water-sluice.
bior-dhruidheachd, *s. f.* Mode of divining by water.
bior-dubh, *s.m.* Stem- or stern-post of a ship, see O1 and N1 p. 73.
bior-eidhe, see bior-deighe.
bior-fheadan, -ain, *s.m.* Water-pipe.
bior-fhiacal, -an-, *s.m.* Tooth-pick.

†bior-fhion, *s.m.* Metheglin, drink made of honey and water boiled and fermented.
bior-fuinn, *s.m.* Landmark, beacon. Bheirinn am bior-fuinn a mach, *I would descry the land-mark.*
biorg, *pr.part.* a' biorgadh, *v.n.* Flow, gush. 2 Twitch suddenly and sorely. 3*Tingle, thrill, feel a tingling sensation. 3††Gall.
———ach, -aiche, *a.* Ecstatic, transporting, rapturous, nervous.
biorgadaich,* *s.f.* Thrilling or tingling sensation.
biorgadh, -aidh, *s.m.* Painful wrench or twist. A' b—, *pr.part.* of biorg. Bhuail biorgadh de'n eagal e, *he was thrilled with fear.*
biorgainn,†† -e, *s.f.* Sharp lancinating pain.
biorganta, *a.* Perplexing. 2 Hampering. 3 Vexatious. 4 Thrilling. 5 Galling.
————ch, see biorganta.
————chd, *s.f. ind.* Perplexity. 2 Entanglement. 3 Intricacy. 4*Degree of thrilling, or tingling sensation.
bior-glantachain, *s.m.* Weeding grubber.
bior-greasaidh, *s.m.* Goad, ox-goad. 2‡‡Awl.
biorguinn, see biorgainn.
bior-iaruinn, *s.m.* Marline-spike. see bàta 29 p. 76.
bior-iasg, -éisg, *s.m.* Bait for fishing. 2 Fish with prickles.
bior leacain,§ *s.m.* (*lit.* the pointed hill-side plant.) Juniper. see aitionn.
bior-linn, see birlinn.
†bior-mhéin, *s.f.* Ooziness, moisture.
bior-nam-bride, see bearnan-Bride.
†bior-oir, *s.f.* Water margin.
†bior-phoit, *s.f.* Urn.
†biorra, see biorra-crùidein.
biorra-an-iasgaire, *s.m.* see biorra-crùidein.

53. *Biorra-crùidein.*

biorra-crùidein,¶ *s.m.* Kingfisher—*alcedo ispida.*
†biorrach, *s.f.* Boat, yawl, skiff. 2‡‡Muzzle.
————dach, -aiche, *a.* see biorach.
————dair, -ean, *s.m.* Tricky fellow, sharper. 2 Petty thief.
biorrach lachan,§ Reed grass, see seasgan.
†biorrag, *s.f.* Soft marshy field or plain.
biorraid, -e, -ean, *s.f.* Helmet. 2 Head-piece. 3 Hat. 4* Cap with a scoop on it. 5 Osier-twig. 7‡‡Cone. 7 *rarely* Strife. Biorraid bu loinntreach snas, *a burnished helmet.*
————each, -eiche, *a.* Conical. 3 Wearing a helmet. 3 Of, or belonging to, a cap. 4 Scooped. 5**High-headed.
biorramaid, *s.f.* Gaelic spelling of *pyramid.*
————each,** *a.* Pyramidical.
†biorran, -ain, *s.m.* Vexation of mind. 2 Top of a small hill.
†————, *v.a.* Distract. 2 Embarrass. 3 Ensnare, entangle.
†————ach, *a.* Distracted.
†————aire, *s.m.* Fomenter of strife.
†bior-ròs,§ *s.m.* White water-lily, see duilleag-bhàite bhàn. 2 Yellow water lily, see duilleag bhàite bhuidhe.
bior-ròslaidh, see bior-ròstaidh.
bior-ròstaidh, *s.m.* Spit.
biorsadh, -aidh, *s.m.* Eager impatience. 2†† Keen wish. 3‡Goading.
biorsamaid,-ean, *s.f.* Roman balance for weighing small quantities. 2 Steel-yard. 3(AH) Term of contempt, applied to a sharp-tongued woman.
bior-shruth, *s.m.* The old bed of a river.
bior-shùil, -ùla, -ùilean, *s.f.* Piercing eye. 2** Quick-sighted eye.
————each, -liche, *a.* Quick-sighted, sharp-sighted. Gabhair bh.. *sharp-sighted goats.*
bior-snaois, *s.f.* Beak. 2 Top of the stem of a boat, see bàta, p. 76.
bior-stùc,** *s.m.* Pyramid.
bios, *v.* see bitheas. †2 *s.m.* Silk.
biosa, (*for* bi thusa) sometimes written *bios* and *bi-sa.*
†biosar,** -air, *s.m.* Silk.
biosgach, *a.* Churlish, niggardly.
biosgail, see biosgach.
biosgair, -ean, *s.m.* Scrub.
————eachd,** *s.f.* Scrubbishness, meanness.
biota, *s.f.* Churn. 2 Pitcher. 3‡Vessel.
biota-bhùirn,(AG) *s.f.* Water-pitcher.
biotailt, *s.m.* Gaelic spelling of *victuals.* 2 Grain of all kinds.
————each, -eiche, *a.* Abounding in victuals, or grain.
biotais, see biatas.
†bioth, *s.m.* The world. 2 Being.
†biothanach, *s.m.* Thief.
†bioth-bhuaine, see bith-bhuantachd.
bìr, *s.m.* Alarm note of the solan geese when attacked at night. 2† see bior.
bireid, see biride.
†bir-fhion, see bior-fhion.
biriche,** *s.m.* see biorach, *s.*
birichean, *s.m.* Conoid.
†biride,(AF) *s.f.* Breeding cow. 2**Shrew.
birlinn, -ean, *s.f.* Galley. 2 Barge, pleasure boat.
————each, *a.* Abounding in galleys or barges.
†birread, see biorraid.
†birt, *s.f.* Hilt, haft, handle. 2‡‡Castle, fortified place.
†birt, *pl.* of beart, Loads, bundles.
birtich, *v.a.* Kindle, excite, stir up. Birtich an teine, *poke the fire.*
†bis, *s.f.* Buffet, box, slap.
b' ise, (*for* bu ise) It was she.
biseach,** -sich, *s.f.* Crisis of a disease.
biseach, -eich, } see piseach.
————d, }
bisidh, Gaelic spelling of *busy.*
biteag,** -eig, -an, *s.f.* see bideag.
biteig, *gen. sing.* of biteag.
bith, *s.f. ind.* Life, existence, being, living. 2 The world. 3‡‡Creature.
†bith, *s.f. ind.* Custom, habit. 2‡‡Order, law. 3 Wound. 4 Blow. 5 Contest. 6 Woman.
bìth, -e, *s.f.* Glue, gum. 2 Bird-lime. 3 Resin. 4 Tar, bitumen. 5 Pith. 6 Caulking.
bìth, *a.* Quiet, peaceable, tranquil, calm. 2 Coy. Bi bìth, *be quiet* ; cho bìth ri uan, *as*
bith-, *prepositive particle* signifying *ever-, always,* as bith-bhuan, *everlasting.*
†bithbheanach, see biothanach.
†bithbheanta, *a.* Stolen.
bith-bheò, *a.* Everliving. 2 Everlasting. 3** Perennial. 4**Evergreen.
bith-bhreun,(DM) see bith-bhreunach.
bith-bhreunach,** *s.m.* Assafœtida.
bith-bhriathrach, -aiche, *a.* Talkative, loquacious, babbling.
————————d, *s.f. ind.* Loquacity.
bith-bhrigh, *s.f.* Essence. 2 Life-blood.

bith-bhuan, *a.* Everlasting, eternal, immortal. 2 Perpetual.
————tachd, *s. f. ind* Eternity, perpetuity.
bith-chainnt, *s. f.* Babblement, senseless ill-timed prate.
bith-chraoibh, -e-e, Gum of trees.
bith-chùram, -aim, *s.m.* Anxiety, continual care or solicitude. 2‡‡Worldly care.
————ach, *a.* Extremely careful.
bith-dheanamh, -aimh, *s.m.* Continual acting.
bith-dheanta, see bitheanta.
————s, see bitheantas.
†bithe, *gen. sing.* of bith.
†bithe,** *a.* Female, of, or belonging to, the female sex.
bìtheach, -eiche, *a.* Bitumenous.
bitheadh, *3rd. pers. sing. & pl. imp.* of bì. Let [him, her, or it]be. Bitheadh e cho math 's a thogras e, *let him be ever so good.*
bitheag,(AC) *s. f.* Life.
bitheam, *1st. pers. sing. imp.* of bì. Let me be.
†bitheamhnach, see biothanach.
†bitheamhnanta, *a.* Thievish.
bìthean,** *s.m.* Bait.
bitheanach,* *a.* see bìtheanta.
bitheanta, *a.* Frequent, continual. 2 Common. 3 Numerous.
bìtheanta, *a.* Glutinous, viscous, tenacious, ropy.
————chd,‡‡ *s. f. ind.* Adhesiveness.
bitheantachd,* see bitheantas.
bitheantas, -ais, *s.m.* Frequently happening. 2**Frequency, commonness. 3**Common occurrence. Am *b.*, *frequently, generally.*
bithear, *fut. impers.* of bì. [It] shall be. [ex. under the word "beus."]
bitheara, see bitheanta.
bitheas, *fut. subj.* of bì. see bhitheas.
bìth-eòin, *s.f.* Bird-lime.
bith-gheal,(AC) *a.* Beauteous. A Bhrìghde bhith-ghil ! *thou beauteous Bridget !*
bith-ghràbhadh, -aidh, *s.m.* Cosmography, description of the world.
bithibh, *2nd. pers. pl. imp.* of bì. Be ye. Bithibh coimeas do cheud, *be a match for a hundred.*
bithid, *for* bithidh iad.
bithidh, *fut. ind.* of bì. Shall or will be.
bithidh, *gen. sing.* of biadh.
bithis, see bidhis. 2‡‡Female
bith-labhairt, *s. f.* Talkativeness. 2 Prattling, perpetual talking.
bith-rè, *s. f. ind.* Life-time.
bith-shìor, *a.* see bith-shiorruidh.
bith-shiorruidh, *a.* Eternal, everlasting.
bìth-thalmhuinn, *s.f.* Bitumen.
†bitiorra, *a.* Cheerful, blythe.
bitis, see biatas.
bitse, see bidse.
——ach, see bidseach.
——achd, see bidseachd.
bitsich, see bidsich.
biu,(AC) *a.* see beò.
biùdhas, -ais, see biùthas.
biùg, *s.m.* Difficulty in speech. Cha d'thubhairt i biùg, *she said nothing.*
biùgadh, -aidh, see biogadh.
biuidh, see biùthaidh.
†biùthaidh, -ean, *s.m.* Hero, champion. 2 Foe. 3 Army.
biùthannas, -ais, *s.m.* Enmity.
biùthantas, see biùthas.
biùthas, -ais, *s.m.* Fame, glory, reputation. 2 Good or bad report. 3* Defamation of the worst kind.
biùthasach,* *a.* Defamatory, libellous in the highest degree.
biùthasachd,* *s.f.* Defamation.
†blà, *s.m.* Town, village. 2 Piety, devotion. 3 Green field. 4 Cry, shout. 5 Offspring. 6 Praise.
†blà, *v.a.* Be it enacted.
†blà, *a.* Yellow. 2 Healthy, well. 3 Safe. 4 see blàth.
blabaran, -ain, *s.m.* Stammerer, stutterer.
blabhdach, -aiche, *a.* see bladach.
blabhdair, see bladair & bladaireachd.
————eachd, see bladaireachd.
blac,(AC) *s.m.* Cream. (? bliochd)
†blachd, *s. f.* Word.
blad, -aid, *s.m.* Mouth. 2 Foul or abusive mouth. 3*Wide mouth. 4**Dirty mouth. 5 (AF)Wolf.
——ach, -aiche, *a.* Garrulous. 2 Abusive. 3 Wide-mouthed. 4**Foul-mouthed. 5 Guttural.
——ach,* *s. f.* Female with a large mouth.
bladaidh,(AG) *s.m.* Flatterer.
bladair, -e, -ean, *s.m.* Flatterer. 2 Babbler. 3 Sycophant. 4 Blockhead. 5 Wide mouth. 6(AF)Wolf. 7‡‡Coward. 8**One of the followers of a Highland chieftain.
————, -air, *s.m.* see blanndar.
————eachd, *s. f.* Flattery. 2 Sycophancy. 3 Babbling. 4 Yelling, howling. 5 Cowardice.
bladairt,* *s.m.* see bladaireachd.
bladar,** -air, *s.m.* Flattery. 2 Hypocrisy, dissimulation.
————ach,** *a.* Flattering, coaxing.
bladh, -aidh, *s.m.* Essence. 2 Juice. 3 Substance. 4 Meaning. 5 ‡‡Flattery. 6 Energy. 7 Fame, renown. 8 Garland. 9 ‡‡Shout. 10 Praise. 11 Blow. 12* Pith. 13 see blàth. Is buaine bladh na saoghal, *renown is more lasting than life*—N.G.P.
†bladh, *a* Smooth. 2 Soft.
†——, *s.m.* see bloigh.
†——, *v.* see bloighich.
blàdhach, *a.* see blàthmhor.
————, -aich, *s.m.* see blàthach.
†bladhachd, *s. f.* Crushing, smashing. 2 Crumbling, breaking into pieces.
bladhail, -e, *a.* [‡bladh, *pith*] Strong, forcible, energetic, sappy, pithy, substantial.
bladhair, -ean, *s.m.* see bladair. 2‡‡Blast. 3 (bladh, 7)‡Boaster.
†————, *v.n.* Boast.
————, -e, *a.* Important, momentous, expressive. 2 Substantial. 3 Significant.
————eachd, see blaghaireachd & bladaireachd.
bladhan, see blaoghan.
bladhantas, see blaghaireachd & bladaireachd.
bladhar, see bladair. 2* Substantial, full of meaning, substance, or importance.
bladhastair, -ean, see blaomastair.
————eachd, see blaomastaireachd.
bladh-leabhair, *s.m.* Contents of a book.
bladh-leasgaidh, see blàth-fhleasg.
bladhm, -a, -annan, see blaom.
bladhmadaich, -e, see blaomadaich.
bladhmadh, see blaomadh.
bladhmag, -aig, -an, see blaomag.
†bladhmaich, *s.* Fame, commendation, praise.
bladhmair, -ean, see blaomair.
————eachd, see blaomadaich.
bladhmannach, -aich, -ean, see blaomannach.
bladhmastair, -e, -ean, see blaomastair.
————eachd, see blaomastaireachd.
bladh-shùgh, *s.m.* Elixir.
blad-shrònach, -aiche, *a.* Flat-nosed.
blad-spàgach, *a.* Flat-footed, plain-soled.
†blagaireachd, *s. f.* Blast. 2 Boasting, blustering, bravado.

blagh, -aigh, see bladh.
†——, v.a. Puff, blow. Gaelic spelling of Sc. blaw.
blàghach,** a. Effectual. 2 Famous, renowned.
————, s. see blàthach.
blaghair,** -ean, s.m. Blast, puff. 2 Blustering wind. 3 Blusterer, boaster.
————eachd,** s.f. Blustering. 2 Boasting. 3 Bravado.
blaghan,(AF) -ain, s.m. Whiting, pollack (fish.)
blaghantach, -aiche, a. Boastful, blustering.
blaghastair, see bladhastair.
blaghmhanach, -aich, s.m. Blustering fellow.
†blai, s.f. The womb.
blaidh, -e, -ean, see bloigh.
blaidh-lìn, see braith-lìn.
blaigh, s.f. see bloigh.
——deach, s.f. & a. bloigheach.
blaighdeachadh, -aidh, s. m. & pr. part. see bloigheachadh.
——deachas, see bloigheachas.
blaighdich, see bloighich.
blaigh-lìn, see braith-lìn.
†blainic, see blonag.
†————each, see blonagach.
blais, pr. part. a' blasad [& a' blasadh,††] v.a. Taste, try by the mouth. 2 Sip. 3 Relish. 'Nuair a bhlais e am fion, *when he tasted the wine.*
blais-bheum, s.m. Blasphemy. 2 Taunt, reproach. 3 Infamy.
————ach, -aiche, a. Blasphemous, given to blaspheme.
blaiseagail, s. m. } see blaiseamachd.
blaiseagraich, } see blaiseamachd.
blaiseamachd,* s.f. Smacking with the lips. A' b—, pr.pt. of blaiseamaich.
blaiseamaich, pr. part. a' blaiseamachd, v.a. Smack with the lips. 2 Taste, try.
blaisidh, fut. aff. act. of blais.
blàiteachadh, -aidh, s.m. Warming. 2 Hatching. 3 Fomenting. 4 Cherishing. 5 Feeling affection for. A' b—, pr.pt. of blàitich. A' blàiteachadh nan uighean breaca, *hatching the spotted eggs.*
†blàith, v.a. Smoothe, plane, level, polish.
†———, a. Smooth, plain, level.
†blaith, s. Blossom.
blàithe, comp. of a. blàth. Warmer, softer, smoother. Warmest, softest, smoothest. Nighean 'bu bhlàithe sùil, *a maid of softest eye.*
blàitheach, } ** a. Bloomy.
blàitheanach, } ** a. Bloomy.
blàithean, -ein, s.m. dim. of blàth. Little blossom. 2 pl. of blàth. Blossoms.
†blaitheasach, a. Smoothed, polished.
blàith-fhleasg, -eisg, -an, s. f. see blàth-fhleasg.
——————aidh, see blàth-fhleasg.
blàithin, -e, -ean, see blàithean.
blàith-leac, -ic, s.f. Polished flag, smooth stone. 2‡‡Pumice-stone.
†blaithmheul,‡‡ s.f. Sea-monster.
blàithteachadh, -aidh, s.m. see blàiteachadh.
blàitich, pr.part. a' blàiteachadh, v.a. Warm, heat, hatch. 2 Foment. 3 Cherish.
blanag, see blonag.
———ach, see blonagach.
†blànc,‡‡ s.m. Farthing. 2 *properly* Plack (⅓d.)
†blannda, a. Gentle, meek, mild.
blanndaidh, s.m. Rotten egg.
————, a. Rotten, stinking. 2 Stale, as milk. Ubh blanndaidh, *a rotten egg.*
blanndair, s.m. & a. see blanndaidh.
blanndar, -air, s.m. Cajoling, flattery. 2 Dissimmulation. 3 Hypocrisy. 4 "Blarney."
blaoc, -oic, see blaoch.
†blaoch, s.f. Whale.

†blaodh, -aoidh, s.m. Shout, loud calling. 2 Breath.
blaodh, pr.pt. a' bladhaich, v.n. Cry, shout.
blaodhag, -aig, -an, s.f. Noisy female.
blaodhaich, s. f. Cry. A' b—, pr. pt. of blaodh, Crying.
blaodh-eun, s.m. Bird-call.
blaodhmanach, -aiche, a. Imprudent, indiscreet. 2 Contemptible. 3 Foolish. 4 Blustering.
†blaodhrach, see blaoghagach.
blaoghagach, -aiche, a. Noisy, clamorous.
blaoghan, -ain, s.m. The fawn's cry. 2‡Calf's cry. 3 see blaghan. [†† says bladhan.]
blaom,* v.a. Stare with the greatest surprise; as when taken unawares. 2 Start.
———, -a, -annan, s. m. Flirt. 2 Start. 3 Boast, brag. 4 Blunder.
———adaich, -e, s.f. Giddy starting. 2 Stupid outcry. 3 Boasting, bragging. 4 Flirting. 5 Blundering. 6*Habit of staring foolishly.
———adh, -aidh, -aidhean, s.m. Foolish excitement. 2 Flush. 3 Loud, senseless talking. 4* Wonderful stare. 5 Starting. 6††Whim; Thug e blaomadh le a dhà shùil, *he stared with both eyes.* A' b—, pr. part. of blaom.
blaomag, -aig, -an, s. f. Blundering stupid woman.
blaomair, -ean, s.m. Blusterer, bragger, swaggerer. 2 Eccentric person. 3*Fellow that stares like a fool. 4*Nonsensical talk.
————eachd, see blaomadaich.
blaomannach, -aiche, a. Inconstant, irresolute, variable. 2 Talking incoherently or inconsistently.
——————, -aich, s.m. Swaggerer, boasting fellow.
blaomastair, -ean, s.m. Stupid fellow, dolt; blockhead. 2 Blusterer, bully.
———————eachd, s. f. ind. Stupid blundering.
†blaor, -aoir, s.m. Cry, shout.
†———, v.n. Cry.
†blaosg, s.m. The skull. 2 see plaosg.
blàr, gen. sing. -àir, n.pl. -àir, -a, & -an, s.m. Plain, field. 2 Ground, floor. 3 White spot on the face of animals, (chiefly applied to cows and horses.) 4*Cow with a white spot on its face. 5 Green. 6 Battle. 7 Battlefield. 8 Peat moss, marsh. An ceud bhlàr a chuir iad, *the first battle they fought*; a' dol sios do'n bhlàr, *going down to the battle-field*; fraoch nam blàr, *the rage of battle*; a muigh air a' bhlàr, *out on the plain*; 'na shìneadh air a' bhlàr, *stretched on the ground* or *on the floor*; chaidh e feadh a' bhlàir, *it spilled on the ground*; sgeadaichear na blàir, *the plains shall be adorned*; réidh a' bhlàir, *the plain of battle*; thoir am blàr ort! *away with you!* tha blàr 'na h-aodann, *she (the cow) has a white spot on her forehead*; o'n bhlàr gu 'bhàrr, *from the ground to its top.*
blàr, -àire, a. White-faced, having a white forehead (applied to cows and horses.) An t-each blàr, *the white-faced horse.*
blàr,(AH) v.a. Chip timber roughly with an axe or adze. 2 Hew a stone slightly.
——adh, -aidh, s.m. Blaze, rough chipping of wood. 2AH Rough hewing of stone.
—— ag, -aig, -an, s. f. White-faced cow or mare. 2**White spot on the face of cattle. An gobhal na blàraig, *between the legs of the white-faced cow.*
——an, -ain, s.m. dim. of blàr. Little plain field. 2 Small level spot. 3 Glade. 4†† Little moss.
——as, -ais, -an, s.m. White spot on the face of an animal.

blàr-chaob, (AH) *s.m.* Snow-ball fight.
—— -fhiathachd, (AH) *s.m.* Confusion, chaos.
—— -fola, (AH) *s.m.* Place where cattle used to be bled annually.
—— -gealachaidh, *s.m.* Bleaching-field.
—— iachd, see blàr-fhiathachd.
—— -mòine, *s.m.* Peat-moss.
—— -mòna,†† see blàr-mòine.
blas, -ais, *s.m.* Taste. 2 Savour. 3 Flavour. 4 Relish. 5 Particle, the least part. 6 Experience. Am bheil blas air gealagan uibhe? *is there any taste in the white of an egg?* cia milis leam blas do bhriathran! *how sweet are thy words to my taste!* is don' am blas a th' air, *it has a bad taste*; cha'n 'eil blas dheth an seo, *there is not a particle of it here*; tha blas na meal' air do phògan, *thy kisses taste of honey* (*lit.* the taste of honey is on thy kisses); do bheul air blas an t-siucair, *thy lips are as sweet as sugar*; is fheàrr blas an teine na blas na gainne, *better the taste of fire than the taste of want*—said when food is served very hot; an déidh na h-uile blas(d), *after all 's said and done.*
blàs, -àis, see blàths.
——achd, *s.f. ind.* Tasting, act of tasting.
——ad, -aid, *s.m.* Tasting, act of tasting. 2 Bit. 2 Drop. Gun am blasad, *without tasting them.* A' b—, *pr.pt.* of blais. [Cha chuala mi blasad dheth—*for* cha chuala mi guth dheth—*lit. I have not heard a taste of it*; *I have heard nothing of it—Sleat, Skye.* J.M.]
——adh, -aidh, *s.m.* Tasting, act of tasting. A' b—, *pr.pt.* of blais.
——ardaich,* *s.f.* Smacking with the lips. 2 Tasting with a relish.
blasbheum,** *gen.sing.* -bhéim, see blais-bheum.
————ach,** -aiche, *a.* see blais-bheumach.
blasd, see blas.
blasda, *a.* Delicious, savoury, tasty. 2 Well-tasted. 3 Tasteful. 4* Agreeable. 5 Eloquent. 6**Seasoned. Dean dhomh biadh blasda, *make me savoury meat*; briathran blasda, *eloquent* or *agreeable words.*
blasdachd, *s.f.* Sweetness, savouriness. 2 Tastefulness. 3*Agreeableness.
blasdag, *s.f.* Sweet-mouthed female.
blasd'or, see blasda.
†**blasgaoin**, *s.f.* Skull.
blasmhoire, *comp.* of blasmhor. More or most sweet.
————achd, *s.f.* Sweetness. 2 Tastefulness.
————ad, -eid, *s.m.* Increase of sweetness or savouriness. A' dol am blasmhoiread, *growing more and more savoury.*
blasmhor, -oire, *a.* Savoury, tasty. 2 Sweet. 3 Tasteful.
blas-phòg, -oig, -an, *s.f.* Sweet kiss.
blàtaich, see blàitich.
blàth, -aith, -a, *s.m.* Flower, blossom. 2 Bloom. 3 Foliage. 4 Colour, hue. 5 Fruit. 6 Effect, consequence. 7 Mark, stain. 8 Form, manner. 9 Devotion. 10 Praise. 11 ‡‡Green field. 12‡‡Sea. 13 see blàdh.—Ged nach toir an crann-fìge uaith blàth, *although the fig-tree shall not blossom*; fo làn bhlàth, *in full bloom*; thig e 'mach mar bhlàth, *he shall come out as a flower*; bithidh a bhlàth ort, *the* (lit. *its*) *effects will be seen in your case*; is léir a' bhlàth ort, *the* (lit. *its*) *consequences are obvious in your case*; daraig a's guirme blàth, *an oak of the greenest foliage*; blàth a dh'fhuirich air na cupaichean, *the stain that remained on the cups*; blàth nan deur mu'n tig an dìle, *the drops show by their appearance that a flood is coming*; blàth fearra-dhris 's a' choilleig, *the hue of the briar-rose in the bud.*
blàth, -àithe, *a.* Warm. 2 Warm-hearted. 3 Pleasant, kind. 4 Affectionate. 5** *rarely* White, clean. Is blàth anail na màthar, *warm is the mother's breath*; tha e glé bhlàth, *he is affectionate enough*; smuainte blàth a steach, *warm* (*tender* or *pleasant*) *thoughts within*; gu bog, blàth, *snug and warm.*
blàthach, -aich, *s.f.* Buttermilk. Deoch blàthaich, *a drink of buttermilk.*
————,** *a.* Efflorescent, flowery.
————adh, -aidh, *s.m.* Warming, fomenting. 2 Cherishing. 3 Hatching. A' b—. *pr.part.* of blàthaich.
————ail,** *a.* Efflorescent, flowery.
†**blàthadh**, *s.m.* Smoothness. 2 Politeness.
blàthaich, *pr.part.* a' blàthachadh, *v.a.* Warm, foment. 2 Cherish. 3 Hatch. 4**Air. 5** Flower, as a plant. [*thig fo bhlàth* is better.] 6**Polish, smoothe.
————te, *pt. part.* of blàthaich. Warmed, fomented, &c.
blàthaid, *comp. of a.* blàth.
blàth-aigneach,* *a.* Enthusiastic.
†**blàthaile**, *s.m.* Mark of a wound.
blàthan, -ain, *s.m.* Small flower. 2††Twig.
——ach, *a.* see blàthmhor.
blàthas, -ais, see blàths.
blàth-bhriathrach, -aiche, *a.* Gentle, kind in speech. 2 Mild, affectionate.
—— -buidhe,§ *s.m.* Dandelion, see bearnan-Bride.
—— -chainnteach, see blàth-bhriathrach.
—— -chridheach,** *a.* Tender-hearted, affectionate.
—— -fhleasg, -an, *s.f.* Garland *or* wreath of flowers.
—— -fhleasgadh, see blàth-fhleasg.
†**blàth-leig**, *s. f.* Pumice-stone.
blàth-leighis, *s.m.* Any medicinal plant.
—— -mhaiseach, *a.* In the bloom of beauty.
blath-mhial, (AF) *s.m.* see †bleidh-mhiol.
blàthmhor, -oire, *a.* Blossomy, flowery.
blàth-mhor, -oire, *a.* Warm.
blàth-nam-bodach, -a-, *s.m.* Red poppy, see meilbheag.
—— -obair, -oibre, -richean, *s. f.* Embroidery, variegated needlework.
—— -oibreachadh, -aidh, *s.m.* Embroidering.
—— -oibrich, *pr, part.* a' blàth-oibreachadh, *v.a.* Embroider.
blàths, -àiths, *s.m.* Warmth, heat. 2 Kindliness, affectionate disposition. Thig tlùs agus blàths, *mildness and warmth shall come.*
blàths-inntinn,* *s.m.* Enthusiasm.
†**bleachd**, see bliochd. 2 Cows.
————air, -ean, *s.m.* Soothing flattering fellow.
————aireachd, *s. f.* Flattery, soothing, cajoling.
bleagh, (‡‡bleaghan) *v.a.* Milk, draw milk. Is ann as a ceann a bhleaghar a' bhò, *you milk a cow just as you feed her* (*lit.* it is from her *head that a cow is milked.* see bleoghainn.
bleaghan, -ain, *s.m.* Dibble used for digging in sand for shell-fish; also for planting kale. 2 ‡Worthless tool.
bleaghainn, *v.a.* see bleoghainn.
bleanach, (AF) *s. f.* Full-faced cow.
†**bleasghanach**,** *a.* Emulgent.
bleath, *v.a.* } see bleith—.
——ach, -aiche, *a.* } see bleith—.
—— -ghlùineach, -eiche, } see bleith—.
†——mhor, *a.* Fruitful, productive, prolific.
bleid, -e, *s. f.* Impertinence. 2 Requesting, soliciting. 3 Cajoling. 4**Larceny. 5**Envy. 6

Spite. 7 Adulation. 8*Importunity.
bleid-chuirm,** *s. f.* Junket.
——each, see bleideil.
——ealachd, see bleidireachd.
——ear,** -eir, *s.m.* see bleidir.
——eil, -e, *a.* Impertinent, troublesome, teazing. 2** Pilfering, thievish. 3** Invidious, spiteful. 4* Begging in a sly way. Fear dubh dàna, fear bàn bleideil, *a black-haired man is bold, a fair-haired man impertinent.*
†bleidh, -e, *s. f.* Cup, goblet.
†——ir, see bladair.
†——mhiol, *s. f.* Whale.
bleidich, *v.a.* Intrude.
bleidir, -e, -ean, *s.m.* Beggar, teazing petitioner. 2 Impertinent fellow. 3 Coward. 4** Pilferer. 5(AF)Wolf. Urram a' bhleidire do'n stràcair, *the sneak's deference to the swaggerer.*
bleidir,¶ *s.m.* Buzzard, see clamhan.
——,* *v.n.* Beg in a genteel way, importune. 2 Tease, trouble.
——each, *a.* Obtrusive.
——eachd, *s. f.* Begging, beggary, solicitation. 2 Impertinence. 3 Obtrusion, intrusion. 4**Thievishness. 5*Importunity. *B.* mholaidh, *impertinent praise.*
bleidir-molach,¶ *s.m.* Rough-legged buzzard—*buteo lagopus.*
—— -riabhach,¶ *s.m.* Honey-buzzard, see clamhan.
—— -tonach,¶ see b— -molach.
†blein, *s. f.* Harbour for boats.
bleith, *pr.pt.* a' bleith, *v.a.* Grind, pulverize. 2 Make meal. Gabh na clachan-muilinn agus bleith min, *take the mill-stones and grind meal.*
bleith, -e, *s.f.* Grinding, pulverizing. A' b—, *pr. pt.* of bleith. Luchd bleith, *grinders, millers.*
——each, -eiche, *a.* Grinding, that grindeth.
——eadh, -eidh, *s.m.* Grinding, pulverizing.
—— -glùineach, *a.* In-kneed, knock-kneed.
—— -mhiol, see bleidh-mhiol.
——te, *past pt.* of bleith. Ground.
bleodhainn, see bleoghainn.
bleodhan, -ain, *s.m.* Wheel-barrow.
bleodhann, see bleoghann.
bleoghainn, *pr.pt.* a' bleoghann, *v.a.* Milk.
bleoghann, *s. f.* Milking. 2 Act of milking. A' bleoghann a' chruidh, *milking the cows*; cuman bleoghainn, *a milk-pail.* A' b—, *pr. part.* of bleoghainn.
bleomhnach,** *s.m.* Sniveller.
bleth, see bleith.
——,(AF) Whale.
†bleun, -a, *s.m.* see blian.
bliadhna, *pl.* -chan, [& -ichean] *s. f.* Year, the space of a year. Eadar seo agus ceann bliadhna, *within a year*; an ceann bliadhna, *in a year's time;* Bliadhn' a' Phrionnsa, *the common name among Highlanders for 1745-6* (*lit.* the Prince's year); bliadhna Chuilfhodair, *the year in which the Battle of Culloden was fought (1746)*; am bliadhna, *this year;* a' bhliadhna ùr, *the New Year;* a' bhliadhn' an àm seo, (bliadhna roimh 'n àm seo - D.M.) *this time last year.* [Generally used in the singular after numerals followed by the plural of other nouns, as, còig bliadhna, *5 years.*]
bliadhnach, -aich, -aichean, *s. m.* Yearling, year-old beast. 2 see blianach.
————, -aiche, *a.* Miserable.
————as,** -ais, *s.m.* Annuity.
————ail, see bliadhnail
bliadhna-chàin,** *s. f.* Annuity.
bliadhnachd,* see bliadhna-chàin.
bliadhnail, *a.* Yearly, annual.
bliadhna-leum, *s. f.* Leap-year.
blialum, -uim, *s.m.* Confused speech, stammering.
blian, *pr.part.* a' blianadh, *v. a.* Bask in the sun—*Skye.* 2AC Blanch.
——, -a, *a.* Lean, starved, wanting flesh. 2 Meagre. 3 Insipid.
——, -iain, [& **blein] *s.m.* Flank, groin, belly. Làimh ris a' bhlian, *near the flank.*
——ach, *a.* Miserable. Is blianach Nollaig gun sneachd, *miserable is the snowless Christmas.*
——ach, -aich, -aichean, *s. f* Meagre, tough or lean carcase. 2 Slow, inactive person. 3AC Fish, bird, or beast that has died from want or disease. 4 Exhausted land, or land covered with drift-sand.—*Uist.* 5‡Lean flesh. Leanaidh blianach ris na sràbhan, *lean flesh cleaves to straw,*—said of worthless people who adhere to one another
——adh, -aidh, *s.m.* Basking. A' b—, *pr.part.* of blian.
blianag, (J.M.) *s.f.* Green level spot of land. Is minic a bha sùil-chruthaich air bliadhnag bhòidhich, *a quagmire is often seen on a bonny green level spot*—applied to people whose character looked fair at a distance. A person walking or riding across the country might be tempted to cross the *blianag,* but would soon find himself in a quagmire.
bligh, see bleagh.
†blimh, *s.f.* Spittle. 2 Froth of a dead body.
†blin,‡‡ *s. f.* Eyelashes of a corpse.
blincean,**-ein, *s.m.* Torch, flambeau. 2 Blink.
blinn, see blimh.
blioch,§ see bliochan.
†blioch, *s.f.* see blaoch.
bliochan,**s.m.* Corn marigold, see bile bhuidhe.
bliochan,(McL & D., & §) -ain, *s.m.* Bog asphodel, or yellow marsh asphodel,—*narthecium ossifragum.* (illust. 54.)
bliochd, *s. f. ind.* Milk. 2 Milkiness. 3 Produce of cows. 4** Profit arising from selling milk, dairy produce. 5 AC Skimmed milk, sour milk, milk that has lost any of its original character. 6 AC Whey when in the curd. 7 AF Kine giving milk.
——ach, -aiche, *a.* Milky, lacteal. 2 Milk-producing, giving plenty of milk. Chinn an spréidh gu bliochdach, *the cattle became teeming with milk*; an coire bliochdach, *the milk-producing dell.*
——ar, *a.* see bliochdach.
——arachd,** see bliochdmhorachd.
——as, -ais, *s.m.* Tendency to milk, lactescence.
bliochd-fochdan, *s.m.* Corn milk-plant, see bliochd fochain.

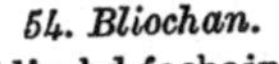

54. Bliochan. *55. Bliochd-fochain.*

bliochd-fochain,§ *s.m.* Corn milk-plant—*sonch-*

us arvensis. (illust. 55.)
bliochd-fothannan, Cow milk-plant, see bliochd fochain.
bliochdmhor, see bliochdach.
——————achd, *s. f. ind.* Abundance of milk, milkiness.
bliogh, see bleagh.
blionach, -aich, see blianach.
blìonadh,‡ -aidh, *s.m.* Basking.—*Isles.*
†bliosan, -ain, *s.m.* Artichoke, see farrusgag.
bliotsan,§ *s.m.* Wall lettuce — *lactuca muralis.* Very rare in the Highlands.
blob, *a.* see blobach.
——ach, -aiche, *a.* Blubber-lipped, thick-lipped.
——achd,** *s.f.ind.* Deformity of blubber-lips.
†blobaran, -ain, *s.m.* Stammerer. 2** Blubber-lipped person.
†bloc, *a.* Round, orbicular.
†bloc, bluic, *s.m.* see ploc.
blocadh,** *s. m.* Crack, (noise.)

56. Bliotsan.

blocan, -ain, *s.m.* *dim.* of bloc, (for ploc) 2 AF see blaghan.
†blochbharr, *v.a.* Turn in a lathe.
†blochd, *s.* see bliochd.
†blodh, see bloigh.
†blodh, *v.* see bloighdich.
†blodhaire, *s.m.* Battery.
blog, see blocan.
bloide, (*for* bloighdean.)
bloidean ,, ,,
bloidh, see bloigh.
bloigh, -e, -ean, *s.f.* Half or part of anything. 2 see bloighd. Bloigh 'nan cadal, *some asleep.*
bloighd, -ean & -ichean, *s f.* see bloigh. 2 Fragment, splinter. 3 **Share, portion. A shleagh 'na bloighdibh, *his spear in splinters.*
————eachadh, -aidh, *s.m.* Halving, dividing, breaking in pieces. A' b—, *pr.pt.* of bloighdich.
————eachas, -ais, *s. f* Act of dividing
————eag, -eig, -an, *s.f.* Little fragment or splinter.
————ean, *pl.* of bloigh. Fragments, splinters.
————ear,** -eir, *s.m.* Battery. 2 Place from which an attack is made.
bloighdich, *pr.pt.* a' bloighdeachadh, *v.a.* Divide, break in pieces, cut asunder.
bloighdichean, *pl.* of bloigh.
bloigheach, *a.* In pieces, in halves. 2††Divisible.
————, *s.f.* Part, portion, instalment.
bloigheachadh, -aidh, *s.m. & pr. part.* see bloighdeachadh.
bloigheachas, -ais, see bloighdeachas.
bloigheag, see bloighdeag.
bloigheil, *a.* see bloigheach.
bloighich, *pr.pt.* a' bloigheadh, see bloighdich.
bloing,** *s.f.* Bubble.
bloinigeach,* *a.* Plump, soft, fat.
bloinigean, *s.m.* Any plant with curled or crisped leaves.
———— -ghàraidh, *s. m.* Spinach—*spinacia oleracea.*
bloinigein,†† *s.m.* Plump, fat child.
blòmas, -ais, *s.m.* Ostentation, pomp.
————ach, -aiche, *a.* Boastful. 2 Fond of show, ostentatious.
blonag, -aig, *s.f.* Fat, suet, lard.
————ach, -aiche, *a.* Full of suet. 2 Greasy. 3 Abounding in fat.
————aich,** *v.a.* Lard.
blonag-rotha, *s.f.* Coom on a wheel.
†blor, -oir, *s.m.* Noise, loud noise. 2 Voice.
†——ach, -aiche, *a.* Clamorous, noisy.
†——ach, -aich, *s.m.* Clamorous noisy fellow.
†——achan, -ain, *s.m.* see blorach.
†blos, *a.* Manifest, open, plain.
†blosg, *v n.* Sound a horn or trumpet. 2 Explode.
blosg, *s.m.* Congregation. 2‡‡Light.
——ach, -aich, *s.m.* Clown, rustic.
†blosgadh,**-aidh, *s.m.* Congregation. 2 Sound, report.
†blosgair, -ean, *s.m.* Collector.
†blosg-mhaor, Crier at court. 2 Collector.
†blot, *s.m.* Cave, den, cavern.
†blotach, *s.m.* **Cave, den. 2 Cave-dweller.
†blotach,** *a* Full of dens or caverns. 2 Like a den or cavern.
blubach,†† *a.* Stammering.
†bluch, *s.m.* Fatness.
†bluirc, *s.m.* Crumb, crumbs, fragment, fragments.
†bluirid, *a.* Pinched.
blunag, see blonag.
†blusar, -air, *s.m.* Tumult, outcry, noise.
bo ! *int.* Bo ! bo ! word to excite terror in children.
bo ! bo ! *int.* Strange ! wonderful !
bó, *s. f irreg.* Cow. 2***rarely* fawn. Declined thus :—

	Sing.	Plur.
Nom.	bó,	bà,
Gen.	bà,[1] *or* boin	bó
Dat.	boin[2] *or* bó,	bà,
Voc.	a bhó !	

[[1] Correct form of *Gen.* bà, [2] of *Dat.* boin, —J.M.]

bó adhairceach, *a horned cow.*
bó-alluidh, *buffalo.*
bó bhailg-fhionn, *white-bellied cow.*
bó bhainne, *milch-cow.*
bó bhreac, *spotted cow.*
bó bhiadhta,(AG) "*mart,*" *for killing.*
bó cheann-fhionn, *white-faced cow.*
bó chais-fhionn, *white-footed cow.*
bó dhruim-fhionn, *white-backed cow.*
bó ghamhna,(AF) *farrow cow.*
bó gheamhraidh, *winter "mart."*
bó ghlas, *grey cow.*
bó laoigh, *cow in calf.*
bó liath,** *grey cow,*—grey with age.
bó mhaol, *cow without horns. 2 Polled cow.*
bó riabhach, *brindled cow.*
bó sheasg, *cow not giving milk. 2 Barren cow.*
Is minic a bha rath air aona bhó na caillich, *the old woman's only cow has often been lucky.* [Many of the Hebridean blessings and charms for cattle begin "an t-eòlas a rinn Calum-cille dh'aona bhó na caillich," *the charm given by St. Columba for the old woman's only cow.*] Ciùin ris a' bhó is garbh ris an each, *gentle to the cow and harsh to the horse*—supposed to be the proper treatment; dh'fhalbh e leis a bhoin,(JM) *he departed with the cow*; bhuail e am bata air a' bhoin, *he struck the cow with the staff.*
boag, -aig, -an, see bodhag.
bó-alluidh, *s. f.* Buffalo. 2AF Furious ox.
bob, AF *s.m.* Worm, caterpillar destructive to bushes, &c.
bobag,†† -aig, *s.m.* Boy, chum. [Used chiefly in the Vocative case,—a bhobaig! a bhobagain !] 2 Fool—*Caraid nan Gàidheal.*
bobaidh,(AG) *s.m.* "Papa."—*Suth'd.*
boban, -ain, *s.m.* Term of affection for a boy. 2††Godfather, term of contempt. 3 "Papa."
boban,‡ -ain, *s.m.* Bobbin.
†bobeloth, Gaelic alphabet.

†bobgurnach, *s.m.* Blast.
bobh, -a, *s.m.* Fright.
bó-bhainne,(AF) *s. f.* Milch-cow.
†bó-bhaith, *s. f.* Cow slaughter.
†bobhdach, *s.m.* Pimp.
†bobhdag, *s.m.* Bawd.
bobhlaireachd, *s. f. ind.* Bowling.
bobhstair, -e, -ean, *s.m.* Gaelic spelling of *bolster.* (adhart.)
bo ! bo ! ** *int.* Strange ! wonderful !
bobug, see boban.
boc, *s.m.* Deceit, fraud. 2 Blow, box, stroke.
boc, buic, *s.m.* Buck, roe-buck. 2 He-goat. 3AF Entire horse. 4**term of *ridicule* for a fop. Boc-earb, *roe-buck* ; fichead boc, *twenty bucks.*
boc, *pr.part.* a' bocadh, *v.n.* Leap or skip, as a deer or roe.
bòc, *pr.part.* a' bòcadh, *v.n.* Swell, blister. 2** Bloat, puff. 3 Grow turgid. 4* Inflame.
bòc, -a, -an, *s.m.* Pimple, pustule.
bocach, -aiche, *a.* Like a roe-buck. 2 Abounding in roe-bucks. A' Bhealltuinn bhocach, *roe-producing May.*
bòcach, -aiche, *a.* Bluff.
bocadh, -aidh, *s.m.* Skipping, as a deer. 2** Discussion. A' b—, *pr.part.* of boc.
bòcadh, -aidh, *s.m.* Eruption, blister, swelling. 2 Frown. A' b—, *pr.part.* of bòc.
bocaid, *s.f.* Whelk.
†bocaide, } *s. f. pl.* Studs or bosses of a
†bocaidean,** } shield.
bòcaidh, -ean, *s.m.* Terrifying object.
——— -fhaileag,(AG) *s.f.* Wild rose-berry
bocail, *s. f. ind.* Skipping. 2 Of, or pertaining to, a roe-buck. 3**Ostentation.
bocain, -ein, see boicionn.
bó-cainneal, see bó-choinneal.
bocam ort ! †† *int.* Threat to children.
bòcan, -ain, *s. m.* Hobgoblin, sprite, spectre. 2 Terrifying object, apparition. 3 Larva of insects. 4**Bugbear.
bòcan,†† -annan, *s.m.* Pimple, pustule.
bocan, -ain, *s.m.* see bacan. 2 see bochdan-bearrach. 3 Little buck.
†bocan, *v.a.* Bend, make crooked.
bocanach, -aiche, *a.* Hooked, bent. 2†† Of, or belonging to, little bucks.
bocan-bearrach, see caochag.
bocan-biorach,‡‡ see caochag.
bocan-loin,¶ *s.m.* Snipe, see gabhar-athair.
bocan-rocais, (JGM) *s.m.* Scarecrow.
boc-Bealltuinn,(AF) *s.m.* Wild or unmanageable entire horse, said to be wilder about midsummer.
boc-caol,(AC) *s.m.* (*lit.* a slim buck) Roe-buck.
boc-cluigeineach,(JGM) *s.m.* Bell-wether.
boc-earba, buic-, *s.m.* Roe-buck. Cho luath ri boc-earba, *as swift as a roe.*
boc-gabhar, } see boc-goibhre.
boc-ghobhar, }
boc-goibhre, buic-, *s.m* He-goat.
boc glas,(AF) *s.m.* Large dog-fish. 2 Shark.
boch,* *s.m.* Great happiness or joy, rejoicing, ecstacy.—*Isles.*
——, *v.* see boc.
—— ! *int.* Hey day !
bochail -chala, *a,* Lively, animated, 2 Nimble. 3 Proud, strutting. 4 Showy, ostentatious. 5 Happy, overjoyed.
bochalachd, *s.f.ind.* Liveliness, animation. 2 Pride of dress. 3 Joy, extreme happiness.
bochan, -ain, *s.m.* see bothan. 2(AH) Vain, affected, impudent person.
———achd, (AH) *s.f.ind.* Vanity in dress or manners. 2 Affectation. 5 Folly. 4 Impudence.
———ta, *a.* Turgent.
bòchar,(JM) *s.m.* Mud, as of a cattle fold late in harvest, when the ground is turned into soft mud by the feet of the cattle.
———ach. *a.* Full of mud.
bòchd, *v.n.* see bòc. 2‡‡Bud, spring.
†bochd, *v.a.* see bochdainnich.
bochd, -a, *a.* Poor. 2 Needy. 3 Wretched. 4 Sick, sickly. 5 Sad. 3 Lean, lank. 7 Dear. Ni làmh na leisge bochd, *the hand of laziness maketh poor* ; tha neach ann a leigeas air a bhith bochd, *there is such that pretends to be poor* ; is bochd an gnothach e, *it is a sad affair* ; is bochd nach d'fhuair sinn e, *it is a pity we did not get it* ; an duine bochd ! *the dear creature !* is bochd a thachair dha, *sadly it happened to him* ; tha e gu bochd, *he is sick* ; crodh bochd, *lean cattle* ; is fheàrr a bhith bochd na bhith breugach, *better be poor than false* ; leaghaidh am bròn am bochd anam, (*or* an t-anam bochd), *sorrow melts the miserable.*
bochd, -a, [AC *gen. sing. & n.pl.—Isles.*] *s.m.* The poor, the parish poor. 2 Poor person. Coinnichidh am beartach agus am bochd a chéile, *the rich and poor meet together;* cuid de bhochdaibh na tìre, *some of the poor of the land ;* a' roinn airgiod nam bochd, *distributing the poor's funds* ; am bochd is an nochd, *the poor and the naked;* treabhadh nam bochd, *the tillage of the poor.* [Declined like boc, *buck* in Barra, &c. Is misde na buic a bhi lìonar, *the poor are the worse of being numerous* ; na beirt a' dol a suas, na buic a' dol a sios, *the rich going up, the poor going down.*—AC]
†bochd,‡‡ *s.m.* Breach. 2 Fire. 3 Reaping, cutting down.
bòchdadh, see bòcadh.
bòchdail,‡‡ -e, *a.* Tumid, turgid.
bochdainn, *s.f.ind.* Poverty. 2 Trouble. 3 Mischief. 4 Bad luck. 5** Mishap. 6 The Devil. Chuir sin e gus a' bhochdainn, *that reduced him to poverty* ; thàinig e gu bochdainn, *he was reduced to extreme poverty* ; is ann airsan a tha blàth na bochdainn, *he has every sign of extreme poverty about him* ; thig am misgear agus an geòcair gu bochdainn, *the drunkard and the glutton shall come to poverty;* chaidh a' bhochdainn uile ort a nis, *you are in a sad plight now*; thàinig bochdainn an rathad an teaghlaich, *the family was visited with affliction,* or *sickness ;* ciod a' bhochdainn a rug ort ? *what the mischief came over you ?* mar a tha a' bhochdainn an dàn dhomh, *as my bad luck would have it* ; mar a bha a' bhochdainn ann, *as bad luck would have it ;* ann am bochdainn, *in trouble* ; gu'n gabh a' bhochdainn thu ! *plague take you !* teagaisg na bochdainn ! *what a preposterous idea !* leth na bochdainn ! *what a remarkable, dreadful thing !*
bochdainneach,** *a.* Causing trouble, poverty, or misery.
———————d, *s. f.* Same meanings as bochdainn.
bochdainnich, *v.a.* Impoverish, make poor, cause poverty.
bòchdan, see bòcan.
bochdan, *n.pl.* of *s.* bochd. 2 see caochag.
bochdan-bearrach, -aich, } see caochag.
——— -beucach, -aich, }
——— -biorrach, -aich, }
bochdas, -ais, *s.m.* Poverty, indigence. 2†† Leanness. Bochdas agus beartas, *poverty and riches.*
bochdrach,** -aich, *s.m.* Beggar.
bochduinn, see bochdainn.

†bochnadh, -aidh, *s.f.* The sea, narrow sea, strait. 2 Mouth of a river.
bó-choilleag, *s. f.* Pastoral, rural dialogue. (Gaelic spelling of *bucolic.*)
bó-choinneal,§ *s.f.* Mullein (*lit.* cow's candle) see cuingeal Muire.
†bocht, *s.m.* see †bochd.
boch-thonn, -thuinne, *pl.* -thonnan, *s.f.* Surge, billow, swelling wave.
boch-thonnan, *n.pl.* of boch-thonn.
boch-thuinne, *gen.sing.* of boch-thonn.
bòchuin, (AC) *s.f.* The sea, ocean. 2 Ripple at the bow of a moving boat.
bòchuin, (AC) *s.f.* Swelling, bursting, protruding.
——— -Muire,(AC) *s.f.* (*lit.* the swelling of Mary.) Month of May.
boc-roin, *s.m.* Prawn. 2 Shrimp.
boc-ruadh,(AC) *s.m.* (*lit.* red buck) Roebuck.
bocsa, *pl.* -aichean, *s.m.* Box, coffer, trunk, little chest. 2‡‡Blow. Bara bocsa, *a rimmed barrow.*
bocsa,§ *s.m.* Box-tree or plant, see aigh-ban.
bocsach, *a.* Boxen.
———an,‡‡ -ain, *s.m.* (*dim.* of bocsa.) Casket.
bocsadh, -aidh, *s.m.* Boxing.
boc-saic,¶ *s.m.* Snipe, see gobhar-athair
bocsaich, *v.a.* Beat, thump, pelt, cuff, buffet.
———ean, *n.pl.* of bocsa.
bocsaid,‡ *s.f.* Thump.
bocsair, -ean, *s.m.* Boxer.
bocsa-na-mionna, *s.m.* Witness-box.
boc-seang, *s.m.* (*lit.* slender buck) Roebuck.
bòcta, *a.* Blown.
bòc-thonn,†† *s.f.* Swelling wave.
———ach,†† *a.* Belonging to swelling waves.
bocum ort ! *int.* see bocam ort !
bod,‡‡ *s.m.* Mentula, membrum virile. 2 Tail.
boda, (AF) *s.m.* Redshank (bird.)
bodach, -aich, *s.m.* Old *or* churlish man. 2 Rustic, countryman. 3 Sorry fellow. 4 Meanness of spirit, niggardliness. 5 Mutchkin, liquid measure a little less than imperial pint. 6 Spectre. 7 Cod-fish. 8 AF Lesser seal. 9‡‡Familiar term in addressing a youth. 10(JM) *originally* married man without family. Cha'n 'eil e 'na bhodach, *he is not a churl*; bodach uisge-beatha, *a mutchkin of whisky* (half a bottle—the mean man would grudge to buy a whole one. It was "biatach a' bhotuil," the man who divided the bottle among his friends that was praised of old.JM) beiridh na bodaich ort, *the bogies will lay hold of you*; is e a chuireadh am bodach á fear a bhitheadh teann, *it (whisky) would drive meanness out of a miser or churl*; sliob bodach is sgròbaidh e thu, buail bodach is thig e gu 'd làimh, *stroke a churl and he will scratch you, strike him and he will come to your hand*; bodach leth bhaireach, *the half-goal man, the odd one who has to change sides when his side wins, an individual between two bands of players*; gean a' bhodaich—as a bhroinn, *the churl's suavity—off his stomach*—this seems to mean that the churlish, greedy old man is never pleased except when his belly is well filled with good things; is tric a bha suaib chuthaich air leanabh bodaich, *there was often a touch of madness on an old man's child.*
bodachail, -e, *a.* Churlish, boorish, clownish, inhospitable. 2 Slovenly. 3 Like an old man.
bodachan, -ain, *s.m.* Little old man. 2 *in derision* squat young fellow.
bodachas, -ais, *s.m.* Churlishness. 2 Brutality. 3 Ruggedness of manner.
bodach-dubh,§ *s.m.* Children's name for ribwort in Perthshire and Argyllshire. see slàn lus.
bodach-fhleasgaich, *s.m.* Bachelor.
bodach-Gallda,(AH) *s.m.* Lowland (Scotch) farmer, applied irrespective of age.
bodach-gorm,§ *s.m.* Field scabious. see gille-guirmein.
bodach-nan-claigionn,§ *s.m.* Yellow rattle, see modhalan buidhe.
bodach-oidhche,¶ *s.m.* Tawny owl, see comhachag dhonn.
bodach-rocais,(AH) *s.m.* Scare-caow.
bodach-ruadh, -aich-ruaidh, -aich-ruadha,*s.m.* Cod-fish. 2(JM) Codling.
bodag, -aig, -an, *s. f.* Rage, anger, short fit of passion. 2 Yearling calf. 3 Heifer. 4** Bawd.
bodagac, *s.f.* Heifer that wants bulling.
bodagach, *a.* Apt to fly into a passion. 2 Like a heifer. 3 Like a bawd, wanton.
†———d,** *s.f. ind.* Rage, anger. 2 Rage for copulation, furor interinus.
bod-agh,(AF) *s.m.* Heifer fit for breeding.
bodair, -e, -ean, *s.m.* Debauchee.
bodaireachd,** *s. f.* Fornication.
bodan, -ain, *s.m.* Membrum puerile.

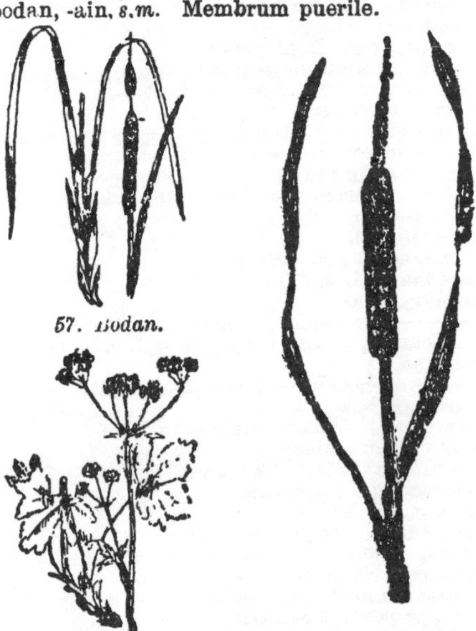

57. Bodan. *58. Bodan-coille.* *59. Bodan-dubh.*

bodan,§ *s.m.* Lesser reed-mace or cat's tail—*typha augustifolia.*
bodan,§ *s.m.* Cat's tail grass *or* timothy—*phleum pratense.* [This has the same name in Gaelic as *typha augustifolia,* as well as *phleum arenarium* and *phleum alpinum.*]
bodan-coille,§ *s. m.* Wood sanicle—*sanicula europœa.*
bodan-dubh,§ *s. m.* Great reed-mace—*typha latifolia.* 2 Yorkshire sanicle (McL & D) Also called cuigeal-nam-ban-sith, *and* bog bhuine, which is not correct.§
bodan-measgain,§ *s.m.* Bog-violet, see lus-a'-bhainne. 2**Butterwort.
†bodar, see bodhar.
bod-chrann, -ainn, *s.m.* Crupper (in harness.)
bod-dà-bhioran, *s.m.* Year-old hart. 2 Kind of sail in a small boat.
bod-dubh-a'-mhùsgain,(AF) *s.m.* Black-skinned spout-fish, pouter fish. 2 Hose-fish.
bodh, see badh.

bodha,* *s.m.* Rock over which the waves break. 2 Breaker over sunken rocks.

bodhag, -aig, -an, *s.f.* Common sandpiper, sea-lark, see luatharan. 2AF Ringed plover. 3 (AG) The bellow one cow gives when gored by another.

bodhaig, -e, -ean, *s.f.* The human body. 2** Skin of the human body. 3††Person. 4(JM) Hulk of a vessel. Òigh a's gloine bodhaig, *a maid of the fairest skin.*

bodhair, *pr. part.* a' bodhradh, *v. a.* Deafen, stun with noise. Cha mhór nach do bhodhair an t-òglach mi le 'raibheiceil, *the fellow almost stunned me with his roaring ;* na bodhair mi le d' dhrabhluinn, *do not stun me with your absurdity.*

bòdhair, -aire, *s.m.* Murrain in cattle.

bodhaire, see buidhre.

bòdhan, -ain, *s.m.* The ham, thigh. 2 Breach, seat. 3 Calf of leg. 4‡‡Breast. 5(JM) Part of the belly of man or beast below the navel, abdomen.

bodhar, buidhre [& bodhaire] *a.* Deaf, dull of hearing. 2 Dull, heavy. Ach mar dhuine bodhar cha chluinn mise, *but as a deaf man I do not hear.*

bodhar, -air, *s.m.* Deaf person. Tha na bodhair a' cluinntinn, *the deaf hear*; cluinnidh am bodhar fuaim an airgid, *a deaf man hears the sound of money ;* cò a rinn am bodhar? *who made the deaf ?* tha na geòidh bodhar a's t-Fhoghair, *the geese are deaf in autumn* (they do not want to hear.)

———ach, -aiche, *a.* Deafening, stunning with noise.

bodhar-chluasail, -e, *s. f.* Dullness in hearing.

†bodh-arfach,‡‡ *s.m.* Destroying of cows.

bodhar-fhead, -a, *s.f.* Dull, heavy sound, as of whistling wind.

————ach, -aiche, *a.* Dull sounding.

bodhar-fhuaim, -e, *s.m.* [& *f.*] Slow, heavy, hollow sound.

————neach, -eiche, *a.* Dull sounding.

bodhbh, see bobh.

bó-dhearc,§ *s.f.* Red whortleberry, cowberry, see lus-nam-braoileag.

bòdhrach,** *a.* Infected with the murrain. Bó bhòdhrach, *a diseased cow.*

bodhrach, see bodhar.

bodhrad,** *s.m.* Degree of deafness.

bodhradh, -aidh, *s.m.* Deafening, stunning with noise. Tha mi air mo bhodhradh leat, *you stun me with your noise* or *importunity.* A' b—, *pr.part.* of bodhair.

†boel, *s.f.* Pith of any stalk.

bog,** buig, *s.m.* Marsh, fen, swampy ground.

bog, buige, *a.* Soft. 2 Boggy. 3 Tender. 4 Silly, foolish. 5 Moist, damp. 6 Mellow. 7 Spiritless. 8**Sweet or soft sounding. 9** Timid, effeminate. A ciabh bhog, *her soft hair* ; a' Bhealltuinn bhog, *moist [showery] May;* 'fhir bhuig ! *O effeminate man !* le 'ribheid bhuig, *with his soft-sounding reed* ; brisidh an theangadh bog an cneadh, *a smooth tongue softens a wound* ; brisidh an teangadh bhog an cnàimh, *the smooth tongue breaks the bone* ; àite bog, *a place where a person or animal is apt to sink* ; cha'n 'eil ann ach duine bog, *he is only a chicken-hearted fellow ;* gu bog blàth, *snug and warm* ; cridhe bog, *a tender heart;* dh'fhalbh e gu bog, balbh, bodhar, *he sneaked away quietly, without a word, tail between legs.*

bog, *pr. part.* a' bogadh, [— a' bogadan & a' bogail] *v.a.* Dip, steep. 2 Move, agitate. 3 Bob. 4 Wag. 5†† see bogaich. Tha'n cù a' bogadh 'earbaill, *the dog wags his tail* ; is fhearr an cù a bhogas 'earbaill na'n cu a chuireas dreang air, *better is the dog that wags his tail than the dog that snarls* ; 'nuair a bhogadh an dram air, *when the whisky would excite him ;* bhogainn anns an allt e, *I would dip him in the burn.*

bogach,** -aich, -aichean, *s.m.* Swamp, quagmire.

bogachadh, -aidh, *s.m.* Softening. 2 Making tender or mellow. 3*Steeping. 4**Making effeminate. 5**Softening into tears. A' b—, *pr.part.* of bogaich. Softening, making timid, &c.

bogachan,¶ *s.m.* Wheat-ear, see brù-gheal.

bogachan,¶ *s.m.* Water-ouzel, see gobha-uisge.

bogadach,** -aich, *s.m.* see bogadaich.

bogadaich, -e, *s.f.* Waving. 2 Shaking. 3 Tremor from heat of passion or impatience. 4** Continued or frequent bobbing, bobbing gesture. 5** Gesture. Anns a' bhogadaich, *bobbing.*

bogadan, -ain, *s.m.* Shaking. 2 Wagging. 3 Bobbing. 4 Waving. 5 Floating, heaving. 6** Fellow who walks with a foppish gait, *in derision.* Tha a' chraobh a' bogadan, *the tree waves.* A' b—, *pr.part.* of bog.

bogadanaich, *s.f.* Continued shaking, wagging, or bobbing.

bogadh, -aidh, *s.m.* Softening, mollifying. 2 Steeping, dipping. 3* Moistening. 4* State of sticking fast in the mire. 5 Wagging, bobbing. 6**Softness, tenderness. 7**Mellowness. Chaidh a' bhò am bogadh, *the cow stuck fast in the mire* ; a' bogadh 'earbaill, *wagging his tail* ; is mithich a bhith 'bogadh nan gad, *it is time to be steeping the withes*, (This saying meant "it is time to be going," and applied to the time when withes of osier, &c. were used for fastenings of harness. These would become dry and brittle if laid by for a time, and would require steeping for a while before taking to horse.—N.G.P.) A' b—, *pr. part.* of bog.

bogadh-leo, *s.m.* Bumpkin.

bogag,‡‡ -aig, -an, *s.f.* Frost-bitten potato.

bog-a'-ghiogain,** see bog-ghiogan.

bogaich, *pr.part.* a' bogachadh, *v.a. & n.* Soften. 2 Mellow. 3 Moisten. 4 Effeminate. 5 Soften or melt into tears. 6 Steep. Bogaich an leathar, *steep the leather.* see bog.

———ear, *fut. pass.* of bogaich. Shall or will be softened.

———idh, *fut.aff. a.* of bogaich. Shall or will soften.

———te, *past part.* of bogaich. Softened, made soft. 2*Moistened.

bogail (a') (AH) *pr.pt.* Bowing, bobbing. A' bogail is a' beiceadh, *bowing and scraping.*

bogainn,* *s.m.* see bogan.

bog-a-loireag, *s.m.* Term of contempt for a long shore sailor.—N.G.P.

bogalta, *a.* Moist, wet, softish, watery.

———chd, *s.f.* Tendency to softness or moisture.

bogan, -ain, *s.m.* Anything soft. 2 Egg in embryo. 3 Quagmire, marsh. 4***rarely* Bacon.

boganach, -aich, *s.m.* Simple fellow 2 Bumpkin, booby. 3 Coward. 4‡‡Vegetable frequently used by coopers. Is minig a thàinig boganach á blàthaich, *buttermilk has often bred bumpkins.*

————, (AF) *s.m.* Young puffin. 2 Any young bird.

————d, *s. f.* Softness. 2 Behaviour of a bumpkin.

bog-an-lochain, *s.m.* ¶Water-ouzel, see gobhauisge. 2(AF) Wheat-ear see brù-gheal.

bog-an-lòin,(AF) *s.m.* Snipe, sandpiper, see cròman-lòin.
bogar, *a.* see bog. 2**Balmy, balsamic. 3** Buttery. 4 Healing.
bogarsaich,* *s.f.* Waving, wagging, bobbing.
bog-bheulach, -aiche, *a.* Soft-mouthed. 2 Mild, kind.
——————as, -ais. *s.m.* Soft or timid speaking.
——————d, *s.f.* see bog-bheulachas.
bog-bhuine, *s.f.* Bulrush(McL & D, **, & *) This name should not be applied to the reed-mace or cat's-tail—‡.
bog-chridheach, -eiche, *a.* Faint-hearted, cowardly, chicken-hearted.
bog-ghiogan,‡ -ain, *s.m.* Sow-thistle,milk-thistle—*sonchus oleraceus.*
bog-ghluasad, -aid, *s.m.* Floating, soft movement.
bog-ghluasdachd, *s. f.* see bog-ghluasad.

60. *Bog-ghiogan.*

†bogh, *v.a.* Bend as a bow.
bogha, -chan, *s.m.* Bow. 2 Bow, bend. 3 Arch. 4 Vault. 5 Rock sunk at sea ("blinder.") 6 Wave called a "beaver. Tha bogh' air, *it has a bend ;* bogha na drochaide, *the arch of the bridge ;* tha bogha mòr air a' bhalla, *the wall has a great bow or bulge ;* mar bhogh' air ghleus, *like a bow on the stretch ;* tha bogh' air a' ghéig, *the branch has a bend in it ;* chuir e 'bhogh' air lagh, *he bent his bow ;* fir bhogha, *archers.*
bogha,* *pr.part.* a' boghadh, *v.a.* Bow, bend.
——— -braoin, *s.m.* Rainbow. Mar b. a' soillseachadh, *as a rainbow shining.*
——— -cath, *s.m.* Battle-bow.
——— -cogaidh, -achan-, *s.m.* Battle-bow.
boghadair, -e, -ean, *s.m.* Archer, bowman.
——————eachd, *s.f.* Archery.
boghadh, (a') *pr. part.* of bogha.
bogha-drochaide,-achan-, *s.m.*Arch of a bridge.
bogha-fìdhle, *s.m.* Bow of a fiddle.
bogha-froise, *s.m.* Rainbow.
boghaich,** *v.a.* Arch.
——————te, *past part.* of boghaich. Arched.
boghainn,* *s.f.* The human body. 2 Person. Is ciatach a' bhoghainn duine e, *he is a handsome person ;* nach ann aige a tha a' bhoghainn ! *what a handsome body he has !*
bó-ghamhna, *s.f.* Farrow cow.
bogha-mucag,(AC) *s.m.* Blue hyacinth.
boghan, -ain, *s.m.* see bòdhan.
———, (*for* boghachan, *pl.* of bogha.)
boghar, see bodhar.
bogha-saighde, -achan-, *s.m.* Archer's bow.
boghata,* *a.* Vaulted.
bogha-uisge, *s.m.* Rainbow. 2‡ Iris, see seilisdeir.
bòghsdair, *s.m.* Gaelic spelling of *bolster.*
boghta,(DU) *s.m.* Swathe of mown hay or corn.
†boghtainn, *s.f.* Building, 2 Roof, vault.
boghun,** -uin, *s.m.* see bàbhun.
boglach, -aich, -aichean, *s.f.* Quagmire, marsh, morass, bog, swamp. 2 Barrow.
bog-ladhrach, -aiche, *a.* Having soft hoofs or claws.
boglag, *s.f.* Softy.
boglainn, -e, *s.f.* see boglach.
bog-luachair §*gen. sing.* -e, & -chrach, *s.f.* Bulrush. see luachair ghòbhlach.
bog-luasgach, -aiche, *a.* Floating, softly moving, waving.
bog-luibh, see bog-lus.
bogluinneach,** *a.* Flabby.
——————d,** Flabbiness.

61. *Bog-lus.*

62. *Bog-uisge.*

bog-lus,§ *s.m.* Ox-tongue—*helminthia echioides.* [‡Not *senecio palludocis* as O'Reilly says] 2 Bugloss, see lus teang' an daimh. 3 Viper's bugloss, see lus na nathrach.
bog mhuine,‡ Bulrush, see luachair-ghòbhlach.
bogsa, *pl.* -an, -achan, see bocsa.
bogsach, *a.* see bocsach.
bog-uisge,‡ *s.m.* Yellow flag or iris—*iris pseudacorus.* [Corruption of *bogh'-uisge.*]
†bogun, *s.m.* Bacon.
†bogur, *s.m.* see bagradh. 2 *v.* see bagair.
†bogus, *for* am fagus.
bògus, -uis, *s.m.* (& *f.*) Timber moth. 2 Bug.
bòichead, see bòidhichead.
boicheal, -eil, *s.m.* Bottle. Boicheal bainne, *a bottle of milk.—Sutherland.*
boiceanach,**-aich, *s.m.* Small boy of 14 years of age.
boiceann,* *s.m.* see boicionn.
——————ach, see boicineach.
——————aich, see boicionnaich.
†boichde, *s.f.* see bochdainn.
boicineach,|| -eich, *s.f.* Smallpox—*Suth'd.* 2* Shingles, herpes.—*Lewis.* [Preceded by the article *a'.*] 3‡‡see boiceanach.
boicionn, -an, *s.m.* Goat-skin. 2**Hide, skin of any kind.
——————aich, *s.m.* Peltmonger.
boicneach,†† *a.* Of, or belonging to, goat-skins.
——————adh, -aidh, *s.m.* Thumping or beating a person. 2* Belabouring furiously till the skin blisters. 3**Thrashing. A' b—, *pr.part.* of boicnich.
boicnich, *pr. part.* a' boicneachadh, *v.a.* Skin. 2 Beat, belabour, flog. 3* Chastise till the skin blisters.
bòid, -e, -ean, *s. f.* Vow, solemn promise. 2 Oath, swearing. Bòid ciaraig ris na fearaibh, is bòid nam fear ri ciaraig, *the swarthy maid's vow against the men, and the men's vow against her—never to marry one of them.*
†——, *v.n.* Vow.
boid,** *s.m.* Bottle. 2** *a,* Neat, trim.
†boideach, *a.* Tolerable.
bòideach, -eiche, *a.* Pertaining to a vow. 2 Like a vow.
boideachan,** -ain, *s.m.* Bodkin.
†boideal, *s.m.* Pudding.
bòidean, *n. pl.* of bòid. Bòidean baistidh, *baptismal vows.*
†boideis, *s.m.* Drunkenness.
†boidh, *a.* Neat, tidy, trim, spruce.
bòidhche, *comp.* of *a.* bòidheach.
bòidhche, } see bòidhichead.
bòidhchead, }

†boidhe, see buidhe.
bòidheach, *comp.* bòidhche, *a.* **Pretty**, beautiful, fair, handsome, comely. 2 Neat. Is ise a's bòidhche, *she is the most beautiful*; cha dean a' ghlòir bhòidheach an t-amadan sàthach, *fine words fill not a fool's belly.*
bòidheachd,* see bòidhichead.
boidheag, *for* buidheag. see lasair-choille.
———an, see buidheagan.
bòidheam,‡‡ *s.m.* Flattery.
†boidheasach, *s.f.* Yellow jaundice.
bòidhiche, see bòidhichead.
bòidhichead, -eid, *s.f.* Beauty, increase of beauty, degree of beauty, handsomeness, elegance. Cha toir a' bhòidhichead goil air a' phoit, *beauty will not boil the pot*; is e do bhòidhichead a leòn mi, *it is thy beauty that has wounded me.*
bòidhicheas,** -eis, *s.m.* Beauty, comeliness. Cha'n e a mheud a *bh.*, *bulk is not beauty.*
†boidhlia, *s.f.* Puddle.
†boidhmhios, *for* buidhe mhìos. (July.)
boidhre, see buidhre.
boidhread, see buidhre.
bòidich, *v. a.* Promise solemnly, vow, swear. 2 Curse. Bhòidich thu bòid do'n Tighearna, *thou hast vowed a vow unto the Lord.*
boidirein, -ein, -ean, *s.m.* Fat, short man.
†boid-reult, *s.f.* Tailed star, comet.
boidsear,* -eir, -earan, *s.m.* Gaelic spelling of *botcher*. 2 Blockhead, stupid fellow.
———achd,* *s.f.ind.* Stupidity, conduct of a blockhead.
†boigbheulachd, *s. f. ind.* Stuttering, stammering.
boige, see buige.
boigean,** *s.m.* Sniveller
bòigear,¶ *s.m* Puffin, ducker, see bùdhaigir.
†boigeun, see boigrean.
†boigh, *s.f.* Teat, dug. 2**Udder.
†boighe, see buidhe.
bòigheach, see bòidheach.
†boigrean,** -ein, *s.m.* Bulrush, see luachair ghòbhlach. 2 Flummery. 3 Anything flabby.
———ach,** *a.* Abounding in bulrushes. 2 Like a bulrush. 3 Like flummery. 4 Flabby.
———,** -aich, *s.m.* Place where bulrushes grow
†boigshibhin, see boigrean.
boil, see boile.
boil-aighir, *s.m.* Over-joy.
boile, *s.f.ind.* Madness, rage, fury, passion, frenzy. 2 see buil. C'arson a ghabh na cinnich boile? *why did the heathen rage?* a chridhe laiste le boile chatha, *his soul highly inflamed with the fury of battle*; tha e air bhoile, *he is in a great passion*; fear na boile, *the passionate man*; is ann orra sud a bha bhoile! *how mad those people were!*
boileach,** *a.* Apt to fly into a rage, furious. 2 see buileach.
boile (air) *adv.* Mad, raging, distracted.
boile-cuthaich,‡‡ *s.f.ind.* Mania.
boilg, see builg. 2 Bubble. 3 Husks of seeds.
†boilgbhiast, *s.f.* Bellyworm.
†boilgein, see balgan.
bòilich, *s.f.* Idle talk. 2 Vain boasting. 3 Blustering, bombast. 4 Telling lies. 6 Flirtation. 7(DU) Talk of a person whose mind is wandering, as in a fever. 8* Ostentation. Tha e cho làn de bhòilich 's a tha 'n t-ubh de bhiadh, *he is as full of romancing as the egg is of meat (substance)*; thoir thairis de d' bhòilich, *stop your romancing.*
boilisg, *s.* Prattling.
†boill, -e, *s.f.* Knob, boss.
†boill-fhada, *for* buill-fhada. Long limbed.
†boillrinn, *s.f.* Ring, circle.
boillsg, -e, -ean, *s m.* Gleam, glare, flash. 2 Effulgence, glitter. 3**Peep. Fo bhoillsg an là, *in the effulgence of day.*
———, *v. n.* Gleam, shine, flash, glitter. 2 Radiate. 3**Peep, look.
———each, -eiche, *a.* Glittering, gleaming, beaming, shining, blazing. 2 Sparkling. 3 **Peeping.
———eachd, *s.f.ind.* Brightness, refulgence. 2* Gaudiness.
———eadh, -eidh, -eidhean, *s. m.* Shining, gleaming, glittering, glaring, flashing, effulgence. 2 Cheering, rousing, lively. 3 Fond of dress, gaudy. A' b—, *pr. part.* of boillsg. Is math an comharra air an t-side shamhraidh, boillsgeadh dearg 'bhi as na soluis fad air falbh, *a good sign of summer weather, when the far away lights have a reddish gleam*; a' boillsgeadh air an t-sliabh, *shining on the mountain.*
†boillsgean, *v.a.* Make round or bulky.
———, -ein, *s.m.* Focus or centre of a fire. 2‡‡Navel. 3 see buillsgean. 4**Mountain.
boillsgeanachd,‡‡ *s.f.ind.* Bulging out.
boillsgeanta, *a.* see boillsgeach.
———chd, see boillsgeachd.
boillsgeil, *a.* Dazzling, flashing, shining, luminous.
†boilrinn, *s.f.* Ring.
boin, *gen.* [*dat.*—JM] *sing.* of bó.
†boineadh, -eidh, *s.m.* Running issue, scrofulous sore. 2 Sprouting, budding.
†boinean, *s.m.* Bud, sprout.
boineanta, see boinneanta.
boineid, -e, -ean, *s.f.* Bonnet. Boineid bhallach, boineid chath-dath, *a tartan bonnet*; is i a' bhoineid bhiorach a ni an gille smiorail, *the cocked bonnet makes the smart lad.* [Boineid is *m.* in Suth'd; boineid biorach, *a Glengarry bonnet.*—AG]
——— -an-losgainn, *s.f.* Brown boletus—*boletus bovinus.* §Also applied to other species of this genus. 2§Puff-ball, see caochag.
———each, *a.* Having bonnets.
———ich,** *v.* Cap.
boineid mhór, *s.f.* *In Islay* something similar to "struileag," an imaginary boat which was sent from one to another, rhyme accompanying it. It was never sent to a friend, and no one cared to keep it long, if he could not make a verse himself, he must get someone else to make one for him, as it could not be passed on by any other means.—*An t-Eileanach.*
boineid-smachain, *s.f.* Mushroom,—*Aberfeldy*, see balg-losgainn.
boinich,(AC) *v.n.* Vow. Boinichidh mi do Mhoire, *I will vow to Mary.*
boinn, *n.pl.* of bann
boinne, *gen.sing.* of bann
boinne, -achan, [& boinnean—DU] *s.f* Drop of any liquid. 2††Current. Gach boinne, *every drop*; cha'n 'eil boinn' agam, *I have not a drop*; boinne fola, *a drop of blood*; 2 *a name for a woman.*
boinne,‡‡ *adv.* On a sudden.
boinneach,‡‡ -eiche, *a.* Sprouting. 2 Dropping.
boinneadh,‡‡ -eidh, *s.f.* Budding, sprouting. 2 Running sore.
boinneag,** -eig, -eagan, *s.f.* Cake. 2(DU) Small drop.
boinnealaich, -e, *s.f.* Dropping of rain previous to a shower.
boinneanta, *a.* Mild, gentle. 2 Stout. 3 Handsome. 4 Healthy. 5 Well-built.

boinneantachd, *s.f.* Mildness, gentleness. 2 Firmness. 3 Stoutness. 4*Handsomeness.
boinneartaich, see boinnealaich.
boinne-bàn, *s.f.* Acrospire.
boinne-fola } *s.m.* Spotted persicaria. see gluineach mhór. 2‡‡Fair one, beauty.
boinne-liath,(DU) *s.f.* Foreshot, first drops of whisky distilled.
boinne-tàig, *s.f.* Rain-drop.
†**boir**, *s.m.* Elephant.
boirb, -e, *s.f.* see buirbe. 2‡‡Brow of a ridge.
boirb-bhriathrach, see borb-bhriathrach.
boirbeachd, see buirbe.
boirche, *s.f.* Elk. 2 Buffalo. 3 Thick edge.
boir-chriadh, *s.f.* Certain species of clay.
boirdheach,** *a.* Hyperborean.
†**boire**,** *s.f.* Hole.
boireal, -eil, -an, *s.m.* Small augur, whimble. 2 Joiner's brace.
boiream,* -eim, *s.m.* Rumour, surmise. 2 Creating hubbub—*Islay.*
———ail,* *a.* Spreading, as a rumour or surmise. 2 Creating great interest.
boireann, see boirionn.
———ach, see boirionnach.
boireanta, *a.* Effeminate. 2 Feminine in *gram.*
boirg,* *s.m.* Little screwed-up mouth.
boirgeach,* -aich, *s.f.* Prating female.
———,* -aiche, *a.* Having a prating mouth.
boirgire,* *s.m.* Fellow with a little screwed up mouth. 2 Tattler.
boiriche, *s.m.* Rising ground, bank.
boirinn,** *s.* Buttock.
boirionn, *a.* Female, of, or belonging to, a female, feminine.
———ach, *a.* see boirionn.
———ach, -aich, *s.m.* Female, woman. *B.* bòidheach, *a pretty woman*; firionnach is boirionnach, *a male and a female*; boirionnach eireachdail, *a handsome female.*
boirionnachd, *s.f.ind.* } Muliebrity, woman-
boirionnas, -ais, *s.m.* } hood, effeminacy. 2 **Adultress.
bois, -e, -ean, *gen. sing.* of bos.
boisceall, -eill, *s.m.* & *f.* Wild man or woman. 2 Hind, deer. 3 Cowardice.
———, -eill, *a.* Uncivilized. Thog thu oirnn gu'n robh sinn boisceall, *you have reported of us that we are savage.*
boiseachd, *s.f.* Palmistry.
boiseag,-eig,-an, *s.f.* Box or slap on the cheek. 2**Slap with the palm of the hand. 3**Little palm. 4††Handful. 5*Palmful of water. Boiseag uisge, *a handful of water.*
———achadh, -aidh, *s.m.* Boxing or slapping on the cheek.
———an, (JM) -ain, *s.m.* Coddle.
boisean,‡‡ see basaidh.
boisean-ionnlaid,‡‡ *s.m.* Washing-basin.
†**boiseid**, -e, -ean, *s.f.* Belt, girdle.
bòiseid, -e, -ean, *s.f.* Purse, budget.
boisg, *v.n.* see boillsg.
boisge, *s.f.* see boillsgeadh & boillsgeachd.
———ach, *a.* see boillsgeach.
boisgealachd, see boillsgeadh & boillsgeachd.
boisgeanta, see boillsgeach.
———chd, see boillsgeadh.
boisgeil, see boillsgeil.
bois-ghaire, see bas-ghaire.
boisileag,(AC) *s.f.* Palmful. 2 Small palmful of water.
boisteadh,** *s.m.* Tincture.
boiteach, *s.f.* Swampy ground.
boiteadh,‡‡ *s.m.* Boiled food for horses.
boit,‡ *s.f.* Taste for. *prov.*
boiteag, -eig, -an, *s.f.* Cauldron. 2 White worm in dung. 3 Earthworm.
boiteal, -eil, *s.m.* see boitean.
———, -eil, *s.m.* Pride, haughtiness,arrogance.
———ach, -aiche, *a.* Proud, haughty, presumptuous, arrogant.
———aich, see boiteanaich.
boitean, -ein, -eanan, *s.m.* Bundle or wisp of straw or hay. 2(AC) Bottle, pottle. A' call nam boitean, a' cruinneachadh nan sop, *losing the bundles, gathering the wisps.*
———ach, *a.* In wisps or bundles, as hay or straw.
———achadh, (a') *pr. part.* Making straw or hay into bundles.
———aich,* *pr. pt.* a' boiteanachadh, *v.a.* Make into bundles or wisps.
——— mearbhail,** *s.m.* Jack-o'-lantern.
boith,* *s.f.* (*for* both) Cottage, hut.
boitidh ! boitidh !* *int.* Call to a pig.—*Skye & Suth'd.*
boitig, *s.* Carriage, see p. 76.
†**bol**,** *s.m.* Poet. 2 Art, skill. 3 Cow.
bòl,‡ -òil, *s.m.* Bowl, cup. 2**Crater.
bol, *pr. part.* a' boladh, *v.a.* Smell, scent.
†**bolachd**, *s.f.ind.* Poetry
boladh, -aidh, *s.m.* Smell, stink, savour. Cha 'n ioghnadh boladh an sgadain a bhi de'n t-soitheach 'sam bi e, *it is no wonder that the herring vessel smells of herring.*—N.G.P.
bòlaich, *s.* Loud speaking. 2(DU)Bombast.
bó-làn,(AF) *s.f.* Full-grown cow.
bó-laun, -a, *s.m.* Cow-house, byre. 2 Fold. 3 ‡‡Ox-stall.
bolanta, *a.* Excellent, consummate, fine, exquisite. Gu bolanta, *exquisitely.*
———chd, *s.f.* Perfection. 2 Exquisiteness.
bó-laoigh, *s.f.* Cow with calf. 2 Milch cow.
bolb, -uilb, *s.m.* Species of worm or caterpillar destructive to bushes.
bolg, -uilg, *s.f.* see balg.
——,‡ *v.n.* see balgaich.
——ach, -aiche, *a.* see balgach.
——ach, -aich, *s.f.* see balgach.
bolgam, -aim, see balgam.
bolgan,* -ain, *s.m.* see balgan. 2**Frock.
bolgan-béiceach, see caochag.
bolgan-beucan,* see caochag.
bolg-an-t-solair, see balg-solair.
bolg-dhubh, -dhuibhe, *a.* see balg-dhubh.
bolg-luachair,} *s.f.* Bulrush, see luachair ghòbhlach.
bolg-saighead, see balg-shaighde.
—— -séididh, *s.m.* see balg-séididh.
—— -solair, *s.m.* see balg-solair.
†**bolguidh**, *for* builg.
†**boll**, *s.m.* Boss of a bridle or gorget.
bolla, *pl.* -chan, [& -ichean,**] *s.m.* Net-, or anchor buoy. 2 Boll (measure of 16 pecks.) 3 ***rarely* Bowl, goblet. Bolla mine, *a boll of meal*; bolla buntata, *a boll of potatoes.* [*B.* is used in the singular after numerals which otherwise govern the plural.]
bolladh, see bolla.
†**bollag**,** -aig, *s.f.* Shell. 2 Skull, top of the head. 3 Heifer. 4 (AF)Bullock.
bollan,(AG) *s.m.* Small tub.
bolla-stiùraidh,** *s.m.* Buoy.
†**bollog**, see ballag.
†**bollsair**,** *s.m.* Citer, crier. 2 Antiquary. 3 ‡‡Teacher, doctor.
bollsg,* *v.n.* Bluster, babble.
———ach,* *a.* Blustering, boasting.
———ach,* *s.f.* Blustering curious female.
†**bollsgair**, *v.n.* Proclaim.
† ———, -ean, *s.m.* Antiquary. 2 Herald crier at court. 3 Boaster, blusterer. 2*Bullying fellow.
† ——— -bùird, *s.m.* Grand carver.

bollsgaireachd,* *s.f.* Habit of blustering or swaggering.
bollsganta,* *a.* Blustering, swaggering, bullying.
bolstar, Gaelic spelling of *bolster*.
bolt, built, *s.m.* see balt.
†——adh, *s.f.* Bolt, bar.
——anach, *a.* Rank, olefactory.
†——anas, -ais, *s.m.* Smell, odour, perfume.
†——nigh, *v.a.* Smell.
boltrach, -aich, *s.m.* Scent, smell, odour, perfume. 2 Volume or bolt of smoke, fire, ashes, &c. Oladh agus boltrach, *oil and perfume.*
————, -aiche, *a.* Scented. 2‡‡Smelling, scenting.
————ail, *a.* see boltrach.
————an, -ain, *s.m.* Scent-bottle. 2 Perfume. 3 Nosegay. 4 Spikenard. 5 Perfumer.
————as, -ais, *s.m.* Perfumery. 2 Fragrance. 3††Scent-bottle. 4††Nosegay.
boltraich,** *v.n.* Smell, scent, perfume, aromatize. †2**Chafe. Bholtraich e boladh, *he smelt a smell.*
————te, *past pt.* Aromatized.
†**boltrunnachadh,**-aidh,*s.m.* Scenting, smelling.
†**bolunta,** *a.* Refined. 2 Excellent, fine, exquisite.
boma, *s.m.* Bomb.
bomach,†† *a.* Of, or pertaining to, a bomb.
†**bomadair,** *s.f.* Vomit.
†**boman,** *v.n.* Boast, vaunt, brag. 2 Exalt.
————,** ain, *s.m.* Boast, bounce.
————ach, *a.* Boasting, vaunting, blustering.
————ach,** *s.m.* Boasting or blustering fellow.
————achd, *s.f.ind.* Habit of bragging, boasting, vaunting or blustering.
bomannach,‡‡ -aiche, *a.* Spotted, chequered.
†**bomluchd,** *s.f.* Cow and profit.
bonaid, see boineid.
boncait,** -ean, *s.m.* Balk.
bonn, -uinn, *pl.* -uinn & bonnan, *s.m.* Heel. 2 Sole. 3 Foundation, found of house. 4 Pedestal, bottom, base, socket. 5 Coin. 6 Boom of a sail. 7‡‡Good, advantage. 8 Tyre of a cycle. Bonn na bròige, *the sole of the shoe;* cha'n 'eil mi bonn ann ad eisimeil, *I am not the least in your reverence, I do not care a straw for you ;* fichead bonn, *twenty sockets ;* fichead bonn airgid, *twenty pieces of silver ;* bonn na beinne, *the base of the mountain* ; fo bhonnaibh 'ur cas, *under the soles of your feet;* bonn leth-chruin, *a half-crown piece*; thug iad na buinn asda, *they took to their heels* ; rothan aig gach bonn, *wheels at every base* ; a chù ri a bhonn, *his dog at his heels* ; á larach nam bonn, *instanter* ; thug e buinn di, *he took to his heels.*
†**bonn,** *a.* Good.
bonnach, -aich, *s.m.* Cake. (Scot. *bannock.*) Mar is miannaich brù bruichear bonnach, *as the stomach craves the scone is toasted.* [Bannach in *Suth'd*—AG.]
————air, -ean,*s.m.* Wandering greedy beggar.
————aireachd, *s.f.ind.* Practice of a wandering glutton.
————an, -ain, *s.m.* Little cake. 2 That part of a spade on which the foot presses.
bonnach an t-sodail,(AH) (*lit.* the cake of flattery) Dh'ith thu bonnach an t-sodail, *you have eaten the cake of flattery*—said to a child when it manifests an undue amount of friendship for anyone.
bonnach-boise,(AC) *s.m.* Cake made on the palm of the hand.
bonnach-cloiche,(AH) *s.m.* Thick oat-meal cake made on the palm of the hand, and not baked on a griddle but in an upright position before a fire.
bonnag, -aig, -an, *s.f.* Jump, spring. 2 Sole of a shoe. 3 see bannag. 4(DU) Little cake. 'Dol air bhonnaig, *going out as guisers on New Year's eve.*
————ach, *a.* Leaping, bounding, jumping.
bonn-a-h-ochd, *s.m.* Piece of eight (the Spanish *peso duro* or "hard dollar."
†**bonnaidhe,** *for* buinn.
bonnail, *a.* see borrail.
†**bonnainne,** *s.m.* Footman, lacquey. 2 Bittern, see corra-ghrian.
†**bonnamh,** *s.m.* Tribe, family.
bonna-mine,(AF) Bittern, see corra-ghrian.
bonnan, -ain, *s.m.* Little sole. †2 (AF) Bittern, see corra-ghrian.
————ach(AC)*s.m.* Short, stout, well-set man.
bonnan-buidhe,(AF) *s.m.* Heron, see corraghlas. 2 Crane, see corra-mhonaidh.
———— -leana, / ———— -liona, }(AF) see corra-ghlas.
bonnanta, *a.* see bunanta.
bonn-a-sè, *pl.* buinn- & bonnacha-, *s.m.* Halfpenny sterling (*lit.* a piece of six, *i. e.* six *peighinn* or Scots pence.)
bonn-a-sia, buinn- & bonnacha-, see bonn-a-sè.
bonn-bog, *s.m.* Cushion-tyre (of a cycle.)
bonn'chan, -ain, see bonnachan.
bonnchart, -airt, -an, *s.m.* Balk, land between two ridges.
bonn-chasach, -aiche, *a.* Stout, strong-legged.
bonn-chumadair, -e, -ean, *s.m.* Shoe-last.
bonn-cruaidh, *s.m.* Solid tyre (of a cycle.)
bonn-crùin,†† *s.m.* Crown piece.
bonn-dubh, *s.m.* Heel—*Lewis & Suth'd.* At a' bhuinn-duibh agus bàs an aona mhic, *the swelling of the heel and the death of the only son—equally painful and difficult to bear*; losgadh buinn-duibh, losgadh gu cnàimh, *burning in the heel, burning to the bone* (expressive of the agony of a sore heel.—NGP.
bonn-mhall, *a.* Steady, firm, constant.
bonnsach, -aich, -aichean, *s.f.* Dart, spear, javelin.
bonnsach,(DU) *a.* Steady, firm.
bonnsachd, *s.f. ind.* Leaping, springing, jumping, vaulting.
bonnsaich, *v.n.* Spring, dart, bounce.
bonnsair,** *s.m.* Thrower.
bonn-shuidheachadh, -aidh, *s.m.* Establishing. 2 Getting a firm footing.
bonn-shuidhich, *v.a.* Establish, found. 2 Get or give a firm holding.
bonntach,-aich, *s.f.* The thickest part of a hide, used for shoe-soles.
†**bor,** *a.* Illustrious, high, noble. 2 Proud. 3 Ostentatious.
†**bor,** *s.m.* Swelling, pride.
boraisd, see barraisd.
†**borb,** -uirb, *s.m.* Tyrant, oppressor.
borb,* *v.a.* Enflame, swell.‡‡ 2 Get enraged. Bhorb a chas, *his foot enflamed* ; bhorb i 'na aghaidh, *she got enraged against him.*
borb, buirbe, *a.* Fierce, furious, violent. 2 Passionate, raging. 3 Outrageous. 4 Strong. 5 Savage. 6 Turbulent. 7 Cruel. 8 Rude, ignorant. 9‡‡Haughty, proud. O'n iorguill bhorb, *from the fierce contest* ; tha 'm fuaim mar an geamhradh borb, *their sound is like the boisterous winter* ; nochd an sluagh borb caoimhneas dhuinn, *the barbarous people showed us kindness* ; is borb an duin' e, *he is a passionate man* ; tha 'n t-amadan borb, *the fool is raging.*
†**borba,** see borbas.
borbachd, *s.f.ind.* Fierceness, furiousness. 2

Barbarity. 3*Cruelty.
borbadh, -aidh, s.m. Raging, swelling. 2 Fierceness. 3 Haughtiness. 4 Enflaming. 5*Enraging, getting furious. Also used for buirbe. A' b—, *pr.pt.* of borb.
borbarra, *a.* Barbarous, wild, fierce, untamed, uncivilized. Gu *b.*, *barbarously*.
borbas, -ais, *s.m.* Strictness. 2 Severity. 3 Rigour. 4 Sharpness. 5 Churlishness. 6 Fierceness.
borb-bhriathar,** *s.m.* Barbarism.
borb-bhriathrach, -aiche, *a.* Speaking fiercely or rudely. 2 Vain glorious. 3*Furious.
borb-choigreach,‡‡ -ich, *s.m.* Foreigner.
borbhan, -ain, *s. m.* Murmur, low sound. 2 Purling of a stream. 3**Humming, grumbling, any continued low sound. 4‡‡Noise of a tempest, or 5†† of small stones falling. 'S fhada bhuam fhéin Bealach a' Bhorbhain, *far from me is "the defile of murmuring" (name of a place in Trotternish, Skye.)*
———ach, -aiche, *a.* Deep, grave, bass.
———ach,** -aich, *s.m.* Bass in *music*.
———achd, *s.f.ind.* Deepness or bassness of sound.
———aich, *s.f.* Murmuring, grumbling, muttering. 2 Gurgling. Ciod a' *bh.* a th' ort? *what are you grumbling about?*
borbnachadh, -aidh, *s.m.* Incitement, encouragement, instigation. 2 Impulse. 3 Swelling with rage. A' b—, *pr.pt.* of borbnaich.
borbnaich, *pr.pt.* a' borbnachadh, *v. a. & n.* Impel. 2 Heave with anger or indignation. 3 *Enrage. 4††Fester.
borb-ràdh,** *s.m.* Barbarism.
borb-smachdail, *a.* Arbitrary, imperious.
bòrc, *pr.pt.* a' bòrcadh, *v.n.* Spring, sprout, bud. 2 Blossom. 3 Swell. 4 Burst.
——ach, -aiche, *a.* Springing, sprouting, budding. 2 Swelling. 3**Tall. 4††Strutting.
——adh, -aidh, *s.m.* Springing, sprouting, budding. 2 Swelling. A' b—, *pr. part.* of bòrc.
bòrd, bùird, *s.m.* Table. 2 Plank, board, deal. 3 Board (directors or managers of company&c) 4 Boarding. Air bhòrd, *boarded, as a boarder*; air bòrd, *on board (a ship)*; cuir air bòrd, *put on board*; mu 'n bhòrd, *about the table*; aig ceann a' bhùird, *at the head of the table*; sgoil-bhùird, *boarding-school*; sgoil a' Bhùird, *a Board-school*; tha e fo 'n bhòrd, *he is dead*; bòrd dà-dhuilleig, *a two-leaved table*; bòrd beulaibh, *the starboard of a ship*; bòrd cùlaibh, *the port of a ship*; cuir air 'bhòrd, *board him, send him to a boarding-house*; cha 'n e am bòrd a theirig dhuit ach am beagan fearainn, *you did not fail because the mould-board gave way, but because the land was too small*; am bòrd mór uaine, see below.
bòrd, *v.a. & n.* Tack. 2 Board (as a ship.) *Bh.* iad an long, *they boarded the ship.*
bòrdadh, -aidh, *s.m.* Tacking, as a vessel at sea. A' b—, *pr.pt.* of bòrd.
bòrdaich, *v.a.* Plank.
bòrdair, -ean, *s.m.* Gaelic spelling of **boarder and of ‡‡border.
bòrdaireachd, *s.f.ind.* see bòrdadh.
bòrd-beulaibh, *s.m.* Starboard side of a ship.
—— -chluich, *s. pl.* Billiards—*Forbes' G.Gr.*
—— -cluiche, *s.m.* Billiard-table.
—— -cùlaibh, *s.m.* Port side of a ship.
—— -luathaidh, *s.m.* Waulking-table.
—— -luinge, *s.m.* Deck of a ship.
—— -mór (am), am Bòrd mór Uaine, *s.m.* The Board of Green Cloth, the highest court of appeal. Théid mise gu lagh leis, agus mur faigh mi ceartas cha stad mi gus an ruig mi am Bòrd Uaine an Lunnainn, *I'll go to law with him, and should I not get justice, I will not rest till I bring my case before the Board of Green Cloth in London.*
—— -na-cìse, *s.m.* Board of customs or excise.
—— -uachdair,(AH) *s. m.* Lid of a chest or coffin.
—— -uaine, *s.m.* The green table, board of green cloth.
—— -uisge,** *s.m.* Flood-gate.
—— -ùrchrainn, *s.m.* Mould-board of a plough, (bòrd-urchair—* ; bòrd ùrach—AM)
†borg, *s.m.* Tower. 2 Village. 3 House.
borlanachd,†† *s.f.* Compulsory labour for a landlord.
bòrlum, -uim, *s.m.* Sudden evacuation. 2 Strip of arable land. 3 Ridge, acclivity. 4 Royal castle lands in the Highlands. 5‖ Sudden flux or vomiting.
†boroimh, *s.f.* Tribute of cattle.
†borr, -a, *s.m.* Knob. 2 Bunch. 3 Grandeur, pride. 4 Greatness, majesty. 5 Swelling tumour. 6 Curled upper lip. 7 Blubber lip. 8‡‡Elephant.
†borr, *a.* Great, noble. 2 Haughty. 3 Splendid, grand.
†borr, *v.a. & n.* Swell. 2 Become big and proud. 3 Scent, as a dog. 4**Bully. 5**Swagger. 6**Parch.
borrach, -aich, *s.m.* †Great, haughty, or proud man. 2 Projecting bank.
borrach,§ -aich, *s.m.* Mat-grass or moor-grass —*Skye*, see beitein. 2 Borage, see barraisd. 3 Sweet meadow-grass, see mislean.
———, *a.* Blubber-lipped. 2††Bullying.
†borracha, *s.m.* Bladder.
borrachas, -ais, *s.f.* Boasting, bullying. 2 Bravado. 3††Blubber-lips.
borradh, -aidh, *s.m.* Swelling. 2 Bravadoing. 3 Parching. 4 Scent, smell—*Skye.* 5††File of soldiers.
†———ach, *a.* Parched. 2 Valiant.
borraidh, *s.f.* Borage, see barraisd.
borrail, -e, *a.* Swaggering, boastful, haughty, proud.
borraileachd, *s. f.* Pride.
borraisd, *s.m.* Borage, see barraisd.
†borral, *s.m.* Brace, pair.
———achd,** *s.f.* see borraileachd.
borran, -ain, *s.m.* Haunch, buttock. 2 Little blubber-lip. 3‡‡see borrach. 4‡‡Anger.
borras, -ais, *s.m.* Protuberance, prominence. 2††Blubber-lip. 3‡‡Solder.
———ach, -aiche, *a.* Blubber-lipped.
borr-fhuaim, *s.m.* Low murmuring noise.
borrghanta, *a.* Swelled, bloated. 2 Pompous. 3 Turgid. 4††Fierce.
borr-shuil, *s.f.* Full round eye.
————each, -eiche, *a.* Full-eyed, round-eyed. 2(AM) Sulky—*Uist.*
†borr-thoradh, *s. m.* Grandeur, magnificence, majesty.
†borruin, see borran.
†borsa,** *s.m.* Purse.
†borsair,** *s.m.* Purser. 2 Bursar.
borsadh,** *s.m.* Bourse.
bos, boise, boisean, *s.f.* see bas.
†bos, *a.* Certain. 2 Abject, low, mean, vile, of low origin.
bos (AH) *a.* Hollow, emitting a hollow sound.
bosag, -aig,-an, *s.f.* Slap on the cheek or mouth. 2 Handful.
———achadh, -aidh, see boiseagachadh.
†bosan, *s. m.* Purse.
bosarguin, *s. f.* †Destruction. 2†† Clapping the hands in grief.
bos-bhuail, see bas-bhuail.
bos-bhualadh, -aidh, *s.m.* see bas-bhualadh.

bosd, *s.m.* see bocsa.
bòsd, *v.n.* Boast, vaunt.
——, -a, *s.m.* Boast, pride, boasting language. 2 Vain-glory. Am bòsd gun fheum, *the useless boast.*
——ail, -e. *a.* Vaunting, boasting, boastful. 2 Vain. Luchd *b.*, *boasters.*
——air, -e, -ean, *s. m.* Swaggerer, blusterer. 2 Bully. 3 Turbulent noisy fellow.
——alachd,* *s. f.* Boastfulness, vain-glory, swaggering. 2 Romance.
bosdan, -ain, *s.m.* Small box. 2**Basket. 3 (AM) Child's coffin—*Uist.*
bosghaird, see basgaird.
————eachas, see basgairdeachas.
————eadh, *s.m. & pr. pt.* see basgairdeadh.
bos-ghaire, see bas-gaire.
boslach, see baslach. 2‡‡Fire. 3‡‡Vault.
bos-luadh, see bas-luaidh.
bos-luaidh, see bas-luaidh.
bos-luath, *a.* see bas-luath.
†————, *s.f.* see bas-luaidh.
bos-mhìn, see bas-mhìn.
————each, *a.* see bas-mhìn.
bosraich, *s.f.* see basraich. 2**Shouting, roaring. 3**Squall, high wind. Mar bhosraich geamhraidh, *like the loud winter gale.*
bòstail, see bòsdail.
bos-uaill, see bas-uaill (appendix)
bòt, -òit, *s.m.* see bòtuinn.
bòt, -a, -an, *s.f.* Vote. **v.n.* Vote.
bot, -a, -achan, *s.m.* Mound. 2 Bothy, house. 3*River bank.
bot, *s.m.* see bod.
†**botach**, *s.f.* Reedy bog, fen. see bothach.
bòtach, *a.* Wearing boots, booted. Gu sporach, *b.*, *spurred and booted.*
bòtaich,** *v.a.* Boot.
bòtaidh, -ean, *s.f.* Wooden vessel of the size of half an anker (5 or 6 gals.)
†**botaigear**, -eir, -an, *s.m.* Fork.
bòtair** -ean, *s.m.* Bootmaker.
bòtais,‡‡ *s.f.* see bòtuinn.
botal, -ail, see botul.
——aich, see botulaich.
†——lach, -aiche, *a.* Violent, furious, turbulent, outrageous.
both, *s.m.ind.* Perturbation. 2 Furious agitation. 3 Declamation. 4 Vehement action of body. A' cur nam both dheth, *in great agitation.*
†**both**, -a, -an, *s.m.* Cottage, hut, tent, bower, bothie, *now* buth. 2‡‡Shade. 3*Plash.
bothach,** -aich, *s.f.* Marsh, quagmire.
————, -aiche, *a.* Full of tents or cottages.
bothadh,(AG) -aidh, *s.m.* Startling. Chuir e bothadh orm, *he startled me.*
bothag,¶ -aig, *s.f.* Ringed plover, see trìleachan-tràighe. 2 see bothan. 3 see bodhag.
————ach,†† *a.* Abounding in huts or booths.
bó-thaigh, -e, -ean, *s.m.* see bàthaich.
bothaireachd,** *s.f.* Prey.
bothan. -ain, *s. m.* Cottage, hut, tent, booth, bower, bothie. Bothan am fasgadh nam fuar-bheann, *a hut in the shelter of the bleak mountains* ; rinn e bothain d' a sprèidh, *he made booths for his cattle* ; mar bhothan a ni am fear-coimhead, *as a booth that the watchman makes* ; cha chuir mi bothan air, *I will not conceal it—Uist* (JM.)
————ach,‡‡ *a.* Bowery, belonging to a cottage.
bothan-àiridhe,(DU) *s.m.* The sheiling.
bothan-faire, *s.m.* Sentry-box.
bòthar,(JM) -air, *s.m.* Soft mud. Rinn iad bòthar dheth, *they made soft mud of it.*
bothar, -air, -airean, *s. m.* Lane, road, street, avenue, alley, passage.
——, *a.* see bodhar.
botrachan, *s.m.* see bod-chrann.
botrumaid, -e, -ean, *s.f.* Slattern, drab, slut, trull, slovenly woman.
——————each, *a.* Drabbish, sluttish.
bòtuinn, -e, -ean, *s.f.* Boot.
————each, *a.* Booted. 2 Thick-legged.
————eachadh, -aidh, *s.m.* Booting.
————ich, *v.a.* Boot, put on boots.
botul, -uil, *s.m.* Gaelic spelling of *bottle.*
——ach, †† *a.* Having bottles. 2 Bottled.
——aich, *pr.pt.* a' botulachadh, *v.a.* Bottle, put into bottles.
————te, *past part.* Bottled.
botulair, see buidealair.
botulan,‡‡ -ain, -an, *s.m.* Small bottle.
botus,‖ -uis, *s.m.* Belly-worm.

63. Botus-each.

botus-each,(D.M.) -uis-, *s. m.* Horse-bot—*gasterophilus equi*,—(an intestinal worm.) [Ill. 63 does not represent *creithleag-nan-each*, which lives on blood of animals, but the fly of botus-each, which does not take any food while in the fly form. It is often called *creithleag* in error. see creithleag.]
bó-ursainn,(AF) *s.f.* Her best cow always taken by the proprietor of old from a newly-made widow.

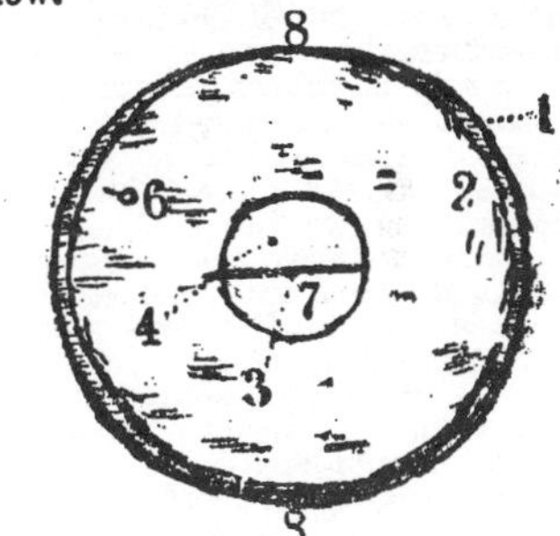

64. Brà.

65. An dòigh air a' bhrà oibreachadh.

brà, *gen.* bràthan, *pl.* bràthntan, *s.f.* Quern

handmill. 2†Brow. 3(AC) Anything round anything that has no end. Is fheàirrde brà a breacadh gun a briseadh, *a quern is the better of being picked but not broken*; bonnach bràthan, *a round bannock*; liabag bràthan, *a round flounder.*

We are indebted to Mr. D. Murray (of Lewis) Aberdeen, for the following names of PARTS OF A QUERN :—

1 A' chlach iochdarach, a' bhrà iosal, *or* a' chlach bhuinn, *the nether stone.*

2 A' chlach uachdarach, *or* a' bhrà àrd, *the upper stone.*

1 & 2 Clachan na bràthan, *the stones.*

3 An dual, *Eye-bar, the cross stick in "eye."*

4 Am mialair, *The bearer, the stick on which the upper stone rests.*

5 An t-aotroman, *Bearing-gear, the stick or wedge that lightens the pressure of the stone on the grain.*

6 An sgonnan, *the handle, by means of which the quern is turned.*

7 Sùil na bràthan, *the eye.*

8 Fiacail, *the tooth.*

9 Bannas, *gum* } The lower side of upper

10 Carbad, *jaw* } stone, and upper side of lower stone.

11 Leth-bhann, leth-bhuinn, *In gear.* A' cur na bràthan air a leth-bhuinn, *putting the mill in working order.* i. e. making one stone to fit the other and to revolve with equal weight on both sides. Chaidh i de a leth-bhann, *it is off one side of the nether* or *sole stone.*

12 Sasag, *large round vessel made of straw, 9in. high and 4ft. in diameter, for holding the meal before sieving.*

13 An loban, *straw vessel smaller than sasag, for keeping the roughest portion of the meal* (garbhann.)

14 An rùsgan, a vessel for holding the husks (cathadh.)

15 Cisean-bafair, a vessel made of sea-bent, from which the quern is fed with one hand while being turned with the other. [Cìsean-mùrain—DM]

16 Craiclonn-bràthan, *Skin spread on the ground under the quern to keep the meal from going on the floor*—"Fionn."

Nos. 12, 13, 14, & 15 are all narrower at the bottom than at the mouth, something after the fashion of a zinc pail. [see muileann.]

braban,§ *s.m.* Purple mealie-grass, see bunglas.

brabhd,* *s.f.* Bandy-leg. 2(CR) Big, clumsy person or thing.

——ach,* *a.* Bandy-legged.

——ach,* *s.f.* Bandy-legged female.

——adh, -aidh, *s.m.* Idle talk, bravado.

brabhdair, *s.m.* Noisy, talkative fellow. 2 Blusterer. 3 Bully. 4 Bandy-legged man.

——eachd, *s.f.* Blustering language, bravado. 2 Swaggering, loud talk. 3 Haughtiness, insolence.

brabhd-chasach, *a.* Bow-legged.

brabhtalachd, see brabhdaireachd.

†brac, -aic, *s.m.* Arm. 2 Shop. 3 *s.f.* Harrow.

†brac, *v.a. & n.* Break, as with a harrow. 2 Embrace.

brac, AC *a.* Rich, as milk.

bràc, (AC) *s.m.* Curve, curve of a wave immediately before breaking. 2 Bellow, roar of a stag. 3 Branch, applied to antlers of a deer. 4 Reindeer, red deer, fallow deer, deer in general. Ceud bràc bruaill an t-samhraidh, *a hundred reindeer intractable in summer.*

†braca, *s.m.* Breaker, harrow.

bracach, -aiche, *a.* Greyish, white and black.

†bracadh,‡‡ -aidh, *s.m.* Cabin. 2 Harrow.

bracaille,** -an, *s.f.* Bracelet. 2 Sleeve.

bracairneach, *a.* Greyish, dusky. Mart *b.*, *a black and white faced cow.*

bracan,** -ain, *s.m.* †Broth. 2 Gauntlet, glove. 3 Handcuff.

brach, *s.m.* Bear. 2(AF) Dog. 3**Lippitude.

brach, *pr. pt.* a' brachadh, *v.a. & n.* Ferment, malt. 2‡‡Rot.

bràch, *a.* (Gu bràch, *adv.*) see bràth.

†brach, -aich, *s.m.* Pimple.

bracha, *gen. sing.* of braich.

brachach, see brachadh.

brachadair, -e, -ean, *s.m.* Maltman.

brachadh, -aidh, *s.m.* Fermenting, fermentation, malting. 2 Tainting, rotting, putrefying. Grùthan na h-earba gun bhrachadh, *the roe's liver untainted*—N.G.P. A' b—, *pr. pt.* of brach.

brachag, -aig, -an, *s.f.* Pustule. 2‖Stye. 3 Ophthalmia, soreness of the eyes. 4 see brachadh.

——ach, -aiche, *a.* Pimply. 2 Ophthalmic.

brachan, -ain, *s.m.* Anything fermented, leaven. 2 Putrefaction. 3*Rubbish.

bràchd, (AC) *s.f.* Putrescence, putrefaction. 2 Effervescence, fermentation. 3 see brùchd.

——, (AC) *a.* Fat, rich. 2 Generous.

†brachd, *s.f.* Drop. 2 Sap, juice. 3 Increase of riches. 4 Reaping, mowing. 5**Hatred.

brachd,* see brachan.

——ach, -aiche, *a.* Substantial, solid, firm.

——ag, -aig, -an, *s.f.* Drab, slut.

brachdlig,(AM) *s.m.* Vile fellow.

brà-cheò, *s.m.* see bràth-cheò.

brach-shuileach, -eiche, *a.* Blear-eyed.

————d, *s.f.ind.* Blear-eyedness.

braclach, see broclach.

bracuirneach, -eiche, *a.* see bracairneach.

bradach, -aiche, *a.* Thievish. 2 Stolen. 3 Roguish. Measar e mar ni *b.*, *it shall be reckoned as stolen goods*; tha thu cho breugach 's a tha 'n luch cho bradach, *you are as untruthful as the mouse is thievish.*

——,** -aich, *s.m.* Thief.

bradag, -aig, -an, *s.f.* Thievish woman. 2 Term of familiarity used for checking a female. 3 Sly young girl. Ceisd bradaig air breugaig, *ask the thief if I be a liar.*

—— -chail,** *s.f.* Cabbage-worm.

bradaiche,** -ean, *s.m.* Thief, robber.

bradaidh, *s.m.ind.* Thief, robber. 2 Familiar term of reproof. 3‡‡Rogue. 4 The Devil (*N. High's.*) Saoilidh bradaidh nam bruach gur gadaichean uile càch, *the thief of the braes thinks all others thieves.*

——eachd, see bradalachd.

bradalach, *a.* Thievish. 2 Haughty. Gu *b.*, *haughtily.*

————d, *s.f.ind.* Theft. 2 Pride, arrogance, haughtiness. 3*Trickiness.

bradan, -ain, *s.m.* Salmon 2 Swelling on the skin, ridgy tumour on the surface of the body.

——ach, -aiche, *a.* Full of salmon. 2†‡ Full of swellings.

—— -bacach, AC (*lit.* halting salmon) *s. m.* Sturgeon.

—— -bràthan, AC (*lit.* round *or* quern-like salmon) *s.m.* Turbot.

—— -breithinn, AC *s. m.* The salmon of knowledge touched by Fionn.

—— -cearr, } (*lit.* left-sided or broad sal-

—— -gearr, } mon) AC *s.m.* Sturgeon.

—— -leathann, AC (*lit.* broad salmon) *s.m.* Sturgeon. 2AF Halibut. 3 Turbot.—*West of Ross* (CR.)

—— -sligeach, *s.m.* Mullet.

bràdh, see brà.
†——,‡ see bràth.
bradh, *v.a.* Oppress.
bradhadair, -ean, *s.m.* Kindling, fire-wood, fuel. 2 Large fire—*Skye.*
bradhan,** *s.m.* Chatwood.
†bradh-rudh, *s.m.* Ambush.
braduidh, see bradaidh.
†brafal, (brath+foille) *s.m.* Deceit.
brag,(CR) *s.m.* Herd of deer, group of stags or hinds—*Athole.*
brag,* *v.n.* Be infected with an epidemic or contagion.
bragàd** -àid, -an, *s.m.* Gaelic spelling of *brigade.*
bragàdach,** *a.* In brigades.
bragainn,** *s.f.* Bragging, boasting, vaunting. Thòisich e air bragainn, *he began to vaunt.*
————,** *v.n.* Brag, boast. 2 Flourish.
bragair, *s. m.* §Leaves of the sea-girdles. 2** Braggadoccio. *In Uist* the seaweed cast ashore in summer, and of which kelp was made—(JM.)
bragaire,§ *s.m.* Barberry (plant)—*Lewis.* 2 (AH) "Topper," an animal belonging to either flock or fold on which its owner bestows exceptional attention in order that it may excel all specimens of its class in the neighbourhood. Rinn thu bragaire de'n ghamhainn ruadh, *you have made a topper of the red stirk.*
————achd, *s. f.* Empty pride, pride above merit, vain-glory, boasting.
bragh, -a, *s.m.* Burst, explosion. 2‡Peal.
——, *a.* see brac.
——achail,** *a.* Purulent.
bràghad, -aid, -an, *s.m.* Neck, throat, windpipe. 2**Back. 3‡‡Breast and upper parts of the body. Lagan a' bhràghaid, *the hollow at the upper part of the breast* ; a bràghad gu sèimh a' soillseachadh, *her neck shining softly* ; rùisgidh brù bràghad, *the belly will strip the neck* ; losgadh bràghad, *the heartburn.*
————, *gen. sing.* of bràighe.
————ach, *a.* Of, or belonging to, a neck or throat, jugular. 2**Having a long neck.
————aich, -e, *s.f.* Crackling, bursting, as in drying of grain. 2 Noise.
braghadh, *s.m.* Purulence. 2 Gore. 3 see bragh. 4‡‡see bràghad.
braghairt, *s.f.* Truss, bundle.
†bragha-ruigheach, see bragha-ruighidh.
†bragha-ruighidh, *s.f.* Gibbet.
bragsaidh, *s.f.* "Braxy," disease among sheep.
†braic, *s.m.* Mouth.
braiceas, -eis, *s.f.* Gaelic spelling of *breakfast.*
braich, bracha, *s.f.* Malt, fermented grain. Àth-bhracha, *a malt-kiln* ; muileann-bracha, *a malt-mill.*
†——, *s.m.* Stag. 2 Buffalo. 3AF Wolf. 4AF Badger.
†braicheam,-eim,*s.m.* Pack-saddle, pannel. 2** Horse-collar.
——eadh, *s.m.* Malting.
†——eamh, *s.m.* see †braich.
——eamhaill, ——eann, ——eas. -eis, } see †braich.
†braicmhias, *s.m.* see braiceas.
†braicne, *s.m.* Cat.
bràid, -e, -ean, *s.f.* Horse-collar, brecham. 2*Collar round a thief's neck.—*Islay.* 3 see bràghad. 4 see bràighe. 5 Mountain, mountainous country. Bràid-chluaisein, *hames* ; bràid phaib, *a horse-collar made of coarse flax.*
braid, -e, *s.f.* Theft. Luchd braid, *thieves* ; saor o bhraid is o antlachd, *free from theft or bad behaviour.*

bràidean, -ein, *s.m.* Little horse-collar. 2 Calf's collar. 3 Thievish fellow.
bràidh, see braigh.
braidhe,** *s.* Blast, bounce, knack, clap.
braidhin,** *s.f.* see brà.
braidhleag, -ig, -an, see braoileag.
————ach, *a.* see braoileagach.
braidseal, -eil, -an, *s.m.* Hill used as a beacon. *This word is now used for a large fire of any kind, particularly in times of rejoicing. 2 Volley. 3 Broadside, scolding. 'S ann agaibh a tha 'm *b.* ciatach ! *what a fine blazing fire you have !* an ceud *bh.* a leig iad, *the first volley they fired* ; 's iad sud a fhuair am *b.*, *what a scolding they got !*
braigail,(CR) *a.* Vain, uplifted.—*Arran.*
bràigh,-e, *pl.* dean, & -de, *s. m.*(*& f.*) Hostage, pledge. 2 Prisoner. Bràighde-gill, *pledges.*
braigh, -e, -dean, *s.m.* Loud report, loud crack or clap. 2 Heavy stroke. 3 Monosyllable. Leig an gunna braigh as, *the gun made a loud report.*
bràigh,* *v.a.* Give a crackling sound, as wood burning, crackle, burst, explode, crash.
bràigh, *gen.sing.*-e & bràghad, *pl.* bràigheachan, *s.m.* The upper part of any thing or place. 2 **Upland country. 3 Cable. 4**see bràghad. 5 see bràid. 6(AH) Chief (upper 3rd, part of shield in *heraldry.*) Bràigh a' chuirp, *the upper part of the breast* ; bràigh dùthcha, *the higher parts of a district* ; Bràigh Lochabair, *the braes* (*lit.* upper part) *of Lochaber* ; bràigh an taighe, *the top of the house* ; bràigh a' chroinn, *the mast-head* ; bràigh a' ghlinne, *the head of the glen* ; bràigh na leapach, *the top of the bed* ; réiteach bràighe, *expectoration* (*lit.* a clearing of the chest,) do bhràigh bhàn, *thy fair bosom* ; bràigh na stairsnich, *landing on a staircase.*

68. Braigh

bràigh-chrann, *s.m.* Top-mast.
bràighde, *pl.* of bràigh.
————ach, aich, -ichean, *s.f.* Horse-collar.
braighdeachd, *s.f. ind.* see braighdeanas.
bràighdean, *pl.* of bràigh.
bràighdean, -ein, -an, *s.m.* see bràidean.
————as, -ais, *s.m.* Bondage, captivity, slavery. Am bràighdeanas, *in captivity.*
†braighdinneach, *a.* Able to obtain or procure.
bràighe, see bràigh. 2‡‡ Means of obtaining.
————ach, -aich, *s.m.* Highlander, mountaineer, specially one belonging to the Braes of Lochaber.
bràigheach,** *a.* Having a long neck. 2 Having a handsome neck. 3 Of, or belonging to, a neck. 4 Uplandish.
braigheach, *a.* Giving a loud report. 2 Explosive.
braigheachan, -ain, -an, *s.m.* Little cable.
braigheachd, *s. m.* Confinement, constraint, imprisonment.
bràighead, -eid, see bràghad.
bràigheadh, *s.m.* Report, explosion, crackling. 2 Blow.
bràigheall,(AF) see broigheal.
†braighean, *s.f.* Debate.
bràigheardaich, *s.f.* Crackling. 2 Blustering, swaggering.
bràigh-ghill, *s.m.* The goal, ascendant or preeminence. Thug thu bràigh-ghill air na chuala mi riamh, *you surpass everything I ever heard;* tha sin a' toirt bràigh-ghill air a h-uile ni, *that excels everything* ; fhuair e *b.* ort gun taing dhuit, *he got the ascendant in defiance of you.*
bràighid, see bràid.
braighirt,** *s. f.* Bundle.

†braigh-ioslaid, *s.f.* Collar.
bràigh-leab,* *s.m.* The wood roof of a house, sarking.
braighleach,* —*Lewis,* see broilleach.
braighleag, see braoileag.
braighlich,* *v.a.* Make a noise. 2 Crackle. 3 Bluster, swagger.
braighlich,* *s.f.* Noise, crackling. 2 Blustering, swaggering.
bràigh-sheol,* *s.m.* Top-sail.
bràigh-shlat,* *s.m.* Top-sail yard.
braight,* see braidseal.
braightseal,* see braidseal.
†brail, *v.n.* Dismiss. 2 Refuse, reject, slight. 3 Feel.
braile, -ean *s.f.* Heavy rain. 2 Violent sudden eruption. 3 Burst of indignation.
braileadh, -eidh, see braile.
brai'-lìn, see braith-lìn.
brailis, *s.f.* Wort of ale or beer.
braim, brama, bramannan, [*gen. pl. in Uist* bràm] *s.m.* Crepitus ventris. Mar tha gille mór nam braim, cha'n fhuirich e thall 's cha'n fhuirich e bhos, *like the ne'er-do-weel, he will stay nowhere.*
braimneach, -eiche, *a.* Addicted to f—g.
†brain, *s.m.* Chieftain. 2 Naval commander, captain of a ship. 3 Front, beginning.
†brain, *s.f.* see broinn. 2 see brà.
†——, *a.* Big, bulky. 2 Abundant, extensive.
†——each, -eich, *s.m.* see brain.
†——each, -eiche, *a.* see brain.
braineach,** -nich, *s.m.* Prow of a ship.
brainn, branna, (*for* broinn) see brù. 2* Bulging.
†brais, -e, *a.* see bras. 2‡‡ Jocose. 3 *rarely* Fabulous, inventive.
brais,* *s.f.* Fit, convulsion. Tha na braisean tric, *the fits return often.*
bràisd, see bràist.
bràisdeach, see bràisteach.
braise, *s.f.ind.* Rashness, boldness, impetuosity, fervour, ardour. 2 Wantonness. 3 Rapidity. 4‡‡Fit of sickness. see braisead. *B.* fola is feòla, (*lit.* heat of blood and flesh) *youthful impetuosity.*
braiseachd, see braise.
braisead, -eid, *s. f.* Degree of forwardness, boldness, rashness, impetuousness, fervour, ardour, wantonness. 2 Rapidity.
†braiseagnach, *s.f.* Unjust accusation.
braisealachd, *s.f.ind.* see braisead.
braiseil, -e, *a.* Keen, bold, fervid, impetuous, forward.
braiseineachd, see braisead.
bràisiche,(JM) *s.m.* A man of 60 or 70 years of age. I have heard a young woman in Lewis asking for her father of another person say, "am faca tu am braisiche againn?"
braisionlach,† see braiseagnach.
braisleach, *s.m.* †Full-formed, bulky man. 2 Fat middle-aged man.
†braislead, *s.f.* Gaelic spelling of *bracelet.*
brais-sgeul, -eoil, *s.m.* Feigned narrative, fable, romance.
bràist, -e, *pl.* -ean & -eachan, *s.f.* Brooch. 2** Bracelet. (see illust. 67.)
——each,†† *a.* Abounding in brooches, pertaining to a brooch.
——eachan, -ain, -an, *s.m.* Little brooch.
braistich, *v.a.* Brooch.
†braith, *v.a.* Inspect, oversee.
bràith-bheartach, -aiche, *a.* Vain-glorious, conceited.
†braithcheam, *s.m.* Stag. 2 Wild ox.
braithean, *pl.* of brath.
†braitheoir, *s.m.* Overseer, inspector.

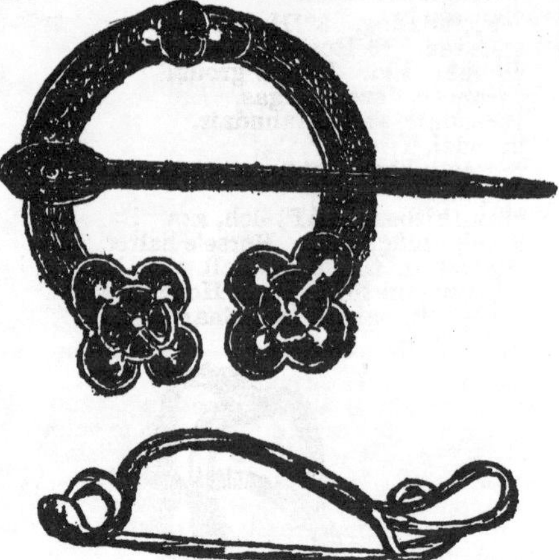

67. Bràistean Gàidhealach.

braith-lìn, *s.f.* Linen sheet, linen cloth.
braithlis, -e, see brailis.
bràithre, *pl.* of bràthair.
——achas, -ais, *s.m.* Brotherhood. 2 Partnership. Cha bhi bràithreachas mu mhnaoi no mu fhearann, *there is no partnership in women or land.*
——achd, see bràithrealachd.
†——ag -eig, *s.f.* Paternal aunt.
——alachd, *s.f.* Brotherhood, brotherly attachment, brotherliness, fraternity, unanimity, harmony.
——an, *pl.* of bràthair.
——ich,(DU) *v.a.* Admit to brotherhood (e.g. masonic.) Tha e air a bhràithreachadh, *he has been admitted a brother craftsman.*
——il, -e, *a.* Brotherly. 2 Affectionate. Gràdh bràithreil, *brotherly love;* agus nach do chuimhnich iad an coimh-cheangal bràithreil, *and that they have not remembered the brotherly contract.*
brallach, (AF) *s.m.* Shell-fish.
bram, see braim.
brama, *gen. sing.* of braim.
brama, *a.* Unpolite, uncivilized, boorish. 2‡‡ Unlucky.
bramach, -aich, see bromach.
bramadaich, *s.f.ind.* State of being swelling, blowing up. 2 Repletion.
bramair,** *s.m.* Flatulent fellow, one addicted to f—g. 2 Unpolished fellow, noisy fellow, boor.
braman,‡ -ain, *s.m.* Misadventure. 2 The Devil. 3**Crupper. 4**Croup.
——ach, *a.* see brama.
——ach, -aich, *s. m.* Noisy fellow, boorish fellow.
——achd,** *s.f.ind.* Noisiness, boorishness. 2 Sulkiness.
——nan, *pl.* of braim.
——ta,** *a.* Boorish, unpolished. 2 Sulky.
bramartaich, *s.f.* Frequent f—g, habit of f—g.
bramasag, -aig, -an, *s.f.* Prickly head of a thistle (burdock.) 2‡Cloth-burr. 3 Flatulence. 4 Disaster, betokened by eating the first bread of the season without butter.
bramsag, see bramasag.
†bran, *a.* Poor. 2 Black.
Bran, -ain, *s.m.* Mountain stream, name of several rivers in the Highlands. 2 Name of

Fionn's dog. 3**Husks of corn, bràn. †4 Raven. †5 Rook.
†branar, s.m. Fallow ground.
†brancas, see brangas.
†brandair, see branndair.
brandal, " "
††brandubhan, -ain, s.m. Spider's web. 2(AF) Spider.
bran-fhitheach,(AF) -ich, s.m. Raven. 2 Rook.
brang, -aing, s.m. Horse's halter. 2‡ Slip of wood in the head-stall of a horse's halter resting on the jaw. 3 Horse's collar.
———ach, -aiche, a. Snarling, growling. 2 Grinning.

68. *Brangas.*

———as, -ais, s.m. Scold's bridle, used for scolding women in the old days. [It was made of iron, came down over the nose in front and kept their chins from wagging.] 2 Padlock. 3‡‡Halter.
†bran-ghàire, s.m. Corpse left in the open air.
brangus, see brangas.
†brann, -ainn, s.m. Firebrand, burning coal 2 Woman.
branna, *gen.* of brainn, (*for* bronn) see brù.
———ch, a. see bronnach.
———ch, s.f. see bronnach.
———ire, s.m. see bronnaire.
†brannamh, -aimh, s.m. Coat of mail. 2‡‡ Chess-man.
branndaidh, s.f. Gaelic spelling of *brandy*. Is mairg a dh'òladh branndaidh ! *pity him who would drink brandy ! (instead of whisky.)*
branndair, -e, -ean, s.m. Gridiron.
———each,†† a. Pertaining to a gridiron, abounding in gridirons.
brannduidh, see branndaidh.
†brannrach, -aich, s.m. Border of a country. 2 ‡‡Pen, fold.
†brannradh, s.m. Trivet, pot.
†brannumh, see †brannamh.
branorgain, (AF) s.m. Raven. 2 Crow.
†braoch, s.m. Confines or border of a country.
braodag,(CR) s.f. Huff. Ghabh e braodag, *he took the huff.*
braodhlach, -aich, see braoilich.
braoghal, -il, s.m. see breitheal.
———aich, s.f.ind. see braoilich.
†braoi, s.pl. Eyebrows.
braoidhlich,†† see braoilich.
†braoighill, v.n. Crack, crumble.
†———e, s.f. Crack, flaw. 2 Heavy shower.
braoileadh, -eidh, -ean, s. m. Great noise, bounce. 2‡‡Furious burst of indignation. 3 ‡‡Crack, flaw.
braoileag, -eig, -an, s.f. Whortleberry. 2 Bilberry. 3 Cranberry—*Lochaber.* 4 Called by Cameron(?) lus-nam-braoileag, which see. 5 Small pieces of dried peat—*Argyll.*
———ach, a. Abounding in whortleberries, &c. Do leacan b., *thy rocks abounding in whortleberries.*
———an, *pl.* of braoileag.
——— -nan-con,** -eig-, -an-, s.f. Red bearberry,? see grainnseag. 2**Dogberry, see caor-chon.
braoilich, s.f. Loud noise, rattling sound. 2 Violent burst of indignation. Ciod a' bhraoilich a tha 'n sud ? *what noise is that ?* ciod a' bh. a th' ort ? *why do you make such a noise ?*
braoim, see braim.
braoisg, -e, s.f. Grin, gape. 2 Distortion of the mouth, as in contempt. 3 *Yawn. Chuir e b. air, *he grinned.*
braoisgeach, -eiche, a. Grinning, gaping. 2 Toothless. 3 Broken-edged. 4** Having a a distorted mouth. Fear braoisgeach, *a man with a distorted mouth ;* a bhodaich bhraoisgich! *you grinning old man !* an claidheamh braoisgeach, *the broken-edged sword.*
———,* s.f. Female with broken teeth. 2 Grinning female.
braoisgean, -ein, s.m. Toothless person. 2 One who grins. 3 One with a distorted mouth.
———achd. s.f. Habit of grinning.
braoisgeil, s.f.ind. Idiotic laughter. 2*Prattling.
braoisgire,* s.m. Grinning fellow. 2 One that distorts his mouth in contempt.
braolaid, -e, s.f. Raving, dreaming.
braon, -aoin, s.m. Drop. 2 Drizzle. 3 Rain. 4 Shower. 5 Dew. Gach braon d' a fhuil; *every drop of his blood ;* le braonaibh na h-oidhche, *with the drops of night ;* braon nan sion, *the drizzling of the blast;* bogha nam braon, *the rainbow,* (am bogha-braoin—*Perthshire.*)
braon, v.a. & n. Drop. 2 Distil. 3 Drizzle.
braonach, -aiche, a. Showery, drizzly, rainy, dewy, dropping. 'Sa mhadainn bhraonaich, *in the dewy morn ;* an duibhre braonach, *the dewy gloaming.*
———d, s.f. Continual drizzling, constant dropping, genial showers, showery weather.
braonan, -ain, s.m. The bud of a brier. 2 see braonan-bhuachaille.
———ach,†† a. Abounding in earth-nuts, of an earth-nut.
——— -bachlaig,? -ain-, s.m. Tormentil or potentil, see leamhnach. 2 Earth-nut, see braonan-bhuachaille.
——— -bhuachaille,§ -ain-, s.m. Earth-nut—*bunium flexuosum.*
——— -fraoich,? -ain-, s.m. Common tormentil, see leamhnach.
——— -nan-con, s. m. Dog-carmillion—*tormentilla erecta.*
braon-bogha,‡‡ -achan-, s.m. Rainbow.
——— -dhealt, s. f. Heavy dew. *B.* na maidne, *the heavy dew of morn.*
braos, -aois, see braoisg. †2 Prosperity, increase. †3 Lie, romance.
†——ach, -aiche, a. see braoisgeach.
——dail,** see braoisgeil.
braosgail, see braoisgeil.
bras, braise, a. Rash, impetuous. 2 Keen, active. 3 Bold, intrepid, daring. 4 Brisk, quick, sudden. 5 Hasty. 6 Wanton. 7 Inconsiderate. 8 Ardent, incautious. Bras le d' bheul, *rash with thy tongue (mouth) ;* each bras, *a mettlesome horse ;* bras bhuilleach, *ready in dealing blows ;* mar steud-shruth bras, *like an impetuous torrent ;* ag ràdh ri 'mhic bhrasa, *saying to his impetuous sons.*
†bras, s.f. Hat.
brasach,** a. Nimble, lively, sudden.
†bras-asgnaidhe,‡‡ s.m. Sophist.
brasailt, s.f. Panegyric. 2 Eulogy.
brasaire-bùird, s.m. Sycophant, one who subsists by flattery.
bras-bhuilleach, -eiche, a. Ready in dealing blows, quick in action, incautious.

bras-bhuinne, *s.f.* Torrent. 2 Strong current. 3 Stormy sea. 4 Whirlpool.
bras-chaoin, -e, *a.* Quick and pleasant.
†bras-chomadh, see †bras-chuma.
bras-chòmhrag, -aig, -an, *s.m.* Ardent fighting. 2 Tilts, tournaments.
†bras-chum, *v.a.* Counterfeit.
†———adh, *s.m.* Counterfeiting.
†bras-fhalt, *s.m.* Hair of the head.
brasgan, -ain, *s.m.* see prasgan.
bras-ghabhail, *s.f.* Quick burning.
bras-ghaille, see bras-ghalladh.
†bras-ghalladh, *s.m.* Declamation.
bras-ghallaimh, see bras-ghalladh.
bras-ghaoir, -e, *s f.* Quick loud noise.
†bras-ghruag, (cas-ghruag) *s.f.* Curled lock, curled hair.
brasguil, see brais-sgeul.
†bras-luidhe, *s.m.* Perjury. Luchd-bras-luidhe, *perjured persons.*
bras-sgeul, -sgeòil, see brais-sgeul.
bras-stròiceadh,‡‡ -eidh, *s.m.* Violent tearing.
†brat,** *s.m.* Judgment.
brat, *gen. sing.* -a, [& brait] *pl.* bratan, *s. m.* Covering, mantle, cloak. 2 Veil. 3 Coverlet, bed-cover, counterpane. 4**Blanket. 5 Curtain. 6*Hair-cloth for a kiln. 7 Apron—*Islay.* 8 Rag. Crochaidh tu am brat, *thou shalt hang the veil* ; agus ghabh iad brat, *and they took a garment* ; brat na h-oidhche, *the mantle of night.*
bratach, -aich, -aichean, *s. f.* Banner, flag, colours, ensign. Bratach shìth, *the fairy flag*, now in Dunvegan Castle, and said to have been brought by the parson of Harris from Constantinople at the time of the Crusades ; a' bhratach mhór aig rìgh nan lann, *the great banner of the king of swords*; bratach àlainn righ nam magh, *the beauteous banner of the king of the plains.*
———, *a.* see bradach.
———ag, -aig, -an, *s.f.* Banneret, pennant.
———ail,‡‡ -e, Bannered.
———d,** *s.f. ind.* Entertainment.
bratag, -aig, -agan, *s. f.* The rough or hairy caterpillar. 2**Rag. 3**Impudent girl. 4 **Canker.
———ach, -aiche, *a.* Abounding with hairy caterpillars.
bărataich, *v.a.* Kindle, rouse, ferment, excite.
brat-bròin, *s.m.* Mort-cloth.
brat-chasach,** *a.* Bow-legged.
brat-dhearg, *a.* Red-veiled, covered or decked with red.
brat-dìona, *s.m.* Awning.
brat-dubhar, *s.m.* Awning.
brat-falaich,* *s.m.* Cloak. 2**Blind man. Mar bhrat-falach do'n dall, *as a cloak for the blind.*
brat-gnùise, *s.m.* Veil for the face.
†brath, *s.m.* Residue, remnant. 2 Fragment.
brath, -a, *s.m.* Knowledge, notice, informing, information. 2 Treachery, advantage by unfair means, betraying, spying. 3 Treason. 4 **Spy. 5 Intention, design. 6 see bràth. 7 Pursuit of information. 7**Expectation. 8 Opinion, idea, guess. 9**Mass, lump. 10** Lie. 11**Dependance. 12 see brà. Am bheil brath aige ? *has he any information ? does he know ?* tha a mhiann air brath a dheanamh ort, *he means to betray you*, or *inform against you* ; ghabh e brath orm, *he took the advantage of me* ; bi air brath, *be in pursuit of information* ; am bheil brath agad c'àit' am bheil e ? *have you any idea where he is ?* 's ann a tha brath amadain agad air, *you take the advantage of him as though he were a fool* ; an d' fhuair thu a bhrath ? *did you get any information of him ?* 's ann aig Dia tha brath, *God alone knows* ; tha e air bhrath, *he is to be found* ; cha bhi am bàrd air bhrath, *the bard shall not be found* ; gun bhrath furtachd, *without expectation of relief* ; cia mar a gheibh sinn brath mar a dh'éireas dhuit ? *how shall we get information of what happens to you ?*
brath, *pr. part.* a' brathadh, *v. a.* Betray. 2 Deceive. 3 Spy. 4 Suppose, guess. 5 Inform against. 6**Design, intend. 7**Entertain an opinion. Brathaidh iad a chéile, *they shall betray one another* ; esan a bhrath e, *he that betrayed him;* a' brath tighinn, *intending to come ;* bha e a' brath mo bhualadh, *he was about to strike me.*
bràth, -a, *s. m.* Judgment. 2 Destruction. [The sense *conflagration* given in the dictionaries is due to Druidic theorisings and is imaginary.—‡] Gu là a' bhràth cha'n éirich Calum, *Malcolm shall not rise again till the day of judgment* ; na tréig mi gu buileach no gu bràth, *do not forsake me utterly nor for ever* ; seachd bliadhna roimh 'n bhràth thig a' mhuir air Eirinn ré aon-thràth, *seven years before the day of judgment the sea at one tide shall cover Ireland ;* cha ghluais e gu cruadal gu bràth, (pron. *gu bràch*) *he shall never move to the perils* (*of war.*)
bràth, *gen.sing.* bràthan, see brà.
bratha, *gen.sing.* of brath.
†brathach,‡*a.* Constant, continual.
brathadair, -ean, *s.m.* Betrayer, informer. 2 Knave. 3 Traitor. 4 Kindling, ††great fire. 5 Fuel.
brathadh, -aidh, *s.m.* Betraying, spying, informing. 2 Treachery. Luchd brathaidh, *spies*, A' b—, *pr.part.* of brath.
brathaidh, *fut.aff.a.* of brath. Shall betray, &c.
bràthair, *gen.* bràthar, *pl.* bràithrean, (& -re), *s.m.* Brother. Is lag gualainn gun bhràthair, *feeble is the arm of him who has no brother.*
——— -altruim, *s.m.* Foster-brother.
——— -athar, *s.m.* Paternal uncle. Bràthair m'athar, *my paternal uncle.*
——— -bochd, *s.m.* Friar. 2 Poor brother, lay-capuchin.
——— -céile, *s.m.* Brother-in-law, wife's or husband's brother.
——— -céirde,‡‡ *s.m.* Brother-craftsman.
———eachd, see bràithreileachd.
———eachas, } see bràithreachas.
———ealachd, }
———ean, *n.pl.* of bràthair.
———eil, -e, *a.* see bràithaireil.
——— -màthar, *s.m.* Maternal uncle. Bràthair mo mhàthar, *my maternal uncle.*
——— -mhort, *s.m.* Fratricide.
——— -suiridhe,‡‡ *s.m.* Rival lover.
bràthan, *gen.sing.* & *n. pl.* of brà.
bràthar, *gen. sing.* of bràthair.
bràth-cheò, *s.m*, Bewilderment. Chaidh e 'na bh., *he got bewildered.*
brath-foille, *s.m.* Intention of betraying. 2 Unfair dealing. 3 Unawares. 4*Disguise.
brath-gabhail, *s.m.* Consideration, forethought. 2(AH) Close application. 3(AH) Determined effort. An làn a' tighinn a staigh cho bras air na faodhlaichean gu'n robh feum air brath-gabhail mu'm faigheadh duine thairis orra, *the tide coming in so briskly upon the sandy hollows, that one had to exercise prompt deliberation in making his way over them.*
brath-lìn, see braith-lìn.
bràth-losgadh,‡‡ -aidh, *s.m.* Furious burning.
brat-laimh,** *s.f.* Hand-towel.
brat-leapach, *s. m.* Counterpane, bed-cover, quilt.

brat-lìn, see braith-lìn.
brat-nasg,‡‡ *s.m.* Brooch, skewer.
brat-roinn, *s.m.* Dividing cloth, partition veil.
brat-sgàile, see brat-gnùise.
brat-spèilidh, *s.m.* Swaddling-cloth.
brat-ùrlair, *s.m.* Carpet.
†**bratalian**,** Gaelic form of *battalion.*
†**bre**, *s.m.* Hill, headland.
breab, -a, -an, *s.m.* Kick. 2 Prance. 3 Spurn. 4 Start. 5(AM) Anger—*Reay Country.* Chuir e breab orm, *he made me angry* ; bhuail e breab air, *he gave him a kick.*
——, *v.a.* Kick. 2 Spurn. 3 Prance. 4 Stamp with the foot. 5 Reject. 6 Start.
——ach, -aiche, *a.* Apt to kick or prance. 2 Elastic. Each breabach, brògach, *a prancing strong-hoofed horse.*
——adaich, *s.f.ind.* Kicking. 2 Prancing, bounding. 3 Starting. 4 Stamping.
breabadair, -ean, *s.m.* Weaver. 2 One who kicks. [In Uist "breabadaireachd" was considered the lowest possible calling in which a man could take part. People seemed even ashamed to mention the word "breabadair." They used to say "breabadair, le cead na cuideachd," *(a weaver, with the company's permission)* ; breabadair nan casan loisgt', *the burnt-legged weaver (used as a term of contempt.)*
——eachd, *s.f.ind.* Trade of a weaver. 2 **Habit of kicking or stamping.
——ean, *n.pl.* of breabadair.
breabadh, -aidh, *s.m.* Kick, kicking. 2 Prancing, prance. 3 Bounding. 4 Starting. 5 Stamping, stamp of the foot. 6**Spurning. A' b—, *pr. pt.* of breab.
breabail, -e, *s.f.* Kicking. 2 Prancing. 3 Spurning. 4 Stamping. 5 Gurgling noise. Tha na sruthan ri breabail, *the streamlets are gurgling.*
breabain, *gen.sing.* of breaban.
breabair,
—— -smògach, } (AF) *s.m.* Spider.
breaban, -ain, -an, *s. m.* Piece on a shoe-sole. 2 Heel-piece—*Islay.* 3‡‡ Patch on the sole within. 4‡‡Any small piece of leather. 5** Patch on tip of a shoe. 6(DU) Any patch hanging on to, or connected with anything. Di-luain a' bhreabain, *the Monday of chastisement,* when boys were whacked with the sole of a shoe. They were very apt to get into mischief on Sunday, and their parents did not like to chastise them till Monday.
breabanach, -aiche, *a.* Kicking. 2 Prancing. 3 Abounding in shoe-patches. 4‡‡Spurning. 5 Jerking.
——d,‡‡ *s.f.* Botchery.
breabanaiche, -ean, *s. m.* Shoe-maker. 2 Cobbler.
breaban-deiridh,‡‡ *s.m.* Heel-piece for a shoe.
—— -toisich, *s.m.* Fore-sole for a shoe.
breabartaich,** *s.f.* Jerking. 2 Kicking. 3 Prancing. 4 Spurning.
breac, brice, *a.* Spotted, speckled, chequered, piebald. 2 Marked with small-pox. Breac le neòineanaibh, *chequered with daisies* ; each breac, *a piebald horse* ; bò bhreac, *a piebald cow* ; fear breac, *a man pitted with the small-pox* ; cù breac, *a spotted dog.*
breac, bric, *s.m.* Trout. 2 Salmon-trout. 3** Salmon. 4***rarely* Badger. 5 **Wolf.
breac, brice, *s.f.* The small-pox. [Preceded by the article *a'* (*bh*—)] 2**Any spotted appearance.
breac, *pr.pt.* a' breacadh, *v.a.* Carve. 2 Chequer. 3 Speckle. 4 Embroider. 5 Set or pick a millstone. 6 Engrave. 7 Cover with devices. 8‡‡Mix. 9‡‡ Cover with freckles. 10 (DU) Cut turf with a spade preparatory to turning the sod.
——ach,‡‡ -aich, *s.m.* Art or act of fishing for trout.
——ach, -aiche, *a.* Abounding in trout. 2 Pock-marked.
breac-a'-chruidh, *s.f.* ‖Vaccination. 2 Cow-pox.
breacadan-buidhe-nan-allt,(CR) *s. m.* Yellow wagtail—*West of Ross.* see breacan-buidhe.
breacadh, -aidh, *s.m.* Spotting, chequering. 2 Carving. 3 Engraving. 4 Embroidering, ornamenting. 5 Picking a mill-stone. 6 Getting freckled. 7 Getting black and white. 8(DU) Breaking the surface of the ground with any sharp instrument. A' b—, *pr.part.* of breac.
—— -muiltein, see breac-a'-mhuiltein.
—— -rionnaich, *s.m.* Dappled sky.
—— -seunain, see breac-sheunain.
—— -sianain, see breac-sheunain.
—— -teine, *s.m.* Shin freckles.
breacag, -aig, -an, *s.f.* Small thin cake. 2 Scone. 3 Pancake. Breacagan neo-ghoirtichte, *unleavened cakes.*
breacaich, *v.a.* Carve. 2 Engrave. 3**Bedrop. 6**Spot, chequer.
——te, *past pt.* Mixed. 2 Chequered, spotted. 3 Carved. 4 Engraved.
breacain, *gen.sing. & n. pl.* of breacan.
breacair, -e, -ean, *s.m.* Graver (engraving tool.) 2 Engraver (person.)
——eachd, *s.f.* Employment of an engraver. 2 Chequering, chequer work.
breac-a'-mheanaidh,‡‡ *s.f.* Freckles on the face.
breac-a'-mhuilinn, see breac-a'-mhuiltein.

69. *Breac-a'-mhuiltein.*

breac-a'-mhuiltein, *s.m.* Dappled sky, kind of clouds known as *cirro-cumulus.*
breacan, -ain, *pl.* -an, [& **-ain] *s.m.* Highland plaid. 2 Tartan. Parti-coloured cloth was used by the Celts from the earliest times but the variety of colours in the *breacan* was greater or less, according to the rank of the wearer. That of the ancient kings had seven colours, that of the druids six, and that of the nobles four. In the days of Martin the tartans seemed to be used to distinguish the inhabitants of different districts, and not the members of different families as at present. He expressly says that the inhabitants of the various islands were not all dressed alike, but that the setts and colours of the various tartans varied from isle to isle. As he does not mention the use of a special pattern by each family, it would appear that such a distinction is a modern one, and taken from the ancient custom of a tartan for each district, the family or clan originally most numerous in each part eventually adopting as their distinctive clan tartan the tartan of such district. Martin's information was not obtained on hearsay, he was born in Skye and reared in the midst of Highland customs.
breacanach, *a.* Tartan. 2 Plaided. Aodach breacanach, *tartan clothes.*
breacan-an-fhèilidh, *s.m.* Belted plaid. This

70. *Breacan singilte mu dhuine* 70. *Breacan dùbailt uime.*

is the original garb of the Highlanders, and formed the chief part of their costume. The *breacan* in its simple form is now seldom used. It consisted of a plain piece of tartan, two yards in width, and four or six in length. In dressing, this was carefully plaited in the middle, of a breadth suitable to the size of the wearer, and sufficient to extend from one side around his back to the other, leaving as much at each end as would cover the front of the body, overlapping each other. The plaid being thus prepared, was firmly bound round the loins with a leathern belt, in such a manner that the lower side fell down to the middle of the knee-joint and then, while there were the foldings behind, the cloth was double in front. The upper part was then fastened on the left shoulder with a large brooch or pin, so as to display to the best advantage the tastefulness of the arrangement, the two ends being sometimes suffered to hang down, but that on the right side, which was necessarily the longer, was more usually tucked under the belt.—*Logan.*

breacanach, *a.* Plaided, dressed in plaids or tartans.

breac-an-anmoich, *adv.* Rather late, latish.

71. *Breacan-baintighearna.*

breacan-baintighearna,¶ *s.m.* Grey wagtail—*motacilla boarula.*

breacan-beithe,¶ *s.m.* Chaffinch—*fringilla cœlebs.* 2 Linnet (McL & D.) 3AF Green lint white. 4††Species of grass.

72. *Breacan-beithe.*

73. *Breacan-buidhe.*

breacan-buidhe,¶ *s.m.* Yellow wagtail—*motacilla flava.* 2(AF) White, grey, or pied wagtail, see breac-an-t-sìl.

74. *Breacan-glas.*

breacan-glas,¶ *s.m.* Spotted fly-catcher—*muscicapa grisola.*

breacan-sgiobalt,¶ *s.m.* Spotted fly-catcher, see breacan-glas.

75. *Breac-an-t-sìl.*

breac-an-t-sìl,¶ *s.m.* White, grey, or pied wagtail,—*motacilla Yarrelii.* 2 Chaffinch (McL & D., 2nd. Part.)

breacarsaich,* *s.f.* Twilight. 2 Middle state, especially of health.

breac-beachdaidh, see breac-beadaidh.

76. *Breac-beadaidh.*

breac-beadaidh, *s.m.* Loach.

breac-bhallach, -aich, *a.* Spotted, speckled.

breac-bhoiceannach,* *s. f.* Herpes, shingles.—*Bute, Cowal & Lochfyneside.*

breac-ceanndac,(AF) *s.m.* Turbot.

breac-chreideamh, *s.m.* Mixed religion.
breac-deamhainn, *s. m.* —*Islay*, see bioran-deamhnaidh.
breac-dhearg, *a.* Spotted with red and some other colour. An tarbh breac-dhearg, *the red and white bull.*

17. Breac-feusagach.

breac-feusagach, *s.m.* Barbel.
breac-fhrangach, *s.f.* The venereal, pox. [Preceded by the article a' (*bh*—.)
breac-geal, *s.m.* Salmon-trout.
†breachaoidh, *s.* Indifference.
†breachd, *s.m.* Doubt.
†breachdan, *s.m.* Wheat. 2 Custard. 3 Fresh butter. 4**Fresh meat. 5 see breacan.
breac-iteach,-eiche, *a.* Having spotted feathers. Glacagan nan eun breac-iteach, *the dells of the spotted birds.*
breac-iteag,** -eig, *s.f.* Spotted or speckled feather.
breac-laogh, -aoigh, *s.m.* Fawn. 2 Speckled calf.
————ach, *a.* Abounding in fawns or spotted calves.
breac-liath, *a.* Greyish.
breac-lion, -lin, -liontan [& **-liontaichean] Trout-net. 2 Drag-net. 3 Landing-net.
breac-luirgneach, *a.* Shin-freckled.
breac-mhac,(AF) Magpie, see pioghaid.
breac-mhara, (AF) *s.m.* Mackerel. 2 Roach.
breac-mhuc, *s.m.* Magpie, see pioghaid.
breac-mhuilinn,** see breac-a'-mhuiltein.
breacnachadh, -aidh, *s.m.* Chequering, spotting. 2 Mingling. 3 Embroidery. 4 Variegating. A' b—, *pr.pt.* of breacnaich.
breacnaich, *pr.part.* a' breacnachadh, *v.a.* Chequer. 2 Mix. 3 Make spotted. 4 Embroider.
————te, *a., & past pt.* of breacnaich. Chequered. 2 Made spotted. 3 Parti-coloured. 4 Embroidered.
breac-nam-bò,* *s.f.* Cow-pox.
breac-òtraich,‖ *s.f.* Chicken-pox. [Preceded by the article *a'*.]
breac-rionnaich, see breacadh-rionnaich.
breac-seunain, see breac-sheunain.
breac-shean, *a.* Oldish.
breac-sheunain,‖ *s.f.* Freckles. [Preceded by the article *a'*.]
breac-shìth, *s.f.* ‖Chicken-pox. 2 Nettle-rash. 3 Livid spots on the skin of a dying person, 4 Hives (McL & D.) [Preceded by the article *a'*.]
breac-shoillsich, *v. n,* Shine faintly. 2 Glimmer as the twilight.
breac-sholus, -uis, *s.m.* Twilight. 2**Daybreak. 3‡‡Glimmer.
breacta, *past pt.* of breac. Spotted, chequered. 2 Embroidered. 3 Carved. 4 Picked, as a mill-stone.
†breac-ughach,‡‡ *a.* Full of spotted eggs.
breacuich, see breacaich.
†bread, -eid, *s.m.* Breach.
†breadh, see brèagh.
————achd, see brèaghachd.
————as, see brèaghad.
brèag, -eig, *s.f., & v.* see breug.
————ach, -aiche, *a.* see breugach.
————adair, *s.m.* see breugadair.
†brèagadh, see breugadh.
brèagag, see breugag.
brèagaire, -e, -ean, *s.m.* breugaire.
brèagan, see breugan.
†brèagarsaidh, *s.f.* Imagination.
brèag-chràbhadh, *s.m.* see breug-chràbhadh.
brèagh, -a, *a.* Fine. 2 Well-dressed. 3 Splendid. 4 Good-looking. 5 Pretty. 6 Beautiful. 7 Surprising. 8 Showy. 9 Pleasant. 10 Specious. Nighean bhrèagh, *a handsome young woman;* là brèagh, *a fine day;* is brèagh nach d'thàinig thu dhachaidh an àm, *it is surprising you did not come home in time* ; gu brèagh anmoch, *pretty late in the evening*; cia brèagh a snuadh ! *how splendid her appearance !* 'nuair a labhras e gu brèagh, *when he speaks fair* ; trì nithean brèagha : long fo sheòl, craobh fo bhlàth, duine naomh air leabaidh a bhàis, *three beautiful things : a ship under sail, a tree in bloom, a holy man on his death-bed.*
————achd, *s.f.* Finery. 2 Prettiness. 3 Ornament. 4 Showiness. 5 Elegance. 6** Speciousness. A bhrèaghachd, *his ornaments.*
brèaghad, -aid, *s.m.* Beauty. 2 Attire. 3 Ornament. 4 Finery. 5**Showiness.
————aich, *v.a.* Adorn, ornament, embellish. 2 Accomplish.
————aichte,** *past pt.* Accomplished.
†breaghaidh, *s.m.* Enthusiast.
brèaghas, -ais, *s.m.* Finery, ornaments, showiness, gaudiness.
†breaghaslach,** -aich, *s.m.* see breisleach.
†breaghaslaich, see breislich.
brèaghchaid,* *s. f.* Degree of beauty. 2 Superiority in beauty.
†breag-luigh, *v.n.* Forswear, perjure.
†breagnuich, *v.a.* see breugnaich.
brèaghoire, see breugaire.
†breall, -eill, *s.m.* Knob. 2 Knob at either end of the sticks of a flail. 3‡Glans mentulæ. 3**Phymosis.
breallach,(AF) *s.m.* Small hose-fish. 2 (AM) Large cockle-shell.
breallach,** *a.* Having a phymosis, of, or relating to a phymosis.
breallan,** -ain, *s.m.* Vessel.
————-dubh,‡ *s.m.* Crowberry, see lus-na-flonnaig.
breamain, *gen.sing. & n. pl.* of breaman.
breaman, -ain, -an, *s.m.* Tail of a sheep or goat. 2 Backside, rump. 3* Train. Barr a' bhreamain, *the tip of the tail.*
————ach, -aiche, *a.* Tailed. 2 Like a tail. 3 Of, or belonging to a tail or train.
———— -fuilteach,‖ *s.m.* Piles.
breamas, -ais, *s.m.* Mischief. 2 Mishap, mischance. 3 Fatality. 4‡The Devil. 5*Blunder. Dh'éirich am breamas dhuit, *mischief has happened to you* ; cha leighis aithreach,

as breamas, *repentance cannot remedy a blunder*; ri breamas, *at mischief.*
breamasach, -aiche, *a.* Unfortunate, unlucky. 2 Fatal. 3 Ruinous. 4 Bungling, blundering.
————d, *s.f.* Fatality. 2 Misfortune. 3 Unfortunate state or condition. 4**Liability to mischance.
breamasag, see bramasag.
brèan, -ein, *s.* & *a.* see breun.
brèanach, brèanadh, brèanan, } see breun—.
†breangal, see brionglaid.
brèantag, brèantas, } see breun—.
†breas, *s.m.* Prince. 2**King. 3 Potentate. 4 Voice. 5 Loud noise, sound.
†——, *v.a.* Reign.
breas, *a.* Illustrious, eminent, great.
——ail,** *a.* Princely, mighty.
†breas-aontaidh, *s.m* The royal assent.
†breas-chathair,-thrach,-thraichean,*s.f.*Throne.
†breas-cholbh, -an, *s.m.* Sceptre.
†breasda, *a.* Principal. 2 Quick. 3 Lively, smart.
†breaslang,** *s.m.* Deceit.
†breas-lann, -ainn, *s.f.* Palace. 2 Court of justice.
†breas-oirchiste, *s.f.* Royal treasury.
†breas-ròd, *s.m.* King's road. Cha'n 'eil breasròd gu cò-mheas, *there is no royal road to (easy way to learn) geometry.*
breath, -an, *s.f.* Row, rank, layer, stratum. 2 Flake. 3 Also used for *breith.* 4**Couch. Tri breathan, *three rows.*
†breath,** *a.* Clean, pure, bright. 2 Innocent.
breathach, *a.* In ranks, in rows. 2**Judicial, critical. 3 see breitheach.
breathal, -ail, *s.m.* see breitheal.
————ach, *a.* see breithealach.
————aich, *v.a.* see breithealaich.
breathamh, see breitheamh.
breathanas,* *s.m.* see breitheanas.
breathas,* -ais, *s.m.* Frenzy, extreme fury, flaming wrath. 2††Infatuation. Tha e air bhreathas, *he is frantic*; tha breathas a' chuthaich air, *he is in a frenzy.*
breathnach,** *a.* Judiciary.
————adh,* *s.m.* see breithneachadh.
breathnaich,* *v.a.* see breithnich.
†breathnas, *s.m.* Bodkin, skewer. 2 Clasp. 3 Tongue of a buckle.
breice,** (breac) *s.f.* Spots, spottedness, maculation. A bhreice, *his (the leopard's) spottedness.*
†breichneoras, *s.m.* Sculpture.
brèid,* *v.a.* Spread peats—*North High's.* 2‡‡ Wear or deck with the *brèid*, or matron's badge. 3‡‡Patch.
——, -e, -ean, *s.m.* Kerchief, napkin. 2 Sail. 3 Patch, piece of cloth of any kind. 4 Woman's head-dress, consisting of a square of fine linen pinned round the head, and fastened with cords of silk or pins of silver or gold, donned by a woman the morning after her marriage, and regarded as the badge of wifehood. 5(DU) Rag, clout.
brèid-air-tòin, *s.f.* Hen-harrier, ring-tail hawk, mouse-hawk.—*circus cyaneus.*
brèid-an-crannaig,AC *s.m.* "Kertch on props."
brèid bàn,AC *s.m.* White kertch.
brèid beannach,(AC) *s.m.* "Pinnacled kertch."
brèid-broige,‡‡ *s.m.* Shoe-patch.
brèid-bronn, *s.m.* Apron.
brèid-cuailein,AC *s.m.* Hair kertch.
brèid cuimir nan crùn,AC *s.m.* Shapely kertch of the crowns. Brèid cuimir nan tri crùin, *the shapely kertch of the three crowns.*
brèideach, -eiche, *a.* Like a kerchief. 2 Ragged, tattered. 3‡‡Of, or belonging to cloth of any kind. 4**Like a woman's head-dress. 5**White-spreading. Ar siùil *bh.*, *our white-spreading sails.*
————, -ich, *s.f.* (*lit.* woman with the *brèid*) Married woman, matron. Bha mi 'nam bhrèidich, 'nam ghruagaich is 'nam bhantraich 'san aon àm, *I was a married woman, a virgin and a widow at the same time.*
brèideachag,AC see brèideag.
brèideadh, -eidh, *s.m.* Dressing of the head. 2 Attiring, clothing. 3 Adjusting the badge of matron. 4 Patching.
brèideag, AC *s.f.* (*lit.* Little woman of the *brèid*) Wifie.
brèidean, -ein, -einean, *s.m.* Little rag. 2 Clout 3 Coif. 4 Web of frieze.
brèidean, *n.pl.* of brèid.
brèidear,‡‡ -eir, -an, *s.m.* Botcher.
brèid geal, *s.m.* White head-dress.
brèid-gheal, -ile, *a.* White-sailed. 2 Having a white handkerchief or napkin. Boirionnach *b.*, *a female with a white head-dress*; luingeas brèid-gheal, crannach, *a white-sailed, high-masted ship.*
brèidich, *v.a.* Patch.
brèid-shoithichean, *s.m.* Dish-clout.
brèid-uchd, *s.m.* Stomacher. 2 Bib.
†breife, †breifne, } ‡‡*s.* Finger-, or-toe-nail. 2 Hole.
†breifneach, *a.* Full of holes.
†————, *s.m.* Rustic, boor.
brèig, *s.f.* ——, *v.a.* } see breug.
†——, *s.m.* Rustic, boor.
brèig-chiabh, see breug-chiabh.
——————adair, -e, -ean, see breug-ch——.
brèige, *gen.sing.* of breug. Beul na brèige, *the lying mouth.*
brèige, *s.f.* see breug.
†breigeadh, -eidh, *s.m.* Violating, abusing.
brèig-fhios, -a, *s.m.* see breug-fhios.
——————ach, *a.* see breug-fhiosach.
†brèignich, *s.m.* Fiction.
brèig-riochdaich, see breug-riochdaich.
†breileach, see braoilich.
†breileadh, see braoileadh.
breill, *gen.sing.* of breall.
breilleis, *s.f.* Delirium, raving.
————each, *a.* Delirious. 2 Causing delirium.
————eachd, *s.f.* Deliriousness. 2 Liability to delirium. 3 Giddiness.
breim, see braim.
brèin, *gen.sing.* of breun.
brèine, *comp.* of breun.
——,* *s.f.* Turbulence, turbulent disposition. 3**Stink. Thig a bhrèine a nios, *his stink shall ascend.*
brèineachd, see breunachd.
brèinead, see breunad.
brèineag, see breunag.
brèinean, see breunan.
———— -brothach, -aich, *s.m.* Ox-eye, see neòinean mór. [Preceded by the article *an.*]
brèinid, see breunaid.
†breis, *s.f.* Tear. 2‡‡Distilling.
†breis, *v.a.* see bris.
breiseachan,** -ain, *s.m.* Still.
†breisg, see brisg.
†————te, *a.* Moved, provoked.
†breisi, *a.* Dropping.
†breisim, *s.f.* War-cry.
breisleach, -ich, *s.m.* Dream. 2 Abashment. 3 Confusion. 4‖Delirium, raving. 5‡Nightmare. Chuir e 'm breislich mi, *he quite confounded*

me ; chaidh mi a'm bhreislich, *I was confounded.*
breisleachadh, -aidh, see breisleach.
————ail, -e, *a.* Confusing. 2 Delirious. 3 Causing delirium.
breislich, *pr. pt.* a' breisleachadh, *v.n.* Rave, talk irrationally. 2 Confuse, confound.
†breismion, *s.m.* Writ, mandamus, royal mandate.
breith, *s. f.* Judgment, sentence, decision. 2 Row, rank. 3 Layer. 4 Birth, descent. 5 Interpretation, signification. 6 Bearing, carrying. 7 Penance. 8 Overtaking. 9** Opinion. 10** Censure. 11** Confidence. Breith air a' phobull bheir thu, *thou shalt judge the people* ; tha Dia ann a tha 'toirt breith air an talamh, *there is a God that judgeth the earth* ; na h-aingidh anns a' bhreith, *the wicked in judgment*; ciod is breith de 'm bhruadair ? *what is the interpretation of my dream ?* thoir breith air mo bhruadair, *interpret my dream* ; a' dol air seacharan o 'm breith, *going astray from their birth* ; o bhreith gu bàs, *from birth to death* ; bithidh breith luath lochdach, *a hasty or faulty judgment will be hurtful.*
breith, (*i.e.* thoir breith) *v.n.* Judge, sentence.
breith (a') *pr.part.* of beir. A' breith air làimh orm, *seizing me by the hand ;* cha b' fhad' bha sinn a' breith orra, *we soon overtook them* ; a' breith air a chéile, *seizing each other* ; tha i a' breith cloinne, *she is bearing children* ; a' breith ughean, *laying eggs* ; a' breith searraich, *casting a foal*; a' breith laoigh, *calving*; a' breith uain, *yeaning* ; a' breith uircean, *farrowing ;* a' breith chuileanan, *whelping*; a' breith phiseag, *kittening.* [For additional examples see under *beir.*]
breith-air-eiginn,†† *s.m.* Violence, deforcement. rapine. 2*Child scarcely alive when born.
breith-buidheachais, *s. f.* Thanksgiving. Agus air *b., and after giving thanks.*
breith-dhìtidh,***s.f.*Sentence of condemnation.
breith-dhligheachd,‡‡ *s.f.* Legitimacy.
breitheach, *a.* Judicial, critical. 2 Exact, accurate.
breitheadaireachd, *s.f.* Interpretation, as of dreams, &c.
breitheal, -il, *s.m.* Confusion, as of mind. 2 Astonishment. 3*Delirium, raving. 4**Terror. 5**Turmoil.
breithealach, *a.* Causing confusion. 2 Apt to be confused. 3 Causing terror.
breithealaich, *v.n.* Hurry. 2 Confuse the mind.
————,** *s.f.* Confusion of mind, flurry.
breitheamh, -eimh, *pl.* -a -an & -nan, *s.m.* Judge. 2 Umpire. 2**Judgment, decision, sentence (more usually *breitheanas.*) Nach dean breitheamh na talmhainn uile ceartas ? *shall not the judge of all the earth do right ?*
breitheamhnas, see breitheanas.
breitheanas, -ais, -an, *s.f.* Judgment, decision, sentence. 2 Faculty of judging. 3 Sudden calamity. Thàinig breathanas ort, *a judgment came upon you*; is fìrinn breitheanais an Tighearna, *the judgments of the Lord are true*; là a' bhreitheanais, *the day of judgment.*
breitheanasach, *a.* Retributive, as a just judgment.
breitheantach, -aiche, *a.* Judicious, prudent. 2 Skilful. 3 Judicial.
breith-fhéillteachd, *s.f.* Birthday solemnity.
†breithiontair, *s.m.* Fuller.
breith-là, -làithean, *s.m.* Birthday.
breithneach, *a.* Imaginative.
breithneachadh, -aidh, *s.m.* Apprehension. 2 Conception, imagination. 3** Way of thinking, idea. 4‡‡Art or faculty of judging. 5‡‡Interpretation. *B.* aisling, *the interpretation of a dream*; a dh' aon bhreithneachadh, *of one way of thinking.*
breithnich, *pr.part.* a' breithneachadh, *v.a.&n.* Conceive, apprehend, imagine, suppose. 2 Judge, opine. 3††Interpret, explain.
breith-réite, *s.f.* Arbitration.
—— -thabhairteach,‡‡ -eiche, *a.* Judicatory.
breitich, *v.n.* Swear.
†breitireachd, *s.f.* Interpretation.
breo, *v.n.* see breoth.
†breò, *s.m.* Fire, flame. †*a.* see brèagh.
breoc,* *v.a.* Patch.
breocaich, *v.a.* Botch, patch.
breòcail, *pr.part.* a' breòcladh, *v. a.* Patch, put together.
†breoch, *s.m.* see bruach.
breòchaid, -e, -ean, *s.f.* Any fragile, tender, or brittle thing.
breochail, (a') AC *pr.part.* Drivelling.
breòchdail, see breòcail.
breòchdlair,†† see breòclair.
breò-chlach, *s.f.* Flint.
breò-choire, *s.m.* Warming-pan.
breò-chual, *s.f.* Funeral pile, bonfire.
breòcladh, -aidh, *s.m.* Clumsy patching. A' b—, *pr.pt.* of breòcail.
breòclaid,‡ *s.f.* Sickly person.
breòclair, -e, -ean,*s.m.* Mender,botcher,patcher.
breodh, see breoth.
———adh, see breothadh.
breò-dhruidheachd, *s.f.* Pyromancy.
breòg, -òig, *s.f.* Leveret.
†breòg, *a.* Feeble, weak, sickly.
†breòg, *v.a.* Pound, bruise. 2 Bake.
†breògach, -aich, -aichean, *s.m.* Baker.
†breògadh, -aidh, *s. m.* Crushing, bruising, pounding.
breògh, *v.n.* see breòth.
†breòghas, see brìoghas.
†breòghasach, see brìoghasach.
breòig,(AH) *s.f.* Feeble, weak, sickly person. 2 Fragile vessel of any description.
breòillean, -ein, *s.m.* Darnel, rye-grass—*lolium perenne* and *temulentum.*
breòilleanach, *a.* Abounding in darnel or rye-grass. 2 Like darnel or rye-grass.
breòinn, (AF) *s.* Cat.
breòite, *a.* Infirm, frail, weak, feeble, sickly, tender. 2**Slender. 3**Bruised. 4‡‡Rotten, putrid. Ged tha mi breòite, *though I be infirm* ; tha mi breòite, tinn, *I am weak and sickly.*
breòiteachd, *s.f.* Infirmity, frailty, weakness, debility. 2 Sickliness. 3**Slenderness. 4‡‡ Rottenness.
breòlaid, -e, -ean, *s.f.* Dotage. 2 ‖Debility. 3 Delirium.
breòlaideach, -eiche, *a.* Delirious, raving. 2 Doting.
breòlamas,‡‡ -ais, *s.m.* Confusion.
†breòn, -òin, *s.m.* Blemish, blur, spot.
†———, *v.a.* Blur, spot, stain. 2 Efface.
breoth, *pr.part.* a' breothadh, *v.a. & n.* Rot, corrupt, putrefy. 2 Bruise, crush. 3 Maim.
breothadh, -aidh, *s.m.* Putrefaction, corruption, putrefying. 2 Wounding, maiming. 3 Bruising, crushing. 4**Decay, consumption. 5**Wound. 6**Crush, bruise. A' b—, *pr.pt.* of breoth.
breothag,(DU) -aig, *s.m.* [*& f.*] Fat, corpulent, middle-aged person.
†breothan, -ain, *s.m.* Wheat.
†bret,** *a.* High.
breth, see breith.

breuban, see breaban.
breug, bréige, breugan *gen.pl.* breug, *s.f.* Lie, falsehood. Saor m' anam o bhilean nam breug, *deliver mysoul from lying lips;* fhuaradh 'sa bhréig e, *he was found out in a lie ;* gheall Dia do nach comasach breug a dheanamh, *God, who cannot lie, promised.*
breug, *pr.part.* a' breugadh, *v.a.* Soothe,amuse. 2 Flatter. 3 Pacify. 4 Cajole. 5 Entice. Breug am pàisde, *pacify* or *soothe the child ;* breug leat e, *cajole him away with you ;* 'g a bhreugadh mar gu'm bitheadh leanabh ann, *cajoling him as though he were a child ;* ma bhreugas peacaich thu, *if sinners entice thee.*
——ach, -aiche, *a.* Lying, false, deceitful. 2 **Flattering,cajoling,soothing. 3**Deceived. Is breugach thu an diugh, *you are deceiving today ;* tha e cho breugach 's a tha an cat cho bradach, *he is as much a liar as the cat is a thief* [an emphatic way of saying a man is a liar] ; tha e breugach, *he is untruthful* ; nach breugach thu ! *how much you lie !* also *you don't mean it !*
——ach,* *s.f.* Lying female.
——achan, *s.m.* Plaything.
——achd,‡‡ *s.f.* Illusiveness.
——adaire, -ean, *s.m.* see breugaire.
——adaireachd, see breugaireachd.
——adan, see breugachan.
——adh, -aidh, *s. m.* Cajoling, flattering, soothing, lulling, amusing. 2* Caressing.
——ag, -aig, -an, *s.f.* Little lie. 2 Lying female.
——aich, *v. n.* Belie, falsify, give the lie. 2 Disprove. 3 Gainsay. Bhreugaich e mi, *he belied me.* breugaich e, *belie him ;* ged éignichear an sean-fhacal cha bhreugaichear e, *though the proverb be gainsaid it cannot be disproved.* [also breugnaich.]
breugaiche,** *s.m.* Same meaning as *breugaire.*
breugaire, -an, *s.m.* Liar. Is fhearr duine bochd na breugaire, *a poor man is better than a liar ;* éisdidh am breugaire teang' an aimhleis, *the liar listens to a corrupt tongue ;* is fheairrde breugaire fianuis, *a liar is the better of a witness.*
breugaireachd, *s.f.* Practice of lying. 2 of contradicting. 3 Vice of lying.
breugan, -ain, -an,‡‡ *s.m.* Child's toy.
——, *n. pl.* of breug.
breug-chiabh, -an, *s. f.* Wig, peruke.
——adair, -e, -ean, *s.m.* Wig-maker.
breug-chràbhach, *a.* Hypocritical, deceitful.
breug-chràbhadh, -aidh, *s.m.* Hypocrisy, dissembling. 2 False devotion.
breug-fhàidheachd, *s. f.* False prophesying.
breug-fhios, -a, *s.m.* Enthusiasm, fanaticism.
——ach, *a.* Enthusiastic.
breuglachadh, -aidh, *s.m.* Fore-swearing, perjuring. 2 Falsifying, gainsaying. A' b—, *pr.part.* of breuglaich.
breuglaich, *pr.part.* a' breuglàchadh, *v.a.* Perjure, forswear, gainsay, belie.
——te, *past pt.* Forsworn, perjured. 2 Gainsaid. 3 Falsified.
breugnachadh, -aidh, *s.m.* Falsifying. 2 Belying, gainsaying. 3 Contradicting. A' b—, *pr. pt.* of breugnaich.
breugnachair,** -e, -ean, *s.m.* Gainsayer.
breugnaich, *pr.part.* a' breugnachadh, *v.a.* Belie, falsify, gainsay, disprove. 2 Contradict. Bhreugnaich e mi, *he belied me.* [also breugaich.
——, *s. f.* Same meanings as breugnachadh. Thug e a' bhreugnaich dhomh, *he belied me.*
breugnaichidh, *fut. aff. a.* of breugnaich.
breugnaichte, *past part.* of ,,
breug-riochd, *s.m.* Disguise. 2‡‡Spectre.
breug-riochdair,* *s.m.* Pretender, disguiser. 2 Traitor.
breun, bréine, *a.* Stinking, fœtid, putrid. 2 Filthy, loathsome, nasty, corrupt. 3* Bold, indelicate, as a female. 4 Of a turbulent, boisterous disposition. 5**Clumsy. 6‡‡Beastly, brutal. Bainne breun, *soured milk*—(AC); o'n òtrach bhreun, *from the stinking dunghill.*
——, *v.a.* Become corrupt. 2 Stink.
——, *s. f.* Stench. 2 Corruption.
——ach,* *s. f.* Turbulent immodest female.
——ach,** -aiche, *a.* Stinking. 2 Nasty. 3 Surly.
breunachd, *s. f.* Corruption, rottenness. 2 Becoming rotten. Stench, stink, bad smell. 4 Degree of turbulence. 5* Indelicacy.
breunad, -aid, *s.m.* see breunachd. 2 A' b—, *pr. pt.* of breun.
breunadh, see breunachd.
breunag, -aig, -an, *s. f.* Dirty female, slattern, drab. 2 Turbulent female. 3††Sulky woman. 4(JM) Lying woman. Aontachadh brionnaig le breunaig,*the flattering woman agreeing with the lying woman*—a common saying in the Outer Hebrides when two bad characters conspire to prove a point or to hide a fault.
breunaid, *s. f.* Stink, putrid smell.
breunair, *s.m.* Turbulent man.
breunan, -ain, *s.m.* Dirty fellow. 2 Dunghill. 3 Any stinking thing. 4 Surly ill-tempered fellow. 5‡‡Inhospitable man.
†breunan, *v.n.* Stink.
breunan-brothach,**-aich,*s.m.* The great daisy. 2(JM) Dirty fellow given to sullen anger, a bad description of anyone.
breun-bhith,** *s. f.* Assafœtida.
†breun-chrann, *s.m.* Kind of tree.
breun-fheòcullan,(AF) *s.m.* Foumart,fulimart, see feòcullan.
breun-ladhrach, -aiche, *a.* Rotten- or stinking-toed.
breuntachd,‡‡ *s. f.* see breunachd.
breuntag,** -aig, -an, *s. f.* Filthy drab.
breuntas, -ais, *s.m.* Filth. 2 Stink. 3 Putrefaction. 4 Any loathsome smell.
breun-ubhal,§ *s. m.* Prickly buckthorn, see ramh-droighinn.
†bri, *adv. & prep.* Near to.
†brì, *s. f.* Anger. 2 Word. 3 Effort. 4 Rising ground. 5 Dignity. 6 Honour. 7 see brìgh.
†bria, *s.m.* Town.
†briadh, *s. f.* Remnant.
briadha, see brèagh.
——chd, see brèaghachd.
——d, -aid, see brèaghad.
——ich, see brèaghaich.
——s, -ais, *s. f.* see brèaghachd.
briag, see breug.
briagh, see brèagh.
†briagh, *s.m.* Wound, mortal wound.
briaghachd, see brèaghachd.
briaghas, -ais, *s.m.* see brèaghas.
briaghchaid, see brèaghad.
brian, -ain, *s.m.* Word. 2 Composition. 3** Warrant. 4**Author. 5 (AC) Angel, archangel, god, divinity, *hence* god of evil. 6(AC) Term of exclamation, a bhriain ! *thou god !* cha luidh Brian leam, *Satan shall not lie down with me.* [** says brian is †]
†——ach, *a.* Fair-spoken. 2 Full of speeches, specious, prosing.
†brianna, *s.m.* Author. 2 Composition. 3 Warrant.
†——, *pl.* Pieces.

†brian-sgaradh, -aidh, *s.m.* Cranny, chink,cleft

†briantadh, -aidh, *s.m.* Bream. [see illust.78.]

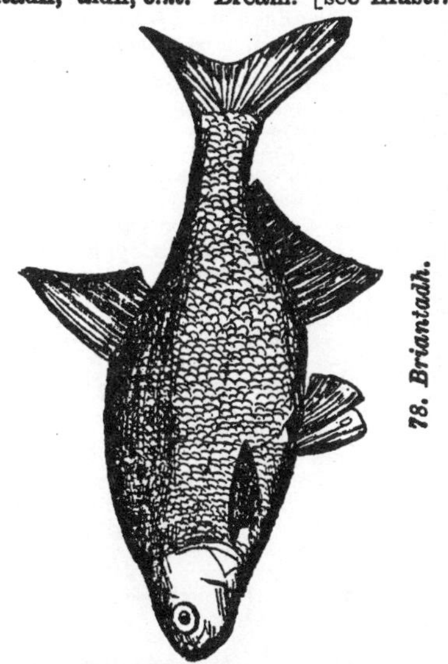

78. *Briantadh.*

†briar, *s.m.* Pin, prickle. [? Eng. *brier*.]

bri'ar, see brighmhor.

briarach, *a.* Thorny, prickly.

briathar, -air, *pl.* briathra & briathran, *s.m.* Word. 2 Saying. 3 Assertion. 4 Oath. 5 Verb. 6 *rarely* Victory, conquest. Air mo bhriathar, *upon my word.*

briathar, *v.* see briathraich.

briathra, *n.pl.* of briathar.

briathrach, -aiche, *a.* Wordy, verbose, talkative, loquacious. 2 Verbal. Ni thu am fear tosdach briathrach, *you make the silent man talkative.*

——————adh, -aidh, *s.m.* Wording. 2 Swearing. 3 Stating.

——————an, -ain, -an, *s.m.* see briathradair.

——————as, -ais, *s.m.* Eloquence. 2 Elocution. 3 Verbosity. 4 Oratory, rhetoric. 5‡‡ Phraseology. 6*Wit.

briathradair, *s.m* *Dictionary, lexicon. 2**Asserter.

——————eachd,* *s.f.* Lexicography, lexicographer's work.

briathradan,* -ain, see briathradair.

briathraich, *pr. pt*, a' briathrachadh, *v. a.* Affirm, maintain, assert. 2 Dictate. 3 Swear to. 4 Set down in words.

briathrail, -e, *a.* Verbal. 2††Verbose. Eadartheangachadh briathrail, *a verbal translation.*

brib, *pr.pt.* a' bribeadh, *v.a.* Bribe, suborn.

brìb, -e, *pl.* [-ean &] ††-eachan, *s. f.* Bribe. 2 Small sum of money—*Islay.* 3 Driblet. 4 Item. Am bheil thu am brath a' bhrìb sin a phàigheadh ? *are you going to pay that trifling sum ?* brìb nach do ghabh, *who has not taken a bribe.*

brìbeadh, -eidh, *s.m.* Bribing, bribery. A' b—, *pr. pt.* of brìb.

bribear,** Gaelic spelling of *briber.*

bribearachd, *s. f.* Bribery, venality.

bribeil,(AM) *a.* Mean. Duine bribeil, *a mean man.*

bri-bheadagan,‡‡ -ain, *s.m.* Word-pedant.

bribid,(JM) *s.f.* Small debt. Tha bribidean fhiach aige a muigh, *he has small debts out i. e. against people.*

bric, *gen sing. & n.pl* of breac. (*s.m.*)

bric-dhearg,** *s.* Ruddock.

brice, *gen.sing.* of breac, (*s.f.*)

brice, *comp.* of *a.* breac.

brice, *s.f.* Spottedness.

brice, *s. f.* Gaelic spelling of *brick.*

bricear, -e, -ean, *s.m.* Brickmaker.

bricein, -ein, *s.m.* Sprat. 2 Small trout.

bricein-, *prefix* attached to certain names of animals, derived from *breac.* [also breacan-]

bricein-baintighearna, see breacan-baintighearna.

bricein-beithe, see breacan-beithe.

bricein-buidhe, see breacan-buidhe.

79. *Bricein-caorainn.*

bricein-caorainn,¶ *s.m.* Mountain finch,—*fringilla. montifringilla.*

bricein-dubh,§ *s.m.* Baldmoney, (plant) see muilceann.

bric-liath, *a.* Greyish.

bric-shorn, -ùirn, *s.m.* Brick-kiln.

†brìd,** -ìde, *s. f.* Bridle.

bride, *s. f.* see frìde.

†brìdeach, -dich, -dichean,** *s.f.*[& *m.*] Dwarf. 2 Bride. 3 Virgin. 4**Grub. Cha bhrìdeach air an fhàich e, *he is not a dwarf on the battle-field ;* carraig Phaidean aig na brìdich, *Padeen's rock in the possession of the dwarfs*—a common saying in Tiree when the weak get possession of what by right belongs to the strong—J.M.

†——————ail, *a.* Dwarfish. 2 Like a virgin. 3 Bridal, like a bride.

brìdeag, -eig, -an, *s. f.* Part of the jaw. 2 Little woman.

Brìdeag,** -eig, *s. f.* Image of St. Bridget, used on that saint's eve by unmarried girls, with a view to discover their future husbands.

bridean, *s. f.*(bird) see gille-brìde.

brìdein, see brìd-eun.

brìd-eun, -eoin, *s.m.* Oyster-catcher *or* sea-piet, see gille-brìde. Cho luath ri brìd-eun 'san tràigh, *as swift as a sea-piet on the shore.*

brìg,* *s. f.* Heap, pile.

——,* *v.a.* Pile, build as a stack of peats.

——eadh, *s.m.* Stacking. A' b—, *pr. pt.* of brìg. A' brìgeadh na mòna, *building the peat-stack —Mull.*

brigean, see briogais.

brìgh, *s. f.* Essence. 2 Substance. 3 Wealth. 4 Sap, juice, pith. 5 Elixir. 6 Vigour. 7 Strength, virtue. 8 Value. 9 Effect, avail, benefit. 10 Juice of meat. 11 Meaning, interpretation. 12 Energy. 13**Relish. 14** Capacity. 15***rarely* Tomb. 16**Miracle. 17 ‡‡Mountain. 18**Valour. 19**Price. Chaill na h-ùbhlan am brìgh, *the apples lost their sap ;* mairt-fheoil gun bhrìgh, *beef without substance ;* craobh gun bhrìgh, *a sapless tree ;* briathran gun bhrìgh, *words without meaning;* innis dhomh brìgh mo bhruadair, *tell me the interpretation of my dream ;* a' caitheadh mo bhrìgh, *dissolving my substance ;* is deacair brìgh do sgeòil, *sad is the substance of thy tale;* b'e seo bu bhrìgh d' an dàn, *this was the*

burden of their song; caithidh cumha gun bhrìgh, *mourning consumes without avail*; do bhrìgh, a bhrìgh, *by virtue of, because*; thubhair triath Eireann bu mhòr bhrìgh, *said Ireland's chief of great energy*; ged gheibhinn brìgh Eireann, *though I were to get the wealth of Ireland*; innis da ar brìgh, *tell him our strength*.
brìgh'ar, *a.* see brìghmhor.
brìgh-àrd, *s.f.* Definition (in *gram.*)
brìgh-chainnt,** *s.f.* Argument.
brìghead, see brìghealachd.
brìghealachd, *s.f.* Substance, substantiality. 2 Vigorousness. 3 Juiciness, pithiness, virtue. 4 State of being full of meaning.
brìgheamh,* see breitheamh.
brìgheil, -e, *a.* see brìghmhor.
brìghich, *v.n.* Strengthen, confirm. 2 Establish.
†**brighide**, *s.f.* Hostage, pledge, security.
brìghinn,* *s.f.* Seasoning. 2 Any fat. 3 Dainties, delicacies. †4 see bruidheann.
———eachadh,* *s.m.* Act of seasoning. 2 Act of feeding on dainties or delicacies.
brìghmhoire, *comp.* of brìghmhor.
———achd,** *s.f.* Substantialness. 2 Juiciness. 3 Vigorousness.
brìghmhor, -oire, *a.* Energetic. 2 Sappy, juicy. 3 Substantial, solid, real. 4 Efficacious, effective, effectual. 5 Full of meaning.
brìgh-sgrìobhaidh,** *s.f.* Argument.
brìgh-tharruing, *s.f.* Abstraction.
brigis, see briogais.
brill, see breall.
brillean,** -ein, *s.m.* The clitoris.
——ach, *a.* Lewd.
brilleineach, *a.* see brilleanach.
brimin-bodaich, *s.m.* Mean, shabby old man. [‡*for* breimein, a side form of *braman.*]
†**brin**, *s.f.* Dream, reverie.
†**brindeal**, *s.m.* Picture.
†**brin-dealan**, *s.m.* Frontlet.
†**brindealbhadair**, *s.m.* Painter. 2 Sculptor.
†**brindealbhadh**, *s.m.* Painting, sculpture, limning, pourtraying. 2 Disguising.
†**brinneach**, *s.f.* Hag, old woman. 2**Mother.
†**brinnichte**, *a.* Hag-ridden.
brìob, *v.a.* see brìb.
——, -a, -an, *s.f.* see brìb.
——achd, see brìbearachd.
brìobadh, see brìbeadh.
brìobair, see brìbear.
———eachd,* see brìbearachd.
†**briochd**, *s.f.* Wound. 2 Art. 3 Trade. 4 Secrecy. 5 Witchcraft. 6 Colour, complexion. 7 Beauty.
†**briochdaic**, *s.f.* Amulet.
brìodail, *pr.part.* a' brìodal & brìodaladh, *v.a.* Caress, flatter, coax, court. 2**Tattle.
brìodal, -ail, *s.m.* Caressing, acts of fondness, expressions of tenderness, soft words, kind speeches, endearing attentions. 2 Flattery. 3 Language and manner of lovers, courting. Do bhrìodal cùil, *thy secret flattery.* A' b—, *pr.part.* of brìodail.
brìodalach, -aiche, *a.* Caressing, fondling. 2 Flattering, inclined to flatter or cajole. 3** Tattling.
brìodalachd, *s.f.* Tattling. 2 Propensity to flatter. 3††Caressing. 4‡‡Amorousness.
brìodaladh, -aidh, *s.m.* Caressing. 2 Cajoling, flattering. 3 Tattling. A' b—, *pr. part.* of brìodail. 'G am brìodaladh, *caressing them.*
brìodalaiche, *s.m.* Flatterer, cajoler. 2** Tattler. 3††Caresser.
————, *comp.* of brìodalach.
brìodalair,** *s.m.* Dallier.
brìodha, see brèagh.
briog, *v.a.* Cut round, hack. 2 Thrust, stab, Gaelic spelling of *prick*. 3††Restrain.
——, *s.m.* Confinement. 2 Restraint.
——ach, -aiche, *a.* Mean, miserly, avaricious. 2 Spiritless.
——achd,* see briogadaich.
briogadaich, *s.f.* Avarice, meanness, sordidness. 2 Ludicrousness, affected capering. 3 ‡‡Hacking, cutting.
briogadh, -aidh, *s.m.* Act of stabbing or thrusting.
briogaid, *s.f.* Elderly woman. 2 Morose old female. Esan a phòsas briogaid, *he who marries a morose old female.*
———each,* *a.* Elderly. 2 Like a little or morose female.
briogaire, -an, *s.m.* Miser, mean shabby fellow, churl.
———achd, *s.f.* Sordidness, avarice. 2 Want of spirit.
briogais, -ean, [*n.pl.* briogsan—DU] *s.f.* Breeches, trousers. Briogais anairt, *linen breeches.*
———each, *a.* Having breeches or trousers.
———ich,‡‡ *v.a.* Breech, put into trousers.
†**briogan**, -ain, *s.m.* see briogais.
———ach, *a.* see briogaiseach.
briogh, see brìgh.
†**brìoghach**, *a.* Hilly, mountainous.
brìoghach, *a.* see brìghmhor.
brìoghail, *a.* ,, ,,
brìoghalachd, *s.f.* see brìghmhorachd.
brìoghas, -ais, *s.m.* Fervour of passion, fondness, dalliance.
———ach, -aiche, *a.* Fond, given to dalliance.
brìoghmhor, -oire, *a.* see brìghmhor.
brìghmhorachd, see brìghmhoireachd.
briollag, -aig, *s.f.* Illusion.
———ach, -aiche, *a.* Illusory. 2 Deceitful.
briollair, -ean, *s.m.* Whoremonger, lecherous fellow. 2**One afflicted with incontinence of urine.
briollan, -ain, *s.m.* Chamber-pot. 2 Urinal. 3 Ignorant stupid fellow.
———ach, -aiche, *a.* Stupid, boorish, ignorant.
———achd, *s.f.* Stupidity. 2 Boorishness, ignorance, rudeness.
†**briollsgaire**, *s.m.* Bully. 2 Interfering, meddling person, busybody.
†**brion**, *s.m.* Fiction, lie. 2 Drop. 3 Gem.
brion,** *s.m.* Disquietude, dissatisfaction.
†**brionach**, -aich, *s.m.* Liar.
brionain-beò, see buinnean-beò.
brional, (AF) *s.m.* Male seal.
†**briondath**, *v.a.* Counterfeit, forge, imitate.
brionglaid, -e, -ean, *s.f.* Confusion, wrangling, disagreement. 2**Dream. 3**Reverie.
brionglaideach, -eiche, *a.* Causing trouble, confusion or mischief. 2 Squabbling, wrangling, quarrelsome. 3**Dreaming.
brionglaideachd,** *s.f.* Chicanery. 2 Quarrelsomeness.
brionglaidich, *v.a.* Cause trouble or embarrassment.
brionglaidiche,* *s.m.* Chicaner.
†**brionn**, see †brion.
brionn,†† *s.f.* Prettiness.
brionn, *a.* see brionnach.
——ach, *a.* Pretty, comely, fair. 2 Flattering. 3 Lying. [‡*from* †brion] 4 Striped with various colours. [‡*from* Eng. *brinded*, now *brindled.*] 5 Shining, glittering.
brionnachd, *s.f.* Prettiness, comeliness. 2 Flattery. 3 Falsehood. 4 Glitter. 5 Variety of colours.
brionnag, -aig, -an, *s.f.* Glitter. 2(JM) Flattering woman. (see note under breunag.) Bha 'n Tràigh-bhàn 'na brionnagan, *the white*

shore was glittering.
brionnal, -ail, *s.m.* Flattery, fawning, sycophancy. 2 Caressing, toying, flirting. Ni e brionnal, *he will flatter ;* ri brionnal, *flirting.*
brionnalach, -aiche, *a.* Flattering, fawning, sycophantic. 2 Toying, flirting.
brionnalachd, *s. f.* Habit of flattering or fawning, sycophancy.
brionndal, -ail, see **brionnal.**
brionndalach, see **brionnalach.**
brionn-shuil, -ula, -ean, *s.m.* Bright, lively eye.
brionn-shuileach, -eiche, *a.* Having bright, quick eyes.
brios, -a, *s.m.* Mockery, derision. 2*Half-intoxication, "breeze."
briosagnaidheachd,** *s. f.* Sophistry.
briosaid, -ean, *s. f.* Belt, girdle. 2* Witch, sorceress.
briosaideach, *a.* Belted, girdled. 2 Like a belt or girdle.
briosag, -aig, -an, *s. f.* Witch, sorceress.
†**briosargnaiche**, *s.m.* Sophist.
†**briosargnaidhe**, *s.m.* see †**briosargnaiche.**
†**briosarguin**, *s.f.* Sophistry.
briosg, *pr.part.* a' briosgail & briosgadh, *v.n.* Start, leap, jerk, move suddenly or quickly through surprise, fear, or joy. 2* Quicken, come alive, as a child in the womb. 3 Crumble. 4* Quiver, as the flesh of an animal immediately after being slaughtered.
briosg, -a, -an, *s.m.* Start, leap, sudden movement, emotion of joy, fear, or surprise. 2 Breve, short mark over a letter in *gram.* 3 ** Very short space of time, instant. 4‡‡ Bony part of the mouth.
briosg, -a, *a.* see **brisg.** 2‡‡Pressed.
briosgachd, see **briosgarrachd.**
briosgadh, -aidh, -aidhean, *s.m.* Starting, sudden motion, leap, springing, jerking. 2 Briskness. 3 Very short space of time. A' b—, *pr.part* of briosg.
briosgaid, -ean, *s. f.* Gaelic spelling of *biscuit.* [‡ by folk-etymology made to agree with *brisg*, brittle.]
briosgaideach, *a.* Abounding in biscuits.
briosgaid-mhara,‡‡ *s.f.* Sea-biscuit.
briosgail,* *s. f.* Sudden start or movement. 2 Quickening, state of coming alive. A' b—, *pr.pt.* of briosg.
briosganta, *a.* see **briosgarra.**
†**briosgarnach**, *a.* Crackling.
†**briosgarnachd**, *s. f.* Crackling.
briosgarra, *a.* Brisk, lively, active, ready, willing. 2 Apt to jerk or start.
briosgarrachd, *s. f.* Alacrity, activity. 2 Readiness, willingness.
briosgartaich,* *s. f.* Starting or jerking movement, as the flesh of an animal newly-flayed. 2 Starting, moving.
briosg-ghlòir, -e, *s. f.* see **brisg-ghlòir.**
briosg-ghlòireach, *a.* see **brisg-ghlòireach.**
briosglach, *a.* Frank.
briosgean,§ *s.m.* Silverweed, see **brisgean.**
briosog, -oig, -an, see **briosag.**
briosuirneach, -eiche, *a.* Ludicrous. 2‡‡Hairy. 3 Muffled up.
†**briot**, *a.* Speckled, spotted, piebald.
briot. *s.m.* [***s.f.*] see **briotal.**
†**briotach**, *a.* Stammering. 2 Chattering, talkative, prone to tattle, prattling.
briotachan, -ain, *s.m.* Prater, tattling fellow.
†**briotaire**, *s.m.* Stammerer.
briotal, -ail, *s.m.* Chit-chat, tattle, small talk. 2 Flattery. 3 Sound made by birds in pursuit of the fry of fish. 4 Meeting or company where everyone is speaking. 5**Caressing.
†**brioth**, *s.m.* Fraction.

bris, *v.a.* Break, fracture, splinter. 2 Burst. 3**Break forth. 4 Exclaim. 5 Become insolvent. 6**Back. Bhris fàire air monadh nan sruth, *the dawn broke on the mountain of streams ;* bhris le guth a gràidh an òigh, *the maid exclaimed with her voice of love ;* bhris e a shleagh, *he broke his spear ;* bhris e, *he failed* ["bhris air" is a better form, and the one in common use all over the W. Isles—JM] brisidh an aimsir, *the weather will turn to rain.*
brisd, *v.a.* see **bris.**
brisde, see **briste.**
brisdeach, see **briseach.**
brisdeadh, -didh, see **briseadh.**
briseach, -eiche, *a.* Brittle, apt to break. 2 Interrupted, broken. 3 Confused, inarticulate. 4**Glimmering. 5**Splintering. 6**Anfractuous. Solus briseach nan reultan, *the broken light of the stars.*
briseachd, *s. f.* Anfractuousness. 2 Brittleness.
briseadair,‡‡ -e, -ean, *s.m.* Infringer.
briseadh, -sidh, -sidhean, *s.m.* Breaking, splintering. 2 Bursting. 3 Break, breach, fissure. 4 Act of breaking. 5 Failure, insolvency. A' b—, *pr.pt.* of bris. Luchd-brisidh mhionn, *breakers of oaths ;* briseadh air bhriseadh, *breach upon breach ;* briseadh air son brisidh, *breach for breach;* troimh bhriseadh nan neul, *through the opening of the clouds.*
briseadh,** *3rd pers.sing. & pl. imp.* of **bris.**
——— -céille, *s.m.* Derangement of mind.
——— -creideis, *s.m.* Bankruptcy.
——— -cridhe, *s.m.* Heart-break, over-powering sorrow, grief, pain, affliction, vexation, continued cause of vexation, dejection of mind. 2**Discouragement.
——— -a-mach, *s.m.* Eruption. 2 Outbreaking of any kind. 3 Rebellion.
——— -pòsaidh,(AM) *s.m.* Adultery.
brisg, -e, *a.* Brisk, lively, agile, active, clever (in Scots sense.) 2 Brittle. 3 Tender, as flesh. 4 Mettlesome, as a horse. 5 Alert, ready. 6 Not stingy, as a person. 7**Hasty.
brisg, *v.n.* see **briosg.**
brisg-bhuille, *s.m.* Smart blow, sudden quick blow. 2**Jerk.
brisge,* *s. f.* Readiness, aptness. 2 Activity, animation. 3 Tenderness. 4 Brittleness.
brisgeachd,* see **brisge.**
brisgead,* see **brisge.**
brisgealachd, see **brisge.**
brisgean, -ein, -einean, *s.m.* Cartilaginous part of a bone. 2 The part of tripe called brisket or gristle. 3§Silverweed, white tansy,—(*lit.* the brittle one)—*potentilla anserina.* 4**Wild skirret—*sium sisarum. B.* milis, *the sweet-bread of any creature.* 5**Moor-grass.

80. *Brisgean (3)*

———ach, *a.* Abounding in gristle, like gristle, gristly. 2 Abounding in silver tansy.
———ach,** -aich, *s. f.* Crackling, rind of roast-ed pork.
brisg-gheal, -ile, *a.* Limpid, clear, transparent.
brisg-ghlòir, *s. f.* Quick utterance, gabble, prattle, loquacity.
———each, *a.* Garrulous, talkative, forward, pert, prating.
brisg-phunc, *s.m.* Crotchet in *music.*
†**brisleach**, *s. f.* Overthrow of an army. 2

Breach.
brislean, -ein, -an, *s.m.* Silverweed, see brisgean.
———ach, *a.* Abounding in, or like, white tansy or silverweed.
brisneach, *a.* see briogaiseach.
brisnean, *pl.* of briogais.[Used only in poetry.]
brist, *v.a.* see bris.
briste, *a.* & *past part.* of bris. Broken. 2*Made a bankrupt, insolvent. 3 Bruised. 4 Wounded. 5**Splintered. Tha mo chridhe briste, *my heart is broken* ; is e iobairt Dhé spiorad briste, *the sacrifice of God is a broken spirit* ; a ghàirdean air clàrsaich bhriste, *his arm on a broken harp* ; fear briste, *a bankrupt.*
briste, *for* brisdeadh, see briseadh.
bristeach, see briseach.
bristeadh, *s.m.*&*pr.part.* of bris, see briseadh.
bris-thraisg, *s. f.* Breakfast.
brith, -e, *a.* see bruich.
†**brith**,** *s.* see breith & breitheamh.
†**britheaghlaidh**, *a.* Kind, gentle.
britheamh, -eimh, -han, *s.m.* see breitheamh.
†**britinneas**, *s.m.* The measles.
†**brium**, *s. f.* Helmet.
†**brò**, *a.* Old, ancient, antique. 2‡‡Much,many.
†**bro**, *s.m.* Champion. 2 Quern, handmill, see brà. 3** Grinding stone.
†**broar**,‡‡ *s.m.* Fault, error.
†**bròas**, *s. f.* Old age.
brobh,§ *s.m.* Sea-scirpus or round-rooted bastard cypress—*scirpus maritimus.*
brobhadan,** -ain, *s m.* Grasshopper.
†**broc**, *a.* Grey, dark grey.
broc, -ruic, *s.m.* Badger, "brock."
brocach, -aiche, *a.* Speckled, freckled, spotted in the face, pock-marked. 2 Greyish in the face. 3 Like a badger. 4 ‡‡Ill-scented. 6‡‡ Dirty. 7**Odious.
bròcail, *pr.part.* a' bròcladh, *v.a.* Mangle, spoil, disfigure, lacerate.
brocair, -e, -ean, *s.m.* Fox-hunter, badger-hunter, destroyer of vermin in the Highlands.
———eachd, *s. f.* Fox-hunting, badger-hunting, vermin-hunting.
brocanta, *a.* Shy, like a badger.
———s,** -ais, *s.m.* Shyness.
bròchail, *pr.pt.* a' bròchladh, *v.a.* see brócail.
brochaill, *s.m.* Banner of Gaul, son of Morni.
brochan, -ain, *s.m.* Porridge. 2 (*Skye, &c.*) Pottage, gruel. Deoch bhrochain, *gruel* ; sodar bhrochain, *thick gruel* ; a' phoit bhrochain, *the porridge-pot* ; agus bhruich Iacob brochan, *and Jacob made pottage* ; brochan tiugh, *porridge* ; brochan tana, *gruel* ; brochan bainne, *milk porridge* ; brochan feòla,*gruel of flesh juice* ; brochan liath, *milk gruel* ; chlisg am brochan nach d' òl mi, *the porridge that I have not sipped trembled*—a far-fetched way of making known that one has got a very bad fright—*Mull* ; brochan reamhar, amh do na gillean, brochan tana, bruich do na h-igheanan, *for the boys, porridge thick and raw,for the girls, well-boiled and thinner far,—Uist.*
brochanach, -aiche, *a.* Gruelly, of, or belonging to gruel or porridge. Bi gu curraiceach, brògach, brochanach 'sa Gheamhradh, *be well capped, shod and fed in winter.*
brochan-bainne,* *s.m.* Milk porridge.
brochan-cruithneachd,* *s.m.* Flummery.
brochan-ghall-pheasair,* *s.m.* Lentil porridge.
brochan-leanna, *s.m.* Ale-berry.
brochd, *s.m.* see broc.
———ach, see brocach.
brochlach,* *s. f.* Woman.
bròchladh, see bròcladh.
bròchlaid, -e, -ean, *s. f.* Trash. 2 Mixture of different meats.
broclach, -aich, *pl.* -aichean [**-aich] *s.f.* Warren. 2 Badger's den. 3††Fox's den.
bròcladh, -aidh, *s.m.* Spoiling, mangling,wasting. A' b—, *pr.pt.* of bròcail.
broc-lann, -inn, *s m.* Badger's den. 2 Den of wild beasts. 3 Cavern. 4*Any stinking place.
broc-luidh, see broc-lann. Tha broc-luidh aig na sionnaich, *the foxes have holes.*
bròcuil, see bròcail.
bròd, -oid, *s.m.* Pride, arrogance, haughtiness. 2**Chastisement. 3 Land—*Mull.* 4 Brood, crowd, band, swarm.—*Argyll.* 5 Children, the rising generation. Féin-spéis agus bròd, *self-conceit and arrogance* ; bròd-gheadh, *a goose that has a brood, a dam.*
brod, bruid, brodan, *s.m.* Goad. 2 Prickle,sting. 3 Choice of anythig. 4 Best quality of grain or of any other article. 5 Lid. 6 Small board. 7*Box handed round a church to collect alms. 8 Pintle of rudder or stern-post, see bàta O7. p.73. 9(DU) Awl. Brod an t-sil, *the best part of the corn* ; brod na poite, *the lid of the pot* ; brod an taighe, *a splendid house.*
†**brod**,‡‡ *s.m.* Spot, blemish.
brod, *pr.pt.* a' brodadh, *v.a.* Stir up, rouse, stimulate, goad, sting, excite. 2* Level or smoothe land with a spade after the first ploughing. 2‡‡Pick or separate the best parts. 3(DU) Stir up in search of anything.
——ach, -aiche,*a.* Stimulant, tending to enliven, stirring up. 2 Goading, prickling.
bròdach, *a.* In crowds, in swarms. 2**Arrogant.
brodadh, -aidh, *s.m.* Goading, spurring, stimulating, stirring up, urging. 2 Compelling. 3 Searching. 4*Levelling land. 5 Poking. 6**Winnowing. A' b—, *pr.pt.* of brod.
†**bròdail**, *a.* Proud, arrogant, conceited, forward. Tha e cho bròdail ris a' mhac mhallachd, *he is as proud as Lucifer.*
bròdalachd,* *s. f.* Arrogance, haughtiness, extreme pride.
brodann,†† *s.m.* Goad, prickle. 2 Staff.
brod-ghaineamh, -eimh, *s.m.* Gravel.
brodaiche,* *s.m.* Bodkin.
†**brodh**, *s.m.* Straw, stem. 2 Atom. 3 Point, spot.
brodhach, -aiche, *a.* see brothach.
†**brodhag**, *s.f.* Bosom, fold of the breast clothes.
brodh-bràighe, *s.m.* Common rush, see luachair.
brod-griasaich,(JM) *s.m.* Poker. Dheanadh a fiaclan b. 'sa ghealbhan, *her teeth (are so long that) they would make a poker for the fire.*
brod-iasg, -éisg, *s.m.* Needle-fish. 2 Sword-fish.
brod-leabag,(AH) *s.m.* Spear for killing flounders.
brod-teine, *s.m.* Poker.
brodunn, -uinn, *s.m.* see brodann.

81. Seann bhrògan Gàidhealaich.

bròg, -òige, brògan, *s.f.* Shoe. 2 Hoof. 3 *By a fig-*

-ure of speech, Foot. 4 Sorrow. 5 DU Fish's roe—*Gairloch, Loch Broom, &c.* [The Highland *bròg* was made of a piece of raw hide with the hair turned outwards and tied before and behind with a thong.] Cuir ort do bhrògan, *put on your shoes*; bròg an eich, *the hoof of the horse*; buailidh e bròg ort fhathast, *you will feel the bad effects (sorrow) of that again*; bhuail an t-earrach seo bròg oirnn, *we have felt the sad effects of this untoward spring*; o mhullach gu bròig, *from head to foot*; brògan air a' chat! na'm bitheadh na h-osain air, rachadh e á cnàimh na h-amhaich, *the cat with shoes on! had he the hose on, he would break his neck (with conceit)*—said of a conceited person who has little to be conceited about; bròg a' chroinn, *a mast-step* (see bàta, p. 76); bròg gun deireadh, *a sandal*, or *slipper*; brògan tionndaidh, *shoes turned inside out after being sewn*; bròg truisg, *cod's roe.*

†brog, *s.f.* House.

brog, see †borg & brugh.

†bròg, *a.* Sorrowful.

brog, *pr.pt.* a' brogadh, *v.a.* Spur, stimulate, goad.

——, -oig, -an, *s.m.* Shoemaker's awl. 2 Probe, poker.

brogach, -aiche, *a.* Sturdy. 2 Lewd, filthy, nasty. 3 Spurring, goading, stimulating.

brògach, -aiche, *a.* Shod, wearing shoes. 2** Having large shoes. 3** Strong-hoofed, in which sense it is applied to one of Cuchullin's horses.

brogach, -aich, *s.m.* Sturdy little boy. 2 Young lively lad—*Provin.*

†brògachadh, *s.m.* Approaching.

brogadh, -aidh,** *s.m.* Goading, stimulating. 2 Conciliation.

brògag, *s.f.* Little shoe.

brògag-na-cu'aig, see bròg-na-cubhaig.

brògaich,* *v.a.* Shoe, supply with shoes.

brogaich, *v.a.* Approach, come near to. 2‡‡ Dig.

brogaidh,** *s.m.* & *f.* Name given to a cow that puts with her horns. 2 *in derision*, Squat, sturdy fellow.

brogail, -e, *a.* Sturdy, lively, active, hale, hearty.**[Always applied to old people.—*] 3‡ "In good form."

brogair,** -ean, *s.m.* Hastener.

brògair, -ean, *s.m.* Shoe-maker, cobbler.

————eachd, *s.f.* Shoe-making, cobbling.

brogalachd, *s.f.* Sturdiness, activity.

brogan, -ain, -anan, *s.m.* Awl.

————ach, -aich, -aibhean, *s.m.* Lively little man. 2 Smart boy. 3**Lively, sturdy fellow.

————ach, -aiche, *a.* see broganta.

broganta, *a.* Sturdy. 2 Lively, jocose, active, brisk. 3‡‡Crooking. Cailleach *bh.*, *a lively old woman.*

brogantachd, *s.f.ind.* Sturdiness. 2 Liveliness, briskness, alacrity.

bròg-bhréid, -e, -ean, *s.m.* Sandal.

bròg-chalpaich,* *s.f.* Boot.

bròg-chlùdair, -ean, *s.m.* Cobbler.

bròg-fhiodha, *s.f.* Sabot, wooden shoe worn by peasantry on the Continent. 2 Clog. 3 Sandal.

†brogh, *s.m.* Filthiness, dirt. 2 see broth.

†broghach, -aiche, *a.* see brothach. 2 Excessive, superfluous.

†broghadh, *s.m.* Increase, profit.

broghail,** *s.* Dirt.

†broghain, *s.f.* Excess, superfluity.

bròg-na-cubhaig, *s.f.* §Heart's ease, pansy—*viola tricolor.* 2§ Bog violet, see mòthan. 3§ Blue-bell, wild hyacinth, see fuath mhuc. 4§ Round-leaved bellflower, see am pluran cluigeannach. 5§ Corn cockle, see lus loibheach. [McL & D. in Gael.—Eng. part gives *butterwort*, and in Eng.—Gael. part *cuckoo flower* and *cowslip.* †† gives *wild violet.* ** gives *butterwort.*]

†brogoid, *s.f.* Bur.

bròg-sgrìob, -a, *s.f.* Kind of shoe.

bròguidh, -ean, *s.m.* Shoemaker.

broice, *s.f.* see broicean.

broicean, -ein, *s.f.* Mole, freckle.

broicne, *s.f.* see broicean.

broicneach, -eiche, *a.* Freckled. Aghaidh bhroicneach, *a freckled face.*

broid,* *v.a.* Embroider.

†broidhlich, *s.f.* see braoilich.

82. *Bròg-na-cubhaig (1.)*

broidileag, see brù-dhearg.

†broid-inneal, -eil, *s.m.* Richly-embroidered garb.

broid-innealta, -eilte, *a.* Embroidered.

broidireachd,* *s.f.* see broidneireachd.

broidneireachd, *s.f.* Embroidery.

broigealachd,* *s.f.* see brogalachd.

broigeanta,* *a.* see broganta.

————chd,* *s.f.* see brogantachd.

broigeil,* *a.* see brogail.

†broigheal, -il, *s.m.* Cormorant, sea-raven.

broighleach, *a.* Bustling, noisy, tumultuous.

broighleadh, -idh, *s.m.* Bustle, confusion, turmoil, loud noise. [also braoilich.]

broighleag, -eig, *s. f.* see braoileag.

————ach, *a.* see braoileagach.

broighlich, *s.f.* Noise, bawling, confusion, tumult. 2* Crackling of wood on a fire. 3** Swaggering.

broigileineach, -eiche, *a.* Substantial.

broileadh, -eidh, *s.m.* see broighleadh.

broilein, -e, *s.m.* Manyplies in an animal's stomach. [The Gaelic Dictionaries erroneously give "king's hood," which is currachd an rìgh.] 2‡ Pig's snout.—*Badenoch.*

————each, -eiche, *a.* Manyplied.

broilich, *s.f.* see broighlich.

broilleach, -lich, -lichean, *s.m.* Breast, bosom, front. A *b.* mar chobhar nan stuadh, *her bosom like the foam of the waves*; an urrainn duine teine a ghabhail 'na *bh.* agus gun 'aodach a bhith air a losgadh? *can a man take fire in his bosom without burning his clothes?* broilleach bàta, *the bow or stem of a boat*, see bàta, p. 76.

broilleach-bothan,¶ *s.m.* Black-throated diver (bird,) see learga.

†broimceadh, *s.m.* see broimseadh.

†broimeis, *s.f.* Anger, boldness.

†broimseadh, *s.m.* Furious burst of anger.

†broin, *s.f.* Height. 2 Large company.

bròin, *gen.sing.* of bròn.

bròin, *v.a.* Mourn, lament, deplore.

broineach,* *s.f.* Ragged woman. 2 Ragged garment or vesture.

————,* *a.* see broineagach.

broineag, -eig, -an, *s.f.* Rag, shred, tatter. 2 Ragged garment. 3**Apron. 4‡‡Ill-clothed woman.

bròineag, see brònag.

broineagach, -aiche, *a.* Ragged, tattered. 2 Full of rags.

bròinein, *s.m.* Sickly person. 2 Querulous, complaining person. 3 Wretch. 4††Poor or sorry person.

broinileag, *s.f.* see brù-dhearg.

broinn, *dat.* of brù. 2 Used *provincially* as *nom.* Belly, &c.
broinn-dearg, } *s.f.* see brù-dhearg.
broinn-deargan, }
†broinn-fhionn, *a.* White-bellied.
bròisde,* see bràist.
broisg, *pn.pt.* a' brosgadh, *v.a.* Excite, incite, stir up, provoke.
†broisnean, -ein, *s.m.* Bundle. 2 Small faggot.
broit, -e, *s.f.* Bosom, breast. *properly* 2 Covering for the breast. Cuir 'n ad bhroit e, *put it in your bosom.* [‡ The word appears to be from brat, *a mantle*, with a leaning for meaning on bruinne, *breast.*]
†broith, *s.m.* Carnation colour.
†broithdheanta, *a.* Flesh-coloured.
broithlein, see broilein.
brolachan,†† -ain, *s.m.* see brollachan.
brolaich, *s.f.* Inarticulate and incoherent muttering, as in sleep. 2††Raving.
bròlainn,-ean, *s.f.* see brothluinn.
brolamas, -ais, *s.m.* Mixture.
brolasg, -aisg, *s.m.* Garrulity, confused loquacity. 2††Flattery.
————ach, -aiche, *a.* Talkative.
————adh, -aidh, *s.m.* Tattling, loquacity.
brolosgach, *a.* see brolasgach.
brollach, -aich, *s.m.* see broilleach. 2††Mess.
brollachan, -ain, *s.m.* Ragged, naked person. 2* Anything entangled or entwined. 3 Shapeless, deformed creature. 4 Clumsy, lumpish, stupid person, but *not* a malicious person. 5 Senseless creature. [** says †]
†brollaigh, *s.f.* Boldness, confidence.
bròluinn, -e, -ean, *s.f.* see brothluinn.
brom, -a, see bramadaich.
bromach, -aich, -aichean [& **-aiche]*s.m.* Colt.
broman, -ain, -an, *s.m.* Rustic, boor, rude person. 3 Booby. 4† see braman.
————ach, -aiche, *a.* Rustic, rude, country, boorish.
————ach,** -aich, *s.m.* Countryman, bumpkin.
†bròn, *a.* Perpetual.
bròn, -òin, *s.m.* Sorrow, grief. 2 Mourning, wailing, weeping. 3* Mourning dress or habiliments. 'S e seo fàth mo bhròin, *this is the cause of my sorrow* ; fo bhròn, *sorrowing, lamenting* ; is beannaichte iadsan a tha ri bròn, *blessed are they that mourn ;* thionndaidh thu dhomh-sa mo bhròn gu dannsadh, *thou hast turned for me my mourning into dancing ;* oladh aoibhneis an àite bròin, *the oil of joy for mourning* ; tha iad 'am bròn, *they are in mourning (apparel)* ; is fhearr dol gu taigh a' bhròin, *it is better to go to the house of mourning* ; mo bhròn ! *alas ! woe is me !*
bròn, *v.n.* Sorrow, grieve, mourn.
——ach, -aiche, *a.* Sad, sorrowful, mournful. 2 Grieved, mourned. 3**Mourning. 4*Mean. Le cumha brònach, *with sad lamentation.*
——adh, (a') *pr.part.* of *v.* bròn.
†bronadh, *s.m.* Destruction.
bronag, -aig, -an, *s.f.* (AF) Gudgeon, gobie. 2† see bronnag. 3‡ *prov.* Crumb.
brònag, -aig, *s.f.* Poor, sorrowful, mournful female. 2**Disconsolate female. 3**Querulous female. 4 for bruanag.
bròn-bhrat, -ait, *s.m.* Mort-cloth, pall.
bròn-chuimhne, *s.f.* Sad remembrance. Bhur bròn-chuimhne, *the sad remembrance of you.*
bròn-cuthaich,‡‡ *s.m.* Melancholy.
†bron-muilinn, *s.f.* for brà-muilinn. Mill-stone.
bronn, *gen.sing.* & *gen.pl.* of brù.
†——, [**-oinn] *s.m.* Gift, favour. 2 Track, mark. 3 Breast.
†bronn, *v.a.* Distribute, divide. 2 Grant, give, bestow, concede.
bronnach,†† -aich, *s.f.* Girth, belt. 2**Belly-band. 3* Corpulent female.
bronnach, -aiche, *a.* Swag-bellied, gluttonous. 2 Bagged. 3 Well-fed. 4 Bellied. Caoraich bhronnach, *well-fed sheep.*
————-diolta, *s.f.* Saddle-girth.
†bronnadh, -aidh, *s.m.* see pronnadh.

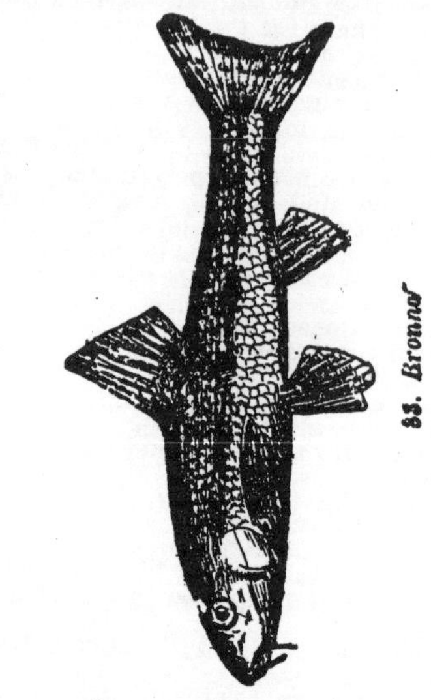
33. Bronnag

bronnag, -aig, -an, *s.f.* Gudgeon. 2 Little bulky female. 3**Apron.
bronnair, -ean, *s.m.* One who divides or gives. 2 Liberal one. 3* Corpulent male. Gheibh bronnair mar a bhronnas e, is gheibh loman an lom dhonas,*the liberal will get as he spends, but the niggard will get more wretchedness.*
bronn-dhearg,** *s.f.* Ruddock (fish)
bronn-ghabh, -ail, *v.n.* see brù-ghabh.
——————ail, *s.f.* see brù-ghabhail. A' b—, *pr.part.* of bronn-ghabh.
bronn-ghabhailte, see brù-ghabhailte.
bronn-sgaoileadh, -lidh, *s.f.* Flux, diarrhœa, dysentery.
bronn-sgaoilte, *a.* Troubled with flux.
——————ach, *a.* Causing a flux or dysentery.
†bronnta, *a.* & *pt.part.* of bronn. Bestowed, given away, distributed.
†bronntanus, *s.m.* see bronntas.
†bronntas, *s.m.* Gift, favour. 2**Fairing. 3 Track.
bronnthach, -aich, *s.m.* see bronnach.
†bròs, *s.m.* Track of a wheel carriage.
brosdachadh, -aidh, *s.m.* see brosnachadh.
†brosdadh, -aidh, *s. m.* Stimulating, encouraging, stirring up.
brosdaich, *v.a.* see brosnaich.
brosdan, -ain, -dannan, *s.m.* Spunk, match. 2 Little sticks to light a fire.
brosduich, see brosnaich.
brosg, *v.a.* see brosnaich.
†brosgach, *a.* Easily frightened.
brosgadh, *s.m.* Exhortation, incitement.
brosgail,** *v.a.* Actuate, incite.
brosgal, see brosgul.
————tach, *a.* Anthypnotic.
brosglach, -aiche, *a.* Lively, active, brisk, prompt, clever (in Scots sense.) 3**Flattering. 4**Loquacious.

brosglachadh, -aidh, see **brosnachadh.**
brosglachd,** *s.f.* Promptitude.
brosgluchadh, -aidh, see **brosnachadh.**
brosgluich, see brosnaich. 2 see **brosguil.**
brosguil, *pr.pt.* a' brosgul, *v.a.* Flatter, cozen, coax. 2‡ Fawn, as a dog.
brosgul, -uil, *s.m.* Flattery, adulation. 2** Lively talk. 3‡ Fawning, as a dog. A' b—, *pr.pt.* of brosguil. Fear brosguil, *a flatterer.*
———ach, -aiche, *a.* Flattering. 2 Coaxing, cozening.
brosgulair,** *s.m.* Adulator.
brosluim, -e, *s.f.* Excitement.
†**brosna**, -ai, *s.m.* Faggot. 2 Armful.
†**brosnach**, *s.f.* River, running water.
brosnachadh, -aidh, -aidhean, *s.m.* Incitement, provocation, spurring on, exhortation, encouragement to heroic actions, cheering. 2 Flattering. 3 Piece of martial music for the bagpipe classed under "ceòl mór." A' b—, *pr.pt.* of brosnaich. *B.* catha, *a battle song.*
brosnachail, *a.* Instigating, encouraging, provocative.
brosnachair,** -ean, *s.m.* Cheerer.
brsnadh, see brosnachadh.
brosnaich, *pr.pt.* a' brosnachadh, *v.a.* Provoke, incite, encourage, bestir, spur on, actuate. Iad-san a bhrosnaich mi, *they that provoked me*; bhrosnaich e ri faicinn an righ, *he cheered up on seeing the king.*
————te, *past part.* of brosnaich. Provoked, incited, actuated.
brosnuchadh, -aidh, *s.m.* see **brosnachadh.**
brosnuich, see brosnaich.
————te, see brosnaichte.
brot, -oit (& -uit), -an, *s.m.* see **brat.**
——, -a, *s.m.* Broth.
——, *v.a.* see brotaich.
——,* *a.* Fat.
brotachadh, -aidh, *s.m.* Thriving, improvement in condition, becoming fat. [Generally applied to cattle of any kind.] 2** Convalescence. A' b—, *pr.pt.* of brotaich.
brotadh, see brotachadh.
brotaich, *pr.pt.* a' brotachadh, *v.n.* Thrive. 2 Mend, improve in condition, grow fat, fatten. 3 Feed grossly. 4††Gluttonize.
brot-biathadh, -aidh, *s.m.* Feeding grossly with intention to fatten.
brot-braigileinach, -eich, *s.m.* Hotch-potch.
†**broth**, *s.m.* Mole. 2 Ditch. 3 Flesh. 4 Fire. 5**Straw.
broth, -a, *s.m.* Itch, eruption of the skin. 2 Mole. 3§Prurigo. 4 for bruth. 5(AC)Breast, breast-bone. 9††Lunar halo. 7‡‡Straw,corn, &c.
brothach, -aiche, *a.* Scabbed, mangy, itchy. 2 Filthy, disgusting. 3(JM) Pertaining to sullen anger. Duine brothach, *a man given to sullen anger* ; cù brothach, *a mangy dog*; caora bhrothach, *a scabbed sheep.*
brothag, -aig, -an, *s.f.* Bosom. 2 Fold of the breast clothes. 3 Little ditch. 4 Little hollow. 5 Dirty wench. 6 for breothag.
†**brothair**, *s.m.* Caldron. 2 Butcher. 3** Bruiser.
brothaireachd, *s.f.* Bruising, mauling, maiming. 2 Butchering.
†**brothaireagadh**, *s. m.* Shambles, butchery. 2**for bruthadaireachd.
†**brothairne**, *s.f.* Down, fur.
†**bròthaigh**, *s.m.* see broth-thaigh.
brothas, -ais, *s.m.* see bruthaist.
†**brothlach**, *s.m.* Pit made in the ground for dressing meat in.
†**brothladh**, *a.* Intent on mischief.
brothlain,** *s.m.* see **broilein.**
†**brothluachair**, *s.f.* **Rush, rushes.**
brothluinn, *s.f.* Agitation, confusion, **struggle.** 2 Meeting of tides. 3** Struggle between wind and tide. 4 Steam. 5 Heat and stink. 6* Disagreeable heat.
————each, *a.* Tumultuous, causing commotion, agitative, disturbed, confused.
broth-thaigh, -thaighean, *s.m.* Slaughter-house, shambles.
†**brotlach**, *s.m.* for brollach(2). 2‡‡Boiling-pit.
brù, *irreg. s.f.* Belly. 2 Womb. 3 Big belly, as a woman with child. 4 Bulge.
Declined thus:—

Nom.sing.	brù	*pl.*	brùthan, [††bronna & bronnaichean.]
Gen.	[1]bronn		bronn
Dat.	broinn		bronnaibh
Voc.	a bhrù !		a bhrùtha !

[1] *Gen.sing.* broinne (DU.)

Tha brù air a' bhalla, *the wall bulges* ; brù-ghoirt, *belly-ache* ; a brù torrach, *her womb pregnant* ; toradh na bronn, *the fruit of the womb* ; air do bhroinn, *on thy belly* ; làn bronn, *bellyful* ; cha lìon beannachd brù, *blessings do not fill a belly* ; is gainne brù na biadh dhuit, *you are scarcer of belly room than you are of food*—applied to a grumbler ; loisg thu do bhrù 's cha d'rinn thu do gharadh, *thou hast burnt thy belly but didst not warm thyself* (this saying can be applied in various ways, for instance, a man makes great efforts to gain a certain object, but comes to grief in his endeavours) ; tha a bhrù air an t-sop, *his belly is on the straw* (this applies to a gluttonous person or animal who would eat till he could not move, and had to lie down, *dh'ith e gus an robh a bhrù air an t-sop.*
†**bru**, *s.f.* Hind. 2 Bank. 3 Country.
bruach, -aich, -an, *s.f.* Bank. 2 Brink, border, edge, brim. 3‡‡Surly boor. 4 see bruthach. Bruach an uillt, *the bank of the river* ; air na bruachan seo, *about these borders* ; bruach dhuine, *a boor of a fellow, a stupid fellow.*
———ach,‡‡ -aiche, *a.* Banked.
———ag, -aig, -an, *s.f.* Little bank.
bruachair, -ean, *s.m.* Surly fellow, person of unamiable disposition. 2 One that hovers about, lounger, hoverer.
————eachd, *s.f.ind.* Hovering about, lounging. 2 Grumbling, sullenness of manner, pouting. 3 Obstinacy.
bruachan,** -ain, *s.m.* Little bank. 2 *rarely* fawn.
bruach-bhaile, *s.m.* Suburbs.
†**bruachdach**, *a.* Magnificent.
bruadair, *pr.pt.* a' bruadar & bruadaradh, *v.n.* Dream. Bhruadair mi an raoir, *I dreamed last night.*
bruadair, *gen.sing.* of bruadar.
bruadal, *s m.* see bruadar.
bruadar, -air, -an, *s.m.* Dream, reverie, vision. A' b—, *pr.part.* of bruadair.
bruadaradh,** -aidh, *s.m.* Dreaming, act of dreaming. A' b—, *pr. pt* of bruadair.
bruadaraiche, -an, *s.m.* Dreamer.
bruadarach, -aiche, *a.* Visionary.
†**bruaidh**, -ean, *s.m.* Peasant.
†**bruaidhe**, see bruaidh.
bruaidlean, *s.m.* see bruaillean. An t-sean fhuil uasal, onorach, cha tàradh bruaidlean conas aisd', *strife would not be evoked from the old, noble, honourable blood by grief or annoyance—Duanaire, p.53.*
————ach, *a.* see bruailleanach.
————achd, *s.f.* see bruailleanachd.
†**bruaigh**,‡‡ *s.f.coll.* Shreds, rags.

bruail,(AC) *s.pl.* **Dreams. Ann mo bhruail,** *in my dreams.*
bruaillean, -ein, *s.m.* **Grief, melancholy. 2 Annoyance, vexation. 3 Confusion, tumult, noise. 4 Murmur. 5 Trouble. 6 Offence. 7 Distraction.** Cò a tha 'cur bruaillein ort? *who is troubling you?* duine gun bhruaillean, *an inoffensive man;* loch gun bhruaillean, *a quiet loch;* is mòr am bruaillean a dhùisg thu, *you have created a great tumult;* mar bhruaillean thonn air druim a' chuain, *as the tumult of waves on the surface of the ocean;* tha bruaillean air aghaidh nan tom, *there is boding gloom on the face of the hillocks;* chuir mi bruaillean air an òigh, *I have troubled the maid.*
bruailleanach, -eiche, *a.* **Disturbing, confounding, deranging. 2 Grieved, vexed. 3 Causing grief or vexation. 4* Riotous, tumultuous. Is** *b.* **m' aigne,** *my thoughts are disturbed.*
——————d, *s.f.ind.* Grief, sadness, melancholy. 2 State of being grieved or vexed, vexation. 3**Disturbance. 4††Confusion.
bruais,‡ *v.a.* Crush to pieces. 2 Gnash. *prov.*
bruan, *pr.part.* **a' bruanadh,** *v.a.* **Break into small pieces or crumbs, crush, crumble, pound,pulverize,smash. 2‡ Thrust. 3 Wound. 4* Disjoint.**
bruan, -ain, -ruanan, *s.m.* **Fragment, morsel, splinter, crumb. 2* Shortbread, cake made of butter, &c. to keep children quiet. 3(DU) Large portion. Thuit bruan de 'n bhalla,** *a large part of the wall fell.*
†bruan, *s.m.* Stab, wound. 2‡‡Thrust.
bruanach, -aiche, *a.* **Causing or tending to crumble, pound, or break. 2 Crumbled, pounded.**
——————, *s.m.* Fragments.
——————d, *s.f.* Continued breaking, smashing, or crumbling. 2 State of being in pieces or fragments. 3* Fragments.
bruanadh, -aidh, *s.m.* **Breaking, crumbling, smashing, pounding. 2** Disjunction. 3** Crashing noise. A' b—,** *pr.pt.* **of bruan. A' bruanadh o na cnocaibh,** *crashing from the hills.*
†bruanadh, -aidh, *s.m.* **Act of stabbing or thrusting.**
bruanag, -aig, -an, *s.f.* **Morsel, crumb, piece, fragment. 2* Little cake. 3‡‡Slight thrust or stab.**
————ach, -aiche, *a.* **Full of crumbs. 2 Apt to fall into pieces or crumbs.**
bruanaibh, *dat.pl.* of bruan.
bruanan, -ain, *s.m.* **Morsel, crumb, piece, fragment.**
bruansgadh,†† -aidh, *s.m.* **Crunching, crushing.**
bruansgail, *s.f.* **Deep crashing or grating noise, clashing noise.**
——————, *pr.part.* a' bruansgal, *v.a.* **Break into fragments, crumble. 2* Make a deep crashing or crushing noise.**
bruansgal, -ail, *s.m.* **Falling in pieces or fragments with a crashing noise. A' b—,** *pr.part.* **of bruansgail.**
bruanspealt,* *s.m.* Splinter.
——————, *pr. pt.* a' bruanspealtadh, *v.a.* Splinter, hew, hack. 2 Smash, break.
——————ach, *a.* Splintering, hacking, hewing. 2 Smashing, crashing, breaking.
——————adh, -aidh, *s.m.* Splintering, hacking, hewing down. 2 Crashing. 3 Smashing. A' b—, *pr.pt.* of bruanspealt. A' *b.* chraobh, *hewing down trees.*
bruanta,** *past part.* **Disjointed. 2 Broken** into fragments. 3 Wounded.
bruasgail, see bruansgail.
bruasgal, see bruansgal.
brù-bhruidhinn,‡‡ *s.f.* Ventriloquy.
brucach, -aiche, *a.* Spotted, speckled, freckled. (particularly in the face.) 2 Foul, squalid, filthy. 3**Pimpled. 4 Gloomy. Là brucach, *a gloomy, lowering day:* caora bhrucach, *a speckled sheep, black-faced sheep;* aodann brucach, *a freckled face.*
brucachadh, -aidh, *s.m.* Act of irregularly digging up the soil. A' b—, *pr.pt.* of brucaich.
brucachd,* *s.f.* Gloominess.
brucag, *s.f.* Chink, cranny. 2 Eyelet. 3 Dirty, drabbish little woman. 4 Leaky boat. 5 **Leaky vessel. 6‡‡Dim candlelight. 7 Little shrivelled horse. Cha bu bhrucag air meirg i, *she was not a rusty, leaky vessel.*
——————ach,** *a.* Crannied.
brucaich, *pr. part.* a' brucachadh, *v.a.* Dig. 2 Turn up the ground imperfectly. 3†† see breacaich.
brucainneach, see brucach.
——————d, *s.f.* Spottedness, freckledness.
brucanaich, *s.f.* Dawn, peep of day. Bi an seo 'sa bhrucanaich, *be here at dawn.—Islay.*
bruchag, *s.f.* see brucag.
————ach, *a.* see brucagach.
brù-chainnt, see brù-bhruidhinn.
brùchd, -a, -an, *s.m.* **Sudden rushing forth, as of a multitude, sally, any sudden burst or disruption. 2‖Belch. 3 Heap, large quantity, glut. 4 Bulge. 5 Rift. 6‡‡Blast. 7 JM In Skye, Lewis, &c., the red sea-weed cast on the shore and collected in heaps and allowed to ferment. [It is called "feamainn dubh" in Uist.] Rinn e brùchd,** *he belched;* thàinig brùchd de na daoine a mach, *a rush of the people came forth;* thuit brùchd de'n mhòine, *a great quantity of the peats fell.*
brùchd, *pr.part.* **a' brùchdail & brùchdadh,** *v.n.* **Sally, rush out, burst forth. 2 Pour. 3 Bulge. 4 Belch. 5 Rift. Bhrùchd na daoine a mach,** *the men rushed forth;* tha e 'bruchdail, *he is belching;* bhrùchd 'fhuil a mach, *his blood rushed out;* bhrùchd iad g'ar còmhnadh, *they rushed to our aid.*
brùchdach, -aiche, *a.* **Pouring, sallying, breaking or bursting forth. 2 Belching. 3 Causing a rift, belch, or sally. 4 Of, or pertaining to, a rift, belch, or sally.**
brùchdadh,-aidh, *s.m.* **Rushing, pouring forth, sallying. 2 Belching. 3* Rifting. 4*Gushing. A' b—,** *pr.pt.* **of brùchd.**
†brùchdag, -aig, *s.f.* **Blast.**
brùchda-dubh, (JM) *s.m.* **Seaweed in a rotten state.—***Uist.*
brùchdail, *s.f.* **Rushing, pouring forth, sallying. 2 Belching. 3 Bilging. 4 Rifting. 5* Gush. A' b—,** *pr.pt.* **of brùchd.**
†brùchdan, *s.m.* see brùchdag.
brùchd-ruadh,‖ *s.m.* **Waterbrash. [see note under ruadhan.]**
——————ain, *s.m.* **Belching from an overloaded stomach.**
brùchd-seile, *s. m.* see brùchd-ruadhain.
bruchlag, -aig, -an, *s. f.* **Mean or wretched hovel. 2 Crumbling, insecure wall. 3††Bad boat.**
——————ach, -aiche, *a.* **Mean, squalid, dirty-looking.**
bruchlas, -ais, *s.m.* **Fluttering of fowls going to roost.**
brù-chorcachd, *s.m.* see brù-chorcan.
brù-chorcan,§ *s. m.* **Heath-rush, stool-bent, dirk-grass.—***juncus squarrosus.*
brù-chorcur, see brù-chorcan.

bruch-shuil, -ula, -uilean, *s. f.* Bird-eye, hole through which light may enter.
————each, -eiche, *a.* Bird-eyed, having quick small eyes.
†brudan,** -ain, *s.m.* Simmering noise. 2 see bradan.
†————og *s.m.* (bradan òg) Salmon trout.
brudh, see bruth.
brudhach, -aich, -aichean, *s.m.* see bruthach.
————ail, see bruthachail.
brùdhachd,‡‡ *s.f. ind.* Prevalence.
brùdhadh, see brùthadh.
brudhainn, see bruth——.
————each, see bruth——.
————eachd, see bruth——.
brudhaiste, see bruth——.
————ach, see bruth——.

84. *Brù-chorcan.*

†brudhaiteach, *s.m.* Thread-bare coat.
†brudhan, -ain, *s.m.* Small bundle of sticks.
brù-dhearg, -dheirge, *a.* Red-breasted.

85. *Brù-dhearg.*

brù-dhearg, -eirge, *s.m.* Robin red-breast.—*erythaca rubecula.*¶
brù-dheargan, *s.m.* see brù-dhearg
brug, *s.m.* see brugh.
bruga dubh, see bruchda dubh.
†brugaidhe, *s.m.* see brughaidh.
brugh, bruighne, bruighnean, *s.m.* Large house. 2 Village. 3 Tower. 4 Fortified town. 5 Fairy hillock. 6 Tumulus. 7 Cave. 8 House half under the surface. 9‡‡ Fort. Sìth bhrugh, *a fairy hillock.*
brùgh, see brùth.
brù-ghabh, *pr.pt.* a' brù-ghabhail, *v. a.* Conceive, as a female.
brù-ghabhail, *s. f.* Conception. A' b—, *pr.pt.* of brù-ghabh.
brù-ghabhailte, *past part.* Conceived.
brughach, *s.m.* see bruthach.
brughadh, -aidh, see bruthadh.
brughaiche, *s.m.* Burgher. 2 Farmer.
†brughaidh, *s.m.* Farmer, husbandman.
†brùghaidhe, *s.f.* Gormandizing, voraciousness, gluttony.
brughan, -ain, *s.m.* see bruan.

86. *Brù-gheal.*

brù-gheal,¶ *s. m.* Wheat-ear (bird)—*saxicola œnanthe.*
bruic, *gen.sing. & n.pl.* of broc.
bruich, *pr.pt.* a' bruich & a' bruicheadh, *v.a.* Boil, seethe, simmer. 2 *rarely* Roast, toast. Bruich e, *boil it* ; tha e bruich, *it is boiled* ; tha e 'ga bhruich, *he is boiling it.*
bruich, *s.f.* Boiling. A' b—, *pr. pt.* of bruich. Is don' a' bhruich a th' air, *how badly it is boiled.*
bruich, -e, *a.* Boiled, seethed. 2 Roasted, toasted. 3** Sultry. 4‡‡ Ruddy-faced, reddened with anger or passion.
————eadh, *3rd. per. sing. & pl. imp.* of bruich.
————eadh, *s.m.* Boiling, seething. 2 Decoction. 3 Any of the various ways of subjecting eatables to the action of fire in cooking. A' b—, *pr.pt.* of bruich.
————ealachd, *s.f.* Sultriness, warmth.
————eil, -e, *a.* Sultry, hot.
————idh, *fut. aff. act.* of bruich. Shall boil.
————te, *a. & pt. pt.* of bruich. Boiled.
bruid, -e, -ean, *s.f.* Captivity. 2 Stab, thrust. 3 Grief, anguish, affliction. 4‡‡Check. 5‡‡ Thorn. 6‡‡ Carrying, bringing. Thug thu bruid am braighdeanas, *thou hast led captivity captive* ; tha thu 'gam chumail ann am bruid, *you keep me in great anxiety.*
brùid, -e, -ean, *s.m.* Brute, beast. 2 Brutal person.
bruid, *pr. pt.* a' bruideadh, *v.a.* Torture, oppress, enslave. 2 Stab. 3* Give the hint by touching. 4 Probe, poke. 5 Dig. 6 Foment. 7 Fire. 8‡‡Stir up.
————eachadh, -aidh, *s.m.* Digging, stirring. 2 Budding of grain. A' b—, *pr.pt.* of bruidich.
————eadh, -eidh, *s.m.* Stabbing, thrusting. 2 Soliciting, enticing. 3*Touching by way of a hint. A' b—, *pr. pt.* of bruid.
brùideag, -eig, *s. f.* Little brute, beast. 2 Brutish woman.
bruideag,‡‡ -eig, -an, *s.f.* Any pointed weapon. 2(DU) Shove, punch, blow.
brùidealachd, *s.f.* Brutality, beastliness. 2 coarseness, savageness, barbarism.
bruidean, *n.pl.* of bruid.
brùidean, *n.pl.* of brùid. 2 *dim.* of brùid.
brùideil, -e, *a.* Brutal, beastly. 2‡‡Unsavoury.
†bruidhe, see †bruighe.
————achd, *s.f.* Colony.
bruidheann, *gen. sing.* -inn & bruidhne, *s. f.* Talk, speech, conversation. 2 Quarrel. 3 Report. 4‡‡ Noise of talk, tumult. Tha mi a' cluinntinn bruidhne, *I hear talking or conversation* ; bruidheann mhór, *loud talk* ; tha an leithid sin de bhruidheann am measg dhaoine, *there is such a report among people* ; chuala mi bruidheann fada uam, *I heard talking at a distance* ; móran bruidhne, *much talking*; cath bruidhne, *much fast and loud talking.*
bruidhinn, see bruidheann.
bruidhinn,* *pr.pt.* a' bruidhinn, *v. a.* Speak, say, talk. Bruidhinn ris, *speak to him* ; bha mi a' bruidhinn ris, *I was speaking to him* ; c' uim' am b' fhiach leat bruidhinn ris ? *why would you condescend to speak to him ?* cha'n 'eil agad ach a bhi bruidhinn, *talk on as you like.*
†bruidhlionta, *a.* Cloyed.
bruidhne, *gen. sing.* of bruidheann. Fear na mór bhruidhne, *the talkative man.*
bruidhneach, -niche, *a.* Talkative, garrulous, loud, loquacious. 2** Querulous. 3 Given to gossip. 'S e siod am fear bruidhneach ! *what a talkative fellow that is !* sgathaidh an Tighearna an teanga bhruidhneach, *the Lord shall cut off the tongue that speaketh proud*

things.
bruidhneachd,* *s.f.* Talkativeness, garrulity, loquacity.
bruidhte, see **brùite.**
bruidich, *pr.pt.* a' bruideachadh, *v.a. & n.* see bruid. 3 Bud, as grain.
bruidil,†† *v.* see bruid.
bruidleachadh, see **bruideachadh.**
bruidlich, see bruid.
†bruigeineach, *a.* Quarrelsome.
†bruigh,** *s.f.* Field.
†bruighe, *s.f.* Farm. 2‡‡ *s.m.* Farmer.
†bruigheadh, *s.m.* Burgomaster.
†bruighean, see bruidheann.
bruigheann, -inn & -ghne, *pl.* -ghnean, *s. m.* †Palace, royal residence. 2 Fairy hill.
†bruigheas,** *s.m.* House.
†bruigheir, *s.m.* Farmer.
†bruighseach, *s.* Womb with young.
†bruighteach, *s.m.* Tyrant, oppressor.
†bruigne, *s.f.* Assault.
brùill, *pr.pt.* a' brùilleadh, *v.a.* Crush, bruise, beat, thrash. 2* Squeeze. Brùillidh mi do chnàmhan, *I will crush your bones.*
brùilleadh, -eidh, *s.m.* Crushing, bruising, beating, thrashing. 2* Crush, squeeze.
brùilleagadh,‡‡ -aidh, *s.m.* Broiling.
bruillich,** *v.a.* Probe.
brùillidh,* *s.m.* see brùillig.
brùillig, -e, -ean, *s.m.* Man of clumsy figure, and of awkward, unwieldy motions.
brùilligeach, -eiche, *a.* Clumsy, unwieldy, awkward.
————d, *s. f.* Clumsiness, awkwardness of gait or movements. 2 Corpulency.
bruilisgeantachd,** *s.f.* Impetuosity.
bruim-fheur,- fheoir, *s.m.* Couch or switch-grass, see feur-a'-phuint.
†bruin, *s.f.* Caldron. 2 Kettle. 3 Belly.
†————, *v.n.* Make a rattling noise.
brùinceach, -ceiche, *a.* Pregnant. 2 Productive.
bruin-deargan, see brù-dhearg.
bruine, see bruinne.
bruine-àrd. *a.* Having a high breast or chest. An ainnir bhruine-àrd, *the high-bosomed maid.*
brùiniceach, see brùinceach.
brùinidh, *s.m.* Spectre. 2 The *brownie* of the Lowlanders.
†bruinne, *a.* Fine.
bruinne, *s. f.* †Belly. †2 Caldron. 3 Waist. 4 Chest.front, breast. Bruinne seang, *a slender waist.*
†————ach, -ich, -ichean, *s. f.* Nurse. 2 Mother. 3 Glutton. 4 (AH) Stout, stupid man. [When used in senses 3 & 4 it is *masc.*]
†bruinneadach, -aich, *s.m.* Apron.
bruinneadh,‡‡ -eidh, *s.m.* The front.
†bruinnean, -ein, *s.m.* Nap or pile of cloth.
————ach,** *a.* Nappy, as cloth.
bruinninn, see bruinnean.
†bruinteach, *a.* Great with child.
bruis, *s.pl.* Shivers, splinters, fragments.
bruis, -e, -ean & -eachan. *s.f.* Brush.
bruis-dreachaidh, *s.m.* Pencil, artist's brush.
bruisinn,** *v.a.* Brush.
————, *s.f.* Gaelic spelling of *brushing.*
bruit, *gen. sing.* of brat.
brùite, *pt.part.* of brùth. Bruised. 2 Broken. 3 Crushed. 4 Oppressed, grieved, sad. Daoine brùite, truagh, *poor, oppressed men*; c'arson an osnaich bhrùite 'ad chliabh? *why the sad sigh from thy bosom?* iadsan a tha brùite 'nan spiorad, *they who are contrite in spirit*; fuil bhrùite, *extravasated blood*; tha m' anam brùite 'am chom, *my soul is oppressed within me.*

bruiteach, -eiche, *a.* Warm, snug, comfortable 2 Contented.
†bruith, *s m.* Flesh.
————, *pr.part.* a' bruith, *v.a.* see bruich.
bruitheadh, see bruicheadh.
bruitheann, -einn, *s. f.* Skirmish. 2‡‡ see bruthainn. 3‡‡ see bruidheann.
†bruithne, *s.m.* Refiner.
bruithneach. -eiche, *a.* see bruthainneach. 2 (AC) Frank.
————————, -eich, *s. f.* see bruthainn.
brù-lìonta, *a.* Satiated, cloyed.
————ch, *a.* Satiating, filling, cloying.
†bruitin, *s.f.* The measles.
†brullsgiantach, *a.* Impetuous.
†brum, *v.* Pede.
†brumair, -ean, *s.m.* Pedant.
†————eachd, *s f.ind.* Pedantry.
†brun, -uin, *s.m.* Firebrand.
brùnaidh, -ean, *s.m.* Corpulent man. 2(DU) *rarely figuratively* Pompous man. 3 Gaelic spelling of Lowland *brownie.*
brundal, see brùnsgal.
brundlais, see pronndail.
brùnsgal,†† -ail, *s.f.* Rumbling noise.
brùs,** *v.n.* Gaelic spelling of *browse.*
†bruscair,** *s.m.* see brusgar.
brusg,†† -uisge, *s.f.* Crumb, bit. 2(AH)Unkempt matted head of hair. Bithidh mi 'nad bhrusg, *I am ready to fright you* (*i.e.* to punish you by plucking your hair.)
brusgach,‡‡ -aiche, *a.* Diminutive, trifling. 2 Blear-eyed. 2 (AH)Shaggy, unkempt.
brusgadh, -aidh, *s. m.* Diminutiveness, meanness. 2 Bleareaness of eyes.
†brusgar, *s.m.* Broken ware. 2 Baggage. 3 Mob.
brutach, -aich, *s.m.* Digging.
brutag,‡‡ -aig, -an, *s.f.* Palmer-worm.
brutaich,‡‡ *v.a.* Dig.
brùth, *pr. part.* a' brùthadh, *v. a.* Bruise. 2 Crush, pound, pulverize. 3 Squeeze, compress. Brùthaidh thusa 'shàil-san, *thou shalt bruise his heel.*
bruth, -a, *pl.* bruithean, *s. f.* see brugh.
brùth. *s.m.* (broth) Bruise.
†bruth, -a, *pl.* bruithean, *s m.* Hair of the head. 2 Heat in the blood or skin, itch. 3‡‡ Anything red-hot. 4‡‡Confined hot place.
bruthach, -aich, -aichean, *s.m.* [& *f.*] Ascent, steep, acclivity, hill-side, brae, precipice. A' dol suas am bruthach, *ascending the brae*; thoir am bruthach ort! *take to your heels!* thug e am bruthach air, *he took to his heels*; le bruthach, *downhill, downwards*; ri bruthach, *ascending, upwards*; fo chreig na bruthaich, *under the rock of the steep*; ruithidh an taigeis féin le bruthach, *even a haggis will run downhill.*
————ag, -aig, *s.f.* Little precipice.
————ail, *a.* Full of precipices or braes. 2 Ascending, steep.
————an, -ain, *s m.* Short ascent.
brùthadair, -ean, *s.m.* Pestle, pounder, bruiser, crusher Le brùthadair, *with a pestle.*
————eachd, *s.f.* Pounding, bruising, crushing. 2 Maiming. 3**Pugilism.
brùthadh, -aidh, -aidhean, *s.m.* Bruising, contusion,‖ crush. 2 Act of bruising, pounding, squeezing, or crushing. A' b—, *pr. part.* of brùth.
————, *3rd. sing. & pl. imp.* of brùth.
brùthaidh, *fut. aff. act.* of brùth.
bruthainn, -e, -ean, *s. f.* Sultry heat, warmth. Nach b'e sin a' bhruthainn! *what sultriness!*
————each, -eiche, *a.* Warm, sultry. 2 **Glowing. 3**Red-hot. Aimsir bh.. *sultry*

weather.
bruthainneachd, *s.f.* Continuance of warmth, sultriness.
bruthaist, *s. f.* Brose, a kind of pottage, used mostly in the Lowlands, and made by pouring boiling water or milk on meal, which is stirred while the liquid is being poured on. 2 Brewage.
bruthaisteach, *a.* Of, or belonging to, brose. 2 Of, or pertaining to, a clumsy or bulky person.
brùthan, *n.pl.* of brù.
bruthan, -ain, *s.m.* Faggot. 2 see brughan.
†**bruthchan,** *s.m.* see brochan.
bruth-chorc, see bruth-chorcan.
————an, -ain, *s.m.* Heath-rush, stoolbent, dirk-grass, see brù-chorcan.
bruthmhaireachd, *s. f. ind.* Fainting through heat.
bù ! *int.* Sound to excite fear in children.
bu, *past ind.* of *defec. v.* is. Was, wert, were. Bu mhi, *I was* ; b' e (*for* bu e) *he was* ; b' i (*for* bu i) *she was* ; b' fhearr leam *I would prefer* ; b' fhearr a bhi gun bhreith na bhi gun teagasg, *better not to have been born than to be unlearned* ; b' fhearr gun tòiseachadh na sgur gun chrìochnachadh, *better not begin than stop without finishing*; b' fhearr a bhi gun fhàinne na fàinne luachrach, *better be without a ring than wear a rush one.* [*Bu* is written *b'* before a word beginning with a vowel or *fh* ; and *b, c, f, g, m, p, s,* & *t* are aspirated after *bu*, as B' aille, b' fhearr leam.] Bu dana e ! *how daring he was !* bu gheur e ! *how sharp it was !* bu mhios' e, *it was worse ;* bu phailt iad, *they were plentiful* ; a laoich bu mhór an sòlas nam fleadh, bu mhór an àm cruadail, *hero who wast great in the joy of feasts and in time of trouble.* For various other idiomatic expressions commencing with *bu*, see under the present tense, *is.*
†**bua,** } (AF) *s. f.* Cow.
†**buabh,** }
buabhall, -aill, -an, *s.m.* Unicorn. 2 Buffalo. 3 Trumpet, cornet, wind instrument. 4 Cowstall. 5‡‡ Horn. 6‡‡ Apron. 7** Any wild horned creature. Mar adharc bhuabhaill àrdaichidh tu m' adharc-sa, *my horn shalt thou exalt as the horn of an unicorn* ; le h-iolach agus le fuaim a' bhuabhaill, *with shouting and with sound of cornet.*
————ach, *a.* Like, of, or pertaining to, a trumpet ; 2 unicorn ; 3 buffalo ; or 4 cowstall.
————aiche, *s.m.* Trumpeter.
buabhall-chòrn, *s. f.* Bugle-horn.
buabhull, -uill, see buabhall.
————ach, see buabhallach.
————aiche, see buabhallaiche.
buac,* *v.a.* Work lime and gravel into mortar. 2 Work clay &c.
†**buac,** *s.m.* Dung used in bleaching. 2 The liquor in which cloth is washed. 3 Unbleached linen, linen in an early stage of bleaching. 4‡‡ Brow of a hill. 5‡‡ Roof of a vault. 6‡‡Settlement. 7**Cap of mist on a hill.
†**buacachan,** -ain, *s.m.* Bleacher.
buacadh, (a') *pr.pt.* of buac.
†**buacais,** see buaic. 2**Confusion.
†**buach,** -uaich, *s.m.* see buac.
†————ach, *a.* Fine, beauish, foppish, gaudy.
buachaill, -e, -ean, *s.m.* Cow-herd. 2 Shepherd. 3 Watch or protector of cattle of any kind. 4 **Youth. Is buachaillean na daoine, *the men are shepherds* ; am buachaill dh' an còir, *the herdsman near them.*
buachaill-an-sgadain,(AF) *s.m.* Large ray *or* skate, northern chimæra—*chimæra monstrosa.*
buachaill-bréige,(AH) *s.m.* Rudely built monument on the crest of a hill.
buachaille, *gen. sing.* of buachaill. [Often used as the nominative.]
buachailleach, -eiche, *a.* Pastoral. 2 Of, or pertaining to, a shepherd or cow-herd.
————d, *s.f.* Herding, watching cattle, occupation of a herdsman. Ri *b.*, or, ris a' *bh.*, *herding.* A' b—, *pr.pt.* of buachaillich.
buachaillich, *pr. pt.* a' buachailleachd, *v.a.* Herd, tend, keep cattle.
buachaill-seòmair,** *s.m.* Valet-de-chambre.
buachair,* *v.a.* Bedaub with dung.
buachar, -air, *s.m.* Cow-dung. 2 Dung of cattle in general. 3**Dunghill. 4**Stall. Buachar bhò, *cow-dung*; dubh-chail' a' bhuachair, *a dung-hill trollop.*
buacharan, -ain, *s.m.* Dried cow-dung used for fuel.
bua-choilleag, Gaelic spelling of *bucolic.*
buadan,** ain, *s.m.* The bone in a horn.
buadh, -aidh, *pl.* -an & -annan,*gen.pl.*buadh,*s.f.* Virtue, excellence. 2 Palm. 3 Endowments, qualifications, talents. 4** Gem. Deagh bhuaidheannan nàdurra, *excellent natural talents* ; deagh bhuaidheannan inntinn, *excellent mental endowments* ; tha buaidh air an uisge-beatha, *whisky has virtue in it* ; fear nam buadh, *the man of accomplishments.*
————, *gen. pl.* of buadh
†————, -aidh, *s.m.* Food, sustenance.
†**buadha,** *a.* Precious.
buadhach, -aiche, *a.* Victorious. 2 Highly-gifted. 3 Virtuous. Connal buadhach, *victorious Connal.*
buadhach, -aich, *s.m.* see buadhaiche.
————adh, -aidh, *s.m.* Conquering. 2 Act of conquering or overcoming. 3 Excellency. 4* Succeeding well in anything. A' b—, *pr. pt.* of buadhaich.
buadhachail,* -e, *a.* Triumphant, victorious, overcoming, subduing.
buadhachas, -ais, *s.m.* Attainment of superiority. 2 Gaining of victories. 3††Luck. 4** Victory, triumph.
buadhaich, *pr.pt.* a' buadhachadh, *v. a. & n.* Conquer, overthrow, subdue, subject. 2 Prevail. 3 Triumph.
buadhaiche, -an, *s.m.* Conqueror, champion, victor. 2**Tribute. Gheibh am buadhaiche e, *the conqueror shall receive it.*
buadhail, -ala, *a.* Victorious, triumphant. 2 Lucky, fortunate.
buadhair,-ean,*s.m.* Conqueror,champion,victor.
buadhairt,** -ean, *s.f.* Hardship, trouble.
buadhal, *s.* see buathal.
†————, *a.* Victorious.
————achd, *s.f.ind.* Superiority. 2 Conquest. 3 Flourishing condition, prosperity. 4*Ascendant. 5‡‡Nature. 6††Luck. Am buadhalachd, *in prosperity.*
buadhannan, *pl.* of buadh.
buadhar, -aire, *a.* see buadhmhor.
buadhar, -air, *s.m.* Adjective in *grammar.*
†**buadharg,** *s.m.* Victorious champion.
†**buadharrtha,** *a.* see †buaidheirthe.
buadhas, -ais, *s.m.* Victory, conquest. 2 Succession of victories.
†**buadh-dharg,** see †buadharg.
buadh-fhacal, *s.m.* Adjective, epithet, qualifying term.
buadh-fhaclach, -aiche, *a.* Triumphant in speech, expressions, or words.
buadhghallan, -ain, *s.m.* Ragweed, ragwort.

buadhghallan buidhe,§ *s.m.* Yellow ragwort,—*senecio Jacobœa.*

buadh-ghuth, *s.m.* Triumphant shouting. 2 Clamour.

†**buadhlain,** *s.m.* Judge.

buadhlan-buidhe, see buadhghallan buidhe.

buadhmhoire, *comp.* of *a.* buadhmhor.

————achd, see buadhalachd.

buadhmhor, -oire, *a.* Victorious, triumphant, successful.

————achd,** *s. f. ind.* Insuperableness.

†**buaf,** *s.m.* Toad. 2 Any ugly venomous creature.

87. *Buadhghallan buidhe.*

†**buafa,** *s.m.* Serpent.

†**buafach,** *a.* Virulent.

†——d, *s.f.* Poison.

†**buafadh,** *s.m.* Poisoning.

†**buafair,** -e, -ean, *s.m.* Viper, adder.

†**buafan,** *s.m.* Snake.

buaf-athair, see buaf-nathair.

buaf-bheist,(AF) *s.m.* Toad. 2 Adder.

buaf-mathair, see buaf-nathair.

†**buaf-nathair,** *s.f.* Adder.

†**buag,** -aig, -an, *s.f.* Spigot, plug. 2 see buaidh. [** says *s.m.*]

†**buagair,** *s.m.* Faucet, pipe inserted in a vessel to give vent to the liquor, and stopped up by a peg or spigot.

†**buagair,** *v.a.* Tap, broach, as a cask. 2 Pierce.

buaghach, *a.* see buadhach.

buaghair, -ean, *s.m.* Cow-herd, herd 2 Shepherd. Thachair orra *b.* bhó, *a cow-herd met them.*

buaghal, see buathal.

buaghallan, -ain, *s.m.* see buadhghallan.

————-buidhe, see buadhghallan-buidhe.

buagharra, *a.* Grieved, vexed. 2 Vexatious, oppressive. 3††Sulky. 4††Boisterous. Mios buagharra, *an oppressive month.*

buaic, -e, -ean, *s.f.* Wick of a candle, lamp, or torch. 2††Tallow. 3‡‡Pinnacle. 4** *rarely* Wave. 5 for buac. 6(DU) Dirt lying thick anywhere.

——, *pl.* of buac. Bleaching lees.

——each, *a.* Of, or connected with, a wick. 2 Having a wick. 3 Giddy, thoughtless. 4 Fluctuating.

buaicean, *n.pl.* of buaic.

buaicean,** -ein, -ean *s.m.* Veil. 2 Lappet. 3 Ltitle wick. 4‡‡Odd laughable little boy. 5(AM) Untidy fellow.

†**buaiceis,** *s.f.* Small wick.

buaichd, -e, -ean, *s.f.* see buac. 2 see buaic.

————, *v.a.* Anoint, besmear, rub over with dung, mud, or oil.

buaichdein, *s.m.* see buaicean.

———— -iall, *s.m.* Piece of unmelted tallow with which brogue-makers rub the thong they sew with. [It used to be in a leather case in the shape of a horn, tied over the left palm, so as to be handy for sticking the awl into when making shoes.—JM]

†**buaicin,** see buaicean.

†————, *v.a.* Blindfold.

buaicneach,‖ *s.f.* Smallpox—*Suth'd.* [Always preceded by the article a' *bh*—.]

————, *a.* Skinny, tough.

†**buaid,**** *s.* Lamp.

buaidh, -e, *n. pl.* -ean -dheanan *s.f.* Victory, conquest, success. Thugadh buaidh 'nam fhianuis 'sa bhlar, *victory was obtained in my presence on the battle-field;* faigh no thoir buaidh, *obtain the victory* or *conquer;* bhuidhinn iad buaidh 'sa chòmh-stri, *they gained the victory in the strife;* beannachd do t' anam is buaidh, *a blessing to your soul and success;* ma gheibh sibh buaidh, *if you obtain the victory;* buaidh-chaithream, *a triumphant shout;* a' deanamh buaidh-chaithreim, *triumphing;* buaidh leat, *success to you;* buaidh no bàs, *conquest or death*—motto of the MacDougalls; gheibh thu bhuam buaidh cnuic agus còdhalach, *thou shalt get for me victory over hills and opposition.—Duanaire, p. 124.*

buaidh,** *v.a.* Conquer, overcome. [Takes *air*, simple or compounded after it, as *b.* orra, *conquer them.*—"thoir buaidh orra" is a more usual expression.]

buaidh-chairm, see buaidh-chaithream.

buaidh-chairt, *s.f.* Trump at cards.

buaidh-chaithream, *s. m.* Triumphant shout. 2 Song of triumph. 3**Triumph.

————————ach, -aiche, *a.* Triumphant, uttering triumphant shouts.

buaidh-chraobh,§ *s.f.* Spurge laurel—*daphne laureola.* Badge of the MacLarens.

88. *Buaidh-chraobh.*

†**buaidheal,** see buabhall 3 & 4.

buaidheam, -eim, *s.m.* Fits of inconstancy or unsteadiness.

————ach, *a.* Giddy, volatile, unsteady.

†**buaidhean,** see buidheann.

buaidhear, *s.m.* see buaidh-fhear.

————achd,* *s. f. ind.* Triumph, victory, coming off victoriously.

†**buaidheart,** -eirt, *s.m.* Tumult, confusion.

†**buaidheirthe,** *a.* Disturbed, agitated. 2 Possessed.

buaidh-fhear, -fhir, *s.m.* Conqueror.

buaidh-fhacal, *s.m.* see buadh-fhacal.

buaidh-ghàir,-e, *s.f.* Shout of victory or triumph.

————each, *a.* Like a shout of triumph. 2 Triumphant.

————eachdaich,** *s.f.* Continued shout of triumph.

buaidh-ghuth, *s.m.* Voice of victory, shout of triumph.

†**buaidhirt,**‡‡ *s.f.* Tumult. 2 Crosses, afflictions.

buaidh-làrach, *s.m.* Decisive victory, gaining of the field, conquest. Buaidh-làrach anns gach strì, *victory in every battle.*

†**buaidhr,** *v.a.* see buair.

†————eadair, see buaireadair.

†————eadh, see buaireadh.

†**buaif-bhiast,** *s.f.* see buaf-bheist.

†**buaifeach,** *a.* Angry, fretting.

†**buaific,** see buaifig.

†**buaifig,** *s.f.* Antidote.

†**buaig,** *s.f.* Cup, chalice.

buaigh, see buaidh.

†——eal, -ean, *s.f.* see buabhall (3 & 4)

buail, *pr. part.* a' bualadh, *v.a.* Strike, beat smite, thrash. 2 Thresh, as corn; beetle, a lint. 3 Thrust. 4 Strike up, as a tune. 5 Attack. 6 Belabour. 7 Knock, as at a door. 8**Touch at, or land at. 9 Proceed. 10 Rush, used to describe rapid motion. 11 Win, as a game at shinty, football, &c. Bhuail e mi, *he struck me* ; tha iad a' bualadh 'san t-sabhal, *they are threshing in the barn* ; tha iad a' bualadh an lìn, *they are beetling the lint* ; bhuail iad oirnn, *they attacked us* ; bhuail chuige Dearg, *Dargo rushed on towards him* ; bhuail iad chun na beinne, *they rushed towards the mountain* ; bhuail e 'chruaidh 'na taobh, *he thrust his steel into her side* ; buailibh clàrsach, *strike up the harp*; an ceud fhear a bhuail an tìr, *the first man that touched the land* ; bhuail iad chun a chéile, *they attacked each other;* bhuail iad chun a' chladaich, *they rushed towards the shore* ; buail an dorus, *knock at the door* ; buailidh e bròg ort fhéin fhathast, *he will hurt yourself yet* (*lit.* strike a shoe on you); buail as, *thrash off* ; bhuail am pathadh mi, *I became thirsty* ; bhuail e air cleasachd, *he began to play* ; bhuail na coin air cobhartaich, *the dogs found prey* ; bhuail mi chugam fo m' asgall e, *I tucked it under my arm* ; bhuail mi mo chuaille 'nam dhorn, *I seized my staff in my hand* ; bhuail mi bàir, *I won a game.*

† buail, *s.f.* Step, degree.

buail-a'-chnag,(AF) *s.* Balm-cricket.

buaile, *pl.* buailtean, *s. f.* Fold for sheep or black cattle. 2 Herd or number of cattle. 3 **Stall. 4**Dairy. 5(AM) Circle, halo. Tha buaile mu n ghealaich, *there is a circle round the moon* ; a' bhó a's miosa 'sa bhuaile, *the worst cow in the fold* ; buailtean spréidhe, *herds of cattle;* bà 'sna buailtibh, *cows in the folds.*

†buaileach, -lichean, *s.f.* Ox-stall, stall. 2** Fold.

————, *a.* Of, or belonging to, a fold.

————an,** -ain, *s.m.* (buaile) Milker of cows. 2 Place where cows are milked.

buaileadair,** *s.m.* Assailant, assailer.

buaileag,* *s.f.* Circlet. 2(DU) Small circular enclosure.

———— -thimchioll, *s.f.* see bualagan-timchioll.

buailear, *fut. pass.* of buail, Shall be struck. 2 used impersonally, as, buailear suas leam, *I proceeded upwards.*

†buail-ghlas, *s.f.* Mill-pond.

buailidh,** *s.f.* Dairy, milk-house. 2 Stall. 3 Fold. A steach do 'n bhuailidh, *into the milking-house.*

buail-sa, *(for* buail thusa) Strike thou.

†buailt,** *s.f.* Cabin. 2 Locker. 3 Niche.

buailte, *past pt.* of buail. Struck, threshed,&c. Cha bhi bail air fodar buailte, *threshed corn is not spared.*

————ach, -tiche, *a.* Liable to, subject to. 2 Obnoxious to. 3 Apt to strike or thrash. 4 Exposed to. 5 Quarrelsome. 6**Amenable. Buailteach do iomadh cunnart, *exposed to many dangers ;* cha'n 'eil e 'na dhuine buailteach, *he is not a quarrelsome fellow* ; gun a bhith buailteach, *not given to striking*; buailteach do chìs, *liable to tax ;* gu mireagach, buailt ach, *playfully beating.*

buailteach, -eich, -eichean, *s. m.* Summer booth or hut for shielings. 2**Dairy-house.

————d,‡‡ *s.f.* Aptness, tendency.

†————an, -ain, *s.m.* Flying camp.

buailtean, *n pl.* of buaile.

————, -ein, -einean, *s.m.* Flail. 2 Supple, that part of a flail which strikes the corn. 3 see bualan. 4 One stick used in threshing corn, similar to a carpet-beater.

buailtear, *s.m.* Thresher. 2**Racket for tennis. 3(AF) Thresher (fish.) 4 see buailtean. 5 Any instrument for striking or beating.

†buain, *s.f.* Equality. 2 Deprivation.

buain, *gen.* buana, *dat.* buain, *s. f.* Reaping, cutting down, as of corn, mowing, harvest. 2‡‡Value. A' dol chun na buana, *going to the reaping* ; a' bhuain-eòrna, *the barley-harvest ;* àm na buana, *harvest-time* ; tha làrach buain fhòid air an athar, *there is a mark of turf-clearing on the sky*, i. e. there will be a good day to-morrow; deireadh buana,*harvest-home*; ge b'e nach cuir 'san là fhuar,cha bhuain 'san là theth, *he that sows not on a cold day shall not reap on a hot one.* A' b—, *pr.pt.* of buain.

buain, *pr.pt.* a' buain, [& a' buaineadh] *v.a.* Mow, reap, cut down. 2 Shear. 3 Pluck. pull, tear by the root. 4**Engage. A' buain na mòna, *cutting peats ;* a' buain sh!at, *cutting twigs;* a' buain chnò, *gathering nuts;* cha bhuain thu gu buileach, *thou shalt not wholly reap* ; buain a' chraobh seo, *cut down this tree*; a' buain na h-àraich, *cutting down* [*the files*] *of battle* ; buainidh aon fhacal ceud, *one sharp, bitter word may provoke a hundred retorts*, or *one word may start a conversation which will extend to a hundred words.*

buaine, *comp.* of *a.* buan. More or most enduring. Daraig a's buaine dreach, *an oak of hardiest form.*

buaine, *s. f.* Perpetuity, durability, lastingness, continuance. 2 Hardiness. Buaine an ni seo, *the durability of this thing.*

buaineachd, *s.f.* see buaine.

buainead, -eid,*s.f.* Degree of durability, or stability, durableness. 2 Hardiness.

buaineadh,**-nidh, *s.m.* Reaping,cutting down. 2 Enjoying, as the fruits of one's labour. A' b—, *pr.pt.* of buain. "Muinntir a' bhuainidh," is given by ** for *the reapers*, but "muinntir na buana" is the correct form.

————, *3rd. sing* & *pl.* of buain.

buainear, *fut. pass.* of buain.

buainiche, -ean, *s.m.* & *f.* Reaper, shearer. Ri taobh nam buainichean, *alongside the reapers.*

buainte, *past part.* of buain. Shorn, reaped. 2 **Torn up by the root. 3**Hewn down.

†buaintear, -eir, -earan, *s.m.* see buanaiche.

buair, *gen. sing.* of buar.

————, *pr.pt.* a' buaireadh. *v.a.* Tempt, allure. 2 Provoke, vex, annoy. 3 Disturb, distract. 4 Madden. 5 Alarm. 6 Make muddy, as water. 'Nuair a bhuair bhur n-aithrichean mi, *when your fathers tempted me* ; bhuair thu an t-uisge, *you have made the water muddy.*

buair, *s.f.* Rage.

buaire', see buaireadh.

buaireadair, -ean, *s.m.* Tempter. 2 Disturber, one who vexes or troubles. Air teachd do 'n bhuaireadair, *when the tempter came.*

buaireadh, -ridh, -ridhean, *s. m.* Temptation, tempting. 2 Trouble. 3 Disturbance. 4 Annoyance, aggrievance. 5 Severe trial. 6 Maddening. 7 Distraction. 8‡‡Passion,rage. A' b—, *pr.pt.* of buair. Mar ann an là a' bhuairidh anns an fhàsach, *as in the day of temptation in the wilderness ;* chum a buaireadh, *to tempt her* ; air a bhuaireadh, *tempted.*

buaireanta, *a.* Tempting, enticing, trying. 2 Inflaming. 3 Annoying, hence, provocative of strife. Duine *b., a quarrelsome fellow.*

buairear,** *s.m.* Kindler.

buaireas, -eis, -an, *s.m.* Tumult, confusion. 2 Anxiety, trouble. 3 Confusion of mind. 4 Ferment. 5‡‡Dismay, terror. Fo bhuaireas,

troubled, annoyed ; a' cur buaireis am measg nan daoine, *creating a disturbance amongst the people*; fion a' bhuaireis, *the wine that disturbs the mind.*
buaireasach, -aiche, *a.* Turbulent, raging. 2 Stormy, tumultuous. 3 Furious, fierce. 4 Inflaming. 5 Anxious. 6 Provoking. 7‡‡Dismaying. Deoch bhuaireasach, *drink that inflames* ; duine buaireasach, *a man that annoys, a tumultuous fellow* ; geamhradh buaireasach, *a stormy winter.*
——————d, *s.f.* Turbulence. 2 Storminess, tumultuousness. 3 Fierceness.
buaireasaiche, *comp.* of *a.* buaireasach.
buairte, *a. & past part.* of buair. Distracted, troubled. 2 Infuriated, enraged. 3 Tempted. 4 Stormy. 5 Made muddy, as water. 6 Disturbed, confused.
buait,** -e, -ean, *s.f.* Lantern.
bual, *s.m.* see buabhall.
†——, *s.m.* Remedy. 2 Physic. 3**Water. 4 ‡‡Urine.
bualachd, *s.f.* Drove of cattle.
bualadach,** *a.* Percutient.
†bualadh, *s.m.* see †bual.
bualadh, -aidh, *s.m.* Striking, beating, knocking. 2 Threshing. 3 Battle. Bualadh nan laoch, *the battle of heroes* ; bualadh arbhair, *threshing of corn* ; "bualadh a mach" *a repetition of the first measure in* ceòl-mór. A' b—, *pr. pt.* of buail.
bualagan-timchioll,‖ *s.m.* Ringworm.
bualaidh, -ean, *s.f.* Cow-stall.
†bualaisle *s.f.* Sea-lark. 2(AF)Wagtail.
bualan,§ *s.m.* Groundsel—*senecio vulgaris.*
†bualchomhla, *s.f.* Sluice.
†bualchrannach,*s.m.* Float,raft.
bualghas, -ais, *s.m.* Mill-pond.
†buall,‖ *s.m.* Healing.
buallachd, *s.f.* see bualachd.
bualtair, see buailtear.
bualtrach,-aich, *s.m.* Cow-dung.
buamasdair, see buamastair.
buamastair, *s.m.* One who talks boisterously. 2 Vain boaster. 3 Dolt, pompous blockhead, booby. 4 Sudden attack—*W. Isles*, probably from "buathan." The general idea expressed by this word in W. Isles is one having a mental defect.—J.M.

89. *bualan.*

buamastaireachd, *s.f.* Boisterous talking. 2 Vain boasting. [Not used in senses 1 or 2 in W. Isles, but to signify the conduct or condition of one somewhat mentally deficient.—J.M.] Ri *b.*, *talking boisterously.*
buan, buaine, *a.* Lasting, durable. 2 Long, tedious. 3 Hardy, tough. Cruaidh mar an fhraoch, buan mar a' ghiuthas, *hard as heather, lasting as pine* : rathad buan, *a tedious way* ; cead buan, *a long farewell* ; bodach buan, *a tough* or *hardy old man.*
†buan, *a.* Good, harmonious.
†buan, -aine, *s.f.* Nurse.
buana, *gen.sing.* of buain.
†buana, *s.m.* Hewer. 2 Reaper.
buanachadh, -aidh, *s.m.* Continuing, continuance. 2 Persevering, perseverance. 3 Obtaining. A' b—, *pr.part.* of buanaich. 'N am brosnachadh nach 'eil mo shùil a' buanachadh ? *in their provocation doth not mine eye continue ?*
buanachail,‡‡ -e, *a.* Perseverant.
buanachas,‡‡ -ais, *s.m.* Perseverance.
buanachd, *s.f.* Reaping. 2 Erroneously used for buannachd.
buanachdach, -aiche, *a.* see buannachd.
buanachdail, -e, *a.* see buannachdail.
buanaich, *pr.part.* a' buanachd & buanachadh, *v.a. & n.* Last, abide. 2 Persevere. 3 Endure, continue. 4 Erroneously used for buannaich.
buanaiche, -an, *s.m.* Reaper, shearer.
buanaichidh, *fut. aff. a.* of buanaich. Shall last, shall persevere.
buanaichte, *pt.part.* of buanaich.
buanas, -ais, *s.m.* Perpetuity, durability, long continuance, duration. 2††Perseverance.
buan-chuimhne, *s.f.* Lasting remembrance, memorial, chronicle. 2 Retentive memory.
——————ach, see buan-chuimhneachail.
——————achail, -e, *or* -ala, *a.* Having a retentive memory. 2 That is long remembered.
buan-dhùrachd,** *s.f.* Assiduity.
——————ach,** -aiche, *a.* Assiduous.
buan-ghàirdeachas, -ais, *s.m.* Continual or perpetual rejoicing.
buan-mhair, *v.n.* Last long, endure.
buan-mhaireachduinn, *s.m.* Enduring, continuing long, everlastingness, continuance, perpetuity. 2 Perseverance.
buan-mhaireannach, -aiche, *a.* Everlasting, durable, perpetual, perennial.
————————d, *s.f.* Perpetuity, durability, eternity.
buan-mharthannach, see buan-mhaireannach.
buan-mheal, *v.a.* Enjoy for ever.
buann,(CR) *pl.* buanntaich, *s.m.* Child—*Perthshire.*
†buanna, -chan, *s.m.* Billeted soldier. 2* Billet master. 3 Idler, straggler. 4‡Mercenary. Sè buannachan deug MhicDhomhnuill, *MacDonald of the Isles' sixteen billet-masters.*
buannachail, *a.* see buannachdail.
buannachas,* *s.f.* Free quarters for soldiers in place of rent.
buannachd, *s.f.* Gain, profit, acquisition. 2 **Acquirement. 3** Availableness. 4 for buaineachd, see buaine. 5 Emolument. 6 Erroneously used for buanachd. Ni gun *bh.*, *a profitless thing.* A' b—, *pr.pt.* of buannaich.
——————ach, -aiche, *a.* Profitable.
——————ail, -e, *a.* Profitable, emolumentary. 2 Available. 3 Useful. 4 Gratis, as a billet.
buannaich, *pr.pt.* a' buannachd, [& †buannachadh] *v.a.* Gain, profit, win, acquire. *Bh.* iad cliù, *they won renown.*
buannaiche, *s.m.* One who enjoys. 2 Winner.
buannaichte, *past part.* of buannaich.
buan-sheas, *pr.part.* a' buan-sheasamh, *v. n.* Persevere. 2††Stand steady.
——————amh, *s.m.* Persevering. 2 Standing for ever. A' b—, *pr.pt.* of buan-sheas.
——————mhach, -aiche, *a.* Firmly-footed. 2 Constant, lasting, perpetual, stable.
——————mhachd, *s.f.* Constancy. 2 Perseverance, continuance, firmness, durability, stability.
buantas, -ais, see buanas.
†buan-thosgach, *a.* Strong-tusked.
†buanuigh, *gen.* of buana.
buar, -air, *s.m.* Cattle, oxen. 2 Herd of cattle. Buair air buailibh, *herds in the folds.*
buarach, -aich, -aichean, *s.f.* Cow-fetter, shackle bound round the hind legs of cows when being milked. 2‡‡Stomach of limpet. 3‡‡ Slovenly, spiritless fellow. 4**Cow-spaniel.
buarach,** -aich, *s.m.* Early feeding of cows. 2 Rising to feed cows.
†buarach, *a.* Early.
buarachan, -ain, *s.m.* Cow-herd.
buarach-bhaoibh, *s.f.* Lamprey. 2 Kind of eel, supposed to inhabit rivers and to possess

magical powers.
buarach-na-baoibh, see buarach-bhaoibh.
buart, see buairte.
†buas, -ais, *s.m.* Belly. 2 Breach. 3 Rout. 4 Trade. 5 Art.
†——ach, *a.* Abounding in cattle.
†——ach, *s.f.* Bluebottle (plant)
†buasair,‡‡ *s.m.* Diaphragm.
buath, -uaith, *s.f.* Rage, madness, frenzy, fury. 2 Mad frolic. Tha buath air, *he is in a rage.*
———ach, -aiche, *a.* Subject to fits of madness. 2 Apt to become enraged.
———adh, -aidh, *s.m.* Mad fit, fury. 2 Wild ramble. 3 Mad frolic. 4 Impetuousness, rushing.
———al, -ail, *s.m.* (AH) Stall in a byre or stable. 2†*Boose. Dh'amais e air deagh bhuathal, *he has found a snug berth.*
†buatham, -aim, -an *s.m.* Bittern.
buatham, (J.M.) -aim, *s.m.* Sudden attack. *B.* doill, *the sudden and furious way in which a blind man would attack anyone who offended him.*
buathar,** -air, *s.m.* Affidavit.
buatharra, (JM) *a.* Impetuously raging. Duine *b.*, *a man of impetuous rage.*
bùb, *pr.part.* a' bùbail, *v.n.* Bellow, roar. 2* Blubber, as a child. 3 Weep in a most melancholy way.
bùb, -a, *s.m.* Roar, bellow, yell. Leig e bùb as, *he uttered a roar*
——ail, -e, -ean, *s.f.* Roaring, bellowing, yelling, blubbering, continued bellowing. 2 Lamenting. A' b - ,*pr. part.* of bùb. Ciod a' *bh.* a th' ort? *what are you bellowing for?* Bùbail tairbh, *the roaring of a bull.*
bùbaire, *s.m.* *Person that blubbers. 2(AF) Common bittern, see corra-ghrian.
————achd, *s.f.* Blubbering.
bùban, -ain, *s.m.* Coxcomb.
———ach, -aiche, *a.* Coxcomical, like, or pertaining to, a coxcomb.
———achd, *s.f.ind.* Behaviour of a coxcomb.
bùbarsaich, *s.f.* see bùbaireachd.
bùc,** *s.m.* Size, bulk.
bucach, -aich, *s.m* Boy. *prov.*
bucach, *a.* see bùcail.
bucaid, -ean, *s.f.* Pimple, pustule. 2 Boss of a shield. 3 Blotch. 4 Gaelic spelling of *bucket.*
†bucaide, *s.f.* Palm. 2 Knob.
bucaideach, *a.* Pimply, full of pimples, causing pimples. 2 Like a bucket. 3**Booming. Sgiath *bh.*, *a booming shield.*
bùcail,** *a.* Bulky, sizeable.
bùcaill, *gen.sing. & n. pl.* of bucall.
bucain, see bucaid.
bùcall, -aill, *pl.* -aill & -an, *s.m.* Buckle. Bùcaill airgid, *silver buckles.*
———ach, *a.* Buckled, having buckles, wearing buckles. Brògan *b.*, *buckled shoes.*
bucar,** *a.* Compact.
bucas, see bocsa.
buchainn, (AC) *s.m.* Swelling. Mios buchainn, *the month of swelling, month of bursting forth (May); called also* buchainn Muire, *the swelling of Mary*; buchainn buidhe Mhoire nam buadh, *the yellow swelling month of Mary of the graces*; buchainn Bealltainn, *the swelling of Beltane*; buchainn buidhe Bealtainn, *the yellow swelling of Beltane.*
————, *a.* Melodious. 2 Warbling. 3††Nestling.
————each, *a.* see buchainn, *a.*
buchallach, *a.* Nestling in the woods. 2†† Melodious.
bùchd, *s.m.* Cover of a book. 2 see bùc.
bùchdail,†† *a.* see bùcail.
———ach, *a.* see bùcail.
buchthuinn, see buchainn.
buchuinn, see buchainn.
bucla, see bùcall.
buclach,‡‡ *a.* Buckled.
buclaich, *v.a.* Buckle up. 2 Tuck up. 3 Trim.
————te, *past part.* of buclaich.
bucsa, see bocsa & aigh-bàn.
bucull, see bùcall.
———ach, see bùcallach.
†bud, *s.m.* see †budh.
bùd, see pùt.
bùdach, see pùtach.
budagoc, *s.m.* Snipe. 2 Woodcock.
†budh, see bu.
†budh, *s.m.* The world. 2 Breach. 3 Rout.
budhag, -aig, -an, *s.f.* Bundle of straw.
budhaigir, -e, -ean, *s.m.* Puffin or coulterneb, see fachach.
†budhail, *s.m.* Place, residence.
budhailt, -e, -ean, *s.m.* Recess on the inside of a cottage wall, wall-"press."
budragoc, see budagoc.
bùdraid, see butarrais.
bùdrais, see butarrais.
bugair, for budhaigir.
bugan,** -an, *s.m.* Unlaid egg.
†bugh, *s.m.* Fear. 2 Leek. 3 see briseadh.
bugha, *s.m.* (CR) Green spot by a stream, side form of "bogha," *a bow*, such spots being made bow-shaped by the windings of the stream.—*Skye.* 2† see bugh.
ughall,* -aill, *s.m.* Pot-hook.
bugsa, see bocsa & aigh-bàn.
†buibiollan, *s.m.* Coxcomb.
buic, *gen.sing. & n.pl.* of boc.
†buicead, *s.m.* Mouthful.
buicean, -ein, *s.m.* Young buck or roe. 2 Little buck or roe. 3 Pimple. 4** Bubble. Buicein bhinneach, *the high-headed young roes.*
————ach, *a.* Like a young buck or hart. 2 Of, or belonging to, a young buck or hart. 3 Pimply.
———— -darach,* *s.m.* Nutgall. [With the article *am.*]
buicein, see buicean.
————each, see buiceanach.
buiceis, *s.f.ind.* Sporting, as of a buck.
————each, -eiche, *a.* Sportive, frisky.
†buich, *s.f.* Breach.
buichd, (AC) *gen.sing. & n.pl.* of bochd.—*Isles.* [Not used between Sound of Barra and Butt of Lewis—J.M.]
†buichin, *s.m.* see buicean.
buid, *gen.sing. & n.pl.* of bod.
buideal, -eil, *s.m.* Cask. 2 Anker. 3 Bottle. 4‡‡Surly person. Mar bhuideal anns an toit, *as a bottle in the smoke.*
————aich, -ean, *s. f.* Blaze of fire. 'Na bhuidealaich, *on fire*; 's ann an sin a tha a' bhuidealaich! *what a conflagration is there!* chaidh e 'na bhuidealaich, *it blazed.*
buidealair, *s.m.* Butler.
buidealaireachd, *s. f.* Butlership, business or occupation of a butler. Chum a *bh.*, *to his butlership.*
†buidh, *a.* Grateful, thankful.
†buidhe, *s.f.* Thanks. Mo bhuidhe ri Dia, *my thanks to God*, a short expressive grace after meat, common in some parts of the Highlands. [Now buidheachas—‡]
buidhe,‡ *part.* of necessity, Glad to, had to.
buidhe, *a.* Yellow, golden. 2 Grateful. 3 Agreeable. 4††Lucky. Grian bhuidhe, *a golden sun*; falt buidhe, *yellow hair*; bu bhuidhe leat a dheanamh, *you were glad to do it*; is buidhe

dhuit, *it is fortunate for you*; bu bhuidhe leis na rùisg itheadh, *he would fain eat the husks.*

buidhe, *s.m.ind.* Yellow colour.

buidheach,‖ -ich, *s.f.* The jaundice. [Preceded by the article *a' bh.*]

———, -eiche, *a.* Thankful. 2 Well-pleased, satisfied, satiated, content. Cha'n 'eil e buidheach dhìom, *he is displeased with me*; bi buidheach, *be thankful*; bu chòir dhuit a bhith buidheach, *you should be thankful*; tha mi buidheach air son sin, *I am pleased at that*; cha'n fhaigh thu sin co dhiubh' bhitheas tu buidheach no diombach, *you will not receive that, whether you are satisfied or otherwise.*

buidheachan-bó-blioch, *s. m.* Cowslip, see muisean.

†**buidheachar**,‖ *s.* Dr. Gillies says—" A disease that played havoc in Ireland about the middle of the 7th. cent. I have not been able to form any opinion as to its identity. The root of the word is evidently bude (buidhe) *yellow*, as in our buidheach, *jaundice*, or *yellow disease.* The disease was evidently epidemic and violent, and it would apply to yellow fever with exactness, if we knew that disease to have been, or to have been possible as, an epidemic in this climate."

buidheachas, -ais, *s.m.* Thanksgiving, thanks, gratitude, acknowledgement. 2 Grace after food. 3 State of being bought but the bargain not concluded, in abeyance. Thoir buidheachas, *give thanks*; buidheachas do Dhia, *thanks be to God;* fo bhuidheachas, ann am buidheachas, *in abeyance*; taing is buidheachas, *many thanks*; buidheachas an fhogharaidh, *harvest thanksgiving.*

†**buidheachd**, *s.f.* Piety.

buidhead, -eid, *s.f.* Degree of yellowness. A' fàs am buidhead, *growing more and more yellow.*

buidheag, -eig, -an, *s.f.* Goldfinch. 2 Linnet. 3 Any small bird of a yellowish colour. 4 Any yellow flower. 5 Yellow seaweed. 6**Daisy. 7**Lily. 8**Cow of a yellowish colour. Gheibh sinn a' bhuidheag 'san lòn, *we shall find the daisy in the meadow.*

90. *Buidheag.*§

buidheag,§ -eig, -an, *s. f.* Creeping crowfoot (*ranunculus repens.*

buidheagach, *s. m.* see feamainn bhuidhe *and* feamainn bholgainn.

buidheagan, *nom. pl.* of buidheag.

———, -ain, *s. m.* Yolk of an egg.

buidheag-an-arbhair,§*s.f.* Scentless May-weed — *matricaria inodora.*

buidheag-an-t-samhraidh, *s f.* Corn-marigold, see bile-bhuidhe. 2 Buttercup. see cearban.

buidheag-bhealaidh,¶ -eig-, *pl.* buidheagan-bealaidh, *s.f.* Yellow-hammer—*emberiza citrinella.* A beautiful bird, but of very evil repute in Highland superstitions. 2‡‡Yellow bunting—*emberiza alba.*

buidheag-bhuachair, see buidheag-bhealaidh. 2‡‡Yellow-hammer—*cenchrymus bellonii.*

buidheag-hearbh, *s.f.* Camomile, see camomhail.

91. *Buidheag-an-arbhair.*

buidhean, -ain, *s.m.* see buidheag. 2 see buidheag-bhealaidh.

buidheann, [-einn &] buidhne, *pl.* buidhnean [& buidhnichean], *s. f.* Company, troop, band, party. 2**Rulers. Buidheann shaighdearan, *a company of soldiers*; rinn na Caldéich tri buidhnean, *the Chaldeans formed three bands*; tha mi a' faicinn buidhne, *I see a company.*

92. *Buidheag-bhealaidh.*

†**buidheannach**, *a.* Agminal.

buidhean-na-coille, *s.f.* Goldhammer. *Yellowhammer* according to ‡‡, which gives "buidhnein-na-coille." 2 ¶Woodpecker, see lasair-coille. 3 Bullfinch, see corcan-coille.

†**buidheannail**, *a.* Agminal.

buidhean-nan-ingean,§ *s. m.* Sea-spurge—*euphorbia paralias.*

buidhe-bhàn, *a.* Buff (colour.)

†**buidhe-Chonnaill**,‖ see †buidheachar.

buidhe-dhonn, *a.* Auburn (colour.)

buidhe-nan-ingean, see buidhean-nan-ingean.

buidhe-ruadh, *a.* Bay (colour.) 2** Auburn. Falt buidhe-ruadh, *auburn hair.*

buidhe-shoilleir, *a.* Amber (colour.) 2 Fallow.

buidhinn, buidhne, *s.f.* Gain, profit, emolument. 2*Quarrying of stones. Is don' a' *bh.* air na clachan sin, *how badly those stones are quarried*; is beag do bhuidhinn dheth, *your profit of it is little.*

———, *pr pt.* a' buidhinn, *v.a.* Gain, get profit, win, acquire. 2 Conquer. 3 Quarry. *Bh.* sinn bàir, *we won a game*; buidhnibh saorsa, *gain liberty.*

93. *Buidhean-nan-ingean.*

buidhinneach,* *s.f.* Quarry for stones, &c.

buidhleis,(AF) *s. f.* Black or rock gobie.

†**buidhlia**, *s.m.* Puddle.

buidh-liath, *a.* Pale yellow (in colour.)

buidh-mhios, *s.m.* (*lit.* the yellow month) July.

buidhne, *gen.sing.* of buidheann & of buidhinn.

buidhneach, -eiche, *a.* Victorious, successful. 2 Numerous. 3 In bands or companies. 4 Acquiring, gainful, profitable. Na laoich *bh.* mhòra, *the high-minded victorious heroes.*

———, -ich, -ichean, *s.f.* Band, company, troop, party. 'Uile bhuidhnichean, *all his bands.*

———,‖ *s.f.* see buidheach. *Suth'd.*

buidhneachd, *s. f.* Victoriousness, successfulness. 2 Gain, profit. 3 Aggrandizement.

buidhnich, *pr.part.* a' buidhneachadh, *v.a.* Arrange into companies or parties. 2 ‡‡Impeople.

buidhnichean, *n.pl.* of buidheann.

buidhnichte, *past pt.* of buidhnich. Arranged or drawn into companies or parties.

buidhnidh, *fut. aff. a.* of buidhinn. Shall or will win, &c.

buidhre, *s.f.* Deafness.

———, *comp.* of bodhar. More or most deaf. Cluinnidh tu air a' chluais a's buidhre e, *you will hear it in the deafest ear.*

buidileir,†† -ean, *s.m.* Gaelic spelling of *butler*.
———eachd,†† *s.f.* Office of a butler.
buidire,(AC) *s.m.* Witling. Bheir *b.* breith ach co a bheir ceartas? *a witling may give judgment but who will give justice?*
buidseach, see buitseach.
———as, see buitseachas.
———d, *s.f.* see buitseachas.
buidseir, *s.m.* Great grey shrike *or* butcher-bird, see pioghaid ghlas. 2 Gaelic spelling of *butcher*.
buig-bhuinne, see bog-bhuine.
buige, *s.f.* Softness. 2 Humidity. 3 Effeminacy.
———, *comp.* of bog. Softer, softest. 2 Smoother, smoothest.
buigeachas,** -ais, *s.m.* Tenderness, pity, compassion. Gun ath-thruas gun *bh.*, *without compassion or pity.*
buigead, -eid, *s.m.* Degree of softness, &c.
buigean, -ein, *s.m.* Soft, effeminate, unmanly fellow.
———ach, see buigean.
buigileag, *s.f.* Bog, soft place, quagmire. 2 Anything very soft. 3 Crab after casting its shell. 4†† Coward, soft unmanly fellow. *B.* bhuntàta. *a soft, wet potato.*
buiginn,†† -e, *s.f.* Morass, marshy ground.
buigire, *s.* see budhaigir. *St. Kilda.*
buigleach, -ich, *s.m.* } see buigileag.
buigleag, *s.f.* } see buigileag.
buiglinn, *s.f* see buigileag.
buigneach, -eich, *s.f.* Bulrushes. 2 Generally any acquatic weeds or plants. 3 Quagmire.
†**buig-shibhin**, *s.f.* see bog-bhuine.
†**buigsin**, *s.m.* Little box.
†**buil**, see boil.
buil, -e, *s.f.* Completion, perfection. 2 Consequence, effect, issue, end, conclusion. 3 Success. 4 Application, use. 5‡‡ Advantage, improvement. Bithidh a' *bh.* dhuit, *the consequence must be obvious in your case*; bheir thu a' bhuil, *you will reap the consequences*; bithidh sin air bhuil, *that will come to pass*; is léir a' bhuil, *the result is obvious*; buil gach aon taisbein, *the effect of every vision*; tha a' bhuil sin air, *the effect of that is obvious on him*; an rud a nithear gu ceart, chìthear a bhuil, *when a thing is properly done, the result will be seen*; a thoirt gu *b.* 'fhacal, *to complete his word*; a bheir a dhroch innleachdan gu buil, *who will bring his evil devices to pass*; dean deagh bhuil dheth, *make good use of it*; buil cheart a dheanamh dheth, *to make proper use of it*; gu buil, (*adv.*) *above*; ni gun bhuil, *a useless thing*; tha a' bhuil air, tha a' bhlàth air, *the mark is on it*, or *it is like it*—a remark often used when good counsel is condemned, and one comes to grief because of the neglect, or it may be reversed to show that foolish counsel was not heeded, and the end justified the means adopted.
buileach, *a.* Complete, whole, total, entire. [Another form of baileach—‡]
———, (gu) *adv.* Completely, wholly, utterly, altogether. Glanaidh e gu ro bhuileach, *he shall thoroughly purge*; na tréig mi gu buileach, *do not forsake me altogether*; cha bhuain thu gu buileach, *thou shalt not wholly reap*; is buileach a dh'fhairtlich e ort, *it has completely defied you*; is buileach a chaidh thu a dholaidh, *you are completely ruined*; gu bileach, buileach, *pick and crumb*.
———adh. -aidh, *s.m.* Bestowing, giving. 2 Assignment. 3 Improving. 4 Finishing completely. 5**Presentation, as of a church living. 6‡‡Treatment, usage. A' *b.* ort, *bestowing on you*; chaidh a *bh.* gu mór, *he was much abused*; nach ann air tha 'm buileachadh? *is he not badly used?* —*Suth'd*; buileachadh math, *a good use*; droch bhuileachadh, *a bad use*. A' b—, *pr.pt.* of builich.
buileachas,** -ais, *s.m.* Frugality.
†**buileamhuil**, *a.* Raging, mad.
buileann, see builionn.
———ach, see builionnach.
bùileasg, -eisg, see bùlas.
buileastair, -e, -ean, *s.m.* see bulaistear.
builg, *gen. sing. & n. pl.* of balg. 2‡‡Bellows. 3‡‡Seeds of herbs.
———, *s.f.* Distemper among cattle through heat or want of water.
builg,* *v.a.* see balg & balgaich. 2* *v.n.* Rise, as a fish in the water, rise to the fly.
———each,‡ *s.m.* Knobbed seaweed, see feamainn bhalgainn.
———eadh, *s.m.* Bubbling up, as water beginning to boil. 2 Blistering.
builgeag, *s.f.* see balgan.
———ach, *a.* see builgeanach.
builgean, -ein, -an, *s.m.* Blister. 2 Pimple. 3 Bubble, bell on liquor. 4 Little bag, bladder. 5**Bellows. 6(AF) Puffin. Mar bhriseadh builgein. *like the bursting of a bubble.*
———ach, -eiche, *a.* Full of blisters, pimples, pustules, or bladders.
builgeanta, *a.* Fat and small, as a dog.—Gael. Soc. of Inv'ss, xv, 53.
†**builgeas**, *s.f.* see builgleas.
———ach, -aiche, *a.* Spotted.
builgein, -e, -ean. see builgean.
———each, -eihhe, *a.* Full of pustules, blisters or small bubbles.
builgeun, (AF) *s.m.* Puffin, see fachach.
†**builghionn**, *s.f.* see builionn.
†**builgleas**, *s.f.* Blister.
†———ach, *a.* Spotted. 2 Blistered.
builich, *pr.pt.* a' buileachadh, *v.a.* Grant, bestow, present. 2 Administer, manage. 3 Spend, dispose of. 4 Improve. 5 Finish completely. 6‡‡Treat or use one well or ill. Gach ni a bhuilich Dia ort, *everything God hath bestown on thee*; *b.* an là, *finish the day completely*; *b* an ùine, *improve the time.*
———te, *past pt.* of builich. Assigned, &c.
†**builid**, *for* (am) bheil iad?
builionn, -inn, -an, *s.f.* Loaf of bread or sugar.
———ach, -aich, *s.m.* Baker.
———ach, -aiche, *a.* Full of loaves.
———aiche, *s.m.* see builionnach.
buill, *gen. sing. & n. pl.* of ball.
buill-bheirt, *s.pl.* Tackling, instruments.
buille, *pl.* -an & annan, *s.f.* Blow, stroke, strike, knock. Buille air son buille, *blow for blow*; fead am builleannan, *the noise of their blows*; buille thall 's a bhos, mar gu'm bitheadh duine a' marbhadh radanan, *a hit here and there, like a man killing rats*—often applied by worthy "Moderates" in the North to the Catechists' style of preaching.
builleach, -eiche, *a.* That gives blows. 2 Prone to give blows or to strike, percutient.
———as, -ais, *s.f.* Act or habit of striking. 2**Boxing 3 Bruising.
builleanach, *a.* Striking, giving blows. Sàthach builleanach, *giving thrusts and blows.*
builleasg, -eisg, *s.m.* see bùlas.
buille-choilleag, *s.f.* Blow given to the ball in playing shinty, sending it beyond the goal and winning the game.
buillis, see buidhleis.
buillsgean, -ein, -an, *s.m.* Middle, centre. 2 Focus. 3 Core. *B.* [illegible] fairge. *the midst of the sea*; am buillsge[illegible] an teine, *in the* ca-

tre of the fire; b srutha, *the vortex of a stream.*
builsgean, see buillsgean.
built, *gen.sing. & n.pl.* of balt.
†buime, *s.f.* see muime.
buimealair, buimilear, } *s.m.* see bumailear.
†buimpis, *s.m.* Pump.
buin, *pr.part.* a' buntuinn, *v.a. & n.* Belong to. 2 Interfere, meddle with. 3 Treat with, deal with. 4 Take away, tear from. 5 Touch, handle. 6 Be related to. Na *b.* da sin, *do not touch that* ; buinidh iad d' a chéile, *they are related to each other* ; 's ann do Dhia a bhuineas slàinte, *to God belongs salvation* ; *b.* gu caoimhneil ri m' ghaol, *deal gently with my love* ; cò dha a bhuineas seo? *to whom does this belong?* cha bhuin e dhuit-se, *it does not belong to you* ; an rud nach buin duit, na buin da, *do not meddle with what does not concern you.* [The Irish *beanaim* is from the *v.* bean, *touch* ; the Scottish Gaelic, which has the idea of relationship or origin (cha *bh.* e dhomh, *he is not related to me*) seems to confuse *bean* and *bun*, stock.—‡]
†buinchios, *s.f.* Pension.
buindeal, see buinnseal.
buine,** *s.f.* Set-off, in basket-making. 2 The thick welt or border finishing any wicker-work. †3 (*s.m.* McL & D) Tap, spigot.
†buineadhach, -aiche, *a.* Warlike. 2 Powerful.
†buinean, *s.m.* Shoot, twig, branch.
†———a, *a.* see boirionn.
buinidh, *fut.aff.act.* of buin. Shall or will belong, &c.
buinig, *v.a.* Conquer, obtain by conquest. buinigear buaidh le foighidinn, *victory is won by patience.*
———, *s.f.* Superiority.
buinn, *gen.sing. & n pl.* of bonn.
bùinne,* *s.m.* Statue, bust. 2 One who stands stock-still. Is tu am bùinne, *you stand stock-still, like a statue.*
buinne, -achan, *s.f.* Border, hem, selvage. 2 Spout, cataract. 3 Rapid current, stream. 4 Strong tide. 5 Confluence. 6 Pool in a river. 7‡‡Drop. 8‡‡Tap, spigot. 9** Billow. 10 *rarely* Sprout, twig. 11**Ulcer, boil. Air *b.* reidh, *on a smooth stream* ; buinnean àrda, *lofty billows.*
——— ach, -ich, *s.f.* Looseness, diarrhœa, flux, dysentry. [Preceded by the article *a' bh.*]
———ach, *a.* Contemptible, abominable. Duine buinneach, *a contemptible person.*
——————-mhór, *s.f.* Cholera-morbus. [Precededby the article *a' bh.*] 2§ Osier-twig, see fineamhuin.
———ag, -eig, -an, *s.f.* Twig. 2 Germ. 3 Sprout. 4††Docken. 5 Young maiden. 6 Familiar term in addressing a female. 7 Sole of a shoe. 8‡‡Hem, border. 9‡‡Sorrel shoot. Cha chuir e *b.* air a bhrògan, *it will not sole his shoes.*
†buinnéamh, -imh, *s.m.* Effusion.
buinnean,** -ein, *s.m.* Shoot, young twig.
buinnean-beò, (AF) *s. m.* Sea animalculæ, phosphorescence.
buinnean-leana, *s.m.* Bittern, see corra-ghrian.
buinne-beò, *s.m.* Beginning of the flow of a spring-tide.
buinne-shruth,** *s.f.* Precipitous stream. 2 Cascade. 3 Rapid tide way. Mar bhuinne-shruth reamhairt (reothairt), *like a spring-tide stream.*
buinnig, *v.a. & s.f.* see buidhinn.
———each, *a.* see buidhneach.
———eachd, *s.f.* see buidhneachd.
buinnir, -ean, *s.m.* see bonnair (appendix.)
buinnse,** Gaelic spelling of *bunch.*
———al, -eil, *s.m.* Ream of paper. 2 Truss. 3 Bunch.
buinnteach, *a.* Causing looseness of the bowels.
——————, -eich, *s.m.* One troubled with a flux, one who is habitually troubled with looseness. 2 Leather for shoe-soles, the thickest part of the hide.
buinnteachd, *s.f.* Flux, dysentery, habitual looseness of the bowels.
buintear, -eir, -eirean, *s.m.* Dunce.
buintinn, *s.m. & pr.part.* see buntuinn.
bùir, *pr. part.* a' bùirich [& bùireadh] *v. n.* Roar, bellow, as a deer or bull.
buirbe, *s.f.* Barbarity, barbarism. 2 Fierceness, wrath, anger, rage, savageness. 3 Severity. 4 Cruelty. 5 Turbulence. 6 Boisterousness. Gun gheilt no buirbe, *without fear or wrath*; mharbh sibh iad le buirbe, *you killed them in a rage.*
———, *gen. sing. f.*, and *comp.* of borb.
———achd, *s.f.* same meanings as buirbe.
buirbean, -ein, *pl.* -einean, *s.m.* ||Cancer. 2†† Savage.
———ach,** *a.* Cancerous.
———achadh,** *s.m.* Canceration.
bùird, *gen.sing. & n.pl.* of bòrd.
bùirdeasach, -aich, *s.m.* Freeman of a city or town, 2 Burgess. 3 Merchant, shop-keeper. 4 Citizen. 5 Boarder. 6 Idler. Bùirdeasaich sgiathach nan speur, *the winged inhabitants of the skies.*
bùire, *s.m.* see bùireadh.
———adh, *s.m.* Wailing, loud weeping, burst of grief. 2 Roaring, bellowing, braying. 3 Rutting. 4*Rutting-place. Poll bùiridh, *the rutting-place of deer*, see dàmhair. Bhris uaipe bùire, *she broke a loud burst of grief.*
†buireadh, -ridh, *s.m.* Gore. 2 Pus, corrupt matter.
bùireadh, *3rd. pers. sing. & pl. imp.* of bùir.
bùrean, -ein, *s.m.* Roar, bellow, as of a deer. 2 Loud noise. 3(AF) Bittern (*lit.* lowing bird) see corra-ghrian. An fhairg' a' teachd le *b.*, *the sea coming with a noise.*
———ach, -aiche, *a.* Roaring, bellowing, noisy, ‡‡mugient.
bùireinich, *s.f.ind.* see bùireadh.
bùirgeiseach, see bùirdeiseach.
buirich, *s.f.* Roaring, as a bull, bellowing. 2 Wailing. 4**Growling. 3 Loud lament. 5 Low murmur.
———, *pr.part*, a' bùrach [& a' bùrachadh] *v.a.* Dig, delve. 2 *v.n.* **Howl, roar, make a loud lament.
———e, *s.m.* Mattock, pickaxe. 2 Hoe. 3 Spade. 4 Dibble. 5 One who delves or digs. 6(AF) Bittern (lowing bird) see corra-ghrian.
———-idh, *fut.aff.a.* of bùirich.
bùiridh, *gen.sing.* of bùireadh.
bùirleadh, -idh, *s.m.* Language of folly or ridicule.
bùirling, *s.f.* see birlinn.
bùirn, *gen.sing.* of bùrn.
bùirseach, -ich, *s.f.* Deluge of rain. 2‡ Rousing fire—*Hebrides.*
bùirte, *s.f.* Gibe, taunt. 2 Sarcasm. 3 Witticism, repartee.
buis,** *s.f.* Kit.
†buiscean, -ein, *s.m.* Thigh, haunch. 2 Thigh-armour.
buisdear, (DU) *s.m.* Wizard. 2 Wicked fellow.
buisdreach, see buitseach.
———d, see buitseachd.
buiseal, *s.m.* Bushel.
buisean, -ein, -an, *s.m.* (*dim.* of bus) Little mouth.

bnisein, see buiseau.
buisgean, -ein, *s.m.* see buillsgean.
buisginn,** *s.* Buttock.
buisinn-iall,* *s.m.* see buaichdein-iall.
buisneachd,‡‡ see buitseachd.
——————ach,‡‡ *a.* Incantory.
†bùiste, -an & -achan, *s.m.* Pouch, pocket, scrip.
†buistin, *s.m.* Fustian.
buistreachd, see buitseachd.
buit, *a.* *Badenoch* for buitidh. 2 "Fugy" as a fowl, see pùt.
†buite, *s.m.* Firebrand.
bùiteach, -ich, -ean, *s.f.* see buidealaich. 2 ‡‡*s.m.* Threat.—*Suth'd.*
†buitealach, *a.* Fierce. *s.f.* see buidealaich.
buithre, see buidhre.
bùitich, *v.a.* Threaten.—*Suth'd.*
buitidh, -e, *a.* Bashful.
†buitse,** *s.f.* Icicle.
buitseach, -ich, -ichean, *s.m.* & *f.* Wizard. 2 Witch. Is *b.* e, *he is a wizard* ; is *b* i, *she is a witch.*
——————as, -ais, *s.m.* Witchcraft, sorcery, magic.
——————d, *s.f.* Witchcraft, sorcery, enchantment.
†buitsear, -eir, *s.m.* Gaelic spelling of *butcher.* 2 Butcher-bird, see pioghaid ghlas.
†——————achd, *s.f.* see feòladaireachd. Ag ionnsachadh na *b.*, *learning the butchery business.*
buitseir, see buitsear.
†bul, *s.m.* Manner, fashion, mode.
bul,* *s.m.* see bùlas.
bula, *s.m.* †Bowl. 2 see bùlas.
bulag, see pulag
bulaistear, see bulastair.
bùlas, -ais, *s.m.* Pot-hook. 2 see †bùlos.
bulastair,†† -ean, *s.m.* Sloe, bullace.—*prunus insititia.* 2 Potato seed.
bulbhag, (balbhag) } (CR) Boulder—*Perthsh.*
bulbhag-cloiche, }
bulg, *v.n.* (balg) Bulge—*Perthshire.*
bulg, builg, *s m.* Ship's bilge-piece, (see bàta F8, p. 73.) 2 Ship's hold. 3 Convexity. 3 see balg
——ach, *a.* see balgach. 2 Convex, bulging out. 3 Capacious. Ceud srian bulgach, *a hundred capacious bridles.*
bulgaich, *v.a.* see balgaich.
bulgan, see builgean.
bulla, *s.m.* Bowl. 2 Ball. 3 Bubble. 4 Pope's bull
†——ch, *a.* Globular, like a globe,. ball or bubble.
†——ch, *s.m.* Connor (fish.)
†bùlos,‡‡ *s.m* Prune.
bulta, (AF) *s.m.* Colt.
bumailear, -an, *s.m.* Bungler.
——————ach,‡‡ -aiche, *a.* Loggerheaded.
——————achd, *s.f.ind.* Bungling, clumsiness, inexpertness, awkwardness.
bumalair, see bumailear.
bun, *pl.* buin & bunan, *s.m.* Root, stock, stump. 2 Bottom, base, foundation, foot. 3 Socket. 4 Mouth of a river. 5 Squat, short person or animal. 6 Dependence, trust, confidence. 7 Affiance. 8‡‡Care, charge, keeping. Bun os cionn, *upside down* ; b. na craoibhe *the root of the tree* ; *b.* na beinne, *the bottom of the hill* ; *b.* na h-altrach, *the foot of the altar* ; spìon as a bhuin e, *root it out* ; na dean bun á gàirdean feòla, *place no confidence in an arm of flesh* ; dean bun á Dia, *place your confidence in God* ; cha'n fhàg e bun no bàrr, *he will leave neither root nor branch* ; am bun an taighe, *taking care of the house*; am bun nan caorach, *tending the sheep* ; asad rinn ar sinnsearan bun, *in thee our ancestors placed their confidence* ; bun eich, *an old stump of a horse* ; bun na cìob, *the root of the mountain grass* ; bun balaich, *a stout squat fellow* ; *b.* a dhà sgéithe, *the sockets of his two wings* ; *b.* an earbaill, *the rump.*
bun,(AF) *s.m.* Northern diver, see muir-bhuachaill.
——abhas, -ais, *s.m.* Element. 2††Buttock.
——abhasach, *a.* Elemental. 2††Pertaining to a buttock.
——ach, -aich, *s.f.* Coarse tow. 2 Tare of flax. 3 Sturdy little person. 4 Cutch, roots of wool to be shaken out of the tufts. 5 Radical, *in politics.*
——ach, -aiche, *a.* Clumsy, not handsome. 2 Squat, short, stumpy. 3**Sturdy. 4††Radical, of, or pertaining to, a root. 5**Chopping.
——achadh, -aidh, *s.m.* Establishing, founding, settling. 2 Taking root. A' b—, *pr.part.* of bunaich.
——achaiunt, *s.f.* Etymology.
bunachar, -air, -an, *s.m.* Foundation. 2 Base, bottom. 3 Root. 4 Authority. 5 Etymology. 6*Dependence, confidence, trust.—*Islay.* 7**Radix. Na dean *b.* sam bith á sin, *place no confidence in that* ; cha'n 'eil *b.* eil' agam, *I have nothing else to depend on—Islay*; O '*bh.* luaisgidh an talamh, *the earth shall quake from its foundation.*
bunachas, -ais, *s.m.* Foundation, root, principle. 2 Etymology. 3 Authenticity, authority. Faclair bunachais, *an etymological dictionary.*
——————ach, *a.* Authentic. 2 Well-founded. 3 Etymological. 4 Radical. 5††Fundamental.
bunadas, -ais, *s.m.* see bunadh.
bunadh, -aidh, *s m.* Origin, stock. 2 Root, foundation. 3††Habitation.
†bunadhas,** -ais, *s.m.* Institution.
†——————ach,** *a.* Institutionary.
bunaich, *pr.pt.* a' buanachadh *v.a.* Found, establish, make firm. 2 Take root. 3 Depend on.
——————te, *a.* & *past pt.* Established, founded, rooted.
bunaideach, *a.* see bunaiteach.
——————d, *s.f.* see bunaiteachd.
bunaidh, *s.m.* Habitation. Gu bunaidh, *for ever.*
bunail, *a.* Radical.
——————t, *s.f.* }
——————teach, *a.* } see bunait——.
——————teachd, *s.f.* }
——————teas, *s.m.* }
bunain,‡‡ *s.pl.* Stubble.
bunait, -e, -ean, *s m.* Steadiness, constancy. 2 Basis, sure foundation 3 Inflexibility, firmness. 4 Perseverance. 5‡‡Dwelling. Bunaitean an domhain, *the foundations of the earth.*
——————each, -eiche, *a.* Steady, grounded, fixed, stable. steadfast, immovable. 2** Authentic. 3**see bunaiteach.
——————eachadh, -aidh, *s.m.* Founding, establishing A' b—, *pr.part.* of bunaitich.
——————eachd, *s.f.* Steadiness, firmness, constancy. 2 Inflexibility. 3 Safety.
——————eas, -eis, *s.m.* Same meanings as bunaiteachd.
——————ich, *pr.pt.* a' bunaiteachadh, *v.a.* Found, establish. 2 Inherit. 3 Possess. 4 Fix an abode. 5* Inhabit.
bunamas, -ais, *s.m.* see bunntamas.
bunamhas,* -ais, *s.m.* see bun-mhàs.
——————achd,** *s.f.* Radicality.

bunan, (*pl.* of **bun**) Stubble.
bunan, -ain, *s.m.* (*dim.* of **bun**) Little root or stump. 2‡‡Stubble root.
bunanta, -ainte, *a.* Strong, stout, steady, sturdy, firm. 2 Well-set, having a good bottom or foundation. 3††Constant, steadfast.
———chd, *s.f.* Firmness, steadiness. 2 Sturdiness.
bunasach, -aiche, *a.* Firm, solid, steady. 2‡‡ Well-founded. 3 Authentic. 4 Stout.
bun-bhean, (declined like *bean*) *s.f.* Female of discreet years.
bun-bhuachaill,¶*s.m.* Northern diver, see muir-bhuachaill.
bunchailleach, -eich, *s.f.* Old woman.
bunchar, -air, -an, *s.m.* bunachar.
bun-chiall, -chéill, *s.f.* Moral having a concealed meaning.
———ach, -aiche, *a.* Concealing a moral, as a fable.
†**bun-chìs**, *s.f.* Chief rent, tribute paid to a monarch. 2 Pension.
———each,** *a.* Pensionary.
bun-chìsear,** *s.m.* Pensioner.
†**bun-chìsiche**, -an, *s.m.* Pensioner.
bun-chùis, -e, -ean, *s.f.* First cause.
bun-chuisleach, -lich, -lichean, *s.f.* Foot-stalk.
bun-dearg,(AC) *s.m.* Red swelling (disease in cattle.)
bun-dubh, -uibh, *s.m.* That part of a root which is underground and comes up by pulling. 2 Lowest tiers of sheaves in a corn-stack. 3DU Roots of bracken, used as thatch for houses or corn-stacks.
†**bundun**, *s. m.* Foundation. 2‡‡Fundament. 3 Blunder.
†———ach, *a.* Ungainly.
bun-feam,(AC) } see bun-feann.
bun-feamainn, }
bun-feann, *s.m.* Tail, root of the rump.
bun-feòir, *s.m.* Hay-stubble, orts.
bun-fhàth, -a, *s.m.* Primary cause.
bunglas,§ -ais, *s.m.* Purple mealie-grass—*molinia cærulea.*
bun-luchd,*s.pl.* Original inhabitants, aborigines.
bun-mhàs, -ais, *s.m.* Buttock.
———ach, *a.* Having large buttocks. 2 Of, or belonging to, the buttocks. 3 Strong in the bottom.
†**bunn**, *s.m.* Work.
bunna,(AF) *s.m.* Northern diver, see muir-bhuachaill.
bunna-bhuachaill,¶ *s. m.* Great auk, see gearra-bhall. 2 Northern diver—*W. Isles* (IM) see muir-bhuachaill.
bunnacha-bac,(AC) *s.m.* The horizon. 2(AH) Eaves of a thatched house.
bunnachas,(AH) -ais, *s.m.* Stability.
bunnan, -ain, *s. m.* Bittern. 2 (AF) Black beetle, crawler.
bùnndaist, -e, -ean, *s.m.* Fee, wage, perquisite, bounty. 2††Thrashing. 3††Grassum. 4‡‡ Weaver's fee, paid in kind.
bùnnlum, -uim, *s.m.* Steadiness, solidity. 2 Self-command.
———ach, -aiche, *a.* Solid, steady.
bun-nòs, -nòis, *s.m.* Old custom.
bùnnsach, -aich, -aichean, *s.f.* Rod. 2 Osier twig, (see fineamhuin.) 3 Place where osiers grow. 4 Sudden rush.
bùnnsag, -aig, -an, *s.f.* see bùnnsach.
———ach, *a.* Twiggy.
bùnnsaidh, -e, *a.* Firm, solid, strong, having a good bottom.
bunntair,(AC) *s.m.* Foundation of a house.
bùnntam, -aim, *s.f.* Solidity, steadiness, sedateness.
———ach, -aiche, *a.* Shrewd, sensible. Steady, sedate.
———as,-ais, *s.m.* Deep discernment, shrewdness. 2 Quickness of comprehension. 3 Solidity, steadiness.
bun-os-ceann, *adv.* Upside down, topsy-turvy.
bun-os-cionn, see bun-os-ceann.
bun-rannsachadh,** *s.m.* Analysis.
bun-rannsachail,** *a.* Analytical.
bun-rannsaich, *v.a.* Analyze.
bùnsach, *s.f.* see bunnsach.
bùnsag, see bùnnsag.
bùnsaidh, see bùnnsaidh.
buntais,***s.pl.* Perquisites.
buntàta, *s.m.* (*s. & pl.*) Potato, potatoes—*solanum tuberosum.* Tha am buntàta bruich, *the potatoes are boiled.*
———-tachair, *s. pl.* Potatoes left in the ground during winter.
———-talmhuinn, DU see bun à a-tachair.
buntuinn, (a') *pr.pt.* of buin. Belonging to, meddling with, touching, taking away. 2†† Dealing. A' b. ris gu nàimhdeil, *persecuting him.*
———eas,** *s.m.* Adjunct, appendage, appurtenance, concomitant. 2 (AH) Blood or family relationship.
†**bunudhasach**, *a.* see bunasach.
†**bùr**, -ùir, *s.m.* Boor, clown, boorish person. 2 Swelling of anger. 3‡‡Sot.
†**bùr**, *poss.pron.* (now bhur Your.
bura-bhuachaill,¶ *s. m.* Northern diver, see muir-bhuachaill.
bùrach, -aich, *s.m.* Searching or turning up the earth, delving, digging. †2 Exploit. †3 File of soldiers. †4 Swelling, tumour, sore.
———adh,** -aidh, *s.m.* Digging, delving. A' b—, *pr.pt.* of bùirich. 'G a *bh.* le 'rùdanan, *digging it with his knuckles.*
buraghlas,(AF) *s.m.* Large dogfish.
bùraich, *v.a.* see bùirich.
———e, *s.m.* bùiriche.
———te, *past pt.* for bùirichte.
buraidh,* *a.* Mouldy, as land, easily delved.
———, *s.m.* see burraidh.
———eachd,* *s.f.* Mouldiness.
†**burba**, see buirbe.
burbaigh,(AF) *s.f.* Whistle-fish, bourbee.
burban, *s.m.* see burmaid.
burbanaich,(JM) *s.f.* Irritation of any open sore. When a wound was too often probed, or an unsuitable remedy was applied, people said "bhurbanaicheadh an lot."—*Isles.*
bur-bhuachaill, -e, -ean, see muir-bhuachaill.
bùrd, see bùrt.
———,* *s.m.* see dùrdan.
burdag,(AF) *s.f.* Minnow. 2 Shrimp.
†**bùrdan**, *s.m.* (MM)Kind of chorus. 2 see dùrdan.
———ach, *a.* Pertaining to a chorus. 2 see dùrdanach.
burdanaiche,** *s.m.* Libeller.
†**burg**, *s.m.* Village, town. 2 Tower, fortress.
burgaid, -e, -ean, *s.f.* see purgaid.
———,†† *s.m.* Awkward or noisy fellow.
———each,†† *a.* Clownish, awkward.
———ich, *pr.pt.* a' burgaideachadh, *v.a.* see purgaidich.
burgair, -ean, *s.m.* Gaelic spelling of burgher.
bùrlam, see bùrnlam.
burmaid,§ *s.f.* Wormwood—*artemesia absinthium.*
burmaill, *s.f.* see burmaid.
bùrn, -ùirn, *s.m.* Water, *not applied to* salt water. Sàil is bùrn, *salt water and fresh water;* ni bùrn salach làmhan glan, *foul water makes clean hands*; cho saor ri *b.*, *as cheap as*

water; chitheam am fuil do bh., would that I saw their blood as water.—AM.
——ach, -aiche, a. Watery.
——lam,†† -aim, s.m. Flood, downpour.
†burr, a. Great.
bùrr,(CR) s.m. Pout, sulky mouth—Perthsh.
burracach,(JM) -aich, s. m. Clownish person.
burracaid,* s.f. Stupid or silly female.
————, s.m. Clumsy, awkward fellow.
————each,-eiche,a.Clownish.

94. Burmaid.

burrach, see burras.
burraghlas, -ais, s.f. Torrent of brutal rage.
————ach, a. Brutally passionate.
burraidh, pl. -nean, s.m. Fool, blockhead, simple, foolish person. 2‡‡Surly, morose fellow. 3(AF) Cat (bye-name.)
burraidheachd,AM s.f. Folly.
————neachd, s.f. Folly, stupidity.
burrail,* v.n. Romp, as children, play rudely.
————eas, (AH) -ais, s f. Inarticulate jabber of a child or a deaf mute.
burrais, gen. sing. & n. pl. of burras. Also used as nom. sing.**
burrait, a. Stupid. 2‡‡Beastly.
burral, -ail, s.m. Howl, burst of grief, weeping, clamorous grief, mournful and loud cry. Chuala na glinn a bh., the glens heard his howl.
————ach, a. Crying. 2 Apt to cry, whine or howl. 3 Sulky.
————adh,* -aidh, s.m. Romping; rude, noisy play.
————aich, s.f. Loud lamentation; loud, continued crying or weeping. 2 Dog's howl, in Uist "sgalartaich," and there "burralaich" is applied to human beings—J.M. Thòisich e air b., he began to howl.
burras, -ais, s.m. Caterpillar. 2(AF) Worm.
————gadh, -aidh, -aidhean, s.m. Burst of rage or passion.
————gaireachd, s.f. Brutality. 2††Fury.
burr'caid, see burracaid.
burrghlas,†† -ais, see burraghlas.
————ach,†† see burraghlasach.
burrsgadh,‡ s.m. Burst of passion.
burruis, s.m see burras.
bùrsach,†† -aich, s.m. Stormy fellow. 2 Torrent of rain.
bursaid, s.f. Worsted.
bur-shuileach,(AC) a. Blear-eyed.
bùrt, -ùirt, s.m. Mockery, ridicule, quizzing, joking. Is fheairrde cuideachd cùis-bhùirt, a company is the better of a laughing-stock.
bururus, -uis, s.m. Warbling, purling noise, gurgling. 2 Infant lisping. Ri b. sèimh, warbling softly.
————ach, -aiche, a. Purling, warbling. 2 Lisping, as an infant. 3††Harsh grating.
bus, -uis, s. m Mouth. 2 Lip. 3 Snout. 4 Ludicrous term for the human mouth. 5** Mouth with very large lips. 6**Kiss. 7** Gaelic spelling of puss. 8‡‡ Pouting of the lips in anger. 9AM Cheek—Uist. Am fear a dh'itheas an ceann dathadh e 'm bus, he that eats the (sheep's) head let him singe the mouth himself; chuir e bus air, he made a grimace.
†bus,‡‡ v. Shall be.
busach, -aiche, a. Snouty. 2 Having a large mouth. 3 Blubber-lipped. 4 Pouting. 5 Sullen.
busach,* s.f. Female having large lips.
busachd,* s.f. Deformity of blubber-lips.
busag, -aig, s.f. Girl with thick lips. 2 Smacking kiss. 3††Blow on the lips.
busaidh,** s.f. Gaelic spelling of pussy.
busair,* -ean, s.m. Man having blubber-lips. 2 Sullen fellow.
bus-dubh, s.m. Surly, dark aspect. 2 Name for a dog [**and a democrat(!)] (black snout or mouth.) 3‡‡Ill-fate.
busg, v.a. Thread a fishing-hook. 2**Hinder. †3Dress, adorn. Gaelic spelling of busk.
——adh, -aidh, s.m. Threading a fishing-hook. 2 Head-dress. 3 Dressing. 4 Adorning the person of a female.
busgaid, -e, -ean, s.f. Bustle, hurry.
busgainn,** s.f. Dressing. 2 Adorning. B. dubhain, the dressing of a fishing-hook.
busgainn,** pr.pt. a' busgainn, v.a. see busgainnich.
————ich, v.a. Dress, adorn. 2 Buckle up, prepare. 3**Dress a fishing-hook.
bus-iall, -éill, -iallan, s.f. Muzzle.
————aich,* v.a. Muzzle.
buslach,(DU) s.f. Small quantity, tuft, handful.
bustail, s.f. Puffing, blowing. 2 Discord, disagreement, fuss.
bustuil, see bustail.
bùt, see pùt.
†bùta, s. Butt, mark, object. 2 Clown. 3‡‡ Short ridge. 4‡‡Tun.
buta, s.m. Difference in price, surplus—Islay, Atholl. 2 CR Luckpenny, discount—Arran. [Bata in Perthshire, only used in gu bata, which is equivalent to gu leòir, but stronger.]
buta,(JM) s.m. Skin float to keep fishing-nets and lines from sinking—Outer Hebrides [in Skye bolla.]
bùta, s.m. Sometimes used for pùt, (fledgling, young of moor-fowl.)
butadh, -aidh, -aidhean, s.m. see putadh.
butag, -aig, -an, s.f. see putag.
————oc, s.f. Snipe, see gobhar-athair.
†butais, see bòtuinn.
†butar, s.m. Gaelic spelling of butter.
butarrais, s.f. Confusion, heterogenous mixture, hotch-potch. 2 Filth. 3 Dross.
bùth, -a, pl. bùthan, [-annan & bùithean,] s.m. Shop. 2 Tent, pavilion, booth. 3 Cot. 4 Ant-hill. Shuidhich e a bh., he pitched his tent; chòmhnuich iad am bùthaibh, they dwelt in tents; sròl as a' bh., crape from the shop.
——ach,‡‡ -aiche, a. Of, or pertaining to, a cottage.
——ach, (JM) -aich, s.m. Instrument to prevent calves from sucking.—Uist.
buthaid, s.f. Puffin (fish.) 2 Puffin or coulterneb (bird), see fachach.
buthaigre, s.f. Puffin, (bird) see fachach.
buthainn, s.m. see bùthuinn.
buthainn,* v.a. see buthainnich.
————eachadh, -aidh, s.m. Thumping, thrashing, beating.
————ich, v.a. Thump, thrash, beat.
bùthal, -ail, s.m. Pot-hook. 2 Fulcrum. B. ràimh, the fulcrum of an oar, rowlock, (see bàta, No. 40 p. 76.)
butha-mucag,(AC) s.f. Blue hyacinth.
bùthan, -ain, s.m. Little booth, pavilion. 2 Tent. 3 Bothy.
————, n.pl. of bùth.
bùthlas, -ais, -an, s.m. see bùthal.
————an, n.pl. of bùthlas.
bùth-leighidheachd,‡‡ s.f. Laboratory.
—— -sheangan,‡‡ s.m. Ant-hill.

buthuinn, *s.f.* Long straw used for thatching, [sputhuinn *in Argyll.*]
butrais, *s.f.* see butarrais.
butta,** *s.* Butt (measure.)

C c

c, Coll, *hazel* ; the third letter of the Gaelic alphabet now in use. When not aspirated, broad *c*; that is, before *a*, *o*, or *u*, sounds like *c* in *cub*. as cù, *a dog* ; small *c* sounds like *c* in *cube* or *k* in *kick*, as cìr, *a comb*. When aspirated, it sounds like the Greek *ch* in chórdē, as moch, *early*; or small, like chĕimŏn, as chì, *see*.
c', (*for* cò ? cia ? ciod ?) *pron.* What ? C'ainm a th' ort ? *what is your name ?* c' àit' an toir mi e ? *where shall I bring it ?*
†**ca**, *s.m.* House.
c' à ? *adv.* (*for* c' àite) Where ? C' à bheil thu ? *where art thou ?*
ca'ab,‡‡ *s.m.* Concord in singing.
cab, *pr.part.* a' cabadh, *v.n.* Indent, notch, as the edge of a bladed weapon. 2 Hack. 3 Break land, dig. Chab thu an sgian, *you have notched the knife.*
càb,‡‡ *pl.* -achan, & -annan, *s.m.* Cap. 2 Cloak.
cab, caib, *s.m.* Mouth. 2 Mouth ill-set with teeth. 3 Gap. 4 Head. 5 Hebrew measure equal to about 2 Scots pints. 6**Aperture. 7‡‡Bit of a bridle.
caba, DU caibe, see caibe.
cabach, -aiche, *a.* Toothless. 2 Ugly-mouthed. 3 Notched, indented, full of gaps. 4**Long-toothed. 5**Babbling, garrulous. 6‡‡Hacked, irregularly cut.
——, *s.f.* Female with broken teeth. 2†† *s.m.* Toothless man. *C.* an dranndain, *a peevish old woman.*
†——, *s.m.* Hostage.
——**adh**, *s.m.* Indenting, notching, indentation. 2 Growing indented or notched. A' c—, *pr.pt.* of cabaich.
†**cabad**, -aid, *s.m.* Head.
cabadh, -aidh, *s.m.* Notching, hacking, indenting. 2 Breaking of land, digging. 3 Gaping. 4‡‡Gasping. A' c—, *pr.pt.* of cab.
càbag, -aig, -an, *s.f.* Cheese.
cabag, -aig, -an, *s.f.* Toothless female. 2 Tattling woman. 3 Any blunt or toothless instrument. 4 Hacked instrument, as a knife, &c. 5** *rarely* Strumpet.
càbagach,†† -aiche, *a.* Abounding in cheeses.
cabaich, *pr.part.* a' cabachadh, *v.a.* Notch, indent. 2 Make blunt.
†**cabaig**, *s.f.* Pillory.
†**cabail**, *s.f.* see cabhlach.
cabain, *gen.sing.* & *n.pl.* of caban.
cabair, *gen.sing.* & *n.pl.* of cabar.
——, -ean, *s.m.* Tattler, gabbler. 2 Toothless fellow.
——**eachd**, *s.f.* Custom of tattling, prattling, or babbling.
cabairneach,(JM) *s.m.* Garrulous little boy or man.
cabais, *s.f.* see cabaireachd.
——**eachd**, *s.f.* see cabaireachd.
——**t**, -e, *s.m.* Gaelic spelling of cabbage.
——**teach**, -eiche, *a.* Of, or pertaining to a cabbage or cabbages.
——**tich**,‡‡ *v.a.* Mash, as cabbage.
†**caball**, see capull.
càball -aill, *pl.* -aill [-llan & -llaichean,] *s. m.* Cable.
——**ach**, *a.* Cabled, abounding in cables.
†**caban**, -ain, -an, *s.m.* Booth, tent. 2 Cottage. 3**Cottager. Gaelic spelling of *cabin.*
càban, -ain, *s.m.* Gaelic spelling of capon.
cabar, -air, *pl.* -air & cabraichean, *s.m.* Horn. 2 Antler. 3 Stake. 4 Pole, rafter. 5 Eminence, height. 6**Deer. 7**Rung. 8**Lath. 9***rarely* Joint, confederacy. 10(AF)see cabhar.† Cabar beinne, *a mountain-top ;* cabair féidh, *a deer's antlers*, (the war-cry, and one of the crests of the MacKenzies) ; *c.* cléibh, *a pannier's ri*
——**ach**, -aiche, *a.* & *s.m.* see cabrach.
cabar-corra,(AH) *s.m.* Odd or superfluous pole or rafter in a house. Tha cabar-corra a staigh, *there is a superflous rafter in the house* —a hint frequently given to a speaker to direct his attention to the fact that a suspected tattler is among those listening to him.
—— -**buaile**,‡‡ *s.m.* Fold-stake.
—— -**droma**, -air-, *s.m.* Ridge-pole (of house.)
—— -**fraighe**,‡‡ *s.m.* Eave-beam.
—— -**oisne**, *s.m.* Corner-pole.
†**cabartha**, *a.* Coupled.
cabasdair, *s.m.* see cabsdair.
cabasdan,** see cabsdair.
cab-dheudach, -aich, *s.f.* Broken teeth, indented teeth.
cabh, *v.n.* see cath.
——**a**, see cathadh.
cabhachan,* -ain, *s.m.* Cuckoo-titterer. (bird)
cabhadh,* -aidh, see cathadh.
cabhag, -aig, *s.f.* Hurry, haste, despatch, speed. 2 Straits, troubles, difficulties. 3** Kind of pillory. Dean cabhag, *make haste* ; tha thu 'nad chabhaig, *you are in a hurry.*
——**ach**, -aiche, *a.* Hasty, impatient, hurried, in haste, causing haste, requiring haste. 2 Abrupt. Gnothach cabhagach, *business requiring haste.*
——**achd**,* *s.f.* Hastiness. 2 Abruptness.
——**aich**,‡‡ *v.a.* Accelerate. 2 Precipitate.
cabhaig, *gen.* & *dat. sing.* of cabhag.
cabhail, -ean, *s.f.* Frame (of a cycle.)
cabhair, caibhre, *s.f.* see cobhair.
——, *v.a.* see cobhair.
——**each**, *a.* see cobharach.
†**cabhan**, -ain, *s.m.* Field, plain.
cabhanach, -aich, see camhanach.
†**cabhan-shail**, *s.f.* Prop or stay of a building.
†**cabhar**, -air, *s.m.* Hawk. 2 Any old bird. 3 see gabhar.
†**cabhara**, see cathbharr.
cabharnach,* -aich, Wicket, bar-gate, gateway.
cabhartach, -aich, see cobhartach.
cabharthach, see cobharthach.
cabhlach, -aich, -aichean, *s. m.* Fleet, navy. 'Na chabhlach làidir, *in his strong fleet.*
——**ail**,‡‡ -e, *a.* Naval.
——**an**,** -ain, *s.m.* Mariner.
cabhlachdach,** *a.* Of, or pertaining to, a fleet. 2 Having a large fleet.
cabhlaich, *gen.sing.* of cabhlach.
——**e**,* *s.m.* Admiral.
cabhnadh, see cathadh.
†**cabhog**, -oig, -an, *s.f.* see cathag. 2‡‡Ransacking, plundering.
cabhra, cabhrach, *gen.sing.* of cabhair.
——, *a.* see cobharach.
†**cabhrach**, *s.m.* see cobharach.
cabhraich, *v.* see cobhair.
càbhruich,‡ *s.f.* Flummery, a mess made of the boiled filtered juice of corn seeds and

called by the Lowlanders *sowens.*
cabhsaidh,* *a.* Snug, comfortable. Gaelic spelling of *cosy*. 2 AH) Tame, docile.
————eachd,* *s.f.* Snugness. 2 Too much fondness for comfort. 3(AH) Docility.
cabhsair, -e, -ean, *s.m.* Causeway, pavement.
————each, -eiche, *a.* Abounding in causeways or pavements, having a causeway or pavement.
————eachd,* *s.f.* Business or act of making causeways or pavements, pavior's work.
cabhsairich,‡‡ *v.a.* Pave.
cabhsairiche, -an, *s.m.* Pavior, maker of causeways.
cabhsanta, *a.* Dry. 2 Snug, comfortable, cosy. 3 Fond of comfort. 4 Effeminate, unmanly.
cabhtair,|| -e, -ean, *s.m.* Issue, drain in the body.
cabhuil, -ean, *s.f.* Kind of creel for catching fish. 2 Hose-net. 3 Basket.
†cablachda, *a.* see cabhlachdach.
càblaid,* -e, *s.f.* Turmoil, tumult.
————each,* *a.* Tumultuous.
càblan, (*for* càbaill) *pl.* of càball.
càbluich, *v.a.* Cable, bind with cables.
càbog, see càbag.
cabon, *s.m.* Capon. 2(AF) Young dromedary. Gaelic spelling of *capon.*
†cabra, *s.f.* Sepulchre.
cabrach, -aich, *s. m.* Deer, stag. 2 Copse, thicket. 3** Timber-moss. An déidh chabrach, *in pursuit of deer*; mar astar doill an c., *as a blind man's progress through a hedge.*
————, -aich, *s.f.* Bold masculine female.
cabrach, -aiche, *a.* Of, or belonging to, poles, rafters or antlers. 2 Branchy, branching. 3 Like a rung or stake, full of rungs. Gu c., *well supplied with antlers.*
†cabradh, *s.m.* Joining, coupling.
†cabram, *v.a., Irish form of pres. aff.* I couple, unite. 2 I concur. 3 I concert.
†cabsanta, *a.* Dry, snug.
cabstair, -ean, *s.m.* Kind of curb. 2 Bit. 3 Bridle. 4 Muzzle.
————each, *a.* Having a curb or bit. 2 Like a curb or bit.
————ich,** *v.a.* Muzzle.
cabsdanaich, see cabsdairich.
cabstair, see cabsdair.
cabstar, ,, ,,
càbull, -uill, see càball.
————ach, *a.* see càballach
cac, -a, *s.m.* Excrement, dung, dirt, ordure, mire, filth.
cac, *v.a. & n. pr. part.* a' cac [& a' cacadh] Go to stool. 2** Avoid.
cac, -a, *a.* Dirty, filthy, foul, vile, nasty.
†càca, *s.m.* Cake.
caca, *a.* see cacach.
cacach, -aiche, *a.* Filthy, dirty, miry, nasty, excrementitious.
†cacadh, -aidh, *s.m.* Yawl.
cacadh,** -aidh, *s.m.* Voiding of excrement. A' c—, *pr.part.* of cac.
cacaidh, *fut. aff. a.* of cac.
cacail, *a.* see cacach. 2 Shabby.
cacan, D.U. -ain, *s. m.* Annoyance, anger. Chuir e c. orm, *he annoyed me, made me angry.*
†cacan, *s.m. dim.* of cac.
cac-an-airgid,** *s.m.* Litharge.
càch, *pron.* The rest, others. Càch a chéile *each other* [*not for* gach a chéile as McL & D has it. *Le 'chéile, ri 'chéile,* &c. prove that *a* stands for *his*, or we should have *leis a chéile*, &c., which is never heard. *Gach* is never aspirated, for example, "do gach fear," *cách* is aspirated, for example, "thug iad na laoigh do chàch a chéile—J.G.M.] ; air thùs chàich, *in front of the rest*; thoir do *ch.* e, *give it to the rest*; thàinig e roimh *ch.*, *he arrived before the rest*; am measg *ch.*, *among the rest.*
cachaileith, -e, -ean, *s. f.* Gate, rustic gate. 2** Temporary breach made in a park wall as a thoroughfare for carts or cattle.
†cachain, *past v.* Can.
†càchan, -ain, Advantage, profit, use. 2** Gate.
†cachd,** *s.f.* Maidservant. 2 Confinement. 3 Fasting. 4 Clamour.
cachdan, -ain, *s.m.* Uneasiness of mind, vexation, chagrin.
cachlaidh, } see cachaileith.
cachliadh, }
cachliag, }
†cacht, *s.f.* The world. 2 Exulting shout. 3 see cachd.
†————, *adv.* Commonly, generally.
†————amhuil, *a.* Servile.
caclach, -aich, *s. m.* Filth, trash, nastiness, dirt.
cacradh, -aidh, *s.m.* Cacophony. Bad sound of words (Fuaim searbh, neo-bhinn.)
cac-shiubhal, -ail, *s.m.* Flux, diarrhœa.
†cacta, *s.m.* Hunger.
†c'ad ? *adv.* How long since ? (cia fhada ?)
†cad, -aid, *s.m.* Friend. 2 *pron.* see ciod.
†càd, *a.* Holy, high, sacred, good.
†cadach, *s.f.* Affinity, friendship. 2 Assistance.
†cadachas, *s.m.* Expiation, atonement.
†cadad, *s.m.* Suppression or ellipsis of a letter. 2** Eclipse.
cadadh, -aidh, *s.m.* Tartan. 2 Kind of cloth particularly used for making hose. Còta de chadadh nam ball, *a coat of spotted tartan.*
cadail, *gen. sing.* of cadal.
————,** *v.n.* see caidil.
†cadaim, *s.* Chance.
cadal, -ail, *s.m.* Sleep, slumber. 2 Delay. Is sèimh do chadal, *gentle is thy slumber*; tha e 'na chadal, *he is asleep*; an cadal dhuit ? *are you sleeping ?* chaidh iad a chadal, *they went to sleep*; cha robh cadal mu 'n righ, *the king was sleepless.*
————ach, -aiche, *a.* Sleepy, drowsy, heavy with sleep, dull, lethargic. 2** Causing sleep, narcotic. 3. Dilatory. Galar *c., lethargy.*
————achd, *s.f.* Sleepiness, drowsiness, heaviness.
————aiche,* *s.m. & f.* Dormant creature like a serpent.
————ag,(AF) *s.f.* Slug.
————an, -ain, *s. m.* Short sleep, nap. 2 §White poppy, see codalan.
———— -deilgneach,|| *s. m.* The pricking sensation in a limb known as "pins and needles." [Preceded by the article *an.*]
———— -eun, -eòin, *s.m.* Mandrake.
cadalan-tràghad,JM *s. m.* Semi-dormant fish found on the shore. When any person was extremely slow at work, he was compared to the cadalan-tràghad.
†cadall, *s.m.* Battle, confused skirmish.
cadaltach, see cadalach.
————d, see cadalachd.
cadaltaiche, see cadalaiche.
†cadam, -aim, *s.m.* Fall, ruin, destruction. 2 Fork of the hair.
†————ach, *a.* Destructive, ruinous.
cadan, -ain, *s.m.* ‡see codan. 2 Pledget.
†cadarus, *s.m.* Contention.
†———— ? *adv.* Whither ?
†cadas,‡‡ -ais, *s.m.* see codan. 2 Friendship. 3 Honour. 4 Bombast.

cadath, *s.m.* see cadadh.
cadha, *s.m.* Narrow pass at the side or foot of a mountain. 2 Narrow ravine. 3 Porch, entry. 4 (CR) Pass—often occuring in place-names, and erroneously translated as "brae" in Sutherland, Ross. and Argyll. Dorus a' *ch.*, *the inner door.*
†cadhachas, -ais, *s.m.* Reconciliation, second agreement.
cadhag, -aig, -an, *s.f.* Swingle-tree wedge. 2 ¶Magpie, see pioghaid. 3** Jackdaw, see cathag.
†cadhal,-ail,*s.m.* Basin. 2 Hide, skin. 3‡‡Rail.
càdhal, *s.m.* see càl.
†cadhal, *a.* Fair, beautiful.
——, *s.m.* Point of the compass, "airt." Ciod e an cadhal as am bheil a' ghaoth ? *what "airt" is the wind from ?—Suth'd.*
cadhan, -ain, *s.m.* see cathan.
cadhas, -ais, *s.m.* Friendship. 2 Honour, respect. 3 Privilege. 4 Attention.
†cadhasach, *a.* Friendly. 2 Respectful. 3 Honourable.
†——d, *s.f.* Friendliness. 2 Respectfulness. 3 Honourableness.
†cadhla, *s.f.* Goat. 2 Gut 3 Fat of the guts.
†——, *a.* Fair, handsome, beautiful. 2 Kind.
†cadhlach, -aich, *s.m.* } Goat-herd.
†——al,‡‡ }
cadh-luibh, *s.f.* see cat-luibh.
†cadhmus, *s.m.* Haughtiness, pride, arrogance.
càdhmus, -uis, -an, *s.m.* Bullet mould.
†cadhus, -uis, see cadhas.
cad-luibh, see cat-luibh.
——each, *a.* see cat-luibheach.
†cado, *s.m.* Blanket.
†cados, -ois, *s.m.* Lawn.
càdran, -ain, *s.m.* see cànran.
†——ta, *a.* see cànranach.
cafag, -aig, *s.f.* see cabhag.
†cagaidh, *a.* Just, lawful.
†——,** *s.f.* Strangeness.
cagail, *v.a.* see coigil.
cagailt, -e, -ean, *s.f.* Hearth. 2**Parsimony, frugality, economy. 3‡‡ Profit, advantage. Corra-*ch.*, *the sulphurous hue seen in hot embers on a frosty night ;* airgiod cagailte, *hearth-money.*
cagainn, *pr. part.* a' cagnadh, *fut.aff.act.* cagnaidh, *v.a.* Chew, gnaw, champ, masticate. 2**Backbite. Cha chagnainn cùl mo chompanaich, *I would not backbite my companion.*
cagair, *v.n.* Whisper. 2 Suggest. 3 Listen to a whisper. 4**Conspire. Trobhad, cagair, *come, hark.*
——, *gen.sing.* of cagar.
cagal, -ail, *s.m.* see cogal.
——lach, *a.* Parsimonious, sparing, economical.
——lach, -aich, *s.m.* Penurious person, economical person.
——lachd, *s.f.* Parsimoniousness, penury.
†cagalt, *s.m.* Frugality.
——ach,** -aich, *s.m.* see cagallach. 2 Economical person.
†cagannach, -aich, *s.m.* Chew, materials for chewing.
cagar, -air, -airean, *s.m.* Whisper. 2 Secret. 3 Darling. 4**Buzzing sound, hum. Gheibhear bean-chagair, ach is ainneamh bean-ghaoil, *a dear-wife may be got, but a love-wife is rare—mo ghaoil* is a warmer expression than *mo chagair* for "my darling."
——ach, -aiche, *a.* Whispering. 2 Auricular.
cagaraich, -e, see cagarsaich.
cagaraiche, *s.m.* Breather, whisperer.
cagaran, -ain, *s.m.* Little darling.
cagar-athair, *s.m.* Wireless telegraphy.
cagarsaich, -e, -ean, *s.f.* Whispering. 2 Suggesting. A' c—, *pr.part.* of cagarsaich. Ciod a' *ch.* a th' ort ? *what are you whispering about ?*
——, *pr.part.* a' cagarsaich, *v.n.* Whisper.
†caghaidh, *s.f.* Right, privilege.
cagnadh, -aidh, *s.m.* Chewing, gnawing, champing, mastication. A' c—. *pr.pt.* of cagainn.
cagnaidh, *fut.aff.a* of cagainn.
cagnar, *fut.pass.* of cagainn. Shall be chewed.
caguinn, see cagainn.
†cagunnach, see cagannach.
†cai, *s.f.* Road, way. 2 House. 3 Titling. 4 AF Cuckoo's bird.
caibdeil, see caibideil.
caibe, *n.pl.* -annan & -achan, *s.m.* Spade. 2 Mattock. 3 The iron part of a cas-chrom, or of any delving instrument, blade of a spade. 4‡ Turf-cutter. Iasaid a' chaibe gun a chur fo thalamh, *the loan of a spade that is not put in the ground.*
caibeal, -eil, -an, *s.m.* Chapel. 2 Family burial ground. 3‡‡Chaplain.
caibeineachd, *s.f.* Gabbling, prattling.
caibe-làir, } (CR) *s.m.* Flauchter-spade,
caibe-sgrath, } breast-plough. The English name "breast-plough" is an absurd one, for the instrument never touches the breast. [*Illustration in appendix.*]
caibheanach, -aich, *s.m.* see caimeineach.
caibheis, *s.f.* Tittering, laughing.
caibhne, *s.f.* see caoimhneas.
caibhre, (*for* coibhre) *gen.sing.* of cobhair.
——ach, -eiche, *a.* see cobharach.
caibhridh, (*for* coibhridh) *fut.aff.act.* of cobhair.
caibhtinn, see caiptean.
caibideil, -il, -ean, *s.m.* Chapter.
†caibineid, *s.f.* Gaelic spelling of *cabinet.*
†caibinneachd, see caibeineachd.
†caibne,** *s.f.* Mouth.
†caic, *a.* Blind.
†caicmhe, *s.f.* Neck ornament.
†caid, *s.f.* see cuid. 2 Rock. 3 Summit.
†caide, see c'àite ?
†caideacha, *s.m.* Spot, stain.
caideag,(AF) *s.f.* Earthworm.
†caideal, -eil, -an, *s.m.* Pump.
caidearach, *a.* see caidreach.
——d, see caidreachd.
†caidh,** *a.* Chaste, immaculate. 2‡‡ Noble.
†——,** *s.* Manner, method.
†caidhe, *s.f.* Spot, dust, dirt, blemish.
†——ach, *a.* Dirty, blemished, polluted.
†caidheachd, *s.f.* Chastity, purity of morals.
†caidheamhuil, *a.* Decent.
†caidhean, -ein, -an, *s.m.* Leader of a flock of goats. 2 Turtle dove.
†——, *a.* Alone, solitary.
†caidheil, *a.* Chaste, decent.
†caidhidhe, *a.* Covered with a hide.
†——, *s.f.* Cover of a house.
†caidhle, *s.f.* Finishing.
†caidhlich, *v.a.* Finish, conclude.
†caidhliche, *s.f.* Thick fur.
†caidhlichte, *past part.* Finished, concluded.
†caidhni, *s.f.* Virgin.
caidhtiche, *a.* Long-enduring.
caidil, *pr.part.* a' cadal, *v.n.* Sleep, slumber, repose. 2**Delay. Cha do chaidil mi neul, *I have not slept a wink;* na caidil ach aotrom, *let thy sleep be light.*
†caidiol, *s.m.* Sun-dial.
caidir, *v.a. & n.* †Permit, cherish. 2 Connive at. 3 *Embrace, hug, fondle, caress. 4 Indulge in. 5**Converse.
caidreabh, -reibh, *s.m.* Fellowship, partner-

ship. 2 Familiarity, friendship, acquaintance, intercourse. 3 Vicinity. 4 Discourse. 5 The embrace, the bosom. 6** Commerce 7**Assemblage. An c. a chéile, *in the bosom of each other.*

————ach, -aiche, *a.* Friendly, kind, familiar, affectionate. 2**Conversant. 3**Fond. 4**Social.

————ach, -aich, *s.m.* †Company. 2**Ally. 3**Acquaintance. 4**Fellow-lodger. 5*Companion, bosom friend.

————achd, *s.f.* see caidreabhas.

————as, -ais, *s.m.* Consanguinity. 2**Alliance, as of states. 3**Familiarity, intimacy. 4 Fondness. 5 Sociability.

caidreach, -ich, *s.m.* Spouse, partner. 2 Companion, acquaintance. Mo chaidreach, *my spouse.*

————, -aiche, *a.* see caidreachail.

caidreachail, -e, *a.* Friendly, familiar. 2 Kind, affectionate. C. ri daoine anns gach dàimh, *friendly to men in every station of life.*

caidreachd,**s.f.* Same meanings as caidreabhas.

caidreadh, -eidh, *s.m.* see caidreabh.

caidreamh, -eimh, see caidreabh.

————ach, -aich, *s.m.* see caidreach.

————ach, -aich, *s.f.* Company.

————ach, -aiche, *a.* see caidreachail.

caidreamhail,‡‡ -e, see caidreamhach.

caidreamhas, -ais, see caidreabhas.

caidrich, *v.a.* Befriend, make friendly. 2 see caidir.

caifean,** -ein, *s.m.* Cypher. 2 Trifling, diminutive fellow. 3 AF (bird) Chiff-chaff, chatterer, wood-chatterer.

————ach,** *a.* Trifling, diminutive, pithless.

caig,†† -e, *s.f.* Rush of conversation.

caig,** *pr. part.* a' caig *v.a.* Teaze, torment. Tha e a' caig orm, *he is teasing me.*

caige,** *s.f.* Teasing.

†caigeal, *v.a.* see caigil.

caigean,** *s.m.* Winnowing-fan.

caigeann,** *v.a.* Couple together, link together.

caigeann, -inn, -an [& caignichean,] *s.f.* Pair, couple, brace, (used only of animals and when bound together.) 2‡‡Couple, machine for taming wild goats by binding them in pairs. [Governs the singular.]

————,†† -inn, *s.m.* Rough mountain pass. [An example of this as a place name occurs near Taigh-a'-chladha, Leadaig.]

caigil,** *v.a.* Gather up. 3 Cover the fire.—*Arran* (Same as coigil—CR.)

caigionn, -inn, -an [& caignichean] see caigeann.

†caigionn, *v.a.* see caignich.

caigleachd,** *s.f.* Commerce, intercourse.

†caigne, *s.f.* Winnowing-fan.

caigneachadh, -aidh, *s.m.* Coupling, linking. A' c—, *pr. part.* of caignich.

caigneadh, -nidh, *s.m.* see caigneachadh.

caignean, *pl.* of caigeann. 2† *dim.* of caigne.

†caignein, see caignean (2)

caignich, *pr.part.* a' caigneachadh, *v.a.* Bind, link, couple together. 2**Fan.

————ean, *pl.* of caigeann.

†cail,‡‡ *v.a.* & *n.* Burn.

càil, -e, -tean, *s. f.* Disposition, temper. 2 Quality, property, condition. 3 Life. 4 Strength. 5 Sense, endowment. 6 Constitution. 7 Voice 8 Appetite, desire, longing for food. 9 Look, appearance. 10*Pith. 11(AC) Anything. Cha'n 'eil càil air failbhe, *there is nothing in the firmament*; tha a chàil air falbh, *his constitution wears away*; gun chàil, *without strength* or *energy*; 'san taigh chaol gun chàil, *in the narrow house (grave) without power of motion, lifeless*; mo chàil 'gam thréigsinn, *my constitution* or *strength failing*; cha'n 'eil c. do bhiadh agam, *I have no appetite for food*; chum molaidh gleusaibh binn ur càil, *to praise attune your voice*; chaill iad càil an léirsinn, *they lost their sense of seeing*; gu'n faithnich naimhdean a càil, *that enemies may feel its temper*; 'nuair a thàinig càil an là, *at the first streak of dawn.*

†càil, -e, *s.f.* Spear. 2 Shield. 3 Assembly. 4 Ward. 5 Commendation. 6 Name. 7 Back.

†càil, *prep.* Behind.

†cailbhe, *s.f.* Mouth, orifice.

cailbhe, -an, *s.m.* (calbh) Partition wall, wattle or clay partition. 2‡‡ House wall from within.

†cailbheach, *a.* Wide-mouthed. 2 Yawning, gaping.

†————d, *s.f.* Continued or frequent yawning.

†cailbhearb, *s.m.* Cow-herd.

cailbhir,** *s.* Calibre.

cailc, *pr.part.* a' cailceadh, *v.a.* Chalk, mark as with chalk.

——, -e, *s.f.* Chalk. 2 Lime. 3 Calx.

†cailc, *s.f.* Shield. 2 Buckler.

cailceach, -eiche, *a.* Like chalk, chalky.

cailceadh, -idh, *s.m.* Chalking, describing or making out, as with chalk. A' c—, *pr. part.* of cailc.

†cailceamhuil, see cailceil.

cailceanta, *a.* Hard, firm.

cailceil, -e, *a.* Chalky, like chalk. 2 Hardy.

cailcein, *s.m.* Disorder in the eyes. 2DU Islet formed when the tide recedes, usually in an estuary.

†cailcin, *dim.* of †cailc.

cailc-thochailtear,** *s.m.* Chalk-cutter.

†càile, see càil.

caile, -an, *s.f.* Vulgar girl, quean, hussy. 2 Strumpet. 3 Any young girl—*Argyll & Perthshire.*

càile,** *s.f.* Capacity.

caileabh,* *s.m.* see cailbhe.

càileach, *s.m.* Refuse. 2 Husks of grain eaten by mice,&c.,"seeds,"chaff. 2‡‡see coileach.

————, *a.* Of, or belonging to, disposition. 2 Being well disposed or tempered.

————d, -an, *s.f.* Natural endowments, genius. 2 Energy, ability. 3 Temper, nature, constitution. 4**Affection. Gun chron chàileachd, *without blemish of temper*; gun fhàillinn 'nur càileachd ged 'shirte sibh, *without a failing in your nature although searched—Moladh an Leòghainn, Filidh, p.64.*

————dach, -aiche, *a.* Having natural endowments, having genius. 2 Accomplished. 3 Elegant. 4††Strong, powerful.

————dan, *n.pl.* of càileachd.

————dail,‡‡ *a.* Constitutional.

caileadair, -e, -ean, *s.m.* Philosopher, stargazer, **dervish. 2 Calendar.

————each, -eiche, *a.* Physical.

————eachd, *s.f.ind.* Star-gazing, prognostication, philosophy. 2 Chemistry.

caileadh, *Islay* for cailbhe.

caileag, -eig, -an, *s.f.* Little girl, "lassie."

————,¶ *s.f.* Black guillemot, see calltag.

————an, *n. pl.* of caileag.

†caileamhuil, *a.* Girlish.

càilean,** *s.pl.* Mental powers.

————, -ein, -einean, *s.m.* Seedling, husk. 2 Prickle. *C.* 'na fhiacail, *a seedling in his tooth.*

càileanach, -aich, *s.m.* Breeze.

————, -aiche, *a.* Husky, seedy, abounding with seeds. Min *ch.*, *meal full of husks.*

caileanta, *a.* Girlish, like a girl. 2**Fond of

girls.
cai'le nta, *a.* **Slow-paced. 2††Hard, firm.
caileas, -eis, *s.m.* Lethargy.
caileasadh, see caileas.
caile-bhalach. *s.f.* Romp, tomboy.
caile-circeiu,** *s.f.* Shuttlecock.
càil-éiginn, *s.f.ind.* Some, somewhat. 2 Small matter. 3**In some degree, in some measure. Tha c. de mhath air, *it is worth something.*
caileil, -e, *a.* Effeminate, womanish, queanlike.
càileil,** *a.* Constitutional.
càilein, see càilean.
†cailein, *s.m.* Scalding of the eyes.
†càileireachd, *s.f.* Cremation, burning of the dead.
†cailg, -e, *s.f.* Sting. 2 Resentment.
†——, *v.a.* Pierce, sting, prick.
†cailgeamhuil, *a.* Pricking, piercing, biting. 2 Pungent.
cailibhear,** *s.* Bore of a gun. Gaelic spelling of *calibre.*
cailidear, -eir, *s.m.* Rheum, phlegm, snot.
†cailidheach, *s.m.* Humourist.
†càilidheachd, *s.f.* Quality. 2 Genius. 3 Qualification.
†càilidheas, *s.f.* Disposition.
caílin, *pl.* cailinean, *s.f.* Girl, damsel, maid, nymph. 2**Company of young women. Cailin ro mhaiseach, *a very handsome damsel;* chum beathachadh do chailinean, *for the maintenance of thy maidens.*
†cailindha, *pl.* Calends (of a month.)
cailis, -ean, *s.f.* Chalice, sacramental cup.
cailise, *s.f.* Nine-pins, kayle.
caill, *pr.part.* a' call, *v.a.* Lose, suffer loss, forfeit Mu 'n caill iad an treòir, *ere they lose their strength.*
†caill, *s.m.* Testicle.
†——, *v a.* Name, call. 2 Emasculate.
caill'chail, -e, *a.* see cailleachail.
†caill'chula, *a,* see cailleachail.
†caille, *s.f.* Hood, veil, cowl.
cailleach, -iche, *pl.* cailleachan, *s.f.* Woman, single woman, old woman. 2 Old wife. 3 Woman without offspring. 4 Nun. 5 Carlin. 6(AC)Supernatural or malign influence dwelling in dark caves, woods and corries. 7 Coward, spiritless, heartless man. 8 The last handful of standing corn on a farm. 9 9 Circular wisp on the top of a corn-stack. 10 (AF) see cailleachag-cheann-dubh. 11 see càileach Ged a bha mi air uiread caillich a dh'arbhar, *though I possessed no more corn than a wisp.* Great emulation was displayed by all in harvest-time so as not to be last. Upon him came the cost of maintaining the other people if a dearth set in in the spring. The *Cailleach* was tied up with ribbons, and hung up on a nail till spring. On the first day of ploughing it was taken down and given as a handsel for luck to the horses—N.G.P.
Cailleach, -lich, *s.f.* The week in spring after "Gearran," *i.e.* from 12th. to 18th. April—*i.e.* First week of April Old Style. 2**see càileach.
caiileachag, -aig, -an, *s.f.* Little old woman.
—————— -cheann-dubh, *s.f.* Cole-titmouse, cole-tit. 2¶ Black-cap,—*parus ater.*
cailleachag-cheann-ghorm,¶ *s.f.* Blue tit-mouse —*parus cœruleas.*
cailleachail, *a.* Like an old woman. 2 Cowardly.
cailleach-an-dùdain, (*lit.* carlin of the mill-dust) AC Curious character dance, described as follows in *Carmina Gadelica.*

95. Cailleachag-cheann-dubh.

cailleach-an dùdain (cont.)—
"It is danced by a man and a woman. The man has a rod in his right hand, variously called *slachdan druidheachd,* (druidic wand), and *slachdan geasachd,* (magic wand.) The man and the woman gesticulate and attitudinize before one another, dancing round and round, in and out, crossing and recrossing, changing and exchanging places. The man flourishes the wand over his own head and over the head of the woman whom he touches with the wand, and who falls down, as if dead, at his feet. He bemoans his dead "carlin," dancing and gesticulating round her body. He then lifts up her left hand, and looking into the palm, breathes upon it, and touches it with the wand. Immediately the limp hand becomes alive, and moves from side to side and up and down. He rejoices and dances round the figure on the floor. Having done the same to the right hand, and to the left and right foot in succession, they also become alive and move. Though the limbs are living, the body is still inert. The man kneels over the woman and breathes into her mouth and touches her heart with the wand. The woman comes to life, and springs up confronting the man. Then the two dance vigorously and joyously as in the first part. The tune varies with the varying phases of the dance. It is played by a piper or fiddler, or sung as a "port-a-beul" (mouth-tune) by a looker-on or by the performers themselves. The air is quaint and irregular" and the words which are curious and archaic commence as follows:—
"Cailleach an dùdain, dùdain, dùdain,
Cailleach an dùdain, cum do dheireadh rium"
cailleachanta, *a.* Cowardly, soft, unmanly.
cailleachantas,** -ais, see cailleachas.
cailleachas, -ais, *s. m.* Conduct of an old woman. 2 Dotage. 3**Cowardice.
—————— -dubh,‡‡ *s.m.* Nunnery (profession of.)
cailleach-baic, (AH) *s.f.* In cutting peats, the outside peat in a bank.
———— -bhàn,¶ *s.f.* Snowy owl, see comhachag-bhàn
cailleach-bheag-an-earbaill, (AF) Long-tailed titmouse, see cìochan.
———— chòsach, see corra-chòsag.
———— -dhubh, *pl.* -eachan-dubha, *s.f.* Nun. 2(AF) Shag-cormorant, see sgarbh.
cailleach-oidhche, *s. f.* Common owl—¶*strix ulula.* 2 Tawny-owl. 3* Spiritless fellow. [see illustration 96.]
—————— bhàn, see c—oidhche-gheal.
—————— -gheal,** *s. f.* White owl.—*strix flammea.*
cailleach-oidhche-mhór,¶ *s.f.* Eagle-owl—*bubo maximus.* [see illustration 97]
cailleach-spuinge, *s.f.* Touchwood, soft tinder —‡*polyporus fomentarius* and *betulinus.*
cailleach-uisg', (AC) *s.f.* Water-woman, wa-

96. *Cailleach-oidhche.*

97. *Cailleach-oidhche-mhòr.*

ter-carlin. 2 Diseased potato containing only water.

cailleadh, -idh, *s.m.* Emasculation, castration. 2 Effeminacy.

cailleag,* -leig, -an, *s.f.* see coilleag. 2** Loss. 3**Detriment.

———ach, -aiche, *a.* see coilleagach.

†cailleago, *s.m.* Gaelic spelling of *calico.*

†cailleamhnach, *a.* Defective. 2 see caillteach.

†cailleamhuinn, *s.m.* Loss, damage.

càillean, -ein, -an, *s.m.* see càilean.

———ach, *a.* see càileanach.

cailleanach, -aich, *s.m.* Loser.

†cailleasg, -eisg, -an, *s.m.* Horse. 2 *s.f.* Mare.

†cailliog, *s.f.* Loss. 3 Detriment.

caillte, *past part.* of caill. Lost. 2 Ruined. 3 Damned. 4**Gelded. Caillte is fa dheòidh air sgeul, *lost and found again.*

caillteach, -eiche, *a.* Ruinous, causing loss. 2 Apt to lose, losing. 3††Hurtful. Brù *ch.*, *a miscarrying womb.*

caillteachd,* *s.f.* Ruination 2 Degree of loss.

caillteanach, -aich, *s.m.* Eunuch.

caillteàrnach, -aich, *s.m.* Shrubbery. †2 see coillteàrnach.

†cailmhion, *s.f.* Light helmet.

càilpeach, -ich, -ichean, *s.f.* see calpach.

†cailpig, *s.m.* Jug, mug.

†cailte, *s.f.* Hardness, firmness.

†——, *a.* see caillte.

†cailtean, see caillteanach.

†cailtin, *s.m.* see calltuinn.

caim, *s.f.* Stain, blot, fault. 2(AC) Loop, curve, circle, sanctuary, guard, imaginary circle described with the hand round himself by a person in fear, danger or distress.

caim-beul, -eòil, see cam-beul.

caimdeal, -eil, *s.m.* Prolixity, tediousness, perplexity. 2 Objection.

———ach, -aiche, *a.* Tedious, round about, perplexing, drawling.

caimdealaiche, *s.f.ind.* Delay, procrastination, dilatoriness.

caime, *s.f.* Crookedness. 2 Blindness of one eye.

——, *comp.* of cam. More or most crooked. Tha 'm bata ni's caime na sin, *the staff is more crooked than that.*

——acan, -ain, ain, see caimeachan.

——achan, -ain, -an, *s.m.* Hump-backed person.

caimead,** *s.* Aduncity.

caimein, -ean, *s.m.* Mote 2 Small stain. 3 **Reproof, blame, reproach.

———,(AC) *a.* Small.

———each, -eiche, *a.* Full of motes. 2 Like a mote. 3 Blemished. 4(AC) Saving, economical. 5(CR) Mottled, spotted—*Skye.*

———each, (CR) *s. m.* Small trout. Cho sona ri c. an sruth, *as happy as a trout in a stream—Skye.*

†caimfear, *s.m.* Champion.

caimh, *v.a.* see caimhil.

†caimhdean, *s.m.* Multitude.

†caimheach, *s.m.* Protector.

caimhear,** -ir, -an, see caimfear.

caimheineach, see caimeineach.

caimhil, (AC) *pr.part.* a' caimhleachadh, *v.a.* Confine.

caimhleachadh,(AC) -aidh, *s.m.* Restraining, confining, hemming in, entrapping. *C.* chaorach, *hemming in of sheep* ; *c.* bhreac, *guddling of trout.* A' c—, *pr. part.* of caimhil.

caimir, AC *s.* Fold, stockade in which flocks were safeguarded. 2 Sanctuary.

†caimis, -mse, *s f.* Shirt, shift. Gaelic spelling of French *chemise.*

caimleid, -e, *s.f.* Camlet, a kind of hard worsted cloth. 2 AC Crook. Anns a' chaimleid, *in the crook.*

caimleir,-ean, *s.f.* Bent stick used by butchers.

†caimneach, *a.* Chaste, pure, free from obscenity. (geamnuidh.)

†caimpear,** -ir, see †caimfear.

†caimse, *gen.* of caimis.

†caimseag, *s.f.* Falsehood, false assertion.

càin, *pr.part.* a' càineadh, *v.a.* Traduce, slander, revile, dispraise. 2 Scold. 3 Satirize. 4‡‡Number, count. Càineam agus aoiream a' bhaoibh a rinn an t-òran, *let me traduce and satirize the fury that made the song* ; chàin e mi gu m' bhrògan, *or* chàin e mi gu cùl mo dhroma, *he traduced me thoroughly.*

càin, cànach [& ††càine], *pl.* càintean, *s.f.* Tribute, tax, toll, kain, rent. 2 Fine. 3 Payment in kind, given to a blacksmith. 4** Slander. A' pàigheadh na cànach, *paying the tribute;* leig càin orra, *make them pay tribute, punish them.*

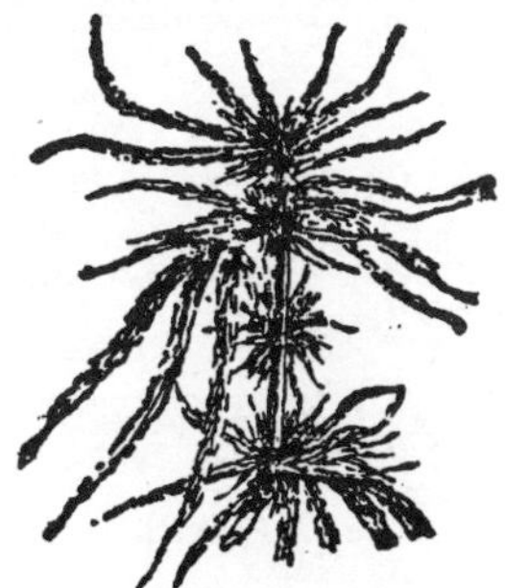

98. *Cainb.*

càin, -e, *a.* White. 2 Chaste. 3 Beloved, dear 4AC Clear, bright, fair, pure. Cù càin [bàn], *a white dog.*
càin-acairseid,(AH) *s.f.* Harbour or pier dues, keelage.
cainb, -e, *s.f.* Hemp. 2 Canvas. 3‡‡ Sack-cloth, covering worn by penitents. 4§ Hemp plant—*cannabis sativa.* See illust. 98.
cainb-aodach, -aich. *s.f.* Canvas, sack-cloth.
cainbeach,* *s.f.* Rope-yarn.
cainbear, *s.m.* Instrument for dressing flax.
cainb-theàrra,* *s.f.* Tarpaulin.
cainb-uisge,§ *s. f.* Hemp agrimony--*eupatorium cannabium.*
cainchean, -ein, *s.m.* see canach.
†caindeal, see coinneal.
caineab,* *Islay* for cainb.
——ach,* *a.* caineabach.
càineach, *a.* Tributary. 2 Like a tribute or fine. 3 Satirical, dispraising. 4 Prone to slander.
†———, *s.f.* Satire, dispraise.
———d, *s. f.* Taxation. 2 Habit of slander, traducing.

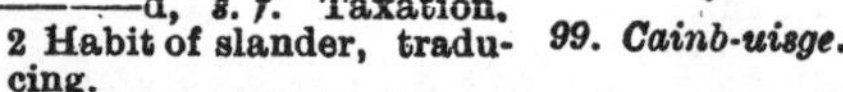
99. *Cainb-uisge.*

càineadh, -idh, *s.m.* Reviling, traducing, slander. 2 Scolding. 3 ‡‡Satire.
†caineag, -eig, -an, *s. f.* see cainneag. 2 Farthing. 3 Barley and oats. 4‡‡Muliebre pudendum.
caineal, -eil, *s.m.* Cinnamon—*laurus cinnamomum.*
cain-éisdeachd, *s.f.* Act of listening.
†cainfic, see cainich.
†caingeal, *s.m.* Hurdle. 2 Reason.
caingeann, -ionn, -an, *s. m.* Prayer, supplication. 2 Agreement. 3 Rule. 4 Cause. 5 ‡‡Fine.
Caingis, *s.f.ind.* Whitsuntide, Pentecost.
càinich, *pr.pt.* a' càineachadh, *v.a.* Impose a tax, tribute or fine.
†cainichein, see canach.
càinichte, *past part.* of càinich. Taxed.
càinidh, *fut.aff.a.* of càin.
cainn, AC see cainnt.
†cainneabhar, *s.m.* Dirt, filth.
cainneag, -eig, -an, *s.f.* Mote, small matter. 2 *Hamper—*Skye.* 3(AF) Small moth. 4(CR) Plait of straw for making into bags.—*Skye.*
cainneal, -eil, -ean, *s.f.* see coinneal. 2** Channel, canal.
†cainnse, *s.f.* The face.
†cainnsear, *s.m.* Scolder. 2 Dagger. 3‡‡Gaelic spelling of *cancer.*
†cainnseireachd, *s.f.* Scolding.
†cainnseoir, *s.m.* see cainnsear.
†cainnseoireachd, see cainnseireachd,
cainnt, -ean, *s. f.* Speech language. 2 Discourse, conversation. 3 Language, tongue. C. bhallsgach, *burlesque* ; droch chainnt, *oaths and curses.*
———each, -eiche, *a.* Loquacious, conversable. 2 Peevish, cross, malicious, carping. Gu c., *peevishly.*
cainnteachas,** -ais, *s.m.* Protervity, peevishness, wantonness.
cainnteachd, *s.f.ind.* Pronunciation. 2 Talkativeness. 3 Peevishness. 4**Asperity, hastiness. 5 Speaking.
cainnteag, -eig, *s.f.* Peevish, cross young female. 2**Canticle.
cainnteal, -eil, *s.m.* Press, crowd. 2 Lump.
cainntean, -ein, *s.m.* Peevish or cross person.
cainntear, -e. -an, *s.m.* Censurer. 2 Reproacher. 3**Babbler. 4**Orator. 5**Linguist.
———achd, *s.f.ind.* Oratory, eloquence. 2 Rhetorical expression. 3 see cann taireachd.
cainnt-fhear, see cainntear.
———achd, see cainntearachd.
†caintic, *s.f.* Song, canticle. 2 Song of Solomon so named.
caipin, *s.* Cap (of a cycle.)
caiptean, -ein, -an, *s.m.* Captain.
caiptein, *gen. sing.* of caiptean.
———eachd, *s.f.* Captaincy. (ceannas-ceud)
càir, *s.f.* Gum. 2 Red blaze. 3 for caoir. 4 Grin. 5 Image. 6 sometimes used for "càthar," *s.m.*
càir, *pr.part.* a' càradh, *v.a.* Dig. 2 Raise. 3 Prepare. 4 Gird on. 5 Bury. 6 Repair, mend. 7 Lay up. 8 Send away. 9 Assert, aver, affirm. 10 Persuade, make to believe. 11 Endear. [Also see càirich.] Càiridh mi a balla, *I will repair her wall ;* chàireadh e orm e, *he would make me believe it.*
†cairb, *s.* Jaw, gum.
cairb, -e, -ean, *s.f.* The bent ridge of a girth-saddle. 2 Fusee. 3 Chariot. 4 Ship. 5 Plank. 6 Plough.
cairbean,** -ein *s.m.* Sailfish.
———ach,(AH) -aiche, *a.* Rough, unsmooth, nodulated. Tha cas na sgine c., *the handle of the knife is rough* or *nodulated.*
———eil,** *s.f.* Large eel.
———ein, see cearban.
cairbh,-e, -ean, *s.f.* Carcase, dead body, corpse. Cairbh spréidhe neo-ghloin, *the carcase of unclean cattle.*
†cairbh, *v.a.* Man a fleet. 2 Shake, quiver.
cairbh-carbad,** *s.m.* Bier.
†cairbheacan, *s.m.* Ship-boy.
cairbheach, *a.* Cadaverous, charnel.
cairbhean, *n.pl.* of cairbh.
cairbheiste, *s.f.* see cairbhist.
†cairbhin, *s.m.* Little ship. 2 The gums.
cairbhinn, -nnean, *s. f.* Carcase of a person, corpse. 2 Lean meat. 3 Carrion. Cairbhinn an righrean, *the carcases of their kings.*
———each, -eiche, *a.* Full of carcases. 2 Of, or pertaining to, a corpse or carcase. 3 **Cadaverous.
———eachd, *s.f.* Slaughtering, massacring. 2 Cadaverousness.
cairbhist, -e, *s.m.*[* *f*] Carriage. 2 Load, baggage, bundle. 3 Feu-duty. 4 Personal service to a landlord. 5 Beating, flogging. Fhuair e deagh *ch., he got a good flogging.*
cairbh-theine,** *s.f.* Bust.
cairbinn, (a') AC *pr.part.* Dragging.
———, -e, -ean, *s.f.* Carbine.
———each, -ich, *s.m.* Toothless person.
———each,** *a.* Toothless.
†cairbne, *s.m.* Charioteer.
cairb-srathrach, see cairb 1.
cairc,* *s.f.* Strait, predicament—*Islay.* 2(AC) Flesh, person. 'S e a bha 'na chairc, *he was in a curious predicament.*
†cairc, -e, *s.f.* Hair, fur. 2**Eagerness.
†——each, *a.* Hairy, rough. 2 Eager. Gu cairceach, *eagerly.*
†cairche, *s.f.* Music.
†cairc heas, *s.m.* Little vessel. 2 Twist.
caircheas, *v.a.* Twist. 2 Contort.
càird, *s.f.* (*contr.* of càirdeas.) Gun *ch., without partiality, without lenity* ; fasgadh is c., *shelter and kindness.*
càird, -e, *s.f.* Delay, respite. 2 Rest. 3 Scruple. Gun chàird, *quickly.*
cairde,AC *a.* Convenient, suitable, appropriate, as being of kin.

càirde, *s.m.* Bosom friend. 2 Relation. 3† Friendship. 4 *nom.pl.* of caraid (*for* càirdean)
———ach, -eiche, *a.* Related, connected by birth or marriage. 2 Friendly. 3 Kindly, favourable. Tha iad *c.* d' a chéile, *they are related to each other*; do na h-uaislean tha thu *c.*, *you are related to the gentry.*
———achas, -ais, *s.m.* see càirdeas.
———alachd, *s.f.ind.* see càirdeas.
———alas, see càirdeas.
càirdean, *pl.* of caraid. Friends, relations, cousins. [In the shape of cousins, bad.—*] Càirdean, mic an dà pheathar, *cousins, the sons of two sisters.*
càirdeas, -eis, *s.m.* Relationship. 2 Friendship. 3 Kindness. 4 Fellowship, friendliness. 5 Benevolence, goodwill. 6**Alliance, as of states. Càirdeas is comain is eòlas, *relationship, obligation, and acquaintanceship*—[a formula to regulate funeral invitations. The "comain," or obligation, is really an act of courtesy— you invite those who on similar occasions have invited you] ; comhdhaltas gu ceud is càirdeas gu fichead, *fostership to a hundred, blood-relation to twenty degrees.* [The closeness of relationship established by fosterage among the Celts is almost without parallel, and this is one of the strongest expressions of Highland opinion on this point.] Càirdeas fola, *blood-relationship; c.* pòsaidh, *affinity.*
càirdeil, -e, *a.* Friendly. 2 Kind, affectionate, tender. 3 Related. Gu *c.*, *kindly.*
càir-dhearg, -eirg, *s.f.* Blush.
——————, -eirge, *a.* Red-blazing.
càirdich, *v.a.* see caidrich.
caireachan, -ain, *s.m.* Wide-mouthed person.
†caireachd, *s.f.* Quirks, sleight, cunning.
caireachd.†† *s.f.* Wrestling.
càireadh,‡‡ -ridh, *s.m.* Insertion.
———, *past subj.* of càirich—Like éirich, fuirich, &c., càirich drops its *ch* in conjugation. 'Sud a' chungaidh 'chàireadh 'm bàta 'choisinn buaidh, *that is the instrument that would shape (or mend) the boat that won fame —Filidh, p. 76.*
càireag, -eig, -an, *s.f.* Prating young girl.
————ach, -eiche, *a.* Prating, applied to a garrulous young female.
caireal, *v. n.* Carol, sing, warble.
caireal, -eil, *s.m.* Noise, clamour. 2 Outcry. 3 Sound of distant music. 4 Harmony, melody. 5 Carol. 6††Chirping of birds.
cairealach, *a.* Noisy. 2 Harmonious. 3 Carrolling. 4 Loud and cheerful. 5 Musical. 6††Chirping.
caireall, see caireal.
————ach, see cairealach.
caireamhachd, *s.f.* Sociableness.
†càireamhan, *s.m.* Shoemaker, cobbler.
càirean, -ein, -einean, *s.m.* Gum of the mouth. 2 Palate. 3 Chap. 4**Taste of the mouth. 5**Grin. 6 (CR) *erroneously used for* càran. Tha càilean 'am chàirean, *there is a seedling in my gum*; do m' *ch.* ni's milse, *to my palate sweeter.*
càireanach, *a.* Having gums. 2 Of gums, gingival.
caireist, -e, see cairbhist.
†càireog, see càireag.
†cair-fhiadh, -fhéidh, *s.m.* Hart. 2 Stag.
cairg, *dat. sing.* of carraig.
cairge, *gen. sing.* of carraig.
cairgein, *s.m.* Sea moss, Irish moss.—*chondrus crispus.* [Always preceded by the article *an.*] So called from Carragheen (*dim.* of carraig) Co. Waterford—.‡

†cairgh, *v.n.* Abstain, forbear.
càir-gheal, -ile, *a.* White-foaming, as a wave.
——————, ghil, *s.f.* Foaming wave.
Cairghios, -is, *s.m.* see Carghus.
cairgneach, *a.* Knotty, having a rough surface. Sgian is cas chairgneach innte, *a knife with a deer-horn handle*—JM
càirich, *pr.part.* a' càradh, *v.a.* Repair, mend. 2 Order. 3 Affix. 4 Lay to one's charge. 5 Aver. 6 Soothe. 7 Place. [The meanings "8 Cajole. 9 Inter, bury. 10**Raise a monumental mound," as given in the dictionaries do not apply to *càirich* used by itself, but to its meanings in conjunction with other words in the context where it occurs.—this remark applies to many words besides *càirich.*] Air a chàradh, *mended*; *c.* an altair, *repair the altar*; na *c.* am peacadh oirnn, *lay not their sins to our charge*; *c.* r' an taobh e, *place it beside them*; *c.* air falbh e, *cajole him away;* chàirich iad 'san uaigh e, *they laid him in the grave*; chàirich mi orra, *I set out (on the journey) resolutely and unflinchingly.*
càirichte, *a. & past part.* of càirich. Repaired, mended. 2 Ordered.
cairid, see caraid.
cairidh, -ean, *s.f.* Mound or wall thrown across the estuary of a river, stream, or arm of the sea, to catch fish. 2 Weir. 3 Tomb. *C.* a chàradh an éisg, *a weir to deceive the fish*; thug pailteas làmh gu cairidh e, *a sufficiency of hands bore him to the tomb.*
†cairigh, *v.a.* see caraich.
cairin, *s. m. & f.* Darling, favourite. 2 see cairbhinn.
cairioil,‡‡ -ill, *s. m.* Cheerful note, carol. 2 Noise.
cairis, -e, -ean, *s.f.* Carcase, corpse.
———each, -eiche, *a.* see caithriseach.
†cairle, *a.* Tumbled, tossed.
†———, *s.m.* Club, staff, stake.
†———, *v.a.* Beat. 2 Toss about.
†cairleacan, *v.* see cairle.
†cair-leum, *v.a.* Tumble or toss about. 2 Beat about.
cairmeal, *s.m.* Tuberous bitter vetch, see carrameille.
càirn, *gen. sing.* of càrn.
———each, -ich, -ichean, *s.m.* Druid, priest. 2 Osprey, see iolair-iasgair. 3 Kingfisher, see biorra-cruidein.
càirneach, -ich, *s.f.* see càrnach. 2 see bàirneach. †3*Osprey.
—————, -eiche, *a.* see càrnach. 2**Fleshy.
càirnean, -ein, *s. m.* Egg-shell. *C.* uigh, *an egg-shell.*
†cairpe, *a.* see coirbte.
†cairptheach, *s.m.* see cairbeach.
†cairptheoir, *s.m.* see carbadair.
cairreall, see caireal.
†cairrig, see carraig.
†———each, *a.* see carraigeach.
†cairrthe, *s.m.* (carra) Chariot. 2 Pillar.
‡cairse, *s.m.* Club.
cairsealan, *s. pl.* see cairtealan.
càirt, *gen. sing.* of càrt.
cairt, *pr. part.* a' cartadh, *v.a.* Muck, cleanse, purge. 2 Tan, as leather. 3 Strip off the bark. Cairt an leathrach, *tan the leather*; tha 'm bàthaich cairte, *the byre is cleaned.*
cairt, cartach [& cairte; cairteach in *Lewis*] *pl.* cairtean, *s. f.* Bark. 2 Cart. 3 Card. 4 Chart. 5 Charter. 6 Deed, bond, indenture. 7** *rarely* Stone, rock. [There are five distinct Gaelic words here—i No 1, ii No 2, iii No 3, iv No 4, v Nos 5 & 6. iii, iv, & v are all from Latin *charta*; v direct

100. Roinnean na Cartach.

from Latin, iv through English *chart*, iii through French and Broad Scots.—CR] Cairt dharaich, *the bark of an oak-tree* ; ag iomairt air na cairtean, *playing at cards.*

NAMES OF THE PARTS &C. OF A CART : (Roinnean na cartach. Earrainnean cairteach—*Lewis.*)

1 Roth, *pl.* -an, *wheel.* [for parts of a wheel see under "roth"

2 Bocsa na cartach, *body of cart.* [bucus na cartach—*Lewis.*]

3 Cluasag, sorchan (DM) *bolster* Brògan, *clogs* (AH) —Pieces of wood severing trams from axle.

3a Na buiun, the two *beams* or *sole-beams*, on each side lengthwise—*Lewis.*

4 Lorg *pl.* luirg, Luirg, *pl.* luirgean, } Shaft, tram—DM Troma, *pl.* tromachan—*Lewis* ; Spòg, *pl.* spògan; (AH)Speicean ("Fionn") Gàirdean, *pl.* gàirdeanan *W. Isles.*—JM

5 Ceapaichean, *top-sides, floats* Sgiathan—*Lewis.*

6 Cromagan na briogais, *breeching-hooks.* Dubhain na briogais,—*Lewis.*

7 Stapull nan spéilearan, *runner-staple.*

7a Udalan, *runner;* Dubhan deiridh—*Lewis.*

8 Cromag-tharruing, *draught-hook.* Dubhan toisich, dubhan guaille—*Lewis.*

9 Dorus cairte, dorus cùil, deireadh cairte, *back.* Deireadh—*W. Isles & Argyll.*

10 Tarrang-aisil, *lynch-pin.* Bouta [Gaelic spelling of *bolt*] na h-aisil, *axle-bolt*,[the bolt that goes through the sole-beams]; *draught-pin* or *-nail.*

10a Piune na h-aisil, *axle-pin* [Pins at each end to hold wheels on.]

11 Dromach, *Saddle-chain,* "*rigbody.*"—*Perthshire* (CR); Bann-droma, *back-strap*—*Lewis.*

12 Ùrlar, *bottom*—*W.Isles* ; Màs—*Lewis.*

13 Toiseach, *front*—*W.Isles.*

14 Bòrd-taoibh, *side-board*—*W.Isles* ; Taobhan—*Lewis.*

15 Sail bhroillich, *front cross-beam*—*W.Isles.*

16 Sail dheiridh, *box*—*W. Isles.* 2 *Hind cross-beam.* ☞ Nos. 15 & 16* connect the soles before and behind.

17 Crann meadhon, *pole* between two horses in a coach or waggon.

18 Sglaigean,** *beam.*

19 Beul, beul na cartach, (AH) *rim of cart.* [Corresponding to gunwale of a boat.]

20 Sailthean màis, *or* sailthean ùrlair, (AH) *stos* [Heavy cross-beams below and supporting bottom.]

21 Cùb,‡‡ *a coup-cart.*

22 Cairt-thaomaidh, *coup-cart*—*Lewis.*

cairt, *s.m.* fee cairteal.

cairt-bhlàir,* *for* cairt-làir. Common tormentil.

cairt-cheap, -chip, *s.m.* see ceap-cartach.

cairt-chluiche, *s.f.* Playing-card.

cairte, *a. & past pt.* of cairt. Cleansed, purged. 2 Tanned. Leathrach c., *tanned leather.*

cairteach, *a.* see cairtidh.

——a,** *s.* Deed.

cairteadh, -tidh, *s.m. & pr. pt.* of cairt, see cartadh.

cairteag, -eig, -an, *s. f.* Small cart. 2 Small card. 3**Tumbrell.

cairteal, -eil, -an, *s. m.* Quarter (¼.) 2**Gill. 3**Lodging. 4**Chartulary. †5**Challenge. 6**Edict.

——, -eil, *s.m.* Water-mint—*mentha aquatica.*

——achd,** *s.f.* Hospitality.

——aiche,** *s m.* Boarder.

——an, *s. pl.* of cairteal. Quarters, lodgings.

cairtear, -ir, -irean, *s.m.* Carter, waggoner. 2 **Barker, as of trees.

——achd, *s.f.* Carter's trade, cartage.

cairtearbhan, see caisearbhan.

cairt-fhear, *s.m.* see cairtear.

cair-thalmhainn,§ *s.f.* Yarrow, milfoil, see luschosgadh-na-fola.

†cairthe, *s.m.* Chariot.

cairtidh, *a.* Swarthy, tawny, bark-coloured, tanned, Truaill *ch.*, *a tanned scabbard.*

——eachd, *s.f.* Swarthiness.

cairt-iùil, *s.f.* Sea-chart. 2 Compass.

cairt-làir,§ *s.* Tormentil, potentil. see leamhnach.

cairt-lann, -lainn, *s.f.* Chartulary, chart-house.

cairt-leamhna, *s.f.* Tuberous bitter vetch.

cairt-locha, (JM) *s.f.* Root of the water-lily the

juice of which, when boiled, was used to fix black dye in wool
cairt-phostail s.f. Post-card.
cairt-shleamhna, (JM) Root of a small plant, used for tanning leather.
†cais, a. Spruce, trim, neat.
†——,** s.f. Regard, love, esteem. 2 Hatred. 3 Eye.
cais,** v.a. see cas, v.
caisbheart, -eirt, s.f. Shoes and stockings. 2 **Greaves. (*lit.* foot-gear, as opposed to head-gear—*ceann-bheart.*)
cais-chiabh, -an, s.f. Curl, ringlet.
——————ach, a. Curly, having ringlets or tresses.
caisd, pr. part. a' caisdeachd, v. n. Listen, hearken. 2 Be quiet. Nach c. thu, *will you not be quiet*; c. a sin thu! *be quiet you there!*
caisd! int. Silence!
caisdeachd, s.f.ind. Listening, act of listening. 2 Silencing. A' c—, p part. of caisd.
caisdeal, see caisteal.
————ach, see caistealach.
càise, s.m.ind. Cheese. Pailteas de ìm is de chàise, *plenty of butter and cheese.*
caise, s.f.ind Impetuosity, shortness of temper, passion. 2 Stream of water. 3 Wrinkle, fold. 4 Natural curling of hair. 5** *rarely* Mushroom. 6**Discord. 7**Privy parts of a female. 8*Steepness. 9*Haste, shortness of time. 'An caise, *in haste*; c. a' bhruthaich, *the steepness of the ascent*; is i do chaise féin is coireach, *it is your own impatience that is the cause*; c. an t-srutha, *the impetuosity of the current;* aghaidh gun sgraing, gun chaise, *a face without frown or wrinkle.*
——, comp. of a. cas. More or most steep or rapid.
càiseach, -eiche, a. Abounding in cheese. 2 Productive of cheese. Aranach, càiseach, *abounding in bread and cheese.*
caiseach, -eiche, a. Wrinkled. 2 Passionate, impetuous.
————d,* (gu) a. Crabbedly.
caisead, -eid, s.m. Degree of steepness, 2 of suddenness, 3 of rapidity, 4 of impetuosity, 5 of crispness. 6 Increase of steepness, &c. 7** see casaid. Dìridh mi a' bheinn air a caisead, *I will ascend the mountain, no matter how steep* (*lit.* on its steepness.)
caiseag,** -eig, s.f. Stem of a weed.
caiseal, -eil, -an, s.m. Bulwark, wall. 2 Castle, garrison. 3 Hurdle. 4 Mound. 5 Cruive in a river for fishing. 6‡‡Ford. 7‡‡ Stone building.
————ach, a. Having bulwarks, walled.
————achd, s.f. Battlement.
caiseamachd, see caismeachd.
†caiseamhan, -ain, s.m. Shoemaker.
caisean, -ein, -an, s.m. Anything curled, wrinkled or hairy. 2 The dewlap or skin that hangs down from the breasts of cows. 3 Surliness. 4* Short-tempered man. Comharradh caisein, *a mark upon cattle by cutting the dewlap.* [Dewlap in Uist is "sprògan"]
†caisean, s.m. Hoarseness. 2 Phlegm.
caiseanach, -aiche, a. Sour, short-tempered.
——————d, s.f.ind. Fretfulness, peevishness, shortness of temper.
caisean-feusaig,* -in-, -an-, s.m. Moustache.
caisean-snidhe,* -in-, -an-, s.m. Stalactite.
caisean-uchd, -in-, -an-, s.m. The breast strip of a sheep killed at Christmas, or on New Year's eve, and singed and smelled by each member of the family, as a charm against fairies and spirits. [MacAlpine adds "in Islay at any time, but never for the sake of the fairies." (!)
càisear,** a. Cheesy.
————,** -ir, s.m. Cheesemonger.
————achd,** s.f. Cheesemongery.
caisearbhan,§ -ain, s.m. Dandelion, see bèarnan-Bride. 2 Chicory, succory, see lus-an-t-siùcair.
——————-nam-muc, ‡‡ s. m. Dandelion, see bèarnan-Bride.
cais'eart, -eirt, s.f. see caisbheart.
caisein-clach, (AF) Stone chatterer, see cloichearan.
cais-fhionn, caisne, a. White-footed.
——————,** s.m. White-legged cow.
Càisg, gen.sing. Càisge, Càsg, Càsga, s f. The Passover, Easter. 2 Feast. Di-dòmhnaich na Càisge, *Easter Sunday.* [Always preceded by the article a' Ch—.]
caisg, pr.part. a' casgadh v.a. & n. Restrain, check, stop, still, calm, quiet, subdue, subside, put an end to. 2*Staunch. *Ch.* an onfhadh, *the storm subsided*; a chaisgeas fuaimneach mara is tuinn, *who stills the roar of sea and surge*; caisg an fhuil, *staunch the blood.*
Càisge, gen. sing. of Càisg.
càisgeach, a. see càisgeil.
caisgear, fut. pass. of caisg.
càisgeil,** a. Paschal.
caisgidh, fut. aff. act. of caisg.
caisiall, -ill, -lan, s.m. Shoemaker's strap.
caisil-chrò, (casair‡) Coffin, bier made of wicker (*lit.* bed of blood.) 2 Circular paling.
caisiol, -il, -ean, s.f. see caiseal.
————achd, see caisealachd.
———-chra, see caisil-chrò.
caisionn, see cais-fhionn.
caisle, see cuisle.
caisleac,** s.f. Stream.
caisleach, -ich, s f. Ford. 2 Foot-path. 3 Smooth place. 4**Smooth path.
caisleachadh, -aidh, s.m. Stirring up, shaking, as of a feather-bed. A' c—, pr. part. of caislich.
caisleach-spuing, s.f. Touchwood, spunk.
†caislean, -ein, s.m. Castle, garrison, tower.
†caislear, -an, s.m. Projector. 2 Castle builder.
†cais-lì, a. Polished, made smooth
caislich, pr. part. a' caisleachadh & caisleadh, v.a. Shake, stir up, as a bed. 2 Rouse. 3†† Smoothe, soften. 4**Polish.
caislichte, a. & past part. of caislich. Shaken, stirred up, roused. 2 Polished, smoothed.
caismeachd, -an, s.f. Alarm, warning. 2 Hint. 3 Highland march or war-song. 4* Beating time to an instrument with the foot—*Islay.* C. bhuadhach, *shouts of victory.*
——————ach, a. Alarming, that alarms. 2 That gives warning or notice.
caismeart, -eirt, -an, s. f. Heat of battle. 2 Armour. 3 Band of combatants.
——————ach, -ich, -ichean, s.m. Armed man.
caisne, comp. of a. cais-fhionn.
caisnich,††pr. part. a' caisneachadh, v.a. Shake roughly, crush.
caisreabhachd, s. f. Legerdemain, juggling conjuring.
caisreabhaiche, s.m. Juggler, conjurer.
caisreag, -eig, -an, s.f. Curl, ringlet. 2 Wrinkle.
caisreagach, -aiche, a. Curled. 2 Wrinkled. 3 Shrivelled. 4**Bushy, as hair.
——————d,** s.f. Crispation.
caisreagaich,** v.a. Curl.
caisreagan, pl. of caisreag.
caisrig, v.a. see coisrig.
———ich, see caisreagaich.
caiste, a. & past. part. of cas. Twisted, curled,

twined. Snàth caiste, *sewing thread.*
caisteal, -eil, -an, *s.m.* Castle, fort, tower, garrison. 2 Turreted mansion 3 Trunk of the body. Bu chaisteal dhomh thu, *thou wert a castle to me* ; caisteal a' chuirp, *the trunk of the body.*
——— -deiridh,** *s.m.* Quarter-deck of ship.
——— -toisich,‡‡ *s.m.* Forecastle of ship.
caistean,** -ein, *s.m.* Crafty fellow.
c'àit', see c'àite.
cait, *gen. sing.* of cat.
†cait, *s.f.* Sort, kind.
caitcheann,(JM) *s.m.* Land common to all the crofters in a township—*Tiree.*
caitchinn,(AC) *a. Tiree* for coitchionn. 2 Striped, cat-head like.
c'àite ? (c'àit' before a vowel) *adv.* for cia àite ? *where ? in what place ?* C'àit' an robh thu ? *where were you ?* c'àit' am bheil e ? *where is he ?* c'àit' an d'fhuair thu e ? *where did you get it ?*
càite, *a.* & *past part.* of càth, Winnowed, sifted.
caite, *a.* & *past part.* of caith, (for caithte.)
càiteach, -ich, ichean, *s.f.* Chaff, husks. 2 Refuse. 3 Measure made of rushes, basket. 4††Winnowing sheet.
———, -iche, *a.* Full of chaff or husks.
†caiteach, *s.f.* Ship's mainsail. 2‡‡Main-sheet.
caiteach, see caithteach.
———as, see caithteachas.
caiteag, -eig, -an, *s.f.* Basket. 2 Butter pot. 3*Leather pot. 4 Basket for trout—*Islay.* 5 **Canister. 6 Place made of straw, to contain oats or barley in a barn. 7 Small bit. 8**Butter. 9(AF) see cuiteag.
†caitean, -ein, *s.m.* Chain.
caitean,§ -ein, *s.m.* Classes of plants called *amentiferæ* and *cupuliferæ.*
———, -ein, *s.m.* see caitein. 2§Blossom of osier. 3‡‡Little cat.
———ach, see caiteineach.
caiteas, -eis, *s.m.* Caddis, scrapings of linen applied to wounds. 2 Refuse from carding wool. 3(AF) Caddis worm.
caitein, -ean, *s.m.* Shag, nap on cloth. 2 Ruffling of the sea surface. 3 Springing breeze. 4 Bad temper. 5(DU) Effect of wear on cloth. Tha caitein air an aodach, *the cloth has a nice nap on it* ; thoir c. air an aodach, *raise the nap;* thoir c. air an duine, *rouse the man's temper ;* caitein gaoithe, *a springing breeze.*
caiteineach, -eiche, *a.* Shaggy, hairy, rough, nappy. 2 Ruffled, as the sea. 3** Rough-skinned. 4**Curled, frizzled.
———,** *s.m.* Hairdresser. 2 Cloth-dresser.
càith,* *gen.* càtha, *s.f.* "Seeds," husks of corn. †2 Chaff. 3†Blemish. Sugh na càtha, *juice of the seeds for making sowens.*
caith,** *s.m.* Pudendum virile.
caith, *pr. part.* a' caitheamh & caitheadh, *v.n.* & *a.* Spend, wear, consume, exhaust. 2 Waste, squander. 3 Cast. 4 Shoot. 5**Drive, as a ship. Chaith e 'shaibhreas, *he squandered his wealth*; chaith e 'aodach, *he wore out his clothes ;* a' caitheamh casaig, *wearing a cloak* ; chaith a' choinneal, *the candle is consumed* ; chaitheadh e, *it is consumed ;* a' caitheadh chlach, *throwing stones* ; a' caitheamh air comharradh, *shooting at a mark* ; gu'm meal 's gu'n caith thu e, *may you enjoy and wear it*—said to anyone who puts on a new article of clothing for the first time.
†caith, *a.* see caidh.
†càith, *v.a.* Winnow, sift.
caith-bheart, -eirt, -an, *s.f.* Battle-armour.
caith-bhràghad, *s.* King's evil—*Arran.*

caitheach, -eich, -eichean, *s.m.* Spendthrift, prodigal, profuse, extravagant.
———, -eiche, *a.* Prodigal, profuse, extravagant.
caitheadh, *s.m.* & *pr.part.* see caitheamh.
caitheamh, -eimh, *s.m* Spending, consuming. 2 Wasting. 3 Casting, putting, shooting. 4 **Extravagance. A' c—, *pr. part.* of caith. Thug iad tri laithean aig a caitheamh, *they took three days driving her (the boat.)*
caitheamh,||-eimh, *s.f.* Consumption. 2**Asthma. [Preceded by the article *a' ch*—.]
——— -aimsire, -aimsreach, *s.f.* Pastime, sport, diversion. 2 Waste of time.
——— -beatha, *s.f.* Moral conduct, behaviour, conversation, mode of living.
caithear, *fut pass.* of caith.
———, caithearra, *a.* Just, well-bestowed.
†caithfear, *v. irr.* & *def.* One must. Caithfeam, *we must* ; caithfidh mi (&c), *I (&c.) must.*
†caithiochd-aimsire, see caitheamh-aimsire.
caithir, -threach, *pl.* caithrichean [& -thriche] see cathair.
càithleach, -ich, *s.m.* see càileach & càtha.
càithlean, -ein, see càilean.
———ach, see càileanach.
caith-mhìleadh, -idh, -ean, *s.m.* Soldier, warrior.
caithne,§ *s.* Strawberry-tree—*arbutus unedo.* 2 (AF) Two-year-old heifer.
caithream,-eim,*s.m.*[*& f.*] Joyful noise. 2 Applause. 3 Shout of triumph or joy. 4 Loud noise. 5 Shout. 6 Beating, as of a drum at regular intervals—*Islay.*

101. Caithne.

7**Symphony. 8** Information, notice. 9 (JGM) Careering pace. 10**Triumph. Chum c. a dheanamh ann ad chliù, *to rejoice in thy praise* ; is c. bròin am beul ar bàird, *and the shout of death in the mouth of our bard* ; mar *ch.* chlàr, *like the symphony of harps* ; sgeul 'tha dubhach le m' inntinn, nach robh sibh anns a' Chaillich fo chaithream an lionadh, *what a pity you were not in the Corryvreckan when the filling neap tide was in full career—Filidh, p. 44.*
caithreamach, -aiche, *a.* Victorious, triumphant. 2 Shouting, making a loud shout. 3* Beating at regular intervals.
———adh, -aidh, *s.m.* & *pr. part.* Triumphing. 2 Shouting.
†caithreamadh, *s.m.* Information.
caithreamaich,†† *s f.* Shouting.
caithreim, see caithream.
———ich, *v.a.* & *n.* Triumph, conquer. 2 Shout.
caithrig,(DU) *v.a.* Take refuse of straw out of grain with the hand.
———ean,(DU) *s.m.* Broken straw separated from grain.
caithrinn,* *s.f.* Refuse of straw taken out of corn after being threshed.
———ich,* *v.a.* Shake straw before bundling it, or making trusses.
caithris, *s.f.ind.* Watching. 2 Circumspection, attention. 3 Watch by night. 4*Excessive fatigue from watching incessantly. 5(AC) Labour required of a crofter holding under a tacksman. 6**Ball (dance.)
———, *pr. part.* a' caithris, *v. a.* Watch, guard, defend, keep. 2(AC) Wake, harass.
———each, -eiche, *a.* Watchful, attentive, circumspect. 2*Fatigued by continual watch

ing. Gu c., *watchfully*.
caithriseachd, *s. f.* Watchfulness, attentiveness, circumspection. 2 Continued or frequent watching.
caithrisich, *v.a. & n.* see caithris.
caithte, *past. pt.* of caith. Spent, wasted, exhausted, squandered. 2 *a.*Lean, lank.
———ach, -eiche, *a.* Lavish, wasteful, prodigal. 2 Consumptive. 3**Wearing. Caithteach air duine, *apt to wear one down soon* ; duine c., *a wasteful person* ; tinneas c., *a wasting disease*.
———achas, -ais, *s.m.* Lavishness, profusion, prodigality. 2 State of wearing or exhausting. 3* Liability to be worn out. 4**Wasting.
———achd, *s.f.* see caithteachas.
caithtein, see caitein.
caithtiche, -ean, *s.m.* Spendthrift, waster, prodigal. 2‡‡Wearing garment.
caitin, see caitean.
———each, -ich, *s.m.* Cloth-dresser.
†caitinn, -e, *s.f.* Often frequenting.
†———each, *a.* Much frequented.
caitleacach, *a.* see catholach.
càl, càil, *s.m.* Kale, cabbage, colewort. 2** Name for all sorts of cabbage. 3** Scotch broth, of which kale is a principal ingredient. 4**Dinner. 5 *rarely* Joke. An d' fhuair thu do chàl ? *did you have your dinner (kale.)* ?
†cal, *s.m.* Sleep, slumber, insensibility.
†cal, *v.a. & n.* Burn. 2 Keep safe. 3 Sleep. 4 Get into harbour.
cal,** *s.m.* Condition of body. 2 Grief, despondency. 3 Darkness. 4†† see ceal. Is math a chal, *he is in good condition* ; mu'm fàs air t'inntinn cal, *ere grief falls on thy mind.*
cala, *s.m.* see caladh.
†cala, *a.* Hard, thrifty, frugal, saving.
caladair, -ean, *s.m.* Calendar, register. 2 Machine for calendering cloth.
caladh,** see cal.
†caladh, *a.* see †cala.
caladh, -aidh, -aichean [calaidh & calachan] *s.m.* Harbour, port, haven, road for ships. 2 Shore. 3 Ferry. 4 Porch. 5 Bay. 6*Land in the distance, as at sea. Fhuair sinn an caladh,*we gained the harbour* ; cha d' thug thu do long gu caladh fhathast, *you have not brought your ship into harbour yet* ; thog sinn c. air an treas là, *we descried land on the third day* ; na Còig Calaidh, *the Cinque Ports;* an c. ait, *the joyful shore* ; cala-dhìreach an long, *slack-sheet.*
cala-dhìreach, *a.* see calg-dhìreach.
calaich, *pr.pt.* a' calachadh, *v.a. & n.* Bring into harbour. 2 Reside. 3 Continue,remain. 4 *Moor, anchor.
†calaim *(for* caidleam,) I am sleeping.
†calainn, *s.f.* Couch.
calainn, -ean, see colann.
†calair, *s.m.* Crier.
†———eachd, *s.f.* Burying, interring. †2 Shouting. †3 Proclamation.
†calaiseachd, *s.f.* Juggler.
†calaist,** *s.f.* Gaelic spelling of *college.*
calaman, see calman.
calameilt,§ Calamint—*calamintha.*
calamh, see caladh.
calanas, *s.f.* Spinning of wool or flax. 2 Working at wool, flax, hemp, &c. For technical terms employed see under "beart-fhigheadaireachd," "cuidheall - sniomh," "cuigeal" &c. [Usual measurements—Five ells, or seven yards make a suit of men's clothes; 6 ells, a lady's costume ; 8 ells a costume, including outdoor cloak or jacket. Amount of materials for a tweed suit—1℔ wool an ell of cloth (a little less for ladies' stuffs); 7 ℔ clean wool makes 3 yards of drugget; 1½ ℔ warp, ½℔ good indigo. Carding and spinning. 8d. ℔ lb., ; weaving, 7d. ℔ yard.]
calanu,†† *s.m.* see calum.
†calb, see †calbh.
calba, *s.m.* see calpa.
calbh, cailbh [& cailbhe] *s.m.* †Head. [2 Erroneously given as "Headland, cape." by ‡—CR.] 3 Bald pate. 4 Hardin ss. 5 see colbh. 6††Scalp.
calbh, cuilbh [& cailbh], *s.m.* Shoot or rising tree, especially of hazel. 2 Rib of an osier basket, &c. 3 Continuous gush or pouring of any liquid, from a cleft or cranny. *C.* fola *streaming of blood from a wound.*
——, *a.* Bald.
——ach. *a.* Causing baldness.
——achd, *s.f.ind.* Baldness.
calbhair, -e, *a.* Eager for food, voracious.—*Suth'd.*‡
†calbhthas, *s.m.* Half-boot, buskin.
càl-bloinigein, *s.m.* Spinach. 2 Colewort.
calc, *pr.pt.* a' calcadh, *v.a.* Caulk. 2 Full, drive, beat, ram, cram, push violently forward. 3** Drive a wad into a gun with a ramrod.
——,** *a.* Hard, obdurate.
——, *s.f.* see cailc.
——ach,¶ *s.m.* Eider-duck, see lach-Lochlannach.
calcadair, see calcair.
calcadh, -aidh, *s.m.* Caulking, driving, beating, ramming, cramming, pushing violently. 2** Driving with a rammer. 3** Oakum. Luchd-calcaidh, *caulkers.* A' c—, *pr. pt.* of calc.
calcadh-bith,(AH) *s.m.* Calking.
calcaich, *v.a.* Same meanings as calc. †2 Harden by tramping. 3**Grow obdurate.
————te, *a. & past pt.* of calcaich. Caulked. 2 Hardened. 3**Obdurate.
calcaidh, *fut. aff. act.* of calc.
calcair, -ean, *s.m.* Caulker. 2 Rammer.
————eachd, *s.f.* Caulking, occupation of a caulker. 2 Ramming.
calcas,* *s.m.* Oakum. 2(MMcD) Tarry hemp used for caulking.—*Lewis.*
càl-ceanann, -ainn, *s.m.* Dish of greens and potatoes boiled and mashed together,
càl-ceirsleach, -eich, *s.m.* Cabbage.
†càl-chearcain, *s.m.* Shuttlecock.
càl-colaig, *s.m.* Cauliflower.
càl-colbhairt,§ *s. m.* Sea-kale or -cabbage, (colbh, *stalk* + art, *flesh*) see praiseach braidhe.
caldach, *a.* Sharp-pointed.
†caldach, see calldach.
cal-dìtheanach, *s.m.* Cauliflower.
calg, cuilg, *s.m.* Awn. 2 Prickle, point. 3 Any sharp-pointed thing. 4 Sting. 5 Beard of corn. 6 Spear, shaft. 7 Arrow. 8 Sword. 9 Hair or fur of animals, especially pile of black cattle, and bristles of pigs. 10**The grain. 11 see colg. 12* Refuse of lint. An aghaidh a' chuilg, *against the bristle*; an cluaran a' call a chuilg, *the thistle losing its prickle* ; iomairt nan calg, *the contest of spears.*
calgach, -aiche, *a.* Bristly, sharp-pointed, prickly. 2 Piercing. 3 Having awns, as ears of barley. 4 Shaggy. 5 Barbed. 6**Sprightly. 7**Passionate, ardent. Le slataibh c., *with piercing lashes* ; armach, calgach, ullamh, *armed, ardent, and ready.*
†calg-ard, *a.* Straight, high.
calg-bhealaidh,§ cuilg-, *s.m.* Butcher's broom,

—*ruscus aculeatus*. [Said to be the badge of the Sutherlands, but it is not indigenous to the Highlands, and it is doubtful if a plant of it existed there when this clan was powerful 500 years ago.]

102. *Calg-bhealaidh.*

calg-bhior, -a, -an, *s.m.* Barbed weapon. 2 Point of a spear.
———ach, -aiche, *a.* Barbed, crenated.
calg-bhrudhainn, *s.m.* Butcher's broom, see calg-bhealaidh.
calg-dhìreach, -eiche, *a.* Direct, straight as an arrow. 2**Contrary, against the grain.
———, *adv.* Directly, quite. 2*Slack sheet, right before the wind. Calg-dhìreach an aghaidh a chéile, *directly opposite each other*.
càl-gruidhean,§ -ein, *s. m.* (gruidhean, *grain-like flowers*). Cauliflower.
càl-gruth, } see càl-gruidhean.
càl-gruthach, }
call, -a, *s.m.* Losing, dropping. 2 Loss, damage, detriment. 3 Calamity. 4 Privation, destitution. Is mór mo chall ris, *great is my loss by it*; call ùine, *loss of time*; a' call na h-aimsir, *losing time*; a' call air, *losing by it*; a' call airgid, *dropping money*. A' c—, *pr.pt.* of caill.
†**call**, -a, *s.m.* Church. 2 Veil. 3 Hood.
calla, *a.* Tame, quiet, not wild, domestic. Beathaichean calla, *domestic animals*.
†**callach**, *s.m.* see cullach. 2 Bat.
———adh, -aidh, *s.m.* Taming, domesticating. A' c—, *pr.pt.* of callaich.
callag, *s.f.* see calltag.
callaich, *pr.part.* a' callachadh, *v. a.* Tame, make quiet, domesticate. Callaichidh am biadh fiadh na beinne, *food will tame the mountain deer*.
———te, *a.* & *past pt.* of callaich. Tamed, domesticated, civilized.
callaid, -ean, *s.f.* Fence, partition, hedge. 2 Lurking-place. 3 Cap. 4 Wig. 5 Funeral cry. 6 Elegy. 7**Wrangling noise. An ti a bhriseas callaid teumaidh nathair e, *he that breaketh a hedge a serpent shall bite him*; c. dhroighinn, *a hedge of thorns*.
callaideach, -eiche, *a.* Fenced, hedged, partitioned. 2 Surrounded. 3 Wearing a cap or wig. 4 Of, like, or belonging to, a fence, hedge, or partition. 5**Obstreperous.
callaidh, -e, *a.* Active, nimble, quick, agile, "clever."
†**callaidhe**, -an, *s.m.* Partner.
callaidheachd, *s.f.* Activity, nimbleness, agility, quickness, "cleverness." 2 Tameness.
callaid-thogail,‡‡ -ean-togail, *s.f.* Circumvallation.
callaig, see calluinn.
callaighe, -an, *s.m.* Divider, distributer.
call-aimsir, *s.m.* Loss or waste of time.
callainn, *s.f.* see calluinn.
†**callair**, *s.m.* Gaelic spelling of *caller*.
callais,** *s.f.* Buffoonery.
†**callait**, see gairm.
†**callamh**, *a.* Supple, flexible, pliant.
callan, -ain, *s.m.* Noise, clamour, shouting. 2 Prating, babbling. 3* Absurd hammering at anything. 4(AH) Constant repetition of a word or phrase. 5(DU) Noisy group, applied to a gossiping assembly. [Sometimes used for *calum*.]
callanach, -aiche, *a.* Noisy, clamorous.
callathar,(CR) Gaelic spelling of "caller." Cho callathar ris a' bhreac, *as healthy as the trout*.
call-chircein, *s.m.* Shuttlecock.
callda, *a.* see calla.
calldach, -aich, -aichean, *s.m.* Loss, detriment, damage. 2 Calamity. 3 Succession of losses. Ni e suas an c., *he will make up the loss*.
———,* *a.* Losing, ruinous.
———d,* see calldach.
calldaich, *v.* see callaich.
calldain, -e, *s.m.* see calltuinn.
càl liath-ghlas,§ *s. m.* White goose-foot, see praiseach fhiadhain. *Argyllshire*.
calloid, -e, -ean, *s.f.* see callaid.
callta, *a.* see calla.
———ch, -aich, -aichean, see calldach.
calltag, -aig, -an, *s.f.* Black guillemot—*uria grylle*.¶
†**calltarnach**, *s.f.* Truss of weeds.
calltuinn, -e, *s. m.* Hazel—*corylus avellana*. [Badge of Clan Colquhoun.] Slatan de 'n ch., *hazel rods*; preas ch., *hazel bush*; cnò ch., *hazel nut*.
Calluinn, -e, *s.f.* New year's day. †2** Collection of dressed victuals made all over the country by the poor on New year's day. 3**Christmas box. [Generally preceded by the article *a'*.] Gillean Calluinne, *Hogmanay lads*—carollers who perambulate the townland at night at the New year.

103. *Calltuinn.*

calm, *a.* see calma.
———,* *s.m.* Thick-set, stoutly-built person. 2 Prop, pillar. 3**Champion.
calma, *a.* Brave, stout, daring, resolute, strong. 2 Thick-set, brawny, robust.
———chd, *s. f.* Stoutness, courage, strength, bravery, personableness.
———dachd, see calmachd.
———das, see calmachd.
———idh, see calma.
———il, see calma.
calman, -ain, -an, *s.m.* Dove, pigeon.
——— -cathaidh,¶ *s.m.* Hoopoe—*upupa epops*. Gob a' chalmain-chathaidh, bithidh tu slàn mu 'm pòs thu, *beak of the moulting dove, you 'll be well before you marry*. The saying is applied to sick children—N.G.P. "Calman-cathaidh" is rendered "hoop" in A. MacDonald's vocabulary.
——— -coille,(McL & D) *s. m.* Wood-pigeon, ring-dove, cushat.
——— -coille-fearan,¶ Ring-dove, see calman-fiadhaich 1.
——— -creige,(AF) Rock-dove. see smùdan.
——— -dé, *s.m.* Butterfly.
——— -fiadhaich,¶ *s.m.* Ring-dove, wood-pigeon—*columba palumbus*. 2 Stock-dove, see calman gorm.
——— -gobhlach,(AF) Fan-tailed pigeon.
——— -gorm,¶ *s. m.* Stock-dove.—*columba œnas*.

104. Calman-cathaidh.

105. Calman-fiadhaich.

106. Calman-gorm.

——— -mara,¶ *s.m.* Rock-dove, see smùdan.
calman-nan-creag,*s.m.*Rock-dove, see smùdan.
——— -taighe, *s.m.* Domestic pigeon.
——— -tùchan, (AF) Turtle-dove. see turtur.
calmar,†† *s.m.* Kind of fish.
calmarra, see calma.
†calmas -ais, *s.m.* see calmachd.
calm-lann, -a, -an [& -lainn**], *s.m.* Dove-cot.
calmunnach, -aiche, *a.* see calma.
càl-na-mara,§ *s.m.* Seakale, see praiseach-tràgha.
calp,* *s.f.* Rivet nail. for calpa 6.
calpa, *pl.* -an [& -annan] *s.m.* Calf of the leg. 2 Pillar. 3 Tier or ply of a rope or cable. 4 Shrouds or standing rigging of a ship. 5 Capital (of money.) 6 Nails, see bàta, p. 76. 7 Shank of an anchor, see under bàta, p.77. *C.* na tàirnge, *a halliard or hoisting rope*; *c.* is riadh, *capital and interest*; meall a' chalpa, *the calf of the leg*; caol a' chalpa, *the small of the leg.*
calpach, -aich, -aichean, *s.m.* [& *f.*] see colpach.
———, -aiche, *a.* Stout-legged, strong-legged.
calpannach, *a.* see calpach.
calpanta,** *a.* Bony.
———s,** -ais, *s.m.* Brawniness.
càl-Phàdruig,§*s.m.* London pride, Peter's kale, none-so-pretty—*saxifraga umbrosa.*
càl-phleadhag, -aig, -an, *s.f.* Gardener's dibble.
cal-shalainn,** *s.* Alkali.
caltuinn,§ s. Southernwood. see meath-chaltuinn.
calum, -uim, *s.m.* ||Corn, hardness on the skin from working with spades, oars, &c., callosity.
calunn, -uinn, see calum.
cam, *v.a.* Bend, curve, make crooked or distorted. 2 Blind. Cham thu am maide, *you bent the stick.* [càm in *Gairloch, &c*—DU.]

107. Càl-Phàdruig.

cam, *gen.m.* caim, *comp.*caime,*a.* Crooked,awry, distorted, curved, bent. 2 Blind of an eye. 3 Ill-directed. 4 Tricky, dishonest, deceitful. Tha e cam, *he is blind of an eye*; maide cam, *a crooked stick*; cha robh cam nach robh crosda, *the one-eyed was ever cross.* [*Càm* in some places.]
cam, see caim.
†cam, *s.m.* Deceit, fraud, artifice.
cam,* -aime, *s.f.* Female blind of one eye.
†cama, *a.* Strong, courageous, daring, bold, brave.
†camabhil, -e, *s.f.* Camomile.
camcag, -aig, *s.f.* Trip, sudden tripping of the heels. Leig e mi le *c.*, *he tripped me up*; cuir *c.*, *trip.*
†camach, *s.f.* Power, influence. 2 Ability.
camachag,†† -aig, -an, *s.f.* Small bay.
cama-chnòdan, see cnòdan.
cama-chraos,(AH) *s.m.* (*lit.* wry mouth) Mendicant expectancy, condition in which one makes a poor mouth.
camadh, -aidh, *s.m.* Bend, bending, curve, curving, crook. A' c—, *pr.pt.* of cam. Air chamadh, *adv. aside.*
cama-dhubh, *s.f.* Arm- or thigh-bone. 2 see cam-dhubh.
camag, -aig, -an, *s.f.* Curl, ringlet. 2 Crook. 3 Clasp. 4 Side of the head, temple. 5 Club. 6 Bay, arm of the sea. 7 Anything crooked or curved. 8 Comma, in writing. 9**Quibble, quirk. 10 Anything undesirable. 11†† Curve. Bhuail e 'sa chamaig e, *he struck him on the temple.*
———ach, -aiche, *a.* Curled, as hair, having ringlets. 2 Crooked. 3**Winding. Do chùl *c.*, *thy tressy ringlets.*
———an, *pl.* of camag.
camagan-sréine, *s.m.* Bit.
camag-ara, see camag-gharaidh.
camag-gharaidh, *s.f.* The temple, hollow above the eye.
camaich,‡‡ *v.a.* Bend.
camaichte,** *past part.* Bent.
camalag,(JM) *s.f.* Curl, ringlet—*W. Isles.*
†cam-all, see càmhal.
cama-lùbach,(AF) Sandpiper, see trileachan-tràighe.
———, *a.* Devious, winding.
camamhil, see camomhail.
caman, -ain, *pl.* -ain [& camanan,] Club for playing shinty, hurley, or golf. Not a cricket-bat, as given in some dictionaries, as *cam an* must have a curve in it. 2(DU) see cam-ag, 4.
———achd, *s.f.* Shinty, hurley, golf.
camar,** *s.m.* Fool, idiot.
———an, see camar.
camart, -airt, *s.m.* Pain or spasmodic affection of the neck, causing the patient to look a-wry. 2 Wry neck.
camas,* -ais, *s.m.* Mould for making bullets. 2

see camus.
——ach, see camusach.
cambar,(AC) s.m. Place of burial.
cam-bheul, -eòil, s.m. Distorted mouth.
————ach, a. Wry-mouthed.
cam-bhileach, a. Wry-lipped.
cam-bhuidhe, a. Yellow-curled, yellow-waving. T'fhalt cam-bhuidhe, *thy yellow curled hair.*
†cam-braic, s.m. Wry mouth.
†cam-ceachdta, s.m. The North Pole.
cam-chas,** s.f. Bandy leg.
————ach, -aiche, a. Bandy-legged.
cam-chòmhdhail, s.f. Unlucky foregathering or meeting. Cam-chòmhdhail ort ! *bad luck to you !*
cam-dhàn, -ain, pl. -dàna, s.m. Iambic verse.
————ach,‡‡ a. Iambic.
cam-dhubh, pl. cama-dhubhna, s.f. Fore-leg of cattle and sheep. There is no white on them, even when the beasts are fat.—JM
†ca-mead, see cia meud ?
cam-glas,¶ s.f. Red-shank. 2(AF) Red-start, red-pole, purple sandpiper.

108. Cam-ghlas.

cam-ghob,¶ s.f. Common crossbill, wrybill,—*loxia curvirostra.*

109. Cam-ghob.

†camh, -aimh, s. m. Power, might, ability, strength. 2 Influence. 3 Gaelic spelling of *cave.*
camh,* *contr.* of camhanach.
†camhach, s.f. Might, power, influence.
camhach, -aiche, a. Loquacious, garrulous, prattling, talkative.
————as, -ais, s.f. Loquacity, garrulity, talkativeness.
càmhair,** s. f. see camh-fhàir.
càmhal, -ail, s.m. Camel. Deich càmhail, *ten camels.*
camhan, -ain, pl. camhanan, s.m. Hollow plain. 2**Little cave, cove. Feadh nan lùb 's nan camhanan, *among the bays and coves.*
camhanach, -aich, s.f. Dawn, early morn. 2 Twilight.
†camhaoir, see camh-fhàir.
camh-fhàir, -e, s.f. Dawn, daybreak.
camhlach, -aich, see cabhlach.
camhul, -uil, see càmhal.

camlag,(CR) s.f. *Skye* for camag 1, see camalag
————ach, a. see camagach.
camlaid, -e, see caimileid.
cam-lorg, -luirg, s.f. Crooked staff. 2 Circuitous road. 3**Crooked or meandering path. Am fear nach gabh comhairle gabhaidh e c., *he that takes not advice will go astray.*
cam-lùb, s. m. Curl.
————ach ‡‡ -aiche, a. In curls.
cam-luirgneach, a. Bow-legged, bandy-legged.
†cam-mhuggarlach, see c— -luirgneach,
cam-mhuin, see cam-mhuineal.
cam-mhuineal, -eil, s.m. Wry neck. 2 The bird wryneck.
————ach, a. Wrynecked.
camog, -oig, -an. see camag.
†camoga, s.pl. The temples of the head.
camogach, a. see camagach.

110. Camomhail.

camomhail, s.m. Camomile—*anthemis nobilis.*
————-fiadhain, s.m. Scentless May-weed, see buidheag-an-arbhair.
camp, -a & caimp, pl. -aichean, [-an & -annan,] s.m. Camp. Am meadhon a' chaimp, *in the middle of the camp.*
——-achadh, -aidh, s.m. Encamping, encampment. A' c—, pr.pt. of campaich. Tha aingeal Dhé a' campachadh, *the angel of God encamps.*
——-aich, pr.pt. a' campachadh, v.a. Encamp.
†campaineach, a. Of Champagne.
campair, -ean, s.m. Camp-master.
campar, -air, s.m. Anger, grief, vexation, uneasiness, sorrow. 2** Camphire. Na cuireadh e c. ort, *do not let it vex you* ; c. inntinn, *vexation of spirit.*
————ach, -aiche, a. Angry, grievous, vexatious, troubled, fretting.
camparaid,* s.f. Bustle.
†camp-thuaim, s.f. Entrenchments.
cam-rath, -a, -an, s.m. Sewer, gutter, dyke.
cam-riaghailt, -ean, s.f. Anarchy, confusion without rule.
cam-sgrìobach, -aiche,‡‡ a. Curvilinear.
cam-shron, -oine, -an, s.f. Crook- or hook-nose.
————ach, a. Hook-nosed. 2 Crook-nosed.
cam-shuil, -ula,-shuilean, s.f. Squint-eye.
————each, a. Squint-eyed. Cailleach chrosda, cham-shuileach, *a cross-grained, squinting dame.*
camus, -uis, s. m. Bay, creek, harbour. 2** Crooked rivulet. 3 The space between the thighs. 4(AH)Stern-seat of a boat, see bàta, p. 76. An camus Clutha nan iomadh stuadh, *in the bay of Clutha of many waves.*
————ach, a. Abounding in bays, creeks, or harbours. 2 Like, of, or belonging to, a bay, creek, or harbour.
can, pr.pt. a' cantuinn, [& cantail] v.a. Sing, rehearse, say, name, call. Can òran, *sing a song* ; can sin fhathast, *repeat that—Glendale.*
†can, a. White.
†can, adv. Whilst, when.
†can, -a, s.m. Moth. 2 Lake. 3 Whelp, puppy.
càn,(AC) see càin.

can, (CR) *s.m.* Business—*Perthshire.* Tha e air a chan féin. *he is in business on his own account* [Scots—he is on his own can.]
cana, *pl.* -chan, *s.m.* Little whale, grampus. 2 *Sturgeon, porpoise. 3 Order of poets third inferior to an *ollamh.*
canabhas, -ais, *s.m.* Sackcloth, Gaelic spelling of *canvas.*
canach,‡ -aich, -aichean, *s.f.* [*m***] Cotton-sedge *or* cat's-tail—*eriophorum vaginatum,* and *eriophorum polystachyon.* [Given by some as the badge of Clan Sutherland.] 2 ‡‡Cotton. 3‡‡Down. Crann canaich, *a cotton-tree.*
†**canach**, *s. m.* Standing water. 2 Bombast. 3 Deceit. 4 Sturgeon. 5 Porpoise.
†-———, *a.* see cannach.
cànach, *gen. sing.* of càin.
canachail, -e, *a.* Cottony.
cànachas, -ais, see cànachd.
cànachd, *s.f.ind.* Taxing, placing under tribute.
cànachus. see cànachd.
canadh, see cana.
canadh,** *s.m.* Chant.
canaib, see cainb.
canaich,** *s.* Dirt.
canaichean,** *s.m.* Cotton, bog-cotton.
cànaichte, see càinichte.

111. Canach.

canaidh, *fut. aff. a.* of can.
†**canaigh**, *s.f.* Dirt.
cànain, -e, -ean, *s.f.* Language, dialect, speech, tongue. 2 Pronunciation, accent.
———each, -iche, -ichean, *s.m.* Linguist, philologist.
———each,‡‡ *a.* Philological.
cànainiche, *gen. sing.* of cànaineach. also 2 same meaning as cànaineach.
canal, -ail, see caineal.
canam, *v.* Let me say. 2 I shall say.
cànamhuinn, see cànain.
†**canan**, -ain, *s.m.* Cannon.
cananach,** -aich, *s.m.* Canon. 2 Canonist.
canar, *fut.pass.* of can. Prionnsa na sìothchainnt canar ris,*he shall be named the Prince of peace.*
cana-siogach, (AF) Wolf cub.
canastair, -e, -ean, *s.m.* Gaelic spelling of *canister*
†**canfam**, for canaidh mi, *fut.aff.:a.* of can.
can-fhonn,** -fhuinn, *s.m.* Song. 2 Precept, canon.
cangairnich, *pr.part.* a' cangairneachadh, *v.n.* Suppurate, gangrene, canker.
cangaruich, *pr. part.* a' cangaruchadh, *v. a.* Fret, vex, agitate.
cangluinn, -e, -ean, *s.f.* Vexation, trouble, uneasiness.
————each, -eiche, *a.* Troublesome, teasing, importunate.
————eachd, *s.f.ind.* Uneasiness, importunity, turbulence.
cànmhuinn, see cànain.
cànmhuinniche, see cànaineach.
†**cann**, *s.m.* Reservoir. 2 Vessel. 3 Full moon.
†**canna**, -chan, *s.m.* Can. 2 Cup. 3 Moth. 4 see †can 3.
———ch, *a.* Pretty. 2 Soft, mild. 3**Kind. 4††Sweet. Gris-dhearg, *c., ruddy and comety.*
cannach, -aich, *s.m.* Sweet-willow. 2‡ Bog-myrtle. 3 Any fragrant shrub.
canndaidh,** *s.f.* Gaelic spelling of *candy.*
cannran, see cànran.
†**cannta**, *s.m.* Lake, puddle.
†**canntach**, *a.* Dirty, nasty, filthy, miry, puddly.
canntail, -e, -ean, *s.f.* Singing. 2 Voting for, as at an auction. 3 Auction. A' c—, *pr.pt.* of can.
canntair, -e, -ean, *s.m.* Chanter, singer.
———eachd, *s.f.* Chanting, singing, warbling. 2**Melodiousness. 3**Song-singing. 4 **Merriment. 5 The ancient Highland manner of noting classical pipe-music by a combination of definite syllables, by which means the various tunes could be the more easily recollected by the learner.

Through the kindness of Chas. Bannatyne Esq., M.B., C.M., Salsburgh, Holytown, we are able to give here the only systematic key to this ancient system of notation for "ceòl-mór" ever published. As MacLeod of Gesto, who published the MacCrimmons' tunes in canntaireachd, took them down phonetically, it is rather difficult to describe the system minutely. This must not be lost sight of in translating tunes. The complete key is here given. A few of the notes resemble one another very closely, but the changes used are indicated, and the pronunciations are given approximately, in brackets. The key note, "low A" is always represented in this notation by *in,* probably a contraction of "an dara aon," *the second one,* to distinguish the key note from the first note of the chanter—"low G." "High A" is always *i,* but in a canntaireachd word it is often denoted by a preceding *l,* thus, *liu,* and so confusion is avoided. "Low A" is either *in, en, em,* or simply *n* after some notes. The alternatives seem to have been used for the sake of euphony. D note is *a* and B note is *a,* but the qualifying effect of the grace notes —"high G" represented by *h,* and D represented by *d* or *h* (the latter a contraction of [a']chorag, the finger playing D) prevents any confusion. The note E is represented by *i.* At the beginning of most of the MacCrimmon tunes and variations is *I,* which gives the key note. It stands for E (soh)the dominant of the "low A" (doh.) Where it does not occur, the tune will be found to start with a word like *hien,* which denotes E with "high G" grace note, and then "low A." The vowel for F note is *ie,* and it also is always made certain by its grace note *d* or *h.* "High G" is *u,* often distinguished by a preceding *h.* "High A" is often *vi,* to distinguish it from E note. When F succeeds "high A" in a tune, the word is often *vie.* Regarding grace notes, *h.* the aspirate, qualifies all notes down to "low A," but often where *ha* obviously means "B" note, it must be concluded that it should have been written *cha.* Similarly *ho ho* should be *ho cho.* The letter *d,* is used, as is *t,* to denote both "high G" and D grace notes, but an examination of the notation word, makes a mistake unlikely, thus, *dieliu* means F with "high G" grace note, and then "high A" and G. *Tihi* means two E's played with two G grace notes. *T* and *d* resemble each other very closely in Gaelic, but the context in canntaireachd makes it always easy to see whether "high G" grace note or D is meant. It is necessary to explain the compound grace note systems. *Dr* is doubling of "low G" by a touch of D grace note, *drin* is doubling of "low G" by a touch of D grace note and open "low A" and so on over the whole scale. The letters *dr* are obviously a contraction of *dà uair,* "two times" or twice.

Tri means doubling of "low G" by D grace note, and as A is opened, double E by F and E and open E. This is a crunluath form. *Tro* is the same, at first, but the doubling of E is done with the grips from *o* or C note. This is "crunnluath a mach" These examples will make the rest easy. In many tunes where a *tr* type occurs, it obviously when translated, should only have been a *dr* type, this confusion being due to the similarity of *d* and *t* in Gaelic. The shake on "high A" is *vivi*. The other shakes are represented by *rr*, according to where the beats or shakes are taken from. This seems to be a contraction of *gearr-adh*, a shake. A simple touch of a note before opening is always represented by a single *r*. For instance, such a word as *radin* signifies that B is to be touched with "low G" (lùdag) before opening; *din* is "low A" with D grace note. *Ho radin*, is the C note *o*, with "high G" grace note keeping the *ra* below D note, also an A note. *Rules for the grace note scheme.* 1. All grace notes and grace note types are forestrokes, that is, they occur before the notes they embellish. They are appoggiaturas or semi-quaver notes, or acciaturas or demi-semi-quaver notes, which predominate. 2. All grace notes in canntaireachd are represented by consonants. 3. All compound forms are made up by combining single forms. 4. All leading or scale notes are represented by vowels. 5. All note forms with *m* or *n* in them contain "low A." 6. Grace notes *h* and *d* are qualifying or modulating grace notes. 7. Doublings are represented by *dr*, triplings by *tr*, compound types by combinations of these. 8. Open doublings above D are represented by *dir*, such as *dirie*, where the note is doubled by itself and the note above it. *Dr* denotes closed doublings, *dir* open doublings.

Grace note forms defined. Grace note forms consist of single, double, and compound. The single group includes all simple forms, together with the "dà-lugh" variation form. The double includes the single and double types of "tri-lugh" and "ceithir-lugh." The single type of tri-lugh is composed of three low A's graced by G, D, and E grace notes, and it precedes the note embellished. An example of this is "hinínindo," the syllable *do* being C graced by D. This type is called *fosgailte* or open, and is opposed by the double or closed form, represented by such a word as "hindirinto." The latter is called *a steach* or inside, when opposed to a type like "hodorito," which is said to be *a mach* or outside, as the grips are taken from the note played. The types last named are also *breabach* forms, having a "kick" note at the finish. The crun-lugh or ceithir-lugh forms are also *fosgailte*, *a mach* and *a steach*. The word "hadatri" is *a steach*, when opposed to "hadatri," which is *a mach*. "Hiodratatiriri" is a pure "cliabh-lugh"—the chest or creel of fingers, because every finger on the chanter is engaged in some way, either acting or acted on. In bagpipe music the variations are all named from the acting fingers, and the old pipers counted their time from the number of fingers engaged in the several parts of a tune. "Chin-drine" may be taken as an example of "leum-lugh," the jump of the fingers. This is low A played by D grace note, then G, doubled by D, low A then opened, and F rapidly opened from it. "Hiriri" is an example of a beat form. The

Note and grace note key to MacLeod's MacCrimmon tunes in Canntaireachd. Basis, a nine line stave or scale, each line representing a note of the chanter.

Key note of chanter : approximately A Major.

Scales		G. ordinals	Vowels	Names of fingers.	Single grace note scales.				Shakes	Doublings	Triplings	Touches	Types
A'	Doh.	an 9.mh.	i (boy)	òrdag, *thumb.*	vi			li	vivi				*ceithir-lugh*
G'	Ta.	an t-8mh.	u (au)	iulugh, *index, leading* or *guiding.*	vu	h	d, t,	lu	riuru	dru	triu	riu	hodatri†
F	Lah.	an 7mh.	ie (ebb)		vie	hie	die, tie	lie	rieri	drie, dirie	trie	rie	hodratiriri‡
E	Soh.	an 6mh.	i (if)		bhi	hi*	di, ti		riri*	dri, diri	tri	ri	hohorieri‡
D	Fah.	an 5mh.	a (awl)	(a') chorag, *first,* (*index, leading*)	bha, *vao*	ha, ch	d, ta		tiriri	drao	trao	rao	*tri-lugh*
C	Me.	an 4mh.	o (son)		bho, *vo*	ho, cho	do, to, tho	lo	roro	dro, dor	tro	ro	hodirit†
B	Ray.	an treas.	a (ale)		bha, *va*	ha, cha	da, ta, tha	la	rara	dra, dar	tra	ra	hodorit‡
A	Doh.	an dara.	en in(ihn) im em			hin, chin	din		rurin	drin, dirit, dirin	tri	rin	hinínindo§
G	Ta.	an ceud.	u (süne)	lùdag lùdan } *little.*		hu, chu	du		ru	dr, dir, dur	tru		

* Beats are combined forms, such as "hiriri." † A steach. ‡ A mach. § Fosgailte.

General structure of "Ceòl-mór" or "piobaireachd."

1 Ùrlar, or ground.
2 Iulugh or dà-lugh, two finger variation. } Ordag. Leumlugh. } Dùbailt, doublin.
3 Tri-lugh, or three finger variation } Fosgailte / a mach / a steach } Breabach
4 Ceithir-lugh, or four finger variation

Key words.

1. Gearradh, *a shake.* 2. Crathadh, *a shake.* 3. Ceileirich, *a warble.*
4. Dà-uair, *twice.* 5. Tri-uairean, *thrice.*

playing of two low A's by touching low G twice with the little finger is "ririn" or "rurin." The prosodic quality of the syllables forming the notation, together with the spacing and punctuation, give the time and rhythm of the tunes. [Want of space forbids our following this important and fascinating subject further.]

†canntal, *v.a.* Sell by auction.
†cann-thigh, *s.f.* Strawberry.
†canoin, -e, -ean, *s.f.* Rule. 2 Song. 3(MM) Canon.
cànran, -ain, *s.m.* Contention, broil, quarrel. 2 Grumbling, murmuring, muttering, wrangling. 3*Reflecting incessantly. 4**Purring. 5**Cackling of geese. 6**Chattering, as of a bird. 7* Bickering, scolding and reflecting incessantly. Mar a' ghaoth ch., *like the murmuring wind.*
cànranach, -aiche, *a.* Grumbling, murmuring, muttering. 2 Cross, fretful, peevish, bickering.
——d, *s.f.* Fretfulness, contention, peevishness.
cànranaich, *pr.pt.* a' cànranachadh, *v.n.* Contend, grumble.
——, *s.f.* Continual grumbling or murmuring.
cant,** *s.* Dirt.
†canta, *s.f.* Quince-tree. *2 Lake. 3 Puddle.
†cantach, -aiche, *a.* Dirty, puddly, miry.
càntach,** *a.* Singing.
†cantaig, -ean, *s.f.* Canticle, song.
†cantaighear, -eir, -an, *s.m.* Accent.
cantail, *pr.pt.* of can.
càntair, see canntair.
cantal, -ail, *s.m.* Grief, weeping, lamentation
†cantaoir, -e,-ean, *s.m.* Press.
†cantlamh, see cantol.
cantoir, -e, -ean, see canntair.
†cantol, *s.m.* Strife. 2 Grief.
cantuinn, -e, *s.m.* Singing. 2 Saying, speaking. A' c—. *pr.pt.* of can.
càinichte, (for càinichte) *past pt.* of càinich.
†canur, see canach.
caob, -aoib, -an, *s.m.* Clod. 2 Lump, as in thread. 3 Nip. 4 Bite. 5 Bit. 6 Piece of anything cut off, as with the teeth. 7 Glebe. Caob sneachdaidh, *a snowball.*
——, *pr.part.* a' caobadh, *v.a.* Clod, strike with clods. 2 Bite, as with the teeth, nip.
——ach, -aiche, *a.* Full of clods, like a clod. 2 Biting.
——adh, -aidh, *s.m.* Clodding. 2 Biting. A' c—, *pr.pt.* of caob.
†caobainn, *s.f.* Prison.
†caobh, *s.m.* Bough, branch, twig.
caobhan,** -ain, *s.m.* Little bough or twig.
†caobhan, -ain, *s.m.* Prison.
caobte, *past part.* of caob. Clodded. 2 Bitten, cut, as with the teeth, into small pieces. [see note at foot of p. 53.]
caoch, caoiche, *a.* Empty. 2 Blind. 3 Hollow. 4 Blasted. 5 (MMcD) see cuthach.
caoch, -oich, *s.m.* see cuthach.
caochad, -aid, *s.f.* Blindness. 2 Emptiness.
caochadh, -aidh, see caogadh.
caochag, -aig, -an, *s.f.* Nut without a kernel. 2 Empty shell. 3 The game "blind man's buff." 4 Puff-ball—*lycoperdon gemmatum.* 5 **Mushroom. [Frequently applied to the whole family of the larger fungi.] 6(AF) Grampus. 7(AF)Mole, blind beast. 8(AF) Spiral shell-fish.

112. *Caochag(4)*

——ach, *a.* Full of nuts without kernels, 2 of turned shells, 3 of mushrooms or puffballs. 4 Like a hollow nut, turned shell, mushroom, or puff-ball.
caochail, *pr.pt.* a' caochladh, *v.a.& n.* Change, alter. 2 Expire. [Used only of human beings in this sense.] 3** Travel. 4**Pass away.
——ear, *fut.pass.* of caochail. Shall be changed.
caochan, -ain, *pl.* caochanan, *s. m.* Eddy of air. 2 Whisky in its first process of distillation (Scot. *wash.*) 3 Streamlet, purling rill. 4 Purling noise, like the sound of worts fermenting. 5(AF) Bird—*Dean of Lismore.* 6** Eddy on the surface of any liquid. 7**Mole. 8**The fundament. Tosgaid chaochain, *a vat or wash-tub, for fermenting worts.*
——ach,‡‡ -aiche, *a.* Brooky.
caoch-chnuasach, -aich, *s.m.* Empty nut.
caochlach, -aich, *a.* Changing, inconstant, variable.
caochladh, -aidh, -aidhean, *s.m.* Change, alteration. 2 Death, dying, passing away. 3 Putrefying. 4(DU) Variety. A' c—, *pr.pt.* of caochail. C. tuineachais, *a change of dwelling*; c. an t-soluis, *the phases of the moon*; air chaochladh dreach, *in a different form*; c. sheòrsachan, *several kinds*; ann an c. àitean, *in various places.*
caochlaideach, -eiche, *a.* Changeable, variable, inconstant, fickle. Uair ch., *changeable weather*; duine c., *a fickle person.*

caochlaideachd, *s.f. ind.* Inconstancy, mutability, changeableness, fickleness.
caochlaidh, *fut.aff.a* of caochail.
———each ‡‡ -eiche, *a.* see caochlaideach.
———ich,‡‡ *v.a.* Interchange.
caochlan, -ain, *pl.* caochlanan [& -ain**], *s.m.* Swift rill or rivulet.
caoch-nan-cearc, *s.m.* Henbane, see gafann.
†caod, *s.m.* St. John's wort, see eala bhuidhe.
†caod, *v.n.* Come.
†caoda ? *adv.* How ?
caodachan,** -ain, *s. m.* Infant beginning to walk.
caod-aslachan-Chaluim-Chille, *s.m.* St. John's wort, see eala-bhuidhe.
caod-Chaluim-Chille, *s.m.* see eala-bhuidhe.
†caod e ? *for* ciod e ?
†caodh, *s.m.* Tear. 2 Good order, condition.
†caodhamhlachd, *s.f* Competency, suitableness, adequateness.
†caodhan, *s.m.* Person in good order or condition.
caog, *pr.pt.* a' caogadh, *v.n.* Wink. 2 Connive. 3 Take aim by shutting one eye. 4**Beckon.
caogach, -aiche, *a.* Winking. 2 Squint-eyed. 3**Blinking 4**Twinkling.
caogad, -aid, *a.* Fifty. Phill iad nan caogadaibh, *they returned in their fifties.* Trì miosan cù, còig caogaid cat, *three months a dog, forty-five days a cat*—referring to the time of going with young—(the translation of this as "five times nine days" in N.G.P. is pure conjecture, the correct reading being apparently "còig á caogad," *five from fifty,* i.e. 45—CR.)
———amh, -aimh, *a.* Fiftieth.
caogadh, -aidh, *s.m.* Wink, winking. 2 Connivance, conniving. 3 **Beckon. A' c—, *pr pt.* of caog. A' caogadh shùl na bitheam, *let me not wink with the eye.*
caogadh, *3rd. pers. sing. & pl. imp.* of caog. Caogadh e, *let him wink.*
caogail, -e, *s.f.* Winking, squinting.
caogair, -ean, *s.m.* Blinkard.
caogluidheachd,‡‡ *s.f.* see caochlaideachd.
caog-shuil, -shul, *s.f.* Eye that winks. 2 Squint-eye.
caog-shuileach, -eiche, *a.* Winking, blinking. 2 Squint-eyed.
caoi, (AF) see caolag.
†caoi, see caoidh. 2 Ways and means.
caoibean, (AC) *s.m.* The first five or six inches of warp uncrossed by the weft at the beginning of the web, thrum.
†caoich, *a.* Blind of an eye.
†———e, *s f* see caoichead.
†———ead, *s.f.* Blindness.
caoichealachd, *s.f.ind.* Noisy, turbulent, obstreperous or clamorous mirth.
caoicheil, -e, *a.* Mad, insane. 2 Abounding in noisy merriment.
caoideag, *s.f.* see cuiteag.
caoidh, -e, *s.f.* Lamentation, weeping, wailing, mourning. 2 Lament, wail, moan. 3**Decency. A' c—, *pr.pt.* of caoidh.
caoidh, *pr.pt.* a' caoidh, *v.n.* Lament, mourn, bewail, weep, wail. Cha chaoidh am prìosanach, *the prisoner shall not mourn.*
caoidh-chòmhradh, -aidh, *s.m.* Mournful expressions. 2 Wailing voice. Dh'fhàilnich a c.-ch, *her wailing voice ceased.*
caoidh-chòradh, see caoidh-chòmhradh.
caoidheach, -eiche, *a.* Mournful, wailing, weeping.
caoidheadh, -idh, *s.m.* Mourning, wailing, lamenting, deploring. A' c—, *pr.pt.* of caoidh. Turlach a' c.a chloinne, *Turlach lamenting for his children.*
caoidheag, see caoineag.
caoidhear,** *s.m.* Bemoaner.
———an, -ain, *s.m.* Wailing. 2 Low murmuring sound. 3 Mournful voice.
———anach,†† *a.* Mournful, plaintive.
caoidh-ghuth, *s.m.* Plaintive voice.
caoidh-ràn, -àin, *s.m.* Moaning.
caoidhrean, -ein, *s.m.* see caoirean.
caoil, *gen. sing. & n. pl.* of caol.
caoil,†† -ean, *s.m.* Twigs, wands.
caoile, *comp.* of caol.
———, *s.f.ind.* Leanness. 2 Smallness. 3 Attenuation. 4 Narrowness. 5 Dearth, want of fodder for cattle. 6 ‖Starvation. 7**Trouble. 8**Destruction 9**Distemper among sheep and goats. 10‡‡Waist. Fhuair e bàs leis a' chaoile, *he died of starvation* ; crodh leis a' chaoile, *the cattle starving for want of fodder.* [In senses 5. 6, & 9, it is preceded by the article, a' ch—.]
caoilead, -eid, *s. m.* Smallness, slenderness, leanness. 2 Fineness, as of linen or yarn, 3 Progression in leanness. A' dol an caoilead, *getting leaner and leaner.*
caoilich,†† *pr.pt.* a' caoileachadh, *v.n.* Make slender, attenuate.
†caoille, *s.f.* Land.
caoillean, -ein, caoilleanan, *s.m.* Small twig or osier used in wicker-work.
caoiltean, *pl.* of caol, *s.*
caoimh, *a.* see caomh.
caoimh, *gen. sing. m.* of caomh.
caoimhe, *comp.* of caomh.
———ach, -aich, *s m.* see caomhach.
———ach, -eiche, *a.* Kind, polite, friendly.
———achan, -ain, *s.m.* Entertainer. 2 Hospitable person. 3 Beloved person.
———achas, *s.m.* Society. 2 Social love. 3 Hospitality.
caoimhne, *s.f.* see caoimhneas. Caoimhne ort, *be gentle, be affable.*
caoimhneag, see caomhnag.
caoimhnealachd, *s.f.* Kindness, benevolence, affability. 2 Courteousness. 3 Agreeableness to the touch.
caoimhnealas, -ais, *s.m.* see caoimhneas and caoimhnealachd.
caoimhneas, -eis, *s.m.* Kindness, mildness, affability. 2* Kind turn. Dean *c.* dhomh, *show kindness to me.*
———ach, -aiche, *a.* Kind, mild, affable. 2 Benevolent.
caoimhneil, -e, *a.* Mild, kind, courteous, genial, gentle, favourable, affable, lenient. 2 Friendly. 3 Obliging. 4 Affectionate. Coltach ris a' Chuan-an-Iar, mar is crosd' i 's ann a's caoimhneile, *like the Western sea, the wilder the kinder*—this is literally true, for the more unsettled the sea, the larger are the quantities of drift-ware and wreckage cast ashore ; an samhradh caoimhneil, *the genial summer;* gu caoimhneil, *kindly.*
caoimh-sgiath, -sgéith, -an, *s.f.* Shield.
†caoimhtheach, *s.m.* Inmate, bed-fellow, lodger.
caoimhtheachas, -ais, see caoimheachas.
†caoimhtheachd, *s.f.* Protection. 2 County.
†caoimin, *s.f.* Eyebright (plant.) 2 The murrain.
†———each, *s.f.* Common for cattle.
caoin, *pr. part.* a' caoineadh, *v.a. & n.* Weep, wail, deplore. 2 Howl. 3 Regret. Cha chaoin òighean, *virgins shall not weep.*
———, -e, *a.* Kind, mild, pleasant, gentle, tender. 2 Delightful. 3 Dry, seasoned, as hay, sheaf-corn, &c. 4 **Smooth, smoothly polished. 5 ** Soft, mellow. 6** Lowly.

Mar aisling ch., *like a pleasant dream* ; caoin-chnàmh, *a polished bone*; a' taghadh chlacha caoin, *choosing smooth stones* ; caoin-sian, *a gentle shower*.
caoin, -e, *s.f.* The exterior surface of cloth, vulgarly called the "right" side 2 Rind. 3 Kindness. 4 Sward. Caoin uaine, *green sward* ; bhris e caoin an leathrach, *he broke the surface of the leather* ; caoin is as-caoin an aodaich, *the "right" and "wrong" side of the cloth*; chuir mi caoin air as-caoin, *I got into a great rage*.
caoin-air-ascaoin, *adv.* Inside out.
caoin-chaithlinn, *s.f.* Name of a star.
caoin-cheann,§ *s.m.* Cotton-sedge (plant), see canach.
caoin-chronachadh,‡ *s.m.* Admonition.
caoin-chronaich,* *v.a.* Admonish.
caoine, *comp.* of caoin.
†**caoineach**, -ich, *s.m.* Stubble. 2 Moss, see còinneach.
caoineachadh, -aidh, *s.m.* Drying, as of hay, exposure to the sun's heat for the purpose of drying. A' c—, *pr.part.* of caoinich. A' caoineachadh na saidhe, *drying the hay*.
caoineachag, see caoineag.
†**caoineachan**, -ain, *s.m.* Polisher of stone.
caoineachas, -ais, *s.m.* Peace, mildness, tranquility. 2 see caoimhneas.
caoineadh, -idh, *s.m.* Weeping, crying, lamentation. 2**Wailing, howling. A' c—, *pr pt.* of caoin.
caoineag,(AC) [*lit.* weeper] *s.f.* Naiad who fortells the death of, and weeps for those slain in battle.
caoinear,* *s.m.* Sheer indifference.
———ach,* *a.* Indifferent, careless.
caoineas,** -eis, *s.m.* Lamenting.
†**caoineasgar**, -air, *s.m.* Fort. 2**Garrison.
caoineis,* *s.m.* Taking off, gibing, jeering.
———each,* *a.* Indifferent, apt to gibe or take off.
———eachd,* *s f.* Assumed indifference, fastidiousness, foolish pride.
caoin-gheal, *a.* White and soft. Do chanach caoin-gheal, *thy soft white mountain-down*.
caoinich, *pr.part.* a' caoineachadh, *v.a.* Dry, expose to dry, season. 2 Make smooth.
†**caoinich**, *s.f.* Cotton.
caoin-iochdach, -aiche, *a.* Compassionate.
caoinleach,** -lich, *s.m.* Corn-stubble.
caoin-mholadh,‡‡ -aidh, -aidhean, *s.m.* Blandation.
caoin-shuarach, -aiche, *a.* Indifferent, careless.
——————d, *s.f.ind.* Indifference, carelessness.
caointeach, -eiche, *a.* Sad, sorrowful, mournful, melancholy, whining. Bha 'acain caointeach, *his moan was mournful* ; c. fad na h-oidhche, *mournful all the night*.
—————, -tich, *s.m.* Mourner, whiner.
—————,* *s.f.* Female fairy or water-kelpie, whose particular province it was to warn the members of her favourite clans of the approach of death, by weeping and wailing opposite the kitchen-door.
caointeachag, see caoineag.
caointeachan, *s m.* see caointeach, *s.m.*
caointeag, (AC) see caoineag.
caoir, -e, -ean, *s. f.* Firebrand. 2 Blaze of fire, fiercely burning, accompanied by noise. 3 Rapid torrent. 4 Foam with sparks of fire in it, as in a stormy sea, phosphorescence. 5‡‡ Coal. 6** Gleams, flames, flashes. 7** Thunderbolt. 8 (AF) see caora. 9†† Red-hot iron. Na tonnan 'nan caoir, *the waves like flame* ; a' choille 'na caoiribh, *the wood in flames*; caoir dhealan, *gleams of lightning* ; a' mhuir 'na caoiribh geala, *the sea in white foam*; slios na beinne 'na aon chaoir gheal, *the hill-side one mass of white foam* (because the rain had so increased the rivulets.)
caoi-ràn, see caoidh-ràn.
caoir-bianag,(MMcD) *s.f.* Phosphorence, gleam in the sea. 2 Effulgence thrown off by decaying fish.
caoir-chon,§ Guelder-rose, see céir-iocan.
caoir-dhris, -e,‡ *s.f.* Thicket of thorns or brambles.
caoireach, *a.* Sparkling, gleaming, flashing, flaming. 2**Fiery, impetuous. 3 Flagrant.
caoireag, -eig, -eagan, *s.f.* Small dry peat. 2 Small piece of coal. 3 Small peat or piece of coal on fire. Cha tuit caoireag á cliabh falamh, *fuel will not fall from an empty creel*.
———ach, *a.* Full of dry peats or small pieces of coal. 2**Crumbled, like peat or coal.
caoireall, see caireal.
caoirean, -ein, -reanan, *s. m.* Plaintive song, plaintive sound. 2 Soft sound, purling sound. 3 Wailing, mournful voice. 4** Murmur, moan. 5**Cooing of a dove. 6**Brawl. 7 see caoireag. *C.* na coille, *the murmur of the wood ;* ri sior-chaoirean, *making a continual plaintive sound, wailing*.
———ach, *a.* Moaning, murmuring, gurgling, purling. 2**Brawling
———achd, *s.f.* Frequent or continued murmuring or moaning, purling noise.
caoir-gheal, -ghile, *a.* Glowing hot, bright flaming, white-hot, heated to incandescence. 2** Emitting sparks.
————,(AH) *s.* White crest of waves in a gale.
caoiribh, see caoraibh.
caoirich, see caoraich.
†**caoirin**, *s.f.* Little sheep. 2 Little berry.
caoirin-leana, *s. f.* Marsh or dwarf valerian—*valeriana dioica*.

113. Caoirin-leana.

†**caoirl**, *v.a.* Beat with a club.
caoir-lasair, -lasrach, -lasraichean, *s.f.* Flaming coal. 2 Sparkling flame.
†**caoirle**, *s.m.* Club.
†**caoirleachd**, *s.f.* Tossing, or driving with clubs.
caoirnean,-ein,-ean, *s.m.* Globule of sheep or goats' dung. 2‡‡ Drop of any liquid.
caoir-sholus, -uis, *s.m.* Gleaming light. 2 Effulgence.
caoirtheach, -eiche, *a.* Fiery, impetuous. 2 Sparkling, gleaming. Sruth *c.* bh'o chruaich nam beann, *a fiery stream from the brow of the mountains*.
caoir-teine, AC) *s.f.* Fire sparkles, blaze of fire. 2 Firebrand. Tha 'n duine 'na chaoire dearga teine, *the man is in red sparkles of fire*.
caoir-theinntidh,** *s.f.* Thunderbolt.
†**caois**, *s.f.* Farrow pig, young pig. 2 Furrow.
†**caoiseachan**, -ain, *s.m.* Swine-herd.
†**caoitein**, -ean, *s.m.* Gaelic spelling of *kitten*.
†**caoithearan**, -ain, see caoidhearan.
caol, caoile, *a.* Small, slender, thin, lean, lank, attenuated, narrow. 2**Shrill-toned. Dh' fhighinn breacan a bhiodh caol dhuit, *I would weave tartan for you that would suit you well;* ceòl caol, *shrill high-toned music ;* is caol an teud as nach seinn e, *it is a slender string that he cannot take a tune from*.
caol,caoil, *pl.* caoiltean, *s.m.* [& -aoil,] Narrow strait, sound, firth. 2**Narrow part of a ri-

ver. 3**Smaller part of anything. 4 (AC) Osiers. 5‡‡Pile. Fo chaol nam marbh, *under the pile of the dead* ; a' seòladh troimh na caoiltean, *sailing through the straits* ; caol an droma. *the small of the back*; caol an dùirn, *the wrist;* caol na coise, *the ankle* ; ceangail a chaoil, *bind him hand and foot* ; an taigh caol, *the narrow house (grave)* ; caol a' chalpa, *the small of the leg.* "Caol ri caol," a rule observed by most writers of Gaelic. It prescribes that the vowels which flank any consonant, should, if narrow on one side, be narrow on the other also, as: buailteach (*liable*) not buailtach ; oillteil, (*shocking*) not oilltail. Grinne caoil, *a bundle of osiers.*

caol-abhainn,** *s.f.* Narrow river.

caolach,** -aich, *s.m.* Wattles.

caolach, *s.f.* Fairy flax. 2 Worst part of corn.

——— -aifrinn, *s.m.* Prayer - or mass-bell.

———adh, -aidh, *s.m.* Act of making small, thin, or slender.

†caoladh-adhbhair, -ean, *s.m.* Less cause.

caolag, } (AF) *s.f.* Cuckoo, see
——— -riabhaich, } cubhag.

caolaich, *pr.part.* a' caolachadh, *v. a.* Make or grow small or slender. 2 Attenuate. 3 Diminish, lessen. 4 Taper. Caolaichidh tu a chasan, *thou wilt make his legs slender.*

———te, *past part.* Made slender.

caolan, -ain, *s.m.* Small gut, tripe, entrail. *C.* -cait, *cat-gut.*

———ach, *a.* Like guts, of, or belonging to a gut, made of guts. 2 Intestinal.

caolas, -ais, -an, *s. m.* Firth. 2 Strait. 3 **Ferry. Snàmhaiche a' chaolais, *the swimmer of the strait.*

caol-chasach, -aiche, *a.* Having small or slender legs. 2 Slim-footed.

caol-chòmhnuidh, *s.f.* Narrow abode, grave.

caol-chorpach, -aiche, *a.* Slender-bodied.

caol-chromadh, -aidh, *s.m.* Narrow curve. *C.* na gealaiche, *the narrow curve of the moon.*

caol-chruth, -an, *s.m.* Slender form.

———ach, -aiche, *a.* Slender-formed.

caol-dearrsa, *s.f.* Name of a star.

†caol-fail, *s.f.* (caol, *slender* + fàil, *spite, malice*) Nettle, see deanntag.

caol-fairge, *s.m.* Strait, firth, narrow part of the sea.

caol-ghealach,** -aiche, *s.f.* The New Moon. 2 The Old Moon. A' chaol-ghealach troimh neul, *the new moon (seen) through a cloud.*

caol-ghleann,** -ghlinn, *s.m.* Narrow valley, glen. Air astar an caol-ghleann, *travelling in the narrow valley.*

caol-ghlòireach, see caol-ghuthach.

caol-ghlòrach, see caol-ghuthach.

caol-ghruagach,** *a.* Thin-maned. Each caol-ghruagach, *a thin-maned horse.*

caol-ghuth,** *s.m.* Shrill voice.

———ach, -aiche, *a.* Shrill, having a shrill voice.

caol-mhala, *pl.* mhalaichean, *s.f.* Finely-arched and narrow eyebrow.

———ch, -aiche, *a.* Having narrow eyebrows.

†caol-mhaor, *s.m.* Apparitor.

†caol-mhìosachan, *s.m.* Purging flax.

caol-mhìosachan,§ *s.m.* Fairy flax, see lìon na mna-sìth.

caol-mhuingeach, -eiche, *a.* Small or narrow maned.

caol-pheirceallach, *a.* Chapless.

caol-shrath, -a, -an, *s.m.* Narrow plain, strath, or valley.

caol-thearnadh, (AH) *s.m.* Narrow escape.

caomh, caoimh, *s.m.* Friend. 2 Beloved object. 3 Kindness, friendship, hospitality. 4** *rarely* Feast. An tog mi mo shiùil 's gun chaomh am fagus? *shall I hoist my sails without a friend being near ?* caomh mo theach, *the hospitality of my house.*

caomh, *v.a.* see caomhain.

†caomh, *s.m.* The follicle or seed-vessel which some fruits and flowers have over them.

caomh, -a [& caoimhe,] *a.* Kind, meek, gentle, mild, tender. 2 Dear, beloved. 3‡‡ Handsome. †4‡‡Noble. Labhair e gu caomh ris a' ghruagaich, *he spoke kindly to the damsel*; cha chaomh leam e, *I do not like him.*

†caomh, *a.* Little.

†caomha, *s.f.* Skill. 2 Knowledge. 3 Poetry, versification.

caomhach, -aich, *s.m.* Friend, bosom friend. 2 Associate. 3 Bed-fellow. 4**Stranger. Gun mhac gun *ch.*, *without son or friend.*

———as,* -ais, *s.m.* Chambering, sensuality, dalliance.

caomhachd,†† see caomhachdas.

———as, -ais *s. m.* Affection, sociality, kindness.

caomhag, -aig, -an, *s.f.* Mildly-tempered, kind female. 2 Affectionate girl. 3(DU) Form of addressing a female. A chaomhag ! *my lassie!*

caomhaich, *pr.pt.* a' caomhachadh, *v.a.* Cherish, fondle. 2††Pacify, sooth.

†caomhaidh, *s.m.* Man expert in feats of arms.

caomhail, -e, *a.* see caoimhneil.

caomhain, *pr.part.* a' caomhnadh, *v.a.* Spare, protect, save. 2 Reserve. 3** Economize. *C.* gus am màireach e, *save it till to-morrow;* na *c.*'e, *do not spare it.*

caomhainn, see caomhain.

caomhalach, -aiche, *a.* Kindly, of a mild, gentle disposition or manner.

———d, *s.f.* Kindness, affability, gentleness. 2††Mildness. Lagh na *c.*, *the law of kindness.*

caomhan, -ain, *s.m.* Noble, affable, kind, friendly man. 2 Beloved person. 3 Friend. †4 Nobleman. A chaomhain ! *my dear sir !*

———ach, -aich, *s.m.* Friend, companion.

———ach, -aiche, *a.* Mild, merciful, benevolent.

———tach, -aiche, *a.* Saving, frugal, economical. 2**Protecting. 3* Stingy.

———tachd, *s.f.ind.* Frugality, economy. 2 Parsimony, saving disposition.

†caomhchladh, see caochladh.

†———ach, see caochlaideach.

caomh-chridhe, -eachan, *s.m.* Tender or affectionate heart.

———ach, *a.* Tender-hearted, kind, affectionate.

caomh-chruth, *s.m.* Slender form or person, as of a female.

———ach, -aiche, *a.* Slenderly formed.

†caomhdha, *s.m.* Poetry, versification.

caomh-ghràdh, -ghràidh, *s. m.* Tender mercy, compassionate kindness.

caomh-lasair, -lasrach, -lasraichean, *s.f.* Pleasing flame.

caomh-leus, -eòis, *s.f.* Pleasant blaze.

†caomhna, see caomhan.

caomhnach, -aich, *s.m.* Friend. 2 Feeder.

———, -aiche, see caomhantach.

caomhnadh, -aidh, *s.m.* Economy, saving, sparing, parsimony, frugality. 2* Reserving. 3***rarely* Protection. A' c—, *pr. part.* of caomhain. Dean *c.*, *spare* ; *c.* math air a' bheagan Beurla agus a' Ghalltachd gu léir romhainn ! *use your little English sparingly with the whole of the Lowlands before us !*

†caomhnam, *v.a.* I spare, save, reserve.
†caomhnasgar, *s.m.* Defence.
caomh-shrath, -a, -an, *s.m.* Pleasant valley.
caomhuinn, see caomhain.
†caon, caoin, *s.m.* Resemblance.
†caon, *v.a.* Resemble. 2 Refer.
caon,** *v.a.* Conceal.
†caonaran, -ain. see aonaran.
caon-bhuidhe, *s.f.* Gratitude.
†caon-dùrachd, *s.m.* Love, devotion.
caonnag, -aig, -an, *s.f.* Fight, skirmish, fray, squabble. 2** Boxing match. 3**Nest of wild bees. Daoine nach d' rinn caonnag, *men who fought not*; dheanadh thu caonnag ri d' dhà lurgainn, *you would quarrel with your own two shins.*
caonnagach, -aiche, *a.* Fond of fighting or boxing. 2 Riotous, quarrelsome.
†caonta, *a.* Private.
caonntach, -aiche, *a.* see caomhantach.
———d, see caomhantachd.
caor, *gen.* caoire, *dat.* caoir, *pl.* caoran, see caoir.
caor, -a [& caoir**], -an, *s.f.* The berry of the rowan or mountain ash. 2(AC) Any red berries, or red bodies of a globular form. 3 see caoir.
caora, *s.f. irreg.* Sheep. 2 (*in derision*) Sheepish person. Declined thus:—

Nom. Sing.	caora,	*pl.* caoraich.
Gen.	caorach,[caoire‡‡ caoir,**]	caorach.
Dat.	caora,	caoraibh.
Voc.	a chaora !	a chaoraich !

Am bun nan caorach,*looking after the sheep*; o chrò nan caorach, *from the sheep-fold.*
NAMES OF SHEEP AT DIFFERENT AGES:—
[*G.* is for Gaelic name; *S.* for Eng. name in Scotland; *E.* for Eng. name in England.]
MALE & FEMALE before weaning—
G. uan,(*s.m.* —*never s.f.*)*S & E lamb.* uan firionn, *a male lamb*; uan boirionn, *a female lamb.*
FEMALE, after weaning till 1st shearing:
G. òthaisg. Ciora, uan—*Lewis.* 2 (If it had a lamb), fiar-òthaisg, *a crooked hogg.* the lamb being called, uan na fiar-òthaisg. If small or inferior, òthaisg is called, seot. *S.& E. ewe-teg, ewe-hogg.*
after 1st shearing:
G. caora bhliadhnach. Tiaraineach, òthaisg bhoirionn—*Lewis.* 2 (If with lamb), òthaisg, the lamb being called, uan òthaisge. *S. gimmer,E.gimmer, theave.*
after 1st. shearing, if not put to ram:—
G. Dìonag.
after 2nd shearing, if with lamb:—
G. caora uain. Dà bhliadhnach—*Lewis. S. twinter*; *E. two-shear ewe.*
after 2nd shearing, if not with lamb:—
G. caora sheisg, *S. barren twinter*; *E. two-shear ewe.*
after 2nd shearing, if not put to ram:—
G. Dà bhliadhnach seasg. Caora-chiatain, (MMcD)—*Lewis. S. eild gimmer*; *E. two-shear ewe.*
after 3rd shearing:—
G. Tri bhliadhnach. In *Lewis* if barren, *crogais*; if with lamb, *caora uain. S. winter ewe*; *E. three-shear ewe.*
after 4th shearing:—
G. crog,(AH) *S. aged ewe, three winter ewe.*
when ceasing to give milk:—
G. caora sheasg, *S. yeld ewe.*
when taken from the breeding flock, regardless of age:—
G. crog,(AH) *S. draft ewe.*
when taken from the breeding flock as unfit to breed from:—
G. crog, *S. draft gimmer.*
MALE (not castrated.)
from weaning till first shearing:—
G. uan reithe, *S. up-hogg*; *E. hogg, hogget, hoggerel, tup teg.*
after 1st shearing:—
G. reithe, bliadhnach reithe. Aona bhliadhnach reithe,—*Lorn.* Tiaraineach, tiaraineach rùid,(MMcD)—*Lewis. S. dimmont tup*; *E. shearling, dimmont tup, one shear tup.*
after 2nd shearing:—
G. dà bhliadhnach reithe. Dà bhliadhnach rùid,—*Lewis. S. two shear tup*; *E. two shear ram,*
after 3rd shearing:—
G. Tri bhliadhnach reithe, seann reithe(AH.) Rùd, seann rùd.—*Lewis. S. aged tup*; *E. three shear ram.*
after 4th shearing:—
G. Seann reithe, ceithir bhliadhnach reithe. Ceithir bhliadhnach rùid, seann rùd—*Lewis. E. four shear ram.*
MALE (castrated.)
from weaning till first shearing:—
G. Uan firionn, uan spothta—*Lewis.* Òthaisg fhirionn, (*s.f.*)—*Lorn. S. he-teg, wether hogg*: *E. wether teg.*
after first shearing:—
G. Bliadhnach mult, Òthaisg fhirionn, tiaraineach mult—*Lewis.* Còig ràitheach mult,(JM)—*Skye.* Sè ràitheach muilt, (spelt according to local pronunciation) bliadhnach muilt, (*lit.* yearling of a wether—DM) *after 1st. Hallowe'en O.S.*—*Lorn. S. dimmont*; *E. shear hogg, wether hogg.*
after 2nd shearing:—
G. mult,—*Lorn.* Dà bhliadhnach mult—*Lewis. S. two shear wether*; *E. two tooth wether.*
after 3rd shearing:—
G. Tri bhliadhnach mult—*Lewis. S. wether*; *E. three tooth wether.*
after 4th shearing:—
G. ceithir bhliadhnach mult—*Lewis. E.four tooth wether.*
Sheep are often described in LORN as:—
Aona bhliadhnach caoire, *one yearling of a sheep*; dà bhliadhnach caoire, *two yearling of a sheep,* &c.
In LEWIS, after 3rd. shearing, the females are generally named according to the number of times they have lambed, till the 7th. or 8th. lamb, when they are called *seann chaora,* and are taken away to be killed. The castrated male after 4th. shearing, is called *ceithir bhliadhnach mult* to *seachd* or *ochd bhliadhnach mult,* when they become useless for wool &c. In Ness, and neighbourhood, the uncastrated male is called *rùda* after 2nd. shearing for the rest of its life.
In PERTHSHIRE the following are the most usual names:—Uan boirionn, uan firionn, uan reithe, *till Nov. 11 then* òthaisg bhoirionn, òthaisg fhirionn, òthaisg reithe, *then* bliadhnach mult, dìonag, reithe. Ath-dìonag, *3-year old*; caora ceithir bhliadhnach, *4-year old*; crog, *cast ewe*; sè raitheach, *six-quarter old gimmer*; deat, *unshorn year-old sheep or wether.*
OTHER NAMES:—
caora bhainne, *milk ewe.*
caora bheannach, *4-horned sheep of Uist &*

St. Kilda.
caora bhrogach,(MMcD) *Speckled or spotted sheep.*
caora càraid, *sheep with twins.*
caora cheaslach, *coarse woolled sheep.*
caora cheannan (ceann-fhionn) *white-faced sheep.*
caora chileach, *piebald or speckled sheep.—Lewis.*
caora dhubh, *black sheep.*
caora dhubh-cheannach, *black-faced or Highland sheep.*
caora gheal, (AH) *white sheep, in contradistinction to the smeared or dipped members of a flock.*
caora mhaol, (*lit. hornless*) *Cheviot sheep.*
caora mholach, *heavy fleeced sheep.*
caora Nollaig, *fat sheep for butcher at Xmas.*
caora reamhar, *fat sheep for butcher.*
caora Shasunnach, *English sheep.*
caora sheasg, *a yeld sheep.*
caora uain, *a breeding sheep.*
ceireag, see ciora.
ceireagan, see ciora. Crò nan ceireagan, (from old *port-a-beul.*)
ciora, *pet ewe-hogg or sheep.*
cireag, see ciora.
ciridh, see ciora.
crog,(AH) *cast ewe, age depending on breed and kind of pasture.*
crog,‡‡ *sheep past bearing.*
deata, *year-old unshorn ewe hogg.*
dìonag, *do. after first shearing.* 2‡‡ 2-year old sheep or goat.
feirmige, *ram with one of its testicles wanting.—Lewis.*
leth uan, *twin lamb.*
reige, *ridgling.*
rige, *ram only partly castrated,—Lewis.*
reithe studhach, see rùda studhach.
rùdan, -ain, -an, *little ram, ridgling.*
rùda studhach, *ram with short tail.—Lewis.*
sagart—*Lewis*, see feirmige.
sùgan, *pet lamb.*

†caora(*for* caoran) Bunches of berries. 2 Grapes
caora-bada-miann,§ *s.f.* Stone-bramble—*rubus saxatilis.*
caora-beanach, (AF) see under caora.
caora-bheanan, for caora-bheanach.
caorach, *gen. sing. & gen. pl.* of caora.
caorachd,** *s.f.* Stock of sheep. 2 Sheep. 3 Cattle. 4 Sheepishness.
caora-dhromain, *s.f.* Elder berry.
caora-feannaig, -aig, -an, *s.f.* Crowberry, see lus-na-feannaig.
caora-feullain,* *s.f.* Ivy berry.
caora-fiadhag, see caora-feannaig.
caora-fithich,†† see lus-na-feannaig.
caorag,** -aig, -an, *s. f.* Small dry peat, dry clod or turf.
caorag-lèana,§ *s. f.* (*lit.* marsh spark) Ragged-robin, see currachd-na-cubhaig.
caoraibh, *dat.pl.* of caora.
caoraich, *n. & dat. pl.* of caora.
caora-mhadaidh, see caor-chon.
caoran, -ain,-an, *s.m.* Third or bottom row of peat cut from a bank with the "toirsgian"—*Lewis* (M. McD.) 2 Dry clod. 3(DU) Small shoal or school of fish, as haddock, &c. 4 Fragment of peat. 5 Ember.

114. Caora-bada-miann.

caora mhaol bhàn,(AH) *s.f.* (*lit.* white Cheviot sheep) Skittish, timid, poor-spirited person, milk-sop.
caoran, *n. pl.* of caor.
caorann, see caorunn.
caora-staoin, *for* caor-aitinn, see aitionn.
caor-bheirteach, *a.* Producing berries, rich in berries.
caor-chon,§ *s.f.* Dogberry—*viburnum opulus.* 2 Guelder rose. 3 Water elder.
caor-dhromain, see caora-dhromain.
caor-feaunaig, see lus-na-feannaig.
caor-gheal,**see caoir-gheal.
†caor-lann, *s.m.* Sheep-fold.
caornag, -aige, *s.f.* Wild hive. 2 see caonnag.
caor-thalmhuinn, see caorunn-thalmhuinn.
caor-theine, see caoir-theine.
caor-theinntidh,**see caoir-theinntidh.

115. Caor-chon.

caorthuinn, *for* caoruinn. 2 Sometimes used for the *nom.* caorunn.
caorunn, -uinn, *pl.* -uinn & -uinnean, *s. m.* Mountain-ash or rowan tree. 2 ‡‡Wood of the mountain-ash tree. [The berry is called *caor*, and the tree *caorunn*. In *Gairloch, &c., caorunn* is the berry, and *craobh-chaoruinn* is the tree—DU.]
caorunn-caoich, -uinn-, *pl.* -uinn- & -ean-, *s.m.* Species of cranberry supposed to be poisonous.
caorunn-talmhuinn, *s.m.* Earth nut. 2 Wild strawberry.
caoth,** *s.m.* Shower.
caothach,‖-aich, see cuthach.
caothach-nan-cearc, *s.* Henbane, see gafann.
caothail(AF) *s.f.* (*lit.* wailer) Long-tailed duck, see eun-buchainn.
†caothruadh, *s.f.* Mildew.
†cap, -a, *s.m.* Cup. 2 *rarely* Cart. 3 Tumbrel. 4 Mouth. 5 Old person.
càpa, *pl.* -chan, *s.m.* Cap. 2 Top.
†capaireadh, *s.m.* Capering, cutting capers.
capalan-a'-chinn-mhóir, *s.m.* Kind of fish.
capall, see capull.
†capan, -ain, *s.m.* Little cup.
capar, -air, -airean, *s.m.* Caper, kind of pickle.
†capat,** -ait, *s.m.* Head.
cap-dheudach, -aiche, *a.* see cab-dheudach.

116. Capull-coille.

capar-coille, see capull-coille.
†cap-fhlath, -fhlaith, *s.m.* Commander-in-chief.
capull, -uill, *s.m.* Mare. 2 *in some places* Horse. 3 Colt. [*Formerly* horse broken to the bit.]
capull-abhainn, *s.m.* Hippopotamus.
capull-coille, -uill-, *s.m.* ¶Capercaillie, great cock of the wood—*tetrao urogallus.* (illust. on p. 166.)
capull-lìn, -uill-lìn, *s.m.* Lint-beetle.
càr, caire, *a.* *1st comp.* cara, Friendly. 2 Related to.
càr, -àir, *s.m.* Friend. 2 Relation. 3 *Mossy plain, fen. Mar chanach cà r, *like the moss cotton*; gu'n cluinn mi mo chàra, *that I may hear my friend*; bi 'nad chàra do 'n rìgh, *be an ally to the king.*
car, *prep.* During, for, whilst, near about, in reference to time. Car tiota, *for a moment*; car oidhche, *for the space of a night*; car uair, *for a time, sometimes*; car mìosa, *for a month*; car greis, *for a while*; car ùine bhig, *for a little while.*
car, cuir, *s.m.* Twist, bend, turn. 2 Winding, meandering, as of a stream. 3 Trick, fraud. 4 Way, course. 5 Bar of music. 6 Motion, movement. 7 Revolution. 8 Case, *in grammar.* 9*String of beads, pearls, &c. 10 Contact, neighbourhood. 11 Direction. 12 Throw. 13 Circular motion. 14**Care. 15‡‡Plait, fold. An *c.* a bhitheas 'san t-sean mhaide, is do-cair a thoirt as, *it is impossible to straighten the twist that is in the old stick*; gach car a th' ann is cleas, *all his wiles and tricks*; thug e an car asam, *he cheated me*; car a' mhuiltein, *a somersault*; thug thu mo char is mo leth-char asam, *you have cheated me in earnest, to all intents and purposes*; na cuir car dheth, *do not overturn it*; gun aon char a chuir dheth, *without moving it*; car chneap, *a string of beads*; car neamhnuidean, *a string of pearls*; thoir an car as, *cheat him*; thoir car mu'n cuairt, *take a turn round*; tha car eile an adharc an daimh, *there is another bend in the bullock's horn*; car eil' air ruidhl' a' bhodaich, *another turn in the old man's reel*—this saying, and the one before it are often used when anything unexpected happens; thèid sinn an car seo, *we will go this way*; car an aghaidh cuir, *twist against turn, diamond cut diamond*; gille nan car, *an artful dodger*; cha robh car ach car gu call, *everything that was done made matters worse*; a' cur nan car dheth, *dancing, very busy*; cha robh car air an t-saoghal a b'fhearr leam seach &c., *there was nothing in the world I was so fond of as &c.*
†càr, *s.m.* Cart, car, raft for carrying things on, 2 see càrr.
†càr, *s.m.* Care. 2 Jaw. 3 Fish. 4 Stone. 5** Scab, mange, itch. 6**Chariot.
†car, *a.* Brittle.
car,** *a.* see carach.
càra, *a., comp.* of càr, *akin.* Bu chàra dhuit t' obair a dheanamh, *it would better become you to do your work.*—J.G.M.
†cara, *s.m.* (ceathramh) Leg, haunch. 2 Jaw, hog's cheek.
càra, *for* càr, *friend.*
carach, -aiche, *a.* Cunning, sly, wily, tricking, deceiving. 2 Meandering, whirling, circling, winding, turning. 3 Changeable, unstable. 4 Acute. 5**see carrach. Tha 'n saoghal seo *c.*, *this world is deceitful*; fear *c.*, *a deceitful person*; cho *c.* ris a' mhadadh ruadh, *as wily as the fox*; am measg osnaich *ch.*, *amid the circling breeze*; am fear a bhitheas *c.* 'sa bhaile seo, bithidh e *c.* 'sa bhaile ud thall, *he that is tricky in this town will be tricky over there too.*
carachadh, -aidh, *s.m.* Moving, stirring, motion, movement. A' c—, *pr.pt.* of caraich. Carachadh céille, *insanity*; oiteag a' *c.* an duillich, *a breeze stirring the leaves.*
càrachadh,** -aidh, *s.m.* Act of burying.
carachail,‡‡ -e, *a.* Motory.
carachair,** *s.m.* Motor, mover.
carachd, *s.f.ind.* Wrestling. 2 Sparring. 3 Deceitfulness. 4 see carachadh. *C.* an t-saoghail seo, *the deceitfulness of this world.*
carachdach, -aiche, *a.* Athletic. 2 Of, or belonging to wrestling.
carachdaich, -e, *s.f.* Wrestling.
†carach-ullamh, *s.m.* Upper garment.
caracin,‖ see cairgein.
†caradach, see cairdeach.
càradh, -aidh, *s.m.* Mending, repairing, adjusting. 2 Usage or treatment, whether good or bad. 3 Condition. 4 Cheating, deceiving. 5**Way, course, direction. 6**Abuse. 7** Turn, winding, twist. Fear-càradh a' bheum, *the repairer of the breach*; is truagh mo chàradh, *sad is my condition*; is don' an càradh a dh'fhàg thu air, *you have left him in a sad condition*; an duine a's miosa càradh, *the man of worst condition.* A' c—, *pr.pt.* of càraich, 2 *pr.pt.* of càir. "Making", as of a bed. Tha i 'càradh na leapa, *she is "making" or shaking up the bed.*
caraibh, (*dat. pl.* of car) An caraibh a chéile, *in contact, in grips*; aom 'nan caraibh, *bend in their direction*; an caraibh a bhroclainn, *in the direction of his den*; gach ni a thig 'ad charaibh, *everything that comes near you*; an caraibh a chéile, *in contact with each other.*
caraiceach,** -eiche, *a.* Hairy. 2 Eager, keen.
caraiceag,** -eig, -an, *s.f.* Pancake.
caraich, *pr. part.* a' carachadh & a' carachdainn, *v.a.* Move, stir. 2 Remove. 3 see càr. Na *c.* e, *do not move it*; cha *ch.* thu as a seo, *you shall not move out of this*; *ch.* iad, *they moved*; mar a charaicheas iolair a nead, *as an eagle stirreth up her nest.*
———e, *a., comp.* of carach.
———e, -an, *s.m.* Wrestler. 2 Tumbler. 3 Sharper. 4**Pugilist.
———te, *past part.* of caraich.
caraid, *dat.* caraid, *pl.* càirdean, *s. m.* Male friend or relation. 2**Cousin. Mo dheadh charaid, *my dear friend*; caraid, mac piuthar athar, *cousin, the son of a father's sister.*
càraid, -e, -ean, *s. f.* Pair, couple, brace. 2 Twins. 3 Married couple. 4‡‡Defence. 'Nan càraidibh, *two by two*; càraid each, *a pair of horses*; càraid-rann, *a couplet*; càraid na maoislich, *roes that are twins.*
———each, *a.* Paired. 2 In couples or braces.
†caraidheach, *a.* Wrestling. 2 Of, or belonging to wrestling. 3 Debating.
†————d, *s.f. ind.* Debate, dispute. 2 Wrangling, wrestling.
càraidich, *pr.part.* a' càraideachadh, *v.a.* Couple, join together in couples or pairs.
caraid-nan-Gàidheal, (AF) *s.m.* Gannet (bird) see tabhs.
†caraigh, see caraich.
càr-aingeal, -eil [& -gil,] *pl.*-glean [& -gle] *s.m.* Guardian angel.
carainnean, *s.pl.* Refuse of threshed barley.
car air char, *adv.* see car mu char.
caraist, *s.f.* ‡Catechism. 2** see cairbhist.
caraiste, see cairbhist.‡
†-———ach, -eich, *s.m.* Carrier.
caramasg, -aisg, *s.f.* Contest. 2 Confusion.
cara-meala, see carra-meille.
càramh, -aimh, see càradh.

caramh, *adv.* see caraibh.
cara-mhil-a' choin,§ *s.* Common tormentil, see braonan-fraoich.
cara-mhill, *s.* Mandrake.
car-a'-mhuiltein, *s.m.* Somersault.
†caran, -ain, *s.m.* Crown of the head.
càran,(CR) *s.m.* Beloved person, darling.(*dim.* of càr, *friend, relation.*)
caran-creige, *s.f.* Sand eel, conger eel. 2(AF) Shrimp, prawn. 3(AF)Stickleback. 4 Only applied to the shoemaker fish in *Lochalsh, Western Isles &c.*, and not to the conger-eel.
carantach, *a.* see carthannach.
———d, *s.f.* see carthannachd.
carantas, -ais, *s.m.* see carthannas.
caranuich, *v.a.* Separate. 2 Stir up.
†caras, -ais, *s.m.* First-rate ship.
carasan, -ain, *s.m.* Hawking.
———aich, *s.* ,,
†carb, cairbe, -an, *s. f.* Basket. 2 Chariot, (cairb.) 3**Plank. 4**Ship.
carbad, -aid, -an, *s.m.* Chariot, coach, chaise. 2 Waggon. 3 Litter. 4 Bier. 5 Any pleasure vehicle. 6 The jaw, upper or lower. 7 Jaw of a quern. Araon c. agus marc-shluagh, *both chariot and horseman*; buail am balach air a' charbad, agus buail am balgair air an t-sròin, *strike the clown on the jaw and the dog on the nose*; c cogaidh, *a war-chariot*; fiacal carbaid, *jaw-* or *cheek-tooth*; c. uachdar, *the upper jaw*; c. iochdar, *the lower jaw*; c. màlaidh, *a mail coach.*‡‡
carbadach,‡‡ -aiche, *a.* Jawed.
————d,‡‡ *s.f.* Aurigation.
carbadair, -ean, *s. m.* Charioteer, driver, coachman.
————eachd, *s.f.* Business of a charioteer or coachman.
carbad-farraidh, *s.m.* Fly.
carbad-smùide,* *s.m.* Railway carriage.
carbair, see corbair.
†carbal, *s.m.* Roof of the mouth.
†carban, -ain, *s.m.* Unlucky person.
†carbanach, -aich, see carbhanach.
car beag, *adv.* Rather little.
†carbh, -airbh, *s.f.* see cairb. 2(AF)Carp (fish.)
carbh,* *v.a.* Gaelic spelling of *carve.*
carbhaidh, *s.f.* Caraway—§*carum carui.*
carbhaig, see carbh.
carbhainn, see carbhaidh.
carbhair, -ean, *s.m.* Gaelic spelling of *carver.* 2 Engraver, sculptor.
———eachd, *s.f.* Carving, occupation of a carver. 2 Engraving. 3 Mangling, mutilating. 4 Massacring.
carbhaist, *s. f.* Heriot. 2 **Drubbing.
carbhan,** -ain, -anan, *s.m.* Little ship. 2 Carp.
———ach, *s.m.* Sea bream. 2††Carp.

117. Carbhaidh.

†carbhanach, -aich, *s.m.* Master of a ship.
carbhanach-uisge, *s. m.* Carp,—*cyprinus carpio.* (illust. 118.) 2 (AF) Fresh-water bream.
†Carbhas, -ais, *s.m.* Lent, see Carghus. 2 Intemperance.
†car-bhodach, -aich, *s.m.* Clown. 2 Sailor.
car-bhriathar,** *s.m.* Antiphrasis.
car-bhriathrach,** *a.* Antiphrastic.
†carboir, -e, -ean, *s.m.* Coachman.
carbuncul, -uil, *s.m.* see carmhogal.
†carc, cairc, *s.m.* Care, anxiety.
carc,(AC) *v.a.* Put in a cell. Cha charcar mi, *I shall not be put in a cell.*

carcair, -e, -ean, *s. m.* Prison. 2 Coffer. 3 Sink or sewer in a byre.
carcais, -e, -ean, see cairbh.
carcaiseach, -sich, *s.m.* Carcase, see cairbh.
carcar,** see carcair.
†carchaill, *v.a.* Destroy. 2 Abuse.

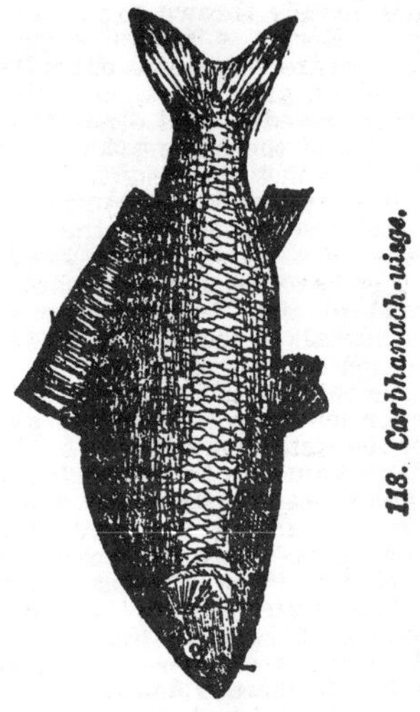

118. Carbhanach-uisge.

car-chuileag,(AF) *s.f.* Humming or singing fly.
càrd, -a [& càird], -an, *s.f.* Wool-card. 2 English gallon or four Scots pints. 3 see càrt.
càrd, *pr.part.* a' càrdadh, *v.a.* Card wool, cotton or flax.
càrdadh, -aidh, *s.m.* Process or act of carding wool &c.
†cardaigh, *s.f.* Flesh.
càrdair, *s.m* Carder or teazer of wool &c.
————eachd, *s.f.* Employment of a carder or comber. Ris a' *ch., at the wool-combing trade.*
càrd-eich,* *s.m.* Currycomb.
car fada, *adv.* Rather long.
car-fhacal, -ail, *pl.* -fhaclan [& -ail], *s.m.* Quibble, prevarication. 2 Antiphrasis. 3 Double entendre. 4 Pun.
car-fhaclach, *a.* Quibbling. 2 Prevaricating. 3 Antiphrastic. 4 Disposed to quibble, prevaricate or pun.
car-fhaclaiche, *s.m.* Quibbler. 2 Prevaricator. 3 Punster.
†cargair, *v.n.* Congratulate.
Carghus, -uis, *s.m.* Lent [Preceded by the article *an.*] 2‡ Torment. An deireadh a' Charghuis, *at the end of Lent.*
Carghusach, *a.* Lenten, quadragesimal.
†carla, -ai, carlan, *s.m.* Wool-card.
†càrlach, -aich, *s.m.* Cart-load.
†————an, -ain, *s. m.* Carder or comber of wool.
càrlag, -aig, -an, *s.f.* Lock or tuft of wool.
carlag,(AF) *s.f.* Black guillemot, see calltag.
càrlagach, *a.* Like a tuft of wool. 2 Of tufts of wool.
†carlair, -ean, *s.m.* Carder.
†carlamh, *a.* Excellent.
càrlas, -ais, *s.m.* Excellence.
carmasg, see caramasg.
carmhanach, see carbhanach.
†carmhogal, *s.m.* Carbuncle (stone.)
†————ach,** *a.* Carbuncular.
car mu char, *adv.* Round and round. 2 Over

and over. Thuit e car mu char leis a' bhruthaich, *he fell down the slope, turning over and over.*

†carn, cairn, *s.m.* Quern, handmill for grinding corn.

†càrn, càrna, *s.f.* Flesh. 2 Booty.

càrn, càirn [& cùirn], *s.m.* Cairn, heap or pile of stones loosely thrown together. 2 Peat-barrow. 3 Rock. 4 Sledge, car. [Cairns and barrows are very numerous in the Highlands, Ireland and Wales, as well as parts of Norway, Sweden, and other Continental countries, and there are a few in America. Some of them measure 300 ft. in circumference at the base and 20 ft. in height. They consist of loose stones, and the whole is in the shape of a cone. In many instances where they have been opened, they contained sepulchral urns, which show that they were memorials of the dead. Many of these piles consist entirely of earth, and this gave rise to the opinion that stone cairns were intended for malefactors, while those of earth were for the victorious and brave. We learn from ancient authors that malefactors were buried under heaps of stone, and it was a common practice among the Druids to erect cairns on spots where criminals had been burnt. Hence "fear air chàrn" means an outlaw, "tha e air a' chàrn," *he is an outlaw.* Is oil leam nach robh do luath fo chàrn, *I do wish your ashes under a cairn;* b' fhearr leam a bhi fo chàrn, *I had rather be under a cairn, (i.e.* be punished as an outlaw.) The ceremony in later times was continued in the Highlands, but its meaning was altered. A sudden death was *bàs gun sagart*, and the dead person's soul was believed to be in the hottest part of purgatory, so every passer by was expected to put a stone on the cairn and to pray for the repose of the soul of the departed—hence the saying "cuiridh mi clach 'nad chàrn," *I will add a stone to your cairn*, which betokens a friendly intention and means that one's remembrance shall be kept alive. When the remains of anyone were carried a long distance for interment, and the bearers had to take some rest on the way, a cairn was put up there also, and those who passed by were expected of their charity to put a stone on it, and pray for the soul of the deceased. Cairns are still frequently erected to mark the spot in which a funeral has rested, and on whatever spot a person is found dead, a few stones are immediately put together.—**]

O iomall nan càrn, *from the edge of the rocks.*

càrn, càirn [& cùirn], *s.m.* Horning. [The Gaelic seems a confusion between *corn*, horn, Eng. *horn, put to the horn*, and *càrn*—‡]

†càrn, *s.m.* Province.

càrn, *pr.part.* a' càrnadh, *v.a.* Heap, pile, accumulate, throw together. A' càrnadh airgid, *accumulating wealth ;* chàrnadh le Daorghlas an t-seilg, *the game was piled up by D.*; ged chàrn e airgiod, *though he accumulate silver.*

carnabhan,(AF) *s.m.* Beetle. also ceardabhan.

càrnach, -aich, *s.m.* Heathen priest. 2 Stony ground. 3 Quarry. [Used as the names of several places having a stony or rocky situation.]

————,** -aiche, *a.* Rocky, stony. 2 Like a cairn, abounding in cairns. 3 Shelvy.

càrnadh, -aidh, *s.m.* Heaping, piling up, accumulating. 2**Riddance. A' c—, *pr. part.* of càrn.

càrnag, -aig, -an, *s.f.* Sand-eel found under stones on sea shore. 2 Conger-eel—*Lochalsh.* 3(AF) She-terrier.

càrnaid, *s f. ind.* Carnation. 2 Cochineal. 3 *Flesh-colour. 4 Certain tint of red, much used in the Highlands.

————ich,* *v.a.* Incarnatine.

†carnal, -ail, *s.f.* Mole *or* small heap of stones.

carnan,(AF) *s.m.* Cockroach. (cearnan)

càrnan, -ain, -an, *s. m.* Little cairn. 2 Any small heap of stones.

————aich, *s.pl.* Highlanders. 2 Inhabitants of any rocky or mountainous country.

càrnan-caochaig, see càrnan-caochain.

càrnan-caochain, *s.m.* Mole-hill.

càrn-aolaich,** *s.m.* Dunghill.

càrn-cuimhne, *s.m.* Monument.

càrn-eaglais, *s.m.* Excommunication.

car-neamhnuidean, *s.m.* String of pearls.

càrn-slaodaidh,* *s.m.* Hurdle, drag, sledge.

càrn-slaoid,* see càrn-slaodaidh.

càrnta, *a. & past part.* of càrn. Heaped, piled up, accumulated.

càrr, càrra, *s.f.* Itch, mange. 2 Any crustaceous roughness on the skin. 3 The curl in potatoes. 4 Rocky shelf, projecting part of a rock. 5 Scald. 6* Scurvy. 7* Leprosy. 8* Dray, chariot, sledge. 9 Flesh of a whale or seal—*Hebrides.* 10‖ Scabbiness. 11 Bran. 12(AC) Flesh, coarse flesh.
Duine aig am bheil *c.*, *a man that has the scurvy* ; plàigh na càrra, *the plague of leprosy;* each anns a' chàrr, *a horse in the dray* or *sledge;* o chàrr monaidh, *from a mountain rock.*

càrr,** càirr, *s.m.* Bog, fen, morass, moss. 2 Spear. 3 (AC) Udder. 4 (AC) Shingle on mountain tops. Mar chanach càrr, *like the moss co ton.*

†carra, *pl.* -chan, *s.m.* see carragh.

carrach, -aiche, *a.* Itchy, mangy, scorbutic. 2 Stony, rocky. 3 Of uneven surface. 4 Cross-tempered. 5 Crustaceous, as potatoes. 6** Curvated.

carrachag, -an, *s.m.* Shell-fish that grows on the lowest part of a rock.

carrachan, -ain, -an, *s. m.* Shoemaker fish. 2 Frog-fish, chub, or ‡cobbler. 3 Wild liquorice root. 4 AF Small angler *or* devil-fish. 5 Swivel—*Lewis*, see bàta No. 28 p. 76. 6* Little old-fashioned fellow. 7(DU) Group, small crowd

———— -cnuacach, *s.m.* see carran-creige.

carrachd,** *s.f.* Ascendancy.

carradh, -aidh, -aidhean, *s.m.* Forming of scab or scurvy. 2**see carragh.

carragh, -aigh, -aighean, *s.f.* Rock. 2 Pillar. 3 Erect stone. 4 Monument. Far an d'ung thu a' *c.*, *where you anointed the monument ;* a thamhaisg nan carragh ! *O spectre of the rocks !* carragh nan tonn,*the rock of the waves;* carragh salainn, *a pillar of salt.*

————ach,‡‡ *a.* Monumental.

————ail,‡‡ *a.* Monumental.

carraicean, -ein, -ceanan, *s.m.* see carra-meille. 2††Knotty stick. 3††Thick man.

carraich, *v.a.* Crust.

carraid, -e, *s.f.* Conflict, strife, riot. 2 Distress, trouble, grief. 3* Fatigue and anguish from watching a sick person. *C.* nan sian, *the conflict of the elements* ; le *c.* ghéir, *with sore fatigue.*

carraideach, -diche, *a.* Troublesome, turbulent, quarrelsome. 2* Fatigued with watching a sick person. 3 Grieved and fatigued. 4 *Afflicting. 5‡‡Distressful, vexatious. 6**

Conflicting.
carraideach, -eich, *s.m.* Turbulent, quarrelsome person.
———d, *s.f.* Fatigue.
†carraidhin, *s.f.* see carraighin.
carraig, -e [& cairge,] -ean, *s.f.* Rock, cliff. 2 Pinnacle. 3 Rock jutting into the sea, serving as a quay or fishing station. 4 Knot of wood. 5‡‡Timber ball used in club playing. 6(AF)Cockroach. 7*Headland. *C.* mo neart; *the rock of my strength*; mar thuinn mu *ch.*, *as waves round a rock.*
———each, -eiche, *a.* Rocky, abounding in rocks or cliffs, of or belonging to a rock or cliff. 2**Rugged.
carraigeag, -eig, -an, *s.f.* Sort of pancake.
carraigean, -ein, -eanan, *s.m.* Knot of wood. 2††see cairgein.
carraigeineach, -eiche, *a.* Knotty, as timber. 2††Rocky.
carraighin,** *s.* Thick part of butter-milk.
carraigneach, -eiche, *a.* see carraigeach.
carraid,§ Gaelic spelling of *carrot*, see curran.
carra-meille,‡ *s.* Wild liquorice, wild pease, heath pease, §tuberous bitter vetch—*orobus tuberosus.*
carran, -ain, *s.m.* Spurrey, a weed growing among corn, see cluain-lìn. 2§ Scurvy grass, see am maraich.
———, -ain, *s.m.* Shrimp. 2 Prawn. 3(AF) Angler-fish. 4‡‡Sillabub. 5 *rarely* see corran. 6(AF) Field-bug.
———ach, see carthannach.
———achaich,(AF) *s.f.* Carp.
———achd, see carthannachd.
——— -buidhe, *s.m.* Charlock.
carran-creige, *s.m.* Lump-fish. 2 Conger-eel. 3 Sea-porcupine (fish.) 4**Shrimp, prawn.
carrannachd, see carthannachd.
carrantach, see carthannach.
———d, see carthannachd.
carrantas, -ais, *s.m.* see carthannas.
carrasan, -ain, *s.m.* Hoarseness. 2 Wheezing in the throat. 3‖ Catarrh. Casd is *c.*, *a cough and hoarseness* ; *c.* a' bhais, *death-rattle.*
———ach, *a.* Hoarse. 2 Wheezing.
———aich, *s.f.* Continued wheezing in the throat. 2 Catarrh. 3 Effects of a catarrh.
†càrr-fhiadh, -fhéidh, *s.m.* see cair-fhiadh.
carr-fhiodh, -a, *s.m.* Knot in timber.
carroid, *s.f.* see carraid.
carrs,(AC) *s.* Buttercup, see cearban.
carrsan, see carrasan.
———ach, see carrasanach.
carrtha, see carragh.
———nas,‡‡ -ais, *s.m.* Kindliness. see carthannas.
carruchadh, -aidh, see carachadh.
carruich, see caraich.
†carruidhe, *s.f.* Scabbedness.
carruig, -e, -ean, *s.f.* see carraig.
carruigeag, see carraigeag.
cars, *s.f.* Gaelic spelling of *carse*, (level fertile tract of country.)
càrsan, -ain, *s.m.* see carrasan.
———ach, -eiche, *a.* see carrasanach.
car-shuil, -shul, *s.f.* Rolling eye.
———each, *a.* Having rolling eyes.
c'ar son? *adv.* Why? for what? wherefore? C'ar son a ghabh na cinnich boil? *why did the heathen rage?*
càrt, càirt, *pl.* -an [& -àirt],*s.f.* Quart. 2 One fourth part of any measure, as of a peck or a yard. 3 Lippy. †4 Cart.
cart, *v.a.* see cairt.
——ach, *gen.* of cairt.
——adh, -aidh, *s.m.* Act of cleansing any place of mire, as a stable or byre. 2 Tanning of leather. 3 Barking of trees. A' c—, *pr.part.* of cairt.
cartair, see cairtear.
cartan, -ain, -an, *s.m.* Sleek brown insect that eats into the flesh, flesh-worm(AF.) 2*Heath-mite. 3‡‡ Sour-tempered, crabbed person. 4 Cattle-bot—*œstrus bovis.* 5 Crab [Gadelicised form of *partan.*]

119. Cartan (4)

———ach, -aiche, *a.* Quarrelsome, ill-tempered.
cartaran, -ain, *s.m.* One-fourth of a stone, (measure for butter, &c.)
carthadh, -aidh, *s.m.* see carragh.
carthan, -ain, *s.m.* Charity, friendship, affection. 2**Prawn. Luchd-carthain, *charitable people.*
———ach, see carthannach.
———achd, see carthannachd.
carthannach, -aiche, *a.* Kind, charitable, affectionate, friendly. 2*Polite.
———d, *s.f.ind.* Charity, friendship, affection, tenderness. 2* Politeness. Blàths is *c.*, *warmth and friendship.*
carthannas, -ais, *s.m.* Same meanings as carthannachd, *C.* fuar, *cold friendship.*
carthanta,* *a.* see carthannach.
———chd,* see carthannachd.
carthuinnich, *v.a.* Separate, part, put asunder. 2 Dwell in a cave. 3 Riddle, winnow.
cart-iùil, see cairt-iùil.
cart-làir,§ *s.* Common tormentil, see braonan-fraoich.
car-tuathal, -ail, *s. m.* Wrong turn. 2 Turn to the left, or contrary to the sun's course. 3 Ill-chance, mishap. 4 Unprosperous course. This term is said by some to have had its origin in Druidical superstition. On certain occasions they moved three times round their stony circles or temples. In performing this ceremony they kept the circle on the right (car-deise) and consequently moved from E. to W., this was called the prosperous course. The car-tuathal, or moving with the circle on the left, was deemed fatal or unprosperous, being contrary to the course of the sun. Car-tuathal t' aimhleis ort! *the left-about unlucky turn to you!*
car uair, *adv.* Sometimes.
caruchadh, -aidh, see carachadh.
caruibh, *adv.* Beside, near. [*Generally* 'an caraibh.]
caruich, *v.a.* see caraich.
caruill, see caireal.
car ùine, *adv.* For a time.
caruinnean, see carainnean.
†caruinnich, *v.* see carthuinnich. 2‡Winnow.
†carull, *s.m.* see caireal.
cas, *gen.* coise, *dat.* cois, *pl.* casan, *s.f.* Foot. 2 Leg. 3 Shaft, haft, handle. 4 Stem. 5 Stalk. 6 Ply or plait in thread. 7 Curl. 8 Wrinkle. 9**Money. Taobh do choise, *the side of your foot* ; cas na sgéine *the handle of the knife* ; cas an ùird, *the shaft of the hammer* ; aig cois na beinne, *at the foot of the hill* ; glan ceann do chasan, *wash your*

feet ; glan do chasan, *wash your legs* (or *your feet*); cas a' falbh agus cas a' fuireachd, *one foot going and the other foot staying,* —said of one who is undecided ; fo chasaibh nan an-laoich, *under the feet of ruthless warriors.*

†cas, *s.f.* Case. 2 Hair of the head.

cas, caise, *a.* Steep. 2 Wreathed, curled, twisted. 3 Sudden, quick, rapid. 4 Hasty, irritable. 5 Rash, passionate. 6 Headlong, abrupt, eager. 7‡‡Wrinkled. Duine cas, *a passionate man* ; sruth c., *a headlong stream, an impetuous current ;* cas air a chéile, *close upon each other* ; bruthach c., aonach c., *a steep* or *headlong acclivity ;* cas gu còmhraig, *eager for battle ;* cùl fainneach, cas, *curled, wreathed hair* ; cas-fhalt, *curled locks* : gu c., *quickly.*

cas, *pr.part.* a' casadh, *v.a.* Gape. 2 Gnash. 3 Turn against. 4 Be angry with. 5 Oppose, thwart. 6 Curl, frizzle. 7 Fire *or* cast, as a stone. 8* Approach. 9 Brandish. 10** Wreathe, twist, bend. 11**Climb. 12‡‡Shoot out the lip in insult or derision. 13‡‡ Stop, hesitate. 14‡‡ Become wrinkled. 15‡‡Wind, wind up. Cas an t-sreang, *twist the string*; chas e m' a làimh e, *he twisted it about his hand ;* chas e 'fhiaclan, *he gnashed his teeth;* chas e 'bheul, *he gaped with his mouth;* a' casadh air a' bhaile, *approaching the town*; chas e ris, *he was enraged against him*; chas e 'shleagh, *he brandished his spear* ; chas e braoisg air, *he screwed up a grimace ;* chas iad oirre, *they closed upon her.*

càs, -àis, -an, *s. m.* Difficulty, emergency, hardship. 2 Plague. 3 Distress. 4 Case. 5 Trying or difficult situation, dilemma, predicament. 6**Anxiety. 7 Respect. 8** *rarely* Fear, pity. 9**Appetite. 10**Misfortune, evil event. Bha e an càs gu'n tigeadh tu, *he was anxious that you would come* ;anns gach càs, *in every emergency*; cha'n e sin an càs, *that is not the difficulty;* cha 'n e an càs e, *it is no difficulty ;* 's ann dhuit is léir mo chàs, *it is thou that seest my distress*; an càs air, *eager for him* or *it.*

†casach, -aich, *s.f.* Ascent.

casach, -aiche, *a.* Having feet. 2 Many-footed. 3‡‡Corrugant. Gu c., làmhach, *exerting legs and hands.*

casach,* -aich, *s.f.* Outlet of a lake. 2 Ford. 3 Hook-line.

casachain-gréine,(AH) *s.m.pl.* Long shafts of light radiating from the sun, and betokening unsettled weather.

†casachdaich, see casadaich.

†casachdaighe,*s.f.* Coltsfoot, see gallan-greannchair.

†casachdas, see casadaich.

casa-corrach, *s.f.* see cas-chorrach.

casad, -aid, *s.m.* ‖Cough. 2 see caisead.

——,* *v.n.* see casadaich.

——ach, -aiche, *a.* Coughing, ill of a cough. 2 Causing a cough. Am mios c., *the cough producing month.*

casadadh,** -aidh,*s.m.* Coughing, act of coughing. 2 Cough.

casadaich, *pr.part.* a' casadaich, *v.n.* Cough.

——, *s.f.ind.* Cough. 2 Act or habit of coughing. 3* Gripes in cattle, making them strike their belly with their feet. 4‡‡Cold, or any disease causing a cough. Ciod a' chasadaich a th' ort ? *why do you cough so ?*

casadh, -aidh, -aidhean, *s.m.* Grinning, gaping. 2 Gnashing. 3 Turning against, opposing. 4 Corrugation, wrinkle. 5**Brandishing. 6**Wreathing, twisting, curling. 7** Climbing. 8*Approaching. Sleagh a' c. 'n a làimh, *a spear brandishing in his hand.* A' c—, *pr. part.* of cas.

casa-feannag, *pl.* Crow's feet. 2 "Crow's-foot" stitching. Fuaigheal chasa-feannag, *the angular stitching on blanket selvidges known as "herring-boning."*

casag, -aig, -an, *s f.* Long coat, cassock, as opposed to a short coat or jacket. Luchd nan casag, *Scottish Lowlanders.*

——ach, *a.* Wearing a long coat. 2 Of, or belonging to, long coats.

——aiche, *s.m.* Man with a long or skirted coat.

—— -mharcachd,‡‡ *s.f.* Riding-coat.

casa-gearra, see casa-goirid.

casa-gòbhlach, *a.* & *adv.* Astride.

casa-goirid, *s.pl.* Short spatter-dashes, spats.

casa-gòrach,(DU) see cas-chorrach.

casaid, -e, -ean, *s.f.* Complaint, accusation, grumbling. 2‡‡Suit-at-law. Dean casaid, *complain;* na gabh casaid, *receive not an accusation.*

——, see casaidich.

——each, -eiche, *a.* Apt to complain, accuse, or grumble, complaining, accusing.

——eachadh, -aidh, *s.m.* Arraignment.

——eachd, *s.f.* Complaining, proneness to make complaints.

casaidich, *pr. pt.* a' casaideachadh [& a' casaidich,] *v.a.* Accuse, arraign, lodge a complaint. Ch. e orm, *he accused me.*

——e, -an, *s.m.* Accuser, complainant. 2 Grumbler.

casair, -e, -ean, *s.f.* Sea-drift. 2 Phosphoric light proceeding from old wood when in the dark. see teine-sionnachain.

†casair, casrach, *s.m.* Thorn. 2 Clasp, buckle. 3 Slaughter, carnage. 4 Shower, hail.

casan, -ain, -an, *s.m.* The supporting beam of a house-top. 2 Path, road. 3 Name given to the Parallel roads in GlenRoy. 4††Treadles of a loom. 5‡‡Prickle. 6†† Post or stick in the inside of a wall. Taigh chasan(AH), *a house built of wattle-work.*

casan, *n. pl.* of cas.

——ach, -aiche, *a.* Having foot-paths, like a foot-path. 2 Parallel in *grammar* (‖.)

casan-cairbe,‡‡ *s.pl.* (*lit.* chariot spokes) Sun's rays as seen breaking through masses of watery clouds. Called "casan caimbe," *hempen legs* in *Uist.*

—— -cama, *s.pl.* Bow-legs.

—— -corrach, *pl.* of cas-chorrach.

—— -eunain,‡‡ *s.pl.* (*lit.* little bird's feet) Shoots from a hazel stump.

—— -làbhach, *s.pl.* Pigeon toes, (feet having the toes turned inwards.)

—— -lùgach, *s.pl.* In-knees, knock-knees.

—— -spàgach, *s. pl.* Splay-feet (flat feet having the toes turned outwards.)

cas-an-teannachaidh,(AH) *s.f.* In roping a house after thatching, the side of the loop or rope which is to be tightened and secured.

cas-an-uain,§ *s.f.* Kidney vetch, see meòir Muire.

casan-uchd,** *s. m.* see caisean-uchd. 2 Knee-strap,—*MacFarlane's Vocab.*

cas-aodannach, -aiche, *a.* Wrinkled-faced.

†casar, *s.m.* Little hammer. 2 see cabhsair.

†——nach, *s.f.* Lightning.

†casbanach, -aiche, *a.* Side by side, parallel.

cas-bhacaig, *s.f.* see camachag.

†cas-bhàirneach, *s.f.* see bàirneach

cas-bhàrd, -bhàird, *s.m.* Satirist.

——achd, *s.f.ind.* Satire, invective, lampooning.

———ail, *a.* Satirical.
cas-bheag,(AH) *s.f.* One of the fore-legs of a young dog, which is tied up to its neck in order to impede the animal's movements. Air an cois bhig 'san tarsuinn, (in reference to the words in a printer's proof) *with the letters upside down and obliquely set*, or *out of the straight line* (technically known as "not ranging.")
cas-bheairt, cas-bheart, cas-bheirt, } *s.f.* see cais-bheart.
cas-bhonnach,** -aich, *a.* Antipodal.
cas-bhonnaich, *s.* Antipodes.
cas-bhrat, -ait, -an, *s.m.* Carpet. 2(MM)Mat.
cas-bhriathar, -air, *s.m.* Hasty, unguarded, or cross expression, intemperate language.
cas-bhriathrach, *a.* Hasty, or intemperate in speech.
cas-bhuidhe, *a.* Having yellow feet. 2 Having curled yellow hair. Cuach fhalt cas-bhuidhe, *curled yellow hair.*
†cas-cailliche, *s.f.* Shaft of a fir-torch.
†cascar, *s.m.* Cup.
cas-chaibe,†† see cas-dhireach. 2 *for* cas-chrom in *Gairloch, &c.*
†cas-chailliche, see †cas-cailliche.
cas-cheum, *s.m.* Foot-path. 2 Steep, or difficult way. 3**Stride, long pace. Cas-cheum nan gann, *a great stride.*
———ach, aiche, *a.* Steep. 2 Difficult to pace. 3**Striding. 4**Having a foot-path.
cas-chiabh, -an, *s.f.* Curled lock, ringlet.
———ach, -aiche, *a.* Having curled locks. 2 Tressy.
cas-chlùd, *s.m.* Door-mat.
cas-choirbeil,†† *s.f.* Roof couple, couple-legs.
càs-choisgeach, -eiche, *a.* Antipestilential.
cas-chorrach, -aich. *pl.*casan-corrach, *s.f.* Stilt.
cas-chreag, -an. *s.f.* Steep rock.
———ach, *a.* Abounding in steep rocks.

120. *Cas-chrom.*

cas-chrom, cois-chruim, *s.f.* The crooked spade, an implement of tillage peculiar to the Highlands, used for turning the ground where a plough cannot work on account of the stony ground. It is of great antiquity, and is described as follows by Armstrong. "It is very inexpeditious in comparison with the plough, eight men being necessary to dig as much with it in one day as a horse would plough in the same time. It is chiefly used for tillage, and consists of a crooked piece of wood, the lower end somewhat thick, about two-and-a-half feet in length, pretty straight, and armed a the end with iron made thin and square to cut the earth. The upper end of this instrument is called the shaft, and the lower, the head. The shaft above the crook is pretty straight, being six feet long, and tapering upwards to the end which is slender. Just below the crook or angle, there must be a hole wherein a strong peg must be fixed, for the workman's right foot in order to push the instrument into the earth; while in the meantime, standing on his left foot, and holding the shaft firmly in both hands, when he has in this manner driven the head far enough into the earth, with one bend of his body he raises the clod by the iron-headed part of the instrument, making use of the heel or hind part of the head as a fulcrum. In so doing, he turns it over always towards the left hand and then proceeds to push for another clod in the same form. To see six or eight men all at work with this instrument, standing all on one leg and pushing with the other, would be a curious sight to a stranger. With all its disadvantages, the cas-chrom is, of all instruments, the fittest for turning up the ground in the country, for among so many rocks a plough can do little or nothing, and where there are no rocks, the earth is generally so marshy that cattle are not able to pass over it without sinking in deeply." It is of pretty general use in the Western Isles, one man being able to turn over more ground with it in a day than four are able to do with a common spade.
Peg of cas-chrom, *sgonnan.*
caschuing, -e, -ean, *s.f.* Anti-asthmatic.
cas-cùirn, *s.f.* Draught-tree or tram of a car or sledge.
casd, *s.m.* see casad. An triugh-chasd; *the whooping-cough.*
——, *v.a. & n.* see casadaich.
†casda, *a.* see casadach.
casdach, *a.* see casadach.
casdadh, -aidh, see casadadh.
casdaich, see casadaich.
cas-dhìreach, *s.m.* Straight delving spade used in the Hebrides.
cas-dhubh, *s.f.* Stem of the mircean (kind of seaweed.)
†cas-dlaoi,‡‡ *s. f.* Curled hair.
cas-dubh, -uibhe, *a.* Having black legs or feet.
———, -uibh, *s.m.* [& *f.*] Black-legged wild goose
cas-fa-chrann, *s.* Honeysuckle—*Skye*, see uilleann.
cas-fhionn, *a.* White-footed, as of cattle. see cais-fhionn. Bha i c., *she was white-footed.*

121. *Cas-dhìreach.*

cas-fhliuch, *a.* Wet-foot. Gille cas-fhliuch, *a member of a Highland chief's retinue who carried his master over streams, fetched home water, &c.*
casg, -a, *s.m.* see cosg, *s.m.*
casg, *v.a.* see caisg.
Càsg, Càsga, } *gen. sing.* of Càisg.
casgach, *a.* see coisgeach.
casgach,(AF) -aich, *s.m.* Red-shank, see camghlas.
casgadair, *s.m.* see cosgadair.
casgadh, -aidh, *s.m. & pr.part.* see cosgadh.
casgaidh, see cosgaidh.
casgair, *pr. part.* a' casgairt [& a' casgradh] *v.a.* Slay, slaughter, butcher, massacre. 2 Mangle. Cò a chasgras an torc? *who will slay the boar?*
———t, *s.f.ind.* Slaughtering, butchering.

massacring, slaughter, massacre. 2 Triumph, rejoicing. A' c—, *pr.part.* of casgair. Casgairt ort ! *may death take you !*
casgan-long, (AF) -ain-, *s.m.* Black guillemot, see calltag.
casgarrach, -aich, *s.m.* Kite. 2 Sanguinary person. 3 Conqueror.
cas-ghaosaid, (DU) *s.f.* Plaited horse-hair attached to a hook.
cas-ghruagach, -aiche, *a.* Curly-haired.
càsgoil,* *s.f.* Dilemma, predicament. 'An càsgoil, *in a dilemma—Islay.*
casgrach, -aiche, *a.* Slaughtering, massacring. 2 Of, or belonging to, slaughter. 3 Destructive. 4 Sanguinary. 5 Victorious. 6††Mangling.
———d, *s.f.ind.* Victory, triumph.
casgradh, -aidh, *s.m.* Same meanings as casgairt. A' c—, *pr.pt.* of casgair. Mheasadh sinn mar chaoraich chum a' chasgraidh, *we were esteemed as sheep for the slaughter.*
casgraiche, -an, *s.m.* Queller. 2 Conqueror. 3 Slaughterer. 4 Sanguinary person.
casgrair, *s.m.* see casgraiche.
casg-thuiteamas,‡‡ -ais, *s.f.* Anti-apoplectic.
casguirt, see casgairt.
†casla, *s.f.* Frizzled wool.
†caslach, -aich, *s.m.* Children. 2 Clan, tribe.
caslachdan,** -ain, *s.m.* I agery.
casladh,** -aidh, *s.m.* Frizzled wool.
†cas laoidh, *s.f.* see cas-dlaoi.
cas-leapa, *s.f.* Bedpost.
cas-leathann, *a.* Broad-footed, web-footed.
cas-lighe, -an, *s.f.* Water of a ford that is rapid. 2 Act of fording.
cas-lom, *a.* Bare-footed. 2 Bare-legged. Caslom, ceann-lom, *bare-footed and bare-headed.*
cas-luath, -luaithe, *a.* Swift-footed.
cas-lùbach, -aiche, *a.* Thickly-curled.
cas-maighiche,§ *s.f.* Hare's foot clover—*trifolium arvense.*
cas-mu-seach, *adv.* Heads and thraws
cas-nàbuidh, -ean, *s.m.* Walking companion.
casnaid, *s.f.* Split wood, chips.
cas-na-tunnaig,§ *s.f.* Charlock, wild mustard, see maragbhuidhe.
caspanach, *a.* Parallel.
†casrach, *s.f.* see casgairt.
cas-rop,‡‡ -an, *s.m.* Stirrup.
cas-ruisg, *v.a.* Make bare the feet or legs, put off one's shoes and stockings.
———, *a.* see cas-ruisgte.
———each, *a.* see cas-ruisgte.

122. Cas-maighiche.

———te, *a.* Bare-footed. 2 Bare-legged. Lomnochd is cas-ruisgte, *naked and bare-footed.*
†cassal, *s.m.* Storm.
cas-shlighe, -an, *s.f.* Foot-path.
cas-stòl, -stoil, *s.m.* Foot-stool.
†cast, *a.* Pure, chaste, undefiled.
casta, *a.* see caiste.
castan, -ain, -an, *s.m.* Chestnut.
castaran, -ain, *s.m.* see cartaran.
castearbhan, *s.f.* Chicory, succory.
castreaghainn, *s.f.* Straw on which grain is laid to be kiln-dried.
†casuigh, *a.* Headlong.
casur,** *s.m.* Knocker.
cas-urla, see cas-urladh.
cas-urlach, -aich, *a.* Having curls, curly-locked. T' òr-chùl 'na shlamagan cas-urlach, *your yellow hair in curled tresses.*
cas-urladh, -aidh, *s.m.* Curled lock, ringlet.
cat, cait, *s.m.* Cat. Faodaidh cat amharc air an rìgh, *a cat may look at the king.*
cata, -n, *s.m.* Sheep-cot.
†càta, càtan, *s.m.* see cata.
càtachadh, -aidh, *s.m.* Taming, domesticating, soothing. A' c—, *pr.pt.* of càtaich.
catadh, see càtachadh.
càtadh, -aidh, *s.m.* see càtachadh.
catag, -aige, -an, *s.f.* Potato-cellar.
———ach, -aiche, *a.* Abounding in potato-stores, Of, or belonging to, a potato-store.
càtaich, *pr.pt.* a' càtachadh, *v.a.* Tame, domesticate, soothe. 2**Honour, reverence.
———te, *past pt.* of càtaich. Tamed, domesticated.
càtaidh,** *v.a.* Domify.
†càtaidh, *s.f.* Generosity, nobility.
†———,** *a.* Generous, noble.
catail,** *a.* Cattish, cross, crabbed.
catalach *s.m.* Sleepy person. 'Nuair a théid crodh a' bhaile dìosg, 'san ann a ni *c.* càise, *not until the milch cows have run dry, does the sleepy-headed person think of making cheese.* [It appears to mean that a "sleepy-head" would neglect the opportunity of making cheese while the cows were giving a plentiful supply of milk, and that only when that supely ceased would he think of making cheese. The word *c.* may be intended for cadalaiche, *sleeper* or *procrastinator.*]
catanach, -aiche, *a.* see caiteineach.
catas, -ais, -an, *s.m.* see caiteas.
cat-cinn, (AC) *s.m.* Catkin; inflorescence on trees and shrubs. 2 Spots in the hair of animals.
cat-cnaige,* *s.m.* Mouse-trap.
†cat-crainn, -oinn, *s.m.* Rat-trap.
cat-criadhaich, (DU) *s.m.* Plaster made of clay or gravel and straw or chaff, laid on partitions. The partition consisted of upright posts closely interwoven with straw- or twig-ropes.
cat-cuthaich, (AF) *s.m.* Wild cat.
cat-dubh, *s.m.* Black cat (fish)—*Lewis.*
cat-fiadhaich, *s.m.* Wild cat.
cath, -a, -an [& annan], *s.m.* Battle, fight, struggle, contest. 2 Company of soldiers. 3 Battalion. 4 Army. Chuir iad cath {air, ris,} *they struggled against him*; n'an teichinn fhéin o 'n chath, *should I myself flee from the battle;* 'gar feitheamh le seachd cathan, *awaiting us with seven companies.*
cath, *pr.pt.* a' cathadh, *v.n.* Fight, carry on war. 2 Contend, strive. 3 Drift, as snow.
càth, *v.a.* Riddle, winnow, sift, fan.
càth, càtha [& càithe] *gen.pl.* càthunn (DU) *s.f.* Seeds, husks of corn. 2 Bran, pollards. 3** Chaff. Poca càthunn, *a bag of husks.*
cath, *adv.* Continually.
——a, *s.m.* see cadha.
——ach, -aiche, *a.* Warlike, of, or pertaining to war, fighting.
càthach, *a.* Chaffy.
——ach, -aich, *s.m.* Warrior, soldier, champion. Seachd cathaich, *seven warriors.*
càthach, *a.* Chaffy. 2††Husky, seedy.
cathachadh, -aidh, *s.m.* Fighting, act of fighting, battling. 2 Struggling, striving, trying. 3 Tempting, provoking. A' c—, *pr. pt.* of cathaich. A chur cathachaidh, *to provoke.*
cathachail, -e, *a.* Militant.
càthadh, -aidh, *s.m.* Winnowing, riddling, sifting. 2 Breach. 3 Defile. 4‡‡ Provocation. A' càthadh 'san t-sabhal, *winnowing in the barn.* A' c—, *pr.pt.* of càth.
cathadh, -aidh, *s.m.* Snow-drift, snow driven

about by the wind. 2 Sea-drift. Tha cur agus c. ann, *it is snowing and drifting*; thig ioma-chathadh, *a whirling drift shall come*; dorus cathadh, *middle door of a kitchen passage.*
——ach,** *a.* Drifty, like a drift, of, or belonging to, a drift.
cathadh-cuir,** *s.m.* Falling snow.
—— -fairge, *s.m.* Sea-drift, spray, spindrift.
—— -làir, (AC) *s.m.* Ground-drift.
—— -mara, *s.m.* see c—fairge.
—— -sian,(AC) *s.m.* Visible storm of rain, white sheet of rain.
cathag, -aig, -an, *s.f.* Jackdaw—¶*corvus gladarius.*

123. Cathag.

cathagach, *a.* Abounding in jackdaws. 2 Of, or like, a jackdaw.
cathag-dhearg chasach,¶ *s.f.* Chough, or red-legged crow—*fregilus graculus.*

124. Cathag-dhearg chasach.

†cathaghadh, -aidh, *s.m.* see cathachadh.
cathaich, *pr.part.* a' cathachadh, *v. a.* Fight, engage, carry on war. 2 ††Strive. 3‡‡Tempt, try,prove,provoke. 4 Accuse. 5 see cothaich.
cathair, cathrach, cathraichean, *s. f.* Chair, seat, bench, throne. 2 Town, city. 3 Fortified city. 4 Gig. 5**Bed of any garden stuff. 6**Stock of colewort or cabbage. 7**Plot. 8 **Sentinel. 9**see càthar. An creamh 'na chathraichean, *gentian in plots or beds*; each na cathrach, *the gig horse.*
†cathair, *s.m.* Guard, sentinel, warder.
càthair, *gen.sing.* of càthar.
cathair-bhreitheanais, *s.f.* Tribunal, judgment seat. Air a' chathair-bhreitheanais, *on the judgment seat.*
cathair-easbuig, *s.f.* Cathedral. 2††Episcopal chair.
cathairiche, -an, *s.m.* Citizen.
cathair-iomchair, -thrach-, -thraichean-, *s. f.* Sedan chair.
cathair-rìgh, see cathair-rìoghail. Chi gach sùil a chathair-rìgh, *every eye shall see his throne.*
cathair-rìoghail, -thrach-, -thraichean-, *s. f.* Throne.
cathair-shuidhe,-thrach-,-thraichean-, *s.f.* Seat.
cathair-thalmhuinn,§ *s.f.* Yarrow, see lus-chosg-adh-na-fola.
cathair-thalmhunda, see c— -thalmhuinn.
†cathais, *s.f.* see caithris.
cathaiseach, *a.* Brave, stout. 2 Warlike. 3 Noisy, clamorous. 4**Quick. Gu *c.*, *bravely.*
cathal, *v.a.* see callaich.
——,(AF) (bird) see caothail.
——adh, -aidh, *s.m.* & *pr. pt.* of cathal, see callachadh.
——ta, *a.* & *past pt.* of cathal, see callaichte.
cathamh,** *s.* see cathadh.
cathan,* *s.m.* Yarn on the warping machine.
——,¶ -ain, *s.m.* Bernicle goose, a species of goose having a black bill—*anser leucopsis.*

125. Cathan.

cathan, *n.pl.* of cath.
——ach, -aiche, *a.* see cathach.
—— -aodaich, *s.m.* Web.
càthar, -air, *s.m.* Mossy, soft ground, boggy ground. 2‡Dry part of a peat-moss. O chàthar 's o chruaich, *from marsh and from mountain.*
càthar, *a.* Husky, seedy, full of seeds or husks. 2 Mossy, soft. Gu gleann càthair, *to a mossy glen.*
cathara, see catharra.
càtharach, -aiche, *a.* Mossy, spongy, boggy, as in hilly ground.
†catharnas, -ais, *s.m.* see carthannas.
catharra, *a.* Strenuous. 2 Fighting bravely or resolutely. 3††Militant. 4‡‡Civil. 5 Reformed. An creideamh c., *the Reformed (Protestant) religion*; cath c., *a civil battle*; creideamh c., *militant faith*; an Eaglais c., *the Church militant.*
——chd, *s.f.ind.* Resolution, bravery.
†cath-bhàrr, *s.m.* Helmet, headpiece. Bhris e an cath bhàrr, *he broke the helmet.*
†cath-bharun, -uin, *s.m.* Commander, officer.
càth-bhruich, -e, *s.f.* see càbhruich.
càth-bhruith, see càbhruich.
cath-bhuadhach,-aiche, *a.* Victorious, triumphant in battle.
cath-bhuidheann,-dhinn, -dhnichean,*s.f.* Party, company or battalion of soldiers.
cath-bhuidhneach, *a.* Regimental.
cath-chrith, -e, *s.f.* Impatience for fighting.
cath-eun, (bird) see cathan.
—— leadain, see cathan.
cath-fhear, -fhir, *s.m.* Warrior, hero, champion.
cath-labhar,†† *s.m.* Inciting speech. 2 Loud and angry talk.
cath-labhradh, -aidh, -aidhean, *s. m.* The speech of a general before or after a battle.
†cathlach, *a.* see catholach.
cathlach-dearg,§ *s. m.* Corn-poppy—*papaver rheas.* (see illust. No. 126)
cath-làgain,** *s.m.* Corn seeds, of the juice of which the Lowlanders make flummery.
cath-làrach, -aich, -aichean, *s.f.* Field of battle.
cathlum, *s.m.* see calum.

126. Cathlach-dearg.

cathlunn, *s.m.* see calum.
cath-mharcach, -aichean, *s.m.* Cavalry soldier, dragoon.
cath-mheal,(AF) *s.m.* Charger, war-horse.
cath-mhileadh, -mhilidh, *s.m.* Military commander. 2 Officer of high rank. 3 Field-officer.
càthmhor, -oire, *a.* Chaffy, husky. 'S e am foghar gaothmhor a ni an coirce càthmhor, *it is the windy harvest that makes the oats husky.*
†cathoir, see caithearr.
catholach, *a.* Catholic, universal.
cathrach, *gen. sing.* of cathair.
————,** *a.* Boggy.
cathraichean, *n.pl.* of cathair.
†cathraigheoir, *s.m.* see cathairiche.
cath-reim, -e, *s.f.* see caithream.
cathu } (AC) *s.m.* Offensive smell, especially from fish newly salted, or from skate when long taken.
cathudh }
†cathughadh, *s.m.* see cathachadh.
cat-luch, cait-, *s.m.* Mouse-trap.
cat-luibh, *s.f.* Cudwort, cudweed, see luibh-a'-chait.
————each, *a.* Abounding in cudweed.
cat-mhara, (AF) Catfish, sea-cat, sea-devil, wolf-fish. 2 Fishing frog, angler—*lophias piscatorius.*
†càtoil, -e, *a.* Luxurious, faring sumptuously.
catran,* -ain, *s.m.* The fourth part of a stone of butter, cheese, wool, &c —*Islay.*
†ca-tràth, *adv.* When ? at what time ?
c' e, *pron. interr. sing.& pl.* Who ? what ? (*for* co e ? *or* cia e ?) Who is he ? what is it ? Also adverbially, (*let me see it.*) C' e do làmh, *give me,* or *reach hither your hand.* see cia. c' e mar, erroneously used for cia mar ? *how ?* c' e fàth ? *why ? how ?*
cè, cèithe, *s.m.* Cream.
cé, *s.m. & f.* Spouse. (*contr.* for céile.)
cé, *s.m.ind.* The earth, the world, see cruinne-cé.
cé, *s.* Night. 2 Pier.
ceaba, ceibe, ceabannan, *s.m.* The iron part of a spade or other implement for digging or turning over the ground. 2 Old-fashioned kind of spade.—*Islay,* (see illust. 127.) 3 see caibe.
ceabag,(DU) *s.f.* Cheese.
ceabain, *s.m.* Gaelic spelling of *cabin.*
ceaba-sìthe, *s.m.* Fairy-stone.
ceabhacdach,** *a.* Arch. 2 Crafty, disingenuous.
ceabhachdair,** *s.m.* Bubbler. 2 Knave, prevaricator.
————eachd,** *s.m.* Disingenuousness, imposture, prevarication.
cèabhar, -air, -an, *s.m.* Light breeze, gentle breeze. 2*State of being slightly intoxicated. 3(AC) Sky, cloud, upper clouds.
ceabhcach, see ceabhachdach.
ceach ! *int.* Expression of dislike, disgust, antipathy, abhorrence of filth, or other disagreeable object.

127. Ceaba (2.)

†ceach, *a. for* gach.
†————ail, *v.a.* Dig, excavate. 2**Hackle. 3** Destroy.
†————aing, *a.* Hard to march, inaccessible.
†————air, *s.f.* Dirt, filth. 2 Penury.
ceacharra, *a.* Dirty, sordid, scurfy, mean, sorry, worthless, stingy. 2(AC) Obstreporous, unmanageable, headstrong. 3††Cowardly. 4 (AH) Simple, gullible, inept, vacant. Cha robh e cho c., *he was not so green* or *so silly;* duine c., *a headstrong man.*
————chd, *s. f. ind.* Dirtiness, meanness, worthlessness.
————n, -ain, *s.m.* Worthless, pusillanimous person.
————nach, -aich, *s.m.* see ceacharran.
†ceachd, *s.f.* see cumhachd.
†————lach, -aich, *s.m.* Coal-black.
ceachladh, -aidh, *s.m.* Digging. A' c—, *pr. pt.* of ceachail.
ceachrach,** *a.* Dirty, filthy. 2 Penurious, stingy.
————d,** *s. f.* Dirtiness, filthiness. 2 Penuriousness, stinginess.
†ceacht, *s.m.* Power. 2 The circle of sciences. 3 Instruction, lesson.
ceachtadair,** *s.m.* Lecturer.
cead, *s.m.ind.* Leave, permission, license. 2 Farewell, adieu. Iarr cead, *ask liberty* or *leave;* gun do chead a' gabhail, *without asking your permission;* an d' fhuair thu cead ? *have you got leave ?* thoir dhomh c., *give me permission;* thoir a chead dha, *set him about his business;* c. dol dhachaidh, *permission to go home;* c. fuireachd, *leave to remain;* gun ch., *without leave;* gabhaidh mi mo ch. dhiot, *I will take my leave of you;* c. buan, *a long adieu* ; leig c. dhiot ! *enough of you !* ; gun a chuir 'nam chead, *without asking me first* ; tha mo chead aige ! *I am very glad he is doing so, well done he* !
†cèad, see ceud.
ceadach, *a.* Talkative, forward.
†————, -aich, *s.m.* Coarse cloth. 2 Veil. 3 Mantle.
ceadachadh, -aidh, *s. m.* Allowing, permitting, permission, granting, liberty. 2 Dismissing. 3(AH) Perplexity, bewilderment, "nut to crack." Tha e 'cur c. orm cia mar a fhuair e an t-airgiod, *it perplexes me how he obtained the money.* A' c—, *pr. pt.* of ceadaich.
ceadachail, -e, *a.* Permissive, lawful, allowable.
ceadachas,‡‡ -ais, see cead.
ceadachd, *s.f.ind.* see ceadachadh.
ceadaich, *pr.pt.* a' ceadachadh, *v.a. & n.* Allow, permit, let, grant, give permission. 2 Dismiss. [This verb has the prep. *do,* simple or compounded, construed with it in its first sense, as, ceadaich do t' òglach, *permit thy servant.*]
————idh, *fut. aff. act.* of ceadaich.
————te, *a. & past pt.* of ceadaich. Permitted, suffered, lawful. Am bheil e c.? *is it lawful ?*
†ceadal, *s.m.* Story, narrative. 2 Malicious report. 3 Singing. 4‡‡Education.
ceadalach, *a.* Malicious, as a story. 2††Crazy.

3†† Subject to fits of sickness.
ceadalaiche, *s.m.* One who raises malicious stories.
céadamas,‡‡ -ais, *s.m.* (ceud+amas) First finding.
———, *adv.* In the first place.
ceadan, -ain, -an, *s.m.* Bunch, lock as of wool. 2††Burden.
céadaoin, -e, *s.f.* see ciadaoin.
cead-bhileach, -lich, *s.f.* see ceud-bhileach.
cead-fadh, -aidh, -an, see ceud-fath.
————ach, *a.* see ceud-fathach
†**ceadfaidheas,** -eis, *s.m.* Sensuality, voluptuousness.
ceadha, -dhan, *s.m.* Share-beam, the part of a plough on which the share is fixed. 2 see ceithe.
ceadhal, -ail, *a.* Blistered, full of sores.
†**ceadhraoidheachd,** *s.f.* Geomancy, art of divining by figures.
†**cead-lomaidh,** see ceud-lomaidh.
ceadna, see ceudna.
†**ceadoir,** *s.f.* see ceud-uair.
†**cead-thomalt,** -ailt, *s.m.* see ceud-lomaidh.
†**cead-thuisneadh,** *s.m.* Firstling, firstborn.
†**cead-thus,** -uis, *s.m.* Principle, element.
ceaduichte, *a. & past pt.* see ceadaichte.
ceafan,‡ -ain, *s.m.* Frivolous person.
ceàird, -e, -ean, *s.f.* Trade, profession, occupation. 2 Handicraft. 3 Art, skill. Ciod e 's ceàird dhuit ? *what is your occupation ?* cha'n uaisle duine na a *ch.*, *a man is not higher than his trade.*
———, *gen.sing. & n. pl.* of ceàrd.
———each, -eiche, *a.* Professional. 2 Having a trade. 3 Expert, dexterous, ingenious. Is an-uasal mac an uasail mur bi e *c.*, *without parts the son of a noble is mean.*
ceairdealachd, see ceàrdalachd.
ceairdeal, see ceàrdail.
ceairidh, (AC) *s.f.* Cirrus clouds.
ceairsle, -ean, *s.f.* see ceirsle.
————ach, *a.* see ceirsleach.
ceairslich, see ceirslich.
†**ceal,** *a.* False.
†**ceal,** *v.a.* Eat. 2 see ceil.
ceal, -a, -an [& -aichean,] *s.m.* Concealment. 2 Forgetfulness. 3 Stupor, torpor. 4 Stupidity. 5 Expression of countenance. 6 Hue or colour. 7 (AC) Cliff, ridge. 8 (AC) End, finish, completion. 9**Powder. 10‡‡Socket. 11 Muliebre pudendum. 12 (AH) State of being lost in thought, preoccupied, or abstracted. Is bochd an *c.* a th' ort, *what a miserable expression of countenance you have* ; na cealaichean, *the cliffs*; cuir *c.* air, *put an end to it.*
ceal, (AC) *a.* Same, similar.
†**ceal,** -a, *s.m.* Death. 2 Heaven. 3 Use. 4 Joint. 5 Fine flour. 6 Covering. 7 Sickness. 8 Prophecy.
cealach, -aich, -aichean, *s.m.* Fire-place of a kiln. *C.* na h-àth, *the fire-place of the kiln.*
————adh, } **cealadh,** } *s.m.* see ceileadh. 2 Eating.
cealaich, *v. a.* *Perthsh.* for ceil. 2 Eat. A chealaich m' aran, *who ate my bread.*
————te, *past pt.* of cealaich.
cealaideach,* *s. m.* [& *f.*] Miserable-looking person.
cealair, see ceallair.
ceal-chobhair, -e, -ean, *s.f.* Sanctuary, asylum.
cèaldair, *s.m.* The Z-like instrument used by housewives for forming hanks of yarn. [also called *crois-iarna.*] 2 (AG) Gnarled old fellow of slow movements.—*Suth'd.*
ceal-fhuath, -fhuatha, -an, *s.m.* Private grudge.
cealg, ceilge, *dat.* ceilg, *s.f.* Hypocrisy, deceit, treachery. 2 Malice. **Spiorad ceilge,** *the spirit of deceit.*
———, *v.a.* Beguile, deceive.
cealgach, -aiche, *a.* Crafty, cunning. 2 Hypocritical, treacherous, deceitful, false. 3 **Malicious. Tha 'n cridhe *c.*, *the heart is deceitful.*
cealgadair, -e, -ean, *s.m.* see cealgair.
————eachd, *s.f.* see cealgaireachd.
cealgadh, -aidh, *s.m.* Alluring, deceiving. A' c—, *pr.pt.* of cealg.
cealgaich, see cealaich.
cealgaiche, -an, *s.m.* see cealgair.
————, *comp.* of *a.* cealgach.
cealgair, -ean, *s.m.* Hypocrite, deceiver, rogue, cheat, traitor. Bàsaichidh dòchas a' *ch.*, *the hope of the hypocrite shall perish.*
————eachd, *s.f.ind.* Hypocrisy, fraud, deceit, treachery. Bithibh air bhur faicill o thaois ghoirt nam Pharasach, eadhon *c.*, *beware ye of the leaven of the Pharisees, even hypocrisy*; ri *c.*, *practising deceit.*
†**cealg-aonadh,** *s.m.* Dissimulation.
cealg-chòrdadh, -aidh, *s.m.* Collusion for fraudulent purposes. 2 Private understanding.
†**cealguidhe.‡‡** see cealgaiche.
ceall, *s.f.* Mast-step.
†**ceall,** cille [& **cealla] *dat. sing.* cill, *n.pl.* cilltean, *s.f.* Cell. 2 Church. 3†† Burying-place.
ceall,∥ *s.f.* Stupor.
†**ceallach,** -aich, *s.m.* War. 2 Contention, strife. 3 Churchman. 4 Monk. 5 *provin.* Peat-cart, creel placed on a sledge to carry peats, manure, &c. 6**Contention.
†**ceallada,** *s.m.* Custody.
ceallaich, see ciallaich.
ceallair, -ean, *s.m.* Superior of a monastery. 2 ††Cellarer. 3 ††Talker.
ceall-ghoid, -e, *s.f.* Sacrilege.
†**ceallmhuin,** *s.f.* Oracle, prophecy.
cealloir, see ceallair.
———-òlach, *s. m.* Mean or nasty person.
†**ceall-phort,** -uirt, *s.m.* Cathedral church.
ceall-shlad, shlaid, *s.f.* Sacrilege. 2**Simony.
ceall-shiod, see ceall-shlad.
†**cealltair,** *s.m.* Spear. 2 Cause. 3 Castle.
†**ceal-stol,** *s.m.* Close stool.
†**cealt,** *s.m.* Apparel, clothes, garments, dress.
cealt, (AF) *s.* Kelt (fish.)
———ar, -aire, *s.* Thick broad-cloth, generally of a grey colour. *provin.* 2 (DU) Web of any kind of cloth.
†**cealt-mhuinnleir,** *s.m.* Fuller.
†**ceamar ?** see ciamar ?
†**cean,** -e, *s.m.* Love, favour, fondness. 2 Desire. 3 Fault, crime. 4**Elegance. 5‡‡Debt. Tha mo *ch.* air an òg-mhnaoi, *my love is for the virgin.* [same as cion.]
ceana ? *adv.* (*for* c' ionad, cia an t-ionad ?) Whither ? 2 see cheana, *and* a cheana. 3‡‡ Even. 4 Lo, already.
†**céana,** see ceudna.
ceanail, -e, *a.* Mild, kind, loving. 2 Civil, well-bred. 3 Elegant. 4**Faulty. 5**Fond.
†**ceanair,** *a.* Hundred.
ceanal, -ail, *s.m.* Kindness, mildness. 2 Politeness, gentility. 3 Elegance. 4††Pleasantry, merriment. 5**Fondness. Beul a' cheanail, *the mouth of mildness.*
ceanalta, -ailte, *a.* Kind, mild, amiable. 2 Polite, genteel. 3 Handsome, comely, fair, clean, seemly. 4 Auspicious. 5†† Humoursome. Gille *c.*, *a handsome lad.*
ceanaltachd, *s.f.ind.* } **ceanaltas,** -ais, *s.m.* } Kindness, mildness, urbanity, complaisance. 2 Handsomeness, comeliness. 3 Polite-

ness.
ceanann, *a.* see ceann-fhionn.
†cean-aois *s.f.* Old age.
céandachd, *s.f.ind.* see ceudnachd.
ceandail,(AF) *s.pl.* Lice.
cean-fhionn, see ceann-fhionn.
†cean-fidhne, see ceann-feadhna.
cean-folaidh, see cion-falaich.
ceangail, *pr.pt.* a' ceangal [& ceangladh,] *v.a* Bind, tie, fasten. 2 Fetter. 3 Article, as an apprentice. 4**Tighten. 5** Oblige. 6** Restrain. Ceangail teann is faigh tearuint, *fast bind fast find.*
———te, *a.* & *pt.pt.* of ceangail. Bound, confined, restrained, tied, fastened. 2**Obliged, compelled.
———teach,** *a.* Astringent.
———teachd-cuim,‖ *s.f.* Constipation.
ceangal, -ail, *pl.* -ail [-laichean & ceangaltaichean], *s.m.* Tie knot, bond, fetter, ligature, bandage, fastening. 2 Restraint. 3 Obligation. 4 Binding. Act of binding. 6**Articulation. Fo cheangal aig duine sam bith, *under restraint to any man;* am fear a cheanglas 's e a shiùbhlas, *he that ties (his bundle) fast can walk without stopping*; ceanglaichean pòsaidh, *marriage-bonds, betrothal*; ceangal nam mionn, *the obligation of oaths*; A' c—, *pr.pt.* of ceangail.
ceangalach, -aiche, *a.* see ceangaltach.
ceangal-pòsaidh, *s.m.* Betrothal. Ni thu ceangal-pòsaidh, *thou shalt betrothe a wife.*
ceangaltach, -aich, *a.* Binding. 2 Connecting. 3 Obligatory, obliging.
ceangaltaichean,* *n.pl.* of ceangal.
ceangaltas, -ais, *s.m.* Tying, binding, fastening. 2††Obligation.
ceanglach, see ceangailteach.
———an, -ain, -an, *s.m.* Bundle, truss, bale. *C.* airgid, *a bundle of silver.*
ceangladair,** *s.m.* Binder.
ceangladh, -aidh, *s.m*, Same meanings as ceangal. A c—, *pr.pt.* of ceangail.
ceanglaiche, -an, *s.m.* Binder.
———an, *n.pl.* of ceanglaiche, & ceangal.
ceanglaidh, *fut.aff.a.* of ceangail.
ceanglair,** *s.m.* Binder.
ceanglar, *fut. pass.* of ceangail.
ceanionn, see ceann-fhionn.
ceann, cinn, *s.m.* Head. 2 Point. 3 Hilt. 4 Top. 5 End. 6 Chief, commander. 7 Headland, promontory. 8 Extremity, limit. 9 Period, expiration. 10*Genius, ingenuity. 11* Attention. 12 Head of yarn (4 to 6 cuts or hanks.) 13**Harvest-home. 14(AH) Head of a plough, on which sock is fixed. Thog tuinn an cinn, *waves reared their heads*; sleagh a's géire ceann, *a spear of the sharpest point*; *c.* nan laoch, *the chief of the heroes*; 'an *c.* bliadhna, *at the expiration of a year*; mu cheannaibh nan crann, *about the tops of the trees;* bi 'nad *ch.* mhath dha, *be kind (good) to him*; 'na dhroch *ch.* dhuit, *very bad for you*; is dona an *c.* sin dhuit, *that is against your health;* bha e 'na dhroch *ch.* dha, *he behaved very ill to him;* a' dol air cheann ghnothaich, *going on business;* cha'n 'eil an droch *ch.* aige, *he is not destitute of genius;* air *ch.* dha tighinn dhachaidh, *preparatory to his coming home*; an *c.* a sè deug, *at long last*; 'an *c.* a chéile, *mixed, assembled*; 's ann agad a tha an ceann! *how shrewd you are!* shiubhail mi Ile bho *ch.* gu *c.*, *I walked from one extremity of Islay to the other;* na cuir *c.* 'na leithid sin, *do not attempt such a thing;* thoir an ceann dheth, *behead him* ; a chur *c.* air strì, *to conclude the strife*; àm a bheir ar n-àmhghar gu *c.*, *a time that will bring our troubles to a close*; *c.* na cìche, *the nipple;* an *c.* tiotaimh, *in a little while*; an *c.* tacain, *in a little while; c.* nan lann, *the hilt of the swords;* ciod e an *c.* a rinn e dhuit? *what attention did he show you?* gus an liath dŏ cheann, *till you are grey-headed*; liath thu mo *ch.*, *your conduct has turned my hair grey;* ghabh e 'n saoghal m' a *ch.*, *he took the range of the wide world*; os ceann an athair, *above the firmament* ; an *c.* shìos, *the farthest off extremity*; an *c.* a bhos, *the nearest extremity;* an *c.* shuas, *the upper extremity*; air mo cheann, *awaiting me*; os do *ch.*, *above your head, over you;* air a' cheann thall, *at long last.*
ceanna-bhàrd, *s.m.* Head bard.
ceannabhard, *s.m.* see ceannard.
ceanna-bhàrr,†† *s.m.* Head-dress, hat, cap.
ceanna-bheart, -eirt, -an, *s.f.* Covering for the head. 2††Helmet.
ceanna-bhiorach,†† *a.* Conical, pointed at the top.
ceanna-bhrat,††-ait,*s.m.* Head-dress. 2 Canopy.
ceannach, -aich, *s. m.* Hire, price, wages. 2 Purchase, purchasing, buying. 3**Bargain. 4 Reward. 5 Bribe. 6**Covenant. 7 Enough. Ceannach geal 'nuair a thig an sneachd, *a white present when the snow comes* [meaning that markets will be cheap]; bu *c.* leam t' ugh air do ghloc, *your egg is dear for so much cackling* ; is *c.* ort an gnothach, *you bother me too much about the business*; tha *c.* agad air, *you have had enough of it, it is a bother to you*, or *you will pay dearly for it.* A' c—, *pr.pt.* of ceannaich.
———achd, see ceannachd.
———adh, -aidh, *s.m.* Buying. 2 Act of buying. 3 Purchase. A' c—, *pr.pt.* of ceannaich.
———air,** see ceannaiche.
ceannachd, *s.f.ind.* Commerce, trade. 2 Merchandise. 3**Buying, purchase. Agus ni sibh ceannachd 'san tìr, *and ye shall trade in the land ;* oir 's fhearr a *c.* na *c.* airgid, *for her merchandise is better than the merchandise of silver.*
ceannachdair, -e, -ean, see ceannaiche.
ceannachdrach, -aich, *s.m.* Upper part of the throat.
ceann-a'-chnac, *s.m.* Thwart-brace of a boat—*Lochbroom.* see p. 76.
ceanna-chnàmhan, *s.m.* Head or ribs of boat see bàta, G 16, p.73.
ceann-achra, *s.m.* Epiphany.
ceann-a'-chraidh, *s.m.* Thwart-brace of boat—*Lewis, &c.* see p. 76.
ceann-adhairt, *s. m.* Pillow. 2 Bed-head. Cnamhadh a' chinn-adhairt, *a curtain lecture.*
ceannag, -aige, -an, *s.f.* Wisp. 2††Head-rig.
ceann-aghaidh, *s. f.* Forehead. 2 Countenance, physiognomy.
ceannaich, *pr.pt.* a' ceannach [& a' ceannachadh] *v.a.* Buy, purchase. 2*Redeem. 3 Traffic. A cheannaich sinn cho daor, *which we purchased so dearly.*
ceannaich,** -aiche, *s.f.* Strife. 2 Contention for supremacy or superiority.
ceannaiche, -an, *s.m.* Purchaser. 2 Shopkeeper. 3 Merchant, trader, whether buyer or seller. 4 Pedlar.
ceannaichte, *past part.* of ceannaich, Bought.
†ceannaide, *s.m.* see ceannaiche.
†ceann'aidh, see ceann-aghaidh.
ceann-aimsir, cinn-, *s.m.* Date, epoch, era. 2 Term, period.
ceann-aimsreach (JM) *s.m.* Term-day.
ceannair,** -ean, *s.m.* Driver, goadsman, 2** Leader of plough-horses.

ceannairc, -e, *s.f.* Rebellion, sedition, mutiny, insubordination. 2**Conspiracy. 3 Perverseness. 4‡ Turbulence. [*C.* has no *pl.*] Làn ceannairc, *full of rebellion.*

——,** *v.n.* Rebel, mutiny.

——each, -eiche, *a.* Rebellious, seditious, insubordinate, mutinous. 2 Perverse. 3 Turbulent.
Daoine dall agus c., *blind and rebellious men.*

——eas, -eis, *s.m.* Proneness to rebel. 2 Insubordinateness. 3††Sedition.

——ich, *v.a.* see ceannairgich.

ceann-air-chrith,§ *s. m.* Quaking grass, see conan.

ceannaird, *gen.sing.* of ceannard.

ceannaire, -an, *s.m.* see ceannair. 2 see geannair.

——achd, *s.f.ind.* Occupation of a goadsman. 2 of leading horses when ploughing.

ceannairge, *s.f.* see ceannairc.

——ach, *a.* see ceannairceach.

——achadh, -aidh, *s. m.* Contention, strife. 2 Rebelling. A' c—, *pr.pt.* of ceannairgich.

ceannairgich, *v.n.* Rebel, contend, revolt.

ceann-airm, *s.m.* General, head of an army.

ceannamhăg,(DU) *s.f.* Part at end of a field where the horses turn in ploughing (*lit.* end-rig)—*W. of Ross.*

ceannamhagan, *s.pl.* Scraps of grass adjacent to growing corn.—*Suth'd.*

ceannamhaide,(AH) *s.m.* Couple-leg in roof of a house.

ceann-aobhair, -e, -ean, *s.m.* Prime cause, first cause.

ceann-aodach, -aich, *s. m.* Head-dress. 2** Mitre. 3**Turban.

ceannarra,(AC) *a.* Strong-headed.

ceannarach, *s.m.pl.* Scraps of grass adjacent to growing corn—*Argyll.*

ceannard, -aird, -an, *s.m.* Chief, chieftain, leader, commander-in-chief.

ceann-àrd, -àirde, *a.* High-headed.

ceannardach, -aiche, *a.* Commanding, ambitious, arrogant, proud, imperious, dictatorial. 2 Confident, dogmatical, influential. 3‡‡ High-headed.

——d, *s.f.ind.* Arrogance, pride, imperiousness, ambition. 2 Superiority, chieftainship.

ceannardas, -ais, *s.m.* see ceannas.

ceann-armailt, *s.m.* General, commander of an army.

ceannas, -ais, *s.m.* Superiority. 2 Chieftainship. 3 Haughtiness, superciliousness, arrogance, forwardness, imperiousness. 4 The upper hand. 5**Ambition. 6 Vaunting.

——ach, -aiche, *a.* Superior. 2 Ambitious, aspiring. 3 Authoritative, commanding. 4 **Haughty. 5**Headstrong.

——achd, *s.f.ind.* Superiority. 2 Ambition. 3 Haughtiness, imperiousness. 4‡‡Despotism.

—— -cinnidh, *s.m.* Chieftainship.

—— -feadhna, *s. m.* Chieftainship of a clan or tribe.

—— -fine, see c— -cinnidh.

ceannasg, -aisg, -an, *s. m.* †The forehead. 2 Coif, hair lace. 3**Cap. 4**Headstall. 5 Band. 6**Government, ruling.

†**ceannath**, *s.m.* Bargain, agreement.

ceann-bàn-a'-mhonaidh,§ *s. m.* Cotton-sedge, see canach.

ceann-barrach, -aich, *s.m.* Jack-fish, pike.

ceann-beag, *gen.* cinn-bhig, *n.pl.* cinn-bheaga, *s.m.* Sheaf out of each shock as cottagers' wages. 2 Certain proportion of crop, dressed in harvest in order to ascertain the probable quantity of the whole, generally called a "proof."

ceann-bhàrr, -a, -an, *s.m.* [& *f.*] Hat, bonnet, cap, any male head-dress. Ceann-bhàrr easbuig, *bishop's mitre.*

ceann-bheairteach, *a.* ceann-bheartach.

ceann-bheart, -bheairt, *pl.* -an [cinn-bheairt & cinn-bheartan,] *s.m.* Helmet, head-piece.

—— ——ach, *a.* Wearing or having a helmet or head-piece.

ceann-bheirteach, see ceann-bheartach.

ceann-bhiorach, -aiche, *a.* Conical, pointed at the head.

——, -aich, *s.m.* see ceann-biorach.

ceann-bhrat, -ait, *s.m.* Canopy.

ceann-bhriathar, -air, -thran, *s.m.* Adverb.

ceann-bhriathrach, *a.* Adverbial.

ceann-bhriathrail, see c— -bhriathrach.

ceann-bhroit, (*for* ceann-bhrait) *gen. sing.* of ceann-bhrat.

†**ceann-bhurgaid**, see ceann-phurgaid.

†**ceann-bhurgair**, *s.m.* Burgomaster.

†**ceann-biorach**, *s.m.* Prow of a ship, generally called "ceann-caol."

ceann-biorach-na-doinionn, (AH) see ceann-biorach-na-stoirm.

ceann-biorach-na-stoirm, (AH) *s. m.* Stormy petrel—*cellaria pelagica.*

ceann-buidhne, cinn-bhuidhne, *s. m.* Captain of a company or party.

ceann-caol, *pl.* cinn-chaola, *s.m.* Prow of a ship. 2 Tapering or smaller extremity of anything, distinguished from "ceann-garbh," the thicker extremity. 3‡‡ The head, in contra-distinction to the lower extremities. 4(AH) The legs in contra-distinction to the head. Seas air do cheann-caol, *stand upon thy head;* tha duine a tha mach air a cheann-caol fad an là feumach air fois 'nuair a thig e dhachaidh, *a man who is out on his legs all day requires rest on coming home.*

ceann-carach,‡‡ *s.m.* Jack (tool.)

ceann-chàrr,** *s.m.* Dandriff.

ceann-chathair, -thrach, -thraichean, *s. f.* Metropolis.

ceann-cheòladair, -e, -ean, *s.m.* Chief musician.

ceann-cheud, *s.m.* Centurion.

ceann-chlaon, *a.* Headlong. 2 Steep.

ceann-chuag,(DU) see ceann-tobhta 1.

ceann-choire, -ean, *s.f.* Capital offence.

†**ceann-chunn**, *s.m.* Goad.

ceann-cinneil, see ceann-cinnidh.

ceann-cinnidh, *s.m.* Chief, chieftain, head of a clan, chief of a tribe.

ceann-còmhraidh, cinn-chòmhraidh, *s.m.* Topic, subject of discourse.

ceann-connspoid, cinn-chonnspoid, *s.m.* Topic of debate.

ceann-crìche, cinn-chrìche, *s.m.* Goal, end of a journey.

ceann-dàn, -dàna, *a.* Pertinacious, stubborn, headstrong.

——adas, -ais, *s.m.* Pertinacity, stubbornness, obstinacy.

ceann-dearg, -eirge, *s.m.* Red-start, red-pole—¶*phœnicura ruticilla.* [** gives *motacilla phœnicurus.*] see illust. 128. 2‡‡Redness of an evening sky.

ceann-deargan,¶ *s. m.* Redstart, see ceann-dearg. 2 Common redpole, see deargan-seilich. 3 (AH) High dawn, redness of a morning sky betokening unsettled weather.

ceann-deiridh, *s.m.* Quarter-deck.

ceann-dubh, -uibhe, *a.* Black-headed, black-haired.

ceann-dubh,¶ *s.m.* Black-cap—*curruca articapilla.* 2 Marsh-titmouse—*parus palustris.* 3

(AF) **Black red-start.**

128. *Ceann-dearg.*

129. *Ceann-dubh (1)*

130. *Ceann-dubh (2)*

ceann-dubhag, see **ceann-dubh.**
ceann-dubhan, *s.m.* **Black-headed gull,** see faoileag.
ceann-dubh-fraoich,(AF) *s.m.* **Reed-bunting,** see gealag-dubh-cheannach.
ceann-éideadh,-idh, *s.m.* **Head-dress. 2 Turban. 3**Mitre.**
ceann-eudach, see **ceann-aodach.**
ceann-fàth, ceann-fàtha [& cinn-fàth] *s.m.* see cion-fàth.
ceann-feachd, cinn-fheachd, *s. m.* see **ceann-feadhna 2.**
ceann-feadhna, cinn-fheadhna, *s. m.* **Chief.** 2 Captain, leader, commander, general.
————chd,** *s.f.* Captainship.
ceann-feadhnas, -ais, see **ceannas-feadhna.**
ceann-feodhna,** see **ceann-feadhna.**
ceann-fhacal, -ail, *s.m.* **Adverb.**
ceann-fhiodh, -a, *s.m.* **Roof timber, rafters.**
ceann-fhionn, *a.* **White-headed, white-faced,** as a cow or sheep. 2 Bald. 3 Grayish.
————,***s.m.& f.* Name given to a white-headed or white-faced cow.
ceann-fine, cinn-fhine, *s.m.* **Chieftain, head of a clan, chief.** Chaill iad ceann-fine no dhà, *they lost a chieftain or two.*
ceann-fineacha,** *s.m.* **Head of a clan or tribe,** head of a nation.
ceann-finid,(AH) *s.m.* **Consummation, culmination, finish, conclusion.**
ceann-fiodha, *s.m.* **End of a ship timber.**
†**ceann-fuirt,** (*for* ceannaird) Chiefs, leaders.
†**ceann-ghalar,** -air, *s.f.* Any disorder of the head, *dolor capitis*||. 2**Dandriff, scales on the head.
————ach, *a.* Subject to diseases of the head. 2 Subject to dandriff.
ceann-gharbh, -airbhe, *a.* **Thick-headed.** 2 Rough- or ragged-headed.
ceann-garbh,†† *s.m.* **Thick end.**
ceann-gheal, -ile, *a.* **White-topped, white-headed.**
ceann-ghlas, -aise, *a.* **Grey-headed.**
ceann-ghorm, -uirme, *a.* **Blue-headed.**
ceann-ghràbh, *s.m.* **Motto.** 2 **Superscription,** title.
————adh, see **ceann-ghràbh.**
ceann-ìleach, -ìlich, *s.m.* **Sword-hilt of a shape peculiar to those manufactured in Islay.**
ceann-iùil, cinn-, *s.m.* **Guide, leader of the way.** 2**Chieftain.
ceann-labhairt,‡‡ *s.m.* **Eloquence.** 2 **Topic of discussion.**
ceann'-laidir, see **ceann-làidir.**
ceann-làidir, *a.* **Headstrong, stubborn, opinionative.** Tha i c., *she is headstrong.*
————eachd, *s.f.ind.* Stubbornness, obstinacy. 2 Opinionativeness. 3**Stiffness.
ceann-liath, -léithe, *a.* **Grey-headed.** 2 Grey-haired.
ceann-litir,ceann-litreach, ceann-litrichean, *s.f.* **Capital letter.**
ceann-lom, *a.* **Bare-headed.** Mo nighean mhiog-shuileach cheann-lom, *my smirking bare-headed maid.*
ceann-maide, ceann-mhaide, *s.m.* **Block, blockhead.**
ceann-mathain, *s.f.* **Name of a star.**
ceann-mathon, see c— -mathain.
ceann-mhàg, -àige, **ceann-mhàga,** *s.m.* **Head-ridge in a ploughed field.**
ceann-molach, *s.m.* **Tufted dun bird,** see curracag.
ceann-muinchill,‡‡ **cinn-mhuinichill,** *s.m.* **Cuff.**
ceann-nan-sìth-mhaor, *s.m.* **The Lyon-king-at-arms.**
ceann-paib, *s.m.* **Tow-head.** Chuir thu ceann-paib air mu dheireadh, *you have put a tow-head on it at last.* [MacIntosh in *Gaelic Proverbs* says, "said of those who destroy all the good they have done by an ill-deed."]
ceann-phollan, -ain, -an, *s.m* **Tadpole.**
ceann-phort, ceann-phuirt, *s.m.* **Head port.**
————, *pl,* cinn-phuirt, *s.m.* ‡‡Founder, author. 2 Director of a choir.
ceann-phurgaid, *pl.* **ceann-phurgaidean,** *s. f.* **Gargarism, gargle.**
ceann-pluic,** *s.m.* **Block, blockhead.**
ceann-puist, *s.m.* **Chapiter, capital of a pillar.**
ceann-ràcain, cinn-ràcain, *s.m.* **Rake-head.** 2 *prov.* Small portion of land.
ceannrach, -aich, -aichean, *s. m.* **Halter.** 2 Horse-collar. 3 Tether. 4 Snare. 5 Fillet. 6‡Bridle.
†**ceannragh,** *s.m.* **Head-stall, halter.**
ceannraig, *s.m.* see **ceannrach.**
†**ceann-reiteachadh,** -aidh, *s.m.* **Propitiation.**
ceann-riabhach, -aiche, *a.* **Brindled in the head.**
ceann-roinge, *s.* **Head or rib of a boat,** see bàta G16, p. 73.
ceann-ruadh, -aidhe, *a.* **Red-headed or red haired.**
ceann-ruadh, *s.m.* **Celandine** *or* **swallow-wort.** [Preceded by the article *an.*] The flower is yellow and not red, although called *ruadh* in Gaelic. see illust. 131.
ceannruisgeach, see **ceannruisgte.**
ceannruisgte, *a.* **Bare-headed.**
ceannruitheach, -eiche, *a.* **Headlong, precipitate, rash.**
ceannsa, see **ceannsach.**
ceannsach, -aiche, *a.* **Continent, temperate.** 2 Mild, gentle. 3**Bashful. 4 Under authority, subordinate.

131. Ceann-ruadh.

ceannsachadh, -aidh. *s.m.* Subduing, commanding, taming. 2 Keeping under authority, 3 Reducing, subjugation, subjection. A' c—, *pr.pt.* of ceannsaich.
ceannsachd, *s.f.* Temperance, continence. 2 Mildness, gentleness. 3 Authority, government. 4 Subordination, condition of being kept under. 5**Docility, meekness. Le c., *with meekness.*
ceannsaich, *pr. part.* a' ceannsachadh, *v. a.* Quell, tame, subdue, conquer, train, discipline, keep under.
————ear, *fut. pass.* of ceannsaich.
————idh, *fut. aff.* of ceannsaich.
————te, *past part.* of ceannsaich. Quelled, subdued, conquered, disciplined, tamed.
ceannsaidh,** *a.* Clement.
ceannsal, -ail, *s.m.* Rule, government, sway, authority 2*Subjection. Fo cheannsal, *subjected*; do m' *ch.* géillibh, *yield (ye) to my authority.*
————ach, -aiche, *a.* Authoritative, commanding. 2 Fit for rule. 3 Prone to rule or govern. 4 Swaying. 5 **Active. 6**Supreme. Ceannard c., *a commanding chief.*
————ach, -aich, *s.m.* Commander, active leader. An c. mileanta, *the brave commander.*
————achd, *s.f.ind.* Rule, government, sway. 2 Supremacy. 3**Authoritativeness. 4 Tyranny.
ceannsaladh, -aidh, *s.m.* Dominion.
ceannsalaiche, -an, *s.m.* Conqueror, governor, subduer. 2**Overbearing man.
ceannsgal, -ail, *s.m* see ceannsal.
————ach, *a. & s.m.* see ceannsalach.
ceann-sgalpan, -ain, *s.m.* see ceann-ghalar.
ceann-sgrìobh, see ceann-sgrìobhadh.
————adh, -aidh, -aidhean, *s.m.* Motto. 2 Title, subject of writing.
————aichean, *n.pl.* of ceann-sgrìobh.
ceann-sgur, -a, cinn-sgur, *s.m.* Period, full stop in *gram.* 2††End.
ceann-simid, *s.m.* Tadpole.
ceann-sìthe, cinn-shìthe, *s.m.* Peace-maker. 2 ††Membrum virile.
ceann-snaodh, (AC) cinn-, *s.m.* Head of band of carol-singers who used to go about at Christmas-time.
ceann-spreadhach, -aiche, *a.* Headstrong.
ceann-stuaidh, -e, -ean, *s.m.* Arch. 2 Gable top or head.
ceann-suic, -e, cinn-shuic, *s.m.* Share-beam, the part of a plough to which the share is fixed.
ceann suidhe, cinn-suidhe, *s.m.* President.
ceann-taighe, cinn-taighe, *s.m.* Chieftain. 2 Head of a family. 3 Master of a house or household.
————achd,‡‡ *s.f.* Chieftainship.
ceann-tàla, *s.m.* Bard.
†ceanntar, *s.m.* Hundred. 2‡‡Side of a country.
ceann-teagaisg, cinn-theagaisg, *s. m.* Text, subject of discourse.
ceann-teurma, (AH) *s. m.* Death-stroke, accident or act of carelessness which results, sooner or later, in the death of a person involved therein.
ceann-tìre, cinn-tìre, *s.m.* Headland, promontory (*lit.* land's end.) 2 Peninsula.
ceann-tobar, *s.m.* Well-cover. 2 Mother spring.
ceann-tobhta, cinn-thobhta, *s.m.* Knee of timber in a vessel, which connects the bench with the gunwale, thwart-brace. 2 Bench-head. 3††Beam-end.
ceann-toiseach luinge, *s.m.* Prow or fore part of a ship.
ceann-treun, -a, *a.* Obstinate, headstrong, self-conceited, foolhardy.
ceann-trom, -truime, *a.* Drowsy, sluggish, heavy-headed, dull.
ceann-troman, (AF) *s.m.* Gurnet, gurnard. (fish)
ceann-uaisgineach, -eiche, *a.* Rash, incautious.
ceann-uallach, -aiche, *a.* Proud, haughty, vain, ostentatious, silly.
ceann-ubhall, cinn-ubhaill, *s.m.* The bowl, ball, or globe on the top of a pillar.
ceann-uidhe, cinn-uidhe, *s.m.* End of a journey, goal, terminus, destination. 2 Hospitable landlord. 3 Dwelling-place. 4**Stage. Ceann-uidhe na bàigh, *the dwelling-place of mercy*; ceann-uidhe na féille, *the head stage of hospitality.*
ceannuigheachd, *prov. for* ceannachd.
ceann-ùr, *s.m.* Paragraph in *grammar* (¶.)
ceann-ùrlair, see under bàta, A1, p. 73.
ceannus, see ceannas.
†ceansal, see ceannsal.
ceap, cip, *pl.* cip ceapa & ceapan, *s.m.* Block. 2 Shoemaker's last. 3 Top, as of a hill. 4 Stocks. 5 Trap, snare. 6 Sign set up, as a rallying point in time of battle. 7 Cap. 8* Clog or stumbling block on a beast's foot. 9 Sort of sofa or couch formed of peats, placed between the fire and the bed in the *bothan-àiridh*, and used as a seat. 10 Nave of a wheel. 11**Head. Leag iad c., *they laid a snare*; peanas a' chip, *the punishment of the stocks*: ceap nam mór chruach, *the top of the lofty hills.*
ceap, *pr.pt.* a' ceapadh, *v.a.* Catch, stop, intercept, obstruct, keep. Ceap e, *intercept him.*
ceapach, -aiche, *a.* Of, or belonging to, stumps or trunks of trees, or lasts.
†————, -aich, *s.m.* Tillage plot of land. 2** *s.f.* Decayed wood.
ceapadh, -aidh, *s.m.* Intercepting, catching or stopping, a flying or falling body, whether animate or inanimate. 2 Act of lasting, binding, or fettering. 3* Carping. A' c—, *pr.part.* of ceap. A' c. chuileag, *catching flies*; bithidh e cho math dhuit an cothrom sin a cheapadh, *it will be as well for you to make the most of that opportunity.*
———— -rann,‡‡ *s.m.* Scanning.
ceapag, -aig, -an, *s.f.* Catch, verse or verses composed impromptu. 2 Wheel of a wheel-barrow. 3 Small pair of stocks. 4††Small turf, *or* sod. 5††Block. 6‡Carelessly sung verse.
ceapaich,** *v.a.* Cap (catch.)
————ean, *s.pl.* Top sides or floats of a cart.
ceapaig, (CR) *v.n.* Catch, stop.—*Perthsh.* (Scot. kep.)
ceapail, *s.m.* see ceapadh.
ceapainn, *v.a.* see ceap.
ceapaire, -an, *s.m.* Bread covered with butter and cheese.
———— -Caluinn, (MM) *s.m.* Christmas bannock of same kind as c— Sàileach.
———— -Sàileach, -an-, *s.m.* (*lit.* the Kintail piece) Slice of cheese covered with butter

of equal thickness—C.G.I. xiv, 148.
ceapan, -ain, *pl.* -an, [& -ain] *s. m.* Little stump, block, or last. 2 Pin.
———ach,†† -aiche, *a.* Of, or pertaining to, little stocks, blocks, or lasts.
———ta, *a.* Stiff, niggardly. 2*Snatching, 3 Carping. 4††Thick, strong. **Gu c.,** *in a niggardly manner.*
ceap-cartach, *s.m.* Nave of a cart-wheel.
ceap-cinn,(MMcD) *s.m.* Peat cut with a spade leaving the grass on the top. 2 The surface cut with a spade when cutting a new peat-bank.—*Lewis.*
ceap-sgaoil, *v.a.* see craobh-sgaoil.
ceap-tuislidh, *s.m.* Stumbling-block.
†cear, *s.m.* Blood, offspring, progeny.
cear,(AF) *s.m.* Stag, roe, hart.
†ceara, *a.* Blood-coloured, red.

132. Cearacan.

cearacan,§ *s. m.* Skirrets,—*daucus carota* and *sium sisarum.* Name applied to the roots of these and curran earraich.
†cearach, *s m.* Wanderer. 2 Indigent person.
†———adh, *s.m.* Wandering, straying. 2 **Deliriousness. (not † in **)
†cearachar, *s.m.* Grave.
cearb, cirbe, *dat.* cirb, *pl.* cearban, *s.f.* Rag, tatter. 2 Skirt. 3 Piece of cloth. 4 Imperfect or ragged piece of dress. 5*Corner. 6 Defect. 7**Lappet. 8‡‡Excrescence. Rug e air chirb, *he laid hold of a skirt*; òran gun c., *a song without defect;* faigh c., *cavil, rail slander;* a' faghail c. orra. *railing at them*; c. nan neul, *the skirt of the clouds.*
†cearb. *s.m.* Cutting. 2 Slaughtering. 3 Money, silver. 4‡‡Contribution, subsidy.
cearbach,-aiche, *a.* Ragged, imperfect in dress. 2 Awkward, clumsy. 3 Not neat, not compact, untidy. 4*Unfortunate. 5 Afterwise. Is c. nach robh thu an seo, *it is a pity you were not here;* is c. an gnothach e, *it is an unfortunate affair*; cho c. ris a' chuileig a chaidh am bainne MhicCodruim, *as awkward as the fly that went into MacCodrum's milk,* [M. the Uist bard, while on a visit to some house, received one day for dinner a barley bannock and a very small quantity of milk. A fly happening to go into the bowl, M. took advantage of the incident to draw attention to the scarcity of the milk; "Tubaist ort, a chreutair chearbaich," ars' esan, "a dhol g' ad bhàthadh fhéin far am faodadh tu grunnachadh?" *"plague on you, you awkward creature," said he, "to go and drown yourself where you might easily have waded"*; the host thereupon said "thoir an còrr bainne do 'n duine," "*give the man more milk;*" M. replied "tha dìol an arain a dh' annlann agam," "*I have enough milk for the bread*"—meaning *I have very little bread either.*]
cearbachd, *s.f.ind.* Awkwardness, clumsiness. 2 Raggedness. 3 Want of neatness.
cearbadan-dé, see dearbadan-dé.
cearbagan,** *s.m.* Frippery.
cearbaiche, see cearbachd.
cearbail, -e, *a.* see cearbach.
cearbair, -ean, *s.m.* Awkward or spiritless person.
———eachd, *s.f.ind.* see cearbachd.
cearbalachd, *s.f.ind.* see cearbachd.
cearban, -ain, -an,*s.m.* Sail-fish, basking-shark. 2§ Buttercup, crowfoot—*ranunculus.*
cearbanach, *s.m.* see cearbhanach.
cearban-feòir,§ *s.m.* Upright meadow crowfoot, —*ranunculus acris.*
cearbhachd,‡‡ *s.f.* Incorrectness.
†cearbhal, *a.* Deceitful. hurtful.
†cearbhall, *s. m.* Massacre, carnage.

133. Cearban-feòir.

cearbhanach, *s.m.* Mullet. [With article *an.*]
cearbuinn, -e, -ean, *s.f.* Gaelic spelling of *carbine.*
†cearbusair, *s.m.* Banker.
cearc, *gen.* circe, *dat.* circ, *pl.* cearcan, *s.f.* Hen. Ceann circe, *a witless head*; cridhe circe an gob na h-airce, *a hen's heart in the mouth of poverty.*
———ach, -aiche, *a.* Of, or belonging to, a hen or hens. 2 Like a hen.
cearcag, -aig, -an, *s.f.* Little hen.
cearcall, -aill, -an, *s.m* Hoop, circle, ring. 2* Circumference. C. fuileach na ré 's i làn, *the bloody circumference of the full moon* ; ged a chuireadh tu c. air Albainn, *though you should include all Scotland.*
———ach, -aiche, *a.* Circular, resembling a hoop, hooped. 2 Having hoops. 3 Rounded. 4‡‡Curled. A braghad c. bàn, *her rounded fair neck.*
———aich, *v.a.* Circle, surround.
———aichte, *past.pt.* Circled.
——— -màis, *s.m.* Lower hoop, as of a cask. Is math an cearcall-màis deagh bhean-taighe, *a good housewife is as necessary to a family as the bottom hoop to a cask;* thilg e a chearcall-màis,—*he threw off all restraint,*—refering to the important part the bottom hoop plays in holding a cask together.
——— -nan-sùl, *s.m.* Iris of the eye.
cearc-choille, *gen.* circe-coille, *dat.*circ-choille, *pl.* cearcan-coille, see cearc-thomain.
——— -chrudhach(AF) *s.f.* Partridge.
——— -chìreach } (AF) Crested hen.
——— -chìreanach, }
——— -feucaig, see c— -pheucaig.
——— -Fhrangach, *gen.* circe-Frangaich, *dat.* circ-Fhrangaich, *pl.* cearcan-Frangach, *s. f.* Turkey-hen.
——— -fhraoich, *gen.* circe-fraoich, *dat.* circ-fhraoich, *pl.* cearcan-fraoich, *s.f.* Moor-hen, female of the red grouse.
——— -ghlopach,** *gen.* circe-glopaich, *dat.* circ-ghlopaich, *pl.* cearcan-glopaich, *s. f.* Hen whose head is covered with down.
——— -ghreannach, *s.f.* Rough-feathered hen, called Russian hens and French hens in parts of the Highlands and Isles, and "frizzles" by fanciers.
——— -ghur, *gen.* circe-guir, *dat.* circ-ghuir, *pl.* cearcan-guir, *s.f.* Brooding-, sitting-, or "clucking-" hen.
†cearchaill, -e, -ean, *s.f.* Pillow, bolster. 2‡‡ Clumsy man.
†cearchall, -aill, *s.m.* Pillow, bolster.

cearc-Innseanach, ** circe-Innseanaich, *pl.* cearcan-Innseanach, *s. f.* Indian hen. 2 (AF)Guinea hen.
cearclach,** *a.* see cearcallach.
cearclag,** *s.f.* Circlet.
cearclaiche,** *s.m.* Hooper.
cearclaichte,** see cearcallaichte.
cearclair,** *s.m.* Hooper.
†cearc-lann, -a, -an, *s.f.* Hen-house. 2** Poultry-yard.
cearc-lobhta,** *s.m.* Hen-roost.
†cearc-loch, *s.m.* Hen-roost.
†cearc-mhànrach, *s.f.* Hen-coop.
cearc-òtrach,(AF) *s.f.* Common or barn-door hen.
cearc-pheucaig,‡‡ *s.f.* Pea-hen.
cearc-riobach, *s.f.* *Argyll* for c— -ghreannach.
cearc-shealbhag,(AF) *s.f.* Hen or fowl paid of old to the falconer of the lord of the manor.
cearc-thomain, *gen.* circe-tomain, *dat.* circ-thomain, *s.f.*-Partridge.—¶*perdix cinerea.* [** gives *tetrao perdix.*]

184. Cearc-thomain.

cearc-thomain dhearg-chasàch,¶ *s.f.* Red-legged partridge—*perdix rufa.*

185. Cearc-thomain dhearg-chasach.

cearc-thopach,** *gen.* circe-topaich, *dat.* circ-thopaich, *s.f.* Tufted hen.
cearc-thopanach,(MM) see c— -thopach.
cearc-uisge,¶ *s.f.* Water-hen.—*gallinula chloropus.* 2 Moor-hen. 3 (AF) Dabchick.

186. Cearc-uisge.

ceàrd, ceàird [& ciùird], *pl.* ceàrdan [ciùird,** ceirdinnean & ceàirdinnean,] *s. m.* Tinker. 2 Smith, brazier, any tradesman working at smith-work of any kind. 3 Mechanic. 4 Blackguard. The word *ceàrd* is seldom used in sense No. 2, except in composition, as, fear-ceàird, *a tradesman*; ceàrd-airgid, *a silversmith*; bràthair-ceàird, *a fellow tradesman.*

ceàrdabhan, *s.m.* Beetle. (also carnabhan.)
ceàrdach, -aich, -aichean, *s.f.* Smithy, forge, smith's shop.
————d, *s.f.ind.* Business of a tinker. 2 Forging. 3 Mechanics.
ceàrdaich, *dat. sing.* of ceàrdach.
†ceàrdaiche, -an, *s.m.* Mechanic.
ceàrdail, *a.* Tinker-like 2 Of, or belonging to a tinker. 3**Artificial. 4**Well-wrought. 5**Commercial. 6 Tradesman-like, business-like.
ceàrd-airgid, *s.m.* Silversmith.
ceàrdalachd, *s.f.ind.* Handicraft. 2 Ingenuity. 3*Shameful conduct. 4††Tinkerishness. 5** Artificialness. 6 Skilfulness, tradesman-like manner.
ceàrdaman,* -ain, see ceàrd-dubhan.
†ceàrdamhuil, *a.* Artificial. 2 Well-wrought.
ceàrdamhlachd,‡‡ *s.f.ind.* see ceàrdalachd.
ceàrd-dubhan, -ain, *s.m.* Dung-beetle 2 Scarabæus. 3 Hornet. 4 see ceàrr-dubhan.
ceàrd-fhiollan, see ceàrr-dubhan.
ceàrd-òir, *s.m.* see òr-cheard.
ceàrd-staoin, *s.m.* Tinsmith.
ceàrd-umha, *s.m.* Coppersmith.
†ceariour, *s.m.* Grave.
†cearl, *v.a.* see ceirslich.
†cearla, *pl.* -n, *s.m.* see ceirsle.
†cearlach, *a.* see ceirsleach.
cearmanaich,(OR) *v.a.* Tidy—*Perthsh.*
cearmanta, *a.* Tidy, spruce, trim, succinct, compact, collected.
————chd,** *s. f. ind.* Same meanings as cearmantas.
————s, -ais, *s.m.* Tidiness, trimness, compactness, succinctness.
cearmontan, -ain, *s.m.* Kind of herb.
†cearmnas, -ais, *s.m.* Lie.
ceàrn, -a, -an, *s.f.* Corner, quarter, region. 2 Kitchen. 3‡‡Man. †4‡‡Victory. 5‡‡Expense. 6‡‡Hold of a ship. 7 Rectangle. Ceàrnan iomallach, *remote corners;* sluagh bho gach c., *people from every quarter;* cò an c. de 'n t-saoghal am bheil e ? *in what quarter of the world is he ?* †c. duais, *an athletic laurel.*
†ceàrnabhan, -ain, -an, *s.f.* Corner. 2 Hornet. 3(AC) see ceàrr-dubhan.
ceàrnach, -aiche, *a.* Angular, cornered. 2 Square. †3 Victorious. 4**Of, or belonging to, a kitchen.
————,*-aich, *s.m.* see ceàrnag-ghloine.
†cearnach, *s.m.* see carnach.
ceàrnadh, see cearn.
ceàrnag, -aig, -an, *s.f.* Narrow or small corner. 2**Little square. 3**Little kitchen. 4**Corner-stone. 5 Square in a town. Ceàrnag an Leas-righ, *Regent's Square.*
————ach,†† -aiche, *a.* Of, or pertaining to, little corners, or to squares.
———— -balla, -aig-, -an-, *s.f.* Corner, or exterior angle of a wall.
———— -ghloine, -aig-gloine, -an-gloine, *s. f.* Pane of glass. 2 (MM) Quarry of glass. 3 Lozenge of glass.
———— -lèigh, *s.f.* Tablet.
ceàrnaichte,** *past part.* Angulated.
ceàrnair, *s.m.* Conqueror.
†ceàrn-airrdhe, *s.f.* Trophy.
ceàrnan, -ain, -an, *s.m.* Quadrangle, square.
cearnan, (AF) *s.m.* Cockroach.
†ceàrn-dhuaichd, *s.f.* see cearn-duais.
†ceàrn-duais, *s.f.* Prize, athletic laurel.
†ceàrn-fearnadh, -aidh, *s.m.* Destroying.
†ceàrn-luach, *s.m.* Prize.
ceàrn-riaghailt, -e, -ean, *s. f.* Square, (joiner's tool.)
†cearr, *a.* Wounding, cutting.

cèarr, -a & ciorra], *a.* Wrong, awkward. 2 Unlucky. 3 Left. 4 Left-handed. †5‡‡Cutting. †6‡‡Wounding. 7 Astray. An taobh c., *the wrong side*; chaidh e c., *he went wrong*; deilg 'nan gualaibh c., *pins in their left shoulders*; a' bheart sin nach faighear ach c. is i foighidinn a's fhearr a dheanamh rithe, *what cannot be helped should be borne with patience ;* is fhaid' an làmh ch. na 'n làmh cheart, *the wrong (left) hand is longer than the right*—a polite way of saying that a person is a thief; tha sinn c. 's gun fhios againn, *we are astray and have lost our bearings.* [The form *ceàrr* given in dictionaries is *prov.*]

——,* *adv.* (i.e. gu cèarr) Improperly. Is c. a fhuaradh thu, *you have acted very improperly.*

——a,* *s.f.* Impropriety, wrongfulness.

cearracan,** *s.m.* Carrot.

cèarrach, -aich, -aichean, *s.m.* Gamester, dexterous player of games, gambler.

————, -aiche, *a.* Expert, skilful.

————d, *s.f.ind.* Dexterity, skill in playing games.

cèarradan,(AC) see cèarr-dubhan.

cèarrag, -aig, -an, *s.f.* The left hand.

————ach,†† -aiche, *a.* Left-handed.

cèarra-ghob,(AF) *s.* Avocet (bird.)

137. Cèarra-ghob.

†**cèarraiche**, *s.m.* Master of one's art or profession. 2 Gamester, gambler, dicer. Cha cheilich c. a dhìsnean, *a gambler will not conceal his dice.*

cèarraman, see cèarr-dubhan.

cèarran, see cèarr-dubhan.

cèarran-cré,(AF) *s.m.* Clay- or earth-beetle.

cearrbhach, -aich, -aichean, *s.m.* see creach.

cèarrbhach, see cèarrach.

cearrbhag, *s.f.* see cèarrag.

†**cèarr'chiall**, *s.f.* Madness, insanity.

cèarr-daolag, see cèarr-dubhan.

cèarr-daolan, see cèarr-dubhan.

cèarr-dubhan,(AC) *s.m.* The sacred beetle.

cèarr-fhiollan, see cèarr-dubhan.

cèarr-làmhach, *a.* Left-handed. 2 Awkward. Fear c., *a left-handed man.*

cèarr-mharcach, -aiche, *a.* Obliquely riding.

cearrsach, (AF) *s.m.* Corn-craik, see treun-ri-treun.

cearsail,** *s. f.* Clew. (ceirsle)

ceart, -eirte, *a.* Right. 2 Just, honest, upright. 3 Proper. 4 Certain. 5 Fair. 6 Correct, exact, identical. Tha thu c., *you are correct*; bha Noah 'na dhuine c. agus iomlan, *Noah was a just man and perfect;* an c. duine, [*a' *ch.* duine,] *the identical man*; an c. ni a bha dhìth orm, *the very thing I wanted* ; air a' ch. là, *on the very same day*; an c. uair, [pronounced *an ceartair*] *this very moment* ; c. mar sin, *just so ;* is c. cho math leam seo ri sin, *I like this just as well as that.*

——, ceirt, *s.m.* Right, justice. 2 Propriety. 3**Righteousness. 4**Redress. Agus rinn e an c., *and he executed justice*; cuir c., *rectify, correct;* brìgh ceirt, *justice.*

——,* *adv.* Equally. 2 Just, exactly, precisely. C. cho math, *equally well;* c. mar a thubhairt thu, *exactly as you said*; c. mar nach tugadh Dia fainear, *just as though God did not observe*; c. mar gu'm bitheadh, *just as if it were.*

†——, *s.m.* Reflection, critical remark. 2** Rag, old garment. 3‡‡Debt, due.

cearta,(DU) *s.f.* Ball of string, twine or yarn. *Gairloch* for ceirsle.

ceartach, -aich, -aichean, *s.m.* see ceartachadh. Ceartaichean, *little domestic jobs.*

————adh, -aidh, *s. m.* Adjusting, rectifying. 2 Mending, trimming. 3 Putting into order. 4 Little domestic job. 5**Paring, pruning, dressing. 6‡‡Rebuking. 7**Accommodation. 8‡‡Amendment. A' c—, *pr.part.* of ceartaich.

————ail, -e, *a.* Rectifiable. 2 Reclaimable. 3 Ready to rectify or adjust. 4‡‡Corrective.

————air, -ean, *s.m.* Adjuster. 2 Rectifier. 3 Regulator. 4**Editor. 5 Printer's reader. C. uaireadair, *a watch- or clock regulator.*

————d,** *s.f.* Adaptation. 2‡‡Allowableness.

ceartaich, *pr.pt.* a' ceartachadh, *v.a.* Adjust, rectify, put to rights, amend. 2**Cut, prune, trim,

————e, -an, *s.m.* Adjuster, correcter.

ceartair *adv.* (generally "an ceartair") The present time. Thig e an c., *he will come in a moment*—(future time)—*Lewis & most parts* ; bha e an seo an c., *he was here just now* (past time—*Harris.*

ceartais, *gen.sing.* of ceartas.

ceartas, -ais, *s. m.* Justice, equity. Dean c., *decide impartially*; 's iad c. agus breitheanas àite-taimh do rìgh-chaithreach, *justice and judgment are the habitation of thy throne*; tha do ch. àrd, *thy justice is high;* c. na cléir ri chéile, *the redress that the clergy give to each other.*

ceart-bheirt,†† *s.f.* Good turn. 2 Good deed.

ceart-bhreith, -e, -ean, *s. f.* Righteous judgment, just decision or sentence. 2**Birthright. [Generally *coir-bhreith.*] Bheir e c. air do shluagh, *he shall pronounce a righteous judgment on thy people.*

————each, -eiche, *a.* Righteous or just in judgment.

————eamh,-eimh, *pl.* -an [-nan & -a] *s.m.* Just judge.

————eanas, -ais, *s.f.* Just or righteous judgment. 2 Just retribution or visitation.

ceart-cheudnachd,‡‡ *s.f.ind.* Identity.

ceart-chainntéach, -eiche, *a.* Grammatical.*

ceart-choimeas,** -eis, *s.m.* Just resemblance, just comparison.

ceart-chreideamh, *s.m.ind.* Sound faith, orthodoxy.

ceart-chreidimhich,***s.* see ceart-chreidmheach

ceart-chreidmheach, -eiche, *a.* Orthodox, of sound faith.

————————, -eich, *s.m.* Orthodox person, one of sound faith.

————————d,‡‡ *s.f.ind.* Orthodoxy.

ceartla, see ceirsle.

————ich, see ceirslich.

†**ceart-lann**, *s.f.* House of correction.

†**ceart-làr**, *s.m.* Centre, middle joint.

ceart-luigheachd, *s.f.* Just recompense or reward.

ceart-mheadhon, -oin, -an, see teis-meadhon.

————————ach, -aiche, *a.* see teis-mea-

dhonach.
ceart-sgrìobhadh, -aidh, *s. m.* Orthography, correct writing.
ceart-sgrìobhaiche, *s.m.* Orthographer, correct writer.
ceart-sgrìobhair, *s.m.* see c— -sgrìobhaiche.
ceart-thomhasadh,** -aidh, *s.m.* Admeasurement, admensuration.
ceartuair, *adv.* see ceartair.
ceartuich, see ceartaich.
†ceas, *s.m.* Gaelic spelling of *case* (receptacle only; and 2 *kiss*.
†ceas, -a, *s.m.* Obscurity. 2 Irksomeness. 3 Sadness. 4‡‡Vision. 5 Ore, metal.
†ceas, ad ceas, (*for* it chunnacas) Was seen.
ceas,†† -an, *s.m.* Coarse tuft of matted wool.
——ach, -aiche, *a.* (DU)Matted. 2 Of, or pertaining to, matted wool. 3 Ungainly, awkward. Clòimh ch., *matted wool.*
——ach, -aich, *s.m.* Ungainly figure—*Argyll* ("Fionn.")
ceasach,* -aich, *s.m.* Temporary bridge or footpath over bogs—*Islay.*
———d, see casaid.
ceasad, -aid, -aidean, *s.m.* see casaid. 2(AH) Concealing or denying one's good fortune or prosperity. 3*Repining, grumbling at one's lot, or share of anything.
———ach, -aiche, *a.* see casaideach. 2*Repining, whining, discontented, displeased with one's share of anything.
———air, *s.m.* see casaidiche.
†ceasadh, -aidh, see ceusadh. 2** Vexation, punishment.
ceasan, see ciosan.
ceasan,** -ain, *s.m.* Coarse wool of the flank.
ceasg, *s. f.* Tuft. 2 (AC) Floss, an animal with long flossy hair or wool, sheep. 3 Supernatural creature of great beauty, half woman, half grilse. 4 Fresh-water mermaid with long and flossy hair. C. lìn, *a tuft of fine lint*; c. sìoda, *a tuft of fine silk;* c. clòimhe, *a tuft of fine wool.*
†ceaslach, -aich, *s.f.* Coarse wool on the borders of a fleece. 2**Fine wool.
†ceaslaid, *s.f.* see ceall-shlad.
†ceasna, *s.m.* Necessity, want.
†ceasnach, *a.* see casaideach & ceasnachadh.
ceasnachadh, -aidh, *s.m.* Examination by questions, questioning, scrutiny, search. A' c—, *pr.part.* of ceasnaich.
ceasnachail, *a.* Interrogatory, inquisitive. 2 Impertinent.
ceasnachair,** *s.m.* Catechist, catechizer.
ceasnachd,** *s.f.* Inquisitiveness.
ceasnaich, *v.a.* Examine, catechize, question, search.
———te, *past pt.* of ceasnaich. Examined, catechized, questioned, searched.
†ceas-naoidhean, *s.f.* Infant weakness, kind of disease.
ceasnuich, see ceasnaich.
———te, see ceasnaichte.
†ceast, *s.m.* Girdle. 2(AF)Sheep.
†ceata-cam, *s.m.* The seven stars "plough," or "great bear."
ceatain, see ceitein.
ceatal,** Gaelic spelling of *kettle.*
†ceatfàdh, *s.m.* see ceud-fàth.
†———ach, *a.* see ceud-fàthach.
†———achd, *s.f.* Lust.
ceatach, *a.* see ceutach.
†ceat-cam, see ceata-cam.
†ceath, *s.f.* Cream (see cè.) 2 Quay. 3 Shower, (ceatha.) 4 *rarely* Sheep.
†——,** *v.a.* Skim, as milk.
ceath,(AF) Jackdaw, see cathag.

†ceatha, *s.f.* Shower.
ceathach, -aich, *s.m.* Mist, fog, vapour. An c. a' seòladh, *the mist gliding;* mar ch. air beanntaibh, *as mist on the hills*; uisge ceathaich, *misty rain*; coire a' cheathaich, *the misty corrie.*
———ail, -e, *a.* Misty, foggy, vapoury, smoky.
ceathair, *a.* see ceithir.
——— -bheannach, *a.* see ceithir-chèarnach.
——— -chasach, *a.* see ceithir-chasach.
——— -chèarnach, *a.* see ceithir-chèarnach.
——— -chosach, *a.* see ceithir-chasach.
——— -deug, *a.* see ceithir-deug.
†ceathair-dhùil, *s.f.* The world as consisting of four elements.
ceathairle, -an, *s.f.* see ceirsle.
———ach, -eiche, *a.* see ceirsleach.
ceathairleag, -eig, -an, *s.f.* see ceirsleag.
ceathairlich, *v.a.* see ceirslich.
———te, see ceirslichte.
ceathairne, *s.f.ind.* Peasantry. 2 Yeomanry. 3 That portion of the male population that is fit to bear arms. 4††Party of men. 5††Stout men.
———ach, *s.m.* see ceatharnach.
———achail,‡‡ *a.* see ceatharnachail.
———achd, *s.f.* see ceatharnachd.
——— -choille, *s.pl.* Freebooters, outlaws, persons under hiding.
†ceatharbh, see ceatharn.
†ceathardha, *a.* Belonging to four.
ceatharlagach, -aiche, *a.* see ceirsleagach.
ceatharn, -airn, -airne, *s.f.* Troop. 2 Guard. 3 Fighting band. 4 Party of freebooters. Mar a dh'fheitheas ceathairne, *as freebooters wait.*
———ach, -aich, *s.m.* Soldier, guardsman. 2 Hero. 3 Stout, trusty peasant. 4 Strong robust man. 5* Freebooter, robber. 6** Boor.
———achail,‡‡ *a.* Plebian.
ceatharnach-coille, *s.m.* Freebooter, outlaw.
ceatharnachd, *s.f.ind.* Valour, heroism. 2 Deed of strength or courage. 3**Freebooting. 4**Peasantry. 5**Yeomanry.
ceatharnail,‡‡ -e, *a.* Peasant.
ceatharnas, -ais, *s.m.* see ceatharnachd.
——— -coille, -ais-, *s.m.* Outlawry.
†ceathar-ràmhach, see ceithir-r——.
ceathmaid, see ceath.
ceathnaid,(AF) *s.f.* Sheep.
†ceathra, *pl.* Four-footed animals, cattle, quadrupeds.
†ceathrachdamh, *a.* Fortieth.
ceathramh, *a.* Fourth. An c. mìos, *the fourth month;* an c. bliadhna, *the fourth year.*
———, -aimh, -an [-amhnan & -annan] *s.m.* Fourth part, quarter. 2 Measure of 8-fourpenny lands. 3 Firlot or four pecks. 4**Bushel. 5 Thigh. 6 Stanza. 7 Leg of beef, pork, or mutton. 8**Lodging. 9(AF) see ceathra. 10 Quarter in *heraldry.*

188. Ceathramh.

ceathramhan, -ain, *s.m.* Quadrant. 2 Cube.
———ach, *a.* Quadrated. 2 Cubical.
ceathramhan-caorach, -ain-, *s.m.* Common orache, see praiseach-mhìn.
ceathramhan-luain-griollag, *s.m.* Common orache, see praiseach-mhìn.
ceathramhnach, *a.* Quarterly *in heraldry.*
ceathramhnan, *s.pl.* Quarters, lodgings.
ceathrar, *a.* Four. [Generally used of persons only.—Followed by genitive plural.] C. mhac,

189. Ceathramhnach.

four sons; c. bhan, *four women* ; c. ag éirigh mu 'ràmhan, *four men rising at his oars.*
———, *s.m. & f.* Four persons. Thàinig c. a staigh, *four (persons) came in.*
cé-chruathachadh, *s.m.* Cosmogony.
†cedas, *adv.* At first, see air tus.
ceideach, (AF) *s.* Pet lamb.
cé-eòlas, -ais, *s.m.* Geography.
cé-ghràbhachd,** *s.f.* } Geography.
cé-ghràbhadh, -aidh, *s.m.* } Geography.
cé-ghràbhair,** *s.m.* Geographer.
ce h-àm? (*for* ce 'n t-àm) *adv.* At what time? when?
ce h-uair? (*for* ce 'n uair) *adv.* At what hour? when?
ceibe, *gen.* of ceaba.
†cèide, *s.f.* Market, fair. 2 Green. 3 Hillock.
†Ceideamhain, see Céitein.
†ceidghrinneachd, *s.f.* Ripeness of age.
ceidhe, -an, *s.m.* Quay, pier. 2††Coulter-holder of a plough.
†ceidiol, *s.m.* Duel, conflict.
ceig, -e, -ean, *s.f.* Mass of matted wool or hair. 2††Lump, bunch. 3 Clumsy, useless appendage. 4 Gaelic spelling of *kick*.
—, *v.a. & n.* Collect into bunches or knots. 2 Gaelic spelling of *kick*.
——each, *a.* Squat, low of stature. 2 Shapeless, clumsily formed. 3 Inactive. 4(AC) Shaggy, having long matted hair or wool. 5 **Canting. 6††Lumpy, bunchy. Dhannsadh na gobhair ch., *the shaggy goats would dance.*
——each, (AC) -gich, *s.m.* Sheep. 2 Goat.
——eadh, -idh, *s.m.* Clotting. 2 Jumbling. 3 Gaelic form of *kicking*.
ceigean, -ein, -an, *s.m.* Diminutive and unhandsome person. 2 Corpulent man, clumsily formed and of low stature. 3** Turd. 4‡‡ Tuft of shag. 5** Affected person. 6‡‡Clot of fat. 7‡‡Bundle, burden of hay, straw, &c.
———ach, *a.* Squat, diminutive in person. 2 Affected, canting. 3**Like a turd. 4‡‡Matted. 5‡‡Corpulent. 6**Trifling, fidgety.
———ach, -aich, *s.m.* Small squat person. 2 Unkempt person. Ceigeanach dubh, ceann gun chìreadh,—said to an unkempt person in *Lewis.*
———achd,** *s.f.ind.* Squatness, stoutness. 2 Diminutiveness. 3 Affectation.
ceigein, see ceigean.
———each,** see ceigeanach.
———eachd, see ceigeanachd.
ceighe, -an, *s.m.* see ceidhe.
ceigich, *n.pl.* of ceigeach.
ceig-rùsgach,‡‡ -aiche, *a.* Thick-fleeced.
ceil, *pr. part.* a' cleith [a' ceileadh, a' ceilteadh, a' ceilteachadh, & a' ceiltinn,] *v. a.* Conceal, hide. 2*Shelter, screen. 3**Deny. Ma cheileas sinn 'fhuil, *if we conceal his blood.* [*Ceil* is generally construed with the *prep.* "air," simple or compounded. Cha cheil sinn e air ar cloinn, *we shall not conceal it from our children;* na c. orm t' àitheanta, *hide not from me thy laws.*]
céil, see céill.
céile, *s.m. & f.* Spouse. 2 Husband. 3 Wife. 4 Equal, match. 5 Servant. Athair c., *a father-in-law* ; màthair ch., *a mother-in-law*; céile-còmhraig, *an antagonist, a match in combat* ; c. a h-òige, *the husband of her youth*; a céile, *her husband* ; a ch. chadail, *the wife of his bosom;* as a ch., *asunder, disjointed*: a chum a ch., *towards each other* ; dh'fhuathaich iad a ch., *they hated each other*; miadhail m' a ch., *fond of each other*; cuir r' a ch. iad, *join them, make them fight*; bho (*or* o) chéile, *asunder, separate*; a' pògadh a ch., *kissing each other;* a' brosnachadh a ch., *mutually urging one another*; thoir o c. iad, *separate them* ; cum o ch. iad, *keep them separated* ; mar a' chìr-mheala silidh do bhilean, a ch! *as the honeycomb thy lips drop sweetness, O spouse!* a' gabhail d' a ch., *belabouring each other* ; thar a chéile, *at variance;* Clanna nan Gàidheal an guallaibh a chéile! *Descendants of the Gael, shoulder to shoulder!* (*lit.* in the shoulders of each other), *also often written* "ri guallaibh a chéile." [The term *Gàidheal* is frequently erroneously translated "Highlander," which is only a political Sasunnach word invented to keep Gaels asunder and consequently comparatively helpless.] Am measg a ch., *confused, huddled*; chaidh iad am badaibh a chéile, *they fought tooth and nail;* le chéile, *together* ; troimh a chéile, *in disorder, in confusion, mixed, stirred about.* [As "match" céile is never used with personal pronouns.]
céile, *adv.* (*for* a chéile) Across.
†ceileabhair, *v. n.* Bid farewell. 2‡‡ Greet. 3 Celebrate.
†ceileabhradh, -aidh, *s.m.* Leave, farewell. 2 Salutation. 3 Conference. 4 Festivity.
ceileach,‡ *a.* Martial.
————adh, *pr.part.* of ceil, see ceileadh.
céileadach,** *a.* Abditive.
céileadail,** *a.* Abditive.
céileadair,* *s.m.* see cileadair.
ceileadh, -idh, *s.m.* Concealing, hiding, screening, covering. 2** Denying. 3** Concealment. 4**Hiding-place. 5**Purloining. A' c—, *pr. part.* of ceil.
cèileann, see cilean.
ceilear, *s.m.* [& *f.*] Light, lively music, commonly applied to the singing of birds, warble, warbling. 2**Sonnet, melody. 3**Concealer, coverer, screener, shelterer. Cluinnidh Gall an ceilear 'na cheò, *Gaul shall hear their warbling and be stupified therewith.*
———ach, *a.* Musical, warbling, melodious. 2††Chirping.
———ach,** *s.m.* Warbling, melody.
———achd,* *s.f.* Chirping.
†ceile-de, *s.m.* Preserver of the fires. 2 Culdee. [*fanciful word.*]
†ceilegheall, *v.a.* Betrothe, affiance.
ceileir, *s.m.* see ceilear.
———, *pr.part.* a' ceileireadh, *v.n.* Chirp, warble. 2 Sing sweetly. Mar smeòrach a' ceileireadh, *warbling like a mavis.*
———each, *a.* see ceilearach.
———eachd, see ceilearachd.
———eadh,†† see ceilear. 2 *pr.part.* of ceileir.
———ean, -ein, *s.m.* see ceilear.
———ich, *v.n.* see ceileir.
ceileiriche, *s.m.* Warbler, songster. 2¶ Blue-throated warbler—*phœnicura suecica.*
ceilg, *gen.sing.* of cealg. [Sometimes used as the nominative.]
céilich, *v.n.* Participate, share in. 2 Eat. 3** see cealaich. 4**see ceil. 5**Purloin.
céilidh, -ean, *s.f.* [*m.* in some places.] Gossiping, visiting, visit. 2 Sojourning. 3 Pilgrimage. Air chéilidh, *on a visit, gossiping*; an fheadh 's [* erroneously gives "neas"] a bhitheas tu an céilidh an t-saoghail, *while your earthly pilgrimage lasts*; earrag chéilidh, *the gossiping stroke* (said of a person who is hurt on a visit.); c. nam ban Slèibhteach, *the visit of the Sleat women*—they stayed too long.
céilidh, *v.n.* Visit.
céilidheach,** *a.* Companionable.

ceilinn, *1st. per. sing, fut. subj.* of ceil, (unaspirated form used in composition) Na'n ceilinn, *If I should conceal.*
——,** *s.m.* Large codling.
†**ceiliubhra**, *s.m.* Concealment.
céill, *dat.* of ciall. [Sometimes used as the nominative.]
céille, *gen. sing.* of ciall.
†**ceilleachd**, *s.f.* Large piece.
†——ach, -aiche, *a.* In large pieces or fragments.
céillidh, -e, *a.* Wise. 2 Sober, steady, sedate. 3 Prudent, discreet. Gu c., *soberly* ; b'fhearr dhuit bhi c., *it were better for you to be prudent.*
ceilp,‡ *s.f.* Kelp.
ceilt,** *s. f.* Concealment, secrecy. 2 Anything concealed or hidden. An ceilt, *in concealment.*
ceilte, *past part.* of ceil. Concealed, hid, secreted. A ghaisgich c., *his heroes concealed.*
——ach, -eiche, *a.* Concealing, reserved, silent. 2‡‡ Penurious.
céilteach, -eiche, *a.* Fond of gossiping or visiting.
——,* -eich, *s.f.* Gossiping female. Cha robh c. nach robh bradach, *there never was a tale-bearer that would not steal.*
ceilteachadh, -aidh, see ceileadh.
ceilteachd,‡‡ *s.f.* Latitancy.
ceilteadh, -tidh, see ceileadh.
céiltidh, *a.* Wise. 2 Sober. (—**bad*)
ceiltinn, *s. f.* Concealing, covering, hiding. Concealment. A' c—, *pr. part.* of ceil.
ceilt-inntinn, -e, see cleith-inntinn.
ceim,** *gen. sing.* of ceum.
céim, *v.a.* see ceum.
——ich, *v.a.* see ceum.
céimeadh, -eidh, *s.m.* & *pr. part.* of ceim (for ceumadh.)
†**ceim-dhealg**, -eilg, *s.m.* (ciabh-dhealg) Hair bodkin.
ceimhleag, -eig, -an, *s.f.* Fillet.
——ach, *a.* Like a fillet. 2‡Abounding in fillets.
†**ceimh-mhileach**, *s.m.* Hair bodkin.
†**ceimh-phion**, *s.m.* Hair bodkin.
céimneachadh, -aidh, *s.m. & pr. part.* of ceimnich, (for ceumadh.)
ceimnich, *v.a.* see ceumnaich.
céin, -e, *a.* Distant, remote, removed, far off. 2 Foreign. Dùthaich chéin, *a foreign country*; an aimsir chéin, *remote time.* (Oblique form of cian.—‡)
céin (an)** *adv.* Far off, far away, afar. 2 Long since. 3 From afar. An céin tha madainn na h-uaighe, *far off is the morning of the grave.*
céin-chagair, *s.m.* Telephone.
ceinide, *comp.* of ciùin. More benign. Gu 'm bu ch. mo chruth, *that my face be more benign.*
†**ceiniol**, *s.m.* see cineal.
céin-thìr, *s.f.* Distant land, foreign land.
——each, *s.m.* Emigrant.
ceinn,** *s.* Laxity.
†**ceinn-liath**, *a.* Grey-headed.
†**ceip**, *s.m.* see ceap.
céir, -e, *s.f.* Wax. 2 Wax candle. 3 Buttock. Mar leaghas teine c., *as fire melts wax*; coinneal ch., *a wax candle*; c. an fhéidh, *the deer's buttock* ; gu ma h-ann [corruption of gu'm bu ann," an old optative subj.] bhios do leac gun fhuaim chlàrsaich, gun lasair chéire, *may your fire-side be without music of harp, or light of candle,—Filidh, p. 51;* bu chòidheis (coimhdheas) céir leat no cabar, *all the same to you whether it is wax or a wooden beam*—meaning that the person spoken to would fashion a wooden beam as easily as a piece of wax.
——, *pr.part.* a' céireadh, *v.a.* Cover with wax, seal with wax. C. an litir, *seal the letter.*
—— -sheulaidh, *s.f.* Sealing-wax.
céir-aodach,‡‡ -aich, -aichean, *s.m.* Cere-cloth.
céir-bheach, *s.f.* Bees' wax. 2 Honeycomb.
†**ceirbheadh**, -aidh, *s.m.* Gaelic form of *carving.*
céir-bhrat,** *s.m.* Cerement.
céir-chluais, see céir-cluaise.
céir-chuachag, -aig, -an, *s.f.* Waxen cell *or* cup.
céir-chùmhnant,‡‡ -aint, -an, *s.m.* Indenture.
céir-cluaise, *s.f.* Cerumen, ear-wax.
cèird, -e, -ean, *s.f.* see cèaird.
——each, *a.* see cèairdeach.
cèirdinnean, (*for* cèairdinnean) *pl.* of ceàrd.
céire, *comp.* of *a.* ciar.
céire,** *s.f.* Buttock, haunch, breech.
céire, *gen. sing.* of céir.
——ach, -eiche, *a.* Waxy, waxen, abounding in wax, of or belonging to, wax.
céiread, -eid, *s.f.* Duskiness, hoariness.
ceirean,-ein,-an, *s.m.* Appendage, tail. 2 Plaster, medicine, poultice. 3* Wafer. 4‡Clout.
——aich,(CR) *v.a.* Fondle, make much of, make comfortable—*Perthshire.*
céireil, -e, *a.* see céireach.
ceirein, *s.m.* see ceirean.
—— -cròin, *s.m.* Leviathan. (McL)
céir-gheal, -ile, *a.* White about the buttocks, as deer or roe.
céirich, *v.a.* see céir, *v.*
——te,** *a.* & *pt.part.* of céirich, Sealed.
céir-iocan,§ *s.m.* Guelder-rose or water-elder. —*viburnum opulus.*
†**ceirn**, *s.m.* Plate, platter, trencher.
†——in, *s.m.* see ceirn.
ceirseach,(AF) *s.* Woodlark, see uiseag-choille.
céirseach, *s.m.* Lightstand, old-fashioned form of candlesticks known as *carles* or *peer-men.*

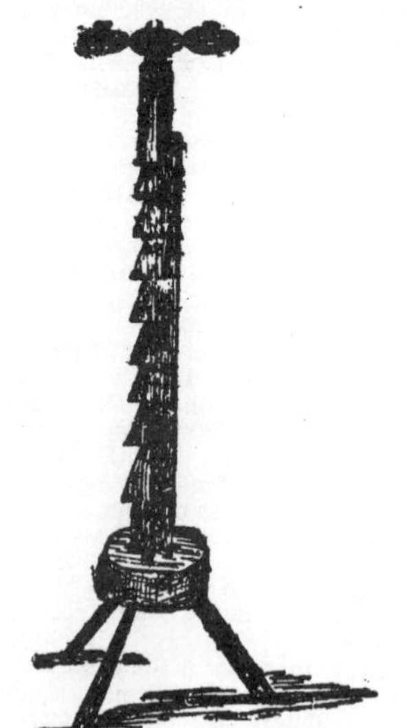

140. Céirseach.

céir-sheillein, *s.f.* Bees' wax.
ceirsle, *pl.* ceirslean, *s.f.* Clew or ball of yarn. 2 Stock, stalk. C. chàil, *a stock of cabbage*; c. snàtha, *a clew of yarn, ball of yarn.*
——ach, *a.* Round, as a clew, resembling a

clew. 2 Abounding in clews.
——achadh, -aidh, *s.m.* Forming of yarn into clews. A' c—, *pr. part.* of ceirslich.
——adh, -lidh, *s.m.* see ceirsle.
——ag, -eig, -an, *s.f.* Little clew.
——agach, -aiche, *a.* Of little clews, abounding in little clews.
ceirslich, *pr. part.* a' ceirsleachadh, *v.a.* Wind up, form into clews. 2 Coil. 3**Conglomerate, conglobulate.
——te, *a. & past pt.* of ceirslich. Formed into clews.
ceirt, *gen.sing.* of ceart. †2 *s.f.* Apple-tree. 3 Rag.
céirte, *a. & past pt.* Waxed, covered with wax, sealed with wax. Aodach c., *wax-cloth*; litir ch., *a sealed letter.*
ceirte, *comp.* of *a.* ceart. More or most just or righteous. Ni bu ch. na mise, *more righteous than I.*
†ceirteach, *a.* Ragged. Gu c., *raggedly.*
†——, *s.f.* Rag.
†ceirteachd, *s.f.* Tawdriness, raggedness.
†ceirteag, -eig, -an, *s.f.* Ragged girl.
ceirtle, -an, *s.f.* see ceirsle.
——ach, see ceirsleach.
ceirtlich, see ceirslich.
ceis, -e, -ean, *s.f.* Gaelic spelling of *case.* (receptacle only.)
céis,‡‡ -e, -ean, *s.f.* Creel, basket, hamper.
ceis, *s.f.* Farrow sow or pig. 2 Grumbling. 3 Loathing. 4 Lance. 5 Spear.
ceis-chrainn, *s.f.* Polypody, see clach-raineach.
ceisd, -e, -ean, *s.f.* Question. 2 Problem, dispute, controversy. 3 Darling. 4 Regard. 5 Anxiety. 6**Puzzle. Agus cha robh c. air a chur air, *and no question was put to him;* tha, gun ch., *yes, indeed, undoubtedly;* tha, a cheisd, *yes, darling.*
ceisdeachadh, -aidh, *s.m.* Questioning, examination. A' c—, *pr. part.* of ceisdich.
ceisdealachd, *s. f.* Fondness. 2 Flirting. 3 Gallantry. 4* Questionableness.
ceisdealaichte,** *a.* Capsulated.
ceisdean, *n.pl.* of ceisd.
ceisdean, *s.m.* Person secretly beloved, sweetheart, admirer.
ceisdear,** -eir, an, *s.m.* Catechist.
ceisdeil, -e, *a.* Questionable, suspicious, doubtful. 2 Beloved. 3‡‡Worthy of regard. 4††Chaste, modest. C. air fiona, *fond of wine.*
——eachd, see ceisdealachd.
ceisdein, see ceisdean.
——each,** *a.* Amorous.
——eachd,** *s.f.* Amorousness.
ceisd-fhacal,‡‡ -ail, *s.m.* Interrogative.
ceisdich, *pr.part.* a' ceisdeachadh, *v.a.* Question, examine, interrogate.
——te, *past part.* of ceisdich. Questioned, examined. 2** *a.* Capsulated.
†ceisdiughadh, *s.m.* see ceasnachadh.
ceisd-leabhar, -air, -bhraichean, *s.m.* Catechism, question-book.
ceisd-phunc, *s.m.* Note of interrogation (?.)
céiseach, -ich, -ichean, *s. f.* Large corpulent woman.
——,‡‡ -eiche, *a.* Full of compartments.
ceiseag, -eig, -an, *s.f.* Small pannier or basket. 2 Hurdle.
céiseag, -eig, -an, *s.f.* ‡‡Slip, sapling. 2 Gaelic diminutive of *case.* (receptacle only.)
ceisean, -ein, -an, *s.m.* see ceiseag.
ceisean, (AF) *s.m.* Young pig.
†ceisneamh, *s.m.* Whining, complaining.
ceist, see ceisd.
——each, *s.m.* see ceisd-phunc.

——eachadh, *s.m.* see ceisdeachadh.
——eachan,†† *s.m.* Catechism.
——ean, see ceisdean.
——eanaiche,** *s.* Catechumen.
——eil,†† -e, *a.* Chaste, modest, of a good character.
——ein, see ceisdean.
——eir, -ean, see ceisdear.
——ich, *pr. part.* a' ceisdeachadh, see ceisdich.
ceistich, see ceisdich.
Céit, *poetical contr.* for Céitean. Madainn chùbhraidh Chéit, *a fragrant May morn.*
†ceitean, *s.m.* Vehicle formed of twigs.
Céitean, -ein, *s.m.* Month of May. 2 Beginning of summer. 3 Spring. 4‡‡Fair weather. 5 ‡‡Favourable season. 'S a' mhadainn bhoidhich Ch., *on the beautiful spring morning;* C. na h-òinnsich, *April 19th. to May 12th.*
——ach, -eiche, *a.* Belonging to May or the beginning of summer.
ceiteanach,* -aich, *s.m.* Coal-fish of next size larger than a cuddy.
ceiteineach,‡‡ see ceiteanach.
ceithe, *s.m.* see ceidhe.
ceithir, *a.* Four. C. taighean, *four houses.*
ceithir-bheannach, *a.* see c— -chèarnach.
—— -chasach, *a.* Four-footed, quadruped.
—— -chasach, *s.m.* Quadruped.
—— -chèarnach, *a.* Four-square, quadrangular, quadratic.
—— -chèarnadh, -aidh, *s.m.* Squaring. A' c—, *pr.part.* of c— -chèarnaich.
—— -chèarnag, *s.f.* Canton in *heraldry.* 
—— -chèarnaich, *pr. part.* a' c— chèarnachadh, *v.a.* Square, shape into a square.
—— -chèarnaichte, *past part.* of c— chèarnaich. Squared, formed into a square.

[141. *Ceithir-chèarnag.*

—— -deug, *a.* Fourteen.
—— -fillte, *a.* Fourfold, quadruple.
————ach, *a.* see ceithir-fillte.
—— -ghobhlach, *a.* Four-pronged.
—— ghobhlanach, see ceithir-ghobhlach.
—— -oisinneach, *a.* Quadrangular, having four angles.
—— -ràmhach, *a.* Four-oared.
—— -ràmhach, *s.f.* Quadreme, four-oared boat. Sgioba na c., *the crew of the four-oared boat.*
—— -shlisneach, *a.* Four-sided, quadrilateral.
—— -shlisneag,** -aig, *s. f.* Quadrilateral figure.
†ceithreachad,** *a.* Forty.
ceithreamh, see ceathramh.
————nan, see ceathramhnan.
ceithreannach, *a.* see ceathramhanach.
ceithreannan, (*for* ceathramhnan.)
ceitleag, (AF) *s.f.* Catfish.
†Céituin, see Céitein.
†cèl, *s.m.* The mouth. Cèl-fàisdine, *prophecy.*
†cel,‖ s. Death.
†cèl-fàisdine, *s.* Prophecy.
cé-mheas, -a, *s.m.* Geometry.
——ach, *a.* Geometrical.
——ach, -aich, -aichean, *s.m.* Geometer.
ceò, *gen.* ceò & ceòtha, *pl.* ceòtha, *s.m.* Mist, vapour, fog. 2* Amazement. 3** *rarely* Milk. Chaidh e 'na cheò, *he got quite amazed*; Gall 'na cheò, *G. amazed (lit.* in his mist); c. teas, *vapour, steam*; an c. a dh'fhàgas an seann solus, 's e sneachd no gaoth a sgapas e, *the mist left by the old moon will be cleared away by wind or snow*; sléibhtean c., air an lear, *mountains of mist on the sea.*

†ceò, *s.m.* Milk.
†ceò, sceò, *conj.* And.
ceò'ach, -aiche, *a.* see ceòthach.
ceò'achd, *s.f.* see ceòthachd.
ceò'ar, -air, *a.* see ceòmhor.
ceòb, -a, -an, *s.m.* Dark nook or corner. 2* Drizzly rain. see caob.
——ach, -aiche, *a.* Cornered, awkward.
†ceòbach, *s.* Drunkenness.
ceòban, -ain, (ceò+buinne) *s. m.* Small drizzling rain, accompanied by mist. 2††Small bay.
———ach, -aiche, *a.* Dewy. 2 Misty, drizzly, moist.
ceòbanach,** -aich, *s.m.* Drizzling rain, moist mist.
————d, *s.f.* Frequent or continual drizzling.
ceòbhach,** -aich, *s.m.* Drunkenness.
ceòbhainne,* *s.m.* see ceò-bhraon.
ceò-bhran, -ain, *s.m.* see ceò-bhraon.
ceò-bhraon, -aoin, *s.m.* Dew. 2 Mist. 3 Drizzling rain.
ceòbnach, *a.* see ceòbanach, *a.*
ceòdhach, ceòdhar, } *a.* see ceòthach.
ceò-eididh, *s.m.* Shroud of mist.
ceò-ghlas, *a.* Grey, as mist.
ceò-ghorm, *a.* Blue, as mist.
ceòl, ciùil [& ceòil] *s.m.* Music, melody. 2 Song. Is e Dia mo ch., *God is my song*; gabh c., *sing a song*; fear-ciùil, *musician, singer.*
ceòlach, -aiche, *a.* Musical.
ceòlan, -ain, *s.m.* Faint music. 2 Tender soft air. 3* Humdrum of a person, one quite bewildered. (ceothallan.) 4**Little bell. 5 see ceòlan-cuilc. Taibhse le 'n c., *ghosts with their music;* fhad's a rinn an c. fuireach, *as long as the air lasted.*
ceòlan-cuilc,(AF) *s.m.* Warbler, reed-warbler.
ceòlar, *a.* see ceòlmhor. 2 Peculiar, odd, eccentric—*W. of Ross.* Duine c., *a peculiar, eccentric man.*
ceòl-beag, *s. m.* The music of marching and dancing, the time being strictly rigid in unison with the beat of the foot.
ceòl-bhinn, *a.* Melodious.
ceòl-chuilm, -e, -ean, *s.f.* see ceòl-chuirm.
ceòl-chuirm, -e, -ean, *s.f.* (*lit.* a musical feast) Concert.
ceòl-garbh, see ceòl-mór.
ceòl-meadhonach, *s.m.* The music of a song played in the free time of singing.
ceòl-mhoire, *comp.* of ceòlmhor.
ceòlmhor, -oire, *a.* Musical. 2 Melodious, abounding in harmony, harmonious, tuneful. 3 Funny, queer. Duine c., *a funny fellow—Harris, Suth'd.*
————achd, *s. f.* Melodiousness, harmony, harmoniousness.
ceòl-mìn, see ceòl-beag.
ceòl-mór, *s.m.* The classical music of the bagpipe which is symphonic, that is, consists of an ùrlar (thema), and variations. It is generally called *piobaireachd.* Its time is very free like that of a song.
ceòlra, see ceòlradh.
ceòlradh,-aidh,-aidhean, *s.f.* Muse. 2 Musician.
ceòlraiche,** *s.m.* Chanter.
ceòlraidh, *s.pl.* The Muses. 2**Musicians, band of musicians. Sguir na c. Ghreugach o 'n dàn, *the Grecian Muses have ceased their strain.*
†ceòl-reim, *v.a.* Modulate, play music.
†ceòl-reimeadh, -aidh, *s.m.* Modulation, musical arrangement of sounds to produce harmony.
ceòmhor, -oire, *a.* Misty, foggy, obscure.
ceòmhorachd, *s.f.ind.* Mistiness, fogginess, obscureness.
ceò-mhil, -e, *s.f.* see ceò-mhillteach.
ceò-mhillteach, -eich, *s.m.* Mildew.
ceòpach, -aiche, *a.* see ceòthach.
ceòpan, -ain, *s.m.* see ceòban.
ceòpanach, see ceòbanach.
ceòpanachd, see ceòbanachd.
†ceòr, -òir, *s.m.* Mass, lump.
ceòs, -eòis, -an, *s.m.* Hip, posteriors, buttock.
ceòsach,†† *a.* Having hips or buttocks. 2 Having large hips or buttocks.
ceòsach,** -aich, *s.m.* Perinæum, posteriors.
ceòsan, -ain, *s.m.* Light down of feathers or flowers. 2**Burr. 3**Prickly head of burdock. Mar ch. air sgiath an fhìreoin, *like bur clinging to the eagle's wing.*
ceò-nach, -aiche, *a.* Broad-skirted. 2 Bulky, clumsy.
ceò-soillse, *s.m.* Misty light.
ceòtha, *gen. sing. & pl.* of ceò. Cearb nan c., *the fringe of mists.*
ceòthach,** -aich, *s.m.* Drizzling rain.
ceòthach, -aiche, *a.* Misty, foggy, drizzling, cloudy, obscure. 2 Of, or belonging to, mist.
ceòthachd,‡‡ *s.f.* Mistiness.
ceòthaich,‡‡ *v.a.* Cover with mist.
ceòthaireachd, *s.f.* see ceòmhorachd.
ceothallan, *s.m.* Dullard, simple person. also ceòlan.
ceothallanach,** *a.* Chuffy.
ceòthar, -aire, *a.* see ceòmhor.
ceò-theas, *s.m.* Steam, vapour accompanied by heat.
ceòthmhor, -oire, *a.* see ceòmhor.
————achd, *s.f.ind.* see ceòmhorachd.
ceòthragach,* *s.m.* see ceòthran.
ceòthragach,* *a.* see ceòthranach.
ceòthragachd,* *s.f.* see ceòthranachd.
ceòthran,-ain, *s.m.* Small drizzling rain, gentle shower. (ceò-bhraon)
ceòthranach, *a.* Showery, drizzly, misty. 2 **Dewy.
————d, *s.f.ind.* Showeriness, drizzliness. 2**Dewiness.
cer, see cear.
c'e 'sam bith, [*for* cia e 'sam bith] *adv.* However. 2 [*for* cò e 'sam bith] Whoever. C'e 'sam bith cho fearail 's a tha iad, *no matter how manly they are.*
cé-sgrìobhachail,‡‡ -e, *a.* Cosmographical.
cé-sgrìobhadh, *s.m.* Cosmography.
cé-sgrìobhair, *s.m.* Cosmographer.
cé-thomhas, -ais, *s.m.* Geometry.
†ceuchd, *s.m.* Plough.
ceud, *pl.* -an, *a.* Hundred. [Governs its noun in the gen. plur. unaspirated when by itself or combined with other numerals, as, ochd ceud, *eight hundred*; it is also used in the singular when governed by numerals otherwise requiring the plural after them, as, trì cheud eun, *three hundred birds—Forbes.* It is aspirated by the four numerals *aon, dà, trì, ceithir*, as, aon cheud, *one hundred*; ceithir cheud fear, *four hundred men.*
ceud, *a.* First. An ceud fhear, (*m.*) *the first man;* a' cheud bhean (*f.*) *the first woman*; 's e an ceud thaom de 'n taigeis a's teotha, *the first helping of the haggis is the hottest.*
ceudach, *a.* Centuple, in hundreds.
ceudamh, *a.* Hundredth.
ceudan, *n.pl.* of ceud.
ceud-bhainne, *s.m.* First milk of a cow after calving, (bainne-nòis,) Sc. beastings.
ceud-bhann-malairt, *s.m.* Debenture.
ceud-bhileach, -ich, *s.f.* Centaury *or* red gentian—*erythræ centauriuui.*

ceud-bhreith, *s.m.* Birthright, priority in birth.
ceud-chathach, *s. m.* Hundred fighter, *i.e.* the fighter of a hundred men, epithet of Conn, an ancient king of the Gaels.
ceud-chuairt, *s.f.* First-footing on New Year's Day.
ceud-cothrom, *s.m.* Hundredweight.
ceud-dhuilleach, *a.* Hundred-leaved.
ceud-dhuilleagach,** see ceud-bhileach.

142. *Ceud-bhileach*

ceud-dreagh,‡‡ *v.a.* Prime.
ceud-fàdh, see ceud-fàth.
ceud-faithne, see ceud-fàth.
ecud-fàth, -an, *s. f.* Sense, faculty. 2* First principle. 3**Conjecture, guess. 4**Judiciousness.
———**ach**,** *a.* Intellectual.
ceud-fhàire, *s.m.* Dawn, first dawn.
ceud-fhàs, -fhàis, *s.m.* First growth, embryo. 2 Spring.
ceud-fhéille-Muire-earraich, *s.f.* The Purification (2nd. February.)
ceud-ghin, *s.m.* Firstborn, firstlings. Ceud-ghin a' threuda, *the firstlings of the flock.*
ceud-laoigh, -e, -ean, *s.f.* Cow that has calved once.
ceud-lomaidh, *s.f.* Breakfast. [Preceded by the article *a' ch—*.]
ceud-luaidh, -e, -ean, *s.m.* Shout of applause.
ceud-lùth, -a, *s. m.* Beginning, first essay, first. 2‡‡Shout of applause.
ceud-mheas, -an, *s.m.* First fruit. 2 Tax. 3 Chief respect, chief honour.
ceudna, *a.* The same, that formerly mentioned, similar. Air an dòigh ch., *in the same way*; mar an c., *also;* an duine c., *the same man;* mar an c. an duine seo, *likewise this man.*
ceudnachd, *s.f.* Identity, sameness.
†**ceudoir**, *for* ceud uair.
ceud-tharruing, -ean, *s.m.* First draught or drawing. 2 First running of spirits in distilling, singlings.
ceud-theagasgach, -aiche, *a.* Institutionary.
ceud-thoiseach, -ich, *s.m.* First principle. 2 first cause, origin, commencement. 3**Rudiments, elements. 4**Archetype.
ceud-thomhailt,** *s.* Breakfast.
ceud-thùs, *s.m.* see ceud-thoiseach.
Ceuduin, see Céitein.
ceum,[-a &] céim, *pl.* ceuman -a, & -annan, *s.m.* Step, as of a stair or ladder. 2 Footstep. 3 Degree. 4 Path. 5**Stride, pace. 6**Pedigree. Trì cheumannan, *three paces ;* tha e c. ni's fhaide mach, *he is a degree farther removed in relationship;* mullach nan c., *on the top of the stairs;* gabh do ch., *go thy way;* c. sràid, *a short walk;* thoir c., *make a stride.*
ceum, *pr.part.* a' ceumadh, *v.a.* Step, measure by steps, pace. 2 Move step by step. Cheum e gu mòr mu'n cuairt, *he walked majestically about.*
ceumach,†† -aiche, *a.* see ceumail.
ceumadh, -aidh, *s.m.* Stepping, pacing, measuring. 2 Walking slowly, strutting, striding. A' c—, *pr.part.* of ceum.
ceumaid, -e, *a.* Swift.
ceumaide,(AC) *comp.* of ceumaid.
ceumail, -e, *a.* Stately in gait, stalking, strutting, majestic, pompous.
ceumanna, *n.pl.* of ceum.
ceumanta, -ainte, *a.* see ceumail.
ceum-cille, *s.m.* Bier-balk.
ceum-inbhe, *s.m.* Degree in rank or dignity. 2††Promotion.
ceumnach, *a.* Gradatory. 2 Ambling, pacing, moving majestically or stately.
ceumnachadh, -aidh, *s.m.* Pacing, striding, strutting, marching, stepping. 2**Prancing. A' c—, *pr.pt.* of ceumnaich.
ceumnachd,** *s.f.ind.* Graduation.
ceumnaich, *pr.part.* a' ceumnachadh, *v.a.* Step, pace, march, advance by steps. 2**Prance.
ceumnaiche,‡‡ -an, *s.m.* Pacer.
ceumnaidheachd, see ceumnachd.
ceum-tuislidh, *s.m.* False step.
ceun', *for* ceudna.
ceus, ceòis, ceusan, *s. m.* The ham or lower part of the body. 2 The coarser parts of wool on sheeps' legs.
ceus, *pr.part.* a' ceusadh, *v.a.* Crucify. 2 Torture.
ceusach, *a.* Crucifying. 2 Torturing. 3 Of, or connected with crucifying or torturing. 4 Crucificatory, like, or belonging to, a cross.
ceusadair, -ean, *s.m.* Crucifier. 2 Tormentor.
———**eachd**, *s.f.* Business of a crucifier or tormentor, crucifying.
ceusadan, -ain, *s.m.* Crucifix.
ceusadh, -aidh, *s. m.* Crucifying, crucifixion. A' c—,*pr.pt.*of ceus. Crann-ceusaidh, *a cross.*
ceus-chrann,(AC) *s.m.* Passion-flower, crucifixion tree, so called from a resemblance of the cross on the flower.
ceusda, see ceusta.
ceuslach, -aich, *s.m.* Wool on a sheep's legs, also the borders and coarser parts of the fleece.
ceusta, *a. & past part.* of ceus. Crucified.
†**ceut**,(AF) *s.f.* Sheep.
ceutabh, *s.m.* (CR) Admiration. 2(DM) Joy, satisfaction. Bu bheag dheth 'san àm mo cheutabh, *I had precious little satisfaction out of it at the time.*
†**ceuta**, *s.m.* Opinion in favour of, approbation, satisfaction, pleasure. Ciod do ch. dheth ? *what do you think of him?* cha'n 'eil c. air an t-saoghal agam dheth, *I do not think much of him—lit.* have no opinion in the world of him.
ceutach, -aiche, *a.* Handsome, goodly, seemly; comely, pleasant, pleasing. 2 Personable. 3 Admirable. 4 Elegant, graceful, engaging. 5 Beautiful. 6**Conceited. 7‡‡Honest. 8 Sensible, intelligent. Luach c., *a goodly price ;* duine c., *a handsome man* ; A Chonnail cheutaich ! *O handsome Connal !* tha e c. as fhéin, *he is conceited.*
ceutachas, -ais, see ceutachd & ceutaichead.
ceutachd,* *s.f.* Amenity, acceptability. 2** Agreeableness.
ceutadh, -aidh, *s.m.* Pleasure, love, admiration, delight. 2**Elegance, gracefulness, comeliness. 3**Pleasantness, seemliness. 4 **Kindness. 5** Satisfaction. 6** Opinion. Cha'n 'eil c. sam bith aige dheth, *he has no great affection for him.*
ceutaich, see ceutadh.
ceutaiche, *comp.* of ceutach.
———**ad**, -hid, *s.m.* Degree of beauty, comeliness, gracefulness, seemliness, decorum or elegance. A' dol an c., *improving in elegance, beauty, &c.* [Like many similar words in Gaelic, this is often used as a kind of double comparative, as, is ceutaichid i an culaidh sin, *that dress renders her more engaging.*]
c'fhada ? *adv. for* cia fhada ?

ch,

for words not given below under *ch*, see under *c*.

cha, *negative particle*, Not. [*Cha* aspirates the *fut. neg.* of a verb, also the initial of words beginning with labials and gutturals, and, in *Argyllshire*, with dentals also, as— cha dhuin an dorus, *the door will not shut*; cha dhaor a phris, *its price is not high*. *Cha* simply negatives the signification of the verb, as,(do) bhuail mi, *I struck;* cha do bhuail mi, *I did not strike*. It becomes *cha'n* before initial vowels or *f* pure, as cha'n òl mi, *I shall not drink*; cha'n fhosgail mi, *I shall not open*. Dr. Gillies remarks that the *n* of *cha'n* in *cha'n 'eil*, "shows the abiding influence of a lost dental *n*,—the *n* doubtless which re-asserts itself before initial vowels—it shows that it is wrong to separate the *n* of *cha'n* as is usually done in writing, as *cha'n*, *cha-n* and *cha n-*." [N is not a dental, and the *n* has as much right to separation as in gu'n dean. *Cha'n* is simply aspirated *gu'n* or *co'n*, only the aspirating influence is lost. It was *no cha'n*, and appears again in *nach*.]
Cha'n 'eil eadar an t-amadan agus an duine glic ach tairgse mhath a ghabhail 'nuair a gheibh e i, *there is no difference between the wise man and the fool, but to accept a good offer when in his power;* cha mhac mar an t-athair thu, *you are not a son worthy of your father*; cha téid e dhachaidh, *he will not go home*; cha tig fuachd gu h-earrach, cruaidh-chàs no droch cheannach, *cold, hardships, and bad bargains do not come till spring*; cha'n fhidir an sàthach an seang, 's mairg a bhitheadh 'na thràill do 'n bhroinn, *the satiated will not sympathise with the starveling, woe to him who is a slave to his belly*; cha'n fhiach duine gun sibht gun seòltachd, *a man without shift and ingenuity is good for nothing*; cha'n 'eil ann ach bó odhar mhaol, agus bó mhaol odhar, *it is only a dun hornless cow, and a hornless dun cow*—Gaelic equivalent of "six of one and half-a-dozen of the other"; cha mhór nach do mharbh e mi, *he almost killed me*; cha chuir mi, *I will not put*; cha dean mi, *I shall not do*; cha d'fhalbh mi, *I did not go*; cha d'éisd mi, *I did not hearken;* cha d'òl mi, *I did not drink*; cha leig mi, *I shall not allow*; cha d'rinn mi ach sgur, *I have only just stopped*; cha robh sgìreachd anns a' Ghàidhealtachd cha mhór anns nach robh e, (*col.* cha mhór gu'n robh sgìreachd &c., *or* 's gann a bha sgìreachd &c.,) *there was hardly a parish in Gaeldom he had not been in*; cha dean mi, *I shall not do*; cha'n fhaod thu, *you must not*; na'm bithinn ag iarraidh cuideachaidh, cha lughaid gu'n rachainn do d' ionnsuidh air son 'fhaotainn, *if I were wanting assistance, not the less would I go to you for it.*

chab, *past aff.* of cab.

cha chreid, *v.* An expression very often used in connection with another negative verb to equal the word *think*, *suppose*, *expect*. Am bheil thu dol ann? *are you going (to it)?* cha chreid mi gu 'm bheil, *I expect not*; cha chreid mi nach 'eil, *I think so.*

chagainn, *past aff.* of cagainn.

chagnadh, *past subj.* of cagainn.

chaidh, *past aff.* of rach. B' ann ortsa chaidh, *it was you that had the worst of it*; chaidh e as, *it went out (as a flame)*; 2 *he escaped*; a' bhliadhna seo chaidh, *last year*; an deach e mach? chaidh, *has he gone out? yes.*

chaill *past aff.* of caill.

chàin, *past aff.* of càin.

chàininn, *1st sing. past subj.* of càin, I would traduce or miscall.

chàirich, *past aff.* of càirich.

chaisg, *past aff.* of caisg.

chaith, *past aff.* of caith.

chaitheas, *fut. subj.* of caith. (That) shall or will consume.

cha mhi, see *v.* is.

cha mhó, *adv.* Neither, none the more. Cha mhó tha mise 'gad dhìteadh, *neither do I condemn thee.*

cha mhór nach, *adv.* Almost. Cha mhór nach do thuit e, *he almost fell.*

chan, *past aff.* of can. 2 Old form of cha'n, see note under cha.

cha'n 'eil (e), *pres.neg.* of bi. (It) is not.

chaob, *past aff.* of caob.

chaochail, *past aff.* of caochail.

chaoidh, *adv.* see a choidhche.

chaomhain, *past aff.* of caomhain.

chàrnadh, *past subj.* of càrn.

chas, *past aff.* of cas.

cheadaich, *past aff.* of ceadaich.

cheana, *adv.* Already, before now. 2 Indeed —*W. of Ross.* Rinn e sin a cheana, *he has done that already*; tha e fuar cheana, *it is cold indeed.*

cheana, see chianamh.

cheangail, *past aff.* of ceangail.

cheangladh, *past pass. aff. & past subj. act.* of ceangail. Was bound. 2 Would bind.

cheannaich, *past aff.* of ceannaich.

cheannsaich, *past aff.* of ceannsaich.

cheannsaicheadh, *past subj.* of ceannsaich. Would tame, would subdue.

cheil, *past aff.* of ceil.

chéile, *adv.* Both. Bha iad le 'ch. lomnochd, *they were both naked*; ghabh iad air a ch., *they fought among themselves*; thar a ch., *in confusion*; fanaibh ri 'ch., *wait for one another*; a réir a ch., *one with another, at an average, on good terms.* [Though chéile is always aspirated, it is due to the effect of the poss. pron. a, which is suppressed in Scottish, though not in Irish Gaelic.]

chéile, *asp.* form of céile, (spouse.)

cheilinn, *1 per. sing. fut. sub.* of ceil. I would conceal.

chéin, *asp.* form of céin, *a.*

chéir, *past aff.* of céir.

chì, *fut. aff.* of faic. Chì mi, *I shall see.* [Often used as a simple present tense, like all future affirmatives, as, chì mi triùir, *I see three persons.*]

chiallaich! †† *s.f.* (*voc.*) Darling!

chianamh, *adv.* (also a chianamh) A little time ago, a little while ago.
Am fear a mharbhadh a mhàthair a chianamh, bheireadh e beò a nis i, *the man who would have killed his mother a little while ago, would bring her alive now*—said when a good day appears after a storm of in any similar circumstances.

chiar, *past aff.* of ciar.

†chim, (*for* chi mi,) I see.

chinnte, *asp. form* of cinnte. Air chinnte, *certainly.*

chinnteach, *asp.* form of cinnteach.

†chiom, see †chim.

chion, *asp.* form of cion, (oftener a chion, *for want of.*)

chionn, *adv. & conj.* (*for* a chionn) Because, for that reason. A chionn gu'n do bhuin e rium gu fial, *because he dealt bountifully with me;* a chionn nach do chreid iad, *because they did not believe*; deas air chionn domh tighinn dhachaidh, *ready by the time of my home-coming;* bha e deas agam air chionn da

dheug ast oidhche, *I had it ready by twelve o'clock at night.*
chiotar, see chithear.
chite, see chiteadh.
chiteadh, *past subj.* of chì, Might be seen.
chitear, see chithear.
chitheadh, *past subj. act.* of faic, Would or could see.
chitheamaid, *1st. per. pl. past subj* of faic. We would see.
chithear, *fut. aff. pass.* of faic. Shall be seen. 2 Is seen.
chithinn, *1st. per. sing. past subj.* of faic. I would see.
chladhaich, *past aff.* of cladhaich.
chleachd, *past aff.* of cleachd.
chlisg, *past aff.* of clisg.
chlisge, *adv.* see a chlisge.
chlisgeadh, *adv.* see a chlisge.
chluinn, *v. irr. past.* Was wont to hear. e.g. in Mary MacKellar's well known song—"Chluinn mi na h-eòin," *I was wont to hear the birds.* It has not the same meaning as chuala.
chluinneamaid, *1st. per. pl. past subj.* of cluinn. We would hear.
chluinnear, *fut. subj. pass.* of cluinn. (Ma) chluinnear mi, (*if*) *I be heard.*
chluinninn, *1st. per. sing. past subj.* of cluinn. I would hear.
chluinnte, *asp. form of past part.* of cluinn. Heard.
chluinnteadh, *past pass. subj.* of cluinn. Would be heard.
chluinntinn, *1st. per. sing. past subj.* of cluinn. I would hear.
cho, *adv.* As, so. Cho dalma, *so presumptuous;* cho cruaidh ris an stàilinn, *as hard as steel;* cha robh mi cho brònach agus cho dall, *I was not so mournful and so blind;* am bheil e cho mór sin? *is it as big as all that?* a cheart cho mór, *every bit as big.* [Cho is always aspirated in modern Gaelic.]
chog, *past aff.* of cog.
choidhche, see a choidhche.
choimeas, *past aff.* of coimeas.
choimhead, *past aff.* of coimhead.
choinnich, *past aff.* of coinnich. Choinnich iad a cheana, *they met already.*
chòir, *prep.* see a chòir.
choisinn, *past aff.* of coisinn.
chon, *adv.* Until. 2 To. *prov.*
†chonnaire, see chunnaic.
cho....ris......, As....as...... Cho cruaidh ris an darach, *as hard as the oak.*
chorrach, (*for* a charachadh) To move.
chrath, *past aff.* of crath.
chreach, *past aff.* of creach.
chreid, *past aff.* of creid.
chreidinn, *1st. per. sing. past subj.* of creid.
chrith, *past aff.* of crith.
chroch, *past aff.* of croch.
chrom, *past aff.* of crom.
chruadhaich, *past aff.* of cruadhaich.
chruinnich, *past aff.* of cruinnich.
†chuabhair, (*for* chaidh sibh) Ye went.
†chuadar, *v.* They went.
†chuaidh, see chaidh.
chuala, *past aff.* of cluinn. Heard. [Written *chual'* before a word beginning with a vowel.]
†chualabhair, (*for* chuala sibh) Ye heard.
†chualadar, (*for* chuala iad) They heard.
chualadh, *past aff. pass.* of cluinn, see chualas.
chualaig, *parts of Argyll* for chuala.
†chualais, (*for* chuala tu) Thou didst hear.
†chualam, (*for* chuala mi) I heard.
†chualamairn, see chualamar.
†chualamar, (*for* chuala sinn) We heard.
chualar, see chualas.
chualas, *past aff. pass.* of cluinn. Was heard.
†chualas, (*for* chuala mi) I heard.
†chuamar, We went.
chuca, *prep. pron.* To them, towards them. Sgrìobh e litir ch., *he wrote a letter to them.*
chugad, *prep.pron.* To thee, towards thee. Chì thu chugad e, 's cha'n fheairrd thu agad e, *you'll see it coming (towards) you, and when you have got it you'll be none the better of it.*
chugaibh, *prep.pron.* To you, towards you.
chugainn, *prep.pron.* To us, towards us, 2 It behoves us. Chugainn a bhi falbh dhachaidh, *it behoves us to go home.*
chugam, *prep.pron.* To me, towards me. Chì mi chugam, chì mi bhuam a' bhogha-frois, *I see the rainbow stretching towards me and from me—i.e.* in both directions.
chuice, *prep.pron.* To her, towards her.
chuige, *prep.pron.* To him, towards him. Thàinig i chuige, *(as a ship) she came to, (as anything else) it improved;* a' dol chuige is uaidh, *going hither and thither;* thàinig e chuige fhéin, *he came to himself, recovered his judgment;* chuir iad chuige mi, *they have severely tried me.*
ch'uile, (*for* gach uile) Generally pronounced and written "a h-uile," which see.
chuilein, (a chuilein!) *int.* see cuilean.
chuimhnich, *past ind.* of cuimhnich.
chuir, *past aff.* of cuir.
chum, *past aff.* of cum.
chum, (see a chum) Thainig e dh'am ionnsaidh a chum furtachd a dheanamh orm, *he came to me for the purpose of aiding me;* a chum mo sgrios, *for the purpose of killing me.*
chum, *prep.* (a chum) For. 2 Towards. 3 Till. 4††In order to. [Governs the genitive case.]
chùm, see chum.
chun, *adv.* To, toward. 2 Thither. 3 Near, almost, on the eve. 4‡‡Until. Chun an taighe, *towards the house;* chun teireachdainn, *nearly exhausted;* chun éirigh, *on the eve of rising;* chun cogaidh, *for war;* chun mo mhic, *to my sons.* [Governs the genitive case—often pronounced and written *thun.***]
chunna, see chunnaic.
chunnacadh, *past aff. pass.* of faic.
chunnacas, *past aff. pass.* of faic. [Used in preference to the regular form *chunnacadh.*] Chunnacas e, *it was seen.*
chunnaic, *past aff.* of faic. Chunnaic mi, *I saw.*
†chunnairc, see chunnaic.
†chunnam, (*for* chunnaic mi.)
chunnas, see chunnacas.
†chunnacabhair, (*for* chunnaic sibh) You saw.
†chunnacadar, (*for* chunnaic iad) They saw.
†chunnacamar, (*emphatic* chunncamair-ne) We saw.
chunnacas, see chunnacas.
ci, (AF) *s.m. & f.* Animal, beast. 2 Hind, roe. 3 Stag, the leader. 4 Noble animal.
c' i ? (*for* cò i ? *or* cia i ?) *pron. interr.* Who is she ?
†ci, *s.f.* Lamentation.
†ci, *v.n.* Lament, wail, weep.
cia ? *pron. interr.* Which ? what? who? 2 How? 3 **Where ? Cia an uair ? *what hour ?* cia an duine ? *what man ?* cia aois thu ? *how old are you?* cia an taobh? *which side?* cia an t-ionad? *what place ?* cia b'e air bith de d' sheirbhisich aig am faighear e, *with whomsoever of thy servants it may be found.*
†cia, *s.m.* Man. 2 Husband. 3 Cream.
cia as ? *adv.* Whence ? Cia as air bith, *whencesoever, from whatever place.*
ciab, *s.m.* Lock of hair, ringlet. 2**Side lock.

ciaban, -ain, -an, see giaban.
ciabh, -a, -an, *s.f.* Side lock of hair. 2 The hair. 3 Ringlet. 4 Tress. Thuit i agus sgaoil a ciabha air an làr, *she fell and her tresses spread on the ground.*
ciabh,* *pr.pt.* a' ciabhadh, *v. a.* Tease, vex, gall. Tha e 'gam chiabhadh, *he is teasing me.*
———ach, -aiche, *a.* Hairy, bushy. 2 Having much or long hair. 3 Having ringlets, tressy.
ciabhag, -aig, -an, *s.f.* Small lock, small ringlet. 2 Whisker. 3* Lock or tress of hair. 4 *pl. only*, Mustachios.
ciabhagach, -aiche, *a.* Bushy, having curls, ringlets, locks or whiskers.
ciabhag-choille, *pl.* -an-coille, *s.f.* Wood-lark, see uiseag-choille.
†ciabharthan, see ceatha.
ciabh-bhachlach,-aiche, *a.*Having curled locks. 2 Tressy. Mo chaileag ch., *my tressy girl.*
ciabh-chasta, -chaiste, *pl.* -an-casta, *s.f.* Curled lock of hair.
ciabh-cheann-dubh, *s.f.* Deer's hair grass, see ciob-cheann-dubh.
†ciach, *s.m.* see ceathach. 2 Sorrow, concern.
†ciad, see ceud.
ciad, (CR) *s.m.* Opinion, impression.—*Strathtay.* Ghabh mi droch ch. dheth, *I formed a bad opinion of him.*
ciadach, see ceutach.
ciadamh,†† see ceudamh.
†ciadan, *s.m.* Height, altitude. 2 Moor.
Ciadaoin, -e, *s. f.* (Di-ciadaoin) Wednesday, (*lit.* day of the first fast‡—di-, + ceud + aoine)
———each, *a.* Falling on a Wednesday. 'Nuair is c. an t-Samhuinn *when Hallowmass falls on Wednesday.*—NGP.
ciad-bhainne, see ceud-bhainne.
ciad-bhileach, see ceud-bhileach.
cia dha? *adv.* see co dha?
ciad-dhuilleach, ciad-fhàire, } see ceud ——.
ciad-fhàs, ciad-ghin, ciad-laoigh, } see ceud——.
ciadlus, -uis, *s.m.* Curiosity.
———ach, ** *a.* Curious.
ciad-mheas, see ceud-mheas.
ciadna, see ceudna.
ciadnaich, see ciadaoineach.
cia fhada? *adv.* How long?
ciagach, *a.* Sly-humoured. *prov.*
cial, *s.m.ind.* Side or brim of a vessel. (see gial.
cia lion? *adv.* How many?
ciall, céille, *dat.* céill, *s.f.* Reason, sense. 2 Opinion. 3 Meaning. 4 Discretion, prudence. 5 Darling. 6*Understanding, wisdom. 7***rarely* Death. 8(AC) Inspiration. As a ch., *out of his senses, mad*; duine gun ch., *a madman*; ceann na céilie, *the prudent man,* (*lit.* the wise head); a chiall mo chridhe! *my heart's darling!* a ch. de na fearaibh! *my beloved of all men!* glac c., *be easy, do not forget yourself;* ciod e is c. dhuit? *what do you mean?* ciod e is c. do na daoine? *what do the people mean?* ciod e is c. dha sin? *what is the meaning of that?* ciod e is c. do m' aisling? *what is the interpretation of my dream?* tha e 'dhith céille, *he lacks understanding*; air bheag céille, *possessing little understanding*; is e 'n c. ceannaichte a's fearr, *wisdom bought (by experience) is best*; air call a chéille, *losing his senses, doting*; mo chiall! *my darling!* coimhead c., *regard discretion.*
[Very generally used as an expression of fondness or term of endearment, also to express desire, as, a chiall, *I would, I wish;* a chiall nach mise bh'ann, *I wish I had been there*; also as an expression of surprise, as, a chiall! *goodness!*]
ciallach,** -aich, *s.m.* Lover.
ciallach, -aiche, *a.* Judicious, rational, prudent, cautious, sensible, discreet. 2 *Sedate 3 Significant. Dean do ghnothach gu c., *do your business rationally;* ceilidh duine c. mas ladh, *a wise man covereth shame;* cho c. r cnoc, *as staid as a hill.*
———adh, -aidh, *s.m.* Meaning, signification, interpretation. A' c—, *pr. part.* of ciallaich. Signifying. Ciod tha thu a' ciallachadh? *what do you mean?* [This is a literal Gaelic translation of the Eng. idiom, the idiomatic Gael. form is given under *ciall.*
———ail, *a.* Emblematical. 2 Rational. 3 Significant, allusive.
———d,‡‡ *s.f.ind.* Advisedness. 2 Ingeniousness.
ciallag, *s.f.* Feminine form of ciallan.
ciallaich, *pr. part.* a' ciallachadh, *v.a.* Signify, mean, allude, design, interpret.
†ciallaideach, -eiche, *a.* see ciallach.
ciallaidheach, *a.* Significant.
ciallail, see ciallachail.
ciallairt, see cialtradh.
ciallan, -ain, -an, *s.m.* Favourite. A chiallain! *my dear!*
ciall-chagair, -air, *s.f.* Watch-word.
†ciall-chaisg, *s.f.* Example. 2 Check, warning.
ciall-chogair, see ciall-chagair.
†cialldha, *a.* see ciallach.
ciall-dhealbh,** *s.m.* Emblem.
ciall-ionnsachaidh, *s.f.* Acquired knowledge.
ciall-nàduir, *s.f.* Natural sense.
ciall-nàdurra, see c— -nàduir.
ciallradh, *s.m.* Full or complete sentence.
ciallsgur, (JGM) *s.* Upshot, final proceeding.
†ciallughadh, see ciallachadh.
†cialluigheach, see ciallach.
cialtradh, -aidh, -aidhean, *s.m.* Sentence. 2 **Proposal.
cia mar? *adv.* How? in what way? in what condition? in what state or manner? Cia mar tha thu? *how are you?* air na h-uile cia mar, *by all means,* (said in answer to *cia mar? in what way?*)
cia meud? *adv.* How many? how much? Cia meud a th' ann? *how many are there?* cia meud bliadhna tha thu? *how old are you?* (*lit.* how many years are you?)
†ciamh, see ciabh.
ciamhadh, *s.m.* Mauling. 2 Pelting—*Islay.*
†ciamhair, *a.* Sad, weary, lonely. Gu c., *sadly.*
†———e, *s.f.* Lamentation, wailing.
ciamhaireachd, *s.f.* Sadness. 2 Weariness. 3 Loneliness.
†ciamhchallach, *a.* Curl-haired.
†ciamhoir, see ciamhair.
cia minic? *adv.* How often?
cian, céine, *a.* Long, tedious, lasting. 2 Vast. 3 Far-distant, remote, foreign. 4**Causing regret or pain. Is c. an oidhche, *dreary is the night*; bu ch. leinn guin am buillean, *lingering was the pain of their blows*; gu c. nan c., *for ever and ever;* is c. mo leannan, *my love is far away*; sgeul cho binn cha chuala sinn o ch., *so sweet a tale we have not heard this long while.*
cian, *adv.* As long as, while, whilst. An c., *long since, long ago*; an c. a bhitheas mi beò, *as long as I live.*
cian, *dat.* céin, *s.m.* Distance of time or place. An céin, *at a distance*; bho chéin, *from afar*; is iomadh c. o nach robh e an seo, *it is a long time since he was here*; gu c. nan c., *to all eter-*

nity.

cianail, -e [& -ala,] *a.* Melancholy, mournful, sad, lamentable. 2 Pensive. 3 Solitary, lonely, lonesome, dreary. 4 Mild, gentle. 5 Loving. 6** Weary, fatigued, fatiguing, tedious, forlorn. 7(DC) *with another a.* Exceedingly. 8(MMcD) Amusing. Is c. m' aigne, *my thoughts are sad*; dà chraoibh ch., *two solitary trees*; c. fiadhaich, *exceedingly stormy—Uist;* duine c,, *an amusing fellow—Lewis.*

cianalach, -aiche,*a.* Solitary, lonely. 2 Pensive. 3 Sad, mournful, lamentable.

——d,* *s.f.* see cianalas.

cianalas, -ais, *s.m.* Melancholy, sorrow, sadness. 2 Mildness. 3 Dulness, pensiveness. 4**Wearisomeness. 5 (MMcD) Home-sickness. 6* Solitariness, loneliness, dreariness. A' cur dhinn ar c., *banishing our dreariness* ; thàinig smal oirnn le c., *we are darkened with sadness*; tha c. air, *he is home-sick.*

cianamh, *adv.* see a chianamh.

cianaran, -ain, -an, *s.m.* Melancholy person.

cian-fhuaim, *s.m.* Telephone.

——neach, *a.* Telephonic.

cian-fhulang, -aing, *s, m.* Patient meek endurance. 2**Perseverance. 3**Longanimity.

——ach, -aiche, *a.* Long-suffering. 2 **Persevering.

——as, -ais, see cian-fhulang.

cian-mhaireannach, *a.* Lasting, durable, continual, perennial.

cian-mhothachaidh,** *s.m.* Apathy.

cianog, -oig, -an, *s.f.* see cionag.

cian-òran, -ain, *pl.* -ain [& -an,] *s.m.* Mournful, plaintive song.

cian-sgeul, *s.m.* Telegram.

cian-sgriobhach, *a.* Telegraphic.

cian-sgriobhadh, -aidh, *s.m.* Telegram.

cian-sgriobhair, *s.m.* Telegraph.

cian-sgriobhadair, *s.m.* Telegraphist.

cian-shanasair, *s.m.* Telegraph, telephone.

cian-shanasach, *a.* **Telegraphic, telephonic.

†ciap, *v.a.* Vex, torment.

†——al, -ail, *s.f.* Strife, debate. 2**Quarrelling. 3**Vexation.

†ciapal, *v.a.* Encounter.

ciapalach, -aiche, *a.* †Contentious, quarrelsome. 2**Militant.

——d, *s.f.* Vexatiousness.

†ciapalaiche, *s. m.* Contentious, troublesome fellow, quarrelsome fellow.

ciapan,(DU) *s.m.* see giaban.

ciar,* *s. m.* Gloominess. 2 Dusk, evening. 3 Darkness. C. nan càrn, *the gloom of the rocks.*

ciar, céire, *a.* Dusky, dark grey. 2 Dark brown, swarthy. 3 Dun. 4 Roan. 5 Sable. 6 Gloomy. 7 Stern. Sléibhte nan earba c., *the hills of the dusky roes*; fonn c. a' bhròin, *the gloomy strain of grief ;* a ghaisgich chiar! *thou stern hero!* ciar imeachd an aineoil, *the dark path of the stranger.*

ciar, *pr.part.* a' ciaradh, *v.n.* Grow dusky. 2 Become grey or brown. 3 Become dark, gloomy or stern. Am feasgar a' ciaradh, *the evening growing dusky.*

ciara, *pl.* of ciar.

ciarach, -aich, -aichean, *s. m. & f.* Swarthy person of either sex.

ciarachadh, -aidh, *s. m.* State of becoming dusky, dark or grey. 2 Dusk. A' c—, *pr.pt.* of ciaraich. Darkening, making or becoming dark or dusky. 'S a' chiaradh, *in the dusk of evening.*

ciarachan,(AC) -ain, *s.m.* Wool-basket. It is open at the top, bulges out in the middle, and tapers in again towards the base. (called *mùrlag (f.)* and *mùrlainn (m.)* in *Argyll.*

ciaradh, see ciarachadh. C. nan speur, *the darkening of the heavens*; c. an anmoich, *the evening dusk.*

ciarag, -aig, -an, *s.f.* Any little dark-coloured creature. 2 Kind of beetle or bug. 3 Chafer. 4**Dark-brown haired girl. 5**Swarthy maid. 6††Any dark-coloured thing. 7‡‡ Dark grey cow. Ex. under bòid.

ciaraich, *pr.pt.* a' ciarachadh, *v.a. & n.* Grow dusky. 2 Make brown, dusky or grey.

†ciarail, *s.f.* Quarrel, brawl, fray.

†ciaralach, -aiche, *a.* Perverse, froward, quarrelsome.

ciaralachd, *s.f.ind.* Perverseness, quarrelsomeness, contentiousness.

ciaran††, -ain, *s.m.* Dark or swarthy man.

ciarcail, *a.* see ciocrach.

ciar-cheò, *s.m.* Dark mist, dusky mist. C. na h-oidhche, *the dusky mist of night.*

ciar-dhubh, -uibhe, *a.* Dark grey.

ciar-imeachd, *s.f.* Dark departure.

†ciarog, see ciarag.

ciarsach,(AF) *s.m.* Thrush, see smeòrach.

†ciarsain, *s.f.* Kerchief.

†ciarsan, -ain, *s.m.* Grumbling. 2**see ciarsain.

ciarsanachd,** *s.f.* Grumbling.

ciar-shuil, -shul, -suilean, *s. f.* Dark eye. 2 Scowling eye.

——each, *a.* Dark-eyed. 2 ‡Having a scowling eye. B'fhada spàirn nan ciar-shuileach, *long was the struggle of the dark-eyed (chiefs.)*

†ciarsuin, see †ciarsain.

†ciarsur, see ciarsain.

†ciarta, *part.* Waxed.

cias, ceòis, ciasan, *s.m.* Border, skirt, fringe, corner. 2†† see ceòs.

——ach, -aiche, *a.* Bordered, skirted, fringed, cornered. 2†† see ceòsach. 3(AH) Tangled wisp of wool or hair.

†ciasail, -ean, *s.f.* Strife, dispute, contention, brawl.

ciasalach, *a.* Quarrelsome, brawling.

ciat,* see ceutadh.

ciata, see ceuta.

ciatach, *a.* see ceutach.

——as, see ceutachas.

——d, see ceudachd.

ciatadh, see ceutadh.

ciataich, see ceutaich.

ciataiche, see ceutaiche.

ciataichead, see ceutaichead.

ciataidh, *gen.sing.* of ceutadh.

ciatamh,‡‡ -aimh, see ceutadh.

ciatfach, see ceutach.

——d, see ceutachd.

ciatfadh, see ceutadh.

cìb, -e, *s.f.* see cìob.

cìb-cheann-dubh, see cìob-cheann-dubh.

cibean, -ein, -an, *s.m.* Rump.

cibein, -ean, *s.m.* see cibean.

cìbeir, -ean, *s.m.* see ciobair.

——eachd, see ciobaireachd.

cibh,* *s.m.* *Skye* for cuithe. Wreath of snow.

cibheall, see giall.

cibhear,* *s.m.* Drizzling rain, drizzle.

cibhearg, -eirg, -an, *s.f.* Rag. 2 Little ragged woman. 3 Wisp of wool, grass, &c. [** gives *s.m.*]

cibheargach, *a.* Ragged. 2 Tawdry.

cibheargan, -ain, *s.m.* Little rag. 2 Little ragged wight.

cibhlean, *s.pl.* Jaws.

cibhrinn,* see cùrainn.

cìbidh, (ciob, *bite*) Mì-run a' mhillteir 'g iarraidh fàth chum do ch.—*Dain Iain Ghobha.*

cich, *dat.sing.* of cioch.
†cich, *s.m.* Greyhound.
ciche, *gen.sing.* of cioch. Ceann na ciche, *the nipple.*
cichean, *n.pl.* of cioch. C. liontach, *full breasts.*
cideach,(AF) *s.m.* Pet lamb.
†cidh, *v.a.* See, behold.
†cidh, *s.f.* Sight, view.
cidheal, see giall.
cidhean,(AF) *s.m.* Fat lamb.
cidhis, -e, -ean, *s.f.* Mask, disguise. 2 Vizor. Luchd cidhis, *masqueraders.*
———ear, -an, *s.m.* One wearing a mask, masquerader.
———earachd, *s.f.* Masquerade. 2**Masking.
cigeall, -gill, *s.m.* see diogailt.
———ach, see diogailteach.
———adh, see diogailteadh.
cigh, see ci. †2 *s.f.* Hind.
——each, (AF) *s.m.* Fat lamb.
cigil, *v.a.* see diogail.
——teach, -eiche, *a.* see diogailteach.
†cil, *s.f.* Ruddle, species of clay. 2 Death.
†cilcheis, *s.f.* Bad wool.
cileach, *a.* Piebald, speckled over the body—*Lewis.*
cileadair,* -ean, Prophet, soothsayer.
cileag, -eig, *s.f.* Thin spare female. 2††Frail old woman. 3(AH) Timid, pliant, irresolute man. Never used in *Lewis* to signify physical frailty, but one easily led, as, cileag dhuine, *a man easily deceived.*
cilean, -ein, -eanan, *s.m.* Large cod fish.—*Skye**
cilean, *s.pl.* see cibhlean.
†cilting, *s.f.* The belly.
cilig, -e, -ean, *s.m.* see cilean.
cill, -e, cilltean [& cillean] *s. f.* Cell, church. 2 Chapel. 3 Churchyard, burying-ground. 4 Grave. 5**Ruddle. 6‡‡Death. Thug am bàs an cuirp do 'n chill, *death has given their bodies to the cemetery.*
†cill, *s.f.* Partiality, prejudice.
Cille-, A form of *cill* prefixed to the names of builders of churches, as, Cille-Mhàilidh, Cille-Bride, Cille-Mhaodain, &c. Before a vowel or *fh* it is written *Cill'.*
cillean,(CR) *s.m.* Scamp.—*Blair Athole.* Is e c. grannda a th' ann, *he is a nasty scamp of a fellow.*
———,** see cillein.
cillein, -e, -ean, *s.m.* Repository. 2 Concealed heap. 3 Anything concealed from observation. 4 (Fionn) Small quantity—*Argyll.* C. eòrna, *a puckle barley;* nach d' rinn riamh de 'n t-saoghal cillean (cillein)—*Duanaire, p. 15.*
cilleorn,(AC) *s.m.* Urn. 2 Sacred vessel.
cillinn,** *s.f.* Chapel.
cill-inntinn, *s.f.* see cleith-inntinn.
cill-mhanach, *s.m.* Abbey, monastery.
cilltean, *n.pl.* of cill.
†cim, *v.a.* Captivate, capture, enslave.
†cim (*for* chi mi) I shall see.
†cim, *s.m.* Drop. 2 Money.
†cimcheartaich, *v.a.* Rifle, pillage.
cimeach, see ciomach.
———as,** -ais, *s. m.* Captivity, imprisonment, bondage, slavery.
cimich, *v.* see ciomaich.
†cimidh, -ean, see ciomach.
cin ? *adv.* Where ? whither ? to what place ? Cin a chaidh e ? *whither did he go ?* (ceana ? in *Argyll.*)
†cine, see cinneadh.
cineadach, see cinneadach.
cineadail, see cinneadail.
†cineadh, *s.m.* Country, nation. 2 Determining, decreeing.
cineal, -eil, -ealan, *s. m.* Offspring, progeny. 2 Sort, species, nature. 3 Extraction, race, tribe, clan. 4‡‡Kindness.
———ach,** *a.* In clans or tribes. 2 National. 3 Clannish. 4 Populous.
cinealta, *a.* see ceanalta. 2**Clannish.
———chd, *s.f.* see ceanaltachd. 2**Clannishness.
———s, -ais, *s.m.* see ceanaltas. 2**Clannishness.
cineamhuinn,** *s.* Random.
————each,** *a.* Fortuitous.
————eachd,** *s.f.* Fortuitousness.
cineanta,(CR) *a.* Agreeable. willing—*West of Ross.*
†cineil, *s.f.* Sort, kind, sex, gender. (see cineal.)
†cineil-Scuit, *s.pl.* The Scots.
†cineil-Sguit, see cineil-Scuit.
†cinfideach, *s.m.* Conception.
†cing, *a.* Strong.
†cing, *s.m.* Gaelic spelling of *king.* 2 Prince.
†cingeach, -eiche, *a.* Brave. 2**Strong. 3**Impetuous.
†cingeachd,** *s.f.* Bravery. 2 Strength. 3 Impetuousness.
†cingeadh, *s.m.* Courage, bravery. 2 Magnanimity.
cingean,** *s.m.* Keg.
Cingeis, see Caingis.
†cinid, *a.* Peculiar to a family.
cinionnan-crò, *s.m.* see cionnan-crò.
†cinmheath, *s.f.* Consumption.
†cinmhiol, *s.m.* Colours.
†———, *v.a.* Paint.
†———adh, *s.m.* Painting, image, picture. 2 Art of painting.
†———air, *s.m.* Painter.
cinn, *gen. sing. & n. pl.* of ceann.
cinn, *pr. part.* a' cinntinn, *v.n.* Grow, increase, become greater or more numerous, multiply, spring from. 2 Vegetate. 3* Result from, happen. 4 Grow taller. 5**Agree to.
†cinn-bheartas, -ais, *s.m.* Sovereignty, dominion.
†cinn-bheirt, *s.m.* Ruler, governor, see ceann-bheart
†————eadh, see ceann-bheartas.
†cinn-bheirteas, *s.m.* Dominion.
cinne, see cinneadh. †2 *s.f.* Megrim.
cinneach, -ich, *s.m.* Nation. 2 Heathen. 3 Gentile. 4 Surname, cognomen. 5*Heathen nation. Air feadh nan cinneach sin, *among those nations.*
cinneachadh, -aidh, *s. m.* Growing, growth. 2 Budding. 3 Vegetating. 4 Prospering. 5** Augmentation. A' c—, *pr.part.* of cinnich.
cinneachdach, -aiche, *a.* Vegetative. 2 Increasing in size.
————,** *s.m.* Accretion.
cinneachdaiche, *comp.* of cinneachdach.
cinneachdainn,** *s.m.* see cinneachadh.
cinneachduinn, *s.m.* Same meanings as cinneachadh. A' c—, *pr.part.* of cinnich.
cinneadach, -aiche, *a.* see cinneasach. 2** Clannish, in clans. Gu c., *clannishly.*
cinneadachd,** *s.f.* Vegetability.
cinneadail, -e, [& -dala,††] *a.* Attached to one's own name and family. 2 Clannish, partial to persons of the same name or clan, fond of a namesake. 3**Accretive. Cinneadail còir, *clannish and hospitable.*
cinneadalachd, *s.f.ind.* Clannishness, partiality for one's own name, clan, or kindred.
cinneadas, -ais, *s.m.* Clan, kindred. 2 Clanship. Do ch. còir, *thine honest kindred.*

cinneadh, -idh, -idhean, *s.m.* Clan, tribe, surname, relations, kin, kindred. 2**Progeny, offspring. 3‡‡ Preparing. 4‡‡ Happening. Fear-cinnidh, *a namesake, clansman;* bean-chinnidh, *a clanswoman ;* ceann-cinnidh, *a chieftain ;* an c. maiseach, treubhach, *the handsome, powerful clan.*

———, *v.n.* Decree.

cinneag, -eig, -an, *s.f.* Spindle—*Sutherl'd.* 2 Tuft of wool, especially wool on the spindle. 3 Coward.

cinnealtas,** -ais, *s.m.* Fondness, affection. 2 Clannishness.

†**cinneamhna**, *a.* Accidental.

†**cinneamhnach**, *a.* Fatal. 2**Accidental.

†**cinneamhuin**, *s.f.* Chance, accident, fortune, fate. Am agus c., *time and chance*; clach na c., (see Lia fàil) *the fatal stone.*

cinneas, -eis, *s.m.* Growth, vegetation. 2 Increase, produce, crop, fruit, production. 3 Access. A ch. agus 'fhochann, *its produce and brier.*

———ach, *a.* Fruitful. 2 Vegetative, inclined to grow, germinative, productive.

———achd, *s.f.* Fruitfulness. 2 Vegetativeness. 3* Vegetation, growth.

cinn-fheadhna, *pl.* of ceann-fheadhna.

†**cinnfhionn**, *a.* Bald-headed.

†**cinnfidh**, *v.n. fut.* (*for* orduichidh) Will order.

cinnich, *gen.sing.* & *n.pl.* of cinneach.

cinnich, *pr.part.* a' cinneachdainn [& a' cinneachadh] *v.a.* & *n.* Grow. 2 Rear. 3 Increase, abound. 4**Make to vegetate. Cha chinnich craobh ni's àillidh, *a fairer tree shall never grow*; an do ch. na caoraich dhuit am bliadhna? *did your sheep do well this year?* (*at the lambing season.*)

cinnidh, *gen. sing.* of cinneadh. 2 *fut. aff.* of cinn.

cinnire-cartach, *s. m.* (*for* ceannaire-cartach) Carter.

†**cinnlitir**, see ceann-litir.

†**cinn-mhire**, *s.f.* Frenzy. 2 Insanity.

cinn-ruidhe, *s.pl.* Timbers in a boat, see bàta.

†**cinnseach**, -sich, *s.m.* Want, need.

cinnseal, -eil, -an, *s.m.* Commencement, origin, beginning. 2 Want, necessity, hardship. 3 *Contact. 4**Desire. 5** Search. 6 (AC) Possession. 7 (DC) Pretence.—*Argyll.* An c. dol do 'n chlachan chaidh e dh' iasgach, *pretending to go to church he went a-fishing*; a' dol an c. gàbhaidh, *getting in contact with danger;* is coma leam dol 'na ch., *I do not like to get in contact with it;* bitheadh Micheal an c. an anama ghaoil, *may M. take charge of the beloved soul.*

cinnt, -e, *s.f.* Certainty. 2 Truth. 3 Confidence, reliance, assurance. Cha'n 'eil c. 'nam beul, *there is no certainty in their lips*; air chinnt, *certainly, most assuredly, decidedly so.*

cinnte, *gen.sing.* of cinnt.

cinnte, *a.* see cinnteach. 2‡‡Continual.

cinnteach, cinntiche, *a.* Certain, positive, assured, sure, confident. 2 Unerring, exact. 3 Plain, evident, obvious. 4 Definite in *gram.* Saighde cho c. ris a' bhàs, *arrows as sure as death*; nach c. a làmh! *how unerring his hand is!* am bheil thu c.? *are you quite sure?* tha mi làn ch., *I am quite certain*; mo ghille c. féin, *my own confidential servant*; tha mi c. as, *I am certain of it.*

———as, -ais, *s.m.* Same meanings as cinnteachd.

———d, *s.f.ind.* Certainty, actuality, assurance, positiveness, confidence. 2 Clearness, unquestionableness. 3 Evidence. 4** Sureness of aim. 5*Demonstration.

cinnteadair, -ean, *s.m.* Insurer, assurer.

†**cinnteagal**, see cinnteagan.

cinnteagan, -ain, *s.m.* Coarse cloak.

cinntealas, -ais, *s. m.* Certainty, assurance. Am bheil cinntealas agad air? *are you sure of it?*

†**cinntich**, *v.a.* Appoint, determine. 2 Ascertain.

cinntinn, *s.m.* Growing, vegetating, increasing. 2 Prospering. 3**Becoming. 4**Growth. A' c—, *pr. pt.* of cinn. [** gives *s.f.*]

†**cinn-treun**, *a.* Headstrong, obstinate.

ciob, -a, *s. f.* Tufted scirpus, deer's hair, heath club rush. see ciob-cheann-dubh. 2 Tow, refuse of flax. 3* Sponge—*Islay.* 4(AF) Sheep. 5 Sheep stock. 6‡‡Hand. C. nan ciar-bheann, *the grass of the dusky hills.*

ciob,* *a.* Spongy, porous. Mòine ch., *spongy* or *porous peats.*

ciob, *v.a.* Bite. 2 Wound, maim.

ciobach, -aiche, *a.* Abounding in tufted scirpus.

cioba-cloimhe, (AF) *s.f.* Woolly sheep.

ciobair, *s.m.* (ciob) Shepherd. Fead c. an aonaich, *the whistle of the mountain shepherd.*

———eachd, *s.f.* Herding of sheep. Ris a' ch., *herding sheep.*

ciob-cheann-dubh,§ *s.f.* Tufted scirpus, deer's hair, *or* heath club rush—*scirpus cæspitosus,* (Badge of the MacKenzies.) 2(AC) Flaky peat.

ciobhal, -ail, cibhlean, see gial. 2††see ciobhull. 3 (DC) Door-catch or "sneck."

ciobhraig, *s.f.* *Skye* for eùrainn.

ciobhull, -uill, *pl.* [-uill &] cibhlean, *s.m.* Jaw-bone. 2††Door-jamb.

†**cioblaid**, *s.f.* Trouble.

†———each, -eiche, *a.* Troublesome, tedious, clumsy.

†**ciobrathach**, *a.* Chattering, twittering.

143. Ciob-cheann-dubh.

ciocar, -air, -an, *s.m.* Hungry, ravenous creature.

ciocarach, *a.* see ciocrach.

ciocaraiche, *comp.* of ciocarach.

†**ciocardha**, see ciocrach.

cioch, *gen.* ciche, *dat.* cich, *pl.* ciochan, [& -a] *s.f.* Woman's breast, pap. 2 Nave of a wheel. Cioch a' mhuineil, *or* cioch a' bhràghaid, *the uvula;* c. an t-sluigein, *the sac that propels the food into the gullet*; leanabh ciche, *a babe*; bainne mo chìocha, *the milk of my breasts.*

ciochair,** *s.m.* Stingy man.

144. Ciochan.

ciochan, -ain, *s.m.* Long-tailed tit-mouse—*parus caudatus.* 2 *n.pl.* of cioch.

——— -fada,¶ *s.m.* Long-tailed tit-mouse, see ciochan.

——— -nan-cailleach-marbha,§ *s.m.* Foxglove, *Skye* for lus-nam-ban-sìth.

ciocharan, -ain, -an, *s.m.* Suckling, infant on the breast.

ciocharanachd, *s.f.* Condition of a babe or suckling. 2 Management of a suckling child.

cioch-bhràghad, ciche-, -an-, *s.f.* The uvula.

cioch-chinn, *s.f.* The uvula.

cioch-mhuineil, *s.f.* The uvula.

ciochrach,(AC) -aich, *s.m.* **Breastling.**
ciochran, see **ciocharan.**
————achd, see **ciocharanachd.**
cioch-shlugain, *s.f.* **The muscular sac which propels the food into the gullet, the uvula.**
†**ciocht,** *v.a.* **Rake, scrape.**
†————, *s.m.* Carver. 2 **Engraver.** 3 **Weaver.** 4 Children.
†————adh, *s.m.* **Engraved work.**
ciocrach, -aiche, *a.* Greedy of food, ravenous, voracious. 2 Longing, as a female. 3**Avaricious. Gu c., *ravenously;* an t-anam c. lionaidh e, *he shall fill the hungry soul* ; Roimhich ch., *avaricious Romans.*
ciorachd,‡‡ *s.f.* see ciocras.
ciocras, -ais, *s.m.* Earnest longing. 2 Hunger. 3 Ravenousness, greediness, avariciousness. 4 Excessive desire. 5**False appetite. Air chiocras fola, *through thirst for blood.*
————ach, -aiche, *a.* see ciocrach.
————an, -ain, *s. m.* Hungry fellow. 2** Greedy fellow.
ciod ? *interr. pron. ind.* What ? Ciod seo ? *what is this?* c. air son? *why ?* c. tha thu ag ràdh ? *what do you say ?* c. ged a tha, *what though there be;* c. ged a bhitheadh, *what though there were;* c. mu dhéidhinn? *what about it ?* c. e an t-astar a tha Caoilte de 'n fhiadh? *or* c. e an t-astar anns am bheil C. de 'n fhiadh? *how far is C. from the deer ?* c. gus an tig e, *what it shall come to ;* an cadal dhuit ? ciod e ma's e ? ma's e, cha bhi, *are you asleep ? what if I am ? if you are, you will not be so long*—Gaelic idiomatic way of saying "wake up, the enemy is near"—*Waifs & Strays.*
†**ciodar,** *adv.* Wherefore.
†**ciodh,** What.
†**ciodhfa** ? (ciod am fàth?) Wherefore ? for what cause ? how many ?
†**ciodhfar** ? (ciod am fàth air ?) see †ciodhfa ?
ciog,(AF) *s.m.* Beast, animal.
ciogail, *v.a.* see diogail.
ciogailt, -e, *s.f.* see diogailt. 2‡‡Terror.
————each, -eiche, *a.* see diogailteach.
†**ciogal,** see cuigeal.
ciogladh, -aidh, *s.m. & pr.pt.* see diogladh.
cioguilt, -e, see diogailt.
†**ciol,** *a.* Squint.
†**ciol,** *s.m.* see cill. 2 Death. 3 **Inclination, propensity.**
†**ciolach,** *s.m.* Small fry.
†**ciolag,** -aig, *s.f.* Hedge-sparrow. 2**Store, provision.
ciolam, -aim, *s.m.* Vessel.
ciolar,** -air, *s.m.* Linsey-woolsey.
ciolarn,** *s.m.* Vase.
†**ciolcach,** *s.f.* see cuilc.
†**ciollach,** *a.* Superior, master of.
ciollam,(DU) see ciorram.
†**ciolrath,**** *v.n.* Chatter, twitter.
†**ciolrathach,** *a.* Chattering.
ciom, -aichean, *s.m.* Comb. 2 Wool-card.
ciom, *pr.part.* a' ciomadh, *v.a.* Comb, card or teaze wool.
————ach,** *a.* Restless.
————ach, -aich, *s.m.* Prisoner, slave, captive. 2**Restless fellow. Ceud-ghin a' chiomaich, *the first-born of the captive.*
ciomachas, -ais, *s.m.* Captivity, slavery, bondage, imprisonment. Thug t' aghaidh gach aon an c., *thy face has brought everyone into captivity.*
ciomadh, -aidh, *s.m.* Fault.
ciomaich, *v.a.* Imprison.
ciomaidh, see ciomach.
cioman, -ain, *s.m.* Comb or card for dressing wool. 2 Kitt. 3**Combing, teazing. 4 Skimming-dish.
ciombal, -ail, -an, *s.m.* **Bell.** 2 **Cymbal.**
————air, -ean, *s.m.* **One who plays on cymbals.**
ciomboll, -oill, -oillean, *s.m.* **Bundle of hay** or straw.—*Hebrides.*
cion, *s.m.ind.* Desire, love, esteem, fondness. 2 **Fault. 3**Cause. 4‡‡Want, defect. C. léirsinn, *want of sight, defect of vision;* an c. air a leannain, *fond of her lovers;* mo ch. ort, *I love thee* ; le c. a bhi 'ga chleachdadh, *in consequence of neglecting to practise it;* c. faobhair, *want of edge, bluntness.*
†**cion,**‡ see ciont.
c' ionadh ? *adv.* Whither ?
cionag, -aig, -an, *s.f.* †Kernel. 2 Small coin. 3 Small piece of land (¼ of a cléiteag and ⅛ of a farthing-land.)
cionail, *a.* Desirous, fond. 2 Defective. 3 Guilty. C. air móran fiona, *fond of much wine.*
cion-aire, *s.f.* Inattention.
————achail, *a.* Inattentive.
cionalta, see ceanalta.
†**cionamhuil,** -e, *a.* Desirable.
cionar, -air, *s.m.* Music, melody, song. Ri c., *singing.*
†**cion-chorran,** -ain, *s.m.* Hook.
cion-cnàmhaidh,‡‡ *s.m.* Indigestion.
cionda, see ceudna.
cion-eòlach, *a.* Ignorant.
cion-eòlais, *s.m.* Ignorance, lack of knowledge.
cionfa, see cion-fàth.
cion-fàbhair,** *s.m.* Disfavour.
cion-falaich, *s.m.* Secret, ardent love.
cion-faobhair, *s.m.* Bluntness, want of edge.
cion-fàth, *s. m.* Occasion, cause, reason or ground of any proceeding or occurrence. 2** Quarrel. C. 'n ar n-aghaidh, *occasion against us* ; gun ch., *without reason.*
cion-fhaobhair,** see cion-faobhair.
cion-fhoighidinn, *s.m.* Impatience.
cion-léirsinn, *s.m.* Blindness, defect of vision 2**Shortness of sight.
cion-maoidheim,** *s.m.* Disfavour.
cion-meirbhidh,* *s.m.* Indigestion.
cion-mhaireann,** *a.* Continual.
cion-mhaireannach,** *a.* Continual.
cionmhor,** *a.* Lovely.
cion-modh,** *s.m.* Bluntness, disrespect.
cion-mothachaidh, *s.m.* Apathy. 2 Insensibility. 3 Want of sense or feeling. 4 (DU) Thoughtlessness.
cionn, *s. m. ind.* Reason, ground, occasion, cause, sake, quest, purpose. A chionn gu, *because that.*
cionn, (os cionn *prep.*) Old dative case of *ceann.*
cionnabharr,* *s.m.* Commode. 2 Hood.
cionnachd, *s.m.* (ceann-aghaidh) Face.
cionnan-cro, *s. m.* The "leader" of a school of whales. Seachd mucan-mara beaga, sàth cionnan-crò, *seven small whales a full meal for a bull whale.*
cionnarra, *a.* Identical. †2(AC) White-headed.
cionnas ? *adv.* How ? in what way or manner ? by what means ? A dh' fhaicinn c. a dh'ainmicheadh e iad, *to see how he would name them* ; c. a thàinig orra claoidh ? *how has trouble come upon them ?* c. a tha thu ? *how do you do ?*
cionnfath, see cion-fàth.
cionnsaich, see ceannsaich.
cion-omhaill,** *s. m.* Recklessness. (cion-umhail)
†**cionradharc,** *s.m.* Fate. 2 Want of sight.
cionradharcach, -aiche, *a.* Deficient in vision.

2 Deficient in foresight. 3‡‡Illiberal, stingy.
†cionran, -ain, *s.m.* Melancholy music.
cion-seirce, *s.m.* Disaffection.
cion-sgeòil,(AC) *s.m.* Propensity.
ciont, -a, *pl.* -a [& -an,] *s.m.* Guilt, crime, sin, fault, blame. Dean c., *sin, offend*; na maith an c., *pardon not their sin*; gun ch., *blameless*
——ach, -aiche, *a.* Guilty, at fault, sinful, criminal.
——ach, -aich, *s.m.* Culprit,criminal,defaulter.
——achadh, -aidh, *s.m.* Trespassing, transgressing, sinning, blaming. 2 Act of contracting guilt. A' c—, *pr.part.* of ciontaich. Le c. am aghaidh, *with trespassing against me.*
——achd,* *s.f.* Degree of guilt. 2 Sinfulness.
——aich, *pr.pt.* a' ciontachadh, *v.a.* & *n.* Trespass, transgress,sin,blame, be guilty. Chiontaich iad am aghaidh, *they sinned against me*; cha ch. sibh, *ye shall not sin.*
ciontaiche,** *s.m.* Aggressor.
cion-teas,** *s.m.* Chilliness.
cion'thar, -air, see cionar.
†cion-tìre, *s.f.* Tax, tribute.
cion-tùir,‡‡ -e, *s.m.* Foolishness.
ciopair,** see ciobair.
†ciopallaich, *s.f.* Galling.
ciopan, -ain, *s. m.* see cipean 1.
†cior, -a, -an, *s.f.* Comb. 2 Jaw. 3 The cud of ruminating animals. 4 Hand. 5 Agent.
†cior, *v.a.* see cìr.
ciora, -an, [*pl.* cioirachan—*Lewis*]*s.f.* Pet lamb. 2 Sheep that feeds with cows. 3 Cud chewer. 4 Ewe-teg.
ciorag, see ciora.
cioralta, *a.* Cheerful.
†ciorb, *v.a.* & *n.* Mangle. 2 Mortify. 3 Become black.
ciorbail, -e, *a.* Snug, close-wrapped.
†ciorbh, *v.a.* Take away, mutilate.
†———adh, *s.m.* Mutilating, mangling.
†———tha, *a.* & *past pt.* of ciorbh, Hurt, lacerated.
ciorcail, -e, *a.* see ciocrach.
†ciorcal, -ail, -an, *s.m.* see cearcall.
†ciorghal, *s.m.* Bravery.
†———,** *a.* Brave, fearless. 2 Strong. Bi c. treubhanta, *be fearless and strong.*
ciorra, (*for* cèarra) *comp.* of cèarr.
ciorraidh ! see ciridh.
ciorram, -aim, -an, *s. m.* Mischief, disaster, accident, mishap. 2 Maim, hurt, defect in a person's body. 3 Damage, wounding.
————ach, -aiche, *a.* Mutilated, maimed, deformed by accident. 2 Pernicious, dangerous, destructive, hurtful. 3 Accidental, untoward. 4* Painful. 5**Mean. 6**Blemished. 7**Causing a flaw or blemish.
————achd,** *s.f.* Lameness. 2 State of being maimed.
†ciorrbhach, -aidh, *s. m.* Wearing, spending, consuming. 2 Mangling.
ciorrtham, -aim, -an, see ciorram.
ciorrumach, *a.* see ciorramach.
ciorusgrach,** -aiche, *a.* Clearing, driving away with the hands.
†ciorusgraich, *s.f.ind.* Clearing, driving away with the hands.
†cios, -a, *s.f.* Wages of a nurse.
†cios, *s.f.* Petition. 2(AC) see cìs. 3‡‡Sin.
†ciosach, -aiche, *a.* Importunate. 2 Sluggish, slovenly. Gu c., *importunately.*
ciosachadh, -aidh, *s.m.* Restraining, act of restraining. 2 Subduing, quieting, calming, appeasing. A' c—, *pr.pt.* of ciosaich.
ciosachdach,** *a.* Importunate. 2 Sluggish. 3 Slovenly.
ciosaich, *v.a.* see ciosnaich,
———e, -ean, see ciosnaiche.
———te, *a.* & *past pt.* of ciosaich, see ciosnaichte.
ciosal,** -ail, *s.m.* Wages of a nurse.
ciosan, -ain, -an, *s.m.* Basket. 2 Corn-skep. 3††Box.

145. Ciosan. (ill. by MMcD)

——— -arain, *s.m.* Bread-basket.
——— -bafair, *s.m.* Vessel made of sea-bent, see brà 15, p. 112.
——— -clòimhe, *s.m.* Large spherical baske with an opening in the side.
——— -mine, *s.m.* Basket circular like a beehive, for holding meal.
——— -mùrain, *s.m.* Another name for ciosanmine.—*Lewis.* 2(DM) Another name for ciosan bafair, (see brà 15, p. 112.)
cios-chàin, *s.f.* Tribute, tax, assessment.
cioslaich, see ciosnaich. O chioslaich am bàs thu, *since death subdued you—Rob Donn.*
cios-mhór, -oire, *a.* Exacting tribute.
ciosnach,†† -aiche, *a.* Tiresome.
ciosnachadh, -aidh, *s.m.* Act of conquering, subduing, appeasing, quieting, calming. 2‡‡ Wearing out, oppressing. A' c—, *pr. pt.* of ciosnaich. Tha 'n tìr air a c., *the land is subdued.*
ciosnachail, *a.* Placable, tranquillizing. 2* Overpowering. 3 Made to pay tribute. 4††see ciosnaichte.
ciosnaich, *pr. pt.* a' ciosnachadh, *v.a.* Overpower, conquer, subdue. 2 Appease, quiet, calm, restrain.
ciosnaiche, *s.m.* Conqueror, subduer. 2 Appeaser.
ciosnaichte, *a.* & *past pt.* of ciosnaich. Conquered, subdued, appeased.
ciosnuich, see ciosnaich.
ciotach, -aich, *s.m.* Left hand.
ciotach, -aiche, *a.* Left-handed. 2 Awkward. 3 Cunning, crafty, designing. 4 Sinister, defective. Duine c., *a left-handed man.*; Colla c., *Colkitto.*
———d, *s.f.* see ciotaiche.
ciotadh,** *s.m.* Pail.
ciotag, -aig, -an, *s. f.* Left hand. 2 Cunning unlooked-for trick. 3 Little plaid or scarf. 4 Rag. Ghabhainn ort le m' chiteaig (chiotaig), *I would take you, fight you, with my left hand.*
ciotaiche, *s.f.* Left-handedness, habit of using the left hand more than the right. 2 Awkwardness.
ciotaiche, *comp.* of ciotach.
†ciotan, *s.m.* see ciotag.
cioth, -a, *s.m.* see cìth.
——ach, see cìtheach.
†ciothramach, -aiche, *a.* see ciorramach. 2‡‡ Mean.
†ciothruimich, *s.pl.* Abject persons.
ciotog, see ciotag.
cip, *gen.sing.* & *nom. pl.* of ceap. 2 Ranks,files.
cipean, -ein, -an, *s. m.* Stump, stake, peg, tether-stake. 2 Stick or dibble for planting. Cuir air c., *tether.*
cìr, *gen.sing.* of cìar
cìr, *pr. pt.* a' cìreadh *v. a.* Teaze or comb, as wool. 2 Curry-comb. 3 Hackle, as wool. Cìr t'fhalt, *comb your hair.*
cìr, -e, -ean, *s. f.* Comb. 2 Honey-comb. 3 Crest of a cock. 4 Cud. 5 Jaw. 6* Part of

a key containing the checks. 7(AC)Sheep. 8 (AC)Cud-chewing animal. Tha a' bhó a' cnàmh na cìre, *the cow is chewing the cud* ; eun cìr-dhearg an aonaich, *the red-crested fowl of the heath*.
†cirb,** *a.* Swift, fleet.
cirb,(AH) *s.f.* Skirt, tail, pendant, appendix, edge. Ghlac mi c. a' chòta aige, *I seized the tail of his coat*.
cirb, *dat.* of cearb.
cìrcean-caorainn,(AF) *s.m.* Mountain finch, see bricein-caoruinn.
circe-ball, *s.m.* Shuttlecock.
circ-fheòil, *s.f.* Flesh of a hen or chicken.
†cird (cèaird) *s.f.* Employment.
cìr-dhearg,‡‡ *a.* Red-crested.
cire, see cìr 7.
cìreach,‡‡ -eich, -eichean, *s.m.* Comb-case.
———, -eiche, *a.* Crested. 2 Having a comb. 3 Of, or belonging to, a comb, or crest. 4** Combing, inclined to comb. Cha mhinnean gorm no coileach c. e, *it is neither a grey kid nor a crested cock*.
cìreachan, -ain, *s.m.* Comb-case.
cìreadh, -idh, *s.m.* Combing, act of combing. 2 Teazing, as of wool. A' c—, *pr.pt.* of cìr. Tha a cuaileanan gèarrte gun chìreadh, *her shorn locks are without combing—Duanaire*, 14.
cìreag, -eig, -an, *s.f.* see ciora. 2††Little comb.
———ach,‡‡ -aiche, *a.* Abounding in little combs.
cìrean, -ein, *pl.* -an [& -einean,] *s. m.* Crest. 2 Metal badge or family crest, as worn on belts, bonnets, &c. 3 Cock's comb. 4 Coaming of a boat, see bàta, F4 p. 73.
———ach, -aiche, *a.* Crested. 2 Of, or belonging to, a comb or crest. 3 Like a crest.
cìreanach,(MMcD) -aich, *s.f.* Short seaweed that grows nearest high-water mark on a beach or shore—*Lewis*.
cìrean-choilich,§ *s. m.* Red campion,—*lychnis diurna*.
cìrean-tarsuing, *s.m.* Coaming of a boat, see bàta, F4 p. 73.
cìr-eich,* *s.f.* Currycomb.
cìreineach, see cìreanach.
cìre-mheal, see cìr-mheala.
ciridh ! *int.* Call addressed to a goat or sheep—*North Highlands*.
ciridh, *s.f.* see ciora. 2 see ceairidh. 3(AC) see cìr 7.
cìr-mheala, *s.f.* Honeycomb. Mar ch., *as a honeycomb*.

146. Cìrean-choilich.

cìs, -e, -ean, *s.f.* Tax, tribute, impost, rent, oblation. 2 Homage, submission, 3 Reverence. 4**Aid. Thoireadh Cuchulainn dhomh c., *let C. yield me tribute* ; fo ch., *under subjection* ; tha 'n dàmh fo ch. aige, *he has brought the stag low* ; thug am bàs fo chìs iad, *death has brought them low* ; seirbhiseach do ch., *a servant to tribute*.
cìs-badhar,‡‡ *s.f.* Excise.
cìs-bhuailteach, *a.* Taxable, liable to tax.
cìs-chachaileith, *s.f.* Turnpike charge.
cìs-chàin,** *s.f.* Tribute, tax. 2 Poll-tax.
cisd, see ciste.
cisde, ,,
cisdeag, -eig, *s.f.* (cisteag) *dim.* of ciste.
†cisdeamhuil, *a.* Capsular. 2 Hollow. 3 Like a chest.
cìs-dhiolach,* *a.* Assessable.
cìseach,†† *a.* Of, or pertaining to, tax or tribute.
†ciseal, *s.m.* Nurse's wages. 2 The Devil.
†ciseal, (co-iosal) *a.* Low, as if between two waters.
†cisean, -ein, *s.m.* Little chest, coffer. 2*Hamper—*Islay*.
cisean-bafair, see ciosan-bafair.
cisean-mùrain, see ciosan-mùrain.
cìsear, -eir, -an, *s.m.* Exciseman, tax-gatherer.
cìsearachd, *s.f.* Business of an exciseman or tax-gatherer.
cìse-bhuailteach, see cìs-bhuailteach.
cis-fheart, *s.f.* Mixed cloth. Ri fuachd Fèill-Bride foghnaidh c., *for Candlemas cold, mixed stuff will do*—N.G.P.
cìsire, see cìsear.
cìs-leagadair, see cìs-leagair.
cìs-leagadh,*-aidh, *s.m.* Assessment, assessing.
cìs-leagair, *s.m.* Assessor.
cìs-mhaor, -mhaoir, *s,m.* Tax-gatherer, †publican. Caraid chìs-mhaor, *a friend of "publicans."*
cìs-righ,* *s.f.* Allegiance. 2 Excise.
ciste, *pl.* cisteachan, *s.f.* Chest, box, coffer. 2 Coffin. 3**Treasure. 4***rarely* Cake.
——ach,‡‡ -eiche, *a.* Chested.
——achan, *n.pl.* of ciste.
cisteag, -eig, -an, *s.f.* Small chest or box.
——— -thàirneach,* *s.f.* Drawer.
cìs-teallaich,* *s.f.* Fumage.
cistean, -ein, *s.m.* *dim.* of ciste. Little chest, little trunk.
†cisteanach, -aich, -aichean, *s.f.* Kitchen.
†cisteanadh, -aidh, *s.m.* Rioting.
cistear, *s.m.* Cashier.
ciste-chaol,(MMcD) *s.f.* Wooden settee, with bottom and sides closed in, and lid on top, about 7ft. long, placed towards the wall and near the fire in a black house—*Lewis*. also "beinge." 2 *poetically* Coffin.
cisteil,** *a.* Capsular.
ciste-mhairbhe,** *s.f.* Coffin. Chuireadh ann an c. e, *he was put into a coffin*.
ciste-mhine, *s.f.* Meal-chest.
cistin, -e, -ean, Gaelic spelling of *kitchen*.
———each, -eiche, *a.* Deriv. of *kitchen*. Culinary. 2 Low bred.
———eadh,** -nidh, *s.m.* Rioting.
citeag, see ciotag.
citean,(AF) *s.m.* Lamb.
†cìtear, see chìthear.
cith,-e,-ean,*s.m.* Shower,heavy rain,mist. 2 Ardour. 3**Havoc. 4**Peal. 5‡‡Particle.—*Sut'd* 6 (AC)Lake. 7 Snow-drift—*Skye*. †8 Rage, fury, ire. This meaning is preserved in "cith-chath," as, chuir e 'na chith-chath e, *he tore it in shreds* (*lit.* the ardour of battle)—*Suth'd* said of anyone impatient to do anything (AG.) ; tha e an cith falbh, *he is eager to be off* ; cith na fola, *the shower of blood*; an cith, *in the mood, attuned* ; *eager to do anything* ; cathadh na fuar chithibh, *drift in cold showers*.
cith-chaolan, -ain, *s.m.* Vomiting.
cith-chath, *s.f.* Ardour or impatience to begin a battle. 2(DMy) Hurry scurry—*Lewis*.
cithe, see cuithe.
citheach, -eiche, *a.* Showery. 2 Destructive, wasteful. 3 Furious, keen.
citheal, see ciall. 2 see giall.
cithean, -ein, *s. m.* Complaining, lamenting, grumbling.
———ach, -aiche, *a.* Complaining, grumbling.
cithein,†† *s.m.* see cithean.
———each,†† *a.* see citheanach.
cithiurach, -aiche, *a.* Showery.
cithris-chaithris, *s.f.ind.* Confusion, tumult, commotion, hurly-burly. 2 ††Loquacity.

citsin, see cistin.
———**each**, see cistineach.
ciùbhrach, -aiche, see ciùbhran. Frasan a thig 'nan c., *showers that come in drizzle.*
ciùbhragaich, *s.f.* see ciùbhran.
ciùbhran, *s.m.* Small drizzling rain.
ciuch, *s.m.* Pass.
ciuchach,(AC) *a.* Plaintive.
ciuchair, *a.* Beautiful. 2 Dimpling.
ciùcharan, -ain, *s. m.* Low-voiced, plaintive lamentation.
†**ciuchlaith**, *v.a.* Hear.
ciùcran,‡‡ see ciùcharan.
ciud-siorraig,(DC) *s.f.* The modern wool-winder with an arrangement of toothed wheels, worked by the revolving winder and with a spring which makes a sound when the number of threads forming a "cut" is wound on the rim of the winder-wheel—*Uist.*
ciùil. *gen.sing.* of ceòl.
†**ciùileabhar**, *s.m.* Greyhound.
ciùin, -e, *a.* Calm, gentle, meek, mild, amiable. 2 Smooth, agreeable to the touch. 3 Unruffled, placid, peaceful, quiet, composed. Agus bha 'n duine Maois ro ch., *and the man Moses was very meek;* feasgar c., *a still evening;* aodach c., *smooth cloth,* [McA says *North* after this, but "aodach mìn" is the correct expression]; cha ch. e, *he is not mild.*
ciùin, *pr.pt.* a' ciùineadh, *v.a.* see ciùinich.
ciùine, *s.f.ind.* Mildness, gentleness, meekness. 2 Calmness, peacefulness, tranquillity. 3 Quietness, repose. 4**Smoothness. 5** Gentle gale. C. mhór, *a great calm.*
——, *comp.* of ciùin. More or most calm.
———**ach**,** *a.* Assuasive.
———**achadh**, -aidh, *s.m.* Appeasing, quieting, calming, pacifying, assuagement. A' c—, *pr pt.* of ciùinich.
———**achail**,** *a.* Appeasable.
———**achair**,** *s.m.* Appeaser.
———**achd**, see ciùineas.
———**ad**, -eid, *s.f.* Degree of calmness. 2 Increase of calmness or smoothness. A' dol an c., *increasing in calmness.*
———**adair**,** *s.m.* Calmer.
———**as**, -eis, *s.m.* Calmness, quietness, mildness, meekness. 2 Gentleness. 3 Smoothness. 4 Composure.
ciùinich, *pr.pt.* a' ciùineachadh, *v.a.* Appease, calm, still, pacify, assuage. Ch. e iad, *he stilled them;* ciùinichidh tìodhlac, *a gift will pacify.*
ciùinichte, *past pt.* of ciùinich. Pacified, appeased, calmed.
†**ciùird**, *prov.* for cèaird. 2 *gen. sing.* & *n. pl.* of cèaird. 3 Covering.
†**ciùirinich**, *v.a.* Cover.
†**ciùirt**, *s.f.* Rag.
†——,** *v.a.* Tatter.
ciùirteach, -eiche, *a.* see ciùrrail.
ciùlan,** *s.m.* Murmur.
———**ach**,** *a.* Murmuring.
ciulcharan,(CR) *s. m.* Warbling, singing of birds.—*West of Ross-shire.*
†**ciumhas**, -an, *s.m.* Border, selvidge, "list" of cloth.
†———**ach**, *a.* Having a border or selvidge.
ciùnachair,** see ciùineachair.
ciùnadair, see ciùineadair.
†**ciùnas**, see ciùineas.
ciùr, see ciùrr.
†**ciùr**, *s.m.* Merchant.
†**ciùra**, *a.* Marketable, merchantable.
ciùrach, -aich, *s.f.* see ciùbhran. 2**Querimoniousness.
———**dan**,** see ciùlan.
———**danach**,** *a.* Murmuring.
———**danachd**, see ciùrach 2.
ciùrair, *s.m.* Gaelic spelling of *curer.*
ciùran,†† -ain, *s.m.* Drizzling rain. *also* ciùbhran. (sgiùran—*Argyll.*)
———**ach**,†† *a.* Rainy.
ciùrlan, see ciùlan.
———**ach**,** see ciùlanach.
———**achd**, see ciùlan.
ciùrr, *pr. pt.* a' ciùrradh, *v.a.* Hurt, torture, agonize. 2††Harm, injure, blemish. 3 Put to pain, smart. 4 Cause loss or damage.
———**ach**,** see ciùrrail.
ciùrradair, -e, -ean, *s.m.* Tormentor, one who hurts or pains.
ciùrradh, -aidh, -aidhean, *s.m.* Hurt, injury, wound. 2 Act of hurting or wounding. 3 Aggrieving. 4**Blemish. A' c—, *pr. pt.* of ciùrr. Chum mo ch., *to my harm;* fhuair e 'ch., *he got himself hurt.*
ciùrraidh,** *a.* Hurtful, destructive. A' ghaillionn ch., *the destructive storm.*
ciùrrail, *a.* Hurtful, destructive, injurious, causing damage or grief, torturing. 2 Bad. 3‡‡Wounding. 4‡‡Ragged. Ana-mhiann c., *a hurtful lust.*
ciùrram,** *s.m.* see ciùrr.
———**ach**, -aiche, *a.* Hurtful. 2 Maimed, lamed. 3 Lame. 4 Maiming. An t-sleagh ch., *the destructive spear.*
———**ach**, -aich, *s.m.* Maimed or lame person.
ciùrramaich,** *v.a.* Damage.
ciùrrta, *a.* & *past pt.* of ciùrr. Hurt, wounded, injured. 2 Blemished. 3 **Offended. Is c. tha mo chridhe, *wounded is my heart.*
ciùrrteach,†† see ciùrrail.
†**ciùrrtha**, *a.* Bought, purchased.
†———**mach**, see ciorramach.
ciùrtach, *a.* see ciùrrail.
———**d**,‡‡ *s.f.* Offensiveness.
ciuthrach,(AF) *s.m.* Red-head (bird.)
†**ciùthramach**, *a.* see ciorramach.
†**ciùthramaich**, *v.a.* Maim. 2 Mutilate.
†**clab**, *a.* Thick.
clab, -aib, -an, *s.m.* Open mouth, gaping garrulous mouth. 2 Thick-lipped mouth (a ludicrous familiar term.) 3**Lip. 4**Gonorrhœa or any venereal affection. 5(AF) Frog-fish, angler. 'S ann ort a tha 'n clab, *how talkative you are*—said to a chatterer ; an dorus air clab a' chraois, *the door wide open.*
——**ach**, -aiche, *a.* Thick-lipped. 2 Open-mouthed. 3 Wide-mouthed. 4 Garrulous.
——**ach**, *s.f.* see clabag.
clàbadair,* see clàbaraiche.
claba-dubaidh, (AF) Cockles, clams.
clabag, -aig, -an, *s. f.* Garrulous female. 2 Thick-lipped female. 3 Large-mouthed female. (cliob—*Argyll.*) 4**Scoff.
clabair, -ean, *s.m.* Babbler, loud disagreeable talker, prater.
———, *gen. sing.* of clabar.
———**eachd**, *s.f.ind.* Babbling, tattling, vice of tattling.
claban, -ain, -ainean, *s. m.* Mill-clapper. 2 clack. 3††Paddle. 4††Rattle.
claban,‡ -ain, *s.m.* Top of the head, brain-pan. 2 Balance—*MacL.*
claban-uaireadair,* *s.m.* Balance of a clock.
clabar,†† -air, -an, *s.m.* Mill-clapper. 2**Clack.
clàbar, -air, *s. m.* Filth, dirt, nastiness. 2 Mire, mud, clay. 3 Puddle. 4**Kennel. C. cré, *miry clay;* c. an t-sràid, *the mire of the street.*
———**ach**, -aiche, *a.* Dirty, filthy, nasty. 2 Miry.

clàbarachd, s. f. Dirtiness, filthiness, nastiness. 2 Miriness.
clàbaraich,‡‡ v.a. Bedraggle.
clàbaraiche, s.m. Scavenger.
clabaran,** s.m. Patten.
clabarsach,(DC) a. Hashing—applied to work requiring exertion and strength—*Uist.*
clabastair, -e, -ean, s.m. Brawler, babbler.
——— -ciocharain, see clab-ciocharain.
clab-ciocharain, pl -an-ciocharain, s.m. Frog-fish. —*Uist.* [griasaiche—*Skye ;* mac-làmhaich —*Argyll.*]
clab-dubh,* pl, claba-dubha, s.m. Mussel (fish.) 2 Phola (shell-fish), the "chubby doo" of the Firth of Clyde.
†clabh, see claimh.
†clabhair, s.m. Mead.
clabhais-feach,¶ s.m. Red-shank (bird) see cam-ghlas.
clàbndain, s.pl. see clàdain. 2**Stilts.
clabhdan, -ain, s.m. Clamp. 2 see clàdan.
clabhrachan,** -ain, s.m. Babbler.
†clabhsail, a. Systematic, quiet, tranquil.
†clàbhuin, s.m. see clàmhuinn.
clabog, -oig, -an, s.f. Good bargain, great bargain. 2 see clabag.
†clabsal, -ail, s.m. Column of a page.
clab-sgàin, -e, -tean, s.m. Open-mouthed noisy fellow.
†clab-sholus,** -uis, s.m. Twilight.
clabstair, s.m. Clatterer.
†clabstur, s.m. Cloister.
clach, cloiche, *dat.* cloich, *pl.* clachan, s.f. Stone. 2 **Pebble. 3**Rock. 4 Stone weight (14 lb.) 5** Monument. 6* *Testicle. 7* Goggle-eye—*Islay.* C. olainn, *a stone-weight of wool* ; clachan an cliù, *the memorials of their fame* ; c. na sùla, *the apple of the eye* ; is fhearr a' chlach na 'bhi gun mhathachadh, *better stones than no manure.*
——, *pr. pt.* a' clachadh, *v. a.* Stone, strike with stones. 2 Kill by stoning.
clach-a'§bhoisgein, s.f. Putting-stone—*Cowal.*
clachach, -aiche, a. Stony, rocky, pebbly.
clachaidh, *fut. aff. a.* of clach. Shall stone.
clach-ailm, s.f. Alum stone.
clachair, *pl.* -ean, s.m. Mason, stone-builder. A' chlach a dhiùlt na clachairean, *the stone which the builders rejected*; c. Samhraidh, diol deirc Geamhraidh, *mason in summer, beggar in winter.*
clachaireach,‡‡ -eiche, a. Masonic.
————d,‡‡ s.f.ind. Masonry, occupation of a mason, stone-building. 2*Architecture. Ris a' ch., *at the masonry business.*
clachairich,‡‡ v.a. Build.
clachan, *n.pl.* of clach.
———, -ain, -an, s.m. Village or hamlet in which there is a parish church, inn, and smithy. 2**Church. 3**Churchyard, burying-place. 4**Druidical circle composed of stones raised on end. 5* Stepping-stones. Didòmhnuich 'dol do 'n ch., *on Sunday going to church ;* baile chlachain, *a name given to a parish village because it contains the parish church, &c.*
clachan-ghadhair, s.m. Early orchis, see mothùrach.
clachar, *fut. pass.* of clach.
clacharan, -ain, -an, s.m. Pavement. 2 Stepping stones across a river, or in boggy ground.
————,¶ s.m. Wheatear, 2 Stonechat, see cloichirean.
clacharra, a. Set with stones. 2 Goggle-eyed.
clach-bhalg, -bhuilg, -an, s.m. Originally a bag with stones in it to scare off birds or horses by rattling. 2 Now applied to any description of rattle, such as those formerly used by the police.
clach-bhannag,(AC) s.f. Bannock-stone, the stone against which the cake is supported before the fire.
clach-bhleath, see c— -bhleith.
clach-bhleith, *pl.* -an-bleith, s.f. Grindstone, whetstone. 2 Dram before meals particularly breakfast.
clach-bhlionain, (DC) *Argyll* for clach-bhleith.
clach-bhogha, s.m. Catapult.
clach-bholg, see clach-bhalg.
clach-bhriseach,§ s.m. (lit. stone breaker) Saxifraga,—*saxifraga.*
clach-bhuadhach, -aich, *pl.* clacha-buadhach, s.f. Precious stone, gem, amulet, charm.
clach-bhuaidh, see clach-bhuadhach.
clach bhuinn, s.f. Nether stone of mill.
clach-bràth, s.f. Judgment stone. 2 Rocking-stone, an immense spherical mass of rock, so situated that the least touch can rock in one certain direction, but which cannot be made to move in any other by all the force that can be applied to it. Such stones were once frequent in Britain. There are stones in Iona called *na clachan-bràth.* They are within the precincts of the burial-ground, and are placed on the pedestals of a cross, and have been, according to Pennant, the supports of a tomb. It is believed by some that the world's end will not come till the stone on which they stand is worn through.
clach-buaidh, see clach-bhuadhach.
clach-cheangail, s.f. Key-stone.
clach-chinn, *pl.* clachan-cinn, s.f. Head-stone. 2 Copestone. 3 Upright grave-stone.
clach-chnotaidh, (DC) *Argyll* for clach-chnotainn.
clach-chnotainn, s.f. Hollowed stone into which barley is put and beaten with a mallet, until freed from the husks. [Generally called *cnotag*, mortar.
clach-chreadha, *pl.* -an-creadha, s. f. Brick. Deanamaid clachan-creadha, *let us make bricks.*
clach-chrìche, *pl.* -an-crìche, s.f. March-stone, landmark.
clach-chrocaidh, }
clach-chrotaidh, } see clach-chnotainn.
clach-chrotainn, }
clach-chrùbain, *pl.* -an-crùbain, s. f. Amulet supposed to cure rheumatic complaints; species of gryphites.
clach-chuarsgaidh, *pl.* -an-cuarsgaidh, s.f. Stone roller.
clach-chuimhneachan, -an-cuimhneachan, s.f. Monument.
clach-dhealbh,‡‡ s. Stone statue.
clach-dheanadach,‡‡ -aiche, a. Lapidific.
clach-dhearg, s.f. Keel, ruddle.
clach-dhualadair,‡‡ s.m. Stone-cutter.
clach-dhùnaidh,‡‡ s.f. Keystone of an arch.
clach-éiteig, s.f. Alabaster. 2(DC) Quartz.
clach-fhàisneachd,‡‡ s.f.ind. Lithomancy.
clach-fhaobhair, s.f. Hone, whetstone.
clach-fhaobhrach, see clach-fhaobhair.
clach-fhuail,‖ *pl.* -an-fuail, s.f. Gravel-stone, stones ejected with urine.
clach-ghaireil, s.f. Freestone.
clach-gheurachaidh, *pl.* -an-geurachaidh, s.f. Hone, whetstone.
clach-ghineadach, -aiche, a. Lapidific.
clach-ghineamhuinn,‡‡ s.f. Lapidification,
clach-ghlaisidh,‡‡ s.f. Keystone of an arch.
clach-ghleusaidh,(MMcD) s.f. Grindstone, hone, whetstone—*Lewis.*
clach-ghorm,(AH) s. f. Lunar caustic, fused

crystals of nitrate of silver.
clach-ghoireil, see clach-ghaireil.
clach-ghràbhadh, -aidh, *s.m.* Lithography.
clach-ghràin, *s.f.* Granite.
clach-ghraineil, see clach-ghràin.
clach-ghuail, *s.f.* Sea-coal. 2 Shale.
clach-ghuiteir, *pl.*-an-guiteir, *s.f.* Gutter-stone.
clach-glùin-a'-choilich, *s.f.* Amulet supposed to cure sundry distempers. [*lit.* the cock-knee stone, so called from the notion that it is obtained from the knee of a cock. It is only a common pebble.]
clach-inne, *s.f.* Gutter-stone.
clach-ìochdarach, *s.f.* Nether mill-stone, see brà, p. 112. ‡
clach-iolaire,* *s.f.* Aetites.
clach-iùil, *pl.* -an-iùil, *s.f.* Loadstone, magnet.
———— -dhealanach, *s.f.* Electro-magnet.
clach-leanraidh, *s.f.* *Perthshire* for clach-liobhaidh.
clach-lèig, *pl.* -an-lèig, *s.f.* Precious stone, gem.
clach-lìobhaidh, *pl.* -an-liobhaidh, *s. f.* Grindstone. 2 Smoothing-stone, polishing-stone.
clach-lìobhair, see clach-liobhaidh.
clach-lìobharain, see clach-lìobhaidh.
clach-lìonraith, *pl.* -an-lìonraith, *s.f.* Rolling whet-stone.
clach-loisgeach, *s.f.* Caustic.
clach-luachmhor, *s.f.* Precious stone, gem.
clach-mhara, *s.f.* Aqua marina (stone.)
clach-mheallain, *pl.* -an-meallain, *s.f.* Hailstone. 2 singular used *collectively*, Hail.
clach-mhìle, *s.f.* Mile-stone.
clach-mhìneachadh, -aidh, *s.m.* Smoothing or polishing of stones.
clach-mhìneachair, *s. m.* Lapidary, stone polisher.
clachmhor, -oire, *a.* Stony.
clach-mhuilinn, *pl.* -an-muilinn, *s.f.* Mill-stone.
clach-mhullaich, *pl.* -an-mullaich, *s. f.* Topstone, abacus, copestone.
clach mu'n cuairt, (DC) *Uist* for clach-bhleith.
clach-na-cineamhuinn, *s.f.* The fatal stone, the stone on which the ancient Caledonian kings were inaugurated. So called from an old belief that wherever the stone remained one of the Scottish race should reign.
clach-nam-buadh,* *s.f.* The philosopher's stone.
clach-na-sùla, *s. f.* The apple or pupil of the eye.
clach-nearaidh,** -an-nearaidh, *s.f.* Grinding-stone.
clach-neirt, *pl.* -an-neirt, *s. f.* Putting-stone, (*lit.* stone of strength.)
clach-oisinn, -an-oisinn, *s.f.* Corner-stone.
clach-raineach,‡ *s. m.* Polypody—*polypodium vulgare.*
clachran,** *s.m.* Pier, landing-place. 2 Stepping-stones in water, or on watery ground.
clach-sgrioban,-an-sgrioban, (DJM) *s. f.* Weight for hand fishing-line.
clach-sgrìobhadh,‡‡ -aidh, *s.m.* Lithography.
clach-shloc, -shluic, -shlocan, *s.m.* Stone quarry. O na clach-shlocaibh,*from the stone quarries.*
clach-shnaidheadair, -ean, *s.m.* Hewer or dresser of stone. 2 Engraver (stone) 3 Sculptor.

147. *Clach-raineach.*

clach-shneachd, cloiche-, clachan- *s. f.* Hailstone, hail. Le c. chruaidh, *with hard hail*
clach-shneachdaidh, see clach-shneachd.
clach-shreathail, *s.f.* Freestone, ashlar.
clach-shùil, -shùla, -ean, *s.m.* Pearl eye. 2 Eye of an infant gazing with pleasure at any object.
———-——each, -eiche, *a.* Having pearl eyes.
clach-smior, *pl.* -an-smiora, *s.f.* Emery.
clach-spor,(AH) *s.f.* Flint.
clach-tabhuill,** *s.f.* Sling-stone.
clach-thàirnge, *s.f.* Loadstone.
clach-theine, *pl.* -an-teine, *s.f.* Flint (stone.)
clach-thochailt, *pl.* -thochailtean, *s.f.* Stone quarry.
————-———iche, -an, *s.m.* Quarrier.
clach-thogalaich, (AH) *s. f.* Stone used in weight-lifting contests.
clach-thomhais, *pl.* -an-tomhais, *s.f.* Weight Clachan-tomhais cearta, *just weights.*
clach-thuislidh, *pl.* -an-tuislidh, *s.f.* Stumbling block, rock of offence.
clach-uachdarach, *s.f.* Upper stone of mill.
clach-uasal, *pl.* -an-uasal, *s.f.* Precious stone.
clach-ultaich,(Fionn) *s.f.* Lift-stone, *i.e.* what a man could lift. "Clach ultaich Iain Ghairbh MhicIlleChaluim Raasaidh" is at Duntuilm, Skye, and is said to weigh about a ton.
clach-ùrlair,(AH) *pl.* -an-ù—, *s.f.* Paving-stone.
clàd, -a, -an, *s.f.* Wool-comb. 2††Mud scraper. 3 Wool hackle.
clàd,†† *pr. pt.* a' clàdadh, *v.a.* Card wool.
cladach, -aich, -ean, *s.m.* Shore, beach, coast, stony beach. 2* Anything scattered. 3** Sandy plain. 4†† Channel of a river. 5†† Death, destruction. Cha suaicheantas còrr air cladach, *a heron on the shore is no odd thing* ; 'sa chladach fheamainn, *in the seaweed shore, i. e.* that part of the shore where seaweed can be gathered.
†clàdach, -aich, *s,m.* Clay, mire.
cladachail,‡‡ -e, *a.* Beachy.
cladach leis, (AH) *s.m.* Lee shore.
clàdadh, -aidh, *s.m.* Combing of wool. 2 Hackling of wool. A' c—, *pr.pt.* of clàd.
clàdain,(AH) *s.pl.* Oar-cleets, see bàta, p. 76.
clàdaire, -an, *s.m.* Wool-comber.
clàdan, -ain, -an, *s. m.* Burr. 2 Flake of snow. 3†† Prickly seed-case of burdock. 4‡ Thing that sticks.
———ach,* *a.* Like burrs. 2 Flaky.
clad-chasach,** *a.* Duck-legged.
cladh,* *pr.pt.* a' cladh, *v.a. & n.* Spawn, as a fish. Tha na bradain a' cladh, *the salmon are spawning.*
cladh, -a [& claidh**], *s.m.* Spawn. 2 Act of spawning. 3 Burying-place. 4 Mound, dyke. 5 Trench. 6 Hollow between two waves. 7** *rarely* Wool-comb. C. a' chùlthuinn, *the back wave hollow.*
cladh-abhainn,** *s.f.* Canal.
———ach, -aich, *s. m.* Digging, delving. 2 Poking. A' c—, *pr.pt.* of cladhaich. A' c. fo 'n bhruaich, (*the river*) *undermining the bank.*
———achadh,** -aidh, *s.m.* Digging. 2 Burying. A' c—, *pr.pt.* of cladhaich. An tulach uaine a' c., *in the green mound a-digging.*
cladhaich, *pr.pt.* a' cladhach & a' cladhachadh, *v.a.* Dig, delve. 2* Poke.
cladhaire, -an, *s. m.* Coward, poltroon. †2 Hero. †3One superintending the burying of soldiers in an army. 4 Grave-digger. 5** Rogue. Ni robh còta dubh air cealgair no còta dearg air cladhair, *may black coat (of minister) never cover hypocrite, nor red coat (of soldier) coward* ; cha teich ach c., *none but a coward will flee.*
cladhaireach, *a.* Cowardly, timorous. 2**

Roguish.
cladhaireachd, *s.f.* Cowardice, cowardliness. 2 Roguery.
cladhan,(AH) -ain, *s.m.* Channel, very shallow stream.
cladharra, *a.* see cladhaireach.
cladh-dùdaidh, *pl.* -an-dùdaidh, *s.m.* Roaring billow.
†cladhe, *s.f.* Genealogy.
cladh-nàire, *s.m.* Modesty, bashfulness.
cladh-shruth,** *s.m.* Canal.
cladh-uisge, see cladh-shruth.
cladrach,* *s.m.* Anything scattered.
cladraich,* *v.a.* Scatter.
clàduinn, see clàd.
clag, cluig, *s.m.* Bell. 2* Crash. 3 Clock. 4 **Loud talk. 5**Mill-clapper. Cluig nan each, *the bells of the horses*; freasdail an c., *answer the bell.*
——, *pr.pt.* a' clagadh, *v.a.* Sound, as a bell. 2 Make a noise.
——ach, -aiche, *a.* Like a bell. 2 Abounding in bells.
——adair,** *s.m.* Bell-founder.
clagadh, -aidh, *s.m.* Ringing, chiming as of a bell. A' c—, *pr.pt.* of clag.
clag-àite, *s.m.* Belfry. 2 Steeple.
clagan, -ain, *s.m.* Little bell. 2 Hand-bell.
———ach,†† -aiche, *a.* Pertaining to small bells or hand-bells.
clagarnach, -aich, *s.m.* Loud noise.
clagarsaich, *s.f.* Clashing noise. 2 Dangling, waving.
†clagartas, -ais, see clagharthas.
clagas,** *s.m.* Belfry.
clag-chumach, *a.* Bell-shaped.
clag-ciùil, *pl.* cluig-chiùil, *s.m.* Music bell.
clagh, see cladh.
claghann, see claon.
clagharra, *a.* Sluggish. 2 Slovenly. Gu c., *sluggishly.*
†clagharthas, *s.m.* Sluggishness 2 Slovenliness.
clag-ionad, see clag-lann.
clag-làimh, cluig-làimh, *s.m.* Hand-bell.
clag-lann, clag-lainn, *s.f.* Belfry. 2 Steeple.
clag-mheur, *pl.* cluig-mheòir, *s.f.* Finger of a clock, (not a watch) also làmh-uaireadair.
clag-smàlaidh,* *s.f.* Curfew.
clag-thaigh, -ean, *s.m.* see claig-theach.
†clagun, -uin, *s.m.* Flagon. 2 Lid.
clagunn, *prov.* for claigeann.
†claibin, *s.m.* Tap, spigot.
†claicheach, *s.f.* Church steeple.
clàideag, -eig, -an, *s.f.* Lock, wreath, ringlet. 2 Erroneously used for clàidheag.
———ach,†† -aiche, *a.* Pertaining to locks or ringlets.
claidean,* *s.m.* Absurd hammering at anything. 2 Dangling.
claideart,(AH) *s.f.* Toil, strain, drudgery, fatigue.
†claidh, *v.a.* Dig. see cladhaich.
†claidhe, *s.m.* Burial.
claidheach, see claidheamhach.
clàidheag, -eig, -an, *s.f.* Last handful of corn cut on the ground, *better* maighdeann-bhuana.
claidheamh, -eimh, *pl.* claidhean [claidhmhnean *claidhmhichean & **cloidhean] *s. m.* Sword. 2 That part of a spinning-wheel which connects the footboard and crank. C. caol, *a small sword, rapier*; c. crom, *a sabre, a scimitar*; c. mór, *a broad-sword, claymore*; c. cùil, *a back-sword*; c. leathann, *a broadsword;* c. dà-làimh, *a two-handed sword,* properly c. mór. Cha'n 'eil fios ciod an c. a bhitheas 'san truaill gus an tàirnear e, *it is not known what (kind of) a sword is in the sheath till it is drawn*; seasamh claidheimh, *standing on one's head*—children in school see who can stand longest on their heads—cò a's fearr a sheasas air an ceann.—*Fionn.*

PARTS OF A SWORD:
1 Lann, *blade.*
2 Truaill, *sheath.*
3 Bàrr, rann, *point.*
4 Dòrn-chuir, dòrn-bheirt, ceann, *hilt.*

Ceann-aisneach, *a basket-hilt;* ceann-Ìleach, *an "Islay"-hilt.*
Crambaid, *ferrule on sheath.*

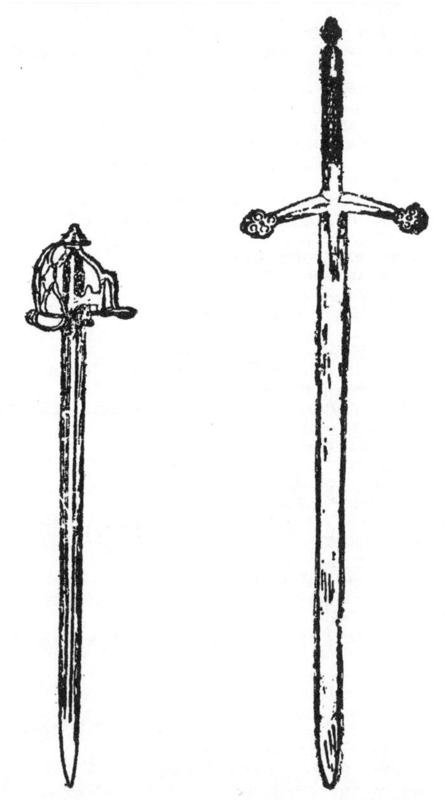

148. Claidheamh-mór. *149. Claidheamh-dà-làimh.*

claidheamhach, -eiche. *a.* Full of swords. 2 Of, or belonging to, a sword.
claidheamhail, -e, *a.* Ensiform, having the shape or appearance of a sword.
claidheamhair, -e, -ean, *s.m.* Swordsman. 2 Fencer.
————eachd, *s.f.ind.* Swordsmanship 2 Fencing.
claidhean, *n.pl.* of claidheamh. *prov.*
————, *dim.* of claidheamh. *s.m.* Little sword, scymitar, bilboe.
clàidhean,‡ *s.m.* Bolt or latch of a door.
———— -doruis, *s.m,* Bolt or bar of a door.
claidheil,** see claidheamhail.
claidreach, *a.* Harassing, fatiguing. 2 Damaging, shattering. 3††Deafening.
claidreadh, -ridh, *s. m.* Shattering. 2 Damaging through toil or fatigue. A' c— *pr.pt* of claidrich

claidrich, *pr.pt.* a' claidreadh, *v. a.* Shatter. 2 Damage. 3 Harass, fatigue. 4†† Deafen.
claig, -e, -ean, *s.f.* Indentation. 2 Dimple.
——each, -ich, *s.m.* see claig-theach.
†claigeag, -eig, *s.f.* Deceit.
claigeann, see claigionn. 2 Head of a rudder, see under rudder, p. 78.
————ach, see claigionnach.
claigionn, -inn, *pl.* claignean, *s. m.* Skull. 2* Scalp. 3 Best field of arable land on a farm. Bhrist e 'ch., *he broke his skull* ; àrd mo ch., *at the top of my voice.*
————,(AH) Stem of a boat, see bàta E1, p. 78.
claigionnach, -aiche, *a.* Of, or belonging to, a skull, abounding in skulls.
———— ——, -aich, *s.m.* Head-stall of a halter. 2 *Best arable land of a district. C. sréine, *headstall of a bridle.*
claigionnachd, *s.f.* Craniology.
claigionnaiche, *s.m.* Craniologist. [** says *s.f.*]
claigionn-deiridh, Stern-post, see O 1, p. 73.
———— -srathrach,‡‡ *s. m.* Timbers of girth-saddle.
———— -stiùrach, *s.m.* Helm-top.
———— -toisich, Stem-post of boat, G 1. p 74.
claig-theach, -an, *s.m.* Steeple, belfry.
†claime,‖ *s.f.* Scabies, leprosy.
claimh, -e, see cloimh.
claimheach, eiche, *a.* see cloimheach.
claimh-each, -eich, *s.m.* Farcy.
claimhean, *s.m.* ‡see clàidhean 2††Latch.
claimh-leighiseach,‡‡ -eiche, *a* Antiscorbutical.
claimhseach,‡‡ -eiche, *a.* Mangy, scorbutic.
————,-ich,-ichean, *s.f.* Scorbutic female.
†clain, *s.f.* Engendering. 2 Children.
clainn, } (for cloinne) *gen.* of clann. 2 Used
clainne, } *prov.* as nominative.
clàir, *gen.sing. & n. pl.* of clàr. Boards, staves, tables. 2* Lids.
†clàir, *pr.pt.* a' clàireadh, *v.a.* Divide, partition.
†clàir-bheul, (clàr-beòil) *s.m.* Lid, cover.
†clàireach, *a.* see clàrach.
†clàireadh,-idh, *s.m.* Division, disjunction, releasing, separating. A' c—, *pr.pt.* of clàir.
†clàirein, *s.m.* Cripple.
clàireineach, -neich, -neichean, *s.m.* Cripple. 2 Dwarf.
————, -neiche, *a.* Broad-bottomed. 2 Flat-nosed.
clàir-eudannach, -aiche, *a.* see clàr-aodannach.
clàir-fhiacaill, -fhiaclan, see clàr-fhiacaill.
clàir-fhiaclach, -aiche, *a.* see clàr-fhiaclach.
clàiridh, -e, -ean, see clàraidh.
†clàirin, see †clàirein.
clàirinn,(DU) see clàirinneach 2.
clàirinneach,** -eiche, *a.* Decrepit. 2 Marbled, mottled, marked with spots of various colours or shades.—D.C.
clàir-iongach, -aiche, *a.* Broad-nailed.
†clàirneach, *a.* Crippled.
clàirseach, -ich, -ean, see clàrsach.
clàirseir, -ean, see clàrsair.
†clàirthe, *past part.* of clàir.
clais, -e, -ean, *s.f.* Furrow. 2 Gutter. 3 Streak, stripe, mark. 4 Pit. 5 Ditch. 6 Hollow, groove. 7 (AH) "Finish," in a ploughed rigg. Gach c. 'na ghnùis, *every furrow in his face* ; anns na claisibh, *in the gutters*; c.-bhlàir, *a trench;* sruth-ch., *a channel.*
clais, *pr.part.* a' claiseadh, *v.a.* see claisich.
†clais, -e, *s.f.* Class.
clais-alpaidh, *s.f.* Mortice.
clais-bhlàir, *s.f.* Trench.

†claischeadal, *s.m.* Psalm-singing.
clàisdeachd, *s.f.ind.* Hearing, sense of hearing. 2 Listening, hearkening. Ann am ch., *in my hearing*; chaill e a ch., *he lost his sense of hearing.*
clais-dhìonaidh, *s.f.* Fortifying trench.
clàisdinn, see claistinn.
claise,** *s.f.* Avoidance.
claiseach, *a.* Furrowed, trenched, full of ditches or hollows. 2 Grooved, fluted. 3 Striped, streaked.
†claiseach, -ich, -ichean, *s.m.* Sword. 2‡‡ Rifle.
claiseadh, *vr.pt.* of clais.
claiseag, *s f.* Rindle.
claisich, *pr.part.* a' claiseadh, *v.a.* Furrow, flute. 2 Dig, trench.
————te, *past part.* of claisich.
claisire,* *s.m.* Trencher.
clais-locair, *s.f.* Mortice-plane.
claisneach,** *a.* Auditory.
————-d, see claisdeachd.
claisniche,** *s.m.* Auditor.
claist, *pr.part.* a' claistinn, [& claisteachd] *v.a.* Hearken.
claisteachd, *s.f.* see claisdeachd.
claist-eòlas, see claist-iùil.
claistine, *s.f.* see claistinn.
claistinn, *s.f.* Hearing, listening, hearkening. A' c—, *pr.pt.* of claist.
claistinneach,** *a.* Auditory.
claist-iùil, *s.m.* Diacoustics.
clàiteach, *s.m.* see clàiteachd.
————d,†† *s.f.* Gentle rain—*Arran.*
clàiteag, (AH) *s.f.* Snowflake.
†claithe, *s.f.* Jest, game, ridicule, sport. 2 Genealogical table.
clambar, -air, *s. m.* Wrangling, clamour. 2 Scramble, scuffle. 3 Evil report, private slander. 4 *Litigiousness. 5** Wrestling, struggling. Ri c., *struggling or wrestling.*
————ach, -aiche, *a.* Litigious, wrangling, slandering.
clambrach, see clambarach.
†clamh, *s.m.* Leper. 2 see cloimh.
†————ach, -aiche, *a.* see cloimheach.
clàmhainn, see clàmhuinn.
————each, see clàmhuinneach.
clamhair, *v.a.* see clamhar.
clamhaire,(MMcD) *s. m.* Greedy, rapacious, grasping person—*Lewis.*

150 Clamhan.

clamhan, -ain, -an, *s.m.* Buzzard,—*buteo vulgaris.* 2**Kite. Am fang agus an c., *the vulture and the kite ;* cha d' thàinig eun glan riamh á nead a' chlamhin, *a clean bird never came from a kite's nest.*
clamhan-fionn.¶ *s.m.* Hen-harrier, see bréid-

air-tòin.
clamhan gèarr, (AF) *s.m.* Broad buzzard.
clamhan-gobhlach,¶ *n.pl.* -ain-gh—, *s.m.* Kite, or salmon-tailed gled—*milvus vulgaris.*
clamhan-loin,¶ *s.m.* Marsh harrier—*circus rufus.*
clamhan-luch,¶ *s.m.* Montague's harrier—*circus Montagui.* 2 Hen-harrier, see breid-airtòin.
clamhan-nan-cearc, (MMcD) *s.m.* Hen-harrier, —*Lewis.*
clamhan-nan-luch, see clamhan-luch.
clamhan-riabhach,¶ *s.m.* Honey-buzzard—*pernis apivorus.*

151. Clamhan-riabhach.

clamhan-ruadh,¶ *s. m.* Kestrel—*falco tinnunculus.*
clamhar, *v.a.* Scratch by shrugging.
———ach, *a.* Shrugging. 2 Prone to shrug. 3 Litigious. 4 Wrangling.
clamhas, -ais, see clamhras.
———ail,* *a* Brawling, clattering.
clamhrach, *a.* see cloimheach.
clamhradh, -aidh, *s. m.* Shrugging, act of shrugging. 2 Scratching by shrugging.
clamhras, -ais, *s.m.* Brawling, chiding, clamour, scolding, altercation. 2 *Unfounded report. 3** Brawl, scold. 4* Clatter.

152. Clamhan-ruadh.

clamhsa, *pl.* -chan [& -aichean] *s. m.* Alley, narrow lane, little court, entry, close, passage [** gives clamhsadh.]
†clàmhuin, *s.f.* Sleet.
clàmhuinn, s.m. Sleet. Sneachd is c. air gach tom, *snow and sleet on every hillock*; ris a' ch., *showering sleet.*
———each, *a.* Sleety.
clampar, -air, *s.m.* see clambar. 2‡‡Injury.
———ach, -aiche, see clambarach.
clamras, -ais, see clamhras.
†clanach, *s.f.* Virtue. 2 Fruitful persons.
clann, *gen.* cloinne [clainn, clanna & clainne] *collective s.f.* Offspring, children. 2 Descendants. 3**Clan, tribe. C. bheaga, *little children*; cleas na cloinne bige, *the manner of little children*; Clann Mhuirich, *the MacPhersons.* Clann Dòmhnuill, *the MacDonalds*; Clann-antoisich, *the MacIntoshes*; c. dìolain, *bastard children;* c. an cloinne, *their children's children;* a ch. nan sonn, *ye descendants of heroes*. thoir seo do 'n chloinn, *give this to the children.* [C. is followed by the adjective in the plural when in nominative case, but in the singular when in other cases. It aspirates a proper name following except one beginning with D. It is preceded by the article in the singular. "Donald's children" may be either "clann Dòmhnuill", with the emphasis on *clann*, or "clann Dhomhnuill" with the emphasis on *Dhòmhnuill.* Clan Donald has the emphasis on "Dòmhnuill." "Donald's children" is generally "clann Domhnuill" in the Gairloch district, and "clann Dhòmhnuill" in Lorn.
clann, -a, -an, *s.f.* Lock of hair. 'Na clannaibh, *in curls, in ringlets.*
clannach, -aiche, *a.* Fruitful, prolific. 2 Hanging in locks, curled. 3 Bushy, clustering, crowding. 4 Luxuriant. Anna ch., *Ann with the many ringlets.*
clannadh, -aidh, *s.m.* Thrusting. 2 Blast, puff. †3* Interment. 4**Child's portion.
clannaich,* *v.n.* Beget children.
clannail, -e, *a.* see clannach.
Clann-an-oistir,** *s. pl.* Ostuarii, doorkeepers to the monastery of Iona. The first of the family came over from Ireland with "Colum Cille," but causing the displeasure of that saint, he invoked a curse on him, by which it was decreed that never more than five of his clan should exist at the same time. Accordingly, when a sixth was born one of the five was to look for death, which always happened until the race was extinguished. A female who died about the middle of the 18th. century, in Iona, was the last person who could trace a lineage to the doorkeepers of this monastery.
†clannar, *a.* Shining, sleek. 2 Hanging in locks or clusters. 3 see clannmhor.
clannmhor, -oire, *a.* Having issue, prolific, fruitful.
†claochladh, see caochladh.
†claochloid, *v. a.* Exchange.
claodhaire, see cladhaire.
———achd, see cladhaireachd.
†claoi, see claoidh.
†claoicheadh, see cladhach.
claoidh, *s.f.* Pain, affliction. [does not mean Sorrow, as given by McL & D—CR] 2 Vexation. 3 Anguish, torment. 4 Defeat. 5* Fatigue, excessive fatigue. 6‡‡Desolation, destruction, consumption. 7* Fagging, fainting. A' c—, *pr. pt.* of claoidh. Gu bràth cha'n fhaicear c., *sorrow shall never be seen.*
claoidh, *pr.part.* a' claoidh & a' claoidheadh, *v.a.* Vex, annoy, harass, trouble. 2 Afflict, torment. 3 Defeat, overthrow. 4 Mortify. 5 Oppress. 6 Exhaust, fag, fatigue. 7** Wound. 8**Consume, overcome. 9**Dazzle, Mar a chlaoidheas teine coillteach, *as fire overcomes wood;* claoidhibh 'ur buill, *mortify your members*; a' claoidh fradhairc, *dazzling the sight;* na c. m' fhacal, *do not contradict me.*
claoidheach, -eiche, *a.* Vexing, annoying. 2 Tormenting, afflictive, painful, troublesome. 3 Harassing, tiresome, overcoming, exhausting. 4**Defeating, overthrowing. 5*Spending.
————d,** *s.f.ind.* Distress, vexation, annoyance, mortification. 2 Continued or frequent distress, continued vexation or annoyance. 3 Fagging, exhaustion.
claoidheadair,* *s.m.* Tormentor.
claoidheadh, -idh, *s. m.* Wearying out, act of frequently oppressing, tormenting, harassing, afflicting, mortifying, or paining. 2 ...

comforting, conquering. 3**Overthrow. A' c—, *pr. part* of claoidh.
†claoidheamh, see claidheamh.
claoidhear,** *s.m.* Afflicter.
†claoidheir, *s.m.* see cladhair.
claoidhte, *past part.* of claoidh. Defeated, overpowered, overwhelmed, conquered. 2 Harassed, wearied out, exhausted. 3 Afflicted, distressed, tormented.
———ach, *a.* see claoidheach.
———achd,* *s.f.* see claoidh, *s.*
claoine, *s.f.* Obliquity, squintness. 2(DU) Obtuseness, stupidity.
———ad, see claoine.
claoin-leathad, *s.m.* Sloping hill.
claoin-leid, *s.m.* see claoin-leathad.
claoin-leud, see claoin-leathad.
claointe, *a.* & *past part.* of claon. Bent. 2 Sloping.
claon, -aoine, *a.* Squint, squint-eyed. 2 Inclining, oblique. 3 Winding, meandering. 4 Perverse. 5 Partial, prone to. 6 Uneven, unequal. 7**Moving obliquely or aslant. 8 (DU) Stupid, dense. Fear c., *a man that squints ;* nithean c., *perverse things.*
———, *pr. part.* a' claonadh, *v. a.* Incline. 2 Go aside, depart, pervert, move aslant or obliquely, make awry. 3 Squint. 4 Decline. 5 Go wrong, rebel. Linne a tha claon 'sa ghleann, *a pool that is transverse in the glen ;* ch. iad uile, *they all went aside*; mar a' ghrian a tha 'claonadh 'sa ghleann, *as the sun that moves aslant in the glen ;* sùil ch., *a squint eye.*
†claon, *s.m.* Partiality.
———ad,** -aid, *s.m.* Proclivity.
———adh, -aidh, -aidhean, *s.m.* Inclination, bending, bend. 2 Squinting. 3 Turning aside. 4 Moving aslant or obliquely. 5** Declining, squinting. 6**Oblique motion, as of the descending sun. Mar sgàile a' c. sìos, *like a shadow declining.* A' c—, *pr. pt.* of claon.
———ag, -aig, -an, *s.f.* Cunning deceitful woman.
———aire, (DU) *s.m.* Stupid fellow, used of a person whose wits are considered to be less sharp than the normal.
———aireachd, *s.f.ind.* Partiality. 2††Inclination.
claon-aontachd,‡‡ *s.f.ind.* Assentation.
claon-àrd, -àirde, -an, *s.m.* Inclining steep.
claon-bhàigh, *s.f.* Partiality, bias, prejudice.
————eil, *a.* Partial.
claon-bhòrd, -bhùird, *s. m.* Sloping table. 2 Desk. 3 Inclined plane.
claon-bhreith, -e, -ean, *s.f.* Prejudice, partiality. 2 Unjust judgment, unfair decision.
————each, -eiche, *a.* Partial, unjust in judging or deciding.
————eachd,‡‡ *s.f.* Partiality.
claon-bhreitheamh, *s.m.* Partial judge.
claon-chòmhnard, -aird, *s.m.* Inclined plane.
claon-mharbh, *pr.pt.* a' claon-mharbhadh, *v.a.* Mortify.
————adh, -aidh, *s.m.* Mortification. A' c—, *pr.pt* of claon-mharbh.
claon-shuil, -shula, -shuilean, *s.f.* Squint eye.
————each,‡‡Squint-eyed.
claor,** *s.m.* Shout.
clap,|| *s.m.* Gonorrhœa [preceded by the art. *an.*]
——, *v.* English word *clap.*
——ach, -aiche, *a.* Clapping.
——aig, (DU) *v.a.* Gaelic form of *clap.* 2 Embrace.
——ail, see clapartaich.
clapartaich, -e, *s.f.* Act of clapping or flapping with the wings. 2 Fondling, caressing.
clap-ciochrain, (DC) *s.m.* Fishing frog or sea angler—*Uist.*
†clap-sholus, *s.m.* Twilight.
†clàr, *v.a.* Deceive, fable.
clàr,* *pr.pt.* a' clàradh, *v.n.* Maintain, contradict, oppose. 2 (Fionn) Make believe, induce one to believe more than is true. Am bheil thu math air claradh ? *are you good at persuading or make believe ?* a' c. orm, *contradicting me ;* 's ann a tha e a' c. orm, *he stoutly contradicts me.*
clàr, -àir, *pl.* clàir and clàran, *s.m.* Any smooth surface or plane. 2 Stave, *in music.* 3 Stave of a cask. 4 Lid. 5 Trough. 6 Wooden tray or plate. 7 Table, desk. 8 Spoke. 9 Sheet, as of paper. 10 Board, deal, plank. 11(AH) Deck of a ship. 12 Catalogue. 13 see clàrsach. 14††Tablet. Cha togadh e salann bhàrr a' chlàir, *he would not lift salt from the table* —said of a very shy person ; clàir cloiche, *tables of stone ;* le clàraibh giubhais, *with planks of fir ;* clàir umha, *plates of brass.*
clàrach, -aiche, *a.* Bare, bald. 2 Of, or belonging to, staves, boards, or planks. 3**Full of tables or plates. 4**In staves. 5‡‡Floored.
clàrach, -aich, -aichean, *s.f.* Woman of clumsy figure, "broad-built. 2 Floor. 3(AC) Small boat.
†clàradh, -aidh, *s.m.* Familiarity. 2 Dividing. A' c—. *pr.pt.* of clàr.
†clàr-aenach,|| *a.* see clàr-aodannach.
clàrag, -aig, -an, *s.f.* Fore-tooth. 2 Frame of hand fishing-line. 3** Wattle-work, as in a sledge. 4 (AH) Square-sterned boat. 5†† Broad woman. 7(JM) Crutch—*Tiree.*
clàr-aghaidh,* *s.m.* Frontispiece.
clàraich,*-e, -ean, see clàraidh.
————,‡‡ *v.a.* Planch.
clàraichean, (DC) *s.pl.* The incisor teeth—*Uist.*
clàraidh,** *a.* Dividing. 2 Of deal or plank. 3 Floating. 4 Row of layers. Urlar ch., *a deal floor*; leabaidh ch., *a deal bed.*
clàraidh, -ean, *s.f.* Partition. 2 Flooring.
clàraineach, *a.* Flat-nosed.
clàr-ainm, -ean, *s.m.* Catalogue.
clàr-ainme, see clàr-ainmeachaidh.
clàr-ainmeachaidh, *s.m.* Title-page. 2**Index.
clàr-ainmiche, see clàr-ainmeachaidh.
clàr-amais, *s.m.* Index.
clàran, *n.pl.* of clàr.
clàran,** -ain, *s.m.* Little table. 2 Little plate. 3 Little stave. 4 Little trough. 5 Little deal or plank.
————ach, -aich, (AC) *s.m.* Boatman.
clàr-an-aodainn, see clàr-aodainn.
clàr-aodainn, *s.m.* Front, visage, brow, forehead.
clàr-aodannach, -aiche, *a.* Broad-faced, flat-faced, broad-browed, broad-visaged. [** gives clàr-aodainneach.]
clàr-beòil, *s.m.* Lid. 2‡‡Forepiece.
clàr-bhuideal,** *s.m.* Bottle-rack.
clàr-bualaidh, *s.m.* Printing-press.
clàr-buideal, *s.m.* Stave of a cask. 2**Bottle-rack. Cho tioram ri c., *as dry as a bottle-rack.*
clàrc, *s.m.* Gaelic spelling of *clerk.*
clàr-chairtean,‡‡ *s.m.* Card-table.
clàr-chas, -chois, -chasan, *s.f.* Splay-foot.
————ach, -aiche, *a.* Splay-footed. 2 Duck-legged. 3 Crump-footed.
clàr-chos, see clàr-chas.
clar-ciocharain, see clab.
†clàr-cisteanach, *s.m.* Dresser, kitchen table.
clàr-cuibhle, *s.m.* Spoke of a wheel.
clàr-cùil, *s.m.* Back piece.
clàr-cunntais, -an-, *s.f.* Abacus.
†clàrtha, *past aff.* of clàr, Divided, parted.
clàr-dhealbh, -a, -an, *s. m.* Painting, sketch

draught, map.
clàr-eudannach, -aiche, see clàr-aodannach.
clàr-fadhairt, s.m. Smith's trough.
clàr-feòirne, s.m. Chess-board, draught-board.
clàr-fhiacaill, -clan, s.m. Fore-tooth, butter-tooth.
clàr-fhiaclach, a. Having large fore-teeth.
clàr-fhuine, see clàr-fuine.
clàr-fodhairt, see clàr-fadhairt.
clàr-fuine, s.m. Kneading-trough. 2††Baking-board.
clàr-fuinidh,** see clàr-fuine.
clàr-ìnnse, see clàr-ìnnsidh.
clàr-ìnnsidh, s. m. Index, contents of a book. 2**Title-page.
clàr-iomairt, s.m, Chess-board, draught-board.
clàr-iongach, see clàir-i—.
clàr-Lochluinneach,(MMcD) s.m. Plank hollowed out in centre in form of a trough. Small shallow holes were cut at intervals in the top edges which were for holding salt. The meal of potatoes was poured into the hollow in the centre, round which the family sat at dinner —*Lewis*.
clàr-maide, (DC) s.m. Stick laid across a doorway to close up the space between door and floor, and exclude wind, rain, &c—*Barra*.
clàr-malairt,* s.m. Counter of a shop.
clàr-mìneachaidh, clàir-, s.m. Glossary.
clàr-na-dèarna, s.m. Palm of the hand.

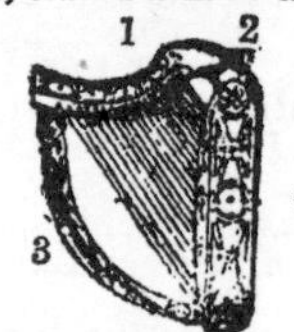

153. *Clàrsach.*

clàrsach,‡ -aich, -aichean, s.m. Harp. Cho caoin ri c., *as soft as a harp.*
PARTS OF A HARP :—
1 Amhach, *neck,*
2 Cnagan, *pins,*
3 Com, *chest,*
4 Làmh-chrann, *tree,*
5 Teudan, *strings.*
clàrsach-ùrlar,* s. f. Old woman in gentlemen's families, kept for telling stories. 2 Witch.
clàrsaich, *gen. sing.* of clàrsach.
clàrsair, -e, -ean, s.m. Harper, minstrel.
———eachd, s.f. Harp-music, harping, employment of a harper.
clàr-seòlaidh, s.m. Guide-post.
clàr-sgéithe, s.m. Field *in heraldry.*
clàr-sh ìthichean, s.m. Cupboard, "press."
clàr-tàilisg, s.m. Backgammon table.
clàr-thomhais, see clàr-tomhais.
clàr-tomhais, s.m. Balance, scale, measure.
clar-uachdair, s.m. Lid of a chest or trunk. 2 (AH) Deck of a ship.
†clas, s.m. see glas. 2 s.f. see glas.
†clas, clais, s.m. Melody. 2 Furrow, pit. 3 see cleas.
clasach,‡‡ s.f. see closach.
†clasach, a. Crafty. 2 Playful. 3 Fat, fatted. 4**Melodious.
†———d, s.f. Craftiness, subtlety.
†clasaiche, s. m. Singer.
claspa,‡‡ -an, s.m. & v.a. Gaelic form of *clasp.*
clàtar, -air, see clàbar 2.
clath-nàire, s.f.ind. Bashfulness, shamefacedness, modesty.
†clè, s.f.ind. (clì) The left hand. 2 Evil, injury. 3 Disposition.
†—, a. Left-handed. 2 Prejudiced, partial.
cleabhaid,** s.f. Slap.
cleabhar, (AF) see gleithir.
cleabhar-caoch,(AF) Corn-craik, see trèun-ri-trèun.
cleachd, -an, s.f. Ringlet of hair, waving lock, tress. 2 Fillet of combed wool. 3 Habit, custom, practice. 4** Exercise. 5** Plait. 6 Ray of the sun. [** says s.m.] Cleachdan na gréine, *the rays of the sun* ; Eilidh nan òr-chleachda, *Helen with the golden locks.*
———, pr.part. a' cleachdadh, v.a. & n. Accustom, habituate, inure. 2 Practise, use. 3**Acquaint. 4**Plait. C. thu fhéin ris, *inure yourself to it* ; ch. mi a bhi, *I was accustomed to be* ; ch. mi moran dheth 'fhaotainn, *I was accustomed to get much of it.*
———ach, -aiche, a. Usual, customary, habitual. 2 Having clustering ringlets or tresses. 3 Waving, flowing, as hair 4**Filleted. 5**Plaited. 6** Accustomed. 7‡‡ Thick, clustering.
cleachdadh,-aidh, pl. -aidhean, [cleachdannan, & cleachdainnean,] s. m. Custom, practice, use, exercise, habit. 2 Accustoming, inuring. A' c—, pr. pt. of cleachd. Is e an cleachdadh a ni teòma, *practice makes perfect.*
cleachdag, -aig, -an, s.f. Ringlet, tress.
————ach, a. Full of curls, ringlets or tresses. 2**Curled. T' òr-chul cleachdagach, *thy curled golden locks.*
cleachdaidh, see cleachdach.
————eachd, see cleachdalachd.
cleachdail, -e, see cleachdach.
cleachdainn, a. see cleachdach.
cleachdainn, -ean, s. m. Custom, habit, practice, use and wont. [** gives s.f.] Is don' an c. sin, *that is a bad custom* ; deagh ch., *a good custom.*
cleachdalachd, s.f. Customableness.
cleachdan, n. pl. of cleachd. Do ch., *thy locks.*
cleachdar,** a. see cleachdmhor.
cleachdmhor, -oire, a. Accustomable.
cleadhdna, see cleachdan.
cleachdta, a. & past pt. of cleachd. Accustomed, wont, habituated, inured, trained. 2 **Expert. 3**Plaited. 4**Secondhand. C. ris an olc, *accustomed to do evil* ; c. an cogadh, *expert in war.*
cleachdte, see cleachdta.
cleachduinn, see cleachdainn.
cleachta, see cleachdta.
cleachte, see cleachdta.
cleadhag, s.f. see cloitheag.
cleamhna, gen. of cliamhuinn.
cleamhnas, ais, s.m. Affinity, bethrothal. 2 Friendship, consanguinity, relationship by marriage. 3* Sexual intercourse, carnal connection, copulation. Dean c., *become connected by marriage;* c. am fagus is goisdeachd am fad, *marriage near and gossiping afar.*
†clearadh, -aidh, s.m. Familiarity.
clearc, -an, s.m. Curl, lock of hair.
———, a. Curled. 2 Bright, radiant, shining. 3**Of a bright yellow.
———, v.a. Spread, curl, arrange. 2 Make into ringlets.
———ach,* a. Curled, in ringlets.
†clear-na-càine, s.m. see under cliar.
cleas, -a, -an, s. m. Play, trick, craft, feat. 2 Gambol. 3 Feat in legerdemain. 4 Stratagem. 5**Warlike exercise. 6**Deeds, movements. Cuchulainn nan c., *C. full of exploits* ; gun ch., (adv.) *above-board* ; c. luchd-tognail na gainneimh, a' faicinn each a chéile dhachaidh gu latha, *the way of sand-carriers, seeing each other home till daylight* ; air chleas

(AC) *like ;* chithear an t-anam air ch. meall soluis ; *the soul is seen like a bright ball of light.*
cleasach, -aiche, *a.* Playful, sportive. 2 Crafty, full of schemes or tricks. 3 Juggling. 4 Performing feats of valour. 5 Frisky, active, brisk.
cleasachail,‡‡ -e, *a.* Pantomime.
cleasachd, *s.f.ind.* Play, diversion, pastime, sport, relaxation. 2 Legerdemain, sleight of hand. 3**Strife. 4††Playfulness. 5‡‡ Performing of heroic deeds. 6 Frolicsomeness, friskiness. Ri c., *playing, sporting* ; dh' éirich iad gu c., *they rose up to play ;* c. dhaoine, *the sleights of man ;* droch ch., *foul play.* A' c—, *pr.pt.* of cleasaich.
cleasachdach, -aiche, *a.* Playful, sportive.
cleasachdaich, -e, see cleasachd.
cleasadh, -aidh, *s.m.* Bounding, leaping, sporting, gambolling. Miolchoin a' c. àrd, *greyhounds bounding high.*
cleasaich, *pr.pt.* a' cleasachd, *v.n.* Play, sport, gambol, perform feats of activity, vault, tumble as a rope-dancer.
cleasaiche, -an, *s. m.* Juggler, conjurer. 2 Buffoon. 3 Mountebank. 4 Stage-player, actor. 5* Cunning fellow.
————, *comp.* of cleasach.
cleasaidheachd, *s.f.ind.* see cleasachd.
cleasanach,‡‡ -aiche, *a.* Apish. 2 Wanton.
cleasanta, see cleasach. Gu c., *playfully.*
————chd, see cleasachd.
cleasan-teine, *s.pl.* Fireworks.
cleasmhor,** -oire, *a.* Agile.
cleath, *s. m.* see cleith. †2 Prince chieftain.
————, (for cleith) *pr. pt.* of ceil.
cleatha, *s.f.* Goad. 2 Rib. 3 Stake. 4 Club or clumsy stick. [†† & * give s.m.]
†————ch, -aiche, *a.* Ribbed.
†cleathaireachd, *s.f.ind.* Rusticity. 2 Boldness.
cleathar, *s.m.* Milch-cow.
†cleathard, *a.* Steep, inaccessible.
† ————, *s.m.* Fame, eminence.
cleathar-lead, } see cleathar.
†———— -sed, }
†cleath-chur, *s.f.* Relation by blood. 2 Genealogical line.
†cleathramh, -aimh, *s.m.* Partiality, prejudice.
cleibe, -achan, *s.m.* Instrument used to catch fish and sea-fowl.
cleibeach,(DU) *a.* Clumsy.
cleibean,(DU) *s.m.* Slow, clumsy, awkward [fellow.
cleibeire, see cleibean.
cleibeirt, see cleibean.
cléibh, *gen. sing.* of cliabh.
†cléibhin, see cliabhan.
cleibideach, *s.f.* Clumsiness, untidiness. 2 (DU) Tossing. Thàinig e anns a' chleibidich, *he came clumsily*—said of one deformed, of an old person, or cripple ; bha biodag anns a' chleibidich air mac a' bhodaich leibidich, *the awkward fellow's son had his dirk dangling.*
cleid, -e, -ean, *s.f.* see cleit. 2 (AC) Quip, prank, trick, fillip, sharp stroke.
cleide,** *s.f.* Fair.
cleideach, -eiche, see cleiteach.
cleideag, -eig, -an, see cleiteag.
————ach, -aiche, see cleiteach.
cleidh,(AC) *s.* Cot. (cleith)
†cleidhe, *s.f.* Chalice, cup.
cléidhseam,(CR) *s.m.* Wrath, fury.—*West of Ross.* Chuir thu an c. dearg air, *you made him perfectly furious.*
cleig, *v.a.* Dishevel, as hair.
cléir, -e, *s.f.* Clergy. 2 Presbytery. A' ch., *the clergy* (collectively.)
†cléirceach, Old misprint for cléireach.
cléir-chuilbheart, -eirt, -an, *s.f.* Priestcraft.
cléireach, *a.* Clerical. 2 Presbyterian.
cléireach, -ich, *s.m.* Clerk. 2 Clergyman. 3 Writer. 4 Proclaimer of banns. 5 Beadle, church-officer. 6**Precentor. Cha'n 'eil c. no pears'-eaglais ann, *there is neither clerk nor clergyman.*
————ail,** *a.* Clerical.
cléireach-cùirte, *s.m.* Actuary.
cléireachd, *s.f.* Scholarship. 2 Clerkship. 3 Condition of a churchman. 4 Body of churchmen.
cléireanach, -aich, *s.m. prov.* for cliaranach.
cléireil, *a.* Presbyterian. An Eaglais shaor ch., *the Free Presbyterian Church.*
cléirich, *gen. & pl.* of cléireach.
cléir-lagh, *s.* Canon.
cléir-shònruchadh,‡‡ -aidh, *s.m.* Ordination.
cléirsinneachd, *s.f.* Clerkship, writing, accountantship. Ris a' ch., *clerking.*
cléir-smachdaichte, *a.* Priest-ridden.
cléirsneachd, see cléirsinneachd.
cléir-uachdaranachd,‡‡ *s.f.ind.* Churchdom.
cleit, -e, -ean, *s.f.* Quill. 2 Feather. 3 Down. 4 Covering of feathers. 5 Rocky eminence. 6 Ridge or reef of sunken rocks —*Islay.* 7 Eaves. 8 Flake, as of snow. 9(AC)Land surrounded by the sea at high-water. 10*Clot. 11(AC) Door-bar.—*Uist.* 12 (AC) Backbone. 13**Penthouse. 14(JM)Cliff on the sea-shore. 15(DU) Gaelic spelling of *cleat,* see bàta, Nos. 6 to 8 p. 75.
[Often appears as a prefix or suffix in names of places, as, Ormacleit, *Orme's ridge ;*] c. na dabhcha, *the ridge of the district ;* c. na comhla, *the bar of the door.*
[McL & D. and ** give "cléit," "cléiteag," &c., but the *e* is short, and "cleit," &c. as given here and by ‡ & †† is correct.—CR. †† gives "cleit" for Nos. 5 & 6, and "cléit" for Nos. 1 & 8, but the accent is omitted by ‡ in both.]
cleite,** *s.f.* Calamus. 2 see cleit.
————ach, -eiche, *a.* Rocky, craggy. 2 Feathery. 3 Flaky. 4 Clotty. 5 Shaggy.
cleiteadh, -idh, -ean, *s.m.* Ridge of rocks in the sea.
cleiteag, -eig, -an, *s.f.* Small flake, quill, or feather. 2 Small clot. 3**Down. 4**Head of the burdock. 5 (DC) Flake of snow—*Perth & Argyll.* Cho pailt ri cleiteagan sneachd, *as plentiful as flakes of snow.*
————ach, -aiche, *a.* Flaky. 2 Downy. 3 Feathery. 4 Craggy, rocky. 5 Shaggy.
cleitean, -ein, -an, *s.m.* see cleiteag. ‡‡Penthouse. 3 Eaves of a roof.
cleith, -e, -ean, *s. f.* & *m.* Stake. 2 Goad. 3 Oar. 4 Roof. 5 Post. 6**Residence. 7** Concealment. 8 Skulking, lurking. 9 Secrecy. 10‡‡Hill, eminence. 11 (AC) Waulking board. 12‡ Wattle. 13 Body of anything. A' c—, *pr.pt.* of ceil. An c., *in concealment ;* cha'n 'eil c. air an olc, ach gun a dheanamh, *the only way to conceal evil is not to commit it;* cleithean righinn, *tough oars.*
cléith, *dat.* of cliath.
cleith, *v.a.* see ceil.
cleithe, *pr. pt.* of cleith.
cléithe, *gen.sing.* of cliath.
cleitheach, -eiche, *a.* Private, concealing, clandestine. Gu c., *clandestinely.*
cléitheach,** *a.* Feathery.
————d, *s.f.ind.* Lurking, skulking. 2 Concealment, secrecy.
cleith-inntinn, *s.f.* Mental reservation, dissimulation.

cleithir,(AF) see gleitbir.
cleith-luaidh, see cleith-luathaidh.
cleith luathaidh,(AC) *dat. sing.* of cliath-luathaidh.
cleith-mhiosguis, *s.f.* Private grudge.
cleitig, -e, -ean *s.f.* One cow's grass. 2 Croft. 3 Measure of land, containing ⅛ pennyland.
cleitinn, see cleitig.
cléit-sgrìobhaidh,** *s.f.* Pen.
†clé làmhach, see clì-làmhach.
†cle mhana, *s.f.* Mischief.
cleòbag,(AF) see cliobag.
———**ach**, see cleòbag.
cleòc, -a, -an [& -annan,] *s.m.* Cloak, mantle. C. nam meanbh bhall ruadh, *a cloak with small red spots.*
cleòc, *v.a.* Cloak, cover with a cloak or mantle, conceal.
——**ach,††** *a.* Mantled, cloaked.
——**an**, -ain, -an, *s.m.* Little cloak or mantle. 2**Scarf.
——**anach,††** -aiche, *a.* Of, or pertaining to, a little cloak.
cleòchd, *s. & v.* see cleòc, *s. & v.*
cleòd,(AF) *s.m.* Horse-fly.
cleubach,** *a.* Dilatory.
clì, clìthe, *s.f.* Vigour, strength, force. 2 Power of motion. 3 Ability. 4 Energy, pith. 5 ***rarely* the body, ribs. Gun ch., *without power of motion*; duine gun ch., *a man without energy;* chunnaic e a' ghaoth gun ch., *he saw the wind was without force.*
clì, clìthe, *a.* Left-handed, left. 2 Awkward. 3 Slow, feeble. 4 Humble. 5**Strong. 6‡‡ Kind. 7††Clever. 8‡ Wrong. A dh' ionnsuidh na làimhe clìthe, *to the left hand*; air a thaobh clì, *on his left side*; c. 's a' chòmhraig, *lame* or *feeble in the strife;* labhair gu c., *speak wrongly*; dh' éirich thu bhàrr do thaobh clì, *you have risen off your left, or wrong side*—generally applied when one is not getting on well, or has a reference to the idea of being lucky or unlucky; ma théid mi c., *if I go wrong.*
†clì, s. *m.* Successor to an episcopal see. 2 Poet of the third order.
†clia, *s.m.* see crùn-luath.
cliabh, -éibh, *s.m.* The chest, the breast. 2 Kind of basket or hamper used in the Highlands for carrying burdens, and generally slung on each side of a horse, creel. 3 Stay. 4 Strait-jacket, strait-vest of wicker-work for a madman. 5††Cheese-chest. 'S ann a tha 'n t-òlach ann an cliabh, *the fellow is mad*; a' taomadh m' a ch., *pouring it on his chest* ; c. gùin, *bodice of a gown*; cliabhan mnà, *stays*; glacadh-cléibh, *rickets.*
PARTS OF A CREEL :—
1 Briagan a' chléibh, taobhaisdean, *holes round the centre.* Mu bhriagan a' chléibh, *about half-full.*
2 Cluasan, *ears*—where the ends of suspender are inserted.
3 Bulais, *suspender.*
4 Iris, iris-mhuineal, (AH) *shoulder-band of creel* (made of rope.)
5 Dula na h-iris, *loop of shoulder-band.*
6 Staingean, *ribs.*
7 An curra, an t-inneach, *the woof or weft.*
8 An dlùth, *the warp.*
9 Màs, *bottom.*
10 Prais, *pot.*
11 Uchdaich, *breast-band to carry creel* (made of woven grass.)
cliabhach, -aiche, *a.* Chested, having a large chest. 2 Of, or belonging to, the chest. 3 Like a hamper or basket. 4 Of, or abounding in, hampers or baskets.
†cliabhach, -aich, *s.m.* Wolf. 2(AF)Fox.
cliabhadair,** see cliabhair.
cliabhair,** *s.m.* Basket-maker.
cliabhairt, *v.a.* Fish thoroughly.
cliabhan, -ain, -an, *s.m.* Small creel, hamper, or chest. 2**Cage.
———**ach,††** -aiche, *a.* Full of small creels or chests.
cliabhan-ceangail,* *s.m.* Bodice.
cliabh-caol. *s.m.* Creel made of wands.
cliabh-chuiseag, *s.m.* Creel made of stalks.
cliabh-fharsuing, -e, *a.* Broad-chested, broad-breasted.
cliabh-fiodha, *s.m.* Creel made of slips of wood.
cliabh-fraoich, *s.m.* Creel made of heather.
cliabh-giomach,(AH) *s.m.* Lobster-creel, lobster-pot.
†cliabhrach, -aich, -aichean, *s.f.* see cliathach.
cliabh-sgeathrach, -aich, -aichean, *s.f.* Vomit.
cliabh-spidrich, *s.m.* Creel for carrying burdens on horseback, having a false bottom fixed with moveable pins. 2 Creel with closed pointed end for catching fish—*Livingstone's Poems.*
cliadan, -ain, -an, *s.m.* Burr, burdock.
———**ach**, *a.* Abounding in burrs, like a burr.
†cliadh, *s.m.* Antiquaries.
clia lùth, *s.f.ind.* see crùn-luath. 2 Musical term for a certain class of fingering, not the same as crùn-luath, nor in pipe-music only—(MM.)
cliamach, ** -aich. *s.m.* Lobster. 2 Ragged child. 3 Surly fellow.
†cliamhach, -aich, *s.m.* Fox.
cliamhnas, -ais, see cleamhnas.
cliamhuinn, *gen.* cleamhna, *pl.* cleamhnan, [& cleimhnean,] *s.m.* Son-in-law. 2**Ally. 3 *Brother-in-law—*Islay.* [In the plural it generally signifies any near relations by marriage.]
———**eas**, -eis, *s.m.* see cleamhnas.
cliar, -eir, [***gen. & pl.* cliair] *s. m.* Poet. 2 Brave man. 3 see cléir. Fuil nan c., *blood of the brave men.* The Cliar Sheanachain, (Senchan's lot) was the mythic bardic company, especially on its rounds—*Gaelic Folk Tales*—‡.
——**ach,**** *a.* Like a poet. 2 Like a brave man. 3 Brave. 4 see cléireach.
——**achas**, -ais, *s.m.* Singing. 2 Bardism. 3 Versification. 4 Heroism. 5 Fighting. 6 Feats of strength or valour. 7*Chorus—*Islay.* Ri c. ré fad an là, *fighting all day.*
cliar,†† *a.* Brave, gallant. 2 Renowned.
——**achd**, *s.f.* see cliarachas.
cliaradh, -aidh, *s.m.* Singing. 2 Music.
cliaraiche, -an, see cliaranach.
cliaraidheachd, *s.f.* see cliarachas.
cliaranach, -aich, *s. m.* Songster, bard, minstrel. 2 Harper. 3 Sword. 4 Swordsman.
†cliar-ealain, *s.m.* Band of bards.
cliata, see cliathta.
cliata,* *s.m.* Meadow. 2 Burr—*Lewis.*
cliatan, -ain, -an, *s.m.* Level plain of ground. 2 **Trellis. 3††Hand.
cliataran,(DU) *s.m.* Crawling.
cliath, *gen.* cléithe, *dat.* cléith, *n.pl.* cliathan [& cléith,] *dat. pl.* cliathaibh, *s. f.* Harrow. 2 Grate. 3 Lattice. 4 Casement. 5 Battalion. 6 Shoal, as of fishes. 7 Darning of a stocking. 8‡ Worm of a still. 9 Body, multitude. 10 Hurdle, as for fulling cloth. 11 Hurdle, as used in fencing. 12 Weir for salmon.— *ewis.* 13 Strong stockade constructed of wood or wattle, and erected in olden times

to protect "meanbh-chrodh" (small cattle,as sheep, goats, &c.,) from the ravages of wild animals. 14††Set of oars. 15‡‡Treadles of a loom. 16 Certain use of the fingers in playing bagpipe and other music. 17 Sometimes used for cliabh. Stann-cléithe, *a worm-vat;* c. éisg, *a creel or school of fish;* c. chliata, *a harrow*; troimh mo chléith, *through my casement;* cuid an t-searraich de 'n chliath, *the foal's share of the harrow—i.e.* idleness, as the foal only follows its mother when at work; thug e leis a' ch. agus na h-ursainnean, *he took the door and lintels with him.*
cliath, *pr.pt.* a' cliathadh, *v.a.* Harrow. 2 Copulate, as fowls. 3 Run or darn a stocking. A' cliathadh nan cearc, *treading the hens*; tha 'n stoirm air a mhuir a' cliathadh, *the storm has smoothed* (*lit.* harrowed) *the sea—Lewis.*
cliathach, -aich, -aichean, *s.f.* Side of the human body. 2 Side of a quadruped. 3 Slope or side of a hill. 4 Battle, conflict, 5 Bilge of a boat. Ri cliathaich na luinge, *to the side of the ship*; ri d' chliathaich, *at your side*; c. a' mhonaidh, *the side of the hill;* leig leis a' ch. e, *let it go overboard.*

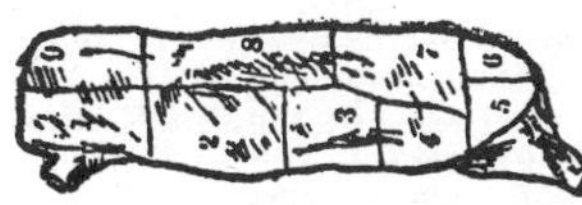

154. An dòigh air cliathach muc-fheòil a ghearradh.

PARTS OF A SIDE OF BACON :—
1 Spòg thoisich, slinnean, *fore hock.*
2 Gearradh meadhonach, an stiallach tiugh, *thick streaky* or *middle cut.*
3 An stiallach tana, *thin streaky cut.*
4 Loch-bhléin, *flank.*
5 Spòg dheiridh, *gammon.*
6 Oisinn na spòige deiridh, *corner of gammon.*
7 Leasradh, *loin.*
8 Druim agus aisnean, *back and ribs.*
9 Amhach, *collar.*

cliathadh, -aidh, *s.m.* Harrowing. 2 Treading, as the males in poultry. A' c—, *pr. pt.* of cliath.
cliathag, -aig, -an, *s.f.* Little hurdle or harrow. 2 The chine.
cliathaich, *gen. sing.* of cliathach.
cliathaidh, *fut. aff. a.* of cliath.
cliathair, -ean, *s.m.* Harrower.
cliathan, -ain, -an, *s.m.* Breast. 2**Breastbone. 3 (JM) Broken side of a ship or boat. 4(MMcD) Timbers placed under the thatch of a house—*Lewis.*
cliath-bharraich, *pl.* -an-barraich, *s.f.* Hurdle or frame of basket-work, chiefly made from branches of the birch-tree, and used as doors for cottages.
cliath-chliata, -an-cliata, *s.f.* Harrow.
cliath-chòmhraig, *pl.* -an-còmhraig, *s.f.* Battalion. 2 Hero.
cliathdan, -ain, -an, see cliadan.
cliath-éisg, *s.f.* Shoal of fish.
cliath-iaruinn, *pl.* -an-iaruinn, *s.f.* Pot-trivet. 2**Hand-harrow.
cliath-làimbe, *pl*, -an-làimhe, *s.f.* Hand-barrow.
cliath-luathaidh,*pl.* -an-luathaidh, *s.f.* Fuller's frame or hurdle, waulking-board.
cliath-lùth, see clia-lùth.
†cliathog, -oig, -ean, *s.m.* The spine or back.
cliath-poite-duibhe,†† *s.f.* Worm of a still.
cliathrach,** *s.m.* Trellis.
†cliathrach, *a.* Breast-high.
cliathraich,** *v.a.* Grate, lattice.
cliath-ràmh, *pl.* -an-ràmh, *s.f.* Set of oars.
cliath-sheanchaidh, *pl.* -an-seanchaidh, *s.m.* Genealogical table.
cliath-sheanchais, *pl.* -an-seanchais, *s.m.* see cliath-sheanchaidh.
cliath-shlat,** *s.* Hurdle.
cliathta, *past pt.* of cliath.
cliath-theine,* *s.f.* Grate, fireplace.
cliath-uinneig, *pl.* -an-uinneig, *s.f.* Lattice. 2 Balcony. Troimh ch.-u., *through a lattice.*
clib, -e, -eachan, *s.* see cliob.
clib, *v.* see cliob.
——each. *a.* see cliobach,
——eadh, -eidh, see cliobadh.
clibeag, -eig, -an *s.f.* Trick, wile, imposition. 2 Accident. 3 Flap. 4 Sometimes used for cliobag.
clibealachd, *s.f.* see cliobaireachd.
clibean, -ein, *s. m.* Dewlap. 2 Excrescence. 3 Any flabby thing. 4 Dupe. 5 Appendage. —*Lewis.* C. na cluaise, *the ear-lobe;* c. àdha, *a piece of liver.*
clibeil, -e, see cliobail.
clibein, -e, -ean, see clibean.
†clibheadh, *s.f.* Stumbling. 2 Stepping.
†clibhiseach, -eiche, *a.* Peevish. 2 Petulant. 3 Waspish.
†————d, *s.f.ind.*Peevishness. 2 Petulance. 3 Waspishness.
clibidich, see cliobaidich.
†clibin, *s.m.* Piece, segment.
†clibis, *s.f.* Tumult, stir, wild commotion.
clibist, -e, -ean, *s.f.* Misadventure. 2 Gudgeon, (not a fish, but in the sense of a simpleton.) 3(JGM) Slut.
clibiste, see cliobair.
————ach, -eiche, *a.* Unfit, awkward, unhandy.
clic, -e, -ean, *s. f.* Iron hook or crook. 2 (AH) Gaff for landing fish. 3 Hinge. 4 Trick. 5**Clasp. 6**Bad trick.
——, *v.a.* Shut up by means of a hook or hooks. 2 Draw towards one with a hook or crook. 3 **Catch with a hook.
——each, -eiche, *a.* Cunning, artful, fraudulent, deceitful.
——each,‡‡ -eiche, *a.* Knavish, wicked.
——eadh,‡‡ -idh, *s.m.* Accroachment.
†clich, *v.a.* Assemble, bring together.
clichd, see clìc.
———each, see clìceach.
———eadh, see clìceadh.
†clicheadh, *s.m.* Assemblage, collection.
clìd,(CR) *s.* Strength. (clì, *vigour.*)
clifeagaich, (AH) *s. f.* School-boy game in which each tries to knock the bonnet off the other.
clifeid, (CR) *s. f.* Sleet, soft snow that melts when it touches the ground—*W. of Ross-sh.*
clig, see clìc.
clì-làmhach, *a.* Left-handed. 2 Awkward. Duine c., *a left-handed man.*
——————d, *s.f.* Left-handedness. 3 Awkwardness.
†clinnceadh, -idh, -ean, *s. m.* Gaelic form of *clinking.*
cliob, *pr. pt.* a' cliobadh[& a' cliobaidich,] *v.a. & n.* Stumble, slip. 2‡‡ Tear in pieces. 3 Nibble, pick with the mouth. 4** Dangle, swing—*Lewis.* Tha earball na bà a' cliobaidich, *the cow's tail is swinging*; leig leam gus an c. mi an cnàimh, *let me alone till I pick the bone* (*with my teeth.*)

cliob, *s.m.* Anything dangling loosely. 2 Excrescence. 3 see cliobadh.
—**ach**, -aiche, *a.* Curled. 2 Rough. 3** Hairy. 4 Clumsy, awkward—*Lewis.* 5‡ Stumbling.
cliobad,†† -aid, *s.f.* Lisping, stammering.
cliobadh, -aidh, *s.m.* Slipping, stumbling. 2 Stumble, slip. 3** Tearing in pieces. 4 Nibbling. A' c—, *pr. pt.* of cliob. Tha iasg 'gam ch., *a fish is nibbling my hook.*
cliobag, -aig, -an, *s.f.* Filly, young mare.
———-**eich**, *s.f.* Shaggy colt.
cliobaidich, *pr. pt.* of cliob.
cliobail, -e, *a.* Clumsy, awkward, silly, helpless. 2 Imbecile. 3 Liable to accidents.
cliobain, -ean, see clibean.
cliobair, -ean, *s.m.* Clumsy, awkward silly person. 2 Simpleton.
———**eachd**, *s.f.ind.* Clumsiness, silliness, awkwardness, helplessness.
cliobalachd, see cliobaireachd.
cliobar, -air, *s.m.* see glìb.
cliobhach, -aiche, *a.* Curled, rough.
cliobhag, *s.f.* Slap with the open hand.
cliòbhaid,(DU) *s.f.* Sleet.
†**cliobhuna**, *s.m.* Rug.
†**cliobsa**,‡ *s.f.* Dejection of countenance.
cliof,‡‡ -a, -annan, *s.f.* Cliff.
clìogair, *v.a.* Croak, make a noise.
clìogar, -air, *s.m.* Croaking.
———**ach**,** *a.* Croaking.
†**clìogarsa**, *a.* That croaks.
†**clìolunta**, *a.* Strong, stout, potent, hearty.
cliopach, -aiche, *a.* Stammering, halting in speech.
cliopach,‡‡ *s.m.* Halt in speech.
cliopad, see cliobad.
cliospach, -aiche, *a.* Lame. 2 Handless. 3 Inactive.
cliostar, -air, -an, *s.m.* Clyster.
cliotach,** *a.* see ciotach.
clip, *pr.pt.* a' clipeadh, *v.a.* Hook, catch with a hook. 2* Pilfer, snatch, steal.
clip,-e, -an,*s.f.* Fraud, deceit,cunning. 2 Hook. 3*Hand-hook, for taking fish into the boat which are too heavy for the line, fish-gaff. 4 ††Piece of fish or white leather used as a bait. 5* Stratagem, deceit, cunning.
—**each**, -eiche, *a.* Deceitful. 2 Unhandy. 3 Having weak hands. 4‡‡Slack. †5**Hooked. 6††Stammering. 7‡‡ Defective.
—**eil**, see clipeach.
clipiche, *s.f.ind.* Defectiveness.
clip-làmhach,-aiche, *a.* Unhandy.
————**as**, -ais, *s.m.* Unhandiness.
clip-làmhaiche, see clip-làmhachas.
clipse,** *s.f.* Gaelic form of Scots *clipps* (an eclipse.)
clis, *v. a.* & *n.* Leap, skip. 2‡‡Frustrate. 3‡‡ Deceive.
clis, -e, *a.* Active, agile, quick, nimble, speedy. Na fir-chlis, *the merry dancers* or *aurora borealis* ; gu c. 'na chéile shàs iad, *they seized each other keenly* ; bradan grad-chlis, *a nimble salmon.* [‡ says †.]
—**beach**, *a.* Unsteady on the feet, apt to stumble 2**Cripple, lame.
—**beachd**, *s.f.* Lameness, unsteadiness.
—**each**,(CR) *s.m.* Side of the human body—*W. of Ross-shire.*
—**each**,* *s.m.* Wicket.
—**eachd**, *s.f.* Presentness, quickness, agility.
—**ead**, -eid, *s.m.* see cliseachd.
—**eadh**, -sidh, -idhean, *s.m.* Leap, skip, jump. A' c—, *pr. pt.* of clis. Leaping, skipping, jumping.
—**eil**, *a.* Nimble. Gu cliseil fearr-ghleusach, brisg fo 'armachd, *nimble, trained, and brisk under arms—Duanaire, 155.*
clisg, *pr.pt.* a' clisgeadh, *v.a.* & *n.* Start, startle, leap through fear. Ch. e, *he started.*
clisg-bhuail,‡‡ *v.a.* Cause to stand agaze.
clisge, *s.f.* Start. 2 Brisk movement. A ch., (*adv.*) *suddenly.*
———**ach**, -eiche, *a.* Apt to start, starting, timid, fearful. 2 Skittish. 3**Skipping.
———**achd**,‡‡ *s.f.* Quickness, activity, nimbleness.
———**adh**, -idh, -idhean, *s.m.* Startling, alarm. 2 In a start, instantly. 3 Skipping. Bi an seo an clisgeadh, *be here instantly;* ch. féidh is earba 'san fhraoch, *startling of deer and roe in the heather* ; bha iad air an c. romhad, *they were afraid of you* ; c. ort ! *the greeting accorded to one who has startled another.* A' c—, *pr.pt.* of clisg.
clisgean,(AF) Swift (bird,) see gobhlan mór.
clisgear, *s.m.* Interjection in *grammar.*
clisneach, -nich, *s.m.* Human body. 2 Carcase. 3 The outward appeapance. 4* Wicket, bargate. 5 Mouth never at rest. 6 (CR) One side or slope of a roof—*Perthshire.*
clisneach, see clisbeach.
cliste, *a.* Active, nimble, supple, swift, dexterous. Gu c., *nimbly.*
clisteachd, *s.f.ind.* Activity, swiftness, dexterity, agility, nimbleness.
clith,** *s.m.* Desire of copulation in cattle.
——, *a.* & *s.* see clì.
——,‡‡ -e, *a.* Close, true. 2 Vile.
†**clitheag**, *s.f.* Gap.
clìth-làmhach, see clì-làmhach.
—————**d**, see clì-làmhachd.
†**clithre**, *s.f.* Guard.
clitig, -e, -ean, see cleitig.
clitinn,†† see cleitig.
cliù, *gen.* cliù [& cliùtha,] *s.m.* Fame, renown. 2 Praise. 3 Character, reputation. Fo dheagh ch., *under a good character* ; cha'n éireadh mo ch. 'na bhàs, *my reputation would not increase by his death* ; is e do ch. do cheud alladh, *the estimate of you goes according to the first report of you.*
cliùar, see cliùmhor.
cliùc, *pr.pt.* a' cliùcadh, *v.a.* Mend or repair nets or shoes.
cliùc,* *s. f.* Stratagem, hellish trick. 2 Deceit, fraud.
———**ach**, -aiche, *a.* Hooked. 2 Cunning, deceitful, deceiving, artful.
———**ach**,* *s.f.* Deceitful female.
———**adh**, -aidh, *s.m.* Mending of nets. A' c—, *pr.pt.* of cliùc.
———**air**, -ean, *s.m.* Mender of shoes or nets. 2 Net-maker. 3 Cunning fellow, strategist. 4 (DU) Double hook or S for keeping net in position while undergoing repairs.
———**aireachd**, *s.f.ind.* Art of mending nets or shoes. 2 Artifice, cunning, deceit, fraud.
cliùchd, &c., see cliùc, &c.
cliùd, -a, -an, *s.m.* Slap on the face. 2 Slight stroke with the fingers, fillip. 3 Children's play. 4 Disabled hand. 5* Small trifling hand.
†**cliùd**, *a.* Squint-eyed.
cliùdan, -ain, *s.m.* see cliùd. 2 Little person disabled in the hands. 3††Little hand. 4* Trifling stroke or blow. 5**Slap on the face. 6**Fillip. C. cliadan, *children's play.*
————**achd**, *s.f.ind.* Continued or frequent slapping on the face. 2 Filliping.
cliùich, see cliùthaich.
cliùin,(AF) *s.* Wolf.
cliùiteach, -eiche, *a.* Famous, renowned, no-

ted, celebrated. 2 Laudable, commendable. Fionn c., *celebrated Fingal*; is cliùiteich' an onair na 'n t-òr, *honour is more commendable than gold.*
——adh, -aidh, *s.m.* Celebrating, praising, lauding, renowning.
——d,** *s.f.* Admirableness, celebrity.
cliùitich, see cliùthaich.
cliùmhor, -oire, *a.* Renowned, famous, noted, celebrated, praiseworthy.
cliùmhoireachd,†† *s.f.* Renown, celebrity.
cliù-òirdheirc, -e, *a.* Illustrious, noble. 2 Conspicuous.
cliùthach, -aiche, see cliùiteach.
cliùthachadh, -aidh, *s.m.* Act of praising, extolling, celebrating or exalting. A' c—, *pr.pt.* of cliùthaich.
cliùthaich, *pr.pt.* a' cliùthachadh, *v.a.* Praise, extol, exalt, celebrate, make famous.
——te, *past pt.* of cliùthaich. Celebrated, praised, extolled.
cliùthar, -aire, *a.* see cliùmhor.
cliuthmhor, see cliùmhor.
——achd, see cliùmhoireachd.
cliù-thoilltinneach, -aiche, *a.* Praiseworthy, commendable, deserving praise.
clò, *gen.* clòtha, *pl.* clòithean, *s.m.* Homespun, coarse home-made cloth. 2 Nail. 3 Pin, peg. 4 Gloom, vapour. 5 Sometimes used for clòdh; also 6 clò-chadal. Clò do 'n t-sùil, *slumber to the eye*; bròn gun ch., *sorrow without rest.*
clò, *v.a.* see clòdh.
†**clò**, *s.m.* Defeat. 2 The sea. 3 Variety, change.
clobha, *pl.* -chan, [& clobhan,] *s. m.* Tongs. Saighdearan a' chlobha, *volunteers* [*lit.* stay-at-home soldiers.]
clobhar-na-maighiche,§ *s.m.* Wood-sorrel, see seamrag.
clobhdach,(CR) *a.* Clumsy—*W. of Ross-shire.*
clobhdair,(CR) *s.m.* Bungler, botcher—*West of Ross-shire.*
clobh-arbhair,** *s.m.* Weed-hook.
clobhsa, -chan, *s.m.* see clamhsa.
clò-bhuail, *v.a.* see clòdh-bhuail.
——te, see clòdh-bhuailte.
——tear, see clòdh-bhualadair.
clò-bhualadh, see clòdh-bhualadh.
clòca, -chan, *s.m.* see cleòc.
clòcach, -aiche, *a.* Slouched.
clocaire,* -an, *s. m.* Rogue, deceitful fellow. 2 Dissembler, pretender.
clocaireachd,* *s.f.* Dissimulation.
cloch, cloiche, -an, *s.f.* see clach. 2§Henbane —*hyocymus niger.*
clochach, see clachach.
clò-chadal, -ail, *s.m.* Dozing, slumber, lethargy. C. na h-aoise, *the lethargy of age.*
clochan, -ain, -an, see clacharan. 2 see clachan.
——, *v.n.* Respire.
clochar, -air, *s. m.* Wheezing in the throat of a dying person. 2 Assembly, congregation. 3 Convent.
——nach, -aich, see clochranaich.
clocharra, *a.* see clacharra. 2 Lively, active, clever. 3** Pertaining to wheezing in the throat.
cloch-bheumnaich, -e, *a.* Stamping, prancing.
cloch-bhrath, see clach-bhrath.
cloch-bhuadha, -an-buadha, see clach-bhuadhach.
cloch-bhuaidh, see clach-bhuadhach.
cloch-chinn, see clach-chinn.
cloch-chnotaidh, see clach-chnotainn.
cloch-chròcaidh,‡‡ see clach-chnotainn.
clochlain,¶ *s.f.* Wheat-ear, see cloichearan.
clò-chlàr, see clòdh-chlar.
clò-chodal, see clò-chadal.
clochran, -ain, -an, see clacharan.
——aich, *s.f.* Wheezing in the throat.
cloch-reathnach, (*for* clach-raineach) see ceischrann.
cloch-shnaidheadair, see clach-shnaidheadair.
cloch-shreathail, see clach-shreathail.
cloch-shùil, see clach-shùil.
——each, -aiche, see clach-shùileach.
cloch-thàirnge, see clach-thàirnge.
clod, *gen.* cluid [& cloda,] *pl.* cluid [& clodan,] *s.m.* Clod, turf, sod. 2** *in derision*, Sluggish person.
clod, *pr. pt.* a' clodadh, *v.a.* Clod, pelt or cover with clods. 2(DU) Lift or remove clods and weeds from ploughed land which is to grow a green crop.
——ach, -aich, *s.f.* Dirt, filth, slime. 2 see cladach.
——ach, -aiche, *a.* Full of clods or turf. 2 Like a clod or turf, cloddy.
clodair, -ean, *s.m.* Pelter with clods. 2 Heavy dull man or beast. C. duine, *dull heavy man;* c. de each, *a dull heavy horse—Lewis.*
——eachd, *s.f.ind.* Clodding, throwing of, or pelting with, clods.
clodan, *n. pl.* of clod.
——, -ain, -an, *s.m.* Little clod.
——ach, -aiche, *a.* Cloddy, full of small clods.
clod-cheann, -chinn, *s.m.* Dull heavy head.
——ach, -aiche, *a.* Dull, stupid, heavy-headed.
——achd,‡‡ *s.f.* Obtuseness.
clòdh, -a, -an, *s. m.* Print, impression. 2 Printing-press. 3 Variety. 4** see clò.
clòdh, *v.a.* See clòdh-bhuail. 2 Conquer.
clodha, see clobha.
clòdhadh, see clòthadh.
clodhachadh,** -aidh, *s.m.* Drawing close together. A' c—, *pr.pt.* of clodhaich.
clodhaich,** *pr.pt.* a' clodhachadh, *v.a.* Draw close together, approach.
clòdhadair, -ean, *s.m.* Compositor, printer.
clòdhair,** see clòdhadair.
——eachd, *s.f.ind.* Business of a printer, printing, typography.
clòdh-bhuail, *v.a.* Print, exercise the art of typography. 2 Stamp, impress.
——te, *past part.* of clòdh-bhuail, Printed.
clòdh-bhuailtear, see clòdh-bhualadair.
clòdh-bhualadair, -ean, *s.m.* Printer.
clòdh-bhualadh, -aidh, *s.m.* Print, impression. 2 Edition of a book. 3 Printing, stamping, typography. A' c—, *pr.pt.* of clòdh-bhuail.
clòdh-chlàr, -air, *s.m.* Copper-plate. 2 Printing-press. 3 Printing-establishment.
†**clòdh-fhàsgadh**, *s.m.* Impression or edition of a book.
clòdh-fhear, see clòdh-bhualadair.
clòdh-ghalar, -air, *s.m.* Dizziness, giddiness, vertigo.
clòdh-mhearachd,** *s.f.* Misprint.
clòdh-sgrìobhadair, -ean, *s.m.* Type-writer.
†**clòdhuich**, *v.a.* Approach, contract.
clog, cluig, *s.m.* see clag. †2 Head.
†**clog**, *v.a.* Sound, as a bell.
†——achd, *s.f.ind.* Belfry.
clogad, -aid, -aidean, *s. m.* see clogaid.
clogaid, -e, -ean, *s. f.* Helmet, headpiece. 2 Cone, pyramid. 3 *s.m.* (DU) Headpiece of a stack of corn.
clogaide, *gen.sing.* of clogaid.
clogaideach, -eiche, *a.* Wearing helmets, armed with a helmet. 2 Belonging to a helmet.

clogais,‡ *s.f.* Wooden clog.
clogan, see **clagan.**
clogarnach, *s.f.* see **clagarnach.**
clogarnaich, see **clagarnach.**
clogas, see **clagas.**
clog-mheur, } *s.m.* Hour-hand of
clog-shnàthad, -aid, -an, } *s.f.* a dial-plate or clock (not of a watch.) *better* **làmh-uaireadair.**
†cloguide, -an, see **clogaid.**
cloich, *dat.* of **clach.**
cloich-bheumnaich, -e, see **cloch-bheumnaich.**
cloiche, *gen.sing.* of **clach.**
†cloichead, -eid, *s.f.* Passport.
cloichear, -eire, *s.m.* see **clochar.**
cloichearan,¶ *s.m.* Stone-chat,—*saxicola rubicola.* Facetiously called Fear na Féill-Padruig, *the one of St. Patrick's day*—because he appears about then.—AC. 2 Wheat-ear, see **brù-gheal.**

155. Cloichearan (1)

cloichirein, see **cloichearan.**
cloich-mheallain, see **clach-mheallain.**
†cloichreach, *s.f.* Stony place.
†cloichrean, *s.m.* see **cloichreach.**
cloich-shneachd, see **clach-shneachd.**
clòidh, *s.m.* see **clòimh.**
†clòidh, *s.f.* Paddock, small enclosure of grassland.
cloidhe, see **cloitheag.**
clòidheag, -eig, see **cloitheag 3,** & **clòimhneag.**
————ach, see **cloitheagach** & **clòimhneagach.**
cloidheamh, -imh, -an [& **cloidhean**] see **claidheamh.**
cloidhean, -ein, *s.m.* Pith of the box-tree. 2 Pith of any shrub tree. 3 see **clàidhean.**
————, *n.pl.* of **cloidheamh.**
————-doruis, see **clàidhean-doruis.**
cloidhibh, (*for* **claidhibh.**) Le c., *with knives.*
†cloigean, see **claigionn.**
†cloigineach, see **cluigeanach.**
†cloigionn, -inn, see **claigionn.**
clòilein, -e, *s.m. dim.* of **clò,** Little web of cloth.
clòimh, *gen.* -e [& **clòmhach,**] *dat.* **clòimhidh,** *s.f.* Wool. 2 Down of feathers. 3 Plumage. 4(AF) Woolly sheep.
Leabaidh chlòimh, *a feather-bed*; ge math c. cha'n ithear c., *wool is good, but one doesn't eat wool*—said by a half-starved woman to a Skye minister who, in response to an appeal for help, had offered her some wool. The saying is a good equivalent for the English proverb, *who gives thoughtfully gives twice*; air thughadh le c., *thatched with down*; tha c. mo chaorach féin ort, *I like you,* (*you cut your jib just like my own friends.*)
cloimh, *s.f.* The itch, scab, mange. [Preceded by the art. a' ch—.]
clòimh, *s.m.* Instrument to dress flax.
clòimh-chat, (AC) *s.m.* Catkin, cat-wool, inflorescence of the birch, beech, willow, &c. The catkin wool was twined into a 3-ply cord and that into a circle to safeguard against unseen powers.
cloimhdeachadh, -aidh, *s. m.* Shrugging. 2 Rubbing of the skin against one's clothes. A' c—, *pr.pt.* of **cloimhdich.**
cloimhdich, *pr. pt.* a' cloimhdeachadh, *v. a.* Shrug the shoulders. 2 Rub the members against one another.
clòimheach, -ich, *s.f.* see **clòimh.** 2(AF) Woolly sheep.
————, -eiche, *a.* Woolly, feathery.
cloimheach, -eiche, *a.* Mangy, scabby, scorbutic.
————d,‡‡ *s.f.ind.* Manginess.
clòimheag, -eig, *s.f.* see **clòimhneag.** 2 see **cloitheag.**
————ach,‡‡ *a.* see **cloitheagach.**
clòimhein, -ean, *s. m.* Icicle. 2 Snot, slaver. 3††Sort of small eel. 4 see **clàidhean.**
————each, -eiche, *a.* Hanging in snots, bubbles or slavers.
clòimheinich,‡‡ *pr.pt.* a' clòimheineachadh, *v.n.* Flutter, fall slowly, as down or feathers.
clòimh-ghargach, -aich, *s.f.* Down.
clòimh-gharrain,†† see **c— -ghargach.**
clòimhidh, *dat.* of **clòimh.**
clòimh-itean, *s.f.* see **clòimhteach.**
clòimh-liath, *s.f.* Mildew, mould—*mucedo.*
clòimhneag,** -eig, -an,** *s.f.* Small feather. 2 Down. 3 Flake of snow.
————ach, *a.* Feathery, downy, flaky.
clòimhteach, -ich, *s.f.* Down of feathers.
cloimhteachadh, *s.m.* see **cloimhdeachadh.**
cloinn, *dat.* of **clann.**
cloinne, *gen. sing.* of **clann.**
clois, -e, *s. f.* Plants of the order *equisetaceæ.* growing in watery places. 2‡‡ Marsh-weed, "horse-tail."
†clois, *v.n.* Hear.
†——dean, see **claistinn.**
cloitheag,‡ -eig, *s. f.* Shrimp, prawn. 2(JM) Small fish of a yellowish colour, found under stones on the sea-shore It has a few black spots on each side of the dorsal fin; spotted blenny. 3 (AF) Gadfly, cleg. 4 Small lamprey. Cuiridh a' ch. an lòn troimh a chéile (*i.e.* a very trifling person may create a disturbance. [This fish is used as a bait while trailing for lythe.]
†cloitheagach, *a.* Full of shrimps or prawns.
†cloithear, -ir, *s.m.* (claidheamh-fear) Champion.
clòithlein, *s.m.* see **clòilein.**
†clòmh, *v.a.* Dress flax.
clomh, (AC) *v. a.* see **clòth.**
——ach, -aiche, see **cloimheach.**
——adh, see **cloth.**
——ais, *s.f.* Cloves.
clòmhar, see **clamhar.**
†clomhas, -ais, *s.m.* Trap.
clo-mheas,** *s.m.* Cloves.
clòmhr,†† *pr.pt.* a' clòmhradh, *v.a.* Scratch by shrugging.
clòmhrachan,†† -ain, *s.m.* Fledgling.
clomhsadh,** see **clamhsa.**
†clonn, -a, *s.m.* Pillar. 2 chimney-piece.
†clòs, *s.m.* Hearing. 2 Report.
clos, *s. m. ind.* Rest, repose, stillness, sleep. 2 Quietness, silence. 3**Report. 4**Hearing. 5 see **clamhsa.** Gabh gu c., *be silent;* a' plosgail gun ch., *panting incessantly.*
——, *pr.pt.* a' closadh, *v.a. & n.* Be calm, be quiet, be still. 2 Hush, quiet. 3 Rest, repose.
——ach, -aich, -aichean, *s.f.* Carcase. 2 Dead body, corpse. C. fiadh-bheathaich, *a wild beast's carcase.* [Illustrations on p. 213.]
——adh, -aidh, *s.m.* Hushing, quieting, being still. A' c—, *pr.pt.* of **clos.**

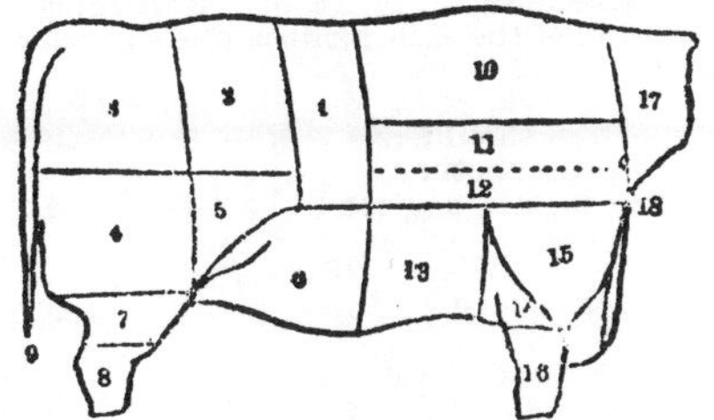

156. An dòigh air an gearrar sìos closach mairt an Albainn.

PARTS OF A CARCASE OF BEEF AS DIVIDED IN SCOTLAND :—

1 Leasradh uachdar ; Losaid—*Lewis*, MMcD *sirloin* or *back sey.*
2 Dubh chléith ; Cruachann—*Lewis*, MMcD, *hook bone.*
3 Màs *buttock.*
4 Bunamhas, sliasaid, *large round.* } Rumball, *rump.*
5 Loch-bhléin thiugh, *thick flank.*
6 Loch-bhléin thana, *thin flank.*
7 Leas ; Leis—*Lewis*, MMcD, *small round.*
8 Iosgaid, *hough.*
9 Earball, *tail.*
10 Slinnean, *spare rib* or *fore sey.*
11 Staoig mhór, *large runner.*
12 Staoig bheag, *small runner.*
13 Na h-aisnean, *nineholes.*
14 Broilleach, *brisket.*
15 Spòg thoisich, *shoulder lyar.*
16 Lurgainn, *nap* or *shin.*
17 Amhach, *neck.*
18 Slugan, *sticking piece.* (up towards the neck) Sprogan—*Lewis*, MMcD.

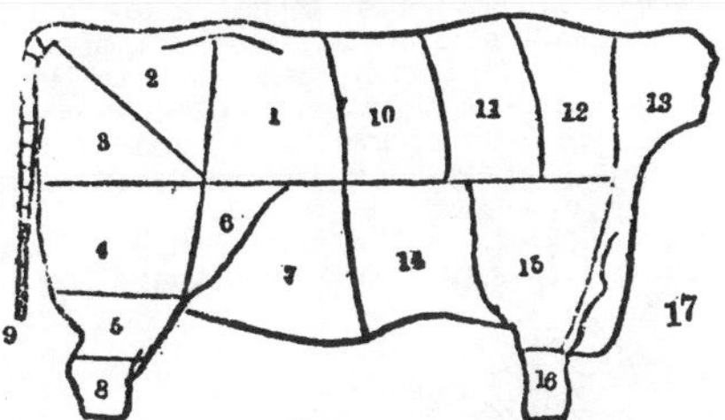

157. An dòigh air an gearrar sìos closach mairt an Sasunn.

PARTS OF A CARCASE OF BEEF AS DIVIDED IN ENGLAND :—

1 Leasradh; Losaid—*Lewis*, MMcD *loin.*
2 Cruachann, *aitch bone.*
3 Màs, *rump.*
4 Bunamhas; Sliasaid—*Lewis*, MMcD *buttock.*
5 Leas; Leis,—*Lewis*, *hock.*
6 Loch-bhléin thiugh, *thick flank.*
7 Loch-bhléin thana, *thin flank.*
8 Lurgainn, *shin.*
9 Earball, *tail.*
10 Aisean dheiridh, *chuck rib.*
11 Aisean mheadhonach, *middle rib.*
12 Aisean thoisich, *fore rib.*

[In *Lewis* the joint between 10 & 11 is cut as a continuation of that between 14 & 15, and the piece then representing 11 & 12 is called " aisean thoisich," and the remainder of 10 " aisean mheadhonach." The division between 1 & 2 is also moved farther forward about one-third, and what is left of 1 is called " leasradh" or " losaid." With these exceptions a carcase of beef is divided in Lewis after the English fashion.—MMcD]

13 Amhach & broillein, *clod, sticking-piece & neck*
14 Broilleach, *brisket.*
15 Spòg thoisich, *leg-of-mutton piece.*
16 Lurgainn, *shin.*
17 Slugan,—*Lewis.*

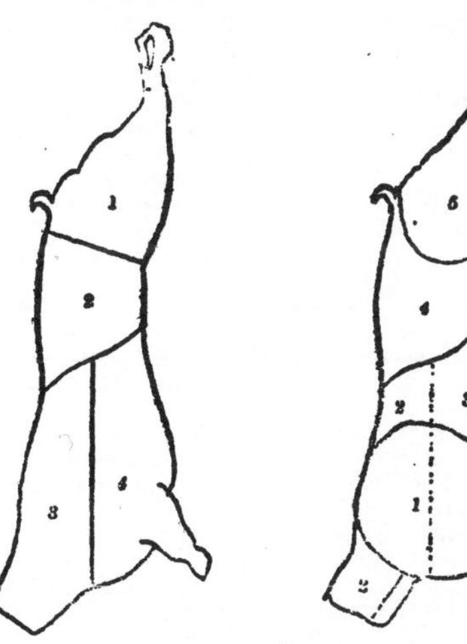

158. 159

158. An dòigh Albannach air caora a ghearradh sìos.

159. An dòigh Shasunnach air caora a ghearradh sìos.

SCOTS METHOD OF DIVIDING A CARCASE OF MUTTON (158)—

1 Spòg dheiridh, Ceathramh deiridh—*Lewis*, *jigot.*
2 Leasradh ; Aisnean cùl *or* droma—*Lewis*, *loin.*
3 Aisnean droma, *back ribs.*
4 Broilleach, *breast.*

ENGLISH METHOD ;—

1 Gualainn ; Slinnean—*Lewis*, *shoulder.*
2, 2, Amhach, *neck.*
3 Broilleach, *breast.*
4 Ceathramh, *hind quarter.* Leasradh—*Lewis.*
5 Spòg, *leg.* Ceathramh deiridh—*Lewis.*

[The carcase of a sheep is cut in Lewis more after the English than the Scots style.]

closaich,* *v.n.* Get lean or gaunt, as a half-starved brute.

clòsaid, -e, -ean, *s.f.* Closet, study.

clò-suaine, *s.f.* Slumber. Ag aomadh gu c., *drooping in slumber.*

†cloth, *a.* Noble, generous.

clòth, -a, *pl.* clòithean [& clòithntean] *s.m.* see clò. 2 Silly man.

†clòth, *s.m.* Victory. 2 Fame, praise. 3 Wind.

clòth, *pr.pt.* a' clòthadh, *v.a.* Mitigate, still, restrain, calm. 2 Counteract, subdue, surmount, overcome.

†clotha, Was heard.

†clòthach, -aiche, *a.* Famous, illustrious, renowned, celebrated.

clòthadair,** *s.m.* Clothier.

————-eachd,** *s.f.* Clothiery.

clòthadh, -aidh, *s.m.* Mitigating, restraining, calming. 2(CR) Gadding, roving. A' c. nan

taighean, *ranging the houses.* **A' c—,** *pr. pt.* of clòth.
clòth-suaine, see **clò-suaine.**
†clù, *a.* Chosen.
†clu, *s.m.* see cliù.
†cluach, *a.* see **clachach.**
†clùach, *s.m.* (cliùthbach) **Hero.**
cluain, -e, -ean [& -tean] *s.f.* **Pasture, green field, meadow, lawn. 2 Bower. 3 Retirement. 4 Ambush. 5 Pacification, quietness. 6**Burying ground. 7**Intrigue, deceit, dissimulation. 8**Flattery. 9(CR) Apprehension, application, attention**—*West of Ross.* Cha'n 'eil c. ann, *he lacks understanding*—said of one who fails to grasp what he is told ; **gun ch.,** *careless about work or business* ; **cuir c. air an leanabh,** *pacify the child* ; **le 'n c.,** *with their dissimulation* ; **air cluainibh an fhasaich,** *on the pastures of the desert.*
——each, -eiche, *a.* **Meadowy, abounding in pastures, grassy. 2**Deceitful, dissembling. 3**Flattering.**
cluaineag, -eig, -an, *s.f.* **Retired field, little pasture, little lawn. 2 Neat little woman. 3 Islet in a river. 4††Deceitful woman.**
cluaineagach, *a.* **Abounding in little lawns or pastures.**
cluainean,** -ein, *s.m.* **Little pasture, little meadow, little lawn, pleasure ground. Fo ch. an fhéidh,** *beneath the deer's pasture-ground.*
cluainear, -eir, see **cluainire.**
————as, see **cluaineas.**
cluaineas, -eis, *s.f.* **Intrigue, artifice, design, hypocrisy, treachery. 2**Gambolling, frisking. Ri c. mhear,** *frisking merrily* ; **mar bhradan air an aigeal a' cluaineis** ; *like a salmon frisking in the pool—Duanaire, p. 84.*
cluaineireach, *a.* **Deceitful, alluring, hypocritical.**
cluaineireachd, *s.f.* **Deceit, flattery, practice of deceit.**
cluaineiseach, -eiche, *a.* **Private, remote, retired, fond of being alone. 2 Intriguing.**
cluainire, -an, *s.m.* **Flatterer, seducer. 2 Hypocrite, fawner, cunning fellow.**
cluain-lìn,§ -e, Corn-spurrey—*spergula arvensis.*
cluainteach, -eiche, *a.* **Cunning.**
cluaintean, *n.pl.* of **cluain.**
cluainteir, see **cluainire.**
————each, see **cluaineireach.**
————eachd, see **cluaineireachd.**
cluais, *dat. sing.* of **cluas.**
cluaise, *gen. sing.* of **cluas.**
——ean, -ein, *s.m.* **Blow, box on the ear. 2 Porringer. 3 Shoe-latchet. 4**Ansated dish. 5**Pillow. Pinne cluaisein,** *tram-pin of a cart.* [‡‡ gives cluaisein as *nom.*]
cluaiseineach,†† -eiche, *a.* **Pertaining to a shoe-latchet.**
cluan, -ain *pl.* -an [& -tan,] *s.f.* see **cluain.**
——ag, see **cluaineag & claonag. 2****rarely* **Joy.**
——agach, see **cluaineagach.**
cluanaire, -an, *s.m.* see **cluainire.**
cluanaiseach,** *a.* **Sauntering, lounging alone.**
cluanas, (AC) *s.m.* **Friendship.**
cluantaireachd, *s.f.* see **cluaineireachd.**
†cluara, *a.* **Steep, inaccessible.**
cluaran, -ain, -an, *s. m.* **Thistle. Used as a general name for all thistles, but especially** *chrysanthemum segetum.* **2 Corn-marigold. 3 Sponge.**
————ach, -aiche, *a.* **Abounding in thistles, thistly. 2 Fungous.**
————ach,** -aich, *s.m.* **Thistle.**
cluaran-cruaidh,§ *s.m.* **Sow-thistle, see bog-ghiogan.**

160. Cluaran (1)

cluaran-deilgneach,§ *s. m.* **Spear - thistle**—*carduus lanceolatus.*
cluaran-leana,§ *s.m.* **Marsh-thistle**—*carduus palustris.*

161. C. deilgneach. *162. C. leana.*

cluaran-òir,§ *s.m.* **Carline-thistle**—*carlina vulgaris.*

163. Cluaran-òir. *164. Cluas-an-fhéidh.*

†cluas, -uais, *s.m.* **Joy, gladness.**
cluas, -aise, -an, *s.f.* **Ear. 2 Handle of a dish, cycle, and most things that may have two handles. 3 Tack of a sail, see p. 76. 4** *pl.* **Ears of a creel, where ends of suspender are inserted. 5 (MMcD) Top corners of a herring net.**—*Lewis.* **C. a' chridhe,** *auricle of the heart* ; **chailleadh tu do chluasan mur bitheadh iad 'an ceangal riut** (*or* **ceangailte riut,**) *you would lose your ears if they were not fixed to you.* [For Gaelic names of various marks on sheeps' ears, see under "comharradh."]
——ach, -aiche, *a.* **Ansated, having ears or handles. 2 Having large ears. 3 Deaf. 4 (DU) Careless, slow. Meadar c.,** *an ansated wooden dish*; **an t-sòbhrag c.,** *the round-leaved primrose.*
cluasachan, -ain, -an, see **cluasag**
cluasag, -aig, -an, *s.f.* **Pillow. 2 Pin-cushion.**

3 Bolster of a cart. C. de fhionnadh ghabhair, *a pillow of goat's hair.*
———ach, *a.* Abounding in pillows. 2 Of, or belonging to, a pillow.
———aich,** *v.a.* Bolster.
——— -ghlùin, ***s. f.* Hassock, cushion.
cluas-aire. ‡‡ *s.f.ind.* Audience.
cluas-an-fhéidh, *s.f.* Melancholy thistle—*carduus heterophillus.* Said to have been the badge of King James I. (of Scotland.) The plant generally used to represent the Scottish heraldic thistle is *onopordon acanthium,* —the cotton-thistle.
cluas-an-luch,§ *s.f.* Mouse-ear- chick-weed—*cerastium alpinum.*
cluas-bhiorach, *a.* Sharp-eared. 2 Pointed-eared.

165. Cluas-an-luch. *166. Cluas-chaoin.*

cluas-chaoin, *s.f.* Wake-robin, lords and ladies, cuckoo-pint—*arum maculatum.*
cluas-chiùil, *s.f.* Musical ear.
cluas-chrochag,** -aig, -an, *s.f.* Ear-ring, ear-pendant.
†cluas-doille, *s.f.* Deafness, dullness of hearing.
cluas-fhail, -e, -ean, *s.f.* (& *m.*) Ear-ring.
cluas-fhàinne, *pl.* -fhàinntean, *s.f.* & *m.* Ear-ring.
cluasgaich,‡‡ *v.a.* Pillow.
cluas-ice,** *s.* Acoustics.
cluas-liath, *s.f.* §Colt's foot—*tussilago farfara.* 2 Mouse-ear, hawkweed, see cluas-luch.
cluas-luch,§ *s.f.* Mouse-ear, hawkweed—*hieracium pilosella.*

167. Cluas-liath. *168. Cluas-luch.*

cluas-mhaothan, -ain, -an, *s.m.* Top of the ear.
†cluasoil, *a.* Loud.
cluas-ri-claisdeachd, *s.f.* Hearkener, character in a romance, one anxious to overhear a conversation.
cluas-sheud, -a, -an, *s.m.* Ear-jewel.
†clùb, *v.a.* Bend, incline.
†clubadh, -aidh, *s.m.* Winding bay.
clùd, -ùid [& -a,] *pl.* -an [& ùid,] *s.m.* Patch, rag, clout.
clùd, *pr.part.* a' clùdadh. *v.a.* Clout, patch, mend. 2**Cover up warm. 3**Cherish.
——ach, -aiche, *a.* Abounding in rags. 2 Patched, clouted, ragged.
clùdadh, -aidh, *s.m.* Clouting, patching, mending, cobbling. A' c—, *pr.pt.* of clùd.
clùdag, -aig, -an, *s.f.* Little clout or rag. 2 Concealment. 3**Store.
———ach, -aiche, *a.* Abounding in little rags or clouts.
clùdaich, *pr.part.* a' clùdachadh, *v.a.* see clùd.
————te, *past pt.* of clùdaich. Clouted, mended, patched.
clùdair, -ean, *s.m.* Patcher, botcher, cobbler.
————eachd,** *s.f.* Patching, clouting, cobbling.
clùdan, -ain, -an, *s.m.* see clùdag.
clùdan, *n. pl.* of clùd.
————ach, -aiche, see clùdagach.
clugan, } (AC) -ain, *s.m.* Figwort. see lus-
————ach, } nan-cnapan.
cluich, -e, *pl.* -ean [-eachan & -eannan,] *s. m.* Play, pastime, sport, game. 2 Funeral games or solemnities. 3 Battle. 4 School vacation. 5**Flirting. 6**Gaming. 7**Theatrical performance. A' c—, *pr. pt.* of cluich.
———, *pr. pt.* a' cluich, a' cluicheachd, & a' cluicheadh, *v.a.* Play, sport, game. 2 Finger a musical instrument. 3**Represent a character. 4††Gamble.
——— -àbhachd,* *s.m.* Comedy.
——— -cneutaig, *s.m.* Tennis.
——— -cnagaire, *s.m.* Cricket match.
———each, -eiche, *a.* Sportive, playful, frolicsome.
———eachd, *s.f.* Playing, sporting, gambolling. 2 Gambling. A' c—. *pr.pt.* of cluich.
———eadair, -ean, *s.m.* Player.
———eadh, -hidh, *s.m.* Playing, sporting. 2 Fingering a musical instrument. 3 Representing a character on the stage. A' c—, *pr. pt.* of cluich.
cluicheag, -eig, -an, *s. f.* Children's play. 2 Pastime. 3 Flirtation. 4 Trick. Ri c., *playing.*
cluichealachd, *s.f.ind.* Playfulness.
cluicheil, -e, *a.* Playful, sportive.
clùid, *gen.sing.* of clùd, sometimes used for the nominative. 2**Nook.
cluidhein, -ean, see claidhean.
cluig, *gen. sing.* & *n. pl.* of clag. 2 Bubble.
———ean, -ein, *s.m.* Icicle. 2 Cluster. 3 Anything hanging or dangling, appendage, pendant. 4 Catkin. 5 Wattle, as of a hen. 6 ** Ear-pendant. 7** Little bell. 8**Bubble. 9(DU) Tassel. C. cluaise, *an ear-pendant;* c. na mnàtha sìthe, *foxglove.*
———eineach, -eiche, *a.* Abounding in clusters, bells or hanging ornaments. 2 Sonorous, jingling, sounding, as bells. Boc c., *a bell-wether*; bàrr c., *bell-topped.*
————eineichte,** *a.* & *past part.* Belled.
cluimh,(AC) *a.* Softly.
clùimh, see clòimh.
————each, see clòimheach.
†cluimhealta, *s.f.* Royston-crow. 2 Flock of birds.
clùin,** *s. f.* Fraud. 2 Enclosure.
†cluin, see cluain.
cluinn, *irreg. v.* Hear, hearken, listen, attend to.

Active Voice—

IND. *past*, Chuala mi, &c. *I &c. heard.*
,, *fut.* Cluinnidh mi. &c., *I &c shall hear.*
INTERR. *past* (cha ch—, an ? nach ?) cuala mi, &c, (*did*) *I &c.* (*not*) *hear ?* (mur) cuala mi, (*if*) *I did not hear.*
,, *fut.* (cha ch—, an ? nach ?) cluinn mi, &c., *shall I &c.* (*not*) *hear ?* (mur) cluinn mi, (*if*) *I do not hear.*
SUBJ. *past*, (ged) chluinninn, (*though*) *I*

would hear.
(ged) chluinneamaid, (*though*) *we would hear.*
(ged) chluinneadh tu, &c., (*though*) *thou &c. wouldest hear.*
„ *fut* (ma) chluinneas mi, &c., (*if*) *I &c. shall hear.*
IMPER. *1st per. sing.* cluinneam, *let me hear.*
INFIN. A chluinntinn, *to hear.*
PRES. PART. A' cluinntinn, *hearing.*
Passive Voice—
IND. *past*, chualadh mi, &c., *I &c. was heard.*
[The form "chualas" is also used, but only in first person, and then not followed by *mi.*]
„ *fut.* cluinnear mi, &c., *I &c. shall be heard.*
INTERR. *past*, (cha ch—, an ? nach ?) cualadh mi, &c., *was I &c. (not) heard?* (mur) cualadh mi,(*if*) *I were not heaad.*
„ *fut.* (cha ch—, an ? nach ?) cluinnear mi, &c., *shall I &c. (not) be heard ?* (mur) cluinnear mi, (*if*) *I shall not be heard.*
SUBJ. *past*, (ged) chluinnteadh mi, &c. (*though*) *I &c. would be heard.*
„ *fut* (ma) chluinnear mi, &c., (*if*) *I &c. shall be heard.*
An ti a shuidhich a' chluas nach c. e ? *he that planted the ear shall he not hear ?* an sin cluinnidh mise, *then shall I hear* ; nach cluinn thu ? *do you not hear ?* an ni a chluinneas na big 'se a chanas na big, *what the young hear they repeat.*
[The following remarks by J.G.M. concerning the form of the verb in *-eas* (*e.g.* cluinneas) should be borne in mind. "In the Gaelic sense it is not subjunctive. The proof is that *cluinnear* does duty for cluinn, cluinnidh and cluinneas in the so-called Passive. Thus *ma*, which in active takes *-eas*, in passive takes *cluinnear* ; *an* and *nach*, which in active take *cluinn*, in passive take *cluinnear*, and the absolute *cluinnidh* is represented in passive by *cluinnear*. The so-called passive is really an impersonal form *e. g.* tillear air 'ais, *he returns home.* How can an intransitive verb have a passive voice ? for instance, *come*, one cannot say *I was comed*, yet in Gaelic we have, *cha tigear as eugmhais na pìoba mòire*, "cannot be comed without the pipes." The Gaelic mind's conception of the subjunctive mood certainly does not cover the same ground as in English. Again, bhatar, *people were*(not *people were'd* or *was'd.*) If *cluinnear* is passive, so is *bhatar.*"]
†cluinneach, -ich, *s.m.* Miner.
cluinneadh, *past.subj.*(*except 1st. per.*) of cluinn.
cluinneam, *1st. per. sing. imp.* of cluinn. Let me hear.
cluinneam (*for* cluinnidh mi) I will hear.
cluinnear, *fut. pass.* of cluinn. Shall be heard.
cluinnte, *a.* & *past pt.* of cluinn. Heard. 2 Attended to.
cluinnteadh, *past. subj. pass.* of cluinn.
cluinntear, (*for* cluinnear) *fut. ind. pass.* of cluinn.
cluinntear, -an, *s.m.* Hearer, listener.
———achd, *s.f.ind.* Listening. 2 Craftiness.
cluinntinn, *s.f.* Hearing, listening. 2 Hearsay. A' c—, *pr.pt.* of cluinn.
cluip, *pr.pt.* a' cluipeadh, *v.a.* Cheat, deceive,
——, *s.f.* Deceit.
——eadair, -eir,-ean, see cluipear.
cluipear, -an, *s.m.* One who cheats, deceiver.
———achd, *s.f.ind.* Deception, villany. 2 Baseness, depravity. C. agus cha bu cheartas, *deception and not justice.*
cluith, see cluich.
———each, see cluicheach.
———eadair, see cluicheadair
———eag, see cluicheag.
cluitheil, -e, *a.* see cluicheach.
cluitheir,‡‡ see cluicheadair.
†clùmh, *s.f.* Cloak.
———ach, see clòimheach, *a.*, & clòimh, *s.*
clumhaidh,(AC) *a.* Cosy. Gu'm bu c. dhuibh gach nochd, *cosy be every exposure to you.*
clùmhar, -aire, *a.* see clù-mhor.
clùmhor, -oire, *a.* Warm, sheltered, snug.
†clumhthach, -aiche, *a.* Hairy, rough.
clù-nead, -nid, *s.m.* Warm, sheltered nest.
clupaid, -e, *s.f.* Swollen throat in cattle.
clùt, see clùd.
——ach, see clùdach.
clùtaireachd, see clùdaireachd.
cluth, see cluthaich.
cluthachadh, -aidh, *s.m.* Clothing. 2‡‡Chasing. A' c—, *pr.pt.* of cluthaich. A' c. nan nochd, *clothing the naked.*
cluthaich, *pr.pt.* a' cluthachadh, *v. a.* Clothe, make warm. 2 Chase.
cluth-aodaich,** *v.a.* Clothe, clothe warmly. Is éiginn duinn bhi air ar cluth-aodachadh, *we must be clothed.*
clùthar, -aire, see clùmhor.
clùth-ghlùineach, -eiche, *a.* In-kneed. see bleith-ghlùineach.
clùthmhor, -oire, see clùmhor.
clùthmhorachd, *s.f.ind.* Warmness, snugness. 2††Shelter.
†cna, *a.* Good, bountiful, gracious, merciful.
cnab, *v.a.* Pull, haul. 2 Batter.
cnabadh, -aidh, *s.m.* Pulling, hauling, battering. A'c—, *pr.pt.* of cnab.
cnabaire, -an, *s.m.* Scoffer, jester. 2 Instrument for dressing flax.
†cnabar, *s.m.* Drowsiness, heaviness.
cnac, *s.f.* Crack, fissure, crevice, breach. 2 Crack of a whip. 3 Any loud report. Bheirinn c. anns na h-àitheantaibh, *I would make a breach in the commandments* ; ann an c., *in an instant* ; leig e c. as, *it gave a crack.*
——, *v.a. & n.* Crack. 2 Break. 3 Crash. 4 Split. 5 Splinter. 6††Snap, as the fingers. 7††Knock.
——adh, *s.m.* Cracking, act of cracking. A' c—, *pr.pt.* of cnac.
cnacail, -e, *s. f.* Crackling noise, continued crackling or splitting.
cnacair, *s.m.* Talker, (Scot. cracker.) 2 Cracker. 3 Cracker of a whip. 4 Knocker.
———eachd, *s.f.ind.* Conversation, chat. 2 **Cracking.
cnacan, -ain, see cnacail.
cnachdair, see cnacair.
†cnadair, -ean, *s.m.* Prating jester, scoffer.
———eachd,** *s.f.* Derision.
†cnàdan, -ain, *s.m.* Frog.
†cnadar-bharca, *pl.* Ships.
†cnadhoil, -e, *s.f.* Whining, complaining.
cnag, -aig, -an, *s.f.* Pin. 2 Peg. 3 Knob. 4 Knock. 5 Thole-pin of a rowing-boat. 6** Wrinkle. 7 see cnac. 8 Plug. 9¶ Pine-grosbeak—*pyrrhula enucleator.* 10**Woodpecker, little wood-rapper.
cnag, see cnac & cnap.
——ach, -aiche, *a.* Knobby. 2 Full of pegs or pins. 3 Like a peg or pin. 4* Knotty.
——achd, *s.f.* Knottiness. 2 Knobbiness. 3 *rarely* sternness.
cnagadh, -aidh, *s. m.* Knocking down, driving down. 2 Making knobby. A' c—, *pr.pt.* of

cnag.
cnagag-choille,(AF) s.f. Pine grosbeak, see cnag.
†cnagaid, -ean, s.f. Rap, knock. 2*Old maid. 3 *Old cow with stumps of horns.
†cnagaidh, a. Bunchy.
cnagair, -ean, s.m. Gill, noggin. 2 Quart measure. 3 see cnacair.
cnagan, -ain, -an, s.m. Little knob. 2 Peg, pin. 3 Earthen pipkin. 4 Thole-pin, see under bàta, No. 39B, p. 76. 5(MMcD) Small earthen drinking cup—*Lewis.*
cnagan-faolaig,(MMcD) s.m. Sea-urchin—*Lewis.*
cnagan-tràghad, (MMcD) s. m. Sea-urchin—*Lewis.*
cnag-bhuilleach, a. Knocking. Gu cnag-bhuilleach, òrdail, *knocking precisely—Duanaire, p. 80.*
cnag-grabaidh, s.f. Sny, toggle, see bàta, 1,p.76.
†cnagsa, v.a. Push.
cnaib-uisge, s.f. Water-necked weed.
cnàid, v.a. Deride, jeer, scoff.
——, -e, -ean, s.f. Derision, jeer, scoff. Na dean c. air an duine bhochd, *do not deride a poor man.*
cnàideach, -eiche, s. f. Vexation. 2 Uneasiness. 3 Sorrow, trouble.
†cnaidhteach, -eiche, a. Fretted, peevish. 2 Angry.
cnàimh, gen. cnàmha, pl. cnàmhan [& cnàimhean,] s.m. Bone. C. an droma, *the spine ;* c. na lurga, *the shin-bone ;* c. mór do dhuine ghionach, *the big bone to the greedy man.*
cnàimh-bhristeach, s.m. Ossifrage, osprey.
cnàimh-built, -ean, see cneaball.
cnàimh-coileir,** s.m. Clavicle.
cnàimh-criche,* s.m. Balk, landmark. 2 Matter of dispute (about boundaries only—MM) —*Islay.*
cnàimh-deud, s.m. Ivory.
cnàimheach, -eiche, a. Bony, having large bones.
————, -eich, s. m. see fitheach. 2 see cnàimhneach 3 Rook. 4 Crow. 5 Jackdaw.
————adh,‡‡ -aidh, s.m. Ossification.
cnàimhean,‡‡ -ein, -ean, s.m. Ossicle.
cnaimhean-glas,(DJM) s.m. Mode of planting potatoes, by which the ground between the drills is left undisturbed. [Cnàimh, bailc, *baulk* or *fallow*+glas, *locked up* or *unused.*—J.G.M.]
cnàimh-fhitheach, s.m. see fitheach.
cnàimh-gheadh, -gheòidh, s.m. Kind of fowl between a goose and a duck.
cnàimh-gheal, -ile, a. White-boned.
cnàimh-ghobhail, s.m. The share-bone.
cnàimhich,‡‡ v.a. Bone.
†cnaimhigheach, s.m. see fitheach.
cnàimhneach, s.m. Skeleton.
cnàimh-nighidh, s.m. Beetle, instrument for beating clothes in the washing.
cnàimh-puirt,‡‡ s.m. Part of a pipe-tune, see ùrlar.
cnàimh-reamhar, -a, a. Thick-, or clumsy-boned.
cnàimh-rionnach, see cnàmh-rionnach.
cnàimhseag, -eig, -an, s.f. Pimple in the face. 2 ‖ The bearberry, . ˙ . *acne vulgaris,* "blackheads." 3 Particles or dregs (crackling) of dissolved fat or tallow.
————ach, -aiche, a. Full of pimples or greasy particles. 2 Abounding in bearberries.
cnaimhte, a. & *past pt.* of cnàmh. Corroded. 2 Consumed.
————ach, -eiche, a. Consuming without flame. 2 Corrosive. 3 Having a strong digestion. 4**Gnawing, chewing.
————achd, ‡‡ s.f. Causticity.

cnaip, gen. & pl. of cnap.
cnaipileis, -e, s.m. Lumps, masses.
cnaire,** s. Buckle.
cnàmh, gen. pl. of cnàimh.
cnàmh, s.m. ‖The digestion. [Preceded by the art. *an.*] 2 see cnàmhadh.
cnàmh, pr. pt. a' cnàmhadh, [& a' cnàmh] v.a. Chew, ruminate. 2 Digest. 3 Consume. 4 Corrode. 5 Moulder, putrefy, decay. 6**Concoct. A' cnàmh na cìr, *chewing the cud;* ch. e a bhiadh, *he digested his food ;* ch. an t-iarrunn, *the iron corroded;* ch. an gealbhan, *the fire wasted.*
cnàmhach, -aiche, a. Wasting slowly. 2‡‡Digestive. 3 Deleterious. 4 Corroding, corrosive. 5 * Consuming. 6 see cnàimheach.
————d, s.f. Deleteriousness. 2 Corrosiveness. 3 Wasting, consuming.
cnàmhadh, -aidh, s. m. Wearing, decaying, consuming, mouldering. 2 Digesting. 3 Chewing, masticating. A' c—, *pr. pt.* of cnàmh. C. a' chinn-aghairt, *bitter reflection.*
cnàmhag, -aig, -an, s. f. Substance. 2 Anything from which juice has been extracted by boiling, maceration or chewing. 3 Remains of corn destroyed by cattle. 4 Refuse of anything. 5 Dying embers or cinders. 6 Pimple. 7 Cracklings of melted tallow. 8 see cruimheag.
cnàmhairneach,* s.f. Small transparent fish, found on the coasts of all the islands, young mackerel. 2 see cnàmharlach.
cnàmhan, -ain, s.m. Corrosive substance. 2 Gnawing pain. 3 Unceasing, vexatious talk. 4**Scolding, rebuking. 5 *n. pl.* of cnàimh.
————ach, -aiche, a. Vexatious, troublesome. 2 Fretting, as a sore. 3 Corroding, consuming. Luibhre c., *a fretting leprosy.*
cnàmharlach, -aich, s.m. Raw-boned, cadaverous person. 2††Skeleton. 3 Halm, succulent stalk, as of peas, potatoes or beans.
cnàmh-chagainn, v.a. Arrode.
cnàmh-chagnadh,‡‡ -aidh, s.m. Arrosion.
cnàmh-chruimh,** s.m. Cankerworm.
cnàmhlach, see cnàmharlach.
cnàmh-lus, s.m. Cudwort, cudweed, see luibh-a'-chait. 2§ Samphire, see saimbhir. [Preceded by the art. *an.*]
†cnàmh-mhargadh, -aidh, -ean, s.m. The shambles.
†cnàmh-nàireach, a. Demure, sober, decent, grave.
cnàmh-rionnach, (AF) s. Horse-mackerel, bone-mackerel.
†cnàmh-ruighe, -an, s.m. Cubit.
cnàmhtach,** a. Wasting without flame. 2 Consuming. 3 Corrosive. 4 Chewing.
cnàmhuinn,‖ -e, -ean s.f. Gangrene, lupus.
†cnaoidhteach, a. Consuming, corrosive.
†cnaoighteach, see cnaoidhteach.
cnap, -aip, -an, s.m. Knob. 2 Button. 3 Lump. 4 Boss, stud. 5 Little hill. 6 Little blow, thump. 7 Potato. 8** Stout boy. 9**Knot in wood.
cnap, pr. pt. a' cnapadh, v.a. Thump, strike, beat, knock, rap. 'Gam chnapadh, *thumping me.*
——ach, -aiche, a. Knobby. 2 Hilly. 3 Lumpy. 4 Bossy. 5 Stout.
——ach, -aich, -aichean, s. m. Youngster, Stout, smart, middle-sized boy.
—— achd,‡‡ s.f. Knottiness.
cnapadair, -e, -ean, s.m. Thumper. 2 see cneapadair.
cnapadh, -aidh, s.m. Thumping, beating, rapping, knocking. 2 Falling with a great

noise. 3**Shrinking, contracting. 4**Crushing. A' c—, *pr. pt.* of cnap.
cnapag,†† -aig, -an, *s.f.* Little stool or block. 2 Shinty ball.
cnapaich, *pr. pt.* a' cnapachadh, *v. a.* Collect into bunches. 2 Accumulate. 3 Emboss. 4 aggregate. 5††Gather into lumps.
cnapain,** see cnapan 5.
cnapain, *gen. sing.* of cnapan.
cnapair, -ean, *s. m.* Stout, strong article. 2 Thumper. 3 Stout fellow.
———neach, -ich, see cnapach.
cnapan, *n. pl.* of cnap.
———, -ain, *s.m.* Little lump. 2 Small knob. 3 Little boss or hillock. 4 Piece of wood to save the edge of a hatchet in cutting or splitting wood. 5(AF) Louse. Is e leigheas a' chnatain c. itheadh, *the cure of a cold is to eat a bit.*
———ach, -aiche, *a.* Knobby. 2 Abounding in little hillocks. 3†† Full of lumps or blocks.
———ach, -aich,*s.m.* see cnapach.
cnapan-dubh, § *s. m.* Knapweed—*centaurea nigra.*

169. Cnapan-dubh.

cnapan-trusgaidh, *s.m.* Button.
cnap-lus,* *s.m.* Marsh-mallow.
cnaparra, *a.* Stout, strong, bulky, sturdy. 2* Falling with a thumping noise. An t-suiridh ch., *the sturdy wooing.*
cnap-gaoithe,(MMcD) *s.f.* Squall, strong gust of wind—*Lewis.*
cnap-saic, -e, *pl.* -ean & -anna-saic, *s.m.* Knapsack.
cnap-starradh, -aidh, *s. m.* Obstruction. 2 Brass ball at the end of a spear, to terrify an antagonist or distract his attention with its noise when shaken. 3‡‡ Interruption. A' dearg-shruthadh mu a ch. phraiseach, *pouring red about his brazen ball.*
cnap-trusgain, see cnapan-trusgaidh.
†cnarra, *pl.* cnarradha, *s.f.* Ship.
cnatan,‖ -ain, *s.m.* Cold. 2††Cough. 3 Obstruction of perspiration. [Preceded by the art. *an.*] Fhuair mi cnatan nach gann, *I got a severe cold (lit.* a cold that is not meagre—*Duanaire. 78.*
———ach, -aiche, *a.* Having, inducing or exposed to a cold (** or cough.) 2 Pertaining to a cold. Mios c., *the cold-causing month.*
cneaball,*s.m.* Garter, belt of thrums tied round the hose.
cnea-chritheach, see cneadh-chritheach.
cnèad, see cneutag.
cnead, -a, -an, *s.m.* Sigh, moan, groan, grunt. 2 Scoff. 3* Sudden sigh or groan, as when one gets a blow unexpectedly. 4*Anything. Cha bhi c. ort, *nothing will be wrong with you;* cha' 'eil c. air, *nothing is wrong with him;* cha'n oil leam c. mo leas-mhàthar, *I pity not the sigh of my step-mother.* [** says *s.f.*]
———, *pr. pt.* a' cneadail & a' cneadadh, *v.n.* Sigh, moan, groan. 2**Scoff.
———ach, -aich, *a.* Sobbing, sighing, groaning, querulous. 2**Asthmatic. 3**Puny.
———ach, -aich, *s.m.* Puny person. 2 One who sobs or sighs. 3 Asthmatic person. Is tric a chinn an c., agus a dh' fhalbh an sodarnach, *often the puny thrived and the vigorous drooped.*
cnèadag, (CR) *s.f.* Fir-cone. 2 Shinty—*Loch Tay & Strathtay.* Cluich-chnèadag, *shinty.*
cneadail, -e, *s.f.* Sighing, groaning heavily and quickly. 2 Oppression of breathing. A' c—, *pr. pt.* of cnead.
cneadh, -eidhe, -an, *s.f.* Wound, bruise, hurt. 2 Disaster. Guirme cneidhe, *the blueness of a wound.*
———ach, -aiche, *a.* Full of wounds, hurts, or sores, wounded. 2 Causing wounds.
cneadhalach, -aich, *s.m.* One who is wounded. 2 Sufferer. Ge b'e an coireach, is mise c., *whoever is to blame, I am the sufferer.*
cneadh-chritheach,(AC) *a.* Wound-quivering.
cneadh-fhiacall, *s.f.* The tooth-ache. 2 Gumboil.
cneadh-shliochd, *s.m.* Scar.
———ach, -aiche, *a.* Full of scars.
cneadraich, -e, *s.f.* see cneadail.
cneamh, -a, see creamh.
†cneamhaire, -an, *s.m.* Artful, designing fellow.
cneamh-mac-fiadh, *s.f.* see Aspàrag. 2 (CR) Elecampane. 3(CR) Hart's tongue.
cneap, -eip, -an, *s.m.* Button. 2 Bead. 3 Spherical gem. 4 Pebble.
———adair,* *s.m.* Button maker.
cneapailt, *Skye & Lewis* for cneaball.
cnéapan,(CR) *s.m.* Stool, low seat—*W. of Ross.*
cneap-tholl, *s.m.* Button-hole.
cneas, -a [& **cneis,] -an, *s.m.* The waist. 2 The human skin. 3 The breast, bosom. 4** Form, body. 5**Neck. C. mo ghràidh, *the form of my love;* is lionmhor c. 'san do chuir e lann, *many were the breasts he stabbed;* léine-chneis, *a bodyguard.*
———achadh, ** -aidh, *s.m.* Sqeeezing, tightening. 2‡‡Healing. Is fheairrd gach cneadh a c., *every wound is the better of being healed;* N.G.P. says, is fheairrde gach c. a ceasnachadh, *a wound is the better of being probed.* A' c—, *pr. pt.* of cneasaich.
cneasaich, *pr. pt.* a' cneasachadh, *v. a.* Cure, heal. 2 Shape. 3 Make slender, as the waist. 4**Straighten, press. 5**Squeeze, tighten. 6 ††Beautify. 7**Shake a person.
cneas-Chuchulainn,§ *s.m.* Meadow-sweet, see lus-chneas-Chuchulainn.
cneasda, *a.* Humane, temperate, moderate. 2 Modest, meek. 3 Pious, religious. 4 Fortunate, auspicious, of good omen. 5 *in the negative only* Ominous. 6 Canny. Gu c., *temperately;* cha'n 'eil seo c., *this is uncanny.*
———ch, see cneasda.
———chd, *s.f.ind.* Humanity. 2 Mildness, meekness. 3 Piety, religion. 4**Temperance, moderation. 5**Modesty. Gun ch., *intemperate.*
cneas-gheal,*-ile, *a.* White-skinned, fair-skinned. 2 White-bosomed. 3 White-bodied.
cneasmhoireachd, *s.f.* Shapeliness. 2 Handsomeness. 3 Humaneness. 4**Mildness.
cneasmhor, -oire, *a.* Shapely, handsome, well-formed. 2 Humane. 3 Modest, mild, meek.
cneas-mara, *s.f.* Firth, strait of the sea.
cneas-mhuir, see cneas-mara.
cneasnachadh, see cneasachadh.
cnea. naich, see cneasaich.
cneasnaidh,* *a.* Delicate, tender. 2* Slender,

cneasnaidheachd,* *s.f.* Delicacy.
cneast, -a, see cneasdachd.
——**achd,** see cneasdachd.
cneasuchadh, see cneasachadh.
cneataich, -e, *s.f.* Sighing, groaning.
cneatan, -ain, see cnatan.
cneatas, -ais, -an, *s.m.* Knitting. 2 Running thread or tape in a woman's head-dress.
cneath, see cneadh.
cneatraich, -e, *s.f.* see cneataich.
†**cneatrom,** *s.m.* Kind of horse-litter.
†**cned,** *s.* Wound.
cneid, -e, *s.f.* see cnàid.
cneidh, *v.a.* Wound.
—— **-chuthach,** *s.f.* Whitlow, kind of sore.
cneidhe, *gen.sing.* of cneadh.
†**cneidheach,** *a.* Wounded.
cneidh-fhiacall, see cneadh-fhiacall.
cneidh-ghalar, *s.m.* Painful complaint—*Dàin Iain Ghobha.*
†**cneidh-shliochd,**** *s.f.* Scar.
†**cneidh-shliochdach,**** *a.* Full of scars.
cneidsinn,* *s.m.* Knitting. 2 Tape.
cneim, *v. & s.* see creim.
cneis, -e, *a.* Tender, compassionate, mild. 2 Feeble.
——**eachd,** *s.f.ind.* Tenderness, mildness. 2 Feebleness.
cneisne, *a.* Slender.
cneut, see cneutag.
cneutag, *s.f.* Small ball, as for shinty, tennis, &c. 2**Football.
cniad, see cneutag.
cniadach, -aiche, *a.* Caressing, patting, soothing, stroking, prone to caress.
——**adh, -aidh,** *s.m.* Caressing, touching or rubbing gently. A' c—, *pr.pt.* of cniadaich.
cniadaich, *pr. pt.* a' cniadachadh, *v.a.* Caress, stroke, touch or rub gently.
——**e,** see cniadaire.
cniadaire, -an, *s.m.* Fondler.
†**cnioc,** *s.m.* Niggard.
†**cniochd,** *s.m.* Knight, soldier.
cniodachadh, see cniadachadh.
cniodaich, see cniadaich.
†**cniopaire, -an,** *s.m.* Poor rogue.
†——**achd,** *s.f.ind.* Roguery.
†**cnis, -e, -ean,** *s.f.* Opening in the warp for the shuttle to pass through the weft.
cnò, *pl.* cnothan [cnòmha & ††cnòmhan], *s. f.* Nut. 2 Filbert. 3 Shell of a species of cockle. Lios nan cnò, *the nut garden* ; coille-chnò, *hazel-wood.*
†**cnò,** *a.* Famous. 2 Excellent. 3 Gruff.
cnò-almoin, *s.f.* Almond.
cnò-bhachaill,(MMcD) *s.f.* Species of nut, sometimes called Mary's nut, found cast up on the sea-shore. It was strung on a string and worn by young women round their necks as a charm.—*Lewis.*
cnò-bhàchair, *pl.* cnothan-bàchair, *s.f.* Acorn. 2‡ Molucca bean.
cnò-bhainne, *s.f.* The milk-nut, a wooden vessel used for carrying home the milk from the *buaile,* and made in the form of a nut.
cnoc, *gen.* cnuic [& cnoic,] *pl.* cnuic [& cnocan] *s.m.* Hill, knoll, hillock, eminence. 2 ‖Heel-kibe. 3(AC) Council, court. 4(AC) Wisdom. C. seallta, *hill of observation* ; cha rachainn gu cùl cnuic leis aig meadhon latha, *I would not go with him behind a hill at mid-day*—said of a doubtful character ; an latha bhatar a' roinn na céille, cha robh mi fhéin air a' chnoc, *the day that sense was apportioned, I myself was not on the hillock* (*i.e.* was not present at the function—alluding to the ancient custom of holding ceremonies of importance in elevated positions); cuirm-chnuic, *a picnic*; ged is ann ris na cnuic a tha mi 'ga ràdh, *though I am saying this between us and the post* (*lit.* to the hillocks.)
cnocach, -aiche, *a.* Hilly, full of knolls. 2 Rugged.
cnocag, see cnomhagan.
cnòcag, see cròcag.
cnocaid, *s. f.* Young woman's hair bound up in a fillet. 2* Landmark. 3 Balk. 4(DC) Swelling, as from a blow with the fist—*Argyll.*
——**each, -eiche,** *a.* Wearing hair bound with fillets.
cnocair, -e, -ean, *s.m.* Saunterer, loiterer. 2 **Crabbed little fellow. 3‡‡see cnoc-faire.
——**eachd,** *s.f.ind.* Sauntering about the hillocks. 2 Walking idly abroad, airing. 3 **Merrymaking.
cnocan, -ain, -an, *s. m.* Hillock, little hill or knoll. 2** Mound, little heap. 3 Barrow (tumulus.) 4(MMcL) Ball of thread.
——**ach, -aiche,** *a.* Abounding in little hills, or knolls. 2**Rugged.
†**cnocc,**‖ *s.m.* "Gibber."
cnò-calltuinn,(WC) *s.f.* Hazel-nut.
cnoc-faire, *pl.* cnuic-fhaire, *s.m.* Alarm-post. 2 ††Watch-hill.
cnò-chanaich, *pl.* -than-canaich, *s.f.* Quince.
cnò-chòmhlach, *pl.* -than-còmhlaich, *s. f.* Hazel double nut.
cnoc-seallaidh, see cnoc-seallta.
cnoc-seallta, *pl.* cnuic-sheallta, *s. m.* Watch-hill.
cnòd, -òid, -an, *s.m.* Patch. 2 Piece on a shoe, 3 Clamp.
cnod, Gaelic spelling of *knot.*
cnòd, *pr.pt.* a' cnòdadh, Patch, repair. 2 Darn. 3(DC) Chew greedily, "gulch"—*Argyll.*
——**ach, -aich,** *s.m.* Acquiring, gaining, collecting together of goods or money by industrious habits. 2 Goods or effects so won. 3(WC) Clothing.
——**ach, -aiche,** *a.* Patched, clouted, patchy. 2††Industrious. 3**Scraping together. 4** Gaining.
cnodach,(WC) *pr.pt.* a' cnodach, *v.n.* Accuse, lay to the charge of (in the sense of guilt.) Bha siod air a chnodach air, *he was accused of that.*
——**achd,**‡‡ *s.f.ind.* Patchiness.
cnòdachadh, *pr. pt.* of cnòdaich.
cnodach.cinn,(WC) *s.m.* Head-dress.
cnòdadh, -aidh, *s.m.* Patching, clouting. 2 Knitting. A' c—, *pr. pt.* of cnòd.
cnòdaich, *pr.pt.* a' cnòdachadh, *v. a.* Acquire, collect, lay up with care. 2**Entangle. 3 ††see cnòd. 4(WC) Dress.
cnòdair,‡‡ **-e, -ean,** *s.m.* Patcher.
cnòdan, -ain, -an, *s.m.* Gurnet (fish) species of the genus *trigla* of Linn. (Scots, *crooner.*)
——**ach, -aiche,** *a.* Dwarfish. 2 Careful. 3 Opinionative.
cnòdhach, -aiche, *a.* see cnòthach.
cnòdhair, -e, -ean, *s.m.* see cnòthair.
cnò-dharaich, *s.f.* Oak apple. 2(Fionn) Acorn.
cnò-Fhrangach, *pl.* -than-Frangach, *s.f.* Walnut.
cnò-gheanmnuidh, *s.f.* Chestnut.
cnò-Ghreugach, *s.f.* see almon.
cnoic, *gen. sing. & nom. pl.* of cnoc.
cnòid, -e, -ean, *s.f.* Splendid present.
cnoidh, *s. m.* Severe pain, throbbing pain. 2 Tooth-ache.
——**each,** *a.* Painful, giving pain. Gu c., lotach, *causing pain and wounds.*

cnoidheag,* see cruimheag.
cnoidh-fhiacall,* see cruimh-fhiacall.
cnoimh,* see cruimh.
——eag,* see cruimheag.
cnòiteachan,(CR) *s.m.* Shrugging—*W. of Ross.*
cnò-leana,§ *s. f.* Marsh-cinquefoil, see còig-bhileach.
cnòmh, -a, -an, see cnò.
†cnomhadh, -aidh, *s.m.* Breaking, as of a nut.
cnomhag, *s.f.* see cnomhagan. 2(MMcL) Blow with one of the fingers. Mharbh mi le c. i, *I killed her with a blow from one of my fingers.*
cnomhagag, -aige, *s.f.* *Skye* for cnomhagan.
cnomhagan, -ain, *s. m.* Large whelk or periwinkle, buckie, conch.
cnò-mheannt,* *s.f.* Nutmeg.
†cnomhuine, *s.f.* Hazel wood.
cnò-shamhna, *s.f.* The Hallowe'en nut, nuts eaten or burnt on Hallowe'en in divination of marriage.
cnò-shearbh, *pl.* -than-searbha, *s.f.* Filbert.
cnò-spuinge, *pl.* -than-spuinge, *s.f.* Molucca-nut; nuts washed by the Gulf-stream across the Atlantic Ocean in the seaweed known as *tùrusgar.* Their kernels are used as a cure for diarrhœa and dysentry.
cnot, Gaelic spelling of *knot.*
cnot, *pr.pt.* a' cnotadh, *v.a.* Unhusk corn.
cnot,* *s.m.* Oarslip—*Skye.* 2 (DC) Door-bar—*Uist & Lewis.*
cnotach, -aich, *s.m.* Nod.
†cnotadh, -aidh, -aidhean, *s.m.* Gaelic form of *knotting.*
cnotag, -aig, -an, *s.f.* Block of stone, or wood, hollowed out for unhusking corn; mortar. 2‡‡Hunch-backed woman.
cnotainn, *v.a.* see cnot.
——,** *s.* Barley hulled by pounding. 2 Broth in which barley so hulled is a principal ingredient.
cnotal, see crotal.
—— -coille, see crotal-coille.
cnoth, see cnò.
cnòthach, -aiche, *a.* Nuciferous, nutty. 2‡‡ Mastful. Coille ch., *a wood abounding in nuts.*
cnò-thalmhuinn, *pl.* -than-talmhuinn, *s.f.* Earth-nut, see braonan-bhuachaille.
cnòthair, -e, -ean, *s.m.* Nut-cracker.
cnòthar,‡‡ -aire, *a.* Nuciferous, nutty.
cnothan, *n.pl.* of cnò.
cnotuinn, *v.a.* see cnot.
†cnotul, see crotal.
cnù, -mha, -mhan, *s.f.* see cnò.
cnuac, -aic, *s.m.* Costard. 2 see cnuachd.
cnuacag, (WC) *s.f.* Thump, smart blow.
cnuacaid, *s.f.* Bang.
cnuacarra,‡‡ *a.* Deep, shrewd.
cnuachd, -an, *s.f.* Lump. 2 Head. 3 Brow, forehead, temple. 4(DC) Rounded hill shaped like a head. A' sgoltadh chnuachd, *splitting heads*; 'nuair a thàirngteadh leibh lanntaidh, 'ghearradh cheann agus chnuac, (chnuachd), *when blades would be drawn by you that would cut heads and crowns.*
cnuachdach, -aiche, *a.* Lumpish. 2 Round, as the head. 3 Deep, shrewd, cunning. 4 Steady. 5**Large browed. 6**Little browed.
cnuachdadh, *s.m.* Munching.
cnuachdair, -e, -ean, *s. m.* Cunning, deep, shrewd fellow. 2 Crumpy fellow.
cnuachdanach,(AH) *a.* Careful, shrewd, astute.
cnuachd-chasach, -aiche, *a.* Crump-footed.
cnuaichdein, -e, -ean, *s. m.* *dim.* of cnuachd. cnuaichdein-giuthais, *a roughly cut piece of bog-fir.*
——each, see cnuachdach.
cnuaipeadh, *s.m.* Munching.

cnuaiste, *past pt.* of cnuas. Gnashed, chewed. 2 Collected, gathered, scraped together.
†cnuas, -ais, *s.m.* Collection, acquisition. 2** Gnashing. 3‡‡Chewing. 4**Scraping. An c. a's fhearr, *the best collection.*
cnuas, *pr.pt.* a' cnuasadh, *v. a.* Gnash, chew voraciously, crunch. 2 Collect, gather, assemble. 3††Ponder, meditate. 4* Quash. 5* Gather eatables.
†cnuas-abuich, *a.* Fruitful.
cnuasach, -aich, *s.m.* Earning. 2 Purchasing. 3 Hoarding. 4 Pondering, ruminating. 5 Investigating. 6 Fruit, growth.
——, *a.* see cnuasmhor.
cnuasachadh,** -aidh, *s. m.* Gathering, accumulation, scraping together. 2 Pondering, ruminating. 3 Gnashing, chewing. 4*Agitation. A' c—, *pr. pt.* of cnuasaich.
cnuasachd, *s.f.ind.* Pondering, ruminating, investigating. 2 Gathering, collecting, compiling, hoarding. 3** Recollection. 4 ** Agitation. 5 Unripe fruit. 6* Gathering eatables. C. le 'n lùbadh slat, *a collection beneath which the bough bends*; c. na gràineig, *the storing up of the hedgehog*—useless labour.
——ach, -aiche, *a.* That gathers, collects, ruminates or investigates. 2** Providing.
cnuasadach,** *a.* Accumulative.
cnuasadair, -e, -ean, *s.m.* see cnuasaiche.
cnuasadh, see cnuasachadh. 2 *pr. pt.* of cnuas.
cnuasaich, *pr. pt.* a' cnuasachadh, *v.a.* Ponder, sift, ruminate, reflect, review. 2 Investigate. 3 Assemble, gather, collect, accumulate, compile. 4 Earn, win. 5 Gnash, chew. 6 **Procure. 7 Aggregate.
——e, -an, *s.m.* Searcher, gatherer, hoarder, scraper. 2 One who ponders or ruminates. 3 Provider.
——te, *past pt.* of cnuasaich. Investigated, pondered, ruminated. 2 Collected, gathered. 3 Earned, won, purchased. 4 Gnashed, chewed.
cnuasair, see cnuasaiche.
cnuasmhor, -oire, *a.* Fruitful, fertile, productive.
†cnuasta, *n.pl.* of cnuas. Gatherers, collectors.
cnuasuichte, see cnuasaichte.
cnubhan,(CR) *s.m.* Knuckle of the second or middle joint of the fingers.—*W. of Ross.*
cnùdan, see cnòdan.
cnùdhach, see cnòdhach.
†cnudhaire, -an, see cnodhaire.
cnugan, see cnubhan.
cnuidh, see cruimh.
cnuimh, -e, -ean, *s.f.* see cruimh.
——ean,(MMcL) *s. pl.* Tips of the fingers gathered together.
cnuimh-fhiacall, see cruimh-fhiacall.
cnuimheach, -eiche, see cruimheach.
cnuimheag, -eig, -an, see cruimheag.
——ach, see cruimheagach.
——an, see cruimheag.
cnuimhean, see cruimhean.
cnuimh-itheach, -eiche, *a.* see cruimh-itheach.
cnuimh-shioda, see cruimh-shioda.
cnumhagan, -ain, *s.m.* Handful.
†cnùs-mhor, -mhoire, see cnuasmhor.
cò? *interr. pron.* Who? 2 Which? Cò e? *who is he?* cò i? *who is she?* cò a sgrìobhas an rann? *who will write the verse?* cò e seo? *who is this?* cò aige tha fios gu'n d'thàinig e? *who knows that he came?* (*lit.* at whom there is knowledge that he came?); *or* cò aig am bheil fios gu'n d' thàinig e? (*lit.* who is [the man] at whom is knowledge that he came? cò an seo a thig leam? *who here will come*

with me?
co, *conj.* As. This word is placed before an *adj.* as, cho mór, *as great*; cho eireachdail, *as handsome*; and it should always be written *cho* when so placed, except after *is*, as, is co lìonmhor osna aig an righ agus aig an duine a's ìsle staid, *the king's sighs are as plentiful as those of a man in the humblest position.*
co, *prefix*, used as a contraction of *comh* -or *coimh-*.
còail, -e, -ean, see còmhdhail.
co'ainm, see comh-ainm.
cò air bith, *comp. rel.* Whoever, whosoever.
co'-àiteachadh, see comh-àiteachadh.
co'-àitich, see comh-àitich.
co'-alta, see comh-dhalta.
co'-altas, see comh-dhaltas.
co'-aois, see comh-aois.
co'-aontachadh, see comh-aontachadh.
co'-aontachd, see comh-aontachd.
co'-aontaich, see comh-aontaich.
co'-arguinn, see comh-arguinn.
co'-astaraich, see comh-astaraich.
còb, -òib, *s.m.* Plenty, abundance.
cobair,** *s.m.* Jockey. 2(CR) Horse-dealer.
còbaraid,* *s.f.* Coffer.
†cobh, *s.m.* Victory, triumph, conquest.
cobhach, -aich, *s.m.* Tribute.
———, -aiche, *a.* Stout, brave, victorious.
co'-bhaigh, see comh-bhaigh.
————each, see comh-bhaigheach.
†co'-bhail, see combhail.
cobhair, *gen. sing.* cobhrach & coibhre, *s.f.* Assistance, relief, salvation, aid. Fear-cobhrach, *a saviour.*
cobhair, *pr. pt.* a' cobhair & a' cobhradh, *fut. aff.* coibhridh, *v.a.* Relieve, help, aid, assist. C. oirnne, *help us*; an luibh nach fhaighear cha'n i a chobhaireas, *the herb that cannot be found will heal no wound.*
còbhair,** -ean, *s. m.* Dry-stone mason, dyke-builder.
còbhaireachd,** *s.f.ind.* Dry-stone building.
cobhais, see cubhais.
†cobhais,(DC) *s.f.* Any foul language—*Argyll.*
cobhaltach, -eiche, *a.* Triumphant, victorious. Gu c., *successfully.*
cobhan, -ain, -an, *s.m.* Coffer, box. 2 Ark. 3 Coffin. 4 Chariot, car. 5 Hollow. 6 Walking side by side. 7 Small creek. Naomh ch., *a shrine.*
————ach, -aiche, *a.* Hollow, eddying. 2†† Full of coffers or boxes.
cobhar, -air, *s.m.* Foam, froth, sillabub. 2 see gobhar. Mar ch. thonn, *like the foam of waves.*
———-ach, *a.* Foamy, frothy. 2 Aiding, relieving. 3 Helpful, supporting, succouring. Fear-c. an righ, *the auxiliary of the king.*
————tach, -aich, *s.m.&f.* Booty, plunder, prey. 2* Any property coming on shore.
————tach, -aiche, *a.* Assisting, aiding, relieving, ready to help.
————tachail,‡‡ -e, *a.* Predatory. 2(DC) Helping oneself.
————tachd,‡‡ *s.f.ind.* Prize, plunder.
————tachd-srutha,‡‡ *s.f.* Alluvion.
————thach, -aich, *s.m.* Saviour, helper, comforter.
————thach, -aiche, see cobhartach, *a.*
†cobhludh, *s.m.* Strength. *a.* United.
†cobhra, *s.f.* Shield, target.
cobhrach, *gen. sing.* of cobhair.
————(AC) *a.* Foam-white. 2**Foamy. 3** Prone to aid.
————ail,‡‡ -e, *a.* Assistant.
cobhragach, -aich, *s.m.* Foam, sillabub.

†cobhsach,** *a.* Victorious, triumphant.
†cobhthach, -aich, *s.m.* Creditor.
†cobhthach, -aiche, *a.* Victorious, triumphant.
co-bhoinn, see comh-bhoinn.
coc, *pr. pt.* a' cocadh, *v.a.* & *n.* Cock. 2*Bristle. 3(MMcL) Make small haystacks. 4*Hold up in defiance. C. do bhoineid, *cock your bonnet.*
coc,** -a, *s. m.* Cocking or stiffening, as of a Highland bonnet. 2(AC) see cochull. 3 Haystack.
còc,** *s.m.* Cooking.
†coc, -a, *a.* Manifest, plain, intelligible.‡
cóca? (*for* co aca?) Which of the two?
†còca, *s.m.* Boat. 2 Cook.
†còca, *a.* Void, empty, hollow.
cocadh, -aidh, *s. m.* Cocking. A' c—, *pr.pt.* of coc.
cocainn, *s.f.* Cocking or dressing of a bonnet. Tha a bhoineid air a cocainn, *his bonnet is cocked.*
còcaire, -an, *s.m.* Cook. Is math an c. an t-acras, *hunger is a good cook.*
————achd, *s.f.ind.* Cookery, cooking. Ris a' ch., *engaged in cooking.*
cocannta, *a.* Airy, perky, gay, jaunty, "cocky." 'Bhi shuas 'na taobh gu cocannta, *to be up in its side jauntily.—Filidh, p. 33.*
†cocar, *a.* Systematic, perfect.
cocàrd, *s.m.* Cockade.
coc-bhran,(AC) *s.m.* Jackdaw, see cathag.
coch, see cochull.
cochall, see cochull.
————ach, see cochullach.
cochionta,†† see coitchionn.
cochla,(AF) *s.m.* Snail.
cochlach,** *s.m.* Hair-lace.
cochlach,** *a.* Braided.
co'-chomunn, -uinn, *s.m.* comh-chomunn.
cochull, -uill, *s.m.* Husk, shell of a nut or grain. 2**Ear or beard of barley. 3 Cap, capsule, hood, mantle. 4* Skin of a snake. 5(AC) Sheath, shrine, screen. 6‡‡ Dust of timber. 7 Shell of a pulley, see ulag, p. 78. 8§Corn-cockle, see bròg-na-cubhaig. Chuir e i á c. a cridhe, *he frightened her out of her senses (lit.* out of the husk of her heart.)
cochullach, -aiche, *a.* Capsular. 2 Husky, branny. 3 Coated with a shell or husk. 4 Bearded, or having ears, like barley.
†cocol, -oil, *s.m.* Cuckold.
cocontachd, *s.f.ind.* Smartness, quickness, forwardness.
cocraich,** *v.a.* Challenge.
coc-shron, -a, -an, *s.f.* Cocked nose.
————ach, -aiche, *a.* Cock-nosed.
†cod, *s.m.* Victory.
†cod, -a, *s.f.* (cuid) Piece, part.
†coda, *s.m.* Law, equity, justice.
†coda, *impers. verb*, It is encumbent.
codach, *gen. sing.* of cuid. Air son mo chodach-sa dheth, *for my part of it.* 2**Share, part, portion. 3(DC) *s.f.* Result of one's labour, as of harvest, &c. 4(DC) Benefit.
†codach, *s.m.* Invention. 2 Piece of art. 3 Friendship.
còdach, see comhdach.
codachadh, -aidh, *s.m.* Sharing, dividing. 2 Accession, addition. 3 (MMcL) Swearing on oath. A thoirt a ch., *to swear on his oath.* A' c—, *pr. pt.* of codaich.
còdachadh, see comhdachadh.
codag, (AF) see cudainn. 2 Haddock.
codaich, *pr. pt.* a' codachadh, *v. a.* Divide, share. 2(MMcL) Swear on oath, give witness.
còdaich, see comhdaich.
codaiche, (a ch— !) *voc. pl.* of cuid.

codaichean, *pl.* of cuid.
codaichte,** *past pt.* of codaich, Divided.
còdaichte, see comhdaichte.
codail, see cadal.
codal, -ail, see cadal.
codalach, see cadalach.
——d, see cadalachd.
codalan,§ *s.m.* Common opium poppy—*papaver somniferum.* 2**Mandrake.
codaleun,** -eoin, *s.m.* see cadalan 2.
codalta, see cadalach.
——ch, see cadalach.
——chd, see cadalachd.
codarsnachd,** *s.f.* Contrariety.
†codh, *adv.* Alike.
cò dha ? *adv.* To whom ?
còdhail, -e, *s.f.* Meeting.
dhail.
còdhalach, -aich, *s.m.* Opposition.
codhan, see cobhan.
co dhiù, *conj.* However.
2 Whether. 3 In any case.
†codhnach, *s.m.* King, lord. 2 Disease in cattle. 3 Wealth, goods.
codla, see cadal.
†codladh, see cadal.

170. Cadalan.

†codlaim, Ir. form of *1st. per. sing. pres. aff.*
codrum, -uim, *s.m.* Sea-calf, seal.
còduich, see còdaich.
†coech,‖ *a.* Blind, see †coic. 2 see caoch.
cofar, Gaelic spelling of *coffer.*
cofaran, *dim.* of cofar.
cofra, see cofar.
†cog, *s.m.* Drink, draught. 2 Mill-cog.
cog, *pr. part.* a' cogadh, *v.a.* War, fight, carry on war. 2* Gibe, jeer. Ch. iad, *they warred*; tha e a' cogadh air, *he is jeering at him*; cò a chogas riut ? *who will fight against thee ?*
cogach, -aiche, *a.* see cogail.
cogadh, -aidh, -aidhean, *s. m.* War, warfare, fighting. A' c—, *pr. pt.* of cog. C.-choilleach, *cock-fighting* ; deanta ri c., *trained to war;* luingeas chogaidh, *a war-ship*; c. no sìth, *peace or war* (motto of the MacCrimmons.)
cogaidh, *a.* Just, lawful.
——, *fut. aff.* of cog.
cogail, *a.* Warlike, belligerent.
cogair, *gen. sing.* of cogar.
cogair, *v.a.* see cagair.
——seach, -eich, *s.m.* Whisperer.
cogais, -e, -ean, *s.f.* see coguis.
cogais,* *s.f.* Prodigiously large red carbuncle nose.—*Isles.* 2 Cog of a wheel. 3 Ludicrous name for a large pinch of snuff. 4 Nose—*Skye.* 5 Nasal canal—*Lewis.* 6 Cork of a bottle—*Ross & Caithness.* 7 Huge frog—*Inverness-shire.* 8 Throttle—*Arran.*
——each, -eiche, *a.* see coguiseach.
cogal, see cogull.
cogall, -aill, see cogull.
cogallach, see cogullach.
cogallaidh, see cugallaidh.
cogan, -ain, *s. m.* Loose husk, covering. 2 Drink, draught. 3 Small drinking dish.
†coganta,** *a.* Bean ch., *a midwife.*
cogar, -air, see cagar.
†cogar, -air, *s.m.* Insurrection. 2**Conspiracy.
cogarach, -aiche, *a.* see cagarach. 2**Auricular.
cogaraich, -e, -an, *s.m.* see cagarsaich. 2 see cagaraiche.
——, *v.* see cagaraich.
†cogaras, *s.m.* Peace, amity.
cogarn,(AF) *s.m.* Large periwinkle.
cogarsaich, -e, *s.f.* see cagarsaich.
——, *v.n.* see cagarsaich.
——e, -an, *s.m.* see cagaraiche.
cogarsnach, see cagarsaich.
coghain,** *v.n.* see congnain.
coghnach,** *a.* congnach.
——ail,** *a.* see congnachail
coghnadair,** *s.m.* see congnadair.
coghnadh,** -aidh, *s.m.* see congnadh.
coghnath, -aith, *s.m.* see congnadh.
——ach,** *a.* see congnathach.
cognadh, -aidh, *s.m.* see cagnadh.
†cogoirse, *s.f.* Regular system.
†cogradh, *s.m.* Conspiracy.
cograich, see cagarsaich.
coguill, *s.m.* see cogull.
coguis, -e, -ean, *s.f.* Conscience. 2‡‡Cogs of a wheel. Agartas coguis, *remorse of conscience.*
coguiseach, -eiche *a.* Conscientious 2‡‡ Coggeo.
——d,‡‡ *s.f.ind.* Conscience, honesty.
cogull, -uill, *s.m.* Tares, the plant cockle. 2 Friction, rubbing. 3 see cochull. 4‡‡ Sawdust. 5** Beard of barley. C. ràmh, *friction of oars on the fulcrum.*
——ach, -aich, *s.m.* Filings.
——ach, -aiche, *a.* Full of tares. 2 see cochullach.
coi-, *contr.* of prefix coimh-.
coi,(AF) *s.f.* Cuckoo, see cubhag.
†coib, *s.f.* Company, troop. 2 Copy. 3 Cope.
†coibh-dean, *s.f.* Troop.
†coibh-dhean, see coibh-dean.
†——achd, *s.f.* Captainship.
†coibh-dhealchadh, *s.m.* Relationship.
coibhearan, (AF) *s.m.* Dog.
—— -dobhar, (AF) *s.m.* Otter.
—— -muirt, (AF) *s.m.* Rabbit.
†coibhgioch, see coimheach.
Coibhi, *s.m.* see †coimhdhe.
†coibh-lighe, *s.f.* (coimh-dhlighe) Law of corelatives as lord and vassel.
coibhneas,†† Same meanings as caoimhneas.
——ach, Same meanings as caoimhneasach.
coibhneil, Same meanings as caoimhneil.
†coibhreachadh, *s. m.* Relieving, comforting. A' c—, *pr. pt.* of coibhrich.
†coibhrich, *pr.pt.* a' coibhreachadh, *v.a.* Comfort, relieve.
coibhseach,†† *a.* Sufficient, proper.
——d, *s.f.* Propriety, decorum.
†coibhthe, *s.f.* Hire.
†coic, *s.f.* Secret, mystery.
——, *a.* Blind.
coiceig,†† *s.f.* Trouble, hindrance.
coich, see cochull. C. anama, *soul-shrine ;* c. chuaiche, *couch-shrining*—prayer before retiring at night.
coicheid -e, -ean, *s.f.* Doubt, suspicion. 2* Objection, obstruction. Cò a chuir c. ? *who objected ?*
——each, -eiche, *a.* Doubting, suspicious. 2 Objecting, hindering.
†coid, *s.f.* Sticks, firewood, brushwood.
coidhean,(AF) *s. m.* Vessel to hold cream, similar to, but much broader at the bottom, and narrower at the mouth than, "cuinneag."
†coidhean, -ein, *s.m.* Barnacle.
coi'-dheas, -dheise, *a.* see comh-dheas.
——achd, see comh-dheasachd.
coidheis,** *a.* Lukewarm, indifferent. Tha mi c. m'a dheidhinn, *I am indifferent about it.* see coingeis.
coidhiseachd,** *s. f.* Convenience. 2 Recklessness.
coidhirp,†† *s.f.* Rivalry, emulation.
coidil, see caidil.

coifi, *Gaelic spelling of* coffee.
cóig, *a.* Five. Car nan c. cuairt, *the turn of the five circuits ;* c.-air-fhichead, *twenty-five;* c. ceud *five hundred.*
cóig-bhileach,‡ *s.m.* Cinquefoil, see meangach.
——————,** *a* Cinquefoliated.
—————— -uisge,§ *s.m.* Marsh cinquefoil—*comarum palustre.*

171. Cóig-bhileach-uisge.

†coigchreach, *s.f.* Plundering, sacking, pillaging.
†coigcreach, *s.f.* see comh-chrìoch.
†coig-criach, see comh-chrìoch.
†coig-crich, *s. f.* Strange country. 2 see comh-chrìoch.
cóig-deug, *a.* Fifteen. An cóigeamh fear deug, *the fifteenth man.*
cóigeach, -ich, *s.f.* Hand ; so named from the five fingers.
cóigead, *s.m.* Fifty.
†coigeal, *s.m.* Noise, outcry. 2 Clap. 3 Thrift. 4 see cuigeal. 5 see coigil.
coigealta, see coigilte.
cóigeamh, *a.* Fifth.
cóigeamh,(DU) *s.m.* Fifth. 2 Province.
coigeann, see caigeann.
cóigear, see cóignear.
coigeart, -eirt, *s.m.* Judgment. 2 Question.
coigil, *pr. pt.* a' coigleadh, *v. a.* Spare, preserve, keep alive,save. 2 Economise. 3 Cover fire to keep it from extinguishing Cagail (c.) an teine, *secure the fire.—Arran.*
coigill, *s.f.* Thought, secret.
coigilte, *past pt.* of coigil. Spared, preserved, saved alive.
†coigle, *s. m.* Companion. 2 Secret. 3 Vassalage. 4 Wisdom.
coigleachd, *s.f.ind.* Sparing. 2 Commerce. 3 Train, retinue.
coigleadh, -idh, *s.m.* Act of sparing or saving alive. A' c—, *pr.pt.* of coigil.
coiglich, *v.a.* Attend, accompany.
cóig-mheòir-Muire,‡ Five-leaved clover, cinquefoil, see meangach.
†coigne, *s.f.* Spear, dart.
cóignear, *s.* Five (generally only used of persons, and is followed by genitive plural.) C. bhan, *five women.*
coigreach, -ich, *s.m.* Stranger, foreigner.
———, -iche, *a.* Strange, foreign. Dùthaich ch., *a strange country.*
————ail, -e, *a.* Strange, like a stranger, foreign.
coigrich, *gen. sing & nom. pl.* of coigreach. 2 ‡‡see comh-chrìoch.
coigridh, (for coigrich) *voc. pl.* of coigreach. Guilibh, a ch., an laoch, *ye strangers weep for the hero.*
coigrigheach, -eiche, *a.* see coigreach.
cóigrinn, see cóig-roinn.
cóig-roinn, *s.f.* Five parts or divisions.
cóigsheag,‡ Marsh cinquefoil, see cóig-bhileach.
cóig-shliosnach, *a.* Pentelateral, pentagonal.
cóig-shliosnag,** *s.f.* Pentagon.
cóig-thaobhach, see cóig-shliosnach.
†coil, *s.f.* see cùil.
——,** *s.f.* Coil. 2 Cock of hay.
——,** *v.a.* Coil or gather hay into cocks.
coilbhein, -in, -ean, *s.m.* Stem, stalk. 2 Small shaft. 3††Small rope for carrying burdens. 4 see coilpein.
coilbhinn,** see coilbhein.
coilbhinn,(AF) *s.f.* Young pig.
†coilce, *s.f.* Bed. 2 Bed-clothes.
————adha, (*pl.* of coilce.) Bed materials put under the sheets or blankets, as, feathers, straw, heath &c. Tri c. na Féinne, bàrr gheal chrann. còinneach, agus ùr-luachair, *the three bedstuffs of the F., fresh tree-tops, moss, and fresh rushes*
coilchean, -ein, -ean, *s.m.* Water gushing from an orifice. 2 Small cock.
coilchinn,(AC)*a.*Stunted Coirce c., *dwarf oats* ; eorna c., *meagre bere*; seagal c., *stunted rye.* This is the name given to corn grown on the sandy machairs of the W. Isles, which is stunted in dry seasons and pulled up by the roots instead of being cut in the usual way.
coi'-leabach, see comh-leapach.
coileach, -lich, *s. m.* Cock. 2 Barn-cock. 3 Rill of water. 4 Eddy, rapids. 5(CR)White crest on the waves—*W. of Ross.* 6(AH)The apex of a thatched hay- or corn-stack. Ann an c. an t-sruith, *in the eddy of the stream ; 2 in a serious predicament;* tha c. air (na tuinn) an diugh,*the waves are white-crested today*; is binn uiseag 'sa chamhanaich, ach 's binne coileach 'sa mheadhon-oidhche, *sweet is the lark at dawn, but sweeter the cock at midnight*—when the cock begins to crow, the ghosts, &c. disappear.
————ach, Like a cock. 2 Of or belonging to a cock. 3 Abounding in cocks.
————, see coilleachadh.
———— -aifrinn, see caolach-aifrinn.
————ail, see coileachach.
————an, -ain, *s. m.* Little cock. 2 Rivulet, rill.
————anach,†† *a.* Like a little cock.
———— -an-dùnain, *s.m.* Barn-door cock.
————anta, *a.* Lively, active. 2 Like a cock.
———— -àrcain, *s.m.* Shuttle-cock.
———— buadha, (AF) *s. m.* Victor in a cock-fight.
———— -catha,¶ *s.m.* Game-cock.
———— -cathaig,(AF) *s.m.* Jackdaw.
———— -coille,¶ *pl.* -ich-choille, *s. m.* Woodcock—*scolopax rusticola.* (see illust. 172.)
coileach-dubh,¶ *pl.* -lich-dhubha, *s. m.* Blackcock—*tetrao tetrix.* (see illust. 173.)
coileach-Dùitseach, *pl.* -lich-Dhùitseach, *s. m.* Curtailed cock.
coileach-dùnain, see coileach-an-dùnain.
coileach-feucaig, see peucag.
coileach-Frangach, *pl.* -lich-Fhrangach, *s.m.*

172. Coileach-coille.

173. Coileach-dubh.

Turkey-cock. 2* Bustard.
coileach-fraoich, *pl.* -lich-fhraoich, *s.m.* Moor-cock, heath-cock, red grouse cock.—*lagopus Scoticus.*

174. Coileach-fraoich.

coileach-gaoithe, *pl.* -lich-ghaoithe, *s.m.* Weather-cock, vane.
coileach-gròid,(AF) *s.m.* Fireplace of a kiln.
coileach-Innseanach, *s.m.* Guinea-fowl.
coileach-lacha, *s.m.* Drake.
coileach-maragan,(WC) *s m.* Boy riding stride-legs on another boy's shoulders. Bha e 'coileach-mharagan, *he was riding stride-legs.*
coileach òg, *s.m.* Cockerel.
coileach-oidhche, see cailleach-oidhche.
coileach-òtraich, *s.m.* Barn-door cock.
coileach-pheucaig,¶ see peucag.
coileach-ruadh, see coileach-fraoich.
coileach-spodhta,(AF) *s.m* Capon.
coileach-sraide, *s.m.* Shuttle-cock. 2(WC) Fireplace of a kiln—*Poolewe.*
coiteach-teas, (WC) *s.m.* Mirage, shimmering effect on a hot day.
coileach-tomain, *pl.* -lich-thomain, *s.m.* Cock-partridge.
coileach-Turcach, see coileach-Frangach.

còileadh,(WC) *s.m.* Romping about in an aimless manner.—*Poolewe.* 'De c. a th' ort? *why are you romping so?*
coileag, -an, *s.f.* Coil. 2 Cock of hay (ruc.)
-———ach,†† *a.* Like a cock of hay.
-———aich, *pr. pt.* a' coileagachadh, *v.a.* Coil, or gather hay into cocks.
còileid, (WC) *s.f.* Romping girl.—*Poolewe.*
coileid, -e, -ean, *s.f.* Stir, movement. 2 Noise.
——each, -eiche, *a.* Noisy. 2 Stirring, in confusion.
coileir, -e, -ean, *s.m.* Collar. 2 Necklace. 3 Neck. 4 Quarry, mine. 5(AH) Brace-stick, see G 2 p. 73.
——each, -eiche, *a.* Collared, abounding in collars.
coilichin, *s.m.* Large cravat or muffler.—*Sgeulaiche-nan-caol, p. 138.*
coilideach,* *a.* Parisyllabical.
coi-lige, see coimhliong.
coiligeann,** -inn, *s.m.* Colic. C. adhairceach, *a ludicrous name for pregnancy, or for the pains of childbed.*
coilinn, see coinneal.
coiliobhar, -air, -ean, *s.m.* see cuilbheir.
coilion, *a.* see coimh-lion.
†coill, *s.f.* Sin, iniquity. Tha e fo 'n ch., *he is an outlaw* (*lit.* under a sense of his guilt.)
†——, *v.a.* Blindfold. 2 Trespass. 3 Castrate.
coille, *pl.* coilltean [& coilltichean] *s.f.* Wood, forest, grove. Caoidhrean na c., *the murmur of the wood*; maor-coille, *wood-keeper;* cearc-choille, *partridge.*
coille, s.*f.* see Calluinn. Dàir na coille, *the night of the fecundation of trees*—the first night of the new year when the wind blows from from the w.)
†coilleach,‡‡ *s.m.* Hog. 2 Wood. 3 Blinding. 4 Infringing. 5 Plundering.
coilleachadh, -aidh, (AC) *s. m* Stretching. A' c— an aodaich, *stretching the cloth after waulking.*
coilleadair, see coinnealair.
†coilleadh, see †coilleach.
coilleag, -eig, -an, *s.f.* Cockle. 2 Smart stroke. 3 Potato sprout. 4 Rural song. 5 Loud and cheerful note. 6 *contr.* for buille-choilleag. 7* Husk of lint. 8**Bucolic. 9(MMcL) Few peats put up together to dry—*Harris.* 'Nuair a sheinneadh tu c., *when thou wouldst sing a song.*
———ach, -aiche, *a.* Full of cockles, 2 of potato sprouts. 3 Sonorous, melodious, musical. 4 Cheerful.
———ach,†† -aich, *s.m.* Song.
coilleannach, -aich, *s.m.* Poltroon, truant.
coilleanta, *a.* Tall, straight, slender.
coillear, -eir, *s.m.* Wood cutter. 2 see coinnleir.
———nach, -aich, *s.f.* Woody place. 2 Shrubbery.
coille-bionan, (AF) *s.m.* Sea animalculæ. 2 (MMcL) Gaseous light. Chunnaic mi mu 'n cuairt dhiom na coille-bionain, *I saw the gaseous lights round about me.*
coille-challtuinn, *s.f.* Hazel wood.
coille-chnò, *s.f.* Nuttery.
coille-chu,(AF) *s.m.* Wolf.
coille-dharaich, *s.f.* Oak wood.
coille-dhearcag, *s.f* Wood where brambles (blackberries) grow.
coille-ghiuthais, *s.f* Pine wood.
coille-shlat,(AH) *s.f.* Wood where wattles may be cut.
coillidh, *prov. form of dat. sing.* of coille.
coillinn, see coinneal.

coilliog, see coilleag.
coill-mhias, *s.f.* Wooden plate. 2 Mess.
coillte' (for coilltean) *n.pl.* of coille.
coillte, *a. & past pt.* of coill. Gelded.
———ach, -eiche, *a.* Woody, wooded, sylvan, woodland. Chlisg na sléibhte c., *the wooded hills startled.*
———ach, -ich, *s. f.* Wood, forest. Mar a chlaoidheas teine c., *as fire consumes a wood.*
———achail, -e, *a.* Woody. 2 Wild, savage. 3 Uninhabited.
coilltean, *pl.* of coille.
————ach, see caillteanach.
coilltear, -an, *s. m.* Absconder, fugitive. 2 Wood-wanderer. 3 Saunterer. [†† gives -eir as *nom.*]
————achd, *s.f.ind.* State of a fugitive or wanderer. 2 Banishment.
coillteil, *a.* Savage, untamed, wild. 2 Sylvan, woodland.
coilltich,** *v.a.* Afforest.
————ean, *pl.* of coille.
coilmein, see coilmhinn.
coilmhinn,(AF) *s.m.* Young pig.
coilpeach, see colpach.
————adh, -aidh, *s.m.* see colpachadh.
coilpein, -ean, *s.m.* Rope, tow.
coilt,** *s.f.* Heifer.
co'imeachd,** *s.f.* Attendance. 2 Company. 3 Train. 'Na c., *in her train.*
coimeas, -eis, *s. m.* Comparison, equality. 2 Equal. 3 Resemblance, likeness. 4 Parable. 5**Mate. Gun a choimeas ann, *without his equal or match;* thusa is coimeas ri creig, *thou who art like a rock* ; gun do ch. ri taobh do shoillse, *without thy mate near thy effulgent light.*
coimeas, *v.a.* Compare, liken, equal.
———, *a.* Co-equal, like, comparative.
———ach,†† -aiche, *a.* Co-equal. 2 Exemplary.
———achd,‡‡ *s.f.ind.* see coimeas.
———aich, *pr.pt.* a' coimeasachadh, *v.a.* see coimeas.
coimeasg, *pr. pt.* a' coimeasgadh, *v. a.* Mix, mingle, confound. 2 Adulterate. 3 Commix, admix, amalgamate.
————, -isg, -an, *s.m.* Mixture, composition, compound. 2**Fight.
————ach,** *a.* Chaotic.
————achd, *s.f.* Composition, mixture.
————adh, -aidh, *s.m.* Mixing, conjumbling, compounding, combination. 2 Mixture, admixture, composition, compound. 3 Batter. A' c—, *pr. pt.* of coimeasg.
coimeasgta, *past part.* of coimeasg. Mixed, confused, adulterated, commingled, commixed, compounded.
coimeasta, *past part.* of coimeas. Likened, compared, of equal worth or value.
†coimeirce, *s.f.* Dedication.
coimh, Prepositive syllable which takes the place of the prefix comh-, in words which, having been originally compounds, with a small vowel in the first syllable of the second element, are now accented on the first element and no longer written with a hyphen, as, comh-lion, *now written* coimhlion. Coimh should never be used as a compound. When coimh is used, it signifies that the compound has become consolidated into a simple word. [This rule is not consistently observed in most Gaelic Dictionaries, so many words given in them as beginning with *coimh,* will be found here under *comh-.*]
†coimh, *s.m.* Protection, guard, defence.
coimh-cheangal, see comh-cheangal.
coimhdeach, -eiche, *a.* Safe, secure.
————d, *s.f.* see coimheadachd.
†coimhdhe, *s.m.* God, the Trinity. [‡The fanciful "Coibhi, the Celtic archdruid," is due to a confusion of the obsolete *coimhdhe* and the Northumbrian *Coifi* of Bede.]
coimhdheas, see coingeis.
†coimhdhreamas, -ais, *s.m.* see comh-dhreimeachd.
†coimhdhreimeachd, *s.f.* Competition.
coimheach, -eiche, *a.* Foreign, strange. 2 Shy. 3 Barbarous. 4 Fierce, cruel. 5 Wrathful. 6* Unkind. 7**Terrible. 8**Bitter. 9**Careless. †10 Safe. †11 Like, alike. 12 AH Inaffable, ungracious, unneighbourly. 13(AH) *prov.* Exceeding, excessive, singular. Tha e c. làidir, *he is exceedingly strong* ; is c. an tom ùire, *strange is the earthy mound;* ged nach bi mi bruidhneach, bithidh mi c., cuimhneach, *though I will not be talking, I'll be shy and mindful;* a h-uile cù air a' chù ch., *all dogs down on the strange dog;* is c. a' bhliadhn' ùr do 'n t-seann duine, *the New Year is unkind to the old man;* duine c., *a strange person*; gnothach c., *a terrible affair;* shéid osnadh c., *a sharp wind blew* ; dia c., *a strange god.*
coimheach, -ich, *s. m.* Stranger, foreigner, alien. Aig na coimhich, *with strangers.*
coimheachas, -ais, *s. m.* Estrangement. 2 Strangeness. 3 Shyness. 4 Fierceness, barbarity. 5 Coldness, unkindness, incivility. 6 ††Frowardness. 7‡‡Strange punishment. 8 **Sharpness, as of wind. 9††Alienated affection, dislike, revulsion. 10* Sourness of disposition. C. an teanga, *the strangeness of their tongue.*
coimhead, *fut. aff.* coimheadaidh (*contr.* coimhdidh), *pr. pt.* a' coimhead, *v.a. & n.* Watch, 2 Keep, preserve. 3 Look, observe. 4**Reserve. 5(CR) Show—*W. of Ross.* 6(CR) Look at, *not* keep—*Perthshire & Lewis.* C. ri, *look for* ; dha coimhideam gràs, *I will keep grace for him;* coimheadaidh mi dhuit e, *I will show it to you;* c. orm, *look at me*; a' c. ri bàs, *expecting death.*
————, -hid, *s.m.* Looking. 2 Watching. 3 Watch. 4 Observing. 5 Inspection. 6 Weaver's laze—*Islay.* 7 Keeping. 8**Reserving. Fear-coimhid (*pl.* luchd-coimhid), *inspector, watch, scout.*
————ach, -aiche, *a.* Wary, vigilant, watchful, circumspect, diligent, attentive.
coimheadach, -aich, *s.m.* Keeper, guard, warder. 2**Attendance. 3(AH) The vagina, especially in cattle and sheep.
coimheadachd, *s.f.ind.* Convoy. 2 Observation, watching. 3 Inspecting. 4 Escorting, attending. 5††Conveying. Luchd c., *an escort, suite, retinue*; thoir c., *convoy.* Ris a' ch., *acting as a township herd.*
coimheadaiche, -an, *s.m.* Keeper. 2 Observer. 3 Inspector. 4 Scout, spy. 5‡‡Grass-keeper. 6††Watch. 7 (DC) Township herd—*Uist.*
coimhearsnach, -ich, *s.m.* Neighbour. C. bun-an-doruis, *or* c. na h-ursainn, *the next-door neighbour.*
——————ail, -e, *a.* Neighbourly, accommodating.
——————d, *s.f.ind.* Neighbourhood, 2* Neighbourly conduct. Air fad na c., *throughout the neighbourhood.*
coimhearsnail, *a.* see coimhearsnachail.
coimheart, -a, -an, *s.m.* Comparison.
coimhearta,†† *a.* Equivalent, equal.
coimheartaich,‡‡ *v.a.* Compare.
coimheartas, see coimheart.

†coimheas, *s.m.* Comparison. 2 see coingeas. 3 see coimheachas.
coimheas,** *a.* Equal. 2 Indifferent. 3 Alike.
———ail,** *a.* Equally respectable. 2 Of equal worth.
———da, *a.* Of equal worth, equivalent, comparable.
coimheasg, *v.a.* see coimeasg.
coimheasgachd, *s.f.* see coimeasgadh.
coimheasgadh, -aidh, see coimeasgadh.
coimheasgaich, see coimeasg.
†coimheasgar, *s.m.* Conflict.
coimheicheas, -eis, *s.f.* see coimheachas.
coimheirbse,‡ *s.f.* see comh-eirbse.
coimheis, *a.* Listless. see coingeis.
coimheiseach,** *a.* Indifferent.
coimheiseachd,** *s.f.* Disinclination.
†coimheud, *a.* Even, equally matched, properly adjusted.
coimhich, *pl.* of coimheach.
coimhichead, -eid, see coimheachas.
coimhicheas, -eis, *s.m.* *Argyll* for coimheachas.
coimhid, *v.a.* see coimhead.
———eachd, see coimheadachd.
coimhileadh, -idh, -idhean, see comh-mhileadh.
coimhiocas, -ais, *s.m.* Retribution, compensation.
coimhirp,†† see coidhirp.
coimhis, *a.* see coingeis.
coimhiseach,‡‡ -eiche, *a.* see coingiseach.
————d,‡‡ *s.f.ind.* see coingiseachd.
coimhlion, -ean, *s.m.* see cuinnean.
coimhlion, *adv.* As many as. 2 As often as. 3 Equal in number. [When aspirated it signifies "such a large quantity," as, bu thruagh leam gu'n robh a ch. loch agus lùb 'san rathad, *I was to be pitied there were such a number of lochs and puddles in the way.*]
coimhlion, *a.* see comh-lìonta.
coimhliong, -inge, -ingean, *s f.* Race. 2 Course. 3 Running together. 4 Career. Ruitheamaid a' ch., *let us run the race.*
coimhliongadh, -aidh, *s.m.* Racing. 2 Conflicting, contending. 3 Regular march of an army.
†coimhneas, -a, -an, *s.m.* Neighbour. 2**Neighbourhood.
†coimhneasda, *s.f.* Neighbourhood.
†coimhreach, -ich, *s.m.* Assistant.
coimhseachadh, -aidh, *s.m.* Perception, comprehension. A' c—, *pr. pt.* of coimhsich.
coimhsead,** *s.m.* Lukewarmness.
coimhseas, *s.f.* Conscience.
coimhseasach,* *a.* Conscientious.
coimhseasachd,* *s.f.ind.* Conscientiousness.
coimhsich, *pr.pt.* a' coimhseachadh, *v.a.* Perceive.
coimhsichte, *a.* & *past pt.* of coimhsich. Perceived, understood. 2 Comprehensible. 3 ‡‡Provident.
†coimhsiughadh, see coimhseachadh.
†coimhteach, *s.m.* Monastery, convent.
†coimin, *s.f.* Common, suburbs.
coimirc, -e, *s.f.* Mercy, sparing, giving of quarter. C. Dhé oirbh, *may God spare you*—said in *Uist* to the cattle as they were driven to pasture ; fo ch. na h-eaglais, *under the protection of the church.*
coimirceadh, -idh, *s. m.* Protecting, act of sparing or saving.
coimire, -an, see coimpire.
†coimire, *s.f.* Brief, abridgment, compendium. [** gives coimirc.]
coimisdear, see comasdair.
coimisdearachd, see comasdaireachd.
coimisear, see comasdair.
coimisearachd, see comasdaireachd.
coimpire, -an, *s.m.* Equal, match. 2 One's equal in rank, abilities or means. 3** One of the same mind with another. Fear a bu ch. dhomh fhéin, *a man who was my equal.*
coimpireachd, *s.f.* Equality in rank, commonwealth.
coimpreadh,** -ridh, *s.m.* Conception.
coimric, -e, see coimirc.
coimrig, -e, -ean, *s.f.* Interruption, impediment. 2 Trouble, embarrassment, strait. 3 see coimirc.
coimrig, *pr.pt.* a' coimrigeadh, *v.a.* Interrupt, impede. 2 Trouble, molest, embarrass, straiten.
coimrigeach, -eiche, *a.* Interruptive, full of obstacles. 2 Troublesome.
coimrigeachd, *s.f.ind.* Troublesomeness.
coimrigeadh, -idh, *s. m.* Troubling, act of troubling, molesting. 2 Interrupting. A' c—, *pr. pt.* of coimrig.
coimrigte, *a.* & *past pt.* of coimrig. Troubled, molested. 2 Interrupted.
†coimse, see cuimse.
coimseach, -eiche, *a.* Indifferent, careless. 2 Deliberate.
coimsich, see coimeas. 2 see coimsich.
coin, *gen. sing.*, & *n.* & *dat. pl.* of cù.
†coinbheadh, see coinbheath.
†coinbheadhach, see coinbheathaiche.
†coinbhearsaid, *s.f.* Conversation.
†coinbheath, *s.m.* Feast, entertainment. [** gives *s.f.*]
coinbheathaiche, *s.m.* Guest at an entertainment.
coin-bhile, *s.f.* Dogwood, cornel-tree—§*cornus sanguinea.*

175. Coin-bhile.

†coin-bhliochd, *s.f.* Conflict, battle.
coin-bhràghad, -aid, *s.m.* Disease in the throat. 2 King's evil.
coin-chriche, *s.pl.* Gag-teeth, canine teeth in in most mammals separating the incisors from the bicuspids.
coin-dealg, -eilg, *s.m.* Similitude, comparison. 2 Criticism. 3 Counsel. 4 Contention. [** marks this †.]
coindealg, *v.a.* Persuade.
coindean, -ein, *s.m.* Kit, small tub. [†† gives coinndean.]
coindid, *s.* Leek, see leigis.
†coindreach, *v.a.* Direct.
coindreach,** *s.m.* Impediment, restriction. 2 Mischief. 3 Instruction, direction.
coin-dris, -e, -ean, *s.f.* Dog-briar, see ròs-nan-con.
còineach,** see còinneach.
coin-droighionn, see ròs-nan-con.
còineachan, -ain, *s. m.* Child stolen by the fairies.
còineachan, (AF) *s.m.* see còinneachan.
coineadach, see coinean.

còineadh, *s.m* Reproof.
còineag, -eig, -an, *s.f.* see còinneag.
coin'eall, see coingheall.
coin'eallach, see coingheallach.
coinean, -ein, *pl.* -a & -an, *s.m.* **Rabbit, coney.** Tha 'n c. neo-ghlan, *the rabbit is unclean.* [†† gives -ein as *nom.*]
———ach, see coinean.
———ach,** *a.* **Abounding in, like, or belonging to, rabbits.**
coinearb,** *s.* Bull-baiting.
coineil, see caoimhneil.
coinein, -ean, see coinean.
———each, -eiche, *a.* Abounding in rabbits or conies. Of, or belonging to, a rabbit or coney.
———each,(AF) *s.m.* see coinean.
†coin-fheasgar, -air, *s.m.* Evening.
†————ach, -aiche, *a.* Late.
coin-fhiacail, -cla, -clan, *s.f.* Dog-tooth. 2 Canine madness.
†coin-fhodhairne, *s. pl.* Otters.
coin-fhuadach,(AF) *s.m.* (*lit.* dog-chaser) Vulture, see fang.
†coinfidir, *s.f.* Roman formula of confession.
†coinfliochd, *s.f.* Debate. 2 Battle, conflict.
†coingbheal, see cumail.
coingeal, *s.m.* Vortex. 2 Whirlpool.
coingeis, -e, *a.* Indifferent, free, independent. 2††Equally ready. Tha mi c., *I am indifferent;* is c. cò aca, *it is no matter;* is c. dhuit, *it is all the same to you* ; an c. cò aca a bheir mi leam? *does it matter to me which of them I take?* is c. leis a' chist a bhi air muir no air tìr, *it is all the same to the (magic) chest to be on sea or land—W. Highland Tales.*
coingeas,** -eis, *s.m.* Coolness, indifference. 2 Equality. 3 Comparison.
coingheall, -ill, *s.m.* Loan. 2**Condition. 3‡‡ Whirlpool. 4(JGM) Dog's collar. Thoir an c., *lend* ; gabh c., *borrow.*
————ach, -aiche, *a.* Accommodating, ready to lend. 2 Of, or pertaining to a loan. 3 Officious. 4**Conditional. Duine a bhitheas c., *a man who is ready to lend.*
————achadh, -aidh, *s.m.* Act of lending or accommodating. 2 Violent quashing or shattering. A' c—, *pr.pt.* of coingheallaich.
————achd,‡‡ *s.f.* Obligingness.
————aich, *pr.pt.* a' coingheallachadh, *v.a.* Lend, accommodate. 2 Quash, shatter.
————aiche,** *s.m.* Borrower.
————aichte, *a. & past pt.* of coingheallaich. Lent. 2 Quashed, shattered.
coingioll, -ill, -an, *s.m.* Qualification. 2 Condition. 3‡‡Pass.
————adh, -aidh, -aidhean, *s.m.* Complaint.
coingir, -ean, *s.f.* Pair.
coingiseach, *a.* Indiscriminate.
————d, *s.f.* Indifference.
coinicear, -eir, *s.m.* Rabbit-warren.
coinigin,* see coinicear.
†coinin, see coinein.
coiniosg, *prov.* for conusg.
coinle, -an, see coinnlein.
†coinleach, see connlach.
coinleag, -eig, -an, *s.f.* Stalk. 2 Bud.
coinlein, -ean, *s.m.* see cuinnean. 2 see coinnlein.
coinlin,** see coinnlein.
coinlion, -lin, -lionn, *s.m.* see cuinnean.
coin-luirg, *s. m.* Lurchers. 2(JGM) Bloodhounds.
coinn, (*for* cuinnean) *s. m.* Nostril. 2 Prow —*Dain Iain Ghobha.*
coinn, *s.m.* Fit of coughing.
coinndean,††-ein, *s.m.* Kit, small tub.

coinne,* *s.f.ind.* Reproach. 2 Imitation. 3 see coinneamh. A' c—, *pr. pt.* of coinne. Cha' n fhaigh mi c. air son m' athar, *I shall never be reproached on account of my father* ; an ann a' c. riums' a tha thu? *are you imitating me?*
coinne,* *pr.pt.* a' coinne, *v.n.* Imitate, follow the example of.
†coinne, *s.f.* Woman. *Scots,* quean.
còinneach, -ich, *s.f.* Moss, fog. 2§ Order of ferns called *bryaceæ.* Air lic chòinnich, *on mossy slopes.*
coinneachadh, -aidh, *s.m.* Meeting, assembly. 2 Act or circumstance of meeting. A' c—, *pr.pt.* of coinnich.
còinneachail,‡‡. *a.* Mossy.
còinneachan,(AF) *s.m.* Wild yellow bee; *Scots,* foggy bee.
còinneach-dhearg,§ *s.f.* Bog-myrtle, see mòinteach-liath.
còinneag, -eig, -an, *s.f.* Nest of wild bees.
coinneal, *gen.* coinnle, *pl.* coinnlean, *s.f.* Candle. 2 Torch. 3 (DC) Straight piece of wood on which, after being waulked, the web of tweed is tightly and evenly wound, thereafter being placed for some days under a heavy weight to press it. When unwound the tweed is found to be much improved in appearance. Cha téid a c. as, *her candle does not go out*; rannsaichidh mi le coinnlibh, *I will search with candles*; las a' ch., *light the candle*; 'nuair a bhiodh an clò deas air son a chur 'sa choinneal, *when the web would be ready to wind round the stick—Sgeulaiche-nan-caol,* p. 46 ; "air coinneal" is the phrase in *Uist*—DC.
————ach, -aiche, *a.* see coinnleach.
————aich,* *v.a.* Brandish, flourish. C. do bhata, *flourish your stick.*
————air, *s.m.* Tallow-chandler. 2 Candlemaker.
———— -bhàite, *a.* Excommunicated.
———— -bhàth, *pr. pt.* a' coinneal-bhàthadh, Excommunicate.
———— -bhàthadh, -aidh, *s. m.* Excommunication. A' c—, *pr.pt.* of coinneal-bhàth.
———— -bhàthaidh, *s. f.* Symbol of excommunication.
———— -bianain,‡‡ *s.f.* Ignis fatuus.
———— -buaic-sitheig,* *s.f.* Rush-light.
———— -chéire, *s.f.* Wax-candle.
————dair, see coinnleir. 2** see coinnealair.
———— -ghiubhais, *s.f.* Fir-candle.
———— -ghlas,(Fionn) *s. f.* Candle made by rolling the refuse of suet (cnàmhag) in a rag.
coinneamh, -imh, -an, *s.f.* Meeting. 2 Assembly, convention. 3 Interview. 4 Facing. 5 Opposing. 6 Assignation. 7‡‡ Supper. 8 Pic-nic party. 9 Party to which everyone brings his own provisions.—*Hebrides.* C. nan càirdean, *the meeting of friends;* rach 'nan coinnimh, *go to meet them*; mu 'ch., *opposite him;* mu 'c., *opposite her* ; cum c., *hold a meeting;* 'sa ch. mhòir, *in the great congregation*; ma tha am barrachd agad mu m' ch., *if you have anything further for me to do—Caraid nan Gàidheal;* cuiridh mi mu d' ch., *I am asking you to do, &c.*

EXPRESSIONS FOR USE AT MEETINGS :—

coinneamh fhollaiseach, *a public meeting.*
coinneamh ghnàthaichte, *a general meeting.*
coinneamh chumanta, *an ordinary meeting.*
coinneamh shònruichte, (c. churamach, *or* c. chomharraichte, c. air leth, c. eugsamhuil) *a special meeting, particular meeting marked*

out for a particular programme.
coinneamh a ghairm (*no* a chumail), *to call* (or *hold) a meeting.*
fear-na-cathrach, *the chairman.*
iomarbhaidh, *debate.*
sgrìobhadh, *document.*
a riaghladh, *to preside over.*
a' chomhairle, *the committee.*
tha a' Chomhairle 'na suidhe, *the council is sitting.*
a' chathair a ghabhail, *to take the chair.*
rinn e gnìomh fear-cathrach dhuinn, *he filled the chair for us, acted as chairman for us.*
dealachadh, *division for taking a vote.*
fear-iarraidh oifig, *candidate.*
inbhe - dreuchda, còir - dreuchda, urram-dreuchda, *ex-officio rank.*
ball, *a member.*
bha e air a thaghadh mar bhall, *he was admitted a member.*
a chur buill an tairgse (*no* ball 'ainmeachadh), *to propose a member.*
fear-dreuchda, ball-dreuchda, *an ex-officio member.*
lìon-comhairle, *quorum.*
lìon-gnothaich, *a business quorum.*
is lìon-gnothaich còignear, *five shall form a quorum.*
an gearr-sheanachas, *the minutes.*
leughadh an rùnair an gearr-sheanachas,*I call on the secretary to read the minutes.*
leughadh gearr-sheanachas na coinnimh mu dheireadh, agus chaidh a dhearbhadh, *the minutes of the last meeting were read and confirmed.*
am bheil duine sam bith 'cur an aghaidh m' ainm a chur ris a' ghearr-sheanachas ? *does anyone object to the minutes being signed ?*
iomchar ghnothaich, *procedure.*
dol a mach na buidhne, *proceedings of the company.*
òrdugh na coinnimh, *programme.*
gnàth-imeachd, gnàth-eagair, *routine.*
briseadh gnàth-imeachd, *infraction of routine.*
rùn a chumadh, *to draft a resolution.*
tairgse, *proposal, proposition.*
rùn, *resolution.*
rudanachd, mion-chùis, *minutiae, details.*
mion-fhiosrachd mu gach rudanachd a bhuineas da, *full information of every point concerning it.*
athair an rùin, athair an leasachaidh, *initiator (mover) of a resolution or amendment.*
na'm biodh esan comhla ruinn, b'ann a b' àirde bhiodh gach gnìomh dhuinn, *were he with us, our proceedings had more weight and efficiency.*
aobhar-rùin (rùn *a resolution*; aobhar-rùin,*the makings of a resolution, i.e. a proposal, a motion*) a leasachadh, *to amend a motion.*
aobhar riaghailt agam dhuibh, *I have to propose a rule* to you.

aobhar / ùghdar / còir / gleus } { leasachaidh,*proposed amendment.* / rùin, *a proposed resolution.* / coinnimh, *makings of a meeting (people.)* / buill, *materials of a member (i.e. (a prospective member.)*

aobhar iomarbhaidh, *or* còir deasboireachd, *a question for debate.*
tuigear sin as, ged nach deach a labhairt os àrd, *that is implied, understood, though not stated formally.*
aobhar a shaoid 's a shiubhail, *materials for his activity and holding forth.*
tarsnachan, dubh-cheisd, *a debateable question.*
cuspair na h-iomarbhaidh, *the subject of debate.*
rannsachadh ceisde, *to debate a question.*
fear-iomarbhaidh, *debater.*
suidheachadh 'san iomarbhaidh, *order in debate.*
ar sruth-rannsachaidh, *the lines upon which the subject is discussed by us.*
bun agus bàrr na cuspair (an sgeòil), mion agus garbh na cùise, fad agus gearr na cùise, smìor a' ghnothaich, *all the substance of the matter.*
an dàil (an luib, fa chomhair, an coinneamh) a' ghnothaich, *in preparation for, in anticipation of the matter.*

—Opening remarks—

a' dol an ceann ar turuis dhuinn,
a' dol an tarruing oibre,
a' teannadh gu feum,
ciod a théid sinn 'na dhàil an toiseach ?
is e is toiseach-gnothaich dhuinn......, *the first business for us to transact is......*
an nì is toiseach seanachais dhuinn, (an nì a tha an uachdar seanachais dhuinn), *the chief matter or subject of our discussion., the burning question of the occasion.*
faigheamaid fios na fìrinn agus cur a' ghnothaich, *let us ascertain the truth and the state of affairs.*
bheireamaid ruith air gach cùis, (cuspair, obair, gnothach, *or* aobhar ar saoid 's ar siubhail), *let us treat of, consider everything, our offairs, &c.*
ceisd r'a rannsachadh, *a question yet to be settled.*
[The following sentences bracketed together all mean "what we are engaged about," &c]

ann an los na coinnimh,
'fhad 's a tha sin 'nar taic ('nar cois, 'nar fochair.)
ar ceann-steidh, fath ar turuis.
an fhéill,(an ceaird) air am bheil sinn.
aobhar ar saoid 's ar siubhail.
ann an lorg an aobhair seo.
am bonn (an car) a th' againn ri 'dheanamh tha ar làmhan 'san taois.

o'n a tha sinn ann an ionad breithneachaidh cò eile a bheir ruith air a chùis duinn ? *since we are in the full swing of debate, will some one else hold forth to us on the matter ?*
tha mi 'cur air Mgr.... a nis mion agus garbh na cùise 'innseadh dhuinn, breithneachadh cothromach—*or* rannsachadh—a thoirt air a' chuspair, a' chuspair a chur air a ballaibh dhuinn, *I now call on Mr.... to give us a full summary of the matter.*
is math an airidh, agus fear-na-cathrach 'ga iarraidh orm, *certainly, seeing that it is the chairman who wishes me to do so.*
bheir mi dhuibh dlùth-chuir air na cùisean seo, *I will give you a close survey of these things.*
cha dean mi car rannsachaidh air, cha rachainn féin an seilbh na h-oibre, *I will not go into the subject at all, I would not undertake such a thing.*

thar rian, *wandering from the point, out of order.*
riaghailt, *order.*
rian is riaghailt ! *order, order !*
cha'n 'eil thu an eiseimeil orduigh no rian, *you have a lordly contempt for order.*
tha 'n gnothach gu riaghailteach uile, *the matter is entirely in order.*

tha 'n gnothach a' dol mu seach oirnn (*or* **cha bhuin sin do 'n chùis**), *the proceeding is out of order.*

tha e 'dol 'sa mhuileann orm, ('dol mu seach orm, a' fairtleachadh orm, 'gam sharachadh) *it flabbergasts, puzzles, dumfounders, baffles me.*

tha mi 'cur an teagamh riaghailt a' ghnothaich sin, *I rise to a point of order.—i.e. I contest the orderliness of the present remarks.*

cha chuir sin an aghaidh an riaghailt, ach fàgaidh e an riaghailt cho slàn 's a bha e, *that is not against the rule at all, but it leaves the rule as unbroken as ever.*

cha chuspair riaghailt sin idir, *that is not a point of order.*

tha mi 'toirt beum do 'n leasachadh sin, is e tha mi togail dhuibh gur briseadh air riaghailt an leasachadh, *I wish to point out that the wording of the resolution is out of order.*

tha sin as ar gabhail, cha'n 'eil sin 'nar taic, *that is not the subject under discussion.*

cha tiochd sin 'san iomarbhaidh. *that is not within the area of the discussion.*

ma chaidh mi cèarr air mo rùn, cha b' ann do m' dheòin, (eadar dhà naigheachd, chaidh guth thairis air a' chuspair againne), *if I have strayed from my motion, it was not willingly, between two discussions our affair has quite been lost sight of.*

chaidh sinn thar ar siubhail, ar sgeòil, *or* **ar gnothuich,** *we have wandered from our subject.*

gabh mu chùl do chruidh agus ar cruidh fhéin, *direct speech to the question.*

cha bhi urram-gnothaich againn air a sin, *we shall not deem that to be business;* **(leigeamaid troimh na meòir e,** *or* **gabhamaid ealla ris,)** *we shall ignore that.*

[The terms in the next bracket are all requests for relevancy.]

cha'n e sin an fhìor-obair a th'againn an dràsd.
tha cuid dheth sin nach 'eil a thaobh a' ghnothaich againn.
tha sinn an grèim (an sàs) ann an ceisd eile an dràsd.
ann am bun ceisd eile.
cha'n i sin a' cheisd a tha 'nar cois: na biodh ruith coin an dà fhéidh againn.
gabh mu chùl do chruidh.
na·bi againn bhos, is thall.
airgiod thall, airgiod a bhos ! *money there, money here !—money is not the question just now.*
càirdeas fad as aig an dara cheisd ris a' cheisd eile.
is bacadh air rùn sin, *that is blocking the proposal or resolution.*

chuireadh sin caochladh cuir an clò Chaluim, *that would confuse our aims and position.*

chuireadh sin car 'san rùn againn, *that would upset, or alter our proposition or resolution.*

bheireadh sin ar n-anam-fàs asainn, *that will prevent us developing, take away our raison-d'etre.*

na tog mi gus an tuit mi, *do not interrupt unless I go wrong, out of order.*

sin an ni is lugha th' air m' aire, b' fhada bhuaidh sin a ghabhainn, *that is far from my intention.*

anns gach dàimh agus suidheachadh, *in all circumstances and relations, on every occasion.*

anns an riochd sin, *in that connection, relation.*

fuaighte, (an comh-cheangal) ris air dha ghleus, *bound up with it in two ways.*

tha 'n dara ni an eiseimeil aon a chéile, *the two things depend upon, arise out of each other.*

tha leanmhuinn a thaobh-eiginn eadar an dà cheisd, *there is a certain amount of connection between the two things.*

thoir an aon ruith da seo,

deanamaid an dalta (tomhas) ceudna da seo, *treat this in the same way.*

cha'n 'eil sin ann an ìnnleachd na coinnimh, *that is not in the power of the meeting to settle.*

air a shon sin dheth, *as far as that goes, touches the matter.*

air son na rinn sinne, *as far as regards what we did in the matter.*

tha sin agus a roghainn aig a' choinnimh, *the meeting can do so if it please.*

---

tha A.B. a' cur suas, agus C.D. a' cur taic ris gu'm...., *it is moved by A.B., and seconded by C.D. that......*

tha mi 'tairgse, *I propose.*

tha mi 'cur suas gu'm.., *I beg to move that..*

tha mi 'cur suas an rùin seo,
is e cead-rùin a tha mi 'g iarraidh ort,
bu mhath leam rùn a chur 'nur cead,
I beg to move the following resolution.

tha mi 'cur f' ur comhair, air bhur beulaobh, *or* **mu bhur coinneamh, mar leasachadh, gu'm fàgar na facail a leanas a mach,** *I move as an amendment, that the following words be omitted.*

tha mi 'cur f' ur comhair, air bhur beulaobh, *or* **mu bhur coinneamh, an leasachadh a leanas a chur air an rùn,** *I move the following amendment to the motion.*

tha mi 'cur suas leasachaidh mar a leanas, *I move that the motion be amended as follows.*

tha mi 'cuideachadh leis an leasachadh sin, *I second that amendment.*

cha bu ruith leam ach leum gu cuideachadh leis an leasachadh sin, (tha mise a' cuideachadh leis a sin le fàilte—*or* **agus beannachd 'na cheann),** *I have much pleasure in rising to support the amendment.*

is tu fhéin a th' ann fhathast, is math a fhuaras tu, tha thu air chùl do sgeòil, buaidh leat ; sgailc thu air ! *hear, hear !*

a' cheisd roimhe, *the previous question.*

tagram (*or* **iarram) gu'n rachadh a' cheisd a chur a nis,** *I beg to move that the question be now put.*

cha leig sinn leò e, *we will not allow them to carry it out.*

cha'n fhaigh thu sin leat, *you will not be able to carry that.*

cha tog sin buannachd dhuinn, *that will not benefit us.*

leasachadh a dhiùltadh, *to reject an amendment.*

rùn a chuir an neo-bhrigh, *to rescind a resolution.*

rùn a dhubhadh as, *to expunge a resolution.*

rùn a dhiùltadh, *to negative a proposition.*

diùltadh (*s.*), **diùltach** (*a.*), *negative.*

an aghaidh an aobhair, *against the proposition.*

gabhaidh sinn an leasachadh de roghainn air an rùn, *we accept the amendment in preference to the motion.*

cha'n fhaod sinn a mhilleadh, (a sharachadh), *we cannot do better than that.*

iarram cead o 'n chathair an aobhar-rùin a tharruing air ais, a dheòin a' chinn-suidhe

cuiridh mi aobhar mo chuspair air chùl, *I beg to withdraw the motion, with the consent of the chair.*

tha nis agam m' ur coinneamh gu'n glac sibh mar rùn leis na leanas, *I now propose to you that you adopt as a substantive resolution what follows.*

bha an tairgse air a chur an cruth rùin, *the proposal was put in the form of a resolution.*

cuireamaid an dara taobh e, *let us settle it, dispose of it.*

b' e 'n turus gun bhuaidh dhuinn a' chòir a thoirt seachad air a cheisd seo, *it were a great mistake on our part, not to deal justly and fairly with this question.*

cuireamaid seachad seo, *let us dispose*, or *get rid of this.*

---

gheibhear deireadh gach sgeòil a nasguidh, *don't hurry, thrash the matter out at leisure.*

comh-dhunadh na h-iomarbhaidh, cur a' ghlas-ghuib orra, *closure of the debate.*

facal ann! *hurry up! finish the discussion; say the final word!*

cràtnamaid an t-slabhruidh-éisdeachd, *call for silence.*

éisd do bheul! *silence!*

o'n a tharla mar seo dhuinn, *since we are so placed, circumstanced.*

leis a h-uile rud a th' ann, *under the circumstances.*

ann a bhi 'togail dhuibh cur na h-iomarbhaigh, (*or* da thaobh na h-iomarbhaigh), *in summing up to you the state, or pros. and cons. of the debate.*

chuala sibh an dà thaobh, 'fheara! tha a chùis 'nur meinn féin a nis, cuir fo 'r smaointean i, dèan bhur roghainn ris! *you have now heard both sides of the affair, think well over it and give your decision, for the issue is entirely in your hands.*

gach duine a tha ag aontachadh leis an rùn seo, abradh e "biodh"—an aghaidh sin "na biodh," *all who are in favour of this resolution, say "aye"—to the contrary, "no."* (*or* cò a chuireas leis an rùn seo? thogadh iad an làmhan, cò tha 'na aghaidh? thogadh iad an làmhan, *whoever is in favour of this let them hold up their hands; against, hold up their hands.*)

aontachadh iomlan, *unanimous consent.*

taghadh folaichte, *voting by ballot.*

taghadh fosgailte, *open voting.*

taghadh a sheachnadh, *to abstain from voting.*

fear-iarraidh a thaghadh, *to vote for a candidate.*

guth fear-na-cathrach, *casting vote.*

iarram (*or* tagram) comh-àireamh, (leig gu ràdh an taghaidh e), *I demand a poll.*

thatar a' glaodhach taghaidh (*or* comh-àirimh,) *they are demanding, clamouring for a poll.*

iarram (*or* tagram) togail làimhe, *I demand a show of hands.*

taghadh, *act of voting.*

fear-taghaidh, *voter.*

cuir gu toil na coinnimh e, *put it to the vote of the meeting.*

breith fear-na-cathrach, *the decision of the chair.*

cha'n 'eil dol thar breith fear na cathrach, *there is to be no disputing the chairman's ruling.*

cha'n ann 'gad sharachadh, *or* a' cur cosg ort a tha mi, *I do not wish to contradict or stop you.*

dearbhadh (*s.*), dearbhtach (*a.*), *affirmative.*

a' bheag chuid, *the minority.*

a' mhòr chuid, *the majority.*

a' bharrachd, *excess of majority over minority.*

tha e rùnichte, dainguichte, gu'm bitheadh, &c., *resolved that, &c.*

cuirtear mac an rùin seo do...., *let a copy of this resolution be sent to....*

mac-an-rannsachaidh seo, *the upshot of this debate.*

leigear a' chuis fa chomhair an rùnair, bidh esan a' freasdal an deis gach ni, *let the matter be referred, delegated, or entrusted to the secretary—he will attend to everything.*

tha a' choinneamh air a cur fa sgaoil, *the meeting is dissolved.*

sguireamaid mar tha sinn, *let us stop at this* (*lit. stop as we are.*)

cò chuireas an aghaidh na Gàidhlig gur a bacadh air gnothach i? *who opposes the use of Gaelic as being a hindrance to business?*

là na coinnimh a shineadh, *to postpone a meeting.*

tha dàil air a chur 'sa choinnimh gu seachduin o 'n diugh, *the meeting is adjourned till this day week.*

sònruicheamaid là do 'n ath choinnimh le cion agus nach 'eil lion-gnothaich againn, *let us fix a date for next meeting, as we have not a business quorum present.*

sìneadh gu dìlinn (gun chàirde, am feasd, *or* gu suthainn) a chur 'sa choinnimh, *to adjourn the meeting "sine die."*

gnàth-riaghailtean, *standing orders.*

na gnàth-riaghailtean a chur an dàil, *to suspend standing orders.*

☞In the above list the reader follows the course of an imaginary debate, and the sentences are divided into five sections for facility of reference, thus;—
(1) Names of processes and equivalents for amendments, &c. (2) Opening remarks, dealing in general with the subject of discussion, and calling upon people to speak. (3) Matters of order and relevancy. (4) Amendments, and the putting and withdrawing of same, and requests for the thorough thrashing out of any matter. (5) Closure and summing up, voting, upshot, sending out notices, dissolving and proroguing. [This is the first such list published in Gaelic.]

coinneanach,* -aiche, *a.* Ruttish.

†coinneas, -eis, *s.f.* Ferret. 2(AF) Dog-weasel.

†———ach, *a.* Abounding in, like, of, or belonging to, ferrets, or dog-weasels.

coinngiallach,‡‡ *s.f.* Complaint.

†coinniceir, *s.m.* Rabbit warren or burrow.

coinnich, *pr.pt.* a' coinneachadh, *v.a. & n.* Meet, face, oppose, encounter. 2**Stop progress of a person or thing. 3* Assemble. Coinnichidh na daoineach cha choinnich na cnuic, *men meet but the hills do not;* coinnichidh an dà fhacal a chéile, *the two words mean the same thing.*

———te, *past part.* of coinnich, Met, opposed, faced, encountered.

coinnimh, *gen.sing.* of coinneamh.

coinnir, -e, -ean, *s.f.* Pair, brace, couple.

coinnle, see Calluinn. 2 *gen.sing.* of coinneal.

coinnleach, -eiche, *a.* Full of candles. 2 Of, pertaining to, a candle. 3 Like a candle.

————adh, -aidh, *s.m.* Winding of cloth on a stick in order to dress it.

coinnleag, -eig, -an, *s.f.* Oily surface of broth. 2 Fiery sparkling of the eyes.

coinnleagach, -aiche, *a.* Having an oily surface, as broth. 2 Bright, sparkling (of eyes.)
coinnlean, see coinnlein.
———— -bianain, *s.m.* Wild fire, phosphoric light seen in the sea, when agitated by oars in the dark. 2(DC) Infusoria.
coinnlein, -e, -ean, *s.m.* Stalk of grain, especially barley. 2**Bud. 3†† see cuinnean.
————each, -eiche, *a.* Stalky.
coinnleir, -e, -ean, *s.m.* Candlestick. Ann an c., *in a candlestick.*
————each, -eiche, *a.* Of, or pertaining to, a candlestick.
————eachd, *s.f.* Office of holding the candle. 2**Candle-making.
coinnlin, -e, -ean, see coinnlein.
coinnlineach, -eiche, *a.* see coinnleineach.
coinnseanta, *a.* Conscientious. 2 see coguiseach.
coinnseas, -eis, -an, *s.f.* Gaelic spelling of *conscience.*
†coinnsi, *a.* Fit, proper.
coinnspeach, -a, -an [& ††coinnspeich], *s.f.* see connspeach.
†coinnt, *s.f.* Woman.
còinnteach, see còinneach.
†coinntibhe, *s.f.* Gibe, scoff, sneer, expression of scorn.
†coinreachd, -a, *s.m.* Law of the chase.
coin-ròs,§ *s.m.* Dog-rose, see ròs-nan-con.
coinseas, Gaelic spelling of *conscience.*
coinsianaich, *v.n.* Conjure.
coinsias, see coinnseas.
————ach, see coinnseanta.
†coint, see coinnt.
†cointean,** -ein, *s. m.* Contentious man, wrangler. 2 Controversy.
cointeanach,** *a.* Contentious.
————d,** *s.f.* Contentiousness, quarrelsomeness.
co'ionann, see comh-ionann.
————achd, see comh-ionannachd.
†coip, *s.f.* see †coib. 2* Heap of foam or froth.
coip, *gen. sing.* of cop.
coip-gheal, -ile, *a.* see cop-gheal.
còir, -e, *1st. comp.* cora, *a.* Just, honest, virtuous, good. 2 Kind, civil. 3 Decent. 4 Easy-minded. 5**Proper. 6** Near. 7 Pious. 8(AG) Benevolent.—*Reay country.* 9†† Affable. 10(DC) *of animals,* Docile, tame, domesticated. 11 Kind-hearted—*Uist.* Duine c., *a pious person*; ged is olc e, tha e glé ch., *although he is wicked, he is very generous*; an duine c.! *the worthy man!* is c. dhomh, *I ought*; bu ch. dha am maille treun, *he ought (would require) to be in strong armour.*
còir, *irreg. s.* declined thus:—

Sing. N. còir,	*Plur. N.* còraichean [còirichean, & còirean,]
G. còrach [& còire]	*G.* còraichean,
D. còir,	*D.* còraichean,
V. a chòir!	*V.* a chòraiche!

Right, justice, equity, probity, integrity. 2 Right, claim, title, charter, 3 see comhair. 4 Authority. 5‡ Share. 6* Franchise. 7** Possession, property. 8**Business. 10**Interest. 11**Custom, usage. Còirichean a' bhaile, *the freedom of the city,* a' cumail na còrach rium, *doing justice to me; maintaining my right, 2 keeping time for me (as in music)*; rinn thu a' chòir, *you have acted with propriety*; coirichean an fhearainn, *the charter of the land*: bheir mi dhuit comhairle na còrach, *I will tell you what you should do,* or *what ought to be done*; tog romham air ch. an sgiath, *carry the shield before me as usual*; mar bu ch. dhuit, *as you ought*; le c., *with authority*; tuilleadh na còrach, tuilleadh 'sa ch., *more than the just quantity*; cùis na corach, *the cause of justice*; cumaibh c. riu, *support their right*; tuilleadh 'sa ch.. (*pres,*) tuilleadh 's bu ch., (*past*) *too much.*
coir, *prov.* for cuir.
coir, *gen. sing.* of cor.
coir, *s.m.* Spear. 2 Fault. 3‡‡Musical air.
còir, (an) *adv.* see comhair.
coirb, -e, *a.* Accursed. 2 Perverse, untractable. 3 Vicious. 4‡‡ Cross-grained.
coirb *v.a.* Corrupt. 2 Abandon.
coirbeach, *a.* Impious, corrupt, vicious.
coirbeachd, *s.f.ind.* Crossness, perverseness. 2 Hostility. 3 Wickedness, corruptness, lewdness, carnality.
coirbidh,¶ *s.m.* Raven, see fitheach.
còir-bhreith, -e, *s.f.* Birthright.
coirbte, *a.* Accursed. 2 Perverse. 3**Corrupt. 4**Cross. 5**Hostile. 6* Abandoned, vicious. An triath bu ch. colg, *the chief of the most implacable wrath.*
coirbteachd, see coirbeachd.
coirce, *s.m.* Oats—*avena sativa.* C.-nan-speur, *manna.*
coirceach, -eich, *a.* Abounding in oats. 2 Of, or belonging to oats. 3 Made of oats.
coirceag, -eig, -an, *s.m.* Bee-hive made of straw. 2 Tub or dish made of straw, to hold seeds, &c.
coirce-circe, *s.m.* Quaking grass, see conan.
coirce-dubh,‹ *s.m.* see coirce-fiadhain. The name "coirce-dubh" is applied to all kinds of oats when black with blight, but especially to *avena strigosa.*
coirce-fiadhain,‹ *s. m.* Wild oats—*avena fatua* and *avena pratensis.*
coirceil,†† *a.* see coirceach.
†coircheann, *s.m.* Spindle.
†coir-cheann, *v.a.* Make round at the top.
†coir'-chléireach, -ich, *s.m.* Dishonest clerk.
còird, *v.* see còrd.
-——ealaiche, -an, *s.m.* Rope-maker.
còirdean, -ein, *s.m.* Small rope. 2**String.
†còirdeas, -ais, *s.m.* Agreement, coalescence. 2 Reconciliation.
†coirdheabh, *v.a.* Fight with a spear.
còirdte, *a.* & *past part.* Agreed.
coire, *pl.* -annan, *s.f.* Fault, offence, charge. 2 Sin, guilt, crime, harm, wrong, trespass. 3 Defect. 4 Complaint. 5* Blame. 6 Damage. Dean c., *offend*; gach gnè c., *every kind of damage*; mur dean mi t' fhaotainn le còir dhaoine, *if I do not get thee owing to the opposition of men;* c. bàis, *a capital crime*; is iomadh c. a gheibhear air an duine bhochd, *many a fault may be found in a poor man.*
coire, *pl.* -achan, *s.m.* Cauldron, kettle, boiler, vat. 2 Bath (in *weaving.*) Cuir air an c., *put the kettle on (the fire.)*
còire, *pl.* -achan, *s. m.* Circular hollow surrounded by hills. 2 Mountain dell. 3 Whirlpool. [Often erroneously pronounced like the last word.]
†coire, *s.m.* Wherry. 2 Ring. 3 Girdle.
†còire, *s.f.* Raw flesh. 2 Syntax.
coireach, -iche, *a.* Full of circular hollows or dells.
coireach, -iche, *a.* Faulty, at fault. 2 Guilty. 3 Criminal. Is tusa 's c., *it is you who are to blame*; *2 it is you that caused it* (without any disparagement); cò air bith is c., is mis' an creanaiche, *whoever is guilty, I am the sufferer*—said by "Seumas a' Ghlinne" at his trial.
coireach, -eich, *s.m.* Defaulter. 2 Guilty per-

son. 3**Aggressor.
coireachadh, -aidh, *s.m.* Blaming, censuring, accusing. 2**Accusation, arraignment. A' c—, *pr.pt.* of coirich.
coireachail, -e, *a.* Apt to blame, censorious.
coireachalachd, *s.f.ind.* Censoriousness.
coireachan, *n.pl.* of coire.
coireachas,‡‡ -ais, *s.m.* Injuriousness.
coireachd, *s.f.ind.* Culpability, blameableness. 2‡‡Honesty.
còiread, -id, *s.f.* Probity. 2 Goodness, kindness. [** gives *s.m.*]
coireadh,** see coire.
coireal,* *s.m.* Loud tone of voice, as of a person scolding or in a passion. 2(JGM) Choir. 3(JGM)Music. 4(DC)Skirling, as of sea-birds.
coireal, -eil, *s.m.* Coral—*corallina officinalis.*
coirealach, *a.* Like coral. 2 Abounding in coral, coralline.
coireall, *s.m.* Quarry.
coireaman,§ -ain, *s.m.* Coriander, see lus-a'-choire.
coireamanach, *a.* Abounding in coriander. 2 Like coriander.
coirean, -ein, -ean, *s.m.* Little circular hollow. 2 Little mountain dell.
cõirean, -ein, -ean, *s.m.* Little cauldron.
coirean-coilich, *s.m.* Wild campion.
coirean-muice, *s.m.* Pig-nut.
coireannan, *n.pl.* of coire.
coireineach, -eiche, *a.* Full of little hollows or dells.
†còireiseach, *a.* Important, with an important air.
coire-togalach, -aich, *s.m.* Brewer's cauldron.
còir-ghniomh, -a, -ghnìomhran *s. m.* Virtuous action. 2‡‡Satisfaction.
†còiriasach, -aiche, *a.* Important.
coirib,** *v.a.* Corrupt.
coirich, *pr.pt.* a' coireachadh, *v.a.* Blame, find fault with, reprove, reprimand. 2 Arraign.
coirich, *pl.* of coireach. *s.pl.* The guilty.
còirichean,** *s.pl.* Records, title-deeds.
coirichte, *past pt.* of coirich, Blamed, charged, reproved, accused.
†coirigh, *s.m.* Ranges, ranks, enclosures.
coirill, see caireal.
coirioll, -ill, *s.m.* see caireal.
coiriollach, -aiche, see cairealach.
†coirip, *v.a.* Corrupt.
†coirleighte, *a.* Correctly written or read.
†coiripidh, -e, *a.* Corruptible, wicked, impious. Gu c., *wickedly.*
†coiripte, *past pt.* of coirp. Corrupted.
†coiriptheachd, *s.f.ind.* Corruption.
†coirm, *s.f.* Kind of beer or ale used of old by the Gael. 2 Pot companion. 3‡‡ see cuirm.
†coirmeach, *s.m.* Drunkard.
‡coirmeag, -eig, *s.f.* Female gossip.
†coirneach, *s.m.* Kingfisher. 2 Part.
†coirneach, *a.* Cornered, angular.
còirneal, -eil, *s.m.* Colonel in the army. 2‡‡ Cornel tree. 3‡‡Corner.
coirnean,** -ain, *s.m.* Curl.
coirneanach,** *a.* Frizzled, curled.
coirneileir, -ean, *s.m.* Colonel in the army. O 'n chaidh an c. fo thalamh, *since the colonel was buried.*
†coirneineach, -eiche, *a.* see coirneanach.
†còirn-stiall, *s.f.* see còrn-stiall.
†coirpeachd, see coirbeachd.
coirpileir, -e, -ean, *s.m.* Corporal.
coirpte, see coirbte.
coir-sgrèachag, *prov.* for corr-sgreuchag.
coirt, *prov.* for cairt.
coirtheach, -eiche, *a.* see coireach.
còirtear, see cairtear,
†coirthigh, *v.a.* Sin. 2 Blame.
†coirthiughadh, see coireachadh.
cois, *dat.sing.* of cas.
còis, *gen.sing.* of còs.
cois (an & ri) *s.* Near, beside, by, along with, close by. An cois na mara, *near the sea;* 'na chois, *near him,* or *it* ; 'nan cois, *near them* ; an cois nan aibhnichean, *close by the rivers*; ri cois na Mara Ruaidh, *near the Red Sea ;* ceud caora 'nam chois, *a hundred sheep along with me;* bithidh beannachd an c. do shaoithreach, *your labour will be crowned with success.*
cois-bheart, -bheairt, see caisbheart.
coisc, see coisg.
cois-chéimnich, see cois-cheumnaich.
cois-cheum, -éim, -an, *s.m.* Step, pace, stride. 2(DC) Footprint—*Bible.*
cois-cheumnach,** *a.* Stepping, pacing.
cois-cheumnaich, *v.a.* Step along, walk, pace. 2 Measure by pacing.
†coisde, *s.f.* Coach. 2 Jury.
còisdeachd, (comh-éisdeachd) *s.f.* Act of hearkening, listening.
coisdearachd, *s.f.ind.* Coach-driving, business of a coachman.
†coisdear, -an, *s. m.* Coachman.
†còisdear, -an, *s.m.* (comh-éisdear.) Juryman.
coisdeargan, -ain, -an, *s.m.* Red-shank (bird) see cam-ghlas.
coise, *gen.sing.* of cas. Do bhonn a choise, *to the sole of his foot.*
coise,** *s.f.* Coach. *prov.*
coiseachadh, -aidh, *s.m.* Walking. 2 Pedestrianism. A' c—, *pr.pt.* of coisich.
coiseachd, *s.f.ind.* Walking. 2 Pedestrianism. A' c—, *pr.pt.* of coisich. Bheir a Callainn a coiseachd dith, *her Hogmanay will make a cripple of her*—said of a woman much given to visiting her neighhours; cia as a thug thu a' ch ?, *where did you walk from ?*
coiseachdail,‡‡ -e, *a.* Pedestrian.
coiseag, -eig, -an, *s.f. prov.* for cuiseag.
còiseag, -eig, -an, *s.f.* Small nook, snug corner.
———ach, *a.* Snug, warm, sheltered.
†coiseamhan, -ain, *s.m.* Shoemaker.
coisean, *s.m.* Stalk, stem.
———ach, -aiche, *a.* Slender-legged. 2 Having a stalk or stem.
———tach,** -aich, *s.m.* Protector.
cois-éideadh, -idh, -ean, *s.m.* Shoes and stockings, boots, greaves, foot-armour.
coiseineal,** *s.m.* see coisiniol.
†coiseun, see coiseunaich.
†———achadh, *s.m.* Preservation, deliverance. A' c—, *pr.pt.* of coiseunaich.
———aich, *v.a.* Conjure. 2 Bless, consecrate.
†———ta, *past pt.* of coiseun. Protected, defended. 2 Consecrated.
———tach, -aidh, *s.m.* Protector, defender.
coisg, *pr. pt.* a' cosg [a' casg & a' cosgadh] *v.a.* Stop, restrain, wean. 2 Quell, suppress, pacify, quench, extinguish, quiet, staunch, subside. 3 Put an end to. Choisgeadh an teine, *the fire was quenched;* choisgeadh an t-uisge, *the water was restrained*; ch. do chathair bho thuiteam, *keep your chair from falling.*
———each, *a.* Quenching, quelling, restraining, staunching.
———eadh, -gidh, *s.m.* see cosgadh.
coisgear, -eir, -an, *s.m.* see cosgair.
coisgear, *fut. pass.* of coisg.
coisgidh, *fut. aff. a.* of coisg.
coisglidh, *a.* Still, quiet. 2 Diligent.
coisgte, *past pt.* of coisg. Quelled, stilled, restrained, pacified, calmed, appeased, quench-

ed, settled, tranquillized, extinguished.
coisich, *pr. pt.* a' coiseachd [& a' coiseachadh], *v.a.* Walk, travel on foot. 2 Move off, depart.
coisiche, -an, *s.m.* Walker, pedestrian. 2 Footman. 3**Traveller. 4††Foot-soldier. Sè mìle c., *six thousand foot-soldiers;* a ch. na beinne! *thou traveller of the hill!* saighdear-coisiche, *a foot-soldier.*
†coisin, -e, -ean, *s.m.* Stem, stalk. 2 Defence.
†coisiniol, *s.m.* Gaelic spelling of *cochineal.*
coisinn, *fut.* coisnidh (*sync.* of coisinidh) *pr.pt.* a' cosnadh, *v. a.* Gain, earn, win, obtain, acquire. 2* Deserve. Tha i aig a cosnadh, *she is at service*—this expression in Gaelic is used to signify domestic service, and is not applied to any one working at a skilled trade. In such cases the name of the trade is always mentioned, as, tha e ris a' chlachaireachd, *he earns his living as a mason;* tha i 'ga chosnadh, *she is earning it.*
coisinn,** *s. f.* Gain, advantage, profit. 2 Earning.
coisinnte, *past part.* of coisinn. Gained, earned, won, obtained, acquired. 2 Expert. Anns gach ceàird tha thu c., *in every trade you are expert.*
coisionta, see coisinnte.
coisiontach, -aiche, *a.* That gains, acquires, or wins.
coisiontair, -ean, *s.m.* Gainer.
coisir, -sre, *s. f.* Choir. 2 Festive party. 3 Wake. 4 Singing of birds. 5 Military band. 6††Party of singers. 7†† Attendants. 8‡ Chorus. 9**Company. 10**Feast.
coisir-chiùil, *s.f.* Choir.
coisireach,‡‡ -eiche, *a.* Choral.
cois-leathann, *a.* Broad-footed.
coisneadh, -aidh, see cosnadh.
coisreach, -ich, *s.f.* Parish feast. 2 Wake. 3 Wedding.
coisreadh, -ridh, -ridhean, see coisir.
coisreagach,** *a.* Bushy, as hair.
coisreagan, -ain, *s.m.* **Consecration. 2(AC) Consecrator. Bana-choisreagan, the woman who leads the singing in the ceremony of consecrating the cloth after waulking.
coisridh, -e, *s. f.* Infantry. 2 Company on foot.
còisridh, -e, *s.f.* **Jovial club. 2**Entertainment. 3**Concert of birds.
coisrig, *pr.pt.* a' coisreagadh, *v. a.* Consecrate, sanctify. 2 Dedicate, as a book. 3**Bless. 4**Anoint. 5**Addict.
coisrigeach, *a.* Consecrative.
coisrigeadh, -dh, *s.m.* Consecrating, act of consecration, sanctifying. 2‡‡Devotedness. 3 **Addiction.
coisrigidh, *fut. aff. a.* of coisrig.
coisrigte, *past pt.* of coisrig. Consecrated, sanctified. 2**Addicted. 3**Anointed. Uisge c., *holy water.*
†coisrioghadh, -aidh, *s.m.* Sanctification.
coisriomhadh, -aidh, *s. m.* Elegant arrangement of feet in verse. 2‡‡Scanning of verse.
coiste, †see cosd. 2 see coisde.
coistear, see coisdear.
————achd, see coisdearachd.
coistre, (AC) *a.* Benign.
coistri, see comh-strì.
coit, -e, -ean [& -eachan] *s. f.* Small fishing boat, canoe. 2 Coracle. 3 Punt. 4 Hut. 5 **Quoit. 6**Dog-hole.
†coit, *s.m.* Word.
coitcheann, -a, *a.* Common, public, communal, general. 2* Exposed to many callers, as a house by the highway. Gu c., *publicly, commonly;* air aithris gu c., *commonly reported.*
coitcheann,(AC) *s.m.* Common grazing.
————ach, -aich, *s.m.* Commoner.
————achd, *s.f.ind.* Community, commonness, generalness. 2 Universality, catholicness.
————as, -ais, *s.m.* Community, state of having things in common. 2 Universality. 3 Exposure. 4* The state of being subject to calling. 5 Public situation, as of a house. 6 Frequency. 7**Co-partnership.
coitcheanta, see coitcheann. Gu c., *adv. commonly.*
coitcheanntachd, see coitcheannachd.
coitcheanntas, -ais, see coitcheannas.
coitchionn, -a, see coitcheann.
coitchionnas,* -ais, see coitcheannas.
coite, *s.f.* see coit.
coiteach,‡‡ -ich, *s. m.* Pressing to take anything.
————adh, -aidh, *s.m.* Pressing to take anything. 2* Contending, as in argument. A' c—, *pr. pt.* of coitich.
coitear, -eir, -an, *s.m.* Cottager, cottar. 2‡‡ Boatwright.
coiteireachd, *s.f.ind.* The state of a cottager or cottar.
†coi-teorainn, *s.m.* Limit, boundary.
†coi-theoran, see coi-teorainn.
coi'thional, see comh-thional.
coitich, *pr. pt.* a' coiteach [& a' coiteachadh], *v. a.* Press to take anything. 2 Urge an argument, contend, maintain.
coitidh,†† *a.* Common, general.
†coiting, *s.f.* Battle, combat.
‡coitinn, see coiting.
coitinn, *a. prov.* for coitcheann.
†coitit, *s.f.* Awl, bodkin.
col, *v.a.* Hinder, restrain. 2 Prohibit. 3‡‡ Plaster.
col, -a, *s.m.* Impediment, obstacle. 2 Prohibition. 3 Incest. 4 Sin, crime, stain.
còla, see còmhla and còmhlan.
col'ach, see coltach—*Dain Iain Ghobha.*
colach, -aiche, *a.* Forbidden, prohibited. 2 Wicked, impious, incestuous. *More usually* collaidh. 3 *Lewis,* for coltach.
colach,** -aich, *s.m.* Flock-bed.
còlach,** -aich, -aichean, *s.m.* see còmhlach.
còlachadh, see comhlachadh.
colachd, *s.f.ind.* Plastering, daubing.
†coladh, *s.m.* Superfluity.
colag,§ -aig, *s.f.* Cauliflower. 2†‡ Cutlet of meat, collop. †3(AF) Young cow.
colagag, see colgag.
†colagan,** -ain, *s.m.* Salmon. 2 Salmon-trout.
còlaich, *v.n.* see còmhdhalaich.
colaidh, see collaidh.
————eachd, see collaidheachd.
còlais,** *s.f.* Cabbage.
colaisde, -an, *s.m.* College, academy.
————ach, *a.* Of, or belonging to, a college, collegiate.
†colam,(AF) *s.f.* Young cow.
†colamadh, *s.m.* Mine.
colamaidh, (AF) *s.* Coal-fish.
colaman, see calman.

176. Colamoir.

colamoir, -ean, *s.m.* Hake, (fish)
còlan, -ain, -an, *s.m.* see còmhlan.

†colan, -ain, *s.f.* Young cow.
colann, *gen.sing.* -ainn [colla & colna], *pl.* collainnean, *s. f.* The body. 2 In good condition of habit or body. 3**Carcase. 4**Flesh. Is math a ch., *he is in good condition.*
co'lannachd, see comh-lannachd.
co'lannaireachd, see comh-lannaireachd.
colar,(AF) *s.m.* Dove, see calman.
colbain,** *s.m.* Rope of a ship.
†colbh, see calbh.
colbh, cuilbh, *s.m.* Sceptre. 2 Post, pillar. 3 Plant, stalk. 4* Front of a bed. 5(AC) Wile. 6**Reed. Bho chuilbh an fhir-cheilg, *from the wiles of the deceiver;* c. nam buadh, *the sceptre of victory.*
†colbh, *v.a.* Sprout, shoot.
†colbha, *s.m.* Love, friendship, esteem, regard.
colbhach, -aiche, *a.* Sceptred. 2 Pillared.
colbhaidh, -e, *a.* Having pillars or columns.
colbhairt,** *s.f.* Colewort.
colbh-seòlaidh, *s.m.* Finger-post, sign-post.
†colbtha, *s.m.* see colpa.
†colbthach, see colpach.
co'leagh, see comh-leagh.
colc, -a, -an, *s.m. & f.* Eider-duck.
colca,¶ *s.f.* Great auk, see gearra-bhall.
†colcach, *s.f.* Bed. 2(AF) Eider-duck, see lach Lochlannach.
colcach bheag, ¶ *s.f.* Little auk—*mergulus melanolencous.*

177. Colcach bheag.

†colcaidh, *s.f.* see colcach.
colcair,¶ *s.* Great auk, see gearra-bhall. 2 (AF) Eider-duck, see lach Lochlannach.
coldach, see coltach.
co'leagh, see comh-leagh.
co-leic', (CR) *s.m.* Cuff, slap.
colg, cuilg, *s.m.* Rage, ardour, wrath. 2 Fierce look. 3‡‡Manly hue, cheerful aspect. 4 see calg.
——ach, *a.* Fierce, furious, wrathful. 2 Fretful. 3 Stern. 4 Ardent. 5 see calgach. A shùl ch., *his fierce eye;* mar thanasg 'na leum ch., *like a furiously bounding spectre.*
colgach,¶ *s.m.* Puffin, see fachach.
————d, *s.f.* Prickliness.
colgag, -aig, -an, *s.f.* Forefinger.
colgaiche, *s.f.ind.* Peevishness. 2 Sourness. 3 Fierceness, wildness. 4 Alacrity.
colgaiche, *comp.* of colgach.
colgaichte,** *a. & past pt.* Barbed.
colgail, -e, *a.* Lively, martial, smart, brisk.
colgair,¶ *s.m.* Puffin, see fachach.
†colgan, -ain, -an, *s.m.* Salmon-trout. 2 Salmon.
†colgan,(AF) *s.m.* Dove, see calman.
colganta, see colgail & colgarra.
colgantachd, see colgarrachd.
colgantas, -ais, *s. m.* Briskness, liveliness, smartness. 2††Wildness. 3**Bitterness.
colgaradh,** *a.* see colgarra.
colgarra, *a.* Fierce, stern, angry-looking. 2** Brisk, lively, smart. 3**Bitter, biting, as frost. 4**Freezing. 5**Prickly. Mios c., *a freezing month.*
————chd, *s.f.ind.* Fierceness, sternness. 2 *New year's eve. 3* Absurd hammering at anything.
†colg-bhealaidh, see calg-bhealaidh.
colg-bhruidhinn, *s.m.* Butcher's broom.
colg-chu,-choin, *s.m.* Hound, fierce-looking dog.
colg-raineach,‡ *s.f.* Holly fern—*Breadalbane,* see raineach-cuilinn.
colg-rasgadh, -aiche, see colg-rosgach.
colg-rosach, -aiche, *a.* Having strong eye-lashes. 2**Prickly.
colg-rosgach, -aiche, *a.* Fierce-looking. 2 Lively eyed.
colg-sheòl, -iùil, *a.* Quick moving sail.
colg-throid, *v.a.* Fight with the sword.
†coll, *s.m.* Hazel. 2 Gaelic name of the letter C. 3 Neck. 4 Destruction.
†coll, *v.n.* Sleep.
colla, *gen.sing. (bad)* of colann.
colla,** *s.* Epicurism.
†collach, -aiche, see collaidh.
†————, *s.f.* Fat heifer. 2 Boar. 3 Yearling calf.
collachail, -e, *a.* Boorish.
collachd, see collaidhneachd.
†colladar, *v.* They lodged.
†colladh,** -aidh, *s.m.* Sleep, rest.
collag, see collag-lìn.
†collag-lìn, *s.f.* Earwig.
collag-lìon, see collag-lìn.
collaid, -e, -ean, *s.f.* Clamour, scolding. 2 Loquacity. 3 Quarrelsome woman. 4 *more frequently "cullach"* Heifer of two years old. 5†† Din.
————each, -eiche, *a.* Clamorous, vehement, quarrelsome, loquacious, turbulent.
collaidh, -a, *a.* Sensual, carnal, lewd. 2 Wicked, impious, incestuous. 3 Forbidden, prohibited. Gu c., *carnally.*
collaidheachd, see collaidhneachd.
collaidhneachd, *s.f.ind.* Carnality, lewdness. 2 Incestuousness.
collaidin-bàn, -e-baine, *s.f.* Opium poppy, see codalian.
†collaim, *v.* I sleep.
Collainn, see calluinn.
collainn, -e, -ean, *s.f.* Smart stroke.
————ich, *v.a.* Strike, thresh, thump.
collaire-bothain,(AF) *s.* Cormorant, shag, see sgarbh.
collas, see coltas.
†coll-chnò, *s.f.* Filbert (cnò-challtuinn.)
†coll-choille, *s.f.* Hazle-wood.
coll-leabaidh, ** *s.f.* Bedstead (of hazel.)
collnach,†† -aich, *a.* Incestuous.
†collotach, -aiche, *a.* Soporific.
colltach,** -aich, *s.f.* Fleet, navy.
colluinn, -e, -ean, see calluinn, colann & calltuinn.
†colm, *s.m.* see calman.
colmach,** -aich, *s.m.* Dove-cot, pigeon-house.
colman, see calman.
colman-coille, see calman-coille.
colman-taighe, see calman-taighe.
colmh, cuilmh, see calbh.
colmhuinn,** see colbh.
————each, see colbhach.
colm-lann, -an, *s.m.* see calm-lann.
colna, *gen.sing.* of colann. 2**Temperament.
colnach, -aiche, *a.* Incestuous.
†colog, *s.m.* see colag.
cologag, see colgag.
†colp, -a, *s.m.* Head. 2 Thigh, haunch.
†colpa, *s.m.* Cow, 2 Horse, colt. 3 see calpa,

colpach, -aich, *s.m.* Heifer. 2 Steer. 3 Bullock. 4 Colt. 5(AF) Cow-calf. 6(AF) Cow that has never calved. Bheirear colpaich dhuit, *heifers shall be given to thee.*
†colpach, *s.m.* Duty payable by tenants to landlords—*Martin.*
colpachadh, -aidh, *s.m.* Equalizing cattle stock. This varies in a slight degree in some of the islands, but the following is fairly representative of the whole Outer Hebrides.
1 horse is equal to 8 foals.
,, ,, 4 one-year-old fillies.
,, ,, 2 two-year-old fillies.
,, ,, 1 three-year-old, and 1 one-year-old filly.
,, ,, 2 cows.
1 cow ,, 8 calves.
,, ,, 4 stirks.
,, ,, 2 two-year-old queys.
,, ,, 1 three-year-old quey & 1 one-year-old stirk.
,, ,, 8 sheep.
,, ,, 12 hoggs.
,, ,, 16 lambs.
,, ,, 16 geese.
2 sheep ,, 3 one-year-old hoggs.
1 ,, ,, 1 two-year-old hogg.
—In *Argyll :*
1 cow is equal to 4 calves.
,, 2 stirks.
,, 1 two-year-old and calf.
,, 1 three-year-old.
,, 5 sheep.
,, 10 hoggs.
,, 20 lambs.
colpach-seamlach,(AF) *s.m.* Uncalved cow.
colpindach, see colpach.
colsach, see coltach.
†colt, -a, *s.m.* Meal, victuals.
coltach, -aiche, *a.* Like, similar. 2 Likely, probable.
coltachail, see coltach.
coltachd, *s.f.* see coltas.
coltair-cheannach,§ Puffin. see fachach.
coltar, -air, *s.m.* Coulter, that part of a plough-iron which cuts the soil.
coltas, -ais, *s. m.* Likeness, resemblance. 2 Likelihood, probability. 3 Appearance. 4 Good-looks. A réir coltais, *in all likelihood*; mar sin bha a choltas, *such was his appearance*; fear do choltais, *a man like thee* ; tha c. millidh air na béistean, *the insects look like doing damage*; tha a choltas sin ort, *you look as if you had*, or *as if you were.*
———achd, see coslachd.
†coltra, *a.* Dark, gloomy.
coltrachan,§ Puffin, see fachach.

178. Coltraiche.

coltraiche, -an, *s.m.* Razor-bill—*alca aorda.*
†coltur, see coltar.
co'luadair, *s.m.* see comh-luadar.
coluaisg, *s.f.* Conquassate.
Coluinn, see Calluinn.
coluinn, see colann.
colum, -uim, *s.m.* see calman.
columan, -ain, *s.m.* see calman.
†columhan, -ain, -an, *s. m.* Pedestal, pillar, prop.
colunn, -uinne [colla & colna,] *pl.* -uinn [& -an,] *s.f.* see colann.
c' om ? for c' uime ?
com, *a.* see coma.
†com, *s.m.* Kindred.
†com, *v.a.* Frame, shape.
com, cuim, *s.m.* The cavity of the chest, the region of the viscera. 2 The trunk of the body. 3** Breast, bosom. 4**Waist. 5** Belly, bowels. 6**Womb. 7**Protection, guard. Corruich a chuim, *the rage of his breast;* chlisg a cridhe 'na com, *her heart started in her bosom* ; tinneas-cuim, *bloody flux*; *2 any disorder of the intestines.*
coma, *a.* Indifferent, not caring, regardless. Is c. leam thu, *I hate you* ; nach c. leat-sa ? *what is that to you ?* is c. dhomh-sa cò aca, *it is no matter to me* (*which of them*) ; is c. leis an righ Eòghann, agus is c. le E. co dhiù, *the king doesn't like Ewen, but E. doesn't care whether the king likes him or not.*
coma, *conj.* However.
†comach,** -aich, *s.m.* Breach. 2 Defeat. 3 Tax, toll.
†comadair, -ean, *s.m.* Romancer, story-teller.
†———eachd,** *s.f.ind.* Fiction, romancing.
comadh,** *a.* Desirous. 2 Lukewarm.
comaidh, -ean, *s.f.* Mess. 2 Eating together or promiscuously of the same food, particuarly if out of the same vessel; bi 'd thosd 's bi 'd chomaidh, *be silent and take your share —ask no questions for conscience' sake*; thoir dhomh c., *give me a share of your food*; gabh c., *take out of the same dish with him;* is sona gach cuid an c., *pleasant is every morsel that is shared.*
comain, -ean, *s. f.* Obligation for favour received. 2**Recompense. 3**Gratuity. Tha mi fada 'nad chomain, *I am much obliged to you*; cha'n 'eil mi 'nad chomain, *I am not obliged to you*; cha b' e do chomain e, *I did not deserve that at your hand*; c. do làimhe féin, *tit for tat;* fo ch. agad-sa, *under obligations to you*; c. an uilc a ni, *reprisals, evil for evil* ; bu ghaol gun ch. mo ghràidh dha-san, *I love him for his own sake, and not for anything he has done for me;* ann an c. nam briathran ceudna, *in much the same words* or *agreeably to what has been previously said;* seallaidh cù air c., *a dog remembers a favour.*
comaineach,‡‡ -eiche, *a.* Obligatory.
comair,†† -ean, *s.f.* Meeting or confluence of waters.
†comair, *v.a.* Liken, compare.
†comair, *a.* see cuimir.
†comairce, *s.f.* see comraich.
comaith,* *s.f.* see comaidh.
†comallnae,‖ *s.* Dropsy.
†conaltach, *a.* Fulfilled, performed.
†comamar, *s.m.* Comparison.
comanach,** see comanachadh.
comanachadh, -aidh, *s.m.* Sacrament. 2 The celebration of the Lord's Supper. 3 Act of partaking of it. Luchd-comanachaidh, *communicants.* A' c—, *pr.pt.* of comanaich.
comanaich, *pr.pt.* a' comanachadh, *v.a.* Communicate, partake of the Lord's Supper.

comanaiche, -an, s.m. Communicant, one who partakes of the Eucharist.
†coman-mionla, s.m. Corn-camomile, see minlacha.
comann, -ainn, see comunn.
†comann-searraich, s.m. Pilewort (plant.)
comannd, -a, s.m. Gaelic spelling of *command.*
comanndair, -ean, s. m. Gaelic spelling of *commander.*
commanta,** s.m. Captaincy.
†comaoine, see comain & comanachadh.
†comaontoir, -ean, s.m. Benefactor.
†comar, -air, -an, s.m. Meeting. 2 Confluence of waters, place where two or more waters meet. 3**Help. 4**Nose. 5‡‡Way. 6‡‡Valley.
comarach,** a. Confluent. 2 Auxiliary, helpful.
comaradh, -aidh, s. m. Anything thrown on the shore. 2 Booty. 3 see comradh.
comarag,(AC) s.f. see comraich.
comaraich, s.f. see comraich.
comaraich, *pr. part.* a' comarachadh, *v. a.* Protect. 2‡‡ Help.
comarath, v.n. Strive.
comarc,** -airc, s.m. Part, share.
†comart, s.m. Death, killing.
†-——, v.a. Kill.
comas, -ais, s.m. Power, authority. 2 Ability. 3 License, liberty, permission. 4 Practicability. 5 Virility. 6 Datum. Gun c. ruith, *without power of running*; thoir c. dha, *give him liberty*; orra chomais, *an amulet to deprive a person of his virility.*
——, -ais, s.m. Pulse.
——ach, -aiche, a. Powerful, able, capable 2 Active. 3 Potential in *gram.* 4*In good worldly circumstances. 5**Effective. Daoine comasach, *effective men.*
——achd,** s.f.ind. see comas.
——aiche, *comp.* of comasach.
——dair, -ean, s.m. Commissary.
——daireachd, s.f. Commissariat, business of a commissary. 2 Commissaryship.
comasg, -aisg, see coimeasg.
——achd, see coimeasgachd.
†comasg-ghnùmh, s.m. Confused mass, chaos.
combach, -aich, s.m. *prov.* for companach. 2** Breach. 3**Defeat. Ceud c. do mhnà, *the first companion (husband) of thy wife.*
combaiche, s.f. Friendship, companionship.
combaiste, -an, s.m. Compass. 2 Circle.
——ach, -eiche, a. Of, or belonging to, a compass.
combanach, see companach.
†combrùghadh, -aidh, s.m. Oppression. 2 Contrition.
com-chochlach, -aiche, a. Wrapping up the body.
comeirce, s.f. given in some Dicts. for coimeirce.
co meud? see cia meud?
comh-, *insep. particle.* "Comh-" should always be used before a hyphen, "coimh" only in composition, when first vowel of next syllable is a small one.
†comh, v.a. Preserve, keep.
comh-abairt, -ean, s. f. Conference, dialogue, conversation.
comhach, -aich, s.m. Prize. 2 Prey. 3 Predatory life. 4**Cense.
comhachadh,‡‡ -aidh, s.m. Dispute, fight. A' c—, *pr.pt.* of comhaich.
comhachag, -aig, -an, s.f. Barn-owl—*strix ulula.* Chualas a' ch. 'á creig, *the owl was heard from a rock.*
——— -adharcaiche,¶ s.f. Long-eared owl, —*otus vulgaris.*
comhachag-bhàn,¶ s. f. Snowy owl—*surnia nyctea.* 2 Barn-owl, see cailleach-oidhche.

179. Comhachag. *180. C.-adharcaiche.*

181. Comhachag-bhàn (1.)

182. C.-bheag.

183. C.-chluasach.

comhachag-bheag,¶ s. f. Little owl—*noctua passerina.*
comhachag-chluasach,¶ s.f. Short-eared owl —*otus brachyotus.*
comhachag-dhonn,¶ s. f. Tawny owl—*syrnium* or *ulula stridula.* (*illust.* 184.)
comhachag-gheal, see comhachag-bhàn.
comhachag-mhór,¶ s.f. Eagle-owl. see cailleach-oidhche-mhór.
comhachag-mhór,(2) s. f. see c— -bhàn.
comhachag-ruadh,¶ s. f. see c— -dhonn.
comhachag-shneachdaidh (AF) s.f. Snowy owl.
†comhachd, see cumhachd†.
———ach, see cumhachdach.
†comh-acmac, s.m. Circuit.

184. Comhaohag-dhonn.

†comh-acmach, see †comh-acmac.
comhad, -aid,-aidean, *s.m.* (comh+fada‡) Comparison, similitude. 2 Elegy. 3**Parable. 4**Two last quatrains of a verse. Gu c., *arow.*
comhad,** *a.* Equal, even, lineal. 2 Like.
———achd,** *s.f.* Equality.
comhadh, see cumhadh.
†comh-agal, -ail, see comh-agalladh.
————ladh, -aidh, *s.m.* Conference. Ann an taigh comh-agallaidh, *in uncertainty.*
comhaib,* *s.f.* Contention about right.
———,* *v.n.* Contend about rights or time to do something.
comhaich,‡ *pr.pt.* a' comhachadh, *v.n.* Dispute, assert, contend. 2**Collect, gather. 3(DU) Defeat. Chaidh a chomhachadh, *he was defeated.*
————eadh,‡‡ -idh, -an, *s.m.* Competition. 2 Contradiction.
comhaideach,** see coimheadach.
————d, see coimheadachd.
comhaidh,** *s.m.* Keeper. 2 Reward.
†comhaidhcheas, -eis, see comh-àiteachas.
comhaidich,** *v.n.* see comhaidrich.
comhaidrich,††*pr.pt.* a' comhaidreachadh, *v.n.* Squire. 2 Convey. 3 Attend.
†comhaightheach, -aich, *a.* see coimheach.
comh-aigne, *s.f.* Similar turn of mind. 2 Similar passion or affection. 3 Fellow-feeling. Duine aig an robh c. ruinne, *a man who had like passions with ourselves.*
————ach, *a.* Having similar passions or affections.
†comhail, -ean, see còmhdhail.
†———, *v.a.* Discharge an office or duty.
†———t, *v.a.* Join.
comhailteach, *a.* Fulfilled, performed, completed.
————d, *s.f.* Convoy, convoying.
†comhaim, *s.f.* Wife, spouse.
†comh-aimseardha, *a.* } see comh-aimsireil.
comh-aimsireach, }
——————,** -ich, *s.m.* Contemporary.
——————d, *s. f. ind.* Concurrence of events happening at the same time.
comh-aimsireil, *a.* Contemporary, coeval.
comh-aimsirich,‡‡ *v.n.* Contemporize.
comh-ainm, -ean, *s. m.* Surname, additional name. 2**Namesake. 3††Anniversary. Is e seo c. là a bhreith, *this is his birthday,* (*lit.* the anniversary of his birth.)
comh-àir, *v.a.* Count, number.
còmhair,** -ean, *s.m.* Dry-stone builder.
†comhair, *s.m.* Certainty, sure sign.
comhair, *s.f.ind.* Direction or tendency—forward, backward, headlong, sideways, &c. 2 Presence. 3††View. 4 Opposite, against, before, over against. An c., *nearly, almost;* an c. a' chinn *headlong;* an c. a' chùil, *backward.* a ch. a bhaile, *near the town;* na tig 'gam ch., *do not come near me.*
comhairc, -ean, *s.f.* Outcry, clamour. 2 Forewarning. 3 Mercy, quarter, protection. 4†† Appeal.
———, *v. a.* Cry out, bewail. 2‡‡Protect, assist.
†comhairce, see comhairc.
†comhaircis, -e, *s.f.* Assistance.
còmhaireachd, *s.f.* Opposition. 2**Dry-stone building.
comh-àireamh, -e, *s.m.* Numbering together. 2 Poll, as of votes.
co'-mhaireann, *a.* Equally lasting. C. ris a' ghréin, *as lasting as the sun.*
†comhair, *s.m.* Certainty, sure sign.
comhairle, -an, *s.f.* Advice, counsel. 2 Council, synod, convocation. Bheir mi comhairle ort, *I will give thee advice;* c. na còrach, *right advice;* is diù nach gabh c., agus is diù a ghabhas a h-uile c., *he is foolish who won't take advice, and he is foolish who takes all advices*—the over-wise in his own conceit, and the man who is too easily led by all influences ; c. càraid gun a h-iarraidh, cha d'fhuair i riamh a meas bu chòir dhi, *a friend's advice unasked is never appreciated;* is ann air c. na gaoithe 'tha 'n cuan, *the wind controls the ocean*—the dwellers in Uist, the land of fords, know this from experience; gabh c., *take advice;* cuir c., *confer, ask advice;* chuir e c. ris na daoine òga, *he consulted with the young men.*
comhairleach, -ich, -ichean, *s. m.* Adviser, counsellor, monitor. 2 Councillor. C. dìomhair, *a privy councillor.*
————,‡‡ -eiche, *a.* Persuasive.
————d,‡‡ *s.f.ind.* Advisedness.
comhairleachadh, -aidh, *s.m.* Advising, act of advising. A' c—, *pr.pt.* of comhairlich.
comhairle-dhìomhair, *s.f.* Private advice. 2 Privy council. Ball na comhairle dìomhair, *a member of the Privy council.*
comhairlich, *pr. pt.* a' comhairleachadh, *v. a.* Advise, counsel, admonish, put on one's guard.
————e, -an, see comhairleach.
————te, *a.* & *past pt.* Advised.
comh-airp, *s.f.* see comh-fharpuis.
————each, *a.* see comh-fharpuiseach.
comh-airpeas, see comh-fharpuis.
comh-airpse, see comh-fharpuis.
comhair-thrà na h-oidhche, *s.f.* Evening twilight.
comh-aistreach, -ich, -ichean, *s.m.* see comh-astaraiche.
comh-àiteachadh, -aidh, *s.m.* Dwelling together.
comh-àiteachas, -ais, *s. m.* Neighbourhood. 2 Colony.
comh-àitich, *v.a.* *pr.pt.* a' comh-àiteachadh, *v.a.* Co-habit, dwell or reside together.
comh-àitiche, *s.m.* Neighbour. 2 Townsman.
comhaitheach, -ich, *s.m.* Competitor.
comhal,** *a.* Brave, courageous.
†comhal, -ail, -an, *s.f.* Waiting-maid. 2 Performance or execution of anything.
†comhal, *v .a.* Keep. 2 Perform. 3 Connect, join together. 4**Heap together.
comhal, -ail, -an, *s. m.* Binding or joining together. Droch c. air, *evil be his fate !* (*lit. may he be bound by death !*)
————aiche, -an, *s.m.* Confederate.
————ta, -n, *s.m.* see comh-dhalta.
————tas, see comh-dhaltas.
comh-altaich,** *v.a.* Join together 2 Congratulate. 3 see comh-dhaltaich.
comh-altrumas, -ais, *s.m.* Mutual fosterage.

comh-amar, see comair.
comhan, -ain, *s.m.* Shrine. 2 Kiln-pot.
comh-aogas,**ais, *s.m.* Equiformity.
comh-aois, -ean, *s.m.* One's equal in age.
comh-aoiseach, -ich, -ichean, *s.f.* One's equal in age. 2 Contemporary.
————, -iche, *a.* Contemporary.
comh-aolachd, *s.f.ind.* College.
comh-aomach,‡‡ *a.* Convergent.
————ail, see comh-aomach.
comh-aom,‡‡ *v.a.* Converge.
comh-aonta, *s.f.* Consent.
comh-aontach, -aiche, *a.* Consenting, agreeing, concordant, concurrent.
————adh, -aidh, *s.m.* Consenting, accord, agreement. A' c—, *pr.pt.* of comh-aontaich.
————d, *s.f.ind.* Agreement, accord, concord, unanimity, consent, agreeableness.
comh-aontadh, -aidh, see comh-aonta.
comh-aontaich, *v.a.* & *n.* Agree, unite, consent. 2 Yield, admit, grant, as a point in an argument.
comh-aontuich, see comh-aontaich.
comh-aosda, *a.* Of equal age. 2**Contemporary, co-eval.
comhar,** *s.m.* Forerunner. 2 Presence. 3 **see comharradh.
comhar (mu) ** Opposite. Mu comhar, *opposite her*; mu 'n comhar, *opposite them.* see comhair.
comhara, see comharradh.
comharachail,** *a.* Assignable.
comharaich, see comharraich.
comharan (*for* comharraidhean) *pl.* of comharradh.
comh-arba, *s.m.* Partner in church lands. 2 Successor. 3 Vicar. 4 Order of monks. †5 Protection.
comh-arbachd, *s.f.ind.* Vicarage (office.)
†comh-arbaich, *v.n.* Succeed.
†comh-arbas, -ais, *s.m.* Succession.
comh-àrd, *a.* Equally high.
comhard, -aird, -airdean, see coimheart.
comh-àrdachadh,‡‡ -aidh, *s.m.* Agreement, correspondence, in poetry.
†comharguin, *s.f.* Syllogism.
†————neach, *a.* Syllogistical.
†comharnais, -e, *s.f.* see comh-fharpuis.
comharrachadh, -aidh, *s.m.* Marking, distinguishing. 2 Spying, descrying. A' c—, *pr. pt.* of comharraich.
comharrachadh-clàir, *s. m.* Staff notation in *music.*

185. Comharraidhean-cluais chaorach.
(ill. by MMcD.)

comharradh, -aidh, -aidhean, *s.m.* Mark, impression, token, sign. 2 The sexual mark. 3 Banner. 4**Print. 5**Vestige. 6**Proof. Mar ch. air am buaidh, *as a sign of their victory*; is olc an c. e, *it is a bad sign*; c.-cluais, *an ear-mark* ; deagh ch., *a good sign* ; droch ch., *a bad sign.*

NAMES OF EAR-MARKS ON SHEEP :—

1 Toll—hole made in the centre of ear.—*hole.*
2 Bàrr—top cut off the ear—*tip, crop.*
3 Ròibeadh—Slit made downwards from the top of ear—*Lewis,—slit.* Sgoltadh (AH)—*Argyll—split.*
4 Sùileag—Top cut off in the form of a V with the apex downwards—"*eal stob,*" *fork* ; *swallow-tail.—Lewis.* Smeòrach (AH)—*Argyll.*
5 Geagan—triangular piece taken from top of the ear—*cut.*
6 Beum—semicircular piece taken from under-side of ear—*hind-bit. —Lewis.* Beum fo chluais(AH), beum cùlaoibh (DM) *back-nip.*
7 Gearradh cruacan—Slit taken diagonally upwards, at the side of the ear.
8 Gearradh—slit made at the side, across the ear.
9 Slisinn, cas,—slice taken from the side of the ear.
10 Amaladh—dovetail-shaped piece, taken from the side of the ear.
11 An t-snàthad—slit made in the centre of ear by bending or doubling the ear lengthwise and cutting down, leaving a tongue like that of a net-needle, from which it takes its name.
12 Bacan àrd,(AH) the fore, or upper half of *bàrr* cut off—*fore-quarter—Argyll.* —*high-notch* (DM.)
13 Bacan iosal,(AH) hind, or lower half of *bàrr* cut off—*hind-quarter—Argyll.* —*low-notch* (DM.)
14 Beum os cionn na cluaise,(AH) Semi-circular piece taken from upper side of ear, like No. 6 on under side—*fore-bit.* Beum beulaoibh,(DM) *fore-nip.*
15 Cas-chaibe, piece taken from side of ear shaped like a cas-chom(DU)—*Gairloch.* In *Argyll*, this mark is taken from the top of the ear, so that when the mark *bàrr* is made, *cas-chaibe* disappears—(DM) *spade-shaft.*
16 Dà-sgoltadh,(DM) two parallel slits made downwards from top of ear—*two splits—Argyll.*
17 Dà-bheum,(DM) [like No. 6 duplicated] —*two nips.*
18 Beum mhéirleich, varies. If a sheep-stealer cuts off a *cas-chaibe* mark, the ear will then be like one marked *bàrr.* When lower marks than *cas-chaibe* have to be removed, a larger part of the ear is cut off, leaving only a stump.

In *Lewis*, the marks 1 to 9 are the old ear-marks, known as "na naoidh deargadh." Nos. 10 & 11 are of modern origin—(MMD)
The "near" ear, is "cluas chlì," or "cluas a' ghlacaidh;" the "far" ear, "cluas dheas."
By combinations of these marks, and the use of either or both ears, a practically endless variety may be obtained.
There are some who put age-marks on their sheeps' ears,—one nip for one-year-old, two nips for two-year-old, and so on up to five-year-old, when the marking ceases—(DM.)
We are indebted to MMcD for names above, against which no references are given.

comharradh-criche, *s.m.* Barrier.
comharraich, *pr. pt.* a' comharrachadh, *v. a.* Mark, point out. 2 Distinguish. 3 Observe, descry. 4 Remark. C. iadsan, *mark them.*
——————e, *s.f.* Index in *gram.* (☞)
comharraichte, *a. & past part.* Marked, pointed out. 2 Noted, singular, notable, notorious, distinguished. 3 Goodly. Duine c., *a goodly man.*
comharsachd, see coimhearsnachd.
comharsanachd, see coimhearsnachd.
comharsanta, see coimhearsnachd.
comharsnail, -e, *a.* see coimhearsnail.
comhart, -airt, -an, *s.m.* Bark of a dog.
————aich, -e, *s.f.* Barking, act of barking. 2(CR) Barking at nothing—barking at some object is *tabhannaich—West of Ross-shire.*
†comhartha, *s.m.* Sign, print, mark, vestige, token, proof.
comharthan, *n.pl.* of comhartha.
†comas, -ais, *s.m.* see companas.
comh-astaraiche, -an, *s.m.* Fellow-traveller.
comh-bhagair, *v.a.* Comminate,‖ threaten, denounce.
——————t, -ean, *s. f.* Commination, threatening, denunciation.
comh-bhagradh, *s.m.* see comh-bhagairt.
comh-bhàidh, -e, *s.f.* Sympathy, fellow-feeling. Tha c. agam ris, *I have a fellow-feeling for him.*
——————each, *a.* Sympathetic, compassionate, tender-hearted.
comh-bhann, -an, *s.f.* Confederacy, league, bond, compact, contract. C. na sìth, *the bond of peace.*
comh-bhan-oighre, *s.f.* Co-heiress.
comh-bheanailteach,†† -eich, *s.m.* Co-tangent.
————————, -eiche, *a.* Co-tangent.
†comh-bheir, *v.a.* Contribute.
comh-bheothachadh, -aidh, *s.m.* Quickening together. 2**Maintaining or feeding together.
comh-bheothaich, *pr.pt.*a' comh-bheothachadh, *v.a.* Quicken together. 2 Revive together. 3 Maintain together.
comh-bheurla, *s.f.ind.* Conference. [McL. & D. gives "conference in the English language;" but *beurla,* means "language," and has no connection with English in this case.]
——————ch, *a.* Closely united. 2 Conjunctive, in *gram.*
——————chadh, -aidh, -aidhean, *s.m.* Conjugation, union.
comh-bhith, -e, *s.f.* Co-existence.
comh-bhitheach,** *a.* Co-existent.
————————adh,‡‡ -aidh, *s.m.* Consubstantiation.
comh-bhith-bhuan, *a.* Co-eternal.
————————tachd, *s.f.* Co-eternity.
comh-bhitheach,** *a.* Co-existent.
comh-bhogartaich, -e, *s.f.* Quivering, shivering, shuddering.
comh-bhoinn, *gen. & dat.* of comh-bhann.* 2 Support. An c. ris, *supporting him—Dain Iain Ghobha.*
comh-bhràithreach, -eiche, *a.* see comh-bhràthaireil.
————————eil, see c— -bhràthaireil.
————————d, *s. f.* see c— -bhràithreachas.
comh-bhràithreachas, -ais, *s.m.* Brotherhood. 2 Fellowship. 3 Consanguinity.
†comh-bhraoch, -aich, -an, *s.f.* The borders of a country. 2 Hills or eminences which separate countries from one another.
†——————ach, *a.* Bordering, contiguous. 2 Marching with each other, as countries.

comh-bhràthair, -thar, bhràithrean, *s.m.* Brother. 2 Companion, fellow, chum.
comh-bhràthaireil, -e, *a.* Fraternal.
comh-bhreith,‡‡ -e, *s.f.* Connascence.
comh-bhrìgheach, *a.* Of the same substance, consubstantial.
comh-bhrìgheachadh, -aidh, *s.m.* Consubstantiation.
comh-bhrìgheachd, *s.f.* Consubstantiality.
comh-bhrìgheil,** *a.* Consubstantial.
comh-bhrighich, *pr.pt.* a' comh-bhrìgheachadh, *v.a.* Consubstantiate.
comh-bhrìoghachadh,see comh-bhrìgheachadh.
comh-bhriseadh, -sidh, -sidhean, *s.m.* Defeat. 2 Flight.
comh-bhrodadh, -aidh, -aidhean, *s. m.* Compunction.
†comh-bhruach, -aich, see comh-bhraoch.
†comh-bhruachach, see comh-bhraochach.
comh-bhrùite,*past pt.* of comh-bhrùth. Contrite.
——————achd, *s.f.ind.* Contrition.
comh-bhrùth, *v.a.* Bruise. 2**Oppress.
——————adh, -aidh, *s.m.* Contrition.
†comh-bhuaidhreadh, -ridh, -ean, see comh-bhuaireadh.
comh-bhuail, *v.a.* Touch upon, come into contact, strike mutually.
comh-bhuailte, *past pt.* of comh-bhuail.
comh-bhuair, *v.a.* Tempt, disturb, trouble, embroil. 2**Raise a tumult.
†comh-bhuaireadh, *s.m.* War, tumult, uproar.
comh-bhuairte, *past pt.* of comh-bhuair. Tempted, embroiled, infuriated.
comh-bhualadh, -aidh, *s.m.* Mutual striking. 2 Contact. 3‡‡Allison. A' c—, *pr. pt.* of comh-bhuail.
comh-bhuintinn,‡‡ *s.m.* Inosculation.
comh-breith, see comh-bhreith.
comh-chagar, -air, *s.m.* Conspiracy.
comh-chaidir, *v.n.* Live, dwell. 2 Unite affectionately. 3 Trade, traffic, correspond.
comh-chaidreach, -eiche, *a.* Corresponding. 2 Linked in affection, companionable. 3 Trafficking. 4 Dwelling together.
comh-chaidreachas, -ais, *s.m.* Close friendship, companionship. 2 Correspondence. 3 Commerce, traffic.
comh-chaidreachd, *s.f.* } see c— -chaidreachas.
comh-chaidreadh, *s.m.* }
comh-chaidreamh, *s. m.* Mate, companion, chum. 2 see comh-chàirdeas.
comh-chainnt, -e, *s. f.* Conference, dispute, dialogue. Cum c., *hold a conference.*
comh-chainnteireachd,see c— -channtaireachd.
comh-chàirdeas, -eis, *s.m.* Correspondence, society, harmony.
comh-chaireachd, see c— -charachd.
comh-chàireadh, *s.m.* Allocation.
comh-channtaireachd, *s.f.* Choir. 2 Choral music.
comh-chaochladh, -aidh, -aidhean, *s.m.* Commutation, exchange.
comh-chaochlaideach, -eiche, *a.* Commutable, exchangeable. 2 Equally subject to change.
comh-chaochlaideachd, *s.f.ind.* Commutability, exchangeableness. 2 Circumstance of being capable of exchange, or liable to change.
comh-chaoidh, *v.n.* Condole, sympathize.
——————, *s.f.*Condolence, sympathy, commiseration.
comh-chaoin, *v.n.* Weep with another, condole.
comh-chaoineadh, -nidh, *s.m.* Weeping together, condolence. A' c—, *pr. pt.* of c—chaoin.
comh-charachd, *s.f.ind.* Mutual struggling. 2 Contortions in wrestling.
comh-charaid, -ean[& -chàirdean,] *s. m.* Mutual

friend.
comh-charaidheachd, *s.f.ind.* see c— chaireachd.
comh-chàrn, *v.a.* Accumulate, heap together.
comh-chàrnadh, *s.m.* Accumulation, act of accumulation. A' c—, *pr.pt.* of c— -chàrn.
comh-chàrnta, *a. & past pt.* Accumulated, heaped together.
comh-charraideachd, *s.f.* Mutual struggle. 2 Violent competition.
comh-cheadachadh, -aidh, *s.m.* Consent. A' c—, *pr. pt.* of comh-cheadaich.
comh-cheadaich, *pr. pt.* a' comh-cheadachadh, *v.a.* Concede, admit, grant.
————te, *past part.* Conceded, admitted, granted.
comh-chealg, -eilg, *s.f.* Rebellion, conspiracy, treason.
comh-cheangail, *pr. pt.* a' comh-cheangal, *v.a* Connect, unite, bind together, couple, league, confederate.
————te, *past part.* of comh-cheangail. Connected, united, bound together. 2 *a.* Corporate.
comh-cheangal, -ail, *s. m.* Tying, binding, uniting or linking together. 2 Covenant, treaty, league. 3** Conspiracy. 4 Conjugation, agreement. A' c—, *pr. pt.* of comh-cheangail.
comh-cheangladh, -aidh, *s.m.* Covenanting. 2 Stipulation, compact, agreement, league. 3 Conspiracy.
comh-cheanglaiche, -an, *s.m.* Link of connection, bond, person or thing that ties together. 2 Conjunction in *gram.*
comh-cheannach, -aiche, see c— -cheannachd.
comh-cheannachd, *s.f.ind.* Commerce, trade.
comh-cheannaich, *v.n.* Trade together.
comh-cheannairc, *s.* Conspiracy, conspirator.
————each, *a.* Conspirant.
comh-chearclach,** *a.* Concentric.
comh-chearrach, -aich, *s. m.* Mate, consort, companion, playfellow, bed-fellow.
comh-chearraiche,** *s.m.* Fellow-player, fellow gambler.
comh-cheart, -eirte, *a.* Fashioned together. 2 Proportioned, adjusted.
comh-cheartaich, *v.a.* Fashion or form equally.
comh-chéilidh, *s.m. & f.* Paramour.
comh-chéimneach, -eiche, *a.* Concurrent, concomitant, conjoined, associated.
————d, *s. f. ind.* Concurrence, union, association, accompanying.
comh-chéimnich, *v.n.* see comh-cheumnaich.
comh-cheòl, -chiùil, *s. m.* Concert. 2 Symphony. 3 Chorus.
comh-cheòlach, -aiche, *a.* Choral.
comh-cheòlraiche,** -an, *s.m.* Chorister.
comh-cheumnaich, *v.n.* Concur. 2 Accompany, convoy. 3 Keep the same pace.
comh-chiallach, *a.* Synonymous. Briathran c., *synonymous words.*
comh-chinneas, -eis, *s.m.* Concretion.
————ach,** *a.* Co-existent.
comh-chinntinneach, *a.* Accretive.
comh-chiontaiche, *s.m.* Accessory.
comh-chìseach, *a.* Contributory.
comh-chliamhuinn, -chleamhna, *pl.* -chleamhnan & -chliamhuinnean, *s. m.* Brother-in-law. 2**Son-in-law.
comh-chnuasach, -aiche, *a.* Mutually investigating, pondering or scrutinizing.
comh-chnuasachadh, -aidh, *s.m.* Mutual investigation, pondering, or scrutiny.
comh-chnuasachd, *s.f.ind.* Mutual collection. 2 Investigation, pondering. 3‡‡Corollary.
comh-chnuasaich, *v.a.* Collect together. 2 Mutually ponder. 3 Sift, investigate.
comh-chnuasaichte, *past pt.* of c— -chnuasaich. Mutually collected, investigated, pondered.
comh-chogadh, -aidh, *s.m.* Opposition. 2 Mutual contention.
comh-chogar, -air, -an, see c— -chagar.
comh-choigreach, -ich, -ichean, *s.m.* Fellow-stranger.
comh-choimeasail,** *a.* Comparable.
comh-chòir, *s.f.* Equal right, title, or claim.
comh-choisiche, *s.m.* Fellow-pedestrian.
comh-choitcheann, *a.* Catholic, universal.
————achd, *s.f.* Universality.
————as, -ais, *s.m.* Universality.
comh-choltas, -ais, see comh-choslas.
comh-chomhairle, -an, *s.f.* Consultation, deliberation.
————ach, -ich, *s.m.* Fellow-counsellor. 2 Fellow-councillor.
————achadh, -aidh, *s.m.* Consultation. 2 Confederation.
comh-chomhairlich, *pr. pt.* a' c— -chomhairleachadh, *v.n.* Advise, consult together.
comh-chòmhnuidh, -ean, *s.m.* Common abode. 2 Co-habiting.
†comh-chomhthrom, see c— -chothrom.
comh-chomunn, -uinn, *s.m.* Fellowship, communion, partnership, society, association.
————achd,‡‡ *s.f.* Corporation.
†comh-chorbadh, -aidh, *s.m.* Destroying.
comh-chòrd, *v.n.* Accord, agree mutually.
————ach, -aiche, *a.* Mutually accordant.
————achd, *s.f.ind.* Agreement, mutual understanding, congruence.
————adh, -aidh, *s.m.* Unanimity, agreement, concord. A' c—, *pr.pt.* of c— -chòrd.
————ail, -e, *a.* Compatible, consistent.
————alachd, *s.f.ind.* Compatibility, consistency.
comh-chorp, -chuirp, -achan, *s.m.* Corporation.
————achadh, -aidh, *s.m.* Incorporation, act of incorporating. A' c—, *pr. pt.* of c— chorpaich.
comh-chorpaich, *pr. pt.* a' c— -chorpachadh, *v.a.* Incorporate.
————te, *past pt.* of c— -chorpaich, Incorporated.
comh-chòs, -òis, -an, *s.m.* Concavity.
————ach, -aiche, *a.* Concave.
————achadh,‡‡ -aidh, *s.m.* Concavation.
————aich, *v.a.* Excavate.
————aichte, *past part.* of c— -chòsaich, Excavated, hollowed.
comh-choslach, *a.* Conformable, like, equal. 2 Bearing a mutual resemblance.
comh-choslachd, *s.f.* Conformity. 2 Equality. 3 Likeness. 4 Assimilation.
comh-choslaich,** *v.a.* Assimilate.
comh-choslas, -ais, *s.m.* Equality. 2 Likeness, resemblance.
comh-chosmhal, see comh-chosmhuil.
comh-chosmhuil, -e, *a.* Alike, similar. 2 Conformable. 3 Equal.
comh-chosmhuileachd, *s.f.ind.* Similarity, consimilitude.
comh-chothrom, -uim, *s.m.* Counterpoise, equality of weight, balance, equipoise, equivalent.
————ach, *a.* Equiponderant.
————achadh, -aidh, *s.m.* Equalizing of weights, balancing. 2 Equipoising. A' c—, *pr.pt.* of c— -chothromaich.
————aich, *pr. pt.* a' c— -chothromachadh, *v.a.* Counterpoise, counterbalance weigh together, equiponderate.
comh-chothromaichte, *past pt.* of c— -chothromaich. Weighed together, equalized, equipoised, balanced.

comh-chràbhadh, -aidh, *s.m.* Social worship.
comh-chraithte, *past pt.* of c— -chrath, Conquassated, shaken together.
†comh-chras, *s. m.* Good fellowship. 2 Mutual agreement or understanding.
comh-chrath, *v.a.* Shake together.
comh-chrathadh, -aidh, *s.m.* Concussion, act of shaking together. A' c—, *pr. pt.* of c— chrath.
comh-chreutair, -ean, *s.m.* Fellow-creature.
comh-chridheach, -eiche, *a.* Agreeing, unanimous, of one mind.
comh-chridheachd, *s.f.ind.* Agreement, unanimity.
comh-chrìoch, -ìche, an, *s.f.* Confines, border, edge, march.
comh-chroch, *v.a.* & *n.* Hang together. 2 Be coherent.
comh-chrochach, -aiche, *a.* Coherent.
comh-chrochadh, -aidh, *s.m.* Coherence, cohering. A' c—, *pr. pt.* of c— chroch.
comh-chrùb, *v.a.* & *n.* Shrivel up, contract.
——————adh, -aidh, *s.m.* Contraction, act of shrivelling. 2 Become shrivelled.
comh-chruinn, *v. a.* Globulate.
comh-chruinn, -e, *a.* Globular. 2**Commeasurable. 3**Concentric.
comh-chruinneach, -ich, see c— -chruinneachadh.
comh-chruinneachadh, -aidh, -aidhean, *s. m.* Collection. 2 Congregation, assembly. A' c—, *pr. pt.* of c— -chruinnich.
comh-chruinnich, *pr. pt.* a' c— -chruinneachadh, *v.a.* & *n.* Collect, assemble, congregate, gather.
comh-chruinniche, -an, *s.m.* Collector, compiler.
comh-chruinnichte, *past pt.* of c— -chruinnich, Collected, compiled, assembled.
comh-chrùpadh, see comh-chrùbadh.
comh-chruth, -a, -an, *s.m.* Sameness of form. 2 Resemblance. 3 Conformation, equiformation.
†comh-chuan-cogaidh, *s.m.* Theatre of war on sea.
comh-chudthrom, -oim, *s.m.* Equiponderance, equilibrium, equal weight, equipoise, counterbalance.
comh-chudthromach, *a.* Equiponderant, equipoised.
comh-chudthromaich, *v.a.* Equalize, equiponderate, poise, weigh together.
comh-chuibhreach, -ich, -ichean, *s.f.* Compound chain, concatenation.
comh-chuibhreachadh, -aidh, *s.m.* Chaining together, act of fettering or chaining together, concatenation. A' c—, *pr.pt.* of c— -chuibhrich.
comh-chuibhrich, *v.a.* Chain together, concatenate.
comh-chuibhrichte, *past pt.* of c— -chuibhrich. Chained together, connected.
comh-chuideachadh, -aidh, *s. m.* Joint assistance, aid, help, act of jointly assisting or helping. A' c—, *pr. pt.* of c— -chuidich.
comh-chuideachail,‡‡ -e, *a.* Contributive.
comh-chuideachd, -an, *s.f.* Association, concomitancy. 2 Company, partnership. 3 Community.
comh-chuideachdach,‡‡ -aiche, *a.* Associated.
comh-chuidich, *pr.pt.* a' c— -chuideachadh, *v.a.* Aid, assist jointly.
comh-chuidiche, -an, *s.m.* Assistant, coadjutor.
comh-chuimsich,‡‡ *v.a.* Attemperate.
comh-chuimte, *a.* Harmonized—*Dain I. Ghobha.*
comh-chuing, -e, -ean, *s. f.* Compound yoke, conjugation.
comh-chuingeachadh, -aidh, *s.m.* Yoking together, act of yoking together. A' c—, *pr pt.* of c— -chuingich.
————————ich, *v.a.* Yoke together, conjugate.
————————ichte, *past pt.* of c— -chuingich, Yoked together.
comh-chuir, *v. a.* Apply. 2 Compose. 3 Arrange, set in order. 4**Dispose.
†comh-chuisnich, *v.a.* Congeal.
†————————te, *past pt.* Congealed.
comh-chum, *v.a.* Conform. 2 Proportion.
comh-chum,** *s.m.* Configuration.
comh-chur, -uir, *s.m.* Application. 2 Composition. 3 Arrangement, allocation. 4 Setting in order.
comh-churaidheachd, see c— -charachd.
còmhdach, -aich, -aichean, *s, m.* Covering, clothing, dress. 2 Shelter. 3 Proof, evidence. 4 Quotation. 5 Envelope of a letter. 6 Solemn declaration—*Dain Iain Ghobha.* Mar ch. air sin, *as a proof of that*; dè 'n c. a bh' air? *what dress had he on?* gorm ch. nam mór chrann, *the green covering of the lofty trees*; c. luirgnean, *armour for the legs.*
——————,(AH) *pr.pt.* a' còmhdach, *v.n.* Dissemble, dissimulate, mis-state, mis-report, fib, fabricate. 'S ann a' c. a tha mi, *I am only fabricating (telling lies.)*
còmhdachadh, -aidh, *s.m.* Cover, act of covering. 2 Shelter. 3 Refuge. 4 Proof. 5 Quotation. 6**Cital. A' c—, *pr.pt.* of còmhdaich.
còmhdachail,** *a.* Convincing.
còmhdachan,¶ *s.m.* Puffin (bird), see fachach.
còmhdaich, *pr.pt.* a' comhdachadh, *v.a.* Cover, clothe, dress. 2 Shelter, screen. 3 Prove. 4 Quote. 5 Witness. 6‡ Allege.
——————te, *past pt.* of còmhdaich. Covered, clothed, dressed. 2 Sheltered. 3 Proved. 4 Quoted. 5 Witnessed.
còmhdhail, -alach [& -ala,] -aichean [& -ean,] *s.f.* Meeting, interview. 2 Assembly, convocation. 3 Opposition. 4* Reproach. 5** Abutment. 6††Luck. 7††see comhairle. 8 (DU) Accommodation, as of wind. Fhuair iad c., *they got a favourable wind*; droch ch. ort! *bad luck to you!*—the wish conveyed is that one may meet a person or animal that it was considered unlucky to meet; Am ch., *to meet me*; thoir c. dha, *reproach him.*
còmh-dhàil, (an) ** *prep.* To meet. 2 In meeting, in opposition.
†comhdhaileam, see comhdhalaich.
comh-dhàimheachd,‡‡ *s.f.* Correlativeness.
comh-dhaingneachadh, -aidh, *s. m.* Confirmation, act of confirming. 2 Strengthening. A' c—, *pr.pt.* of comh-dhaingnich.
comh-dhaingnich, *pr. pt.* a' comh-dhaingneachadh, *v.a.* Confirm, strengthen.
comh-dhaingniche, -an, *s.m.* Confirmer.
†comhdhais, -e, *s.f.* (coltas) Resemblance.
†comhdhal, *s.f.* see còmhdhail.
†comhdhala, *s.m.* Statute, law.
còmhdhalach,(DU) *a.* Accommodating, favouring.
còmhdhalach, *gen.* of còmhdhail.
——————adh, -aidh, *s.m.* Meeting, act of meeting, or assembling. 2 Encounter. 3 Opposing, intercepting.
còmhdhalaich, *v.a.* & *n.* Meet. 2 Coincide. 3 Oppose, stop the progress of a person or thing. 4 Interpret.
còmhdhalaiche, -an, *s.m.* Meeter, one who meets. 6(DU) One who favours or accompanies, companion.
comh-dhalta, -a, *s.m.* Foster-brother. 2 Foster-sister. 3 Highland cousin. Is caomh le

fear a charaid, ach 's e smior a' chridhe an c., *dear is a kinsman, but the pith of the heart is the foster-brother* (NGP) ; an nuair a théid a' ghrian fodha, teichidh m' fhaileas, ach grian ann no as, cha teich mo ch., *when the sun sets, my shadow forsakes me, but in shade or shine true is my foster-brother*. [Chieftains of the Gael were in the habit of fostering their heirs with such of their vassals as had a promising family of sons, in order that mutual attachment might secure fidelity and friendship in future years.

comh-dhaltaich,** *v.a.* Rear children together.

comh-dhaltas, -ais, *s. m.* Relationship of fosterage. 2 Sucking the same breast.

comh-dhanns, *v.a.* Dance with another.

comh-dhannsadh, *s.m.* Dancing in company. 2 Mixed or promiscuous dancing.

comh-dhannsair, -ean, *s.m.* Fellow-dancer.

comh-dhaoine, *s.pl.* Contemporaries.

comh-dhas, -ais, *s.m.* Equal right.

comh-Dhé, see coimhdhe. 2 The Trinity.

comh-dhealbh, *v.a.* Configure, construct, delineate.

comh-dhealbhadh, -aidh, -aidhean, *s.m.* Configuration, construction, delineation. 2 Act of constructing, delineating. 3**Political constitution. A' c—, *pr.pt.* of c— -dhealbh.

comh-dhealradh, -aidh. *s.m.* Coradiation.

comh-dhean, *v.a.* Compose, settle, adjust.

——————adh, see comh-dheanamh.

——————amh, -aimh, *s.m.* Act of composing, adjusting, composition. A' c—, *pr. pt.* of comh-dhean.

——————ta, *past pt.* of comh-dhean. Composed, adjusted.

——————tachd, *s.f.ind.* Composition, adjustment.

comh-dhearbh, ‡ *v.a.* Prove fully or satisfactorily, confirm by evidence, comprobate.

——————adh, -aidh, -aidhean, *s.m.* Complete proof, full evidence.

——————ta, *past pt.* of comh-dhearbh. Demonstrated, clearly proved.

comh-dhèarrsadh, *s.m.* Coradiation.

comh-dheas, -eise, *a.* Convenient, ambidextrous, well adapted. 2 Handsome. 3 Complete. 4 Commodious. 5(AH) Endowed with an appetite that refuses no kind of food. 6 As ready to perform or accept one thing as another, indifferent.

——————achadh, -aidh, *s.m.* Accommodation, adjustment. A' c—, *pr.pt.* of comh-dheasaich.

——————achd, *s.f.ind.* see comh-dheasachadh. 2‡‡Neutrality.

comh-dheasaich, *pr. pt.* a' comh-dheasachadh, *v.a.* Accommodate, supply.

——————te, *past part.* of comh-dheasaich. Accommodated, supplied.

comh-dheas-làmhach,‡‡ *a.* Ambidextrous.

——————d,‡‡ *s.f.* Ambidexterity.

comh-dheas-làmhaiche,(AH) *s.m.* Man ready to undertake any kind of work, person not liable to be defeated in any struggle.

comh-dheuchainn, -e, -ean, *s.f.* Competition, trial of valour, rivalry.

——————aiche, -an, *s.m.* Competitor.

†comh-Dhia, see coimhdhe.

comh-dhilseachd,‡‡ *s.f.ind.* Correlativeness.

comh-dhìol, *pr.pt.* a' c— -dhìoladh, *v.a.* Compensate, remunerate, make amends for. 2 Retaliate.

comh-dhìoladh, -aidh, *s.m.* Compensation, act of compensating. 2 Remuneration. A' c—, *pr.pt.* of c— -dhìol.

comh-dhìreach, -eiche, *a.* Straight,direct,plain.

comh-dhlighe, -an, *s.f.* Equal right.

——————ach, *a.* Equally privileged.

comh-dhlùithte, *a.* Assembled. 2 Bound together.

comh-dhlùth, -ùithe, *a.* Compact.

comh-dhlùtha, *a.* see c— -dhlùithte.

——————chd,‡‡ *s.f.ind.* Contiguity.

——————chadh, -aidh, *s.m.* Binding together, compact. 2 Contribution. A' c—, *pr.pt.* of comh-dhlùthaich.

——————dh, see c— -dhlùthachadh.

——————ich, *v.a.* Frame, conjoin, bind together.

comh-dhoilgheas, -eis, *s.m.* Condolence, commiseration.

comh-dhreachta, *a.* Conformed, resembling. 2 **Proportioned.

comh-dhualadh, -aidh, *s.m.* Embroidery. 2 Sculpture.

comh-dhùin, *pr.pt.* a' c— -dhùnadh, *v.a.* Close, bring to an end, conclude. 2 Close together.

——————te, *past pt.* of c— -dhùin, Concluded, closed.

comh-dhùnach, -aiche, *a.* Conclusive.

comh-dhùnadh, -aidh, *s.m.* Conclusion. 2 Act of concluding. 3 Act of closing together. A' c—, *pr.pt.* of c— -dhùin.

comh-dhùthchas, -ais, *s.m.* The circumstance of belonging to the same country, connection with the same country.

——————ach, -aiche, *a.* Of, or belonging to, the same country.

†——————ach, -aich, *s.m.* Countryman.

comh-eagar, -air, *s.m.* System, order.

——————ach, -aiche, *a.* Systematic, methodical.

comh-eagnadh, -aidh, *s.m.* Complex wisdom, privileges. 2 Knowledge of contemporaries.

comh-éiginn, *s.f.* Force, constraint, compulsion.

comh-éigneachadh, -aidh, *s.m.* Constraining. forcing, urging, compelling. 2** Constrainment, compulsion. A' c—, *pr.pt.* of comh-éignich.

comh-éignich, *pr.pt.* a' comh-éigneachadh, *v.a.* Compel, constrain, force, urge.

comh-éignichte, *past part.* of comh-éignich. Constrained, compelled, forced, urged.

comh-eirbse, *s.f.ind.* Wrangling, disputing, quarrelling.

comh-eirbseach, -eiche, *a.* Contentious,quarrelsome.

comh-éirigh, -e, *s.f.* Insurrection, rebellious commotion.

comh-eòlach, -aiche, *a.* Conscious, equally knowing, equally informed. 2** Mutually acquainting.

comh-eòlas, -ais, *s.m.* Consciousness. 2 Interknowledge. 3 Mutual acquaintance.

co mheud ? see cia meud ?

comh-eud, -a, *s.m.* Emulation, rivalry. 2 Mutual jealousy or suspicion.

comh-eudmhor, *a.* Mutually jealous.

comh-eugas,** see comh-aogas.

comh-fhacal, -ail, *pl.* -ail & -clan,*s.m.*Synonym.

comh-fhaclach, -aiche, *a.* Synonymous.

comh-fhad, *a.* Equal, even, equally long. 2 Lineal.

comh-fhad-thràth, *s.m.* The equinox, at which time days and nights are of equal length. C.-f.-t- an earraich, *the vernal equinox*;c.-f.-t.- an fhogharaidh, *the autumnal equinox*.

comh-fhad-thràthach, *a.* Equinoctial.

†comh-fhagharach, see comh-fhoghar.

comh-fhagus, -uise, *a.* Equally near.

comh-fhagusgach, -aiche, *s.m.* Mutual relation,

†comh-fhaighleadh, *s.m.* Conference.

comh-fhàilteachd, *s.f.ind.* Congratulation. 2 Mutual salutation.
comh-fhàiltich, *v.a.* Congratulate. 2 Salute.
comh-fhàir, -e, *s.f.* Twilight, dawn.
comh-fhaire, *s.f.ind.* Watching, waking or sitting up together.
comh-fhaireachadh, see c— -fhaire.
comh-fhan, see c— -fhuirich.
comh-fharpuis, -e, -ean, *s.f.* Emulation,rivalry. competition. 2* Gibing, jeering, taking off.
comh-fharpuiseach, -eiche, *a.* Emulative, disposed to competition. 2* Imitative.
comh-fharpuiseachd,** *s.f.* Emulativeness. 2 Frequent or continued emulation.
comh-fhàs, *v.n.* Grow together, increase together.
comh-fhàs, -a, *s.m.* Growing together. 2 Concretion.
comh-fhàsach, *a.* Co-existent.
comh-fhàsail, *a.* Accretive.
†comh-fhàsg, *v.a.* Embrace.
comh-fheadhainn,-fheadhna, -an, *s.f.* Company, troop, assembly.
comh-fheall, -a, *s.f.* Conspiracy.
comh-fhealltach,‡‡ -aiche, *a.* Conspirant.
comh-fhear, -fhir, *s.m.* Equal, fellow.
comh-fhearsnach, see coimhearsnach.
——————d, see coimhearsnachd.
comh-fhill, *v.a.* Convolve. 2**Complicate.
comh-fhilleadh,** *s.m.* Complication 2 Folding together.
comh-fhillich, *v.a.* Fold together.
comh-fhillte, *a.* Folded.
comh-fhillteadh, -idh, see c— -fhilleadh.
comh-fhilltich, *v.a.* see c— -fhillich.
comh-fhios, *s.f.* Conscience. 2 Consciousness. An inntinn agus an c., *their mind and conscience.*
——————ach, -aiche, *a.* Conscientious.
——————rach, -aiche, *a.* Conscious.
——————rachd,** *s.f.ind.* Consciousness.
comh-fhlaithe, *s.m.* see c— -fhlaitheachd.
comh-fhlaitheach, *a.* Democratic, republican. 2**Aristocratic.
comh-fhlaitheachd, *s. f. ind.* Democracy, republic, commonwealth. 2 Republicanism. 3**Aristocracy.
comh-fhlaitheas, see comh-fhlaitheachd.
comh-fhlannas,** *s.m.* Consanguinity.
comh-fhlath, -aith, -aithean, *s.m.* Fellow-ruler. 2 Demagogue. 3‡‡Vanguard.
comh-fhocal, see comh-fhacal.
comh-fhoclach, see c— -fhaclach.
comh-fhoghair,** see c— -fhoghar.
——————each,** see c— -fhogharach.
comh-fhoghar, -air, -airean, *s.m.* Consonant. 2 Consonance. 3* Resound, mutual stroke and sound. 4**Chime, as of bells.
comh-fhogharach, -aiche, *a.* Consonant. 2 Chiming.
comh-fhoghar-chlag, *s.m.* Chime of bells.
comh-fhoghlum, -uim, *s.m.* The circumstance of being educated together, receiving the same education.
comh-fhoghlumaiche, -an, *s.m.* Schoolfellow, fellow-learner.
comh-fhogus, -uise, *a.* see c— -fhagus.
comh-fhogusach, -aich, see c— -fhagusach.
comh-fhois, -e, *s.f.* Rest, mutual rest.
comh-fhoiseachadh, -aidh, *s.m.* Resting or settling together. 2 Act of mutually ceasing. A' c—, *pr.pt.* of c— -fhoisich.
comh-fhoisich, *pr.pt.* a' c— -fhoiseachadh. *v. n.* Repose, or rest with. 2 Mutually cease.
comh-fhola, *gen. sing.* of c— -fhuil.
comh-fhonnmhorachd,‡‡ *s.f.* Chime.
comh-fhreagair, *pr. pt.* a' comh-fhreagairt [& a' comh-fhreagradh], *v.a.* Correspond, agree, suit. 2 Resound, echo. Ch. gach tulm agus cnoc, *every hill and knoll resounded.*
comh-fhreagairt, -e, -ean, *s.f.* Consonance, correspondence, conformity, suitabl ness, congruence, congruity, fitness, propriety, agreement, uniformity, symmetry. 2* Re-echo. A' c—, *pr. pt.* of comh-fhreagair.
comh-fhreagairtear,** *s.m.* Correspondent.
comh-fhreagarrach, -aiche, *a.* Corresponding, fitting, suitable, proper, answerable, fit, responsive, commensurable.
comh-fhreagarrachd, *s.f.* see comh-fhreagartas.
comh-fhreagartas, -ais, *s.m.* Symmetry. 2** Correspondence. 3**Fitness.
comh-fhreagradh, -aidh, *s. m.* same meanings as comh-fhreagairt.
comh-fhreagraiche,** *s.m.* Correspondent.
comh-fhuaigh, *v.a.* Sew together.
comh-fhuaigheal, *s.m.* Sewing together.
comh-fhuaighte, *past pt.* of c— -fhuaigh. Sewed together.
comh-fhuaim, *s.m.* Musical concordance, equitone, harmony, consonance.
comh-fhuaimneach, -eiche, *a.* Consonant, harmonious, sounding together, agreeing in sound.
comh-fhuaimneach, *s.m.* see c— -fhuaimneachd.
comh-fhuaimneachd,‡‡ *s.f.ind.* Assonance, harmony.
comh-fhuaimnich, -e, -ean, *s.f.* Sounding together.
comh-fhuaimnich, *v.a.* Attune.
comh-fhuasgladh, -aidh, *s.m.* Joint relief.
comh-fhuil, -fhola, *s.f.* Consanguinity, relationship.
comh-fhuileach, -ich, *s.m.* Relation by blood.
comh-fhuileach, -liche, *a.* Related by blood.
comh-fhuiling, *v.n.* Suffer with, feel with, condole with, sympathize with.
comh-fhuireach, -ich, *s.m.* Staying with or together. 2(AH) Brief delay, act of waiting for one who is coming on behind.
comh-fhuirich, *v.n.* Wait, wait together.
comh-fhulang, -aing, *s.m.* Fellow-suffering.
——————ach, -aiche, *a.* Suffering with, condoling, sympathizing. 2 Feeling, tenderhearted.
——————aiche, } *s.m.* Fellow-sufferer.
——————air,
——————as, -ais, *s.m.* Sympathy, compassion, fellow-feeling. Tha c. aige, *he has a fellow-feeling.*
comh-fhurtachadh, -aidh, *s.m.* Aiding, helping, consoling, comforting. A' c—, *pr.pt.* of c— fhurtaich.
comh-fhurtachail, -e, *a.* Comfortable. 2 Analeptic. 3**Consolatory.
comh-fhurtachd, *s.f.ind.* Aid, help, assistance. 2 Consolation, comfort, comfortableness.
comh-fhurtaich, *pr.pt.* a' c— -fhurtachadh, *v.a.* Aid, assist. 2 Comfort, relieve, console.
comhfhurtaich, see comh-fhurtaich.
comh-fhurtaichte, *past pt.* Aided. 2 Relieved, comforted, consoled.
comhfhurtair, -e, -ean, *s. m.* Comforter, consolator.
†comh-ghabhail, *s.f.* Harmony. 2 Love.
†comh-ghail, *a.* Of the same family. 2 Fellow-heroism. 3 Battle, conflict.
comh-ghàir, *v.n.* Shout together.
——————, -e, *s.f.* Conclamation, simultaneous shout. 2 Congratulation.
comh-ghair, *v.n.* Convoke.
comh-ghàirdeachadh, -aidh, see c— -ghàirdeachas.
——————deachail,‡‡ -e, *a.* Congratulant,

comh-ghàirdeachas, -ais, s.m. Social joy, mutual solace. 2 Congratulation.
comh-ghàirdich, v.n. Congratulate, wish joy.
comh-ghàirich, -e, s.f. Shouting aloud, as of crowd or multitude.
comh-ghairm, -e, -ean, s.f. Convocation. 2** General shout.
comh-ghairm, v.n. Convoke, call together.
comh-ghal, -a, see c— -ghul.
comh-ghaol, -aoil, s.m. Mutual love. 2**Consanguinity.
†comh-ghaolta, s.m. Kindred.
comhghar, -aire, s.m. Nearness, juxtaposition. 2**Instrument.
comhgharach, -aiche, a. Near to.
comh-gheall, v.a. Perform a promise, implement an agreement, fulfil an engagement.
comh-ghealladh, -aidh, -aidhean, s.f. Performing a promise.
comh-ghèarr, pr. pt. a' comh-ghearradh, v. a. Cut short.
————adh, -aidh, s.m. Curtailing, cutting off, concision. 2 Reckoning, score.
comh-ghiol, s.m. Condition.
comh-ghleachd, -an, s. m. Struggle, combat, conflict. 2 Wrestling. 3 Competition. A' c—, pr. pt. of c— -ghleachd.
comh-ghleachd, pr. pt. a' comh-ghleachd. v.n. Struggle. 2 Wrestle together. 3 Conflict. 4 Compete.
†comh-ghleic, see comh-ghleachd.
†comh-ghleus, v.a. Compose, adjust.
comh-ghleusaiche, -an, s.m. Composer.
comh-ghlòir, -e, s.f. Equal glory. 2 Conference. 3 Consonance.
————each, -eiche, a. Consonant.
comh-ghlòrach, see c— -ghlòireach.
comh-ghlòrmhor, -oire, a. Equal in glory.
comh-ghluasachd, s.f. see c— -ghluasad.
comh-ghluasad, -aid, s.m. Simultaneous movement. 2 Commotion. 3 Fermentation.
————ach, -aiche, a. Fermentative.
comhghnath,** s. m. Assistance. A ghaoil, comh-ghnàths, -àis, s.m. Even temper.
comh-ghnàthsach, -aiche, a. Genteel.
dean mo ch., *my love, assist me.* [*generally* còmhnadh.]
†comh-ghnè, s. f. Historical knowledge. 2 Genealogy of contemporaries. 3 Homogeneousness, like or similar nature.
comh-ghnèitheach, -eiche, a. Homogeneous, congenial.
comh-ghnèithealachd, s. f. ind. Homogeneousness.
comh-ghnèitheil, -e, see comh-ghnèitheach.
comh-ghnìomhar, s.m. Adverb, in *gram.*
comh-ghnothach,‡‡ -aich, -aichean, s. m. Negotiation.
†————adh, -aidh, s.m. Conversation.
comh-ghràdhaiche, -an, s.m. Rival in love.
comh-ghramach, -aiche, a. Adhesive.
————adh, -aidh, s.m. Adhesion, act of adhering. A' c—, pr. pt. of c— -ghramaich.
comh-ghramaich, pr. pt. a' c— -ghramachadh, v. n. Adhere, cling to, fasten to, cohere, grasp mutually.
comh-ghreamach, -aiche, a. see c— ghramach.
————adh, -aidh, see comh-ghramachadh.
comh-ghreamaich, } see comh-ghramaich
comh-ghreimich, }
comh-ghrianach,‡‡ -aiche, a. Rising or setting with the sun.
comh-ghuil, pr. pt. a' c— -ghul, v.n. Weep together, condole.
†comh-ghuin, -e, s.f. Compunction.
comh-ghul, -uil, s.m. Condolence, weeping with one another.
comh-ghuth, -a, s.m. Consonant.
————ach, -aiche, a. Consonant, sounding with.
comh-iadh,‡‡ pr. pt. a' comh-iadhadh, v. a Close round, environ.
comh-iadhadh, -aidh, -aidhean, s.m. Conspiracy. 2 Enclosing, encircling, environing. A' c—, pr.pt. of comh-iadh.
comh-iasad, ‡‡ -aid, s.m. Mutation.
comh-iath, see comh-iadh.
comh-iathach,‡‡ -aiche, a. Conspirant.
comh-imeachd, s.f.ind. Marching, walking or going together.
comh-imeachdach,** a. Attendant.
comh-imrich, -e, -ean, s.f. Commigration.
————, pr. pt. a' comh-imrich, v.n. Commigrate.
comh-inbheach, a. Co-ordinate.
————d, s.f. Co-ordination.
comh-iomair, pr. pt. a' c— -iomradh, v.n. Row together.
comh-iomlaid, -e, -ean, s.f. Commutation.
comh-iomlaideach,‡‡ -eiche, a. Interchangeable, exchangeable. 2 Commutable.
comh-iomlaideachd,‡‡ s.f.Interchangeableness. 2 Commutabitity.
comh-iomlaidich,* v.a. Bandy, exchange.
comh-iomlan, -aine, a. Perfect, complete.
comh-iomlanachd, s.f.ind. Completeness, perfection.
comh-iomradh,(WC) s.m. Rowing competition. Bha e a' c., *he was in a rowing competition.* A' c—, pr. pt. of c— -iomair.
comh-ionann, a. Alike, co-equal, same.
comh-ionannachd, s.f. } Equality. 2**Similarity.
comh-ionnas, -ais, s.m. }
comh-ionannas, -ais, see comh-ionnas.
comh-ith, v.n. Eat with, partake of food. see comaidh.
————eadh, -eidh, s. m. Eating together. Taigh comh-itheidh, *an eating house.*
comh-itheannaich, } see comh-itheadh.
comh-ithinnich, }
comh-ith-thaigh,** s.m. Eating house.
còmhla, -aidh, pl. -aidh & -chan [& -ichean], s.m. Door-frame, door-leaf, gate. 2(DC)One half of a door—*Uist.* 3(DC) Outer door of a house. 4 Barrier, obstacle. 5 Guards. 6 Horn. 7**Sluice. 8**Valve. 9* Shutter. A dh'fhosgladh nan c., *to open the two-leaved gates;* còmhlaichean de 'n òr bhuidhe, *doors of yellow gold.*
còmhla, adv. (comh+làmh) Together, in company. 2 At one time. Thigibh c., *come together;* falbh c. riumsa, *come along with me;* dh' ith e na trì tràithean mar ch., *he ate the three meals at one whack.*
comh-labhair, v.a. Speak together, converse, confer.
————t, s.f. Speaking together. 2 Dialogue. 3 Conference. 4(AH) Debate, disputation.
còmhla-bhigein,(DC) s.m. Trap set to capture small birds, consisting of a riddle resting on the ground and with one end held up by a stick; seed is placed under the riddle and the stick snatched away by a string attached to it as soon as the birds begin to eat the seed—*Uist.*
comh-labhradh, -aidh, s.m. Dialogue, conversation, speaking together.
còmhlach, s.f. see connlach. 2 (AF) Sucking-pig.
————daidh, see còmhlach.
†còmhlachadh, -aidh, s.m. see còmhdhalach.

adh. 2 Meeting. 3 Opposing, intercepting.
còmhlachdaich, *s.f. & pr.pt.* of còmhlaich.
còmhlachdaidh,(AF) *s.f.* Sucking-pig.
†**còmhlachduichte**, *a.* Reared by the same nurse.
còmhlaich, *pr.pt.* a' còmhlachadh & còmhlachdaich, *v. a.* Meet, intercept, oppose, stop the progress of an object.
còmhladh, -aidh, -aidhean, *s.m.* see còmhla, *s.*
còmhladh, *adv.* see còmhla, *adv.*
còmhla-lùthaidh, *s.f.* Folding-door.
còmhla-lùthainn, see còmhla-lùthaidh.
còmhlamh, *prov.* for còmhla.
comh-làmhaiche, -an, *s.m.* Helpmate,colleague, coadjutor.
còmhlan, -ain, -an, *s.m.* see còmhlann.
còmhlann, -a, -an, *s.f.* Duel, combat, fray. 2 Hero. 3 Companion, colleague. 4 Companion in arms. 5 Assistant. 6 Procession. 7 Troop, band, complement of men. 8‡‡Hill. 9‡‡Couple. C. grinn, *a nice company;* c. mór, *a large assembly.*
còmhlannach, -aich, *s.m.* Duellist. 2 Combatant.
———ach, -aiche, *a.* Quarrelsome, turbulent.
———achd, *s. f. ind.* Duelling, fighting with swords or spears.
comh-lannair, *pl.* -ean, *s.m.* Swordsman, swordplayer. 2**Prize-fighter.
———eachd, *s.f.* Swordsmanship. 2 Sword or spear exercise. 3**Fighting with spears.
comh-laoch, -aoich, *s.m.* Fellow-warrior, companion in arms.
comh-lasach,** *a.* Conflagrant.
comh-lasadh, -aidh, -aidhean, *s.m.* Lighting together, illumination, conflagration.
comh-lasaich, *v.a.* Light together.
còmhlath, see còmhla, *adv.*
comh-leabach, -aich, *s.m.* Bed-fellow. 2 Concubine.
comh-leabachas, -ais, *s.m.* Concubinage.
comh-leagadh, -aidh, *s.m.* Parallelism, laying together in the same direction.
comh-leagh, *v.a.* Melt together, amalgamate, colliquefy.
comh-leaghadh, -aidh, *s.m.* Amalgamation, act of melting together, colliquefication. A' c—, *pr.pt.* of comh-leagh.
comh-leaghan, -ain, *s. m.* Amalgam, the mixture of metals produced by amalgamation.
comh-leagta, *a.* Parallel.
comh-lean, *v.n.* Cohere.
———ailt, -e, *s.f.* Sticking together, coherence.
———ailteach, -eiche, *a.* Consecutive, consequent.
———mhuinn, -e, *s.f.* Consequence.
———mhuinneach, *a.* Continuous.
comh-leapach, -aich, *s.m.* see c— -leabach.
comh-leapachas, -ais, see comh-leabachas.
comh-leasachadh, -aidh, *s.m.* Requital, compensation. A' c—, *pr. pt.* of c— leasaich.
comh-leasaich, *pr.pt.* a' comh-leasachadh, *v.a.* Make up, compensate. 2 Restore, requite.
comh-leasaichte, *past part.* of comh-leasaich. Made up, compensated.
comh-leig, (DC) *pr. pt.* a' comh-leigeadh, *v.n.* Strive together—*Barra.*
†**comh-lin**, *s. f.* Assembly.
†**comh-linn**, see comh-lin.
comh-linnteach,** *a.* Coeval.
comh-lìon, -lìne, -lìnean, *s.m.* Complement. 2 Multitude.
———, *v.a.* Fill up, fulfil, accomplish, perform, complete. 2 Absolve,

comh-lìonachd, see comh-lìontachd.
———adh, -aidh, *s.m.* Fulfilling, accomplishment, fulfilment. A' c—, *pr.pt.* of comhlìon.
comh-lìonta, *a. & past pt.* of comh-lìon. Perfect, complete, mature. 2 Perfected, completed. 3 Fulfilled, accomplished. 4 Absolute. 5** Upright.
comh-lìontach,‡‡ -aiche, *a.* Adscititious.
comh-lìontachd, *s.f.ind.* Completeness, completion, perfection, fulfilment, accomplishment, consummation.
comh loma luath, (*for* co loma luath) As soon as.
comh-lorg, -luirg, *s.f.* Consequence, result. 2 Effort. An c. sin, *in consequence of that.*
comh-losgach, see comh-lasach.
comh-losgadh, -aidh, *s.m.* Conflagration.
comh-luadar, -air, *s.m.* Company, party. 2 Communication, conversation, fellowship. Truaillidh droch ch., *evil communication corrupts.* [* gives -air as *nom. case.*]
†**comhluadar**, *v.n.* Converse. 2 Accompany.
comh-luadrach, -aiche, *a.* Conversable, talkative.
comhluath, *adv.* Whenever, at the same time. 2 Abreast of. 3**Together.
comhluath agus, *adv. for* cho luath agus.
comh-luathghair, -e, -ean, *s.f.* Joint congratulation, repeated shouts of joy.
comh-luchd, *s.pl.* Partners, associates, allies. C. oibre, *fellow-labourers.*
comh-luibeach,** *a.* Equi-angular.
comh-luidhe, *s.m.* Lying together. 2 Alliance, partnership, association.
———, *v.n.* Co-habit. 2 Lie together.
comh-meas, -a, *s.m.* Comparison, consideration.
comh-meas, *a. & v.a.* see coimeas.
comh-measach, *a.* see coimeas.
comh-measda, *a & past pt.* see coimeasgta.
comh-measg, see coimeasg.
comh-mhacnus, -uis, *s. m.* Sporting together, dallying.
comh-mhalairt, *s. f.* Counterchange, barter. Dean c., *make an exchange.*
———each,** *a.* Commutable.
———eachd,** *s.f.* Commutability.
———ich,‡‡ *v.n.* Interchange.
comh-mharbh, *v.a.* Massacre, kill together.
comh-mharbhadh, -aidh, *s.m.* Massacre, mutual killing, internecion. 2 Battle. A' c—, *pr. pt.* of comh-mharbh.
comh-mharbhtach,‡‡ *a.* Internecine.
comh-mharcach, -aich, -aichean, *s.m.* Fellow-rider.
———d, *s.f.ind.* Riding in company.
comh-mharcaiche, -an, *s.m.* Fellow-rider.
comh-mhartach,‡‡ -aiche, *a.* Latrant.
comh-mheas, see coimheas.
comh-mheasail,** *a.* Equally respectable, of equal worth.
comh-mheasair,** *s.m.* Collator.
comh-mheasda, *a.* Of equal worth, equivalent. 2**Comparable.
comh-mheasg, *v.a.* see coimeasg.
———adh, -aidh, *s.m. & pr.pt.* of comhmheasg, see coimeasgadh.
comh-mheasgta, *past pt.* of comh-mheasg, see coimeasgta.
comh-mheigheachail,‡‡ -e, *a.* Libratory.
comh-mhileadh, -idh, -idhean, *s.m.* Fellow-soldier.
comh-mhilleadh,‡‡ -idh, *s.m.* Internecion.
comh-mhillteach,‡‡ -eiche, *a.* Internecine.
comh-mhionnachadh,** -aidh, *s.m.* Conspiring, conspiracy.

comh-mhionnaich, *pr.pt.* a' comh-mhionnachadh, *v.n.* Conspire.
comh-mhire, *s.f.* Mutual flirtation.
comh-mhisgeachd, *s.f.ind.* Composition.
comh-mhisgich,‡‡ *v. a.* Immix.
comh-mhol, *v.a.* Praise together.
comh-mhothachadh, -aidh, *s. m.* Sympathy, commiseration, compassion, sympathizing, fellow-feeling.
comh-mhothachail, -e, *a.* Sympathetic, compassionate.
comh-mhothaich, *v.a.* Sympathize.
comh-mhothuich, see c— -mhothaich.
comh-mhùiteach, *a.* Commutable.
comh-mhùthadh, -aidh, *s.m.* Commutation.
comh-mhuthaich, see c— -mhothaich.
comh-mortas, -ais, *s.m.* see comh-ortas.
còmhnachail,* *a.* Conducible.
còmhnadail,* see còmhradh.
còmhnadalach, *a.* see còmhraiteach. Duine còir c., *a decent conversable man.*
còmhnadh, -aidh, -aidhean, *s.m.* Aid, assistance, help, relief.
còmhnaich, *v.a.* Favour.
†còmhnaidh, -e, *s.f.* Leisure.
còmhnaigh, see còmhnuidh.
comh-naisg, *v.a.* Knit together, tie, connect.
———eadh, *s.m.* Knitting together. A' c—, *pr.pt.* of comh-naisg.
còmhnard, -airde, *a.* Level, plain, even, equal, smooth. Rathad c., *a level road;* siùil c., *equal sails.*
———, -aird, -an, *s. m.* Plain. 2 Level ground, field.
———achd, *s.f.ind.* Equality.
———aich,‡‡ *v.a.* Ballast a ship.
———aiche, -an, *s.m.* Roller, leveller.
comh-nasgadh, see comh-naisgeadh.
comh-neart, -eirt, -an, *s.m.* Compound force.
comh-neartachadh, -aidh, *s. m.* Confirmation, confirming. 2 Strengthening, reinforcing, increase of force. A' c—, *pr. pt.* of comh-neartaich.
comh-neartachail, *a.* Corroborant.
comh-neartaich, *pr. pt.* a' comh-neartachadh, *v.a.* Strengthen. 2 Confirm. 3 Reinforce.
comh-neartaichte, *past part.* of comh-neartaich. Confirmed. 2 Strengthened.
comh-neartmhor, -oire, *a.* Strong, firm.
còmhnuich, *pr. pt.* a' còmhnuidh, *v.n.* Dwell, inhabit, reside, abide, continue, stand still.
còmhnuiche, -an, *s. m.* Dweller, inhabitant, resident.
còmhnuidh, -e, -ean, *s.f.* Dwelling, habitation, house, abode. An c., *habitually, always, continually.* A' c—, *pr. pt.* of còmhnuich.
còmhnuidheach, -eiche, *a.* Steadfast, firm, permanent.
†còmhnuigh, *v.n.* see còmhnuich.
comh-obair, -oibre, -oibrichean, *s.f.* Joint work, the same employment.
comh-ogha, *s.f. & m.* First cousin.
comh-òglach, -aich, *s.m.* Fellow-servant(male.)
comh-oibreach, -eiche, *a.* see c— -oibreachail.
———adh, -aidh, *s. m.* Working together, co-operation. A' c—, *pr.pt.* of comh-oibrich.
———ail, -e, *a.* Co-operative, working together. 2 Co-efficient.
comh-oibrich, *pr.pt.* a' comh-oibreachadh, *v.n.* Co-operate, work together, assist.
———e, -an, *s. m.* Fellow-labourer. 2 Coadjutor. 3 Co-operator, accomplice.
comh-oighre, -achan, *s.m.* Co-heir, co-parcener, joint partner.
comh-oighreachas, -ais, *s.m.* } Co-heirship, co-
comh-oighreachd, *s.f.ind.* } parceny.
comh-oisinneach, *a.* see comh-oisneach.
comh-oisneach, *a.* Equi-angular.
comh-òl, -òil, *s.f.* Compotation.
comh-òlair, -ean, *s.m.* Pot-companion, fellow-tippler.
comh-olc,(WC) *s.m.* Anger. Chuir o c. orm, *he made me angry, offended me—Poolewe.*
comh-olcas, -ais, *s.m.* Malice, malignity,spleen.
comh-ortas, -ais, *s.m.* Comparison, emulation.
co'mhothachadh, see comh-mhothachadh.
comh-phàirt, *s.f.* Partnership, share, participation, community. 2‡‡League. Luchd-c., *partakers.*
comh-phàirteach, -eiche, *a.* Participating, sharing. 2**Portionable, divisible. 3**Communicable, willing to share or communicate.
comh-phàirteachadh, -aidh, *s. m.* Communicating, sharing, dividing, partaking.
comh-phàirteachail,‡‡ -e. *a.* Attributive.
comh-phàirtear, -an, *s.m.* Accessory. 2 Partner.
comh-phàirtich, *pr.pt.* a' comh-phàirteachadh, *v.a. & n.* Communicate, share, divide, partake.
comh-phàirtiche, see comh-phàirtear.
†comh-phais, see comh-fhulang.
comh-phàrtuchadh, -aidh, see c— -phàirteachadh.
comh-phàrtuich, see comh-phàirtich.
comh-phòitear, -an, *s.m.* Drinking companion.
———achd, *s. f. ind.* Drinking together.
comh-phrìosanach, -aich,*s.m.* Fellow-prisoner.
†comhra, *s.m.* Companion. 2 Coffin.
còmhra, see còmhradh.
còmhrachadh, -aidh, see comharrachadh.
còmhradh, -aidh, -aidhean, *s.m.* Conversation, dialogue. 2**Speech, language.
còmhrag, -aig, -an, *s.f.* Combat, fight, battle, struggle, strife. Dealan na c., *the lightning of battle* ; C. a' Choin Duibh, *the Black Dog's Fight*—a well-known folk-tale.
còmhragach, *a.* Warlike. Sluagh garg c., *a fierce warlike people.*
còmhragair, -ean, *s.m.* Fighting man, warrior. 2**Encounterer.
còmhrag, ‡‡ *v.a.* see còmhraig.
comhraidhteach, see comhraiteach.
còmhraich, see comharraich.
còmhraig, *s.* see còmhrag.
còmhraig, *v.n.* Fight, war, combat. 2* Fight, as black cattle.
còmhraig, *gen.sing.* of còmhrag.
còmhraiteach, -eiche,*a.* Conversable, talkative.
còmhraitiche, -an, *s.m.* Talkative person.
còmhrannaich,** *s.* Community.
———,** *a.* Conjoint.
comh-reatain,** *s. m.* Coition.
comh-réidh, -e, *a.* *for* co réidh, *or* cho réidh.
†comh-réimnich, *v.a.* Assemble.
comh-réir, -e, *s. f.* Construction. 2 Syntax.
comh-réite, *s.f.* Agreement, reconciliation.
comh-réith ri, *adv.* As plain as.
comh-reult, -a, -an, *s.f.* Constellation.
comh-reusan,** *s. m.* Deduction.
comh-riachdanas, -ais, *s. m.* Great want, distress.
†comh-riachduin, *s.f.* Engendering.
comh-rian, *s.m.* System.
comh-riarachadh, -aidh, *s. m.* Sharing among all, equal division or distribution. A' c—, *pr. pt.* of comh-riaraich.
comh-riaraich, *pr. pt.* a' comh-riarachadh, *v.a.* Share or divide equally among all.
comh-rialtain,** *s.* Copulation.
†comh-rith, see comh-ruith. 2‡‡Concur.
†comh-ròc, *v.n.* Belch, retch. 2 Meet.

comh-roghainn, *s.f.* Election, choice. 2**General election. 3 Unanimous election.
comh-roghnaich, *v.n.* Elect unanimously.
————te, *a.* & *past pt.* of comh-roghnaich. Elected unanimously.
comh-roighnich, see comh-roghnaich.
comh-roinn, -e, -ean, *s.f.* Share, proportion, dividing, contribution. 2**Participation, division, partnership. C. de 'n toradh, *a share of the fruits.*
comh-roinn, *v. n.* Share, divide, distribute. 2**Participate.
————teach,‡‡ -eiche, *a.* Participant.
comh-rol, *v.a.* Roll together.
————adh, -aidh, *s.m.* Rolling together. A' c—, *pr. pt.* of comh-rol.
comh-ruagach, -aiche, *a.* Pursuing together.
comh-rùisgte, *a.* Equally bare or naked.
comh-ruith, -e, *s. f.* Race, running together. Ri c. timchioll nan raon, *running together around the fields.*
————, *v. a.* Run together, run at the same time. 2 Concur. 3‡‡Converge.
comh-rùn, -ùin, *s.m.* Conspiracy, joint design.
————achadh, -aidh, *s.m.* Conspiring, act of conspiracy or joint designing. 2**Communication. A' c—, *pr.pt.* of comh-rùnaich.
comh-rùnaich, *pr.pt.* a' comh-rùnachadh, *v. n.* Conspire. 2 Communicate designs. 3**Concur. Ch. mi leis, *I conspired with him.*
comhsachadh, see connsachadh.
comhsaich, see connsaich.
comh-samhuil, -e, *a.* Like, resembling.
†comhsanach, *a.* Perpetual, everlasting.
comh-sgoilear, -eir, -an, *s.m.* School-fellow.
comh-sgrìobh, *v. n.* Correspond.
comh-sgrìobhadh, *s.m.* Composition.
comh-sgrios,‡‡ -a, *s. m.* Internecion.
comh-sgriosail,‡‡ -e, *a.* Internecine.
comh-shaighdear, -eir, -an, *s.m.* Fellow-soldier. Mo chomh-shaighdearan ! *my fellow-soldiers !*
comh-shamhlach, *a.* Comparative.
comh-shamhlachadh, -aidh, *s. m.* Comparing, comparison.
comh-shamhlaich, *v.a.* Compare together.
————te, *a.* & *past.pt.* of comh-shamhlaich. Compared.
comh-sheanachas, *s. m.* Conversation.
comh-shearmonaiche, -an, *s. m.* Fellow-preacher.
comh-sheasamh, -aimh, *s. m.* Consistency, equipoise, equilibrium. 2(AH) Connection, relation. Anns a' ch. seo, *in this connection.*
comh-sheasmhach, -aiche, *a.* Constant, steady, consistent.
comh-sheasmhachd, *s.f.ind.* Constancy, consistency. 2 Contradiction.
comh-shéid, *v.a.* Blow together, conflate.
————eadh, -idh, *s.m.* Conflation, act of blowing together. A' c—, *pr.pt.* of c— -shéid.
comh-sheinn,†† *v.a.* Intonate.
comh-sheinn,** *s. f.* Chorus.
comh-sheirbhis, -ean, *s.f.* Joint service.
————each, -ich, *s.m.* Fellow-servant.
————eachd,** *s.f.* Fellow-service.
comh-sheirm, -e, -ean, *s.f.* Concert. 2 Harmony. 3** Accordance, accord. 4††Choir. Cànaibh comh-sheirm ciùil, *sing in concert.*
comh-sheirmeach, -eiche, *a.* Harmonious, in concert.
comh-sheirmich,‡‡ *v.n.* Sound in harmony.
comh-sheise,** *s. m.* & *f.* Antagonist, opponent. 2 (DC) Match.
comh-sheòd, -sheòid, *s.m.* Fellow-champion. 2 **Brother hero. Innisidh e 'n sgeul d' a chomh-sheòid, *he will tell the tale to his brother-heroes.*

comh-sheòladh, -aidh, -aidhean, *s. m.* Direction. 2 Conveyance. 3 Sailing in company. 4 Boat or ship race.
comh-shèomraiche, -an, *s. m.* Fellow-lodger, room-companion, comrade, chum.
comh-shìn, *v. a.* Stretch in one direction, lay parallel. 2 (DU) *v.n.* Coincide.
comh-shìneadh, *s.m.* Extending, lengthening in the same direction. A' c—, *pr. pt.* of comh-shìn.
comh-shìnte, *a.* & *past part* of comh-shìn. Extended together in one direction, parallel. 2 (DU) Coinciding.
comh-shìnteachan, -ain, *s. m.* Parallelogram.
comh-shìon, *s.f.* Calm weather.
comh-shìorruidh, *a.* Co-eternal.
comh-shìorruidheachd, *s. f.* Co-eternity.
comh-shlìogte, (DC) *a.* Drawn out or combed in the same direction, *hence* 2 Agreeing in nature.
comh-shlisneach, *a.* Equilateral.
comh-shnaim, -e, *s.f.* Knitting together, alliance, union.
comh-shnàmh,‡‡ -a, *s.m.* Swimming together.
comh-shnìomh, *s.m.* Convolution.
comh-shnìomh, *v. n.* Convolve.
comh-shocair, -e, *a.* Completely at ease.
comh-shocrachadh, -aidh, *s. m.* Settling, arranging, fixing. A' c—, *pr.pt.* of comh-shocraich.
comh-shocraich, *pr. pt.* a' comh-shocrachadh, *v.a.* Settle, arrange, fix.
comh-shoillse, -shoillsean, see comh-sholus.
comh-sholus, -uis, -an, *s.m.* Constellation.
†comh-shreabh, *s.m.* Confluence of streams, tides or currents.
comh-shreip, -e, *s. f.* Rivalry.
comh-shruth, *v. n.* Stream or flow together, converge.
————, -an, *s.m.* Confluence of streams.
————adh, -aidh, *s.m.* Junction or union of two or more streams. 2 Circumstance of flowing together. A' c—, *pr. pt.* of comh-shruth.
comh-shuain, *v.n.* Sleep together.
comh-shuain, *s.m.* Sleeping together. A' c—, *pr.pt.* of comh-shuain.
comh-shùgradh, -aidh, *s.m.* Playing, sporting together. 2**Play, pastime.
comh-shùgraiche, -an, *s.m.* Play-fellow.
comh-shuidhe, *s.f.ind.* Sitting together, session.
————achadh, -aidh, *s.m.* Constitution, system, order.
comh-shuidhich, *pr.pt.* a' comh-shuidheachadh, *v.a.* Settle, constitute, methodize, compose.
————te, *past pt.* of c— -shuidhich, Settled, organized, composed, constituted.
comh-shuirbhe, -an, see comh-shuirdhe.
comh-shuirbhiche, -an, see comh-shuirdhiche.
comh-shuirdhe, -an, *s.f.* Competition in courtship, rivalry in love.
comh-shuirdhiche, -an, *s.m.* Rival in courtship.
comh-shuirich, see comh-shuirdhe.
comh-shusbainteach, *a.* Consubstantial.
————adh, -aidh, *s.m.* Consubstantiation, substantial identity.
comh-shuthainn, *a.* Co-eternal.
†comh-smug, *v.n.* Expectorate, vomit.
comh-spàirn, *v.n.* Wrestle with.
————, *s. f.* Emulation, rivalry. 2 Wrestle. 3 Mutual struggle.
————each, *a.* Emulous. 2 Wrestling. 3 Struggling.
————eachd, *s. f. ind.* Emulousness. 2 Frequent or continued competition. 3 Continued wrestling.

comhspaid, see connspoid.
————each, see connspoideach.
comhstach,* *a.* Obliging, accommodating. 2 Useful, convenient.
————,* *s.f.* Concubine. 2 Whore.
còmhstadh, -aidh, *s. m.* Accommodation, obligation. 2 Loan. 3 Favour.
————ach, -aiche, *a.* Obliging, accommodating. 2 Friendly.
comh-stàth, see comh-stadh.
comh-streup, -a, *s.f.* see comh-shreip.
comh-strì, -the, -thean, *s. f.* Strife, battle. 2 Broil, quarrel. 3 Contest, struggle, rivalry.
comh-strìgh, -e, -ean, *s.f.* see comh-strì.
comh-strìth, -e, -ean, see comh-strì.
————each, -eiche, *a.* Contentious, emulous.
————eachd, *s.f.ind.* Pugnacity.
comh-stuthachadh, -aidh, *s. m.* Consubstantiation.
comh-stuthachd, *s.f.ind.* Consubstantiality.
comh-stuthaich,** *v.n.* Consubstantiate.
comh-stuthail, *a.* Consubstantial.
comh-thabhartas,‡‡-ais, -an, *s.m.* Contribution.
comh-thach, -aich, *s.m.* see comh-thathach.
comh-thagairt, -e, *s.f.* see comh-thagradh.
comh-thagradh, -aidh, *s.m.* Joint pleading.
comh-thaigheas, *s.m.* Co-habitation, living together.
————ach, *a.* Co-habiting.
comh-thaingeachadh, -aidh, *s.m.* Congratulation.
comh-thaingich, *v.a.* Congratulate.
comh-thàirng, *v.a.* Nail together.
————te, *a.* & *past pt.* of comh-thàirng. Nailed together.
comh-thairnte, see comh-thàirngte.
comh-thaithte, *past part.* of comh-thàth. Joined. 2 Articulated. 3 Soldered.
comh-thalach, *for* còmhdhalach, *gen. sing.* of còmhdhail, (meeting.) Far am bi na laoich cumail comh-thalach (còmhdhalach), *where the heroes (huntsmen) will be holding a meet.* —*Beinn Doran.*
comhtharrachadh,-aidh, *s.m.* & *pr.pt.* see comharrachadh.
comhtharradh, -aidh, -aidhean, *s.m.* see comharradh.
comhtharraich, *v.a.* see comharraich.
comhtharraichte, see comharraichte.
comh-tharruing, *v.a.* Contract. 2 Draw together, pull at the same time.
————each, -eiche, *a.* Contractive. 2 Having the power of contraction.
————te, *a.* & *past pt.* of comh-tharruing. Contracted, drawn together. 2 Drawn at the same time.
comh-thàth, -a, -an, *s.m.* Seam, joint. 2 Enclosure.
————, *v.a.* see comh-thàthaich.
————ach, -aich, *s.m.* Companion, chum.
————aich, *v. a.* Join. 2 Articulate. 3 Solder, put together.
————aich, -ean, *s.f.* Mutual acquaintance or familiarity. 2 Mutual visiting.
comh-thàthadh, -aidh, *s.m.* Articulation. 2** Cementing. 3 Soldering. 4 Joining together. 5**Joint. 6**Syntax.
comh-thathte, *past part.* of comh-thath. Joined. 2 Articulated. 5 Soldered.
comh-theach, *s.m.* House where several families dwell.
comh-theachaiche, -an, *s. m.* Inhabitant of the same house with another. 2 Inmate.
comh-theachas, -ais, *s.m.* Cohabitation, living together.
comh-theagasg, *s. m.* Context.
comh-theànal, -ail, -an see comh-thional.
†comh-thìtheach, -ich, see coimneach.
comh-thigheas, see comh-thaigheas.
comh-thigheasach, see comh-thaigheasach.
comh-thimchioll, -an, *s.m.* Circuit. 2 Act of moving round anything.
comh-thionail, *pr. pt.* a' comh-thional, *v.a.* & *n.* Assemble, gather together, congregate. 2 Convoke.
comh-thional, -ail, -an, *s. m.* Assembly, congregation, gathering. 2(DM) Variety of pipe-music for gathering the clans to battle. A' c—, *pr. pt.* of comh-thionail.
comh-thìreach, -rich, *s.m.* Countryman, compatriot.
comh-thog, *v.a.* Raise. 2 Construct together. 3 Rear together, educate, bring up together. Ch. e sinn, *he brought us up together.*
————ail, -ean, *s.m.* Raising. 2 Constructing. 3 Rearing together, bringing up, or educating together.
†comh-thoilich, *v. a.* Please. 2 Mutually agree to.
comh-thoimhseach, -eiche, *a.* Commeasureable, reducible to a general measure, commensurable.
————d, *s.f.ind.* Commeasurability, commeasurableness, commensurability.
comh-thoinn,‡‡ *v.n.* Convolve.
comh-thoisgte, *adv.* As early as.
comh-thorrachd, *s.f.* Commerce.
comh-thras, *s.m.* Sweet flavour. 2** Sweet smell.
comh-throm, *a.* Equally heavy, equipoised. 2** Even, equal.
————, -uim,-uimichean,*s.m.* see cothrom.
————ach, -aiche, see cothromach. 2†† Rich.
————achadh, -aidh, *s.m.* & *pr. pt.* see cothromachadh.
comh-thruacanta, *a.* Compassionate, merciful, tender.
comh-thruacantachd,*s.f.*see comh-thruacantas.
comh-thruacantas, -ais, *s. m.* Compassion, mercy, tenderness, commiseration, pity.
†comh-thruaighe, *s.f.* Compassion, fellow-feeling, sympathy.
comh-thruas, -ais, *s.m.* Compassion, sympathy.
†comh-thrus, *v.a.* & *n.* Collect together, contract. 2**Truss up together.
comh-thuiniche,** *s.m.* Cohabitant.
comh-thulgadh, -aidh, -aidhean, *s.m.* Agitation, defeat.
comh-uchdach, *a.* Having breast to breast.
————, -aich, *s.m.* Co-sine. Tha 'n gath-riaghailt 'san inbhe mheadhonaich eadar a' chomh-uchdach agus an sgrìob-ghearraidh, *the radius is a mean proportional between the co-sine and the secant.*
†comh-uidiche, -an, *s.m.* Attendant.
comh-uileannach,** *a.* Equi-angular.
†comhursa, *s.m.* see coimhearsnach.
co'mhuthaich, see comh-mhothaich.
comith, *s.f.* see comaidh.
comlachdaigh,(AF) *s.f.* Young pig.
†commaithcheas, -eis, *s.f.* Neighbourhood.
†comor, *v.a.* Gather together.
†comoradh, *s.m.* Assembly, meeting.
comortas, -ais, *s.m.* see comh-ortas.
compach, -aich, see companach.
compailt,** *s.f.* Company.
compàirt, -e, -ean, *s.f.* see comh-phàirt.
————each, -eiche, *a.* see comh-phàirteach.
————eachd, *s.f.* see comh-phàirteachd.
————ich, *v.a.* see comh-phàirtich.
————iche, -an, *s.m.* see comh-phàirtiche.
compaiste, -an, *s.m.* see combaiste.

compan,** -ain, *s.m.* see companach.
companach, -aich, *s. m.* Companion, mate, chum, associate. 2 Husband. C. nan amadan, *the companion of fools*; is c. do neach a nàdur, *a man's nature sticks to him.*
companaich,‡‡ *v.n.* Make a partner of.
companas, -ais, *s.m.* Companionship, fellowship, society, intercourse.
companta, *a.* Sociable.
————s, -ais, *s.m.* see companas.
compàrtaich, see comh-phàirtich.
compàrtachadh, -aidh, *s.m. & pr. pt*, see comh-phàirteachadh.
†**compas,** -ais, *s.m.* Compass. 2 Ring. 3 Circle.
†**compraid,** *s.f.* Comparison.
†**compuir,** *s.f.* The body, chest, trunk. 2 Heart.
†**comrac,** *s.m.* Part, share.
†———air, *s.m.* Protector.
comradh, -aidh, *s.m.* Aid, assistance, help.
comraich, -e, -ean, *s.f.* Protection, favour, obligation. 2 Sanctuary, asylum. 3 Condition, stipulation, 4‡‡Reverence, faith. Mo ch. ort, oir is tu Fionn, *I ask your protection, as you are Fionn.*
†**comraigheas,** *s.m.* Form, fashion.
†**comrannach,** *s.m.* Comrade, companion.
†**comuc,** *s.m.* Bodily need.
comunach, -aich, see comanachadh.
————adh, see comanachadh.
comunn, -uinn, *s.m.* Company, society, club. 2 Fellowship, intercourse. 3** Confederacy. 4**Meeting. C. liath nan sean-fhear, *the grey meeting of aged men*; càirdeas no c., *friendship or fellowship;* C. Gàidhlig Inbhirnis, *The Gaelic Society of Inverness;* is coma leam c. an òil, *I dislike the friendship that is formed in liquor.*
comunnach,†† -aiche, *a.* Civil.
————adh, -aidh, *s.m.* Associating. A' c—, *pr. pt.* of comunnaich.
comunnaich, *pr. pt.* a' comunnachadh, *v.n.* Associate. 2 see comanachadh.
comus, -uis, -an, see comas.
———ach, -aiche, *a.* see comasach.
con-, (with) see coimh & comh-.
con,(AF) *s.m.* Squirrel. 2 Wolf.
con, *gen. pl.* of cù. Chum nan con, *to the dogs*; mo chuid ch., *my dogs.*
†**con,** *s.m.* Sense, meaning. 2 Appetite.
†**cona,** *s.f.* The Scots fir.
cona, *s.m.* see canach. 2 Cat's tail grass, see goin-fheur.
con-abhann, *s.m.* (comh-abhainn) Confluence.
conablach, -aich, *s.m.* Mangled carcase. 2 Anything mangled. 3**Carcase.
————adh, -aidh, *s. m.* Mangling, act of mangling, tearing asunder, disfiguring, lacerating. A' c—, *pr. pt.* of conablaich.
————ail,** *a.* Cadaverous.
conablaich, *v.a.* Mangle, lacerate, disfigure.
————te, *past.pt.* Mangled, lacerated.
†**conach,** -aich, *s.m.* Property, affluence. 2 Shift, smock. 3 Murrain in cattle.
conach,§ *s. m.* Flax dodder—*cuscuta epilinum.*
conach, -aiche, *a.* †Rich. 2 Prosperous. 3 Canine.
———ag, -aige, *s.f.* see cnomhagan.
conachair,* *s. m.* Sick person who gets neither worse nor better. 2 see conghair.
conachlon, -oin, *s. m.* Equal, companion. 2 Kind of Gaelic verse.
conachuileag, -eig, *s.f.* Fly. 2 Murrain of flies.

186. Conach.

conadal,†† -ail, *s. m.* Conversation. 2 (AF) Stray sheep. 3 Strangers.
conadh, -aidh, see comhghnath.
†**conadh,** *s.m.* see conbhadh. 2**Prosperity.
†**conadh,** *conj.* So that.
conaghair, *s.f.* see conghair.
cona-ghaothach, *s.m.* Raging gale, tempest.
conagladh, -aidh, *s. m.* Teasing. Is miann leis a' chat a ch., *the cat loves to be teased.*
†**conaidh,** *a.* Enchanted. 2 Soft, gentle. 3 Affable.
conaig,(CR) -ean, *s.f.* Knuckle of the first or root joint of the fingers—*W. of Ross-shire.*
conaigh, for còmhnuidh.
conail,** *s.f.* Plague that once raged in Ireland.
†**conailbhe,** see †conall.
†**conailbheach,**** *a.* Friendly. 2 Upholding.
conair, -e, -ean, *s.f.* Way, course, path. 2 Haven. 3 Crown. 4(AC) Blessing. 5 (AC) Plant. 6 (AC) Circle. 7†† Help. 8††Set of beads. Iomhaigh is c. Moire, *image and rosary of Mary;* bu cham leò gach c. gus ...., *every short cut seemed crooked (round about) to them (in their haste) to....*
†**conairde,** *adv.* As high as.
†**conaire,** *conj.* Therefore.
conaire,§ *s f.* Loosestrife, see lus-na-siothaimh. 2(AF) see conairt.
conairt, *s.f.* Hunting with hounds. 2 Pack of hounds. 3 Rout of wolves. 4* Barking of many dogs. 5 Scolding in a high key.
†**conairt,** *v.n.* Hunt with hounds.
†**conais,** *v.a.* Dispute. 2 Number.
†———leach, *a.* Busy.
conalach, *a.* Brandishing.
conalaich,†† *pr.pt.* a' conalachadh, *v.a.* Brandish, swing.
†**conall,** -aill, *s. m.* Love, friendship. 2 Fruit. 3 Fruitfulness. 4 Ear of corn. 5 (AC) The Guardian Spirit of childhood. 6(AC) The Cupid of the Gael.
conall,(AC) *v.n.* Endow. Brighde bhith 'ga chonall dhomh, *calm Bridget endowing it to me.*
conaltrach, -aiche, *a.* Social, fond of company, conversable. Do chuirm ch., *thy social feast.*
conaltradh, -aidh, *s.m.* Conversation. 2 Company. Cum c., *keep company;* 'na ch., *in his company.*
conan,* -ain, *s.m.* Peevish person. 2§ Crested dog's tail, see goinfheur. 3 Quaking grass—*briza.* C. cumanta, *briza media*; c. beag, *briza minor.*
conanachd,* *s.f.* Venery—*Lochaber.* C. nàdurra—*Argyll.*
conan-coille, (AF) *s.m.* Wood-wren.
conan-conaisg,(AF) *s.m.* Willow wren, see crionag ghiuthais.
conan-crion, (AF) *s.m.* Wren, see dreathann-donn.
conan-mara, (AF) *s.m.* Sea-urchin or hogg. 2 Sea-egg.
†**conaraiths,** *s.m.* Offensive object, nuisance. 2 Expression of contempt or execration. C. ort; *a plague upon thee!* (*lit.* dog's mockery.)

187. Conan (S.)

conartaich,** *v.a.* Bait (with dogs.)
conas, *pr. pt.* a' conas, *v.n.* [followed by *air.*] Tease—*Argyll.* C'arson tha thu a' c. air? *why are you teasing him?* 2 Oppose. 3 Quarrel, fight.
conas, -ais, *s. m.* Quarrel, fight. 2 Dispute, wrangle. 3**War, battle. 4**Carcase. 5 see conasg. 6 Mischief. A' c—, *pr. pt.* of

conas. A' c. ri chéile, *opposing each other*; bheireadh tu c. as do leth-luirg, *you would quarrel with one of your legs.*
conasach,* *a.* Fretful, peevish, short-tempered, apt to take offence. 2 Contentious, striving, quarrelsome. 3 see conasgach.
——achd, *s.f.* Hastiness of temper. 2‡‡Contentiousness.
conasag,(AF) *s.f.* Whinchat, see gocan
conasan, *s.m.* see conasag.
conas-beach, (AF) see coinnspeach.
conasg, -aisg, *s. m.* Furze, whin, gorse—*ulex europœus.* [Badge of the MacLennans.]
——ach, -aiche, *a.* Abounding in furze; of, or pertaining to furze, like furze.
conasgag, see conasag.
conasrach, (AF) -aich, *s. m.* Flea.
†conbach, -aich, *s.f.* Hydrophobia.
conbhach, -aiche, *a.* Furious.
conbhadh, -aidh, *s.m.* Rage, fury. 2 Ravenous appetite. C. acrais, *raging hunger.*
conbhair, -e, -ean, *s.f.* Dog-kennel. 2 The man who looks after the dogs, dog-boy.

188. Conasg.

†con-bhàiscne, -an, *s. f.* Dog berry tree, see coin-bhile.
conbhallach, -aiche, *a.* Having buttresses. 2 Of, or belonging to buttresses. 3 Steady, well-proportioned. 4 Sound, as in health. 5 (WC) Having uniformity and symmetry. Slàinte ch., *sound health.*
——d,‡‡ *s.f.* Firmness.
conbhalladh,** -aidh, *s.m.* Buttress. 2 Battlement.
conbhallas,‡‡ -ais, see conbhallachd. 2** Prop, support, buttress.
conbharsaid,** *s.f.* Conversation. 2 Conduct, demeanour.
conbhliochd,** *s.f.* Battle, conflict.
†conbhuidheann, *s.f.* Guard.
†concharra, *a.* Dog-like.
†conchas, *s.m.* Punishment, torment, torture.
†concoicceartar, *v.* Be it righted.
†cond, *s.m.* Keeping, protection.
†condaghais, *s.f.* Gaelic spelling of *countess.*
condasach, -aiche, *a.* Furious, enraged. Gu c., *furiously.*
——d, *s.f.ind.* Rage, fury, ire.
condrachd, see contrachd.
con-dris, see coin-ròs.
condual, condualadh, } see comh-dualadh.
co-neartaich, see comh-neartaich.
†confa, *s.m.* see confhadh.
confadh, see confhadh.
confhadh, -aidh, *s.m.* Rage, madness, boisterousness, eagerness, fury, ire. 2 Roaring, howling. 3 see onfhadh. C. ro dhian, *impetuous fury.*
——ach, -aiche, *a.* Furious, raging, boisterous, enraged.
confhliochd, see conbhliochd.
confuadhach,** *s.m.* Vulture.
†conga, *s.m.* Contemporary. 2‡‡Instrument. 3**Antlers of a buck.
congailt,(AF) *s.f.* Monster.
†congain, *s.f.* Help, aid.
†congantach, -aich, *s.m.* Assistant.
congart,** -airt, *s.m.* Command.
†congasach, *s.m.* Kinsman.
congbhail, -e, *s.f.* Keeping house. 2 Habitation.
congbhallach,** *a.* Tenacious.
congbhallas, -ais, *s.m.* Stay, help, support.
†conghaidhe, *s.f.* Relationship.
conghail, *s.f.* Gallantry, bravery.
conghair, -e, *s.f.* Uproar, clamour. 2 Confusion, tumult. 3 Shout, outcry, conclamation. 4* Fury. 5**Faction. 6**Acclamation.
——each, *a.* Clamorous, tumultuous, factious.
——eachd, *s.f.ind.* Clamorousness, tumultuousness, factiousness.
conghaireadh,‡‡ -idh, *s.m.* Roaring.
conghart, *s.m.* Rout.
conghlas,(CR) -ais, [*pron.* canalas, *n* long] *s.m.* Bandage or swathe round the jaws and the crown of the head, such as is used to keep the jaw from falling down after death, hence the imprecation, conghlas ort! a chonghlas air!; a' mharbh-phaisg air a' chonghlas.—*West of Ross-shire.*
conguachal,** *a.* Auxiliary.
congnadoir,** *s.m.* Auxiliary.
còngnadh, -aidh, *s. m.* Abetment, aid. see còmhnadh.
——ach, -aiche, *a.* Auxiliary.
congnain,** *v.n.* Abet, side with.
còngnamh, see còngnadh.
congnath, see congnadh.
——ach, see congnadhach.
congraim, *s.f.* Cunning. craft. 2 clothing, apparel.
†congramh, -aimh, *s.m.* Activity, agility.
cònlach, -aich, *s.f.* see connlach.
cònlan, -ain, *s.m.* Assembly. (còmhlan)
†conlann, -ainn,*s.m.* Hero, companion in arms.
conlapach, -aiche, *a.* see connlapach.
conn, cuinn, *s.m.* Reason, sense, meaning. 2 Prudence. 3 The frame, body. 4 Lease-band or water-band, dividing the cuts in a hank of yarn. 5 Thread tying a hundred of yarn for weaving, base-bands. 6 Principle. 7**Pleasantry. 8(AC)Control. Dà-chonn, *heer-band, band for 2 cuts of yarn*; duine gun ch., *a man without principle or sense*; òinid gun ch., *a senseless idiot*; tha 'n cridhe fo d' ch., *their hearts are under thy control*; cuiridh aon bheairt as gu lòm do dhuine 's gun a ch. fo chéill, *one deed may a man undo when his reason ruleth not.*
connadh, -aidh, *s.m.* Fuel. 2 Firewood, wood. Cual chonnaidh, *a faggot of firewood.*
connail, *a.* Pleasant. 2 Intelligent, reasonable, rational.
†connairc, *v.n.* See, behold.
connalach, -aich, *s.f.* Stubble.
connan, -ain, *s.m.* Lust.
——achd,‡‡ *s.f.* see conanachd.
connar, *a.* see connmhor.
connlach, -aich, *s. f.* Straw, hay. fodder. 2 Aliment. Tha c. againn, *we have fodder.*
connlain-glacaireachd,** *s.m.* Press-gang, *for* còmhlan-glacaireachd.
conlann, -lainn, *s.m.* see còmhlann.
conn-lapach, -aiche, *a.* Feeble.
connmhor, *a.* Intelligent, reasonable, rational. 2**Cheerful, pleasant. Gu c., *cheerfully*; is c. fonnmhor thu, *thou art pleasant and sprightly.*
——achd, *s.f.ind.* Intelligence, reasonableness. 2**Cheerfulness, pleasantness.
connrag, *s.f.* Consonant in *gram.*
connsach, see connsachadh.
——adh, -aidh, *s.m.* Disputing, arguing. 2 Quarrelling. 3**Dispute, contention, dissension. A' c—, *pr. pt.* of connsaich.
connsachail, *a.* Controversial, disputatious, quarrelsome.

connsachair, -ean, *s.m.* Disputant, wrangler, quarrelsome person.
connsachd,‡‡ *s.f.* Quarrelsomeness.
connsaich, *v.n.* Dispute, wrangle, quarrel, strive.
connspaid, *s.f.* see connspoid.
————each. see connspoideach.
connspair, *s.m.* Wrangler, contentious person, disputant, reasoner, one fond of argument or disputation.
————eachd, *s.f.* Disputation.
conspàirn, *s.f.* Rivalry, emulation. 2 Mutual struggle.
connspanach, -aiche, *a.* Contentious.
connspeach, -an, *s.f.* Wasp. 2 Hornet.
connspoid, *s. f.* Dispute, strife, controversy, row, wrangling. Le c. 's le h-an-iochd, *with strife and cruelty.*
————, *v.n.* Dispute, argue, wrangle, quarrel.
————each, *a.* Quarrelsome, contentious, litigious, wrangling.
————eachd, *s.f.ind.* Contentiousness.
————ich,‡‡ *v.a.* Contest.
————iche, *s.m.* Wrangler, contentious person.
connspullach, -aiche, see connspunnach.
————d, see connspunnachd.
connspunn, -uinn, *s.m.* Hero.
————ach, -aiche, *a.* Heroic, warlike.
————achd, *s.f.ind.* Heroism, bravery.
conntachan,¶ -ain, *s.m.* Puffin, see fachach.
conn-taod, -aoid, see con-taod.
conntom, -ùim, see con-tom.
conntràigh, see contraigh.
con-nuallaich, -e, *s.f.* Barking of dogs.
connuibhe, *s.m.* see conuibhe.
†connuimh, *v.a.* Keep.
conphocan, -ain, *s.m.* The shellfish "buckie."
†conrach, *s.m.* Coffin-maker.
————, *a.* Of, or pertaining to, a coffin.
†conradh, -aidh, -ean, *s.m.* see cùnnradh.
†conradoir, -e, -ean, *s.m.* Bearer at a funeral.
cònsachadh, see connsachadh.
cònsachail, see connsachail.
cònsaich, see connsaich.
cònsbeach, -a, -an. *s.f.* see connspeach.
con-shàthadh, -aidh, *s.m.* Canine appetite.
cònsmann, -ainn, see connspunn.
cònsmunn, -uinn, see connspunn.
————ach, -aiche, see connspunnach.
cònspair, see connspair.
————eachd, *s.f.* see connspaireachd.
cònspoid,‡‡ see connspoid.
————each, -eiche, see connspoideach.
————iche, -ean, see connspoidiche.
conspull, -uill, *s.m.* see connspunn.
————ach, *a.* see connspunnach.
conspunn, see connspunn.
constabal, -ail, *s.m.* Gaelic spelling of *constable*; Township-bailiff.
constaballach,** -aich, see constabal.
————, -aiche, *a.* Of, or pertaining to, a constable.
constaileach, -eiche, *a.* Stiff, opinionative.
†constal, -ail, *s.m.* Advice, counsel.
†contabhairt, *s.f.* Chance, peril, hazard, venture. (cunnart) Gun ch., *doubtless.*
†————each, see cunnartach.
contagair, *pr. pt.* a' contagairt, *v.a.* Affirm, allege.
contagairt, -e, *s.f.* Affirmation, allegation, alleging, affirming. A' c—, *pr. pt.* of contagair.
con-taod, -aoid, *s.m.* Dog-thong or -string.
†contar, -air, *s.m.* Doubt.
contarach,** *a.* Gaelic form of *contrary.*
†contath, *s.f.* County.
con-tom, -tuim, *s.m.* Dog-hillock.

contrachd, *s.f.ind.* Mischief, mishap. 2**Imprecation, curse. C. ort ! *a form of execration.*
contrachd, *a.* Evil, wicked, mischievous. Is e miann an duine lochdaich càch uile a bhi c., *the wicked man wishes all to be on a level with himself.*
contraigh, *s.f.* Neap-tide.
con-tràigheachan,(AF)*s.m.* Coulterneb, puffin, see fachach. 2 Eider-duck, see lach Lochlannach.
contraill,** *s.f.* Opposition.
†————eachd,** *s.f.* Contrariety.
contran, -ain, *s.m.* Wild angelica.
contruagh, *a.* Lean, poor, slender, emaciated.
contuinneach,** *a.* Fiery.
conuibhe, -ean, *s.m.* Hornet. Cuiridh mi conuibhean, *I will send hornets.*
conuich, -ean, see conuibhe.
cònuidh, -ean, see còmhnuidh.
conus, -uis, *s.m.* Crossness, bad-temper.
————ach, -aiche, *a.* Bad-tempered.
————an, -ain, -an, *s.m.* Bad-tempered person.
conusg, -uisg, see conasg.
————ach, *a.* see conasgach.
co'oibrich, *v.n.* see comh-oibrich.
————e, -an, see comh-oibriche.
co'oighre, -achan, see comh-oighre.
————achd, see comh-oighreachd.
co-oisinneach, see comh-oisneach.
co-olcas, see comh-olcas.
cop, *v.n.* Foam, froth.
cop, -oip, (cuip) *s.m.* Foam, froth, spume. 2** Boss of a shield. A chraos fo chop, *his mouth foaming.*
cop,* *s.m.* see copan.
cop,* *v.a.* Capsize. 2††Pour out. 3††Foam.
copach, -aiche, *a.* Foamy. 2 Hollow. 3 Bossy. 4**Campanulated. 5**Bellied. 6**Like a cup.
copadh,* *s.m.* Capsizing. A' c—, *pr. pt.* of cop.
copadh, -aidh, *s.m.* Foaming, frothing. A' c—, *pr.pt.* of cop.
copag, -aig, -an, *s.f.* Dock—*rumex obtusifolius*, *r. crispus* and *r. conglomeratus.* (Scots, *docken.*) 2**Dock-leaf. C. chamagach, *rumex crispus* ; c. leathann, *rumex obtusifolius* ; c. bhagaideach, *rumex conglomeratus* (ill. *191.*)

189. Copag chamagach.

190. Copag leathann.

copagach, -aiche, *a.* Abounding in docks, or 2 dock-leaves.
————, -aich, *s.f.* Dock, see copag. 2 Place where docks grow. 3**Crop of docks.
copagach-dhearg,§ *s. f.* Blood-stained dock—*rumex sanguineus.* [Preceded by the art. *a' ch.*] ill. *192.*
copag-shràide,§ *s.f.* Common sorrel, see samh.
copag-thuaitheal, *s.f.* Bur, burdock.
copaibh, *dat. pl.* of cop.
copain, *gen.sing. & n.pl.* of copan.
còpair,* *s.m.* Fishmonger. 2**Buyer, seller or dealer, especially of horses. 3**Truckster.
————eachd,** *s.f.* Dealing in horses. 2**Truck-

191. Copagach bhagaideach.

192. Copagach-dhearg. *193. Copan-an-driùchd.*

ing.
co-phàirt, see comh-phàirt.
————each, see comh-phàirteach.
————ich, see comh-phàirtich.
————iche, see comh-phàirtiche.
copan, -ain, -an [& -ain] *s.m.* Boss of a shield. 2 Cup. 3**Bowl. 4**Flagon. 5 Dimple. 6 Pan of the head. 7 Anything curved. C. sréine, *the boss of a bridle.*
——ach, -aiche, *a.* Bossy. 2 Dimpled. 3 Of, or pertaining to a cup or ladle. Sgiath ch., *a bossy shield.*
——aichte, *a.* Bossed.
copan-a'-ghlùine,(WC) *s.m.* Knee-cap. patella.
copan-an-driùchd,§ *s.m.* Common lady's-mantle, (illust. 193.)—*alchemilla vulgaris.*
copan-Muire,(JM) *s.m.* Small limpet, thinner and finer in shell than ordinary limpets—*Uist.*
copar, -uir, *s.m.* Copper, copperas.
——-dubhaidh,‡‡ Copperas. Sulphate of iron. (*lit.* substance for producing black dye.)
coparach, *a.* Cupreous.
coparran-Muire,(AF) *s. m.* Kind of limpet—*Eriskay.* see copan Muire.
cop-gheal, -ile, *a.* White-foamed. 2**Foamy. A' mhuir ch., *the foamy sea.*
co-phoiteir, see comh-phoiteir.
co-phrìosanach, see comh-phrìosanach.
coprach, see coparach.
cor, *gen.* [cor, coir &] cuir, *s. m.* Condition, state, situation, circumstance. 2 Method, manner. 3 Custom. 4 Surety. 5 Term or condition of a treaty. 6‡‡ Progress. 7 (AF) Spider. 8‡‡see car. 9(AF) see corr. Air ch., *so that;* cha dean mi sin air ch. 'sam bith, *I shall not do that on any condition* ; air na h-uile c., *by all means*; air ch. air bith, *anywise;* is truagh mo ch., *sad is my condition:* cò a dh' fhidireas mo chor? *who will sympathize with my condition?* is e sin mo ch., *that is my condition*; ciod e is c. da? *how is he?* c. na talmhuinn, *the custom of the land;* air chor's gu'n tig thu, *on condition that you come* ; air chor 's nach, *so that not* ; air choraibh sgéithe, (see corr) *;* na guilibh air aon chor, *weep not on any account.*
cor, (*for* car.) 2 see corr.
còr,** còir, *s.m.* Music. 2 Choir.
còra, *comp.* of còir. More or most fitting, &c. Bu chòra dhuit dol dhachaidh, *it were more befitting that you should go home.* see cora.
còrach, *gen.sing.* of còir. 2 see curach. Slighe na c., *the path of justice;* a thuilleadh na c., *over and above enough.*
coracha,* see còrach.
corach-shuil,(AF) *s.* Sole (fish.)
coradh, see curaidh.
còradh, -aidh, -aidhean, *s. m.* Choir. 2 see còmhradh.
coradhan,** -ain, *s.m.* Coral.
coradh-uisge,(AF) *s.m.* Fishing-weir.
corag, -aig, -an, see corrag.
còrag, see còmhrag.
còragach,** see cobhragach.
coragach, *a.* see corragach.
corag a' chroinn, see corrag a' chroinn.
coragadh, -aidh, *s.m.* Neatness, trimness.
cora-ghleus, see corra-ghleus.
còraich,(AC) *v.a.* Claim. Gu'n c. an Ti naomh mi, *may the Holy One claim me.*
còraiche, [a ch!] *voc. pl.* of còir.
————an, *pl.* of còir.
còraicheas,** -eis, *s.m.* Surety, protection.
còraid, *s.f.* †Cheese-rennet. 2 *s.m.* see càraid.
†coraidh, see curaidh.
————eachd,** see curaidheachd.
coraig, *gen.sing.* of corag.
†corais, -e, *s.f.* Curtain.
còraiteach, see còmhraiteach.
còram,* -aim, *s.m.* Faction, set. 2 Quorum. 3 Bad set of people.
coran, see corran.
coranach, *s.m.* see corranach.
cora-uisge, see coradh-uisge.
†corb, cuirb, -an, *s.m.* see carbad.
corb, *a.* see coirb.
corb, *pr.pt.* a' corbadh, *v.a.* Consume, waste. 2††Corrupt, spoil, ruin.
——adh, -aidh, *s.m.* Wasting. 2 Cast, throw. 3 see coirbeachd. A' c—, *pr.pt.* of corb.
†————-cùil, *s.m.* Incest.
†corbaidh, -e, *s.f.* The cramp.
†corbair, -e, -ean, *s.m.* Cartwright. 2 Charioteer, coachman. 3 Waggoner.
†corbhadh, *s.m.* see carbhadh.
corbha,(AC) *s. pl.* Crests. Air c. nan neul, *on the crests of the clouds.*
corc, -a, -an, *s.m.* *Fairy-bull, water-bull. 2* Gaelic spelling of *cork.*
corc, cuirce, *dat.* cuirc, *pl.* -an, *s. f.* Sheath-knife, butcher's cleaver, (Scots, *whittle.*) 2 *rarely* Cauldron, pot. 3 *Uist & round Inverness* for coirce. C. an ionad cuinnseir, *a knife in the place of a whinger.*
corc, see corcach.
corca, *Ullapool, Lewis, &c.* for coirce.
corcach, -aiche, *a.* Of, belonging to, or like, a fairy- or water-bull. Laogh corcach, *a calf having small ears like the water-bull,* (a presage of evil.) [In *Uist* laogh corc-chluasach]
corcach, -aiche, *a.* Oaten.
†——, *s.m.* Moor. 2 Marsh.
còrcach,§ -aich, *s.f.* Hemp, carle, see cainb. Buill de 'n chaol-chorcach, *tackling of hempen ropes.*
———— chalcaidh, *s.m.* Oakum.
———— coille,§ *s.m.* Red campion, (plant) see cirean-choilich. 2 (bird) see corcan-coille.
corcag, -aig, -an, *s.f.* Little knife. 2 see coirceag.

corcair,** *v.a.* see corcuir.
———eachd, *s.f.* Working with a knife. (Sc. whittling.)
corcais, -e, -ean, *s.f.* see corc.
corcan, -ain, -an, *s.m.* Little cork. 2**Boat. 3** Pot.
——— -coille, *s.m.* Bullfinch—*pyrrhula vulgaris.* 2 see corcach-coille.

194. Corcan-coille.

——— -glas,(AF) *s.m.* Green bullfinch.
corcas, -ais *s.m.* Cork—*Harris.*
corc-chluasach, *a.* (AC)Purple-eared. 2 Knife-eared.
cor-chopag,§ *s.f.* Water-plantain (cor, *weir*+ copag)—*alisma plantago.*
————ach, *a.* Abounding in water-plantain.
corcra, *a.* see corcurach.
———n,** -ain, *s.m.* Small pot.
corcuir, *v. a.* Make red, crimson, or purple. Is iomadh sleagh a chorcradh leis, *many a spear was made bloody by him.*
———, *gen.sing.* of corcur.
———,** *a.* Red, purple. 2 Bloody.
corcur, -uir, *s.m.* Scarlet, crimson, purple. 2 The mossy white scurf adhering to large stones, from which the Gael make a pleasing crimson dye. It is first well dried in the sun, then pulverized and steeped, commonly in urine, and the vessel made air-tight. In this state it remains for three weeks, when it is fit to be boiled with the yarn it is to colour. 3 Cudbear—*lecanora tartarea.*
corcurach, -aiche, *a.* Purple, red, crimson. 2 Of. abounding in, or belonging to, pudple or crimson.
————d, *s.f.* Purple colour.
corcuraich,** *v.a.* Empurple.
còrd, -ùird, *s.m.* Cord, rope, string, line. 2** Cable. C. sgéinnidh, *a string of twine.*
———, *v.n.* Agree, settle, adjust, arrange. 2** Reconcile. 3**Rope, bind, secure with ropes.
corda,§ *s.* The genera *scirpus* and *shœnus* of plants, both being formerly used in making ropes.
còrdach, -aiche, *a.* Corded, of, or belonging to a cord. 2 Consistent.
————d,** *s.f.* Agreeableness.
còrdadh, -aidh, *s. m.* Agreement, agreeing, contract. 2 Good terms, good understanding. 3 Apposition in *gram.* 4 Roping, fastening with ropes. 5 Betrothal. A' c—, *pr. pt.* of còrd. Droch ch., *dispute, disagreement*; c. a reubas reachd, *concord (or compromise) that rends the law* [*Scots*—law's costly, let's tak' a pint an' gree—N.G.P.]
còrdaidh,‖ *s.m.* Spasms. [Preceded by art. *an.*] 2 *gen.sing.* of cordadh.
còrdaidh, *a.* Agreeable. 'S iad tha c !. *how agreeable they are !*
còrdail,** *s.f.* Lace. 2 Cordage. Le c., *with lace.*
co-réir, see comh-réir.

còrd-failbheig, *s.m.* That part of a cable fastened to the ring of an anchor.
cor-ghleus, *s.m.* Good condition.
————ach, -aiche, *a.* Well prepared. 2 In extra good condition. 3‡‡Flustered.
————ach, -aich, *s.m.* Tongue prepared for scolding.
còrlach, -aich, *s.m.* Bran, refuse of grain. 2 **Apotome. †3**Arrearage. 4**Grit.
†corm, -a, *s.m.* Kind of beer or ale.
cormach, -aich, *s.m.* Brewer.
†corm-nuall,′ *s.m.* Noise of drunkards.

195. Còrn. *196. Còrn.*

còrn, -ùirn, *s. m.* Drinking horn or cup. 2 Trumpet. 3 Robe. 4 The plant cornus. 5 Bale of cloth. 6**Flagon. 7**Cruise. 8** Convex surface. 9‡‡ Straw or prickle, used to provoke sneezing or vomiting. Talla nan c., *the hall of revelry (cups)* ; neart nan c., *the strength of the drinking-horns (strong drink.)* All the northern nations formerly drank out of horns which were commonly those of the urus or European buffalo. These horns were carefully dressed up and their edges lipped all round with silver. One of these immense horns, at least, an ox-horn of prodigious size, is still preserved in Dunvegan Castle. It was only produced before guests, and the drinker, in using it, twisted his arm round its spi es, and turning his mouth towards the right shoulder, was expected to drain it off.
còrn, *v.a.* Plait, curl. 2* Fold cloth.
còrnach, -aiche, *a.* Of, or pertaining to drinking-horns, &c. 2 Festive. 3 Like or of a sounding-horn. 4 Curled. 5 Waving. T' òr-chul casurlach c., *thy waving, curled yellow locks.*
còrnadh, -aidh, *s.m.* Folding of cloth, rolling, plaiting. 2 Corner. 3 Skirt. 4 Curl. 5 Fold. 6 Plait.
còrnair, -ean, *s.m.* Wrapper, folder.
còrnan, *s.m., dim.* of còrn.
còrnan-caisil, *s.m.* Wall-pennywort (plant.)
còrnan-fàil, -ean, *s.m.* Hemlock.
còrn-caisil, see cornan-caisil.
còrn-chlàr, -chlàir, *s.m.* Cupboard, buffet, dresser.
còrn-eun, -eòin, *s.m.* Royston crow, hooded crow.
còrn-stiall,** *s.m.* Cupboard.
còrnta, *past. pl.* of còrn. Folded, plaited, curled.
còrnuil,‖ -e, *s. f.* Retching, vehement coughing.
coron, -oin & -an, *s. m.* Crown, coronet. 2 Chaplet. C. òir, *a crown of gold*; c. Muire, *a rosary of beads* (*lit.* Mary's coronet.)
coronach, -aiche, *a.* Coronal, of, or belonging to a crown or chaplet. 2 Having a crown or chaplet.
coronaich,‡‡ *v.a.* Enwreathe.

coronair,** *s.m.* Coroner.
corp, -uirp, *s.m.* Body, carcase (in distinction to soul.) 2 Corpse. C. airm, *the main body of an army*; c. Chriosd, *the Eucharist, Lord's supper*; c. na h-oidhche, *midnight, the midnight watch.*
corpach, -aiche, *a.* ††Corpulent.
———,** -aich, *s. m.* Ground under which there is decayed wood.
———d,‡‡ *s.f.* Bodilyness.
corpag, -aig, -an, *s.f.* Tiptoe. Tha e ag imeachd air a chorpagaibh, *he is walking on tiptoes.*
corpaich,(CR) *v. n.* Be disgusted at, revolt from. Ch. mi ris, *I was disgusted at him.*
———te, *a.* Corporate.
corpailear, see coirpileir.
corpan, -ain, -an, *s.m.* Little body. 2**Miserable body. 3**Corpuscule.
corpanach,†† *a.* see corpanta.
corpanta, *a.* Bulky, corpulent, solid.
———chd, *s.f.* Bulkiness, corpulence.
corp-criadhach,(WC) *s.m.* Clay corpse. When a witch desired to destroy any one to whom she had an ill-will, she often made a corpse of clay resembling the unfortunate one, and placed it in some out-of-the-way burn under a precipice, in such a way that the water trickled slowly on it. As the clay body wasted so the live body of the person it resembled was also supposed to waste away. Were the body found, it was carefully preserved, and so the spell of the witch was broken. Sometimes pins were stuck in the clay body to make the death of the doomed one more painful. Several such bodies have been found, even of late years.
corp-eòlas, -ais, *s.m.* Anthropology.
corp-ghabhail,‡‡ *s.m.* Incarnation.
còr-phairteach,** *a.* Aliquant.
corp-làidir,‡‡ -e, *a.* Able-bodied.
corp-léine, -léintean, *s. f.* Winding-sheet, shroud.
corpordha, *a.* see corporra.
———chd, *s.f.* see corporrachd.
corporra, *a.* Bodily, corporeal, material, gross, not spiritual. Gu c., *bodily.*
———chd, *s.f.ind.* Materiality, corporeity, not spirituality.
corp-rannsachair,* *s.m.* Dissector, anatomist.
corp-rùsgadh, -aidh, *s. m.* Despoiling of the dead.
corp-sgian,* *s.f.* Scalpel, dissector's knife.
———adair,* *s.m.* Dissector, anatomist.
———adaireachd,* *s.f.* Anatomy, dissection.
corp-shnasach, *a.* Anatomical.
———d, *s.f.* Anatomy, dissection.
corp-shnasadair, see corp-shnasair.
———each, see corp-shnasach.
———eachd, see corp-shnasachd.
corp-shnasadh, -aidh, *s.m.* Anatomy, dissection.
corp-shnasaiche,** *s.m.* Anatomist.
corp-shnasair, -ean, *s.m.* Anatomist, dissector. 2* Body polisher, statuary.
———each, see corp-shnasach.
———eachd, see corp-shnasachd.
còrr, -a, *a.* Excellent, great, eminent. 2 Extraordinary. 3 Odd, not even. 4**Remaining. 5**Upwards of, more than. 6**Stately. 7**Lofty, vast. 8**Beauteous. 9**Stormy. 10‡‡Long. 11‡‡Dismal. Bliadhna ch., *an extraordinary year*; duine c., *a singular man*; a' ghiuthas ch., *the stately fir*; uimhir ch., *an odd number*; c. is mìle fear, *upwards of a thousand men*; fichead fear is c., *twenty men and upwards*; còrr-gaoithe nan speur, *the stormy winds of heaven*; iasgach amadain, c. bheòthach mór, *a fool's fishing, an occasional big fish*—only fools despise littles—NGP.
corr,(AF) *s.m.* Any undersized or diminutive animal. 2 Odd or exceptional looking creature. see corra.
còrr, *s.m.* Odds, excess, surplus, overplus, remainder. 2 Snout, bill. 3 Horn. 4‡‡End, corner, limit. Thoir dhomhs' an c., *give me the remainder*; air chòrraibh an sgiath, *on the extremities of their wings*; air ch., *especially.*
corra, -n, *s.f.* Heron, hern. 2**Stork. 3***rarely* Waterpiet. 4(AF) Crane. Cha suaicheantas c. air cladach, *a heron on the shore*—a likely sight, and no sign of anything unusual about to happen.
corra-beada, see corra-biod.
corra-beaga, see corra-biod.
corra-bhainne,(DU) *s. f.* The insect cranefly, "daddy long-legs."
còrra-bhàn,¶ *s.f.* White heron—*ardea alba.* 2¶ White stork—*ciconia alba.* 3**Crane.
corra-bheinn,†† *s.f.* Steep hill.
corra-bide, see corra-biod.
corra-biod, -a, *s.m.* Certain posture of standing or cowering, which prepares the person assuming it for an instant start or spring. 2 (with *air*—air corra-biod) Tip-toe. 3 Watchfulness. 4 Impatience. 5 Niceness, fastidiousness. 6 Anxiety to find fault. [†† gives corra-bioda.]
corrach, -aiche, *a.* Steep, precipitous. 2 Erect. 3 Abrupt, passionate, angry. 4 Inconsistent. 5 Wavering. 6**see carach. 7(AH)Unsteady, unstable, affording insecure foothold. 8** Rolling, as the eye. Àite c., *a steep place*; 2 *a shaking place*—*Lewis*; is c. gob an dubhain, *fishing is a precarious livelihood.*
corrach, -aich, *s.f.* Fetter, shackle. 2 Bog, marsh. 3‡‡Boat.
corrachadh, -aidh, see comharrachadh.
corra-chagailte, -n-cagailte, *s.f.* Salamander. 2 Fluctuating sulphureous figures, observed among hot embers on frosty nights. 3 (WC) Person given to constantly sitting by the fire. 4 Coward, fireside soldier.
corracha-margaidh,(AF) *s. pl.* Jailbirds (i.e. market herons, birds or people, who haunt markets or places where they are likely to pick up something or find employment.) see corra-margaidh.
corrachan,(AF) *s.m.* Stilt.
corrachan,¶ *s.m.* Daw—*Iona & Mull*, see cathag.
———, *n.pl.* of corra.
corrachan, *n.pl.* of corr.
corra-chaoghal, *pl.* -chan-caoghail, *s.f.* Grasshopper.
corrachas,‡‡ -ais, *s.m.* Crankiness. 2 Steepness.
corrachd,(AC) *s.f.* Very sacred promise or entreaty, death promise.
———an,(AF) *s.m.* Chicken.
corra-cheann, -chinn, *s.m.* Dunderhead. 2** Giddy head.
corra-cheannach, *a.* Light-headed, giddy, inconstant.
corra-cheòsach, see corra-chòsag.
corra-chòsach, see corra-chòsag.
corra-chòsag, -aig, -an, *s.f.* Cheslip, small insect found in chinks.
corra-chrithich,¶ *s.f.* Heron, see corra-ghritheach.
corrach-shod, § *s. f.* Marsh-marigold—*caltha palustris.* [Preceded by art. *a' ch*—.] see illust. 197.

197. *corrach-shod.*

corra-dhuil, -e, *s.f.* First effort of an infant to articulate.
corra-diosag,(AF) *s.f.* Cheslip.
corrag, -aig, -an, *s.f.* Finger. 2 Fore-finger. 3 Left-hand stilt of a plough, plough-tail. Cha dean c. mhilis im, *a sweet finger will never make butter.*
——**ach**, -aiche, *a.* Fingered, having fingers.
——**achadh**, -aidh, *s. m.* & (A' c—,) *pr.pt.* of corragaich. Fingering.
corragaich, *pr.pt.* a' corragachadh, *v.a.* Finger, handle.
corrag-croinn, *s.f.* Plough-handle or stilt.
corra-ghabhan, see corra-ghobhlach.
corra-ghlas,¶ -ais, *s.f.* Common heron. 2 Stork, see corra-ghritheach. 3* Crane, see corra-mhonaidh. 4** Bittern, see corra-ghrian. Sgiathan na corra-glaise, *the wings of the stork.*
corra-ghleus,†† *s.m.* Good condition, prime.
————**ach**,†† *a.* Primed.
corra-ghòbhlach,(AF) *s.f.* Earwig.
corra-ghrain, *s.m.* Heron, see corra-ghritheach.
corra-ghrian, *pl.*-an- & -achan-grian,*s.f.* Bittern —*botaurus sellaris.* 2(AF)Swan. 3(AF)Turtle-dove.
corra-ghribheach, see corra-ghritheach.
corra-ghriodhach, see corra-ghritheach.
corra-ghritheach, *s. f.* Heron, stork, crane— *ardea cimerea.* [Griathach is from Early Irish grith, *a scream.*]

198. *Corra-ghrian.* 199. *Corra-ghritheach.*

corrag-shacaiche, -an-sacaiche, *s.f.* Sort of hurdle, set on the back of a horse to carry grain, &c.
corra-iasg,(AF) *s.f.* Crane, stork.
corraichead,‡‡ -id, *s.f.* Crankiness. 2 Steepness.
corrail,(DC) *a.* Fretful, (applied to a child)— *Uist & Lewis.*
còrralach, -aich, *s.m.* Remainder, excess, surplus, overplus, odds.
corralachd,(DC) *s.f.* Fretfulness—*Uist.*
corra-leisg,* *s.f.* Sloth. [Preceded by art. *a' ch.*]
corra-maothar,* *s.m.* Sea-pike (fish)—*Islay.*
corra-margaidh, -n- & -chan-margaidh,*s.m.* The rabble.
corra-meille,* see carra-meille.
corra-mheagan,(MMcD) *s.m.* Bilberry, whortleberry—*vaccinium myrtillus.*
corra-mheur,* *s.f.* Little finger. 2††Odd finger.
corra-mhona, see corra-mhonaidh.
corra-mhonaidh, *pl.* -chan-monaidh, *s.f.* Crane —¶*grus cinerea.* 2**Stork. 3**Heron.

200. *Corra-mhonaidh.*

corran, -ain, *s. m.* Reaping-hook, sickle. 2 Point of land running far into the sea. 3 Point of a weapon. 4 Spear. 5 Barbed arrow. 6 Beard. 7(WC) Island which comes in sight at low tide at the mouth of a river. —*Poolewe.* 8** Prickle. 9** Sharp-edged weapon. [The meanings given in some dictionaries as "Narrow passage through which the tide runs swiftly," "semi-circular bay," and "bend" are not the equivalents of corra which signifies the promontory which contracts the passage, or which bounds the bay. Mu ch. a mhionnaich, *on the bend of his stomach;* gach té le a c. cam *every woman with her crooked sickle;* c. saighde, *the point of an arrow.*
corranach, -aiche, *a.* Barbed. 2 Prickly. 3 Notched. 4 Sharp. 5 Destructive. 6 Of, like, or pertaining to a reaping-hook or sickle. 7 Hooked, crooked. 8††Circular. Do shaighde c., *thy barbed arrows.*
corranach, -aich, *s.f.* Crying, loud weeping, the funeral cry of the Gael. 2**Mournful ejaculation. 3** Singing at funerals. [**Gives "Bagpipe-music when used at funerals or on mournful occasions," but this should be *cumha.*] The c. of the Gael is a panegyric on the deceased, with a recital of the bravery or worth of his ancestors.
corra na h-easgann,(AF) *s.f.* Crane, bittern.
corran-bearraidh, -ain-, *s.m.* Pruning-hook.
corran-coille, see corcan-coille.
corran-creige,(DC) *s.m.* Stickleback—*Uist.*
corran-gart-ghlanaidh, *s.m.* Weeding-hook, hoe.
corran-greusaiche,(AF) *s.m.* Small catfish, angler.—*Argyll.*
corran-lìn, *s.m.* Corn-spurrey, see cluain-lìn.
corran-sgathaidh, *s.m.* Pruning-hook. 2 (M. McL)Hook for cutting the lower part off sheaves of corn for thatch.
corran-shioman,†† *s.f.* see cor-shiomain.
corranta, *a.* see corranach.
corra-riabhach, -aich, *pl.* -n-riabhach, *s. f.* Heron, crane—*ardea major*, see corra-ghritheach.
corra-sgreuch, see corra-sgreuchag.
corra-sgreuchag, *s. f.* Screech-owl. 2(AF) Heron.

corra-sgritheach,(WC) *s.f.* Heron. [Always called thus at *Poolewe*, from an imitation of the bird's cry.]
corra-shìomain, see cor-shìomain.
corra-shòd, see corrach-shod
corra-shùghadh, *s.m.* The backward swell from the shore after a wave has spent its strength on the beach. 2 Trough of the high waves out at sea. A h-uile rud tosdach, sèidh, ach corra-shùghadh a bheireadh stuth air na boghachan *everything calm and quiet, except an occasional murmur from the sea-swell on the sunken reefs.—Sgeulaiche-nan-caol, p. 128.*
corra-shùgain, *s.m.* Flickering figures, caused by reflected rays of light on roofs or walls of houses. (*Scots*, glaiks.) 2 see corra-shùgan.
corra-shùgan,* *s. f.* Twist-handle, also cor-shìomain.
corra-spiod, see corra-biod.
corra-thòn-dubh, *pl.* -n-tòn-dubh. *s.f.* Crane.
corra-thulchainn,(AH) *s.f.* In roof of a house with sloping gable, the beam extending from middle of end wall to the apex of the nearest couple.
còrr-bheann, *a.* Long-sheeted.
còrr-bheinn, -e, *pl.* -bheanntan, *s.f.* Steep hill.
corr-chagailte, see corra-chagailte.
còrr-cheann, -chinn, *s.m.* Empty head.
——————ach, -aiche, *a.* Empty-headed.
còrr-chlaonadh, -aidh, *s.m.* Bias, leaning.
corr-chopag, *s. f.* Water-plantain — *alisma plantago.*
——————ach, *a.* Abounding in water-plantains.
corr-fhàd,(MMcD)*s.m.* First or outermost peat cut from a peat-bank.
corr-fhòd, -fhòid, *s.m.* The concluding or outermost furrow of a ridge or field.
corr-ghleus, see cor-ghleus.
——————ach, -aiche, *a.* see cor-ghleusach.
——————ach, -aich, *s. f.* see cor-ghleusach.

201. Corr-chopag.

corr-ghlùineach, -eiche, *a.* Long-kneed. 2 Having sharp-pointed knees.
corr-ghòbhlach, -aich, *s.m.* Earwig.
còrr-ghrian, see corra-ghritheach.
corrghuil, -e, *s.f.*Murmur, muttering, chirping.
còrrlach, -aich, *s.f.* Coarsely ground meal. 2 Overplus, remainder.
corr-léine, *s.f.* Shirt of armour.
corr-marguidh, see corra-margaidh.
corr-meille, see carra-meille.
corr-mheille, see carra-meille.
còrr-mheur, -mheòir, *s.m.* Odd finger. Cha chuir mi mo ch. air, *I will not touch it.*
†**corr-mhiann**, *s.f.* Conceit.
corr-mial,(AF) *s.* Gnat. 2 Hornet. 3 Horse-fly.
corr-phàirteach, *a.* Aliquant.
corr-riabhach, see corra-riabhach.
còrr-sgreuchag, -aig, see corra-sgreuchag.
còrr-sgriachag, see corra-sgreuchag.
corr-shùgan, see corra-shùgan.
còrr-shuidhe, *s.* Discumbency.
corr-thùlchann, see under taigh.
†**corrughadh**, -aidh, see carachadh.
corruich, -e, *s.f.* Anger, wrath, ire. 2* Offence. Tha c. air, *he is offended*; na gabh c., *do not be offended*; 'na ch. ghéir, *in his fierce anger.*
——, *v.a.* see caraich.
†**corruidhe**, see corruighe.
†**corruigh**, *v.a.* Stir, move.
†**corruighe**, *s.f.* Trouble, disorder.
†**corruigheach**, *a.* Moving.
corruil, -e, see coirioll.
corr-urraidh, -ean, *s.m.* Surety.
còrsa, -n (& -chan), *s.m.* Coast, shore. 2**District. 3(MMcD) That part of a sail betwеen the upper reef-points and yard. Air c na Frainge, *on the coast of France*; air ar còrsaibh, *on our coasts.*
còrsachadh, -aidh, *s.m.* Coasting, cruising. A' c—, *pr.pt.* of còrsaich.
còrsachd,‡‡ *s.f.ind.* Sponginess.
còrsadh, see còrsa.
còrsaich, *v.a & n.* Coast, cruise.
còrsair, -ean, *s.m.* Coaster, cruiser. 2**Pirate, corsair.
——————eachd, *s.f.ind.* Cruising, coasting. 2 Piracy.
cor-shìomain, -ain, *s.m.* Twist-handle, (*Scots*, thraw-crook) for making straw-ropes.
†**cortas**, -ais, *s.m.* Debt.
corthachd,** *s.f.ind.* Lassitude.
†**corughadh**, -aidh, *s.m.* Armament, armour
cor-urraidh, see corr-urraidh.
cos, coise, *dat.* cois, *pl.* cosan, *s.f.* see cas.
còs, -òis, -an, *s. m.* Hollow, crevice, recess. 2 Cavern, cave, hole. 3* Sponge—*Islay.* C. mo shuain, *the cavern of my rest*; a' leum o 'n còsaibh, *bounding from their holes.*
cosa, (*for* casa) *pl.* of cas.
còsach, -aiche, *a.*Cavernous, abounding in hollows, recesses, or crevices. 2 Snug. 3 Spongy, porous. 4** Bibulous.
cosach, -aiche, *a.* see casach.
còsachd, *s.f.* Sponginess, porousness.
cosag, -aig, -an, see casag.
còsag, -aig, -an, *s.f.* Small crevice, cavern, cave, or cell.
——ach, *a.* Full of holes or crevices. 2 Snug. warm, cosy, sheltered. 3 Spongy.
cosagach, see casagach.
cosa-gòbhlach, see casa-gòbhlach.
còsaiche, *s.f.ind.* see còsaichead.
——————ad, -eid, *s.m.* Hollowness. 2 Degree of sponginess.
cosail, -e, *a.* see cosmhail.
†**cosain**,** *v.a.* Defend, keep off. 2 Preserve. 3 Avouch, maintain.
cosaint,** *s.f.* Reply. 2 Defence. 3 Averment
cosair,** *s.m.* Feast. 2 Bed.
cosalachd, see cosmhalachd.
†**cosam**, *v.a.* Defend, keep off, preserve.
cosamal, see cosmal.
cò 'sam bith, *comp. rel.* Whoever, whosoever.
cosamhlachadh, -aidh, *s.m.* Allusion, act of alluding, comparing, likening. A' c—, *pr.pt.* of cosamhlaich.
cosamhlachd, see cosmhalachd.
cosamhlaich, see comh-shamhlaich.
——————te, *a.* & *past pt.* of cosamhlaich, see comh-shamhlaichte.
còsan, -ain, -an, *s.m.* Little hollow or crevice. 2**Cell. 3 *n.pl.* of còs.
——ach, -aiche, *a.* Full of little hollows.
cosan,** -ain, *s.m.* Footpath.
——, *n. pl.* of cos, (*for* cas.)
cosanta, *a.* Industrious, diligent. 2**Defended. 3**Perplexed, entangled. 4(AH) Sturdy, vigorous, weatherproof, sound of wind and limb.
cosantach, -aiche, *a.* see cosanta.
——————,** -aich, *s.m.* Defender, in a process.
cosar,** -air, *s.m.* Coat, mantle.
cosarach,** *s.pl.* Fetters.
†**cosbair**, -e, -ean, see cuspair.
cosbheairt, see caisbheart.
coscach,(MMcL) *a.* Spongy.
cos-cheum, -a, -an, see cas-cheum.

cosd, *pr. pt.* a' cosd, *v.n. & a.* Spend, waste, cost, squander. 2 Wear, tear. Cò 'tha 'cosd air seo ? *who is paying for this ?* (not *squander*)—*i.e.* leave my affairs alone ; na c. t' airgiod, *do not squander your money.*
cosd, *s.m.* Cost, expense, expenditure, extravagance. A' c—, *pr. pt.* of cosd.
cosdail, -e, *a.* Expensive, extravagant, prodigal, profuse. 2 Dear, costly.
cosdalachd, *s.f.ind.* Expensiveness, costliness. 2**Preciousness, valuableness.
cosdas, -ais, *s.m.* Expense, price, cost, expenditure. 2 Extravagance. Is ionann c. gun chosnadh agus anshocair gun leigheas, *aye spending and never earning is like an incurable disease* ; fear cosdais, *an extravagant man.*
cosdasach, -aiche, *a.* Expensive, costly. 2** Extravagant. 3 Precious, valuable.
———d, same meanings as cosdalachd.
cos-diollaide, *s.m.* Saddle-pillar of a cycle.
†**cosd-thaigh**, -e, -ean, *s.m.* Inn.
cos-dubh, see cas-dubh.
cosg, *pr.pt.* a' cosg, see cosd.
cosg, *s.m. & pr.pt.* of coisg, see caisg.
cosgach,** *a.* Assuasive. 2 Expensive, wasteful.
cosgadair, -ean, *s.m.* Assuager, mollifier.
cosgadh, -aidh, *s.m.* Quenching, stopping, curbing, staunching, appeasing, restraining. 2 Act of quenching, staunching, ceasing, &c. A' c—, *pr.pt.* of coisg. An fhuil a' ruith gun luibh 'ga cosgadh, *the blood flowing and no herb to stop it.*
cosgail, -e (& -ala), *a.* see cosdail.
cosgair, *s.m.* Queller, pacifier.
cosgair, *v.* see casgair.
cosgairt, see casgairt.
cosgar, -air, *s.m.* see casgairt. 2**Triumph, rejoicing.
———ach, -aiche, *a.* see casgrach. 2**Triumphant.
cosgarachd, see casgrachd.
cosgaradh, -aidh, *s.m.* see casgradh.
cosgaraiche,** see casgraiche.
cosgarra, see casgrach.
cosgarrach, *s.* see casgarrach.
———, *a.* see casgrach.
cosgas, see cosdas.
cosg-leigheas,** *s.* Antidote.
cosgrach, see casgrach.
cosgradh, see casgradh.
cosgraiche, -an, see casgraiche.
cosguirt, see casgairt.
cosguis, -e, *s.f.* Periodical allowance to servants sent to their houses. 2(MMcL) Expenditure—*Lewis.*
cosgus, -uis, see cosdas. (cosgas—*Uist.*)
còslach, (CR) *a.* Spongy, as bread, peats, or any dry thing.—*W. of Ross-shire.*
coslach, -aiche, see coltach.
coslachd, see cosmhalachd.
coslas, -ais, see coltas. Is fhearr e na a ch., *he is better than his appearance.*
cos-leathann, see cas-leathann.
cos-lom, see cas-lom.
cos-lomnochd, see cas-lom.
cos-luath, see cas-luath.
cosmail,†† -e, *s.f.* Rubbish, refuse of meal, straw, &c.
———each,†† *a.* Worthless.
cosmal,* -ail, *s.m.* Rubbish. *also* cosmail.
cosmhail, -e, *a.* Like, similar, resembling.
cosmhal, see cosmhail.
———achd, *s.f.ind.* Likeness, resemblance. 2 Probability. 3 Comparison. 4 Parable. 5 Appearance. 6 Agreeableness. C. 'nur n-aghaidh, *a proverb against you.*
cosmhalas, -ais, see cosmhalachd.
cosmhuil, see cosmhail.
———eachd, see cosmhalachd.
———eadh, -idh, -idhean, see cosamhlachadh.
cosmuil, -e, *s.f.* see cosmal.
cosmul, -uil, see cosmal.
cos-nàbuidh, see cas-nàbuidh.
cosnach, -aich, *s.m.* Labourer, workman, day-labourer. 2 Defendant. 3(CR) Wage-earner, provider (for his own family.) Comharradh an deagh chosnaich, cadal fada ri gaoith mhóir agus a' chlann a chumail a mach o 'n teine, *the mark of the good servant, to sleep long when the wind is high and to keep the children from the fire*—the good servant has everything safely secured before night comes, and thus, having an easy mind, he sleeps soundly, even through a storm, also, he keeps the house well supplied with fuel, so that the fires are big, and the children forced to keep at a safe distance.
cosnachail,‡‡ -aile, *a.* Peasant.
cosnadh, -aidh, *s.m.* Gaining, earning, act of gaining, getting or winning. 2 State of servitude, occupation and state of a menial. 3 Service, employment, work. 4* Accomplishment. 5**Defence. 6**Preservation. A' c—, *pr. pt.* of coisinn. [see note under coisinn.] Dubh-chosnadh, *outdoor or field-labour, as planting potatoes, spreading peats, &c.* ; 2 (*WC*) *working very hard;* is bochd am pòsadh nach fearr na'n dubh-chosnadh, *it is a poor marriage that is not better than field-work*—seldom desirable for women.
cosnaiche, *s.m.* see cosnach.
†**cosnamh**, -aimh, see cosnadh.
cos-nochdte, *a.* see cas-rùisgte.
cosoil, -e, *a.* see cosmhail.
cosrach, -aich, *s.m.* Slaughter, havoc. 2 Fetters. A deanamh cosraich, *slaughtering.*
cos-rùisgte, see cas-rùisgte.
cos-shlighe, -an, see cas-shlighe.
còs-shruth, -a, -an, *s.m.* Stream running partly underground, or forming hollows in its course.
cos-stòl, -òil, see cas-stòl.
cost, -a, *s.m.* see cosd. 2‡‡ see cosguis.
cost, *v.a. & n.* see cosd.
costach, *a.* see cosdail.
costadhach, see còmhstadhach.
costag,§ -aig, *s.f.* Chervil—*anthriscus cerifolium, a. vulgaris,* and *a. temulentum.*
costag a' bhaile gheamhraidh, see costag.
costag-fhladhain, *s.f.* Wild chervil — *chœrophyllum sylvestre.*
costail, -e, *a.* see cosdail.
costalachd, *s.f.* see cosdalachd.
costas, -ais, see cosdas.
co'strì, see comh-stri.
co'strigh, see comh-stri.
co strìgheach, -eiche, *a.* see comh-stritheach.
costus, -uis, see cosdas.
costusach, -aiche, *a.* see cosdail.

202. *Costag-fhiadhain*

cos-uisge, *s.f.* Sweet cicely, great chervil—*myrrhis odorata.* (illust. 202.)
cosumail, -e, *s.f.* see cosmal.
†**cot**, -a, -an, *s.m.* Small boat. 2 Part, share, portion.
cot, -a, -achan, *s.m.* Gaelic form of *cottage.*
còta, -aichean, *s.m.* Petticoat. 2 Coat. 3**Covering. 4‡ Alpine lady's mantle (plant), see

trusgan.

còta-bàn, *s.m.* Flannel petticoat. 2 Groat (4*d.* piece.) 3 Fourpence-land. Leirtheas, *two fourpenny-lands*; ochdamh, *four fourpenny-lands*; ceathramh, *eight fourpenny-lands.*

còta-bior,(DC) *s.m.* Flannel or plaiding petticoat—*Argyll.*

còta biorach dubh, *s. m.* Black tailed coat, "morning coat,"

còta-bhioran,†† -ain, *s.m.* Knitted petticoat.

còta-cathdath, *s.m.* Tartan coat.

còtach,†† *a.* Of, or pertaining to, a coat or petticoat. 2 Coat-wearing.

còta-craicinn, *s.m.* Coat of skins.

còta "croisidh,"(MMcL) *s.m.* Crotchet petticoat.

còta-fada,(AH) *s.m.* Frock-coat.

còta-gearr,(AC) *s.m.* Short coat or doublet like an "Eton" jacket with short cut-away tail. It was made of tartan or scarlet cloth, which was called cath-dath (war colour) or cath-dath rìoghail (royal war colour.)

còta-glas, *s.m.* Grey coat. Cha tig an c. glas cho math do na h-uile fear, *the grey coat becomes not every man alike.* Mackintosh says, "King James the V's wearing a grey coat when in disguise might probably give rise to this saying.

còta-goirid,** *s.m.* Jacket.

còtaich, *v.a.* Provide with a coat. 2 Cover, envelop.

còtaichean, *pl.* of còta.

†cotaig, *s.f.* Harmony. 2**Good understanding.

còta-mòr, *pl.* còtaichean-móra, *s.m.* Surtout, top-coat, greatcoat.

cotan, -ain, *s.m.* Cotton. 2(MMcL) Small fold for a calf.

còtan, -ain, *s.m.* Little petticoat. 2 Little coat. 3**Little pile. 4**Part, portion.

còtanach,†† *a.* Of, or pertaining to, little-coats.

cotanach,‡‡ -aiche, *a.* Cottony.

còta preasach nighinn an rìgh, *s. f.* Lady's mantle—*alchemilla vulgaris.* see copan-an-drùchd.

còta-uisge,(AH) *s.m.* Waterproof coat.

†coth, *s.m.* Meat, victuals.

†coth,(AF) *s.m.* Cat.

còthach,(CR) *a.* Spongy, as a decaying turnip, or any wet thing—*W. of Ross-shire.*

cothachadh, -aidh, *s.m.* Earning, support. 2 Dispute, contention. 3 Competition. 4 Obstinacy, pertinacity. 5 see cathachadh. 6 (AH Banter, badinage, sally, repartee, A' c—, *pr.pt.* of cothaich. Is àrd t' iarrtas os cionn na tha 'nam chomas a chothachadh, *your desire is beyond what I am able to satisfy;* ainmich na duilgheasan, leig leam an c., *name the difficulties, let me overcome them;* a' c. riut, *struggling against you.*

cothadh, -aidh, *s. m.* Support, protection. 2 Preservation.

203. Cos-uisge.

204. Cotharach.

co'thaghadh, -aidh, *s.m.* Syntax, proper choice and construction of words.

cothaich, *v.a.* Gain, get, earn, win. 2 Contend, strive. 3 Try, tempt. 4**Debate. 5**Struggle, fight.

cothaiche, -an, *s.m.* Earner. 2 Disputant, contender.

cothaidh,(CR) *a.* Soft, spongy—*Glenmoriston.*

cothan, -ain, *s.m.* Cough. 2 Anhelation. 3 Asthma. 4 Froth. 5 (AH) Decayed, corroded timber. 6‡ Pulp. 7 (DC) Shrine, reliquary box—*Argyll.*

cothanach, -aiche, *a.* Frothy. 2 Asthmatic. 3 (AH) Corroded, decayed.

————d, *s.f.* Frothiness, anhelation.

cothannach, *s.f.* Froth, spray, foam.

cothar, -air, -airean, *s.f.* Coffer.

cothar, -air, *s.m.* see cobhar.

cotharach, -aich, *s.f.* Water scorpion-grass, forget-me-not—*myosotis palustris.*

co'thional, -ail, *s.m.* see comh-thional.

cothlaim, *pr. pt.* a' cothlamadh, *v.a.* Mix together.

cothlamadh, -aidh, *s.m.* Things of different kinds or colours mixed together. 2 Act of mixing together different sorts of wool as black and white. 3 Wool-mixture. A' c—, *pr.pt.* of cothlaim.

†cothlon, -oin, *s.m.* Victuals for a journey.

cothrom, *a.* see cothromach.

cothrom,-uim,-an, *s.m.* Equipoise, equilibrium. 2 Weight, any certain weight. 3 Justice, equal terms, as of combat, fair-play. 4 Comfort. 5 Opportunity. 6 Ability, power. 7 Advantage. 8**Support. 9**Mercy. Ar n-airgiod 'na làn chothrom, *our money in full weight*; far am bi càil bidh c., *where there's a will there's a way*; c. na Féinne, *the Fingalian fair-play*; —i.e. one to one, gaisgeach air gaisgeach agus laoch ri laoch—N.G.P.; a' dol a dh'ionnsuidh a' chothroim, *going to seek justice*;an ceud ch. a gheibh mi, *the first opportunity I get ;* tha e an c. math, *he is in comfortable circumstances.* ; *2 in good health*—(*Lewis*); fhuair e a h-uile c. d' a mhac, *he got the best education for his son* ; cuin c. rium, *support me*; c. agus ceart, *justice and equity.*

cothromach, -aiche, *a.* Just, equitable. 2 Upright, honest. 3 Comfortable, in easy circumstances. 4 Weighty. 5*Parallel, equal, even with, level. 6 Of the same size. 7**Firm, firmly situated. 8‡‡ Easily accomplished. 9 Righteous. Athair ch., *O righteous father!* Duine c., *a man in easy circumstances* ; *2 influential person*; *3 religious person* ; meidhean c., *just weights* ; cha'n 'eil an slighe c., *their way is not equal* ; calpa cruinn c., *brawns, well rounded and firm.*

————adh, -aidh, *s. m.* Weighing, act of weighing. 2 Poising, balancing. 3 Pondering. 4 Settling, placing on a firm foundation. A' c—, *pr.pt.* of cothromaich. A' c. nam bròg, *paring the shoes.*

cothromachd,‡‡ *s. f. ind.* Appropriateness. 2 Equality.

cothromaich, *pr. pt.* a' cothromachadh, *v. a.* Weigh. 2 Poise. 3 Ponder, consider. 4 Establish, settle. 5* Make even with. 6*Make of the same size. C. na sgleatan, *make the slates of one size.*

cothromaiche, -an, *s. m.* Weight. 2 Balance. 3 Weigher.

cothromaichte, *past pt.* of cothromaich. Weighed. 2 Poised. 3 Measured. An talamh c., *the poised earth.*

còt'-iochdair, còtaichean-, *s.m.* Undercoat. 2 Under-petticoat.

còt'-uachdair, *pl.* còtaichean-, *s. m.* Upper or

outer coat, overcoat.
†cotun, -uin, *s.m.* Coat, coat of mail.
crà (AC) *s.* Blood; *hence* 2 Red.
crà,(CR)*s.m.* Cruive for catching salmon—*W. of Ross-shire.*
cràbhach, -aiche, *a.* Devout, religious, pious, austere, hypocritical.
cràbhach, -aich, *s.m.* see cràbhaiche.
cràbhachd, *s.f.* see cràbhadh.
cràbhadair,* *s.m.* Monk. 2 Austere religious devotee, puritan.
cràbhadh, -aidh, *s.m.* Religion. 2 Devotion. 3** Hypocrisy.
cràbhaiche, -an, *s.m.* Devout man, devotee. 2 Worshipper. 3 Hypocrite.
cràbhaichean, *s.pl.* see crabharsaich.
cràbhaidh, -e, *a.* see cràbhach.
cràbhair, see cràbhadair.
crabharsaich,*s.pl.* The smaller articles of household furniture. 2 Small wares.
cràbhat, -an, *s.f.* Gaelic spelling of *cravat.*
cràcach, -aiche, see cròcach. 2(DU) Tousled, curly.
crac, *v.* & *s.* see cnac.
cracail, -e, *s.f.* see cnacail.
cracaire, -an, *s.m.* see cnacair.
———achd, see cnacaireachd.
cracairiche, *s.m.* see cnacair.
cracair-neòil,** *for* cnacair-neòil, *s.m.* Balloon, (in *fireworks.*)
cracan, -ain, *s. m.* Hill-side. 2 Vexation. 3 see cnacail.
cracas,‡ -ais, *s.f.* see cnacaireachd.
crachann, -ainn, *s.m.* see creachann.
crachd, see cnac.
crachdadh, see cnacadh.
crachdail, see cnacail.
cràc-dhamh, (AF) *s.m.* Stag.
crà-chluasach, *a.* (AC) *a.* Red-eared.
crà-chù, (AC) *s.m.* (*lit.* red dog) Fox.
cràdh, *v.a.* see cràidh.
cràdh, -aidh, *s. m.* Pain, anguish, torment, pang. Cùis mo chràidh, *the cause of my anguish* ; móran cràidh, *much pain* ; c. cridhe, *mental anguish.*
cràdhadh, -aidh, *s.m.* Act of tormenting, vexing, harassing. 2**Vexation. A' c—, *pr.pt.* of cràidh.
cràdhaich, see cràidh.
———te, see cràidhte.
cràdhair,** *s.m.* Afflicter.
cràdhar, *fut. pass.* of craidh.
crà-dhearg, -dheirge, *a.* Red-footed. 2 Blood-red.
cràdh-gheadh,¶ -gheoidh, *s. f* Common sheldrake—*tadorna bellonii.*

205. *Cràdh-gheadh.*

cràdh-lot, -an, *s.m.* Painful wound. 2 Mental anguish, torment, agony. Cùis mo ch., *the cause of my distress.*
cràdh-lot, *v.a.* Inflict a grievous wound.
———ach, -aiche, *a.* Of, or connected with, a painful wound.
cràdh-shlat,* *s.f.* Sort of pillory or tread-mill, used by the Gael of old. 2 see cràdh-lot. A mo ch., ! *alas, my torment !*
crà-dhubh, (AC) *a.* & *s.m.* Dark red.
crà-fhaoileag,(AC) *s.f.* Red gull. 2 (AF)Black-headed sea-gull.
crag, -aige, -an, see creag.
crag, *v.a.* Knock, see cnac.
—, *gen. pl.* of craig.
cràg, -àige, -an. *s.f.* see cròg.
——ach, -aiche, *a.* see crògach.
cragach, -aiche, *a.* see creagach.
cragadh,‡‡ -aidh, *s.m.* Collision, knocking, see cnagadh.
†cràgair, *vr.pt.* a' cràgairt, *v.a.* Handle awkwardly or inelegantly.
cràgair, -ean, *s.m.* Pawer. 2 (MMcL) Person with large clumsy hands.
———eachd, *s.f.ind.* Act of pawing. 2 Act of handling awkwardly.
cràgairt, *s.f.* Handling awkwardly or indelicately. A' c—, *pr.pt.* of cràgair.
cràgan, *n.pl.* of cràg.
cragan, -ain, -an, see creagan. 2 *n. pl.* of crag. 3‡‡ Little pipkin (earthen vessel.)
———ach, -aiche, *a.* see creaganach.
cràganach, -aich, *s. m.* In-footed or in-toed person. 2**Splay-footed person.
cragan-feannaig,(AF) *s.m.* Sea-urchin. 2 Large periwinkle.
cragan-tràghad,(MMcD) *s.m.* Sea-urchin.
cràg-chasach, *a.* In-footed. 2 Splay-footed.
crà-gheadh, see cràdh-gheadh.
crà-gheal,(AC) *a.* & *s.m.* Light red.
cragmhor, -oire, *a.* see creaganach.
cràgnadh, -aidh, see cràgairt.
cràic, -e, -ean, *s.f.* see cròic. 2(DU)Tousled, matted head of hair.
cràiceadh, -idh, *s.m.* see cròiceadh.
craiceann, -inn [& -cne], -cnean, *s.m.* Skin. C. caorach, *a sheep-skin;* c. coin, *dog-skin;* c. cait, *cat-skin;* c. bràthan, see under brà.
——— ———aiche, *s.m.* Skinner.
craiceann-fionnaidh,* *s.m.* Fur.
craicionn, see craiceann.
craicionn-fionnaidh, see craiceann-fionnaidh.
craicne, *gen.sing.* of craiceann.
———ach, -eiche, *a.* Of, or belonging to skins.
craicnibh, *dat.pl.* of craiceann.
cràiteach, see cràidhteach.
cràidh, *pr.pt.* a' cràdh, *v.a.* Torment,pain,gall, harass, vex. Rè a làithean uile craidhear an t-aingidh, *the wicked travaileth with pain (shall be tortured) all his days.*
cràidh, *gen. sing.* of cradh.
craidheal, see creadhal.
craidhleag, -eig, -an, *s.f.* Basket, creel, egg-shaped receptacle for balls of worsted. 2†† Skull.
craidhneach, -ich, -ichean, *s.f.* Skull. 2 Skeleton. 3 Collection of bones. 4 Meagre-looking person, lean, gaunt figure. 5 (MMcL) Anything about to fall to pieces.
craidhneadh, -idh, *s. m.* Drying, decaying. 2 lessening, wearing out.
craidhneag, -eig, -an, *s. f.* Fragment of dried peat. *prov.*
———ach, -aiche, *a.* Full of peat fragments.
craidseach,(DC) *s.m.* Clumsy person, ungainly lout—*Perthshire.*
cràidseag,(DC) *s.f.* Clumsy woman—*Perthshire.*
craigear, -eir, *s.m.* Cricket (game.)
craidhnich, *pr.pt.* a' craidhneachadh, *v.a.* & *n.* Make lean. 2 Grow lean. 3 Tire.
cràidhte, *past pt.* of cràidh. Tormented, pain-

ed, afflicted, galled. 2 Shrunk.
cràidhteach, -eiche, a. Tortured, miserable. 2 Afflicting, grievous, painful. 3 Causing affliction, grief, or pain.
———ach,* v.n. Ache.
———achd, s.f.ind. Vexation, misery, grief. 2 Affliction. 3 Pain.
craig, see creag.
cràigeach,(AF) s.m. Black guillemot. 2 Splay-footed person.
craigeach, -eiche, a. see creagach.
cràigean, s.m. Splay-footed person. 2 Frog. 3 (AF) Toad. 4 (AF) Sea-serpent.
———achd, s.f. Splay-footedness, gait of a splay-footed person.
craigheach, see cràganach & cràigean.
craighte, s f. see croit.
———ar, s.m. see croitear.
cràileag, ‡‡ -eig, -ean, s.f. see craidhleag.
craimb-iasg,** -éisg, s.m. Cramp-fish, torpedo.
craimcean,(CR) s.m. Little stout man—*Suth'd.*
craimh-chadal, see cràmh-chadal.
craimheach, -ich, s.m. see cnàimheach.
craimhinn, -ean, s.m. Cancer.
craimhseag, see cnaimhseag.
craimneach, -eiche, a. Scarred. 2 Rough surfaced. 3 Botched.
craimpiasg,** see craimb-iasg.
craimscean, *for* craimcean.
cràin, -e, -tean, s.f. Sow. 2(AF) Litter of pigs. 3(AF)Female of any animal.
craindidh,* a. Cross-grained.
cràineag, s.f. see gràineag. 2 Urchin.
crainn, *gen.sing. & n.pl.* of crann.
crainn,* s.f. The queen of the hive. 2 Ugly old woman—*Islay.* 3 see cràin.
crainngidh, see crainntidh.
crainn-ghridh, -e, s.f. Mast-rigging.
crainnseag, -eig, -an, see cnaimhseag.
crainn-seile,** s.f. Tough phlegm.
crainnteachd, see crainntidheachd.
crainntidh, -e, a. Parching,withering,pinching, shrivelling. 2 Piercing. 3 Quick-tempered. 4(WC) Sour-tempered. Tha e 'na dhuine c., *he is a sour-tempered fellow.*
crainntidheachd, s.f.ind. Drought. 2 Effect of cold winds.
crainnt-sheile, s.m. Tough phlegm.
cràinteach,†† a. Of, or pertaining to, sows or pigs.
crait, s.f., *W. of Ross* for croit.
cràite, a. see cràidhte.
———ach, see cràidhteach.
———achd, s.f. see cràidhteachd.
cràiteag, -eig, -an, s.f. Niggardly woman.
cràitheach, -ich, s.m. One disabled by wounds or sores.
craithleag, see craidhleag.
craitneag,(AF) Bat (bird.)
cràlad, -aid, s.m. Woe, torment. [cràdh-lot]
cràlaidh,* s.m. Crawl, crawling, [*from* Eng. crawl.]
crà-leaba, s.f. Bier, hearse.
cràlot, see cràdh-lot.
cramag, (AF) s.f. Snail.
cramaist,(CR) s.f. Crease in cloth caused by folding—*Skye.*
cramasgadh, (CR) s. m. Creasing. Air a chramasgadh, *creased—Skye.*
cramb, pr.pt. a' crambadh, v.a. Squeeze, press.
cramb, -aimb, s.f. Cramp-iron,holdfast, clincher. 2 Knot. 3 Quarrel.
———ach, -aiche, a. Griping, clenching. 2 Quarrelsome. 3††Pertaining to clamp-irons.
———adh, -aidh, s.m. Quarrel. 2 Holding fast, fixing, clinching. 3 Stiffness of the joints. 4** Knotting.
crambaid, -e, -ean, s.f. Metal on the end of a sword-sheath or -stick, ferrule. 2 Cramp. 3 Objection. 4** Buckle, hasp. 5 Hook or catch, by which anything like a buckle is held in place. Gun chrios gun ch., *without belt or buckle.*
cràmh, v.a. see cnàmh.
cràmhag, -aige, -an, s.f. see cnàmhag. 2‡‡ Dead embers.
cràmhan, -ain, -an, see cnàmhan.
cramhan,** s.m. Rebuke, scold. 2††Continued grumbling.
cràmharlach, -aich, see cnàmharlach.
cràmh-chadal, (CR) s. Slumber, dose—*West of Ross.*
cràmhor, -oire, a. see cnàimheach.
†crampa,‡‡ s.m. Knot.
crampadh, -aidh, -aidhean, see crambadh.
crampag, -aig, -an, s.f. Noose.
crampaid, -e, -ean, see crambaid.
cranachan, see crannachan.
cranag, see crannag.
†cranaiche, s.m. Decrepit old man.
crangaid, s.f. Crank.

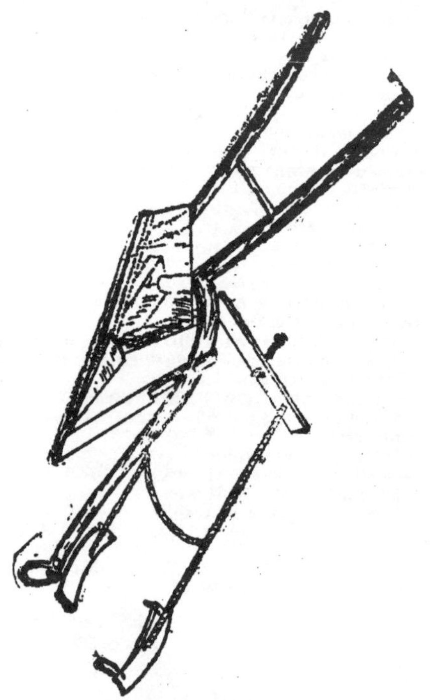

206. Crann Gàidhealach.

crann, [-ainn &] -oinn s. m. Plough. 2 Bar, bolt. 3 Tree. 4 Beam. 5 Mast. 6 Shaft. 7 Lot. 8 Measure for fresh herrings (cran.) 9* Chance, risk, ballot. 10* Partiality, side, interest. 11‡‡ Membrum virile. 12 Saltire *in heraldry*—St. Andrew's Cross—the National Badge of Scotland. 13 see crann-arain—*Astron.* Cuir na h-eich 'sa chrann, *yoke the horses in the plough*; cuir an c. air an dorus, *bar or bolt the door*; c. na luinge, *the ship's mast*; thàinig an c. air, *he was chosen by ballot*; cha'n 'eil cuid no c. agad 'sa ghnothach seo,

207. Crann

you have neither lot nor part in this affair; tha Dia Iehobhah air mo ch., *the Lord Jehovah is on my side;* cò a bhitheas air do ch. ? *who shall be your friend ?* ; ma bhitheas tusa air mo chrann, *if you befriend me;* gabh cuid do chroinn, *take your chance* ; ma 'se sin do ch., *if that be your lot*; ris a' ch., *at the plough, ploughing*; Lebanon nan c., *woody L.*; an c. meadhonach, *the middle bar*; còig croinn, *five bars;* tilg croinn, *cast lots.*

PARTS OF A PLOUGH :—

[A more detailed list will be found under "crann-nan-gad."]

1 Ceann, *head—to which the soc is fixed.*
2 Uaidne, *pl.*-an, Corrag-a'-chrainn, *handle, stilt.* (AH) Spàg, *pl.* -an, *stilt* ; corrag, *handle.*
3 Urchaill, *furrow-board, mould-board.*—(AH) Sgiath.
4 Druide-bòrd, *earth-board.*
5 Earrghas, *mainpiece.*
6 Ceidhe, ceighe, ceadha, ceann-suic, *share-beam part to which the share is fixed.*—(AH) Druim.
7 Amhach, (AH) Part extending from upper corner of furrow-board to the muzzle-holder.

crann, *pr.pt.* a' crannadh, *v.a.* Bar, bolt, barricade, as a door. 2 Wind about a beam, as a web. 3* Shrivel, decay, wear off. 4** Plough. 5†† Fit with masts. A' crannadh, *shrivelling, dying by inches* ; c. an dorus, *bolt the door.*

cranna-cas, *s.pl.* Weaver's treadles.

crannach, -aiche, *a.* Full of trees or masts.

———, -aich, *s.f.* Plough-gear. 2 Dwarfish decrepit person. 3(DC) Rogue—*Argyll.*

crannachan, -ain, -an, *s.m.* Crane, for raising weights. 2 Kind of churn, called also "bite" in *Lewis.* 3 (AF) Beaten milk, a Hallowe'en treat, into which a ring &c. is put.

crannachu, see crann-chu.

crannadh, -aidh, *s.m.* Shrivelling, decaying. 2|| Withering. 3 Choosing by lots. 4 Winding warp about the beam of a loom. A' c—, *pr.pt.* of crann. A' c. aodaich, *winding cloth about the beam.*

crannadhail, (AC) *s.f.* Framework of a coracle. 2 Any skeleton-like, odd contrivance.

crannadh-aodaich, *s.m.* Act of winding the warp about the beam of a loom.

crannag, -aig, -an, *s.f.* Pulpit. 2 Round top of a mast. 3 Cross-trees of a ship. 4 Hamper. 5 Fillet used of old in dressing a woman's hair, snood. 6* Churn. 7 Bar, in *law.* 8‡‡ Mill-clapper. 9‡‡ Hollow of a shield. 10‡‡ Kind of wicker or wooden frame suspended over the fire, on which fir-roots used for candles are set to dry. 11(AH) Fortified island in a lake, partly natural and partly artificial. [An ancient artificial islet on Loch Tollie, Poolewe, is called *A' Chrannag.*] 12 Applied to many kinds of wooden structures in Gaeldom. 13 Boat. C. air a stiùradh leis a' ghaoith, *a boat steered by the wind.*

crannaich, *pr.pt.* a' crannachadh, *v.a.* Fit with masts. 2 Bolt, bar.

crannaiche, ‡‡ *s.m.* Decrepit old man.

crannaichte, *past pt.* of crannaich. Fitted with masts. 2 Bolted, barred.

crann-aimhreidh, *s. m.* Spindle for twining thread (fearsaid)—*Livingstone's Poems.*

crannair, *s.m.* Plougher.

crann-àirneag, ** *s.m.* Sloe-tree.

crann-aisil, *s.m.* Axle-tree.

crannalach, -aiche, -aichean, *s.m.* Carpenter. 2 Wreck, ruins of anything. Chaidh i 'na c., *she went to pieces (as a ship.)*

crann-aodaich, *s. m.* Cloth-beam of loom, see under beart-fhigheadaireachd.

crann-àraidh, *s.m.* Plough.

crann-arain, *pl.* croinn-, *s.m.* Plough. 2 Baker's bread shovel, thin piece of wood for turning bread on a gridiron. 3 "The Plough" Charles' wain, or the Baker's bread-shovel, —the seven stars in the constellation of the Great Bear.

crann-arbhair, croinn-, *s.m.* Plough, see crann-arain.

crann-àrcain, *s.m.* Cork-tree—*quercus suber.*

crann-àrd, *s.m.* Top-mast.

crann-aruir, see crann-arain.

crannas, -ais, *s.m.* see crannadh.

crann-athair, * *s.m.* *Mull* for crann-arain.

crann beag Gàidhealach, see crann-nan-gad.

crann-beith, ** *s.m.* Birch-tree.

crann-bhràid, -ean, *s.m.* Hames.

crann-bocsa, *s.m.* Box-tree.

crann-calltuinn, *s.m.* Hazel-tree.

crann-canaich, *s.m.* Cotton-tree.

crann-caorainn, *s.m.* Wild ash-tree, service-tree.

crann-ceusaidh, croinn-ch—, *s. m.* Gibbet for crucifixion, cross. 2** Crucifix.

crann-ceusda, croinn-ch—, see crann-ceusaidh.

crannchan, -ain, *s.m.* Old crooked stick—*MacFadyen.*

crannchar, -air, -airean, *s.f.* see crannchur.

crann-chu, (AF) -choin, *s.m.* Lap-dog.

crannchuir, *v.a.* Cast lots (*better* tilg croinn.) 2** Ballot.

crannchur, -uir, -an, *s.m.* Casting of lots. 2 Lot, portion, share. 3 Fortune, whether good or evil. 4* Fate, destiny, predestination. 5** Ballot. Bocsa crannchuir, *ballot-box*; paipear crannchuir, *ballot-paper;* Ma 's e sin mo ch., *if that be my fate* ; cuir c., *refer to the ballot* ; gach tuiteamas thig 'na ch., *every occurrence that may fall to his lot.*

crann-coirneil, *s.m.* Cornel-tree.

crann-cosgair, *s.m.* Laurel.

crann-cothromachaidh, *s.m.* see crann-cothromaiche.

crann-cothromaiche, croinn-ch—, *s. m.* Balance-beam.

crann-crithinn, ** *s.m.* Aspen-tree. 2 Poplar.

crann-cuilce, croinn-chuilce, *s.m.* Cane.

crann-cuilinn, ** *s.m.* Holly-tree, see cuilionn.

crann-cuinnse, ** *s.m.* Quince-tree.

crannda, *a.* Decrepit, frail.

———idh, *a.* Excessively cold and withering, as weather in the spring. 2†† Frail. 3†† Dry, withered.

———idheachd, *s.f.* Cold, withering weather. 2 The withering blast.

crann-dall, croinn-dalla, *s.m.* Bowsprit of a ship.

crann-daraich, *s.m.* Oak-tree.

crann-dealbha, see crann-deilbhe.

crann-deilbhe, croinn-dealbhaidh, *s.m.* Warping frame.

crann-deiridh, croinn-deiridh, *s. m.* Mizzen-mast.

crann-dlù, *s.m.* Warp-beam—*Argyll mainland*

†**crann-dòrdain**, *s.m.* Sort of music produced by applying the hand to the mouth.

crann-doruis, croinn-, *s.m.* Door-bolt.

crann-dromain, ** *s.m.* Bore-tree, elder-tree.

crann-druididh, croinn-d—, *s.m.* Bar, bolt.

crann-dubhan, (AF) *s.m.* Black-headed gull.

crann-dùrdain, ** see crann-dòrdain.

crann-eboin, ** *s.m.* Ebony-tree.

crann-faidhbhile, § *s.m.* see craobh-fhaidhbhile

crann-fàisneachd, ‡‡ *s.f.* Sorcery.

crann-fèarna, *s.m.* Alder-tree.

crann-fhaoileag, ¶ *s. m.* Little gull—*larus mi*

nutus.

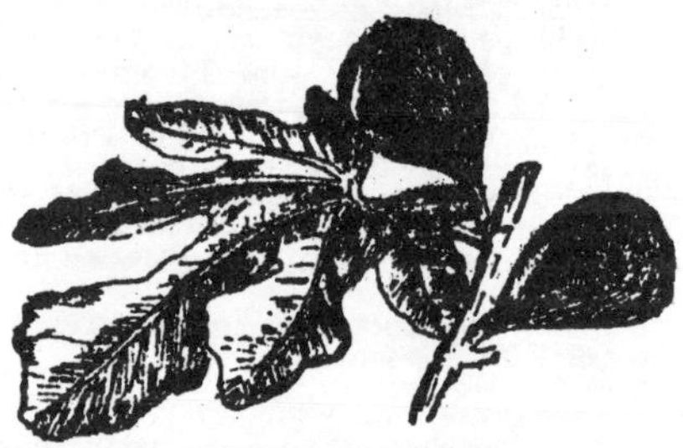

208. *Crann-fìge.*

crann-fìge, *s.f.* Fig-tree—*ficus carica.*
crann-figis, see crann-fìge.
crann-fiodha,(AH) *s.m.* Wooden plough.
crann-fìona, croinn-fhìona, *s.f.* Vine—*vitis vinifera.*
crann-forca, croinn-fhorca, *s.m.* Prong, fork.
crann-fuine, croinn-fh-, *s.m.* Baker's rolling-pin.
crann-gafainn,** *s.m.* Henbane.
crann-gatha, croinn-gh-, *s.m.* Spear-shaft.
crann-ghallchnò,** *s.m.* Walnut-tree.
†crannghail, -e, -ean, *s. f.* Mast-rigging. 2 Mortification. 3 Pulpit. 4 Lattices before the altar. 5 Bow.
crann-ghiuthais,** *s.m.* Fir-tree. 2 Pine. see giuthas.
crann-gràin-ubhal, *s.m.* Pomegranate.
crann-iubhair,** *s.m.* Yew-tree. [Badge of the Frasers.]
crannlach, -aich, *s.f.* Boughs, branches, brushwood. 2(AH) Large, lank, lean man.
——,(CR) *s.m.* Tulchan calf, figure of a calf made of a skin stretched on a frame of wood, used for setting beside cows to induce them to yield their milk—*W. of Ross.*

209. *Crann-lach.*

crann-lach, -aich, -aichean, *s. f.* Teal—*anus crecca.* 2(AF) Wild duck. 3(AF) Red-breasted merganser.
crann-laoibhreil,§ *s.m.* Laurel. 2**Bay-tree. see craobh-laibhreis.
crann-laoicionn,†† *s.m.* Tulchan calf.
crann-leamhain,** *s.m.* Elm-tree, see craobh-leamhain.
†crann-leathann, *s.m.* Ancient Irish silver coin.
crann-liomain,‡ *s.m.* Lemon-tree—*citrus limonum.*
crann-lìthe, *s.m.* Carpenter.
crannlochan, -ain, -an, *s.m.* Churn, *prov.*
crann-luch,* *s.m.* Peewit, see adharcan-luachrach.
crann-mhailp, see craobh-mhalpais.
crann-malpais, see craobh-mhalpais.
crann-meadhoin, croinn-mh-, *s.m.* see crann-mór. 2 Pole between two horses in a waggon or coach.
crann-meas,** *s.m.* Fruit-tree.
crann-meidil,‡ *s.m.* Medlar-tree.—*mespilus germanica.*
crann-mhaol-dhearc,§ Common mulberry-tree, —*morus nigra.*
crann-mór, croinn-mhóra, *s.m.* Main-mast of a ship. 2 Iron or Lowland plough.—*Lewis.*
crann-mullaich, *s.m.* Top-mast.

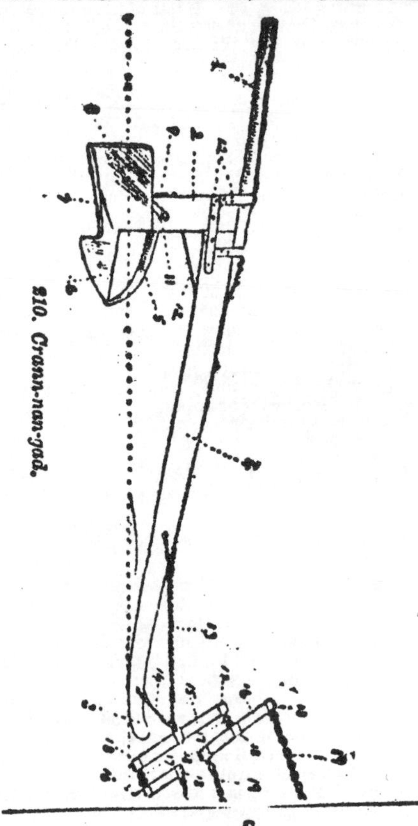

210. *Crann-nan-gad.*

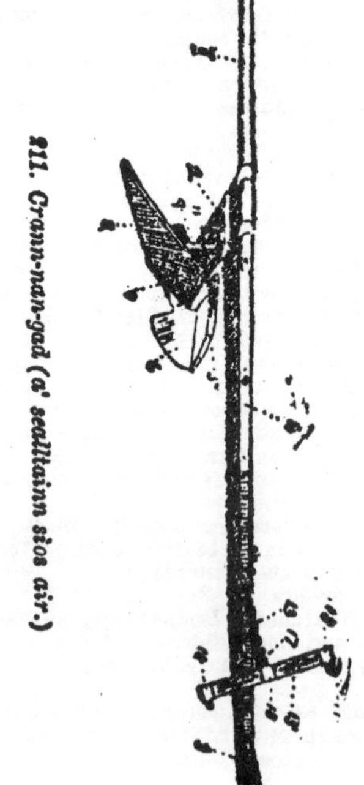

211. *Crann-nan-gad (a' sealltainn sìos air.)*

crann-nan-gad, *s. m.* Kind of plough, seldom used now, though at one time common enough, especially in the Western Isles. The parish of Barvas is the only part of Lewis where it is still used. It is usually drawn by one horse, though two can be used. From its construction it is especially suited to the stony ground of the crofts, and its gradual disappearance is a cause of great regret, as there is no other implement, equally convenient to take its place. It possesses a great advantage over the common iron plough, in that, as the point runs along the ground behind the horse, it serves the two-fold purpose of keeping the plough steady, and when the share comes in contact with a stone, by lifting the handle, or *làmh-chrann* upwards like a lever, the share and sock can be lifted clear of the obstruction. The ploughman uses only one hand, and walks on the left side of the implement, instead of behind, as is now usual in ploughing.

PARTS OF CRANN-NAN-GAD :— (see illst. 210 & 211.

1 Làmh-chrann, *handle.*
2 Màs a'chroinn, *rearpiece.*
3 Sròn, *point.* It is shod with iron, and runs along the ground behind the horse.
4 Earrghas, *body* or *mainpiece*, between *màs* and *sròn.*
5 Coltair, *share* (of iron.)
6 Soc, *sock* (of iron.)
7 Ùirthilleach, *the piece of hard wood with iron sheath on it, on which the mould-board rests,* held in by "maide-a'-chroinn-sparraidh," by passing a thong through the mould-board and round the stick; the stick, or "maide-a'-chroinn-sparraidh," being inserted in the "lùbach" of the "ùirthilleach" and pressed below "tarrag-a'-chroinn-sparraidh."
8 Bòrd-ùireach, *mould-board.*—Bòrd (CR.)
9 Maide-a'-chrann-sparraidh, *the stick for holding mould-board* in its place, by one end being fixed in a loop of iron in the "ùirthilleach" called "lùbach na h-ùirthilleach," the other end being pressed below "tarrag-a'-chroinn-sparraidh"—[sparr cruaidh e, *press it hard*—hence the name.]
10 Tarrag-a'-chroinn-sparraidh.
11 Tarrag-mhaide-a'-chroinn-sparraidh, nail to which the bi-forked end of the stick is pressed under.
12 Na goid, *bands of iron* which bind the *màs* and *earrghas* together. [These were originally of withes, hence their name.]
13 An druim mór, *long part of rope by which the plough is drawn.*
14 An druim beag, *short part of rope, which steadies the* sròn.
15 Amall, *main swingle-tree.*
16 Na greallagan, *swingle-trees next the horses* to which the "sliosan" are attached by means of a "lùbach" and "cadhag" to each "slios."
17 Na cadhagan, *iron links* in the form of an S, between swingle-tree and plough, or between two swingle-trees. 2 *Swingle-tree wedges.*
18 Na lùbaichean, *loops* of iron, one on each end and one in the centre of each swingle-tree, in which the "cadhagan" are inserted.
19 Na sliosan, na sìntean, *drag-ropes* or *traces*, on each side of horse, and attached to each end of swingle-trees.—Gearraiseach (*sing.*)—CR.

The following parts are best explained by reference to illustrations 212 & 213.

19a Lùbach na h-ùirthilleach, the part where the lower end of "maide-a'-chroinn-sparraidh" is inserted.
20 Meirgeal, the stick or iron which attaches the sock and "ùirthilleach" to the "màs," by one end being inserted in a hole through the lower end of the "màs" and the other end into "ailean an t-suic" along with the "ùirthilleach."
21 Ailean an t-suic, the space into which the "meirgeal" and "uirthilleach" are put in the sock. The illustration shows them inserted.
22 Òrdag an t-suic, *toe of sock,* which is inserted in a small hole in the point of the share.

Iall, *thong,* which passes through a couple of small holes in the mould-board, and is tied to "maide-a'-chroinn-sparraidh" behind, in order to keep the mould-board steady.

Na géinntean, *wedges,* which tighten the coltair, share and "meirgeal."

Clasan, *iron sole,* fixed on the bottom of the "màs" or rear-piece, to protect it from injury.

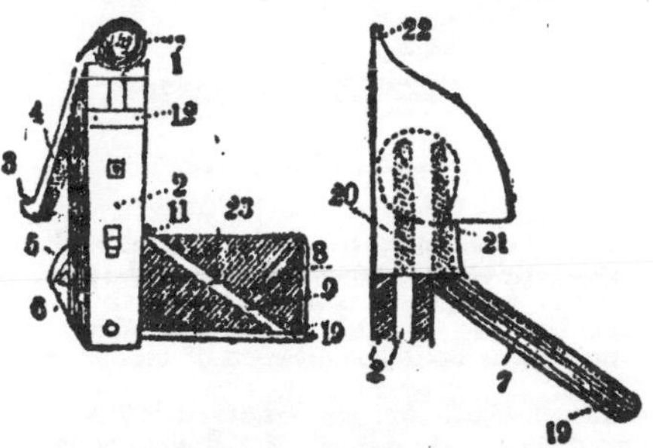

212. Crann-nan-gad bho 'n taobh-chùil. | *213. A' sealltainn sìos air an t-soc.*

Ill. 210 shows the space called "ailean an t-suic," in the under side of sock (shaded.) It is drawn looking from top or upper part of sock, so that the space may be seen plainly through it, though it would not be seen in actual fact as shown in this sketch.

[We are indebted to Mr. D. Murray, Aberdeen, for many of above terms, and to Mr. M. MacDonald, Stornoway for illustrations and additional information.]

crann-neochdair,** *s.m.* Nectarine-tree.

crann-ola,†† see crann-olaidh.

crann-olaidh,‡ croinn-, *s.f.* Olive-tree—*olea europœa.*

crann-pailm,‡ *s.m.* Date-palm—*phœnix dactylifera.* (see ill. 214.)

†**crann-phìosan,** *pl.* croinn-, *s.m* Kind of missive weapon.

crann-pìce, *pl.* croinn-ph-, *s.m.* Pick-shaft.

crann-reultach, see crann-arain.

crann-riaghailte, *s.m.* Regulator of a watch.

crann-riaslaidh, see crann-ruslaidh.

crann-ristil, see crann-ruslaidh.

crann-ruslaidh, *s.m.* Sort of rude plough, used for paring an uneven surface, by means of a sharpened share and without a coulter, the common plough following in its track. The

214. *Crann-pailm.*

215. *Crann-ruslaidh.*

idea of combining ploughshare and coulter in one implement does not appear to have occurred to the agricultural mind when this was in general use, or the roughness of the ground may have made the division of labour necessary.

crann-rustlaidh,‡‡ see crann-ruslaidh.
crann-seilg, *s.m.* Arrow. 2 Hunting-spear.
crann-seilich,** *s.m.* Willow-tree, sallow-tree.
crann-seudair, see crann-sheudair.
crann-seunta, *s.m.* Sacred wood.
crann-sgòide, *pl.* croinn-, *s.m.* Boom.
crann-shaor, *pl.* croinn-shaoir, *s.m.* Carpenter. 2 Mast-wright. 3 Plough-wright.
crann-sheudair,** *s.m.* Cedar-tree—*cedar*.
crann-shlat, -ait, -an, *s.f.* Withered wand.
——————ag, *s.f. dim.* of crann-shlat.
crann-shneachda, *s.f.* Laying on of snow. 2 Snow-plough.
crann-siris,‡‡ *s.m.* Cherry-tree.
crann-sitroin,** *s.m.* Citron-tree.
crann-siùil, *pl.* croinn-sh-, *s.m.* Mast. Air bàrr croinn-shiùil, *on the top of a mast.*
crann-sleagh,** *s.m.* Pike-staff.
crann-snàth, *s.m.* Warp-beam in a loom—*Hebrides*, see beart-fhigheadaireachd.
crann-spreòid, *pl.* croinn-s-, *s. m.* Bowsprit.
crann-tabhuill, *pl.* croinn-t-, *s. m.* Sling. 2 Shaft of a sling. Luchd nan c., *the slingers.*
cranntach,(AF) Curlew, see guilbneach.
cranntachan, -ain, *s.m.* Churn-stick.
crann-tachrais, s.m. Winding-wheel (for illust. see liaghra.) 2††Reel.
cranntail, -e, *s.pl.* Trees.
crann-tàir, see crann-tàra.
crann-tàirnean, *pl.* of crann-tarrang.
crann-tàra, *pl.* croinn-th-, *s.m.* The gathering beam, a signal formerly used on occasions of insult or impending danger, to summon a clan to arms. It was a piece of wood, half burnt and dipped in blood, in token of the revenge by fire and sword awaiting those clansmen who did not immediately answer the summons. It was handed from one permanently appointed messenger to another, and in this manner the alarm was spread through the largest districts in an incredibly short time. In 1745 the *crann-tàra* traversed the wide district of Breadalbane, upwards of 30 miles, in three hours. 2 Fiery-cross. 3 Fire kindled on an eminence to notify alarm or danger.
crann-tàraidh,†† see crann-tàra.
crann-tarraig, *Uist* for crann-tarrang.
crann-tarrang, *gen.* -tàirnge, *pl.* -tàirnean, *s.f.* Wooden pin or bolt fastening the couples or joists of a house, see under taigh. 2 Tree-nail, wooden pin used in ship-building. 3 Choosing by lots. 4 Lynch-pin. 5 Draught-tree or shaft. 6**Peg.
crann-tarsuinn, *s.m.* Cross-bar. 2 Diameter.
crann-tarung, } see crann-tarrang.
crann-tarunn, }
crann-teach, *pl.* croinn-theacha, *s.m.* Arbour.
crann-teannta, see crann-teannachaidh.
crann-teanndaidh,** *s.m.* Calender (for cloth)
crann-teile, *s.m.* Lime-tree.
crann-teannachaidh, *pl.* croinn-th-, *s.m.* Printer's press. 2 Bookbinder's press. 3 Rack-pin.
crann-togalach, *s.m.* Crane, lever.
crann-toisich, *pl.* croinn-th-, *s.m.* Fore-mast.
crann-ton, -oin, *s.f*, Pink stern, sharp bottom.
crann-tuilm,** *s. m.* Holm oak, see craobh-thuilm.
crann-tùise,** *s.m.* Frankincense-tree.
crann-ubhail, *pl.* croinn-ùbhail, *s.m.* Apple-tree.
crann-uinnsinn,** *s.m* Ash-tree.
crann-uisge, *pl.* croinn-uisge, see crann-spreòid.
craobh, -aoibhe, -an, *s.f.* Tree, bush. 2‡‡Relation. 3 Ear of oats (craobh coirce.) 4(DC) Streaming clouds, rising from the horizon and spreading wide as they ascend to the zenith.—*Uist*. This word (or *crann*) is always prefixed to the names of trees in Gaelic when speaking of growing timber. Meas craoibhe, *the fruit of a tree.*
craobh, -aoibhe, *s.f.* Foam or globules ("bell") on the surface of liquids. Cha chum e c., *it will not retain the foam.* 2**Richness.
craobh, *v. n.* Branch out, sprout, bud, shoot forth, gush out. 2 Propagate. 'Fhuil a' craobhadh mu thalamh, *his blood gushing forth and ramifying.*
craobh-abran,§ *s.f.* Laburnum.
craobhach, -aiche, *a.* Woody, wooded, full of trees. 2 Of, or belonging to trees. 3 Having tall trees. 4 Flowing, branching, spreading, rilling, ramifying in ramifying gushes, as blood. 5 Flowing in a branching or forked stream. 'Fhuil ch., *his streaming blood*; mo dhùn c., *my woody hill*; an t-sleagh ch., *the tree-like spear.*
craobhachd, see craobhaidheachd.
craobhadair,** *s.m.* Arborist.
craobhag, -aig, -an, *s. f.* Small tree, bush. 2 Bunch.
——————ach,†† *a.* Pertaining to small trees.
craobhaidh, -e, *a.* Nervous. 2 Tender. 3 Shivering.
craobhaidh fuar,(CR) *a.* Piercingly cold, shiveringly cold—*W of Ross-shire.*
craobhaidheachd, *s. f. ind.* Lassitude, infirmity. 2 Tremor, nervousness.
craobh-àirneag,** *s.f.* Sloe-bush.
craobharnach, *s. m.* Shrubbery. 2 Hedge of

thorns, whins, &c.

craobh-bheithe,** *s.f.* Birch-tree.

craobh-bhròin,§ *s. f.* Cypress-tree—*cupressus sempervirens.* [Badge of the MacDougalls.]

craobh-challtuinn,** *s.f.* Hazel-tree, see calltuinn.

craobh-chanaich,** *s.f.* Cotton-tree.

craobh-chaorainn,§ *pl.* -an-, *s.f.* Mountain-ash or rowan-tree, see luis. 2** Service-tree, see craobh-cheòrais.

craobh-cheòrais,‡ *s. f.* Service-tree—*pyrus torminalis—Perthshire.*

216. Craobh-cheòrais.

craobh-chòinneach, *s.f.* Catling.

craobh-choirneil, *s.f.* Cornel-tree.

craobh-chòmhraig, *pl.* -an-, *s. f.* Hero, [*lit.* branch of war.]

craobh-chosgair, *pl.* -an-, *s. f.* Laurel-tree. 2 Trophy.

craobh-chrithinn, *s. f.* Aspen-tree, see critheann.

craobh-chuilinn, *s.f.* Holly-tree, see cuilionn.

craobh-chuinnse,§ *s.f.* Quince-tree,—*pyrus cydonia.*

217. Craobh-chuinnse.

craobh-chuir, *pl.* -an-c-, *s.f.* Planted tree.

craobh-dharaich, *pl.* -an-d-, *s. f.* Oak-tree—*quercus robur.*

craobh-dhearg, -eirge, see crò-dhearg. 2††Red-streaming.

craobh-ealp,* *v.a.* Ingraft, graft.

——————air,* -ean, *s.m.* Grafter.

craobh-eòlas,* *s.m.* see eòlas-chraobh.

craobh-fhaidhbhile,§ *s. f.* Beech-tree —*fagus sylvatica.*

craobh-fhèarna, *s.f.* Alder-tree.

craobh-fhiadhain,‡ *s.f.* Wayfaring-tree—*viburnum lantana.* (see ill. 218.)

craobh-fhiodhag,‡ *s. f.* Bird-cherry—*prunus padus.* 2 **Hardberry-tree. (see ill. 219.)

craobh-fhiona, *s.f.* Vine, see crann-fiona.

craobh-geanmchno,‡ *s.f.* Common chestnut-tree

218. Craobh-fhiadhain.

219. Craobh-fhiodhag.

—*castanea vesca.*

craobh-geanmchno-fhiadhaich,‡ *s. f.* Horse-chestnut-tree—*æsculus hippocastanum.* [Introduced into Scotland in 1709.]

craobh-ghallchno,§ *s.f.* Walnut tree—*juglans regia.*

craobh-ghinealaiche, *pl.* -an-g-, *s.f.* Genealogical tree.

craobh-ghiuthais, *s.f.* Fir-tree. 2 Pine-tree, see giuthas.

craobh-ghrain-ubhal, *s.f.* Pomegranate.

craobh-iubhair,** *s.f.* Yew-tree.

craobh-laibhreil, see craobh laibhreis.

craobh-laibhreis, *s.f.* Laurel-tree.

craobh-leamhain, *s.f.* Elm-tree.

craobh-learaig, *s.f.* Larch-tree, see learag.

craobh-liath-ghorm,‡ *s. f.* Lilac-tree—*syringa vulgaris.*

craobh-liomain, *s.f.* Lemon-tree, see crann-liomain.

craobh-mhailp,‡ see craobh-mhalpais.

craobh-mhalpais,‡ *s.f.* Common maple-tree—*acer campestris.* (see illust. 220.)

craobh-mhaol-dhearc,** *s. f.* Mulberry-tree, see crann-mhaol-dhearc.

craobh-mheas, *pl.* -an-m-, *s.f.* Fruit-tree. C. a bheir measan, *a fruit-tree that beareth fruit.*

craobh-mheidil, *s.f.* see crann-meidil.

craobh-na-geanmnachd, *s.f.* Agnus castus.

craobh-nan-smeur,‡ *s.f.* The "mulberry-tree" of Scripture, supposed to be the aspen (critheann.)

craobh-neochdair, *s.f.* Nectarine-tree.

craobh-òmair, *s.f.* Amber-tree.

220. *Craobh-mhalpais.*

craobh-phailm, *s.f.* Palm-tree, see crann-pailm.
craobh-pheurain-fhiadhain,§ *s.f.* Wild pear-tree, *pyrus communis.*
craobh-phobuill,§ *s.f.* Poplar-tree—*populus alba.*
craobh-pleantrainn, see craobh-shice.
craobh-sgaoil,* *s. f.* Crawling, sprawling. 2 Torture.
craobh-sgaoil, *pr. pt.* a' craobh-sgaoileadh, *v.a. & n.* Spread abroad, diffuse, propagate. 2 Branch, ramify. 3**Sprout.
craobh-sgaoileadh, -idh, *s. m.* Propagating, publishing, spreading abroad. 2 Branching. 3 Sprouting. A' c—, *pr. pt.* of craobh-sgaoil.
craobh-sgaoilteach, -eiche, *a.* Propagative, publishing. 2 Branching.
craobh-sheanchuis, *pl.* -an-s-, see craobh-ghinealaiche.
craobh-sheilich,*s.f.* Willow-tree. 2 Sallow-tree.
craobh-sheudair,** *s.f.* Cedar-tree.
craobh-shice, *s. f.* Sycamore-tree.—*acer pseudo platanus.* [Badge of Clan Oliphant.]

221. *Craobh-shice.*

craobh-shiris, *s.f.* Cherry-tree—*prunus cerasus.*
craobh-shitroin,§ *s.f.*Citron-tree—*citrus medica.*
craobh-shlighe,** *s.m.* Avenue.
craobh-theile,§ *s.f.* Lime-tree, linden—*tilia europœa.*
craobh-thuilm,§ *s.f.* Holm-tree (evergreen oak) *quercus ilex.*
craobh-thuinidh, *pl.* -an-t-, *s.f.* Tree of descent, genealogical tree.
craobh-thuise,** *s.f.* Frankincense-tree.
craobh-uaine-ghiuthais,§ *s.f.* see craobh-bhròin.
craobh-ubhail,** *s.f.* Apple-tree.
——— -fhiadhain, *s.f.* Wild apple-tree—*pyrus malus.* [Badge of Clan Lamont.]
craobh-ubhlan, see craobh-ubhail.
craobh-uibhear,** *s.f.* see craobh-iubhair.
craobh-uinnsinn, *s.f.* Ash-tree,—*fraxinus excelsior.* [Badge of Clan Menzies, according to some.]
craoim, *v.a. & s.* see creim.
craois, *gen. sing.* of craos.
———each, see craosach.
craoiseag, *s.f.* Whortleberry—*Lochaber*, see cnaimhseag (appx.)
craoisein, -ean, see craosair.
craoit, see croit.
craon, *s.m.* Torture, agony.
craonach,** *a.* Throbbing.
craos, -aois [& -ach], -an, *s.m.* Wide mouth. 2 Ludicrous term for the human mouth. 3 Mouth of a beast, particularly a voracious beast. 4‡ Open mouth. 5 Gluttony, appetite, debauchery, revelry, excess, gross sensuality. Luchd craois, *gluttons* ; a ch. fo chòip, *his mouth covered with foam;* tha 'n dorus air clap a' chraois,*the door is wide open*; cha bhi mi 10 ghearan chraosach, *I will not allow my appetite to dominate me.*
craosach, -aiche, *a.* Gluttonous, voracious. 2 Wide-mouthed. 3**Bibulous.
———, -aich, *s.m.* Spear, dart. Crath do ch., *shake thy spear.*
———, *s.m.* see craosair.
———,* *s.f.* Wide-mouthed female.
———d, *s,f.* Gluttony, greediness, voracity. 2 Sensuality.
——— -dhearg, -aich-dheirg,-aichean-dearga, *s.f.* Burning spear.
craosail,(CR) *s.f.* Gaping mouth—*Skye.* 2** Gluttony.
craosair, -ean, *s.m.* Glutton. 2 Epicure. 3 Sensualist. 4 Wide-mouthed fellow. 5** Gaper, 6**Blubber-lipped fellow.
———eachd, see craosachd.
craosal,** -ail, *s.m.* Gluttony. 2 Drunkenness, revelry, excess in eating or drinking. 3 Carousal.
craosan, -ain,-an, *s.m.* see craosair.
craosan,** *n.pl.* of craos. 2 *dim.* of craos.
craos-ghàire,** *s.f.* Horse-laugh.
craos-ghlan, *v.a.* Gargle, cleanse the mouth.
craoslach, -aiche, *s.f.* see craosach.
craosnach, -aich, *s.m.* see craosach, *s.f.*
craos-òl, -òil, *s.m.* Drunkenness.
craos-shlugadh, -aidh, *s.m.* Gormandizing.
craos-shlugair, -ean, *s.m.* Glutton.
craos-shluig, *v.a.* Swallow greedily, gormandize.
crap,‡‡ *v.a.* Crush.
crapadh, see cnapadh.
craparra, *a.* see cnaparra.
crap-lùth, -a, *s.m.* Curl in pipe-music.
crapluich, *v.n.* Fetter, bind.
crapta,‡‡ *past pt.* of crap, Crushed.
crà-rionnach,(AC) *s.* Red mackerel, tunny fish.
†**cràs**, -àis, -an, *s.m.* Body.
†——ach,** -aiche, *a.* Corpulent, bulky.
†——achd,** *s.f.* Corpulence, bulkiness.
crasagan, *s.pl.* Order of plants known as *crassulaceæ.*
†**cràsan**, *s.m. dim.* of cràs. Little body.
crasg, *s.f.* Cross. 2 Crutch. 3 Across place. 4 Club (in cards.)
crasgach, -aiche, *a.* Corpulent, bulky. 2 Uncombed. 3 Ill-natured. 4 Lying cross-way. 5* Crawling, or walking, as a person feeling torturing pain. 6* Branching, as stamped cloth. 7**A-kimbo. 8‡‡Clumsy. 9‡‡Slow. 10‡‡Thwart. 11 (MMcL) Going on crutches. 12††Contrariwise.
———d, *s.f.* Crossness.
crasgadh, -aidh, *s.m.* Box, coffer.
crasgag,(CR) *s.f.* Star-fish—*W. of Ross-shire.*
——— -thràghad,((JM) *s.f.* Star-fish.

craggan, -ain, -an, s.m. Any object of a cruciform shape.
crasgaoil,* v.a. & s.m. see craobh-sgaoil.
cratach,(CR) s.m. Back, of a person—*Skye.* 2 Side—*Glen Moriston & W. of Ross.*
cratan, see cnatan.
———ach, see cnatanach.
crath, v.a. & n. Shake. 2 Tremble. 3 Quiver. 4 Wave. 5 Brandish. 6 Sprinkle. 7**Churn. C. do cheann, *shake your head* ; ch. e 'bhata. *he flourished his staff;* crath uisg' air, *besprinkle it with water* ; c. ris, *wave to him* ; mar a chrathas na beanntan an cranna, *as the hills shake their woods.*
——ach, -aiche, a. Shaking, quivering, brandishing.
——adh, -aidh, s.m. Shake. 2 Brandishing. 3 Waving. 4 Act of shaking, brandishing or waving, as trees. 5**Sprinkling. 6**Churning. A' c—, pr. pt. of crath. C. bainne, *churning.*
crathaidh, fut. aff. a. of crath.
crathanach, -aiche, a. see crathach.
crathar, fut. pass. of crath.
crath-ghlan, v.a. Clean by shaking or shifting.
cràthrach, -aich, -an, s.f. Boggy place, marsh.
crè, s.f.ind. Clay, dust. †2 Creed. †3 Keel of a ship. 4 see creubh. Fhuair iuthaidh a ch., *an arrow found his breast.*
creabaire,(AF) s.m. Gadfly.
creabail, -aill, s.m. Garter. see cnèaball.
———ach, a. Gartered, having or wearing garters.
———aich,** v.a. Fasten with garters, provide with garters.
———aichte, past.part. of creabalaich.
creaban,** -ain, s. m. see cnèapan.
†creabh, v.a. Dun. 2 Gaelic spelling of *crave.*
creabhach, see creubhach.
creabhach,** -aich, s m. Brushwood, dry brushwood.
————, -aiche, a. Full of brushwood, dry as brushwood.
creabhag, -aig, -an, s.f. The body. 2 Constitution. 3 Young woman. 4**Twig.
creabhaichean,* -ain, s.m. Bandy.
creabhaidh,** a. Frail, not stout.
creabhar,(AF) s.m. Woodcock, see coileach-coille.
creabuill,(DM) -ean, s.m. Garter, *prov.*
creacar,** s.m. Shrine, vestry.
creach, creiche, -an, s.f. Plunder, booty, pillage. 2 Ruin, devastation. 3‡‡Host, army. 4† *for* creag. 5 *rarely* Wave. Mo chreach! mo chreach! *my ruin, alas! and alas!* cha tuig a' bhan-Leòdhasach a c. gus an tig i chum an doruis, *the Lewiswoman never realizes her loss until it comes to her door*—which shows the stolidity of the Lewiswoman. "Creach" is a stronger word than loss, but in this case at any rate, not quite so strong as ruin. Tha mo ch.-sa deanta, *I am done for, as good as dead* ; ag éigheach a c., *shouting that she was ruined* ; a' togail na creiche, *carrying away the plunder.*
creach, pr. pt. a' creachadh [& a' creach,] v.a. Plunder, spoil, pillage, rob, ruin. 2*Harry a nest, rob birds of their young. Ch. thu mi, *you have ruined me.*
†———, a. Blind. 2 Grey.
†———,** creich, s.f. Scallop-shell, large ribbed shell-fish. 2 Cockle. 3 Cup.
creachach. -aiche, a. Plundering, rapacious. 2 Abounding in scallop-shells, shellfish or 3 Cups.
creachadair, -ean, s.m. Plunderer, depredator, freebooter, spoiler, robber. Creachadairean an-iochdmhor, *merciless robbers.*
————eachd, s.f. see creachadh.
creachadh, -aidh, s. m. Preying, plunder, plundering, spoil. 2 Act of spoiling, plundering or pillaging. 3 Freebooting. 4**Ruining, ruin. 5‡‡ Execution on a musical instrument. A' c—, vr.pt. of creach. Theab e mo ch., *he had almost ruined me.*
creachag, -aig, -an, s f. Cockle, scalloped shell. 2(AF) Mole. 3 Large ribbed shellfish. C. aisneach, *a ribbed cockle.*
·———ach, -aiche, a. Abounding in ribbed cockles.
creachag-seisreach. see creachag.
creachaidh, fut. aff. a. of creach.
creachair, v.a. Stigmatize. 2 Mark, scar.
·————eas, -eis, s.m. Sculpture.
creachan, -ain, -an, s.m. Pudding made of calf's entrails. 2**Flask. 3 Ruin on a small scale. 4** Cup.
creachann, -ainn, -an, s.m. Rock. 3 Summit of a rock. 3 Mountain. 4 Hard rocky surface without foliage. 5‡‡Stony declivity of a hill. 6**Scallop shell. 7* Large ribbed cockle. Slige-chreachainn, *scallop shell used as a drinking-cup.*
†creachar, -air, s.m. Vestry. [**gives creacar.]
†-————, fut. pass. of creach.
creach-cheilgneach,(AC) s.m. Arch-deceiver.
creachd, see creuchd.
creachlach-dearg, s.m. Bloody crane's-bill [*lit.* the red wound-healer—*geranium sanguineum.*

222. *Creachlach-dearg.*

creachta, *past part.* of creach. Spoiled, plundered, ruined, robbed. An creachta an aghaidh an tréin, *the spoiled against the strong.*
crèadh, -a, see crè. Uidhe gach aon chreadha, *the goal of every body*—the grave.
crèadh,(AF) s.m. Swan.
creadha, a. Clayish, of clay.
†creadhach, a. see cneidheach.
creadhadair, s.m. Potter.
——————eachd, s.f. Potter's trade.
creadhal, -ail, s.m. †Austerity. 2 see creithleag. 3 see creathall.
†————, -aile, a. Religious, worshipping.
creadh-chumadair, -ean, s.m. see crè-chumadair.
crèadh-ghlaodh, s.m. Lute.
†creadhla, s. . see cléir.
creadhn,‡‡ v.a. Pain, torment. see crein.
creadhonadh, see creaghonadh.
creadh-thaois,‡‡ s.f. Clay for soldering.
†creadradh, -aidh, s.m. Chariot.
creafag, -aig, -an, see creubhag.
creag, -eige, -an, s.f. Rock, crag. 2 Cliff. 3 Precipice. 4 Quarry. 5 Hill. Taobh na creige, *the side of the precipice* ; bhuail e a ch., *he struck the rock* thuit mi leis a' chreig, *I fell down the rock* ; bile na creige, *the edge of*

the precipice.
——ach, -aiche, *a.* Rocky, craggy, cliffy. 2** Stony. 3 Lapideous. Air àitibh c., *on stony places.*
creagachas, -ais, *s.m.* } Craggedness.
creagachd, *s.f.ind.* } Craggedness.
creagag, -aig, -an, *s.f.* Conger. 2 Perch—*labrax lupus.* 3 Name of a famous rowing-song or iorram. [Mac Alpine says this never means *conger.*] 4 (AF) Grey plover, rock-goose, sheildrake, see trilleachan. 5 (DU) Little ball of yarn.
creagagach, †† *a.* Pertaining to congers or perch.
creagag-uisge, *s. f.* Freshwater perch—*perca fluviatilis.* 2 (AF) Perch, conger. 3 Black-goby, wrasse, rock-fish.

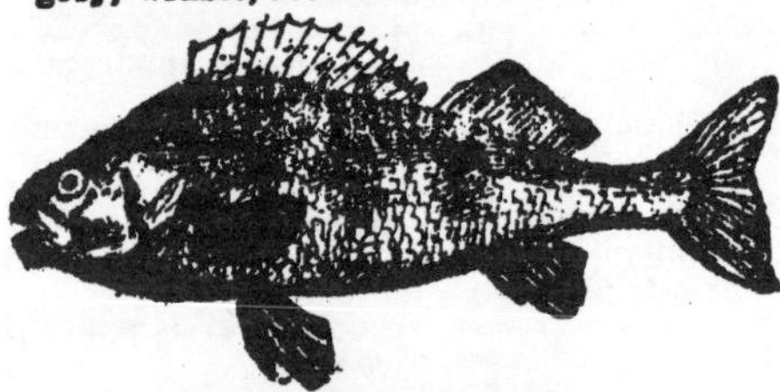
223. *Creagag-uisge.* (1.)

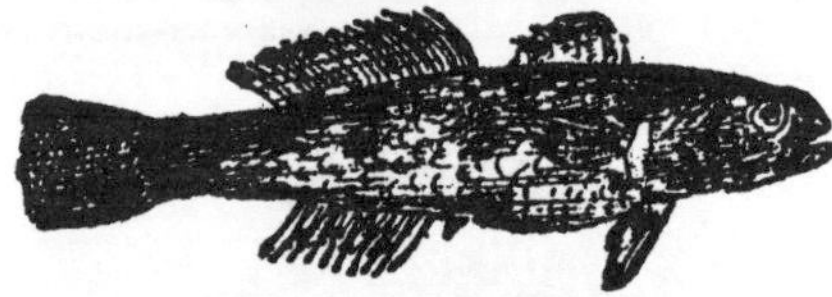
224. *Creagag-uisge.* (3.)

creagair, ** *s.m.* Grapnel.
creagan,-ain,-an, *s.m. dim.* of creag. Little rock, rocky place. 2 *n. pl.* of creag, rocks, &c.
creaganach, -aich, *a.* Rocky.
creaghonadh, -aidh, *s.m.* Twitching, piercing pain.
creag-shalann, ** -ainn, *s.f.* Saltpetre, nitre. Air ch., *on nitre.*
creag-ùillidh, ** *s.m.* Petroleum.
cream, see creim.
creamadair, see creimeadair.
————eachd, see creimeadaireachd.
creamh, -a, *s.m.* Gentian, see lus-a'-chrùbain. 2 Hart's tongue fern, see creamh-na-muice-fiadhaich. 3 Garlic, see gairgean. 4* Leeks. 5 Elecampane, see aillean. 5 Beer. An c. 'na chathraichibh, *gentian in beds or plots.*
creamhach, *a.* Abounding in, or belonging to, wild garlic or gentian.
crèamhach,†† -aich, *s.m.* see cnàimheach.
creamhachd,†† -a, -an, *s.f.* Stock, stump.
————an, -ain, *s. m.* Root of a tree, stump, block of wood, faggot, clump.
creamh-ghàraidh, *s.m.* Chives, see feuran. 2 Leek.
creamh-mac-féidh, (McL.) *s.m.* Asparagus, see creamh-na-muice-fiadhaich, and aspàrag. 2 Hart's tongue fern. 3 (CR) Elecampane.
creamh-na-muice-fiadhaich, *s.m.* Asparagus—*asparagus officinalis.* (illust. 225.) 2 Hart's tongue fern—*scolopendrium vulgare.* (illust. 226.)
creamh-nan-creag, *s.m.* Rocambole (*lit.* rock garlic)—*allium scorodoprasum.* (illust. 227.)
†creamh-nuall, -nuaill, *s.m.* Noise of carousers.
†crean, *v.a.* Consume, remove.
†crean,** -ein, *s.m.* Purchase. 2 Market-place.

225. *Creamh-na-muice-fiadhaich* (1.)

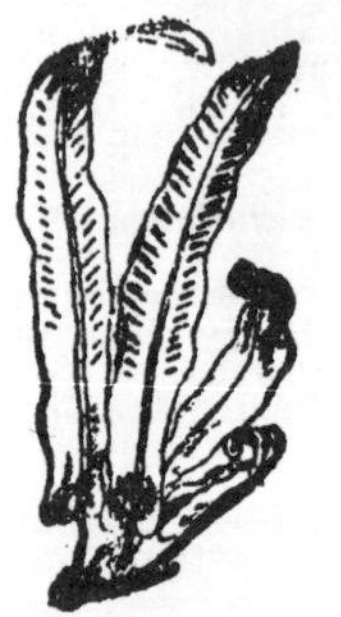
226. *Creamh-na-muice-fiadhaich* (2.)

227. *Creamh-nan-creag.*

crean,* *v. a.* see crein. 2**Consume. 3**Remove.
creanach, *s.m.* see creineach.
————adh, -aidh, *s.m.* see criothnachadh.
creanadh, *pr. pt.* of crean, see creineadh.
creanaich, *v.a.* see criothnaich.
creanaiche, *s.m.* see creineach.
creanaichte, *past part.* of creanaich, see crioth naichte.
creanair, *s.f.* Sedition. 2 Tumult.
†creanait,** -eachan, *s.m.* Market-place.
creanas, -ais, *s.m.* Whetting, hacking of sticks
————, *a.* Handy, "neat-handed."
crè-an-fhùcadair, *s.f.* Fuller's earth.
creangan, *-ain, *s.m.* Deep wound.
crèanluadh, -uaidh, see crunnlùth.
creanta,* *past part.* of crein. Dearly bought or suffered for—*Isles.*
†creapadh,-aidh, *s.m.* see crupadh.
†creapail,** *v.a.* see creapuill.
creapall,-aill, *s.m.* Entangling, stopping, hindering. 2†† Lump, let, hinderance.
creapan,**-ain, *s.m.* Stool, low stool. *Scots* creepie. see cnèapan.
creaplaichte, *past part.* of creapuill. Entangled
creapuill, *v.a.* Stop, hinder, impede.
creapull,** -uill, *s.m.* Garter.
†crear, *s.m.* see criathar.
†crearadh, -aidh, *s.m.* Bending, crooking.
†crearal, ail, *s.m.* Retaining, witholding.
crea-rionnach, see cnàmh-rionnach.
†creas, *s.m.* see crios.
†creas, *a.* Narrow, strait.
creasach,** -aich,-aichean, *s.m.* see craosach.
creasan, -ain, -an, *s.m.* see criosan. 2 Penitent. 3 Faith.
†creasgoin, *v.a.* Wound.
†creasmhuir, -mhara, *s.f.* Strait, arm of the sea.
creat, see cnead.
creatach, see cneadach.
————,** -aich, *s.m.* Hurdle.

creatachan,** -ain, *s.m.* Churning-stick.
creath, see creadh.
————ach, aiche, *s.f.* Underwood. 2 Brushwood, faggots. 3** Pollenger. [** gives *s.m.*, and *gen. sing.* -aich.]
————ail, see creathall.
————air,** -ean, *s.m.* Extortioner. 2 see criathair.
————all, -thlach, [‡‡ -eithle,] *pl.* -thlaichean, & ‡‡ -eithlean, *s.f.* Cradle. 2 Grate. 3 see creithleag.
creathall, -aill, *s.f.* Lamprey.

228. Creathall.

creathar, (AF) *s.m.* Woodcock, see coileach-coille.
†**creath-fonn,** *s.f.* see crith-fuinn.
creathlach, *gen. sing.* of creathall.
creathlaichean, *n. pl.* of creathall.
creathnachadh, -aidh, *s.m.* see crith. 2** Emotion.
creathnaich, *v.n.* see criothnaich.
creatrach, -aich, -ean, *s.f.* Wilderness.
creatuir, -e, -ean, *s.m.* see creutair.
crè-chumadair, -ean, *s.m.* Potter.
creic, *pr.pt.* a' creic, *v.a.* Sell, dispose of, barter, exchange.
creiceadair, *s.m.* Seller.
creiceal, *s.m.* Wheeze, caused by breath being impeded by phlegm.
creicealach, *a.* Wheezing.
creicealaich, *v.n.* Wheeze.
————————e, *s.m.* Wheezer.
creich, -e, *s.f.* see creach.
creiche, (AF) *s.f.* Selling cattle.
creid, *pr. pt.* a' creidsinn, *v.n.* Believe, feel convinced. 2** Credit. 3** Confide, trust, rely. Cha chreid mi nach...., *I rather think....*
————each, -eiche, *a.* see creidmheach.
————each, -ich, *s.m.* see creidmheach.
creideadh, *s.m.* see creideamh.
creideamh, -eimh, *s.m.* Faith. 2 Religious belief. 3 Tenets of a religious sect or persuasion, creed. 4** Trust, credit, confidence. Is iomadh duine laghach a mhill an c., *religion has spoilt many a nice man*—an old heathen's wail.
creideamh-a'-bhata-bhuidhe, *s.m.* The religion of the yellow stick. A Coll priest of former times was accustomed to drive recalcitrant natives to church by a smart application of his walking stick, those who yielded were thus said to come under "creideamh a' bhata bhuidhe." Another version says Hector, son of Donald Maclean, of Coll, was the one who applied the yellow stick. Hector was laird in 1715, and as the religion of the yellow stick was introduced into Rum in 1726, it is beyond dispute that Hector was the author, or propagator, of it. He was dignified in appearance and stern in manners and could no doubt wield the yellow stick gracefully and with efficiency.
creideamhach, see creidmheach.
creideamh-galar,‖ *s.m.* Religious mania. [*bad.*]
creideas, -eis, *s.m.* Credit, esteem, good repute. 2** Trust, confidence. 3** Belief. Thar c., *incredible.*
————ach, -aiche, *a.* Creditable, accredited. 2 Credited, responsible, respectable, credible, reputable.
creideasachd,** *s.f.* Creditableness, reputableness.
creideasaiche,** *s.m.* Creditor.
creideir,** *s.m.* Botcher.
†**creidhm,** see creim.
————each, see creimeach.
creidhmeadh, -idh, *s.m.* & *pr. pt.* see creimeadh.
——————— -chire, †† see creimeadh-chìre.
creidhm-raineach, *s.f.* Sweet mountain fern—*lastrea oreopetris.* see crim-raineach.
creidimh, *s.m. gen. sing.* of creideamh.
creidmheach, -aiche, *a.* Believing, having faith, faithful.
——————, -ich, *s.m.* Believer. C. no ban-ch., *a man or woman that believes.*
creidsin, see creidsinn.
creidsinn, *s.m.* Believing, act of believing. 2 Trusting, confiding. A' c—, *pr. pt.* of creid.
creidte, *past pt.* of creid. Believed. 2 Confirmed.
creig, *dat. sing.* of creag. [Used provincially as the *nom.*]
creige, *gen. sing.* of creag.
creigeag, -eig, see creagag.
creigeir, -e, -ean, *s.m.* see creagair.
creim, *pr. pt.* a' creimeadh [& a' creimeartaich,] *v. a.* Nibble. 2 Crop grass, as cattle. 3 Pick, gnaw, as a bone. 4 Erode. 5 Become scabbed. 6** Chew. 7* Nip. Is lom leac air nach c. thu, *it is a bare stone from which you will pick nothing.*
creim, *s.f.* Nibble. 2 Erosion. 3 Scab, scar. 4 see greim. 5‡‡ Disease.
————each, -eiche, *a.* Scabbed, mangy, full of sores. 2 Nibbling.
————eachas,‡‡ -ais, *s.m.* Mordacity.
creimeadair, -e, ean, *s.m.* Picker. 2 Carper, biter, verbal critic. 3 see greimiche.
——————eachd, *s.f. ind.* Picking, gnawing. 2 Carping, captious criticism.
creimeadh, -midh, *s.m.* Gnawing, chewing, picking, nipping, nibbling. 2** Erosion. A' c—, *pr. pt.* of creim. A' c. na cìre, *chewing the cud.*
creimeadh-chìre, *s.m.* Chewing of the cud.
creimeartaich,* *s.f.* Picking. A' c—, *pr.pt.* of creim.
creimneach, -niche, *a.* Knotty surfaced, scarred, blotched, mangy, full of sores, itchy, rough. 2 Nibbling. 3 Carping.
crein, *pr.pt.* a' creineadh [& a' creineachdainn,] *v.n.* Smart, suffer for. 2 (AC) Quake, tremble. 3 (AC) Upheave, tear up, excavate. Cò a chreineas air sin? *who shall suffer for that?*
creineach,* *s.m.* Sufferer, loser.
creineachan, -ain, *s.m.* Chastisement. 2 Suffering for past conduct.
creineadh, -idh, *s.m.* Act of suffering for, undergoing punishment. A'c—, *pr. pt.* of crein.
créis, -e, *s. f.* Grease, tallow, fat. 2 Narrow strait. 3 Narrow defile, *cañon.*
créis,†† *pr.pt.* a' créiseadh, *v.a.* Grease.
————each, -iche, *a.* Greasy, daubed with grease or tallow. 2 Squalid.
créiseadh, -idh, *s. m.* Greasing, smearing with fat.
créisean, -ain, -an, *s.m.* Piece of oatcake dipped in fat. 2 see creadhal.
créisidh, *a.* see créiseach.
creithil, -e [& -thlach,] -lichean, *s.f.* see creathall.
†**creithir,** *s.f.* Cup.
creithire, see gleithir.
creithleag, -eig, -an, *s.f.* Gad-fly, cleg, an insect that torments cattle.
creithleagach, †† *a.* Pertaining to gad-flies.
creithleag-mhór, (DM) *s.f.* Oxfly.
creithleag-nan-each, (DM) *s. f.* Horse-fly.

horse-cleg.
creithnich, see criothnaich.
creubhar,¶ s.m. Woodcock, see coileach-coille.
creuddach, (AC) s.m. Paralysis of the limbs in horses.
creoithtiche,* s.m. An invalid person getting better one day, and worse the next.
creòn, v.n. Put over or by.
†creon, a. see crion.
creònadh,††-aidh, s.m. Paining, torturing.
†creòp, v.a. Seduce.
†creòpach, -aich, s.m. Seducer.
creotachadh,(AH) s.m. Torturing, act of inflicting much pain or torture.
creotachd,(AH) s.f.ind. Pain, torture.
creoth, v.a. Wound, hurt. Skye.
creòth,* s.m. Wound hurt. Skye.
——ach, a. Wounding, hurting.
creothar, -air, s.m. see coileach-coille.
creòthluinn, s.f. Bier. 2 Sickly person—Islay.
crespeis, (AF) s.f. Whale.
creubh, v.a. Crave. 2 Dun.
creubh, [**-a] -eibh, -an, s.m. Body, corpse. 2** Clay (crè.) 3** Breast. 4** Being, person. 5 (AF) Animal.
——ach, -aich, s.f. see creathach, creubh and crè.
——ach, -aich, s.m. Pudding made with calf's entrails—prov. 2† Withered wood or branches, firewood, dry sticks.
——ach, -aiche, a. Infirm—Lewis. Bha e 'coiseachd c., he was walking unsteadily—as one walking with bare feet on a rough road.
——achan, -ain, -an, see creubbach.
creubhag, -aig, -an, s.m. Body, small body. 2 Little woman. 3 Twig. 4 Beloved little female. 5(AH) Boiled chicken, as distinct from its soup. O mo ch., an exclamation of disappointment or sudden fright.—Lewis.
creubhaidh, -e, a. Delicate in health. 2 Irritable.
creuch, creich, s.f. see crè, criadh and creubh 2** Mortar.
creuchach, see criadhach.
creuchaidh,** a. Clayey.
creuchd, -a, -an, s.f. Wound, hurt, sore, scar. A' ch. a bha 'na chliabh, the wound that was in his breast.
——, v.a. Wound, hurt.
——ach, -aiche, a. Wounding, hurtful. 2 Destructive, bloody. 3 Sinful. 4 Full of sores or scabs. Còmhrag c., a battle full of wounds; an leòghann c., the bloody lion.
——adh, -aidh, s.m. Wounding, act of wounding. A' c., pr. pt. of creuchd.
——air,* -ean, s.m. Invalid.
creuchd-lorg,** s.f. Cicatrice.
†creuchd-lorgach, a. Full of scars.
creud ? (for ciod ?—cia [cè] rud)
creud, -a, -an, s.f. Creed. 2 Belief. Tha barrachd agus a' chreud agus a' phaidir aige, he knows more than his creed and paternoster (i.e. has had intercourse with the Devil, or is a wizard, or merely, is "knowing.)
creudag,** -aig, -an, s.f. see cneutag.
creufag, -aige, -an, s.f. see creubhag.
creug, see creag.
creugach, see creagach.
creugan, see creagan.
creumhach, -aich, s.m. see cnàimheach.
†creun,** s.m. Body. 2 Skull.
creupan,** -ain, s.m. see cneapan.
creutair, -ean, s.m. (& f.) Creature, being, person. 2 Body. An c. truagh, the poor body.
creutair-talmhaidh, (AF) s.m. Creature.
creuthach, -aich, s.f. see creubhach.
creuthachas,(CR) -ais, s.m. Disgust. Chuir e c. orm, it disgusted me, made me shudder—Std.
cri (poetical for cridhe.)
criabhar, see criathar.
criabus, (AF) s.m. Pig.
criabus-mara, (AF) s.m. Porpoise.
criach, -a, -an, s.f. prov. for crìoch.
criach, pr.pt. a' criachadh, v.a. see crìochnaich. 2‡‡Propose to one's self.
criachadh, -aidh, s.m. see crìochnachadh, 2‡‡ Proposing to one's self, intending. A' c—, pr. pt. of criach.
criadh, gen. -a, dat. criadhaidh, s.f. Clay, dust. 2 Body, being. Clàbar c., miry clay.
——a, gen. of criadh.
——ach, -aiche, a. Clayey, earthen, clayish, argillaceous.
——ach, s.f. see criadh.
——achd,** s.f.ind. Crockery.
——adair, -e, -ean, s.m. Potter.
——adaireachd, s f. Potter's trade, pottery. 2 Pottery (place.)
criadh-an-fhùcadair,* see crè-an-fhùcadair.
criadh-aol, -aoil, s.m. Mortar.
criadh-cheangail, v.a. Cement, lute.
criadh-chlachair,** s.m. Bricklayer.
criadh-dhuslach, s.m. Brickdust.
criadh-fhear, s.m. see criadhadair.
criadh-loisgear,** s.m. Brickmaker.
criadh-loisgte, s.f. Brick (lit. burnt clay.)
criadh-luch, -a [& -aidh,] s.f. Mole.
————ag, see criadh-luch.
criadh-mhathachaidh,‡‡ s. f. Marl. 2 Earth used as manure.
criadh-reamhar,‡‡ s f. Marl.
criadh-thaigh, -e, -ean, s.m. Clay house, earthen house. 2 The Grave. Sìth ann ad ch. caol, peace in thy narrow dwelling of clay—grave.
criadh-umha, s.f. Brass-ore.
crian, see crion.
crianag, see crionag-ghiuthais.
crianta, see crionta.
†criapach, -aiche, a. Rough.
criair, v.a. see criathair.
criarach, see criathrach.
criaradh, -aidh, see criathradh.
criatach,** see cniatach.
——adh, see cniatachadh.
criataich, see cniataich.
criatag, -aig, see cneutag.
criatair, see cniatair.
criath, -a, s.f. see criadh.
——ach, -aiche, a. see criadhach.
——air, pr.pt. a' criathradh, v.a. Sift. 2 Examine minutely. 3 Filter.
——airte, past pt. of criathair. Sifted, &c.
criathar, -air, -an [& -thran,] s.m. Sieve, riddle, cribble.
criathar, see criathair.
criatharadh, -aidh, see criathradh.
————an, -ain, -an, s.m. Little sieve.
———— -meala, s.m. Honeycomb.
criathrach, -aich, -aichean, s.m. Wilderness. 2 Marshy ground, swamp.
————, -aiche, a. Like, of, or belonging to, a sieve or riddle.
————adh, -aidh, s. m. Sifting, filtering, minute examination. A' c—, pr.pt. of criathraich.
————ail,* a. Marshy.
criathradh, -aidh, s.m. Sifting, act of sifting. A' c—, pr. pt. of criathair. 2* Shrugging.
criathrag,** s.f. Filter.
criathraich, pr.pt. a' criathrachadh, v.a. Sift, examine. 2 Filter.
————te, a. & past pt. Sifted, examined.

criathran,** -ain, *s.m.*, *dim.* of criathar. 2 *n. pl.* of criathar.
†crib, -e, *s.f.* Swiftness, speed. 2 Comb.
crich, *dat. sing.* of crioch.
criche, *gen. sing.* of crioch.
cridhe, *pl.* -achan, *s.m.* Heart. 2**Understanding. 3**Courage. 4‡‡ Centre. 5 ‡‡Kind of buckle. 6 Presumption, courage, cheek, nerve. A chiall mo ch. ! *my dearest dear !* ; a mhic ch. ! *my dear sir !* a nic cridhe, *my dear madam !* ; fhir mo chridhe, *man of my heart* —a common way our forebears had of expressing themselves on meeting a friend they held dear ; air c. do dhèarnaidh, *on the middle* (*lit.* heart) *of your palm—W. of Ross-shire* ; cha dean c. misgeach breug, *a drunken soul tells no lies*; nach ann aige tha 'n cridhe ! *how hardened he is !* ; bha mi mar mo chridhe air son sin, *I did my utmost for that*; bha e mar a ch., *he was very keen for it*; is aon an c., *their hearts are one* ; dè a' ch. a bh' agad ! — (i. e. de chridhe a bh' agad,—*a'* is not the article, but what remains of the prep. *de*);*how dare you presume !*; cha'n 'eil a' ch. agad, *you dare not*; cha'n 'eil a' ch. no a dh'anam agad, *you dare not for your life* ; buinidh an gnothach sin do d' ch. féin, *that is a matter for your own consideration*; gun ch,, *without understanding*.
———ach,** -dhich, *s.m.* Hearts, at cards. Aon a' chridhich, *the ace of hearts*.
———ach, -dhiche, *a.* see cridheil.
———achan, -ain, -an, *s.m.* Small brooch or buckle worn at the breast. 2‡‡Little heart.
———ag,** -eig, *s.f.* Mistress, female favourite.
cridhealachd, see cridhealas.
cridhealas, -ais, *s.m.* Cheerfulness, merriness, hilarity, state of being touched with drink. 2* Kind or hearty reception, as by a host.
cridhean, *s.m.* Gallant, favourite. [†† cridhein.]
cridhe-chrìonachd, *s.f.* Systole, contraction of the heart.
cridheil, -eile [& -eala,] *a.* Hearty, cheerful. 2 Courageous, bold. 3* Kind. Bha iad c. maille ris,*they were merry with him*.
crileag,†† -eig, *s.f.* Small sprinkling, few grains.
crilein, -e, -ean, *s.m.* Box, small coffer. 2 †† Small creel. 3 Small quantity. 4(AH)Small quantity of any granular substance, as meal, sugar, or salt.
crimeagach,** *a.* (criomag) Carping.
crim-raineach,‡ *s.* Sweet mountain fern—*aspidium oreopteris*.

239. Crim-raineach.

crin, -e, *a.* Niggardly.
crinbhriathrach,* *a.* Silly, talking foolishly.
crinceanachd,** *s.f.* Humourousness.
crindreas,** -dris, *s.m.* Bramble.
crine, *s.f.ind.* Niggardliness, meanness. 2 Withering. 3 Rottenness. 4 Littleness. 5‖ Consumption. Cridhe na crine, *a niggard*.
crine, *comp.* of crion.
———achd, *s.f.* see crine.
crinead, -eid, *s.f.* see crine.
crineam,** -eim, *s.m.* Fall.
†crineamh, -eimh, *s.f.* Fate, destiny.
†———, *s.m.* Fall.
†———uin, see crineamh, *s.f.*
crinean, -ein, -an, *s.m.* Miser. [†† gives *n.sing.* crinein, and *n.pl.* crineinean.]
cringeanach,** *a.* Crabbed.
———d,** *s.f.ind.* Crabbedness.
crinlein, -e, -ean, *s.m.* Small writing desk.
†crinteach, -tiche, *a.* Fretful, anxious.
†criobh, -a, -an, *s.f.* Jest. 2 Trifle.
crìoch, -ìche, -an [& -a,] *s. f.* End, limit. 2 Boundary, frontier, land-mark,march, border. 3 Conclusion. 4** Brief. 5**Preferment. 4 Design, intention. 5 Country. 6 Death. 7 ‡‡Copse. Mu na crìochan, *about the borders* ; cuir c. air, *finish it* ; *2 kill him* ; tha 'n là a' tighinn gu crìch, *the day is drawing to a close* ; c. deas na gréine, *the Tropic of Capricorn* ; c. m' athar, *my father's boundary*; crìochan ciana, *distant countries*.
———adair, -ean, *s.m.* Borderer. 2 Finisher. 3 Gag-tooth, (coin-chriche.)
———ail,‡‡ -e, *a.* Limitaneous.
———air, *s.m.* Border keeper, margrave.
———alachd, see crìochnachadh.
crìochan, -ain, *s.m.* Strife. 2 Querulous tone. 3 *n.pl.* of crìoch. Na Garbh-chrìochan, *the tract of country lying between Loch Suineart in the South, and Loch Hourn in the N.E.* (*lit.* the rough boundaries.)
crìochar,** *a.* Briery.
crìoch-chaithriseach,‡‡ -eiche, *a.* Limitary.
crìoch-chluiche,** *s.f.* Epilogue, end of a play.
crìochdair,** -ean, see crìochadair.
crìoch-fhradhairc,‡‡ -e, *s.f.* Horizon.
crìochnach, *a.* Come to years of maturity or discretion. 2 Desistive.
crìochnachadh, -aidh, *s.m.* Finishing, completing, concluding. 2 Act of finishing or concluding, completion. A' c—, *pr. pt.* of crìochnaich.
crìochnachair, ** *s.m.* Accomplisher. 2 Closer.
crìochnaich, *pr. pt.* a' crìochnachadh, *v.a.* End, finish, conclude. 2 Fulfil, accomplish. 3 Die. 4 Propose to oneself. Ch. e an raoir, *he died last night*.
———e, -an, *s.m.* Finisher.
———te, *past part.* of crìochnaich. Finished, completed, fulfilled. 2 Mature,perfect. Duine c., *a full grown man*.
crìochnaidheach, -eiche, *a.* Finite. 2 Desistive.
———d, *s.f.ind.* Finitude, finiteness, quality of having an end.
crìochnaigheach, see crìochnaidheach.
———d, see crìochnaidheachd.
crìochnuich, see crìochnaich.
crìochnuigheachd, see crìochnaidheachd.
crìochran,(AF) *s.m.* Stonechat, see cloichearan.
crìoch-sgeòil,** *s.f.* Epilogue, end of a tale.
crìoch-smachd, -a, -an, *s.m.* Government.
criodaich,* *v.a.* see cniadaich.
criodair,** -ean, *s.m.* Fondler.
criodhail, -e [& -dhala] see cridheil.
criodhalachd, *s.f.ind.* see cridhealas.
criodhalas, -ais, see cridhealas.
criodhaltas, -ais, see cridhealas.
criodhar,(AF)*s.m.* Woodcock,see coileach-coille.
†criodhar, -air, -airean, *s.m.* Leech.
criodhdaich,* see cniadaich.
criogag,†† -aig, *s.f.* Very slight knock.
†criol, -a, *s.m.* Chest, coffer, basket.
†——ach, -aich, *s.f.* Repository. Graibh ch., *a repository of archives*.
criom, *pr.pt.* a' criomadh, *v.a.* see creim.
———achd, *s.f.* see creimeadh.
criomadan, -ain, -an, *s.m.* see criomag.
criomadh, -aidh, *s.m.* & *pr. pt.* of criom, see creimeadh.
criomag, -aige, -an, *s.f.* Small bit of anything, fragment, tatter, shiver, shred, morsel. 2** Tit-bit. 3**Mouthful. A' dol 'na chriomagan, *falling to pieces*.

criomagach,†† a. In small bits.
———achadh, -aidh, s.m. Reducing to bits or crumbs. 2 Act of pounding or crumbling. A' c—, pr. pt. of criomagaich.
———aich, pr. pt. a' criomagachadh, v. a. Crumble, pound. 2 Divide into bits or fragments. 3* Nibble. 4* Tease, gall.
criomagaichte, past pt. of criomagaich. Reduced to fragments, pounded, crumbled, torn into pieces.
criomair, -ean, s.m. Nibbler, picker, nipper.
†criomairt, -e, s.f. Second milk, cream.
crioman, -ain, -an, s. m. Bit, morsel, small piece of anything. 2**Crust. 3**Splinter. 4** Mouthful. C. arain, *a piece of bread*; c. crion, *a little bit*.
———ach,‡‡ -aiche, a. Piecemeal.
criomb,* v.a. see creim.
———air,* -ean, s.m. Miser, churl.
———anta,* a. Niggardly, mean.
———antachd,* s.f. Niggardliness, meanness, want of spirit.
criomchag,** s.f. Fault. 2 Invective.
criomhan,(AF) s.m. Fox. 2 Wolf.
criomthann, see criomhan.
crion,**-a, s.m. Split in wood produced by heat.
crion, crine, a. Little, mean, trifling, diminutive. 2 Niggardly. 3 Dry, withered, parched, shrunk. 4**Decayed. Balach c., *a little boy*; duilleag ch., *a withered leaf*; sìor fhàs fuilt, crìon fhàs cuirp, *overgrowing of the hair means the under-growing of the body*—these are some of the signs noted of the progress made in other things as well as in the human body.
crion, pr. pt. a' crionadh, v. . & n. Wither, fade, decay. 2 Blast. 3 Repress growth by oppression. 4** Depress 5(AC) see crein.
——ach,** -aiche, a. Withered, rotten, as brush-wood.
——ach, -aiche, s.f. Withered tree. 2 Withered leaves. 3 Brushwood, firewood. 4 Decay. 5 Withering. 6 Term of extreme, personal contempt. 7 Withered branches, firewood. 8**Littleness of mind. 9**Pusillanimous person. 10††Rotten tree. A chrionaich nam Fiann ! *thou disgrace of the Féinne*; cual chrionaich, *a faggot of firewood*.
crionachadh, -aidh, s.m. Withering, decaying, fading. 2 Circumstance of withering, decaying or fading. 3**Blasting or scorching with heat. A' c—, pr. pt. of crionaich.
crionad, -aid, s.m. Littleness.
crionadh, see crionachadh. Air c., *withered*.
———, *3rd. sing. & pl. imper.* of crion. C. e, *let it wither*.
crionag-bhuidhe,¶ s. f. Golden-crested wren, —*regulus cristatus*.

230. Crionag-bhuidhe. 231. Crionag-ghiuthais.

crionag-ceann-bhuidhe,(AF) s. f. Wren, mite-bird, yellow-headed mite.
crionag-ghiuthais,¶ s. f. Willow-wren—*sylviæ trochilus*.
crionaich, pr. pt. a' crionachadh, v.n. Wither, decay, fade. 2 Scorch.
crionaidh, fut. aff. a. of crionaich. 2 gen. sing. of crionadh.
crionaidh, a. Withered, decayed. 2 Scorched, 3 Little, pusillanimous.
crion-allt, -uillt, s.m. Small rill. 2 Exhausted rill, stream nearly dried up by the sun's heat, stream that dries in summer.
crionan,(AH) -ain, s.m. Matter ejected by cows when in heat and before calving.
†crioncain, v.n. Strive, contend.
†crioncan, -ain, s.m. Strife, tumult. 2 Murmur.
crioncanach,** a. Quarrelsome, relating to a quarrel.
—————adh, see crioncanachd.
—————d, s.f.ind. Striving. 2 Quarrelsomeness, wrangling.
crion-chaith,‡‡ v.a. Absume, consume.
crion-chur, -uir, -e, s.m. Laying on of snow or small hail.
crionda, a. prov. for crionna.
crion-dhuilleach,-ich,s.m.& f. Withered foliage.
crion-dhuilleag, -eige, -an, s.f. Faded or withered leaf. Thuit e mar ch., *he fell like a withered leaf*.
crion-dris, -e, -ean, s.f. Bramble.
crion-fhaoileag,¶ s. f. Little gull, see crann-fhaoileag.
crion-fhiodh, -a, s.m. Decayed wood.
criodglach,(AH)s.m. Culprit. 2 One made to pay a penalty, see creineach.
crionlach, -aich, s.f. Brushwood, firewood.
crion-lach, -laich, s.f. Teal, see crann-lach.
crion-lus, -uis, -an, s.m. Withered herb.
crion-mhial, -a, -an, s.f. Wood-louse, wall-louse.
—————ach, a. Abounding in wood-lice.
crionna, a. Cautious, wise, prudent. 2 Penurious, parsimonious, niggardly. 3 Old, ancient. 4 Advisable. 5 Advised. 6* Attentive to the minutest articles of gain. 7**Discreet. Gu c. glic, *cautious and wise*.
crionnachd, s.f.ind. Caution, wisdom, prudence, sagacity. 2 Wit. 3 Penuriousness, sordidness. 4* Minuteness 5**Antiquatedness. 6 **Advisableness. Coimhead c., *regard discretion*.
crionnta, a. see crionna.
———chd, s.f. see crionnachd.
crionntag,†† -aig, s.f. see criontag.
crion-shearg, v.a. see crion-shearg.
crion-sgamhanach,** a. Asthmatical.
crion-sgolt, see crion-sgoltadh.
crion-sgoltach, -aiche, a. Splitting, causing fissures and cracks as in wood.
crion-sgoltadh, -aidh,s.m. Fissure in wood caused by heat or age. 2 Crack in any surface caused by heat.
crion-shearg,v.n. Wither, decay, fade. 2**Scorch.
criontach,** -aiche, a. Saving, parsimonious, niggardly.
criontachd,** s. f. Parsimony, saving spirit. Cinnidh a' ch., ach théid a' ro-chriontachd a dholaidh, *the saving will increase his store, the too saving will destroy it*.
criontag, -aige, -an, s. f. Sorry or parsimonious female.
criontaireachd, see criontachd.
criopag, -aige, -an, s.f. Wrinkle, as in the skin. 2 Clew of yarn.
———aich, v.a. & n. Wrinkle, rimple.
crioplach, see cripleach.
———adh, see cripleachadh.
———d, see cripleachd.
crioplaich, see criplich.
———te, see cripleachta.
criopus,(AF) s.m. Stag.
crios, -a, -an [& -achan,] s.m. Belt, girdle. 2 Strap. 3 Zone, band. 4 The waist. †5 Sun. C.-claidheimh, *sword-belt*; c.-guailne, *shoulder-belt*; c.-muineil, *neck-band*; c.-spéillidh, *swad-*

dling-band; tha tlachd fuaighte ri crios na h-oibre, *it is very interesting if done thoroughly*; léine chrios, *body-guard, circle of immediate followers*; cha'n 'eil mo theanga fo d' chrios, *my tongue is not under your girdle*.
——, *v.a.* Gird, belt, border. 2**Envelop. 3** Bend round.
——ach, -aiche, *a.* Girdled, belted. 2 Succinct. 3 Like, of, or belonging to, a belt or girdle, 4**Tight. 5**Striped.
——achadh, -aidh, see crioslachadh.
criosadair, -ean, *s. m.* Belt-maker. 2†† One that belts.
————eachd, *s.f.* Belt-making, occupation of a belt-maker.
criosaich, see crioslaich.
————te, see crioslaichte.
criosan, -ain, -an, *s.m.* Small belt. 2 Slender waist. 3* Apron.
————ach,†† *a.* Pertaining to a small belt.
crios-ceangail, *s.m.* Belt, swaddling band.
crios-chomhchuluinn, see crios-Chuchulainn.

232. *Crios-Chuchulainn.*

crios-Chuchulainn, *s.m.* Meadow-sweet, queen of the meadow, "my lady's belt,"—*spiræa ulmaria*.
crios-claidheimh, *s.m.* Sword-belt.
Criosd, -a, *s.m.* Christ, Our Saviour.
†criosda, *a.* Swift, quick, nimble, active, smart.
Criosdachd, *s.f.* Christianity. 2 Christendom. 3* Benignity. A' Ch., *Christendom.*
Criosdaidh, -e, -ean, *s.m.* Christian.
————eachd, see Criosdachd.
Criosdail, -e [& -ala,] *a.* Christian, Christian-like.
†criosdal, -ail, *s.m.* Ring of thong or withe.
Criosdalachd, *s.f.ind.* Christian disposition and behaviour.
Criosd-athair, -athar, -thraichean, *s.m,* Godfather.
Criosduidh, see Criosdaidh.
————eachd, see Criosdaidheachd.
crios-féile, (AC) *s.m.* Kilt-girdle.
crios-guaille, see crios-guailne.
crios-guailne, *pl.* -an-guailne, *s. m.* Shoulder-belt.
crios-gualann, -ainn, see crios-guailne.
crioslach, -aich, -aichean, *s.f.* Girding of the loins. 2 Bosom-belt, girdle. 3**Border. 4‡‡ Apron.
————adh, -aidh, *s.m.* Girding, belting, tightening. 2 Act of girding, belting or tightening. 3**Bordering. A' c—, *pr.pt.* of crioslaich.
————an, -ain, (AC) *s.m.* Bag suspended from the "crios" or girdle. C. chnò, *a girdleful of nuts.*
crioslaich, *pr. pt.* a' crioslachadh, *v.a.* Gird the loins. 2 Belt, bind. 3 Tighten. 4 Limit, determine. 5 Border.
————te, *past pt.* of crioslaich, Girded, belted, begirt, bordered.
criosluich, see crioslaich.
————te, see crioslaichte.
crios-meadhon-an-t-saoghail, *s.m.* The Equator or equinoctial line (*lit.* the middle belt of the world.)
crios-mhuir, -mhara, *s.f.* Strait, arm of the sea.
crios-muineil, *s.m.* Necklace. 2 Neck-band.
crios-na-gréine, see grian-chrios.
crios-nèimhe, *s.m.* The zodiac.
criosolit, *s.f.* Gaelic spelling of *chrysolite.*
crios-pasgaidh, *s.m.* Swaddling-band.
crios-pheilear, *s.m.* Bandolier.
criosrachadh, -aidh, see crioslachadh.
criosraich, see crioslaich.
————te, see crioslaichte. 2 *a.* Succinct.
crios-roinn, *s.m.* Shield divided by band or band, party per bend in *heraldry.*
crios-spéillidh, *s.m.* Swaddling-band.
crios-tarsainn, *s.m.* Shoulder-belt.
criosta, see criosaichte.
criostal -ail, -an, *s.m.* Gaelic spelling of *crystal.* Sruthan criostail, *crystal streamlets.*

233. *Crios-roinn.*

————ach, -aiche, *a.* Transparent, translucent 2 Crystalline.
criot, -a, -achan, *s.f.* Earthen vessel, *prov.*
criotach, *prov.* for criadach.
criotaich, *prov.* for criadaich.
†criotail, *a.* Earthen, made of clay.
criothach, see critheann.
†crioth-chumadair, -e, -ean, see creadhadair, (cré-chumadair.)
criothuach, -aiche, *a.* see critheach.
————adh, -aidh, see crith.
————ail, *a.* see critheach.
criothnaich, *v. a. & n.* see crith. Shake. 2 Tremble.
†crioth-stabhair, -ean, *s.m.* Potter.
crioth-thalmhuinn, *pl.* -anna-t-, see crith-thalmhuinn.
criothuun, -uinn, *s.m.* see critheann.
cripleach. -ich, *s.m.* Cripple.
————adh, -aidh, *s.m.* Laming, act of laming or crippling. 2 Craziness. A' c—, *pr. pt.* of criplich.
————d, *s.f.ind.* Lameness, decrepitude.
————ta, *past pt.* of criplich. Crippled.
criplich,†† *pr.pt.* a' cripleachadh, *v.a.* Make lame, cripple.
criplich, *s.m.* see cripleach.
crislean, *s.pl.* Sinews.
†crislion, -in, see crislean.
crisgein-craisgein,†† *s.m.* Starfish.
crit, -e, -ean, see croit.
†criteagan, -ain, *s.m.* Dwarf.
crith, -e, -ean, *s. f.* Trembling. 2 Tremor—*paralysis agitans.* 3 Fit of ague. [Preceded by the article *a' ch*—] 4 (DU) Shivering, 5 (DU) Disease of sheep. Air chrith, *trembling.*
crith, *pr.pt.* a' crith, *v.n.* Tremble, shake, quiver. An talamh air ch., *the earth trembling*; geilt ch., *trembling from terror;* cuir air ch., *shake, cause to shake.*
crith, -e, *s. f.* Trembling, act of trembling or shaking. A' c—, *pr. pt.* of crith.
crith-chath, -e-, *s.m.* Battle-panic.
crith-cheann, -chinn, *s.m.* Shaking head.
————ach, *a.* Shaking in the head, nodding, paralytic.
crith-cheòl, -chiùil, *s.m.* Warbling, 2 Quavering. 3 Musical trills.
crith-chosg.** *a.* Antiparalytic.
crith-chreideach, -dich, *s. m.* see crith-chreidmheach.
crith-chreideamh, *s.m.* Quakerism.
crith-chreidmheach, -ich, *s.m.* Quaker.

crith-dhealbhair, see criadhadair.
crith-dhealrach, -aiche, a. Radiant.
crith-dhealradh, -aidh, s.m. Tremulous radiance.
crithe, gen. of crith.
——ach, -aiche, a. Shaking, quaking, quivering, aguish.
——ach, -ich, s.m. see critheann.
——achadh,** -aidh, s.m. Trembling, terror. A' c—, pr. pt. of crithich.
critheachan,¶ s.m. Wheatear, see brù-gheal.
critheadh,‡‡ -idh, s.m. Quaver.
crith-eagal, -ail, s.m. Astonishment accompanied by extreme terror. 2 Consternation, trembling.
crith-eaglach, -aiche, a. Astonishing, dismaying. 2 Terrified, trembling, quaking. 3** Causing extreme terror.
critheanach, -aiche, a. Causing or inducing tremors. 2 Aguish. 3(DU) Shaky, insecure. Am fiabhrus c., ague; c. air a chasan, shaky on his feet.
——d, s.f. Aguishness.
critheanaich,†† s.f. Trembling, paralysis.
critheann,§ -inn, s.m. Aspen-tree—populus tremula. 2 Poplar. [With art. an.] Badge of Clan Fergusson according to some. Mar ch. 'san t-sìne, like an aspen in the blast.
——, a. Aspen.
——ach,‡‡ -aiche, a. Aspen.
—— -chladaich, s.m. Erigo (plant.)
crithear, -ir, s.m. Spark of fire. 2 Drinking-cup.
crithein,(AF) s. m. Common sandpiper, see trilleachan-tràighe.
crith-fheur,§ s.m. Quaking grass, see conan.
crith-fhuachd,** s.f. Chilliness.
crith-fuinn, s.f. Earthquake.
crith-ghalar, -air, s.m. Palsy. 2‖Paralysis. †3 ‡Ague.
crithich, pr.pt. a' critheachadh v.n. see crith.
crithidh, fut. aff. a. of crith.
crithionn, -inn, see critheann.
crith-làmh, -làimh, -an, s.f. Trembling hand.
——ach, aiche, a. Having trembling hands.
——achd, s.f.ind. Trembling of the hands.
crith-mhosgladh, -aidh, s.m. Awaking in terror.
crithneachan,(AF) s.m. Wheatear, see cloicheiran.
crith-neul, -eòil, s.m. Shower.
——ach, -aiche, a. Showery.
crithnich, pr.pt. a' crineachdainn, v.n. see crith.
crith-oillt,** s.f. Shudder.
†crithre, s.pl. Small sparks from the collision of arms. 2 Small particles of anything.
crith-reodhadh, -aidh, s.m. Hoar-frost. 2 Mildew. 3 Blasting mist. 4 Weak ice, frost. Mar dhuilleach 'sa ch., like leaves in hoar-frost; ma bhitheas c. ann, if there be mildew.
crith-reothadh, -aith, see crith-reodhadh.
crith-shùileach, -eiche, a. Having tremulous eyes. 2 Dim-sighted. 3 Blear-eyed. 4 Purblind.
crith-snàgadain,(DU) s. f. Rattling of teeth against each other through cold or fear.
crith-snàgadan,‖ s. m. "The pins and needles." [Preceded by the article an.]
crith-thalmhuinn, crithe-t-, pl. crithean-t-, s.f. Earthquake.
crith theas, s.m. Mirage, the tremulous exhalation observed near the surface of the ground on a hot day.
crith-thinneas, see crith-ghalar.
criudarnach, -aich, s.m. The hiccough.
criun,(AF) see criomhan.
cro,(AF) s. Pig.
crò, -òtha, -òithean [& -òitean,] s.m. Circle. 2 Sheep-cot, pen or fold, wattled fold. 3 Stall. stable. 4 Hut, hovel, cottage. 5 Witchcraft. 6 Eye of a needle. 7 rarely Group of children. 8 High wattled cart rim. 9 see cnò. 10 see crodh. 11§ Saffron, see crò-chorcur. 12(AC) †Heart. 13†Death. 14 see crà. 15‡‡ Iron bar. 16**Crop. C. na mòine, the peat-cart; crò crodh-bainne, a fold of milch cows; a Chriosda Chrò-naoimhe, O Christ of the Holy Blood; crò chaorach, a sheep-fold; cho fad 'sa bhitheas monadh an Ceann-tàil, cha bhi Mac-Coinnich gun àl 'sa chrò, as long as there are moors in Kintail, MacKenzie will not want cattle in the pen—c. has a double meaning here, being also the name of a place in Kintail, girt with hills, and from which the river Crò is named.
crò, v.a. Fold, enclose in a fold. 2 Hem in together.
crò, crotha, a. Strait, narrow. 2 Close. 3 see cròdha.
cro'an, -ain, -an, s.m. see crodhan.
crobh, -a, s.m. Hand. 2** Claw, paw. 3**Hoof. Ge b'e air bith tha thu ag itheadh no ag òl, is léir a bhlàth air t' aghaidh gu'm bheil aghaidh do chrobhan ri d' chraos, whatever your meat and drink be, it is very clear from your face that your hands and your mouth are good friends—said by a master to a servant, who protested that she ate nothing but bread and milk.
crobhagan,‡ s.m. Handful.
crò-buntàta,(AH) s.m. Small enclosure for potatoes.
†crobhall, -uill, s.m. Genitalia.
crobhan, see crodhan.
——ach, see crodhanach.
crobh-priachain, s.f. The herb Crane's bill.
crobhsag,(CR) s. f. Variation of groiseid—W. of Ross-shire.
cròbhtach, a. Tender-soled.
cròc, v.a. Beat, pound, prov.
cròc, -òic, -òicean [& -òcan], s.m. Deer's antler. 2 Given by ** in error for crog.
croc, see cnoc.
crocach, see cnocach.
cròcach, -aiche, a. Branched, antlered. 2 Horny, having large horns.
cròcach††, s.m. Spiked instrument to keep calves from sucking.
†crocad, -aid, s.m. Barley-broth, pottage.
crocadul,†† -uil, s.m. Crocodile.
cròcag,(DU) s.f. Crook handle of a stick. 2‡‡ Pothanger.
crocaid,** -ean, s.f. Cockernony.
crocaireachd see cnocaireachd.
cròcan, -ain, -an, s.m. Crook, hook. 2(MMcD) see mac-an-òg.
crocanach,* -aiche, a. Crooked.
crocan-cairt,(MMcD) s.m. Implement made of iron with wooden handle, used for digging or dragging the roots of the "cairt-làir" from the ground—Lewis.
crocas, -ais, s.m. Cork—Gairloch.
cròc-cheannach, -aiche, a. Antlered, horned. 2 Having branching horns.
cròc-dhearg, -dheirge, a. see crà-dhearg.
cròch, -òich, s.m. Saffron, see crò-chorcur. 2 Red-colour. Léine c., ancient Highland mantle.
cròch, a. Saffron-coloured, red, crocus.
croch, pr.pt. a' crochadh, v.a. & n. Hang, suspend. 2 Punish by hanging. 3 Depend. 4 Linger, hover. Ch. iad e, they hanged him; c. an còta, hang the coat.
cròchach, -aiche, a. Saffron-coloured, cornigerous.
crochadach,‡‡ -aiche, a. Pensile.

crochadair, -ean, *s.m.* Hangman.
crochadaireachd, *s.f.ind.* Business of a hangman. 2 Hovering or lounging about.
crochadan, -ain, *s.m.* Pendulum. 2 Pendant. 3 Tassel.
crochadas,** -ais, *s.m.* Appendage.
crochadh, -aidh, *s.m.* Hanging. 2 Act of hanging or suspending. 3**Suffocation. 4**Hovering. 5**Grief. A' c--, *pr. pt.* of croch. An c. ris, *depending on it*; c. pòite, *a meal, one potful.*
crochag, -aig, -an, *s.f.* Ear-pendant. 2**Pendulum.
crochaid,** -ean, *s.f.* Frontlet, particular form of dressing a young woman's hair.
crochaire, -an, *s.m.* Villain, (one deserving to be hanged.) 2**Idle fellow. 3**Hangman.
———achd, *s.f.* Villany. 2 Idleness. 3 Lounging.
crochan, -ain, -an, *s.m.* Pothook.
croch-aodach, -aich, *s.m.* Hangings.
crò-chaorach, *s.m.* Sheep-fold.
crochar, -air, -airean, *s.m.* Bier. 2 Horse-litter. 3 Body.
†cro-charb, -airb, -airbean, *s.m.* Bier.
cro-charbad,** -aid, *s.m.* Hearse.
†crocharsach, -aich, *s.m.* Sheep-fold.
croch-bhrat, -ait, -an, *s.m.* Hanging tapestry. 2 **Curtain. 3**Screen. 4**Blind. 5 Drop-scene.
cròchd, -òichde, -òchdan, *s.f.* see cròc, *s.m.*
crochd, see cnoc.
cròchdach, -aiche, *a.* see cròcach.
crochdach, see cnocach.
crochdaid, -aide, -aidean, see crochaid.
crò-chorcur,‡ *s. m.* Saffron crocus, meadow-saffron—*crocus sativus* or *colchicum autumnale.*

234. Crò-chorcur.

crochta, *past pt.* of croch. Hung up, suspended. 2 Hanged.
crò-chuilc,(AF) *s.* Recessed pen, pen in the hollow between two or more hills. 2 Place-name.
crodal, see crotal 4.
cròdan, see cnòdan.
crodh, cruidh, *s.m.* Cattle, especially black cat- 2 *pl.* Herds. 3 Dowry, portion. 4 The fine imposed by the ancient Scots on one who was guilty of murder. It differed for every man murdered according to his rank. The c. of a king was 1,000 cows, of an earl 140, of a thane (earl's son) 100, of a villain or plebeian 16.
cròdh, *v.* see crò.
cròdh,** fee cròdhan.
cròdh,‡ *s.f.* Saffron crocus, meadow saffron, see cro-chorcur.
cròdha, *gen.*crodhaidh[& croidhe,] *pl.* croidhean, (DU) *s.f.Gairloch & W. of Rossshire* for crudha.
cròdha, -òidhe, *a.* Valiant, heroic, brave. 2** Powerful. 3**Hardy 4**Active. 5**Clever. 6**Effective. 7††Stout, valorous.
———chd, *s.f.ind.* Valour, bravery, prowess. 2 Hardihood. 3**"Cleverness," activity.
cròdhadh, -aidh, *s.m.* Contraction, act of contracting. 2 Gathering in of corn. 3 Gathering into a fold. 4 Rebuke.
crodhaich, (C R) *s.* Something that adulterates the milk, said locally to be a disease of the shaws of potatoes, when black spots or lumps form and the top falls down—*Suth'd.*
†crodhaiche, -an, *s.m.* Heir.
crodhal,(AC) *a.* Valiant. Micheal c., *valiant M.*
———achd, *s.f.* see cròdhachd.
crodhall, see croghall.
crodhan, -ain, -an [& -ain,] *s.m.* Parted or divided hoof, as of sheep or cows. 2**Paw. 3 **Claw. 4 Clumsy hand. 5 (AF) Piece of wood fixed in or tied to the mouth of a calf like a bit and round the back of the head, to prevent it sucking its mother when following. Reubaidh e an crodhain, *he will tear their claws*; an c. mo làimhe, *in the palm of my hand.*
———ach, -aiche, *a.* Having parted hoofs, cloven-footed. 2 Having claws or paws. 3 Like a claw or hoof. Tarbh c., *a bull that has hoofs.*
crodh-bainne, *s.m.* Milch-cattle.
crodh-caoch,(AF) *s.m.* Hornless cows.
crodh-chorcur, see crò-chorcur.
crò-dhearg,** -dheirg, *s.m.* Saffron. 2 Crimson.
———-——, -dheirge, *a.* see crà-dhearg.
crò-dhion,(AC) *s.m.* Sanctuary.
crodh-fhionn, see croidh-fhionn.
crodh-gamhnach, *s.m.* Farrow cattle (giving milk, but not with young.)
crodhlainn,‡‡ -e, -ean, *s.f.* Decrepit old woman.
crodh-mara,(AC) *s.pl.* Sea cows.
crodh-reic,(AF) *s.m.* Selling stock.
crodh-seasg, *s.m.* Barren cattle.
crodh-sìth,(AF) *s.m.* Fairy cattle, said to have been of a dun colour in *Harris*, and speckled red in *Skye*. Their calves had short ears, as if the upper part had been cut off with a knife and a slit made in the top—corc-chluasach.
crog, -a, *pl.* -achan & -aichean, *s.f.* Aged or effete ewe, sheep past bearing. 2 Three-winter ewe. 3 Draft ewe, draft gimmer.
cròg, -òige, -an, *s.m.* Large or clumsy hand. 2 Clutch. 3 Palm of the hand. 4 Paw. 5** Claw. 6** Fist. Làn mo chròige de 'n òr bhuidhe, *my fist full of the yellow gold.*
crog, -a, -achan, *s.m.* Earthen vessel,crock,jar.
crògach, -aiche, *a.* Having large clumsy hands. 2 Having paws. 3 Like a paw. 4‡‡Clutched.
crogach, -aiche, *a.* Of, connected with, or full of, earthen vessels or crocks.
crògach, *s.f.* Female with large hands.
crogaichean, *pl.* of crog.
crogaid,* *s.f.* Beast having small horns.
crògair,* *v.a.* Handle awkwardly, bungle.
crògaire, -an, *s.m.* One who searches or handles awkwardly, bungler. 2* Man having large hands.
———achd, *s.f.ind.* Act of searching or handling awkwardly, or with foul hands or fingers. 2**Pawing.
crogairneach, -nich, *s.m.* Rocky ascent.
crogairsich,* *s.f.* Rough handling. 2 Bungling, spoiling.
crògairt, *s.f.* see crògaireachd.
crogais, -e, -ean, *s.f.* Barren winter ewe, three-shear ewe—*Lewis.*
crogan, -ain, *pl.* -ain & -an, *s.m.* Pitcher, little earthen dish. 2 Lean, little person. 3*Little horn. 4 Muck-fork, (gràba-crom.) 5(AF) see cragan-feannaig. 6††Twisted and shrivelled branch. C. caillich, *a shrivelled old woman*; c. tràghad, *sea-urchin.*

croganach, -aiche, *a.* Shrivelled up, scraggy, lean, shrunk. 2††Pertaining to jars or pitchers.
crògarsaich, *s.f.* see crògaireachd.
cròghadh, -aidh, see cròdhadh.
crogball, -aill, *s.m.* Crocodile. 2 Alligator.
croghall mór,** *s.m.* Alligator.
cròglach, -aich, *s.m.* Handful.
crògnachadh, -aidh, *s. m.* Pawing, handling awkwardly or indelicately. 2 Act of pawing or handling indelicately. A' c—, *pr.pt.* of crògnaich.
crògnaich, *pr.pt.* a' crògnachadh, *v.a.* Handle indelicately or clumsily.
cròg-ri-fraigh, -e, *s.f.* The shadow of a hand upon the wall to frighten children.
croibheal, -eil, *s.m.* see coireal.
cròic, -e, -ean, *s.f.* Deer's antler. 2 Rage. 3 Foam on the surface of spirituous liquors. 4 Skin, hide. 5 ‡Cast sea-weed. 6 Difficulty, hardship, hard task. 7** Venison feast. 8 Sometimes used as the *nom.* case in place of cròc, instead of as its *gen.* Cha ch. sin air, *or* cha ch. air sin, *that is no task to him.*
croic, *gen. sing.* & *n. pl.* of croc.
—— -cheannach, -aiche, *a.* see cròiceach.
——each, *a.* Rising into foam. 2 Abounding in cast seaweed. 3**Meadowy. 4 see cròcach.
——eadh, -idh, *s.m.* Act of branching out, like horns or antlers.
croich, -e, -ean, *s.f.* Gallows, gibbet. 2**Cross.
cròich, (CR) *s. f.* Difficulty of breathing, as from asthma or from cold. 2 Wheezing—*W. of Ross-shire.*
croicheil,‡‡ -e, *a.* Patibulary, pertaining to a gibbet or gallows.
croicionn, -inn [& -cne,] *pl.*-cnean, see craiceann.
————ach, see craicneach.
croicne, (for craicne) *gen.sing.* of craiceann.
croicneach, -iche, see craicneach.
croicneag, *s.f.* Integument.
croicnean, see craiceann.
croicnibh, see craicnibh.
cròid, -e, -ean, *s.f.* see cuòid.
cròidh, *v. a.* Coop, contract, house. 2 House corn. A' cròidheadh an arbhair, *housing the corn* [in *Harris*—a' dlùitheadh an arbhair* ;] a' cròidheadh nan caorach, *penning the sheep.*
croidhbheal, *s.m.* see coireal.
croidh-chasach, *a.* Crump-footed.
†**croidhe**, -achan [& -an,] see cridhe.
————ach, -ich, *s.f.* Portion, dowry.
————achd, *s.f.ind.* see croidheach.
cròidheachd, *s.f.ind.* Bravery.
croidheag,** -eig, *s.f.* Sweetheart, mistress.
croidhean,** -ein, *s.m.* Gallant, lover.
croidh-fhionn, -a, *a.* White-hoofed.
croidhle,** see craidhleag.
croidhleag, -eig, -an, *s.f.* see craidhleag.
croidhlean, *s.m.* see cròilean.
croidhlear,** *s.m.* Basket-maker.
cròig, *dat.sing.* of cròg.
cròileagan, -ain, *s.m.* Ring, or circle of people, generally used of children. C. tuatha, *an assemblage of tenantry.*
cròilean, -ein, -an, *s.m.* Little fold. 2 Group, little circle or ring of children. 2**Cage. 3**Cluster. 4*Game of touch. [††gives cròilein as *n.sing.*, & cròileinean as *n.pl.*]
†**croilige**, *s.f.* Blood-letting.
croiligh,** *s.f.* Pain, infirmity.
†**croiligheach**, -eiche, *a.* Sickly.
croimheag, -eige, -an, see cruimheag.
croimheal, see coireal.
cròin-fhionn, *a.* Grey-headed or -haired. 2 White-headed or -haired.
†**croinic**, *s.f.* Chronicle, annal.
croinic,** *v.a.* Paint.
————eachd,** *s.f.* Painting.
croinn, *gen. sing.* & *n.pl.* of crann.
croinn-chas, *s.pl.* Pedals of a loom.
croinn-chluiche, *s.m.* Lottery.
croinn-chluithe, see croinn-chluiche.
croinneach,* *s.f.* Old worn-out animal.
croinn-grith, *s.* Mast rigging of a ship.
croinnseag,** *s.f.* Crackling, see cnàimhseag.
crois, -e, -ean, *s.f.* Cross. 2 Any object in the form of a cross. 3 Misfortune, mishap. 4 Obstacle, obstruction. 5 Hank-reel, yarn-windlass. 6 Obelisk in *writing* (†.) 7**Market-place. 8 Fork, see glac, p. 76.
†**cròis**,‖ *s.f.* Gluttony.
crois, *pr.pt.* a' croiseadh, *v.a.* Form a cross. 2 Forbid, cross, thwart. 3 Wind or reel yarn. Croiseam ort ; *the Cross be between us !* croiseam sgiorradh ! *the Cross between me and mishap !*
crois-Aindrea, *s. f.* St. Andrew's cross, see crann.
crois-bhogha, *s.f.* Cross-bow.
————-dair,** *s.m.* Cross-bowman.
————-air, see crois-bhoghadair.
crois-Chriosda, *s.f.* The cross of Christ.
crois-Dheòrsa, see crois-Sheòrais.
croiseadh, -idh, *s. m.* Crossing. 2 Hindering, thwarting. 3 Forbidding. 4 Difficulty, obstruction. 5 Act of crossing, hindering or obstructing. 6 Reeling (hank 300 yards.) A' c—, *pr. pt.* of crois. Air a chroiseadh, *forbidden, set round.*
croiseag, -eig, *s.f.* Little cross, crosslet.
croiseid,** -ean, *s.f.* Rail. 2 Barrier.
crois-fhiacaill, -fhiaclan, *s.f.* Gag-tooth.
†**croisg**, *v.a.* Cross, go across. 2 Cut across.
crois-ghèarr, *v.a.* Cross-cut.
croisgileid, -e, -ean, *s.f.* Cross cloth or triangular piece of linen, tied about an infant's forehead, child's head-dress.
crois-iarna, -n, *s.f.* Hank-reel. A rudimentary form of the *ciud-siorraig.* It consists of a stick of a certain length, with a cross-piece at each end, set at right angles to each other. The yarn is coiled on the cross pieces off the spool of the spinning-wheel, so many threads or turns round the cross-pieces, which threads are counted, make an old yard of cloth, i. e. 46 in. of a constant width such as the loom in use suffices to weave—*Uist* (DC.)
croislin, -e, -ean, *s.f.* Diameter (distance across a circle.)
————each, -niche, *a.* Diametrical, pertaining to a diameter.
crois-na-tràgha, (AF) *s.f.* Starfish.
crois-riaghlaidh, *pl.* -ean-, *s.f.* Regulating cross. 2 Criterion.
croisrich, *v.a.* Envelop. 2 Involve.
crois-Sheòrais, *s.f.* Cross in *heraldry.* i.e. St. George's cross [the National badge of England.]
crois-sheunaidh, *s. f.* Crucifix. 2 Act of crossing oneself as a charm against harm.
crois-shlighe, -an, *s. f.* By-path, cross-road.
crois-tàra, see crann-tàra.
crois-tàraidh, see crann-tàra. 2* Signal of defiance before commencing a battle.

235. Crois-Sheòrais.

crois-thachrais, *s.f.* Winding-reel, worsted-winder. 2 Yarn windlass.
croit, -e, -ean, *s.f.* Hump on the back. 2 Ludicrous term for the back. 3* Cringing attitude.

4 Hunch-back. 5 Little eminence, hillock. 6 Croft, small piece of arable land. 7 (AH) Crook-backed attitude assumed by man and beast when exposed to a cold piercing wind.
croit-fhearainn,(CR) *s.f.* Croft—*W. of Ross.*
——each,** *a.* Gibbous.
cròiteach, *a.* Humpbacked.
croiteag,-eige,-an, *s.f.dim.* of croit. 2 see crotag.
——ean,** *s.m.* Hump-backed person. 2 (AF) Gurnet (fish.)
——ear, -eir, -an, *s. m.* Crofter, one holding a croft of land. 2**Peasant. [The modern crofters or small tenants appear very little in evidence before the beginning of the 18th. century. They were tenants at will under the tacksman and wadsetters, but practically their tenure was secure enough. The first evidence we can find of small tenants holding directly of the proprietor is in a rental of the estates of Sir D. MacDonald in Skye and N. Uist in 1718—*Clan Donald, iii.*] †† gives croiteir as *n. sing.*
——eireachd, *s.f.ind.* Occupation of a crofter.
cròithean,†† *n. pl.* of crò.
croit-ministeir,** *s.f.* Glebe.
crò-laogh,(AC) *s.m.* Calves cot.
crò-leaba, (DC) *s.f.* Bier. Used in Skye, Uist, &c., where it is still the custom to carry a coffin to the grave without the use of horse or conveyance. 2* Bier to carry a wounded person.
crò-léine,(AC) *s.m.* Shroud.
†croloc,** *s.m.* Place where malefactors were executed.
crò-lot, *v.a.* Wound dangerously.
†crom, *s.m.* Nose. 2 Slough.
crom, -uime, *a.* Crooked, bent, curved, not straight. 2**Bending, winding. 3**Eddying. 4††Having crooked horns, as sheep. 5**Concave. 6* Sloping. An tacan a bhitheadh a cheann-san c., *while his head was bent down (to feed)*; croit ch., *a crooked back*.
——, -uim, *s. m.* Circle. 2**Bending, curvature. 3**Bend, curve. 4††Ridge of hills. 5 **Concavity. C. nan speur, *the concavity of the heavens.*
——, *pr.pt.* a' cromadh, *v. a. & n.* Bend, incline. 2 Stoop, bow. 3 Descend. 4 Make crooked. C. do cheann, *bow your head.* C. air an abair, *set to work, "wire in;"* crom le, *descend, as a hill.*
cromachas,†† -ais, *s.f.* Bandy-leg.
————ach,†† -eiche, *a.* Pertaining to a bandy-leg.
cromadh, -aidh, *s.m.* Bending, making crooked. 2 Stooping, bowing. 3 Drooping. 4 Inclination, inclining. 5 Act of bending, stooping, or bowing. 6 Measure, the middle finger's length. 7**Kneeling. 8** Bend, curvature, curve, turn, winding. 9**Concavity. A' c—, *pr. pt.* of crom. Tha a' ghrian a' cromadh, *the sun descends*; fo ch. an taighe, *under the roof of the house*; c. gun ghainne 'sa chaol, *a full finger-length to the small*—part of a rhyme called "Cumadh an triubhais; c. a' chuain, *the bending of the sea, a boy, headland;* deanar c. leinn, *let us kneel.*
cromag, -aige, -an, *s.f.* Any little crooked thing. 2 Hook. 3 Clasp. 4 Crook. 5 Catch. 6 Gallows. 7 Tache. 8§ Skirret (plant.) 9 Clip, see No 13 p. 76. 10* Peg. C. òir, *a tache of gold;* cromagan na briogais, *breeching-hooks of a cart.*
————ach, -aiche, *a.* Hooked, crooked. 2 Of, or belonging to, anything hooked or crooked. 3 Full of skirrets. 4††Pertaining to clasps.
————an, *s.pl.* Crotchets in *grammar* [ ].
cromag-an-aithreachais, *s.f.* Crozier.
cromag-ghuaille,** *s.f.* Clavicle.
———— -tharruing, *s.f.* Draught-hook.
crom-aisinn, see crom-aisne.
crom-aisne, -an,& -aisnichean,*s.m.*The little rib.
croma-lòin, -e, -anan-, *s.m.* see croman-lòin.
croman, -ain, *s.m.* Kite. 2 Large hawk. 3 Crooked, hump-backed man. 4 The hip-bone. 5 The hip. 6 Hoe. 7 Crooked graip, an implement used in digging dung-heaps. 8 The s of a plough.
———— -beag,¶ *s.m.* Jack-snipe, see gobhragbheag.
corman-coillteach,** *s.m.* Woodcock—*scolopax rusticola.*
crom-an-donais, *s. m.* Bungler. 2 Impotent, unfortunate or unsuccessful person. 3*Dolt.
———— -gobhlach, see clamhan-gobhlach.
———— -lachdunn,¶ -ain-, *s.m.* Kite, see clamhan-ghobhlach. 2 Small water-fowl.
———— -lochaidh, *s.m.* Kite—*falco milvus.*

236. Croman-lochaidh.

237. Croman-lo...

croman-lòin, -ain-, *s.m.* Snipe—*scolopax gallinago.* 2 AF) Marsh-harrier, see clamhan-lòin 3(AF) Woodcock, see coileach-coille.
———— -luatha, *s. m.* Wooden ash-rake. 2** Wooden fire-shovel.
———— -luch, -ain, *s. m.* Kite, kestrel, see clamhan-ruadh.
———— -luchaidh,¶ *s. m.* Kite, see clamhan gobhlach.
cromartaich, *s.f.* Shield.
crom-bhileach, -iche, *a.* Anything with curved borders or skirts.
——— -chas, -choise, -an, *s.f.* Bandy-leg, crooked leg.
——— -chasach, -aiche, *a.* Bandy-legged.
——— -cheannach, -aiche, *a.* Bent-headed.
——— -chòmhdach,** *s.m.* Canopy.
——— -ghlùineach, -niche, *a.* see cluth-ghlùineach.
——— -ghobach, -aiche, *a.* Curve-billed.
——— -ghobach,** -aich, *s.m.* Bird with a crooked bill.
——— -leac, -lic, -an, *s.f.* Flat stone in an inclined position, supported by three stones placed perpendicularly, commonly supposed to be druidical remains. One in Alsace measures 36ft. round, 12ft. broad, and more than

4ft. in thickness, is raised on other stones several feet from the ground; another in Pembrokeshire is 28ft. high, and 20ft. in circumference, and one in Poictiers is 60ft. round and is placed on five large stones.

crom-leachd, see crom-leac.

—— -lus, -uis, -an, *s.m.* Poppy.

—— -nan-cearc,(AF) *s. m.* Hen-harrier, see bréid-air-tòin.

—— -nan-duilleag, -an-, *s. m.* Woodcock, see coileach-coille.

—— -nan-gad, see crann-nan-gad.

—— -odhar, cruim-odhair,*s.m.* Membrum virile.

—— -ruaig, -e, -ean, *s.f.* Chase through a crooked path.

—— -sgiath, -sgéithe, -an, *s.f.* Sort of crooked shield.

—— -shliabh, -ibh, -shléibhtean, *s.f.* Druidical chapel.

—— -shlinneineach, -niche, *a.* Bent-shouldered. round-shouldered. 2**Hump-backed.

—— -shoc, -shuic, -an, *s.m.* Crooked snout.

—— -shocach, *a.* Curve-snouted.

—— -shrònach, -aiche, *a.* Bent-nosed. 2 Hook-nosed, aquiline.

—— -shrònach, -aich, *s.m.* Person with a hooked or aquiline nose.

—— -shùileach, -liche, *a.* Bent-eyed.

†cròn, -òin, *s.m.* Time. 2 Explanation. 3 Head.

†——, *a.* Ready. 2 Brown, swarthy.

cron, -oin, *s. m.* Fault, defect. 2 Harm, mischief. 3 Blame, imputation of wrong. 4 **Hurt. 5 *rarely* Sign, mark. Tha a (*not* a') chron sin ort, *the blame of that lies on you.*

†cron, *v.a.* Explain. 2 Bewitch. 3 Blush.

cron, see cronaich.

cronach, see corranach.

cronach,** *a.* Aching.

cronachadh, -aidh, *s.m.* Rebuking, reproving, finding fault with. 2 Checking, check. 3 Reproof, blame. 4**Harm, hurt. 5**Chastening. A' c—, *pr. pt.* of cronaich. C. soilleir, *a public rebuke.*

cronachail,‡‡ -e, *a.* Corrective.

cronachair,** *s.m.* Carper.

cronachan, -ain, -an, *s.m.* see cronachadh. 2 (AH) Incantation, exorcism. Eòlas a' chronachain, *counter-charm.*

cronadair, -ean, *s.m.* Reprover, critic, one who finds fault. Is fhearr an cumadair na 'n cronadair, *the maker is better than the critic.*

crònag, -aige, -an, *s. f.* Hum, noise of many voices. 2 Circle. 3 Fortress.

cronaich, *pr. pt.* a' cronachadh, *v.a.* Rebuke, reprove, blame. 2* Hurt with an evil eye. 3 Chide, check, reprimand. Ch. e mi, *he reprimanded me.*

————te, *past pt.* of cronaich.

cronail, -e, *a.* Hurtful, harmful, mischievous, pernicious. 2 Diseased. 3*Offensive.

cronalachd, *s.f.ind.* Harmfulness, hurtfulness, perniciousness, harm. 2*Offensiveness.

crònan, -ain, *s.m.* Dull note. 2 Mournful tune. 3 Any low murmuring sound. 4 The buzzing of a fly. 5 The humming of a bee. 6 The purring of a cat. 7 Purling sound of a brook. 8 Bass in *music.* 9 Dirge. 10 Pathetic ode. (*Scots*, croon.) 11**Sound of a bagpipe drone. 12 Bellowing of a deer. 13 Lulling voice. 14 (AH) Wheezing in the throat, as in asthma or bronchitis. C. an uillt, *the murmur of the mountain stream;* seillean le c., *the bee with a humming sound.*

————ach, -aiche, *a.* Humming, buzzing, purling, purring, murmuring. 2 Lulling. 3 Gurgling. †4 Brown. Damh c. dearg, *a bellowing red-deer.*

crònanaich, -e, *s.f.* Continued humming, purring, murmuring, gurgling or buzzing sound. 2 Bellowing of deer. 3* Dirge. 4 Bass in *music.*

Cro-naomh,(AC) *s.m.* The Sacred Heart. Cha tugainn do 'n Ch. thu, *I would not give thee to the Sacred Heart.*

cronnach, -aiche, *a.* Mournful, melancholy, lamentable.

cronnag, -aige, -an, see crannag, 4.

†cronnt, *a.* Green. 2 Grey.

†————aich, *v.a.* Loathe, abhor, detest.

cron-seanchais, -e, -ean, *s.m.* Anachronism. 2 Error in words.

cron-sgrìobhaidh, -ean, *s.m.* Mistake in writing.

cronuich, see cronaich.

————e, see cronaiche.

cropan, -ain, *s.m.* Deformed person.

†cros, *s.m. & v.a.* see crois.

crosach, -aiche, *a.* Crossing, thwarting, hindering. 2 Streaked, striped.

crosadh, -aidh, *s.m. & pr.pt.* see croiseadh.

crosag, -aige, -an, *s.f.* see croiseag. 2 Frame of a fishing-line. 3** Small cross. 4** Small cup. 5**Perverseness.

crosan, -ain, -an, *s.m.* Peevish man. 2**Cross-grained person.

crosan, (AF) *s.m.* Puffin, see fachach.

————ach, -aiche, *a.* Cross, perverse, obstinate, peevish, fretful, froward. Gu c., *perversely.*

————achd, *s.f.ind.* Perverseness, obstinacy. 2 Fretfulness, crossness. 3 Adversity, misfortune. 4 Bickering, picking a quarrel as children. 5 Certain mode of versification.

crosanta, -ainte, *a.* Troublesome, vexatious, perverse, cross-grained, obstinate.

————chd, see crosanachd.

crosda, *a.* Cross, perverse, fretful. 2 Obstinate, froward. 3 Peevish, ill-natured. 4 Prohibited. 5 Troublesome, vexatious. Té ch., *a cross female.*

————chd, *s.f.ind.* Perverseness, fretfulness. 2 Ill-nature. 3 Peevishness.

crosdag,(AH) *s.f.* Cross, peevish female.

crosda-traghad,(AF) *s.* see crois-na-tràgha.

crosdan, -ain, -an, *s.m.* Cross or peevish person.

cros-dhàn,** *s.* Acrostic.

crosg, -oisg, see crasg.

cròsgach, -aiche, *a.* see crasgach.

crosgag, see crois-na-tràgha.

crosgag-thràghad,(DC) *Uist* for crois-na-tràgha.

crosgan-crasgan,(AF) *s.m* Starfish.

crosg-chainnt,** *s.f.* Antithesis.

crosg-cheasnachadh,see cruaidh-cheasnachadh.

crosg-cheasnaich, see cruaidh-cheasnaich.

crosg-lìn,** see crois-lìn.

†crosra, *s.m.* Cross road, by-path.

cro-sheilg,(AC) *s.m.* Hiding-place for hunters.

cros-shùileach, -liche, *a.* Squint-eyed.

crosta, see crosda.

crostachd, see crosdachd.

crostal, -ail, see crotal.

crostan, see crosan.

crot, see cnot.

crotach,(AF) *s.m.* Curlew, see guilbneach.

crotach, -aiche, *a.* Hump-backed. 2**Bandy-legged. 3**Crooked-backed, gibbous. Duine c., *a hump-backed man.*

crotach, *a.* for cnotach, deriv. of cnot.

————d, *s.f.ind.* Prominence, protuberance. 2 Unevenness. 3 Hump-backedness, gibbosity.

crotach-mara, -aichean-mara, *s.f.* Curlew, see guilbneach.

crotag, -aige, -an, *s. f.* Crooked little woman. 2 Sort of plover. 3 Slang term for a sixpenny-piece. 4 Mortar for making barley ready for broth—eòrn'-chrotag, 18 inches in height, 15 inches in diameter, with round opening in centre about 1 ft. deep, and 7 or 8 inches wide. The barley is mixed with water, pounded with hammer-shaped mallet, stirred occasionally, and then dried and winnowed.

crotaiche, *s.f.ind.* Gibbosity, hump-backedness. 2 Prominence, protuberance.

crotainn, see cnotainn.

crotair, -ean, *s.m.* Crooked, hump-backed man.

———eachd,** *s.f.ind.* Infirmity of a hump-back. Ag imeachd 'sa ch., *walking like a hump-backed person.*

crotal, -ail, *s.m.* Awn, husk, pod. 2 Rind of a kernel. 3 Cymbal. 4 General name for the varieties of lichen used for producing dyes of various shades of red and brown. The colour produced from these is not so fine as that obtained from the *corcur.* 5 The lichen, stone-, or heath-parmelia—*parmelia saxatilis* and *omphalodes.*

———ach,** *a.* Dyed filemot. 2 Like filemot. 3 Like, pertaining to, or abounding in, any of the lichens used in dyeing.

——— -coille, *s.m* Lungwort—*stricta pulmonacea.*

——— -nam-madadh-ruadh,§ *s. m.* Club-moss—*lycopodium clavatum.* [Badge of Clan Munro.]

crotan, -ain, *s.m.* see crotal, croitean, & clàdain. 2 Box of an oar.

†**croth**, *s.m.* see cruth. 2 *s.f.* see cnò.

cròth, *pr.pt.* a' cròthadh, *v.a.* Confine in a coop, house, fold or pen.

cròthadh, -aidh, *s.m.* Enclosing. 2‡‡ see crathadh. A' c—, *pr. pt.* of cròth. A' c. uan, *enclosing lambs*; a' c. arbhair, *enclosing corn, ingathering corn.*

238. *Crotal-nam-madadh-ruadh.*

crothaid,** *s.f.* Gravel.

cròthan, for cnòthan.

cròthan, -ain, *s.m.* Cribbage (game at cards.)

†**crothar**, -air, *s.m.* Bier. 2 Vehicle.

†**cru**, *s.m.* Gore, see crà.

†**cruabair**, *v.a.* Chew.

cruabair,** *s.m.* Cruncher. 2 One who chews awkwardly.

———eachd,** *s.f.* Crunching. 2 Chewing.

cruac, -aice, -aicean, see cnuachd.

cruacach, -aiche, see cnuachdach.

cruac-chasach, -aiche, see cnuachd-chasach.

†**cruach**, *a.* Red.

cruach, -aiche, -an, *s.f.* Pile, heap. 2 High stack of corn or hay. 3 Rounded hill standing apart. 4** Mountain, pinnacle. 5* Stack of peats. 6* Heap above the brim of a vessel. Gu cruaich fhichead tomhais, *to a heap of twenty measures*; c. agus càrn air gach taobh, *hill and rock on every side*; ithear c. 'na breacagan, *a stack may be eaten in cakes;* air cruaich nam beann, *on the pinnacle of the mountains.*

cruach, *pr.pt.* a' cruachadh, *v.a.* Heap, stack, build into ricks or stacks. 2 Accumulate, gather into a heap, pile.

———ach, -aiche, *a.* Of, or belonging to mountains, heaps, stacks or ricks. 2** Full of heaps or hills, hilly. 3 Lofty. 4** Accumulative.

———adh, -aidh, *s.m.* Heaping up, accumulating. 2 Stacking. 3 Heaping above the brim of a vessel. 4 Act of heaping or accumulating. A' c—, *pr.pt.* of cruach. 'Ga ch., *making it into stacks.*

———ag, -aige, -an, *s.f.* Little rick or stack.

cruachainn, *gen. sing.* of cruachann.

————each,** *a.* Having large thighs or hips. 2 Of, or pertaining to, a thigh or hip.

cruachan, -ain, -an, *s.m.* (*dim.* of cruach) Conical hill or mountain-top, &c. 2 see cruachann. 3 *n.pl.* of cruach.

cruachann, -ainn, -uaichnean, *s.f.* The haunch, thigh, hip. Os cionn na cruchainn, *above the hip;* tharruing e 'lann o 'chruachainn, *he drew his sword from his side.*

cruachas, -ais, -an, *s.m.* see cruaidh-chàs.

cruachd, -aichd, see cnuachd.

———ach, -aiche, *a.* Knobby, brawny.

———alach, -aiche, *a.* Coarse.

cruach-luachair,§ see ciob-cheann-dubh.

cruach-Phàdruig,§ Greater plantain, see cuach-Phàdruig.

†**cruad**, -uaid, *s.m.* see cruaidh. 2‡‡Stone.

cruadail, *gen. sing.* of cruadal.

cruadal, -ail, *s.m.* Difficulty, distress, adversity, hardship, danger, trial. 2 Courage, bravery, valour. 3 Virtue. 4 Firmness, hardihood. 5**Stinginess. 6(AH) Privation. Ròs a's fearr cruadal, *a rose (youth) of the greatest hardihood*; ri uchd cruadail, *on an occasion of danger*, or *when actually facing danger.* [* says it never means Virtue.]

———ach, -aiche, *a.* Dangerous, hazardous. 2 Distressing, grievous, dismal, trying. 3 Puzzling. 4 Courageous. 5 Hardy, energetic. 6 Patient of hardship or pain. 7 Inhuman, barbarous, unfeeling, ruthless, hard-hearted. 8 Niggardly. 9 Desperate. 10 Adverse. 11 Calamitous. Duine c., *a hardy, energetic man*; is c. an ni e, *it is a calamitous circumstance.*

———achd, *s.f.ind.* Hardship, danger. 2 Hardihood, endurance. 3* Bravery. 4†† Firmness.

———aich,** *pr.pt.* a' cruadalachadh, *v.a.* Inure, harden, habituate. 2††Dry.

———as,‡‡ -ais, *s.m.* Courageousness.

cruadhach, *gen.* of cruaidh. De smior na c., *of the best steel.*

cruadhach,** *a.* Of, or pertaining to steel.

————adh, -aidh, *s.m.* Enduration. 2 Hardening, drying. 3 Act or state of hardening. 4 Drying, as of grain in a kiln. A' c—, *pr. pt.* of cruadhaich. Àth-chruadhachaidh, *a drying-kiln;* cha'n e cruadhachadh na h-àtha sealltainn foipe, *looking under the kiln does not dry the corn.*

cruadhachair,** *s.m.* Hardener.

cruadhachas, -ais, *s.m.* Rigour, hardness, hardship, trial.

cruadhag, -aig, -an, *s.f.* Distress, difficulty, affliction. An t-anfhann 'na chruadhag, *the weak in his distress.*

cruadhaich, *pr.pt.* a' cruadhachadh, *v.a.* Harden. 2 Dry, parch. 3**Make hardy. 4**Make insensible or unfeeling.

cruadhaichte, *past part.* of cruadhaich. Hardened. 2 Parched. 3**Baked. 4**Made insensible. 5**Made hardy. 6 Dried. Gràn c., *dried corn.*

cruadhail,** *s.f.* Danger. 2 Hardship. 3 Inhumanity.

cruadhalach, -aiche, *a.* Inhuman, barbarous, hard, unfeeling. 2 Niggardly. 3**Poor. 4** Difficult.

—————d,** *s.f.* Hardness, rigour. 2 Niggardliness.

cruadhalta, *a.* see cruadalach.

cruadhas, -ais, *s.m.* see cruas.

cruadhchradh, -aidh, *s.m.* Austerity.

cruadhlach, -aidh, *s. m.* Rocky acclivity. 2 Hard stony ground. 3*Hard bottom, (*boglach* is a soft bottom.)

cruadhmhor, -oire, *a.* Corpulent.

cruagalach, -aiche, *a.* Hard, rigid, severe.
†cruaghadh, -aidh, *s.m.* see cruadhachadh.
cruaic, see cnuachd.
cruaich, *gen. sing.* of cruach.
cruaidh, -e, *a.* Hard, firm. 2 Difficult. 3 Painful, distressing. 4 Scarce, not plentiful. 5 Narrow-minded. 6 Niggardly, parsimonious. 7 Severe. 8 Stiff, stubborn. 9 Vexatious, annoying. 10 Calamitous. 11 Energetic. 12 Forcible. 13 Unreasonable, unjust. 14 Irksome. 15**Made of metal (especially steel.) Àite c., *a hard place;* ni c., *a distressing thing* ; bliadhna ch., *a scarce year* ; duine c., *a niggardly narrow-minded man;* is cruaidh na dh' fheumar, *what's needed is hard.*
cruaidh, cruadhach, cruadhaichean, *s.f.* Steel. 2**Spear, sword, arms. 3**Metal. 4**Armour. 5 Declivity of a hill, hill-side. 6 Stone used in place of an anchor for a small boat. [used then with the article, a' *chruaidh.*] C. agus dearg, *steel and fire,* used to kindle a fishing-torch at night. *prov.* Le farum nan cruaidh, *with the clangour of arms.*
cruaidh-bheum, -éim, -bheuman [& -bheumannan] *s.m.* Hard or severe stroke. 2 Disaster.
——nach, -aiche, *a.* Giving hard or heavy blows. 2 Wounding. 3 Satirical. 4 **Felling.
cruaidh-chàs, -àis, -an, *s.m.* Peril, danger. 2 Hard case. 3 Emergency. 4 Difficulty, distress, hardship, adversity. Là mo chruaidh-chàis, *the day of my adversity.*
cruaidh-chàsach, -aiche, *a.* Perilous, dangerous. 2 Trying, distressing. 3 Difficult, perplexing. 3**Calamitous.
cruaidh-cheangail, *pr.pt.* a' c— cheangal, *v. a.* Bind or tie firmly.
cruaidh-cheangal, -ail, *s.m.* Hard bond. 2 Tying or binding firmly. A' c—, *pr. pt.* of cruaidh-cheangail.
cruaidh-cheasnachadh,** *s.m.* Cross-examination.
cruaidh-cheasnaich,** *v.a.* Cross-examine.
cruaidh-cheisd, -e, -ean [& -eachan,] *s.f.* Hard question. 2**Riddle.
cruaidh-chòmhrag,** -aig, *s.f.* Hard contest. 2 Hottest part of the battle.
cruaidh-chràbhach,** *a.* Ascetic.
cruaidh-chridheach, *a.* Hard-hearted. unfeeling. 2**Niggardly.
cruaidh-chuing,** *s.f.* Hard slavery. 2 Rigorous service. 3 Heavy or oppressive yoke.
cruaidh-chùis, -e, -ean, see cruaidh-chàs.
——each, -aiche, see cruaidh-chàsach.
cruaidh-fhortan, -ain, -an, *s.m.* Misfortune. 2 **Hard fortune.
——ach, -aiche, *a.* Unfortunate.
cruaidh-fhuachd,†† *s.f.* Keenness of cold.
cruaidh-ghleachd, -a, *s.m.* Hard conflict. 2 Agony.
cruaidh-ghlaodh,(AH) *s.m.* Loud shout. 2 Cry of pain or distress.
cruaidh-ghreimeach, *a.* Brawny.
cruaidh-làmhach, -aiche. *a.* Hard-handed.
cruaidh-leum, *s.* Bound, as when a deer runs lifting all four feet at once. Dh' fhalbh e 'na chruaidh-leum, *he bounded away.*
cruaidhlinn, see cruailinn.
cruaidh-losgadh, -aidh, -aidhean,*s.m.* Searing, branding, burning with a red-hot iron.
cruaidh-lus, -uis, -an, *s.m.* Sneezewort—*achillea ptarmica.* [McL& D gives *white hellebore.*]
cruaidh-mhuineal, -eil, -an, *s.m.* Hard neck. 2 Stiff, stubborn neck.
——ach, *a.* Hard-necked, 2 Stiff-necked, stubborn.
——achd, *s.f.ind.* Stubbornness. 2 Inflexibility. 3††Hardihood.
cruaidh-mhuinealaiche, see c mhuinealachd.
cruaidh-naisgte, *a.* Entangled.
cruaidh-rathad, -aid,*s.m.* Hard road. 2 Causeway.
cruaidh-reodhadh, -aidh, *s. m.* Hard frost.
cruaidh-ruith, *v.a.* Run hard, run at full speed. 2 Pursue at full speed. Gadhair 'gan c., *hounds pursuing them at full speed.*
cruaidh-ruithe, *s.m.* Swift running. 2 Running at full speed. 3 Race. Each 'na c., *a horse at full speed.*

233. Cruaidh-lus.

cruaidh-sgrùd**, *v.a.* Cross-examine.
cruaidh-sgrùdadh,** *s. m.* Cross-examination.
cruaidh-shion, -shine, [*s.m. & f.*] Dry wind or weather.
cruaidh-shnaim, -e, -ean, *s.f.* Hard knot, i.e. not a running knot. 2 Double knot.
cruaidhte, see cruadhaichte.
cruaidh-theinn, -e, *s.f.* Severe affliction or trial. 2 Straits, distress.
cruaidh-theud, -an, *s.f.* Wire.
cruaidh-throd,†† -oid,*s.f.* Daggers' drawing.
cruailinn, *s.f.* Mountainous rocky ground, hard ground.
cruailinn,† *a.* Hard, rocky.
crualach, -aich, *s.f.* see cruailinn *s.* & cruadhlach.
†cruan, -a, *a.* Of a blood-red colour.
cruas, -ais, *s.m.* Hardness, rigour. 2 Trial, hardship, distress, difficulty. 3 Hardihood, durability. 4 Strength. 5 Crisis. 6 Niggardliness. Thug e mach a h-uile ni le a ch. féin, *or* le c. nan dorn, *he accomplished everything by his own energy* ; c. do chridhe, *the hardness of thy heart.*
cruas, *v.* see cnuas. 2 see cruasb.
cruasachd, see cnuasachd.
cruasb,** *v.n.* Crunch.
cruasbail,** *s.f.* Munching.
cruathas, see cruas.
crùb, *pr.pt.* a' crùbadh, *v.n.* Sit, squat. 2 Creep. 3 Stoop, crouch. 4 Contract, shrink. 5 Crinkle. 6*Cringe. Ch. e mar leòghann, *he crouched like a lion.*
crùb,(AC) -a, *pl.* -annan [& -achan,] *s.* Bed recess in the thickness of the wall, with entrance a little above the floor, not to be seen now except in old St. Kilda houses and sheiling bothies in Lewis. 2(AH) In old Highland houses, an upright beam, meant as a support to each couple-leg, strongly nailed thereto, and extending therefrom to within a foot or two of the ground. It was partly or wholly imbedded in the masonry.
crub, -uibe, -ean, *s. f.* Part of a mill. 2 see crubh. 3** Contraction. 4**Wrinkle. 5** Croup. 6* Lame foot. 7* Halt.
crùba, *gen. sing.* of crùb.
crùbach, -aiche, *a.* Lame, halt, cripple. 2 Awkward. 3** *rarely* Difficult.
crùbach, -aiche, *a.* Restringent, contracting, shrivelling.
crùbach, -aich, *s m.* Cripple, lame person.
crùbadh, -aidh, *s.m.* Bending, act of bending. 2 Contraction, contracting, shrinking. 3 Crouch. 4 Crinkle. A' c—, *pr. pt.* of crùb.
crùbadh-féith, -aidh-fh—, -aidhean-f—, *s. m.* Spasm.
crùbag, -aig, -an, *s.f.* Thrum, knot in a thread in weaving. 2 Crooked woman. 3††Lame woman. 4 Hook. 5 Wooden frame placed on

a horse's back for the purpose of carrying anything bulky, as hay, corn, &c. 6 Crab of a brown colour, 10 or 12 in. by 5 or 6 in. [*Partan* is black, and 3 or 4 in. long by 2 or 3 in. broad, and quicker in motion than c.]
crùbagach, *a.* Cancerous.
crùbag-ghuail,* *s.f.* Chafing-dish.
crùbaiche, *comp.* of crùbach.
crùbaiche, *s.f.ind.* Lameness.
crùbaidh, *fut. aff. a.* of crùb.
crùbain, *pr. pt.* a' crùban & a' crùbanadh, *v. n.* Creep, crouch. 2 Cringe. 3 Shrug the shoulders, as with cold.
crùban, -ain, *s.m.* Crouching or cringing attitude. 2 Sitting squat. 3 Creeping. 4 Crab. 5 Disease in the legs of animals. 6 Any crooked creature. A' c—, *pr.pt.* of crùbain. Anns a' ch., *in a crouching attitude*; dean c., *crouch down.*
crùbanach, -aiche, *a.* Of, or belonging to, crouching, creeping, &c.
crùbanachd, *s.f.* Crouching, creeping.
crùbanadh,** -aidh, *s.m.* Act of creeping, cringing, crouching, or couching.
crùban-cait,(AF) *s.m.* Wild melitot (plant.)
crùban-coille,‡‡ *s.m.* Tortoise.
crùban-na-saona, *s.f.* §Cloudberry, see foighreag. 2 Dwarf mountain-bramble.
crubh, -a, -an, *s. m.* Horse's hoof. 2 Claw, fang. 3 Nave of a wheel. [**gives *gen. sing.* cruibh.]
crubhach, -aiche, *a.* Having hoofs, &c.
crubh-an-leòghainn,§ *s.m.* Common lady's mantle, see copan-an-driùchd. [McL & D gives vervain for "crubh-leòmhainn."]
†crubhas, -ais, *s.m.* Crimson colour.
crubhasg,** *s.f.* Crimson colour.
crubha-cait,(AH) *s.m.* The tips of the thumb and of all the fingers, set together in the form of a cat's paw.
crubha-sìthne, *s.m.* Haunch of venison.
crubh-eòin,§ *s.* Fenugreek, see deanntag-Ghreugach. 2**Birdsfoot (herb.)
crubh-leòghainn,§ *s.m.* Common lady's mantle, see copan-an-driùchd. 2**Vervain.
crùbog, see crùbag.
crùbta,** *a.* Diminutive.
†cruca, *s.* Hook.
crucach,** -aich, *s.m.* Heap.
crùdan, see cnòdan.
crudh, see crudha.
crùdh, *pr.pt.* a' crùidheadh, *v.a.* Shoe, as a horse. 2††Hoop a cart-wheel.
crudha, cruidhe, cruidhean, *s. m.* Horse-shoe. 2††Iron heel. 3††Hoop of a cart-wheel.
crudhach, *a.* Shod, as a horse. 2**Well-shod. Each c., *a well-shod horse.*
crudhan, *s.m.* see crubh.
crugh, see gruth.
†crughalach,** see cruadhalach.
cruibh,(AF) *s.* Cat.
crùibte, *past pt.* of crùb. Cramped, contracted, crippled, shrunk, shrivelled.
crùidein, *s.m.* Kingfisher, see biorra-crùidein.
cruidh, *s.f.* Vaccine.
cruidh, *gen.sing.* of crodh.
crùidh, *v.a.* see crùdh.
crùidheach, *a.* †† see crùidhte. 2‡‡Shod.
crùidhean, -dheinean, *s.m.* Paw. 2 Small trifling hand. 3 As much as can be lifted by the five fingers of any pulverised substance.
crùi-dhearg, see crà-dhearg.
cruidhleag, *s.f.* Rick.
crùidhte, *a.* & *past pt.* Shod.
crùidse, *s.m.* see crùisle. O'n a dh'fhàgadh 's a' chrùids' thu, *since you were left in the church vault—Duanaire*, p. 8.
cruime, *s.f.* Bend, curvature. 2 Crookedness.
——, *comp.* of crom.
†cruimeacuda, *s.* Crow. 2(AF) Sow.
cruimead, -eid, *s.f.* see cruime.
†cruimeadannach, -aiche, *a.* Whole, entire.
cruimeal, -ail, *s.m.* Tall bent person.
cruimh,‡ -e, -ean, *s.f.* Worm, maggot. 2 Insect. 3**Pain, suffering. Ghin e cruimhean, *it bred worms*; bithidh a' ch. dheireannach cràidhteach, *the last pain shall be grievous.*
cruimh-chàil, *s.f.* Caterpillar.
——each, -eiche, *a.* Wormy, maggoty, full of worms.
cruimheach,(AF) -eich, *s. m.* Rook. 2 Crow, see cnàimheach.
cruimheag, -eige, -an, *s.f.* Worm, little worm, maggot. 2 (AF) Insect, moth. 3* Niggardly female.
cruimheagach, -aiche, *a.* Wormy, full of maggots.
cruimheagan, *pl.* of cruimheag.
cruimhean, *n.pl.* of cruimh.
cruimh-fhiacaill,‖ *s. f.* Tooth-ache. 2 [* gives cnoidh-fhiacaill, *gum-boil.*
cruimh-gheala,(AF) *s f.* Glow-worm.
cruimh-goile, *s.f.* Maw-worm.
cruimh-itheach, -eiche, *a.* Insectiverous.
†cruim-leachta,(AF) *s.* Sow.
cruimh-lobhta,(AF) *s.f.* Palmer-worm, canker-worm, crump.
cruimh-shìoda, *s.f.* Silkworm.
cruim-shlinnean, *s.m.* Protuberance on the back, roundness of shoulders.
cruim-shlinnein, see cruim-shlinnean.
————each, -eiche, *a.* see crom-sh—.
†cruimthear, -ir, *s.m.* Priest.
crùin, *gen. sing.* & *n.pl* of crùn.
cruineachd, see cruithneachd.
cruinn, -e, *a.* Round, circular, globular. 2 Well-rounded. 3 Succinct, neat. 4 Gathered, assembled, collected. 5 Scant. 6**Sound, sane. 7†† Compact, neat. "Cruinn, cothrom" is said of a through train in *MacTalla*; cearta, cruinn, còmhla, *all the whole lot together*; ni an t-each mìle a dh'astar 'na chruinn-leum, *the horse will do a mile galloping*; maide c., *a round stick*; tha 'n saoghal c., *the world is round*; tha 'm pobull c., *the people are assembled*; tha 'm bàrr gu math c., *the crop is somewhat small in bulk*; tha 'm bàrr c., *the crop is secured*; gu c., *succinctly.*
cruinne, *s.ind.*, *m.* in *n. sing.*, *f.* in *gen.* Roundness, rotundity, circularity. 2 The world, the globe. 3**Circumference, circle. Gu crìch na c., *to the ends of the earth*; cha'n 'eil do leithid 'sa ch., *your match is not on the face of the earth*; an c., *the world.*
cruinne, *comp.* of cruinn.
cruinneacan,** -ain, *s.m.* Coronal, coronet.
cruinneach,** -nich, *s.f.* Dew, mist, fog.
cruinneachadh, -aidh, *s.m.* Gathering, assembling. 2 Assembly, act of gathering or assembling. 3 Collecting, adding. A' c—, *pr. pt.* of cruinnich.
cruinneachail,** *a.* Accumulative.
cruinneachan, -ain, *s.m.* Any round heap.
cruinneachd,†† *s.f.* Convexity. 2 see cruithneachd.
cruinnead, -eid, *s.m.* Circularity, roundness. A' dol an c., *increasing in roundness.*
cruinneadach,** *a.* Accumulative.
cruinneadair, *s.m.* Geometrician.
cruinneadaireachd, *s.f.* Geometry, spherics. 2 Geography.
cruinneadh, -idh, *s.m.* see cruinne.
cruinneag, -eige, -an, *s.f.* Neat, tidy girl. 2** Little plump young female. 3** Young wo-

man. Mac-samhuil na cruinneige, *the maiden's equal.*
cruinneagach, *a.* Of, or relating to, young women. 2**Fond of young women.
cruinneagan, -ain, *s.m.* Mass, heap.
cruinnealas,* -ais, *s.m.* Tidiness, economy.
cruinnean,* *s. m.* All the fingers put together. 2 The quantity the fingers can hold. 3**Tuft.
cruinne-cé, *s., m.* in *n. sing., f.* in *gen.* The world, the earth, the universe. [With art. an] Gach ni 'sa ch., *everything in the world.*
cruinne-ghràbhair,** *s.m.* Geographer.
cruinneil,* -e, *a.* Tidy, economical.
cruinneineach, -ich, *s.m.* Stout boy. 2 Anything round. 3‡‡Sizeable person or thing.
cruinn-eòlach, -aiche, *a.* Skilled in spherics. 2**Having a knowledge of geography.
cruinn-eòlaiche, -an, *s.m.* Master of spherics.
cruinn-eòlas, -ais, *s.m.* Address. 2 Knowledge of spherics. 3**Geography. 4 Geology.
cruinne-sheòladair,** *s.m.* Circumnavigator.
cruinne-thomhas, -ais, *s.m.* Geometry.
cruinne-thomhasach, *a.* Geometrical.
cruinne-thomhasair, *s.m.* Geometrician.
cruinn-fhad,‡‡ -aid, *s.m.* Oblongness.
cruinn-fhada, *a.* Oblong. 2‡‡Cylindrical.
cruinn-ghluasad,** -aid, *s.m.* Circulation. [not a good word.]
cruinnich, *pr. pt.* a' cruinneachadh, *v.a.* Collect, accumulate. 2 Gather, assemble, convene. 3 Make round. 4 Draw close. 5 Sweep together.
cruinniche, -an, *s.m.* Gatherer, collector.
cruinnichte, *past pt.* of cruinnich. Gathered, assembled. 2 Collected, accumulated.
cruinnire, -an, *s.m.* Turner.
cruinn-leum, -léim, -an [& -annan,] *s.m.* Leap without a run, standing jump. 2 Bound. 3 Horse's gallop.
cruinnseag, -aig, -an, see cnaimhseag.
cruinn'-thomhas, see cruinne-thomhas.
crùinte, see crùnta.
crùintean, *n. pl.* of crùn.
cruipean,** -ein, *s.m.* Crupper.
crùisgean, -einean, *s.m.* Oil-lamp. 2 Cruse. 3‡‡ Small jug, pitcher. 4‡‡Potsherd. Oladh an c., *oil in a cruse.*
crùisgein, see cruisgean.
crùisgein-craisgein, see crìsgein-cràisgein.
crùisgeineach,†† *a.* Of, or pertaining to, cruses, &c.
crùisle, -an [& -ichean,] *s.m.* The hollow vault of a church, mausoleum.
crùisleach, -lich, -lichean, *s.m.* Recluse. 2 Sluggard. 3‡‡Inhabitant of a church vault. 4 (AH) Big, slow, unwieldy fellow.
cruislean, see crùisgean.
crùistean,** -ein, *s.m.* Little lamp or cruse.
cruit, -e, -ean, *s.f.* Crowd. 2 Violin. 3 Cymbal. 4 Lute. 5 see croit. [The c. was a six-stringed instrument, used of old in Scotland and Ireland, but now confined to the mountains of N. Wales.] C. an aonaich, *the ridge of the hill;* meòir a' sguabadh na cruite, *fingers sweeping along the crowd.*

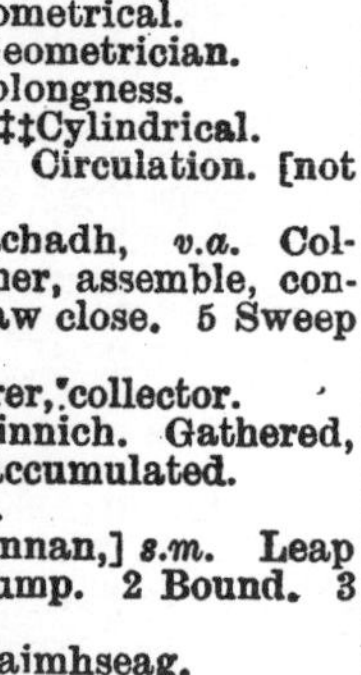

240. Crùisgean.

cruit-chiùil, -ean-ciùil, *s.f.* Musical instrument, especially crowd. 2 Violin.
cruiteachan,** -ain, *s.m.* Dwarf. 2 Hunchback.
cruiteach-mhara, see crotach-mhara.
cruiteag, -eige, -an, *s.f.* Little crowd or violin. 2**Female performer on the crowd or violin. 3**Hump-backed female.
cruiteal,** *a.* Lively, pleasant, sprightly.
cruitealachd, *s.f.ind.* Pleasantness, liveliness.
cruitean, -ein, *s.m.* Kingfisher, see biorra-cruidein. 2** Hump-backed person. 3**Little hump. 4**Little ridge.
cruiteanach,** *a.* Humpbacked.
cruitear,-eir,-an, *s.m.* Crowder. 2††Fiddler. 3** Musician. 4 see cruitein.
cruiteil, -e, *a.* see cruiteal.
cruitein, *s.m.* see cruitean.
cruiteineach, -eiche, *a.* see crotach.
cruiteireachd, *s.f.* Performance on the crowd. 2 Occupation of a crowder. 3‡‡ Minstrelsy.
cruit-eun, *s.f.* see biorra-cruidein.
cruit-fhilidh,** *s.m.* Lyric poet.
crùith,** *a.* Lively. 2 Ingenious, expert. 3 Prudent.
crùithe,** *s.f.* Prudence, liveliness.
cruitheach, -eiche, *a.* see crùidheach.
cruitheachd, *s.f.ind.* Form, complexion, conformation. 2 The exact figure, identity of a person. 3 Creation. 4 The universe.
crùitheachd,** *s.f.ind.* Prudence. 2 Liveliness. 3 Expertness.
cruitheamh,(AF) *s.m.* Insect.
cruithear, see cruith-fhear.
cruith-fhear, -fhir, *s.m.* Creator.
†cruithin-tuath,‡‡ *s.* The Pictish nation.
cruithneachd, *s. m. ind.* Wheat—§*triticum æstivum.* Smìor c., *the best part of wheat.*
cruithneachd-buidhe, *s.m.* Buckwheat.
cruithnichd,‡‡ -e, *a.* Wheaten.
crùlaist, -e, -ean, *s.m.* Rocky hill.
crullsach,†† see cruthlach.
crum, *v.* see crom.
crumag, -aig, -an, *s.f.* Skirret, see cromag.
cruman, -ain, *s. m.* Hip-bone. 2 Instrument used by surgeons.
crumanaiche, -an, *s.m.* Turner.
crum-dubh, *a.* Black and crooked. Didomhnuich c., plaoisgidh mi 'n t-ubh, *on Crooked black Sunday I'll shell the egg.* This saying is obscure. Crum-dubh apparently for crom-dubh, is known in Ireland as the name of the first Sunday in August, but in Lochaber it is applied to Easter.—N.G.P. [Crum-dubh was a Celtic god, see *Voyage of Bran, II. p. 149,* where the dinnshenchas of Mag Slecht is quoted as mentioning the Crom Croich, or king idol of Erin. This Crom Croich is, on pp. 213, 214, identified with Crum-Dubh.]
crùmh, -a, -an, *prov.* for cruimh.
†crumhor, *a.* Bloody, gory.
crum-shùileach, *a.* Frowning.
crum-shùileachd, *s.f.ind.* Sourness of look.
crùn, -ùin, -ùintean, *s.m.* Crown. 2 Garland of flowers. 3 Boss of a shield. 4 Five-shilling piece. 5 Crown of the head. C. na h-airte, *ornament in the description of a shield;* gu seirbhis a' chrùin, *to the service of the crown;* bonn crùin, *a five-shilling piece.*
crùn, *pr. pt.* a' crùnadh *v.a.* Crown.
crùnadh, -aidh, *s.m.* Coronation, act of crowning. A' c—, *pr. pt.* of crun. C. an rìgh, *the coronation of the king.*
crùnair,‡‡ -e, -ean, *s. m.* Coroner.
crùnan, see cnòdan.
crùn-easbuig, *s.m.* Bishop's mitre.
†crunnach, -aich, *s. m.* Dwarf.
crunnan, -ain, -an, *s.m.* see grunnan.

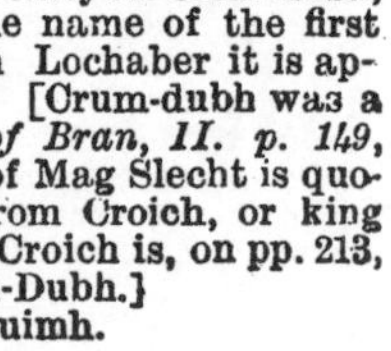

241. Crùn-easbuig.

crunn-lùth, -ùith, *s. m.* Quick measure in

bagpipe-music and formerly in harp-music. 2 * Seal.
crùn na h-airte, *s.f.* Ornament in the description of a shield.
crùn-sagairt,** *s.m.* Sacerdotal cap.
crùn-sgéithe, *s.m.* Shield-boss.
crùnta, *a.* & *past pt.* of crùn. Crowned. 2 Finished.
crùp, *s.m.* Part of a house, see under taigh.
crup, see crub.
crùp, see crùb.
crùpach, see crùbach.
crupach, see crubach.
crùpadh, -aidh, *s.m.* The croup. 2 see crùbadh. A' c—, *pr.pt.* of crùp.
crùpadh-féithe, -aidh-fh-, -aidhean-, see crùbadh-féithe.
crùpag, see crùbag.
crupag, -aige, -an, *s.f.* Wrinkle, fold, plait, gather.
crupagach, -aiche, *a.* Wrinkled, plaited. 2 Causing wrinkles. 3 Like a wrinkle.
crùpaich, *v.a.* see crùb.
crup-phutag,** -aig, -an, *s.f.* Blood-pudding.
crùpta, *past pt.* of crùp, see crùibte.
crusaidh,** *s.f.* Cruse (crùisgean.)
crùsbal, *s.m.* Gaelic spelling of *crucible.*
cruscladh, -aidh, -ean, *s.m.* Wrinkling.
crusgadh, -aidh, *s.m.* Box, small coffer.
†cru-sgaoileadh, -aidh, *s.m.* Bloody flux, dysentery.
†crut,‡‡ *s.m.* Hand.
crutach, see crotach.
crutair, see cruitear.
crutaireachd, see cruiteireachd.
cruth, -a, -an [& -annan], *s. m.* Form, figure, shape. 2 Countenance. 3 Personal appearance. 4 Expression of countenance. 5**Person. 6**Phantom. 7(AC) Pedal harp. Cò thug dhi a c. ? *who gave her her shape ?*
——ach, -aiche, *a.* Real, resembling, identical. 2**Having shape or figure. 3††Full of shapes or forms. Cho c., *so identical ;* gu c., *really, actually.*
——ach, (AC) *s.m.* Placenta of a mare.
——achadh, -aidh, *s. m.* Creation, created being, creature. 2 Forming, inventing. 3 The universe. 4 Creating. 5 Asserting, assertion. 6 Proof. A' c—, *pr. pt.* of cruthaich. An c. féin, *the creature himself.*
cruthachail, *a.* Plastic. 2‡‡Creative.
cruthachd, see cruitheachd.
cruthadair, -e, -ean, see cruith-fhear.
cruthaich, *pr. pt.* a' cruthachadh, *v.a.* Create, make, form. 2**Figure. 3**Assert.
cruthaichte, *past pt.* of cruthaich, Created, &c.
cruthaidheachd, see cruitheachd,
cruthaidh-fhear, see cruithear.
crùthaig, (CR) *s. f.* Distress, strait, necessity. Is e an caraid caraid na crùthaig, *a friend (to one) in need is a friend indeed—W. of Ross.*
cruthaighear, -ir, see cruith-fhear.
cruthail, -e [& -ala,] *a.* Shapely, well-formed, comely.
cruthalachd, *s.f.ind.* Shapeliness, comeliness.
cruthann, (AH) *s.m.* Form, shape, person.
cruth-arraichte, see cruth-atharraichte.
cruth-atharrachadh, -aidh, *s.m.* Transfiguration, transformation, changing of shape or appearance, metamorphosis. 2 Act of transforming or changing. A' c—, *pr. pt.* of cruth-atharraich.
cruth-atharrachail, *a.* Transformative, transfigurative.
cruth-atharraich, *pr. pt.* a' cruth-atharrachadh, *v. a.* Transfigure, transform, metamorphose, change shape or appearance.
cruth-atharraichte, *a.* & *past pt.* of cruth-atharraich. Metamorphosed, transfigured, transformed, changed in form or appearance.
cruth-chaochail, *pr.pt.* a' cruth-chaochladh, *v.a.* Same meanings as cruth-atharraich.
cruth-chaochladh, -aidh, -aidhean, *s.m.* & *pr. pt.* Same meanings as cruth-atharrachadh.
cruth-chaochlaideach, -diche, *a.* Changing forms, causing change of forms or appearance, of, or pertaining to, transformation.
cruth-inntinneach,‡‡ -eiche, *a.* Imaginable.
cruthlach,* *s.m.* Tall, bent person. 2††Large, clumsy person. 3 Ghost. 4 Fairy.
cruth-lachd, *s.f.* Belt. 2 Sword-girdle.
cruth-shuidhich,‡‡ *v.a.* Organize.
†cu, *s.f.* & *m.* Champion, hero.
cù, *irreg.s.m.* Dog. 2(AF) Moth, (*i.e.* clothes-dog or gnawer.) 3(DU) Dog-fish. 4(WC)Timber-dog, used in saw-mills, scaffolding, &c.
Declined thus :—

	Singular.	*Plural.*
Nom.	cù,	coin,
Gen.	coin,	chon,
Dat.	cù,	coin,
Voc.	a choin !	a chona !

For kinds of dogs and compounds of cù, *see alphabetical order below.*
C. cuthach, *a mad dog ;* mial-chù, *a greyhound*; mo ghaol air do dhà shùil, ged bhiodh do bhrù aig "na coin," *I like your two eyes, though "the dogs" should have the rest of you*; mo chuideachd fhéin, "coin" Throtairnis, *my own company, the "dogs" of Trotternish,* "the dogs" being a nickname for the people of Trotternish; dà chaol-chù, *two gaunt dogs ;* taigh-chon, *a kennel*; taigh nan con, *the kennel*; c. dubh Eadailteach, *sleuth-hound*; coin dubha Ghriogarach, *kind of blood-hound, used of old for tracking deer; also used by their enemies for tracking fugitives of the Clan Gregor*; coin-fhodair, *fleas—*Mull*;* is fheairrde h-uile cù a dhìon a chinn a dhranndan, *a dog's snarl defends his head ;* cho sgìth ri c., *as tired as a dog ;* is e duine a ni, is e cù a dh' innseas, *he is a man who acts, but a cur who tells.*
†cua, *s.m.* Flesh.

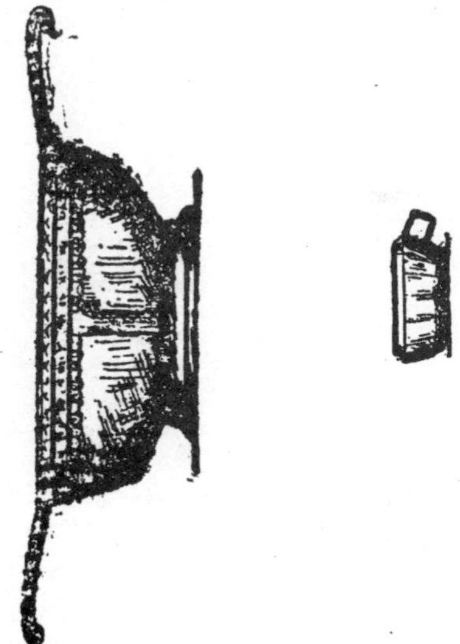

242. Cuachan Gàidhealach.

†cua-bhacan, -ain, *s.m.* Flesh-hook.
†cuabhach, -aiche, *a.* Fleshy.
†cua-bhreid, *s.f.* Itch. 2 Lechery.
cuacair, *s.m.* Slouch.
cuach, -aich, -an, *s.f.* Drinking cup, bowl, goblet. 2 Coil, fold, plait. 3 Curl, curl of hair. 4 Hollow or bosom of a hill. 5 Hollow part of a bird's nest. 6(AF)Cockle (fish.) 7††Pail. 8††Cap. Ma dhiùltas iad a' ch., *if they refuse the cup.* [Ills. of *cuach* on p. 283.]
cuach,¶ *s.f.* Cuckoo, see cubhag.
cuach, *pr.pt.* a' cuachadh, *v.a.* Fold, plait, curl.
cuachach, -aiche, *a.* Abounding in, of, or belonging to, plaits, folds, cups, hollows, pails, &c. 2 Plaited, folded, curled. 3 Crisp. 4**Frizzled. 5 Concave. 6** Like, of, or belonging to, a cuckoo. Is math thig breacan c. ort! *how well the folded plaid becomes you!*; an cìrean c., *their curled crests.*
cuachadh,** -aidh, *s.m.* Crispation.
cuachag, -aige, -an, *s.f.* Little cup. 2 Little curl. 3 Neat young girl. 4 Female with curled hair. 5 Spiral shell. 6 Cuckoo, see cubhag. 7††Little plait.
———ach, -aiche, see cuachach.
———achd, *s.f.ind.* Crispness.
cuachaich, see cuaichnich.
cuachan, -ain, -an, see cuachag. 2**Bird's nest.
———ach, -aiche, see cuachach.
cuach-bhleoghainn, *pl.* -an-b—, *s.f.* Milking-pail or cog, a vessel that superseded the *cno-bainne,* and is itself now replaced by the tin pail.
cuach-chiabh, -an, *s.f.* Curled lock, ringlet.
cuach-chlàr, see còrn-chlàr.
cuach-fhalt, -uilt, *s.m.* Curled hair. 2 Waving locks. Do ch. bàn, *thy fair waving hair.*
cuach-ghorm, *s.f.* Remedy for chest complaints, made by melting butter and adding the juices of certain herbs.
cuach-mhullach,** *s.f.* Dome.
cuach-Phàdruig, *s.f.* Greater plantain — *plantago major.* 2 Banana tree. [In some places, cruach-Phàdruig.]
†cua-chromag, -aig, -an, *s.f.* Flesh-hook.
cuach-shrann,** -ainn, *s. m.* Violent snoring.
cuadan,** *s.m.* Complaint.
†cuadh, *v.a.* Tell, relate.
†cuadhaire, -an, *s.m.* Newsmonger.
cu'ag, -aig, -an, see cubhag.
cuag, -aig, -an, *s.f.* Awkward curve or bending. 2 Excrescence on the heel. 3 (AF) Pine grosbeak, see cnag. 4**Kink.

243. Cuach-Phàdruig.

cuagach, -aiche, *a.* Awkwardly bent or curved. having unshapely curves. 2 Having excrescences or tumours on the heel. 3 Crump-footed. 4 Limping or halting—*Lewis.* 5(JM) Lame—*Uist.* Is c. ceartas an eucoirich, *the justice of the unjust is twisted.*
cuagair, -ean, *s.m.* Awkward slovenly man. 2 Crump-footed man. 3 Lame person—*Lewis.*
———eachd, *s.f.ind.* Awkwardness, clumsiness, slovenliness.
cuagan,** -ain, *s.m.* Hind part of the heel. †2 ‡‡Hind-head.
cuagas, -ais, *s.m.* Crippleness.
cuag-chas, -choise, -chasan, *s.f.* Foot with the heel swollen. 2 Crump-foot.
cuag-chasach, *a.* Very deformed in the legs.
cuaichean, -ean, *s.m.* Curl. 2 Seam. 3††Nest.
———ach, -aich, *a.* Plaited. 2 Tight. 3 Compact. 4 Curly-headed. 5††Abounding in nests.
cuaichneachadh, -aidh, *s.m.* Curling, plaiting act of curling or plaiting. A' c—, *pr. pt.* of cuaichnich.
cuaichnich, *pr. pt.* a' cuaichneachadh, *v. a.* Plait. 2 Frizzle. 3 Crisp. 4 Curl.
cuaichnichte, *past pt.* of cuaichnich. Plaited. 2 Curled. 3 Frizzled.
cuaigean, -ein, -an, *s.m.* Splay-footed man. 2 (AH) Small, squat, sturdy man. 3(AH)Term of endearment, frequently used in addressing a little boy.
cuail,** *s.f.* Impediment to marriage. (col.)
cuail, *gen. sing.* of cual.
cuailean, -ein, -an, *s.m.* The hair. 2 Lock, curl, 3 Wreath. 4 Small stick, used by Highland women for adjusting the *bréid* or head-dress. 5* Cue, plaited hair. C. amlach, *curled locks.*
———ach, -aiche, *a.* In curls or ringlets. 2 Of, or belonging to, the hair, curls or ringlets.
cuailein, see cuailean.
———each, see cuaileanach.
cuaille, -an [& -achan,] *s.m.* Club, baton, bludgeon. 2 Ponderous staff or cudgel, pole, stake, post. 3 Fool. 4 Rafter. Eadar ch. agus chlach, *both rafter and stone*; c. bata, *a cowl-staff*; sireadh caimein an cònlaich (connlach) sanas a thoirt do ch., *searching for a mote in straw, hinting to a fool*; c. math daraich, *a stout oak stick*; is treasa slat na c., *a rod is more effectual than a club*—meaning that moderate punishment is best.
cuain, -e, *s.f.* Litter of whelps or pigs. 2 (AF) Pup. 3 †Corner. †4 Angle. 5 *gen. sing.* of cuan.
———te, see cuanta.
cuair, *s.* Gaelic spelling of *quire* (of paper.)
cuairealta,** *a.* Curious. 2 Exquisite.
cuairean, *s. pl.* for cuarain, *n.pl.* of cuaran.
cuairsg, *pr. pt.* a' cuairsgeadh, *v. a.* Roll up, wreathe, twist, wrap, coil.
———each, -giche, *a.* Coiled, rolled, wrapped up. 2 Tressy. 3 Circuitous. 4 Twisted. 5 Wreathed. 6**In rolls or volumes.
———each, *s.m.* Wrapper.
cuairsgeadh, -gidh, *s.m.* Volume. 2 Rolling, act of rolling, wrapping or coiling. 3 Wreath. 4 Circuit. A' c—, *pr.pt.* of cuairsg.
cuairsgeag, *s.f.* Tress.
———ach, see cuairsgeach.
cuairsgean, -ein, -an, *s.m.* Wrapper, envelope. 2 Felloe of a wheel. 3 Heart or core of a fruit. 4¶ Roller (bird,)—*caracius yarrula.*
cuair-sgiath, -sgéith, *s.f.* Crooked target.
cuairsgte, *past pt.* of cuairsg. Rolled, wrapped up.
cuairt, -e, -ean, *s.f.* Circle, circuit, cycle, zone, circumference. 2 Circulation. 3 Round. 4 Expedition, excursion, tour, journey, walk. pilgrimage. 5 Visit, sojourning. 6 Repetition. 7 Circumlocution. 8 Tier of planks in shipbuilding. 9 Pommel. 10 Round ball or knob in architecture. 11 Whirl, eddy. 12 Set of tunes on the pipes. 13 Compass. 14 **General gathering of sheep. 15‡‡Anus. C. na gaoithe, *the eddy of the wind*; tri chuairt, *thrice*; luchd-faire air cuairtibh, *watchmen on their rounds*; a' cheud ch., *the first round*; cha'n 'eil annainn ach luchd-cuairt air an talamh, *we are only travellers on the earth*; chaidh sinn air ch. do 'n Ghalltachd, *we went on a tour to the Lowlands*; cainnt gun ch., *language without circumlocution*; c. na fola, *the circulation of the blood*; theirig mu 'n cuairt, *get round about*; mu 'n cuairt de dheich bliadhna, *about ten years*; air ch., *sojourning*; thoir c. air a' phìob, air an fhidhill, *take a turn at the pipes, at the violin*; car mu'n cuairt aca, *they taking turns at it, tak-*

ing it alternately.

cuairt, (mu 'n) *adv.* **Round, around. 2 About.** Chaidh an t-slige mu 'n cuairt, *the shell went round.*

——— -beòil, *s.f.* Saxboard, see under bàta, E8, p. 73. 2 Top-stroke, p. 76.

——— -bheag, *s.f.* Brace-stick of a boat, see under bàta, G2, p. 73.

cuairt-chainnt,‡‡ -e, *s.f.* Circumlocution.

————each,‡‡ -eiche, *a.* Circumlocutory.

cuairt-char,‡‡ -uir, *s.m.* Meander.

cuairt-cladaich,(AC) *s.f.* Shore circuit, a practice prevalent in the Western Isles of going daily round the sea-shore on the chance of picking up flotsam.

cuairt-claidh, (AC) *s.f.* Circuit of the burial-ground.

cuairt-dhurrag,‖ *s.f.* Ringworm. [Preceded by the article *a' ch—.*]

cuairt duine,(AC) *s.f.* Man's time.

cuairteach, -tiche, *a.* Circular, round. 2 Circuitous, circumambient. 3 Ambient. 4 Full of circles. 5**Mazy.

————,‖ -tich, -tichean, *s.f.* Epidemic disorder. [Preceded by the article *a ch—.*] A' ch. sgàrlaid, *scarlet fever—Gairloch & W. of Ross-shire.*

————adh, -aidh, *s.m.* Surrounding. 2 Act of surrounding, encircling, encompassing, or enclosing. 3 Whirling. 4 Circulation. 5 Compass, compassing. 6 Visiting. 7 Tour. 8 Circuit. 9 Circumlocution. 10 Investing. 11 Enclosure. 12 Siege, besieging. 13(AC) Sanctuary. A' c—, *pr.pt.* of cuairtich. C. chaorach, *a general gathering of sheep into a fold.*

cuairteachadh-teaghlaich, (AC) *s. m.* Family worship.—*Ross, Sutherland & Caithness.*

cuairteachas, -ais, *s.f.* Journeying, tour, round of visiting, gossiping.

cuairteag, -eige, -an, *s.f.* Little circle. 2 Round hollow. 3 Little whirlpool. 4 Bird's nest. 5 Fillet in architecture. 6 Wheel. 7 Eddy. 8 Gulf. Eun an fhraoich 'na ch., *the heath-fowl in its nest.*

cuairteagach, -aiche, *a.* Circular, round. 2 Eddying. 3 Globular. 4 Circling. 5 Gulfy. Aitreabh c., *a circular dwelling, a nest.*

cuairteagan, *s.pl.* Fruit of the apple-tree.

cuairteag-shluganach,** *s.f.* Little whirlpool.

cuairt-ealain,‡‡ *s.f.* Cyclopædia.

cuairtean, -ein, *s.m.* Little circle. 2 Little circuit. 3 Maze, labyrinth. 4**Whirlwind. 5 **Eddy. 6 Period in *writing* (.) 7 *n. pl.* of cuairt. 8 Strakes in boat, see bàta, G12, p.73.

cuairteanach,** *a.* see cuairteach.

cuairtear, -eir, -eirean, *s.m.* Tourist, visitant, sojourner, pilgrim.

cuairt-eòlais,‡‡ *s.f.* Cyclopædia.

cuairt-ghaoth, -ghaoithe, -an, *s.f.* Whirlwind, eddying wind. 'Sa chath mar ch., *in battle like a whirlwind.*

cuairtich, *pr. pt.* a' cuairteachadh, *v. a.* Surround, enclose, encompass on all sides, environ, make a circuit. 2 Gather in, collect, as cattle. 3‡‡Fillet, in architecture. 4(WC)Engage, perform. 5(WC) Find—*Lewis.* C. do dhleasdanas, *do your duty* (very imperative); bithidh sinn a' cuairteachadh an aoraidh-theaghlaich, *we shall engage in family worship*; cha bhi mi fada 'ga chuairteachadh, *I shall not be long in finding it.*

cuairtichean,(AC)*s.pl.* Circuiters, men from each of two families taken in rotation, chosen to patrol the townland at night to keep deer and other vermin from the crofters' crops, before the security of tenure recently obtained by them enabled them to erect fences round their holdings.

cuairtiche-sgàrlaid,‖ *s.f.* Scarlet fever. [Preceded by the article *a' ch—.*]

cuairtichte, *past pt.* of cuairtich. Surrounded, enclosed, encompassed on all sides. 2 Collected. 3 Filleted, in architecture.

cuairt-imeachd,** *s.* Circulation.

cuairt-iùil, *s.f.* Cyclopædia.

cuairt-labhairt,‡‡ *s.m.* Circumlocution.

cuairt-labhrach,‡‡ -aiche, *a.* Periphrastic.

cuairt-lìn,** *s.* Circumference.

cuairt-linn, -linntean, *s.f.* Whirlpool.

cuairt-lùb, *s.m.* Circumflex accent in *writing* (â.) 2‡‡Meander.

cuairt-Mhìcheil,(AC) *s.f.* Circuit made round burial-grounds on St. Michael's day.

cuairt-ràdh, *s.m.* Circumlocution.

cuairt-shàbh,‡‡ -aibh, -an, *s.m.* Compass-saw.

cuairt-sheòl,** *v.a.* Circumnavigate.

cuairt-shiùbhlach,‡‡ -aiche, *a.* Circumrotary.

cuairt-shlugan, -ain, -an, *s.m.* Whirlpool, eddy, vortex.

cuairt-shluganach, -aiche, *a.* Abounding in whirlpools.

cuairt-shruth, -shruithean, *s. f.* Whirlpool or eddy in a stream. 2 Stream abounding in whirlpools or eddies.

cuairt-shuidheachadh,** *s.m.* Circumposition.

cuairt-thoisich, *s.f.* Brace-stick of a boat, see under bàta, G2, p. 73.

cuairt-tìme,(AC) *s.f.* Time-circuit.

†cuaith, -e, *s.f.* The country.

cual, -uail, -uailtean, *s. f.* Faggot. 2 Burden of sticks. 3 Back-load. 4(AF)Herds, cattle. †5 see gual. C. chonnaidh, *a faggot of firewood*; cleas gille nan c., cual bheag is tighinn tric, *the carriers' motto—little at a time and coming often*; a' ch. chrò, *a door of heather,* always used in the sheep-folds and in the airidhs and in old houses in Gaeldom—cuir a' ch. (*or* a' ghual) 'san dorus, *shut the door* —(WC.) [** gives "an c. chrò, *the sheep fold,*" which appears to be incorrect both in gender and meaning.] C. fhraoich, *bundle of heather* of certain dimensions, tied up with ropes made of birch switches (a' bharrach.) The ropes were exactly six feet long with loops at end for tying—(WC.)

cuala, *past interr.* of cluinn. Nach cuala mi? *have I not heard?*; is fada bho 'n a chuala mi.. ., *I have always heard....*, (generally said of a proverb); tha mi far nach cuala mi riamh e, *well, well, I never heard of such a thing!*

cualach,†† -aich, -aichean, *s.m.* Great burden of sticks. 2 Act of gathering sticks. 3 see cuallach.

————, -aiche, *a.* Having many faggots, burdened.

cualag, -aige, -an, *s.f.* Little burden, bundle. 2 Hard task. Cha ch. sin air, *that is no task to him. 2 that were no indignity to him, he took it quite as an ordinary affair.*

cualan,** -ain, *s.m.* Little burden. 2 Faggot. 3 *W. of Ross* for cuailean.

cualas, *past pass.* of cluinn. Was heard. Gus an c. mu 'bhuaidh, *till we have heard of his victory.*

cual-chnàmh,(AH) *s.f.* Anything shattered to very small pieces. Bhuail e a' phoit leis an òrd agus rinn e c. dhi, *he struck the pot with the hammer and smashed it to atoms.*

cuallach, -aich, *s.m.* Herding, tending of cattle 2 Keeper of cattle. 3(AF)Cattle, stock cattle. 4 see cualach. Agus e a' c. na spréidhe, *and he tending the cattle.* A' c—, *pr.pt.* of cuall-

aich.
cuallach, -aich, *s. f.* Corporation, society, fraternity, company. 2 Family.
————adh, -aidh, *s. m.* Tending of cattle, herding. A' c—, *pr.pt.* of cuallaich.
† ————d, *s.f. ind.* Dependants. 2 Herding. 3 *rarely* Colony.
cuallaich, *pr. pt.* a' cuallach & a' cuallachadh, *v.a.* Tend or herd cattle, *prov.*
————e,** *s.m.* Keeper of cattle. 2 Society. †3 Companion.
cù-allaidh,(AF) *s.m.* Wolf.
cuallaidheachd, *s.f.* Society.
†cuallas, -ais, *s.m.* Assembly.
†cua-mhargadh, -aidh, *s.m.* Shambles. 2** Flesh-market.
†cuamhor, *a.* Fat, corpulent.
cuan, -ain, cuantan [-uaintean & -uanta,] *s.m.* Sea, ocean, the deep. 2** Large lake. 3** *rarely* Harbour, haven, bay. 4**Deceit. 5** Multitude. 6(AF) Pack of hounds or wolves. An t-àrd-chuan, *the high sea;* air|àrd a' chuain, *on the high seas.*
cuanairt, *s.f.* Pack of hounds.
cuanal, -ail, -an, *s.m.* Company. 2 Band of singers, choir. 3* Group of children living on the best of terms. 4(AC) Flocks, cattle, horses, sheep, goats.
cuanar, -aire, *a.* Soft, calm. 2††Handsome, fine, trim.
cuan-ard, -aird, -an, *s.f.* Stormy, tempestuous sea.
cuan-choire, *pl.* -choireachan, *s.m.* Gulf, whirlpool.
cuanda, see cuanta.
cuan-mara,(AF) *s.m.* Sea-urchin.
cuanmhor,‡‡ see cuannar.
cuanna, see cuannar.
cuanna, *s.m.* Hill.
cuannal, see cuanal.
cuannar, *a.* Handsome, neat, fine, showy, engaging, elegant. 2 Snug, comfortable. Bean bu ch. càil, *a woman of the most engaging temper.*
cù-an-òtraich,(WC) *s.m.* Mongrel dog.
cuanta, *a.* Able. 2 Robust. 3 Handsome, elegant, trim, tight, tidy. 4**Fine, showy, engaging. 5‡‡Prolific.
cuanta, *n.pl.* of cuan.
cuantach, -aich, *s.m.* Seafaring man. 2††Inhabitant of the sea-coast.
————, -aiche, *a.* Sea-bred.
————d, *s.f.* Daintiness. 2**Handsomeness, fineness, neatness, tidiness, showiness.
cuantaibh, *dat. pl.* of cuan.
cuantaiche, *s.m.* Rover.
cuantal, -ail, *s.m.* Group. 2 Rapid torrent of language, *prov.*
cuantan, *n. pl.* of cuan.
†cuar, *a.* Crooked, perverse. 2(AC)Venomous.
——,(AC) -air, -airean, *s.m.* Distress. †2Worm, screw. 3†Flesh. Gach c. agus cunnart, *every distress and danger.*
cuar,†† *pr.pt.* a' cuaradh, *v.a. & n.* Torment. 2 Feel sorely.
†cuara, *s.m.* Vessel.
cuaradh, -aidh, *s.m. prov.* for ciùrradh.
cuarag, -aige, -an, *s.f.* Knapsack. 2††Sock. 3 **Shoe made of untanned leather with hair on.
cuaran, -ain, *s.m.* Sock. 2 Brogue of untanned skin, commonly worn with the hairy side outwards. 3 Sandal. 4 Buskin. 5 Bandage on a wounded finger or toe, finger-stall. 6** Any part of a shoe. 7 Slipper. Feumaidh fear nan cuaran éirigh uair roimh fhear nam bròg, *the man of the sock must rise an hour before the wearer of shoes*—the lacing of the *cuaran* was a tedious affair—N.G.P.
————ach, -aiche, *a.* Socked, of, or belonging to, a sock, brogue or sandal. 2 Wearing hairy brogues. 3 Buskined.
————ta, *a.* Hardy.
cuaras,-ais, *s.m.* Lover. Stocainnean do m' ch., *stockings to my lover.—Lewis.*
cuarsgach, -aiche, *a.* Wrapped, enveloped. 2 Crooked, bent. 3 Round, circular. 4 Twisted, twirled, curled.
cuarsgadh, -aidh, *s.m.* Rolling, act of rolling. A' c—, *pr. pt.* of cuairsg.
cuarsgag,†† -aig, *s.f.* Curve, circle. 2*Eddy. 3* Curl.
————ach,†† *a.* see cuairsgeach.
cuart, see cuairt.
——ach, *s.m.* Fever. 2 Current.
——achadh, see cuairteachadh.
cuartachail,** *a.* Ambulatory.
cuartag, -aige, -an, see cuairteag.
————ach, -aiche, see cuairteagach.
cuartaich, see cuairtich.
————,** *s.m.* Farm servant in the Hebrides, whose sole business is to preserve the grass and corn of his employer. His wages are, grass for four cows, and as much arable land as one horse can plough and harrow.
cuartalan, -ain, -an, *s.m.* Turning round, act of turning round circularly, circuit, circuitous route.
cuartan, -ain, -an, *s.m.* Maze, labyrinth.
†cuartughadh, see cuairteachadh.
cuas, -ais, -an, *s.m.* Cave. 2 Any hollow or cavity. 3**Hollow of a tree. Bu ch. e, *it was a cave.* see còs.
——ach,** *a.* Cavernous. 2 Full of hollows or holes. 3 Concave.
——achd,** *s.f.* Hollowness. 2 Subterraneousness. 3 Concavity.
†cuasag, -aige, -an, *s.f.* Bees' nest. 2 Honeycomb in hollow trees. 3 Apple. 4 Egg. 5** Little cave.
cuasan,** -ain, *s.m.* Hole, cavity. 2 *n. pl.* of cuas.
cuat,(AC) *s.m.* Lover, sweetheart, bosom friend.
cùb, -ùib -an & -a, *s.f.* Sledge. 2 Pannier. 3 Box-cart. 4 Coup-cart. 5 Tumbril. 6 Gaelic spelling of *coop.* Fasan ùr aun am measg nam muillear, briseadh nan cùban, *a new fashion among the millers, breaking their carts, barrels, &c.—Duanaire, p. 38.*
cùb, -ùib, *s.m.* see cùbadh.
——, *pr. pt.* a' cùbadh, *v.n.* Crouch, stoop, bend. 2**Yield. 3**Lie down. 4 Shrink from fear. 5 Feel the utmost torment of mind.
——a, -n, *s.m.* Bed.
cùba-chùil, -n-cùil, *s.f.* Bed-chamber.
——ch, -aiche, *a.* Bent. 2 Hollowed. 2 Belonging to sledges or panniers.
——dh, -aidh, *s.m.* Bending. 2 Shrinking for fear. 2**Stooping. 3**Yielding. A' c—, *pr. pt.* of cùb.
cubadh, -aidh, *s.m.* Spelling.
cùbag, -aige, -an, *s.f.* Small pannier.
cùbaid, -e, -ean, *s.f.* Pulpit. 2 Precentor's desk.
————h, -e, -ean, *s.f. Ross & Suth'd* for cùbaid.
cùbainn, *Lewis* for cùbaid.
cùbair, -ean, *s.m.* Cooper. 2‡‡Black-cock. 3 Shabby, sneaking fellow.
————eachd, *s. f. ind.* Occupation of a cooper. Ris a' ch., *working as a cooper.*
cùbait,** -ean, *s.f.* Gaelic spelling of *cubit.*
cubhag, -aige, -an, Cuckoo. 2 Snipe. 3 Wagtail. 4***in derision,* Person affected with itch. 5(DU) Silly woman. Cuir air ruith na cubhaige, *send on a fool's errand on 1st. April, make an April fool of* ; greim cubhaige, *a piece*

244. *Cubhag.*

of food to be eaten early, in order not to hear the cuckoo's call on an empty stomach; chuala mi a' ch. gun bhiadh 'nam bhroinn, *I heard the cuckoo before tasting food*—considered a sign of an unlucky year to follow.

———ach,** *a.* Like a cuckoo, abounding in cuckoos. 2 Crump-footed. The saying "cho clomhach ris a' chubhaig," which means, as full of itch as the cuckoo, should doubtless be "cho clòimheach ris a' chubhaig," *as downy as the cuckoo.*

——— -chluaise, *s.f.* Tell-tale. Ge binn leinn a' chubhag cha bhinn leinn cubhag-chluaise, *we like the cuckoo but not the "ear-cuckoo."*

cubhag-ghliogarach,** *s.f.* Snipe.

cubhaidh, -e, *a.* Decent, fit, becoming, seemly. 2* Hereditary, having a just claim to. 3 **Compatible. Cha bu ch. dhuit, *you had no family right to it*; tha thu mar bu ch. dhuit, *you are just as one would expect (from such parents)*; mar bu ch. do mhnathan pòsda, *as befitting married women.*

†cubhaidh, *s.f.* Honour.

cubhaidheachd, *s.f.* Seemliness, decentness, fitness, decency. 2** Compatibility. 3**Justness.

†cubhail, *s.m.* Religious habit.

cubhaing, -ean, *s.f. & a.* see cumhang.

†cubhais, *s.f.* Oath. 2 Conscience.

†cubhal, -ail, *s.m.* Religious habit.

cubhann, -ainne, *a. prov.* for cumhang.

cubhar,** -air, *s.m.* Corner. 2 see cobhar. 3 (AF) Hawk, see cabhar.

cubhas,** -ais, *s.m.* Word, promise. 2 Tree, block.

†cubhnachail, see cùba-chùil.

cubhrag,†† -aig, -an, *s.f.* Infant's flannel shawl.

cùbhraich,** *v.a.* Aromatize.

———te, *past pt.* Aromatized.

cùbhraidh, -e, *a.* Fragrant, balmy, perfumed. 2 Having a pleasant flavour. Fàile ch. de d' anail, *a fragrant smell off thy breath*; 'sa bheithe ch., *in the fragrant birch*; rinn mi mo mo leabadh c., *I have perfumed my bed.*

———eachd, *s.f.ind.* Fragrance, perfume.

cùbhraig,‡ -e, -ean, see cuibhrig.

cùbhrainn, -e, -ean, *s.f.* see cùrainn.

———ich, see cùrainnich.

cuchailte, *s.m.* Seat, residence.

cuchair, *s.m.* Hunter.

cù-chaorach,(AH) *s.m.* Sheep-dog, shepherd's collie.

cù-choille,(AC) coin-ch—, *s.m.* Wolf.

cu-chullain, *s.m.* Yellow bed-straw.

cù-cnàmha,(AF) *s.m.* Louse.

cudag, see cudainn.

cudaig, -e, -ean, see cudainn.

cudainn, -e, -ean, *s. m.* Cuddy, coal-fish till the New Year, saithe, lythe, &c.

cùdainn, -ean, *s.f.* Tub or dish of large size. 2‡‡Bowl. 3 Tumbler with round or pointed bottom, to prevent its being set down till quite empty. Clach na cùdainn, *the rocking-stone of Inverness.*

———each,†† *a.* Pertaining to large tubs or dishes.

†cudal, *a.* Bad, wicked.

cudal, *s.m.* see cuiteal.

†cudam,** -aim, *s. m.* Scar on the head. 2 Fault in the hair of the head. 3 Dandriff. C. an t-sléibhe, *the mountain eruption.*

†cudamach, -aiche, *a.* Frail, corruptible. 2 Liable to error, fallible.

cudamachd,** *s.f.ind.* Frailty, fallibility, corruptibleness.

cudamaiseach,** *a.* Epileptic.

cudan, see cudainn.

†cudarman, -ain, *s. m.* The vulgar.

cù-donn, *pl.* coin-donna, *s.m.* Otter, *prov.*

cudrom, see cudthrom.

cudthrom,‡-uim, *s.m.* Weight, heaviness. 2 Burden, load. 3**Importance. Leig do ch. orm, *lean on me.*

———ach, -aiche, *a.* Heavy, ponderous, weighty, burdensome. 2 Important, momentous. 3**Grave, sedate. 4**Just. 'S ann a tha 'n gnothach sin c., *that is a momentous affair.*

———achd, *s.f.ind.* Weightiness. burdensomeness. 2 Importance, gravity. 3 Weighing.

———aich,‡‡ *v.a.* Poise.

——— -siùdain, *s.m.* Pendulum.

——— -socrachaidh,(AH) *s.m.* Ballast.

cù-dubh,(CR) *s.m.* Blood-hound—*W. of Ross-sh.*

cù-dur,(AF) *s.m.* Otter.

cù-eunaidh,(AF) *s.m.* Pointer. 2 Spaniel. 3 Setter. 4 Retriever.

cù-fada,(AF) *s.m.* Greyhound.

cù-fionn,(AF) -a, *s.m.* Greyhound.

cù-fionn,(AF) *s.m.* Moth.

cù-faol,(AC) *s.m.* Wolf.

cù-fàsach, } (AF) *s.m.* Wolf.
cù-fàsaich, }

cù-feòladair, (AF) *s.m.* Bull-dog. (*lit.* flesher's dog.)

cù-fhind, see cù-fionn.

cugainn, see cugann.

cugallach,(AC) *a.* Precarious, unstable, uncertain. Is c. an t-sealg, *hunting is precarious.*

cugallaidh,(MMcL) *a.* Liable to accidents.

cugann, -ainn, *s.m.* Rich milk. 2 Milk set for cream. 3 Delicacy, kitchen.

cugar,(AC) *s. m.* Male cat, tame or wild. 2 Hero, gallant, champion.

cugarbhad, see cugar. C. mór nan cat, *the chief of the cats.*

cù-gèarr,(AC) *s.m.* Wolf.

cù-ghearraidh,(WC) *s. m.* Critic, backbiter. Nach b'e sin na coin-ghearraidh! *what backbiters they were!*

cughainneach,** -ich, *s.m.* Mixing together, as of wool.

cughainnaich,** *v.a.* Mix together, as wool. 2 Tighten, circumscribe.

cù-gorm,(AF) *s.m.* Greyhound.

cù-gortach, (AF) *s.m.* Greyhound.

cughann, *a.* see cumhang.

———,** *s.m.* Bay.

———achadh,** *s.m.* Circumscription.

†cugull, -uill, see cochull.

cù-ian, see cù-eunaidh.

cuib, *s.* (AF) Dog. 2 Greyhound. 3**Phial.

†cuibeanach, *a.* Ill-favoured.

cuibh, *s.f.* *Muzzle-bar, splinter. C. mhór, *one for four horses*; gearra ch., *one for two horses—Islay, Lochaber, Cowal & mainland of Argyll.* 2 (AF) Dog, greyhound. 4 see cuidh.

†cuibhe, -an, *s.m.* see cuithe.

cuibhe,‡*a.* see cubhaidh.

———achd, see cubhaidheachd.

cuibheall, see cuidheall.

cuibheas, -eis, *s. m.* Enough, sufficiency. 2*

Moderation. Cha'n 'eil sin 'na ch., *that is beyond all moderation* ; cha'n 'eil thu 'nad ch., *you are not easily dealt with*, (*Scots*, ye'r nae canny) ; tha c. air a h-uile rud, gu ruig òl a' bhrochain, *there is reason in everything, even in supping porridge.*
cuibheasach, -aiche, *a.* Sufficient. 2 Tolerable, middling, average. 3* Easily dealt with.
————ach, -aich, *s.m.* Moderate person.
————achd, *s.f.* Average. 2††see coibheasachd.
cuibhill, *v.* see cuidheall.
cuibhioll, cuibhle, cuibhlichean & cuibhleachan, *s.f.* see cuidheall.
cuibhle, *pl.* -achan & -ichean, see cuidheall.
——, *v.* see cuidheall.
——adh, -leidh, *s.m.* & *pr.pt.* see cuidhleadh.
cuibhleag,(DC) -an, *s.f.* Beam of a kiln—*Uist.*
cuibhlean, see cuidhlean.
cuibhle-mhór,(AF) Moth—*Arran.* 2(CR)Night-jar—*Jura.* [Preceded by the article *a' ch.*]
cuibhlich, *v.a.* see cuidheall.
cuibhlig, *prov.* for cùbhraig.
cuibhne, *pl.* -an & -nichean, *s. f.* Antler of a deer. 2 Dart.
cuibhreach, -rich, -richean, *s. m.* Bond. 2 Chain. 3 Trammel. 4*Harness of a plough-horse. 5**Cover. 6** *as a collective s.*, Slavery. An c. cruaidh, *in hard chains, in slavery*; c. righrean, *the bond of kings.*
————adh, -aidh, *s.m.* Binding, fettering, act of binding or fettering, bondage. 2 Entangling. 3** Clothing. A' c—, *pr. pt.* of cuibhrich.
cuibhrich, *pr.pt.* a' cuibhreachadh, *v.a.* Bind, fetter, chain, put in bonds or irons. 2 Entangle. 3**Cover.
————te, *past pt.* of cuibhrich. Chained, fettered, bound. 2 Entangled. 3 Covered.
cuibhrig, -e, -ean, *s. m.* Coverlet, plaiden, coarse home-made flannel, quilt. 2††Lid, cover. C. poite, *a wooden pot-lid* ; c. bolla, *the wooden covering lid of a buoy*; c. na poite bige am beul na poite móire, *the lid of the little pot in the mouth of the large pot*—said of anything very unsuitable.
cuibhrig, *pr.pt.* a' cuibhrigeadh, *v.a.* Cover, conceal, hide, coat.
————each,†† *a.* Pertaining to a lid, cover or quilt.
————eadh, -gidh, -gidhean, *s.m.* Cover, covering, act of covering. 2 (DC) Bed-cover—*Uist.*
————te, *past pt.* of cuibhrig. Covered, concealed, hidden. 2 Restricted.
cuibhrinn, -ean, *s. f.* see cuibhrionn. 2 see cùrainn.
————eachadh, -aidh, -aidhean, *s.m.* Welt, cover. 2 Binding, act of binding. 3 Welting.
cuibhrionn, -inn, *pl.* -ean &-an, *s.m.* Part, portion. 2 Lot of land. 3 Allotment. 4**Allowance.
cuibhseach, -ich, see cuibheasach.
————d,‡‡ *s.f.ind.* Average, mean.
†cuibhte, *a.* see cubhaidh.
†cuice, *adv.* see chuice.
cuichean,(AH) -ein, *s. m.* Private confidential interview, tête-à-tête.
cuicheanachd, *s. f.* Gentle banter, teasing of lovers, hob-nobbing.
cuid, *irreg. s. f.* Declined thus:—

	Sing.	*Plur.*
Nom.	cuid,	codaichean,
Gen.	codach,	chodaichean,
Dat.	cuid,	codaichean,
Voc.	a chuid !	a chodaiche !

Share, part, some. 2 Victuals, food. 3 Property, effects, means, substance. 4†† Lodging, quarters. 5 ** The privy parts. 6(AC) Clothes of deceased persons, which became the perquisite of the clergy. Is e seo mo ch.-sa, *this is mine*; a' chuid a's mó, *the greater part*; cuid do chroinn, *your chance, your lot* ; mo ch.-sa dheth, *my part of it* ; c. oidhche, *a night's entertainment or lodging* ; c. an tràth, *what serves for a meal of meat*; mo ch. de 'n t-saoghal, *my all;* air son mo chodach-sa dheth, [*better* air mo chuid-sa dheth] *for my part of it;* c. duine chloinne, *the share of one of a family*; cha toir muir no monadh a ch. bho dhuine sona, *dangers by sea or land cannot deprive a fortunate man of his lot;* a ch. mhac, [in *Poolewe* they say, a chuid mac] *his sons;* a c. mac, *her sons;* c. de na daoine, *some of the men* ; a' ch. eile, *the other part* or *the rest*; am bheil do làmhan-sa glan ? tha mo ch.-sa salach, *are your hands clean ? my own are dirty*; b'e a bhi 'buaireadh an Fhreasdail cuid a' chunnart a ghabhail d' a leithid sin a dh' àite, *it were tempting Providence to run such a tremendous risk by going to such a place* ; a' pàigheadh cuid fiach na mnà agam, *such is my lot, to pay my wife's debts.* [The peculiar use of *cuid* in the last two examples should be noted, as it is not, as is usual in such a context, associated with possession.] A c. àlaich, *her litter* ; a' gharbh ch., *the greater part;* an dà chuid......agus......, *both......and.......*

Aon chuid......no......, *either......or......*, [when associated with a negative verb =neither...... nor....] Dara would be impossible in the following examples : 'nuair a chaidh an sgeulachd mu 'n cuairt, cha robh aon ch. aige sgeulachd no òran, *when the tale went round, he had neither tale nor song* (*to give*) ; nach labhair thu ri Iacob aon chuid math no olc, *that you speak not to Jacob either good or bad* ; gu'n d' rinn e aoradh dhaibh, aon ch. do 'n ghréin, no do 'n ghealaich, no do..,*that he worshipped them, either the sun or the moon, or....* ; ni 's oillteile na bha i aon ch. do Tholamsan no do Bhreac-ghlun, *more repulsive than she was either to T. or B.* ; cha d' fhoghlum e eòlas, air an aon chuid no air a' ch. eile, *he got no learning, either the one way or the other.* [" Aona chuid " which is often met with, is simply the product of a drawling pronunciation.]

An dara cuid....no......, *either ......or ......*; an dara c., bithidh fuath aige do neach aca agus gràdh do 'n fhear eile, no.., *either he will hate the one and love the other, or ....*, an dara c. deanaibh a' chraobh math agus a toradh math, no deanaibh ...., *either make the tree good and its fruit good, or make ....*; 'nuair a tha mi an am bruadair, tha mi an dara c. ri camanachd air an raon, no ri luingearachd air a' chaol, no ri...., *when I dream, I am either playing shinty on the plain, or boating on the narrows, or ....*; éighibh le guth àrd, oir is dia e ! an dara c. tha e 'beachd-smuainteachach, no tha e air toir, no...., *cry aloud, for he is a god ! either he is talking, or he is pursuing, or....* [Dara does not associate with a negative verb.]
cuid, *s. indef.* Some, certain number.
——eachadh, -aidh, *s.m.* Help, relief, assistance, aid, act of assisting or helping. A'c—, *pr. pt.* of cuidich.
——eachaidh,** *a.* Auxiliary.
——eachail, -e, *a.* Assisting, helping, auxiliary, supporting. 2 Prone to help.
——eachair,** *s.m.* Auxiliary, helper.
——eachd, *adv.* Also, likewise. 2 Together, in company. 3 In contact. Thàinig esan c., *he*

came too; c. rium, *along with me;* theann i an lomairt c., *she squeezed the fleece together.*
cuideachd, -an, *s.f.ind.* Troop, company, throng. 2 Society, intercourse. 3 Friends, relations. 4**Private company. 'Nam ch., *in my company*; c. shaighdearan, *a company of soldiers*; a ch. a' chridhe, *my dear people*; bheir e e féin as gach c. le ceòl 's le conaltradh, *he would acquit himself well in any company in music or conversation*; ged a tha e math 'ga thoirt féin á c. tha e motha 's math 'ga chuir féin ann, *though he can acquit himself well in company, he is better at getting himself invited*—he is too forward or cheeky; cha'n ann de 'm ch. thù, *you are not of my flock*—an imitation of the cooing of a pigeon.
————aich, *v.a.* Accompany.
————ail, -e, *a.* Social, entertaining, sociable. 2 Assistant, helpful.
cuideag, -eig, -an, *s.f.* Small portion. 2†† Small effects. 3 Spider. 4(AC) see cuiteag.
cuideal, -eil, *s.m.* see cuidealas.
———ach, *a.* Proud, haughty.
———achd,** *s.f.* Pride.
———as, -ais, *s.m.* Pride, conceit, forwardness.
cuideam, *prov.* for cudthrom.
———ach, -aiche, *prov.* for cudthromach.
cuidear rium, *prov.* for cuide rium.
cuideil, -deala, *a.* Proud, conceited, forward, vain, prim.
cuide ri, *prep.* With, along with, C. rium, *along with me*; c. riut, *along with thee*; c. ris, *along with him*; c. rithe, *along with her*; c. rinn, *along with us*; c. ribh, *along with you*; c. riu, *along with them*; c.ri chéile, *with each other.*
cuidh,‡ -e, -ein, *s.f.* Enclosure. 2 Cattle-fold, pen—*Barra.* 3 Enclosed field—*Eigg.* 4(DC) Trench, hollow artificially formed as a sheltered place to milk cows in on the grazing ground, and save the trouble of driving them to and from the byre. This word enters largely into place-names—*Uist.*
†cuidhbheach, -eiche, *a.* see cubhaidh.
cuidhe, see cuithe.
†cuidheachd, *s.f.* Decency.

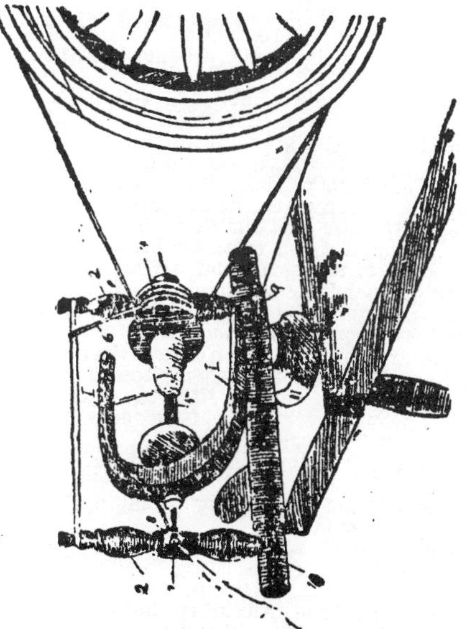

245. *Cuidheall-shnìomha.* (*MMcD*)

cuidheall, -dhill [& cuidhle], -dhleachan, *s. f.* Wheel. 2 Coil. 3** Spinning-wheel, see cuidheall-shnìomha. 4**Reel, yarn-windlass. 5**Whirl, whirling, reeling. 6** Cock of hay. 7 Circle. 8 Circular motion. Saor-chuidhleachan, *a wheelwright.*
————, *pr. pt.* a' cuidhleadh, *v.a.* Wheel. 2 Roll. 3 **Whirl, twirl. 4 Hurl. 5 Coil. 6 Gather into cocks, as hay.
————aireachd, *s.f.ind.* Wheeling. 2 Rolling. 3 Spinning.
———— -iarna, *s.f.* Hank-reel.
cuidheall-shnìomha, *gen.* cuidhle-, *s.f.* Spinning-wheel.

PARTS OF A SPINNING-WHEEL :— (ill. 245.)
1 Teic, seic,†† *flyer.* Séicle—*Uist.*
2 Maighdeanan, gàirdeanan. *sing.* maighdeag & maideag.
3 Iuchair na cìche, *nave.* [deag & maideag.
4 Rolan, *wheel which turns the flyer.* Rathan—*Poolewe* (WC.)
5 Piorna, [pùirne,] *pirn, reel.*
6 Bann beag, *little band.* [A' bhann bheag, (*s.f.*) in *Poolewe* (WC.)]
7 Dealgan, *spindle.*
8 Cluas na cuidhle, *ears,* rests of leather fixed to maighdeanan, and through which dealgan-an-t-seic revolve. [A' chluasag—*Poolewe* (WC.)
9 Iuchair, *key.*
10 Beairt mheadhon, *bar.*
11 Stoc, *main body.*
12 Com, *body.*
13 Aisnean, aisnichean, *ribs* or *spokes* of large wheel.
14 Iuchair, *pin* for tightening bann beag.

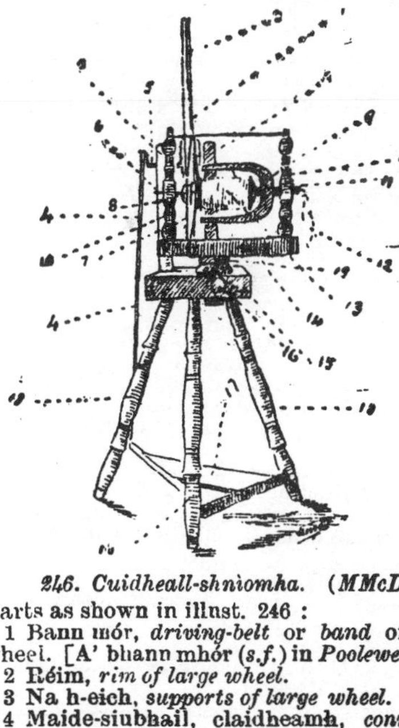

246. *Cuidheall-shnìomha.* (*MMcD*)

Parts as shown in illust. 246 :
1 Bann mór, *driving-belt* or *band* of large wheel. [A' bhann mhór (*s.f.*) in *Poolewe* (WC.)]
2 Réim, *rim of large wheel.*
3 Na h-eich, *supports of large wheel.*
4 Maide-siubhail, claidheamh, *connecting-rod,* one end of which is attached to the crank of the large wheel, and the other to the foot-board. An t-amadan—(WC.)
5 Deil, *crank.* Deil is aisil, *crank and axle* of large wheel.
6 Aiseil an-t-seic, *axle of flyer.*
7 Bann beag, *little band,* regulating string to prevent pirn from revolving. [*s.f.*—*Poolewe.*]

8 Roileinean, *rollers.*
9 Teic, seic, *flyer.*
10 Maighdeanan, gàirdeanan, *supporters of flyer*, resting on beairt-mheadhon.
11 Sùil na cuidhle, *eye*, hole in the axle, through which the unspun wool passes.
12 Clòimh, *wool.*
13 Snàth, *thread* wound on pirn.
14 Beairt mheadhon, *bar* on which the maighdean rests.
15 Stoc, com na cuidhle, maide-buinn, *body.*
16 Iuchair na cìche, key in form of a handle projecting from end of body.
17 Stol-cois, seòl-cois, lobht, *foot-board.* Siol-caise,(JM) ; cleasachan.
18 Casan, *legs.*
19 Cìoch, round piece of wood, that attaches the thread-making part to the body.
20 Roth na cuidhle, *flywheel.*
21 Bann-nam-maighdeanan, *cord* tying the tops of the supports (maighdeanan,) and to which the bann beag is attached.
22 Glas, *lock.*
23 Dealgan na teic, *spindle of flyer.*
24 Bior na banna bige, *the tension-key*, for regulating the fineness of the thread (WC.)
25 Fiaclan na teic, *the teeth of the flyer.*
[We are indebted to Mr.D. Murray, Aberdeen, for many of above terms, and to Mr. M. MacDonald, Stornoway, for terms and diagrams.]

cuidhil, see cuidheall.
cuidhle, *gen.sing.* of cuidheall. A' biadhadh na c., *feeding the wheel.*
cuidhleachan, *n.pl.* of cuidheall.
cuidhleadh, -lidh, *s.m.* Wheeling, coiling. A' c—, *pr.pt.* of cuidheall.
cuidhleag,** -eig, -an, *s.f.* Cock of hay.
cuidhlean,** -ein, *s.m.* Little wheel.
cuidhlearachd,** *s.f.* Wheeling, rolling. 2 Hurling. 3 Spinning on a wheel.
cuidhle-mhór,(AF) *s.f.* see cuibhle-mhór.
cuidhlidh, *fut.aff.a.* of cuidhil.
cuidhte, *a.* & *past pt.* of cuidhtich. Quit, freed, rid of; tha mi cuiteas e (cuidht' agus e) *I have done with him, am free from it.*
cuidhteach, -tiche, *a.* That quits, frees, leaves, abandons, or 2 recompenses.
cuidhteachadh, -aidh, *s.m.* Quitting, parting with, abandoning, leaving. 2 Act of quitting, compensating, repaying. 3 Compensation, recompense. A' c—, *pr. pt.* of cuidhtich.
cuidhteag,(CR) *s.f.* *W. of Ross* for cuiteag.
cuidhteas, *s.m.* Quittance, receipt.
cuidhtich, *pr.pt.* a' cuidhteachadh, *v.a.* Recompense, restore, repay, requite. 2** Consign. 3 Quit, abandon. 4**Avoid.
————eas, *fut. pass.* of cuidhtich.
————te, *past pt.* of cuidhtich. Left, abandoned, forsaken. 2 Quit of.
cuidich, *pr.pt.* a' cuideachadh, *v. a.* Help, assist, relieve. 2 Countenance, favour. C. has often the *prep.* le, simple or compounded, put after it, as, c. le Seumas, *help James*; c. leam, *help me.*
————e, -an, *s.m.* Helper, assistant.
————idh, *fut. aff. a.* of cuidich.
————te, *past pt.* of cuidich. Helped, assisted, aided.
cuidreach, -riche, *a.* Forcible, powerful. 2 In partnership. 3††Corroborative.
cuidreamach, -aiche, *a.* see cudthromach.
cuid ri, see cuide ri.
cuidridh, *a.* Common.
cuid-roinne, *s.f.* Portion, share, lot.
†cuife, -an, *s.f.* Pit. 2 Den.
cuife,(CR) *s.m.* Ninny, *Scots*, coof.
——an, *s.m.* see cuife.
cuifean, -ein, *s.m.* Wad of a gun.
†cuig, *s.f.* Counsel, advice. 2 Secret, mystery.
cùig, *a.* see còig.
cùig-bhile, see còig-bhileach.
cùig-bhileach, see còig-bhileach.
cùig-deug, *a.* see còig-deug.
cùigeadh, *a.* see còigeamh.
c'uige, see chuige.
†cuigead, *adv.* Therefore.
cùigeadh, see còigeamh.
cuigeal, -eil & -alach, *pl.* -an & -aichean, *s. f.* Distaff, hand-rock. 2**Flax put on a distaff. Greim de 'n chuigeil, *hold of the distaff* ; c. is fearsaid, *distaff and spindle ;* cinneag, *spindle —Sutherland.*
————ach, -aich, *s.f.* Wool or flax prepared for the distaff. 2 Task in spinning. 3 *gen. sing.* of cuigeal.
————ach, -aiche, *a.* Of, or belonging to, a distaff. 2 Having distaffs or rocks.
————-an-losgainn,§ *s. f.* Early orchis, see maoth-ùrach.
————-nam-ban-sìthe,§ *s.f.* Great reed-mace, see bodan-dubh.
————nan-losgann,§ *s. f.* Great reed-mace, see bodan-dubh. [Not the same as cuigeal-an-losgainn.]
cùigeamh, see còigeamh.
cùigear, see còignear.
cuigeil, *gen.sing.* of cuigeal.
cuigh,(AF) *s.m.* Bird. 2 Cock.
†cùigh, *s.f.* Bed-chamber.
cùignear, see còignear.
cuigse, *s.f.* Whig. Na bha dh' armailt air a chuigse, *what there was of an army turned whiggish—Donnachadh bàn.*
cuigseach, *a.* Whiggish.
————d, *s.f.* Whiggism.
cuil, *s.f.* Fly, (for cuileag.)
cùil, -e, *pl.* -tean [& -ean,] *s.f.* Corner. 2 Niche, nook. 3 Couch. 4 Closet, any retired, obscure or private place. 5** Angle. Mheall thu le d' bhrìodal cùil, *thou didst deceive with thy secret flattery* ; cùil-mhòna, *peat-corner* ; c. a' chadha, *a corner in the kitchen* ; seòmar c., *a back room, an inner chamber.*
cuilbh, *s.f.* Capital.
————ean,(DC) *s. m.* Cup-shaped whirl in a stream or eddy.
cuilbhear, -eir, -an, *s.m.* Gun, fowling-piece, musket. 2**Calibre or bore of a gun. 3(CR) Anything big—*W. of Ross-shire.* C. mór bhoirionnaich, *a very big woman* ; c. sgéine, *a carving knife, cleaver* ; le 'n cuilbhearan gleusta 'nan làimh, *with their cocked guns in their hands.*
————eart, -eirt, -eartan [& -eirtean,] *s.f.* Wile, trick, deceit, cunning, craft.
————eartach, -aiche, *a.* Deceitful, fraudulent, wily.
————eartachd, *s. f. ind.* Craftiness, wiliness, trickiness, deceitfulness, cunning. 'Nan c. féin, *in their own craftiness.*
————eartaich,‡‡ *v.a.* Juggle.
————eartair,** *s.m.* Artificer.
cuilbheireach, -riche, *a.* Having guns, armed with guns.
cuilc. -e, -ean, *s.f.* Reed, bulrush, cane. 2 Cane to bottom chairs with, cut from the gobhal-luachair. 3(MMcD) Bamboo. Is mór toirm cuilce gun dol troimhpe, *the storm of reeds is loud till you go through them*—more formidable in sound than in reality ; cobhan cuilce, *an ark of bulrushes.*
————-chrann,§ -chroinn, *s.m.* Sweet flag cane, see cuilc-mhilis.
————each, -ciche, *a.* Reedy, abounding in

reeds or bulrushes.

cuilceach, -eich, s.m. Reedy fen. 2 Any place where reeds grow. 3**Crop of reeds. 4** Veil. 5**Hood. 6**Steeple.

——eag,(AF) s.f. Reed-warbler.

——ean, s.m. see cuilceag.

——earnach, -aich, s.f. Place where reeds grow.

cuilc-fhear,§ s.f. Wood small reed—*calamagrostis epigejos.*

†cuilcheannag, -aig, s.f. Bribe.

247. Cuilc-fheur.

248. Cuilc-mhilis.

cuilc-lorg,** s.f. Cane.

cuilc-mhilis, -ean-milis, s.f. Sweet flag cane—*acorus calamus.*

cùildich,‡‡ v.a. Absent, conceal.

cuile, -an [††-ich & -ichean,] s.f. The part of a cottage in which the stores are kept, cellar, see cuilidh. 2 Rocky corrie. 3 Meadow or morass with rocky boundaries. 4 (WC) The "but" or the "ben" of a house. Dorus na cuile, *the door of the "ben."*

cuileabannach,(CR) *Suth'd* for guilbneach.

cuileabhar,(AF) s.m. Dog, greyhound.

cùileach,** a. Angular.

cuileachan, -ain, s.m. Deep wicker basket.

cùileachd,** s.f. Angularity.

cuileag, -eige, -an, s.f. Common fly. 2 Artificial fishing-fly. 3**Gnat. Sgaoth ch., *a swarm of flies.*

——ach, -aiche, a. Full of flies. 2 Of, or belonging to, flies. 3**Like a fly. 4**Lively, frisky.

cùileagan, -ain, s.m. Private feast, secret treat.

cuileag-an-Frangach, s.pl. Cantharides.

—— -dhubh,(AF) s.f. Beetle.

—— -lìn,(AF) s.f. Earwig.—*Arran.*

—— -shionnachain,** s.f. Glow-worm.

—— -shnìomhain, -an-s—, s.f. Glow-worm.

—— -Spainndeach,** s.f. Spanish fly, cantharides.

—— -theallaich, s.f. Cricket, beetle.

cuilean, -ein, -an, s. m. Whelp. 2 Puppy. 3 Cub. 4 Leveret. 5 Frequently used for a dog of full growth, or of any age. 6 Darling, term of familiar endearment. 7 Skinflint—*Suth'd.* 8‡‡Staple in a wooden lock. 9(AF) Young seal. 10(WC) Small bone in ankle or wrist. 11 see cuilfhionn. Cuileanan na coise, *the small bones in the ankle*; cluich a' chuilein ris a' mhial-chù, *the puppy's play with the greyhound;* c. na muice-mara, *the whale's whelp*; c. bioraiche, *a young dog-fish.*

—— -coin, s.m. Puppy, any young dog.

—— -leòghainn, s.m. Lion's whelp.

—— -maighich, s.m. Leveret.

—— -math-ghamhuinn, s.m. Bear's cub.

—— -muice, s.m. Young sow—*Lewis.*

cuileann, -linn, see cuilionn.

——ach, see cuilionnach.

cuilean-ròin, s.m. Young seal—*Lewis.*

cuileasg,** -eisg, s.m. Jade. 2 Horse.

cuilein, see cuilean.

cuilfhinn, -e, a. Handsome, lovely.

cùil-fhionn,** a. Fair-haired.

cuilfhionn, s. Term of endearment. 'Se 'chuilfhionn, *yes, dear*; 'n e 'chuilfhionn, *indeed! is that so?*; and an exclamation, O chuilfhionn! *O dear!*

cuilfhionn, -inn, see cuilionn.

——ach, see cuilionnach.

—— -tragha, see cuilionn-tràgha.

—— -mara, see cuilionn-tràgha.

cuilg, *gen.sing. & n.pl.* of calg. An aghaidh chuilg, *against inclination.*

——ean, ean, s.m. Small beard or awn, as of barley. 2††Prickle. 3‡‡Small bristle.

cuilgearra,** a. Sharp-pointed. 2 Prickly. 3 Keen. 4 Spirited.

cuilgein, see cuilgean.

——each, -iche, a. Bristly, prickly, full of awns.

cuilg-sruth-eich,§ s.pl. Horse's water- or stream-bristles — *equisetum fluviatile, e. palustre, e. ramosum, & e. arvense.* [Illust. is *e. arvense.*]

†cuiliasca, s.f. Hazel rods.

cuilidh, -ean, s.f. Cellar. 2 Hollow. 3 Lockfast place, press. 4(AC)Retreat, sanctuary. 5 Treasury. 6 Treasure. Cha bhi e an àird no an ìosal nach faic sùil an Ìlich, cha bhi e an cùil no an cuilidh nach faic sùil a' Mhuilich, *there is nought in height or hollow but the Islayman's eye will see, there is nought in nook or store but the Mullman's eye will see.* [Cùilidh, as given by McL & D., may be due to a supposed connection with *cùil*, whereas the connection in fact is with *cuile.*]

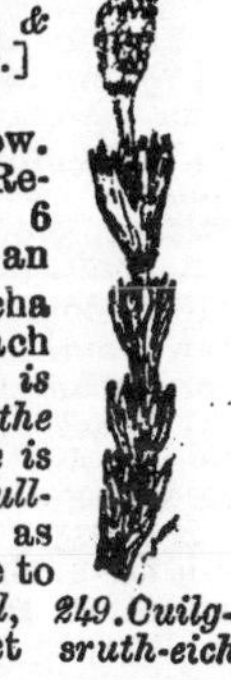

249. Cuilg-sruth-eich.

cuilidh, (a chuilidh!) *int.* Call to a dog when its name is not known.

cùilidh-rath,(AC) s.f. The sea. (*lit.* the treasury of prosperity.)

cùilidh-Moire,(AC) s.f. The sea (*lit.* the treasury of Mary.)

cuilidh-siùchaireachd,(CR) s.f. Doing things in a corner, sly work.

cuiliobhair, see cuilbhear.

cuilionn,§ -inn, s.m. Holly—*ilex aquifolium.* 2** Elm. Fo chrannaibh chuilinn, *under elms.* 3§Name given in Bible to the Teile or turpentine-tree. [Holly is the badge of the MacMillans.]

——ach, -aich, s.f. Place where holly grows. 2 Mavis, thrush.

——ach, -aiche, a. Abounding in hollies, of, or belonging to hollies. 2** Abounding in elms. 3** Of, like, or belonging to an elm.

250. Cuilionn.

—— -mara, see cuilionn-tràgha.

—— -tràgha,§ s, m. Sea-holly—*eryngium maritimum.* [illust. on p. 292.]

†cuiliosal, a. Vile, worthless, useless.

cuille,** s.f. Calamus. 2 Quill. 3 Black cloth.

cuillean,(DU) see cuinnean.

†cuillear, s m. Quarry.

cuilleasg,** s. pl. Hazel rods or twigs.

251. Cuilionn-tràgha.

cuillidh, *s.m.* Horse. Cuir an c. 'san fheun, *put the horse in the cart.—Strathtay.*
cuillsean,** *s. m.* Quill. 2 Quilt or tick of a bed.
cuilm, -e, -ean, *prov.* for cuirm.
———ean, *s.m.* Atom.
cùil-mhionnachadh,** -aidh, see cùl-mhionnachadh.
cùil-mhionnaich, *v.a.* Abjure.
—————te, *past pt.* Abjured.
cùil-mhionnan,** see cùl-mhionnan.
cùil-mhùtaire, *s.m.* Smuggler.
cùil-sheòmar, -air, -raichean,*s.m.* Bed-chamber. 2**Back room.
†cuilt, -e, -ean, *s.f.* Gaelic spelling of *quilt.*
cùilteach, -tiche, *a.* Retired, set apart, obscure, private. 2 Having corners or niches, angular. 3 Dark, dismal. 4**Skulking.
————, -tich, -tichean, *s.f.* Bedroom. 2 Bed. 3 Place having corners, recesses or niches. 4 *Skulker. 5 *rarely* Bakehouse. 6††Cellar. 7 ††Backbone. 8* Skulking female.
cùilteag, -eige, -an, *s.f.* Concealment. 2 Small corner. 3 Whiting, for cuiteag—*W. of Ross.*
cùiltean, *n.pl.* of cùil.
cùiltear, -eir, -eirean, *s.m.* Skulker. 2 Smuggler.
cùilteireachd, *s.f.ind.* Skulking. 2 Low cunning. 3* Smuggling. [** gives cùiltearachd.]
cuilthinn, *a.* see cuilfhinn.
†cuim, *s.f.* Shirt. 2 Feast. 3 Mercy. 4 Protection.
cuim, *gen. sing.* of com, *s.* 2(AC) see guim.
†cuim-dhealbhadh, -aidh, *s.m.* Feigning.
c'uime ? *adv.* (for cia & cò uime ?) For what ? of what ? about whom ? of whom ? why ? wherefore ? C' uim' am b' fhiach leat ? *why should you condescend ?* ; c' uim' a thréig thu mo chluas ? *why hast thou left mine ear ?*
cuimear,** *a.* Brief.
cuimeir, see cuimir.
cuimean, -ein, *s.f.* Cummin (plant.)
cuimeis, see cuimse.
cuimhealta,** *a.* Bruising.
cuimheas,** see cuimse.
————ach, see cuimseach.
cuimhne, *s.f.ind.* Memory, remembrance, recollection. 2** Record, memorial. An c. leat ? *do you remember ?* is c. leam, *I remember ;* cha ch. leam, *I do not remember ;* ma 's. c. leat, *if you recollect* ; ma 's math mo ch., *if I recollect aright* ; a réir c. dhomhsa, *to the best of my recollection* ; cum 'nad ch., *keep in remembrance ;* c. nan gaisgeach a thriall, *the memory of departed heroes* ; cuir an c., *remind ;* leabhar c., *a note-book* ; is fhearr meomhair luchd an tagraidh na c. luchd nam fiach, *the memory of creditors is better than that of debtors.*
————ach, -niche, *a.* see cuimhneachail.
————achadh, -aidh, *s.m.* Remembering, recollecting. 2 Act of remembering, keeping in remembrance. 3**Commemoration. A' c—, *pr.pt.* of cuimhnich.
————achail, -e [& -ala,] *a.* Keeping in mind, mindful, not forgetful. Cò e an duine, gu'm bitheadh thusa c. air ? *what is man, that thou shouldst be mindful of him ?* gu c., *mindfully.*
————achair, see cuimhniche.
————achan, -ain, *s.m.* Memorial. 2 Medal. 3* Token of respect or gratitude. 4**Keepsake. 5**Remembrance. 6**Memorandum. Mar ch. orm-sa, *in remembrance of me.*
————achd,‡‡ *s.f.* Mindfulness.
———— -feidh,** *s.f.* Attire.
cuimhnich, *pr.pt.* a' cuimhneachadh. *v.a. & n.* Remember, bear in mind, recollect, recall to memory.
————e, -an, *s.m.* Recorder, chronicler, remembrancer.
————ear, *fut.pass.* of cuimhnich.
———— -fhear, see cuimhniche.
†cuimide, *s.f.* Appointed time.
†cuimil, *v.a.* Touch, rub.
cuimin, *s.m.* see cuimean. 2 Little coffer or chest. †3 Suburb.
cuimir, -e, *a.* Short, brief, concise. 2 Well-proportioned. 3 Trim, neat, exact, tidy. 4 Handsome, elegant. 5 Equally filling, of exactly the same size.
———eachd, *s.f.ind.* Neatness. 2 Handsomeness. 3 Symmetry. 4 Same size or proportion. 5**Precision.
†cuimleadh, -lidh, *s.m.* Intermeddling. 2 Performance, fulfilling.
cuimreach,** -rich, *s.m.* Assistant.
————d,‡‡ *s.f.ind.* Aim.
cuimrich,* *v.a.* Size, as slates. 2 Pare, as shoes.
cuimrig, *v.a.* see coimrig.
————, -e, -ean, *s.f.* see coimrig.
————each, see coimrigeach.
————eadh, -gidh, see coimrigeadh.
————ich, *v.a.* see coimrig.
————te, see coimrigte.
cuimse, -an, *s.f.* Aim, mark, hit. 2 Moderation, sufficiency, mediocrity, moderate portion. 3 Any measuring instrument. 4(DU) Measure, as for a suit of clothes. Ni gun ch., *a thing without moderation*; dean c. air siod, *aim at that;* tha c. agamsa, *I have sufficiency*; cha'n 'eil c. agad, *you have no moderation ;* ghabh e mo ch., *he took my measure.*
cuimseach, -siche, *a.* Moderate, in a state of mediocrity. 2 Sure of aim, unerring. 3 Indifferent. 4 Mean, little. 5* Befitting, suitable to one's case. 6**Adjusted. Bogha bu ch. beachd, *a bow of sure aim*; sealgair c., *a good hunter, a good shot*; rinn iad c. math, *they did fairly well (at fishing or anything)* ; tha e c. gu leòir, *he is moderate enough*; *2 he is but indifferent ;* is c. dhuit sin, *it is but proper that you should be so.*
————adh, -aidh, *s.m.* Aiming, hitting. 2 Adapting. 3 Measuring. 4 Act of aiming. hitting or measuring. A' c—, *pr. pt.* of cuimsich. A' c. air comharradh, *aiming or shooting at a mark.*
————d, *s.f.* see cuimse.
cuimsich, *pr.pt.* a' cuimseachadh, *v. a.* Aim. 2 Hit, as a mark. 3 Fit, adapt. 4††Point. 5‡‡ Bound. C. ris e., *aim it at him* ; ch. na fir-

bhogha e, *the archers hit him.*
cuimsiche, -an, *s.m.* Aimer. 2 Guesser.
cuimsichte, *a. & past pt.* of cuimsich. Well-aimed. 2 Hit after being aimed at. 3 Proportioned, truly guessed.
cuimte, see cumta.
cuin ? *adv.* When ? at what time ? Cuin a dhùisgeas esan o 'shuain ? *when shall he awake from his slumber ?* [Written *cuine* when not followed by a vowel.]
cùin, *v.a.* see cùinn.
——eadh, see cùinneadh.
cuineag, -eige -an, *s.f.* see cuinneag. 2**Copy.
cuineal,(AF) *s.m.* Pig.
——— -Mhuire,** *s.m.* see cuingeal-Muire.
†cùineas, see ciùineas.
cuing, -e, -ean, *s.f.* Yoke. 2 Bond, obligation. 3 Restraint, hinderance. 4 Stoppage. 5 Captivity. 6 Strait, difficulty. 7 Yoke of a rudder, see rudder 1, p. 78. 8* Asthma. Fo ch. agad-sa, *under your tyrannical sway ;* fo ch. nan coimheach, *under the yoke of strangers*—said of a person in the employment of strangers.
cuing,‖ -e, -ean, *s.f.* Asthma. [Preceded by the art. a' *ch*—.]
cuing-analach, *s.f.* Shortness of breath, asthma. Tha e làn c., *he is quite asthmatic.*
——— -cheangail, *v.a.* Yoke together.
——— -cheangal, -ail, -glaichean, *s. m.* Bond used to fasten a yoke to the neck of an animal. 2 Servitude, bondage.
cuinge, *s.f.ind.* Narrowness. 2 Narrow strait or passage. 3 Distress, difficulty. 4***rarely* Solicitation, entreaty. C. garbhlaich, *a stony narrow channel.*
———, *comp.* of cumhang.
†———, *s.f.* Solicitation, entreaty.
†———ach, -ich, *s.f.* Pair, couple.
cuingeach, -giche, *a.* Asthmatical.
————-adh, -aidh, *s.m.* Act of abridgment, lessening or straitening. 2 Abridgment.
————-air,** *s.m.* Abridger.
cuingead, -gid, *s.f.* see cuinge.
cuingealach, -aich, *s.f.* Yoke. 2 Straitness, narrowness. A' ch.chleibh, *asthma.*
cuingealach,(DU) *a.* Restricting, restraining.
cuingeal-Muire, *s.f.* Mullein, hog's taper, cow's lungwort, Aaron's rod, Adam's flannel, blanket leaf, Jacob's staff, shepherd's club, torches, or lady's foxglove, —*verbascum thapsus.*
cuingeil, *a.* Tyrannical, arbitrary.
Cuingeis, -e, *s.f.* see Caingis.
cuing-fhuail, *s.f.* Strangury.
cuingich, *pr. part.* a' cuingeachadh. *v.a.* Yoke, subjugate. 2 Abridge, lessen, straiten. 3* Tyrannize. 4 ††Hamper.
————te, *past pt.* of cuingich. Yoked, abridged, straitened.

252. Cuingeal-Muire.

cuingid, *s.f.* see cuinge.
†cuingir, *s.f.* Couple.
cuingiseach,‡‡ -eiche, *a.* Pentecostal.
cuingleachadh, see caimhleachadh.
†cuingreach, -rich, *s.f.* Cart, waggon.
cùinidear, -eir, -an, *s.m.* see cùinneadair.
cuinn, *gen.sing. & n.pl.* of conn.
cùinn, -e, -tean, *s.f.* Coin. C. òir, *a gold coin.*
———, *pr.pt.* a' cùinneadh, *v.a.* Coin. 2‡‡Forge. 3††Shape, form.
cuinn, -e, *s.f.* see cuinnean.
†cuinne, *s.f.* Corner, angle. 2 Meeting.
cùinneach, -niche, *a.* Of, or abounding in coin.
cùinneadair, *s.m.* Minter.
cùinneadh, -nidh, *s.m.* Coining, act of coining. 2 Coinage. 3 Coin. A' c—, *pr. pt.* of cùinn.
cuinneag, -eige, -an, *s.f.* Small pail. 2 Milk-pail. 3 Bucket to carry water in. (*Scots*, stoup.) 4 Churn. 5 **Barrel, cask. Min ann an cuinneig, *meal in a barrel.*
————ach, -aiche, *a.* Abounding in, or pertaining to, pails, buckets or churns.
————an, *n. pl.* of cuinneag.
———— -bhleoghainn,(AF) *s.f.* Milking-pail.
———— -bhùirn, *s.f.* Water-pail.
———— -mhighe,** *s.f.* Wild angelica—*angelica sylvestris.*
———— -thuaitheal, *pl.* -an-t—, *s.f.* Whirlpool, vortex.
cuinnean, -ein, -ean, *s. m.* Nostril. Ann an cuinneinibh a shròine, *in his nostrils.*
cuinneineach, -niche, *a.* Having nostrils. 2 Having wide nostrils. 3(AH) Huffy, touchy, susceptible, "thin-skinned."
cùinnich,‡‡ *v.a.* Stamp, coin.
cuinnlein, -ein, see coinnlein & cuinnean.
————each, -niche, *a.* see coinnleineach & cuinneineach.
cuinnse, -an, *s.f.* Quince.
————ach,†† *a.* Pertaining to quinces.
cuinnsear, -eir, -an, *s.m.* Dagger, sword, poniard. 2 Hanger. A' chorc 'an ionad a' chuinnseir, *the knife in place of the sword*—a sign of peace.
————ach, -raiche, *a.* Armed with swords or daggers.
cuinnseas, see coinnseas.
cuinnseir, -ean, see cuinnsear.
————each, see cuinnsearach.
cùinnte, *past pt.* of cùinn. Coined, forged. Breug ch., *a false tale.*
cuinseal,** *s.m.* Face. 2 Remembrance.
cùinte, see cùinnte.
cuip, -e, *pl.* -ean & -eachan, *s.f.* Whip. 2 Stratagem, deceit. 3**Foam, froth. [** gives cuipe as *nom.*]
cuip, *gen. sing.* of cop.
cuip, *pr. pt.* a' cuipeadh, *v.a.* Whip, flog, lash.
cuipeach,†† *a.* Pertaining to a whip.
———an, *n. pl.* of cuip.
cuipeadh, -pidh, *s.m.* Whipping, flogging. 2 Act of whipping or flogging.
cuip-gheal, -ile, *a.* Foamy, white with foam. Muir ch., *a foaming sea.*
cuipinn, Gaelic spelling of *whipping.*
————, *v.* Whip, lash. Derivative of *whipping.*
————te, *past part.* of cuipinn.
cuir, *pr. pt.* a' cur [& a' curadh,**] *v. a.* Put, place. 2 Lay. 3 Send. 4 Invite. 5 Sow. 6 Act upon. 7 Produce an effect. 8 Influence. 9 Tire—*Lewis.* 10* Snow.

Cuir enters into such a number of idiomatic phrases in Gaelic that it has been found necessary to annex a somewhat lengthy list for beginners.

cuir a bhàn, *put down.*
c. a' bhuntàta, *plant the potatoes.*
c. a dh' iarraidh, *send for.*
c. a dholaidh, *spoil, abuse.*
c. a ghul, *set a-crying.*
c. air, *prevail. 2 molest. 3 beach, as a boat.* Cha chuir e air, *it will not annoy him*; c. air laidhe chuige, *make the ship lie-to* ; is beag tha 'cur orm, *I am quite well, all right;* c. an t-eathar air, *beach the boat.*
c. (an sgeul) air a bhallaibh, *tell, relate adequately.*
c. air adhart, *forward, promote.*
c. air aimhreidh, *put wrong.*

c. air ath là, *delay.*
c. air bonnaibh, *describe.* Is deacair domhsa a cur air a bonnaibh, *it is very difficult for me to describe her adequately.*
c. air chois, *institute.* 2 *set on foot.* 3 *erect.* 4 *rouse out of bed.*
c. air chrith, *cause to shake.*
c. air chuimhne, *put in remembrance, remind.*
c. air cùl, *abrogate,put behind,abandon, forget, discard.*
c. àird (air,) *prepare (it.)*
c. air dioghladh, see c. bho 'n deoghal.
c. air falbh, *put or send away, discharge.*
c. air gnothach, *send on a message.*
c. air lagh, *prepare, adjust as a bow, cock as a gun.*
c. air leth, *separate, appropriate, set apart.*
c. air mhire, *transport with joy.*
c. air mhisg, *make drunk.*
c. air riadh, *put to usury.*
c. air sheòl, *put in good tune.*
c. (air,) teicheadh, *put (him) to flight.*
c. air 'thapadh (e,) *encourage (him.)*
c. air thioramachadh, *put out to dry, as washing.*
c. aithne air, *get acquainted with, renew acquaintance with.*
c. alladh (air,) *libel him.*
c. a mach, *publish as a book.* 2 *extinguish, put out.* 3 *vomit.*
c. a mach (air,) *set (him) at variance, quarrel with (him.)* 2 *disagree.* Chuir iad a mach air a chéile, *they disagreed.*
c. am farsuingeachd, *enlarge, extend.*
c. am fiachaibh, *bind one to act in a given manner.*
c. am mearachd, *misdirect, misadvise, deceive.*
c. am mugha, *render useless.*
c. an aghaidh, *oppose.* Cuir 'na aghaidh, *oppose him.*
c. an àirde, *put up, exalt.*
c. an amharus, *doubt.*
c. an céill, *declare, describe, confess.*
c. an clòdh, *print, set up in type.*
c. an geall, *bet, mortgage.*
c. an gnìomh, *put into action.*
c. an ire, *cause to believe.* 2 *lay on, as a duty, compel.*
c. ann, *further, promote.* 2 *reinstate.* Chuir e ann dhomh, *he promoted my interest* ; c. ann do 'n mhath, *promote good.*
c. an neò-bhrigh, *make of none effect.*
c. an neo-phris, *despise.*
c. an omhail, *treat as nothing.*
c. an suarachas, *slight, make light of.*
c. an suim, *execute.*
c. an seilbh, *instal.*
c. an umhail, *suspect.*
c. as a ghabhail (e,) *disappoint (him.)*
c. as a phoinc (e,) *disappoint (him.)* 2 *convince (of error of his opinion.)*
c. as (da,) *extinguish (it.)* 2 *devour or destroy (him.)* Cuir as do 'n olc, *prevent evil.*
c. a shean, *spend extravagantly.*
c. a staigh (air,) *make friends with him.* 2 *overtake him*—(WC.)
c. as (mo) leth, *accuse (me.)*
c. athchuinge suas, *pray, supplicate.*
c. beannachdan, *send compliments.*
c. bho 'n deoghal, *wean.*
c. bhuait, *put away from you.*
c. campar (air,) *ruffle or vex (him.)*
c. car dhiot, *bestir yourself.* Gu de an ath char a chuir thu dhiot? *what was your next move?*
c. cath, *fight.*
c. ceart, *put to rights.* Cuir-sa ceart na chì thu tuaitheal, *put right what you see wrong.*
c. crìoch (air,) *finish (it)* ; *kill (him.)*
c. chuige, *urge, exert ; prosecute.* Cuir chuige am bàta, *make the boat lie-to.*
c. comhairle ri, *confer, consult.*
c. cuidheall dhiot, *wheel about.*
c. cùl ri, *forsake, abandon.*
c. dàil (ann,) *delay, forsake (it.)*
c. deagh chath, *fight a good battle.*
c. deatach, *emit smoke.*
c. deuchainn air, *put to trial.*
c. (dhiot,) *put off, as an article of clothing.* 2 *descant, deliver, as a speech.* Bha e 'cur dheth, *he was talking away,* or *talking to himself* ; cuir dhiot do chòta, *take off your coat.*
c. dòchas ann, *hope, confide, trust in.*
c. doilgheas (air,) *grieve (him,) cause (him) to mourn.*
c. dragh (air,) *trouble him.*
c. druigheachd (air), *bewitch (him.)*
c. (eatorra,) *separate (them.)* 2 (DU) *cause a quarrel between them.*
c. fàilt' (air,) *salute (him.)*
c. faire, *place a watch, observe.*
c. fàs, *lay waste.*
c. fa sgaoil, *release, let go.* Bidh gùn is gùn 'gan cur fa sgaoil chum aodaich do na caileagan, *dress after dress will taken to pieces for frocks for the little girls.*
c. feadh a chéile, *mix, disarrange.*
c. fios air, *or* c. fios air chugad, *send for (him.)* Cuir fios air an leabhar, *send for the book* ; c. fios a nìos air, *send word for him to come up.*
c. fios d' a ionnsuidh, *or* c. fios chuige, *send word to him* (not desiring his presence.)
c. fodha, *sink.*
c. fodhad, *put under thee* ; *weather, as a boat.* c. fodhad an rudha sin, *weather* or *get past that cape.*
c. fo mhionnaibh, *adjure by oath.*
c. geall, *bet, wager.* Cuiridh mi geall riut nach robh, *I'll bet you it was not so.*
c. glan a dholaidh, *spoil completely.*
c. gu bàs, *kill.*
c. gu buil, *occupy, employ to some purpose* ; 2 *give effect to.*
c. gu fulang, *put to trial or suffering.*
c. gu taic, *trim, manage, give a dressing to.*
c. gu taobh, *put by.* Cuir a dh' aon taobh, *put all on one side* ; cuir an dara taobh, *dispose of completely, set in the proper direction.*
c. impidh (air,) *constrain (him.)*
c. (leam,) *favour (me,) support (me.)*
c. mar fhiachaibh (air,) *pretend, make (him) believe* ; *make incumbent upon (him.)*
c. mu seach, *lay by, accumulate.*
c. na lìontan, *shoot the nets.*
c. (ort,) *put on you.* Cuir ort do bhrògan, *put on your shoes.*
c. réis, *run a race.*
c. ri, *add to.* 3 *importune.* 3 *hasten, apply.* 4 *be active, be diligent.* 5 *study.* 6 *exaggerate.* 7 *worry.* 8 *master.* 9 *baffle.* Cuir riut, *eat somewhat, get on with your food.*
c. ris na ràimh, *take to the oars.*
c. romhad, *resolve, propose.*
c, (roimhe,) *prompt (him,) dictate to (him.)*
c. sàradh, *arrest (in law.)*
c. seach, see c. seachad.
c. seachad, *hoard, lay by.* 2 *avoid.* C. seachad gach spàirn 'bheireadh ort, *parry with ease every stroke aimed at you.*
c. sìol, *sow seed.*
c. sìos air, *abuse.*
c. smugaid (air,) *spit on (it.)*

c. smùid, *emit smoke.*
c. sneachd, *snow.* Tha e 'cur an t- sneachd, *it is snowing;* tha e 'cur is 'cathadh, *or* tha cur is cathadh ann, *it is snowing and drifting.*
c. stad (air,) *stop (him.)*
c. suarach, *despise.*
c. suas, *set up, establish, constitute.*
c. suas air, *praise*—(DU.)
c. suas athchuinge, *pray, supplicate.*
c. suas (leis,) *bear with (it or him.)*
c. sùrd air, *prepare.*
c. teicheadh air, *put to flight.*
c. thairis, *put over, overflow; pass as time.*
c. troid, *fight, oppose.*
c. (umad,) *put on, about*(*you,*) *dress*(*your*)*self.*
c. ùbhla (air,) *fine (him.)*
An ni a chuir iad ri an sùil, *the thing that they had definitely concluded to do*; c. ris an iasgaich, *employ yourself as hard as you can at fishing;* a' mheud mhór gun ch. leatha, *the great boasting without anything to support it*; ch. sinn iad, *we invited them*; cò tha 'cur ort? *who molests you?* cuiridh mise riut, *I will master or manage you*; cò 'tha 'cur dragh' ort? *who molests you?* c. e, *invite him*; tha mi air mo chur, *I am tired*; c. 'sna casan, *take to your heels*; c. 'sna ràimh, *row hard*; c. t' òrdag fo m' chrios, *submit, yield*; tha caochladh cuir air clò Cnaluim, *Malcolm's cloth is of a different set*; b' olc an t-eòlas a chuir e orra, *it was rather a bad thing for him to have ever become acquainted with them*; ch. mi eòlach air a chéile iad, *I introduced them to each other*; c. air laidhe chuige, *make him heave-to*; chuir e cluas air féin rium, *he turned an attentive ear to me*; 'se 'chuir na cluasan air, *it greatly surprised him*; chuir e dà chluais air, *he was greatly astonished* (on hearing something wonderful.)

cuir, *gen.sing. & nom. pl.* of car. **Na cuir a chuir e dheth,** *the tumbles he got.*
†cuirb, -e, *a.* Cursed.
†———sire, -an, *s.m.* Brewer.
cuirc, *gen.sing. & n.pl.* of corc.
†cuirc, *s.f.* Multitude. 2 Head, crest, comb, top-knot.
cuirceag, -eig, -an, *s.f.* Hive.
†cuirchle, *s.f.* Sorcery.
cuircinn, -e, -ean, *s. m.* Kind of female head-dress, (*Scots,* courche.)
cùird, *gen.sing. & n. pl.* of còrd. 2 see càird.
cùir-dhris,§ -e, -ean, *s.f.* Sweet-briar, see dris-chùbhraidh.
†cuire, *s.m.* Caldron. 2 Throng.
cuireadach,** *a.* Sly, wily, cunning. 2 Inviting. Gu c., *slyly.* (cuireideach.)
cuireadh, -idh, -ean, *s.m.* Invitation. 2**Inviting. 3**Placing, laying. 4 **Sending. 5** Deputation. Thig gun ch., *intrude*; thoir c. dhaibh, *invite them*; là chuiridh, the day on which a bride and bridegroom take their rounds, inviting their acquaintances to the wedding; c. cùl na coise, *back-leg invitation*—that of a person who gives a faint invitation, and escorts one out of the house saying, "I am sorry you could not stay"; c. MhicPhilip,—gabh no fàg, *MacKillop's invitation—take or leave;* is duine dona gun fheum a chuireadh cuireadh orm fhéin is caitheamh, *he is a pitiful fellow who would invite me and leave me to pay*: c. pìobaire, *late invitation to a marriage,* or any invitation at the last moment (WC.)
cuireall, -eill, *s.m.* Kind of pack-saddle.
———ach, -aiche, *a.* Resembling a pack-saddle, abounding in pack-saddles.
cuirean, see cuireid.

cuireid, -e, -ean, *s.f.* Turn, wile, trick, strategem 2 Coquettish conduct.
———each, -diche, *a.* Tricky, cunning, full of wiles. 2 Full of turns or twists. 3**Frisky. 4(AH) Forward, conceited.
———each,* *s.f.* Coquette, flirt, wily girl.
———eachd,* *s.f.* Flirtation. 2**Friskiness, nimbleness, playfulness. 3**Craftiness.
cuirean, -ein, -einean, *s.m.* Little turn or trick.
cuireineach, -iche, *a.* Full of little turns.
cuiridh, -ean, see curaidh.
———, *fut. aff. a.* of cuir. 2 *gen. sing. & n. pl.* of cuireadh.
cuiridin,§ *s.f.* Dutch rushes or share-grass, see a' bhiorag.
cuirinnein, -e, -ean, *s.m.* White water-lily, see duilleag bhàite bhàn.
cuirlidh-siùcaireachd, *Strathtay* for cuilidh, *s.*
cuirm, -e, -ean [& -eannan.] *s.f.* Feast, banquet. 2**Entertainment. 3**Kind of beer or ale once used by the Gael, a powerful intoxicating liquor made from barley, and being of course used at all feasts, the word c. came ultimately to mean a feast. It is supposed by some to have been the same as whisky, but the process of brewing being so much easier and cheaper than distilling, it was more probably a strong kind of beer.
——— -bhliadhnail, *s.f.* Anniversary-feast.
——— -chiùil, *s.f.* Concert.
——— -chnuic, *s.f.* Picnic.
———each,** *s.m.* see cormach.
———each,‡‡ *a.* see cuirmeil.
———eachd,** *s.f.* Festivity.
———eag,** *s.f.* Cup-gossip.
———eil,‡‡ -e, *a.* Convivial.
cuirmear, -eir, -ean, *s.m.* Host, entertainer, one who gives a feast.
cuirmire, see cuirmear.
cùirn, *gen.sing. & nom.pl.* of càrn.
———eachadh, see cùrainneachadh.
———eag,** *s.f.* Dew.
———ean, -ein, -an, *s.m.* Small heap, as of stones. 2 Particle. 3 Spangle. 4*Dew-drop. 5 Small curl, ringlet. 6 Head of a pin—*Islay.* 7**Brooch. 8**Knoll. Mar ch. daoimein, *like a diamond brooch;* tha cuirnean falluis air, *he has drops of sweat on his face.*
cùirneineach, -iche, *a.* Abounding in small heaps. 2 Full of ringlets. 3 Covered with dew-drops. 4 Like a brooch. 5**Wearing a brooch. 6**Knolly.
cùirnich, *pr.pt.* a' cùirneachadh, see cùrainnich.
cuirp, *gen.sing. & nom.pl.* of corp.
†——eachd, *s.f.* Wickedness, corruption.
cuirpean, -ein, *s.m.* Crupper.
cuirpear,** -eir, *s.m.* Carper.
cuirpidh, -e, *a.* see coiripidh.
cuir-sa, (*for* cuir thusa) Send thou.
cuirreadh, *s.m.* Woof—*Lewis.* Gheibh dlùth c., *warp will get woof.*
†cuirt,** *s.f.* Apple-tree. 2 Wilding.
cùirt, -e, -ean, *s.f.* Court. 2 Palace. 3 Privilege, honour. 4 Area, yard. 5** Circus. 6(DU) *used contemptuously,* B' e sin a' chùirt, means "I don't care," "what does it matter?" "that 's a heat." 7 (AH) Frame of a sieve or riddle. Fhuair e c. air, *he has gained court or favour;* c. mu choinneimh an taighe, *an area* or *yard opposite the house;* puist na cùirte, *the pillars of the court*; c. nam Morairean Dearg, *circuit court.*
——— -cheartais, *s.f.* Court of justice.
——— -dlighe, *s.f.* Assizes.
cuirte, *a. & past pt.* of cuir. Put, placed. 2 Sent. 3 Laid. 4 Planted, sown. 5 see curr-tha.

cuirteag,** -eig, *s.f.* Phial. †2 Wild apple-tree.
cùirtealachd, *s.f. ind.* Courtliness, courteousness, urbanity, politeness, affability.
†**cùirteamhuil,** *a.* see cùirteil.
cùirtean, *n.pl.* of cùirt.
cùirtean, -ein, -einean, *s.m.* Curtain. Cùirtein-ean ciatach nan speur, *the beauteous curtains of the skies.*
cùirtear, -eir, -an, *s.m.* Courtier. 2 Plaiding. 3 Same meaning as English customer, fellow, chap, person, beggar, "bloke," &c.
cùirteas,-eis, *s.f.* Courtesy, urbanity, politeness, gallantry. 2*Currying favour. 3 Ceremony.
———ach, -aiche, *a.* Ceremonious. 2 Polite, courtly, courteous. Gu c., *courteously.*
———achd, *s.f.ind.* Courtesy, practice of courtesy. 2 Ceremony. 3 Courtliness.
cùirteil, -e [& -ala] *a.* Courtly, polite, courteous, complaisant, affable, petted. 2 Honourable, worthy of esteem.
cuirteinnich,†† *v.a.* Curtain.
cuirteir, *s.m.* Serge cloth.
cùirteir, see cùirtear.
———eachd, see cùirtealachd.
cùirteiseach, see cùirteasach.
—————d, see cùirteasachd.
cùirtfhear, -ir, see cùirtear.
cùirtin, -ean, see cùirtean.
cùis, -e, -ean, *s.f.* Matter, affair, circumstance. 2 Cause, reason. 3 Subject. 4* The side one takes in a game, particularly shinty or cricket. 5*Fate. Cha'n e sin a' ch., *that is not the case* or *point of discussion*; millidh tu a' ch., *you will spoil the business*; bithidh e air ch. na còrach, *he will support the cause of right*; c. a b-aisling, *the subject of her dream*; bu ch. dhomh anart is uaigh, *my fate would be a winding-sheet and a grave*; fa ch., *because of.*
c.-airtneil, *cause of depression* or *weariness.*
c.-bhròin,†† *subject of sorrow.*
c.-bhrosnachaidh, *provocation.*
c.-bhùrta, *laughing-stock, buffoon.*
c.-chasaid, *ground of accusation.*
c.-chleith, *private affair.*
c.-chruaidh, *hard cause.*
c.-dhìtidh, *cause of condemnation.*
c.-dèisinn, *an object of disgust.*
c.-eagail, *cause of fear, terrible object, bugbear.*
c.-fharmaid, *cause of envy.*
c.-ghearain, *cause of complaint.*
c.-ghràin, see culaidh-ghràin.
c.-ghrath, *a horrible sight*—(WC)
c.-lagha, *action-at-law, process.*
c.-mhagaidh, -fhochaid, or -fhanoid, *laughing-stock, cause of derision.*
c. mhaslaidh, *cause of reproach.*
c.-mhiosguinn, *a blameable affair.*
c.-sgreat, *a nuisance.*
c.-thogail, *appeal.*
c.-thogair, *s.m. appellant.*
c.-truais, *an object of pity.*
c.-uamhais, *cause of terror, horror dread,* or *wonder.*
cuis,†† -ean, *s.f.* Narrow sea-stream. 2 see cuisle. 3 Jet from a vein or artery.
cùis-bhùirt, see cùis-bhùrta (under cùis.)
cuisdeag, -aige, -an, *s.f.* The little finger.
cuisdeog, -oige, see cuisdeag.
cuiseach, -eiche, *a.* Discreet, staid—*Lewis.* 2(WC) Comfortable, careful, thrifty. Tha e cho c. ri cnoc, *he is as staid as a hill*—generally said of youngsters.
———,§ *s.m.* Darnel or rye-grass, see breoillean. 2 see cuiseag.
cuiseadair,(WC) *s.m.* In olden times blood-letting of a certain vein in the arm was very common for nearly all troubles. An expert in the operation was called cuiseadair.
cuiseag, -eige, -an, *s.f.* Species of grass having a slim straight stem. 2 Stalk. 3 Plant stem. 4**Reed. 5** Rush, bullrush. 6 (CR) Stick, switch—*W. of Ross.* 7(DW)Dock. 8 In *Gairloch* applied to the stem of the dock. 9)CR) Ragwort—*Perthshire & Gairloch.* Le cuiseagaibh an lìn, *with the stalks of flax.*
———ach, -aiche, *a.* Full of slender stalks or stems. 2**Abounding in reeds or rushes. 3** Like a reed or rush. Gleannan c. mo ghràidh, *my beloved little glen, where reeds do so abound.*
——— -bhuidhe,§*s.f. Ragwort, see buaghalan-buidhe.
cuiseal,(WC) *a.* Thrifty. 2 Well-off. Nach e 'tha c.? *isn't he well-off,* or *comfortable?*
†**cuisean,** -ein, *s.m.* Crime. 2 (WC) see cuislean.
cùisear, *s.m.* Subject of a sentence in *gram.*
cuisil, see caiseal, caisil & cuisle.
cuisilin, *dim.* of cuisle.
†**cuision,** Gaelic spelling of *cushion.*
cùisire, -an, *s.m.* Casuist, client. 2* One who employs a lawyer.
cuisle, -ean, *s.f.* Vein, blood-vessel. 2 Artery. 3 Pipe. 4 Stream of water. 5*Layer of ore, as in a mine. 6 Narrow passage of the sea through which the tide runs swiftly. 7 Term of endearment. 8 Pulse. Troimh chamchuislibh bhad-chrann, *through the crooked veins of tufted trees.* [This form, which is generally used as *nom, sing.,* is really the *gen.,* the correct form of the *nom.* being *cusail.*]
cuisleach, -liche, *a.* Full of veins, veinous, arterial. 2 Veined, having veins or arteries. 3**Like a vein or artery. 4**Blustering. 5** Freezing.
cuisleach,* *s.f.* Lancet. 2 Lance.
———ail, *a.* see cuisleach.
cuisleag, -eige, -an, *s.f.* Lancet. 2 Little vein or artery.
———ach, *a.* Full of, or pertaining to, little veins or arteries.
cuisle-aibheach, -eich, *s.f.* Liver-wort.
cuislean,** -ein, *s. m.* Little vein or artery. 2 Chanter. 3 Little pipe. 4 *rarely* Cattle. 5 Pulse. 6 *n. pl.* of cuisle.
cuisleanach, -aich, *s.m.* Piper, one who plays on a reed.
cuisleannan, *pl.* of cuisle.
cuisle-chinn,** *s.f.* Aorta.
cuisle-chiùil, -annan-c—, *s.f.* Musical vein. 2 Musical wind-instrument. [*better form,* cusail-chiùil.]
cuisle-mhór, -óir, *s.f.* Artery, great artery.
†**cuislin,** *s.* Pole. 2 Flute. 3 Hautboy.
cùis-mhagaidh, *s.m.* see under cùis.
†**cuisne,** *s.f.* Ice, frost.
cuisneach, -eiche, *a.* Freezing, congealing, frosty.
cuisnich, *v.a.* Freeze, congeal.
———te, *past pt.* of cuisnich.
cuist,(MMcD) *s.f.* Arithmetical question.
cuist! *inter.* You don't say so! 2 Hush! 3 (AH) Shut up!
cùiste, -an, *s.f.* Couch.
†**cuite,** *s.f.* The head.
cuite, *a.* & *past pt.* of cuitich, see cuidhte.
——ach, *a.* see cuidhteach.
——achadh, -aidh, see cuidhteachadh.
cuiteag, -eige, -an, *s.f.* Whiting (fish.) Tha dà bhall dubh air an adaig is earball fad' air a' chuiteig, *there are two black spots on the haddock, and the whiting has a long tail.*
cuiteal,(AF) *s.m.* Cuttle-fish.
cuith, see cuidh and cuithe.
cuithe, -achan, *s.f.* Trench, pit. 2 Deep moist

place. 3 Wreath of snow. 4 Cattle-fold or -enclosure. 5(AC) Stronghold. 6(AC) Mass, quantity. 7(AC) Drizzle. 8*Pit. C. bùirn, *a mass of water;* c. sneachd, *a wreath of snow,* c. ceò, *a bank of fog;* an c., *the world, the mass.*
——ach, -hich, *s.m.* see cuthach. 2**Foam.
——ach, -eiche, *a.* Abounding in snow-wreaths.
——adh, -eidh, *s.m.* Hedging, enclosing.
——amh, -eimh, -ean, see cuithe.
cuitich, see cuidhtich.
——ear, see cuidhtichear.
——te, see cuidhtichte.
cùl, -ùil,-ùiltean,*s.m* .Back of anything. 2 Hinder part, not the front. 3 Hair of the head. 4 Aftertime. 5(AF) see cull-bhoc. 6‡‡Guard. 7 Custody. 8(DU) Matter for thought, food for reflection. 9(CR) Care, anxiety. Chuir e c. orm, *it made me anxious, it troubled me ;* chaidh esan 'bha treun air ch., *he who was strong has perished* ; is buaine c. na aghaidh, *back lasts longer than front*—a cheese, stack of peats, &c. would be more freely used at first than at last—the moral is that feuds last longer than friendship ; c. gaoithe agus aghaidh gréine, *back to wind and face to sun*—a pleasant retreat; air mo ch., *behind me ;* c. na beinne, *the back of the mountain;* c. a' chinn, *the back part of the head* : cuir c. ri, *forsake;* c. buidhe dualach, *yellow curled hair*; bithidh mis' air do ch., *I will be behind you, ready to support you* ; gu c., *thoroughly, completely ;* is tu an cù g' ad ch., *you are a dog every inch of you*; cùl ri cùl, *back to back;* gu c. Calluinn, *till after the New Year*; air c. do naigheachd ! *tell away !* ; cum c., *support, countenance* ; air c. lainn, *handling a weapon* ; c. an dùirn, *the back of the fist*; c. ri d' charaid no ri d' nàmhaid, c. riut fhéin, *to turn your back on friend or foe is to unman yourself* ; tha thu air ch. do ghnothaich, *you are managing your affairs well ;* gabh mu ch. do chruidh, *get to the rear of thy cattle*—come to business, come to the point, do not wander ; leòn e mi o thaobh mo chùil, *he wounded me from behind*—treacherously.
cùl, (gu) *adv.* Completely, perfectly, to the back. Chunnaic mi 'anam gu cùl, *I saw his soul perfectly* ; stàillinn gu c., *steel every inch of it.*
culach, -aiche, *a.* In good condition, fat, plump. 2 Well-dressed. Tha e c., *he is fat.*
cùlachadh, -aidh, *s.m.* Forsaking, renouncing, abandonment.
cùlachair, *s.m.* Refuser.
cula-cheann, see cullach-cheann.
cùlachrach,(DU) *a.* Reticent, secret, dour.
culadh, -aidh, -aidhean, *s.m.* Good condition of body, fatness, plumpness, used chiefly of cattle. 2** see culaidh.
cùlag, -aige, *s.f.* Back tooth. 2 Turf placed at the back of a peat-fire, large flat peat cut with a common spade, which dries much quicker than an ordinary peat. 3 One who rides behind another on horseback, generally a woman sitting sideways behind a man. 4 Back stroke from the horn of a ram, instead of a fronting box or budge—*Lewis.* 5 Stroke with the back of the hand, back stroke, slap. 6 ("Fionn") Back-stroke with a shinty. Thòisich e leis na cùlagan, *he began with the back strokes*—indicating that the ram was to come off second best.
culag,** -aig, *s.f.* Collop. 2 Piece of flesh. 3 (DC) see colag.
cùlagach, -aiche, *a.* Abounding in turf, of or belonging to turf, or 2††Back teeth.
cùlagan, *n.pl.* of cùlag, Grinders, back teeth.
cùlaibh,†† *s.m.* Back, back parts.
Cùlaibh an taighe, *behind the house,* or *the back part of the house* ; cùlaibh is beulaibh, *back and front* ; ag aomadh air craoibh o 'chùlaibh, *leaning on a tree from behind* ; c. air beulaibh, *vice versa,* any garment put on back to front.
cùlaich, *pr. pt.* a' cùlachadh, *v.a.* Forsake, renounce. 2 Turn the back upon. 3**Put behind.
culaidh, -e, -ean,*s.f.* Garment. 2 Suit of clothes, dress apparel. 3 Accoutrements. 4 Armour. 5 Protection, support. 6 Instrument, tool or tools. 7 Boat, coble. 8 Subject. 9 Object. 10**Kept miss. 11†† see culadh. 12‡‡Any convenient or useful thing. 13* Materials. C. is the word for a fishing boat in Sutherland, the word *bàta* being seldom heard there; na'm bitheadh a' ch. agam, *had I the materials* ; a c. bantraich, *her widow's garments*; gabhaidh c. mhath a chur air a' bhoin roimh Nollaig fhathasd, *the cow can be fattened up well yet before Christmas comes.*
c.-àbhachdais, *object of mirth.*
c. a dhùsgadh nan deamhan, *a means to rouse the devils.*
c.-aodaich, *suit of clothes.*
c.-bainnse, *wedding suit.*
c.-bhrosnachaidh, *incentive, provocation.*
c.-bhùird, *or* c. bhùrta, *butt, laughing-stock.*
c.-chiùil, *musical instrument.*
c.-eagail, *object of fear.*
c.-fhanoid, *mocking-stock.*
c.-fharmaid, *object of envy.*
c.-ghràbhalaidh, *engraving tool.*
c.-ghràin, *eyesore.*
c.-leighis, *medicine, antidote.*
c.-mhagaidh, see c.-fhanoid. 2 *object of merriment.*
c.-mhaitheis, *business.* 2 *level best.* Ni mi mo c.-mh., *I will do my level best.*
c.-mheallaidh, *dupe.*
c.-mhì-thlachd, *object of disgust.*
c.-shiùil, *canvas, materials for making sails,&c.*
c.-thàlaidh, *decoy.*
c.-thruais, *object of pity.*
cùlaig, -e, -ean, *s.f.* Hinderance, burden, drawback, impediment to one's prosperity or comfort in life.
culair,** *s.f.* Throat. 2 Palate. 3 Chops.
cùl-air-thòin, *adv.* Inverted.
cùlaist, *s.f.* (AC) Back place. 2 Back wing to a dwelling. 3††Recess, wall-press. 4(CR) Inner apartment of old cottages in Gaeldom, best room, "parlour"—*Skye & W. of Ross.* [*s. m.* in *Poolewe*—(WC)]
cùl-àit', see cùlaist.
cùlan, -ain, *s.m.* Hair, tresses. 2 Of two waves on the sea, this is the second one. 3††Crust.
——ach, -aiche, *a.* Behind the back. 2 Belonging to the back or background. 3††Coming behind.
——ach, -aich, *s.m.* Backing, security. 2 The second son of a family. 3‡‡Back wave.
—— -caise, *s.m.* Small crust of cheese—(Fionn)
cùl-an-éisg,(WC) *s.m.* Corner of the bag-net in which salmon are caught.
cùlantas, -ais, *s.f.* Bashfulness, backwardness.
cùlaobh, see cùlaibh.
†cular, -air, -airean, *s.m.* Flag, banner. Gaelic spelling of *colour.*
cularaibh, *dat.pl.* of cular.
cularan, -ain, -an, *s. m.* Cucumber—*cucumis sativus.*
cùl-armachd,‡‡ *s.f.* Backpiece (of armour.)
cùl-bheum, -eim, -an, *s. m.* Back stroke. 2

Calumny. 3 Act of slandering.
cùl-bhoc,** -bhuic, see cull-bhoc.
cùl-chabag, (WC) *s. f.* Shell-fish, similar to cockle but much larger.
cùl-caise,(WC) *s.m.* Rind of a cheese. Cha do thachair a leithid bho là a' chùl-caise, *the like did not happen since the day of the cheese-rind*—said of any rare occurrence.
cùl-chagnaidh,(WC) *s.m.* Object of backbiting or contempt. Nach bu mhi an c. ? *was I not an object of contempt ?*
cùl-chàin, *v.a.* Backbite, slander, calumniate.
———each,‡‡ -eiche, *a.* Detractive.
———eadh, -nidh, *s.m.* Backbiting, detraction, slander, calumny. 2 Act of backbiting, slandering or traducing. A' c—, *pr.pt.* of cùl-chàin.
cùl-chainnt, -e, *s.f.* Calumny, slander.
————each, -tiche, *a.* Traducing, calumnious, slanderous. 2**Tattling. Cailleach chabach ch., *a toothless tattling old woman.*
————ear, -eir, -ean, *s.m.* Backbiter, calumniator. 2 Tattler.
cùl-cheum,** -cheim, *s.m.* Back step.
————nachadh, -aidh, *s.m.* Tergiversation. A' c—, *pr.pt.* of cùl-cheumnaich.
cùl-cheumnaich, *pr. pt.* a' cùl-cheumnachadh, *v.n.* Go backwards, retrograde.
cùl-choimhead, -hid, *s.m.* Rearguard. 2 Retrospection, looking behind.
cùl-chuideachd, *s.f.* Rearguard. 2 Reserve, company to assist.
cùl-chur,‡‡ -uir, *s.m.* Abandonment.
cùl-cinn,(DC) *s.m.* Outrun, common grazing ground of a township—*Uist.* 2 (AH) Oats or barley of the first or best quality.
cùldaich, see cùilteach.
cùl-earalais,** *s.m.* Body of reserve.
cùl-earbsa, *s.m.* Reservation.
cùl-fhiach,‡‡ -a, -an, *s.f.* Arrear.
cùl-fhradharc, see cùl-radharc.
————ach, see cùl-radharcach.
cùl-ghairm, -e, *s.f.* Recalling, revoking. 2 Calling from behind.
————, *v.a.* Recall, call back, revoke. 2 Call from behind.
cùl-ithe, *s.f.* Backbiting, slander.
†culla, see culladh.
cullach, -aich, *s.m.* Boar. 2 Yearling calf. 3 Impotent man, eunuch. 4 Pole-cat—*Mull.* 5 (AF) Fat heifer. 6(AF) Male cat. 7(AF)Bat. 8(AF) Stallion. 9(AF) Conger-eel. Greim cullaich 'na thaic, *a piece of bacon along with it*—*Sgeul.-nan-caol.*
———as, -ais, *s.m.* Impotence.
cullach-cheann,(AF) *s.m.* Boar (leader)
cullach-cuain,(AF) *s.m.* Male seal.
cullach-ròin,(DMy) *s.m.* Male seal.
†culladh, -aidh, -aidhean, *s.m.* Hood, cowl.
cullag, see culag.
cullaich,* *v.a.* Line, as a boar.
cullaid,** *s.f.* Noise, tumult, uproar, brawl. 2 (WC) Noisy party. 3(WC) Gossiping untidy female. Nach b' e a' ch. i ? *isn't she a gossip ?*
———each,** -diche, *a.* Noisy, tumultuous, quarrelsome.
cullaidh, see cuillidh.
cull-bhoc, -bhuic, *s.m.* Wether-goat.
culm,(CR) *s.m.* Energy, push, liveliness (about business)—*Perthshire.* 2 Gloom, haze, darkness of atmosphere—*W. of Ross-shire.* Tha c. air a' ghréin, *the sun is hazy.* (gulm)
———,(MMcD) *v. a.* Break into small pieces—*Lewis.*
culmach,(DU) *a.* Hazy, applied to a heavy sky. 2(WC) Surly, gloomy. Duine c., *a surly fellow.*
cùl-mhionnachadh, -aidh,*s.m.* Abjuration, oath
cùl-mhionnaich, *v.a.* Abjure, deny.
—————te, *a. & past part.* Abjured, denied.
cùl-mhionnan, *s.m.* Oath of abjuration. Thug e a ch., *he gave his oath of abjuration.*
cùl-mhùtaire, -an, *s. m.* Mutineer, plotter. 2 Backbiter. 3**Smuggler.
————achd, *s.f.ind.* Mutiny, plotting in private, conferring. 2 Backbiting. 3 Smuggling.
culmor,(CR) *a.* Vigorous, active—*Perthsh.*
cù-lomna,(AF) *s.m.* Tied dog.
cù-lorgaidh,(AF) *s.m.* Beagle.
cùl-radharc,** *s.m.* Retrospection, looking-behind. 2**Circumspection.
————ach, -aiche, *a.* Circumspect, retrospective, looking behind.
cùl-raoinidh, *s.m.* Goal-keeper—*Suth'd.*
cùl-sgrìobh, *v.a.* Superscribe, endorse. 2* Direct, address, as a letter.
————adh, -aidh, *s. m.* Direction, as on a letter.
————ta,* *past pt.* Directed.
cùl-shleamhnach, *a.* see cùl-sleamhnach.
—————adh, see cùl-sleamhnachadh.
cùl-shleamhnaich, see cùl-sleamhnaich.
—————e, see cùl-sleamhnaiche.
cùl-sleamhnach, -aiche, *a.* Backsliding. 2 Prone to backslide.
—————adh, *s. m.* Backsliding, act of backsliding, falling back. 2 Apostatizing. A' c—, *pr.pt.* of cùl-sleamhnaich.
—————air,** -ean, see c.-sleamhnaiche.
cùl-sleamhnaich, *pr.pt.* a' c.-sleamhnachadh, *v. n.* Backslide, fall back,fall off, become worse, 2 Apostatize.
—————e, -an, *s.m.* Backslider.
cùl-spor, -uir, -ean, *s.m.* Spur.
cùl-staidhir, -dhre, -dhrichean, *s.m.*Back-stairs.
cùl-taghail,(WC) *s.m.* Full-back at shinty or football, goal-keeper.
cùl-taic, -e, *s.m.* Support, backing. 2 Patron. 3 Patronage. 4**Defence. 5**Supporter. 6 Abettor. 7**Authority.
†culthaideach, *a.* Preposterous.
cùl-thaobh, see cùlaibh.
cùl-tharruing, -e, *s.f.* Drawing back, retracting. 2* Sly insinuation—*Islay.*
————,** *v.a.* Retract.
cù-luirge, *s.m.* Beagle, bloodhound, gaze-hound.

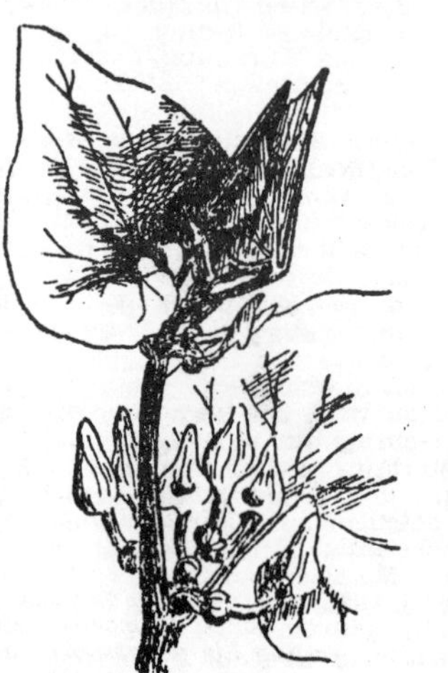

253. Culurain.

254. Culuran.

culurain,§ *s.m.* Birthwort—*aristolochia clematitis.* [ill. on p. 298.]
culuran, -ain, -an, *s.m.* Swinebread, sowbread, cyclamen—*cyclamen hederæfolia.* [ill. p. 298.]
c'um, see c'uime.
cum, see chum.
cum, *pr. pt.* a' cumail, *v.a.* Keep, hold, withhold, retain. 2 Restrain. 3 Observe, celebrate, as a holiday. 4 Contain, as a dish, &c. 5 Detain, obstruct—*Isles.* 6**Comprise. 7** Preserve. 8**Uphold, maintain. Cum seo, *hold this;* cumaidh an soitheach seo e, *this dish will hold it;* c. oirre, *crowd all sail on her* (the boat). *2 keep the boat going in the same way as she is going.*
c. agad, *hold, refrain thyself. 2 avast, avast heaving, &c.*
c. air t' aghaidh, *keep on, go forward.*
c. air t' ais, *keep back, hold back.*
c. air do làimh, *restrain thy hand.*
c. air falbh, *keep off.*
c. a mach, *hold forth, maintain.*
c. còdhail, *keep an appointment.*
c. do theanga, *keep quiet.*
c. fodha, *back water with the oars.*
c. greim air, *keep hold of him.*
c. ort, *forbear. 2 restrain.*
c. ris, *keep up to him, do not yield to him.*
c. roimh, *prop, hold against.*
c. suas, *keep up. 2 support, maintain.*
c. uaith a thuarasdal, *withhold his wages.*
c. o 'n òl, *refrain from drinking.*
a' cumail là na féille, *keeping the holiday;* am fear aig am bheil, cumadh e, *he that has, let him keep.*
cum, *pr. pt.* a' cumadh, *v.a.* Frame, shape, form. 2‡‡Compose.
†cùm, -uim, see còm.
†cum, -a, *s.m.* Battle, fight, duel.
cuma, *a.* see coma.
cuma, see cumadh.
cumach,** -aich, *s.m.* Breach, derout.
cumachd, *s.f.ind.* see cumadh.
†cumachda, see cumhachd.
cumachdail,* -dala, *a.* Well-shaped, well-proportioned. Garbh c., *thick and shapely.*
cumadail, *a.* Plastic. 2**Shapely, well-formed, or proportioned. 3** Equal (in parts.) Do chalpannan c., *thy shapely calves;* sgiath ch., *a well-formed shield.*
cumadair, -ean, *s.m.* Shaper, former, fashioner. 2 Frame. 3(AH) Paper pattern for lady's or gentleman's article of dress.
————eachd, *s.f.ind.* Framing, forming. 2 Act of framing or forming. 3** Device, invention.
cumadalachd, *s.f.ind.* Shapeliness, elegance of form. 2 Symmetry, proportion.
cumadh, -aidh, *s. m.* Shape, figure, form, proportion, pattern. 2 Shaping. 3 Act of shaping, framing or fashioning. 4 Contriving. 5 Act of contriving. 6 Trunk of the body. 7 ‡‡Degree. A' c—, *pr.pt.* of cum. C. do mhìn-chalpanna, *the shape of thy smooth calves;* gun ch., *shapeless.*
cumaidh, *fut. aff. a.* of cum.
cumaidheachd, *Suth'd & W. of Ross* for cumachd.
cumail, cumalach, *s.f.* Holding, witholding, restraining, refraining. 2 Act of observing or celebrating. 3 Containing, comprising. 4 Detaining, detention. 5 Maintaining, supporting. 6 Keeping. 7††Lease. A' c—, *pr. pt.* of cum. Mo ch. suas, *my support or sustenance;* ciod a tha 'gad chumail? *what is keeping you?;* 'gam ch. suas, *supporting me;* a' c. làimh rithe, *paying his addresses to her* (*lit.* keeping near her); is math a tha thu a' c., *you wear well.* [These examples from other dictionaries all appear to be mere translations of English idioms.]
cumail,** *v.a.* Touch, wipe, rub off.
cumailt,** *s.f.* Touching, wiping.
————each, -tiche, *a.* Tenacious, adhesive.
————eachd, *s.f.* Tenaciousness, adhesiveness.
cumaint, *prov.* for cumanta.
———— (an), *adv.* for an cumanta.
cumair, *a.* see cuimir.
————eachd, see cumadalachd.
†cumaisg, *v.a.* see coimeasg.
†————te, see coimeasgta.
cumait,** *a.* Neat, well made, handsome.
————eal,(WC) *a.* Neat, tidy.
†cumal, -ail, *s.m.* Price of three cows. 2 Three cows.
cumalas, -ais, *s.m.* Support, stay.
cumaltachd,†† see cumailteachd.
cuman, -ain, *s. m.* Milking-pail. 2 Circular wooden dish without a handle, *Scots,* cogue. †3 Shrine. 4**Skimmer. 5(AF) Angler (fish)—*Caithness.* A c. eadar a dà ghlùn, *her pail between her knees.*
cumanda, see cumanta.
cumanta, *a.* Common, general, customary, ordinary, plebeian. Gu c., an c., *commonly;* aon de 'n phobull ch., *one of the common people.*
————chd, *s.f.* Same meanings as cumantas.
————s, -ais, *s.m.* Commonness, usualness. An c., *generally, usually.*
†cumar, -air, -airean, see †comar.
cù-mara, *pl.* coin-mhara, *s.m.* Sea-dog, dog-fish, angler, ranger. 2 Slow- or sleuth-hound. 3 (AF)Seal.
†cumaraich, *s.pl.* Inhabitants of a country abounding in valleys and hills.
cumas, see comas.
————ach, see comasach.
————g,* -aisg, *s.f.* Tumult. 2 Brose. 3 Mixture, amalgam, medley. 4**Battle. Cumasg sluaigh, *a mixture of people.* †5 Contention. 6 Melée. 7**Confusion
————gach, -aiche, *a.* Tumultuous. 2**Confused, mixed, disordered. 3 Causing confusion or disorder. Is tric a dhearbh an cruaidh-chuis 's na buan ruagaibh cumasgach, *who oft proved their hardihood in the long confused pursuits—Filidh,* p. 66.
————gadh, -aidh, see coimeasgadh.
cumasgta,***a.* Mixed, confused, in a medley.
†cumca,‖ *s.* Constriction.
cumha, *pl.* -chan, *s.m.* Mourning, lamentation, sorrow. 2 Elegy, poem in praise of the dead, eulogy. 3* Epic poem. 4††Dirge. 5**Doleful voice. Cumha Mhic MhicAlasdair, *Glengarry's lament*—a noted pipe-tune; c. ro gheur, *very bitter lamentation.*
————, -chan, *s.f.* Condition, stipulation, covenant. 2 Reward, bribe. Cha d' thug Fionn riamh blàr gun ch., *F. never fought a battle without offering terms;* air a' ch. seo, *on this covenant.*
†cumhac, see cumhang.
cumhach, -aiche, *a.* Sorrowful, mournful, sad, disconsolate. 2**Wailing. 3**Bribing.
————adh, see cumhachd.
————ag, see comhachag.
————d, -an, *s.m.* Power, authority, might, strength, ability. 2 Virtue, medicinal virtue. 3* Permission. 4* Influence. Toil nan c. air neamh, *the will of the powers in heaven.*
————dach, -aich, s.m. Mighty man.
————dach, -aiche, *a* Powerful, mighty, strong. 2 Having great authority or influence. Duine c., *a mighty man;* gu c., *powerfully.*

cumhachdaiche, *comp.* of cumhachdach.
———dair, -ean, *s.m.* Commissioner, person high in authority. 2 Delegate, agent.
cumhadair,** *s.m.* Bemoaner.
cumhadh, -aidh, see cumha.
cumhag-bhogadh-tòine,(AF) *s.f.* Water-wagtail.
cumhaing, *pr.pt.* a' cumhangachadh, see cumhangaich.
———e, see cuinge.
———ich, see cumhangaich.
cumhainn, see caomhain.
cumhais, *s.f.* Selvage as of cloth.
†cumhal,(AF) *s.m.* Price of three cows. 2 Subjection, slavery. 3**Maidservant, bondmaid. 4**Obedience.
cumhanach,(AC) see camhanach.
cumhang, [1st. *comp.* cuinge, 2nd. *comp.* cuingeid, 3rd. cuingead] *a.* Narrow, strait, contracted. 2 Narrow-minded. 3**Tight, close. 4**Powerful. Is goirt 's is cumhang a bhualadh, *sore and powerful is its blow.*
———, -aing, *s.m.* Strait, defile. 2**Power, strength.
———achadh, *pr.pt.* of cumhangaich.
———achd, *s. f.* Narrowness, straitness. 2 Tightness, closeness. 3**Difficulty. Ann an c., *straitened.*
———aich, *pr. pt.* a' cumhangachadh, *v. a.* Make narrow, straiten. 2 Tighten.
———aichte, *past pt.* Straitened. 2 Tightened.
cumhann, *s. & a.* see cumhang.
cumhannaich, see cumhangaich.
———te, see cumhangaichte.
cumhasag, *s.f.* Barn-owl, see comhachag.
cumhdach, see comhdach.
cumhdaich, see comhdaich.
cumhlach,(AF) *s.m.* Sucking-pig.
†cùmhlaich, *v.a.* Fulfil, perform.
cùmhlaichean, *s. pl.* Stipulations, bonds—*Dàin I. Ghobha.*
†cùmhlaichte, *past pt.* of cùmhlaich. Fulfilled, performed.
cumhlaid, *s.f.* Gift. Gheibh thu uam mar chumhlaid, *you shall get as a gift from me—Duanaire,* p. 124.
cùmhnadh, -aidh, see còmhnadh & caomhnadh.
cùmhnant, -aint, *pl.* -a & -an, *s. m.* Covenant, contract, compact, article, agreement, bargain, engagement. 2* League. 3** Stipulation, condition. 4 Marriage contract. A réir ceannaibh a' chùmhnaint, *agreeable to the terms of the agreement ;* an c. a rinn e riu, *the covenant he made with them* ; air a' ch. seo, *on this condition.*
———ach, -aiche, *a.* Federal. 2 Of, or belonging to, contracts, bargains, leagues or covenants. 3* Stingy, unaccommodating. Duine cruaidh c., *a niggardly, stingy fellow.*
———ach, -aich, *s.m.* Covenanter.
cùmhnantaich, *v.a.* Bargain, covenant, article, **articulate.
cùmhnantaiche,** *s.m.* Bargainer.
cùmhnantaichte, *past pt.* Affied.
cùmhnantail, -tala, see cùmhnantach.
†cùmhra, see cùbhraidh.
cùmhrachadh, -aidh, *s.m.* Encumbrance.
cùmhrachd, see cùbhraidheachd.
cùmhradh, -aidh, -aidhean, see cùmhnant and cùnnradh.
cumhrag, see cubhrag. 2**Sweet apple-tree.
†cumhtha, *s.m.* Proffer.
†cumhul, -uil, *s.f.* Handmaid.
cumlach, see cumhlach.
†cumoradh, -aidh, *s.m.* Emulation.
cùmpaich, *a.* Well-shaped.
†cumpluchd, -an, *s.m.* Crew, gang.
cumraich, *v. a.* Cumber, encumber, impede, incommode.
cumraidh, see cubhraidh.
cumraig, see cumraich. 2 *Suth'd* for coimrig.
†cumsanad, *s.m.* Rest.
†cumsgadh, -aidh, *s.m.* Ringing.
cumta, *a.* & *past pt.* of cum. Well-shaped, suited, adapted, proportioned. 2 Artificial. 3** Set, as a task. Bhur n-obair ch., *your set tasks.*
cumtadh, *past subj. & pass.* of cum.
cumusg, -uisg, -an, see coimeasg.
cun, *s.m.* Body. 2 Time. 3 Hour.
cunablach, -aich, see conablach.
cunadh,(AF) -aidh, *s.m.* Stock, cattle.
cunbhaidh, see cumaidh.
cunbhail, *s.f.* see cumail. 2††Sense, wit.
———teach, -tiche, see cunbhalach.
———teachd, see cunbhalachd.
cunbhalach, -aiche, *a.* Constant, steady, firm, durable. 2††Sensible, witty. 3 Even—*Lewis.* 4(DU)Regular, uniform. 5(AH)Trim, tidy, snug. Gu c., *firmly* ; tha 'n sìol air a chur gu c., *the seed is sown evenly*; tha e 'tighinn gu c., *he is coming regularly.*
cunbhalachd, *s.f.* Constancy, steadiness, firmness, durableness. 2††Sense, judgment. 3 Evenness. 4(AH) Tidiness.
cunbhalas, -ais, *s.m.* see cunbhalachd.
cunbhas, *for* a chumas, see cum.
cung, -uing, -an, *s.f.* Medicine, drug. Droch chungan, *bad medicines.*
cungaidh, -ean, *s. f.* Tool, instrument, implement. 2 Materials, ingredients. 3 Baggage. 4††Medicine. 5 Stuff, texture, as of cloth. 6 Rennet. 7**Privy parts. 8** Assortment. Tha 'n deagh ch. ann, *it is good stuff* ; 'nam bitheadh a' ch. agam, *had I the materials;* c.-leighis, *medicine, salve.*
cungaisich, *pr.pt.* a' cungaiseachadh, *v.a.* Help, co-operate, assist. 2* Subdue, overcome. 3 ††Provide with tools.
†cunganta, *s.f.* Help, assistance. 2 Keeper, assistant.
†cunganta,** *a.* Ready to help. Bean ch., *a midwife.*
†cungantach, -aiche, *a.* Helpful.
cungantair,** *s.m.* Helper, assistant.
cungarach,** *a.* Exigent.
———d,** *s.f.* Exigence.
cunglach, -aich, -aichean, *s.m.* Narrow defile. 2**Cleft.
cunglaichean, *n.pl.* of cunglach.
cunglait,(AC) *s.f.* Narrow. Anns a' ch., *in the narrows.*
cunmhalach, see cunbhalach.
cunn,* *v.a.* see cum & cunnt. C. an còta, *shape the coat.*
cunna,* *Isles* for cumadh.
cunnabhallach,* see cunbhalach.
cunnabhallachd,* see cumadalachd.
cunnadh, see connadh.
cunnail, *s.f.* see cunnuil.
†cunnairc, see chunnaic.
cunnarach,** *a.* Cheap.
———, -aich, *s.m.* Bargain. 2 Bad bargain. 3**Purchase. 4**Pennyworth. 5‡‡Membrum virile. Is geal gach c. a thig am fad, *sweet is the pennyworth that comes afar.* [N.G.P. gives cùnradh.]
cunnart, -airt, -an, *s.m.* Danger, risk. 2 Jeopardy. 3***rarely* doubt. Cuir an c., *take risk, endanger.*
cunnartach, -aiche, *a.* Dangerous. 2**Hazardous. 3***rarely* Doubtful. 4(DU) *rarely* Lively, wild. Duine c., *a lively fellow.*
cunnartachail,‡‡ -e, *a.* Challengable.

cunnartachd,** *s.f.* Hazardousness.
cunnartaich,‡‡ *v.a.* Imperil. Chunnartaicheadh dol 'nan ordugh, thoirt do chòrach mach a dh' aindeoin, agus hò Mhòrag!
†cunnahail, *v.a.* Grasp hard, keep a firm hold of.
†cunnbhalach, *a.* Firm, strong, sturdy, having a firm grasp. Fir ch., *strong men.*
†cunnla, *a.* Modest, bashful.
cunnmhalas, -ais, see cunbhalas.
cùnnradh, -aidh, *s.m.* Good bargain. 2 Covenant, agreement, compact. 3 Condition, stipulation.
cùnnradhach, -aiche, *a.* Federal, of, or belonging to, agreements, compacts, or covenants.
†cunnsan, -ain, *s.m.* Noble person.
cunnt, *pr.pt.* a' cunntadh, *v.a.* Count, number, reckon, tell, calculate, compute. Am fear nach c. rium, cha chùnntainn ris, *he who keeps no account of his good actions to me, I will repay without measure* ; is gann an t-earrach anns an cunntar na faochagan, *it is a scarce spring when even the whelks are counted.*
†cunntabhairt, see cunnart.
cunntach, -aich, *s.m.* Numeral. 2(WC)Thrifty person.
cunntadh, -aidh, -ean, *s.m.* Counting, numbering, act of counting, numbering, reckòning, telling. A' c—, *pr.pt.* of cunnt.
cunntadhach,(WC) *a.* Careful, reckoning. Tha e glé c.air a' ghnothach, *he is very careful in reckoning the affair.*
cunntair, -ean, *s.m.* Accountant. 2 Arithmetician. 3**Reckoner.
———eachd, *s.f.* Counting, reckoning, numbering.
cunntart, -airt, -airtean, see cunnart.
cunntas, -ais, -an, *s.m.* Counting, act of counting, reckoning, calculating, telling or numbering. 2 Arithmetic, art of counting. 3 Account. 4 Settling or adjustment of account. 5**Number. 6**Detail, narration. 7 Abbreviated *cuns.* for a/c. 8(DU) Explanation. Thoir c. ort fhéin, *give an account of yourself* ; ris a' ch., *at arithmetic* ; triath gun ch., *chiefs beyond number* ; pàidh do ch., *pay your account*; gu 'm b' olc gu c. fearainn i, *she (the boat) coasted very slowly.—Uist Bards.*
cunntasach, -aiche, *a.* Keen, sharp, exact, precise. 2 Narrow. 3**Calculating. 4(DU) Responsible.
cunntasan, *n.pl.* of cunntas.
cunntas-eag, *s.m.* Tally.
cunntas-fearainn, *s.m.* Progress of a boat as it passes along the coast.
cunnuil, -e, -ean, *s.f.* Objection, check. 2** Exception.
cunnuileach,** -eich,*s.m.* Exceptor. 2 Objector.
cunnuileach, -eiche, *a.* Objectionable. 2**Objecting, inclined to object. 3**Wrangling.
cunnuilich, *v.a.* Object. 2 Dispute. 3 Wrangle.
————e,** *s.m.* see cunnuileach.
cunradh, -aidh, -aidhean, see cùnnradh.
cunradhach, -aiche, see cùnnradhach.
cunraich,** *s.* Covenant.
cunraiche, *s.m.* Covenanter.
cunthart, see cunnart.
cù-odhar,(AC) *s.m.* Otter. 2 Beaver.
cùp, cùpa, see cùba. 2 see cupa.
cupa, *pl.* -chan, -paichean, *s.m.* Cup. 2 Vial.
cupach, -aiche, see copanach.
cupaichean, *n.pl.* of cupa.
†cupaid, *s.m.* Cupid.
cupair, -ean, *s.m.* Cup-bearer.
cupaireachd,†† *s.f.* Cup-bearing.
cupall, see cupull.
cupan, -ain, -an, *s.m.* Cup, little cup.
cupanach,†† *a.* Pertaining to little cups.
†cupar, *s.m.* Conception.
cuphair,§ *s.m.* Cypress tree.
cupla, see cupull.
cuplach, see cupullach.
cuplachadh, -aidh, *s.m. & pr. pt.* of cuplaich. Coupling.
cùplaich, *pr. pt.* a' cuplachadh. Couple, join.
cuplaich, *s.* Shroud.
cupuill, *s. pl.* Shrouds.
cupull, -uill, -uill &-plaichean, *s.m.* Couple,pair. 2 Couple, the arched standing timber that supports the roof of a house. 3 Dog-chain. 4 *pl.* Shrouds of a ship (p. 76)
cupull, *v.a.* Couple, pair.
cupullach, -aiche, *a.* Abounding in pairs, roof-couples, or dog-chains.
cùr, *Suth'd.* for cùbhraidh.
cur, -uir, *s.m.* Placing, setting, sending, sowing. 2**Laying, pouring. 3 Falling of snow, raining. 4 Throwing. Àm a' chuir, *seed-time;* àm c. a' choirce, *oat-sowing season*; c. is cathadh, *a fall of snow and drift.* A' c—, *pr. pt.* of cuir.
cur, -uir, *s.m.* Power, virility. 2 Weariness. 3 Defeat. 4 (AF)Horse.
†cur, *a.* Difficult.
†cur, *s.m.* Present time. 2 Surety, pledge.
cùra, *s.m.* Guardian, protector. 2 Protectorship. Bithidh e 'na ch. orra, *he will be a protector to them.*
cura,(AF) *s.* Sheep.
cùrabh, see cùradh.
curacag,** *s.f.* Lapwing, see adharcan-luachrach.
curach, -aich, -ean, *s.f.* Boat made of wicker, and covered with skins or hides, coracle. 2 Canoe, skiff. 3**Marsh, fen, bog. The c. or boat of leather and wicker, may seem to moderns a very unsafe vehicle to trust to in tempestuous seas, yet our forefathers fearlessly committed themselves in these slight pinnaces to the mercy of the most violent weather. They were once much in use in the Western Isles, and are still found in Wales. The framework is called crannaghal, a word now used in Uist to signify a frail boat. [†† gives *s.m.*]

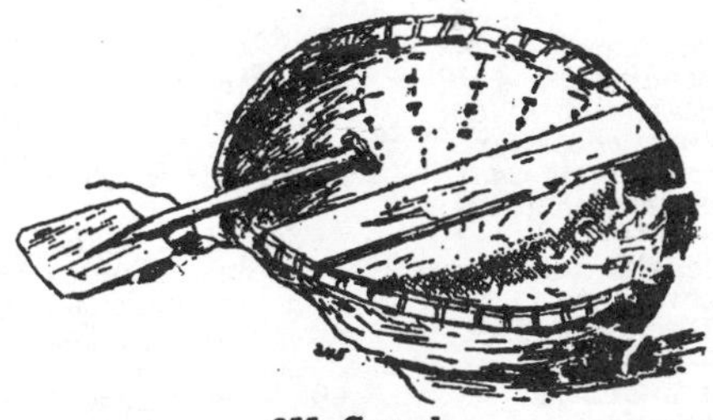

255. Curach.

curach-àile, *s.f.* Balloon.
curachan, -ain, -an, *s. m.* Little coracle, little wicker boat. 2**Skiff, canoe.
curachan-na-mnà-sìth,(AC) *s. m.* Shell of the blue valilla.
curachd, *s.f.* Sowing, act of sowing. 2 *Quantity to be sown. 3 Seminary. 4 see currac. A réir a churachd, *according to its sowing.*
curach-na-cubhaige, see currac-cubhaige.
cùradair,* *s.m.* Curator.
cùradh, -aidh, *s. m.* Obstacle, impediment,hinderance, difficulty. 2 Severe distress. 3** Agony. 4**Anxiety.
curadh,** -aidh, *s. m.* Act of sowing, see cur. A' c—, *pr. pt.* of cuir.

†curagh, -aigh, *s.m.* Burial-place.
curaicich,** *v.a.* Cap.
curaich,** *v.n.* Agonize.
cùraichean, *s.pl.* Rights—*Dain I. Ghobha.*
curaid,** *s.m.* Gaelic spelling of *curate.*
curaideach, -diche, see cuireideach.
curaideachd, see cuireideachd.
curaidh, -nean, & -dhean, *s.m.* Champion, hero, warrior. 2**Giant. Curaidhnean na Craoibhe Ruaidhe, *the warriors of the Red Branch.*
curaidh, *s.f.* (AH) Wherry. 2** see curraidh.
cùraidh, see cùbhraidh.
curaidheachd,** *s.f.* Heroism. 2 Recognizance.
†curaigheachd, see curachd.
†curaighir, *s.m.* Mug.
cùraing, see cùrainn.
cùrainn, -e, -ean, *s. f.* Counterpane, coverlet, quilt. 2 Coarse woollen cloth or flannel. 3 Serge, felt, plaiding. 4 Support, prop.
cùrainn-chneas, *s.f.* Flannel.
cùrainneachadh, -aidh, *s.m.* Covering, as a table. A' c—, *pr. pt.* of cùrainnich.
cùrainnich, *pr.pt.* a' cùrainneachadh, *v.a.* Cover.
cùrainnichte, *past pt.* Covered.
†curaist, Gaelic spelling of *courage.* 2 (DU) Presence of mind, sense.
†curaisteach, *a.* Courageous. 2 Strong, capable—*Suth'd.*
curaisteachd,** *s.f.* Courageousness, boldness, bravery. †2 Curacy.
curair,(AF) *s.m.* Horse.
cùram, -aim, -an, *s. m.* Care, anxiety, solicitude. 2 Charge, trust, command. 3 Office, employment. 4 Responsibility. 5 Prize. 6‡‡ Prey. 7 Family. Air mo ch.-sa, *under my charge* ; na biodh c. ort, *never mind* ; is beag mo ch. air a shon sin, *I feel no uneasiness on that score* ; bithidh iad fo ch., *they will feel anxiety, or be anxious* ; gabh c., *take care* ; ciamar tha 'n c. ? *how is the family ?* ; air an c.-sa, *under their charge* ; tha e fo ch., *or* tha c. air, *he is a converted man—Lewis.*
——ach, -aiche, *a.* Careful, solicitous, anxious, attentive. Gu c., *carefully* ; b'e siod an t-slàinte c., *yon was the responsible toast.*
——achd, *s.f.ind.* see cùram.
——as, see cùram.
curan,** -ain, *s.m.* Brave man.
cùranaich, see cùrainnich.
————te, see cùrainnichte.
curanta, *a.* Heroic, valorous, brave, courageous. 2 Powerful.
curantach, see curanta.
————d, *s.f.ind.* Bravery, courage, boldness, intrepidity.
curasan,** -ain, *s. m.* Milk-pail. 2 Firkin for butter. Cuach is curasan, *a cup and a milk-pail.*
curata, see curanta.
curcag, see curracag.
curcais, *s.f.* Hair. 2 Bulrush. 3 Genus of plants called *scirpus.* 4 see gobhal-luachair.
cur-ghalan,** *s.m.* Bucket.
cùrnaich, see cùrainnich.
curpur,(CR) *Lewis* for corcur.
cùrr, -a, -achan, *s.f.* Corner. 2 End. 3 Pit. 4 Fountain, well. 5 Situation, site. †6 Back.
cùrra, see còrra.
†curra, *s.m.* Sowing. 2 Little farm.
curra, *s.m.* Woof. [pron. *cuire* in *Lewis.*] An dlùth 's an c., *the warp and woof.*
currac, -aic, -aicean, *s.m.* Cap, woman's head-dress. 2 Servant's cap.
——ag, -aige, -aigean, *s. f.* Peat heap. 2 Rick. 3 Hood, woman's cap.
——ag, -aige, -an, *s.f.* Bubble on the surface of liquids. 2 Cock of hay or barley, when built in little cocks on the rigs or ground. 3¶ Tufted dun bird, pochard—*fuligula cristata.* 4 (JM) Lapwing, so called on account of the tuft of feathers at back of head resembling the "curraicean" worn by women in olden times, see adharcan-luachrach. 5**Sandpiper. An uair a bhios c. air Cruachan, cha bhi pathadh air Urchaidh, *when there is a cap (of clouds) on Ben Cruachan, the River Orchy will not suffer from thirst.*
curracagach,†† *a.* Pertaining to hay-cocks, bubbles, &c.

256. Curracag (3.)

curracan,(DU) *s.m.* Little mutch. It does not have the frilling and laces forming the border of the mutch proper, but is an "undress" head covering.
currac-an-easbuig,§ *s. m.* Field gentian, see lus-a'-chrùbain.
——— -an-rìgh, *s.m.* Caul. 2 Kingshood in an animal's stomach.
——— -bhain tighearna,§ *s.m.* Great tit-mouse, (bird)—*parus major.*
——— -cubhaige,§ *s. m.* Ragged robin—*lychnis floscuculi.* 2 Bluebottle, see gorman. 3** Small leaved bell-flower. 4* Harebell.

257. Currac-cubhaige.

——— -dubh,(AH) *s.m.* Judge's black cap. 2 Witch's wishing cap.
——— -manaich, Monkshood, see fuath-mhadaidh.
——— -na-cubhaige, see currac-cubhaige.
——— -sagairt, (AC) Monkshood, see fuath-mhadaidh.
——— -sìde,(AF) *s.m.* Blue-bonnet (bird.)
——— -oidhche, *s.m.* Night-cap.
——— -rath, (*lit.* lucky cap, lucky cowl.) The caul or membrane occasionally covering the head of a child at birth, and frequently used as a talisman.
†currach, -aich, -an, *s.m.* Bog, fen where shrubs grow. 2**Burying-place.
currachag, see curracag.
currachd, see currac.
————ag,* *s.f.* Peat-heap.
curradh, -aidh, *s.m.* Crowding together, collecting into one place.

curraq, -aige, -an, s.f. see curraс.
curra-ghalan,** s.m. Didapper, diver (water-fowl.)
curraiceach, -ciche, a. Wearing a cap or caps. 2 Of, belonging to, or full of caps. 3**Hooded, bonneted. 4**Like a hood or bonnet. Bi gu c., *mind you are well protected with head-gear.*
curraichdeach, see curraiceach.
curraidh, -e, a. Exhausted, weary. 2 Difficult, stiff. Tha seo c. r' a dhìreadh, *this is difficult to climb.*
———,(CR) v.n. Sit on the heels as sailors and colliers do, called in the S. of Scotland the "colliers' curry," (pron. *coorie*, e.g. coorie doun=*cower down.*)
———, s.m. Cower, "curry." Dean c.,*squat.*
curraighin, -e, -ean, s.m. Can, tankard.
currail, a. Manifest, plain, evident.
curral, -ail, see curran.
curran,§ -ain, -an, s.m. Carrot—*daucus carota.* 2 Pannier slung on horses for carrying bulky loads, as hay, corn, &c. 3** Flannel. 4** Root of the carrot or radish kind—*daucus.*
———ach, -aiche, a. Of, or belonging to, carrots, panniers or radishes.
curran-buidhe,** s.m. Carrot.
——— -cruaidh, (AC) s. m. (*lit.* hard carrot,) Hemlock—*Uist.*
——— -dearg,** s.m. Radish.
——— -earraich,§ s. m. Silverweed—*potentilla anserina.* [The flower is called bàrra-bhrisgein, which see for illust.]
——— -Frangach,(MMcL) s.m. Carrot.
——— -geal,§ s. m. Parsnip, see meacan-an-rìgh.
——— -petris,§ *Harris* for meacan-an-rìgh.
curranta, a. see curanta.
currasan,†† -ain, -an, s.m. Large deep vessel, pail.
†curraghalan, -ain, s.m. Bucket. 2 Didapper.
currtha, a. Wearied, fatigued.
currucadh, -aidh, s. m. Cooing of pigeons. 2 (MMcL) Making corn-ricks.
currucag -aig, -an, s.f. Lapwing, see adharcan-luachrach.
currusan, -ain, -an, s.m. s.m. see curasan.
†curs, -a, -an, s.m. Horse.
cùrsa, Gaelic spelling of *course.*
cùrsa,** s.m. Course, direction. 2 Order,rank, row. 3 Manner. 4 Coursing, race. Òirleach d' a cheart ch., *an inch of his straight course.*
cùrsach, -aiche, a. Winding, meandering. 2 Folding. 3 In courses, ranks or rows.
———, s.m. see cùrsair & cùrsan.
———adh, -aidh, s. m. see cùrsadh. 2** Curse. A' c—, *pr. pl.* of cùrsaich.
———d, s.f. Traversing, scampering, coursing. 2 Travelling. 3 Meandering.
cùrsadh,** -aidh, s.m. Coursing, traversing. 2 Meandering. 3 Direction, course. 4 Order, manner. 5 Row, rank.
cùrsaich, *pr. pt.* a' cursachadh, v.a. Course, traverse. 2 Arrange in ranks or rows.
cùrsair,- e, -ean, s.m. Horse, courser. 2 Courier, messenger. [McL & D gives 2 as *cùrsaire.*)
———each,†† a. Of, or pertaining to a courser.
———eachd, s.f. ind. Coursing. 2 Traversing.
cùrsan, -ain, s.m. Race. 2 see cùrsair.
———ach, -aich, s.m. see cùrsan.
———ach, a. see cùrsaireach.
——— -srann,(AF) s.pl. Snorting steeds.
curt,** a. see curta.
curta, a. Bad, infamous, shocking. 2 Rank. 3 Excessive. 4 Wearied, overcome. Is c. am balach thu, *you are a bad (cursed) fellow.*
curtag-mhór-a'-chuain,(AF) s.f. Sea-serpent.
†curu, see caora.
†curuinn, s.f. Objection.
†curunn, -uinn, s.m. Thunder.
curusan, -ain, s.m. see curasan.
cus, cuis, s.m. Enough, sufficiency. 2 Subsidy, tax, tribute. 3 Superfluity, too much. 4 (DU) Used as a term of incredulity, equivalent to "no fear." 5**Quantity.
cus, a. Many.
†cusadh, -aidh, s.m. Bending, inclining.
cusag, -aig, s. f. Wild mustard, see maragbhuidhe.
———ach, -aiche, a. Abounding in wild mustard.
cusail, This is the correct form of *n. sing.*, its place generally being taken by *cuisle*, which is the *gen. sing.* Vein, artery, pulse.
——— -chiùil, cuisle-, s.f. Musical wind-instrument.
†cusal, s.m. Courage, boldness.
†———ach, a. Caurageous.
cusb, -a, see cusp.
———ach, see cuspach.
cusbair, -ean, s.m. see cuspair.
———eachd, see cuspaireachd.
cù-seilge,(AF) s.m. Hunting dog.
cù-sìthe,(AC) s.m. Fairy dog.
cusmunn, -uinn, see cuspunn.
cusp, *pl.* -an, [& -aichean] s.f. Kibe, ulcerated chilblain on the heel. An t-ainm a's uaisle air a' chusp—milleadh bròige, *the politest name for a chilblain—a boot-sore.* [Meant to apply to people who try to minimize a disaster by giving it the mildest possible name, e. g. "untoward incident."] †† gives *cuspa.*
———ach, s.m. see cusp.
cuspach, -aiche, a. Kibed, having kibes.
cuspaich, see cusp.
cuspair, -ean, s.m. Mark to aim at. 2 Subject, object. 3 Lover. 4 see cuspairiche. 5‡ Customer. Mo ch., *or* c. mo ghràidh, *my lover—Lewis* ; c. mo smuaintean, *the subject of my thoughts* ; seadh a ch. ! *well sir* !
———each,‡‡ -eiche, a. Objective.
———eachd, s.f.ind. Archery. 2 Aiming or shooting at a mark. 3 Objection. 4 Argument. 5 Officiousness. Ri c., *firing or throwing at a mark.*
——— -deuchainn, *pl.* -ean-d—, s.m. Criterion. 2**Subject of experiment.
———ich, v.a. Aim, shoot or throw at a mark. 2 Meddle with.
———iche, -an, s. m. Opponent, adversary. 2 Marksman. 3††Archer.
cusparach, a. Objective (case in *grammar.*)
cuspunn, -uinn, s.m. Custom, tribute, impost, tax.
†cust, s.m. Skin.
†———air, -ean, s.m. Tanner.
cut, *pr.pt.* a' cutadh, v.a. Gut, as a fish. 2†† Dock, shorten.
cut, -a, -achan, s.m. Bob-tail. 2 Piece. 3 ††Short log. 4 Skein of yarn [There are four cuts or skeins in a hank, and sixty threads in a cut.]
cutach, -aiche, a. Short, diminutive. 2 Docked, shortened. 3 Bob-tailed. 4 Curtailed, concise. 5 Pertaining to a short log or skein of yarn.
cutach,* -aiche, s.f. Little woman.
———adh, -aidh, s. m. Elision. 2 Curtailing, curtailment. A' c—, *pr.pt.* of cutaich.
cutadh, -aidh, s.m. Gutting, disembowelling, as of fish. A' c—, *pr. pt.* of cut. A' c. an sgadain, *gutting the herring.*
cutag, -aige, -an, s.f. Little dumpy female. 2

Short tricky female. 3(MMcL) Gutting-knife. 4 Short spoon or tobacco pipe. 5**Short horn spoon. 6 Circular kiln. 7(AF) Coot, plover.
cutaich,** *pr. pt.* a' cutachadh, *v.a.* Shorten, curtail, dock.
———ead,** *s.m.* Shortness.
†cutaidh, *s.m.* Wake-robin.
†cutalaiche, *s.m.* Companion, partner.
†cuth, *s.m.* The head.
cutha, see cuthach.
cuthach, -aich, *s. m.* Madness. insanity. 2 Hydrophobia. 3 Foam, froth. Air ch., air a ch., *insane, mad* ; chaidh e air a ch,, *he went wild, he was very angry ;* is e 'n t-eud c., *jealousy is rage.*
cuthach, -aiche,ia. Infuriated.
———ail, -e, [& -ala,] *a.* Outrageous.
cuthadh, -aidh, *s.m. & pr.pt.* see cutadh.
cuthag, -aige, -an, see cubhag.
-———ach, see cubhagach.
-——— -bhogaidh,‡‡ *s.f.* Water-wagtail.
cuthaich, *gen.sing.* of cuthach.
———, *a.* Mad, frantic, insane.
———,‡‡ *v.n.* Be mad.
———te, *a.* Raging, mad, furious, insane.
cuthaidh,§ *s.* Wake-robin, see cluas-chaoin.
†cuthaileach, *a.* Bashful, modest, timid.
cuthaileachd, *s.f.ind.* Bashfulness, modesty, timidity.
cuthann, see cumhang.
†cuthar, see cobhar.
cutharlan, -ain, -an, *s.m.* Earth-nut, pig-nut, see braonan-bhuachaill. 2 Onion, see uinnean.
-———ach, -aiche, *a.* Of, or belonging to, earth-nuts or onions.
†cuth-bhàrr, -airr, *s.m.* Helmet, head-piece.
cuth-bharran, -ain, *s. m.* Sort of cap, "Monmouth" cap.
cuth-darun, -uin, see cuth-bharran.
†cutt,** *a.* Short.
cù-uisge, *s.m.* Spaniel, water-dog. 2 Newfoundland dog.

D d

dair (darach, *oak*) the fourth letter of the Gaelic alphabet now in use. The letters *d* and *s* at the commencement of a word often give it opposite meanings, as, daor, *dear* ; saor, *cheap.*

D has various sounds : (1) *Broad*—more dental, e.g. more explosive than in English, and with the tip of the tongue right up to the teeth, as in dàn, *a song* ; duine, *a man*; dlagh, *a handful.* (2) *Small* like *g* in genius, when flanked by a small vowel (e, *or* i,) that is when small vowels are the nearest to it, as, faide, *length*; cèaird, *a trade.* (3) D after *ch* sounds like *k* in English, thus lochd is pronounced *lochk*, the combination *chd* is thus the exact equivalent of final or medial *c.* (Boc, *a buck*, and bochd, *poor*, sound exactly the same.) (4) Dh, when broad, is very soft and resembles a soft English *g.* Thus, MacDhonnachaidh, *a son of Duncan*, usually Englished as Robertson, has also crept into English as MacConachy. MacDhaibhidh, *a Davidson*, has also been Englished as MacKay, so that some suppose that it was the MacKays who fought at the North Inch of Perth, whereas a little knowledge of Gaelic would have shown that it was the Davidsons. As a final, broad *dh* usually gets its full value in pronunciation, thus, Odh has practically the force of *O* only, as in Loch Odha, the best English representation of which is Lochow. Odha, *a grandson*, is well known in Lowland Scots as *oë.* Bodhar, *deaf ;* odhar, *dun-coloured* ; modh, *politeness ;* crodh, *cattle;* are practically pronounced *bohr, ohr, mow* and *crow.* In *Skye*, however, in some words, as, fiodhol, fiodha, the *odh* gets its full value. Adh when medial, as in adharc, *a horn* ; cladhach, *digging* ; sounds as though the speaker checked or interrupted his breathing, besides which, the first *a* is sounded like *ao.* (5) Dh, when narrow, sounds like English *y*, as, dheth, *off him*; dhi, *off her*, (*pron.* yea, ye.) When final, as, in buailidh, *shall strike*; fàidh, *a prophet ;* aghaidh, *face ;* it has the same *y* sound, except in *Skye, Mull*, and some other parts, where a final *idh* is pronounced almost as if written *ich.* Dh followed by *l*, or *r*, has no similar sound to them in English. The nearest approach to explaining it is to say that it is much softer than the softest English *g*, as in, a dhlighe, *his right* ; dhrùidh, *did penetrate, did impress.*

In Old Gaelic the article sometimes ended in *d.* In Skye that *d* of the article has sometimes been retained before *fh*, as, an d fhàidhe, *of the prophet* ; and sometimes the *d* is absent, as, an fhir, *of the man.* This *d* appears with great irregularity in connection with feminine nouns, as, an d-fhois, *the rest* ; an d-fhairge, *the sea.* Traces of *d* before initial vowels as in the old language, also occur. as, ceann an d-aigh, *the heifer's head ;* sgòthan air an d-athar, *clouds on the sky.* Fèile, *kilt*, in Skye has *nom. sing.* an t-éile, *gen. & dat.* an d-fheile. "Dobhran donn and sruth" is another example. We do not know the precise circumstances under which this *d* of the article appears.

The *n* of *cha'n* frequently becomes *d* before verbs beginning with *t*, especially irregular ones, thus, cha d'thoir, cha d'thig, cha d'teid, which are usually thus spelt, should be cha dtoir, cha dtig, cha dteid. This is called the eclipsis of t. D can also suffer eclipsis, as, a dh' aindeoin, *in spite of*, (*pron.* a ganyon.) Nan damh is pronounced *nan amh* in many parts of the North, is eudar dhomh, *I must*, is also sometimes contracted *is eudar 'omh.*

'd, (for iad) They, them. Ni 'd gàirdeachas, *they shall rejoice.*
'd, *contr.* (for ciod ?) 'd é ? (i.e. ciod e ?) *what ? what is it ?*
d', *contr.* for do. 1 *pron.* Thy. [Used before words beginning with a vowel or *f* aspirated. Dr. Stewart does not approve of the custom, of writing *t'* where in other circumstances *d'* is used for *thy*, but *t'* is correct, both on account of pronunciation and derivation.] 2 *prep.* To. 3 *Not* the sign of the past tense of verbs, as mentioned in some dictionaries. It precedes verbs in the past tense. The real past tense sign is preserved in *robh*, spoken by some *air an d'robh.*
da, *prep.pron.* (for do e) To him, to it. Bu phaillinn dha, *his pavilion was* (*lit.* it was a pavilion to him.) Though generally written (da) without the accent to distinguish it from the numeral dà (*two*,) it sometimes requires it in metre.
d' a, (for do a) To his or its. Chaidh e d'

a chois, *he went on foot* ; d'a shaoradh, *to deliver him.* [*De*, of his or its, is written *de'* when the possessive pron. is understood.]
d' a, (for do a) To her. D' a h-inghein, *to her daughter.* [*De*, of her, is written *de'* (*h*-) when the possessive pron. is understood.]
†da, *adv.* If, whence.
†da, *a.* Good (deagh.)
dà, *a.* Two, In counting in Gaelic, for 1, 2, 3, &c., it is usual to say, a h-aon, a dhà, a trì, &c. [Dà aspirates a noun following, as, dà dhuine, *two men ;* dà thaigh, *two houses* ; dà shaighdear, *two soldiers.* *Dà* governs a noun following it in the *dat. sing.* and the adjective qualifying that noun in the *n. sing. fem.* The dative so-called is really the accusative of the old dual number in such an expression as, chunnaic mi *dà* chloich, *I saw two stones*, and *dà* properly speaking has no governing influence. The nom. dual fem. was like the dative singular, and the genitive dual was like the genitive singular. For all practical modern purposes, however, it will be easiest for beginners to follow the rule as usually expressed, and put a noun following *dà* in the *dat. sing.*, and its qualifying adjective in the *nom. sing. fem.* Dà mhnaoi (*better* dithis bhan) *two women* ; dà sheachdain, *two weeks* ; dà chaol-chu, *two gaunt hounds* ; cò an dà luundaire mhór seo ? *who are these two great loons ?* dà fhear dheug is pìobaire, *twelve men and a piper* (here *deug* is an adj. to *fear*); an dà mhnaoi mhór, *the two big women.* This curious government gives way upon occasion, when other influences are too powerful, as, buinn mo dhà bhròige,*the soles of my two shoes*; ruith coin an dà fhéidh, *the running of the dog of the two deer*—said of people with divided aims; rudha nan dà ghleann deug, *the promontory of the twelve glens* ; is e coslas dà bhean-uasal a th' ann, *it seems to be two ladies ;* is duine còir fear dà bhò, *the man who has two cows is a decent man.* When used absolutely, e.g. without a noun, *dà* becomes *a dhà*, as, tha a dhà agam, *I have two* ; a nuas a dhà dhiubh, *bring down two of them.* When combining with deug, *ten*, and no noun being expressed, it is both aspirated and aspirating, as, aon bhò a bhriseas an gàradh, agus a dhà dheug a leumas, *one cow breaks the dyke, and a dozen leap it.* When used to express multiplicity, a dhà uiread agus ...., *twice as much as*, is said ; (here the *a*, and the aspirate in *dhà* are the sign of the old possessive masculine or neuter, used proleptically. The literal meaning, therefore, is, *its twice as much as.*)]
da, *prov.* form of verbal particle *do*, used in *Suth'd.* "An t-àit an da throg (thog) e," *the place where he built.*
d'a However. *prov.* "Is d'a olc gu'm bi an grunnd," *and however bad be the soil.*
dà-adharcach, *a.* Two-horned, bi-cornous.
dà-ainmeach,‡‡ *a.* Binominous.
dà-aodannach,(AH) *a.* Double-faced, hypocritical, false.
dabh, *prov.* for doibh (to them.)
dabh,(AF) *s.m.* Cow.
dabhach, -aich, *pl.* dabhcha & -aichean, *s.f.* Vat, mashing vat. 2 Large tub. 3 District of a country, lot, portion of land or farm to carry 60 cows or head of cattle, davoch. MacBain gives " either one or four ploughgates, according to locality and land." [A ploughgate contains 100 Scots acres.] Watson in *The Place Names of Ross & Cromarty*, says "usually four ploughgates." Skene in *Celtic Scotland*, says, " In the eastern district there is a uniform system of land denomination consisting of dabhachs, ploughgates and oxgangs, each dabhach consisting of four ploughgates, and each ploughgate containing eight oxgangs. As soon as we cross the great chain of mountains separating the eastern from the western waters, we find a different system equally uniform. The ploughgates and oxgangs disappear, and in their place we find dabhachs, and pennylands. The portion of land termed a *dabhach*, is here also called a *tirung*, or ounce-land, and each dabhach contains 20 pennylands." Prof. MacKinnon in *Place and Personal Names of Argyll*, says " In Pictland the unit of land measure was the dabhach, a word which properly denotes a liquid measure. An old farmer in Western Gaeldom frequently speaks of his fields, not as containing so many acres of land, but as " the sowing of so many bolls of oats," "the bed of so many barrels of potatoes," &c. Accordingly, from a measure of capacity, dabhach came early to be used as a measure of land surface. In Gaeldom, where the arable land is scant and scattered, the variations in the acreage of particular dabhachs or ounces must have been very great, still the extent of land represented by these terms seems to have been, as a rule, about 104 Scots acres, or 120 English acres. 4* Huge woman. A legend says that "an Dabhach" was the name of Ossian's wife. She was big, burly, and fat (mór, màsach, agus mèith.) When he was old and blind they fell out, he threw a deer's shin-bone at her and missed her, hence the saying, urchar an doill mu 'n dabhaich, *a throw or blow at a venture ;* d. fìona, *a wine-press.*
dabhan, -ain, *s.m.* Pitcher, bucket.
dabhan-alluidh, -ain-, } *s.m.* see damhan-alluidh.
dabhan-eallaich, -ain-, }
dabhar, -air, -an, see dabhan.
dabhasg, -aisg, -an, see dathas.
dabhd, *s.m.* Sauntering.
——, *pr.pt.* a' dabhdail, *v. n.* Prowl, saunter, loiter.
——**ag,** -aige, -an, *s.f.* Fragment.
——**ail,** *s.m.* Prowling, sauntering, loitering. A' d—, *pr.pt.* of dabhd. [dawdle.]
dà-bheathach, *a.* Amphibious.
————, *s.m.* Amphibious animal.
————**as,**** -nis, *s.m.* Amphibiousness.
dà-bheum, *s.m.* Kind of ear-mark on sheep, see under comharradh-cluais.
dà-bhileach, see dà-dhuilleach.
dà-bhliadhnach, -aich, *s.m.* see dò-bhliadhnach.
dabhoch, -oich, *s.m.* see dabhach.
dàcha, see dòcha.
†dàchadh, -aidh, *s.m.* Opinion, conjecture, likelihood.
dàchadh,** *a.* see dàchail.
dachaidh, -ean, *s.f.* Home, dwelling-place, residence, domicile. G' a dhachaidh féin, *to his own home.*
————, *adv.* Home, homeward. A' dol dhachaidh, *going home.* [Generally aspirated.]
dàchail,** *a.* Probable.
————**eachd,**** *s.f.ind.* Probability.
dà-chasach, *a.* Two-footed.
————, -aich, *s.m.* Biped. Gach d. a th' agam, *every biped I have.*
dà-cheannach, *a.* Having two heads, bicipitous. 2 Two-topped. Beannan d., *a two-topped hill.*
dà-chòmhlach, *a.* Bivalvular.
dà-chorpach, *a.* Having two bodies, bicorporal.
dà-chosach, see dà-chasach.
dà-chrannach, *a.* Biaxial. 2 Two-masted.

dà-chruthach, *a.* Doubly formed, compounded of two forms, biformed.
dà-chumachd, *s.f.ind.* Biformity.
dad, *s.& a.* Aught, anything. 2 Whit, trifle, jot. Cha'n 'eil dad math air, *it is not worth anything*; 'd è a th' ort? *what is wrong with you?* cha'n 'eil d., *nothing* (is wrong with me); d. a's leat-sa, *anything of yours*; cha'n abair mi d., *I will say nothing*; fear gun d., *a poor man*; cha robh e d. na bu mhiosa, *he was none the worse.* [Always used after an interrogative or negative clause.]
dadam, see dadum.
——unn, see dadmunn.
——unnach, see dadmunnach.
dadan, -ain, *s.m.*, *dim.* of dad.
dadhas, -ais, see dathas.
dà-dhathach, -aiche, *a.* Parti-coloured, bi-coloured.
dà-dhealbhta, *a.* Biformed.
d' a dheòin, *adv.* Spontaneously.
dà-dhuilleach, *a.* Bifoliated. 2 Two-folded, as a door.
——, *s.m.* Tway-blade—*orchis* or *listera ovata.* 2**Any bifoliated herb.

258. Dà-dhuilleach.

dadmunn, -uinn, *s.m.* Mote, atom, jot. 2** Anything. 3** Some little thing. 4 (AF) Mite, very small insect.
——ach, -aiche, *a.* Atomical. 2 Corpuscular.
——ach, -aich, *s.m.* Atomist.
——aiche, see dadmunach, *s.* 2 *comp.* of dadmunach.
dadum, -uim, *s. m.* Mote, atom, whit, jot. 2 Anything. 3 Some little thing. 4 Gloom.
——ach,†† *a.* Pertaining to motes, &c.
dà-fhaobhair, *a.* Two-edged.
dà-fhaobhrach, see dà-fhaobhair.
dà-fhiaclach, *a.* Having two teeth, bidental.
dà-fhichead, *a.* Forty.
dà-fhillte, *a.* Double, two-fold.
dà-fhoghair, *s.m.* Diphthong.

259. Dagaichean Gàidhealach.

dag, daige, *pl.* -an, -achan, & -aichean, *s. m.* Pistol. D. dìollaide, *a holster-pistol, blunderbuss*; paidhir dhag, *a pair of pistols.* [The change of meaning from *dagger* to *pistol* is one which occurs in the history of *pistol* itself, which originally meant a dagger.]
daga, see dag.
dagach, -aiche, *a.* Having a pistol or pistols. 2 Of, or belonging to, pistols. Gu gunnach d., *armed with guns and pistols.*
dagachan, **dagaichean**, } *n.pl.* of dag.
dagar dùbailt, *s.m.* Double dagger in *writing* (‡.)
dag-dialta, see dag-dìollaid.
dag-dìollaid, -achan-d-, *s.m.* Holster-pistol.
dagh, *a.* see deagh. *v.a.* †Dye
——adh, -aidh, *s.m.* see dathadh.
daghdag, see dabhdag.
dà-ghuth, *s.m.* Diphthong. 2**Empyreuma.
——ach,** *s.m.* Diphthong.
daibh, see doibh.
daibhear, -eire, *a.* see daibhir.
——,* -eir, *s.m.* Bankrupt.
daibheid,* *s.m.* Self-command, circumspection.
——each,* *a.* Self-denying.
†daibhleag, -eig, -an, *s.m.* Place of worship.
daibhreach, -reiche, *a.* see daibhir.
——d, *s.f.ind.* Poverty, necessity, want.
daibhreas, -eis, *s.m.* Poverty, want. (opposite of saibhreas.)
daibhir, *a.* Poor, needy, destitute. 2 Uncomfortable. 3* Adverse. D. no saibhir ge 'n robh mo chor, *let my lot be prosperous or adverse.*
——, *s.m.* The common or worst pasture of a farm ("Innis" is the best pasture. 2 Poor person.
daibhireach, see daibhreach.
dàich,** *s. f.* Beauty, comeliness, handsomeness.
——ealachd, *s.f.ind.* Handsomeness, beauty, gracefulness. 2 Dignity. 3 Plausibility. 4 False appearance.
dàicheil, -eala, *a.* Handsome, graceful. 2 Genteel. 3 Majestic, stately, dignified. 4 Haughty, proud. 5 Strong. 6 Keen. 7 Severe, hard. 8 Well appointed. 9 Bold—*Dain I. Ghobha.* 10 Queer—*The Aird.* 11* Plausible. 12 Outwardly a hero, inwardly a coward. [Has various meanings in different districts.] Is minic a bha 'n Donas d., *the Devil has often been found plausible*; le ceum d., *with a stately step*; is ann bòidheach 's cha'n ann d., *bonnie rather than graceful.*
daidean, -ein, *s.m.* Daddy. (child's prattle.) 2 Foster-father.
daidhbhir, -e, *a.* see daibhir.
daidhbhreas, -ris, see daibhreas.
daidhear, see daoidh.
†daidhm, -e, *a.* Poor, spoiled.
daididh, *s.m.* Daddy. (child's prattle.)
†daif, *s.m.* Drink. [** gives *s.f.*]
daigear,** -eir, *s.m.* Gaelic spelling of *dagger.*
daigeil,†† -eala, *a.* Firm, strong.
†daigh, *s. m.* Fire. 2 Pain. 3 Matter, cause. 4 Hope, confidence. (*now* dòigh.) 5‡‡Plunder. 6‡‡Slaughter. [** gives *s.f.*]
†daigh, *v.a.* Give, grant.
†——-bhiorasg, *s.m.* Fuel.
†daigheadh, -idh, *s.m.* Giving, delivering, granting, bestowing. 2**Great odds. A' d—, *pr pt.* of daigh.
daigheann,** see daingeann.
daighear, -ir, -an, *s.m.* see daoidh.
——ra, *a.* see daoidhearra.
daighneach, -ich, -ichean, see daingneach.
——adh, see daingneachadh.
daighnich, see daingnich.

daighnichte, see daingnichte.
dail, -e, -ean, *s.f.* Kind of wooden collar for cattle. 2 Stall-halter for a cow.
dail, dalach, -lthean, *s.f.* Field, dale, meadow, plain.
†dàil, *s.f.* Portion, share. 2 Tribe.
dàil, dàlach, dàlaichean, *s.f.* Delay, procrastination. 2 Meeting, convention, congress. 3 Attempt. 4 Friendship, attachment. 5 Fortress, fastness. 6 Credit, trust. 7 Preparation. 8 Interval. 9 Intermediate space between the rafters of a house. 10 Contact. 11 **Decree. 12**Nearness, neighbourhood. 13 **Desire, willingness. 14‡‡Account, history. 15‡‡Relation, friend. 16‡‡Sparingness. 17‡‡ Giving, bestowing. 18 *in government with the prep.* an, Hostile opposition. 19 Ox-bow. Thig gun d., *come without delay* ; d. eadar an dà làmhnain, *the space between the two couples* ; d. shia mìosan, *credit for six months* ; is coma leam dol 'na dh., *I don't like to get in contact with him*; feumaidh sin rudeigin an d. an Dòmhnaich, *we must have something in preparation for the Sabbath* ; cuir d. ann, *delay, procrastinate* ; thoir d., *give on trust or credit* ; chaidh sinn an d. a chéile, *we rushed towards each other* (to fight) ; le 'curach chaidh i 'na dh., *in her skiff she went to meet him* ; an rud anns an téid d., théid dearmad, *delay brings neglect.*
dail, *v.a.* see dailich.
dail-bhuntàta, *s.f.* Potato-field. Cha reic e a dh. air a tarsuinn, *he will not sell his potato-field cross-wise* (in such a way that the buyer can see the weak spots in it.) If he looked across (air a tarsuinn), the buyer would see the blanks, but he could not do so if he looked along the rows.
dail-chatha, *pl.* dailthean-c-, *s.f.* Pitched-battle. 2 Battle-field.
dail-chuach,§ -an, *s. m.* Dog-violet—*viola canina.*

260. Dail-chuach.

dàileach, -liche, *a.* Dilatory, tardy, procrastinating. 2††Pertaining to meetings.
———adh,** *s.m.* Adjournment, delay. A' d—, *pr.pt.* of dàilich.
daileachadh, -aidh, *s.m.* Distributing, act of distribution. A' d—, *pr.pt.* of dailich.
daileadh, -lidh, *s.m.* Tradition. 2 Affiance.
daileag, -eige, -an, *s.f.* see crann-pailm. 2 Little dale or meadow.
———ach, *a.* Abounding in little dales or meadows.
dailean, -ein, *s.m.* Scoff.
dailgheach, -ich, -an, *s.m.* The withy attached to a cow's collar, *prov.*
dailgionn, -inn,(AC) *s.m.* Prophecy, foretelling.
dailgneachd,(AC) *s.f.* Auspices, prophetic vision
dailich, *pr.pt.* a' daileachadh, *v.a.* Distribute, deal. 2 Give, deliver.
dàilich, *pr.pt.* a' dàileachadh, *v. a. & n.* Delay, procrastinate, postpone, prorogue. 2 Linger.
daille, see doille.
daillidh,** *a.* Corpulent.
dailte, *past pt.* of dailich.
dailtean, -an, *s.m.* Stripling. 2 Coxcomb, puppy, jackanapes. 3**Rascal.
———ach, -niche, *a.* Coxcomical.
dailteanas, -ais, *s.m.* Impertinence. 2 Foppery, coxcombry. 3**Scurrility.
dailthe, *prep.* After. see daithle.
dailtheach,†† *a.* Abounding in fields or plains.
dailthean, *n.pl.* of dail.
daimh, *gen. sing. & n.pl.* of damh.
dàimh, *s.m. & f.* Relationship, connection, affinity, friendship. 2**Kindness. 3**Friend. 4‡‡Relative situation. Cò ris tha do dhàimh? *with whom is thy connection?* mar ni athair d., *as a father befriends* ; an còmhstrì ri d., *in contest with friends;* dlùth an d., *closely connected* ; fad' a mach an d., *distantly related.*
†daimh, *a.* Troublesome.
†dàimh, *s.m.* Church. 2 House. [** gives *s.f.*] 3 People. 4 Assent, free will. 5 Poet. 6 Learned man. 7 Guest, stranger. 8(AH) Man who eats or otherwise helps himself to excess.
———each, -ich, *s.m.* Relative, friend. 2 Associate, companion. 3 Guest.
———each, -iche, *a.* Having many relations or friends. 2†† Related.
dàimhealachd, *s.f.ind.* Relationship. 2 Friendship, kindness. 3* Kindred disposition.
dàimheil, -heala, *a.* Affectionate towards one's relations. 2 Related, relative, connected. 3 Friendly. 4 Kind, benevolent. Gu d., *in a friendly manner.*
daimh-fheòil, -fheòla, *s.f.* Beef.
daimhich, *n. pl.* of daimheach.
†daimhleag, -eig, *s.f.* Place of worship.
daimsean, see daimsin.
———ach, see daimsineach.
daimsear, *s.m.* Rutting of deer. see bùiridh.
daimsin,§ *s.m.* Damson—*prunus damascena.*
———each, *a.* Abounding in, of, or like damsons.
daimsir, *s.m.* Mud.
dàin, *gen. sing. & n.pl.* of dàn.
daindeoin, see dh' aindeoin.
dàine, *comp.* of dàna.
daingean, -ein, -ngnean, *s.f.* see daingneach.
daingean, see daingeann.
daingeann, -geinn & daingne, *a.* Strong, firm. 2 Fortified. 3 Unmoveable, tight. 4**Tightly bound. 5††Straight. Gu d. làidir, *firmly and strongly.*
daingeann an ceart, *adv.* In thorough earnest.
†daingeann, *s.m.* Assurance, contract.
daingionn, *a.* see daingeann.
daingne, *comp.* of daingeann.
daingneach, -iche, -ichean, *s. f.* Stronghold, castle, fortification, fastness, garrison, fort. 2 Prison. 3**Compact, assurance. 4**Bulwark. 5**Ratification. Mo charraig 's mo dhaingneach, *my rock and my fortress* ; mar chrannaibh daingnich, *like the bars of a castle.*
———adh, -aidh, *s. m.* Fortifying. 2** Binding, fastening. 3**Establishing a ratification. 4**Fortification. 5**Constipation, constipating, constringating. 6 Confirming. 7 Founding. 8 Sanctioning. 9 Obliging, compelling. 10 Strengthening. A' d—, *pr.pt.* of daingnich.

daingneachail,** *a.* Affirmable, affirmative. 2 Corroborative.
———air,** *s.m.* Affirmer. 2 Corroborator.
———as, -ais, *s. m.* Same meanings as daingneachd.
daingneachd, *s.f.ind.* Strength, firmness, tightness. 2 Confirmation. 3**Fortification, bulwark. 4**Compact, ratification, affirmance, assurance, security. 5 Surety.
daingnich, *pr.pt.* a' daingneachadh, *v.a.* Strengthen, fortify, confirm, establish, found. 2 Bind, fasten, tighten. 3** Confirm, ratify, sanction. 4**Oblige, constrain. 5**Constipate.
———idh, *fut. aff. a.* of daingnich.
———te, *past pt.* of daingnich. Confirmed, fortified. 2 Established, founded. 3 Bound, tightened. 4**Obliged, constrained. Baile d., *a fortified town.*
dainn,* *s.f.* Rampart, barrier.
———each,* see daingneach.
———eachas, -ais *s.m.* see daingneachd.
dainnion, see daingeann.
†dain-oide, *s.m.* Schoolmaster.
†dair, -e, -ean, (darach) *s.f.* Oak.
dàir, dàra, *s.f.* Pairing of cattle, also dàireadh. 2(MMcD) Calving—*Lewis.* Bliochd is d. air an ni, *the cattle teeming with milk and calving.* When a cow is brought to the bull, they say in W. Isles, *tha 'n d. oirre* ; in Wester Ross, *tha i fo dhàir* ; in Argyll, *tha i air theas.*
dàir, *pr.pt.* a' dàireadh, *v.n.* Rut, copulate.
dairb,(AC) *s. f.* Insect of the beetle tribe.
———eag, -eige, -an, *s.f.* Tadpole. 2(AF) Minnow. 3 Any very small fish.
———eart,(AC) *s.m.* Water-beetle.
dairbh, *a.* see doirbh.
———, *s.m.* see doirb. 2 **Little slender person.
———re, *s.f.* Oak. 2 Nursery or grove of oaks.
daire, [-an &] -achan, see doire.
dàireach, *a.* Rutting, copulating, breeding.
dàireadh,** -ridh, *s.m.* Bulling, copulation, copulating. Bó air d., *a cow that is a-bulling.*
dairghe,** *s.f.* Oak-apple.
dairireach, -ich, -ichean, *s.f.* Loud rattling noise, noise of shooting. 2 Volley. 3 Smart blow.
dairirich, -e, *s.f.* see dairireach.
dàir-na-coille, *s. f.* The first night of the New Year, when the wind blows from the West—the night of the fecundation of trees.
dairt, -e, *s.f.* Heifer. 2**Clod.
dàirte, *s.f. & past pt.* of dàir.
———ach,** *a.* Of clods, full of clods.
dais, -e, -ean [& -eachan,] *s.f.* Heap or mow of peats or corn. 2*Pile of seasoned fish. 3 (M McL) Haystack.
———, *v.a.* Mow or pile, as seasoned fish. 2 Trample hay.
———, -eachan, *s. m.* Fool, blockhead. 2 (AC) Musical instrument. 3 (AF) Fallow deer or buck.
———each, -eiche, *a.* Having mows of hay or corn.
———eachan, -ain, *s.m.* Insipid rhymer, low-witted poet.
daisgean,** -ein, *s.m.* Writing-desk.
dait, *s.m.* Daddy—child's prattle.
dàite,†† *a.* see dòthta.
daite, *a. & past pt.* of dath. see dathta.
———ach, -iche, *a.* Fresh-coloured, fair-coloured. 2††Much coloured.
———an, -ein, *s.m.* "Daddy." †2 Foster father. †3 Foster child.
†daith, *a.* Quick, nimble, active, supple.
†———e, *s.f.* Revenge.
daithead, -eid, -an, *s.f.* Gaelic spelling of *diet.* (*Perthshire* dìot.) Meal, as dinner, &c. 2 (MMcL) Sufficiency.
dàithealachd, see dàichealachd.
daithear,** -eir, *s.m.* Avenger. 2 Revengeful men.
†daitheasg,** -eisg, *s.f.* Eloquence. 2 Speech 3 Remonstrance.
dàitheil, see dàicheil.
†d'aithle, *prep.* After.
daithte, see dathta.
———achan,* -ain, *s.m.* Miserable sized looking person.
daitidh, *s.m.* Daddy. Gaelic form of Welsh *tad.*
†dàl, see dàil.
†dala, *s. m.* News. 2 Oath. 3 Espousals. 4 Wedding.
dàla, *gen. sing.* of dàil.
dala, see dara. An dala, *the one of two.* †2 see dàil. †3 *adv.* As to, as for. 4 *gen.sing.* of dail
dàlach, *gen.* of dàil.
———d, *s.f.ind.* Delaying, act of delaying.
†dalaigh, *v.a.* Assign, appoint.
dà-làimh, *a.* see dà-làmhach. Claidheamh d., *a two-handed sword.*
dà-làmhach, -aiche, *a.* Ambidexter, equally expert with both hands.
———d, *s.f.* Ambidexterity.
dalan-dé, -ain-, see dearbadan-dé.
dalba, *a.* see dalma.
———chd,** *s.f.ind.* Impudence, pertness, forwardness.
†dalbh, *s.m.* Lie, contrivance.
dalbhadh,** -aidh, *s.m.* Sorcery.
dà-lid, *s.f.* Diæresis over a letter in writing(ä.)
dall, *pr. pt.* a' dalladh, *v.a. & n.* Blind, make blind. 2 Mislead. 3 Deceive. 4**Puzzle. Dallaidh tiodhlac, *a gift blindeth* ; dhall iad air an fhaghail, *they made for the ford* ; dh. iad air, *they attacked him severely.*
dall, doill, *s.m.* Blind person. Radharc iùil do 'n dall, *a guiding vision to the blind.*
dall, doille, *a.* Blind. 2 Ignorant. 3 Obscure. 4 Dark. 5**Misled. 6**Puzzled. 'San oidhche dhoirche dhaill, *in the pitchy dark night.*
dallabhrat,†† -an, *s.m.* Blinding bandage.
dallachran,†† -ain, *s.m.* Ignorance. 2 Blindness.
dallachreideamh,†† *s.m.* Blind faith.
dalladh, -aidh, *s.m.* Blinding. 2 Misleading. 3 Act of blinding or misleading. 4 Darkening. 5**Blindness. A' d—, *pr.pt.* of dall. D. na h-inntinn, *a blinding of the mind* ; a' d. a léirsinn, *darkening his vision* ; bha e air a dh., *he was blin' fou* ; air a sheann dh., *use and wont in drinking.*
——— -eun, -aidh-eun, *s. m.* Purblindness, defect of vision.
dallag, -aige, -an, *s.f.* Shrew-mouse—*sorex araneus*, dormouse. 2 Mole. 3 Leech. 4 Any little blind creature. 5 (DJM) Spotted dog-fish.—*scyllium catulus.* 6 Young dogfish. 7 Small shark. 8**Buffet. 9 (AF) King-fish.
———ach, *a.* Like, or pertaining to, a shrew-mouse, dormouse, mole or leech. 2**Buffeting.
——— -an-fheòir, *s. f.* Dormouse. 2 Mole. (AC) Grass mouse, shrew.
——— -an-fhraoich, *s.f.* Shrewmouse, field shrew.
——— -feòir, see dallag-an-fheòir.
——— -na-h-urlaich, see dallag.
dallaig, *gen. & dat. sing.* of dallag.
dall-aigeantach, -aiche, *a.* Dull, slow-witted, stupid.
dallan, -ain, *s. m.* Winnowing fan. 2 Blind person. **3 Short-sighted person. 4**Improvident person. 5**Blindfolded person. 6 ‡‡Great bulk.
———ach, -aich, *s.f.* Large winnowing fan (*Scots*, wecht.) 2 Volley, broadside. Leig

iad d., *they fired a volley or broadside.*
———ach, -aich, *s.m. & f.* Inebriation, state of complete intoxication. Air an d., *"blin' fou.*
———ach,†† *a.* Abounding in winnowing fans.
dallanachd,** *s.f.ind.* Winnowing with a large fan.
dallan-cloiche, -ain-ch-, *s.m.* Monumental stone.
dallan-dà, *s.m.* The game Blind man's buff. 2 (AH) Spider.
dallan-dait, see dallan-dà.
allan-dé, see dearbadan-dé.
dallan-nan-caorach,§ *s.m.* Large fuzz-ball, see beach.
dallaran, -ain, -an, *s.m.* Blind person. 2 Confused, stupid person.
———achd, *s.f.ind.* Blindness. 2 Confusedness. 3 Groping in darkness.
dall-bhrat, -an, *s.m.* Blinding bandage. 2 Dark covering or mantle. D. na h-oidhche, *the dark mantle of night.*
dall-cheo, *s.m.ind.* Dark thick mist. 2‡‡Gross darkness.
dall-cheòthar, -aire, *a.* Very misty.
dall-chreideamh, *s.m. & f.* Implicit faith.
dall-chreidmhiche,** *s.m.* Bigot.
dall-inntinneach, -niche, *a.* Stupid, weak-minded, dull-witted. 2††Dark-minded, blind.
dall-luch, *s.f.* Dormouse.
dall-oidhche, *s.f.* The darkest time of night. 2 Dark night. O' n òg-mhaduinn gu d., *from early morn till dark night.*
dall-sgiomh, -a, *s.m.* The alloy in metals.
dall-shùil, *s. f.* Dim eye. 2 Sightless eye. Meallaidh gach neul a dh., *every cloud deceives his dim eye.*
dallta,**s.m.* The very same case,way or method.
———,* *adv.* In the very same way or manner. D. Sheumais, *just as James would do* ; d. an fhir nach maireann, *just as he that is no more would have done.*
———ch, *a.* Tricky.
dalma, *a.* Bold, forward, audacious, impudent. 2**Stout. 3‡‡ Obstinate. Gu d., *stoutly, haughtily.*
———chd, *s. f. ind.* Impudence, audacity, forwardness, boldness, temerity. 2** Stoutness. 3‡‡Obstinacy. 4 Haughtiness.
dalta, [-an -achan &] -aichean, *s. m.* Foster-child. 2 God-child. 3 Step-child. 4‡‡Disciple.
dalta-baistidh, *s. m. & f.* God-son. 2 God-daughter.
dalta-boirionn,‡‡ *s.f.* Foster-daughter. 2 Step-daughter.
daltach, -aiche, *a.* Betrothed. 2 Of, or belonging to, a foster-child.
———an, *pl.* of dalta.
daltadh, see dalta.
daltan, -ain, -a, *s.m. dim.* of dalta. 2 Foster-son. 3**Disciple. 4‡‡Stripling.
dàm, -àim, *s.m.* Reservoir, conduit, mill-dam. 2 Black mud, mire—*Suth'd.*
damacraich,(CR) *s.f. & pr.pt.* Hesitating. 2 (DU) Walking unsteadily and clumsily. Tha e a' d. *he is undecided* ; ciod e an d. a th' ort ? *what makes you hesitate ?—W. of Ross-shire.*
damain,* *v.a.* Gaelic form of *damn.*
———te, *a. & past pt.* of damain. Accursed, most abandoned.
dàmais, -ean, *s. f.* Draughts (game.) Bòrd d., *a draught-board.*
damaisear,(CR) *s.m.* Mud, mire—*W. of Ross-sh.* 2 (AH) Large ugly pool of muddy water standing where it ought not to be, e.g. near a dwelling-house or farm-steading.
†damaiste, -an, *s.m.* Gaelic spelling of *damage.*

damanta, *a.* see damainte.
d'amh, (for domh) see do.
dàmh, *s.m.* Learned man 2***rarely* Learning.
†damh, *v.a.* Give, grant, permit.
damh, -aimh, *dat. pl.* daimh, *s.m.* Ox. 2 Hart, stag. 3 Male of the red deer. 4 Buck. 5 Beam, that part of a harrow in which the teeth are fixed. 6* Mast—*Ossian.* 7 Joist. †8‡‡ Earthquake. D. sùirn, *a kiln-joist* ; thuit an d., *the buck fell.*
———ach, *a.* Of, or belonging to, an ox or hart. 2 Full of oxen or harts.
———ach,** -aich, *s.m.* see dabhach.
†———adh, -aidh, *s.m.* Granting, giving, permission.
———aich, *gen.sing. & n.pl.* of damhach.
———ail, [-e &] -hala, *a.* Stupid, boorish. 2 Of, or belonging to, oxen.
———ail,** -ean, *s.m.* Student.
dàmhair, -e, *a.* Earnest, keen, eager, zealous. [** giues damhair.]
———, -ean, *s.f.* Rutting of deer. 2 Rutting-time. 3 The month of October [preceded by the art. *an.*] 4**Noise. 5 (CR) Time—*about Inverness & W. of Ross-shire.* Mu 'n d. seo an dé, *about this time yesterday* ; facal an d., *a word in season.* 6‡‡ Earnestness, keenness, 7 Rutting riot—*Dain Iain Ghobha.* Bhuail chuca an d., *the noise came suddenly upon them*; an d. a' mheadhon oidhche, *in the dead of night.* 8 Middle. An d. a' chuain, *in the middle of the ocean.*
———each, -riche, *a.* Keen, earnest, endeavouring, industrious, diligent. 2**Noisy. 3††Rutting.
———eachd, *s. f. ind.* Keenness, eagerness, diligence, industry. 2**Noisiness.
damhais,* *v n.* see danns.
damh-allaidh,(AF) *s.m.* Wild ox. 2 Wild stag. 3 Pygarg.
†damhamhail, *s.m.* Student.
damhan,** -ain, *s.m.* Spider.
damhan-alluidh, -ain-, *pl.* -ain, [& -a-,] *s. m.* Spider. Lìon an damhain-alluidh, *the spider's web.*
damhan-eallaich, see damhan-alluidh.
damhas, see danns.
damhasg, see dathas.
damh-cabrach,(AF) *s.m.* Antlered stag.
damh-dearg,(AF) *s.m.* Stag of red deer.
damhdha,** *a.* Scholastic.
damh-féidh,** *s.m.* Hart, stag, buck.
damh-fiadhaich,(AF) *s.m.* Wild ox, buffalo. 2 Pygarg.
damh-imir, *s.m.* Twenty-acre field.
damh-lann, -lainn, *s.m.* Ox-stall.
†damhliag, -aig, -an, *s.m.* Cathedral.
damhnadh,** -aidh, *s. m.* Band, tie. 2 Matter out of which anything is formed.
†damhna, *s.m.* Cause, reason.
damh-nartaidh,(AF) *s.m.* Bullock.
dà-mhogullach,(AF) *s.m.* Bivalve shell-fish.
dà-mhogullach,‡‡ *a.* Bivalve.
†damh-oide,** *s.m.* Doctor. 2 Teacher, school-master.
†———achd, *s.f.* School-instruction.
damhra,(AF) *s.m.* Wild beast.
damhs, *v.n.* see danns.
damhsa, *s.m.* see dannsadh.
d'amhsa, (for domh-sa, *emphat.* of do.)
damhsa-clis,* see dannsadh-clis.
damhsair, -ean, see dannsair.
damh-shùileach,‡‡ *a.* Ox-eyed.
†damhtha, *a.* Scholastic. 2 *s.m.* Scholar.
damh-ursainn, *s.m.* (*lit.* door-posts ox, i.e. the supporting ox) The best or only ox of a widow, taken by the proprietor on the death

of her husband.
damnach,** *a.* Condemnatory.
————adh,** -aidh, *s. m.* Condemnation, condemning. 2 Doom. A' d—, *pr. pt.* of damnaich.
damnadh, -aidh, *s.m.* Cursing. damning. Condemnation, condemning. 3* Doom, judgment, punishment.
damnaich, *pr.pt.* a' damnachadh, *v.a.* Condemn, doom, judge, punish. Damnar e, *he shall be damned.*
————te,** *past pt.* of damnaich. Condemned, doomed, judged. 2 Punished.
dà-mogullach,(AF) see dà-mhogullach.
damuinte, see damaint.
dàn, -àin, *pl.* dàin dàna & dàintean, *s.m.* Poem. 2 Song. 3**Verse. 4 Treasure. 5 ‡‡Work. Ma tha sin an d., *if that be ordained*; bha sin an d. dhomh, *that was my fate*; seann dàin le Oisean, *Ossian's ancient poems*; is duilich cur an aghaidh dàin, *to oppose fate (or destiny) is difficult*; ma tha e 'n d. dhomh a bhi beò, *if it be destined for me to live*; am fear do 'n d. an donas, 's ann da bheanas, *it is he that will suffer for whom evil is destined.*
dàn, -àin, *s.m.* Fate, destiny. 2 Decree, predestination.
——, *a.* see dàna.
dàn, -a, *a.* Bold, daring, intrepid, resolute. 2 Confident, audacious, presumptuous, forward, impudent. Cha d. leam innseadh dhuit, *I do not think it presumptuous in me to tell you;* cho d. 's a chaidh e air aghaidh! *how impudently he behaved!* or *how resolutely he went forward!* d. mar leòghann, *bold as a lion.*
Dana,(CR) *s.f.* The Evil One. Tha e 'dol thun na Dana, *he is going to ruin.*
dànach, -aiche, *a.* Poetical, of, or connected with, poems, metrical.
——,** -aich, *s.m.* Fatalist.
dànachd. *s.f.ind.* Poetry. 2 Poesy, art of composing poetry. 3 see dànadas.
dànadail,** *a.* Fated, destined.
dànadas, -ais, *s. m.* Assurance, presumption, audacity, boldness. 2 Familiarity. 3‡‡Security. Agus mar an ceudna o pheacadh dànadais cum t' òglach air 'ais, *keep back thy servant also from presumptuous sin*; am bheil d. agad mo bhualadh? *have you the boldness to strike me?*
dànaich, *pr. pt.* a' dànachadh, *v.a.* Defy, challenge, dare. 2 Adventure.
†danaigh, see danaich.
†danair, *s.m.* Stranger. 2 Foreigner. 3 Guest.
†——eachd,** *s.f.ind.* State of being strange or foreign.
dàn-aoghaireil, *s.m.* Pastoral poem.
danar,(AF) *s.m.* Peregrine, see seabhag.
danaradh, see danarra.
danardha, see danarra.
————chd, see danarrachd.
danarra, *a.* Stubborn, obstinate, contumacious, presumptuous, opinionative. 2 Impudent, forward. 3 Firm, steady. 4 Bold, resolute, undaunted. 5‡‡Froward.
————chd, *s.f.ind.* Stubbornness, obstinacy, contumacy. 2 Presumption, forwardness, impudence. 3 Boldness, resolution. 4 Opinionativeness.
dàn-cluiche, *s.m.* Dramatic poem.
dàn-cruite, *s.m.* Lyric poem.
dàn-mór, *s.m.* Epic poem.
dannarra, see danarra.
†dànndha, *a.* Fatal.
danns, *pr.pt.* a' dannsadh, *v.n.* Dance, hop, skip.
——a, *s.m.* see dannsadh.
——adh, -aidh, *s.m.* Dancing, act of dancing. 2**Ball. A' d—, *pr.pt.* of danns. Le d., *with dancing*; maighstir-dannsaidh, *a dancing master;* seòmar-dannsaidh, *a ball-room.*
dannsadh-clìs, *s.m.* Corant.
——adh-deise,** *s.m.* Strathspey.
——adh-nan-clag, *s.m.* Morris-dance.
——aidh, *gen. sing.* of dannsadh. 2 *fut. aff. a.* of danns.
——ail,** *a.* Fond of dancing.
——air, -ean, *s.m.* Dancer. D. dubh an uisge, *a water-spider*; deagh dh., *a good dancer.*
——aireachd,** *s.f.ind.* Dancing.
†dant, -aint, *s.m.* Morsel. mouthful. 2 Share, portion.
dàntuigheacad, see dànachd.
dàntachd, *s.f.ind.* Fatalism. 2**Poetry (dànachd.)
dao,‡ *a.* Obstinate.
daobhaidh, -e, *a.* Wicked. 2 Perverse, stubborn.
daoch, *s.f.ind.* Strong dislike, disgust, antipathy. 2 Horror, fright.
——,** -oich, *s.m.* Periwinkle, sea-snail.
——ag,** -aig, -an, *s. f.* Small periwinkle or sea-snail.
——ail, -ala, *a.* Disgusting, exciting great aversion. 2 Confounded.
——al,** -ail, *s.m.* Morsel, bit.
——alachd, *s.f.ind.* Disgustfulness.
†daochan, -ain, *s.m.* Vexation. 2 Anger, fit of passion.
†————ach, *a.* Angry, passionate.
daoi, *a.* & *s.m.* see daoidh.
d'aoibh, for d' uibh.
daoibhir, *a.* see daibhear.
daoidh, -e, *a.* Wicked, foolish, perverse, turbulent, worthless. 2 Weakly, feeble. 3(AH) Adverse to taking medicines, cordials or special diets in sickness, when coaxed to do so by nurses or friends. Tha e cho daoidh (daobhaidh) 's ged bu phàisd e, *he is as difficult to coax as a child would be.* Cuideachd dhaoine d., *the company of foolish men.*
——, -e, -ean, *s.m.* Wicked man, reprobate, rogue. 2**Foolish man. 3**Vain man. 4(AF) Wild beast. Comhairle nan d., *the council of the wicked*; rug e air an d., *he seized the vain man.*
——eachd, *s.f.ind.* Wickedness, folly, worthlessness. Moladh na daoidheachd, *praise from the worthless.*
——ear, *s.m.* Rogue, wicked man.
——earra, *a.* Sly.
daoifhearachd, see daoidheachd.
daoighear, see daoidh.
daoil, -ean, *s.f.* see deala. 2 *gen.sing.* of daol.
——each,** *a.* Like, or of, a leech. 2 Full of leeches.
daoimean, -ein, -an, *s.m.* Diamond.
————ach, *a.* Tesselated. 2 Full of diamonds. 3 Of or like diamond.
†Daoin, *s.f.* Thursday.
daoine, *pl.* of duine. Móran dhaoine, *many people.*
————ach, -iche, *a.* Populous, numerous.
————achd, *s.f.ind.* Population.
————as, -eis, *s.m.* see duinealas.
daoin'-itheadh,‡‡ *s.m.* Anthropophagy.
daoire, *comp.* of daor, Dearer, dearest. Ni 's d., *dearer.*
——,* *s.m.* Extreme dearness. 2 Dearth.
——ad,** *s.m.* Dearth, A' dol an d., *getting dearer and dearer.*
——id, *comp.* of daor. Is d. e sin, *it is dearer on that account.*
——achd,‡‡ *s.f.* Chargeableness.

daoireagan, -ain, *s.m.* *prov.* for doireagan.
daoir-fhine,** *s.f.* Subjected or enslaved people.
daoirich, *gen.* & *dat. sing.* see daoraich.
daoir-mhaighstir, see daor-mhaighstir.
daoirse, *s.f.ind.* Dearth, scarcity. 2 Famine. 3**Captivity, slavery, see daorsa.
——ach,** *a.* Afflicted with dearth or famine. 2 In captivity or slavery.
——ach,** *s.m.* Captive, slave.
daoirsinn, *s.f.* see daorsainn.
daoite, (ma dhaoite—for math dh' fhaoiteadh) Perhaps.
daol, -oil, *s.f.* Beetle, chafer. 2 Bug. 3**Worm. 4** Caterpillar. 5(AF) Fierce animal. An d. a réir a ghnè, *the beetle after his kind.*
daolag, -aige, -an, *s.f.* Little beetle or chafer. 2 Bug. 3 Miser. 4 *in derision* Slovenly woman. 5 Lazy young female. 6**Worm. 7** Caterpillar. Gun bhi ro chaithleach no 'm dh., *without being a spendthrift or a miser.*
daolagach, -aiche, *a.* Abounding in beetles, worms or caterpillars. 2**Vermicular.
daolag-bhreac, -an-breaca, *s.f.* Lady-bird, lady-cow.
daolag-bhreac-dhearg, -an-breac-dearga, *s.f.* Lady-bird, lady-cow.

261. Daolag-bhreac-dhearg.

daolag-bhuidhe,* *s.f.* Chafer.
daolag-dhearg-bhreac, see daolag - bhreac-dhearg.
daolag-ghorm,(AH) *s.f.* Cockchafer.
daolair, -e, -ean, *s.m.* Lazy, inactive man. 2 Mean, sneaking, grovelling fellow. 3††Miser.
——each,** *a.* Lazy, lounging.
——eachd, *s.f.ind.* Penury. 2 Laziness, inactivity. 3**Frequent lounging. 4 Meanness.
daol-bhreac,(AH) *s.f.* Lady-bird. 2 Beetle.
daol-bhuidhe,(AF) *s. f.* Yellow worm or caterpillar.
daol-chaoch, (AF) *s.f.* Blind stag-beetle.
daol-dhubh,** *s.f.* Black-beetle, cockroach.
daomhais,** *v.a.* Ruin, demolish.
†**daon**, *v.a.* Ruin, demolish.
daonachd, see daonnachd.
daonail,(AC) *s.* Mankind. Roimh dh., *against mankind.*
daonalt,** *adv.* *prov.* for daonnan.
——a,** *adv.* Perpetually.
daonda, see daonna.
daondach, see daonnachdach.
daondan, see daonnan.
d' aon fhuil,** *a.* Akin, allied, related.
daonna, *a.* Human. 2 Humane, charitable, liberal. 3 Hospitable. 4 Civil An cinne d., *mankind.*
——ch, -aiche, *a.* see daonna.
——chd, *s.f.ind.* Humanity, charity, benevolence, liberality, hospitality. 2**Civility. Fear na d., *the humane man* ; an d., *in liberality.*
daonnachdach, -aiche, *a.* Liberal, benevolent, hospitable, charitable, almsgiving. 2**Civil.
daonnachdail,** *a.* Same meanings as daonnachdach.
daonnairceach, -eiche, *a.* see daonnachdach.
daonnan, *adv.* Always, continually, at all times, habitually.
daonnanach,‡‡ -aiche, *a.* Continual.
daonndach, -aiche, *a.* Humane.
daonntach, see daonndach.
daontan,(CR) *Suth'd* for daonnan (& *aspirated*) Is tha 'nis 'nan cuideachd dhaontan, *and he is always in their company now.*
daor-, †† *intensive particle.*
daor, -aoire, *a.* Dear, costly, scarce, precious, 2 Enslaved, bound firmly. 3 Imprisoned. 4 Condemned. 5 Deeply involved. 6 Guilty. 7* Most abandoned, completely corrupted. 8††Slavish. Chuir e ceangal gu d. air an righ, *he bound the king firmly* or *in subjection* ; bliadhna dh., *a year of scarcity;* d. shlaightear, *a most abandoned rascal* ; d. mheirleach, *a most abandoned thief*; d. bhodach, *a complete churl*; d. bhalach, *a complete boor*; mar dhaoine d., *like bondmen* ; bean d., *a bondwoman* ; gu d., *dearly*; is d. leam e, *I think it dear;* is tuilleadh 's d. leam e, *I think it too dear;* tha d.-an-ceannach aig an duine bochd eadhon air cadal na h-oidhche, *the poor man pays dearly even for his night's rest*—he would need to be working even at night to make both ends meet.
——,** -oir, *s.m.* Slave. †2 Earth, land.
——, *v.a.* & *n.* Raise the price, make dearer. 2 Sentence, doom, condemn. 3 Enslave.
——ach, -aich, *s.f.* Intoxication, drunkenness. Air an daoraich, *drunk*; cha'n fhaicear d. air 's cha'n fhaicear aodach air, *he 's never seen drunk and he 's never seen properly clad*—said of a person who is by no means a spendthrift, and yet is ever in difficulties ; tha 'n d. air, *or* tha e fo 'n d., *he is drunk.*
——achadh, -aidh, *s.m.* Act of raising the price or enhancing the value of anything. 2 Act of condemning, condemnation. A' d—, *pr.pt.* of daoraich.
daorad, -aid, see daoiread.
daoradh, see daorachadh.
daoraich, *pr. pt.* a' daorachadh, *v.n.* Make dearer, enhance the value of.
daorair,** *s. m.* Slave, bondman. 2 Captive. 3 Oppressed man. 4 Oppressor.
daoranach, -aich, *s. m.* Slave, bondman. 2 Captive.
daor-bhalach, -aich, *s.m.* Man-slave, captive. 2 Unmannerly, low-bred fellow, churl.
daor-bhean, *s.f.* Bondwoman.
daor-bhodach, -aich, *s.m.* Slave. 2 Churl.
daor-chlann,** *s. pl.* Slaves. 2 Servants. 3 Plebeians.
daor-éigeantas, -ais, *s. m.* Absolute necessity.
daorgan, *corruption* of an t-adharcan.
daor-ghille,** -an, *s.m.* Man-slave.
daor-mhaighstir,** *s. m.* Taskmaster. 2 Oppressor.
daormunn, -uinn, -an, *s.m.* Dwarf. 2 Miser, niggard. 3 Curmudgeon.
——ach, *a.* Dwarfish.
daor-òglach, -aich, *s. m.* Slave, bondman. 2 Captive.
daorsa, *s.f.ind.* Bondage, captivity. 2 Dearth, famine. Ar clann an d., *our children in captivity.*
daorsadh, -aidh, *s.m.* see daorsa.
daorsa-geamhail, *s.f.* Bondage of fetters.
daorsainn, *s. f.* Famine, dearth. 2 Bondage, slavery.
daorsann, -ainn, *s.f.* see daorsa.
daorta, *past pt.* of daor. Condemned, convicted.
daor-thaigh, -ean, *s.m.* Prison, house of bondage.
daosgar,** -air, *s.m.* Refuse, remainder.
——,** *a.* Unteachable.
——ach,** *a.* Mobby.
—— -sluaigh,** *s.m.* Mob, populace.

daoth, *a.* Obstinate, stubborn.
†daothain,** *s.f.* Sufficiency, enough. Dh' ith e a dh.. *he ate enough.*
dà-pheighinn, *s.m.* Ancient coin of two pennies Scots, or one-sixth penny sterling.
dà-phunc,** *s.m.* Diphthong.
————ach, -aich, *s.m.* Diphthong.
————ach, -aiche, *a.* Diphthongal.
dar, *prov.* for 'nuair. *adv.* When, while.
dar, *prep.* By, through. [Used only in swearing, as, dar mo làimh, *by my hand.*]
da 'r, *prep.* (for do ar, *to our.* Sometimes used in error for de ur.) 2 (for do bhur,) *to your.*
dara, *a.* Second, either, either of two. An d. h-uair, *the second time*; an d. h-àite, *the second place*; an dara là mu dheireadh de 'n mhios a dh'fhalbh, *the last day but one of last month* ; chaidil mi dara leth na h-uine, *I slept half the time* ; an e ministear a tha anns an dara fear aca seo ? *do you mean to say that one of these two men is a minister ?* ; bheir thusa air an dara fear, agus beiridh mis' air an fhear eile, *you catch one, and I will catch the other.* D. does not aspirate, cha d' fheum i riamh an dara gluasad, *she never required a second urging* ; thoir dhomh an dara fios ma's falbh thu as a seo, *tell me one way or the other before you leave here* ; exceptions,—an d. mhàireach, *the second morning*** ; togaidh mi thu an dara mhàireach—*Bishop Carsewell.* For " an d. cuid" see notes under *cuid.* Abbreviated 2nd. 2ra.
darab, (do+an+robh) *v.* To whom was.
dar-abhall, see dar-ubhall.
darach, -aich, *s. m.* Oak-tree—*quercus robur.* Badge of the Camerons. 2 Oak-timber. 3 Oak-wood. 4 *by metaphor,* Ship. Craobh-dharaich, *an oak-tree* ; sròn daraich, *an oak prow.*
dàrach, *a.* see dàireach. Gu bliochdach, dàrach, sruth-bhainneach, *milky, breeding and milk-flowing.*
darach-buidhe, *s.f.* Wainscot.
darach-sìor-uaine,§ *s. m.* Evergreen oak, see craobh-thuilm.
daradh, see dara.
dàradh, see dàireadh.
darag,§ -aige, -an, *s.f.* Oak-tree. 2 Oak wood. 3* Stump of a tree. 4 Small stone.
———-thalmhuinn, *s.f.* Germander,—1 Plant 2 Bird.
dà-ramhach, *s.m.* Two-oared boat, see bàta,p.78.
dararach, see dairirich.
dararaich, -e, *s.f.* see dairirich.
†daras, -ais, *s.m.* Home, dwelling.
†darb, -a, *s.m.* Worm, reptile.
†darbh, -airbh, *s.m.* Coach, chariot.
darcain, *gen. sing. & n. pl.* of darcan.
darcan, -ain, *s. m.* The hollow of the hand. 2 Acorn. 3**Teal, coot. 4††Pine-cone. †5 Mast.
————ach,** *a.* Abounding in acorns or teals.
darcon,** *s.* Dram, (measure.)
†dardal, *s.m.* Storm. 2‡‡Weather. 3 Severe season.
dar-daoil,(AF) *s.f.* Venomous beetle.
da rìreadh,* *adv.* In earnest, seriously. An ann an d. a tha thu ? *are you in earnest ?*
†darn, -airn, *s.m.* School.
dàrna, *a.* see dara.
———dh, see dara.
darnaig,‡ *s.f.* Gaelic spelling of *darning.*
dàrail, -e, *a.* Libidinous.
darsa, see daras.
darsan,** see dearrasan.
†dart, -airt, *s.m.* Dart.
†dart, *v.a.* Bull a cow.
dartach,(AF) -aich, *s.m.* Two-year-old bull.
dartaidh,(AF) *s.m.* Heifer.
dartaidh-Inide, (AF) *s.m.* Heifer three years old at Shrovetide.
dartaig,(AF) *s.f.* Yearling cow.
dartan,** -ain, *s.m.* Herd, drove. 2 Two-year-old bull.
——— -eallaigh.(AF) *s.m.* Herd, drove.
†dartluich, *a.* Impossible, see fairtlich.
dar-ubhall, -aill, -ubhlan, *s.m.* Oak-apple. 2 Gall-nut.
†das, -ais, *s.m.* see dasg.
dàsachd, *s.f.ind.* Fierceness, furiousness, madness, rage, fury. 2**Impertinence.
————ach, -aiche, *a.* Fierce, furious, mad. 2**Impertinent, assuming.
dàsaidh, -e, *a.* Furious. 2(DU) Audacious.
da-san, *prep. pron. emphat.* (do+esan) To himself. [Generally aspirated.] Thoir dha-san e, *give it to himself.*
†dasan, *a.* Binocular.
dàsan, -ain, *s.m.* Fury, frenzy.
———ach, -aiche, *a.* Cunning, wily. 2 Presumptuous. 3 Furious, fierce, frantic.
———achd,** *s.f.ind.* Furiousness, fierceness, frenzy.
dasg, -aisg, -an, *s.m.* Gaelic spelling of *desk.*
dà-sgiathach,** *a.* Bipennated, two-winged.
dà-sgoltadh, *s.m.* Ear-mark on sheep. [For its position see comharradh-cluais.]
dà-sheadh, *s.m.* Ambiguity.
————ach,‡‡ *a.* Ambiguous.
dà-shealladh, -aidh, *s. m.* Secondsight, see sealladh.
dà-shiolach, *a.* Dissyllabic
dà-shioladh,** *s.m.* Dissyllable.
dà-shligheach,‡‡ *a.* Bivious.
dà-shùileach,** *a.* Binocular. 2 Having two loops.
dasunnach, see dàsanach.
†data, *a.* Pleasant, handsome, agreeable.
datan, see daitean.
dàth, see dòth.
dath, *v.a.* Colour, dye, tinge stain.
——, -a, -an [& -aithean,] *s.m.* Colour, stain, dye, tincture. 2 Colouring, appearance. Cha luidh d. air dubh, luidhidh dubh air gach d., *black materials will not dye a colour, but any colour will take black* ; do ghruaidh air d. na céire, *thy cheeks coloured like red wax* ; d. bréige, *a false dye* ; dathan eug-samhuil, *various colours.*

The following are the principal native vegetable dyes used in Gaeldom, with the colours they produce. Several of the tints are very bright and pretty, but have now, unfortunately, in many cases been superseded by foreign mineral dyes.

Claret—corcur—a lichen scraped from the rocks and steeped in urine three months,then taken out, made into cakes and hung in bags to dry. When used, these cakes are reduced to powder and the colour fixed with alum.

Black (finest) —Common dock root with copperas. 2 Darach, *oak* bark and acorns, with copperas. 3 (or grey) Seilistear, *iris* root. 4 Sgitheach, *hawthorn* bark with copperas. 5 Alder bark with copperas. 6 (bluish) Common sloe—*prunus spinosa,* preas-nan-àirneag. 2 (bluish) Red bearberry—*arbutus uva ursi,* grainnseag.

Blue—blaeberry, with alum or copperas. 2 Elder, with alum. 3 Ailleann, *elecampane.*

Brown—Common yellow wall-lichen—*parmelia parietina.* 2 Dark cnotal —*parmelia cetarophilla.* 3 Duileasg, *dulse*—kind of seaweed. 4 Currant with alum. 5 Darach (*oak*) bark, or berries of craobh-an-dromain, *elder.* 6 (*Dark chestnut*) Roots of rabhagach, *white water-lily.* 7 (*Dark*) Blaeberry with nut-galls. 8 (*Reddish*) The dark purple lichen, 'cen cerig cen du'—(gun chéire gun dubh—*neither crimson nor black*) treated in the same manner as the lichen for *claret* dye. 9 (*Philamot*) — yellowish (dead leaf coloured) cnotal—*parmelia saxatilis.*

Drab or *Fawn,*—Birch bark, *betula alba.*

Green—Ripe privet berries with salt. 2 Wild mignonette, *reseda luteola,* lus buidhe mór, with indigo. 3 Rùsg conuisg, *whin* bark. 4 Cow-weed. 5 (*Lively*) Common broom. 6 (*Dark*) Heather, *erica cinerea,* fraoch bhadain, with alum. The heather must be pulled before flowering, and from a dark shady place. 7 Iris leaf, duilleag seilisteir.

Magenta—Dandelion,—*contodon taraxacum,* bearnan Brìde.

Orange—Ragweed (stinking Willie)—*senecio Jacobœa,* buaghallan. 2 Barberry root—*berberis vulgaris,* barbrag. 3 (*dark*)—Bramble—*rubus fruticosus,* preas smeur.

Purple—Euonymous (spindle-tree,) with salammoniac. 2 Sundew—*drosera rotundifolia,* lus-na-feàrnaich. 3 Blaeberry—*vaccinium myrtillis,* with alum.

Red—Tormentil—*potentilla tormentilla,* leanartach. 2 Rock-lichen — *ramalina scopulorum,* cnotal. 3 White cnotal—*lecanora pallescens,* cnotal geal. 4 (*fine*)—Rue—*gallium virum,* ladies' bedstraw. A very fine red is obtained from this. Strip the bark off the roots, then boil them in water to extract the remainder of the virtue, then take the roots out and put the bark in and boil that and the yarn together, adding alum to fix the colour. *Gallium boreale* treated in the same way alsc produces a red dye. 5 (*purple*)—Blaeberry, *vaccinium myrtillis,* lus-nan-dearc, with alum, verdigris and sal-ammoniac. 6 (*crimson*)— cnotal corcur—*lecanora tartarea,* white and ground and mixed with urine. This was once in great favour for producing a bright crimson dye. 7 (*scarlet*)—limestone lichen—*urceolaria calcaria,* cnotal clach-aoil. Used by the peasantry in limestone districts, as Shetland. 8 (*scarlet*) Ripe privet berries with salt.

Violet—Wild cress—*nasturtium officinalis*—biolair. 2 Bitter vetch—*orobus tuberosus*—cairmeal. 3 Bilberries fixed with alum.

Yellow—Apple-tree, ash and buckthorn. 2 Poplar and elm. 3 Roid, *bog-myrtle.* 4 Ash roots. 5 Teazle—*dipsacus sylvestris*—lus-anfhùcadair *or* leadan. 6 Raineach mhór, *bracken* roots. 7 Cow-weed. 8 Tops and flowers of fraoch, *heather.* 9 Wild mignonette—*reseda luteola,* dried, reduced to powder and boiled. 10 Leaves and twigs of beithe beag, *dwarf birch* 11 (*bright*) Sundew with ammonia.—*drosera rotundifolia* — lus-na-feàrnaich. 12 (*rich*) Achlasan Chalum Chille, *St.John's wort,* fixed with alum. 13 (*dirty*) Peat soot. 14 Rhubarb, (monk's)—*rymex alpinus*—lus-na-purgaid.

The process employed is to wash the thread thoroughly in urine long kept (fual,) rinse and wash in pure water, then put into the boiling pot of dye which is kept boiling hard on the fire. The thread is lifted now and again on the end of a stick, and again plunged in until it is all thoroughly dyed. If blue, the thread is then washed in salt water, but any other colour in fresh.

dàtha-bàn,§ *s.m.* Dropwort—*œnanthe.*

dathach, -aiche, *a.* Coloured. 2 Of various colours. 3**Colouring. 4**Apt to tinge.

———-adh,** -aidh, *s.m.* Colouring, dyeing, staining. A' d—, *pr. pt.* of dathaich.

dathadair, -ean, *s.m.* Dyer. Fitheach dubh air mullach an taighe, fios gu nighean an dathadair, *a black raven on the roof, a warning to the dyer's daughter—a death omen, suggesting the probability of there being clothes to dye black.*

————eachd, *s. f. ind.* Trade of a dyer. 2 Process of dyeing. Ri d., *dyeing;* ris an d., *at the trade of a dyer.*

dàthadh, -aidh, *s.m.* Singeing, act of singeing, see dòthadh.

dathadh,** -aidh, *s.m.* Dyeing, tincturing. 2 Dye, colour, tincture. A' d—, *pr. pt.* of dath.

dathag,** -aig, -an, *s. f.* Worm in the human body.

———-ach,** *a.* Abounding in worms, as a body. 2 Like a worm.

——— -mhortach, *a.* Destructive as worms.

dathaich,** *pr. pt.* a' dathachadh, *v.a.* Colour, dye, tincture, stain.

———-te,** *past pt.* of dathaich.

dathaidh, *fut. aff. a.* of dath.

-———, see dachaidh.

dathaigh, see dachaidh.

dathail, *a.* Coloured. 2 Well-coloured. 3 Decent, comely. 4 Agreeable.

———eachd,** *s. f. ind.* Pleasantness, comeliness, decentness. 2 Finery.

dathais, -e, -ean, *s.f.* see dathas.

dathan, *n.pl.* of dath.

dathas, -ais, *dat.pl.* dathasaibh, *s. m.* Fallow-deer, buck of the fallow-deer.

dath-chlodhach, -aiche, *a.* Parti-coloured.

†dathnaid, -ean, *s.f.* Foster-mother.

dath-reodha,(AF) *s.m.* Mole.

dath-ruadh,(AH) *s.m.* Saw-dust of Californian red-wood tree, used for dyeing purposes.

dà-theangach, *a.* Bilinguous, bi-lingual.

dàthta, see dòthta.

dathta, *past pt.* Coloured, stained.

dè ? *int.pron.* What? Dè sin ? *what is that?* dè 'b' aill leat ? *what is your will ?* Curtailed form of ciod e ? *what is it ?* Dè an t-each a th' agad ! *what an extraordinary horse you have !*

de, *prep.* Of, off. According to MacBain, the peculiar custom of confusing this word with do, *to,* in speaking Gaelic, extends back to Old Irish in pre-accentual *de* compounds, but the erroneous practice has no doubt largely been increased by the publishers of the Gaelic Scriptures, the instances of the use of *do,* instead of *de* making the meaning of the text in Gaelic just the opposite of what the original conveys. It is strange how tenacious some Gaelic writers are of the pernicious custom of using *do* for both *de* and *do,* while it is quite plain that the meaning of one is just the opposite of the other. It is no excuse to say that it is often spoken so (in some places *de* is practically obsolete) for it is the duty of scholars and those who write or speak Gaelic, to do so correctly, and so help to correct popular errors instead of perpetuating them. This is only one case among many, where any unprejudiced person can see the absolute necessity of Gaelic being taught in every school, at least in Gaelic-speaking districts, to prevent its becoming a mixture of exceptions like English.

An gabh thu roinn dheth sin ? *will you take a part of that ?* bheir mi 'a ghlas de 'n dorus, *I will take the lock off the door* ; thug mi 'n ceann de m' òrdaig, *I took the tip off my thumb.* If *do* be substituted for *de* in each of above examples, the result is mere nonsense.

De mar a bha mo dhalta de 'n chomhraig? *how did my foster-son come off in the battle?* [*De* becomes *dh'* before a vowel, and *a dh'* if also following a consonant, it aspirates everything following it, and governs the Dative case.]
Armailt mhór de dhaoinibh agus a dh' eachaibh, *a great army of men and horses*; làn de reubainn agus a dh' aingidheachd, *full of ravening and wickedness.*
De is thus declined in conjunction with the personal pronouns:
Sing. diom, *of me*, *Plur.* dinn, *of us*,
diot, *of thee*, dibh, *of you*,
deth, *of him*, diubh, *of them*,
dith, *of her*. *m. & f.*
The initial *d* is generally aspirated (dhiom, dhiot, &c.) in composition.
de', *prep.* Of or off his or its. [Used before a word beginning with a vowel, or when *poss. pron.* is understood.]
de' h-, *prep.* Of or off her, (*poss. pron.*) [Used before a word beginning with a vowel, or when *poss. pron.* is understood.]
dé,** *s.m.* Day.
Dé, *gen.sing.* of Dia.
dé, *adv.* (an dé) Yesterday. Air bho 'n dé, *the day before yesterday.*
deabastach,‡‡ -aiche, *a.* Bawdy.
dèabh, *pr.pt.* a' dèabhadh, *v.a.* & *n.* Drain, dry up, shrink. 2**Battle. †3 Encounter. †4 Hasten. [pronounced *dè-u.*]
——ach,** *a.* Contentious. 2 Litigious. 3 Causing haste. 4 Apt to dry up.
——adh, -aidh, *s.m.* Drying, draining. 2 Evaporating. 3 Shrinking, as the staves of a dish. 4 Circumstance of becoming dry, having shrunk or become parched. 5 Hasty encounter. 6**Wrangling. †7 Skirmish, battle. †8 Haste, despatch, hurry. Thun ar fuil a dh., *almost drying up our blood.* A' d—, *pr. pt.* of dèabh. A Lochbroom rhymer says "'Se d. sluagh an t-saoghail thu," by which he seems to mean, *you are of the scum of creation*, This word does not appear to be used in this sense elsewhere.—D.U.
——aidh, *fut. aff. a.* of dèabh. 2 *gen.sing.* of dèabhadh.
deabhunn, *s.m.* Horse-fetter.
deabhlach, see deabhthach.
dèabhta, *past pt.* of dèabh. Parched, shrunk, dried up.
†deabhthach, -aiche, *a.* Contentious. 2 Litigious.
†deacaid, -e, -ean, *s.f.* Jacket. 2 Waistcoat. 3 *Bodice. 4 Corsets.
————each,** *a.* Having a waistcoat.
deacair, -e, *a.* Difficult, hard, abstruse. 2 Sad, mournful, grievous. 3 Surly, gloomy. 4 Sorry, grieving, sorrowful. 5** Wonderful, strange, rare. 6**Powerful. 7**Terrible. 8**Abstracted. 9**Thorny. 10* Sore. Is d. brìgh do sgeòil, *sad is the substance of thy tale*; is d. leinn 'achmhasan, *his reproofs are grievous to us.*
————eachd, *s.f.ind.* Difficulty, hardship. 2 Sorrow. 3**Wonderfulness. 4**Grievousness. 5**Terribleness. 6 Essay.
deacait, -ean, *s.f.* see deacaid.
———each, *a.* see deacaideach.
deach, *past interr. & neg.* of rach. see deachaidh. An deach e dhachaidh? *has he gone home?*
——, *a.* see deagh. †2 Profitable.
†——, *s.m.* Movement.
deachadh, *past subj. neg. & interr.* of rach.
————,(DC) *a.* Addled. Ugh d., *an addled egg—Uist.* (Ugh deachaidh in *Gairloch.*)
deachaidh, *past neg. & interr.* of rach. An d. tu? *hast thou gone?*; cha d. mi, *I have not gone, no*; gu'n d. na daoine a mach, *that the men went out.*
deachaidh, *a.* *Gairloch* for deachadh, *a.*
deachainn, see deuchainn.
†deachair, -e, *a.* Bright, glittering.
†deachair,** *s.f.* Separating. 2 Separation. 3 Brightness.
†deachair, *v.n.* Follow.
deachamh, -aimh, -aimhean, see deicheamh.
————aich, *v.* see deicheamhaich.
deachd, *v.a.* Dictate, indite. 2 Inspire. 3 Make completely certain, assure positively. 4 **Interpret. 5**Debate. 6**Teach.
——,** -a, -an, *s.f.* Dictate. 2 Word. 3 *for* diadhachd.
——achadh,** -aidh, see deachdadh.
deachdadair, *s.m.* see deachdair.
————each, see deachdaireach.
————eachd, see deachdaireachd.
deachdadh, -aidh, -aidheadh, *s.m.* Inditing. 2 Act of dictating. 3 Dictate, thing dictated. 4 Infusion. 5**Inspiring. 6**Law. A' d—, *pr. pt.* of deachd.
deachdaich, *v.a.* Dictate, indite.
————te, *past pt.* of deachdaich, Dictated.
deachdainnear,** *s.* Lexicon, dictionary.
————achd,** *s.f.ind.* Lexicography.
deachdair, -ean, *s.m.* Dictator. 2 One who dictates. 3**Teacher. 4**Doctor.
————each,** *a.* Dictatorial.
————eachd, *s.f.ind.* Dictatorship, act of dictating. 2 Dictation. 3**Teaching.
deachdannair, see deachdainnear.
deachdta, *past pt.* of deachd. Quite certain. Gu d., *most certainly, most assuredly.*
deachlach,** *a.* Hard, difficult.
deachmhaich, *v.a.* see deichmhich.
†deachmhor, -oire, *a.* Smoky.
deachmhoradh,** -aidh, *s.m.* Courtesy, affability.
†deachosa, *int.* Lo! behold! there! see!
†deachradh,** *s.m.* Indignation, anger.
deacra, *comp.* of deacair.
———ch,** *a.* see deacaireach.
———chd, see deacaireachd.
dead,** *a.* Meet, proper, decent, becoming. 2 Hereditary.
dead, déid, *s.m.* see deud.
——ach,** see deudach.
†deadh, -a, *s.m.* End, purpose.
deadh, *adv.* (air dheadh) Otherwise, else. Rach ann am màireach na dheadh cha'n fhaic thu e, *go to-morrow else you will not see him.* [Air deodh & air dheodh in *Perthshire*, and na dheadh in *Suth'd.*]
——, *a.* see deagh.
deadh-, For words beginning thus, see deagh.
deadhachd, see diadhachd.
deadhail,** *s.f.* Separation of night and day, dawn of day, twilight. 2 Releasing. 3 Weariness. D. na maidne, *morning dawn.*
deadhair,** *a.* Swift.
deadhan, see deaghan.
————achd, see deaghanachd.
deadhman, (AF) *s.m.* Moth.
deadla,** *a.* Bold, confident.
deadlas,** *s.m.* Confidence.
deagaid, see deagha.
deagailt,** *s.f.* Separation. 2 Divorce.
d' eagal, *conj.* For fear, lest, in case. D' eagal gu, *for fear that*; d' eagal nach, *for fear that not.*
deagal,* *s.m.* see deaguil.
deaganach,** -aich, *s.m.* see deaghan.
deagh, *a.* Good, excellent, worthy. Dà dheagh

mheann, *two good kids*; d. dhuine, *a good man.* [Always precedes its noun, which it aspirates. It never predicates of its noun, thus you never meet with "tha thu deagh," nor yet "is deagh thu."]
dĕägh, (mu'n) *for* mu'n rachadh. Mu'n deagh 'n glacadh no 'n tarraing, *ere they would be caught or drawn—Dàin I. Ghobha.*
deagha,** *s.m.* Banewort. [Preceded by the article *an.*] 2 (AF) Chafer, bug.
deagha-buidhe,§ Yellow centaury, perfoliate yellow-wort—*chlora perfoliata.*
deaghad,‡ *s.m.* Living, diet, morals—*Uist.*
deagha dearg,§ *s.m.* Red centaury, see ceud-bhileach.
deaghaidh, -e, -ean, *s. f.* see déigh.
deagh-ainm, -ean & -eannan, *s.m.* Good name.
deaghan, -ain, *s.m.* Dean. 2 Any noted person.
———achd,** *s.f.* Deanery.
deagh-bheachd, -an, *s. m.* Due attention or consideration. 2**Civility. 3††Good intention. 4(AH) Vivid recollection, certainty, assurance, conviction.
deagh-bheart, -airt, -an, *s.f.* Virtue, good deed.

262. *Deagha-buidhe.*

deagh-bheus, -an, *s.m.* Good morals, good behaviour, virtue, virtuous habits, morality.
———ach, -aiche, *a.* Well-behaved, virtuous, moral, well-bred.
deagh-bhlas, -ais, -an, *s.m.* Good taste, relish.
———da, *a.* Well-tasted, pleasant to taste, dainty, well-relished.
———ta, see deagh-bhlasda.
deagh-bholadh, -aidh, -aidhean, *s. m.* Sweet smell or odour, fragrance. Àileadh deagh-bholaidh, *an odour of sweet smell.*
deagh-bholtan,** -ain, } *s. m.* see deagh-
———as,** -ais, } bholadh.
deagh-bholtrach, -aiche, *a.* Aromatic, perfumed, fragrant.
———, -aich, -aichean, *s.f.* Sweet flavour.
———as,‡‡ -ais, *s.m.* Odoriferousness.
deagh-bholtraich,** *v.a.* Perfume, scent, aromatize, cense.
———te, *a. & past part.* of deagh-bholtraich. Perfumed, fragrant. 2 Sweet-flavoured.
deagh-bhuil, -e, *s. f.* Good management, good disposal. good use. 2 Economy. 3 (MMcL) Good result. Cuir gu d., *put to good use*; tha d. air, *it shows a good result.*
———each, -iche, *a.* Economical, well-disposed of.
———eachadh, -aidh, *s.m.* Economy, frugality. 2 Act of putting anything to a good use, proper disposal of anything, proper management. A' d—, *pr. pt.* of deagh-bhuilich.
———eachas,** -ais, *s.m.* Economy, proper management, good usage.
deagh-bhuilich, *pr. pt.* a' deagh-bhuileachadh, *v.a.* Bestow well, manage well.
deagh chainnteach, -iche, *a.* Eloquent.
deagh-chliù, *s.m.* Good repute.
deagh-choingheallach,-iche, *a.* Humane, benign.
deagh-chridheach, -iche, *a.* Good-hearted, kindly disposed, benevolent.
deagh-chruth, *s.m.* Handsome form or shape.
———ach, -aiche, *a.* Shapely, well-formed. 2 Handsome.
deagh-fhaclach, -aiche, *a.* Eloquent, well-spoken, fair-spoken.
deagh-fhonn, -fhuinn, *s. m.* Good mood, good humour, good tune. 2 Good disposition, good principle.
deagh-fhuinn,** *s.f.* Good-will.
deagh-fhulang, -aing, *s.f.* Patience under suffering, patient endurance.
———ach, -aiche, *a.* Patient under suffering. 2 Hardy. 3 Persevering.
deagh-ghean, -a, *s. m.* Good will, favour. 2 Benevolence. 3 Grace. 4 Good humour, good mood. D. dligheach, *due benevolence.*
deagh-ghlòir, -e, *s.f.* Affability, courteousness.
deagh-ghlòireach, -iche, *a.* Affable, courteous, condescending.
deagh-ghnè,** *s.* Candour.
deagh-ghnìomh,‡‡ -a, -ara, *s.m.* Benefaction.
deagh-ghnùis,** *s. f.* Pleasant countenance, good face.
deagh-ghràdh,** -ghràidh, *s.m.* Sincere attachment, ardent love.
———aich, *v.a.* Love ardently, sincerely or fervently.
deagh-ghuth,** *s.m.* Good word. 2 Good voice. 3 Euphony.
———ach, -aiche, *a.* Sweet-voiced.
deagh-iomchar, -air, *s.m.* Good comportment, proper bearing, good conduct.
deagh-ith,** *s.f.* Toothache. see déideadh.
deagh-labhairt,** *s.f.* Elocution. 2 Eloquence good utterance.
deagh-labhartach, *a.* see deagh-labhrach.
deagh-labhrach, -aiche, *a.* Well-spoken, eloquent.
———, -aich, *s.m.* see deagh-labhraiche.
deagh-labhraiche, -an, *s.m.* Orator.
deagh-laoch,** *s.m.* Good soldier.
deagh-mhaise,** *s.f.* Handsomeness, comeliness, excellence.
———ach, -aiche, *a.* Good-looking, handsome, comely. 2**Excellent. 3 Decent, becoming.
———achadh, -aidh, *s.m.* Ornamenting, adorning, decorating. 2 Improving one's personal appearance. A' d—, *pr. pt.* of deagh-mhaisich.
———achd, *s.f.ind.* Beauteousness.
deagh-mhaisich, *pr. pt.* a' deagh-mhaiseachadh, *v.a.* Adorn, decorate.
———te, *past pt.* Adorned, ornamented.
deagh-mhisneach,** -nich, *s.f.* Good courage. 2 Confidence.
———ail, -ala, *a.* Of good courage. 2 Confident, bold, hopeful.
deagh-mhùinte, *a.* Well-bred. 2 (MMcL) Well-educated.
†deaghnad, -aid, *s.m.* Frost.
deagh-obair,** -oibre, *s.f.* Good work. 2 Good deed.
deagh-oideas,** -eis, *s.m.* Good education.
———ach,** *a.* Well-educated. 2 Discreet.
deagh-òrduich,** *v.a.* Methodize, arrange.
———te, *a.* Well-ordered, methodized. 2 Prudent, provident.
deagh-thagarrach, *a.* Argumentative.
deagh-thairgneach,‡‡ -aiche, *a.* Of good omen.
deagh-theis,** *s.f.* Good report. 2 Good testimony.
———teas,** -eis, *s. m.* Good testimony, favourable evidence
deagh-théisd, see deagh-theis.
deagh-thoil, -e, *s. f.* Sincere desire. 2 Good will, benevolence. 3**Gratuity. 4** Accept-

ance. Dh'fhalbh e le d., *he left with good-will.*

deagh-thoileach, -iche, *a.* Favourable, friendly, benevolent. 2 Voluntary, gratuitous, willing.

deagh-thoill, *v.n.* Deserve well, merit.

————tinneach, *a.* Meritable.

deagh-thriall, *s.m.* Good gait, portliness.

deagh-thuigse, *s. f.* Good understanding. 2 Knowledge, wisdom.

————ach, -iche, *a.* Of good understanding. 2 Of quick apprehension. 3 Prudent, wise, sensible.

deagh-uair, *s.f.* Good season, goód time, good opportunity.

deaguil, *s.f.* Twilight.

deailgne,(AC) see dailgionn. 2(DC)Soothsaying *Argyll.* Már a thùbhradh anns an d., *as was spoken in the prophecy.*

deainte, see deanta.

deairbean,(AC) *s.m.* Glow-worm.

deaith,** *s.f.* Wind.

———each, *a.* Windy.

deal, -a, *a.* Zealous, keen, eager, earnest. 2 Friendly. 3††Relative. Mo dh. charaid, *my true friend.*

deal, *s.f.* see deala.

deala,‡‡ -n, *s.f.* Link.

deala, -n & -chan, *s.f.* Leech. 2 Cow's dung. 3 Sheep's teat. 4 Nipple. 5(AF) Eel. 6(AF) Lamprey. Tha 'n d. 'snàmh, thig frasan blàth roimh fheasgar, *the leech is swimming, warm showers will come ere evening*—N.G.P. [** gives *s.m.*]

——, *comp.* of deal.

——, *s.m.ind.* Kindred, friendship. 2 Refusal, denial.

dealachadh, -aidh, *s. m.* Parting, separating. 2 Act of parting,separation,division. 3 Space. 4 ‡‡Schism. 5 Divorce, divorcing. 6**Farewell. 7**Difference. A' d—, *pr.pt.* of dealaich. D. dà rathad, *a place where two roads diverge* ; balla dealachaidh, *a partition wall* ; cuir d. eatorra, *separate them* ; d. nan tràth, *the morning and the evening twilight.*

dealachail, -ala, *a.* Separating, causing separation, separable. 2 That may be separated. 3 Liable to separation.

dealachd, see dealachadh.

deala-eich, see deala.

dealag, -aig, see dealg.

dealagach, see dealgach.

dealagan, see dealgan.

dealaich, *pr.pt.*a' dealachadh, [a' dealachdainn, a' dealachdan & a' dealaichdean—*Suth'd.* a' dealaicheadh,] *v. a.* Separate, divide. 2 Divorce. 3** Make a difference. [This verb takes *ri* or *ris* after it, either simple or compounded, as, d. ri t' airgiod, *part with thy money;* d. riu, *part with them.*]

————ear, *fut.pass.* of dealaich.

————te, *past pt.* of dealaich. Separated, divided. 2 Divorced.

dealaidh, -e, *a.* Keen, zealous. 2 Affectionate, fond, dear. 3††Relative. 4††Friendly. 5†† More related.

————eachd, *s.f.ind.* Keenness, zealousness. 2 Affectionateness. 3††Kindred, relationship. 4††Loyalty.

dealair,* *v.* see dealraich.

dealan, -ain, -an, *s.m.* Lightning. 2 Nocturnal brightness in the heavens. 3 Wooden bar of a door. 4**Coal. 5**Flaming coal. 6‡‡Wooden peg fastening a cow-halter round the neck. 7 see deala. †8 (WC) Blister. 9 (WC) Mark left on hand or face, caused by the bite of an insect, as a midge. 10 (DC) Electric spark—*Uist.* D. bàis, *lightning of death.*

dealanach, -aich, *s.m.* Lightning. 2 Electricity. Bha dealanaich mhór' ann, *there were vivid flashes of lightning.*

————ach,** -aiche, *a.* Like lightning. 2 Flashing. 3 Electric, electrical. 4 Pertaining to a door-bar.

————achd, *s.f.* Electrification.

————aich, *pr.pt.* a' dealanachadh,*v.n.* Lighten, flash as lightning. 2 Electrify.

————air, *s.m.* Electrician.

dealan-dé, *s.m.* The appearance produced by shaking a burning stick to and fro, or by whirling it round. 2 *s.f.* see dearbadan-dé.

dealan-doruis, -ain-, -an-, *s.m.* Latch, door-bolt.

dealann, see deileann.

dealan-spéid, *s.f.* Telegraph.

dealas, -ais, *s.m.* Zeal, vehemence, keenness, hurry, speed, eagerness. 2 Affection, loyalty. 3** Contention. 4* Keenness of a woman spinning, or in household affairs.

————ach, -aiche, *a.* Zealous, vehement, fervid, keen, eager, earnest, acute. 2 Friendly.

————achd, *s. f. ind.* Zealousness, quickness, speediness, eagerness, keenness, ardour, fervour.

————aiche, *comp.* of dealasach.

deala-tholl,(AF) *s. m.* Leech, see deala. 2** Lamprey—*lampetra.*

dealb,(AF) -eilb, *s.* Water-beetle.

dealbh, -a [& deilbh,] -an, *s.m.* Image. 2 Statue. 3 Picture, delineation. 4 Photograph. 5 Appearance, form, figure, shape. 6**Face. 7 Contemptible, unsubstantial person. 8 Spectre, spectral-looking person. 9 Frame (of a cycle.) 10 Order, arrangement. 11 Abb, warping, stitches "cast on" for knitting. 12 Mould. 13 Warping-frame.

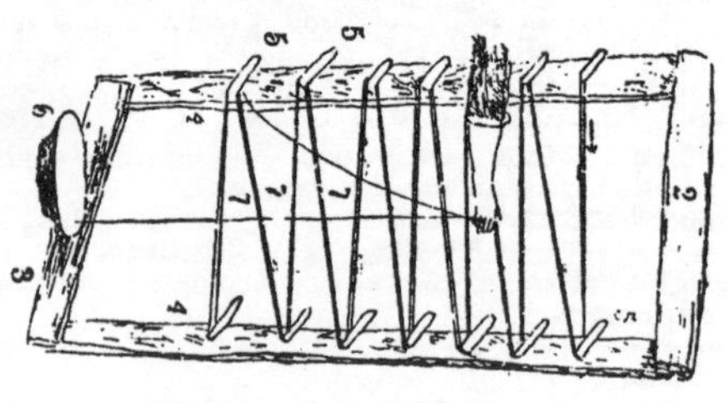

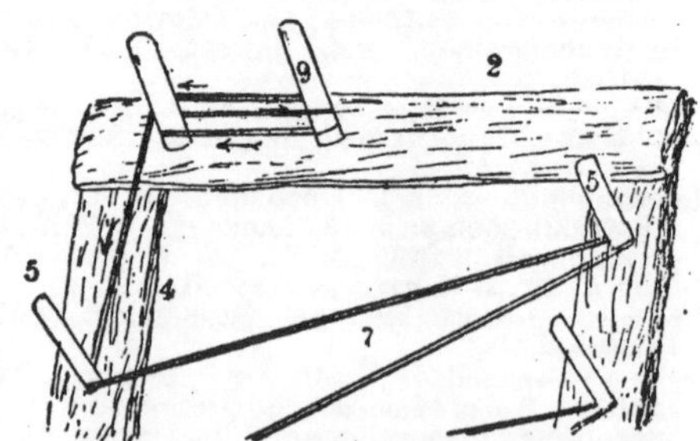

263. Dealbh (13.) Dealbh-àrd.
263a. Suidheachadh na creiseim.

The warping-frame shown in illust. is known in Uist as "deilbh àrd," and the term *deilbh* (dealbh) is seldom used in this connection alone. It is called *deilbh àrd* because the old original, and still usual manner, of warping the thread is by fixing the *fuaintean* in the clay floor. Consequently, when a frame was constructed and raised up against the wall, it received the name of "deilbh àrd."

PARTS OF A WARPING-FRAME :—

1 Crann-deilbhe, crann-dealbha, *or* beart-dheilbh, *frame.* [*bar.*
2 Spàrr-mullaich, sail-mhullaich, *upper cross-*
3 Spàrr buinn, sail-bhuinn, *lower cross-bar.*
4 Bacain, puist, na sailthean cliathaich, *side sticks of frame, uprights, posts.*
5 Fuaircean, fuaintean, pinneachan, fuaidnean (*sing.* fuaidne) *pins or pegs.*
6 Bocsa na deilbhe, bocsa na céirsle, *box for holding the clew.*
7 Croisean, *threads on frame.* Croiseadh an t-snàtha, is the name of the operation shown here. Double threads are used, and when finished, half the threads are on each side of the creiseim-stick.
8 Dealbhach, *thread on frame.*
9 Creiseim. These two pegs on upper cross-bar, as in second illust., and two similar ones on lower cross-bar, explain the old form of dealbh formerly in use in *Lewis,* but the form shown in first illust., is that generally used elsewhere. For modern form as used in *Lewis* see appendix. The form of winding thread on two top and bottom pegs in lower ill. is called *creiseim* in *Lewis.*

Ghoid Rachel na dealbhan, *Rachel stole the images* ; agus bha 'n talamh gun dealbh, *and the earth was without form* ; gnothach gun d., *an absurd thing* ; is beag d. a th' air, *it is out of form* or *arrangement ;* cuir air d., *or* cuir d. air, *arrange, adjust, put in order* ; maiseach 'na dealbh, *comely in her person* ; le dà dhealbh chuilean, *with the remains of two dogs—Leabh. na Féinne*, p. 164.

†dealbh,** *a.* Poor, miserable. 2 Spectral.

dealbh, *pr.pt.* a' dealbhadh, *v.a.* Form, figure, shape, mould. 2**Construct, make, build. 3 Delineate. 4 Contrive, plot, devise, feign. 5 Warp, weave, make abb of. 6 "Cast on" stitches for knitting. Dh. i a h-eachdraidh, *she wove her history ;* curach a dh. m' athair, *a boat constructed by my father* ; mu 'n do dh. thu an talamh agus an cruinne, *ere thou hadst formed the earth and the world* ; glacar iad 'sna h-innleachdan a dh. iad, *they shall be taken in the devices which they have imagined*; tha i a' dealbhadh, (a' deilbh—*Uist*) *she is warping*, or *making abb.*

———ach, -aiche, *a.* Shapely, symmetrical. 2 Handsome. 3 Evident, manifest, probable, likely, congruous. 4 Specious, ingenious, inventive. 5 Like a picture. 6 Allegoric. 7** Sagacious. 8**Resembling.

———ach,* -aich, *s.f.* Abb. (yarn on a weaver's warping-frame.)

dealbhachadh, -aidh, *s.m.* Forming, act of forming, framing, delineating, picturing. A' d—, *pr.pt.* of dealbhaich.

dealbhadair, -ean, *s.m.* Framer, inventor, contriver. 2 Statuary. 3 Painter, delineator. 4 Warper.

———————eachd, *s.f.ind.* Art of painting. 2 Statuary, moulding, delineation, framing. 3 Warping. 4**Framework.

dealbhadan, -ain, -an, *s.m.* Mould or frame in which to cast anything.

dealbhadh, -aidh, *s.m.* Forming, shaping, painting, delineating. 2 Contriving, planning, feigning, devising. 3 Statuary. 4**Imagining, imaginable. A' d—, *pr. pt.* of dealbh.

dealbhag,** -aig, *s.f.* Picture, miniature. 2 Statue.

dealbhaich, *pr.pt.* a' dealbhachadh, *v.a.* Same meanings as dealbh.

dealbhaiche, *comp.* of dealbhach.

dealbhaidh, *s.f.* Web of cloth.

dealbhail,** *a.* Shapely. 2 Spectral, ghost-like. 3 Like an image.

dealbhair, -ean, *s.m.* Photographer. 2 Painter. 3 Statuary.

dealbhaireachd,** *s.f.* Painting, delineation. 2 Statuary.

dealbhan, *s.m.* Little image, statue or picture. 2 *n.pl.* of dealbh.

·——— -dé -ain-, -an-, see dearbadan-dé.

dealbhas, -ais, *s.m.* Misery. 2 Poverty. Cha'n 'eil ac' ach an d., *they have nothing but poverty.*

————ach, -aiche, *a.* Poor. 2 Miserable. 3 Causing poverty or misery.

dealbh-bhruis,** *s.f.* Artist's "pencil" or brush.

dealbh-chaochladh, -aidh, -aidhean, *s.m.* Transfiguration.

dealbh-chluiche, -an & -annan, *s.f.* Play, stage-play, drama. [actor.

——————adair, -ean, *s.m.* Stage-player,

dealbh-chluith, -e, -ean, *s.f.* see dealbh-chluich.

——————eadair, see dealbh-chluicheadair.

dealbh-dùthcha, *s.m.* Map.

dealbh-inntinneach, -eiche, *a.* Ideal.

dealbh-lìobhair, -ean, *s.m.* Painter.

dealbh-sgrìobhadh, -aidh, -aidhean, *s. m.* Hieroglyphic.

dealbh-sgrìobhaidh, *s.m.* Etching.

dealbhta, *past pt.* of dealbh. Formed. 2 Built, constructed. 3 Woven, warped.

deal'-each, -eich, *pl.* dealachan-each, *s.f.* Horse-leech.

dealg, -eilg, -an, *s.f.* Pin, skewer, wire. 2 Thorn, prickle. 3 Bodkin. 4** Needle, knitting-needle, "stocking-wire." 5 *Skye* for (and) ealag (an dealg). 6 Pin of a pulley, see under ùlag, p. 78. 7 Goad. 8 Brooch-pin. D. gualainn, *a pin to fasten the plaid on the left shoulder.*

———ach, -aiche, *a.* Prickly. 2 Stinging. 3 Of, like, or belonging to, pins, skewers, wires, &c. 4*Thorny.

———achadh, -aich, *s.m.* Skewering. 2 Pinning. A' d—, *pr.pt.* of dealgaich.

———achd, *s.f.ind.* Prickliness.

———adh, -aidh, *s.m.* Act of prickling. 2 Stimulating, urging.

———aich, *pr.pt.* a' dealgachadh, *v.a.* Skewer. 2 Pin.

dealgain, *gen.sing.* & *n.pl.* of dealgan.

dealgan, -ain, [*pl.* -ain-&] an, *s.m.* Spindle,—*Bible.* Used in ancient times for spinning thread. 2 Small spindle. 3 Little pin or skewer. 4 Collar-bone. 5**Thorn, prickle. 6**Needle. 7 *n. pl.* of dealg.

dealganach, -aiche, *a.* Full of, or like, little prickles, spindles, skewers, pins, &c.

dealgan-gabhar, (AF) *s.m.* Lizard.

dealg-bhacaidh, *s.f.* Sny, toggle, see bàta, No. 1. p. 76.

dealg-cheangail, *s.f.* Belaying-pin, see No. 2 p. 76.

dealg-chluais,** *s.f.* Ear-picker.

dealg-doruis, (WC) *s.f.* Door-bar, latchet.

dealg-fhiacall,** -aill, *s.f.* Toothpick.

dealg-fhuilt,** *s.f.* Hair-pin.

dealg-gualainn,‡‡ *s. f.* Pin or brooch by which the plaid is fastened on left shoulder.

dealg-maraig, (PM) *s. f.* Wooden pin, used in fastening ends of white or black Scots puddings.

†dealgnaiche, *a.* Unjust. 2 Unlawful.

†————, *s.m.* Outlaw, rebel.

dealg-snaime, *s.f.* Belaying-pin, see No. 2, p. 76.

dealg-ursainn, (WC) *s.f.* Peg used of old for holding one side of a two-leaved door, now superseded by the iron bolt.

†deallas, *s.m.* Zeal, quickness, hurry.

†-———ach, ‡‡ *a.* Hasty, quick.

dealman-dé, see dearbadan-dé.

deal-mhara,(AF) *s.f.* Sea-leech. 2 Skate-worm.
dealrach, -aiche, *a.* Bright, radiant, shining, refulgent, gleaming, brilliant, beaming. 2 Clear, resplendent. Cia d. glòir a' mhath-shluaigh ud! *how bright the glory of those saints!*
dealrachadh, -aidh, *s.m.* Shining, gleaming, resplendence. 2 Act of shining, gleaming or beaming. A' d—, *pr.pt.* of dealraich.
dealrachd, *s.f.* see dealradh.
dealradh, -aidh, *s.m.* Brightness, effulgence, lustre, light, radiance, splendour, shining. 2 Act of shining or gleaming. D. glan do ghnùis, *the clear light of thy countenance.*
———ach, -aiche, *a.* see dealrach.
dealraich, *pr.pt.* a' dealrachadh, *v.a. & n.* Shine, radiate, gleam, flash, beam, brighten, glitter. 2 Emit rays.
———ead, -eid, *s.m.* Degree of brightness. A' dol an d., *growing brighter and brighter.*
———idh, *fut.aff.a.* of dealraich.
dealraidheachd, *s.f.* see dealradh.
dealrait, *Suth'd* for dealraichte.
dealruich, see dealraich.
dealt, -a, -an, *s.f.* & ††*m.* Dew. 2 Drizzle. 3 Rain glittering on the grass.
———ach, -aiche, *a.* Dewy. 2 Drizzly. 3 Rainy.
dealtag,(PM) *s.f.* Small quantity of rain—*Uist.*
dealtag, ——— -anmoch, } *s.f.* *Badenoch* for ialtag.
dealtair,* *v.a.* Glitter. 2 Gild, see dealtraich.
dealt-dhaolag, *s.f.* Dew-worm.
deal-tholl, see deala.
dealt-lus,‖ *s.m.* Moon-wort, see **luan-lus.**
dealtmhor, *a.* see dealtach.
dealtrach, *a.* see dealtach.
dealtradh, -aidh, *s.m.* Besprinkling, spangling, gilding, bedropping, lacquering, varnishing, glittering. A' d—, *pr.pt.* of dealtraich.
dealtraich, *pr.pt.* a' dealtradh, *v.a.* Gild, bedrop, lacquer, varnish.
dealt-ruaidhe,‖ *s.f.* Round-leaved sundew, see ròs-an-t-soluis.
dealuich, see dealaich.
———te, see dealaichte.
dealuigheach, -iche, *a.* Separable.
dealunn, -uinn, *s.m.* see deileann.
†deamal, -ail, *s.m.* Demon.
†deamh, *s.* Want, deficiency.
deamh,** *a.* Wicked.
deamhais, *pl.* deimhsean, [& deamhaisean] *s.m.* see deamhas.
deamhais, *gen. sing.* of deamhas.
deamhan, -ain, *s.m.* Demon, devil, evil spirit. 2‡‡Person bent on mischief. Tha d. aige, *he is possessed of a devil.*
———aidh, *a.* see deamhnaidh.
——— -eolas, -ais, *s.m.* Demonology.
†deamharruin, -e, -ean, *s.m.* Mystery.
†deamharun, -ùin, -ùintean, see †deamharruin.
deamhas, -ais, *s.m.* [†† *f.*] Pair of sheep-shears. 2 Scissors.
deamhnaidh, -e, *a.* Devilish, malicious, designedly wicked.
deamhsadh, -aidh, *s. m.* Fleecing, plying of shears in sheep-shearing. 2‡‡Working with all one's might.
dèan, *v.irreg.* Do, make, act, work, perform. 2 *Suppose, imagine, think. Conjugated thus:

Active Voice—

IND. *past*, rinn mi, &c., *I did.*
,, *fut.* ni mi, &c., *I shall do.*
INTERR. *past*, (an? nach?) d' rinn mi, &c. *did I (not?)* NEGATIVE, cha d' rinn mi, &c., *I did not.*
,, *fut.* (an? nach?) dean mi, *shall I(not) do?* NEGATIVE, cha dean mi, *I shall not do.* [cha dhean (*asp.*) in *Suth'd.*]
SUBJ. *past*, (ged) dheanainn, (*though*) *I would do*; (ged) dheanamaid, (*though*) *we would do*: (ged) dheanadh tu, e, i, sibh, iad, (*though*) *thou, he, she, ye, they would do.* [Cha dheanadh (*asp.*) in *Suth'd.*]
,, *fut.* (ma) ni mi, &c., (*if*) *I do.*
IMPER. *1st.p.sing.*, deanam, *let me do.*
"INFIN.," a dheanamh, *to do.* [properly *its doing.* There is no Infinitive in Gaelic, but unfortunately the Gaelic Verbal Noun frequently appears in places where in English infinitives would be used. A true infinitive cannot govern the genitive case. A participle is a noun, and therefore governs the genitive case, an infinitive is a verb, and therefore cannot govern a noun in the genitive. When one sees a thing *called* "an infinitive" governing something in the genitive, it may be concluded that it is a noun, *not* a verb, and, consequently, *not* an infinitive. Bonnach a mhealladh na cloinne, is *a bannock for deceiving of* (NOT *to deceive*) *the children*; bu mhath leis an rìgh Pàdruig a theachd, is translated, *the king wished Pat to come*, whereas what is meant is, *the king wished Pat to coming.* That *teachd*=coming and not *come*, This appears from the following, which occurs in *MacTalla.* "Bu mhath leam iad a dh' fhàgail nan each," *I wish them to leave* (*to leaving*) *of the horses.* Now, *nan each* is incontestably a genitive case, therefore it must have been governed by a noun, *not* by a verb. The Latin *amare* was an infinitive, so it could not govern a genitive, but *amatum* was a noun and declinable like a noun. So was the old Celtic gerund, or verbal noun, equally declinable, and many of them showed a dative case after the preposition *do. Cuir* in the dative, is, to this day, *cur*, which is its dative. But further, what about "bu mhath leam iad dha m' fhàgail," (some write "ga m' fhàgail")? If *fàgail* equals in this case an infinitive, i. e. if it is to be translated *to come*, we shall have *my to come.* In other words, because *fàgail* is qualified by a possessive pronoun, or by a possessive adjective, we see that it is a noun, *not* a verb. *My coming, my leaving*, are possible, *my to come, my to leave*, are inconceivable. As every one of the so-called infinitives can (1) take a possessive adjective, and can (2) govern a noun in the genitive, the conclusion is that these "infinitives" are all nouns and not verbs.]

PRES. PART., a' deanamh, *doing.*

Passive Voice— [properly a GRAPHIC or HISTORIC voice, not "PASSIVE." No intransitive verb can have a passive voice, but all intransitive verbs in Gaelic have an impersonal or graphic form. Chualas a bhi 'fosgladh an doruis, *I heard (people) opening the door;* dh'iarr a' mhuir a bhi 'ga taghal, *the sea wished people to resort to her.* Here "a bhi aig" seems to include a subject (people.) However, this is not revelant, see *MacTalla*, vi. p. 50 "Deanar caol-dìreach air an aite," *(they) made straight for the place.* "Deanar" is an intransitive verb, like "go." Translate it for a moment as "go." If it be passive, then the sentence means (*they*) *are go-ed* (or *went-ed*) *straight* &c. Again, cha tigear as eugmhais na pìoba, (*people*) *cannot get on without the bagpipe*—"tigear" is passive, then the sentence means *without the bagpipe it will not be comed.* Tachrar maighdean Eilean-an-éisg orra, thuit i an trom ghaol air D., *the maiden of Eilean-an-éisg meets them, she falls in heavy love on D ;* NOT *the maiden will be met on them,* NOT *she will be fallen in heavy love on D.*]

IND. *past*, rinneadh mi, &c., *I was made.*
,, *fut.* nithear mi, &c., *I shall be made.*
INTERR. *past*, (an ? nach ?) d' rinneadh mi, *was I (not) made ?* NEGATIVE, cha d' rinneadh mi, *I was not made.*
,, *fut.* (an ? nach ?) deanar mi, &c., *shall I (not) be made ?* NEGATIVE, cha deanar mi, *I shall not be made.*
SUBJ. *past*, (ged) dheanteadh mi, (*though*) *I should be made.*
,, *fut.* (ma) nithear mi, &c., (*if*) *I shall be made.*
PART., deanta, *done.*
d. aithreachas, *repent.* [=gabh aithreachas.]
d. aoibhneas, *rejoice.*
d. athchuinge, *supplicate.*
d. breug, *tell a lie.*
d. bròn, *mourn.*
d. bun, *trust, confide.*
d. cabhag, *hasten, make haste.*
d. cadal, *sleep.*
d. caithream, *triumph.* 2 *applaud.*
d. ceannairc, *rebel.*
d. ceartas, *decide impartially.*
d. còmhnadh (leinn,) *aid* (*us.*)
d. còmhnuidh, *dwell.*
d. dàil, *delay.*
d. deifir, *hasten, make haste.*
d. dhe, *receive, show hospitality to.* Rinn e glé mhath dhiom, *he received me well, treated me hospitably.*
d. dìchioll, *endeavour.*
d. dìmeas, *despise.*
d. do bhiadh, *make or cook your food.*
d. do chasan, *run away, (make use of your feet.)*
d. do chluasan, *hearken, (use your ears.)*
d. do chrochadh, *hang thyself.*
d. do shùilean, *look, attend, (use your eyes.)*
d. éigin, *compel.*
d. eòlas do, *heal by counteracting incantation.*
d. fadal, *delay.*
d. faire, *watch.*
d. fàisneachd, *prophesy.*
d. fanoid, *mock.*
d. fianuis, *bear witness.*
d. fìrinn, *speak the truth.*
d. foighidinn, *have patience.*
d. fòirneart, *oppress.*
d. fuasgladh, *release, deliver.*
d. fuireach, *stay.*
d. furtachd, *delay.* 2 *give relief.*
d. gàirdeachas, *rejoice.*
d. gu réidh, *do at leisure.*
d. guth aige 'san dol seachad, *call on him in passing.*
d. iochd, *pity.*
d. iomlaid, *exchange.*
d. iomradh (air,) *speak of.*
d. iteag, *fly.*
d. iùl, *guide.*
d. luaidh (air,) *speak of.*
d. luidhe, *lie down.*
d. magadh, *mock.*
d. masgul, *flatter.*
d. mìr, *make a piece, help yourself.*
d. mire, *play, sport.*
d. moille, *delay, stop.*
d. mulad, *be sorry.* [=bi muladach.]
d. òran, *compose a song.*
d. réite, *make peace, reconcile.*
d. sanas, *whisper.*
d. seasamh, *stand.*
d. sgeul (*air*), *declare.*
d. sgur, *cease.*
d. socair, *do at leisure.*
d. sòradh, *hesitate.*
d. spàirn, *strive.*
d. stad, *stop.*
d. strì, *try, strive, compete.*
d. suas, *make up, compensate.*
d. subhachas, *be glad.* [=bi subhach.]
d. sùgradh, *sport.*
d. suidhe, *sit down.*
d. sùil ri, *lay an evil eye upon.*
d. tàir, *despise.*
d. t' anail, *rest yourself, draw your breath.* [*better* leig t' anail.]
d. tarcuis, *despise.*
d. truas, *show pity.*
d. uaill (air *or* as), *boast, be proud of.*
d. ùrnuigh, *pray.*
D. air do shocair, *or* d. air t' athais, *do at leisure* ; cha d. cas luath maorach, *or* cha d. bean luath tràigh, (*one with*) *a hasty foot will not get shellfish* ; ge b' e cò rinn dhuit an t-sùil, *whoso laid on thee the (evil) eye* ; tha mi a' deanamh dheth, *I suppose* ; am bheil thu a' deanamh dheth ? *do you suppose ?* d. dhomh, *make for me* ; d. fasdadh, *hire yourself* ; d. suas càirdeas, *make up friendship* ; deantar truas rium, *let pity be shown to me* ; bha e 'n dùil gu 'n deanadh e an rathad dhachaidh leis fhéin, *he thought he could find the way home by himself.*

†dean, *s.m.* Colour.
deanabh, for deanadh.
deanachdach, -aiche, *a.* see déineachdach.
deanachdachd,* *s.f.* see déineachd and deanadachd.
deanachdas, -ais, *s.m.* see déineas & déineachd.
deanadach, -aiche, *a.* Laborious, industrious, diligent, active, endeavouring, busy. 2 †† Thrifty. Òganach d., *an industrious youth.*
————d, *s.f.* Agency. 2 Industry, activity, exertion. 3 Perseverance, diligence. 4 Conduct, behaviour. 5 Industries (in trade.)
deanadaich,(CR) Shin e air deanadaich, *it has begun to rain—Suth'd.*
deanadaiche, see deanadair.
deanadair,** *s.m.* Achiever.
deanadas, -ais, *s.m.* Industry, activity, exertion. 2 Conduct, behaviour, doings, act. 3* Perseverance, diligence. 4 Result.
deanadh, see deanamh.
deanaich,(CR) *pr.pt.* Working. Am bheil e a' d. an dràsd ? *has he got employment, has he a job at present ?* ; or of a mill, *is it going at present ?* in opposition to being closed and disused—*Perthshire.* [In the first example *obair* is understood, in the second one, *mine*, Perthshire Gaelic is often so much contracted.]
deanam, *1st.per.sing. imp.* of dean. Let me do.
————aid, *1st,per.pl.imp.* of dean. Let us do.
deanamh,-aimh, *s.m.* Doing, acting, performing. 2‡‡Form, figure. A' bith-dheanamh uilc, *always doing evil.* A' d—, *pr.pt.* of dean.
deanananaich,** *s.f.* Doings, behaviour.
deanannas,** -ais, *s.m.* Doings.
deanar, *fut.int.pass.* of dean.
deanas,* -ais, *s.m.* see deanadas. 2**Space, while, interval. D. (deanadas) a meòir, *the work of her fingers.*
————ach, -aiche, *a.* see deanadach.
————achd,* *s.f.* see deanadas.
†deanbh, -an, *s.f.* Effect.
dean-chlodhach,** *a.* Of changeable colours.
dean-choire,** *s.f.* Caldron.
deang, *v.a.* see diong.
deangan, see seangan.

deanmhas,** *s.m.* Consequence, effect.
deanmhasach,** *a.* Prim, spruce. 2 Coy.
deanmhasachd,** *s.f.* Primness. 2 Coyness.
deangalta,** *a.* see diongalta.
deann, -a, -an, *s.f.* Force. 2 Haste, velocity, hurry,speed. 3 Particle,very small quantity of anything comminuted. 4 Rush or dash, rapid motion. [No direction implied, as in *MacAlpine*, but simply the idea of "running amok."] 5**Noise. 6**Colour. 7**Figure. 8** Pinch, as of snuff. †9 Mist. †10 Gibe. 11**Impetuosity. Cha'n 'eil d. snaoisein agam, *I have not a particle of snuff*; thàinig e a steach 'na dh., *he came rushing in*; an t-each 'na dh., *the horse at full speed*; a' leum thar sàile 'na d., *bounding speedily over the deep*; dearg dh., *violent speed*; deanna-nam-bonn, *as fast as the feet can carry*; tha na clachan-meallain a' cur d. as an talamh, *the hail-stones are spattering (putting mist out of) the ground;* mar dh. a bheir dà òrd, *like the noise of two hammers.*
deanna,** *s.m.* Clap.
deannach, -aich, *s.f.* Dust, mill-dust. Sguab deannaich, *whisk.*
deannachdach,‡‡ } *a.* Dusty.
deannachdaidh, }
deannadh,* -aidh, *s.m.* Sweep. 2**Career.
deannag, -aige, -an, *s.f.* Very small quantity of any comminuted matter. 2 Pinch, as of snuff. 3 Small grain.
deannagach, -aiche, *a.* In small quantities. 2 In pinches, as snuff, or any pulverized substance.
deannaibh, *dat.pl.* of deann. Tha e 'na dh., *he is running with all his might.*
deannal, -ail, *s.m.* Conflict, onset, contest,stir. 2 Haste,hurry. 3 Shot. 4 Flash. 5*Spell or little while at anything with all one's might. Le d. nan gàirdean ann an d. nan claidheamh, *with the force of the arms in the clash of swords*; thug sinn d. cruaidh, *we made a furious onset.*
deannalach, -aiche, *a.* Impetuous, vehement, hasty. Gu d., *impetuously.*
deannalachd, *s.f.ind.* Impetuosity,vehemence, hastiness.
deannan, -ain, -an, *s.m.* see deannag. 2 *dim.* of deann. 3**see deuran. 4 *Lewis* for deannruith. Is mairg a chrathadh a dh. salainn air, *pity anyone who would sprinkle his salt on him*—said of a doubtful character; thàinig iad 'nan d.,(d.-ruith),*they came at utmost speed.*
deannanach,‡‡ -aiche, *a.* Atomical.
deann-ruith, -e, *s.f.* Great hurry, velocity, impetuosity, utmost speed.
deanntag, -aige, -an, *s.f.* Nettle—*urtica urens* and *urtica dioica.*
————ach, -aiche, *a.* Abounding in nettles. 2 Like a nettle, of nettles.
————ach, -aich, *s.m.* Place where nettles grow. 2 Tuft of nettles.
deanntag-arbhair, *s.f.* Corn-nettle, caltrop.
deanntag-bhàn,§ *s. f.* White dead-nettle, see teanga-mhìn.
deanntag-dhearg,§ *s. f.* Red dead-nettle—*lamium purpureum.* see ill. 264.
deanntag-Ghreugach,§ *s.f.* Fenugreek—*trigonella ornithopodioides.* see illust. 265.
deanntag-mharbh,§ *s.f.* White dead-nettle, see teanga-mhìn.
deanntag-rògach, (MMcD) *s.f.* Corn-nettle, caltrop.
deant', see deante.
deanta, see deante.
deantach, -aiche, *a.* Practical, practicable, possible.
————, -aich, *s.m.* Agent, one who acts or

264. Deanntag-dhearg.

265. Deanntag-Ghreugach.

performs, doer. 2 Industrious man.
deantag, see deanntag.
deantanas, see deanadas.
deantar, *3rd.per.sing.imper.pass.* of dean.
deantas, -ais, -an, *s.m.* see deanadas. 2 Poetry, rhyming.
————ach, -aiche, *a.* see deanadach.
deante, *past pt.* of dean. Done, made, performed, finished. D. ri cogadh, *trained to war;* duine d., *a grown-up man.*
deaorachan,** -ain, *s.m.* see deurachan.
dear, see deur. 2** *s.f.* Refusal, denial. 3** Daughter.
——,** *a.* Great, large, prodigious.
——ach, see deurach.
——ach,** -aich, *s.m.* Destruction. 2 Pillage.
dearadh, -aidh, *s.m.* see dearcadh.
dearag-thalmhuinn,§ see lus-deatach-thalmhuinn.
dèarail, [-e &] -ala, *a.* Beggarly, poor, wretched. 2††Feeble, dependant.
dèaralachd, *s.f.ind.* Want, defect. 2 Destitution.
†dearaointeach, *a.* Despairing.
dearasan,* for deireasan, *pl.* of deireas.
dearb,(AC) *s.* Kind of beetle.
dearbadan, -ain, *s.m.* see dearbadan-dé.
dearbadan-dé, -ain-, *s.m.* Butterfly. [Butterflies are very frequently confounded with moths, which are a different kind of insect altogether.]

The following Gaelic names of the principal varieties of butterflies are from Forbes' *Gaelic Names of Beasts, &c.*

An t-ailean donn,—*hipparchia janira*—meadow brown.
àrd-sheoladair bàn,—*limenitis sibylla*—white admiral.
argus beag,—*lycœna agestis*—small argus.
argus Albannach,—*erebia blandina*—Scots argus.
argus donn,—*polyommatus agestis*—brown argus.
am baintighearna dreachmhor,—*cynthia cardui*—painted lady.
an t-iompaire corcurach,—*apatura iris*—purple emperor.
dealbhan gorm airgiodach,—*polyommatus œgon*—silver-studded blue.
dealbhan fad-earr,—*lycœna œgon*—long-tailed blue.
dealbhan gearr-earr,—*lycœna bœtica*—short-tailed blue.
dealbhan mór an fhraoich,—*hipparchia tithonus*—large heath.
dealbhan beag an fhraoich, — *cœnonympha pamphilus*—small heath.
dealbhan breac na coille—*lasiommata egeria*—speckled wood.
Diùc Bhurgundi,—*hemeobius lucina*—fritillary

Duke of Burgundy.
an donnag bhallach, *or* donnag a' bhalla,—*lasiommata megæra*—wall butterfly.
an donnan Arainneach,—*erebia ligea*—Arran brown.
an donnan tuathach,—*erebia æthiope*—northern brown.
am faineag,—*hipparchia hyperanthus*--ringlet.
faineag a' mhonaidh,—*erebia cassiope*—mountain ringlet.
faineag bheag,—*cœnympha davus*—small ringlet.
an glaisean,—*hyparchia samele*—grayling.
an gorman, — *polyommotus alexis* — common blue.
gorman na caile,—*inatus corydon*—chalk-hill blue.
an gorman beag,—*polyommatus alsus*—little blue.
marsairionach mór nan creag,—*polyommatus acis*—blue mazarine.
an grìs-fhionnach geal,—*arge galathea*—marbled white.
an leumadair beag,—*pamphila linea*—small skipper.
an leumadair breac-bhallach,—*steropes paniscus*—chequered skipper.
an leumadair lachdunn,—*thanaos tages*—dingy skipper.
an leumadair grìs-fhionn—*pyrgus alveolus*—grizzled skipper.
Lulworth mór Shasunnach—*pamphila actæon*—Lulworth skipper.
an litir bhàn,—*thecla w. album*—white letter hair-streak.
an roinne donn stiallach, — *thecla betulæ*—brown hair-streak.
an roinne dubh stiallach, —*thecla pruni*—black hair-streak.
an roinne stiallach chorcurach,—*thecla quercus*—purple hair-streak.
an roinne stiallach uaine,—*thecla rubi*—green hair-streak.
an t-umhach beag,—*chrysophanus phlœas*—small copper.
[Description and illustration of every native British butterfly may be found in "British Butterflies."]

dearbh, *pr.pt.* a' dearbhadh, *v.a.* Prove,confirm. 2 Try. 3**Experience. 4**Demonstrate. 5 **Ascertain. 6**Affirm. 7**Attest. 8**Tempt. 9**Put to the test. D. sin, *prove that.*

dearbh,** -an, *s.m.* Proof, demonstration. 2 Experiment, test, trial. 3 Churn. 4 Milk-pail. Cuir gu d., *put to the test.*

dearbh, -a, *a.* Sure, certain. 2 Particular, peculiar, identical. 3 Demonstrative (in *gram.*) 4**True, genuine. 5**Fixed. An d. ni a bha dhìth orm, *the very thing I wanted* ; an d. dhuine, *the identical man* ; tha gu dearbh, *yes indeed* ; gu dearbh fhéin seadh,—a very emphatic affirmative.

dearbh (gu) *adv.* Truly,really, certainly,indeed. Is d. gu'm bheil, *it is truly* or *positively so.*

———ach, -aiche, *a.* Sure of. 2 Confirmatory. 3 Affirmative. 4**Demonstrative. 5 Capable of proof.

———achadh, -aidh, *s.m.* Proving, confirming, attesting. 2 Act of confirming or attesting. 3**Protesting. 4**Swearing. 5**Allegation. A' d—, *pr.pt.* of dearbhaich.

———achail,‡‡ *a.* Conclusive.

dearbhachd, *s. f.* Experience. 2 Proof, testimony, demonstration. 3 Experiment. 4 Assurance.

———adaich, *v.a.* Demonstrate, prove, confirm.

dearbhadair,** *s. m.* Affirmer, alleger. 2 Approver. 3 Ascertainer.

dearbhadas, -ais, *s.m.* Capability of proof. 2* Way of leading proof.

dearbhadh, -aidh,-aidhean, *s.m.* Evidence,proof. 2 Proving, act of proving. 3 Trying, confirming, test, trial. 4 Demonstrating. 5**Certainty. 6**Approbation. 7‡‡Experience. 8 see dearbhag. 9 (MMcD) Disputing, arguing. Mar dh. air sin, *as a proof of that* ; a' d. na cùise, *confirming the fact, proving the case.* A' d—, *pr.pt.* of dearbh.

——————-sùl,** *s.m.* Autopsy.

dearbhag, -aige, -an, *s.f.* Touch-stone.

dearbhaich, *pr.pt.* a' dearbhachadh, *v.a.* Prove. 2 Confirm, attest. 3 Swear.

dearbhail,** *a.* Affirmable. 2 Affirmative.

dearbhair, see dearbhadair.

dearbhann, -ainn, -ainnean, *s.f.* Axiom, proposition evident at first sight, truism.

dearbhar, *fut. pass.* of dearbh.

dearbh-art, -airt, *s.m.* see dearbhag.

dearbhas, -ais, -an, *s.m.* Proof.

————ach, -aiche, *a.* Capable of proof.

dearbh-bhann, -ainn, -an, see dearbhann,

dearbh-bheachd, -an, *s.m.* Certainty, assurance, confidence, confident hope. 3**Full view. 4 ††Full aim. 5††Full notice. Làn d., *full assurance.*

——————air,** *s.m.* Assurer.

dearbh-bhràthair, -thar, -àithrean, *s.m.* Brother, full brother, own brother.

dearbh-bhràthair-athar,** -ar-, -àithrean, *s. m.* Full uncle on the father's side.

dearbh-bhràthaireachd,** *s.f.* Brotherhood. 2 Society.

dearbh-bhràthair-màthar, -ar-, -àithrean-, *s. m.* Full uncle on the mother's side.

dearbh-bhriathar, -air, -thran, *s. m.* Axiom, truism, dogma, true saying.

dearbh-bhriathrach, -aiche, *a.* Dogmatical, axiomatic.

dearbh-chinnte, *s.f.* see dearbh-chinnteas.

——————ach, -tiche, *a.* Sure, certain, beyond doubt.

——————as, -eis, *s.f.* Certainty, full assurance.

dearbh-chlach, -chloich, -chlachan, *s.f.* Touchstone.

dearbh-chliamhuinn, -ean, *s.m.* Son-in-law.

dearbh-dheante, *a.* Accurate, correct.

dearbh-fhios, *s.m.* Certain knowledge, correct knowledge. 2**Assurance. 3**Certain news.

——————rach, -aiche, *a.* Absolutely certain, having certain knowledge, well assured, convinced.

dearbh-ràdh,** *s.m.* Axiom.

dearbhtach, -aiche, *a.* Capable of proof, or of demonstration.

dearbhte, *a. & past. pt.* of dearbh. Proved, confirmed, tried, ascertained, affirmed, attested, established. 2**Demonstrated. 3**Approved. 4**Tempted.

dearbhthachd, -an, *s.f.* see dearbhachd.

dearbh-theachdair, -an & -draichean, *s.m.* Sure or trusty messenger.

dearc, -an, *s.f.* Berry (general term.) 2 Grape. 3 Lizard. 4(AF)Speckled serpent. 5(AF)Dart. Fàgaidh thu dearcan, *thou shalt leave grapes.*

†dearc, *s.* Eye. 2 Cave, grotto. 3 Hole. 4 Grave.

dearc, *pr.pt.* a' dearcadh, *v.a.* Behold, look, observe. 2 Look keenly or piercingly, examine, inspect. 3 Fix the mind on intensely, watch. Dearcam ort do gnàth, *I will make thee the subject of my meditations continually* ; dh. mi le sòlas, *I looked with delight.*

dearcach,** *a.* Abounding in berries, bearing

berries, like a berry, relating to a berry. 2 Watchful, observant. 3†† Abounding in, of, or relating to, lizards.

dearcadh, -aidh, *s. m.* Advertence. 2**Looking, inspecting, examining, beholding. 3** Look, inspection, examination. A' d—, *pr. pt.* of dearc.

dearcag, -aig, -an, *s.f.* Little berry.

———ach, -aiche, *a.* Full of little berries.

——— -choille, *s.f.* Hurtleberry.

——— -Fhrangach, see dearc-Fhrangach.

——— -fhiadhaich,** *s.f.* Heathberry.

——— -fhraoich,** see dearc-fhraoich.

——— -mhonaidh, *s. f.* Bilberry, blaeberry—*Lochaber.*

dearcaidh, *fut. aff. a.* of dearc.

dearc-aitinn, -an-aitinn, *s.f.* Juniper berry.

dearcam, *1st.p. sing.* of dearc. Let me look. 2 (*for* dearcaidh mi) *fut. aff. a.* of dearc, I will look.

dearcan, *n. pl.* of dearc. 2 see deargan.

——— -allt, see deargan-allt.

——— -alltaidh, see deargan-allt.

——— -fithich,§ *s.m.* Whortleberry, see lus-nan-dearc.

——— -suiriche,** *s.m.* Bur.

dearc-bhallach, -aiche, *s.f.* Speckled serpent. 2 Lizard.

dearc-dharaich, -an-daraich, *s.f.* Acorn.

dearc-dhearg, -an-dearga, *s.f.* see raosar-dearg.

dearc-dhubh, -an-dubha, see raosar-dubh.

dearc-eighinn, -an-eighinn, *s.f.* Ivy berry.

dearc-fhìona,-an-fìona, *s.f.* Grape. 2 Crowberry.

dearc-Fhrangach, -an-Frangach, *s. f.* Red or white currant, see raosar-dearg & r.-geal.

dearc-fhraoich, an-fraoich,*s.f.* Blaeberry, heathberry, cowberry, bilberry.

dearc-fithich,§ *s.f.* Crowberry, see lus-na-feannaig.

dearc-iubhair, -an-iubhair, *s.f.* Yew berry.

dearc-luachair, see dearc-luachrach.

dearc-luachrach, -an-luachrach, *s. f.* Lizard, asp—*lacerta agilis.*

266. Dearc-luachrach.

dearc-luachrach uisge, *s.f.* Asker.

dearcnach, -aiche, *a.* Goodly, handsome. 2 Likely.

———adh, -aidh, *s.m.* Act of marking with emphasis. 2 of examining, of inspecting keenly. 3 of confirming by observation. 4* Of criticizing. A' d—, *pr.pt.* of dearcnaich.

dearcnaich, *pr.pt.* a' dearcnachadh, *v.a.* Mark with emphasis. 2 Confirm by observation. 3 Examine keenly, inspect. 4††View. 5*Criticize.

dearc-na-sùla, *s.f.* Apple of the eye.

dearc-ola, -an-ola, *s. f.* Olive.

dearc-roide,§ -an-roide, *s.f.* Bog-myrtle berry—*vaccinium uliginosum.* McL & D gives bilberry. [Badge of Clan Buchanan.]

dearc-ubhal,** -ail, *s.m.* Oak-apple.

dear-dhun,** -uin, *s.m.* Penitentiary, oratory. [dear-theach.]

dearg, deirge, *a.* Red, ruddy. 2 Flaming. 3 Red-hot. 4 Real, very, intense, inveterate. 5 Violent. 6 Downright mad. 7*Most abandoned, or notorious. 8 Com-

268. Dearg.

267. Dearc-roide.

plete. 9** Bitter. 10** Severe. 11**Turned or ploughed. 12†† Impetuous. 13 Gules, in *heraldry*, represented by perpendicular lines, see illust. D. amadan, *a complete fool* ; d. mhèirleach, *a notorious thief* ; d. strìopach, *a most abandoned strumpet* ; d. mar fhuil, *red as blood* ; air an d. chuthach, *stark mad* ; talamh d., *turned or ploughed land* ; feòil dh., *red* or *raw flesh.* [*Dearg* is often prefixed to a noun, when it is required to express an extraordinary degree of guilt, &c., as, tha 'n dearg-chiontach saor, *the glaringly guilty is free* ; tha 'n d. chuthach air, *he is mad with rage.*]

dearg, *pr. pt.* a' deargadh, *v. a. & n.* Redden, make red. 2 Blush. 3 Plough. 4 Make an impression. 5**Kindle. 6** Burn. 7***rarely* Make, prepare. 8‡‡Draw blood. 9(AC)Wound. Cha d. e air, *it makes no impression on him* ; cha d. iubhair mi, *no arrow shall wound me.*

dearg, deirg, *s.m.* Red colour, crimson. 2 Red deer, mountain deer, roe. 3 Right hand side of land ploughed, as distinguished from *bàn*, the left hand side. 4 (AC) Impression, see deargadh. 5(AC)Wound. 6(AC)Creature. 7 Red mark on sheep. 8 *not* " a single fish." as given by ††. Cha d' fhuaradh d. éisg air an loch, means, (*they*) *did not find any fish at all on the loch.* Cha'n 'eil d. an abhainn, *there is not a fish in a river* ; aonach nan d., *the hill of deer* ; sruth an deirg, *the deer's brook* ; tha d. air an t-slinnean oirre, *it* (*the sheep*) *has the red mark on its shoulder.*

deargachadh, *pr.pt.* of deargaich.

deargad, *s.f.* see deargann.

deargadh, -aidh, *s.m.* Reddening, act of making red. 2 Act of blushing. 3 Ploughing, act of ploughing. 4 Impression. 5 Act of making an impression. 6**Kindling. 7(JM) The smallest of the dorsal fins, i.e. the one near the tail—*Hebrides.* 8 Ear-mark; for *na naoi deargadh*, see p. 238. 9 Creature. A' d—, *pr.pt.* of dearg. Cha toir mi d. air, *I cannot make an impression on it* ; cha d' fhuair sinn d. éisg, *we did not get any fish.*

deargaich, *pr.pt.* a' deargachadh, *v.a. & n.* Redden, make red. 2 Blush.

deargain, *gen. sing.* of deargan.

dearg-ainmhidh,(AF) *s.m.* Red cattle.

deargan, -ain,-an, *s. m.* Red stain, red dye, rouge. 2 Crimson. 3 Purple. 4 Essence. 5 Reality. 6 Bream (fish.) 7 (AF) Kestrel, hawk, falcon, red-necked phalarope, stenchel, redstart. †8 *s.f.* see deargann. 9††Red spot.

dearganach, -aich, *s.m.* Red-coat (cant term for a soldier.) 2 (DU) Mouse or rat before hair has grown on it.—d. lucha, d. radain. An aimsir a dhearbhar na dearganaich, *the time when the Whig soldiers were tested.*

dearganaich, *n.pl.* of dearganach.

deargan-aitinn, *s.m.* Juniper starter, bird found in Lewis.

deargan-allt, -ain-allt, -ganan-allt, *s.m.* Kestrel, see clamhan-ruadh. 2(AC) Redstart. 3 ¶Red-necked phalarope—*phalaropus hyperboreus.*

————aidh, see deargan-allt.

deargan-coille,(AF) *s.m.* Bullfinch.

deargand, see deargann.

deargan-doirionn,* *s.m.* Nebula.

deargan-fraoich, -ain-, -anan-fraoich, *s.m.* Goldfinch. 2 Bullfinch, see corcan-coille.

deargan-ghiuthais,¶ *s.m.* see cam-ghob.

deargan-leadh, (AF) *s.m.* Red cattle.

deargann, -ainn, -nnan, *s. f.* Flea. Rinn e luath is deargannan ann, *he made ashes and leas there,* i.e. he stayed there long enough—J.G.P.

————ach,** -aiche, *a.* Full of fleas.

deargann-tràghad,(AF) *s.f.* Seashore flea, multipede.

deargan-seilich,¶ *s.m.* Common red-pole—*linota linaria.*

deargan-sneachda,¶ *s.m.* Redwing, see sgiath-deargan. 2 Snow-bunting,*s.m.*see eun-buidhe-an-t-sneachdaidh.

deargant, -aint, -an, *s.f.* see deargann.

dearg-chneadh, -chneidh, *s. m. & f.* Bloody wound, severe wound.

————ach,** *a.* Causing bloody wounds. 2 Full of deep wounds.

dearg-chreadh, -a, *s.f.* Ruddle. 2**Ochre.

dearg-fhraoich, see deargan-fraoich.

†dearglaice, *s.f.* Offer, bribe.

dearg-las, *v.n.* Blaze up, break into flames. 2 Give out red flames.

————ach, see dearg-lasrach.

————rach, -aiche, *a.* Red-flaming. 2 Red-hot.

————adh, -aidh, *s.m.* Red-flaming, emitting red flames.

dearg-léigh, *s.m.* Surgeon.

————eachd,** *s.f.* Surgery.

deargnaich,‡‡ *v.a.* Impurple.

deargnaidh, *a.* Unlearned.

dearg-shoilleir, *a.* Fallow.

dearg-shùil, -shùla, -shùilean, *s. f.* Red eye, blood-shot eye. 2**Flaming eye. A dh. fo dheòir, *his red eyes in tears.*

————each, -iche, *a.* Having red eyes. 2 Having blood-shot eyes.

dearg-theinn,(AC) *s.* Great difficulty.

dearlaic,** *s.f.* Gift.

dearlan, see dèarr-lan.

dearlanachd, see dèarr-lànachd.

dearmad, -aid, -an, *s.m.* Omission, negligence, neglect, forgetfulness. 2 Inattention, slight. Cuir air d., *neglect, forget*; ge dàil do fhear an uilc cha d., *though the wicked man's (punishment) is delayed, it is not forgotten*; na ma h-e do dh. a thoirt leat, *do not forget to bring it with you.*

dearmad, *pr. pt.* a' dearmad & a' dearmadadh, *v.a. & n.* see dearmaid.

————ach, -aiche, *a.* Forgetful, negligent, careless, inattentive.

————achd, *s.f.ind.* Negligence, carelessness, forgetfulness, inattentiveness, omission.

————aich, *v.* see dearmaid.

————ail, -dala, *a.* see dearmadach.

dearmaid, *pr.pt.* a' dearmad & a' dearmaideadh, *v.a. & n.* Neglect, fail to perform, disregard, forget, omit, slight, overlook.

dearmail, -e, -ean, *s.f.* Anxiety, solicitude. 2†† Worldliness.

†————, *a.* Anxious.

————each,†† *a.* Anxious. 2 Worldly.

————eachd,‡‡ *s.f.ind.* Anxiety.

dearmal, see dearmad.

————ach, -aiche, *a.* Anxious, solicitous. 2‡‡ Forgetful.

†dearmhail, *a.* Huge, very great.

†dearmhair, *a.* Huge, very great. 2 Excessive, violent, vehement.

†dearmharadh, -aidh, *s.m.* Wonder.

dèarn, see dèarnadh.

dèarn, *v.n.* Do, act, accomplish.

dèarna, *pl.* -rnan & -naichean, see dèarnadh.

dearnad, see deargann.

dèarnadair, -ean, *s.m.* Palmist, one who practises divination by palmistry. 2 Chiromancer.

————eachd, *s.f.ind.* Palmistry. 2 Chiromancy.

dèarnadh, -aidh, -aidhean, *s. f.* Palm of the hand. 2 Palm-ful. Air dèarnaibh mo dhà làimh, *on the palms of my hands.*

dèarnag, see dearnagan.

dèarnagan, -ain, -an, *s.m.* Small cake made on the palm of the hand. 2 Wafer. 3 Little hand. 4 *n.pl.* of dearnag. D. neo-ghoirtichte, *unleavened cakes.*

dèarnan,* *s.m.* Shoemaker's waxed thread.

†dearrach, -aich, *s.m.* Apartment in a monastery consecrated for prayers.

dearrais,(AF) *s.* Serpent, winged serpent.

dearral, see dearralach.

————ach, -aiche, *a.* Beggarly, wretched, poor.

————achd,** *s.f.ind.* Want. 2 Wretchedness. 3 Defeat.

dearras, -ais, *s.m.* see diorras. 2 *s.*(AC)Serpent. 3 *a.*(AC) Venomous.

dearras, (an) After. 2 Since, seeing that. An d. dhuit sin a dhèanamh, *since you have done that.*

dèarrasach, -aiche, *a.* Obstinate. 2 Fretful. 3 Keen, eager.

dearrasain, *gen. sing. & n. pl.* of dearrasan.

dearrasan, -ain, *s. m.* The noise of anything crackling, burning or roasting. 2 Hurling. 3 Gurgling. 4 Hissing, buzzing, rustling. 5 Snarling. 6 Flapping noise of a banner. 7** Balm cricket. 8**Hurry.

dearrasanaich, -e, *s.f.* see dearrasan.

dearrasan-uisge,(WC) *s.m.* Heavy shower of rain.

dèarr-làn,†† *s.m.* Complete fill.

————, *a.* Brimful

dèarr-lànachd, *s.f.* Brimfulness.

dèarrs, *pr. pt.* a' dèarrsadh, *v.a. & n.* Shine, beam, gleam, radiate, emit rays. 2 Burnish.

dèarrsach, -aiche, *a.* Shiny, bright, beaming, radiant, gleaming, effulgent, glittering, resplendent.

————,(DC) -aich, *s.f.* Heavy rain—*Uist.*

dèarrsachd,***s.f.*Shining,gleaming. 2 Vigilance.

dèarrsadh, aidh, -aidhean, *s.m.* Brightness, radiance, splendour, effulgence. 2 Shining beaming, flashing, gleaming. 3 Sun-beam. 4 *Gleam, ray. A' d—, *pr. pt.* of dèarrs. D. na maidne, *the morning ray.*

dèarrsaich, *pr.pt.* a' dèarrsadh, *v. a. & n.* see dèarrs. 2** Watch, observe, be vigilant.

dèarrsaidheachd, *s.f.ind.* Vigilance, watchfulness. 2 Brightness.

dèarrsanta, see dèarrsach.

dèarrsg, *v.a.* Polish, burnish, make bright. 2** File. 3**Command. 4**Surpass.

dèarrsgach,** *a.* Polished, burnished. 2 Filed.

dèarrsgnach,** *a.* Polite, polished, excellent, complete, accomplished.

dèarrsguach,** *s.m.* Polished or accomplished man.

dèarrsgnachadh, -aidh, *s.m.* Polishing, act of polishing, burnishing, brightening. A' d—*pr.pt.* of dèarrsgnaich.

dèarrsgnachd, *s.f.ind.* Politeness, excellence,

accomplishment.
dèarrsgnaich, see dèarrsg.
———e, -an, *s.m.* Polisher. 2 Polished, accomplished man.
†dèarrsgnaidn, -e, *a.* Wise, prudent.
dèarrsgnaidh, -e, *a.* Burnished, polished. 2** Polite. 3** Bright, of good parts, accomplished.
dèarrsguuidh, *s.m.* see dèarrsgnaiche. 2 Science.
———eachd, *s. f. ind.* Polish, elegance, neatness. 2 Excellence.
dèarrsgta, *past pt.* of dèarrsg.
dèarrsnaiche,* see dèarrsgnaiche.
dèars, see dèarrs.
dèarsach, see dèarrsach.
dèarsadh, see dèarrsadh.
dèarsaich, see dèarrs.
dèarsaigheachd, see dèarrsaigheachd.
dèarsanta, -ainte, *a.* see dèarrsach.
dèarsgaich, see dèarrs.
†dèarsgnaidh, -e, *a.* Excellent, perfect. 2 Wise, prudent.
dèarsnaich, *v.* see dèarrsg.
†deart, *a.* Shining.
dearta ? contraction of " de thubhairt thu ?"
dèar-theach,** *s.m.* Apartment in a monastery appropriated for prayers and acts of penitence.
Deas, -eise, *s.f.* The South (*for* an àirde deas) 2**Pew. 3***rarely* Order, rule, method. Bho 'n D., *from the South.*
deas, deise, *a.* South. 2 Right-hand (side.) 3 Ready, prepared. 4 Dexterous, skilful, expert. 5 Proper, fit. 6 Easily accomplished. 7 Pretty, handsome. 8 Trim, having an appearance of activity. 9**Portly. 10*Well-shaped, elegant. 11**Active. An làmh dh., *the right hand*; gaoth dh., *or* gaoth á d., *a south wind;* rinn thu sin gu d., *you have done that properly*; duine d., *a well-shaped, personable individual*; *2 a prudent man—Lewis*; am bheil thu d. (in *Lewis & Uist* deiseil)? *are you ready? have you done?* bu d. dhomh sin a dhèanamh, *I could easily accomplish that*; bu d. dhomh mo làmh a ghlacail, *I could easily engage*, or *close a bargain*; fhreagair e mi gu d., *he answered me readily;* d. dheth, *finished with it*; air an deise dh'éireadh fonn, *who would most readily raise a song—Gu ma slàn a chì mi.*
deas,** *v.n.* Remain, abide.
deasach, *a.* Southerly.
deasach, -aich, *s.m.* South-countryman. 2 Native of Southern Gaeldom. 3 (MMcD) Loch Fyne type of fishing-boat.—*Lewis.*
———adh, -aidh, *s.m.* Preparation, dressing. 2 Act of preparing or dressing. 3 Baking. 4 Batch of bread. 5 Adorning. A' d—, *pr.pt.* of deasaich. Rinn e d., *he made preparation*; d. an fhùineadair, *the baker's dressing.*
———d,* *s.f.ind.* Aptitude, qualification, quality.
deasad, -aid, *s.m.* see deisead.
deasadan, -ain, *s.m.* Common-place book, book of reference. 2**Repository.
deasaich, *pr. pt.* a' deasachadh, *v.a.* Prepare, get ready. 2 Dress, cook. 3 Bake. 4 Gird. 5**Mend. 6**Correct. 7**Attemper. 8**Accomplish. 9**Adorn. D. do chlaidheamh, *gird on your sword.*
———e, *s.m.* Cook, baker. 2 Editor.
———te, *past pt.* of deasaich, Prepared, made ready. 2 Dressed. 3 Cooked. 4**Corrected. 5 Adjusted, amended.
deasail, see deiseil.
deasal, -aile, see deiseil.
———an, -ain, *s.m.* see deisealan.
———as, see deasalachd.
deasbair, -ean, *s. m.* Disputant. [** gives —e as *nom. sing.*]
———,* *v.a.* Argue, dispute.
———each, -aiche, *a.* Argumentative.
———eachd, *s.f.ind.* Dispute. 2 Reasoning, conference, debate, pleading, argumentation. 3 Wrangling. 4 Act of disputing or arguing, disputation. Mór dh., *much reasoning.*
———ich, *pr.pt.* a' deasbaireachadh, *v.n.* Dispute, plead, argue, wrangle.
———iche,** *s. m.* Disputant, pleader, arguer, wrangler.
deas-bhriathrach,(WC) *a.* Eloquent.
deasbud, -uid, -an, *s.m.* Dispute. 2††Debate, conference.
deascadh, -aidh, see deasgainn.
deas-chainnt, -e, -ean, *s.f.* Eloquence.
———each, *a.* Eloquent, witty, ready in replying.
deas-cheumach, -aiche, *a.* Stately in gait. 2 Having a neat manner of walking.
deas-fhacal, -ail, -clan, *s. m.* Ready word. 2 Smart reply.
deas-fhaclach, -aiche, *a.* Ready-witted. 2 Eloquent, ready-worded.
deas-fhear,‡‡ *s.m.* Ambidexter.
deasg, *v.n.* Parch.
deasgachd, *s.f.ind.* Parchedness.
deasgadh, -aidh, -ean, *s.m.* see deasgainn. †2 Lees, dregs. D. an t-sluaigh, *the rabble, the mob.*
deasgainn, -e, -ean, *s.f.* Rennet. 2 Yeast. 3 Lees, dregs, refuse.
———each,** *a.* Full of dregs, or lees. 2 Yeasty, barmy.
deasgainnean, given by * for deasgainn.
†deasgair,** *v.a.* Pluck off the ears.
deasganan, *Lewis* for deasgainn.
deasgann, -ainne, -an, see deasgainn.
deasghabhail, *s.f.* Ascension-day.
deasghair, -e, *a.* On the right hand.
deas-ghluasad,‡‡ *s.m.* Proper gestures.
deas-ghnàth, -àith, -an, *s.m.* Ceremony. 2 Custom, usage. Lagh nan d., *the ceremonial law.*
———ach, -aiche, *a.* Ceremonious, ceremonial. 2 Customary.
———achd, *s.f.ind.* Ceremony.
deas-ghnàth-tòrraidh, *s. m.* Obsequies, funeral rites or ceremonies.
deasgraich, -ean, *s.m.* Heterogeneous mass.
deasguinn, see deasgainn.
———each, see deasgainneach.
deas-iomairt,‡‡ *s.f.* Proper gestures.
deas-iùil,** see deiseal.
deas-labhairt, *s.m.* Eloquence, address, fluency of speech. 2‡‡Elocution.
deas-labhrach, -aiche, *a.* Eloquent, having a command of language.
deas-labhradh, -aidh, see deas-labhairt.
deas-lamh, -laimh, *s.f.* Right hand.
———ach, -aiche, *a.* Right-handed, ambidexterous. 2 Dexterous, "neat-handed." 3 Ready-handed. 4 Of, or pertaining to, a right hand.
———achd, *s.f.ind.* Ambidexterity. 2 Dexterity, "neatness" of hand.
deasmaireachd, see deasmireachd.
deasmaireas, see deismireachd.
deasmas, -ais, *s.m.* see deasmireachd.
deasoireach, -aiche, *a.* Spicy.
———d,** *s.f.* Spiciness.
deasp,(MMcL) *s.* Chain of a padlock.
deaspoireachd, see deasbaireachd.
deaspoirich, see deasbairich.
deaspud, -uid, see deasbud.
deasuchadh, see deasachadh.
deasuich, see deasaich.
deat, -a, *pl.* deathaid, *s.m. & f.* Unshorn year-

old ewe *or* wether Cosmhuil ri d., *like an unfleeced year-old sheep.*

deatach, -aiche, -aichean, *s. f.* Smoke. 2 Vapour, steam, exhalation, fume. 3* Smoke on the point of breaking into flame. 4 Gas. Cuir d., *emit smoke* ; a' cur na deataich, *emitting smoke* ; breislich á deataich, *drunkenness from the fumes* (*of whisky* ; fhuair e car troimh 'n deataich, *he got a toss in the smoke.*—referring to a stroke of good luck. If you heard of anyone having £1,000 come in a windfall to him, you would say " Fhuair e car troimh 'n deataich," or " is ann roimhe a dh' éirich an naosg."

†deatacha, see deatachail.

deatachail, -ala, *a.* Smoky. 2**Misty. 3**Full of vapour or exhalation.

deatachair, -e, *a.* see deatachail.

deatachan, -ain, -an, *s.m.* Chimney, vent.

deatach-thalmhuinn, -aich-, *s.m.* Fumitory, see lus-deatach-thalmhuinn.

deataich, *gen. sing.* of deatach.

deatam, -aim, *s.m.* Anxiety, eagerness, solicitude. 2*Keenness.

———ach, -aiche, *a.* Anxious, eager, solicitous. 2* Necessary, needed—*Islay*. 3*Keen for the world—*Skye*.

deatamas,* -ais, *s,m.* Requisite, family necessity or want.

deathach, see deatach.

———ail, -ala, see deatachail.

——— -thalmhuinn, see lus-deatach-thalmhuinn.

deathadh,(CR) *subj.* of rach, Would go—*Suth'd.*

deathaid,(AF) *s.f.* Two-year-old sheep.

deathnaid,(AF) *s.f.* Sheep separated from flock.

decreut,** *s.m.* Gaelic spelling of *decree.*

dée, *pl.* of dia. Ainm an dée, *the name of their gods.*

deibh, see mu dhéidhinn. 2 see diathaibh.

†deibhe, *s.f.* Care, diligence.

deibheach,** *a.* Hasty, hurried, flurried. 2 contentious. 3 Passionate.

———d,** *s. f.* Hastiness, hurriedness. 2 Contentiousness. 3 Passionateness.

†deibheadh, -eidh, *s.m.* Debate. 2 Battle. 3 Haste, speed.

deibhidhe,** *s.f.* Kind of verse or *dàn dìreach*, having several rules to be observed, among which are that the first quatrain shall end in a minor termination, and the second in a major termination. [This word, given by **, does not appear to be used in Scotland.]

déibhinn, see mu dhéidhinn.

déibhleach, *a.* Diminutive.

déibhleid, -e, -ean, *s.f.* Feeble, awkward, unhandy person.

déibhleidheachd, *s.f.ind.* Inability, awkwardness, wretchedness, clumsiness, helplessness.

déibhlin, -linne, *s.f.* Poverty.

déibhreagach,‖ *s.m.* Whitlow. [Preceded by the article *an.*]

deic, -e, *a.* Convenient, fitting. 2* Due. 3 Legal, lawful. 4 Sufficient. †5 Hairy. 6 Easy. Cha d. a dhol dhachaidh, *it is not easy to go home* ; cha d. luathas na h-earba gun na coin a chur rithe, *the swiftness of the roe is known without the loosening of the hounds*—N.G.P.

deich, *a.* Ten. D. clachan, *ten stones* ; d. fir, *ten men.*

deich-bhrigh, *s.f.* The decalogue.

———te, see deich-bhrigh.

deicheach, see deich-fillte.

deicheamh, *a.* Tenth. An d. fear, *the tenth man.*

———, -eimh, *s. m.* Tithe, the tenth part. 2 Decimal. 3 " Ten " at cards. Bheir mi d. dhuit, *I will give you a tenth part.*

———achd,** *s.f.ind.* Decimation.

———adh, *s.m.* see deicheamh, *s.*

———aich, *v. a.* Decimate, addecimate, tithe, divide into tenths.

deich-fillte, *a.* Ten-fold, decuple.

deichimnich, see deicheamhaich.

†Deichmhios, -a, *s.m.* December.

deichnear, *s.m.* Ten persons. 2 Decade. Air sgàth dh., *for the sake of ten persons* ; cha robh air fhàgail ach aon deichnear, *there were only ten left.* [Followed by the *gen. pl.*]

deich-ràmhach, Kind of boat, see p. 78. [A certain man when ordering a boat said, " siaràmhach a dhion ochd-ràmhach, a dhèanamh feum deich-ràmhach, 's nach fhàgadh a bheag de luchd bìrlinn dà-ràmh-dheug ri là math soirbheis." At that time the price of a boat depended on the number of oars she carried, so the man wanted a 12-oared boat for the price of a 6-oared one.]

deich-roinn, -e, -ean, *s.f.* Decimal, tenth part.

———each, *a.* Decimal.

deich-shlisneach, -niche, -nichean, *s.f.* Decagon.

———, *a.* Ten-sided.

deich-shlisneag,** *s.f.* see deich-shlisneach.

deich-thaobhach, -aiche, *a.* Ten-sided.

———, -aich, -aichean, *s.m.* Ten-sided figure, decagon.

deicir, -e, see deacair.

déid (for téid) see under rach & theirig.

†deid, *s.f.* Obedience, submission. 2 Care, diligence.

déid-chnàimh, see deud-chnàimh.

déide, see déideadh. 2** *rarely* Submission, obedience.

deide, see deid.

déideadh,‖ -idh, *s.m.* The toothache. [Preceded by the article *an.*]

déideag, -eig, -an, *s.f.* Pebble. 2 Toy, bauble. 3 Little fair one. 4 Ribwort, see slàn-lus. 5 ††Gift. 6††Darling one.

déidh, -e, -ean, *s.f.* Wish, desire, longing. 2 Contention. 3**Fondness, love. 4** *rarely* Protector, defender. A dh. air òl, *his great propensity for drink*; tha e an d. oirre, *he is very fond of her.*

déidh, *prep.* After. 'Na dh. sin, *after that;* 'na d., *after her;* 'nar d., *after us*; m' ar d., *about* or *concerning us*; 'nam dh.,*after me*; chuir mise 'nan d. mo ghlaodh, *I called after them.*

déidh-bhodach,** *s.m.* Old lecher. 2 Dotard.

deidhe,** *s.f.* Pair.

déidhealachd, * *s.f.ind.* Extreme or degree of desire or propensity. 2 Enthusiasm. 3 Industry.

déidheanach,**-aiche, *a.* Fond, loving, amorous. 2 Pretty. 3 Late, last, hindermost. 4 Dilatory.

déidheil, -eala, *a.* Desirous, fond of, addicted to. 2 Enthusiastic. 3 Persevering. D. air an uisge-bheatha, *fond of whisky ;* cho d. aig a ghnothach, *so enthusiastic at his business.*

déidhinn, see mu dhéidhinn.

déidh-làimh,* (an) *adv.* Too late, afterwards. 2 After-hand, behind. 3 In arrears.

déidhs,(CR) *s.f.* Gaelic spelling of *dais*—*Gairloch.*

deifir, -e, *s.f.* Haste, speed, hurry, expedition, despatch. 2 (PM) Difference. Cha'n 'eil e gu d., *it does not matter.* [A Gaelic form of *difference.*]

——each, -iche, *a.* see deifreach.

——ich, *v.a.* see deifrich.

deifreach, -riche, *a.* Hasty, in haste, speedy, expeditious. 2 Causing hurry or despatch. 3 Requiring expedition. 4 (PM) Eccentric. Gnothach d., *an affair requiring the utmost expedition ;* fhreagair mi gu d., *I answered*

speedily; duine d., *an eccentric* or *peculiar man.*
———-adh, -aidh, *s.m.* Hastening, hurrying, act of hastening, hurrying or bestirring. 2 Haste, expedition. A' d—, *pr.pt.* of deifrich. A' d. gu mór, *hastening greatly.*
deifreadh,** -eidh, *s.m.* Haste. 2 Difference.
deifrich, *pr.pt.* a' deifreachadh, *v.a.* & *n.* Hasten, hurry, speed, bestir, make haste. D. ort, *be quick.*
———te, *past pt.* & *a.* Hastened.
deigh, -e, *pl.* -ean [-eachan & -eannan] *s.f.* see eigh. [Final *d* of the old article has been attached in *déigh.*]
déigh, *prep.* see déidh.
deigh, *a.* More fit.
deigheach, -iche, *a.* see eigheach.
déigheanach, see déidheanach.
deigheanach,** -aich, *s.m.* see eigheanach.
deigheann,(DU) -inn, *s.m.* Shackles for a horse. Each air deighinn, *a shackled horse.*
déigheil, see déidheil.
déighinn, *for* mu dhéidhinn.
deighinn,(DU) *v.a.* Shackle, tie the legs of a horse to prevent it wandering far.
déigh-làimh, see déidh-làimh.
deighlean, -ein, -an, *s.m.* Quire of paper.
deighnich, *v.a.* Fetter feet of cattle, &c.
deil, -e, -ean, *s.f.* Turner's lathe. 2 Axle. 3 Sharp iron rod. 4 Mare. 5**Cow's udder. 6 (AF) Two-year-old sow or pig. 7 see deala. 8 Two, double. 9 see dealas. 10**Twig. 11 see déile. Fo sparradh an deile, *in the coffin.*
——, *a.* see déidheil. 2 see dil.
deil,** *v.a.* Turn with a lathe.
deil-aodannach, -aiche, *a.* Two-faced.
deilb,(AF) see dealb.
deilbh, -e, -ean, *s.f.* see dealbh. 2 *gen.sing.* of dealbh.
——, *v.a. pr. pt.* a' deilbh. see dealbh. Tha i 'deilbh an aodaich, *she is warping.*
†——, *a.* Fine, fair, sprightly. 2 Brave. 3 Sightly.
deil'-bhainne, (AF) *s.* Milk-dish *or* cup.
†deilbh-bhog, -oig, -oigean, *s.f.* Seal.
deilbh-chaochladh, see dealbh-chaochladh.
deilbheag, -eig, see dealbhag.
†deil-bhealach, -aich, *s.m.* Meeting of two ways.
deilbhean, -ein, see dealbhan. [†† gives —ein as *nom.sing.*]
deilbhich, *v.a.* see dealbh, *v.*
deilbhidh, see dealbhaidh.
deilbhin, -e, -ean, see dealbhan.
deilbhte, see dealbhta.
deilchead,** *a.* Ill. 2 Bad. 3 Sad.
deil-cheannach, -aiche, *a.* Two-headed, double-topped.
'deile? (for ciod eile?) *interr.pron.* What else? 'D. a th' air t' aire? *what else do you mean?*; d. a dheanainn? *what else could I do?*; d. a dheanadh e? *what else would he do?*
deile,* see déidhealachd.
deile, *gen.sing.* of deil.
déile, -idh, [-an &] -leachan, *s.f.* Deal, plank. 2 Plank on which a corpse is laid. 3 Pale in *heraldry*, to represent a narrow board as used in fencing. Tha e air an d., *he is stretched*—dead; fo sparradh nan déilean, *in the coffin.*
déileach, *a.* Planked.
———adh, -aidh, *s.m.* Contabulation.
———an, *n.pl.* of déile.
déileadair, -ean, *s.m.* Turner. 2 Sawyer.

269. *Déile.*

———eachd, *s.f.ind.* Turnery, business of a turner, or 2 of a sawyer.
déileag, -eige, -an, *s. f.* Little deal, board or lath. 2**Rod.
déileagach,†† *a.* Abounding in little deals.
†deileala, *s.f.* Space of two years.
deilean,** -ein, *dim.* of deil. Little lathe. 2 (AF)Gunnel (fish.) 3 see deileann.
deileang,(AF) *s.m.* Pig. 2 Young sow, two-yr. old sow.
deileann, -linn, *s.m.* Loud sharp barking, as of a dog. 2 Whining. Bha 'n cù a' d. fad na h-oidhche, *the dog was whining all night;* a' tabhannaich le deifir a bhi deileann air an tòrach, *briskly barking with eagerness to be at full bay in the chase.*
deile-aodannach,** *a.* see deil-aodannach.
deileas, -eis, see dealas. 2**Grudging through avarice.
———ach,(CR) *a.* Convenient, advantageous, having easy access to conveniences or advantages—*Skye.*
déile-bhogadain,(DC) *s.f.* See-saw—*Uist.*
deile-mhuc,(AC) *s.f.* Two-year-old sow
deile-roinn, *s.f.* Party per pale, in *heraldry.*
deile-thorc,** -thuirc, *s.m.* Two-year-old hog.

270. *Deile-roinn.*

deilf,(AF) *s.f.* Dolphin.
deilg, *gen.sing.* of dealg.
deilge, *gen.sing.* of dealg.
deilginneach,* *s.* Shingles. 2 Small-pox.—*Islay.*
deilgionnadh, -aidh, *s.m.* Waste, havoc. 2 Depopulation.
deilgne, *s.pl.* Thorns, prickles.
———ach, -niche, *a.* Thorny, prickly. Cadal d., *the "pins and needles."*
———ach, -nich, *s.m.* Spear-thistle.
deil-gréine, *s.m.* see deò-ghréine.
deilich, *v.a.* see dealaich. 2**Board (with wood.) 3**Contabulate.
†deilidh, -e, -ean, *s.f.* Pursuit.
déilig, -ige, -ean, *s.m.* Gaelic spelling of *dealing.*
———, *pr. pt.* a' déiligeadh, *v.a.* & *n.* Deal, transact business, treat with.
———eadh, -idh, *s. m.* Transacting business. A' d—, *pr. pt.* of déilig.
deilin,** *s.f.* Trespass.
deilinn, *v.n.* Yelp, bark, as a dog.
†deill, *v.n.* Lean upon.
deillseag, -eige, -an, *s.f.* Blow with the open hand. 2**Slap on the breech. 3**Box on the ear or cheek.
†deilm, *s.f.* Noise, rumbling, trembling.
†deil-oidhche, *s.f.* Space of two nights.
†deilt, -e, *s.f.* Separation.
deil-tharruing, *s.f.* Trigger. 2 Iron nail.
deil-theine,(AH) *s.f.* Iron rod, used when heated, for boring holes in wood.
deiltre, † *s.m.* Druid idols. 2 School of magic.
———ach,†† *a.* Gilt.
———adh, -aidh, *s.m.* Gilding, lacquering.
deiltrich,** *v.a.* Gild.
———e,** *s.m.* Gilder.
†deim, *s.f.* Lack, want. 2 Failing, deficiency.
deimh, -e, *a.* Dark, hidden.
†deimhe, *s.f.* Darkness. 2 Defence, protection.
deimheas, -eis, -easan, see deamhas.
deimhinn,** *v.* see deimhinnich.
———, -e, *a.* True, certain, of a truth, sure. Gu d., *truly, indeed, certainly*; gu d., d., tha mi ag ràdh riut, *verily, verily, I say unto thee*; d. sgeul, *a true story*; tha a' dh. agam gu..., *I know for a fact that...*
déimhinn, -e, *s.f.* Desire or concern about anything.
———each,** *a.* Affirmative.
———eachd, *s.f.ind.* Certainty, proof.
———ich, *pr.pt.* a' deimhinneachadh, *v.a.*

Affirm, confirm, ascertain, prove, verify, demonstrate, assure.
†deimhne, *s.f.* Assurance, certainty. 2 Truth. 3 Edged tools.
deimhneach,** *a.* Affirmative.
deimhnich, see deimhinnich.
†dein, *s.f.* Lack, want.
†dein, -e, *a.* Clean, neat. 2 Strong, firm.
déin, -e, *a.* Vehement.
déine, *comp.* of dian. More or most keen or eager. Mu choinneamh a' chath a's d., *pending* or *about to engage in the hottest battle.*
——, *s.f.ind.* Eagerness, keenness, vehemence, ardour, violence, impetuosity. 2**Neatness. 3**Cleanness. 4 Sometimes used for teine.
déineachd, *s.f.ind.* Keenness, violence, emphasis, vehemence, impetuosity, eagerness, fierceness, ardour.
————ach, -aiche, *a.* Rude, rough. 2 Vehement, violent, urgent, fierce. 3 Bold. 4 Keen. 5 Grievous. 6 Cruel. 7 Incessant. 8 Emphatic, (as speech.) 9 Mad. Uisge d., *incessant rain* ; labhair e gu d., *he spoke emphatically.*
déinead, *s.f.* Same meanings as déine.
déineas, -eis, *s.m.* Eagerness, keenness, vehemence, fierceness. 2* Faint attempt to be diligent or eager. 3 Impetuousness, violence. [* gives deineis as *nom.sing.*]
————ach, -aiche, *a.* see déineachdach.
————achd, *s.f.* see déineachd.
déineis, see déineas.
deinib, see deirbh.
deinmheach,** -hiche, *a.* Vain, frivolous. 2 Void.
—————air,** *s.m.* Toyman, pedlar. 2 Trifling, vain fellow.
†déinmheas, -eis, *s.m.* Vanity, self-conceit. 2 Frivolousness.
déinmheasair, -ean, *s.m.* Vain, frivolous fellow.
deinmhich,** *v.n.* Vanish.
†deinmhin, -e, -ean, *s. m.* Vain fellow, trifler.
†deinmne, *a.* Swift, active.
deir, *v.n., pres. ind.* Say. Used thus, A deirim, *I say;* a deir thu, *or* deir thu, e, i, sinn, &c., *thou, he, she, we, &c. say.*
deir, -e, *s.f.* The Shingles, St. Anthony's fire.
deir-ainfhiach,** *s.pl.* Arrears.
†deirbh, *s.f.* Churn.
†deirbhe, see dearbhadh.
déirc, -e, -ean, *s.f.* Alms, charity. Thoir d., *give alms ;* naomh-dh., *alms collected at church;* mo dh. ort ! *give me alms !* ; chaidh mi air an d., *I took to begging ;* diol-déirc, *an object of pity.*
——each, -ich, *s.m.* Object of charity. 2 Beggar. Bu tu fuasgladh nan d., *thou wert the needy's aid.*
——each, -iche, *a.* Poor, penurious. 2 Ready to give alms, charitable. 3 Of, like, or pertaining to, alms or charity. 4**Seeking alms.
déirceachail, -hala, *a.* Charitable, almsgiving.
déirceag, -eige, -an, *s.f.* Term of contempt or ridicule for a parsimonious female. 2 **Female mendicant.
déircear, -eir, -an, *s. m.* Almoner. [†† gives -eir as *nom. sing.*]
deirciche, see deircear.
deircire, -an, *s.m.* see deircear.
déirc-Pheadair,(AC) *s.f.* (St. Peter's tribute.) The fish caught in the Isles on Xmas Day, and given to the poor.
déirc-roinneadair,** *s.m.* Almoner.
†deirdeas, *v.* They say.
deir-dhunnan,** *s.m.* see deir-thunnan.
†deire, *s.f.* Abyss, pool. 2 The deep.
déireach,(DU) *s.f.* Thrill, dirl, as the result of a sharp blow.
deire, -annan, see deireadh.
deireadh, *a.* see deireannach.
deireadh, -ridh, -ridhean, *s.m.* End, conclusion. 2 The end, rear, hindmost part of anything. 3 Stern of a ship. 4**Extremity. 5 Back of a cart.—*W. Isles, Argyll, &c.* D. na bliadhna, *the year's end* ; ceann deiridh, *hinder part, stern, posteriors* ; air dh., *behind;* air d., *last* ; d. feachd, *the rear of an army;* d. an ni seo, *the end of this thing;* d. na luinge, *the stern of the ship ;* d. cuaiche, *a round stern,* d. poite, *lees;* mu dh., *at last :* toiseach tighinn is d. falbh, *first to come and last to go* (motto of Goll MacMorna) ; feith ri a' dheireadh, *respice finem* ; aig d. an là is math na Domhnullaich, *the MacDonalds can be relied on at the end of the day* ; is beag an ni nach d. a's t-Fhoghar, *it is a little thing that is not a hindrance in Autumn.*
————-buana,‡‡ *s.f.* Harvest-home.
————-cairte, *s.m.* Back of a cart.
————-chrè, (PM) *s.m* In Uist, applied to the ingathering of the potato and turnip crop. The ordinary *deireadh-buana* comes first, followed by the d.-chrè, when the potatoes are secured.
————-cuaiche, *s.m.* Round stern of a ship.
†deiream, *v. pres. aff. a.* I say.
deireannach, -aiche, *a.* Last, hindmost, latter. 2 Late, tardy, slow, dilatory, behind. 'S na laithean d., *in the latter days*; an neach d., *the last individual.*
—————d,** *s.f.* Backwardness.
deireannan, -ain, *s.m.* Dessert.
deireas, -eis,-an, *s.m.* Injury, harm, hurt. 2 Loss, calamity. 3 Defect, damage. 4 Mischief. 5 Requisite, convenience. 6 Want, scarcity. Deireasan; *domestic requisites or conveniences* ; tha mi gun d., *I am quite well* ; cha robh dìth no d. oirre, *she wanted nothing.*
deireasach, -aiche, *a.* Damaged, hurt, lame. 2 Mischievous, detrimental. 3*Very requisite, needful. 4 Defective. 5**Calamitous. 6** Injurious, hurtful.
deireasachd,** *s.f.* Injuriousness, hurtfulness, calamitousness.
deir'-fhiachan, *s.pl.* Arrears.
deirge, *comp.* of dearg. More or most red. Fìon a's d. dreach, *wine of the reddest hue.*
deirge, *s.f.* Redness, ruddiness. 2 Red, vermilion. D. shùl, *redness of the eyes.*
deirgead, -eid, *s.f.* Degree of redness, red. A' dol an d., *growing redder and redder.*
deirgid, *second comp.* of dearg. Is d. e seo, *it is the redder for this;* cha d. e sin, *it is not the redder for that.*
†deirginnleadh, -idh, *s.m.* Red cattle.
deirid,** *s.f.* Mystery. 2 Secret.
deirideach,** *a.* Secret, hidden, private.
deiridh, *gen. sing.* of deireadh.
deirim, see deir.
deirionnach, -aiche, see deireannach.
†deirire, *s.m.* Clamour.
deirse,** -an, *s.f.* Goal, gate.
†deirte, *past part.* Was said.
deir-thunnan, -ain, *s.m.* Dessert, collation.
dèis, *s.f.* Pew. Gaelic spelling of *dais.*
déis *adv.* An déis, (*not* for an déidh. Old Gaelic was " daneis," *after them.*‡) After. 2†† Afterwards.
déis,* *v.a.* Skelp the breech.
déis, *dat.sing.* of dias.
deis, *dat. sing. f.* of *a.* deas. 2 *gen. sing.* of *s.* deas, see deise.

deisboireachd, see deasbaireachd.
deisceart,** *s.m.* The southern point, the south quarter.
deisciobul, -uil, *s.m.* Disciple.
————achd,** *s.f.* Discipleship.
deiscir,* *a.* Active, nimble. 2 Quick, fierce, sudden.
deiscreideach,** *a.* Discreet, prudent. 2 Grave, sober.
deis-dé,(AC) *s.* Girth, sanctuary, godwards, place of safety. 2 Spot in game " tig " where the player within is secure and cannot be touched.
deis-dé,†† *int.* Halt ! Mu'n abradh tu " deas-dé," *before you had time to speak, before you could say " Jack Robertson."*
déisdinn, see déisinn & déistinn.
————each, see déisinneach.
déise, *gen. sing.* of *s.* dias.
deise, *gen. sing. f.* of *a.* deas. A dh'ionnsuidh na làimhe deise, *to the right hand.*
deise, *comp.* of deas. Is i a' Ghàidhlig ni 's d. dhomh na a' Bheurla, *Gaelic comes more readily to me than English.*
——,‡‡ *a.* Dual. An t-àireamh d., *the dual number.*
deise, -achan, *s.f.* Suit of clothes.
deise,** *s.f.* Couple, pair, two persons. 2 see deisead.
deiseach,** *a.* Southern, Southerly, towards the South.
deiseachadh, -aidh, *s.m.* Dressing. 2 Going in full dress. 3 Decoration, ornament.
deiseachan, *n.pl.* of deise.
deiseachd, *s.f.ind.* Convenience, neatness, elegance, handsomeness, ornament, dress. D. muineidh, *the ornament of learning.*
deisead, -eid, *s.f.* Neatness, elegance. 2 Readiness. 3* Symmetry of body, proportionable parts. 4**Cleanness. 5**Appositeness. Cha'n fhaca mi a leithid air dh., *I never saw its match for elegance.*
déiseag, -eige, -an, see déillseag.
déiseagaich,‡‡ *v. a.* Breech. 2 Whip on the breech.
déiseag-thubaist, *s.f.* Accidental slap with the open hand.
deiseal, -eala, *a.* Towards the South. southward. 2 Having a southern exposure. 3‡‡ Lucky. 4 Dexter in *heraldry.* 5 Ready, prepared. 6 Finished. Am feadh 'sa bhitheas a' ghrian a' dol d., *while the sun goes southwards*; d. air gach ni, *the sunward course with everything—south course, right direction;* cuimhnich am beagan a bha eadarainn, gu'm beil e d. dhomhs' agad, *remember that there is a little outstanding between us, you ought to have it ready for me.* Prosperous course, turning from east to west in the direction taken by the sun. D. air gach ni, *the sunward course (is the best) for everything.* This is descriptive of the ceremony observed by the Druids, of walking round their temples, by the south, in the course of their divinations, keeping the temple always on their right. This course was deemed prosperous, the contrary (tuathal) fatal, or at least, unpropitious. From this ancient superstition are derived several customs which are still retained amongst us, as drinking over the left thumb, as Toland expresses it, or according to the course of the sun. Martin says," some of the poorer sort of people in the Western Isles retain the custom of performing these circles sunwise about the persons of their benefactors three times, when they bless them, and wish good success to all their enterprises. Some are very careful, when they set out to sea, that the boat be first rowed sunwise, and if this be neglected, they are afraid their voyage may prove unfortunate. I had this ceremony paid me when in Islay by a poor woman, after I had given her an alms. I desired her to let alone that compliment, for that I did not care for it ; but she insisted to make these three ordinary turns, and then prayed that God and MacCharmaig, the patron saint of that island, might bless and prosper me in all my affairs. When a Gael goes to drink out of a consecrated fountain, he approaches it by going round the place from east to west, and at funerals, the procession observes the same direction in drawing near the grave. Hence also is derived the old custom of describing sunwise a circle, with a burning brand, about houses, cattle, corn and corn-fields, to prevent their being burnt, or in any way injured by evil spirits, or by witchcraft. This fiery circle was also made around women, as soon as possible after parturition, and also around newly-born babes. These circles were, in later times, described by midwives, and were deemed effectual against the intrusion of the *daoine sìth* or *sìthichean*, who were particularly on the alert in times of childbed, and not infrequently carried infants away, according to vulgar legends, and restored them afterwards, but sadly altered in features and in personal appearance. Infants stolen by fairies are said to have voracious appetites, constantly craving for food. In this case it was usual for those who believed that their children had been taken away, to dig a grave in the fields on quarter-day and there to lay the fairy skeleton till next morning, at which time the parents went to the place, where they doubted not to find their own child in place of the skeleton. "
deisealachd, *s.f.ind.* Readiness, circumstance of being prepared. 2 Convenience.
deisealan, -ain, *s.m.* Box or slap on the ear.
deisealas, -ais, see deisealachd.
déisean, -ein, *s.f.* see déisinn.
deisear, -eire, *a.* see deisearach. Fonn gun d. gréine, *land without a southern exposure.*
deisear, *s.m.* Place having a southern exposure. The north side of the country round Loch Tay is called Deisear, and the south side, Tuathar.
deisearach, -aiche, *a.* Sunny. 2 Having a southern exposure. 3* Conveniently situated, handy. 4 Applicable. D. air an sgoil, *near the school*; taobh d., *a countryside which has a southern exposure.*
————.—d,* *s.f.* Convenience in point of situation. 2 Applicability.
deisear-gréine, *s.m.ind.* Southern exposure.
deisearra, *a.* see deisearach.
deisearrach, see deisearach.
deiseil, -e, *a.* see deiseal.
deiseir, see deisear.
deise-mharcachd,** *s.f.* Riding-habit.
déisg,†† *pr.pt.* a' déisgeadh, *v.a.* Crack, split, dry up.
déisgeadh, -idh, -idhean, *s.m.* Chink, crack, fissure.
deisgeanan, *s.pl.* see deasgainn.
deisgiobul, -uil, see deisciobul.
†deisibh,** *s.pl.* Lands.
deisich, see deasaich.
deisimeireachd, see deismireachd.
déisinn, -e, *s.f.* Dislike, disgust. 2 Abomination, abhorrence. 3 Enormity. 4**Sadness. 5**Squeamishness. 6**Numbness. 7**Fright. 8‡‡Pity. 9* Disgust at the conduct or con-

sequences of skelping the breeches. 10 Physical weakness. Shil mo dheòir le d., *my tears dropped with sorrow;* tha d. air t' fhiaclaibh, *thy teeth are numbed,* or *on edge.*
déisinn,** *v.a.* Hate, abhor, detest.
———each, -niche, *a.* Ugly, horrible, frightful, disgusting, shocking. 2 Sorrowful, sad. 3**Squeamish.
———eachd, *s.f.ind.* Disgustfulness, ugliness, frightfulness. 2**Sorrowfulness. 3**Squeamishness.
deis-iùil,** *s.f.* see deiseal.
deisleann, -ein, *s.m.* Beam or ray of light, proceeding from any luminous body.
†deismich, *v.a.* Dress, adorn.
deismireach, -iche, *a.* Curious, inquisitive.
———d, *s.f.ind.* Curious prolix talk, curiosity. 2 Quibble. 3 Quotation.
deismireas, -eis, *s.m.* see deismireachd.
déisneach, -niche, see déisinneach.
déis-nòin,‡‡ *s.* Afternoon.
déistean, -ein, -einean, see déisinn.
———ach, see déisinneach.
deisthinn, see déisinn.
———each, see déisinneach.
deisthinneachd, see déisinneachd.
déistinn, see déisinn.
———each, see déisinneach.
———eachd, see déisinneachd.
deith, *s.f.* Iron rod, used when heated for boring holes in wood.
†——bhir, -e, *a.* Legal. 2 *s.f.*Charge, custody.
†——bhrigh, see deifrich.
·——ear, *Cowal* pron. of deifir.
†——idhe, *s.f.* Separation. 2 Care, diligence.
.——ionn,(DC) *s.m.* *Harris, Skye & Lewis* for deubhann.
deithineach, -niche, *a.* Dainty.
deithleann, see deileann.
deithlinn, see deilinn.
deithneamach, -aiche, *a.* Worldly, avaricious, too eager for gain.
deithneas, -is, *s.f.* Haste, speed.
———ach, -aiche, *a.* Keen, hasty.
de-meine,(AC) *s.* God-like mind.
deò, *s. f.* Breath. 2 Air. 3 The vital spark, life. 4 Ray of light. 5 Vision. 6**Place where a stream falls into the sea. Gun d., *breathless ;* cha'n 'eil aige na chumas an d. ann, *he has not what will keep the vital spark in him;* tha e an impis an d. a chall, *he is on the eve of giving up the ghost ;* cha'n 'eil d. gaoith' ann, *there is not a breath of wind ;* d. gealbhain, *a spark of fire ;* d. soluis, *a ray of light ;* cha tig d. de 'n ghréin a steach, *a single ray of sunshine shall not enter ;* an fheadh 'sa bhitheas an d. annad, *while you breathe ;* gun d. léirsinn, *without a ray of vision, stone-blind;* glacaibh mo dh., *take hold of my departing spirit* or *ghost ;* thug Abraham suas an d., *A. gave up the ghost.*
deòbhail, see deoghail.
deobhal, -ail, see deoghal.
———ach, see deoghalach.
———adh, see deoghaladh.
deoc,(CR) *v.* Suck—*Lewis.*
deocadan,(AC) -ain, see deocan.
deocan, -ain, *s.m.* Valve. 2*Noise in sucking. 3(AC) Sponge-like substance coughed up by a new-born foal. 4 The five-leaved shamrock, supposed to grow out of this substance after it is buried.
——— -an-gamhnach, (MMcD) *s. m.* Honeysuckle.
deocan-dearga,§ *s. m.* Red clover, see seamrag chapuill.
deoch, *irreg.s.f.* Thus declined:

	Sing.	*Plur.*
Nom.	deoch,	deochan, deochannan,
Gen.	dighe, [*not* dibhe]	dheochan, dheocannan,
Dat.	deoch,	deochan, deochannan,
Voc.	a dheoch !	a dheocha !

Drink, potion, draught. 2 Any kind of strong liquor. Thoir dhomh d., *give me a drink;* thoir d. as, *take a draught out of it ;* d. m' eòlais ort ! *may we be better acquainted !* (the drink of my acquaintance on you) .
deoch,†† -a, -annan, *s.f.* Drink, dram.
†——,** *v.a.* Embrace tenderly.
——air,** *s.f.* Difference, distinction.
——al,** -ail, *s.m.* Grudging.
——an, *n.pl.* of deoch. Spirits, all sorts of drinks, liquors.
—— -an-doruis, *s.f.* Stirrup-cup, parting drink.
—— -bhàn,(MMcD) *s.f.* Gruel, oatmeal drink.
—— -bhiugh,¶ *s.* Greenshank—*totanus glottis.*
—— -cadail,‡‡ *s.m.* Sleepy dose.
—— -Chloinn Donnachaidh, *s.m.* Stirrup-cup, parting drink.
deoch-eiridinn,* *s.f.* Potion, draught.
deoch-eòlais,* *s.f.* The first glass drunk to a stranger.
deoch-ìobairt,‡‡ *s.m.* Drink offering.
deoch-làidir, *s.m.* Strong drink.
deoch-leighis,‡‡ *s.m.* Medicinal potion.
deoch-maidne, *s.f.* The morning drink among the better-class Gaels of old, being an egg switched in a glass of milk, with a little whisky added—*Gael. Soc. Inv.*, xiv, p. 147.
deoch-mairt, *s.f.* Huge drink (*lit.* cow's drink.)
deoch-réite,‡‡ *s.m.* Friendship bowl.
—— -rèith,‡‡ *s.m.* Flummery, sowens.
—— -sgliap,‡‡ *s.m.* Drink at other's expense.
—— -slàinte, *s.f.* Health, toast. Dh' òl (*or* ghabh) e mo dh., *he drank my health.*
—— -thumte,‡‡ *s.m.* Decanted drink.
—— -uasal,‡‡ *s.m.* Costly drink, foreign drink.
deodh, *a.* Everlasting.
deòdhas, -ais, *s.m.* see deòthas.
deoghaidh, see déidh (after.)
deoghail, *pr.pt.* a' deoghal, *v.a.* Suck, as infants, or the young of quadrupeds. 2**Imbibe.
deoghal, -ail, *s.m.* Suckling. 2(AF) Sucking calf.
———ach, -aiche, *a.* Sucking, suckling, apt to suck or suckle.
———adair,** -ean, *s.m.* Sucker.
———adh,** -aidh, *s.m.* Sucking. 2 Imbibing. 2 Suction.
———ag, -aige, -an, *s. f.* Honeysuckle, see uilleann.
———agach,** *a.* Like honeysuckle. 2 Full of honeysuckle.
deoghladair,** -ean, *s.m.* Sucker.
deoghann, (mo dheoghann) see mu dhéidhinn.
deòghlair,‡‡ -e, -ean, *s.m.* Imbiber.
deò-ghréine, *s.f.* The name of Fingal's banner. 2 Ray, sunbeam. D. MhicCumhail, *Fingal's banner.*
deòidh, (fa) *adv.* (*or* fa dheaghaidh) At last, finally.
deòigh, *adv.* see deòidh.
deòin, -e, *s.f.* Accord, assent, will, purpose. A dheòin, *willingly ;* am (= do m') dheòin-sa *with my consent* or *concurrence ;* le d. Dhé, *God willing,* ("D. V.") ; a dh. no a dh' aindeoin, *nolens volens ;* cha b' ann am dh. a rinn mi e, *I did not do it intentionally,* or *on purpose (I was forced to do it)* ; nach seachnadh le d. an àrach, *that would not willingly shun the field* (*of battle.*)
———-bhàidh, -e, *s.f.* Strong attachment. 2‡‡

Indulgence.
deòinich, *v.a.* see deònaich.
deòir, *gen. sing. & n. pl.* of deur.
†deòir,** *s.f.* Will,pleasure,inclination,purpose.
deòireachd, *s.f.ind.* Proneness to tears, *prov.*
deòirid, see deòiridh.
deoirideach, *s.m.* see deòiridh.
deòiridh, -e, -ean, *s. m.* Melancholy, tearful creature, see deurach. 2††Poor desolate creature.
†———, (given by ** as deòraidh,) -e, -ean, *s.m.* Disobedience. 2 Surety who withdraws himself. 3 Stranger. 4 Guest. 5 Exile. 6 Vagabond. 7(MMcL) Pilgrim.
†deòirseach, -ich, *s.m.* Slave. 2 Porter, doorkeeper.
deòl, *contr.* for deoghail.
deòlach, *a.* see deoghalach.
deòlachadh,‡‡ -aidh, *s.m.* see deoghaladh.
deolaidh,** *s.* Aid. 2 Dowry. 3 Grace, pardon.
deolag,** *s.f,* Honeysuckle, see uilleann.
———an,** *s.m.* Honeysuckle, see uilleann.
deolchadh,** -aidh, *s. m.* Sotting, drinking copiously.
deolchar,** -air, *s.m.* Present.
deònach, -aiche, *a.* Agreeable, willing, granting. Gu d., *willingly* ; an d. leat? *art thou willing?*
deònach,* *adv.* Most willingly, voluntarily. Is d. a dheanainn-sa e, *most willingly would I do it.*
deònachadh, -aidh, *s.m.* Granting, act of granting, giving consent. 2 Bestowing, bestowal, A' d—, *pr. pt.* of deònaich.
deònachas, -ais, *s.m.* see deòntachd.
†deonachd, *s.f.* Pudendum.
deònaich, *pr. pt.* a' deònachadh, *v.a.* Grant, vouchsafe. 2 Give consent, approve. 3** Bestow, impart. 4**Allow,permit. D. dhuinn gàirdeachas do shlàinte, *vouchsafe unto us the joy of thy salvation*; gu'n deònaicheadh Dia, *God grant.*
————te, *past part.* Allowed.
deòntach, -aiche, *a.* see deònach.
deontachd, *s.f.* see deòntas.
deòntas, -ais, *s.m.* Willingness.
deònuich, see deònaich.
deòr, -òir, see deur.
deòr, *s.m.* Feeble man.
deòir, *pl.* deòra, Almoner.
deòra, *s.m.* see deòradh.
†deòrach, -aiche, *a.* see deurach.
————adh, -aidh, *s.m.* Banishing, banishment. 2 Act of banishing or exiling. A' d—, *pr.pt.* of deòraich. Fhuair e d., *he got himself banished.*
————an, *s.m.* see deurach.
deòrachd, *s. f. ind.* Banishment, exile. 2 Pilgrimage. 3 Affliction. Air d., *in banishment.*
deòradh, -aidh, *pl.* -aidh & -aidhean, *s.m.* Alien, stranger. 2 Helpless, afflicted, forlorn being. 3**Fugitive, outlaw.
deòraich, *pr.pt.* a' deòrachadh, *v.a.* Banish, expel.
deòraidh, -e, -ean, see deòiridh. 2 *gen. sing. & n. pl.* of deòradh.
†————, -e, *a.* Strong, stout, robust.
————eachd, *s.f.* see deòrachd.
deòrail,** *a.* In tears, wretched.
deòranta,** *a.* Exotic, extraneous. 2 Banished, expelled. 3 Strange.
deoth,** *a.* Active, clever, manly.
deòthadh,§ *s.m.* Henbane, see gafann. 2 Drying up, as of water, evaporation. see dèabhadh.
deothaidh, (deoghaidh) 'S minn bheag as an deothaidh 'gan deoghal mu'n chrò, *and little kids following and sucking them about the fold.* *Donn. Bàn*, p. 109, 5th. Ed.
deothail, see deoghail.
deothal, see deoghal.
deòthan,‡‡ -ain, *s.m.* Air in gentle motion.
deòthas, -ais, *s.m.* Desire, longing, lust, great affection. 2**Fervour. 3‡ Eagerness. 4** Longing, as of a calf for its mother.
————ach, -aiche, *a.* Eager, fiery. 2 Fond, affectionate. 3* Very lustful, appetible, desirous, fervent, amorous. 4**Keen, as a calf for its mother.
————achd,** *s.f.ind.* Appetibility, avidity. 2 Earnestness.
deòthasaiche,** *s.m.* Amorous fellow, lecher.
————,** *comp.* of deòthasach.
deòthlag, *s.f.* Woodbine. 2**Honeysuckle.
————an,** -ain, *s.m.* Honeysuckle.
de 'r,(*for* de ar) Of our. 2 (*for* de ur) Of your.
†des, *s.f.* Land. 2 Spot, speckle.
†dese, *s.m.* Number.
†desreith, -e, -ean, *s.m.* Judge.
†det, *s.m.* Victuals. see diot.
deteigheach, -iche, see de-tigheach.
deth, *prep. pron.* Of him, of it. 2**From. 3** From off. 4**From among. Tog dh. ! *cease, nonsense !*; air mo shon-sa dh., *for my part of it.*
dethealaich,(JM) *s.f.* *Uist* for deith.
dethealaidh,(MMcL) see deith.
detheine, *s.f.* Boring-iron, *prov.* see deith.
detheodha, *s.f.* Henbane.
detheodhach,†† *a.* Abounding in hemlock.
deth-tigheach, *s.f.* *Uist* for de-tigheach.
detheogha, see detheodha.
de-tigheach, -iche, *s.f.* The weasand, gullet, windpipe, œsophagus, gorge, epiglottis.
deubh,* *s.f.* see deubhann.
deubh,* *v.a.* see dèabh.
deubhadh, -aidh, -aidhean, *s.m.* see dèabhadh. †2 Fight, quarrel. 3(MMcL) Dregs, lees. Tha a' chuinneag a' d. (dèabhadh), *the pitcher is leaking.*
deubhann, -ainn, -an, *s.f.* Horse-fetter.
deubhoil,* *s.f.* Enthusiasm, eagerness.
————,* *a.* Keen, enthusiastic—*Islay.*
deuch,* *v.a.* Taste, try. 2 Sort.
deuchainn, -e, -ean, *s. f.* Trial, hardship. 2 Experiment. 3 Attempt, endeavour. 4 Probation. 5 Proof. 6 Essay. 7 Distress. Fhuair mi d. dheth, *I got a taste* or *trial of it* ; thoir d. dha, *give it a trial.*
deuchainneach, -aiche, *a.* Trying, difficult, hard, distressing.
deuchainneachadh,‡‡ -aidh, *s.m.* Molestation.
deuchainnich,‡‡ *v.a.* Molest.
deuchainniche, *s.m.* One taken on trial, probationer, candidate. 2 Competitor.
deuchainnichte,** *a.* Approved.
deud, *s.m.* Tooth. 2 see deudach.
deudach, -aich, *s.m.* The teeth. 2 Set of teeth. 3**Jaw. 'Ga chagnadh fo d' dheudaich, *to chew it under thy teeth* ; mur comas duit teum, na ruisg do dheudach, *if you cannot bite, do not show your teeth.*
deudach,* -aiche, *s.f.* Tooth-brush.
deudach, -aiche, *a.* Of, or belonging to, teeth, dental. 2 Having a good set of teeth. 3 Dentated. 4 Of ivory. 5 Large-toothed. De chnàmha d., *of ivory.*
deudadh,** -aidh, see déideadh.
deudaiche,** *s.m.* Dentist.
deudair,** *s.m.* Dentist.
deud-cheartachadh, -aidh, *s. m.* Setting the teeth right.
deud-cheartachd,** *s.f.* Dentistry, business of a

dentist.
deud-cheartaich,** *v. a.* Set the teeth right, as a dentist.
deud-chnaimh,** *s.* Ivory. Adharcan d., *ivory horns.*
deud-gheal,†† *a.* White-toothed.
deudhan, see deubhann.
deug, *a.* Ten. [Used only in composition, as, Tri taighean deug, *thirteen houses.*]
†deunach, *a.* Sad, heavy, melancholy.
†———as, -ais, *s.m.* Sadness, heaviness, melancholy.
deur, deòir, *s.m.* Drop. 2 Tear. 3 Any small quantity of liquid. 4**Brine. A' sileadh nan deur, *shedding tears;* cha'n 'eil d. an seo, *there is not a drop here;* a deòir a' snitheadh, *her tears trickling.*
———ach, -aiche, *a.* Tearful, weeping. 2 Sad, mourning. 3 Dropping.
deurach, -aich, *s.f.* Burning pain, caused by a blow, lash, or sudden exertion. 2 Stunning report. Dlùths na d., *the closeness of the report of musketry, a rapidity of firing.*
———adh, see deurach.
———an, -ain, *s.m.* Pain occasioned by cold in one's finger ends.
deuradh, -aidh, *s.m.* Bed-clothes, *prov.*
deurail, -ala, *a.* see deurach.
deuran,** -ain, *s. m.* Little drop. 2 Small quantity of any liquid.
deur-lus,§, *s.m.* Moonwort, see luan-lus.
deur-shùil, -shùla, -shùilean, *s.f.* Blear-eye. 2 Tearful eye.
————each, -iche, *a.* Blear-eyed. 2 Apt to weep. 3 Having tearful eyes.

dh, For words commencing with *dh* and not to be found below, see in their plain form under *d.*

dh' (*for* do) Used before certain tenses of a verb beginning with a vowel or *fh.*
dhà, *a.* Two. A dhà no |a trì, *two or three.*
dha, *asp. form.* of da. Thoir dha sin, *give that to him;* leig dha (*or* leig leis,) *let it alone;* cha bu leis bu dha, *he did not like it.*
dh' a, *prep+poss.pron.* To his, her, their.
dha, see da, *to.*
dhachaidh, *s.* Home. 2 *adv.* Homewards, to one's own habitation, to one's own country. [also dachaidh.]
dhabh, *prov.* for dhaibh.
dh' adhlacadh, (a) *infin.* of adhlaic, To bury.
dh'adhlaic, *past aff. a.* of adhlaic, Buried.
dh' aidich, *past aff. a.* of aidich, Confessed.
dh'aindeoin, *adv.* In defiance, in spite of.
dha-san, *emphat. form* of dha.
Dhé, *gen. & voc. sing.* of Dia. Taigh Dhé, *the house of God.*
dhe, *asp. form* of de. Am fear a's àirde dhe'n triùir, *the tallest of (from among) the three.*
dheanainn, *1st. pers. sing. past subj.* of dean, I would do.
dheanamaid, *1st. pers. pl. past subj.* of dean. We would do.
dheanteadh, *past subj. pass.* of dean. Would be done.
dh' easbhuidh, *prep.* For want of.
dhéibhinn, see déidhinn.
dheo, (air), see air neo.
dheth, *prep. pron., asp. form* of deth.
dh'fhaoidteadh, *adv.* Perhaps. Dh. gu'n tig e, *perhaps he will come* ; ma dh., *perhaps.*
dh'fhios, for do fhios.
dhi, *asp. form* of di, *to her.*
Dhia, *gen. & voc.* of Dia.
dhibh, *asp. form.* of dibh. *emphatic,* dhibhse.
dhinn, *asp.form* of dinn. *emphatic,* dhinne.
dhìom, *asp. form* of dìom. *emphat.* dhìomsa.

dh' ionnsaidh, *prep.* Towards, unto, to.
dhìot, *asp. form* of diot. *emphat.* dhiotsa.
dhìse, *asp. & emph. form* of di.
dhith, (a), Without. 2 For want of. Chaidh sin 'nam dhith, *I lost that.*
———, *asp. form* of dith.
dhithse, *asp. & emph. form* of di.
dhiù, see dhiubh.
dhiubh, *asp. form* of diubh. Cò dh.? *which of them?* ; cuid d., *some of them* ; aon d., *one of them, emphatic.* dhiubhsan [& dhiubhsa.]
dhleasadh, *impers. v.* see dleas, *v.*
dhò, *a.* see dhà.
dho, for da.
dhoibh, *asp. form* of doibh. *emphat.* dhoibhsan.
dholaidh, see dolaidh.
dhomh, *asp. form* of domh. *emphat.* dhomhsa.
dhòsan, see dha(san.)
dhuibh, *asp. form* of duibh. *emphat.* dhuibhse.
dhuinn, *asp. form* of duinn. *emphat.* dhuinne.
dhuit, *asp. form.* of duit. *emphat.* dhuitse. Sin duit-sa, *that is for yourself* ; ciod sin duit-sa? *what is that to you?* sin duit, *behold, there's for you.*
dhut, *asp. form* of dut. *emphat.* dhutsa, see duit.
di, *prep.pron.* To her, to it (*f.*) Ni slàinte tearmunn di, *salvation shall be a bulwark to her* ; ri sealltainn di, *while looking at her*; air sealltainn di, *after showing her.*
dì, *s.m.* see dìth.
di-,‡ *negative prefix,* also diom-, and dim-.
Di-, *or* Dia, -day, prefix in the names of the days of the week.
Dia, *s.m. irreg.* Declined thus :

	Sing.	*Plur.*
Nom.	Dia.	diathan, [dée & *déidh]
Gen.	Dhé, Dhia,	dhia, [& dhée]
Dat.	Dia,	dée, [déibh & diathaibh]
Voc.	a Dhé ! a Dhia !	a dhiatha !

God. 2 Divinity. 3 False god. 2 used as an *emphatic particle.* D. tha, *it is indeed* ; an d. cha robh, *in sooth it was not.*
dia-àicheadh, -idh, *s.m.* Atheism.
dia-àicheanach,** *a.* Atheistical.
dia-àicheanaiche,** *s.m.* Atheist.
dia-aitheas, -eis, *s.m.* Blasphemy.
dia-athair, -thar, -thraichean, *s.m.* God-father.
dia-bheum, *s.m.* Blasphemy.
————ach, *a.* Blasphemous.
diabhlachd, see diabhlaidheachd.
diabhlaidh, -e, *a.* Devilish, diabolical. 2 Demoniac. 3 Hellish.
————eachd, *s.f.ind.* Devilishness, demonism, extreme iniquity.
diabhluidh, see diabhlaidh.
diabhol, -oil, -bhlan [& -oil], *s.m.* Devil. An d. toirt leis thu, *the Devil take you;* an d. mìr dhiot, *devil an inch of you* ; an d. toirt, *the Devil may care.*
†———nach, -aich, *s.m.* Necromancer.
diabhuilidh, see diabhlaidh.
†diabladh, -aidh, *s.m.* Twice as much, double.
diachadaich, *adv.* Especially—*Hebrides.*
diachainn, see deuchainn.
diachair, -e, -ean, *s.f.* Sorrow, grief.
diacharach, -aiche, *a.* Sorrowful, sad, oppressed with grief. Gu d., *sorrowfully.*
diacon,** -oin, *s.m.* Gaelic spelling of *deacon.*
diadha, *a.* see diadhaidh.
diadhach, -aiche, *a.* see diadhaidh.
————, -aich, *s.m.* Religious person, divine, clergyman.
————adh, -aidh, *s.m.* Deification, act of deifying. 2 Apotheosis. A' d—, *pr.pt.* of diadhaich.
diadhachd, *s.f.ind.* Deity. 2 Godliness. 3

Religion, theology. 4**Godhead. Anns an uile d., *in all godliness.*
diadhaich, *pr.pt.* a' diadhachadh, *v.a.* Deify, adore as a god.
diadhaidh, -e, *a.* Godly, Godlike, pious, divine. 'Nan giùlan d., *godly in their conduct ;* gu d., *piously;* a ghluais gu d., *who walked righteously.*
——————eachd, *s.f.ind.* Piety, godliness.
diadhair, -ean, *s.m.* Divine, minister of the gospel. 2**Theologian.
——————eachd, *s.f.ind.* Divinity, theology.
diadhalachd, *s.f.ind.* Godliness, piety.
dia-dhean, *v.a.* Deify.
——————adh, see dia-dheanamh.
——————amh, -aimh, *s.m.* Deification, apotheosis.
diadhuidh, -e, see diadhaidh.
——————, *s.f.ind.* see diadhaidheachd.
dia-dhuine, *s.m.* God-man, Christ, our Saviour.
Dia-dòmhnuich, see Di-dòmhnuich.
diag, see deug.
diaghaltach (air), (CR) *a.* Fond of anyone or anything—*Perthshire.*
Dia-haoine, see Di-haoine.
diaigh, see déidh.
diail,** *a.* Quick, immoderate. 2 Soon.
di-àirmhe, see di-àirmheadh.
di-àirmheadh,** *a.* Innumerable.
†dial, *s.m.* Weaning.
dial,** *v.a.* Wean.
dialadh,** -aidh, *s.m.* Weaning. Cuir air d., *wean.*
dialan,** *s.m.* Diary.
†diall, *s.f.* Submission. 2 Breech.
diall,* *s.m.* Attachment, fondness. 2 Continuance. see dìol.
——,** *v.a.* Attach, get fond of, as a child, &c.
——ag,** -aig, see dialtag.
diallаdair, -ean, see dìollaidear.
diallaid,‡ -e, -ean, see dìollaid.
——————eachadh, see dìollaideachadh.
——————eachd, see dìollaideachd.
——————ear, see dìollaidear.
——————ich, see dìollaidich.
†dialon, -oin, *s.m.* Diary.
dialta, *gen.sing.* of diallaid.
dialtag, -aige, -an, *s.f.* see ialtag. 2**Species of bonnet-grass. 3* *Vespertinus murinus.*
——————ach,†† *a.* see ialtagach.
—————— -anmoch,(CR) see ialtag.
Dia-luain, see Di-luain.
Dia-màirt, see Di-màirt.
†diamann, -ainn, *s.m.* Food, sustenance.
diamha,(AC) *s.* Grief. Á taigh nan diamha dùbhra, *from the house of grief and gloom.*
diamhain, -e, see dìomhain.
diamhair,‡ -e, *a.* Secret, private. 2**Mysterious, unintelligible. 3**Solitary, lonely. 4** Dark. Gleannan d., *a solitary little glen ;* rùn d., *a secret purpose.*
——————eachd,‡ *s.f.ind.* Privacy, mystery, secrecy. 2 Recess, lonely place. 3 Loneliness, solitude, concealment, obscurity. 4 Darkness.
——————eas, -eis, *s.m.* same meanings as diamhaireachd. 2(AH) Piece of important and exclusive information confided by a person to another under a promise of secrecy.
——————ich,‡ *v.a.* Secrete, hide, make private.
Dia-mhallachadh, -aidh, *s.m.* Blasphemy.
Dia-mhallaich,* *v.a.* Blaspheme.
diamhanach, -aiche, *a.* see dìomhanach.
diamhanas, -ais, see dìomhanas.
Dia-mhaoin, -e, *s.f.* Church-property. 2**Charity given in church. 3 Deodand.
diamhar, see diamhair.

dìamharan,** -ain, *s.m.* Mystery. 2 Hermit. 3 Hermit's cell.
Dia-mhaslach, -aiche, *a.* Blasphemous.
——————adh, -aidh, *s.m.* Blasphemy. 2** Blaspheming.
——————air, -ean, *s.m.* Blasphemer.
Dia-mhasladh, see Dia-mhaslachadh.
Dia-mhaslaich, *v.a.* Blaspheme.
dia-mhàthair, -ar, -mhàthraichean, *s.f.* Godmother.
diamhlachadh,** -aidh, *s. m.* Darkening. 2 Growing dark or coloured.
†diamhladh, -aidh, *s. m.* Place of retreat or refuge.
†diamhlaich, *v.a.* Make dark.
dian,(AF) *s.m.* Worm.
dian, déine, *a.* Hasty, vehement, eager, keen, headlong, precipitant. 2 Violent, furious. 3 Nimble, brisk. 4**Strong. 5**Sad. [Often used before the noun it qualifies.] Osag dh., *a violent blast ;* tòrachd dh., *eager pursuit ;* gach neach d., *every hasty person ;* d. fhearg, *fiery indignation ;(adv.)* d. theth, *intensely hot;* d. iarr, *importune;* d. loisg, *burn vehemently;* d. mhear, *furiously lustful;* tha thu tuilleadh d. orm, *you press me too hard ;* 'na dhian-mhiamhuil, *meowing dreadfully.*
dian-abaich,** *a.* Precocious.
dian-abachd,** *s.f.* Precocity.
dian-achanaich,†† *s.f.* Earnest supplication or prayer.
dianadach, see deanadach.
dianag, -aig, -an, *s.f.* see dìonag.
dianaich,‡‡ *v.a.* see dìonaich.
dian-airm,** *s. m.* see dìon-airm.
dianas, -ais, see déineas.
——————ach, see déineachdach. Gu d., *ardently.*
dian-astarach, *a.* Active-footed. 2 Quick-moving.
dian-athchuinge, -an, *s.f.* Importunate request, fervent prayer.
——————ach,** *a.* Importunate, fervent in prayer.
dian-bharalach,‡‡ -aiche, *a.* Assertive, conceited in one's own opinion.
——————d, *s.f.* Peremptoriness.
dian-bhriathraich, *v.a.* Asseverate.
†diancecht,‖ *s.m.* God of the powers—*deus salutis*—name for the sage of leech-craft.
dian-chnusachadh,‡‡ -aidh, *s.m.* Plodding.
dian-chòmhla, see dìon-chòmhla.
dian-chorruich,** *s.* Fierce wrath.
dian-dheothas,** *s.m.* Fervent zeal. 2 Bigotry.
——————ach,** *a.* Fervent. 2 Bigoted. 3 Zealous. Gu d., *fervently.*
dian-fhearg, -fheirge, *s. f.* Great indignation. 2 Fiery wrath.
——————ach,** *a.* Wrathful, in a great rage. Causing great wrath.
dian-fhòireigneadh, -idh, *s.m.* Close pursuit. 2 Oppression.
†dian-ghalar, *s.m.* Fast consuming disease.
dian-ghluasad,** -aid, *s.m.* Violent motion. 2 Great agitation.
dian-iarr,‡‡ *v.a.* Implore.
——————tachd, *s.f.ind.* Importunity.
dian-imeachd,(PM) *s.f.* Fast walking.
dian-liosdach,** *a.* Importunate. Gu d., *importunately.*
——————d,** *s.f.* Importunacy.
dian-loisg, *v.a.* Burn vehemently.
——————each, -iche, *a.* Burning vehemently.
dian-lorgadh, *s.m.*Keen search. 2 Act of searching keenly or eagerly.
dian-lorgaich,** *v.a.* Pursue hotly. 2 Persecute.
dian-lorgair,** *s.m.* Persecutor. 2 Pursuer.

dian-lorgaireachd, *s.f.* see dian-lorgadh.
dian-losgadh, -eidh, *s. m.* Vehement burning. 2 Act or circumstance of burning vehemently or fiercely. A' d—, *pr.pt.* of dian-loisg.
dian-mhagadh, -aidh, -aidhean, *s.m.* Keen derision, mockery.
dian-mhear, *a.* Extremely merry.
dian-ruagadh, -aidh, *s.m.* Close pursuit, keen pursuit.
dian-ruith, -e, *s.m.* Keen running, rushing, running at full speed. 2 Eager, impetuous motion.
——— —,‡*v.n.* Run impetuously.
dian-shruth, *s.m.* Rapid stream, torrent.
dian-smuainich,‡‡ *v.n.* Apply, study.
dian-sparradh, -aidh, *s.m.* Urgent demand, injunction, pressing order.
dian-theas, *s.m.* Intense heat, fervent heat. 2 Fervent zeal.
dian-theth,** *a.* Intensely hot.
dian-thograch,** *a.* Ambitious. 2 Extremely covetous. 3 Keen.
dian-thogradh,** -aidh, *s.m.* Ambition. 2 Extreme covetousness. 3 Keenness.
diardan, -ain, *s.m.* Anger, surliness, snarling.
———ach,** -aiche, *a.* Angry, surly, snarling. Gu d., *in a surly manner.*
———achd,** *s.f. ind.* Angriness, surliness, churlishness.
Diardaoin, *s.m.* Thursday. D. a' bhrochain mhóir, *Maunday Thursday.* It was at one time a custom in the Long Island, if the usual drift of seaweed were behind time, to go on Maunday Thursday and pour an oblation of gruel on a promontory, accompanying the ceremony by the repetition of a certain rhyme.—N.G.P.
dia-riaghladh, *s.m.* Theocracy.
diarmad,** see dearmad.
di-armaich, *v.a.* Disarm.
diarras, -ais, *s.m.* see dìorras.
———ach, -aiche, *a.* see dìorrasach.
dias, see dithis.
——, déise, *dat.* déis, *pl.* diasan, *s. f.* Ear of corn. 2** Corn. 3** Blade of a sword. Seachd diasan, *seven ears of corn*; fo dhéis, *in ear*; fàs déis, *the growth of corn.*
diasach, -aiche, *a.* Of, or belonging to, ears of corn. 2*Luxuriant, as a crop. 3**Bladed, as corn. Coirc d., *bladed oats.*
diasad,** -aid, *s. f.* Ear of corn. 2 Blade of corn.
———ach, *a.* see dias-fhada.
diasag, -aig, -an, *s.f.* Little ear of corn. 2 Ludicrous name for a satirist's tongue.
diasaich,** *v.* Fork.
diasair, *v.a.* Glean, as a corn-field.
diasan, *n.pl.* of dias.
Dia-Sathuirn, see Di-Sathuirn.
diasdach, -aiche, *a.* see diasach.
dias-fhada, *a.* Long-bladed.
diasradh, -aidh, *s.m.* Gleaning.
diathaibh, *dat. pl.* of Dia. Gu d. eile, *to other gods.*
diathan, *n. pl.* of Dia.
di-bàigh,(AC) *a.* Loveless, merciless. 2(PJM) Impartial.
†dibeadach,** *a.* Negative.
dibearra,‡‡ *a.* Banished. 2 Uncertain.
———ch, *s.* & *a.* see dìobarach.
———chd, see dìobarachd.
———iche, *s.* see dìobarach, *s.*
dibeartha, see dibearra.
———ch, -aich, see dìobarach.
di-beathte,(CR) *past pt.* & *a.* Welcome—*W. of Ross-shire, Uist, Suth'd. &c.* Tha sibh d., *you are welcome.* [Not a good form, but a phonetic spelling of *deagh-bheatha-te*, the *deagh* of which is pronounced *dì* in some parts.] Pronounced *di-beatht'* in *Lewis.*
†dibeoil, -e, *a.* Mute, dumb.
dibh, *prep.pron.* Of you, from you, off you.
dibh, Given by ** in error as *dat. sing.* of deoch.
†dibh, *s.f.* Farm.
di-bhall,** *v.a.* Dislimb.
———aich,** *v.a.* Dislimb.
dibh-bhruaineach,(AF) *s.m.* Mite.
dibh-chailin,(AF) *s.* Mite.
dìbhe, erroneously used for dìghe.
†dibheal, *a.* Weak. 2 Old.
dibheach, -ich, *pl.* -a & -an, *s.m.* Ant.
dibhealaich,** *a.* Without way or passage. 2 Pathless. 3 Impassable.
†dibhearadh, -aidh, *s.m.* Consoling, consolation.
dibheargach, -aiche, *a.* Vindictive. 2 Wrathful.
———, *s.m.* Robber. 2 Fugitive.
dibhearsain, Gaelic spelling of *diversion.*
dibh-fhearg, -fheirge, *s.f.* Vengeance. 2 Wrath, rage, indignation.
dibh-fheirg, see dibh-fhearg.
†dibhirce, *s.f.* Endeavour.
dibhirceach, -ciche, *a.* Diligent. 2 Fierce, violent, unruly.
di-bhladhaich,** *v.a.* Repeal, abrogate.
dibhleachadh,** -aidh, *s.m.* Abrogating, abrogation, repeal.
di-bhlasda,** *a.* Insipid, tasteless.
di-bhrìgh,** *s.f.* Contempt. 2 Neglect.
di-bhrògach, -aiche, *a.* Unshod, without shoes.
di-bhruaineach,(AF) *s.m.* Mite.
dibh-se, see dibh.
dì-bidh,(DU) *s.* Mild form of cursing. D. ort! *confound you!*
di-bidhidh,(PM) *s.* *Uist* form of dì-bidh.
†dibineachd, *s.f.* Extremity.
dìbir, see dìobair.
dibir,** *s.f.* Abandonment. 2 Neglect, forgetfulness.
dibirt, -e, see dìobairt.
dì-bith,(AC) *a.* Lifeless. 2 Luckless.
dibleachd, see dìblidheachd.
dibli, see dìblidh.
diblich,** *v.a.* & *n.* Make vile. 2 Become vile or wretched. 3 Demean, lower. 4 Become drooping.
dìblidh, -e, *a.* Vile, mean, abject. 2 Bashful. 3**Wretched, poor. 4**Vulgar, worthless. Do 'n anrach dh., *to the destitute wanderer.*
———eachd, *s. f. ind.* Meanness, abjectness. 2 Wretchedness. 3**Poverty. 4 Bashfulness.
dìbreachan, -ain, see dìobarachan.
dìbreadh, -idh, see dìobradh.
dìbrigh, -e, *s.f.* Contempt. 2 Disrespect.
———eil, -eala, *a.* Contemptible, contemptuous.
Di-ceadoine, see Di-ceudaoin.
Di-ceudaoin, *s.m.* Wednesday. D. na luaithre, *Ash Wednesday*; D. seo chaidh, *last Wednesday*; D. seo tighinn, *next Wednesday*, "*Wednesdayfirst;*" Là ceudaoin, *on a Wednesday.*
dìchairt, *v. a.* Peel, take off the bark, decorticate.
dì-chaisg, *a.* Uncontrollable.
di-chathairich,** *v.a.* Disenthrone.
dìcheall, -eill, see dìchioll.
———ach, -aiche, see dìchiollach.
———achd, see dìchiollachd.
†dichealtair, *s. m.* Deer-park. 2 Shaft of a spear.
dì-cheann, *v.a.* Behead.
———ach, -aich, *s.m.* Beheaded man.
———achadh, see dì-cheannadh.
———achd, *s.f.ind.* Decapitation.
———adh, -aidh, *s.m.* Decapitation, act of

beheading. A' d—, *pr.pt.* of dì-cheann.
dì-cheannaich, *v.a.* Behead.
————aichte, *past pt.* of dì-cheannaich.
————ta, *past pt.* of dì-cheann.
dì-cheartachadh,** *s.m.* Disfranchisement.
†dicheil, *s.f.* Disguise.
dìchill, *gen. sing.* of dìchioll.
———, *s.f.* Protection.
dìchioll, -ill, *s.m.* Diligence. 2 Attempt, endeavour. 3 Utmost endeavour. 4**Perseverance. 5*Forlorn effort. Le móran d., *with much diligence.*
————ach -aiche, *a.* Diligent, industrious, endeavouring, persevering, careful.
————achd,** *s.f.ind.* Practice of diligence. 2 Industry. 3 Perseverance. 4 Carefulness.
dìchiollaich, *v.n.* Endeavour.
dì-chliù,** *s.* Disrepute.
dì-chòireachadh, -aidh, *s.m.* Disfranchisement.
dì-chòirich,** *v.a.* Disfranchise.
dì-chrannachadh, -aidh, *s.m.* Dismasting.
dì-chrannaich, *v.a.* Dismast.
——————te, *past pt.* of dì-chrannaich.
dì-chreid, *v.a.* Disbelieve.
————eamh, -imh, *s.m.* Disbelief, unbelief, scepticism, infidelity.
————mheach, -iche, *a.* Unbelieving, incredulous, sceptical.
————mheach, -ich, *s.m.* Unbeliever, infidel, incredulous person.
————te, *a.* Incredible.
dì-chuimhne, *s.f.* Forgetfulness, oblivion, neglectfulness. Tìr na d., *the land of forgetfulness*; air dh., *forgotten*; leig air d., *forget.*
——————ach, -iche, *a.* Forgetful, heedless, oblivious.
——————achadh, *pr. pt.* of dì-chuimhnich.
——————achd,** *s.f.ind.* Carelessness.
dì-chuimhnich, *pr.pt.* a' dì-chuimhneachadh, *v.a.* Forget. 2**Neglect.
——————eadh, -aidh, *s. m.* Forgetting, act of forgetting, forgetfulness.
Di-ciadain, see Di-ceudaoin.
Di-ciaduin, see Di-ceudaoin.
diclìt,(AH) *s.f.* Gaelic spelling of *decree.*
dì-cnamhaidh,** *s.* Indigestion.
dìd, -e, -ean, *s.f.* Peep.
dìd,* *a.* Worse.—*Islay.* Is beag is d. (misd') thu sin, *you are little the worse for that.*
dìdeag, *s.f.* Peep. 2**Sly look. 3**Small candle. D. ort! *I am peeping at you.*
———ach, *a.* Peeping.
———aich, *s.f.* Peeping. Ciod an d. a th'ort? *what are you peeping at?*
dìdean, -ein, -einean, *s.f.* Fort, rampart. 2 Protection, defence, sanctuary, refuge. 3 **Preservation. 4**Safety. Fo dhìdein, *in safety*; is d. glìocas, *wisdom is a defence*; a' guidhe an dìdein, *begging their defence.*
————ach,** *a.* Protecting, affording protection or shelter. 2 Ready to shelter or protect.
————achadh, -aidh,** *s.m.* Protection, protecting, fortifying.
————aich, *pr. pt.* a' dìdeanachadh, *v.a.* Defend, protect, fortify.
————aichte, *a.* & *past pt.* of dìdeanaich. Defended, protected.
————air,** *s m.* Defender. 2 Fortifier.
dìdeann, see dìdean.
————, *v.a.* see dìdeanaich.
dìdeanta, *a.* & *past pt.* of dideann.
dìdearachd,(PM) *s.f.* Peeping—*Uist & Skye.*
dìdein, *gen. sing.* of dìdean.
———ich,†† see dìdeannaich.
dì-dhaoineachadh, -aidh, *s. m.* Depopulation, act of depopulating.
dì-dhaoinich, *v.a.* Depopulate, lay waste, extirpate.
dì-dhìol,** *s.m.* Arrears.
dì-dhuilleach, *a.* Without leaves or foliage.
dìdil, *s. f.* Act of peeping, looking slyly, as through a hole. 2**Great love. 3 Kindness.
dìdinn, *s.f.* see dìdean.
————, *v.a.* Defend, protect.
dìdionn, -inn, see dìdean.
————air, -ean, *s.m.* Protector, guardian.
dìdneadh, -idh, *s.m.* Protection, defence. A d—, *pr.pt.* of dìdinn.
dì-dhuilleach,** *a.* Without leaves or foliage.
Di-dòmhnuich, *s.f.* Sunday. D. crum-dubh, see crum-dubh. Là Dòmhnuich, *a Sunday.*
dì-fhrìthich,** *v.a.* Disforest.
dì-fhulang, *a.* Intolerable.
difir,‡ *s.* Gaelic form of *differ.*
dìg, -e, -eachan, *s.f.* Ditch, drain. 2 Mound to keep out an inundation. 3 Wall of loose stones, dike. [The word *dike* is applied to a ditch or mound in England, but only to a wall in Scotland.] Thuit e 'san d. a rinn e, *he fell into the ditch which he made.*
dìg,* *v.a.* Dress, hoe up, as potatoes. 2 Furrow. 3 Drain.
†digealre,‖ *s.* Health.
†dìge, see dìghe & deoch.
dìgeach, -iche, *a.* Full of, or like, ditches or dikes.
dìgear, -eir, -ean, *s.m.* Ditcher.
digeireachd,†† *s.f.ind.* Ditching.
digh,* *s.f.* Conical mound built by the Danes. 2 Fairy-hillock. 3 Rampart. D. mhór Thallanta, *a noted fairy knoll in Islay.*
digh, *v. n.* Come, arrive. Gu'n d. thu féin dhachaidh, *welcome home—Lewis.*
dìghe, *gen.sing.* of deoch.
†dighe, *s.f.* Succour, help. 2 Satisfaction.
†dighe, *a.* Condign, adequate.
†dighin, *v.a.* Suck.
†dighiona, *a.* Morose, surly.
dighne, *s. m.* Degenerate *or* dwarfish race.
dì-ghreanna,** *a.* Bald.
——————chd, *s.f.ind.* Baldness.
dìgire, see dìgear.
Di-haoine, *s.m.* Friday. Di-haoine gu fàs 's D-imàirt gu buain, ach obair a thòisichear Di-luain bidh i luath no bidh i mall, *on Friday sow, and mow on Tuesday, but the work begun on Monday will be either quick or slow.* Monday, being the first free day of the week, gives a good chance for getting on with work, but if one relies too much on having abundance of time, the work will probably be put off. D. seo chaidh, *last Friday*; D. seo tighinn, *next Friday*, "*Friday first.*"

Though Friday has always been held an unlucky day in various Christian countries, and even among such people as the Brahmins, still in the Hebrides it is supposed to be the lucky day for sowing the seed in the ground. Good Friday in particular is a favourite day for potato planting—even strict Catholics make a point of planting a bucketful on that day. Probably the idea is, that as the Resurrection followed the Crucifixion and Burial, so too in the case of the seed, that after death will come life.
dil,(DU) *s.f.* Very small quantity, drop of liquid. Cha'n 'eil d. uisge agam, *I haven't a drop of water.*
dìl, *s.f.* see dìle.
dìl, *s.* Attention.
dìl,* *a.* Diligent, persevering, zealous—*Islay.* 2 Keen, close.
dì-lachdach, -aich, *s. m.* see dilleachdan.
dì-làrachadh, -aidh, *s.m.* Depopulation.

dì-làraich, *v.a.* Utterly destroy, annihilate.
dì-làthaireach, *a.* Absent.
————d, *s.f.ind.* Absence.
dì-làthairich, see dì-làirich.
dìle, *gen.* dìleann, *dat.* dìlinn, *s.f.* Flood, deluge. 2 Heavy rain. 3**Blast. 4**The Earth. An d. ruadh, *Noah's flood* ; an searbh dh., *the bitter blast* ; ged thigeadh d., *though rains were to come*; ged nach tigeadh dìleann a thigeadh tu, *though you should never come*—*Lewis.*
dile, *comp.* of dil.
dile,§ *s.m.* Strong-scented or common dill—*anethum graveolens.*
dile, *s.m.* Wort.
†dile, *s.f.ind.* Love, friendship, affection.
dìleab, -eib, *s.f.* Legacy. Mar dh., *as a legacy.*
———ach, -aich, *s.m.* Legatee, heir.
———ach, -aiche, *a.* Of, or belonging to, a legacy.
———aiche, -an, *s. m.* Testator. 2 Legatee. Cha d' eug duine riamh gun d., *no man ever died without an heir.*
———air, *s.m.* see dìleabaiche.
dileach, -aiche, *a.* Beloved, affectionate.
dìleach, *a.* Deluging, rainy.
dìleag, -eig, -an,†† *s.f.* Blossom, flower.
dileag, -eig, -an, *s.f.* Drop, small quantity of liquid.
dìleagach,†† *a.* Abounding in flowers.
dileagach,†† *a.* Abounding in small drops of liquid.
dileagh,** *v.a.* Digest food.
†dileaghadh, -aidh, *s.m.* Digestion.
dileaman,** -ain, *s.m.* Love, affection. 2 Kindness.
dìleann, *gen.* of dìle.
dileann,(PJM) *s.m.* Rope used to tie the forelegs of a horse, to prevent its jumping over dikes—*Lewis.*
dìleant, -a, *a.* Profound. 2 Inundating, rainy. Gu d., *for ever.*
dìleas, dìlse, *a.* Beloved. 2 Faithful, loyal, trusty. 3 Favourable, faithful. 4 Nearly related or connected. 5‡‡Just. 6**Friendly. 7 Real, as opposed to spurious. Bi d. do 'n rìgh, *be loyal to the king* ; d. dhomh, *nearly related to me* ; d. do d' mhaighstir, *faithful to your master* ; na 's dìlse, *more loyal* ; gach d. gu deireadh, *the best loved last* ; tearmunn d., *a trusty refuge* ; airgiod d., *real silver* ; is d. duine dha fhéin, *a man is faithful to himself.*
†dìleas-choimhead, *s.f.* Protection.
di-leum,‡ (accent on leum) *s.m.* Shackle. 2(DC) Horse-fetter—*Uist.*
dilghean, *s.m.* Affection. 2 Suppression.
dilgheann, -inn, *s.m.* Destruction, plundering, pillaging.
†dilgionadh, -aidh, *s.m.* Emptying.
dilib, see dìleab.
——each, see dìleabach.
dìlich,** *v.a.* Digest, as food.
———te,** *past part.* of dìlich.
dilimich,(AC) *v.a.* Endow.
dìlinn, *dat.* of dìle. Gu d., *ever* ; gu d. cha dùisg thu, *thou shalt never awake* ; gus an caillear an d. aois, *till age is lost in the flood of time* ; cha d. a thig e, *he shall never come.*
——, *a.* Endless. 2 *in situ.* 3 see diolain. Leac d., *a stone in situ, a rock appearing above ground.*
—— each,** *a.* Deluvian, inundating.
dìlionnach, -aiche, *a.* Deluging.
dìlionn, see dìleann.
dìliseachd, see dìlseachd.
dilit,** *s.m.* Peewit, see adharcan-luachrach.
dìlleachd, see dìlleachdan.
————ach, -aiche, *a.* Fatherless.
————an, -ain, -an, *s.m.* Orphan. 2**Little orphan.
————anachd,** *s.f.* Orphanage.
————as,‡‡ -ais, *s.m.* Orphanage.
dilleann,(PM) *s.m.* The depth of the earth. As an d., *out of the depth of the earth!* (as a spring.) —*Uist.*
dilmain,** *a.* Meet, proper, fit, becoming.
dilse, see duileasg.
dìlse, -an, *s.m.* see dìlseachd.
——, *comp.* of *a.* dìleas. More or most faithful, related, or friendly.
——,** see dìlsean. 'Nuair a thig thu chum mo dh., *when you come to my kindred.*
——achd, *s.f.ind.* Affection, love. 2 Friendship. 3 Relationship. 4 Faithfulness, fidelity, loyalty. 5**Esteem. 6**Subjection, subordination. 7**Propriety. 8**Relations, kindred. Mo dh., *my relations*; do dh. chuir mi an céill, *I have shown thy faithfulness.*
——ad, -eid, *s.f.* see dìlseachd.
——an,** *n. pl.* of dìlse. Relations, kindred, connections, "friends."
†dilte, *s.f.* Nutriment.
dilteadh, see dìoladh.
Di-luain, *s.m.* Monday. D. seo chaidh, *last Monday* ; D. seo tighinn, *next Monday*, "*Monday first*" ; D. bannaig, *the first Monday after Christmas*, D. an t-sainnseil, *the first Monday after the New Year.*
dì-luchdachadh, -aidh, *s.m.* Disencumbrance. A' d—, *pr.pt.* of dì-luchdaich.
dì-luchdaich, *v.a.* Disencumber. 2 Unload
Di-màirt, *s.m.* Tuesday. D. Inid, *Shrove Tuesday* ; 2 *The Carnival.*
dim-bàigh, see di-bàigh.
dimbith, see di-bith.
dimbrigh, see dì-brìgh.
————each, see di-brìgheil.
————eil, -eala, see dì-brìgheil.
dìm-buaidh, -e, *s.f.* see diom-buaidh.
————each, -iche, see diom-buaidheach.
dìmeas, *v.a.* Despise, slight, undervalue.
——, *s.m.* Contempt, reproach, disrespect, disesteem. 2**Bad name, bad character. 3 Scarcity of fruit. Dean d., *despise* ; cuir air d., *despise* ; fo dh., *despised.*
———ach, -aiche, *a.* Despicable, contemptuous, contemptible, mean, disrespectful.
———da, *a.* Despised, slighted, undervalued.
———dachd, *s. f.* Disrespect. 2 Disrespectfulness. 3 Disrepute.
dìmheas,** *s. m.* see dìmeas. 2 Scarcity of fruit. [** gives Great honour, high esteem, but *dìmheas* in that case is a phonetic spelling of a provincial pronunciation of *deagh-mheas.*]
————ach, -aiche, *a.* see dìmeasach. 2 Proud, contemptuous, servile.
————ail, see dìmeasach.
————da, see dìmeasda.
————dachd, see dìmeasdachd.
dì-mhill, *pr.pt.* a' dì-mhilleadh, *v. a.* Destroy, abuse.
————eadh, -idh, *s.m.* Destroying, destruction, act of destroying. A' d—, *pr. pt.* of dì-mhill.
————teach, -ich, see dì-mhilltear.
————tear, -eir, -eirean, *s.m.* Destroyer. 2* Miserable person.
dì-mhilltear, *fut.pass.* of dì-mhill. Shall be destroyed.
dimhin, see deimhinn.
dimhin,** *s.* see dimhineachd.
————eachd,** *s.f.* Provision. 2 Caution. 3 Heed. 4 Confidence.
dì-mhisneachadh,‡‡ -aidh, *s.m.* Brow-beating. 2 Discouragement.

dì-mhisneachail,(PM) *a.* Faint-hearted.
†dimhneachd, *s.f.* Confidence.
dimhnich, see deimhnich.
dimhnidheach,** *a.* Sad. Gu d., *sadly.*
——————d,** *s.f.ind.* Sadness.
di-mhol,** see di-mol.
————adair, see di-moltair.
di-mholtair,** *s.m.* Slanderer.
dì-miadh, -miaidh, *s.f.* Disrespect, irreverence, dishonour.
dì-mill,†† see dì-mhill.
di-millteach, -ich, *s.m.* Glutton, *prov.* 2 Cow or horse that breaks through fences.
†dimnidheach, *a.* Sad, sorrowful.
†——————d, *s.f.* Sadness, sorrowfulness.
dimreas,** -eis, *s.m.* Necessity, want.
di-mol, *pr.pt.* a' di-moladh, *v.a.* Dispraise, underrate, abuse, disparage.
di-moladair, see di-moltair.
di-moladh, -aidh, *s. m.* Dispraise, act of dispraising, abusing, disparaging or underrating, disparagement, slander. A' d—, *pr. pt.* of di-mol.
dì-molta,** *a.* Dispraised, blamed, censured, disparaged, slandered.
di-moltair, -ean, *s.m.* Dispraiser, disparager, slanderer.
†din, *a.* Pleasant, delightful, agreeable.
†din, *s.* Sucking.
†din, *v.a.* Drink, suck.
di-nàire,** *s.f.* Shamelessness.
di-nàireach,** *a.* Shameless.
†dì-naisg. *v.a.* Disjoin, loosen, undo.
dinait,** *v.a.* Desolate. 2 Dislocate.
————eadh,** -eidh, *s.m.* Dislocation.
din-aodach,** -aich, *s.m.* Frock.
dì-nasgach,** *a.* Dissolute.
dì-nasgadh,** -aidh, *s.m.* Untying, loosening. 2 Disjoining,
†dine, *s.f.* Generation, age. 2 Beginning.
dineach,** -ich, *s.m.* Salutary draught.
dineamait, *s.f.* Gaelic spelling of *dynamite.*
†di-neart, for Dia-neart.
dì-neart, -eirt, *s.m.* Imbecility. 2** Infirmity.
————aich, *v.a.* Weaken, enfeeble. 2 Flank.
din-eudach, see din-aodach.
ding, *v.a.* see dinn.
——, *s.f.* see dinn.
†dinge, *s.f.* **Thunder. 2 *s.pl.* Dictates, doctrine. 3 Oppression, tyranny.
———adh, -idh, *s.m.* see dinneadh.
dingir, *s.f.* Custody. 2 Incarceration. 3 Place of confinement.
———e, -an, *s.m.* Paver's rammer. (dinnear.)
diniath,** *s.* Headpiece.
dinib,** *s.* Drinking.
dinidh,(AF) *s.m.* Lamb.
†dinimh, *s.f.* Weakness. 2 Diminution.
dinn, *prep. pron.* Of us, from us, concerning us, from amongst us.
dinn, *s.f.* Wedge. †2 see dùn.
——, *pr. pt.* a' dinneadh, *v. a.* Press, force down, cram, stuff. 2 Trample. 3 Wedge. 4 **Invade, encroach.
dinne, *prep. pron., emphat.* of dinn.
———ad, *s.f.* see déinead.
dinneadh, -idh, *s.m.* Pushing in, stuffing, forcing down. 2 Act of pressing, trampling or stuffing. 3**Depression. 4** Encroaching. A' d—, *pr.pt.* of dinn.
dinnean, -ein, *s.m.* Small heap. 2 Pittance. 3 ††Small quantity, as of meal.
dinnear, -an, *s.m.* Paver's rammer. 2 Wedge. 3 Ramrod.
dinneasg, -eisg, -an, *s.f.* Mischief, mishap.
dinneir, dinnearach, [-ean &] -ichean, *s.f.* Dinner. An déidh tràth dinnearach, *after dinner-time.*
dinnire, see dinnear.
†dinnis, *s.f.* Oath. 2 Contempt.
dinnsear, see dinnear.
————, -eir, -eirean, *s.m.* Ginger.
————ach,†† *a.* Gingery.
dinnte, *a. & past pt.* of dinn. Pressed, closely stuffed, packed.
———achd,* *s.f.ind.* Condensity.
dinseadh,** -idh, *s.m.* Contempt.
†diobadh, -aidh, *s.m.* Point. 2 Edge. 3 Prick. 4 Thorn.
dìobair, *pr.pt.* a' dìobradh, *v. n.* Desert, quit, abandon, forsake. 2 Omit. 3 Neglect. 4 Fail. 5* Extirpate, expel, root out. 6 Depopulate. 7 Banish. 8**Forget. 9**Depart. 10**Put away in anger. 11**Circumvent. Na d. a bhi mar iadsan, *do not forget to be like them* ; na flathan a dh., *the nobles who have departed ;* an d. màthair a cìochran ? *can a mother forget her suckling ?* ; dh. mi an deanntag, *I have extirpated the nettle.*
—————each, -ich, see dìobarach.
dìobairt, -e, *s.m.* same meanings as dìobradh.
—————e, *past part* of dìobair.
diobanach, see diobarach.
diobar,** -air, *s.m.* Disrespect, contempt.
diobarach, see dìobarach.
dìobarach, -aich, *s.m.* Deserted, forlorn person. 2 Outcast. 3 Exile. 4 Orphan. Dìobaraich Israeil, *the outcasts of Israel.*
—————,** -aiche, *a.* Banished. 2 Needy. 3 That banishes.
dìobarachan,** -ain, *s.m.* Wanderer, outcast, exile,destitute person. 2 Orphan.
dìobarachd, *s.f.ind.* The condition of a forlorn, deserted or banished person. 2 Banishment, exile. 3**Want. Fhuair e 'dh., *he was banished.*
†dìobhadh, -aidh, *s.m.* Destruction. 2 Death. 3 Inheritance, any transitory or worldly inheritance. 4 Dowry, portion.
†dìobhaidh,** *v.a.* Destroy, ruin.
dìobhaidh,** *a.* Impious. 2 Destructive. 3 Ruinous.
dìobhail, -alach [& -e,] -ean, *s.m.* Loss. 2 Defeat. 3 Destruction, ruin. 4 Mischief,harm, calamity, distress. 5 Pity. 6 Want. 7** Robbery. 8** Profusion. 9**Frenzy. 10** Injury. Thàinig an d., *their destruction came*; d. misnich, *want of courage ;* mo dh. ! *my ruination !* is mór an d., *it is a thousand pities ;* a dh. làimh, *without a hand, with the loss of a hand.*
dìobhaileach, see dìobhalach.
——————adh, -aidh, *s.m.* Compensation. A' d—, *pr.pt.* of dìobhailich.
——————d, see dìobhalachd.
dìobhailich, *pr.pt.* a' dìobhaileachadh, *v.a.* Impair. 2 Recompense, compensate, make up deficiencies.
dìobhair, *pr.pt.* a' dìobhairt & a' dìobhradh,*v.n.* Throw up, vomit.
————t, *s.m.* Vomiting, act of vomiting. A' d—, *pr.pt.* of dìobhair.
dìobhalach, -aiche, *a.* Destructive. 2 Robbed, spoiled, damaged. 3 Profuse. 4 Detrimental. 5 Extravagant. 6 Adverse. 7 Abortive. 8 Ablative. 9 Mischievous, hurtful, pernicious. 10*Heart-rending.
†——————, -aich, *s.m.* Ablative case.
——————d,** *s.f.* Privation. 2 Robbery. 3 Damage. 4 Destruction. 5 Ablation.
dìobhalaich,‡‡ *v.a.* Impair.
——————e, *s.m.* Impairer.
dìobhall, *a.* Old, ancient, antique.
dìobhanach,** -aich, *s.m.* Outlaw.

———————, -aiche, *a.* Lawless, unruly.
———————d, *s.f.ind.* Lawlessness, unruliness.
dìobhar,** *s.m.* Disrespect. 2 Omission.
dìobhargach, -aiche, *a.* Keen, fierce.
dìobhargadh, -aidh, *s.m.* Persecution. 2 Captivity, slavery.
dìobhathadh, -aidh, *s.m.* Destruction.
——————as,** -ais, *s.m.* Ingratitude.
dìobhlach,** *a.* Prodigal.
——————d, *s.f.* Prodigality.
†dìobhladh, *s.m.* Accusing.
†dìobhlaiseach, *a.* Prodigal.
dìobhlas,** -ais, *s.m.* Prodigality.
†dìobhraice, *a.* Warlike. 2 Destructive.
†dìobhrath, *v.a.* Discover.
dìobhruaineach,(AF) *s.m.* see di-bhruaineach.
†dìobhuan, -ain, see diom-buan.
diobhuantachd, see diom-buanachd.
†dìobhuidhe, *s.f.* Ingratitude.
dìobhuidheach,** *a.* Ungrateful, thankless. Gu d., *ungratefully.*
dìobhuidheachas, -ais, *s.m.* Ingratitude.
dìobhuir,* *pr.pt.* a' dìobhairt, see dìobhair.
——————t, see dìobhairt.
diobrach, see dìobarach.
——————an, see dìobarachan.
diobradh, -aidh, *s.m.* Forsaking, abandoning, deserting, failing. 2 Banishing. 3*Extirpating. 4**Banishment. 5 (PM)Lessening.—*Uist.* A' d—, *pr.pt.* of dìobair. Cha'n 'eil d. air an uisge, *the rain is not abating.*
diocail, *pr.pt.* a' dìocladh, Lower, diminish, assuage. 2 Abate, as rain.
dìochain, -e, see dì-chuimhne.
dìochairt, see dì-chairt.
dìochanach, see dì-chuimhneach.
diochd, -a, *a.* Small.
†diochoisgeach, -iche, *a.* Implacable.
diochrach,** *a.* Diligent, zealous.
†diochron, *a.* Immediate, without time.
†diochuidh, *a.* Small.
dìochuimhne, see dì-chuimhne.
——————ach, see dì-chuimhneach.
dìochuimhnich, see dì-chuimhnich.
diocladh, -aidh, *s.m.* Act of lowering, diminishing, assuaging. 2 Abatement. Uisge gun d., *incessant rain.*
diocras,** *s.m.* Inappelancy.
†diocuir, *v.a.* Drive.
†diocuireadh, -idh, *s.m.* Driving, expulsion.
diod,* *s.f.* Drop, spark. [** gives *s.m.*]
——ag, -aig, -an, *s.f.* Sip. 2**Drop of water.
——agach, ** *a.* Guttulous.
‡diodhailin, *s.* Mote, atom.
†diodhaoineachadh, *s.m.* Depopulation.
†diodhaoineadh, *s.m.* Depopulation.
†*iodhma, *s.m.* Fort, fortification.
†dìodhnadh, *s.m.* Satisfaction, comfort.
diofhlainn,** *a.* Pale, bloodless.
†diofhulaing, -e, *a.* Intolerable.
diog, -a, *s.m.* Syllable. 2 The least possible effort of speech. 3 Breath. 4 Life. Na h-abair diog, *do not say a syllable* ; cha'n 'eil d. ann, *he is breathless* ; cha'n 'eil d. innte,—applied to a cow found to be without calf after taking the bull—*Lewis.*
diog, see dìge.
——ail, *pr.pt.* a' diogladh, *v.a.* Tickle. 2 Suck closely.
——ailt, -e, *s.f.* Tickling. 2 Terror. 3 Crisis of timerous determination. Cuir d. ann, *tickle him.*
——ailteach, -aiche, *a.* Tickling. 2 Ticklish, difficult, dangerous.
diogair, -e, *a.* Eager, keen, vehement.
diogalach,** *a.* Sucking closely. 2†† see diogailteach.
diogaladh, -aidh, *s.m. & pr.pt.* see diogladh.
dìogan, -ain, *s.m.* Revenge. 2 Severity. 3 Spite. 4 Grief, sorrow. 5 Cruelty.
dìogana, *a.* see dìoganach.
——————ch, -aiche, *a.* Fierce. 2 Revengeful, spiteful. 3*Severe. 4*Cruel. Gu d., *revengefully, vindictively.*
——————achd, *s.f.* Revenge, spite. 2 Cruelty. 3**Fierceness.
dìoganta, see dìoganach.
dìogantach, see dioganach.
——————d, see dìoganachd.
diogar,** *a.* Eager, intent, vehement.
†diogha, *a.* The worst.
dìoghail, *v. a.* Revenge, avenge, retaliate, repay, requite. 2 (AH) Pay or settle, as in a commercial transaction.
——————t, *s. f.* Revenge, vengeance, spite. 2 Grief, sorrow. D. fear na dàlach, *the tardy man's revenge.*
——————te, *a.* & *past pt.* of dìoghail. Revenged, avenged, retaliated.
†dioghais, *a.* High, tall, stately.
dìoghalt, -ailt, see dioghaltas.
——————a, *past pt.* see dìoghailte.
——————ach, -aiche, *a.* Revengeful, vindictive. 2**Fond. 3* Requiring much.
——————ach,** -aich, *s.m.* Avenger. 2 Revengeful person. An d. mi-cheart, *the unjust avenger.*
——————achd, *s.f.ind.* Revenge, spite. 2 Cruelty.
——————aiche, -an, see dìoghaltach.
——————air, -ean, *s.m.* Avenger. 2**Revengeful man.
——————as, -ais, *s.m.* Vengeance, punishment, revenge, spite. 2 Grief, sorrow. Dean d., *revenge.*
——————asach, -aiche, *a.* see dìoghaltach.
†dioghann, *a.* Plentiful, not scanty.
dioghaoth,** -aoithe, *s.m.* Blast in corn.
†dioghart,** *s.m.* Decollation.
†dioghbhail, see dìobhail.
dìoghbhalach, *a.* see diobhalach.
dìoghladair,** *s.m.* Bridle-cutter.
dìoghladair, see dioghaltair.
——————eachd, see dioghaltachd.
dìoghladh,** -aidh, *s.m.* Avenging, revenging, repaying. 2 Revenge, requital. 3 Injustice. 4(AH) Act of settling or paying, as in a commercial transaction. A' d—, *pr.pt.* of dìoghail.
dìoghlaidh, *fut.aff.a.* of dìoghail. D. coireach no neo-choireach ris, *the guilty or innocent will suffer.*
dioghlagan,** *s.m.* Weanel, weanling.
dioghlais,** *s.f.* Abuse, defamation.
dìoghluim, *pr. pt.* a' dìoghlum & a' dìoghlumadh, *v.a.* Glean, cull, gather minutely. 2** Lease. 3**Weed.
dìoghlum, -uim, *s. m.* Gleanings, the thing gleaned or gathered.
——————aich, see dìoghluim,
——————air,** -ean, *s.m.* Gleaner. 2 Weeder.
dioghlus,** -uis, *s.m.* Darkness.
dìoghnadh,** -aidh, *s.m.* Contempt.
†dioghnas, *a.* Rare.
dioghradh,** -aidh, *s.m.* Moroseness. 2 Rudeness. †3 Hatred.
——————a, see dioghradhach.
——————ach, *a.* Morose, rude, unlovely.
†dioghrais, *adv.* Constantly, frequently.
dioghraiseach,** *a.* Beloved.
dioghras,**-ais, *s.m.* Zeal. 2 Uprightness.
——————ach,(PM) *a.* Excessively keen.
†dioghrog,** *v.n.* Belch.
——————,** *s.* Eructation.
dioglach, see diogailteach.
diogladh, -aidh, *s.m.* Tickling, act of tickling or

sucking closely. A' d—, *pr. pt.* of diogail. Seillean a' d. cluarain, *a bee sucking the thistle flower.*
diograis,** *s.f.* Diligence, secret.
diogras,** -ais, *s. m.* Honesty, integrity, uprightness. 2 Zeal.
dìol, *pr.pt.* a' dìol & a' dìoladh, *v.a.* Avenge, revenge. 2 Pay, render. 3 Fill, satisfy. 4 Ransom. 5 Restore, renew. 6 Recompense, requite. 7** Empty. 8**Change. 2 Wean. Dh. thu sin, *you have recompensed that*; d. dhomh, *pay me*; dìolamaid do 'n iompachan, *let us pay to the penitent*; dìolaibh a' ghloine gu bonn, *drain the glass to the bottom.*
dìol, -a, *s.m.* Recompense, satisfaction, retribution. 2 Reward, pay, hire. 3 Satiety, sufficiency. 4 Object, end proposed. 5 Fate, destiny. 6 The act of weaning, as a child. 7 *Condition, state. 8 Complement, proportion. 9**Use. 10**Selling. 11**Restitution. Is bòidheach a dh., *he is in a pretty condition*; tha mo dh. agam-sa, *I have my satisfaction* or *abundance*; a dh. ùin' aige, *he has plenty of time*; clach càise le a d. de dh' ìm, *a stone of cheese with its complement of butter*; d.-déirce, *an object of charity*; bu dubh a dh., *black was his fate*; chuireadh air d. e, *he was weaned*; mo dh. mhnatha, *rather too much of a wife for me*; is mór an d. a th' aige air an uisge, *there is a great continuance of rain*; 'se rinn an d. air, *he gave him an awful mauling.*
†diol, *a.* Worthy, sufficient.
dìolachd,** *s. f.* Requital. 2 Restoration. 3 Recompense. 4 Satisfaction. 5 Payment. 6 Orphan.
dìoladair, -ean, see dìoghaltair.
———eachd, see dìoghaltachd.
diola-deirce, see dìol-déirce.
dìoladh, -aidh, *s. m.* Paying. 2 Filling, satisfying, requiting, restoring. 3 Payment. 4 Requital. 5 Ransoming. 6 Yielding. 7 Restoring, restitution. 8 Atonement. A' d—, *pr. pt.* of dìol. D. iomlan, *full restitution.*
dioladh-deirce, see diol-deirce.
——— Pheadair, *s.m.* The fish caught in the Isles on Christmas Day and given to the poor.
†———mhàil, *s.m.* Receipt, discharge.
diolaid, see doillaid.
dìolaidh, *fut.aff.a.* of dìol. 2 *gen.sing.* of dìoladh.
———eachd, see dìoghaltachd.
diolaim, see dìoghluim.
dìolain, -e, *a.* Illegitimate, unlawfully begotten, bastard. Mac d., *an illegitimate son* or *bastard.*
———each,** *s.m.* Bachelor.
dìolair, -nan, *s.m.* Avenger, restorer, requiter. 2 Rewarder. 3 Amender.
———eachd, *s.f.ind.* Conduct of an avenger or requiter. 2**Requital. 3**Revengefulness.
dìolam, see dìoghluim.
diolamair, see dìoghlumair.
†diolamhnach, *s.m.* Hireling, soldier.
diolan, see dìolain.
———achd, *s.f.* see dìolanas.
———as, -ais, *s.m.* Fornication, bastardy, illegitimacy. 2**Celibacy. Rugadh an d. e, *he was born in fornication*; fhuair i urra le d., *she got a child by fornication.*
diolanta, ** *a.* Brave, manly, stout. 2 Generous. 3 Hospitable.
———s,** -ais, *s. m.* Manhood, bravery. 2 Generosity. 3 Hospitality.
diolar, *fut.pass.* of dìol.
dio-làrachadh,** -aidh, see dì-làrachadh.
dio-làrachd,** *s. f. ind.* see dì-làrachadh.
dio-làraich,** *v.a.* see dì-làraich.
†diolas, see dìleas.

dio-làthaireachd,‡‡ *s.f.* Absence.
†diolbhrugh, -a, *s.f.* Shop.
†diolchomhan, -an, *s.m.* Confederacy.
diol-chuan,** -ain, *s.m.* Shop.
diol-déirce, -an, *s. m.* Beggar. 2 Object of charity. 3*'Giving of charity.
diolfar, see dìolar.
†diolg,** *v.a.* Dismiss. 2 Forgive.
———ad, -aid, *s.m.* Forgiveness, remission.
†———adh, -aidh, *s.m.* Dismissal. 2 Forgiveness. 3 Dismissing, forgiving.
†diolgion, *v.a.* Empty.
diollad, see dìollaid.
———achadh, see dìollaideachadh.
dìolladair, -ean, *s.m.* Saddler.
———eachd, see dìollaideachd.
dìollaid, -e, -ean, *s.f.* Saddle.
———each, *a.* Of, or pertaining to, saddles.
———eachadh, -aidh, *s.m.* Saddling. A' d—, *pr.pt.* of dìollaidich.
———eachd, *s. f. ind.* Saddlery, saddler's business. Ris an d., *at saddle-making.*
———ear, -eir, see dìolladair.
———ich, *pr. pt.* a' dìollaideachadh, *v. a.* Saddle.
†diolmhannach, *s.m.* see diùlannach.
diolmhaoin,** *s.f.* Alimony.
dìolta, *past pt.* of dìol.
dìolta, *s.m.* Girth.
dìoltag, see ialltag.
dìoltair,** *s.m.* Seller.
dìoltair, *s.m.* see dìolladair.
dìol-thuarasdal,** -ail, *s.m.* Reward, recompense, wages.
dìoluim, see dìoghluim.
diolunta, see diùlanta.
———s, see diùlannas.
dìom, *prep. pron.* Of, off or from me. 2 Concerning me. Ghabh e truas dh., *he took pity on me.*
dìom, see diomb.
diom, -a, *s.f.* see diombadh.
diomach, -aiche, *a.* see diombach.
diomadh, -aidh, *s.m.* see diombadh.
diomail, see di-mol.
diomain, -e, *a.* see diom-buan.
diomaladh, -aidh, *s.m.* & *pr.pt.* see di-moladh.
diomaltair,** *s.m.* Glutton.
diomarag,‡ *s.f.* Clover seed.
diomas, -ais, *s.m.* Pride, arrogance. 2**Defiance.
———ach, -aiche, *a.* Proud, arrogant, bold, haughty, defying. 2**Disrespectful.
diomb, *s.m.* Hatred, disdain, dislike. 2 Indignation, dissatisfaction, offence, resentment, displeasure. Na toill d. duine sam bith, *do not incur the displeasure of any person.*
———ach, -aiche, *a.* Displeased, dissatisfied, discontented. 2* Indignant. 3**Sorrowful, mournful. Gu d., *unthankful*; d. ri m' [*or* de mo] mhàthair, *displeased with my mother.*
———achd, *s.f.ind.* Reluctance. 2* Indignation.
———adh, -aidh, *s. m.* Anger. 2 Discontent, displeasure. 3 Indignation. 4 Offence. 5 Pain. 6**Grief, trouble. 7 Spite. 8 Hatred. Móran diomaidh, *much trouble.*
———aiche, *comp.* of diombach.
diom-bàigh, see di-bàigh.
diombas, -ais, *s.m.* Lasciviousness.
———uadhach, -aiche, see diom-buaidheach.
———uaghail, -ala, *a.* see diom-buadhach.
diom-buaidh, -e, *s.f.* Unsuccessfulness, bad luck, 2‡‡Displeasure. 3** Defeat. 4**Mishap, misfortune. 5 **Crime.
———each, *a.* Unsuccessful, luckless, unfortunate.

diom-buainead, -eid, see diom-buanachd.
diom-buan, -uaine, *a.* Fading, fleeting, transitory, transient, not durable. Is d. gach cas an tìr gun eòlas, *the foot is ever moving in the land of strangers*—where there are no friends to visit, the traveller quickly passes.
diom-buanachd, *s. f. ind.* Transitoriness, evanescence, shortness of continuance.
diom-buanas, -ais, see diom-buanachd.
diombuidheach, see diombach.
diom-buil, -e, *s.f.* Prodigality, waste. 2 Profusion. 3* Misapplication. 4 Abuse.
diom-buil, *v.* see diom-builich.
diom-buileach,** *a.* Wasting, extravagant, prodigal, giving without discretion.
——————adh,‡‡ -ridh, *s.m.* Abuse.
diom-builich, *v.a.* Waste, consume. 2 Put to bad use, abuse.
diomgha, *s.f.ind.* see diomb.
diomhagad, *s.m.* Enfranchisement, liberty, freedom.
diomhaidis, see dìomhanach.
dìomhain, -e, *a.* Idle, lazy. 2 Frivolous, vain, trifling, unavailing, nugatory, useless, to no purpose. Beairt dh., *vain doings* ; iasgair d., *an unsuccessful fisher* ; *2 a bird, see under* iasgair ; gu d., *vainly.*
dìomhaineach, -eiche, *a.* Larkish.
dìomhair, -e, *a.* see diamhair.
dìomhaireach, see diamhair.
dìomhaireachd, see diamhaireachd.
dìomhaireas, -eis, see diamhaireas.
dìomhairich, see diamhairich.
diomhaltas, -ais, *s.m.* Caution, notice.
dìomhan, see dìomhain.
————ach, -aiche, *a.* Idle, lazy. 2 Vain, in vain. 3**Trifling, frivolous. 4**Nugatory. Is d. dhut teannadh ris, *it is idle* (or *vain*) *for you to attempt it*; cainnt dh., *idle talk*; breugan d., *lying vanities.*
dìomhanachd, *s.f.* Inactivity.
dìomhanaiche, -an, *s.m.* Idler.
dìomhanas, -ais, *s.m.* Vanity, idleness, laziness. 2 Emptiness. Dìomhanasan breugach, *lying vanities.*
diomhar, see diamhair.
diomharachd, see diamhaireachd.
diomharan, -ain, see diamharan.
†diomharg, *v.a.* Quench. 2 Suppress.
†diomhothuigheach, -eiche, *a.* Stupid.
†diomhrachd, see diamhaireachd.
†diomhran, -ain, *s.m.* Mystery. 2 Cell.
diomhuinn, see dìomhain.
diomol, see di-mol.
———adair, see di-moladair.
———adh, see di-moladh.
———ta, see di-molta.
———tair, see di-moltair.
diomrac, -aic, *s.m.* Temple.
dìon, -a, *s.m.* Shelter, protection, covert, fence. 2 State of being wind and water tight. 3** Second semi-metre or leth-rann of a verse. 4 **Apology. 5 Defence (in law.) Fo dh. do sgéithe, *under covert of thy wing* (or *shield*) ; air son mo dhìona, *for my defence* or *protection*; tha d. 'san taigh, *the house is wind and water tight* ; cum d., *shelter, protect.*
dìon, *pr.pt.* a' dìon & a' dìonadh, *v.a.* Defend, protect, shelter, shield, guard, save. D. thu fhèin, *defend yourself* ; d. mi le d' sgéith, *defend me with thy shield.*
dìonach, -aiche, *a.* Close-joined, air-tight, water-tight, water-proof. 2 Safe, secure. 3 Reserved, 4 Sheltered. laid up. Taigh d., *a water-tight house ;* long dh., *a ship without a leak*; àite d., *a sheltered place.*
dìonachadh, -aidh, *s.m.* Tightening, defending. 2 Act of securing, tightening or rendering water-tight. 3**Caution, bail. 4**Sheltering. 5**Security. A' d—, *pr.pt.* of dìonaich.
dìonachas, see dìonachadh.
dìonachd, *s. f.* Security, shelter. 2 Circumstance of being water-tight.
dìonadach, *a.* Preventive.
dìonadair, -ean, *s. m.* Protector, defender. 2 Fender. 3 Fend-off, see under bàta, 17—20, p. 76.
dìonadh, -aidh, *s.m.* Protecting, defending, sheltering, shielding. 2** Defence, shelter, security. A' d—, *pr. pt.* of dìon.
dìonag, -aige, -an, *s.f.* Two-year-old sheep or goat. 2**Hoggerel. 3 Dimmont, see under caora.
dìonaich,†† *v.a.* Make water-tight, caulk. 2 3 Join closely, as a vessel. 4 Shelter. 5 Secure.
dìonaiche, *comp.* of dìonach.
dionaire, see di-nàire.
————ach, see di-nàireach.
dìon-airm, -e, *s.f.* Place of refuge, sanctuary. 2 Depôt.
†dionaisg, see dì-naisg.
dìon-aite, -aiteachan, *s.m.* Place of refuge, shelter, sanctuary.
dìon-amhaiche, *s.m.* Habergeon.
dionasach,** *a.* see dianasach.
dionasgach, see dì-nasgach.
dionasgadh, see dì-nasgadh.
dìon-bhothan,** *s.m.* Cloister.
dìon-bhréid, -ean, *s.m.* Apron.
dìon-chainnt, -ean, *s.f.* Speaking in defence.
dìon-charn,** -chuirn, *s.m.* Fort.
dìon-chòmhla, *s.m.* Aide-de-camp. 2 Officer of life-guards.
dìon-fheachd,** *s.f.* Fencibles.
diong, -a, -an, *s.f.* Hillock. 2 Immoveable object. 3 Worthy. 4 *s.m.* see gliong.
diong, *pr.pt.* a' diongadh, *v.a.* Join. 2 Match, equal, pair. 3 Overcome, conquer. 4 Effect, accomplish. 5 Pay, recompense. Is iomadh ceud a dh. thu, *many a hundred hast thou conquered*; diongam-sa rìgh Innis-con, *let me match the king of Inniscon*; as a seo cha diongadh e, *out of this he could not drag* ; diongam fear ma dh' fhuiricheas mi, agus fuilingeam teicheadh, *I'll match a man if I stay, and I can suffer a retreat*—N.G.P.
diong, *v.a. & n.* see gliong.
diong, -a, *a.* Worthy. 2* Immoveable.
diongach, -aiche, *a.* Able to accomplish, to match or to overcome, matching. 2**Suitable, proper, meet, worthy.
diongadh, -aidh, *s.m.* Matching, act of matching, overcoming, conquering. 2††Effecting. concurring. A' d—, *pr. pt.* of diong.
diongail,** *a.* Worthy, fit, proper, suitable, fit to bear.
diongail, *s.f.* see gliong.
diongalta, see diongmhalta.
diongaltas, see diongmhaltas.
diongar,(DU) *a.* Persistent, stiff.
dionghair,** *s.f.* Tribute, benevolent succour.
diongmhail, -e, *s.f.* Effect, sufficiency, efficiency.
——————, *a.* see diongmhalta.
†diongmhalar, *a.* Worthy.
diongmhalta, *a.* Firm, tight, strong. 2 Perfect, sufficient, substantial. 3 Effective. 4 Worthy, meet, proper, suitable. 5 Completely certain. 6 Able-bodied. 7(AH) Trustworthy, reliable. Seachd cathaich d., *seven able-bodied warriors.*
diongmhaltachd, *s.f.ind.* same meanings as diongmhaltas.
diongmhaltas, -ais, *s.m.* Firmness, tightness. 2 Perfectness, efficiency, sufficiency. 3 State of being fast, fixed or firmly bound.

diongnach, -aiche, *a.* Fortified.
dìon-làthaich, -a-, *s.m.* Mud-guard.
dìon-long-phort,** -uirt, *s.m.* Harbour garrison.
†dionn, -a, *s.m.* Hill.
dionnal, -ail, -an, see deannal.
†dionnan, -ain, *s.m.* Little hill.
†dionnsuighe, for dh' ionnsuidh.
dìon-oglachas,** -ais, *s.m.* Heroism.
dìonta, *past pt.* of dìon. Defended, protected.
†dior, *a.* Meet, proper, decent.
†dior, *s.m.* Law.
†diorach, *a.* see direach.
dìorachd, *s.f.ind.* Ability, power, capability of performing or enduring. 2‡‡Inveteracy.
†diorachrach, *a.* Lawless.
†diorang, *v.n.* Belch.
dirras, see diorras.
diorbhsail, *s.* Snarling of a dog.
†diorgas, -ais, *s.m.* Uprightness, integrity.
†diorma, *s.* Troop, crowd.
†diormach, *a.* In troops, in companies. 2 Crowded. 3 Numerous. 4 Infinite. 5 Unfit to walk.
†diorna,** *s.* Quantity.
†diorr, *s.* Spark of life.
dìorrais,(CR) *s.f.* Perpetual work, bustle.
dìorras, -ais, *s.m.* Stubbornness, obstinacy. 2 Crossness, irascibility. 3 Vehemence, keenness, enthusiasm. 4* Tenacity, pertinacity. 5 Childish efforts. Am fear a ni d., is iomadh a ni d. ris, *he that is obstinate will often find his match.*
dìorrasach, -aiche, *a.* Stubborn, obstinate. 2 Cross, irascible. 3 Vehement, forward, rash, fierce, keen. 4*Tenacious. 5 Opinionative. 6 Striving in vain.
dìorrasachd, *s.f.* Extreme pertinacity or tenacity. 2**Irascibility, hastiness, rashness, forwardness, fierceness.
diorrasail,(DC) *v.n.* Spatter, hiss, crackle. 2 Nag peevishly.
diorrasan, -ain, *s.m.* Fretful person. 2 Grasshopper. 3 Snarl. Fraoch an diorrasain, *a kind of heather that sparkles when burning,* (called also *fraoch spreadanach.*)
————ach, *a.* Irascible. 2 Fretful. 3 Snarling.
————aich, *s.f.* Irascibility. 2 Snarling. 3 **Crackling.
†diorrasg, -aisg, *s.m.* Suddenness. 2 Fierceness. 3**Hastiness of temper. 4 Rashness.
†————ach, -aiche, *a.* Forward. 2 Sudden, rash. 3**Irascible, fierce.
†diorsan, -ain, *s.m.* Bad news.
dioruanach, see di-bhruaineach.
diosd, *v.a. & n.* Jump. 2 Kick with the heels.
dìosg, *a.* Barren, dry, applied to a cow that gives no milk.
diosg, -a, -an, *s.m.* Dish, plate, platter. 2†† Any quantity of water or liquor in a dish. 3 (AF) Barren cow. Is bràthair do 'n d. an tuairnear, *the turner is brother to the dish ;* chaidh am màrt an d., *the cow has become dry.*
diosg, *v.a. & n.* Creak, as hinges. 2 Gnash, as teeth.
dìosgadh, -aidh, *s.m.* State of being barren or dry, not giving milk, as a cow, barrenness, dryness. 2**Grating or squeaking noise.
dìosgaidh-dàsgaidh, (CR) *s. f.* Sucking sound, as made by walking with water in the shoes —*Suth'd.*
diosgail, *s.f.* Creaking noise, as of withes or iron joints when put in motion.
diosgan, -ain, *s.m.* Creaking noise, as of rusty hinges. 2**Grating of the teeth. 3**Gnashing. 4**Crashing. D. air gach maide, *every timber creaking.*
diosganach,(CR) -aich, *s.m.* Boarded-out dipsomaniac—*Skye & Harris.*
dìosganaich, *s.m.* see dìosgan.
diosgar,** -air, *s.m.* Mob, rabble.
diosgarnach,** -aich, *s.m.* Mob, rabble. 2 One of a mob.
†diosla, *s.m.* Die.
diosmuig, see dì-smuig.
diosnaidhm, see dì-snaidhm.
diospoireachd, see deasbaireachd.
diot, *s.f.* Gaelic spelling of old pronunciation of *diet.* [*Diot* is restricted to one particular meal (dinner) when not qualified by an adjective, as, d. mhór, *dinner* ; d. bheag, *breakfast. Tràth* is applied to any meal.—*W. of Ross.*]
diot, *prep. pron.* From thee, of thee, off thee. Cuir dh. do chòta, *put off your coat.*
diot, see diod. Cha'n 'eil d. ann, *there is not a drop in it.*
diotag, see diodag.
dìoth, see dìth. †2 *v.n.* Die, decay.
dìothachadh, see dìtheachadh.
diothadh,** -aidh, *s.m.* Decaying, dying, withering. 2 Decay. 3 Death. A' d—, *pr. pt.* of dioth.
dìothadh, -aidh, see dìtheachadh.
dìothaich, see dìthich.
diothaireach,** *a.* Emetic.
†diothramh, -reimh, see dìthreabh.
diothruaill, *v.a.* Unsheathe.
†diothughadh, see dìtheachadh.
diot-mhór, -a-móire, -an-móra, *s.f.* Dinner.
dìpin, -e, -ean, *s.m.* Certain measure of a net, usually a herring-net. 2‡ Deepening in a net.
dìpinn, see dìpin.
†Diplinn, -e, see Giblinn.
†dir, *s.f.* Letters. 2 Pimples.
dìr, *pr. pt.* a' dìreadh, see dìrich.
dirb, see darb.
†dire, *s.f.* Tax, tribute.
dìreach, -iche, *a.* Straight. 2 Perpendicular, upright. 3 Just, right, equitable. 4 Positive, certain. 5 Direct. 6 Frugal. An ni sin tha cam, cha ghabh e deanamh d., *that which is crooked, cannot be made straight*; d. sin, *just that* ; is d. Dia, *God is upright* ; air ceumaibh d. réidh, *on a straight, plain path* ; tha 'dheanadas d., *his work is right* ; caol d., d. air adhairt, *straightforward* ; d. glan, *exactly so* ; d. 'na sheasamh, *standing upright* ; dàn d., *verse,* or *metre of a certain class.*
dìreach, *adv.* Directly, exactly so. D. mar a thubhairt thu, *just as you said* ; d., *or* seadh d ! *just so !*
†dìreach, *s.m.* Dwarf.
dìreachadh, -aidh, *s.m.* Making straight, becoming straight. A' d—. *pr.pt.* of dìrich.
dìreachan, -ain, *s.m.* Perpendicular.
dìreachas, -ais, *s.m.* Uprightness. 2 Straightness. 3 Honesty. 4 Perpendicularity.
dìreachd,** *v.a.* Geld.
————as,** -ais, *s.m.* Act of gelding.
dìreadh, -idh, *s. m.* Ascending, act of ascending, ascension, mounting, climbing. 2**Direction. 3**Panegyric. 4‡‡Prevailing. A' d—, *pr.pt.* of dìr. A' d. a' bhruthaich, *ascending the brae* ; ceò a' d. aonaich, *mist ascending a hill.*
dì-riaghailt,‡‡ *s.f.ind.* Asymmetry.
†diribe, *a.* Bald.
dìrich, *pr.pt.* a' dìreachadh, *v.a.* Straighten, make straight, even, or perpendicular. 2‡‡ Direct. Am fear nach d. a dhruim, *he that will not be at the trouble of straightening his back.*
dìrich, *pr. pt.* a' dìreadh, Ascend, go up, mount,

climb. 2 Surmount. Cha d. thu am fireach, *thou shalt not climb the steep*; dh. e an carbad, *he mounted the chariot.*
dìriche, *comp.* of dìreach.
dìrichead, *s.f.* Erectness. 2 Straightness.
dìrichear, *fut. pass.* of dìrich. Also used impersonally, as d. [leinn] am monadh, *let us ascend the hill.*
dìrichte, *past pt.* of dìrich.
dìrid, *s. f.* Lapwing, see adharcan-luachrach. 2 (MMcD) Puffin—*W. Suth'd.*
†dirim, *a.* Numerous, plentiful. 2 Great.
†dirtheach, *s.m.* Feast, solemnization.
dis, -e, *a.* Susceptible of cold, incapable of bearing cold. 2 Delicate, tender. 3 Chill. 4 Miserable. 5 Poor.
Dis,* *s.m.* Celtic deity.
dìs, see dithis.
Di-Sathuirn, *s. m.* Saturday. D. seo chaidh, *last Saturday* ; là Sathuirn, *a Saturday;* thàinig e D. [not *air* D.,] *he came on a Saturday.*
disbeirt,** *a.* Twofold, double.
discir, see disgir.
†discréide,** Gaelic form of *discretion.*
disd, -e, -ean, *s.f.* Mow, rick. 2 Layer of stacked peats or turf. 3 see disinn.
di-se, *emphat.* of di, *prep. pron.*
dise,** *s.f.* Mow, rick.
diseachan,(AH) -ain, *s.m.* Person who is exceptionally susceptible to, or afraid of cold.
disear, *s. m.* Susceptibility to cold, delicateness—*Lewis.*
disgir, -e, *a.* Sudden, fierce, nimble, active. 2 ‡‡Cruel.
dìsinn, dìsne, dìsnean, *s.m.* Die [*pl.* dice.] 2 Cube. 3 Wedge, as in the shaft of anything. Ag iomairt air dìsnean, *playing at backgammon.*
dis-lann,** *s.m.* Gaming-house.
dìsle, *comp.* of dìleas.
dìsle, see dìlseachd.
dìsleach, -iche, *a.* Stormy. 2 Uncouth. 3 Straggling.
disleachadh,(PM) -aidh, *s. m.* Benumbing or overcoming with cold.
dìsleachd, *s.f.ind.* see dìlseachd.
dìslead, -eid, see dìlseachd.
dislean, *s. pl.* Relatives. 2** see dìsnean.
disleanaiche,** *s.m.* Player of dice. 2 Gambler.
dislein, see dìsnean.
di-sligheach,** *a.* Devious, straggling. 2 Impervious. 3 Immethodical. 4 Uncouth.
dì-smuig, *v.a.* Snuff, as a candle.
di-snaidhm,** *a.* Smooth, without knots.
dìsne, *gen, sing.* of dìsinn. [given by †† and ‡ as *nom. sing.*]
dìsneach, -aiche, *a.* Tesselated, variegated by squares. 2††Abounding in dice or cubes, diced. 3 ‡‡Cubic.
dìsneag, -eig, -an, *s. f.* Little die.
dìsnean, *pl.* of dìsinn. Dice.
dìsnean, -ein, *s.m.* Dice-box. [†† gives -ein, as termination of *nom. sing.*]
dìsnear,** -eir, *s.m.* Dice player.
dìsnibh, *dat.pl.* of dìsinn. Deud shnaithte mar dh., *teeth polished like dice.*
dìsnich,* *v.n.* Raffle.
disread,** -rid, *s.m.* Aspergillum, used at mass to sprinkle holy water on the people.
dìst,** *s.f.* Mow, rick. 2 Die. 3 Gaelic spelling of *joist.*
dìstean,** see dìsnean.
dìstear,** see dìsnear.
dit, *pr. pt.* a' diteadh, *v.a.* Condemn. 2 Sentence. 3 Reproach, despise. 4**Surrender. 5††Rebuke. Cò a dhìteas iad ? *who shall condemn them ?* an d. mi air son sin, *reproach me not for that.*
dìteach, -eiche, *a.* Accusable.
dìteachail, -e, *v.* Libellous.
dìteadh, -tidh, -idhean, *s. m.* Sentence, sentencing, judgment, act of condemning, reproaching, condemnation. 2** Surrender. 'S e seo an d. gu'n d' thàinig an solus do 'n t-saoghal, *this is the condemnation that light is come into the world.* A' d—, *pr.pt.* of dìt.
dìteag, see dìdeag.
dìteagaich, see dìdeagaich.
dìteam, *1st.pers. sing. pres. aff.* of dìt. I sentence. 2 *for* dìtidh mi, *I will sentence.*
dìtear,** *s.m.* Accuser.
dìth, -e, *s.m.* Want, defect. 2 Failure, deficiency. 3 Destruction. D. céille, *want of sense ;* cha'n 'eil d. air, *he wants for nothing ;* dè tha dh. ort ? *what do you want ?* is mór a tha dh. orm, *I want much*; chuir thu seo a dh. orm, *you deprived me of this* ; is mór tha sin a dh. orm, *I want that very much ;* is beag a tha sin a dh. ort, *you have very little need of that* ; théid iad a dh. orm, *I shall be deprived of them ; 2 they shall become useless to me ;* a dh. fasgaidh, *for want of shelter* ; tha móran a dh., *there is a great deficiency.*
dìth,†† *pr. pt.* a' dìtheadh, *v.n.* Die, perish, wither away. Tuirc nach faodadh airm a dh., *boars that arms may not kill.*
dith, *prep.pron.* Of, off, *or* from her, *or* it (*f.*)
dith, *pr.pt.* a' ditheadh, *v. a.* Press together, press, squeeze, compress. †2 Suck.
dith,* *pl.* -ean & -eanan, *s. f.* Layer, course, streak. 2 Stratum, vein, as in a mine. D. mu seach, *layer about ;* dithean saille, *layers or streaks of fat,* as in beef ; ditheanan luaidh is airgid, *veins of lead and silver.*
dìth-armaich, see dì-armaich.
dithbhir, see deifir.
dìth-bhith,†† *s. f.* Annihilation. D. ort ! (an imprecation.)
dìth-bhrògach, see dì-bhrògach.
dìth-chealtair,** *s. m.* Necromantic veil that renders things invisible.
dìth-cheann, see dì-cheann.
dìth-cheannadh, see dì-cheannadh.
dìthchioll, see dìchioll.
dìthchiollach, see dìchiollach.
dìthchiollaich, see dìchiollaich.
dìth-chreideamh, see dì-chreideamh.
dìth-chreidmheach, see dì-chreidmheach.
dìth-chuimhne, see dì-chuimhne.
dìth-cnamhaidh, see dì-cnamhaidh.
dìtheach, -ich, *s.m.* Beggar. 2 Needy person.
dìtheach, -iche, *a.* Empty. 2 Indigent, poor.
dìtheachadh, -aidh, *s.m.* Abolition. 2 Destruction, destroying. 3**Causing to cease. 4** Failing. A' d—, *pr. pt.* of dìthich.
dìtheachail, -e, *a.* Lossful.
dìtheadh, -idh, *s.m.* Hoarding up. 2 Concealing. 3 Pressing. 4 Destruction.
dìthean,‡ -ein, *s. m.* Daisy, darnel. 2 Blossom, any flower, see breòillean. 3††Wild marigold. 4(PJM) Knoll. 5(PJM) Place on top of head towards back, where the hair naturally parts, forming shape of a daisy. Dìthean nan gleann, *the flowers of the valleys.*
dìthean-Abraoin,§ *s.m.* Hepatica—*hepatica.*
dìtheanach, -aiche, *a.* Abounding in darnels or flowers, of or belonging to, darnels or flowers. 2††Abounding in corn-marigolds.
dìthean-mór, -ein-mhóra, *s.m.* Ox-eye.
dìthean-òir, (an)§ *s.m.* Corn-marigold, see bile-bhuidhe.
dìthean-ùr, *pl.* -eanan-ùra, *s.m.* Fresh flower.
dìth-fhear,‡‡ -fhir, *s.m.* Bankrupt.
dìthich, *pr.pt.* a' dìtheachadh, *v.a. & n.* Destroy,

extirpate, root out, cause to cease, destroy utterly. 2**Fail, cause to fail. 3†† Die, perish. Dìthichidh mi an ìomhaighean, *I will root out their images*; dh. mo chàirdean, *my friends have failed.*
†dithimh, *s.f.* Heap. (hemp in ‡‡)
†dithinge, *a.* Dumb, mute.
dithis, *a.* Two. [Used only of persons, and followed by the *gen. pl.* Erroneously applied to two of anything in some parts.] Thàinig d., *two (persons) came*; 'nan dithisean, *in pairs*; d. fhear, *two men*; 'nar d., *we two together.*
——each, *a.* Mutual.
dithisd, see dithis.
dìth-làrachadh, dìth-làraich, dìth-làthaireach, dìth-làthaireachd, dìth-làthairich, see dì-l—.
dithleach,** *a.* Forgetful, neglectful.
dith-luchdaich,* *v.a.* see di-luchdaich.
dithmeas, see dìmeas.
———dachd, see dìmeasdachd.
dìth-mhill, *v.a.* see di-mhill.
———eadh, see di-mhilleadh.
———tear, see di-mhilltear.
dith-mhol, see dì-mol.
dith-mothachaidh, *s.m.* Inattention. 2 (PM) Want of common sense.
dìthreabh, -eibh, *s.f.* Desert, wilderness. 2 The higher and less cultivated parts of a district. 3**Hermitage. 4**Hermit.
———ach, -aich, *s.m.* Hermit, anchorite, ascetic.
———ach,** *a.* Desert, uncultivated, solitary. 2 Bleak.
———achd,** *s.f.* Bleakness.
dìthreachdach, -aiche, *a.* Lawless, insubordinate. Gu d., *insubordinately.*
dìthreamh, see dìthreabh.
dith-reodha,(AC) *s.* see dubh-threabha.
dìtidh, *fut. aff. a.* of dìt.
dìtig, *Lewis* for dìrid.
diù, *a.* Worth. 2 Due. 3**see diùbhaidh. Cha d. leam sin, *that is beneath me*—not good enough for me to do.
diu, *adv.* see diugh. †2 Long since.
diù, *s.m.* Long time. 2 see diùbhaidh. 3 (DU) Care. D. nam beathach fìrionn, *the refuse of male animals*; is d. teine fearn ùr, is d. duine mi-rùn, is d. dìbhe fìon sean, ach 'se d. an domhain droch bhean, *worst of fuel alder green, worst of human malice keen, worst of drink wine without life, worst of all things a bad wife.* Fìon sean is literally *old wine*, but the Celts certainly knew what was what in wine as in other things—N.G.P.
diubh, *prep. pron.* Of, off or from them. 2 From among them. Cuid dh., *some of them*; aon dh., *one of them*; cò dh.? *which of them?*
diùbhaidh, -ean, *s.m.* The refuse, worst. 2 Object of contempt. Roghainn is d., *pick and get the worst*; cha d. idir e, *it is no object of contempt.*
———, *a.* Low, worthless, abject.
diùbhail, -alach, -ean [& -aichean,] see dìobhail.
———each, *a.* see dìobhalach.
diubhair,** *s.m.* Discrepancy.
diùbhalach, -aiche, see dìobhalach.
———adh, see dìobhalachadh.
diùbhalaich, see dìobhalaich.
diubhar, *s.m.* see diubhras. Cha dean e d. sam bith, *it will make no difference.*
———aich, *v.n.* Contradistinguish.
———aiche,** *s.m.* Distinguisher.
diubhrais, for dìamhaireas. Cha d. eadar dithis no idir eadar triùir, *betwixt two a secret is unsafe, and among three persons it is no secret at all—Sgeulaiche nan caol, p. 133.*
diùbhras, -ais, *s.m.* Difference.
———ach, -aiche, *a.* Differential, making difference. 2 Auricular.
———achd,** *s.f.* Privateness.
diubhsan, *emphat. form* of *prep. pron.* diubh.
diuc, -a, *s.m. & f.* The pip, a sickness in fowls.
*diùc, *v.a. & n.* Exclaim, cry out. 2 Approach. 3 Present one's self.
diùc, -an, *s.m.* Duke.
†diùcadh, -aidh, *s. m.* Coming to, presenting one's self.
diùcail, *a.* Ducal.
diùcair, -ean, *s.m.* Bladder or small buoy, used to keep fishing nets at the right depth, ducker.
diuchaidh, -e, *a.* Addled, of no value, what proves useless in corn, eggs, &c.
diuchair,** *v.a.* Drive away, keep off.
diuch-bhlian,(CR) *W. of Ross-sh.* for dubh-bhlèin.
diùchd, -an, see diùc.
diùdan, -ain, *s.m.* Giddiness, thoughtlessness. 2 Thoughtless person.
———ach, -aiche, *a.* Giddy, thoughtless, *prov.*
diudhal,** -ail, *s.m.* see dìobhail.
diug! *inter.* Chuck! cry to gather fowls. Na h-abair d. a choidhche ris an eun gus an tig e as an ugh, *never say "chuck" to the chick before it is out of the egg.*
diug,** *v.n.* Cluck, cackle.
diugadh,** -aidh, *s.m.* Clucking, as of a hen.
diugan, -ain, *s.m.* Mischance, misfortune.
———ta, *a.* Unfortunate.
diugh, *adv.* "an diugh" to-day. An diugh fhein, *this very day.*
diugha, *a.* see diùbhaidh.
diughlar, see dìolar.
diùid, -e, *a.* Tender-hearted, flexible, timid. 2 *Fearful, bashful, awkwardly sheepish. Fear gun rud aige, is d. a chéilidh anmoch, *an empty hand makes a long visit unpleasant—(lit. a man having nothing, bashful is his late visit.)*
diùid, -e, -ean, *s.m.* Awkward spiritless fellow. 2 Silliness. 3(PM) In *Uist* Bashful, shy, coy, and *not* meanings 1 or 2. Is d. fear na h-eisimeil, *the dependant is timid*—N.G.P.
——, -e, -ean, *s.f.* Pain. 2 Sorrow. †3 Succour.
diuide, *comp.* of diùid.
diùide,* *s.f.* see diùideachd. †2 Continuance.
——ach, -iche, *a.* Sneaking, mean-spirited. 2 Silly, shy, timid, bashful. 3**Tender-hearted. 4**Flexible.
——achd, *s. f. ind.* Bashfulness, backwardness, sneakingness, shyness, timidity, diffidence.
diùididh, -e, *a.* Shamefaced, bashful, shy, timid.
diuir, see deor.
diùireas,** -eis, *s.m.* Any worthless thing. 2 The worst part of anything. Gach d. gu deireadh, *the worst is always reserved till last.*
diul, see deoghail. 2 see dìol.
diùlach,* see diùlannach.
diùlam,(DU) -aim, *s.m.* Sense of shame, modesty, reserve. Duine gun d., *a man without shame.*
diùlannach, -aich, *s.m.* Hero, bravo man. 2 Good man. 3**Handsome man. 4** Stout man. 5**Hireling, mercenary. A liuthad d. ainnis, *many a poor youth.*
diùlannas, -ais, *s. m.* Manliness. 2 Activity. 3 Heroism, bravery. 4 Stoutness. 5 Generosity, hospitality.
diùlanta, *a.* Manly. 2 Brave, heroic. 3 Active. 4 Stout, lusty. 5 Generous, hospitable.
———s, see diùlannas.

diùlnach, see diùlannach.
diùlnas, see diùlannas.
diùlt, *pr.pt.* a' diùltadh, *v.a.* Refuse. 2 Misgive, reject, deny, disown. Nach diùltadh strì, *who would not refuse battle*; is tearc each a dhiùltas a mhuing, *seldom will a horse refuse his mane.*
——,** *s. m.* Refusal, denial. 2 Negative. Fhuair e an d., *he got a refusal.*
——ach, *a.* Negative in *grammar.*
——adh, -aidh, -aidhean, *s.m.* Refusal, denial, act of refusing or denying. 2**Negative. A' d—, *pr.pt.* of diùlt. Is buaine aon d. na dàthabhartas-deug, *one refusal is longer remembered than a dozen offers.*
diùmach, see diombach.
diùmb, see diomb.
diùmbach, see diombach.
diùmhlach, -aich, see diùlannach.
diùmhlannach, -aich, see diùlannach.
diùmhlannas, -ais, see diùlannas.
†diùn, *a.* Gaelic spelling of French *jeune*, young.
diùnach, see deònach.
diunanachadh, -aidh, *s. m.* Walloping, drubbing. A' d—, *pr.pt.* of diunanaich.
diunanaich,* *pr.pt.* a' diunanachadh, *v.a.* Wallop, drub.
diùnlaoch,* -aoith, see diùlannach. Ceum air adhart aig gach d. (diùlannach), *each hero marching forward.*
†diùr,** -a, *a.* Bad. 2 Difficult, hard, dire. Bu d. an gàbhadh, *it was a dire necessity.*
diurasan, see dearrasan.
†diùrn, *v.a.* Drink greedily, gulp. 2 Swallow.
diurnach, -aich, *s.m.* One who drinks or swills.
diùrr,* *s.f.* Vital spark. Cha'n 'eil d. ann, *he is quite dead*; na h-abair d., *say not a wheest.*—P.J.M.
diùrrais,* *s. f.* Secret, mystery. 2(PJM) Desire to bite, as a child when teething. An d., *as a secret.*
——each,* *a.* Secret, private, requiring secrecy.
†diùs, *s.m.* Protection.
diù-san, see diubh-san.
diute, see diutidh.
diutha, *prov.* for diubh.
†diuthach,‖ *s.m.* *Nomen doloris,* produced by rubbing the thighs in travelling.
diùthadh, *a.* see diùbhaidh.
diùthaidh, see diùbhaidh.
†diuthan, see †diuthach.
diutaidh,(DC) *a.* *Uist* for diùididh.
dlagh,*-aigh, *s.m.* Natural order. 2 see dlòth. As a dh., *out of its natural order* or *arrangement.*
dlaigh, *gen. sing.* of dlagh.
dlaimh,** *s.f.* Darkness.
dlaogh, see dlagh.
dlaoi, see dlóth.
dleachd, see reachd.
——air, see reachdadair.
dleas,* -a, -an, *s.m.* Right, due, merit, desert. 2††Office. 3 see dleasnas. Mo dh. fhéin, *my own due* or *right.*
——,* *a.* Due, deserved, merited, incumbent, in duty bound. Is d. dha sin, *that is due to him*; ma tha sin d. dhut, *if that be due to you*; an d. dhomh sin a dheanamh? *is it incumbent on me to do that?*
——, *pr. pt.* a' dleasadh, *v.a. & n.* Merit, deserve. 2*Owe, extort. 3* Procure. Na d. ni do dhuine sam bith, *owe no man anything*; dleasaidh airm urram, *arms procure respect.*
——ail, -ala, *a.* Dutiful.
——alachd, see dleasnachd.
——annach, -aiche, *a.* see dleasnach.
——annas, -ais, see dleasnas.
dleasdanach, see dleasnach.
dleasdanas, see dleasnas.
dleasnach, -aiche, *a.* Dutiful, dutious. 2 Affectionate. 3**Rightful.
dleasnas, -ais, *s.m.* Duty, filial duty. 2 Affection. 3 Obligation. 4**Right. Rinn mi mo dh., *I did my duty*: a réir mo dhleasnais, *according to my duty.*
dligead,** -eid, *s.m.* Separation.
dligh, *v.n.* Owe, be indebted. Ma dhligheas mi ni sam bith, *if I owe anything*; thoir moladh dhasan do 'n dlighear e, *give praise to him to whom it is due*; dlighear mo thaing dha, *my thanks are due to him.*
dlighe, *s.f.ind.* Law, ordinance. 2 Duty. 3 Right, due. 4 Tribute, custom. 5 Perquisite 6 Property. Is e seo mo dh., *this is my due*, le d. cheirt, *with just right.*
——ach, -iche, *a.* Lawful, rightful. 2 Legitimate. 3** Right, due. 4**Dutiful. Oighre d., *a rightful heir*; clann d., *legitimate children*; ma 's d. dhuit sin, *if that be due to you.*
——achail, see dligheil.
——achas, -ais, *s.m.* Duty. 2 Lawful right 3 Absoluteness.
dligheachd-breithe,‡‡ *s.f.* Legitimacy.
dligheadh, -idh, see dlighe.
dlighean-air-leth, *s.m.* By-laws.
dlighear,** *a.* see dligheach.
——, *fut. pass.* of dligh.
——, -ir, *s.m.* Lawyer. 2 Magistrate, justice of the peace. 3††Creditor.
dligheil, -e & -gheala, *a.* Just. 2 Obedient to law, lawful. 3 Rightful. 4**Skilled in law. 5**Litigious. Duine d., *a litigious man.*
dlighe-thabhairt,‡‡ *s.m.* Legitimation.
†dlighleanuigh, -ean, *s.m.* Lawgiver.
dlightheach, -iche, *a.* see dligheach.
dlisteanach,** *a.* see dligheach.
dlisteanas, see dligheachas.
dlithe, see dlighe.
dlitheach, *a.* see dligheach.
dlithear, see dlighear.
dlò, -tha, -than, *s.f.* see dlòth.
dlochd, -an, *s. m.* Strainer. 2 Colander. Snare.
dlochdair, see dlochd.
dlochdair, *v.a.* Strain, press, squeeze.
dlochdan, see dlochd.
dlodan,** -ain, *s.m.* see dlochd.
dlogh,* *s.m.* Wart. 2 see dlòth.
dloghainn,* *s.f.* Sheaf-corn half thrashed, given to cattle when fodder is scarce.
dlòintibh, *dat. pl.* of dlòth.
†dlomh, *v.n.* Tell. 2 Refuse, deny. 3 Make evident or plain.
†dlomh, *s.m.* Refusal.
dlomhadh,** -aidh, *s.m.* Refusal, denial.
†dlomhaisinn, *s.f.* Destruction.
dlòth, -a & -ann, *dat.* -ainn, *pl.* dlòintean, *s.f.* Handful of corn or grass cut with one stroke of the reaping hook. 2**Lock of hair. D. gruaige, *a lock of hair*; cuid de na dlòthaibh, *some of the handfuls.*
——ach, *a.* Pertaining to, or full of handfuls of corn.
dlù, see dlùth.
dlug,** -uig, *s.f.* Avarice. 2 Penury.
dluigh, see dluigheil.
dluigheachd, *s.f.* Activity, nimbleness.
dluigheil,‡ *a.* Handy, active. 2 Prepared. 3 Tidy, trim, neat. 4††Thrifty.
dluimh, *s.f.* Cloud, darkness. 2 Blaze of fire.
dlùith,* *v.a.* see dlùthaich.
dlùithe, *comp.* of dlùth. More or most fast, or near.
dlùitheachd, *s.f.ind.* Closeness, nearness. 2

Thickness. 3 Quickness, fastness.
dlùithead, -eid, see dlùitheachd.
dlùitheadh, see dlùthadh.
dlùithean,** s.m. Closet, little study.
——,(PJM) s.pl. Relatives.
dlumh,** s. Much, plenty.
dlùs, see dluths.
dlùth, -ùithe, a. Near, close to, close. 2 Thickly set, dense, tight, confined. 3 Quick. 4** Incessant. 5 Related, nearly connected. 6 **Nimble. Neòil a tha d. mu 'n cuairt, *clouds that are thick around*; uisge trom d., *heavy incessant rain*; a' choille thiugh dh., *the thick close wood*; 'gad phògadh gu d., *kissing thee incessantly*; 's mi 'falbh leam fhéin gu d., *and I walking along communing with myself*, (*in a brown study*.) [*Dlùth* takes after it in government the preposition *air*, *do*, *an* or *ri*, simple or compounded.] Is d. aoibhneas do bhròn, *joy is close upon grief*; d. ri chéile, *close to each other*; d. an dàimh, *nearly related*; d. orm, *near me*; d. air an là, *near daylight*; d. air a chéile, *near* or *close upon each other*.
dlùth, -a, s.m. Warp of cloth. Gu leòir de dh. is fuigheal innich, *abundance of warp and remainder of woof*—i. e. enough and to spare, something to go and come upon; gheibh bean bhaoth d. gun cheannach, 's cha'n fhaigh i inneach, *a silly woman will get the warp without paying, but won't get the woof*; d. glic agus inneach gòrach, *said of a person who seems foolish but is really wise*.
dlùth, -ùith, s.m. Joining. 2 Enclosure, fence. 3 Cloister.
dlùth, v. a. House corn—*Harris & Uist*. 2 see dlùthaich.
dlùthachadh, -aidh, s.m. Approaching, act of approaching. 2 Joining, joining closer. 3 Crowding. 4 Contracting. 5**Warping, as of cloth. 6 Knitting. A' d—, *pr. pt.* of dlùthaich.
dlùthachd, see dlùitheachd.
dlùthadh, -aidh, s.m. Building of corn-stacks. 2 Housing of corn. 3‡‡ Pounding of clods. 4 see dlùthachadh. A' d—. *pr. pt.* of dlùth.
dlùthaich, *pr. pt.* a' dlùthachadh, *v. a.* Approach, draw near. 2 Join, adhere, join closely together. 3 Warp. 4 Press together, pack together. Dh. iad ris a' bhaile, *they approached the town*.
dlùthaicheadh, see dlùthachadh.
dlùthaichear, *fut. pass.* of dlùthaich.
dlùthaichidh, *fut.aff.a.* of dlùthaich.
dlùthaichte, *a.* & *past pt.* of dlùthaich. Made close, cemented, glued, pressed, joined, compressed, knit.
dlùth-aireach, *a.* Intense.
dlùthas, -ais, *s. m.* Nearness,[1] closeness, propinquity, neighbourhood. 2(PM) Denseness. D. nan craobh, *the closeness of the trees*.
dlùth-bhailtean,** *s.pl.* Suburbs.
dlùth-bharrach, *s.m.* Brushwood.
dlùth-bheachd, -an, *s.f.* Meditation.
dlùth-bhuidhneach, -eiche, *a* Close-banded.
dlùth-chàirdeas, *s.m.* Intimacy.
dlùth-charcair, -ean, *s.m.* Labyrinth.
dlùth-cheangail, *v.a.* Bind firmly.
dlùth-cheangladh, -aidh, *s.m.* Binding firmly.
dlùth-chinneas,** *s.m.* Aggeneration.
dlùth-chlòdh, *v*, & *s.m.* Stereotype.
dlùth-dhuilleach, -eiche, *a.* Close-leaved.
dlùth-eòlach,** *a.* Intimate, acquainted, familiar.
dlùth-eòlas, -ais, *s.m.* Intimacy, familiarity.
dlùth-fhàs,** *s.m.* Aggeneration.
dlùth-fheachd, -an, *s.f.* Phalanx.
dlùth-fhraoch,§ *s.m.* Smooth-leaved heath, see fraoch-a'-bhadain.
dlùth-ghleus, -eòis, -an, *s.m.* Gathered form.
dlùth-impidh,‡‡ *s.f.* Adhortation.
dlùth-lean, *pr.pt.* a' dlùth-leanail & -leantuinn, Cleave unto, stick close to, adhere. 2 Follow closely, pursue.
dlùth-leanachd,** *s.f.* Adherence.
dlùth-leanailteachd, *s.f.ind.* Adherence.
dlùth-leanmhuinneach,‡‡ -eiche, *a.* Continuous, dogging.
dlùth-leanmhuinneachd, *s.f.* Continuity.
dlùth-oidhirp, -ean, *s.f.* Assiduity.
dlùth-phreas,** -phris, *pl.* -phris & -phreasan, *s.m.* Thicket. 2 Thick bush.
dlùth-phreasach, ** *a.* Full of thickets or of thick bushes.
dlùth-phreasarnach, *s.m.* Brushwood.
dlùths, dlùiths, see dlùthas.
dlùth-sheanachas,(PM) -ais,*s.m.*Close conversation.
dlùth-shéidrich,** *a.* Asthmatical.
dlùth-stòl, -stòil *s.m.* Close-stool.
dlùth-smuainich,*v.a.* Revolve in mind, consider.
dlùth-smuainteach, -eiche, *a.* Abstracted (in mind only.)
dlùth-spàgach, -aiche, *a.* Palmipede.
dlùth-thàirngeach, -iche, see d— tharruingeach.
dlùth-tharruing, *v.a.* Attract.
dlùth-tharruingeach, -eiche, *a.* Drawing closely. 2 Attractive. 3 Magnetic.
dlùth-tharruingeachd,** *s.f.ind.* Magnetism.
dlùth-tharruingeadh,** *s.m.* Attraction.
dlùth-theann, *pr. pt.* a' dlùth-theannadh, *v. a.* Press close upon, draw near. 2**Crowd together, approach in crowds.
dlùth-theannadh, -aidh, *s. m.* Pressing close upon, hard pressing, act of pressing closely. A' d—, *pr.pt.* of dlùth-theann.
†dò, *a.* see dà.
do, *prep.* To (i.e. unto.) [Aspirates word following, and governs the Dative case. It is often *dh'*, or redundantly *do dh'*, or *a dh*, before a word commencing with a vowel. In other cases it is often *a*, or is omitted entirely. Chaidh e dh' Eirinn, [*or* do dh' Eirinn, *or* a dh' Eirinn,] *he went to Ireland*; chaidh iad a Phort-rìgh, *or* chaidh iad Phort-rìgh, *they went to Portree*.

Do is joined with the personal pronouns thus :—domh, *to me*; duit, *to thee*; da, *to him*; di, *to her*; duinn, *to us*; duibh, *to you*; doibh, *to them*. These prepositional pronouns are generally aspirated.

Do is a remarkable preposition too subtle to analyze, but the examples given below give a fair idea of its different meaning in various contexts. Do 'n duine, *to the man*; do d' mhàthair, *to thy mother*; do mo réir-sa, *according to my views*; gùr pailt liagh do na ràmhan na lùnn, *the blades of the oars are too big for the oars*!; a dh' olc no a dh' eiginn [*or* a chòir no a dh' eugcoir, *or* a dheòin no a dh' aindeoin,] *somehow or other, by hook or by crook, willy nilly*. As a prepositional pronoun :—Is aithne dhomh sin, *I know that*; is math dhomh sin, *that is well (good) for me*; is léir dhomh, *I can see*; leig dhomh, *permit me*; dé 'dh' éirich dhuit? *what has befallen thee?* nach ann domh a dh' éirich! *to me what evil has befallen!* cha'n 'eil dhomh ach—, *all that is necessary for me is*—; leig dhomh, *let me alone*, (*also* leig leam); roimh tighinn dhuinn, *before we came*; mhothaich e da ged a bha e uaigneach, *he perceived (to) it though it was in secret*; is dona an ceann sin dhuit, *that is against your health*; an urrainn duit ceann a thoirt dhaibh? *are you able to vanquish them?* (*lit.* a head to give them), [also *are you able to face them ?*] ; oidhche dhomh 'sa bheinn-sheilg, *I being one night in the hunting mountain* ; ri teachd dhomh, *just as I was arriving* : an déidh dhomh falbh, *after I had gone* ; an àm dhomh dol sìos, *when I go down (to battle)* ; an dùsgadh no an cadal duinn, *both when we are asleep and awake* : a' falbh á Loch-nam-madadh dhuinn, *when we, going from Loch Maddy* ; cia as duit ? *whence have you come ?* also *where was your birth-place ?* bhiodh an àireamh diom-buan doibh, *their number would soon be reduced for them* ; is dithis duinn sin, mu 'n dubhairt an fheannaig mu a casan, *they 're a pair, as the crow said of her legs* ; bu lìon-mhoire dhuit 'shracadh ann, na cunntas shlat an cliabh, *you could find more rents in it than withies in a basket* ; gur e dhùisg mo sheanachas domh...., *what caused my muse to awake is..* .; 'nuair dhùisgear ascaoin duit, *when your anger be awakened* ; theirig gual domh, *my coal has given out*; cha'n e am bòrd a theirig dhuit, ach am beagan fearainn, *it is not the plough that failed you, but that there was not enough land* ; a réir fios domh, *as far as I know* ; ma 's fìor daibh féin, *if they may be believed* ; fhuair mi fios bho phiuthar dhomh, *I got word from a sister of mine* ; chuala mi an t-òran sin aig caraid domh, *I heard that song being sung by a friend of mine* ; ma 's e bàs dhomh gu ma h-e dhuit e ! *if it be a case of death for me may it be so to you !* is pailte brù na biadh dha,—*said to a glutton* ; mar a chìthear dha, *as circumstances may warrant.*

For note on the pernicious practice of confounding *do* and *de*, see under *de.*

do, *poss.pron.* Thy, thine. [Aspirates its noun, and there is a pernicious practice of dropping the *o* after prepositions ending in vowel, even before consonant initials, as do d' mhac, *to thy son*, which must be guarded against.] Do làmh, *thy hand* ; do fhreagairt, *thine answer.* [*T'* before a vowel, t' athair, *thy father.*]

do, *particle*, placed before verbs, but not the sign of the past tense, as is often stated. An do fhreagair e ? *did he answer ?*

do, worn down in most districts to *dh'* or *a*, is still retained in *Suth'd* before the infinitive, and in certain phrases. Nach 'eil thu dol do shuidhe ? *are you not going to sit ?* ; tha e dol do shealltainn ort, *he is going to see you* ; do dh' fheuchainn (for *a dh'*) ; dol do ghabhail, *going to take.*

do, substitute for *a dh'* in Suth'd. Cha toir a' bhò am bainne d' easbhuidh fiach, *the cow will not give her milk without its equivalent.*

do-, *negative initial particle* of the same import as Latin and English *in-*, or English *un-*, implying sometimes difficulty, sometimes impossibility. [Aspirates consonants following.] Compounds of *do* not found below, can be translated by finding the meaning of the second portion, and placing *in-* or *-un* before it.

doacal, -ail,** *s.m.* Affliction.

do-àichidh, *a.* Incontestable.

do'ail, see domhail.

do-àill, -e, *a.* Close, compact. 2 Boisterous, raging.

do-ainmeachadh,** *a.* Indefinable.

do-àireamh, *a.* Difficult to count. 2 Numberless, innumerable.

do-àireamhach, -eiche, *a.* see do-àireamh.

do-àireamhtachd, *s.f.* Innumerability,

do-aisigeachd,†† *s.f.ind.* Irrevocableness.

do-aithneachadh,** *a.* Not easily known.

do-aithnichte,(PM) ‡*a.* Unknowable.

do-aithriseadh,** *a.* Not easily repeated.

do-aomadh, -aidh, *a.* Immovable, inflexible, inexorable.

———eachd, *s.f.* Inexorability.

do-aslachaidh, *a.* Inexorable.

do-atharrachadh, *a.* Immutable, not easily changed or altered.

do-atharraichidh, *a.* see do-atharrachadh.

do-atharraichte,‡‡ *a.* Immutable.

†**dob**, doib, *s.m.* River, stream.

†**dòb**, *s.m.* Plaster. 2 Gutter.

†**dòb**, *v.a.* Plaster, bedaub, cement.

†**dòbadh**, *s.m.* Daubing over.

†**dòbail**, see †dòbadh.

dobair, -ean, *s.m.* Plasterer.

dobh, -a, *a.* see dòbhaidh.

——achd,(AC) *s.f.* Unrighteousness. Air cuan na d., *on the sea of unrighteousness.*

dòbhaidh, *a.* Boisterous, stormy. 2**Raging, swelling, destructive. 3 Terrible, dreadful, awful. 4**Felling. Is d. an companach an t-acras, *hunger is a violent companion* ; oidhche dh., *a boisterous night*; buillean trom d., *heavy, felling blows.*

†**dobhair**, *s.m.* Border of a country. 2 Water. 3** Territory.

†**do-bhàis**, *a.* Immortal.

dobhar,** *a.* Dark, obscure.

do-bharalachaidh,‡‡ *a.* Inconceivable.

dobhar-chù, -choin, *s.m.* Otter. 2 Otter-hound. 3(AF) Beaver. Iasg a teicheadh o 'n d., *a fish fleeing from the otter.*

dobhar-lus, -uis, -an, *s. m.* Water-cress, see biolair. 2 Any aquatic plant, name applied to all cresses.

dobhar-shoitheach, -ich, -ichean, *s.m.* Bucket, pail, pitcher.

do-bheachdachaidh,** *a.* Unimaginable, not easily perceived.

dò-bheart, -bheairt, -an, *s.f.* Bad deed, vice. 2 Iniquity, mischief, prank. Leth do dh., *the half of thy vice.* [†† gives do-bheirt as *n.sing.*]

———ach, -aiche, *a.* Wicked, vicious.

dò-bhliadhnach, -ich, *s.m.* Animal of two years of age, said of cattle and sheep in Outer Isles and Argyllshire, for dà-bhliadhnach. Also applied to certain fish, as d. piocaich, *a two-year-old coalfish.* Pronounced " dorlunn-ach" and " dobh'lunnach" in Isles, but as spelt here in Argyllshire.

dò-bholadh,** -aidh, *s.m.* Stench.

dòbhrach,§ -aich, *s.m.* Cress of any kind, see biolair. D. ballach mìn, *smooth-spotted water-cress.*

dòbhrach-bhallach, -aiche, *s.f.* Orchis.

dòbhran, -ain, *s.m.* Fresh-water otter—*mustela lutra.* 2**Dog. 3(AF) Beaver. Ball dòbhrain, *a freckle* or *mole on the skin.*

———ach, -aiche, *a.* Dry, distant, shy, stiff. 2 Abounding in, or like otters.

——— -donn, *s.m.* see dòbhran.

——— -leaslan,** -ain, *s.m.* Otter.

——— -leas-leathann, -ain-, *s.m.* Beaver.

dò-bhinntichte,‡‡ *a.* Incoagulable.

do-bhrisidh,‡‡ *a.* Infrangible.

———eachd,‡‡ *s.f.* Inviolability.

do-bhrìgh, *adv.* Because, as, for the reason that.

do-bhròn, -òin, *s.m.* Sorrow, grief, sadness, melancholy. 2 Great grief.

———ach, -aich, *a.* Sad, sorrowful, melancholy, dejected. Gu d., *sorrowfully.*

do-bhuidheachas, -ais, *s.m.* Ingratitude.

do-bhuileachaidh, *a.* Incommunicable.

†**docail**, see docair.

——each, see docair.

——eachd, see docaireachd.

docair, -ean, *s.f.* Trouble, uneasiness, agitation of mind, affliction, restlessness. 2 *Annoy-

ance. Ceum docair, *an annoying occurrence*.
——, -e, *a.* Hard, grievous, painful. 2 Difficult. 3 Uneasy. 4 Sullen. 5 Intractable. 6 Not settled. Àite-suidhe d., *an uneasy seat* ; socair no d., *either easy or uneasy.*
——eachd, *s.f.* Difficulty.
†doch, *s.f.* One's native country.
dŏcha, *comp.* of *a.* toigh. More or most dear, esteemed, valued or preferable. Is toigh leam thusa, ach is d. leam esan, *I like you, but I prefer him.*
dòcha, *comp.* of *a.* dogh. More or most likely or probable. Is d. gu 'm bheil, *probably it is so* ; 'se seo a's d., *this is more probable* ; is d. leam, *I presume,* or *I suppose.*
dòcha, *s.* Likelihood, probability.
†dochad, †dochaide, } *adv.* Rather.
dochadh, dochaidh, } *a.* see docha.
do-chaillte, *a.* Imperdible, unlosable.
dochainn, *pr.pt.* a' dochainneachadh, & a' dochnadh, *v.a.* Hurt, injure, wound, bruise. 2 Annoy.
———, *gen. sing.* of dochann.
dochainneadh, *s. m.* Injuring, act of injuring, hurting or damaging. A' d—, *pr. pt.* of dochainn. Chaidh a chliabh a dhochainneadh, *his breast has been wounded.*
dochair, -e, -ean, *s.f.* Hurt, damage, injury, wrong. 2 Misery, sorrow. 3 Pain. 4 Wound. 5**Loss. 6 Fault. 7**Discontentedness. Dè do dh, ? *what has hurt you?*
———,* *v.a.* see dochainn.
———,(DU) *a.* Same meanings as dochaireach. Tha thu d., *you are wrong.*
———each, -iche, *a.* Wrong. 2 Hurtful. 3 Uneasy, troubled, agitated. 4 Injurious. 5 Grievous. 6**Preposterous. 7**Athwart. Is e an suidhe d. 'san taigh-osd' a's fhearr, *the uneasy seat in the ale-house is best.*
———eachd, *s.f.ind.* Incorrectness. 2 Injuriousness.
———eas, -eis, *s.m.* Hurt, wrong, injury, damage. 2 Sorrow, pain.
———ich,** *v.a.* Disadvantage.
†dochairt, -e, *a.* Sick.
do-chaisgte, *a.* Invincible.
do-chaitheamh, *a.* Inexhaustible.
————achd, *s.f.* Inexhaustibleness.
dochann,(DC) *v.a.* Punish. 2 Thrash—*Uist.*
———, -ainn, -an, *s.m.* Hurt, injury, damage. 2* Harm, mischief. 3 Agony. 4**Mishap, calamity. Á d. bàis, *from the agony of death* ; fhuair e d., *he got a hurt* ; a thaobh dochainn, *on account of damage.*
———ach, -aiche, *a.* Hurtful, mischievous, injurious, causing pain or damage. 2 Prejudicial.
———achd,** *s.f.* Hurtfulness, mischievousness, injuriousness.
———aich,** *v.a.* see dochainn.
———aiche,** *s.m.* Injurer.
do-chaochlaidheach,‡‡ -eiche, *a.* Incommutable.
————————d,‡‡ *s.f.* Incommutability.
dochar, see dochair.
docharach, -aiche, see dochaireach.
do-charachadh,* *a.* see do-charaichte.
docharaich, *v.a.* see dochainn.
docharaiche, *comp.* of docharach.
do-charaichte, *a.* Unmoved. 2 Immovable.
dochartach, *s.* see dochartas.
dochartach, -aiche, *a.* Sick, very ill.
dochartas, -ais, *s.m.* Sickness.
dòchas, -ais, -an, *s.m.* Hope, expectation. 2 confidence, trust. 3 Conceit, notion, presumption. Tha mi an d., *I hope* ; gun d., *without hope* ; an d. do theachd, *in expectation of thy coming* ; do dh., *your conceit* or *presumption* ; dè an d. a ghabh thu a nis ? *what has come into your head now ?* ; beò-dh., *a lively hope.*
dòchasach, -aich, *a.* Hopeful, confident. 2 Vain, conceited. 3* Presumptuous. 4 Confiding. 5‡‡Droll. 'S e fear d. e, *he is a conceited fellow*; tha thu d., *you are confident.*
————d,* *s.f.* Confidence, hopefulness. 2 Conceitedness.
do-chasg, *a.* see do-chasgadh.
do-chasgadh,-aidh, *a.* Unruly, turbulent, unmanageable. 2 Unquenchable. 3 Invincible.
do-chasgaidh, see do-chasgadh.
†dochd, *a.* Strait, narrow, close.
do-cheangal, *a.* That cannot be bound, not easily bound.
do-cheannsach, see do-cheannsachadh.
do-cheannsachadh, -aidh, *a.* Untameable, uncontrollable, unmanageable, unruly. 2 Invincible.
do-cheannsachd, *s.f.* Incorrigibleness.
do-cheannsaichte, *past pt.* Unruly, forward, unappeasable, unmanageable.
do-cheannsail, -sala, *a.* see do-cheannsachadh.
do-chìosnachadh, *a.* Invincible, unconquerable. 2 Indefatigable.
do-chìosnaichte, see do-chiosnachadh.
do-chiùrraidheachd, *s.f.ind.* Invulnerableness.
do-chlaoidh, see do-chlaoidheadh.
do-chlaoidheadh, *a.* Insuperable. 2 Indefatigable. 3**Invulnerable, invincible.
do-chlaoidheachd,** *s.f.* Invincibility.
do-chlaoidhte, *a.* see do-chlaoidheadh.
do-chlaoidhteachd, *s.f.* Insuperability. 2 Invincibility.
doch-luachair,(AF) *s.m.* Lizard, newt.
†dochma, *a.* Weak, incapable.
do-choimeasgta, *a.* Immiscible, that cannot be mixed.
do-choimisgte, see do-choimeasgta.
dochoir, -ean, see dochair.
dochoireach, see dochaireach.
do-choireachaidh, *a.* Irreprovable, irreproachable.
do-chomhairle, -ean, *s.f.* Bad advice.
do-chomhairleach, -iche, *a.* Incorrigible, that will not be advised. 2 Untameable.
——————d,** *s.f.* Incorrigibleness.
do-chomhairleachadh, see do-chomhairleach.
do-chomhairlichte,†† *a.* Incorrigible, unadvisable.
do-chòmhdachaidh, *a.* Indemonstrable.
dochrach, -aiche, see docair & dochaireach.
dochrachd, *s.f.ind.* Hardship, difficulty.
dochraid,** *s.f.* Servitude.
dochraidh,** *s.f.* Lust.
do-chreidsinn, *a.* Incredible, improbable. Mar ni d., *as an incredible thing.*
do-chreidsinneach,(PM) *a.* Inconceivable, beyond belief.
do-chronachaidh, *a.* Irreprovable.
†docht, *v.* see tachd.
†dochta,** *a.* Learned, instructed.
dochtair,** -ean, Gaelic spelling of *doctor.*
dochtrail,** *s.f.* Luxury.
dochuinn, *v.a.* see dochainn.
do chum, see a chum.
dochunn, -uinn, see dochann.
do-chunntaidh, *a.* Innumerable.
docoisle,(AF) *s.* Whale.
docrach, -aiche, *a.* see dochaireach. 2**Mortifying.
docran, -ain, *s.m.* Sorrow, vexation, distress. 2 Fit of anger.
docranach, -aiche, *a.* Troubled, vexed, distressed. 2 Causing sorrow or vexation.

docras,** s.m. Discontent, discontentment.
dochraid,** s.f. Servitude.
dod, -oid, s.m. Peevishness, the pet, the dumps. Tha 'n d. air a' bhò mhaol, cha'n ith i fodar no fraoch, *the hornless cow has taken the dumps, she'll eat neither straw nor heather*—said to a child remaining in the dumps after being promised "something nice;" gabh an d., *take the pet.*
do 'd, *or* do d' (for do do) To thy or thine. 2 *not* Of thy or thine, which is *de* do.
dodach, -aich, *a.* Morose, peevish, pettish.
dodachd, *s.f.ind.* Pettishness.
do dh', *prep.* Used before *fh* or a vowel redundantly. Do dh' fhear, *to a man,* [*Dh'* is *do,* with *d* aspirated and *o* dropped before the following *fh* or a vowel.]
†dodhail, s. Bad news.
dò-dhathach, -aiche, see dà-dhathach.
do-dhèabhaidh,‡‡ *a.* Inexhalable.
do-dhealachaidh,** *a.* Inseparable, indissoluble, not easily parted.
do-dhealaichte, *a.* Indissoluble. 2 Inalienable.
do-dhealbhach, -aiche, *a.* Unlikely, improbable. 2 Not easily painted or delineated.
do-dheanamh, *a.* Impracticable, difficult to be done. 2**Impossible.
do-dheanta, *a.* Impossible, not practicable, difficult.
do-dheantachd, *s.f.* Impossibility.
do-dheantas, -ais, *s.m.* Impracticability.
do-dhideannachaidh,‡‡ *a.* Indefensible.
do-dhìonaidh, *a.* Indefensible.
do-dhìthichte,‡‡ *a.* Inconsumptible.
dò-dhiùltach,-aiche,*a.* Irrefragible,irrefutable. 2(PJM) Irresistable.
do-dhruigheachd,‡‡ *s.f.* Impenetrability.
do-dhuine,** dhaoine, *s.m.* Bad man, rogue.
dod-stùirtealachd, *s.f.* Heaviness. 2 Moroseness.
dodum,‡ *s.m.* Teetotum.
†doer-galar,‖ *s.m.* Head-ache.
†doeth, *s.f.* Sickness, disease.
do-fhaghail, -e, *a.* Hard to find, difficult to come at, scarce.
do-fhaicinneach, -iche, see do-fhaicsinneach.
do-fhaicsinn, see do-fhaicsinneach.
do-fhaicsinneach, -iche, *a.* Invisible. 2††Hard to be seen.
——————d,** *s.f.* Invisibility.
do-fhairsuingeachadh,(PM) *s.m.* Impossibility to widen or broaden.
do-fhaisneis, -e, *a.* Unspeakable.
do-fhalachaidh, *a.* Inconcealable.
do-fhalbhuichte, *a.* Inexhaustible.
do-fhaothachaidh,‡‡ *a.* Implacable, inexorable.
do-fhàsgaidh,‡‡ *a.* Incompressible.
——————eachd,‡‡ *s.f.* Incompressibility.
do-fhogharach, -aich, see dà-fhoghair.
do-fhreagarrachd,‡‡ *s.f.* Irresponsibility.
do-fhuasgladh, -aidh, see do-fhuasglaidh.
do-fhuasglaidh, -e, *a.* Inextricable. 2 Insoluble. 3‡‡Irrelievable.
——————eachd,‡‡ *s.f.* Irresolubleness.
do-fhulang, *a.* Intolerable, not easily borne.
do-fhulangach, see do-fhulang.
do-fhulangachd,‡‡ *s.f.* Insupportableness.
dog,‡ -a, *s.m.* Bit, junk, short thick piece of anything. 2 Thickset person. D. buill, *a junk of rope.*
dog, *v.a.* Gaelic spelling of *dock.*
dogail, -ala, *a.* Cynical, dry, *prov.*
†dogaladh, -aidh, *s.m.* Revenge, revenging.
dogaltach,-aiche, *a.* Revengeful, *prov.* for dioghaltach.
dogan,†† -ain, *s.m.* Stot, steer.
dògan, *s.m.* Sort of oath, *prov.* [" dog-on-it."]
dogan, -ain, *s.m.* *dim.* of dog. D. maraig, *a bit of pudding.*
doganta, *a.* Fierce, ferocious. 2**Revengeful. 3*Thick-set, stumpish. Gu d., *revengefully.*
dogantachd, *s.f.ind.* Brutality, canine ferocity, fierceness. 2**Revengefulness.
dogh,* *s.m.* Opinion. Am dh.-sa gu'm bheil, *in my opinion it is.*
dogh,* *a.* *1st. comp.* docha. Like, probable. Is d. nach 'eil, *it is probably not so*; 's e seo is dòcha, *this is more probable.*
dogh, *v.a.* see dòth.
dogha, *s.m.* (meacan-dogha) Burdock.
doghadh, see dòthadh.
doghaltas,** -ais, *s.m.* Revenge.
do-ghiùlainteachd,‡‡ *s.f.* Insupportableness.
do-ghiùlan, -aine, *a.* Insupportable, intolerable, insufferable. 2‡‡Importable.
do-ghlacaidh,** *a.* Not easily taken, impregnable.
dòghlas, -ais, see dòlas.
do-ghleusadh,** *a.* Untuneable.
do-ghlideachadh,** *a.* Immoveable.
do-ghlideachd, *s.f.* Immobility.
do-ghluaiste, *a.* Immovable.
do-ghluasad, *a.* Immovable, not easily moved.
do-ghluasadach, -aiche, *a.* Constant.
——————d,‡‡ *s.f.* Impassiveness.
dòghlum,* *a.* Needy.
doghnasach,** *a.* Ill-favoured.
do-ghnàth, *adv.* Always.
do-ghnàthach, -aiche, *a.* Uncommon, unpractised.
do-ghnìomh, *s.m.* Injury.
doghradh,** -aidh, *s.m.* Sorrow, sadness. 2 Dulness, stupidity.
dò-ghrainn, -e, -ean, see dòruinn.
†do-ghreas, see do-ghnàth.
do-ghrisleachadh, *Lewis* for do-ghlideachadh.
doghruinn, -e, -ean, see dòruinn.
dòghruinneach, -iche, *a.* see dòruinneach.
doib, *s.f.* Plaster, daub.
doibealach, *a.* Plastering, daubing.
doibealadh, -aidh, *s.m.* Daubing.
doibh, *prep. pron.* To them. Thoir dhoibh e, *give it to them.*
doibhear, -eire, *a.* Rude, uncivil, boorish. 2 Sullen.
doibhear,(DC) *s.m.* Miserly churl—*Argyll.*
doibheart, see dò-bheart.
doibheas, -eis, *s.m.* Vice.
doibhir,(DC) *a.* Greedy, seeking too much.
†doibhre, *s.f.* Sacrifice.
†doibil, *v.a.* Bedaub.
†doibleadh, -idh, *s.m.* Daubing.
†doibrith, *s.m.* Sowens, gruel.
doich, *pr.pt.* a' doichioll, *v.a.* Hasten.
†doich, -e,‖ *a.* Swift, quick. 2 Early.
†doiche, *s.f.* Hope, confidence.
doicheall, -ill, *s.m.* Churlishness, boorishness, inhospitableness. 2 Grudging. 3 (PJM) Unwillingness to receive on the part of a guest. A' d—, *pr. pt.* of doichill. Cadal an doichill, *the sleep of churlishness.—A' Chailleach Bheurr.*
doicheallach, -aiche, *a.* Churlish, inhospitable, boorish, sordid, niggardly. 2 Angry, enraged.
doicheallachd, *s.f.* Inhospitableness.
†doicheidhe, *adv.* Rather.
doi-chiallach, -aiche, *a.* Ambiguous, obscure.
doichill, *pr.pt.* a' doicheall, *v.n.* Grudge, begrudge, be churlish. 2(DC) Treat exclusively, boycott. Cha'n ann 'ga dhoicheall dhuit a tha mi, *I am not grudging it to you.*
doichinmheal,** s. Enamel.
doichinmhil,** *v.a.* Enamel.

doichioll, -ill, *s.m.* see doicheall. 2 *pr. pt.* of doich. 3 Warning.
doichiollach, -aiche, *a.* see doicheallach.
dòid, -e, -ean, *s.f.* The hand, grasp. 2 Little farm. 3*Croft. 4 Pendicle. 5**see dòit. D. gheal, *a fair hand.*
dòideach, -iche, *a.* Frizzled up, shrunk (of hair) *prov.*
dòideach, -iche, *a.* Strong, muscular. 2†† Handed. 3 Strongly grasping. 4 Fond of dress. Le 'n gairdeanaibh d., *with their muscular arms.*
Doideag, *s.f.* Famous Mull witch.
dòid-gheal, -ghile, *a.* White-handed, fair-handed.
d' oidhche, *adv.* (dh' oidhche) By night.
dòi-dhiùltach, see dò-dhiùltach.
doidhreau, -ein, *s.m.* Duel.
doidire,* *s.m.* Crofter, cottager.
doidse, *s.f.* Dint.—*Badenoch.*
†doif, -e, -ean, *s.f.* Potion.
dòigh, -e, -ean, *s.f.* Manner, method, knack, ways and means. 2 Case, trim, condition, state, order. 3 Good order. 4 Proper arrangement. 5 Hope, confidence, trust. 6**Fire. 7** Supposition, opinion. 8 Guess. 9 Testimony. Tha d. air a h-uile ni—tha d. air buan an fhraoich, *there's a knack in everything, there's a knack in pulling heather*; air an d. seo, *in this manner*; dè an d. a th' ort ? *how are you ?* cuir air d., *arrange, adjust, put in order;* cuiridh mi mo dh. an Dia, *I will put my confidence in God ;* gun d., *out of order, absurd ;* co-ionnan air gach d., *in every way equal* ; ciod an d. a th' ort ? *how are you ?* ma's olc no math mo dh., *whether my condition be good or bad ;* tha d. mhath orra, *they are in good* or *comfortable circumstances* ; 'se th' air a dh., *he is very pleased* or *happy.*
†dòigh, -e, *s.f.* Guess, opinion. 2 Testimony. 3 Fire.
dòigh,** *a.* Sure, certain, of direct aim. 2(PM) Contented—*Uist.* Gu d., *certainly.*
dòigh-bhriathar, -air, *s.m.* Phrase, idiom, byword, proverb.
dòigh-bhriathrach, *a.* Proverbial.
dòigheadh, -idh, *s.m.* Hoping. 2 Adjusting.
dòighealachd, *s.f.* System, regulation, arrangement. 2 Capability of adjustment.
doighear, -ir, *s.m.* Spear.
dòigh eigiun,* *adv.* Somehow, somehow or other.
do-ghniomh, *s.m.* Injury.
dòigheil, -eala, *a.* Systematic. 2 Well-arranged, well-appointed. 3 Good-tempered. 4 Convenient. 5 Hopeful, confident. 6††Accommodating. 7**Decent. 8(DC) Suitable—*Uist.* 9 (DC) Tradesmanlike—*Uist.* 10* In good trim or condition. 11 Well-off, in good circumstances. Am bheil thu gu d. ? *are you in good trim ?*
†doighir, *s.f.* Flame.
dòigh-leug, *s.* Touchstone.
doi-ghniomh, see do-ghniomh.
doilbh, -e, *a.* see doirbh.
doilbhe, *s.f.* see doirbhead.
doilbheachd,** *s.f.* see doirbheachd.
doilbheas, -eis, see doirbheas.
†doileag, *s.f.* Stone.
doilean, -ein, *s. m.* Eddying wind, circling breeze.
doileanach, *a.* Eddying, circling, as wind.
doileas, -eis, *s.m.* Injury. 2 Prejudice. 3 Difficulty, hardship.
doileasach,†† *a.* Injurious.
doilghe, *a.* see duilich.
doi-leighis, -e, see do-leighis.
doilgheas, -eis, *s.m.* Sorrow, affliction, mourning, vexation, melancholy. 2 Bitterness. Fògraidh e d., *he will banish sorrow;* na biodh d. oirbh, *be not grieved.*
doilgheasach, -aiche, *a.* Grievous, sorrowful, afflicting. 2**Troubled. 3**Causing trouble or sorrow.
doilghios, see doilgheas.
doilghiosach, see doilgheasach.
doiliag, *s.f.* see doigh-leug.
doilich, -e, see duilich.
doilicheachd, *s.f.* Forwardness.
doilicheadas, see duilicheadas.
doilichinn, -ean, see duilichinn.
doilidh, see duilich.
doilinn, *s.f.* Grief, dolor,—*Dàin Iain Ghobha.*
doilisg,(AC) *s.f.* Vexation, annoyance. 2 State of death.
doill, *pl.* of dall.
doille, *s.f.ind.* Blindness. 2 Darkness, dimness. 3*Stupidity. Bhuail e iad le d., *he struck them with blindness*; d. na h-oidhche, *the darkness of night.*
doille, *comp.* of *a.* dall. More or most blind, stupid or ignorant.
doillead, -eid, *s.m.* see doille, *s.f.*
doilleir, -e, *a.* Dim, dark, shaded, sombre. 2 Obscure, ambiguous. 3 Scarcely visible. 4 Mysterious, mystical. Bha 'n oidhche d., *the night was dark;* is aoibhinn ge d. an cuimhne, *pleasant though indistinct is the remembrance of them* ; duine d., *a stupid fellow.*
doilleireachadh, -aidh, *s.m.* Darkening, state of becoming dark. 2 Shading. A' d—, *pr.pt.* of doilleirich.
doilleireachd, *s. f.* Dimness, darkness, shade, obscurity, cloudiness. 2 Ambiguity. 3 Mysteriousness. 4 Stupidity.
doilleiread, -eid, *s.m.* Degree of darkness.
doilleirich, *pr.pt.* a' doilleireachadh, *v.a.* Darken, obscure, cloud. 2 Become dark. 3 Perplex. 4 Foul, soil.
doilleirichte, *past pt.* of doilleirich. Darkened, obscured, shaded, clouded. 2 Perplexed. 3 Fouled.
†doim, -e, *a.* Poor, slovenly.
do-imeachd, *a.* Passless.
do-imeachdail, *a.* Passless.
doimeag, -eige, -an, *s.f.* Slut, slattern. Is mòr le doimeig (*al.* donnaig) a cuid abhrais, *spinning troubles a drab.*
doimeagach,†† *a.* Slatternly.
doimh, -e, *a.* Gross, cumbersome, clumsy, bulky. 2 Unshapely. 3 Poor, needy. 4 Galling, vexing. 5 Inconvenient. Gu dòmhail d., mar a bhitheas màthair fhir-an-taighe an solus na cloinne, no an rathad nan eun, *crowding, cumbersome, as the husband's mother in the light of the children, or in the way of the fowls.*
doimhe, *a.* Intractable.
doimheachd,‡‡ *s.f.ind.* Bluffness.
doimheadach,* *a.* Vexing, galling. Is d. an ni e, *it is a vexing thing.*
doimheadas,* -ais, *s.m.* Vexation, grief.
doimheal, *a.* Stormy.
doimheamh,†† -eimhe, *a.* Vexed, grieved, sad.
doimhne, *comp.* of domhain. Deeper, deepest.
doimhne, *s.f.ind.* Depth, profundity. 2 *with the article,* The deep, the sea. D. a' gairm air d., *the deep calling unto the deep* ; air gnùis fhoisneach na d., *on the still face of the deep ;* 'san d., *in deep water.*
doimhneachadh, -aidh, *s.m.* Deepening. 2 Act of deepening. 3 Fathoming. A' d—, *pr. pt.* of doimhnich.
doimhneachd, *s.f.ind.* Depth, deep. 2**Deepness, profundity. 3**Deep water. 'San d., *in deep water* (air an tanalach, *in shallow water*) ; á d. mhòir, *from a great depth ;* doimh-

neachdan na fairge, *the depths of the sea.*
doimhnead, -eid, *s.f.* Deepness, depth, degree of deepness.
doimhnich, *pr.pt.* a' doimhneachadh, *v.a.* Deepen. 2 Hollow. 3 Fathom.
doimhsheamh, -eimhe, *a.* see doimheamh.
——————dach,(PM) *a.* Vexed—*Uist.*
——————das, -ais, *s.m.* Vexation, chagrin.
doin-dearg, see donn-dhearg & donn-ruadh.
doineach,** *a.* Sorrowful, sad, mourning. 2 Calamitous. 3 Baneful. Tha 'n dùthaich uile d., *the whole country is sorrowful.*
————as,** -ais, *s.m.* Sorrow, mourning.
doineann, -inn, *s. f.* Inclement weather, tempest, storm. 2 Storminess. 3 Force, power. Thàinig d. a' gheamhraidh, *the inclemency of winter has come ;* gach d. 'gar léireadh, *every storm distressing us.*
————ach, -aiche, *a.* Tempestuous, stormy, blustering. Gu d., *tempestuously.*
————achd, *s.f.* Storminess.
doineanta, *a.* Stormy, boisterous, *prov.* 2‡‡Sullen. 3 Dogged.
doinne, *s.f.* Brownness, brown colour.
————, *comp.* of donn. Browner, brownest. 2 see duinne.
do-innse, see do-innseadh.
do-inniste, see do-innseadh.
do-innseadh, *a.* Unspeakable, inexpressible, unaccountable.
dointe, *a.* ‡‡Intelligible. 2**Unintelligible.
dointe,(AF) *s.* Small black insect.
do-iomachar, -aire, *a.* Intolerable, not to be borne.
——————ach, -aiche, see do-iomachar.
do-iomchair, -e, *a.* Intolerable.
——————eachd,‡‡ *s.f.* Insupportableness.
do-iompachadh, *a.* *Perverse. 2** Inconvertible.
do-iompaichte, *a.* Inconvertible. 2 Unconverted.
doirb, -ean, *s.f.* Worm, vermicule. 2 Minnow. 3**Any small fish. 4**Attempt. 5 *in derision* pithless, diminutive person. 6(MM) Diminutive *or* insignificant creature.
————eag, -eig, -an, *s.f.* Minnow. 2 see dairbeag. 3**Worm, reptile.
————ean, see dairbeag.
doirbh, -e, *a.* Hard, difficult. 2 Peevish. 3 Dissatisfied. 4 Stormy, boisterous. 5 Wild, ungovernable. 6 Grievous, intolerable 7** Quarrelsome. 8**Bitter, sour, ill-natured. 9 Cynic. Céist dh., *a difficult question* ; cha 'n 'eil i dàna no d., *she is neither forward nor peevish* ; oidhche dh., *a boisterous night* ; cha 'n 'eil mo reachd-sa d., *my law is not grievous;* duine d., *a turbulent, incorrigible person.*
doirbhe, *comp.* of doirbh. More or most difficult.
————, *s.f.* see doirbhead.
doirbheach, -ich, *s.m.* Mischief, *prov.*
doirbheachd, *s.f.ind.* Peevishness. 2 Difficulty, hardship. 3**Sourness. 4**Quarrelsomeness. 5**Dissatisfaction 6††Roughness. 7 *Turbulence. 8**Grievousness.
doirbhead, -eid, *s.f.* Hardness, difficulty, degree of difficulty,peevishness, sourness, quarrelsomeness, *or* roughness, boisterousness, indocility.
doirbheadas, -ais, *s.m.* see doirbheachd.
doirbheag, -eig, -an, *s.f.* Ill-tempered, cross woman.
doirbhean, -ein, *pl.* -ean & -an, *s.m.* Churl.
——————ach, see doirbhean.
doirbheas, -eis, *s.m.* Mischief. 2 Sorrow, distress, grief, anguish. 3 Difference. 4* Difficulty. 5 Boisterousness. 6**Keenness. 7** Adversity. 8 Mischance. Là an doirbheis, *the day of adversity ;* a' dol gu d., *getting obstreperous* or *unmanageable* ; ciod an d., *what the mischief !*
————ach,** *a.* Adverse, calamitous.
doirbhein, -ean, *s.m.* see doirbhean.
doirbheineachd, *s.f.ind.* Churlishness, unamiableness.
doirch, *gen. sing.* of dorch.
doirch, *v.n.* Get dark. Dh. an oidhche dhuinn, *we were benighted* (the night darkened on us.)
doirche, *comp.* or dorch. Darker, darkest.
————, *s.f.* see dorchadas.
doircheachd, *s.f.* see dorchadas.
doir'-choille, -choilltean, *s.f.* Grove, forest.
doire, *pl.* -an, & -achan, *s.f.* [*m.* in many places] Grove, thicket. 2 Insulated clump of trees, properly of oaks. 3 Bent timber in a boat, see bàta, D, p. 73. 4 (DU) Swelling on young cattle, usually on the belly similar in nature to a wart. Shuidhich Abraham d. chraobh, *A. planted a grove of trees;* gach coire 's gach d., *every wood and grove.*
doire,§ *s.f.* *Skye & Lismore* for stamh. Sea-girdles, oar-weed stalks.
doireach, -iche, *a.* Woody, abounding in woods, groves or thickets. 2 Of, or belonging to, a grove, wood or thicket. 3* Wild.
————an, *n.pl.* of doire.
doireagan,¶ *s.m.* Lapwing, see adharcan-luachrach.
doirean,§ *s.pl.* Sea-girdles—*Lismore,* see stamh. 2(PM) Mange-like spots round the eyes, head, and neck of young cattle—*Uist.*
doireann, see doineann.
————ach, see doineannach.
————achd, see doineannachd.
doireanta,* *a.* Sullen. 2**Dogged.
doirearach, see dairirich.
doire-òigh, *s.f.* Dryad.
doiriarach,** *a.* Difficult. 2 Ungovernable.
†doiriata, *a.* Lewd.
doirionn, -inn, -an, see doineann.
————ach, see doineannach.
————achd, see doineannachd.
doirionta, see doineanta.
doirireach, -ich, see dairirich.
doirling, -e, -ean, *s.f.* Isthmus. 2 Peninsula. 3 Stream. 4 Gulf. 5* Islet to which one can wade at low water.—*Mainland.* 6 Pebbly or stony part of a shore—*Isles.* 7**Promontory. 8(AH) Narrow sound separating an islet from the mainland, and liable to ebb dry.
————each, -iche, *a.* Belonging to an isthmus, peninsula, gulf, stream, &c. 2 Abounding in promontories. 3**Peninsular.
doirlinn, see doirling.
————each, see doirlingeach.
doirneag, -eige, -an, *s.f.* Round stone of a size to fill the fist, or that can be thrown without inconvenience. 2 Pebble, round pebble, cogglestone. 3 Oar-handle. Fras nan d., *the shower of stones* ; bho 'n is e is nì do Chlann Néill na doirneagan, gabhadh iad d' an ionnsuidh, *since the property of the MacNeills consists of pebbles, let them take to them.*
————ach, -aiche, *a.* Abounding in round stones or pebbles, pebbled, like a pebble, calculous, gravelly.
doirneanach dhuine,(CR) *s. m.* Thickset man —*W. of Ross-shire.*
doirse, (*for* doruis) *gen.sing.* of dorus.
————ach, -iche, *a.* see dorsach.
————ar, -eir, -an, see dorsair.
doirseir, -ean, see dorsair.
————eachd, see dorsaireachd.
dòirt, *pr.pt.* a' dòrtadh, *v.a.* Spill, shed, pour out 2 Stream. 3 Rush forth, as a multitude.

4* Scatter. Dh. e 'fhuil, *he shed his blood ;* dh. e m' a cheann e, *he poured it on his head;* dh. iad chun a' chladaich, *they rushed towards the shore* ; dh. e 'fhuil air son Thearlaich, *he spilt his blood for (Prince) Charles.*
dòirte, *past pt.* of dòirt. Spilt, poured out, &c.
——ach, -iche, *a.* see dòrtach.
——ach, -ich, *s.m.* Spiller, pourer, shedder, as of blood. 2 Dative case in *grammar.*
——ach,* *s.f.* Flood, sudden pour of rain.
——al, -eil, -an, *s.m.* Sink, sewer, drain.
——ar, *fut. pass.* of dòirt. Shall be spilt.
——ar,** -eir, *s.m.* Spiller.
——il, see dòirteach.
doirtheas, see doirbheas.
dòirtidh, *fut. aff. a.* of dòirt.
doisheamh, see doimheamh.
dòit,‡‡ -e, *s.f.* Mite, small coin one-twelfth of a penny (*Scots*, doit.)
doit,‡‡ -e, *s. f.* Darnel, cockle.
—, *a.* see doite.
doite, *a.* Foul. 2 Dark-coloured. 3 Grim.
dòite, *a.* Singed, scorched, burnt. Is d. ceann gach firich, *scorched are the tops of every hill.*
doiteachan, see daithteachan.
doiteag,(CR) *s.f.* Stout little woman—*Arran.*
Doiteag Mhuileach, *s.f.* Celebrated Mull witch.
doithcheall, see doicheall.
doithcheallach, -aiche, see doicheallach.
doithchearnas,** -ais, *s.m.* Churlishness, niggardliness. 2 Abhorrence.
doithir, *a.* Dark, gloomy, obscure. 2 Ill-featured, ugly. 3 Deformed. 4**Dull, unpleasant. 5**Ill-humoured.
†doithir, s. Contract, covenant.
dol, *s.m.ind.* Going, travelling. 2 Proceeding. 3 Ways. 4 Walking. 5 Space, distance. 6* Condition, state. A' d—, *pr.pt.* of rach. [*Dol* and *rach* have no connection etymologically.] A' dol dhachaidh, *going home*, dol fodha na gréine, *the setting of the sun* ; a' d. iomraill air a chéile, *missing each other ;* a' d. as, *escaping, going out, as a fire or light*; a' d. sìos, *going down*, (of stairs and battle only) ; a' dol le, *descending* ; a' dol suas, *going up* (of stairs only) ; a' dol ri, *ascending* ; tha dol aige air glé mhath, *he has a good grip of the matter*; an d. a dh' fhàg thu air, *the state in which you left him ;* is bòidheach an d. a th' air, *it is in a pretty condition ;* dol an t-saoghail, *the state of the world* ; cha'n 'eil d. as aige, *he has no way of escape*; is e seo a bu dol dhaibh aig gach siubhal, *this was the method of their going at every trip they took* ; mhothaich mi rud a' dol mu'm chasan, *I noticed that my foot had caught in something.*
†dòl, *s. m.* Grief. 2 Cunning. 3 Trap. 4 Kind of fishing net.
do là, *adv.* By day.
do-labhairt, -e, *a.* Ineffable, unspeakable, inexpressible.
————eachd, *s.f.ind.* Ineffableness.
do-labhrach, see do-labhairt.
dòlach, -aiche, *a.* Destructive, pernicious, grievous. 2* Indifferent. 3**Each, individual. 4 **Single. 5 Mean, poor, wretched.—*Dàin I. Ghobha.* Gach d. là, *every single day* ; duine dona d., *a bad* or *indifferent man.*
dolach,(AC) see dòrlach.
dolaid,¶ *s.f.* Oyster-catcher, see gille-brìde.
dolaidh, *s.f.* Harm, loss, injury, damage, defect. 2 Detriment. 3*Mischief. Cuir a dh., *ruin , spoil the well-being of ;* is beag an d., *it is no great harm ;* dè an d. a rug ort ? *what the mischief came over you ?* cha'n 'eil d. ann, *there is no harm done* ; is sàmhach an obair dol a dh., *going to ruin is silent work ;* is iomadh deagh ghnìomh a dheantadh mur b' e a dh., *many a good deed would be done but for miscarriage.*
dolaidh,** *a.* Impatient, restless.
do-làimhseachaidh,(PM) *a.* Beyond control, generally applied to grown-up children—*Uist.*
dolair, (AC) *v.a.* Withhold.
dol a mach,** *s.m.* Carriage, behaviour, conduct. Dè an dol a mach a th' air ? *what carry on has he ?* ; dol a mach na cuideachd, *the proceedings of the meeting.*
dò-làmhach, -aiche, *a.* see dà-làmhach. 2**Not easily handled.
——————d, *s.f.* see dà-làmhachd.
dolar, -air, *s.m.* Gaelic spelling of *dollar.*
dòlas, -ais, *s.m.* Woe, grief, mourning, 2 Mishap, harm. 3 Dissolution, destruction. 4 Loathing, abhorrence. 5 Disdain. 6‡‡Desolation. 7††Pain. 8(DU) Cause of evil. Fògraidh e gach d., *he will drive away all grief.*
dol as,** *s.m.* Escape.
dòlasach,-aiche, *a.* Disastrous. 2 Sad, melancholy, mournful, grieved, grievous. 3 Baneful, hurtful. 4 Destructive. 5**Sick. Gu d., *sadly.*
————d, *s.f.* Sadness, melancholy, mournfulness. 2††Torment, pain.
dò-lasair, -lasrach, *pl.* -lasraichean, *s.f.* Inauspicious or destructive flame.
do-lasta,** *a.* Not inflammable. 2 Not easily blown to a flame.
†dolbh, s. Witchcraft, sorcery.
†dolbhad, -aid, s.m. Fiction.
do-leaghadh,** *a.* Not easily melted.
do-leanachd, *a.* see do-leanmhuinn.
do-leanmhuinn, *a.* Inimitable, that cannot be followed, difficult to be followed.
————————eachd, *s.f.* Inimitableness.
do-leantalach, -aiche, *a.* Inimitable.
——————d, *s.f.* Inimitableness.
do-leantalaiche, see do-leantalachd.
do-leas, -leis, see doileas.
————ach, see doileasach. 2 see do-leasaichte.
————achadh, -aidh, *a.* Irreparable, that cannot be helped. 2 Incurable.
do-leasaichte, *a.* Irreparable. 2 Incurable.
do-leigheas, -is, *a.* Irremediable. 2 Invulnerable. 3 Incurable. Creuchd d., *an incurable wound.*
—————ach,†† *a.* Irremediable.
—————eachd, *s.f.ind.* Incurableness. 2 Irrecoverableness.
do-leighiseach, see do-leigheasach.
do-léirsinn, see do-léirsinneach.
——————each, *a.* Invisible, dark, hidden. 2** Inexplicable. Iomadh sloc d., *many a hidden gulf.*
——————eachd, *s.f.* Invisibility.
do-leònaidh, *a.* Invulnerable.
do-leòntachd, *s.f.* Invulnerableness.
do-leubhadh, see do-leughta.
do-leubhta, see do-leughta.
do-leughadh, see do-leughte.
do-leughte, *a.* Illegible. [see foot-note p. 53.]
——————chd, *s.f.* Illegibility.
do-lionadh,‡‡ *a.* Insaturable. 2 (DC) Insatiable.
do-loghaidh,‡‡ *a.* Irremissible.
——————eachd, *s.f.ind.* Irremissibleness.
do-lorgachaidh,** *a.* Difficult or impossible to be traced.
do-losgaidh,‡‡ *a.* Inremable, unburnable. 2 (MM)Inflammable.
do-lotaidh,‡‡ *a.* Invulnerable.
——————eachd, *s.f.ind.* Invulnerableness.
†doltrum, -uim, *s.m.* Grief, vexation, anguish. 2 Terror. 3††Gloom. Gaelic spelling of *dol-*

drum(s.)
doltrumach,** -aiche, a. Grievous, vexatious.
do-luaidh, -e, a. Unspeakable, unutterable, unmentionable.
do-luaidhte, (PM) a. Unwaulkable, impossible to be milled.
do-luasaichte, a. Inadmissable.
do-lùbachd,** s.f.ind. Inflexibility, stiffness. 2 Stubbornness, inexorableness.
do-lùbadh, see do-lùbaidh.
do-lùbaidh, -aidhe, a. Stubborn, obstinate. 2 Inflexible, rigid.
do-lùbtachd, see do-lùbachd.
doluidh, -ean, see dolaidh.
dòlum, -a, a. Surly, morose, peevish. 2 Mean, penurious. 3 Rigid. 4 Scarce, poor—*Dàin I. Ghobha.* O 'n bha thusa d., *as thou wert surly.*
——, -uim, s. m. Wretchedness, misery, ill. 2 Poverty. 3††Murmuring.
——ach, -aiche, a. Wretched, miserable. 2 Indigent.
dolus, see donas.
do 'm (*for* do am) To their. [Not *of* their.] Do 'm bailtibh, *to their towns.*
do m' (*for* do mo) To my. [Not *of* my.] Do m' mhàthair, *to my mother.*
dom, -a & duim, s.m. Gall, gall-bladder. †2** House.
domail, -e & -alach, -ean, s.f. Loss, damage, injury, *particularly damage by cattle, as to corn, &c.
——each, -iche, a. Hurtful, causing loss, injurious.
†domain, a. Transitory.
domairm, s.f. Armoury, magazine, depôt. 2** *rarely* Speech.
domar,(MM) *Badenoch* for domail.
domblachd,* see domhlachd.
domblas, -eis, s.m. Choler, gall, anger. 2 ‖Bile, biliousness. [Preceded by the article *an.*]
———ach, -aiche, a. Biliary. 2 Disgustful. 3 Ill-tempered. 4**Unsavoury. 5**Choleric.
———achd, s.f.ind. Bitterness. 2 Nauseousness. 3 Turbulence of temper, choler.
†domblas ae, Bitterness of liver, bile. 2††Anger.
domblas-àighe,†† s.m. Gall-bladder.
domblasda, a. see domblasach.
————chd, see domblasachd.
domblas-sàth,* s.m. Gall-bladder.
dombuidheach, -iche, same meanings as diombach.
†dombuileach, -iche, a. Prodigal, wasting.
domh, *prep. pron.* To me. Cha'n fhios domh, *I know not.*
†domh, s.m. House.
domhach, -aich, -aichean, s.m. Savage.
dòmhail, -ala, a. Bulky, corpulent, thickset. 2 Crowded. 3 Dense. 4 Clumsy. 5 Inconvenient. 6 Suffocating—*Dàin I. Ghobha.* 7(AH) Pregnant. Taigh d., *a crowded house*; dubh dh., *dark and dense*; gun bhi meanbh no d., *without being puny or bulky*; cuideachd d., *a crowded company*; Mòd nan Crìochan Dòmhail, *the Congested Districts Board.*
domhaileachd, s.f.ind. Lustiness.
domhain, doimhne, a. Deep, profound. 2** Double-minded. 3**Hollow.
———, *gen. sing.* of domhan.
domhainn, see domhan.
dòmhainneachd, see doimhneachd.
do-mhaithidh,‡‡ a. Irremissible.
do-mhaithte, a. Irremissible, unpardoned.
dòmhalachd,** s.f. Crowdedness. 2 Bulkiness.
dòmhalas,** -ais, s. m. Crowd, throng. 2 Crowded condition.

domhan, -ain, s.m. The world, the universe, the globe. [Preceded by article *an.*] An d. 's na bheil ann, *the universe and all it contains*; an d. mu 'n iadh grian, *the globe round which the sun revolves*; Rìgh an Domhain, *the King of the World.*
———-sgrìobhadh, -aidh, s.m. Cosmography.
domhar, see †dobhar, s.
do-mharbhadh, see do-mharbhte.
do-mharbhte, a. Immortal. [see foot-note p.53.]
do-mhearachdas,‡‡ -ais, s.m. Infallibility.
do-mheasgaichte, see do-mheasgaidh.
do-mheasgaidh,‡‡ a. Immiscible.
—————eachd, a. Immiscibility.
do-mheasraichte,‡‡ a. Incalculable.
†domhghnas,** s.m. Inheritance, patrimony.
†—————, a. Hereditary.
do-mhillte,‡‡ a. Imperdible. 2(PJM) Indestructible.
do-mhìneachaidh, a. Inexplicable.
——————eachd, s.f. Inexplicableness.
dòmhlachadh, -aidh, s.m. Thickening, crowding. 2 Crowd. 3 Affluence. A' d—, *pr. pt.* of dòmhlaich.
dòmhlachd, s.f. Bulk, thickness. 2 Crowd, throng. 3** Weight. 4 Clumsiness. D. shluaigh, *a large crowd of people.*
dòmhlad, -aid, s.m. Girth.
———as, -ais, s.m. see dòmhlachd.
dòmhlaich, *pr.pt.* a' domhlachadh, v.a. Crowd. 2 Assemble, gather in crowds. 3 Swell, increase in bulk. 4††Thicken.
dòmhlas, -ais, s.m. see dòmhlachd.
†domh-lios,** s. m. House surrounded by a moat or watered trench as a means of defence.
dòmhluich, see dòmhlaich.
Dòmhnach, -aich, s.m. Sunday. see Di-dòmhnaich. 2** *rarely* Church, great house. †3 Lord. D. Càisg, *Easter Sunday*; D. Inid, *Shrove Sunday*; D. Caingheis, *Whit Sunday.*
dòmhnach, -aiche, a. Sabbatical. 2 Lamentable, sad.
†domhnus, s.m. Place of residence.
dò-mhogullach, see dà-mhogullach.
do-mhothachaidh,** a. Imperceptible. 2 Callous, unfeeling.
do-mhùchadh, -aidh, a. Inextinguishable, not easily smothered.
do-mhuinte, a. Intractable, indocile, perverse. 2††Unlearned.
domhun, -mhuinne, a. see domhain.
do-mhunaidh, a. see do-mhuinte.
do-mhùthaidh,‡‡ a. Intransmutable, inconvertible. 2(PJM) Unchangeable.
domlas, -ais, see domblas.
domlas-sàth, see domblas-sàth.
†don, s. Water.
don, -a, s.m. Defect, want. 2 Mischief, evil. D. bidh ort! *ill betide thee (lit.* may you want food.)
do 'n, (*for* do an) To the. 2 To their. [Not *of* the, *of* their, which is *de 'n.*]
don,* v.a. & n. Make worse. 2 Deteriorate. Don-bidh, don-fhardaich, *vile food, wretched hearth.*
dona, *1st. comp.* dona, *2nd. comp.* donaid, *3rd. comp.* donad. a. Evil, bad. 2 Contemptible. 3**Sad. 4**Dangerous. 5**Awkward. 6** Mean. 7 **Pusillanimous. 8** Unlucky, unfortunate. A' dhonainn dh., *the good-for-nothing wretch*; an dubhra d., *the sad darkness*; a dhonainn dhona! *oh good-for-nothing wretch!* bu dona mo ghnothach ris, *it were not for me to tackle it, not in my province, it were presumption on my part.*

donachas, -ais, see donas.
donad, -aid, *s.m.* Degree of badness or vileness.
donadas, -ais, *s. m.* Badness, evil. 2**Miserableness. 3 Contemptibleness. A' dol an d., *deteriorating.*
donadh, -aidh, -aidhean, *s.m.* Hurt, evil, mischief.
donadh, *a.* see dona.
donaich,** *v. a.* Deteriorate, depreciate. 2 Hurt, damage. 3 Make bad or worse. 4 Destroy.
donamharc,** *s.* Naughtiness.
donas, -ais, *s. m.* Mischief, harm, hurt. 2 Bad luck, mishap. 3 The Devil. 4 Worthless fellow. 5* Badnsss. Tha d. fo 'theangaidh, *there is mischief under his tongue*; a dhonais chrine; *you little devil!*; thoir an d. ort! *go to the devil!*; cha bhi d. toirteach, *a worthless fellow is not ready to give*; thig an d. ri iomradh, *speak of the devil and he will appear*; an d. bonn a bhiodh agam, *devil a coin would I have*; tha 'n d. ort, *the devil is in you.*
donasach, -aiche, *a.* Cross.
donasan, -ain, -an, *s.m.* Little devil or mischief.
don-fhois,‡‡ -e, *s.f.* Intranquillity.
dongaidh, -e, *a.* Moist, humid. [*pron.* tongaidh in *Lewis.*—PJM.]
don-innleachd,‡‡ *s.f.* Indexterity. 2(PJM)Resourcelessness.
don-ionnsachadh,(PJM) -aidh, *s.m.* Naughtiness, bad-breeding.
don-ionnsaich, see don-ionnsachadh & don-ionnsaichte.
——————te,(MMcD) *a.* Bad-mannered, impertinent.
don-mathais,(CR) *s.m.* Bad requital for labour or kindness.—*W. of Ross-shire.*
don-mhodh,‡‡ -a, -an, *s.m.* Incivility.
donn, duinne, *a.* Brown, brown-coloured. 2 Brown-haired. 3 Surly, bad-tempered. 4* Indifferent, bad. 5***rarely* Pregnant. 6 Dun. Diarmad d., *brown-haired D.*; nighean d. an t-sùgraidh, *the brown-haired flirting girl*; each d., *a bay horse*; cha'n 'eil ann ach duine d., *he is only an indifferent man*; le sgiath duinn na doininn, *with the dusky wing of the storm*; is tu a's duinne de 'n triùir, *you are the greenest of the three*; dìreach d., *instantly.*
donn, *pr.pt.* a' donnadh, *v.a.* Imbrown, make brown. 2 Bronze. 3 Grow brown. 4††Singe. 'Nuair a dhonnadh na speuran, *when the heavens were darkened.*
donnachadh, -aidh, *s. m.* Embrowning. 2 Growing brown or dun.
donnadh, (a'), *pr. pt.* of donn.
donnag, -aige, -an, *s.f.* Large kind of cockle. 2 Hose-fish. 3 Young ling (fish.) 4 Hedge-sparrow, see gealbhonn-nam-preas. 5**Brown cow. 6 Drab, slut. 7‡‡Brown-haired woman. [ex. under doimeag.]
donnaich, *v.* see donn, *v.*
donnal, -ail, -an, *s.m.* Complaint. 2 Howl of a dog. 2 Loud cry.
donnalach,** *a.* Apt to howl. 2 Howling as a dog.
donnaladh, -aidh, see donnalaich.
donnalaich, *pr.pt.* a' donnalaich, a' donnalachadh & a' donnaladh, *v.a.* Howl or bark as a dog. 2**Yell.
——————, *s.f.* Continued howling, slow drawling barking. 2 Loud wail. 3 Burst of lamentation. 4**Yell. A' d—, *pr.pt.* of donnalaich. Ciod an d. a th' ort? *what are you howling for?*
donnan, -ain, *s.m.* (Bird) see donnag.
donn-chleachda,** *s.m.* Brown-hair.
donn-chleachdach,** *a.* Brown-haired.
donn-dhearg, *a.* see donn-ruadh.
donn-eun, *s.m.* Hedge-sparrow, see gealbhonn-nam-preas.
donn-ghlas, *a.* Ash-colour.
donn laogh-na-h-éilde, *s.m.* Fawn-brown colour.
donn-lus,§ *s.m.* Figwort, see lus-nan-cnapan.
donn-ruadh, -ruaidh, *a.* Bay or chestnut-coloured.
donn-rusg,§ *s.m.* Bird-cherry—*prunus padus.*
donn-shùileach, *a.* Brown-eyed.
donn-uaine, *s.f.* Olive-brown colour.
donus, -uis, see donas.
do oidhche, (a dh' oidhche) By night.
do-phàirteachaidh, *a.* Incommunicable.
do-phianta,‡‡ *a.* Impassible.
——————chd, *s.f.* Impassibility.
†dor, *s.m.* Door, confine.
dora, see dorra.
dorachar, see dorchar.
†doradh, -aidh, *s.m.* Line, rule.
doraghadh,(AC) *s.m.* see dorghadh & dorghach.
doraidh,** *s.f.* Strife, dispute, controversy, wrangling.
doraingeachd,** *s.f.* Forwardness.
dòrainn, see dòruinn.
————each, see dòruinneach.
————eachd,†† *s.f.* Torment.
dòraman, see dòrraman.
————ach, see dòrramanach.
dòran, see dòbhran.
doran, -ain, *s.m.* see dorran.
dòran-donn, see dòbhran.
dorangach, -aiche, *a.* Froward.
dòran-leas-leathann, (AF) *s. m.* see dòbhran-leas-leathann.
do-rannsachaidh, *a.* Inscrutable, unsearchable.
do-rannsaichte, see do-rannsachaidh.
†dorar, -air, *s.m.* Conflict, scuffle, battle.
doras, see dorus.
dorathach, see dorghadh.
dorbh, doirbh [& duirbh] see dorgh.
dorbhach, see dorghach.
dorc, *s.m.* Piece.
dorcan,** *s.m.* Yearling bull-calf.
dorch, -a [& duirche,] *a.* Dark, black, dusky. 2*Mysterious, doubtful. 3 Obscure. 4 Proud. 5* Gloomy. 6**Stern. [*1st. comp.* dorcha *or* duirche; *2nd. comp.* dorchaid *or* duirchid; *3rd. comp.* dorchad *or* duirchead.] Is d. do mhala 's duirche do ghnè, *dark is thy brow and darker thy temper*; oidhche dhubh dh., *a pitchy dark night*; asgailt dh. na h-iargailt, *the black bosom of the storm.*
dorch, *v.a.* see dorchaich.
dorcha, *1st. comp.* of dorch.
dorchachd, see dorchad.
dorchad, -aid, *3rd. comp.* of dorch, & *s.m.* Darkness.
dorchadas, -ais, *s.m.* Darkness, degree of darkness. 2 Obscurity. 3 Gloominess. 4 Duskiness. 5 Mysteriousness.
dorchadh, -aidh, *s.m.* Darkening, obscuration, shade. 2 State or act of darkening. 3** Gloom. 4**Eclipse. 5**Darkness. 6* Mystifying. A' d—, *pr.pt.* of dorchaich. A bhròn a' d., *his sorrow darkening.*
dorchaich, *pr. pt.* a' dorchadh, *v.a.* Darken, cloud, obscure, shade, sully. 2**Grow dark. C' uim' an d. thu laithean na h-aois? *why wilt thou darken the days of age?*
————te, *past pt.* of dorchaich. Darkened, clouded, obscured, shaded, sullied.
dorchaid, *2nd. comp.* of dorch.
dorchar,(AC) *s.m.* Darkness. 2 Dark man.
dorch-chainnt, -e, *s.f.* Ambiguity in speaking.
——————each,** *a.* Ambiguous.
dorchraich,(DU) *Gairloch* form of dorchaich.

dorch-thuigseach,‡‡ -eiche, *a.* Blind of understanding.
dòr-chù, see dòbhar-chù.
dòrd, see dùrd.
——ail, see dùrdail.
dòrdalan, see dùrdalan.
dòrdan, see dùrdan.
dordha, see dorcha.
———chd, see dorchadas.
dòr-dhuille,** *s.m.* Folding-door. 2 Leaf of a door.
do-reamhraichte,(PM) *a.* That cannot be fattened—*Uist.*
do-reicte,(PM) *a.* Unsaleable, unmarketable—*Uist.*
do-réidhtichte, see do-réitichte.
do réir, *prep.* According to, agreeably to. Do réir t' iarrtais, *according to your request.*
do-réiteachaidh, } *a.* Implacable, irreconcil-
do-réiteachail, } able, not easily disentangled, not easily made clear, smooth or level.
do-réiteachas, -ais, *s.m.* Irreconcilability, implacability. 2(PJM) Inability to disentangle.
do-réitealachd, *s.f.* see do-réiteachas.
do-réitichte, *a.* Irreconcilable, implacable.
do-reothaidh,‡‡ *a.* Incongealable.
do-riarachadh,†† *a.* Insatiable. 2 Ungovernable.
dorga,** *a.* Despicable. 2 Crusty.
——, see dorgh.
dorgadh,** -aidh, *s. m.* see dorgh. †2 Fishing-net.
dorganach,** *a.* Recusant.
dorganta,** *a.* Discourteous, surly.

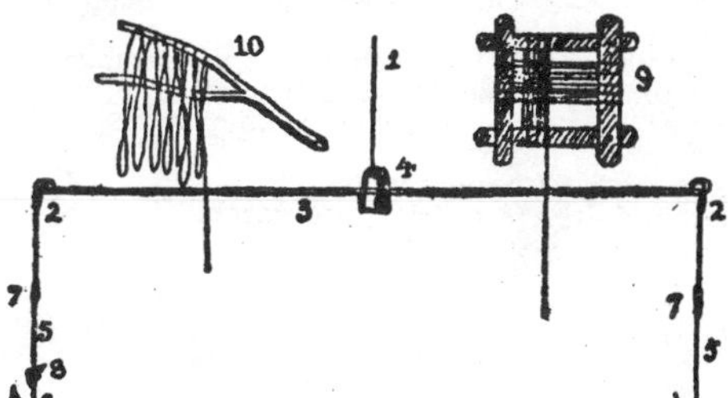

271. Dorgh.

dorgh, duirgh, *s.m.* Handline for fishing, as applied to the whole arrangement by means of which a piece of wire or whalebone is used to connect the lines to which the hooks are attached with the line held in the hand. †2 Mason's line.
[*also spelt* dorbh, dorga, dro, drobha, and drogha.]
PARTS OF A HANDLINE (DORGH):—
1 Sreang. In *Gairloch,* streang, *part of line held in the hand.*
2 Bodag, *loop of string at each end of* meigh.
3 Meigh, *piece of streng wire.*
4 Clach-luaidhe, *lead.*
5 Cas-ghaoisid, *part of line attached to hook, usually in two parts, each called* snòthd.
6 Dubhan, *hook.*
7 Snaim, snaime-gaoisid, *knot.*
8 Snàthgaladh, *the thread wound round the* cas-ghaoisid *and* dubhan, *to attach the latter to the hair line.*
9 Clàrag,square *frame,*on which line is wound.
10 Cròcan, *or* gòbhlag, *fork-shaped twig,* barked or otherwise, for the same purpose. When neither frame nor twig is used, the line is hanked and called *conn.*
dorghach, -aich, *s.m.* Act of fishing with handlines.
dorghach, -aiche, *a.* Of, or belonging to hand lines. 2(DJM) Bottom-fishing.
dorghadh, -aidh, *s.m.* see dorghach, *s.*
do-riaghlachadh, see do-riaghlaidh.
do-riaghlaichte, see do-riaghlaidh.
do-riaghlaidh, *a.* Ungovernable, unmanageable.
do-riarach, see do-riarachaidh.
———aidh, *a.* Insatiable. 2‡‡Insaturable. 3 Surly, discontented, peevish, ungovernable.
———d, *s.f.ind.* Surliness, peevishness, discontent, insatiateness.
do-riaraichte,same meanings as do-riarachaidh.
do-riarthachd, see do-riarachd.
do-riaruichte, see do-riaraichte.
dorlach, -aich, *s.m.* Handful. 2 Bundle, good deal, considerable quantity or number. 3 Sheaf of arrows. 4 Quiver. 5 Hilt of a sword. 6* Cluster. 7(MMcL) Sheaf of corn. [D. eòrna was 60 sheaves.] D. sluaigh, *a number of people;* d. airgid, *a handful of money;* d. sìl, *a handful of corn.* The *dorlach* was a kind of truss or wallet worn of old by the Gael in the army in place of the knapsack or valise.
dorn, duirn, *s.m.* Fist. 2 Blow or box with the fist, buffet. 3 Hilt, haft, handle. 4* Hold of an oar. 5 Short cut or piece of anything. 6**Agonist. Làn a dhuirn, *his handful;* an d. clì, *the left fist;* thug e d. dha, *he gave him a box* or *thump;* chaidh d. air ghaisge, d. air tréine, 'us d. air thapachd, an uair a chaidh na trì duirn an ceann a chéile, *I called up my utmost energies, pulled myself together, and felt strengthened.* [Duirn, & dorn and its compounds, although given in all the dictionaries as *dùirn* and *dòrn,* should be written without the accent, for it is the liquids *rn* that are long, and not the *u* and *o.*]
——, *pr. pt.* a' dornadh, *v.a.* Thump. 2 Strike with the fist. 3 Box. D. e, *box him.*
——ach, -aiche, *a.* Of, or belonging to fists.
——ach, -aich, *s.m.* see dornair.
——achadh,** -aidh, *s.m.* Boxing. 2 Bruising with the fist.
——adair, see dornair.
dornadaireachd, see dornaireachd.
dornadh, -aidh, *s.m.* Striking or thumping with the fist. 2 Act of striking,thumping or boxing. A' d—, *pr.pt.* of dorn.
dornag, -aige, -an, *s.f.* Glove, gauntlet. 2 see doirneag.
dornaich, see dorn.
dornaiche,‡‡ -an, *s.m.* Pugilist.
dornaidh,** *s.f.* Narrow channel of the sea, where it flows and ebbs, and where at full tide, a vessel can be towed to either side of the harbour.
dornair, -ean, *s.m.* Boxer, pugilist.
———eachd, *s.f.* Pugilism, boxing. 2 Bruising with the fists. 3 *Thumping. Làmhainn d., *a boxing glove.*
dornais, *s.* Link.
dornan, -ain, -an, *s. m.* Small fist. 2 Small handful. 3 That part of an oar grasped in the hand in rowing. 4 * Handful of lint. 5 (AC) Glove without separate fingers. 6(AC) Handful of corn cut with one stroke of the reaping-hook. 7‡‡Sheaf of barley. 8(MMcD) Small rope with eyelets in each end, which goes round the head-post in a byre, and to which the neck-rope of a cow is tied, the end being reeved through the eyelets.—*Lewis.* 9 **Small bundle.
———ach,†† *a.* Pertaining to small fists.
dornasg,** see dorn-nasg.
dorn-chùl,** -chùil, *s. m.* see dorn-chur.
dorn-chur,** -chuir, *s.m.* Sword-hilt. 2 Haft or

handle of any bladed weapon. 3 Oar-handle. An d. an déidh na loinne, *the haft after the blade.*
dorn-churaidh,** *s.m.* Pugilist, pugilistic champion.
dorn-fhùar,(MMcL) *s.m.* The feat of twisting a cow's foot off without cutting the skin.
dorn-gheal, -ghile, *a.* White-handed.
dornlach, see dorlach.
dorn-locar, -air, -an, *s.f.* Hand-plane.
dorn-nasg, -naisg, *s.m.* Bracelet. 2 Manacle.
do-roinneadh, see do-roinnte.
do-roinnte, *a.* Indivisible, not easily divisible.
———achd,‡‡ *s.f.ind.* Imparity. 2 Imperviousness.
doromhach,(DJM) -aich, *s.m.* see dorghach.
dorr, *a.* see dorrach.
†dorr, *s.m.* Anger. 2 Displeasure. *a.* Indocile, harsh.
dorra, *1st. comp.* of duilich. More or most difficult. 2 More or most sorry or vexed.
dorrach, -aiche, *a.* Rough, rugged. 2 Austere. 3**Surly, uncivil. 4**Cruel.
dorrachd,** *s.f.* Harshness of temper. 2**Surliness. 3 Austerity. 4 Ruggedness. 5 Cruelty.
dorrad,** -aid, *s.m.* Badness. 2 Difficulty. A' dol an d., *growing more or most difficult.*
dorradas, -ais, *s.m.* Hardship, difficulty. Tha d. agam air a shon, *I am sorry for him.*
dorraid, *2nd. comp.* of duilich.
dòrraman,* -ain, *s.m.* Person alone, hermit, recluse—*Argyll.*
———ach, *a.* Of, or pertaining to, a hermit.
———achd,* *s.f.* Hermitage. 2 Living or wandering alone, seclusion.
dorran, -ain, -an, *s.m.* Vexation, anger. 2* Offence at a trifling cause. 3* Anguish, mental heaviness. Trom dh. nan laoch, *the deep wrath of the heroes.*
———ach, -aiche, *a.* Galling, vexatious. 2 Angry, vexed.
———achd,‡‡ *s.f.ind.* Difficulty. 2 Pettishness.
———aich, *pr. pt.* a' dorranachadh, *v.a.* Vex, gall, grieve.
dorrda, see dorrach.
dorrtha,** see dorrach.
dorsa, *n.pl.* of dorus. (*for* dorsan.)
dorsach, -aiche, Full of doors. 2 Open. 3 Obnoxious. 4* Exposed to the blast, as a house, field of corn, &c.
dorsaiche,* *s.f.* Exposure to the blast. 2 Exposed situation.
dorsair, -ean, *s.m.* Door-keeper, porter.
———eachd, *s.f.ind.* Door-keeping, office of a porter. 2 Porterage. Bu docha leam a bhi (ri) d., *I had rather be (at) door-keeping.*
dorsan, *n.pl.* of dorus.
———, -ain, *s.m.* see diurrasan.
———ach, *a.* see dorsach.
——— -lùdhaidh, *s.pl.* Folding-doors.
dorseir, see dorsair.
†dòrt, see dòirt.
dòrtach, -aiche, *a.* Ready to spill or shed. 2 Spilling, dropping. 3 Not water-tight. 4* Not keeping or retaining. 5**Barren. Brù dh., *a barren womb.*
dòrtadh, -aidh, *s.m.* Spilling, shedding, pouring. 2 Act of spilling, shedding. 3 Very heavy rain. 4**Rushing forth. D. fola, *bloodshed, 2 an issue of blood.* A' d—, *pr. pt.* of dòirt.
†dorubha, -n, *s.m.* Line. [see dorgh.]
do-ruigheachd, see do-ruigsinn.
do-ruigsinn, -e, *a.* Unattainable, approachless, that cannot be reached. 2 Difficult to be reached, inaccesible.
———eachd,‡‡ *s.f.ind.* Inaccessibility.

dòruinn, -e, -ean, *s.f.* Pain, torment, anguish, vexation, perplexity. 2**Tribulation. 3** Danger. D. is dorran a' chléibh, *the anguish and trouble of his breast.*
———each, -iche, *a.* Pained, tormented, excruciating. 2**Dangerous. 3**Perplexed. 4 **Perplexing. 5* Tormenting. 6**Wretched. 7 Vexed.
———eachd, *s.f.ind.* Painfulness, torment, anguish. 2**Calamity. 3**Wretchedness.
†dorum, -an, *s.m.* Mean wretch.
dorus, -uis, dorsan, *s.m.* Door. 2 Wicket gate. 3 Opening. 4 Orifice, as of a wound. Dùin an d., *close the door*; deoch-an-doruis *stirrup-cup*; neasgaid làn dhorsan, *a boil full of orifices*; fàilte na circe mu 'n àrd-dhorus, *the hen's salute at the lintel*; cha do dhùin d. nach d' fhosgail d., *no door ever shut but another opened—i. e.* when troubles come, a way will be provided to meet them, *or* when one aspect of a matter is settled, another appears.
——— a' chadha, *s.m.* Middle door, door between the front door and that of the kitchen.
——— beòil, *s.m.* Front door of a house.
——— cairte, *s.m.* Back of a cart.
——— cathamh, see dorus a' chadha.
——— cùil, *s.m.* Back of a cart. 2 Back door of a house.
——— iat,(MMcL) Back-door.
——— lùdhainn, *or* lùdhaidh, *s. m.* Folding door.
——— mór, *s.m.* Front door of a house.
dos, dois, *pl.* dois & dosan, [*n. pl.* of Nos. 6 & 7 is generally duis.] *s. m.* Bush, thicket. 2 Anything bushy. 3 Cluster. 4 Tuft. 5 Plume, bow, cockade. 6 Hunter's horn. 7 Drone of a bagpipe. 8 Antler of a deer. 9 Bunch of hair. 10 Forelock. 11 Tassel. 12 Mane. 13**Bramble. 14**Froth, scum. 15 *figuratively* Thick body of men. 16(DU) *figuratively* Attentiveness, watchfulness, expectation. 'S ann ort a tha 'n d., ! *how expectant you are !*; dosan nan ruadhag, *the thickets of the roes*; dosan nan càrn, *the bushes of the rocks*; d. na ceann-bheairt, *the plume of the helmet*: gleadhraich nan dos, *the skirling of the pipe-drones*; d. de 'n t-sìoda, *a tassel of silk.*
dosach, -aiche, *a.* Bushy, full of bushes of thickets. 2 Branchy. 3 Plumy. 4 Tufty. 5 Having a flowing mane. 6 see dosgainneach. 7(DC) Haughty. Uaill dh., *unreasonable pride.*
dosaich,‡‡ *v.a. & n.* Plume.
†dòsal, see dùsal.
dosan, -ain, -an, *s.m.* Little bush. 2 Little clump or tuft, as of hair or heath. 3 Plume. 4**Mane. 5 *n. pl.* of dos. 6‡‡Tassel. 7 Hair on the forehead. 8 Cluster.
dò-san, see dà-san.
dosanach,** *a.* Full of little tufts. 2 Full of thickets. 3 Bushy.
dosanachd,‡‡ *s.f.* Bushiness.
dosan-banntraich, *s.m.* Braid.
dosdan, -ain, *s.m.* Kind of food given to horses.
dosgach, -aiche, *a.* Calamitous, unfortunate, liable to accidents or damage. 2** Sad, mournful, deplorable. 3**Morose.
dosgadh, see dosgaich.
dosgaich,* -ean, *s.f.* see dosgainn.
dosgaidh, -ean, see dosgaich.
dosgaidheachd, *s.f.* Moroseness. 2 Wrong. 3 **Mischief. 4**Troublesomeness. 5**Sadness. 6 *Extravagance.
dosgainn, -ean, *s.f.* Misfortune. 2 Loss of cattle. 3 Accident. 4 Damage. 5 Liability to damage or misfortune. 6**Trouble, mischief. Gu'n éirich d., *that mischief may arise.* In *Uist* applied solely to loss of farm-stock, par-

ticularly cattle or horses.—(PM)
dosgainneach, -niche, a. Unfortunate, liable to misfortunes, ill-fated, calamitous, hurtful.
——————d, ‡ s.f. Privativeness.
do-sgàineachd,‡‡ s.f. Imperviousness.
do-sgairte, a. Inseparable. 2 Not easily separated.
do-sgaoileadh, -idh, a. Indissoluble.
do-sgaoilte, a. Not easily spread. 2 Inseparable. 3 Indissoluble. 4 Inevitable.
do-sgaraidh,‡‡ a. Indiscerptible, inseparable.
—————eachd,‡‡ s.f. Indiscerptibility.
do-sgaranta, see do-sgaraidh.
—————chd,‡‡ see do-sgaraidheachd.
do-sgarradh, a. see do-sgaraidh.
do-sgartha, see do-sgaraidh.
do-sgàthach, -aiche, a. Improvident, extravagant, profuse. Gu d., *improvidently.*
do-sgeul,** -sgeòil, s.m. Fictitious tale,romance, novel.
do-sgioblaichte,(PM) a. Unadjustable, as dress —*Uist.*
do-sgrioste, (see foot-note, p. 53) a. Indelible. 2(PJM) Indestructible.
do-sgrùdaidh, -e, a. Unsearchable, inscrutable.
dosguidheach, a. Extravagant.
dosguidheachd, s.f. Extravagance.
dosguinn, see dosgainn.
dosguinneach, see dosgainneach.
do-shaithte,‡‡ a. Impenetrable.
do-shamhlachail,‡‡ a. Inimitable. 2 Unsurpassable.
do-shamhlachas,‡‡ -ais, s.m. Inimitability.
do-sharachaidh,‡‡ a. Indefatiguable.
do-shàrte, (see foot-note p. 53.) a. Troublesome, difficult.
do-shàruichte, a. Indefatigable.
do-shàsachaidh, a. Insatiable.
do-shàsaidheachd, s.f.ind. Insatiableness.
do-shàthaichte,(PM) a. Insatiable.
do-sheachanntach, see do-sheachanta.
do-sheachanta, a. Inevitable, unavoidable, fatal.
do-sheachnach,‡‡ see do-sheachanta.
do-sheachnachd, s.f.ind. Infallibility. 2(PJM) Inerrancy.
do-sheachnadh, a. see do-sheachanta.
do-sheallte, (see foot-note p. 53.) a. Invisible. 2(PJM) Indemonstrable.
do-sheòladh, -aidh, a. Unnavigable. 2 That cannot be guided or directed.
do-shìor, adv. Always, continually, for ever.
do-shiubhal, a. Impassable, not easily travelled.
do-shiubhalachd, s.f.ind. Impassableness.
do-shiubhlach, a. do-shiubhal.
do-shlànachaidh,‡‡ a. Cureless.
do-shònrachaidh,‡‡ a. Indeterminable.
do-smachdabh, -aiche, a. Ungovernable.
do-smachdachadh, -aidh, a. Incorrigible, obstinate, stubborn, unmanageable.
do-smuainteachadh, -aidh, a. Inconceivable,incomprehensible, difficult to understood.
do-smuaintichte, a. Incomprehensible.
do-spìonaidh,‡‡ a. Inextricable.
do-spionte, (see foot-note p. 53.) a. Not to be rooted out. 2**Unsearchable.
do-spriochta,** a. Stubborn, untractable.
dosrach, -aiche, a. Bushy, branchy. 2 Plumy. 3*Tufted, plumed. 4* Luxuriant, flourishing, as corn, trees, &c. A' cinntinn gu d., *growing luxuriantly* ; ite dosrach an fhìrein, *the eagle's plumy feather.*
dosraich, -e, s.f. Luxuriance of branches, tufts, or plumes. 2 Buffeting, as of water. 3 Rising and foaming, as of water against a ship's prow. 4* Branching appearance. 5** Floundering. D. thonn, *the buffeting of waves.*

dostan, -ain, s.m. see dosdan.
do-stiùraidh, a. Untractable, unmanageable. 2 Not easily steered.
dot, see dod.
dòtaman, s.m. see dòtuman.
dotarra, a. Sulky. 2(PM) Smart in appearance (applied to old people)—*Uist.*
doth, -a, a. Doting upon one.
dòth, pr.pt. a' dòthadh, v.a. Singe, scorch,burn.
dòthach,†† a. Singed, scorched.
dothachadh,(PM) s.m. Well seasoning, as of corn or hay—*Uist.* Arbhar air a d., *well-seasoned corn.*
dòthadh, -aidh, s.m. Singeing, scorching. A' d—, pr. pt. of dòth.
dòthag,** -aig, s. f. Slight singeing, slight scorching.
dothaman,(AH) s.m. Puny, shiftless, spiritless person, milksop, one who cannot say "bo" to a goose.
dothan, see domhan.
†dothar, see †dur.
†dothar-chlais,** s. m. Conduit, water-pipe, channel.
do-theagaisgeach, -eiche, a. Indocile.
————————d, s.f.ind. Indocility.
do-theagaisgte, a. Indocile.
do-theagasg, -aisg, a. Indocile, intractable. 2**Unteachable.
do-theannachaidh,‡‡ a. Incompressible.
————————eachd,‡‡ s. f. Incompressibility.
do-theanntachail, see do-theannachaidh.
do-thiomnaidheach,‡‡ -eiche, a. Intestible.
do-thionndaidh,‡‡ a. Inconvertible.
do-thiughachaidh,‡‡ a. Incoaguable.
do-thogail, a. Difficult to be lifted. 2 Difficult to be reared.
do-thograidh,‡‡ a. Censorious, hypercritical, difficult to please.
do-thollaidh,‡‡ a. Unpierceable, impenetrable, as a suit of armour.
do-thomhaiseachd, s.f.ind. Immensurability.
do-thomhaiste, a. Immeasurable.
do-thomhas, -ais, a. Immeasurable, immensurable, difficult to measure.
do-thraighte,(PM) a. Undrainable, that cannot be exhausted, as a well.
do-thraoghadh,‡‡ a. Inexhaustible.
do-thraoghaidheachd,‡‡ s. f. ind. Inexhaustibility.
dòthta, see dòthte.
dòthte, (see foot-note p. 53.) *past pt.* of dòth. Singed, scorched, burned.
†dothuar, s. f. River. for dobhar.
do-thuigsinn, -e, a. Unintelligible, hard to be understood. Cuid de nithibh d., *some things hard to be understood.*
——————each, -eiche, a. Incomprehensible.
——————eachd, s.f.ind. Incomprehensibility.
dòtuman,‡‡ -ain, -an, s.m. Whirligig. 2 Boy's top.
dò-uair, -e, -ean, s. f. Unfavourable weather, stormy weather. 2 Evil hour. 3**Blight. Is caoin do bhlàth, ach is fagus d., *thy blossom is sweet, but the blight is near.*
douran, see dòbhran.
drab,* s.f. Offal. 2 see dràbag.
†drab, s.m. Spot, stain, blemish.
dràbach, -aiche, a. Dirty, nasty, slovenly. 2 Oozy.
dràbag, -aige, -an, s.f. Slattern. 2 Obscene-tongued female.
dràbair, -e, -ean, s.m. Dirty, slovenly fellow.
dràbaireachd, s.f. Slovenliness.
drabas, see drabhas.
drabasda, a. Dirty, obscene, filthy, smutty,

indelicate. 2**Uncouth. 3(MMcL) Crabbed.
drabasdachd, *s.f.ind.* Obscenity of language, smuttiness. 2**Uncouthness.
drabh, -aibh, *s.m.* Draff, grains of malt after the juice is extracted. 2***rarely* Cart. 3(PM) Untidy person—*Uist.* 'Nuair a bhitheas a' mhuc sàthach, cinnidh an d. (*or* an treasg) goirt, *when the sow is full, the draff grows sour.*
drabh, *v.a. & n.* Dissolve. 2 Solve. 3 Decay. 4*Scatter, as a multitude. 5 Bulge, as a wall. [Gaelic form of *draw.*]
dràbh,* *s m.* Ruin. Chaidh e do dh., [*or* 'dh.] *he has gone to pigs and whistles* or *ruin.*
dràbhach, -aiche, *a.* Rifted, fissured. 2 Ill-cemented. 3††Diverging.
dràbhachd,(AC) *s.f.* Debauchery. 2 Indelicacy.
drabhadh, -aidh, *s.m.* Separating, as a crowd. 2 Dissolving. 3 Running out. 4 Decaying. 5 Act of separating, separation. 6 Bulging, as a wall. A' d—, *pr.pt.* of drabh.
dràbhag, -aige, -an, *s.f.* Dregs, lees, sediment, refuse. 2 Little filthy slattern. 3*Market thinly attended. 4* Scattered multitude.
——— -shiùcair, *s.f.* Treacle.
———ach, -aiche, *a.* Full of dregs, foul. 2 **Like lees or sediment.
drabhailt, *s.f.* Grain-holder, for feeding the mill when grinding corn—*Lewis.* [*also* trabh-ailt.]
drabhais, *s.pl.* Dregs—*Dàin I. Ghobha.* 2 (PJM) Off-scourings of society.
drabhall, see draibhill.
drabhas, -ais, *s.m.* Filthiness of speech, smut. 2 Turbulence. 3 Filth. 4 Foul weather. 5 (PM) Filthy man—*Uist.*
———-ach, -aiche, *a.* Foul, turbulent (of weather.) 2 Filthy, indelicate, obscene (of speech.)
———achd,** *s.f.* Filthiness of speech, obscenity.
drabhasaich,‡‡ *v.a.* Bespurt, make foul.
drabhasda, see drabasda.
drabhc,(CR) *s.m.* Lazy or stupid worker—*W. of Ross.*
drabhluinn, -ean, *s. m.* Trifler, idler. 2*Absurdity, sheer nonsense.
———each,* -iche, *a.* Absurd, very nonsensical.
———each, -eich, *s.m.* Absurd person.
———eachd, *s.f.ind.* Drollery, ludicrous exhibition, absurd conduct, farce, *prov.*
dràc, dràic, -an, *s.m.* Drake.
—ach,** *a.* Abounding in drakes, like a drake. An coire d., *the dell abounding in drakes.*
dradh, -a, *s.m.* see dragh.
———ais, Gaelic spelling of *drawers.*
drag, -aig, see dreug.
†drag-aigheann, -aighne, *s.f.* Fire-shovel.
dragart,** -airt, *s.m.* (drag+art) Flint.
†drag-bhod,** -bhuid, *s.* The constellation the Little Bear.
dragh, *s.m.* The rope of straw or hay, which keeps the ends of the heather-rope loops in their places on a thatched roof. 2 (DU) Line attached to a fishing-rod, fishing (rod) tackle.
dragh, -a, *s.m.* Trouble, vexation, annoyance. Na cuir d. air, *do not trouble him* ; cha ruig thu leas a' dhragh sin a ghabhail, *you need not be at the trouble* ; ged éireadh d., *though trouble should arise* ; cha bhi uaill gun d., 's cha bhi sinn a' draghadh ris [NGP gives rithe,] *pride is not without trouble, so we won't be troubled with it.*
dragh, *pr. pt.* a' draghadh [& a' draghachadh,] *v.a.* Part, separate. 2 Gaelic form of *drag.*
draghachadh, see draghadh, (1).
draghadair, see draghair.
draghadh, -aidh, *s.m.* Parting, separating. 2 Dragging, pulling. A' d—, *pr.pt.* of dragh.
draghail, -ala, *a.* Troublesome, vexatious, annoying, teasing.
draghair, -ean, Gaelic spelling of *dragger*, and hence of *dray.* 3 Teasing fellow. 4**Troublesome fellow.
———eachd, *s.f.* Gaelic form of *dragging.*
———eachd, *s.f.ind.* Teasing, troubling, annoying.
draghaistich,* *v.a.* Drag in an absurd or childish way [Eng. word.]
draghalach, -eiche, see draghail.
———d, *s.f.ind.* Troublesomeness, annoyance, teasing.
draghlainn,‡ *s. f.* Slovenly person. 2 Mess. *prov.*
dràgon, -oin, -an, *s.m.* Dragon. 2†† Paper kite.
dràib, *s.* see dràbag.
———each, *a.* see dràbach.
draibh, *gen & pl.* of drabh.
draibhill, (PM) *s.m.* Most untidy worker—*Uist.*
draic, see draig.
dràic, -ean, *s.f.* Slattern, drabbish, unthrifty person.
———each,** see dràiceil.
———ealachd, *s. f. ind.* Sluttishness, drabbishness.
———eil, *a.* Sluttish, drabbish, unthrifty.
draig,** *s.m.* Spendthrift, unthrifty person. 2 (AF) Dragon. Bhiodh sonas aig d., n'am faigheadh e mar dhòrtadh e, *the spendthrift would be happy, if he got as he squandered.*
draigh, see droigheann.
†——— -bhiorasg, -aisg, *s.m.* Fuel.
———eann, see droigheann.
———ionn, see droigheann.
draighearnach, see droighneach.
draighilc,†† *s, f. ind.* Trollop, draggle-tail.
draighneach,* *s.f.* Lumber. 2 Absurd detention. 3 see droighneach. 4**Loud rumbling noise, as thunder.
draighneag, see droighneach.
draillseanach, } see trillseineach.
draillseanta, }
draillsein, see trillsein.
———each, -iche, *a.* see trillseineach.
draimheas, -eis, -an, *s.m.* Foul mouth.
———ach, -aiche, *a.* Having a foul mouth.
dràin, -e, *s.m.* see dréin.
———eag, see gràineag.
draing, -e, *s. f.* Snarl, snarling. 2*Grin. 3** Peevishness. Chuir e d. air rium, *he snarled at me.*
draingeag,(DC) *s.f.* Peevish, fault-finding woman. [The *ng* is elided in speech—*drai'ag.*]
draingean,(DC)*s.m.* Peevish, fault-finding man.
draingeanta,** *a.* Snarling, cross, peevish.
———chd,** *s. f. ind.* Peevishness. 2 Snarling. 3 Cross, peevish temper.
draingeis,* *s. f.* Snarling, carping. 2 Childish bickering.
———each,* *a.* Grinning. 2 Snarling. 3 Bickering.
drainn, *s.m.* see dréin. 2 see droinn.
draint,** *s.f.* Snarl. 2 Peevishness.
draip, -e, *s. f.* Hurry. 2 Strait, difficulty. 3 Confusion. 4 **Vexation. 5**Calamity. 6** Slut.
draipealachd, *s. f. ind* Hurriedness. 2 Confusedness, embarrassment.
draipeil, -ala, *a.* Hurried. 2 Confused, embarrassed.
dràis,** *s.pl.* Gaelic spelling of *drawers.*
drallainn,(AH) *s.m.* Man who works or talks without method.
†dram, *s.m.* Much, plenty.

dram, -a, -annan, *s.m.* Dram. 2 Drachm weight. D. mar lìnig cléibh. *a dram to line the thorax*; tachas an drama, *itching for a dram*; leith-sgeul an drama, *an excuse for a dram*; na gabh an dram gun fhios, *do not make a practice of taking drams secretly*.
——ach,†† *a.* Abounding in drams.
——ach,(DC) *s.m.* Mixture of meal and water.
dramag, -aige, -an, *s.f.* Foul mixture. 2** Dram of spirits. 3 "Crowdie." [‡ gives dramaig as *nom.sing.*]
dramaig, -e, -ean, see dramag.
†**dramh**, *s.m.* Wry-mouth.
dramhd,‡‡ *v.n.* see drannd.
——an, see dranndan.
dràn, see dàn.
drànag, see dàn.
drand, see drannd.
drann,* *s.m.* see drannd & dranndan.
drannadh, -aidh, -ean, *s.m.* Grinning. 2*Word.
drannag, see dronnag.
drannd, -a, -an, *s.m.* Small quantity, the least bit. 2 Word, syllable. 3 Chirp. 4**Hum, murmur. 5‡ Snarl. Cha d' fhuair sinn d., *not a word was said to us*; cha chluinn e d., *he is stone deaf*.
dranndail, *s.f.* Grumbling. 2 Snarling.
dranndan, -ain, *s.m.* Hum, humming, as of bees. 2 Snarling, growling. 3 Grumbling, bickering, murmuring. 4 Whistling of the wind. 5 Querulous complaint. 6* Teasing. 7**Gurgling.
——-teallaich, *s.m.* Fireside grumbling, domestic jarring.
——ach, -aiche, *a.* Humming, inclined to hum. 2 Grumbling, murmuring, complaining, querulous, prone to grumbling, inclined to murmur or grumble. 3 Growling, snarling. 4 Buzzing. 5 Envious. 6 Gurgling. Am beach d., *the buzzing bee*; alltan d., *a gurgling brook*.
dranndanachd, *s.f.ind.* Grumbling, complaining, murmuring, querulousness 2 Humming. 3 Buzzing. 4 Snarling, growling. 5 *Gurgling noise, as of a brook.
dranndanaich, *s.f.ind.* see dranndanachd.
——,‡‡ *v.n.* Buzz, hum.
drannd-eun, -eòin, *s.m.* Humming-bird. [Preceded by the art. *an*.]
drannd-sgàit, *s.m.* *Lewis* for dronn-sgàit.
draoch, -aoich, *s. m.* Hair standing on end. 2 Pale, fretful, *or* ghastly look. 3 see driùchd.
draoidh, -ean, see drùidh.
——each, -iche, *a.* see drùidheach.
——each, -ich, *s.m.* see drùidheach.
——eachd, see drùidheachd.
——neach, -ich, *s.m.* see drùidhneach, *s.*
draoightear, -ir, *s.m.* Enchanter. 2 The Evil One.—*Dàin I. Ghobha.*
†**draoilinn**, *s.f.* Tediousness, delay. 2 Inactivity.
draoin, *s.m.* see dréin. 2 (AC)Sculptor.
draoisg, -e, -ean, see braoisg.
——each, see braoisgeach.
draoitheachd, see drùidheachd.
draoluinn, -e, *s.f.* Drawling, tediousness, delay.
——each, -iche, *a.* Tedious, drawling, inactive.
——eachd, *s.f.ind.* Prolixity.
draonnag,* see dronnag.
draos, -aois, *s.m.* Trash. 2 Filth. 3**Obscenity, ribaldry.
draosda, *a.* Obscene, smutty, lewd. 2(MMcL) Ugly-looking—*Harris*.
——chd, *s.f.ind.* Smut, obscenity, ribaldry, filthiness, lewdness.
——il, -ala [& -aille,] *a.* see draosda.
draosdair, -ean, *s.m.* Whoremaster.
draosdaireachd, see draosdachd.
draoth,** -a, *s.m.* Pull, tug, pluck. [*Eng.draw.*]
draoth,* -aoith, *s.m.* Good-for-nothing person, humdrum, wastrel, spendthrift. 2 One shamelessly vicious or profligate. 3‡‡ see drùidh.
draothadh, -aidh, *s. m.* Twitch. 2 Pulling, tugging, plucking.
drapuinn,‡ *s.* Tape.
dràs, see dràsda.
dràsda, (an dràsda—*for* an tràth seo) *adv.* Now, the present time, at this time.
dràsdaich, (an dràsdaich) *prov.* for an dràsd.
drathainn, see dreathan-donn.
drathais, -ean, *s.f.* Gaelic spelling of *drawers*. 2* Old patched pair of trousers.
†**drè**, *s.m.* Gaelic spelling of *dray*.
dreach, *pr. pt.* a' dreachadh, *v.a.* Figure, delineate, shape. 2 Adorn, polish, dress. 3 Colour, paint.
dreach, -a, -an, *s.m.* Form, figure, image, shape. 2 Fashion, appearance. 3 Seemliness, beauty. 4 Colour. 5 Aspect. 6 Vision. 7 Hue of the complexion. 8* Probability. Air chaochladh d., *in a different form* or *shape*; òr a's deirge d., *the purest-coloured gold*; deud air dh. cailce, *teeth as white as chalk*; air dh. an fhithich, *having the appearance of a raven, as black as a raven*.
dreachach, -aiche,** *a.* That dresses or polishes. 2 Polishing, figuring, delineating, adorning. 3 Ornamental. 4 Drawn, figured, delineated. 5 Fair, handsome, of good appearance.
dreachadair, -ean, *s.m.* Painter. 2 Sculptor, statuary. 3**Dresser. 4**Polisher.
——eachd,** *s.f.ind.* Occupation of a painter, or statuary. 2 Polishing. 3 Dressing, ornamenting.
dreachadan, -ain, *s.m.* Mould.
——ach,†† *a.* Pertaining to a mould.
dreachadh, -aidh, *s.m.* Portraiture. 2 Polishing, dressing, adorning. 3 Figuring. 4 Act of pourtraying, polishing, &c. A' d—, *pr. pt.* of dreach.
dreachail, -ala, *a.* Comely, good-looking, handsome, personable, having a good appearance, showy.
dreachalachd, *s.f.ind.* Comeliness, handsomeness, personableness.
dreach-bhuidhe, *a.* Beautifully yellow.
dreachar, *prov.* for dreachmhor.
drèachd, -an, *s.f.* see dreuchd.
dreachd, -an, *s.f.* Wile, trick, stratagem, *prov.*
†**dreachd**, *s.f.* see dreach. 2 Poem.
†**dreachda**, *s.m.* Troop.
†**dreachdaire**, -an, *s.m.* Historian.
dreachlagh,(MMcL) *s. m.* Change of appearance. Thug e d. air, *he made its appearance change*.
dreach-lùbach, -aiche, *a.* Serpentine.
dreach-mhìn, -e, *a.* Beautifully smooth. 2 Attractive, mild. 3 Graceful.
dreachmhor, -mhoire, *a.* Comely, graceful, handsome, shapely, showy, specious.
——achd,** *s.f.* Beautifulness.
†**dreacht**, *s.f.* Poem. 2 Draught. 3 Pattern.
dreadhan, -ain, *s.m.* see dreathan-donn.
dreug, dreige, *s.f.* Meteor. 2 Falling star. 3 Fireball. 4 (AH) Corpse-candle. 6(DU)Portent. Cruas na creige is luathas na dreige, *the hardness of the rock and the speed of the meteor*.
†**dreag**, *v.a.* Fight, wrangle. 2 Certify. 3** Signify, give notice.
†**dreagadh**,** -aidh, *s.m.* Advertisement.
dreagail, -ala, *a.* Meteorological.

dréagan, *s.m.* Gaelic spelling of the Scots pronunciation of *dragon.*
dreaganta, *a.* Fierce, perverse, cross, wrangling, captious, peevish.
———chd,** *s.f.ind.* Captiousness, wrangling, peevishness.
dreaghain, see droigheann.
dreaghann, -ainn, see dreathan-donn.
drèagon, -oin, *s.m.* see dràgon.
dreall, -ill, *s.m.* Blaze, torch. 2 see droll.
dreallach,†† *a.* Abounding in door-bars.
dreallag, -aige, -an, *s.f.* Swingle-tree, *prov.* 2 Swing for play. 3 Any swinging machine. 4 Absurdity.
dreallaire, -an, *s.m.* Idler, saunterer, lounger.
———achd, *s.f.ind.* Idling, sauntering.
dreallaman, (AH) *s. m.* Unskilled, awkward workman.
dreallan, *dim.* of dreall.
dreallanaiche, -an, *s.m.* Augur, seer.
dreallan-doiuinn,†† *s.m.* Stormy petrel.
dreallan-teasbhuidh, see dreòlan-teasbhuidh.
dreallsach* -aich, *s. m.* Blazing fire. 2 The face blazing with liquor.
dream, *s.m.ind.* Tribe. 2 People, folk. 3 Family. 4 Company, band. 5 Handful, as of corn. 6††Distorted mouth. 7 Bundle. Gluaiseadh gach d., *let every tribe advance* ; an d. a bha dlùth do 'n bhàis, *the people who were near to death* ; chì mi mo dh., *I see my band* ; is rìoghail mo dh., *my race is royal*—motto of the MacGregors.
dream, *v.a.* Grin, smile distortedly. 2 Snarl.
——ach, -aiche, *a.* Grinning. 2 Snarling. 3 Peevish, morose, boorish. Dh' fhàgadh tu suairc fear d., *you would make a surly man mild.*
——achd, *s.f.ind.* Moroseness, peevishness, boorishness.
——adh, -aidh, *s.m.* Grinning, snarling. 2 Act of grinning. A' d—, *pr. pt.* of dream.
——ag, -aig, -an, *s.f.* Handful, as of hay or corn, used as a decoy for a horse. 2 Peevish female.
——aiche, *s.f.ind.* Peevishness, moroseness.
——aiche, *comp.* of dreamach.
——air, -ean, *s.m.* Barker. 2 see dreimire.
dreaman, -ain, *s.m.* Madness, furiousness. 2** Fit of passion. 3**Fanaticism. 4 Handful, as of hay or corn. 5** Climax. 6(PJM) Irritable, snarling person.
———ach, -aiche, *a.* Mad, frantic, furious. 2 Fanatical.
dreamanaiche, see dreamanach.
dreamasach, -aiche, see dreamach.
dream-chraos, -aois, *s. f.* Distorted, snarling mouth.
dreamasgal, see dreamsgal.
†**dreamhnach**, -aich, *s.m.* Fop, coxcomb.
†**dreamhnach**, -aiche, *a.* Perverse, foolish.
dreamlach, -aiche, *a.* see dreamlainneach.
dreamlainn, *s.f.* Snarling, grumbling. 2 Grinning. [*Used for drabhluinn in *Skye.*]
————each, -iche, *a.* Morose, peevish, snarling.
dreamsgal, -ail, *s.m.* Heterogeneous mass. 2 (DU) Rubbish of any kind.
————ach, -aiche, *a.* Foully mixed, heterogeneous.
†**drean**, -ein, *s.m.* Strife, debate, wrangling. 2 see dreathan.
†**drean**, *a.* Bad.
dreanach,** *a.* Despicable.
dreang,* *s. f.* Snarl, girn. 2 Girning expression of countenance.
dreang,* *v.a.* see dream, *v.*
dreangad,(AF) *s.* Flea.
dreangaire,* *s.m.* Snarler.
dreangais,* *s.f.* Snarling.
dreangan, -ain, -an, *s.m.* Snarler. 2 Trifling, insignificant, tiresome, peevish person.
————ach, -aiche, *a.* Snarling, grumbling, cross, peevish.
dreangcuid, see dreangad.
†**dreann**, *s.m.* Haste. 2 Contention, battle. 3 Grief, pain. 4 Skirmish, scuffle.
†**dreann**, *a.* Good.
†**dreannach**, *a.* Repugnant, opposite, contrary, perverse. 2 Contentious.
dreannad, -aid, *s.m.* Rashness.
dreap, see streap.
——air, see streapair.
——aireachd, see streapaireachd.
dreas,§ drise, -an, *s.f.* Brier, bramble, see dris. 2**Place, stead.
dreas, *v.* Gaelic spelling of *dress.* Air an "dreasadh," (! !) *dressed up, decorated.*
dreasach, -aiche, *a.* see driseach.
dreasadh, see under dreas, *v.*
dreasag, -aig, -an, *s.m.* Little brier, little bramble.
dreasail,** *s.pl.* Shreds. 2 Small teats.
————, -ala, *a.* see driseil.
dreasamhuil, -ala, *a.* see driseil.
dreasar,(AH) *s.m.* Gaelic spelling of kitchen *dresser.*
dreasarnach, -aich, *s.f.* see drisearnach.
dreas-choill, -e, see dris-choill.
dreas-chùbhraidh, see dris-chùbhraidh.
dreasgaidh, -e, *a.* see driseach.
dreas-nan-smeur, see dris-smeur.
dreaste, Gaelic spelling of *dressed.* Anartan d., *dressed linen.*
dreathan, -ain, *s.m.* Wren, see dreathan-donn. An d. talcarra, *the plump wren.*
dreathan-a'-chinn-bhuidhe, -ain-, *s.m.* Golden-crested wren, see crionag-bhuidhe.

272. *Dreathan-donn.*

dreathan-donn, -ain-, *s.m.* Wren—*traglodytes vulgaris.*
dreathlann-donn, see dreathan-donn.
dreibhse, see treis.
dreicis, Gaelic spelling of *dregs.*
dreige, *gen.sing.* of dreag.
dreigeas, -eis, *s.m.* Grin. 2 Peevish face.
————ach, -aiche, *a.* Cross-grained, peevish.
dreigeil, (PM) *a.* Perverse, cantankerous. Duine d., *a perverse man—Uist.*
dreigeis, (PM) *a.* Perverse.
dreigeiseach, see dreigeasach.
†**dreim**, *s.f.* Endeavour, attempt.
†**dreim**, *v.n.* Climb, clamber, scramble.
dreimear,** *s.m.* Climax.
†**dreimhne**, *s.f.* Warfare.
†**dreimire**, -an, *s.m.* Ladder, stair. 2 Scrambler, climber.
dreimire-buidhe, *s.m.* Yellow centaury, yellow wort§—*chlora perfoliata.* [Not found in Scottish Gaeldom.]
dreimire-gorm,§ *s.m.* Woody nightshade, bitter sweet, dulcamara, felon-wood—*solanum dulcamara.*

dreimire-Muire, *s.m.* Dwarf tufted centaury, see dreimire-mara.
dreimire-mara,§ *s.m.* Dwarf tufted centaury.—*erythræa littoralis.*
dreinisg duine, *s. m.* Peevish man—*Lewis.*
dréin, -e, -ean, *s. f.* Grin. 2** Grinning. 3 (TS) Snarling expression.
dréineach, -iche, *a.* Grinning.
dréineag, -eige, -an, *s.f.* Grinning female.
dreingein, see dreangan.
dreis, -e, -ean, *s.f.* see dris. 2 *W. of Ross* for greis.
dreisd, Gaelic spelling of *dressed.* see dreaste.
dreiseag, see greiseag.
dreòcam, -aim, *s. m.* The crying of deer. 2 **Purring.
dreochail, (AC) *pr. pt.* A' d., *floundering.*

273. Dreimire-mara.

dreòdag, see streòdag.
dreòdan, -ain, *s.m.* Little louse.
†dreogh, *v.a. & n.* Rot. 2 Wear out.
†dreòighte, *past pt.* of dreogh. Rotten.
dreòlan, -ain, *s.m.* Silly, inactive person, see droll. 2††Dwarf. 3 Wren, see dreathan-donn.
——— -teasbhuidh, -e, *s.m.* Grass-hopper.
———ach,** *a.* Silly. 2 Like, of, or belonging to, a wren.
———achd, *s.f.ind.* Silliness, triflingness. 2 Imbecility.
dreoll, -a, *s.m.* Paltry, worthless fellow. 2 see dreall.
———an, -ain, see dreòlan.
———anachd, see dreòlanachd.
dreòllan-teasbhuidh, see dreòlan-teasbhuidh.
dreòs, -eòis, *s.m.* Blaze. 2 Taper.
———ach, -aiche, *a.* Blazing, pertaining to a blaze.
dreòsgach,(CR) *a.* Open, loosely-woven, as canvas.—*W. of Ross-shire.* 2 (PJM) Having a rough surface.
dreòs-theine, *s.m.* Blazing-fire.
dreuchd,‡ *s. f. ind.* Trade, business. 2 Office, duty. D. an t-sagairt, *the priest's office* ; luchd d., *office-bearers, officers.*
———ach, -aiche, see dreuchdail.
———ail, -ala, *a.* Official. 2 Fond of office. 3 Of, or belonging to, office.
dreuchd-chainnt, -e, -ean, *s.f.* Cant.
dreug, see dreag.
dreug, *s. f.* Mare, old and done. Bheir seann dreug bhàn na bhitheas dh' oighreachdan air Bealach chun na Cille, *an old white worn out mare will carry all [the last of] the heirs of Taymouth to the tomb.*
dreugan, -ain, see dràgon.
driachadach,** *a.* Stiff. 2 Inflexible. 3 Obstinate.
driachadaich, *s. m.* Stiffness. 2 Inflexibility. 3 Obstinacy.
driachaire, -ean, *s. m.* Persevering, patient plodder.
———ach, *a.* Stiff. 2 Inflexible. 3 Obstinate.
———achd, *s.f.ind.* Patient plodding. 2 Stiffness. 3 Inflexibility. 4 Obstinacy.
driachan, -ain, *s.m.* Persevering, constant labour, plodding, drudgery. 2 Obstinacy.
———ach, -aiche, *a.* Sickly, peevish, ailing, fretful. 2††Plodding.
———achd, *s.f.ind.* Sickness. 2 Fretfulness. 3††Plodding. 4††Botching.
driamlach, -aich, -aichean, *s. f.* Fishing-line, line for a fishing-rod, made of old from the long hairs of a horse's tail twisted together. 2 Tall, clumsy, disproportioned fellow. 3 Sea-laces, kind of seaweed.—*chorda filum.*
†drib, *s.f.* Filth. 2 Snare. 3 Danger.
†dribhleach, -eich, *s.f.* Cowl.
dric,(AF) *s.* Dragon. 2 Winged serpent.
drifeag, -eige, -an, *s f.* Hurry, confusion, tumult.
dril, -e, *s.f.* Drop, as of dew or rain, sparkling in the sun. 2 Spark, twinkle. 3 Glimpse. 4 *State of being slightly intoxicated.
dril,** *v.n.* Drop, drizzle.
drileanach, *a.* Shining, sparkling.
drilleach,†† *a.* Abounding in drops or sparks.
———, *s.m.* Anything sparkling. Cho chùbhraidh ri ùbhlan a' ghàraidh air drilleachan cuirteil, *as fragrant as garden apples on sparkling dishes of crystal.*
drilleachan, -ain, *s.m.* Oyster-eater, see trilleachan.
drillin, see drithleann.
———neach, see drithleannach.
drillsein, see trillsean.
drilseach, -iche, *a.* Radiant, dazzling, glittering. 2 Drizzling, dropping, rainy, dewy. 3* Glimmering. 4 Flashing. Na sradan d. 'thig o 'chruidhean, *the flashing sparks that come from his shoes—Filidh.*
drilsean,* *s.m.* see trillsean.
———ach, see trillseineach.
drim, droma, see druim.
drimneach, -iche, *a.* Of many heights. 2 Striped, streaked. 3 Parti-coloured, pie-bald. 4 Ribbed, as stockings.
driobaid, -e, -ean, *s.f.* Drop.
driobhail-drabhail, *adv.* Hurly-burly.
driobhunn, see droigheann.
driodairt, (form of driod-fhortan) Trifling accident, mishap. Cha d' éirich d. do neach, *no mishap befel anyone—Sgeul.-nan-caol, p. 92.*
driodamhartan, -ain, *s.m.* see driod-fhortan.
driodar, -air, *s.m.* Lees, dregs, refuse. 2 Corrupt matter. 3 **Gore.
———ach, -aiche, *a.* Dreggy, full of lees. 2 **Gory.
driodartha, *a.* see driodarach.
driod-fhortan, -ain, *s.m.* Misfortune, trifling mishap, or disappointment. 2 Anecdote. Ag innseadh dhriod-fhortan, *relating anecdotes.*
———ach,†† *a.* Unfortunate.
driod-shùileach,* *a.* Having a twinkling eye.
driog, -a, -an, *s. m.* Drop. 2 Tear. 3 see triuthach.
driog, *v.a.* Drop, distil.
driogach,†† *a.* Dropping slowly.
———d, *s.f.ind.* Distillation.
driogair, -ean, *s.m.* Distiller.
driom, see druim.
drioman-dubh,(AF) *s.m.* Black cow having a white back.
driongam, *s.m.* (DC)Disputing. 2(TS)Drinking. 'S tra 'chaidh sinn gu driongam, *'tis quickly we set to disputing—Duanaire, p. 22*
driongan, (CR) -ain, *s.m. & pr.pt.* Pottering, trifling. Tha e a' d. fad an là, *he is pottering about the whole day—W. of Ross.*
driongan, -ain, *s.m.* Slowness.
———ach, -aiche, *a.* Slow, tardy. 2 Unceasing.
———ach, *s.m.* Slow, tardy person.
———achd, *s.f.ind.* Slowness, tardiness.
driop,** *v.a.* Climb.
driop, *s.m.* see drip, 1.
driopail, *a.* see dripeil.
driopall, -aill, *s.m.* Mixture, anything confused.
———ach, -aiche, *a.* Confused.
driothlag,* -aige, *s.f.* Glimmering fire.
driothlunn, -uinn, see drithleann.

driothlunnach, -aiche, *a.* see drithleannach.

drip, -e, *s.f.* [* gives *s.m.*] Bustle, hurry, haste, confusion. 2 Want. 3 Affliction. 4 Snare. [* says, snare intended for another but ensnaring the author of it.] 5 Combat, fight. 6* Predicament, perplexity. Tràth thuiteas daoidh 'san drip, *when the wicked fall into the snare*; daoine faoine an drip, *foolish men in perplexity*; cha'n fhacas riamh muc gun d. oirre, *you never saw a sow that was not in a hurry.*

dripeil, -eala, *a.* Hurried, busy. 2 (DC) Industrious, assiduous—*Uist.* 3 Confused, embarrassed. 4 Unfortunate. 5 Indigent.

274. Dris.

dris, -e, -ean, *s. f.* Common bramble, brier, blackberry or thorn.—*rubus fructicosus.* [The badge of a branch of Clan Maclean.—§] An d. a' fàs gu h-ùrar, *the brier freshly growing*; an àite dhroigheann agus dh., *instead of thorns and briers*; mar theine dh., *as a fire of thorns*; am fear a théid 'san droighinn dhomh, théid mise 'san d. da, *who goes through the thorns for me, I will go through the briers for him*; ge milis a mhil, cò dh' imlicheadh bhàrr na dris i? *sweet as is honey, who would lick it off the brier?*

dris-choill, -e, -choilltean, *s.f.* Thicket of briers or brambles.

dris-chùbhraidh,§ *s f.* Sweet brier or eglantine.—*rosa rubiginosa.*

driseach, -siche, *a.* Brambly, briery, thorny. 2 Prickly. 3 Cross, fretful.

driseachan, (AF) *s.m.* Blood pudding, formerly given to the family water-carrier when a sheep was killed.

275. Dris-chùbhraidh.

driseag, -eige, -an, *s.f.* Small bramble or brier. 2 Little fretful female.

———ach,†† *a.* Abounding in little thorns.

driseamhuil, *a.* see driseil.

drisean, *n.pl.* of dris.

———ta, *a.* Thorny, brambly. 2 Cross, fretful. Gu d., *fretfully.*

drisearnach, -aich, *s.f.* Thicket of brambles or briers. 2 Place where brambles or briers grow.

driseil, -eala, *a.* Prickly. 2 Thorny. 3 Full of briers.

drisleach, *s.f.* -ich, see drisearnach.

———, *a.* see drilseach.

dris-mhuine,§ *s.f.* Common bramble, see dris.

dris-smeur,§ *s.f.* Common bramble, see dris.

dritheanaich, *s.pl.* Spasms—*Arran.* [Preceded by the article *na.*]

†drithle, *s.f.* Sparkle.

drithlean, -ein, -an, *s.m.* Rivet.

drithleann, -inn, *s. m.* Sparkle, flash, ray. 2 Radiance.

———ach, -aiche, *a.* Sparkling, gleaming, glistening, flashing.

drithlich, *v.a.* Sparkle, flash, gleam, shine.

drithlinn, see drithleann.

———each, *a.* see drithleannach.

drithlis, -e, -nan, *s.f.* Sparkle.

driubhlach, -aich, *s.m.* Cowl.

driùcan, -ain, -an, *s.m.* Beak, snout. 2*Incision under one of the toes—*Islay & Lewis.*

driuch,* *s. m.* Activity, energy. 2**Peevish look. 3 Peevishness, fretfulness. 4 Hair standing on end. 5**Beak, snout. Cuir d. ort, *bestir yourself.*

———,** *v.n.* Stand on end, as the hair of the head.

———adh,** *s.m.* Standing on end, as the hair of the head.

———ail,* -ala, *a.* Active, lively.

†driuchal,** -ail, *s.m.* Anger.

†driuchail, *a.* Angry.

driuchalach,** *a.* Angry, fretful, peevish.

———d,** *s.f.* Angriness, fretfulness, peevishness.

driuchan,* -ain, *s.m.* see triuchan.

driuchanach,* -aiche, *a.* Striped.

driùchd, -an, *s.m.* see drùchd. 2**Hair standing on end

driùchdach, see drùchdach.

driu'-chasd, (triuch-chasd) *Perthsh.* for triuthach.

driùchd-a'-mhonaidh, see drùchdan-monaidh.

driùchdach, -aiche, *a.* see drùchdach.

driuchdail, -ala, *a.* see drùchdach.

driùchdan, see drùchdan.

driug, -a, -an, *s.f.* see dreug. 2 (CR) Any illness, the name and cause of which are unknown. Ghabh e d., *he had* [or *took*] *an illness.*

driùlagan, *s.m.* Mishmash.

dro, *s.m.* see dorgh.

dròbh, -òibh, -an, *s.m.* Drove of cattle. 2 Market—*Lewis.* 3 Crowd. 4**Calvacade. Thig d. nam mart, *the drove of cattle shall come.*

drobha, see dorgh.

dròbhach,†† *a.* Full of cattle-droves.

drobhach, see dorghach.

dròbhair, -ean, *s.m.* Drover. 2 Cattle-dealer. 3* Man at a market.

———eachd, *s.f.ind.* Business of cattle-dealing, occupation of a cattle-dealer. 2* Sauntering at a market.

drobhlas, -ais, *s.m.* Profusion. 2**Misery.

———ach, -aiche, *a.* Profuse. 2 Miserable, pitiable.

droch, *a.* Bad, evil, wicked. 2 Mischievous. 3 Sad, calamitous. [Always placed before its noun. Numbers of words with *droch* prefixed are inserted in other Gaelic Dictionaries, and for that reason are reprinted here. These words might certainly be omitted, excepting a few, like *droch-bheart* and *droch-ghean* in which the accent has transferred itself to *droch.*] Droch bhean, *a bad woman*; droch fhear, *a bad man*; d. rùn, a *wicked intention*; droch-bheart, *mischief*; d. là, *a bad day*; cha'n 'eil an droch fheum aige air, *he is sorely in need of it* [droch fheum, *no need;* cha'n 'eil an droch fheum, *there is not no need=there is great need.* Compounds formed with *droch* whose second element begins with *c* should always have the *c* aspirated, as, droch-chleachdadh, *not* droch-cleachdadh, as in McL & D.

†droch, *a.* Right, straight, even, direct.

†———, *s.m.* Coach-wheel. 2 Death. 3(AF) Moth, cloth- or wood-worm.

droch-àbhaist, -ean, *s.f.* Bad custom, bad habit.

droch-àbhaisteach, -iche, *a.* Having bad habits. 2 Mischievous, vicious. 3** Idle.
drochaid, -e, -ean, *s.f.* Bridge. Bogha drochaide, *an arch* ; balla drochaide, *parapet of a bridge.*
——each, -iche, *a.* Of or belonging to a bridge. 2 Full of bridges.
drochaid-fhiodh,** *s.f.* Wooden bridge.
drochaidich,* *v.a.* Overarch, bridge.
drochaid-thogalach,** *s.f.* Drawbridge.
droch-aigeantach, -aiche, *a.* Furious, violent, mad.
droch-ainm, *s.m.* Bad name.
droch-airidh, *a.* Unworthy, undeserving.
droch-àisteach, see droch-àbhaisteach.
droch-àistean, *for* d— -àbhaistean,*n.pl.* of droch-àbhaist.
drochait, see drochaid.
droch-bhail, see droch-bhuil.
droch-bharail, -alach, -alaichean, *s.f.* Bad prejudice or opinion. 2 Bad guess. Tha d. agam air, *I have a bad opinion of him.*
droch-bhàs, -bhàis, *s.m.* Bad death, used as an imprecation— Droch-bhàs ort ! *bad death to you* !
droch-bheart, -eairt, -an, *s.f.* Vice, evil deed, wickedness, mischief. Ri droch-bheart chuir sinn cùl, *we have forsaken wickedness.*
droch-bheartach, -aiche, *a.* Wicked, vicious, evil-doing, immoral, mischievous.
droch-bheulach, -aiche, *a.* Foul-mouthed.
droch-bheus, -an, *s.m.* Bad behaviour, misconduct, bad breeding, bad morals.
droch-bheusach, -aiche, *a.* Immoral, ill-behaved, ill-bred.
droch-bhlas,** *s.m.* Bad taste. 2(PJM) Disgust. Ghabh mi d. dheth, *I got disgusted with him.*
droch-bholadh, -aidh, -ean, *s.m.* Bad smell, stink.
droch-bhriathar, -air, -an & -thran, *s.m.* Evil expression, bad word.
droch-bhuil, -e, *s.f.* Improper disposal of anything. 2 Evil end, event or fate. 3 (PJM) Want of economy, extravagance. Tha 'n d. air, *he now suffers the evil consequences.*
droch chadal ort ! (imprecation) Bad sleep to you.
droch-chaidreamh, -eimh, *s.f.* Evil communication.
droch-chaingeall,‡‡-eill, -an, *s.m.* Bad covenant.
droch-chainnt, -e, *s.f.* Bad language, swearing.
droch-chlaonadh, -aidh, -ean, *s.m.* Evil inclination, tendency to evil.
droch-chleachdas, see droch-cleachdadh.
droch-chòmhnil, see droch-chòmhdhail.
droch-chomhairle, -an, *s.f.* Bad advice.
droch-chomhairlich,** *v.a.* Misadvise.
droch-chleachdadh,-aidh,-ean & -eachdainnean, *s.m.* Bad practice.
droch-chomhar,** -air, *s.m.* Bad sign.
droch-chomharradh, -aidh, *s.m.* Bad mark, as from a blow.
droch-chòmhdhail, -alach, -ean & -alaichean, *s.f.* Ill-omened meeting. 2‡‡Used as an imprecation.
droch-chomhluadar,-air,*s.m.* Bad conversation. Truaillidh d. deagh-bheusan, *evil communications corrupt good manners.*
droch-chonaltradh,-aidh,*s.m.* Bad conversation.
droch-chreideamh, -eimh, *s.m.* Heresy, unbelief.
droch-chreidmheach, -mhich, *s.m.* Heretic.
——, -mhiche, *a.* Heretic.
droch-chuimhneachan, -ain, -an, *s.m.* Bad remembrance, bitter remembrance.
drochd,** *a.* Black, obscure.
drochdail,** *s.pl.* Bad news.
droch-dhiol, -a, *s.m.* Evil entreating, ill-usage. 2††Used as an imprecation.
droch-dhuine, *pl.* -dhaoine, *s.m.* Bad man, reprobate.
droch-fhacal, -ail, -clan, *s.m.* Bad word, curse, oath, malediction. 2 Bad character of one.
droch-fhàistinn,** *s.f.* Bad report, misinformation. 2 False prophecy. 3 Gloomy prophecy.
droch-fhradharcach, -aiche, *a.* Dim-sighted.
droch-ghaile, see droch-ghoile.
droch-ghean,** *s.m.* Bad humour.
droch-ghnìomh, -a, -aran, *s.m.* Misdeed, crime.
droch-ghnùiseach, -iche, *a.* Ill-favoured, ugly.
droch-ghoile, *s.f.* Dyspepsia, ill-digestion.
——ach, *a.* Dyspeptic.
droch-ghuidhe, -achan, *s.f.* Evil wish. 2 Imprecation. 3 Malediction, curse.
droch-inntinneach, -iche, *a.* Ill-minded, evil-disposed.
droch-iomchar, -air, *s.m.* Ill-conduct, mis-conduct, misdoings. 2 Malapert.
droch-iomradh, -aidh, *s.m.* Evil report, bad fame.
droch-labhartach, *a.* see droch-labhrach.
droch-labhrach, -aiche, *a.* Ill-spoken.
droch-mhanachail,‡‡ *a.* Portentous.
droch-mharbhadh, -aidh, *s.m.* Murder, treacherous homicide.
droch-mheas,‡‡ *s.* Bad opinion, disregard.
droch-mheasta, *a.* Ill-reputed, of bad fame.
droch-mheitealtach, -aiche, *a.* Alloyed.
droch-mhèinn, -e, *s. m.* Grudge, ill-will, malice, spite. 2 Irritability.
droch-mhèinneach, -iche, *a.* Envious, grudging. 2 Touchy, irritable. 3 Malicious. 4 Sinful. 5 Despiteful.
droch-mhèinneachd,** *s.f.* Envy. 2 Despite.
droch-mhisneach, -ich, *s. f.* Pusillanimity. 2 Despondency, low spirits. 3 Cowardice. Cha robh an droch-mhisneach aige, taigh a chur an ordugh, agus gun sgeoil aige air bean, *what a mighty cheek he had, to arrange things (as though all were settled) when he had, as yet, no word of a wife*—i.e. he thought himself cock-sure of victory as a suitor.
droch-mhisneachail, -ala, *a.* Low-spirited, pusillanimous, desponding.
droch-mhisneachd, see droch-mhisneach.
droch-mhuinte, *a.* Malicious, wicked, sinful, vicious. 2 Insolent, ill-bred. 3*Perverse. Air daoinibh d., *on wicked men.*
droch-mhuinteachd,‡‡ *s.f.ind.* Lewdness, wickedness.
droch-mhunadh, -aidh, *s.m.* Bad breeding, insolence. 2*Malice.
droch-nòs,** *s.m.* Bad habit.
droch-nòsach, -aiche, *a.* Immoral.
droch-obair, -oibre, -oibrichean, *s.f.* Bad work. 2 Evil doing, crime. 3 Bad job.
droch-ràit, -e, -ean, *s.f.* Evil saying.
droch-ràitean,(AH) *s.pl.* Fraud, deceit, guile, chicanery, mendacity.
droch-rathaidean, see droch-ràitean.
droch-riaghladh, -aidh, -ean, *s.m.* Misrule, bad management.
droch-rùn, -ùin, -ùintean, *s.m.* Malice, ill-will.
droch-rùnach, *a.* Malicious. 2 Grudging, envious.
droch-rùnachd,** *s.f.* Maliciousness.
droch-sgeul,-sgeòil,*s.m.*Bad story. 2 Bad news or report. 3 Detraction.
droch-shion, -shioin, -shiontan, *s.m.* Bad weather.
droch-sheanachas, *s.m.* Bad language, swearing.
droch-shùil, -shùla, -shùilean, *s. f.* Evil eye, blasting eye.

droch-shùileach, -iche, *a.* Having an evil eye.
droch-spiorad, -aid, -an, *s.m.* The Devil. 2 Any evil spirit. 3 Bad temper.
droch-tharagrach, -aiche, *a.* Ominous.
droch-theanga,†† *s.m.* Bad tongue. 2 Reviling.
droch-theangach, -aiche, *a.* Ill-tongued.
droch-thionnsgnadh, -aidh, -aidhean, *s.m.* Ill-commencement. 2 Evil imagination, conspiracy.
droch-thoillteannach, -aiche, *a.* Ill-deserving.
droch-thoillteannas, -ais, *s.m.* Demerit. 2(PM) Bad crime—*Uist.*
droch-thuairisgeul, -eòil, -an, *s.m.* Bad report, ill-fame. 2** Misinformation.
droch-thuar, -thuair, *s.m.* Bad appearance, bad colour. 2 Bad sign, ill-omen.
drochta-bainne, (AF) s. Milk-tub.
droch-thuigsinn, *s.f.* see mi-thuigsinn.
droch-uair, -e, -ean, *s.f.* Evil hour. 2 (PJM) Danger in a storm on sea or land. [Always used with *a'st* or *a's.*] Puirt a's d., *how very inappropriate* ; gu dè a's d. ach ...., *what happened in an evil moment but....*
†drog, *s. m.* Agitation or motion of the sea, land-swell.
drògaid, -e, -ean, *s.f.* Drugget. 2 Linsey-wolsey. 3 Russet. 4* Anything spoiled by being mixed.
drògh, see dròbh.
drogha, -chan, see dorgh.
†droibheil, *a.* Hard, difficult. 2 Grievous. see draghail.
†droich, *v.n.* Do evil, do wrong. 2 Abuse.
droich, -ean, *s.m.* see troich
droichealachd,* *s.f.* Dwarfishness.
droicheanta, *a.* see droicheil.
†droichead, see drochaid.
droicheil, -ala, *a.* Dwarfish. 2 Hump-backed.
droichein, *dim.* of droich.
†droicheoin, *s. pl.* Deep waters. 2 The deep. 3 Depth.
droichilein, *dim.* of droich. see troichin and troichilein.
droidheachd, see drùidheachd.
†droighean, -in, *s.* The deep. 2 Depth.
droigheann, -inn & **droighne, *s. m.* Thorn, bramble. 2 Blackthorn, sloe. Pàirc an droighne, *the bramble field.*
———— -mu-chrann, *s.m.* Honeysuckle—*Skye.*
———— -dubh,§ *s.m.* Blackthorn, see preas-nan-àirneag.
———— -geal,§ *s.m.* Whitethorn, see sgitheach-geal.
†droigheil, *a.* Active, nimble. 2 Affecting.
droighionn, -inn [& droighne,] see droigheann.
droighneach, -ich, *pl.* -ichean, *s.m.* Thorns. 2 Place where thorns grow. 3 Lumber in one's way. 4 Brake fern. Fuaim droighnich, *the sound of thorns* ; croinn droighnich o 'n ear 's o 'n iar, *thorn trees on either side.*
droighneach, -iche, *a.* Thorny, abounding in thorns, brambly.
droighneag, -eig, *s.f.* Blackthorn, sloe.
droighnean, -ein, *s. m.* Thicket of blackthorn. [Some give -ein, as *n.sing.* and -eine, as *gen.*]
dròilean, -ein, *s.m.* Slow, unhandy person. 2 Cluster.
droimlein, -e, -ean, *s.f.* Alder. 2 Alder bush.
droineach, -iche, *a.* Ragged, *prov.* 2 (PM) Worried with the world—*Uist.*
droineach,**s.f.* Ragged garment.
droineap,* *s.m.* Ragged person. 2 Anything ragged. 3**Tackle, tackling. 4††Sails, canvas. 5††Rag. Gach d. a chrochas ri 'r crannaibh, *every tackle that hangs to our masts.*
droing, -e, *s.m.* People, race, tribe, persons, folk. [** gives *s.f.pl.*]
droinip, see droineap.
droinnse, *s.* Fardel.
droinnseach, see droinnse.
droitseach,(AH) *s. f.* Good deal, considerable quantity or number.
†dròl, -òil, *s.m.* Bay. 2 Plait. 3 Look. 4 Trick, stratagem.
drola, -chan, *s.m.* Pot-hook. 2 Handle of a pot or pan. 3 Chain. 4 Link of a chain. 5(M McL) Noose, loop.
drolabha,(AH) *s.f.* Tug-of-war.
drolabhaid, -e, -ean, *s.f.* Intricacy. 2 Unnecessary lumber, *prov. Drialabhaid* in *Lewis.* 3(PJM) Incorrigible or noisy following. Tha i tighinn, agus an d. 'na déidh, said of an unwelcome visitor, who comes to a house and is followed by several of her family.
drolabhais, -e, *s.f.* see drolabhaid.
dròlabhan, -aid, *s.m.* Good-for-nothing fellow, trifler.
drola-bùlais, s.m. Pot-hook—*Lewis.*
drolach, -aich, *s.m.* Pair of pot-hooks.
drolach, *a.* Abounding in pot-hooks.
drolachan, -ain, -an, *s.m.* Button-neck.
drolag, -aige, -an. *s.f. dim.* of drola Swing. 2 Pastime of moving in a swing. 3 Fulcrum. 4 ††Chain-link.
droll, druill, *s m.* Tail of an animal. 2 Unwieldy stick. 3 Door-bar. 4 Awkward sluggard, idle, inactive person. 5* Back of a beast. 6 Rump. 7 High dudgeon. Cho corrach ri ugh air d., *as tottering, as an egg on a staff.*
drolla,** *s.m.* Pot-hook. 2 **Pair of pot-hooks. 3**Handle of a pot or pan. 4 Loop to go over a button—*Lewis.* D. an osain, *the loop or point of headless stockings, to go over the second and third toes.*
drollach,* *a.* Apt to take great offence.
drollag, see drolag.
drollaire, -an, see dreallaire.
————achd, see dreallaireachd.
drollanta,(PM) *a.* Wanting in energy or spirit —*Uist.*
————chd, *s.f.* Want of energy or spirit—*Uist.*
drolmad-bhainne,(AF) *s.m.* Milk-pitcher.
droma, *gen.sing.* of druim.
dromach,* *s.f.* Back-band of a horse. 2(CR) Saddle-chain of a cart.
————, *a.* see dromanach.
————d,** *s.f.ind.* Affirmation.
dromadair, -ean, see droman. 2**Drummer.
dromainn, *s.f.* see droman (2.)
dromairt,‖ *s. f* Lumbago. [Preceded by the article *an.*]
dromaltach, *s.m.* Vertebra.
droman, -ain, *pl.* -ain & -nan, *s.m.* §Dwarf elder-tree, bore-tree, see ruis. 2 Ridge. 3 Back. 4 Dromedary. 5** Back-band of a horse, when in a cart. 6††Little hill or eminence. Ann an dromannan a chéile gabhar iad, *in the backs of each other (=to grips) they take.*
————ach, -aiche, *a.* Ridgy, ridged, furrowed. 2 Hilly. 3 Like a dromedary. 4 Made of elder-wood, of, pertaining to, or abounding in elder. 5(AH) Back-band of a horse when in a cart.
————ach,** -aich, *s.m.* Place where elders grow. 2(DU) Wooden staple, used for fixing laths over thatch, made of bog-fir and formed by twisting the middle while soft and pliable.
———— -alluidh, see damhan-alluidh.
————na, [a dh— !] *voc. pl.* of druim.
————nan, *pl.* of druim.
dromanta,** *a.* Hunched, humped. 2 Ridged.
†dron. *a.* Right, straight. 2 Sure, steadfast.

†dron, *v.a.* Affirm, assert.
†dronadh, -aidh, *s.m.* Direction.
†dron-dùnadh, -aidh, *s. m.* Shutting, stopping.
drong,† -oing, *s.m.* see droing. 2**Chest, box.
drongair, -ean, *s.m.* Gaelic form of *drunkard.*
———eachd,*s.f.ind.*Drunkenness. [Eng.word.]
†drong-chlann, *s.pl.* Soldiers.
dronn, -uinn & -oinn, *s.f.* Rump, the bard's portion of the mutton. 2 Ridge. 3 Back. 4 Summit. 5 At weddings, the man to whom the *dronn* would come was obliged to make a verse, or *an dubh chapull* would be on him. 6**Hunch. Bho dh. gu troigh, *from ridge to basement (of a house.)*
dronnach,** -aich, *s.m.* White-backed cow.
———, -aiche, *a.* White-backed or rumped. 2 Ridgy. 3**Convex.
———d,‡‡ *s.f.ind.* Convexity.
dronnag, -aige, -an, *s.f.* Ridge of the back. 2 Loin (of flesh.) 3 Hump. 4 Knoll. 5 Chine. 6††Bank. 7 Small burden. 8 Dorn (fish.) 9 Creel-pillow or -pad, placed between creel and back of bearer.—*Lewis.* 10**Summit, highest point of a ridge. 11††Small height or ridge. 12**Cow having a hunched back. 13 (DU) Swing, as used by children—*Gairloch.* Cuan meamnach nan d., *the bounding ridgy ocean.*
dronnagach, -aiche, *a.* Bunchy, ridgy, humped. 2 Full of backs or heights.
dronnain, *gen.sing. & n.pl.* of dronnan.
dronnan, -ain, *s.m.* Back. 2 Ridge. 3 Back or ridge of a hill. 4**Hump on the back.
dronn-chruinn,** *a.* Convex.
dronn-chruinnead,** *s. f.* Convexity.
dronn-chuachach,** *a.* Convexo-concave.
dronn-chuairteach,** *a.* Convex.
dronng, *s.m.* Gaelic form of *trunk.*
———air, *s.m.* see drongair.
———aireachd ‡‡ see drongaireachd.
dronn-sgàit, *s.m.* Trunk of a skate.
dronn-uileann,** *s.f.* -inn, Right angle.
—————each,** *a.* Rectangular.
—————ag,** -aig, *s.f.* Rectangle.
drothan, -ain, -an, *s.m.* Gentle breeze.
———ach, -aiche, *a.* Breezy.
———ach,* -aich, *s.m.* see drothan.
drothlair,** -ean, *s.m.* Carpenter. 2 Waggon-maker. 3 Waggoner.
———eachd,** *s.f.* Occupation of a carpenter or waggon-maker ; or 2 Waggoner.
†dru, *s.m.* Oak.
druabag, -aig, -an, see drùbag.
druablach, *s.f.* see druaip.
druablaich,†† *s.f.* Muddy water, lees.
druablas, -ais, *s.m.* Muddy liquor.
†druadh, *s.m.* see druidh.
druaip, -e, *s.f.* Lees, dregs, sediment. 2 Tippling, debauchery, drinking in bad company. 3 Debauchee. 4**Slops, sloppy potion.
———each, -iche, see druaipeil.
———ear, -eir, -an, *s.m.* Tippler.
———eil, -eala, *a.* Turbid. 2 Addicted to tippling. 3**Having sediment. 4**Sloppy.
———eireachd, *s.f.ind.* Practice of tippling.
†druath,** -aith, *s.m.* Fornication.
drùb, -a, *s. m.* Wink of sleep. 2‡ Mouthful of liquid. Cha d'fhuair mi d. chadail, *I did not get a wink of sleep.*
drùbag, -aig, -an, *s.f.* Little mouthful of liquid.
drùbanta, *a.* Drowsy, sleepy, slumbering.
†drubh, *s.m.* House. 2 Chariot.
drùbhag, -aige, *s.f.* see drùdhag.
†drubhair,** *s.m.* Charioteer. 2 Cartwright, coach-builder. [eer.
drubhaireachd,** *s.f.* Employment of a chariot-2 Occupation of a cartwright or coach-builder.
drùblach, see drùb-shùileach.
drùbladh,(AH) *s.m.* Decanting to the last drop, as liquor from a bottle.
drùb-shùileach, -iche, *a.* Dull-eyed, sleepy-eyed. 2**Dozy.
†druchd, *s.m. & f.* Heaving. 2 Rising up.
drùchd, -an, *s.m.*[**&*f.*] Dew. 2**Drizzling rain. 3 Tear. 4 Sweat. D. gean, *a tear of joy.*
———,* *v.a. & n.* Ooze, emit drops.
———ach, -aiche, *a.* Dewy, like dew. 2 **Drizzly, rainy. 3 Tearful. 4 Oozing. Duilleach d., *dewy foliage.*
———ail,* see drùchdach.
———an, -ain, *s.m.* Drop. 2 Whey. 3(PJM) Hacking of the skin under the great toe in dry weather.
drùchdan-monaidh, *s.m.* Round-leaved sundew, —used for dyeing hair.
drùchd-na-maidne,§ *s.m.* Round-leaved sundew, see ròs-an-t-soluis.
drùchd-na-mòna, see drùchdan-monaidh.
drud, -uid, *s.m.* Enclosure.
drùdh, *v.a. & n.* see drùidh.
drùdhadh, -aidh, see drùidheadh.
drùdhag, *s.f.* Sip, small drop, weak drink.
drug,** *s.* see driug.
drugair,‡ -ean, *s. m.* Drudge, slave, mean swiller.
———eachd, *s.f.ind.* Drudgery, slavery.
drùghadh, -aidh, see drùidheadh. 2**Ascendancy, superiority. 3**Auspice.
druibheal,** -eil, *s.m.* Dark place, recess.
druibhleagan,** *s.m.* Mishmash.
druibleach, see drùb-shùileach.
druichd-a'-mhonaidh, see drùchdan-monaidh.
druid, *pr.pt.* a' druideadh, *v.a.* Shut closely. 2 Cover. 3 Enclose, surround. 4 Advance, come up. 5 Join. 6**Hasten. 7‡‡Step forward. 8**Approach, draw near. Druid-sa gu m' làimh, *hasten to my hand.*
druid,¶-e, -ean, *s.f.* Starling,—*sturnus vulgaris.* 2 Thrush.
druid-bhreac, *s.f.* see druid.
druid-dhubh, *s.f.* see druid. 2 see dubh-chreige.
druideadh,* -idh, *s.m.* Shutting, covering. 2 Act of shutting or covering. 3 Coming forward, approaching. 4* Conclusion, close. A' d—, *pr.pt.* of druid. Naimhdean a' druideadh oirnn, *foes closing in upon us* ; àm druideadh a' gheata, *the time of closing th gate.*
druideag, -eige, -an, *s.f.* Little starling. 2 Little thrush, young thrush.
druidean, *s.m.* see druideag.
druidear, *fut.pass.* of druid. Shall be shut, &c. [** says "Also used impersonally ... prep. *le*, simple or compounded being exp...ed or understood. Druidear (leam) an dorus, *the door shall be closed (by me.)*" All verbs are used impersonally, the prep. *le* being sometimes used, but sometimes not even understood, whereas these remarks seem to show that only *druid* is so treated.]
druide-bòrd, -bùird, *s.m.* Left earth-board of a plough.
drùidh, *v.a. & n.* Penetrate to the skin. 2 Pierce, make an impression, bore through. 3 Drain, pour forth the last drop. 4**Ooze. 5 **Operate upon. 6**Affect, influence. 7**Drop. 8**Distil. Dh. an t-uisg' orm, *the rain has penetrated to my skin* ; 's ann mar sin a dh. e air, *that is how it impressed him,* (or *how he felt it*) ; dh. e an soitheach, *he poured forth the last drop in the dish* ; drùidhidh achmhasan air duine glic, *reproof will affect a wise man.*
druidh, -ean, *s.m.* Druid, magician. 2 Conjurer. 3 Philosopher. 4††Morose person.

No direct native information is available concerning druidism in Scotland or Ireland,

and it is only when Christianity had been long established and druidism had become a thing of the remote past, that we have writers who speak of the druids, and then only refer to them as magicians and diviners, sometimes only as conjurers ; there is no hint of either philosophy or religion in Druidism. They surrounded kings and chiefs. The power of the Tuatha Dé Danann, the pre-eminent masters of druidic art, over the forces of nature shows them to have been degraded gods. The Druids opposed Columba and Patrick with darkness. A blow from their wand caused transformation and spells. Their sacred wood was not the oak, as in Gaul, but yew, hawthorn and especially the rowan. Divination by watching smoke and flame, chewing raw flesh (cf. Fionn's thumb), &c., was one of their chief occupations. Bards were sometimes diviners, thus apparently showing an ancient connection with the Druids. Sometimes we have an echo of the time when Druidism was something more than mere wizardry, and even when human sacrifices were offered (for example, the Columba and Odhran story.) Prof Rhys sums up :— At the time of Cæsar, the Druids were a powerful class—soothsayers, magicians and priests. In Gaul, under the influence of Mediterranean civilization, they were also philosophers, and discoursed on the stars, the world, the nature of things and the power of the gods. Rhys thinks Druidism non-Aryan, MacBain does not.

The following remarks by foreign writers were made while druidism was still practised and full particulars easily obtainable. The accuracy of Latin writers on the military and domestic arrangements of the Celts is well known, so their remarks about the druids are probably quite as reliable.

Diodorus Siculus calls attention to the druidic doctrine that the souls of men were immortal, and that after the lapse of an appointed number of years they came to life again, the soul then entering another body.

Julius Cæsar says the Druids were occupied with religious matters, conducted public and private sacrifices, and interpreted omens. They were the teachers of the country, and judges in public and private disputes, awarding damages and penalties. Any contumacy in reference to their judgments was punished by exclusion from the sacrifices—the severest punishment among Gauls. Men so punished were treated as outlaws. There was one supreme head over the Druids, who, on his death was succeeded by the nearest in dignity, or if several were equal, the successor was chosen by the vote of the Druids. Sometimes the primacy was not decided without arbitrament of arms. Cæsar mentions the belief that their doctrines originated in Britain, and were carried from thence into Gaul. The Druids were immune from military service and payment of tribute. They were said during their training, which sometimes lasted twenty years, to learn by heart a large number of verses. They held it wrong to put their religious teaching in writing. Their cardinal doctrine was the transmigration of souls, and this was a supreme incentive to valour, by making the fear of death count for nothing. They discussed the stars and their motions, the size of the universe and the earth, the nature and the might and power of the immortal gods. They presided at the human sacrifices, which might be public or private.

Cicero says the Druids possessed knowledge of natural science, and foretold the future.

Origen says they practised sorcery.

Strabo refers to them as judges, philosophers and divines, says they were held in exceptional honour, and mentions their belief in immortality. No sacrifice could be made without the presence of a Druid. They were in great request in time of war, being consulted alike by the enemy and those of their own side. Even when two armies were on the point of going to battle, Druids have been able to stop them.

Lucan refers to the seclusion of the Druids' groves and their belief in immortality.

Pliny refers to their veneration of the mistletoe, and the tree on which it grew (if an oak,) hence their predilection for oak-groves, and the requirement of oak-leaves for all religious rites. He mentions a serpent-egg, produced from the frothy sweat of snakes writhing together in a ball.

Ammianus Marcellinus says they were closely linked together into confraternities, and declared the soul immortal.

Cæsar includes under the term *druid* all non-military professional classes—whether priests, seers, teachers, lawyers or judges. To others, druids are philosophers and teachers, and distinguished from seers. To others again, such as Pliny, they were the priests of the oak-ritual, whence their name was derived.—*Extracts from art. by Dr. MacBain in Celtic Mag. 1883-4, and Celtic Religion by Prof. Anwyl.*

druidheach, -iche, *a.* Druidical, magical.
————-d, -an, *s.f.ind.* Magic, sorcery, druidism, enchantment, witchcraft. 2** Charm. Cò a chuir d. oirbh ? *who has bewitched you ?*
drùidheachdainn,* *s.f.* see drùidheadh.
drùidheadh, -idh, *s.m.* Penetrating, piercing. 2 Soaking, oozing through. 3* Impression. 4 Influence. 5**Affecting, as of the feelings. 6**Distillation. Cha d' rinn e an d. a bu lugha air, *it did not make the smallest impression on him.* A' d—, *pr. pt.* of drùidh.
druidhean,§ *s.m.* The stem of the marine plant bàrr-staimh.
druidhean, *nom. pl.* of druidh.
druidheann, see droigheann.
drùidheil, -eala, *a.* Penetrating. 2 Impressive. 3 Bewitching, magical, druidical, pertaining to sorcery.
druidhil, *v.a.* see druighil
druidh-lus,§ *s.m.* Mistletoe, see uil'-ioc.
druidhneach, -ich, *s.m.* see druineach.
drùidte, *past pt.* of drùidh. Penetrated, oozed through.
drùidhteach, -iche, *a.* Impressive, emphatic. 2 Penetrating. 3**Oozing. 4**Enticing. 5 Attractive. 6**Distilling, dropping. Cainnt dh., *impressive* or *emphatic language.*
drùidhteachd, *s.f.ind.* Pathos.
drudidh, *fut. aff. a.* of druid.
druid-mhonaidh, -e-, -ean-,*s.f.* see dubh-chreige.
druidte, *past pt.* of druid. Shut, closed, shut up closely.
druigh, see druidh.
drùigheadh, see drùidheadh.
druighil,** *v.a.* Troll, hurl. 2 Roll together, mix by rolling together. see druithlig.
druighleach, *s.m.* Dregs.
druighleadh,** -idh, *s.m.* Trolling, hurling. 2 Rolling together.
drùighteach, -iche, *a.* see drùidhteach.
druighleagan, -ain, *s.m.* Meal and water

hens' food. (*Scots*, drummock.)
drùighteachd, see drùidhteachd.
druil,** *v.a.* see druighil.
druilinn,** *s.f.* Sudden flash, especially that of iron heated to incandescence, when it is first struck on coming from the forge-fire.
druim, *s.m.irreg.* Declined thus :—

	Sing.	*Plur.*
Nom.	druim,	dromannan,
Gen.	droma,	dhromannan,
Dat.	druim,	dromannan,
Voc.	a dhruim !	a dhromanna !

Back of men or of animals. 2 Ridge of a hill. 3 Roof. 4 Keel of a ship, see bàta, F9, p. 73. 5**Surface. 6(CR) Beam of a plough. 7 (CR) First furrows of a ridge. [6 & 7 *W. of Ross-shire.*] 8 (AH) Crown, in ploughing. Cuir a staigh d., *form a crown* (*in ploughing*); cnàimh an droma, *the back-bone* ; Taigh-an-droma, *the place-name Tyndrum* (the house of the ridge) ; do dhruim nan amadan, *for the back of fools* ; gun d. ach athar, *without roof but the sky* ; air d. a' chuain, *on the face of the sea, in the offing* ; d. nan speur, *the vault of heaven* ; air claisneach a dhroma air leacan loma an ùrlair, *on the furrow of his back on (the) bare flags of the floor* ; d. uachdarach a' chàirein, *the palate or roof of the mouth* ; ann an dromannan a chéile, *wrestling* ; an d. fada, *name of a hill in Corpach.*
druim-bogha,** *s.f.* Vault.
druim-bhreac,** *a.* Having a spotted or speckled back. Bradan d., *a spotted-backed salmon.*
druim-chroinn,** *s.f.* Beam of a plough.
druim-dhonn, *a.* Brown-backed.
druimean,** -ein, *s.m.* Ridge, hill.
————ach, see druimneach. 2**White-backed.
druimfhionn, *a.* White-backed, as of cattle. 2 White-crested, as a wave.
druimionn, see druimfhionn. 2**Ridgy.
druim-luinge,** *s.f.* Keel of a ship.
druimneach, -iche, *a.* Ridged, furrowed. 2 Striped. 3††Full of eminences or backs.
druim-robach, -aiche, *a.* Foul-ridged.
druin,** -e, *s.f.* Needlework, embroidery.
drùin, *v.a.* see dùin.
druineach, Watson in *Place Names of Ross & Cromarty* says, " Sometimes equated with *druidh*. It is based on Old Irish *druin*, glossed *glice*, wise, clever, and *druineach* in Irish means an embroideress. The exact significance of it in our place-names is far from clear. Logan in *Scottish Gael*, takes it to mean cultivators of the soil, as opposed to hunters, which may represent a genuine tradition. Martin makes mention of little round stone houses in Skye, capable of containing only one person, and called *Tey-nan-druinich. Druineach*, says Martin, signifies a retired person much devoted to contemplation.
druinn, *s.m.* Hunch on the back.
druinneach, -ich, *s. m.* see druineach. 2** Artist. 3**Mantua-maker, milliner. 4**Embroiderer. 5**One who works with a needle.
————as,** -ais, *s.m.* Embroidery, tapestry, needlework, tambouring. 2 Millinery, mantua-making.
druinnean, -ein, *s.m.* Little back. 2 Lowest part of the back.
druinnein, *gen. sing.* of druinnean, sometimes used as the *nom.*
————each, -iche, *a.* Hump-backed. 2†† Having a little back.
druinnse, -an, *s.f.* see druinnseach.
druinnseach, -ich, -ichean, *s.m.* Burden.
drùinnsear,** *s.m.* Kidder.
druipe,** *s.f.* Drudge.
drùis, -e, *s.f.* Lust, lasciviousness, lechery. 2 Exudation, perspiration.
drùis,(WC) *s.m.* Noise as of fish frying in a pan. —*Gairloch.* Bha e cho blian nach d' rinn e d., *it was so lean it did not frizzle at all.*
drùis,** *v.n.* Play the wanton, prostitute. Dh. i i-féin, *she prostituted herself.*
druis, see dris.
drùisdear, see drùisear.
————eachd, see drùisearachd.
drùiseach, -iche, *a.* Libidinous, lustful, lecherous. 2**Dewy. 3 Disordered, disorderly.
————, -ich, *s.m.* Lecher.
drùiseadh,** -idh, *s.m.* Whoring, wantoning.
drùiseadh,(WC) *s.m.* Frizzling noise, caused by the contact of such as a red-hot iron with the flesh. Thug an t-iarunn dearg drùiseadh air mo làimh. [*Drùis* is never used in this sense, but *drùiseadh* is sometimes used in the sense given under " druis."] —*Poolewe, &c.*
drùiseag,** -eig, -an, *s.f.* Little prostitute. 2 Young prostitute.
drùisealachd, *s.f.ind.* Lewdness, wantonness, lecherousness. 2 Perspiration. 3* Moisture. 4**Dewiness. 5**Sap.
drùiseamhlachd, see drùisealachd.
†drùiseamhuil, -e, *a.* see drùiseil.
drùisear, -eir, -an, *s.m.* Whoremonger, lecher, fornicator.
————achd,** *s.f.* Whoremongering, lecherousness.
drùiseil, -eala, *a.* Pithy, juicy. 2 Humid. 3 **Dewy. 4 Lustful, libidinous, lascivious.
drùiseir, see drùisear.
drùis-ghalar,‡‡ -air,-an, *s.m.* Venereal affection.
drùis-ghuirean, *s.m.* Pimple.
drùis-lann, *s.m.* } Brothel.
drùis-thaigh, *s.m.* } Brothel.
drùit, *past pt.* see drùidhte.
drùiteach, see drùidhteach.
druiteag,(DU) *s. f.* Driblet, small quantity, usually applied to anything carried on the back. D. mhìne, *a little meal in a bag.*
druithleagan,(CR) *s.m.* Oatmeal dough for feeding chickens—*Perthsh.*
druithlig,(CR) *v.a.* Drill about, drive round about—*Perthsh.* [Scots, dreel.] see druighil.
druith-mhangair, *s.* Pander.
druma, -chan [& -ichean,] *s.f.* Drum. Chluinntear pìob is drumaichean, *pipes and drums might be heard.*
drumach,* see druman.
————,†† *a.* Abounding in drums.
drumadair,** *s.m.* Drum-maker.
drumain, *gen.sing.* of druman.
drumair, -ean, *s.m.* Drummer.
————eachd, *s.f.ind.* Drumming, business of a drummer. 2*Absurd hammering. 3 Noise. 4**Battering. Ciod an d. a th' ort ? *what are you drumming for ?* ri d., *beating the drum.*
druma-lachdan,|| *s.m.* Pain in the spine. [Preceded by the article *an.*] [see drumlachdan.]
druman, -ain, *s.m.* Ridge. 2 Hill. 3 Summit. 4 Little back. 5 Back-band of a cart-horse. 6 § Common elder, bore-tree, boor-tree. 7 Wood of the bore-tree.
————ach, -aich, *s.f.* Ridge-band of a cart. 2 (DU) Wooden staple used in thatching, see dromanach. 3 Elder-tree.
†drumchull, -uill, *s.m.* Topmost thatch.
drumlach, *s.m.* Fishing-rod tackle or line.
————dan,(CR) -ain, Swelling and stiffening of the wrist from unaccustomed work—*W. of Ross-sh.*
drumlaichean, *s.m.* Kind of long sea-weed, of no use, except as manure when nothing else

was obtainable, sea-laces.
drùnadh, -aidh, *s.m. & pr.pt.* see dùnadh.
drunnsail,* *s.f.* Tintillation.
drùs, -ùis, *s.f.* see drùis.
drusag,(WC) *s.f.* Small quantity. D. eallaich, *a little burden,—Poolewe, &c.*
drusdair, see trusdar.
———eachd, see trusdaireachd.
drusdar, see trusdar.
drùs-lann, see drùis-lann.
drùs-thaigh, see drùis-thaigh.
drutaireachd,** *s.f.ind.* Fornication. 2 Filthiness, filth.
drutan,** -ain, *s.m.* Drudge.
drutar, -air, -an, *s.m.* Fornicator. 2 Person of dirty habits.
drùth,‡ *a.* Lecherous, lascivious. 2 Foolish.
drùth,* *s.f.* Harlot.
drùth,** *v.n.* see drùidh.
———ach, -aiche, *a.* Obscene. 2 see drùidhteach.
———achdainn, see drùidheadh.
———aich, -e, *s.f.* Obscenity.
———aidh, *fut. aff. a.* of drùth.
———aidheachd, *s.f.ind.* Obscene *or* filthy language.
drùthail, -ala, *a.* Lascivious, obscene.
druthan, (AF) *s.m.* Snail.
drùthanag,** -aig, -an, *s.f.* Harlot, bawd.
drùth-bhosgair, -ean, *s.m.* Pimp, pander.
drùth-labhair, *v.n.* Blab out.
drùth-lann, see drùis-lann.
drùth-leanabh,** *s.m.* Bastard.
drùth-mhac, -mhic, *s.m.* Bastard son.
drùth-mhangair, see drùth-bhosgair.
drùthta, see drùth.
†drutoir, -e, -ean, *s.m.* Fornicator.
du-,‡ *prefix*, Badness of quality.
du-, *negative prefix*, see do.
†du,** *s.m.* Land, country. 2 Habitation. 3 Place of abode.
dù, *a.* see dùth.
dù, *s.m.* see dùth.
du, *s.m.ind.* see dubh.
duabharachadh,(AH) *s.m.* Vilification, asperation, slander, calumny.
duabharaich, (AC) see duibhrich. 2(AH) Traduce, calumniate, slander, cast asperations.
duad,** *s.m.* Labour. 2 Hardship, difficulty.
†duadh,** -aidh, *s. m.* Labour, hardship. 2 Eating.
†duadhal, *a.* Hard, difficult, laborious.
†———achd, *s.f.* Hardship, difficulty, laboriousness.
†duadhmhor,** *a.* Laborious.
duadh-obair,** -oibre, *s. f.* Hard labour. 2 Handicraft.
†duagh, -an, *s.m.* Cross, affliction, fatigue.
†duaibhseach, -eiche, *a.* Gloomy. 2 Horrible.
duaiceil, -eala, *a.* see duaichnidh.
duaichneachadh, -aidh,*s.m.* Act of making ugly, disfiguring, disfiguration. A' d—, *pr. pt.* of duaichnich.
duaichneachd, *s. f. ind.* Deformity, disfigurement, crookedness. 2 Ugliness. 3**Horridness. 4**Mask. Gu d., *to corruption.*
duaichnich, *pr. pt.* a' duaichneachadh, *v. a.* Deform, deface, disfigure, make ugly, corrupt. 2 Darken. 3**Mask. 4**Delete.
duaichniche,** *s.m.* Disguiser.
duaichnidh, *a.* Deformed, disfigured. 2 Ugly. 3 Gloomy, horrible, dismal, black. 4 Ghastly, death-like. 5**Masked. Tha iad d., *they are black.*
duaichnidheachd, see duaichneachd.
duaidh, -e, -ean, *s.f.* Contest, fight, battle. 2 Evil, mischief. 3 Terrible event, catastrophe. 4 Dreadful scene. Anns an d. sin, *in that dreadful scene.*
———each, -iche, *a.* Mischievous, calamitous.
duaigh, see duaidh.
duaile, *s.f.ind.* Propriety.
duailean, -ein, -an, *s.m.* Little lock of hair.
duailisg,(AC) *s.f.* Fraud, deceit. 2 Stubbornness.
†duaillbhearta, *s.m.* Dialect.
duain,(CR) *pr.pt.* a' duanadh, *v.a.* Close, shut. [Rare in *Suth'd*, common in *Caithness.*]
duain, *gen.sing.* of duan.
duaineil,(CR) *a.* Ugly, ill-looking.—*Suth'd.*
duainidh,(CR) *a.* Bad, ill of look or of conduct. —*W. of Ross.* 2(MM) Fading, going into consumption, (*Scots*, dwine.) Is e rinn d. air, *how badly he treated him*, (e.g. of one who cheated another;) duine d., *a repulsive man— Lewis.*
duairc, -e, *a.* Unpolished, uncivil, unamiable, surly. 2**Stern.
duairc, -e, -ean, *s.m.* Rude, unpolished person, uncivil, stupid person. 2 Unpolished stone. 3* (*s.f.*) Surliness. 4††Vice.
———each, -iche, *a.* Surly, uncivil, unamiable, 2**Stern. 3**Squabbling.
———eag, -eige, -an, *s.f.* Senseless, awkward woman. 2 Surly, ill-natured unamiable woman.
———ean, -ein, *s.m.* Surly, base fellow.
———eas, -eis, see duaireachas.
———eil,* *a.* Unamiable.
———ein, see duaircean.
duaireachadh, -aidh, *s. m.* Slander. Sgeul duaireachaidh, *a slanderous tale.* A' d—, *pr. pt.* of duairich.
duaireachas, -ais, *s.m.* Sternness. 2 Commotion, 3 Sedition. 4 Squabble. 5 Slander. 6**Fray. A' deanamh duaireachais, *raising sedition.*
duaireasach,** *a.* Ungovernable.
————d,** *s.f.* Ungovernableness.
†duairfhine, *s.pl.* Poets.
duairidh, see dubhairidh.
d' uairibh, *adv.* At times, sometimes.
duairich,(DMy) *pr. pt.* a' duaireachadh, *v. n.* Cause one to forsake a familiar haunt. Dh. thu air an taigh e, *you have driven him from the house.*
duais, -ean, *s. f.* Reward, wages. 2 Prize. 3 Bribe. 4**Gains. 5* Premium, present. A' toirt d. seachad, *giving wages ;* d. an uilc, *the wages of sin.*
duais-bhrath,** -bhraith, *s.f.* Bribe, bribery, gains of treachery, traitor's hire.
duais-dhéidheil,‡‡ -e, *a.* Mercenary.
duaiseach, -iche, *a.* Giving a reward. 2 Generous, liberal. Of, or connected with, rewards, wages or bribes.
duaisich,‡‡ *v.a.* Reward. requite.
———e,** -an, *s.m.* Hireling, hired servant.
duaisire,* *s.m.* Rewarder.
duais-thoillteanais, -eis, *s.m.* Merit.
†duaithrichte, see dutharaichte.
dual, -uail, -an, *s.m.* Lock of hair, plait, curl, ringlet. 2 Plait, fold, or strand, in ropes or thread. 3 Braid. 4‡‡Device. 5 Eye-bar of a quern. Còrd thri dual, *a three-plaited cord ;* ceann maiseach nan d., *the handsome head of ringlets.*
dual, -ail, -an, *s.m.* Due, hereditary right. 2 Duty. 3 Office. Bu d. da sin, *that was his birthright.*—This is one of the most familiar and characteristic sayings in Gaeldom, where belief in blood and hereditary tendencies and claims is exceptionally strong. It is difficult to translate literally, but might be paraphrased, " that is what you might ex-

pect of his father and mother's son"—N.G.P. esan do 'n d. am bàs, *he whose due is death* ; bu d. athar dhuit sin, *you inherited that from your father* ; mar bu d. dha, *as was hereditary to him* ; nam b' e nach bu d. da, *if it were (or so happened) that it was not hereditary to him* ; mur b' e gu 'm bu d. da, *were it not that it was hereditary to him* ; do 'n d. gach cliù, *to whom every praise is due.*

dual, -ail, -an, *s.m.* Law. 2‡‡Study.

dual, *pr.pt.* a' dualadh, *v.a.* see dualaich.

dual, *a.* Hereditary. 2 Usual. 3 Natural, due. 4 Probable. Cha bu d. a bhi gun aoidheachd, *it was absolutely opposed to use and wont to be without hospitality.*

dualach, -aiche, *a.* Braided, falling in locks or braids (of hair.) 2 Having luxuriant hair, beautiful. 3*Plaited, in folds. 4**Curled, bushy, as hair. 5**Tressy, 6‡‡Tortuous. 7‡‡ Carved. Falt dubh d., *black and curled hair* ; a chiabhan d., *his bushy locks* ; còrd d., *a plaited rope.*

dualach,‡‡ -aiche, *a.* Hereditary.

dualachan,** -ain, *s.m.* Toil-maker.

dualachas, -ais, see dualchas.

dualadair, -ean, *s.m.* Embroiderer. 2 Carver. 3 Plaiter, one who plaits. 4 Cordwainer.

————eachd,**s.f.* Business of a cordwainer. 2**Plaiting. 3**Carving. 4**Embroidery, embroidering.

dualadh, -aidh, *s. m.* Carving, act of carving. 2 Plaiting. 3**Embroidery. 4** Fold, plait. 5**Ringlet. A' d—, *pr.pt.* of dual. 'Na dh. liath, *in his grey ringlets.*

dualaich, *pr.pt.* a' dualachadh, *v.a.* Twist, plait. 2 Carve. 3 Braid. 4**Loop, curl, as hair. 5 **Engrave. 6**Weave. 7 Fold. 8††Link.

————, *gen. sing.* of dualach.

————e, -an, *s. m.* Carver. 2 Engraver. 3 Sculptor. 4 Plaiter.

————eas, *s.m.* Sculpture. 2 Engraving.

dualan, -ain, -an, *s. m. dim.* of dual. Little lock, tress or ringlet.

————ach, *a.* Abounding in small locks, tresses or ringlets.

dual-bheurla, see dual-chainnt.

————ch, -aiche, see dual-chainnteach.

dual-bhruidhinn, -inn, *s.f.* see dual-chainnt.

dual-chainnt, -e, *s.f.* Dialect, branch of a language.

————each, -iche, *a.* Dialectic.

dualchas, -ais, *s.m.* Hereditary disposition or right. 2 (DMy) Imitation of the ways of one's ancestors. 3 Bias of character. 4**Nature, temper. 5**Native place. 6**Hire, wages, dues. 6**Duty. 'S e do dh. a bhi duineil, *it is thy (hereditary) nature to be manly.*

————ach, -aiche, *a.* Derived from ancestors, acquired by birth or parentage.

†duam,** -aim, *s.m.* City.

duan, -ain, *pl.*-ain, *s.m.* Poem, canto. 2 Ode, song, ditty. 3 Oration, harangue. D. molaidh, *a panegyric* ; d. mórdha, *an heroic poem* ; duan bhreug, *a rhyme of lies, a false story.—Poolewe.*

duanach, -aiche, *a.* Of, or belonging to, poems, odes, songs or harangues. 2 Poetical, in verse 3 Melodious, tuneful.

————adh, -aidh, *s.m.* see duanaireachd.

————d, see duanaireachd.

duanag, -aige, -an, *s.f. dim.* of duan. Little song, ode, little poem, catch, glee, sonnet, ditty, canto.

————ach,†† *a.* Abounding in little songs or odes.

duanaiche, see duanaire.

duanaire, -an, *s.m.* Chanter, reciter of rhymes. 2 Rhymer, bard, versifier, songster.

duanaireachd, *s. f. ind.* Chanting, rhyming, poetry, versification.

†duanartach,** *s.m.* Senator.

†duan-chruitheachd, *s.f.* Policy.*

duan-mór, -ain-mhóra, *s.m.* Epic poem. (*lit.* a great poem.)

duan-nasg, -naisg, -an, *s.m.* Collection of poems

duantach, -aiche, see duanach.

duantachd, see duanachd.

duantaireachd, see duanaireachd.

†duar, -air, *s.m.* Word, saying. 2 Verse, metre

duarman, -ain, -an, *s.m.* Murmur, growl.

————ach,** *a.* Murmuring.

————achd, see duarmanaich.

————aich, -e, *s.f.* Murmuring, grumbling, expression of discontent.

duarmanaiche,** *s.m.* Grumbler.

†duas, -ais, *s.m.* Poet.

duasach,** *a.* Inauspicious.

————d, *s.f.* Inauspiciousness.

duathar, -air, *s.m.* see dubhar.

————ach, -aiche, see dubharach.

†dub,‖ s. Bile.

†dub, *v.a.* Dip. 2 Dub.

†dubadh, -aidh, *s.m.* Pond.

dùbail, *pr.pt.* a' dùbladh, *v.a.* see dùblaich.

————te, *a.* & *past pt.* of dùbail. Doubled. 2 Ambiguous. 3 Double-minded. 4**Cunning, false. 5 Double, twofold. Duine d., *a deceitful person* ; uisge-beatha d., *double-distilled whisky*—this ex. from ** is a translation from English, the correct Gaelic form being *uisge-beatha da-tharruingte* or *air a dha-tharruing.*

————teachd, *s.f.ind.* Disingenuousness, dissimulation, duplicity, deceit. 2**Ambiguity.

dubairt,** *s.f.* Earnest prayer.

dubh, duibhe, *a.* Black. 2 Dark. 3 Sad, mournful. 4* Disastrous. 5 Lean, as flesh. 6 Sable, *in heraldry.* 7**Dark-haired. 8**Wicked. 9***rarely* Great. Bu d. a sgeul, *sad was his tale* ; daol d., *a black beetle* ; is d. an t-sùil a tha 'nad cheann, *black is the eye in your head*—this expression is used when it is wished to imply that some one concerned in a misdemeanor escaped scatheless—cha d'thubhairt e rium is d. an t-sùil a tha 'nad cheann, *he was not able to congratulate me on my escape* ; neòil dubha (*not* dhubha) na Càisge, *the five days before Easter Sunday.* D. is also used for emphasis, thug iad géill agus dubh ghéill, *they gave it up, yielded totally.* 276. Dubh.

dubh, duibh, *s.m.* Blackness. 2 Darkness. 3 Ink. 4 Pupil of the eye. A' cur an duibh air a' ghcal, *putting black on the white*—prevaricating, telling lies ; cha robh a dhubh no a dhath ri fhaicinn, *he was not to be seen anywhere (alive or dead.)*

dubh, *pr.pt.* a' dubhadh, *v.a.* Blacken. 2 Blot out. 3 Darken. 4 Condemn. 5**Stain.

dubhach, -aiche, *a.* Sad, mournful, sorrowful, melancholy. 2 Disastrous. 3 Dark, gloomy. 4**Frowning. Aodach d., *mourning clothes* ; òighean d., *mourning maidens* ; a shùil a' siubhal gu d., *his eye moving darkly* or *frowning.*

dubhach, -ich, *s.m.* Blacking. 2**Ink. 3 Inkstand. 4 Black dye. 5**Tub. D. bhròg, *shoe-blacking* ; d. cobhain, *lamp-black.*

dubhachail,** *a.* Hypochondriac.

dubhachais, *gen.sing.* of dubhachas.

dubhachas, -ais, *s.m.* Sadness, sorrow, melancholy. 2 Darkness, duskiness. 3**Bitterness.

dubhadair,** *s.m.* Ink maker.

dubhadan, -ain, *pl.* -an & -ain, *s.m.* [* gives *s.f.*] Ink-holder, standish. 2**Soot. 3**Blacking.

4**Ink.
———ach,** *a.* Inky. 2 Black. 3 Sooty.
dubhadh, -aidh, *s.m.* Act of blacking, or darkening. 2 Any kind of substance that dyes black. 3**Mourning. 4**Obscurity, darkness, blackness. 5**Ink. 6**Any black substance. 7**Blotting. 8**Staining. 9**Condemning. A' d—, *pr.pt.* of dubh. D. nan speur, *the darkness of the skies.*
dubhag, -aig, -an, *s.f.* Kidney. 2**Name given in disrespect to a young female. 3 Deep, dark pool. 4(AF)Little black cow. Thèid d. ri dualchas, *like mother like daughter.*
———an, -ain, *s. m.* Deep gulf. 2 Deepest part of a stream or pool. 3**Ink. 4**Blacking. 5**Pupil of the eye. 6**Ink-standish. D. na sùla, *the pupil of the eye.*
dubh-aghaidh,** *s.m. & f.* Black or dark visage. 2 Dark aspect. 3 Dark surface.
dubhaich, *v.a.* Blacken, darken, blot out, shade.
———, -e, see dubhachas.
———e, *comp.* of dubhach.
dubh-aigeann, *s.m.* The deep, the ocean. 2 Abyss. 3 Bottom of an abyss. D. na fairge, *the bottomless depths of the sea.*
dubhailc, -e, -ean, *s. f.* Vice, wickedness. Comharraichte an d., *noted for vice.*
———each, -iche, *a.* Vicious, wicked.
———each, -ich, *s.m.* Wicked person.
dubhailt,** *s.f.* Darkness, gloom.
———each, -iche, *a.* Sorrowful, sad. 2 Dark, gloomy.
———each, -eich, *s.m.* Sorrow, sadness.
dubhain, *gen.sing. & n.pl.* of dubhan.
dubhair, *v.a.* Darken, shade.
———, *gen.sing.* of dubhar.
———iche,** *s.f.* Jointress.
———idh, *s.f.* Dowry.
dubhairt, (*for* thubhairt) *past interr. & neg.* of abair.
dùbhaith, -e, -ean, *s.f.* Pudding.
†dubhalladh, -aidh, *s.m.* Want.
dubhan, -ain, *s.m.* Hook, fishing-hook. 2 Hooked claw, as of cats. 3* Clutch. 4**Snare. 5 **Kidney. 6**Darkness. 7**Soot. 8 (AF) Blackbird—*Dean of Lismore.* 9(AF)Spider. 'Nad dhubhain, *in thy clutches;* d. busgainte, *a baited fishing-hook* ; d. cuileig, *a fly-hook ;* dubhain na briogais, *breeching-hooks of a cart —Lewis* ; d. an t-siuil, *the sail-hook.*
———ach, -aiche, *a.* Hooked, of, belonging to, or abounding in, hooks or claws.
———achadh,(AH) -aidh, *s.m.* Set to, shindy, spar, pugilism, wrestling.
dubhanaich,(AH) *v.a.* Exchange fisticuffs, spar, wrestle, strive, struggle, scramble.
——— -alluidh, see damhan-alluidh.
dubhan-ceann-còsach, [dubhan, *kidney*+ceann, *head*+còsach, *spongy.*§] Self-heal — *prunella vulgaris.* [Also called, devil's bit and all-heal.]

277. *Dubhan-ceann-chòsach.*

278. *Dubhan-nan-caorach.*

dubhan-deiridh, *s.m.* Runner of a cart—*Lewis.*
——— -guaille, Draught-hook of a cart—*Lewis.*
——— -iasgaich,** *s.m.* Fishing-hook.
——— -nan-caorach,§ -ain-, *s. m.* Sheep-bit—*jasione montana.* [Also called, sheep-scabious.]
——— slabhruidh,(WC) *s.m.* Hook for hanging a pot over the fire.
——— -toisich, *s.m.* Draught-hook of a cart—*Lewis.*
dubhanuith,§ see dubhan-ceann-chòsach.
dubhar, -air, *s.m.* Shade, darkness. 2 Eclipse. 3**Gloom. Tha anam an rìgh mar dh. na h-uaighe, *the soul of the king is like the darkness of the grave* ; d. an fheasgair, *the dusk of evening;* d. a' cheò, *the darkness of mist* ; fo dh. géige, *under the shadow of a branch.*
———ach, -riche, *a.* Shady, shading, shadowy, opaque, dusky, dark, cloudy, gloomy. An oidhche dh., *the gloomy night.*
———ach, -aiche, *s.f.* see dubharachd.
———achd, *s.f.* Shade, darkness. 2 Shady or dusky place. 3 Opacity. 4 Eclipse of the sun or moon. 5**Duskiness. 6**Cloudiness.
———adh,** -aidh, *s.m.* Shadowing, darkening. 2 Darkness, shade, duskiness. 3 Eclipse. D. gréine, *a solar eclipse* ; d. gealaich, *a lunar eclipse.*
dubharaich,* see duibhrich.
———te, see duibhrichte.
dubharaidh, -ean, see dubhairidh.
dubharan, *n.pl.* of dubhar.
dubhas,** -ais, *s.m.* Sorrow.
dubh-bhannach, -aiche, *s.f.* Gun.
dubh-bhileach, *s.m.* Club (in playing-cards.)
dubh-bhlianach, -aiche, *s.f.* Lean carcase. 2†† Lean or meagre flesh.
dubh-bhreac, -bhric, *s. m.* Black trout. 2†† Large trout. 3**Smelt. 4**Spirling.
dubh-bhrochan, (AH) *s. m.* Very thin porridge, porridge of a liquid consistency.
dubh-bhròn, -òin, *s.m.* Deep sorrow.
———ach, *a.* Disconsolate.
dubh-bhuidhe,** *a.* Livid. 2 Dark yellow. 3 Black and yellow. Chinn an speur gu d., *the sky became a dark yellow.*
dubh-bhuille,** *s.m.* Fatal blow.
dubh-chaile, -an, *s.f.* Scullion, trollop. 2 Girl of the lowest rank of peasantry. D. a' bhuaraich, *the dunghill trollop.*
dubh-chall, -a, *s.m.* Perdition.
dubh-chapull, *s.* Chuir e 'n dubh-chapull air, *he quite outdid him.* This is a Lochaber phrase of unknown origin. It used to be the practice at weddings to have a pleasant competition in singing between two parties—often the bride's against the bridegroom's. The side that held out longest would then say to the others "an dubh-chapull oirbh !"
dubh-chasach, -aiche, *s. f,* Black spleenwort — *asplenium trichomanes.* 2 Maidenhair, maidenhair spleenwort. 3**Black-foot, black-leg.
———, *a.* Black-legged, black-footed.
dubh-cheannach, -aich, see faoileag.
———, -aiche, *a.* Black-faced. Caora dh., *a black-faced sheep.*
dubh-cheathach,** -aich, *s. m.* Black mist, thick mist.
dubh-cheist, ** -ean, *s, f.* Puzzle, enigma. 2 Motto, superscription.

279. *Dubh-chasach.*

dubh-chiabhach, -aiche, *a.* Black- or dark-haired.

dubh-chìos, -a, see dubh-chìs.
dubh-chìs, -e, *s.f.* Tribute, tax. 2 Black-mail.
dubh-chladach, *s.m.* Flood-mark. 2 High-water mark of ordinary spring tides.
dubh-chleas,** *s.* Feat in legerdemain or black-art.
dubh-chleasachd,** *s.f.* Black-art.
——————ail, -e, *a.* Necromantic.
dubh-chleasaiche,** *s. m.* Adept in black-art, conjurer.
dubh-chléin, -e, -ean, *s.f.* The flank, spleen.
dubh-choimeasg,** *s.m.* Chaos [Preceded by art. *an.*]
dubh-choitchinn, see dubh-choitchionn.
dubh-choitchionn, -a, -an, *s.f.* Common prostitute.
dubh-chosach,** see dubh-chasach.
dubh-chosnadh, *s.m.* Field-work. Is bochd am pòsadh nach fearr na 'n d., *it is a poor marriage that is not better than field-work.*
dubh-chreag, *s.f.* Gloomy rock.
dubh-chreige, -an, *s.f.* Ring-ouzel or mountain blackbird—*turdus torquatus.* 2**Gloomy rock.

280. Dubh-chreige.

dubh-chriothnaich, *v.a.* Convulse.
dubh-chùil, *s.f.* Beetle.
dubh-chomharrachaidh, *s.m.* Marking-ink.
dùbhdach, see dùdach.
dùbhdair, see dùdair.
————eachd, see dùdaireachd.
dùbhdan, -ain, *s.m.* Smoke. 2 Smothered flame. 3 Cinders of burnt straw. 4‡ Soot.
————ach, -aiche, *a.* Sooty. 2 Smoky.
dubh-dhaol, -aoil, -an, *s.f.* Beetle.
dubh-dhearg, -dheirge, *a.* Dark red, liver-colour. [** gives *auburn, russet, dark brown.*]
dubh-dhonn, -dhuinne, *a.* Dark brown. 2 Auburn, russet. 3* Drab, dun, dusky. Falt d., *auburn hair.*
dubh-dhorch,** *a.* Pitchy dark.
dubh-dhorcha,‡‡ -dhuirche, *a.* Pitchy.
——————das, -ais, *s.m.* Pitchiness, pitchy darkness.
dubh-dhruim,†† -dhroma, *s.f.* Dark surface. 2 Dark height. 3 Black back. 4 Black ridge. D. na mara, *the dark surface of the sea.*
dubh-eun,** *s.m.* Diver (bird.)
————ach(AF) *s. m.* Razor-bill, see coltraiche.
dubh-fhacal, -ail -fhaclan, *s.m.* Riddle, puzzle, enigma, parable, dark saying. 2 Bad expression.
dubh-fhaclach, -aiche, *a.* Obscure, enigmatical.
dubh-fhàd, *s.m.* Second or lowest peat—*Suth'd.*
dubh-fhalt,** -fhuilt, *s.m.* Black hair.
dubh-fhaoileann,(AF) Large gull.
dubh-fhiamhach, -aiche, *a.* Blackish.
dubh-fhiodh,§ Ebony—*diospyros ebenus.*
dubh-fhuathaich,‡‡ *v.a.* Loathe.
dubh-ghalar, -air, -an, *s.m.* Looseness, disease in cattle, see dubh-thuil.
Dubh-Ghall, -aill,*s.m.*[*&*f.*] Lowlander,foreigner. 2 Dane. 3††Real Lowlander. 4 *in contempt* Mean-spirited fellow.
dubh-ghlac, -aic, -an, *s.f.* Dark valley. [†† gives dubh-ghlaic as *nom.*]
dubh-ghlas, -aise, *a.* Dark grey, dark drab.
dubh-ghleann,** -ghlinn, *s.m.* Gloomy vale.
dubh-ghnosach,** *a.* Black-mouthed.
dubh-ghnùiseach, -eiche, *a.* Blackfaced.
dubh-ghorm, -ghuirme, *a.* Dark blue, black and blue.
dubh-ghormadh,** -aidh, *s. m.* Making dark blue, making black and blue, generally applied to change of colour through cold.
dubh-ghràin, -e, *s.f.* Abhorrence, extreme disgust.
——————ealachd,** *s.f.* Abhorrence, abomination.
——————eil, -eala, *a.* Abhorring, extremely disgusting.
——————ich,* *v.a.* Detest, abhor.
dubh-ghruaim, -e, *s.f.* Dark frown.
dubh-ghruamach, *a.* Dark-frowning.
dubh-là, -laithean, *s.m.* Mournful day, day of temptation or trial. Cumaibh an d. air chuimhne, *keep the mournful day in mind.*
Dùbhlach, -aich, *s.m.* see Dùdlachd.
dubh-lach,(AF)*s.f.* Bald coot, see lach-a'-bhlàir.
dùbhlachadh,** -aidh, *s.m* see dùblachadh.
dubh-lachadh,** -aidh, *s.m.* Coot.
dùbhlachd, *s.f.ind.* see Dùdlachd.
————ail,* *a.* Wintry.
dùbhlaidh, -e, *a.* Gloomy, dark. 2 Wintry. 3 Dark-coloured. 4**Tempestuous. Gu d., *darkly.*
————eachd,* *s.f.ind.* Darkishness. 2 Dark blue. 3**Wintriness, tempestuousness.
dùbhlaith, -e, *a.* Melancholy.
————each,** *a.* Melancholic.
dùbhlan, -ain, *s.m.* Challenge, defiance. 2*Hardihood, capability of bearing cold, hardship and want. Cuir gu d., *set at defiance* ; 'nuair a théid duine g' a dh., *when a person is roused* ; a' toirt dùbhlain, *challenging.*
————ach, -aiche, *a.* Defying, challenging, 2 Bold, fearless, daring, brave. 3*Capable of bearing cold and fatigue. Gu d., *proudly, in defiance.*
————achadh, -aidh, *s.m.* Challenging, defying. A' d—, *pr.pt.* of dùbhlanaich.
————achd, *s.f.ind.* Challenging, defiance. 2 *Hardihood, degree of bravery, fearlessness.
dùbhlanaich, *pr. pt.* a' dùbhlanachadh, *v.a.* Challenge, defy, set at defiance.
——————te, *past pt.* of dùbhlanaich.
dubh-latha, see dubh-là.
dubh-leann, *s.* Melancholy, see leann-dubh.
——————ach, -aiche, *a.* Melancholic.
——————achd,*s.f.ind* Woe, sorrow, melancholy, depression of spirits.
dubh-leum, see duibh-leum.
dubh-liath, -léithe, see dubh-chléin.
——————, *a.* Ash-coloured, dark grey.
dubh-lith, -e, *a.* see dubhlaidh.
dubh-liunn, see leann-dubh.
dubh-lochan,(AF) *s.m.* Trout.
dubh-loisg,* *v.a.* Burn to a cinder.
——————te, *a.* & *past pt.* Burnt black, burnt to a cinder.
dubh-losgadh, -aidh, *s.m.* Thorough burning,incineration.
dubh-mhèarsadh,** -aidh, *s.m.* Procession.
dubh-neul, see duibh-neul.
Dubh-nimhe, *s.* The name of Caoilte's banner.
dubh-ogha, *s.m.* Great grandson's grandson. [*Dubh* is used to add a step to *fionn-ogha,* though *fionn* here is really a prep. and not fionn, *white.*]

dùbhra, duibhre, see dùbhradh.
———,** *a.* Dark, gloomy.
dùbhrach, -aiche, *a.* see dùbharach.
———d, -an, *s.m.* see dùrachd.
———dach, -aiche, *a.* see dùrachdach.
dubhradan, -ain, *s. m.* Sable. 2 Used by * for dùradan.
dùbhradar, *impers. v.* They said (abair.)
dùbhradh, *v.* It was said.
dùbhradh, -aidh, -aidhean, *s.m.* Shade, shading, shadiness, gloom, darkening, darkness. 2 Sternness. 3* Dark object in the distance. 4 **Spectre. D. m' an gruaidh, *sternness in their visage.* A' d—, *pr.pt.* of dubhair.
†dubhram, (*for* thubhairt mi) I said.
dubh-rann, *s.m.* Blank verse.
dubhras,** -ais, *s.m.* Gloomy wood. †2 House, room, habitation.
†dubhras (*for* thubhairt mi.)
dubh-reabha,(CR) *s.m.* Mole.
dubh-reabhgan, *s.m.* Mole.
du'-bhreac, see dubh-bhreac.
dubh-reotha, see dubh-reabha.
dubh-reothadh,** *s.m.* Black frost. Smùidrich an dubh-reòthaidh, *the mist of black frost.*
———,** *s.f.* Mole.
du'-bhròn, -bhròin, see dubh-bhròn.
———ach, -aiche, *a.* see dubh-bhrònach.
dubh-ruadh, -ruaidhe, *a.* Dark red, *auburn.
dubh-ruith, -e, *s.f.* Swift running, running at full speed, furious running.
dubh-sgiathach,** *a.* Dark-winged.
dubh-sgithich, *v.a.* Harass, overlabour.
dubh-shiubhal,** -ail, *s.m.* Dark stream. 2 Progress of a dark stream. 3 Dark path. 4 Miserable journey. D. na linn, *the dark rolling of the abyss.*
———, -aile, *a.* Dark rolling, as of waters.
dubh-shiùbhlach, -aiche, *a.* Dark-rolling.
———,* -aiche, *s.f.* Strolling female or gipsy.
dubh-shnàmh, *v.a.* Dive.
———aiche, -an, *s.m.* Diver, (waterfowl.)
dubh-shnàmhair, see dubh-shnàmhaiche.
dubh-shùileach, -iche, *a.* Black-eyed.
dubh-shnagan,¶*s.m.* Water-rail, see snagan-allt.
dubh'e, *past pt.* of dubh. Cancelled, blotted, blackened. [see foot-note, p. 53.]
dubhtach, see dùdach.
dubhtharach, -aiche, see dubharach.
dubh-thoill, *s.f.* Hæmorrhoids.
dubh-thonn, -thuinn, *s.* Gloomy wave.
dubh-thràth, *s.m.* Evening twilight.
dubh-threabha,(CR)*s.m.* Ground mole—*Perthsh.*
dubh-thriall,** *s.m.* Procession. [art. *an.*]
dubhthuil,|| *s. f.* Diarrhœa. [Preceded by the
dùblachadh, -aidh, *s.m.* Double, duplicate. 2 Act of doubling or folding. 3* Distilling the second time. 4 Copying. A' d—, *pr. pt.* of dùblaich.
dùbladh, -aidh, -aidhean, *s. m.* Doubling. 2 Covering, lining. 3**Sheath, scabbard, case.
dùblaich, *pr.pt.* a' dùblachadh, *v. a.* Double, fold. 2 Repeat. 3 Distil a second time.
———te, *past pt.* of dùblaich.
dùblainn,** *v.a.* see dùblaich.
———,** *s.* Double quantity, as much again.
dublas,(AH) *s.m.* [sometimes *f.*] Distasteful, unpalatable infusion, as badly made tea, soup or broth.
dù'-breac, see dubh-bhreac.
dù'-brònach, see dubh-bhrònach
dùc, -a -an, *s.m.* Heap, hillock, *prov.*
dùcain, *gen. sing. & n.pl.* of dùcan.
dùcait, -ean, *s.f.* Ducat (coin.)
dùcan,** -ain, *s.m.* Little heap, little hillock—*Perthshire.* D. dubh -threabha, *a mole—Perthshire.*
dùcanach, -aiche,***a.* Full of hillocks or heaps.
dùcan-faimh, *s.m.* Mole-hill.
dùcan-uir-faimh, *s.m.* Mole-hill.
duch,(CR) *s.m.* Nightfall (only in the phrase "bho mhuch gu duch," *from morning till night.—Suth'd & Perthsh.* [*Generally* o mhoch gu dubh.]
ducha, *for* dùtha, *comp.* of dùth.
†duchan, -ain, *s.m.* War.
dùchannaibh, (*for* dùthchannaibh.)
dùchas, -ais, see dùthchas.
dùchasach, see dùthchasach.
dùd, dùid, -an, *s.m.* Tingling of the ear. 2 The ear. 3 Horn. 4 Blast of a horn. 5* Hollow sound. 6**Rag. 7††Word, sound.
dud,* *s.m.* see tudan.
dudach,** -aiche, *a.* Ragged. 2 Thin-skinned. Cho d. ri circ, *as thin-skinned as a hen.*
dùdach, -aiche, -aichean, *s.f.* Sounding horn, bugle, war-horn, trumpet. D. sheilge, *a hunting horn.*
dùdag, -aige, -an, *s.f.* Little horn, little bugle.
dudag,** -aige, -an, *s.f.* Rag. 2 Small cup. 3 Measure of liquids, containing a drachm, and commonly made of horn. 4 Slight stroke on the ear. 5 Ragged girl.
dùdair, -ean, *s.m.* Trumpeter. [†† & * give -e as *n. sing.*]
———eachd, *s.f.ind.* Noise of horns or trumpets. 2 Act of sounding a horn. 3**Sound of a hunting horn.
dùdan, -ain, *s.m.* Mill-dust. 2 Beard of dried oats. 3 (MM) Short pipe [*Irish,* dùidín.]
dudarlach, -aich, *s.m.* Paltry wretch.
dù-dhearg,* *a.* see dubh-dhearg.
dùdlach, -aich, *a.* Stormy, wintry, gloomy, dark, dismal.
Dùdlachd, *s.f.ind.* Depth of winter. 2 Tempestuous weather. 3 Gloominess, dreariness. 4 Month of December [preceded by the art. an.] 5††Storm. D. a' gheamhraidh, *the depth of winter.*
dùdlaich, *v.a.* Darken, make gloomy. 2 Frown.
dùdlaidh, -e, *a.* Dark, gloomy, sad.
dùgh, see dùth.
dùghaich, *s.f.* One of the intestines—*Sgeulaiche nan Caol.*
dughall, -aill, see dubh-ghall.
dugharra, *a.* Stubborn.
dùghlas, see dubh-ghlas.
duibh, *prep. pron.* To you. *Emphatic form,* duibh-se. An cadal duibh ? *are you asleep ?*
duibh, *gen. sing. m.* of dubh.
duibhe, *comp.* of dubh. Is d. na neul fo 'ghaoith, *darker than the wind-driven cloud.*
duibhe, *s.f.ind.* Blackness, darkness, inkiness. 2**Ink. 3(AC) Spaul.
———ad, -eid, *s.m.* Degree of blackness. A' dol an d., *growing blacker and blacker* ; air a dh., *however black it be.*
duibheagan,** -ain, *s.m.* Abyss. 2 Dagger, short sword.
†duibhearach,** *a.* Vernacular.
duibheid, -ean, *s.f.* Flat turf used for covering cottages, " divot."
———ich,** *v.a.* Cover with turf, as the roof of a cottage.
duibhir,** *a.* Melancholy. 2 Anxious. 3 Gloomy.
†duibheilneach, -ich, *s.m.* Necromancer.
†duibhghean, -ein, *s.m.* Sword, dagger.
†duibhghein, -e, -ean, *s.m. & f.* Foreigner.
duibh-leas, see duibh-leus.
duibh-leum, -léim, *pl.* -a, & -annan, *s.m.* Leap in the dark. 2* Bound, leap. 3* Sudden leap

—*Argyllshire.* [†† gives *s.f.*] Feithidh fear sona ri sìth, ach bheir am fear dona d., *a well-advised person will bide his time, but a fool will leap in the dark.*

duibh-leus, -leòis, *s.m.* Shade, cloud.

———ach, -aiche, *a.* Cloudy, shadowy.

duibh-neul, -neòil, *s.m.* Dark cloud. 2**Dark colour. 3**Swarthy complexion. 4 Gloomy aspect.

duibh-neul,** *v.a.* Darken.

———ach, -aiche, *a.* Dark clouded, murky, 2 Dark visaged. 3 Frowning.

duibhre, *s f. ind.* Gloom, shade, obscurity, darkness. 2 Melancholy, sadness. An d. bàis, *in the darkness of death* ; mar bhruaich 'san d., *like a precipice in the dark.*

duibhreas, -eis, *s.m.* Darkness. 2 Mysteriousness, secrecy, secret.

duibhrich, *v.a.* Shade, eclipse, darken.

———te, *past pt.* of duibhrich. Shaded, darkened, eclipsed.

duibh-rith, -e, *s.f.* see dubh-ruith.

duibh-se, *emphatic* form of duibh.

duibleid,** *s.f.* Gaelic spelling of *doublet.*

duibreac,* *s.m.* Spirling.

duidhean, *s.m.* The stem of the langadar, a kind of seaweed. J. Cameron (§) seems to be in error when he confounds this with *stamh.*

dui-eunach,¶ *s.m.* Razor-bill, see coltraiche.

†**duigh**, *v.n.* Cluck, as a hen.

dùigh,** *s.* Poison.

dùil, -e, -ean, *s.f.* Hope, expectation. 2 Belief. 3 Supposition. 4 Desire. 5 Delight. Tha d. againn, *we expect* ; tha mi 'n d., *I expect, imagine, suppose, hope* ; am bheil d. agad ? *do you suppose ?* an d. r' a theachd, *in expectation of his coming* ; thug sinn ar d. dheth, *we lost all expectation of him* ; is beag d. a bh' agamsa, *little did I expect* ; tha d. agam ris, *I expect him* ; am bheil d. agaibh ris ? *do you expect him ?* chaill sinn ar d. dheth, *we lost all expectation of him* ; cha'n 'eil d. no sùil agam ris, *I neither hope nor look for him* ; is d. leam nach cian an t-àm, *I expect the time is not distant.*

dùil, -e, *n.pl.* dùilidh, dùil, dùilinn, dùiltean & dùilean, *gen. pl.* dùl, *s.f.* Element. 2 Animal, being, creature. 3 Nature. 4**Partition. Na duil ! *poor creatures !* gach d. bheò, *every living creature* ; leaghaidh na dùilidh, *the elements shall melt.*

dùil,* *v.a.* Hoop or thread, as a hook—*Perthsh.*

duilbhear,** *a.* Sad, anxious, melancholy, cheerless, unpleasant. [The opposite of suilbhir.]

———achd,** *s.f.* Sadness, anxiety, suspense, melancholy. [The opposite of suilbhearachd.]

———ra, *a.* Sad, anxious, melancholy, cheerless, unpleasant. [The opposite of suilbhearra.]

———rachd, *s.f.* Dolefulness, cheerlessness, unpleasantness, sadness, anxiety.

dùil-bhriseadh, *s.m.* Disappointment.

dùile, *gen. sing.* of dùil. 2**Poor creature. 3 ††Weak person. 3‡‡Pleasure. 4 see duilleag.

dùileach, -iche, *a.* Elemental.

dùileachan, (AF) *s.m.* see dubh-lochan.

duileachd,* *s.f.* Doubt, suspicion, as of a child. 2**Hopelessness. 'Ga chur an d., *suspecting that the child is not your own.*

dùileag, -eige, -an, *s.f.* Poor little girl, term of affection. 2 see duilleag.

†**duileamh**, *s.* God.

duileann,* *s.m.* Perquisite, present, tribute. Mòran dhuileannan eile, *a great number of other perquisites.*

duileasg,§ -isg, *s.m.* Dulse, kind of seaweed—*rhodymenia palmata.* 2§ Pepper-dulse—*laurentia pinnatifida.*

duileasgach,** *a.* Abounding in, or like, dulse.

——— na h-aibhne,§ *s.m.* Broad-leaved pondweed—*potamogeton natans.*

duileasg-nam-beann,§ *s. m.* Mountain dulse—*palmella montana.*

†**duileil**, *a.* Skilled.

dùile-theannsgnaidh, see dùil-thionnsgnaidh.

duileum, see duibh-leum.

dùil-fheitheamh,‡‡ -imh, *s.m.* Expectation.

duilghe, *s.* see duilghead.

———, *comp.* of duilich.

duilghead, -eid, *s.m.* Degree of difficulty or sadness.

———as, -ais, *s.m.* Sorrow, difficulty. Cha chuir sin mòran duilgheadais roimhe, *that will not cause him much sorrow.*

[*281. Duileasg-na-h-aibhne.*]

duilgheas, see duilgheadas.

duilghid, *2nd. comp.* of duilich.

†**duilgne**, *s.pl.* Wages, hire, premium.

duiliasg, see duileasg.

duilich, *a.* Difficult, hard. 2 Sorry, grieved. Thus compared :—*1st. comp.* duilghe *or* dorra, *2nd. comp.* duilghid *or* dorraid, *3rd. comp.* duilghead *or* dorrad. [Duilghe, duilghid, used in the two senses of *hard* and *sorry.* Dorra only in the sense of hard or difficult in *W.* of *Ross-shire*—(DU.) Ceisd dh., *a difficult question* ; is d. leam, *I am sorry* ; is d. leis, *he is sorry* ; is d. dhuit 'fhàgail, *it is a pity for you to leave him* ; sgeul a bu d. leinn, *news for which we were sorry* ; is d. leam gur fìor, *I am sorry it is true* ; na's duilghe, *more difficult* ; tha seo d., *this is difficult* ; tha mi d. air do shon, *I am sorry for you.*

duilichead,** *s.m.* Arduousness.

———as,** *s.m.* Arduousness.

duilichinn, -e, -ean, *s. f.* Sorrow, vexation. 2 Compassion. Tha e fo mhòran d., *he is very grieved (under much grief)* ; is beag d. a th' ort *you do not seem to be the least sorry for it.*

†**duilieachd**, *s.f.* see duileachd.

dùilinn, *s.pl.* The elements. 2***s.f.(sing.)* Tax, tribute.

duilinne, -an, *s.f.* Tribute, tax. *pl.* Customs.

dùilinnean, see dùilinn.

duilinnean, *s., pl.* of duilinne.

duiliomral,** -ail, *s.m.* Error.

duiliosg, *s.m.* see duileasg.

duill-chuil, (AF) *s.* Beetle, black-beetle.

duill-dhaol, (AF) *s.* Beetle, black beetle.

duille, -an, *s.f.* see duilleag. 2 Sheath, as of a knife or dagger. 3**Blade. 4‡‡Vagina. Gun d. chall no blàth, *without losing leaf or blossom* ; d. sgèine, *the blade of a knife.*

†**duilleabhar**, -air, *s.f.* Foliage.

duilleabhrach, -aiche, *a.* see duilleagach.

duilleach, -ich, *s.m.* Foliage, leaves. 2**Withered leaves.

———, -iche, *a.* see duilleagach. 2†† Sheathed.

———adh, -aidh, *s.m.* Flourishing, vegetating, putting forth leaves. A' d—, *pr. pt.* of duillich.

———an, -ain, *s.m.* Book, pamphlet, sheet.

duilleag, -eige, -an, *s.f.* Leaf, as of a tree or plant. 2 Leaf, as of a door or book. 3* Leaflet. 4**Fold. 5** Scabbard. Taobh duilleige, *a page* ; d. còmhla, *a leaf of a door, flap of the breast* ; d. luaineach, *a fluttering leaf* ; dà dh. aon chòmhla, *the two leaves of one door* ; d. leabhair, *the leaf of a book*; an d., *the diaphragm.*

duilleagach, -aiche, *a.* Leafy, abounding in leaves, having foliage. 2**In folds, as a door. Dorus d., *a folding door.*
duilleag a' chruineachd,*s.f.* Common liver-wort.
duilleag-bhàite,§ *s.f.* Water-lily—*nymphæa.*
———— bhàn,§ *s.f.* White water-lily—*nymphæa alba.*
———— bhuidhe,§ *s.f.* Yellow water-lily—*nuphar luteum.*
duilleag-bràghad,§ *s.f.* Nipple-wort, see duilleag-mhath.
duilleag-Bhrighde, *s.f.* see duilleag-mhath.
duilleag-mhath,§ *s. f.* Nipple-wort—*lapsana communis.*

282. *Duilleag-mhath.*

283. *Dùil-mhial.*

duilleag-mhìn,§ *s.f.* see duilleag-mhath.
duillean,** -ein, *s.m.* Spear.
†duillear, -eire, *a.* Leafy.
duille-doruis *s.f.* The leaf of a door.
duille-sgéine, *s.f.* The sheath of a knife.
duillich, *v.n.* Sprout, put forth leaves, infoliate. 2 Flourish.
duillinnean, see duilinnean.
duilliur-féithlean,§ *s.m.* Honeysuckle, see uilleann.
duilliur-spuinc,§ -e, *s.m.* Coltsfoot, see cluasliath.
†duill-mhial,(AF) -an, *s.m.* Caterpillar.
duill'-thaobh, -thaoibh, -an, *s.m.* Page of a book. 2 Side of a leaf.
dùil-mhial,§ *s. f.* Great bindweed—*convolvulus sepium.* 2**Caterpillar.
dùil-theannsgnaidh,** -tean- *s. m.* see dùil-thionnsgnaidh.
dùil-thionnsgnaidh,-e, -ean, *s.f.* Element.
†duim, -e, *a.* Poor, needy.
dùin, *pr.pt.* a' dùnadh, *v.a.* Shut, close. 2 Enclose, surround. 3 Lace or button, as boots or shoes. 4 Darken, obscure. Dh. ceò bhliadhna air a dhèarrsa, *the mist of years has shrouded his splendour ;* d. an dorus, *close the door.*
dùin, *pl. & gen. s.* of dùn.
duine, *gen.sing.* duine, *pl.* daoine, *s.m.* Man. 2 Person, body, individual. 3 The oldest man of a village. D. gun mhath gun chron, is mó 'chron na 'mhath, *a man that's neither good nor ill is more ill than good*—duine gun mhath gun chron, is also applied to a shiftless,thriftless sort of man who is otherwise quite decent; an duine, *the good-man of the house ;* an d. agamsa, *my husband—d.* is often applied to either men or women,as,am bheil d. a staigh ? *is anyone in ?* ; is fhèarr d. na daoine, *a proper person is better than many men* ; ro-dh., *an excellent man, man of rank* ; fiadh-dh., *wild man, satyr ;* d. gaoil, *a male relative*; d. math, *good man;* duine-nan-clag, *the bell-man.* Fear de m' dhaoine, *one of my men,* is a good example of the difference between *fear* and *duine.* [The following remarks apply to *W. of Ross-shire. Duine* means, emphatically a married man. An unmarried man of any age is *gille. Fear* is as colourless, except as to sex, as "individual," "person," or "one," and is generally little more than a peg on which to hang an attribute. Cha robh e 'na dh. aig an àm sin, *he was not a (married) man at that time ;* A native would never commit himself so far as to ask "cò e an d. sin ? *who is that man ?*" Bean is duine, is *husband and wife* (*lit.* wife and husband.) The precedence of the wife is possibly a relic of Pictish custom. The phrase occurs in other parts, for example Perthshire, which was also in Pictland. In Arran [& Argyllshire—AH] "fear agus bean" is the invariable usage. In Gairloch both phrases are used. In Lewis the latter, and more rarely "duine agus bean" are used. "Cà bheil na fir ud ?" *where are those fellows ?* used, for example, in reference to two boys, aged respectively two and three.—C.R. in *Gael. Soc.*, xxiv, 368.]
†duineabhadh, -aidh, *s.m.* Manslaughter.
duineachan, -ain, *s.m.* Little man, manikin.
duineadas, -ais, *s.m.* see duinealas.
duinealachd, *s.f.ind.* see duinealas.
duinealas, -ais, *s.m.* Manliness. 2 Warmth of heart. 3**Boldness. 4**Decision of character.
duinean,** -ein, *s.m.* Manikin.
dùinear *fut.pass.* of dùin.
†duine-bad,‖ *s.* Plague or general destruction of the people.
duineil, -eala, *a.* Manly, firm, like a man. 2 (AH) Dutiful. Bi d., *be manly.*
duine-mharbhadh,** -aidh, *s.m.* Manslaughter.
duine-mharbhaiche,** *s.m.* One who has committed manslaughter. 2 Murderer.
duine-oirceneach, -ich, *s.m.* Assassin.
duin'-iaruinn,(DU) *s.m.* Windlass in a fishing-boat. This is the name always used in *Gairloch.* [The mechanism at a distance bears a close resemblance to a man.]
dùinidh, *fut. aff.* of dùin.
†duinionga, *s.f.* Onyx stone.
duin'-itheach, -ich, *s.m.* Cannibal, man-eater.
duinn, *prep.pron.* To us, *emphatic* form, duinne. Gu slàinte 'thabhairt dhuinn, *to give us salvation* ; is còir dhuinn, *we ought.*
duinne, *comp. & gen. fem.* of donn.
———, *s.f.* Brownness.
———ad, -id, *s.f.* Degree of brownness.
dùinte, *a. & past pt.* of dùin. Shut, closed. 2 Not communicative, reserved. 3 Niggardly.
dùinteachd,** *s.f.* Closeness.
dùintean, *n. pl.* of dùn.
Duir, *s.f.* Old name of the letter D. 2 Oak.
†duirbh, -e, *s.m.* Disease.
†duirc, *a.* see duairc.
———, *s.f.* Gaelic spelling of *dirk.*
———,†† *s.f.* Pine-cone. 2 Acorn.
——— -daraich, *s.f.pl.* Acorns.
duirce,** -an, *s.f.* Acorn.
duirceall, *s.f.* Spud. 2 Rusty knife. 3‡‡Acorn.
duircean,** -ein, *s.m.* Diminutive naughty person. 2 *dim.* of duirc††. 3 *pl.* of duirc††.
duircein, see duircean.
duirche, *comp.* of dorch.
———,** *s.f.* Darkness, gloom. Thional an d., *the darkness gathered.*
———ad, see dorchad.
duirchid, *2nd. comp.* of dorch.
dùire, *comp.* of dùr. More or most obstinate, unmanageable or impenetrable.
duire, see doire.
dùire, *s.f.ind.* Hardness. 2 Obstinacy, indocility. 3 Stupidity.
dùiread, -eid, *s.f.* Stubbornness, degree of stubbornness, obstinacy or indocility. 2 Hard-

ness. 3 Stupidity. A' dol an d., *growing harder and harder.*

——, *2nd. comp.* of dùr. Is d. e sin, *he is the more obstinate for that.*

†dùir-fheur, *s.m.* Wet grass.

dùirig, *v.n.* see dùraig.

duirn, *gen. sing. & n.pl.* of dorn. Làn duirn, *a fistful.* Is fheàrr làn an duirn de cheaird na làn an duirn de dh' òr, *a hand ful of trade is better than a handful of gold*—N.G.P. says "this is undoubsedly a borrowed proverb, the trade of the smith or armourer being the only one that the Gael of old looked upon with any respect."

duir-shian, -tan, *s.m.* Tempest.

duirt, (*for* d' thubhairt) *past interr. & neg.* of abair.

duis, *gen. sing. & n.pl.* of dos.

dùis, -eachan, *s.f.* see duais. 2** Jewel. 3** Crow. 4**Gloom. 5**Mist. 6‡‡Chief. 7‡‡ Dust, dross. 8(DMy) Lights, entrails of a cow or sheep, with all the fat attached to it. D. bà, d. caorach.—*Lewis.*

duis-chill,** *s.f.* Asylum, sanctuary.

duiseal, -eil, *s.m.* Spout. 2 [* gives *s.f.*] Whip. 3 see duisiol.

dùiseal, -eil, *s.m.* Cloud. 2 Gloom, heaviness. 3 Dulness. 4 Spell of work. 5 Slumber, drowsiness. Gun d. 'san iarmailt, *without a cloud in the firmament*; gun d. cadail, *without the heaviness of sleep.*

——ach, -aiche, *a.* Cloudy. 2 Sleepy.

——ach,** -aich, *s.m.* Rain.

duisealadh, -aidh, *s.m.* Flogging, whipping.

duisealan, see duisleannan.

duisealtach,** see duisealach.

dùisg, *pr. part.* a' dùsgadh, *v.a. & n.* Awake, awaken, rouse up. 2 Rouse, excite.

dùisgear, *fut.aff.pass.* of dùisg. Shall be awakened.

dùisgidh, *fut.aff.act.* of dùisg.

duisgioll,** -ill, *s.m.* Client.

dùisgte, *past pt.* of dùisg. Awakened, roused, 2 Excited.

†duisich, *v.a.* Awake, arouse.

†duisighe, see dùisgte.

duisiol, -il, *s.f.* Flute, pipe.

duisleag,** -eig, -an, *s.f.* see duileasg.

duisleannan, *s. pl.* Ill-natured pretences, false complaints, freaks. 2 Obstinacy. 3 Dissimulation. *prov.*

duis-neul, -neoil, *s.m.* see duibh-neul.

——ach, see duibh-neulach.

duis-òglach, -aich, *s.m.* Client.

dui-suineach,¶ see coltraiche.

duit, *prep.pron.* To thee, for thee, unto thee.

duiteag,(CR) *Perthshire* for doiteag.

duit-se, *emphat.* form of duit.

duitseach,** *a.* Curtailed, docked, as a fowl. Coileach d., *a docked cock*; cearc dh., *a docked hen.*

dul, *s.m. prov.* for dol.

dul,* *s.m.* see dula.

dùl, *gen.pl.* of dùil, *element.* †2 used as *n. sing.* Dia nan dùl, *the God of the elements.*

dùl,** -ùil, *s.m.* Terraqueous globe, universe.

dul,** *v.a.* Loop, catch with a loop.

dul,(MMcD) *s.m.* Eyelet in dornan (which see), —*Lewis.*

dula, -chan, *s.m.* Noose, slipping loop. 2 Hollow. 3 Pin, peg. 4**Trap, gin. 5**Satirist. 6**Hook. 7††Swivel. 8 Lock of hair. 9** Fishing with nets.

——ch,** *a.* Full of loops, snares, gins or swivels.

Dùlach, see Dùdlachd.

Dùlachd, see Dùdlachd.

dulag, -aige, -an, *s. f. prov.* see dallag. 2** Little loop. 3**Little snare.

——ach,** *a.* Full of little loops. 2 Full of little gins or traps.

——an,(AC) *s.m.* Holiness. D. nan seachd sagart, *the holiness of the seven priests.*

dùlaidh, *a.* see dubhlaidh.

dùlan, -ain, -an, *s.m.* see dùbhlan.

——ach, -aiche, *a.* see dùbhlanach.

——achadh, see dùbhlanachadh.

——achd, see dùbhlanachd.

——aich, *v.a.* see dùbhlanaich.

dulbhar,** *a.* see duilbhearra.

——achd, see duilbhearrachd.

dulchann,** -ainn, *s.f.* Avarice, covetousness. 2 Miserableness.

——ach,** *a.* Avaricious, covetous. 2 Miserable.

——achd,** *s.f.* Covetousness.

dul-chaoin,** *s.f.* Lamentation, wailing.

——teach,** *a.* Lamenting, wailing.

dulchuis,** *s.f.* Earnestness, diligence, perseverance. 2(PJM) Gumption.

——each,** -siche, *a.* Earnest, diligent, persevering.

dulchunn, -uinn, see dulchann.

dùldach, see dùdlach.

Dùldachd, see Dùdlachd.

dùldaich, see dùdlaich.

dùldaidh, see dùdlaidh.

——eachd, see Dùdlachd 2 & 3.

du'liath, -a, see dubh-liath.

dullag, see dallag.

dùllaigh, -e, *a.* see dùbhlaidh.

†dùllaigh, -e, -ean, *s.f.* Winter.

dùmhail, dùmhala, *a.* see dòmhail.

dùmhalachd,** see dòmhalachd.

dùmhalas,** *s.m.* Grossness.

dùmhchas, -ais, *prov.* for dùthchas.

dùmhlachadh, see dòmhlachadh.

dùmhladas, -ais, see dòmhlachd. D. dòrainn, *a weight of grief*; a' dol an d., *growing more bulky and clumsy*; d. mór sluaigh, *a large concourse of people.*

dùmhlaich, see dòmhlaich.

dùmhlas, -ais, *s.m.* see dòmhlachd.

dùn, -ùin, *pl.* dùin & dùintean, *s.m.* Heap. 2 Hill, hillock, mound. 3 Fortified house or hill. 4 Fortress, castle. 5 Fastness. 6 Tower. 7**Hedge. 8(AH)Dunghill (at a farm steading.)

dùnach,** *a.* Hilly, full of heaps or knolls. 2 Full of towers or forts. 3 Like a tower or fort.

dunach, *gen. sing.* of dunaidh.

dùnadh, -aidh, *s.m.* Shutting, act of shutting or closing. 2 Lacing, binding, buttoning, as shoes. 3 Barricading. 4 *rarely* Camp, dwelling. 5 Multitude. 6††Termination, closing. A' d—, *pr.pt.* of dùin.

dunaich,* *s.f.* see dunaidh.

dunaidh, *s. f.* Woe, disaster, misfortune. 2** Perplexity. 3**Mischief. Dè an d. a thàinig air? *what the mischief came over him?*

dùnan, -ain, *s.m. dim.* of dùn. Little castle. 2 Small heap, knoll or hill. 3 Dunghill. 4** Little fort. 5 *n. pl.* of dùn.

——ach,** *a.* Knolly. 2 Full of little heaps, little hills or little forts.

dùn-aolaich, *s.m.* Dunghill.

dùn-àros,** -àrois, *s.m.* Dwelling-place.

dun-bhalach, *s.m.* Mere fellow.

dùncan,** *s.m.* Fortlet.

dùn-catha,** *s.m.* Bulwark. 2 Sconce.

dùn-feamainn,‡‡ *s.m.* Dunghill of seaweed.

dùn-Iuchair,‡‡ *s.m.* August dunghill.

dùn-lios, -lis, -liosan, *s. m.* Palace. 2 Palace-yard. 3 Fort garden. 4**Garrison.

dun-lus, -luis, -an, *s.m.* (*for* donn-lus) see lus-nan-cnapan.
dun-mharbh, *v.a.* Murder.
†**dun-mharbhach**, } -aich, *s.m.* Man-slayer.
†**dun-mharbhtach**, }
†**dun-mharbhadh**, -aidh, *s.m.* Homicide, massacre. A' d—, *pr.pt.* of dun-mharbh.
†**dunn**, -uinn, *s.m.* Teacher, doctor.
dunnsag,(CR) *s.f.* Large stone or boulder—*W. of Ross.*
dùn-rainiche,‡‡ *s.m.* Dunghill of moss and fern.
dùn-sheangan, *s.m.* Ant-hill.
dunt, *s.m.* Thump. 2 Blow producing a hollow sound. 3††Thud. *Scots*, dund.
duntag,†† -aig, -an, *s.f.* Plump little article or person. 2 (Fionn) Short knife with a blunt point, often consisting of a razor-blade fixed in a wooden handle.
duntail,* *s.f.* & *pr.pt.* Thumping.
dupadaich,(CR)*s.f.* Staggering or tottering from weakness—*W. of Ross.*
dùr, -ùire, *a.* Dull, stupid. 2 Stubborn, untractable, indocile, obstinate. 3 Surly. 4 Cold, indifferent. 5 Steady, persevering, earnest, eager, attentive. Gu d., *attentively*; duine d., *a surly fellow.*
dur, *adv.* *Prov.* for 'nuair, uair, trà or tràth.
†**dur**, -uir, *s.m.* Water. 2§Oak, see darach.
dùrachd, -an, *s.f.* Diligence, earnestness, sincerity. 2 Intention, good-will. 3 Expression of good-will, good wish. 4 Inclination. 5 Luck-penny. 6**Daring, courage. Am bheil e an d. mhath dhuit? *has he good intentions towards you? does he mean well?* gun d. cron, *without inclination to harm;* le d. cridhe, *with sincerity of heart;* maille ri d., *with diligence*; cha'n 'eil a' dh. agam, *I have not the courage.*
dùrachdach, -aiche, *a.* Diligent, earnest, sincere. 2 Urgent. 3 Fervent. 4**Industrious, assiduous, persevering. Neo-dh., *careless.*
dùrachdaiche, *comp.* of dùrachdach.
dùrachdainn,** *s.f.* Daring, courage. 2 Secret wishing. 3 Venturing.
dùrachdan-monaidh, *s. m.* Round-leaved sundew, moor-grass.
dùrad,‡‡-aid, *s.m.* Contumacy.
dùradan, -ain, -an, *s.m.* Mote, atom, particle of flying dust. 2 Pepper-corn. 3(AH) Moth. 4(DH) Small insignificant man. Chaidh d. 'nam shùil, *a mote stuck in my eye.*
———,¶ *s.m.* Wood-pigeon, dove, see calman-fiadhaich.
———ach,†† *a.* Abounding in motes or atoms. 2 Covered with dust.
durag,** *s.f.* Canker.
——— -chàil,** *s.f.* Cabbage-worm.
——— -mharbhach,** *a.* Anthelmintic.
dùraichd, *v.a.* see dùraig.
dùraig, *pr. pt.* a' dùraigeadh & a' dùrachdainn, *v.a.* Wish, incline, desire. 2**Dare. 3**Venture, adventure. Cha d. i pòg dhomh, *she has no desire to kiss me*; dhùraiginn marbh thu, *I would wish thee dead*; cha d. mi dol do 'n t-sabhal air eagal a' bhodaich, *I dare not go into the barn for fear of the spectre.*
———,** *s.f.* Attempt.
dùran, -ain, *s.m.* Morose fellow. 2 Obstinate fellow.
———ach, -aich, *s.m.* Obstinate blockhead.
duranta, see durranta.
———chd, see durrantachd.
duras,** -ais, *s.m.* House. 2 Room.
durb,** -uirb, *s.m.* Disease, distemper.
durbadan, see dùradan.
dùr-bhalach, see dùr-bhodach.
dùr-bhodach, -aich, *s.m.* Dunce. 2 Stupid old man. 3 Clown. 4††Stiff old man.

†**dur-bhuth**. *s.m.* Cell.
durc,** -a. *s.m.* Lump or piece of anything. 2 Clumsy knife, dirk. 3‡‡Truncheon. D. arain, *a lump of bread*; d. cloiche, *a lump of stone.*
durcais, -e, -ean, *s.f.* Pincers, nippers, *prov.* [durcaisd in MacL & D. and ‡.]
———each,†† *a.* Abounding in pincers or nippers.
durcan, *dim.* of durc. 2 (AF) see dorcan.
dùr-chluasach, -aiche, *a.* Hard of hearing.
dùr-chridheach, -iche, *a.* Hard-hearted.
dùr-chù, see dobhar-chù.
dùrd, -ùird, *s.m.* Word. 2 Syllable. 3 Hum, buzz. 4** Muttering. 5** Sullenness. 6 †† Sound.
——, *v.a.* Hum, buzz. 2 Mutter.
——ach, -aiche, *a.* Syllabic.
——ail, -e, *s.f.* Murmuring, grumbling. 2 Cooing. 2 The cushat's note. 4 The black-cock's note. 5 Querulousness. 6 Buzzing, humming, purring. Ri d., *cooing*; an d. mhùirneach, *the pleasant murmur.*
dùrdain, *gen.sing.* of dùrdan.
dùrdalan, (MMcL) *s.m.* Cockchafer. [Preceded by the art. *an.*]

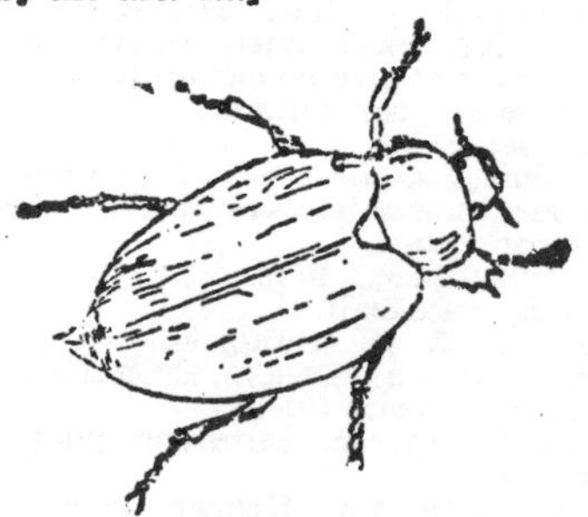

284. Dùrdalan.

dùrdan, -ain, *s.m.* Humming, murmur, cooing, purring. 2**Gibe. 3 Sing-song. 4**Bit of dust, mote, atom. 5*Teasing. Coileach-dubh ri d., *a black-cock making a murmuring noise*; 'nuair a bhitheas ni aig a' chat ni e d., *when the cat has got hold of anything it purrs*—said of those who speak much of their riches.
———ach, -aiche, *a.* Humming. murmuring. 2 Querulous. 3** Gibing. 4 Cooing. 5†† Abounding in motes or atoms. 6 Covered or sullied with dust. An calman d., *the cooing pigeon.*
———aich, *s.f.* see dùrdail.
dùr-fheur-fairge,§ *s.f.* Sea hard-grass—*lepturus filiformis.*
dùr-fhoghar,(CR) *s.m.* Dog-days.—*Suth'd.*
durga, *a.* Surly, sour, forbidding, repulsive, grim. 2††Grumbling.
———nta, *a.* see durga.
———ntachd, *s.f.* Surliness, moroseness, grimness.
dur-lus,§ -luis, *s.m.* Water-cress, especially *nasturtium officinalis*, but applied to all cresses, see biolair.
dùrn, -uirn, see dorn.
dùrradan, see dùradan.
———ach, see duradanach.

285. Dùr-fheur-fairge.

durradh! durradh!* *int.* Call to a pig—*Argyll.*
durradh, *s.m.* see durraidh.
durrag, -aige, -an, *s.f.* Worm-grub, maggot. 2‡ Worm. 3 Little pig. Fùdar nan d., *worm-powders.*

durragach, -aiche, *a.* Wormy, vermicular, abounding in worms, like a worm or maggot.
———-an, *s.pl.* of durrag.
——— -bhracha, *s.f.* Bound.
——— -chòmhlaich, (AF) *s. f.* Door- or house-worm.
——— -fheòla, *s.f.* Flesh-maggot.
durraghan, -ain, *s.m.* Grunting of a dog.
durraidh, -e, *s.f.* Sow, pork. *prov.*
durranta, *a.* Stiff, rigid. 2 Rigorous. 3 Morose, churlish. 4 Obstinate.
———chd, *s.f.* Moroseness, churlishness. 2 Rigidness. 3 Obstinateness, stiffness. 4 Austerity.
durrasan, (AF) -ain, *s.m.* Grasshopper.
durrasgach, -aiche, *a.* Quick, nimble. *prov.*
durrghail, -e, *s.f.* Cooing of a dove or black-cock. 2 Grunting of a dog. 3 Purring of a cat. Tha 'n cat a' d., *the cat is purring.*
durrghail, see durdail.
dursan,** -ain, *s.m.* Crack, report.
dursann, -ainn, -an, *s. m.* Unlucky accident, mishap. 2 Unhappiness.
dùr-shnaim, -e, -ean, *s.f.* Hard knot.
†**durtach**, †**dur-theach**, *s.* Church, foundation. 2**Cell, hut. 2**Pilgrim.
dùr-thuinn, *s.pl.* Surly waves, short choppy waves that give no chance to a small boat.
durunta, *a.* see duranta.
dus, see gus.
dus, duis, *s. m.* Dust. 2* Smithy ashes. 3 Remains of animals or plants. Neulta duis, *clouds of dust.*
dus,** -uis, *s.m.* Fort.
dusach, see dusail.
dusachd, *s.f.* Watchfulness.
dusail, -ala, *a.* Dusty. 2** Earthy, earthlike.
†**dusair**,** *s.m.* Client.
dusait,** -ean, *s.m.* Sanctuary, place of refuge, safety.
———iche,** *s.m.* One who takes refuge in a sanctuary.
dùsal, -ail, *s.m.* see dùiseal. 2 (AC) Quirk. 3 Dust, dustiness. Rinn iad d., *they slept.*
———ach, -aiche, *a.* see dùisealach.
dusan, -ain, *s.m.* Dozen. 2**Certain quantity of yarn.
———ach,†† *a.* In dozens.
dùsgach, *a.* Rousing, wakening. 2 Stimulating.
dùsgadh, -aidh, *s.m.* Awaking, awakening. 2 Act of awaking, rousing or arousing. 3* Excitement, exciting. A' d—, *pr. pt.* of dùisg. Ni mi cadal gun d., *I will sleep without awakening.*
dusgairm, *s.f.* Calling, appellation.
duslach, -aich, *s.m.* Dust, earth, ground. Is d. thu, *thou art dust.*
———ail, -ala, *a.* Dusty. 2 Earthy, like earth.
duslaing, *s.f.* see duslainn.
duslainn, -e, -ean, *s.f.* [* gives *s.m.*] Gloomy, solitary place. 2 Dark place. 3 Dust. 4 Thicket.
———each, -iche, *a.* Gloomy. 2**Deserted, as a house. 3 Dusty. 4 Earth-like, terrestrial, made of earth.
duslann, see duslainn.
———ach, see duslainneach.
dusluingeach,** *a.* Bushy.
dustach, see dusail.
dustadh, Gaelic form of *dusting—W. of Ross.*
dustail, see dusail.
dut, *prep. pron.* see duit.
dùth, -a, *a.* Natural, hereditary, native. 2 Meet, just, proper, fit, suitable, befitting one's case. Cha d. dha sin, *that cannot be expected of him* ; tha e mar is d. dha, *he is as you would expect* ; an d. dhomh-sa sin ? *can that be expected of one situated as I am* ; is d. dha gu 'm bheil e mar sin, *it is befitting his case that he should be so.*
——,* *s.m.* Complement, proportion, equitable share, proportionate quantity or number. Tha mo dh. féin agam-sa, *I have my own proportion* ; clach ìme le a d. de chàise, *a stone of butter with its complement of cheese* ; na 'm faighinn mo dh. féin, *were I to get my own equitable share*; tha a dh. sin a dhìth orm, *I want a proportionate share of that, the equivalent of that is lacking*; Gaidheal d' an d.buaidh, *a Gael whose due is victory.*
dùthaich, dùthcha, dùthchannan, *s.f.* Country, land, native-land, district, territory. Air an d., *in the country* ; muinntir mo dhùthcha, *my country-folk.*
duthaich, -e, -ean, *s.f.* The great gut. 2 Sausage. 3*The anus.
duthail, (AF) *s. f.* see dubhthuil.
dùthail,* *a.* Hereditary. 2 Giving just grounds to anticipate or expect. 3 Quite natural, reasonable. Is d. dùthchas im ùr a bhith air blàthaich, *it is quite natural that new-churned milk should produce fresh butter.*
duthainn, (AC) *adv.* For evermore.
†**duthamhail**, *a.* Of a good family.
†**duthan**, *s.m.* Nation.
duthar, -aire, *a.* Grim, stern, rough.
dùthcha, *gen.sing.* of dùthaich.
———il, *a.* Rural. 2**National. 3 Of good family.
———lachd, see dùthchasachd.
———nna, *pl.* of dùthaich.
———nnaibh, *dat. pl.* of dùthaich.
———nnan, *pl.* of dùthaich.
dùthchas, -ais, *s.m.* Place of one's birth. 2 Heredity, native or hereditary temper, spirit or blood. 3**Visage, countenance. 4 Hereditary right. Théid d. an aghaidh nan creag *hereditary tendencies go against rocks,* i. e. against all obstacles, " birth tells "; cha bhi d. aig mnaoi no sagart, *women and priests have no birth-tie,*—i. e. the woman that marries takes her husband's settlement, the priest's must be where the Church bids.
———ach, -aiche, *a.* Of one's country. 2 Native, natural, indigenous. 3 Hereditary. 4 Natural to one's family. 5**Patriotic, fond of one's native land. Bu d. sin dha, *that was hereditary in his family.*
———ach, -aich, *s.m.* [& *f.*] Native. 2 Aboriginal. 'Nuair a thréigeas na dùthchasaich Ìle, beannachd le sìth na h-Alba, *when the natives forsake Islay, farewell to the peace of Scotland.*
———achd, *s.f.ind.* Nativity, natality, nationalness. 2 Circumstance of being hereditary. 3*Hereditary right, privilege or failing.
dùthrachd, -an, *s.f.* see dùrachd.
———ach, -aiche, *a.* see dùrachdach.
du-thràth, see dubh-thràth.
duthuil, -e, see dubhthuil.
dut-sa, (*for* duit-sa) *emphatic* form of duit.

E e

Eadha, *the aspen*, the old name of the fifth letter of the Gaelic alphabet, and one of the Small vowels. It has various sounds. With the grave accent, (è) it sounds like *e* in *there*, as è, *he*; with the acute accent (é), like *ai* in *fail*, as, té, *a female*; cé, *the earth*. At the end of a word, it sounds like *e* in *brother*, as, duine, *a man*; roghnaichte, *chosen*.

è! *inter*. Ay! ay!; è! è! exclamation of surprise.

è, *pers.pron*. He, him, it. Written sè when it precedes *e*. [This is an artificial rule and has rarely been followed.] Marbhaidh sè è, *he will kill him*. "Gu ma h-è dhuit" alone, may be used as a threat; when followed by *gu'n* and a clause, it expresses an earnest hope, as, gu ma h-e dha gu 'n tig e, *God grant that he may come*.

ea, the 22nd. letter of the old Gaelic alphabet according to the Book of Leacan.

ea-, *privative prefix*, see eu-.

eabair, *pr.pt*. ag eabradh, *v.a*. Besmear, daub with mud. 2* Make slimy, as mud, by continual tramping. 3 Roll in the mud.

eaban, -ain, see eabon.

eabar, -air, *s.m*. Mud, puddle, slime, mire, sedimet, filth, kennel. 2 see abar.

——**ach**, -aiche, *a*. Muddy, miry, filthy. 2 Grovelling, dirty, wallowing. 3 Prone to wallow.

eabhadh,§ (eadha) *s*. Aspen, see critheann.

eabhall, -aill, *s.f*. see éibheall.

——**ach**, -aiche, see éibhleach.

eabhlach, -aiche, see éibhleach.

†**eabhron**, see iarunn.

eabon, -oin, *s.m*. Ebony.

——**ach**,†† -aiche, *a*. Ebony.

eabrach, -aiche, *a*. see eabarach.‖

eabradh, -aidh, *s. m*. Besmearing with mud, wallowing in mire. 2 Grovelling. 3**Kennel. †4 *rarely* Iron. A chum a h-e. 'san làthaich, *to her wallowing in the mire*. Ag e—, *pr.pt*. of eabair.

eabraich, *v.a*. Mangle.

†**eabron**,‖ -oin, *s.m*. Pan, caldron.

eabur, -uir, *s.m*. Ivory.

——**ach**,†† -aiche, *a*. Ivory.

eacal, -ail, *s.m*. see eucail.

†**eacaoin**, see acain.

eacart, -airt, see eu-ceart.

†**eacartha**, *a*. Stupid.

†**eacconn**, *s.m*. Rage, madness, want of sense.

†——**ach**, -aiche, *a*. Mad, absurd.

†**eaccosg**, -oisg, -an, *s.m*. see aogasg.

†**eaccosmhuil**, -e, *a*. see eu-cosmhuil.

ea-ceart, -ceirte, *a*. see eu-ceart.

ea-ceartas, -ais, see eu-ceartas.

ea-céillidh, -e, *a*. see eu-céillidh.

286. Buill eich.

each, eich, *n. pl*. eich, *dat. pl*. eachaibh, *s. m*. Horse, 2* Brute.

PARTS OF A HORSE (BUILL EICH);

1 Gàmùidh, *crest*. (Muing, *mane*.)
2 Slinneanan, *withers*.
3 Braman, *croup, rump*.
4 Féith-lùthaidh, féith-na-h-iosgaid, spéir, *spearralach, *ham-string*.
5 Iosgaid, *hough*.
6 Luirg, lurgainn (hind leg only) *cannon, shank*.
7 Luighean-deiridh, *fetlock*.
8 Rùdan, ruitean, fiarag [fiar, *slanting*,—CR] *pastern*.
9 Crubh, ionga, bròg, *hoof*.
10 Luighean-toisich, *coronet*.
11 Gàirdean, *arm*.
12 Sgòrnan, *gullet*.
13 Bus, craos, *muzzle*.

Caol na coise *is between* fetlock *and* hoop; ubhal a' chruachainn *or* ubhal na cruachainn *is at upper part of haunch*; lùgh na sléisde *at top of hind-leg thigh*.

each bàn, *a white* or *cream-coloured horse*.
each beilichte, *a muzzled horse*.
each blàr, *a horse with a white spot on the forehead*.
each breac, *a piebald horse*.
each buidhe, *a cream-coloured* or *dun horse*.
each buidhe-ruadh, *a bay horse*.
each buidhe-dhonn, *a bay horse*.
each cartach, *a cart horse*.
each ceannaich, *a post-horse*.
each coimhliongadh, *a dromedary*.
each-dìollaid, *a riding-horse*.
each donn, *a brown horse*.
each donn-dhearg, *a bay horse*.
each-féin, *a cart-horse*.
each fuadain, *a stray horse*.
each geal, *a white horse*.
each gearrte, *a castrated horse*.
each glas, *a grey horse*.
each gorm, *a dapple-grey horse*.
each-iaruinn, *a bicycle*. 2 *railway-engine*.
each-mara, *sea-horse, morse, great walrus*.
each marcachd, *a saddle-horse*.
each meamnach, *a mettlesome horse*.
each meileige, *a muzzled horse*.
each odhar, *a dun-coloured horse*.
each-oibre, *a working* or *broken horse*.
each réidh, *a hackney*.
each ruadh, *a bay horse*.
each ruith, *a roadster*.
each seabhaid *or* saibhd, *a stray horse*. each-seabhain—*Lewis*; each seabhaid—*Skye*.
each-shasaid, *a riding-horse*.
each sìth, *a fairy horse, kelpie*.
each spothte, *a castrated horse*.
each srathach, *a pack-horse*.
each sréine, *a bridle-horse, courser*.
each-steud, *a race-horse*.
each-trotain, *a trotting horse*.
each-uisge, *a water-horse*.

Air muin eich, *on horse-back*; 'nam each 's 'nam dhìollaid, *ready in my saddle*.

†**each**, see neach.

eachach, -aiche, *a*. Having many horses, abounding in horses.

eachail, -ala, *a*. Horse-like, brutal.

eachalachd, *s.f.ind*. Brutality, coarseness.

eachan, -ain, -an, *s.m*. Little horse. 2 Instrument used in winding yarn. 3 *Swifts. 4 Smooth cockle. 5**Blast. 6 Windle. E. gaoithe, *a blast of whirlwind*; e. tachrais, *a worsted winder*.

——**ach**,** *a*. Windy, stormy, blasty. 2†† Abounding in little horses, or winding-horses.

eachanachd,** *s.f.* Windiness.
each-aodach, -aich, -aichean, *s.m.* Horse-furniture, caparison, horse-cloth.
eacharais, *s.f.* see eachrais.
eacharnach, *s.f.* Park for horses.
each-bhalach,-aich, *s.m.* Groom, jockey, stable-boy.
——————an, -ain, see each-bhalach.
each-chir, -e, -ean, *s.f.* Horse-comb,curry-comb.
eachd, -a, -an, *s.m.* see euchd.
eachda,** *a.* Clean, neat, spruce, trim. 2 Pure. 3 Comely, decent.
eachdail,** *a.* Conditional. 2 Cleanly, neat, comely. Gu h-e., *cleanly*.
eachdair, -e, -ean, *s.m.* History, story, relation. 2**Historian, recorder, chronicler. [some give eachdaire as *n. sing.*]
————eachd, see eachdraidheachd.
eachdaran, -ain,*s.m.* Pen for confining straying cattle or sheep, pin-fold.
eachdarra, *s.m.* see eachdaran.
eachdrachail,‡‡ *a.* Narrative.
eachdra, see eachdaran.
eachdradh, see eachdaran.
eachdraich,* see eachdraidh.
eachdraiche, -an, *s.m.* Historian.
eachdraidh, -e, -ean, *s.f.* History, chronicle, record, tale, narrative.
——————eachd,*s.f.ind.* History,historiography.
eachdranach, -aich, *s.m.* Foreigner.
——————,** *a.* Foreign.
eachdrath, see eachdaran.
each-fodair,(AH) *s. m.* Term applied in derision and contempt to a coarse, churlish man.
each-fuinn, *s.m.* Calp, herezeld. This, in early times, was the symbol of dependance paid by the native man to his lord, but in later ages it was exacted by the chief from his vassals. On the death of a tenant the best horse had to be given over. The custom was forbidden by law in 1617, but like most Celtic customs it survived long after, being still recognized in 1710—*Clan Donald, iii.* [also each-ursainn.]
eachlach, -aich, *s.m.* see each-laoch.
eachlair,* *s.m.* Brutish fellow. 2††Hostler.
————eachd,* see eachalachd.
eachlais,* *s.f.* Passage, entry.
each-lann, -ainn, *s.m.* Stable.
each-laoch,-laoich, *s.m.* Groom,jockey, post-boy.
eachlaraiche, -an, *s.m.* Unfeeling churl.
each-lasg, -laisg, -an, *s.f.* Lash, horse-whip.
each-léigh, -e, -ean, *s.m.* Farrier, veterinary. 2(AF)Horse-leech.
——————eas, -ghis, *s.m.* Veterinary art.
eachliath, -aith, *s.f.* Horse-rack, manger.
each-loinn, -e, *s.m.* Horse-litter.
each-maide,(Fionn) *s.m.* Mason's tress.
each-mhuileann, -linn, -mhuillnean, *s.f.* Horse-mill.
eachradh, see eachraidh. 'Nuair a chithear an t-eachradh air an raon, *when the cavalry are seen on the field.*
eachraidh, *s.m.pl.* Horses, cavalry. 2 Stud of horses. Acfhuinn na h-e., *the harnesses of the stud.*
eachrais, -e,*s.f.* Confusion, disturbance, bustle, mess. 2 Lumber. †3 Fair. †4 Rowing. †5 Method.
————each,†† *a.* Confused, bustling.
eachrann,§ *s.m.* Place where brambles grow. 2 Bramble. 3 Impediment, stumbling-block.
eachras,** *s.m.* Fair. 2 House.
eachruidh, see eachraidh.
each-saic,* *s.m.* Sumpter.
each-seamrag,)AF) *s.f.* Horse-clover.
each-shlighe, -ean & -eachan, *s.f.* Horse-road, horse-path.
each-siamar, see each-seamrag.
†eacht,** *s.f.* Condition.
eachta,(AF) Kind of bird,—*Dean of Lismore's Book.*
eachtradh,** -aidh, *s.m.* Adventure, enterprise.
eachtran, see eachtrannach.
————nach, -aiche, *a.* Foreign. 2 Adventurous, enterprising. Gu h-e. eadar-bhuaiseach, *adventurously and victoriously.*
eachtrannach, -aich, *s.m.* Foreigner. 2 Adventurer.
each-uisge, *s.m.* Water-horse, kelpie (fabulous.)
each-ursainn, *s.m.* The best horse on a farm, always claimed by a proprietor on the death of a tenant. [see each-fuinn.]
ea-cinnt, -e, see eu-cinnt.
————each, -iche, see eu-cinnteach.
————ealas, see eu-cinntealas.
eacnach,** -aich, *s.m.* Blasphemy.
ea-cneasda, see eu-cneasda.
——————chd, see eu-cneasdachd.
ea-coir, -corach, -ean, see eucoir.
ea-conn, -a, see eu-conn.
————ach, -aiche, see eu-connach.
ea-corach, -aiche, *a.* see eucorach.
ea-còrdadh, -aidh, see eu-còrdadh.
ea-cosmhuil, -e, see eu-cosmhuil.
——————each, see eu-cosmhuileach.
——————eachd, see eu-cosmhalachd.
ea-cosmhalas, see eu-cosmhalas.
ea-crionna, *a.* see eu-crionna.
——————chd, see eu-crionnachd.
ea-crionnta, see eu-crionna.
——————chd, see eu-crionnachd.
ea-cubhaidh, -e, *a.* see eu-cubhaidh.
èad, *s.m.* see eud.
†ead, see †eid.
èadach, -aich, *s.m.* see aodach.
èadachadh, -aidh, see eudachadh.
èadaich, *v.a. & n.* see eudaich & aodaich.
eadail, see feudail.
eadaileach, see feudaileach.
Eadailis,** *s.f.* The Italian language.
ea-daingean, *a.* see eu-daingean.
ea-daingneachd, see eu-daingneachd.
†èadaire, see eudaire.
†eadal, -ail, *s. f.* Profit, advantage. 2 Prey, spoil.
eadan, eadann, } see aodann.
eadannan, see aodannan.
eadar,*prep.* [Governs a substantive in the nominative. Combined with the personal pronouns thus :— eadarainn, *between us* ; eadaraibh, *between you* ; eatorra, *between them.*] 1 Between, betwixt. Eadar thusa is mise, *between you and me* ; eadar long agus laimhrig, *between the cup and the lip* (*lit.* between the ship and the quay) ; e. feala-dhà is dà-rìreadh, *between jest and earnest* ; e. am bogh' agus an t-sreang, *with much ado, making both ends meet with much difficulty*; e. an dà chuid, *between the two* ; e. chlàr is ursainn, *between the door and the post* ; 'se chaidh e. thu 's do rùsg, *it has gone between you and your clothes* (*lit.* your fleece—you have very much at heart); a' cur e.,*causing us to disagree*; thàinig rudeigin e., *we disagreed about something*; e. sinne agus sibh-se, *between us and you* ; leig e. sinn féin 's na biodagan, *let us fight it out with dirks, none interfering.* 2* Among. Eadaraibh fhéin fhuaradh e, *he was found among yourselves.* 3 Both. [When signifying *both*, it does not admit the article between itself and the noun ; but aspirates both its nouns, as, eadar cheann is chasan, *both head and feet* ; eadar bheag agus mhór, *both great and*

small; eadar mhath is olc, *both good and bad.*
eadaradh, -aidh, *s.m.* Division. 2 Interest. 3 see eadradh.
eadaraibh, *prep. pron.* Between you.
eadar-aimsir,‡‡ -e, -ean, *s.f.* Intermission.
eadarainn, *prep. pron.* Between us.
eadar-aisneach,‡‡ -eiche, *a.* Intercostal.
eadar-astar,‡‡ -air, -ean, *s.m.* Interval.
eadar-bhacain, *s.* Space between the row-locks or thole-pins in a boat.
eadar-bhalla,‡‡ -chan, *s.m.* Mid-wall.
eadar-bhuaidh, *s.f.* Defeat, rout. 2**Victory.
†eadar-bhuais, *s.f.* Agony. 2 Dismay, confusion.
†eadar-bhuaiseach,***a.* Discomferting, routing. 2 Victorious. 3 Of, or belonging to, a rout or defeat. Gu h-eachtrannach e., *adventurously and victoriously.*
eadar-chasaideachd, *s.f.ind.* Discord.
†eadar-cheanas, *s.m.* Distance.
eadar-cheangail, *v.a.* Interjoin.
eadar-cheart, -cheirt, *s.m.* Equal distributive right.
eadar-cheart-fhacal, -ail, *s.m.* Right interpretation.
eadar-chluich,‡‡ -e, -ean, *s.m.* Interlude.
eadar-choimhearsnachd,‡‡ *s.f.ind.* Intercommunity.
eadar-chòmhradh,* -aidh, -aidhean, *s.m.* Interlocution.
eadar-chomunnachadh, -aidh,‡‡ *s.m.* Intercommunity.
eadar-chraicneach, -eiche, *a.* Intercutaneous.
eadar-chuir, *v.a.* Interpose.
eadar-chur, -chuir, -ean, *s.f.* Interjection. 2 Interposition.
eadar-dhàil, -dhàlach, -dhàlaichean, *s.f.* Interval. 2 Interposition.
eadar-dhà-lionn, *adv.* Between sinking and swimming, floundering.
eadar-dhà-shian,(DU) *s.* (Between two pelts of rain) Applied to a fine day following a succession of wet ones which are likely to continue, hence *a.* Exceptional. [*pron.* "eadarra(th)-shian," the aspirate being very slight.]
eadar-dhà-thuinn, *Poolewe, &c.*, for eadar-dhà-lionn.
eadar-dhealachadh, -aidh, *s.m.* Difference, distinction. 2 Distance. 3 Separating, act of separating, distinguishing, parting, dividing. 4 Divorcing. 5**Faction. 6‡‡Sedition. Cha'n 'eil e. ann, *there is no difference.* Ag e—, *pr. pt.* of eadar-dhealaich.
eadar-dhealachail,** *a.* Causing separation. 2 Causing divorce. 3 Like a separation or divorce.
eadar-dhealaich, *pr. pt.* ag eadar-dhealachadh, *v.a.* Separate, part, divide. 2 Distinguish. 3 Divorce.
eadar-dhealaichte, *past pt.* of eadar-dhealaich. Separated, parted. 2 Distinguished. 3 Divorced.
eadar-dhealbhadh, -aidh, *s.m.* Distinction.
eadar-dhealrach,‡‡ -aiche, *a.* Interlucent.
eadar-dhlùthaich,‡‡ *v.a.* Interjoin.
eadar-dhol,‡‡ *s.m.* Transit.
eadar-dhuilleagaich,‡‡ *v.a.* Interleave.
†eadar-dilgin, *s.f.* Devastation, ravaging.
†eadar-easga, *s.f.* Change of the moon.
†eadar-eug, *s.f.* Change of the moon.
†eadar-fhàs, -fhàis, *s.m.* Space, distance.
eadar-fhigh,‡‡ *v.a.* Interweave.
eadar-fhigheadh,‡‡ *s.m.* Intertexture. 2 Interweaving. Ag e—, *pr.pt.* of eadar-fhigh.
eadar-fhill,‡‡ *v.a.* Intervolve.
eadar-fhonn, *s.m.* Space, distance.
eadar-fhosgladh,‡‡ *s.m.* Interstice.
eadar-fhrasach, -aiche, *a.* Between showers.
eadargain, -e, -ean, *s.f.* see eadraiginn.
eadargaineach, see eadragainneach.
eadar-ghaire, see eadar-ghèarradh.
eadar-ghèarr, *v.a.* Intersect.
eadar-ghèarradh, -aidh, *s.m.* Divorce. 2 Separation. 3 Intersection.
eadar-ghèarrtach,‡‡ *a.* Intersecant.
eadar-gheanas, -ais, *s.m.* Distance.
eadar-ghlacach,‡‡ -aiche, *a.* Intercipient.
†eadar-ghlaodh, *v.a.* Judge, decide.
eadar-ghnàth, *s.m.* Ingenuity.
†eadar-ghnàth, *v.a.* Know, distinguish.
eadar-ghnàthach, -aiche, *a.* Ingenious. Gu h-e., *ingeniously.*
eadar-ghuaille, -ghuailne, -ghuailnean, *s.f.* The space between the shoulders.
eadar-ghuidh,* *v.a.* Intercede, make intercession.
eadar-ghuidhe, *s.f.* Intercession, mediation. 2 Supplication.
eadar-ghuidheach,** *a.* Intercessory, mediatory.
eadar-ghuidheadh, -idh, *s.f.* see eadar-ghuidhe.
eadar-ghuidhear, -eir, -eirean, *s.m.* Intercessor, mediator.
eadar-ghuidhearachd,***s.f.ind.* Intercessorship.
eadar-ghrab,‡‡ *v.a.* Interpose.
eadar-iomlaideach, -eiche, *a.* Intermutual.
eadar-ionad, -aid, -an, *s.m.* Interval.
eadar-labhair, *v.a.* Intertalk.
eadar-labhrach, *a.* Interlocutory.
eadar-labhrair, -ean, *s.m.* Interlocutor.
eadar-làmh, -làimh, *s.f.* Temporary happiness.
eadar-luaths, -luaiths, *s.m.* Hurly-burly.
eadar-luighe, *s.f.ind.* Interjacency.
eadar-luigheach, *a.* Interjacent.
eadar-mhala,** *s.m.* Distance between the eyebrows.
eadar-mhalairteach,‡‡ -eiche, *a.* Intermutual.
eadar-mheadhon, -oin, *s.f.* Mediation. 2 Middle.
eadar-mheadhonach, -aiche, *a.* Mediatorial, intercessory. 2 Indifferent, middling. 2 Like a go-between.
eadar-mheadhonaich,* *s.f.* Middling state. Tha e 'san e., *he is but very indifferent.*
eadar-mheadhonair, -ean, *s.m.* Mediator, intercessor, reconciler, go-between, arbiter. 2 Interpreter.
eadar-mheadhonaireach, -iche, *a.* Intercessory, mediatorial.
eadar-mheadhonaireachd, *s.f. ind.* Mediation, intercession, continued mediation, practice of intercession.
eadar-mhìneachadh, -aidh, *s.m.* Interpretation. 2* Annotation, explanation. 3**Translating. Ag e—, *pr.pt.* of eadar-mhìnich.
eadar-mhìneachair, -ean, *s.m.* see eadar-mhìniche.
eadar-mhìnich, *pr. pt.* ag eadar-mhìneachadh, *v.a.* Interpret, translate. 2* Explain.
eadar-mhìniche, -an, *s.m.* Interpreter, translator. 2 Explainer.
eadar-mhìnichear, see eadar-mhìniche.
eadar-mhìnichte, *a.* & *past part.* of eadar-mhìnich. Interpreted, translated.
eadar-mhùth, *v.a.* Alternate.
eadarnach,** *a.* Fraudulent, malicious. Gu h-e., *fraudulently.*
eadarnaidh,** *s.f.* Fraud, double-dealing. 2 Malice.
eadar-phill,‡‡ *v.n.* Intervene.
eadar-phongaich,‡‡ *v.a.* Interpoint.
eadar-phòs,‡‡ *v.n.* Intermarry.
eadar-phòsadh,‡‡ *s.m.* Intermarriage.
eadarrach,‡‡ -aiche, *a.* Intermediate.
eadarrachd,‡‡ *s.f.* Interjacency.

eadar-riaghladh,‡‡ *s.m.* Interregnum.
eadar-rioghachd, *s.f.* Interregnum.
eadar-ruitheach,‡‡ *a.* Intercurrent.
eadar-ruith-fhear,‡‡ *s.m.* Internuncio.
eadar-sgàin,** *s.f.* Interposition. 2 Reconcilement. 3 Parting. 4 Greeting.
eadar-sgaoil,‡‡ *v.a.* Intersperse.
eadar-sgap, *v.a.* Intersperse.
eadar-sgapadh,‡‡ *s.m.* & *pr.pt.* Interspersion.
eadar-sgar,* *v.a.* Separate. 2 Divorce. 3 Pull asunder. 4 Analyze.
eadar-sgarach, -aiche, *a.* Separating, causing separation. 2 Divorcing, causing divorce. 3 Intersectant.
————dainn, -e, -ean, *s.f.* Separating, separation. 2 Divorce, divorcing. 3 Analysis.
eadar-sgaradair, *s.m.* Interpolator.
eadar-sgaradh,-aidh, *s.m.*see e— -sgarachdainn.
eadar-sgrìobh, *v.a.* Interline.
————adh,‡‡ *s.m.* Interlineation.
————ta, *a.* Interlinear.
eadar-shìon, *s.m.* Pet day (*lit* between weathers.
eadar-shlighe, -an, *s.f.* Intercurrence.
————ach, -eiche, *a.* Intercurrent.
eadar-shoillse, see eadar-sholus.
————ach, -iche, *a.* Having a glimmering light, as twilight.
eadar-shoillsich, *pr.pt.*ag eadar-shoillseachadh, *v.n.* Glimmer, as in twilight or dawn. 2** Dawn. 3 Shine between.
eadar-sholus, -uis, *s.m.* Twilight. 2**Dawn.
————ach,** *a.* Having twilight. 2 Glimmering, as twilight.
eadar-shreathach, -aiche, *a.* Interlinear.
eadar-shreathadh, *s.m.* Interlineation.
eadar-shreathaich, *v.a.* Interline.
eadar-shruth,(DC) *s.m.* Slack tide.
eadar-shruthach, *a.* Interfluent.
eadar-shuidheachadh, *s.m.* Interlocation.
eadar-thamull, -uill, *s.m.* Interval of time. 2 Interval between two remote distances.
eadar-theachd, *s.f.ind.* Intervention.
————ail, *a.* Intervenient.
————air, *s.m.* Internuncio.
eadar-theangachadh, -aidh, *s.m.* Interpretation, translation, version. 2 Act of interpreting or translating. Ag e—, *pr. pt.* of eadar-theangaich.
eadar-theangachair, see e— -theangair.
eadar-theangachd, *s.f.* see e— -theangachadh.
eadar-theangaich, *pr. pt.* ag eadar-theangachadh, *v.a.* Translate, interpret.
————te, *a.* & *past pt.* of eadar-theangaich. Translated, interpreted.
eadar-theangaidh,** *s.f.* Translation.
eadar-theangair, -ean, *s.m.* Interpreter, translator.
eadar-theangaireachd, *s.f.* see e— -theangachadh.
eadar-thig, *v.a.* Intervene.
eadar-thìreach, -iche, *a.* Mediterranean.
eadar-thoinn, *v.a.* Intertwine.
eadar-thràth, -àith, -àithean, *s.m.* Interval of time. 2**Noon. 3 Mid-day milking. Dòmhnach an eadar-thràith, *a certain Sunday in May when cows were brought to the milking-place for the first time in the year.*
eadar-thriath, -an, *s. m.* Interregnum. 2 Regency. 3 Regent.
eadar-thuinn, (AH) *s. f.* Hollow between two succeeding waves.
eadaruibh, *prep. pron.* see eadaraibh.
eadar-uidhe, *s.f.* Interval.
————ach, *a.* Interstitial.
eadar-ùine, *s.f.ind.* Intermission.
————ach, *a.* Intermittent.
eadaruinn, *prep. pron.* see eadarainn.
eadh, *adv.* It. Used adverbially, as, Seadh (is eadh) *yes, it is so*; an eadh ? *is it so ?* cha'n e., ni h-e., *it is not so*; an e nach cronaich e ? *is it that he will not rebuke ?* [not " an eadh nach cronaich e ? " as given by **]
eadh,‡ *s.m.* Space, time. 2 Opportunity.
eadh,(CR) *Suth'd.* for feadh, (extent.)
eadha, *s.f.* The aspen-tree, old name of the letter E. 2 The depth.
eadha, -chan, *s.m.* see eighe.
———dh, -aidh, -aidhean, see eadha.
eadhain,* see eadhon.
eadhal, -ail, *s.m.* Brand. 2 see éibheall. 3 (DMy) Udder of a heifer before calving.
eadhann, -ainn, *s.f.* Joy. 2 see eidheann.
eadhon, *adv.* To wit, namely, even, " viz. " (videlicet). Bheir mise, e. mise dìle air an talamh, *I, even I will bring a flood upon the earth.*
èadmhor, -oire, see eudmhor.
———achd, see eudmhorachd.
èadnan, see aodann.
èa-dòchas, -ais, see eu-dòchas.
———ach, see eu-dòchasach.
èa dòchasachd, see eu-dòchasachd.
èa-domhain, see eu-domhain.
†eadrad, (*for* eadar thu.) Eadrad agus mise (eadar thus' agus mise) *between you and me.*
eadradh, -aidh, -aidhean, *s.m.* Division of time. 2 Morning time of milking, or folding of cows, goats, sheep, &c. 3* Noon. 4**Lust, adultery. 5(DC) Process of milking—*Uist.* Mu e., *about noon.* [see eadar-thràth.]
eadraig, *pr.pt.* ag eadraiginn, *v. a.* Interpose, separate two combatants.
eadraiginn, -e, -ean, *s.f.* Act of interposing in order to separate two combatants. 2* Interference. Is minic a fhuair fear na h-eadraiginn buille, *often has the queller of strife been struck.* Ag e—, *pr.pt.* of eadraig.
———each, *a.* Interposing, parting, quieting, of or pertaining to a reconciliation, like a reconciliation.
èadrom, -uime, *a.* see aotrom.
———an, -ain, -an, see aotroman.
eadruinn, see eadarainn.
eadthorras, see eatorras.
eadtlaith, see eadtlathach.
eadtlathach, -aiche, *a.* Courageous, strong, undaunted. Gu h-e., *courageously.*
eadtreoir, -e, see eudtreoir.
èag-, *priv. prefix,* Variously spelt, eug-, ea-, eu-, ao-. see eu-.
eag, eige, -an, *s. f.* Nick, hack, notch, gap. 2 Slip. 3**Chap. †4 Moon. [†† gives *gen.* eig.]
èag, -a, see eug. [** gives éig for *gen.*]
eagach, -aiche, *a.* Notched, indented. 2** Deep. Glacag e. nan neòinean, *the deep dell of the daisies.*
eagachadh, -aidh, *s.m.* Hacking, notching. 2 Act of hacking or notching. 3**Dovetail. Ag e—, *pr.pt.* of eagaich.
eagaich, *pr.pt.* ag eagachadh, *v.a.* Hack, notch, mark with notches, nick, indent. 2* Imbed. 3**Dovetail.
———te, *a.* & *past part.* of eagaich. Hacked, notched, marked with notches. 2*Dovetailed.
eagail, *gen. sing.* of eàgal.
eagair,* *v.a.* see eagaraich.
eagal, -ail, *s. m.* Fear, timidity, fright, dread, terror. 2 Superstition. Dé is eagal duit ? *what harm can happen to you ?* ni h-e. leam, *I am not afraid*; tha eagal orm, (temporary), is eagal leam (permanent), *I am afraid*; is mór m' e., *I am much afraid*; cò a chuireas e. orm ? *who shall make me afraid ?* is beag m'

e., *I am not the least afraid* ; tha e. a chridh' air, *he is terrified out of his wits ;* an e. domhsa do chruth ? *am I afraid of your spectre ?* cha'n e. duit, *there is no fear of you ;* chuir an t-e. ás da, *superstition deprived him of his senses ;* uallach an eagail, *the burden of fear* ; air eagal gu'n tig osag, *for fear* (*or lest*) *a blast should come* ; air e. gu'n tuit e, *lest he fall* ; e. urramach, *reverence ;* e. tràilleil, *slavish fear ;* ghabh e e., *he took a fright.*
———ach, -aiche, *a.* Fearful, timid, cowardly. 2 Terrible, dreadful. 3 Causing fear. 4* Superstitious. 5**Skittish. Ni e., *a dreadful thing ;* duine e., *a terrible man, a superstitious person ;* tha e e., *he is superstitious* ; duine leth-eagalach, *a half-timid* or *cautious man.*
———achd,* *s.f.ind.* Terribleness, dreadfulness, apprehensiveness. 2 Superstitiousness.
eagalaich,‡‡ *v.a.* Intimidate.
eagall, -ail, see eagal.
———ach, -aiche, see eagalach.
eag-amhairc, see eug-sùl.
eagan, *adv.* Perhaps, see theagamh.
eagan,** -ain, *s.m.* Gizzard. 2 Depth. 3 Bottom. 4(AF) Salmon.
eagar, -air, *s.m.* Order, art, class, row, array. 2 Tenor, appointment. 3* Regular building, as of peats, hewn stone, &c. An cath an e., *the battle in order* ; eagar-cath, *battle-order.*
———ach, -aiche, *a.* Systematic, methodical, precise, well-ordered, arranged, in ranks, rows, or files. 2 Digestive.
———achadh, -aidh, *s.m.* Act of arranging, setting in order. Ag e—, *pr.pt.* of eagaraich.
———achd, *s.f.ind.* Correctness.
eagaradh, *s.m.* Digestion.
eagaraich, *pr.pt.* ag eagarachadh, *v.a.* Digest. 2 Set in order or rows, arrange. 3 Draw up in files, as an army. 4* Build as peats.
eagarair,** *s.m.* Digester.
eagarra, *a.* Exact, precise, methodical. 2 Artificial, by rule.
éag-bhroth,** *s.m.* Carrion.
éagcoir, see eu-coir.
éagcosg, -oisg, see aogasg.
éag-cosmhuil, see eu-cosmhuil.
—————eachd, see eu-cosmhuileachd.
éag-cruaidh, -e, *a.* see eu-cruaidh.
éag-cruas, -ais, see eu-cruas.
éag-cubhaidh, see eu-cubhaidh.
eagh, see eadha.
eaglach, -aiche, see eagalach.
eaglain, *s.m.* Tag of a lace.
eaglais, -e, -ean, *s.f.* Church, temple. An e. chathach, *the church militant* ; an e. neamhaidh, *the celestial church*; an e. bhuadhach, *the church triumphant* ; an E. Chaitleach, *the Catholic Church* ; an E. Easbuigeach, *the Episcopal Church* (the term " E. Shasunnach," is often applied by Gaelic speakers to the Scots Episcopal Church, which is not correct) ; an E. Chléireach, *the Presbyterian Church ;* an E. Stéidhichte, *the Established Church* ; an E. Shaor, *the Free Church* ; an E. Shaor Chléireach, *the Free Presbyterian Church ;* an E. Shaor Aonaichte, *the United Free Church* ; E. Bhaisteach, *a Baptist Church ;* E. Choimhthionalach, *a Congregational Church* ; e. fhàs, [or, more generally, e. bhàn,] *a vacant church.*
———each,** *a.* Ecclesiastical. 2 Like a church.
———each, -ich, *s.m.* Ecclesiastic, churchman.
———ear,* *s.m.* see eaglaiseach.
———eil, -eala, *a.* Ecclesiastical.
———iche,** *s.m.* see eaglaiseach.
†eaglam, -aim, *s.m.* see greim.
eaglan,** -ain, *s.m.* Biting.
†eaglasda, *a.* Ecclesiastical.
†eagma, *s.m.* Order, arrangement.
eagmhais, see eugmhais.
————each,** *a.* Famous, great. 2 Admirable.
————eachd,** *s.f.* Admirableness.
†eagmin, -ean, *s.m.* Winding, circuit, meander. E. mall, *a slow meander, winding of a river.*
eagna, *s.f.* Wisdom, prudence.
eagnach,** -aich, *s.f.* Blasphemy. 2 Complaint. 3 Resentment. 4 Cause of grief.
————, -aiche, *a.* see eagnaidheach.
————d, *s.f.ind.* Prudence. 2 Cunning. 3 Wisdom.
eagnadh, -aidh, -aidhean, see eagna.
eagnaidh, -ean, *s.m.* Philosopher, wise man. 2**Prudence. 3**Wisdom. 4**Caution, subtlety, sharpness. Comhairle o 'n e., *counsel from the wise.*
————, *a.* Wise. 2 Prudent. 3 Precise, accurate, punctilious, attentive to nick-nacks, extremely careful. 4**Subtle. Gu h-e., *exactly, accurately.*
————each, -eiche, *a.* Wise, prudent. 2 Precise, accurate, punctilious. 3 Subtle. 4 Sharp. Gu h-e., *prudently* ; duine e., *a prudent man.*
————eachd, *s.f.ind.* Wisdom, prudence. 2 Punctuality, exactness. 3 Pointedness about the minute articles of gain. 4 Subtlety, sharpness.
†eagnairc, *s. f.* Love. 2 Querulousness. 3 Complacency.
eagnuidh, -e, see eagnaidh.
————eachd, see eagnaidheachd.
eagonach,** *s.m.* Caitiff.
————,** *a.* Foolish.
éag-samhlachadh, see eug-samhlachadh.
éag-samhlachd, see eug-samhlachd.
éag-samhlaich, see eug-samhlaich.
éag-samhlas, -ais, see eug-samhlas.
éag-samhluidh, see eug-samhuil.
éag-samhuil, -e, see eug-samhuil.
—————eachd, see eug-samhlachd.
eag-sùl, *s.f.* Loop.
èairleigeach,* *a.* Urgent.
èairleigeadh, -idh, *s.m.* Temporary want. 2 Immediate need.
èairleis, see eàrlas.
èairlig, -e, -ean, *s.f.* Want, poverty.
èairlin, -e, -ean, *s.f.* Kelson of a boat, see bàta F9, p.73. 2 Bottom. 3 End or limit of anything. [†† gives éairlinn.]
èairneis, -ean, see àirneis.
————each, -iche, see àirneiseach.
————ich, see àirneisich.
eal,** *s.* (*for* neul) Swoon, trance.
eala,¶ -aidh, ealachan, *s.f.* Mute swan—*cygnus olor.* [‡‡ gives *sylvestris olor, s.m.*] 2(AC) Pillared stone. 3(AC) Sanctuary.
ealabar, *Laggan* for earball.
eala-bhàn, -aidh-bàine, -chan-bàna, *s.f.* Wild swan, hoopoe—*cygnus ferus.*
eala-bheag,¶ *s.f.* Bewick's swan—*cygnus Bewickii.*
eala-bheag an sgadain, (AF) *s.f.* Black guillemot, see calltag.
eala-bhuidhe,§ *s.f.* Perforated St. John's wort —*hypericum perforatum.* Badge of the Mackinnons. 2 Common hypericum. [illust.287.]
ealach, -aiche, *a.* Abounding in swans. Of, or belonging to, a swan.
———, -aiche, -aichean, *s.m.* Peg to hang anything on, as clothes, arms, &c.
———ag, -aige, -an, *s.f.* see ealachainn. This form (ealachag) is always used in *Poolewe* for a block or hacking-stock—W.C.

287. Eala bhuidhe. *288. Eala fleadh.*

ealachainn, -e, -ean, *s.f.* Armoury, ward-room, keeping-place, repository. 2 Peg, pin, hook, crook, bracket. 3 Stand for arms, stand to lay a gun upon. 4 Platform in a travelling crane. 5 Furnace, particularly of a distillery. 6 Fulcrum. 7* Hearth.

————each, *a.* Full of hooks, pegs, &c. 2 Of, or pertaining to, hooks, pegs, &c.

ealachd (an), *adv.* Presently. Is mór an ceò a thig as an e., *great will be the smoke from it presently* ; gu'm faic thu 'n tràigh an e. ann, *that you will see the ebb presently—Filidh, 80.*

ealachuinn,(DC) *s.f.* Disgust, scunner—*Argyll.*

ealadair,* *s.m.* Prowler.

ealadh, *s.f.* *prov.* for eala.

èaladh, -aidh, *s.m.* Creeping, crouching, as to get within reach of game. 2**Stepping softly. 3**Desertion.

ealadh, see ealdhain.

eala-dhà, see feala-dhà.

ealadhan, see ealdhain.

————ach, see ealdhanach.

ealadhanachadh, -aidh, see oileanachadh.

ealadhanta, see ealdhantach.

ealadhantach,** *a.* see ealdhantach.

ealadhantair,** *s.m.* see ealdhantair.

eala-dhonn,(AF) *s.f.* Cygnet, (*lit.* brown swan.)

eala-fhiadhaich,(AF) *s.f.* Wild swan, see eala-bhàn.

eala-fleadh, *s. f.* Stinking goose-foot—*chenopodium vulvaria* or *olidum.* [illust. 288.]

ealag, -aige, -an, *s. f.* Little swan. 2 Block, hacking-stock. 3** Bracket. Is math an e. a' chlach gus an ruigear i, *the stone is a good chopping-block till it is reached*—N.G.P.

——ach,** *a.* Like a block.

eala-gheal,(AC) *s.f.* White swan.

eala-ghlas,(AC) *s.f.* Cygnet, grey swan.

eala-ghual, *s.m.* Peat-charcoal used of old by the blacksmiths in Gaeldom instead of coal-dross.

ealaidh, -e, -ean, *s.f.* Ode, song. 2 Music. 3 Merriment. 4 Art, science. 5 Knack. Far an greadhnach luchd-e., *where the sons of mirth are glad* ; seòlta air e., *understanding science.*

èalaidh, *pr.pt.* ag èalaidh, & ag èaladh (MMcL) *v. n.* Creep, crawl, skulk, stalk. 2**Watch jealously. 3**Steal away, desert.

èalaidh (ag) *pr. pt.* of èalaidh. Creeping, stealing softly.

————each, -iche, *a.* Creeping, crawling. 2** Stealing softly, sneaking. 3**Jealous. 4** Deserting. Gu h-e., *jealously.*

————each, -ich, *s.m.* Deserter, revolter.

ealaidheachd,** *s.f.* Creeping softly, sneaking. 2 Propensity to jealousy.

ealain, see ealdhain.

——each, -iche, see ealdhanach. 2††Musical.

ealainn, *s.* Ditty, song.—*Dàin I. Ghobha.*

ealamh, -aimhe, *a.* Quick, nimble, ready. 2 Expert.

ealamhachd, *s.f.ind.* Alertness, quickness. 2 Acumen. 3*Expertness. An e., *soon, quickly.* [see ealachd.]

ealan, see ealdhain.

——ach, see ealdhanach.

——achd, see ealdhanachd.

†ealang, -aing, -an, *s.f.* Fault, flaw.

ealanta, see ealdhanach.

————chd, see ealdhantachd.

————s, see ealdhantachd.

†ealar, -air, *s.m.* Salt.

ealbh,‡ *s.* Bit, tittle.

——,(AF) *s. m.* Herd or drove of cattle.

——a, see ealbh.

ealbhar,‡ *s.m.* Good-for-nothing fellow—*Suth'd.*

ealbhuidhe,§ see eala-bhuidhe.

ealc,** *a.* Malicious, envious, spiteful.

ealchadh, -aidh, *s.m.* Grain pounded in the corn-pounder, previous to being ground—the pounding makes it easier to grind on the quern—DC. Ma's ealchadh a th' agad no gradan, *whether you have pounded or parched grain.*

ealchainn, -ean, see ealachainn. 2‡‡Arm-pit.

ealcmhor,** *a.* Malicious, spiteful, envious. 2 Lazy, sluggish.

ealdhain, -e, -ean, *s.f.* Learning, art, science. 2 Skill, ingenuity. 3 Poesy. 4*Trade, profession, occupation. 5**School, academy. 6 Trickery—*Gairloch.* [spelt *eallainn* here, the liquid *ll* and not the *ea* being long—DU.] Dé 'n e. a tha e a' leantainn ? (*or* a th' aige) *what is his occupation ?* a réir ealdhain an léigh, *according to the apothecary's art* ; fear e., *an artist, a mechanic.*

———— -chéirde,‡‡ *s.f.* Mechanics.

———— -ghluasadachd,‡‡ *s.f.* Mechanism.

———— -sgrìobhaidh,‡‡ *s.f.* Orthography.

ealdhanach, -aiche, *a.* Ingenious, expert, clever. 2 Alert. 3 Technical, scientific. 4 Artificial. 5 Curious.

ealdhanta,** *a.* Same meanings as ealdhanach.

————ch, see ealdhanach.

————chd,** *s. f.* Ingenuity, expertness, cleverness. 2 Quickness.

ealdhantair, *s.m.* Artificer.

ealdhantas, -ais, *s.m.* Same meanings as ealdhantachd.

†ealg, eilge, *a.* Noble, excellent. 2* Expert.

eal-ghrìs, -e, *s.f.* Horror. 2 Deadly paleness.

eall,** *s.m.* Essay, trial, proof.

ealla, *adv.* Nothing ado. Gabh e. ris, *have nothing ado with him* ; modh na crice, gabhail e. rithe, *hen politeness, letting her alone* ; 2 (MMcL) Gabh e. ris, *take stock of him, watch him.*

eallaban, -ain, see allaban.

†eallabhair, -e, *s.f.* Vast number. 2 Multitude.

†eallach, -aich, *s.m.* see meadhon.

†————, -aiche, *a.* Gregarious.

eallach, -a, *pl.* -an & eallaichean, *s. f.* [Always *m.* in *W. of Ross-shire*—WC.] Burden, armful, load. 2 Trick. 3 Battle, charge. 4**Bracket. 5(CR) Herd. 6(AF)Cattle given as tocher or dot.

————ail,* *a.* Hard, grievous. 2††Cumbersome.

eallag, -aig, see ealag.

eallaiche,** *s.f.* Household stuff, furniture.

eallaidh, *s.m.* Cattle.

†————e, *a.* White.

———— -mèithe,(AF) *s.m.* Fat cattle.

†eallaighe, *s.f.* see eallaiche.

eallainn, *Gairloch* for ealdhain.

eallamh,** -aimh, *s.m.* see eallach 6. 2 Wonder, astonishment.

eallan, -ain, *s.m.* Elecampane.
eallbha, see ealbh.
eallsg, -an, *s.f.* Termagant, scolding female.
——ail, -ala, *a.* Scolding. 2 Inclined to scold.
ealp, -an, *s.f.* Chip from an axe.
ealpadh, *a.* Notched.
ealpait(AF) *s.f.* Monster.
ealt, -a, ealtan, *s.f.* Covey or flight of birds; number of quadrupeds, as drove of cattle, trip of goats, rout of wolves, pace of asses, sounder of swine. E. eun, *covey of birds* ; e. asal, *a pace of asses.*
†ealt, *s.m.* Repentance.
——a, see ealt.
——ach, -aiche, *a.* Gregarious. 2**Flighty, as a flight of birds.
ealtag, see ialtag.
——-leathraich,(CR) *Arran* for ialtag.
——-leuthraigh,(AF) *s.f.* Bat.
ealtain, *s.* The bird world.
ealtainn, -e, -ean, *s.f.* see ealt. 2 see ealtuinn. Toirm ealtainn eun, *the noise of a flight of birds.*
————each, -iche, *a.* In flights, as birds.
ealtar, -air, *s.f.* Drove.
ealtraidh,(AC) *s.* Mischance.
ealtuinn, -e, -ean, *s. f.* Razor. 2 Any sharp-edged instrument. 3 see ealt. Mar e. ghéir, *like a sharp razor.*
————each, -aiche, *a.* Like a razor. 2 Sharp. 3 see ealtainneach.
ealuidh, see ealaidh.
eaman, see feaman.
†eamhainse, *s.f.* Wisdom.
†eamhan, -ain, *s.f.* see dias.
eamhanta,** *a.* Double.
†eamhuadh, -aidh, *s.m.* The connection of two things inseparable.
èan, see eun.
†èan, *s.* Water. *a.* One.
eanach, -aich, *s.f.* Dandriff. 2 Bounty. 3 Praise, renown. 4* Hat. 5 Scarf. 6 Scurf between the bark and trunk of a tree. 7 Down, wool.
——, -aich,§ *s.f.* The plant *nardus stricta.*

289. Eanach.

eanachaill,** *s.f.* see eanchainn.
eanach-gàraidh, -aiche-, *s.f.* Endive,—*cichorium endiva.*
eanag,(AF) *s.f.* Plover.
éanaidh, *Suth'd* (*Rob Donn*) for ainmhidh—*heifer.*
eanaraich, see eanraich.
eanasg, -aisg, -an, *s.m.* Tie, engagement.
eanbhruith, -e, see eanraich.
eanchaill, see eanchainn. Chaidh an t-e. as, *he was brained* ; ceanna gun e., *a brainless fellow—Gairloch.*
eanchainn, -e, -ean, *s.f.* Brains, the brain. 2 *Impudence, audacity. 3 Ingenuity, genius, capacity. Dh'fhàgadh e 'e., *he would leave his brains.*
————each, -iche, *a.* Of, or belonging to, the brain. 2 Ingenious. 3 Bold, impudent. 4**Clear-headed. 5** Cerebral. Gu h-e., *ingeniously.*
eanchainneachd,** *s.f.* Ingeniousness.
†eanda, *s.m.* Simple in medicine.
eandag, see deanntag.
————ach, see deanntagach.
ean-dealbhach, -aiche, see eun-dealbhach.
eang, -a, -an, *s.f.* Leg, foot, hoof. 2 Track, footstep. 3 Point of land. 4 Skirt, nook, corner. 5 Small portion. 6 Mark on an archer's bow, to guide the aim, also applied to the whole strength of the weapon. 7 The twelfth of an inch. 8 Gusset. 9**Nail. 10 *rarely* Year. 11 (AH) Muscle. 12 (DU) Any organ of the body. Cha ghluais e eanga, *he cannot move a limb* ; ghabh e a rithisd gu gluasad nan eang, *he betook himself again to exercise at running*; leum nan ceithir eang, *an agile standing leap*, in which the whole powers of a man's body were exercised. Sometimes used for *ionga.* 13* Mesh of a net.
eangach, -aiche, *a.* Hooked. 2 Nailed. 3 Nimble-footed. 4**Having a gusset. 5**Having headlands. 6**Full of footsteps. 7**Talkative. 8 see iongach.
————, -aich, -an, *s. f.* Fetter, snare. 2 Train of herring- or salmon-nets. 3 Drag-net. 4**Large fishing net. 5 Net-bladder. 6 Tuck. 7**Babbler. Eangaich bàis, *the agony of death.*
eangag, -aige, -an, *s.f.* Little foot. 2 Slender leg.
eangaich-bàis, *s.* Agony.
eangan, *pl.* -a, *s.m.* Mesh—*Dàin I. Ghobha.*
eangarra, *a.* Nimble, agile, quick. 2 Spirited, lively. 3 Stout. 4 Persevering. 5 Well-hoofed. 6 Cross-tempered, fretful, ill-natured.
————chd, *s. f. ind.* Nimbleness, agility. 2 Ill-nature.
eangbhaidh, -e, *a.* High-mettled, hard to tame.
eanghach,** -aich, *s.m.* **Bladder. †2 Babbler.
ean-ghabhrag, -aige, -an, *s.f.* Snipe, so called from its habit when mounting in the air of making sounds with its wings resembling the bleating of a goat.
eanghlas, -aise, *s.f.* Gruel. 2**Any weak drink. 3**Milk and water. Deoch eanghlais, *a drink of milk, meal and water.*
eanghnamh,** *s.* Liberality.
eanghnath,** *s. m.* Prudence. 2 Dexterity, cleverness. 3 Generosity.
————ach,** *a.* Prudent. 2 Dexterous, clever. 3 Generous. Gu h-e., *prudently.*
eangla,** *s.* Anniversary feast.
eangladh, -aidh, *s.m.* Entanglement. Tha e air e., *it is entangled.*
eang-ladhrach, -aiche, *a.* Well-hoofed.
eanlair, see eunlair.
eanlaith, see eunlaith.
eannach,** -aich, *s.f.* Innocence, spotlessness.
————,** *a.* Innocent.
eannraidh,(AF) *s.* Heifer—*Suth'd.*
eannsaich, *prov.* for ionnsaich.
eanntag, -aige, see deanntag.
————ach, -aich, *s.f.* see deanntagach.
————ach, *a.* see deanntagach.
eanraich, -ean, *s.f.* Kind of soup, flesh-juice, broth, gravy. Am fear a dh'itheas a sheanmhair, faodaidh e a h-e. òl, *he that eats his grandmother, may sup her broth.* When Fearchar lighiche had tasted the bree of the serpent, his master, who knew that his apprentice now had his eyes opened to see the secrets of nature, and his ears to understand the language of birds, threw the pan at him in wrath saying, Ma dh' òl thu an sùgh, ith an fheòil, *if you have supped the juice, eat the*

fesh—N.G.P.
eanruic, see ionraic.
ean-ruith,* see eun-bhrigh.
†eantar, see eadar.
eantog, see deanntag.
†eanmair, *s.f.* Bad weather. 2 Ill-luck.
ear, *s.f.ind.* The East, eastward. O 'n ear, *from the East*; an ear-thuath, *the North-East*; an ear-dheas [in *Gairloch & Lewis* an earra-dheas,] *the South-East*; gaoth an ear, *the East wind*; an ear 's an iar, *on every side*.
†ear, *s.m.* Head.
ear,†† *a.* Easterly.
earabhruich,** *a. & past part.* Parboiled. 2 Fomented.
———, *past pt.* earabhruich, *v.a.* Parboil. 2 Foment.
———te,** *past part.* see earabhruich.
earacais,(MMcL) *s.f.* Strait. Ni e 'chuis an e., *it will do for a shift.*
earach,** *a.* Feigned.
——ainn,(CR) *Reay country* for eanchainn.
earachall, see earchall.
earadh, see euradh. 2 see earradh.
———ain,** *s. f.* Bit, bridle. E. sréine, *the reins of a bridle.*
earag, *s.f. Suth'd.* for adharc. 2(AF)Squirrel.
earail, earalach, earalaichean, *s.f.* Exhortation, urging. 2 Importunacy. 3 Caution, warning. 4 Provision. 5* Guard. 6**Reproof. 7 Bidding. Rinn e ro-earail, *he urged.*
——, *v.a.* see earalaich.
——each, see earailteach.
——ich, see earalaich.
earailt,* see earail.
——each, -iche, *a.* Cautious, circumspect. 2 Ready to exhort, exhorting. 3 Cautioning, warning. 4 Importunate. 5 Providing, provident, foreseeing.
——eachd,* *s.f.* Cautiousness. 2**Exhortation. 3 Importunacy. 4**Warning.
earair,†† *pr.pt.* ag earaiadh, [pron. uraradh in *Gairloch.*] *v.a.* Parch or dry corn.
†earais, *s.f.* End, conclusion. 2 Tail.
earal, -ail, see earail.
——ach, -aiche, see earailteach. Gu h-e., *importunately.*
——achadh, -aidh, *s.m.* Exhorting, act of exhorting. 2*Putting one on one's guard, warning. 3**Importunacy. Ag e—, *pr.pt.* of earalaich.
earaladh,** -aidh *s.m.* Cautioning. 2 Importunacy. 3 Exhortation.
earalaich, *pr.pt.* ag earalachadh, *v.a.* Exhort, urge, press. 2 Caution, warn. 3 Entreat. Dh' e. mi air, *I cautioned him.*
———e, -an, *s.m.* Exhorter.
———idh, *fut. aff. a.* of earalaich.
———te, *past pt.* of earalaich.
earalas, -ais, *s.m.* Foresight, precaution. 2 Sagacity. 3 Provision. 4 Caution. 5 Exhortation.
——ach, -aiche, *a.* Cautious, circumspect.
earar, *adv.* (an earar) The day after to-morrow.
earārach, *a.* Eastern—*Islay.*
———, -aich, *s.m.* see earāradh 4.
earāradh, -aidh, *s. m.* Seeking, searching. 2 Night watching of the dead. 3 Parching of corn for the quern, by putting it in a pot over the fire. 4 Corn so prepared. Ag e—, *pr. pt.* of earair. Air earāradh, *on the search*; e. maidne, *morning search*; e. chlòimh, *wool-search*; e. dhaoine, *seeking people.*
earārais, (an earārais) which see.
earas,** -ais, *s.m.* End, conclusion. 2**Consequence.
earasaid, -e, -ean, *s.f.* Square of cloth, usually

290. Earasaid.

tartan, worn over the shoulders of females, and fastened before with a brooch, female robe. 2 Ornament. 3 Petticoat. 4 Simar. 5 Hoop. [** says the e. covered the whole body, and was worn without any underclothing.] Cha choisinn balbhan e., 's cha'n fhaigh amadan oighreachd, *a dummy won't win a mantle, nor a fool get an inheritance.* The use of the word *earasaid* here is peculiar, the article of dress it denotes being known to us only as feminine. The second half of the proverb means that no fool can *win* a fortune —N.G.P.
ear-astar,‡‡ -air, *s.m.* Longitude.
earb, *pr.pt.* ag earbsadh, *v.a. & n.* Trust, confide, hope, rely. 2 Bid, command. 3***rarely* Tell, relate. Earbam ris, *I confide in him*; earbam riut, *I confide in you*; na h-earb as a sin, *do not depend on that*; earbaibh á Dia, *trust ye in God.*
earb, -a, *pl.* -aichean, ††& -an, Roe. 2***rarely* Command. 3 Offer. 4 Employment. Mhosgail an e., *the roe awoke.*
——ach,* *a.* Full of, or like roes. 2 Of, or belonging to, a roe.
earbag, -aige, -an, *s. f.* Young roe. 2 Little roe. An e. a' clisgeadh a leabaidh, *the young roe starting from its bed.*
——ach,†† *a.* Abounding in little roes. 2 Like little roes.
earbaidh, *fut.aff.a.* of earb.
earbail, -e, *s.f.* Trust.
earbais, -e, -ean, *s.f.* Inhibition, command.
earball, -aill, *s.m.* Tail. 2* Ludicrous name for the train of a dress. E. an eich, *paddock-pipe, horse-tail*; bun an earbaill, *the rump*; e. sguabach, *a bushy tail.*
——ach,** -aiche, *a.* Long-tailed. 2 Like a tail. 3 Of, or belonging to, the tail.
——-eich,§ Plants of the order *equisetaceæ* growing in the drier places.
—— -iasaid,‡‡ *s.m.* Affix. [cuil.
—— righ,§ *s.m.* The herb Robert, see righeal
earbar, *fut.pass.* of earb.
earbchean, (*for* earbaichean) *n.pl.* of earb.
earbsa, *s.f.* Confidence, hope, trust, reliance. Na cuir e. ann, *do not trust him.*
earbsach, -aiche, *a.* Confident, relying, trusting. 2 Accredited. E. 'na casaibh, *trusting to her legs* (*swiftness.*) [This ex. given by ** is not a Gaelic idiom, but only a translation

from English.]
earbsachd,* see earbsalachd.
earbsach, -aidh, *s.f.* see earbsa.
earbsadh, see earbsa.
earbsail, -ala, *a.* Trusty, confident.
earbsalachd, *s.f.ind.* Complete confidence, fullest assurance, trust.
earbull, see earball.
———ach, see earballach.
†earc, *s.f.* Cow. 2(AF) Heifer. 3 (AF)Trout. 4**Bee. 5**Honey. 6**Dew. 7**Salmon. 8 **Tax. 9**Heaven.
†—, *a.* Speckled. 2**Red.
earcail,** *a.* Pleasant, sweet, agreeable.
†earca-iucna, *s.pl.* White cows with red ears, notched cattle, fairy cattle.
†earcan, *s.pl.* Sweets, dainties, delicacies.
†earcdhath, *a.* Coloured red.
earc-dhruchd,** *s.f.* Mildew. Ma bhitheas e. ann, *if there be mildew.*
earchaill,** *s.f.* Prop, post, pillar. 2 Barring, hinderance.
earchall,** *a.* Evil.
earchall, -aill, *s. m.* Misfortune. 2 Loss by death of cattle. 3(DU) Sudden and unexpected loss of cattle. 4**Detriment. 5**Mischief. 6**Suffering. Is fad' a lean e. ris, *long has misfortune pursued him.*
———ach, -aiche, *a.* Subject to loss by death of cattle. 2**Calamitous, unfortunate.
earchanaich, *v.n.* Reflect.
†earchaomh, *a.* Noble.
earc-iucna, see earca-iucna.
earc-luachrach, see dearc-luachrach.
†eardach, -aich, *s.f.* Feast, solemnity.
eardanal,** -ail, *s.m.* Piper. 2 Trumpeter.
ear-dheas (an), *adv.* The South-East.
earfhitheach, *s.* Glede—*Dean of Lismore.*
ear-fhlaitheachd,** *s.f.* see iarlachd.
ear-fhlath, *s.m.* see iarla.
†earg, *v.a.* Build, frame, make up.
ear-ghabh,** *v.a.* Arrest, apprehend, make prisoner.
————ail,** *s.f.* Miserable captivity.
earghair,** *s.f.* Embargo, prohibition.
————,** *v.a.* Congratulate. 2 Forbid, prohibit.
earghalan,** -ain, *s.m.* Piper.
————,** *a.* Noisy, clamorous.
earghalt,(CR) *s.m.* Arable land.
†earghlais, -ean, *s.f.* Horror.
†earghlaiseach, -eiche, *a.* Horrible, nauseous.
ear-ghóbhlach, see earr-ghóbhlach.
eargnachadh, -aidh, *s. m.* Irritation, painful swelling. Ag e—, *pr. pt.* of eargnaich.
eargnadh,** -aidh, *s.m.* Conception, quickness of apprehension. 2**Devastation, destruction.
eargnaich, *pr. pt.* ag eargnachadh, *v.a. & n.* Inflame, enrage, cause or feel rage.
earghnaidh, *a.* Magnificent. 2 Worthy. 3 Virtuous. 4**Munificent.
—————,** *s.f.* Munificence.
†eargnamh, *s.f.* see aithne.
†————, *a.* see uasal.
†eargnumh, see gniomh.
earlach,** *a.* Diffusive.
earlachadh, -aidh, *s.m.* Preparing of food, i.e. the culinary preparations, and not the same as the southern word *deasachadh—Suth'd.*
èarlaid, -e, -ean, *s. f.* Expectation, hope. 2 Dependence, trust, confidence. 3††Land. 4(AH) The right sometimes sold by an outgoing to an incoming tenant to enter into possession of the arable land early in spring—the incomer doing the ploughing, sowing and planting, and subsequently claiming the resulting crop. It is in vogue only in places where Whitsunday is the removal term for farmers.
èarlaideach,** *a.* Expectant. 2 Dependent, confident.
†earlamh, *a.* Noble, grand, august.
èarlas, -ais, see àirleas.
†earmadh, see arm.
earn,¶ see iolair-mhara.
†earn, see eòrna.
earna,(AC) *s.* Invocation. E. Mhoire, *an invocation to the Virgin Mary.*
†earnach,‡‡ -aich, *s.m.* Iron.
èarnach, -aich, *s.f.* Red-water in cattle. 2* Murrain, bloody-flux.
——— -dhearg, (AC) *s.f.* Red murrain.
——— -dhubh,(AC) *s.f.* Black murrain.
earnadh,(AF)*s.m.* Black spawl, disease of cattle.
earnadh,** -aidh, *s.m.* Payment. 2 Assessment. 3 Promulgation. 4**Extension. 5** Prophecy.
earna-dhearg, see èarnach-dhearg.
——— -dhubh, see èarnach-dhubh.
èarnag, -aig, see àirneag.
———ach, *a.* see àirneagach.
earnaid,(AC) *s.f.* Fairy wort.
——— -shith, see earnaid.
earnail,** *s.f.* Part, share.
earnail,** *s.f.* Endowment. 2 Department of any science.
earnais, see àirneis.
†earnbhàs, -àis, *s.m.* Death by steel.
èaroch, see under beart-fhigheadaireachd.
èarr,** *v.a.* Clothe, array.
èarr, -a, -an, *s.m.* [*f.* in *Badenoch.*] End, conclusion. 2 Extremity, limit, boundary, bottom. 3 Tail, as of salmon. †4 Champion. 5 ‡‡Heroism. 6 see earran-geal. 7(AH)Deadwood in stern of a boat, see O 3, p.73. 8* Extremity of a barrel. 9 (DMy) Chimb of a tub or barrel. 10 (DMy) Rock submerged on a promontory. 11 (AH) Butt of a gun. Gu'm bu tapaidh thu féin air èarr a' ghunnaghlaic, *how expert you were at the butt of the gun !*
†èarr,** *a.* Noble, grand.
—ach, -aiche, *s.f.* Bottom of a dish. 2 Lower extremity. 3* Chimb of a tub or cask.
—ach,** *a.* Tailed. 2 Having a long tail. 3 Limited, bounded. Am bradan e., *the long-tailed salmon.*
Earrach, -aich, *s.m.* Spring (season.) [Among the old Gaels it was divided into two parts, E. Geamhraidh and E. Samhraidh.
Earrachail,* *a.* Spring-like.
earrachail,* *s.m.* Loss of cattle in Spring—*Skye.*
èarr-a'-chridhe, *s.f.* Kind of creeping plant.
earradh, aidh, -aidhean, *s.m.* Dress, habit, clothing. 2 Armour, accoutrements. 3 Wares, goods, commodities. 4**Tail. 5**Conclusion. 6**Limit, border. E. rìgh. *a king's robe* ; e. stàta, *a robe of state.*
————, see earradhubh.
earradhris,§ -e, -ean, *s.f.* Dog-brier, see ròs-nan-con.
earradhubh, -uibh, *s.m.* Wane. 2 The waning moon. 'San e., *on the wane.*
—————,** *a.* Waning. A' ghealach e., *the waning moon.*
earrag, -aige, -an, *s.f.* Taunt. 2‡ Blow. 3 see earag. 4‡ Shift, refuge, attempt. E. chéilidh, *a gossiping stroke*—said of a hurt received by one when visiting.
earragach, -aiche, *a.* Taunting.
èarragheall,* see èarr-gheal.
èarra-ghlan, *a.* Shapely-tailed. Thig bradan iteach, è., *a finned and shapely-tailed salmon shall come.*
earra-ghlòir, -e, *s.f.* Bold or taunting language.

2*Gibberish. 3‡ Vain glory. [*also* fearra-ghlòir.
———each, *a.* Foolishly talkative. 2 Vain-glorious.
earra-ghobhlach, see èarr-ghòbhlach.
èarraich, *a.* Bottom-most. Thilg e 'n cearcal è., *he has cast the bottom hoop*—said of one losing his chief support or honour.
earraid, -ean, *s.m.* [*s.f.* in *W. Ross-shire.*] Tipstaff, officer of the law. 2 King's messenger. 3 Notary public. 4 Sheriff-officer. †5**Mistake, fault.
———each, -iche, *a.* Pertaining to messengers. 2 Quarrelsome. 3**Erroneous.
earraig, -e, -ean, *s.f.* Shift. 2 The last shift, great deal ado, greatest strait.
———each, -iche, *a.* Ingenious. 2*Straitened.
earraigh, -ean, *s.m.* Captain, commander.
earrailteach,** *a.* Hospitable.
earran-gheal,(AF) *s.m.* Gazelle (*lit.* white tail.)
earrann, -ainn, -an, *s.f.* Share, portion, section of land, division. 2 Province. 3 Paragraph, clause. Ceithir earrannan, *four parts.* [Earr-ainn is used as *nom.* in *Gairloch.*]
earrannach,* *s.f.* Fleece, wool.
———adh, -aidh, *s.m.* Division. 2 Act of dividing, or making into shares. Ag e—, *pr.pt.* of earrannaich.
earrannaich, *pr. pt.* ag earrannachadh, *v.a.* Share, divide.
———e, -an, *s.m.* Sharer, divider.
earraradh, see earararadh.
earras, -ais, -an, *s.m.* Wealth, treasure, richness, property, goods, portion. 2 Provision, precaution. 3 The person secured or the principal. Théid Eilidh 'sa h-earras dhach-aidh, *Helen and her marriage-portion shall go home* ; cha'n fhèarr an t-urras na'n t-earras, *the security is not a whit better than the principal (the one secured)* ; gun òr, gun e., *penniless and without property.*
earrasach, -aiche, *a.* Rich, wealthy. 2**Having goods or commodities. 3**Of, or pertaining to goods or commodities.
earrasaid, *s.f.* see earasaid.
earrasgaidh, *s.f.* Superfluity.
èarr-bhruich, *v.a.* Stew.
èarr-dhearg,¶ *s.f.* Redpole, see ceann-dearg. 2 (McL & D)Redstart, see cam-ghlas.
èarrdhris, *s.f.* see ròs-nan-con.
èarr-dhubh, see earradhubh.
èarr-fhighe, -an, *s.f.* Weaver's tenter.
èarr-ghainmhich,¶*s.f.* Sandpiper, see luatharan.
earrghas, *s.m.* Mainpiece of plough.
èarr-gheal, -ile, -an-geala, *s.f.* The bird white-tail. 2 The pygarg of Scripture, a kind of antelope. [** gives *s.m.*]
earr-ghlòir, -e, see earra-ghlòir.
———each, see earra-ghlòireach.
èarr-ghóbhlach, -aiche, *a.* Fork-tailed. Na bric e., *the fork-tailed trout.*
èarr-ite, -an, *s.f.* Tail-feather. 2(AH) The caudal (sometimes the anal) fin of a fish.
èarr-iteach,†† *a.* Having tail-feathers.
earrlaich,‡‡ *v.a.* Kiln-dry.
earrlain,(AC) see èirlin.
earrlainn,** *s.f.* Limit of anything. 2 End,conclusion, close.
earrlait,(AC) *s.f.* Rich soil, ground manured one year and productive the next. 2 Productive animals. 3 Prosperous undertaking.
èarr-loisgeach, -iche, *a.* Nipping. 2 Taunting.
èarr-loisgidh, (AH) *a.* Pleasant. 2 Shrewd, quick of apprehension, discerning, perspicacious. [Applied to persons.]
èarrnag, -aige, -an, see àirneag.
èarr-thalmhuinn,§ *s.f.* Yarrow, see lus-chosg-adh-na-fola.
†earsail, *s.m.* Song.
earthrath, *adv.* for an earar.
ear-thuath, *s.f.* The North-East. [Ear-thrŏth in *Gairloch*, the o being full like English, but short, as in *bow, low.*]
eas, -a, -an, *s.m.* Waterfall, cataract. 2 Cascade. 3**Stream with high precipitous banks. Gach coille, gach doire 's gach e., *every wood, grove and waterfall.*
eas,** *s.f.* see neas. 2(AF) Eel.
eas-, *privative prefix*, signifying *in-*, *un-*, as, eas-aonachd, *disagreement.*
†eas, *v.a.* Do, make.
easach, -aich, -achean, *s.m.* Thin water-gruel. 2**Panada, bread boiled in water, saps. 3** Dark, deep, rocky stream. 4**Cataract, cascade. Mar thoirm easaichean, *like the roar of cataracts.*
———, -aiche, *a.* Abounding in waterfalls.
———,* *s.f.* see eas, *s.m.*
†easadh, -aidh, *s.m.* Sickness, disease.
easag, -aige, -an, *s.f.* Pheasant—*phasianus colchicus.* 2 Squirrel. 3**see neasag. 4**Shrew-mouse. 5(AF) Stoat. 6(AF)Ermine.
———ach,†† *a.* Abounding in pheasants, squirrels, &c.
easaich, *gen.sing.* of easach.
easaichean, *n. pl.* of easach.
easaille,** *s.f.* Dispraise, disparagement.
easair,** *s.f.* Excess.
easair,(AH) *v.a.* Roll in mud, bespatter.
easal,** -ail, *s.m.* Tail.
eas-amail, -e, *a.* Unseasonable.
easamh, see eis-dhamh.
easamplair, -ean, see eisimpleir.
easamplar, -air, -airean, see eisimpleir.
easan, -ain, -an, *s. m.* Little waterfall or cascade. 2 *variant* of esan. 3(AF) Squirrel. 4(AF) Little weasel. 5(AF)Stoat. 6(AF)Ermine. 7(AF)Launce eel. 8††Thin gruel. Crònan t' easain srùthlaich, *the murmur of thy flowing cataracts.*
easaonach, see eas-aontach.
———d, see eas-aontachd.
easaont, -a, *s.f.* Dissention, disagreement.
———ach, -aiche, *a.* Dissenting. 2 Disobedient, rebellious. 3 Guilty, transgressing. 4**Repugnant. Gu h-e., *disobediently.*
———achadh, -aidh, *s.m.* Disagreeing. 2 Act of disagreeing. Ag e—, *pr.pt.* of eas-aonaich.
———achd, *s. f. ind.* Disagreement, discord, schism, factiousness, dissent. 2 Disobedience, insubordination, rebellion.
———aich, *pr.pt.* ag easaontachadh, *v.a.* Disagree, discord, secede.
———as, -ais, *s.m.* Disobedience, transgression, trespass, iniquity. 2**Discordance, faction. Air son easaontais, *on account of transgression.*
easar,‡ see eas, *s. m.* 2 Surface drain in a byre or stable to carry away the water.
———adh,(AH) *s.m.* The having of mud clinging to all parts of one's attire, bespattering. Ag e—, *pr.pt.* of easair.
———aich, -e, -ean, *s.f.* The boiling of a pool where a cascade falls. 2 Bustle, tumult, confusion, noise. 3* State of requiring much attendance and service without moving from your seat. 4(WC) Sportive leap, as of a fish playing itself. Dè an e. a bh' air ! *what sportive leaps it was making !*
——— -chasain, *s.f.* Thoroughfare.
easard,** -aird, *s.m.* Quarrel. 2 Cataract. 3 Fowl-house.
†easarg, -an, *s.m.* & *f.* Tumult.
easargain,** *s.f.* Contrition.

easarguin,** *s.f.* Tumult, confusion. 2 Mob. 3 Quarrel.
easarlaich,** *v.a.* Philtre.
easarluidbeachd,** *s.f.* Incantation.
†easba, *s.m.* Want, scarcity, defect. 2 Vanity. 3**Idleness. 4**Absence. [easbhuidh.]
——— -bràghad, -aid, *s.m.* King's evil.
easbach,(PM) *s.m.* Iron loop or chain used for securing doors or gates.
easbadh,** -aidh, *s.m.* Vanity. 2 Idleness.
——— -brothach,§ *s.m.* Ox-eye, see neòinean mór.
easbal, see abstol.
———air,* *s. m.* Trifling, tall, slender, handsome, good-for-nothing fellow.
easbaloid, -e, *s.f.* Absolution.
———each,** *a.* Pertaining to absolution.
easba-riaghad, see easba-bràghad.
easbarta, *s.pl.* Vespers, evening prayers.
eas-bhacaig,** *s.f.* Obstacle.
easbhuidh, -e, -ean, *s. f.* Want, defect. 2 Necessity. 3 Caret in *writing* (^) Dè tha a dh' e. ort ? *what do you want ?* gun e. gheibh e, *he will receive without fail.*
———each, -iche, *a.* Poor, empty, needy, lacking, wanting, deficient. Duine e., *a needy man.*
easbuig, -ean, *s.m.* Bishop. E. na Ròimhe, *the Pope.*
——— bàn,§ bàin, *s. m.* Great ox-eye, see neòinean mór.
———each, -aiche, *a.* Episcopal. An eaglais Easbuigeach, *the Episcopal church.*
———eachd, *s. f. ind.* Bishopric, seat of a bishop. 2 Prelacy, episcopacy.
———ich,‡‡ *v.a.* Bishop.
†easbul, -uil, see abstol.
†———achd, see abstolachd.
†easc, see uisg.
†eascaich, *s.f.* Quagmire, fen.
eascain, -e, -ean, *s. f.* *Imprecation, cursing, blasphemy, envy, slander. †2 see ascaoin. Le h-e.'s le mallachadh,*with slander and cursing.* [eascainnt in *Uist*—PM.]
eascair,** *s.f.* Storm, blustering wind. 2 Surprise. 3 Warning.
———deach, -iche, *a.* Inimical, hostile. 2 Inveterate. Gu h-e., *hostilely.*
———dean, *n.pl.* of eascaraid.
———deas, -eis, *s.m.* Enmity,hostility. Luchd eascairdeis, *private enemies.*
———deil, -e, *a.* Opponent.
eascann, see easgann.
eascaoin, -e, *a.* see ascaoin. 2* ‡Unsound, as grain—*Islay.*
eascaoin,* *s.m.* Unsoundness, as of meal, grain, &c.—*Islay.* 2 for ascaoin.
———each,** *a.* Malignant, malicious, envious. Gu h-e., *malignantly.*
———eachd,** *s.f.* Malignity, maliciousness, enviousness.
†eascar, *s.m.* Fall. 2 Shooting into ears, flourishing.
eascar, -air, *s.m.* see eascaraid. Cia an t-e. ? *who is the enemy ?*
eascara, -an, see eascaraid.
eascaraid, -cairdean, *s.m.* Adversary, enemy. Pòg e., *an enemy's kiss.*
eascard, -aird, see ascart.
eas-chridheach, -iche, *a.* Discordant.
———d, *s.f.ind.* Disagreement.
eascnadh, -aidh, see asgnadh.
eascoin, see eascaoin.
———each, see eascaoineach.
———eachd, see eascaoineachd.
eas-comain, -e, -ean, *s.f.* Ill-requiting, ungrateful return.
†eascoman, *a.* Dirty, nasty, filthy.
†easconn, -oinn, *s.f.* Moon. 2 Old man.
†eascra, *s.m.* Cup, drinking vessel.
†eascradh, -aidh, *s.m.* Walking, stepping,marching.
†eascu, *s.f.* Eel. [*for* easgann.]
easdradh,* *s.m.* see easradh.
easg,* -a, -an, *s.f.* Ditch formed by nature. 2 Fen. 3 Bog. 4 see easgann. 5 see easga.
†easga, *s.f.* The Moon. [This word was in use in Braemar in the 18th. century.]
easgach,* *a.* Full of ditches. 2**Like an eel. 2**Abounding in eels.
easgaid, -e, -ean, see iosgaid. 2 see neasgaid.
———each,* -iche, *a.* see iosgaideach, *a.*
———each,* -ich, *s.* see iosgaideach, *s.*
easgaidh,** *s.f.* Quagmire.
èasgaidh, -e, *a.* Ready, nimble, active. 2 Willing to oblige. 3*Officious. 4 Nimble to do a thing you do not need to do, but neglectful of duty. 5**Obsequious. 6 Laborious. Is e. an droch ghille air chuairt, *the lazy servant is active from home.*
———eachd, *s.f.ind.* Nimbleness. 2 Readiness to oblige. 3* Officiousness, excessive readiness of a lazy person to do what he does not need to do.
easgainn, see easgaidh.
easgairc,** *s.f.* Quagmire, bog, fen.
easgall,** -aill, *s.m.* Storm, blustering wind. 2 Wave. 3 Noise.
———ach,** *a.* Stormy, blustering. 2 Billowy. 3 Noisy.
easgan, *n.pl.* of easg. 2 see iosgaid.
easgann, -ainne, -an, *s. f.* Eel. 2 Grig. 3 Merry creature. 4 Anything below natural age. 5 see iosgaid. Là fhéill Mo Cheasaig bithidh gach e. torrach, *on St. Kessock's day every eel is pregnant.* In a MS. collection of proverbs *easan* is substituted for *easgann.* This is intelligible, though the use of the word *torrach* as applied to water is anomalous, the reference to eels is more singular, that fish being of ill-repute in Gaeldom—N.G.P. [A " band " of eels is 250, a " stick " 25.]
———ach, -aiche, *a.* Lively, supple or slippery as an eel. 2 Anguliform. 3 Wanton.
easgann-bheag, (AF) *s.f.* Grig.
——— -bhreac,(AF) *s.f.* Lamprey.
——— -faragaidh,(AF) *s.f.* Eel.
——— -mhara,(AF) *s.f.* Conger eel.
†easgar, -air, *s.m.* The plague. 2 Grain of corn. 3 Kernel.
easgar,** *s.* Fall.
†easg-bhàineach, -eiche, *a.* Lunatic.
easg-bheag,(AF) see easgann bheag.
——— -bhreac, see easgann bhreac.
eas-ghleusadh, -aidh, *s.m.* Confusion.
easg-mhara, see easgann-mhara.
easgonnach, -aiche, see easgannach.
†easgradh, -aidh, *s.m.* Cup, drinking vessel. 2 Grain of corn. 3 The plague.
easgraich, -e, -ean, *s. m.* Torrent. 2 Coarse mixture.
easg-shùileach,** *s.f.* Conger eel.
easguid, -e, -ean, see iosgaid.
———each, see iosgaideach.
èasguidh,** see èasgaidh.
†easguinn, -e, *a.* see easgaidh.
easgull, see easgall.
easgunn, see easgann.
†eas-idhe, *a.* Conspicuous.
eas-ionraic, -e, *a.* Dishonest. 2**Faithless. 3 **Wicked.
eas-ionracas, -ais, *s.m.* Dishonesty. 2 Faithlessness. 3**Wickedness.
ea-sìth,** *s.f.* Mischief. 2 Disturbance.

easlabhra,** *s.m.* Bounty, courtesy, affability.
easlach, see easloch.
easlain, see easlan.
ea-slaine, *s.f.* see easlaint.
easlaint, -e, -ean, *s.f.* Infirmity, ill-health, sickness. Luchd-easlainte, *invalids, sick people.*
———each, -iche, *a.* Invalid, sickly, infirm. Gu h-e., *unhealthy.*
———eachd. *s.f.ind.* Morbidness, sickliness, infirmity. 5 Unwholesomeness.
———ich, *v.a.* Indispose.
ea-slainnt, see easlaint.
easlan, -aine, *a.* Infirm, sick, not healthy. Bha mi e., *I was sick.*
eas-leine, -léintean, *s.f.* Shroud, winding-sheet. [see eislinn.]
easloch, *s.m.* Lake, pool.
easmaidh,** *s.f.* Lath. 2 Spear.
easmail, -malach, see eisimeil. †2 Reproach, reproof.
———teach, -ich, *s.m.* see eismeilteach.
easanadh,** -aidh, *s.m.* Time. 2 Music, melody. 3 Song.
†easmoid, -e, *s.f.* Disrespect, dishonour.
†———each, -eiche, *a.* Disrespectful.
easmunn, see easgann.
ea-snàth,** -snaith, *s.m.* Want of sufficient web for the loom.
easomaid,** *s.f.* Disrespect, dishonour.
———each,** *a.* Disrespectful, disobedient.
easoman,** -ain, *s.m.* Welcome.
eas-onoir, -e, *s. f.* Dishonour, abuse. 2**Disgrace. 3**Reproach. 4**Dishonesty.
eas-onorach, -aiche, *a.* Dishonourable. 2 Abusive. 3 Ill-bred. 4**Disgraceful. 5** Reproachful. 6**Dishonest.
———adh, -aidh, *s.m.* Dishonouring. 2 Disgrace. 3 Abuse. 4 Act of dishonouring or disgracing. Ag e—, *pr.pt.* of eas-onoraich.
eas-onoraich, *pr. pt.* ag eas-onorachadh, *v.a.* Dishonour, abuse. 2**Disgrace.
———te, *a. & past pt.* Dishonoured, abused.
†easontach, -aiche, *a.* Rude, guilty.
easontachd, see easaontachd.
eas-òrdach, -aich, *a.* Factious, unruly. 2** Irregular.
eas-òrduchadh, -aidh, *s.m.* Disarranging, disordering. 2 Act of disordering or confusing. 3 Disorder, confusion, disarrangement, anarchy. Ag e—, *pr.pt.* of eas-òrduich.
eas-òrdugh, -uigh, -uighean, *s.m.* Disorder, anarchy, confusion, irregularity, unruliness, ado.
eas-òrduich, *pr. pt.* ag eas-òrduchadh, *v.a.* Disarrange, confuse.
easorgain,** *s.f.* Contrition.
†easorgnadh, -aidh, *s.m.* Squeezing, crushing.
easpuig, see easbuig.
———each, see easbuigeach.
———eachd, see easbuigeachd.
easradh, -aidh, *s.m.* Ferns or heather to litter cattle.
easraich, -e, -ean, *s.f.* see easaraich. 2 Sowens —*Arran.*
easran, -ain, *s.m.* Dispersion.
†easrannachadh, -aidh, *s.m.* Decaying substance.
eastarruing, -e, -ean, see as-tharruing.
†eastraloch, -oich, *s.m.* Astrologer.
easuain,** *v.a.* Scum, skim.
eas-ùmhail, -ala, *a.* Disobedient, stubborn, insubordinate, rebellious. 2 Irreverent. E. do pharantan, *disobedient to parents* ; gu h-e., *disobediently.*
eas-ùmhlachd, *s.f.ind.* Disobedience, contumacy, obstinacy, rebelliousness, insubordination. 2 Disloyalty. 3 Irreverence. Luchd na h-e., *the insubordinate.*
eas-ùmhlaich, *v.a.* Disobey.
eas-urram, -aim, *s.m.* Disrespect, contumacy, dishonour, disgrace, reproach.
———ach, -aiche, *a.* Disrespectful, contemptuous. 2 Stubborn. 3 Dishonourable, disgraceful, causing dishonour or disrespect.
———achadh, -aidh. *s.m.* Disobedience, act of disobeying or rebelling. 2**Degrading, disgracing or treating contemptuously. Ag e—, *pr.pt.* of eas-urramaich.
———achd, *s.f.ind.* Contumacy, stubbornness. 2††Dishonour, disrespect.
———aich, *pr.pt.* ag eas-urramachadh, *v.a.* Condemn. 2**Dishonour, treat with contempt, degrade, despise.
†eata, *a.* Old, ancient, antique.
†eatach, -aich, *s.m.* Elderly person. 2 Elder.
†eatal, -ail, *s.m.* Flight. 2 World. 3 Pleasure, delight.
†eatha, *s.f.* Cattle. 2 *s.m.* Corn.
eathaidh,(AF) *s.pl.* Birds.
eathar, -air, -thraichean, *s. m.* [Always *f.* in *Gairloch*, and the *gen. sing.* frequently eathrach—DU.] Generally used as the name for a small fishing-boat in *W. of Ross-shire*, the word " bàta " being seldom heard there. 2 **Skiff, barge, vessel. 3**Cup. E. iasgaich, *a buss* ; e. ùr is seana chreagan, *a new boat and old rocks*—suggestive of a thousand tragedies beyond the mere literal translation. Both rock and boat are personifications ; the rock is old and cunning and unscrupulous, the boat is young and simple and unsuspicious, and when the two come into collision, the boat goes down.
———-àile,** *s.m.* Balloon.
———-trithinn,(WC) *s.m.* Boat on hire which is paid for with a share of the fish caught—*Poolewe, &c.*
†eathla, *s.pl.* Prayers.
eathlamh, -aimhe, see ealamh.
———achd, see ealamhachd.
eathrach, *gen. sing.* of eathar, in *Gairloch.*
eathraichean, *n.pl.* of eathar.
†eatla, *s.m.* Boldness. 2 Sadness.
eatlathach,** *a.* Bold, intrepid. 2 Sad. Gu h-e., eugmhaiseach, *in a bold and singular manner.*
———d,** *s. f.* Boldness, intrepidity. 2 Sadness.
eatorra, *prep. pron.* Between them. 2 Among them. E. fhéin, *among themselves*; thàinig e., *they quarrelled.*
éa-torrach, *a.* see neo-thorrach.
eatorras, -ais, *s.m.* Mediocrity. 2*Middle state of health. Tha mi an e., *I am tolerably well, in tolerable health.*
éa-tràthach, -aiche, see eu-tràthach.
ea-treòir, see eu-treòir.
éa-treòrach, -aiche, *a.* see eu-treòrach.
éa-treun, -éine, see eu-treun.
éa-tròcair, see eu-tròcair.
———each, -iche, see eu-tròcaireach.
éa-trom, -truime, see aotrom.
———achadh, see aotromachadh.
———aich, see aotromaich.
———aichte, see aotromaichte.
———an, see eutroman.
———uich, see aotromaich.
ea-truime, see aotruime.
———ad, see aotruimead.
†eatuaithcheall, *s.f.* Imprudence, folly.
†eatualaing, -e, -ean, *s.f.* Injury.
ebeir, see eabar.
†ecconta, *a.* Silly, unwise, see eu-connta.
†eccnionne, see ecconta.
‡echt, *s.m.* Death, murder. 2 Exploit. [euchd.]

†echtge,(?) (AF) s. Cow, cattle.
†ecmacht,‖ a. Impotent.
†econn,‖ s.m. Lunatic, idiot. [euconn.]
†ecsidhe, a. Apparent, clear.
†ed, see feudail. 2 see eit. 3 see eid.
†ed, v. Make. 2 Receive. 3 Handle.
†edal, s.f. see feudail. [eudal.]
†edearbh, a. Uncertain.
†edeighneach,(AF) s.m. Gelded horse.
†edidh, -e, see eitigh.
†edir, see eadar.
†edire, s.pl. Hostages.
ei-, see eu-.
eibeantach, a. Faulty, inferior, faint, wishy-washy—*Rob Donn.*
éibh, see éigh.
eibheadh, -idh, s.f. see eadha.
éibheall, -bhle & -bhill, pl. -bhlean, [*nom.* in *Gairioch* eibhill—*bh* silent.] s. f. Live coal. 2**Flame. 3**Hearth-fire. Mar é. 'sa bhealach, *like a fire in the pass.*
eibheis, see aibheis.
éibhinn, -e, a. Odd, curious. 2 see aoibhinn. 3 Delightful. 4(PM) Jolly and witty—*Uist.*
———, s.f. see aoibhinn.
Is é. an gill thu, *what a funny fellow you are!*
———each, -iche, see aoibhneach.
———eachd, see aoibhneas.
eibhir, s.f. Granite.
eibhle,* see éibheall.
éibhleach, -iche, a. Of, or abounding in live coals.
éibhlead, see éighlead.
———ach, see éighleadach.
éibhleadh, -idh, see féileadh.
éibhleag, -eige, -an, s.f. Burning coal. 2 Little fire. 3††Small ember. Mhùch iad m' é., *they have quenched my fire.*
éibhleagach, -aiche, a. Of or belonging to burning coal, like a burning coal.
éibhlean, n.pl. of éibheall.
éibhlich,** v.n. Sparkle, kindle, flame.
†éibhlich, v.n. Sparkle.
†eibhligh, see eibhlich.
†eibhling, v.n. Spring off or on.
éibhlisg,(CR) s.f. Slow or stupid woman—*W. of Ross.*
éibhneach, -iche, see aoibhneach.
———d,†† s.f. Joyfulness.
éibhneas, -eis, see aoibhneas.
éibhrionn,* see eibhrionnach.
eibhrionnach, -aich, s.m. Castrated goat, wether goat.
eibhrionta, see eibhrionnach.
†eibir, -e, -ean, s.f. Report, character.
eiblit,** s.f. Interjection.
†eibteadh, for ràdh.
†eiceas, -eis, s.m. Art, science.
eiceart, -eirte, see eu-ceart.
———as, see eu-ceartas.
eich, *gen.sing. & n. pl.* of each.
éich, see éigh.
†eicsidhe, a. Apparent, manifest.
†eid,** int. Word used on discovery of any animal of prey, or game, meant to give notice to the hunting companion to be in readiness to seize the animal.
†eid, -e, s.f. Tribute, tax, subsidy. 2 see feudail.
éid, v.a. Clothe, dress. 2 Accoutre, put on a uniform. 3 Mount, as with silver. 4 Mount, as swingles. 'Ga éideadh féin, *putting on his accoutrements, dressing*; ged éid thu thu féin le corcur, *though thou clothe thyself with crimson.* pr.pl. ag éideadh.
eid-bheann,* Clough.
éide, see éideadh.
——ach, -iche, a. Clothed, harnessed, accoutred, armed.
éideadh, -idh, -ean, s.m. Clothing, apparel. 2 Act of clothing. 3 Armour. 4 Act of arming. 5*Uniform. 6 The garb of the Scottish Gael. 7**Dressing. 8**see eige. É. anairt, *a web of linen*; é. thùilinn, *a web of twilled linen*; é. làimhe, *a gauntlet*; 'na é. soillse, *in his armour of light*; ar n-é. cuirp, *our body garments*; gun é. gun each, *without horse or armour*; 'nuair a rachadh tu 'd é., *when you arrayed yourself in all your panoply*; é. calpa, *greaves*; é. uchd, *a breast-plate*; é. bròin, *mourning dress*; é. muineil, *gorget*; é. Gàidhealach, *the garb of the Gael*; é. droma, *back-piece*; é. amhaich, *cravat.* Ag é—, pr.pt. of éid.
éideag, s.f. White pebble. 2 (Fionn) White quartz—*Argyll.*
———ach, -aiche, a. Pebbly.
éideam, 1st. sing. pr. aff. of éid. I clothe. E. na nèamha, *I clothe the heavens.* [Irish form.] 2 1st. sing. imp. of éid. Let me clothe. 3 (*for* éididh mi) *I will clothe.*
eidean,** s.m. Receptacle.
———n,†† -inn, -an, s.f. Suit, equipment.
eidear, see eadar.
†eidearbh, -a, a. False.
eidh, v.n. Go—*Suth'd.* Dh'eidhinn, *I would go.*
eidhe, see deigh.
eidheachail, see deigheach.
eidhean, -eidhne, see eidheann.
———ach, -aiche, a. see eidheannach.
———an, s.m., *dim.* of eidheann. Ivy bush.

291. Eidheann.

eidheann, -eidhne, s.f. [* gives m.] Ivy—*hedera helix.* Badge of the Gordons. Spion an e. bho [*or* bhàrr] a craoibh, *tear the ivy from its twigs.*
———ach, -aiche, a. Of, or belonging to ivy, ivied.
———ach, -aich, s.f. Ivy—*Arran & Argyllsh.* 2 Ice—*Islay.*
———ag, -aige, s.f. Ivy branch or bough.
——— -thalmhainn,§ s. f. Ground-ivy, see iadh-shlat-thalmhainn.
eidheinean, see eidheanan.
eidhionn, see eidheann.
——— -mu-chrann,(AC) see eidheann.
eidhneach, a. see eidheannach.
eidhnean,** -ein, s.m. Bough or branch of ivy. 2 Young ivy.
——— -thalmhuinn, s. f. Ground ivy, see iadh-shlat-thalmhuinn.
eidhre, s.f.ind. see eighre. 2**Burden.
eidhreadhail, a. see eighreadail.
eidhreannach, -aich, s.f. Icicle.
eidhreanta, a. see eighreadail.
eidh-shlat, see iadh-shlat.
eididh, *Perthsh.* for eidhreannach.
éididh, s.m. see éideadh. 2 see eige. 3 a. see éitigh.
†eidimhin, a. Doubtful, uncertain. 2 Fluctuating, changeable.

†eidir, *v. impers.* Ni h-eidir [leis,] [*he*] *cannot.*
†eidir, see eadar.
†eidir, *pl.* -e, *s.m.* Captive, hostage.
eidir-cheart,** -cheirt, *s. m.* Equal distribution.
éifeachd, *s.f.ind.* Effect, avail, consequence, efficacy. Gun e., *without effect.*
éifeachdach, -aiche, *a.* Effectual, efficient, of avail. A' ghairm e., *effectual calling*; gu h-e., *effectually.*
éifeachdail, see éifeachdach.
éifeasach, *a.* Serious.
eig, *dat.* of eag. †2 see easg.
éig, *gen.sing.* of eug.
†eigcneasda, *a.* see eu-cneasda.
eige, *gen. sing.* of eag.
eige,* -achan, *s.f.* Web. E. de chlò, *a web of homespun* ; pinne na garmain agus an e., *the pin of the beam and the web.*
eigeach,* *s.f.* Abb.
†eigeal, *s.m.* see torran. 2 Furrowed rock or eminence.
éigean, see éiginn.
eigean,** *a.* Lawful, rightful, just.
éigeannach,* see éiginneach.
————-.—adh, see eigneachadh.
éigeanntach,* *a.* see éiginneach.
—————adh, *s.m.* see éigneachadh.
éigeantach, -aiche, *a.* see éiginneach.
éigeantas, -ais, *s. m.* Necessity. 2*Miserable shifts. 3 State of requiring every kind of shift.
†eigeas, *s.m.* Bard, learned man.
éigh, *pr. pt.* ag éigheach, *v. a.& n.* Call, shriek, shout, cry in a slow, swelling manner. 2** Proclaim. 3**Sound. Éighibh caismeachd, *sound an alarm* ; cha'n éighear cath, *battle shall not be called—they shall not call battle.*
éigh, -e, -ean & -eachan, *s. f.* Cry. 2* The death-watch, a tingling noise in the ear, supposed to portend news of death. 3 Long continued swelling cry, as of women when hearing of some disastrous catastrophe. Is fhad' an é. o Loch Odha, *it is a far cry from L.Awe* —expressive of its remoteness ; tha 'n é. 'nam chluais, gu'n gleidheadh Dia na's caomh leam, *the death-watch is in my ear, may God keep all that are dear to me* ; é. nam ban Muileach, 's iad a' caoineadh 's a' tuireadh, *the lamentation of the Mull women, mourning and lamenting,* [this is given by * under éibh, but the correct form of the saying is " gaoir nam ban Muileach " &c.] ; é. a' bhàis, *the lamentable cry of death* ; thoir an éigh " shiod thu," *shout out " that's you "* ; é. còmhraig, *war-cry, shout of battle.*
eigh, -e, -ean -eachan & -eannan, *s.f.* Ice. 2 (AF) Roe.
eigh-bheinn,(WC) *s.f.* Ice-berg.
éigh-còmhraig,** *s.f.* War-cry.
eighe, -achan, *s.f.* File, especially a 3-corner one. 2††Peat-cutter. Bha e. aca, *they had a file.*
éigheach, -ich, -ichean, *s.f.* Cry, earnest entreaty. 2**Proclamation. 3**Shout. 4** Wail. 5**Loud voice. 6**Act of crying, calling, shouting, bawling or proclaiming. Ag e—, *pr. pt.* of éigh. 2 *pr.pt.* of éighich. É. mhór, *great wailing*; is aithne dhoibh t' é., *they know thy call.*
————, -iche, *a.* Clamorous, vociferous, noisy. 2**Crying, shrieking, shouting, bawling.
eigheach,‡‡ -eich, *a.* see deigheach.
éigheachd,‡‡ *s. f. ind.* Proclamation. 2 (DU) Shouting, clamour.
eigheadail, -ala, *a.* Icy. 2 Abounding in ice. 3 Ice-built. 4 Glacial.
éigheadair,** *s.m.* Crier, proclaimer.
éigheamh, -imh, *prov.* for éigheach.
eigheanach, -aich, *s.m.* Icicle.
eighean-làir, *s.* Gill.
eigheann, see eidheann.
.————ach, see eidheannach.
†eighi, *s.f.* Science.
éighich, *pr.pt.* ag éigheach, *v.n.* Call, cry, shout, shriek, bawl. 2 Proclaim.
éighlead,** -eid, *s.m.* Interjection.
————ach,** *a.* Interjectional.
éighneachair,** *s.m.* see éigneachair.
eigh-mhòine, (CR) *s. f.* Peat-cutting spade—*Perthsh.*
eighneadh, see deigh.
eighre,†† *s.f.* Ice. 2 Frost. see deigh.
eighreach, see deigheach.
eighreadail, see deigheach.
eighreadh, see deigh.
eighreag,‡ see oighreag.
eigh-thogte,‡‡ *a.* Ice-built.
éigin, see éiginn.
éigineach, -iche, *a.* see éiginneach.
eiginn,*pron.indef.sing. & pl.* Some. Cuid-eiginn, *some person* ; fear-eiginn, *some man* ; rud-e., *something* ; té-e., *some female* or *woman.* In all such compounds the *e* of this word is hardly sounded, thus *cuid'*eiginn, not cuid-*éiginn.* [We could say *fear-éiginn*, &c. with the same meanings.]
éiginn, *s. f.* Force, violence, compulsion. 2 Straits, hardship. 3 Difficulty. 4 Necessity, distress. 5 Rape. 6 Oppression. 7 (TS) Steep hillside nearly impassable. Thug e a h-é., *he committed rape, he violated her* ; tha e 'na é., *he is distressed*; thog e air é. a shùil, *he raised his eye with difficulty* ; beò air é., *just alive and that is all* ; air e., *with much ado, scarcely, with difficulty*; 'nuair is é., *when it is necessary* ; tein'-éiginn, *forced fire,* [for particulars see under tein'-éiginn] ; bu rabhadh na h-é. e, *it was an emergency warning* ; an rud a chuir an earb air an loch—an e., *what made the hart take to the loch—necessity.*
——— -fhuail, *s.f.* Dysury.
————each, *a.* Necessary, indispensable, requiring every kind of shifts. 2 Oppressive. 3 Needy, needful, poor. 4** Indisputable, certain. 5** Compulsive. 6** Ravishing, forcing. 7**Critical. 8 (AH)Niggardly, parsimonious.
————eas,** -eis, *s. m.* Force, violence. 2 Necessity, need. 3 Compulsion. 4 Rape.
————teach, see éiginneach.
éigiontach, -aiche, see éiginneach.
eigir,(AC) *a.* Small, insignificant. Iasg e., *a dwarf fish* ; iasgach e., *a poor fishing—Arran*; ugh e., *a small egg* ; uighean e., *the eggs of the smallest birds—Barra* ; teòm e., *a small dole* ; deirc e., *miserable alms* ; tiodhlac e., *an illiberal religious oblation.*
——, -ean, *s.m.* Small insignificant person. 2 (AF) Small gull, kittiwake, see seagair. E. giollain, *a puny boy* ; e. bodaich, *a miserable carle* ; e. duine, *a mean, miserable man.*
eiglidh,** *a.* Mean, abject, feeble.
———eachd, *s.f.ind.* Abjectness, feebleness.
eigne,(AF) *s.* Salmon.
éigneach, -iche, *a.* see éiginneach.
————, -ich, *s.m.* Oppressor. 2 Compeller.
————adh, -aidh, *s.m.* Forcing, compelling, constraining. 2 Ravishing, compulsion, rape. 3 Act of forcing, compelling, or ravishing, rape. Ag e—, *pr.pt.*of éignich.
————air,** -ean *s.m.* Oppressor. 2**Ravisher, constrainer, compeller.
éignich, *pr. pt.* ag éigneachadh, *v. a.* Compel, force, constrain. 2 Ravish. 3** Oppress.

4**Take by force. Agus dh'é. na h-Amoraich Clann Dain, *and the Amorites forced the children of Dan* ; -dh' é. thu mo chridhe, *you have ravished my heart.*
-———ear, *fut. pass.* of éignich. Shall be ravished.
-———te, *a. & past pt.* of éignich. Forced, constrained, compelled. 2 Ravished.
eignidh, see eagnaidh.
eigse,** *s.f.* Art, science. 2 Knowledge.
-——ach,** -aich, *s.f.* School, study.
éil,(AC) *for* éill, *gen.* of iall.
'eil, (*for* bheil) see bi, *v.*
†eil, *v.a.* see eilc.
†eilc, *v.a.* Rob, spoil.
éilde, *gen.* of eilid.
-——ach, -iche, *a.* Abounding in hinds. 2 Of, or belonging to hinds. Gleann é., *the valley of hinds.*
éildeag, -eige, -an, *s.f.* Young hind or roe. (female of stag or red-deer.) [The doe is the female of the fallow-deer.]
——ach,†† *a.* Abounding in young hinds or roes.
éild, *Harris* for eilid.
éildear -an, *s.m.* Gaelic spelling of *elder*.
———-achd, *s.f.* Office of an elder.
éile, *Skye, Badenoch & N. Argyll* for féileadh.
eile, *pron.indef.* Other, another. 2 The other of two. see dara. 3**Else. Duin' eile, *another person* ; ni e., *another thing* ; neach e., *another individual* ; agus rud e. dheth, *and more than that, (another thing of it)* ; cò e.? *who else?*
†eile, *s.f.* Prayer, entreaty. 2 Oration. 3 Lowing of deer.
†eileabair, *s.f.* Hellebore.
eileabanachd,(MMcL) *s.f.* Mockery, making a fool of anyone.
eileach, -ich, -ichean, *s.m.* [** gives *s.f.*] Milldam. 2 Mound, bank. 3††Rock. 4(CR) Weir, bank of stones to guide fish into a *cabhuil* or bag-net. 5(CR) Any place where water can be crossed on stones. [Last two meanings both *W. of Ross.*] E. na muilne, *the channel bringing the water to the mill.*
†eileachadh,** -aidh, *s.m.* Accusing, accusation.
eileachair,** *s.m.* Impeacher.
éileachanaichte,** *a.* Numb.
éileadh, *Skye & N. Argyll* for féileadh.
éileadh, -idh, -idhean, *s.m.* Folding, plaiting.
éileag, -eige, -an, *s.f.* see éibhleag. †2 V-shaped structure, wide at one end and narrow at the other, into which deer were driven and shot with arrows as they came out.
——ach, -aiche, *a.* see éibhleagach.
eilean, -ein, -an [*pron.* eilea'an in *Suth'd, &c.*] *s.m.* Island, isle, islet. 2 see oilean. E. àraidh, *a certain island* ; a null do na h-eileanan, *away to the isles* ; e. lòn, *a mud island—Arran.*
——, see oilean.
——ach, -aich, *s.m.* Islander, inhabitant or native of an island, especially one of the Hebrides. 2 Generous man. Ban-e., *an Hebridean woman.*
——ach, -aiche, *a.* Abounding in islands, insular. 2 Like an island. 3 Peninsular. 4 Generous, liberal, munificent.
——achd,* *s.f.ind.* Generosity, liberality, munificence. 2 Insularity.
eilear,* see eilthìr. 2 **Deer's walk.
eilear,‡ *s. m.* Crose, notch on the staves of a cask where the bottom is fixed.
eileineach, -ich, see eileanach.
eileinich, *v. n.* see oileinich. 2 (PM) Abuse, thoroughly villify, also often applied to physical punishment—*Uist.*
eileir, -ean, see eilthìr.
eilgheadh, -idh, *s.m.* Levelling a field for sowing. 2 Fallow ground. 3 First ploughing of land that requires a second to prepare it for seed. 4 Ploughing of stubble—*W. of Ross-sh.* 5**Burial, interment.
————,††*v.a.* Plough for a second ploughing.
eile-trom,(DC) *s. m.* see eilitriom.
eile-trium, *Lewis* for eilitriom.
eilibear,** *s.f.* Hellebore.
eilich,** *v.a.* Accuse, charge, call to account.
eilid, éilde, éildean, *s.f.* Hind, female of the red deer, roe. Laidh an e. air an fhuaran, *the hind lay at the spring well* ; e. ag iarraidh a h-annsachd, *a hind in search of its mate.*
——each, -iche, *a.* Full of hinds. 2 Of, or relating to hinds.
eilidh,** *s.* Fallow ground.
eilig,‡ -e, *s.f.* Willow herb, see seileachan.
†eilightheoir, -e, -ean, *s.m.* Creditor. 2 Accuser.
eilitriom, -an, *s.m.* Plank or board on which a dead body is placed—*Uist.* 2†† Hearse.
eill,** *s.f.* Precipice. 2 Advantage. 3 Flock.
eillbhuinn, -e, *s.f.* Sensation of burning, as of a barefooted person treading on a live coal. Cuspach is gàg is e., 's mairg an spàg air am beireadh iad, *kibe and crack and burning heel, pity the foot they come on*—these are only experienced by those who go barefooted.
éille, *gen.* of iall.
eillimh,** *s.* Plea.
†eiligheadh, *s.m.* Burial.
eillteil, -eala, see oillteil.
eilltich, see oilltich.
†eilminte, Gaelic form of *element.*
eilne,** *s.f.* Uncleanness, pollution.
eilnich,** *v.a.* Corrupt. 2 Soil. 3 Violate.
†eilnighte, *a. & past pt.* Corrupted.
eilteachadh, -aidh, *s. m.* Rejoicing, gladness, act of rejoicing. Ag e—, *pr. pt.* of eiltich.
eilteir, -ean, see éildear.
eilthir,(AG) *Reay country* for oirthir.
eil-thìr, -ean, *s.m.* Sequestered region or district. 2 Coast, sea-coast. 3**Foreign land, strange country. 4*Desert. 5**Pilgrim.
eilthire, see eilthireachd.
eilthireach, -ich, *s.m.* Pilgrim, stranger, sojourner, alien, foreigner.
————, -eiche, *a.* Foreign, strange. 2 Of, or belonging to, a pilgrim.
eilthireachd, *s.f.ind.* Pilgrimage, sojourning.
eiltich, *v.a.* Rejoice, be glad. 2 Exult.
†eim, *s.m.* see ìm.
eimh,** *a.* Quick, active, brisk. 2 *Gairloch pron.* of amh, *raw.*
†eimh, -e, *s.f.* Haft. 2 Tail. 3 Sanctuary.
†eimhe, see éighe.
eimheach,** *a.* Nimble, swift.
eimheachd,** *s.f.* Obedience, compliance.
†eimhidhe, -an, *s.f.* Proclamation.
eimhilt,** *a.* Slow, tedious.
éimhleag, see éibhleag.
†ein, see aon.
ein,(AC) *s.* Sap. Mar e. nan sugh, *as the sap of strawberries.*
†einchineadh, (*for* aon chineadh) One family.
eineach -ich, *s.m.* Bounty, goodness, courtesy. 2 Affability. 3** Truce, armistice. 4**Shirt. 5**Smock. 6 Fine countenance. 7 Face. 8 Any body. (Irish form of *aon neach.*)
éineach,(MMcL) *s.m.* Stalks of heather.
eineachas, -ais, see eineach.
eineach-lann, -lainn, *s.f.* Protection, defence, safeguard. 2 Attribute.
†ei-neart, -neirt, *s.m.* Weakness.

†eing, *gen. sing.* of eang.
eingeal, see aingeal.
†einghin, for aon-ghin.
einglich,* *v.a.* Benumb.
†einmheid, *a.* Of equal size. (aon mheud.)
einnid, *s.f.* Generosity.
eintridh, Gaelic spelling of *entry*.
eipistil,** Gaelic spelling of *epistle*, see litir.
†éir,** *v.a.* Rise, mount, ascend.
†eirb, *s.f.* Quickness.
†eirbhe, *s.f.* Fence, wall. Camus na h-eirbhe, *a place name near Callart*.
eirbheach,** *s.f.* Wasp. 2 Hornet.
†eirbhearn, *v.a.* Transgress, break.
eirbheirt, -e, *s.f.* Moving, stirring. 2 Power of motion. 3 Endeavour. 4**Burden. 5††Activity. Tha comas eirbheirt aice, *she is able to move about.*
†———, *v.a. & n.* Move. 2 Carry.
eirbhir,* *pr.pt.* ag eirbhir, [*ag eirbhirt,] *v. n.* Seek in an in direct way. Cò tha ag eirbhir sin ort? *who asks that of you*, or *who insinuates that?*
eirbhir, -e, *s.f.* Act of asking or blaming indirectly. Ag e—, *pr.pt.* of eirbhir. Bha e. nan corp air a cheann, *he was indirectly blamed for the dead bodies—for their being dead bodies —Call Ghaig.*
———each, -ich, *s.m.* Person that questions or blames indirectly.
eirbhirt, *pr. pt.* of eirbhir.
eirbhrith, *s.f.* Drying by fire.
eirbleach, *a.* Decrepit, infirm, crippled.
eirbleach,(PM) *s.m.* Decrepit man or beast—*Uist.* Cha'n fhac'' thu e. riamh ach e, *you never saw a more miserable object.*
eircbheach, see eirbheach.
eirc-chòmhla, *s.m.* Portcullis.
eirceach, see eiriceach.
eirceachd, see eiriceachd.
éire, *s.f.* Burden. 2 *for* eighreadh, see deigh. Is e. mo sgiath, *my shield is a burden*; och agus ochain nan och éire! *alas! alas!* bithidh mi an e. sin ri m' bheò, *I shall feel the effects of that as long as I live.* 3 Effect.
éireach, -iche, *a.* Burdensome, heavy.
eireachd, -an, *s.f.* Assembly, meeting. 2 Congregation. 3 Heresy. 4††Elegance, beauty.
———ail, -ala, *a.* Handsome, beauteous, comely, seemly, graceful, fair. 2 Decent, becoming, proper, as dress. 3**Specious.
eireachdas, -ais, *s.m.* Handsomeness, showiness, good appearance. 2 Good breeding. 3 Congregation. 4*Decency, suitableness to appear in company with. A' dol a dh' e. leis, *becoming quite handsome with it, cutting a dash with it*; gleann air an robh e. thar gach gleann, *a glen that was beauteous beyond all others.*
éireadail,†† *a.* Burdensome.
eireadail, -ala, *a.* Frosty, pinching, severely cold, see deigheach.
éireadh, *3rd. sing. & pl. imper.* of éirich. É. e, *let him arise.*
éireadh, see éire.
éireag, see oighreag.
eireag, -eige, -an, *s. f.* Young hen, pullet.
———ach, *a.* ††Abounding in pullets.
éireagach, see oighreagach.
eireallach, -aich, *s.m.* Clumsy old man. 2 Monster.
eireannach,(CR) *s.m.* Plunger churn—*Gairloch.*
eirearaich, -e, see earraradh.
†éirghe, see éirigh.
†eirgionnach, -aich, *s.m.* Pursuer.
éiribh, *dat.pl.* of éire.
éiribh, *2nd.imp. a.* of éirich. Rise ye.

éiric, -e, -ean, *s.m.* éirig.
eiriceach,** -eich, *s.m.* Heretic, unbeliever.
———,** -eiche, *a.* Heretical, unbelieving.
———d, *s.f.* Heresy.
eiriceil,* *a.* Heretical.
éirich, *pr. pt.* ag éirigh, *v.a.* Rise, ascend. 2 Rise out of bed. 3** Befall, happen. 4** Rebel. É. tràthail 'sa mhadainn, *rise early in the morning*; dh' é. e air an obair, *he started the work*; é. air, *go at it*; 'nuair a dh'éireas maduinn, *when morning shall rise* or *dawn*; is bochd mar a dh' é. dhuit, *sad is that which has befallen you*; dh' leis, *he succeeded* or *prospered*; é. air, *set to*—said, for example, as an encouragement to a singer about to commence; é. ort, *arise*; dh'é. Fionn 'na comhair, *F. rose to meet her*; éiridh mi, *I shall rise.*
———idh, *fut.aff.a.* of éirich. [Erroneously given by ** for éiridh, which is the correct form.] Shall or will rise.
eiridh, see deigh.
éiridh, *fut. aff. a.* of éirich. 2 Often erroneously used for éirigh, *pr.pt.*
eiridinn, *s.m.* Nursing, attendance on the sick. 2 Person so attended, patient. 3(MMcL) Medicine. Deòch e, *a potion.* Ag e—. *pr.pt.* of eiridnich.
———, *v.a.* see eiridnich.
eiridinneach, see eiridneach.
eiridneach, -iche, *a.* Cherishing, affectionate.
eiridneach,* -ich, *s.m.* Patient.
eiridneachadh, -aidh, *s.m.* Cherishing, nursing. Ag e—, *pr. pt.* of eiridnich.
eiridneadh, *s.m.* see eiridneachadh.
eiridnich, *pr. pt.* ag eiridneachadh & ag eiridinn, *v.a.* Cherish, nurse, foster.
éirig, -e, -ean, *s.f.* Ransom, forfeit, reparation, amercement, fine. An é. m' anama, *in ransom for my soul*; an é. a ghràidh, *in return for his love.* [For amounts of *éirig* according to rank, see under crodh.]
†eirige,** *s.f.* Command, government.
éirigeach,* *a* As a ransom. 2‡‡Piacular.
———,* -ich, *s.m.* Heretic, captive, bondsman. Duine a tha 'na e., *a man that is a heretic.*
†eirigeachd, see eirige.
éirigeil, *a.* Redemptory.
éirig-fheumnach, see éirigeach, *s.*
†eirigh, -e, -ean, *s.m.* Viceroy, chief governor.
éirigh, *s.f.ind.* Rising, mounting. 2 Rise, act of rising, ascension. 3*Rebellion, mutiny. Àm é., *time of rising*; am bheil thu air é.? *have you risen, are you out of bed?* é. na gréine, *sunrise*; bha gach ni ag é. leis, *everything was prospering with him.* Ag é—, *pr. pt.* of éirich.
éirigheachd,** *s.f.* Ascension.
éirionnach, -aich, see éibhrionnach.
eirirt, *s.f.* Advancement—*Dàin I. Ghobha.*
†eiris, *s.f.* Era. 2 Friend. 3 Mistrust. 4 Heresy.
†eirle, *s.f.* Fragment.
†eirlioc, -oic, -an, *s.f.* Flake of ice.
eirlioch,** *s.m.* Destruction.
eirmis, *pr. pt.* ag eirmeas, *v.a.* Find out, hit, find out by searching. Dh' e. mi air, *I found him.*
eirmiseach, -iche, *a.* Quick, expert, good at finding, searching or aiming. E. air a theangaidh, *quick in repartee.*
eirmiseachd, *s.f.* Finding after a search.
eirneadh,** *s.m.* Gift.
èirneis, see àirneis.
†eirr,** *s.f.* Shield. 2 End. 3‡‡Snow. 4‡‡ Ice. 5 *gen.sing.* of earr.
†eirt, -e, *s.f.* Strength.

eirthir, -e, -ean, see oitir. Coast, used in place-names about Gairloch.
eirthireach, see oitireach.
éis, -e, -ean, *s.f.* Delay, detention, hindrance. 2 Rest, respite. 3 Defect, want. 4* Obstruction—*Lewis.* 5** Band, troop. 6 Footstep, trace. 7 (Fionn) Trouble, annoyance. 8(M McL) End—*Lewis.* Bho thùs gu é., *from beginning to end*; air é.,*back,backwards*; cha'n 'eil agam da éis sin, *I have nought in consequence*; na bi deanamh é., *do not delay* ; dè tha cur é. ort ? *what is annoying you?* cha'n 'eil é. mòine 'n Uidhist, *there's no lack of peats in Uist.*
éis, *pr.pt.* ag éiseadh, *v.a.* Hinder, prevent, obstruct. 2 Trace, search.
éis-bhreith, -e, -ean, *s.f.* False judgment.
eisceach, -eich,** *s.m.* Exception, exclusion.
eis-chinnealachadh, -aidh, *s.m.* Degeneracy.
éisd, *pr. pt.* ag éisdeachd, *v. n.* Hear. 2 Hearken, listen. 3 Be slow to obey. 4 Take no heed. Éisdibh uile shluagh, *hearken all ye people* ; éisd ! *hist ! be silent ! obey !* a chluas, nach é. thu ! (ironical) =*what nonsense* ; é. do bheul ! *be quick !*
éisdeachd, *s.f.ind.* Hearing, hearkening. 2 Act of hearing, hearkening or listening. 3 Attention. 4**Audience. 5**Auditory. 6‡‡ Confession. Ag é—, *pr.pt.* of éisd. Luchd é., *hearers, audience* ; an ti a bheir é., *he that hears* or *listens* ; ag é. ri caoirean na coille, *listening to the murmur of the wood* ; thoir é., *listen* ; an t-slabhruidh é., *the audience chain,* —rattled to secure a hearing. [Often pron. éisneachd in *Gairloch.*]
éisdeam, *1st.sing.imp.* of éisd. Let me hear *or* listen. [*not for* éisdidh mi, as given by **,— that should be éisdim.]
éisdear, -eir, -ean, *s.f.* Hearer, hearkener.
éisdeir, see éisdear.
eis-dhamh,(AF) *s.m.* Ox.
éisdich, see éisd.
éisdim, *v.* (*for* éisdidh mi,) *I shall hear.*
eise,(AF) s. Fish.
eiseach,* *s.* see eisleach.
éiseach, see éiseil.
éiseadh,** -idh, *s.m.* Seeking, hunting after, tracing, research. Ag é—, *pr. pt.* of éis.
eiseairt, *a.* Poor destitute, feeble.
eiseamplair,* see eisimpleir.
eisean, *prov.* for esan.
eisear,* see eisir.
eisearach,‡‡ -aiche, *a.* Destitute.
eisearadh, -aidhe, *a.* Poor, destitute. 2 Feeble.
éiseil, *a.* Obstruent, hindering.
eiseimeileachd, see eisimeil.
eiseirghe, see aiseirigh.
eiseolach, see aineolach.
eiseòlas, see aineolas.
éisg, *gen. sing.* of iasg. Gach seòrsa é., *every kind of fish.*
eisg, -e, -ean, *s.f.* Satirist, lampooner, scurrilous poet. 2 Scold. 3 *Suth'd* for aisg. 4** Lampoon, satire. Àrd-eisg nan droch fhilidh ! *thou supreme failure of all lampooning bards !* [** gives *s.f.* for 4, and *s.m.* for 1.]
eisgeach, *a.* see eisgeil.
eisgeach,** *s.m.* Study.
eisgeadh,-idh,-idhean, *s.m.* Satirizing,censuring.
eisgealachd, *s.f.ind.* Scurrility, satire.
eisgeanta, *a.* Satirical, scurrilous.
eisgear, -eir, -eirean, *s.m.* Satirist, lampooner, scurrilous poet. 2 Scold.
eisgearra,** *a.* Bitter, satirical, scurrilous. 2 Unsociable.
eisgearrachd,** *s.f.ind.* Bitterness of language, scurrility, satire, lampooning.
†eisgeartha, see eisgearra.
eisgeil, -eala, *a.* Satirical, scurrilous. 2* Flippant.
éisgin, -e, -ean, see éisglinn.
eisgir, *s.* Ridge of mountains.
éisglinn, -e, -tean, [** gives *pl.* -linnticheanl]*s.f.* Fish-pond.
†eisil, *a.* Ignorant, rude.
eisimealach, -aiche, *a.* Dependent, under obligation or subjection. 2 Reverent, respectful. 3 In one's debt or reverence. 4 ††Biassed.
eismealachd, *s.f.ind.* Same meanings as eisimeil. 2* State of dependence or 3 poverty.
eisimeil, eisimealach, [eisimeil—N.G.P.] *pl.* eisimealaichean, [‡‡ gives *gen.* eisimeile, *n. pl.* eisimeilean,] *s.f.* Dependence, reverence, obligation. 2 Partiality, bias to one side of a question. 3* Power. 4‡‡Courage. 5(DU) Respect, Is diuid fear na h-e., *the dependent is timid* ; cha'n 'eil mi an e. do chuid Beurla, *I can do very well without your English* ; cha 'n -eil mi 'nad e., *I am not in your reverence* ; gun e. gun ùmhlachd, *without reverence or obedience* ; ni mi e gun e., *I can do it without being in the reverence of anyone for help* ; cha'n 'eil mi bonn 'nad e., *I am not a whit in your reverence* ; thoir e., *show respect.*
———each, see eisimealach.
eisimeilteach, -ich, *s.m.* Reproachful person.
†eisimh, *a.* Near, close at hand.
eisimpleir, -ean, *s.m.* Example, pattern, ensample. 2 Model. 3**Copy. 4**Parable. Gu'n robh sibh 'nur n-eisimpleiribh, *that you were examples.*
eisimpleireach, -aiche, *a.* Exemplary. 2‡‡ Precedented.
eisimpleireiche,** *s.m.* Copyist.
eisinn, see eislinn.
†eisinnil,** *a.* Weak, infirm.
†eisiodhan, *a.* Unclean.
eisiomail, see eisimeil.
eisiomalach, see eisimealach.
eisiomlair, see eisimpleir.
eisiomlaireach, see eisimpleireach.
eisiomplair, see eisimpleir.
————each, see eisimpleireach.
————eiche, see eisimpleiriche.
eisir, -ean, [(AF) eisiridh, *eisrean,] *s.m.* Oyster. [eisire in *Gairloch.*]
eisireach, -iche, *a.* Of oysters, abounding in oysters.
eisirean,** -ain, *s.m.* Scallop, clam. 2 *nom. pl.* of eisir. 3 *dim.* of eisir.
eisireineach, see eisireach.
eisiridh, see eisir.
eisith,** *s.f.* Debate, disagreement.
eisleach, -ich, -ichean, *s.f.* Crupper. 2 *pl.* (CR) Stretchers of withe or cord, from the ends of the tail-beam to the corresponding sides of the saddle.
†eisleadhach, -aiche, *a.* Feeble, weak, unwarlike.
éislean, -ein, *s.m.* Grief, sorrow, affliction. 2 Heaviness, doowsiness, melancholy, dulness, stupor. 3 Infirmity. 4††Hinderance. Làn éislein, *full of sorrow.*
éisleineach, -iche, *a.* Sorrowful, wretched,languid, melancholy, sickly, heavy, dull, drowsy, distressful.
eisleir, -ean, *s.m.* Defect, damage, detriment.
eislig, see eislinn.
eisling, see eislinn.
eislinn, -ean, *s.f.* Plank or couch on which a corpse is laid—*Argyll.* 2 Shroud, winding-sheet.
———each, -eiche, *a.* Assailable.
†eislis, *s.f.* Neglect. 2 Mistake. 3 Forgetfulness.

eismeach,** *a.* Lying, false. 2 Unready.
eismeil, see eisimeil.
eisreachd.** *s.f.* Orphan.
eisreadh,** *s.m.* Research.
eist, see eitionach.
éist, see éisd.
eisteachd, *s.f.* Death.
eit,(AF) *s.* Cattle.
eite,‡ *s.m.* Unhusked ear of corn.
éite, *s.m.* see éiteadh. 2 *s.f.* see ite. 3**Piece added to a ploughshare when worn.
eiteach, -ich, *s.f.* Wings, fins.
éiteach, -ich, *s.m.* Denial, refusal. 2 Lie. 3 Root of burnt heath. 4 Asthma. 5††Consumption. 6 see éitig.
éiteach,†† *a.* Consumptive. 2(MMcL) Insignificant. Duine é., *an insignificant person*
éiteachadh, -aidh, *s.m.* Denying, refusing. 2 Act of swearing. 3 Confirming. 4 Denial, refusal. Ag é—, *pr. pt.* of éitich. Ag é. o ar bòrdaibh, *banishing from our tables.*
éiteachail, -ala, *a.* Tabid, wasting away from disease.
éiteadh, -idh, *s.m.* Stretching, extending.
eiteag, see iteag.
éiteag, -eige, -an, *s. f.* White pebble. 2 Fair maid. 3 (DU) White quartz. 4‡ Precious stone.
——ach,†† *a.* Abounding in white pebbles or fair maids.
eitealaich, see itealaich.
†eiteam, -im, *s.m.* Danger, hazard.
eitean, -ein & eitne, -ean, *s.m.* Kernel, nucleus. 2**Grain, as of corn. E. chnò, *kernel of a nut* ; e. peasrach, *grain of peas, a pea* ; e. peubair, *a peppercorn* ; e. paidirein, *a bead.*
——ach, *a.* Kernelly.
eiteodha, *s.f.ind.* Hemlock.
†eiteog, see iteag.
eith,‡ *v.n.* see eidh.
eith, see deigh. 2**see eighe. Mar mheall e., *like a lump of ice.*
eitheach, -ich, *s.m.* Lie. 2 False oath, perjury. 3**Mistake. Thug e mionnan eithich, *he perjured himself* ; luchd eithich, *perjurers.*
†eitheach,§ *s.* Oak, see darach.
eitheadh, see eighe (file.)
eitheann, -inn, see eidheann.
————-ach, see eidheannach.
eithear, -eir, -thraichean, *s.m.* see eathar. 2** Liar.
eithich, -e, *a.* False. 2 Of, or connected with perjury. 3**Perverse. Mionnan e., *a false oath.*
———, *v.n.* Lie. 2 Swear falsely, perjure, deny, refuse.
eithichibh, see feudail.
eithir, see oitir.
eithre, *s.f.* **Tail of a fish. 2(AF)Salmon. 3 (AF) Ox, bull, cow. 4**see eighre. 5** Burden 6**Conclusion.
———ach, *a.* see deigheach.
———ach,** -rich, *s.f.* Wilderness.
———ag, -eige, -an, see oighreag.
———agach, -aiche, see oighreagach.
eitibh, see feudail.
eitich, see eiteach. 2* see eithich.
éitidh, -e, *a.* see éitigh.
———eachd, see éitigheachd.
eitidh, see feudail.
eitig,(DC) *s.f.* Fault, flaw—*Uist.* 2 (DU)Disease, germs of disease, applied to any long standing illness in man or beast. Làn eitig, *full of disease* ; tha droch e. anns an each, *the horse is far from sound.*
éitig,‖ -e, -ean, *s.f.* Consumption. 2 Tendency to decay.

†eitig, *v.n.* Foreswear, abjure. 2 Refuse. 3 Contradict.
éitigeach,‡‡ -eiche, *a.* Consumptive.
éitigh, -e, *a.* Fierce, angry. 2 Boisterous, stormy. 3 Dreadful. 4 Ugly. 5 Dismal. Tannasg e., *a frightful spectre.*
eitigheach, -ich, *s.m.* see de-tigheach.
éitigheachd,** *s.f.* Dismalness. 2 Frightfulness, ugliness.
eitionach,(AF) *s.m.* Gelded horse.
eitleag, -eig, -an, } *s.f.* see ialtag.
eitleog, -oig, -an, } *s.f.* see ialtag.
eitne, *gen.sing.* of eitean.
†eitre, *s.f.* Trench, furrow.
eitreach,‡ *s.m.* Storm. 2 Sorrow.
eitreòrach, -aiche, *a.* see eu-treòrach.
eitrich,* see séidrich.
eitridh,** *s.f.* Ditch.
†ela, see eala.
†elc, see olc.
elebor,§ *s.m.* Green hellebor—*helleborus viridis.*
elebor geal,§ *s.m.* White helleborine—*epipactis latifolia.*

292. Elebor.  *293. Elebor geal.*

elta,(AF) *s.* see ealt.
eltlagh,(AF) *s.m.* Flock, herd.
enach-ghàraidh, see eanach-ghàraidh.
enig, *Suth'd.* for aing. 2 *prov.* for eiginn, e, g. duin'-einig.
enigeach, *Suth'd.* for aingeach.
enigidh, *Suth'd.* for aingidh.
†eo,(AF) *s.* Salmon. 2**Peg. 3 Thorn. 4** Pin. 5**Grave.
†eo, *a.* Good, worthy.
†eobhrat, -ait, *s.m.* Head-dress, cap, coif.
eochair, *s.f.* Brim, brink, edge. 2 Tongue. 3 Young plant, sprout. 4 see iuchair.
eog,(AF) *s.m.* Salmon.
†eoghunn, *s.m.* Youth.
eoilse, see eòlas.
eòin, *gen.sing.* & *n.pl.* of eun.
eòinean, -ein, *s.m.* Little bird. 2 *Gairloch* for neòinean.
eòin-fhiadhaich, *s. pl.* Wild fowl.
eòin-fhiadhachd,** *s.f.* Fowling.
eòin-shealgair,**, -ean, *s.m.* Fowler, bird-catcher.
——————eachd,** *s.f.* Fowling, bird-catching.
eòin-taigh, -e, -ean, *s.m.* Hen-house, hen-coop.
eòir,(AC) *s.* Spell, charm, incantation—*Lewis.*
eòisdinn, *s.* Quietness.
eòisle, an, *s. f.* see eòlas 6. (Metathesis of eòlas.)
eòl, *s. m. ind.* Knowledge, discernment. 2 Science. 3 Art, charm. 4**Nostrum. Is eòl dhomh, *I know. classic.* [*seldom used.]
†eòl, *a.* Expert, knowing.
eòlach, -aiche, *a.* Knowing, acquainted, cunning, skilled, expert. 2* Intelligent. Tha mi e. air, *I am acquainted with him* ; am bheil thu eòlach air ? *are you acquainted with him ?*

duine e., *a man well acquainted, an intelligent man* ; rinn mi e, air a chéile iad, *I introduced them to each other* ; maor e., maor a's mios' a théid an crò, *a bailiff acquainted with the stock, the worst to send among the flock*—NGP.
eòlach, -aich, *s.m.* Adept, guide. 2 Acquaintance.
eòlaiche, *comp.* of eòlach.
eòlais, *gen.sing.* of eòlas.
eòlan, -ain, *s. m.* Lamp-oil. 2(DU) Preparation of fish-oil, &c., sprinkled on wool before carding. 3 Sore with broken skin and raw flesh, putrefying sore.
eòlas, -ais, -an,†*s.m.* Knowledge. 2* Acquaintance. 3 Intelligence. 4 Skill,art. 5 Science. 6 Enchantment, spell, incantation. Dìth eòlais, *ignorance* ; an tìr m' eòlais, *in my own country* ; chaidh e air 'e., *he strayed to the place he knew before*—said of cattle ; e. nan sùl, *a spell to get free of a mote in the eye* ; e.-adhair, *aerology* ; e.-bhithean, *ontology* ; e.-cogaidh, *tactics* ; e.-daingneachd, *fortification* ; e.-inntinn, *metaphysics* ; e.-meudachd, *geometry* ; e.-nàduir, *physics* ; e.-seòlaidh, *intuition;* cuir e. air, *get acquainted with him.*
eòlasair,‡‡ *s.m.* Necromancer.
eolchaire,** *s.f.* Sorrow, grief, mourning, concern.
———ach,** *a.* Sad, sorrowful.
†eòlgach, -aiche, *a.* Knowing, skilful.
eollach, -aich, see eallach.
†eòlmhor, -oire, *a.* Wise.
eòluidhe, -an, *s.m.* Guide. 2 Doctor.
eònadan, -ain,** see eunadan.
eòrlain, *s.* The three planks on each side of the keel of a boat—eòrlain na h-eathair. 2 Floor, bottom. 3 Lower part of a glen that slopes to a narrow compass.
eòrna, *s.m.ind.* Barley—*hordeum distichon.* An lìon 's an t-e., *the flax and the barley* ; e. fo dhéis, *barley in ear* ; Eilean ìosal an eòrna,*the island of Tiree* ; feitheamh fada ri e. na gainmhich,=*barley sown in sand comes to nothing;* a' cur eòrna, *sowing barley.*
eòrnach, -aiche, *a.* Of, or connected with barley, abounding in barley.
———,* *s.f.* Barley-land.
eorrlain, see eòrlain.
eorrtha,(DU) *s.f.* Spell, charm.
eòsag -aig, -an,** *s.m.* see uiseag.
†eoth, *s.* Horse.
eothanachadh, -aidh, *s.m.* Languishing.
eothanaich,†† *pr.pt.*ag eothanachadh, *v.n.* Languish, decay.
†eothan-bànag,(AF) *s.m.* Weak white animal.
†er, *a.* Great, noble.
†era, *s.m.* Denial, refusal.
†erc, see earc.
†eribeirt, -e, -ean, *s.f.* Burden. 2 Carriage.
†———each, -eiche, *a.* Burdensome.
†err, see eàrr.
es,(AF) s. Ox, see is.
es', esa, see esan.
esan, *emphat. form* of *pers.pron.* e.
†ess, *s.f.* Ship, vessel. *s.m.* Death.
†essid, *s.* Unrest.
†etenge, *a.* (eu+teanga) Mute.
†étrad, *s.* Lust.
escung,(AF) *s.* Fen snake.
eu-, *neg. particle,* also eug-, ea-, ei-, and a-.

eu, The following remarks about the distinguishing features between the North and South dialects of Scottish Gaelic through the occurrence of *eu* or *ia* in various words, are extracted from an article by Rev. C. M. Robertson, in *Celtic Review, October, 1906.* Most Gaelic Grammars and Dictionaries say that the North and South dialects of Gaelic are distinguishable by their respective uses of *eu* and *ia* in certain words, but no detailed list is ever given.

"Dr. MacBain says the crucial distinction between the two main dialects of Gaelic consists in the different way in which the dialects deal with *é* derived from compensatory lengthening—in the south it is *eu,* in the north *ia.* Another characteristic of the words in which this change is found is that their original stems ended in *o* or *a.* There are exceptions, drawn in,perhaps,by the influence of analogy.

The vowel that changes to *ia* in the north is usually written *eu,* but it occurs also as *èa, èi* and *è.* In southern pronunciation it generally has the sound that is called open *e,* and that resembles, except that it is long, that of *e* in English *let.* The close sound *e,* like that of *e* in English *whey* or of *a* in English *fate,* occurs occasionally in words that have *ia* in the north, but in general is confined to those words in which diphthongisation is not found, as, beum, ceum, treun, beud. In contact with nasals diphthongisation is found as a rule only in those instances in which the vowel is nasalised in the south, *e.g.* in eun, meur, but *not* in beum, treun.

Of the words that have *ia* in the north, the following are found with *é* in the south—
Ceudna 'ceunna,' 'féirseag' (for feursann), geur, reustladh (for reusladh), sleuchd, in Arran.
Deug, feun, geug, leubh, in Arran & Islay.
Feudail, gleus, reul, in Arran, Islay & Perth.
Peur (a pear), in Arran, Islay & Glenlyon, eud in Arran & East Perth, Seumas in Arran & Glenlyon.
Sgeun ('sgéan') and déabh in Islay, geuban in Islay & Perth.
Céud (first) and céud (hundred) in Mid-Argyll.
Créadhach (crè), in Perth.

In Strathspey and in Sutherlandshire there are fewer instances of *é* than in Arran. The only words showing the change to *ia,* that are not known to have *è,* in place of *é,* in some district or other, are ceud, ceudna, deug, feudail, feun, geuban, peurtag, reul, reusail, and reusan, and of these, three are borrowed words, while the diphthongisation of at least two others, feudail and reul, is local and exceptional. The association of the change to *ia* with the open sound *è* is thus very close. The tendency, apparently, when the vowel happens to be left undiphthongised in the north, is to sound it *é,* and further, the vowel is apt in such cases to be *é* also in Arran and Islay, but *è* in Perth, Strathspey and Sutherland. Beurla, *e.g.* is béurla in Arran. Islay, North Argyll, part of Skye, North Inverness and West Ross, but bèurla in Perth and Sutherland ; geug is géug in Arran,Islay, part of Skye and Lewis, but gèug in Perth, Stathspey and Sutherland.

The vowels that are subject to diphthongisation are arranged in the following groups to show the occurrence of the change in the southern dialect, in Arran, Islay and Perthshire, and in the northern dialect in the following districts in order, North Argyll (Appin and Sunart), Skye (Sleat), North Inverness-shire(the Aird, south and east of Beauly), West Ross-shire, and Lewis. The pronunciation given in MacAlpine's *Dictionary* is, in general, that of his native island and is that given here under the name Islay. The absence of a word from the list for any particular district does not in all cases imply non-diphthongisation of the vowel in that district; it may mean that there is some other alteration on the word, or that the attempt to ascertain its pronunciation has not been attended with success. Smeuraich, for example, is smeòraich in Sutherland and Lewis. Feusgan, *mussel*; fè, *a calm;* and muir-tèachd, *a jelly-fish*, (II. iii. below), are not in Dr. Henderson's list for the Aird, and were unfamiliar as Aird words to an aged farmer from the district. Cè, *cream*, is unknown in several districts, uachdar or bàrr being used instead, and smeur, *bramble*, is unfamiliar in Lewis. Geug, *branch*, no doubt owes its non-diphthongisation in parts of the northern Hebrides to its disuse during a treeless period and its subsequent adoption from literature. In West Ross-shire, giag was not disused, but was degraded during the treeless period, and now means, in part at least of the district, a stalk of heather, while a branch of a tree is called meur (' miar ').

Southern Dialect—

I. Ceud (hundred), ceud (first), Di-ceudaoin, ceutach, ceutadh (sense, impression), ceudna, deug, brèagh.

North Argyll et seq.—

II, i. Beul, breug. deuchainn, deur, dreuchd, eudach (jealousy), eulaidh (stalk game, &c.), eun, feuch, feur, feusag, freumh, geuban (ciaban in Skye and onwards), geur, greusaich, leugach (clammy, &c., leug, leugaire), leus (torch, &c.), meud or meudachd, cia meud, meur, neul, reub, seud (hero), seun, breac-sheunain, sgeul, sgreuch, crè (clay), dèan, èasgaidh, gèadh, lèad, mèanan, sè (six), sglèata, tèaruinn,

North Argyll et seq. except Lewis—

II. ii. Beuc, ceus (ham, coarse part of fleece), geug, reusail (ill-use), smeur (bramble), smeuraich (grope), speuc, sèap.

North Argyll et seq. except Inverness—

II iii. Feusgan, fè (calm), lèana or lèanag, rèap (a slattern, rèapach *adj.*, rèapail *verb*), muir-tèachd.

Skye et seq.—

III. Loch-bhlèin or dubh-chlèin (flank, loin), sgeun (fright), smeur or smiùr (to smear), mèith, sèamarlan.

North Inverness et seq.—

IV. Feursann (warble), speuclan (spectacles), teuchdaidh (viscid, &c., 'tiachaidh ' N. Inverness).

North Inverness &c.—

V. i. Feunaidh (peat-cart, from feun), peurtag (partridge), cè (cream).

V. ii. Peuras (a pear), seum or seumaich (enjoin, &c.), Seumas (James), leubh (read) clach-nèaraidh (grindstone), trèasg (shrivel.)'

V. iii. Sleuchd, nèarachd.

Various—

VI. i. Beurla, eud, m' fheudail, càl-feurain (cives), gleus (trim, &c.), spleuc (stare), teuchdadh (parching,) lèabag, piata, trèan-ri-trèan.

VI. ii. Earlais (arles), reusan (reason).

Group I. contains words that are diphthongised in the South; all have *ia* (or *iao*) in Perthshire, all but the last in Islay, and all but the last three in Arran. MacAlpine gives ' a cheud ' or ' a chiad.' The diphthong is *ia* in all the instances in Arran, and in Glenlyon in Perthshire; in East Perthshire and in the North generally in those words, with the exception of brèagh, it is *iao, i.e.* the second constituent of the diphthong is not *a*, but the Gaelic *ao* sound. Ceudna varies; ' ciaodna ' N. Argyll, 'cianda ' N. Inverness, West Ross, Sutherland, ' ciaont ' Lewis, ' ciaodainn ' East Perth, Strathspey, ' céunna ' Arran, ' ciaonna ' Skye. MacAlpine gives ' cianna ' and apparently ' ceudna.'

In addition, dreuchd, omitted by MacAlpine, has *ia* in Arran, and èarlais and reusan, Group VI. ii., have *ia*, the former in Arran and Islay, and, the latter throughout Argyll and in West Perth (' riaosan ' in N. Argyll). Nèaraidh (V. ii.) has *ia* in Perthshire.

Groups I. and II. i. have the diphthong in N. Argyll, Skye, N. Inverness, W. Ross and Lewis; Group II, ii. in N. Argyll et seq., except Lewis, and Group II. iii. in N. Argyll et seq.. except N, Inverness. Group III. falls to be added to the number in Skye and onwards, and Group IV. in N. Inverness and onwards. The words in V. i. ii. and iii. all have *ia* in N. Inverness, and those in V. ii. in West Ross also. Trèasg in N. Argyll, and sleuchd in Skye have *ia*. Nèarachd is ' niarachd' in N. Argyll, ' miarachd ' in Skye, and ' meurachd ' according to MacAlpine (sub néarachd) in Argyll.

The words of VI, i. have *ia* as follows:—Eud (and eudmhor, ' iadar ') càl-feurain, spleuc, and lèabag in N. Argyll.

Spleuc, teuchdadh, lèabag and trèan-ri-trèan (' trianaidh-trian ') in Skye.

Beurla (' biaorla ' or ' biaolla ' so also Lochbroom), eud ('iad ' in Barra also) 'm' fheudail, gleus, and teuchdaidh in Lewis.

' Piata ' a puny child, N. Inverness and W. Ross, has been explained by Dr. Henderson as a by-form of peata, English ' pet '; in Lewis ' piatan ' is used affectionately of one craving for a drink.

Eud in the North generally means zeal, while jealousy is ' iadach ' (in Glenlyon 'eudach ').

Diphthongisation of the vowel *è* thus appears to be most prevalent in the central Highlands, and somewhat less so in N. Argyll and Lewis. It has extended strongly into Rannoch which breaks away from the rest of Perthshire in this respect, and is sharply distinguished from Glenlyon and the parish of Blair-Atholl, bounding it respectively on the south and east, and is in full force in Badenoch and Strathdearn, its eastern limits. On the other hand, Strathspey, which means in local usage the part of the valley of the Spey below Rothiemurchus, and lies in an angle between Badenoch on the south-west, and Strathdearn on the north-west, differs from both districts, and agrees closely with the South. Far north Sutherlandshire also, with the exception perhaps of the Assynt quarter of the county, claims to stand with Strathspey and the south in this matter. The words in which *ia* has been found in Strathspey are:—

Ceud, ceud, ceudna, Di-ceudain, deug sgreuch, brèagh, sè, ceutach, seun.

With the exception of the two last, those words are diphthongised in Sutherlandshire —Creich, Kildonan, and Strathy—and with the following list, they exhaust the known instances of that vowel change in the south-east and in the north of that county :—

Deuchainn, feuch, feusgan, cia meud, reul, crè.

Beul, neul, sgeul, 'cial.'

Ceutach and feusgan have the diphthong in Creich, deuchainn and feuch in Creich and Kildonan, reul ('rialt' or more frequently 'rialtag') in Kildonan, and crè ('criaodhach') in Kildonan and Strathy. Ceutach and ceutadh apparently are diphthongised by some speakers and not by others ('cèutach' and cèutu') in the Strathy district.

The southern *è* of beul, neul, and sgeul is changed in Sutherland, not into *ia*, but into *à*, so that the words would be written respectively, beàl, nyàl, and sgeàl, and are pronounced byàl, nyàl, sgyàl. Cial, *brim of a vessel*, is also changed into ceàl in Sutherland. Though this resembles in the result the change in Arran of brèagh, cè *cream*, crè, gèadh, and sè, respectively into breàgh (brè *or* bryà, *MacAlpine)*, ceà, creà, geàdh, seà (br'à, cyà, cr'à, gyà, shà), it is no doubt to be compared rather with the transference in Gaelic generally, of the pronunciation from *e* to *a* in such words as geal, ('gyal,') seal, ('shal,') &c.

A substitution of other sounds for *è* sometimes occurs. Lèabag is leóbag ('lyóbag') in N. Inverness, W. Ross, Lewis, and Sutherland ; feusag is feòsag (fyòsag) in Sutherland ; and rèapach is reòpach in N. Inverness. Teuchaidh *viscid*, in N. Inverness tiachaidh, is teaochaidh in Creich, and beurla is beaorla in Strathspey, and in parts of Skye and Lewis. The name for the landrail—trèan-ritrèan—is traon in Lewis and, according to MacAlpine, in Skye ; in Ireland it is traona, [but pronounced *trevna*, in *Uist* treona.]

It is not an unknown thing that a word should come to have two pronunciations accompanied by some differentiation in meaning or usage. In N. Argyll, Skye, N. Inverness, W. Ross, and Lewis, *seud*, when it means jewel, is 'séud,' but when it means hero it is 'siad.' The word is everywhere in those districts familiar in the latter sense. As séud, *jewel*, it is not at all so frequently used, and may have been adopted from literature. Meud is undiphthongised throughout Sutherland, except in the phrase 'co miad' *how much*. The phrase is 'ce mìod' in Skye and Lewis, while the word otherwise is both 'mìod' and 'miad' in Lewis, and 'miadachd' in Skye, and also in N. Argyll. MacAlpine gives 'meud' and 'mìod.' The undiphthongised form of deug is kept in Perth, Strathspey, W. Ross, and Lewis in 'da uair dhéug,' often preceded by the article and compressed 'an da'r 'éug' *the twelve o'clock ;* in Sutherland 'an da'r 'iaog.' In Irish 'dareug' means twelve persons.

Similar diphthongisation is found in Munster in such words as ceud, deug, eun, feuch, feur, and also in words in which it is unknown in Scotland, as breun, eug, treun, and even eudochas, eudtrom, *light*, eugcóir, *injustice*, eugmhais *want*, and others. To Scottish Gaels the diphthongisation of eucoir and eugmhais, not to speak of eudochas or aotrom (for eutrom), seems a sheer impossibility, and yet it is found with us in the word èasgaidh, *i.e.* eu-sgìth, of exactly similar formation."

eubarlag, (AH) *s.f.* Ragged, emaciated creature.

eubh, -a, -an, *s.f.* see éigh.

——, -aidh, -ean, see eadha.

——, *v.n.* see éigh.

eubhach, -aich, -aichean, *s.m.* see éigheach.

eubhadair, see éigheadair.

eucag, -aige, -an, *s.f.* see euchdag. 2 see peucag.

eucail, -alach, -ean, *s.f.* Disease, infirmity, distemper. Neart m' eucalach, *the strength of my disease* ; gach e. 'na aoraibh, *every disease in his constitution* ; aon de na h-eucailibh, *one of the diseases*.

eucail, -ala, *a.* see euchdach.

eucaileach, -iche, *a.* Diseased, infirm. 2 Causing disease. 3 Unhealthy. 4**Infectious.

————d,* *s. f. ind.* State of disease or distemper. 2 Infectiousness.

eucailich,** *v.a.* Disease.

eu-càirde, *s.f.ind.* Enmity.

eucairdeach, -iche, *a.* Inimical, hostile.

eucairdeas, *s.f.ind.* Enmity, unfriendliness.

eu-càirdeil,†† *a.* Unfriendly.

eucairteachd, *s.f.ind.* Unlawfulness.

eucalach, *gen.sing.* of eucail.

eu-ceart, -eirte, *a.* Unjust, unfair. 2 Iniquitous. 3 Injurious.

————,** -eirt, *s.f.* Injustice, unfairness. 2 Iniquity.

————ach,†† *a.* Unjust.

————as, -ais, *s. m.* Injustice. 2 Iniquity. 3 Oppression. Luchd eu-ceartais, *unjust people*.

eu-céillidh, -e, *a.* Mad, insane. 2 Foolish, giddy, thoughtless. Gu h-e., *foolishly*.

————eachd, *s.f.ind.* Irrationality.

euchall, see earchall.

euchar, see iuchar.

euchd, -an, *s.m.* Feat, exploit, achievement. 2 **Mournful event. 3**Valour. Cuimhne e. no treubhantais, *a memory of exploit or achievement* ; iorghail nam mór e., *the strife of mighty feats*.

————ach, -aiche, *a.* Heroic, valorous, performing achievements. 2*Daring, brave. Daoine treubhach, e., *heroic, chivalrous people* ; bàs a' ghaisgich euchdaich, *the death of the chivalrous hero* ; dùisg ! a leóghainn euchdaich ! *wake ! thou bold lion !*

————ag, -aige, -an, *s.f.* Charmer, fair or lovely female.

————ail, -ala, *a.* see euchdach.

————alachd, *s.f.ind.* Heroism, bravery. 2 Performance of feats. 3**Achievement.

eu-ciall, -céill, see mi-chiall.

————ach, *a.* see mi-chiallach.

eu-cinnt, -e, *s.f.* Uncertainty, doubt.

————each, -iche, *a.* Uncertain, doubtful, hesitating.

————ealas,** -ais, *s.m.* Uncertainty, doubtfulness.

eu-cneasda, *a.* Inhuman, cruel. 2 Intemperate. 3 Rude, impolite. Gu h-e., *inhumanly*.

————chd, *s.f.ind.* Inhumanity, cruelty. 2 Intemperance. 3 Rudeness.

eucoir, -corach, -ean, *s.f.* Injury, wrong, injustice. 2 Guilt. 3 Impropriety. Ris an e., *acting unjustly*.

eu-coireach, -iche, *a.* Innocent, blameless, see neo-choireach.

————d, *s.f.ind.* Injuriousness. 2†† Injustice.

eu-coirich,** *v.* Aggrieve.

eu-coltach, -aiche, *a.* Unlikely, improbable. 2 Dissimilar. 3 Inconsistent.

eu-coltas, -ais, *s.m.* Unlikeliness, improbability. 2 Dissimilarity, unlikeness. 3 Inconsistency. E. a' ghnothaich sin, *the improbability of that thing*.

eu-comas, (PM) *s.m.* Inability.

————ach, (PM) *a.* Impossible.

eu-conn, -a, *s.m.* Madness, insanity.

eu-connach, -aiche, a. Mad, insane.
eucorach, -aiche, a. Unjust, wrong. 2 Injurious. Gu h-e., *unjustly*.
————, -aich, s.m. Unjust, wicked, or evil person. 2††Devil.
eu-còrdadh, -aidh, s. m. Dissension, discord, disagreement, jarring, quarrel.
†eu-cosg, -oisg, -an, see aogasg.
eu-cosmhail, -e, a. Dissimilar. 2 Improbable. 3**Unequal.
eu-cosmhalach,** a. Dissimilar, unlike, unequal. 2 Unlikely.
————d, s.f.ind. Dissimilarity.
eu-cosmhalas,** -ais, s. m. Dissimilarity, inequality. 2 Improbability, unlikeliness.
eu-cosmhuil, -e. a. Dissimilar.
eu-crionna, a. Imprudent, thoughtless, foolish. 2 Intemperate, immoderate. Gu h-e., *imprudently*.
————chd, s.f.ind. Imprudence. 2 Intemperance, intemperateness, immoderateness.
eu-crìonachd, s.f.ind. Vastness, immensity.
eu-cruaidh, a. Sick, weak, feeble, impotent, delicate. 2** Soft, not hard. 3**Effeminate.
————,** s.m. Delicate person.
eu-cruas, -ais, s.m. Sickness, feebleness. 2** Softness, effeminateness. 3**Delicateness.
eu-cuandachd, s.f. Deformity.
eu-cubhaidh, -e, a. Unfit, improper.
eud, s.m. Zeal. 2 Jealousy. [E. in the North generally means *zeal*, while jealousy is *iadach*, —in Glenlyon *eudach*.] 3 Grudge. 4*Malice at another's success. Eud do theach-sa, *the zeal of thine house* ; thig tri nithean gun iarraidh, an t-eagal, an t-iadach (eud) 's an gaol, *three things come without seeking, fear, jealousy, and love* ; e. bean a' chlàrsair, a' chlàrsach fhéin, *the harper's wife's jealousy, the harp*.
eudach,** -aiche, a. Zealous. 2 Jealous. Gu h-e., *jealously*.
————, -aich, s.m. Jealous man. 2* Jealousy between man and wife. Ag e. rithe, *accusing her of being unfaithful to his bed*.
————, -aich, s.m. see aodach.
————adh,** -aidh, s.m. Jealous watching. 2 Stepping or stealing softly. Ag e—, *pr. pt.* of eudaich. 3 see aodachadh.
————ail,* a. see eudmhor.
eudaich, *gen. sing.* of eudach (*for* aodach.)
————,* v.a. Watch jealously. [*zealously.] 2 see aodaich.
————te, *past pt.* Watched. 2 see aodaichte.
eudail, -ean, s.f. see feudail.
————each, -iche, a. see feudaileach.
eu-daingeann, -daingne, a. Weak, infirm, defenceless.
eu-daingneachd, s.f.ind. Weakness, defencelessness. 2 Nakedness.
eudainn, *gen. sing.* of eudann (*for* aodainn.)
————ean, *n. pl.* of eudann (*for* aodannan.)
eudaire, -an, s.m. Jealous person.
†eudairmeas, -ais, s.m. Act of invention.
†eudal, -ail, see feudail.
eudanan, -ain, see aodannan.
eudan, } s.m. see aodann.
eudann, }
————ach, -aiche, see aodannach.
————an, -ain, see aodannan.
†eudaoigh, -e, a. Uncertain.
eud-fhulang, -ainge, a. Intolerable.
eu-dìon, s.m. Leak.
————ach, a. Leaky.
————achd, s.f.ind. Leakiness. 2 Leakage.
eud-mheadhonach, -aiche, a. Immediate.
eudmhoire, *comp.* of eudmhor.
————achd, see eudmhorachd.
eudmhor, -oire, a. Zealous. 2 Jealous.
eudmhorachd, s.f.ind. Zealousness. 2 Jealousy.
eu-dòcha, *comp.* a. Less probable.
eu-dòchas, -ais, s.m. Despondency, despair, melancholy, dejection. 2 Distrust.
————ach, -aiche, a. Despairing, hopeless, despondent, melancholy.
————ach,** -aich, s.m. Person in despair.
————achd, s.f.ind. Despondency, melancholy, hopelessness.
eu-domhain, -doimhne, a. Shallow.
eu-dorcha, -doirche, a. Clear, plain, manifest.
eudrom, -uime, a. see aotrom.
eug-,‡ *neg. particle*.
eug, éig, s.m. Death. 2**Ghost, spectre. Suain an éig, *the sleep of death*.
eug, *pr.pt.* ag eug & ag eugadh, *v.n.* Die, perish, expire, give up the ghost. 2 Fail, give way. 3††Decay, Dh' e. i, *she died* ; an dòigh 's an d' e. i, *the manner in which she died* ; eugiadh strì a choidhche, *strife shall die away for ever*.
eugach,* a. Death-like. 2 Deadly. 3**Ghastly. Buille eagalach e., *a terrible deadly blow*.
eugaidh,** a. Ghastly, spectral, death-like. 2 Hearse-like.
————, *fut.aff.a.* of eug. Shall or will perish.
eugail, -e, -ean, see eucail.
————,** a. see aogail.
————eachd, see aogaileachd.
eugais, see eugmhais.
eugalachd, s.f.ind. Ghastliness.
eugas, -ais, -an, see aogas.
————ach, a. see aogasach.
————g, -aisg, -an, see aogas.
eug-bhoil,** s.f. Deadly wrath. Bi treun 'nad e., *be strong in thy deadly wrath*.
eug-coir, -e, -ean, see eucoir.
eug-corach, -aiche, see eucorach.
eug-cruaidh, -e, a. Soft.
eugh, see éigh.
————ach, a. & s. see éigheach.
eug-lios, -is, -an, s.m. Burying ground, churchyard, cemetery.
eugmhail, (CR) s.f. Harm, evil—*Skye*.
eugmhais, s. f. Possession. 2 Presence. 3** Privation. 4** *rarely* Fame. As e., *without, deprived of*.
————e, -an, s.f. Defect, blemish.
————each, -iche, a. Calamitous. 2 Famous, remarkable, illustrious, great.
eugnachadh, -aidh, s.m. Dying. 2 Going into decay. 3 Becoming pale or ghastly. Ag e—, *pr.pt.* of eugnaich.
eugnaich, *pr. pt.* ag eugnachadh, *v.n.* Die, decay. 2 Make pale or ghastly.
eugnaidh, -e, a. Death-like, pale, withered. 2 Going into decay. 3**see eagnaidh.
†————, a. Insane.
eugsamhlachadh, -aidh, s.m. Diversifying, varying, mixing. 2 Chequering. 3 Diversity, variety. Ag e—, *pr.pt.* of eugsamhlaich.
eugsamhlachd, s.f.ind. Variety, change, changeableness of appearance. 2 Excellency. 3 Strangeness.
eugsamhlaich, *pr.pt.* ag eugsamhlachadh, v. a. Vary, diversify, change. 2 Spot, chequer.
eugsamhluidh, see eugsamhuil.
eugsamhuil, -samhla, a. Various, manifold, different. 2 Incomparable, matchless. 3* Mournful. 4** Mixed. 5**Chequered. 6** Strange. Dathan e., *various colours* ; ceòl e., *incomparable music* ; duine e., *a man whose like cannot be found*.
euladh, -aidh, s.m. see èaladh.
eulag,** -aig, s.f. Escape.
eulaghadh, -aidh, see èaladh.
eulaigh, v.n. see èalaidh.

eulaigheach, -ich, see èalaidheach.
eumhann, -ainn, -an, *s.m.* Pearl. 2†Jewel.
eun, eòin, *s.m.* Bird, fowl. 2*Chicken. 3** Pout (fish.) E.-siubhail, *a bird of passage, a straggler.*

294. Buill eòin.

PARTS OF A BIRD (BUILL EÒIN) :—
1 Dìon cluaise, *ear-covert,* soft feathers covering external organ of hearing.
2 Slinneanaich, *scapulars,* feathers which cover shoulders and shoulder-blades.
3 Sgiath mheallltach, *bastard wing,* a number of feathers bearing a resemblance to the true wing.
4 Dìon-sgéith beag, *lesser wing-coverts.*
5 Prìomh dìon-sgéith, *greater do.*
6 (DC) Itean gàirdeanach. (DMy) Prìomh itean sgéith, itean móra na sgéith, *primaries,* or principal quills, (the termination of the wings, and the strongest feathers on the bird.)
7 Dara itean sgéith, *secondaries,* or second quills of the wings.
8 Treas itean sgéith, *tertiaries,* or third quills of the wings.
9 Prìomh itean an earbaill, itean mór' an earbaill, *rump feathers and upper tail-coverts.*
10 Fo-itean an earbaill, itean beag' an earbaill, *vent feathers and under tail-coverts.*

eunach, -aich, *s.m.* Fowling, shooting, hunting. Cù eunaich, *a pointer.*
———, -aiche, *a.* Full of birds. 2 Of, or belonging to, birds.
———adh,** -aidh, *s.m.* Act of hunting, or of fowling.
———an, -ain, see eòinein.
eun a' chrùbain,¶ *s. m.* Guillemot, see eun dubh an sgadain.
eunadair, -ean, *s. m.* Fowler. 2 Gamekeeper. 3**Bird-catcher. O lìon an e., *from the fowler's snare ;* an t-e. mallaichte, *the Devil.*
———eachd, *s.f.ind.* Fowling, shooting, occupation of a fowler or bird-catcher. 2 Gamekeeping.
eunadan, -ain, *s.m.* Aviary. 2 Cage. E. do gach eun, *a cage for every bird.*
eunag,** -aig, *s.f.* Young bird.
eunaich,** *v.n.* Fowl.
eun aille,(AF) *s.m.* Guillemot, see eun-dubh-an-sgadain.
eunan,* *gen.* eòinein, *n. pl.* eòineinean, *s. m.* Humming-bird. 2 *dim.* of eun, Little bird.
eunan-dé see dearbadan-dé.
eunan-àir,(AF) *s.m.* Bird of prey.
eun-an-sgadain, see eun-dubh-an-sgadain.
eun-an-t-sneachda,¶ *s.m.* Snow-bunting—*plectrophanes nivalis.* 2 Redwing.

295. Eun-an-t-sneachda.

eunarag,¶ *s.f.* see gobhar-adhair.
eun-ballach-a'-ghart, (AF) Common bunting, see gealag-bhuachair.
eun bàn an sgadain,¶ see sulaire.
eun bàn an t-sneachda, (AF) *s.m.* Ptarmigan, see tarmachan.
eun-Bealltuinn,¶ *s. m.* Whimbrel—*numenius phœopus.*
eun-bhiadh, -bhìdh, *s.m.* Birds' meat, bird-seed.
eun-bhrìgh, -e, *s. m.* Chicken-broth. 2†Soup, gravy, see eanraich.
eun-bhrigheach, eiche, *a.* Of, or pertaining to, chicken-broth.
eun-bhualadh, -aidh, *s.m.* Palpitation, fluttering.
eun-binn,(AC) *s.m.* Long-tailed duck.
eunbhruich, see eanbhruich.
eun-bruidhne,(AF) *s. m.* (*lit.* speaking bird) Parrot.
eun-buchainn,¶ *s.m.* Long tailed duck, " coal an' can'le licht,"—*fuligula glacialis.*
eun-chridhe,** *s.m.* Faint heart, chicken-heart.
———ach, -iche, *a.* Timid, hen-hearted.
eun-crom, *s.m.* Fulmar,—*Lewis.*
eun-dealbhach, -aiche, *a.* Painted with pictures of birds.
eun-druidh,** -ean, *s.m.* Augur. 2 Augurer.
———eachd, *s.f.ind.* Augury.
eun-dubh,¶ *s.m.* Blackbird, see lon-dubh.
eun-dubh-a'-chrùbain,¶ see eun-dubh-an-sgadain.
eun-dubh-an-sgadain,¶ *s.m.* Common guillemot —*uria troile.* (illust. 296.) 2 see coltraiche.
eun-fionn,¶ see clamhan-fionn. 2(WC) Ptarmigan, see tarmachan. Nach ann air dh' éirich an t-ian-fhionn ! (eun-fhionn),—said of a greedy person doing an unusual act of kindness, *also,* nach tu a chunnaic an t-ian-fhionn ! said to a person who was telling a friend that a miserly person gave her (or him) a gift or a sum of money—*Poolewe,* (WC.)
eun-fhiosachd, *s.f.ind.* Auspice.
eun-foghladh,(AF) *s.m.* Horned owl, see comhachag.

296. Eun-dubh-an-sgadain.

eun-foirthir, (AF) *s.m.* Bird of passage.
eun-fraoich,¶ see coileach-fraoich and cearc-fhraoich.
eun-ghobhrag,¶ *s.m.* see gobhar-adhair.
eun-ghurag, -aig, -an, see gobhar-adhair.
eun-glas-an-sgadain,(AF) *s.m.* Great northern diver, see bur-bhuachaill. 2 " Holy Carrara."
eun-gur-le-gùg, (AF) *s. m.* Storm petrel, see luaireag.
eunlach,(DC) *s.m.* Fowls about a house, as hens, ducks, turkeys, &c.
eunlaidh,* *v.n.* Creep, sneak, as a bird-catcher or fowler.
eunlainn, *s.pl.* see eunlaith.
eunlaireachd,** *s.f.* Fowling.
eunlaith, *s.pl.* Fowls, birds, all the feathered tribes. Ealt e., *or* sgaoth e., *a flight of birds;* e. a réir an gnè, *fowls after their kind.*
eun-lann, *s.m.* Aviary.
eun-leadain,(AF) *s.m.* War-bird, barnacle-goose.
eun-liath,(AF) *s.m.* Black grouse.
eun-lìon, -lìn, -liontan, *s. m.* Fowler's net, bird-net.
eun-mór-an-fhàsaich, *s.m.* Pelican, see pealag.
eun-òtrach,(AF) *s.m.* Barn-door fowl.
eun-rap,(AF) *s.m.* Landrail, see trèan-ri-trèan.
eun-ruadh,(AF) *s. m.* Grouse, see coileach-fraoich & cearc-fhraoich.
eun-snàmh,(AF) *s.m.* Aquatic bird.
eun-snàmhach,¶ *s.m.* Coot, see lacha-bhlàir.
eun-uasal, *s.m.* Foreign bird, rare bird.
eun-uisge, eòin-, *s.m.* Waterfowl.
†eur, *a.* see uasal.
eur, *pr. pt.* ag euradh, *v.a. & n.* Refuse. 2** Deny. Cha d' eur an rìgh dha, *the king refused him not.*
euradh, -aidh, -aidhean, *s. m.* Refusal, denial. 2 Refusing, denying. Eadar an t-e. is an t-aimbeairt, *between denial and want;* cha d' thug Fionn an t-e. do dhuine riamh, *Fionn never refused anyone.* Ag e—, *pr. pt.* of eur.
eurmaireachd,** *s.f.* Galloping, riding.
eusaontas, -ais, see easaontas.
†eusgad, -aid, -an, see iosgaid.
euslaint, see easlaint.
————each, -iche, *a.* see easlainteach.
————eachd, see easlainteachd.
————eil,** *a.* see easlainteach.
————ich, see easlaintich.
euslan, see easlan.
——achd, see easlainteachd.
eusontach,** *a.* see easaontach.
eusontas, see easaontas.
†eusploid, -e, *s.f.* Absolution.
eu-tairiseachd, *s.f.ind.* Alienation, ill-will.
†eutlach, -aithe, *a.* Not tame, courageous.
†————ach, -aiche, *a.* Not tame, courageous.
eu-torrach,†† -aiche, *a.* Barren, unfruitful.
eu-tràthach, -aiche, *a.* Late. 2 Tempestuous.
eu-treòir, -e, *s.f.* Imbecility, weakness, incapacity, pithlessness.
eu-treòrach, -aiche, *a.* Irresolute, weak, imbecile, silly, powerless, feeble. 2 Ungirded. 3 Unguided.
eu-treun, -tréine, *a.* Weak, silly, powerless.
eu-tròcair, *s.f.* Cruelty, want of mercy, mercilessness.
————each, -eiche, *a.* Cruel, unmerciful, unfeeling. Gu h-e., *cruelly.*
————eachd, *s.f.ind.* Unmercifulness, unfeelingness. 2 Practice of cruelty.
eutrom, -uime, *a.* see aotrom.
————achadh, -aidh, *s.m. & pr.pt.* see aotromachadh.
————achd, see aotromachd.
————ad, -aid, *s.f.* see aotromad.
————aich, see aotromaich.
————aichean, see aotromaichean.
————aichidh, see aotromaichidh.
————aichte, *past pt.* of eutromaich.
————an, see aotroman.
————as, -ais, see aotromas.
eutruime, *s.f. ind.* see aotromachd.
————, *comp.* of eutrom, see aotruime.

F f

F, fèarn, *the alder*, the sixth letter of the Gaelic alphabet now in use. It is sounded like *f* in English, but when aspirated, that is, when followed by *h*, it is always silent, except in the three words fhathast, fhéin and fhuair, in which *fh* sounds like *h* in English.
f',** *for* fa or fo.
fa,** *prep.* On, upon, above. Fa làr, *on the ground, omitted, neglected*; fa 'n aobhar ud, *on that account;* ciod fa 'n abradh iad? *wherefore should they say?*
fa, *prep.* see fo. Used in adverbial expressions. Aspirates an indefinite noun, as fa dheireadh, *at last.* Fa 'r casaibh, *under our feet*; fa sgaoil, *at liberty.*
fà, see fàth.
†fa, *v.* see bha.
fàbh,* *s.m.* Thick cake, thick bread.
——achd, *s.f.* see fabh.
fàbhair, *pr.pt.* a' fàbharadh, *v.a.* Favour, prefer, oblige.
————,(CR) *s.m.* Faint rumour—*Perthshire.*
————t, *s.f.ind.* see fadhairt.
†fabhal,** -ail, *s.m.* Fable, romance, 2 Journey.
†fabhall, -aill, *s.m.* Report, account.
†fabhaltas, -ais, *s.m.* Profit, benefit, gain, advantage.
fàbhan,(WC) *s.m.* Hint. Thug e f. dhomh, *he gave me a gentle hint—Poolewe.*
fàbhar, -air, -an, *s.m.* Favour, friendship. 2 Sign, badge, cockade. 3 (PM) Hint.
————, *v.n.* Favour, befriend.
fabhar, -bhra, -bhran, *s. m.* Eye-lid. [see fabhra.]
fàbharach, -aiche, *a.* Favourable. 2* Kind, disposed to befriend.
————d,** *s.f.ind.* Favourableness. 2 Disposition to befriend, kindliness.
fabhd,* *s.m.* Fault, blame.—*Perthsh., Lewis.*
fabhda,** *s.* Crime.

†fàbhor, see fàbhar.
fabhra, *n.pl.* -n, -innean & -nnan, Eyebrow. 2 Eyelid. 3 Veil, curtain. 4 Fringe. 5* Flounce.
——, *s.pl.* The eye-lids. 2 Hairs of the eye-lids.
†Fabhra, *s.m.* February.
fabhrach,** *a.* Having eye-lids. 2 Having large eye-lids. 3 Of, or belonging to, an eyelid, ciliary.
fabhrad, -aid, -an, *s.m.* see fabhra.
fabhradh, -aidh, -aidhean, *s.m.* see fabhra. 2 (AC)Swirl, eddy, whirl. F. nimheil na gaoithe 'n ear, *the venomous swirl of the east wind.*
fabhraiche,** *s.* Blazer.
fabhraidh, *s.pl.* see fabhra.
fabhranta, } *a.* Having large eye-lashes or
————ch, } eye-lids.
fabhsadh,(AC) *s.m.* Eddy.
fabht, *s.* Error, flaw,—*Dàin I. Ghobha.*
fabhtas, *Lewis* for fabht.
†fabhthoirseach, -eiche, *a.* Negligent.
fabhunn,** *s.m.* Surmise, rumour.
fabhur, see fathann.
faca, *past interr.* of faic.
facach¶, *s.m.* see sgraib.
facadh, *past interr. pass.* of faic.
facain, *Suth'd* for acain, *moaning.*
facal, -ail, *pl.* -ail & -clan, *s.m.* Word. 2 Solemn oath. Thoir t' fh., *swear.*
—— -aonaidh, *s.m.* Conjunction.
—— -buaidhe, *s.m.* Epithet.
—— -comharraidh, *s.m.* Countersign.
—— -comh-bhoinn, *s.m.* Conjunction.
—— -faicill, *s.m.* Countersign.
—— -fhreumh,** -fhreimh, *s. m.* see freumh-fhacal.
————ach,** *a.* see freumh-fhaclach.
————achd, *s.f.ind.* see freumh-fhaclachd.
————aiche,** *s. m.* see freumh-fhaclaiche.
facall, -aill, see facal.
†facamar, *past synthetic* of faic (*for* chunnaic sinn.)
fach,** -aich, *s. m.* Hole of a lobster. 2 see faochag.
——ag, see faochag.

297. *Fachach.*

fachach,¶ -aich, *s.m.* Puffin, coulterneb, shearwater,—*fratercula arctica.* [A small bird with a yellow beak, which carries sand-eels or small herrings in its mouth to its young every morning, having been gathering them all night. The tails of the fishes are hanging out on both sides of its bill, and 20 or 30 of them packed in its mouth.] The young is called "gille bog" *soft, fat fellow* (DMy.) 2 (AF) The young of these and other sea-birds. 3(DC) Sand-martin—*Argyll.* 4 Mole.
fachail, -e, *s. f.* Strife, contention, dispute, struggle.
————each, -aiche, *a.* Litigious.
†fachaill, *a.* Full of words.
fachainnt, -e, *s.f.* Scoffing, derision, ridicule, mockery, sneering. [‡ gives fachaint.]
————e, *a.* see fachainnt.
————each,** *a.* Derisive, scoffing, apt to sneer.
fachanta, -ainte, *a.* Insignificant, petty, puny.
————chd, *s.f.ind.* Insignificancy, puny appearance or size.
†fachd, *s.m.* Fight.
fa cheud, *adv.* One hundred times.
fachlas, -ais, *s.m.* Reward for valour. Fìon is f. is feòil, *wine, a prize and meat.*
fa-choill,** *s.f.* Thick wood.
————,** *a.* Full of woods.
fa chomhair, *adv.* Opposite to, or before him or it (*m.*) 2 In anticipation of, in preparation for.
fa chùis, *adv.* By reason of, because.
fa chùl, *adv.* Backwards, behind. Fa 'n cùl, *behind them.*
faclach, -aiche, *a.* Wordy, full of words.
————adh, -aidh, *s.m.* Expressing by words. 2 Diction. 3 Etymology. A' f—, *pr. pt.* of faclaich.
faclaich, *pr.pt.* a' faclachadh, *v.n.* Word, indict, express by words, speak. Cha d' fh. e orm, *he did not speak to me.*
————e, *s.m.* Good speaker. 2**Spokesman.
facladair, -ean, *s.m.* Lexicographer.
————eachd, *s.f.ind.* see faclaireachd.
faclair, -ean, *s.m.* Vocabulary, dictionary. 2 **Lexicographer.
————eachd, *s.f.ind.* Lexicography.
fa comhair, *adv.* Opposite or before her or it (*f.*)
facon,¶ -oin, *s.m.* Gaelic spelling of *falcon.*
fad,‡‡ *pr.pt.* a' fadail, *v.a.* Kindle, see fadaidh.
fàd, -àid, fòid. 2(DMy) Furrow of the plough. 3 Single peat. F. mòineach, *a peat.*
fad, *s.m.ind.* Length. 2*Distance. 3*Tallness. *prep.* During, over. 2 Throughout. 3** Altogether, wholly. 4**Longitudinally.

fada, faide, *a.* Long, of great length, the opposite of short. 2 Of long continuance, for a long time. 3* Distant.

[This is the way *fad* is treated in the other dictionaries, but the different significations of the word in different positions are more clearly explained by grouping the various examples given according to the different meanings of *fad*, rather than according to its parts of speech, thus,]

(*a*) *Length, longitude—*
Fad is leud an taighe, *the length and breadth of the house;* a' dol am fad, *getting longer;* air fhad, *lengthwise, longitudinally;* cuir am f., *lengthen;* rathad fada, *a long way.*

(*b*) *Subordinate to Length, longitude—*
Air fad an t-saoghail, *throughout the world;* air fad, *altogether, wholly;* fìor air fad, *just wholly.*

(*c*) *Distance—*
Fad as, *afar off;* fad air astar, fad air falbh, *far away, at a great distance;* o thìr fhada, *from a distant country;* fada bhuam, *far from me;* cian fhada, agus fada nan cian agus làn fhada.

(*d*) *Time—*
Fad an là, *all day long;* fad fìnn foineach an là,' *throughout the live-long day;* fad làithean mo bheatha, *throughout my whole life;* is fad' an là dha-san nach do chuir blas na h-oidhche â 'bheul, *long is the day to a hungry*

man, (*lit.* to him who hasn't put the taste of the night out of his mouth); is fhad' a dh' fhan thu, *you stayed long*; cia fhad ? *how long ?* am fad, *whilst*; 'fhad 's a bhitheas mi, *as long as I am*; o chionn fada, *long ago*; cha tig e gu ceann fada, *he will not come for a long while*. Baile fada-gu-là, *the township of the long night* (*lit.*the long-till-day township.) The reference is to Paible, N. Uist. Long ago a stranger, happening to spend a night in the place, some mischievous lads covered up his bedroom window from the outside, with the result that the night was lengthened by many hours. Several times the astonished stranger was heard to mutter " b' e seo am baile fada-gu-là !" *what a long-till-day township !*

[Fad is always aspirated in sentences of comparison, but like other adjectives, it is not aspirated by *cho*, as, air cho fad ? *how long ?*]

fàdach, *a.* see fòideach. 2††Abounding in peats.

fadachadh, -aidh, *s.m.* Lengthening, extending. 2 Act of lengthening, prolonging or stretching. A' f—, *pr.pt.* of fadaich.

fadachd,(CR) *s.f.* *Skye, Uist & W. of Ross* for fadal. An robh thu 'gabhail fadachd rium ? *were you wearying for me ?*

fadadh, -aidh, *s.m.* Act of kindling, lighting or inflaming. 2* Blowing into a flame. 3 Fire-place of a kiln. 4 Pan of a gun. A' f. gealbhain, *kindling a fire*; a' f. bhur n-ana-miannna, *inflaming your lusts*; f. cluaise, *the priming of a gun, match*; f. cruaidh, *part of a rainbow seen by sailors in stormy weather, called " a dog-tooth "*; f. spuing, *touchwood, tinder*. A' f—, *pr.pt.* of fadaidh. [Sometimes spelt fàdadh.]

fadaich, *pr.pt.* a' fadachadh, *v. a.* Lengthen, extend, stretch out, prolong. 2 Grow long.

fadaich, *v.a.* see fadaidh.

fadaichear, *fut. pass.* of fadaich.

fadaichidh, *fut. aff. a.* of fadaich.

fadaichte, *a. & past pt.* of fadaich. Lengthened, extended. 2**Kindled.

fadaidh, *pr.pt.* a' fadadh, *v.a.* Kindle, as a fire, inflame. 2 Blow into a flame.

fadail, *gen.sing.* of fadal. 2 *pr. pt.* of fad.

fadair,** *s.m.* Match-maker.

fadal, -ail, -an, *s.m.* Delay, tediousness. 2 Longing, weariness, anxiety, ennui. 3 Prolixity. 4 Appetite. Na gabh f., *do not weary*; tha f. orm, *I am wearying*; a' gabhail fadail, *wearying*.

——ach, -aiche, *a.* Tedious, lingering, wearisome, late. 2 Dreary, slow, tardy. Oidhchechan f., *dreary* or *tedious nights*; tha thu f., *you are late*.

——achd, *s.f.ind.* Prolixity, tediousness.

fad-altach, -aiche, *a.* Long-jointed.

fad-anaileach,-liche & -alaiche, *a.* Long-winded.

fad as, *adv.* Afar off.

fada-spuinge, see fadadh-spuinge.

fàd-bhuinn,(AC) *s.m.* (*lit.* Sole-sod) Door-step. The name originated when a grassy turf was, as it still occasionally is, the door-step. 2 Wooden step. 3 (DC) Stick laid across a doorway, to close up the space between the door and floor, to keep out draughts, rain, &c. (called a threshold berge.)—*Uist.*

fad-chasach,¶ *s. m.* Black-winged stilt, see luirgneach.

fad-cheannach,* *a.* Long-headed, sagacious, shrewd.

fad-cheum,** *s.m.* Long step or pace, stride.

————ach,* *a.* Striding, bounding, bouncing, taking long steps.

fad-chluasach,* *a.* Long-eared.

fa d' chomhair, *adv.* Opposite thee, in front of thee.

fà-déistinn, *s.f.* see fàth-déistinn.

fad-fhoidhidinn, -e, *s.f.* Patience, longanimity.

————each, see fad-fhoidhidneach.

fad-fhoidhidneach, -iche, *a.* Patient, longanimous.

fad-fhuilingeach, -eiche, see fad-fhulangach.

fad-fhulang, -aing, *s.m.* Long-suffering, forbearing, patience, longanimity.

————ach, -aiche, *a.* Long-suffering, forbearing, patient. Gu f., *patiently*.

————achd, *s.f. ind.* Long-suffering, patience.

————as, -ais, *s.m.* Same meanings as fad-fhulang.

fad-gheugach, -aiche, *a.* Long-branched.

†fadh, *s.m.* Science.

fàdh,† *gen. pl.* of fàidh. 'Nam bitheadh fios nam fàdh agam, *had I the gift of prophecy* (*of the prophets.*)

fadh,(AF) *s.m.* see famh.

fădhadh,(WC) -aidh, *s.m.* Little handful of anything, as meal. Crath f. air, *shake a little on it*.

fadhail, -dhlach, -dhlaichean, *s.f.* Extensive beach. 2 Hollow in the sand, formed by and retaining water, after the egress of the tide. 2 Ford, space between islands when rendered passable on foot through the tide receding. The hollowed out rhines are called *dìgean*.

fadhairt, -e, *s.f.* The temper of a cutting instrument. 2 Forging, moulding, hammering. Gun fh., *blunt*.

————e, *past pt.* Tempered. 2 Sharpened.

————each, -iche, *a.* Tempered, as steel. 2 Well-tempered.

————ich,* *v.a.* Temper.

fadharsach, -aiche, *a.* Trifling, paltry, mean, of little value. Gu f., *in a trifling manner*.

fadharsachd, *s. f. ind.* Insignificancy, paltriness, meanness.

†fadhbach, see saoghlach.

†fadhban, -ain, *s.m.* Mole hillock. 2 Tossing.

fadhbh,* *s.f.* see famh.

fadhbhag, -aige, -an, *s.f.* see faobhag.

fadhdach,(AC) *s.m.* Black, blackness. 2 Confusion.

fa dhéigh, *adv.* see fa dheòigh.

fa dheire, *adv.* see fa dheireadh.

fa dheireadh, *adv.* At last, at length, at the end.

fa dheòidh, see fa dheòigh.

fa dheòigh, *adv.* At last, finally, after all, at length. F. air sgeul, *found at last*.

fadhlach,†† -aiche, *a.* Having an extensive beach.

fadhlainn, *s.f.* Exposed place beside the shore, covered with small white stones.

†fa dhò, *adv.* Twice.

fa dhruim,** *adv.* Backwards.

fadhtag, see faobhag.

fad-labhairt,(PM) *s.f.* Loquacity. Generally preceded by the article, as, 's ann ort a bha an fhad-labhairt, *how loquacious you were !*—said to one repeating secrets.—*Uist.*

fad-làmhach, -aiche, *a.* Long-handed, thievish, dishonest. Gu f., *thievishly*.

fad-monadh,¶ *s. m.* Little grebe, dabchick, see spag-ri-tòin.

fad-seilbh,(AC) *s.m.* Possession, infeftment. 2 The sod or handful of earth, given by the seller to the buyer of land.

fad-shaoghalach, -aiche, *a.* Long-lived. Gu ma f. thu ! *long may you live !*

fad-shaoghalachd, *s.f.ind.* Longevity.

fad-sheallach, -aidhe, *a.* Prospective. 2 Long sighted.

fad-tharruing,* *s. f.* Dilatoriness, drawling, procrastination.
————each,* -iche, *a.* Dilatory, procrastinating.
fad-theangach, -aiche, *a.* Long-tongued.
fàfann, -ain, *s.m.* Gentle breeze.
fàfannach, -aiche, *a.* Breezy.
fàg, *pr.pt.* a' fàgail, *v.a.* Leave, quit, abandon, forsake. 2* Relinquish. 3 Outrun, outstrip. 4 Render, make, effect. 5 Cackle, as a duck. Dh' fhàg e i, *he forsook her, he abandoned her*; dh' fhàg an dara bàt' an té eile, *the one boat outstripped the other* [when a boat is sailing she is *feminine* in Gaelic, thus while "bàta math" is *a good boat*, they always say "is math a sheòlas i!" *how well she sails!*; dh' fhàgadh tu am buamastair treubhach, *thou wouldest render the blockhead heroic*; fàg m' fhianuis, *get out of my presence!* fàg mis' am aonar, *leave me alone*; fàg an t-àite 's am bheil thu 'nad shuidhe, *leave your seat*—of the same import and of similar application to "fliuch do shùil."
fàg, *pr.pt.* a' fàgail, *v.n.* Father upon, accuse of, lay to the charge. Dh' fhàg iad sin air, *they fathered that upon him, they laid that to his charge*; dh' fhàg iad am pàisd' air, *they fathered the child upon him.*
fagaid,** Gaelic spelling of *faggot.*
fàgaidh, *fut. aff. a.* of fàg.
fàgail, -e, -ean, *s.f.* Leaving, quitting, abandoning, act of leaving. 2* Rendering. 3††Custom, habit, failing. A' f—, *pr.pt.* of fàg.
fàgail, *s.f.ind.* Anything left. 2* Curse. 3* Fatality, destiny, fate. 4 Bias, disposition—*Dàin I. Ghobha.* Tha 'fh. féin aig gach neach, *everyone has his own fate*; is bochd an fh. a th' agad, *there is a sad fatality following you.*
fagaire,* -an, *s.m.* Wag, wit, though nothing like such.
fagaireachd,* *s.f.* Waggery or witticisms of a person, from whom nothing of the kind is to be expected.
fàgalach, -aiche, *a.* Ready to fail or desert.
fàgam, *1st. per. sing. imp.* of fàg. Let me leave. †2 (*for* fàgaidh mi) *1st. fut. aff. a.* I will leave.
fagannta,* *a.* Slow and drawling, yet witty and waggish.
fàgar, *fut. pass.* of fàg.
†fàgbhuid, *for* dh' fhàg iad.
†fagha, *s.m.* Spear. 2 Attempt. 3 Offer.
faghaid, see foidhidinn.
faghaid, -e -ean, *s. f.* Hunting. 2 Game. 3 Starting of game. 4 Chase, hunt. 5 Hunting party. 6 Men who start the game. Tha f. a' bhaile 'na déidh, *all the dogs in the village are in pursuit of her*; f. an réidh, *the chase of the plain*; f. fàsaich, *a forest hunt.*
————each -eiche, *a.* Hunting. 2 Connected with hunting or game. 3**Carniverous.
————each, *s.pl.* Carniverous birds.
faghail, *s.f.ind.* see faotainn. A' f—, *pr. pt.* of faigh. A' f. cuideachd, *getting help*; a' f. bàis, *dying.*
faghail, -lach, -laichean, *s.f.* see fadhail.
faghainn, *s.f.ind.* see faighinn.
faghairt,†† *s.f.* see fadhairt.
faghairt,†† *v.a.* see fadhairtich.
†faghal, -ail, *s.m.* see fadhail.
faghaltach,** *a.* Profitable, gainful, lucrative. Gu f., *profitably.*
faghaltas,** -ais, *s.m.* Profit, gain, advantage.
faghar,†† -air, *s.m.* see foghar.
fagharach,†† -aiche, *a.* see fogharach.
fagharsach, *a.* see fadharsach.
fagharsachd, *s.f.* see fadharsachd.
fagmaid, *1st. pers. pl. imp.* of fàg. Let us leave.
fàgta, *past pt.* of fàg. Left, abandoned.
fagus, faisge, *a.* Near, nigh. 2 Nearly related. Fagus orm, fagus dhomh, *near me*; am fad 's am f., *far and near*; f. air a bhi deas, *or* f. do bhi deas, *nearly ready*; na 's fhaisge, *nearer.* [*Fagus* takes the prep. *air* or *do*, simple or compounded, after it, as, fagus do 'n bhàs, *near death*; ged is fagus "duinn," is faisge "oirnn," *though "near us" be nigh, "upon us" is nigher.*]
fagusach, -aiche, *a.* Adjacent.
fagusachd, *s.f.ind.* Adjacency, nearness.
fagus air, *adv.* About. 2 *prep.* By.
fagusg, see fagus.
faibhile, see faidhbhile.
faic, *irreg. v.* See, look, behold. 2*Observe. 3 (CR) Show.—*W. of Ross.*
Active Voice—
IND. *past*, Chunnaic mi, &c. *I &c. saw.*
,, *fut.* Chì mi, &c., *I &c. shall see.*
INTERR. & NEG. *past*, am ? (nach fh— ? cha'n fh—,) faca mi, &c. *Did I &c. (not) see ?*
,, *fut.* am ? (nach fh— ? cha'n fh—) faic mi, &c., *Shall I &c. (not) see ?*
SUBJ. *past*, (ged) chithinn, (*though*) *I would see*; (ged) chitheamaid, (*though*) *we would see*; (ged) chitheadh tu, e, i, sibh, iad, (*though*) *thou, he, she, you, they would see.* [Another form after interrogative or negative particles—am ? (nach fh— ? cha'n fh—, mur,) faicinn, *would I (not) see ?*]
,, *fut.* (ma) chì mi, &c., (*if*) *I &c. shall see.*
IMPER. *1st. per. sing.* Faiceam, *let me see.*
INFIN. A dh' fhaicinn, [& a dh' fhaicsinn] *to see.*
PRES. PART. A' faicinn, [& a' faicsinn] *seeing.*
Passive Voice—
IND. *past*, chunnacadh mi, &c. *I, &c. was seen.* [Chunnacas is generally used in preference to chunnacadh.]
,, *fut.* chithear mi, &c., *I &c. shall be seen.*
INTERR. & NEG. *past*, am ? (nach fh— ? cha'n fh—,) facadh mi, &c.
,, *fut.* am ? (nach f— ? cha'n fh—) faicear mi.
SUBJ. *past*, (ged) chiteadh mi, &c. (*though*) *I &c. would be seen.*
,, *fut.* (ma) chithear mi, &c. (*if*) *I, &c. shall be seen.*
PAST PART. faicte, *seen.*
[Parallel passive impersonal forms—o'n chiteadh, *since it would be seen*; but, nach faicteadh ? *would it not be seen ?*
Chì mi dhuit e, *I will show it to you*; faic dhomh e, *show me it*; faiceam do phìob, *let me see your pipe.*
faic ! *int.* See ! behold ! lo ! Faic mo dheòir, *observe my tears.*
faic, *fut. interr.* of faic.
faic, -e, -ean, *s.f.* Hiding-place, den, hole. 2 **Sparkle.
faice, *s.f.* see aice, 3. 2**Tatter.
faicealach, -aiche, *a.* see faicilleach.
faiceall, see faicill.
————achd,** see faicilleachd.
faiceam, *1st. sing. imp. a.* of faic.
faicean,** *s.m.* Swaddling-band, child's blanket.
faiceanaich,** *v.a.* Swaddle.
faiceanaichte, *past part.* of faiceanaich.
faicear, *fut. interr. & neg.*, and *imperf. pass.* of faic. F. t' obair, *let thy work be seen*; cha'n fh. an ceum na 's mó (tuilleadh), *their approach shall no more be seen.*
faiceil,** *a.* Momentary, in a trice.
faich,‡‡ -e, -ean, see faiche.
faichd, -e, -ean, *s.f.* see faic.
faiche, -an, *s.f.* Field. 2 Field where soldiers

are reviewed. 3 Plain, meadow, green. 4 The burrow of a shell-fish. 5**Forest. 6‡ Green by the house. F. giomaich, *a lobster's burrow*; f.-bhuill, *bowling-green*; saidhe na faiche, *meadow-hay*.

faicheach, -iche, *a*. Lawny. 2 Agrarian.

——d,** *s.f.* Traversing the fields. 2 Field sports. 3 Stately gait. 4 Field manœuvring, drilling of soldiers, parading.

faichealachd, *s.f.ind.* Showiness.

†faicheall, -ill, *s.m.* Wages, reward, salary.

faicheallach,** *s.m.* Lamp, candle.

————, *a*. †Luminous.

————d, see faicilleachd.

faichean, see faicean.

fàicheil,** *a*. Graminivorous.

faicheil, -eala, *a*. Stately, trim, showy. 2* Tidily and cleanly dressed, as soldiers, and at the same time proud of such. 3**Agrestic.

†faichilleach, -ich, *s.m.* Hired servant.

faichilleach, see faicilleach.

faichuach,** *s.f.* see fail-chuach.

faicibh, *2nd. pl. imp.* of faic. See you or ye.

faicill, -e, *s.f.* Caution, guard, watchfulness, precaution. 2 Care. 3**Attention. 4**Chariness, circumspection. 5**Evidence. Trid f. mhaith, *by means of great attention*; air 'fh., *on his guard*; f. ort! *take care! be on your guard!*

faicill,** *a*. see faicilleach.

——each, -iche, *a*. Cautious, wary, watchful, observant. 2 Careful. 3**Attentive. 4** Evident, manifest. 5‡‡Provident. Gu f. *circumspectly, warily*; tha 'n aois f., *age is circumspect*.

——eachd, *s.f.ind.* Attentiveness. 2 Cautiousness, circumspection, observance. 3** Evidence.

faicinn, *s.f.ind.* Seeing, perceiving, act of seeing. 2 Vision. 3**Sight. 4**Observation. 5 View. 6**Visibility. A' f—, *pr. pt.* of faic. Leig fhaicinn dhomh, *show me*.

——, *irreg. past subj.* form of faic.

——each, -iche, *a*. see faicsinneach.

faicleach, -iche, *a*. see faicilleach.

faicse,** (faic thusa) *v*. See thou, behold, observe.

faicsinn, *s.f.* see faicinn. 2 A' f—, *pr.pt.* of faic.

————each, -iche, *a*. Visible. 2**Conspicuous. 3**Watchful, observant. 4**Wrathful. 5††Evident, manifest. 6*Notorious. An eaglais fh., *the visible church*; f. agus neo-fhaicsinneach, *visible and invisible*.

————eachd, *s.f.ind.* Conspicuity, conspicuousness. 2**Visibleness. 3 Clearness.

†faicsiona, *s.m.* Fashion, form, pattern.

faicte, *past pt.* of faic.

faid, *s.m.* see fàidh.

faide, *s.f.ind.* Length, degree of length. 2 Tallness of a person.

——, *comp.* of fada. Longer. 2 Longest. A's fhaide gu mór, *longest by far*; 's e a's fhaid' a mhaireas, *he will last the longest*; mar a's fh. chì mi, *the longer I can see*.

faidead, -eid, *s.m.* Distance. 2 Length, degree of length. 3 Longitude. Air f. bhur saoghal, *no matter how long you may live*.

faideag,** -eig, -an, *s.f.* Lot. 2 Chance. 3 see feadag (plover.)

†faidear, *adv.* see fainear.

faidh, see faigh.

fàidh, -e, -ean, *s. m.* Prophet, seer. 2 Soothsayer. Tha 'm f. breugach, *the prophet is lying*. [*gen.pl.* sometimes fàdh—in *Gairloch*, fàth.]

faidhbhile, -an, *s.f.* Beech-tree.

faidhbhile dhubh,§ *s.f.* The black beech-tree —*fagus sylvatica* var. *atrorubens*.

————ach, -iche, *a*. Beechen.

fàidheachd, see fàidheadaireachd.

fàidheadair,** -ean, *s. m.* Prophet.

fàidheadaireachd, *s. f. ind.* Prophesying, prophecy, prediction, divination.

†fàidheamhuil, *a*. Prophetic. 2 Critical.

fàidheil,* *a*. Prophetic, like a prophet. 2**Apt to criticise. 3** Happy in expression. 4**Witty.

298. Faidhbhile dhubh.

faidhidinn, see foidhidinn.

faidhinn, see faighinn & faidhrean.

faidhir, -dhreach, -dhrichean, *s.f.* Fair, market. 2 Fairing. Là na faidhreach, *the market day*; f. na feòla, *the flesh-market*; f. an éisg, *the fish-market*; f. nan luideag, *the rag-market*.

faidhneachd, see faighneachd.

faidhreach, *a*. Showy, fit for sale or show. 2 Of, or pertaining to, a fair.

————ail, -ala, *a*. see faidhreach.

faidhreag, -eige, -an, see oighreag.

faidhrean, -ein, *s.m.* Fairing, present purchased at a fair.

faidhrichean, *n.pl.* of faidhir.

faidhrionn, -inn, -an, *s.f.* see oighreag.

fàidse,* -achan, *s.m.* Lump of bread, "piece." 2**Budge. 3 (MM) Pancake about two inches thick.

fàidseach, -iche, *a*. Lumpish. 2 Clumsy.

————,†† -ich, -an, *s.f.* Lumpish girl. 2 Bout, hard spell—*Gairloch*.

fàidseachd,** *s.f.* Lumpishness.

†fàig, see fàidh.

†faigean,** *s.m.* Sheath, scabbard. 2 Vagina.

faigh,** *s.f.* Begging by licence. 2 Thickster.

faigh, *irreg. v.* Get, obtain, acquire. 2 Find. 3**Reach.

Active Voice—

IND. *past*, fhuair mi, &c., *I, &c. got*. [*fuair*, not aspirated in *Suth'd.*]

,, *fut.* gheibh mi, &c., *I, &c. shall get*.

INTERR. & NEG. *past*, (an ? nach ? cha) d' fhuair mi, &c., *did I, &c. (not) get ?*

,, *fut.* am ? (nach ? cha'n fh—,) faigh mi, &c., *shall I, &c. (not) get*.

SUBJ. *past*, (ged) gheibhinn, *(though) I would get*; (ged) gheibheamaid, *(though) we would get*; (ged) gheibheadh tu, e, i, sibh, iad, *(though) thou, he, she, you, they would get*. [Another form used after interrog. and neg. particles—'nam ? (nach ? cha'n fh—, mur) faighinn, *(if) I would (not) get*, save personal terminations, as "gheibhinn."

,, *fut.* (ma) gheibh mi, &c., *(if) I, &c. shall get*.

IMPER. *1st. per. sing.* faigheam, *let me get*.

INFIN. a dh' fhaotainn [a dh' fhaghail & a dh' fhaighinn††] *to get*.

Passive Voice—

IND. *past*, fhuaradh *or* fhuaras mi, &c., *I, &c. was got*.

,, *fut.* gheibhear mi, &c., *I, &c. shall be got*.

INTERR. & NEG. *past*, an ? (nach ? cha) d' fhuaradh mi, &c., *shall I, &c. (not) be got ?*

SUBJ. *past*, (ged) gheibhteadh mi, &c., *(though) I, &c. would be got*.

,, *fut.* (ma) gheibhear mi, &c., *(if) I, &c. shall be got*.

PAST PART., faighte, *got*.

[Parallel passive impersonal forms—(ged) gheibhteadh, *(though) it would be got;* (mur) faighteadh, *(if) it would not be got*.

[*Faigh* in its impersonal forms has the meaning of *do, achieve, exert*, as, is math a fhuaras tu ! *how much you have achieved* ; and, is math a gheibhear thu, *you would do much*.] Fhuair sinn, *we have found* ; faigh a mach, *find out* ; faigheam do lorg, *let me get thy staff* ; fhuair iad a mach thu, *they found you out* ; cha d'fhuair mi faighneachd gus a seo, *I did not get (a chance) to enquire till now* ; a' bheairt sin nach fhaighear ach cearr, *the loom that is awry* ; cha mhath a fhuaras Lachlann ort, *L. treated you badly*, or *outdid you* ; a h-uile olc ge 'n d' fhuaras mi, *in spite of every disadvantage I laboured under* ; fhuaras i an àit' a fir, *she was found in her husband's place*.

faighbhile, see faidhbhile.

faighdhe, see faoighe.

faighe, *s.f.* see faoighe.

faigheam, *1st. per. sing. imp.* of faigh. Let me get.

faighear, *fut. interr. pass.* of faigh. Tha e far am f. e, *it is where it shall be found*. 2 *imp. pass*. Faighear mi, *let me be found*.

faighean,** *s.m.* Scabbard.

faighid, *s.f.* see foidhidinn,

———inn, *s.f.* see foidhidinn.

faighidinneach, *a.* see foidhidneach.

faighidneach, *a.* see foidhidneach.

faighileach, -iche, *a.* Acquirable.

faighinn, *s.f.ind.* Getting, obtaining, acquiring. A' f—, *pr. pt.* of faigh.

faighinn, *irreg. past subj.* of faigh, which see.

faighir, see faidhir.

†faighleadh,** -idh, *s.m.* Ivy. 2 Conversation.

faighneach, *a.* Inquisitive.

faighneachadh,** -aidh, *s. m.* Enquiring, asking. A' f—, *pt. pt.* of faighnich.

faighneachd, *pr.part.* a' faighneachd, *v.n.* Ask, enquire, question. This verb takes the prep. *de*, simple or compounded, after it, as, f. de Sheumas, *enquire of James* ; f. dheth, *ask of him*.

faighneachd, *s.f.ind.* Asking, questioning. 2 Inquisitiveness. A' f—, *pr. pt.* of faighneachd and faighnich.

————ach, *a.* see faighneach.

————ail, -ala, *a.* see faighneach.

————as, -ais, *s.m.* Inquisitiveness.

faighnich, *pr. pt.* a' faighneachd & a' faighneachadh, *v.n.* Ask, enquire, question.

faighreag, see oighreag.

faighrean, -ain, see faidhrean.

faighrichean, see faidhrichean.

faighte, *past. pt.* of faigh. Got.

———adh, *past subj. pass.* of faigh.

———ear,** see faighear.

faigse,* *s.m.* see faisge.

——, *a.* see faisge.

fail, *pr.pt.* a' faileadh, *v.a. & n.* Corrupt, putrefy. 2 Make bald or bare. 3 Loosen the hair by maceration or putrefaction.

fail,* *adv.* see far.

fail, *v.a.* Confine in a sty.

†fail, -e, -ean, *s.f.* Sty. 2 Hiccough. 3** Den. F.-chon, *a dog-kennel* ; f.-mhuc, *a pig-sty*.

fail, -e, -ean, *s.f.* Ring, wreath, bracelet. 2 Earring. 3*Mark, print, trace. 4 Beautiful collar—*Dàin I. Ghobha*. 5 *rarely* Company, society. 6 see fàile. 7* see fàl. F. do làimhe, *the print of your hand* ; f. do choise, *the print of your foot* ; mar fh. òir, *like a jewel of gold*.

fàil, *gen. sing.* of fàl.

†fàil,** *a.* Fatal. 2 Generous, liberal. see Lia fàil.

failbhe, *s.f.ind.* Emptiness. 2 Exhaustion. 3 The aërial expanse. A' snàmh 'san fh. mhóir, *swimming in the great firmament*.

failbhe, -an, for fail, *ring*. 2(AH)Ring-bolt.

†failbhe,** *a.* Lively, sprightly.

failbheadh,** -idh, *s.m.* Vegetation.

failbheag, -eige, -an, *s.f.* Ring, bolt-ring for a rope. 2 (DU(Curl. 3**Ring of any metal. Failbheagan òir, *gold rings*.

————ach, -aiche, *a.* Full of rings. 2 Like a ring.

failbhean, -ein, see failbheag.

failbheas,** -eis, *s.m.* Liveliness, sprightliness.

failbheig,** *gen. sing.* of failbheag.

†failbhich,** *v.a.* Quicken, enliven.

failbhisg, *a.* see failmisg. Dh' fhogair iad cuid gu bàs, is cuid gu àitean failbhisg, *they compelled some to go to their death, and some to places much exposed to bad weather*—Joseph Mac-Kay's elegy on John Grant, Reay country, speaking of the clearances.

failc,** -e, *s.f* Gap, opening. 2 Hairlip. 3 Bath, bathing. 4(AC) Flood, flooding. F. theth, *a hot bath*.

——, *pr.pt.* a' failceadh, *v.a. & n.* Bathe.

——each,* *s.f.* see failceadh.

——each,** *a.* Like a bath. 2 Having a bath.

——eadh, -idh, *s.m.* Bath, bathing. 2 Cleaning of the hair by bathing. 3**Lye of potash. F. de dh' iubhar beinne, *bath of the juice of the juniper*—a popular remedy for head-ache. A' f—, *pr.pt.* of failc.

failcean,‡ *s. m.* Pot-lid. 2 Rotula or whirl bone of the knee. 2 see falman.

fail-chon, *s.f.* Dog-kennel.

fail-chuach,§ -uaiche, -an, *s. f.* Sweet violet—*viola odorata*.

299. Fail-chuach.

failcin,* *s.m.* see falman, failcean and faircill.

failcire,* *s.m.* Bather.

failcis,** -e, -ean, *s.f.* Pit.

failcte, *past pt.* of failc. Bathed.

fàile, *pl.* fàileachan, *s.m.* see àileadh.

†faileabadh, -aidh, *s.m.* Death.

faileach,* -aiche, *a.* Rank.

faileach,†† *a.* Abounding in styes.

faileach,†† *a.* Abounding in rings.

————an, -ain, *s.m.* Ear-ring.

————d,(CR) *s.f.* Hiding, concealment. Tha e air f., *he is in concealment*,—said e. g. of a boy who has been in mischief and is keeping out of sight, (*from* falach)—*W. of Ross-sh.*

fàileadh, *s.m.* see àile. 2**Putrefying, putrefaction.

faileadh, -idh, *s.m.* Corrupting, putrefying. 2 ††Soddening. 3 Said of a creature that lies dead till the hair falls off. 4 (CR) Moulting. Tha na cearcan air f., *the hens have moulted*—*W. of Ross*. A' f—, *pr. pt.* of fail. In *Poolewe*—na caoraich fhailidh, tha iad air faileadh, *the sheep are scabby, and losing their wool (from some disease)* ; tha na cearcan fo na h-itean gorma, *the hens are moulting*—WC.

faileag, *s.f.* see aileag. 2**Hump, hillock. 3 (AC) Little lawn, little meadow.

fàileag, -eige, -an, *s.f.* Dog-briar berry. 2 *Uist* for fàireag.

fàilean, -ain, *s.m.*, *dim.* of fàl. Little sod.
——ach,* -aiche, *a.* Turfy. 2††Smelling.
fàileanta, *a.* see àileanta.
faileantan, *s.m.* Honeysuckle—*Arran & Lorn.*
faileas, -eis, -an, *s.m.* [*s.f.* in *Badenoch.*] Shadow. 2* Reflected image. 3** Shade. 4**Spectre, ghost. Mar fh. teichidh tu, *as a shadow thou shalt fly* ; mar fh. ar làithean, *our days are like a shadow* ; f. an ré, *the reflected image of the moon.*
faileasach, -aiche, *a.* Shadowy, causing a shadow. 2 Polished. 3 Reflecting. 4**Spectral. 5 Air-built. Iuthar f., *polished yew.*
faileasachd,** *s.f.* Shadowiness. 2 State of being polished.
faileasaiche, -an, *s.m.* Stile or gnomon of a sun-dial.
fàileineach, -iche, *a.* Fragrant.
fàile-raineach,§ see creidhm-raineach.
faileus, *s.m.* see faileas.
——ach, *a.* see faileasach.
failgeach,** *a.* Poor, necessitous.
failghe, -an, see fail (ring.)
fàil-gleidhte, *s.m.* Hedge.
————ach, see fàil-gleidhte.
fàil-gleusta, *s.m.* see fàil-gleidhte.
fàil-gleuta, see fàil-gleidhte.
failich,(MMcD) *v. Lewis* for fairtlich.
†**fàilidh**, *a.* Gentle, unperceived.
failidh,(WC) *a.* Scabby and losing the wool, as sheep.
fàilig, see fàillinn.
fàilingeach, see fàillinneach.
fàilingeachd, see fàillinneachd.
fàilingeadh, see fàillinneadh.
fàilinn, see fàillinn.
†**faill**,** *s. f.* Opportunity. 2 Advantage. 3 Leisure. 4 Kernel. 5 Precipice, see †àill. 6 Branch, twig, sprout. 7‡‡Hard lump of flesh. 8 Danger. 9 Decay. Cha d' thug mi f. eagalach da, *I did not give him time to get afraid.*
failleach,** *a.* Branchy, abounding in twigs. 2 Sprouty. 3 Like a sprout, branch or twig. 4 (DU) Uncomfortable, not feeling at home.
————d,(DU) *s.f.* Uncomfortableness, feeling of not being at home.
failleadh,** -eidh, *s.m.* Neglect,omission,failure.
failleagan,‡ *s.m.* see faillean.
faillean, -ein, -an, *s.m.* Sucker of a tree. 2 Bud. 3 Young branch, twig. 4 Root of the ear. 5 *Drum of the ear. A' chluas o 'n fh., *the ear from the root.*
failleanach, -aiche, *a.* Full of young suckers or branches. 2 Like a twig. 3 Sprouting.
————d,** *s. f.* Branchiness. 2 State of sprouting. 3 Tendency to sprout.
failleanaich, *pr.pt.* a' failleanachadh, *v.n.* Germinate.
faillein, see faillean.
fàillich,** *v.n.* Fail, neglect, decay.
†**faillidheach**,** *a.* Drowsy.
fàillig, *pr.pt.* a' fàilligeadh, *v.n.* see fàillinnich. [*Fàillig* is the form always used in *Lewis.*]
——each, see fàillinneach. Duine f., *a physically weak or frail man—Uist.*
——eadh,(PM) *s.m.* Mental deficiency—*Uist.* A' f—, *pr.pt.* of fàillig. Bha f. mór anns an duine, *the man was very mentally deficient.*
fàilling, -e, -ean, see fàillinn.
——each, -iche, *a.* see fàillinneach.
fàillingich, see fàillinnich.
fàillinn, -e, -ean, *s. f.* Failing. 2 Fainting-fit. 3**Falling off. 4**Lack. 5**Blemish, fault. Thàinig f air, *he fainted* ; thig ort f. tuigse, *a failing of judgment shall come over thee* ; gun fh. truacantachd, *without lack of compassion* ; cha d' aithnich mi f. ort, *I never knew a blemish in thee* ; gun fh., *without fail.*
fàillinneach,** -nich, *s.m.* Defaulter.
————, -iche, *a.* Failing, fallible, liable to error. 2 Neglectful. 3**Weak, faint, delicate, frail. 4 Decaying. 5 Languid, falling off. 6* Wanting.
fàillinneachd, *s.f.ind.* Defectiveness. 2 Fallibility, faintness. 3 Falling off, failing.
fàillinneadh, -idh, *s.m.* Failing. 2 Fainting. 3 Tendency to decay.
fàillinnich, *v.n.* Fail. 2 Fall off. 3 Decay.
————e,** *s.m.* Defaulter.
fàillne, see fàillinn.
fàillnich, *pr.pt.* a' fàillneachadh, see fàillinnich.
faillseach,** *a.* Sudorific.
faillsich,** *v.a.* Sweat, perspire.
failm, -e, -ean, *s. f.* Helm of a boat or ship. 2 Tiller of a rudder, see rudder 5, p. 78. Glac an fhailm, *steer, take your turn at the helm.*
failmeach,††*a.* Pertaining to a helm.
failmean, -ain, see falman.
failmhe, see failbhe.
fail-mhuc,** *s.f.* Pig-sty.
fail-mhuineil,** *s.f.* Collar.
failmisg, *a.* Stormy, as weather. 2 Fierce, as a man—both *Suth'd.* 3 Unprotected, as a place.
failmisg,(DMC) *s.f.* Wickedness. F. ort ! *may evil take you !*
failmse,†† -ean, *s.f.* Mistake, blunder. 2 *Skye* for ailmse—Gael. Soc. Inv. xxiii, 80. A f., *unawares.*
failmseach,†† *a.* Blundering, mistaking.
fàilneach, *a.* see fàillinneach.
fàilneachadh, -aidh, *s.m.* Failing, act of failing. 3 Decaying, giving way. A' f—, *pr.pt.* of fàilnich.
fàilnich, *v.n.* see fàillinnich.
failreag,** -eig, *s.f.* Lump. 2 Hillock.
fàil-shlatan, *s.m.* Honeysuckle—*Arran.*
fàilt ! *int.* Hail !
fàilte, -an, *s.f.* Salutation, welcome, hail, salute. Chuirinn f., *I would hail* or *salute*; ceud f. a rìgh ! *a hundred welcomes,O king* ! f. shìth, *a salutation of peace* ; cuir f. air, (oirre,) *salute him (her)* ; f. do 'n là, *hail to the day* ; f. na maidne dhuit ! *good morning to you* ; f. na Nollaige ort ! *Gaelic form of " a merry Christmas to you* ; f. na Bealltainn ort ! may also be heard.
fàilteach, -iche, *a.* Welcoming, saluting. 2 Receiving kindly. 3**Hospitable. 4**Welcome.
fàilteachadh, -aidh, *s.m.* Saluting, greeting, act of saluting. 2 Welcoming, hailing. 3 Salute, welcome, kind reception. A' f—, *pr.pt.* of fàiltich.
fàilteachail, -ala, *a.* Prone to salute. 2 Ready to welcome, hospitable.
fàilteachas,*s.m.Same meanings as fàilteachadh.

300. Failtean-fionn.

failtean,** -ein, -teana, *s.m.* Head-band. Na faiiteana, *the head-dress.*
failtean-fionn,§ *s.m.* Maidenhair fern—*adiantum capillus veneris.* (see illust. 300) [Often erroneously applied to trichomanes (dubhchasach.)]
fàiltich, *pr. pt.* a' fàilteachadh, *v.a. & n.* Greet, welcome, salute, hail. Le 'r n-ait hosanna fàiltichidh sinn e, *with our glad hosannas we shall welcome him.*
fàim, *s. & v.* see fàitheam.
fàimeach, -eiche, } *a.* see faitheamachail.
fàimeachail, -ala, }
faimear, see faitheamar.
faince, }
fainche, } (AF) *s.m.* Fox.
fain-chu, }
fàine, *s.f.* see fàinne.
fàine,(CR) *a.* Lower—*Suth'd.*
faineachadh, -aidh, see aithneachadh.
faineachas, -ais, see aithneachas.
fainear, *adv* (fo 'n air') Under consideration, into consideration. 2**Under observation, attention, heed, or notice. Bha 'n t-olc f. dhaibh, *they had evil intentions;* mise f. dha sin, *I brought that about.*
faing, *gen.sing.* of fang. [Used in *Gairloch* as *nom.*]
fainich *v.* see aithnich & fairich.
fainleag, -aige, -an, *s.f.* Swallow, see gobhlangaoithe. 2 (AF) Storm petrel, see luaireag.
fàinne, *pl.* -achan & -an, *s.f.* Ring, circle. Thug iad leo fàinneachan, *they brought rings;* f.-pòsaidh, *a wedding-ring.* [*m.* in many places, e. g., f. mór, in *Argyll.* *Fàinnte* in *Gairloch.*]
fainne, *s.f.ind.* Weakness, weakening. 2 Languishment, languor. 3 Debility. †4 Ignorance.
fàinneach, -iche, *a.* In rings. 2 Abounding in rings or ringlets, curled. A cùl f., *her curled locks.*
†fainneadh, see fionnadh.
fàinneag, -eige, -an, *s.f., dim.* of fàinne. Little ring, ringlet, annulet.
fainneagach, -aiche, *a.* In ringlets.
fainneal, -eil, *s.m.* Ignorance. 2 State of being astray. 3 Bewilderment. 4**Fannel, handful of straw used in thatching. Air f., *astray, bewildered.*
fainneamh, *Gairloch* for fannadh.
fàinneil,** *a.* Annular.
fàinnich, *pr.pt.* a' fàinneachadh, *v.a.* Curl, ring.
fàinnte, *pl.* fàinntichean, *Gairloch* for fàinne.
fair, *pr.pt.* a' faireadh, *v.def.* Give me, bring. F. a nall an t-searrag, *hand over the bottle.*
fàir,‡ see fair.
fàir, *s. f.* Ladder—*Dàin I. Ghobha.*
fàir, -e, *s.f.* see fàire.
fàir, -e, -ean, *s.f.* Dawn. 2 (AC) Horizon. 3 Sky-line. 4 Height, hill, ridge. Briseadh na f., *the dawn;* tha 'n fhair' a' briseadh, *the dawn is breaking;* fhuair mi f. orra, *I spotted them on the horizon;* is luath fear air f. ri là fuar earraich, *swift moves a man over the mountain ridge on a cold spring day.*
fair-ainm,* see for-ainm.
fairbheach,** *s.m.* see foirfeach.
fairbhiteach,(DC) *s. m.* Township constable, bailiff in charge of social arrangements under the estate factor.
†fairbre, *s.f.* Notch, impression. 2 Fault. 3 Stain.
fairc,‡ *s.f.* Links, land sometimes covered by the sea. 2 Hole—*Bute.* 3 Rammer. 4** Hammer.
fairc, see failc.
fairce, -an, *s.m.* see fairche. †2 Extent.
fairceadh, -idh, see failceadh.
fairceall, -ill, -an, *s.m.* Reward. 2**see faircill.
———ach, see faircilleach.
fairche, -an, *s.m.* Hammer, beetle, mallet. 2 Diocese. 3 Parish. 4**Choice. 5(AF)Death-watch beetle. F.-chlach, *a rammer.*
faircheach,†† *a.* Abounding in mallets. 2 Pertaining to a mallet.
faircheadh, -idh, *s.m.* Beating with a mallet.
fairchean, *s.m.* see fairche.
fairchil, see farch-chuil.
faircill, -ean & fairclean, *s.m.* Lid of a cask or pot.
faircilleach,** *a.* Having a lid.
faircle,** *s.f.* The uppermost. 2 Extremity. 3 Choice.
faircte, see failcte.
fàirdeach, -iche, a. see farraideach.
fairdeadh, see farraideadh.
fàirdean, -ein, -deinean, *s.m.* see feòirling.
——— ach, *a.* Abounding in farthings.
fairdhris, see fearra-dhris.
fairdinn, see feòirling.
faire, *v.n.* Properly fairich *or* dean faire.
faire, *s. f.* Watching, watchfulness. 2 Watch (division of time.) 3 Watch, sentinel, guard. 4* Attention, circumspection. 5**Watch-hill. 6 see fàir. 7(PM) Wake—*Uist.* Cuir f. air, *set a watch* or *guard on it;* cnoc-f., *a watch-knoll;* taigh na f., *the wake-house;* f. chliadh, *a churchyard watch;* dè a th' air t' fhaire? *what do you mean?* thoir an fh., *take care, be circumspect, be upon the watch;* cum fair' air sin, *attend to that;* 's e sin a bh' air m' aire, *that is what I had in view;* a' deanamh f. na h-oidhche, *watching by night.*
fàire, *s.m.ind.* see fàir.
faire! faire! *int.* Aye! aye! so! so! heyday! what! pronounced in a tone of anger and surprise. 2(DU) *as applause,* Well done! hear, hear!
faireach, -iche, *a.* see faireil.
———, see faireachadh.
faireachadh, -aidh, -aidhean, *s.m.* Waking, awakening, 2 Watching. 3 Sitting up. 4 Feeling. 5 Warning, alarm. Am bheil thu 'nad fh., *are you awake?* eadar cadal agus f., *between sleeping and waking.* A' f—, *pr. pt.* of fairich.
faireachail, -ala, *a.* Given to watching. 2 Feeling. 3 That has feeling. 4**Watchful, observant, attentive. Gu f., *watchfully.*
†faireachas, -ais, *s.m.* Watching.
faireachdainn, -e, -ean, *s.f.* Feeling, perception. 2 Act of feeling. A' f—, *pr. pt.* of fairich.
faireadh,** -ridh, *s.m.* Watching. 2 Watchfulness, attention. 3 Sentinel. 4 see fàire. Ri f., *keeping watch;* fear-fairidh, *watchman, sentinel.* A' f—, *pr. pt.* of fair.
faire-claidh,** *s.f.* Spectre's watch over a grave.
fàire-druim, -droma, -ean, *s.m.* Saddle-back.
fàireag, -eig, -an, *s.f.* Gland, hard lump between flesh and skin. 2 Wax-kernel. 3**Hump. 4 ** Hillock. 5 (DMy) What the plough or spade would leave unturned of the furrow when it had too broad a piece to turn. 6(DU) Sod. F. am bun na teanga, *almonds of the throat or tongue;* ‖fàireagan, *swollen glands.*
faireag,¶ *s.f.* Kittiwake, see seagair. 2 Lapwing, see adharcan-luachrach.
fàireagach, *a.* Glandular. 2**Kernelly.
fàireagaich,** *v.a.* Kernel.
faireagan! *int.* Bravo! F. a Mhóraig; *bravo Morag!*
fàireamh, -eimh, -an, *s.m.* see fàire.
faireil, -eala, *a.* Watchful, circumspect. 2 Wakeful.

fairge, *pl.* -achan & -annan, *s.f.* Sea, the sea. 2 **Oc an. 3 *Wave. 4‡‡ Swelling of the sea, storminess. 5 (CR) Angry sea—*W. of Ross.* Tha 'n fh. mór, *the sea is rough*; tha f. air a' chladach, *there is a sea on the beach*; 'san fh., *in the sea*; thar f., *across the sea*; annradh f., *a storm at sea*; an fh. mhór, *the great ocean.* [* gives *pl.* fairgeachan.]
fairgeach, -aiche, *a.* Marine. 2 Pelagic, inhabiting the deep sea.
———an, *n.pl.* of fairge.
fairgean,* *s.m.* Mallet.
fairgear, -an, *s.m.* Sailor, seaman.
———ach, *a.* Of, or pertaining to, seamen.
———achd,†† *s.f.* Seamanship.
fairgeir, *s.m.* see fairgear.
fairgneadh, -idh, *s.m.* Hacking. 2‡‡Sacking.
†fairgneamh, -imh, *s.m.* Building.
fairic, see failc.
fairich, *pr. pt.* a' faireachadh & faireachduinn, [faireachdain in *Suth'd.*] *v.n.* Feel. 2 Perceive, observe. 3 Watch. 4**Awake, arouse, bestir. 5**Smell. 'Dè a dh' fhairich thu? *what did you feel? what do you mean? what ails you?* f. as do shuain, *awake from your profound sleep*; teich no f. m' fhearg, *flee or feel my wrath*; dh' fh. e boladh, *he smelled a smell*; dh' fh. mo chridhe, *my heart felt.*
fairich,* *s.f.* see fairche.
———ear, *fut.pass.* of fairich.
———idh, *fut. aff. a.* of fairich.
———te, *past pt.* of fairich.
fairig,* *v.a.* see failc.
———,(AC) *s.f.* Dead bird, dead fish, any dead creature found on the sea or shore.
———ean, *int.* see faireagan.
fairir,(AC) *s.f.* Border, coast. see oirthir.
fairis, see thairis.
fairisgneadh, *s.m.* Peeling.
fairleag,** -eig, *s.f.* see adharcan-luachrach. 2 Swallow.
———ach,** *a.* Abounding in lapwings or swallows. 2 Like a lapwing or swallow.
fàirleas, -eois, an, *s.m.* Object seen on an eminence in contact with the sky.
fairleus, *s. m.* Smoke-hole in the ridge of a house, for egress of smoke and ingress of light.
fairmeil, *a.* Noisy, merry—*Dàin I. Ghobha.*
fairneachd,** *s.f.* Meeting.
fàirneag, -eige, -an, *s.f.* see àirne.
†fairnic,** *v.a.* Get, obtain. 2 Invest. 3 Devise, contrive.
†fairrigeoir, -e, -ean, see fairgear.
fairsbeag,** -eig, -an, *s.f.* Large gull.
———ach,** *a.* Abounding in large gulls.
†fairsgin, *a.* Viewing, espying.
fairsing,‡ *a.* see farsuing.
fairsing, *v.a.* see farsuingich.
———each,†† -eiche, *a.* see farsuingeach.
———eachadh, -aidh, *s.m.* see faisuingeachadh.
———eachd, *s.f.ind.* see farsuingeachd.
———ead, see farsuingeachd.
———ich, *pr.pt.* a' fairsingeachadh, *v. a.* see farsuingich.
fairsinn, see farsuing.
fairsleachadh, see fairtleachadh.
fairsleag, *s.f.* Large gull.
fairslich, *v.a.* see fairtlich.
fairsneachd, see farsuingeachd.
fairsnich, *pr.pt.* a' fairsneachadh, *v.a.* see farsuingich.
†fairspeag, -eig, -an, see farspach.
†fairtne, *s.f.* Feast.
fairtleachadh, -aidh, *s. m.* Overcoming, overpowering, act of overcoming. 2 Conquering, conquest. A' f—, *pr. pt.* of fairtlich.
fairtleachair,** *s.m.* Baffler.
fairtlich, *pr.pt.* a' fairtleachadh, *v.a.* Overcome, overmatch. 2* Defy. 3 Worst, baffle. Dh'fh. e orm, *he* or *it defied me*, or *worsted me.* [Takes the prep. *air* after it, simple or compounded. Spelt failich in *Uist.*]
†fais-bheò, *s.pl.* Vegetative tribes.
faiscre,** *s.f.* Compulsion, violence, force.
†faisdine, -an, see faisneachd.
fàiseach,(CR) *a.* Easy—*W. of Ross.* Cha'n 'eil sin f., *that is not easy* (*to do or bear.*) In *Gairloch* "cha b' e sin a faiseach," is the form used, making f. a substantive.—DU.
faiseachail, -ala, *a.* Mitigant.
fàis, *a.* see fàs. Feadaireachd mu 'n bhuaile fh., is gàradh mu 'n chnàmhag, *whistling round the empty fold, and wall round the refuse corn.*
fàisg, *pr. pt.* a' fàsgadh, *v. a.* Squeeze, wring, compress, press, squeeze by twisting, as water out of cloth. 'Ga fhàsgadh eadar a làmhan, *compressing it between his hands*; fàisgidh iad oladh, *they shall squeeze* (*make*) *oil*; a dheasgann fàisgidh daoine daoi, *the wicked shall wring its dregs.*
fàisg,* *s.m.* Cheese-press, chesit. 2**Penfold. 3**Band. 4**Tie.
†faisg, -e, -ean, see faisgeadh.
faisg, *pr.pt.* a' fasgaidh, *v.n.* Pick off vermin.
faisg, -e, *a.* see fagus. Chunnaic iad i a' tighinn f. orra, *they saw her coming near them.*
faisge, *s. f.* Nearness, proximity. 'Fh. air a' bhaile, *his nearness to the town.*
faisge,** *s.f.* Cheese. 2 Pressure. 3 Violence. 4 Extortion.
faisge, *comp.* of fagus. Nearer, nearest. Is esan a's fhaisge, *he is nearest.*
fàisgeach,* see fàisgean.
faisgeachd, *s.f.ind.* Nearness, proximity.
faisgead, -eid, *s.m.* see faisgeachd.
fàisgeadair, -ean, *s.m.* Presser.
faisgeadh, -gidh, -gidhean *s.m.* see fasgadh & fàsgadh.
fàisgean, -an, *s.m.* Cheese-press. 2 Sponge.
———ach,** *a.* Spongy. 2 Fungous.
fàisgear,** *fut.pass.* of fàisg.
fàisgeil, *a.* Flat, compressed.
fàisgidh, *fut.aff.a.* of fàisg.
fàisgneach, -ich, -an, *s.f.* Cathartic.
faisgre,** *s.f.* Cheese. 2 see faisge.
fàisgte, *past pt.* of fàisg. Squeezed, wrung, compressed.
fàisinneachd, see fàisneachd.
fàisinniche, -an, see fàisniche.
fàisne,‖ -an, *s.f.* Wheal, pimple. 2 Measles.
fàisneach,** see fàisneachail.
fàisneachadh,** -aidh, *s.m.* Prophesying, divining. 2 Prophecy, divination. A' f—, *pr.pt.* of fàisnich. A' f. aislingean bréige, *prophesying false dreams.*
fàisneachail, -ala, *a.* Prophetic, divining, ominous.
fàisneachd, *s.f.ind.* Prophecy. 2 Soothsaying. 3 Omen. Droch fh., *a bad omen.*
fàisneag,** -eig, -an, *s.f.* Pimple.
———ach, *a.* Pimply.
fàisnear,** -ir, *s.m.* Prophet, soothsayer.
faisneas, see faisneis.
faisneigh, *v.* see fàisnich.
fàisneis,** *v.n.* Detect.
———, *s.f.ind.* Speaking, whispering. 2 Small talk. 3 Friendly or secret hint. 4**Intelligence. 5 Rehearsal, relation. [* gives faisneas, *s.m.*]
———,** *a.* Speakable, utterable.
fàisnich, *pr.pt.* a' fàisneachadh, *v.n.* Prophesy, foretell, divine, forebode. 2**Certify. 3**

Tell. 4**Prove. 5**Abide.
fàisniche, -an, *s. m.* Prophet, soothsayer. 2** Wizard.
fàisnichidh, *fut.aff.a.* of fàisnich.
fàisnis, see fàisneis.
†faisteanair, -ean, *s.m.* Soothsayer, prophet.
fàistinn, -e, -ean, *s.f.* Prophecy, omen. Luchd fàistinne, *wizards* ; droch fh., *a bad omen.*
———each, -iche, *a.* Prophetic. 2 Ominous.
———each, -ich, *s.m.* Wizard, prophet, diviner. 2 Augur.
———eachd, *s.f.ind.* Prophecy, divination. 2 Ominousness.
———ear,** *s.m.* Augur.
faitcheas, -is, see faiteas.
———ach, see faiteasach.
faitchios, see faiteas.
faite, -ichean, *s.f.* Smile. 2 Timidity, shyness. [In *W. of Ross* f.-gàire is *a smile*, f., alone never being used there in the sense of *smile.*]
——ach, -iche, *a.* Fearful, timorous, shy, diffident. 2 Smiling. 3 Delicate. Gu f., *timidly.*
fàiteachas, -ais, see faiteas.
faiteal, -eil, -an, *s.m.* see aiteal. 2 Influence.
——ach, see aitealach.
——achd, see aitealachd.
faiteachan, *s.m.* Timid person. 2‡‡see aiteal.
faiteas, -eis, *s.m.* Fear. 2 Bashfulness, delicacy of sentiment, shyness. 3**Reluctance. Cha ruig thu leas f. sam bith a bhi ort, *you need not feel the least bashful.*
——ach,** *v.* Apprehensive, timid.
faitgheas, -eis, see faiteas.
†faith, *v.a.* Clothe.
†faith, *s.f.* Heat, warmth. 2 Apparel. 3 Field.
†faith-bheadh, see flamh.
†faithche, see faiche.
faithche, *s.* Lawn—*W. of Ross-shire.*
†faithe, see faitheam.
†faitheach, *s.m.* see athach.
faitheam, -eim, -an, *s.m.* Hem or border of a garment. 2 Seam. 3 Circumspection. Cuir f. air do theanga, *be circumspect in what you say.*
———, *v.a.* Hem, as a garment. 2 Surround. A' faitheamadh 'aodaich, *hemming his garments.*
———achail, -ala, *a.* That which surrounds or hems in. 2 Hemmed, as a garment. 2 Hemming. 4 Surrounding.
———ar, *fut.pass.* of faitheam.
———te, *past pt.* Edged.
faithiltear,* *s.m.* Broker.
faithir, *s.* The shelving slope between an old raised beach or other plateau, and the present beach—*W. of Ross-shire.*
faithirleag, (AF) *s.f.* Green plover, see feadag.
faithleagh,§ see eidheann.
†faith-lios,** -an, *s.m.* Wardrobe.
fàithn, *Suth'd & Badenoch* for àithne.
faithne, -an, *s.m.* see foinne.
faithnich, *Skye* for aithnich.
faitichean, *pl.* faite, Smiles.
†faitigheas, *s.m.* Reluctance.
†faitse, *s.f.* The South, South point.
——ach, *a.* Southward, southern.
fàl, -àil, *s. m.* Pen-fold for strayed cattle or sheep. 2 Circle. 3 Wall, hedge, dike. 4 Divot, sod. 5 Scythe. 6 Spade. 7*Bow. 8 Peat-spade. 9*Bow.
†fàl, *s.m.* Noble. 2 King. 3 Plenty. 4 Malice. 5 Trifle. 6‡‡Guarding.
fàl, *v. a.* Scythe, mow. 2 Cut peats. 3 Enclose, hedge. 4**Cover with turfs.
fal,** *a.* Ominous.
fala, see fola. see faladh.
falach, -aich, *s.m.* Veil, covering, case, caul. 2 Hiding, secreting, concealment. 3*Place of concealment. 4**Garment. 5**Military colours. 6‡‡What remains in a milked cow's udder, afterings. 7 Emptying. A' f—, *pr. pt.* of falaich. Tha e am f., *he is concealed* ; f. fead, *bo-peep, hide and seek.*
———adh, -aidh, *s.m.* Hiding, concealing, covering. 2 Cover. 3 Concealment. 4‡‡Emptying. A' f—, *pr.pt.* of falaich.
———aidh,†† *a.* Hiding, secret.
———air,** *s. m.* One who conceals or hides.
———an, -ain, -an, *s.m.* Hidden treasure. 2 Concealment. 3 Place where treasure is hidden.
——— -cuain, *s.m.* Marooning. 2 Outdistancing. When one boat under sail outdistances another so as to lose sight of her, they say "rinn i falach-cuain oirre," (lit. *she made sea-hiding with her*)—an expressive way of describing a thorough beating.
———d, -an, *s.f.* see folachd.
fàlachd,(DMC) *s.f.* Rise and fall of a person riding on horseback. 2 Limping.
falachdach,** *a.* Feudal. 2 Grudging. 3 Apt to grudge. 4 Causing feud. 5 Prone to feud.
falach-fead, *s.m.* The game of hide and seek, "high-spy".
falach-fuinn,(AC) *s.m.* Land-hiding. Thàinig ceò draogh air na fearaibh, agus rinn iad f., *a magic mist came over the men, and they made land-hiding*—taking advantage of every natural feature in the landscape to hide themselves.
fàladair, -ean, *s.m.* Scythe. 2 Mower. 3 Orts. 4 Bare pasture. Iarunn f., *a scythe.*
———each, -riche, *a.* Of, or belonging to, scythes. 2‡‡Armed with scythes.
———eachd, *s.f.ind.* Operation of mowing or working with a scythe. Ris an fh., (*at the*) *mowing* (*of*) *grass.*
faladas, -ais, *s.m.* see foladas.
fàladh, -aidh, *s.m.* Enclosing or covering with turf. 2 see foladh.
fala-dhà, see feala-dhà.
falaich, *pr.pt.* a' falach & a' falachadh, *v.a.& n.* Hide, conceal, cover, veil. 2 Keep secret. 3 *Lewis* for fairtlich.
———te, *past part.* of falaich, Hidden.
fàlaid, *s.f.* Reaping-hook—*Dàin I. Ghobha.*
falaid, -e, -ean, *s. m.* Varnish, gloss, polish. 2 **Veil. 3 see fallaid. 4(DU) Mockery, derision. A' falaid, *mocking.*
———ich, *v.a.* Varnish.
———iche, *s.m.* Varnisher.
falaigheach, -iche, *a.* Secret.
———d,** *s.f.* Secrecy. 2 Skulking.
falaimhe, *comp.* of falamh. More or most empty.
———ad, -id, *s.f.* Emptiness.
falain,** -e, -ean, *s.f.* Whale.
falair, -e, -ean, *s.f.* Interment, funeral entertainment.
falair, -e, -ean, *s.m.* Ambler, pacer (of a horse or mare.)
falaireach,†† *a.* Prancing.
———d, *s.f.ind.* Ambling, pacing, curvetting, stately motions of a war-horse, prancing. 2 Canter.
falairich, *v.a.* Amble.
falairidh,(PM) *s.f.* *Uist* for falair (funeral entertainment.)
falaisg, -e, -ean, *s. f.* Moor-burning, heath-burning. 2 Mountain conflagration. 3 Festive fire. A' leum o fh. an aonaich, *bounding from the heath-burning.*
———each, *a.* Of, or pertaining to, heath-burning.
———eadh, -idh, *s.m.* Heath-burning.

falamair, see falmair.
falaman, see falman.
falamh, -aimhe, *a.* Empty, void. 2 Poor. 3 in want. 4 Unoccupied. 5 Wanting substance. 6 Vain. Taigh f., *an unoccupied house* ; soitheach f., *an empty dish* ; air àite f., *in a void space* ; is fheàrr fuine thana na bnith uile f., *a thin batch is better than to want bread altogether.*
———achd, *s.f.ind.* Emptiness, voidness, vacancy. 2**Void, gap. 3‡‡Penury, poverty.
———aich, *v.a.* Empty, make void. Dh' fh. i a soitheach, *she emptied her vessel.*
———aichte,** *past pt.* of falmhaich.
falanach, *a.* Pertaining to blood. Is orra pathadh f., *and the thirst of blood on them.*
falaoisge, see falaisg.
falar, -air, -an, see falair.
——achd, see falaireachd.
——aich, see falairich.
——as, -ais, *s. m.* Pacing, ambling. 2 Horsemanship.
falasg, see falaisg.
falatas,** *s.m.* Chastisement.
falbh, *pr.pt.* a' falbh, *v. a.* Go, begone, walk. 2 Depart. 3 Retire. 4 Perish. F. romhad ! *go about your business ;* caoidh an t-sionnaich air a' chaora mhairbh, nach d' rug i 'n t-uan mu'n d' fhalbh i, *why the fox laments the dead sheep, because she did not drop her lamb before she died.*
falbh ! *int.* Away with you !
falbh, *s.m.* Motion, going, departing, walking. 2 Act of departing or walking. 3**Withdrawing. 4**Gait, air. A' f—, *pr. pt.* of falbh. F. nam fear cròdha, *the departure of the brave*; cia mórdha a f. ! *how majestic her gait ! ;* fad' air f., *far away ;* tonnan a' briseadh 's a' f., *waves breaking and retiring.*
falbhach, -aiche, *a.* Moving, walking, travelling. Is éiginn do 'n fheumach a bhi f., *the needy must be moving.*
†———,** -aich, *s.m.* Body, carcase. 2 One troubled with hiccough.
falbhadair, -ean, *s.m.* Walker, ambulator. 2‡‡ Rudder.
falbhag, *Arran* for failbheag.
———, -aige, *s.f.* Sand-swallow, sea-swallow.
——— -mhara,(AF) *s. f.* Sea-swallow. 2 Storm-petrel, see luaireag.
falbhaich,(AC) *s. pl.* (*lit.* restless ones) Swallows.
falbhaiche, *s.m.* see falbhadair.
falbhaidh, *fut.aff.a.* of falbh.
falbhair, -ean, *s.m.* Young of cattle, follower, as calf, foal, &c. 2 Wanderer, mover, follower, creeper.
falbhaiteach, -eiche, *a.* Moving from place to place. Ma gheibh duine idir rud, 's e firionnach f., *if anybody can get anything, it's the man that keeps moving.*
fal-bhalach,(DMy) *s.m.* Lad undeveloped into a man.
falbhan, -ain, *s.m., dim.* of falbh. Moving about, easy walking, habit of walking, motion, agitation, locomotion, creeping, continual motion. F. a chiabh, *the agitation of his locks*; tha e air f., *he is able to get about, he walks about.*
———ach, -aiche, *a.* Ambulatory, in motion.
———ach, -aich, *s.m.* Wanderer, mendicant.
———achd, *s.f.ind.* Travelling. 2 Habit of travelling or wandering. 3 Motion, ambulatoriness, locomotion. 4**Struggling.
fàl-bheart, -bheirt, -an, *s.f.* see feall-bheart.
————ach,†† *a.* see feall-bheartach.
falc,* *v.* see failc.
falc,‡ -aichean, *s. Hebrides* for falcag. 2(AC) Razorbill. 3(AC) Guillemot.
†falc, -ailc, *s. f.* Flood. 2 Frost. 3 Barrenness from drought.
†——. *a.* Sterile, barren. 2 Parched, as ground through heat.
falcadh, -aidh, *s.m. & pr. pt.* see failceadh.
falcag, -aige, -an, *s.f.* Common auk.
falcair,§ *s.m.* Pimpernel or poor man's weather-glass—*angallis arvensis.*

301. Falcair.

falcaire, *s.m.* see failcire. 2**Scoffer. 3** Cheat. 4(AF) Horse. 5(AF) Mole.
falcaireachd,** *s.f.ind.* Scoffing. 2 Cheating.
falcair-fiadhain, *s.m.* see falcair.
falcair-fuar, see falcair.
falcanach, -aiche, *a.* Foamy. 2 Bristling—Gael. Soc. Inv. xv, 52.
falcanaich, *s.f.* Dashing, splashing.
falcas, -ais, *s.m.* Shade, shadow.
falchaidh, -e, *a.* Lurking, concealing, dissembling. 2 Secret, concealed.
falchaig, *s.f.* Work from which profit directly results, e.g. harvest, seaware gathering, digging potatoes, and the like. A special use of the word is *a raid* or foraging expedition, still used in falchaig chnò, *a nutting expedition.* 2(DMC) Small point of land projecting into the sea. Bha gach duin' a mach air falchaig, *every man was out a-gathering,—Duanaire, 151.*
fal-cheumnaich, *v.a.* March.
†falcus, -uis, -an, see faileas.
fal-dhà, see feala-dhà.
fàl-dhos, -ois, *s.m.* Thorn-hedge.
fal-dhuine,(DMy) *s.m.* Unmanly man.
fàl-dos, -ois, see fàl-dhos.
fa leath, see fa leth.
fa leith, see fa leth.
fa leth, *adv.* Individually, apart, one by one, separately.
fàl-fuinn, -àil-, *s.m.* Hoe.
fàl-gleuta, -àil-, *s.m.* see fàil-gleidhte.
†falladh, -aidh, *s.m.* Dominion, power, rule.
fallag,¶ *s.f.* Sand-martin, see gobhlan-gainmhiche.
fallaid, -e, -ean, *s.f.* (WC) Light shake or dip of anything. 2 Dry meal put on cakes when being fired. Fallaid is the refuse of meal left on the baking-board after a batch of bread has been baked. An interesting custom prevails in the Outer Hebrides, any remains of meal on the board being made into a cake in the palm of the hand, and set to fire among the other and larger cakes. The custom has its origin in a superstitious belief, that doing thus with the remains keeps the store of meal from wasting. No thrifty wife would think of dusting the baking-board into the meal girnel.—DC.
———each,†† *a.* Pertaining to dry meal put on cakes.
fallain, -e, *a.* Sound, healthy. 2 Wholesome. 3**Salubrious. Duine f., *a healthy man ;*

biadh f., *wholesome food* ; àileadh f., *salubrious air*; cridhe f., *a sound heart* ; teanga f., *a wholesome tongue* ; gu slàn f., *sound and healthy*.
fallaine, *comp.* of fallain. More or most healthy or wholesome. Is esan a's f., *he is the most healthy*.
——, *s.f.ind.* see fallaineachd.
fallaineachd, *s.f.ind.* Healthiness, soundness, wholesomeness. 2 Salubriousness. F. 'nam fheòil, *soundness in my flesh;* f. inntinn, *soundness of mind*.
fallaineas, -ais, *s.m.* see fallaineachd.
fallainn, see falluing.
†**fallamhnachd**, *s.f.* Rule, dominion.
†**fallamhnas**, -ais, *s.m.* Kingdom, dominion.
fallan,* *a.* (fo+slan‡) The correct form according to its etymology of the adjective generally spelt fallain.
fal-loisg, -e, -ean, see falaisg.
———**each**, -iche, *a.* Combustible.
fal-losgadh, -aidh, *s.m.* Setting on fire, burning, combustion. 2 Heath-burning. 3**Fire of joy or triumph.
fallsa, *a.* False, deceitful, treacherous, sham, Am measg bhràithrean f., *among false brethren*.
——**chd**, *s.f.ind.* Deceitfulness, fallaciousness, falsity. 2**Treacherousness, falsehood, treachery. 3** False philosophy. 4‡‡Sloth, sluggishness.
fallsail, *a.* see fallsa. Gu f., *falsely*.
fallsaire, -an, *s.m.* Sophist, false philosopher. 2 **falsifier. 3**Liar, deceiver, traitor.
———**achd**,* *s.f.ind.* see fallsachd 3.
fallsan, -ain, -an & -ain, *s.m.* Sluggard.
fallsanach,* -aich, see fallsair.
fallsanachd, see fallsachd.
falluing, -e, -ean, *s.f.* Mantle, garment, robe. 2 **Hood. 3‡ Alpine lady's mantle (plant) see trusgan. Sliabh na falluinge duirche, *the dark mantled hill* ; f. an fhir, *the man's mantle*.
———**each**, -iche, *a.* Mantled, cloaked. 2 Furnished with mantles, cloaks or garments. 3*Like a mantle or garment.
falluing Muire,§ *s.f.* Common lady's mantle, see copan an drùchd.
falluinn, see falluing.
———**each**, see falluingeach.
fallus, -uis, *s.m.* Sweat, perspiration. Tha mi 'nam làn fh., *I am covered with perspiration* ; f. do ghnùis, *the sweat of thy brow* ; tha mi 'm fhliuch fh., *I am perspiring all over* ; cuir f. dhiot, *perspire*.
fallusach, -aiche, *a.* Sudorific, sweaty, perspirable, perspiring.
fallusaich,** *v.n.* Perspire, sweat. 2 Cause to perspire.
fallusail,* *a.* see fallusach.
falm,* *s.m.* see alm.
falm,* *s.f.* Elm-tree, see leamhan. 2 see failm. Mucagan failm, *elm-berries*.
falmach, see almach.
falmadair, -ean, *s.m.* Rudder, helm. 2 Tiller. 2 see fulmair. Cha robh f. gun sgoltadh, *there was not a rudder unsplit*.
falmadaireach,†† *a.* Having helms or rudders.
falmair, -ean, *s.m.* Hake—*merluccius vulgaris*.
falman, -ain, -an, *s. m*, The knee-pan. 2** Whirlbone of the knee. 3**Lid.
falmanta,** *a.* Aluminious.
falmhachadh, -aidh, *s.m.* Emptying, pouring out, act of emptying. A' f—, *pr.pt.* of falmhaich.
fàl-mhagadh, -aidh, -aidhean, *s. m.* Mockery, sneering.
falmhaich, see falamhaich & falbhaich.
falmhaichte, see falamhaichte.
falmhuich, see falamhaich.
falmhuichte, see falamhaichte.
fàl-mòine, *s.m.* Peat-spade.
fàl-mònadh, see fàl-mòine.
fàl-ni,** *s.m.* Trifle, trifling matter. Air f. na caith do chuid, *do not waste thy substance on trifles*.
faloisg, see falaisg.
faloisge, see falaisg.
faloisgeach,** *a.* Combustible.
falosgadh, -aidh, *s.m.* Combustion.
fal-rìreadh,** *s.m.* Earnest, anything but jest.
falsachd, see fallsachd.
falt, fuilt, fuiltean, *s.f.* Human hair. 2 Locks, ringlets. 3 Tail. 'Fh. òr-bhuidhe, *his golden locks* ; cuach fh., *curled hair*. [The hair of any part of the human body other than the head is *gaoiseid*, *fionnadh* or *ròinnean*.]
faltach, -aiche, *a.* Hairy.
faltag, -aige, -an, *s.f.* Tendon. *prov.*
faltan, -ain, -an, *s. m.* Tendon. 2 Welt, belt. 3 Ribbon. 4*Snood, hair-belt.
faltanach,†† *a.* Welted. 2 Having ribbons.
faltanach, -aich, *s.f.* Mountain bulrush, *prov.*
faltanas,** -ais, *s. m.* Occasion, pretence. 2 Quarrel. 3 Enmity.
faltan-fionn, *s.m.* Tendon.
falt-dhealg, -dheilge, *s.f.* Hairpin.
falthunn, *s.m.* Talk.
faltraich, see fartlaich.
faluing, see falluing.
faluisg, see falasg.
fa m' (*for* fo mo) Under my. 2 Upon my.
fa m' chomhair, *adv.* Opposite to me. Fineamhain fa m' chomhair, *a vineyard opposite me*.
fàman, (WC) *s.m.* Gentle breeze, e.g. F. gaoithe.
famh, -aimh *s. f.* Mole. 2 (AC) Man addicted to burrowing underground.
famhair, -ean, *s.m.* Giant. 2 Champion. 3 Mole-catcher. 4 (DC) Bogle.—*Uist*. [*Fuamh* is a giant in *Uist*.] Ban-fhamhair, *a giantess*.
famhaireach,** *a.* Gigantic.
famhaireachd,* *s.f.* Giganticness. 2 Prowess of a giant.
famhalan, (AF) *s. m.* Water-vole. 2 Earth-mole.
famh-bhual, (AC) *s.f.* Water-vole. 2 Mole. 3 Shrewmouse.
famh-fhual, see famh-bhual.
famhlag, (AF) *s.f.* see falbhag.
famhlagan, (AF) *s.pl.* for falbhagan.
famhlag-mhara, (AF) see falbhag-mhara and luaireag.
famh-thalmhainn, *s.f.* Ground-mole.
famh-thòrr, -a, -an, *s.m.* Mole-hill.
famh-ùir, (AC) *s.f.* Earth-mole.
fan, *pr.pt.* a' fantuinn [a' fanachd & a' fanailt,] *v.n.* Stay, wait. 2*Stop. 3 Continue. 4 Remain. 5 Endure. 6 Recognize. F. an seo, *wait here* ; f. ort, *stop, wait a little* ; f. ris or air, *wait for him* ; dh' fh. sinn, *we stayed* ; fanaidh bhur mnathan, *your wives shall stay*, fanaibh-se an seo, *tarry ye here*; f. agad fhéin, *keep by yourself, keep your distance*.
fàn, fàine, *a.* Low. An rùm a's fhàine fo 'n ùir, *the lowest room underground—the grave—Rob Donn*.
fa 'n, Under the. 2 Upon the.
†**fàn**,** *s.m.* Declivity, steep inclination. 2 Level plain, gentle slope.
†**fan**,** -ain, *s.m.* Temple, chapel.
†**fan**, *s.m.* Wandering, peregrination.
fan, *a.* Prone,—*Suth'd.* 2 Propense.
fàn,** *a.* Headlong. 2 Steep.
fanachd, *s.f.ind. & pr.pt.* see fantainn.
fanadh, see fan.

fànaich, *s.* Place of the flat.
†fanaictheach, -eiche, *a.* Mad, frantic. 2 Fanatic.
fanaid, *v.a.* see fanaidich.
fanaid, -e, *s.f.* Mockery, ridicule, derision, scoffing, scorn. Ri f., *mocking* ; dean f., *mock.*
fanaideach, -iche, *a.* Deriding, mocking, ridiculing, scoffing.
fanaidh, *fut.aff.a.* of fan.
fanaidich, *v.a.* Mock, deceive, deride, ridicule.
fanaidiche, -an, *s.m.* Mocker, scoffer. 2 Lampooner. 3 Mimic.
fanaigse, -an, *s.f.* Dog-violet.
fanailt, -e, see fantuinn.
fanaiseach, *a.* Mocking—*Arran.*
fanam, *1st. sing. imp.* of fan. Let me stay. 2 for fanaidh mi, *1st. sing. fut. aff. a.* of fan. I shall stay.
fànas, -ais, *s.m.* Void space. 2* Opportunity. 3 Sly kind of undue advantage. 4 (DMy) Rent in a wall.
fa 'n comhair, Opposite them, before them, in front of them.
fanear, see fainear.
fang, -ainge, -an, *s.f.* Sheep pen, fold or fank. 2 Poind-fold. 3**Place for catching cattle. 4 Confinement. 5 Strait, difficulty, hardship. 6 Irish coin. 7** Gold-leaf, silver-leaf. 8†† Prison. Ann an fh., *in custody.* [†† gives *s.m.*]
fang, *v.* see fangaich.
fang, -ainge, -an, *s.f.* Vulture. 2**Raven.
——ach,** *a.* Like a vulture. 2 Rapacious, ravenous. 3 Full of folds or pens. 4 Like a fold or pen. 5 Of, or belonging to, vultures, folds or pens.
fangachadh, -aidh, *s. m.* Penning of cattle or sheep. 2 Driving into a fold. A' f—, *pr. pt.* of fangaich.
fangadh, -aidh, see fangachadh.
fangaich, *pr. pt.* a' fangachadh, *v.a.* Enclose, pen, fold.
————ear, *fut. pass.* of fangaich, Shall be pent.
————te, *past pt.* of fangaich. Pent, enclosed, as sheep, folded.
fanlag *s.f.* Sea-swallow, see luaireag.
fanlanta,** *a.* Slender, small.
fàn-leac, -lic, *s. f.* Altar of rude stones. 2 Stone in an inclined position.
fann, -a & fainne, *a.* Faint, languid, weak, feeble. 2 Infirm. 3**Helpless. Duine f., *a feeble person* ; is f. do ghuth, *languid is thy voice* ; cridhe f. is com gun treòir, *a faint heart and pithless frame.*
fann,* *v.a.* Fish while boat is being rowed slowly—*Islay.* 2 while stationary—*Skye.* A' fannadh, fishing with the artificial fly, or playing a fish on the line, while the boat proceeds slowly ; when under great weigh is sìobladh. [In *Lismore* sìobladh=fishing with a fly when the boat is under sail.—DC]
fannachadh, -aidh, *s.m.* Faint, act of fainting. 2 Circumstance of becoming weary, languid or faint. 3**Giving up through fatigue. Tha e air f., *he is worn out with fatigue* ; tha e a' f., *he is getting more feeble*, or *making more feeble.* A' f—, *pr. pt.* of fannaich.
fannachail,** *a.* Laborious.
fannachdas, -ais, *s.m.* Imbecility.
fannad,** -aid, *s.m.* Weakness, langour.
fannadh, -aidh, *s.m.* Faintness, weakness, langour. 2 Fishing with a feathered hook. 3 Mode of rowing by which a boat is kept almost stationary when fishing. [fainneamh in *Gairloch*—DU. In *Lewis*—a' f. an t-sruth, *rowing strongly enough to keep the boat over the same ground* ; a' f. nan lìon, *rowing the boat as fast as the lines are hauled.*] 4**Slackening, relaxing of exertion. 5**Remission. 6 **Intermission. 7 Fainting. A' —, *pr.pt.* of fann. Cha robh f. air a' chòmhraig, *the battle continued without intermission.*
fannaich, *pr.pt.* a' fannachadh, *v.a. & n.* Faint, become weak. 2 Make weak or faint. 3** Give up with fatigue. 4** Grow weary. Fannaichidh spiorad na h-Eiphit, *the spirit of* (*the people of*) *Egypt shall fail.*
————te, *past pt.* of fannaich.
fannan, -ain, -an, *s.m.* Gentle breeze. F. de ghaoith 'n ear leannan an t-sealgair, *a breeze from the East is the sportsman's favourite* [*lit. sweetheart*—not *feast* as given by **.]
————ta, *a.* Faintish, weakish, infirm.
fann-ghaoth, -ghaoithe, *s.f.* Soft breeze.
fann-gheal, -ghile, *a.* Pale, whitish.
fann-ghlaodh,‡‡ -aoidh, -aoidhean, *s.m.* Faint cry.
fann-ghuth, -an, *s.m.* Faint voice, weak note. Fhreagair e le f.. *he replied with a faint voice.*
fannlag,** *a.* Weak, languid. 2 Fatigued.
fannlanta, -ainte, *a.* Slender, weak.
fannlas, -ais, *s.m.* Fatigue, wearying. 2 Worrying. 3 Destroying. F. chorp, *carnage in battle.*
fann-leisgeul, -eil, -an, *s.m.* Pretext.
fann-shealladh, -aidh, -aidhean, *s.m.* Glimmering.
fann-sholus, -uis, -an, *s.m.* Glimpse. 2††Weak or dim light.
fanntais, -e, *s.f.* Weakness, faintness. 2 Languishing.
fanntalach, -aiche, *s. f.* Faintish, inclined to faint.
fanntas, see fanntais.
————ach,** *a.* Weak. 2 Causing weakness.
†fannuigh, *v.a.* see fannaich.
fanoid, -e, *s.f.* see fanaid.
——, *v.a.* see fanaidich.
————each, -iche, *a.* see fanaideach.
————ich, *v.a.* see fanaidich.
————iche, see fanaidiche.
fantalach, -aiche, *a.* Waiting, resting, 2 Inclined to wait or rest. 3 Permanent, stable, lasting, durable. 4 Steady. 5 Persevering. 6* Dilatory.
————d,** *s.f.* Permanence, stability, durableness.
fantuinn, *s.f.ind.* Staying, delaying. 2 Remaining, abiding, continuing, lasting, waiting, tarrying. A' f—, *pr.pt.* of fan.
†fànus, -uis, *s.m.* Descent, declivity.
fànus, -uis, *s.m.* The sky-line—*Islay.* Am fosgladh os ceann nam f., *the space above the skyline.*
faob, faoib,-an, *s.m.* Excrescence, lump. 2 Knot on a tree-branch. 3 Acorn. 4 Large one. 5**Any round lumpy substance, as a potato.
——ach, -aiche, *a.* Tuberous. 2 Knotty. 3 Lumpy.
——aire, -an, *s.m.* see faobairneach.
——airneach, -ich, *s.m.* Lump, as a large-sized turnip or potato. 2 Large-boned person. 3†† Anything large or lumpy.
——an, -ain, -an, *s.m.*, *dim.* of faob. Little knob or excrescence.
faobanach, -aiche, *a.* Tuberculous.
faob-cheann, -chinn, *s.m.* Jolt-head, lump-head.
————ach, -aiche, *a.* Jolt-headed.
faobh, -oibh, *s.m.* Spoil, booty. 2**Conquest. 3**Dead men's clothes. 4**Carcase. 5 (CR) Windfall, any unlooked-for good fortune.—*W. of Ross.* Triath nam f., *the chieftain of spoils* or *victories;* faoibh nan nàmhaid, *the carcases*

of the enemies.
faobh,** *v.n.* Shout, cry aloud, proclaim.
faobhach, -aiche, *a.* Abounding in spoil. 2 Victorious. 3** Brave. 4 Plundering, spoiling.
faobhachadh, -aidh, *s.m.* Spoiling, plundering. 2 Robbery, plunder. 3‡‡Stripping the slain. A' f—, *pr.pt.* of faobhaich.
faobhadh,(AC) *s.m.* Swirl.
faobhag, -aige, -an, *s.f.* Common cuttle-fish.
faobhaich, *pr.pt.* a' faobhachadh, *v.a.* Despoil. 2 Strip, disrobe. 3 Plunder. 4 Strip by force. 5**Lay waste. Dh' fh. iad e, *they stripped him.*
——te, *past pt.* of faobhaich. Despoiled. 3 Disrobed, stripped.
faobhair, see famhair.
faobhairt, -e, -ean, *s.f.* see fadhairt.
——e, *past pt.* see fadhairte.
——each,** *a.* see fadhairteach.
faobhar, -air, -an, *s.m.* Edge. 2 Edge, as of a sword or cutting instrument. 3 **Ridge of a hill. 4**Edge or brink of a precipice. 5**Surface. 6 see famhair. Air fh., *edgewise ;* le f. a' chlaidheimh, *with the edge of the sword ;* air f. bheann, *on a ridge of mountains ;* f. a' chuain, *the surface of the sea ;* air bheag f., *blunt ;* f. nan neul, *the edge of the clouds.*
——ach, -aiche, *a.* Edged, sharp. 2 Keen, earnest. 3 **Satirical, pointed. 4** Active, nimble.
——achadh, -aidh, *s.m.* Sharpening, act of sharpening. A' f—, *pr.pt.* of faobharaich.
——aich, *pr. pt.* a' faobharachadh, *v. a.* Sharpen, whet, set, as a razor, hone. F. an sgian, *sharpen* or *whet the knife.*
——aichte, *past pt.* of faobharaich. Whetted, sharpened.
faobh-bhleoghainn, *s.f.* Stealing the milk out of the udder of a cow or goat.
faobhluinn,(DC) *a.* Mock, pretended. Saor f., *a would-be joiner ;* dotair f., *a mock doctor—Uist.*
——,(PM) *s.m.* Novice, man devoid of qualifications for his work. Cha'n 'eil ann ach am f., *he is only a novice.* Generally used as a noun.
faobhraich, see faobharaich.
faoch, -aoiche, *s.f.* see faochag. 2**Field. 3 (AC) Curve.
——ach,** *a.* Abounding in shellfish.
——adh, -aidh, *s.m. Uist* for faothachadh.
——ag, -aig, -an, *s. f., dim.* of faoch. Periwinkle (fish.) 2 Whelk. 3 Any small shellfish. 4 Eye. 5 Whirlpool. 6 Eddy or curl on the surface of a running stream. 7(DU) Arrangement of the hair on the top of the head, so called from being in the shape of a spiral. 8* Weaver's thrum. 2 Periwinkle (plant)—*vinca minor.* [Badge of the MacLachlans.] Tràigh nam f., *the shore of the shellfish ;* oitir fhaochag, *a whelk reach ;* "na faochagan," nickname for the natives of the Mackinnons' country—Strath in Skye ; f. an t-sruith, *the vortex of the stream ;* f. mhullach a' chinn, *the top of the head ;* f. na sùla, *the round of the eye ;* a' dol air fh., *facing danger ;* f. thuaichill, *an eddy, a small whirlpool.*

302. Faochag.

faochagach, -aiche, *a.* Abounding in periwinkles, like a periwinkle. 2 Full of eddies. 3 Of, or belonging to, any small shellfish.
faochag-bhàn, *s.f.* Pale whelk.
—— -chuairtein, *s.f.* Whirlpool.
—— -dhubh, *s.f.* Black whelk.
—— -mhòr, *s.f.* Whelk.
—— -nan-gille-fuinnbrinn, see faochag.
—— -smeòraich, *s.f.* The smallest kind of whelk, usually found above high-water mark.
faochainn,* *v.a.* Entreat most earnestly, urge. 2 ††Struggle, strive.
faochaire,(AC) *s.m.* see faoch. 2 Knave, betrayer, perjurer.
faochan, see faochag.
——aich, *v.n.* Ripple.
faoch-mór,(AF) *s.m.* Loon, roaring buckie.
faochnach,* *a.* Earnest, urgent in requesting. Ni f., *an urgent affair.*
faochnadh,* -aidh, *s.m.* Most earnest request or petition. 2 Urging. 3 Persistent effort. A' f—, *pr.pt.* of faochainn. A' f. orm dol leis, *vehemently urging me to go with him.*
faochnaich,* *v.a.* Urge, entreat perseveringly, be not refused.
faod, *v.aux.* May, can. 2**Must. Faodaidh mi an t-each a reic, *I may sell the horse ;* dh' fhaodainn an t-each a reic, *I might have sold the horse ;* am f. mi bhi ? *may I be ? ;* cha'n fh. mi bhi, *I may not be ;* am f. mi falbh ? faodaidh, *may I go ? yes (you may.)*
——aidh, *fut.aff.a.* of faod.
——ail, -ala, -alach, *s.f.* Goods found by chance. 2 Thing found. 3 Stray treasure. 4 Waif. Spealtaidh e an fh. le 'ghial, *he will tear the treasure-trove with his jaw—i.e.* in his eagerness to get it; cha'n e sealbh na faodalach a faotainn, *the advantage of the treasure-trove does not consist in the getting of it—to find goods is not to own them.*
faodailiche, -an, *s.m.* see faodalach.
faodalach, -aich, *s.m.* Foundling. 2 Anything found.
†faodh, -oidh, *s.m.* Voice.
——, *gen. sing.* of faodail.
faodhail, -alach, -alaichean *s.f.* see fadhail.
†faogh, -oigh, *s.m.* Punishment.
faoghailt, -e -ean, see faghaid.
faoghaid, -e, -ean, *s.f.* see faghaid.
faoghaid, -e, *s.f. prov.* for foidhidinn.
fagohaideach, -iche, *a. & s.* see faigheadach.
faoghaidiche, see faghaideach.
faoghail, -alaichean, *s.f.* see fadhail.
——t, -e, -ean, see faghaid.
faoghal, *s.m. Uist* for fadhail.
faoghar, -air, *s.m.* see foghair.
faoghluimte, see foghluimte.
faoghlumaich, *v.a.* see foghlumaich.
†faoi, *prep.* see fuidh.
†faoi, *s.* Noisy stream.
faoibh, *gen. sing. & n pl.* of faobh.
faoich, *gen. sing.* of faoch.
†faoidh, -e, -ean, *s.f.* Noise, sound. 2 Voice.
faoidh,** *s.m.* Messenger, express. 2 Courser. 3 Departure. 4 see faoighe.
†faoidh, *v.n.* Go. 2 Send. 3 Sleep, rest.
faoidhe, see faidhe.
†faoidheamh, -imh, *s.m.* Messenger.
faoidhreag, *s.f.* see oighreag.
faoighe, *s.f.ind.* Asking for aid in shape of corn, wool, and sometimes cattle, a custom once very common. 2 Gift. 3 Generosity. Cha'n

th. e, *it is not a thigging* ; f. eòrna, *barley thigging* ; f. chruidh, *cattle thigging* ; f. do MhacGriogair, is leig leis fhéin a togail, *give a gift to a MacGregor, and let him help himself to it*,—*i. e.* he will not be bashful in doing so ; f. fir gun chaoraich, *the generosity of a man who has nothing to give* ; air f. nam bannag, *going about begging for bannocks* ; cha'n e rogha nam muc a gheibh fear na faoighe, *it is not the pick of the swine that the beggar gets.* [N.G.P. says "The practice of going 'air faoighe' was common in the Highlands, and was also known in the Lowlands of Scotland. In the 'good old times,' when dearth was as common as a bad season, it was not considered degrading for respectable people to go foraging among their friends for grain, wool, &c. This kind of begging was also practised by or for young couples about to marry, or newly married, to help them in setting up house. The custom is now (1880), I think, obsolete. It was still partially practised in 1830."]

†faoighle, *s.pl.* Words, expression.

faoighleann, -leinn, -an, see faoileann.

faoighreadh, *s.m.* Gift gathering, genteel begging—*Dàin I. Ghobha.*

faoil, -e, *a.* see faoilidh.

——, -e, *s.f.* Hospitality. [* gives profuse hospitality.] 2 Generosity. 3**Mildness, kindness. 4 Welcome, affability. [** gives faoile as *n. sing.*]

——, -e, *s.f.* Gull, *poetical—Gairloch.*

——e, *a.* see faoilidh.

——each, -iche, *a.* Glad, joyful, cheerful. 2 Generous. 3 Thankful.

——each,** *s.f.* Holidays, feastdays, carnival. †2 Supplement.

Faoileach, *Gairloch* for Faoilteach.‖

faoileachd,** *s.f.* Gladness, joyfulness, thankfulness. 2 Generosity, kindness.

faoileag,(WC) *s.f.* White crest on the waves—*Poolewe.* Tha f. air a' mhuir, *there are white crests on the waves.*

303. Faoileag.

————,¶ -eige, -an, *s.f.* Black-headed gull—*larus ridibundus.* F. an droch chladaich, *the gull of the bad shore*—applied to poor creatures still preferring their wretched home.

————ach,†† *a.* Abounding in gulls.

———— -bheag,¶ *s.f.* Little gull, see crannfhaoileag.

———— bheag,¶ see sgaireag.

———— -dubh-cheannach,¶ see faoileag.

———— -mhór,¶ *s.f.* Glaucous or great white gull *or* burgomaster—*larus glaucus.* (illust. 304.)

faoileann,¶ -inn, -an, *s.f.* Common white gull,—*larus canus.* (illust. 305.) 2* Mew. 3(AF) see fadhlainn.

————ach,** *a.* Like a sea-mew. 2 Abounding in sea-mews.

304. Faoileag mhór.

faoileag-mhór,¶ see farspach.

305. Faoileann.

faoilich, *v. a. & n.* Rejoice, be merry. 2 Entertain.

faoilidh, -e, *a.* Hospitable, generous. 2 Mild. 3 Glad, joyful, cheerful. 4* Profusely liberal. Coire f., *an inviting dell* ; gu f., *mildly.*

————eachd, *s.f.ind.* Hospitality. 2 Affability, 3**Gladness. 4**Thankfulness. 5**Generousness. 6**Mildness. 7**Kindness.

†faoiligh, *v.n.* Rejoice, be glad.

faoilinneach, see faoileannach.

†faoill, see foill.

Faoilleach, see Faoilteach. Faoilleach in *Lewis* begins on the Friday nearest three weeks before the end of January, and ends on the Tuesday nearest the end of the third week of February—Di-haoine a thig 's Di-màirt a dh' fhalbhas, *comes on Friday and goes on Tuesday*—three weeks of Winter, and three weeks of Spring—(DMy.)

faoilt, see faoilte.

faoilte, *s.f.* Delight. 2 Cheerfulness, 3 Joyful salutation at meeting. 4 Welcome, welcoming. 5**Invitation to a feast. 6**Hospitality.

Faoilteach, -tich, *s.m.* The last fortnight of winter and first fortnight of spring (Old Style), proverbial for variableness.—McL & D. Season of the wolf-ravage‡‡. It corresponded roughly to the present month of February. Sometimes the first half was called "Am F. Geamhraidh" and the second half "Am F. Earraich." Is còir 'san Fh. na trì claisean taobh-ri-taobh a bhi làn uisge is làn sneachda is làn tugha nan taighean, *or* trì làin anns na claisean; uisge, sneachd, is tugha nan taighean, *in February the three furrows side by side should be full of water, full of snow, and full of house-thatch* ; cha'n 'eil port a sheinneas an smeòrach 'san Fh. nach guil i seachd uairean mu 'n ruith an t-Earrach, *for every song the mavis sings in February, she'll lament seven times ere spring be over.* The Gael of old regarded stormy weather toward the end of January as prognostic of a fruitful season to follow, and vice versâ, as shown in the

above proverbs. Smeuran dubha 'san Fh., *black bramble-berries in February*—applied to anything very improbable or out of season. Na faoiltich, *the equinoxes ;* see *am Feillire.*
faoilteach, -iche, *a.* Happy at meeting. 2 Hospitable, generous, inviting. 3 Welcoming. Fhir a's fhaoiltiche gun fheall ! *thou most generous without deceit !*
faoilteachd,** *s.f.* Practice of hospitality. 2 Welcoming. 3 Readiness to welcome. Le h-aighear 's le f., *with joy and welcoming.*
faoilteas,** -eis, *s.m.* Gladness. 2 Hearty welcome, kind reception.
Faoiltheach, see Faoilteach.
faoiltich, *v.a.* Receive kindly. 2 Rejoice at meeting. 3 Become cheerful.
faoin, -e, *a.* Vain, foolish. 2 Idle. 3 Unavailing. 4 Empty. 5 Light. 6** Lonely. 7 **Trifling. 8**Useless. 9**Sloping. Ni f., *a trifling affair ;* is f. dhuit, *it is unavailing for you ;* duine f., *a silly fellow ;* tha thu f. 'nad bharail, *your opinion is unfounded ;* beanntan f. a dhùthcha, *the lonely hills of his country.*
——-bheachdail, -ala, *a.* Foppish.
——-bheanntan, *s.m.* Sloping hill.
†**faoinbhleaghain**, *s.f.* Gentleness, mildness.
faoin-bhrèagh,** *a.* Tawdry, 2 Foppish.
faoin-bhrèaghas,** -ais, *s.m.* Tawdriness. 2 Foppishness.
faoin-bhreith, *s.f.* Abortion.
faoin-chainnt, *s.f.* Idle talk, vain boasting, babble, babblement.
——————each, -iche, *a.* Prone to foolish talking.
——————eachd, *s.f.* Same meanings as faoin-chainnt.
faoin-cheann, -chinn, *s.m.* Empty head.
——————ach, -aiche, *a.* Empty-headed.
faoin-chòmhradh,** -aidh, *s.m.* Vain talk, babbling, tattle. A' seachnadh faoin-chòmhraidh, *shunning vain talk.*
faoin-dreuchd,** -an, *s.f.* Sinecure.
faoine, *comp.* of faoin. More or most vain.
———, *s.f.ind.* Same meanings as faoineas.
———achadh, -aidh, *s.m.* Making vain. A' f—, *pr.pt.* of faoinich.
faoineachd, *v.a.* see faighnich.
————, *s. f. ind.* Vanity, folly, silliness, lightness, emptiness, vacuity, bauble, silly manner. 2 Toying, trifling. Luchd f., *silly people ;* clachan na f., *the stones of silliness.*
faoineadh, -nidh, -nidhean, *s. m.* Indulging, humouring of one, indulgence.
faoineag, -eige, -an, *s.f.* Vain silly woman. 2 Vanilla (plant.)
faoinealach, -aich, *s.m.* Silly man.
faoinealachd, *s.f.ind.* see faoineas.
faoineas, -eis, *s.f.* Vanity, bagatelle, idleness, uselessness, silliness, vacuity, trifling, toying. Ri f. riu, *trifling with them.*
faoinein, *s.m.* see faoinealach.
faoineis, *s.f.* see faoineas.
————eachd, see faoineachd.
faoin-ghalar,** -air, *s.m.* Feigned or imaginary sickness.
faoin-ghlòireach, -iche, *a.* Vain-glorious.
faoinich, *v.a.* Make vain. 2** see faighnich.
faoin-leisgeul, see fann-leisgeul.
faoinreadh, see faondradh.
faoin-sgeul, -sgeòil, *s. f.* Vain or idle talk. 2 Fiction.
——————ach, -aiche, *a.* Idly talkative.
——————achd, *s.f.ind.* Telling of idle tales. 2 Idle tale. 3‡‡Mythology.
——————aiche, -an, *s.m.* Mythologist.
faoin-sheanchaidh, see faoin-sgeulaiche.
faoin-smuain, ** *s. f.* Foolish thought, idle thought. 2 Delusion. 3 Brown study. 4 Chimera.
faoireag, see oighreag.
faoisdinn, -e, -ean, see faoisid.
faoiseadh,** -eidh, *s.m.* Helping. 2 Recovering. 3 Recovery from sickness. 4 Aid.
faoiseid, see faoisid.
faoisg, *pr.pt.* a' faoisgeadh, *v.a.* Unhusk, take the husk off, hull, as of nuts. 2*Chink, gape, leak, as a dish.
faoisgeag, -eige, -an, *s.f.* Filbert. 2 Unhusked nut. [** gives Ripe filbert.]
————ach,** *a.* Abounding in filberts.
faoisgneach,** *a.* Ripe, as a nut. 2 Bursting, as a nut from the husk.
——————adh, -aidh, see faoisgneadh.
faoisgneadh, -neidh, *s.m.* Unhusking, unpodding. 2 Bursting from the husk, as a nut. 3 Emerging, as a heavenly body from behind a cloud. 4 Appearing on the horizon, as the sun. 5*Chinking, as a dish. A' f—, *pr. pt.* of faoisgnich. Tha a' chuinneag air f., *the water-pitcher chinks* or *leaks ;* a' ghrian a' f., *the sun appearing.*
faoisgnich, *pr.pt.* a' faoisgneachadh & a' faoisgneadh, *v.a.* Squeeze out. 2 Unhusk. 3* Chink, gape, leak, as a dish.
faoisid, -e, -ean, *s.f.* Confessing, confession. 2 Avowal, acknowledgement. Cha'n aideachadh no f. e, *it is neither acknowledgement nor avowal ;* dean t' fh., *confess to the priest.*
———each,** *a.* Confessional.
———ich, *v.a. & n.* Confess.
faoisneadh,*-idh, *s.m.* Bursting from the husk.
†**faol**, -oil, *s.m.* Patience, forbearance. 2**Prop, support. 3 Wolf. 4 (AF)Wild dog. 5**Whelp.
faol, -a, *a.* Wild.
——ach,** -aich, *s.m.* Bird of prey.
——adh,** *s.m.* Doctrine.
——ag, see faoileag.
——asg, see falaisg.
——bhaidh,(AF) *s.* Wolf. 2 Wild dog.
——chon, -choin, *s.m.* Falcon.
†**faol-chu**,*-choin, -chona, *s.m.* Wolf.
faol-fhulang,** -aing, *s.m.* Prop.
faol-iasg,(AF) *s.m.* Wolf-fish.
faol-shnamh,** *s.m.* Swimming.
faol-ulaith, *s.* Wolf, wild dog.
faolum, see fòghlum.
————aich, *v.a.* see fòghlumaich.
†**faomach**,** -aiche, see umhail.
faomadh, see aomadh.
†**faomh**, -aoimh, *s.m.* Consent, permission.
†**faomh**, *v.n.* Assent. 2 Consent. 3 Bear with, permit.
faomhar,(CR) [*ao* short & *mh* sounded] *s. m.* Harvest—*Arran.*
faon, see faoin.
faonach,** *a.* Mild, meek.
faonbhach, -aiche, *a.* Mild, meek. 2 Silent.
faondrach, -aiche, *a.* Wandering, unsettled. 2 Irregular. 3 Defective. 4 Erroneous. 5 Neglected. 6 Straggling, apt to go astray, erring.
faondradh, -aidh, *s.m.* Exposure. 2 Wandering, straying. 3 Desert, waste. 4**Straggling. 5*Neglect. 6*Unsettled state.
faontrach, -aiche, see faondrach.
faontradh, see faondradh.
faontradhach, -aiche, see faondrach.
faontraigh, -e, -ean, *s. f.* Exposed place, the open shore.
faor,(AC) *s.m.* Blade (of grass.)
faosad,* see faoisid.
faosadh,** -aidh, *s. m.* Protecting, relief. 2 Collecting.
faosaid, -e, -ean, see faoisid.

faosaideach, see faoisideach.
——ich, see faoisidich.
faosg,(AF) *s.f.* Snipe, see croman-lòin. [An fhaosg, is often written "an naosg."]
——nach,** *a.* Auspicious.
——nachd,** *s.f.* Auspiciousness.
——nadh,** *s.m.* Auspice. 2 see faoisgneadh.
faotail, -talach, *s.m.* see faodail.
faotainn, *s.f.ind.* Getting, obtaining. 2 Finding. 3 Act of getting. 4* Accomplishment. 5**Receiving. 6**Winning. A' f—, *pr. pt.* of faigh. A' f. seo, *getting this.*
faotalaiche,** -an, *s.m.* Foundling.
faothach, -aich, *s. m.* Alleviation—*Dàin Iain Ghobha.*
faothachadh, -aidh, *s.m.* Relief from suffering, alleviation of suffering. 2 Relief, lightening. 3**Rest, leisure. A' f—, *pr.pt.* of faothaich. Fhuair e f., *he got relief*; gun fh. fad an là, *without alleviation the livelong day.*
faothachail, -ala. *a.* Anodyne. 2 Mitigant.
faothaich, *pr.pt.* a' faothachadh, *v.a. & n.* Relieve, alleviate, be relieved, as from fever, &c.
faothaid, see faghaid.
faothaistean,(MMcL) *s.m.* Open space in creel for lifting it.
faotuinn, see faotainn.
far,*adv.* Where. Far am bheil e, *where he is*; cha bhi loinn ach far am bi thu, *there will be no joy but where thou art.*
far-, *a.* Additional, extra, as far-ainm, *nickname.*
far, *v.def.* see fair.
far, *prep.* (*for* mar) With, along with, in company with. Co théid far rium? *who will go along with me?*
far, *Islay, Mull, &c.* for bhàrr—*Sgeulaiche-nan-caol.*
far,†† *pr.pt.* a' faradh, *v.a.* Freight, as a ship.
far? ‡‡ *adv.* Why? Wherefore?
far,(AC) *prep.* On (used in compounds.)
far, fàr, } *Suth'd* form of tàir. *get, obtain. 2 come.* Used after nach. (Nach fhar *or* nach fhàr.)
fara-bhradan,)AC) *s.m.* Spent salmon.
fara-bhreac,(AC) *s.m.* Spent trout.
farach,** -aich, *s.m.* Mallet, beetle.
farachaidh-chnocaidh,*s.f.* Mall, stone for grinding barley—*Arran.*
farachan,‡ -ain, *s.m.* Death-watch beetle. 2†† Mallet, beetle. 3**Rammer.
farachdach, -aich, *s.m.* Mallet, beetle.
farach-donn,(AC) *s.* see lus-nan-cnapan.
farach-dubh, -duibhe, *s.m.* Fig-wort, see lus-nan-cnapan. [McL & D gives Kernel-wort.]
fara-chrann, see farch-chrann.
fàradh, -aidh, -aidhean, *s.m.* [*f.* in *Perthshire.*] Ladder. 2 Shrouds of a ship.
faradh, -aidh, -aidhean, *s.m.* Hen-roost. 2 Loft made of sticks covered with divots. 3 Freight, ferriage. 4 Gallery. 5**Litter in a boat to receive horses or cattle. 6 Sometimes used for fàrradh. Pàidh f., *pay the freight*; air an fh., *on the cock-loft*; f.-luing, *a ship's load.*
faragair,** *v.n.* Welter. 2 Flounder. 3 Bathe.
fara-ghaol,(AC) *s. m.* False love.
fara-ghruag, *s.f.* Peruke.
faragrach,** *a.* Weltering. 2 Floundering.
faragradh,** -aidh, *s.m.* Weltering. 2 Floundering. 3 Bathing. 4 Report.
faraiche, -an, *s.m.* Cooper's wedge. Rinn e f. de 'n fharaich, *he made a plug of the punch*—driving out a plug with another and that other sticking in its place—i. e. he is as badly off as ever.
faraid, see farraid.
farail, -alach, -alaichean, *s. f.* Visit, enquiry after health.
far-ainm, -ainmeannan, see fath-ainm.
——each, see fath-ainmeach.
faraire, -an, *s. f.* Night-watch, watching a corpse. 2 The entertainment on such occasions, wake.
faralach, -aiche, *a.* Squeamish. †2 Like.
fara-laogh,(AC) *s.m.* False calf, monstrosity.
faram, -aim, -an, see farum.
faramach, -aiche, *a.* see farumach.
faran,§ *s.m.* Garlic, see gairgean. 2**see farran. 3(AF) Turtle-dove, see turtur. 4**Turtle.
——aich,* *v.a.* see farranaich.
faraon, *adv. & conj.* see araon & maraon.
†fàras, -ais, *s.m.* Reason, argument.
farasda, -aisde, *a.* Solid, sober, composed. 2 Mild, gentle, tranquil. 3* Soft. Gu f. fòil, *solemnly and softly.* [F. is often confused with furasda.]
——chd, *s.f.ind.* Solidity, composure, easiness, gentleness. 2††Softness. 3**Soberness.
farasg,(AC) *s.m.* False fish, fish found dead on the sea or shore.
farbhail, -e, *pl.* -ala & -ean, *s.f.* Lid, covering. F. nan sùl, *the eyelids.*
farbhalach, -aich, *s.m.* Stranger, foreigner. 2 ††Big clown.
farbhalla, -chan, *s.m.* Buttress.
——ch,** *a.* Having a buttress. 2 Like a buttress. 3 Of, or belonging to, a buttress or rampart.
——dh, see farbhalla.
farbhas, -ais, -an, *s.m.* Surmise, guess. 2 Report, rumour. 3 Destruction. 4 Attack, assault. 5 Coarse mixture. 6 Loathsomeness —*Dàin I. Ghobha.*
——ach, -aiche, *a.* Guessing, surmising. 2 Rumouring.
far-bheann,** -bheinne, -bheanntan, *s.f.* Cliffy mountain. 2 Pinnacle. 3 Mountain ridge.
——ach,** *a.* Cliffy, rocky. 2 Pinnacled.
far-bhonn, -bhuinn, *s.m.* Fore-sole of a shoe. 2 ††Inner sole.
far-bhriathar,** see for-bhriathar.
far-bhualadh, -aidh, *s.m.* Striking backwards.
far-bhuille, -an, *s.f.* Back-blow.
farca, -n & -chan, see farchan.
farcan,** -ain, *s.m.* Oak. 2 Corn on the hand or foot.
farch,(AC) -a, *s.f.* Kind of musical instrument, probably the lyre, possibly the lute.
farchachan, see farchan.
farchan, -ain, -an, *s.m.* Mallet.
farch-chrann,(AC) *s.m.* Bread-toaster.
farch-chiùil,)AC) *s.f.* see farch. Bu bhinne na f. do ghuth, *sweeter than the lyre thy voice.*
farchin, see far-chrann.
far-chluais, see far-cluais.
far-chraiceann,** *s.m.* Epidermis.
far-cluais, -e, *s.f.* Listening unperceived, eavesdropping, overhearing. 2 Hearkening.
——ich,** *v.n.* Overhear, eavesdrop, listen under windows. 2 Listen.
fàrdach, -aich, -aichean, *s.f.* House, dwelling, lodgings, quarters, mansion, hearth, home. F. oidhche, *a night's lodging*; taobh cùil na fàrdaich, *the back part of the house*; t' fh., *thy dwelling*; théid 'fh. bun os ceann, *his dwelling shall be overturned.*
fàrdadh, -aidh, *s.m.* The bark of alder, used in dyeing black.
fàrdal, -ail, -an, *s. m.* Delay, hinderance. 2 Detention. 3**Longing. Obair gun fh., *a work without delay.* [†† gives *pl.* fàdailean.]
——ach, *a.* Slow. 2 Late, tardy. 3**Dilatory. 4 Obstructing. Gu f., *dilatorily.*

fàrdan,‡ -ain, *s.f.* see feòirling.
fàrdath,* *s.m.* Lye or any colour in liquid. F. gorm, *liquid blue.*
fàrdoch, -oich, see fàrdach.
far-dorus, -uis, *s.m.* Lintel of a door.
fardrach, *s.f.* see fardach. Teasraig an teach 's an fh., *protect the house and household.*
farfas,(CR) *s.m.* Loathing, nausea—*Lochbroom.*
fàr-fhuadach, -aich, *s. m.* Banishing, forcing away.
————adh,** -aidh, *s.m.* Banishing, displacing, ejectment, displacement. A' f—, *pr. pt.* fàr-fhuadaich.
fàr-fhuadaich,** *v.a.* Banish, displace, drive away by force.
fàr-fhuadaiche,** *s.m.* Exile.
farfonadh,‡ -aidh, *s.m.* Warning.
fargradh, -aidh, -aidhean, *s.m.* Report, rumour. 2 Surmise. Tha f. ann, *it is reported.*
fa ri chéile, *adv.* see under far ri.
far-ionga, -an, *s.f.* White swelling. 2‡‡Agnail. *prov.*
farlas, see fairleus.
fàrlus, -uis, -an, see fairleus.
farmachan, -ain, *s.m.* Sand-lark.
farmad, -aid, *s.m.* Envy, grudge at another's success. 2 Malice. Cùis fharmaid, *an enviable object*; gabh f. ris, *envy him*; is e f. a ni treabhadh, *emulation makes ploughing*—one man's achievements spurs on his neighbour to similar deeds; an cunnart a chaidh seachad, is cùis fharmaid e, *a past danger is an enviable danger*—enviable in the sense that it is nice to talk about it.
———ach, -aiche, *a.* Envious. 2**Malicious. 3‡‡Enviable.
farmail, -alach, -an, *s.f.* Large water pitcher—*Hebrides.*
———, *a.* Enviable. 2 (DC) Business-like, of successful intention. An tìr ro fharmail, chliùteach, ainmeil, *the land that is much to be envied, famous and celebrated—Filidh*, p.21.
far-mhaladh,** -aidh, -aidhean, *s.m.* Eye-lid.
farpas, -ais, see fortas.
———ach, -aiche, *a.* see fortasach.
farpuis, -e, -ean, *s.f.* Contest, strife, emulation.
———each, -iche, *a.* Contending, emulative.
fàrr! *inter.* Off! be off!
farrabhalladh, -aidh, -aidhean, see farbhalla.
farrabhonn, -uinn, see farbhonn.
farrach, -aich, *s.m.* Force, violence. 2 Act of forcing. A' f—, *pr.pt.* of farraich. Na bi 'ga fh., *do not press him.*
farrachd,(DMC) *s.f.* Enquiring. A' f. air a shon, *enquiring for him.* A' f—, *pr.pt.* of farraid—*Uist.*
farrachan,(AF) -ain, *s.m.* see farachan.
farradh, -aidh, *s.m.* Crop raised by a married farm-servant for his own use. Strictly speaking, it means the tilling done by the wife, while the husband is attending to the *gràithseach*, the master's crop. Occasionally a very active woman might get through more work than her less active husband, in which case it would be said, is mó am f. na 'ghràithseach, *the servant's crop is bigger than the master's.*
fàrradh, -aidh, *s.m.* Litter, straw or brushwood laid in a boat.
†farradh, *s. m.* Company, vicinity. 2**Comparison. 3**Force.
†farradh, *prep.* Along with.
farra-dhruim, see forra-dhruim (A4 under bàta.)
farragan,‡ -ain, *s.m.* Ledge—*Arran.*
farraich, *pr. pt.* a' farrach, *v. a.* Force, urge, press, prevail.
———e, *s.m.* see fairche.
farraid, *pr.pt.* a' farraid, (also farrachd—*Uist*) *v.a.* Ask, enquire, question, ask for or after.
———, -e, -ean, *s.f.* Enquiry, act of enquiring, asking for or after, A' f—, *pr.pt.* of farraid. Cha d' thug e f. orm, *he made no enquiry of me;* cha d'rinn iad m' fharraid, *they did not ask for me.*
———each, -iche, *a.* Inquisitive, prying, curious, meddling. 2 Mocking—*Arran.*
———eachd,** *s. f. ind.* Inquisitiveness, curiousness, prying habit.
———ich, *v.a.* see farraid.
fàrrais, see pàrras.
farral, -ail, *s.m.* see farran.
———ach, -aiche, *a.* see farranach.
farran, -ain, *s.m.* Anger. 2 Pettishness. 3 Vexation. 4 Regret. 5* Slight offence. 6** Disquietness. 7 Incommodiousness. 8 *rarely* Force. Mu'n tig f. air 'aodann, *ere vexation fall on his brow.*
farranach, -aiche, *a.* Vexatious, provoking, annoying. 2 Proud, haughty. 3 Meddling. 4**Vexed. 5 Incommodious.
————d, *s.f.* same meanings as farran.
————adh, -aidh, *s.m.* Exasperation, provocation, vexation, annoyance. 2 Provoking, teasing. A' f—, *pr.pt.* of farranaich.
farranaich, *pr. pt.* a' farranachadh, *v.a.* Vex, exasperate, tease, pester, gall, annoy, anger. 2**Discompose.
farranaiche, *comp.* of farranach.
farranaichte,** *a.* Chagrined, soured.
farranta, *a.* Neat. 2 Stout, great. 3 Lofty. 4 Stately. 5**Generous. 6**Brave.
————chd,** *s. f.* Stoutness. 2 Bravery. 3 Generousness.
farrantan,** *s.pl.* Tombs.
farrantas, -ais, *s.m.* Power. 2 Stoutness. 3 Manliness. 4 Bravery. 5**Generosity.
fàrras, *s.f.* see parras.
farrbhalladh, see farbhalladh.
farr'bheinn, -e, -bheanntan, see far-bheann.
————each, see far-bheannach.
farr-bhonn, see far-bhonn.
far ri, *adv.* With, in company with. Far rium, *with me*; far riut, *with you*; far rithe, *with her;* far ri (*for* mar ri) chéile, *together.*
farruinn,‡ *s.f.* see fàruinn.
far ruinn, *for* maille ruinn, & mar ruinn, see under far ri, with us, together with us.
farrusg, -uisg, -an, *s. m.* Peeling. 2 Inner rind. 3 Cuticle of diseased flesh. 4 Scales. 5 Refuse of anything. 6 (DMC) Short new wool under the old fleece—*Uist.*
farrusgag,‡ -aige, -an, *s.f.* Artichoke—*cynara scolymus.* [F. and *bliosan* are applied to Jerusalem artichoke (*helianthus tuberosus*) and *plùr-na-gréine* to the flower, from the popular error that the flower turns with the sun.]
————ach,** *a.* Of artichokes. 2 Abounding in artichokes.
farsaing, -e, see farsuing.
†farsan, -ain, *s.m.* } Explication, parsing.
†farsanachd, *s.f.ind.* } Explication, parsing.
farsanach, (DC) *a.* Given to straying or wandering.
farspach,¶ -aiche, -aichean, *s.f.* The great black-backed gull—*larus marinus.*
———— -bheag, *s.f.* Lesser black-backed gull, see sgaireag.
farspag, -aige, -an, see farspach.
farsuing, -e, *a.* Large, wide. 2 Liberal, open. Gu fada f., *far and wide.*
————each,†† -eiche, *a.* Wide, extensive.
————eachadh, -aidh, *s.m.* Widening, enlarging. 2 Act of widening, enlargement. A' f—, *pr. pt.* of farsuingich.

farsuingeachd, *s.f.ind.* Width, extent, largeness.
———ead, Same meanings as farsuingeachd.
———ich, *pr. pt.* a' farsuingeachadh, *v.a.* Widen, increase, enlarge.
farsuinneachd, *s.f.* see farsuingeachd.
farsuinnich, see farsuingich.
far-thagh, (AC) *s.m.* Certain amount of farm-produce allowed to farm-servants in olden times.
far-thìr, (AC) *s.f.* Border, coast. 2 Out-of-the-way place.
far-thìreach, (PM) *s.m.* Foreigner, stranger.
far-thobhta, -chan, *s.f.* Buttress.
fartus, -uis, see fortas.
fàruinn, -ean, *s.f.* Pinnacle. F. na beinne, *an opening between mountains.*
faruinn, see far ruinn.
far-uinneag, -eige, -an, *s.f.* Lattice, casement.
———ach,** *a.* Latticed.
†faruisg, see farrusg.
farum, -uim, *s. m.* Noise, report. 2 Percussion. 3* Sound of the tramping of horses. 4 Clangour, clashing. 5 Rustling. 6 Burliness. 7(AC) Figwort, see lus-nan-cnapan. F. an stàilinn, *the clangour of their steel ;* f. an duillich sheargta, *the rustling of their withered foliages.*
†farum, *a.* Merry.
farumach, -aiche, *a.* Noisy. 2**Loud. 3**Sonorous. 4**Rattling. 5 Beating at regular intervals. 6 Energetic. 7* Merry. A' dol air aghaidh gu f., *going forward merrily* ; beucadh an cuan gu farumach, *let the sea roar mightily.*
———d, *s.f.ind.* Noisiness.
farusg, -uisg, -an, see farrusg.
———ag, -aige, -an, see farrusgag.
fàs, -àis, *s.m.* Growth, increase. 2 Growing, increasing, becoming, state or act of growing. 3* Produce. F. an fhuinn, *the produce or increase of the land ;* cha'n 'eil f. aig ni 'sam bith, *there is no vegetation of anything* ; teachd an fhàis mu dheireadh, *the shooting of the latter growth* ; f. is gnàths is toradh, *growing, indigenous and fruit-bearing*—on New Year's morning a branch or twig having these three characteristics was taken into houses in olden times, as a token of wished-for prosperity during the coming year. The twig required to have life in it, i.e. it must be plucked off the tree. It required to be a native tree, no exotic or introduced tree would do, and it would require to bear fruit in its season. Fàs a' ghruinnd a réir an uachdarain, *the yield of the ground is according to the landlord.* A' f—, *pr pt.* of fàs.
fàs, *pr.pt.* a' fàs, *v.n.* Grow, vegetate. 2 Increase. 3 Become great or little, good or bad. 4*Rise. Dh' fh. e mór, *he grew tall ;* dh' fh. sléibhtean ceò air an fhairge, *mountains of mist rose on the sea ;* f. reamhar, *get* or *become fat ;* dh' fh. an t-eòrna, *the barley vegetated.*
fàs, -a, *a.* Empty, vacant, hollow, void. 2 Waste. 3 Laid waste, desolate. 4*Unoccupied. 5 Uncultivated. 6 False, hollow. 7** Addle. 8** Addle-pated. Taigh f., *an unoccupied house ;* fearann f., *waste* or *uncultivated land ;* ni thu e f., *thou shalt make it hollow* ; rinn mi f. an sràidean, *I have laid their streets desolate ;* thug e ceum f., [thug e ceum fallsa], *he took a false step ;* is f. a' chùl as nach goirear, *deserted is the corner whence no (voice of bird) is heard ;* cuir f., *lay waste.*
†fas, *s.m.* Homestead, abode.
fasa, *comp.* of furasda. Easier.
fàsach, -aich, -aichean, *s.m.* (except *gen. sing.* which is *f.*, but *f.* in all cases in *Badenoch.*) Desert, wilderness, solitude, desolation. 2 Mountain, hill, "forest." 3 Stubble. 4 Choice pasture. 5‡‡Edge, border. 6‡‡Mark, spot. 7** Grassy headland of a ploughed field. F. fiadhaich, *a terrible wilderness ;* féidh na fàsaich, *the forest deer ;* luchd-còmhnuidh na fàsaich, *the dwellers of the desert.*
fàsach, -aiche, *a.* Desolate, untrodden.
———d, *s. f. ind.* see fàsalachd & falmhachd. 2††Growth.
———adh, -aidh, *s.m.* Depopulation. 2 Act of depopulating or laying waste. A' f—, *pr.pt.* of fàsaich.
fasachadh,** -aidh, *s. m.* Encumbrance. 2 Encumbering.
fàsachail, -ala, *a.* see fàsail.
fasad, *3rd. comp.* of furasda.
fàsadach,‡‡ -aiche, *a.* Crescent.
†fasadh, -aidh, *s.m.* Dwelling.
fàsadh, -aidh, -aidhean, *s.m.* Protuberance.
fàsag, *s.f.* Plug-hole in a boat. 2(MMcL) Plug, —*Moidart.* 3 (DU) Pea-pod ih early stages, (before the peas have assumed anything like full size.)
fàsaich, *pr.pt.* a' fàsachadh, *v.a.* Depopulate, lay waste, desolate. 2 Afforest. 3 Destroy. 4 Encumber. Dh' fh. e an dùthaich, *he depopulated the country.*
———ear, *fut. pass.* of fàsaich.
———te, *past pt.* of fàsaich. Depopulated, laid waste, desolated.
fasaid, *2nd. comp.* of furasda.
fàsail, -ala, *a.* Desert, desolate. 2 Solitary, lonely. 3**Wild. 4**Growing. Sruthan f., *a lonely brook ; a dry brook.*
fàsaidheachd, *Suth'd.* for fàsachd (barrenness.)
fàsair, (DU) *s.m.* Boat-plug. Toll(a) fàsair, *plug-hole.*
fasair, *v.a.* see asairich.
———, -srach, -sraichean, *s. f.* Luxuriant pasturage. [Also asair.]
———eadh, (AG) *Reay country* for fasanadh (pasturing.)
fasairich, *v.a.* see asairich.
fàsalach,†† -aich, *s.m.* Void.
———d, *s.f.ind.* State of lying waste, desolation, emptiness, solitude. Là f., *a day of desolation.*
fàsam, for fàsaidh mi, I will grow.
fàsan, -ain, *s. m.* Refuse of grain.
fasan, -ain, -an, -an, *s. m.* Fashion, custom, manner. 2 Homestead and cultivated ground around it. 'San fhasan, *in fashion ;* as an fh., *out of fashion.*
———ach, *a.* see fasanta. Gu f., *fashionably.*
fasanadh, -aidh, *s.m.* The old custom of giving an hour's grazing to milch cows on the green patches (ceannamhagan) adjacent to the corn prior to their being sent to the hill for the day.
fasanta, *a.* Fashionable, in fashion. 2 Customary, habitual. 3**Fond of fashion. Baintighearna fhasanta, a *fashionable lady.*
———chd, *s.f.ind.* Fashionableness. 2 Adherence to fashion or custom.
fàs-bheann, *s.f.* Desert hill. Cìob nam f., *the rank grass of the desert hills.*
fas-bhuain, -bhuana, *s.f.* see asbhuain.
fàs-charn,** *s.m.* Cenotaph.
fàs-cheannach, -aiche, *a.* Barren, dull.
fàs-cheilg,** *s. f.* Hollow guile, low cunning. Labhair e gun f., *he spake without guile.*
fàs-choille, -choilltean, *s.f.* Young grove, grove or wood in the first few years of its growth. 2††Wilderness.
fàsd,** *s.* Seizure.
fasda, (PM) *s. m.* Rope used in towing large lumps of seaweed called *maois* and *ball* after boats.—*Uist.*

fasdachadh, see fasdadh.
fasdadh, -aidh, *s.m.* Hiring, binding, as a servant, for a stated term. 2 Stoppage, seizure. A' f—, *pr. pt.* of fasdaidh. Biodh siod air t' fhasdadh 's lann chinn-aisnich, 's gàirdean gasda leanadh i, *that will be part of your wage, and a fluted sword and strong arms to wield it—Filidh, p. 11.*
fasdaich, *v.a.* see fasdaidh.
fasdaid, *a.* Fee'd, as at market—*Arran.*
fasdaidh, *pr.pt.* a' fasdadh, *v.a.* Hire, engage. 2 Bind, secure, make fast. tie.
fasdail, -alach, -ailean, *s.f.* Dwelling. 2* Dome.
fàs-dhiobhuirt,‖ *s.m.* Retching.
fa seach, *adv.* Apart, distinctly, separately, individually. 2 Alternately. Ceòl is cuirm fa seach, *music and feasting by turns.*
fasg,* *v.a.* see faisg.
fasg,** -aisg, *s.m.* Prison. 2 Band, bond. 3 (DC) Cot in which to confine a sheep with a foster-lamb, to induce each to take to the other—*Argyll.*
——ach, -aiche, *a.* Sheltering, well-sheltered. 2**Screening. 3**Calm. Àite f., *a well-sheltered place.*
fàsgach, -aiche, *a.* Wringing.
fàsgadair, see fàisgeadair.
fasgadair,¶ *s.m.* Arctic gull, Richardson's skua, —*lestris Richardsoni.* [This name is sometimes applied to the *fasgadan.*] 2‡‡One that picks off or destroys vermin.

302. Fasgadair.

fasgadan, -ain, *s. m.* Umbrella. 2 Sun-shade, parasol.
fasgadan, -ain, *s.m.* Common skua—*lestris catarractes.*
fasgadh, -aidh, -aidhean, *s. m.* Protection, shelter, screen. 2**Refuge. 3**Shadow. 4** Sparks from red-hot iron. 5 Fold. 6 Penfolding of cattle. 7 *Blair Atholl* for fasdadh. F. na daraich, *the shelter of the oak;* a dhìth fasgaidh, *for want of shelter;* taobh an fhasgaidh, *a lee side.*
fàsgadh, -aidh, *s.m.* Wringing, squeezing, pressing. A' f—, *pr. pt.* of faisg. An ni nach gabh nigheadh cha ghabh e f., *what will not wash will not wring;* f. samhlach, *a copying-press;* cha'n ionann do fhear na neasgaid agus do fhear 'ga fhàsgadh, *it's different with the man of the boil and the man that squeezes it*—N.G.P.
fasgadh, -aidh, *s.m.* Cleansing from vermin. A' f—, *pr.part.* of faisg.
fasgadhach,** *a.* Sheltering, protecting.
fasgaich, *v.a.* Imbower, shelter.
fasguidh,†† *s. f.* Cleaning off vermin. A' f—, *pr.pt.* of faisg.
————,** *a.* Sheltered. 2 Calm.
fasgain, *pr. pt.* a' fasganadh & a' fasgnadh, *v.a.* Winnow. 2 Sift.
fasgainte, *past pt.* Winnowed. 2 Sifted.
fasgair,** *s.m.* Gaoler. keeper.
fasgan,** -ain, *s.m.* Winnow. 2 Sieve. 3 Muscle. F. an diomhanais, *the sieve of vanity.*
fasganadh,(MMcD) *s.m.* Separating the husks from the seed in a strong wind, winnowing. A' f—, *pr.pt.* of fasgain.
fasgath, -aith, -aithean, *s.m.* see fasgadh.
————ach, -aiche, *a.* see fasgach.
fàs-ghlac, -ghlaice, -an, *s.f.* } Desert vale.
fàs-ghleann, -ghlinn, *s.m.* } Desert vale.
fasgnadair,(CR) *s.m.* Winnower.
fasgnadan,* -ain, *s.m.* Ventilator.
fasgnadh, -aidh, *s.m.* Winnowing, cleansing of grain out of doors. The process of cleaning grain by throwing it up with a sieve and catching it again, thus bringing the bad seed and chaff to the surface, after which it is lifted with the hand, and separated from the good grain—(DC.) 2 Sifting. A' f—. *pr. pt.* of fasgain. Cailleach-fhasgnaidh, *fanner.*
fasgnag, -aige, -an, *s.f.* Corn-fan, winnowing-fan. (beantag.)
————ach, *a.* Of or belonging to a hand-winnow. 2 Like a hand-winnow.
fa-sgrìobhadh,** -aidh, *s.m.* Appendix.
fa sheachd, *adv.* Seven times.
fàslach, -aich, -aichean, *s.m.* Hollow, vacuum, void, space, interstice. 2 Instigation. 3 see furail.
†faslairt, *s.* Encampment.
fàs-lomairt, -ean, *s.f.* Preparation of victuals in the fields or hills. 2 Hasty meal. 3**Expeditious method of cooking victuals in the stomach of an animal, once practised in Gaeldom. 4 Temporary habitation.
fàsmhoire, *comp.* of fàsmhor.
fàsmhor, -mhoire, *a.* Growing, thriving, vegetative. 2 Desert, desolate, lonely, waste.
————ach, -aiche, *a.* see fàsmhor.
————achd *s.f.ind.* State of growing, growth, increasing, thriving.
fasnag, *prov.* for fasgnag.
fàs-na-h-aon-oidhche,§ *s.*Mushroom, see agairg & balg-bhuachaill.
faspan, -ain, -an, *s. m.* Difficulty, embarrassment.
——ach, -aiche, *a.* Difficult, embarrassing.
fasradh, -aidh, see asradh.
fasraichean, *pl.* of fasair (*for* asair)
fast,(AF) *s.m.* Reindeer.
fasta, *s.* see fasdadh.
fastachadh, see fasdadh.
fastadh, -aidh, -aidhean, see fasdadh.
fastaich, see fasdaich.
fastaidh, *v.a.* see fasdaidh.
fàsuich, *v.a.* see fàsaich.
fàth, *s.m.ind.* Cause, reason, object. 2 Opportunity. 3 Ambuscade, principle. 4**Poem. 5 **Field. 6**Heat. 7 Breath. 8 (AC) Vista, perspective. 9(AC) Long narrow glen. 10** *rarely* Skill. F. mo dhuilichinn, *the cause of my sorrow;* f. iongantais, *a cause of wonder;* gabh f. air sin, *watch an opportunity for that;* f. air son fola, *an opportunity for bloodshed;* f. fad air falbh, *a view far away;* chì mi f. air an fhiadh, *I see a distant view of the deer;* ni 'm faic mi f. dhiubh, *nor do I see a view of them.*
fath,** *s.* Advantage.
fath,‡ -ach, -achan, *s. f.* see famh. [*gen.* fathann, *pl.* fathan—*Gairloch, &c* (DU)
fath,* *v.a.* see fàth-fheith.
fàth, *Gairloch for* fàdh, *gen.pl.* of faidh.
——ach, -aich, *s.m.* see fàth.
——ach, -aich, *s.m.* Giant, monster, genius. F. was invariably used in the old tales, and through ignorance of grammar the *fh* has been dropped in many places, and the *gen.*

with the article is used instead of the *nom.*—guth an fhathaich, *the giant's voice*, is thus erroneously written *guth an athaich*. The same thing has happened to many other words as, eagal, &c.
†fathach, -aich, *s.m.* Prudence, knowledge.
fàthach,†† *a.* Pertaining to cause, reason or opportunity.
fàth-ainm, -eau & -eannan, *s.m.* Nick-name.
————each,** *a.* Nicknaming, apt to nick-name.
fathamach,†† *a.* Fearful, reverent, obedient.
fathamas, -ais, *s. m.* Degree of fear, reverence, awe, obedience. 2 Warning. 3 Occasion, opportunity. 4 Indulgence, partiality. 5 Mitigation. 6††Sparing. 7 (DMC) Reprieve, respite—*Uist*. Gun fh. do dhuine seach duine, *without partiality to one man more than another.*
fathan, -ain, *s.m.* Journey. 2§ Colt's foot, see cluas liath. 3 (AH) Light wind.
———ach, -aiche, *a.* Trifling, silly, of mean appearance.
-———achd, *s.f.ind.* Silliness of appearance.
fathann,†† -ainn, *s.m.* Rumour, news.
———ach,†† *a.* Pertaining to rumours or news.
fathas,** -ais, *s.m.* Skill. 2 Poetry. 3 Prudence.
fathasdaich, *Suth'd &c.* for fathast.
fathast, *adv.* Yet, as yet. 2 Still, notwithstanding. Thig e fhathast, *he will come yet*; is aoibhinn leam fhathast t' fhuaim, *thy sound is still pleasant to me*; 'n ann fhathast? *still? do you still persist?* [Generally aspirated.]
fathbh, see famh.
fathbhan, -ain, -an, *s.m.* Mole-hill. [famhan.]
fath-bheathach,(AH) *s. m.* Puny, half-starved animal.
fath-chainnt, -e, *s.f.* see fachaint.
fath-déistinn, *s.m.* Cause of abomination.
fath-dhorsach,** *a.* Having small doors or wickets.
fath-dhorus, -uis, -dhorsan, *s. m.* Small door, wicket.
fath-each, *s.m.* Make-shift horse. Am fear a cheannaicheas am fath-each ceannaichidh e an t-ath each, *he that buys a make-shift hack will have to buy another horse.*
fath-fhaim,** *s.f.* see faitheam.
fàth-fheith, *pr.pt.* a' fàth-fheitheamh, *v.a.* Way-lay, beset. 2**Ensnare.
————eamh,** *s.m.* Ambuscade. A' f—, *pr.pt.* of fath-fheith.
fath-ghabhail,‡‡ *s.* Ambush.
fath-loisg,** *v.a.* Char. 2(DMC) Burn heather.
fathmas, see fathamas.
fath-mhùgach, *s.f.* see famh.
fàth-oide, -an & -chan, *s.m.* Schoolmaster, preceptor. 2**Usher.
fathrag,** -eig, *s.m.* Bath.
fathraig,‡ *pr.pt.* a' fathragach, *v.a.* Bathe.
fathraire, see faraire.
fa thrì, *adv.* Thrice.
fath-rud,** *s.m.* Appendage.
fath-rusgach,‡‡ -aiche, *a.* Paleous.
fath-sgrìobh, *v.a.* Subscribe, subjoin, write as a postcript. [fo-sgrìobh.]
————adh, -aidh, *s. m.* Subscribing, subjoining. 2 Act of subscribing or subjoining. 3 Appendix. 4 Postscript. A' f—, *pr.pt.* of fath-sgrìobh.
fa-thuaiream, *prep.* Towards. 2 About. Buille fa th., *a chance trial.*
fathunn, -uinn, *s.m.* see fathann.
———ach, -aiche, *a.* see fathannach.
fathur,** -uir, see fathunn.
fé. *Arran* for fèin.
fé,** *a.* Wild, inconsistent in a fury.
fè, *s.f.ind.* see fèath. 2 see feith. 3**Quagmire. 4**Park. 5**Fold. 6***rarely* Measuring-rod. 7**Hedge.
†feabh, *s.f.* Conflict, storm. 2 Means, power, faculty.
feabha, One of the *comp.* forms of math.
———id, *2nd. comp.* of math.
feabhas, *3rd. comp.* of math, or *s.m.* (*gen.* -ais.) Superiority. 2 Goodness. 3 Beauty, comeliness. 4 Convalescence. 5**Improvement. 6 7**Excellence. 8**Better, best. 9 Decency. Cha'n fhaic mi 'fh., *I cannot see its superior*, or *better than it*; an duine d' a fh., *no matter how good the man may be*; air son 'fh., *for its superiority*; air 'fh. gu'm faighear thu, *no matter how much you exert yourself*; tha 'n duine tinn a' dol am f., *the sick man is getting better* or *convalescent*.
feabhasach, *a.* Better, improved, ameliorated.
feabhasaich, *v. a. & n.* Ameliorate, correct, amend.
feabhlau, see faoileann.
Feabhradh,** -aidh, *s.m.* February.
†feabhsach, *a.* Cunning, skilful.
fèach, *v.a.* see feuch.
†feach, *s.* Journey. 2 Spade. 3 Handle of a spade.
feachadh,** -aidh, *s.m.* Spade. 2 Mattock. 3 Pick-axe.
fèachainn, see feuchainn.
feachd, -an, *s.f.* Army, host, forces, levy, trained bands. 2 War. Bliadhn' an fh., *the year of the war (1745)*; an làithibh cath is f., *in the days of battle and warfare*; f. nan sonn, *the battle of the brave*; f. oileinichte, *a trained army*; far nach bi na mic-uchd, cha bhi na fir-feachd, *where there are no boys in arms, there will be no armed men.*
———, *v.a. & n.* Bend, bow. 2 Yield. 3 Swerve. Ceannabhard nach gabhadh f., *a chief who would not yield*; esan a dh' fh. o 'n chòir, *he that swerved from the path of rectitude.*
†feachd, *s. f. ind.* Bend, curve. 2 Cramp. 3 Danger. 4 Journey. 5 Alternative time, turn. 6 *rarely* Deeds.
feachda,* *a.* Regimental.
feachdach,** *a.* Crooked, bent. 2 Pliable. 3 Having armies.
feachdadh, -aidh, *s.m.* Bending, bowing. 2 Act of bending. A' f—, *pr.pt.* of feachd.
feachdail,** *a.* Hostile.
feachdaire, -an, *s.m.* Warrior.
feachd-aitreabh, -an, *s.f.* Barracks.
feachd-cheum,‡‡ -éim & -a, *s.* March.
feachd-dhaingnich, *s.f.* Garrison.
feachd-dìon, *s.f.* Fencibles.
feachd-dùthcha, -an-, *s.f.* Militia.
feachd-imeachd, *s.f.* March.
feachd-imich, *v.a. pr.pt*, a' feachd-imeachd, *v.a.* March.
feachd-mara, *s.f.* Armada, fleet, navy.
feachd-mharasgal, -ail, *s.m.* Field-marshal.
†feachdnach,** -aich, *s.m.* Prosperity, luck. 2 Manhood.
feachdraidh, *s.pl.* Armed infantry.
feachdta, *a. & past pt.* of feachd. Bent, bowed, crooked.
feachd-tìre, *s. f.* Militia. 2(AH) Army—foot, horse, and artillery.
fead, -an, *s.f.* Whistle. 2 Hiss, hissing noise. 3 **Shrill voice. 4 Blast. 5 Smart blow. 6** Bustle. 7**Fathom. 8**Island. 9***rarely* Bulrush. F. 'san leth-cheann, *a blow on the cheek*; f. air fuar-luirg, *whistling on a cold track*=" a wild goose chase "; f. an aonaich, *the whistling of the wind on the heath*; dean f.,

whistle; ni e f., *he shall whistle:* gearr f., *whistle—Uist.*
fead, *pr.pt.* a' feadail, *v.n.* Whistle, hiss.
†fead, *v.a.* Tell, relate.
fead,§ *s.f.* Soft rush, see luachair bhog.
feada-coille, *s.f.* Wood-sorrel, see seamrag. 2 **Bulrush.
feadadh,** -aidh, *s.m.* Whistling. 2 Relation, rehearsal.
feadag, -aige, -an, *s.f.* Flute. 2 Whistle. 3 The third week of February. 4 Plover—*charadrius pluvialis.* 5**Flageolet. Le feadagaibh, *with flutes*; cha d' thugainn f. ort, *I don't care a whistle for you.*
——ach,†† *a.* Abounding in whistles, or plovers.
—— -bhuidhe, (AF) see feadag 4.
—— ghlas,¶ *s.f.* Grey plover, *308. Feadag.* see trilleachan.
—— -riasgach,(AF) *s.f.* Lapwing, see adharcan-luachrach.
feadaidh, *fut.aff.a.* of fead. Shall whistle.
féadail, -alach, *s.m.* see feudail.
feadail,** *s.f.* Whistling. 2 Hissing.
A' f—, *pr.pt.*of fead. Òganach a' f. 'sa mhagh, *a youth whistling on the plain.*
feadail, *a.* Whistling. 2 Of, or pertaining to, a whistle.
——ich,* *s.f.* see feadalaich.
feadain,** *v.n.* Pipe, whistle.
——, *gen. sing. & n. pl* of feadan.
——e,(AC) *prov. pl.* of feadan (crevice.)
feadaire, -an, *s.m.* Whistler, piper.
——achd, *s.f.* Whistling. Thòisich e air f., *he began to whistle.*
feadalaich, *s.f.* Whistling.
feadan, -ain, -an, *s.m.* Fife, flute. 2 Chanter of the bagpipe. 3 Reed. 4 Spout. 5 The calibre of a gun. 6 Barrel. 7 Crevice through which the wind whistles. 8 Oaten-pipe. 9 Discharge of a still. 10**Canal. 11 Water-pipe. 12**Flageolet. 13(DMC) Opening in the wall of a barn to let in the wind for winnowing grain. 14(DMC) Opening in the wall of a byre. 15(DMC) Aqueduct under a road. F. na bàthaich, *the byre-runnel;* f. taomaidh, *a pump;* ceòl an fheadain tlàth, *the music of the soft reed.*
——ach, -aiche, *a.* Of, like, or pertaining to, pipes, flutes, chanters, whistles, conduits, reeds, waterpipes or crevices.
——ach, -aich, *s.m.* see feadanaiche.
——achd,** *s.f.ind.* Playing on a flageolet or pipe.
feadanaiche, -an, *s.m.* Pipe-chanter. 2††Piper. 3**One who plays on a flute, flageolet, &c.
feadan-uisge,** *s. m.* Water-pipe, gutter or rone of a house. 2 (AH) Small cascade or waterfall.
feadar, *v.impers.* see feudar.
——,** -air, *s.m.* Pass.
feadaran,** -ain, *s.m.* Mirth.
feadarsaich,(DMC) *s.f.* Whistling—*Uist.*
†feadarthachd, *s.f.* Possibility.
fead-ghoile,** *s. m.* Noise in belly of horses when trotting.
fead-ghuil,** *s.m.* Lamentation.
feadh, *s.m. ind.* [Governs the *gen.*] Extent, length. 2 Fathom. 3 Whilst,during,through, throughout. 4 Among, amid. 5 So long as. F. ghleanntan fàsail, *through desert valleys*; f. gach tìr, *throughout every land;* f. an là, *during the day-time;* f. gach rè, *for evermore;* f. gach linn, *through every age;* f. 's is beò mi, *while I live;* f. 's a bha mis' a' tighinn, *while I was coming.* [*Am feadh,* and *air feadh* are often shortened to *feadh* by the omission of the prep.] Feadh 's a mhaireas an ruaig, *while the chase lasts;* air f. a chéile, *mixed up together;* air f. an arbhair, *among the corn;* tha na radain air f. an fhodair, *the rats are swarming in the hay;* feadh mo choise, *the length of my foot-print—Suth'd.*(DC)
feadhachan,* -ain, *s.m.* see feadhanach.
feadhail, *pl.* feadhlaichean, *s.f.* see fadhail.
feadhain,(AF) *s.m.* Team of horses.
feadhainn, -dhna, -dhnach, *s.pl.* People, folks. 2 Band, troop, company. 3 Group of persons or things. 4* Some, others, those. An fh. a thàinig a staigh, *the people that came in;* f. eile, *others;* an fh. a dh' fhàg sinn, *those we left;* an fh. dhiubh a thig, *those of them that mean to come;* cuid na feadhnach seo, *the property of these;* ceann-feadhna, *a chieftain.*
feadhair,** *a.* Wild, savage.
——eachd,** *s.f.* Gift, present. 2 Strolling, sauntering, idling.
†feadhan, -aine, *a.* Wild, savage.
fèadhan,(AF) *s.m.* Wild goose leader.
——ach, -aich, *s.m.* Soft breeze, breath of wind. F. gaoithe, *breeze of wind.*
feadhlan,(AF) see faoileann.
†feadhma, *s.f.* Service, superintendence.
feadhmach,** *a.* Powerful. Gu f., *powerfully.*
——,** -aich, *s.m.* Governor, overseer. 2 Steward, bailiff.
feadhmanta,** *a.* Official.
——chd, *s.f.* see feadhmantas.
——s,** -ais, *s. m.* Superintendence, overseeing, stewardship.
†feadhm-ghnàthachadh, -aidh, *s.f.* Usurpation.
feadhna,** *s.m.* Commander, chief, captain.
——, *gen.* of feadhainn.
——chd, *s. f. ind.* Captainship, captaincy, chieftainship, command.
feadraich, -e, *s.f.* Whistling.
feag, -an, *s.f.* see eag. 2***rarely* Tooth. 3** Offence.
—ach,** *a.* Crenated.
—aich, see eagaich.
—aichte, see eagaichte.
feagal, -ail, *s.m. Badenoch, &c.* for eagal.
feagamh, see theagamh.
feagh, -a, *s.f.* see feadh 2.
†feagha, *s.f.* Beech-tree.
fèairde, see fèairrd.
——achd,* see fèairrdeachd.
fèairrd, *comp.* of math. [Described thus in all Gaelic grammars, but féairrd and math have really no connection etymologically.] Is fh. thu sin, *you are the better of that;* cha'n fh. thu stuth dheth sin, *you are nothing the better of that.*
fèairrde,(DMC) *s.f.* Betterment. Cha'n 'eil f. dhomh ann, *it does me no good.*
——achd,* *s.f.* Improvement, convalescence. 2 Superiority, excellence. Cha'n fhaic mi fhéin f. sam bith air, *I don't see any symptom of convalescence* or *improvement.*
feairsid, see fearsaid.
feairt, see feart.
†feal, *s.f.* Art, science. 2 Treason.
——, -a, *a.* Bad, evil.
feala-bheadradh, } *s.m.* Mirth.
feala-chluich, }
feala-dhà, *s.f.ind.* Joking, irony, jest, mirth. Ri f., *jesting, playing the fool.*
fealan, -ain, -an, *s.m.* see fiolan. 2 Itch, hives. 3**Fleshworm. 4**Furuncle, bile. 5 Rash on face or body.—*Badenoch.* Duine aig am bheil

am f., *a man who has the itch.*
——ach,** *a.* Affected with itch. 2 Full of, or like, fleshworms.
feala-rìreadh, *s. f.* Earnest. Is tric a chaidh feala-dhà gu feala-rìreadh (*or* feala trì), *joking has often ended in earnest.*
feala-trì, *s.f.* Earnest.
†fealb, -a, -an, *s.m.* Kernel. 2 Lump in the flesh.
†——has, -ais, *s.m.* Evil vision. 2 Misinformation.
fealcaidh, -e, *a.* Austere. 2 Knavish, deceitful. 3 Unpleasant.
————eachd, *s.f.ind* Sharpness, sourness. 2 Knavery, deceitfulness. 3 Dispute, debate.
————eas,** -eis, *s.m.* Debate, dispute.
feall, *s. f. ind.* Treason. 2 Treachery, conspirracy, trickery, deceit, falsehood. Ri f., *practising guile.*
feall,* *a.* False.
feall, *v. a.* Deceive, betray, fail, impose upon.
fealladh, -aidh, *s.m.* Deceit, desertion, failure. A' f—, *pr.pt.* of feall.
fealla-dhà, see feala-dhà.
fealladh-bog,§ *s.m.* Water-hemlock—*cicuta virosa.*
feallair,** *s. m.* Deceiver, traitor. 2 Liar. 3§Water-hemlock, see fealladh-bog.
——eachd,** *s.f.* Deceiving, deceitfulness. 2 Falsehood.
feall-aithris, *s.f.* Pretence.
feallan, -ain, *s.m.* Felon, traitor. see fealan. see fiolan.
fealla-rìreadh, see feala-rìreadh.
fealla-trì, see feala-trì.
feall-bheart, -bheairt, -an, *s.f.* Deceit.
————ach, *a.* Deceitful.

304. *Fealladh-bog.*

feall-chomhairlich, *v.a.* Plot.
feall-chruth,** *s.* Disguise.
feall-chùinn, *v.a.* Counterfeit, forge.
feall-chùinneadair,‡‡ -e, -ean,*s.m.* Counterfeiter.
feall-chùinneadh, -idh, *s.m.* Counterfeiting, forgery, act of counterfeiting or forging.
feall-chùinnte, *past.pt.* Counterfeited, forged.
feall-dhealbh, *v.a.* see feall-chùinn.
————ta, see feall-chùinnte.
feall-duine, *pl.* -daoine, *s.m.* Worthless man. 2 Deceiver, traitor.
feall-faire,(DMC) *s.f.* Waylaying.
feall-fheitheamh,**-eimh, *s. m.* Lying in wait, ambush, ambuscade. Ri f., *lying in wait.*
feall-fhios,(AH) *s.m.* Extravagant or lying story, canard.
feall-fholach, -aich, *s.m.* Ambush, ambuscade.
————ail,** *a.* Treacherous. 2 Prone to lie in wait.
feall-fholaich, *v.a.* Lie in wait.
feall-ghnàthachd, *s.f.ind.* Affectedness, affectation.
feall-ghnìomh, -aran, *s.m.* Deceitful action, swindle, trick.
————ach,** *a.* Base in action, swindling, cheating.
feall-innleachd,** *s.f.* Deceit, guile, snare.
feall-léigh, -ean, *s.m.* Quack doctor, medicaster.
feall-lighiche, see feall-léigh.
†feall-mhac, -mhic, *s.m.* Learned man, scholar.
feall-mhiann, -an, *s.f.* Conspiracy, deceitful intention.
feallsa, *a.* Mendacious. 2 see fallsa.
feallsachd, *s.f.ind.* Mendacity, deceit.
†feallsadh,** -aidh, *s.m.* Philosophy. 2 Learning. 3 Literature.
†feallsaidh, *s pl.* Philosophers.
feallsaimh, -ean, *s.m.* Philosopher.
feallsamhna, *s.pl.* Philosophers.
————ch, -aich, see feallsanach.
————chd, *s.f.ind.* see feallsanachd.
feallsanach, -aich, *s.m.* Sophist, quack, false philosopher.
————d, *s. f. ind.* Philosophy. 2 Learning. 3 Literature. 4 Sophistry. Trid fh. dhìomhain, *through vain philosophy.*
feallta, *a.* see fealltach.
fealltach, -aiche, *a.* Treasonable, false, deceitful. Gu f., *treacherously.*
fealltachd,** *s.f.* Treason, treacherousness, deceitfulness.
fealltail,** *a.* Traitorous, treacherous, deceitful. 2 Murderous.
fealltair, -ean, *s.m.* Traitor, villain. 2 Quack, rogue, deceiver.
————eachd,** *s.f.ind.* Conduct of a traitor. 2 Roguery, villany, deceitfulness.
fealltanach, -aich, see fealltair.
†fealmhac, see feall-mhac.
feam,* *s.* see feaman.
——ach,** *a.* Gross. 2 Dirty. 3 Silly. 4 Superfluous. 5 Having a large rump.
——achail, *a.* Dirty, nasty. 2 Clumsy, inelegant. 3 Gross. 4 Stupid.
——achas,** -ais, *s.m.* Grossness. 2 Dirtiness. 3 Silliness. 4 Superfluity.
feamaid,(DC) *s.f.* Seaware—*Uist.*
feamain,* *s.* see feaman.
feamainn,§feamnach, *s.f.* Seaweed of all kinds, cast ware, whether growing on the rocks or cast ashore. 2§ Rosebay,see seileachan Frangach—a common name for plants growing near water, especially if long-stalked. [Badge of the MacNeills.]
[In *Skye*, *Lewis*, *&c.*, the red or tangle seaweed is called *bruchd*, and the cutting seaweed *an fheamainn*. In *Uist* the red seaweed is called *feamainn dearg*, as distinguished from the black seaweed, which they cut on the rocks round the shore, and which is called *feamainn dubh*. *Feamainn* is the general name for all kinds of seaweeds, but there are names for the different kinds. *F. dearg*, or *bàrr dearg*,as it is sometimes called, is red seaweed. In *Uist* the red seaweed, which is cast ashore in May, June and July, and of which kelp was made, is called *am bragaire*. The cutting seaweed, *an fheamainn ghearraidh*, is known as (*a*) *feamainn dubh*, which does not float, it includes *aona-chasach* and *baiteach*—(PM) ; (*b*) *feamainn bhuidhe* or *bhuidheagach*, which floats ; (*c*) *gleadhrach*, which also floats; and (*d*) *feamainn chìrean* or *chìreag*. It is known as *feamainn chìreanach* in *Uist*, and *f. chìreag* in *Skye* and *Lewis*. It is only a few inches in length,and grows only on rocks that are seldom under the water during neap-tides. It has a strong laxative property, often being plucked off the rocks and boiled, when it is given to cattle that are suffering from dryness—JM. In *Harris* the long seaweed that can be reached when the tide is very low is called *langadal*, in *Uist rochd.*—(DMC) In *Loch Ewe* red tangle is called *feamainn dearg* and *barra-stamh.*—(DU) All seaweed cast ashore is called when in a heap on beach *bruchd*, otherwise it is *feamainn churra*. The very same seaweed if cut from the rock by hand is called *feamainn ghearrta.*—(DMy)]
————, *pr.pt.* a' feamnadh, *v.a.* Manure with seaweed. 2 (DMC) Carrying the seaweed from the shore to the land. A' feamnadh an fhearainn, *manuring the land.*
————-bhalgainn,§ *s.f.* Knotted seaweed, bladder-wrack—*fucus nodosus.*

feamainn-bhuidhe,§ see feamainn-bhalgainn. 2 Applied to all olive-coloured kinds of seaweed.
——— -bhuilgeanach, see feamainn-bhalgainn.
——— -cheilp,(AH) *s.f.* see f— -bhuidhe.
——— -chìr, see feamainn-chìrean.
——— -chireag, see feamainn-chirean.
——— -chirean, *s.f.* Channelled fucus—*fucus canaliculatus.* The short crisp seaweed near high-water mark.
——— -chireineach, see feamainn-chirean.
feamainn-chura, *s.f.* Seaweed cast ashore when ripe, ripe seaweed.
——— -dearg, *s.f.* All the red kinds of seaweed.
——— -dubh,§ *s.f.* Serrated seaweed—*fucus serratus.* 2 All the dark green kinds of seaweed.
——— -phuil, *s.f.* Decomposed seaweed, used to manure the ground after it had become rotten.
———each, -eiche, *a.* Abounding in seaweed. 2 Like seaweed.
feaman, -ain, -an, *s.m.* Tail, rump.¶
———ach,** *a.* Tailed. 2 Having a long tail. 3 Having a large rump.
———ach,** -aich, *s.f.* Quantity of sea-ware sea-ore or dulse. 2**Hind.
feamnach, *gen.sing.* of feamainn.
feamnadh, -aidh, *s. m.* Driving of sea-weed from the shore. 2 Manuring with seaweed. 3‡‡Disarranging.
feamrach, *Arran* for feamainn.
feamuinn, see feamainn.
fean, see feun.
feannach,** *a.* Rough, hairy, as a quadruped.
feanachas,** -ais, *s.m.* Genealogy.
feanadh, see feun.
feann, *a.* Shortening or growing less by degrees. Mar chloich a' ruith le gleannan tha feasgar f. foghair, *like a stone running down glen is the shortening autumn evening.*
feann, *pr.pt.* a' feannadh, *v.a.* see fionn.
feannad, *s.m.* The surface "peat," as opposed to "dubh-fhad," the second or lowest "peat," So called from fionn,*white*, now obsolete here, it not being so black as the under peat from the presence in it of grass roots—*Suth'd.* 2 (DMC) The turf covering the peat.
feannadh, -aidh, *s. m. & pr. pt.* of feann, see fionnadh.
feannag, -aige, -an, *s.f.* ¶Carrion-crow—*corvus corone.* 2** Rook. 3 Rig, a ridge of ground generally used for growing potatoes, and sometimes also for raising corn, the seed being laid on the surface and covered with earth dug out of trenches along both sides. The term "lazy-bed" applied to it in English is merely a southern odium on the system of farming in Gaeldom, where soil was scarce, and where bog-land could not be cultivated in any other way. Gheibheadh tu na feannagan-fìrich, *you would find the forest crows*—said to persons who boast of doing impracticable things; ars' an seòladair anns a' chrannaig—"tha e ro mhòr do fheannaig, agus ro bheag do fhearainn," *quoth the sailor in the cross-trees—"it is too much for a rig and too little for a lot."* This sentence is translated in Campbell's *West Highland Tales* "it is too big for a crow, and too little for land." A.F. gives a modern application of this saying from personal experience, which makes the meaning clearer, and as he narrowly escaped with his life on the occasion, the words and their application are indelibly fixed in his memory. When out fishing in the Sound of Sleat, in his youth, and overtaken by a storm, an old fisherman who was at the helm told the boys who were rowing to keep a sharp look-out for land, as the evening twilight was fast failing. One of the latter suddenly cried out "Chì mi feannagan A Néill! tha sinn faisg air a' Chill bhig." After taking a deliberate survey (no easy matter in the circumstances), N. replied "Cha'n 'eil fhios am an e, 'illean, tha e ro mhór de dh' fheannag agus ro bheag do dh' fhearran, ach dh' fhaodadh gur e an t-eilean mór a th' ann," (I don't know, boys, it seems too big for a rig and too small for the land, but perhaps it's the large island)—which it was.

305. Feannag. *306. Feannag-ghlas.*

feannag,** *s.f.* Whiting.
feannagach, -aiche, *a.* Of, or pertaining to carrion crows; or 2 Rigs.
feannag-fhìreach,(AF) *s.f.* Forest-crow.
feannag-ghlas,¶ *s.f.* Hoodie—*corvus cornix.* 2** Carrion crow.
feannag-uisge,¶ *s.f.* see gobha-uisge.
feannaidh, *fut. aff. a.* of feann. see fionnaidh.
feannan *a.* see feann.
feannar, *v. & a.* see fionnar.
———achd,* *Cantyre* for fionnarachd.
———aich, see fionnaraich.
feanndag, -aige, -an, *s.f.* see deanntag.
———ach, -aiche, *a.* see deanntagach.
——— -Ghreugach, see deanntag-Ghreugach.
feannsair,** *s.m.* Gaelic spelling of *fencer.* 2 (DC) Bullying fellow.
———eachd,** *s. f. ind.* Fencing, sword-playing.
feanntach,(DU) *s.m.* Turf taken off peat-bog before commencing to cut peats.
fè'ar, -aire, *a.* see fèathail.
fèar, *s.m.* see feur.
†fear, *a.* see feàrr.
fear, *s.m.* Man. 2 Husband. 3 Any object or person of the masculine gender. 4 Male.
Thus declined:

Indefinite.

N.	*Sing.*	fear,	*Plur.*	fir,
G.		fir,		fhear,
D.		fear,		fearaibh,
V.		fhir!		fheara!

Definite.

N.	*Sing.*	am fear,	*Plur.*	na fir,
G.		an fhir,		nam fear,
D.		(do) 'n fhear,		(do) na fearaibh,

[Firibh, given by ** as *dat. pl.* is wrong.]

Cath an fhir mhóir, *the hero's battle;* fear dhiubh, *one of them*; an torc a lot t' fhear, *the boar that wounded thy husband;* am Fear Math, *God—Arran*; am fear dona, *the devil—Arran;* am f. mór, *the devil—Argyll, Skye, Uist;* mac an fhir mhóir, *a son of the devil;* an fear mór port no port a gheibh sibh bhuam an nochd, *de'il a tune will you get from me to-night;* am fear ud, *the devil—Uist;* am fear ud troidh *de'il a foot.* [Generally used to signify *a single* or *individual man*, in contradistinction to duine, which means *a human being*. Tha aon dhiubh seo aig gach fear, *every man (but not woman) has one of these;* tha aon aig gach duine, *every man (and woman) has one.*

Compound words beginning with fear, form their plural with *fir* when men only are intended, but with *luchd* when women as well as men may be included, as, fear-ciùil, *pl.* luchd-ciùil, *musicians.*

f.-ain-cheairt, *a buffoon, puppet.*
f.-ainneirt, *a tyrant.*
f.-airm, *a soldier.*
f.-aiseig, *a ferryman.*
f.-amhairc, fir-a—, *an overseer.* 2 *scout.*
f.-an-taighe, *the "goodman" of the house.*
f.-astair,** *a traveller, pedestrian.*
f.-baile, *a farm-tenant.* f. a'-bhaile, *the farm-tenant.* 2 *tacksman, one allowed to sub-let his land.*
f.-bainnse, *a bridegroom;* f. na bainnse, *the bridegroom.*
f.-ballain, *a cupper.*
f.-bàta, *a boatman.*
f.-bogha,* *an archer.*
f.-brataich, *an ensign (officer's rank.)* 2 *a standard-bearer.*
f.-brath, *a spy, traitor.*
f.-brionsgail, *a dreamer.*
f.-brosgail, *a flatterer.*
f.-buitseachd, *a wizard, sorcerer.*
f.-caidridh, *an accompanier.*
f.-cartach, *a carter.*
f.-casaid, *an accuser.*
f.-casaidh, *an assailant.*
f.-cèaird, *a tradesman, mechanic, artificer, travelling tinsmith.*
f.-cheistean, *a catechist.*
f.-cinnidh, *a kinsman, clansman.*
f.-chrìochnachaidh, *a finisher.*
f.-chur, *a champion.*
f.-ciùil, *a musician.*
f.-ciùird, see f.-cèaird.
f.-cluig, *a bell-man.*
f.-cobhair, *a helper.*
f.-cogaidh, *a soldier.*
f.-coghnaidh, see f.-còmhnaidh.
f.-coimhid, *a watchman, scout, overseer.*
f.-còmhnaidh, *a contributor, helper.* 2 *dweller.*
f.-comaraidh, *a patron.*
f.-comuinn, fir-chomuinn, *an associate.*
f.-connspaid, *a wrangler.*
f.-cosnaidh, *a worker, working man, bread-winner for a family.*
f.-cuairt, fir-chuairt, *a sojourner, visitor, tourist.*
f.-cuideachaidh, *a helper.*
f.-cuideachd, fir-ch—, *a buffoon; droll, jovial companion, bottle companion.*
f.-cuidich, *a helper, assistant.*
f.-cuir, *a sower.*
f.-cuiridh, *an inviter.*
f.-cùirn, *an outlaw.* 2 *absconder.*
f.-cùl-chàinidh, *a slanderer.*
f.-cumaidh, *an artificer, former, framer.*
f.-cumail suas, *a sustainer.*
f.-cunntais, *an accountant.*
f.-dàin *or* f.-dàna, *pl.* fir-dhàin *or* fir-dhàna, *a poet.*
f.-dàna *an adventurer.*
f.-deasboireachd, *a debater.*
f.-deilbhe, *an artificer, artist.*
f.-dìona, *a defendant.*
f.-droch-bheairt, *an evil doer.*
f.-duan, see under f.-fuinn.
f.-eadhlain, *an artisan.*
f.-eadraiginn, *a reconciler.*
f.-faire, fir-fhaire, *a watchman, sentinel, sentry.* F.-faire na h-aon sùla, *the one-eyed watcher*—a legendary character.
f.-farcluaise, *an eavesdropper.*
f.-fàsaich, *an ascetic.*
f.-fasgnaidh, *a fanner.*
f.-feachd, *a soldier.*
f.-fearainn, *a landed proprietor.*
f.-fiacha, *a creditor.*
f.-foghluim, *a teacher.*
f.-fòirneirt, *an oppressor, robber, violator.*
f.-fritheil, see f.-frithealaidh.
f.-frithealaidh, *an attendant.*
f.-fuadain, fir-fhuadain, *an outcast, fugitive, straggler, vagabond, exile.*
f.-fuinn, *a chorus-man*, one of a band of men who went about singing carols. Their leader was called *fear-duan.*
f.-gairm-cùirte, *a court crier.*
f.-gleidhidh, *a keeper.*
f.-gnìomha, *a workman.*
f.-gu-breith, *a dictator or judge* (Cæsar's "Vergobretus," appointed by the Gael of old to take supreme command in case of emergency against a common enemy—*Gàidheal*, ii, 129.
f.-iasachd, *a borrower.*
f.-innleachd, fir-innleachd, *an artist, engineer, ingenious person.*
f.-innsidh, *a teller.*
f.-iomachair, *a bearer.*
f.-iomaill, *an accolent.*
f.-ionaid, *an agent, attorney.* 2 *lieutenant.*
f.-ionaid rìgh, *a viceroy.*
f.-iùil, *a pilot.* 2 *a guide.*
f.-labhairt, fir-l—, *a speaker, spokesman.*
f.-lagha, *pl.* fir-l— &, luchd-l—, *a lawyer.*
f.-làimh-chèirde, fir-l—, *an artist.* 2 *artisan, mechanic.*
f.-laoidh, *a hymnist.*
f.-leisgeul, *an excuser.*
f.-na-fàrdaich, *the host of the house.*
f.-nuadh-pòsda, *a bridegroom.*
f.-oibre, luchd-oibre, *an artisan, artificer.*
f.-pòsda, fir-phòsda, *a bridegroom.* 2 *married man, husband.*
f.-ràiteachais, *a boaster.*
f.-réite, *a reconciler.*
f.-riachaid, *a steward.*
f.-riaghlaidh, *a magistrate, ruler, governor, overseer.*
f.-rùin, *a confidant.*
f.-sanais, *an advertiser.*
f.-saoraidh, *a redeemer.*
f.-sàrachaidh, *an oppressor.*
f.-seòlaidh, fir-sheòlaidh, *a director, guide, steerer, helmsman.*
f.-sgrìobhaidh, fir-sgrìobhaidh, *a writer.*
f.-sgrùdaidh, fir-sgrùdaidh, *a searcher, scrutinizer.* 2 *critic.*
f.-siubhail, fir-shiubhail, *a traveller.*
f.-solar-lòin, *a caterer.*
f.-sodail, *a flatterer.*
f.-stiùraidh, fir-stiùraidh, *a steersman, regulator, guide.*
f.-suilbheachd, *an overseer.*
f.-suiridh, fir-shuiridh, *a sweetheart, wooer.*
f.-sùl, & f.-sul-bheachd, *an observer.*
f.-tagair, see f.-tagraidh.
f.-tathaich, *a visitor.*
f.-tagraidh, *a pleader, defender, pursuer.* 2 *advocate.*
f.-taighe, *a husband.*
f.-tàimh, *an abider.*

f.-tàmna, see f.-tàimh.
f.-talaich, *a grumbler.*
f.-tathuinn, *a barker.*
f.-teòma, *an artist.*
f.-togalach, *a bearer.* 2 *uplifter.* 3 *a builder.*
f.-togal-fuinn, *a precentor, leader of a choir.*
f.-tuaileis, *a backbiter.*
f.-tuiniche, *an abider.*
f.-turuis, fir-thuruis, *a wayfaring man, traveller.*
f.-uibe, *a wizard.*
f.-uidhe, *a traveller.* 2 *pedestrian.*
f.-ùmhlaidh, *an amercer.*
f.-urrais, *a surety.*‡
fear,* *v.a.* Follow, as a chief. 2 Claim kindred with. A' dh'aindeoin có a dh' fhearas ort, *in defiance of any person that will take your part.*
——ach,** *s. m.* War-cry among the ancient Irish.
——ach, *a.* †Wild.
——achail,(DMC) *a.* Manly, brave.
——achas, -ais, *s.m.* **Adultness, manhood. 2 *Act of claiming kindred or siding with. 3 Following, as a chief. 4 see fearalachd. 5** Membrum virile. Mar leòghann le f., *like a lion for boldness.*
——achas-taighe,** *s.m.* Frugality.
——achd, *s.f.ind.* Feat of manhood. 2 Power, strength. 3 Manliness.
——achdain,* see fearachas.
fearachlais-ùrlair, *s. m.* Folding screen, fire-screen.
fearaid,** -ean, *s.f.* Gaelic spelling of *ferret.*
fearail, -ala, *a.* Manly, masculine. 2 Brave. 3 ‡‡Mighty. Gu f., *courageously.*
fearain, see fearan.
fearainn, *gen.sing.* of fearann.
†fearach,** *a.* Wild.
fearalachd, *s.f.ind.* Manliness, courage, boldness. 2 Activity, vivacity
fearalas, -ais, *s.m.* Same meanings as fearalachd.
†fearamhachd, *s.f.ind.* Force, might, power.
†fearamhalachd, see fearamhachd.
fearan, -ain, -an, *s.m.dim.* of fear. Mannikin, little man.
fèaran, *s.m.* see feuran. 2 (AC) Dove, stock-dove, wood-pigeon. F.-eidheann, *turtle-dove.*
fearanach, *a.* Abounding in little men.
fearan-breac, } (AF) *s.m.* Turtle-dove, see
fearan-eidheann, } turtur.
†fearanda, *s.m.* Countryman, boor, farmer.
fearann, -ainn, *s.m.* [*s.f.* in *Badenoch.*] Land, country. 2 Estate. 3 Farm. 4**Earth, land, in contradistinction to water. F. saor, *freehold land ;* f. bàn, *lea-ground,* 2 *vacant* (i. e. temporarily unoccupied) *land ;* f. treabhta, *ploughed land ;* f. àlainn na h-Eireann, *the fair country of Ireland ;* f. tioram, *dry land ;* ann am f. fàs, *in a desert land ;* f. comhroinn, *suburbs;* f. oighreachd, *a manor ;* f. coillteach, *wood-land ;* f. dlighe, *manor.*
fearannach, -aiche, *a.* Of, or pertaining to land. 2 Agricultural.
fearannail, *a.* see fearannach.
fearann tuatha, *s.m.* Ancient Celtic tribeland customs, known later as the "run-rig system." By it there was no individual or isolated tenure. The peasantry lived in a village or township, and the surrounding lands and pasture were held, the latter in common, and the former—the cultivated part—was divided every year under the supervision of a village officer called "maor," and in later times "constable."
fearanta, *a.* Masculine.

fearas, *Suth'd* for furasda.
fearas, -ais, *s. m.* see fearachd & fearachas. F., *art of ;* eòlas, *science of.*
†——adh, -aidh, *s.m.* Imitation.
†——air, -ean, *s.m.* Imitator, mimic.
†——aireachd,** *s.f.* Mimicry.
fear-asal, -ail, -an, *s.m.* Male ass.
fearas-bogha,** *s.m.* (Art of) archery.
——— -chlaidheamh, *s.m.* Sword-combat, gladitorial combat—*Dàin I. Ghobha.*
——— -chuideachd, *s.f.* Diversion, wit, raillery, joking. Ri f., *joking.* (art of company.)
——— -dana,‡‡ *s.m.* Poetry.
——— -taighe, *s. f.* Domestic economy, house management. 2**Husbandry, croft management.
†fearb,** *s.f.* Cow. 2 Excrescence. 3 Pimple. 4 Goodness. 5 Word.
fearban,** -ain, *s.m.* Crowfoot (plant.)
fear-bhoc,(AF) *s.m.* Hare.
fearbholg,** -bhuilg, *s.m.* Scabbard, sheath. 2 Budget.
fear-bhuilleach, -iche, *a.* Manly in action. 2 Inflicting manly blows.
fear-boc, *s.m.* Roebuck.
fear-bréige, *s. m.* Puppet. 2 Heap of stones, used as a landmark.
fear-chù, *s.m.* Greyhound. 2 Male fox. 3 Male dog.
fear-choinean, *pl.* fir-ch—, *s.m.* Buck-rabbit.
fear-cuir, see feur-cuir.
feardha,* *a.* see fearail. Clann fh. tapaidh, *a brave and active clan.*
feardhachd,** *s.f.* Bravery. 2 Manliness, manhood.
feardhalach, see fearail.
————d, *s.f.* Manhood.
fear-feòirne, fir-fheòirne, *s. m.* Die. 2 Chessman. 3 Draughts-man.
fearg, feirge, *s. f.* Anger, rage, ire, passion, wrath, displeasure. F. dhoinionnach, *stormy wrath ;* a' cur feirg' air, *irritating* or *provoking him ;* am feirg, *in a passion, furious ;* 'nuair a thraoghas 'fhearg, *when his passion subsides.* [** gives *s.m.* and *gen.sing.* feirg.]
fearg,** *s.m.* Passionate person. 2 Warrior, champion.
fearg,** *v.a.* Irritate. 2 Provoke, incite.
feargach, -aiche, *a.* Angry, passionate, enraged. 2* Furious, outrageous. 3 Raging. 4 Irritated. 5 Causing irritation. 'San doinionn fheargaich, *in the raging storm ;* an dà rìgh feargach, *the two kings in a passion ;* duine f., *a passionate man.*
————adh, -aidh, *s.m.* Irritating, making angry. 2 Irritating, as of an ulcer, irritation. A' f—, *pr.pt.* of feargaich.
————as,‡‡ -ais, *s.m.* Cholericness.
————d, *s.f.ind.* Anger, heat, passion. 2 Irritation, irritableness. 3 Moodiness.
feargaich, *v.a.* Provoke, fret. 2**Vex, enrage, anger. 3 Fester.
fear-ghleus, -eòis, -an, *s.m.* Manly achievement.
————ach, -aiche, *a.* Of, or pertaining to, manly achievements.
feargnachadh,(AH) -aidh, *s.m.* Fighting, striving, or contending against a superior force with perseverance and pluck.
feargnadh,‡ -aidh, *s.m.* Provocation.
fearg-thàmailt, -ean, *s.f.* Indignation.
———— each, -iche, *a.* Indignant.
fear-iasg, *s.m.* Male fish.
fèarlagan,(CR) *s.m.* Field mouse—*W. of Ross.*
feàrna,§ *s. f.* Alder—*alnus glutinosa.* 2 Old name for the letter F. 3 Shield. 4**Mast. Leis am bristear gach f., *by whom every shield shall be broken ;* cabar feàrna, *a rung*

or rafter of alder; is diu teine f. ùr, *new alder, worst of fuel;* cliath-fh-, *a wattle made of alder;* gach fiodh as a bhun, ach am f. as a bhàrr, (*split*) *all wood from the top, but alder from the root.* [*Not* elder, as gven by **.]

307. Feàrn.

feàrnach,** *a.* Aldern, abounding in, or made of alder.
fearnaidh,** *a.* Masculine.
fear-nimhe, *s.m.* Serpent. [*lit.* the poisonous one. Preceded by the art. *am.*]
†fearndi, *gen.* of feàrn. 2 Buckler.
fear-ogha, -oghachan, *s.m.* Grandson.
fèarr, *comp.* of *a.* math. Better, best. 2 Preferable. 'S fhèarr dhuit falbh, *you had better go*; an fh. dhomh falbh? 's fhearr, *had I better be going? yes*; b' fh. leam, *I had rather, I prefer.*
fearra,(AF) *s.* Cow not milking.
fèarrad,** -aid, *s.m.* Improvement, amelioration. 2 Convalescence. 3(DC) Good quality. 'S e f. na h-acfhuinn a thug roimhe e, *the good quality of the gear brought it through*; a' dol am f., *getting better.*
feàrra-dhris,§ -e, -ean, *s.f.* Bramble-briar, dog-briar, dog-rose, see ròs-nan-con.
fearra-ghlòir, see earra-ghlòir.
fearraid, Gaelic spelling of *ferret.*
fearrasaid,* *s.f.* see earrasaid. 2 see fearsaid. 3**Tunic, Roman jacket.
fèarrdachd,‡‡ *s.f.ind.* see fèairrdeachd.
fearrdhalach, -aiche, see fearail.
feàrr-shion, *s.* Rain.
fearsach,** *a.* Full of little ridges in the sand.
fearsa, Gaelic spelling of *verse.*
†fearsad, *s.m.* Estuary, sandbank.
feàrsaid, -ean, *s.f.* Spindle. [The spindle is for winding thread, the ring on it to weight it, so that it may gather momentum when twirled between the thumb and fingers.] 2 Axle of a cycle. 3 Dart. 4 Spear -shaft. 5‡‡ Sand-pit. 6‡‡Wallet. F. na làimhe, *one of the bones of the fore-arm, the ulna.*
fearsaideag,§ -eige, -an, *s. f.* Thrift, sea-gilly-flower, rocket—*cavile maritimum.*
†fearsaidh, -an, *s.m.* Sage, wise man.
fearsan, see fearsa.
†fearsda, -n, *s.f.* Pool, standing water.
fear-shionn, see fearthainn.
feart, -airt, *s.f.* Attention, notice, carefulness, heed. 2 Predicate in *grammar.* †3 Grave. Na toir f. air, *do not heed him.*

308. Feàrsaid

——, -a, -an, [*pl.* in *Suth'd* also feartainn,] *s.m.* Virtue, inherent quality. 2 Efficacy. 3 Attribute, repute. 4 Miracle. 5 Country, land. †6 Grave, tomb. 7 Field. 8 Fair-green. 9‡‡ Action, deed. 10**Forces, host. Le f. do fhrasaibh blàtha, *by the virtue of thy warm showers*; feartan buairidh, *tempting qualities*; Dia nam feart, *God of (many) attributes.*
feartach, -aiche, *a.* Full of virtue or energy. 2 Effectual. 3 Virtuous, reputable, renowned. 4 Infinitive (of mood in *grammar.*) 5 Substantial. 6**Powerful, having forces. 7 Valorous. Toradh f., *substantial crops.*
feartag,(CR) *s.f.* Thrift, sea-pink—*W. of Ross.* [not fearsaideag there.]
feartaich,** *v.a.* Accomplish.
————te, *past pt.* Accomplished.
feartail, -ala, *a.* Reputable. 2 Valorous. 3 **Miraculous, wonder-working. 4* Having good qualities.
†feartaille, *s.m.* Funeral oration.
feartalachd, *s.f.ind.* Efficacy, virtue, energy. 2 Miraculous quality.
feartan, *n.pl.* of feart.
feartas, -ais, *s.m.* Manly conduct.
feart-bhriathar, -air, -thran, see for-bhriathar.
feart-bhriathrach, -aiche, see for-bhriathrach.
feart-fhacal, *s.m.* Adjective.
feart-ghràbh, *s.m.* Epitaph.
fearthainn, *s.f.* Rain. 2 (AF) see feartuinn.
——————each, -iche, *a.* Rainy.
†feart-laoidh, -ean, *s.f.* Epitaph.
feart-mholadh, -aidh, -aidhean, *s.f.* Funeral oration. 2 Panegyric, epitaph.
feartuinn,(AF) *s.f.* Salmon.
†feas, see fios.
†——ach, see fiosach.
†fèasag, see feusag.
feasan,§ *s.m.* Adder's tongue fern, see lus-na-nathrach.
feascorluch, see feasgar-luch.
feascradh, -aidh, *s.m.* Shrivelling. 2 Decaying.
feasd, see am feasd.
feasdrach,** -aich, *s.m.* Muzzle. 2 Bridle-bit.
feasgal,** -ail, *s.m.* Gaelic spelling of *fiscal.*
————aiche, *s.m.* Herald.
feasgand, see feusgann.
feasgar, -air, -graichean, *s.m.* Afternoon, evening. Air f., *on an evening;* beul an fh., *the evening twilight*; mìr f., *an evening meal.*
————ach, -aich, *a.* Of, or pertaining to, the afternoon or evening, vespereal. 2**Late.
————an, -ain, *s.m.* Vesper, evening-song.
———— -luch, *s.f.* Dor-mouse. 2 Field-mouse. 3**Cockchafer. 4**Beetle.
†feas-ghlanadh, -aidh, -aidhean, *s.m.* Gargarism.
†feasgor, -oir, *s.m.* Separation.
fèasog, see feusag.
————ach, -aiche, see feusagach.
feasradh,(DU) *Gairloch* for easradh.
feastrach, -aich, -aichean, *s. f.* Muzzle. 2 Bridle, bit.
fèath, -a, -an, *s. m.* [*f.* in *Argyll* amd some other parts.] Calm, tranquillity. 2 Learning, skill, knowledge. 3 Gentle breeze. 4 ** see féith. 5‡‡Bog. Thàinig f. oirnn, *we were becalmed;* tràth thig am f., *when the calm comes*; tha 'n oidhche 'na f., *the night is a dead calm*; fhuair e f., *he got a respite, his fever abated a little;* f. dubh *or* f. geal, *a perfect calm;* finn-fhèath, *a perfect calm—Lewis;* glag fh., *a dead calm—Uist.* [see note under fèath-nan-eun.]
featha,(AC) *s.m.* Moorland. F. fada farsuing, *the moorland far and wide.*
fèathach,(DU) *a.* Calm.
feathachan,†† -ain, see feothachan.
fèathail, -ala, *a.* Calm, still, quiet.
†feathadh, -aidh, *s.m.* Sight.
†feathal, -ail, *s. m.* Bowl. 2 Cup. 3 Fur. 4 Face, countenance. 5 Figure.
fèathalachd, *s.f.* Calmness, stillness, quietness
fèathamhlachd, see fèathalachd.
fèathamhuil, see fèathail.

fèathan, -ain, *s.m.* Fur, hair.
fèathanach,** *a.* Having fur, hairy.
fèath-ghàire,†† *s. m.* Smile.
fèath-nan-eun, *s.m.* Calmness. **Fèath nan eun mar sgàthan**, *as calm as a mirror.* **Fèath nan eun fionn**, in the tale Gaisgeach na sgéithe deirge, is a euphemism for a hurricane. In some districts, the phrase means a perfect calm, the *fèath geal* of the sea-folk, and the *fèath dubh* of the hill-folk.
†**féathsgaoileadh**, -eidh, *s m.* Palsy.
†**fed**, *s.m.* Narrative, relation.
†**fed**, *a.* Hard, difficult.
†**feibh**, *s.f.* Riches, goods. 2 Long life.
†**fèich**, -e, -ean, *s.f.* Sinew, see féith.
féich, *gen.* of fiach.
feichd, Gaelic form of *effect.*
féicheadair, see féichnear.
féicheamh, -eimh, see féichnear. 2 Debt.
————ach, *a.* Pertaining to a debt.
féicheamhnach, -aich, see féichnear.
féicheanas, (MMcL) *s.m.* Friendly dispute.
féicheannach, -aich, see féichnear.
féichnean, *n.pl.* of fiach.
féichnear, -eir, -eirean, *s.m.* Debtor. [Abbreviated Fr.=Dr.]
féichnibh, *dat.pl.* of fiach.
feideag, see feadag.
féidh, *gen. sing. & n. pl.* of fiadh.
féidh-fheòil, (CR) *s.f.* Venison—*W. of Ross.*
féidheil, see féidh-fheòil.
féidhich, *s.pl.* Deer.
féidhmealachd, see feumalachd.
féidhmeil, see feumail.
†**feidil**,** *a.* Gaelic form of *faithful.*
†**feidir**, *a.* Able, possible.
†———, *s.* Power, possibility.
†**feigh**,** *s.f.* see feith. 2 *a.* Bloody, sharp.
feighe, *s.m.* Warrior, champion. 2 Top of a house. 3 Hill, mountain. 4**Slaughterer.
feighreag, -an, see oighreag.
feilbheachan, (MMcL) *s.m.* Ear-ring.
féild, -e, -ean, *s.f.* see filleadh. [* says "a philosopher—*Irish.*"]
féile, *gen.sing.* of fial. Talla na f., *the hall of of hospitality*; Righ na f., *the King of promise (Christ)*; cridhe na féile, *the liberal soul.* [Also used as *nom. (f.)* Is dona 'n fhéile 'chuireas duine fhéin air an iomairt, *it's an unhappy generosity that drives a man to his shifts.*]
féile, -achan, *s.m.* see féileadh.
†**feile**, *s.f.* Charm, incantation.
feile, (AC) *a.* Grassy. Faileagan f. fo 'r casan, *grassy meads beneath your feet.*
†**feileacan**, (AF) *s.m.* Butterfly, may-bug.
féileach, -liche, *a.* see fialaidh.
————an, *n.pl.* of féile or féileadh.
————d, *s.f.* see fialaidheachd.
féileadh, -lidh, -leachan, [*pl.* féilidhean—*W. of Ross.*] *s. m.* The kilt, that part of the dress of the Gael from the waist to the knee.
féileadh-beag, -idh-bhig, -eachan-beaga, *s. m.* The kilt in its modern form.
féileadh-bhreacain,** *s. m.* The kilted plaid. This consisted of twelve yards or more, of narrow tartan, which was wrapped round the middle, and hung down to the knees. It was most frequently fastened round the middle by a belt, and then it was called "breacan-an-fhéilidh," or "féileadh-bhreacain." The breacan, or plaid part of this article of dress, was, according to occasion, wrapped round the shoulders, or fastened on the left shoulder with a brooch (bràisd) of gold, silver or steel, according to the wealth of the wearer. By this arrangement there was nothing to impede the free use of the sword-arm.
féileadh-mór, -idh-mhòir, -leachan-móra, *s. m.* The kilt in its primitive form, consisting of one piece, generally of tartan, covering, when spread, the whole body, and girt round the waist.
feileag,** -eig, *s.f.* Honeysuckle.
———an,** *s.m.* Butterfly. 2 Diminutive person.
féileas,** -eis, *s.m.* Trifle. 2 Vanity. Luchd féileis, *triflers.*
———ach,** *a.* Frivolous, vain. Gu f., *frivolously.*
féileasachd,** *s.f.* Frivolousness. 2 Vanity.
féile-faraich, *s.* Unexpected encounter, unlooked-for meeting, accident. 'N déis na b' eudar dhomh 'ghabhail le féile-faraich de 'n dram, *what I was compelled to receive, owing to an unlooked-for drain of drink—Duanaire, 187.*
†**feilfios**, *s.m.* Secondsight.
féill, -e, -ean & -tean, *s.f.* Feast, festival. 2 Fair, market. 3 Holiday. 4**Vigil of a festival. 5**Banquet whereat the chief presided. 6**Company at such a banquet. F. an roid, or f. roid, *the autumnal equinox, rood-day*; làithean f., *holydays*, also *days of folly*; cum an fh. air an là, *keep the festival on the right day*—very seasonable advice at the present time, when owing to the completion of the 19th. century there is now an additional day between the Old and New Styles, (New Year's Day Old Style now being Jan 14th.) and in some parts of Gaeldom the dates of festivals being still kept according to 19th. century Old Style reckoning, there are three styles in use at present! "Cum 'an fh. air an là," also signifies *pay* or *keep the engagement on the stipulated day.* [Féill does not aspirate a proper noun following in Scotland, although it does in Ireland.] Féill Brìde, *February—Arran*; F. Bealltainn, *May—Arran.* Eadar Nollaig 's F. roid, eadar F. roid 's F. Briain, =*all the year round.*
féill-bhliadhnail, *s.f.* Anniversary.
féill-Brìde, *s.f.* Candlemas. [Preceded by the art. AN FH—] Là fh.-Brìde, *Candlemas day.*
féilleachadh, -aidh, *s.m.* Keeping of holidays or holydays.
féilleachd,** *s.f.* Festivity.
féilleil, *a.* (DU) Desirable, much sought-after, valuable. 2 (PM) Marketable. Beathach f., *a marketable beast.*
féill-Eòin, ** *s.f.* St. John's day or feast. [Preceded by the art. AN FH—.]
féillire, -an, *s. m.* Almanac.
féill-Martuinn,** *s.f.* Martinmas. [Preceded by the art. AN FH—.]
féill-Micheil, *s.f.* Michaelmas. [Preceded by the art. AN FH—.]
féill-nan-rìgh,** *s.f.* Epiphany.
féill-Samhna,‡‡ *s.m.* All Hallows. [Preceded by the art. AN FH—.]
féillteach, *a*, see féilteach.
————d, see féilteachd.
féilteach, -iche, *a.* Of, or belonging to, fairs or markets. 2**Hospitable. 3**Festal. 4** Fond of feasting.
————d, *s.f.ind.* Feasting, festivity. 2 Keeping of holidays or holydays. 3**Hospitableness.
feilteag,** -eige, *s.f.* Cód.
feiltire, see feillire.
féim, -eannan, *s.m.* see feum.
feim,** *s.f.* Woman, female, wife.
——each, -iche, *a.* see feumach.
——each, -ich, *s.m.* see feumach.
——ean,** -ein, *s.m.* The feminine gender.

fèin, *pers.pron.* Self. Used only as an adjunct to nouns or other pronouns. Mi-fhèin, *myself*; thu-fhèin, *thyself*; iad-fhèin, *themselves*. When combined with a possessive pronoun it may be translated by *own*, as mo mhac-fèin, *my own son*; siod fhèin e mar iolair, *that same is he, like an eagle*; mar seo fhèin, *in this very way*; an seo fhèin, *in this very place*; an sin fèin, *then and there*; an diugh fèin, *this very day*; 'cheana fèin, *already*; cha'n fhaigh duine an t-uisge fèin 'san àite seo gun a cheannach, *one cannot get even water here without paying for it*; is duine dona gun fheum, a chuireadh cuireadh orm fhèin is caitheamh, *he is a pitiful fellow who would invite me and leave me to pay*—a strange use of *fèin*.

It is a peculiarity of the Northern dialect of Gaelic that it makes a distinction in the pronunciation of *fèin* when that word is used with the first personal pronoun. Generally it is *fhìn* in that connection, as, mi-fhìn, sinn-fhìn, orm-fhìn—thu fhèin 's mi-fhìn. In *Suth'd* from Strathy Water to Durness, instead of either *fhèin* or *fhìn* with the first person, they say *fhèin*, mi-fhèan, &c., and in the remainder of Strathy and in the S.E. of the county, they say fhian, mi-fhian, leam-fhian, sinn-fhian, ni mi mo sheunadh fhian, *I will charm myself*. In other connections the word is *fhèin* in the North, as it is in all connections in the South.

fèin, -e, *s.f.* Selfishness.
fèin-agartach,** *a.* Full of compunction, remorseful.
fèin-agartas,** -ais, *s.m.* Self-reproach, compunction, remorse. Saor o fh.. *free from self-reproach*.
fèin-aicheadh, *s.m.* Self-denial.
fèin-bharalachd, *s.f.ind.* Positiveness.
fèin-bheachd, *s.f.* Self-conceit.
fèin-chiontach, -aiche, *a.* Self-reproached.
†**feine**, *s.m.* Boor, ploughman, farmer.
fèineachas, -ais, *s.f.* see fèinealachd. 2**History. 3**Genealogy.
fèineachd, *s.f.* Personality, egotism.
fèinealachd, *s.f.ind.* Selfishness.
fein-eallach,(AF)*s.m.*Cattle given in restitution.
fèinear,** -eir, *s.m.* Egotist.
feinecreasadh,(AF) *s.m.* Ferret.
fèineil, -eala, *a.* Selfish, self-interested.
fèin-fhios, *s.m.* Consciousness. 2**Experience, knowledge acquired by experience.
——————ach, *a.* see fèin-fhiosrach.
——————rach, -aiche, *a.* Conscious. 2 Experienced. Tha mi f. air, *I am conscious of it.*
——————rachadh, -aidh, *s. m.* Consciousness, self-knowledge. 2 Experience.
——————rachd, *s.f.* see fèin-fhiosrachadh.
fèin-fhoghainteach, -tiche, *a.* Self-sufficient, self-confident.
——————————d, *s. f. ind.* Self-sufficiency, self-confidence.
fèin-fhoghainteas,-eis, see fèin-fhoghainteachd.
fèin-fhoghantas, -ais, see fèin-fhoghainteachd.
—— -ghabhaltas, -ais, *s.m.* Intrusion.
—— -ghluasach, -aiche, *a.* Automatic, automotous.
—— -ghluasad, -aid, -an, *s.m.* Self-motion.
—— -ghluasadach, see fèin-ghluasach.
—— -ghluasadh, -aidh, *a.* Automatous, self-moving.
—— -ghluaisear, -eir, -ean, *s.m.* Automaton.
—— -ghluas-rud,** *s.m.* Automaton. 2 Perpetuum mobile.
—— -ghràdh,** -ghràidh, *s.m.* Self-love. 2 Selfishness.
—— -ghràdhach,** -aiche, *a.* Selfish, self-interested. Fear f. *a self-interested man.*
fèin -irisiol, *a.* Humble, condescending.
—— -irisleachd, see fèin-irioslachd.
—— -irioslachd, *s.f.ind.* Condescension, humblemindedness.
feinistear, -eir, Gaelic spelling of French *fenestre*, a window.
fèin-mharbhadh, -aidh, see fèin-mhortadh.
—— -mheas, *s.f.* Self-conceit.
—— -mheasail,** *a.* Self-conceited, vain.
—— -mhort, see fèin-mhortadh.
—— -mhortadh, *s.m.* Suicide, act of self-murder.
—— -mhortail,** *a.* Suicidal.
—— -mhortair, -ean, *s.m.* Self-murderer,suicide.
—— -mhothachadh, -aidh, *s.m.* Conviction.
Fèinn, -e, *s.pl.* The Fingalians. 2 The country of the Fingalians, which included the greater part of Gaeldom.
fèinneachas,** *s.m.* Militia.
fèin-reubach, -aiche, *a.* Self-lacerating.
—— -riaghladh, -aidh, *s.m.* Continence.
—— -shealbhaich,** *v.a.* Possess by prescriptive right.
—— -smachd, see fèin-riaghladh.
—— -spèis, -e, *s.f.* Self-conceit, self-love, self-interest.
—— -spèiseil, -eala, *a.* Selfish, self-conceited, self-opinioned.
—— -thoil, -e, *s.f.* Arbitrament. 2**Self-will, wilfulness. Aoradh fèin-thoile, *will-worship.*
—— -thoileach, -eiche, *a.* see fèin-thoileil.
—— -thoileil, *a.* Arbitrary. 2** Self-willed, wilful, opinionative. 3 Spontaneous. Gun bhi f., *without being self-willed.*
—— -thoilich, *s.pl.* Voluntaries, in an ecclesiastical sense.
†**feir**, *s.f.* Bier.
†**fèird**, -e, -ean, *s.f.* Track or rut, made by wheels of a cart.
fèirdeachd, *s.f.* see fèairrdeachd.
feir-dhris, *s.* Bramble.
feireag, ‡ -eig, -an, *s.f.* Cloudberry, see oighreag.
feiread, -eid, Gaelic spelling of *ferret.*
feirg, *gen.sing.* of fearg.
feirgneachadh, see feargnachadh.
feirm, Gaelic spelling of *farm* or *form.*
feirmeal,(DMC) *s.m.* Boasting, bragging.
feirmealaiche,(DMC) *s. m.* Boaster, braggart, man of great professions.
feirmige, *s. m.* Ram with one of its testicles wanting—*Lewis.*
†**feirsde**,** *s.pl.* Pits or dibs of water on the sand at low tide.
fèirseag,(CR) *Arran* for feursann.
feirsidh,** *s.f.* Strength. 2 Courage.
feirt,** *s.f.* see fèird.
feis,(AF) *s.* Pig, swine.
fèis, see fèisd.
†**feis**, *s.f.* **Convocation. 2**Synod. 3** Carnal intercourse.
fèisd,§ *s.f.* Feast, as applied to grass—*festuca.*
——, *v.n.* Feast.
——, -e, -ean, *s. f.* Entertainment, feast, banquet. Là fèisde, *a feast-day.*
——e, *s.f.*(DMy) Tether for cattle, to keep them from the corn—*Lewis.*
——eachd, *s.f.ind.* Feasting, banqueting, entertainment.
fèisdear, -eir, -an, *s.m.* Entertainer.
fèisdeas, *s.m.* Entertainment, accommodation. F. oidhche, *a night's lodging.*
fèisdeil,** *a.* Feasting. 2 Hospitable.
fèisdeireachd,** *s.f.* Banqueting.
fèisdire, see fèisdear.
feiseag, -eig, *s.f.* see piseag.
fèist, see fèisd.

féisteas, see féisdeis.
féisteil, see féisdeil.
feith, *pr.pt.* a' feitheamh, *v.a. & n.* Wait, remain, stay, attend. F. requires the prep. *air*, or *ri*, simple or compounded, after it, as, f. air, *wait on*; f. rium, *wait for me.*
fèith, *s.f.* see fèath.
féith, -e, -ean, *s.f.* Sinew. 2 Vein. 3 *pl.* (féithichean—DMy) Rents in moor- or bog-land made by water. There is no grass in these hollows, and they look very like sinews at a distance—*Lewis.* An fh. a chrùb, *the sinew that shrank.*
——, -e, -eachan, [*gen.sing.* féithe, *pl.* féithichean—*Gairloch.*] *s.f.* Bog, quagmire, fen, moss. 2 Bog-channel. Am fear a bhitheas 's an fhéith, cuiridh a h-uile duine a chas air, *everyone puts his foot on (as a stepping-stone) him who sticks in the mud.*
feith,§ *s.f.* Honeysuckle, see uilleann. 2(AH) Relief, alleviation, easement. F. roimh 'n bhàs, *relief preceding death*; fhuair e f. ghasda, *he experienced a welcome relief.*
féith-chrùbadh, -aidh, *s.m.* Spasm, convulsion.
feithde, see feitheideach.
féitheach, -iche, *a.* Sinewy, nervous, tendonous, muscular. 2**Having large veins. 3**Boggy, marshy.
————an, *n.pl.* of féith (bog.)
————as, -ais, *s.m.* Nervousness.
————d, *s.f.ind.* Muscularity, wiriness.
feitheadh, see feitheamh.
feitheamh, -himh, *s.m.* Waiting, attending. 2 Expecting. 3 Attendance. 4**Delay, lingering. A' f—, *pr.pt.* of feith. A' f. ri gaoith, *waiting for a (favourable) wind*; a' f. am fàth, *lying in wait.*
————air, -ean, *s.m.* Overseer, watchman, waiter. 2‡‡Seer, augur.
féithean,** -ain, *s.m.* Sinew, tendon.
————ach, -aiche, *a.* Sinewy, muscular.
féithear, *a.* see féitheach.
feitheid,* *s.m.* Beast or bird of prey. 2 Vulture.
————each,* -aiche, *a.* Like a beast or bird of prey.
————each,*-ich, *s.m.* Person ready to pounce on anything, like a vulture or bird of prey. 2 (AF) Beast.
fèitheil, -eala, *a.* see fèathail. Oidhche fh., *a calm night.*
fèith-ghàire, *s.f.* see fèath-ghàire.
fèithich,** *v.* Becalm.
fèithid, see feitheid.
†feithil, *v.a.* Gather. 2 Keep.
feithis, *v.a.* Gather, assemble. 2 Keep, preserve.
féithleag,‡ *s.f.* Honeysuckle, see uilleann. 2 Pod of any leguminous vegetable.
féithlean, *s.m.* Honeysuckle, see uilleann.
féith-lianan, *s.f.* see lìonan-féitheach.
féith-lùthaidh,** *s.f.* Sinew. 2 Ham-string.
féithmealachd, see feumalachd.
†fel, *s.f.* Strife, debate.
†fem, Gaelic spelling of French *femme.*
†fen, *s.m.* Air.
feò,(CR) *s.m.* Air in gentle motion—*Loch Tay & Strathtay.* F. fuar a' chamhanaich, *the cold morning air.* [‡‡ & †† give *s.f.*] (see feòchan.)
feobha, see feabha.
feobhaid, see feabhaid.
feobharan. -ain, *s.m.* Pith. 2 Puff.
feobhas, see feabhas.
————aich, see feabhasaich.
feòcalan, see feòcullan.
feoch,** *v.n.* Droop, fade, decay.
————adan, -ain, *s.m.* Corn-thistle—*carduus arvensis.* see aigheannach.
feòchan, -ain, *s.m.* Air, gentle breeze, breath of wind. 2**Decay.
feachdan, § *s.m.* Corn-thistle, see aigheannach.
feòcullan, -ain, *s.m.* Polecat, *Sc.* foumart. 2** Sneaking fellow. 3(AF)Weasel. 4(AC)Ferret.
†feodaidh, *a.* Hard.
feòdaire, -an, *s.m.* see feòdarair.
feòdar, -air, *s.m.* Pewter.
feodarach,** *a.* Stannary.
feòdarair, -ean, *s.m.* Pewterer.
feòdarra, see feòdarach.
feodhachadh,** -aidh, *s.m.* Drooping.
feodhaich,‡ *v.a.* Decay, fade.
feodhail, *s.f.* Shallow estuary—*Gairloch.* [for fadhail.]
feodhainn, see feadhainn.
feodhas, see feabhas.
feodhnach,** *a.* Feudal.
feodhradh,** -aidh, *s.m.* Manner, fashion.
feoghain, see feadhainn.
feòil, *gen.* feòla, *dat.* feòil, *voc.* 'fheòil, [*gen.* feòladh in *Skye & Lewis.*] *s.f.* Flesh. 2 Flesh in a theological sense in contra-distinction to spirit. Mart-fh., *beef*; muilt-fh., *mutton*; circe-fh., *chicken*; tha a fuil 's a f. 'na craiceann fhéin, *her flesh and blood are in her own skin*—said of a woman who has borne no children.
—— -bhocta, *s.f.* Baked flesh.
—— -chnoidheag, see feòil-chruimheag.
—— -chruimh, *s.f.* Flesh-worm, maggot.
—— -chruimheach,** *a.* Having maggots. 2 Pertaining to maggots.
—— -chruimheag, -eige, -an, *s.f.* Flesh-worm, maggot.
—— -dhath, -aith, -an, *s.m.* Carnation (colour.)
—— -dhaithte, *a.* Flesh-coloured.
—— -dhìonair, *s.m.* Creosote.
—— -fhrigheanaichte, *s.f.* Fried flesh.
—— -ghabhail, -alach, *s.f.* Incarnation, the act of assuming body. An fh., *the incarnation.*
—— -itheach, -iche, *a.* Carnivorous. Eun f., *a carnivorous bird.*
—— -réiste,(MMcD) *s.f.* Flesh which is dried and smoked.
—— -theirce, *s.f.ind.* Leanness.
————ach, -iche, *a.* Lean, having little flesh.
feòir, *gen.sing.* of feur.
feòirlig, see feòirling.
feòirling, -ean, *s.f.* Farthing sterling. 2 Farthing Scots, one twelfth of a penny sterling, "turn-odhar." 3 see feòrlan. 4†† Small peice of land (¼ of a "peighinn.")
feòirlinn, see feòirling.
feòirne, *s.m.ind.* Chess. 2**Grass. Fear-f., *a chess-man.* Gearradh f., *a hack under the toes.*
————achan, (AC) *s. m.* Fairy mouse, lesser shrew.
————an, -ein, *s.m.* Pile or blade of grass. 2** Cock of hay. 3**Straw. 4**Buckle. Nach dean f. lùbadh, *that will not bend a blade of grass.*
————ineach, -iche, *a.* Grassy. 2** Strawy, light as straw. 3**In heaps or cocks.
†feòite, *a.* Faded, decayed.
feòla, *gen.sing.* of feòil.
feòlacan,(PJM) *s.m.* Dormouse—*Lewis.*
————ch, -aich, *s.m.* Carnage, slaughter.
————dair, -ean, *s.m.* Butcher, flesher.
————daireachd, *s.f.ind.* Butchery. Ris an fh., *butchering.*
feòladh, *gen. sing.* of feòil—*Skye.*
feòlan, -ain, *s.m.* Proud flesh, flesh growing beyond the skin, ‖ excoriation.
feòlar, see feòlmhor.

feòlmhach,** -aich, *s.m.* Flesh-meat.
feòlmhoire, *comp.* of feòlmhor.
——achd, see feòlmhorachd.
feòlmhor, -oire, *a.* Fleshy, fat. 2* Lustful, carnal. An inntinn fh., *the carnal mind.*
——achd, *s.f.* Lust, carnality; fleshiness. bestiality.
feòrachadh, -aidh, *s.m.* Enquiry, act of enquiring, questioning, asking. A' f—, *pr.pt.* of feòraich.
feòrachail, -ala, *a.* Curious, inquisitive.
feòrachas,** -ais, *s.m.* Curiosity, inquisitiveness.
feòrachd, see feòrachadh.
feòrag, -aig, -an, *s.f.* Squirrel. Cho grad ri feòragan Céitein, *as nimble as squirrels in May.* [Sometimes applied in error to the ferret.]
——ach,†† *a.* Abounding in squirrels.
feòraich, *pr.pt.* a' feòraich & a' feòrachadh, *v.a.* Enquire, ask, question. Dh' fh. mi dhi, *I enquired of her.*
——, *s.f.* Enquiring, asking. A' f—, *pr. pt.* of feòraich.
feo'ran, see feobharan.
feòran, -ain, -an, *s.m.* Green. 2 Mountain valley. 3 Green land adjoining a brook. 4 Gentle breeze.
feòran-curraidh, *s.m.* Water hore-hound—*lycopus europæus.*
feòras,§ -ais, *s.m.* Common spindle-tree, see oir.
feòrlan, -ain, -an, *s.m.* Firlot. 2 Bushel, four pecks.
feòrnachan, see feòirneachan.
feòrnan,** -ain, *s.m.* see feòirnean.
——ach,** *a.* see feòirneineach.
feòsag, -aige, -an, see feusag.
——ach, -aiche, *a.* see feusagach.

309. Feòran-curraidh.

†feoth, *v.n.* Wither, fade.
feothachan,‡ -ain, *s.m.* Little breeze.
feothan, *s.m.* Dormouse.
feothas, see feabhas.
——aich, see feabhasaich.
feubh, *v.* *prov.* for feith.
feucagach, -aiche, *a.* see peucagach.
feuch! *inter.* See! behold! lo! Feuch ris! *what do you think of him!* =*isn't he the brave man!* feuch riut! *look you! believe me!*
feuch, *pr.pt.* a' feuchainn, *v.a.* See, behold. 2 See, take care. 3 Show. 4 Taste, try. 5 Give. F. gu'm pill thu, *see (take care) that you return;* f. dhomh mo threun, *show me my hero;* feuchaibh an toiseach, *try in the first place;* f. ris, *give it a trial, try it;* f. greim arain, *try a piece of bread;* feuchaidh mi fhathast thu, *I'll test you yet;* a dh' fheuchainn a chéile, *to compete with each other;* feuchaidh seo riut fhéin, *this will test your powers considerably,*
feuchadair, -ean, *s.m.* Wizard, seer. 2 Tester, assayer. 3 Competitor. 4 Rival.
feuchainn, *s.f.* Trying. 2 Seeing. 3 Tasting. 4 Showing. 5 Disclosing. 6 Trial, attempt. 7 Look, aspect. A' f—, *pr.pt.* of feuch.
feuchainneach,* -aiche, *a.* Trying.
feuchar,** *fut. pass.* of feuch. Shall or will be shown. 2 *imp. pass.* Let (it) be shown. F. dhomh an òigh, *let the maid be shown to me. F.* is also used impersonally with the prep. *le,* simple or compounded, expressed or understood. Feuchar ris (leam) mu dheireadh, *it will be tried (by me) at last.*
feud, *v.* May, can, ought, behove. 2 Must, (in a negative sentence only.) Feudaidh gach neach dol as, *everyone may escape;* feudaidh e bhith, *maybe, perhaps;* ma's fheudar tuiteam, *if we must fall.* [also faod.]
feudail! *inter.* Dear me!
feudail, -alach, -an, *s.f.* Treasure, cattle, prey, spoil, booty. 2 Profit, benefit, advantage. 3 Term of endearment. M' fheudail, *my darling,* [also m' eudail, *my object of jealousy*]; toradh na feudalach gun am faicinn, *the fruit of the cattle that have not been seen.*
——each, -iche, *a.* Rich, having treasure, abounding in cattle. 2 (DMC) Precious. Nach e tha f. agad, *how precious it is to you.*
feudal, see feudail.
feudar, *s.* May, can. 'S fh. dhomh, *I must;* ma 's fh. dhuit, *if you must.*
feudmhach, -aiche, *a.* Potent.
†feugmhas, -ais, *s.m.* Absence. 2 Want.
feulainn,* *s.f.* Honeysuckle, see iadh-shiat.
feum, *v.a.* & *n.* Be in want of, be in need of, must, needs must. Feumaidh mi falbh, *I must go;* am feum mi falbh? *must I go?;* cha'n fheum mi falbh, *I need not go;* dh' fheumadh thu dol dhachaidh, *you would require to go home;* am fear a théid 'san dris, feumaidh e tighinn aisde mar a dh' fhaodas e, *he that goes among briers must come out as he can.*
feum, -a & féim, *s.m.* Need. 2 Use, usefulness. 3 Dire necessity. 4 Poverty. 5 Worth. 6 Occasion. Dè is f. dha? *what is the use of it?* cha'n 'eil f. ort, *there is no occasion for (or need of,) you;* cha dean e f., *he, (or it) will not do;* cha'n 'eil f. annad, *there is no use in you;* is beag feum a th' ort, *you are quite useless;* ann am fheum, *in my time of need;* 's e am f. a thug air sin a dheanamh, *dire necessity made him do that.*
feumach, -aiche, *a.* Needy, necessitous. F. air biadh, *in need of food.*
——, -aich, *s.m.* Needy person.
feumaich, *v.a.* Employ, use. *prov.*
feumail, -ala, *a.* Needful, necessary, useful. Ro fh., *very useful.*
feumalach, -aiche, *a.* see feumach.
——d, *s.f.ind.* Use, utility, necessity. 2 **Advantageousness. Fhuair mi m' fh., *I have got what serves my purpose;* f. an ni seo, *the utility of this thing.*
feumalan, (CR) s.m. Thistle—*Arran.*
feumanach, *a.* Having a keen sense of smell.
feumanach, -aich, *s. m.* Needy person. *prov.* 2 Beggar. 3**Tool. Cuid an fheumannaich, *the portion of the poor;* ni e f. dhiot-sa, *he will make a tool of you.*
——d,** *s.f.ind.* Beggarliness.
feumannach, -aich *s. m.* Superintendent. 2 Inspector. 3 Steward.
feum-sgaoilte, *a.* Extensively useful.
feun, *gen.* -a & -éin, -an, *s. m.* Cart, waggon, wain. 2**War-chariot. 3(AC) Arm. 4 Hand, hollow of the palm. 5 (CR) pronounced "feuinn." Load, what a person can carry—*Arran.* F. uisge, *a "gang" of water.*
——adair, -ean, see feunair.
feunadh, see feun.
feunaidh, -ean, *s.f.* Little cart. 2 Peat cart—*Inverness.* 3**Cart-horse.
feunair,** -ean, *s.m.* Carter, waggoner, carman.
——eachd,** *s.f.ind.* Waggon-driving, business of a waggoner.
feur, feòir, *s. m.* Grass. 2 Herbage. 3 Hay. F. tioram, *hay;* cruach fheòir, *a hay-rick;* f. gorm, *green grass;* bhàrr an fheòir, *off the grass, from grazing.*

feur, *v.a.* Feed on grass, graze.
feurach, -aiche, *a.* Grassy, abounding in grass or hay. 2**Verdant. 3(AH)Grazing. Cnocan buidhe f., *a yellow verdant knoll*; pàidhidh am feaman am f., *the tail (manure) will pay the grazing.*
———, -aich, *s.m.* Pasture. 2**Hay-loft. 3** Hay-yard.
feurach, *s.m. & pr.pt. Uist* for feurachadh. A' f. na bà, *grazing the cow.*
———adh, -aidh, *s.m.* Feeding on grass, grazing, pasturing. A' f—, *pr.pt.* of feuraich. A' cur an eich air feurachadh, *putting the horse to pasture.*
———air,** *s.m.* Fodderer.
feurachas, -ais, *s.m.* see feurach.
feuraich, *pr.pt.*a' feurachadh, *v.a.*Feed on grass, graze, pasture.

310. Feuran.

311. Feur-a'-phuint.

feuran, -ain, *s.m.* Green, grassy field.
feuran,§ -ain, *s.m.* Chives, wild garlic—*allium schœnoprasum.*
feur-a'-phuint,§ *s.m.* Couch-grass—*triticum repens.*
fear-caonaichte,(AH) *s.m.* Hay.
feur-chaorach,§ *s.m.* Sheep's fescue grass—*festuca ovina.*
feur-cuir, *s.m.* Rye-grass.
feur-ghartadh,(CR)*s.m.* The keeping of his own cattle next to the crops by the crofter whose turn it is to do the herding of the township—*W. of Ross.*
feur-gortach, see conan.
feur-itheach, *a.* Graminivorous. Beathaichean f., *graminivorous beasts.*
feur-lann, -an, *s.m.* Hay-house. 2 Hay-stack-yard.

312. Feur-chaorach.

feur-lobht, -a, -an, *s.m.* Hay-loft.
feur-loch, -an, *s.m.* Grassy lake. 2 Reedy lake. 3* Morass, marsh, swamp. 4 ‡ *confervæ,* fucus.
———an, -ain, *dim.* of feur-loch. *s.m.* Grassy pool, morass, marsh.
feurmhor, *a.* see feurach.
feur-nan-con, see feur-a'-phuint.
feursa, -an, *s.m.* Canker. 2†† see feursann.
feursag, *dim.* of feursa, see feursann.
feur-saidhe, *s. m. ind.* Hay. 2 (AH) Natural grass, as distinct from rye-grass.
feursann, -ainn, -an, *s.f.* Worm in the hide of cattle.
feursdag, *prov.* for feursann.

feur-shion,** *s.f.* see fearthainn.
feur-sithein-sithe,§ see conan.
feursnan,(CR) *Skye & Lewis* for feursann.
fèurtainean,(CR) *Reay country* for feursann.
feur-thuinn,** *s.f.* see fearthainn.
———-———each,** *a.* see fearthainneach.
feur-tioram, *s.m.* Hay.
feur-uisge,‡ *s.m.* Sweet water-grass, see milsean uisge. 2 Confervæ.
feusag, -aige, -an, *s.f.* Beard. 2 Barb.
——— ach, -aiche, *a.* Bearded. 2*Hairy. 3 *Barbed.
——— -bheòil, *s.f.* Moustache.
feusd, see féisd.
———a, -an, *s.f.* see féis.
feusgan, -ain, *s.m.* Mussel.
———ach, -aiche, *a.* Abounding in mussels. 2 Of, or pertaining to, mussels.
feusta, see féis.
feuth,* *s.* Ditch, slough. 2 (PJM) Moor hag.
———ach,* -aiche, *a.* Sloughy.
fh, is silent except at the beginning of the words fhathast, fhéin and fhuair, when it is pronounced like *h* in English *house.*
fh, For all words beginning with *fh,* except the following, see under *f.*
fhad's, *adv.* (fad+agus) While.
fhal, for falach.
'fheòil ! *voc. sing.* of feòil.
[☞ Although the three following words are treated by Gaelic grammars as variations of *faigh,* they are not connected with it etymologically.]
fhuair, *past aff.* of faigh. Got.
fhuaradh, *past aff. pass.* of faigh. Fh. e, *it was got.*
fhuaras, *past aff. pass.* of faigh. Is math a fh. thu ! *how well you succeeded !*
†fi, *s.m.* Anger, indignation.
†fi, *a.* Bad, corrupt.
†fia, *a,* The farthest.
fiabhras, -ais, -an, *s. m.* Fever. 2 Ague. 3 Confusion. 4 Later stage of fever—*Arran.*
———ach, -aiche, *a.* Feverish, of or connected with fever, aguish.
———achd,** *s.f.* Aguishness.
——— -bainne,‖ *s.m.* Milk fever. [Preceded by the art. AM.]
——— -buidhe,‖ *s.m.* Yellow fever. [Preceded by the art. AM]
——— -cleibhe, *s.m.* Pneumonia. [Preceded by the art. AM.]
——— -chosg,** *s.m.* Febrifuge.
——— -chosgach,** *s.m.* Antifebrile.
——— -critheanach,‖ *s.m.* Ague. [Preceded by the art. AM.]
——— -dearg,‖ *s.m.*Scarlet fever. [Preceded by the art. AM.]
——— -dubh,‖ *s. m.* Typhus. [Preceded by the art. AM.]
——— -loisgeach,** *s.m.* Burning ague.
fiabhruidh, *v.n.* Ask—*Arran.* [fiafraigh.]
fiabhrus, see fiabhras.
fiacaill,-cla, -clan, *s.m.* Tooth. 2 Cog of a wheel. 3 Dovetail in *joinery.* 4**Husk. 5 Tooth of a quern. 6 Jag of a saw, or any dentated instrument. 7 Fluke of an anchor. 'S fhaide t' fhiacaill na t' fheusag, *your tooth is longer than your beard*—a remark sometimes made to a boy with a hungry look ; cha tig d' a fhiaclan ach na thàinig, *they have come all that will come of his teeth*—a remark often applied to one making a prudent answer or statement ; fiaclan a' ghliocais, *wisdom teeth;* is geur f. á fraoch, *one is always hungry when coming from the hill* (*lit.*sharp is the tooth from heather.)

fiacaill-carbaid, *s.m.* Cheek-tooth.
fiacaill-criche, *s.m.* Eye-tooth, gag-tooth [also coin-chriche.]
fiacaill-cùil, *s.m.* Back tooth.
fiacaill-forais, *s.m.* Late-grown tooth, wisdom-tooth.
fiacaill-goibhre,(AF) *s.m.* Name given to a man who holds out against his neighbours.
fiacaill-leòghainn, *s. m.* Dandelion, see bèarnan-Brìde. [Gaelic translation of the French name *dent-de-lion.*]
fiacais, in the conversational Gaelic of *Eigg & Uist*, is the more or less courteous retort to inquisitive folk—c' àit' an robh thu ? bha, aig cùl na fiacais, *where have you been ? at the back of the fiacais ;* dè th' agad an sin ? tha, greim de 'n fhiacais, *what have you got there? a piece of the fiacais.* In some places an expostulatory exclamation—fhiacais,na bath an teine ! *dear me, do not drown the fire !* "Fh. phrìseil !" is a common expression of surprise in *Argyllshire.*
fiacas,(CR) *s.m.* Small fish allied to the dog-fish.
†**fiach**, see fitheach. 2 Wrath.
fiach ! *int.* see feuch.
fiach, féich, fiachan, *s.m.* Value, price, worth. 2**Hire. 3 *pl.* Debt, arrears. F. shè sgillinn, *sixpence-worth ;* an fh. e ? *is it worth, is it good ;* an d' fhuair thu 'fh. ? *did you get its value ?* c'oma am b' fh. leat labhairt ris ? *why would you condescend to speak to him ?* cha b' fh. leam e, *I would scorn it ;* am bheil sin mar fhiachaibh orm ? *am I under obligations to do that ?* am bheil e am fiachaibh ort-sa seo a dheanamh ? *is it obligatory on you to do this ?* cuiream mar fhiachaibh oirbh, *let me charge you ;* tha e 'cur mar fhiachaibh orm-sa, *he would fain make me believe ;* b' àill leis a chur mar fhiachaibh orm-sa gur càise mo shròn, *he would fain make me believe that my nose is cheese ;* gun fh., *without debts*, also *worthless ;* dh' fhiachaibh, *incumbent, obligatory ;* maith dhuinn ar fiachan, *forgive us our debts.*
fiach, -a, *a.* Worthy, valuable. 2 Good. 3 Deserving. 4 Proper. *prov.* Cha'n fh. seo, *this is of no value ;* ma 's fh. an duine a tha do ghnothach ris, *if the man you have to do with is a respectable person* ; an geall na 's fh. e, *almost done for ;* an fh. dhuit do shaothair ? *is it worth your while ?* ma 's fh. an teachdaire 's fh. an gnothach, *if the bearer is respectable the message is important ;* cha 'n fh. sin idir, *that is not proper at all* ; ma 's fh. leat, *if you condescend to such ;* is fh. thu do chairbhisd, *you are deserving of a beating ;* cha 'n fh. leam e, *it is beneath me.*
fiachach, -aiche, *a.* see fiachail.
fiachaicht', *a.* Ransomed—*Dàin I. Ghobha.*
fiachail, -ala, *a.* Worthy, dignified. 2 Virtuous. 3 Having rank or influence. 4 Valuable, relating to a debt. 5* Important. Duine f., *a respectable man ;* ni f., *an important affair.*
fiachalachd, *s.f.* Worthiness, value.
fiacham,* *s.m.* Pretension. Cuir mar fh., *pretend, assume.*
fiachan,* *s.m.* Value, debt.
fiachan, *pl.* of fiach. Debts. Fear f., *a creditor.*
fiach-giùlain, -an-, *s.m.* Fare.
fiaclach, -aiche, *a.* Toothed, having teeth. 2 Jagged, dentated. 3 Pronged. 4**Serrated.
fiaclachadh, -aidh, *s. m.* Showing the teeth. 2 Getting angry. 3 Indenting. 4 Notching. 5 Dove-tailing. 6**Serrating. 7 Grinning. 8 Gnashing of the teeth. A' f—, *pr. pt.* of fiaclaich.
fiaclachan, -ain, *s.m.* Saw-fish. 2 (DC) Iron garden rake—*Argyll.*
fiaclach-coille, -aich-, *s.m.* Wild boar, wild pig.
fiaclaibh, *dat. pl.* of fiacal.
fiaclaich, *pr.pt.* a' fiaclachadh, *v.a.* Grin, show the teeth. 2 Be angry. 3 Indent. 4 Notch. 5 Dove-tail. 6 Serrate.
fiaclair, *s.m.* Dentist.
fiaclan, *n. pl.* of fiacal.
†**fiadh**, *v. a.* Relate, tell.
†**fiadh**, *s.m.* Lord. 2 Land. 3 Meat, victuals.
fiadh, féidh, *s.m.* Deer. Mar fh. air fireach, *like a deer on a mountain.*

NAMES OF DEER AT VARIOUS AGES :

Males—Red deer. [Damh—stag.]
Young—Laogh, *calf.*
1 year—Laogh, *calf.*
2 years—Mang, *brocket.* Procach—*Suth'd.*
3 years—Cnochdach, bod-da-bhioran, *spayad.*
4 years—Stopannach,Damh, damh-féidh, *stag.*
5 years—Damh cabrach, *great stag.*
6 years—Làn damh, *hart.*

Males—Fallow deer. [Boc—buck]
Young—Meann-earb, *fawn.* Laogh—*Lochaber.*

Males—Roedeer. [Boc—buck]
[No Gaelic names exclusively used for fallow deer and roe deer have been obtained and if such exist they are local and not general.]

Female of red deer—Agh-féidh, and after 1 year Eilid, *hind ;* eildeag, grioch(MMcL) —*Lewis, roe.*

Female of fallow deer and roedeer—Earb, *roe.*

Cry of the stag—Langan, langanaich. In the rutting season *bùirich* and *raoicich*—AH. *bray* or *bellow.* Langanaich in *Lewis* is the cry of deer in general—MMcD.

Cry of the roebuck—Nualan. Beucaich, raoicich—AH. Bodhar-gheum—DC. *bell.*

fiadha, *a.* see fiadhaich.
fiadh-abhal, -ail, -bhlan, *s.m.* Crab apple, crab tree.
fiadhach, -aich, *s.m.* Hunting, especially of deer. 2 Venison. 3**Herd of deer. 4**Lord. 5**see fiadhachas. 6 Deer-forest.
†**fiadhach**, *a.* Detestable.
fiadhach, -aiche, *a.* Abounding in deer. 2 Of, or belonging to deer. 3 see fiadhaich.
——————**adh**,** -aidh, *s.m.* Deer-hunting. 2 Deer-hunt. 3 Roe-hunt. 4 (AH) Act of inviting or offering hospitality. 5 Invitation to a wedding, funeral, &c. A' f—, *pr. pt.* of fiadhaich. A' f. bheann, *hunting in the mountains;* là dhuinn a' f., *one day as we were hunting.*
——————**as**, -ais, *s.m.* Wildness, shyness.
——————**d**, *s.f.* see fiadhachas. 2 Hunting, especially of deer. 3**Chase.
fiadhadan, -ain, *s.m.* Witness.
fiadhag, -aig, -an, see fiantag.
fiadhaich,** *pr. pt.* a' fiadhachadh, *v.a.* Hunt deer, hunt, chase. 2(CR) Invite, make welcome, give welcome to—*Skye & Lewis.* 3(DC) Invite to a wedding or funeral—*Uist.* 4 (PJM) Challenge to fight.
fiadhaich, -e, *a.* Wild, untamed, savage. 2 Fierce. 3 Tempestuous, boisterous. 4**Uncultivated, in a state of nature. Daoine f., *savages ;* cat f., *a wild cat.*
——————**e**, -an, *s.m.* Huntsman, hunter. 2†† Wildness.
——————**e**, *comp.* of fiadhaich.
——————**eachd**, see fiadhaichead.
——————**ead**, -eid, *s.f.* Savageness, wildness. 2 Shyness.
fiadhaich-ghearr,(AF) *s.m.* Wolf.

fiadhaidh, see fiadhaich.
fiadhaidheachd, see fiadhaichead.
†fiadhaile, -an, *s.f.* Weed.
fiadhain, -e, *a.* Wild, untamed, savage. 2 Bitter, sour—*Dàin I. Ghobha.* Ubhal f., *a crab apple.*
fiadhair, -dhrach, *s. f.* Lea land. 2 Green sward. Bean fh., *a barren woman—Uist.*
———e,(DMC) *s.f.* Hard moorland grass.
———each,†† *a.* Abounding in lea land.
fiadh-àite, -achan, *s.m.* Wilderness, wild desert place.
fiadhan, -ain, *s.m.* see fiadhachas. 2 Evidence.
fiadhanta, *a.* Wild, shy. 2 Savage. 3 Fierce. 4 Cruel. Gu f., *wildly.*
fiadhantachd, *s.f.* see fiadhantas.
fiadhantas, -ais, *s.m.* Fierceness, wildness. 2 Shyness. 3 Savageness. 4 Cruelty.
fiadh-asal, -asail, -an, *s.m.* Wild ass.
fiadh-bheathach, -aich,-aichean,*s.m.*Wild beast.
fiadh-bheist, *s.f.* Wild beast.
fiadh-bhoireann,(AF) *s.f.* Hind.
fiadh-bhriathar,** *s.m.* Barbarism.
fiadh-chat,** *s.m.* Wild cat. 2 Pole-cat.
fiadh-chleasachd,* *s.f.* Antic.
fiadh-chu, -choin, *s. m.* Wild dog. 2 Wolf. Fiadh-choin nan càrn, *the wolves of the rocks.*
fiadh-chullach, -aich, *s.m.* Wild boar.
fiadh-dhuine, -dhaoine, *s.m.* Wild man, savage. 2 Satyr. Glaodhaidh am f.. *the wild man shall cry.*
fiadh-fhàl, -àil, -an, *s.m.* Deer-park.
fiadh-fionn,(AF) *s.m.* Young roebuck.
fiadh-fireann,(AF) *s.m.* Hart, male deer.
fiadh-ghath, -aith, -an, *s.m.* Hunting spear.
fiadh-ghearr,(AF) *s.f.* Wolf.
fiadh-ghobhar, -uibhre, *s. f.* Wild goat, see gobhar-fhiadhaich.
fiadh-ghleann, -linn, *s.m.* Wild glen. 2 Glen where deer herd together.
fiadh-ghullach, see fiadh-chullach.
fiadh-lann, -lainn, -an, *s.f.* Deer-park.
fiadh-lorg, -luirg, *s.f.* Hunting pole. 2 Slot or track of a deer.
fiadh-mhuc, -uice, -an, *s.f.* Wild sow. 2 Wild boar.
fiadhmhuin,(AF) *s.m.* Any wild animal. 2 Hare.
fiadh-òg, *s.m.* Fawn.
†fiadhnais, see fianuis.
†———, *v.* see fianuisich.
fiadh-radh,** *s.m.* Barbarism.
fiadh-roidis,** *s.f.* Wild radish.
fiadh-ròs, -an, *s.m.* Wild rose.
fiadh-seang,(AC) *s.m.* Roebuck.
fiadhta, *a.* Froward. 2 Wild, fierce. 3 Shy. 4 Surly, unsocial.
———chd,** *s.f.* Wildness, shyness. 2 Surliness. 3 Fierceness, asperity.
fiadh-thorc, -uirc, *s.m.* Wild boar.
fiadh-ubhall, see fiadh-abhall.
fiadhuire, -an, see fiadhair.
†fiafrabh, *a.* Inquisitive.
fiafraich, see feòraich.
fiafraigh, see feòraich.
fiag, -a,** *s.f.* Rushes peeled and prepared. 2 Candlewicks.
fiagh, féigh, *s.m.* see fiadh.
fiaghair,(DC) *s.m.* see fiadhair.
fia-ghàire, see fèath-ghàire.
fiaile,** *s.pl.* Weeds.
fial, -a & féile, *s. f.* Bounty, hospitality. 2 Liberality. 3 Liberal man. 4**Ferret. †5 Veil of a temple.
Clàr na féile, *the table of hospitality ;* bha fleadh, bha fial, bha dàn ann, *there was feasting, hospitality and song.*
fial, -a & féile, *a.* Generous, liberal, bountiful. 2 Good. 3 **Modest. 4 Hospitable. T' fhàrdach f. gach uair, *thy dwelling always hospitable ;* an t- anam f., *the liberal soul.*
fialachd, see fialaidheachd.
fialaidh, -e, *a.* Bountiful, hospitable, liberal. Gu f., *hospitably.*
———,** *s.f.* Relationship, consanguinity, affinity.
fialaidheachd, *s. f. ind.* Bounty, hospitality, liberality. 2 Banqueting, feasting.
fial-chridheach, -iche, *a.* Open-hearted.
————d, *s.f.* Open-heartedness.
fialas,** -ais, *s.m.* Tribe.
fiallach, -aich, *s. m.* Hero, champion. 2 Knight-errant.
fiallachd, *s.f.* Heroism, bravery. 2 Knight-errantry.
fialmhaitheas, -eis, *s.m.* Munificence.
fialmhoire, *s.f.* Bounty, liberality. 2 Heroism.
fialmhor, -oire, *a.* Bountiful, generous, munificent. 2**Heroic.
———achd, *s.f.ind.* Liberality.
fial-teach,** *s.m.* Place where ferrets are bred.
fialtus, -uis, *s.m.* Protection. [** gives fialtas.]
fiaman, see fiadhmhuin.
fiamarach, -aich, *s.m.* Glutton.
fiamh, -a, *s.m.* Fear, awe, reverence, trepidation. 2 Hue, colour, aspect, tinge. 3 Chain. 4 Trace. 5 Track. 6 Footstep. 7 Chair. F. dearg, *a red tinge ;* f. gorm, *a blue tinge ;* air f. an òir, *of the colour of gold ;* gabhaidh e f., *he shall take fright.*
†fiamh, *a.* Ugly, disgusting, horrible.
fiamhach, -aiche, *a.* Fearful, timid, modest, shy. 2**Skittish. Is f. an t-sùil a lotar, *the eye that has been wounded is ever fearful of harm.*
fiamhachd,*s.f.* Modesty, shyness, awe,timidity, 2 Complexion. 3 Resemblance. 4 Skittishness.
fiamhadh, -aidh, *s.m.* Tracing, pursuing.
fiamhaidh, -e, *a.* Fearful, timid, shy, modest. 2**Skittish.
fiamhail, -ala, *a.* see fiamhaidh & fiamhach.
fiamhan, -ain, *s.m.* Heinous crime. 2**Fear.
fiamharach, -aich, *s.m.* Glutton.
————d, *s.f.* Monstrousness. 2 Monster. 3 Monstrous deed.
fiamh-bhothan, -ain, *s. m.* Tent, hut, booth, cottage.
fiamh-ghàire, see fèath-ghaire.
fiamh-ghàireach, -iche, *a.* Smiling.
fiamhlachd,(DC) *s.f.* Fright, skittishness, as of a horse. Tha f. air, *he is skittish.*
fiamh-lochd, -an, *s.m.* Heinous crime. 2 Fear.
†fian, *s.m.* General.
fianach, (MMcL) s.m. Moor-grass—*Lewis.*
fianaidh, *dim.* and *N. Inverness-shire* local form of feun. Peat cart.
†fian-bhuth, s.m. Hut, cottage, booth.
†fianlach, -aich, *s.m.* Fear, scaring.
†fian-laoch, *s.m.* Champion.
fiann,** *s.m.* Giant. 2 Warrior. 3 Fingalian, (this the correct *nom.* case—Féinne is a *gen.*) Flath nam f., *the chief of warriors.* [see Féinne]
fiannach, *a.* August.
fiannach, -aich, *s.m.* Month of August.
fiannach,** *a.* Heroic, gigantic. 2 Like a Fingalian. 3 Of, or pertaining to, a Fingalian.
fiannachail, -ala, *a.* Like a Fingalian. 2 Gigantic. 3 Heroic. 4 August.
fiannag, -aig, *Gairloch, &c.* for fineag.
fiannagach, *a.* see fineagach.
fiannaidh, -ean, *s.m.* Fingalian. 2 Giant. 3 Hero. 4(CR) *s.f.* Thin, slender person.
Fianntachan,* *s.m., dim.* Dwarf of the Finga-

lians.
fianntan, *n.pl.* of fiann. Fingalians. 2 Champions.
fiantag, -aige, -an, *s.f.* Black heath-berry.
fiantaiche, see fiannaidh.
fianuis, -ean, *s.f.* Witness, evidence, testimony. Presence. Thog iad f. 'na aghaidh, *they bore testimony against him;* mar fh. air sin, *as evidence of that;* aon de na fianuisean, *one of the witnesses;* mach á m' fh. ! *or* as m' fh ! *out of my presence!* tog f., *or* thoir f., *bear record;* tha mi a' deanamh f., *I bear record;* am f., *in sight, in sight of;* f. bhréige, *a false witness.*
fianuis, *v.a.* see fianuisich.
fianuiseach, -iche, *a.* Present, witnessing, being a witness. 2* Capable of bearing testimony. Is f. thus' air sin, *you are able to give evidence in this instance.*
fianuiseach,* -ich, *s.m.* see fianuis. Aon de na fianuisich, *one of the witnesses.*
fianuiseachadh, -aidh, *s.m.* Witnessing, bearing witness, giving evidence as a witness. A' f—, *pr.pt.* of fianuisich.
fianuiseadh, -ich, *s.m.* & *pr.pt.* see fianuiseachadh.
fianuisich, *pr.pt.* a' fianuiseachadh & a' fianuiseadh, *v.a.* Witness, bear witness, give evidence.
fianuis-shùl, *s.m.* Eye-witness.
fiar, -a, *a.* Crooked, curved, bent, not straight. 2 Perverse. 3 Wicked, unjust. ‖4 Oblique. 5 Fluctuating. 6 Winding. 7 Wild, fierce. Cuir f. e, *place it obliquely* or *crosswise;* mar bhogha f., *as a bent bow;* an gleanntaibh f., *in meandering valleys;* duine a tha f. 'na shlighibh, *a man that is perverse in his ways;* steud na fiar-ghaoithe, *the steed of the wild wind.*
fiar, *pr. pt.* a' fiaradh, *v.a.* & *n.* Bend, twist, make crooked. 2 Pervert. 3 Go astray or aside. 4*Beat against the wind.‖go obliquely, as a ship. 5 Squint. 6**Wrest. Cha'n fh. thu breith, *thou shalt not pervert judgment.*
fiar, *a.* & *s.* see iar.
fiar, *s.m.* see feur.
fiar,** *adv.* Aside.
fiarach, -aiche, *a.* Inclining, slanting. 2 Twisting, wreathing.
———, *s.m.* see feurach.
——— -tarsuing, see fiodhrach-tarsuing.
———adh,** -aidh, *s.m.* Slanting. 2 Bending. 3 Perverting. 4 Wresting. 5 Slant. 6 Bend. 7 Perversion. A' f—, *pr. pt.* of fiaraich.
fiarachd, *s.f.ind.* Crookedness.
fiaradh, -aidh, *s. m.* Inclination, slanting, going off from the straight line. 2 Bending. 3**Twisting. 4 Whirling. 5**Perverting. 6 **Wreathing. 7** Perverseness. 8**Bend, turn. 9**Meander. 10**Cadence of a strain. A' f—, *pr.pt.* of fiar. A' f. na firinn, *perverting the truth;* f. nam fonn, *the variations of the music;* f. na gaoithe, *the whirling of the wind;* f. luchd-dò-bheirt, *the perverseness of transgressors;* is glan am f. a tha 'nad mhalaidh, (agus ho Mhórag), *exquisitely curved is the sweep of thine eyebrow;* a' f. a' bhruthaich, *climbing the brae in zig-zags;* cha d' thug sin f. as. *that did not make him alter his ways;* f. na h- oidhche, *the twilight;* na cuir f. ann, *do not bend it.*
fiarag, -aige, -an, *s.f.* Slant line, line or rope cast over the corn stack to secure it during winter storms. Two of them are placed to each of the four points of the compass and when there is a storm a heavy stone is attached to them on the side from which the storm is blowing. 2 Fetlock. 3 (Fionn) Bandage over a sore eye or brow, generally eye, tied at back of head. 4(AH) Sly hint. 5(DC) Bursts of petty temper.
fiaraich, *v.a.* see fiar.
fiaras, -ais, *s.m.* Crookedness. 2 Perverseness.
fiarasach,-aiche,*a.*Crooked, curved,not straight. 2 Curve-necked. Each f.,*a curve-necked horse.*
fiar-char, *s. m.* Crank.
fiar-ogha, *s.m.* Given by ** for iar-ogha.
fiar-òthaisg, *s.f.* Year old ewe.
fiar-rabhadh, -aidh, -aidnean, *s.m.* Inuendo.
fiar-shùil, -ùla, -shùilean, *s.f.* Squint-eye.
———each, -iche, *a.* Squint-eyed, looking askance.
———iche, *s. f.* Squinting in the eyes.
fiarslanan, (CR) for feursann.
fiarsnan,(MMcL) *s.m.* Flesh-worm in lean cattle.
fiartanan, (CR) *N. Inverness-sh.& Lewis* for feursann.
fiasag, see feusag.
†**fiasdar**, -air, *s.m.* Anger.
fiasgan, -ain, see feusgan.
fiasganach, -aiche, see feusganach.
fiaslanan,(CR) *Gairloch* for feursann.
fiat, see fiadhta.
fiata, *a.* see fiadhta.
fiatach,(CR) *a.* Quiet, sly, stealthy.—*Skye.*
fiatachd, see fiadhtachd.
fiatail,** *s. f.* Species of weed. 2 Vetches. 3 Tares.
fiatanach, -aiche, *a.* Peevish,waspish. 2(AH) Wild, untractable.
fiatghal, -ail, *s.m.* Vetch—*vicia sativa.*
fiath, *Gairloch &c.* for fèath.
——ach, *a.* see fèathach.
fiathachadh, -aidh, *s.m.* Invitation. F. an rathaid mhóir, neo 'r thaing ciamar tha thu 'n diugh 's cia mar tha iad agaibh, *the highway invitation, any amount of enquiries as to how you are to-day and how your folks are*—but no offers of hospitality. 2 (DMC) Challenging. 'Ga fh. gu sabaid, *challenging him to fight.*
fiadhaich,(DU) *v.a.* Welcome.

313. Fiatghal.

fiathail, see fèathail.
fiathalachd, see fèathamhlachd.
fib,§ see lus-nam-braoileag.
fibin, *s.f.* Rabies,
fich ! *int.* Nasty. Fich ort ! an expression of disgust or contempt.
†**fich**, s. Country village. 2 Castle.
fichead, -chid, *a.* Twenty. [Followed by a noun in *gen. pl.*] F. fear, *twenty men;* aon fhear thar fhichead, *twenty one men;* trì fir fhichead, *twenty three men;* trì fichead clach, *sixty stones.*
†**ficheall**, -ill, *s.m.* Buckle.
ficheadamh, *a.* Twentieth.
fideadh, -idh, -idhean, *s.m.* Bending. 2 Suggestion. 3 Whisper. 4(DMC) Belief, credence. Na toir f. air, *do not believe him.* 5(PM)Short time—*Uist.*
fideag, -eige, -an, *s. f.* Small worm. 2 (AF) Ringworm. 3 Small pipe or flute. 4 Reed. 5 Whistle. 6 (herb,) see fiteag. 7**Kind of bird. Cluich na fideige, *the game* "hunt the whistle;" *in shinty.* the act of throwing up the ball, hitting it while still in mid-air, and sending it, at a somewhat high trajectory, to the other end of the field.—AH.

fideagach, *a.* Like a small worm. 2 Full of little worms.
fideag-cham, see **fiteag-cham.**
fidealadh,(AH) -aidh, *s.m.* Confused and irregular intertwining, intertexture, transversion.
fideil,(AH) *v.a.* Entwine, intertwine, twist. 2 Weave, inweave. 3 Tangle, entangle. 4 Ravel, dishevel. 5 Knot.
fidean, *s.m.* Green islet or spot uncovered at high-tide. 2 Web of sea-clam.—*Isles.*
fideis,(PM) *v.a.* Meddling or playing with work.
fidh, see **figh.**
†**fidh**, *a.* Faithful.
fidheadair, see **figheadair.**
fidheall, see **fiodhull.**
fidhle, *gen. sing.* of **fiodhull.**
fidhleir, -ean, *s.m.* Fiddler, violinist.
———**eachd**, *s.f.ind.* Performance on the violin. 2 Business of a fiddler, fiddling. Ag ionnsachadh na f. *learning to play the violin.*
fidileir, -ean, *s.m.* Bad violinist. 2 Restless fidgetty person.
———**eachd**, *s.f.* Bad fiddling. 2 Restlessness.
fidilin, -ean, *s.f.* Small fiddle.
fidir, *pr.pt.* a' fidreadh, *v.a.* Consider, weigh. 2 Try. 3 Search narrowly, examine. 4 Sympathize. 5 Advert. 6**Prove by trial. 7(M McD) Perceive, notice. Cha'n fh. an sàthach an seang, *the satiated will not sympathize with the starveling ;* f. is ceasnaich mi, *prove and examine me ;* an d' fh. sibh an cabhlach ud ? *did you examine that fleet ?* 'nuair a dh' fhidireas mi m' athair, *when I shall have sounded my father ;* dh' fh. mi rud a' gluasad, *I became aware of something moving.*
fidir, *s.m.* Teacher.
fidleireachd, *s.f.* Restlessness.
[The five following words are given by ** with an extra *i*, thus, fidireach, &c.]
fidreach,** - iche, *a.* Considerate, thoughtful. 2 Prying, inquisitive.
———**adh**, -aidh, *s.m.* see **fidreadh. A' f—**, *pr.pt.* of **fidrich.**
———**ail**, -ala, *a.* Inquisitive.
———**d**,** *s.f.* Considerateness. 2 Minuteness. 3 Inquisitiveness.
fidreadh, -reidh, *s.m.* Considering. 2 Prying, examining. 3 Experience. 4 Agitation. A' f—, *pr.pt.* of **fidir.**
fidrich, *pr.pt.* a' fidricheadh, see **fidir.**
———**e**, -an, *s. m.* Examiner, enquirer, trier, weigher, searcher,
———**te**, *past pt.* of **fidrich.**
†**fig**, -e, *s.f.* Slit.
fige, -an, *s.f.* Fig. 2 Fig-tree.
figeach, -giche, *a.* Having figs. 2 Of, or belonging to, figs.
fige-Indeach,§ *s.f.* Fig of India—*ficus Indicus.*
figeireach,(AC) -rich, *s.m.* Fiend.
figh, *pr.pt*, a' fighe & a' figheadh, *v.a.* Weave. 2 Braid. 3 Knit. 4** Twine, twist, wreathe. F. an eige, *weave the web ;* f. an stocain, *knit the stocking ;* f. an t-sreing, *plait the cord.*
fighde, -an, see **fighdeach.**
fighdeach, -ich -ichean, *s.m.* Links, land sometimes covered by the sea. Fighdean Lite, *Leith links.*
fighdean, *n.pl.* of **fighde.**
figheachan, -ain, -an, *s.m.* Garland. 2 Web. 3 Little web. 4 Weaving. 5 Hanging. 6 Wreath, wreathings.
figheachas, -ais, *s.m.* see **figheadaireachd.**
figheadair,-ean, *s.m.* Weaver. 2 Plaiter, twister. 3* Knitter.
———**eachd**, *s.f.* Weaving, occupation or trade of a weaver. Ris an fh., *at the weaving trade.*
figheadair-fodair(CR) *s.m.* Spider—*Glenlyon.*
figheadh, -idh, *s. m.* Weaving. 2 Knitting A' f—, *pr.pt.* of **figh.**
figheag, see **fuigheag.**
†**figheall**, -ill, *s.m.* Buckler.
figheis, *s.* Spear. 2 Lance.
fighil, *s.f.* Prayer.
fighte, *past.pt.* of **figh.** Woven, twisted, twined, wreathed.
figis, *s.f.* Fig. [For illust. see **crann-fige.**]
fil,(AF) *s.* Elephant.
fil, *v.* for (am) **bheil.**
†**filbin**,(AF) *s.* Lapwing, see **adharcan-luachrach.** 2 Woodcock, see **coileach-coille.**
file, -an, *s.m.* see **filidh.**
fileab-a'-chléite,(AF) *s.* Magpie.
fileachd, *s.f.* Poetry, poesy.
filead, -eid, -an, *s.f.* Gaelic spelling for *fillet.*
———**ach**,** *a.* Filleted.
fileadh, -lidh, -lidhean, see **filidh.**
———**achd**, see **fileachd.**
fileanta, *a.* Ready-worded, fluent. 2 Eloquent. 3 Poetical. 4 Tuneful, melodious.
fileantachd, *s.f.ind.* Fluency of speech, command of language. 2 Eloquence. 3 Melodiousness, tunefulness, execution of music.
filear,** *s.m.* Spruce fellow. 2 Crafty man.
fileil,** *a.* Poetical, poetic, bardic.
fileir, -ean, see **fidhleir.**
†**filibeart**, Gaelic spelling of *filbert.*
filidh, -ean & -nean, *s.m.* Poet, bard, minstrel. 2**Inferior bard. 3 Warbler, songster. 4 Philosopher. 5 Orator. Gu f., *tunefully ;* filidhean binn nan coilltean, *the melodious warblers of the woods.* [Miss Eleanor Hull's *Textbook of Irish Literature* says " The *file* is to be regarded as in the earliest times combining in his person the functions of magician, lawgiver, judge, counsellor to the chief and poet. Later, but still at a very early time, the offices seem to have been divided, the brehons devoting themselves to the study of law, and the giving of legal decisions, the druids arrogating to themselves the supernatural functions, with the addition, possibly, of some priestly offices, and the *fili* themselves being regarded henceforth principally as poets and philosophers. This division seems to have already existed in Ireland in the time of St. Patrick, whose preaching brought him into constant opposition with the druids, who were evidently, at that time, regarded as the religious leaders of the nation, though there does not seem to be much sign that they were, as they undoubtedly were, even at an earlier age in Britain and Gaul, sacrificing priests. We have already spoken of the belief in transmigration, as being a part of the early mythology both of Britain and Ireland. It is to be understood that the Irish pagan belief does not exactly correspond with Cæsar's observations regarding the teaching of the druids in Gaul. In the pagan literature of Ireland, we find no trace of a belief in a life after death. The mortals that went into Magh Mell, or the Irish pagan Elysium, did not go there by means of, or after, death ; they went as visitors, who could at will return again to earth. The distinction is essential. Until after the introduction of Christian teaching, the idea of a life after death seems to have been non-existent. Both the re-incarnations and the entrance into Magh Mell were made during the continuance of mortal life ; they have no refer-

ence to a life beyond the grave. Outside the sphere of the ancient mythology, the belief in transmigration is found also to persist ; it re-appears in semi-historic times."

Pomponius Mela speaks of the druid doctrine of immortality in Gaul, but says nothing as to the entry of souls into other bodies. He cites as proof, the practice of burning and burying with the dead things appropriate to the needs of the living. He wrote about A.D. 44.

filidheach, *a.* Poetic, rhyming. 2 Tuneful.

filidheachd, *s.f.ind.* Versification, poetry, rhyming. 2 Tunefulness.

filit,*s.f.* see fuar-lite.

fill, *pr.pt.* a' filleadh, *v. a.* Fold. 2 Plait. 3 Imply. 4‡‡Contain, include. F. an t-aodach, *fold the cloth ;* tha sin a' filleadh a staigh, *that implies ;* air am filleadh anns a chéile, *folded together.*

fill, *pl.* -ean, *s.f.* Collop. 2 Steak. Fillean saillte, *collops of salted meat.*

fill, *pl.* filltean, *s.f.* Fold, plait. Le filltean teine, *with folds of fire ;* tri-fillte, *three-ply.*

filleadh, fillidh, filltean & filleachan, [*pl.* fillidh & fillidhean in *Gairloch.*] *s. m.* Fold, plait, 2 Ply. 3 Folding, plaiting, wrapping. 4 Implying. 5** A cloth. A' f—, *pr.pt.* of fill. Beagan fillidh, *a little folding.*

filleadh-beag, see féileadh-beag.

filleag, -eig, -an, *s. f.* Shawl, wrapper, little plaid. 2 Little fold or plait. 3 Doublet. 4 Scarf. 5 Covering. 6(AH) Light, slight, shabby cloth covéring, see pilleag.

filleagach,** *a.* Having folds or plaits.

fillean, -ein, *s.m.* see filleag.

fillean, -ein, *s.m.* Species of worm that breeds in the human head and neck causing painful swellings.

fillean, -ein, *s.m.* Collop. 2 see filleag.

fillear, *fut.pass.* of fill. Shall be folded.

fillidh, *fut.aff.a.* of fill. Shall fold.

fillidh, *gen.sing.* of filleadh.

fillt', see fillte.

fillte, *a. & past pt.* of fill. Folded, plaited. 2 Implied. 3 Plied, as wool.

fillte, *a.* Deceitful, treacherous.

fillte, -an, *s.f.* Fold, ply. Tri-fillte, *three-ply.*

fillteach, -iche, *a.* Implicative.

fillteachadh, -aidh, *s.m.* Folding. 2 Multiplying. A' f—, *pr.pt.* of filltich.

filltich, *pr. pt.* a' fillteachadh, *v.a.* Fold, multiply.

filltiche, -an, *s.m.* Multiplier.

filltichte, *past pt.* of filltich.

†fim, *s.f.* Drink, wine.

fimeanach, -aich, *s.m.* Hypocrite.

————, -aiche, *a.* Hypocritical.

————d, *s.f.* Hypocrisy.

†fimh, *s.f.* Drink, potion, wine.

fimridh, *v.aux.* Must, need. *past aff.* dh' fhimir mi, *I must ; pass.* (*impers.*) dh' fhimireadh; *fut. aff.* fimiridh mi, *I must ; pass.* (*impers.*) fimirear ; *Subj. past*, dh' fhimirinn, *I would need ; pass.* (*impers.*) dh' fhimirteadh ; *Inter.* am fimir mi? *must I? ; pass.* (*impers.*) am fimirear ? ; *Neg.* cha'n fhimir mi, *I must not ; pass.* (*impers.*) cha'n fhimirear.

†fin, *a.* Fine.

fine, -achan, *s.f.* Tribe, family, kindred, clan. 2 Nation. 3 Soldier. 4 Surname. Na fineachan Gàidhealach, *the clans of Gaeldom ;* gach f. gairmidh e, *he shall call every tribe ;* ciod is f. dhuit ? *what is your surname ?*

fineach, *a.* In tribes or clans. 2 Clannish. †3 Frugal.

fineach,(CR) *s.m.* Rank moor-grass,—*Lewis.*

fineachail,(DMC) *a.* Heathenish.

fineachan, *n.pl.* of fine. 2 Heathens, gentiles. A réir nam f., *according to their nations ;* thàinig na f., *the heathen came.*

fineachas, -ais, *s.m.* Kindred, relationship, consanguinity. 2 Inheritance. 3 Nation. 4 Law.

fineachd, *s.f.* Same meanings as fineachas.

fineadach, *a.* Wise, prudent, sagacious. 2 Cunning. 3 Clannish.

fineadach, -aich, *s.m.* Clansman.

fineadail, -ala, *a.* National. 2 Clannish.

fineadalachd, *s.f.* Nationality. 2 Clannishness.

fineadh, -idh, *s.m.* see fine. 2 Cast.

fineag, -eige, -an, *s.f.* Cheese-mite. 2 Animalcule. 3 Miser, niggardly person. 4 Crowberry. Làn fhineag, *full of mites.*

fineagach, -aiche, *a.* Abounding in mites. 2 Miserly, niggardly. 3 Full of crowberries. Càise f., *cheese abounding in mites.*

fineal,§ *s.m.* Fennel—*fœniculum vulgare.*

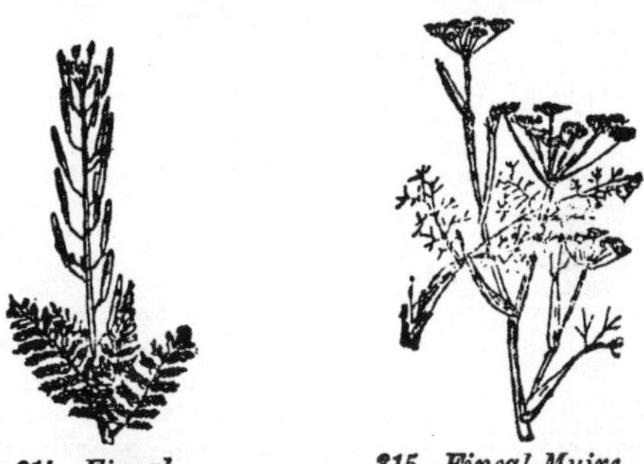

314. Fineal. *315. Fineal-Muire.*

fineal-athaich,§ *s.m.* Fennel giant—*ferula communis.* [Not found in Britain or Ireland.]

fineal-cùbhraidh, *s.m.* Sweet fennel.

fineal-Greugach,§ *s.m.* Fenugreek, see deanntag-Ghreugach.

fineal-Muire,§ *s.m.* Flixweed—*sisymbrium sophia.*

316.Fineal-sràide. *317. Fineamhuin.*

fineal-sràide,§ *s.m.* Hog-fennel, sow-fennel, sulphur-wort—*peucedanum officinale.* [Not found in Scotland.]

finealta, -ailte, *a.* Fine,elegant, handsome. 2 Tidy. 3 Brave. 4 Well-dressed. 5 Polite. 6(DMC) Gentle. Aghaidh fh., *a gentle face ;* foinneamh f., *portly and well dressed.*

finealtachd, *s.f.* Fineness, elegance, handsomeness. 2 Tidiness. 3 Bravery. 4 Fondness for dress. 5 Politeness, polished manners.

fineamhnach, -aich, *s. f.* Place where vines grow.

fineamhnach, -aiche, *a.* Full of vineyards. 2 Like a vineyard.

fineamhuin,§ *s.f.* Osier-willow or cooper's wil-

low—*salix viminalis.* 2 Vine. 3 Vineyard. 4 Twig. 5 Any small rod. F. fa m' chomhair, *a vine opposite to me.*
——————each, see fineamhnach.
fineant, see finealt.
fineun, -eòin, *s.m.* Buzzard.
†fineur, *s.m.* Stock, lineage.
fin-foinneach, Completely, from edge to edge. Foinneach is a contraction for foireannach. Fin-foinneach an là, *the livelong day.*
finic, -e, *a.* Black as jet.
finic, *s.f.* Jet.
finiche, *s.m.ind.* Jet. Cho dubh ri f., *as black as jet.*
finid, -ean, *s.f.* End, close, conclusion. Cuir ceann f. air, *bring it to an end.*
finideach, -iche, *a.* Wise, prudent. 2 Bringing to an end. Gu f., *wisely.*
finn, *a.* Distant. An leathar fhinn 's an leathar fhaisg (*col.* am fad 's am fagus,) *far and near.*
†finn, *s.* Milk. *a.* see fionn.
†finndeol, *v.a.* Enslave.
finn-dhìol, *v.a.* Enslave.
finne, *gen.sing.* of fionn.
finne, -an, *s.f.* Maid, maiden. 2**Beautiful woman. 3**Whiteness, fairness. 4**Attendance. 5**Testimony, evidence.
†finneal, -eil, *s.m.* Shield.
finnean-feòir, -ein-, see fionnan-feòir.
†finnein, -ean, *s.f.* Shield.
finneun, -eòin, -an, *s.m.* Buzzard.
fin-neul, -neòil, *s.m.* White cloud.
finn-gheal, *v.a.* Profess. 2 Promise.
†finnidheach, *a.* Vigilant, prudent, cautious.
finnidheachd, *s.f.* Vigilance, prudence, caution. 2 [given by ** for féinneachas (militia.)]
finn-reic, *s.f.* Proscription.
finn-reic, *v.a.* Enslave. 2 Proscribe.
finn-sgeul, -sgeòil, *s.m.* Romance, tale, fiction.
†fiob, -a, -an, *s.f.* Small battle-axe.
†fiobhar, -air, -airean, *s.m.* Edge, whetting.
†fioch, *s.m.* Choler, wrath. 2 Land.
†fiochach, -aiche, *a.* Fierce, angry.
†fiochadh, -aidh, *s.m.* Spring. 2 Generation.
†fiochail, *a.* Angry, fierce, choleric. 2 Brindled.
fiochar, *a.* Angry.
fiochdha, *a.* Angry, fierce, froward.
fioch-mhor, -oire, *a.* see fiochdha.
†fiochmhorachd, *s.f.* Anger, fierceness.
fiochradh, -aidh, *s.m.* Anger, choler.
fiodadh, -aidh, *s.m.* Laughter.
fiodh, -a, *s.m.* Timber, wood. 2 Wilderness. 3 **Tree. An t-sail as an fhiodh, *the log out of the timber ;* nochd e f. dha, *he showed him a tree.*
fiodhach, -aich, *s.m.* Shrubs. 2 Shrubbery, copse. (AF) Cheese-vat or wooden press.
fiodhach, -aiche, *a.* Abounding in timber or shrubs, copsy. 2 Wooden.
fiodhag, -aige, -an, *s.f.* Bird-cherry. 2 Wild fig. 3 Hard-berry.
fiodhagach, *a.* Abounding in bird-cherries, wild figs or hard-berries.
fiodhagach, *s.m.* see fiodhag.
fiodhagaich, *s.f.* see fiodhag.
†fiodhain, see fianuis.
†fiodhais, *s.pl.* Shrubs.
fiodhall, see fiodhull.
fiodh almuig,§ *s.m.* Sandal wood—*santalum album.*
fiodhan, -ain, -an, *s. m.* Cheese-vat or press.
fiodhannan, *s.pl.* Timbers of a boat in general.
†fiodhbhadh, -aidh, see fiùbhaidh.
fiodh-chait,** *s.m.* Mouse-trap.
†fiodh-cheail, *s.m.* Chess-play.
fiodh-chonnadh, -aidh, *s.m.* Brushwood, fuel, cordwood.
fiodh-ghait, see fioghait.
fiodh-ghual, -ail, see gual-fiodha.
fiodh-ghualach, *a.* Carbonic, abounding in charcoal.
†fiodhlair, *s.m.* see fidhleir.
†fiodhnach, *a.* Manifest, plain.
fiodhnasach, *a.* Conspicuous.
fiodhrach, -aich, *s.m.* Timber. 2 Increase. F. a thoirt do Lochabar, *to bring wood to Lochaber,*—Gaelic equivalent of " to bring coals to Newcastle." [** gives " timber for vessel-building."]
fiodhrach-tarsuing, *s. pl.* Cross timbers in a boat, see under bàta. 2 Cross-sticks of a kiln.
fiodhradh, -aidh, -aidhean, *s. m.* Impetuous rushing forward. 2**Testimony. 3**Fashion.
fiodh-thime,§*s.m.* Thyme-wood—*thuja articulata.*
fiodhull, fidhle, fidhlean, *s.f.* Fiddle, violin.
†fiog, *s.m.* Wall. 2 Wreath, braid.
fiogach,(AF) *s.m.* Dog-fish.
fiogag, -aige, -an, see fige.
fiogair, -ean, see fioghair.
†fiogh, fighe, *s.m.* Braid. 2 Wreath.
†fiogha, *s.m,* Weather or windward side.
fioghair, -ean, *s.m.* Figure. 2 ††see fiughair.
fioghait, -ean, *s.f.* Quadrangle, square.
fioghaiteach,** *a.* Quadrangular, square.
fioghal, *a.* Quadrangular, square. Feun f., *a quadrangular chariot.*
†fioghradh, -aidh, see fioghair.
fioghuir, see fioghair.
fioguis, -ean, see figis.
fioguiseach, *a.* Abounding in figs.
fiolag,(AC) *s.f.* Fly, flighty person.
fiolagan,‡ -ain, *s.m.* Field mouse.
fiolag-fheòir, see fiolan-feòir.
fiolair, see iolair.
fiolan, -ain, -an, *s. m.* Fly, worm, insect, animal, parasite, bot-fly. 2†† Earwig. [** gives fiolann.]
fiolan-donn, *s.m.* Earwig.
fiolan-fada, *s.m.* Centipede.
fiolan-feòir, *s.m.* Shrew.
fiolan-fionn, *s.m.* Parasite. 2 Gad-fly.
fiolan-luachair, *s.m.* Lizard.
fiolar, -air, -an, see fiolan. 2 see iolair.
fiolcanach, *a.* Foamy. 2 Bristling.
fiolcanaich, *s.f.* Dashing, splashing.
fiolc-fhuilteach, -iche, *a.* Bloody.
fiollan, see fiolan.
fiomhalach, -aich, *s.m.* Giant, person of extraordinary size.
†fion, *a.* Old. 2 Small. 3 Few.
fion, -a, *s.m.* Wine. †2 Truth. Ol f., *drink wine.*
fionach, -aiche, *a.* Winy, full of wine.
†fionach, *a.* Old, ancient, antique, old-fashioned.
fionachduinn, *s.f.* Experience.
fionag, -aige, -an, see fineag.
——ach, -aiche, *a.* see fineagach.
†fionais, see fianuis.
fional,** *s.m.* Mulct.
fion-amar, -air, -mraichean, *s. m.* Wine-press. As an fh., *out of the wine-press.*
fionan, -ain, *s.f. & m.* Vine, see crann-fiona. 2 Vineyard, vinery, see fion-lios. Tir nam f. trom, *the land of the heavy vines.*
——ach, -aiche, *a.* Of, or belonging to, vines.
†fion-bhuth, *s.m.* Tent, booth.
fion-chaor, -aoir, -an, *s.m.* Grape.
fion-chrann, -chroinn, see crann-fiona.
fion-dearcag,** *s.f.* Grape.
fion dearg, *s.m.* Port wine.
fion-dhearc, -an, *s.f.* Grape. Fion-dhearcan marbhtach, *poisonous (deadly) grapes.*

fion-dhuille,†† s.f. see fion-dhuilleag.
fion-duilleag, -an, s.f. Vine-leaf.
fion-eun,(AF) s.m. Small bird.
fion-fhàisgean, -ein, -an, s.m. Wine-press. [** gives fion-fhàsgan, pl. -ain.]
fion-fhàsgaire,* see fion-fhaisgean.
fion-fhogharadh, -aidh, s.m. Vintage.
fion-fhuil,†† -fhala, s.f. Pure, uncorrupted blood.
fion-fionn,** s.m. White wine.
fion-foirneannach, see fin-foineach.
fion-geal, s.m. White wine.
fion-geur,** s.m. Vinegar.
†fionghail, -e, s.f. see fionghal.
†fionghal, -ail,** s.m. Treason. 2 Murder of a relative.
fionghalach, a. Murderous. 2 Bloody.
————, -aich, s.m. Murderer, parricide.
————d, s.f. Murder. 2 Bloodiness.
fion-ghàradh, -aidh, -aidhnean [**-ghàrachan,] s.m. Vineyard.
fion-ghort, -airt, -an, see fion-ghàradh.
fion-lios, -an, s.m. Vineyard.
fion-liosach, a. Having vineyards.
fion-mailmhaiseach, s.m. Malmsey wine.
fion-mheug, -mhéig, s.f. Wine-whey.
fionmhor, -oire, a. Abounding in wine.
†————, -oir, -oirean, s.m. Winebibber.
fionn, -a, a. White, fair, pale. 2 Sincere, true, certain. 3 Small. 4 Fine, pleasant. 5 Pale, wan. 6 Lilac. 7 Degree of cold. 8 Resplendent, bright. 9 Known. 10 Prudent. 11 see feann. Aon ni is f. duinn, *one thing we know for certain* or *by experience;* an t-eun f., *the ptarmigan* (*white bird.*) [see note under eun-fionn.]
fionn, *pr.pt.* a' fionnadh, *v. a. & n.* Flay, skin. 2 Examine. 3 Behold, look, see. 4 Know by investigation. 5(DMC) Remove turf in order to get at the peat underneath. (also feann.)
fionn, s.m. Chief, head.
fionn, s. f. Milk. † 2 Cow. 3 Cataract in the eye. 4 (AF) Sow. 5 (AF) Hen-harrier, (bird.)
fionn,‡ *prefix,* To, against.
fionn, finne, s.f. Pretty female (fair one.)
fionna, see fionnadh.
fionnach,§ s.m. Mat-grass, see beitein.
fionnach, -aiche, a. Hairy, covered with hair or pile. 2 Rough, shaggy. †3 Old, antique.
fionnachas, -ais, s.m. Bravery.
fionnachd,* see fionnarachd. 2 Refreshment (coolness.)
fionnachdainn,** s. f. Experience. 2 Knowledge. 3 Investigation.
†fionnad, -aid, -aidean, s.m. Waggon, chariot.
fionnadh, -aidh, s. m. Flaying, skinning. 2 Trying. 3 Searching. 4 Examining. 5** Hair of a quadruped. 6** Beard. 7**Fur. 8 Fur (article of dress.) 9‡ Pile, as of cloth. 10(DMC) Removing the turf to get at the peat underneath. A' f—, *pr.pt.* of fionn.
fionnadh-balgain, s.m. Mode of skinning a carcase by a cut round the neck and without cutting down the breast or belly.
fionnadh-builg,(Fionn) *parts of Argyll* for fionnadh-balgain.
†fionna-fada, s.m. The middle finger.
fionnag, -aige, -an, s.f. White trout. 2 Young salmon. 3* Whiting. 4**see feannag. 5** Mite, see fineag.
————ach, see fineagach.
fionnagan,†† s.m. Crowberry, see caora-fionnaig.
fionnag-feòir, s.f. Fairy mouse, lesser shrew.
fionnaidh, a. Antique.
fionn-àirc, -e, -ean, s.f. *Suber album,* a white corky substance, or kind of fungus, growing on trees, and used as a styptic, also for tinder and as a razor-strop.
fionnaire, *comp.* of a. fionnar.
fionnaireachd, see fionnarachd.
fionnairead, -eid, s.m. Degree of coolness.
fionnairidh, -ean, s.f. Watching. Bheir fear na moch-eirigh buaidh air fear na f., *the early riser will beat the late watcher.*
fionnaltachd,** s.f. Fineness.
fionnamhach, -aiche, a. Hairy. 2 Rough, shaggy.
fionna-mhiong,(AC) s.f. see fionn-mhèag.
fionnan, -ain, s.m. One single hair.
fionnan-aolta, a. Whitewashed.
fionnan-feòir, -ain-fheòir, s.m. Grasshopper. 2 Balm-cricket.
fionnan-geal, -ain-ghil, *pl.* -ain-gheala,§ s.m. Grass of Parnassus, see fionnsgoth.
fionnaobh,** a. Neat, clean. 2 "Clever."
fionn-aolta,** a. Whitewashed with lime.
fionnar, *fut. aff. a.* of fionn. Shall be flayed.
fionnar, -aire, a. Cool, fresh, cold. 2 Agued. Gu f., *coldly ; with indifference.*
fionnarachadh, -aidh, s.m. Becoming cool. 2 Making cool. 3 Cooling, refreshing. 4**Refrigerating. A' f—, *pr.pt.* of fionnaraich.
fionnarachd, s.f.ind. Cool, coolness. 2 Cool breeze. Am f. an fheasgair, *in the cool of the evening.*
fionnaraich,†† *pr.pt.* a' fionnarachadh, *v.a. & n.* Cool. 2 Refrigerate. 3 Be cool.
fionnasga,s.pl. Bands with which vines are tied.
fionnas-gàraidh, s.m. Parsley, see pearsal.
†fionn-bhruinne, s.m. Fine brass.
fionnchair,** s.f. Wisdom.
fionn-chasach, a. White-footed. 2 White-legged, (cais-fhionn.) 3 Rough-legged.
†fionn-choille, s.f. Flourishing wood.
fionn-chòinneach, -ich, s.f. White moss.
†fionnchor, s.m. Wisdom, knowledge.
fionn-chosach, see fionn-chasach.
†fionn-chosmhalachd, s.f.ind. Probability.
fionn-chosmhuil,** a. Probable, like.
fionn-chu,(AF) s.m. Greyhound.
fionndach,‡‡ -aiche, a. Hairy.
fionndadh, s.m. *prov.* for fionnadh.
fionndairneach, -ich, s. m. Rank grass. 2 Downy beard.
†fionndruinne, see †fionn-bruinne. 2 (White) bronze.
†fionnfadh, -aidh, see fionnadh.
fionn-faoilidh,(AC) s. Plant
fionn-fheòir, see fionnan-feòir.
fionn-fholaidh,(AF) s.m. White kine.
fionn-fhuachd, s.f.ind. Coolness, coldness.
fionn-fhuaire, see fionnarachd.
————, *comp.* of fionnar (fionn-fhuar
————achd, see fionnarachd.
————ad, -eid, see fionnairead.
fionn-fhuar, a. see fionnar.
————achadh, see fionnarachadh.
————adh, -aidh, s.m. Cooling, refreshing. 2 Refreshment.
————aich, v. see fionnaraich.
fionnghail,** -e, s.f. see fionghal.
fionnlach,§ -aich, s. m. Bog-myrtle, see moin teach-liath.
fionnlaid,(CR) s.f. Wooden lever.
fionn-mhèag, -mhèig, s. m. White whey, whey wrung from cheese when pressed in the vat.
fionn-ogha, -oghachan, s. m. & f. Grandchild's grandchild.
†fionnrach, -aich, s.f. Daylight. Fad fionnrach mhoireach an là, *all the livelong day.*
fionnsadh,(AC) s.m. Whirl.
fionn-sgeul, -sgeòil, s.m. Fable, romance. 2 Legend. Chàin thu e mar fh., *thou hast reviled*

it as a fable.

——ach, -aiche, *a.* **Romantic.** 2 **Fabulous.**

——aiche, -an, *s.m.* **Romancer.**

fionn-sgiath, -sgéith, *s.f.* **White wing.** 2 **White shield.**

——ach,** *a.* **White-winged.** 2 **White-shielded.**

318. Fionn-sgoth. *319. Fioran.*

fionn-sgoth,§ *s.m.* **Grass of Parnassus**—*parnassia palustris.*

fionn-sgothach,** *a.* **Pertaining to grass of Parnassus.**

fionn-staoig, -ean, *s.* **The diaphragm.**

fionnta,** *a.* **Hairy, rough, shaggy, furred.** Leathar f. an daimh òig, *the hairy hide of the young bullock.*

fionntach, -aiche, *a.* **Hairy, having hair on the body.** 2****Rough, shaggy.** 3 **Furred.** 4** **Woolly.** 5†† **Having pile, as cloth.**

Fionntaidh, *s.pl.* **The Fingalians.**

fiontach, -aiche, *a.* see fionntach.

fion-teantach,** *s.m.* **Tent wine.**

fion-ubhal, -ail, *s.m.* **Grape.**

†**fionuir**, *s.f.* **Vine.**

fior,(AF) *s.m.* **Milk.**

fior, -a & fire, *a.* **True.** 2 **Genuine, pure.** 3 **Sterling (of its kind.)** 4****Just.** 5****Real.** 6 ****Perfect.** 7****Notable.** Am bheil e f. *? is it true ?* is f. e, *it is true enough* ; f. ghrùnnd an loch, *the very bottom of the loch* ; duine f., *a just man* ; f. bhochd, *very poor* ; f. chosmhuil, *very probable* ; f. mhath, *just so, very well* ; f. shlaoightire, *a complete villain* ; is f. an sean-fhacal, *the proverb holds true* ; f. dhìleas, *very nearly connected* ; suaimhneas f., *true peace* ; gu f., *truly, indeed.*

fior,** *v.a.* **Verify.**

fiorach, *s.* **Inside.** Fo 'n fhiorach no fo 'n fhuarachd, *inside or outside.*

fioradh, -aidh, *s.m.* **Verifying, certifying.**

fior-agh,(AF) *s.m.* **Two-year-old cow.**

fioraich, *v.a.* **Justify.**

fioraidheach,** *a.* **Veritable, true.**

†——d,** *s.f.* **Veracity, truth.**

fior-aithris, -ean, *s. f.* **Veracity, speaking of truth, true tale.**

fioran,§ -ain, *s.m.* **Fiorin grass**—*agrostis alba.* 2 (DC) **Muran cuartach or creeping bent-grass, a variety of sea-bent.** 3 ****Welcome.**

fior-athrais, see fior-aithris.

†**fiorcan**, -ain, -an, *s.m.* **Knot.**

fior-charaid,** *s.m.* **True friend.**

fior-chinnteach, -tiche, *a.* **Faithfully true.** 2 **Absolutely certain.**

fior-chion, *s.m.* **Appetite.**

fior-chosmhalach,** *a.* **Probable, likely.**

——d, *s.f.ind.* **Probability, likelihood.**

fior-chrann, -ainn & -oinn, *s.f.* **Sycamore tree,** see craobh-sice.

fior-chreideamh, *s. m.* **Orthodoxy.** 2****Sound faith.**

fior-chreidmheach, -mhich, *s.m.* **True believer.** 2 **Orthodox divine.**

——, -mhiche, *a.* **Orthodox.** 2 **Believing, faithful.**

fiordha,** *a.* **Sincere, true.** 2 **Religious.**

fior-dhìleas, -dhìlse, *a.* **Genuine, true.** 2 **Sincere.** 3 **Very faithful.** 4 **Near akin.**

fior-eun,†† -eòin, *s.m.* **Eagle.**

fior-fhuil, -fhala, *s.f.* **Noble blood.**

fior-ghlan, -ghloine, *a.* **Pure, clean.** 2 **Sincere.** 3 **Bright, spotless.** 4 **Blameless.** 5 **Transparent.** Le h-òr f., *with pure gold.*

fior-ghloine, *s.f.ind.* **Perfect purity or cleanness.** 2 **Spotlessness.** 3 **Blamelessness.** 4 **Brightness.** 5 **Transparency.** 6‡‡**Quintessence.** 7 ‡‡**Sincerity.**

fior-ian, -eòin, *s.* see fir-eun.

fior-iasg,(AF) *s.m.* **Salmon.**

fior-iochdar, -air, -an, *s.m.* **The very bottom.** 2 **Basis, lowest part.** F. na h-uchdach, *the very bottom of the ascent.*

fior-iochdrach, *a.* **Lowest.**

fior-iomall, -aill, *s.m.* **The utmost limit.**

fior-leamh, -a, *a.* **Very impertinent, impudent, rude or petulant.** 2(AH)**Overweening, shamelessly pert and forward.**

——adas, -ais, *s.m.* **Extreme impertinence, impudence, rudeness or petulance.**

fiormann,§ *s.m.* **Wheat,** see cruithneachd.

fior-mhath, *a.* **Perfectly good, very good, excellent.**

fior-mhaitheas, -eis, *s.m.* **Real goodness, excellence.**

†**fiornan**, -ain, *s.m.* **French wheat.**

fior-naomh, *a.* **Truly holy.** Bitheadh e f., *let him be truly holy.*

——achd, *s.f.* **True holiness.**

fior-òthaisg, see fior-uan.

fior-ordha, *a.* **Truly noble, illustrious, excellent.**

†**fiorraideach**,** *a.* **Frivolous, trifling, contemptible.** Gu f., *frivolously.*

†——d, *s. f.* **Frivolousness, insignificance.**

†**fior-raidhteach**, -aiche, *a.* **Truthful.**

†**fiorsa**, *s.m.* **Necessity.**

fior-shamhlachalachd, *s.f.* **Characteristicalness.**

†**fiort**, -an, see feart.

fiorthan,§ **Fiorin-grass,** see fioran.

fior-thobar, -air, -braichean, *s.m.* **Spring well.** 2 **Perennial well.**

fior-thobrach, -aiche, *a.* **Abounding in perennial springs or spring-wells.**

fior-uachdar, -air, *s.m.* **Top, summit.**

fior-uasal, *a.* **Truly noble, genteel, polite.**

fior-uan,(AF) *s.m.* **Hog that has had a lamb.**

fior-uisge, -uisgeachan. *s.m.* **Spring-water, perpetual fountain.** 2 **Fresh-water, in contradistinction to sea-water.** Lochan f., *a fresh-water loch.*

fios, -a, *s. m.* [*s. f.* in *Badenoch.*] **Knowledge, information.** 2 **Notice, intelligence.** 3 **Word, message.** 4‡‡**Science.** 5 **Art, understanding.** 6‡‡**Vision.** Fhuair mi f., *I got word* ; thoir f., *inform, give notice* ; fhuair sinn droch fh., *we received sad intelligence* ; am f. duit ? am bheil f. agad ? *do you know ?* tha f. agam, *I know* ; c' uin' a fhuair thu f. ? *when did you get information ?* a réir f. domh-sa, *to the best of my knowledge* ; a' s fh. do 'n bheò, *what the living know* ; 'ga f., *to her knowledge* ; 'ga fh., *to his knowledge* ; thàinig e staigh gun fh. da, *he came in unknown to him* ; gun fh. nach tig e, *not knowing whether he may come ;* gun fh. dè a ni mi, *not knowing what I shall do ;* gun fh. c'ar son, *without knowing why* ; thàinig f. ort, *a message came for you ;* f. an torraidh, *an invitation to the funeral ;* f. fuadain, *a flying report ;* f. nam fàidh, *fore-knowledge ;* am f. a bu lugha, *the slightest knowledge ;* f. air an fh., *repeated information; an urgent invitation ;* is beag f. dhomh-sa, *little do I know;* f. freagairt, *an answer to a letter ;* tha f. fithich agad, *you have a raven's knowledge*—supposed to be supernatural ; also said to cheeky children ; foighneachd air f., foighneachd a's mios' a th' ann, *asking what is well known, the worst of asking* ; chuir mi fios air a nios chugam, *I sent word to him to come from below to me.* [see ex. under dathadair.]

fiosach, -aiche, *a.* see fiosrach.

———ail, -e, *a.* Knowing.

———d, -an, *s.f.* Augury, foretelling, divination, sorcery, fortune-telling. Cha téid gu buidsiche nach fhaigh f. searbh, *who interviews a witch will get bitter news indeed.*

fiosaiche, -an, *s.m.* Fortune-teller, soothsayer, augur, diviner, sorcerer.

fiosdaidheachd, see fiosachd.

fiosail, -ala & -aile, *a.* Knowing, expert.

fios-dhearbhadh, -aidh, *s.m.* Demonstration, corroboration.

fiosnachail, see fiosrachail.

fiosrach, -aiche, *a.* Knowing, expert, well-informed. 2 Intelligent. 3 Conscious. 4 Inquisitive, prying, busy. 5 Convinced. Tha mi f., *I am conscious ;* is f. mi, *I am fully aware ;* duine f., *an intelligent man* ; am f. thu air sin ? *are you aware of that ?* mar is fhiù is mar is fhiosrach mi, *to the best of my knowledge and belief.*

———adh, -aidh, *s.m.* Inquiry, act of inquiring, questioning or ascertaining. 2**Examining. 3 Knowledge. 4 Experience. O m' fhéin-fhiosrachadh, *from my own experience ;* a' f. a mach, *ascertaining.* A' f—, *pr. pt.* of fiosraich.

fiosrachail, -ala, *a.* Knowing, intelligent. 2 Inquisitive.

fiosraich, *pr.pt.* a' fiosrachadh, *v. a.* Inquire, ask, inquire after, investigate. 2 Try, examine. 3**Visit. 4 Ascertain. Cha'n fhiosraich, mur feòraich, *nothing ask, nothing learn.*

fiosraiche, *s.m.* Critic.

fiothal,(AF) *s.m.* Calf.

fiothnaise,** *s.f.* Sorcery. 2 Poison. 3 Bad news, detestable news.

fiothran, see fioran.

fir, *gen. sing. & n. pl.* of fear. For compounds of fir, not given below, see under fear.

†**firb**, *s.* Swiftness, rapidity.

fir-bhogha, *s.pl.* Archers.

fir-bhréige, *s.pl.* Puppets.

Fir-bholg, *s.pl.* The Belgæ. 2 The ancient Irish.

fir-cheart,** -cheirt, *s. m.* Justice, righteousness.

fir-chlis, *s.f.* The Northern lights, aurora borealis, "merry dancers." [Preceded by the art. NA.] An uair a bhios na fir-chlis ri mire 's gann nach dean iad milleadh, *when the merry-dancers play they are like to slay*—the playfulness of the merry-dancers is supposed to end occasionally in quite a serious fight. Next morning, when children see red patches of lichen on the stones, they say among themselves, thug na fir-chlis fuil á càch-a-chéile an raoir, *the merry-dancers bled each other last night.* [The appearance of these lights in the sky is considered a sign of the approach of unsettled weather.]

fir-chlisneach, *s.f.* see fir-chlis.

fir-chneatain, *s.pl.* Backgammon-men.

fir-chrann, *s. f.* (fior-chrann) Sycamore-tree, see craobh-sice.

fir-dhris,** *s.f.* Bramble.

fir-dhuan, *s.pl.* see under fear-fuinn.

fìre, **fìreachd**, } ‡‡ *s.f.* Truth. 2 Event.

fìre-faire ! *inter.* Ay, ay, what ! what a pother ! Is fheàrr "fìre-faire" na "mo thruaigh," *better to be envied than pitied.*

fireach, -ich, -ichean, *s.m.* Hill, moor, mountain, acclivity. 2 Top of a hill. 3 High barren ground. 4 Name of a dog. Air f. an fhéidh, *on the deer-moor ;* gheibheadh tu feannagan firich, *you would find the forest crows*—said to those who boast that they can obtain impossibilities.

———ail, -ala, *a.* Manly. 2 Cheerful. 3 Showy. 4 Of a good address. 5 Active, nimble. 6 Barren. 7 Moorish, upland.

firead, -eid, -eidean,*s.f.* Gaelic spelling of *ferret.*

———ach ** *a.* Like a ferret. 2 Abounding in ferrets.

fireadh,** -ridh, *s. m.* Bottom. 2 Truth. 3 Flower.

firean, -ein, *s.m.* Manikin, dwarf.

fìrean, -an, *dat.pl.* fìreanaibh & fìreantaibh, *s.m.* Righteous man. Aoibhneas air an fh., *the righteous rejoicing.*

fìreanach, -aiche, *a.* Righteous. 2 Honest.

———, -aich, *s.m.* see fìrean.

———adh, -aidh, *s.m.* Justification. 2 Act of justifying. A' f—, *pr. pt.* of fìreanaich.

fìreanaich, *pr. pt.* a' fìreanachadh, *v.a.* Justify, excuse. 2 Confer righteousness.

———te, *past pt.* Justified, verified.

†**fireann**, *s.m.* Chain, garter.

fìreann,** *a.* Upright, righteous, just. 2 see fìrionn.

fìreannach, see fìrionnach.

fìreannachail, -ala, *a.* Justificative.

fìreannachair,** *s.m.* Avower.

fìreannachd, *s.f.* see fìrionnachd.

fìreannachd, *s.f.ind.* Justification.

fìreanta, *a.* True, just, righteous. 2 Loyal. Gu f., *faithfully.*

———chd, *s.f ind.* Righteousness, integrity, honesty, uprightness, sincerity, truth. 2 Faithfulness, loyalty.

fìreantaibh, *dat.pl.* of fìrean.

fìreas, *Loch Ness* for pìreas.

firein, -ean, *s.m., dim.* of fear. Manikin.

fireineach,†† *a.* Abounding in manikins.

fìr-eun, -eòin, *s.m.* Eagle, see iolair-bhuidhe.

fìreunachadh, -aidh, see fìreanachadh.

fìreunta, see fìreanta.

fìr-iasg, see fìor-iasg.

fìrich, *gen.sing.* of fìreach.

fìrinn, -ean, *s.f.* Truth, verity. 2 Faithfulness. 3 Righteousness. Tròcair is f., *mercy and truth.*

fìrinn, *s.f.* Girl. 2 Maiden—*Braemar.*

fìrinneach, -iche, *a.* True, just, honest. 2 Upright, righteous. 3 Exact. 4 Faithful. 5 Sincere, loyal, Gu f., *faithfully.*

———, -ich, *s.m.* Justified person, one of the righteous.

———adh, -aidh, *s.m.* Justification. 2 Act of justifying. A' f—, *pr. pt.* of fìrinnich.

fìrinneachd, *s.f.* Truth, veracity. 2 Justification. 3 Righteousness. 4 Sincerity, loyalty.

fìrinnich, *pr.pt.* a' fìrinneachadh, *v.a.* Justify, excuse, absolve from accusation. 2 Verify. 3 Confer righteousness. 4 Affirm.

fìrinnichte, *a. & past pt.* of fìrinnich. Justified, verified.

firinn-shuidhichte, *s.f.* Aphorism, axiom.
firinteachd, see fìreantachd.
fìr-ìochdrach, see fìor-ìochdrach.
fìr-iomall, -aill, see fìor-iomall.
fir-ionadach, *s.pl.* Lieutenants.
firionn, *a.* Male, masculine. F. boirionn, *hermaphrodital.*
——,** *s.m.* Male. F. 'na threud, *a male in his flock.*
——ach, -aich, *s.m.* Male. 2 Man.
——achd, *s.f.ind.* Manhood. 2 Virility. 3 Male species.
firlion, *v.a.* Multiply.
——aich, -aidh, *s.m.* Multiplying. A' f—, *pr. pt.* of firlion.
firmidh, *Badenoch* for imiridh.
†fìs, -e, *s.f.* Colour, dyeing. 2 Dream. 3 Knowledge.
fise faise ! *int.* Noise of things breaking. 2 Clandestine private talk.
fiseag, see piseag.
fit,(DC) fiteach, *pl.* fitean & fiteachan, *s.f.* see fidean.
†fit, -e, *s.f.* Life, living. 2 Breakfast, collation.
fiteag-na-machrach,§ *s. f.* Field foxtail-grass.—*alopecurus ægrestis.*
fiteag-an-lòin, *s.f*, Meadow foxtail grass—*alopesurus pratensis.*
fiteag-cham,§ *s.f.* Kind of grass called *alopecurus geniculatus.*

320. Fideag-na-machrach. *321. Fideag-an-lòin.*

fitean,** *s.m.* Quill.
fith, *s.f.* Land.
†fith-cheall, -chioll, *s.m.* Philosopher.
†fithchil, *s.pl.* Tables, chess-board.
fithchiod, *a.* see fichead.
†fithchioll, -a, *s.m.* Chess-board. 2 Complete suit of armour.

322. Fiteag-cham. *323. Fitheach.*

fitheach, -thich, *s.m.* Raven—*corvus corax.* Tha fios fithich aige, *he has raven's knowledge*—supposed to be supernatural ; fios fithich gu ròic, *raven's knowledge to a feast*—said of one arriving accidentally and opportunely ; thug na fithich aran ann, *the ravens brought bread.* [The raven, the Clan MacDougall bird, was considered sacred in Scandinavia, and is supposed to have been introduced into the clan by a daughter of Olave the Red.] [** gives Vulture.]
fitheach-fairge, see fitheach-mara.
——— -garbh,(AF) *s.m.* Vulture.
——— -mara,(AF) *s.m.* Cormorant.
fithean,(AF) -ein, *s.m.* Hog, boar.
†fithil, *s.m.* Poetaster.
fithreach, *s.m.* Species of edible seaweed, see duileasg.
fithriach, *s.m.* see duileasg.
fiù, *a.* Worthy, estimable, worth. 2 Deserving. †3 Like, alike. †4 Edible. Cha'n fh. e dad, *it is not worth anything ;* cha'n fh. e air, *he is not deserving of it ;* cha'n fh. e mise, *he is not worthy of me ;* mar is fh. is fhiosrach mi, *to the best of my knowledge and belief.*
fiù, *s.m.ind.* Worth, value, price. 2*Knowledge. Is beag t' fh., *you are worth little.*
†fiùbhaidh, *s.f.* see fiùthaidh.
————, -ean, *s.m.* Prince. 2 Valiant chief. 3††Hero. 4 Company.
fiùbhas, -ais, *s.m.* Dignity, worth.
fiuch, *v.a.* Boil, simmer. 2 Estuate. 3 Spring forth.
——ach,** *a.* Boiling. 2 That boileth.
——adh,** -aidh, *s.m.* Boiling, simmering. 2 Regurgitating. 3 Heat.
——aireachd,** *s.f.* Boiling rage.
——ar,(CR) *a.* Dapper, nimble—*W. of Ross.*
fiùdhail, see fiùghail.
fiùgh, *a.* see fiù.
——aidh, -ean, *s.m.* see fiùthaidh.
——ail, -ala, *a.* Worthy.
fiughair, -ean, *s. f.* Earnest expectation, hope, longing. 2**Memory. 3** Regard, respect. Cha'n 'eil f. againn ris, *we do not expect him.*
————each, -iche, *a.* Full of hope, cheerful, happy, expectant. 2 Having a good memory. Gu f., *hopefully.*
————eachd, ** *s.f.ind.* Hopefulness, expectancy. 2 Reminiscence.
fiughalach, *a.* see fiùghail.
————,(DMy) *s.m.* Worthy man.
————d, *s.f.ind.* Worthiness. 2 Considerableness.
fiughan, see fiodhan.
fiùghanta, *a.* see fiùghantach.
————ch, *a.* Generous, liberal, benevolent, charitable. 2 Brave, heroic. 3**Ample. 4†† Worthy. Gu f., *generously ;* cridhe f., *a generous heart.*
————chd, *s.f.ind.* Generosity, benevolence, charity, practice of benevolence. 2 Bravery. heroism. 3**Ampleness. 4††Worthiness.
————s, -ais, *s.m.* see fiùghantachd.
fiughar, see fiughair.
fiùi, see fiùghaidh.
fiull, see feall.
fiultag, *s.f.* Fetter on two lambs or sheep, to keep them together, a fore-foot of each being tied to either end.
fiun,(AF) *s.f.* Cow, see fionn.
fiùnas,** -ais, *s.m.* Worth, price, value.
fiundach,** *a.* Worthy, deserving.
fiundas,** -ais, *s.m.* Merit, worth. 2 Dignity.
fiundruin,** *a.* Polished, smooth. An roth f. *the polished wheel.*
fiuntach, see fiundach.
fiùrach, -aich, -aichean, *s.f.* see iùbhrach.
——— -tarsuing, see fiodhrach-tarsuing.
fiuradh,** -aidh, *s.m.* Satisfaction. 2 Comfort. 3 Completion. 4 Sufficiency.
fiùran, -ain, *s.m.* Sapling, branch. 2 Straight free-growing young tree. 3 Blooming or handsome youth. 4§ Cow-parsnip, see odharan. 5

Tendril, germ, sprout. 6** Bud of a wild briar. 7**Hunter, huntsman. 8 (DU) *metaphorically* Hero. F. seasmhach, *a stout stripling*; a' cur sùgh 's na fiùrain, *putting sap in the tendrils*; f. aigeantach, *a mettlesome youth*.

——ach, -aiche, *a.* Flourishing, blooming, youthful. 2**Strong. 3 Like a twig or sapling. 4††Full of young trees.

——ta, *a.* see fiùranach. 2(DMC) Active, smart in walking.

fiusach,** -aiche, *a.* Earnest. Gu f., *earnestly.*

fiùthaidh, -ean, *s.m.* Subject, matter. †2 Timber for boats. †3 Arrow. †4 Sheaf of arrows. †5 Gun. †6 Spear. †7 Poet. †8 Boat. F. is bolg, *an arrow and quiver.*

fiùthail, *a.* see fiùghail.

flaiche, *s.f.* Sudden gust of wind.

——ach, -iche, *a.* Windy, gusty, squally.

flaindearg, see flann-dearg.

†flaith, *s.f.* Milk.

flaith, *gen. sing.* of flath.

†——, -ean, *s.m.* Flower. 2 Strong ale.

flaith-chiste, -eachan, *s.f.* Royal treasure.

flaitheachd, -an, *s.f.* Government, supremacy. 2**Aristocracy.

flaitheamhlachd, see flathalachd.

flaitheamhnas, -ais, see flaitheanas.

flaitheamhuil, see flathail.

flaithean, *n. pl.* of flath.

flaitheanas, -ais, *s.m.* Heaven. 2 Sovereignty, dominion, 3**Kingdom. 4**Reign.

flaitheas, -eis, *s.m.* Sovereignty, dominion. 2 Kingdom. 3 see flaitheanas. Os ceann nam f., *above the heavens.*

————ach, -aiche, *a.* Heavenly. 2 Princely, noble, stately. Talla f., *a princely hall.*

flaitheil, see flathail.

flanainn, *s.f.* Gaelic form of *flannel.*

†flann, *a.* Red, blood-red.

†——, *s.m.* Blood.

flannach, *a.* Purple, red.

flann-bhuinneach, -ich, *s.f.* Bloody flux. 2 Dysentry.

flann-dhearg, *s.m.* Purple. 2**Red. 3 Staynard colour in *heraldry*, used to express some disgrace or blemish in a family.

flann-fhuil, -fhola, *s.f.* Clotted gore.

flann-sgaoileadh,** *s.m.* Dysentry.

flann-shùileach, -iche, *a.* Red-eyed.

flasg, -aisge, *pl.* -an & -aichean, *s. f.* Gaelic spelling of *flask.* 2**Basket. 3**Vessel made of wicker. 4**Bottle covered with wicker.

flath, -aith, *pl.* -an & flaithean, *s.m.* King. 2 Prince, chief, commander. 3 Hero, champion. F. nan dùl, *God*; f. de 'n fhine làimh-thréin, *a commander of the strong-armed clan.*

——ail, -ala & -e, *a.* Princely, stately. 2 Showy, gay. 3 Elegant. 4 Victorious. 5 Illustrious. 6 Noble. 7 Splendid, magnificent. 8 Heavenly. 9 August. Gu f., *nobly, in a princely manner*; ceum f., *a stately step.*

——aileachd, see flathalachd.

flathalachd, *s.f.ind.* Augustness. 2 Princeliness. 3 Stateliness, pomp. 4 Showiness. 5 Courteousness. 6††Gracefulness.

flathan, *n.pl.* of flath.

flathas, see flaitheanas.

————ach, -aiche, *a.* Elegant. 2 Splendid, showy. 3**Stately, majestic. 4**Victorious. 5**Heroic. 6††Divine.

————achd, ** *s.f.* Princeliness. 2 Stateliness. 3 Elegance. 4 Victoriousness. 5 Heroism.

flath-fhaclach, -aiche, *a.* Happily expressed.

flath-innis, *s.f.* see flaitheanas.

flath-mhaise,** *s.f.* Princeliness. 2 Nobleness. 3 Stateliness. 4 Bravery.

————ach, -iche, *a.* Brave, heroic. 2 Princely, noble. 3 Stately. Gu f., *in a princely manner.*

flath-mhòd, *s.m.* Diet (meeting.)

flath-shonas, *s.m.* see flaitheanas.

flath-threun, *s.m.* Demi-god.

fleachdail, -ala, *a.* Flowing in ringlets.

fleadh, -a, -an, *s. m.* Feast, banquet, entertainment, carousal. 2 Company at a feast. 3(DMC) Spell. F. do m' réir, *a feast worthy of me.*

————ach, -aiche, *a.* Of, or connected with feasting, banqueting, or carousing, convivial, prone to entertain. Aodach f., *dress clothes*; cota f., *a dress coat.*

————achas, -ais, *s.m.* Feasting, banqueting, conviviality, carousal, revelry.

————achd, *s.f.* see fleadhachas.

fleadhadh, -aidh, *s.m.* Brandishing.

fleadh-oidhche, *s.m.* Soirée.

fleagh, see fleadh.

————ach, see fleadhach.

————achas, see fleadhachas.

fleann-uisge,§ *s.f.* Water crowfoot, rodewort, ram's-foot—*ranunculus aquaticus.*

[324. *Fleann-uisge.*

fleasg, -a, -an, *s.f.* Rod, wand. 2 Garland, wreath. 3 Fillet. 4 Crown. 5 Ring. 6 Chain. 7***rarely* Sheaf. 8**Moisture. 9 Bottle, flask. F. òir, *a crown of gold.* [The *fleasg* was, of old, the sign of manhood. No one could wear any head-dress until he proved himself by testing his strength that he was able to fill a man's place, hence *fleasgach.* The lift-stones (clachan-togail) are still to be found in many parishes near the church—DC.

fleasgach, -aich, -aichean, *s.m.* Young man. 2 Handsome youth. 3 Bachelor. 4 Best man at a wedding. 5** *rarely* clown. 6**Cornfield. 7**Fiddler. 'Nuair a bha thu 'nad fh. òg, *when you were a stripling*; f. fear na bainnse, *the best man at a wedding.*

————an, -ain, *s.m., dim.* of fleasgach. Little stripling. 2**Rustic. 3**Mean fellow.

fleasgaich, *gen.sing. & n. pl.* of fleasgach.

fleasgairt, -ean, *s.f.* Vessel, barge. 2 Vessel hung with festoons.

fleasgan,** -ain, *s.m.* Treasure. 2 *n.pl.* of fleasg.

fleigire,(AF) *s. m.* Cormorant.

fleisd,** *v.a.* Slay, slaughter, butcher.

fleisdear, -eir, -an, *s.m.* Arrow-maker. [fleisdeir also used as *nom.*]

————achd, *s.f.* Art or business of arrow-making.

†fleisdeoir, *s.m.* see fleisdear. 2 Gaelic form of *flesher.*

†————eachd, *s.f.* Gaelic form of *fleshery.*

fleodag,(DC) *s.f.* Snowflake. [Pleodag in *Uist.*]

fleòdar, -air, *s.m.* see feòdar.

————ach, see feòdarach.

fleòdradh, -aidh, *s.m.* Floating. 2 Buoyancy. Tha mi f. le fallus, *I am in a bath of perspiration.*

fleodruinn, -ean, *s.f.* Buoy.

fleog,* *s.m.* Sole (fish.) 2††Flounder. 3††Fluke.

——an, -ain, *s.m.* Untidy person. 2 Flabby person. 3**Any flat fish. 4**Sole. 5**Fluke. 6**Flounder.

——anach, -aiche, *a.* Untidy, tawdry, unshapely. 2 Flabby. 3 Like a flat fish. 4 Abounding in flat fish.

——anachd,** *s.f.* Flabbiness.

fleoidhte, *a.* Flaccid, flabby.

fliche, *s.f.ind.* Moisture, phlegm. 2**Humours.

3**Water. 4 Wetness.
fliche, *comp.* of fliuch. Wetter. 2 Wettest.
flicheachd,** *s.f.* Humour of the body. 2 Moistnre, ooziness.
flichead, -id, *s. f.* Moisture, ooziness. 2 Degree of moisture or wetness.
flicheann,** -flichne, see flichne.
fliche-inneal,** *s.m.* Hygrometer.
flichmheas, *s.m.* Any measure for liquids.
flichmheidh,‡‡ see flichmheas.
flichne, *s.m.ind.* Sleet—*Cowal, Coll.*
flichneach, -eiche, *a.* Sleety. 2 Wet. 3 Phlegmy.
————d, *s.f.ind.* Sleet. 2 Ooziness, moisture. 3 Cold weather.
flichneadh, -nidh, *s.m.* Sleet. 2 Oozing. 3 see flichneachd.
flichneadh-sneachd,(CR) *s.m.* Sleet—*W. of Ross.*
flichneadh, see flichneachd.
flichnidh, -e, *a.* see flichneach.
————, *s.* see flichneadh.
flige,§ *s. f.* Sandwort—*arenaria alsine.* 2 see fliodh.
flin,(DMy) *Lewis* for flinne.
flinne,* *s.m.* Sleet—*Islay, Arran.*
———achd, see flichneachd.
fliochd,** *s. f.* The second dram taken after breakfast. [see note under friochd.]
fliodh, -a, *s.m.* Chickweed—*stellaria media.* 2 ‖Wen. 3 Excrescence. Duine air am bi f., *a man who has a wen.*

325. Flige. *326. Fliodh.*

327. Fliodh-a'-bhalla. *328. Fliodh-an-tugha.*

fliodh-a'-bhalla, -a-, *s.m.* §Dwarf elder—*sambucus ebulus.* [* gives Danewort.]
fliodhach, -aiche, *a.* Wenny. 2 Abounding in chickweed.
fliodhan, -ain, -an, *s.m.* Little wen or excrescence.
————ach, -aiche, *a.* Full of little wens. 2 Like a little wen.
fliodh-an-tugha,§ -a-, *s.m.* Species of fumitory —*corydalis claviculata.* So called because it is frequently found on old thatched roofs. It has long fragile stems and small whitish flowers.
fliodh-mór, *s.m.* see fliodh-an-tugha.

fliodh-na-nathrach, *s.m.* Adder's wort.
fliothasg,(CR) *s.f.* Earthworm—*Suthd.*
†flitheachd, *s.m.ind.* Matter.
flithne,(CR) *s.f.* Sleet—*Skye, Arran.*
flithne-sneachda, flithne-uisge, } (DC) Sleet—*Uist.*
fliùc, *s.f.* Fluke of an anchor.
fliuch, fliche, *a.* Wet, moist, damp, oozy. Là f., *a rainy day*; fuar, f. gun deò léirsinn, *cold, wet and stone blind*; bàta f., *a boat given to taking waves on board.*
fliuch, *pr.pt.* a' fliuchadh, *v.a.* & *n.* Wet, make wet, moisten. 2 Water. 3(DC) Make drunk —*Uist.* Fliuch e, *wet it.*
———ach, -aiche, *a.* Wet, rainy, humid, oozy.
———adh, -aidh, *s.m.* Wetting, act of wetting or watering. 2 Wet weather, moistening rain. A' f—, *pr.pt.* of fliuch. 'Ga fhliuchadh, *wetting it.*
———aidh, *fut.aff.a.* of fliuch. Shall wet.
———ain,** *s.f.* Juice, moisture, wetness.
———alachd, *s.f.ind.* Rainy weather, wetness, moistness.
———an, -ain, *s.m.* Wet spot. 2 Mark caused by wetting. 3 Drop of any fluid.
fliuch-bheulach, -aiche, *a.* Watery-mouthed. 2 That spits much about. 3 That tipples. 4 That ships water.
fliuch-bhileach,** *a.* see fliuch-bheulach.
fliuch-bhòrd, -bhùird, *s.m.* The plank of a boat next the keel, keel-board.
fliuchlachd,** *s.f.* Wet weather, continued rain. 2 Puddle.
fliuchneachd, see fliuchlachd.
fliuchras, -ais, *s.m.* Moisture.
fliuch-shneachd, -a, *s. m.* Sleet, moist snow. [*pron.* flichneachd.]
fliuch-shrònach, -aiche, *a.* Phlegmatic, snotty.
fliuch-shùil, -shùla, -shùilean, *s.f.* Blear-eye.
—————each, -aiche, *a.* Rheum-eyed. 2 Having blear-eyes. 3 Tearful. 4 Ophthalmic.
—————eachd, *s.f.ind.* Bleaeredness of the eyes. 2 Running of water from the eyes. 3 Ophthalmia.
fliug,(DC) *s.f.* Sleet—*Barra.*
fliuiche, *s.m.* see fliche.
fliuiche, (*for* fliche), *comp.* of fliuch.
fliuichead,†† *s.f.* Wetness, moisture.
flò, *s.f.ind.* Hallucination, infatuation, stupefaction. Thàinig flò-chadail air, *he dozed* or *slumbered*; chuir e f. orm, *it amazed* or *dazed me.*
flocas,** -ais, *s.m.* Lock of wool.
†floch, *a.* Lax, soft.
flod, -a, *s.m.* State of floating. 2 see plod. 3‡†Fleet. Air f., *floating.*
flod, *v.a.* Float. An do fh. am bàta? *has the boat floated?*
flodach, -aiche, *a.* see plodach.
flodadh, -aidh, *s.m.* Floating. 2 State of floating.
flòdar, *Kiltarlity* for feòdar.
flùirean, -ein, see flùran.
flùireineach, -iche, *a.* see flùranach.
flùr, -ùir, *pl.* flùirean & flùraichean, *s.m.* Flour. 2 Meal. 3 Flower. 4 Nosegay.
——ach, -aiche, *a.* Floury. 2 Mealy, like meal. 3 Pulverized. 4 Flowery.
——an, -ain, *s.m.* Floweret, blossom. 2 Nosegay.
——an, *n.pl.* of flùr.
——anach, -aiche, *a.* Flowery, full of blossoms.
——anachd,** *s.f.* Floweriness. 2 Botany. 3 Horticulture.
——anaiche,** *s.m.* Botanist. 2 Florist.
——an-cluigeanach,§ see plùran-cluigeanach.
flùr-a'-Phrionnsa,§ *s.m.* The Prince's flower—*calystegia soldanella.* A kind of pink convolvulus, originally sown by Prince Charles in

1745 when he landed in Eriskay, and still growing in that island.
flusg,** -uisg, *s.m.* Flux.
fluth, -uith, *s. m.* Chickweed. 2 Wen.
——ach, -aiche, *a.* see fliodhach.
fò,(AC) *s.m.* Brink. Fò a' bhàis, *the brink of death.*
fo, *prep.* Under, beneath, below. 2 At the foot of. 3 ‡‡ Towards. Aspirates a noun sing, definite or indefinite, and governs the dative case. Tha tighinn fodham, *it is my intention,* or *I am inclined to;* fo chìs, *tributary;* fo bhròn, *mournful* ; fo leòn, *wounded* ; fo fheasgar, *before evening* ; caidleam fo 'n fheur, *let me sleep beneath the turf* ; dà thoman fo dharaig, *two little mounds at the foot of an oak* ; bheir mi an saoghal fo 'm cheann, *I will go abroad and take the world for my pillow—i.e.* I will run away and take my chance in the world.

329. Flùr-a'-Phrionnsa.

Combined with the personal pronouns thus: fodham, *under me* ; fodhad, *under thee* ; fodha, *under him* ; foipe, *under her* ; fodhainn, *under us* ; fodhaibh, *under you* ; fopa, *under them.*
†fo. *s.m.* King, sovereign. 2 Honour. 3 Regard, esteem. 4 Decency.
†fo, *a.* Good. 2 Unconcerned. 3 Easy, quiet. 4 Powerful.
†fo, *v.* see bha.
†foain, *s.f.* Swarm, crowd.
fob, *v. Suth'd* for ob. (Cease, give over, faint, refuse.)
fobair,** *s.f.* Advancement. 2 Rencontre. 3 Undertaking.
fobhaidh,** *a.* Swift, rapid, quick, nimble.
fo-bhaile, -bhailtean, *s.m.* Suburb.
fobhair,** *s.f.* Salve, ointment. F. shùl, *an eye-salve.*
†——, -e, *a.* Sick, weak.
†——t, -ean, *s.f.* Drenching. 2 Salve.
fobhannan, -ain, *s.m.* see fòthannan.
fobhar,* (*bh* sounded *v*) *s.m.* Harvest.
fobharradh,* see fogharadh.
fobh-thomain,(AF) *s.f.* Dormouse.
fo-bhuail, *v.a.* Strike gently, pat. 2 Strike below.
fo-bhualadh, -aidh, *s.m.* Striking gently, stroking. A' f—, *pr.pt.* of fo-bhuail.
fo-bhuidhe,** *a.* Tawny, yellowish.
fo-bhuille, -ean, *s.f.* Gentle blow, slight stroke. 2 Understroke.
fobhurtach, -aiche, *a.* Quick, nimble, sudden.
foc,** see fogha.
†fòc, *s.m.* Voice.
focal, -ail, -clan, *s.m.* see facal.
—— -aonaidh, see facal-aonaidh.
—— -freumhachd, see facal-freumhachd.
—— -freumhaiche, see facal-freumhaiche.
focalach, -aiche, see faclach.
focalaiche, see faclaiche.
fòcalan, see feòcullan.
focall, -aill, see facal.
fochaid, -e, *s.f.* Scoffing, mocking, scorn, ridicule, derision. Fear f., *a mocker* ; fear na f., *the mocker.*
fochaid, *v.a.* see fochaidich. This verb takes the prep. *air* after it, simple or compounded, as, f. air, *mock him.*
fochaide, *s.f.* Disease, disorder.
fochaideach, -iche, *a.* Scoffing, mocking, ridiculing, deriding, inclined to scoff or mock.
fochaideachd,** *s.f.* Apishness.
fochaidich, *v.a.* Scoff, jeer, scorn, mock, deride, ridicule.
†fochain, *s. f.* Cause, motive, reason. 2 Disturbance.
†fochaidin, -ean, *s.f.* Disturbing.
fochair, *s. m.* Presence, company, nearness, neighbourhood. 2 Conjunction. Dithis 'nam f., *two in contact with them;* am f., *near to, in presence of* ; 'nam fh., *in my presence* ; 'na f., *in her presence.*
†fochall, -aill, *s.m.* Dirt, filth.
fochallan, see foicheallan.
fochann, -ainn, *s.m.* Young corn in the blade. 2**Plant. 3**Food, provender. 4**Chit. Fo fh., *in blade* ; tha f. air an eòrna, *the barley has bladed.*
————ach, -aiche, *a.* Of, or pertaining to, growing corn. 2††Brairded.
fochar, *s.m.* see fochair. †2 Wind.
fochas,§ -ais, *s.m.* Marsh-mallow, see leamhadh. [*lit.* the itch, so called from being used as a remedy for that disorder.] 2**Voraciousness.
†fo-chathair, -thraichean, *s.f.* Suburb.
fo-cheannard, -aird, -an, *s.m.* Lieutenant.
†fochd, *s.m.* Interrogation.
fochd,(DC) *s.f.* Hole where a crab or lobster retires—*Uist.* [faichd.]
fòchdalan, -ain, -an, see feòcullan.
†fochla, *s.m.* The common people.
fochla,(AF) *s.m.* Lion's den.
†fochlach,** -aich, *s.m.* Lowest order of poets or philosophers.
fochladh,** -aidh, *s.m.* Den, cave. 2 Palace. 3 Value or worth of anything. 4 Offering.
fochlas,** -ais, *s.m.* Prize. 2 Gift. 3 Reward for valour. Fìon is f. is feòil, *wine, a reward of valour and venison.*
fochnadh,** -aidh, *s.m.* Dry rotten wood.
fochradh, see fògradh.
fochraic,** *s.f.* Happiness, bliss, felicity.
fochras,** -ais, *s.m.* Bosom, breast.
fo-chrodh,(AF) *s. m.* Inferior, little, mean or small cattle.
fochuidhe,** *s.f.* Flout, jeer, derision, scorn.
†fochuidmheach, -eich, *s.m.* Joking. 2 Mocker.
fochuin, see fochain.
fochunn, see fochann.
————ach, see fochannach.
focla, *pl.* of focal, for faclan.
†focla, *s.m.* Proposition, maxim.
foclach, -aiche, see faclach.
foclachadh, -aidh, see faclachadh.
focladair, -ean, see facladair.
————eachd, see faclaireachd.
foclaich, *v.* see faclaich.
foclaiche, -ean, see faclaiche.
foclair, -ean, see faclair.
————eachd, see faclaireachd.
foclairiche, see facladair.
foclan, see feòcullan.
focull, -uill, see facal.
focullan, see feòcullan.
fo'd, (for fothad), under thee.
fo d' (fo do) Under thy, beneath thy.
fòd, *s.f.* see fòid. †2 *s.m.* Art, science, skill.
†fòdach, -aiche, *a.* Wise, discreet.
†fodachadh, -aidh, *s.m.* Obstruction.
fodair, *gen.sing.* of fodar.
fodair, *v.a.* Fodder, give food to cattle.
fodar, -air, *s.m.* Straw, hay, provender, fodder. [*gen.* in *Suth'd.* fodrach.]
fodarach,** *a.* see fodrach.
†fodh, *s.m.* Knowledge, skilfulness.
fodha,(AH) *s.m.* Sunken rock. 2 Surface (of the sea.)

fodha, *prep.pron.* (fo+e) Under him or it, below him or it. 2 Under his command. Tha 'n là ag brath leigeil fodha, *the day is well nigh past*, [* translates this as, *this day is likely to rain;*] tha a' ghrian a' dol f., *the sun is setting.* When two men are rowing, if the one in charge wants to stop the boat he says "leig f." "cum f." *or* "dean f." *back water ;* if he wishes to stop quickly, or even put the boat backwards, he says "dean f. gu math," or "f. na 's fhèarr" ; chaidh e fodha, *he sank.* [*emphatic*, fodha-san]

fodhad, *prep. pron.* Under thee, below thee, beneath thee. An leabaidh a ta f., *the bed which is under thee.*

fodhaibh, *prep.pron.* Under you, beneath you, below you.

fodhail,** *s.f.* Division. 2 Dissolving. 3 Releasing. 4(DC) Homage.

†**fodhail**,** *a.* Loose, release, untie.

fodhaileach,(DC) *a.* Rendering homage.

fodhainn, *prep. pron.* Under us, beneath us, below us. *emphatic*, fodhainne.

fodhair,** *s.f.* Froth.

fodham, *prep. pron.* Under me, beneath me. 2 Under my command. *emphatic*, fodhamsa. Thàinig sin fodham, *I was so disposed ;* thàinig f. falbh, *I determined to go ;* tha tighinn f. èirigh, *I am inclined to rise, it is my intention* or *purpose to rise.* [*emphatic*, fodham-sa.]

†**fodhb**, -a, *s.m.* Cutting down.

†**fodhla**, *a.* Learned.

fo-dhord, *s.m.* Loud noise. 2 Conspiracy.

†**fodhòrd**, *s.m.* Humming of bees, whispering. 2 Conspiracy, plot.

fo-dhorsach, see fath-dhorsach.

fo-dhorus, see fath-dhorus.

fodhpa, see fopa.

fo-dhuine, -dhaoine, *s.m.* Dwarf. 2 Servant. 3 Plebeian. 4‡‡Ploughman. 5 Farmer.

fo-dhùrdan,** -ain, *s.m.* Humming, low murmur. 2 Conspiracy.

fodrach,** *a.* Having much straw or fodder.

fodradh, -aidh, *s.m.* Giving of provender, hand-feeding of cattle.

fodraich,* *pr. pt.* a' fòdradh, *v.a.* Give provender, fodder.

†**foduair**, *s.f.* Caution, notice.

†**foduchadh**, -aidh, *s.m.* Obstruction.

†**fodurluasach**, -aiche, *a.* Busy.

fo eagal, *adv.* Aghast.

fo-fheasgar, Towards evening.

fo-fhlaitheachd, *s.f.ind.* Lieutenancy.

†**fogail**, *v.a.* Teach. 2 Dictate. 3 Loosen, untie.

fogair,** *s.f.* Proclamation, command.

†**fògair**, -ean, *s.m.* Exile (person.) [spelt fògaire by McL & D.]

fògair, *pr.pt.* a' fògradh & a' fògairt, *v.a.* Expel, banish, drive away forcibly. 2 Chase, pursue. 3 Warn, order.

fogair,** *v.a.* Warn. 2 Order, command.

fògairt, *s.f.ind.* Banishment, exile, expulsion. 2 Chasing, pursuing, driving away forcibly. 3 Banishing, expelling. A' f—, *pr.pt.* of fògair. Air f., *in exile.*

fògarach, see fògrach.

fògaradh, see fògradh.

fògaraiche,** *s.m.* Bandit.

fògaraichte, *past pt.* of fògair. Banished, exiled, expelled.

fògarrach, *s.m.* see fògrach.

†**fogartha**, *a.* Gracious.

fogasg, see fagus.

fogh, *a.* Careless, unconcerned, indifferent, easy.

†**fogh**, *s.m.* Attack. 2 Rape. 3 Hospitality. 4 Pirate.

fogha,** *a.* Suffrage.

foghail, -ean, *s.f.* Hostile incursion. 2 Plunder, spoil, robbery. 3 Offence, offensiveness. 4 Sorrow, grief, vexation. Gun àrdan gun fh., *without pride or offensiveness.*

fòghail, -ean, *s.f.* Noise, bustle. 2(DMC) Delight. 3(DMC) Excitement.

foghail,** *v.a.* Plunder, spoil. 2 Make a hostile incursion.

———iche,** *s.m.* Plunderer, spoiler.

foghain, *pr.pt.* a' foghnadh, *v.a.* Suffice, be sufficient. 2 Avail. 3 Do for, kill. 4 Finish. Foghnaidh seo, *this will be sufficient ;* foghnaidh mi dhuit, *I will finish you ;* cha'n fhoghnadh a sgiath dha air a tiuighead, *the thickness of his shield could not avail him ;* f. da, *do for him*, i. e. *kill him.*

foghaint, see foghain.

———,‡‡ *s.f.* Heroism. 2 Cleverness.

———each, -iche, *a.* Brave, valorous, heroic. 2* Sufficient, fit. 3**Prosperous. 4**Ample. 5(CR) Generous—*Arran.* Duine f., *a valorous, brave person ;* daoine f., *able men ;* bitheadh a làmhan f., *let his hands be sufficient.*

———eachd, *s.f.ind.* Sufficiency, valour, fortitude, bravery. 2**Stoutness. 3**Prosperity.

———eas, -eis, *s.m.* see foghainteachd.

foghair, -ean, *s.f.* Tone, accent. 2 Vowel. 3 Resound, re-echo. 4 Blow that causes a sound. 5(DC) Thud.

foghair,** *v.a, & n.* Make a noise. 2 Tingle.

fo-ghàire, *s.m.* see fèath-ghàire.

foghairt,** *s.f.* Chasing, pursuing. 2 Banishing.

†**foghaluidhe**, -an, *s.m.* Robber.

foghann, } -ain, *s.m.* see fòthannan.
———an, }

foghannas,* -ais, see foghainteachd.

foghanta, *a.* see foghainteach.

———ch, see foghainteach.

———chd, see foghainteachd.

†**foghantaidhe**, -an, *s.m.* Servant.

foghantas,* see foghainteachd.

†**fo-ghaoth**, -aoithe, *s.f.* Gentle wind.

foghar,‡‡ -air, *s.m.* Sound, noise. 2*Note. 3 Vowel. 4* Blow that causes a noise. 5 Favour. 6 Froth.

foghar, -air, *s.m.* Harvest. 2 Autumn. 3 (DC) Crop. F. an eòrna, *the barley-harvest ;* f. a' chruithneachd, *the wheat-harvest;* f. na saidhe, *the hay-harvest ;* air an fh., *out harvesting ;* meadhon an fhoghair, *the middle of autumn ;* rè an fh. uile, *during the harvest*; a's t-Fhoghar, *in Autumn ;* f. nam ban brèid-gheal, *the harvest of young widows*—a prophecy of a time when all men would be slain in battle.

———, -air, -an, *s.m.* see foghair. 2**Favour. 3**Froth.

———ach, *a.* Autumnal. 2 Harvest. 3**Loud, noisy, clamorous. 4**Echoing.

———achadh,** -aidh, *s.m.* Working at harvest, harvesting.

———achd,** *s.f.* Autumnal labour.

———adh, -aidh, *s.m.* Often used for foghar, but foghar is *harvest-time*, and fogharadh is *the produce of the harvest.*

fogharaich,** *v.a. & n.* Hire for harvest-work. 2 Work at harvest.

fogharaidh, see fogharach.

fogharail,** *a.* Autumnal.

foghard,** -aird, *s.m.* Tingling noise.

fòghbhannan, -ain, *s.m.* see fòthannan.

fòghlach,(CR) *s. m.* Rank grass growing on dunghills, manured grass, grass growing on manured land. [forlach in *Argyll.*]

†**foghladh**,** -aich, *s.m.* Trespass, offence. 2 Robbery.

foghlaich,** *v.a.* Rob, pillage, plunder.
——e,** *s.m.* Robber, plunderer.
fòghlainte, *s.m.* see fòghlumaiche.
——ach, *s.m.* see fòghlumaiche.
foghlas,** *v.n.* Grow pale.
foghlmuine, see foghlumaiche.
foghluich, see foghlaich.
——e, see foghlaiche.
foghluidhe,‡‡ -an, *s.m.* Robber, sea robber.
foghluidheach,** *a.* Piratical, rapacious.
fòghluim, *pr.pt.* a' fòghlum, *v. a.* Learn. 2 Teach, instruct.
——te, *a. & past pt.* of fòghluim. Learned, 2 Taught, instructed, trained, disciplined.
fòghluimeach, -ich, *s.m.* see fòghlumaiche.
fòghlum, -uim, *s.m.* Learning, instruction. 2 Acquired knowledge. 3 Act of training, teaching. 4 Learning. 5**Discipline. 6** Edification. 7* Intelligence. A' f—, *pr.pt.* of fòghluim.
——ach, -aich, *s m.* see fòghlumaiche.
——ach, -aiche, *a.* Instructive, edifying. 2 Of, or belonging to, teaching or learning. 2 Academic.
——adair,* see fòghlumaiche.
——aiche, -an, *s.m.* Learner, novice, scholar, student, apprentice. 2 Teacher, instructor. 3 Man of learning.
——aid,* *s.f.* College, university, place of learning.
——ail,** *a.* Doctrinal.
——anaiche, see foghlumaiche.
fòghlunta, see fòghluimte.
——chd, *s.f.ind.* Education, learning.
foghmhair, -ean, see famhair.
——eachd,** *s.f.* Piracy. 2 Plundering. Le f. air tràigh 's air muir, *with plundering by sea and land.*
——iche, *s.m.* Corsair, pirate.
foghmhar, -air, *s.m.* *S. Argyll & Arran* (as in Ireland) for foghar. [*ogh* is sounded with *ao* short—written *fobhar* and *fobharradh* by *.]
fòghnadh, -aidh, *s.m.* Sufficiency. 2 Slavery, servitude, service. 3* Use. 4**Improvement. 5**Availing. Fhuair e 'fh., *he got what did for him.*
——, *3rd. sing, imp.* of fòghain. F. seo, *let this suffice.*
fòghnaidh, *fut.aff.a.* of fòghain.
†foghnamh, -aimh, see fòghnadh.
foghnan, see fothannan.
foghnar, see fothannan.
fòghnas,** -ais, *s.m.* Profit, gain, advantage. 2 Sufficiency. Tha m' fh. agam, *I have enough.*
foghrachail,** *a.* Autumnal.
foghraidh, *s.f.* Warning, charge, caution, proclamation.
foghraimh,** *s.f.* Diploma.
fognamh, *s.m.* Use, improvement. 2‡‡ Servitude, slavery. 3‡‡Assistance.
fògrach, -aiche, *a.* Of, or relating to, banishment or exile, expelling, expulsive. 2**Warning, cautionary, admonitory.
——, -aich, *s.m.* Outlaw, exile, outcast, vagabond.
fògradh, -aidh, -aidhean, *s.m.* Exile, banishment. 2 Act of expulsion, pursuing, ejecting or driving away. 3**Warning, charge, proclamation, decree, ordinance. 4**Robbery. 5** Trespass. A' f—, *pr.pt.* of fògair.
fògraibh, *2nd. pl. imp.* of fògair. Expel ye.
fògraichte, *past pt.* of fògair. Banished, exiled, expelled. 2 Persecuted.
fograidh,** *s.f.* see fògradh.
fògraidh, *fut. aff. a.* of fògair.
fògrar, *fut. pass.* of fògair.
foguisge, see fagusachd.
——ad, -eid, see fagusachd.
fogus, see fagus.
fogusg, see fagus.
foi, (fuidh) for fodha & fo.
foicheall, -ill, *s.m.* Day's hire, wages or salary. *prov.*
foicheallan,(DC) -ain, *s.m.* Useless fellow, lout.
——ach, *a.* Loutish.
foichean,‡ *s.m.* Wrapper, infant's napkin. 2 Piece of cloth wrapped around the foot over the stocking, when men wore *cuarain*, or shoes of untanned leather.
foi-chéimneachadh, -aidh, *s.m.* Series.
foichein, see foichean.
foi-cheumnadh, -aidh, *s.m.* Gradation. 2 Series.
foichill, *v.a.* Provide, prepare.
foichirean, *s.m.* Herb growing on dunghills.
foichleadh, -idh, *s.m.* Wages, *prov.*
foichlean, *s.m.* Sprout, blade of young corn appearing above ground. 2**Chit.
fòid, -e, -ean, *s.f.* Clod. 2 Peat. 3 Turf, sod. 4* Land, country. 5**Glebe. Gus an càrar mi fo 'n fh., *till I am placed under the turf;* o 'n thàinig e do 'n fh., *since he came to the country* ; f. mhòine, *a single peat ;* f. chùlaig, *a peat placed at the back of the fire ;* f. a bhreith 's a bhàis, *the spot where a man is destined to be born or to die ;* tha e nis air f. na fìrinne, *he is now on the sod of truth—dead.*
——each, -iche, *a.* Turfed, abounding in turf.
——ean, -ein, *s.m., dim.* of fòid. Little peat or turf.
——eanach, *a.* Abounding in little peats.
fòidear,(DMC) *s.m.* Man who works with a spade after the plough.
fòid-fàil, *s. m.* Turf. see under taigh.
foidhe, see foipe.
fòidheach, -ich, *s.m.* Beggar, *prov.*
fòidheachas, -ais, *s.m.* Mendicancy.
foidheam, *s.f.* Inference. 2(DC) Rumour. Is e sin an fh. a thug mi as, *that is the inference I drew from it.*
foidhearach, -aiche, *a.* Naked, *prov.*
†foidhneul, -neòil, *s.m.* Glance.
†foidhreach, -eich, *s.f.* Little image.
†foidhreachd, -an, *s.f.* Likeness.
foigh, see faigh.
foighe, see faighe.
——an,** *s.m.* Green, mead, lawn.
†foighid, *v.a.* Bear, suffer, endure, put up with.
foighid, see foighidinn.
——e, see foighidinn.
foighideach, -iche, *a.* see foighidneach.
foighidinn, *s.f.ind.* Patience, forbearance. Glac f., *have patience ;* beiridh f. air a' bhliadhna nach d' thàinig, ach cha bheir i air a' bhliadhna 'chaidh seachad, *patience will overtake the coming year, but not the past year ;* rug an fh. air an lon againn, *patience overtook our eagerness*—a remark used in describing how we have been saved from probable or certain trouble by not saying or doing this or that ; cha'n 'eil f. agad, *you have no patience.*[*pron.* fo(gh)ailtean in *Gairloch.*]
——each, -iche, *a.* see foighidneach.
foighidneach, -aiche, *a.* Patient, enduring, forbearing, long-suffering.
——ail, -ala, *a.* see foighidneach.
foighin,** *s.f.* Green plot, mead.
†foighiontach, *a.* Ample.
†foighiontas, -ais, *s.m.* Amplitude.
foighir, see faidhir.
†foi-ghliocas, -ais, *s.m.* Low cunning. 2 Great prudence.
foighneachd, see faighneachd.
foighnich, *v.a.* see faighnich.
foighreag,§ *s.f.* Cloudberry, see oighreag.

foigse, see faisge.
———achd, see faisgeachd.
foighteag, *s.f.* see faoiteag.
foil, *pr.pt.* a' foileadh, *v.a.* Roast or boil hurriedly upon embers. 2 (DMy) Pilfer, steal by instalments. Dh' fhoil e leis, *he pilfered.*
foil, -e, -ean, *s.f.* see fail.
foil, *v.a.* see fail.
fòil, -e, *a.* Patient, tranquil, gentle, mild, soft. 2 Slow, stately. 3 Solemn in gait.
fòil, -e, -ean, *s.m.* While, little while.
†foilbheum, -eim, see oilbheum.
†———ach, -aiche, *a.* Fierce, cruel.
†foilcheas, *a.* Dark, obscure. 2 *s.* Mystery.
foileabaidh, ** -leabach, -leabaichean, *s. f.* Truckle bed.
foileachan, -ain, *s.m.* see foileag.
———, see feileachan.
foilead,** -eid, *s.m.* Fillet, coif.
foileadh, -idh, *s.m.* Act of roasting or broiling hastily on embers. 2 Acting hurriedly or imperfectly. 3††Develop slowly without forcing. 4(DMy) Gradual stealing or pilfering. A' f. bonnaich, *toasting a cake in a hurried manner.*
foileag, -eige, -an, *s.f.* Cake suddenly and imperfectly toasted. 2 Little cake. 3††Hastily-made cake. [fòileag in *Poolewe.*]
———ach, -aiche, *a.* Abounding in little cakes. 2 Like a little cake.
foilean,** *v.a.* Follow after. 2 Hang after. 3 Hanker.
———,(AF) *s.m.* Foal, filly.
†foilearbadh, -aidh, *s.m.* Death.
foilearm, see faoileann.
†foileasan, -ain, see fuileasan.
foileid,** *s.f.* Wimple. 2 Muffler.
foileum,** *s.f.* Leap, skip, bounce.
foilidh, *s.f.* Gaelic spelling of *filly*, foal.
foill, -e, *s. f.* Deceit, fraud, treachery, wrong. 2 *rarely* Leisure. Labhair e le f., *he spoke with deceit*; ri f., *practising deceit, playing unfair*; cha lugha an fh. na 'm freiceadan, *the treachery is not less than the guard—i. e.* however much the enemy are to blame for adopting treacherous tactics, the guard are quite as bad; gabh brath-foill air, *devise deceitful measures against him.*
fòill, -e, *s.m.* Composure, tranquility. 2 Leisure.
fòill,** *s.f.* Pursuit, chase. 2 Enmity. 3 Enemies.
†foille, *s.f.* Smallness, littleness.
†fòilleachd,** *s.f.* Track, footstep. 2 Tracing.
foilleachdach, -aich, *s.m.* Research.
foillealachd, *s.f.ind.* Deceitfulness, falsehood, treachery.
foillear, -eir, -eirean, *s. m.* Cheat, deceiver, knave. 2**Traitor.
foillear,** -eir, *s.m.* Bud of a flower.
foilleil, -ala, *a.* Deceitful, fraudulent, unfair, treacherous, wrongful. Tha a mhic f., *his sons are treacherous.*
foilleir, see foillear.
foill-fhalach, see feall-fhalach.
foill-fhalachadh, see feall-fhalach.
foill-fhalachail, see feall-fhalachail.
fòill ! fòill ! *int.* Stay ! not so fast !
foillidh, *a.* Hidden, latent, that does not externally appear.
———each, *a.* Negligent. 2 Sluggish.
———eachd, *s.f.* Negligence. 2 Sluggishness.
foill-mharbhadh,** *s.m.* Assassination.
foill-mhortadh,** *s.m.* Assassination.
foill-mhortair,** *s.m.* Assassin.
foillse,** *s.f.* Light. 2 Manifestation.
———ach,** *a.* Declaratory.
foillseachadh, -aidh, *s.m.* Revelation, disclosure, declaration, manifesto, discovery, manifestation. 2 Act of revealing, disclosing, manifesting or discovering. 3 The Apocalypse. A' f—, *pr. pt.* of foillsich. Fear-foillseachaidh, *a publisher, one who reveals.*
foillseachail,** *a.* Apocalyptical, revealing, disclosing, explanatory.
foillseachas,** -ais, *s.m.* Revealment, manifestation, disclosure.
foillsich, *pr.pt.* a' foillseachadh, *v. a.* Reveal, publish, discover, manifest, declare. 2 Lay open. 3 Express. 4 Allege.
———ear, -eir, -eirean, *s.m.* Publisher.
———ear, *fut.pass.* of foillsich. Shall be revealed.
———te, *past pt.* of foillsich. Revealed, declared, manifested, laid open.
†foilmean, -ein, *s.m.* Bad dress.
†foilmhich, *v.* see falmhaich.
foiltean, see failtean.
†foimeal, -a, *s.m.* Consumption.
†foineach, -nich, -an, *s.m.* Demand. 2 Question.
foineachadh, see faighneachadh.
foineachd, *s.f.* see faighneachd.
†foineall, -eill, *s.m.* Fool.
foineasach, -eiche, *a.* see faighneachdail.
†foineul,** -neòil, *s.m.* Little cloud. 2 Gleam. 3 Trance.
†———ach, *a.* Glittering.
foinich, *v.* see faighnich.
†foinn, -e, *s.m.* Matter, importance. Cha'n 'eil f. air, *it is no matter.*
foinne, -an, *s.m.* Wart. Am f. mu'n iath a' ghlac, is niarachd mac air am bi, am f. mu'n iath a' bhròg, is niarachd bean òg air am bi, *wart on palm luck to lad, wart on instep luck to lass.*
———ach, -aiche, *a.* Having warts, of, or belonging to warts, warty, chitty.
———achadh, -aidh, *s.m.* Tempering. A' f—, *pr.pt.* of foinnich.
———al,** -eil, *s.m.* Fool.
———amh, -a, *a.* Handsome in shape, stately, comely, portly, elegant, genteel. 2 Active, lively. F. finealta, *portly and well-dressed;* f. mileanta, *handsome and brave.*
foinneamh, *s.m.* see foinne.
foinneasach, -aiche, *a.* Sightly, well-favoured, slight, genteel. Gu f., *slightly.*
foinne-lus, *s.m.* Spurge, see spuirse.
foinnich, *v.a.* Temper, as a weapon.
———te, *a.* & *past pt.* Tempered.
foinnidh, -e, *a.* see foinneamh.
†foinnse, *s.f.* Ash-tree.
†foinnseag, -eig, *s.f.* Ash-tree.
†foinnsidh, *s.pl.* Springs, wells, fountains.
foipe, *prep. pron.* Under her, beneath her. 2 Under her command. *emphatic* foipe-se. When a cow is near calving they say, "tha i 'ieigeil foipe. [see notes under fodha.]
fòir, *pr.pt.* a' fòirinn, *v.a.* Help, save, deliver, 2 Relieve. 3 Wait on. 4**Heal. 5**Bless. [Used with *prep.* air.] F. le tròcair orm, *mercifully save me.*
foir,** -e, *s.f.* Ship's crew. 2 Crowd of people. 3 People crowded together.
fòir, -e, *s.f.* Help, deliverance, aid, relief. 2** Border, edge, rim, brink. Furtachd is f., *help and deliverance.* Dean f. air, *help.*
foir-,‡ *prefix*, "Super-."
foir,(AF) *s.m.* Pig. 2 Dog.
†foir-àillich, *v.a.* Decorate, adorn.
foir-ainm, *s.m.* Epithet. 2 Pronoun. 3 Nickname.
†foirb, -e, *s.m.* Land.
foirbh,** *v.a.* Adorn, deck. 2‡‡Attend on. 3‡‡ Wait on.
foirbh, see fairbhiteach.

foìrbhaillidh,** *a.* Acceptable.
foirbheach, -ich, *s. & a.* see foirfeach.
———d, see foirfeachd.
foirbheart, -eirt, -an, *s.f.* Help, assistance.
———ach, -aiche, *a.* Aiding, assisting.
———ach,** -aich, *s.m.* Assistant.
foirbheiteach, (DMC) -eich, *s. m.* Wanderer, vagabond.
foirbhidh, see foirfe.
foirbhillidh, *a.* see foirbhilteach.
foirbhilteach, -iche, *a.* Acceptable.
foirbhiteach,(DC) *s. m.* District oversman, ground officer. The equivalent *in Uist* is *constabal*, but the office is now obsolete.
fòir-bhrath,(AH) *s.m.* Cruel betrayal.
fòir-bhreath, -an, see fòir-bhreith.
———nuchadh, see fòir-bhreithneachadh.
———nuich, *v.n.* Divine,guess,conjecture.
fòir-bhreith,** *s.f.* Conjecture. 2 Random prophecy, guess. 3 Prejudice.
———nich, *v.n.* Divine, guess, conjecture, prophecy.
———nicheadh, -aidh, *s.m.* Divining, conjecturing. A' f—, *pr.pt.* of fòir-bhreithnich.
†fòir-bhriach, *s.m.* Power, authority, strength.
fòir-bhriathar, -air, -thran, *s.m.* Adverb. 2 Adjective.
fòir-bhriathrach, -aiche, *a.* Adverbial.
†foirbhriogh, -a, *s.m.* Power, force.
fòir-bhruach, -aiche, *s.f.* Pinnacle. 2 Precipice. 3 Edge of a precipice.
foirceadal, see foircheadal.
foircealadh,(DMC) *s. m.* Truthful disposition, Cha'n 'eil f. agad, *you have no regard for the truth.*
foircean,** -ein, *s.m.* Embrocation.
———nach, see foircheannach.
foirch, see forach.
foirche, (AC) *s.f.* Reef. Sorchair orm gach f., *illumine to me every reef.*
foircheadal, -ail, -an, *s.m.* Instruction, exhortation, admonition, lecture. 2 Doctrine. 3 Essay. 4**Warning, caution. 5 Catechism.
†———, *v.a.* Teach, instruct, admonish.
foircheadalair, -ean, *s.m.* Preceptor, teacher.
foircheann, -chinn, *s.m.* End, conclusion.
foir-cheann, -chinn, *s.m.* White head. 2 White face.
———ach, *a.* White-faced. 2 White-headed.
———ach, -aich, *s.m.* White head.
†foir-cheimnich, *v.n.* Proceed, advance.
foirchinnteachd, *s.f.ind.* Predestination.
foir-chroiceann, -inn, -an [& -chroicnean,] see roimh-chraiceann.
†foircinn, *s.f.* Embrocation. 2 Fomentation.
†foirciobal, -ail, *s.m.* Reinforcement.
†foirciosach, -aiche, *a.* Fat, oily.
foircnich,** *v.a.* Foment, apply embrocation.
foir-dhealbh, -a, -an, *s.m.* Scheme. 2 Schedule, drawing, plan.
———, *v.a.* Scheme, plan, draw out a scheme or plan.
———adair, -ean, *s.m.* Schemer, planner.
———air,** *s.m.* Designer.
foir-dheirc,** *a.* see oirdheirc.
———eas, -eis, *s.m.* see oirdheirceas.
foir-dhorus, -uis, -dhorsan, see for-dhorus.
foir-dhris,** see fearra-dhris.
†foire, *a.* Separated, consecrated. Làithean f., *holy days.*
foireagan,(CR) *s. m.* Playing with, teasing, tormenting,—*Arran.*
foireagh, see far-thagh.
foireann, -inn, *pl.* foirne, *s.m.* Auxiliary band. 2 Brigade. 3 Troop. 4 Crew of a ship. 5 Dweller, inhabitant. 6 Crowd, multitude. Foirne fearail, *a manly crew.*
———ach,** *a.* Marginal.
foirear,** -ir, *s.m.* Watchman.
foireigean, see foireigin.
———tair,** -ean, *s.m.* Obstructor. 2 Oppressor.
foireigin, *v.* see foireignich.
———, *s.f.ind.* Violence, oppression. 2 Ineffectual effort to force a door. 3 Attack. 4 **Tyranny, compulsion. 5 Constraint. Luchd-f., *oppressors.*
foireigneach,** -niche, *a.* Oppressive, tyrannical. Gu f., *oppressively.*
foireigneachadh, -idh, *s.m.* Rapacity, violence.
foireigneadh, -idh, *s.m.* Oppression, extortion, violence. 2 Act of oppressing. 3**Tyranny. 4 Compelling, constraining. A' f—, *pr.pt.* of foireignich. Fear foireignidh, *an extortioner.*
foireignich, *pr.pt.* a' foireigneachadh, *v.a.* Oppress,harass. 2 Extort. 3**Compel, constrain.
———e, -an, *s.m.* Oppressor, tyrant.
———te, *past pt.* of foireignich. Oppressed, constrained, forced, harassed.
foreil,** *a.* Steep, headlong. †2 Clear, evident.
†foireinneachadh, -aidh, *s.m.* Travelling.
foirfe, *a.* Perfect, good, faultless. †2 Old, ancient. 3 Come to man's estate or years of maturity. Duine f., *a full-grown man ;* gu f., *perfectly, faultlessly.*
foirfeach, -ich, *s. m.* Elder of the church. 2** Full-grown person.
———,* *a.* Come to years of discretion or maturity.
———d, *s.f.ind.* Perfection, completeness, excellence. 2**Maturity. 3 Old age. Tha e air teachd gu f., *he has arrived at maturity.*
†foirfeadh, -eidh, *s.m.* Harrowing.
foir-fhiacaill,** -cla, -clan, *s.m.* Fore-tooth.
foir-fhiaclach,** *a.* Having fore-teeth, having large fore-teeth.
foirfich, *pr.pt.* a' foirfeachadh, *v.a.* Perfect, accomplish. 2 Perform, execute.
foirfidh, see foirfe.
———eachd, see foirfeachd.
†foirgeall, -eill, *s.m.* Truth.
foirgheall,** -a, *s.m.* Pledge for protection. 2 Hostage for safety.
foirghioll,** -ghill, *s.m.* Declaration, proclamation. 2 Assertion. 3 Proof, witness. 4 Decision, judgment. F. na fìrinn, *the manifesta- of the truth.*
———,** *a.* Clear, evident.
———,** *v.a.* Prove. 2 Declare.
foirghlac,** *v.a.* Occupy, possess.
†foirghlidhe, *s.f.* Nobility. 2 Truth.
†foirgneachadh,** -aidh, *s.m.* Building.
†foirgneadh, -idh, *s.m.* Building.
foirgneadh-fuinn,** *s.m.* Timber necessary for the use of a farm. 2 Fabric.
†foirgnich,** *v.a.* Build.
foiriarach,** *a.* Preposterous, eccentric. 2 Troublesome, not easy to be served.
foirich,** *v.* see fuirich. 2 Enchase.
———,(AC) *s.m.* Lump. 2 Mallet. 3 Pestle, the stone used in crushing corn in the corn-mortar. [see fairche.]
———e, see foirich.
———e, see forach.
foirichean,* *s.pl.* Borders, boundaries. 2 Suburbs, environs. Mu na f. seo, *about these borders* ; f. a' bhaile, *the suburbs of the city.*
†foirichinn, *s.f.* Help.
foiridinn,** *s.f.* Pursuit.
fòirinn, -e, -ean, *s.f.* Supply, aid, help. 2 Remedy. 3 Strength. 4 Comfort. 5(AC) Border land, debatable land.
foir-innis,** *v.a.* Predict.

foir-inniseach,** *a.* Predictive.
foir-iomall, -aill, -mlaichean, *s.m.* Limit, boundary. 2**Frontier. 3**Territory. 4**Circumference of a circle. F. nan sliabh, *the utmost boundary of the hills.*
———ach, -iche, *a.* On the outmost limit. 2 Bordering. 3 Outward. 4 On the frontiers, extrinsic. 5**Territorial.
foir-iomallach, *s.m.* Utmost boundary, frontier.
foir-iomradh, -aidh, -ean, *s. m.* Ceremony. 2 Compliments.
foir-iomraiteach, -iche, *a.* Ceremonious. 2 Complimentary.
foir-iongantach, -aiche, *a.* Prodigious, wonderful, strange.
foir-iongantas, -ais, -an, Prodigy. 2 Phenomenon.
foirionn, -an, *s.m.* see foireann.
foirireadh, see foiriridh.
foiriridh,(AC) *s.f.* Keen observation. 2 Anxious waiting. 3 Wake, watching a corpse.
foirithin, see fòirin.
foir-leathad, -aid, *s.m.* Expanse.
foir-leathann, *a.* Very broad, spacious, extensive, large. 2 General.
————ach,** *a.* Periphrastic.
————achadh,** -aidh, *s.m.* Periphrasis.
foirleud, -leòid, *s.m.* Expanse, extent.
foirlion,** *a.* Much, great, plenty.
foir-lion, *v.a.* Complete, make perfect, fulfil, supply, fill up. †2 Multiply.
foirlion,* *s.m.* Crew.
———adh, -aidh, *s. m.* Completion, supplement, reinforcement, appendix, act of completing, perfecting. A' f—, *pr.pt.* of foirlion.
———ta, *a. & past pt.* of foirlion. Completed, complete, perfected, filled up.
foirm, -e, *s.m.* see fuirm. 2 Pomp, display, ostentation—*Dàin I. Ghobha.* 3 (AH) Dash, swagger. Thàinig e a staigh le f., *he came in with pomp.*
†foirm, *a.* Dark, obscure.
foirmealach,(CR) -aich, *s.m.* Formalist in religion, stickler for forms.
foirmealach, -aiche, *a.* see foirmeil.
————, -aich, *s.m.* Proud, vapid fops. 2 Conceits—*Dàin I. Ghobha.*
————d, *s. f.* Formality, ceremony, pompousness, forwardness. 2 Cleverness.
foir-mheang,** *v.n.* Prevaricate.
foirmeil, -eala, *a.* Brisk, lively, *Scots* clever. 2 Forward, pompous, ceremonious. 3 Noisy. 4 (DU) Remarkable, noteworthy, applied to a person.
fòirn,†† *pr.pt.* a' fòirneadh, *v.n.* Intrude, press. 2 Be arrogant.
foirne,** *s.* Fodder. 2 see foireann. 3 see foirnidh.
†foirne, *s. pl.* Dwellers, inhabitants.
foirneachan,** *s.m.* Roller.
fòirneadh, -idh, *s.m.* Intruding, intrusion, act of intruding. 2 Arrogance. 3 Inclination, sloping. 4††Forcing. 5(DC) Intrusive exhortation. A' f—, *pr. pt.* of fòirn. A' f. gu dàna, *intruding boldly.*
foirneal,** -eil, *s.m.* Appearance, colour.
———ach, see foirmealach.
foirneanta, *a.* Conspicuously brave. 2 Forward, arrogant. 3 Stout. 4 Firm, steady.
————chd, *s.f.* Bravery. 2 Stoutness. 3 Firmness, steadiness. 4 Forwardness, arrogance.
fòirneart, -eirt, *s.m.* Oppression, violence, force. 2 Fraud. 3 Attack. F. m' eascaire, *my enemy's oppression.*
———ach -aiche, *a.* Oppressive, violent. 2 Fraudulent. 3 Overbearing. Aintighearnan f., *oppressive tyrants.*
————achadh, -aidh, *s.m.* Oppressing, act of oppressing or overbearing. 2 Defrauding. A' f—, *pr. pt.* of fòirneartaich.
————aich, *pr. pt.* a' fòirneartachadh, *v. a.* Oppress. 2 Force. 3 Overbear. 4 Defraud.
foirneata,‡ *a.* see foirneanta.
†fòirneil, -e, *a.* Open, manifest.
foirneis, -ean, *s.f.* Gaelic spelling of *furnace.*
foirnidh, *s.pl.* see foireann.
foirseadh,** -eidh, *s.m.* Harrowing.
foirsear,** -sir, *s.m.* Harrower. 2 Rummager, searcher. 3 Constable.
foirsearachd, *s.f.* Rummaging, searching.
foir-sheòmar, *s.m.* Lobby. 2 Ante-chamber.
†foir-shiol,** *v.a.* Propagate.
†———adh,** -aidh, *s.m.* Propagating, propagation.
†foir-shuidh, *v.n.* Preside.
————ear, -eir, -irean, *s.m.* President.
foirtealachd, see foirteileachd.
foirteil,** *a.* Brave, hardy. 2 Patient. 3 Strong. Gu f., *bravely.*
———eachd,** *s.f.* Bravery, hardihood. 2 Patience. 3 Strength.
foir-theachdair,** -ean, *s. m.* Usher. 2 Forerunner.
foir-theagasg, -aisg, -an, *s.m.* Rudiments, introduction to any part of learning.
foir-thìr,** *a.* Farther, remote. 2 Foreign.
———, *s.f.* Remote or foreign country.
foirthir,(AF) *s.m.* Bird of passage.
†foirthoirt, -e, *a.* Bold, stout. 2 Active.
†foirtil, -e, *a.* Able, strong, hardy.
†———e, *s.f.* Patience, courage.
†———each, -eiche, *a.* Patient. 2 Courageous.
fois, -e, *s.f.* Leisure, rest. 2 Tranquility. 3 Habitation, dwelling. Gabh gu f., *be quiet;* f. do t' anam, *peace to thy soul;* f. anama, *soul's peace*—a death blessing; f. do bhonn a choise, *rest for the sole of his foot;* is beag f. a fhuair e, *little rest did he get;* aig f., *at rest.*
foisciönn,** *s.m.* Malice, backbiting.
foiscionnach,** *a.* Malicious, apt to backbite.
————,** *s.m.* Malice. 2 Cry.
————d, *s.f.* Maliciousness, backbiting.
foisdin, -e, *s.f.* Taciturnity, government of the tongue, quietness.
———each, -iche, *a.* Quiet, silent, calm. 2 At rest. [* gives *s.m.*]
———eachd, *s.f.ind.* Calmness, sedateness, composedness, tranquillity, peaceableness, arrangement.
foiseachadh, -aidh, *s.m.* Stopping, resting. A' f—, *pr.pt.* of foisich.
foisead,** -eid, *s.m.* Faucet.
foiseamh, -imh, *s.m.* Recovery.
foisg, see faisg & fagus.
foisge, *comp.* of faisg & fagus.
foisgeachd,** *s.f.* Closeness.
foisgeil,(CR) *a.* Frank, free, open-handed.—*Suth'd.*
foisgich, *v.a.* Approach, draw near.
foisich, *pr.pt.* a' foiseachadh, *v.n.* Stop, rest.
foisneach, -iche, *a.* Quiet, composed, sedate, serious, tranquil, peaceable, arranged in order. Duine f., *a sedate man, a man of rest;* gnùis fh. na doimhne, *the tranquil face of the deep;* f. fàilteach, *peaceable and hospitable.*
————d, see foisdineachd.
†foiste, *s.f.* Resting, residing.
†———achair -e, -ean, *s.m.* Hireling.
foisteadh, -idh, *s.m.* Wages, salary. 2 Hire.
foisteanach, -aiche, *a.* Serious, arranged in good order. 2 (DMC) Restful, reposeful.
foistine, *s.f.* Rest, dwelling.

foistinn, *s.f.* Quiet—*Dàin I. Ghobha.*
——each, -iche, *a.* see foisdineach.
——eachd, see foisdineachd.
†foitheal, -eil, *s.m.* Plunder, prey.
foithearachd,** *s.f.* Touchiness.
foithre,** *s.pl.* Woods.
fol, see foladh.
†fola, *s.m.* Garment.
fola, *gen.sing.* of fuil.
folabh, see falbh.
fo-labhairt, *s.f.* Speaking under one's voice.
fo-labhradh, ** -aidh, *s.m.* Good speech, pleading, reasoning. 2 Low language. 3 Insidious question.
fòlach, -aich, *s.m.* Rank grass growing on dunghills, manured grass.
folach,** *s.m.* see falach.
——adh, see falachadh.
——an, -ain, -an, see falachan.
——d, -an, *s.f.* Feud, spite, grudge, malice. 2 Treachery. 3 Extraction. 4**Bloodiness. Àrd am f., *of noble extraction* or *descent;* iosal am f., *of base extraction;* f. eadar chàirdean, *feuds among relations;* gach f. air chùl, *every grudge forgotten;* is buan meacan na folachd, *long lasts the rod whose root sprang from blood.*
——dan, -ain, *s m.* Water-salad, water-parsnip—*sium augustifolium.* [‡ gives folachdainn as *nom.*]
folach-fead, see falach-fead.
foladair,** *s.m.* One who sheds blood.
foladas, -ais, *s.m.* Spite, grudge, feud. 2 Chastisement.
foladh, -aidh, -ean, *s.m.* Power, ability. 2** Hatred. 3** Grudge, feud. 4(AF) Cattle, dowry of cattle. 5 see falach. 6 Cover, covering, screen. †7 Garment, robe.
folaich, *v.* see falaich.
——ear, see falaichear.
——te, see falaichte.
folaid, see falaid.
folaigheach, -iche, see falaigheach.
†folair, *s.m.* Command. 2 Offer, proffer.
folais, *s.* *Reay country* for bùlas. 2 see follais.
folamh, -aimhe, *a.* see falamh.
folamhaich, *v.* see falmhaich.
†folaradh, -aidh, *s.m.* Command, order.
folarnaidheach,** *a.* Equal.
————d,** *s.f.* Equality, parity.
folartair, *s.m.* Emperor. 2 Commander.
†folas, -ais, *s.m.* Shoe, slipper, sandal.
folbh, see falbh.
folbhach, see falbhach.
folbhair, see falbhair.
folbhan, see falbhan.
folc, see failc.
folcadh, -aidh, see failceadh. 2 Ley of potash.
foldath, -aithe, *a.* Generous.
fo-leabaidh,** -leabach, *s.f.* Truckle-bed.
†folfaidh, *a.* Whole, entire.
folg, *a.* Active, nimble, quick.
†follach, -aich, *s. m.* Covering, garment. 2 Military colours.
†follach, -aich, *s.m.* Water gruel. 2 see falach.
†——dain, -e, *s.f.* Sufferance. 2 Patience.
folladh,** -aidh, *s.m.* Government.
follais, *a.* see follaiseach.
——,** *s.f.* Openness. 2 Publicity. 3 Conspicuousness. 4 Evidentness. 5 Clearness. Am f., *evident, clear;* thoir am f., *make manifest;* thig e am f., *it will come to light.*
——each, -siche, *a.* Public, conspicuous. 2 Clear, evident, open, manifest, known, public. Ionad f., *a public place.*
——eachd, *s.f.* Publicity, clearness. 2Evidence. 3 Conspicuousness.
——ich, *v.a.* see foillsich.
follamh,** -aimh, *s.m.* Ancestors.
follamhan, -ain, *s.m.*Grace, ornaments.
follas, -ais, *s.m.* Publicity, state of being public, being well known.
follas,** *a.* Manifest, evident. Dean f., *make public, proclaim.*
——ach, -aiche, *a.* see follaiseach.
follasgain,§ *s.f.* Goldilocks—*ranunculus auricomus.*
follsgadh,** -aidh, *s. m.* Scalding.
folluis, see follas.
——each, see follaiseach.
——eachd, see follaiseachd.
——ich, see foillsich.
follus, see follas.

330. Follasgain.

†follusghlan, -aine, *a.* Clear, shrill.
folmhaise,** *s.f.* Advantage, opportunity.
†folmhein, *s.f.* Thunderbolt.
folmhuich, see falmhaich.
————te, see falmhaichte.
folosg, -oisg, *s.m.* see falaisg.
——ain, *s.f.* see follasgain.
fo-losgann, -ainn, *s.f.* Tadpole.
folrachd,** *s.f.* Gore.
folt, fuilt, *s.m.* see falt. 2**Wages. 3 Deceiving. 4**Falling. F. bàn, *fair hair;* f. dualach, *curly hair;* f. dubh-dhonn, *dark brown hair;* fhir an fhuilt bhàin, *thou fair-haired man.*
foltach, -aiche, see faltach.
†foltach, -aich, *s.m.* Vassal, hireling.
foltan, -ain, see faltan.
folt-chib, -e, -ean, *s.f.* Leek.
folt-dhealg, -dheilge, see falt-dhealg.
foluaimean,** -ein, *s. m.* Giddy motion. Running. 3 Skipping.
foluaimneach,** *a.* Moving, stirring. 2 Fickle. 3 Active. 4 Prancing.
foluaineach, see foluaimneach.
fo-luaisg,** *v.a.* Rock gently, dandle.
†foluar, -air, *s m.* Footstool.
fo-luasgach,** *a.* Rocking, dandling.
fo-luasgadh, -aidh, *s.m.* Rocking, dandling.
foluich, see falaich.
†foluidheach,* see falaidheach.
†————d, see falaidheachd.
fòluimte, see foghluimte.
folum,(AF) *s.m.* Cat.
foluman,** -ain, *s.m.* Bad clothes.
fo 'm (fodham), Under me, beneath me.
fo m', (fo mo) Under my, beneath my. Fo m' cheann, *under my head.*
fomas,** -ais, *s.m.* Obedience, submission.
——ach,** *a.* Obedient, submissive. Gu f., *obediently.*
fomh, see famh.
fomhach, see famhair. 2**Pirate.
fomhorach,** -aich, *s.m.* Pirate. 2 Giant.
fomhair, see famhair.
fo-mhaol,** -mhaoil, *s.m.* King's slave.
fo-mhar, see foghar.
fo-mhisg,** *s.f.* Tipsiness.
fo-mhisgeach, -iche, *a.* Half drunk, tipsy.
fo-mhisgear,** -eir, *s.m.* Tippler.
fònadh, -aidh, see fòghnadh.
fonagradh,(MMcL) *s.m.* Disturbing.
fònaich, see foghain.
fònaidh, see foghnaidh.
fonail,** *s.f.* Chilliness.
†fonal, -ail, *s.m.* Cold, rigour.
fonamhad,** -aid, *s. m.* Mockery, derision. 2 Sneer.
————ach,** *s.m.* Jester. 2 Sneerer.
————ach,** -aiche, *a.* Jeering, sneering.

fo 'n choill, (*W. Isles*—JM.) Outlawed. 'Nuair a bha Prionns' Tearlach fo 'n choill, *when Prince Charles was an outlaw.*
fo-neul, -neòil, *s.m.* Little cloud. 2 Thin cloud. 3 Trance.
——ach,** *a.* Somewhat cloudy. 2 Apt to fall into a trance. 3 Like a trance.
fonn, fuinn, *s.m.* Land, earth, plain. 2 Region, district, country. 3 Delight, pleasure, 4 Desire. Longing, carnal inclination, excitation. 5 Frame of mind, temper, humour. 6* Air, tune, music. 7**Drone of a bagpipe. 8(DU) Chorus. Trì ruinn 's am f., *three verses and the chorus* ; dè f. a th' ort ? *how do you do ?* tha f. ciatach air, *he is in grand humour* ; f. clàrsaich, *harp-music* ; dh' éirich f. air, *desire awakened within him* ; f. diadhaidh, *a hymn* ; f. cadail, *a lullaby* ; cheum e troimh 'n fh., *he marched over the plain* ; chriothnaich am f., *the earth trembled* ; f. is cuan, *land and sea.*
†fonnadh,** -aidh, *s.m.* War-chariot. 2 Journey. 3 Proficiency. 4‡‡ Club. F. fleghal, *a quadrangular chariot.*
fonnar,* see fonnmhor.
——achd, see fonnmhorachd.
fonn-cadail, *s.m.* Lullaby.
fonn-chrith, *s.m.* Trembling, impatience.
fonn-duain, *s.m.* Recitative.
fonn-ghràdhaiche, -an, *s.m.* Patriot.
fonnmhor, -oire, *a.* Tuneful, melodious, musical. 2 Willing, inclined. 3 Desirous. 4 Forward. 5 Merry, gleesome, cheerful. 6 Meek, dispassionate. Aite f., *a cheerful situation.*
————ach, -aiche, see fonnmhor.
————achd, *s.f.ind.* Melody. 2**Melodiousness. 3 Inclination, propensity. 4 Meekness. 5††Mirth, humour, cheerfulness, gaiety. 6 Gravity.
fonnsa, *s.* Rim of a cycle. †2 Troop, band.
†fonnsair,* -ean, *s.m.* Trooper. 2**Cooper.
fonntan, *Arran & N. Argyll* for fòthannan.
fopa, *prep. pron.* Under them.
†for, *s.m.* Discourse. 2 Protection. 3 Enlightening, illumination. 4(DMC) Intention, idea, thought. 5(AH) Heed, attention. 6 AF) Dog. Cha d' thug mi f. air, *I did not think about it* ; tha d' thug thu for, *you paid no heed* —*Uist,*
for-,‡ *prefix,* Super-.
fora,** *s.* Bench, seat.
for-abaidh, *a.* Early, ripe before the time.
forach, *s. m.* (AC)Projection, swelling. 2 Rock or reef in the sea. †3 Dispute, controversy. 4(AH) Act of fishing for news or stories.
forachair,** see forair. †2 see furachair.
†forachras, see furachras.
foradh,** -aidh, *s. m.* Purveying. 2 Forcing. 3 Seat, bench.
fora-dhruim, see under bàta. A4.
foragan,** -ain, *s.m.* Rustling noise. 2 Keenness. 3 Anger.
————ach,** *a.* Causing a rustling noise. 2 Angry, passionate. 3 Keen.
†foraich, *v.n.* Watch, wait. 2(AH) Fish for news or stories.
†——, *s.f.* Wages.
foraidheach,** *a.* Wild, fierce. 2**Cruel.
——————d, *s.f.* Wildness, fierceness. 2 Cruelty.
forail, -ean, *s.m.* Command. 2**Gift. †3 Excess, superfluity. 4 Offer.
——,** *a.* Imperious. 2(DC) Attentive.
——, *v.a.* Command. 2 Offer.
foraileach, -iche, *a.* Imperious, imperative.
————d, *s.f.ind.* Imperiousness. 2 Excessiveness.
†foraileamh, *a.* Imperative.

foraim, see foir-ainm.
foraimh,** *s.m.* Journey. 2**Excessiveness.
for-ainm, see foir-ainm.
forair, -ean, *s.m.* Watchman, guard. 2 Night watch, watching, wake.
foral,** -ail, *s.m.* Head of a spindle wherein is a groove in which the string or band plays which gives it motion.
——amh,** -aimh, *s.m.* Anger, wrath, vengeance.
†foran, -ain, *s.m.* Anger, wrath.
fo-rann, -rainn, *s. m.* Short verse or poem. 2 Versicle, stanza. [tuous.
foranta, *a.* Angry. 2 Resolute. 3 Presumpfor-aois, -aoise, *s.f.* The verge of old age.
†foraos, -aois, *s.m.* Forest.
foraosglach,** *a.* Old, ancient.
————,** *s.m.* Old man.
for-aradh,* *s.m.* Balcony.
†for-arbhais, -e, *s.f.* Mischief.
foras, see forfhais.
†——, Law. 2 Increase. 3 Ford of a river. 4 Depth. 5 Foundation, bottom. 6 Armistice.
foras,* *s.m.* Assumed airs or importance of a trifling person. 2 Denomination.
——,** *a.* Old, antique, ancient.
——ach,* -aiche, *a.* Assuming airs.
forasda, *a.* Grave, sedate, sensible, see farasda.
————chd, *s.f.ind.* Gravity, sobriety. 2** Mildness, suavity.
forasaglach,** *a.* Old, ancient.
————,** -aich. *s.m.* Old man.
†forasartha, *a.* Grave, sedate.
forasna, *a.* Illustrated.
†forb, fuirb, *s.m.* Landlord. 2 Land. 3 Glebe land.
forbach,** -aich, *s.m.* Funeral entertainment.
forbadh, -aidh, *s.m.* Cutting. 2 Slaughtering. 3 Flaying. 4 Spending. 5 Finishing. 6 Tax. 7 Land, glebe land.
forbaidh,** *s.m.* Superior.
†forbailteach, -aiche, *a.* Acceptable.
†forbair, *v.* Grow, increase.
forbairt, -ean, *s.f.* Increase, profit. 2 Emolument.
forbais,** *s.f.* Conquest.
forban,** -ain, *s.m.* Excess. 2 Extravagance.
forbann,** -ainn, *s.m.* Marriage banns.
†forbhailtigh, -e, see forbailteach.
†forbhaiseach, see farbhasach.
forbhas, -ais, *s.m.* Snare, ambush, surprise.
————ach,** *a.* Ensnaring, full of snares, treacherous.
for-bhrat, -ait, -an, *s.m.* Cloak, upper garment. 2 Wrapper.
for-bhriathar, -air, -thran, *s.m.* Adjective. 2** Adverb.
for-bhriathrach, -aiche, *a.* Eloquent, persuasive.
for-bhruach, -bhruaiche, *pl.*-bhruachan & -bhruaichean, *s. f.* Pinnacle. 2 Steep ascent. 3 Edge of a precipice.
forc, fuirc, *pl.* -an & forcaichean, *s.f.* Fork. 2 Prong. 3 The cramp [with the art. AN.] An fhorc, *the cramp* ; f.-saidhe, *a hay-fork.* [** gives 1 & 2 as *s.m.*]
forc, *pr. pt.* a' forcadh, *v. a.* Push hard with hands or feet, as a person dragged against his will. 2 Get a purchase with hands or feet. 3 Pitch with a fork. 4 Press, crush. †5 Teach, instruct.
†forc, -a, *a.* Firm, steadfast.
forc,** *s.m.* Top, summit.
forcach, -aiche, *a.* Forked. 2†† Having the cramp.
————adh, see forcadh.
forcadh, -aidh, *s.m.* Forking, pitching with a fork. 2 Pushing. A' f—, *pr.pt.* of forc.

forcan, -ain, -an, *s.m.*, *dim.* of forc. Little fork.
forcaich,** *v.a.* Fork, pitch with a fork.
†**forcaidh,**** *s.m.* Superfluity, excess. 2 Rising or dawning of day.
forcail,** *a.* Forked, forky. 2 Pronged, furcated.
†**forcar**, -air, -airean, *s.m.* Violence. 2 Wooden hook.
forch, see forach.
forchaoin,** *s.f.* Catch in words, quibble.
forchar,** see forcar.
——— -gobhlach,(AF) *s.m.* Earwig.
forchan,** -ain, *s. m.* Instruction. 2 Sermon.
for-chathraichean, *s.pl.* Suburbs.
for-cheumnachadh,‡‡ -aidh, *s.m.* Series.
for-chiunteachd, *s. f. ind.* Predestination. 2 Prescience.
for-choimhead, -id, *s.m.* Watching, lurking for.
for-chongradh,** *s.m.* Persuasion, advice, indulgence. 2 Command.
for-chraicionn, -inn & -cne, see roimh-chraiceann. 2 Scurf.
†**forcuidh**, *s.f.* Superfluity. 2 Rising or dawning of day.
fòrdal, -ail, *s.m.* Erring, straying. 2 Mistake. 3 Delay, hinderance.
———ach, -aiche, *a.* Erroneous. 2 Wandering, astray.
†**fordharc**, -airc, *s.m.* The light (see fradharc.)
†**fordharc**, *a.* Manifest.
for-dhorus, -uis, *pl.* [-dhorsa &] -dhorsan, *s. m.* Porch, vestibule. Troimh 'n fh., *through the porch.*
for-dhroin,** *s.f.* Womb. 2 Loin.
for-dhubh,** -dhuibh, *s.m.* Lid, cover. F. an sùl, *their eyelids.*
†**fordul**, -uil, see fordal.
for-eigean, see foireigin.
†**forf**, *s.m.* Guard.
†**forfaire**, *s.m.* Watch, guard.
†**forfaireach,**** *a.* Vigilant, observant.
†————, *s.m.* Watchman.
for-fhacal, -ail, -clan, *s.m.* Proverb. 2 By-word.
for-fhaclach, -aiche, *a.* Proverbial.
†**for-fhaire**, see forair.
forfhaireach,** *a.* Vigilant, observant.
————,** *s.m.* Watchman.
forfhais, -ean, *s.f.* Inquiry. 2 Knowledge, information. Air f. an taighe, *in search of the house.*
————each, -siche, *a.* Inquisitive.
————ich,** *v.n.* Ascertain.
for-fhuasgladh, -aidh, -ean, *s.m.* Vanquishing, defeating.
for-fhuinneag, see for-uinneag.
forgamh, -aimh, *s.m.* Blow, thrust, wound.
forgan, -ain, *s.m.* Keenness. 2 Anger. 3 Rustling noise. 4 Chime.
———ach,** -aiche, *a.* Rustling. 2 Keen. 3 Angry, passionate.
forganta * *a.* Rigid.
†**forghabhail**, *s.f.* Forcible possession.
for-ghairm, *v.a.* Provoke.
————, -e, -eannan, *s.f.* Convocation.
forghall,** -aill, *s.m.* Lie, fable, romance.
forgladh,(DMy) -aidh, *s.m.* Commotion caused by a person coming in unexpectedly.
forghart,** -airt, *s.m.* Forepart of the head.
forghlac, *v.a.* Prevent, hinder. 2 Catch.
forghuin,** *s.f.* Wound. 2 Sharp pain, beating pain.
forgnadh, see foirgneadh.
forgradh, see fargradh.
fo-riarach,** *a.* Preposterous.
fòrlach, -aich, *s.m.* Pass, furlough. 2 Passport.
forlach, *Argyll* for fòghlach.
fòrladh, -aidh, *s.m.* see fòrlach.
forlaimh,** *s.f.* Leaping, bounding.
forlamhas,** -ais, *s. m.* Possession. 2 Force, power. 3 Conquest. 4 Pain. 5 Superfluity.
†**forlan,**** -ain, *s.m.* Power, force. 2 Pain. 3 Superfluity, excess. 4 Conquest.
†———gus, -uis, *s.m.* Banishment.
forlonn, *s.f.* see forluinn. †2 Attack.
forluinn, -e, *s.f.* Spite, grudge. 2 Hatred.
†**formach**, -aich, *s.m.* Increase, swelling.
formad, -aid, see farmad.
———ach, -aiche, see farmadach.
formail,** *a.* Shapely, sightly, of good form or figure.
————,** *s.f.* Hire, wages.
formaise,** *s.f.* Ornament.
†**formalach**, -aich, *s.m.* Hireling.
forman, -ain, -an, *s.m.* Type, mould. 2 Sound, noise. 3(DMC) Gaelic form of *foreman.*
forn,* *s. m.* Furnace. 2 Ship-well. [* gives Shop-work, and ** Shipwreck.]
†**fornaidheach**, *s.m.* Glutton.
fornair,** *s.m.* Command. 2 Offer.
for-oideas,** -eis, *s.m.* Rudiment, elements of knowledge. 2 Tradition.
—————ach,** *a.* Elemental, elementary. 2 Traditionary.
for-òrduchadh, -aidh, *s.m.* Predestination.
forrach,(AF) -aich, *s.m.* Perch (fish.) 2 Angling rod. 3 Perch (land measure.) 4 Oppression, compulsion. [** makes all meanings obsolete.]
forradh, -aidh, -ean, *s. m.* Gain, emolument. 2 Culling hastily. 2‡Excrescence. 4 Shift.
forra-dhruim, *s. f.* Slip-keel, false keel, see bàta, A4, p. 73.
†**forraid**, *adv.* Near, hard by.
forr-dreas, see dreas-chubhraidh.
forran,** -ain, *s.m.* Oppression. 2 Destruction.
———ach, *a.* Oppressive.
†**forrudh**, -uidh, -uidhean, *s.m.* Fringe.
forrumha,** *s.pl.* Fringes.
†**forrus**, -uis, *s.m.* Increase.
forsail,(CR) *a.* Well-to-do, prosperous. Tuathanach f., *a prosperous farmer.*
forsair, -ean, *s.m.* Forester, one who watches a deer-forest.
———eachd, *s.f.ind.* Forestry, the keeping of a forest, the business of a forester.
for-shoitheach, -hich, -hichean, *s.m.* Basin.
for-shuidhear, -an, see ceann-suidhe.
forsmaltadh, -aidh, *s.m.* Injustice.
fortachd,** *s.f.* Comfort.
fortail, -ala, *a.* Strong, hardy. 2 Patient. 3** Brave.
fortalachd,** *s.f.ind.* Strength, hardihood, bravery.
†**fortamhuil**, see fortail.
fortan, -ain, *s. m.* Fortune, luck. Deagh-fh., *good fortune ;* droch-fh., *bad luck ;* mar bha 'm f., *as good luck would have it.*
———ach, -aiche, *a.* Fortunate, lucky. Gu f., *luckily.*
———achd, see fortan.
fortas, -ais, *s.m.* Straw, litter, orts, refuse of fodder.
———ach, -aiche, *a.* Abounding in refuse.
†**forthan**, -ain, *s. m.* Plenty. 2 (AF) Stud of horses.
for-theachdair, -ean, *s.m.* Usher, under teacher. 2**Squire.
for-theagasg, -aisg, -an, *s.m.* see foir-theagasg.
fortraidh, *s.f.* Rising. F. na maidne, *the rising dawn.*
fo-ruadh, -ruaidhe, *a.* Reddish, of a bastard red, reddish-brown.
for-uinneag, -eige, -an, *s.f.* Balcony. 2 Lattice. 3 Window-shutter.
—————ach, *a.* Having a balcony, belong-

ing to a balcony.
forum, -uim, -an, *s.m.* see farum. 2(AC) Figwort, see lus-nan-cnapan.
-——ach, -aiche, see farumach.
†forus, -uis, *s.m.* Dwelling, abode. 2‡‡Knowledge.
fòs, *adv.* Moreover, too, yet, still. Mu'n do ghineadh f. na cnuic, *before ever yet the hills were formed ;* fòs tamuill beag, *yet a little while* ; ach fos, *but still, but yet.*
fos, *Badenoch* for os, *above.*
†fòs,* *v.* for foisich. 2 Prop, stay. 3 Pitch. 4 Lead.
†fos, see fas.
†fos, -ois, *s,m.* Ditch. 2 Wall. 3 Buttress.
fosadh, -ean, *s.m.* Desisting, cessation, recess, respite. 2 Concord, confederacy.
†fosadh,** -aidh, *s.m.* Cessation, rest, respite. 2 Delaying. 3 Staying. 4 Atonement. 5 Prop, buttress. 6**Sloping. Cha sluagh gun chruaidh a bheireadh f. orra, *it would not be unarmed people that could make them cease.*
fosadh-airm, (fois air airm=fainits, cease) *s.m.* Parley.
fosadh-comhraig, see fosadh-airm.
fosair,* *v. a.* Labour awkwardly in dressing food. 2 Pound bark.
fosaradh, -aidh, -aidh, *s. m.* Deep ploughing, trenching.
fosdadh, -aidh, *s.m.* Steadiness.
†fosdoigh, *v.* see fasdaidh.
fosg,(AC) *s.m.* Space. Am f., *the space above us;* am f. os ceann nam fànus, *the space above the sky-line.*
fosg,(AC)*s.m.* The lark. (bird of the open space.)
fosgadh, see fosdadh.
fosgadh, -aidh, -aidhean, see fasgadh.
fosgag,(AC) *s.f.* Little lark.
fosgag-Moire,(AC) *s.f.* Skylark.
fosgail, *pr.pt.* a' fosgladh, *v.a.* Open, disclose. 2 Unlock. 3 (DU) Introduce a discussion. Am fear nach f. a sporan, fosglaidh e a bheul, *he who will not open his purse will open his mouth*—most people when hearing of distress will be profuse in their expressions of regret, but how very few will express their sympathy in the smallest sum of hard cash.
——te, *a. & past pt.* of fosgail. Opened, that hath been opened. 2 Disclosed. 3 Unlocked. 4 Public.
——teachd,* *s.f.* Airiness. 2 Openness, candour, fairness.
fosgaireachd, see fosgarrachd.
fosgaldair, *s.m.* Broacher.
fosgar, *s.m.* Grunting noise made by some persons when eating.—*Suth'd.*
fosgarra, *a.* Open, frank, free. 2 Cheerful.
————ch, -aiche, *a.* see fosgarra.
————chd, *s.f.* Candour, openness, affability, frankness.
————dh, see fosgarra.
fosghair, *a.* Energetic, strong, irrestrainable. A thlachd bhi 'sgoltadh le roinn fosghair. *his delight was to cleave (the billows) with sturdy prow.—Filidh, p. 62.*
fos-ghàir, *s.* Clamour.
fosglachd, see fosgailteachd.
fosgladh, -aidh, -aidhean, *s.m.* Opening. 2 Unlocking. 3 Breach. 4 Act of opening. 5 Act of making a breach. 6(DU) Sheet lightning—*Gairloch.* 7 (DU)Introduction to a discussion, treatise. A' f—, *pr. pt.* of fosgail.
fosglan,(AC) -ain, *s.m.* Porch.
fo-sgrìobh, *v.a. & n.* Subscribe.
————adh,* -aidh, *s.m.* Postscript. 2 Appendix.
†foslong,** *s.m.* Mansion, dwelling-house.
†——phort, -phuirt, *s. m.* Harbour. 2 Encampment, camp.
†———phortach, *a.* Having harbours.
fosradh, -aidh, *s.m.* (AF) Grazing of cattle when tethered. 2 Hand feeding for cattle. 4**Release. 4** Dissolution. 5**Dwelling. 6 **Bed. 3** Pounded bark to stop leaks. 8 Anything to tighten a leaky dish. 9**Knowledge. 10** Clasp, cramp. 11(WC) Scraps, mixed food for cattle, scraps given to pigs. 12 Refuse of straw. Cha robh ann ach f., *there was only food composed of refuse of various kinds (when fodder was getting scarce.)*
†fost, *v.a.* Hire.
†fost, *s.m.* Prop.
fostadh, -aidh, *s.m.* Securing. 2 Pacifying.
†fosuign, -ean, *s.f.* Lodge.
†fot, *s.m.* Giant.
†fot, *a.* Raging.
fòt,* see foid.
fòtas, see fòtus.
fotha, see fodha.
†fotha, *s.m.* Foundation. 2 Cause.
fothach, -aich, *s.m.* Kind of cough. 2 Glanders in horses. 3 Lake, marsh, pond. 4 Wilderness, waste 5**Giant. 6**Cry, shout.
————,** *a.* Glandered, as a horse.
†fothadh, -aidh, *s.m.* Birch.
fothair, see fòir.
fothal,(DMC) *s.m.* Gossip.
fothalach, *a.* Gossiping.
fothalag, *s.f.* Gossiping woman.
fòthalan,(CR) *s.m.* *W. of Ross* for fòthannan.
fothalan, -ain, *s.m.* Untruthful fellow. 2(DMy) Restlessness.
————ach, *a.* Restless. Leanabh f., *a restless child.*
fotham, see fodham.
fothamas, -ais, see fathamas.
fòthannan, -ain, *s.m.* Thistle.
————-breac, Mary's thistle, see fòthannan beannaichte.
————-beannaichte,§ *s.m.* Mary's thistle—*carduus Marianus.* The leaves of this plant are blotched as if with milk being spilt on

331. Fòthannan beannaichte.

them, the superstition being that they are spotted with the Virgin Mary's milk—hence its other names, f. Muire and f. breac. Its name of bearnan breac is from the peculiar notched shape of the edges of the leaves.
—— ——-Muire,§ see fòthannan beannaichte.
———— ——-soilleir, *s.m.* Carline thistle.
fothantan, (CR) *Shiskine, Arran* for fòthannan.
fothargadh, -aidh, *s.m.* Bath. 2 Well of purification.
†fothlainteach,** -aich, *s.m.* Novice. 2 Apprentice.
fothlus,(AC) *s.m.* Figwort, see lus-nan-cnapan.
fothrag, see fathrag.

fothraig, see fathraig.
fothram, -aim, see farum.
†fothughadh, -aidh, *s.m.* Beginning. 2 Power.
fotlus, for fothlus, see lus-nan-cnapan.
fotrum, -uim, *s.m.* Great figwort, kernel-wort.
fotrus, -uis, see fortas.
fòtus, -uis, *s. m.* Refuse. 2 Corruption. 3 Flaw, blemish. 4 Rotten pus. 5 (AH) Leavings of cattle when fed with straw or hay. 6 see fortas. Dream rìoghail gun fh., *a royal and spotless clan.*
——ach, -aiche, *a.* Full of refuse. 2 Corrupt, blemished. 3 Causing blemishes.
——achd,** *s.f.* State of being blemished.
fo-uachdran, -ain, *s.m.* Lieutenant, deputy governor, viceroy.
————achd, *s.f.* Subordinate command or authority, viceroyalty, lieutenancy.
fo uamhann,** *adv.* Aghast.
frabhas,†† -ais, *s.m.* Refuse. 2 Small potatoes.
frac,** *s.m.* Bleakness.
†frach, -aich, *s.m.* Bleakness.
———ail,(DC) *s.f.* Vestiges,trifling appearances. Tha f. oibre ann, *there are trifling jobs of work to be had.*
frachd,‡ -an, *s.f.* Freight.
frachd,(DMC) *s.m.* Rags. 2 What is left of wool after the best has been pulled out.
fradhaidh, *Suth'd* for rabhadh.
fradharc, -airc, see radharc.
———ach, -aiche, see radharcach.
fràg, -àige, *s. f.* Hand. 2 Woman, wife. 3 Shield, buckler 4‡‡Kind wife.
fragh, see fraigh.
fraghaidh, see rabhadh.
fraidh, -ean, see fraigh.
fraigealach, -aiche, *a.* Ostentatious of personal strength.
†fraigealachd, *s.f.* Show of personal strength.
fraigean, -ein, *s.m.* Smart, little, brisk, warlike fellow, little man with an erect martial gait. [-ein, is also used as *nom.*]
———ach, *a.* Squat and strutting.
fraigeasach, -aiche, *a.* Smart, lively.
————, -aich, *s.m.* Lively little man.
†fraigeil, -e, *a.* see fraigealach.
fraigh, -e, -ean, *s.f.* Partition-wall, side wall. 2 Wattled partition. 3 Border, edge, rim. 4 Border of a country. 5 Frame. 6 Arch. 7 Skirt. 8 Shelf. 9 Wall-press, pantry. †10 Bush of hair. 11***rarely* the sea. 12*Roof. Fraighean na Criosdachd,*the borders of Christendom ;* is duilich beanas-taighe a dheanamh air na fraighean falamh, *it is hard to keep house with empty pantries ;* cròg fraigh, *picture formed by the shadow of the hand on the wall.*
fraigheach, *a.* Having borders or rims, bordered, rimmed, skirted, labiated. 2 Having sidewalls, pantries, &c.
fraighean, *n.pl.* of fraigh.
fraighnich,* *s.f.* see fraigh-shnighe.
fraighnidh, see fraigh-shnighe.
fraigh-shnighe, *s. m.* Water oozing through a wall. [** gives *s.f.*]
fraileach, -ich, *s.f.* Sea-weed.
fraineach, *Suth'd* for raineach.
fraings', *s.f.* Scouring-brush made of cross-leaved heath—*Badenoch* [variant of *roinnse, ruinnse* in *Bodenoch, rainnse* in *Perthshire.*] fraoch-frangach.
fraith, see fraigh.
framadh,** -aidh, *s.m.* Frame.
framh, see freumh.
framhach, see freumhach.
Frangach, *a.* French. Coileach f., *a turkey-cock.;* cearc-fh., *a turkey-hen ;* an galar f., *the venereal.*
Frangachail,** *a.* Frenchman-like.
frangalus, -uis, *s.m.* Tansy—*tanacetum vulgare.* [lus-na-Fraing§.]
————ach, *a.* Abounding in, made of or like tansy.
fraoch, -aoich, *s.m.* Anger, fury. 2 Hunger. 3 Girning expression of countenance. 4 Ripple on the surface of water. Laoch bu gharg f., *a hero of fierce wrath.*
fraoch, -aoich, *s.m.* Ling, heather—*calluna vulgaris.* Air feadh an fhraoich, *among the heather ;* coileach-fraoich, *a heather-cock. grouse.*
fraoch ! *int.* Heather ! A war-cry of the MacDonalds.
fraoch-a'-bhadain,§ *s.m.* Smooth-leaved heath —*erica cinerea.* [Given in error by § as the badge of the Robertsons instead of the bracken.]

332. Fraoch. 333. Fraoch-a'-bhadain.

fraochach, -aiche, *a.* Heathy, heath-covered. 2 Passionate, wrathful, angry, fretful. 3 Raging, stormy. Beanntan f., *heath-covered mountains.*
fraochag, -aige, -an, *s.f.* Cranberry, see muileag. 2††Whortleberry.
———ach, -aiche, *a.* Of, or belonging to whortleberries, abounding in whortleberries.
fraochaich, *v.a.* Enchafe.
fraochaidh, *a.* Angry, fretful, passionate, furious. 2 Stormy.
fraochail, -e, *a,* see fraochach and fraochaidh. Gu f., *angrily.*
fraochan,§ -ain, *s.m.* Whortleberry, see lus-nan-dearc. 2**Bilberry.
fraochan, -ain, *s.m.* Toe-cap, patch on the toe of a shoe, to prevent its wearing by rubbing against the heath. 2 Slight fit of passion. 3 Part of a deer.
————ach, -aiche, *a.* Patched as shoes. 2 Fretful. 3 Passionate. 4 Rippling.
————achd, *s.f.* Fretfulness.
————aich, see faochanaich.
fraoch-an-dearrsain,§ *s.m.* Smooth-leaved heath. (*lit.* the heath in which the wind makes a buzzing sound, or which crackles when being burnt.) also fraoch-a'-bhadain.
fraoch-an-dearrsain geal, *s.m.* White heath.
fraoch-an-ruinnse,§ *s.m.* Cross-leaved heath, see fraoch Frangach.
fraocharnach, -aich, *s.f.* Heathy hill.
fraoch-bhadain, see fraoch-a -bhadain.
fraoch-bheann, -bheinne, -eanntan, *s.f.* Heathy hill.
fraoch-chearc, -chirce, -an, *s.f.* Grouse-hen, female of the red grouse.
fraoch-Dhaboch,§ *s.m.* St. Dabeoc's heath—*dabeocia polifolia.* [Native of west Ireland, but not of Scotland or England.]
fraoch-Eireannach,§ *s. m.* Irish heath—*erica Hibernica.* [Not found in Scotland or England, but in Ireland and on the shores of the Mediterranean.]

334. Fraoch-Dhaboch. *335. Fraoch Eireannach.*

fraoch-Frangach,§-aich, *s.m.* Cross-leaved heath—*erica tetralix.* [McL & D and * give *cat-heather.*]

fraoch geal, *s. m.* White-flowering variety of common ling.—*calluna vulgaris alba.*

336. Fraoch-Frangach. *337. Fraoch-a'-Mheinnearaich.*

fraoch-gorm,§ *s.m.* Ling, see fraoch.

fraoch-mara,§ *s.m.* Kind of seaweed-*polysiphonia fastigiata.*

fraoch-meangain,* see fraoch-Frangach.

fraoch-a'-Mheinnearaich, *s. m.* Menzies' heath—*phyllodoce menziesia.* [So named after the naturalist Archd. Menzies. It is not the badge of Clan Menzies.]

fraoch-nan-curra-bhitheag, *s.m.* see fraochan.

fraoch-sgriachain,†† *s.m.* Crackling heath, see fraoch-a'-bhadain.

fraoch-spreadanach,§ *s.m.* Smooth-leaved heath, see fraoch-a'-bhadain.

fraoghaidh,** *s.f.* Warning.

fraoichean,(AF) *s.m.* Heather chatterer, whinchat.

fraoidh, see fraigh.

fraoidhleadh, -idh, -idhean, see fraoileadh.

fraoidhneadh, -idh, *s.m.* see fraoidhnidh. 2†† Embroidery.

fraoidhneas, -eis, -an, *s.m.* Fringe. 2 Tassel. 3 Embroidery.

——————-ach, -aiche, *a.* Waving, flourishing. 2 Richly fringed. 3 Full of embroidery or fringes.

fraoidhnidh, -ean, *s.m.* Flourishing appearance or hue.

fraoighlich,* see fraoileadh.

fraoileach,** *a.* Tipsy.

fraoileadh, -lidh, -lidhean, *s.m.* Flustering by liquor, tipsiness. Tha f. ort, *you are tipsy.*

fraoineasach, *a.* Waving, flourishing. 2 Calm. 3 Sheltered.

fraon, -aoin, *s.m.* Place of shelter in the mountains, or in a rock. 2 Low-lying valley.

———aiseach, see fraoineasach.

fras, froise, -an, [*pl.* frasdan—*Arran.*] *s. f.* Shower of rain or hail. 2 Small shot. 3 Seed of plants. 4 Any small round grain, as of flax. F. feòir, *grass seed*; f. 'sa ghunna, *small shot in the gun*; f. lìn, *flax-seed*; le cas is f., *corn-growth* (*lit* with foot and root); frasan sneachd, *falls of snow*; an lìon fo fhras, *the flax bolled* or *podded*; f. corcaich, *hemp-seed*; f. lìn, *lint-seed;* bogha-froise, *rainbow*; fras-luaidhe, *small shot.* [** gives *gen.* frois & *s.m.*]

†**fras**, *a.* Ready. 2 Active.

fras, *pr.pt.* a' frasadh, *v.a.* Shower, rain. 2 Scatter. 3 Dash. 4(DU) for frois. Frasaidh mi aran, *I will rain bread.*

frasach, -aiche, *a.* Showery, rainy. 2 Fruitful, prolific. 3 Imbriferous. 4 In flower, as flax.

frasach, -aich, *s.f.* Shower. 2 Manger. (prasach.)

frasachd, *s. f. ind.* Rain, showers. 2 Showery weather. 3 Showeriness. F. a' Chéitein, *the showers of Spring*; bheir mi dhuibh f., *I will give you showers.*

frasachdach, *a.* Showery. Là f., *a showery day.*

frasadh, -aidh, *s. m.* Showering. 2 Act of Showering. 3(DU) for froiseadh. A' f—, *pr. pt.* of fras. A' f. fola, *showering blood.*

fras-fhliuch, -fliuiche, *a.* Moistened by a shower.

frasrachd, see frasachd.

†**freac**, *a.* Crooked, bent, bending.

freacadan, -ain, -an, see freiceadan.

————ach, -aiche, *a.* see freiceadanach.

————aiche, -an, see freiceadanaiche.

freacadh, *s.m.* Attendance.

†**freacair**, *s.m.* Use, practice. 2 Attendance.

†**freacar**, -air, *s.m.* Witness. 2 Testimony, evidence. 3 Practice, frequency.

†**freacaraich**, *v.a. & n.* Wrestle. 2 Exercise. 3 Accustom.

freacaraiche, *s.m.* Wrestler 2 Exerciser.

†**freacaran**, -ain, *s.m.* Wrestling school. 2 Place for exercise.

freachnamh, -aimh, *s.m.* Labour.

†**freachnamhach**, *a.* Cautious, careful. Gu f., *cautiously.*

freachnamhachd, *s.f.ind.* Cautiousness, carefulness.

†**freacnairc**, *s.m.* Conversation.

†**freacuaire**, *s.f.* The present time.

freacuaireach, *a.* Modern.

freacuarach, see freacuaireach.

†**freadh**, *s.m.* Pillaging, plundering. 2 Booty.

freagair, *pr. pt.* [a' freagradh, &] a' freagairt, *v.a. & n.* Answer, reply. 2 Suit, fit. 3 Correspond. 4 Obey. F. an duine, *answer the man;* am bheil an còt' a' freagairt ? *does the coat fit ?* c'ar son nach f. thu mi ? *why will you not obey me ?*

freagairt, -ean, *s.f.* Answer, reply. Answering, act of answering, obeying, suiting or fitting. A' f—, *pr. pt.* of freagair. Fios f., *an answer to a letter*; cha d' thug e f. dhomh, *he gave me no reply.*

freagairte, *past pt.* of freagairt. Answered. 2 Suited, adapted, fitted.

freagar, see freagairt & freagradh.

freagaraich, *v.a.* see freagraich.

freagarair, *s. m.* Respondent, defender, answerer.

freagarrach, -iche, *a.* Answering, that answers or replies. 2 Answerable. 3 Suited, suitable. 4 Accountable, liable, responsible. 5 Accurate.

freagarrachd, *s.f.ind.* Congruity. 2 Accountableness. responsibility, answerableness. 3 Accuracy. 4 Agreeableness. 5 Fitness.

freagarraich, see freagraich.

freagnadh, -aidh, *s.m.* Labour, work, employment.

freagnairc, *s.f.* Conversation.

freagrach, *a.* see freagarrach.
freagrachd, see freagarrachd.
freagradh, -aidh, -aidhean, *s. m.* Answer, reply. 2 Act of answering. 3 Suiting, fitting. A' f—, *pr.pt.* of freagair.
freagraich, *v.a.* Answer. 2 Suit, fit, adapt.
————te, *a. & past pt.* of freagraich. Answered, suited, adapted, fitted.
freagram, *1st.sing. imp.* of freagair. Let me answer. 2 For freagraidh mi, *I will answer.*
frèamh, -an, see freumh.
———ach, see freumhach.
frèamhadh, -aidh, see freumhadh.
frèamhaich, *v.* see freumhaich.
freang, *s.m.* Hide, skin.
†**freang**, *v.a.* Make crooked, bend, twist.
freangach, *a.* Crooked, bent, twisted, winding, turning.
freangach,(AF) *s.m.* Pin-fish.
freapadh, -aidh, *s.m.* Bouncing, kicking, skipping. †2 Medicine.
frearag, (*e* close) *Suth'd* for frádharc.
freasdail, *pr. pt.* a' freasdal [& a' freasdaladh] *v.a.* Attend, wait on. 2 Depend on. 3 Relieve. 4 Provide, prepare. 5 Take precaution. F. do' n bhòrd, *wait at table ;* cò a fh. ? *who relieved ?*
freasdal, -ail, *s.m.* Serving, attending, waiting. 2 Providence. 3 Fate, lot. 4 Guardian angel. 5 Visitation. 6 Charge. F. Dhé, *God's providence ;* choimhead do fhreasdal, *thy visitation has preserved ;* is fheàrr f. na gàbhadh, *foresight is better than falling into danger.* A' f—, *pr.pt.* of freasdail.
freasdalach, -aiche, *a.* Provident, foresighted. 2 Attentive. 3 Providential.
—————adh, -aidh, *s.m.* Attendance. 2 Act of making provision. A' f—, *pr. pt.* of freasdalaich.
freasdaladh, -aidh, *s. m.* Providing, making provision. A' *pr. pt.* of freasdail.
freasdalaich, *pr. pt.* a' freasdalachadh, *v. a.* Provide, make provision. 2 Serve, wait, attend upon.
†**freasg**, *v.a.* Climb, ascend, mount.
freasgabhail, *s.f.* Ascension to heaven.
freaslach, -aich, *s.m.* Anger, resentment, displeasure.
freastal, -ail, see freasdal.
freatachadh, -aidh, *s.m.* see freiteach.
freiceadain,* *v.* Watch narrowly and slyly.
freiceadan, -ain, -an, *s.m.* Guard, watch. 2 Watching most attentively or narrowly. 3** Regiment. 4 Sentinel. Am F. Dubh, *the Black Watch* or *42nd. Regiment of foot,* now *the Royal Highlanders ;* ceannard an fhreiceadain, *the captain of the guard.*
freiceadanach, -aich, *a.* Of, or relating to sentinels, guards, &c, 2 Regimental.
——————d, *s.f.* Watching, guarding, continued watching.
freiceadanaiche, *s.m.* Sentry, guard.
freigh, see fraigh.
freimeiseanta,* *a.* see freimseil.
freimh, see freumh.
freimseadh, -sidh, *s. m.* Great huff or offence for little or no cause. 2††Fuss, pother.
freimseil,* *a.* Hale and hearty though very old. 2**Jolly.
freineach, *Badenoch* for raineach.
freislidh, *s.f.* Anger, vexation.
freiteach, -tich, -tichean, *s.m.* Vow, valedictory resolution. 2 Oath. Thoir f. nach dean thu eucoir, *make a vow that thou shalt not do evil;* cha chum freiteach ach deamhain, *none but devils keep rash vows.*
———adh, *s.m.* Abjuration.
freitich, *pr.pt.* a' freiteachadh, *v.n.* Vow, swear, resolve to abstain from something, as drink.
freòine, *s.m.ind.* Fury, rage.
freothainn,†† -e, *s.f.* Bent grass—*Argyll.*
freothal, -ail, *s.m.* Whirl. 2 Eddy. Mar fh. na mara, *like the eddy of the sea.*
————ach, *a.* Whirling. 2 Eddying, full of eddies.
freumh, -a, -an [& -aichean], *s.m.* Root, stem, stock. 2 Lineage. 3 *rarely* Sound sleep. Spìonar a fh. á bun, *his root shall be torn up.* [** gives *gen. sing.* freimh, and *s.m.*]
freumh, *v.a.* Take root, establish.
freumhach, -aich, -aichean, *s.f.* Root, stem. 2 Origin. 3 Lineage, pedigree. Dìridh snothach o 'n fhreumhaich, *sap shall ascend from the roots ;* a chionn nach robh f. aige, *because it had no root.*
freumhach, -aiche, *a.* Full of roots, rooted. 2 Steady, well founded. 3 Fibrous. 4 Fundamental.
freumhachadh, -aidh, *s.m.* Taking root, rooting. 2 Propagating. 3 Derivation in *grammar.* A' f—, *pr.pt.* of freumhaich. Air dhuibh bhi air bhur f., *on your being rooted.*
freumhachas, -ais, *s.m.* Firmness of root. 2 Etymology.
freumhachd, -an, *s.f.* Original cause or origin. 2 Rootedness. 3 Etymology.
freumhag, -aige, -an, *s.f.* Fibre, root. 2(CR) Portion,measure. Na'm biodh f. slàint' agam, *if I had a measure of health—W. of Ross.*
freumhaich, *v.a.* Take root, radicate.
——————te, *past pt.* of freumhaich. Rooted. F. 'na chridhe, *rooted in his heart.*
freumhaichean, *n.pl.* of freumh.
freumhail, -e, *a.* Radical. 2‡‡Constitutional.
freumhair, -ean, *s.m.* Etymologist.
freumhaireachd, *s.f.* Etymology.
freumh-fhacal, -ail, -clan, *s.m.* Primitive word, etymon, radical term.
freumh-fhaclach, *a.* Etymological.
freumh-fhaclachd, *s.f.* Etymology.
freumh-fhaclaiche, *s.m.* Etymologist.
freumh-fhaclair, *s.m.* Etymologist. 2 Etymological dictionary.
freumh-uibhir, -ean, *s. f.* Primary or cardinal number.
freumhuinean, -ein, *s.m.* Sucker, sprout.
freunaich, *v.a.* Found, establish.
frì, see frìd. *prep.*
†**frialta**, *a.* Free, freed. 2 Fried.
friamh, *pl.* friamhan [& friamhaichean,] see freumh.
frìd, see frìde.
frìd, *prep.* Through. Air m' onair gu'n deach e frìd a' bhealaich mhóir, *'pon my conscience he took leg-bail.*
frìde,‖ *s.f.* The itch. 2 The insect acarus scabei. 3 Tetter. 4 Ringworm, fleshmite. 5 Pustule. 6 Small pimple. 7 (AC) Gnome, pigmy, elf, rock-elfin.
frìdeach, *a.* Pimply. 2 Like a pimple. 3 Pustulous.
frìdeag, -eige, -an, *s. f.* Small ringworm. 2 Pimple, small pustule. 3 see frìde 6.
frìdeagach, *a.* Pimply, full of small pimples.
frìdeam, -eim, *s.m.* Attention, support. 2(DMC) Sufficiency, suitability. Cha dean e f., *it is quite inadequate ;* cha'n 'eil f. agam air, *I don't care a fig about it.*
frìdeamach -aiche, *a.* Officious, attentive, supporting.
frìdean, see frìde 6.
frìdean-fionn, (AF) *s.m.* Wren-mite.
frìdh, -e, -ean, *s.m.* see frìth, *s.f.*
frìdh-ghaduiche, -ean, *s.m.* see frìth-ghaduiche.
frìdhire, see frìthire.
frìdh-mheirleach, see frìth-mhèirleach.

fridich, see fride 6.
†**fridiomb**, *s.m.* The use of another's house as your own for a limited time, kindliest hospitality, see fridean.
fridiombach, -aiche, *a.* Quite at home, under no restrait in another's house.
frigh, see frith.
frigheannachadh, -idh, *s.m.* & *pr.pt.* see frighigeadh.
frighig, *v.a.* Fry.
frighigeadh, -idh, *s.m.* Frying, act of frying. A' f—, *pr.pt.* of frighig.
frighigichte, *past pt.* Fried.
frilisg,(CR) *s.f.* Earthworm used as bait for trout —*Gairloch & Lochbroom.*
frineas, -eis, see frionas.
frineasach, *a.* see frionasach.
friobhag, -aige, *s.f.* see frith-bhac.
friobhruth, *s.m.* Refusal, denial.
friochanntaireachd, *s.f.* Recantation.
friochd, -an, *s. m.* Second dram, nip, half-glassful, after a "sgailc" or morning bumper. [It was usual for a guest in a house in Gaeldom to take when he awakened :—
1 An sgailc-nide,
2 An friochd ullinn,
3 An deoch chas-ruisgte, *and*
4 An deoch bhleth,
before he partook of food in the morning.]
friochd, *v.a.* Lance, pierce or probe quickly, as with an awl, pin, &c.
friochdadh, -aidh, *s.m.* Quick stab, stabbing quickly and painfully.
friochdail, -ean, *s.m.* see friochdan.
friochdan, -ain, *s.m*, Frying-pan.
friochnach,***a.* Diligent. 2 Careful, circumspect. Gu f., *diligently.*
friochnadh, -aidh, *s.m.* Care, consuming care, diligence.
friochnamhach, *a.* Careful.
friochoidheas, -is, *s.m.* Antipathy.
friodhan, -ain, see frioghan.
friodhanach, *a.* see frioghanach.
friodh, see frioghan.
friogh,(DMC) *s.m.* Angry countenance, accompanied by sharp, cutting language.
friogh,** *a.* Sharp, keen, piercing. 2 Bristly. Gu f. nàmhach, *sharply and hostilely.*
frioghach,** *a.* Sharp, keen, piercing. 2 Bristly.
frioghach, -aiche, *a.* see frioghanach.
frioghail,** *a.* see friogh & frioghach. Gu f., *sharply* ; cho f. ris na leòghainn, *as keen as the lions.*
frioghalachd,** *s. f.* Sharpness, keenness. 2 Bristliness. F. t' inntinn, *the sharpness of thy wit.*
frioghan, -ain, *s.m.* Sow's bristle. 2 Edge. 3 Gloom. 4 Frown. 5 Sharp cold. 6‡‡Anger. 7 Barb. 8(AH) Layer of thatch resting on the ridge of a house. 9(DC) Stubble.
frioghanach, -aiche, *a.* Bristly, bristling, rough. 2 Frowning, as winter, wintry. 3 Angry.
frioghanachd,** *s.f.* Bristliness.
frioghanaich,** *v.* Bristle.
frioghlaisg,(CR) *s.f* Shred of skin turning up at the base of the finger-nail.—*Perthshire.* 2 Barb of a hook also—*Loch Tay.*
friolaisg,** *s.f.* Small splinter rising on the surface of deal, or on the skin.
friolanna, *s.pl.* Streamers.
frioluaisg,** *v. a.* Turn down and open the mouth of a bag or sack. 2 Move up and down.
frionas, -ais, *s.m.* Fretfulness, anger. 2 Chagrin, vexation.
frionasach, -aiche, *a.* Angry, vexed. 2 Fretful, peevish. 3 Impatient. 4** Bitter. Na bi -sa f., *be not impatient* ; gu f., *fretfully.*
frionasachd, *s.f.* Fretfulness, peevishness. 2 Impatience. 3 Cholericness.
friosg,** *v.a.* Turn down and open the mouth of a bag or sack.
friosg,** *a.* Nimble, active.
friosg, (AF) *s.f.* Earthworm—*Lochalsh.*
friot,** -a, *s.* Fret, fit of fretfulness.
friotach, -aiche, *a.* Fretful. 2 Angry. 3 Ill-natured, hasty. Gu f., *fretfully.*
friotachas, -ais, *s.m.* Ill-nature, anger.
friotal, -ail, *s.m.* Word. 2 Interpretation. 3 Fret.
friotalach, -aiche, *a.* see friotach. Gu f., *fretfully.*
friotalachd,** *s.f.* Fretfulness. 2 Angriness.
frioth, *a.* see frith.
friothail, *v.a.* see fritheil.
friothailt, see fritheilt.
friothailteach, -iche, *a.* see fritheilteach.
friothaindeach,* see frith-ainmheach.
frioth-ainm, see frith-ainm.
friothair, -e, *a.* Passionate, touchy, frettish.
friothaireachd, *s.f.* Crossness.
friothaladh, -aidh, *s.m.* & *pr.pt.* see frithealadh.
friothalaich, *v.* see fritheilich.
friothalaiche, -an, *s.m.* see fritheiliche.
friothan, see frioghan.
friotharach, *a.* Contradictory.
friotharachd, *s.f.* Captiousness.
friotharadh, *s.m.* Contradiction.
†**friseeart**, -eirt, *s. m.* Answer.
frisealair, *a.* see friotalach.
frisgis, *s.f.* Hope, expectation.
frith, -a, *a.* Small, little, trifling. [Always used before the noun qualified.]
frith, -e, -ean, *s.f.* Forest (of deer, *not* of trees.) 2 Heath, moor. 3**Deer-park. Mo chàirdean 'san fh., *my friends in the deer-forest.*
frìth, -e, -ean, *s.f.* Rage, anger. 2 Augury, divination. 3‡ Incantation to discover if far-away persons live. 4 Fate. 5‡ Sour or angry look. 6 *prov.* Profit, gain, advantage.
†**frith**, *s.f.* The mouth of a river, firth. 2 Suit, attendance.
frith-, *prefix* equal to the prep. *ri*, which see.
frith-aghann, -aighne, *s.f.* Warming-pan.
frith-ainbheach, *s. m.* Arrears, trifling debts, remainder of a debt.
frith-ainm, -eannan, *s.m.* By-name, nickname.
———**each**, *a.* Nicknaming.
frith-ainmich, *pr.pt.* a' frith-ainmeachadh, *v.a.* Nickname.
frithaireach, *a.* Hasty. 2 Peevish. Gu f., *fretfully.*
frithaireachd, *s.f.* Hastiness. 2 Peevishness.
frith-bhac, -aic, -an, *s.m.* Barb of a hook, arrow or anchor.
frith-bhacach, -aiche, *a.* Barbed.
frith-bhaile, -bhailtean, *s.m.* Suburb. 2 Hamlet, village. Anns na frith-bhailtean, *in the suburbs.*
frith-bhailteach, *a.* Abounding in hamlets. 2 Having suburbs. 3 Suburban.
frith-bharail, *s.f.* Paradox.
frith-bharaileach, *a.* Paradoxical.
†**frith-bheart**, *v.a.* Contradict. 2 Object.
frith-bhruidheann, *s.m.* Chat.
frith-bhuail, *pr.pt.* a' frith-bhualadh, *v.n.* Palpitate, vibrate. 2 Strike back. 3 Strike softly.
frith-bhuailteach, *a.* Repercussive. 2 Vibrative.
frith-bhualadh, -aidh, *s.m.* Palpitation. 2 Pulsation. 3 Striking softly. 4 Repercussion. A' f—, *pr.pt.* of frith-bhuail. Tha mo chridhe a' frith-bhualadh, *my heart palpitates.*
frith-bhuille, -an, *s.m.* Little stroke. 2 Back stroke. 3 Vibration.
frith-channtair, -ean, *s.m.* Recanter.
frith-channtaireachd, *s.f.* Recantation.

frith-chasd,(AH) *s.m.* Short, dry, intermittent cough. 2(DC) " Kinks " in whooping cough.
frith-cheannaiche, *s.m.* Hawker, cadger.
frith-cheòl,(AC) *s.m.* Low music.
frith-cheum, -annan, *s.m.* By-walk, by-road.
frith-choille, -lltean, *s.f.* Underwood, brushwood, copse.
frith-chòmhradh, see frith-bhruidheann.
fritheachd, *s f.* Coming and going. 2 Returning.
frith-eagal, -ail, -an, *s.m.* Slight degree of fear, panic, sudden terror. 2 Surprise.
frith-eagalach, *a.* Causing a panic. 2 Apt to be startled.
frithealach, *a.* Waiting, attending. 2 Officious. 3 Attentive. Gu f., *officiously*.
frithealaiche, *s.m.* Administrator.
frithealachd,(DMC) *s.m.* Enough, sufficiency. Tha f. agam dheth, *I have what will do of it.*
frithealadh, -aidh, *s. m.* Attending, waiting, ministering. 2 Dispensation. Bean-fh., *a midwife* [*bean-ghlùin* is better]; fear-frithealaidh, *an accoucheur, attendant, waiter.* A' f—, *pr. pt.* of fritheil.
frithealaich, see fritheil.
frithealaichte, see fritheilichte.
frithear, see frithir.
fritheárach, -aich, *a.* Uneasy. 2 Peevish, morose, cross, impatient. 3 Fervent.
frithearachd, *s. f.* Peevishness, moroseness, crossness, fretfulness.
frithearra, *a.* Peevish. 2*Whimsical.
fritheil, *pr. pt.* a' frithealadh, *v. a.* Attend, wait upon, minister, serve. 2* Attend a woman in child-bed.
fritheileach, *a.* Officious. 2 Attending, waiting on. 3 Attentive.
———d, *s.f.* Officiousness. 2 Attendance. 3 Attentiveness.
frith-eilean, -ein, -nan, *s.m.* Small island. 2** Floating island.
———ach, -aiche, *a.* Having small or floating islands. 2 Of, or pertaining to, small or floating islands.
fritheilich, *v.a.* Same meanings as fritheil.
———e, *s.m.* Attendant. 2 Administrator.
———te, *past pt.* of fritheilich. Attended, waited upon, served.
fritheilt, -e, -ean, *s.f.* Attendance on a woman in child-bed.
———each, -eiche, *a.* Attentive in waiting.
———eachd, *s.f.ind.* Obsequiousness. 2 see fritheilt.
frith-fhacal, -ail, -clan, *s.m.* By-word.
frith-fhill, *v.a.* Turn down and open the mouth of a bag.
frith-fhroineach, see frith-raineach.
frith-ghaduiche, -an, *s.m* Poacher.
frith-ghaol,(AC) *s.m.* Small love.
frith-ghaoth,(AC) *s.f.* Weak wind.
frith-ghàradh, *s.m.* Old or small fence. Aig taobh an fh., *beside the old fence.*
frith-ghearan, -ain, -an, *s.m.* Habit of complaining, querulousness.
———ach, -aiche, *a.* Querulous, complaining.
frith-gheumnaich,(AH) *s.m.* Act of lowin noisily while walking or running. Thàinig am mart dachaidh 'san fh., *the cow came home lowing demonstratively.*
frith-iasg, -éisg, *pl.* -a, -éisg &- iasgan, *s.m.* Small fry of fish. 2 Bait for fish. Generally applied to garvies, matties and immature fish—AC. 3 Ink-fish, cuttle-fish—*Lewis.*
frithich, *v.a.* Afforest.
frithil,†† *a.* Angry.
†**frithing**, *s.f.* Relapse.
frithir, -e, *a.* Earnest, eager, fervent. 2 Intractable, furious. 3††Fretful.
frithir, *s.m.* Impatient man. 2 Augurer. 3 see frithearachd.
frithire, *s.m.* Forester.
———achd, see frithearachd. 2(AC) Augury.
frith-lagh, *s.* By-law.
frith-léim, see frith-leum.
frith-léimneach, -eiche, *a.* see frith-leumnach.
frith-léimnich, see frith-leumnaich.
frith-léimrich, see frith-leumnaich.
frith-leum, *s.m.* Quickstep. 2 Skip, bound, hop.
frith-leum, *v.n.* Skip, leap, bound, hop.
frith-leumartaich, *s.f.* Skipping, bounding, hopping. Ri f., *skipping.*
frith-leumnach, -aiche, *a.* Skipping, bounding.
frith-leumnaich, *s.f.* Skipping, bounding, capering, hopping.
frith-leumraich, see frith-leumnaich.
frithlisg, *s.f.* Splinter.
frith-mhaighstir, -ean, *s. m.* Under-master, usher.
frith-mhinistear, -an, *s.m.* Curate.
frith-mhinistrealachd, *s.f.* Curacy.
frith-mhuir, -mhara, *s.f.* Salt-water loch, arm of the sea.
frithne, *s.f.* Uninhabited place. 2 Unfrequented place.
———asach, *a.* see frionasach.
frith-mhèirleach, *s.m.* Poacher.
frith-phunc, -phuinc, *s.m.* Quaver in *music.*
frith-raineach,‡ -nich, *s.f.* [Bladder-fern, dwarf fern—*cystopteris fragilis.*

338. Frith-raineach.

frith-rathad, -aid, *pl.* -thadan & -aidean, *s. m.* By-road. 2 Foot-path. 3 Short cut, near way.
frith-rathadach, *a.* Having by-roads or short cuts.
frith-rod, see frith-rathad.
———ach, see frith-rathadach.
frith-sheirc, *s.f.* Return of affection, mutual affection.
frith-sheòmar, -air, -mraichean, *s.m.* Side room, small apartment.
frith-shlàinte, *s.f.* Convalescence.
frith-shràid, *s.f.* By-street. 2 Alley, lane.
frith-staidhir, -dhreach, -dhrichean, *s.f.* Back stairs.
frith-thràigh, (AC) *s.f.* Small ebb.
fro, *a.* Hoarse—*Dàin I. Ghobha.*
fròg, -òige, -an, *s.f.* Hole, chink, niche, nook, cranny. 2 Marsh, fen. 3 Retired habitation. 4 ‡Den. 5* Dismal, dark hole, ugly place. 6 Anger. Am frògaibh nan toll, *in the clefts of the caverns.*
frog,(CR) *a.* Active, energetic. 2 Good or quick at work. Ged tha e beag, tha e f., *though he is little, he is able—Lochbroom.* (*grideil* in *Gairloch.*)
frògach, -aiche, *a.* Full of holes. 2 Fenny, marshy. 3* Full of ugly crannies. 4*Having ugly sunk eyes.
frògach, -aich, *s.m.* Hollow. 'S móran frògaich 'nad aghaidh, *and many hollows in thy face.*

frògag, -aig, -an, s. *f.*, *dim.* of fròg. Little hole. 2 Fen.
frògagach, -aiche, *a.* Full of little holes or fens.
frogail, *a.* Merry, cheerful. 2 Tipsy, maudlin. Ag éirigh gu f., *rising merrily.*
frogalachd, *s.f.* Merriness, cheerfulness. 2 Tipsiness.
frogan, -ain, *s.f.* Liveliness, cheerfulness. 2 Degree of tipsiness. 3 Merry fit. 4 Anger, slight fit of anger.
froganach, see froganta.
——————d, see frogantachd.
froganta, *a.* Pert, lively, merry. 2 Tipsy, maudlin. Gu f., *merrily.*
frogantachd, *s.f.ind.* Merriness, cheerfulness, liveliness, pertness. 2 Tipsiness.
fròg-na-cubhaig, *s. f.* Cuckoo-flower—*Arran.* [bròg-na-cubhaig.]
frogoiseach, -siche, see froganta.
fròg-shuil, -ula, -ean, *s.f.* Surly eye.
fròg-shuileach, -eiche, *a.* Surly-eyed.
froidhleach, -iche, *a.* see froganach.
froidhneadh, -nidh, -nidhean, see fraoidhneas.
fròig, -e, -ean, see fròg.
froigh, -e, -ean, see fraigh.
froighnighe, *s.m.* Wetness oozing through a wall.
froineach, see raineach.
froineadh, -idh, -idhean, *s.m.* Sudden tugging or plucking. 2 Rushing at or to. 3††Shake. 4††Drubbing.
froinich,* *s.f.* see fraoidhneas.
froinis, -e, -ean, see fraoidhneas.
froinnseach, *a.* see fraoidhneasach.
froinse, *gen.* of froinis (fraoidhneas.)
frois, *pr.pt.* a' froiseadh, *v. a.* Cast seed from overripeness, spend, as standing corn. 2 Give off as thread. 3 Untwine yarn from clew. 4 Scatter. 5††Run out, as a stocking.
frois,†† *s.f.* Shower of grain of other articles (not rain.)
frois,(AC) *s.f.* Top. Bho fh. m' aodainn, *from the top of my face.*
froiseach, -eiche, *a.* Scattering in every direction, wide scattering. 2 Shaking off, as corn. Gaoth fh., *a sweeping blast.*
froiseadh, -sidh, -sidhean, *s. m.* Wide scattering, dispersion. 2 Shaking off, as of corn. 3 Rain. 4 Blast. 'Ga fhrasadh m' a chluasan, *scattering it about his ears.* When oats are stripped of their ears by a storm, it is said, "chlaidh an coirc' a fhroiseadh."
froisean,(DC) *s.m.* see roisean.
froisnein, -ean, *s.m.* Grain of seed.
froithlin,** *s.f.* Whirl.
†fromadh, *s.m.* Trial.
fròmh,* *s.m.* Hoarseness, cold.
†fromh, *v.a.* Try, taste. 2 Enquire. 3 Examine.
fromhach, -aich, *s.m.* Glutton.
†fromhadh, -aidh, *s.m.* Trial, tasting. 2 Enquiry.
fròmhaidh, -e, *a.* Hoarse. Guth f., *a hoarse voice, a deep-toned voice.*
fròmhail,(CR) *s.f.* Croaking of frogs—*Islay.*
fròn, -òin,** *s.m.* Nose.
fronnsa, *s.m.* Kind of play or mock-wedding at wakes.
fros, -oise, -an, see fras.
†fros, *a.* Dark, obscure.
frosach, -aiche, see frasach.
frosachd, see frasachd.
frothal, -ail, *s.m.* Whirl, whern.
frothalach, *a.* Whirling.
fruan,(AC) *s.m.* Acclivity, steepness, steep hill.
fruchag, -aig, -an, *s.f.* Cranny.
fù, *prep.* see fo.
†fuabart, -airt, *s.m.* Attack. 2 Spoiling.
fuach, -aich, *s.m.* Word.
†fuachaidh,-e, -ean, *s.f.* Jilt, tricking strumpet. 2 Coolness, displeasure.
fuachaideach, *a.* Jilting. 2 Like a jilt. Gu f., *jiltingly.*
fuachaideachd, *s.f.* Jilting.
fuachas, -ais, -an, *s.m.* Cry, outcry. 2 Cold. 3 (AF) Fox's den.
fuachasach, *a.* Making an outcry, tumultuous. 2 Cold. Gu f., *tumultuously.*
——————, *s.m.* Den, cave, hole. 2 Fox's den.
fuachasach, *a.* Full of caves. 2 Very, exceedingly. F. làidir, *very strong.*
fuachasachd, *s.f.* Outcry, tumult, continued tumult. 2 Tendency to tumult.
fuachd, *s. f. ind.* Cold, coldness, chilliness. 2* Obstructed perspiration.
fuachdan, -ain, *s.m.* Any sore occasioned by cold. 2 Chilblain.
fuachdas-làmh,(AH) *s.m.* The degree in which one's hands are susceptible to cold. Tha fuachdas-làmh math aige, *his hands are seldom affected by extreme cold;* tha droch fhuachdas-làmh aige, *his hands are (habitually) readily affected by cold.*
fuachd-ghuirean, *s.m.* Chilblain.
fuad, *v.a.* Elope, run away with. 2 Impress.
fuadach, -aich, see fuadachadh. Dh' fhalbh i am f. leis, *she eloped with him;* cù fuadaich, *a driving dog.*
fuadachadh, -aidh, *s.m.* Running away. 2 Driving, or chasing away. 3 Banishment. 4 Rapine. 5 Elopement, eloping. 6 Driving a vessel out of her course. 7 Estrangement of affections. A' f—, *pr.pt.* of fuadaich.
fuadachd,* see fuadachadh.
fuadaich, *pr. pt.* a' fuadachadh, *v. a.* Put to flight, expel, drive away, banish. 2 Carry off by force. 3 Elope. 4 Ravish. 5 Impress. 6 Drive out of the proper course or channel. 7 Estrange the affections. Gu 'm f. e, *that he will drive out;* f. le fonn a ghruaim, *drive away his frown with a song;* a dh' fhuadachadh bhan, *to carry off (elope with) females.*
fuadaichte, *past part.* of fuadaich. Put to flight, expelled, banished. 2 Taken or snatched away clandestinely.
fuadain, -e, *a.* Exiled. 2 Foreign. 3 Fleeting, transitory, momentary. Sgàil f., *a fleeting shadow.*
fuadan, -ain, *s.m.* Wandering. 2 Carrying clandestinely as a horse. 3 State of straggling or straying. 4 Exile. 5 (AH) Wanderer, friendless person. Is coma leam fear-fuadain is e luath a labhar, *I don't like a wayfarer who talks loudly and volubly*; naigheachd fuadain, *a side-wind story;* air fhuadan, *astray;* aodann f., *a mask used at Samhuinn time.*
fuadar, -air, *s.m.* Haste. 2 Preparation to do anything.
fuadarach, -aiche, *a.* Active, diligent. 2 Hasty, in a hurry.
fuadh, *s.m.* Bier. 2 Foe. 3 Horrid sight, demon, ghost. 4 Slender, ghastly person. 5 see fuath.
fuadhaiche,†† *s.m.* Scarecrow, bogle.
fuadhmhar, -aire, see fuathmhor.
fuadradh, -aidh, *s. m.* Bier. 2 Hindering. 3 Crossing. 4 Forbidding.
fuaduichte, *past pt.* see fuadaichte.
fuagair, *pr.pt.* a' fuagradh, *v.a.* Proclaim. 2 Denounce. 3 Placard.
fuagarthach, -aich, *s.m.* Exile, banished person.
fuagairt, *s.f.* Adjuration, warning.
fuaghal, see fuaigheal.

fuaghladh, -aidh, *s.m.* Bastinade. A' f—, *pr. pt.* of fuaghail.
fuagradh, -aidh, *s.m.* Exile.
fuagradh, *s.m.* Proclaiming, proclamation. 2 Denouncement. A' f—, *pr.pt.* of fuagair
fuagradh, -aidh, *s.m.* *s.m.* Proclamation, edict.
fuagraich, *v.a.* see fuagair.
fuaghail, *v.a.* see fuaigh.
fuaid, *s.f.* Remnant.
fuaideach, *a.* Having remnants.
fuaidearag,(AF) *s.f.* Minnow. Ag iasgachadh le fuaidearaig, *trolling for lythe by line and sinker dragged astern of a boat.*
fuaidheal, see fuaigheal.
fuaidh, see fuaigh.
fuaidhlean, -ein, *s.m.* Anger, fury.
fuaidhte, see fuaighte.
fuaidne, -an, *s.f.* Peg in a warping-frame. 2 Knot. 3 Pillar, post. [fuaidhne in *Uist.*]
fuaidnean, *s.pl.* Warping-pins in *weaving.*
fuaidreag, *s.f.* Eel or natural fly used in fishing. —*Argyllshire.*
fuaigh, *pr. pt.* a' fuaigheal, *v. a.* Sew, stitch, knit, connect. 2* Seam or nail, as planks in a boat. 3**Bastinade. Fuaighidh tu suas, *thou shalt sew up.*
fuaigheal, -eil, *s.m.* Seam. 2 Sewing or stitching, act of sewing or stitching. A' f—, *pr.pt.* of fuaigh. Àm gu f., *a time to sew.*
fuaigheam, -eim, *s.m.* see fuaigheal.
fuaighil, *pr. pt. v.a.* Bastinade.
fuaighte, *a. & past pt.* of fuaigh. Stitched, sewed. 2*Nailed, pegged, as timbers in a boat.
fuaigh-shlat, s. Temporary stock of a ship while building.
fuail, *gen.sing.* of fual.
fuail-fheadan, -ain, see fual-fheadan.
fuailisg,(AC) *s.f.* Hatred.
fuail-uisge, see fual-uisge.
fuaim, -e, -ean, *s. m. & f.* Sound, noise. 2 Echo. 3 Accent. 4 Voice. F. an cliù, *the noise of their fame* ; ri f., *sounding.*
fuaim, *v.a.* see fuaimnich.
fuaim-an-t-siorraimh,§ *s. m.* Fumitory, see lus-deatach-thalamhainn, (a play on the Latin name)—*fumaria officinalis.*

339. Fuaim-an-t-siorraimh.

fuaimeal, -eile, see fuaimeil. Gu f., *noisily.*
fuaimear, see fuaimearra.
fuaimearra, *a.* Reverberant, sounding, noisy, sonorous.
fuaimeil, -e, *a.* Sounding, resounding, noisy, sonorous. 2 Echoing. Tràigh fh., *a sounding shore* ; gu f., *noisily.*
fuaim-iùil, *s.m.* Diacoustics.
fuaimneach, -niche, *a.* Sonorous, noisy. 2 Echoing. Gu f., *noisily.*
fuaimneach, -neich, *s. f.* Great noise, frequent noise, continued noise. F. shleagh, *the noise of spears.*
fuaimneachd, *s.f.ind.* Noisiness.
fuaimnich,†† *s.f.* Great noise.
fuaimnich, *pr.pt.* a' fuaimneachadh, *v.a.* Blow. 2 Sound, resound. 3 Echo.
fuaimreag, *s.f.* Vowel, in *grammar.*
fuaim-sgrìobhair, *s.m.* Phonograph.
fuaim-sgrìobhadh, *s.m.* Phonography.
fuaintean, *s.pl.* Pegs in a warping-frame. 2(DMC) Handles of a plough.
fuair, *s. f.* Sound.
fuair,(CR) *v.* [aspirated *fh*uair, everywhere except in *Suth'd.*] Fuair mi e, *I got it* ; is e sin na fuair e, *that is all he got.*
fuaircean, *s.pl.* Pins or pegs in a warping-frame.
fuaire, *comp.* of fuar. Colder, coldest.
fuairead, -id, *s.m.* Coldness, degree of coldness. A' dol am f., *growing colder and colder* ; air fh. 's ge' m bi an t-earrach, *however cold the spring may be.*
fuaireadach, -aiche, *a.* Chilly.
fuairid, *comp.* of fuar. Colder. Is f. e sin, *it is the colder for that.*
fuairsgeul, -sgeòil, *s.m.* Silly story.
fuais, *gen.sing.* of fuas.
†**fuait**, *s.f.* Judgment.
fuaithne, see fuaidne.
fual, -ail, *s.m.* Urine, water.
fualach, -aiche, *a.* Nephretic.

340. Fualachdar. *341. Fualachtar.*

fualachdar,§ -air, *s.m.* Water speedwell—*veronica anagallis.*
fualactar,§ -air, *s.m.* Marsh-wort—*heliosciadium inundatum.*
fualan, -ain, -an, *s. m.* Urinal. 2 Pimp. 3 Chamber-pot.
fualas, -ais, *s.m.* Tribe, family.
fual-bhrosnach, -aich, *s.m.* Diuretic.
fual-bhrosnach, -aiche, *a.* Diuretic.
fual-bhrosnaidh, *a.* Diuretic.
fual-fheadan, -ain, *s.m.* The urethra.
†**fualiosg**, *s.f.* Strangury, see cuing-fhuail.
†**fualiosgach**, *a.* Strangurial.
fual-losgach, *a.* Causing heat in urine.
fual-losgadh, -aidh, *s.m.* Heat in urine.
fual-phoit, -eachan, *s.f.* Chamber-pot.
fual-ruithe, *s.f.* Diabetes.
fual-uisge, *s.m.* Stranguary, see cuing-fhuail.
fuaman -ain, *s. m.* Shadow, shade. 2 Whiteness. 3 Rebound.
fuamh, for fuath.
fuamhair, -ean, see famhair.
fuamhaireach, *a.* see famhaireach.
fuamhaireachd, see famhaireachd.
fuan, -ain, *s.m.* Veil, cover, mask. 2 Cloth. 3 Mercy. F. air lochd, *veil on a fault.*
fuan, *v.* Veil, cover, mask.
fuar, -aire, *a.* Cold, chilly. 2 Stinging.
fuar, *s.m.* Cold. Cha dean f. bliochd, *cold will not make milk.*
fuar, *v.a.* Get a-head, get before the wind of another ship or boat. 2 Get to windward of a point. Feuch am f. thu a' charraig, *try and weather the point.*
fuar-achadh, *s.m.* Untilled land—*Arran.*
fuarachadh, -aidh, *s.m.* Cooling, act of cooling. 2 Ease, relief. A' f—, *pr.pt.* of fuaraich. Dean do gharadh far an d' rinn thu t' fh., *warm*

yourself where you grew cold.
fuarachas, -ais, *s.m.* Coldness.
fuarachd, *s.f.* Coldness, cold, chilliness. Cròdhaidh f. iad, *the cold shall crowd them together.*
fuarachd, *s.f.* (CR) Dampness. 2(AH) Chilblain, generally used in the *pl.* 3 (DC) Mildew on cloth, books, &c. Tha f. ann, *it is damp*—said e. g. of a house, wall or floor—*W. of Ross.*
fuarad, -aid, *s.m.* see fuairead.
fuaradh, -aidh, *s.m.* The windward or weather side. 2 Blast. 3 Cooling breeze. 4 Draught, as from a door or window. 5 (DMC) Anticipation of coming evil. 6 (AH) Reaching, in sailing. Air f. ort, *on your starboard;* leis ort or leis dhiot, *on your port;* air taobh an fhuaraidh is air an taobh leis, *beating, as a ship just before a shower;* f. cluais, *a ship's earring;* sùil ri f., *an eye to windward;* cum an t-eathar bho chladach an fhasgaidh, agus cumaidh i fhéin bho chladach an fhuaraidh, *keep the boat from the lee shore, and she 'll keep herself from the wind shore.*
fuaradh-froise,†† *s.m.* Breeze which precedes a shower.
fuarag, -aig, -an, *s.f.* ‡Mixture of meal and water or milk, hasty pudding. *Scots,* crowdie. 2 Poultice. also stapag.
fuaragan, -ain, *pl.* -ganan & -gain, *s.m.* Fan. 2 Ventilator.
fuaraich, *pr.pt.* a' fuarachadh, *v.a. & n.* Cool, become cool. 2 Refrigerate.
fuaraich, (MMcD) *s. f.* Black soot dripping through the thatch after a heavy shower—*Lewis.*
fuaraichear, -eir, -eirean, *s.m.* Cooler.
fuaraichte, *a. & past pt.* of fuaraich. Cool, cooled. 2 Refrigerated.
fuaraidh, *a.* Coldish, chill. 2 Cool in manner. 3 (CR) Damp.—*W. of Ross.* Tha 'n oidhche f., *the night is cold;* talamh f., *damp or wet soil.*
fuaralach, -aiche, *a.* Cold, chilly. 2††Indifferent. Gu f., *coldly.*
———d, *s.f.ind.* Coldness, chilliness. 2†† Indifference.
fuaran, -ain, -an & -ain, *s.m.* Well, spring, fountain. 2**Pump-well. 3**Pool for cattle to stand in to cool themselves. F. nan càrn, *the spring of the rocks;* greidh air t' fhuarain, *a troop of horses on the space of thy pools.*
———ach, -aiche, *a.* Abounding in springs.
———ta, *a.* Chill, cold, grown cold. Gu f., *coldly.*
†fuarasdair,** *a.* Judicious.
fuar-bheann, *gen.pl.* of fuar-bheinn.
fuar-bheinn, *gen.pl.* fuar-bheann, *s.f.* Cold, bleak mountain. A' siubhal fhuar-bheann, *traversing the cold mountains.*
†fuar-bhodradh,** -aidh, *s.m.* Benumbing.
fuar-bholadh, -aidh, *s. m.* Unpleasant smell, stench.
fuar-bhòrd, *s.m.* Weather-board.
fuar-bhuille,(WC) *s.f.* Fatal blow, death-stroke. Cò a thug an fh. dhi? *who gave her the death-stroke?*
fuar-chasach, -aiche, *a.* Cold-footed.
fuar-chràbhach, -aich, *s.m.* see fuar-chràbhaiche.
———, -aiche, *a.* Hypocritical. Gu f., *hypocritically.*
fuar-chràbhadair, see fuar-chràbhaiche.
fuar-chràbhadh, -aidh, -aidhean, *s.m.* Hypocrisy, false devotion. 2‡‡Superstition. Luchd fuar-chràbhaidh, *hypocrites.*
fuar-chràbhaiche, *s.m.* Hypocrite. 2 Superstitious person.
fuar-chrapadh, -aidh, *s.m.* Benumbing.
fuar-chridhe,** *s.m.* Cold heart.
———ach, -eiche, *a.* Cold-hearted, unfeeling.
fuar-chrith, -e, *s.m.* Shivering with cold, cold shivering. Tha i 'na f., *she is in a cold shiver.*
———each, *a.* Shivering with cold. Gu f., *unfeelingly.*
fuardachd,** *s.f.* Coldness, chilliness.
fuar-dhealt, -a, *s.m.* Mildew. 2**Blight. 3** Cold dew. Le f., *with mildew.*
———ach, -aiche, *a.* Mildewy, blighty, blighting.
fuar-fhead, -an, *s.f.* Cold whistling, as of wind.
fuar-ghreadadh,** *s.m.* Blast.
fuar-ghreann, *s.f.* Scowl, cold, shivering look.
fuarlanach, -aiche, *a.* Cold. 2 Unfeeling, malign, invidious. 3 Neglectful, unkind. Gu f., *unfeelingly.*
———,** -aich, *s.m.* Malignity, hatred.
———d, *s.f.ind.* Coolness. 2 Malignity, hatred. T' fh. dh' Albainn, *thy hatred for Scotland.*
fuar-làrach,(AH) *s. f.* Cold, empty dwelling, house at meal-time without any fire or signs of food.
fuar-leabadh,(DC) *s.f.* Plank on which a dead body is laid—*Skye.*
fuar-léine,(TS) *s.f.* Shroud.
fuar-lite, -ean, *s.f.* Cataplasm, poultice. 2 *Lewis* for fuarag.
fuar-lorg, -luirg, *s.m.* Retracing, cold scent.
fuarmadh,** -aidh, *s.m.* Form, seat.
fuar-mharbh,** *a.* Starved with cold. 2 Cold in death.
———,** *v.a.* Starve with cold.
———adh,** -aidh, *s.m.* Perishing with cold.
———tachd,** *s.f.* Numbness.
fuarnach,** -aich, *a.* Controversial, wrangling, quarrelsome.
fuarnadh,** -aidh, *s.m.* Controversy, argument. 2 Paper war.
fuarrach,** *a.* Helping, assisting.
fuarrachd, *s. f. ind.* Moisture, dampness. 2* Chill.
fuar-rag, -raige, *a.* Numb.
fuarraidh, see fuaraidh.
———eachd, see fuaralachd.
fuarralanach, *s.m.* see fuarlanach.
fuar-sgallais,** *s.* Game.
fuartanach, *a.* Anodyne.
fuas, -ais, *pl.* -ais & -uasan, *s.m.* see fuathas.
fuas, see fuathasach.
fuasach, -aiche, see fuathasach.
fuasan,** -ain, *s.m.* Gainsaying, contradiction.
fuasgail, *pr.pt.* a' fuasgladh, *v. a. & n.* Loose, untie. 2 Unlock. 3 Liberate. 4* Unriddle, guess, solve. 5 Unyoke. 6 Relieve, aid, assist. 7 Redeem. 8 Absolve. 9 Explain. F. an t-sreang, *loosen the cord;* f. an toimhseachan, *solve the riddle;* f. air, *relieve him;* daoine a dh' fhuasgladh gach snaoim, *men who could solve every difficulty*—untie every knot. [In *Gairloch* tuasgail, where the *t* is also retained in derivatives—WC]
———te, *a. & past pt.* of fuasgail. Loosed, untied, freed, liberated. 2 Unconstrained. 3 Active, having command of one's limbs, nimble. 4 Absolved. 5 (WC) Senseless, simple. Neach f., *a person devoid of perfect sense.*
———teach, -eiche, *a.* Active, nimble, unconstrained. 2**Loose, licentious. 3**Giving or causing freedom. 4**Aperient. 5**Having free use of one's limbs.
———teachd, *s.f.ind.* Ease, looseness. 2 Freedom of action. 3 Use of one's limbs. 4 Activity, unconstraint, unrestrictedness. 5 Absoluteness. 6**Openness. 7**Simplicity.
†fuasgair,** *v. a.* Terrify. 2 Put to flight. 3

Scare off.
fuasgaladh, see fuasgladh.
fuasgaldach,** *a.* Aperient.
fuasgaldair,** *s.m.* Saviour, deliverer, redeemer. F. a' chinnidh dhaoine, *the Saviour of the world.*
fuasgar,** -air, *s.m.* Dispersion, total rout.
fuasglach,** *a.* Loosening. 2 Absolving. 3 Ransoming. 4 Delivering.
fuasgladh, -aidh, -aidhean, *s.m.* Loosing, untying, act of loosing. 2 Relief, assistance, redemption. 3 Guessing. 4**Ransoming. 5 Deliverance, ransom. 6** Explanation, exposition. 7** Loosening of the bowels. F. deas, *ready deliverance;* thoir f. dhòmh, *set me free;* 'ga fh., *loosing* or *freeing him;* a' f. air, *relieving him;* thug e f. dha, *it gave him relief;* f. na ceisd, *the answer of the riddle;* f. briogs', *being at stool, moving of the bowels.* A' f—, *pr.pt.* of fuasgail.
fuasglaidh, *fut.aff.a.* of fuasgail.
fuasglair, -ean, *s.m.* Redeemer, ransomer.
fuasgradh,** -aidh, *s.m.* Fright.
fuaslagadh,** -aidh, *s.m.* see fuasgladh.
fuaslaig,** *v.a.* see fuasgail.
———,** *s.f.* see fuasgladh.
fuasmadh,** -aidh, *s.m.* Blow.
fuasnach,** *a.* Terrible, frightful. 2 Tumultuous.
fuasnadh,** -aidh, *s.m.* Astonishing, astonishment. 2 Driving forward. 3 Tumult.
fuatarach, see fuadarach.
———d, see fuadarachd.
fuath, -a, *s.m.* Hatred, aversion, abhorrence. 2 Hateful object. 3 Scarecrow. 4 Diminutive, insignificant person. 5 Apparition, spectre, ghost, demon, spirit. 6 Kelpie. 7 Spite. Dùisgidh f. e, *hatred shall stir him up;* le 'm briathraibh f., *with their words of spite;* frith nam f., *the forest of the spectres.*
fuathach, -aiche, *a.* Hateful, abhorrent, averse. 2**Spectral, demoniacal.
———, -aich, -aichean, Monster. 2††Spectre.
———adh, -aidh, *s.m.* Detesting, abhorring, abhorrence. A' f—, *pr. pt.* of fuathaich.
fuathachail, -e, *a.* Loathsome.
fuathachair,** *s,m.* Hater.
fuathachd, *s.f.* see fuathmhorachd.
fuathadair, -e, -ean, *s.m.* Hater.
fuathadh,** -aidh, *s.m.* Detesting, detestation, abhorrence.
fuathaich, *v.a. & n.* Hate, detest, abhor.
fuathaiche, -an, *s.m.* Hater.
fuathaichte, *past pt.* of fuathaich. Hated, abhorred, detested.
fuathail, -e, *a.* Spectral, ghostly, ghastly. 2 Frightful. 3 Hateful. 4 Diminutive, insignificant.
fuathais, *gen.sing.* of fuathas. †2 *s.f.* Den.
fuath-a'-mhadaidh, *s.m.* Monkshood—*aconitum napellus.* 2‡‡Wolf's-bane. (ill. 342.)
fuathar, *a.* Antipathetical.
fuath-arrachd,(AF) *s.f.* Monster.
fuathas, -ais, *s. m.* Spectre, apparition. 2 Prodigy. 3 Fright, sudden alarm. 4††Great quantity, great degree of. Chunnaic iad f., *they saw an apparition.*
fuathasach, -aiche, *a.* Dreadful, horrible, terrible. 2 Wonderful, prodigious.
fuathasaich, *v.a.* Terrify, horrify.
fuath-gorm,§ *s.m.* Woody nightshade, bittersweet, see searbhag-mhilis.
fuath-mhadaidh, see fuath-a'-mhadaidh.
fuathmhoireachd, see fuathmhorachd.
fuathmhor, -oire, *a.* Hateful, disagreeable. 2 Terrific. 3 Horrible. 4 Hating, disliking. 5 **Spectral. 6**Unclean. Gach eun f., *every*

342. Fuath-a'-mhadaidh.

unclean bird.
———achd, *s.f.ind.* Hatefulness.
fuath-mhuc, *s.f.* Bluebell, wild hyacinth—*scilla non scripta.* 2 Hare-bell.

343. Fuath-mhuc.

fuath-radain, *s.m.* Rat's-bane.
fuaths, see fuathas.
fuath-shlat, -shlait, *s.m.* Thing in its primordial state. 2††Temporary hoop. 3 (AH) Framework, as the ribs and hoop of a basket. 4(D My)—fuath-shlatan—said of the long legs or thighs of a tall man.
fuath-thannasg, -aisg, *s.m.* Hideous spectre.
fuath-thogalachd, *s.f.* Invidiousness.
fuath-thoilltinneach, -aiche, *a.* Hateful, abominable, deserving of hatred.
fùc, *v.a.* see pùc.
fùc, *pr.pt.* a' fùcadh, *v.a.* Full, waulk, as cloth.
fùcadair, -ean, *s.m.* Fuller of cloth.
———eachd, *s.f.* Fulling of cloth.
fùcadh, -aidh, *s.m.* Fulling of cloth. 2(CR)Pushing or moving heavily. Cha b' e an clò ciar-dubh nach fhiach 'fhucadh, *it is not the dark home-made cloth that deserves not fulling*—alluding to the change of cloth which came into fashion in 1746, when the use of the Gael's beloved tartan was forbidden by a despicable Act of Parliament.
fù'd, *cont.* for fothad. Under thee.
fudag, -ain, -an, *s.f.* Shoe-strap. *prov.*
fudaga dud! *int.* Fie! for shame!
fudagag,(AC) *s.f.* Woodcock, see coileach-coille.
fudaidh, -ean, *s.m.* Vile, worthless fellow, the refuse of his kind. Breunan is F. an cuideachd a chéile, *Dirty and Rubbishy going together*—a Lewis proverb, taken from a verse

by J. Morrison of Bragar on having sent two servants to pull heather :
Chuir mise Breunan is Fucaidh
A bhuain fraoich an cuideachd a chéile ;
Thug Breunan dhachaidh an cudthrom,
'S thug Fudaidh dhachaidh na geugan,
(I sent B. and F. to pull heather together ; B. brought home the weight, and F. brought home the boughs.)—NGP.

fudaidh, -e, *a.* Mean, vile, contemptible, trifling, worthless.

fùdar, -air, *s.m.* Powder, gunpowder. Mheil e gu f. e, *he ground it to powder ;* f.-dhurrag, *a worm-powder ;* f.-cluaisein, *priming*; f.-sròine, *hellebore.*

———ach, -aiche, *a.* Powdered, of, or pertaining to powder.

———aich, *v.a.* Powder, pulverize. 2*Urge on to do mischief, instigate. Is tusa a dh' fh. e, *it is you that urged him to do it.*

fudlan, -ain, -an, see udalan.

fudradh, -aidh, *s.m.* see fuidreadh.

fùdraic, -e, *a.* Smart, brisk, lively. 2 In good condition, in good health.

fùdraich, see fudraic.

fufaireachd,** *s. f.* Irish cry or *conclamatio* at funerals.

fugasg,** -aisg, *s.m.* Patience. 2 Persecution. 3 Steadiness.

†fughall,** -aill, *s.m.* Judgment.

fughar, see futhar.

fuiceag, -eig, see fuidheag.

fuich ! *int.* see fich !

fuicheachd,** *s.f.* Lust, lechery.

fuicheall,** -ill, *s.m.* Reward, hire, wages.

fuideallan,(DMC) *s.m.* Part of a tether between the swivel and the animal's neck or leg—*Uist.*

fuidh, *prep.* see fo.

fuidh ! *int.* see fich.

fuidheach,** *a.* Thankful. 2 Joyful.

fuidheag, -eig, -an, *s.f.* see fuigheag.

fuidheall, -ill, see fuigheall.

†fuidhir,** *s. f.* Gain. 2 Wages. 3 Word. 4 Vassal. 5 Hireling. 6 Servitude. 7 Veil.

fuidhleach, see fuighleach.

fuidhn', *prep.* for fodhainn, see under fo.

†fuidhne, see fuithreach.

fuidhpe, see foipe.

fuidhre, see fuidhreach.

———ach,** *s. pl.* Attendants. 2 Establishment of servants.

———,** *a.* Naked, exposed.

fuidhreachdach, -aiche, *a.* Quarrelsome. 2 Treacherous.

fuidhreachd, *s.f.* Mixture. 2 Mixing.

fùidir,* *v.a.* Besprinkle.

———,(AC) *s.m.* Fool, lout, clown.

fuidir, *v.a.* Fumble.

fùidreadh, -idh, *s.m.* Commixing. 2 Pounding, pulverizing. 3 Heterogenous mixture. 4 Turning hay in the sunshine to dry it, tedding. 5*Sprinkling. 6**Paste.

fuidreadh, -idh, *s.m.* Fumbling.

fùidrichte, *a.* Mixed.

fùidse,** *s.m.* Coward. 2 Conquered dispirited cock. 3 (DMC) Challenge. A' toirt f. dha, *challenging him.*

fùidsidh, *a.* Craven. Coileach f., *a craven cock, the vanquished one in a cock-fight.*

fuiflen, *s.m.* Blister on the breech.

fuigh, *v.a.* see faigh.

†fuighbheatha, *s.m.* Vital sap.

fuigheag,-eig,-an,*s.f.* Thrum, the warp thread in weaving, 10 or 12 inches long, remaining unwoven at the end of the web.

———ach, -aiche, *a.* Of, or belonging to thrums, like a thrum.

fuigheall, -ill, *s.m.* Remainder, remains, remnant, refuse. 2**Relic. Is math f. na foighidinn, *the final results of patience are excellent;* f. an t-sluaigh, *the remnant of the people;* cha d' fhàg claidheamh Fhinn riamh f. beuma, *Fingal's sword never had to cut twice ;* is fheàrr f. na braide na f. na sgeige, *the residue of theft is better than that of scorn.*

fuigheall-margaidh, *s.pl.* Rabble, refuse of a multitude, worthless persons.

fuighleach,-ich,-ichean, *s.m.* Remains, leavings, refuse. F. bìdh, *refuse of meat ;* cha'n 'eil de mhath air f. a' chait ach a thoirt dha fhéin, *the cat's leavings are fit only for himself*—applied to men who would palm the dregs on others after they have drunk the cream.

fuil, *gen. sing.* fola, *dat.* fuil, *voc.* fhuil ! *s. f.* Blood. 2 Family, tribe, kindred. 3*Bloodshed. 4‡‡Wound. 5(DC) Breeding. 6 (DMC) Temper, nature. A' dòrtadh fola, *shedding blood* ; rinn iad f., *they made bloodshed ;* o 'n fh. rìoghail gun smal, *from the royal extraction uncontaminated ;* f. bhrùite, *extravasated blood ;* gu f. is gu bàs, *to blooashed and death* ; feadh fola is àir, *amid blood and slaughter* ; fàth air son fola, *opportunity for bloodshed ;* is milis fuil nàmhaid, ach is milse fuil caraid, *sweet is the blood of an enemy, but sweeter still the blood of a friend*—friendship is stronger than enmity—in the olden times, it was no uncommon thing for the Gael of wild passions to drink the blood of a dear friend who had died a violent death, in token of undying love; nach ann tha 'n droch fh. ! *what an evil temper he has !*

†fuil, see bheil ?

fuilbhean, *s.m.* Atom.

———ach, -aiche, *a.* Atomical.

fuil-bhrùite, *s.f.* Extravasated blood.

fuil-chiont, *s.f.* Blood-guiltiness.

———ach, *a.* Bloody, blood-guilty.

fuil-dhòrtadh, -aidh, *s. m.* Bloodshed, blood-spilling.

fuil-dhòrtair, *s.m.* Spiller of blood. 2 Sanguinary person.

fuileacan, (AF) *s.m.* Asp.

fuileach, -eiche, *a.* Bloody, gory, sanguinary. 2* Cruel. 3 (DC) Fat, full-blooded. Còmhrag f., *a bloody battle ;* a righ a's fuiliche lann ! *O king of the most sanguinary sword !*

———adh, -aidh, *s.m.* Drawing of blood. A' f—, *pr.pt.* of fuilich.

fuileachd, *s.f.ind.* Bloodshed. 2 Bloodiness. 3 Atrocity. 4* *s.m.* Extraction.

———ach, -aiche, *a.* Bloody, sanguinary. 2 Cruel. 3 Ravenous. An duine f., *the bloody man ;* do 'n eunlaith fh., *to the ravenous birds.*

———ach, -aich, *s.m.* Extraction.

fuileadh,** -idh, *s.m.* Increase, profit, gain.

fuileamain,* *s.m.* Blister on the toe.

fuilear, *s.* Too much. *Fuilear* is used to express necessity, need or obligation,and forms a verb, which is Englished by *must, need,* or *require.* Cha'n fhuilear dhuibh a bhi cinnteach á sin, *you require to be sure of that ;* cha mhór nach b' fhuilear dhomh e, *it was no more than it could be*—i. e. I am almost entirely dependent on it ; cha'n fhuilear dha punnd eile, *he will require another pound* ; cha b' fhuilear dhaibh tighinn aig aon uair, *they would need to come at one o' clock ;* cha'n fhuilear dhuit a bhi an seo, *you would require to be here ;* cha b' fhuilear dhuinn cogadh no fàilneachadh, *we were obliged to fight or yield ;* cha b' fh. uiread eile, *as much again is necessary. Cha'n fhuilear* is rendered affirmatively, and *is uilear* negatively in English, as, cha'n fh. dha tasdan air as tunnaig, *he requires a shilling for the duck*; is uilear dha tasdan air an tunnaig, *he does not require (so much as) a shilling for the duck*; tha thusa mar a bha thu an uiridh, 's ged bhiodh tu na b' fheàrr cha b' fhuilear, *you are as you were last year, and if you were better, it would be no more than was needed.*

†fuileasan,** *s.m.* Asp.

fuile-thalmhainn, *s.m.* Bulbous crowfoot—*ranunculus bulbosus.*

fuilich,* *pr.pt.* a' fuileachadh, *v.n.* Bleed, draw blood. Dh' fhuilich e gu bàs, *he bled to death;* dh' fh. e air, *he drew blood from him.*

fuiliche, *a.* Blood-red. 2 *comp.* of fuileach.

fuilidh,** *a.* Bloody. 2 Blood-red.

fuilig, see fulaing.

fuiling, see fulaing.

———each, -eiche, see fulangach.

fuilleadh,** -idh, *s.m.* Reward. 2 Gain. 3 Increase.

fuilmean,** -ein, *s.m.* Toe bleeding by striking it against a stone.

fuil-mios,* *s.f.* Menstrual discharge.

fuil-nan-sluagh,(AC) *s.f.* (*lit.* the blood of the hosts—fairies) Red crotal of the rocks melted by frost. In *Argyllshire,* the saying when one sees red crotal is, thug na daoine beaga cath an raoir, *the little men (fairies) fought a battle last night.*

fuil-siofraith, -e, *s.f.* Pumice-stone.

fuilt, *gen.* of falt.

fuilteach, -eiche, *a.* Bloody. 2 Atrocious. 3 Cruel.

———ail, -e, *a.* see fuilteach.

———as, -ais, *s.m.* Bloodshed, slaughter. 2 Villiany. 3* Extreme cruelty.

———d, *s.f.ind.* see fuilteachas.

fuiltean, -ein, *pl.* -eana & -eine, *s.m.* Single hair. 2 Quoif. 3 Snood. 4**The hair of the female head. Tog do bhréid is t' fh., *lift thy head-dress and snood;* fuilteine bhur cinn, *the hairs of your heads.*

———ach,†† *a.* Containing single hairs. [†† gives fuilteineach.]

fuiltein, see fuiltean.

fuiltionnach, -aiche, *a.* see fuilteach.

†fuin,(AF) *s.f.* Cow.

†fuin,** *s.f.* End or termination of a thing. 2 Will, purpose. 3 Veil, covering.

fuin, *pr.pt.* a' fuineadh, *v.a.* Bake bread. 2 Knead.

fuince,(AF) *s.* Fox.

fuine, *s.f.* see fuineadh. 2 *Lewis* for foinne.

fuineachan, -ain, *s.m.* Kernel. 2**Baker.

fuineadair, -ean, *s.m.* Baker.

———eachd, *s.f.ind.* Trade or business of a baker.

fuineadh, -idh, *s.m.* Baking, act of baking. 2 Batch of things baked, as loaves. 3 Kneading. 4‡‡Boiling. A' f—, *pr.pt.* of fuin. Na mnathan a' f. na taoise, *the women baking the dough;* 's fheàrr f. tana na bhi uile falamh, *better a scanty baking than to be without bread altogether.*

fuineall, -ill, *s.m.* Funnel.

fuinear, *fut. pass.* of fuin.

†fuingeall,** -ill, *s.m.* Idiot, simpleton.

fuinidh, *fut.aff.a.* of fuin.

†fuinn, *s.f.* Conclusion.

fuinn, *gen. sing. & n. pl.* of fonn.

†fuinne, *s.m.* The setting of the sun, the West.

fuinneag, -eig, *s.f.* see uinneag.

———ach, *a.* see uinneagach.

fuinnseach,§ -aich, *s.m.* Enchanter's nightshade —*circœa lutetiana & c. alpina.* (ill. 344.)

fuinnseann,§ -ainn, *s.m.* Ash, see craobh-uinnseann.

344. Fuinnseach.

fuinseag-coille,§ *s.f.* Golden rod—*solidago virgaurea.* 2 Mountain ash, see luis. [Name given by Shaw to *virgo pastoris.*]

345. Fuinseag-coille.

fuinte, *a. & past pt.* of fuin. Baked. 2 Kneaded.

fuipe, *prep. pron.* see foipe.

fuir,** *s.* Sign, token.

fuirbearnach, -ich, *s.m.* see fuirbidh.

fuirbirneach, see fuirbidh.

fuirbidh, *s.m.* Strong man, remarkably powerful man.

fuireach, -ich, *s.m.* Delaying, staying, waiting, lingering. A' f—, *pr. pt.* of fuirich. Gu dè am f. a th' ort? *why are you waiting?*

fuireachadh, -aidh, *s.m.* see fuireach.

fuireachail, see furachail.

fuireachair, see furachail.

fuireachd, *s.f. prov.* for fuireach.

†fuireadh,** -idh, *s.m.* Preparation. 2 Feast.

†fuireann,** -einn, *s.m.* Crowd, multitude. 2 Ship's crew. 3 Furniture.

fuireanal, -ail, *s.m.* Urinal.

fuireann,** -inn, *s.f.* Ballast.

fuirearach,** *a.* Attentive, vigilant.

fuirearadh,(DC) see fuirireadh.

fuireas,** -eis, *s.m.* Entertainment. 2 Feast.

fuirfheitheamh, -imh, *s.m.* Overseeing.

fuirich, *pr.pt.* a' fuireach [& a' fuireachd,] *v.n.* Stay, wait, delay, linger. 2 Abide. 3 Dwell. 4**Deliberate. Cha'n fh. mi, *I will not stay;*

fuirich beagan, *stop a little;* guidheam ort f., *I pray thee stay;* f. ort! *wait thou!* f. orm! *let me see a moment, wait till I remember!*
fuiril,(AC) *s.f.* Lyre. Ainnir na fuiril, *the damsel of the lyre.*
fuirionn,** *s.m.* see fuireann. 2**Land.
fuirireadh,(AC) -idh, *s.m.* Parching corn, mode of drying corn to make the cakes used at Christmas and other festivals. Mìn fh., *parched corn-meal.*
fuirleach, *s.f.* Parchment or skin to cover a milk-dish.
fùirleachadh, -idh, *s.m.* Overcoming, victory.
fùirlich,** *v.a.* Overcome, defeat.
fuirm, ‡-e, -ean, *s. f.* Form, manner, fashion, usage, ceremony. 2 *gen.sing. & n. pl.* of furm. 3 Pomp. 4 Activity, "cleverness." 5 Noise. Thug e cuirm le f., *he gave a banquet with pomp.*
†fuirmeadh,** -idh, *s.m.* Humiliation. 2 Lessening. 3 Travelling.
fuirmealachd, *s.f.ind.* Preciseness, *prov.*
fuirmeil, -e, *a.* Precise.
fuirmheadh, -eidh, *s.m.* Seat, foundation.
†fuirmhidh, *a.* Hard.
fùirneis, -ean, *s.f.* Furnace, stove. 2 see àirneis.
————each, *a.* Like a stove. 2 Furnished with stoves.
fùirneisich, *v.a.* see àirneisich.
†fuis, *a.* Active, thrifty.
fuiseag, see uiseag.
†fuite, *s.* Sound, reiterated noise.
fuiteachadh, *s.m.* Coaxing one to take or to do anything—*Badenoch.*
†fuith, *s.f.* Rag of cloth.
fuith! *int.* see fich!
fuithe, *prep.pron.* see fodha.
fuitheag, see fuigheag.
fuithein, *s.m.ind.* Galling, taking off the skin by riding. 2††Trifling sore.
†fuithir, *s.f.* Good land. Far am faighear famh bidh f., *where a mole is found, good land will be.*
fulachd, see folachd.
————ach, *a.* Patient.
————as, -ais, see fulangas.
fulag, -aige, *s.f.* see ulag. 2 Swivel—*Uist.*
fulaing, *pr.pt.* a' fulang, *v.a.* Suffer, endure. 2 Permit, allow. 3 Bear. Fulaing dhomh, *permit me;* cha'n fh. an gnothach e, *the matter will not admit of it;* cha'n fh. mi dhuit, *I will not permit you.*
fulair,** *s.m.* Occasion, necessity. 2 Obligation.
———,** *a.* Necessary. 2 Urgent. (fuilear.)
fulaisg, *v.a.* Rock, move backwards and forwards.
fulamair, see fulmair.
fulang, -aing, -an, *s.m.* Patience, forbearance. 2 Patient suffering. 3 Capability of enduring. 4 Act of suffering or bearing. 5**Passion. 6 **Feeling. 7**Foundation. 8**Shore. 9** Prop,buttress. 10**Stud, boss. 11*Hardihood. A' f—, *pr.pt.* of fulaing.
———ach, -aiche, *a.* Patient, enduring, suffering. 2 Hardy, tough. 3 Passive in *grammar.* 4**Armed with spear or shield. Gu f., *patiently;* na croinn fh., *the tough, enduring masts.*
———achd, *s.f.ind.* Passiveness.
———aiche, *comp.* of fulangach. More or most capable of enduring or bearing.
fulangaiche, -an, *s.m.* Sufferer, patient. 2 Person of feeling.
fulangas, -ais, *s. m.* Suffering, endurance. 2 Patience. 3 Passion. 4 Feeling. Fad-fh., *long-suffering, longanimity.*
Fulang dorrain, *s.m.* The banner of Fergus, i.e. the banner of one who could sustain a defeat, and play a losing game when necessary, contrary to the English idea that the Gael can only make one rush and are soon disheartened.
†fulangtha, *s.m.* The passions.
fulang-ùird, *s.f.* Malleability.
fulannach, -aiche, see fulangach.
————d, see fulangachd.
fulannaiche, see fulangaiche.
fulannas, -ais, see fulangas.
fulasg,* see fulaisg.
fulasgach, -aiche, *a.* Moving backwards and forwards, agitated, rocking.
fulasgadh, -aidh, *s.m.* Rocking, act of rocking or moving backwards and forwards, tossing. A' f—, *pr. pt.* of fulaisg.
fulbh, -uilbh, *s.f.* Gloom.
†fulladh,** -aidh, *s.m.* Lie. 2 Leaping, skipping.
fullan,** -ain, *s.m.* Ornament.

342. ¹Fulmair.

fulmair, -e, -ean, *s.m.* Fulmar petrel—*procellaria glacialis.* [eun crom in *Lewis*—DMy] 2 (AF) Polecat.
fulpannach, -aich, see fulpannachd.
————, *a.* Restless. An fhairge fh. fhalpannach, *the restless splashing ocean.*
fulpannachd, *s. f. ind.* Articulation, joining of things together.
†fulrath, *s.m.* Corruption.
fulshruth, *s.m.* Corruption. 2 Gore.
fu'luaisg, see fo-luaisg.
fuluing, see fulaing.
fum, see fodham.
†fumair, -ean, *s.m.* Large lump.
funn, see fonn.
funntachadh, see funntainn.
funntaich,†† *pr. pt.* a' funntachadh, *v.a. & n.* Chill, grow cold.
funntail,** *a.* Frosty. 2 Benumbing. Rè là fuar, f., *during a cold, frosty day.*
funntainn, -e, *s. f.* Excessive cold, extreme severity of wintry weather. 2 Stiffness. 3 ‖Foundering. 4**Chilledness, benumbedness. Le f. an fhuachd, *with the benumbing power of cold.*
————each,** *a.* Cold, benumbing, chill. Aimsir f., *benumbing weather.*
†fur, -uir, *s.m.* Thief, robber.
†fur, *s.f.* Preparation.
fur,* see furan.
furachail, -e, *a.* Attentive, carefully observing, looking keenly, observant, vigilant. Gu f., *attentively.*
furachair, -e, *a.* see furachail. F. mu m' cheuma, *watchful about my steps;* gu f., *diligently.*
————eachd,** *s.f.* Alertness.
furachas, -ais, *s.m.* Watching, expectation, vigilance. 2 Care, attention, attentiveness. Faiceall is f., *circumspection and attention.*
furachras, -ais, see furachas.
furadh, see fuireadh.
furail, *v.a.* Offer. 2 Incite, provoke, urge, exhort, persuade. 2 Command.
furail,†† *a.* Welcoming, hospitable.
furail, -alach, *s.f.* Offering. 2 Command. 3 Incitement, exhortation, persuasion. Rinn e

ro-fh. air, *he urged him.*
———eamh, see furail, s.
furailt, see furmailt.
———each, see furail. 2 Courteous, affable, hospitable, welcoming.
———eachd, *s. f.* Kindness. 2 Civility, courteousness, affability. 3 Hospitality.
———eas, see furailteachd.
furain, *s.f.* Plenty, abundance. 2 *gen. sing.* of furan.
———, *pr.pt.* a' furanadh & a' furan, *v.a.* Invite, press hospitably, welcome. 2 Salute.
furan, -ain, *s.m.* Welcome, salutation, expression of kindly recognizance. 2 Hospitality. 3 **Joy. 4 Fondling. 5 Entertainment. Le f. mór, *with much welcome;* is f. a thog mo lann, *hospitality has raised my sword;* is faoin t' fh., *vain is thy fondling.*
———ach, -aiche, *a.* Saluting kindly. 2 Courteous, civil. 3 Joyful at meeting. 4**Hospitable. Tha thu f. truacanta, *thou art courteous and compassionate.*
furanachd,* *s.f.ind.* Complacency.
furanaich, *v.a.* Invite, welcome.
furaradh, see fuirireadh.
furas, -ais, *s. m.* Patience. 2* Leisure. Am bheil f. ort? *have you leisure?* a' cheud f. a bhitheas orm, *the first leisure I get.*
furas, *a.* see furasda.
furasda, *a.* Easy, of easy accomplishment. *1st. comp.* fasa, *2nd. comp.* fasaid, *3rd. comp.* fasad. Tha eòlas f., *knowledge is easy;* cha'n f. géill thoirt o òigh, *it is difficult to obtain a virgin's assent;* cha'n fh. leam t' fhàgail, *I am loath to leave you.*
———chd, *s.f.ind.* Facility, easiness in doing.
furbaidh,‡ see furban.
furbairneach,** *a.* see fuirbearnach.
furban, -ain, *s. m.* Wrath, fervour of rage. 2 Fits of indisposition. 3††Disturbance of mind. 4(AH) The restlessness and uneasiness which sometimes accompany or characterize extreme sickness.
———ach, -aiche, *a.* Raging, provoking to wrath. 2 (AH) Extremely restless and perturbed.
furbhailt, see furmailt.
———each, -eiche, see furmailteach. 2(PM) Attentive.
———eachd, see furmailteachd.
———eas, see furmailteas.
fur-bhuachaill,¶ *s. m.* Great northern diver, see muir-bhuachaill.
fur-bhuachaill,¶ *s.m.* Black-throated diver, see learga.
†**fur-fhogradh**,** -aidh, *s.m.* Warning of removal. 2 Precaution.
furghall, -aill, -ean, *s.m.* Suggestion.
furlachadh,** -aidh, *s.m.* Detestation.
furlachail,** *a.* Detestable.
fùrlaich, *v a.* Hate, detest. [This verb takes the *prep.* ris after it, simple or compounded, as, dh' fh. i riu, *she detested them.*]
furm, -uirm, *pl.* -uirm & -uirmean, *s.m.* Form, stool.
furmach,†† *a.* Abounding in stools.
furmailt, e, -ean, *s.f.* Welcome, reception. 2 Complacency, urbanity. 3**Affability. 4** Hospitality. 5**Ceremony. [-e also used as *nom.*] Le f. is le mùirn, *with courtesy and joy.*
furmailt,(DC) *s.m. prov.* for burmaid or buraban (wormwood.)
———each, -eiche, *a.* Heartily welcome. 2 Courteous, complacent, polite, affable. Gu f., *courteously.*
furmailteachd, *s.f.ind.* Civility, courteously, affability, hospitableness.
†**furnaidhe**, *s.f.* Dwelling, residence.
furnais, see fùirneis.
furralanach, -aiche, *a.* see fuarlanach.
furran,§ see craobh-dharaich.
fursan, -ain, *s.m.* Flame of fire.
fur-shùileach, (AC) *a.* Keen-eyed. 2 (DMC) Observant, watchful.
furt,(AC) see furtachd.
——ach, -aiche, *a.* Ready to assist, aiding, helping, relieving, comforting.
furtach, *s.m.* see furtachd.
———adh, -aidh, *s.m.* Helping, relieving, comforting, relief, aid. A' f—, *pr. pt.* of furtaich.
———ail, -e, *a.* Helping, comforting, apt to help. 2 Anodyne.
———air,** *s.m.* Helper, reliever, comforter.
———d, *s.f.ind.* Relief, ease, help. 2 Consolation, comfort. 3**Deliverance, release. 4** Ease at the crisis of a sickness. F. is fòir, *help and comfort.*
furtaich, *pr.pt.* a' furtachadh, Help, relieve, aid, assist, comfort. 2**Deliver, release. This verb requires the *prep.* air, simple or compound, after it. F. air an duine sin, *deliver that man;* f. oirnne, *deliver us.*
furtaiche, see furtachair.
furtaichear, *fut.pass.* of furtaich.
furtaichidh, *fut.aff. a.* of furtaich.
furtaichte, *a. & past pt.* of furtaich. Comforted, helped, relieved, delivered.
furthain, *s.f.* Satiety, sufficiency.
furthainach,** *a.* Plentiful. Gu f., *plentifully.*
fusa, (*for* fasa) *comp.* of furasda.
fusad, (*for* fasadh) *3rd. comp.* of furasda. Degree of easiness.
fusachd,†† *s.f.* Easiness, facility.
fusadh, see fasa.
fusaid, (*for* fasaid) *2nd. comp.* of furasda.
———, see usaid.
———each, see usaideach.
fusbaireachd, *s.f.ind.* Deep ploughing or trenching.
fùsban,†† -ain, *s.m.* Awkward bungler.
fusgan, -ain, -an, *s.m.* Heather brush.
futadh, -aidh, *s.m.* Blustering.
futail,** *a.* Foppish, airy, showy. Gu f., *foppishly.*
futalachd,** *s.f.ind.* Foppery, airiness, showiness.
fùtar, -air, see fùdar.
futh,* *s.m.* Wen.
futha, see fodha.
futhad, see fothad.
futhar, (CR) *s.m.* Mark or scar of a wound or sore. (pudhar.)
futhar,(CR) *s.m.* Dog-days—*Perthshire.* F. an fhoghair, *the height of autumn; latter half of Aug.—N.Arg.* (DC); f. an earraich, *the height of spring;* f. an t-samhraidh, *the latter half of July—N. Argyll* (DC.)
futhpa, see fopa.

G g

g, gort, *ivy*, the seventh letter of the Gaelic alphabet now in use. When this letter is followed by one or more of the vowels *a, o, u,* it sounds nearly like *g* in *gap, goose,* or rather, it is sounded harder than *g,* and not so hard as *c. G,* at the end of a word, if preceded by one or more of the vowels *a, o, u,* or a liquid, sounds most frequently like *k* in *rook, hook,* as, rug, *bore;* thug, *gave;* (pron. *rook, hook.*) *Gh,* before *a, o* or *u,* has an aspirated power, to which there is no correspondent sound in English, but when followed by *e* or *i*, it sounds like *y* in *ye*, as, gheibh, *will get*. *Gh*, at the end of words or syllables is seldom pronounced at all, as, faigh, *get*; rìoghachd, *a kingdom*. When *g*, is preceded by *i*, or followed by *e* or *i*, it has a mellow sound, like *g* in *girl*, as, gin, *produce*; géire, *sharpness*. In conversation *g* is often elided in agam, agad, againn, agaibh. In *Arran*, it is elided also in Gilleasbuig, Eanruig, thàinig, Domhnas Càsg (*Easter Sunday*), and in *sealg* in *là shealg na cubhaige*; is preserved in Sasgunn, though not in Sasunnach; and in some instances it has become *t* or *d* after *s* at the end of a syllable, as uiste (for uisge, *water*); sothaisdean (for sothaisgean, *primrose*.)

g, (*for* ag) *prep*. At. This prep. when prefixed to infinitives or verbal nouns gives them the force or meaning of the present participle. 'G is used between two vowels, as, tha mi 'g ol, *I am (at) drinking*; cò seo 'g aom air 'luirg? *who is this bending over his staff?* though *ag* might well be written in all such instances in prose. When preceded by a consonant, or followed by a vowel, it is written entire, as, bha 'anam ag éirigh gun fhiamh, *his soul was rising fearlessly*. *Ag* is sometimes used, even though followed by a consonant, as, gathanna lìomhta ag tearnadh, *polished darts descending*. Between two consonants the *g* is often dropped, as Turloch a' caoidh a chloinne, *T. bewailing his children*.

g', *conj*. (*for* gu)

g', *prep*. (*for* gu.)

'g a, (*for* aig a) With whom, with which, to whom, to which. 'G am bheil an cridhe briste, *who has the broken heart*.

'g a, (*for* aig a) At him, at her. 'G a leadairt, *drubbing him*; 'g am bheil cinnte air gach ni, *who has complete certainty about everything*

g' a, (*for* aig a) To his, her or its. G' a cheann, *to his head, to its extremity* (*m*.); g' a ceann, *to her head, to its extremity* (*f*.)

ga,** *conj*. see ged.

†ga, *adv*. see c' a.

ga, *s.m*. see gath.

gab, -aib, *s.m*. Tattling mouth. 2 see gob.

gabach,* -aich, *s.f*. Tattling female.

gabach,* -aiche, *a*. Garrulous, scolding, talkative, querulous. 2 see gobach.

gabachd,** *s.f.ind*. Talkativeness. 2 Incontinence of tongue. 3 Inability to keep a secret.

gabag,†† *s.f*. Chattering woman.

gabagach, -aiche, see gabach.

gàbaidh,** *s.f*. Riddle.

gabair, -ean, *s.m*. Chattering talking fellow, prattler. 2 Chatterer (bird.) 3‡‡Interpreter.

——eachd, *s.f.ind*. Talkativeness, impertinent tattle, loquacity. 2 Gibberish.

gàbairt, see gàbart.

†gabaist, see cabaiste.

gabar, see gobhar.

gàbart, *s.m*. Big unwieldy person. 2 Open boat used for ferrying sheep and cattle. 3 Transport, broad-bottomed sloop, gabart. [‡ gives gàbairt as *nom*.]

gab-èasgaidh, gaib-, *s.m*. One who is too ready to speak. 2 Sharp or snappish person.

gabh, *pr. pt*. a' gabhail, *v.a*. & *n*.

Some idiomatic connections of gabh *grouped under the various meanings*:

1 Take, accept, receive—
G. seo, *take this, accept of this*; ghabh iad am baile, *they took possession of the town*; g. cead, *take leave*; g. mo leithsgeul, *excuse me*; g. naigheachd dheth, *enquire of him for news*; gh. an caladh an long, *the harbour received the ship*; g. radharc, *take a view*; g. cothrom air, *take advantage* or *opportunity of*; g. a' ghaoth do, *disappear into air*; gh. e a' ghaoth dha fhéin, *he vanished into air, disappeared*.

2 Contain, hold—
G. biadh, *fill out, as corn*; cha robh an t-arbhar a' gabhail bìdh, *the corn was not filling out*; gabhaidh seo tuillidh, *this will hold more*; cho mór 's a ghabhas e, *as big as it can manage*.

3 Sing, say, deliver—
G. altachadh, *say grace*; g. ceòl, *sing*; g. òran, *sing a song*; g. oraid, *deliver an oration*; guth dhaoine a' gabhail ciùil, *the voice of men singing*.

4 Emotions—
G. comhairle, *be advised, take counsel*; g. cùram, *be concerned about, meditate about*; g. aithreachas, *repent*; g. fearg, *become angry*; g. iongantas, *be surprised*; g. neònachas, *be surprised*; g. truas de, *pity*.

5 Infection—
Gh. e a' bhreac dheth, *he was infected of the small-pox by him*.

6 Assume, pretend—
G. ort féin, *pretend*; gh. e air féin, *he pretended, he assumed to himself, he presumed*; gabh ort gu 'm fac thu mi, *pretend that you saw me*; a' gabhail orra a bhi 'gluasad ann an riochd na Gàidhlig, *posing as champions of the Gaelic cause*.

7 Burn, kindle, ferment—
An caochan a' gabhail, *the wash fermenting*; gabhaidh an teine, *the fire will kindle*; gh. an t-aingeal, *the fire kindled*.

8 Undertake, endeavour, be concerned with—
G. gnothach ris, *meddle with*; na g. gnothach ris, *do not meddle with him* or *it*; g. iolla ris, g. ealla ris, *look at it, but have nothing else to do with it* (iolla=*a look*, ealla =*letting alone*); g. os làimh, *undertake, engage, take in hand*; g. mu, *endeavour, go about*; gh. e mu'n òrdugh le toirt, *he set himself thoroughly about obeying the order*; gh. iad orra fhéin, *they undertook*.

9 Arrange—
Chuir thu as mo gh. mi, *you have disappointed, distracted me, made me wander from the point, caused me to go astray*; air a' gh. sin biodh, *let it be done on that understanding, let that be the arrangement*.

10 Must, compelled to—
Ghabhainn a bhi 'falbh, *I would require to be going*.

11 Enlist, engage as a servant—
Gh. e 'sna saighdearan, gh. e 'san arm, *or* gh. e an t-airgiod, *he enlisted*; g. agamsa, *engage with me*; g. aig, *engage with (a master) for hire*.

12 Make secure—
Gabh aig, *make snug*; g. aige, *secure it*. 2 *modify a statement*; is math tha e air gabhail aige, *it is well secured* or *seen to*.

13 Entertain, treat—
Fhuair mi gabhail agam gu math 's gu ro mhath, *I was most hospitably entertained*; G. umam, *see to me, take care of me*, g. roimh, *entertain*. 2‡‡ *receive or treat me kindly*; gh. e rium, *he received me kindly*.

14 Acknowledge—
G. ris, *acknowledge him, receive him*; g. ris a' phàisd, *father the child*; cha do gh. e ris a' ghearan ach mall, *he did not pay much*

attention,did not concern himself greatly with the complaint.
15 To worry—
Tha mo chas a' gabhail rium o cheann seachd bliadhna,*my foot has troubled me for seven years.*
16 Conceive, become pregnant—
Gh. i ri cloinn, *she conceived.*
17 Beat, belabour—
G. air, *strike him* ; gh. an t-amadan air féin, *the fool struck himself* ; a' gabhail dhomh, *beating me* ; gh. iad orra, *they struck them;* g. orm, *strike me.*
18 Betake, repair, proceed, go, (motion)—
G. mu 'n cuairt air, *go round* ; g. seachad, *pass by* ; g. suas, *go up* ; g. air t' aghaidh, *pass on, go forward* ; g. an t-aonach, *repair to the hill* ; g. chun a' mhonaidh, *betake yourself to the hill* ; g. chun an doruis ! *be off, leave my presence* ; g. gu fleadh na h-òighe,*repair to the virgin's feast;* g.do cheum, *go thy way* ; g. (an) rathad, *take the road, march off* ; gh. e roimhe, *he went his way* ; g. romhad ! *begone !* g. romham, *lead the way*; g. roimh,*intercept, check.* 2 *go forward* or *in advance* ; g. uam ! *away, begone !* bho'n is e is ni do Chlann Néill na dòirneagan, ghabhadh iad d' an ionnsuidh, *since the property of the MacNeills consists of pebbles, let them take to them* ; mar tha 'n àird an ear 's an iar a' gabhail fad o 'chéil', *as far as the east stretches away from the west* ; is fada bhuaidh sin a ghabh mi, *that is not at all what I mean, wish to convey* (cf. the English idiom " I will go farther and say....") ; g. le, *side with, be satisfied with;* g. leis, *side with him* ; g. leis *that will do* ; g. an ruaig, *take to flight;* g. (an) teicheadh, *take to flight.*
19 Rest—
G. mu thamh, *go to rest;* g. gu clos, *be at peace, be quiet* ; g. fois,*rest thyself.*
Gabh is also an auxiliary verb, ceannard nach g. lùbadh, *a chief who cannot be made to yield* ; cha ghabh sin deanamh, *that cannot be done* ; gabhaidh sin deanamh, *that can be done.*

gabh, *s.m.* Spear, hook, gaff—*Dàin I. Ghobha.*
gabha-bheil, see gabhadh-bheil.
gàbhach,** -aich, *s.m.* see gàbhadh.
gàbhach, -aiche, *a.* see gàbhaidh.
gabhachd.(AC) *s.f.* Greediness.
†gabhadach, -aich, *a.* Cunning, artful.
gabhadair,** *s.m.* Accepter.
gabhadan, -ain, -an, *s.m.* Receptacle. 2 Storehouse. 3‡‡Accipient.
gàbhadh, -aidh, -aidhean, *s.m.* Peril, danger, any kind of danger or emergency, hazardous situation, or hazard of such a nature that one's escape is a miracle. 2**Jeopardy. 3** Want. 4**Surprise, wonder. Ri àm gàbhaidh, *in time of need* ; g. cuain, *perils by sea* ; an g. 's gach uair, *in jeopardy every hour.*
gabhadh, *3rd. sing. & pl. imp.* of gabh. G. e, *let him take* ; g. iad, *let them take.*
gàbhadh-bheil,* *s.m.* Druidical ordeal by fire. ?
gabha-dubh, *s.m.* Balm-cricket. 2 (DC) Storm-riders,the undulations seen in rain accompanied by high wind.
gabhagan,¶ -ain, -an, *s.m. & f.* Rock-pipit—*anthus petrosus.* 2 Titling, tit, tit-lark. (ill.347.)
gabhaibh, *2nd. pl. imp.* of gabh. Take ye.
gàbhaidh, -e, *a.* Perilous,dangerous. 2 Strange, wonderful, odd. 3 Terrible, fearful. 4 Hard, severe. 5 Austere,stern,tyrannical,dreadful. 6††Tempestuous, boisterous, inclement. 7** Surprising. 8**Frugal. Is g. leam thu, *I am surprised at you;* duine g., *an austere* or *tyrannical fellow* ; uair g., *tempestuous weather* ; àmannan g., *perilous times* ; bu gh. 'imeachd, *dreadful was his conduct* ; is g. an ni e, *it is a wonderful thing.*

347. Gabhagan.

gàbhaidh, *gen.sing.* of gàbhadh.
gabhaidh, *fut. aff. a.* of gabh.
gàbhaidheachd,* *s. f.* Austerity, tyrannical manner, tyranny. 2 Inclemency, boisterousness. ‡3 Dreadfulness, terribleness. 4‡‡Perilousness.
gabhail, -alach, -alaichean, *s.f. &'m.* Portion of work performed by cattle at one yoking. 2 Lease, feu, tenure. 3 Farm. 4 Course, direction, bearing of a ship. 5 Tack, as a ship. 6 Spoil, booty. 7 Conquest. 8**Barm. 9**Seizure, capture, taking. 12**Catching. 11** Accepting. 12**Receiving. 13**Kindling. 14 ‡‡ Colonization. 15 Stirrup-strap. Am bochd a' gabhail seachad, *the poor passing by;* gun gh. ri saorsa, *without accepting salvation;* a' g. na pìoba, *smoking the pipe* ; air a' gh. seo, *on this tack* ; mol a' gh., *keep a sharp lookout* ; a chumas a g. gun dad luasgain, *to preserve her course without deviation* ; chuir thu as mo gh. mi, *you have disappointed me* ; na cuir as a gh. e, *do not disappoint him* ; a' g. d' a chéile, *belabouring each other* ; cuir an g., *kindle, set on fire* ; an robh g. mhath orra ? *were they taking well ?*—said of fish taking bait. A' g—, *pr.pt.* of gabh.
gabhail, *a.* Receptive.—*Dàin I. Ghobha.*
gàbhail, *a.* Austere, tyrannical—*Dàin I.Ghobha.* 2(PM) Greedy—*Uist.*
gabhail-cine, *s.f.* Gavelkind, a tenure now only recognized in Kent by which the owner at fifteen can sell the estate or devise it by will. The estate cannot escheat, and on an intestacy the lands descend from the father to all the sons in equal portions.
gabhail-fearainn, *s.f.* Farm. 2 Lease.
gabhail-fuachd,(DMC) *s.f.* Catching cold.
g(h)abhainn, *1st. sing. past subj.* of gabh. I would take.
gabhainn, see gamhainn. 2 see gobhainn.
gabhal, -aibhle, -aibhlean, *s.m.* see gobhal.
——**ach**, -aiche, see gabhaltach.
——**tach**, -aich, *s. m.* Lessee (in *Scotland*, tacksman,) renter, farmer.
——**tach**, -aiche, *a.* Capacious. 2 Infectious. 3 Contagious. 4**Ready to grasp or catch. Galar gabhaltach, *a contagious disease.*
——**tachd**, *s.f.ind.* Capacity, largeness. 2 Contagion. 3 Infection. 4 Capriciousness. 5 Readiness to grasp or catch. 6‡‡Inflectiveness.
gabhaltaiche, *comp.* of gabhaltach. More or most capacious or infectious.
————,* *s.m.* Renter. 2 Farmer.
gabhaltair,** *s.m.* Accepter.
gabhaltas, -ais, *s.m.* Land rented from a land-

lord. 2 Land in tack. 3 Division of land among a tribe. 4 Conquest, invasion. 5 Land obtained by conquest. 6 Tenement.
gabham, *1st. sing. pr. imp.* of gabh. Let me take.
gabhann, -ainn, *s.m.* Flattery, adulation, sycophancy. 2 Gall. 3**Prating, tattling, gossip. 4**Gaol, prison. 5 Henbane, see gafann. Làn de gh., *full of smooth flattery;* is mil o 'n bheartach an g., *sweet is the prating of the rich.*
————ach, -aiche, *a.* Flattering. 2**Tattling, cajoling, gossiping. 3**Of, or pertaining to flattery. 4**Like a prisoner. 5** Of, or belonging to a prison. Mar an ceudna g., *also given to tattling.*
————aiche, *comp.* of gabhannach.
gàbhanta, *a.* Gruesome. see gàbhaidh.
gabhar, *fut. pass.* of gabh. Shall or will be taken. *Gabhar* is often significant of motion, and in this sense it is used impersonally, with an active present and affirmative meaning, as g. suas leam, *westwards* or *upwards I proceeded;* g. suas leinn gu mullach an t-sléibhe, *we took to the top of the mountain.*
gabhar, -air, *s.m.* Light, illumination. 2 Conflict. 3**Comfort. 4** *s.f.* Goal.
gabhar, gaibhre, -air, *s. f.* Goat. 2 (AF) Hawk. 3 (AF) Any old bird. 4(AF) Mackerel. 5 (AF) Shad (fish.)
————ach, -aiche, *a.* Of, or belonging to a goat. 2 Skipping.
————ag,(AF) *s.f.* Gurnard.

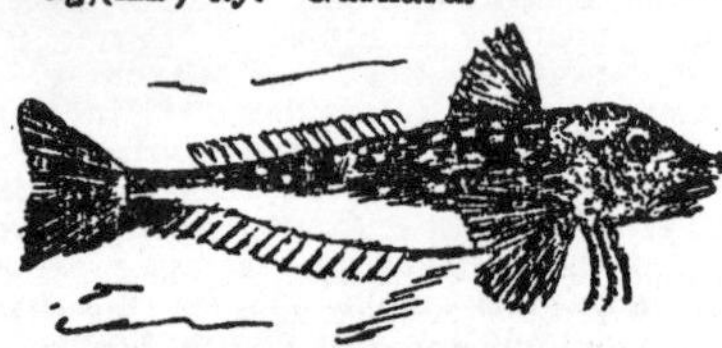

348. Gabharag.

gabhar-alluidh, *s.f.* Chamois.
gabhar-athair, *s.m.* Snipe,—*scolopa gallinago.*
gabhar-bhacach,(AF) *s.f.* Name given in some parts to the last handful of corn to be cut.
gabhar-bhreac, -ic, *s.f.* Buck-snail.
gabhar-cheann,(AF) *s.f.* Leader of goats.
gabhar-chrò, -oithean, see gabhar-lann.
gabhar-fhiadh, (AF) *s.f.* see g.-fhiadhain. 2 *of old,* Horse.
————————ain,(AF) *s.f.* Wild *or* rock goat.
gabhar-fhiadhaich, *s.f.* Antelope.
gabhar-lann, -lainn, *s.f.* Goat-pen.
gabhar-mhór, *s.f.* Crayfish, crawfish. 2 Lobster.
gabhar-oidhche, Snipe, *s.f.* see gabhar-athair. 2 Nightjar.
gabhd, -an, *s.m.ind.* Crafty trick, craft. 2 Lie, fallacy.
———ach, -aiche, *a.* Cunning, tricky. 2 Giddy, coquettish. 3**Plausible. 4**Greedy. 5‡‡ Lying. 6(WC) Trifling.
———ach,* -aich, *s.f.* Coquette. 2 Shrew.
———achd,** *s. f.* Plausibleness, slyness, deceitfulness. 2 Low cunning. 3 Greediness. 4††Cheat.
———adh, -aidh, *s.m.* Cunning. 2 Low trick. Ri g., *engaged in trickery.*
———aiche, *comp.* of gabhdach. More or most deceitful, plausible or cunning. Am fear a's g. de 'n triùir, *the most deceitful of the three.*
gabhdaichead, *s.* Slyness, cunning. 2 Degree of cunning. A' dol an g., *increasing in cunning.*
gabhdair, -ean, *s.m.* Cunning, plausible, tricky fellow, cheat.
gabhdaire,(WC) *s.m.* Trifler, fussy person who manages to accomplish nothing—*W. of Ross.*
gabhdaireachd, *s.f.* Low cunning, habit of lying or using low artifices, plausibleness.
†gabhla, *s.f.* Spear, javelin, lance. 2 Cow with calf.
gabhlach, -aiche, *a.* see gobhlach.
†————adh, *s.m.* Propagation. 2 Genealogy. A' g—, *pr.pt.* of gabhlaich.
————an, -ain, see gobhlachan.
gabhladh, see gobhal.
†gabhlaich, *v.a.* Sprout, bear. 2 Propagate.
gabhlaiche,** *comp.* of gobhlach.
—————ad, see gobhlaichead.
gabhlag, -aig, -an, see gobhlag.
gabhlan, -ain, -an, *s. m.* Wandering man devoid of care. 3 Loquacious, cunning, tricky body. 4**Little branch. 4 see gobhlan. *prov.*
gabhlanach, -aiche, *a.* Wandering, restless. 2 Tricky. 3 Loquacious. 4 see gobhlanach. *prov.*
——————d,†† *s.f.* Idle roving.
gabhlanaich,†† -nach, see gabhlanachd.
gabhlas,** -ais, see gamhlas.
————ach, *a.* see gamhlasach.
gamhna, *gen. sing.* of gabhainn.
gabhnach, -aich, see gamhnach.
gabhrach, *a.* Abounding in goats.
—————,** -aich, *s.m.* Flock of goats.
gabhrag, -aig, -an, *s.f.* (AF) Flock of goats. 2 Sheaf of corn bound slightly near the top, and left standing in the field to dry.
————an, *n. pl.* of gabhrag.
———— -bheag, *s. f.* Jack snipe—*gullima scolopax.*
gabhran, -ain, *s.m.* Little goat.
gabht,* *s.m.* Links—*Cowal.*
———a, *past pt.* of gabh. Taken. 2 Conceived. 3 Captured. 4 Engaged. Tha thu g. agam-sa, *you are engaged with me.*
———ach,** *a.* Ready to take or grasp. 2 Of a grasping or greedy disposition. Gu g. gionach, *grasping and greedy.*
———tach,** -aich, *s.m.* Person in want.
gabhte, see gabhta.
gabhuidh, see gabhaidh.
gabhuinn, gabhna, see gamhuinn.
gàbhunn, -uinn, *s.m.* Captation, claw.
gabhunn,(CR) *s.m.* see gabhann.
————ach.(CR) *a.* see gabhannach.
gabla,** *s.m.* Gaelic spelling of *cable.*
gàc, *v.n.* Cackle, as a hen. (gloc.)
gàcail, *s.f.* Cackling (glocail.)
gach, *pron.in'ef.* Each, every, all. Gach coille, gach doire 's gach eas, *every wood, every grove and every cataract.* [The prepositions ann, á, le, ri and gu, take *s* before *gach.* Gach cannot be aspirated.]
gachar,§ *s.m.* Wake-robin, lords-and-ladies, see cluas-chaoin.
gachunnach, *a.* Harsh. 2 Applied in *Eigg* to a drink strong enough to make one gasp.
gad, *conj.* see ged.
gad, *gen.* gaid & goid, *pl.* gaid, goid & gadan, *s.m.* Withe, twisted twig. 2 Switch. 3 (AH) Number of fish, as carried home on a string or withe. Gad mór, equivalent to a large basket. 4 Bend on anything. Tha gad air bàrr mo shlàite, *there is a bend on the point of my rod,* as when a fish is hooked and being drawn out of the water; cha'n 'eil agam ach an g. air an robh an t-iasg, *I have only the bend made by the fish (on which the fish was)*—referring to a fish hooked and lost in landing—said when anything is lost suddenly (D My.) also used to indicate the disappointment of a person who has been over-reached or deceived. Seachd goid, *seven withes;* cha téid g. air gealladh, *a promise cannot be hand-cuffed;* g.

air sporan (*lit.* withe on purse) *an ironical name for a miser ;* is mithich a bhi 'bogadh nan gad, *it is time to be steeping the withes*—a native Gaelic saying, meaning " it is time to be going," belongs to the time when withes of birch or osier were used for halters and all the fastenings of horse-harness. These withes would become stiff an brittle if laid by for some time, and would therefore be steeped for a while before taking to horse—NGP.

gad, *v.a.* Lop. 2 Pull. 3 Dig.

gàd, -a, -aichean, *s.m.* Iron bar. 2 Large, thick piece of anything. 3*Stalk. 4 Inherent propensity, in a bad sense. G. siabuinn, *a bar of soap* ; g. siùcair duibh, *a stalk of liquorice;* g. tarruich, *a girth ;* g. uchd, *a breast-thong;* tha droch g. ann, *he has a bad turn of mind ;* rathad nan g., *the railroad.*

g ad (*for* ag do) At thy. 'G ad fhiosrachadh, *inquiring for thee.*

gadachd, see gaduigheachd.

gadag, -aig, -an, *s.f.* Originally a rope of twigs. 2 Straw rope or halter. G. 's a dà cheann sgaoilte, *a straw-rope with both ends loose*—applied to a slovenly woman.

gàdag, -aig, -an, *s.f.* Switch—*Dàin I. Ghobha.*

gadaiche, -an, *s.m.* Thief, robber. Mar gh., *like a thief.*

gadaigheachd, *s.f.* Theft, robbery. 2 villiany. Air son a gh., *on account of his robbery.*

gadair, *v.a.* Hopple, tie fore-feet of a horse, to prevent its straying. 2‡‡ Tie horses head to tail. *prov.*

gadan, -ain, -an, *s.m. dim.* of gad. Little withe or twig. 2 *n.pl.* of gad.

†gadan,** -ain, *s.m.* Voice. 2 Continued noise.

†——ach, -aiche, *a.* Noisy, causing a continued noise.

gadanach,†† *a.* Abounding in withes.

gàd-droma,(MMcD) *s.m.* Ridge-pole of a roof.

gàdh, -àidh, -àidhean, see gàthadh. †2 see guidh.

gadhar,-air, *s.m.* Lurcher dog. 2 Cross-bred dog, being half greyhound and half foxhound. 3 *anciently* Greyhound. 4 Mastiff. †5 see gaoir. G. is fiadhchon nan càrn, *the hounds and wolves of the rocks.*

——ach, -aiche, *a.* Of, or belonging to lurchers or greyhounds. 2 see gaotharach.

——an, see gadhran.

gadhar bior-shuileach,(AF) *s.m.* Gazehound.

gadhran, (AF) *s.pl.* Goats.

gadhran,(AF) *s.m.* Lapdog, spaniel.

gadluinne, -an, *s.m.* Slender, feeble fellow. 2 Salmon after spawning.

gadmunn, -uinn, *s.m.* Hair insect, nit. 2(DMC) Atom.

——ach, -aiche, *a.* Full of nits.

gadradh, -aidh, *s.m.* Tying or fettering of horses.

gàdraisg, -e, -ean, *s.f.* Tumult, confusion. 2 Drunken riots.

——each, -eiche, *a.* Tumultuous, confused.

gadruich,(AC) *pl.* of gadaiche.

gàdruisg, see gàdraisg.

gaduiche, -ean, see gadaiche.

gàes, see gàis.

†gaet, *s.* Wound. see gaoid.

†gaf, -a, *s.m.* Hook, any crooked instrument.

†gafal, -ail, *s.m.* Nerve.

gafann, -ainn, *s.m.* Henbane,—*hyoscyamus niger.* (ill. 349.)

gàg, -àig, -an, *s.f.* Cleft, chink. 2 Chap or fissure on the skin, caused by heat. 3 Painful hack on the toes or sole of the foot. 4**Notch. 5**Knot in timber. Cha'n 'eil aige ach ceum air ghàig; *he takes an unwilling step.*

gàg, *pr. pt.* a' gàgadh, *v. n.* Split or go into chinks or flaws. 2 Notch.

349. Gafann.

gag,** -aig, *s.m.* Lisp, impediment in speech. Gag-beòil, *a lisp.*

gag,(DC) *a.* Tender-footed, footsore, walking gingerly.

gàgach, -aiche, *a.* Abounding in clefts or chinks. 2 Having rents in the skin. 3 Chapped. 4** Leaky.

gagach, -aiche, *a.* Stuttering. stammering in speech. 2(DMC) Slow, hesitating.

——,* -aich, *s.f.* Stuttering female.

gagachd,* *s.f.ind.* see gagaiche.

gàgadh, -aidh, *s. m.* Growing into chinks, fissures or rifts. 2**Splitting. 3**Leaking. 4 ††see gagaiche. A' g—, *pr. pt.* of gàg.

gagaiche, *s.f.ind.* Stammering, defect in speech. 2**One who lisps or stammers in his speech, or who cannot pronounce certain letters.

——, *comp.* of gagach. More or most subject to stuttering or stammering.

gagaid, *s.f.* Agate.

gàgaidh, *fut. aff. a.* of gàg.

gagail, *s.* Haw.

gagail,** *a.* Stammering, lisping. 2 Cackling. G. nan eearc, *cackling of hens.*

gagaire, -an, *s. m.* Stammerer, stutterer. 2(DMC) Idler, slow-going person.

——achd, *s.f.ind.* Stammering. 2 (DMC) Hesitating.

gagalan, (AF) *s.m.* Number of small articles stringed or otherwise hanging together as beads on a cord.

gàgan,(CR) *s. m.* Cackling—*Arran.* [In this sense in *Gairloch* 1st. *a* is long and nasalised —WC.] 2 Noisy speech. 3 Knot in timber.

gagan, -ain, -an, *s.m.* Cluster or bunch, as of heath. 2 see gafann. Gaganan, *clusters.*

gaganach, -aiche, *a.* Hanging in clusters or bunches, in ringlets, as hair.

gaganach,** *a.* Knotted, as timber. 2 Noisy, cackling. 3 Garrulous. A fhraoich gh. ! *thou knotted heath !*

——,** -aich, *s. m.* Noisy speech. 2 Garrulity.

gaibheach,** -ich, *s.m.* Needy person. 2 Craver. 3 Complainant.

†gaibhinn, -e, -ean, *s.f.* Little study, closet.

gaibhne, *gen. sing. & n. pl.* of gabhainn, see gobhainn.

——achd, see goibhneachd.

——an, see goibhnean.

gaibhre, *gen.sing. & n.pl.* of gabhar.

gaibhteach, -eiche, *s.m.* Person in want. 2 Craver. 3 Complainant.

gaibhtheach, -eiche, *a.* Stormy. 2 High, lofty.

gaibhthealach, -aiche, *a.* Exposed to want. 2 Inconvenient. 3 Perplexing. 4 Wild, fierce.
gàid, *n.pl.* of gàd.
gaid, *gen.sing. & n.pl.* of gad.
gaid, *v.* see goid.
——ean, -ein, *s.m.* (*dim.* of gad) Small band of twigs. 2 Small withe.
gàidsear, *s.m.* Gaelic spelling of *gauger.*
——searachd, *s.f.* Gauging, business of an exciseman.
gaig,** *s.m.* Fop, proud coxcomb.
gaige, *s.f.* Stammering, stuttering, lisping.
gaighear,(AF) *s.f.* Bitch.
gail, *v.& s.* see goil.
†gail, -e, *s.f.* Slaughter, bloodshed. 2 Bravery. 4 Smoke, fume, vapour.
gailbheach, -eiche, *a.* Stormy. 2 Wrathful, fierce, enraged. 3 Extraordinary, prodigious as to size or power. 4** Boisterous at sea. 5* Enormous, as price. 6* Austere, as a person. 7* Terrible. Ur làimh ri lic ghailbhich, *your hands about a ponderous stone* ; là g., *a stormy day.*
————d,‡‡ *s.f.ind.* Boisterousness.
gail-bheinn, -e, -bheanntan, *s.f.* Great or rocky hill. 2 Huge billow. 3 see gaillionn.
gailbhiche, *comp.* of gailbheach.
————ad,** -id, *s.m.* Storminess, degree of storminess. Tha 'n là 'dol an g., *the day is growing more and more stormy.*
gailbhinn, see gaillionn.
gailc,(CR) *s.* Excitement, agitation, flurry—*W. of Ross.* 2 Sad predicament. Chaidh e 'na gh., *he went into a flurry, became agitated or flurried.*
†gailchinn,** *s.f.* Fine for manslaughter.
gaile, -an, see goile.
gaileachd, see goileachd.
gaileadh,** -idh, *s.m.* Evaporation.
gaileag,(AF) *s.f.* Badger, 2 Cockle (fish.)
gailean, -ein, see goilean.
gaileiridh, Gaelic spelling of *gallery.*
†gailia, *s.* Headpiece.
†gailin, -e, -ean, *s.f.* Parasite.
†gailineach, -eiche, *a.* Flattering.
gaill, *s.f.* see goill.
gaill-chearc, -cuirc, -chearcan, *s. f.* Duck.
†gaille, -an, *s.f.* Rock.
———ach,†† *a.* Large-cheeked.
———ach, -ich, -ichean, *s.m.* Gum. 2 Jaw—*Dàin I. Ghobha.* 3 Disease of the gums to which cattle are subject. 4 The joining of the outer and inner bark of trees. 5 Seam between welt and sole of a shoe. 6††Seam of shoe-uppers.
gàilleach, *s.* Barbel. 2‡ see gailleach. 3 (DMy) Gill of a fish—*Lewis.*
gailleag, -ig, -an, *s.f.* Cuff, blow on the cheek. 2 (Fionn) Caper—*Mull.* A' gearradh ghailleag, *cutting capers, romping.* 3 (DMC) (gearradh-ghailleig) Cracking of middle finger and thumb, usually done by children in a class to show that they know the answer to a question.
gailleann, see gaillionn.
gailleart,* *s.f.* Masculine woman.
gaill-eun, -eòin, *s.m.* Strange or foreign bird.
†gailliann,** *s.m.* Dart, arrow.
gail-iasg, -éisg, -iasgan, *s.m.* Pike.
gaillionn, -inn, *s.f.* Storm, tempest. 2 Impetuous blast. 3(AH) Snow-storm, snowy weather, " white ground." G. nan sliabh, *the mountain-storm* ; mór-ghaillionn nan stoirm, *the mighty force of storms* ; gur gil' thu na 'gh., *whiter art thou than the snow-blast—Duanaire, 81.*
————ach, -aiche, *a.* Wintry. 2 Stormy, tempestuous.
gailllseach, -ich, -ichean, *s.m.* Earwig. 2 Mouth overcharged. 3 Large mouthful of flesh.
gaillseag, -eig, -an, *s.f.* Earwig.
————ach, *a.* Full of earwigs, like an earwig.
gaill-shion, -shìne, *s.m.* see gaillionn.
————ach, see gaillionnach.
†gaimhean,** -ein, *s.m.* Skin, hide.
gain,*** *s.f.* Sand. 2 Clapping of hands, applause.
†gainbheach, see gainmheach.
†gain-cheap,*-chip, *s.f.* Pair of stocks, pillory.
†gaincoir, *s.m.* Archer.
gaine, *s.f.* see gainne. 2 see gàinne. 3 Fin. G. éisg, *the fin of a fish.*
gaineach, see gaineamh.
————, *a.* Finny.
gaineachaidh, *a.* see gaineamhach.
gaineamh, -eimh, *s.f.* Sand. 2 Gravel. 3 The sea-shore. 4 Sandy beach. Garbh gh., *gravel.*
————ach, -aiche, *a.* Of, or relating to, sand, gravel or sandy beaches. 2 Calcareous.
————an,* *s.m.* Sandy bottom (of the sea.)
———— -art,** *s.m.* Sandstone.
———— -chlach, -chloiche, *s.f.* Sand-stone.
———— -chlachach, -aiche, *a.* Of, or belonging to, sand-stones.
gaineamhuinneach, see gainmheineach.
gainear, see gainnear.
†gaing,** *s.f.* Jet. 2 Agate.
gainmheach, see gaineamh.
————, *a.* Barren.
gainmhein, -e, -ean, *s. f.* Sandy beach. 2 Grain of sand. 3 (DMC) Particle, smallest portion. Cha'n fhaigh thu g. dheth, *you won't get a bit of it.*
————each, -eiche, *a.* Sandy.
gainmhidh, see gainmheach, *a.*
†gainn, -e, -ean, *s.f.* Nook.
gainne, *s. f. ind.* Want, scarcity, fewness. 2 Want, hunger. 3 Parsimony, mean saving. 4 Famine.
———, *comp.* of gann.
gàinne, -an, *s.f.* Dart, arrow. 2 Shaft. 3 Reed. 4††Arrow-head. 5**see gaine 2.
gàinneach, *a.* Like a reed, arrow or shaft. 2 Abounding in reeds. 3 Shafted.
————,** *s.m.* Place where reeds grow.
gainneanach,†† -aich, *s.m.* see gainnineach.
gainnead, -id, *s.m.* Scarcity, scarceness, degree of scarceness.
gàinnear,** -eir, *s.m.* Archer. 2 Spearman.
gainneasag, see gainnisg.
gainnineach, -ich, *s.m.* Scrub, miser.
gainniseach,(DMC) *a.* Poor, half-starved, living in poverty.
gainnisg,§ *s.f.* Common sedge—*carex vulgaris.* 2(AC) Small divinity, dwelling among reeds and marshes on the borders of lakes and rivers, who moans and wails before storms for the deaths that are to follow.
————eag, *dim.* of gainnisg.
gainntear, -ir, *s.m.* see gainne.
gainntir, -eir, ean *s.f.* Prison, place of confinement, gaol. 2 (DMC) Corner, narrow place, uncomfortable place for cattle. Sloc na gainntire, *the prison dungeon.*
————each, -eiche. *a.* Like a prison, of, or belonging to, a prison. 2 Wanting, destitute.
————eachd,‡‡ *s.f.* Imprisonment.
————eachadh, -aidh, *s. m.* Incarcerating, incarceration. A' g—, *pr.pt.* of gainntirich.
————ich, *pr. pt.* a' gainntireachadh, *v.a.* Imprison.
————iche, -an, *s.m.* Prisoner. 2 Gaoler.
gàinrich, *v.a.* Defile—*Dàin I. Ghobha.*
gair, see gar.
gàir, see gaireach.

gair, *pr.pt.* a' gairsinn, *v.n.* see goir.
gàir, *pr. pt.* a' gàireachdaich, a' gàirsinn & a' gàireachdainn, *v.n.* Laugh. 2 Shout, cry. 3 Make a noise. 4 Resound. Gàiridh am fitheach air do ghruaidh, *the raven shall croak on thy cheek* ; g. bàite, *the roar of drowning people* ; g. na fairge, *the noise of the sea.*
gàir, -ean, *s.m.* Outcry, shout. 2 Din, murmur or noise of many voices, whether of men or beasts.
gàir, *s.f.* see gàire.
gairbh, -e, *s.f.* Greedy stomach. 2 Paunch or intestines of a deer.
———e, *s. f. ind.* Roughness, grossness, rudeness, coarseness, harshness. 2 Fierceness.
———e, *comp.* of garbh. More or most gross.
———ead, -eid *s.m.* Roughness. 2 Degree of roughness, coarseness, harshness or grossness. 3** Thickness. A' dol an g., *growing thicker and thicker.*
———ead, *comp.* of garbh. Is g. e sin, *it is the thicker for that.*
gairbhdheisinn (CR) *s. f.* Disgust, repulsion, such as would be excited by the sight of filthy food, a mangled body, &c. Chuir e g. orm, *he horrified me*—*W. of Ross.* see gairisinn 1.
†gairbheadach,‡‡ -aich, *s.m.* Coarse garment.
gairbheal, *s. m.* Quarry. 2**Free-stone. 3 Coarse sand, gravel.
————ach, -aich, *s.m.* Stony or rocky ground.
————ach, -aiche, *a.* Stony, gravelly, rocky.
————ta,** *a.* Gravelly.
gairbhean,(CR) *s.m.* Complaining, ailing—*Arran.* 2(DMC) Storm, 3(DMC) Roughness. 4(WC) Gills of fish.
———— -creagach, -aiche, *s.m.* Bruise-wort, —*saponaria.*
gairbheil, *s.m.* see gaireal.
————,* *a.* Rough-tempered.
†gairbheoil, -e, *a.* Large-limbed. 2 Of large body or size.
gairbhtheann, -inn, *s.m.* Species of wild grass.
—————ach, -aiche, *a.* Abounding in wild grass.
gairbh-shian, -shein, *s.m.* see garbh-shìon.
gairceil, *a.* Bulky.
gàircean, see gàirghin.
gàir-chatha,** see gaoir-chatha.
gàir-chreag,** *s.m.* Echo. (mac-talla.)
gàir-chuain, *s.f.* Noise of the sea.
gàird,** *s.f.* Arm. 2 Hand.
†gàirde,** *s.f.* see gàirdeachas.
gàirdeach, -eiche, *a.* Festive, joyous, glad.
————adh, -aidh, *s.m.* Rejoicing, act of rejoicing, congratulating, making merry. A' g—, *pr.pt.* of gàirdich.
————ail,* *a.* Congratulatory, joyous, joyful, glad.
————as, -ais, *s.m.* Joy, gladness, rejoicing, pleasure, gratification, congratulation. Guth gàirdeachais, *a voice of joy* ; a' deanamh gàirdeachais, *or* ri gàirdeachas, *rejoicing.*
gàirdean, -ein, *pl.* -an & -deana, *s. m.* Arm. 2 Hand. 3 *in pl.* Part of a spinning-wheel.
————ach, -aiche, *a.* Having long or powerful arms, large-armed, brawny.
gàirdeas, see gàirdeachas.
gàirdein, *gen.sing.* of gàirdean.
————each, -iche, *a.* see gàirdeanach.
gàirdich, *pr. pt.* a' gàirdeachadh, *v.n.* Rejoice, be glad. 2 **Congratulate.
gairdin, *s.m.* Gaelic spelling of *garden.*
gaire, *s. f.* Nearness. An g. dhuit, *near* or *nigh thee.*
gàire, *s.f.ind.* Laugh, laughter, smile. Dean g., *laugh* ; g. fanoid, *a scornful laugh* ; fiamh g., *or* snodha g., *soft, more or less restrained laughter* ; glag g., *or* rochd g., *guffaw, rough, raucous laughter* ; g. mu aobhar a' ghuil, *laughing at the cause of weeping* ; g. ri do mhi-chialadh, *laughing at your shame* ; cha'n ann do 'n ghuin a' gh., *smiles do not suit with pain.*
†gaire,** *s.f.* Reparation, amendment. 2 Good luck. 3 Auspices.
gàireach, -eiche, *a.* Laughing, merry. 2 Noisy, sounding, murmuring, resonant, roaring, as the sea.
————ail, *a.* see gàireachdail.
————daich, *s.f.* Laughter, act of laughing. A' g—, *pr. pt.* of gàir. Ciod a' gh. a th' ort? *what are you laughing at ?*
————dail, *a.* Laughable, risible.
gàireachdainn, see gàireachdaich.
gàireachdair,‡‡ -ean, *s.m.* Laugher.
gàireachraich, *Poolewe* for gàireachdaich.
†gaireadh,** -idh, *s.m.* Vault. (garadh)
gaireal, -eil, *s.m.* Freestone. 2 Gravel. 3 Hard sand.
————ach, -aiche, *a.* Gravelly, abounding in gravel or freestone, stony.
————ach, -aich, *s.m.* Stony ground.
gàiream,** *1st. sing. imp.* of gàir, Let me laugh. 2 *not for* gàiridh mi, *fut. aff. a.* of gàir, as given by **—that should be *gàirim.*
gaireas, -eis, see goireas.
————ach,* see goireasach.
gàir-éibhinn,‡‡ *s.m.* Shout of joy.
gàire-fanoid,** *s.m.* Scornful laugh.
gaireil, -e, *a.* Snug. 2 Commodious, suitable, convenient. Gu f., *snugly.*
gairetheann,* -ainn, *s.m.* Garbage.
gair-fhitheach, -fhithiche, *s.m.* Raven. 2 Vulture.
gairg, see garg.
gairg,** *s.f.* Cormorant. 2 Diver.
gairge, *comp.* of garg. More or most fierce or tart.
———, *s. f. ind.* Fierceness. 2 Bitterness of taste or flavour. 3 Sourness, sharpness. 4** Harshness, roughness, rudeness. 5**Satiricalness.
———achd, *s.f.* see gairge.
———ad, -eid, *s.m.* Degree of fierceness, bitterness or sourness. A' dol an g., *growing more and more sour.*
gairgean, -ein, *s.m.* Broad-leaved wild garlic, ramsoms—*allium ursinum.* (ill. 350) 2(DMC) Angry-looking or irritable person.
gairgean, *s.m.* Dung, ordure. 2 Stale urine.
————ach, -aiche, *a.* Abounding in garlic.
———— -creagach,§ *s.m.* Samphire—*crithmum maritimum.* (ill. 351.)
———— -gàraidh,§ *s.m.* Garden garlic.
———— -Muire,§ -ein-, *s.m.* Crow garlic, see garlag Muire.
gairgeann,** -inn, *s.m.* Diver. 2 Cormorant.
————ach, *a.* Like a cormorant, abounding in cormorants. 2 Greedy.
gàir-gheal, *a.* Foam-white.
†gairgheala, *s.m.* Outcry.
†gairghean, -ein, *s.f.* Niece. see gair-inghean.
gairghin,§ *s.* Crowfoot.
gartghlan,(*pron.* gartlan)CR *v.a.* Weed—*Arran.*
gairginn,** *s.f.* see gairgean. 2 Pilgrim's dress.
gàir-ghuil, *s.f.* Lamentable weeping.
gairgne, *s.f.* see gairge.
†gairgniomhach, -aiche, *a.* Bigoted.
gairgre,** *s.f.* Pilgrim's dress.
gàirich, -e, *s.f.* Shouting for joy. 2**Continued wailing. 3**Murmur. 4**Raging, roaring, as of the sea. G. a' chuain, *the raging of the sea;* g. siunnsair, *the skirling of a chanter.*
————,** *a.* Shouting. 2 Loud. 3 Noisy. 4

350. Gairgean.

351. Gairgean-creagach.

Roaring. 5 Raging. Sruth g. na h-oidhche, *the roaring torrent of night.*

gàirichdich, see gàireachdaich.

gairid, giorra, *a.* see goirid.

gairidean,** *s.m.* Periwinkle.

gair-inghean,** *s.f.* Niece.

gairios, -is, -an, see goireas

——-ach, -aiche *a.* see goireasach.

gairiseag,** -eig, -an, *s.f.* Wanton, prostitute.

gairisinn, *s. m.* Horror, detestation, disgust. 2 Lewdness. 3 Noisiness. Tha thu 'cur g. orm, *you make me shudder.* [** gives *s.f.*]

gairisneach, -aiche, *a.* Nasty, shocking, abominable. 2 Lewd, debauched. 3 Detestable, Gu g., *bawdily.*

————d,** *s.f.* Lewdness, bawdiness, debauchery, indecency.

gairisnich,** *v.a. & n.* Abhor, detest. 2 Shudder with fear or horror.

gairistinn, *s.m.* see gairisinn.

gairleach-callaid, §*s.m.* Garlic mustard, sauce alone, see garbhraitheach.

gairleag,* -eig, *s.f.* Garlic.

————-Mhuire, see garlag-Muire.

gairlear,(CR) *Aberfeldy* for gàirneilear.

gairm *pr.pt.* a' gairm, *v.a.* Call. 2 Invite. 3 Crow as a cock. 4* Proclaim banns in a church. 5**Bawl, shout. 6**Qualify. 7** Name. 8 Call to beasts, hens, &c. G. air, *call him;* g. gaisgich o bhad 's o choille, *call warriors from thicket and wood.*

gairm, -e, *pl.* -ean & -annan, *s.f.* Call, calling. 2 Act of calling. 3 Title, name. 4 Proclamation of banns. 5**Noise. 6**Shouting. 7 Qualification. A' g—, *pr. pt.* of gairm. G.-phòsaidh, *a marriage-proclamation;* thugadh g., *proclamation was made;* g.-choilich, *a cock-crowing;* g. ghallan, *the noise of hounds in the chase*—bitches giving tongue.

———each, -aich, *s.m.* Vocative case in *grammar.* 2 Appellative. 3 Calling. 4 Invitation.

gairmeadair, -ean, *s.m.* Crier, proclaimer.

gairmeadh, -eidh, *s.m.* & *pr. pt., prov.* for gairm.

gairmean, see garman.

————ach, -aich, see gairmeach.

gairmeanach,** *a.* Beaming.

gairmear, -eir, *s.m.* Crier, advertiser, bell-man.

gairme-gallanaich, *s.f.* Youth's shout. Le fuaim na gairme-gallanaich, *with the sound of the young men's shout.*

gairm-fhitheach,(AF) *s.m.* Crow.

gairm-ghille,‡‡ *s.m.* Crier.

gairmheach, *Suth'd* for gainmheach.

gairmionnach, -aich, see gairmeach.

gairneag,** -eig, *s.f.* Noisy little stream.

gàirneal, -il, -an, *s.m.* Large chest used to hold meal.

gàirneid, *s.f.* The stone garnet.

gàirneil,(CR) *Strathtay* for gàirneilear.

gàirneilear, -ir, -ean, *s.m.* Gardener.

————achd, *s.f.* Gardening.

gàirnlear,(CR) *Strathtay* for gàirneilear.

gairreas,** *s.m.* Apparatus.

gairrigeach, see carraigeach.

gairseach, -eich, -eichean, see gaorsach.

gairseachd,
gairsealachd, } see gaorsachd.

gairsean, -ein, *s.m.* Scold, shrew.

gairseil,** *a.* Lewd, whorish, indecent. 2 Nasty.

gairsg, *s.m.* Horror. 2 Fiendish look. 3 Dishevelled hair.

gàirsgeal,** -eil, *s. m.* Rabble, band of worthless persons.

gairsinn, see goirsinn.

gairsleag,** *s.f.* Strumpet.

gairsneach, -eiche, *a.* see goirisneach.

————d, *s.f.* see goirisneachd.

gairsneag, -eig, -an, *s.f.* Lewd female, bawd.

gairt, see gart.

gairte,** *s.f.* Narrow path.

gairteag,** -eig, *s.f.* Crab tree—*pyrus malus.*

†gairteil, -ean, *s.m.* see gartan.

gairtheach,** *s.m.* Clamour.

gair-theas, *s.m.* Scorching heat. 2 Reflected heat. 3 Glittering reflection of the sun, as from the surface of water.

gàir-thonn, *s.m.* Noise of waves.

gàis,(CR) *s.f.* Loathing—*Arran.* 2 Wisdom. 3 *Surfeit.

gais, -e, -ean, *s.f.* †Torrent, stream. 2 Surfeit. plenty, abundance. 3 Craft, cunning. 4 Generalship. 5 Spear, weapon. 6 Lace. 7 Toil. 8 Spear-haft. 9 Flag-staff. 10 Potato disease. G. na brataich, *the staff of the banner.*

gais, *pr.pt.* a' gaiseadh, *v. a.* Shrivel up, blast. corrupt, wither away. 2 Daunt.

gaisde, -an, *s.f.* Gin, trap, snare. 2 Wisp of hay or straw. 3**Wile, cunning, trick.

gaisde,** *a.* Armed, accoutred.

———an,** -ein, *s.m.* Cunning fellow. 2 Deceiver, cheat. 3 Snare.

†gaisdiche,** *s.m.* Deceiver. 2*Painter.

†gaisdidheach, -ich, *s.m.* see gaisgeach.

gaise, *s.f.* Daunting. 2 Flaw, blemish, injury. 3 see gaisge. 4**Withering, blasting. 5 Qualm. Cha do chuir e g. air, *it did not daunt him in*

the least.
gaiseach,** *a.* Blemished, injured. 2 Blasting, withering.
———d,** *s.f.* Qualmishness.
gaiseadh, -idh, -idhean, *s.m.* Defect in crops, state of their being blasted, shrivelled up, or corrupted. 2** Flaw, injury. 3 Blemishing. 4(PM) Potato blight—*Uist.* A' g—, *pr. pt.* of gais. Aotrom gun gh., *lively without blemish ;* b'iailidh se e le g., *he will strike him with blasting.*
†gaisean, -ein, *s.m.* Scanty crop.
gaisean, -ein, *s. m.* Bush. 2 Tuft or bunch of heath or broom, or of any other low-growing tufty plant. G. iosal, *a low bush.*
———ach, *a.* Tufty, bunchy, in tufts or bunches. Am fraoch g., *the tufty heath.*
gaisge, *s.f.* Bravery, valour, boldness. 2 Feats of arms. 3**Might. 4**Slope. Do gh. féin, *your own valour* ; clann na g., *the sons of bravery.*
———ach, -ich, *s.m.* Champion, hero, warrior. G. liath, *a hoary warrior.*
———achd, *s.f.ind.* Heroism, bravery, the doing of valiant deeds.
gaisgealachd, *s.f.* Heroism, valour, intrepidity.
gaisgeanta, -einte, *a.* Heroic, warlike, valorous. Gu g., *bravely.*
gaisgeil, -e, *a.* Heroic, warlike, valorous, brave. Is g. 'ur mór-thionail cheud, *brave are your gatherings of hundreds.*
gaisgidh,** *s.m.* Stream, current.
gaisidh, (an)‡*s.m.* Potato disease—*Suth'd.*
gaisidh, see gaisgidh.
gaisreadh, -idh, *s.m.* Warlike troops. 2 Attendants. 3(DC) Crew of a ship.
gaist,** *v.a.* Ensnare, trepan, deceive, trick.
gaiste, see gaistean & gaisteag.
———ach,** *a.* Full of snares. 2 Entrapping. 3 Cunning, wily.
gaisteag,** -ein, -an, *s.f.* Snare, gin, trap. 2 Trick, wile. 3**Cunning female.
———ach, *a.* Cunning.
———an, -tein, -an, *s.m.* Straw. 2 Small bundle of straw or hay. 3 Small quantity of anything. †4 Deceiver, wily fellow.
gaistean-cloich,** *s.m.* Tom-tit.
gaitean,** -ein, *s.m.* Brief, abridgment.
gaithean, -ein, *pl.* -an, *s.m., dim.* of gath. Little dart. 2 Straight branch. 3**Oar. A gaithean réidhe, *her smooth oars.*
———ach,†† *a.* Abounding in little darts, &c. [†† spells this gaitheineach.]
gal,** -ail, *s.m.* Smoke, vapour. 2 Gale, puff. 3 Blast or flame of straw. 4 Kindred. †5 Warfare. †6 Slaughter. †7 Valour.
gal, see gul.
gal, *v.n.* see gul.
galabhas,** -ais, *s.m.* Parasite. 2 Glutton. 3 Flatterer.
galach, -aiche, *a.* Valiant, brave. 2 see gulach.
†———, -aich, *s.m.* Valour, courage, fortitude.
galad, *s.f.* Familiar term of address to women and girls, used only in the vocative case, "a ghalad !" [Addressed to both boys and girls in *Uist.*] 2 (DMC)Term of sympathy or pity, A ghalad ! *poor creature !*
———ach,** *a.* Girlish. 2 Queanish.
———achd, *s.f.* Girlishness. 2 Queanishness.
galain, *gen.sing.* of galan.
galan, -ain, -an, *s.m.* Gallon measure. 2 Noise, tumult. 3 see gallan.
galan,** -ain, *s. m* Sudden blast. 2 Sudden glimpse. 3 Chivalry.
galanach, *a.* Stalky. 2 Noisy. 3 Tumultuous. 4 *prov.* for gulanach.
galan-greannchair, see gallan-greannchair.
galann,** -ainn, *s.m.* Enemy.
galapainn, *s.f.* Gaelic spelling of *galloping.*
galapainn, *v.a. & n.* Gallop.
galar, -air, *pl.* -a & -an, *s.m.* Disease, distemper, malady. G. fad' is eug 'na bhun, *a long illness and death at its end ;* cha galar aon duine e, *it is not one man's disease only*—said to any one speaking of their troubles as though there were no worries in the world besides their own ; gur e mo shlàinte mo ghalar, *it is my trouble that sustains me.*

g. araidh, *cholera.*
g. ban-sìth, *sickness of the fairies.*
g. bonn, *bruised soles,* disease in hoof of cattle caused by walking on hard stony ground.
g. buidhe, *jaundice.*
g. buinneach, *diarrhœa.*
g. cam,, *disease in cattle,* whereby the affected animal has a twist in its neck, and walks in a circle.
g. chinn, *headache.*
g. dearg, *or* g. na beinne, *red disease* (in cattle.)
g. dibhe-ruithe, *diabetes.*
g. donn, *brown disease* (in cattle.)
g. Frangach, *venereal.*
g. fuail, *the gravel, dysury.*
g. gasda, *flux, dysentry.*
g. glòig, } *mumps—Arran.*
g. glòigeach, }
g. gluc gloc, *throat-disease.*
g. goilleach, *the mort.*
g. greidh, *fives, strangles.*
g. inne, *bowel complaint.*
g. iongach, *agnail.*
g. lioil, *the water disease.*
g. lom, *disease of cattle,* whereby the skin becomes corrupt and the hair falls off.
g. mialach, *phthyriasis, lousy disease.*
g. mìosa, *menstruation.*
g. mór, *the plague, pestilence.*
†g. n-eclis,‖ *stomach disease.*
†g. noitid,‖ *pregnancy.*
g. plocach, }
g. pluice, } *quinsy, mumps.*
g. pluiceach, }
†g. pòil,‖ *epilepsy.*
g. sploiceach, (AH) *mumps.*
g. sùl, *eye-disease.*
g, tarsuinn, *disease in the head of sheep.*
g. teth, *rot, clap.*
g. tholl, *diarrhœa.*
g. tuiteamach, *epilepsy.*
g. uasal, *venereal.*

galarach, -aiche, *a.* Diseased, distempered. 2 Causing disease. Caora gh., *a diseased sheep.*
———d, *s.f.* Tendency to disease. 2 Condition of being diseased.
galaran, *n.pl.* of galar.
galar-eòlas, *s.m.* Nosology.
galar-ghabhail,‡‡ *s.m.* Infection.
galba, see galbha.
galbha,** *a.* Hard, vigorous, stout, brawny.
———, *s.* Rigour, hardness.
———idh, *s.f.* Heat, warmth.
galc, *pr. pt.* a' galcadh, *v.a.* Thicken cloth by fulling.
———ach, *a.* Stout. 2 Warlike.
———adair, -ean, *s.m.* Fuller of cloth.
———adh, -aidh, *s.m.* **Champion. 2 Act of fulling cloth. A' g—, *pr. pt.* of galc. Muileann galcaidh, *a fulling-mill.*
———anta, *a.* Thick, stout, strong. Fear g., *a man of stout form of body.*
†galchind, see galar-chinn.

galg, see galgadh.
——ach, *a.* Stout, warlike.
——adh, -aidh, *s.m.* Champion.
gall, -aill, gailleachan, *s.m.* Rock, stone. 2 Stone vase or boiler.
†gall, *s.m.* Cock. 2 Swan. 3 Milk.
Gall, Goill, *s.m.* Foreigner, stranger, especially a native of the south of Scotland, or a Scot that cannot speak Gaelic. Buaidh air clannaibh nan Gall, *a victory over foreigners* ; gall mhuileann, *wheel-mill.*
gallach, see gall-luch.
gallachrann, see gall-chrann.
galla, -chan, *s.f.* Female dog, bitch.
†galladh, -aidh, *s.m.* Beauty, brightness. 2 see gallag.
gallag, -aig, -an, *s.f.* Little bitch.
gallaidh, *a.* Hot.
gallan, -ain, -an, *s.m.* Branch, stalk. 2 Youth, handsome or tall young man. 3**Rock. 4 (AF) Whale—*Lewis.* 5††Straight young tree. 4 (DC) *pl.* Heroes. Tha 'n g. ag aomadh, *the branch is bending.*
——ach, -aiche, *a.* Full of boughs or branches. 2 Youthful.
gallan-gainmheich, see gallan-greannachair.
gallan-greannach, see gallan-greannchair.
————air, *s.f.* Colt's foot, see cluasliath. 2* Burdock,
gallan-mór, -móire, *s.f.* Butter-bur or pestilence-wort—*petasites vulgaris.*

352. Gallan mór.

gallantachd, Gaelic spelling of *gallantry.*
galla-thòlair, *s.* Brach.
galla-tholl, (AF) *s.* Bot-worm.
gall-bhalgach, -aich, *s.f.* French-pox, venereal. Gu soithich leis a' gh., *ill of the venereal.*
gall-chnò, -chnòtha *s.f.* Walnut.
gall-chrann, -ainn & -oinn, *s.m.* South-country plough, as distinguished from the kind formerly used in Gaeldom.
Gallda, *a.* Foreign, strange. 2 Surly, poor-spirited. 3 Of, or pertaining to the South of Scotland, or its inhabitants, "Lowland." 4 Unable to speak the Gaelic language.
galldachd, *s.f.* English connection. 2 Association with the English or "Lowland" Scots.
gall-druma, -chan, *s.f.* Kettle-drum.
gall-fheadan, -ain, *s.m.* Flageolet.
gall-ghiuthas, -ais, *s.m.* Pine-tree.
gall-luch, *pl.* -aidh, *s.m.* Rat.
gall-mhuileann, -inn, -uillnean, *s. m.* South-country mill, in contradistinction to the quern or native mill of Gaeldom.
galloban, -ain, see galoban.
gall-òglach,** -aich, *s.m.* Cuirassier. 2 Armour-bearer. 3 Freebooter of Gaeldom armed with Lochaber-axe or sword. The ceatharnach wore a sgian-dubh or dirk. A chieftain's armour-bearer was called gall-òglach. He was chosen on account of his boldness and bravery, and his business was to prevent his employer being taken by surprise. He had a double allowance of food, called *beatha fir*, or a champion's portion.
gall-pheasair,§ *s.m.* Vetches, lentils, see peasair-an-arbhair. 2**Lupine.
gallrach, *a.* Infectious.
gallrachadh, -aidh, *s. m.* Crucifying. 2 Tormenting. 3 Portending.
gallradh, -aidh, *s.m.* Infection. 2 Disorder.
gallraich,** *v.a.* Punish. 2 Torture. 3 Portend.
gall-sheileach,§ -ich, *s.f.* Cooper's willow, osier willow, see fineamhuin.
gall-sheilistear, -an, *s. m.* Flag bullrush. 2 Sedge, see seisg.
galltach, *a.* Tricky.
galltanach, -aiche, *a.* Envious.
————d, *s.f.* Hatred. 2 Envy.
galltanas, -ais, *s.m.* Hatred. 2 Envy. Luchd galltanais, *envious people.*
gall-tromp, truimp, *s.f.* Trumpet. 2 Clarion. 3 Cornet. Fuaim na gall-truimp, *the sound of the cornet.*
galluch, see gall-luch.
gall-uinnseann,§ *s.* Quickbeam—*pyrus aria.*

353. Gall-uinnsean.

gallunach, -aich, *s.m.* Soap.
galluran, -ain, *s.m.* Wild angelica—*ægopodium podagraria.* 2‡‡Lingwort.
galmas, -ais, *s.f.* In old Scots law, a satisfaction for slaughter.
galnas, see galmas.
galoban, -ain, *s.m.* Dwarf.
galraich, see gallraich.
galraidh, *s.f.* Bodement.
galuban, -ain, -an, *s.m.* Band that muffles the dugs of a mare, to prevent the foal from sucking.
'g am, (*for* ag mo) At my. 2 At their. Esan a tha 'g am shàrachadh, *he who oppresses me—lit.* is at my oppressing.
gamag, (DMy) *s.f.* Large mouthful, as of cattle among corn. 2 Man hurrying to get his food finished. Dh' ith e 'na ghamagan e, *he ate it in big mouthfuls.*
gàmag, -aig, -an, *s.f.* Stride, span, long step or bound in running at full speed. 2(DC) Shoemaker's nippers, strong nippers.
gàmagach,†† *a.* Striding, spanning.
gamaineach, *a.* Few, scarce.
gàmairle,** *s.m.* Fool.
gàmal, *s.m.* see camhal.

gamal, -ail, *s.m.* Fool, stupid person.
gàmaltan,(DC) *s.m.* Sumph, slow-witted man.
gàman, -ain, see gàmag.
gamasach,** *a.* Proud in gait.
†gamban, -ain, *s.m.* Leg, arm.
†gamh, -aimh, *s.m.* Winter. 2 Cold. 3 Woman.
gamhainn, *gen. sing.* -aimhne & -amhna, *pl.* -aimhne & -gamhna, *s.m.* Year-old calf. 2** Six-months-old cow. 3**Stirk, steer, young bullock. 4**Yearling deer. 5*Stupid fellow. G. tairbh, *a year-old bull*; g. ruadh, *a yearling deer*; oidhche Shamhna, theirear gamhna ris na laoigh, oidhch' Fhéill-Eòin, theirear aighean ris na gamhna, *on Hallowe'en the calf is called a stirk, on St. John's eve the stirk is called a heifer.*
gamhaldas, *Suth'd* for gamhlas.
†gamhann,** -ainn *s.m.* Stitch. 2 Ditch.
gamhchogus,** -uis, *s.m.* Dent, notch.
gamhlas, -ais, *s.m.* Malice, revenge, desire of revenging. 2 Aversion, hatred. 3* Envy. Ghluais mo gh., *my hatred began to rise*; luchd-gamhlais, *envious people.*
———ach, -aiche, *a.* Envious, hating. 2 Of a revengeful disposition, vindictive.
———achd, *s.f.* Enviousness.
gamhna, *gen.sing.* of gamhainn.
gamhnach, -aich, -aichean, *s. m.* Farrow cow, cow with a year-old calf and still being milked, stripper.
gamhnach,* *a.* Farrow. Tha i g., *she is farrow.*
——— -aigh,(MMcD) *s.f.* Cow that has been one year without calving—*Lewis.*
gamhuinn, see gamhainn.
gàmus, *s. m.* (CR) Bullet-mould—*W. of Ross.* [camus or fòs in other parts.]
'gan, (for ag an) 'Gan ruagadh, *pursuing them.*
'gan, (*prep.* aig+*art.* or *poss. pron.* an.)
gan, see gun.
ganaid,** *s.f.* Railing, fence, hedge. 2 Fold.
gandal,** -ail, *s.m.* Gander.
gangaid, -e, -ean, *s.f.* Falsehood, deceit. 2 Bustle. 3 Light-headed female, naughty female. 4 Deceiver, *prov.* 5 **Mean trick, craft.
———each, -eiche, *a.* False, deceitful. 2 Light-headed, giddy, *prov.* 3**Mean. Gu g., *deceitfully.*
——— eachd, *s.f.* Craft, knavery, deceit. 2 Light-headedness, *prov.* 3**Meanness, narrowness.
gangaraid,(DC) *s.f.* Disorderly crowd of women.
gangarais,***s.f.* Rout (crowd.)
gann, gainne [& goinne,] *a.* Scarce. 2 Little, small. 3 Rare, few. 4**Difficult. 5** *rarely* Stout, thick. Sruth g., *a scanty stream*; ach gann, *almost*; bliadhna gh., *a year of scarcity;* ni g., *a rare thing*; mic nan anma ganna, *sons of the pusillanimous souls*; gun iongantas g., *with no small wonder*; is g. a' ghaoth ris nach seòladh tu, *light would be the breeze that you couldn't sail in*—applied to trimmers and time-servers.
†gann, *s.m.* Poverty. 2 Scarcity. 3 Jug. 4 Fort.
gann, *a.* Scarce, scarcely, hardly. 'S g. a ràinig mi an uair ...., *I had scarcely arrived when* ....; is gann a ni e feum, *it will hardly do.*
gannail,** *s.pl.* Lattices.
ganndar, *a.* Scarce, rare.
———, -air, *s.m.* Scarcity. 2 Hunger.
ganndas, -ais, see gamhlas.
———ach, see gamhlasach.
gann-fhortanach,‡‡ -aiche, *a.* Unfortunate.
gannlas, -ais, -an, see gamhlas.
———ach, -aiche, see gamhlasach.
gànnraich,** *s.f.* Noise, tumult, din, clamour. Mar gh. eun, *like the noise of birds.*
ganntachd, *s.f.* Scarcity. 2 Poverty.
ganntair, see gainntir.
ganntar, -air, see ganntachd.
———ach, -aiche, *a.* Miserly, mean.
ganntas, -ais, *s.m.* see ganntachd.
gànradh, -aidh, -aidhean, *s.m.* Gander.
gànraich, -e, *s.f.* Roaring noise, clamour, clatter, loud murmuring sound, as of billows or of birds, romping, screeching.
———, *v.n.* Clamour.
ganraich,(PM) *v. a.* Bespatter with dirt, disgrace.—*Uist.*
gantair, see gainntir.
†gaod, -aoid, *s.f.* Swan. 2 Goose. 3 Leech.
†gaod, *v.a.* Wound. 2 Blemish.
gaodadh, -aidh, *s. m.* Wounding, wound. 2 Blemishing, blemish.
gaodhar, see gadhar.
gaog, -aoig, -an, *s.m.* Defect, lump or inequality of fineness in yarn, or cloth. 2**Defect of any kind. 3**Evaporation. 4**Staleness. 5 **Flatness. 6**Squint of the eye.
——ach, -aiche, *a.* Unequally spun. 2 Having defects. 3 Flat, stale. 4 Squint-eyed.
——ag, -aig, -an, *s. f.*, *dim.* of gaog. Too much slenderness in a portion of thread.
——an, -ain, *s.m.* see gaogag.
†gaoi, *s.f.* Wisdom. 2 Falsehood.
gaoid, -e, -ean, *s.f.* Blemish, defect. 2 Stain. 3 Disease. 4* Flaw, particularly in cattle. 5‖ Potato disease [with the art. a'] 6 *rarely* Wind, blasts, flatulence. Gun gh. gun ghalar, *without blemish or disease.*
———each, -aiche, *a.* Defective.
———eanta, *a.* Unsound at the core. 2 Idle, slothful, sluggish.
———eantachd, *s.f.* Idleness, slothfulness, sluggishness.
gaoideil, *a.* Diseased, tabid. 2 Blemished.
gaoidhean, *s.m.* False colour, counterfeit.
gaoil, *gen. sing.* of gaol.
†gaoil, *s. f.* Family, kindred. [in this sense it is the *n. pl.* of gaol.] 2 Wound. 3 Violent anger, see goil.
———ean, -ein, -ean, *s. m.* Darling. [†† gives -ein as *nom.*]
†gaoine, *s.f.* Goodness, honesty.
gaoir, -e, -ean, *s.f.* Noise. 2 Loud and continuous murmuring sound. 3 Pain, feeling of pain. 4* Noise of steam escaping, or of liquors fermenting, "singing" of a kettle, noise of frying. 5* Spigot of a cask. 6**Cry of pain or alarm. 8 Cry of woe. 9 (AH) Derisive cheering—*Uist.* 7**Throbbing pain of the toothache. Is goirt leam gaoir nam ban muileach, *painful in my ears is the Mull women's cry of woe*; g. eòin na tuinn, *the noise of the sea-fowl*; g. 'sa mhaduinn, *a cry in the morning*; g. 'n a chluais, *a tingling in his ear*; gaoir chatha, *a battle-cry*; thoir a' gh. as a' bhuideal, *take the spigot out of the cask.*
gaoirbh, *s.f.* see gairbh.
gaoir-chatha, *s.f.* Battle-cry, war-cry, shout set up on the eve of engaging in battle. 2 Din of arms. Cha chluinnteadh g., leibh, a remark made by anyone who is disturbed by the din of peoples' voices.
gaoirdean, see gàirdean.
——— ach, -aiche, *a.* see gàirdeanach.
gaoireach, -eiche, *a.* Sounding, resounding, noisy.
gaoirean, -ein, -an, *s.m.* Noisy, empty fellow.
gaoirich, *s.* Wailing, loud muumuring noise. Air a h-uilinn ri gaoirich, *leaning on her elbow, wailing.*—*Fìnah, p.* 85.
gaoirneal, -eil, } see gairneal.
gaoirnealair, }
gaoirnean,†† *s.m.* see gaorr. [†† gives -ein.]

gaoirnean, -ein, see gaorr.
gaoirreas ** *s.* see goireas.
gaoirsg, see gairsg.
gaoirsinn, see goirsinn.
gaoir-theas,* *s.f.* Gossamer, flickering sheet of cob-webs, seen on the grass in autumn, portending rain—called croisean Moire (Mary's crosses) in *Uist.* 2 Visible throbbing near the ground on a very hot day.
†**gaois**, -e, *s.f.* Wisdom, prudence, discretion. 2 Science.
gaoisd, -e, -ean, see gaoisid.
gaoiseadach,‡‡ -aiche, *a.* Hairy.
gaoisdeach, -eiche, see gaoisideach.
gaoisdean, see gaoisnean.
gaoiseach, -ich, *s.f.* The bolt that fixes a gun-barrel in the stock.
gaoisean, see gaisean.
———ach, see gaiseancah.
gaoisid, -e, *s. f.* Horse-hair. 2 The hair of beasts, hair of mane and tail. 3 Hair of any part of the human body but the head. G. an eich ghlais, *the grey horse's hair.*
———each, -eiche, *a.* Hairy, as a beast. 2 Having long or much hair.
gaoisneach, -eiche, see gaoisideach. Le 'n gàirdeanaibh g., *with their hairy arms.*
gaoisnean, -ein, -einean, *s.m.* Single hair. 2 Thin, slender person.
gaoistean, -ein, -ean, *s.m.* Crafty, tricky fellow. 2 see gaoisid.
gaoith, sometimes used for gaoth.
gaoith, *a.* see gaothaidh.
gaoithe, *gen.sing.* of gaoth.
———an, -ein, -einean, *s.m.* Fop, light-headed, giddy or superficial person, talkative fellow, windbag. 2**Changeling. 3 see gaothaire.
gaoitheanach, -aiche, *a.* Airy, foppish, giddy.
gaoitheanachd, *s.f.* Flatulence, giddiness.
gaoithreag, -eig, -an, *s.f.* Blast, blowing. 2(DC) Whirlwind—*Uist.*
———ach, -aiche, *a.* Of, or relating to blasts of wind or squalls.
gaoithseach,* *s.m.* Sheaf put as thatch on a little shock. [A shock consists of 12 sheaves, and takes its Gaelic name, adag from the sheaf that is fixed on the top like a little hat.]
gaol, -aoil, *s.m.* Love, fondness. 2 Beloved object or person. 3**Liking. 4** *rarely* Kindred. 5††Lover. A ghaoil, *my darling!*; a mhic mo ghaoil! *my beloved son!*; luchd mo ghaoil, *my kin*; am fac' thu mo gh.? *did you see my beloved one?*; clann mo mhàthar ghaoil, *my beloved mother's children*; a nighean mo ghaoil, *my beloved maiden*; thug mi g. da rireadh dhuit, *I loved you most truly*; an g., *in love*; air g. an Ni Mhaith, *for the love of God*; g. fola, *love of relationship*; gheibhear bean-chagair, ach 's ainneamh bean-ghaoil, *a dear-wife can be got, but a love-wife is rare*—"a ghaoil" is a warmer expression than "a chagair."
gaolach, -aiche, *a.* Lovely, dear, loving, beloved, affectionate. G. am bròn, *lovely in grief;* Ardar g., *beloved Ardar.*
———, -aich, *s.m.* Beloved object. 2 Term of kindly familiarity. A ghaolaich! *my darling*; 2 *my good fellow.*
———d, *s.f.* Affectionateness.
gaolaich, *gen.sing.* of gaolach.
———e, *comp.* of gaolach. More or most lovely, loving or beloved.
gaolar,** *a.* Amorous.
gaolan, -ain, *s.m.* Beloved person.
gaor, see gaorr & gadhar.
gaoran, -ain, *s.m.* Glutton. 2 Little glutton.
gaorasgiach,** *s.m.* Bog.
gaor-bhronnach, *a.* Pot-bellied.
gaornanach,(AC) *a.* Fluxy.
gaorr, -a, *s.m.* Gore. 2 Filth. 3 Fæces, ordure on the intestines. [In part of *Argyll* pronounced with a northern *ao* sound, in the North pronounced with *ao* broad, as in Argyll., ** gives *gen.* as gaoirre.]
gaorr, *pr.pt.* a' gaorradh, *v. a.* Gore, pierce, thrust into the side after the manner of cattle. 2 Cram, glut. 3* Lap.
———ach,†† *a.* Gory, filthy.
———adh, -aidh, *s.m.* Thrust, act of thrusting. 2 Glut, act of glutting, or cramming. 3(DMC) Fighting. A' g—, *pr.pt.* of gaorr. A' g. air a chéile, *fighting one with another, more in play than in earnest.*
———an, -ain, *s.m.* Little glutton. 2 Big belly.
gaorsach, -aich, -aichean, *s.f.* Wanton girl. 2 Slut. 3 Bawd, drivelling prostitute.
———d, *s. f. ind.* Wantonness, lewdness. 2 Debauchery. 3*Prostitution.
†**gaorsta**, *s.f.* Whirlwind.
gaort, -oirt, -an, *s.m.* see giort.
gaos, -aois, *s.m.* Wisdom, prudence.
gaosmhor, -oire, *a.* Wise, prudent.
gaoth, gaoithe, *pl.* -an & gaoithean [*Suth'd* gaoitean,] *s. f.* Wind. 2§ Flatulence [with the art. *a' gh—*,] 3**Shooting pain, stitch. 4 **Airiness. 5**Vanity. An ni a thig leis a' ghaoith, falbhaidh e leis an uisge, *what comes with the wind goes with the rain*; cuir ri gaoith, *weather as a ship*; *2 sow in windy weather*; g. chuairtein *or* ioma-gaoithe, *a whirlwind*; a' ruith na gaoithe, *on a vain pursuit*; coileach gaoithe, *a weathercock*; gaoth an ear, *the east wind*; a' gh. deas, *the south wind*; g. an iar, *the west wind*; g. an ear-dheas, *the south-east wind*; g. an iar-dheas, *the south-west wind*; g. an ear-thuath, *the north-east wind*; g. an iar-thuath, *the north-west wind*; g. ruadh, *a blasting wind*; (cf. tuil ruadh, *a devastating flood.*)
†**gaoth**, *s.f.* Dart. 2 Sea. 3 Theft.
†———, *a.* Prudent.
†**gaotha**, *s.* Streams left at low water.
gaothach, *s.* see gaothanachd.
gaothach, -aiche, *a.* Windy.
gaothaiche, -an, *s.f.* Hollow open reed. 2 Drone reed of a bagpipe. 3 Chanter reed.
———, *comp.* of gaothach. More or most windy.
gaothaidh, *a.* Airy. 2 Flighty, giddy. 3 Windy.
gaothaire, -an, *s.m.* Wind-piece or mouth-piece of a bagpipe. 2 Vent. 3 Vapour. 4 Empty, windy talker. 5** Blowing reed.
gaothan, see gaothanachd.
gaothan, see gaoithean. 2 *pl.* of gaoth.
———ach, -aiche, *a.* see gaothach.
———achd, *s.f.* Flatulence. 2 Giddiness.
gaoth-an-tràtha, *s.f.* Monsoon.
gaothar, *a.* see gaothmhor.
———, *s.m.* see gadhar.
———ach, -aiche, *a.* see gadharach.
———achd, *s.f.* see gaothmhorachd.
gaotharan, *s.m.* see gaothran.
gaoth-innisean, -ein, *s.m.* Anemoscope.
gaoth-mheidh, -e, -ean, *s.f.* Wind-gauge, anemometer. [better, meidh-ghaoithe.]
gaothmhor, -oire, *a.* [*pron.* gaothar,] Windy. 2 Blustering. 3 Flatulent. 4 Painful. Seacharan na h-oidhche g., *the wanderings of the windy night.*
———achd, *s.f.* Windiness. 2**Storminess. 3**Flatulence. 4**Shooting pain. 5**Anguish.
gaothrachadh, -aidh, *s.m.* Winnowing. A' g—, *pr.pt.* of gaothraich.
†**gaothraich**, *pr.pt.* a' gaothrachadh, *v.a.* Winnow,

gaothran, -ain, -an, *s.m.* Fan. 2 Giddy fellow.
gaoth-ruadh,** -aidh, *s.m.* Blasting wind, mildew.
gaoth-sgeulachd, *s.f.* Description of the winds.
gaoth-thomhaisear, *s.m.* Auemometer.
gàpaidh,** *s.* Riddle for winnowing.
gar, *pr.pt.* a' garadh, *v.a.* Warm. 2 Ferment. 3 Cherish. G. thu féin, *warm yourself*; garaidh se e féin, *he shall warm himself*; g. do làmhan, *warm your hands.*
gar, *v.a.* Gratify. 2 Accommodate.
gar,†† *s.f.* Proximity. Am ghar, *within hail of me.*
gar, gair, *s.m.* Accommodation. 2 Desert, merit, profit.
gar, *conj.* for ged nach. Gar an tig e, *though he come not*; gheibh mi baolum ort gar am marbh, *I will get a knock at you though I kill (you) not—Duanaire, 301.*
'g ar, *prep.* + *pron.* 'G ar toirt, *bringing us*; 'g ar léireadh, *tormenting us.*
'g ar, *erroneously* for aig + bhur, see **'g ur.**
gàr, see gàradh.
†**gar**, *a.* see gearr.
†**garab**, see darab.
garaban, -aig, *s. m.* Rude fellow, clown, boor. 2(DMy) The rough part in the throat of fish as cod, ling, &c.
———, *a.* Brave.
———ach, *a.* Rude, boorish, clownish. 2 Raw, inexperienced.
garabhan, -ain, *s.m.* Bran.
garach,** -aich, *s.m.* Brawl. 2 see garrach.
garach, -aich, *a.* Useful.
———an, *s.m.*, *dim.* of garach.
———dail,** *a.* Huge.
———dalachd,** *s.f.* Hugeness.
gàradair, -ean, *s.m.* Gardener.
———eachd,** *s.f.* Gardening.
garadan,** -ain, *s.m.* Register, minute-book. 2 Note-book.
gàradh, -aidh, *pl.* -aidhean, -aidhnean, & gàrachan, *s. m.* Garden. 2 Wall, dyke. 3 Mound. 4**Gratuity. G. luibhean, *a garden of herbs*; rinn mi gàrachan, *I made gardens*; g. càil, *a kitchen garden*; g. droighinn, *a hedge of thorns*; g. crìche, *limit, landmark, barrier*; balla a' ghàraidh *and* g. an liosa, both mean *the garden-wall.*
gàradh,(MMcD) *s. m.* The second row of peats taken from a bank with the toirsgein. Fàdadh a' ghàraidh, *a peat taken from the second row—Lewis.*
garadh, -aidh, -aidhean, *s.m.* Den, cave. Tha garaidhean aig na sionnaich, *the foxes have holes.* [*Garaidh* is often used as *nom.*]
garadh, -aidh, -aidhean, *s. m.* Warming, act of warming. A' g—. *pr.pt.* of gar. Dean do gh., *warm yourself.*
gàradh-arbhair,(CR) *s.m.* Corn-yard, stackyard, —*Suth'd.*
——— -an-arbh,(MMcL) *s.m.* Dyke surrounding arable land.
——— -baic,(WC) *s.m.* Peats laid out on the edge of the bank, one over the other, in such a way as to dry rapidly.
——— -cinn,(DMC) *s.m.* The dyke separating the arable land from the moor or common pasture.
——— -crìche, *s.m.* Barrier. 2 Boundary dyke between two properties.
——— -droma,(MMcL) *s.m.* Turf-dyke.
——— -fàil,(AC) *s.m.* Turf-dyke.
——— -gléidht', *s.m.* Defending wall. 2(AH) The embodiment of security, economy or parsimony. O 'n chuir sneachda nan sléibhtean gàradh-gléidht' orm cho teann, *since I was snowed-up, since the snow of the mountains put a defending wall around me so close.—Duanaire, 57.*
——— -griocaig,(DMC) *s.m.* Tottering wall.
——— -na-h-eaglais, *s.m.* Churchyard—*Arran.*
——— -theud,(DMC) *s.m.* Wire fence.
——— -tobhta, *s.m.* Turf-wall.
garag, see garrag.
garaich,* *v. & s.* see gànraich.
garaid,** -ean, *s.f.* Noise, clamour, confusion. 2 Garrulous woman. 3 Gaelic spelling of *garret.*
gàraidh, *gen. sing.* of gàradh.
———eachd,** *s.f.* Merit.
†**garail**,* *a.* Snug, comfortable. 2**Near, neighbouring. 3** Warm. 4 Commodious. 5‡‡ Useful.
garait, see garaid.
garaitiche,** *s.m.* Garreteer.
garalachd,* *s.f.ind.* Snugness.
gar am, } *conj.* Although not. Gar an do
gar an, } thòisich........, *although .... did not begin*; ma 's e gar an e, *whether it is so or not.*
garan, -ain, -an, *s.m.* Grove, forest. 2 Thicket, underwood. 3 see guirean. †4 Crane.
gar-athair, -ar, -thraichean, *s.m.* Grandfather.
†**garb**,‖ *s.* Scabies.
garbag,(AF) *s.f.* Flounder. 2 Plaice.
garban, see garaban.
———ach, see garabanach.
garbh, gairbh, *a.* Thick, not slender. 2 Rough, of unequal surface. 3 Boisterous, stormy. 4 Harsh, haughty, ungentle. 5 Hoarse, sounding harshly. 6 Coarse. 7 Rough, not fine. 8 Fierce, terrible. Maide g., *a thick stick*; duine g., *a harsh, brawny*, or *vulgar man*; àite g., *a rough* or *rugged place*; guth g., *a hoarse voice*; anart g., *coarse linen*; oidhche gh., *a boisterous night*; g. 'na chainnt, *vulgar in his expressions*; a' gh. chuid dhiubh, *the majority of them*; ni na's gairbhe na na leasraidh, *a thing that is thicker than the loins*; gu g., *roughly, severely*; tha sin g., *that is dreadful.*
garbh, gairbh, *s. m.* Thick. 2**Scab. 3**Warfare. 4**Courage. An g. 's an caol, *the thick and the thin*; g. agus mion na cùise, *the general outlines besides the details of the matter.*
garbhacail, *Lochbroom* for garbhaiceil.
garbhach,** -aich, *s.m.* Grandson.
———adh,‡‡ -aidh, *s.m.* Asperation.
———d, *s.f.ind.* Thickness, coarseness, roughness, greatness. 2**Asperity. 3**Rocky place.
garbhad,* see gairbhead.
garbhag, -aig, -an, *s.f.* Sprat. 2 Small herring. 3 Garvie. 4 Plaice, spotted flounder. 5**Savory.
garbhag-an-t-sléibhe, -aig-, *s.f.* Fir club-moss—*lycopodium selago.* [Badge of the MacRaes.]
garbhag-ghàraidh, -aig, *s.f.* Garden savory—*satureja hortensis.*
garbhag-nan-gleann,§ *s.f.* Club-moss, see crotal nam madadh ruadh.
garbhaiceil,(CR) *s.f.* Gulping, bolting, devouring food—*W. of Ross.*
garbhaich,** *v.a.* Roughen, asperate.
garbhainn, *a.* Ill, sick, complaining—*Arran.*
garbh-aite, *pl.* -àitean & -àiteachan, *s.m.* Rough place, rocky place.
garbhalach,** *a.* Rocky, stony. Anns a' choire g., *in the rocky dell.*
———,** -aich, *s.m.* Stony or rocky ground.
———d,** *s.f.ind.* Abruptness. 2 Cragginess.
garbh-allt, *s.m.* Impetuous torrent.
garbhan, -ain, -an, *s.m.* Gills of a fish. 2 Bran.

3 Orts of ill-ground meal. 4 Coarse meal, groat. 5* Grit. 6††Minnow. 7††Garvie, sprat. 8(AF) Sea-urchin—*Lochcarron*. 9**Dog-bolt.

———ach, -aiche, *a.* Coarse, rugged. 2 Brawny, having brawn, like brawn. 3††Full of orts. 4**Rude, inexperienced.

———ach, -aich, *s. m.* Stout tall man. 2 ‡Sea-bream—*Arran*. 3(AF) Silver haddock.

garbh-bhallach, -aiche, *a.* Having large limbs.

garbh-bhuille,** *s.f.* Heavy blow.

———ach, -eiche, *a.* Fetching or striking great blows.

garbh-chath, *s.m.* Severe combat, heat of battle.

garbh-chearbach, -aiche, *a.* Broad-skirted.

garbh-chlachaireachd,** *s.f.* (?) Fretwork.

garbh-choimeasg,(MS) *s.m.* Balderdash.

garbh-chludach,** -aich, *s.m.* Coarse blanket, coverlet.

garbh-chnàimheach, -eiche, *a.* Large-boned.

garbh-chòmhrag, -aig, *s.f.* Furious engagement, fierce struggle, heat of battle.

garbh-chreuchd, *s.f.* Deep wound, severe bruise.

———ach, *a.* Inflicting deep wounds. 2 Having deep or dangerous wounds or bruises.

garbh-chrìoch, -chrìche, -an, *s.f.* Rugged country. For "Na Garbh-chrìochan" see under crìochan.

garbh-chuan, -ain, -chuantan, *s. m.* Rough or stormy sea. An crann nach lùb an g., *the mast that will stand a storm.*

garbh-chulaidh, -ean, *s.f.* Frieze coat.

garbh-churaidh, *s.m.* Fierce warrior. 2 Strong-bodied warrior.

garbh-dhabhach, -aich, -aichean, *s. m.* The mountainous interior of a country.

garbh-eas,** *s.m.* Cascade, rough torrent, boisterous abyss or linn.

garbh-fhras, -ais, -an, *s.f.* Boisterous or heavy shower.

———ach, -aiche, *a.* Abounding in boisterous showers, very rainy. Am mìos g., *the boisterous month.* [February.]

garbh-ghaineamh, -imh, *s. m.* Coarse gravel, coarse sand.

garbh-ghaoisneach, -eiche, *a.* Having coarse hair (of animals.)

garbh-ghaoth, -gaoithe, *s.f.* Rough blast, furious wind, hurricane. Mar gh. nam beann, *like the furious mountain-wind.*

garbh-ghnìomh, -ghnìomharan,*s.m.* Mighty deed or feat. Do gh., *thy feats in battle.*

garbh-ghrinneal,†† *s.m.* Gravel.

garbh-ghucag, -aig, *s.f.* The bell or globule on the surface of whisky, taken to indicate its strength.

garbh-ghuthach, -aiche, *a.* Hoarse, rough or strong-voiced.

garbhlach, -aich, *s.m.* The more rugged part of a country. 2 Stony or rocky bed of a river. 3 *Rank moor-grass.

garbh-làimhsich,‡‡ *v.a.* Bang, handle roughly.

garbh-laoch, -laoich, *s. m.* Fierce warrior, impetuous hero. Garbh-laoich a's cruadalaiche beum, *fierce warriors of the most deadly blows.*

garbh-leac,** *s.f.* Rugged part of a country.

garbh-leas,** *s.m.* Shout.

garbh-linn,** *s.f.* Rough sea, pool or stream.

†garbh-loc, *s.* Crag. 2 Thicket.

garbh-luch, see gar-luch.

garbh-lus, -luis, -an, *s.m.* Goose-grass, cleavers, hay-ruff, catch-weed—*galium aparine.*

garbh-mac-fiadh, *s.m.* *prov.* for creamh.

garbh-rabhadh, (DMC) *s. m.* Strongly-worded warning.

garbhraitheach,§ *s. m.* Garlic mustard, sauce alone—*erysimum alliaria.*

354. Garbhraitheach.

garbhreac, *s.f.* Ducker (bird.)

garbh-sgrìobh,** *v.a.* Engross.

———air,** *s.m.* Engrosser.

garbh-sheòd, -sheòid, *s.m.* Fierce warrior. Anamannan nan g., *the souls of the fierce warriors.*

garbh-shìan, see garbh-shìon.

garbh-shìon, -ìne, *s.m.* Rough weather, storm.

———tach, *a.* Stormy, blasty. Là g., *a stormy day.*

garbh-shleagh,** *s.f.* Thick spear. Gach g. is iùthaidh, *each thick spear and arrow.*

garbh-shlios, -a, -an, *s.m.* Rough side of a hill or country.

———ach, -aiche, *a.* Having a rough declivity.

garbh-thonn,-thuinn,-an, *s.m.* Boisterous wave, breaker.

———ach, -aiche, *a.* Surgy, stormy, billowy, raging as the sea.

garbh-uchd,** *s. m.* (*lit.* fierce breast) Fierce mind. 2 Rough or turbid bosom. G. nan speur, *the turbid bosom of the sky.*

———ach, *a.* Having a rough breast. An cuan g., *the rough-breasted sea.*

gàrcail, *s.f.* see garcan.

gàrcan, -ain, *s.m.* Querulous sounds of a hen.

———ach, *a.* Querulous, as a hen.

†gàrd, *s.m.* Garden. 2 Fenced place. 3 Guard.

gàrdraich,** *s.pl.* Troop, company.

garg, gairge, *a.* Fierce, angry, wrathful. 2 Bitter, tart, acrid. 3 Pungent. 4 Turbulent. 5**Satirical. 6**Sore. 7 Irritating. 8††Wild, terrible. Duine g., *a turbulent person*; blas g., *a pungent taste*; na's gairge, *more acrid*; briathran g., *rough words.*

gargachd, see gairge.

gargad, -aid, see gairgead.

gargaich,** *v.a.* Acidate.

gargail,** *a.* Fierce, keen. An laoch g., *the fierce warrior.*

gargalachd, *s.f.* Acrimony.

gargan,** -ain, *s.m.* Dung, ordure, manure.

garg-chòmhrag, -aig, -an, *s. f.* Fierce engagement.

garg-chosgach,** *a.* Ant-acid.

garg-chronachadh, -aidh, *s.m.* Act of rebuking severely. 2 Harsh rebuke or reprimand.

garg-chronaich,** *v.a.* Rebuke severely. Na g. seanair, *do not rebuke an elder.*

gàrlach, -aich, -aichean, see gàrlaoch.

garlag-Muire,§ *s.f.* Crow-garlic—*allium vineale.*

gàrlaichean, *n.pl.* of gàrlach.

gàrlag, see gairgean.
gàrlaoch, -aoich, *s. m.* Screaming infant. 2 Little villain or rogue. 3 Dwarf. 4 Starving child. 5 Cipher (useless fellow.) 6 ** Bastard. 7**Term of great personal contempt. 8(AF) see gar-luch. 9* Most impertinent fellow. 10(DMC) Weakling in body or mind. 11 (DMC) Coward.
gar-luch, -lucha, -an, *s.m.* Mole. 2 Rat.
———ag, -aig, *s.f.* Young mole. 2 Young rat. 3 Little mole or rat.
gar-luchaidh, *dim.* of gar-luch.
garmach, -aiche, see gairmeach.
garmadair, see gairmeadair.
garmadh, see gairmeadh.
garmainn, see garman.
garmaisg,(AC) *s.* Sprite.
garman, -ain, -an, *s. m.* Weaver's beam. 2 Post, pillar. 3 Gallows.
garman-bhall,* *s.m.* Windlass.
garman-uchd,(AC) *s.m.* Breast-beam—*Argyll.*
gar-mhac, -mhic, *s.m.* Grandson.
†gar-mhàthair, -mhàthar, *s. f.* Grandmother.
garmunn, -uinne, see garman. Dhealbh e a gharmuinne, *he formed its pillars.*
garnanach,(AC) *a.* Pellety.
gàrnardaich,(CR) *s.f.* Yawning—*Suth'd.*
gar-ogha, *s.m.* Grandchild's grandchild.
†garoid, -e, *s.f.* Splutter, noise.
gàrr, see gaorr.
garr, -a, *s.m.* Gorbelly. 2 The belly of a spoiled child or starveling.
——ach, -aiche, *a.* Gorbellied, greedy, voracious. 2 Having a bad odour.
——ach, -aich, -aichean, *s.m.* Glutton, gorbelly. 2 Dirty little worthless creature. 3††Wretch. 4* Gorbellied child. 5* Most impertinent fellow. 6 Carrion-crow, see feannag.
garrachadh, -aidh, *s.m.* Soiling, dirtying. A' g—, *pr.pt.* of garraich.
garrachdadh,(WC) *s.m.* Rebuke shouted or uttered roughly. Thoir g. air, *rebuke him sharply.*
garrachdail,†† *a.* Rough, rugged, coarse.
garrach-glas, see garrag-ghlas.
gàrradair, -ean, see gàradair.
gàrradh, see gàradh. Ri a h-uchd bha g. gu h-àrd mar bhruaich, *there was a wall (of waves) like a brae to her breast.—Dàin I. Ghobha.*
garrag, -aig, -an, *s.m. & f.* see feannag. 2 Unfledged bird, young bird. 3 (AF) Dog ruffled after fighting.
garrag, -aig, -an, *s.f.* Sudden yell, unseemly howl.
garragadaich,(DU) *s.f.* Emitting of hoarse yells.
————, *pr.pt.* a' garragadaich, *v.a.* Emit hoarse yells.
garra-gart,(CR) *s.m.* Corn craik—*W. of Ross.*
————an, see garra-gart.
garrag-ghlas, see feannag-ghlas.
garraich, *pr.pt.* a' garrachadh, *v.a.* Soil, foul. Tha mi oir mo gharrachadh, *I am dirtied*—(DMy.)
garraicleis, -e, *s.f.* Noise of wild geese or swans.
garraid, *s.f.* Splutter, noise. 2 Inquiry.
garran, -ain, -an, see gearran.
garran,** -ain, -an, *s.m.* Den. 2 Thicket, grove. 3 Copse, underwood. 4 Gorbelly, glutton.
———ach, *a.* Woody, having groves, thickets or copses. 2 Having dens.
garran-gaineamhaich, *s.m.* Angler (small fish.)
garran-gaineimh, see garran-gaineamhaich.
garr-bhuaic, *s.f.* The morbid ooze in the skin of a sheep. 2 Filth about a sheep-fold. 3** Noise, clamour. 4**Assembly.
————each, -eiche, *a.* Covered with filth or sheep's dung. 2** Noisy, clamorous.
gàrrlaig, *s.f.* Spurious breed. 2 In some places the idea *dwarfish* is inferred—*Dàin I.Ghobha.*
garrochan,(AF) *s.m.* Angler (fish.)
garrthaich, -ean, *s.f.* see gàrthaich.
garrunach, -aiche, *a.* Dirty, nasty, shocking, horrible.
†garsan, -ain, *s.m.* Lad. (*Irish*, garsoon.)
gart, -airt & -a, *s.m.* Gloom, surly aspect, threatening look. G. a' chuain, *the threatening aspect of the sea.*
gart, -airt, *s.m.* Standing corn. 2 First shoots of sown corn. 3* Vineyard. 4**Garden enclosure. 5(CR) Field, corn-field, field of standing corn. 6(DMC) Belt.
†gart, -a, -an, *s. m.* Head. 2 Resistance. 3 Liberality.
gartain, *gen.sing. & n. pl.* of gartan.
†gartan, -ain, -an, *s.m.* Bonnet, cap. 2 see garra-gart.
gartan, -ain, *pl.* -an & -ain, *s.m.* Garter. Osain ghoirid is gartain, *short hose and garters.*
gartan,(CR) *s.m.* Tick, insect found on deer and dogs, but larger on cattle.
———ach, -aiche, *a.* Wearing garters. 2 Of, or belonging to garters. 3 Like a garter. Osain gh., *gartered hose.*
———achadh, -aidh, *s.m.* Gartering.
———aich,** *v.a.* Garter.
———aichte, *past pt.* of gartanaich.
gartar, see gartmhor.
gart-eun, -eòin, *s.m.* Quail.
gart ghlainn, see gart-ghlan.
gart-ghlainte, *past pt.* of gart-ghlan. Weeded, cleared of weeds.
gart-ghlan, *pr.pt.* a' gart-ghlanadh, *v.a.* Weed, clear of weeds. 2**Examine.
————adh, -aidh, *s. m.* Weeding, act of weeding. 2 Clearing from small stones. 3** Examining. A' g—, *pr. pt.* of gart-ghlan.
†gartha, see gàir and gairm.
gàrthaich, *s.f.* Loud tumultuous shout, clamour, any loud noise, continued din. Fearg agus g., *wrath and clamour.*
garthal,** *a.* Snug, warm, comfortable.
gartlainn,* *v.* see gart-ghlan.
gartlann,* *s.m.* Weeds. 2 Weed-hook, hoe.
gartlann, -ainn, -an, *s.m.* Corn-yard.
gartmhoire, *comp.* of gartmhor.
————achd, *s.f.* Munificence, liberality.
†gartmhor, *a.* Munificent.
garturan, (AF) *s.m.* Dog-louse.
garuidh, -ean, see gàradh.
garunnach,** *a.* Dirty, horrible, shocking.
gas, -aise & -ois, *pl.* -an & gaisean, *s. f.* Stalk. stem of a herb. 2 Bough, twig. 3 Bunch. 4 Young boy. 5‡‡Military servant. 6*Particle. 7 Broom, brush. 8**Copse. G. a sguabadh an taighe, *a broom to sweep the house*; g. càil, *a stock of kale*; gach g., *every particle*; o chàrn nan g., *from the copsy rock.*
†gas, -ais, *s.m.* Strength. 2 Wrath.
gas, *adv., conj. & prep.* see gus.
gas,** *v.n.* Shout. 2 Sprout, branch. 3 Look.
†gasach, *a.* Angry, indignant.
gasach, -aiche, *a.* Branchy, bushy, having many boughs, tufty, bunchy, copsy.
———d,** *s.f.* Branchiness, bushiness, tuftiness, bunchiness.
gasag, -aig, -an, *s.f.*, *dim* of gas. Little branch, stalk, stem or bough.
———ach,†† *a.* Abounding in little stalks, &c.
gàsaid, *s.f.* Fray—*Dàin I. Ghobha.* 2(WC) War-story. 3 Gaelic spelling of *gazette.*
gasair,* *v.a.* Line, as a bitch.
gasan, -ain, -an, *s.m.*, *dim.* of gas. Little branch. 2 Young man, stripling, youth. 3 Tuft. 4** Little copse. 5**Tendril. 6††Pert youth. 7 (DMC) Courtier, one who courts.

gasanach, *a.* Abounding in little branches, youths, &c.
gasar,* -air, -an, *s.m.* Pert fellow.
gasbadan,** -ain, see gasbaid.
gasbaid,** *s.f.* Wasp. 2 Hornet.
gasbuidean, see gasbaid.
gasda, *a.* Excellent. 2 Handsome, beautiful. 3 Clever, expert, ingenious, skilful. 4 Generous, open-handed. 5**Chaste. 6**Gallant, brave. 7**Neat. A bhean gh., *his beautiful wife ;* is gasd' am balach thu, *you are a fine fellow ;* am bheil thu gu g. (*or* gu math)? *are you quite well ?* duine g., *an open-handed and open-minded man—Reay country ;* also *a well-shaped or handsome man ;* ni g., *a fine thing.*
——chd, *s.f.ind.* Excellency, beauty. 2 Cleverness, expertness, skilfulness. 3 Bravery. 4 Neatness. 5(MS) Affectedness. 6 (DMC) Jesting with a view to irritate. Bha e mór 'na gh., *he was very brave.*
gasdag, -aig, -an, *s.f.* Wile, trick, snare.
gasdair,** *s.m.* Active man. 2 Prater.
gasg, -aisg & -a, *pl.* -aisg & -an, *s.m.* Tail, appendage.
†——ach, *a.* Having a tail.
——ag,‡ -aig, -an, *s.f.* Step, stride—*Badenoch.*
gasgan, -ain, *pl.* -ain & -an, *s.m.* Puppy (dog.) 2 Puppy (petulant fellow.) 3 Straight sapling. 4 Tail, extremity. 5 Place where a plateau runs to an acute angle, and narrows down to the vanishing point. 6 Rushy hollow—*Gairloch.* 7(DU) Scrubber made of heather for cleaning cooking-pots &c. [*dim.* of gasg.]
——ach, -aich, *s.m.* see gasgan. 2**Macaroni.
——ach, -aiche, *a.* Pert, petulant, conceited. 2 Many-ringleted—*Agus ho Mhórag.*
—— -coin,(AF) *s.m.* Puppy dog.
gasgara,** *s.pl.* The posteriors.
gasrach, -aiche, *a.* Salacious. 2**Proud. 3** Fiery, hot-tempered.
gasradh, -aidh, *s.m.* Salacity in female dogs. 2 see gasraidh.
gasraidh, *s.f.* Mean company, people, crowd, rabble. 2**Domestic soldiers. 3 Mercenary soldiers. 4**Salaciousness. A' bhàt' is a g., *the vessel and her crew ;* galla air gh., *a bitch on heat.*
gast, see gasda.
gast,** *s.f.* Old woman. 2 Whore. 3 Snare. 4 Wile. 5 Puff, blast.
gastachd, see gasdachd.
gastag,** -aig, *s. f.* Little slut. 2 Whore. 3 Trick, wile.
gàt, -a, -aichean, see gàd.
gàta, see gàd.
gata,(AF) *s.* Pig.
gàtach,(DMy) *a.* Lazy. Duine g., *an awkward or lazy man.*
gàtachan, -ain, -an, *s.m. dim.* of gàt.
gatachan,** -ain, *s.m.* Little boy.
gàtaire,(DMy) *s.f.* Slothfulness.
gath, -a, *pl.* -an, -annan & -achan, *s.m.* Sting. 2 Dart, arrow, javelin of any kind. 3 Ray, ray of light, sunbeam. 4 Beard. 5 Inner row of sheaves in a corn-stack. 6* Snub. 7 Barb of an arrow. 8**Knot in wood. 9 Spoke of a cycle-wheel. G. an t-seillein, *the bee's sting;* g. gréine, *sunbeam,* also *one of the names of Fingal's banner ;* gath dubh, *foundation sheaves ;* g. òige a' dol seachad, *the ray of youth passing by ;* g. na gealaich, *the moonbeam ;* g. tannaisg, *a spectre's spear.*
gàth,§ *s.m.* [with art. *an.*] Ivy, see eidheann.
gathach, -aiche, *a.* Of, or pertaining to, darts, javelins or stings. 2 Aculeate, prickly.
gathaichte, *past pt.* Barbed.
gathan, -ain, -an, *s.m. dim.* of gath. Little sting. 2 Oar.
——ach, -aiche, *a.* see gathach.
—— -òmair, *s.pl.* Röntgen rays. (Dark or invisible rays, emitted under the influence of an electric current.)
gathan-giuthais, *s.m.* Shoot of fir.
gathan-òmair, see gathnn-dealain.
gath-bhalg, -bhuilg, *s.m.* Quiver.
gath-bolg,** *s.f.* Fiery dart.
gath-buafach, -aich, *s.m.* Poisoned dart.
gath-buidhe,§ *s.m.* Large-flowered hemp-nettle, —*galeopsis versicolor.* [Preceded by art. *an.*]
gath-cuip, -e, -an-cuip, *s.m.* Medical tent, roll put into a wound.
gath-diurd,(WC) *s.m.* Small peg of wood on which bobbin in weaver's shuttle revolves.
gath-dòrain, *s.m.* Gaff.
gath-doinionn,(AH) *s.m.* Stump of a rainbow, seen on the horizon in stormy weather called a dog-tooth—*Mid Argyll.* see fadadh-cruaidh.
gath-dubh, -uibhe, -an-dubha, *s. m.* Beard of oats. 2 *in pl.* The storm-riders, the dark undulations seen in falling rain, when gusts of wind compress and scatter the rain like the waves of the sea. 3 Foundation sheaf of a stack. 4(AF) Midge. Cho luath ris na gathan-dubha, *as swift as the storm-riders ;* cho lìonmhor ris na gathan-dubha, *as numerous as the black darts*—variously interpreted, and may be held descriptive of midges darting to and fro in myriads, or of the black spikes of small oats.—NGP.
gath-dubh,§ *s.m.* Common hemp-nettle—*galeopsis tetrahit.* [Preceded by art. *an.*]

355. *Gath-dubh.*

gath-fruighe,** *s.m.* Poisoned arrow.
gath-gealaich,** *s.f.* Moonbeam. Mar gh., *like a moonbeam.*
gath-gréine, *s.f.* Sunbeam. 2 One of the names of Fingal's banner. B' ise an g. am measg bhan, *she was a sunbeam among women.*
gath-làir, *s.m.* Direct spoke of a cycle-wheel.
gath-linn,** *s.m.* North Polar star.
gath-mór,§ see an gath buidhe.
gath-muigh, see gath-muinge.
gath-muinge, -an-, *s.m.* Mane. 2(DMy) The end of mane next the shoulders.
gath-muingeach, *a.* Maned.
gath-muinne, -an-muinne, *s.m.* see gath-muinge.
gath-riaghailt, -e, -an-, *s.m.* Measuring-rod. 2 ‡‡Radius of a circle.
gath-soluis,** *s.m.* Sunbeam. 2 Ray of light. 3 Pencil of rays.
gath-tearradh,** *s.f.* Whitlow. 2 Agnail.
gath-teth,** *s.m.* Fiery dart.
ge, (ge b'e) *pron.indef.* Whoever, whatever. Ge

as air bith, (ce *or* cia as air bith) *whencesoever*.
ge, *conj.* see ged. *Ge* is always used before an adjective or personal pronoun, as, ge mór is ge glic, *although great and wise;* because *ged* is composed of *ge do—do* the particle preceding the rest.
gé, see cé.
geabhag,(CR) *s.f.* Twist, distortion—*Perthsh.*
———ach,(CR) *a.* Awry, askew—*Perthshire.*
geabhair, -ean, *s.m.* Carper.
geabhroc,(AF) *s.* Sea-swallow.
geacach,‡ *a.* Sententious, pert.
gead, -id, -an, *s. f.* Small spot of arable land, ridge, "lazy-bed." 2* Bed in a garden. 3 Lock of hair. 4 Star or spot in a horse's forehead. 5 Buttock, haunch. 6**Pike (fish.)
gead, *pr.pt.* a' geadadh, *v.a.* Clip off the hair, as of a horse.
——ach, -aiche, *a.* Abounding in little fields. 2 Having the hair in tufts or bunches. 3** Patched. 4**Spotted. 5**Ridgy. 6**Like a pike, abounding in pikes.
——adh, -aidh, *s.m.* Act of cutting off the hair. or 2 (DMy) Corn when not ripe enough to be all cut.
A' g—, *pr. pt.* of gead.
——ag, -eig, -an, *s.f., dim.* of gead. Small spot or ridge of arable land. 2 (?)Large trout. 3 (AH) Grilse or salmon, three or four years old when returning from its first season in the sea. **4 Young pike. 5 ††Lock of hair.
geadagach, -aiche, *a.* Abounding in small spots of arable land or ridges. 2 Abounding in large trout. 3**Spotted, patched.
geadan, -ain, -an, *s.m., dim.* of gead. Small tuft or bunch of hair.
————ach, -aiche, *a.* Abounding in tufts or bunches of hair.

356. *Geadas.*

geadas, -ais, -an, *s. m.* Pike fish (called *jack* when young, *pickerel* when larger, and *luce* when old.) 2 Tufty head.
geadas,* -ais, *s.m.* Coquetry.
geadasach, -aiche, *a.* Tufted. 2 Abounding in pikes. 3 Of, or belonging to pikes. 4*Coquettish, flirting.
geadasg, see geadas.
gead-cheann, -chinn, *s.m.* Tufty head.
—————ach, -aiche, *s.m.* Tufty-headed.

gèadh, -eóidh, *s.m. & f.* Goose. 2 Lump of the finest part of meal, made by children. 3 Tailor's goose (iron.) Ugh-na circe dol a shireadh ugh a' gheóidh, *the hen-egg going to seek the goose-egg*—said when poor people give small gifts to be doubly repaid.
geadh,* *v.a.* Propel a boat by means of a boat-hook or pole.
geadh,(DU) *s.m.* Iron rod about 6 ft. in length with end bent into an oval to serve as a handle, used for determining the presence of fir-trees in a peat-moss.
geadha, -n & -chan, *s.m.* Boat-hook, boat-pole, see bàta, Nos. 3 & 4, p. 76.
gèadhach, -aiche, *a.* Abounding in geese.
————, -aich *s.m.* Goose-quill.
geadhachail,* *s.pl.* Domestic jobs or messages.
geadhall,* *s.f.* Field, "park." 2 Ploughed field,
gèadh-amaill, *s.m.* Iron band round a swingle-tree.
gèadh bheag fhionn,‡‡ *s.m.* Barnacle (species of fungus.)
gèadh-bhlàr,¶ *s.m.* White-fronted goose—*anser albifrons.*

357. *Gèadh-bhlàr.*

gèadh-dubh, *s.m.* Solan goose.
gèadh-gaob,(AC) *s.m.* Rain-goose.
gèadh-glas,¶ *s. m.* Grey-legged goose or grey-leg—*anser ferus.*
gèadh-got,¶ *s.m.* Brent goose—*anser greuta.*
gèadh-lann, -lainn, -an, *s. m.* Inclosure for geese. 2 Goose-quill.
gèadh-taighe,(DMC) *s.m.* Tame goose, as distinct from a wild goose (gèadh fiadhaich.)
gead-iasg, see geadas.
†geadt, -an, *s.m.* Atom.
geag, see geug.
——ach, see geugach.
——an, *s.m.* Kind of ear-mark on sheep, see under comharradh-cluais.
geal, -a, -achan, see deal.
geal, gile, *a.* White. 2* Fond of. 3 Clear, bright, radiant, glistening. 4††Pure. Cha'n 'eil e g. da, *he is not fond of him ;* a làmh gh., *her white hand ;* là g. (*coll.* là brèagh) *a fine day ;* mo laoigh geal ! *an address of much affection among the Gael ;* mar charraig ghil, *like a white rock ;* eich gheala, *white horses ;* mo ghille geal, *my brave fellow ;* foghar g. grianach, *a fine sunny autumn ;* is g. an airidh air an aran sgalagan a' chliathaidh, *well worthy of their bread are the farm-servants of the harrow ;* is g. a choisinn e a dhuais, *how well he earned the reward he won ! ;* cha chuir thu an g. air an dubh dhomh-sa, *you shall not make me think that black is white.*
geal, gil, *s.m.* Anything white. 2 Mark to shoot at. 3*The white part of anything. 4(DU) Slice from the flank of another fish of the same species, used as bait. G. na sùla, *the white of the eye.*
geala, see gealadh.

geala-bigein, see gealag-bhuachair.
geala-bhreac, *s.m.* Salmon-trout.
geala-bhricein,(AF) *s.m.* Sea-trout.
gealach,-aich, *s.f.* The moon. [with art. *a' gh*—.] Sud agaibh a' ghealach ùr—Rìgh nan Dùl 'g a beannachadh ! *there is the new moon—the king of the elements bless it* ; said in the Hebrides, in Protestant as well as Catholic districts when one notices the new moon for the first time; gealach a' bhruic,*the badger's moon*, i. e. the October moon, during whose light the badger is said to dry grass for its nest ; [in *Suth'd* the October moon is known as "gealach bhuidhe buain a' choirc," *the yellow moon of the oat-harvest* ;] atharrachadh nan sìon ri g. a' bhruic, *change of weather with the badger's moon* ; g. air na sléibhtean, *the moon on the hills* ; mar a' ghealaich, *like the moon* ; triall na gealaich, *the moon's path* ; a' gh. ùr (an solus ùr), *the new moon* ; g. bhuidhe na Féill Mìcheil, *the yellow moon of Michaelmas;* g. fhionn na Féill Mìcheil, *the fair moon of Michaelmas* ; g. bhuidhe nam broc, *the yellow moon of the badgers*; g. bhuidhe an abachaidh, *the yellow (September) moon that helps to ripen the corn*—AH.
gealachadh, -aidh, *s.m.* Whitening, bleaching. 2 Act of whitening or bleaching. A' g—, *pr.pt.* of gealaich. Blàr gealachaidh, *a bleaching ground.*
gealachag, see gealag.
gealachail, -e, *a.* Lunar.
gealachair,** *s.m.* Bleacher.
gealachd,‡‡ *s.f.* Whiteness.
gealadair,‡‡ -ean, *s.m.* Bleacher.
gealadh, -aidh, *s.m.* Blight. 2**Act of whitening. 3**Whiteness. 4**see deal.
gealadhain, see gealdhain.
geal-adhairc,** *s.m.* Animal with a white horn. 2 Name given to a white-horned cow.
geal-adharcach, -iche, *a.* White-horned.
gealag, -aig, -an, *s.f.* Sea-trout. 2 White trout. 3 Salmon-trout. 4 Whiting. 5* Grilse. 6 (AF) White-throat (bird,) see gealan-coille. 7 White pike. 8(AF) Leech. 9(AF) Eel.
———ach, -aiche, *a.* Abounding in salmon, trout or grilse.
gealagair,(AF) *s.m.* Leech.
gealagan, -ain, -an, *s. m.* White of an egg. 2 White of the eye. 3 *n.pl.* of gealag. 4(AF) see gealag. G. an uighe, *the white of the egg;* g. na sùla, *the white of the eye.*
gealag-an-t-sneachd,*s.m.* Snow-bunting, see eun an-t-sneachd.
gealagan-uighe, *s.m.* The white of an egg.
gealag-bheinne,(AF) *s.f.* Ptarmigan

358. Gealag-bhuachair.

gealag-bhuachair, -aig-, -an-buachair, *s.f.* Bunting—¶*emberiza miliaria.*

359. Gealag-dhubh-cheannach.

gealag-dhubh-cheannach,¶ *s.f.* Black-headed or reed-bunting—*emberiza schœniclus.*
gealag-làir,§ *s.f.* Snowdrop—*galanthus nivalis.*

360. Gealag-làir.

gealag-lòin,¶ see gealag-dhubh-cheannach.
gealaich, *pr.pt.* a' gealachadh, *v.a. & n.* Whiten, bleach, make or become white, blanch.
———, *gen. sing.* of gealach.
———ear, *fut. pass.* of gealaich. Shall be bleached.
———te, *past pt.* of gealaich. Whitened, bleached. Anart g., *bleached linen.*
gealain, *gen. sing. & n. pl.* of gealan.
†**gealairgidh**, *s.f.* Prickle.
gealan, -ain, -an, *s.m.* White of an eye. 2 White of an egg. 3 **Sparrow. 4 Linnet, see gealan-lìn.

361. Gealan-coille.

gealan-coille,¶ *s.m.* White-throat—*curruca cinerea.*
gealan-lìn,¶ *s.m.* Common linnet—*linota cannabina.*

362. Gealan-lìn.

gealbhan, -ain, -an, *s.m.* Fire. 2 Little fire on the hearth. 3 Fire for drying corn. 4**Common fire, bón-fire.

363. Gealbhonn.

gealbhonn, -uinn, -an, *s. m.* House-sparrow—*passer domesticus.* 2 (AF) Linnet. 3 (AF) Swallow.
gealbhonn-cuilionn, *s.m.* Bullfinch.
gealbhonn-gàraidh, *s.m.* Hedge-sparrow.
gealbhonn-lìn, *s.m.* Linnet, lintwhite.

364. Gealbhonn-nam-preas.

gealbhonn-nam-preas,¶ *s.m.* Hedge-sparrow—*accentor modularis.*

365. Gealbhonn-nan-craobh.

gealbhonn-nan-craobh,¶ *s. m.* Tree-sparrow—*passer montanus.*
gealbhonn-sgiobuill,** *s.m.* Bunting.
gealbh-roc,(AF) *s.* Sea-swallow.
geal-bhroilleach, *a.* White-bosomed.
†gealc, see gealaich.
gealcadh, -aidh, *s.m.* Whiteness.
geal-chasach, -aiche, *a.* White-legged or -footed.
geal-chéireach, -eiche, *a.* White-buttocked, of deer.
geal-chlaidheamh, -eimh,** *s.m.* Bright sword.
gealdhain,(AH) *s.f.* Lull or intermission in a rain-storm.
gealdruidh,** *s.* Round-leaved sundew.
geal-ghlac, -aic,** *s.m.* Fair hand. A ribhinn nan g. ! *thou fair-handed maiden !*
geal-ghréine (an), *s.m.* Fingal's banner.
geal-gheugach (an), *s.m.* Fingal's banner. [Corrupt word occuring in ballads.]
geall, gill, *s.m.* Pledge. 2* Mortgage. 3 Bet, wager. 4 Prize, reward. 5 Desire, love. 6 Notch. Thoir dhomh g., *give me a pledge* ; cuir g., *lay a bet* ; mo gheall-sa nach faic thu e, *I pledge my word you will not see him ;* tha e an g. oirre, *he is excessively fond of her ;* is iomadh fear a tha 'n g. air drama, *many are they who like their dram ;* thiginn g' ad choimhead ged bhitheadh na tri gill 'san aon mhaide, *I would come to see you although there were three notches on the one stick*—referring to the old practice of listing engagements by means of notches made on sticks ; tha e an g. na 's fhiach e, *everything he has is at stake* ; *2 he is dying,* or *nearly dead ;* làmh an earball a' ghill, *holding the pledge by the tail*—NGP.
geall, *pr. pt.* a' gealltainn & a' gealladh, *v. a.* Promise, wager. 2 Pledge, vow. Geallaidh iad gealladh, *they shall vow a vow.*
-——achas,* -ais, *s.m.* Prospect, success.
-——adh, -aidh, -aidhnean, *s.m.* Promise, vow. 2 Mortgage. 3 Promising, vowing. 4 Betting. 5 Pledging. G. breige, *a false promise ;* g. gun a chomh-ghealladh, *a promise without its fulfilment ;* bheir mi mo gh. dhuit, *I promise you ;* tìr a' ghealladh, *the land of promise* A' g—, *pr.pt.* of geall.
gealladh-pòsaidh,* *s.m.* Betrothment.
geal-làmh, -làimh, *s.f.* Fair hand.
geall-barantais, gill-, *pl.* gill-bh-, *s.m.* Pledge. 2 Mortgage. 3 Bet.
geall-cheannaiche,‡‡ -an, *s.m.* Pawnbroker.
geall-chinn, see geall-cinnidh.
geall-cinnidh, *s.m.* Fine paid by one guilty of manslaughter to kinsmen of deceased. That of an earl was 66⅔ cows, of a thane or earl's son 44 cows, 20 pence and two-thirds of an obolus or bodle, of a thane's son 11 cows and 5¼ pence, and so on, according to the rank of deceased. For fines in cases of murder, see under eiric.

geall-daingneachaidh, gill-, *s. m.* Pledge, earnest, earnest-money.

geall-daingnich, *pr. pt.* a' geall-daingneachadh, *v.a.* Pledge, promise.

————, *s.* see geall-daingneachaidh.

geall-diolaidh,‡‡ *s.m.* Mortgage.

geall-fuiachan, *s.m.* Mortgage.

geall-meas, *s.m.* Compensation for anything carried away or destroyed. 2**Estimate.

geallmhor, -oire, *a.* Desirous, fond.

————achd, *s. f. ind.* Desire, fondness. 2 Aspiration. 3††Promising.

geallmhuin,** *s.f.* Promise, promising.

geall-réis,(WC) *s.m.* Racing competition, games.

geall-spréidh (*no* cruidh), (WC) *s.m.* Cattle-show.

geall-strith,(MS) *s.* Agonism.

————each,(MS) *s.m.* Agonistes.

geallta, *a. & past pt.* of geall. Promised, vowed, pledged. 2 Betted.

gealltainn, *s. m. ind.* Promising, act of promising, vowing, pledging. A' g—, *pr. pt.* of geall.

————each,** *a.* Promissory.

————te,** *past pt.* Affianced, affied.

gealltanach, -aich, *s.m.* One making promises.

————, -aiche, *a.* Promising. 2 Hopeful. 3 Auguring well, boding. 4(DMC) Desirous, fond. Tha mi glé g. air, *I am very fond of it.*

gealltanas, -ais, *s.m.* Promise, pledge.

geall-treabhaidh,(WC) *s.m.* Ploughing-match.

gealltuineas,** -eis, see gealltanas.

geal-sheileach,§ *s.m.* Sallow tree, see sùileag.

geal-shion, *s.f.* Hail.

geal-shùil, -shùla, -shùilean, *s. m.* White eye, moon eye.

————each, -eiche, *a.* White eyed, moon-eyed.

gealt, geilt, see geilt.

gealta, *past pt.* Whitened, bleached.

———ch, -aiche, *a.* Cowardly, timorous, fearful. 2**Skittish. 3‡‡Jealous. 4‡‡Astonished. Thill e g. gu dlùth, *he turned fearful and fast;* gu g., *timidly.*

———chd, *s.f.ind.* Cowardice, timorousness, timidity. 2** Skittishness. 3 (MS) Baseness. Eadar nàir' agus g., *between shame and timidness.*

gealtaich,‡‡ *v.a.* Intimidate.

————e, see gealtachd. 2 see gealtair.

————e, *comp.* of gealtach. More or most cowardly or timid.

gealtaiute, *past pt.* see gealltainnte.

gealtair, -ean, *s.m.* Coward, timid fellow. 'S tric a bha claidheamh fad' an làimh gealtair, *oft has a long sword been in a coward's hand.*

————each,** *a.* Cowardly, timorous.

————eachd, *s.f.* see gealtachd.

gealtan, *s.m.* Harlequin.

geal-tholl, -thuill, -an-tolla, see deal-each.

gealtran,** -ain, *s.m.* Coward, timid person.

geamach,** *a.* Blear-eyed.

geaman,**-ain, *s.m.* Servant, useful person.

————ach,** -aich, *s.m.* Servant, lacquey. 2 Stout young fellow.

geamann, *s.* Gammoning-iron, see I p. 73. 2 Knighthead, see K2, p. 73.

geamanta,(DMC) *a* Tricky, crafty.

†geamh,** -eimh, *s.f.* Branch. 2 Slip.

geamha,* *s.m.* Pledge, compensation. Cha bu g. leam, *it would be no compensation to me;* am bu gh. dhomhs' air an t-saoghail? *would the whole world be a compensation to me?*; cha bu gh. leam sin air fichead nòt, *I would not do that for twenty pounds.*

geamhal, geimhle, geimhlean & geamhlan, *s. m.* see geimheal.

geamhar,** -air, *s.m.* Blade of corn. 2 Corn in blade.

geamhd,* see geamhta.

————a, *s.* Thick, short block.

geamhlach,** *a.* Sandblind.

geamhladh, -aidh, see geimhleadh.

geamhlag, -aig, -an, see geimhleag.

geamhloch, see geamhlach.

geamhrach,* -aiche, *s.f.* Winter park.

————adh, -aidh, *s.m.* Wintering, feeding during winter, as sheep or cattle. 2** Winter quarters. 3 Feeding stuff for winter. A' g—, *pr.pt.* of geamhraich.

————ail, see geamhrail.

geamhradail, -e, *a.* see geamhrail.

geamhradh, -aidh, -aidhean, *s. m.* Winter. Roimh ghaoith a' gheamhraidh, *before the winds of winter;* bó gheamhraidh, (*or* mart geamhraidh), *a wintermart, heifer slain for winter food.*

geamhraich, *pr.pt.* a' geamhrachadh, *v.a. & n.* Winter, pass or spend the winter. 2 Winter, provide food for the winter.

————te, *past pt.* Wintered.

geamhrail, -e, *a.* Wintry. 2 Cold. 3 Stormy.

geamhrauta, -ainte, *a.* see geamhrail.

geamh-shùileach,** *a.* Pink-eyed.

†geamht, *s.m.* Boy—*Argyll.*

†geamhta, -n, -chan, *s.m.* Anything short and thick. 2††Thick-set person. 3††Junk.

†————ch, -aiche, *a.* Short and thick.

†————ir, -ean, *s.m.* Short thick person.

geamnachd, *s.f.* see geamnaidheachd.

geamnaidh, -e, *a.* Chaste. 2 Abstemious, sober. 3 Womanly, modest. 4 Continent.

————eachd, *s.f.ind.* Chastity. 2 Soberness. 3 Womanliness. 4 Modesty. 3 Continence.

geamnuidh, see geamnaidh.

————eachd, see geamnaidheachd.

gean, *v.a.* see gin.

gean, -a, *s.m.* Good humour, cheerfulness. 2 Mood or frame of mind. 3 Favour, love, fondness. 4 Approbation. 5 Pleasure. 6 Smile, 7 Greed. Cha bhi g. air Cloinn-Dòmhnuill gus am faigh iad an diota, *the MacDonalds are never happy till they get their dinner*—N.G.P. applies this saying to the Grants, MacKenzies, &c., in the case of the MacDonalds, however, the dinner they were supposed to long for was a taste of the Campbell blood; g. math, *good will;* làithean ar g., *the days of our pleasure;* droch gh., *bad humour.*

†gean,** -ein, *s.f.* Woman.

geanach, -aiche, *a.* Of a pleasant or cheerful humour. 2** Fond. Bitheamaid maranach, g., *let us be hospitable and good-humoured.*

————, -aich, *s.m. & a.* see gionachd and gionach.

————d,** *s.f.* Chastity. 2 Womanliness. 3 Continence.

geanaiche, *comp.* of geanach.

geanail, -e, *a.* Cheerful, pleasant. 2 Graceful, comely. 3 Womanly, modest. 4 Fond. 5 (DMC) In good humour. 6(MS) Humane, kind.

†Gèanair, *s.m.* Month of January

geanais,§ *s.* Wild cherry *or* gean tree,—*prunus avium.*

geanalachd, *s.f.ind.* Comeliness, gracefulness. 2 Pleasantness. 3 Womanliness. 4 Modesty. 5(MS) Acceptability. 6†† Cheerfulness, good humour.

geanalas,(MS) -ais, *s.m.* Acceptability.

geanalta,(MS) *a.* Acceptable.

†geanamh, -aimh, *s.m.* Sword.

geanas,** -ais, *s.m.* Chastity. 2 Pleasant humour.

————ach,** *a.* Chaste. 2 Continent. 3 In

a pleasant humour.
geanasachd,** *s.f.* Chasteness, purity. 2 Continence. 3 Womanliness.
geang,** *v.a.* †Strike, beat. 2(DMy) Kick, as a horse.
geang, -an, *s.m.* Kick, as of a horse.
geang, Gaelic spelling of *gang.*
geangach,†† -aich, *s.m.* Crooked dumpy person.
——, -aiche, *a.* Crooked. 2 Thick and short. 3 Apt to strike. 4 Apt to kick, as a horse.
——d, *s.f.* Comeliness, beauty. 2 Striking.
geanm, see geamnaidheachd.
gean-math, *s. m.* Goodwill, good pleasure. 2 Gratuity, donation, bounty. Mar gh., *as a matter of bounty;* cha'n 'eil do gh. ort, *you are not in good humour.*
geanm-chnò, -than, *s.f.* Chestnut. De chraoibh nan g., *of the chestnut tree.*
geanmhuinneach, *a.* Joyful, merry.
geanmnachd, see geamnaidheachd.
geanmnaidh, see geamnaidh.
——eachd, see geamnaidheachd.
geann, see geinn.
geannair, -ean, *s. m.* Hammer. 2 Mallet. 3 Kind of wedge.
——eachd, *s.f.ind.* Hammering. 2 Sharpening.
geanta, *a.* see geamnaidh.
——chd,* *s.f.* Abstinence. 2 Modesty. 3 Self-command, continence. G. na faoilinn, *the abstinence of the sea-mew*—which eats a full-grown fish at a gulp, and makes three portions of a sprat.
gear, see geur.
gear, see geàrr.
gearain, *gen. sing.* of gearan.
gearain, *pr.pt.* a' gearan, *v.n.* Complain, murmur, grumble, moan. 2 Accuse, complain against, appeal. 3 Remonstrate.
gearait, *s.f.* Virgin. 2 Saint. 3 Warrior.
†gearait, *a.* Holy. 2 Prudent.
gearan,‖ *s. m.* Dog-lichen, see lus-ghoinnich. [** gives Dog's-ear.]
gearan, -ain, -an, *s.m.* Complaint, murmur, discontent, murmuring. 2 Supplication, remonstrance. 3 Appeal. 4 Sigh, groan, moan. 5 Accusation. 6**Cry. Dean do g. ris, *apply to him for redress;* cha ruig thu leas a bhi 'g., *you need not complain;* fulaing dhomh mo gh. a dheanamh riut-sa, *permit me to appeal to you;* cha'n 'eil stàth dhuit a bhi 'g. ris, *it serves no end to appeal to him;* rinn iad g., *they murmured;* ri g., *complaining;* bha e 'g. feadh na h-oidhche, *he was moaning during the night.* A' g—, *pr.pt.* of gearain.
gearanach, -aiche, *a.* Complaining, plaintive, discontented, apt to complain, querulous. 2 Sighing, groaning. 3**Sad. 4**Ailing. 5** Accusative. Sgeul mu na daoine g., *news about the men who are apt to complain.*
——d,‡‡ *s.f.ind.* Dolefulness.
gearanaich, *pr.pt.* a' gearanaich, *v.n.* see gearain. 2** Condole.
——e, *s.m.* Accuser. 2 Bemoaner, murmurer.
gearasdan,‡ -ain, -an, *s.m.* Garrison. G. Inbhirlòchaidh, *Fort William fort* (lit. *the garrison of Inverlochy)*; is mis' am bodach liath a bha riamh anns a' gh., *I am the gray-headed old carle who has ever held the fort*—a phrase in a boys' game, now applied to a person who has been long in a responsible position.
†gearb, *s.* Scab, scar. 2 Mange, itch. 3 Tumour. 4 Bran.
†——, *v.a. & n.* Grieve. 2 Hurt, wound.
gearbach,** *a.* Scabbed. 2 Mangy, itchy. 3 Rugged.
gearbag,** -aig, *s.f.* Scab.
gearbh,** *s.* Scab.
gearbhul,¶ -uil, *s.m.* see gearra-bhall.
gearrach,** -aiche, *s. m.* Nestling, unfledged bird.
gearcaig,** *s.f.* Brood.
gearcan,** *s m.* Nestling.
†gear-chuis, *s.f.* see geur-chuis.
†gear-chuiseach, -eiche, *a.* see geur-chuiseach.
geard,** *s.m.* Gaelic spelling of *guard.* Bi air do gh., *be on your guard;* geardan an righ, *the king's guards.* [Anglo-Gaelic from Armstrong.]
gearg,** -eirg, *s.f.* Botch. 2 Boil. 3 Suppuration.
geargach,** *a.* Like a botch or boil. 2 In a state of suppuration.
gear-leanmhuinn, see geur-leanmhuinn.
geàrr, *pr. pt.* a' geàrradh, *v. a.* Cut. 2 Bite, gnaw. 3 Taunt, satirize. 4* Describe, as a circle. 5**Engrave. 6 Shear, as grass. 7 (DU) Emasculate an animal, geld.
g. as, *cut off,* g. a bhàn, *cut down,*
g. goirid, *cut short,* g. sìos, *cut down,*
g. sùrdag, *frisk, trip;* a' geàrradh shùrdag, *frisking;* g. tarsuing an achaidh, *take a short cut across the field.*
geàrr, -a, -an, *s.f.* Hare, *prov.* 2 Weir for catching fish.
geàrr, *1st. comp.* giorra, *2nd. comp.* giorraid, *3rd. comp.* giorrad, *a.* Short, not long. 2 Of short continuance, transient. 3 Laconic. 4 Deficient. 5 Not reaching the intended part. 6 (AC) Thick-set, squat, strong. G. gu 'n robh 'aois, *short be his life;* is g. a dheàrrsadh, *transient is his shining;* thàinig iad g. air, *they came short of it;* cainnt g. tharbhach, *laconic and pithy language;* is gh. gus am bi am minnean na 's miosa na 'n t-seana bhoc, *the kid will soon be worse than the old buck;* an uine gh., *in a short time;* cù g., *a short-tailed dog;* is g. gu bàs fear de a mhuinntir, *someone of his people will soon be dead.*
geàrr,* *s.m.* Abridgement. 2 (AC) Grilse. G. a' ghnothaich, *an abridged statement of the affair;* an còrr 's an g., *the odds and ends—the two extremes.*
gearra-bhall,(AC) *s.m.* Gair-fowl, great auk—*alca impennis.*

366. Gearra-bhall.

gearra-bhoc,(CR) *s. m.* Sea-urchin—*Lochbroom.*
geàrra-bhodach, *s.m.* see geàrr-bhodach.
geàrra-bhonn,* see geàrr-bhonn.

gearradaireachd, *s. f.* Keen, cutting talk, satire. 2 Satirical poems. Anns a' ghearradaireachd gheur, *using cutting expressions—Rob Donn.*
gearra-breac, (AC) *s. m.* Lesser black-headed guillemot.
geàrrach, -aich, -aichean, *s.f.* ¶see turtur. 2 Flux, diarrhœa. 2 Dysentery. 3 Gripe. [With the article *a' gh—.*] Geàrrach-fola, *hæmorrhage.*
gearrach,(CR) *s.m.* Harrow-rope, short trace attaching a harrow to the swingle-tree—*W. of Ross.*
gearra-chasach,** *a.* Duck-legged.
gearra-chlamhan, see clamhan-geàrr.
geàrra-chomharradh,** *s.m.* Apostrophe.
gearra-chòt', see còta-geàrr.
gearr-a'-chuain,(AC) *s.m.* Grilse.
gearra-chuibh,* *s.f.* Muzzle-bar for two horses.
gearradair, -ean, *s.m.* Cutter, hewer. 2 Carver, one who carves. 3 Satirist. 4**Engraver. 5 Lapidary. 6* Cutler. Gearradairean-chlach, *stone-hewers, lapidaries.*
————eachd, *s.f.ind.* Cutting, act of cutting. 2 Satire. 3 Business of a lapidary.
gearradan,** -ain, *s.m.* Register. 2 Note-book.
gearradh, -aidh, -aidhean, *s. m.* Cut, cutting, act of cutting. 2 Satirizing. 3**Biting,gnawing. 4**Hewing, slicing. 5** Mowing. 6** Carving, engraving. 7**Taunt. 8** Tear, rent. 9** Toll, tribute, tax. 10 Cutting in pipe-music. 11 Ear-mark on sheep, see under comharradh-cluaise. 12*Bowel-complaint, flux. 13 (DMC) Morsel, small bit of anything. 14 (DMC) Cutting of seaweed. 15 (DMC) Sarcasm. Nach ioc iad g.? *will they not pay toll?* air a bheul bha gearraidhean, *on its mouth were gravings;* cha'n fhaigh thu g. dheth, *you won't get a bit of it;* an àm a' ghearraidh, *at the time of cutting the seaweed.* A' g—, *pr.pt.* of geàrr.
————, -aidh,-aidhean, *s.m.* Summer grazing-place for cattle—*Lewis.* [Gearraidh is also used as the *nom.*]
gearradh-arm, -airm, *s.m.* Armorial bearings.
gearradh-breac, -bric, *pl.* -aidhean-breaca, *s.m.* Ringed guillemot—*uria lacrymaus.* 2 (AF) Redshank. 3 Guillemot, see eun-dubh-an-sgadain.

367. Gearradh-breac.

gearradh-cainnte,(DMC) *s.m.* Loquacity. 'S ann ort tha 'n g., *how loquacious you are*—you have too much to say.
gearradh-choileir,-ean,*s.m.* Cut-throat,assassin.
gearradh-cròcan, *s. m.* Ear-mark on sheep, see under comharradh-cluaise.
gearrach-dialtaig,(DU) *s.m.* Cut at the base of the toes.
gearradh-dubh-nan-allt,(AF) *s.m.* Water rail.
gearradh-feòirnein,‖ *s.m.* Grass-cut.
gearradh-ghobaich,(MMcL) *s.f.* Sharp wit.
gearradh-glas,(AF) *s.m.* Black guillemot.
gearradh-gort, -aidh-ghort, *pl.* -aidhean-gorta & -aidh-goirt, *s. m.* Quail—*coturnix vulgaris.* Thàinig na gearradh-goirt, *the quails came.*
gearradh-uchd, *s.m.* Dewlap.
geàrrag, -aig, -an, *s.f.* Wafer. 2 Young hare, leveret. 3**Thin scone. 4** Fortune, fate, destiny. Geàrragan neo-ghortaichte, *unleavened wafers.*
gearragach,†† *a.* Abounding in young hares.
gearragan,** -ain, *s.m.* Wafer.
gearra-gort, see gearradh-gort.
gearraich, *v.a.* see giorraich.
gearraidh,* see geàrr. 2 Mole. 3 Rat.
gearraidh,(DC) *s. m.* Point or knuckle-end of land, often used in place-names in *Uist,* as Hougharry, Tigharry, gearraidh dubh, &c. 2 Green pasture-land about a township. 3 The land between the *machair* and *monadh,* the strip where the houses stand—*Lewis.* 4 Fenced field. 5 (CR) Enclosed grazing between the arable land and the open moor. 6(DMC) Common grazing and arable land between the moor and the crofts. 7 (PJM) Place where the sheilings are built.
————ean, *n.pl.* of gearradh. Air na h-uile làmhan bithidh gearraidhean, *on all hands there shall be cuttings.*
gearraiseach, -eich, *s.m.* The chain or rope from the swingle-tree to the horses. 2(CR) Hare—*Suth'd.* 3 Swingle-chain, the chain between the swingle-tree and the plough or harrows.
gearra-mhuc, *s.f.* Guinea-pig.
gearran, -ain, *s. m.* Gelding, horse, hack, "garron." 2 Tit.
Gearran, -ain, -an, *s.m.* Period as to the duration of which authorities vary considerably. ‡‡, ††, McL & D, and * all say it is from 15 Mar. to 11 Apl. inclusive. (OS.) Dr. Norman MacLeod, in *Teachdaire Ùr Gàidhealach,* applies it to the Month of February. 2 The nine days after "faoileach." Mios faoilich, naoidh là Gearrain—*Old saying.* 3 (TS) Last half of February. [Preceded by the art. *an.*]
gearranach, -aiche, *a.* Horse-like, of or relating to, geldings. 2 Clownish.
geàrr-anail,** -analach, *s. f.* Asthma, broken wind.
geàrr-analach, *a.* Asthmatic, broken-winded. Each g., *a broken-winded horse.*
gearran-àrd, *s.m.* Hobby (bird), see obag.
gearran-olach,(AF) *s.m.* Foal.
gearrar, *fut. pass.* of gearr. Shall be cut.
gearrastain, *Duanaire, 48,* is for gearasdan.
geàrr-bhall, see gearra-bhall.
geàrr-bhliadhnach,** *s.m.* One-year-old animal.
geàrr-bhochdan,§ *s.m.* Sea-gillyflower, see fear-saideag.
geàrr-bhodach,* -aich, *s.m.* Young middle-sized cod.
geàrr-bhonn, -uinn, -uinnean, *s. m.* The half sole of a shoe.
geàrr-bhòrd, *s.m.* Keel-board of a boat,(G8,p.73.)
geàrr-bhriathrach,‡‡ -aiche, *a.* Sententious.
geàrr-bhrìgheach, *a.* Compendious.
gearrcach,(AF) *s.m.* Turtle-dove, see turtur.
geàrr-chasach, *a.* Short-legged. 2 Short-footed.
geàrr-chlamhan, see clamhan.
gearr-choileir,** *s.m.* Assailant.
geàrr-chòt', see còta-gearr.
geàrr-chù,(AF) *s.m.* Wolf.
geàrr-chuisle,** *s.f.* Venesection, phlebotomy.
geàrr-daol, see cèard-dubhan.
————ag, see cèard-dubhan.
————an, see cèard-dubhan.
geàrr-dhearc, *s.f.* Cranberry. 2 Barberry, see lus-nan-dearc. 3**Bilberry.
————ag, *s.f.* Barberry.
geàrr-dhuan, *s.m.* Epigram.
geàrr-dubhan, see cèard-dubhan.
geàrr-earbull, -uill, *s.m.* Bobtail.
geàrr-earblach, -aiche,*a.* Short-tailed,bobtailed,

docked.
gearr-fhacail,(AH) *s.pl.* **Raillery, chaff, badinage, banter, ready wit. [Distinct from geur-fhacail.]**
gearr-fhaclach, *a.* **Witty, nimble-witted, quizzical, scurrilous.**
geàrr-fhiadh, -fhéidh, *s.*. **Hare. Mar gh. air mullach sléibhe,** *like a hare on the mountain tops.*
geàrr-fhionn, *s.m.* **Short hair, as of quadrupeds.**
————ach, *a.* **Short-haired, as cattle.**
geàrr-fhoirm,** *s.* **Compendium, abridgement, abstract, brief.**
geàrr-ghath, -a, -an, *s.m.* **Short spear, javelin.**
————ach, -aiche, *a.* **Having a short spear.**
geàrr-gheal,(AF) *s.* **Mountain hare.**
geàrr-ghlas, see gearradh-glas.
geàrr-ghobach, *s.m.* **Sharp witted person, wit, banterer. Geàrra-ghobaich Mhucàrna,** *the sharp witted people of Muckairn.*
†geàrr-ghuin, *s.* **Horse-leech.**
geàrr-ghunna, *pl.* -chan, *s.f.* **Short gun, carbine.**
geàrr-luch, see gàr-luch.
geàrr-mhagach,** *a.* **Satirical, sarcastic, ironical. Té ghobach, gh.,** *a gabbling, sarcastic woman.*
geàrr-mhagadh,** -aidh, *s.m.* **Satire, sarcasm, irony, bitter jest.**
geàrr-mhàsach, -aiche, *a.* **Short-bottomed.**
geàrr-mhàrnach, -aiche, *a.* **Short-flanked.**
geàrr-mhìneachadh, -aidh, *s.m.* **Short explanation.**
geàrr-miola-dearg,(AF) *s.m.* **Pig.**
geàrr-osan, -ain, *s.m.* **Sock.**
geàrr-phoc,** *s.m.* **Satchel.**
geàrr-sgian, -sgìne & -sgèine, *pl.* -an & sgeanan, *s.f.* **Dirk. 2**Stiletto.**
geàrr-sgrìobhadh,** *s.m.* **Shorthand.**
geàrr-shaoghal, -ail, *s.m.* **Short life.**
————ach, -aiche, *a.* **Short-lived, of a few days.**
————achd, *s.f.* **Short-livedness.**
geàrr-sheabhag,¶ *s.f.* **Ger falcon, see seabhag-mhór-na-seilge.**
geàrr-sheallach, -aiche, *a.* **Short-sighted.**
geàrr-shealladh,‡‡ -aidh, *s.m.* **Short-sightedness.**
geàrr-shùileach, -aiche, *a.* **Short-sighted.**
geàrr-smachd, *s.f.* **Severity. 2 Wrath. 3 Over-bearance.**
geàrr-sporan, -ain, *s.m.* **Cut-purse.**
geàrr-suim, -e, *s.f.* **Entrance-money. 2 Difference in money.**
geàrrta, *past pt.* of geàrr. **Cut. 2**Shorn. 3 **Mown. 4**Graven. 5**Carved. 6**Sliced. 7(DU) Satirical, sharp-witted. G. air na clàraibh,** *graven on the tables;* **feur g.,** *mown grass;* **g. fuar,** *piercingly cold.*
geàrrtach, -aiche, *a.* **Incisive.**
gearrthach, see gearrach.
gearsum, -uim,* *s. m.* see geàrr-suim.
†geart, *s.m.* **Milk.**
geartach,* *s.f.* **Trip, excursion, short time. G. do 'n Ghalltachd,** *a trip to the low country.*
geas, -eis & -a, *pl.* -an, *s. f.* **Charm. 2 Sorcery, enchantment. 3 Oath, vow. 4 Metamorphosis. 5 Religious vow. 6**Guess, conjecture. Nighean rìgh fo gheasaibh,** *a princess metamorphosed ;* **chaidh e fo gheasaibh,** *he was metamorphosed ;* **tha mi a' cur mar gheasaibh ort,** *I solemnly charge you ;* **shaoil leis gu'm bu leis an cuan fo 'gheasaibh,** *he thought the ocean his own under his spells*—**applied to persons with an overweening or insane idea of their own importance—NGP.**
geas, *v.* Gaelic spelling of *guess.*
geasach,** *a.* **Enchanting, charming. 2 Guessing, conjecturing. 3 Like a charm or enchantment.**
geasachail,‡‡ -e, *a.* **Incantatory.**
geasachd,** *s.f.* **Enchantment, charm, conjuration. 2 Vow. 3(MS) Astrology. 4 Superstition. C' àit' an robh an fhàinne g.?** *where was the enchanted ring ?*
†geasadach, *s.m.* **Peacock**—*Dean of Lismore.*
geasadair, -ean, *s.m.* **Wizard, charmer, conjurer, sorcerer.**
————eachd, *s.f.* **Enchantment, sorcery.**
geasadan,** -ain, *s.m.* **Shrub. 2**Arrow. 3** Lance.**
geasa-dioma, *s.m.* **Kind of Druidic sorcery. (?)**
geasag, see giseag.
————ach, see giseagach.
geasalanachd,(DMC) *s.f.* **Superstition.**
geasan, *n.pl.* of geas.
————,** -ain, *s.m.* **Oath. 2 Charm. 3 Sorcery. 4(AF) Saith. Nathraichean air nach luidh g.** *serpents that cannot be charmed.*
geasdag, ** *s.f.* **Pike. G. òg,** *a jack.*
geasrag, -aig, see giseag.
————ach, *a.* see giseagach.
————achd, see giseagachd.
†geast, -eist, *s.m.* **Gaelic spelling of** *yeast.*
†————al,** -ail, *s.m.* **Deed. 2 Fact. 3 Want, necessity.**
geat,(AF) *s.* **Curds.**
geat, *s.m.* see gead.
geata, *pl.* -n & -chan, *s.m.* **Gate. 2 Sort of play 3*Stick. Dhùin iad an geata,** *they shut the gate.*
geatach,‡‡ -aiche, *a.* **Gated.**
geatachan, *n.pl.* of geata.
geatadh, -aidh, *s.m.* see geata. **Geataidh an ionracais,** *the gates of righteousness.*
geatair,** *s.m.* **Small cake.**
geatha, *s.m.* see geadha.
geathadaich,†† *s.f.* **Hopping, jogging.**
geatrach,** *a.* **Fearful, timid.**
ge b'e,†† *conj. (for* ce b'e) **Whoever, whatever.**
ged, *conj.* **Though, although. 2**But. Ged a chrochar mi,** *though I were hanged;* **ged tha,** *though it be, notwithstanding.* **[Does not aspirate adjectives, but aspirates all initial consonants of verbs, except** *bu—ged* **being ge+do, it is** *do* **that aspirates.]**
†geibheal, -il, *s.m,* see geall & geimheal. **2 (M McD) Gable of a house. 3 Side rope of a herring-net.**
geibhionn, see geimhlean. **2**Great distress.**
geibhis,** *s.f.* **Valley.**
geibhleach, *a.* see geimhleach.
————adh, -aidh, see geimhleachd.
geibhlean, see geimhlean.
geibhlich, see geimhlich.
†geibleid,** -ean, *s.f.* **Sloven, slattern, drabbish female. 2 (DMC) Disabled female.**
†————each,** *a.* **Slovenly, drabbish. Gu g.,** *drabbishly.*
————each,(DMC) *s.m.* **Disabled man.**
†————eachd,** *s.f.* **Slovenliness, drabbishness.**
†geideal,** -eil, *s.m.* **Fan.**
†geidhne, *s.f.* **Violence.**
geigean, *Uist* for ceigean.
geil,(AC) *s.* **Fountain, well, spring.**
geilb, -ean, *s.f.* see gilb.
geilbhean, *s.m.* **Fawner**—*Badenoch.*
géile, *gen.sing.* of giall.
geilios,***s.m.* **Traffic, commerce, intercourse.**
géill, *pr.pt.* a' géilleachdainn, a' géilleadh, & a' géilltinn, *v.n.* **Yield, submit, cede. 2 Serve, obey, do homage. 3**Fail. 4(DMC) Break gradually under strain or pressure. Dorcha, doirionnta, dubh, a' chiad trì làithean de 'n Gheamhradh, ge b'e bheir géill do 'n spréidh, cha tugainn fhéin gu Samhradh,** *dark, sullen, and black, the first three days of winter, who-*

ever depends on the cattle, I would not till summer—I would not rely much upon the cattle succeeding, although it was considered a good sign to have the winter beginning with dark weather; tha mi a' géilleachdainn da sin, *I admit that*; dha 'n g. mór ghaillionn, *to whom yields the great tempest*; a' géilleachdainn d' a reachd, *yielding assent to his law.*

géill, -e, *s.f.* Yielding, submission, obedience. 2 Homage. 3 see ciall. 4 **The thing yielded or given up. 5 Admission. Na toir g. d' a leithid sin, *yield to no such thing; 2 do not believe it; 3 do not rely on it*; na toir g. dha, *do not believe him*; bheir e leis ar géill, *he will take away our captives.*

†**geille**, *s.pl.* see geimhle.

géilleachdainn, *s.f. & pr. pt.* of geill. Yielding, obeying, serving. A' g. d' a reachd, *yielding to*, or *admitting the uprightness of his law*; cò a bhios a' g. dha-san? *who will pay any heed to him?*

géilleadh, -idh, *s.m. & pr. pt.* of géill, see géilltinn. Ciùinichidh g., *yielding pacifies.*

géillidh, *fut.aff.a.* of géill.

géilligean, *s. pl.* Fat, flabby jaws, *prov.* 2(DMC) Tufts of feathers on the lower part of a fowl's head.

géillios,** *s.f.* Kindness, friendship. 2 Submission.

géilltinn, *s.f.* Yielding, obeying, serving. A' g—, *pr.pt.* of géill.

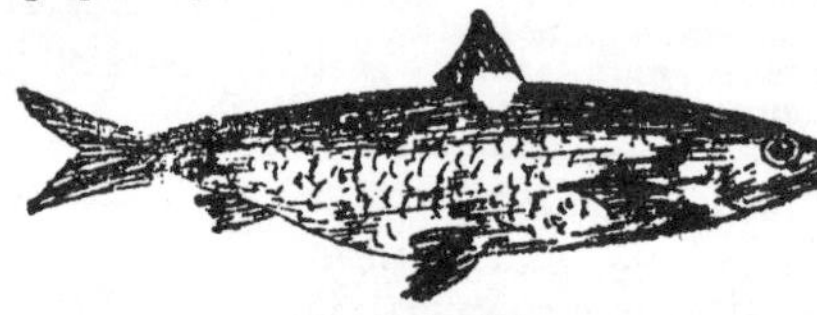

368. Geilmhin.

geilmhin,** *s.* Pilchard.

geilt, -e, *s.f.* Terror, fear, dread. 2**Cowardice. 3**Skittishness. 4 Timidity. Criothnaich le g., *shake with fear;* na biodh g. orm, *let me not be afraid.*

geilt, *s.m. & f.* (AF) Untamable animal. 2** Wild man or woman. 3 One who dwells in woods or deserts. 4 Bird—*Dean of Lismore.*

—, *a.* Mad.

— -chrith, *s.f.* Quaking with fear, extreme terror.

—each,†† *a.* Fearful, in terror. 2 Timid.

— -ghlacte, *a.* Afraid.

—ich, *v.a. & n.* Terrify, intimidate.

— -uisge, *s.f.* Hydrophobia.

geiltrich,(MS) *v.a.* Deaurate.

geiltrigeadh, *s.m.* Enamel.

geiltrig,(MS) *pr.pt.* a' geiltrigeadh, *v.a* Enamel.

geiltrigich,(MS) *v.a.* Enamel.

géim, *v. & s.* see geum.

geimeartach, *a.* Swift.

geimh, -e, *s.f.* see giomh.

——eal, -eil, -mhlean, *s.m.* Fetter, chain. 2 Custody.

geimhean,** -ein, *s.m.* Restraint, bondage.

geimhle, see geimheal.

geimhleach,** *a.* Fettering, like a fetter. 2 Oppressive. 3 Enslaving.

————, -lich, *s.m.* Slave, captive.

gèimhleach,(AH) *s.m.* Man who eats or otherwise helps himself to excess.

geimhleachd,** *s.f.* Bondage, slavery. 2 Chain, fetter. Ann an g., *in bondage, in chains.*

geimhleadh, -eidh, *s.m.* Chaining, binding with chains. A' g—, *pr.pt.* of geimhlich.

géimhleag,‡ -eig, -an, *s.f.* Crowbar, lever. 2(CR) Iron lever—*W. of Ross.*

géimhleagach,** *a.* Like a lever.

geimhlean, *n. pl.* of geimheal. 2 Custody. Le geimhlibh umha, *with fetters of brass.*

geimhlich, *pr.pt.* a' geimhleachadh, *v.a.* Chain, bind with chains. 2**Fetter. 3**Enslave. 4 **Mortgage.

————te, *past pt.* of geimhlich. Chained, bound with chains. 2 Fettered.

geimhneachd, see geamnaidheachd.

geimnich, see geumnaich.

geimnidh, see geamnaidh.

————eachd, see geamnaidheachd.

†**gein**, *s.m.* Sword.

gein, *v.a.* see gin.

geine,(AF) *s.* Swan.

geinealaich, *v.a.* see ginealaich.

geineamhuinn, see gineamhuinn.

geinearalt,** *s.m.* Gaelic spelling of *general.*

geineil, *a.* see gineil.

geingeach, see geinneach.

geinide,(AC) *comp.* of geamnaidh. More chaste.

geinn, -e, -ean, *s.m.* Wedge. 2 Wooden wedge for fastening cow-fetter. 3 Large or thick piece of anything, chunk. 4* Anything firm. Is e geinn dheth fhéin a sgoltas an darach, *it requires a wedge made of oak to split oak.*

geinn, *pr. pt.* a' geinneadh, *v.a.* Wedge, tighten by means of wedges. 2 Press, squeeze.

——each, -eiche, *a.* Abounding in, or supplied with wedges. 2 Wedged. 3**Cuneiform. 4** Pinned. 5 Firm, stout, strong, compact.

——eadh, -idh, *s.m.* Wedging. 2 Pressing, squeezing. A' g—, *pr.pt.* of geinn.

——eag, -eig, -ean, *s.f.* Stout little woman. 2**Little wedge. 3 Bud, germ. 4 Button, as of a coat.

——eagach,** *a.* Short, squat. 2 Full of little wedges.

——eal,** -il, *s.m.* Cuneiform phalanx, order of battle in the form of a wedge.

——ealachd,** *s.f.* Stoutness, firmness, compactness.

——eanta, *s.* Dumpy, firm, stout.

——ear,** -eir, see geannair.

——earachd, *s.f.* see geannaireachd.

——eil, -e, *a.* see geinneach.

——ich,‡‡ *v.a.* Plug.

——te, *past pt.* of geinn. Wedged, tightened by means of wedges.

geinnte, *s.m.* *Uist* for geinn.

geintear, -eir, *s.m.* Planter, sower.

geintileach, -ich, *s.m.* Gentile, pagan, heathen.

————, *a.* Gentile, pagan, heathen.

————d, *s.f.* Paganism, heathenism, idolatry.

geintileas, -eis, see geintileachd.

geintleach, -ich, see geintileach.

geintleachas, -ais, see geintileachd.

geir, *v.a.* Grease, besmear or anoint with grease.

geir, -e, *s.f.* Tallow, grease. 2 Suet. G. cartach, *cart grease.* Is coma leam comunn gille na geire, ge math a thoiseach, bu ro olc a dheireadh, *I like not the tallow lad's company, however good at first, very bad at last*—N.G.P. says " a Lewis and Long Island saying of which no explanation has been given. "

géire, *s.f.ind.* Sharpness, subtlety. 2 Intellectuality, acuteness, discernment. 3 Sourness, bitterness. 4 Gaelic spelling of *gear*, appliances. 5 Sharpness of edge. 6 Witticism.

géire, *comp.* of geur. Sharper, sharpest. 2 Sourer, sourest. Triath a's g. cruaidh, *chief of the sharpest sword.*

geireach, -aiche, *a.* Abounding in tallow, greasy. 2 Full of suet or fat.

géiread, -id, *s m.* Sharpness. Is g. e sin, *it is the sharper for that.*

géireanachd, *s.f.* Satirical turn, bickering sort of wit.
géireas, see géire.
géir-inntleachd,** *s. f.* see geur-innleachd.
geir-mhuc, *s.f.* Lard.
geirnean, -ein, *s.m.* Gin, trap, snare.
——ach, *a.* Full of traps or gins. 2 Like a trap or gin.
geirse, *s.f.* Madness—*Suth'd.*
——ach, -ich, *s.f.* Young girl.
——ag, -eig, *s.f.* Young girl.
géis, *s.f.* Spear, javelin. 2 Fishing spear. 3 (AC) Milk, milk produce. 4 Gestation.
geis,** *s.f.* Custom. 2 Swan. 3 Prohibition. 3 see geas.
†**geiseadh**,** -idh, *s.m.* see geas. 2 Imposing tribute.
géisg, -e, -ean, see giosg.
——, *v.n.* see giosg.
——each, *a.* see giosgach.
——eadh, -idh, } see giosgadh.
——eil, }
†**geisneach**,** *a.* Enchanted, like a charm. 2 Enchanting. 3 Conjuring.
gemeac, *s.* Distortion of the features—*Suth'd.* 2(DMK) Black eye.
†**gen**, *s.m.* Sword. 2 Hurt, wound (guin.)
geò, see geodha.
geòb, -a, -an, *s.m.* Wry mouth. 2* Little mouth. 3*Gaping mouth. 4 Creek.
geòb, *pr.pt.* a' geòbadh [& a' geòbail], *v.n.* Make wry mouths. 2 Gape with the mouth, as fish when losing the vital spark.
——ach, -aiche, *a.* Wry-mouthed.
——adh, -aidh, *s.m.* Making a wry mouth. A' g—, *pr.pt.* of geòb.
geòbail,* *s.m.* Gape. A' g—, *pr.pt.* of geòb.
geòbraich,‡‡ *s.f.* Idle talk.
geoc, -a, -an, *s.m.* Wry neck.
geòc,* *s.f.* see geòcaireachd.
geocach, -aiche, *a.* Wry-necked.
geòcach, -aiche, *a.* Gluttonous, ravenous, voracious. 2**Parasitical. 3**Strolling. 4 *Blair Athole* for geabhagach.
——, -aich, *s.m.* see geòcair.
——d, see geòcaireachd.
geòcaich,** *v.n.* Gormandize. 2 Devour. 3 Stroll.
——e, *s.f.ind.* Insatiableness.
geòcail,* *a.* see geòcach.
geòcair, -ean, *s.m.* Glutton. 2 Spendthrift. 3 **Parasite. 4 Vagabond. 5 Rebeller. 6 Debauchee.

369. Geocair.

geocair,¶ -ean, *s.m.* Wry-neck—*yunx torquilla.*
geòcaireach, -eiche, *a.* Intemperate, gluttonous.
——d, *s.f.ind.* Gluttony, debauchery. 2 Depravity. 3 Revelry.
geochail, *pr. pt.* Snivelling.
geochdach, see geòcach.
geodal,(DMy) *s. m.* Flattery. Tha mi eòlach air do gh., *I am acquainted with your flattery.*
geòdh, see geòdha.
——a, -n, -chan, *s.m.* Creek or cove formed by surrounding rocks. 2**Bay. Thug iad an aire do gh., *they observed a creek.*
—— ach, -aiche, *a.* Abounding in creeks or hollow rocks, gulfy.
geodh-lann, see gèadh-lann.
geoic, see geoc.
geòic, see geòc. 2 *Blair Athole* for geabhag.
——each, see geòcach.
geóidh, *gen.sing. & n.pl.* of geadh.
geòileam,* see goileam.
——aiche,* see geòlamaiche.
geòin,** *s.f.* Fool, foolish person. 2 Confused noise. 3 Derision. 4 Assurance, proof.
geòire, *comp.* of geur. Sharper, sharpest.
——ad, *3rd. comp.* of geur. Degree of bitterness or sharpness.
geoirean,(DU) *s.m.* Common sorrel—*rumex acetosa & rumex acetosella.*
geòirid, *2nd. comp.* of geur.
geòis, *s.f.* Flat belly.
geòla, -chan, *s.f.* Yawl, see p. 78. 2 Ship's boat. 3 Small barge. G. chaol, *a river-cutter.*
geòlach, *a.* Pertaining to a yawl or ship's boat.
——, -aich, *s.m.* Wooden frame on which a coffin is borne at funerals, bier, *prov.* 2 Bandage put round the shoulders and arms of the dead in former times, shoulder-belt. G. ort ! *a form of imprecation* (*lit.* the death-belt on thee !)
geòladh, see geòla.
geòlag, -aig, -an, *s.f.dim.* of geòla. Little boat or yawl.
geòlam,* -aim, see goileam.
——aiche, see goileamaiche.
geolan, -ain, -an, *s.m.* Fan.
geol-mhac,** *s.m.* Jowl.
geon,* *s.m.* Avidity, keenness.
†**geon**, -oin, *s.m.* Oath. 2 Security. 3 Proof.
geonaidh, see gonaidh.
geonail,* *a.* Keen with avidity.
geòp,(DU) *s.m.* Fast talk, generally unintelligible.
geòpraich, *s.f.* Torrent of idle talk.
georas, -ais, *s.m.* Sorbus (plant.)
geòsach, -aich, *s.m.* see ceòsach.
geòsadan, -ain, -an, *s. m.* see gaoisnean. 2** Shaft. 3**Arrow. 4 Stalk.
†**geòsan**, -ain, *s.m.* Belly. 2 Glutton.
geòsgail,* *s.f.* Blustering talk.
geostan,(CR) *s.m.* Ragwort—*Arran.*
geòta, *s.* Stagnant water and mud—*Islay.*
geòtair,(WC) *Poolewe* for geòta.
geòtan, -ain, -an, *s.f.* Spot of arable ground. 2 *Driblet. 3 Trifling sum or debt. 4 Item. 5 Small quantity. 6 Pendicle. A' cruinneachadh gh., *collecting trifling debts.*
geòtar,(DU) *s.m.* Gutters (mud and water)—*Gairloch, &c.*
geòtha, -chan, see geòdha.
geòthach, *a.* see geòdhach.
——an, *n.pl.* of geòtha, for geòdhachan.
geòthadh, see geòdha.
geuban, -ain, see giaban.
——ach, see giabanach.
geug, -éige, -an, *s.f.* Branch, sapling. 2 Young superfine female, nymph. 3**Man's arms. 4†† Sun's ray. 5(DMC) Sprig. Bàrr-geug, *belle*; fo dhubhar a geugan, *under the shadow of her branches*; a' gh. àillidh, *the beauteous maid*; g. fraoich, *a sprig of heather.*
——, *v.n.* Branch, sprout, propagate.

——ach, -aiche, *a.* Branchy, abounding in branches, ramifying. 2 Having long branches. Air craoibh gheugaich, *on a branching tree.*
——ag, -aig, -an, *s. f., dim.* of geug. Little branch. 2 Little girl.
——agach, -aiche, *a.* Abounding in little branches, *or* 2 Little girls.
——ail, *a.* see geugach.
——aire,** *s.m.* Brancher.
—— -dhuilleagach,* *s.f.* Frond.
geuire,(AC) for géire, *comp.* of geur.
geulran, -ain, see geòlan.
geum, -éim & -a, -an, *s.m.* Low, bellow. 2 Lowing of a cow. 3 Roar. 4 (MS)Blatter. An dean damh g.? *will the ox bellow?*
——, *pr.pt.* a' geumnaich, *v.n.* Low, as a cow. 2 Bellow. 3 Roar.
——nach, -aiche, *a.* Lowing.
——naich, *s.f.* Lowing, act of lowing. 2 Bellowing. 3 Roaring. A' g—, *pr.pt.* of geum. G. a' chruidh, *the lowing of the cattle;* anns a' gheumnaich, *bellowing.*
geumraich, *Gairloch, &c.* for geumnaich.
geur, *a. 1st. comp.* géire *or* geòire, *2nd. comp.* géirid *or* geòirid, *3rd. comp.* geurad, géiread *or* geòrad. Sharp,sharp-pointed or edged. 2 Acute in mind, shrewd, ingenious. 3 Acute of vision, sharp-sighted. 4 Quick of hearing. 5 Severe, cruel. 6 Rigid. 7 Painful, afflicting. 8 Fierce, ardent, fiery, eager, keen, vehement, 9 Sharp set. 10 Shrill, penetrating. 11 Acrid, sour, bitter, tart, sharp, acid. 12 Sarcastic. Ann am briathraibh g., *in bitter words;* an iomaguin gh., *in keen affliction;* fuaim g., *a shrill sound;* gu g., *sharply, severely, quickly;* sgian gh., *a sharp knife;* sleagh gh., *a sharp-pointed spear;* duine g., *a shrewd, ingenious fellow;* sùil gh., *a keen eye;* blas g., *a bitter* or *acrid taste;* bainne g., *milk of an acrid taste;* fìon g., *vinegar, sour wine;* tha e tuillidh 's g., *he is too severe* or *keen;* cho g. ri sùgh nan sealbhag, *as sour as sorrel juice;* a' geur-amharc, *looking keenly;* is g. fiacaill á fraoch, see under fiacaill.
geur, géire, *s.m.* Edge, sharpness.
geura, see geurad.
geurach, -aiche, *a.* see geur.
————,* *s.f.* Agrimony (plant.)
————adh, -aidh, *s.m.*Sharpening,act of sharpening. 2**Setting, as of a bladed instrument. 3**Souring, growing sour or bitter. 4 (MS) Attenuation. A' g—, *pr. pt.* of geuraich.
————d,* *s.f.* see geurad.
geur-achmhasanaich,‡‡ *v.a.* Scold, chide.
geurad, -aid, *s.m. & 3rd. comp.* of geur. Sharpness, sourness, pungency. acerbity, acetosity, 2 Acuteness, sharpness. 3 Degree of sharpness or sourness. A' dol an g., *growing sharper or sourer.*
geuradas,(MS) -ais, *s.m.* Acumen.
geuradh,**-raidh, *s.m.* Edge of a bladed weapon. 2 Sharp point. 3 (AH) Ridge of a hill. G. na cruaidhe, *the sharp edge of the steel (sword.)*
geurag,** *s.f.* Acid. 2(DMC) Keen appetite.
———— -bhileach, -ich, *s.f.* Agrimony.
geuraich, *pr.pt.* a' geurachadh, *v. a.* Sharpen. 2 Hone, whet. 3 Sour. 4 Embitter. 5 Make rigid. 6 Make smart, quick or clever. 7 ** Acidulate. A' g. na sgéine, *sharpening the knife;* tha 'm bainne a' g., *the milk is souring.*
geuraichte, *past pt.* of geuraich. Sharpened. 2 Set. 3 Soured. 4(MS) Attenuated.
geuraid, *2nd. comp.* of geur.
geur-aire, *s. f.* Marked attention, particular attention. Thoir g., *mark well.*
geuralachd, see geurad.
geur-amhairc, ** *v.n.* Look sharply or minutely. 2 Search minutely.
geur-amharc,-airc,*s.m.* Sharp or minute search, sharp look-out.
geuranach,-aiche, *a.* Sarcastic. 2 Argumentative, full of arguments. 3**Witty.
————d, *s.f.* Argumentation. 2 Passing of witticisms or repartees.
geur-bheachd,‡‡ -an, *s.f.* Judgment.
geur-bhile,** *s.f.* Foul mouth. 2 Sour leaf or blade.
————ach,§ *s.f.* Agrimony, see muir-dhroighinn.
————ach, *a.* Bitter in speech, acrimonious. 2 Having a pointed leaf or blade. 3 Having an acrid leaf or blade.
geur-bhileag, -eig, *s.f.* Sour leaf or blade.
geur-bhreithneachadh,‡‡ -aidh, *s.m.* Criticism.
geur-bhreithnich, *v.a.* Criticize.
geur-chluas, -ais, *s.f.* Quick hearing. 2 Sharp ear. 3 Short notice.
————ach, -aiche, *a.* Quick of hearing. 2 Having pointed ears.
geur-chosgach,** *a.* Anti-acid.
geur-chronaich,‡‡ *v.a.* Chide.
geur-chuis, -e, *s. f.* Subtlety. 2 Sagacity. 3* Acuteness, ingenuity. 4(MS) Aptness, genius. 5* Mental energy. Fear na geur-chuise, *the cunning fellow.*
————each, -eiche, *a.* Ingenious, shrewd, inventive. 2 Penetrative, sharp. 3 Subtle. 4 Strict, rigorous.
geur-dhearc,§ *s.* Whortleberry, see lus-nan-dearc.
geur-fhacal, -ail, -clan, *s.m.* Witticism, gibe.
————ach, -aiche, see geur-fhaclach.
geur-fhaclach, -aiche, *a.* Witty, satirical.
geur-fhiaclach, *a.* Sharp-toothed. 2 Serrated. Corran g., *a serrated sickle.*
geur-fhios,‡‡ -a, *s.m.* Familiar aquaintance.
————,** *s.f.* Intelligence, clear knowledge.
————rach, -aiche, *a.* Fully knowing. 2 Thoroughly intelligent.
geur-fhradharcachd,‡‡ *s.f.ind.* Perspicuity.
geur-fhuathachadh,‡‡ -aidh, *s.m.* Abhorrence.
geur-fhuathaich,‡‡ *v.a.* Abhor.
geur-ghaoth, *s.f.* Sharp or biting wind.
geur-ghath, -a, -an, *s.m.* Sharp dart or sting.
————ach, -aiche, *a.*Armed with sharp darts or stings.
geur-ghoimh, *s.f.* Severe pain, throb of anguish.
————each, *a.* In severe pain, throbbing with pain. 2 Causing severe pain.
geur-ghoith, see geur-ghoimh.
geur-ghuin,** *s.* Agony.
geur-innleachd, -an, *s.f.* Subtlety. 2 Cleverness, ingenuity. 3 Invention, contrivance.
————ach, -aiche, *a.* Subtle. 2 Inventive. 3 Sagacious.
geur-lann,** -lainn, *s.m.* Sharp sword. 2 (AF) Sheep-louse. Iomairt gh., *the play of sharp swords.*
————ach, *a.*Wearing or armed with a sharp sword.
geur-lean, *pr.pt.* a' geur-leanmhuinn, *v.a.* Persecute. 2 Harass. 3 Pursue hotly.
————achd, *s.f.* Persecution. 2 Hot pursuit.
————mhuinn, -ean, *s.m.* Persecution, act of persecuting. 2 Hot pursuit. Dean g., *persecute;* g. no gort, *persecution or famine.* A' g—, *pr.pt.* of geur-lean.
————mhuinneach,** *a.* Persecuting, prone to persecute. 2 Like, of, or pertaining to persecution.
————mhuinniche,** *s.m.* Persecutor.
geur-mhagadh, -aidh, -aidhean, *s.m.* Sarcasm, bitter jest.
geur-mheasach, -aiche, *a.* Neat.

geur-mhothachadh, -aidh, -aidhean, *s.m.* Lively feeling, lively perception. 2 Full conviction.
geur-oisinn, *s.f.* Acute angle.
geur-rannsachadh, -aidh, *s.m.* Diligent searching, act of searching diligently. 2‡‡Criticism. A' g—, *pr.pt.* of geur-rannsaich.
geur-rannsaich, *pr.pt.* a' geur-rannsachadh, *v.a.* Search diligently.
geur-sheallach, *a.* Sharp-sighted, clear-sighted.
geur-shrònach, -aiche, *a.* Sharp-nosed.
geur-shùil, *s.f.* Sharp, keen, or penetrating eye.
————each, -eiche, *a.* Sharp-sighted, having a quick eye.
————eachd,‡‡ *s.f.ind.* Perspicuity.
geur smachd, -a, *s.m.* Severity.
———— ————ach, -aiche, *a.* Severe, stern. 2 Rigid.
geur-theann, *a.* Rigid.
geur-thogradh, *s.m.* Keen aspiration.
geur-thuigseach,‡‡ -eiche, } *a.* Acute.
geur-thùrail, -e, }

gh, For words beginning with *gh*, and not inserted here, see under *g*.
gheabh, for gheibh.
gheibh, *fut. aff.* of *irr. v.* faigh. Shall get.
———eadh, *2nd. & 3rd. sing., past subj.* of faigh. Would get.
———eamaid, *1st. pl. past subj.* of faigh. We would get.
———ear, *fut. ind. pass.* of faigh. Is math a gheibhear thu, *you will do well ;* also used in a present sense, *bravo ! you are doing well.*
———inn, *1st. sing. past subj.* of faigh. I would get.
———teadh, *past subj. pass.* of faigh. Might, could, would or should be found.
ghios, for a dh' fhios.
gì, see ged.
giaban, -ain, -an, *s.m.* Gizzard, fowl's stomach.
———ach, -aiche, *a.* Of, or relating to gizzards. 2 Having a large gizzard.
giabhair, *s.f.* Prostitute.
————eachd, *s.f.* Prostitution.
giadh, see gèadh.
giadh-gaob, see gèadh-gaob.
gial, see giall.
gialach, see giallach.
†**giall**, -a, -an, *s.* Hostage, pledge.
giall, -a & gèille, -an, *s.f.* Jaw, cheek. 2 Gill of a fish. 3 Cheek or jaw of a boat, see H2, p.73. Bhuail thu an g., *thou hast struck their cheeks*; cnàmh-géille, *a jaw-bone.*
——ach, -aiche, *a.* Having gills, cheeks, or jaws. 2 Of, or connected with, gills, cheeks, or jaws. 3 Having large gills, cheeks or jaws.
—— -bhrat, -ait, *s.m.* Neck-cloth, cravat.
giaman, see geaman.
———ach,(DMC) *s. m.* Good specimen of any creature. 'S e g. a th' annad, *you are a stalwart fellow ;* g. bric, *a splendid trout.*
giamh, -eimh & ††-a, -an, *s. m.* Defect, fault, blemish. 2 Fear. 3** see ciabh.
———— ach, -aiche, *a.* Faulty, defective. 2 Fearful, fearing.
————achd,** *s.f.ind.* Faultiness, defectiveness. 2 Timidity.
gianach,** -aiche, *a.* Lazy, inactive.
————as,** -ais, *s.m.* Laziness, inactivity, indolence.
gianair,** -ean, *s.m.* Sluggard.
———— eachd,** *s.f.* Sluggishness.
giar, see geur.
gibeach, -eiche, *a.* Rough, hairy. 2 Having the hair in bunches. 3 Fringed. 4 Pretty. 5 Neat, tidy. 6(DU) Having ragged, untidy clothes. 7(AH)Spry, active, agile. An fhairge gh., *the rough sea.*
———as, -ais, *s.m.* } Neatness, tidiness, spruce-
———d, *s.f.* } ness. 2 Hairiness, roughness.
gibeag, -eig, -an, *s.f.* Rag. 2 Bundle, bunch, particularly of flax. 3 Little sheaf. 4 Fringe, flounce. 5** Largesse, boon. 6**Gipsy. 7 (DMC) Ringlet or tuft of hair or wool. 2(DMC) Shaggy little animal. 9(PJM) Small neat woman. Mo gh. air an ùrlar, *my neat one on the (dancing) floor.*
———ach, -aiche, *a.* Ragged. 2 Abounding in excrescences. 3 In little sheaves or bundles 4**Having a fringe or flounce. 5(DMC) Shaggy, having long hair or wool.
gibeagachadh,** -aidh, *s.m.* Tying up in small bundles, as of unmilled flax. 2 Fringing.
gibeagaich, *pr.pt.* a' gibeagachadh, *v.a.* Tie in small bunches or handfuls, as unmilled flax. 2 Fringe.
gibeagan,¶ -ain, *s.m.* Ruff—*machetes pugnax.* 2 **Fringe.

370. Gibeagan.

gibeal, -il, -an, *s.m.* see gioball.
gibean, -ein, -ean, *s.m.* Hunch on the back. 2 Grease from the solan goose's stomach—*St. Kilda.* 3 Kind of pudding made in the Hebrides. 4††Piece of flesh. 5 (DU) Poor ragged fellow. 6(DMC) Person soaked through and dripping with rain, 7(DMC) Tuft.
———ach,†† *a.* Abounding in pieces of flesh.
——— -suiriche,** *s.m.* Bur.
gibearnach, *s.m.* John MacFadyen, author of *Sgeulaiche-nan-caol*, says erroneously translated " cuttle-fish " by Gaelic Dictionaries, instead of " squid, or ink fish." The latter, although belonging to the same family, has little or no resemblance to the former, except that it has feelers and can squirt black liquid. It is about a foot long, and has one jointless bone not unlike a shoe-horn in shape.
†**gibhis**, *s.f.* Valley, glen.
gibhte,** *s.f.* Gaelic spelling of *gift*.
———alachd,** *s. f.* Condition of being gifted with good qualities.
———amas,** -ais, *s.m.* Donation, gift.
———ach,‡‡ -eiche, *a.* Belonging to gifts. [This and the last three are given by ** and ‡‡, but are all English.]
gibiche, *s.m.* see gibichead.
————ad, -id, *s.m.* Raggedness, shagginess, roughness, degree of roughness. 2 Neatness. 3 Prettiness. A' dol an g., *growing rougher and rougher.*
Giblean, -ein, *s.m.* Month of April. [Preceded by the art. *an.*]
Giblin, see Giblean.
giblion, *s.m.* Entrails of a goose.
gibne,** *s.* Thread. 2 Greyhound. 3 Cub. 4 Cupping-horn.

gibneach, -ich, *s. m.* see gibearnach. 2 (AF) Sea-urchin.
gibne-gortach,(AF) *s.m.* Greyhound, cub.
gibne-praiseach,(AF) *s.m.* Greyhound, cub.
gid, *gen.sing. & n.pl.* of gead.
gidh, see gidheadh. [although.
gidheadh, *conj.* Yet, nevertheless. 2 Though,
gidhis, see gighis.
gidhisear, see gighisear.
gidhrean, see giodhran.
gig,** *s.f.* Tickling.
gigeach,(MMcL) *a.* Hard-muscled.
gigeal, see diolgadh.
gigean, -ein, -an, *s.m.* Dwarf. 2 Term of contempt. 3‡ Little mass.
gigeanach, -aiche, *a.* Dwarfish.
gigearsaich, *s.f.* Levity.
gigein, see gigean.
gighis, -ean, *s.f.* Masquerade, mask, disguise.
——**ear**,** -eir, *s.m.* Man in a mask, masquerader.
——**earachd**,** *s.f.ind.* Masquerading, masking, going about in a mask.
†gil, *s.f.* Water.
gil, *gen. sing.* of geal.
gil,(AC) *s.f.* Watercourse on a mountain-side. 2 Rift. 3 The moon.
gilb, -e, -ean, *s.f.* Chisel.
gilb-chruaidh,†† *s.f.* Cold-chisel, steel chisel.
gilb-chruinn, *s.f.* Gouge.
gilbeach,†† *a.* Abounding in chisels.
gilb-thollaidh, *s.f.* Mortice-chisel. 2* Gouge.
gilceag,(AH) *s.f.* Little finger or toe.
gile, *s.f.ind.* Whiteness, fairness, clearness. Gile an anairt, *the whiteness of the linen.*
gile, *comp.* of geal. Whiter, whitest. Na's g., *whiter.*
gileab, see gilb.
gilead, -id, *s.m.* Whiteness, degree of whiteness.
gileim, see giolam.
gile-ghréine (a' gh—), *s.f.* One of the names of Fingal's banner.
gill, *gen.sing. & n.pl.* of geall.
gille, -an, *s.m.* Boy, lad, youth. 2 Man-servant. 3 Ploughman. 4 Bachelor—*Arran.* [Gille is used in addressing a young man or youth, as ciamar tha thu 'ille ? *how are you lad !*]; g. muinntir, *a family-* or *farm-servant ;* dh'fhàs na gillean, *the boys grew ;* leanabh-gille, *a male child ;* na leig do làmh air a' gh., *do not harm the lad ;* g. firein is e 'fàs dh' itheadh e mar mheileadh brà, *a growing lad would eat as much as quern would grind.*
gilleacha-fionn, *s.m.* see gille-fionn.
gilleachas,** -ais, *s.m.* Agency.
gilleachafionntruinn, see gille-fionn.
gilleachd,** *sf.* Service. 2 Management of an affair. 3 Conduct.
gilleadas,** -ais, *s.m.* Bachelorship. 2 Celibacy.
gilleagan, -ain, -an, *s.m.* Doll.
gille-airm,** *s.m.* Armour-bearer.
gillean,** -ein, *s.m.* Eunuch.
——, *n. pl.* of gille.
gilleas,** *s.m.* Condition of a manservant.
gille-boidhre,(AF) *s.m.* Fox.
gille-bhròg,** *s.m.* Shoeblack.
gille-Brighde, -ean-,*s.m.* Oyster-catcher, sea-piet —*hœmatopus ostralegus.* [see illust. 371.]
gille-brìdein,¶ *s.m.* see gille-Brighde.
gille-Caluim, *s.m.* Sword-dance. So called from the first two words of a song generally associated with the tune to which it is danced.
gille-cas-fliuch,** *s.m.* Attendant of a chieftain who carried his master over streams, and when necessary, into and out of boats.
gille-cleas, *s.m.* Play-actor.
gille-coise, -ean-, *s.m.* Footman.

371. Gille-Brighde.

gille-comh-sreathainn,** *s. m.* Attendant of a chieftain who took care of his master's horse.
gille-craigein,(AF) *s.m.* Frog. 2 Toad.
gille-cuim,†† *s.m.* Body-servant.
gille-cum-sréine, see gille-comh-sreathainn.
gille-cupa, -an-, *s.m.* Cup-bearer.
gille-cupain,* see gille-cupa.
gille-driùchd, (plant) see lus-na-fearnaich.
gille-each, -an-, *s.m.* Groom. 2 Stable-boy. 3 (DMK) Ploughman.
gille-feadaig,¶ *s.m.* Dunlin, (bird) see pollaran.
gille-fiondrainn, see gille-fionn.
gille-fionn, -an-fionna, *s.m.* Large periwinkle, white buckie, whelk. [*pl.* also gilleacha-fionn —AF.] 2(DMK) Small white periwinkle—*W. coast of Ross.*
gille-fionn-brinn, see gille-fionn.
gille-fionn-truim, see gille-fionn.
gille-fiunnd, see gille-fionn.
gille-fìdir,(DU) *s.m.* Message-boy, courier.
gille-gnothaich,* *s.m.* Messenger.
gille-gormain, see gille-guirmein.
gille-gràidh,** *s.m.* Secretary, chief servant.
gille-greasaid, -ean-aid, *s.m.* see gille-greasaidh.
gille-greasaidh, -an-aidh, *s.m.* Postilion. 2 Cooper's hammer or driver.
gille-guirmein,§ -ean, *s.m.* Field-scabious, cornfield knautia—*knautia arvensis.* 2§ Blue-bottle, see gorman.

372. Gille-guirmein.

gille-marcachd, see gille-greasaidh, 1.
gille-màrtuinn, -ean-, *s.m.* Fox.
gille-mirein, -ean-, *s.m.* Tee-totum, whirligig.
gille-mùchain, *s.m.* Chimney-sweep.
gille-mu-leann, see gille-mu-lunn.
gille-mu-lunn,§ *s. m.* The seaweed sea-laces—*chorda filum.* This plant is frequently from 20 ft. to 40 ft. in length.

gille-mu-lunng, *Gairloch, &c.* for gille-mu-lunn
gille-na-cubhaige,¶ (bird) see geòcair.
gille-neamhag(AF) *s.m.* Water-adder.
gille-òg,(AF) *s.m.* Salmon.
gille-piobair,** *s. m.* Piper's attendant, who carried the pipes when not being played upon He formed one of a chieftain's train in former times, for the piper being then acknowledged as a gentleman and not, as at present, a servant, thought it degrading to carry the instrument about with him.
gille-pinn, *s.m.* Clerk.
gille-ruadh,(AF) *s.m.* Salmon parr.

373. Gille-ruadh.

gille-ruithe, -an-, *s.m.* Courier, runner. 2**Footman. 3** Postman.
gille-sabhail,(AH) *s.m.* Man that works in a [barn.
gille-sguain, *s.m.* Train-bearer
gille-shalm, -an-, see fear-togail-fuinn.
gille-stàbuill, *s.m.* Stable-man.
gille-suiridhe, -an-, *s. m.* Courtier suitor. 2†† Lover's spokesman. 3(MMcL) Best man. 4 Flatterer.
gille-truis-airnis, *s. m.* Courier, messenger 2 Attendant of a chieftain who carried his baggage or wallet.
gillin,(AF) *s.m.* Horse.
gilm, -ean, *s.m.* Buzzard.
gilmean, -ein, -an, *s.m.* Dainty, spruce, talkative fellow, flatterer, fop. 2††Sycophant 3 (DMC) Small green knoll or patch of ground.
———ach, -aiche, *a.* Dainty, spruce, trim, foppish. Gu g., *sprucely.*
†gimleach, -ich, *s.m.* One fettered or chained.
gimleid, -ean, *s.f.* Gimlet.
———each, †† *a.* Abounding in gimlets.
gin, *pr.pt.* a' gintinn a' gineadh & a' gineamhainn, *v. a.* Beget, produce. O 'n a ghineadh e, *since he was begotten ;* mu 'n do ghineadh na cnuic, *before the hills were produced ;* ghin an crodh, *the cattle gendered.*
gin, *s.f.* Anyone. 2** Being, substance, production. 3**Sort, kind. 'Gin sam bith, *any one whatever* , cha'n 'eil gin ann, *there is not any ;* cha d' thàinig g., *no one came ;* am bheil g. agad ? *have you any ?*
†gin, *s.* Mouth.
gin, *s.f.* Gender.
gineadach,** *a.* Creative.
gineadail,‡‡ -e, *a.* Procreant.
gineadair, -ean, *s m.* Progenitor, parent.
gineadalachd, *s.f.ind.* Procreativeness
gineadan,** *s.pl.* The genitals.
gineadh, -idh, *s.m.* Begetting. 2**Cast. A' g—, *pr.pt.* of gin. [Used only in its aspirated and passive form—‡‡.]
gineag, -aig, *s.f.* Acrospire. 2 Tendril, twig, sprout. 3**Germ. 4**Scion.
———ach,** *a.* Having germs or sprouts. 2 Like a germ or sprout.
gineal, -eil, an, *s.m. & f.* Offspring, race, lineage. 2**Children. 3 Generation. 4*Growth of corn in the stack or shock. Do gh., *your offspring ;* a' gh. dhubh, *the black race ;* dannsaidh an g., *their children shall dance.*
ginealach, -aich, -aichean, *s.m.* [*s.f.* in *Suth'd* proper—DMu] Race, offspring, generation, single succession. 2 Genealogy, pedigree. G taghta. *a chosen generation.*
——— d, *s.f.* see ginealach.
ginealaich. *v.a.* see gin. 2 Grow, as corn in shocks 3**Vegetate 4** Branch out, as a tree or family.
†gineamhair *s.m* January.
gineamhuinn. *s.m.* Begetting. state of being begotten. 2 Conception. 3 Producing. 4 Sprouting 5 Production. 6 Birth. 7 Bud, sprout A' g—, *pr.pt.* of gin. O 'n gh., *from the conception*
———-———each, -ich. *a.* see ginteach
———-———eachd,** *s.f.* Productiveness, state of being prolific, generativeness, genitiveness.
ginean, -ein, -an. *s.m. & f.* Diminutive creature. 2 Fœtus
-———ta. *a* Easy of growth, prolific.
-———tachd, *s.f* State of being prolific, genitiveness, generativeness
gineideach,** -eiche, *a.* Prolific, generative, productive.
gineil,** *a.* Prolific, genial, generative. 2 Stout, compact.
gingein, *s.m.* Cask, barrel 2‡ Thick-set person.
gini, Gaelic spelling of *guinea.*
ginis,(TS) *s.f* Gean.
†ginneal, -il, -an, *s.m.* see geinn.
ginte, *past pt.* of gin. Begotten.
ginteach, -ich, *s.m* The genitive case,
———, *a.* Breeding, breedy. 2 Buddy. 3 Prolific.
gintealach, -ich, *a.* see geintileach.
gintealas, -ais, *s.m.* see geintileachd.
gintear,** -ir, *s.m.* Father, parent. 2(MS) Ancestor Umhal do d' ghintearaibh talmhaidh, *obedient to thy earthly parents.*
gintinn, *s.m.ind.* Begetting, procreating, producing A' g—, *pr.pt.* of gin.
†giob,* *s.f.* Shag, hairiness. 2**Tail, 3**Rug. 4‡‡ Gluttony.
—,** *s.m.* Pluck, pull.
—,** *v.a.* Pull, pluck.
—ach, -aiche, *a.* see gibeach.
†—ach, -aich, *s.f.* Coarse rug.
giobach,** *s.m.* Fur.
giobachas, -ais, see gibeachas.
giobadh, -aidh, *s.m.* Pull, tug.
giobag,** -aig, *s.f.* see gibeag.
———ach, *a.* see gibeagach.
———achadh, see gibeagachadh.
———aich, see gibeagaich.
———an, -ain, *s.m.* see gibeagan. 2 *n.pl* of giobag.
giobairneach,* *s. m.* see gibearnach. 2 Solan goose—*Uist Bards.*
giobaiche, see gibichead.
-———ad, see gibichead.
giobalag,(CR) *s. f.* Overwrought woman. 2 Down-trodden woman—*W. of Ross-shire.*
gioball, -aill, *s.m.* Vesture. 2 Canvas. 3 Cast clothes. 4 Fur, hair. 5 Rag, clout. 6‡Chap, odd fellow, term of disrespect. 7* Odd lady. 8* Mantle, shawl. Mar gh. sean, *like an old garment.*
———ach, -aiche, *a.* Full of hairs, hairy. 2 Ragged. 3**Rough.
———ach, -aich, *s.m.* Ragged person. 2 Rough or hairy man.
———achd, *s.f.ind.* Raggedness. 2 Hairiness, roughness.
gioban,(AF) *s.m.* Sand-eel.
gioban-Iortach,(AF) *s.m.* Oil from the fat of the solan goose, used as a cure for various ills in man and beast.
gioban-suiriche,** *s.m.* Bur.
giobarsaich,* *s.f.* see gibichead.
gioblait,(DMC) *s.f.* Person wearing a long rag-

ged garment.
giobuil, -uill, see gioball.
gioburlag,(MMcL) *s.f.* Little, insignificant and untidy woman, slut.
giodal, -ail, *prov.* for miodal.
——ach, -aiche, *a prov.* for miodalach.
——achd, see miodalachd.
giodalaiche, *prov* for miodalaiche.
giodar, -air, *s.m.* Dung, ordure. *prov.*
——ach, -aiche, *a.* Full of, or covered with dung.
giodh, see gidheadh & ged.
giodhran, -ain, -an, *s.m.* Barnacle (fish.) 2 Instrument placed on the nose of an unruly horse. 3 Barnacle goose.

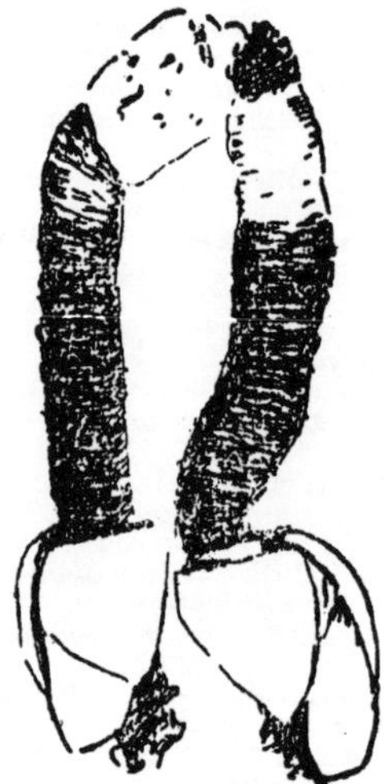

374. Giodhran (1.)

giodhrnan, giodhrsan, } see giodhran.
†giofach,** *a.* Dutiful. 2 Officious. 3 Attentive.
†——d, *s.f.* Dutifulness. 2 Attentiveness. 3 Officiousness.
†giofag, -aig, -an, *s.f.* Female client. 2 Officious woman, gipsy.
†giofair, *s.m.* Client.
†——eachd, *s.f.* Officiousness.
giog, *s.* Prickle of the teazle.
giog, *pr.pt.* a' giogadh, *v.n.* Cringe, fawn, flatter. 2* Peep, steal a look at. Gh. e staigh air an uinneig, *he peeped in at the window*· cha ghiogainn do dhuine, *I would not cringe to any man.*
——ach, -aiche, *a.* Prone to flatter, cringe or fawn. 2 Cringing, fawning.
†giogach, -aich, *s.m.* Budget, bag.
giogadh, -aidh, *s.m.* Cringing, act of cringing, flattering or fawning. A' g— *pr.pt.* of giog.
†giogail, *v.a* Follow, pursue.
giogaileid,(MS) *s.f.* Giglet.
giogaill, *v.a.* see diogail. 2(MS) Giggle
giogair,* *s. m.* Cringer, fawner. 2**Uneasy person.
giogal, *s.m.* see diogladh. 2**Pursuit.
giogan, -ain, -an, *s m* Thistle 2 (CR) Sea-urchin—*W. of Ross.* 3** Flattery. 4 (MS) Bur. 5(DMC) Brooch in the side of a Glengarry bonnet. Bog-gh., *sow-thistle*, see cluaran.
——ach, -aiche, *a.* Full of thistles. 2 Flattering.
giogladh, -aidh, *s.m.* Pursuing. 2 see diogladh.

gioirneanach see giornanach.
giol,* *s.f* see deal.
gioladh,** -aidh, *s.m.* Leaping nimbly.
giolag, see cuilc.
giolaid,** *s.f.* Inlet, little creek.
giolam, -aim, *s.m* Tattling. G. goileam, *tittle tattle.*
——ach, -aiche, *a.* Prone to tattling 2**Gabbling, prating.
——achd, *s.f.ind.* Tattling.
——an, -ain, -an, *s.m.* Little petulant fellow. 2** Tattler, prater.
——anachd,** *s.f* Tattling, prating.
giol-bhéist,** *s.f* Naiad.
giolc,* *v.a. & n.* Bend, stoop. 2 Aim at. 3 **Move nimbly. 4**Make a sudden darting movement. 5‡‡Pop. Giolcam ort, *let me try to hit you.*
†——, -an, *s.m.* **Broom. 2 see cuilc.
giolcach, *a. & s.f* see cuilceach.
—— -sléibhe, *s.m.* Broom, see bealaidh.
giolcadh, -aidh, *s.m.* Nimble motion. 2 Bolting forward. 3 Flippancy.
†giolcag, see giolc.
giolcaidh, -e, *a.* see cuilceach.
giolcail, *a.* Broomy. 2 see cuilceach.
giolcair, -ean, *s.m.* Flippant fellow. 2 Intruder.
——eachd, *s.f.ind.* Flippancy, garrulity.
giolcam-daobhram, -aim, *s.m.* The smallest supposable living thing, animalcule.
giolcanach,** *a.* Flippant.
——d,** *s.f.* Flippancy.
giolla, -an, *s.m.* see gille. 2 Ploughman—*Arran.*
——ch, -aiche, *a.* see giullach.
——chd, *s.f.* see giullachd.
giollaich, see giullaich.
——d, see giullachd.
giollan, see giullan.
giolman, -ain, see giolaman.
——ach, see giolamach.
——achd, *s.f.* see giolamachd.
giol-tholl,* *s.f.* see deal-each.
giomach, -aich, *s.m.* Lobster
——ail, -e, *a* Lobster-like
—— -cuain, see giomach-spàinteach.
—— -spàinteach,(AF) *s.m* Crayfish.
—— uisge,*see giomach-spàinteach
gioma-goc-ard,(AH) *s.m.* Act of setting a child astraddle on one's neck, with its legs hanging in front, cocky-ridy. "Gioma-goc" is always used without "ard" in the Strathglass and Beauly districts.—WC.
giomaich, *gen.sing & n. pl.* of giomach.
giomanach, -aich, *s.m.* Hunter, sportsman. 2* Masterly fellow in anything. 3††Gun. G. a' ghunna, *the masterly marksman.*
giomh, a, *s m.* see giamh.
giomhach, *a.* see giamhach.
——d, see giamhachd.
giomhas, -ais, *s.m* Fringe.
giomhanach,(DC) *s. m.* One who is timid. 'S ordugh teann ag iarraidh sithne 'cur nan g. nan éigin, *and a strict order to procure venison, placing the timid (deer) within danger*—*Donn. Bàn, 5th. ed. p. 46.*
giomlaid,* see gimleid.
gion,* *s.m.* Excessive love or desire, appetite. 2 Avarice. 3 Swallow Tha mo gh. ort, *I am excessively fond of you.*
——ach, -aich, see gionachd.
——ach, -aiche, *a.* Greedy, avaricious, gluttonous, ravenous. 2 Appetised. 3 Ambitious. 4 Keen.
——achd,* *s.f.* Greed, hunger, gluttony, avidity, voracity, avarice. 2 Ambition.
——aiche, *s.m.* see gionachd.
——aiche, *comp.* of gionach.

gionaichead,** *s.m.* Avidity.
gionair, -ean, *s.m.* Glutton, greedy-gut.
Gion-bhair,** *s.m.* January.
gionc, see gion-chu.
gion-chu,(AF) *s.m.* Dog, greedy or ravenous dog. Cha'n fhàg g. an druaip, *the greedy dog won't leave even dregs.*
giontuinn, see gintinn.
gioradan, -ain, -an, *s.m.* Periwinkle, sea-snail. 2(AF) Lamprey.
giorag, -aig, -an, *s. f.* Dread, fear, panic, affright. 2 Noise, tumult. 3** Cause of dread or fear. 4 Babble. 5 (PJM) Sudden start. Nàmhaid gun gh., *a fearless enemy* : fo gh., *troubled, afraid* ; chuir thu g. orm, *you gave me a start.*
——ach, -aiche, *a.* Timid, fearful, panic-struck. 2 Noisy, talkative. 3** Distrustful, jealous. G. roimh lotaibh, *afraid of wounds*
——aich,(MS) *v.a.* Affright, appeal.
——aiche,** *s.m.* Chatterer.
——an,** -ain, *s.m.* Babbler.
gioraic,(AF) *s.* Greyhound.
gioraig, *v.a.* Babble.
gioraman, -ain, *s.m.* Hungry fellow, greedy-gut.
gioramhach,** *a.* Greedy,gluttonous, insatiable, covetous.
——d,** *s.f.* Greediness, gluttony, covetousness.
giornanach,(AC) *a.* Spiral.
giornailear, see girneilear.
giorr,** *v.a.* Glut, sate.
giorra, *comp.* of geàrr & goirid. Shorter, shortest. 2 Sooner, nearer. 3 More lately. Na 's g., *shorter* ; is e a's g. de 'n triùir, *he is the shortest of the three* ; is g. a chunnaic mi Domhnall na thusa, *I have seen Donald more lately than you have;* is geàrr bhuam am bàs, *I am near death*—said by the devil when some-one had ill-treated him, and he received the reply, gu ma giorra bhuat na sin e, *may you be nearer it than that.*
——, *s.f.* see giorrad.
giorrach, -aich, *s.m.* Short and dry heath or hair. 2**Stubble.
——adh, -aidh, *s. m.* Shortening, act of shortening, abbreviation. A' g—, *pr. pt.* of giorraich.
——an,** -ain *s.m.* Abridger, curtailer. 2 Abridgement.
——d. *s.f.* see giorrad
giorrad, -aid, *s.m.* Shortness, degree of shortness 2* Fewness 3 Abridgement. G. làithean *no* g. shaoghail, *fewness of days, shortness of life* ; a thaobh a ghiorraid, *by reason of its shortness.*
giorradair, see giorraiche.
giorradan, -ain, -an, *s.m.* Compendium, abbreviation. 2** Kind of periwinkle, see faochag.
giorrag, see giorag.
giorraich, *pr.pt.* a' giorrachadh, *v.a.* Shorten, abbreviate, curtail.
——e, -an, *s.m.* Curtailer.
——te, *past pt.* of giorraich. Shortened, abbreviated, curtailed, docked.
giorraid, *s.m.* see giorrad. Is giorraid e sin, *it is the shorter of that.*
giorraiseach,(CR) *s.m.* Hare—*Farr & W. of Ross.*
†**giorraisg,** -e, *a.* Inconsiderate, imprudent.
giorra-shaoghail,†† *s.f.* Short life. G. ort! (a malediction) *short life to you!*
giorrta, see giorraichte.
giorruin, see giodhran.
giorsadh,†† *s.m.* Pinching of the skin by salt-water or cold.
giort, -a, -an & -achan, *s.f.* Saddle-girth, belly-band. 2 Haunch, buttocks. 3(DC)Edge,rim.
giort,** *v.a.* Gird, tie, lace.
——ach, -aiche, *a.* Of, or belonging to girths. 2 Having many girths.
giortag, *s.f.* Buttock. Na laoigh bhreaca, bhallach, le 'n giortagan *the spotted and dappled young deer with their white buttocks—Beinn Doran.*
giortaich, *v.a.* Gird, tie with girths.
——te, *past part.* of giortaich. Girded, girt.
giortaideach,** *a.* Having large buttocks.
†**giortail,** *v.a.* Patch, mend.
giort-gheal, *a.* White-edged.
†**giosg,** *s.f.* Yeast, balm.
giosg,* *pr.pt.* a' giosgail, *v.n.* Creak. 2 Crash G t' fhiaclan, *gnash your teeth.* [dìosg in *Uist.*]
——. *s.m.* Creaking noise, creak, roar.
gìosgach,** -aich, *s.m.* Wavering. 2 Wavering fellow.
——, *a.* Crashing. 2 Causing a crashing or creaking sound.
gìosgadh,** -aidh, *s. m.* Crashing. 2 Creaking. A' g—, *pr.pt.* of gìosg. Crainn a' g. le dealan, *trees crashing with lightning.*
gìosgail,** *a.* Crashing. 2 Causing a crashing or creaking sound.
——,* *s.f.* Creaking, gnashing. 2 Roaring, clangour. A' g—, *pr.pt.* of gìosg.
giosgain,** *s.m.* Barm.
gìosgan, -ain, *s.m.* Gnashing. 2 The creaking noise of hinges or wheels. G. fhiacal, *gnashing of teeth.* [dìosgan in *Uist.*]
——ach,** -aich, *s.m.* Waddler.
——aich, *s.f.* see gìosgan.
†**giost,**** Gaelic form of *yeast.*
†**giostaireas,**** -eis, *s.m.* Old age.
giostal, -ail, see geastal.
giotadh,** -aidh, *s.m.* Appendage. 2 Dependance.
giotanach,(DC) *s.m.* Sorner (term of contempt.)
gìr, -ean, *s.f.* see githir.
gircean, *s.m.* Pigmy. 2 Fribbler. 3 Shrimp.
gircean,** *s.m.* Grig.
——ach,** *a.* Pigmean, diminutive.
——achd,** *s.f.* Diminutiveness.
giread(AF) *s.m.* Pike (fish.)
girenan, *s.m.* see geadh-got.
girlinn, *s.f.* see giodhran.
girneilear,(MS) *s.m.* Granary. 2*Hutch.
girt, -ean, *s.m.* Defence, protection, bulwark. 2 see giort.
girteach, -eiche, *a* see giortach.
girteag, -eig, -an, *s.f. dim.* of girt. Little girth. 2 Light spot or streak on the hand.
girtich,** Gird. 2 Defend.
gis,* see giseag. 2 see geas. 3 Gaelic spelling of *guess.* [Armstrong gives "feuch an gis thu e, *try and guess it,*" and "doctair bi gis, *a quack,*" (a doctor by guess !!) but the only three words of which the latter is composed being English ones in Gaelic dress we must conclude that it was concocted by one who was a Gaelic scholar "by guess."]
gise, Gaelic spelling of *guise.*
giseag, -eig, -an, *s.f.* Charm, spell, superstitious ceremony. 2(DMC) Witchcraft—*Sutherlandshire.* 3(DU) Kiss—*Gairloch.*
giseagach, -aiche, *a.* Superstitious. 2 Like a charm. 3**Ceremonious. Gu g., *superstitiously.*
giseagachd, *s.f* Superstitiousness. 2 Superstitious ceremonies.
giseal, -eil, *s.m.* Line.
gìsear,** *s.m.* Disguiser. Gaelic form of *guiser.*
gisreag, see giseag.
gisreagach, see giseagach.
gith, -ean, *s.m.* Shower. 2 Series, numbers. 3 Pain in the wrist caused by spraining, and

common among seamen, reapers, navvies, &c. 4 Humour. 5††Blast. 6(AH) Snow-shower.
gith,** s. Maggot.
githear,(MMcL) *s.m.* same as gith 3.
githeilis, *s.f.ind.* Running to and fro on trifling errands.
githil, *Reay country* for githir.
githir, -ean, *s.m.* Pain in the wrist, see gith, 3
giuban, see giubhan.
giubhal, -ail, *s.m.* Chirping of birds
giubhan, -ain, *s.m.* Fly.
giubhas, see giuthas.
giubhasach, -aich, see giuthasach.
giugaire, see giogair.
giùd, *gen.* giùide & -a, *pl.* an, *s.m.* Wile, stratagem, evil contrivance, deceit. 2(DMC) Worthless fellow.
giùdach,†† *a.* Abounding in deceits or stratagems.
giudal, -ail, *s.m.* Prattle, tattle.
giùg, *v.a.* Cringe, flatter.
giùgach,* -aiche, *a.* Drooping 2 Bending awkwardly with the head on one side. 3††Cringing, fawning. 4‡‡Starving. 5**Jolt-headed. 6**Drooping with cold.
giùig, -e, -ean, *s.f.* Drooping of the head to one side, as of a person sheltering himself from rain 2 Chilly attitude. 3 Shrinking of the body from cold. 4 Crouch. 5 Jolt-head. 6 ‡Langour.
giùigire,†† *s.m.* Cringer, coward, spiritless fellow.
giùir, -e, *s.f.* Gill of a salmon or trout. [* gives same as giùig.]
giùirideach,*-ich, *s.m.* Cringing, drooping, miserable-looking person
giùirne, *s.f.* Rocky hillock or knoll, on the side or summit of a mountain.
giùlain, *pr.pt.* a' giùlan, *v.a.* & *n.* Carry, bear, acquit. 2 Endure. 3 Permit. 4 Support 5 Conduct. 6 Behave. G. an gunna seo, *carry this gun* ; g. thu fhéin, *conduct or behave yourself* ; cha'n urrainn mi sin a gh., *I cannot bear that* ; g. leam, *put up with me.*
giùlan, -ain, -an, *s.m.* Bearing, act of bearing, carrying. 2 Enduring, suffering. 3 Permitting. 4 Supporting. 5 Tolerating. 6 Behaving. 7 Conduct, behaviour. 8 Corpse. 9 Bier. 10(PJM) Funeral. Do gh. fhéin *you own conduct* ; a' g. a chlàrsaich. *carrying his harp* ; atharrachadh giùlain *a change of conduct.* A' g—, *pr. pt.* of giùlain.
giùlanair, *s.m.* Bearer.
giùlanta, *a.* Well-behaved.
giulla, -n, *s.m.* see giullan. 2 (MMcD) Fly-fishing from a boat.
giullach, -aiche, *a.* Having many male servants. 2 Genial. 3 Fostering, cherishing.
giullachadh, -aidh, *s.m.* Cherishing, fostering, nursing.
giullachd, *s.f.* Management. 2 Usage. 3 Conduct. 4 Serving, guiding. 5* Preparing, dressing. 6 Improving. 7 Manufacturing 8 Nourishment, nursing. 9 (DMC) Treatment. 10(MS) Economy. A' g—, *pr. pt.* of giullaich. Ruigidh an ro-gh. air an ro-ghalar, *good nursing will remove a bad complaint* ; a' g. leathrach, *dressing leather* ; a' g. bhuntàta, *dressing potatoes in the field* ; a' g. lìn, *dressing lint* ; rinn a droch gh. air, *he treated him badly* ; cha'n 'eil thu eòlach air a' gh.-each, *you are not skilled in horse management.*
giullaich, *pr.pt.* a' giullachd, *v.a.* Manage well, use well. 2 Cherish. 3 Dress, prepare. 4** Foster, rear. Giullaichidh e i, *he shall foster her.*
giullan, -ain, -an, *s.m.* Boy, little boy. 2 Lad, youth. 3 Servant. Maide giullain, *a boy's staff.*
giumhas, -ais, *s.m.* see giuthas.
giùmsgal,-galach, -aichean, *s.f.* Adulation, flattery.
giùmsgail, *v.a.* Flatter, fawn upon.
giùmsgaileach, -eiche, *a.* Flattering, fawning upon.
giunnach, -aich, *s.m.* Hair.
giùr, see giùran.
giùrain, *gen.sing.* & *n.pl.* of giùran.
giurainnean,(MS) *s.m.* see giodhran 1.
giùram, -aim, *s. m.* Complaining or mournful noise.
giùran, -ain, -an, *s. m.* Fennel (plant.)—*fœniculum vulgare.* 2 Gills of a fish 3 *prov.* for giodhran. Bric le ball-bhreac gh., *trout with spotted gills.*
giùran, *s.m.* Barnacle, see giodhran.
giùrnan,(AF) *s.m.* Beetle, horned beetle, butterfly.
giùirne-mu-ghiùirn, *s.* Auger-dust. Cò dhiubh is fhasa, bata a dheanamh de 'n ghuairne-mu-ghuairn, no cuaille de 'n ghiùirne-mu-ghiùirn ? *whether is it easier to make a stick of the quill-pith or a cudgel of the auger-dust !*—another version of Tweedledum and Tweedledee, the phrases used having reference to the use of a turning lathe.
gius, *s.f* Sow, pig.
gius, *int.* Call to a pig
giùsach, -aich, see giùthsach.
giusaidh, *s.f.* Sow, pig. [*s.m.* in *E. Perthshire*, as, an do bhiadh sibh an g. ? *have you fed the pig !* ; but the pronoun may be *fem.*, as, an d' thug sibh a biadh do 'n gh. ? *have you given the pig her food ?*]
giusaidh, *int* Call to a pig.
†giusta, *s.m.* Can, tankard
giustag,** -aig, *s.f.* Thick-bodied girl.
giustal, -ail, *s. m.* Games or athletic exercises used by the Gael of old at their public meetings.
giùt,(AH) *s.m.* Dodge, wile, trick.
giùtair,(AH) -ean, *s m.* Crafty person.
——-eachd,(AH) *s.f.* Craftiness.
giùthail, *v.a.* Cackle.
giùthail, *s.* Cackle.

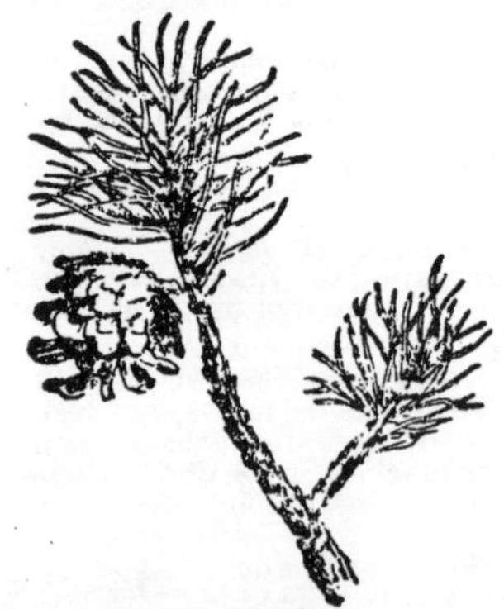

375. Giuthas.

giuthas, -ais, *s.m.* The Scots fir—*pinus sylvestris.* G. nam mór-shliabh, *the firs of the mountains.* [Badge of Clan Alpine. Badge of the Farquharsons. The foxglove was also worn by the Farquharsons when in season.]
giuthasach, -aiche, *a.* Abounding in fir or pine. 2 Like fir, piny.
giuthas bàn,(MMcL) *s.m.* Silver pine.

giuthas blàir,(WC) *s.m.* Bog-fir.
giuthas dearg,(MMcL) *s.m.* Red pine.
giuthas-geal,§ -ais-gil, *s. m.* Silver pine—*pinus pieea.* [First planted at Inverary castle, 1682.]
giuthas-learaig, *s.m.* see learag.
giuthas-Lochlannach,§ *s. m.* Spruce fir.—*abies communis.*
giuthas-Sasunnach,*s s.m.* Weymouth pine—*pinus strobus.* [*lit.* English pine,—it is not an English but a N. American tree.]
giùthsach, *a.* see giuthasach.
giùthsach, -aich, *s.f.* Fir or pine forest. Teine anns a' ghiùthsaich chòrr, *fire in the stately pine wood.*
glabair, *s.m.* Blab.
glabhaig, *Arran* for gloic.
glabhchdaire,†† *s. m.* Nonsensical talker, bladderskite.
glac, *pr.pt.* a' glacail & a' glacadh, *v.a*, Take, seize, catch. 2 Snatch. 3 Apprehend. 4 Feel. 5 Receive, accept. 6 ††Resume. Ghlac iad a' phoit ruadh,*they seized the still* ; gh. iad e, *they took him prisoner* ; esan a ghlacas baile, *he who takes a town* ; g. thusa foighidinn, 's glacaidh tu iasg, *you have (get) patience and you 'll get fish.*
glac, glaice, -an, *s.f.* Hollow valley, defile, narrow valley. 2 Hollow of the hand. 3 Bosom. 4 Embrace. 5 Handful. 6 As much of anything as can be caught between the thumb and middle finger. 7 The span between the thumb and middle finger. 8(AC) Handful of corn cut at one stroke of the reaping hook. 9 Grasp. 10 Prong, fork, see bàta, p. 76. 11 Quiver. 12 Apprehension. 'S a' ghlaic seo, *in this hollow;* g na beinne, *the defile of the mountain* ; fuar gh. a' bhàis, *the cold embrace of death* ; is gann a chitear tom no g., *scarcely could hill or dell be seen* ; an glacaibh a chéile, *wrestling with each other* ; sgaoil e a ghlacan, *he spread his arms* ; mile marbh-phaisg air an t-sabaid 'chaidh feadh ghlac mi m' ònrachd, *a thousand shrouds on the fight that proceeded whilst I realized my aloneness—Duanaire, 179.*
glacach,†† -aich, *s.m.* Swelling in the hollow of the hand. 2 Sprain of the hand. 3*Palmful, handful. 4 Form of consumption.
glacach, -aiche, *a.* Full of hollows or narrow valleys. 2 Grasping, snatching, catching. 3 Ready to seize. 4 Forked. 5††Of, or pertaining to, the hollow of the hand.
glacadh-an-óig, *s.m.* Death-decline.
glacadair, -ean, *s.m.* Catcher, seizer, one who catches or seizes. 2 Receiver.
glacadan, -ain, -an, *s.m.* Repository, receptacle. 2 Trap.
glacadh, -aidh, *s. m.* Taking, seizing, act of seizing, snatching, catching. 2 Receiving. 3 Grasp. 4 Forked part. 5 Acceptance. 6 Feeling. 7 Attachment. A' g—, *pr.pt.* of glac.
glacadh-chléibh, *s.m.* Catching or stitch in the side. The name for massage as formerly practised in Gaeldom for consumption was " a' toirt nan clachan-cléibh dhe 'n ghille," *taking the creel stones off the lad—Gael. Soc. Inv.*, xiv, 301.
glacag, -aig, -an, *s f., dim.* of glac. Little valley or dell. 2 Little handful. 3 Little palm. 4 Bundle. 5 Trigger. Glacagan diomhair, *lonely dells.*
glacagach, -aiche, *a.* Full of little valleys.
glacaichean-cléibh,‖ *s.pl.* Pleurodynia. [Preceded by the art. *na*]
glacaid, -e, -ean, *s.f* Handful. Thug an talamh mach 'na ghlacaidibh, *the earth produced in handfuls.*
glacaidh, *gen.sing.* of glacadh. 2 *fut. aff. a.* of glac.
glacail,(MS) *a.* Acute.
glacail, -e, *s.m.* see glacadh.
glacair, -ean, *s.m.* One who seizes or catches, catcher, seizer, apprehender.
glacaireachd, *s.f.ind.* Seizure, impressment,act of seizing or impressing. 2 Handling.
glacais, *s.f.* Grasping, wrestling, grappling.
glacaiseach, *a.* Grasping, wrestling, grappling. 2 Athletic.
glacamhuil,(MS) *a.* Apprehensive.
glacan, -ain, *s.m.* Little palm. 2 Little grasp. 3 Little dell. 4 Bundle. 5 Prong, fork.
glacanach, -aiche, *a.* Full of little valleys. 2 Forked, as a tree.
glacar, *fut. pass.* of glac. Shall be caught.
glaclach, -aich, *s.m.* Handful. 2 Bundle.
glac-leabhar, -bhraichean, *s.m.* Pocket-book. 2 Portable book. 3 Manual.
glacmhor, -oire, *a.*Holding fast, grasping firmly. 2††Catching, seizing. 3 Fit to catch.
glac-nan-cuileag, *s. m.* Spotted flycatcher, see breacan-glas.
glacta, see glacte.
glacte, *past pt.* of glac. Caught, seized, apprehended. Cha d' fhuair coigreach riamh mi g., *a stranger never found me captive.* [see note on p. 53.]
†**gladair**, -ean, *s.m.* Gladiator.
gladaireachd, *s.f.* Gladiatorship. 2 Sword fencing.
gladamair, see gladaman.
gladaman,(AF) *s.m.* Wolf.
glafaid,‡‡ -e, *s.f.* see glafarnach.
glafair, *s.m.* Babbler. 2(AH) Blustering, noisy, overbearing fellow.
glafar,‡‡ -aire, *a.* Noisy, chattering.
glafarnach, -aich, *s.m.* Noise, din. 2 Prating, chatting.
glag, -aig, *s.m.* The noise of anything falling, particularly of a carcase. 2 Horse-laugh. 3 Babble, loud talk. 4 see clag. 5(DMC) Any rattling noise. 'Na ghlag-phaiseanaidh, *in a dead faint* ; 'na ghlag-starraidh, *falling on his back with a crash.*
glagach, -aiche, *a.* Clumsy, tottering, unsteady. 2 Noisy, loquacious, garrulous, gabbling, babbling. 3 see clagach.
glagadaich, *s.f.* Loud talk, vociferation. 2 Scraping, scratching. 3††Continuous knocking. 4 (DMC) Noise made by a cart on a rough road. G. nam faoileag, *the noise of the gulls.*
glagaid, -ean, *s.f.* Clamorous noisy woman,blustering female.
glagain, *v.a.* Cackle.
glagair, -ean, *s.m.* Impertinent talker. 2 Noisy garrulous fellow, blusterer. 3 Racket, for games like tennis.
glagaireach,‡‡ *a.* Obstreperous.
glagaireachd, *s.f.ind.* Foolish or impertinent talk. 2 Noisiness, garrulity.
glagais, *s.f.* Loquacity, gabbling, verbosity,prattle. 2(AH) Intricate machinery, especially when not in working order. 'S ann ort tha a' gh., *how you do prattle !*
glagan, -ain, -an, *s.m.* Clapper of a mill or bell. 2 Knocker of a door. 3 Rattle. G. doruis, *the knocker of a door.*
glaganach, -aiche, *a.* Noisy, rattling. 2 Like a door-knocker, or 3 mill-clapper. see claganach.
glagan-gnathaichte(DC) *s.m.* Constant theme of talk. 2 Continuous jeering.
glagarra, *a.* Sluggish, dull, slow. 2 Flowing. 3 Loud, noisy, garrulous. Gu g., *loudly.*
glagarsaich,* *s.f.* Crashing, clangour, blustering, horse-laughter.
glag-fheath,(DC) *s.m.* Sudden calm in stormy

weather—*Uist.*
glag-gàire,†† *s.m.* Horse laugh, guffaw.
glaghaic,†† see gloic.
glàib, -e, *s.f.* Dirty water, puddle. 2 Bog.
glaibeach, *a.* Puddly, boggy.
glaibeil, see glaibeach.
glaic, -e, -ean, *gen. sing.* of glac. Sometimes used as a *nom.* (*s.f.*)
glaiceasach, -eiche, *a.* Athletic.
glaiceis, *s.f.* Grasping, wrestling, grappling.
glaiceiseach, *a.* Grasping, wrestling, grappling.
glàichd, -ean, *s.m.* see gloic.
glaicte, see glacte.
glaidean, -ein, *s.m.* Glutton.
glaideanach, *a.* Gluttonous.
glaideanachd, *s.f.* Gluttony.
glaigeilis, *s.f.* Clattering.
glaigis, *s.f.* see glagais.
glaim, -e, -ean, *s.f.* Large mouthful. 2 Great noise. 3 Piteous complaint. 4 Howling, yelling, howl, yell. 5 Common report. Is olc a' gh. a tha muigh air, *there is a bad report abroad concerning him.*
glaim, *v.a.* Seize upon voraciously. 2 Usurp.
glaimh, see glaim.
glaimh,(CR) *s.m.* Glutton—*Arran.*
glaimhean, -ein, *s.m.* Spendthrift. 2††Glutton.
glaimhear, -eir, -an, *s.m.* Spendthrift. 2 Glutton.
glaimhich, see glaimhnich.
glàimhear, -ean, see glamhsair.
glàimhearachd, *s.f.* see glamhsaireachd.
glaimhnich, *v.n.* Roar, cry out, howl.
glaimseach, -ich, *s. f.* Gluttonous woman. 2 Gulp. 3 Ingurgitation.
glaimseir, -ean, see glamhsair.
glaimsich, -ean, see glamhsair.
glaine. *s.f.ind.* Cleanness, purity. 2 Brightness, clearness. G. na sìthe, *the purity of peace* ; g. air mala na h-oidhche, *brightness on the brow of the night.*
glaine, *comp.* of glan. Cleaner, cleanest.
——, *s.* see gloine.
glaineach, *a.* Pellucid. 2 Clean. 3 see gloimeach.
glaineachd, *s. f.* Cleanness, purity, neatness, brightness.
glainead, -id, *s. f.* Cleanness, degree of cleanness, purity, cleanliness. Air gh. an tobair bidh salachar ann, *no matter how clean the well there will be some impurity in it.*
glainean,(WC) *s.m.* Roof of the mouth.
glainid,(DC) *comp.* of glan. Is g. e sud, *it is the cleaner for that.*
glainidh, see gloinidh.
glainne, see glainead. 2 see gloine.
glainnteach, see gloineach.
glais, *gen.sing.* of glas.
glais, *pr.pt.* a' glasadh, *v. a.* Lock, secure. 2 Lock, embrace. 3 Fold. 4 Fetter.
glaisbheinn,‡‡ *s.f.* Grey hill.
glaisdidh, -e, *a.* see glasdaidh.
glaise, *s.f.ind.* Greyness, hoariness. 2 Poverty. 3 Strait. 4**Pale or wan colour. 5**Grey colour. 6**Azure hue. 7**Greenness. 8**Shade. 9**Eclipse. 10 **Verdure. Am mìn-fheur 'na gh., *the rush in its greenness.*
glaise, *comp.* of glas.
glaiseach, -ich, *s.m.* Foam (cobhar.) 2 Lockfast place.
glaiseachd, *s.f.ind.* Greyness, hoariness, paleness. 2**Greenness. 3**Verdure. 4**Eclipse.
glaisead, -id, *s.m.* Hoariness, greyness, paleness, degree of hoariness.
glaisean, -ein, -an, *s.m.* Grey-headed man. 2 Coal-fish in its second and third year. 3 Kind of finch. 4** Green linnet. 5** Sparrow. 6‡‡ Lark. 7(DC) Chaffinch—*Uist.* 8 (AF) Grey fish. 9(DMC) Pale-faced child.
glaisean-coille, *pl.* -an-coille, *s. m.* Wood-sparrow. 2 Jackdaw.

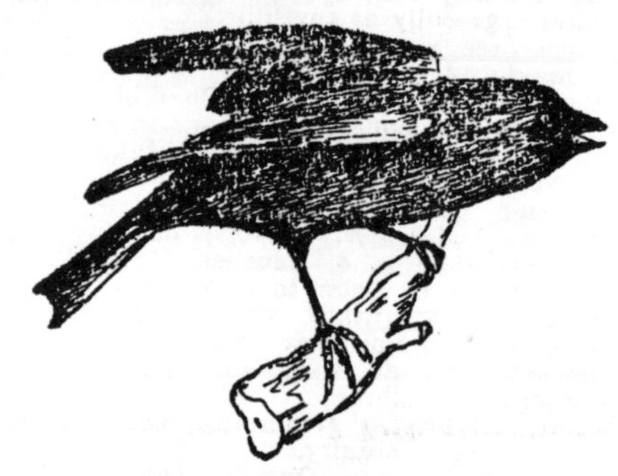

376. Glaisean-daraich.

glaisean-daraich, -ein-, *pl.* -an-, *s.m.* Greenfinch —*coccothraustes chloris.* McL & D gives Greyfinch.
glaisean-seilich, -ein-, *pl.* -an-, *s.m.* Pied wagtail, see breac-an-t-sìl.
glaisear,(DMC) *s.m.* Grass-land, green field.
glaisear, *fut.pass.* of glais.
glais-eun, -eòin, see glaisean.
glais-iasg,(DMC) *s.f.* Grey fish.
glaisleun, -leòin, *s.m.* Lesser spearwort. 2 Pepper-grass.
†glaisneant,(AF) *s.* Cat.
glais-neulach, -aiche, *a.* Pale-complexioned, wan.
glais-neulachd, *s.f.* Paleness.
glaisrig,* *s.f.* Female fairy, half-human, half-beast. 2 Gorgon. 3(DMC) Pale person. see glaistig.
glais-shile, *s.* Water-brash.
glaistic, see glaistig.
glaiste, *past pt.* of glas. Locked.
glaistig, -ean, *s.f.* Supposed she-devil or hag in the shape of a goat. 2 (AH) Beautiful female fairy, usually attired in a green robe, seldom seen except at the bank of a stream, and engaged in washing, also known as maighdean uaine.
glàm, *pr.pt.* a' glàmadh, *v.a.* Eat greedily, gobble, devour. 2 ††Seize voraciously, as a dog. 3 Bawl, cry out. 4 Glut. 4 Handle awkwardly.
glàm, -àim, *s.m.* Cry, outcry. 2 Noise. 3 Large mouthful.
glàmach, *a.* Edacious, ravenous, gluttonous. 2 Censorious.
glàmach,(DC) *s.m.* Greedy man, sorner.
glàmag,(DC) *s.f.* Greedy woman.
glàmadh, -aidh, -aidhean, *s.m.* Voracious bite, as of a dog seizing food or prey. 2 Large mouthful suddenly snatched. 3 Gobbling. 4 Censuring.
glàmaich,** *v.* Gormandize.
glàmair, -ean, *s.m.* Glutton. 2 Noisy silly fellow. 3 Smith's vice. 4 Shoemaker's vice. 5 *Chasm. 6 Lurcher.
glàmaireach,‡‡ -eiche, *a.* Carnivorous.
glàmaireachd, *s.f.ind.* Voracity, gluttony. 2 Continual babbling. 3**Continued noisy talk.
glamaras, see glamras.
glàmasair, ean,†† *s.m.* Voracious eater,glutton.
glambar, -air, -an, see clambar.
glàmh, *s. & v.* see glàm.
glàmhach, -aiche, see glàmach.
glàmhadh, see glàmadh.
glàmhaich, see glàmaich.

glàmhair, see glàmair.
glàmhaireachd, see glàmaireachd.
glamhan, -ain, *s.m.* Spendthrift. 2 One who catches greedily at anything.
glamhas, see glomhas.
glamhasg, *s.f* Greedy catch.
glamhsa, *s.m.ind.* Snapping. 2 Snatching greedily with the mouth, as a dog. 3 Snapping of the mouth. 4 Biting, as a mouthful of bread. 5‡‡Noise, bawling.
glamhsair, ean, *s. m.* Voracious, gluttonous person. 2 Muncher. 3 Noisy, bawling, complaining fellow. 4 Usurper. 5* One who seizes upon, or wishes to monopolize booty.
glamhsaireachd, *s.f.ind.* Voracity, gluttony. 2 Munching. 3 Noisiness. 4‡‡Bawling.
glamhsan, -ain, -an, *s.m.* Great noise. 2 Murmuring, complaining.
glamht,(AH) *pr.pt.* a' glamhtadh, *v.a.* Bolt food with extreme voracity.
glamhtaire,(AH) *s.m.* Onewho bolts food in a ravenous manner.
glamhus, -uis, *s.m.* Wide gap. 2 Open jaws. 3 (DC) Strong pair of pliers, pincers.
glamhusach, -aiche, *a.* Wide-gaping, having wide jaws.
glamradh, -aidh, -aidhean, see glàmair.
glamras,** *s.m.* Chiding. 2(MS) Clencher, vice.
glan, -aine, *a.* Clean, pure. 2 Innocent, uncorrupted. 3 Sincere. 4 Righteous. 5 Clear, bright, radiant, resplendent. 6 Shrill. 7 Willing. G. mar a' ghrian, *clear as the sun*; a't glaine am measg bhan, *purest among women*; a chlaidheamh glan gorm, *his bright blue sword*; cha chuir an t-each glan a chur chuige, *the willing horse should not be driven.*
glan, *adv.* Thoroughly, wholly, completely. 2 Cleanly. 3 Purely, brightly. G. mharbh, *completely dead*; g. rùisgte, *quite bare*; cuir g. a dholaidh, *spoil completely.*
glan, *pr.pt.* a' glanadh, Clean, purify, cleanse, wash, wipe. 2* Free from scandal. 3 Purge. 4 Blaze, brighten, beam. 5 Weed. 6 Winnow.
glanadach, *a.* see glanail.
glanadail, *a.* Abstergent, cleaning, purifying.
glanadair, -ean, *s. m.* Cleanser, purifier, burnisher, washer.
glanadaireachd, *s.f.* Cleansing, scrubbing, purification, winnowing. 2 Cleanliness.
glanadh, -aidh, *s.m.* Cleaning, cleansing, act of cleaning, purifying. 2 Weeding. 3 Washing. A' g—, *pr.pt.* of glan. Coltach ris a' chat a' glanadh 'aodainn, *like the cat cleaning its face* —i.e. scheming or planning. Thoir ruith ghlanaidh air, *give it a good clean up.*
glanaich,(AC) *prov.* for glan, *v.*
glanaidh, *gen. sing.* of glanadh. 2 *fut. aff. a.* of glan. Fuil a glanaidh, *the blood of her purification.*
glanail, -e, *a.* Having a cleansing or purifying tendency. 2 Abstergent. 3 Cleanly.
glanas, -ais, *s.m.* Cleanness. 2 Purity.
glanbhan, -ain, *s.m.* Clean wheat.
glan-bhàrr, -àirr, *s.m.* Clean crop. 2 Clean head of hair.
glang, -a, -an & -achan, *s.m.* see gliong.
†glang, -aing, -a, -an, *s.m.* Shoulder.
glangach, -aiche, *a.* see gliongach. 2 Broad-shouldered.
glan-labhrach, -aiche, *a.* Clean-spoken, eloquent.
glan-labhradh, -aidh, *s.m.* Clearness of expression.
†glanlach, -aich, *s.m.* Fence, dyke.
†glanlaich, *v.a.* Fence, enclose. 2 Trench.
glan-ruis,§ Eyebright, see lus-nan-leac.
glan-rùisgte, *a.* Quite naked. Rinneadh do bhogha g., *thy bow was made quite naked.*
glan-shnuadhach,‡‡ -aiche, *a.* Beautiful.
glan-shoillsich, *v.a.* Outshine.
glan-shuath, *v.a.* Absterge.
glanta, *past pt.* of glan. Purified, cleansed, cleaned, brightened.
glantair, *s.m.* see glanadair.
glantaireachd, *s.f.ind.* Cleansing, act of cleansing, purifying. 2 Weeding.
glante, see glanta.
glan-thoileach, -iche, *a.* Quite willing. 2 Curious.
glaodh, -aoidh & -an, *s.m.* Cry, shout. 2 Glue. 3 Cement. 4 Bird-lime. 5 Batter. 6 Grief. 7 (PJM) Tingling noise in the ear, supposed to be a forerunner of death news, if the noise is heard in the right ear the news to be expected from the south, and *vice versa.* Glaodhan bròin, *the cries of grief*; g.-coilich, *cock-crow*; dean *or* thoir g., *cry.*
glaodh,‡‡ -aoidh, -an, see glaodhan.
glaodh, *pr.pt.* a' glaodhach & a' glaodhaich, *v.a.* Cry, shout. 2 Proclaim, as marriage-banns, or peace after war. 3 Publish. Gh. e le glaodh mór, *he cried with a loud voice.*
glaodh, *pr.pt.* a' glaodhadh & a' glaodhaich, *v.a.* Cry. 2 Glue, cement.
glaodhach, -aiche, *a.* Of, or pertaining to crying. 2 Of a glutinous nature.
glaodhach, -aich, *s.m.* Crying, act of crying, bawling, calling. 2 Proclamation, as of banns. 3 Publishing. A' g—, *pr.pt.* of glaodh. Anns a' ghlaodhaich, *shouting.*
glaodhachadh, -aidh, *s.m.* Glueing, act of glueing or cementing. 2 Publication, as of banns. Chaidh an g, *their banns were proclaimed.* A' g—, *pr.pt.* of glaodhaich.
glaodhachail, -e, *a.* see glaodhach.
glaodhadair,‡‡ -ean, *s.m.* Crier.
glaodhadh, -aidh, *s.m.* Glueing, cementing, agglutination. A' g—, *pr.pt.* of glaodh.
glaodhaich, *s.m.* & *pr.pt.* of glaodh. Same meanings as glaodhach.
glaodhaich, *gen.sing.* of glaodhach.
glaodhaich, *pr. pt.* a' glaodhachadh, *v.a.* Glue, cement. 2 Cry, shout.
glaodhaichte, *a.* & *past pt.* of glaodhaich. Cemented, glued.
glaodhair, *s.m.* Advertiser.
glaodhan, -ain, *s. m.* The remaining part of a potato when the seed-slips have been cut off. 2 Pith of wood. 3 Pipes, tubes. 4‡‡Mixture of flour or meal and water, used as paste. 5(DC) Means by which a benefit is brought. Suighidh an g., *the pith of wood shall suck the juice.*; an g. le 'n do ghabh i ris, *the means by which she accepted him.*
glaodhan, *n.pl.* of glaodh.
glaodhanach, -aiche, *a.* Pithy, as of a tree. 2 Murmuring. 3 Glutinous.
glaodhanta, *a.* Viscous.
glaodhar, -air, *s.m.* see gleadhar.
glaodh-chlàr, *s.m.* Pasteboard.
glaodh-éisg, *s.m.* Isinglass.
glaodhran, -ain, -an, *s.m.* see gleadhran.
————ta, *a.* see glaodhranach.
glaodhte, *past pt.* of glaodh, Glued. 2 Cemented.
glaogh, see glaodh.
glaoghan, see glaodhan.
glaoic, see gloic.
———ealachd,(MS) *s.f.* Foolery.
glaoidh, see glaodh.
glaoidh, *s.f.* Heap, pile.
glaoidheaman,(AF) *s.m.* Wolf.
glaoidhseach, -aiche, *a.* Crying, roaring, sounding high, making a needless noise.
glaoidhseach, -eich, *s. m.* Noisy, senselessly

clamorous person.
glaoim, *s.f.* Tingling sound in the ears. 2 Noise. 3 Report. 4 Common rumour.
glaois, *s.f.* Glue, paste.
glaoine, see gloine.
glaoiteanaich, *v.a.* Paste.
glaomar,‡ -air, -an, *s.m.* Foolish person. 2(W C) Imperfect speaker.
glaoran, -ain, *s.m.* Wood-sorrel. 2 Flower of wood-sorrel. 3(DC) Yellow rattle (plant.) 4 ‡‡Noise.
glaoranach, *a.* Like wood-sorrel. 2 Abounding in wood-sorrel. 3(DC) Abounding in yellow rattle.
glaoranta, *a.* Noisy, prattling.
glaothar, *a.* Noisy, clamorous. 2 Prating.
glaothar, -air, *s.m.* Noise, clamour. 2 Prating.
glaothran, -ain, *s.m.* Rattle.
glas, -aise, *a.* Grey, pale, wan, ashy, sallow. 2 Poor. 3 (DC) Green, as grass, unripe corn, &c. Bu gh. a chiabh, *grey were his locks*; tùr gh., *a grey tower*; a chnoca glasa, *ye green hills*; is g. mo luaidh, *pale is (my love) the subject of my praise*; cho g. ris a' chàl, *as green as kail*—said of anyone looking pale; Gàidheal g., *a true Gael*; Gall g., *a sallow "Lowlander"*—but, dubh Ghall, *a thorough "Lowlander."* NGP says the term *glas* is never applied to an Englishman, but we have come across instaces of its being so applied, even by natives of Nicolson's own island.
glas, -aise, -an, *s. f.* Lock to fasten doors. 2 Fetter. 3 Green surface. 4 Green. 5 (AC) Water. 6 Key of rudder on stern-post, see p. 78. G. crochaidh, g. chrochta *or* dorn gh., *a padlock*; chuir mi a' ghlas-ghuib air, *I muzzled him, put him to silence, applied the closure to him*; g. a' chroinn, *the mast-lock of a ship*.
glas, *v.a. & n.* Become grey, pale or green 2 Make grey, make pale. 3 Dawn. 4 see glais. Gh. a' mhaduinn, *the morning dawned.*
glasach, -aich, -aichean, *s. m.* Lea or fallow land. 2 Green field.
glas-a'-chroinn, *s.f.* Mast-lock.
glasadh, -aidh, *s.m.* Locking, making fast. 2 Making pale. 3 State of becoming gray or pale. G. na cubhaige, *a slight fall of snow in early summer*; translated by NGP. as "*the cuckoo's greening* or *preparation-time*—the time following the 4th. week in March"; g. an la, *the dawn*; g. na Feill Micheil, *28th. Sept. the preparation for, or day preceding Michaelmas.* A' g—, *pr.pt.* of glas.
glasag, -aig, -an, *s. f.* Pied water-wagtail. 2 Female of the salmon. 3 The green ulva (seaweed)—*ulva latissima.* 4 Applied also to other edible seaweeds. 5††Small lock. 6 (AF) Coal-fish. 7 Any kind of salad. 8 (DMy)The fish rae before it has come to maturity.
glasagach, *a.* Abounding in edible seaweed. 2 Abounding in salad.
glasag-coille, see glasair-coille.
glasag-muineil, -an-, *s.f.* Locket.
glasaich, *sf.* Lea field—*Ross-shire.* [Often used as *nom.* instead of glasach.]
glasaidh, *fut.aff.a.* of glas. Shall lock.
glasail, -e, *a.* Greyish, pale, wan.
glasair, -ean, *s.m.* Prater. 2 Any kind of salad.
glasair-coille,§ *s.m.* Betony, see lus Beathaig.
glasan, -ain, *s.m.* Same meanings as glasag.
glasanach, -aich, *s.m.* Grassy plain. 2 Dawn of day. G. na cubhaige, *the grey sky of the cuckoo's advent.*
glasanaich,(MS) *s.f.* Greyness.
glasar, *fut.pass.* of glas. Shall be locked.
glas-bhalach,(DU) *s.m.* A mere boy.
glas-bhàn, *a.* Pale, wan.
glas-bheann, -bheinne, -bheanntan, *s. f.* Grey mountain.
glas-bhreac, *s.m.* Young salmon, samlet. 2 Salmon-trout.
glas-charbad, -aid, -an, *s.f.* Lock-jaw. Duine air am bi g., *a man having lock-jaw.*
glas-charbadach, *a.* Having lock-jaw. 2 Causing lock-jaw.
glas-cheò, *s.m.* Grey mist.
glas-chiabh, -an, *s.f.* Grey lock, grey hair.
glas-chiabhach, -aiche, *a.* Grey-locked, grey-haired.
glas-choire, see glas-choirean.
glas-choirean, -ein, -an, *s.m.* Little green valley.
glasdach, -aiche, *a.* see glasdaidh.
glasdachd, see glasdaidheachd.
glasdaidh, *a.* Greyish, wan, ashy, pale. 2 Surly. 3(MS) Bleak. 4(MS) Grizzled.
glasdaidheachd, *s.f.* Paleness. 2 Greyness.
glas-darach, *s.m.* Peeled oak.
glas-duirn,(DMC) *s.f.* Padlock.
glas-éideadh, *s.f.* Grey shroud. 2 Suit of grey clothes. Taibhse nan g., *the grey-shrouded spectre.*
glas-eun, *s.m.* ¶Rock-pipit, see gabhagan. 2¶ Tree-sparrow, see gealbhonn-nan-craobh. 3¶ Sedge-warbler, sedge-bird, sedge nightingale, sedge wren—*salicaria phragmitis.* 4(AF) Falcon, kite. 5(DC) Chaffinch.
glas-fhairge, *s.f.* The green sea. A' ghlas-fhairge a' sìor-chopadh, *the green sea perpetually foaming.*

377. Glas-fhaoileag.

glas-fhaoileag,¶ *s.f.* Herring-gull—*larus argentatus.*
glas-fheur, -fheòir, *s.m.* Seawheat grass—*triticum junceum* 2 Green grass. 3 Grey grass.
glas-fhothannan, -ain, *s.m.* Green thistle.
glas-ghairmeach, *Poolewe* for glas-ghuib.
glas-ghèadh, -gheòidh, *pl.* na glas-gheòidh, *s.m.* Wild goose, grey goose. 2 Grey lag goose.
glas-ghiall, *s.f.* Lockjaw—*Dàin I. Ghobha.*
gas-ghort, -oirt, -ean, *s.m.* Piece of lea ground. 2 Green, green spot. 3 Fodder.
glas-ghnùiseach, -eiche, *a.* Pale-faced.
glas-ghuib, -e, -an-guib, *s.f.* Muzzle. 2 Gag to prevent eating or speaking.
glas-iasg, -éisg, *s.m.* White fish, as cod, ling, haddock, &c, as distinct from iasg-dearg (red fish) belonging to the family *salmonidæ.* 2†† Coal-fish.
glas-labhraidh, *s.f.* Tongue-tie. G. air nighinn, gun fhios, teang' an abhra dh'iomraicheas, *when a maid is tongue-tied, her eye-lids tell a tale.*
glaslach,(MS) *s.m.* see glas-talamh.
glas-lach,¶ *s.f.* Widgeon—*anas penelope.* see illust. 378.
glas-làmh, -làimhe, -an-làmh, *s. f.* Handcuff, manacle.
glas-lann, *s.m.* Stonecrop, wall-pepper, see grafann-nan-clach.
glas-leau, *s.* Stonecrop, see grafann-nan-clach. 2 Green spot.
glas-leun,§ *s.m.* Lesser spearwort—*ranunculus*

378. Glas-lach.

flammula.

glas-liath, *a.* Greyish.

glas-luachair,(AH) *s.f.* Rough bearded variety of rushes.

glas-lus, *s.m.* Woad, see guirmean.

glas-mhagh, -a, -an, *s. m.* Lea field, green field, green plain.

glas-mhaghach, -aiche, *a.* Abounding in lea fields or green fields.

glas-mheur, -mheòir, *s.f.* A well-known tune in ceòl-mór, the finger-lock. [Preceded by the art. *a' gh—.*] 2 Manacle. 3 Thumb-screw. 4(DC) Cramp in the fingers.

glas-mhogail,(WC) *s.f.* Entanglement made in a net by a conger.

glas-mhuingeach, -aiche, *a.* Grey-maned.

glas-mhuinneach, see glas-mhuingeach.

glas-mhuir, -mhara, *s.f.* The green sea.

glas-neul, -neòil, *s.m.* Pale colour, pale or wan complexion. 2 Grey cloud.

glas-neulach, -aiche, *a.* Pale, wan, sallow. 2 Having grey clouds.

glas-neulachas, *s. m.* Bleakness. 2 Paleness, wanness.

glas-neulachd, *s.f.* Same meanings as glas-neulachas.

glas-neunt,(AF) *s.m.* Cat.

glasra, see glasrach.

glasrach, -aich, *s. m.* Uncultivated land 2 Green plot.

glasrach, -aiche, *a.* Abounding in lea, or unploughed land. 2 Green. 3 Having green groves or meadows. 4 Abounding in pot-herbs.

glasradh, -aidh, *s.m.* Pasture land, verdure. 2 Green grove. 3 Pot-herb. G. na cubhaige, see under glasadh.

glasraich, *pr.pt.* a' glasrachadh, *v.a. & n.* Convert into meadows or pasture land. 2 Become grey or pale. 3 Make green. 4 Prepare green thread for use.

glasruich, *s.f.* Greens or vegetables to eat. 2 Green groves. 3 Pot-herbs.

glas-sheabhag,¶ *s.f.* Goshawk.

glas-shile,‖ *s. f.* Waterbrash. [Preceded by the art. *a' gh—*]

glas-shruthach, -aiche, *a.* Of, or belonging to, grey or azure streams.

glas-stig, *s.f.* see glaistig.

glas-stuadh, *s.m.* Grey gable. 'S tha Caol-chuirn nan g. ag aomadh 's a brachadh, *and Caol-chùirn of the grey gables is bending and wearing down* (lit. *fermenting*)—*Filidh, 60.*

glas-talamh, -lmhainn, *s.m.* (*f.* in *gen.* usually, but *m.* in *Poolewe*) *pl.* glas-talmhuinnean, Unploughed or pasture land, lea ground.

glas-tarruing,* *v.a.* Remove sheaf-corn when cut.

glas-tarruing,* *s.f.* Act of removing sheaf-corn when cut.

glaste, *pr.pt.* Locked. 2 Clasped.

glas-tugha,§ *s.* Soft rush, see luachair bhog.

†glastum,§ *s.m.* Woad, see guirmean.

glas-uaine, *a.* Greyish-green, faintish green. 2 Azure, as the sea. 3 Cerulean.

glé, *a.* Very. 2 Sufficiently, enough. 3 Perfectly. Glé gheal, *sufficiently white, very white;* glé mhath, *very good.* [Aspirates word following it.]

†glé, *a.* Real, pure, clean, good. 2 Open, plain.

gleac, *s. m.* Fight, conflict, battle. 2 Wrestling, struggling. 3 Act of wrestling, struggling fighting, striving or endeavouring, sparring. 4 Agony. A' g—, *pr. pt.* of gleac. A' g. ris a' bhàs, *in the agonies of death;* le iomadh gh., *with many a struggle;* sluagh a bu gharg gh., *people who fought fiercely;* thugainn a gh., *come to wrestle.*

gleac, *pr. pt.* a' gleac, *v.a.* Fight, wrestle, struggle, strive. Gh. mi ri m' phiuthair, *I wrestled with my sister;* chòmhlaich sinn 'sa ghleac, *we met and fought.*

gleacach, *a.* Wrestling, struggling. 2 see cleachdach.

gleacadair, -ean, *s.m.* Wrestler.

gleacadh, -aidh, *s. m.* Wrestle, wrestling, struggling, fighting.

gleacail, *a.* Gymnic.

gleacair,** -ean, *s.m.* Shout, loud cry. 2 see gleacadair.

gleacaireachd, *s. f.* Act or habit of wrestling or striving.

gleacanach, *s. f.* Wrestling, struggling. 2 Rivalry.

gleacas, -ais, *s.m.* Wrestling.

gleacanas, -ais, *s.m.* Keeping, custody.

†gleachas, -ais, *s.m.* Gallery.

gleachd, see gleac.

gleadh, -a, -an, *s.m.* Onset, attack. 2 Deed, exploit. 3 Tricks, sham, humour. 4 (DMC) Quarrel. 5 see gléidheadh.

gleadh, see gléidh.

gleadhach, -aiche, *a.* Furious, wrathful.

gleadhadh, -aidh, see gleidheadh.

gleadhar, -air, -an, *s.m.* Noise. 2 Prating. 3 Rattling. 4 Clang of arms. 5 Collision. 6** Rude blow, strike. 7*Noisy blow. 8 (DC) Clamorous talk—*Argyll.* [‡ gives gleadhair.]

gleadhna, *s.m.* Tricks, humour.

gleadhrach, -aich, *s. m.* Kind of knotted seaweed used for cutting.

——,(DMC) *s.f.* Noisy, prattling woman.

——, -aiche, *a.* Making a shrill or loud noise. 2 Rattling. 3 Giving hard blows. 4 Obstreperous. 5(DC) Clamorous, loud-tongued.

——d,‡‡ *s.f.ind.* Obstreperousness.

gleadhradh, -aidh, *s.m.* Blow. 2 Noise. Thug e g. dha, *he gave him a blow.*

gleadhraich, -ean, *s.f.* Loud noise, rattling. 2 Clang of arms. 3 Collision. 4**Child's rattle. 5* Rustling noise. G. nan còrn, *the rattling of the drinking cups;* ciod e a' gh. a th' ort? *why do you make such a noise?* 's ann ort a tha a' gh.; *what a noise you make!*

gleadhran, -ain, -an, *s.m.* Rattle, noise. 2** Child's rattle.

——,§ -ain, -an, *s. m.* Yellow rattle, see modhalan. 2§ Wood-sorrel, see seamrag.

——ach, -aiche, *a.* Sounding, as a rattle. 2 Noisy. 3 Making a rattling sound. 4 Prattling.

gleadhtach,** *a.* see gléidhteach.

†gleam, -a, -an, *s.m.* Loud noise. 2 Resounding echo.

gleamach,(WC) *a.* Slow, tedious and uninteresting. Duine g., *a tedious uninteresting man.*

†——anach, -aiche, *a.* Noisy. 2 Resounding, loud echoing.

gleamhsa,** *s.m.* Slow long draught of liquor.

——ch,** -aiche, *a.* Slow, tedious. 2 Disagreeable.

gleamhsan,** -ain, *s.m.* Continued talk, tiresome talk. 2 Talkative person.
†glean,** *v.* see lean.
gleang, -a & -ing, -an, *s.* see gliong, *s.*
gleang, *v.* see gliong.
gleangarsach, see gliongartach.
gleangarsaich, see gliongartaich.
gleann, *gen.* glinn & glinne, *pl.* glinn, gleanna, gleannan, gleanntaidh, glinnte & gleanntan, *dat- pl.* gleanntaibh, *s.m.* Valley, opening between two heights. 2 Glen, dell, dale. Bho ghleann nan ruadh-bhoc, *from the valley of roebucks ;* air feadh a' ghlinne, *throughout the valley.*
——ach, -aiche, *a.* Abounding in glens or dales. 2 Of, or belonging to a glen. 3**Steep, shelving.
——ain, *gen.sing. & n. pl.* of gleannan.
——an, -ain, -an, *s.m.* Little valley or glen. 2 Dale. 3** Defile. An g. mòdhar, *in a little peaceful valley.*
——anach, -aiche, *a.* Abounding in little glens or valleys.
——taibh, *dat.pl.* of gleann.
——taidh, *n.pl.* of gleann.
——tail,†† *a.* Full of valleys. 2 Haunting or fond of roaming in valleys.
——tan, *n. pl.* of gleann.
†glear,** *v.a.* Follow.
glearach, *a.* see gleadhrach. A' bhean ghlearach, lonach, shanntach, *the clamorous, greedy and envious woman—Donn. bàn, p. 186.*
†glearrach, *a.* Flexible, pliant.
gleas, see gleus.
gleasd, see gleusd.
——achd, see gleusdachd.
gleaslann,** -ainn, *s.m.* Storehouse.
†gleastadh,** -aidh, *s.m.* Provision.
gleastair,** *s.m.* Farrier.
gleathair, see gleithir.
gleicean, -ein, *s. m.* Shuttlecock. 2 (DC) Sly boy—*Skye.*
——ach,** *a.* Like a shuttlecock.
gléidh, *pr.pt.* a' gléidheadh, *v.a.* Keep,preserve. 2 Retain, hold. 3 Defend, protect. 4 Tend, as cattle. 5** Detain. 6‡‡ Get, provide. 7 (CR) Get, find. Falbh is g. e, *go and find it ;* but, g. sinne ! *keep us !* gléidhidh mi do threud, *I will tend thy flock.* Applied also to meat, fish, &c. in a fresh state, as, an g. e ? *will it keep (without salt) ?*
——eadair,‡‡ ean, *s.m.* Curator.
——eadaireachd, *s.f.ind.* Curatorship.
——eadh, -idh, *s.m.* Keeping, preserving. 2 Act of keeping or preserving 3 Holding, retaining. 4 Good turn. 5**Tending. 6**Industry. 7**Frugality. 8* Preservation. 9* Detaining. A' g—, *pr.pt.* of gléidh.
——ear, *fut.pass.* of gléidh.
——idh, *fut. aff. a.* of gléidh.
——te, *past pt.* of gléidh. Kept, preserved, retained. 2 Protected.
——teach, -eiche, *a.* Careful, close-handed, saving, frugal. 2* In safe custody or keeping. 3**Industrious. 4(MS) Conservative. 5 (DC) Securely protected, as a garden by a wall. Tha sin g., *that is in safe keeping ;* duine g., *a careful* or *frugal man;* gu g., *frugally* ; cha 'n 'eil diochuimhn' ann na's boidhche na diochuimhne g., *the finest forgetfulness, forgetting what was kept.*—N.G.P.
——teachas, -ais, *s.m.* Anything saved or not spent. 2 Store.
——teachd, *s.f.ind.* Carefulness, frugality. 2 Safe custody. 3 State of preservation or keeping. 4**Industry. 5**Disposition to hoard up.
——tiche, *comp.* of gléidhteach.
——tiche, -an, *s.m.* Provider, careful person, keeper.
gleighteachd.(MS) *s.f.* Scantiness.
†gleileachd,** *s. f.* Whiteness. 2 Pureness.
†gleire,** *s.f.* Choice, selection. 2** Chastity.
gleitean,** -ein, *s.m.* Hard fight.
gleith, see gléidh.
†gleithe,** *s.f.* Grazing, feeding.
gleitheadh, *s.m. Gairloch &c.* for gleachd.
gleithire, -ean, *s. m.* Gadfly. 2 Gnat. 3** Grazer, animal that grazes.
gleò, *pl.* -than, *s.m.ind.* Dazzling kind of haziness about the eyes, as of a person losing sight, or threatened with cataract. †2 Fight, uproar, tumult, disturbance. †3 Sigh. †4‡‡ Judgment, decision. †5 Heroic exertion. 6 (DMC) Calm or still condition. Cò a chuir eadh orra g. ? *who would disturb them ?* a' mhuir 'na g., *the sea a dead calm.*
†gleodh, *v.a.* Cleanse, scour, polish.
gleodh, -a, *s.m.* Cleansing, scouring, polishing. 2 Sigh. 3 Slumber. 4 Groan.
——ach, *a.* Mournful.
——adh,* -aidh, *s.m.* Tipsiness.
——aman, see gleòman.
——amanach, see gleòmanach.
——amanachd, see gleòmanachd.
gleog, -oig, -an & -achan, *s.m.* Blow,bang,slap. 2 Drooping, silly look. 3†† Noise of anything falling. G. 'san leth-cheann, *a slap on the side of the head.*
——ach, -aiche, *a.* Silly, timid. 2 Lethargic, dull, lazy.
——aid,(DMC) *s.f.* Slow, idle woman. 2 (DC) Silly, stupid woman.
——air, -ean, *s.m.* Stupid, dull fellow. 2 Talkative fellow. 3 Arrogant fellow. 4 Lazy fellow. 5††Sloth. 6 (DMC) Trifler.
——aireachd, *s. f. ind.* Stupid behaviour. 2 Idle talk. 3 Awkward gestures. 4††Sloth. 5 **Arrogancy. 6** Talkativeness.
gleogaman,** -ain, *s.m.* Stupid drowsy fellow.
gleogartaich, see gliogartaich.
gleogh, see gleodh.
gleoghach,(MS) *a.* Ropy.
gleoghrach, see gleadhrach.
gleòid, -ean, *s.m. & f.* Sloven. 2 Slattern. 3 *Bewildered female.
——eachd,** *s.f.* Slovenliness.
——eil, -e, *a.* Slovenly. 2 Like a slattern. 3†† Silly.
——seach,* see gleòisg.
——sear,* see gleogair.
gleòis, *gen.sing.* of gleus. 2** *s.f.* Babbling. 3 (WC) Certain signs of drink in the eye. 4 (WC) Bright fire.
gleòisg, -ean, *s.f.* Vain, silly, blustering woman. 2 Slovenly woman. 3††Slut.
——eil, -e, *a.* Like a silly female. 2 Apt to talk idly.
gleòite,** *a.* Neat, trim, tight. 2 Handsome. 3 Curious.
gleòman, -ain, *s.m.* Silly stupid fellow. 2 Sluggish man, drowsy person. 3††Dull person.
——ach, -aiche, *a.* Drowsy, sluggish. 2 stupid, silly. Gu g., *sluggishly.*
——achd, *s.f.ind.* Drowsiness, sluggishness. 2 Stupidity, silliness. 3**Sluttishness. 4†† Dullness. 5 (DC) Becoming faint, as with fright. Bha e 'sa gh. gu tuiteam, *he was like to fall.*
gleorachan,(MS) *s.m.* Gewgaw.
gleorag, -aig, *s.f.* The lark.
gleorais,(DMC) *s.f.* Slow, dull female.
gleòramas, -ais, see glòramas.
gleoran,(DMC) *s.m.* Motionless person. 2 Snail-like speed.

gleòrann,§ -ainn, *s. m.* Cuckoo flower, ladies' smock, see plùr-na-cubhaig. 2§ Nasturtium. 3§ Wood angelica, see lus-nam-buadh. 4 This name is applied to various kinds of cresses.
gleòs, -òis, *s.m.* Lamentation.
gleòsg, -eòisg, -a & -an, see gleòisg.
———ach, -aiche, *a.* see gleòisgeil.
———aid, -ean, see gleòisg.
———air, -ean, see gleogair. NicGleòsgair mhór, a famous rock in the sea off Skye.
———aireachd, see gleogaireachd.
gleothaisg, -ean, see gleòisg.
†gleothan,** -ain, *s.m.* Clue.
gleus,-eòis & -a,*s.m.* &*f.*Order,manner,condition, trim. 2 Mean, means. 3 Activity. 4 Action. 5 Provision,ration, 6 Furniture. 7 Readiness or preparation of any kind. 8 Lock of a gun. 9 Key or gamut in music. 10*Screw of a spinning-wheel. 11 Occasion (want.) 12** Work. 13(CR) Wound—*Suth'd.* 14** Strength. 15 Exercise, as for one learning a language. Dè an g. a th' ort? *how are you?* tha iad air gh., *they are in trim;* cuir air gh., *prepare, make ready;* thug aois dhiom g., *age has deprived me of my readiness for action;* chaidh e air gh., *he prepared himself;* fiodhull air gh., *a violin in tune;* gu g. bàis, *to the work of death;* is trom dithis air an aon mhèis, gun ac' ach an t-aon gh., *two are heavy on one dish when there is but one ration;* is math an g. toil, *will is a good putter-in-trim;* g. Gàidhlig, *a Gaelic exercise.*
gleus, *pr.pt.* a' gleusadh, *v.a.* Adjust, mend. 2 Put in tune. 3 Trim, prepare. 3(DMC)Sharpen. G. an fhiodhull, *tune the violin;* gleusaibh bhur cridheachan gu ceòl, *attune your hearts to music;* ghleus iad na h-eich, *they harnessed the horses.*
gleusadair, -ean, *s.m.* Tuner. 2 Trimmer.
gleusadh, -aidh, *s.m.* Tuning, act of tuning,adjusting. 2 Mending repairing, ordering, trimming. 3 (DMC) Sharpening. 4 Preparing. A' g—, *pr.pt.* of gleus.
gleusaich,** *v.a.* Prepare, trim.
gleusda, *a.* & *past pt.* of gleus. Prepared, ready, tuned. 2 Clever, expert. 3 Neat, trim, tidy. 4 Well exercised. 5 Diligent, industrious. 6 Endeavouring, keen, eager, active. 7 (MS) Adventurous. 8**Bent, as a bow. 9**Cocked, as a gun. 10**Braced. 11‡‡ Swift. 12 (CR) Kind—*Arran.* 13 (DMC) Cunning, shrewd 14 In humour, in good condition. Giullan g., *a diligent boy;* coin gh., *keen dogs;* is g. a gheibhear e, *he does well, he is clever;* am bheil thu g.? *are you tolerably well?*
———chd, *s.f.ind.* Preparation, readiness. 2 Order, arrangement. 3 Neatness, tidiness. 4 Expertness, cleverness. 5 Alacrity. 6 Diligence, attention. 7 Keenness, eagerness, activity. 8 Alertness.9 Penetration. 10**Good humour. 11 (DMC) Shyness. 12 Shrewdness
gleus-fhear,‡‡ *s.m.* Ambidexter.
gleus-làimh,‡‡ -an-, *s f* Mechanics.
gleusmhor,** -oire, *a.* Mannerly, orderly.
gleusta, see gleusda.
———chd, see gleusdachd.
gliadar,** -air, *s.m* Loquacity, pertness.
gliadrach,** -aich, *s.f.* Drab, slattern.
———,** *a.* Glittering. 2 Sprightly. 3 Wanton,
gliasda, see gleusda.
†gliath,** *s.m.* War, battle.
gliathrach,** -aich, *s.m.* Drab. 2 Common prostitute.
glib, -e, *s.f.* Sleet. 2 Lock of hair, ringlet. 3 Slut. 4 Raw weather. 5**Glebe, portion of land allotted by the kirk to its ministers.
glibeil,* *a.* Sleety and showery with hail now and then.
glibheid,* *s.f.* Weather in which a curious mixture of rain, sleet and hail prevails.
———each,* -iche, *a.* Rainy, sleety, thawing.
†glib-shleamhainn,** *a.* Slippery with sleet.
glic, -e [& glioca] *a.* Wise, prudent, sagacious. 2**Steady. 3**Cunning. 4**Cautious. Bi g., *be wise;* gu g., *wisely;* g. gun mhoille, *cautious without dilatoriness.*
glic-bhriathrach,‡‡ -aiche, *a.* Apophegmatical.
glice, *comp.* of glic. More or most wise or prudent.
—ad, -eid, *s.m.* Degree of wisdom. A' dol an g., *getting wiser and wiser;* air a gh. 's ge 'm bheil e, *however wise he be.*
glid, (WC) *s.f.* Sleet, showers of soft wetting snow.
†glid, see glidich.
glideachadh, -aidh, *s.m.* Moving, stirring. 2 Act of moving. 3 Power of moving or stirring. 4**Budging. 5 **Motion. Cha b' urrainn dha g., *he could not move.* A' g—,*pr.pt.* of glidich.
glideachair,** *s.m.* Budger.
glideachd,** *s.f.* Motion. 2 Commotion. 3** Power of motion or stirring.
glidich, *pr.pt.* a' glideachadh, *v. n.* Move, stir, budge. 2††Impress upon. Nach g. thu? *will you not budge?*
gliduich, see glidich.
glifeid, *s.f.* Sleet—*Suth'd.* for clifeid.
glifid,** *s.f.* Noise. 2 Voice.
†glin, *s.* see glùn.
†glinn,** *s.* Sky. 2 Light. 3 Fortress.
glinn, *n. pl.* of gleann. Rugadh thu 'sna g., *thou wast born in the glens.*
glinn, -e, *a.* see grinn.
glinne, *gen.sing.* of gleann.
†glinne,** *s.f.* Habit, coat. 2 Bail, as in law.
glinneach,** *a.* Clear, manifest. 2 Pliable, flexible. 3 Full of valleys.
———adh,** -aidh, *s. m.* Making evident, clearing up.
glinnich, *v.a* & *n.* Make evident, clear up. 2 Observe closely. Gh. an là, *the day cleared up.*
———te, *past pt.* of glinnich. Made evident, cleared up.
glinnidh,** *a.* Clear, manifest.
glinnseach, -eiche, *a.* see gleannach.
glinnte, *n pl* of gleann. A' ruith gu g., *running towards the valleys.*
gliob, -a, *s m.* see glib.
gliobach,** *a.* Hairy.
gliobar, -air, see gliobas.
gliobas, -ais, *s m.* Sleet.
———ta, aiste, *a.* Draggled, drenched.
glioca, see glice.
gliocaire, *s.m* Wise man. Togaidh an gòraiche caisteal, is ni an g. còmhnuidh ann, *the fool builds a castle, the wise man dwells in it*—the meaning is that it is cheaper to buy a house than to build one, which is certainly not always the case.
gliocas, -ais, *s m.* Wisdom, prudence. 2**Cunning 3**Wit 4**Steadiness. 5**Sagacity. Is esan ceann a ghliocais, *he has wisdom.*
gliocasair, ean, *s m.* Wise man 2 Philosopher.
gliofaid,(CR) *s.f.* Chatterbox—*Arran.*
gliofan,(CR) *s m.* Chatterbox—*Arran.*
gliog, -a, -an, *s m.* Sound of water falling by drops. 2*Motion. 3††Clink, tinkling, see gliong. 4 (DU) Clicking sound, applied to a shorter metallic sound than gliong. 5 (DC) Tick. as of a clock, crack, as of something breaking. Cha toir e g. as, *he cannot move it;* cha'n 'eil g. agam, *I haven't a copper*—common in *W. of Ross.*

gliog, *v.n.* Click. 2 Tinkle.
——ach, -aiche, *a.* Clumsy. 2 Feeble, staggering. 3 Lazy, inactive. 4 (MS)Inarticulate. 5 Clinking, tinkling, see gliongach. 6‡ Unstable.
gliogadaich,†† *s.f.* Clinking.
gliogag, *s.f.* G. nan dramag *or* dlamag, *clumsy bad woman—Arran.*
gliogaiche, *comp.* of gliogach. More or most clumsy, feeble or lazy.
gliogaid, -e, -ean, *s.f.* Person clumsy about the knees. 2 Sluggish woman. 3 (DC) Anything in a broken-down condition.
———each, -eiche, *a.* see gliogach.
gliogair, *gen.sing.* of gliogar, see gliongair.
———, *v.n.* Tinkle, ring.
gliogan, see gliongan.
gliogar, -air, -an, see gliongar. 2 Slowness.
-———ach, *a.* Making a tinkling noise, ringing.
-———saich, see gliongartaich.
-———snaich, see gliongartaich.
gliogartaich, see gliongartaich.
gliogradh, -aidh, see gliongadh.
gliogram, -aim, *s.m.* Staggering. 2 Contemptuous name for a staggerer.
———— -chas, *s.m.* Long-limbed person.
———— -chois,(MM) (leggeram cosh—*Burns*) Name of the tune " Quaker's wife."
gliom, *s.m.* Mild tussle—*Suth'd.*
gliomach,** -aich, *s.m.* Sloven. 2 Long-limbed person. 3 see giomach.
————, -aiche, *a.* Slovenly, sluttish, drabbish.
————as, -ais, *s.m.* Slovenliness, sluttishness.
———— -Spàinndeach, *s.m.* see giomach-uisge.
gliong, -a, -an, *s. m.* Ringing noise, clash of metals, jingle, clink, clang, clangour.
——, *pr.pt.* a' gliongadh, *v.n.* Tinkle, ring as metal, clang.
———ach, -aiche, *a.* Tinkling, jingling, clinking, ringing, clanging.
———adaich,(DU) *s.f.* Clinking, clanging.
———adh, -aidh, *s. m.* Tinkling, act of tinkling, clinking or rattling. A' g—, *pr. pt.* of gliong.
gliongag, -aig, -an, *s.f.* Slight degree of drunkenness.
gliongair,** *v.n.* Tinkle, ring.
———, -ean, *s.m.* Empty prattler, trifling, prating fellow. 2††Tinkling noise.
gliongan, -ain, *s.m.* Tinkle, tinkling or jingling noise. 2 (MS) Click. 3 Anything that produces a tinkling sound. 4 Cymbal.
-————aich, *s.f.* see gliongan.
gliongar, -air, -an, *s.m.* Tinkling ringing noise. 2**Slowness.
————ach,** *a.* Making a tinkling noise, ringing.
————aich,** *s. f.* Continued jingling noise, tinkle.
————aich,** *v. n.* Clang, make a jingling sound, tinkle. Gh. an claidheamh, *the sword clanged.*
————sach,** *a.* see gliongartach.
————saich, see gliongartaich.
————snach,** -aich, *s m.* Tinkling noise.
gliongartaich, *s. m.* Tinkling noise. 2††Slight inebriety.
gliongnaich,(MS) *v.n.* Ring.
†gliosair,** *s.m.* Prattling fellow, tattler.
———eachd,** *s.f ind.* Prating.
gliosdar, see cliostar.
gliosg, *s.m.* Glance. 2 Twinkling. Ann an g., *in a twinkling.*
———artaich, see gliongartaich. 2**Glancing or glittering light. 3** Tremulous motion, dangling.
gliostair, -ean, see cliostar.

†gliphit, *s.* Torment.
gliùc, *s.m.* Blubbering, crying, sobbing. 2* Bumper. 3 Gulp.
———ach, -aiche, *a.* Blubbering. 2 Given to blubbering. 3 (DMC)Having drooping wings.
———aich, see gliùc.
gliugail,** *s.f.* Clucking, as of a hen.
†gliumh Gaelic spelling of *glue.*
gliusta, see gliustach.
-———ch, *a.* Slow.
-———chd,** *s.f.* Slowness, tediousness.
†glo, *s.m.* Veil, covering, hood.
glòbach,** *a.* Having a head covered with down, as a hen.
glòbag, -aig, *s.f.* Stupid quean.
gloc, *pr. pt.* a' glocail, Swallow greedily. 2 Cackle, as a broody hen. 3 Gulp.
gloc, gloic, *s.m.* Clucking of a hen. 2**Cackle. 3 Noise, loud note. 4**Loud, confident talk. 5**Garrulity. 6**Large wide throat or mouth. 7**Bung of a cask. 8 Gaelic spelling of *clock* (time-piece.) 9††Loud cry. 10 (DU) Guffaw. [** gives *s.f.*]
glocach, -aiche, *a.* Given to cackling. 2**Clucking. 3**Garrulous.
glocadaich, (a' g—) *s.m.* & *pr. pt.* Guffawing.
glocadh, *s.m.* Gulp.
glocail, *s.f.* Clucking, as of a broody hen. 2** Garrulity. 3**Loud prating. 4††Bawling. A' g—, *pr. pt.* gloc.
———,** *a.* Clucking. 2 Garrulous.
glocair, -ean, see glogair.
-————eachd, see glogaireachd.
glocan,* -ain, *s.m.* Bung. 2 Bird cherry, see craobh-fhiodhag. 3**Sling. 4**Fork. 5** Wide throat. 6***dim.* of gloc. 7‡‡Opening or angle where branches meet.
glocar, *a.* Garrulous. 2 Apt to cluck. 3 Apt to talk loudly and confidently.
gloc-gaire,(DMK) *Caithness* for lachan-gaire.
glochar, -air, *s.m.* Wheezing. 2 Difficult respiration, rattling in the throat. 3**Asthma. 4**Snoring.
————naich,** see glochar.
glòchdan, -ain, -an, *s.m.* Wide throat.
gloc-nid, *s.m.* Morning dram taken in bed.
glodh,** *s.m.* Slime. Laogh anns na glodhan, said of a calf before being licked by its mother after birth.
-———ach,** -aich, *s. m.* Slimy matter coming from a cow before calving.
glodhraich,(MS) *v.n.* see glomhraich.
glodhar,(MS) *s.m.* see glomhar.
glog, -oig & -a, -an, *s.m.* Soft lump. 2*Sudden hazy calm or sleep. 3 Dozing.
glogach, -aiche, *a.* Soft, blubbery, heavy. 2 Of a dull stupid look. 3 Heavy, unwieldy, lumpy. 4 Pale, cadaverous. 5**Skinny, flabby.
glogach,(WC) *s.m.* Choppy sea.
glogag, -aig, -an, *s.f.* Dull woman. 2 Bubble, small bladder of water.
———ach, -aiche, *a.* Abounding in bubbles. 2 Bearing bubbles. 3††Pertaining to a dull or stupid woman
glogaid,* *s.f.* Lubberly female.
glogaidh-hòmh, *s.m.* Term expressive of great contempt, unmanly, sottish, useless fellow. 2 Imbecile.
glogainn,* *s.f-* see glogluinn. 2 Sudden hazy kind of calm with occasional soft puffs of wind. 3 Stupor, dozing slumber
glogair, -ean, *s.m.* Heavy, dull, stupid fellow. 2 Lubberly coward 3** Chattering fellow. 4††Bawling fellow. 5††Sottish man. Cha d' thubhairt " mo thogair " riamh ach an fhìor gh., *none ever said " what do I care ?" but a real boor*

glogaireachd, *s. f. ind.* Dulness, stupidity. 2 Offensive idle talk. 3** Lubberliness. 4** Cowardliness. 5**Gasconading. 6**Chattering. 7 Cackling noise. 8††Sottishness.
glogais, *s.f.* Senseless talk —*Dàin I. Ghobha.*
glogan, **-ain, -an**, *s. m.* Soft lumpish man. 2 Little soft lump.
glogluinn, *s.f.* The rolling of the sea in a calm. 2**Agitation of a vessel caused by such rolling. 3††Noise of water.
glograich, *s.f.* The collision of soft substances. 2 The noise produced thereby.
glog-shùil, **-ùla, -shùilean**, *s.f.* Hollow, inanimate eye. 2 Soft eye.
———each, **-eiche**, *a.* Hollow-eyed. 2‡‡ Full-eyed.
glòic,†† *s.f.* Full or tufted cheek.
gloic, **-ean**, *s.f.* Idiot. 2 Foolish or senseless woman. 3**Slattern. 4**Stupid quean. Tha thu 'nad sheann gh. le aois, *age has made an old fool of you.*
——each, **-eiche**, *a.* see **gloiceil.**
glòiceach,†† *a.* Having full cheeks. 2 Having hanging cheeks, as hens.
gloicealachd, *s.f.* Idiotism, stupidity. 2 Sluttishness. 3**Queanishness.
gloiceil, **-e**, *a.* Foolish, idiotic, stupid. 2** Sluttish. 3**Queanish. 4†† Having full or tufted cheeks.
gloc-gaire, *s.f.* Horse-laugh, see **lachan-gaire.**
gloich, see **gloic.**
gloichd, see **gloic.**
gloicnid,** *s.f.* see **gloc-nid.**
gloidhc, see **gloic.**
gloidhchd, see **gloic.**
————each, see **gloiceil.**
————ealachd, see **gloicealachd.**
————eil, see **gloiceil.**
gloidhseam,(CR) *s.m.* Fright. 2 Folly —*W. of Ross-shire.* 3 (DU) Rage, frenzy, also pronounced *cleidhseam.*
gloin, see **gloine.**
gloin,** *v.a.* Glaze. 2 Vitrify.
glòin, *a.* Squint-eyed.
gloin'-amharc, *s.f.* Spy-glass, telescope.
gloine, *s.f.* see **glaine.**
gloine, (*for* glaine) *comp.* of glan. **An t-òr a's g.**, *the purest gold.*
gloine, **-an & -achan**, *s. f.* Glass. 2 Drinking glass. 3*Bumper. 4 Window-glass. 5(DMC) The measure of a drinking-glass. **Gloin' uinneig**, *a pane ;* **cinnidh uisge 'na gh. cruaidh**, *water shall turn into hard glass* ; **g. nan druidh**, *the druids' glass* or *druids' egg*—called in the south of Scotland, *adderstanes ;* **g. uisge-beath**, *a glass of whisky.*

[*Gloine-nan-druidh* was in high esteem among the Druids. It was one of their distinguishing badges, and was accounted to possess the most extraordinary virtues There is a passage in Pliny's Natural History, book xix, minutely describing the nature and properties of this amulet. The following is a translation of it. "There is a sort of egg in great repute among the Gauls, of which the Greek writers have made no mention. A vast number of serpents are twisted together in summer, and coiled up in an artificial knot by their saliva and slime ; and this is called *the serpent's egg.* The Druids say that it is tossed in the air with hissings, and must be caught in a cloak before it touches the earth. The person who thus intercepts it, flies on horseback ; for the serpents pursue him until prevented by intervening water. This egg, though bound in gold, will swim against the stream. And as the magi are cunning to conceal their frauds, they give out that this egg must be obtained at a certain age of the moon. I have seen that egg as large and round as a common-sized apple, in a chequered cartilaginous cover, and worn by the Druids. It is wonderfully extolled for gaining law-suits, and access to kings. It is a badge which is worn with such ostentation, that I knew a Roman knight, a Vocontian, who was slain by the stupid emperor Claudius, merely because he wore it in his breast when a law-suit was pending." Huddleston's edition of Toland gives some very ingenious conjectures on the subject of this enigmatical Druids' egg. The amulets of glass and stone, which are still preserved and used with implicit faith in many parts of Scottish Gaeldom, and are conveyed, for the cure of diseases to a great distance, seem to have their origin in this bauble of ancient priestcraft.—**]

gloineach, *a.* Glassy, vitreous.
————adh,** **-aidh**, *s. m.* Glazing. 2 Vitrifying. 3 Vitrification. 4 Paning, as of a window.
gloinead, **-eid**, *s. m.* Degree of cleanness or cleanliness. **A' dol an g.**, *growing cleaner and cleaner ;* **is g. e an sgròthadh sin**, *it is the cleaner for that scrubbing.*
gloineadair,* **-ean**, *s.m.* Glazier. 2 Glass-blower.
—————eachd,** *s.f.* Glaziery, business of a glazier. 2 Glass-blowing.
gloine-deilbh, *s.f.* Camera.
——— -fhad-sheallaidh,‡‡ *s.f.* Telescope
——— -loisgeach,‡‡ *s.f.* Burning glass.
——— -losgaidh, see **gloine-loisgeach.**
——— -lughdachaidh,‡‡ *s.f.* Microscope. [So given by H. S. Dict., but the author must have been looking through the wrong end of the microscope when he translated this word !]
——— -mhara,‡‡ *s.f.* Sea-glass.
——— -mheudachaidh,‡‡ *s.f.* Magnifying glass, microscope.
——— -mheudaiche,(MS) *s.f.* Magnifier.
——— -òil,(WC) *s.f.* Drinking-glass or horn.
——— -rionnaig,‡‡ *s.f.* Astronomical glass.
——— -shìde, *s.f.* Barometer.
——— -theas, *s.f.* Thermometer.
gloinich, *pr.pt.* **a' gloineachadh**, *v.a.* Glaze. 2 Vitrify. 3 Pane, as a window.
————ear, *fut. pass.* of **gloinich.**
————idh, *fut.aff.a.* of **gloinich.**
————te, *past pt.* of **gloinich.** Vitrified. 2 Glazed. 3 Paned.
glòir, *s.f.* Glory. 2 State of bliss. 3**Praise. 4**Honour 5‡‡Tongue, speech. 6‡‡Boasting. 7(DC) Torrent of coarse language—*Skye.* 8 *gen. sing.* of **glòr.** **Treun thar g.**, *powerful beyond praise.*
—— -bhinn, **-e**, *a.* Sweetly sounding.
—— -dhìomhain, *s.f* Vain-glory.
gloireachadh, see **glòrachadh.**
glòiream, **-eim**, *s.m.* Taunting language. 2†† Pomp, pageantry.
————ach,†† *a.* Taunting. 2 Fond of pomp or pageantry, pompous.
————as, **-ais**, *s.m.* Stultiloquence.
glòireis, **-e**, *s.f.* Boasting, prating, vain talk.
————each, **-eiche**, *a.* Boasting, babbling, prating, verbose.
————eachd,** *s.f.* Boastfulness, verbosity.
glòir-fhionn, **-a**, *a.* Spotted in the face or forehead. *Scots,* Ringle-eyed, as a horse. 2* Of an ugly drab colour.
glòir-ghleusta, see **glòir-fhionn.**
glòirich, see **glòraich.**
————te, see **glòraichte.**

glòirionn, see glòir-fhionn.
glòirmeas, see glòramas.
†gloirlionta,** *a.* Crammed, stuffed, choke-full. 2 Thick-set.
glòir-mhiann, -a, *s.m.* Ambition, desire for glory. 2 Pride.
———ach, -aiche, *a.* Ambitious, desirous of glory. 2 Proud. 3 Vain-glorious. Fear g., *an ambitious man.*
glòir-mhóir, see glòrmhor.
glòir-réim, *s.m.* Pomp, triumph, pageantry.
———each, -eiche, *a.* Pompous.
gloite,** *s.f.* Gluttony.
———ar,** -eir, -an, *s.m.* Glutton.
———arach, *a.* Greedy, gluttonous, voracious. Gu g., *greedily.*
†———arachd, *s.f.* Gluttony, voraciousness.
glòm,(CR) *s.m.* Abyss, gulf, chasm—*W. of Ross-shire.* Hence Glòmach Falls, Kintail.
glomach, *a.* Nasal. 2 Pronouncing the letter *l* like *gh*, thick of speech, as though the tongue were too big for the mouth.
glòmadh, -aidh, *s. m.* The evening twilight, *Scots*, gleaming.
glòmag, *s.f.* Handful of oatmeal eaten dry—*Caithness, Suth'd & Lewis.* (also gròmag.) 2 (DC) Pool in a stream or river—*Argyll.*
glomaiche,*s.f.ind.* Defect in speech, that makes one pronounce *l* like *gh.*
glomainn, see glòmadh.
glomanaich, see glòmadh.
glomar,** -air, *s.m.* Bridle.
glomhar, -air, -mhraichean, *s.m.* Piece of leather or wood, or sometimes a pine cone, with a sharp peg placed in it point upwards, which used to be placed on the snouts of lambs to keep them from sucking the mother. This was used when it was the custom to milk sheep as well as goats. Thàinig an g. as, *he is ungagged.*
glomharaich, see glomhraich.
glomhas, -ais, -an, *s. m.* Rock-cleft, fissure, chink, chasm. 2 (DC) Wide mouth—*Argyll, & Uist.*
glomhraich, *pr.pt.* a' glomhrachadh. *v.a.* Gag.
glomnaich,* see glòmadh.
glomuin, -e, see glòmadh.
glòn,(DMK) *a.* Cross-eyed. 2 Having much of the white of the eyes visible—*Caithness.*
glonach, *a.* Avaricious.
glonaid,** *s.f.* Multitude, crowd.
glong, -a, -an, *s.m.* Slimy, clammy substance, 2††Spittle. 3 Snot.
———ach, -aiche, *a.* Slimy, clammy.
———aiche, *s.f.ind.* Clamminess, glutinous property, tendency to become clammy.
glongaire,†† -an, *s.m.* Dull, weak fellow.
glonn, -a, -an, *s.m.* Deed of valour, exploit. 2 Fact, deed. 3 Loathing, qualm. 4 Boasting. 5**Calf. Oscar nam mór g., *mighty Oscar.*
glonnach, -aiche, *a.* Having an inexpressive, stupid or swollen face, see glonnmhor.
glonnar, see glonnmhor.
glonngag,(DMy) *s.f.* Sling for throwing stones, made of a piece of leather with string at each end.
glonnmhor, -oire, *a.* Heroic, valiant, performing heroic deeds. 2 Loathing, qualmish. 3 Boasting.
glonnrach,** *a.* Glittering, resplendent.
glonnradh,** -aidh, *s.m.* Fulgency, splendour.
glòr, *s.m.* see glòir. 2‡‡ Speech, language, utterance. 3**Noise. 4**Idle talk. C'ait' am faighear g. dhomh? *where can I find language?* Connal bu mhìn g., *C. the mild in speech.*
†glòr, *a.* Clean, neat, trim. 2 Clear.
†glòrach, *a.* Noisy, clamorous. 2 Talkative, garrulous.
glòrachadh, -aidh, *s.m.* Glorifying, act of glorifying.
glòraich, *pr. pt.* a' glòrachadh, *v. a.* Glorify, praise, bless.
———te, *past pt.* of glòraich. Glorified.
glòrais, see glòireis.
———each, *a.* see glòireiseach.
glòramach,†† *a.* Full of pomp.
———d, see glòramas.
glòramas, -ais, *s.m.* Boasting talk, idle talk. 2 ††Pomp, pageantry. 3**Vain boaster. 4**Idle talker.
gloran,(MS) *s.m.* Hopper.
glòrmhor, -oire, *a.* Glorious, illustrious. 2 Excellent. A chumhachd g., *his glorious power.*
glòtair, *s.m.* Glutton.
———eachd, *s.f.* Gluttony.
†glotan -ain, *s.m.* Bosom, breast.
gloth, *s.* see glo.
†———, *a.* Wise, prudent, discreet.
†———, *s.f.* Veil.
glothag, -aig, see glothagach, *s.*
glothagach, -aich, *s.m.* Frog's spawn.
———,** *a.* Abounding in, or like frog's spawn.
glothair, see glomhar.
glothraich, *pr. pt.* a' glothrachadh, *v. a.* see glomhraich.
†gluair, *a.* Clear, bright, gleaming. 2 Clean. 3 Splendid.
†———eachd, *s.f.* Clearness, brightness.
gluais, *pr.pt.* a' gluasachd & a' gluasad, *v.a.& n.* Move, go, walk. 2 Advance, proceed, march. 3 Affect, agitate, put in motion. 4 Affect, touch pathetically. 5 Afflict, provoke. 6 Bestir, make a motion, get up.
G. as a seo, *move out of this*; g. gu blàr, *march to the battle-field*; gh. o 'n ear a' mhaduinn ghlan, *the radiant morn advanced from the east*; bha 'n rìgh air a ghluaiseadh, *the king was agitated*; gh. iad chun a' bhaile, *they proceeded towards the town*; an ni nach cluinn cluas, cha ghluais e cridhe, *what does not reach the ear cannot affect the heart*; gh. e an t-uisge, *he agitated the water*; 'sa mhaduinn 'nuair a ghluaiseadh Di-màirt, *in the morning when Tuesday was ushered in*; o 'n cheud là a gh. i air tùs air thalamh, *since the first day she ever appeared on life's scene*; na glinn 's an do gh. mo shinnsir, *the glens in which my ancestors flourished.*
gluais, *s.f.* Device, invention. 2 Gloss, interpretation.
gluaisdeach, *a.* Moving, stirring, agitating. 2 Causing motion. 3 Affecting, pathetic.
gluaise, *s.f.* Neatness, trimness. 2 Cleanness.
———adair,†† *s.m.* Mover.
———adh, see gluasad.
———ar, *fut.pass.* of gluais.
———ar, -eir, *s.m.* Mover. 2 Agitator.
gluais-fhear, see gluaisear.
gluaisidh, *fut. aff. a.* of gluais.
gluaisneach,(MS) *a.* Active. 2 Busy.
gluaiste, *past pt.* of gluais. Moved, stirred, affected, agitated.
gluarach,** *a.* Pure. 2 Glorious. 3 Vociferous.
gluasachd, -an, *s.f.* see gluasad. 2 *pr. pt.* of gluais.
gluasad, -aid, -an, *s. m.* Moving, movement, motion. 2 Act of motion. 3* Agitation. 4 Conduct, behaviour. 5 Gesture. 6 Gait, carriage. 7**Provoking. 8 Pathos. Gun gh., *without motion*; gun gh. a nunn no a nall, *without moving hither or thither*; 'nad gh., *in your behaviour*; tha g. mnà-uaisle aice, *she has a lady's gait*; a' g. a bhilean,

moving his lips. A' g—, *pr. pt.* of gluais.
gluasadach, -aiche, *a.* Moving, locomotive, capable of motion. 2 Moving, unsteady. 3 Affecting, moving, disquieting, agitative.
gluasadair,** *s.m.* Agitator. 2 Motor.
gluasadh, -aidh, *s. m.* Moving, motion. 2 Agitation. 3 Gait.
gluasag, -aig, *s. f.* Water-wagtail (bird.) 2 Restless girl.
gluasair,** *s.m.* Interpreter.
gluas-rud,** *s.m* Projectile.
gluc, -uic, -an, *s.f.* The socket of the eye. 2 (DMC) Clucking of a broody hen.
glucaid,** *s.f.* Bumper.
glug, -uig, -an, *s.m.* Noise of a fluid confined in a vessel when agitated, or escaping from a narrow aperture 2 Gulp, noise of liquid in the act of being swallowed or gulped. 3* Rumbling stutter or stammer. 4 (DU) Clucking of a hen. Cearc air gh., *a clucking hen ;* cha robh coille riamh gun chrionaich, no linn gun ubh-gluig, *never was wood without dry brushwood, nor brood without addled egg.*
glug,** *v.a.* Swallow with a gulping noise. 2 Gulp. 3 Gurgle. 4* Stammer, Gh. e air a h-uile deur dheth, *he gulped down every drop of it.*
glugach, -aiche, *a.* Making a noise as of fluid when moved in a close vessel not quite full. 2 Stammering. 3 Speaking thickly and imperfectly. 4 Clucking. 5**Lisping. 6 Gurgling. 7(MS) Dull. 8(MS) Pot-bellied.
———, -aiche, *s.f.* Stammering female. 2* Rumbling noise. 3* Stammer.
glugaiche, *s.f.* Same meanings as glugaireachd.
———, *comp.* of glugach. More or most imperfect in speech.
glugail,** *s.f.* Gurgling. 2 Swallowing with a gurgling noise.
glugair, -e, -ean, *s. m.* Stammerer, one who speaks imperfectly. 2 One who talks nonsense, prater. 3 Soft, cowardly fellow. 4* Rumbler.
glugair,** *v.a.* Gargle.
———eachd, *s. f. ind.* Stammering, lisping. speaking inarticulately. 2 Foolish, incoherent talk. 3 Cowardice.
glugairneach,(MS) *a.* Pot-bellied.
glugalaich, see glugaich.
glugaman, (DMC) *s.m.* Unstable condition. Air gh., *in an unstable condition.*
———aich,(DMC) *pr.pt.*a' glugamanachadh, *v.a.* Rock, shake.
glugan, -ain, -an, *s.m. dim.* Faint noise of a fluid confined in a vessel. 2** Gurgling noise of water against the side of a vessel. 3 Rumbling in the intestines. 4 Rolling motion, as of a ship at sea. 5 The uvula. 6 Gurgling noise.
———ach, -aiche, *a.* Rolling, as a ship, unsteady, tottering. 2**Gurgling.
———adh,(DU) *s.m.* Process of making butter from a small quantity of cream by putting it in a bottle and shaking it till the butter forms.
———aich, *pr. pt.* a' gluganaich & a' gluganachadh, *v.a.* Make butter by shaking cream in a bottle.
gluganaich, *s.f.* (MS) Gurgle. A' g—, *pr.pt.* of gluganaich.
glugaran,** *s,m.* Gargle.
glugraich, *s.f.* Rumbling. 2 Superabundance of fluid.
glùig, -e, -ean, see gloic.
gluig, *a.* Addled, as an egg. 2**Unsound, rotten.
glùine, *gen. sing.* of glùn.
glùin, *n.pl.* of glùn.

glùineach, -eiche, *a.* Having large knees. 2 Abounding in joints, as certain kinds of plants. 3 In-kneed, knock-kneed. 4 (DMy) Weak-kneed.
glùineach,‖ -eich, *s.f.* Morbus genuum [preceded by the art. *a' gh—.*]
glùineach,‡‡ -ich, *s.f.* Milkwort. 2 In-kneed female. 3 Large-kneed female.
———, -ich, *s.m.* Any illness causing weakness of the joints or knees. 2 Name given to the potato at its first introduction, from its supposed tendency to weaken and cause debility of the body
——— -an-uisge,§ *s.f.* Amphibious persicaria—*polygonun amphibium.*
——— -bheag,§ *s.f.* Knot-grass—*polygonum aviculare.*

378. Glùineach bheag.

——— -dhearg,§ *s.f.* Amphibious persicaria see glùineach-an-uisge. McL & D. gives " knot-grass."

379. Glùineach dhubh.

——— -dhubh,§ *s. f.* Climbing persicaria, black bindweed. climbing buckwheat—*polygonum convolvulus.*
——— -mhór,§ *s.f.* Spotted persicaria—*polygonum persicaria.*
——— -theth,§ *s. f.* Water-pepper, water knot-grass, lake-weed, see lus-an-fhogair.
glùineag, -eig, -an, *s.f.* Blow with the knee in fighting or wrestling.
glùinean, -ein, -an, *s.m.* Garter, hose-tie on the leg, coarse garter.
———.—ach, -aiche, *a.* Gartered, wearing gar-

ters.
glùineas, -eis, *s.m.* Gout in the knee.
glùineineach, -eiche, see glùineanach.
†gluing,** *s.f.* Shoulder.
glùintean, *n.pl.* of glùn.
glùintibh, *dat.pl.* of glùn. Air do gh., *on thy knees.*
gluis, *s.f.* Slush. 2 Liquid food. —*Arran.*
†gluis-gheugach, -aiche, *a.* Full of green boughs.
glum,* *s.f.* see glàm. 2(MMcD) Deep pool.
glumach,(DU) *a.* Dark, dull, cloudy.
glumadh,†† -aidh, *s.m.* Big mouthful of liquid. 2 Plunge. G. na fuaradh, *a lurch to the weather side*—when a boat is too heavily ballasted on the weather side in a rough sea.
glumag,(WC) *Poolewe* for glumadh 1.
glumag, -aig, -an, *s.f.* Puddle. 2 Deep pool, deep pit full of water, usually applied to a pool in running water. 3 Deep hole.
———ach, -aiche, *a.* Of, or relating to, pools of water. 2 Abounding in such pools. 3 Full of deep holes.
glumagan, -ain, -an, *s.m.dim.* of glumag. Little pool. 2 Deep pool. 3 Deep hole.
glumaid,(DMy) *s. f.* Deep pool in a river or burn—*Lewis.*
glumraidh, *s.f.* Hungriness, voraciousness.
———, *a.* Devouring, engulphing. 2 Applied to the sea when it is bulging heavily in rolling waves.
glùn, -ùin & -ùine, *pl.* glùinean & glùintean, *s. m.* [*s. f.* in *Badenoch.*] Knee. 2 Joint. 3 Generation, race, 4**Step, degree, in a pedigree. 5 Descendant. 6 Joint in reeds. 7 (AH)Beam-knee in boat, see under bàta, p 76. Bean-ghlùin, *a midwife ;* an t-aon nach teagaisgear ris a' ghlùn, cha'n fhoghlumar ris an uilinn, *the child that is not taught at the knee, cannot be taught at the elbow ;* sios air do ghlùinibh ! *on the knee ! ;* aon gh., *first cousin;* dà gh., *second cousin ;* lùbadh gach g., *let every knee bow.*
glùnach, see glùineach.
———an,†† -ain, *s.m.* Knee-cap.
glùnan,** -ain, *s.m.* Little knee. 2 Garter.
glùn-bhleathach, -aiche, see glùn-bhleitheach.
glùn-bhleitheach, -aiche, *a.* In-kneed.
glùn-bhrat, *s.m.* Bass.
†glùndas, *a.* Knock-kneed, bandy-legged.
glùn-dos, *a.* glùn-dosach.
———ach, *a.* Bandy-legged.
glung,(CR) *s. m.* Hollow sound as from an empty vessel—*W. of Ross-shire.* 2(MM) The noise a bottle makes when being emptied.
glungan,** -ain, *s.m.* Clink.
glùn-ghinealaich, -tean-,‡*s.m.* Pedigree.
glùn-lùb,** *v.n.* Kneel. 2 Curtsy as a female.
———ach,** *a.* Kneeling. 2 Genuflecting. 3 Curtsying.
———adh, *s. m.* Genuflexion, kneeling. 2 Curtsy.
glupad,(AC) *s.m.*Dropsy in the throat, affecting cattle and sheep, due to decay in the liver and kidneys. see clupaid.
†glus, -uis, *s.m.* Light, brightness.
glusar,** *a.* Bright, glossy.
glut, -a, *s.m.* Voracity, gluttony. 2*Gulp, glut. 3 (DU) Greed.
glut, *pr.pt.* a' glutadh, *v.a.* Glut, devour, gormandize. 2†† Drink with noise or greedily, gulp.
gluta,(DMy) *s.* Deep round pool—*Lewis.*
glutach, -aiche, *a.* Gluttonous, edacious. 2 (DU) Greedy.
glutadh, -aidh, *s.m.* Glutting, act of glutting. 2 Eating to excess. 3 Gulping food voraciously. 4††Drinking with a noise. A' g—, *pr. pt.* of glut.
———, *Barra* for glut-lìonadh.
glutaich, *v.n.* Gormandize, glut, devour.
glutail, *a.* Intemperate.
glutair, -ean, *s.m.* Glutton. 2 One greedy of gain.
———eachd, *s.f.ind.* Gluttony, avarice, greed.
glutan,(DU) *s.m.* Deep narrow valley, gully.
glut-lìon,(DC)*pr.pt.*a' glut-lìonadh & a' glutadh, *v.a.* Pack inside of a wall with gravel—*Uist.*
———adh,(DC) *s.m.* Packing of gravel, put in the middle of house-walls to fill up the space between them.—*Uist.* These walls are dry-built and hollow, and from 6 ft. to 10 ft. in thickness. A' g—, *pr.pt.* of glut-lìon.
gnà, see gnàth.
gnàbh-lus, -uis, *s.m.* Cudweed, see lus-a'-chait.
gnà-bhogha,‡‡ -achan, *s.m.* Arcade.
gnàda, -àide, see grànda.
gnadan,(CR) *s.m.* Murmuring, complaining—*Arran.*
gnàdran, -ain, see gràdran.
gnàdranach, see gràdranach.
———adh, see gràdranachadh.
gnàdranaich, see gràdranaich.
†gnae,‡‡ *s.f.* Woman.
gnag, *pr.pt.*a' gnagail, *v.n.* Make a small crackling noise.
gnagail,‡‡ *s.m.* Crackling. A' g—, *pr.pt.*of gnag.
gnàidead, -id, see gràindead.
†gnais, *s.f.* Pars nefanda mulieris.
gnàithseach,‡ -aich, *s. m.* Arable land under crop. 2 (DC) Cultivator of the soil, farmer. Ceum a' ghnàithsich, *the ploughman's step*—heavy and solid.
gnàithsear,* *s.m.* Husbandman. 2 Countryman.
gnamhan, -ain, -an, *s.m.* Periwinkle, sea-snail.
gnamhanach, *a.* Abounding in periwinkles.
†gnamhuil, -e, *a.* Peculiar, proper.
gna-mhuinntir, *s.pl.* see gnàth-mhuinntir.
†gnaoi, *a.* Pleasant, courteous. 2 Gentle. 3 Respectable. 4 Ingenious.
†gnaoi, *s.f.* Countenance. 2 Grin. (see gnùis.)
†gnaoi-fhiosachd, *s.f.* Physiognomy.
†gnaoi-fhiosaich, -ean, *s.m.* Physiognomist.
gnàs, -àis, *s.f.* see gnàths.
gnàth,-a, -than & -annan, *s.m.* Manner, fashion, custom, usage. †2 Stature. †3 Lowing of cows. †4 Bleating of sheep. †5 Soothing voice. 6**Experience. Mar bu gh. leis, *as his custom was ;* talla do 'n g. na cuirm, *halls where feasting* (*hospitality*) *was the fashion ;* eòlach air gach g., *acquainted with every custom ;* a gh., do gh., *continually, usually ;* a réir an g., *according to their manner.*
gnàth, -a, *a.* Usual, common. G. obair, *constant work ;* g. chleachdainn, *habitual practice ;* a' gh. Fhéinn, *the standing army of the Féinne.*
gnàth, (i.e. do ghnàth, a ghnàth) *adv.* Always.
———ach, -aiche, *a.* Customary, ordinary, common. 2 Continual, constant, habitual. 3** Active. 4 Industrious.
———achadh, -aidh, *s. m.* Practising, act or habit of doing a thing. 2 Practice, custom, manner. 3 Behaviour. 4**Way, course. 5 (MS) Management. A réir gnàthachadh an t-saoghail, *according to the ways of the world;* do dhroch gh., *your bad behaviour.* A' g—, *pr. pt.* of gnàthaich.
gnàthachas, -ais, *s.m.* Invariableness.
gnàthachd, *s.f.ind.* Customariness.
gnàthaich, *pr. pt.* a' gnàthachadh, *v. a. & n.* Accustom, use, inure, exercise, practise. 2 Behave. G. thu fhéin gu ceart, *behave yourself properly ;* a' gnàthachadh tombaca, *using tobacco ;* is dona a gh. e i, *he behaved very badly to her.*

gnàthaichear, *fut.pass.* of **gnàthaich.**
——ear, -eir, *s.m.* Practitioner.
——te, *a.* & *pr. pt.* of gnàthaich. Used, exercised, practised. 2 Common, usual, accustomed.
gnàthail, *a.* Usual, customary. 2 Peculiar, proper.
gnàth-ainm, *s.* Usual or common name.
gnàthalachd,(DMC) *s.f.* Naturalness.
gnàthanna *n. pl.* of **gnàth.**
gnàthas, -ais, see gnàths.
gnàth-bheurla, *s.f.* Vernacular tongue.
gnàth-chainnt, *s.f.* Phraseology. 2** Vernacular.
——each, -eiche, *a.* Idiomatical.
gnàth-chuimhne, *s. f.* Tradition. 2 Constant remembrance.
gnàth-eòlach, *a.* Experienced.
gnàth-eòlas, -ais, *s. f.* Experience, knowledge got by experience.
gnàth-fhacal, -ail & -clan, *s.m.* Proverb, phrase, by-word. Bithidh e 'na gh., *he shall be a by-word.*
gnàth-fhaclach, *a.* Proverbial.
gnàth-fhiabhras, -ais, -an, *s.m.* Unremitting fever, constant fever.
gnàth-fhuaim, *s.f.* Continued noise, constant clack, din.
——neach, *a.* Making a continued noise.
gnàth-ghlas, *a.* Evergreen.
gnàth-leughach, -aiche. *a.* Bookish.
gnàth-mhaireannach, -aiche, *a.* Perpetual, everlasting.
gnàth-mhuinntir, *s.pl.* Natives.
gnàth-oidhirpeach, -eiche, *a.* Indefatigable.
gnàths, -ais, *s.m.* Custom, practice, habit, bent. 2 (DMC) Nature. Cha'n 'eil sin 'na gh., *that is not in his nature.*
gnàth-shàrachail, -e, *a.* Importune.
gnàthta,* *a.* Arable. Talamh g., *arable land.*
gnàth-ùrnuigh, *s.f.* Frequent prayer.
gnè, *s.f.ind.* Kind, sort, species, nature, quality. 2 Natural temper or disposition. 3 Countenance. 4 Form. 5 Appearance, outward sensible sign, complexion. 6* Slight degree of the nature of anything. 7 Tinge. 8 Tincture. 9**Manner. Is dona' a' ghnè a th' air, *what a bad expression of countenance he has!*; ainnir a bu mhìne gnè, *a virgin of the mildest expression* [** translates this "*of the softest temper*"]; g. chreadha, *a slight degree of clay, clayish (as soil)*; g. deirge, *a tincture* or *tinge of red*; gach creutàir a réir a ghnè, *every beast after its kind.*
gneag,‡‡ -a, -an, *s.m.* Knock.
gneathail, see gnèidheil.
gnèidneach, -eiche, see **gnèidheil.**
gnèidhealachd, *s.f.ind.* Kindness, tenderness, good nature, generosity. 2 Mannerliness. 3 Shapeliness. 4 Inateness.
gnèidheil, -eile, *a.* Genial, generous, tender, kind. 2 Shapely, well-proportioned, urbane. 3 Mannerly. 4 (DU) Endowed with natural affection. Gu g., *good-naturedly.*
gnèith, see gnè.
gnèitheach,(MS) *a.* Inate, see gnèidheil.
gnèitheachas, -ais, *s.m.* Inateness, see gnèidhealachd.
gnèithealachd, *s.f.* Inateness, see gnèidhealachd.
gneitheil, see **gnèidheil.**
gnèithich,(MS) *v.a.* Assimilate.
gnè-mhill,** *v.a.* Disfigure, deform.
gnèth, see gnè.
gnèthealachd, see gnèidhealachd.
gneutail, *s.m.* see gneutair.
gneutair,(DMu) *s.m.* Native race—*Suth'd.* Am bheil e dhe gneutair an àite ? *does he belong to the native race of the place ?*
†**gnia**, *s.* Voice. 2 Knowledge. 3 Tree. 4 Judge. 5 Knowing person. 6 Servant.
gniamh, see gnìomh.
†**gnie**, *s.f.* Knowledge.
gniobann,(MMcD) *s.m.* Rock-fish.
gnìomh, *pl.* -a, -mhtharra, -an, -annan & -mharan, *s.m.* Deed, action. 2 Office. 3 The 7th. sheaf as payment to the hinds that work the farm of tenants or landlords. 4 The building of a peat-stack or of hewn stones. [In *Gairloch*, applied to a temporary peat-stack, where the peats are built up to dry before being built into the permanent stack. The word is also applied to corn similarly dealt with. The meaning appears to be a "show" rather than reality.—DU.] 5 Exploit. 6††Business, avocation, work. 7††Word. 8***rarely* Fear. 9 **Parcel of land. †10 The 12th. part of a ploughland. G. mnà-glùine, *the office of a midwife*; chronaich mi an g., *I blamed the deed*; droch gh., *a bad deed*; g. duine, *the work* or *office of any man*; cuir an g., *perform, operate*; g. a làimhe, *his handiwork*; macgnìomharan Fhinn, *the exploits of Fionn's boyhood.*
gnìomh,* *v.a.* Build or pile, as a peat-stack.
gnìomhach, -aiche, *a.* Active, busy. 2 Diligent, industrious. 3 Actual. 4 Laborious. 5 Operative. 6†† Thrifty. 7 * Making great or good deeds. An seillean g., *the busy bee.*
——adh, -aidh, *s. m.* Performing, performance, execution, agency. 2(DMC) Outside building of a peat-stack. A' g—, *pr. pt.* of gnìomhaich.
——ail,‡‡ -e, *a.* Busy, active.
gnìomhachas, -ais, *s.m.* Activity. 2 Agency. 3 Industry, doings, business, work, performance. 4* Office of an overseer.
gnìomhachd, *s.f.* Efficiency. 2 Activity. 3 Industriousness.
gnìomhaich, *pr.pt.* a' gnìomhachadh, *v. a.* Act, perform, effect, operate, work. Ormsa gh. e beud, *to me he has wrought harm.*
——e, -an, *s. m.* Agent, actor, performer of an action, doer.
gnìomhail, -e, *a.* Actual, active.
gnìomhair, -ean, *s.m.* Actor, agent.
gnìomhar, -air, -an, *s.m.* Verb in *grammar.*
——ach, *a.* Active, actual.
——aich,‡‡ *v.a.* Officiate.
——aiche, *s.m.* Operator.
——an, *n.pl.* of gnìomh.
gnìomharra, *n.pl.* of gnìomh.
——, *a.* see gnìomhach.
gnìomharrach, -aiche, see gnìomhach.
gnìomharran, *n.pl.* of gnìomh.
gnìomh-chomasach, -aiche, *a.* Able to work. 2 Powerful, mighty. 3 Executive.
†**gnis**, *v.a.* Effect, bring to pass.
†**gnithe**, *s.pl.* Transactions, business.
†**gnò**, *s.m.* Jeering, mocking. 2 Sea.
†**gno**, see gnothach.
gnò, see gnòdh.
gnob, -oib, -an, *s. m.* Bunch. 2 Tumour. 3 Hillock, knoll.
gnobach, -aiche, *a.* Bunchy. 2 Tumorous, covered with little swellings. 3††Knolly.
gnoban, -ain, -an, *s.m.*, *dim.* of gnob. Little hill, knoll or heap. 2 Swelling.
——ach, -aiche, *a.* Abounding in little hills, knolls or heaps.
gnòdh, *a.* Gruff, surly, gloomy, down-looked. 2 Notable, remarkable, famous. 3**Jeering. see gnù Iomadh bodachan g., *many a gruff little old man*; bu gh. an geamhradh, *gloomy*

was the winter
gnòdh, *s.m.* Frowning, stern, fierce look.
gnodhan, -ain, *s. m.* Angry frown 2 Growl, moan. 3 Noise. 4 (DMC) Humming of a song.
gnog, *v.a.* Knock. 2 Knock with the hand or knuckles. 3 *Knock down. 4 *Kill
gnog, -oig, -an, *s.m.* Frown, sullen look. 2 Knock. 3 Knock with the knuckles 4 Sudden shove. 5 Jolt.
gnogach, -aiche, *a.* Pettish, sulky, frowning 2 Fickle, ready to take offence. 3††Shy. 4** Jolting. 5**Knocking Gu g., *sulkily*
gnogadh, -aidh, *s.m.* Knocking A' g—, *pr. pt.* of gnog.
gnogag, -aig, -an, *s.f. dim* of gnog. Little pettish female. 2 Little sulky female. 3 Slight knock on the head with the knuckles.
gnogaiseach, -eiche, *a.* Peevish, pettish.
————d, *s.f.ind.* Peevishness, pettishness, sulkiness.
gnoig, *gen.sing.* of gnog.
gnoig, -e, -ean, *s.f.* Surly frown, gloomy sulky look. 2 Surly, old-fashioned face on a young person. 3 Sulks. 4†† Head.
-——each -eiche, *a.* Frowning, sulky, gloomy.
-——eag, -eig, -an, *s. f.* Little sulky frowning woman.
——ean,(CR) *s.m.* Ball of worsted and tar, put on the points of the horns of vicious cattle—*Skye*.
-——eas, -eis, *s.m.* Sulkiness, pettishness, peevishness, sulks.
-——easach, -aiche, *a.* Sulky, frowning, peevish, as a young person. 2 Grim.
gnoigeis, see gnoigeas.
gnòimh, *s.f.* Visage 2 Grin. 3 Ludicrous name for a person with a grinning countenance 4 (CR) Sulky look—*Perthshire* Chuir e g air, *he made faces.*
gnoin,* *pr.pt.* a' gnoineadh, *v. a.* Shake and scold a person at the same time.
gnois, *gen.sing* of gnos
gnòmh,* *v.a.* Grunt like a pig.
——,‡ *s.m.* Grunt of a pig.
gnomhach, see gnothach.
gnomhan, see gnamhan.
gnòmhan, -ain, -an, *s.m.* Groaning, groan.
——·——ach, -aiche, *a.* Groaning.
gnos, -ois, -an, *s.m* Snout or mouth of a beast, especially a pig 2 Derisive term for the human mouth. 3**Bill G. tunnaig, *a duck's bill* [this ex is given by **, but is bad Gaelic] ; g. muic, *the snout of a pig.*
gnosach, -aiche, *a* Having a snout. 2 Having a large mouth 3††Sullen, grumpy surly.
———, -aich, *s.m.* Forward,interfering person.
gnòsad, see gnosd.
gnosad,(MS) *s.m* Hum
gnòsadaich, *s.f.* Querulous low noise or moan made by a cow or ox, approaching to lowing. 2 Roaring, as a bull. 3 Snoring noise.
gnosail, *s.f.* Grunting of a sow
gnosair,** *s.m.* Man with a large mouth. 2 Blubber-lipped man.
————eachd, *s.f.ind.* Muttering. 2 Blubberliness. 3 Mouthing.
gnòsd, *s.f.* Lowing, bellow 2 Snoring noise 3 Deep groan, grunt. 4 Low made by a cow to her calf. 5 The subdued noise a cow utters as her ordinary expression of feeling. 6** Hollow roar of a bull.
gnòsd,** *v.n.* Low, bellow 2 Groan. 3 Snore. 4* Grunt. 5**Make a hollow roar, as a bull.
gnòsdaich, gnòsdail, } see gnosadaich.
gnothach, -aich, -aichean, *s.m.* Business, avocation. 2 Affair, matter, circumstance. 3 Errand. 4 Call of nature. Ni e 'n g., *it will do*; a. gabhail gnothaich ri, *meddling with, being a busybody* ; a' dol air g., *going on an errand* ; na biodh gnothach agad ris, *have nothing to do with him* ; tha g. agam riut, *I have some business to transact with you, I have something to say to you* ; dean do gh., *do your business* ; gille-ghnothaich, *an errand-boy* ; a dh' aon gh., *on purpose* ; g. na cubhaige, *a fool's errand* ; là g. na cubhaige, *all fools' day* (*April 1st.*)
gnothaich, *gen. sing.* of gnothach.
————ean, *n.pl.* of gnothach.
gnothuch, see gnothach.
gnothuich, see gnothaich.
gnù. *a.* Famous, remarkable, notable. 2 Worldly, parsimonious. 3 Grippy. 4††Surly, gruff. 5 Envious. Cho g. ri broc, *as surly as a badger.* (see gnòdh.)
†gnuach, *a.* Leaky.
gnùdhachd,(MS) *s.f.* Gruffness.
gnùgach, -aiche, *a.* Surly, sulky, scowling. 2 ††Worldly, parsimonious.
gnùgag, -aig, -an, *s.f.* Dejected, poor female. 2 Sulky female.
gnùgair, -ean, *s.m.* Surly fellow.
gnùig,* *s.f.* Surly lowering expression of countenance, scowl.
gnùigean, -ein, *s.m.* Sorry wretch. 2 Pitiful miser. 3‡‡Miserable hut.
gnùigeineach, -eiche, *a.* Wry-mouthed, sorry, mean. 2 Morose.
gnùis, -e, -ean, *s.f.* Face, countenance. 2 Surface. 3 Love, favour. 4 Aspect. 5**Appearance. Sheall e 'nam gh., *he looked in my face.*
†gnùis, *s.f.* Hazard, jeopardy. 2 Notch.
gnùis-aognachaidh, *s.m.* Ghastliness.
gnùis-bhrat, -ait, -an, *s.m.* Veil for the face.
gnùis-bhreith, *s.f.* Judging by the look.
——·———eamh, -eimh, -nan, *s.m.* Physiognomist.
gnùis-chiontach, *s.f.* Guilty countenance.
gnùiseach, -eiche, *a.* Aspected.
gnùis-fhionn, -a *a.* White-faced.
gnùis-fhiosachd, *s.f.* Physiognomy. Fear g., *a physiognomist.*
gnùis-fhiosaiche, *s.m.* Physiognomist.
gnùis-mhalda, *s. f.* Modest countenance, face expressive of gentleness of disposition.
———·———, *a.* Of a modest appearance. Mo chaileag g., *my modest faced girl.*
gnùis-mheall, *v.a.* Counterfeit, put on a false appearance, dissemble.
————·——ach, -aiche, *a.* Counterfeiting, apt to deceive by a fair appearance.
———·——adh, -aidh, *s. m.* Counterfeiting, dissimulation. 2**Disguise, mask. Rinn iad g *they dissembled.*
——·———ta, *a.* Counterfeit, fictitious.
——·———tair, -ean, *s.m.* Deceiver, dissembler. counterfeiter
gnùis-naire *s.f.ind.* Bashfulness, shamefacedness.
gnùis-naireach, -eiche, *a.* Bashful. Gu g., *bashfully*
gnùis-naireachd, *s.f.* Bashfulness, shamefacedness, demureness.
gnùis-shubhach, -aiche, *a.* Merry-faced, having a merry countenance.
†gnumh, *s.m.* Notch, dent. 2 Heap, pile.
†gnumh, *v.a.* Heap up, pile, amass.
gnùmhail, *s.f.* Grunting, groaning.
gnumhan, *Gairloch* for gnòmhan.
gnusad, gnusadaich, gnusadh, } see gnòsadaich.

†gnusadh, -aidh, *s.m.* Notch, dent.
gnùsd, see gnòsd.
——adh, see gnosd.
gnùsdaich, } see gnòsadaich.
gnùsdail, }
gnusgalach, see grùnsgalach.
gnùsgail, see grùnsgal.
gnùsgal, see grùnsgal.
——aich, see grùnsgal.
gnùth, -ùith, -ùithe, & gnùtha, *s.f.* see gnòdh
gnutha,(MS) *a.* Niggardly.
——il, see gnùmhail.
go, see gu.
gò, *s.m.ind.* Lie, deceit, hypocrisy. 2 Fault, blemish, defect. 3 Guile. 4 Grudge. 5** Airy gait. 6 Wisdom. 7**Fraud. Duine gun ghò, *a guileless man* ; dà reithe gun ghò, *two rams without blemish.*
gò, *s.m.* †Sea, †2 Spear. 3 Fool.
gŏ, *v. Lochalsh, Suth'd, Torridon & Lewis* for gabh.
gob,** *s.* Babble. 2 Pee of an anchor, see p.77.
gob, guib, *s.m.* Bill or beak of a bird. 2 Mouth. 3 see gab. 4 Garrulity. 5 (DMy) Point. G. an rudha, *the point of the headland* ; g. na snàthaid, *the point of the needle* ; g. a' phrìne *the pin's point* ; g. na cuiteige, *the mouth of the whiting* ; duilleag 'na ghob, *a leaf in its bill* ; g. circe, *a hen's bill* , glas-ghuib, *the closure.*
gobach, -aiche, *a.* Beaked, snouty, having a long bill. 2 see gabach. 3 (DU) Tell-tale. G. cireanach, *long-billed and crested.*
——, -aiche, *s.f.* Prating female, chatterer, gabbler, scold. 'Nuair a phòs mi a' gh. àrd-anach nach obadh cnàmhan rium, *when I married the irritable chatterer, who would not cease from gnawing at me.*
gobach,¶ -aich, *s. m.* Hawfinch--*coccothraustes vulgaris.*
gobachadh,(MS) *s.m.* Growth.

380. Gobach.

gobada-liridh,(CR) *s.m.* Sandpiper—*W. of Ròss.*
gobag, -aig, -an, *s.f.* Dog-fish—*squalus acanthias.* 2(AF) Sea-dog. 3 (AF) Little gab (fish,) 4**Sand-eel. 5 Kiss. 6 Little bill. 7 Garrulous female. 8 Period of the year, lasting according to some, three days, according to others a week, coming in, apparently, between the *Feadag* and the *Gearran* and so ending on 14th. March. Feadagan is Gobagan e tuilleadh gu Féill Pàdruig, *whistling and biting winds on to St. Patrick's day.* Carmichael in *Carmina Gadelica*, explains *A' Ghobag* as the day before an Fhéill Brìghde (p. 276.)
gobag, *s.f.* Staple (DMK)—*W. coast of Ross.* 2 ††Kind of bird. 3 (DU) Little hook, such as is used for keeping a cupboard-door closed.

381. Gobag (1)

gobàgach, -aiche, *a.* Abounding in dog-fish. 2 Like a dog-fish. 3 see gabach.
gobaich,‡‡ *v.a.* Peck.
gobaiche, *comp.* of gobach.
gobair, -ean, see gabair.
——eachd, see gabaireachd.
gobais, *s.f.* see gabaireachd.
goban,(AF) *s.m.* Young sea-gull or fowl.
goban, -ain & guibein, *pl.* -an, *s.m dim.* of gob. Little bill or beak. 2 Garrulous mouth. 3 Muffle. 4 External hinderance to speech.
gobanach, -aiche, *a.* Prattling. 2 Having a little bill.
gobanach, -aich, *s.m.* Prattler.
goba-sàil, (AF) *s. m.* Seal, fat sea-lump.
gob-babharrtha,¶ see cam-ghlas.
gob-cabharrta,(AF) *s. m.* Redshank.
gob-cathainn *s.m.* Spoonbill.
gob-cèarr, (AF) *s.m.* Avocet (bird.)
gob-èasgaidh, see gab-èasgaidh.
gobh, see gabh.
gobha, see gobhainn.
gobha-bhreac, (AF) *s.f.* Buck, or buckie-snail (striated.) [Some writers give "gobha breac," *s.m.*]
gobhachan-allt, *s. m.* see gobha-uisge. 2 (AF) Little grebe.
gobhachan-dubh, } see gobha-uisge.
gobhachan-uisge, }
gobhachan-uisge,¶ see biorra-cruidein.
gobhadh, see gobhainn.
gobha-dubh-a'-mhonaidh, *s.m.* Mountain-ouzel, blackbird.
gobha-dubh-an-uisge, -an-dubha-, *s. m.* Water-ouzel, see gobha-uisge. 2 Balm-cricket.
gobhagan, see gabhagan.
gobhaich, *v.a.* Peck.
gobhainn, *pl.* goibhnean,*s.m.* Smith, blacksmith.
gobhainn-chruidhean, *s.m.* Farrier.
gobhainneachd, see goibhneachd.
gobhainnean, *s.m.* Cockchafer.
gobhail, *gen.sing.* of gobhal. 2 *Lewis* for gabhail.
gobhairnear,(MS) *s.m.* Prefect.
gobhal, -ail & goibhle, *pl.* -bhlean, *s.m.* Fork, 2 Prop, post, pillar. 3 House-support. 4 Forked supporter. 5 Fork of a cycle. 6 Any furcated instrument. 7 Bifurcation. 8 The perinæum. 9 Descendant, branch. 10 Yoking. 11 Day's labour. 12* Pair of compasses. 13* Crutch. 14**Forked part of anything. 15 Prong. G. na briogais, *the crutch of the trousers* ; g. a' chroinn, *the space between the plough-handles.*
gobhallan, *s.m.* Fool.
gobhal-luachair,§ *s.m.* Bulrush, lake scirpus, see luachair-ghòbhlach.
gobhal-reang, see gobhàl-roinn.
gobhal-roinn, -ail-roinne, *s.m.* Compasses, callipers.
gobhann, -ainn, *pl.* goibhean, see gobhainn.
gobhar, *gen.* -air & goibhre, *pl.* -air, *s.f.* Goat. 2 Sort of branching river.—*Perth.* 3 (AF) Shad (fish.) 4 (AF) Mackerel. 5 The sign Capricornus (♑) of the zodiac. 6 (DC) Sheaf of corn—*Skye.* (also gabhar.)
gobharach, *a.* Of, or belonging to, a goat. 2 Skipping.
gobhar-alluidh, *s.m.* Chamois.
gobhar-athair, *s.m.* Snipe—*scolopax gallinago.*
gobhar-bhacach,(AF) *s.f.* Name given in some

parts (e. g. *Skye*) to the last handful of corn to be cut.

gobhar-bhreac, *s.f.* Buck-snail.

gobhar-cheann,(AF) *s.m.* Leader of goats.

gobhar-chrò, see gobhar-lann.

gobhar-fhiadh, gobhar-fhiadhaich, *s.f.* gobhar-fhiadhain, } Antelope. 2(AF)Wild or rock goat. 3 *of old* Horse.

gobhar-lann, *s.m.* Goat-pen.

gobhar-mhór, *s.f.* Crawfish, crayfish. 2 Lobster.

gobhar-oidhche,¶ *s.f.* Snipe, see gobhar-athair. 2 Night-jar.

gobharr, *s.m.* Periwig.

gobharrta,(AF) *s.* Redshank.

gobha-uisge,¶ -n-uisge, *s. m.* Dipper, water-ouzel—*cinctus aquaticus.* 2 Kingfisher.

382. Gobha-uisge.

gòbhlach, -aiche, *a.* Forked, pronged. 2 Long-legged. 3 Bow-legged. 4 Straddle, astride. Sporain gh. do dh' òr a' Phrionnsa, *forked purses of the Prince's gold*—a Lochaber saying alluding to the purses in use in 1745 ; clamhan g., *a kite ;* a' marcachd casa-g., *riding astride.*

gobhlachan,¶ -ain, *s. m.* Turnstone, Hebridal sandpiper—*strepsilas interpres.* 2 Dipper, water-ouzel, see gobha-uisge. 3 (AF)Cricket (insect.)

383. Gobhlachan (1.)

gòbhlachan, -ain, -an, *s.m.* Person sitting astride. 2 Crane-fly, daddy long-legs. 3 Earwig. 4 Shad (fish.) 5 Young trout. 6 Stickleback. 7 Large minnow. 8 Mackerel. 9 Parr, samlet. 10 Swallow. 11 Iron joining furrow-board to lefthand board of plough. 12 (DU) Centipede.

384. Gobhlachan (4.)

gobhlachan-gaoithe, -ain, -ain-gaoithe see gobhlan-gaoithe.

gobhlach-innse,(AH) *s.f.* Cow after giving birth to her third calf, and before giving birth to her fourth.

gobhladh, -aidh, see gobhal.

gobhlag, -aig, -an, *s.f.*, *dim.* of gobhal. Dung fork. 2 Graip. 3 Any two-pronged instrument. 4 Any forked piece of timber. 5 *in ridicule,* Bow-legged female. 6(AF) Earwig. 7 Stick with forked end for turning hay. 8 Fork-shaped twig on which to wind a fishing-line.

gobhlag-fheòir,‡‡ *s.f.* Hay-fork.

gobhlaichead, *s m.* Degree of furcation or forkedness. A' dol an g., *growing more and more furcated.*

gobhlaichid, *comp.* of gobhlach. Is g. e am buille sin, *that blow has made it more forked.*

gobhlaisdeach, *adv.* Astride.

gobhlaisdeach, *s.m.* Clipt of a boat, see H1,p.73.

gobhlaisgeach, -aich, *s.m.* Long-legged person.

gobhlan, -ain, -an, *s.m., dim.* of gobhal. Prong. 2 Small fork. 3 Weeding hook. 4 Little branch. 5 Swallow. 6 Earwig. 7 (DC) Estuary of a river or burn, where the stream divides on the shallows near the sea.

gobhlanach, -aiche, *a.* Pronged, forked. 2 Two-headed. 3 Divided. 4 Branching.

gobhlanachd, *s.f. ind.* Bifurcation.

gobhlan-bharta, (AF) *s.m.* Redshank.

gobhlan-dubh,(AF) *s. m.* Great martin, black martin.

gobhlan-gainmhich, -ain-ghainmhich, *s.m.* Sand-martin (species of swallow)—*hirundo riparia.*

385. Gobhlan-gainmhich.

gobhlan-gaoithe,¶ -ain-gh., -an-g., *s. m. & f.* Swallow—*hirundo rustica.* 2 Fork-tailed petrel—*thalassidroma Leachii—Barra.* 3 see gobhlan-taighe.

gobhlan-mara, *s.m.* **Redshank. 2(AF) Fork-tailed petrel.

gobhlan-monaidh,¶ *s.m.* Alpine swift—*cypselus alpinus.*

gobhlan-mór,¶ *s.m.* Swift—*cypselus apus.*

386. Gobhlan mór.

gobhlannaidh,** *s.f.* Hollow between two hills.

gobhlan-nan-creag, ¶ *s. m.* Alpine swift, see gobhlan-monaidh.

387. Gobhlan-taighe.

gobhlan-taighe,¶ *s.m.* Martin—*hirundo urbica.*

gobhlan-uisge,(AF) *s.m.* Little grebe, dabchick.

gobhrach,†† see gabhrach.

gobhrag, see gabhrag.

gobhragan, see gabhragan.

go hrag bheag,¶ *s.f.* Jack snipe, see gabhrag bheag.

gobhraidh,(MMcD) *s.pl.* Compasses, callipers—*Lewis.*

gobhran, see gabhran.

388. Gobhrag bheag.

gobhta, see gabhte.

gob-labharta,(AF) *s. m.* Redshank.

gob-labhradh, *s.m.* Redstart (bird.)

goblachan, see gobhlachan.

gobhlachan-uisge, see spag-ri-tòn.

389. Gob-leathann.

gob-leathann, guib-,¶ *s.m.* Spoon-bill—*platalea leacorodia.*

390. Gob-leathann (2.)

gob-leathann,¶ -uib-, (2) *s.m.* Shoveller—*anser clypeata.*

goc, -a, -an & -achan, *s.m.* Pipe or faucet put into a cask to give passage to the liquor. 2 **Stop-cock, tap. 3(DC) Finials on the ridge of a house. 4 (DC) Buds of trees, flowers, &c., before bursting.

goc, *v.* see gogaich.

gocach, -aiche, see gogach.

gocag,(DC) *s.f.* Pert, forward girl.

gòcaman, -ain, *s.m.* Usher, attendant. 2 Warder, domestic sentinel, 3* One on the look-out in a mask, spy, scout. 4 Fool. 5 An officer employed in the Hebrides in the days of Martin, who saw a *gocaman* at the house of MacNeill of Barra. He was stationed at the top of the house, where he watched night and day, and strangers were never allowed to draw near the house until they gave satisfactory answers to his questions concerning the purport of their visit.

gocam-gò,* *s.m.* Spy, scout. 2 Fellow perched on any place. see gòcaman.

gocan, -ain, -an, *s. m.* Little attendant. 2†† Pert, conceited little person. 3 Titlark. 4 see gabhagan. G. na cubhaige. *the cuckoo's attendant.*

391. Gocan.

gocan, *s.m.* Whin-chat—*saxicola rubetra.*

gocan-cònuisg,(AF) *s.m.* Whin-chat.

gocan-cubhaige,(DMC) *s.m.* Titlark, little bird always following the cuckoo.

goc-fola,(WC) *s,m.* Blood spurting out.

gochdan, see gocan.

gochdmunn, -uinn, see gocaman.

goch-ghèadh, see gob-ghèadh.

god,* *v.a.* see gog.

gòd, -òid, *s.m.* Show, ornament. 2 Coquetry.

godach, -aiche, *a.* see gabhdach.

gòdach, -aiche, *a.* Showy, dressy. 2‡Coquettish. 3 Giddy.

godadh, -aidh, *s.m.* see gogadh.

gòdag, -aig, -an, *s.f.* Coquette, *prov.*

godagach, -aiche, *a.* Coquettish.

godail,(MS) *s.f.* Talkativeness.

godhan, -ain, *s.m.* Cask, barrel.

gog, *s.m.ind.* Little syllable. 2 Nod. 3 Tossing of the head. 4 Cackling or clucking of a hen. 5 Cooing of a pigeon.

gog,* *pr.pt.* a' gogail & a' gogadh, *v.a.* Cackle, as a hen. 2 Toss.

gogach, -aiche, *a.* Nodding, wagging, as the head. 2 Fickle, wavering. 3 Reeling. 4(DC) Stammering, stuttering—*Perth.*

gogadh, -aidh, *s.m.* Nodding. 2 Tossing of the head. A' g—, *pr. pt.* of gog. Cha'n e gogadh nan ceann a ni an t-iomram, *it is not the nodding of the heads that rows the boat.*

gogag, -aig, -an, see gogaid.

gogaich, *v.a.* see coc.

gogaid, -e, -ean, *s.f.* Light-headed woman, coquette, giddy female, stupid trull.

gogaideach, -eiche, *a.* Light, airy, gay, vain, coquettish, giddy, foolish, light-headed. Generally applied to a female.

gogaideachd, *s.f.ind.* Light airy behaviour, flirting, coquetry, capriciousness, womanish vanity or folly, giddiness.

gogaidh,(CR) *s.* Egg (a nursery word)—*Arran.*

gogail, *s. f.* see gogadh & gogaid. 2 Clucking or cackling of a hen. 3 Cooing of a pigeon. 4‡‡Noise of liquor issuing from a cask or bottle. A' g—, *pr. pt.* of gog.

gogaild, -ean, see gogail.

gogailich, *s.pl.* Blinders, in horse's harness.

gogaill, -ean, see gogaid.

gogailleach, -eiche, see gogaideach.

gogailleachd, see gogaideachd.

gogair,(MMcD) *s.m.* Stupid fellow, fool.
——ehchd, *s.f. ind.* Act of making a fool of anyone. La na g., *All fools' day—Lewis.*
gogain, *gen.sing. & n.pl.* of gogan.
gogallach,** -aich, *s.f.* Cackling of poultry.
gogan, -ain, -an, *s.m.* Small wooden dish made of staves and with one handle. 2 Kit. 3 Pail. 4 *rarely* Prating, cackling Laogh-gogain, *a hand-reared calf ; 2 lout of a lad.*
goganach, -aiche, *a.* Of, or belonging to, wooden dishes. 2 see gog-cheannach.
gogar, -air, *s.m.* Light.
gog-cheannach, -aiche, *a.* Light-headed. 2 Nodding. 3 Tossing the head in walking, as deer.
gog-ghèadh, -eòidh, *s.m.* Gosling, young goose.
gog-shùil, -ùla, -ean, *s.f.* Goggle-eye.
gog-shùileach, -eiche, *a.* Goggle-eyed, having wandering eyes.
gog-shùilich, *s.pl.* Blinders.
goguideach, -eiche, see gogaideach.
goguideachd, see gogaideachd.
goibean, *dim.* of gob. see goban & gobag.
goibh,** Old Gaelic name of the letter G, see gath.
goibheinn,** *s.f.* Little hill.
goibhlich,* *v.a.* Prop, buttress.
goibhneachd, *s. f. ind.* Smith-work, trade of a blacksmith.
goibhnean, *n.pl.* of gobhainn.
goibhre, see gobhar.
goibhrios, *s.m.* False colour.
goibin, -ean, *s.m.* Sand-eel. 2 see goban. 3 see gobag.
goic, -e, *s.f.* Tossing up of the head in disdain 2 Scoff, taunt. 3* Wry-neck. G. moit, *tossing up of the head with pride.*
goicealachd,*s.f.ind.*Scornful tossing of the head.
goicean,(DC) *s.m.* Short, stout man—*Uist.*
goiceil, -a, *a.* Scoffing, taunting, disdainful. 2 Scornfully tossing the head.
goid, *s.pl.* Part of a plough, see goid.
goid, -e, *s.f.* Theft, stealing, pilfering. 2 Creeping, slipping away cautiously. A' g—, *pr.pt.* of goid. Am bheil thu ri g. ? *dost thou steal ?*
goid, *pr.pt.* a' goid, *v.a.* Steal, pilfer. 2 Creep, steal, slip, sneak Goididh an doinionn e, *the storm shall steal him ;* gh. e orm, *he crept softly upon me ;* gh. e a' chlach orm, *he stole the stone from me ,* g. a staigh, *slip in ;* g. air falbh, *abduct.*
goid, (*for* gaid) *n.pl.* of gad.
goideach,** *a.* Inclined to pilfer.
goideadh,** -idh, *s.m.* Act of stealing, theft. 2 Stealth. (Generally goid)
goideadh, *3rd sing. & pl. imp.* of goid. G. iad, *let them steal.*
goidean, -ein, -an, *s.m* Little withe.
——ach, *a.* Abounding in little withes.
goidnich,** *s.f.* Theft, stolen goods.
goigean, ein, an, *s.m.* Bit of fat meat. 2 Cluster. 3 Coxcomb. 4‡ Kink or tangle in thread.
goigeanach, aiche, *a.* Abounding in bits of fat. 2 Clustering, dangling 3 Coxcombical.
goigeanachd, *s.f.ind.* The behaviour of a coxcomb.
goigleis, *s.f.* Tickling.
goil, -e, *s.f.* Boiling, act or state of boiling. 2 Smoke, vapour, fume 3 Battle. 4 Rage,fury. 5 Powder. 6 Valour. 7 Power. 8 Effervescing. 9‡‡Grief. 10 (DC) Swirling of stream in a tideway. A' g—, *pr. part,* of goil Gach anam air g. gu h-àr, *every soul boiling for bloodshed ;* air g., *boiling, on the boil ;* tha 'n coir' air g., *the kettle is boiling :* an g. an t-sruith, *in the swirling of the stream.*
goil, *pr.pt.* a' goil, *v.a. & n.* Boil, as a liquid. 2 Boil with rage. 3 Cook by boiling. 4 Effervesce.
†**goil**, *s.* Prowess, chivalry.
goile, -an & -achan, *s. f.* [*s. m.*—WC] The stomach. 2 Appetite. 3 Throat. 4 Swarm, as of vermin. 5 Fowl's crop. 6 Gizzard. 7‡‡ Gluttony. 8 see goil. Air son do gh., *for thy stomach.*
goileach, -eiche, *a.* Boiling. 2 Hot, as boiling water. Uisge g., *boiling water.*
goileach, -ich, *s.m.* Glutton.
gòileach,(DC) *s. m.* Forward, impudent boy, " sneak "—*Argyll.*
goileachan-éisg, *s.m.* Stomach of a fish stuffed with livers of fish minced with oatmeal and spices—*Caithness, Suth'd & Lewis.*
goileachd, *s.f.ind.* Gluttony. 2 Flattery, the conduct of a parasite.
goileadair, -ean, *s.m.* Boiler. 2 Kettle.
goileadh, -idh, *s.m.* Boiling, regurgitation.
gòileag,‡ -eig, *s.f.* Haycock, cole—*Badenoch.*
goileag, -eig, *s. f.* Flirt. 2 Staggering gait, drunkenness—*Suth'd.* 3 The globules of fat circling on the surface of a pot of broth—*Lochcarron.* see coinnleag. Tha g. air, *he is drunk ;* nach e a ghabh a' gh. a' tighinn ! *what a roundabout way he came !*
goileam, -eim, *s. m.* Prating, chattering, vain tattle. 2 Flattery. 3 Verbiage. 4 Fast and senseless talk. 5(AC) Fire, fire-kindling. 6* Incessant high-toned chattering.
goileamach, -aiche, *a.* Prating, tattling. 2 Adulatory. Gu g., *pratingly.*
goileamachd,‡‡ *s.f.ind.* Petulancy.
goileamag, -aige, -an, *s.f.* Female prater, loquacious girl.
goileamaiche, *s.m.* Prater, tattler.
goileaman, -ain, see goileamaiche.
goileamhuin, *s.f.* Grief, sorrow.
goilean, -ein, *s. m.* Gourmand, greedy-gut. 2 Parasite.
goilean, *s.pl.* State of boiling. Air na g., *boiling, very hot, as liquid.*
goileanach, *a.* Parasitical. 2 Gluttonous. 3 Flattering.
goilear, *s.m.* see goileadair.
goilibheir, Gaelic spelling of *cleaver* (knife.)
goill, -e, *s.f.* Hanging lip. 2 Shapeless mouth. 3 Face distorted by grief or sullenness. 4 Angry or sullen look. 5 Distortion of mouth. 6 Blubber cheek. 7 *rarely* War. 8 Any cause of grief. Is ann air a bha a' ghoill ! *what a distorted mouth he had.*
†**goill**, -e, *s.m.* Shield. 2 War, fight. 3 Any cause of grief.
goilleach, -eiche, *a.* Sulky, sour-looking. 2 Blubber-lipped or cheeked. 3 Having a swollen or distorted face.
goilleag, -eig, -an, *s.f.* Blow on the cheek, slap on the face.
goillear, -eir, -an, *s m* Blubber-lipped person. 2 Man with a distorted mouth or face.
goilleas, -is, see goill.
goilleasach, -aiche see goilleach.
goillseach, -eiche, see goilleach.
goillir, -ean, *s. m.* Petrel. 2 Lewis bird of the size of the swallow, said never to come ashore, except in the month of January.
goimh, -e, *s.f.* Anguish 2 Agonizing pain, pang, throb. 3 Excessive vexation 4 Grudge, hatred, spite, malice. 5 Hurt, damage. 6** Storm. 7 Frown. 8(AF) Leech. 9(AF) Worm. Ceann g. air maduinn Earraich 's mairg a chailleadh a chaomh charaid *a spring morning with a stinging head, who would lose his loved friend*—N.G.P. says the meaning appears to be, that as a bitter spring morning

is often followed by a fine day, so is the displeasure of a friend not to be taken as a ground for serious quarrel, do chridhe gun g, *thy heart without anguish (or without malice.)*

goimh-chridheach a Keen, ardent Gu g guais-bheartach, *keenly and daringly.*

goimheach, a. see goimheil

goimhealachd, s.f.ind. Soreness

goimheil, -e, a. Painful, pinching, causing pain or anguish, inflicting pangs 2 Throbbing 3 Bearing hatred, or grudge, spiteful, malicious. 4‡‡Surly 5* Venomous 6 Vexatious

goin, -e, s.f Wound, hurt 2 Lancinating pain 3 Sting 4 Lance 5 Delusion 6 Paragraph. 7††Fascination 8††Blasting Cha b' fheairrd mo gh. e, *my wounds were not the better for it.*

goin, v.a. Wound, hurt 2 Cause a sudden smarting 3 Fascinate

goineach, -eiche, a. see guineach 2 Painful, throbbing. 3 Prickly, stinging 4 Agonizing, vexatious. 5 Angry (in surgery) 6 Keen eager Gu g., *painfully.*

gòineach, a. see gòinneach.

goinead, -id, s.m. Painfulness, throbbing. 2 Vexatiousness.

goineag, -eig, s.f. Pang, twitching of pain.

goinean, s.m. Couch-grass, quickens—*Perthsh* 2(DC) Withered grass gathered after a harrow or grubber—*Argyll.* 3 (DMy) Growth inside a cow's mouth, which hinders her chewing. It is often cut with scissors.

goineanta, -inte, a. Keen, wounding, piercing.

goinear, s.m. see goin-fheur.

goineideach,* -eich, s.m. Person bewitched, or influenced by the evil eye.

goin-fheur, fheòir,§ s. m. Crested dog's tail, couch-grass—*cynosurus cristatus.* 2 see goinean 2.

goin-làmhach, -aiche, a. Wounding with the hand.

goinneach,(CR) a. Unkempt, shaggy, untidy, uncared for—*W of Ross-shire.*

gòinneag,(CR) s.f. Dowdy, slattern, untidy woman—*W. of Ross-shire.*

goinnean s.m. *Blair Athole* for gonan.

goinntean, s.m. Confinement—*Dàin I. Ghobha.*

goinntir. see gainntir.

goin-olann,* s.f. Bad kind of wool next to the skin of the sheep.

goin-shùil, -shùla, -shùilean, s.f. Blasting eye. 2 Fascinating eye. Goin-shùil na righ-nathrach, *the fascinating eye of the cockatrice.*

goin-shùileach, a. Having a blasting eye 2 Having a fascinating eye.

gointe, *past pt.* of gon. Bewitched, infatuated, fascinated, "fay" 2 Wounded. 3* Hurt with an evil eye. 4* Galled to the core.

goir, *pr.pt.* a' goirsinn, *v.a.* Cry, call. 2 Crow, as a cock, cry, as the cuckoo. [* says ' to apply it to a person is neither good nor polite.'"] 3 Name, style, bestow a name. 4 Talk loudly and pertly. 5‡‡ Shriek, cry with a shrill piercing voice Gh. an coileach, *the cock crew:* fàth mu'n g a' chorr, *the reason why the heron cries.* (also gair.)

goir see gair.

†goir,** a Near.

goire, see gaire.

goireag. *Suth d* for gòileag.

goireal,‡‡ eil, s m. Crow of a cock.

gòirealas, ais, s.m see goraiche

goiream, *1st. per. sing. fut aff* of goir *for* goiridh mi *I will cry.* 2 *1st. sing, imp.* Let me shout.

goireas, -is, s. m. Apparatus, tools. 2*Family necessary—*Islay* 3 Furniture. 4 Moderation, moderate quantity 5 Cheer. 6‡ Convenience. 7 Advantage, benefit Tha g. agam *I have a moderate quantity or a sufficiency*

goireasach aiche a. Convenient, handy, useful. near at hand 2 Moderate, temperate. 3 Needful 4**In moderate quantity

goireasachd s.f ind. Advantageousness.

goireasaich v a Accommodate

goireil. -e, a see gaireil

goirgeach,** a Foolish 2 Doting.

goirgeachd,** s.f Foolishness. 2 Dotage

goirid, a Short, not long. 2 Scarce, scanty 3 Brief. Thus compared :—*1st. comp.* giorra, *2nd.* giorraid, *3rd* giorrad. An ceann g., *in a short time*, o cheann g., *a short time since:* fear g., *a man of low stature ; cha bu bheag* orra bhith g dhomh idir *they did not at all object to being near me*

goiridh, *fut.aff.a.* of goir

goiriosach, -aiche, see goireasach.

goiriseadh, -idh, s.m Target.

goirisinn see gairisinn

goirisneach, -eiche, a see gairisneach.

gòirleis,†† s.f. Foolishness, childishness.

goirmean-searradh,§ s. m Pansy heartsease—*viola tricolor.*

392. Goirmean-searradh.

goirmein, see guirmein

goirn,(AF) see goirnead

goirnead, -id, s.m. Gurnet.

gòirseideach, see gòrsaideach.

goirrid, see goirid.

goirridh,(AC) a. Fox-coloured. M' aghan g., *my fox-coloured heifer*

goirrig,** s Fool. dolt

gòirseadh, -eidh. s.m. Target.

goirsinn, -e, s.f Crying, crowing 2 Act of crying or calling, as of a cock or cuckoo 3 Naming. 4 Boast, loud, pert talking A' g—, *pr.pt.* of goir.

goirt, -e. a. Sore, painful 2 Mournful. 3 Sour. 4 Acid, bitter 5 Salt, salted 6 Hard, sad. 7 Poor-spirited 8 Narrow 9 Mean. 10* Severe 11 High," applied to game, &c. Le amhghar g. *with sore distress ;* acain gh., *bitter sobbing ;* leann g., *sour beer :* is g. a' chùis, *it is a hard case ;* cas gh., *a sore foot ;* deuchainn gh., *a severe trial ,* bainne g. *sour milk (Argyllsh* for blathach), *butter-milk ;* sgadan g (for sgadan saillt,) *salt herring.*

goirt, -e, s.f see gort 2 *gen.sing.* of gort.

goirt-bhriseadh idh, s m. Calamity 2 Misery

goirt-dhearc, *s.f.* Bearberry. Red bearberry—*arctosaphylos uva ursi*; black bearberry—*a. alpina.*
goirte, *s.f.* Saltness. 2 Sourness.
goirteach, -eiche, *a.* see gortach.
goirteachadh, -aidh, *s.m.* Hurt. 2 Act of hurting. 3 Making, or state of becoming sour, acid or bitter. 4(DMC) Leavening. A' g—, *pr. pt.* of goirtich.
goirteachd, *s.f.* Acidity, acerbity.
goirtead, *s. m.* Sourness, saltness, bitterness, acidity. 2 (DU) Soreness 3 (DC) Chagrin G. do chorraig' nad chuimhne, *the soreness of your finger still in your memory.*
goirteag, -eig, *s. f.* Crab-apple, see craobh-ubhal fhiadhain. 2 Stingy female. 3**Acid.
goirtean, -ein, -ean, *s. m.* Little corn-field. 2 Small patch of arable land 3**Little field, enclosure, "park." 4** Little farm. 5 (MS) Croft.
goirteanach, -aiche, *a.* Abounding in little fields, crofts or patches of arable land.
goirteas, -eis, *s.m.* Pain,painfulness. 2‖ Disease [Preceded by the article *an.*] 3*Acidity. 4* Soreness. 5*Sourness. 6*Saltness.
goirteas-nàrach (an), *s.m.* see an tinneas-nàrach.
goirtein, -ean, see goirtean.
goirtich, *pr.pt.* a' goirteachadh, *v.a. & n.* Hurt, pain, cause pain. 2 Make sour. 3 Become sour or acid, acidulate. 4 Leaven. Goirtichear e, *he will be hurt.*
goirtichte, *a. & past pt.* of goirtich. Hurt, pained. 2 Soured, made or become sour. 3** Leavened. Aran g., *leavened bread.*
goisdidh, see goistidh.
goisean, *s.m.* Tuft. 2**Bush.
goisear,(AC) -an, *s.pl.* Waits, young men who go about singing carols at Christmas, New Year and other great festivals. *Scots*, guiser.
goiseid, *s.f.* A horse's or cow's hair. Lùbag gh., *a horse-hair snare for catching birds*; cas-gh., *a fishing-sned*; buarach gh., *cow-fetter made of horse-hair*—WC.
goisir, -e, -ean, see goisinn.
goisinn, goisne, *pl.* -ean & -nicheau, *s.f.* Snare, noose, gin, trap. 2 Fox-trap. 3 (MS)Mouse-trap.
———**each**,** *a.* Full of gins or traps. 2 Like a gin or trap. 3 Ensnaring.
goisne, see goisinn. 2 (MS) Trammel.
goisneach, *a.* see goisinneach.
gòisneach,(DMC) *s.m.* Single loop in the snare.
goisneadh,(DC) *s.f.* Particle, minute part. Cha 'n 'eil g. agam, *I have not a particle*—applied only to straw, and not to meal, &c. in *Uist*—DMC.
goisnean, -ein, -an, *s.m. dim.* of goisinn. Little snare. 2 (DMC) A single straw.
———**ach**,†† *a.* Abounding in little snares.
gòisnibh. *s.pl.* Nets, snares.
gòisnich, *v.a.* Decoy, enmesh. 2(MS) Tangle.
goisridh, see gasraidh.
†**gòiste**, -an & -tichean, see goisinn. 2 Halter.
goisteachd, see goistidheachd.
gòistean, -in, -an, see gaoisnean.
goistidh, -ean, *s. m.* Gossip. 2 Godfather. 3 Father of a child to whom one is godfather.
———**each**, *a.* Gossiping.
goistidheachd, *s.f.ind.* Office or duty of a godfather. 2 Gossipping. Ri g., *assuming the office of a godfather*; cleamhnas am fagus is g. am fad, *affinity at hand and sponsorship afar off.*
†**goithne**, *s.f.* Lance, spear. 2 Quick gait.
gol, *s.m.* see guil & gal.
gola, *s.m.* see goile.
gola-bhigein,(AF) *s.* Common bunting.
†**goladh**,** -aidh, *s.m.* Gluttony.
golag, -aige, -an, *s.f.* Nip, pinch with the nails or teeth. 2 Budget. 3 (WC) Any little fish. 4(DMy) The spaces between the peats when laid upon the fire.
golaidh, -aidhean, *s.f.* Clumsy clasp-knife. *Scots*, gully
golan,(AH) *s.m* Forward, insolent fellow.
gòlanach, *a* Two-headed.
golanach, see gobhlanach.
†**golghair**,** *s.f* Lamentation, loud wail.
†**golghaireach**, -eiche, *a.* Lamenting, wailing, mournful. 2 Causing lamentation.
golibheir, see goilibheir.
†**goll**,‖ *a.* Blind.
gollach, *a.* Gluttonous.
golum, *s.m.* Trifling flattery—*Arran.*
gòm,(DMC) *s.m.* Throat trouble, caused by eating oats or unripe corn.
gòmadaich,(DMC) (a') *pr. pt.* Gaping, opening the mouth wide, as one about to vomit.
gòmag, -aig, -an, *s.f.* Nip, pinch with the nails. 2 (MMcL) Blade of grass
———**ach**, -aiche, *a.* Pinching, nipping with the nails.
———**aich**, *v.* Bepinch. 2 Nip. 3 Sting, stab, gore.
gomhainn, *W of Lewis* for gamhainn.
gon, *pr.pt*, a' gonadh, *v.a.* Wound, wound sorely, stab, lance. 2 Bewitch, destroy by enchantment, hurt by the evil eye. 3 Starve to death by cold. 4 Blast. 5 Pique or gall to the core. 6**Charm, fascinate. 7††Annoy. An ni a gh. thu, *the thing that galled you.*
gon, *prov.* for gus, Gon an till mi nall, *till I return hither.*
†**gon**, *prep.* With, with them.
gon,** -oin & -a, *s.m.* Wound, sting, stab,lance. 2 Stinging, stabbing, lancing. 3 Stinging pain, throb. 4 Charm. 5 Fascination. Naoi gona, *nine wounds.*
gonach, -aiche, *a.* Sharp, keen. 2 Wounding, stinging, stabbing. 3†† Bewitching.
gonachas, -ais, for donachas, see donas.
gonadair,** *s.m.* Wounder, piercer. 2 Annoyer, afflicter. 3 (DC) Man with an evil eye, one who can bewitch—*Argyllsh.*
gonad-fhear, see gonadair.
gonadh, -aidh, *s.m.* Wounding, act of wounding, stinging, stabbing. 2 Bewitching. 3 Fascinating. 4 Starving. 5 Lanciuating. 6 Lancing. 7 Wound. 8 Lancinating pain. A' g—, *pr pt.* of gon. Gonadh ort ! (an imprecation), *may you perish.*
gonadhaire, *s.f.* Wounding, stinging, stabbing.
gonag, -aig, -an, *s.f.* Bite or pinch with the teeth or nails. 2 Stab. 3††Witch. 4††Miserable woman. 5††Spell, enchantment. 5 (DMC) Small bit. Bha gonagan is friodhain air a' chù, *the dog was showing his teeth and his hair was bristling.—S.-na-caol p. 75.*; cha'n fhaigh thu g. dheth, *you won't get a bit of it.*
gonaich,** *v.a.* Annoy.
gonaidh, (AF) *s.f.* Leech.
gonaim, (for gonaidh mi) *v.* I will wound.
gonair,** see gonadair.
gonais. *s.f.* Sting, prick, wound.
gonan,(CR) *s.m.* Grass roots. (see goinean.)
gon-iasg,(AF) *s.m.* Cramp-fish, torpedo.
gonn, see gon, *prep.*
gonta, see gointe.
gontach, -aich, *s.m.* Old coarse coverlet.
gòr, *pr.pt.* a' gòradh, *v.a.* Peep.
†**gor**, *s.m. & f.* Profit. 2 Laughter. 3 Pleasure. 4 Pus. 5 Light. 6 Heat.
gòrach, -aiche, *a.* Silly, foolish. 2 Insane, mad. 3 Inconsiderate, thoughtless, unwise.

'Nuair a bha mi òg is gòrach, *when I was young and foolish ;* na innis do rùn do charaid g., *tell not thy mind to a foolish friend.*
gòrachan,* -ain, *s.m.* Young male, silly fellow.
gòrachd, *s.f.* Foolishness, idiocy.
goradair,(MMcD) *s.m.* Spy.
———eachd, *s.f.* Spying, peeping.
gòradh, -aidh, *s.m.* Peeping, spying, 2 (DU) Hurried look. 3 (DMC) Listing, bending, as if about to fall. A' g—, *pr pt.* of gor. Bha e a' g. orra, *he was watching them on the sly—W. of Ross.*, thug mi g. air, *I made a short call on him.* [3 Whipping
†goradh, -aidh,‡*s.m.* Blush, heat. 2 Warming.
gorag, -aig, -an, *s.f.* Foolish woman. 2 Sheaf of corn standing upright and isolated on a field in harvest. 3 *Young she-crow. 4(DMy) Scare-crow, made of sticks dressed up as a woman, to frighten birds from the corn. Tapan gòraig air cuigeil criontaig, *a foolish woman's flax on the wise woman's distaff.*
†gòraiceadh, -idh, *s.m.* Croaking, croaking voice or shout
goraiceil, *a.* Croaking, screeching.
gòraiche, *s f.* Folly, silliness. 2 Insanity. Mo gh. is coireach rium, *my own folly is the cause;* cha'n 'eil ann ach g., *it is but folly.*
goraiche, *comp* of gòrach.
———. see gòraichead.
gòraichead, -id, *s.f.* Folly, degree of folly or madness. A' dol an g., *growing more and more foolish*
goraicleis, *s.f* Croaking. 2 Shouting, shout.
gòraidear, see goradair.
gòralas, -ais, see gòraiche.
goramhach, *a.* Greedy, hungry, Gu g.,*greedily.*
goramhachd, *s.f* Greediness, hunger, gluttony.
goramhan,** -ain, *s m.* Hungry fellow, glutton.
goran, -ain, see guirean.
gorg, *a.* see garg.
†gorgach, *a.* Foolish. 2 Peevish.
†gorgachas, -ais, *s.m.* Foolishness. 2 Peevishness. 3 Dotage.
gorgaich, *v.a.* Hurt, injure, annoy.
gorghlan,*v.a.* see gart-ghlan.
gorghlanadair, *s.m.* see gart-ghlanadair.
gòrlais,†† *s.f.* Folly.
gorm, guirme, *a.* Blue, azure, blue of whatever shade. 2 Green, as grass, verdant. 3** Hot. 4 *rarely* Great, illustrious. 5 Azure, in *heraldry*, represented by a shading formed of horizontal lines. 7 Green, in the sense of unsophisticated 8* (DU) Mean, spiritless. Nach e tha g. ! *how green he is !* feur g., *green grass :* each g., *a dark grey horse ;* aodach g., *blue cloth ;* na speuran gorma, *the blue heavens ;* cho g. ris a' chàl, *as green as kale ;* fear g. *a negro ;* bean gh., *a negress.*
gorm, guirm, *s. m.* Blue or azure colour. 2 Green. 3 Grassy or green plain. An g. is an dubh, *the blue and the black ;* Irt nan caorach gorma, *St. Kilda of the black-faced sheep.* —DMy.
gorm, *pr. pt.* a' gormadh, *v. a.* Make blue or azure. 2 Make green. 3 Become blue or green. 4 Grow green, as grass. 5 (DU) Starve with cold, benumb. Gh. am feur, *the grass grew green.*
gormachd, *s.f.* Blueness.
gormadh, -aidh, *s. m.* Act of making blue or green. 2 State of becoming blue or green. 3 Growing green. 4‡‡Daybreak. 5 Blue colour or shade. A' g—, *pr. pt.* of gorm. Tha e air g., *he is benumbed with cold ;* fo gh. nan sgiath,*beneath the blue colour of the shields;* g. an là, *twilight, daybreak.*
gorglais,(CR) *s. f.* Croaking of frogs—*Arran.*

gormag,¶ -aig, *s.f.* The hobby bird—*falco subbuteo.*

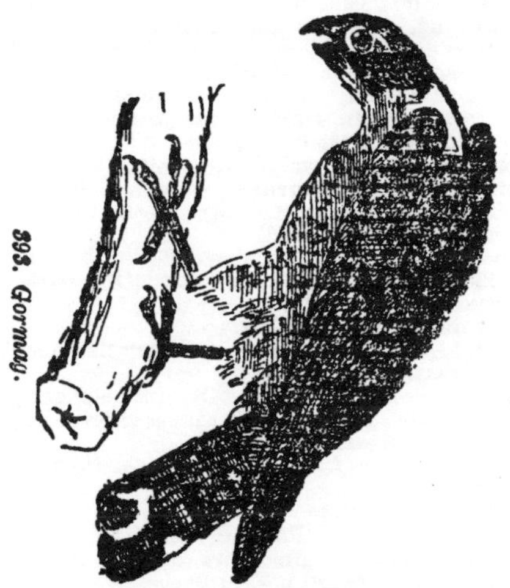

393. Gormag.

gormag-liath, *s.f* Coltsfoot (plant.) *prov.*
gorman, -ain, *s.m* Blue-bottle, bluet, cornflower—*centaurea cyanus.* 2 Woad, see guirmean. 3**Green knoll

394 Gorman.

gorm-aotrom,** *s m.* Light blue.
gormanach, -aiche, *a* Full of green fields. 2 Having green knolls
gormanaich,(AH) *s.f* Grey of the dawn. Anns a' gh *at the first streak of day.*
gorm-bhallach,** *a* Blue-spotted. 2 Blue-bossed. Cuchuilinn nan gorm-bhallach sgiath, *C. of the blue bossed shields.*
gorm-bhileach, -eiche, *a* Blue-edged.
gorm-cheathach,** -ich, *s.m.* Blue mist. An g. a' snàmh, *the blue mist floating.*
gorm-chruaidh,** *s.f.* Blue steel. 2 Blue armour 3 Blue sword. Feachd nan g., *the blue-armed host.*
gorm-aotrom, *s.m.* Light blue colour.
gorm-ghlas, -ghlaise, *a.* Of an azure or blue colour, cerulean. 2 Of a sea-green colour. 3 Slate-drab.
gorm-mhac,** -mhic, *s.m.* Brave servant, sturdy domestic.
gorm-phreas, -phris, -an, *s.m.* Green bush. G.

na bruaich, *the green bush of the bank.*
gorm-rathad, *s.m.* Green path. 2 Passage through the sea, track of a ship on the water.
gorm-ròd, *prov.* for gorm-rathad.
gorm-shléibhteach, -eiche, *a.* Green hilled.
gorm-shùil, -shùla, -shùilean, *s.f.* Blue eye.
gorm-shùileach, -eiche, *a.* Blue-eyed.
gorm-shùileach, -eich, *s. m.* Blue-eyed person An g. treun, *the blue-eyed warrior.*
gorm-thalamh, *s.m.* (*f.* in *gen.*) Blue land.
gorm-thalla, -thallaichean. *s.m.* Blue hall. 2 Poetical name for the sky. 3 see gorm-thalamh.
gorn, guirn, *s.m.* Ember. 2 Fire-brand. 3 The force of poison. 4**Murdering dart.
gorrach, see gòrach.
gorraidear, see goradair.
gòrsaid, -ean, *s.f.* Gorget, military defence. 2 Cuirass.
——each, -eiche, *a.* Of, or belonging to, cuirasses or gorgets. 2 Like a cuirass or gorget. 3 Wearing a cuirass.
†**gort**, -oirt, *s. f.* Ivy. 2 Old Gaelic name f the letter G.
gort, *a.* see goirt.
gort, -a, -oirt, *s.f.* Famine, scarcity. 2** Hunger. 3‡‡Sore. Bha gort 'san tìr, *there was famine in the land.*
†**gort**, -oirt, *s.m.* Standing corn. 2 Garden, field, enclosure. 3 Crop of corn or grass.
gorta, *s.f.* see gort.
gortach, -aiche, *a.* Hungry, starving. 2 Sparing, miserly, parsimonious, penurious, scant. 3**Causing famine. 4** Greedy Bliadhna gh., *a year of famine.*
——, -aich, *s.m.* Hungry person. Cha'n 'eil nàir' air a' ghortach, *the hungry has no shame.*
gortachadh, -aidh, see goirteachadh. 2 Famishing, starvation. 3 Oppression.
gortachas,** -ais, *s.m.* Illiberality.
gortachd, *s.f.ind.* Penury, starvation, scarcity.
gortadh, -aidh, *s.m.* Famine. Air son a' ghortaidh, *by reason of the famine.*
gortag, -aig, -an, *s.f.* Hungry or starving woman. 2 Stingy parsimonious or parsimonious woman. 3**Crab-tree.
gortaich, *pr.pt.* a' gortachadh, *v.a.* see goirtich. 2**Famish, starve. 3**Oppress, wrong.
——te, *a.* see goirtichte. 2 Famished, starved. 3 Oppressed. 4 Soured.
gortaighean,** *s. m.* The universal language before the confusion of tongues of Babel.
gortaladh,** -aidh, *s.m.* Patching, mending.
gortan, -ain, -an, *s.m.* Hungry, starving fellow. 2 Stingy, penurious fellow.
gortas,** -ais, *s.m.* Famine, hunger, starvation. Bhàsaich e le g., *he died of hunger.*
gort-ghlan, see gart-ghlan.
——adh, see gart-ghlanadh.
†**gort-reabadh**,** -aidh, *s.m.* Misery.
gort-threabhadh, -aidh, *s.m.* Act of ploughing. †2 Misery.
gortuchadh, see gòrtachadh & goirteachadh.
gortaich, see gortaich.
†**gosda**, Gaelic spelling of *ghost.*
gosganach, *a.* Tufty.
†**gos-sheabhag**, -aig, -an, see glas-sheabhag.
†**gost-aois**, *s.* Old age.
†**gost-aosmhor**, *a.* Aged.
got-gheadh, see geadh-ghot.
goth, *v.a.* Toss the head contemptuously or giddily.
†**goth**, *a.* Straight, even.
†**goth**, -a, -an, *s.m. & f.* see gath. 2 Vowel.
gòth, *s.m.* Airy gait. 2 (DMC) Taunt, gibe. 3 "Go." Nach ann aige tha 'n g.! *what an airy gait he has!* (or *what "go" he has;*) tiugainn a ghabhail gòth, *come, let us walk about.*
goth, *s.m.* Bagpipe reed.
gòthach,** *a.* Airy, having a smart or airy gait.
gothach, for gothaiche—*Sàr-Obair.*
†**gòthadh**, -aidh, *s.m.* Smart gait. 2 Bending or rushing forward. †3 Appendix. 4 (DMC) Pounding bark.
gothaiche,†† -an, *s.m.* Drone-reed. [This is what the dictionaries give, but g. is evidently meant for "gaothaiche," *mouthpiece.*]
gothail, *a.* Airy, giddy.
gòthan, -ain, *s.m.* Anker, keg. 2 Airy youth.
——ach,** -aich, *s.m.* Smart, lively lad, young man with an airy gait.
——ach, -aiche, *a.* Airy in gait, lively, smart. 2††Envious, malicious.
gothanach, -aiche, *a.* Opprobrious, scurrilous. 2††Envious, malicious.
gothlam, -aim, *s.m.* Noise, prating, tattling. see goilean.
——ach, -aiche, *a.* Prating, noisy.
goug, see guga.
†**grab**, *s.m.* Tooth. 2 Dent, notch.
grab, -a, -achan, *s.m.* see grabadh.
grab, *pr.pt.* a' grabadh, *v.a.* Interrupt, impede, hinder, stop, oppose, prevent from doing or going. 2** Entangle. †3 Notch, indent. Gh. e maomadh na feachd, *he stopped the on-rush of the army.*
†**grabach**, -aiche, *a.* see gròbach & grabalach.
grabadh, -aidh, -ean, *s.m.* Hinderance, stopping, impediment. 2 Act of hindering, preventing, interrupting, stopping, opposing. 3 Notching, indenting. 4 Entanglement. 5 Bar. 6 Protest. A' g—, *pr.pt.* of grab.
grabail,‡‡ -e, *a.* Preventive.
——, (MS) *s.f.* Impediment.
grabair,* -ean, *s. m.* Obstructer, hinderer, opposer. 2 Entangler. 3 Jester, droll. 4 Prattler.
grabaireachd,** *s.f.* Entanglement. 2 Opposition. 3 Idle talk, gibble gabble.
grabalach, *a.* Barful, debarring.
grabalaich, (MS) *v. a.* Blench. 2 Impede. 3 Perplex.
graban,§ -ain, *s.m.* Wormwood, see burmaid.
grabh, -a, -an, *s.f.* Abhorrence, dread, dislike, horror. 2 Cause of abhorrence or dislike. 3 *Horrid thing. Righ nan G., *the King of Terrors.*
gràbh, *pr.pt.* a' gràbhadh, see gràbhail.
——adair, *s.m.* Engraver. 2 Graver (tool.)
——adaireachd, *s.f.* Engraving, business of an engraver.
gràbhadh, -aidh, -aidhean, *s. m & pr. pt.* see
grabhail, -e, *a.* Horrible, causing horror, aversion or strong dislike.
gràbhail, *v.a.* Engrave. 2 Embroider. 3 Carve.
——te, see gràbhalta.
gràbhair, *s.m.* Graver.
gràbhal, -ail, *s. m.* Engraving, carving. 2 Sculpture.
——achd, *s.f.* Carving, engraving.
grabhalachd, *s.f.* Horribleness, matter of aversion, or strong dislike.
gràbhalachd-cloiche, *s.f.* Lithography.
gràbhaladh, -aidh, *s.m.* Writing. 2 Engraving. 3 Sculpture. A' g—, *pr.pt.* of gràbhail. Obair gràbhalaidh, *carved work.*
——-malairt, *s.m.* Bill of Exchange.
——-soluis, *s.m.* Photograph.
——-slàinte, *s. m.* Bill of health.
——, -reic, *s.m.* Bill of sale.
gràbhal-cloiche, *s.m.* Lithograph.

gràbhalaiche, *s.m.* Engraver.
gràbhalair, *s.m.* Engraver.
gràbhalta, *past pt.* of gràbhail. Engraved, carved, sculptured.
gràbhaltach, -aiche, *a.* Of, or pertaining to writing, &c.
gràbhaltaiche, -an, *s.m.* Engraver, sculptor.
——— -cloiche, *s.m.* Lithographer.
——— -soluis, *s.m.* Photographer.
gràbhaltair, see gràbhaltaiche.
grabhan, -ain, *s.m.* Grubbing-axe.
gràbhan-bàn,§ -ain-bàin, *s. m.* White horehound —*marrubium vulgare.*

395. *Gràbhan-bàn.*  396. *Gràbhan-dubh.*

gràbhan-dubh,§ *s.m.* Stinking horehound—*bollota niger.*
gràbhan-nan-clach,§ *s.m.* Stonecrop, wall-pepper—*sedum acre.*
grabhat, Gaelic spelling of *cravat.*
†grabhlochd, *s.f.* Blot, fault, error.
———ach, *a.* Faulty, full of errors, blotted.
‡grabhshorb, see grabhlochd.
gràc,(DC) *s.m.* Cry of a duck—*Argyll.*
grac,†† *pr. pt.* a' gràcadh, *v. a.* Frighten or silence a child by frowns.
gràcan, -ain, *s. m.* Querulous sounds uttered by a hen. Far am bi cearcan bidh g., *where there are hens there will be cackling.*
———ach,†† *a.* Querulous.
†gràd, -a, *s.m.* Degree.
grad, graide, *a.* Sudden, quick. 2 Hasty, irascible, short-tempered. 3 Agile, nimble, "clever." 4**Unexpected. 5**Speedy, soon. Gu g., *speedy, soon, early*; is g. do chaochladh, *thy death is early*; g. 'na ghnothachaibh, *quick in his business*; cho grad 's a dh' éirich e, *he rose so suddenly*; ghrad chlisg e, *he quite of a sudden started.*
gràda, see grànda.
gradag, -aig, -an, *s. f.* Quickness, nimbleness. 2*Hurry, haste, jiffy. 3††Quick woman. 4†† Gun. Cha tig e an gradaig, *he will not come in a hurry*; bi an seo an gradaig, *be here instantly*; an gradaig, *quickly, in a short time.*
gradaig, (i.e. an gradaig) *adv.* Anon.
gradain, *pr.pt.* a' gradanadh, *v.a.* Parch grain preparatory to grinding it
———te, *past pt.* of gradain. Parched as corn.
gradan, -ain, *s. m.* Expeditious mode of drying grain for the quern by burning the straw. 2 The meal obtained from such grain. 3 Snuff hastily prepared by pounding dry leaves of tobacco in a mortar. 4‡‡ Kind of snuff called "Lundifoot." "*Gradan* was corn or meal prepared after the ancient custom of the Gael. A woman sitting down, took a handful of corn and holding it in her left hand by the stalks, she set fire to the ears, which were at once in a flame. In her right hand she held a stick, with which she dexterously beat the grain out the very instant the husks were quite burnt. By this simple process, corn may be cut down, winnowed, ground, dried and baked within half-an-hour. In separating the meal from the husks, instead of sieves, they made use of a sheepskin stretched on a hoop, minutely perforated by a small hot iron. The bread which is thus made is considered very salubrious, and is extremely pleasant to the palate of the Gael" —* In *Uist*, where the three processes, ealachadh, eararadh and gradan, may still be seen practised, the means employed are practically the same as described above. The grain end of the sheaf is put into the flame of the fire; when the chaff and ends of the straw are well alight, the sheaf is held over a clean-swept part of the hearth, or over some vessel, when the grain drops off.—DC.
gradan, -ain, -an, *s. m.* Severity, rigour. 2 Danger, hazard.
———achd, *s.f.ind.* Quickness, alacrity, despatch. 2 see gradan.
gradanadh, -aidh, *s.m.* Act of hastily parching corn. 2 Hasty parching and grinding of tobacco leaves. A' g—, *pr. pt.* of gradain.
gradan-uisge,(DMu) *s.m.* Blink of sunshine before a summer shower.—*Suth'd.*
grad-bheairteach, -aiche, *a.* Soon prepared or accoutred, active, "clever."
grad-bhris,‡‡ *v.a.* Burst, break suddenly.
———eadh,‡‡ -idh, -idhean, *s.m.* Abruption.
grad-bhuille,‡‡ -an, *s.f.* Jerk.
grad-charach, -aiche, *a.* Nimble, quick. 2 Fidgetting. 3††Shy. Gu g., *nimbly.*
———d,* *s.f.* Agility.
grad-cheumach,‡‡ -eiche, *a.* Light-legged.
grad-charaich,‡‡ *v.a.* Jerk.
grad-chleas, *s-m.* Clever trick or movement, hocus-pocus trick.
———ach, *a.* Nimble, active. Gu g., *nimbly.*
grad-chlisg, *v.a. & n.* Startle, convulse.
———each, *a.* Convulsed, convulsive. 2 Startling.
grad-choilleag,‡‡ -eig, -an, *s.f.* Bounce.
grad-dhealachadh,‡‡ -aidh, *s.m.* Abruption.
grad-fhaclach,‡‡ -aiche, *a.* Flippant
grad-fhuasgail,‡‡ *v.a.* Burst.
†gradh, *s.m.* Degree, gradation.
†gradh, *a.* Noble. 2 Valiant. 3 Dear.
gràdh, -àidh, *s. m.* Love, fondness. 2 Lover, beloved object. 3 Charity, benevolence. 4 Virtue of universal love. D' an d' thug m' anam g., *whom my soul loved*; tha g. aige dhi, *he loves her*; tha g. agam ort; *I love you*; a ghràidh! *my love! my dear!* Used in the vocative case as a term of endearment.
gràdhach, -aiche, *a.* Loving, beloved, dear, lovely. 2*Amiable. An éilid gh., *the loving hind*; a cneas g., *her amiable form.*
———, -aich, *s. m.* Beloved object. *prov.* [Generally used in the vocative singular only —a ghràdhaich! *my dear!*]
———adh, -aidh, *s.m.* Love, act of loving. 2 Admiring, admiration. A' g—, *pr. pt.* of gràdhaich.
———d,* *s.f.* Extreme love, endearment.
gràdhadair, -ean, *s.m.* Lover.
gràdhag, -aig, -an, see gràidheag. 2 (DMC) Term of endearment applied to a woman, and

containing the idea of sympathy with, or gratitude to, the person addressed.
gràdhaich, *pr.pt.* a' gràdhachadh, *v. a.* Love, esteem, admire.
———e, -an, see gràdhadair.
———e, *a. comp.* of gràdhach.
———ear, *fut. pass.* of gràdhaich. G. e, *he shall be loved.*
gràdhaichte, *past pt.* of gràdhaich. Loved, beloved. 2 Admired.
gràdhail, *a.* Lovely.
gràdhaileachd, *s.f.* Loveliness. 2 Amiableness.
gràdhair,** *s.m.* Adorer.
gràdhan, -ain, -an, *s. m. dim.* of gràdh. Little darling. see gràidhean.
gradhan,(CR) *s.m.* Darling—*Suth'd.*
gràdharachd, see gràdhmhorachd.
gràdhdan, -ain, see gràdran.
gràdh-dhaoine, *s.m.* Philanthrophy.
gràdh-gheasag,‡‡ *s.f.* Love-charm.
gràdh-laiste, *s.m.* Fervent love.
gràdhmhoire, *comp.* of gràdhmhor.
gràdhmhor, -oire, *a.* Loving, lovely, greatly beloved. 2 Affectionate. Gu g., *lovingly.*
gràdhmhorachd, *s.f.* Loveliness, lovingness. fondness, affectionateness.
gràdhran, see gràdranaich.
gràdh-shealladh, *s.m.* Sheep's eye.
gràdhtainn,*s.m.* for ag ràdhtainn, *pr.pt.*of abair.
gràdhuchadh, see gràdhachadh.
gràdhuich, see gràdhaich.
grad-leum, *s.m.* Quick spring, jump, bound.
grad-leum, *v.n.* Spring, jump quickly. Gh. e, *he sprung quickly.*
gràdran, -ain, *s.m.* see gràdranaich.
———ach, *a.* Noisy, clamorous. 2 Cackling.
———aich, *s. f.* Peculiar complaining noise made by hens. 2 Murmuring. 3 Continued complaining. 4 Prolonged cackle. 5 Chattering. A' g—, *pr. pt.* of gràdranaich.
gràdranaich, *pr.pt.* a' gràdranaich, *v. a.* Cackle, chatter, make a complaining noise, like hens.
gràdranaich, *a.* Noisy, clamorous. 2 Cackling.
grad-theich, *v.a.* Fly quickly, retreat precipitately.
grad-thog, *v.a.* Raise quickly.
grad-thuit,‡‡ *v.n.* Plunge.
grad-thulgadh, -aidh, *s.m.* Jerk.
‡graf, see gràbh.
†grafa, -n, *s.m.* Graft, scion.
†grafadh, see gràbhadh.
†grafan, -ain, see gràbhan.
†graf-chuir, *v.a.* Ingraft.
†graf-chur, -uir, *s.m. & pr.pt.* Ingrafting.
†graf-churta, *past pt.* Ingrafted.
gràg, -aig, -an, *s.m.* Croaking of crows, cawing. 2 Shout.
gràg, *pr.pt.* a' gràg & a' gràgail, *v.n.* Cry out bawl, croak, caw.
gràgail, *s.f.* Cackling, croaking. A' g—, *pr.pt.* of gràg.
gragair, -ean, *s.m.* Glutton.
gràgallaich, *s.f.* Clucking of a hen. 2 Croaking or cawing of a crow.
†gragan, -ain, *s.m.* Manor. 2 Village. 3 District. 4 Bosom.
gràgan, see gràdran.
———ach, see gràdranach.
———aich, see gràdranaich.
†gragh, -aigh, -ean, see greigh.
†grai, *a.* Old.
†graibh, *s.* Almanac.
†graibhre, *s.f.* Loud laugh. 2 Word, utterance. 3 Dignified expression.
gràic, *s.f.* Rough scolding voice. Thug e g air, *he spoke harshly to him.*
gràiceach, *a.* Harsh.
graid, see greigh.
graide, *s.f.* see graidead. 2(MS) Parlousness. 2 Vividness. G. nàduir, *shortness of temper.*
graide, *comp.* of grad.
graideach, Misprint in Gaelic dicts. for graidheach.
graideachd, see graidead.
graidead, -id, *s.m.* Quickness, degree of quickness, haste, hastiness. 2 Acuteness.
graideal, see groideal.
graidh, -e, -ean, see greigh.
gràidh, see gràdhaich.
graidheach, see greigheach.
gràidheag, -ig, -an, *s. f.* Sweetheart, beloved female. 2 Lovely young female. see also gràdhag.
gràidhean, -ein, -an, *s.m.* Lover, sweetheart, admirer. 2 Term of endearment addressed to a man.
————ach, *a.* Gallant, wanton, amorous.
————achd, *s.f.* Gallantry, intrigue, amour.
gràidhear, -ir, -irean, *s.m.* Lover, sweetheart, admirer. 2 Beloved person.
graidhire, see greigheach.
graifear, see gràbhair.
†graifne, see graifneachadh.
graifneach, -eiche, *a.* Alarming, sounding an alarm.
graifneachadh, -aidh, *s.m.* Riding, horsemanship. 2 Alarm.
graige,** *s.f.* Superstition.
———ach, *a.* Superstitious.
———achd, *s. f.* Superstition, superstitious usages.
graigean, -ein, *s.m.* Gluttonous swag-bellied young person.
————ach, *a.* Gluttonous.
————achd, *s.f.* Gluttony. 2 Infirmity of a swag-belly.
————as, -ais, *s.m.* Gluttony.
graigh, see greigh.
———each, -eiche, see greigheach.
graighear, -ir, see greighear.
grailbeag,¶ *s. m.* Wood-cock, see coilleach-coille.
grailleag,(AF) *s.f* Dunlin (bird.)
gràilleag,(CR) *s.f.* Morsel, little bit, as of meat cheese, &c.—*W. of Ross-shire.*
graillean,** -ein, *s.m.* Scimitar.
grailneag,(AF) *s.f.* Winged animal. 2 Bat.
graim, see greim. 2 (CR) Expression of a crying child—*Arran.*
gràin, -e, *s.f.* Disgust, abhorrence, loathing, abomination. 2 Deformity. 3 (DMC) Hatred. G. de bhiadh, *a loathing for food* ; thusa le 'n g. iodhalan, *you who abhor idols* ; is fheàrr na fochaid g., *abhorrence is better than mockery.*
gràin-abhall, see gràn-ubhall.
gràin-aigean, see gràn-aigein.
gràin-chàileach, -eiche, *a.* Antipathetic.
——————d,(MS) *s.f.* Antipathy.
gràinde, *comp.* of grànda. More or most ugly.
gràindead, -id, *s.f.* Degree of ugliness.
gràine, *s.f.ind.* Ugliness.
gràine, see gràinne.
gràineach, -eiche, *a.* see gràinneanach.
gràineachadh,-aidh, *s.m.* Abhorring, loathing, disdaining. 2 Act of causing to abhor, loathe, or disdain. 3 **Granulation. 4(DMC) Alienating. A' g—, *pr. pt.* of gràinich.
gràinead,** -eid, *s.m.* Ugliness. 2 Disgust.
gràineag, -eig, -an, *s. f. dim.* Hedgehog. 2 Bittern, see corra-ghràin. 3**Wild duck. 4 ‡‡Little grain. Cnuasachd na gràineig (the hedgehog's hoard) expressive of the folly of

worldly-minded people who part with all at the grave, as the hedgehog is compelled to drop its burden of crab-apples at the narrow entrance to its hole.
gràineagach, -aiche, *a.* Of, or pertaining to, hedgehogs. 2 Like a hedgehog. 3 Bristly. 4‡‡Of, or pertaining to, little grains.
gràinealachd, -an, *s.f.* Abominableness, detestableness, loathsomeness hatefulness. 2 Abomination.
gràineasadh, -aidh, *s.m.* Glanders in horses.
gràineil, -e, *a.* Abominable, hateful, loathsome, odious, disagreeable, detestable, abject 3 Nasty. Nach gràineile an duine? *is not man more abominable!*
gràineileachd, see gràinealachd.
graing, -e, *s.f.* Disdain. 2 Frown. 3 see gràin.
graingeach, -eiche, *a.* Causing disdain. 2 Frowning.
graingead, see gràinde.
gràingich, see gràinich. 2 Frown.
gràinich, *pr. pt.* a' gràineachadh, *v.a.* Impress with dislike, aversion or disgust. 2 Loathe, abhor, detest, hate, disdain. 3 (DMC) Alienate.
gràinichte, *a.* & *past pt.* of gràinich. Disgusted, impressed with disgust or aversion, loathed, detested.
gràinne, -an & -achan, *s.f.* Grain, single grain. 2 Grain or pellet of shot. 3 Sight on a gun-barrel. 4 Small quantity of any granulated substance. 5** Small number, as of people. G. de shìol, *a grain of seed.*
gràinneach, -eiche, *a.* Full of grain. 2 Granulated, granulous.
gràinneachadh, -aidh, *s.m.* Granulating, granulation.
gràinnean, -in, -an, *s.m., dim.* of gràinne. Little grain. 2 Single grain. 3 Small quantity of any granulated or pulverized substance. 4 Small quantity of anything.—*Argyll.* 4 (DU) Small collection of men or animals. G. fùdair, *a little powder;* g. eòrna, *a small quantity of barley.*
gràinneanach, -aiche, *a.* Grained. 2 Gritty. 3**Pulverized.
gràinneanaich,* see gràinnich.
gràinnein, *gen. sing.* of gràinnean.
gràinne-mullaich, *s.f.* Top grain on a stalk.
gràinnich, *pr.pt.* a' gràinneachadh, *v.a.* Granulate. 2 Pulverize.
gràinnichte, *a.* & *past pt.* of gràinnich. Granulated.
gràinn-itheach,** *a.* Eating granulated or pulverized food, granivorous.
grainnse, see grainnseach.
grainnseach, -sich, -sichean, *s. f.* Grange or corn farm. 2 Granary.
——————, (AH) *a.* Relating to the production of grain. 'Se àite g' math a th' ann, *it is a good grain-producing place.*
grainnseag, -eig, -an, *s.m.* Cracklings, refuse of rendered tallow. 2** Cracknel, hard brittle cake. 3 Red bear-berry—*arbutus uva ursi.*—Badge of Clan Colquhoun. 4 (DMD) Pimple. 5(DMy) Refuse of fish-livers after the oil has been taken from them.
grainnseagach, -aiche, *a.* Of, or belonging to, cracklings, cracknels or bear-berries. 2 (DMC) Full of pimples.
grainnseag-dhubh,§ -ig-dhuibhe, -an-dubha, *s.m* & *f.* Black bear-berry—*arbutus alpina.*
grainnsear, -ir, *pl.* -an, & -eirean, *s.m.* Farmer. 2 Farm-servant. 3 Agriculturist. 4 Corn-dealer. 5**Grieve, overseer.
grainnsearachd, *s.f.ind.* Occupation of an agriculturist, agriculture. 2 Employment of a grieve, overseeing.
grainnseireachd, see grainnsearachd.
graip, see gràp.
grais, -e, *s.f.* Prosperity, success. 2 Blessing.
gràiseag, *s.f.* Crackling.
graisear,(MS) *s.m.* Overseer, see grainnsear.
graisg, -e, *s.f.* Rabble, low people, worthless people, offscouring, canaille, riff-raff, mob. Far am bi g. bi gleadhar, *where the rabble is, there will be noise;* na earb thu féin ri g., *do not rely on the mob.*
gràisg-chòmhradh, *s.m.* Cant.
gràisgealachd, *s.f. ind.* Vulgarity. 2 Blackguardism. 3*Turbulence.
gràisgeil, -e, *a.* Vulgar, mean, low, gross, blackguardish.
gràisg-fhlath,‡‡ -aith, -aithean, *s.m.* Demagogue.
graisg-fhlaitheachd, *s.f.* Democracy.
gràitinn, Improper form of "ag ràdh," *pr.pt.* of abair.
gramachadh, -aidh, *s.m.* Fastening, tightening. 2 Holding fast, clenching, grasping. G. bàrr òrdaig, *holding on by a thumb-top*—with difficulty. A' g—, *pr.pt.* of gramaich.
grama-chas, -chois, *s. m.* Sure-foot. 2 Sure footing.
grama-chasach, -aiche, *a.* Sure-footed.
gramadach, -aich, *s.m.* Grammar. 2**Philologist.
——————, -aiche, *a.* Philological.
gramadh, see greimeadh.
gramag,** -aig, -an, *s.f.* Hook. 2 Buffoon. 3 Jester.
gramaich, *pr.pt.* a' gramachadh, *v.a.* Hold fast, take hold, cling to. 2 Tighten. 3 Clench, grasp. 4 Fasten, adhere. Ris an do gh. an sealgair, *which the hunter grasped.*
gramaiche, -an, *s.m.* One that keeps a good hold. 2 Flesh-hook. 3 Hook of any kind. 4 Smith's vice. 5 Pincers. 6 Grapple. 7‡‡ Chape of a buckle. 8 Cleat, see bàta, Nos. 6 to 10, p. 76. 9 (AH) Table-fork. G. feòla, *a flesh-hook.*
gramaichte, *past pt.* of gramaich. Fastened, clenched, laid hold of, grasped.
gramail, -e, *a.* Strong, firm. 2 Muscular. 3 Vigorous, resolute. 4 Trusty. 5 Tightened, fastened, clenched. 6 Holding fast. 7(MS) Agglutinative. Thugaibh ionnsaidh gh., *make a vigorous onset.*
gramaisg, *s.f.* Mob, rabble.
gramalachd, *s.f.ind.* Firmness of body or mind. 2 Vigorousness, strength, muscular vigour.
gramalas, -ais, *s.m.* Muscular power or strength. 2 Vigour or firmness of body or mind. 3 Power of grasp. Cha'n fhacas do leithid air gh., *thine equal for firmness was never seen.*
gramannan, *pl.* of greim.
gramar, -air, *s.m.* Grammar.
gramasg, -aisg, *s.f.* Morsel, handful. 2 Small bit of food.
gramasgar, -air, -airean, *s.m.* Flock, company. 2 Fry.
gramhaisg, -e, -ean, *s.f.* Rude association.
gramur, -uir, *s.m.* Refuse of grain.
gràn, -ain, *s.m.* Kiln-dried grain. 2 Corn. 3 Hail. 4 Shot of lead. G. cruadhaichte, *dried corn;* g. gradain, *parched corn.*
gràn-abhal, see gràn-ubhal.
gràanach, -aiche, *a.* Grained.
gràanachd, see gràndachd.
gràanaich, *v.a.* Corn, granulate.
gràn-aigein, *s.m.* Common pilewort, lesser celandine—*ranunculus ficaria.* see illust. 397.
gràanalach, -aich, *s.f.* Grain.
gràn-aobrainne, *s.* The glanders.
gràn-arcain,§ see gràn-aigein.

397. *Gràn-aigein.*

gràn-chist, -e, *pl.* -ean & -eachan, *s.f.* Garner 2 Granary. 3 Corn-chest.

grànda, gràinde, *a.* Ugly, ill-favoured. 2 Shameful, causing shame. 3 Unseemly. 4 Nasty. 5 Grim. G. ri 'm faicinn, *ugly to be seen* ; is g. leinn e, *we think it unseemly.*

gràndachd, *s.f.ind.* Ugliness. 2 Unseemliness.

grànlach,** -aich, *s.m.* Corn, grain.

gràn-lachàn,§ *s.m.* Duck-weed, see mac-gun-athair.

gràn-lagain, *s.m.* The grain that falls through the straw when it is placed in the kiln.

grannna, see grànda.

————chd, see grandachd.

grannaidh,** *s.m.* Long hair.
3 Grimness. 4 Nastiness.

grannda, -ine, *a.* see grànda.

granndachd, see grandachd.

grant,** *a.* Grey, green.

gràn-ubhal, -ubhala & -ubhlan, *s.m.* Pomegranate—*punica granatum.* Mar gh., *like a pomegranate.* [Written " pomgranat " in recent editions of the Bible.]

graodha, an galar graodha, *s.m.* Strangles—*Skye.*

graoine,** *s.f.* Joy.

†graoine, *a.* Joyful, cheerful, bright.

†graoineachas, -ais, *s.m.* Joyfulness, cheerfulness. see greadhanachas.

graoineag, -eig, *s.f.* Irritation, provocation.

graoineis* *s.f.* Joy.

graoineagaich, *v.a.* Provoke, irritate, incense.

†graoinich, *v.a.* Provoke, irritate, incense.

graoltas, -ais, *s.m.* Obscenity.

graosda, see graosdach.

graosdach, *a.* Filthy, obscene.

graosdachd, *s.f.* Filthiness, obscenity, ribaldry

gràp,** *v.a.* Climb.

gràp, *s.m.* see gràpa.

gràpa, -n & -chan, *s.m.* Graip, iron dung-fork.

gràpadh, -aidh, *s.m.* see gràpa.

gràs, -àis, -an, *s.m.* Grace, favour. 2 Divine favour. 3 Aid, help. 4 Grace in the soul. 5 Fortune, luck. 6 *Free love. G. Dhé, *God's grace.*

gràsaich,** *v.a.* Give thanks.

gràsail, -e, *a.* see gràsmhor.

gràsalachd, see gràsmhorachd.

gràsda, -àisde, *a.* Compassionate. 2 Gracious. 3 see grànda. 4(DMy) Rugged-faced.

gràsdachd, *s.f.ind.* Compassionateness. 2 see grandachd.

gràsmhoire, *comp.* of gràsmhor.

gràsmhor, -oire, *a.* Gracious, merciful. 2 Favourable. 3 Having the graces of the Holy Spirit. 4 Graceful. A Dhé gh. ! *gracious God !*

gràsmhorachd, *s.f.* Graciousness, benignity. 2 Gloriousness. 3 Gracefulness, grace. 4 Mercifulness.

gràst, see gràsda.

gràsta, -àiste, see gràsda.

gràstachd, see gràsdachd.

gràt, Gaelic spelling of *grate.*

grath, -a, *s.m.* Fear, terror. *prov.* 2 (DU) Abhorrence, feeling of repulsion. Tha thu a' cur g. orm, *you disgust me.*

grath, *a.* Fearful, ugly.

grathail, -e, *a.* Terrific, dreadful. 2(DU) Disgusting, revolting, repulsive.

grathann, see grathunn.

gratharra, *a* Squeamish.

grath-muing, see gath-muinge.

grathunn, -uinn, -uinnean, *s.m.* Space of time, while. 2 Considerable time. 3 Turn. Eadar seo agus ceann grathuinne, *in a while after this* ; gabh g. dheth. *take a while of it* ; gabh do gh. dheth, *take your turn of it* ; g. math, *a good while,* [Armst. gives grathuinne, as *nom.* and marks it *f.* ; ‡‡ has *nom.* grathunn, *gen.* -uinn, *s.m.*, ‡ has *nom.* grathuinn, and gives no *gen.* or gender.]

gràturnach, *a.* see gràdranach.

gràturnaich, *s.* see gràdranaich.

graufal, *a.* Revolting. (now gràineil.)

†gré, *s.m.* Nature, essence. (gnè.)

†gré, *a.* Gaelic spelling of *grey.*

greab, *prov.* for grab.

greabadh, *prov.* for grabadh.

greaban,§ -ain, *s.m.* Dropwort—*spiræa filipendula.*

greabhailt, *s.f.* Helmet, *prov.*

†greach,** *s.m.* Nut.

†greachd, *s.f.* Outcry.

†gread, *pr.pt.* a' greadadh, *v. a.* Wound, torment. 2 Whip severely. 3 Blight, blast. 4 Burn, scorch.

gread, *s.m.* see greadadh.

greada, see greadadh.

greadadh, -aidh, -aidhean, *s.m.* Tormenting, beating, whipping, drubbing. 2 Hardship, misfortune. 3 Impatience. 4 Anxiety, 5 Burning, scorching. 6 Piercing pain. 7** Stroke, blow. 8 Wound. 2 Aridity. 10 Sorrow. Aobhar mo ghreadaidh, *the cause of my wound.*

greadag,** -aig, *s.f.* Gridiron. 2 Girdle.

greadair,** *s.m.* Warming pan.

greadan, -ain, *s.m.* see gradan. 2 Considerable time spent with all one's might at anything. 3**Quarrel. 4 Thumping, blow. 5**Creaking. 6 (AF) Mule. 7 (DMC) Cause to regret. 8 Painful result. 8 Bitter sorrow or pain. 10††Burning. G. feasgair is cead dol dachaidh, *evening spurt and leave to go home* ; is goirt an g. a fhuair an dùthaich, *the country has received a severe blow* ; thoir g. air, *belabour it awhile, give it (try it) awhile* ; g. gaoith, *a very strong gale of wind.*

greadanach,-aiche, *a.* Babbling, chattering, 2 Obstreperous. 3 Quarrelsome. 4 Hot, scalding, burning. 5 Fighting, dealing blows, thumping. 6**Clamorous.

greadanachd, see gradanadh.

greadanta, -ainte, *a.* Hot, scalding. 2 Hard, difficult. 3 Vehement. 4††Beating. Gu g., *vehemently.*

greadh, *s.f.* *Joy, happiness. 2 see greigh. 3 **Baking, batch of bread.

greadh, *pr.pt.* a' greadh, *v.a.* Prepare food,boil, knead. 2 Winnow. 3 Thrash, thump. A' g. na cuilm, *preparing the feast.*

greadhadh, -aidh, *s.m.* Dressing or preparing of food, *or* 2 of grain. 3 Winnowing.

greadhadair, -ean, *s.m.* Dresser of victuals. 2 Winnower.

———————eachd,(DC) *s.f.* Act of winnowing corn—*Argyll.* 2**Dressing of food or grain

greadhair, *s.m.* Stallion, entire horse—*Islay.* 2 Groom—*Lochaber.* 3 Brutish fellow—*Perth.* see greidhear.

greadhainn, see **greadhan.**

greadhaireachd,** *s.f.* Covering a mare.

greadhan, -ain, -an, *s.m.* Band, troop, group. 2 Jovial band. 3 Great noise. G. mu 'n bhòrd, *a company around the table.*

greadhanachd, *s.f.* Drolling, going about in companies or groups. 2‡‡Pageantry.

greadhanadh,(DMC) *s. m.* Slow progress with any kind of work. 'S ann ort tha 'n g. ris; *what a long time you are taking at it!*

greadharra, *a.* Pretty.

greadhnach, -aiche, *a.* Joyful, cheerful, bright, merry, exulting, social. 2 Magnificent. 3 Pompous. An cùirtibh g., *in joyful courts.*

greadhnach, -aich, *s.m* Merrymaking. 2 Adorning, making showy.

greadhnachd, *s.f.* Going about in companies or groups. 2‡‡Pageantry.

greadhnachas, -ais, *s.m.* Joy, festivity, sociality, conviviality. 2 Pomp, august appearance, solemnity, parade. 3 Brightness, magnificence. Le mór gh., *with much pomp.*

greadhnas, -ais, see **greadhnachas.**

greadhte, *past pt.* Boiled.

greadhuinn, -e, -ean, see **greadhan.**

greagag, -aig, -an, see **griogag.**

greagh, see **greigh.**

greaghlain,* *s.m.* Old starved horse. 2 Donkey. 3 Old sword.

greallach, -aiche, *s.f.* Entrails, intestines, garbage. 2 Purtenance. 3 Pluck, 4 Cart-saddle. 5 Chain. 6 Clay. Nighidh tu a gh., *thou shalt wash its entrails;* maille ri 'ghreallaich, *with its purtenance.* [WC gives *s.m.*; H.S.D. and McL & D both spell greallach, *s.*, with one *l*, but McL & D gives two *l*'s in greallach, *a.* As pronounced in *Suth'd*, greallach should have one *l*.]

greallach, -aiche, *a.* Dirty, nasty, filthy.

greallag, -aig. -an, *s.m.* Swingle-tree next the horses, splinter-bar. 2 Swinging rope. 4** Swing. 5 Yoke. 6 see grealach. 7 (MS) Sling. Ann an g., *in a swing;* greallagan a' chroinn, *the plough's swingle-trees.*

greallagach, -aiche, *a.* Of, or belonging to, swingle-trees, *or* 2 swinging ropes.

greallagan, *s.pl.* Treadles to draw heddles of weaver's loom up and down.

greallaich,** *s.f.* Clay, mud, dirt, mire.

grealnach,(AF) see **grealsach.**

grealsach,(AF) -aich, *s.m.* Grilse (fish.) 2 Salmon. 3 see **greusaiche.**

gream, -a, -an, see **greim.**

greama, *s.m.* see **greamach.**

greàmach (AF) *s.m.* Streaked cow.

greamach, *a.* Grinding, biting. 2(DC) Forbidding, tousie, as hair.

greamaich, *v.a.* see **gramaich.**

greamaichte, see **gramaichte.**

†**greaman**, *s.pl.* Shreds.

greamannan, (for greimeannan) *pl.* of **greim.**

†**grean**, *s.m.* Gravel.

†**grean**, *v.a.* Carve, engrave, emboss.

†**greanachadh**, -aidh, *s.m.* Exhorting, exhortation.

greanachair, *s.m* Exhorter.

greanadh, see **greannachadh.**

†**greanaich**, *v.a.* Exhort.

†**greann**, *v.a.* Engrave.

greann, grinn, *s. m.* [*f.* in *Badenoch, North Argyll and Poolewe, m.* in *Coigach,*] Grim surly scowl, angry look, appearance of rage. 2 Hair. 3 Hue, colour. 4 Collision, act of striking. 5 Courage, boldness. 6 Bristling of the hair, as on an enraged dog. 7*Ripple on the surface of water. †8 Uncombed hair. 9**Beard. †10 Fair hair. 11** Gloom. †12 Noise, clangour, blast. 13 Siren (creature.) †14 Friendship, love. 15 Joke. 16 Cloth. 17 Rough-piled clothing. 18* Head having the hair standing on end. Tha g. air an fhairge, *the sea has a rippled, scowling aspect;* bho gach g. 'bhiodh teann do m' thòir, *from every siren hard pressing me;* dh' fhàs air cith is greann, *he became angry and scowling;* mar gh. a bheireadh dà òrd, *like the clangour of two hammers;* is iomadh corp a chaochail a gh., *many a body changed its hue;* pòr a's beadaraiche g., *a race of the loveliest hue;* mar gh. reòtaidh, *like a wintry blast.*

greannachd,(MS) *s.f.* Hairiness.

greannach, -aiche, *a.* Hairy, rough, bristly. 2 Rough, uncombed, having dry, bristling hair. 3 Crabbed, morose, irascible. 4 Gloomy, frowning. 5 Lowering, as weather. 6 Mean, of little worth. 7**Ruffled by the wind, as the surface of a lake. 8 (AH) Breezy and very cold. Claigeann g., *a hard, dry-haired scalp;* duine g., *a fiery person;* feasgar g., *a lowering threatening evening;* aois gh., *gloomy old age.*

greannachadh, -aidh, *s.m.* State of becoming hairy or bristly. 2 Standing of hair on end. 3 Irritating, act of irritating. 4 Frowning. 5 Gloominess, appearance of a rising storm. 6**Growing rough or shaggy. A' g—, *pr. pt.* of greannaich.

greannadh, -aidh, *s.m.* Graving.

greannag, -aig, -an, *s.f. dim.* of **greann.** Few straggling hairs.

greannagach, -aiche, *a.* Having few or straggling hairs.

†**greanna-chluich**,‡‡ -ean, *s.m.* Comedy.

greannaich, *pr.pt.* a' greannachadh, *v. a.* Become hairy or bristly, bristle. 2 Frown, lower, scowl. 3 Irritate, provoke. 4 Shrivel, parch. 5 Defy. 6 Grow gloomy. Gh. gach tulach, *every hillock has grown gloomy;* gh. e rium, *he became angry with me.*

greannaichte,(CR) *a.* Bristling—*Arran.* Tha e g. fuar, *it is bitterly* or *piercingly cold.*

greannan,†† -ain, *s. m.* Shrivelled, ill-favoured creature. 2 (DU)Crabbed fellow.

greannar, see **greannmhor.**

————achd, see **greannmhorachd.**

greanndag, (AC) *s.f.* Piece of cloth, rag, tatter.

greann-ghaoth, -aoithe, -an, *s.f.* Cold, parching wind. 2 Boisterous wind, rough breeze

greannmhor, oire, *a.* Neat, comely, lovely, pretty. 2 Brisk, lively, pleasantly droll, facetious, witty. 3 Sweet, agreeable. 4 Discreet [McL & D says "applied to females only."]

—————achd, *s f* Neatness, comeliness. 2 Pleasantness, affability. 3 Discretion. 4 Loveliness.

greannta, *a.* Neat, handy. 2 Handsome, comely, becoming. 3 Carved, engraved. Gu g., *handsomely.*

—————chd, *s.f.* Neatness, handiness. 2 Handsomeness, comeliness. 3 Carved work. 4 Disagreeableness.

greanntasan, -ain, *s.m.* Graving, carving.

greannuich, *v.a.* see **greannaich.**

greanta, *a.* Exact.

greantachd, *s. f.* Cleanness, cleanliness.
greap, see grap.
gréas, see greis. †2 Guest. †3 Protection. 4† Manner.
greas, *pr.pt.* a' greasad, a' greasachd & a' greasadh, *v.a.* & *n.* Hasten. 2 Drive, urge, as a horse. 3 Despatch. 4 Promote. 5 Prepare, dress, accoutre. 6 (DU) Setting a dog at a thing, forcing or hurrying a dog. G. iuthaidh sìos, *speed an arrow downwards ;* ghreas i oirre, *she hasted ;* greas ort ! *hurry up!*
greas,** *a.* see greasach.
greasach, *a.* Common, usual.
———adh, -aidh, *s.m.* Hastening. 2 Inciting.
greasachd, see greasad & greusachd.
greasad, -aid, *s.m.* Hastening, act of hastening. 2 Driving, act of driving. 3 Preparing, dressing, accoutring. 4 Despatch, hurry. 5 (DU) Setting on a dog. A' g., *pr.pt.* of greas. A' g. a' choin, *setting the dog on.*
greasadach,†† *a.* Impulsive.
greasadair,** *s.m.* Carrier.
greasadh, -aidh, see greasad.
grèasaich, *v.a.* Hasten. 2 Incite.
greasaiche, -an, *s.m.* see greusaiche.
———eachd, see greusaicheachd.
†greasailt, -ean, *s.f.* Inn.
†greasair, -ean, *s.m.* Innkeeper, host.
greasan, -ain, *s.m.* Web.
greasdachd, see greasad.
greastachd, (for greasachd) see greasad.
great, *s.m.* Soap-sud—*Badenoch. Scots,* graith, —warm water so wrought up with soap as to be fit for washing clothes.
†greath, *s.m.* Noise, cry, shout.
greath, *v.a.* see greidh.
greathachd, *s.f.* Surliness, moroseness, churlishness.
greathlach, -aich, see greallach.
†grech,‡‡ -ich, *s.m.* Garden. 2 Nut. 3 Salt.
†grech, -eich, } *s. m.* Dog, hound. Gach g.
gregh, -eigh, } bha 'n ar mùr, *every dog within our house.*
†greid, *s.f.* Stroke, see gread.
†greideadh, -idh, *s.m.* Second stroke of infection.
greideal,‡ -eil & alach, *s. f.* Gridiron. 2 Girdle. Dubh na greidealach, *the smut of the gridiron.*
greideilein, see greidlean.
gréidh, *s.* see gréidheadh.
greidh, see greigh.
———, *s.m.* Treatment. 2 Beating, thrashing.
gréidh, *pr.pt.* a' gréidheadh, *v. a.* Prepare or dress victuals. 2 Winnow. 3 Whip, flog, thrash. 4 Toast, as bread. 5 Knead. 6‡‡ Dress leather. 7 (MS) Dry. 8 Treat *or* use well.—*West Gaeldom.* 9(DMC) Season, cure.
———eadaireachd,†† *s.f.* Winnowing.
———eadh, -idh, -idhean, *s.m.* Dressing, act of dressing victuals. 2 Dressing of leather. 3 Winnowing. 4 Whipping, flogging, thrashing, punishing.—*North.* 5 Toasting, of bread. 6 Treatment. 7 Treating kindly or liberally. 8 Act of curing, toasting, &c. 9 State of being cured, toasted, &c. 10 Seasoning, preserving. A' g—, *pr.pt.* of gréidh. Droch gh., *bad treatment ;* fhuair e a dheagh gh. *he got a good thrashing ;* a' g. an arain, *toasting the bread ;* a' g. an éisg, *curing the fish ;* a' g. 'san t-sabhall, *winnowing in the barn.*
gréidhear, *s.m.* Grieve, man in charge of farm-work under a manager or farmer.
greidheirne,(AF) see greidh.
gréidhte, *past pt.* of gréidh. Prepared, dressed, as of victuals or leather. 2 Whipped, flogged—*North.* 3 Baked. 4 Kneaded. 5‡‡ Treated kindly—*West.* 6 (DMC) Dried, seasoned, in a good state of preservation, as of peats, corn, &c. Aran g., *baked bread.*
greidlean, -ein, -lan, *s.m.* Bread-stick, instrument for turning bannocks on the girdle in baking. 2 Peel. 3 Scimitar. 2 Name of Pleïades. 5 (DMy) Pot-stick for porridge.
greigh, -e, -ean, *s.f.* Herd, flock, as of deer, stud of horses. G. each air t' fhuarain gnorma, *a troop of horses on thy green fountains.*
———, *s.f.* Gadfly.—*Kintyre.* [Spelt *gréigh* by * but the vowel is short in Kintyre.—greighire is the correct spelling.]
greigh,* *s.f.* Uncommon heat of the sun after bursting out from behind a cloud.
———each, -eiche, *a.* Abounding in studs of horses, armental.
———each, -ich, *s.m.* Stallion, see òigeach.
———ear, -ir, -an, *s.m.* Groom, one who tends horses. 2 Horseman. 3(CR) Stallion—*Arran.*
greigheire, see greighire.
greighire,* *s.* Gadfly.
gréighte, see gréidhte.
greillean, -ein, *s. m.* Dagger. 2 Old rusty sword.
greim, *gen.* -reime & -ama, *pl.* -eanna & gramannan, *s.m.* Hold, holding, custody, grasp, gripe. 2 Bite, morsel, piece of bread. 3 Stitch in sewing. 4 Stitch, throb, pang. 5 Bite with the teeth or nails. 6**Difficult expression, hard word. G. bidh, *a morsel of food ;* g. 'san aodach, *a stitch in the cloth ;* tha 'n deagh gh. aige, *he has a good hold ;* cha'n 'eil g. agad air, *you have no hold on him ;* am fear nach cuir a shnaim, caillidh e a cheud gh., *he who knots not his thread, will lose his first stitch ;* chaidh a chuir 'na gh., *he was reinstated ;* tha e an g., *he is in custody ;* cha'n 'eil g. ri ghabhail air uisge no teine, *fire and water cannot be grasped*—i.e. *are good servants and bad masters ;* ann an g. *fixed, held fast ;* gabh g., *take hold ;* g. fola, *pleurisy ;* gach fear 'na gh. ! *all hands to quarters !*
——— -acair, -acraichean, *s.m.* Grapnel.
——— -an-diabhuil,§ *s.* Devil's bit scabious, see ura-ballach.
——— -bàis,‡ *s.m.* Death-throe. 2 Mortal disease.
——— -cluaise,‖ *s.m.* Ear-ache.
———eachadh, -aidh, see gramachadh.
———eachail,(MS) *a.* Ansated.
———eadas,* -ais, *s.m.* Hold, tenement.
———eadh, -idh, *s.m.* Grasping, biting.
———ealas, -ais, see gramalas.
———eanna, *n.pl.* of greim. Grasps, holds. 2 Morsels, bits, pieces. 3 Gripes, sudden pains in any part of the body.
———eannach, *a.* Pleuritic.
———eil, -e, *a.* see gramail.
———eilteach, *a.* see gramail.
——— -fàis, *s.m.* "Growing pains."
——— -fola, *s.m.* Pleurisy.
——— -fuachd, *s.m.* Chilblain, see meilicheart.
———ich, -ean, *s.m.* see gramaiche.
———ich, *v.a.* see gramaich.
———iche, *s.m.* Anchor. 2 Cleat of a boat, (Nos. 6 to 10. p. 76,)
———ichte, see gramaichte.
———ir, -ean, *s.m.* Grappling-iron. 2 Pincers.
†greimisg,** *s.f.* Old garments. 2 Trash, trumpery, lumber.
———ear, *s.m.* Higgler.
———earachd, *s.f.* Higgling.
greim-lòinidh, *s.m.* Rheumatic twinge.
greim-mionaich, *s.m.* Colic.
greim-mór,(DMy) *s.m.* Pleurisy.
greim-neirt, *s.m.* Strengthening muscle—***Arran.***
greim-neòin,‡‡ *s.m.* Luncheon.

greim-sic,‡‡ *s.m.* Pain in the anterior part of the body.
gréinbheach, see grian-chrios.
gréine, *gen.sing.* of grian.
†**greineachadh**, -aidh, *s.m.* Effort.
gréin-ghil, *gen.sing.* of grian-gheal.
gréis, *v.a.* see créis.
†**greis**, -ean, *s. m.* Champion. 2 Protection. 3 Pillage.
greis, -e, -ean, *s.f.* Prowess, strength. 2 Battle, contest, onset, attack, engagement. 3 Virtue, efficacy. 4 Slaughter. 5 While, space of time. 6 Hero. 7††Fit of coughing. G. air fìona's g. air branndaidh, *a while at wine and a while at brandy ;* car gh., *for a while ;* fè na g., *the interval between actions ;* thoir g. air t' obair, *work a while ;* g. mhath, *a good while ;* o cheann gh., *a while ago.*
gréis, -e, *s.f.* Needle-work, embroidery. 2 Furniture. 3**Tambouring. 4** Fine clothes. G.-obair, *embroidery ;* obair-gréise, *embroidered work.*
†**gréis**, *v.a.* Embroider. 2**Adorn. 3**Dress.
gréis-bhean, *s.f.* Milliner.
†**greischill**,** *s.f.* Sanctuary.
gréise, *gen.sing.* of greus.
greiseach,** *a.* Soliciting, enticing.
greiseachd,** *s. f.* Solicitation, enticement.
gréiseadair,* *s.m.* Embroiderer.
———————eachd, *s.f.* Embroidery.
gréiseadh,** -eidh, *s. m.* Embroidery. 2 Act of embroidering.
greiseag,(DC) *s. f.* Wanton woman, "rantin' widow"—*Uist.*
greiseag, *s.f.* Little while.
gréisg, see créis.
gréisg,(CR) *s.f.* Loathing, nausea.—*W. of Ross.*
———ean,(CR) *s.m.* Repulsive food—*W. of Ross.*
———eanach,(CR) *a.* Fastidious, squeamish, easily nauseated.—*W. of Ross.*
gréiste, *past pt.* Embroidered.
gréiste, *past pt.* Greased.
†**greistear**,** -ir, -an, *s.m.* Carter.
†**greit**, *s.m.* Champion, warrior.
gréite, see gréidhte.
†**greith**,** *s.f.* Jewel, ornament. 2 Dress. 3 Gift.
greòd,(CR) *s. m.* Group, company, crowd—*Skye & Argyll.* Gaelic form of *crowd*—not common.
greòig,* *s.m.* Botcher.
———ean,* -ein, *s.m.* Dabbler.
———ich,* *v.a.* Bungle, botch. 2 Dabble.
greollach, see greallach.
greollan, -ain, *s.m.* Cricket (insect.)
greòs, -eòis, *s.m.* Expansion of the thighs.
———ach, -aiche, *a.* Devaricated, expanded in the thighs.
———gach, -aiche, *a.* Grinning, apt to grin. 2 (MS)Rough. Gaire g., *a forced laugh.* Leac gh., *a rough slab ;* làmhan g., *hands rough through hard work.*
greus, *v.a.* see gréis.
greus, -a & -éis, *s.m.* see gréis.
greusachd, *s.f.ind.* Shoemaking trade. 2 Shoemaking work.
greusadaireachd,** *s.f.* see gréiseadaireachd.
greusadh, -aidh, see gréiseadh.
greusaiche, -an, *s.m.* Shoemaker. 2 Cobbler-fish, also known as, frog-fish, lump-fish, chub, bull-head, miller's thumb, sea-devil, and angler. (illust. 398.)
greusaidheachd, *s.f.* see greusachd.
greus-obair, for gréis-obair.
griachan,(MMcL) *s.m.* Warfare.
griam, *s.m.* Kind of lichen growing on stones and trees—*Suth'd.*

398. Greusaiche.

griaman, -ain, *s.m* Kind of lichen.
†**grian**, grein, *s.m.* Ground or bottom of the sea. 2 Bottom of a lake or river. 3 Land.
grian, *v.a.* Bask in the sun, expose to the sun.
grian, gréine, *s.f.* The sun. 2 Light of the sun. A gh. na h-òg-mhaidne ! *thou sun of early morn ! ;* éirigh na gréine, *sunrise ;* luighe na gréine, *sunset ;* aomadh na gréine, *the oblique descending of the sun ;* O ! nach d' eug thu mu 'm facas grian ! *O that thou didst not die ere thou sawest the sun's light ;* gath-gréine, *a sunbeam.*
grianach, -aiche, *a.* Sunny. 2 Coloured by the sun. 3 Bright, shining. 4 Warm. 5(MS) Airy. 6 Abounding in sunny spots. Dealbhan g., *sun-images ;* mu d' bhlàthaibh g., *about thy sunny blossoms.*
————adh, -aidh, *s. m.* Solar warmth. 2 Basking or drying in the sun. 3‡‡Isolation. A' g—, *pr. pt.* of grianaich.
grianachd, *s.f.* see grianachadh.
grianadh, -aidh, *s.m.* see grianachadh. Pàirt 'san raon a' g., *some basking in the sun.*
grianaich, *pr.pt.* a' grianachadh, *v. a.* Bask or dry in the sun. 2**Expose to the sun or air. 3‡‡Isolate.
————te, *past pt.* Dried in the sun.
grianair,* *v.a.* see grianaich.
†**grianair**, -ean, *s.m.* Sun-dial.
grianan, -ain, -an, *s.m.* Sunny spot. 2 Summer-house. 3 Peak of a mountain. 4 Palace, any royal seat. 5 Green. 6 Place where peats are dried. 7**Court. 8 Hall, tent. 9 Round turret. 10 Sunny eminence. 11 Exposure. 12‡‡Arched walk on a hill commanding an extensive prospect. 13 Any place suited for exposing to the heat of the sun. An g. còir, *the beauteous hall ;* g. àrd 'sam biodh na féidh, *a sunny eminence where the deer would be.*
griananach, -aiche, *a.* see grianach.
griananta, -ainte, *a.* see grianach.
grianar, *a.* see grianach.
†**grianarc**, -airc, -aircean, *s.f,* Sundial.
grian-bheum,** *s.m.* Sun-stroke.
grian-chearcall,** -aill, *s.* Solar halo.
grian-chlach,** -chloiche, -an, *s.f.* Sun-dial.
grian-chrios, -an, *s.m.* Zodiac.
———————ach, *a.* Zodiacal. Comharan (*no* ceuman) na g., *the signs of the zodiac.*
grian-chuairteag,** -eig, -an, *s.f.* Solar halo.
grian-dhealrach, -aiche, *a.* Sun-bright.
grian-dheatach, -aich, *s. f.* Exhalation. 2** Vapour.
†**grian-ghamh-stad**, -staid, *s.m.* Winter solstice.
grian-ghath,** *s.m.* Sunbeam. 'Gan tiormachadh 'sna grian-gathaibh, *drying them in the sunbeams.*
———————ach, -aiche, *a.* Emitting sunbeams, sunbright. 2 Radiant, effulgent.
grian-gheal, -ile *a.* Sun-bright.
grian-lasta, *a.* see grian-gheal.

grian-loisgte, *a.* Sun-burnt.
grian-luibh,** *s.* Heliotrope, (flower.)
grianmhor, -oire, *a.* see grianach.
grian-mhuine,§ *s.* Common bramble, see dris.
grian-neòinean,- ein, -an, *s.m.* Turn-sol or sun-flower.
grianrachadh, -aidh, see grianachadh.
grianrachd,** *s.f.* Warmth of the sun. 2 Sun-rising.
grianradh,* -aidh, *s.m. & pr.pt.* see grianadh.
grianraich, see grianaich.
grian-riochd,** -an, *s.m.* Image of the sun.
grian-ròs,§ -òis, -an, *s.m.* Rock-rose—*helianthemum vulgare.* Badge of the Fergussons. 2 Heliotrope.
grian-sgàil,** *s.f.* Parasol, any shade for the face against the sun's heat.
———ean, *s.m.* Little parasol or umbrella.
grian-sgar, -air, see grian-sgaradh.
grian-sgaradh, -aidh, -aidhean, *s.m.* Fissure or chink in anything caused by the sun's heat. 2 Breaking into chinks with the sun's heat.
†grian-shamh-stad,-staid, *s.m.* Summer solstice.
grian-stad, *s.m.* Solstice. G. geamhraidh, *winter solstice ;* g. samhraidh, *summer solstice.*
grian-thìr,** *s. f.* Sunny-land. Grian-thìr is uaine còta, *a sunny, green-mantled land.*
grianuisg,(AC) *s.* Fay. 2(DC) "Silly."—*Argyll.*
grias,* *v. a.* see griòs.
——ach, see griòsach.
——adh, -aidh, see griòsadh.
——aiche, -an, see greusaiche.
griathran, see greollan.
†grib, *a.* Swift, quick.
grib,** -e, *s.f.* Hinderance, impediment. 2 Dirt, filth. 3 Feathers on the legs or feet of birds. 4 Manger. 5(AF) Griffin.
gribeach,** *a.* Having feathers on the legs, as some kinds of fowls.
gribeach,** -eich, *s.m.* Hunting nag.
gribeadh, -eidh, *s.m.* Manger.
†gribh, *s.m.* Griffin. 2 Warrior. 3 Finger.
gribheag, -ig, -an, see griobhag.
———ach, -aiche, see griobhagach.
grìbhean,** -ein, *s.m.* Griffin.
gribh-iongach, -aich, *s.m.* Griffin.
grìd, -e, *s. f.* Substance, quality. 2 Good quality. 3 Disposition, temper, faculty. 4 Very keen penurious woman. 5††Colour.
grìdealachd, *s.f.ind.* Goodness of quality.
grìdeil, -e & -eala, *a.* Of a good quality, genuine. 2 Substantial. 3 Very keen or industrious. 4†† Penurious. Ged tha e beag, tha e g., *though he is small, he is "gritty"—Gairloch.*
grifeag, -ig, -ean, see griobhag.
———ach, see griobhagach.
grigeag, -eig, -an, see griogag.
———ach, see griogagach.
Grigirean, -ein, *s.m.* Pleiades. [*not* The constellation "Charles' wain," which is "an crann-arain."]
grigleach, *a.* Clustered, in festoons or clusters.
grigleachan, -ain, -an, *s. m.* Cluster of stars, small constellation. 2 see Grioglachan.
Griglean, -ain, *s.m.* see Grigirean.
grigleann,§ *s.m.* Quaking grass—*Breadalbane.* see conan.
grìleag,‡ -e, -ean, *s.f.* Grain of salt. 2‡‡ Any small matter. 3 (DC) Small potatoes—*Uist.* see crileag.
——ach, -aiche, *a.* Abounding in grains of salt.
——achadh, -aidh, *s.m.* Breaking into small grains.
grillus,(AF) (for griullus) *s.m.* see greollan.
†grim, *s.f.* see griam. 2 see griom.
grim-challair,** *s.m.* see griom-challair.
†grim-charbad, -aid, *s.m.* War-chariot.
grim-chliath, -chlèithe, *s.f.* Hurdles used in seiges as coverts. 2 Penthouse.
grimeach, -eiche, *a.* Grim, surly. 2 Rugged. 3 Barren. 4††Thin-haired.
grimeasach, -aiche, *a.* see grimeach.
grimeil, -e & -eala, *a.* Valiant. 2 Martial, warlike. 3**Skilful.
†grimisgear, -eir, *s.m.* Pedlar.
†grìn, *s.f.* Piece, bit, morsel.
grìn, -e, *s.m.* Gaelic spelling of *green,* plot of ground.
grìnean, *s.m., dim.* of grìn.
grinn, -e, *a.* Handsome, elegant, beautiful. 2 Neat, clean. 3 Well or neatly made, formed, or arranged. 4 Excellent. 5* Very kind. 6 Very polite. 7**Artificial. 8**Workmanlike. 9**Of an imposing appearance. 10**Pleasant. †11**Serious, attentive, diligent, deliberate, profound. 12††Fine in texture, as linen, &c. Duine g., *a very kind person ;* anart g., *very fine linen ;* na's grinne, *finer, politer ;* do thaigh g., *thy beauteous house.*
grinn, *s. f.* Piece, morsel. 2 Decency. † 3 Beard. †4 Garrison.
grinn (gu), *adv.* Neatly, elegantly. 2 Seriously. 3 Profoundly.
grinne,* *s.f.* Girning expression of countenance.
grinne, *comp.* of grinn. More or most fine. 2 Beautiful. 3 Neat.
grinneach, -ich, -an, *s.m.* Fop, young spark. 2 ††Stripling.
———adh, -aidh, *s.m.* Making neat, ornamenting or finishing with elegance. 2 Dressing, decorating. 3**Decoration. 4**Striving, effort. 5‡‡Pressing, squeezing. A' g—, *pr.pt.* of grinnich.
———as, -ais, *s.m.* Jemminess.
grinnead,-id, *s.m.* Degree of neatness, &c., see grinneas.
†grinneadh, -idh, *s.m.* Dying, perishing.
grinneal, -eil, *s.m.* Bottom of the sea, a river, or a well. 2 Gravel. 3**Channel. 4**Abyss. 5**Pool. G. gaineimh, *a bottom of sand ;* lion air uchd a' grinneil, *a net on the bosom of the pool ;* cha ruiginn g. mo ghràidh, *I would not torment my love.*
———ach, -aiche, *a.* Deep, gulfy. 2 Gravelly, sabulous. 3 Calculous.
———achd, *s.f.* Grittiness.
†grinneanachadh, see grinneachadh.
grinneas, -is, *s.m.* Neatness, elegance. 2 Gentility. 3* Kindness. 4**Finery. 5**Delicateness. Am bòidhchead 's an g., *in beauty and elegance ;* a thaobh grinneis, *by reason of delicateness ;* cha bhi luathas is g., *there cannot be expedition and neatness.*
———ach, -aiche, *a.* Neat, clean, elegant, fine.
grinneinich, see grinnich.
———te, see grinnichte.
grinn-eòlas, -ais, *s. m.* Erudition, profound knowledge.
grinnich, *pr.pt.* a' grinneachadh, *v.a.* Polish, make neat, improve, finish, beautify, adorn. 2**Dress. 3 *rarely* Gather. 4 Pierce.
———te, *past pt.* of grinnich. Polished, finished, ornamented.
grinn-obair,(MS) *s.f.* Mechanics. 2 Mechanism.
grinn-làmhachas,(MS) *s.m.* Mechanicalness.
griob, *pr.pt.* a' griobadh, *v.a.* Nibble, as a fish a hook.
grìob, } (DC) *s.m.* Coast precipice, part of
grìoba, } sea-coast where it is rocky and difficult to land—*Uist.*
griobach,‖ -aich, *s.m.* The itch.

griobadh, -aidh, *s.m.* Nibbling, bite, act of nibbling. A' g—, *pr.pt.* of griob.
griobh,‡ *s.m.* Pimple. 2(AF) Osprey. 3 (AF) Griffin.
grìobh, *s.m.* Gaelic spelling of *grieve.*
griobhach, see griuthach.
grìobhachan, *s., pl.* of griobh. Overseers—*Rob Donn.*
griobhachd, *s.f.* Office of a grieve.
griobhag, -aig, -an, *s.f.* Hurry, confusion. 2 Timidity. [* gives Genteel hurry.]
———ach, -aiche, *a.* Hurried, confused. 2 Flurried. 3 Timorous. 4* In a hurry-burry about trifles or nothing at all.
griobharsgaich,* *s.f.* Rash of pimples through the skin. 2 *Fucus confervæ,* see lianach.
griobhlach, see griuthach.
griobhrach, *prov.* for griuthach.
grioblas,** -ais, *s.m.* Closeness.
griocas,** -ais, *s.m.* Rumbling noise.
grìoch, -ich, -an, *s.m.* Consumptive or lean young deer.
grìochair, -e, -ean, *s.m.* Sickly, consumptive person. 2 Mean, miserly person.
grìochan,‖ -ain, *s.f.* Consumption. [Preceded by the art. *a' gh—.*]
griodar, -air, *s.m.* Great noise.
griofach,(MS) *Kintyre* for griuthach.
griogach,** *a.* Pebbly.
griogag, -aig, -an, *s.f* [McL & D gives *s.m.*] Bead. 2 Pebble. 3 Crystal. *Lewis, Lochaber, &c,* 4* Small cheese—*Islay.*
———ach, -aiche, *a.* Of, or pertaining to, beads or pebbles.
†griogchan, *s.m.* Constellation.
———ach, *a.* Twinkling like stars, blazing, dazzling.
Grioglachan, -ain, *s.m* Pleiades [*not* the constellation called "Charles' wain," as given by some—that is "an crann-arain."]
grioglachanach, -aiche, *a.* Glittering like stars.
griog-shùil, -shùla, -shùilean, *s.f.* Little round lively eye.
———each, -eiche, *a.* Having small round lively eyes.
†griom, *s.m.* War, battle.
grioma,(AF) *s.f.* Streaked cow.
griomach, -aiche, *a.* see grimeach.
griomacach, -aiche, *a.* Thin-haired.
griomagach, -aich, *s.m.* Shrivelled grass.
griomail, -e, *a.* see grimeach.
grioman,? -ain, *s.m.* Lungwort lichen, see crotal-coille. 2 Malt bud or growth.
griom-challair,** *s. m.* Herald, one who proclaims war or peace.
†griom-charbad, see grim-charbad.
†griomh,** *s.m.* Nail. 2 Talon. 3 Claw.
griomh, see gniomh.
griomhach,** *a.* Having claws or talons.
griomhag,** -aig, *s.f.* Hurry, flurry. 2 Timidity. Foighidneach gun gh., *patient without timidity.*
griomh-shrònach,** *a.* Hawk-nosed.
†griongal, -ail, *s.m.* Care, sorrow. 2 Assiduity. 3 Industry.
†———ach,** *a.* Anxious, sorrowful. 2 Assiduous. 3 Industrious.
———achd, *s.f.* Continued care or sorrow 2 Assiduity.
grionnal, see grinneal.
grìos, *pr.pt.* a' grìosadh, *v.a.* Entreat, pray, solicit. 2 Abet, encourage, aid. 3**Adjure. 4 *rarely* Provoke, whet. 5‡ Rake up a fire. 6* Blaspheme. G. air, *beseech him.*
grìos, -a, *s.f.* Heat. 2(AC) Profane swearing, swearing by God, Christ or any of the host of heaven.
grìosach, -aich, -aichean *s.f.* Burning embers. 2 Hot battle. 3 Volley. 4**Fireside. 5 Squall. Aghann grìosaich, *a frying-pan;* 'nuair a thigeadh i 'na grìosaich, *when it (the wind) would come in squalls;* air a' ghrìosaich, *on thy embers;* eadar a' gh. 's an stairsneach, *between the fireside and the threshold.*
grìosach,** *a.* Imploring, supplicating, (also griosail.) 2 (TS) Imprecating.
———,(TS) -aichean, *s.m.* Adjuration.
grìosachadh, -aidh, *s.m.* Frying. 2 Stirring up, as of a fire. 3 Provocation. 4 Exilement.
grìosad, -aid, *s. m.* Conjuration. 2 (MS) Request, invocation, orisons.
———achd, *s.f.* Blasphemy. Ri g., *blaspheming.*
———air,* *s.m.* Blasphemer.
griosadh, -aidh, *s. m.* Entreating, act of entreating, beseeching, praying, supplicating, adjuration, solicitation. A' g., *pr.pt.* of grios.
grìosaich, *v.a.* Entreat. 2 Stir up the fire. 3 Provoke. 4**Fry 5**Grow hot. 6(TS) Imprecate.
———te, *past pt.* of grìosaich. Fried. 2 Kindled
griosail, -e, *a.* Supplicatory.
griosair, *s.m.* Implorer. 2**Frying-pan.
grios-nàimhdeas, -eis, *s.m.* Inveterate enmity.
†grios-nàmhach, *a.* Inveterately hostile.
grìosta, *past pt.* of grios. Stirred up, provoked. 2 Beseeched, implored.
†grioth, *s.* Sun.
grioth,* *s.f.* Gravel-pit. 2 Pebble.
———alach,* -aich, *s.m.* Gravel—*Islay.*
gris, -e, *s.f.* Horror, shuddering. 2 Pimples produced on the skin by heat. 3 Redness. 4 Fire. 5 The horrors. 6**Tremor. 7**Terror. 8** Cuticular inflammation. 9 Shiver. 10 Prickly heat. 11* Perspiration or sweat produced by the idea of horror. 12 Horrified expression or appearance. G. fhuachd, *a cold shiver;* thug e g. orm, *he made me shudder.*
gris,** -e, *a.* Grey.
gris-dhearg, -dheirge, *a.* Red mixed with white. 2 Roan-coloured. 3 Ruddy. 4**Liard, colour formed by mixing red and grey. Gruaidh g., *a ruddy cheek.*
grise, see crèis.
griseach,* *a.* Shivering, fond of the fireside—*North.* 2 Fatty, oily.
———d, *s.f.* Oiliness.
grisean, *s. m.* One of a rabble A gh! *you worthless fellow!—Gairloch.*
gris-fhionn, *a.* Kind of brindled colour, mixture of black and white. 2 Grizzled. 3 Roan. 4 Spotted. Breac agus g., *spotted and grizzled.*
grisg,** *v.a.* Roast. 2 Fry. 3 Broil.
——ean, -ein, *s.m.* Roasted meat. 2 Boiled meat.
grisich,(MS) *v.a.* Begrease, besmear.
grisionn, *a.* see gris-fhionn.
grisnich,(MS) *v.a.* Besmear.
grith,** *s.f.* Knowledge. 2 Learning. 3 Outcry.
——each, *a.* Knowing, learned, wise, discreet.
——eil, *s.f.* Grunting of young pigs.
griùbhrach,(TS) *Inverness* for griuthach.
griugadan, -ain, see grigirean.
griuilleag,(DU) -eig, -an, *s.f.* Small potato. 2 *in pl* Dross of potatoes.
griùllach, *Harris* for griuthach.
griullus, see greollan.
griun, *s.m.* Hedgehog, porcupine.
griùrach, -aich, *Skye, Uist, W. Isles, &c.* for griuthach.
griùragan, -ain, *s. m.* Infinitely small particle, mote. 2 Pustule on the skin.

griùraganach, -aiche, *a.* Full of small particles or pustules.
griuthach,‖ -aich, *s.f.* Measles. [Preceded by the article *a' gh—.*] Tha e 'sa gh., *he has the measles.*
griuth-làmhach, *a.* Quick, expert, ready-handed. Gu g., *expertly.*
griuthrach, -aich, see griuthach.
gròb, *pr.pt.* a' gròbadh, *v.a.* Join by indentation. 2 Serrate, groove. 3 Join or sew together awkwardly. 4 Dig with the hands, grub. 5 (MS) Purse. 6††Cobble.
——, *s. m.* Channel or sewer of a cow-house. —*Arran.*
——ach, -aiche, *a.* Serrated. 2 Indented. 3 Wrinkled. 4 Joined by serration. 5** Digging, grubbing.
grobach, -aich, *s.m.* Sea-ware, see propach.
gròbadh, -aidh, *s.m.* Act of joining by serration. 2 Serrating. 3 Grooving. 4 Rebate in *carpentry.* 5**Digging, grubbing. A' g—, *pr.pt.* of gròb.
——ag, -aig, -an, *s.f.* Poor shrivelled toothless woman. 2* Little tooth.
grobais,§ *s.* The plants mallows—*malvæ.*
groban, -ain, -an, *s.m.* see gnoban.
gròban, -ain, -an, *s. m.* Mugwort—*artimisia vulgaris.*
grobhd,(CR) *s.* Chunk, thick piece. G. arain, *a chunk of bread—W. of Ross.*
gròc, *pr. pt.* a' gròcadh & a' gròcail, *v.a. & n.* Croak. 2 Roar with a hoarse low voice. 3 Frown on, frighten, threaten in order to frighten children. 4 (AH) Scold noisily and passionately.
gròcadh, -aidh, *s.m.* Roaring, act of roaring. 2 Croaking. 3 Frowning. 4(AH) Scolding with noise and passion. A' g—. *pr.pt.* of gròg.
gròcail, -e, *s.f. & pr.pt.* see gròcadh.
grod, -a & -oide, *a.* Rotten, putrid. 2 Proud. 3 Smart. 4(DC) Unreasonable, cross-tempered. Mar fhiodh g., *like rotten wood* ; ugh g., *a rotten egg* ; duine g., *an ill-tempered man.*
grod, *pr.pt.* a' grodadh, *v.a. & n.* Become putrid, rot. 2 Cause to rot.
†grod, -oid, *s.m.* Foam.
grodachd,‡‡ *s.f.ind.* Putridness.
grodadh, -aidh, *s.m.* Rotting, state or act of rotting or becoming putrid.
grodag, -aig, -an, *s.f.* Depraved woman.
grodaidh, *a.* see grod.
grodair,* *s.m.* Putrid fish. 2 Stinking fellow.
grodan,** -ain, *s.m.* Boat.
grodh,** *s.m.* Lever. 2 Gaelic spelling of *crow.*
grodh-iaruinn,** *s.m.* Iron crow.
grodlach, -aich, *s. f.* Rotten tree. 2 Mass of rottenness.
gròdlan,(MS) *s.m.* Hum.
gròdlanadh, -aidh, *s.m.* Grunting, as a pig.
gròdlanaich, *v.n.* Grunt, as a pig.
grog,** -oig, *s.m.* see gnog.
†grog, -oig, -an, *s.m.* see gruag.
grogach,* -aiche, *a.* see gnogach.
grogag, *s.f.,dim.* of grog.
grògair, see gròigean.
groganach, -aiche, *a.* Wrinkled, stunted, as heather.
gròibleach,** *a.* Long-nailed. 2 Having talons.
groideal, -oidle & -oidleach, see greideal.
groidheal,** -il, *s.m.* Coral.
groidlean, *s.m.* Spirtle, pot-stick—*Arran.*
gròig, -e, *s.f.* Awkwardness. 2 Perverseness. 3**Scrawl. 4(DU) Mess. Tha e 'na ghròig, *it is a perfect mess.*
groig,** *s.* see gnoig.
gròig,* *v.a.* Bungle, botch.
gròigean, -ein, -an, *s.m.* Awkward, unhandy person. 2 Botcher, bungler, dabbler.
————achd, *s.f.ind.* Awkwardness, unhandiness, helplessness.
gròigeil, -e, *a.* Awkward, helpless, unhandy.
gròigeileachd, see gròigeanachd.
gròigeileas, see gròigeanachd.
gròigeineachadh, -aidh, *s.m. & pr. pt.* Gnarling.
gròigich,* *v.a.* Botch, bungle, dabble.
groilean,** -ein, *s.m.* Bilbo.
groilleach,** -eich, *s.f.* Coarse cloth.
gròilleach,(DMu) *a.* Muddy. Tha 'n rathad glé gh., *the road is very muddy—Black Isle.*
groim, see greim.
groimh, *s.f.* Grin. 2 Visage. 3 Nickname for a person with a grinning countenance.
grois, see gnois.
groiseag, *Blair Athole* for gròiseid.
groiseanach,** *a.* see gnoiseanach (appx.)
gròiseid, -e, -ean, *s.f.* Gooseberry.
————each, -eiche, *a.* Of, or relating to, gooseberries, abounding in gooseberries.
groisgeach,** -eich, *s.m.* Droll, hare-devil.
grollan, see greollan.
gròm,(CR) *s. m.* Minute shellfish that cover tidal rocks and stones—*W. of Ross-shire.*
gròmag,(CR) *s.f.* Small rock-fish that feeds on the grom—*W. of Ross-shire.* 2 Mixture of oatmeal and churned cream. 3 Mixture of oatmeal and whisky, with or without sugar.—*W. of Ross-shire.*
gromag,** -aig, *s.f.* Prating girl.
gròm-dearg,(DU) *s. m.* Small red variety of coral.
gròmhan, -ain, see gnòmhan.
†gron, -oin, *s.m.* Stain, blot, blemish.
gronnsal,** -ail, *s.m.* Grunt.
grontach,** -aiche, *a.* Corpulent, gross.
gronustal,** -ail, *s.m.* see pronnasg.
gropach,(MMcD) *s.f.* Seaweed, light brown in colour, and used with "slaodach" as food for cattle. It is not found so high up on the shore as "cìreanach."
gropadh,** -aidh, *s.m.* Gully, sewer.
gropais, see grobais.
gros, -ois, see gnos.
grosach, see gnosach.
grosadh, -aidh, *s.m.* Gross (twelve dozen.)
gròsaid, see gròiseid.
————each, see gròiseideach.
grosair, see gnosair.
grosaireachd, see gnosaireachd.
grosanach, see gnosach.
gròsd, see gnòsd.
gròta, -chan, *s.m.* Groat, silver coin value 4d. sterling. Is don' am pàigheadh an g., *a groat is but poor pay.*
grothach, -aich, see gnothach.
grothal, -ail, *s.m.* Sand, gravel.
grothalach, see grothlach.
grothan,** -ain, *s.m.* Purring. 2 Moan, groan. 3 Complaining.
grothlach, -aich, *s.m.* Gravel-pit.
————, -aiche, *a.* Gravelly.
grotonach,** -aiche, *a.* Corpulent. 2 Heavy-breeched. *prov.*
gru,(AF) *s.m.* Greyhound.
grù, see gnù.
gruadhach, -aich, -aichean, *s.f.* see gruaidh.
gruag, -aig, -an, *s.f.* Wig. 2 Hair of the head, especially of a female. 2 Anything resembling hair. 4 Lock of hair. 5**Woman. 6** Wife. G.-bhréige, *a wig.*
gruagach, -aich, -aichean, *s.f.* Young woman, maiden, virgin. 2 *in derision*, Man with long hair. 3 Bridesmaid. 4 ** Bridegroom's maid. 5** *rarely*, Chief of a place. 6 Supposed household goddess. 7†† *s.m.* Brownie.

8 Horizontal bar bearing supports of flyers of spinning-wheel. Ghràdhaich e a' gh., *he loved the virgin ;* na gruagaichean laghach, *the pretty maidens ;* cha ghruagaichean gu léir air am bi am falt féin, *all are not virgins who wear their own hair*—of old, young women in Gaeldom were wont to go bare-headed until after marriage or after child-bearing.
————, -aiche, *a.* Hairy, having much hair. 2 Having ringlets. 2 Womanly.
gruagag, -aig, -an, *s.f., dim.* of gruag. Little wig. 2 Small lock of hair.
gruagair, -ean, *s.m.* Hair-dresser. 2*Wig-maker.
gruag-Muire,§ *s.* Goldilocks, see follasgain.
gruaidh, -e, *s. f.* Cheek. 2 Countenance. 3 Brow. 4 Edge of a furrow. 5 Profile. 6 Temple of the head. 7 Liver. Coslas a' bhàis 'na gh. *the likeness of death in his face*; rughadh g., *a blush.*
gruaidhean, *n. pl.* of gruaidh.
————,** see grùthan.
gruaidh-lagan,** -ain, *s.m.* Dimple on the cheek.
gruaigean,§ -ain, *s.m.* Badderlocks, hen-ware—kind of sea-ware—*Skye*, *birses, see mircean.
———— -éisg,(DMy *s.m.* Round tasselled ball between a fish's stomach and entrails.
————ach, -aiche, *a.* Abounding in seaweed.
gruaim, -e, *s. f.* Gloom, surly look. 2 Sullenness. 3 Sadness, melancholy. 4 Ill-humour. 5 Darkness. Fo dhòruinn 's fo gh., *in sorrow and gloom.*
gruaim-bheinn, -bheanntan, *s.f.* Dark hill. 2 Gloomy mountain. O ghuallaibh nan g., *from the shoulders of the gloomy mountains.*
gruaimean, -in, -an, *s.m.* Gloomy, sullen, morose fellow. 2 Man with a frowning visage. 3**Frown. 4**Gloom.
gruaimean,** *a.* Surly. 2 Frowning.
gruama, *a.* see gruamach.
gruamach, -aiche, *a.* Sullen, gloomy, morose, surly. 2 Dark, sad, sorrowful. 3 Gloomy, obscure, cloudy. Bu gh. an tuar, *gloomy was their aspect.*
————, -aich, *s.m.* Forbidding face.
————d, *s.f.ind.* Sullenness, gloominess, surliness, melancholy. 2 Sternness, grimness, austerity. 3 Habit of frowning, continual frowning. 4 Cloudiness. 5* Unhappy temper.
gruamadh, *pr.pt.* Darkening, as the evening.
gruamag, -aig, -an, *s.f.* Grim, frowning, morose woman.
gruamaiche, *comp.* of gruamach.
————, *s.f.* Gloominess, gloom. 2 Sternness. 3 Surliness. 4 Grumbling.
gruaman, -ain, *s.m.* Gloomy sadness, dudgeon, melancholy, dejection. 2 Slight frown. 3** Man who frowns. Na biodh oirbh g., *let there be no frown upon you.*
————ach, -aiche, *a.* Vexed, dejected, sad, displeased.
grùan, see grùthan. 2* Deep moan
grùanach, see grùthanach.
grùbhan, see grùthan.
†gruc, *s.* Wrinkle.
grùdair, -ean, *s.m.* Brewer, mashman. 2 Distiller. 3††Tavern-keeper, victualler. 4 Mean drinker.
————eachd, *s. f.* Employment of brewing, brewery. 2 Employment of distilling, distillery.
grùg, -ùige, *a.* see gnùg.
grùg, -ùig, *s.f.* see gnùg.
grùgach, -aiche, *a.* see gnùgach.
————,* -aich, *s.f.* see gnùgag.
grugadan, (WC) *s. m.* The seven stars (Seven Sisters.)
grùgag, see gnùgag.
grùgair, -ean, see gnùgair.
grùid, -e, *s.f.* Lees, dregs, grounds, sediment. 2**Malt.
——each, *a.* Full of grains. 2 Malty. 3 Full of dregs.
gruidhear, -an, *s.m.* Overseer.
grùig, -e, -ean, *prov.* for grùg. 2 Churlishness, inhospitality. 3 Shrinking of the shoulders, as from cold, drooping attitude 4(DU)Churlish look. Tha g. air a' bhoin, *the cow has a pugnacious look.*
grùigean -ein, see gnùigean.
grùigeineach, -eiche, *a.* see gnùigeineach.
gruigh, see gruth. 2* Dish of curds dressed with butter, &c.
gruileag, see griuilleag.
gruilleamach, -aiche, *a.* Prancing, leaping suddenly.
†gruin, -e, -ean, *s.f.* see gràineag.
gruin,(AF) see griun.
gruip, *s. f.* see gròb. 2 Gaelic spelling of *grip.*
gruitheach, -eiche, see gruthach.
gruitheam, -im, *s.m.* Curd-butter (that is, half butter and half curd finely mixed.) 2††Crowdie. 3 *Curd-pie.
gruithim, see gruitheam.
gruitin,(AF) *s.* Salt, old or sour butter.
grullagan,* -ain, *s. m.* Circle, ring of people. 2 see grioglachan.
grullan, -ain, see greollan.
grumach, *a.* see gruamach.
grumadh, -aidh, *s.m.* Gaelic noun formed from Eng. *groom.*
grumastal,(CR) *Torridon* for pronnasg.
grùmna,(DU) *a.* Sour-looking. 2 Churlisn.
grùmhan,(DU) *s.m.* Grunt, moan.
†grunn, *s.m.* Crowd, group. 2 see grunnd. G. dhaoine, *a crowd of people ;* lìontan ghrunna, *ground nets.*
grunnachadh, -aidh, see grunndachadh.
grunnadh, see grunndadh.
grunnaich, see grunndaich.
————e, see grunndaiche.
————te, see grunndaichte.
grunnail, *a.* see grunndail.
grunnal,** *s.m.* Bottom.
grunnan, -ain, -an, *s. m.* Cluster, handful, group. 2 Little heap. 3 Hillock. 4 Parcel. 5 Group of animals.
grunnanach,†† *a.* Abounding in clusters.
grunnanaich, *pr. pt.* a' grunnanachadh, *v. a.* Group, collect in groups.
grunnas, see grunnasg.
grunnasg, -aisg, -an, *s.f.* Groundsel, see buaghalan. 2‡‡Dregs, sediment.
————ach, -aiche, *a.* Of, or abounding in, groundsel. 2‡‡ Full of dregs or sediment, draffy.
grunnastal, *prov* for pronnasg. [In *Gairloch* this is the only form used—DU.]
grunnastan, *Reay Co.* for pronnasg.]
grunnd, -uinnd & -a, -an, *s.m.* Ground, bottom, 2 Base. 3†† Sense. 4 Thrift, carefulness, economy. 5 Decision of character. 6**The nether world. 7* Attention. G. an domhain, *the bottom of the deep ;* g. a chléibh, *the bottom of his breast ;* a chumhachdan dubha a' ghruinnd, *ye gloomy divinities of the nether world ;* dean le g. e, *do it carefully ;* duine gun gh., *a man without decision of character ;* làmh a' ghruinnd, *a thrifty person.*
grunndachadh, -aidh, *s.m.* Grounding. 3 Sounding, fathoming. Cord grunnachaidh, *a sounding line.*
grunndadh, -aidh, *s.m.* Heaping up, gathering together, accumulation.
grunndaich, *pr.pt.* a' grunndachadh, *v.a.* Sound

the depth, fathom. 2(DC) Wade—*Uist.* Feuch an g. e, *try if the lead touches the bottom (of the water.)*

————e,†† -an, *s. m.* Sinker, weight for a fishing-line.

————te, *past pt.* of grunndaich. Sounded, measured, (of depth.)

grunndail, -e, *a.* Having a good foundation. 2 Frugal, solid, economical. 3 Very attentive and punctual. 4**Careful. 5**Sensible. Gu g., *frugally.*

———— -fuar,(CR) *a.* Somewhat cold—*W. of Ross.*

grunndalachd, *s.f.ind.* Solidity, firmness. 2 Carefulness, frugality. 3 Economics. 4 Sense. 5 Decisive character. 6 Attention to business. 7 Good management.

grunndalas, -ais, *s.m.* see grunndalachd.

grunndas,** -ais, *s.m.* Good management. 2 Carefulness, frugality. 3 Dregs, lees.

————ach, -aiche, *a.* Abounding in dregs, feculent.

grunnd-lagh, *s.m.* Fundamental law.

grunnd-luchd, *s.m.* Ballast.

grunnd-luchdaich, *v.a.* Ballast.

grunnstal, *Helmsdale* for pronnasg.

grunnstalach, *a.* Brimstony.

grùnsgal, -ail, *s.m.* Grunting, snarling, growling.

————ach, -aiche, *a.* Snarling, growling,grunting.

gruth, -uith, *s.m.* Curds. Cho geal 's an g., *as white as curds.*

———ach, -aiche, *a.* Curdled, abounding in curds. 2 Curdling, curd-producing.

grùthan, -ain, -an, *s.m.* The liver.

————ach,‡‡ -aiche, Livered, belonging to the liver, heptic.

gruth-im, *s.m.* see gruitheam.

gu, *prep.* To, towards. Cuiridh mi litir chugad, *I will send a letter to you* ; chuige is uaithe, *to and fro* ; gu fichead, *to twenty.* [Governs dative case.] *Gu* is generally omitted in *Argyllshire* when speaking of the cardinal points, as tha mi 'falbh an iar, *I am going (to the) west* ; tha mi 'sealltainn deas, *I am looking toward the south* ; but in *Skye* and the North the *gu* is generally inserted, as, tha mi dol gu deas, *I am going to the south.* In *Gairloch, Lochalsh & Lochbroom* they say "a' dol gu deas" and "gu tuath," but "a' dol an ear agus an iar (gu pronounced dho.) *Gu* in these cases is not good idiom ; *gu* implies reaching your destination, but you can never reach the N., S., E. or W. It may be mentioned here, under *gu*, that a strange effect of the migrations from the south side of the Moray Firth is heard in a common English expression among the people of E. Ross generally where they use such comical phrases as, *I am going west to the kitchen, I am going east to the room,*—but the place indicated as *east* is often almost due north. [In certain districts of Perthshire all places are either *east* or *west.*] This disappearance of *to* in English when speaking of the cardinal points is worth noting. At first sight it appears as though the Gaelic idiom of the south had been translated into the English of the north, but the English idiom has really no connection with Gaelic.

Gu is used locally in *Suth'd* in place of the usual *a* before infinitives, as, gu àrach an anma, *to nourish their souls.*

G. seilg nan sliabh, *to the mountain-chase* ; g. crìch mo shaoghail, *to my life's end* ; air dol gu neo-ni, *gone to nothing* ; gu là bràth, *for ever* ; bliadhna gu leth, *a year and a half.* [*Gu* here does not mean *to*, but is a remnant of con, *with*, and is only found in a few sentences, as, "bliadhna gu leth," "gu Mac 'Ic Alasdair 's Lochial."]

When *gu* comes before an adjective, the adj. is translated into English as an adverb, as, math, *good*, gu math, *well* ; buileach, *effectual*, gu buileach, *effectually.* Armstrong says "*Gu* has often a similar effect on a substantive, as, beachd, *observation*, gu beachd, *clearly;* dearbh, *proof*, gu dearbh, *truly, indeed,*" but both words are adjectives—"gu beachd" is an Irishism in the Psalms, "beachd" being an adjective in Irish. Chi thu chugad e, 's cha'n fheàirrd thu agad e, *you'll see it coming to you, and you'll be none the better when you have got it.*

gu, *adv.* Till, until.

gu, *conj.* That, to the end that. Used to signify a wish or idea, and implies that a sentence which is not expressed precedes the clause it introduces. (Tha e fìor) gu'n tugadh crodh Chailein dhomh bainn' air an raon, (*it is true*) *that Colin's cattle would give me milk on the plain* ; (is e mo mhiann-sa) gu'n robh mòran maith agad,(*it is my wish*) *that you may have good*--a way of returning thanks ; (is e mo mhiann-sa) gu'm bu slàn a chì mi thu, (*it is my wish*) *that I may see you well !* gu ma fada beò an rìgh ! *long live the king !* slàn gu'n robh an Gàidheal gasda, *may the gallant Celt be hale. Gu* is used in poetry if the nominative precedes the verb, and also to give greater emphasis, as, fiamh aiteis àird, gu'n robh 'na ghnùis, *an appearance of exceeding joy was in his face ;* nam bu duine eile gu'n deanadh, bu mhise gu'n dìoladh, *had another man done it, it's I would avenge it.* In negative expressions *nach* takes the place of *gu*, O ! (is truagh) nach robh mi 'nam chalman, *O ! (it is sad) that I were not a dove.—MacKay's Easy G. Syntax.*

†gu. *s.m.* Lie.

guag, -aig, -an, *s.m.* Giddy, whimsical fellow, unsettled, capricious person. 2 Splay foot. 3 (DC) Lameness. see cuag. Tha g. ann, *he is lame.*

——ach, -aiche, *a.* Capricious, giddy, whimsical. 2 see cuagach.

guagair, see cuagaire.

guaid, *pr.pt.* a' guaideil, *v.* see guait.

guaideil, *pr. pt.* see guaiteil.

guaigean, -ein, -an, *s.m.* Thick little round cake. 3(DC) Short, stout man or boy—*Argyll.*

————ach, -aiche, *a.* Thick, little and round.

guail, *gen.sing.* of gual.

guailisg,(AC) *a.* False, distorted, displaced, out-of-order morally, mentally or physically.

guaille, *gen.sing.* of gualainn.

guailleach, -ich, -ean, *s. f.* Cord tying the shoulders of the dead. 2* Shoulder-strap or chain of a horse. 3 *pl.* in the sense of Shoulders—*Arran.*

—————an, -ain, -an, *s.m.* Woman's tunic. 2 Companion. 3**Shoulder-piece. 4**Mantle. 5(CR) Draught-chain of a cart.

guaillean, -an, *s.m.* Coal of fire, cinder. 2 *pl.* of gualann.

————ach, -aiche, *a.* Full of cinders. 2 Like a cinder.

guaillear, -eir, -an, (gual) *s.m.* Collier.

————, -eir, (gualann) *s.m.* Comrade, chum.

————achd, *s. f.* Employment of a collier, colliery.

guaillfhionn, -a, *a.* White-shouldered.

—————, *s.m.* Name given to a cow with

white shoulders.
guaillibh, *dat.pl.* of gualann. Clann nan Gàidheal ann an [*not* ri, which is the Eng. idiom translated] guaillibh a chéile, *children of the Gael shoulder to shoulder.*
guaillich, *v.a.* Go hand in hand and shoulder to shoulder. 2 Accompany. 3**Elbow.
guailliche,** *s.m.* Colleague.
guailliinneach, see guailleach.
guaillionn, see guaillfhionn.
guaillneach, -eiche, *a.* Shouldered.
guaillnean, *n.pl.* of gualann.
———, *s.m.* Cinder.
guailneanan, *s.pl.* Traces of a carriage, &c.
guaim,* *s. f.* Economy, attention to minute articles of gain, prudence, good management, thrift. Cha'n 'eil móran g. innte, *she is not a good manager.*
———eas, -is, *s.m.* Quietness. 2 Comfort. 3** Neatness.
———easach, -aiche, *a.* Quiet. 2 Comfortable. snug. 3 Neat. Gu g., *neatly.*
guain,* *s.f.* see guaineas.
guaineag, -eig, -an, *s.f.* Minx.
guaineas, -is, *s.m.* Liveliness, briskness, giddiness. 2 Affectedness. 3 Buxomness. 4 Colt's tooth.
———ach, -aiche, *a.* Brisk, lively, giddy, sportive. 2 Affected.
guaineileas, -eis, *s.m.* Sporting, frisking, restlessness, frolicking.
guaineis,(MS) *s.f.* Levity. see guaineas.
guairdean,‡ *s.m.* Vertigo.
†guaire, *s.f.* Hair of the head. 2 Point of anything. 3 Bristle. 4 Roughness.
†guaire, *a.* Noble.
guairne,* *s.f.* Unshapely, unmannerly woman.
———ach, -eiche, *a.* Spherical.
guairne-mu-ghuairn, *s.* Quill-pith, see guirne-mu-ghiùirn.
guairsgeach, -eiche, *a.* Hairy. 2 Curled, in rings or ringlets. 3 Bristly.
guairtean, see cuairtean.
†guais, *s.* Danger, hazard. 2 Enterprise, venture. 3 Fatigue.
guais-bheart, -eirt, *s.m.* Enterprise, adventure, dangerous enterprise, hazardous attempt. 2 Feat.
guais-bheartach, -aiche, *a.* Enterprising, adventurous, daring, fool-hardy, hazardous. Gu goimh-chridheach, g., *keenly and daringly.*
guaiseach, -eiche, *a.* Dangerous.
———d, *s.f.* see guais.
guaismhoire, *comp.* of guaismhor.
guaismhor, -oire, *a.* Dangerous, hazardous, critical. 2 Enterprising, daring, fool-hardy.
guait,‡ *pr. pt.* a' guaiteil, *v.a.* Leave off, let alone, quit, desist. Used principally, if not solely in Gabh no g. e, *take or leave it.*
———eal, -eil, *s.m.* Desistance.
———eil, (a') *pr.pt.* of guait. Letting alone. 2 Refusing *Arran.*
gual, -ail, *s.m.* Coal. 2 Coal-fire. 3 (AC)Grief, consuming by grief as by fire. Deagh theine guail, *a good coal-fire* ; toll-guail, *a coal-pit* ; g.-fairge, *sea-coal* ; g.-ceardach, *smithy-coal.* Làmh dheas a dheanadh an gniomh' 's nach bu tais a shéideadh an g., *a right hand for action and able persistently to blow the fire.*
gual,* *v.a.* Gall, pain intensely.
gual, *pr.pt.* a' gualadh, *v.a. & n.* Blacken with coal. 2 Burn to coal. 3 Become coal.
guala, see gualann.
———ch, -aiche, *a.* Abounding in coal, coaly. 2 Like coal.
———chan, -ain, *s.m.* Stout young fellow.
———chadh,(MS) *s.m.* Calcination.
gualadair, *s.m.* see gualair.
gualadh, -aidh, *s.m.* Act of blackening with coal. 2 State of burning into coals. 3 Torturing, torture, greatest pain, tormenting. 4 (DU) Act of coaling. A' g—, *pr.pt.* of gual. Mo chridhe 'ga gh. 's 'ga losgadh, *my heart being tortured and burnt.*
gualag, -aig, -an, *s.f. dim.* of gualann. Little shoulder.
gualaich, *v.a.* Tuck. 2 Blacken as with coal. 3 Burn to cinders, calcine, carbonize, char.
———te, *past pt.* Burnt to a cinder, carbonized.
gualair, see guaillear.
gualann, -ainn & -uailne, *pl.* -uailnean & -uaillean, *dat. pl.* guaillibh, *s.f.* Shoulder. 2 Elbow or corner of a mountain. 3 Bend of a ship's bow. 4 Crank of a cycle. 5 Corner, angle. 6 Arm. 7* Stamina. Soitheach air a gualainn, *a vessel on her shoulder;* g. deas an taighe, *the right corner of the house ;* crios guailne, *a shoulder-belt ;* is lag g. gun bhràthair an àm do na fir teachd an làthair, *weak is shoulder without brother when men are meeting one another.*
gual-bhrau,** -ain, *s.m.* Firebrand.
gual-fhionn, *a.* see guaillfhionn.
gual-fhiodha, *s.m.* Charcoal.
guallach, see guailleach.
guallaich, *s.pl.* Shoulders—*Arran.*
guallann, see gualann.
guamach, -aiche, *a.* Thick, plentiful. 2 Smirking. 3 Careful, exact. 4 Nodding, waving. 5*Neat, snug. 6**Well-formed. 7**Pleasant. 8(CR) Managing, thrifty—*Arran.* 9‡ Plentiful. Beul g., *a smirking mouth ;* fàsach g., *a pleasant moor.*
———d, *s.f.ind.* Trimness. 2 Economy.
guamag, -aig, -an, *s.f.* Neat, tidy woman. 2** Smirking girl.
———ach, *a.* Neat, trim, tidy. 2 Smirking, as a female.
guamaiche, *comp.* of guamach.
———ad, -eid, *s. m.* Neatness, degree of neatness. A' dol an g., *getting neater and neater.*
guamaiseach, *a.* see guaimeasach.
guaman, -ain, *s.m.* Cheek.
guamnach, -aich, *s.m.* Lamentation.
guan, -ain, *s.m.* Fool.
guanach, -aiche, *a.* Light, giddy, fickle, affectedly apish, light-headed. 2 Active. 3 Unsteady, nodding, wavering. Maoisleach a' chinn ghuanaich, *the light-headed roe ;* air a' chreig ghuanaich, *on the nodding rock.*
guanachas,(MS) -ais, *s.m.* Airiness.
guanachd, *s.f.ind.* Giddiness.
guanadh, -aidh, *s.m.* Lightness, unsteadiness, giddiness.
guanag, -aig, -an, *s.f.* Light coquettish girl. 2 (MS) Prude. [** gives "guamag" for a smirking girl.]
guanais, *s.f.* Lightness, unsteadiness, giddiness. Air son bhi guanais feadh nan caol, *for gadding about* or *for pleasure-sailing among the kyles* ; air beagan staid no g., *with but little affectedness or airs.*
———each, *a.* Light, active. 2 Light-headed. 3 Unsteady, nodding, wavering. G. òg, *light-headed and young.*
———eachd, *s.f.* Lightness, activity. 2 Light-headedness. 3 Unsteadiness.
guanalas,* -ais, *s.m.* Giddiness, unsteadiness. 2 Light-headedness. 3 Wavering. 4 Strolling. [* gives *nom.* as -ais.]
guarag,(AF) *s.f.* Name of a cow.
——— -bhleothainn, *s.f.* Milch-cow.

†guas, -ais, *s.m.* Danger, jeopardy.
†——ach, *a.* Hazardous.
†——achd, *s.f.* Danger, jeopardy. 2 Perilous situation. 3 Perilous adventure.
guasachdach, -aiche, *a.* Dangerous, dreadful, painful. 2 Perilous, hazardous, forlorn. 3 Enterprising. It is used in the last sense in old medical MSS.
gubarnach,(AF) *s.m.* Devil-fish, angler. 2(DC) Cuttle-fish—*Argyll.*
———— -meurach,(AF) *s.m.* Octopus. 2(DC) Cuttle-fish—*Argyll.*
gu beachd, *adv.* Truly.
gu beagnaich,(DC) *adv.* Almost, nearly—*Uist.*
†gubha, *s.* Lamentation. 2 Battle, conflict.
†gubhach, -aiche, *a.* Mournful, sorrowful.
gubhannach, -aiche, *a.* Slanderous.
†gubhb, -a, -an, *s. m.* Study. 2 Schoolhouse. 3 Armoury.
†——ach, -aiche, *a.* Studious, assiduous.
gu bràth, *adv.* For ever, ever (future time only.)
gu buileach, *adv.* Altogether, quite.
guc, -an, *s. m.* Bell, bubble, drop. 2 Germ. 3 Sprout, bud. 4 Corolla of any flower. 5 Bumper. 6 Acrospire. 7 Bell-flower. 8** Flower of any leguminous vegetable. 9(DU) Egg-shell. 10 Cyst. 11(DU) Bead on whisky. Bàrr-guc, *the flower of any leguminous vegetable, as peas ;* g. uighe, *an empty egg-shell.*
gucag, -aig, -an, *dim.* of guc.
———ach, -aiche, *a.* Bearing bells, bubbles or drops. 2 Clustering, sprouting. 3 Full of buds. 4 Curling, as a wave. 5 Blooming, flowery, in flower, as a leguminous vegetable. Mar thonn g., *as a curling billow.*
gucagaich,(MS) *v.a.* Plower.
gucan, *s.m.* Flowret.
———achd, *s.f.ind.* Floweriness.
gu cruinn, *adv.* About.
gùda, -n & -chan, *s.m.* Gudgeon (fish.)
gudabochd, *s.* Woodcock.
guda-leum,†† *s.f.* Bound, wild leap—*Argyll.*
gu dé ? Form of ciod e ? [The old neuter interrogative pronoun still surviving.]
gu dearbh, *adv.* Indeed. [Pronounced *gu dearra-hoo* in Ross-shire and some other parts of the North—probably a corruption of " gu dearbh fhéin."]
gu dilinn, *adv.* For ever. [Used in negative only.]
†gufarghoill, *s.f.* False testimony.
gug, see gog.
guga, -n & -chan, *s.m.* Solan goose, see sulaire. 2 Young of the solan goose—*Lewis.* 3 Fat, clumsy fellow. 4(DMy) Gannet, young of the solan goose.
gugachan, *pl.* of guga.
gugail, see gogail. [†† gives " cackling of solan geese."]
gugaill,(CR) *s.f.* Crouching or sitting down on the heels—*W. of Ross-shire. Scots,* corrie-hunkers.
gugaille, -an, *s.m.* Silly, slovenly person.
gugairneach,†† -aich, *s.m.* Fledgling bird.
gùgan, *s.m.* Daisy—*Arran.*
gugan, -ain, -an, *s.m.* Bud. 2 Flower.
———ach, *a.* Budding, flowering. 2 Abounding in buds, flowers or daisies.
gugarnaich, *prov.* for gugail.
gugurlach, -aich, *s.m.* Lumpish corpulent man, &c. 2(AF)Useless bird.
gugurla-fuich,‡‡ *s.m.* Certain vile trick.
gu h-àraidh, *adv.* Above all.
gu h-àrd, *adv.* Above, aloud.
gu h-iosal, *adv.* Below.
gu h-osgarra, *adv.* Aloud.
guibean, -in, -an, *s.m., dim.* of gob.

guidh, *pr.pt.* a' guidhe, *v.a. & n.* Pray, entreat, beseech, wish earnestly. 2 Imprecate. G. mallachd air, *imprecate a curse on him.*
guidhe, -achan, *s.m.* [*f.* in *Badenoch, Gairloch, Lochbroom, &c.* Common in the latter in *pl.* meaning Swearing.] Wish, act of wishing. 2 Beseeching, praying, prayer. 3 Curse, imprecation. 4**Intercession. A' g—, *pr. pt.* of guidh. Droch gh., *an imprecation ;* a' g. slàn leis, *wishing him well at parting.*
guidheach, *a.* Prone to beseech. 2 Imploring. Sealladh g., *an imploring look.*
————-air, *s.m.* Supplicant,petitioner, swearer.
————-an, -ain, *s.m.* Earnest prayer,petition, imprecation.
————-an, *s.pl.* Imprecations, oaths, curses.
guidheadh, -idh, *s.m.* Beseeching. 2 Imprecating. 3 Obsecration.
guidheam, *1st. sing. imp.* of guidh, Let me beseech.
guidhear,** *s.m.* Asker.
guidhidiun,* *s.f.* see guidhe. Tha mi a' cur mar gh. ort, *I entreat you most earnestly.*
guidhim, (for guidhidh mi) I shall beseech.
guidseal, *s.* Gaelic spelling of *cudgel.*
guil, *pr. pt.* a' gul, *v.n.* Weep, cry, lament. 2 Wail, mourn. Ait' anns an guileadh e, *a place where he might weep.*
guilbearnach, -aich, see guilbneach.
guilbinn, see guilbneach.
guilbinneach, (AF) *s. m.* Whimbrel, see eun Bealltainn.
guilbneach, -ich, *s.m.* Curlew—*numenius arquata.* Coire 's am bidh guilbnich, *a corrie or gorge where curlews are found.*

399. Guilbneach.

guileach, see gulach.
guileag, -ig, -an, *s.f.* Swan's note. 2 Singing, warbling, chirping. 3 Shout of joy, exultation. 4(AF) see guilleag. [Shaw has guillag, *chattering of birds.*] 5*Drawling screech, supposed to resemble the swan's note. 6(DC) Wailing.
————ag, -aig, -an, *s.f., dim.* of guileag, 1 & 2. 2 *v.* see *Moladh Mòrag.*
guil-ghearan,‡‡ -ain, *s.m.* Bitter lamentation.
†guilimne, *s.f.* Calumny, reproach.
guilimneach, *a.* Calumnious, reproachful. Gu g., *calumniously.*
guilimnich, *v.n.* Calumniate, reproach.
guilleag,(AF) *s.f.* Leech.
———— -chapuill,(AF) *s.f.* Horse-leech.
———— -nan-each, *s.f.* Horse-leech.
guilneach, -ich, see guilbneach.
guim,(CR) *s.m.* Artifice, trick, plot—*Skye.* 2 (AC) Conspiracy, revolt, rebellion. Tha iad a' deanamh g. an aghaidh a' mhaoir, *they are hatching a conspiracy against the ground-officer.*
†guimean, -ein, *s.m.* Holy relic.

guin, -ean, *s.m.* Pain, momentary pain, sting, sharp pain, pang. 2 Arrow, dart. 3 Sharp point. 4 Wound. 5 Fierceness. 6**Trouble. 7**Barb. 8 (DC) *s.f.* Shoemaker's awl. G. gheur, *a sharp awl;* g. na ré, *the falling sickness;* g. saighde, *barb of an arrow.*
guin, *a.* Stinging.
guin, *pr.pt.* a' guineadh, *v. a.* see gon. Sùil mheallach a ghuin mi, *an enticing eye that wounded me.*
†**guin**, -e, *s.f.* Woman.
guin-chridheach, *a.* Ardent, keen. G., guaisbheartach, *keen and daring.*
guin-cheap, -chip, -cheapaichean, *s.m.* Pillory.
guineach, -eiche, *a.* Sharp-pointed. 2 Keen, eager. 3 Bitterly malicious. 4 Wounding. 5 Lancinating, causing sudden pain. 6** Like a dart. 7* Venomous. 8*Fierce, acute.
———, -eich, *s.f.* Arrow, dart. 2**Weapon.
———as, -ais, *s.m.* Sharpness.
guineadachd, *s.f.ind.* Fierceness.
guineas,‡‡ -ais, *s.m.* Violence of a malady, acuteness.
guiniche, *comp.* of guineach.
guinideach, -eiche, *a.* Ready to gore or thrust, as a bull.
guinideachd,‡‡ *s.f.ind.* see guineadachd.
guinneir,** *s.f.* Epilepsy.
†**guinnire**, see guinneir.
guin-scead,** *s.m.* Scar.
———an, -ain, *s.m.* Little scar.
guinte, see gointe.
gùinteach, -eiche, *a.* Having gowns. 2 Dressed in gowns.
gùintean, *n.pl.* of gùn.
guir, *a.* Broody, (as a bird.)
guir, *gen. sing.* of gur.
guir, *pr.pt.* a' gur, *v.n.* Lie or sit upon eggs, as a bird, hatch, brood. 2 Fester. 3* Watch strictly. 4 Clock, call or cluck, as a hen.
guir-bhris, *v.a.* Exulcerate, break out into pimples.
———eadh, -idh, *s.m.* Exulceration, breaking out in pimples.
guirean, -ein, -an, *s.m.* Pimple, spot, blain, pustule. 2 Scab. 3 *in derision,* Sickly looking person. 4 (AF) Eggs of the moth. 5* Bladder. Atadh no g., *a swelling or scab.*
guireineach, -eiche, *a.* Full of spots, blains, pimples or pustules. 2 Scabbed, pustulous.
guirm, see gorm.
guirme, *comp.* of gorm. More or most blue or green.
guirme, *s.f.ind.* Blueness. 2 Greenness. †3 Inn. G. cneidh, *the blueness of a wound.*
———achd, *s.f.* see guirmead.
———ad, -id, *s.m.ind.* Degree of blueness or greenness. A' dol an g., *getting greener or bluer.*
guirmean, -ein, *s.m.* Indigo, dark-blue dye. 2 Washing-blue. 3 Dyer's woad—*isatis tinctoria.*
———ach, -aiche, *a.* Abounding in indigo or woad.
———aich,* *v.a.* Tinge with blue, as linen.
guirminn, see guirmean.
———ich, see guirmeanaich.
guirnead, -eid, *s.m.* Gurnard.
gùirneal,(AH) *s.m.* Guest who outstays his welcome, and sits stolidly in a position where he is in everyone's way.
guirnean,(AF) *s.m.* Brent goose.
———ach,(AC) *a.* Globular.
guis, *s.f.* Leak.
——, *v.n.* Gaelic spelling of *gush.*
guisdean,(AF) *s.m.* Gaelic spelling of *gudgeon.*
guiseach, *a.* Leaky, full of chinks, not air-tight or water-tight.
guisead, -eid, -an, see guiseid.
guiseag, see cuiseag.
——— -rainich, *s.f.* Bracken—*Arran.*
guisean, *s.m.* Bracken—*Arran.*
guisear, -eir, *s.m.* Stocking.
guiseid, *s.f.* Gusset, as of a shirt. 2 Clock of a stocking.
———each,†† *a.* Having gussets.
guit, -e, -eachan, *s.f.* Corn-fan, winnowing-fan, made of sheep-skin stretched on a hoop, somewhat resembling the head of a drum. 2(AH) Ash-shovel without a handle, made of sheepskin stretched over a wooden hoop. 3 (CR) Small corn-basket—*W. Ross-shire.*
guit-dhruma, *s.* Tambourine.
guiteach, -eiche, *a.* Abounding in, or relating to, corn-fans.
guiteachan, *n.pl.* of guit.
guiteadh, -idh, *s.m.* Winnowing, act of winnowing.
guiteag, -eig, -an, *s.f.* Little corn-fan.
guiteanach, *a.* Bashful, timid.
guitear, -ir, -an, *s.m.* Gutter, conduit, sewer, kennel. 2 Sink, drain.
———ach, -aiche, *a.* Abounding in gutters or sewers.
guiteas, -eis, *s.m.* Denial, refusal.
guiteirich, *v.a.* Drain, as a field. 2 Make sewers or drains.
———e, *s.m.* Drainer, ditch-maker.
———te, *past.pt.* Drained, having sewers.
guitich,††*pr.pt.* a' guiteachadh, *v.a.* Winnow, fan.
†**guitineach**, -eiche, *a.* Bashful.
guitseal,** *s.* see guidseal.
gul, -uil, *s.m.* Weeping, crying, act of weeping. A' g—, *pr.pt.* of guil. Àm gu g., *a time to weep.*
gu labhradh,** *adv.* Aloud.
gulach, -aiche, *a.* Lamenting, tearful.
gulanach, -aiche, *a.* Weeping, crying. 2 Noisy.
†**gulba**, *s.m.* Mouth.
gulbanach, *s.m. prov.* for guilbneach.
gul-chaoin, *s.m.* Lamentation.
gul-dheur, -dheòir, *s.m.* Tear.
gu léir, *adv.* Altogether, completely. Chuir seo iongnadh gu leòir air a' chuideachd gu léir, *this made the entire company greatly astonished.*
gu leòir, *adv.* Enough.
†**gulfa**, *a.* Narrow.
gulfhart, see ulfhart.
———aich, see ulfhartaich.
gul-ghàir, *s.f.* Loud lamentation.
———each, *a.* Weeping aloud.
gul-ghearan, -ain, *s.m.* Bitter lamentation.
gulm, -uilm, *s.m.* see glum.
gulmach, -aiche, *a.* see glumach.
gulmag,(AF) *s.f.* Sea-lark.
gu'm, *conj.* That, in-order-that. [Used instead of gu'n, before *b, f, m* or *p.*] Gu'm faigh e e, *that he will get it.*
gu 'm (gu+am) To their, to the. Gu 'm bailtean a ghlacadh, *to take their towns;* gu 'm fearann a sgriosadh, *to lay waste the land.*
gu minig, *adv.* Often, frequently.
gun, *prep.* Without. G. amharus, *without doubt;* g. fhios, *without knowledge, 2 unwittingly, unconsciously, 3 privately, clandestinely;* ; g. eòlas, *ignorant;* g. fhios ciod a ni mi, *not knowing what I shall do;* is truagh g. thu agam! *alas that I am without thee!* g. fhios domh, *without my knowledge;* gun fhios nach fhaic e thu, *in case he may see you.* [Aspirates consonant following, except *d, n, t,* as, gun cheann, *without head.*]
gu'n, *conj.* That, in-order-that. 2 Till, until.

Air chor 's gu'n dean se e, *that he may do it.* [When *gu'n* is followed by the past tense of verbs. *do* is sometimes erroneously elided.] Gu'n robh math agad ! *thank you !*
gu 'n, (gu+an) To their, to the.
gùn, -ùin, *pl.* -achan, gùntaichean & gùintean, *s.m.* Gown. G.-oidhche, *a night-gown.*
gun, -uin, *s.m.* Breach.
gùnach, -aiche, *a.* see gùinteach.
———an,†† *s.m.* Little gown.
gunaideach, -aiche, *a.* see guinideach. 2 Wicked, vicious. 3 Apt to thrust, as a bull.
———d, *s.f.ind.* Viciousness.
gùuan, -ain, -an, *s.m.* Little gown.
gunbhuine, *s.f.* Dart, javelin.
gun chàird, *adv.* Speedily. 2 Incessantly.
gun cheist, *adv.* Without doubt.
gunlann, see gunnlann.
gunn, -uinn, *s.m.* Prisoner, hostage.
gunna, *pl.* -cnan & -ichean, *s. m. & f.* Gun, musket. 2 Cannon. Glacag, *trigger of a gun.*
——— -barraich, see gunna-sgailc.
——— -bhiodaig, -aig, *s.m.* Gun on which to fix a bayonet. 2 Bayonet.
——— -caol, *s.m.* Fowling-piece.
gunnach, -aiche, *a.* Of, or belonging to, guns 2 Armed with a gun. G., dagach, *armed with gun and pistol.*
———an, -ain, *s. m., dim.* of gunna. Little gun.
———an-sputachain,§ *s.m.* Cow-parsnip, see odharan.
——— -mòra,†† *s.pl.* Artillery.
gunnadair, -ean, see gunnair.
gunna-diollaid, *s.m.* Holster-pistol.
——— -dùbailt, *s.m.* Double-barrelled gun.
——— -froise, *s.m.* Shot-gun as distinct from a rifle.
——— -gaoithe, *s.m.* Air-gun.
——— glaice, *s.m.* Fowling-piece, shot-gun.
gunnair, -ean, *s. m.* Gunner. 2 Musketeer, rifleman. 3 Marksman.
———eachd, *s.f.ind.* Gunnery. 2 Cannonading, firing of guns. 3 Shooting. 4 Shooting-match.
———ich, *v.a.* Cannonade.
gunna-marcaich, *s.m.* Carbine.
gunna-mòr, *s.m.* Cannon.
gunna-peilear, *s.m.* Rifle.
gunnars,(CR) *s.m.* Whins, gorse—*Farr & W. of Ross, & Suth'd.*
gunnas,(CR) *s.m.* Whins, gorse—*Black Isle.*
gunna-sgailc, *s.m.* Pop-gun, air-gun.
gunna-Spàinndeach, *s.m.* Long musket.
gunna-spùt, *s.m.* Syringe, squirt—*Arran.*
———ain, *s.m.* Syringe—*Argyll.*
gunna-steallair, *s.m.* Syringe—*Arran.*
gunn' athair, *s.m.* Air-gun.
gunn-bhuine, see gun-bhuine.
gunn'-eunaich, *s.m.* Fowling-piece.
gunnlann, -ainn, *s.m.* Prison. 2 Pound for cattle.
gunnraich,** *s.m.* Artilleryman.
———,** *v.a.* Cannonade.
gunnraidh,** *s.f.* Artillery.
†gunragach,** *a.* Straying. 2 Apt to wander or go astray.
†gunragadh,** -aidh, *s.m.* Straying, wandering.
gun-spùtachan, see gunna-spùt.
gun stad,(CR) *adv.* Immediately—*Arran.*
†gunta, *s.m.* Man of experience. 2 Skilful man. 3 Prying man.
†gunta, *a.*. Wounded. 2 Pained. 3 Prepared. 4 Skilful.
———ch,** -aich, *s.f.* Costiveness.
gun taing, In defiance of. Gun taing dhuit, *in spite of you.*
†gur, *a.* Sharp. 2 Gallant.
gur, -uir, *s.m.* Brood of birds, hatch, incubation. 2 Festering, matter of a fester. 3 †Blotch, wheal. †4 Man. 5 Cover. 6 Pimple. A' g—, *pr.pt.* of guir. Mar chearc a ni g., *as a hen that hatcheth ;* de 'n ghur rìoghail, *of the royal race.*
gur, *v.n.* see guir.
'gur, (aig+bhur) At your. 'Gur bualadh, *striking you* (*lit.* at your striking.)
gur, *conj.* That. Thubhairt e gur math e, *he said that it was good.*
gur, Or not. [Used with *is* only.]
gur, Ach gur, *until.*
gu'r, (gu+ar) To our. Gu'r dùthaich a mhilleadh, *to destroy our country.*
gu'r, (gu+bhur) To your. Gu'r sgriosadh, *to destroy you.*
guraban, -ain, see gurraban.
gurach,(MS) *a.* Broody.
guradan,* see gurraban.
†guradh, -aidh, *s.m.* Hatching. A' g—, *pr. pt.* of guir.
guragag,¶ *s.f.* Ring-dove, wood pigeon, see calman fiadhaich.
guraiceach, -ich, see gurraiceach.
†gur-chliathach, -aich, *s.m.* Palisade.
gùrd, *s.m.* Gourd.
gur-le-gùg,** *s.m.* Hatch-with-song. This name has been given to the kind of cooing uttered during hatching-time by the small sea-fowls called Mother Cary's chickens, see luchaidh-fairge. 2(AF) Stormy petrel.
†gurna, -aidh, *s.m.* Den, cave, place of concealment.
gurpan,‡ -ain, *s.m.* Crupper.
gurraban, -ain, *s.m.* Crouching, posture of crouching, "hunkering." 2(AH) Tall, slen-column of rock often found on foreshores and elsewhere, monolith. G. beag caillich, *a crouching little woman.*
gurracag, -aig, -an, *s.f.* Shock of corn peculiarly constructed. In *Skye*, when weather is uncertain, the sheaves of corn are temporarily built up into a circular stack-like heap, overlapping each other like slates on a house, to cast off the rain, about three score sheaves being placed in each heap—DC. 2††Gurgle. 3 ††Froth bells. 4 Blot—*Argyll.*
———ach, -aiche, *a.* Abounding in shocks of of corn.
gurrach, -aich, see gurraiceach. 2†† One in a crouching posture. 3 "Hunkering."
gurradan, see gurraban.
gurraiceach,(MS) *a.* Hairbrained, queer.
———, -ich, *s.m.* Blockhead. 2 Big, awkward fellow. 3(AF) Unfledged bird. 4 Dotterel.
gurraiceideach, *s.m.* Dotterel.
gurraiceil, -e, *a.* Foolish, stupid.
gurraidh, see gurraban. *Scots*, coorie.
gurran, -ain, *s.m.* Grunting. 2 Lowing. 3 Bellowing.
gurt, -a, & guirt, *s.m.* Fierceness, sternness of look. 2 Pain, trouble, twinge of pain.
———,** *a.* Fierce. 2 Terrible.
———ach, -aiche, *a.* Fierce, cross, angry, in bad temper.
gu ruig, *prep.* Until, as far as.
gus, *adv.* Until, so. G. an till iad, *until they return ;* g. am faic mi thu, *till I see you;* g. am bi mi, *till I be ;* g. an àm seo an ath bhliadhna, *till this time next year ;* seachduin g. an dé, *yesterday se'ennight ;* ach gus, *until.*
gus, *prep.* To, unto, as far as. 2 So that, in-order-that. G. nach cluinnt' e, *so that he could not be heard ;* g. a seo, *as far as this ;* g. nach tigeadh e staigh, *so that he could not*

come in ; g. am b' fhearr dhomh, *so that it was better for me.* Gus=*or not,* not used with *is,* as, ge b' e théid gus nach téid, *whoever goes or does not go.* [Governs *nom.* case in a definite noun, but *dat.* in an indefinite noun.] G. a' chlach, *to the stone.*
†gus, -uis, *s.m.* Weight. 2 Force. 3 Death. 4 Anger. 5 Deed. 6 Inclination, desire. 7 Sharpness, smartness.
†gus, *a.* Sharp, keen, smart. 2 Strong.
gusar,** *a.* see gusmhor. 2 Sharp, smart. [‡ gives gusair.]
gusdal,** -ail, *s.m.* Burden.
gu seo, *adv.* Hitherto.
gusg, see gusgan.
gusgal, see gusgul.
gusgan, -ain, -an, *s.m.* Bumper, hearty draught, swig. Fhuair thu fhéin an ceud gh. dheth, *you got the first bumper of it yourself.*
gusgar,** -air, *s.m.* Roaring. 2 Loud wailing. Cuiridh g. neach 'na bhreislich, *loud lamentation confounds one.*
gusgarlach, see gusgurlach.
gusgul, -uil, *s.m.* Refuse, husks, filth. 2 Idle words. 3*Blubbering. 4**Roaring, bawling. 5 Clatter—*Sàr Obair.*
gusgulach, -aiche, *a.* Filthy. 2 Trifling. 3 Roaring. 4 Lamenting loudly. 5 Abounding in husks.
————d, *s.f.* Continued roaring. 2 Loud lamentation.
gusgurlach, -aich, *s.m.* Keen sharp fellow.
gu siorruidh, *adv.* For ever.
gu siorruidh ! *int.* Well ! well !
gusmhor, -oire, *a.* Valid, strong, powerful, capable. 2**Keen.
gustag,** *s.f.* Clumsy girl.
gustal, -ail, *s.m.* Burden, pledge. 2 Protection. 3 Ability, affluence.
gu suthain, *adv.* For evermore, eternally.
gut,** *s.m.* Gaelic spelling of *gout.*
gutach, *a.* see cutach. 2 Arthritic.
gutalaiche *s.m.* Cuckold maker.
gutalach, -aiche, *a.* Cuckold.
————, -aich, *s.m.* Adulterer.
————d,** *s.f.* Cuckoldom.
gutalag,** -aig, *s.f.* Adulteress.
gu taobh, *adv.* Apart. 2 Aside. Rach gu taobh, *stand aside.*
guth, -a, *pl.* -an, -anna & -annan, *s.m.* Voice. 2 Word, syllable. 3 Taunt, defamation. 4 Calumny. 5 Mention, report, warning. 6 Vote. 7 Vowel. 8 Sound. 9 Ill-name. 10 Bard. †11 Erudition. Chuala e g., *he heard a voice ;* dean g. rium, *speak a word to me ;* cha chuala mi g. air riamh, *I never heard the slightest mention of it ;* dh' aithnich mi a gh., *I recognized his voice* ; na toir g. air a leithid sin, *never mention such a thing;* g. caointeach, *a plaintive voice ;* thàinig g. d' a ionnsuidh, *a voice from the dead warned him ;* guthan a' bhàis, *the sounds of death;* am meadhon a gh., *in the middle of his speech ;* gun guth mór, gun droch fhacal, *without uproar, without strong language ;* dean g. aige 'san dol seachad, *call in on him when going by;* is fheàrr g. na meidh, *a word is better than a balance*—probably meaning that the voice of a powerful friend is of more value than strict impartiality.
guthach, -aiche, *a.* Endowed with a voice. 2 Noisy, vocal. 3**Having a voice or vote. 4†T Wordy.
————,** *s.f.* see cubhag.
————adh, -aidh, *s.m.* Calling. A' g— *pr.pt.* of guthaich.
guthaich, *pr.pt.* a' guthachadh, *v.a. & n.* Call upon, call from a distance. 2 (MS) Vocalize.
guthaid, see guth-àite.
guth-àite, -achan, *s. m.* Oraculum. 2 Confessionary. 3 Oratory—*Dàin I. Ghobha.*
guthalachd, *s.f.* Vocality.
guthan, *n.pl.* of guth.
guth-ghleus,** *s.* Accent.
guth-leagadh,‡‡ -aidh, *s.m.* Cadence.
guth-le-gùg, *Luing* for conachag.
guthmhor, -oire, *a.* Loud-voiced.
————achd, *s.f.ind.* Loudness of utterance.
gu timchiollach, *adv.* About.
gu tur, *adv.* Quite, entirely, altogether.

H h

h, Uath, *the hawthorn-tree.* The eighth letter of the Gaelic alphabet now in use. It is used in Scottish Gaelic not properly as a letter, for no word commences with it, but simply as a sign of aspiration, in the same way as the dot is used over consonants in Irish Gaelic. When it is prefixed to a word beginning with a vowel, it has the same degree of aspiration as *h* in *hall, hurt*—na h-òighean, *the maids ;* na h-oidhche, *of the night.* It is also required between the negative *ni* and the following word, if it begin with a vowel—ni h-e, *not he ;* ni h-eadh, *no ;* ni h-iad, *not they* ; ni h-fheudar, *must not.*

Before an initial vowel, *h* is sometimes inserted, and sometimes not, after certainwords. In Skye, the tendency is to insert that letter as shown by Mary MacPherson in her book of poems—after prepositions, le h-aiteas, pp. 35, 110 ; re h-ùine, p. 44 ; after *gur, mur & ge,* gur a h-e, and gur h-e, *that it is,* both p. 289 ; gur h-ise bhios sona, *that it is she that will be happy,* 91 ; 's gur h-onair dha ar dùthaich thu, 38 ; gur h-uallach mo nighean dubh, 307; mur a h-e, 276 ; ge h-iomadh, *though so many, notwithstanding how many,* 37, 49.

I i

i, Iogh, *yew,* the ninth letter of the Gaelic alphabet now in use. *I* has two sounds—(1) both long and short, long like *ee* in *deem,* as, sìn, *stretch ;* cìr, *comb ;* short like *ee* in *feet,* (only as *feet* is pronounced by a Scotsman) as, bith, *existence ;* sir, *seek.* (2) short and obscure, like *i* in *miss,* as, is, *am, art, are,* in which particular case it does not give the *sh* sound to *s.*

Gun ì, gun ó, gun aobhar, *said when anything is apparently done without rhyme or reason.*
i, *pers. pron., f. ind.* She, her, it. Bhuail si i, *she struck her.* [*emphatic,* ise & i-féin, *herself.*]
ì, *s.f.ind.* Island.
ì,‡ *s.f.ind.* see igh.
†i, *s.f.* Art, science.
†i, *a.* Low, shallow.
†ia, *s.* Country.
iach, éich, -an, *s.m.* Scream, yell. 2 Exclamation. †3 Salmon. 4(AF) Cat. [** gives *s.f.* for No. 1.]
iach,** *v.a.* Cry, scream, shout, yell, bawl.
iachadh, -aidh, *s.m.* Crying, screaming, yelling. 2 Cry, scream, yell. Ag i—, *pr.pt.* of iach.
iachal, -ail, *s.m.* Cry, scream, yell, noise.
iachdar, see iochdar.

iachdarach, see iochdarach.
iad, éid, see eud.
iad, *per. pron.* They, them. [*emphatic*, iad-san, & iad-féin, *themselves*.] Iad sud, *those yonder;* iad seo, *these here ;* iad sin, *those there.*
iadach, -aich, *s.m.* Jealousy. [Generally used in the North with this meaning, but in Glenlyon and the south generally *eudach* is used.]
——, -aiche, *a.* Jealous.
——adh, -aidh, *s.m.* Jealous watching. 2 Jealousy.
iadaich,** *v.a.* Watch jealously.
iadal,** -ail, *s.m.* Disease.
iadh,†† iaidh, *s.m.* Enclosing. 2 Hovering.
iadh,§ *pr.pt.* ag iadhadh, *v.a.* Encompass, circle, shut round, enclose. 2 Bind. 3 Overtake. 4 Hover. 5**Wind, roll. 6 Join. 7 Take a circuitous route. An saoghal mu'n i. a' ghrian, *the world which the sun compasses ;* dh'iadh na tuiltean mi, *the floods surrounded me.*
iadhach,** *a.* Ambient. 2 Circumstant. 3** Meandering, as a stream.
iadhadh, -aidh, *s.m.* Surrounding, act of surrounding, enclosing. 2 Binding. 3 Overtaking. 4 Meandering, as a stream. 5**Winding, rolling. 6 Fluttering or hovering round. 7** Stretching, as of a bow. 8**Circuit. 9** Circumference. 10**Circuitous route. 11** Adjunction. Ag i—, *pr.pt.* of iadh. Ag i. mu 'n tràigh, *winding along the shore ;* a gorm-shùil ag i., *her blue eye rolling ;* bàs ag i. mu 'shleagh, *death hovering about his spear ;* i. do luing, *the circuit of thy ship.*
iadhaidh, *fut.aff.a.* of iadh.
iadhaim, (*for* iadhaidh mi), *I shall surround.* I. ur braighde, *I will surround your captives.*
iadhain, see eidheann.
iadhan, -ain, *s.m.* Parenthesis.
iadhar, *fut. pass.* of iadh. Shall be surrounded.
iadhastar, see aghastar.
iadhladh, see iadhadh.
iadh-lann, -lainn, -an, see iodhlann.
iadh-lus,§ *s. m.* Small bindweed—*convolvolus arvensis.*
iadh-shlat,§ -ait, -an, *s.f.* Honeysuckle, woodbine, see uilleann. 2 Ivy. Mar i. ri stoc aosda, *like ivy to an aged trunk.*
———— -thalmhainn, *s.f.* Ground-ivy,—*nepeta glechoma.*

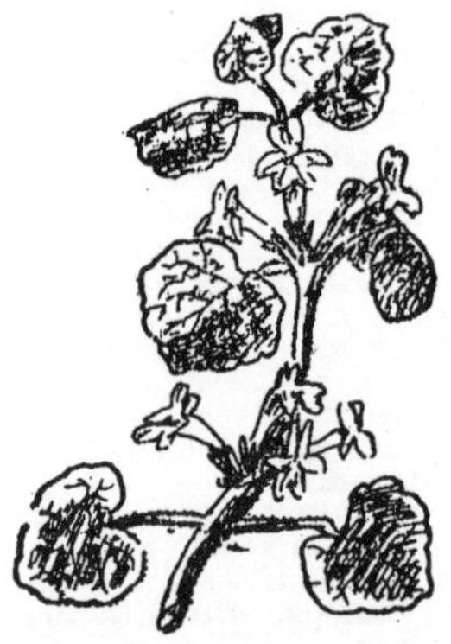

400. *Iadh-shlat-thalmhainn.*

iadhta, *past pt.* of iadh. Encompassed, surrounded, closed, hemmed in, &c.
iad-san, *emphat. pron.* They themselves.
iag,(AF) *s.* Salmon.
†iagh, *s.m.* Island.
iaghastar, see aghastar.
†ial, see iol.
ial, -a, *s. f.* Moment, time, season. 2 (MS)Intermission. 3 Gleam of sunshine. 4**Light. 5**Age, generation. 6** Sunny interval between showers. [‡ says a poetic word—seemingly a metaphoric use of iall.] Gach i., *every moment ;* foghar an aigh—ial is fras, *finest autumn—sun and shower.*
ialach, -aiche, *a.* Shining, bright, clear, luminous. 2**Sunny, having serene intervals, gleamy, as the sun in the interval of showers.
ialadh, see èaladh.
——,(DC) *s.m.* Fair spell between showers—*Argyll*, see ial 6.
ialaidh, see ealaidh.
†iall ! *int.* God forgive you !
†iall,‡‡ -a, -an, *s. m.* Flock of birds. 2 Herd, drove.
iall, éille & -éill, -an, *s.f.* Leather thong, lace, leash. 2 String. 3 Ribbon. 4 Part of crann-nan-gad, see p. 263. 5* Leather strop. I. bròige, *a shoe-lace* or *latch ;* an i. ris an d' earb thu, *the string to which you trusted ;* le h-éill ghuirm, *with a blue lace ;* i. de ghorm, *a ribbon of blue ;* iallan fada de leathar chaich, *long thongs of other people's leather*—expression applied to a person generous with another's goods ; i.-shuisde, *a flail-thong.*
iallach, -aiche, *a.* Abounding in thongs, thongy. 2 Jaunty, lithe.
——,** -aich, *s.m.* Thong. 2 Assortment of thongs. An t-i. cruaidh, *the hard thong.*
iallachrann, *s.pl.* Shoes.
iallag, -aig, -an, *s.f.dim.* of iall. Little thong. 2 Shoe-lace, latchet. 3 Thread. 4**Shoemaker's thread.
——ach, -aiche, *a.* Abounding in little thongs.
iallaich, *v.a.* Bind with thongs.
iallan, -ain, *s.m.* Thong. 2 Shoemaker's thread. 3 *n.pl.* of iall.
——, *s.f.* Honeysuckle.—*Sgeulaiche-nan-caol.*
iall-chasaidh, *s.f.* Martingale.
iall-cuipe,(CR) *s.f.* Lash.
iall-sréine,(CR) *s.f.* Bridle-rein.
iall-sròine, (CR) *s. f.* Musrole, band over a horse's nose.
ialltaich, *s.f.* Howling of dogs—*Suth'd.*
iall-theannaidh, *s.f.* Brace, p. 76.
ialt, see ialtag.

401. *Ialtag.*

ialtag, -aig, -an, *s.f.* Bat, rearmouse—*vespertimus murinus.* 2(MS) Titmouse.
——ach, -aiche, *a.* Abounding in bats, batty. 2 Of, or pertaining to, bats.
ialtag-anmoch, } *s.f.* Bat.
—— -leathair, }
†—— -leuthraigh, }
ialtag-oidhche,(DMu) *s.f.* *Suth'd* for ialtag.
ialuinn, -e, *s.f.* see iadh-shlat.

iamhann,(MS) *s.m.* Pearl.
iamhunn,(MS) *s.m.* Margarite.
ian, eòin, *s.m.* see eun. †2 Vessel. 3 Blade of a weapon. 4 Weasel.
ianach, see eunach.
ianaich, see eunaich.
ian-buchainn, see eun-buchainn.
ian-dubh-an-sgadain, see coltraich.
ian-glas-an-sgadain, see bur-bhuachaill.
ian-ghobhrag,(AH) *s.f.* Snipe, see gobhar-athair.
ianlaith, see eunlaith.
iannraidh, see eanraidh.
ianrag, *s.f.* Snipe, see gobhar-athair.
iapal, -ail, *s.m.* Dispute.
iar, *s.f.ind.* The West. †2 The end. 3 Everything last. †4 Bird. An i., *westward;* an i. 'san iar-dheas, *west-by-south;* an àirde an iar, *the west;* osag o 'n i., *a blast from the west.*
iar, see iarag.
iar, *adv.* West, westerly.
†iar, *prep.* After, second in order. Iár sin, *after that.* 2‡‡Backwards.
†iar, *a.* Dark, black, dusky.
iara,(AF) *s.m.* Cat.
iarach, *s.m.* see iùbhrach.
iarag,** -aig, -an, *s. f.* Weasel. 2 Any little creature of brownish hue. 3 Anguish, grief. 4**see eireag.
iaran, see iarunn.
iaran-gràbhalaidh,*s.m.* see iarunn-gràbhalaidh.
iar-aois, *s.f.* After age, succeeding age, after times.
iar-astar,‡‡ -air, *s.m.* Longitude.
iarbhail, -e, *s.f.* Anger, fury, ferocity. 2 Remains of a disease. 3 Issue of an affair, consequence.
iarbheil, see iar-bheò.
iar-bheò,** *a.* Surviving, still alive.
iar-bhleoghann, -ainn, *s. m.* Second or aftermilking.
iar-bhreith, -e, *s.f.* After-birth.
iar-bhuille, -an, *s.m.* Second stroke. 2 Stroke from behind.
†iar-chara,‡‡ *s.collect.* Posterity.
iar-cheann, -chinn, *s.m.* Hindhead, noddle.
iar-cheann-suidhe, *s.m.* Vice-president.
iar-chléireach, -ich, *s. m.* Under-secretary, under-clerk.
iar-chléirsinneachd, *s.f.* Under-secretaryship, under-clerkship.
iar-chuan, -ain, *pl.* -chuantan, *s.m.* The Western sea.
iar-chuimhne, *s.f.ind.* Indistinct recollection.
iar-chullach,(AF) *s.m.* Wild boar. 2 Monster.
iar-dheas, -dheis, *s.m.* The South-west. [Preceded by the art. *an.*] Chum an i., *to the south-west.*
iar-dhonn, *a.* Brownish black, dusky, blackish, dark brown.
iar-dhraoi,** *s.m.* Remnant. 2 Posterity.
iar-fheur,** -fheòir, *s.m.* After-grass.
iar-fhlaitheach, *a.* Aristocratic, oligarchal.
———d,** *s. f.* Vice-royalty. 2 Earldom. 3 Aristocracy.
iar-fhlaithiche, *s.m.* Aristocrat.
iar-fhlath, -aith, *s.m.* Viceroy. 2 Feudal lord dependent on a greater. 3 Earl.
iargail, -ean, see iargall.
iargaill, see iargall.
iargain, *v.a.* Deplore, miss, bewail the loss of a friend. 2 Feel pain.
———, -ean, *s.f.* Sorrow, grief, smart of sorrow. 2 Pain. 3 Bewailing, lamenting. 4 Danger, peril. 5 Dying groan. 6 Burden, load. 7 Dregs, sediment. 8* Evil effects of anything. Innis t' i., *tell thy trouble;* ionnsachadh làn iargain, *learning full of useless knowledge.*
———each, -eiche, *a.* Uneasy, in great pain, afflictive. 2 Moaning, lamenting. 3 Having dregs or sediment. 4**Distressful. 5** Languishing, troubled. Leabaidh a thinneis iargainich, *the bed of his languishing sickness.*
———eachd,** *s.f.* Painfulness. 2 Distress. 3 State of being troubled or distressed.
iargal, -ail & -aile, *s.f.* The west. 2 Evening. 3 Twilight.
iargall, -aill, -an, *s.f.* Skirmish, battle, strife, contest, fray. 2 Tumult, uproar, bustle. 3 Storm. 4**Concourse. 5 Distress, calamity.
iargallach, -aiche, *a.* Warlike, contentious. 2 Quarrelsome, noisy, fierce.
iargalta, -ailte, *a.* Churlish, inhospitable. 2 Angry. 3 Surly, not affable. 4 Turbulent. 5 Obstinate. 6 Distressing. 7 Backward. 8 (DU) Forbidding, as a haunted place, eerie.
iargaltach, see iargalta.
iargaltachd, see iargaltas.
iargaltaiche, -an, *s.m.* Churl.
iargaltas, -ais, *s.m.* Churlishness, moroseness, surliness. 2 Turbulence. 3 Backwardness. 4(MS) Rudeness. 5**Obstinateness.
iargan, see iargain.
———ach, see iargaineach.
———achd, see iargaineachd.
iarganaich,(MS) *v.n.* Groan.
iar-ghaoth, -ghaoithe, *s.f.* West wind.
iar-ghille, -an, *s.m.* Under servant. 2 Minor.
iarghuil, -ean, *s.f.* Sound, noise, report.
iarguil, see iargall.
———leach, see iargallach.
iarguin, -ean, see iargain.
———each, see iargaineach.
———eachd, see iargaineachd.
iargunach, see iargaineach.
iarla, -an, *s.m.* Earl. (iar-fhlath.)
———chd, *s.f.ind.* Earldom.*
iarlas, see èarlas & àirleas.
iarmad, -aid, -an, *s.m.* Offspring, race, posterity, branch. 2 Remnant, remainder. I. mo shluaigh, *the remnant of my people;* a chogadh ris an iarmad mheanbh, *to fight with the pigmy race.*
———ach, *a.* Having remnants. 2 In remnants. 3 Like a remnant. 4 Having posterity.
iarmaid, *gen.sing.* of iarmad.
iarmailt, -ean, *s.f.* Sky, firmament. 'San i. ùrair, *in the pure firmament;* na h-iarmailtean, *the skies.*
———each, -eiche, *a* Of, or belonging to, the firmament, aërial.
iarmair,** *s.f.* Remnant, remainder.
†iarmantach, -aiche, *a.* Favourable,prosperous. 2 Furious.
iarmart, -airt, *s.m.* Result, consequence of an affair. 2 Riches. 3 Offspring. see iarmad.
iarmheirghe, *s.f.* Matins. 2 Morning. 3 Rising early.
iarna, -ichean, *s.f.* Hank of yarn (300 yards.) 2 Skein of thread. 3 Confusion. An àireamh =5 threads, in counting off the *crois-iarna.*
iarnach, -aiche, *a.* Abounding in hanks of yarn. 2 see iarunnach.
iarnachadh, -aidh, *s. m.* Smoothing, ironing. 2 Act of smoothing with an iron. Ag i—, *pr. pt.* of iarnaich.
iarnachan, -ain, *pl.* -chanan & -ain, *s.m.* Little dressing iron. 2 Any iron tool.
iarnadh, -aidh, see iarna.
iarnag, -aig, -an, *s.f., dim.* of iarna.
———ach, *a.* Abounding in little hanks.
iarnaich, *pr. pt.* ag iarnachadh, *v. a.* Smooth with an iron. 2 Make hanks.

iarnaichean, *n.pl.* of iarna.
iarnaichte, *past pt.* of iarnaich. Ironed, smoothed with an iron, as linen. Anart i., *ironed linen.*
iarnaidh, -e, *a.* Of, or like iron. 2 Iron-coloured. 3 Hard, like iron. 4 Miserly. 5 Chalybeate, having an iron taste. Uisge i., *chalybeate water.*
———eachd, *s.f.* Hardness. 2 Squalid colour. 3 Miserly disposition.
iarnaig, see iarnaich.
———eadh, see iarnachadh.
iarnair,** *s.m.* Ironmonger.
iarnaireachd, *s.f.* Ironmongery.
iarnallach, -aich, *s.f.* After-birth, secundine.
iarnan, -ain, see iarna.
iarn-aois, see iarunn-aois.
iarndobh, (AF) *s.* Fawn.
iar-ogha, -aichean, *s. m. & f.* Great-grandchild. Fionn-ogha *or* ionn-ogha, *a grandson's grandson;* b' i féin is mo mhàthair na h-iar-oghachan, *she and my mother were second cousins.*
iarr, *pr.pt.* ag iarraidh, *v,a.* Ask, request. 2 Seek, search, look for. 3 Pain or purge, as medicine, 4 Probe. 5**Invite. 6**Demand. I. e gu fleadh, *invite him to a feast;* cha'n fhaic 's cha'n iarr iad, *they shall not see nor enquire. Iarr*, in the sense of *bidding* or *desiring*, takes the prep. *air*, compounded or understood, as, iarr air, *desire him;* i. orra, *desire them.*
iarradach,†† *a.* Of a candidate, seeker, &c. 2 Invitatory.
iarradaiche, *s.m.* Probe, feeler. 2 Petitioner.
iarradair, -ean, *s.m.* Seeker, one who seeks. 2 Beggar, petitioner. 3**Candidate.
iarraidh, -ean, *s.m.* Request, petition. 2 Desire, longing. 2 Act of asking, seeking, searching or enquiring. 4 Invitation. Ag i—, *pr.pt.* of iarr. Freagraidh cruachan an i., *hillocks shall respond to their inquiries;* tha 'fhuil air a h-i., *his blood is sought;* ag i. gu bealach, *moving towards the pass.*
———, *a.* Desirable, tolerable. An i. ghleusda, *pretty well;* tha mi an i., *I am pretty well.*
———, *fut.aff.a.* of iarr.
———each, -aiche, *a.* see iarradach.
———eachd,‡‡ *s.f.* Inquisitiveness.
iarraim, *1st. sing. fut. aff.* of iarr (*for* iarraidh mi) I shall ask.
iarram, *1st. sing.imp.* of iarr.
iarratas, -ais, see iarrtas.
iarr-fhionn, (MS) *a.* Rubican.
iarrnaig,‡‡ see iarnaich.
iarrtach, -aiche, *a.* Soliciting, importunate, continually requesting. 2 Desirous, willing.
iarrtachail, see iarradach.
iarrtachd, see iarrtas.
iarrtaiche, -an, *s.m* Seeker. 2 Petitioner, importunate person. 3 Probe. 4**Descenants, posterity. 5 Domestics 6‡‡Feelers of shell-fish. 7**Dun.
iarrtanach, -aiche, *a.* Optative.
iarrtas, -ais, -an, *s.m.* Petition, request, asking. 2 Desire, command, instance. I. faoin, *a vain request;* cha toil i. achmhasan, *request deserves no blame.*
iarrtasach, -aiche, *a.* Frequently soliciting, requesting.
iarrtus, -uis, -an, see iarrtas.
iarsalach, *a.* Covetous.
———, -aich, *s.m.* Covetous person.
iarsceart,** -ceirt, *s.m.* The West. 2 The North-west.
————ach, *a.* West. 2 North-west.
iarsmach,** *a.* Generous.
iarsmadh,** -aidh, *s.m.* Remnant, remainder. 2 Relic. 3 Burden, encumbrance. 4 New Year's gift.
iarspealadh, -aidh, -aidhean, *s.m.* After-grass, after-math, second crop of grass, rowen.
iartaiche, see iarrtaiche.
†iar-taighe, *s.collect.* Descendants, posterity.
iartas, see iarrtas.
iar-thir,** *s.f.* West country.
iar-thrath, -aith, *s.m.* see (an) earar.
iar-thuath, *s.f.* The North-west. [Preceded by the art. *an.*]
iar-thoiseach, -ich, *s. m.* Captain of the van-guard.
iartuinneas, -eis, see iarrtas.
iarunn, -uinn, -an, *s. m.* Iron. 2 Iron tool of any kind. 3 (CR) Blade of a scythe. I. gràbhaidh, *a graving tool;* i. as an talamh, *iron out of the earth;* gad iaruinn, *an iron bar;* i. fàil, *a scythe;* i. casaidh, *a crisping-iron.*
———ach, -aich, *s.m.* Iron, irons. I. seisearaich, *plough-irons.*
———ach, *a.* see iarnaidh.
iarunnaidh, see iarnaidh.
iarunn-amaill, *s.m.* Iron for swingle-trees, generally used in the *pl.*—iaruinn-amuill.
iarunn-anairt, *s.m.* Smoothing-iron.
——— -aois, *s.f.* The iron age.
——— -borrais, *s.m.* Soldering-iron.
——— -earra, *s.m.* Catch of the lock of a gun. 2(AH) Iron used for cutting grooves round inside of casks, &c. to receive bottoms or heads. Bhiodh rùdan air an tarruinn leis an lùbt' an t-iarunn-earra, *a finger-point would be on the trigger, by which the catch would be acted on.* —*Beinn Doran, Donn. Bàn.*
——— -ghreallaig, *s.m.* Iron for trestle-tree of a plough.
——— -gràbhalaidh, *s.m.* Burine.
——— -na stiùireach, *s.m.* Pintle of a rudder, see Rudder, No. 2, p. 78.
——— -tàthaidh, *s.m.* Soldering-iron.
——— -tochailt, (MS) *s.m.* Hoe-iron.
iasachd, *s.f.* see iasad. Gabhaidh e i., *he will borrow.*
iasachdach, *a.* Ready to give on loan. 2 Prone to ask on loan.
iasachdaiche,** *s.m.* Creditor.
iasad, -aid, *s.m.* Loan. 2 The thing borrowed. 3 Profit, advantage, 4 Credit. Millidh airc i., *necessity spoils credit;* ghabhadh e cridhe 'an iasaid, *he would take a heart on loan,* or *heart of grace*—an exaggerated way of saying that one would borrow anything; bu chòir an t-iasad a chur dhachaidh a' gàireachdaich, *the loan should be sent laughing home*—to lend freely is to send the borrower home smiling, to send the loan back laughing is to repay liberally; is tric a fhuair gunna urchair-iasaid, *a gun has often got a loan-shot* —a warning against careless use of fire-arms; na toir iasad air an iasad, *do not lend the loan.* [†† gives *s.f.*]
iasadach, -aiche, *a.* Lending, granting of a loan. †2 Squeamish.
iasadaiche, -an, *s.m.* Creditor. 2 One who lends. 3 Borrower.
iasadail, -e, *a.* see iasadach.
iasad-bhriathar,‡‡ -air, -thran, *s.m.* Quotation.
†iasalach,** *a.* Easy. 2 Feasible, practicable.
iasalachd, *s.f.* Frailty. 2 Facility.
iasan, -ain, *s.m.* Petulance. 2 Sauciness. 3 Petulant person.
———ach, *a.* Petulant. 2 Saucy.
———achd, *s.f.* Petulance. 2 Sauciness.
iasg, -éisg, -an, *s.m.* Fish. Iasg dubh, *salmon on its return from the sea;* i. air chladh, *fish at spawning;* na h-iasgan, *the sign Pisces* (♓)

in the zodiac; ma tha i. a dhith orm, cha'n i. leam sgat, *if I want fish, skate is no fish to me* —the skate is most unjustly underrated by the natives of the West coast of Scotland.
iasgach, *a.* Fishing, angling. 2 Art of fishing or angling. 3 Take of fish. 4**Fishery. Ag i—, *pr.pt.* of iasgaich. Is daor a cheannaich mi an t-iasgach, *dearly have I bought the fishing.*
————, *a.* Abounding in fish.
————adh, -aidh, *s.m.* Fishing, angling. Ag i., *pr.pt.* of iasgaich.
————d, *s.f.* & *pr.pt.* of iasgaich.
iasg-a'-chlaidheimh, *s.m.* Sword-fish.
iasgaich, *pr.pt.* ag iasgachd & ag iasgachadh, *v.a.* Fish, angle.
iasgaiche,‡‡ -an, *s.m.* Fisher.
iasgaidh, see easgaidh.
iasgail, *a.* Fishy.
iasgair, -ean, *s.m.* Fisher, fisherman. 2 Angler.
iasgair-càirneach, *s.m.* Kingfisher, see biorracruidein. 2**Osprey.
iasg-air-chladh,(AF) *s.m.* Spawning fish.
iasgair-dìomhain,¶ *s.m.* Kingfisher, see biorracruidein. 2 Common gull, see faoileann. 3** Unsuccessful fisher.
iasgarach,‡‡ -eiche, *a.* Fishing.
————d, *s.f.ind.* Trade of fishing. 2 Act of, or amusement of fishing. 3 Fishery. 4 Art of angling.
iasgairean, *n.pl.* of iasgair.
iasgair-slaite,* *s.m.* Angler. [* spells iasgair iasgaire.]
iasgan, -ain, *s.m.* Little fish. 2 see feusgan.
iasg-an-donais,(AF) *s.m.* Devil-fish.
iasg-dearg, *s.m.* Fish of the salmon kind, as distinct from white fish.
iasg-deilgneach,(AF) *s.m.* Stickleback.
iasg-driomanach,(AF) *s.m.* Surmullet, red mullet, marked salmon.
iasg-driomman, see iasg-driomanach.
iasg-druimein,(AF) *s.m.* Salmon.
iasg-dubh, *s.m.* Salmon on its return from the sea.
iasg-eigir,(AF) *s.m.* Small or dwarf fish.
iasg-geal,(AH) *s.m.* Any sea-fish not of the salmon kind.
iasg-itheach, *a.* Piscivorous.
iasg-itheanaich,‡‡ *s.m.* Ichthyophagy.
iasg loch, -an, *s.m.* Fish-pond, loch abounding in fish. *Iasg-loch*, with hyphen and consequent accent on *loch* means a fresh-water or loch-fish.
iasg-lochan, -ain, *s.m.* Fish-pond.
iasg-mara,(AF) *s.m.* Porpoise.
iasgmhor, -oire, *a.* Fishy, abounding in fish, piscatorial.
iasg-Pheadail, see iasg-Pheadair-rùnaich.
iasg-Pheadair-rùnaich,(AC)*s.m.* (Loving)Peter's fish. The fish caught in the W. Isles on Christmas Day, and given to the poor.
iasg-seigir, see iasg-eigir.
iasg-shlat, -shlait- *s.f.* Fishing-rod. I. 'sa Cheitein, *a fishing-rod in spring.*
iasg-sligeach, -ich, *s. m.* Shell-fish, see maorach.
iath, *v.a.* see iadh.
†——, *s.m.* Land.
iathadh, see iadhadh.
iathladair,(MS) *s.m.* see èaladair.
ialaideach,(MS) *a.* see èalaideach.
iathlaidh, *a.* see èalaidh.
————, *v.a.* see èalaidh.
iath-lann, see iodhlann.
iathlu,(AF) *s.m.* Cat.
iath-shlat, see iadh-shlat.
iathta, see iadhta.
†ibh, -e, *s. f.* Drink, see dibh. 2 Country people. 3 Tribe of people.
†ibh, *v.n.* Drink.
ibhig,§ *s.* Shield-fern—*polystichum aculeatum, lobatum & angulare.*
ibhne, *s.f.* Drinking.
ibhteach, *a.* Dry, droughty. 2 Soaking. 3 That imbibes water.
†ic, -e, -ean, *s.f.* Cure, remedy, balm. Ic air son a leòin, *a balm for his wound*; gabhaibh ic, *take (ye) balm.*
ic, -e, -ean, *s.f.* Affix. 2 Supply. 3 Appendix. 4(AC)Frame put under a bee-hive. Ic na cuinneig, *edge outside the bottom of a pitcher or barrel.*
ic, *v.a.* Heal, cure. 2 Affix. 3 Supply, eke.
'ic, (for mhic) e. g. Mac 'Ic Alasdair for Mac Mhic Alasdair.
iceach,** *a.* Balmy. 2 Salutiferous. 3 Remedial. 4 Medicinal.
iceadh, -idh, *s. m.* Healing, act of healing. 2 Remedy. 3 Supply, eke. Ag i—, *pr. pt.* of ic.
iceil, *a.* Healing.
ich, see ith.
ichd, see ic.
ic-iarn-nac, *adv.* At any rate.
ic-lus, -uis, -an, *s.m.* Medicinal herb. 2 Healing by herbs.
————ach, *a.* Abounding in medicinal herbs.
ic-shìol,** *s.* Affix.
†id, *a.* Honest, good, just.
†id, *s.m.* Ring. 2 Use.
idearmanachd, *s.f.* Hydromancy.
†idh,** *s.f.* Wreath. 2 Fine chain. 3 Ridge. 4 Use.
†idhal, -ail, see iodhal.
†idid, *a.* Cold, chill.
†idid ! *int.* Exclamation denoting cold.
idir, *adv.* At all. 2**Yet. Cha'n 'eil idir, *not at all*; cha tig e idir, *he will not come at all*; cha'n e idir, *that is not it at all*; no idir air a bhruicheadh, *nor even boiled*; cha'n 'eil e gu math idir, *he is not at all well*; cha deanainn idir e, *I would not do it on any account.*
idireug,** *s.* Change of the moon.
†idneadh, *s.* Weapons, arms.
idnearach,** *a.* Prosperous. 2 Happy, merry. Gu h-i., *prosperously.*
————d, *s. f.* Prosperity. 2 Happiness, mirth.
†idu,‖ *s.* Pain, pang.
†ifinn, *s.f.* Gooseberry.
ifreannta, *a.* see ifrinneach.
ifrinn, -ean, *s.f.* Hell. (I+fuar) The Hell of the old Celts was a cold dark region, abounding in venomous reptiles and wild beasts. The Gael still retain the name, although it is no longer the custom to consider that cold forms any part of infernal punishment.
————each, -eiche, *a.* Hellish,fiendlike,infernal. stygian, extremely wicked.
————each, -eich, *s.m.* Hellish fellow, wicked wretch, fiend, demon.
ifrionda, *a.* ifrinneach.
ifrionn, see ifrinn.
————ach, see ifrinneach.
igh, *s.f.* Burn, small stream with green banks —*Suth'd.*
ìgh, -e, *s.f.* Tallow. 2**Fat of any slaughtered quadruped. +3**Ring. Ghabh e an igh, *he took the tallow (fat.)* [** gives *s.m.*]
ighe, -an, *s.f.* Island.
ighe,(MS) *s.f.* Grease.
†igheach, *a.* Abounding in fat, fat, tallowy.
ighean, ighne, -an, *s.f.* see inghean.
ìgheil, *a.* Tallowy.
†il, ile, *s.m.* Plenty. 2 Difference, diversity. 4

Multitude. 4 Composite particle. 5 see iol. 6 Used as a prefix.
il-, For words beginning with il, see under iol.
ilbhinn, -ean, *s.f.* Craggy mountain.
ileach, -iche, *a.* Variegated, diversified. 2 Neat.
——,** -ich, *s.m.* Ordure, dung.
ileas,** -eis, *s.m.* Diversity, difference.
ilimeag, *Laggan & all W. Ross* for imleag.
ilimich, *Laggan & all W. Ross* for imlich.
ilisgean, *s.pl.* Taunts, nicknames, reflections on one's conduct—*Sar-Obair.*
†ill,** *s.m.* Ill, ruin.
'ille,** (*for* a ghille) *voc. sing.* of gill.
ìllse, *comp.* of ìosal, see ìsle.
ìlsich, see ìslich.
——ear, see ìslichear.
ilmeag, -eig, -an, see imleag.
ìlse, *comp.* of ìosal. see ìsle.
im-, *prefix*, Much, many. 2 About. see iom- & iomadh. [It is the prefixive form of *prep.*mu.]
ìm, -e, *s.m.* Butter. Sruthan ìme, *brooks of butter;* fear an ìme mhòir 's e a's binne glòir, (lit. *the man of much butter, his voice is the sweetest) the rich man's voice prevails ;* cha bhi an t-ìm sin air an roinn sin, *that butter will no be so divided ;* ìm ri ìm, cha bhiadh 's cha'n annlann e, *butter to butter is neither food nor kitchen.*
imbhristeadh,(MS) *s.m.* Flutter.
imbhuideal,(CR) *s.m.* [pronounced, imideal, *m* long.] Wooden keg or pail for carrying home milk and cream on the back from the sheilings. Sometimes carried on horseback, slung one on each side.—*W. of Ross.* The piece of skin tied over its mouth is called *iolaman*,and the piece of of string that ties the *iolaman* is *snathainn imbhuideil.* 2 (DC) In *Uist*, applied not to the pail or keg, but to the dressed skin used as a lid for the keg, and fastened, on the mouth of it by the snàthainn imbhuideil, a strong supple thong, which secures the skin lid, by tightening it between the two hoops on the edge of the pail or keg. When so fastened, the keg could be carried on one's back without spilling any milk, &c., it contained. The usual manner of carrying the kegs so secured, was in a "plaid" or sack made of muran or sea-bent sewn together. They are still made and used in some parts of Uist. 3(AF) Softy of a fellow.
im-chéimnich, *v.a. & n.* Walk round.
imchéin, see im-chian.
imcheist, -ean, *s.f.* Anxiety, perplexity, doubt, distraction. 2** Dilemma, jeopardy. An i., *perplexed.*
———each, -eiche, *a.* Doubtful, anxious, distracted, perplexed. 2 Causing perplexity or doubt.
im-chian, -chéine, *a.* Far, remote, foreign.
———, -chéin, *s.m.* Distance. O i., *from a distance.*
im-chubhaidh, see iomchuidh.
—————eachd, see iomchuidheachd.
†im-dheagal,** -ail, *s.m.* Protection.
†imdheanta,‡‡ *s.m.* Fashion, figure.
im-dhearbh, see iom-dhearbh.
imdheargaich,(MS) *v.a.* Dishonour.
im-dhidean,** -ein, *s.m.* Protection. 2 Protector.
im-dhorus, see iom-dhorus.
imeacach, -aiche, *a.* see ìmeach.
ìmeach, -eiche, *a.* Abounding in butter, buttery. 2 Like butter. 3 Producing butter. I. càiseach, *abounding in butter and cheese.*
imeachd, *s. f. ind.* Journey. 2 Act of going, walking or departing. 3 Departure. 4 Company. 5 The very spot. 6 Distinction. 7†† Boundary, circuit. 8**Pace, progress. 9** Course. 10**Moving. 11 Advancing. 12 Travelling. Ag i –, *pr.pt.* of imich. Mu 'n i. seo, *hereabouts ;* dé 'n i. mu 'n d' fhàg thu e ? *whereabouts did you leave it ? ;* bu garad a h-i., *quick was her pace ;* t' i. an saoghal chéin, *thy travelling in a distant world ;* ag i. an raoin, *traversing the heath;* cha'n 'eil aon 'gan i., *no one walks on (traverses) them ;* bi ag i., *begone, be off.*
imeachdan,** -ain,*s.m.* Child on leading strings.
imeachtraidh,(AF) *s.* Plough-bullocks.
imeall, see iomall.
im-easargain,** *s.f.* Striking on all sides.
im-easarganach,** *a.* Striking on all sides.
ìm-éiginn, *s.m.* Substitute for butter, made with milk and eggs and a little salt stirred together over the fire for a few minutes ; custard, omelette.
imfhios, see impis.
imich, *pr.pt.* ag imeachd, *v. n.* Go, depart. 2 Walk. 3 Stir, budge. 4 Advance. 5 Come. I. gu d' shruthain dhìomhair, *begone to thy lonely streams ;* dh' imich an laoch, *the hero has departed.*
imideal, *s.m.* see imbhuideal.
imileadadh, -aidh, *s.m.* Unction.
imir, *v.a. & n.* Need, behove, must, require. 2 (AC) Deliver. Imiridh mi falbh, *I must go ;* i. do Dhia, *deliver to God ;* an i. mi 'dheanamh ? *must I do it ? ;* cha do thaisg riamh nach d' i., *no man ever laid up a thing who did not find use for it ;* imiridh mi e, *I shall need it ;* dh' i. mi tòiseachadh, *I was obliged to begin ;* an i. mi falbh ? imiridh, *must I go ? yes.*
imir, -e, -ean, *s. m.* Balk or ridge of land. 2 Field.
imirc, *s.f.* see imirceadh.
imirceadh, *s.m.* Journey, departure, flitting.
imir-chuimir,* *adv.* Wholly and solely, most completely or thoroughly. Tha iad mar sin gu imir-chuimir, *they are so wholly and solely.*
imireach, -eiche, *a.* Abounding in ridges.
————adh, see imreachadh.
imirich, *v.a. & n.* see imrich. 2**Ridge, make a ridge, as in ploughed land.
———-te, *past pt.* see imrichte. 2 Ridged or furrowed, as ploughed land.
imiridh, *fut. aff. a.* of imir.
imirt, see iomairt.
imis, see impis.
imisear, *Suth'd.* for aimsir.
imisg, -e, -ean, *s.f.* Sarcasm. 2 Scandal, bad report, disgrace. 3 (CR) Proximity, nearness.—*W. of Ross.* Cha robh e an i. do 'n àite, *he was not near the place ;* cha tig e an i. dha, *he does not approach him, is not to be compared to him ;* is beag an i. nach tilg lethbheisd, *little is the scandal (or fault) that a half idiot will not cast up.*
———each, -eiche, *a.* Sarcastic. 2 Scandalous, disgraceful, given to scandal.
imleach,* see imlich.
———adh, -aidh, *s. m.* Licking. 2 Lapping with the tongue.
imleag, -eig, -an, *s.f.* The navel. 2 Nave of a wheel. 3 Name of the cup-shaped thong,from which the long thongs of the sea-weed *hemanthalia lorea* spring. Eadar m' i. agus m' àirnean, *between my navel and my kidneys.*
———ach, *a.* Umbilical, like a navel. 2 Of, or pertaining to, the navel.
———an, see imleag.
imlich, *pr. pt.* ag imlich, *v.a.* Lick with the tongue. 2 Lap. 3‡‡Sweep off with the finger. Imlichidh iad an duslach, *they shall lick the dust.*

imlich, -e, *s.f.* Licking, act of licking. Ag i—, *pr.pt.* of imlich.
——ear, *fut.pass.* of imlich.
——te, *past pt.* of imlich. Licked.
imlid, see imideal.
†immsruth, *s.m.* Diarrhœa.
imnidh, -e, *s.f.* Care, diligence. 2 Solicitude. 3 **Sadness. 4 (DMy) Anxiety. Gun i. gun eagal, *without care or fear.*
——each, -eiche, *a.* Careful, anxious,diligent. 2 Uneasy. 3 Sad. 4 Vigilant.
——eachd, *s.f.* Care, uneasiness.
impeachadh, -aidh, *s.m.* Persuading, beseeching, converting, constraining.
impich, see iompaich.
——ear, see iompaichear.
——te, see iompaichte.
impidh, -e, -ean, *s.f.* Prayer, petition, supplication, entreaty. 2 Exhortation. 3 Urging, persuasion, constrainment. 4 Means, medium, instrumentality. 5 Conversion. 6 **Twig, rod. Cuir i. air, *urge him ;* le h-impidhibh, *with entreaties.*
——each, -eiche, *a.* Persuading, persuasive, supplicatory, constraining, urging, exhorting, beseeching. 2 Converting. 3 Intercessory, mediatory.
——each, -eich, *a.* Petitioner. 2 Deprecator. 3 Exhorter, one who persuades. 4 Intercessor. 5 Converter.
——eachd, *s.f.* Persuasion. 2 Petitioning. 3 Intercession.
impis (an), *adv.* Almost, on the eve of, like. An i. dol fodha, *almost sinking ;* an i. teicheach, *on the eve of scampering ;* an i. a chiall a chall, *almost losing his reason ;* an i. a bhi sgàinte, *like to burst.*
impis, *s.* Imminence.
imreachadh,* -aidh, *s.m.* Walking in ranks or procession. 2 Procession. 3 Bearing, carrying. I. an tòrraidh, *the funeral procession—Islay.*
imreasan, -ain, -an, *s.m.* Dispute, controversy.
——ach, -aiche, *a.* Disputing, given to controversy.
im-réimnich, *v.n.* Go about.
imrich, -e, -ean, *s.f.* Removal, changing of residence. 2 Effects or furniture so removed. 3 **Emigration. Ag i—, *pr. pt.* of imrich, Air i., *emigrated ;* chuir e air i. iad, *he removed them ;* théid e i. thar a' chuain, *he shall emigrate beyond the sea ;* ni an imrich thric an àirneis lom, *constant flitting makes the furniture scarce ;* is buidhe le amadain i., *fools are fond of removing.*
imrich, *pr. pt.* ag imrich, [ag imreachadh & ag imrichd,] *v.a.* Carry, bear. 2*March, walk in ranks or processions. 3 Procession. 4 Remove furniture, "flit." 5 Change, alter.
——te, *past pt.* of imrich. Carried, changed, altered. 2 Wielded.
imseach, -siche, *a.* Revengeful. 2 Furious, enraged. Gu h-i., *furiously.*
——an,** -ain, -an, *s. m.* Rage, fury.
——d,** *s.f.* Revenge, revengefulness.
†imseachtrach, -aich, *s.m.* Project.
†imshniomh, -a, *s.m.* Heaviness, sadness, care. 2 Diligence.
†——ach, -aiche, *a.* Anxious, solicitous, uneasy.
imtheachd, -an, see imeachd.
im-thus,** *s.* Progress. 2 Adventure.
in-, *prefix*, of the same force as Latin *in-*.
†in, ine, *s.f.* see ionga.
†in, *a.* Fit, proper. (for ion.)
†in, *s.f.* Country. 2 Island.
†in, *prep.* see ann.

inbhe, -ean, *s. f.* Quality, dignity, rank. 2 Eve. 3 Condition, maturity, state of advancement or progression. 4 Size. 'Dé an i. am bheil thu ? *how far have you advanced ?* tha mi an i. mhath, *I have made considerable progress ;* tha mi deas gu h-inbhe deich, *I am prepared within ten ;* bha mi an i. 's an dorus a dhùnadh, *I was on the eve of shutting the door, I was hesitating whether to shut the door;* am bheil iad an inbh' a bhi deas ? *are they near the close ? ;* thàinig i gu h-i., *she grew up to size or stature ;* seasaidh aon suas 'na h-inbhe, *one shall stand up in her stead ;* an i. mhòir, *in great dignity.*
inbheach, -eiche, *a.* Eminent, in high rank. 2 Noble, exalted. 3 Mature, ripe. 4 Sizeable. 5 Advanced in station or condition. 6 Chief. Duine i., *a man of mature age,* [** gives *a man of rank, a man high in office*] ; àite i., *an exalted place ;* a b' inbhiche, *who was most exalted.*
——as, -ais, *s.m.* Fondness for being high in rank. 2 Fondness for high office.
——d, *s.f.ind.* Quality, dignity, rank. 2 Height of rank or office. 3 Nobleness. 4 Maturity, perfection, years of discretion. 5 Aggrandizement.
inbhear, -ir, see ionbhar.
inbheirt,** *s.f.* A perfect birth.
inbhich, *v.a.* **Exult, aggrandize. 2 see ineach.
——te, *past pt.* Aggrandized.
inbhidh,* *a.* see inbheach.
——eachd, see inbheachd.
inbhir, -ean, *s.m.* see ionbhar.
inc,** Gaelic spelling of *ink.*
inchinn, -ean, *s.m.* see eanchainn.
†in-chomharraichte, *a.* Notable.
†indearbh, *v.a.* Prove.
†indlobor, *a.* Weak.
†indlobre, *s.* Weakness.
ine, see ionga.
ine, see iodha.
ineach,** *s.m.* Chopping-block. Is math an t-i. a' chlach gus an ruigear i, *the stone is a good block till it is reached.*
ìneach, *a.* ††see iongach. 2 see iodhach.
ineach,** -ich, *s.f.* see inneach. 2 Generosity. 3 Hospitality. 4 Good management in housekeeping.
——ail,** *a.* Generous. 2 Hospitable. Gu càirdeil i., *friendly and hospitable.*
†——ras,** -ais, *s.m.* Fair. 2 Public meeting.
ineadal, see imideal.
inealta, -ailte, see innealta.
——ir, see ionaltair.
inealtradh, see ionaltradh.
inean, *n.pl.* of ionga.
†in-fhaicsinn, -e, *a.* Remarkable, worthy of notice, notable.
infhir, *a.* Nubile.
†ing,** *s.f.* Force, compulsion. 2 Stir. 3 Neck of land. 4 Danger.
ingealtas,** -ais, *s.m.* Pasture ground, ground fit for feeding cattle.
inghar, -eir, -an, *s.m.* Plumb, mason's line. 2 *Level. 3**Perpendicular. 4 Anchor. 5** Chain or cord to measure with.
——ach,** *a.* Level. 2 Perpendicular.
ingheach,** -ich, see inneach.
ingheann, -an, *pl* ìnghnean, *s.f.* see ighean. A' chlann nighean, *Lewis* for young women as a species.
†inghilt, see ingilt.
in-ghreim,** *s. m.* Clutching grasp. 2 Ravening. 3 Persecution. 4 Extreme avarice.
——each, *a.* Clutching. 2 Ravenous. 3 Clawing. 4 Persecuting. 5 Avaricious. 6

Plundering.
———each,** s.m. Persecutor.
ingilt,** s.f. Feeding, grazing. 2 Pasture. see inilt.
ingir,** s.f. Sorrow, affliction. 2 see ingear.
inglan,** a. Dirty, filthy, nasty.
ingneach, see iongach.
†ingor, s.m. Torment.
iniatar,** -air, s.m. Bowel, entrail.
inich, -e, a. Neat, tidy. 2 Lively. 3 Firm. 4 Handy. 5 Strong. 6 Sufficient. 7 Eager. 8 Effectual. Gu h-i., *sufficiently.*
inich,(CR) s. f. Floor of a cattle-stall, elevated above the *carcair* or *grip—W. of Ross-sh.*
inichead,-id, s.m. Neatness, degree of neatness. 2 Liveliness.
in-ichte,‡‡ a. Edible, eatable.
Inid, -e, s.f. Shrove-tide. Di-màirt na h-Inide, *Shrove Tuesday.*
Inid bheadaidh, said when the full-moon of Shrove-tide comes a few days after An Fhéill Brighde (Feb. 1), then comes "Earrach fad' an déidh Càisge." An I. bheadaidh thar gach féill, 's olc an aimsir duine ghionaich thig 'na déidh, *early Shrove-tide of all feasts, evil days come on a greedy man after it*—there would be a long tail of spring and lean days after Easter.
inilt, s.f. Bondmaid. 2**Pasture. 3**Fodder. 4(AF) Cattle. Tha 'n crodh air an i., *the cattle are on the pasture.*
——, v.a. Feed cattle. 2 Pasture, graze.
inirte,** s.f. Laziness, inactivity. 2 Feebleness.
inis, innse, see innis. †2 Distress, sorrow.
inisg, -e, -ean, s.f. Reproach, bad name, upcast, fling, personality, 2* Libel, calumny, defamation. A' tilgeadh inisgean, *defaming, reproaching*; an i. 'ga cur 's a bun aig a' bhaile, *the reproach getting spread and its root at home.*
inisgeach, -eiche, a. Reproachful, defamatory, disgraceful.
inisiol,** s.m. Servant.
†in-ite, see inithe.
†in-ithe, a. Edible, eatable.
inleighis, -e, a. see ion-leighis.
inmhe, -an, see inbhe.
———ach, see inbheach.
inmheachd,** s.f. Concoction.
in-mheadhonach, -aiche, a. Mean, moderate. 2 Inward, inmost.
inmheallta, a. Deceivable.
inmheasda, a. Commendable.
†inn, see ann.
inn-, *prefix*, of same force as Latin *in-*.
†inn,** I. Now used only in composition with a verb, as, dheanainn, *I would do*; bhualainn, *I would strike.* 2 Us, we.
†inn, -ean, s.f. Wave.
inndrig, *pr.pt.* ag inndriginn, v.a. Enter.
inne, s.f. Byre-channel or gutter, see p. 79.
inne, see ionga.
inne, *dat.pl.* innibh, see innidh.
inneach, -ich, s.m. Woof of cloth. 2 see ineach. 3**Curse. 'San dlùth no 'san i., *in the warp or woof*; 'nam dhlùth 's 'nam i. air, *I, the heart and soul of the affair.*
——,* -iche, a. Black, dirty. 2 Having nails. Thig bradan tarra-gheal, inneach, mealgach, *the white-bellied black salmon full of roe shall come—Filidh, p. 22.*
inneachadh, -aidh, s.m. Agitating.
inneachas, -ais s.m. Scramble. †2 Choice.
inneachd, s.f. Blow.
inneadh, -idh, s.m. Want, deficiency.
inneailt,(MS) v.a. Keep. (corrupt word.)
inneal, -il, *pl.* -an & innil, s. m. Instrument of any kind. 2 State, condition. 3 Mien, carriage, deportment. 4 Order or disposition of anything. 5 Dress, attire, caparison. 6 Service, attendance. 7 Restraint. 8 Machine, apparatus. 9 Implement, tool. 12** Array. Na'm bitheadh an t-i. agam, *had I the means;* i. bu sheinnteach fuaim, *a loud sounding instrument.*
———ach,‡‡ -aiche, a. Mechanical. 2 Organical.
———adh, -aidh, s. m. Ordering, preparing, adjusting, furnishing.
———aich,** v.a. Wield an instrument.
——— -buill,* s.m. Windlass.
——— -ciùil,* s.m. Musical instrument.
——— -cogaidh, s.m. Weapon, arms.
——— -coise, s. m. Footstep of a spinning-wheel.
——— -draghaidh,** s.m. Capstan.
——— -fàsgaidh,** s.m. Press.
——— -glacaidh,** s.m. Trap.
——— -iomchair,** s.m. Vehicle.
——— -mairbh** s.m. Instrument of death.
——— -smàlaidh, s.m. Extinguisher.
——— -stoith,* s.m. see inneal-toit.
———ta, -ilte, a. Well ordered or adorned. 2 Conformed to art. 3 Ingenious. 4(MS) Artificial. 5**Neat. 6**Well made. 7**Sprightly. 8**Handsome. 9**Elegant. 10**Active. 11**Artistic. Deudan an ordugh i., *teeth in elegant array.*
———tachd, s.f.ind. Neatness. 2 Conformity to art. 3 Ingenuity, fitness, aptness. 4 Handsomeness. 5 Sprightliness. 6 Elegance. 7**Activity. 8 (MS) Artificialness. see fi-ealtachd.
——— -tarruing,* s.m. Capstan.
——— -togail, s.m. Crane.
——— -toit,* s.m. Steam-engine.
innealtradh, see ionaltradh.
†inneamh,** -eimh, s.m. Increase, augmentation.
innean, -ein, -an, s.m. Anvil. 2 Rock, hill. 3 **Navel. 4***rarely* Middle of a pool. 5 Ankle. 6(CR) Protuberance at root-joint of little toe—*Farr.* Mar i. nan òrd, *like the sounding of an anvil*; adharc innein, *the horn of an anvil*; chaidh e dhe 'innean, *he dislocated his ankle* (lit. *went off his ankle.*)
———ach,†† a. Abounding in anvils. 2 Like an anvil.
———adh, -aidh, s.m. Deficiency of yarn in weaving.
innear, see inneir.
innearach, *gen.sing.* of inneir.
———, a. Full of dung, mucky.
inneil, see ionnail.
innein, -ean, see innean.
inneir, innearach, -eirean, s. f. Dung, manure. Cairt innearach, *a dung-cart*, or *a cart-full of dung*; dùn innearach, *a dunghill.*
——ich, v.a. Dung. 2‡‡Muck.
innich,* v.n. Scramble, struggle.
innidh, *dat.pl.* innibh, s.f. Bowel, entrail, intestines. 2** Compassion. 3 Byre-channel. O t' innibh, *from thy bowels.*
——,* a. Expert, clever, smart. Gille i., *a clever, active young man.*
——eachd,* s.f.ind. Expertness.
innil, -e, a. Active, prone to, ready.
innil, *n.pl.* of inneal. Gins, snares, &c.
——, *pr.pt.* ag innileadh, v.a. Prepare, equip.
†innill,** s.f. Fort. 2 Gin, snare.
innilt,** -e, -ean, s.f. Handmaid, maid-servant.
innis, innse, *pl.* innsean & innseachan, s. f. Island. 2 Sheltered valley protected by a wood. 3 Field to graze cattle in. 4 Pasture, resting place for cattle. 5 Choice place—*Islay.* 6

Headland. 7 Haugh, riverside meadow. 8 In *Ross & Suth'd* applied to a low-lying and sheltered place, where cows are gathered to be milked, and where they lie out at night 9**Distress, misery. I. nam bò laoigh 's nam fiadh, *a resting-place for milch-cows and deer.*
innis, *pr.pt.* ag innseadh, *v.a.* Tell, declare, relate, report, inform. I. dhomh. *tell me;* ciod a's fhearr a dh' innseas an cladh na 'n eaglais? *what better guide to the churchyard than the church?*
inuisg, -ean, see inisg.
——each, see inisgeach.
innis-mhuir, *s.f.* Archipelago.
innleachd, -an, *s.f.* Device, contrivance. 2 Ingenuity. 3 Invention. 4 Evil device or stratagem. 5 Machine. 6 Art. 7(MS)Adroitness. Cha'n 'eil e am i.-sa sin a dheanamh, *it is not within the power of my invention to do that;* dealbhamaid innleachdan, *let us devise devices;* ni airc i., *necessity is the mother of invention;* am bheil e 'nad i. mis' a leigeil air falbh? *is it within the compass of your invention to let me go?* droch i., *a wicked contrivance;* cha'n fhiach duine gun neart gun i., *a man is of little worth without strength or device.*
————ach, -aiche, *a.* Ingenious, inventive, adept. 2 Subtle. 3 Cunning. 4 Cunningly contrived. 5 Artificial. 6 Sagacious. Gu h-i., *ingeniously.*
————aiche, *s.m.* Contriver, inventor, designer, deviser, ingenious person.
————aiche, *comp.* of innleachdach.
————ail, see innleachdach.
————air, *s.m.* Inventor.
————an, *n. pl.* of innleachd.
————as,-ais, *s.m.* Artificiality. 2 Mechanics.
innleadh, -idh, *s. m.* Aiming, purposing, projecting, preparing, preparation.
innleag,* *s.f.* Child's doll.
innlich, *v.a.* Aim, project, devise. 2‡ Desire.
†innlidh, *s.f.* Forage.
innlinn, -e, *s.f.* Forage, provender, fodder. 2 The third part of the straw left by the tenant who is removing for the one entering the farm, for bedding to the cattle to help manure. Os ceann 'innlinn, *over its fodder.*
———each, -eiche, *a.* Abounding in provender.
innlis,** *s.f.* Lamp, lantern.
innrig,(MS) *v.a.* Begin.
——eadh,(MS) *s.m.* Beginning. 2 Adit. 3 Access, induction.
innse, see innseadh.
——ach, -eiche, *a.* Abounding in islands. 2 Insular, peninsular. 3‡‡Having good pasture. 4 Tattling, given to telling or relating.
——achail,‡‡ -e, *a.* Indicative.
innseachan, *n.pl.* of innis. Islands 2 The Indies.
innseadh, -aidh, *s.m.* Telling, act of telling, informing, rehearsing, relating, intelligence, information. 2 Report. 3 Sign. Is don' an t-i. ort, *it is a bad report of you;* fear-innsidh nan uisgeachan *or* fear innsidh na h-aimsir, *a look-out man in a boat.* Ag i—, *pr. pt.* of innis.
innseag, -eig, -an, *s. f. dim.* of innis. Little island. 2 Ait or isle in a river, 3 Detached field or pasture. 4(MS)Tale. 5**Little patch of arable ground, as in hilly or wooded countries.
———ach, -aiche, *a.* Abounding in small islands, little fields, or level downs.
———ail,‡‡ -e, *a.* Telling of tales, lodging of complaints.
———an, *n.pl.* of innseag.
innsean, *n pl.* of innis.
innseanach, *s.m.* Islander. 2 Indian.
innsear, *fut. pass.* of innis. Shall be told.
innsgeanach, see innsgineach.
innsgin, -e, *s.f.* Mind, courage, vigour.
innsgineach, -eiche, *a.* Sprightly, vigorous, lively, energetic, cheerful. 2 Sagacious. 3 Ingenious. 4 Vehement.
————d, *s.f.* Sprightliness, liveliness, airiness, cheerfulness.
innsidh, *fut.aff.a.* of innis. 2 *gen. sing.* of innseadh.
innsreadh,(MS) *s.m.* Apparatus.
innsridh*,* *s.pl.* Effects, furniture, movables.
innsrumaid, see ionnsramaid.
innt-, ‡ The form taken by the prep. *inn-* before *s.* (in old Gaelic only.)
innte, *prep.pron.* In her, in it (*f.*) 2 In her power.
†innte, *s.f.* Kernel.
innteach, -ich, *s.m.* Way, road, gate.
innteart,* see inntreadh.
inntil,** *s f.* Budget, wallet, satchel.
inntile, see imideal.
inntinn, -ean, *s.f.* The mind. 2 Intention, purpose. 3 Will, pleasure. 4 Intelligence. 5 Ingenuity. Sùil bhur n-i, *the eyes of your mind;* i. dhùbailt, *a double mind;* a dh' aon i., *with one mind or accord.*
————each, -eiche, *a.* Sensible, wise, intellectual. 2 High-minded, high-spirited. 3 Hearty, merry, sportive, jolly. 4 Earnest. 5 Conceited.
inntinneachd, *s. f.* High-mindedness. 2 Conceitedness. 3 Sprightliness.
inntinneas, -eis, *s.m.* Jollity.
inntinneil,‡‡ *a.* see inntinneach.
inntinn-eòlas, *s.m.* Metaphysics.
———— -eòlaiche, *s.m.* Metaphysician.
inntir,* see inntrinn.
inntleachd, see innleachd.
————ach, see innleachdach.
†inntliomh,** *s.* Treasury.
inntreachduinn, *s.f. & pr.pt.* of inntrinn.
inntreadh, -idh, *s.m.* Beginning, commencement. 2 Act of beginning or entering upon. 3 Entering, entrance. Ag i—, *pr. pt.* of inntrinn.
inntreas,** -eis, *s.m.* Entrance-money.
inntric, see inntrig.
inntrig, see inntrinn.
———eadh, see inntreadh.
inntrinn, *pr.pt.* ag inntreadh & ag inntreachduinn [ag inndreachdan in *Suth'd*] *v.a.* Begin, originate. 2 Enter.
————,** *s.f.* Entrance, admittance. 2 Commencement. Cha'n 'eil i. an seo, *there is no admittance here.*
————eadh, *3rd. sing. & pl. imp.* of inntrinn. I. e, *let him enter;* i. iad, *let them enter.*
insgineach, see innsgineach.
————d, see innsgineachd.
insgne,** *s.f.* Sex, gender. 2 Speech.
insiubhal, -aile, *a.* see ion-siubhal.
intleachd, see innleachd.
————ach, see innleachdach.
intreabh,** *s.m.* Want, poverty.
iob,†† -a, -annan, *s.f.* see ubag & uibe. 2(DC) *s.f.* Forward woman, hussy—*Perthshire.*
iob, -a, -an & -achan, *s.m.* Lump of dough. 2 Cake before being fired. 3***rarely* Death.
iobach,†† *a.* Full of, or pertaining to lumps of dough or unbaked cakes.
iobag, see iobalag.
iobair, *pr.pt.* ag iobradh, *v.a.* Sacrifice, immolate. Dh' i. iad uan, *they sacrificed a lamb;* cha'n i. sibh, *ye shall not make an offering.*
iobairt, -e, -ean, *s.f.* Offering, sacrifice. Faigh ear gu h-i. tri uain, *let three lambs be got for*

sacrifice. Rinn thu ì. dheth, in *Blair Atholl* means *you have made a muddle* or *a hash of it.*
——— -buidheachais, *s.f.* Thank-offering.
———each, *a.* Abounding in sacrifices.
———eachadh,(MS) *s.m.* Immolation.
———ear, *s.m.* Sacrificer.
——— -fhìon, *s.f.* Wine-offering.
———ich, see ìobair.
——— -loisgte, / ——— -losgaidh, } *s.f.* Burnt-offering.
iobalag,(CR) *s.f.* Dowdy, untidy woman—*W. of Ross-shire.*
iobartan, -ain, *s.m.* Means to do evil.
iobhlair, see iolair.
iobrachadh, *s. m.* Act of immolating. 2(MS) Mactation.
ìobradh, -aidh, *s. m.* Sacrificing, sacrifice. 2 Act of sacrificing. Ag ì—, *pr. pt.* of ìobair.
———, *3rd. sing. & pl. imp.* of ìobair. Ì. e, *let him sacrifice ;* ì. iad, *let them sacrifice.*
iobraim, (*for* ìobraidh mi) I will sacrifice.
ìobram, *1st. sing. imp.* of iobair. Let me sacrifice.
ioc, ice, *s.m.* Rent, payment. 2 Medicine, healing, remedy. 3 Requital. 4 Compassion, clemency, humanity, mercy, kindness, good nature, generosity. 2 *rarely* Children. I.-éiric, *kindred-money, ransom ;* dean do ghearan ri fear gun i. is their e "tha thu bochd," *complain to a man without compassion, and he will say "you are poor" ;* dean i., *have pity.*
ìoc, *pr. pt.* ag iocadh, *v. a.* Pay, render, retribute. 2 Heal, cure. 3 Reward. 4 Suffer, endure. Ìocaidh iad umhla, *they shall pay a fine.*
ìocach, *a.* Ready to pay or requite.
ìocadh, -aidh, *s. m.* Paying, payment, rendering. 2 Act of rendering. 3 Requital. 4 Curing. 5 Rewarding. 6 Suffering. Ag ì—, *pr. pt.* of ìoc.
ìocadh, *3rd. sing. & pl. imp.* of ìoc. Ì. e, *let him pay !* ì. iad, *let them pay !*
ìocaidh, *fut. aff. a.* of ìoc. Shall pay.
†iocaidh, -ean, *s.m.* Tenant, farmer.
ìocail, -e, *a.* Merciful, compassionate, tenderhearted.
ìocalachd, *s.f.* Mercifulness, compassion, tenderheartedness.
ìocar,‡‡ -aire, *a.* That pays rent or tribute. 2 Submissive.
ioc-ar-nac, Willy-nilly.
iocas, -ais, *s.m.* Payment. 2 Requital, remuneration.
†ioc-éiric, *s.m.* Kindred-money, ransom.
ìochd, *s. f. ind.* see ioc.
ìochdail, see iocail.
ìochdar, -aire, *a,* see iocmhor.
ìochdar, -air, -an, *s.m.* The bottom, lowest part. 2 Foundation. An ì. dheth, *under, worsted, cheated ;* ì. is uachdar, *top and bottom ;* ì. nan cnoc, *the foundation of the hills ;* ì. a' ghlinne, *the lowest part of the valley ;* tha e an ì., *he is beneath.*
iochd-ar-n-achd, see ioc-ar-nac.
ìochdarach, -aiche, *a.* Lower, the lower, nether, nethermost. A' chlach-mhuilinn ì., *the nether millstone ;* ifrinn i., *the lowest hell ;* ionaidean ì. na talmhainn, *the nether places of the earth.*
ìochdaran, -ain, *s.m.* Inferior, subject, subaltern, underling.
ìochdaranach, *a.* Inferior.
ìochdaranachd, *s.f.* Inferiority.
ìochdaranta, *a.* Deputed. 2 Tributary.
ìochdar-chanuis,‡‡ *s.m.* Bass in music.
iochdmhor, see iocmhor.
iochd-ochd,(CR) Nolens volens—*W. of Ross.* see ioc-ar-nac.
ìochdrach, see ìochdarach.
ìoc-luibh, -ean, see ìoc-lus.
ìoc-lus, -uis, -an, *s.m.* Medicinal herb. 2 Healing by herbs. Ì. an aonaich, *the healing herb of the plain.*
ìoc-lusach, -aiche, *a.* Abounding in healing herbs.
iocmhoire, *s. f.* Mercifulness, compassionateness.
iocmhoire, *comp.* of iocmhor.
iocmhor, -oire, *a.* Merciful, clement, humane, compassionate, kind. Rìghrean ì., *merciful kings.*
iocmhorachd, *s.f.ind.* Compassion, clemency, mercy, kindness, regard.
ìoc-shlàint, -e, -ean, *s. f.* Balm, salve, cordial, balsam, remedy, nectar, healing draught, medicine. Bheirinn mar ì. mo chìochan do 'm ghaol, *as a cordial I would give the milk of my breast to my love ;* b' e sin an ì., *that was the cordial ;* beagan ì. *a little balm ;* ì. chluas, *acoustics.*
ìoc-shlàinteach, -eiche, *a.* Healing, cordial, soothing, alleviating, salutary. 2 Balsamic. 3 Abounding in cordials. 4 Benign.
iod ! *int.* Alas !
iodaltach,(MS) *a.* Lazy.
†iodh,(AC) *s.* Corn, food.
iodh,‖ -a, *pl.* -anna & -annan, *s. f.* Cramp, spasm. 2(MS) Fit. 3**Rheumatic affection. 4 Pang. 5 Any severe pain. 6**Chain, collar.
iodh, see iogh.
iodha,(MS) *s.* Pinch.
iodhach, -aiche, *a.* Spasmodic.
iodhal, -ail, -an, *s.m.* Image, idol.
iodhalach, *a.* Idolatrous. 2 Full of idols.
iodhalachd, *s.f.* Idolatry.
iodhal-aorach, -aiche, *a.* Idolatrous.
iodhal-aoradair, -ean, *s.m.* Idolater.
iodhal-aoradh, -aidh, -ean, *s. m.* Idolatry. Luchd iodh al-aoraidh, *idolaters.*
iodhal-aoraidh, -an-aoraidh, *s.m.* Image to be worshipped.
iodhalt, *Suth'd* for iodhal.
iodhan, -ain, *s.m.* Spear, pike, javelin. 2 Affection. 3 Obedience. 4(AC) Small strip of land under corn. †5 Confirming.
†iodhan, *a.* Sincere. 2 Pure. 3 Clean.
iodhan,†† -ain, -an, *s.m.* Throes of child-birth.
iodhanna, *n.pl.* of iodh.
iodhanadh,(MS) *s.m.* Torture.
iodhannach, *a.* Spasmodic.
iodh-chosgach, *a.* Anti-spasmodic.
iodh-chraobh, *s.f.* Cypress.
iodhlach, see iodhlachadh.
iodhlachadh,(AC) *s.m.* All handling of corn from cutting to stacking—*Skye.*
iodhladair, see iodhal-aoradair.
iodhladaireachd, see iodhalachd.
iodhlain, *v.a.* Leap, skip.
iodhlan, -ain, *s.m.* Leap, hop, skip. 2 Hero.
iodhlanadh, -aidh, *s.m.* Skipping, leaping.
iodhlann, -ainn, -an, *s.f.* Corn-yard, stack-yard. 2 Circle (enclosure.) 3**Any fenced place.
———ach, -aiche, *a.* Abounding in corn-yards or stack-yards.
iodh-leigheasach,‡‡ -siche, *a.* Anti-spasmodic.
†iodhna, -ai, *s.m.* Spear, lance. 2 Protection, safeguard. 3 Brightness, purity.
†iodhnach, -aich, *s.m.* Gift.
†———, *a.* Valiant, warlike, martial. 2 Like a lance or spear.
iodhnadh,‖ -aidh, -ean, *s. m.* Pangs of childbirth, see iodhan.
iodhol, see iodhal.
iog,** *s.f.* Deceit, cunning. 2 *rarely* Mother.
iogach, *a.* Deceitful, cunning.

iogan, -ain, -an, *s.m.* Deceit, fraud. 2 Bird's claw. De 'n i., mhallachadh 's de ghò, *of deceit, cursing and fraud.*
ioganach, -aiche, *a.* Deceitful, false, treacherous. 2 Reluctant. 3 Like the claw of a bird. 4 Having a claw. Mionnan i., *false oaths;* gu h-i., *deceitfully.*
ioganaich, *s.f.* Reluctance, backwardness, timorousness, indecision, flinching.
iogannachd,** *s.f.* Deceitfulness, falseness.
iogara,** *a.* Low, humble.
iogaras,** -ais, *s.m.* Uprightness, honesty.
iogarnach, *a.* see ioganach.
iogarnachd, *s.f.* see ioganachd.
iogh, see iodh.
iogh, *s.* The yew-tree, old Gaelic name of the letter I.
iogha, see iodh.
ioghair, see iongar.
ioghanna, *n.pl.* of iogh.
ioghannan, *n.pl.* of iogh.
ioghar, -air, *s.m.* see iongar.
ioghlacadh, *a.* Tractable, easily caught.
ioghnadh, -aidh, -ean, see ionghnadh.
ioghnadh,(MS) *s.m.* Pageant.
ioghoile, *s.* Pylorus, lower orifice of the stomach.
ioghrach,** -aich, see iongarach.
ioghrachadh, -aidh, see iongrachadh.
ioghraich, see iongraich.
ioghras, -ais, *s.m.* Uprightness.
iognach, *a.* Covetous.
iol-,‡ *prefix*, Many.
iol,** *v.a.* Vary, change, chequer. 2 *s.* see iola.
iola, -chan, *s.f.* Fishing station, fishing-rock on shore, fishing-bank at sea.—*Isles.* 2 (DMy) Fishing with rods in a boat.|
iolacadh, see tiodhlacadh.
iolach, -aich, -aichean, *s.f.* Shout, cry, crying in exultation or triumph. 2 ††Roar. 3**Damage, loss. I. bhròin, *a shout of grief;* an i. bhrònach is ait fa seach, *the shout joyful and sad by turns.*
iolachdach, -aiche, *a.* Shouting for joy, merry. 2 Disastrous, destructive.
iolachdadh, see tiodhlacadh.
ioladh, -aidh, *s.m.* Fun, merriment, raillery, merrymaking. Cuir air i., *make light of, make fun of.*
ioladhach,** *a.* Merry. 2 Sprightly. 3 Humorous.
iolagall,** -aill, *s.m.* Damage. 2 Dialogue.
iolaic, see tiodhlaic.
iol-ainmeach, *a.* Polyonymous.
iolainn, see iodhlann.
iolainneach, see iodhlannach.
iolair,‡‡ *a.* Plural, of the plural number.
iolair, -e & iolarach, *pl.* -ean, *s. f.* Eagle. 2 Swift. Do luathas mar iolair, *thy speed like an eagle;* aghaidh iolarach, *the face of an eagle.*
†iolair, *s.m.* Much, diversity, plenty.
iol-àireamh, *v.* Annumerate.
iol-àireamh, -eimh, *s.m.* Annumeration.
iolair-bhàn, -e-bàine, -an-bàna, see iolair-mhara.
iolair-bhreac,¶ -e-brice, -an-breaca, *s. f.* Spotted eagle—*aquila nævia.* Chiefly found in *Skye.*
iolair-bhuidhe,¶ -e-buidhe, -ean-buidhe, *s. f.* Golden eagle—*aquila chrysaëtos.*
iolair-chladaich, *s.f.* White-tailed eagle, see iolair-mhara.
iolair-dhubh, see iolair-bhuidhe. 2 Ring-tail eagle.
iolaireach, *a.* Abounding in eagles. 2 Like an eagle.
iolair-fhionn, *s.f.* Gier-eagle.—*falco ossifragus.*

402. Iolair-bhuidhe.

2(AF) Ossifrage. 3 see iolair-mhara.
iolair-Ghreugach,(AF) *s.f.* Gier eagle.
iolair-iasgaich, *s. f.* Osprey—*falco haliaëtus.*

403. Iolair-iasgaich.

iolair-iasgair, see iolair-iasgaich.
iolairig, *s.f.* V-shaped structure, not necessarily artificial, wide at one end and narrow at the other, into which deer were driven, and shot with arrows as they came out.
iolairin,(AF) *s.* Eaglet.
iolair-mhaol,¶ -e-maoile, -an-maola, *s.f.* Bald eagle.
iolair-mhara, -e-m-, -an-m-, *s.f.* Sea-, or white-tailed eagle—*haliaëtus albicilla.*
iolair-mhonaidh, see iolair-bhuidhe.
iolair-riabhach, see iolair-mhara.

404. Iolair-mhara.

iolair-shùil, -shùl, *s.f.* Eagle-eye. I. na gréine, *the eagle eye of the sun.*
iolair-shùileach, *a.* Eagle-eyed.
iolair-sùil-na-gréine, see iolair-mhara.
iolair-thimchiollach, *s.f.* Gier eagle, see iolair-fhionn.
iolair-uisge, *s.m.* Osprey, see iolair-iasgaich.
iolaman,(CR) *s.m.* Piece of skin tied over the mouth of the imbhuideal with strong thread.
iolan,** *a.* Sincere.
iolanach,** *a.* Ingenious, learned, skilful.
iolanachd,** *s.f.* Ingenuity, learning.
iolann, see iodhlann.
iolar, *adv.* Downwards—*Perthshire.* see ioras. I. shìos, *down below,*
iolar,(DC) *s. m.* Bottom of water, or of a loch. 2 Foot of a hill or rock—*Perth, N.Argyll.* I. na beinne, *the foot of the mountain.*
iolar,** -eir, *s.m.* Variety, plenty, much, diversity.
iolarach, *gen.sing.* of iolair.
iolarach, *a.* Various, varied, variegated, chequered.
iolath,** *s.m.* Disport.
iol-bhéist, -e, -ean, *s.m.* Serpent, snake, adder. 2††Wild beast.
iol-bheusach, -aiche, *a.* Versatile, various in manner. 2 Arch, sly. 3 Multifarious. Gu h-i., *archly.*
iol-bhuadh,** -aidh, *s.m.* Victory, triumph.
iol-bhuadhach, -aiche, *a.* Victorious, triumphant, gaining many victories.
iol-chainnteach,** *a.* Polyglot.
iol-chèard, -èird, *s.m.* see iol-chèardach.
———ach, *s.m.* Jack-of-all-trades.
iol-chèarnach, -aich, *s.m.* Polygon.
iol-chèarnach, -aiche, *a.* Polygonal, multangular.
iol-chèarnag, *s.f.* see iol-chèarnach, *s.*
iol-choimeasgta,** *a.* Mixed, miscellaneous.
iol-chosach, *a.* Many-footed.
iol-chosach, -aich, *s.m.* Centipede.
iol-chridheach, -eich, *a.* Fickle, inconstant, deceitful, double-hearted.
iol-chruthach, -aiche, *a.* Multiform, various. 2 Inconstant, changeable, as clouds. 3 Well-proportioned, well-featured, comely. Gu h-i., *changeably.*
iol-chuire,** *s.f.* Sadness, lamentation.
iol-chumasg,** *s.* Miscellany.
iol-danach, -aiche, *a.* Ingenious, well-gifted. Gu h-i., *ingeniously.*
iol-danach,** -aich, *s.m.* Jack-of-all-trades.
iol-dannsa, -ichean, *s.m.* Ball. 2 Promiscuous dance. 3 Country dance.
iol-dathach, -aiche, *a.* Many-coloured. 2 Discoloured.
ioldhathach, see iol-dathach.
iol-dealbhach, -aiche, *a.* Well-favoured or featured. 2††Multiform.
iol-dhùil, *s.f.* Great desire, avarice.
iol-fhilleadh,** *s.m.* Complication.
iol-fhillte,** *a.* Complex, complicated.
†iolga,** *s.pl.* Tongs.
iol-ghilleach, -eiche, *a.* Complex.
iol-ghineach,** *a.* Heterogeneous. Gu h-i., *heterogeneously.*
iol-ghleusach, -aiche, *a.* Manifold, complicated.
iol-ghnèitheach, -eiche, *a.* Of all kinds, various, heterogeneous. 2 Many-coloured. Gu h-i., *diversely.*
iol-ghnìomhach, -aiche, *a.* Ingenious. 2†† Industrious.
iol-ghonach, -aiche, *a.* Vulnific. 2 Painful. Gu h-i., *painfully.*
iol-ghràineach, -eiche, *a.* Very ugly, horrid, causing disgust.
†iol-ghreasach,** -aich, *s.m.* Inn, lodging.
iol-ghuth, *a.* see iol-ghuthach.
iol-ghuthach, -aiche, *a.* Of various tongues, polyglot. 2**Having a great compass of voice. 3**Having various voices, as a vocal mimic.
iolla,* *s.f.* Sight, view. Gabh i. ris, *just look at it.* 2 see iola.
iolla, *s.* Fishing rock generally covered at high tide.
iolladh,(DC) *s.m.* Fishing ground—*Uist.*
iollag, *s.f.* see iullag.
iollagach, -aiche, see iullagach.
iollagachd, see iullagachd.
iollain, -e, *a.* Expert, mechanical.
iollairce, *pl.* -an, Hiding-hillock in deer-hunting.
iollaisg,(DU) *adv.* Wrong, astray. Chaidh e i., *he went astray* or *wrong.*
iollan, see iollain.
iollanaiche,** *s.m.* Expert of any art.
iollapach, see iullagach.
iol-leabhar, -air, -bhraichean, *s.m.* Volume.
iol-mhaitheas,** -eis, *s. m.* Much good, great advantage.
iol-mhaoin, -e, *s.f.* Opulence, riches.
iol-mhaoineach, -eiche, *a.* Opulent, rich.
iol-mhodhach, -aiche, *a.* Manifold, various.
iol-oilean,** *s.* Polymathy.
iol-phòsadh, -aidh, *s.m.* Polygamy.
iol-phòsda,** *a.* Often married.
iolrach, see iolair.
iol-shioladh,** -aidh, *s.m.* Polysyllable.
iol-shlisneach,** -ich, *s.m.* Polygon.
iol-shlisneach,** *a.* Polygonal.
ioltag, -aig, -an, *s.f.* see ialtag.
iol-thilgte,** *a.* Amphibolous.
iom-, *or* ioma-, *a.* Used as a prefix in compounds (the broad vowel form of the prefix *im-*.)
iom-, *prefix,* About, round. 2 Entire. Iomlan, *quite complete;* iomaghaoth, *whirlwind.*
ioma, *a.* Much, many, numerous. also iomad, iomadh & iomadaidh.
ioma-bhallach, *a.* Circummured.
ioma-bhiorach, *a.* Prone to rebuke or check. Causing a rebuke.
ioma-bhreitheach,‡‡ *a.* Multiparous.
ioma-bhriathrach, -aiche, *a.* Multiloquous.
ioma-bhruidhneach, -eiche, *a.* Multiloquous.
iomacach, -aiche, see imeach.
iomach,** -aich, *s.m.* Colt.
iomach, see iomadh. 2 Parti-coloured, of various colours.
iomachagair, *s.f.* Kind regards, compliments.
iomachain, see iomaguin.
iomachaineach, see iomaguineach.
ioma-chainnteach, *a.* Having many languages.
ioma-chànaineach, *a.* Having many languages.
iomachar, see iomchar.
iomacharag, -aig, -an, *s.f.* Compliments, friend-

ly message,
ioma-chasach, *a.* Polypous, many-footed.
iomachd, see imeachd.
ioma-cheallach, -aich, *s.m.* Any close private place.
ioma-cheannach, *a.* Many-headed.
ioma-chearnach,** *a.* Many-cornered.
ioma-chèarnachd,‡‡ *s.f.* Multangularness.
ioma-chéin, see im-chian.
ioma-cheist,** see imcheist.
ioma-cheisteach, see im-chèisteach.
ioma-chiallachd,** *s.f.* Amphibology.
ioma-chian, see im-chian.
ioma-chladhadh, *s.m.* Circumvallation.
iom-choire, see iomchar. Beul na h-iomchoire, said of one prone to find fault.
ioma-chomhairle, -an, *s.f.* Doubt, suspense. 2 Perplexity, indecision, halting between two opinions.
ioma-chomhairleach, -eiche, *a.* Doubtful, unsteady, undecided, fickle.
ioma-chrith,** *s.f.* Trembling, tremor, violent tremor. 2 Earthquake. Air i. chum dioghailt, *trembling for revenge.*
ioma-chruth,†† *a.* Multiformed, various.
ioma-chruthach, -aiche, *a.* Multiform, various.
ioma-chruthachd,‡‡ *s.f.* Multiformity.
ioma-chuidheachd,(MS) *s.f.* Pertinentness.
ioma-chuimhn', see iomaguin.
ioma-chuimhneach, see iomaguineach.
iomachuinge, *s.f.* Narrowness, extreme narrow-mindedness.
iomachumhann,* *a.* Very narrow, narrow-minded, niggardly.
ioma-chladhaich, *v.a.* Circumvallate.
iomad, see iomadh.
iomadach, -aiche, *a.* Numerous, many, abundant. 2** Too many. I. uair, *often ;* i. té, *many a female;* i. fear, *many a man ;* i. seòrsa, *many a kind ;* na slòigh gu h-i., *the people in numbers.*
iomadachadh, -aidh, *s.m.* Multiplying, multiplication. 2 Numbering. Ag i—, *pr. pt.* of iomadaich.
iomadachd, see iomadalachd.
iomadaich, *pr. pt.* ag iomadachadh, *v.a.* Multiply, increase.
iomadaidh, -e, *s.f.* Multitude. 2 Too much, superfluity. Is co math na's leòir is i., *enough is as good as superfluity.*
iomadaidh, *a.* Manifold, several, superfluous. 2 Frequent. Nèamhnaid nan i. buaidh, *a pearl of manifold virtues.*
iomadaidheach, -eiche, *a.* Legionary.
iomadaidheachd, *s. f.* Abundance, plurality, multiplicity. 2 Superfluity, redundance.
iomadail,-e, *a.* Multiplicable. 2‡‡Miscellaneous.
iomadalachd, *s.f.* Multitude, abundance, plurality, numerousness. 2 Increase, multiplication. 3 Multifariousness. 4‡‡Miscellaneousness. Oir thig aislingean le i. ghnothaichean, *for dreams come through a multitude of business.* [Not good Gaelic idiom.]
iomadan, -ain,-an,*s.m.* Concurrence of disasters. 2 Lamentation, mourning. 3**Anxiety, solicitude. 4 Restlessness, discomfiture. 5 Sadness. 6**Changeable or fickle fellow. 7 ††Moving, flitting. Air i., *adrift ;* leòn no i. no bròn, *neither wound nor anxiety nor grief.*
iomadanach, -aiche, *a.* Pressed by disaster. 2 Sorrowful, sad. 3 Changeable, fluctuating. 4 Restless, unsettled. 5 Moving to and fro, fickle. Gu h-i., *changeably.*
iomadanach, -aich, *s.m.* Fickle fellow.
iomadanachd, *s.f;* Changeableness, fickleness.
iomadas,(MS) -ais, *s.m.* Abundance.
iomadh, *a.* Much, many, divers. 2 Plural in *grammar.* I. saoidh is òigh, *many a hero and maiden.*
iomadhall,** -aill, *s.m.* Sin, iniquity.
iomadhathach, -aiche,*a.* Parti-coloured, changeable.
ioma-dhathte, *past pt.* Many-coloured, dyed with many colours.
ioma-dhòrtach, -aiche, *a.* Circumfusive.
ioma-dhòrtadh, -aidh, *s.m.* Circumfusion.
ioma-dhruid, *pr. pt.* ag ioma-dhruideadh, *v. a.* Enclose, besiege, shut up close.
————eadh, -idh, *s.m.* Enclosing, act of enclosing. 2 Besieging. 3 Siege. 4 Enclosure.
————te, *past pt.* Circummured.
iomad-labhrach,(MS) *a.* Multiloquous.
ioma-fhilleadh. *s.m.* Circumplication.
iomag, -aig, *s.f.* Margin, border.
iomagail, *s.f.* Dialogue. 2 Dispute.
iomagain, -e & -ain, *pl.* see iomaguin.
iomagaineach, -eiche, see iomaguineach.
†iomagallaimh, *s.f.* Counsel, advice.
iomagan,** *s. m.* Restlessness, anxiety. 2 Flitting.
ioma-ghaoth, -aoith, -an, *s. f.* Whirlwind, eddywind. I. fo a sgiathaibh, *a whirlwind under his wings.*
ioma-ghaothach, *a.* Squally, whirling as an eddy-wind.
ioma-ghlac, *v.a.* Grip, grasp, embrace.
ioma-ghnèitheach, -eiche, *a.* Various, manifold. 2 Party-coloured.
iomaghonach, -aiche, *a.* Giving many wounds.
iomaguin, -e & -ain, *pl.* -an, Anxiety, grief. 2 Solicitude. 3 Distress. 4 Agony. Sheas i le h-i., *she stood perplexed ;* an i. gheur, *in sore distress ;* fo i., *solicitous.*
iomaguineach, -eiche, *a.* Anxious, solicitous, distracted, perplexed. 2 Causing pain, distress or anxiety.
————d, *s.f.* see iomaguin.
†iomaich, *s.f.* see iomaigh.
†iomaidh,** *s.f.* Envy.
†iomaidhbhear, *v. a.* Check, rebuke.
iomaidheachd,(MS) *s.f.* Diversity.
iomaididh, see iomadaidh.
iomaigh,** *s.m.* Border. 2 Open champaign ground.
iomaill, *gen.sing.* of iomall.
iomain, *pr.pt.* ag iomain, *v.a.* Urge, drive slowly as cattle. 2 Toss, whirl, roll. 3 Conduct. 4** Drive anything forward on the ground, kick forward, as a football. 5 Play as at shinty,football, or any driving game. Iomainidh iad, *they shall drive ;* 'gan i. 'sa chath, *driving them backward in battle ;* am bheil thu dol a dh' iomain ? *are you going to play?* ciod e an iomain ? *what game ? ;* a dh' i. chaman, am ball iomain, *or* am ball iomanach, *shinty.*
iomain, -e & -each, -ean, *s. f.* Driving, act of driving or urging. 2 Drove of black cattle. 3 Tossing, act of tossing. 4 Whirling, rolling. 5‡‡ Crowd. 6** Drove of sheep. 7**Sounder of swine. Ag i—, *pr.pt.* of iomain. Gach i. leatha féin, *each drove by itself ;* a' leantuinn nan iomaine, *following the droves ;* lorg-iomain *or* slat-iomain, *an ox-goad ;* is leòir a tha thu a' gabhail iomain, *you are being driven back badly.*
iomain-cuain, *a.* Driven by the storm.
iomaineach, -eiche, *a.* Coercive.
iomainiche, -an, *s.m.* Driver of cattle, drover. 2 Player.
iom-ainmeach,‡‡ -eiche, *a.* Multinominal.
iomair. *v.* see imir.
iomair, -ean, *s.m.* see imir. Iomairean cian, *long ridges.*

iomair, *pr.pt.* ag iomairt, *v. a.* Employ, exercise, use. 2 Conduct, behave. 3 Contest, engage. 4 Wield, play, as in fencing. 5 Play at cards, backgammon, &c. 6 Frolic. 7‡‡Need. 8††Move. 9 Serve. I. i 'san àrach, *wield it in the battle-field.*
iomair, *pr.pt.* ag iomram, ag iomradh & ag iomairt, *v.a.* Row, as a boat. I. am bàta, *row the boat;* an ràmh a's fhaisge i., *row the nearest oar;* i. 'Eachainn, dean fodha a Ruairidh, *row Hector, back water Rory.*
iomairc,* see imrich.
iomaire, see imir.
———ach,†† *a.* Abounding in ridges of land.
———achd,** *s.f.* Courting
———ag,** -eig, *s.f.* Skirmish.
iomairg,** *s. f.* Plundering, devastation. 2 Plunder. 3 Skirmish.
iomairich, *s.* see imirich.
———, *v.* see imirich & imrich.
———te, see imirichte.
iomairidh, see imiridh.
iomairl, see iomrall.
iomairt, -ean, *s. f.* [McL & D gives *s.m.* but -e for the *gen. sing.*] Employing, exercising, act of employing. 2 Conduct, behaviour. 3 Engagement, contest, conflict. 4 Bustle, agitation, confusion. 5 Playing, gaming. 6 Frolic. 7**Exertion. 8**Labour. 9**Restlessness, fidgeting. 10 Distress. 11** Moving. 12 Wielding. 13**Making use of. 14**Operation, process. 15‡‡Rowing. 16* Danger. Ag i. air na cairtean, *playing at cards;* 's ann orra a bha 'n i., *they were greatly confused;* ciùin, tlàth ann a h-i., *mild and gentle in distress;* ag i. saighde mar lann, *using an arrow like a spear;* am bheil thu ag i. seo? *are you using this?* i. nan laoch, *the exertion of the heroes;* i. nan tonn, *the agitation of the waves;* is ann ort tha 'n i.! *how you do fidget;* i. nan lann, *the playing of swords.* Ag i—, *pr.pt.* of iomair.
———,(AC) *s.* Cloth striped lengthwise only, not both ways like tartan.
———each, -eiche, *a.* Employed, active. 2 Playful. 3*Betting, laying wagers. 4 Lavish. 5**Bustling, agitating. 6**Fidgeting. restless. 7††Stirring. 8††Thrifty. 2 Industrious.
———eas, -eis, see iomartas.

iomairt fhaochag, *s.f.* Whelk game, or chuckie stanes, a girl's game, played with small whelk shells. Alexander Morrison in an article on Uist Games in *Celtic Review, No. 16,* says:—

"I have taken some trouble to understand this intricate game, but have not succeeded. I have done the next best thing, however, for I have got all the different moves, which none but a feminine mind could remember.

	1	2
(*a*)	Sgabadh aon	Sgabadh a dhà
(*b*)	Dubhas a h-aon	Dubhas a dhà
(*c*)	Trithis a h-aon	Trithis a dhà
(*d*)	Cairteal a h-aon	Cairteal a dhà

	3	4
(*a*)	Sgapadh a trì	Sgapadh a Ceithir
(*b*)	Dubhas a trì	Dubhas a Ceithir
(*c*)	Trithis a trì	Trithis a Ceithir
(*d*)	Cairteal a trì	Cairteal a Ceithir

	5	6
(*a*)	Sgapadh a Còig	Sgapadh a Gobagan
(*b*)	Dubhas a Còig	Gobagan a h-aon dhiu
(*c*)	Trithis a Còig	Gobagan a dhà dhiu
(*d*)	Cairteal a Còig	Gobagan a trì dhiu
		(*e*) Gobagan a ceithir dhiu
		(*f*) Gobagan a còig dhiu

7	8
Sgapadh na Goraiche	Sgapadh a h-aon
Goraich i fhéin	Dubhas a h-aon
	Trithis a h-aon
	Cairteal a h-aon

9	10
(*a*) 'S a bhireach	'S a Seachdadh

11
Sgapadh a h-aon déin chriche
Dubhas a h-aon déin chriche
Trithis a h-aon déin chriche
Cairteal a h-aon déin chriche
Còig a h-aon déin chriche

12
Sgapadh a Gobacan déin chriche
Gobacan a h-aon déin chriche
Gobacan a dhà déin chriche
Gobacan a trì déin chriche
Gobacan a ceithir déin chriche
Gobacan a còig déin chriche
13 Sgapadh an goraich déin chriche
Gorach i fhéin déin chriche
14 'S a bhireach déin chriche
15 'S a seachdadh déin chriche
16 Sgapadh do m' bhig
17 Sgapadh na reis (=span)
18 Reis a h-aon liobag
19 Reis a h-aon bhocag
20 Reis a dhà liobag
21 Reis a dhà bhocag
22 Sgapadh a h-aon
Dubhas a h-aon
Trithis a h-aon
Cairteal a h-aon

I shall not attempt to describe these steps, for I cannot. They are all variations of Sgapadh a h-aon or the common "chuckie-stanes" method."

iomairtiche, -an, *s.m.* Gambler. 2 Busy fellow.
†iomaith,** *v.a.* Check, rebuke.
———bhiorach, -aiche, *a.* That checks or rebukes.
——— fhear,** -fhir, *s.m.* Man who rebukes, or chides.
——— -fhearach, -aiche, *a.* That checks or rebukes.
ioma-labhairt, *s.f.* Circumlocution.
ioma-labhradh, *a.* Circumlocutory.
iom-àlach, -aiche, *a.* Multiparous.
ioma-lìonach, *a.* Circumfluent.
iomall, -aill, -an, *s.m.* Border, extremity, limit. 2 Suburbs of a town. 3 Fault. 4* Refuse, remainder. 5 Coast. 6**Frontier. 7**Rim, edge, border of a vessel. 8**Skirt. 9**Heddles of a loom. 10**Fringe. An i. na dùthcha, *in the outskirts of the country;* i. a' bhaile, *the suburbs of the town;* aon i. a bhios aca, *any refuse they may have;* crùn òir d' a i., *a golden crown for its border;* i. nan stuadh, *the border of the waves, the shore;* i. a' chùirn, *the extremity (verge) of the cairn;* gu i. na talmhainn, *to the ends of the earth.*
———ach, -aiche, *a.* Remote, uttermost, utter, distant. 2 External. 3**On the frontiers. 4 Having borders.
———aiche, *comp.* of iomallach. O na h-àitibh a's i., *from the uttermost parts;* a' chuid a b' iomallaiche de 'n t-sluagh, *the uttermost of the people.*
———aiche,(MS) *s.m.* Accolent.
———anach,(MS) *s.m.* Accolent.
———as,(CR) -ais, *s.m.* Hesitation, uncertainty—*Perthshire.*
iomall-soillse,** *s.m.* Twilight.
iomall-tràigh,** *s.m.* Sea-side, edge of the shore.

iomaltar,** -air, *s.m.* Centre.
ioma-lùbach, -aiche, *a.* Intricate.
ioman, see iomain.
iomanaiche, *s.m.* Driver. 2(AH) Shinty-player.
iomansachd,** Gaelic spelling of *immensity.*
ioma-phòsadh,** -aidh, *s.m.* Polygamy.
iomarach,** -aich, *s.f.* Border, margin. I.-na-ban-righinn, *the place-name Queensferry.*
iomaraiche, *s.m.* Rower.
iomaral, see iomrall.
iomarasg,** -aisg, *s.* Prophecy.
iomarbhaidh, -ean, *s.f.* Struggle, strife, controversy, debate. 2* Hesitation. 3 Confusion. 4**Skirmish. 5**Lie. 6**Deceit. 7**Comparison. 8 see iomramh. [** gives iomarbhadh, *s.m.* e. g. Seachd oidhche ag iomarbhadh, *seven nights contending.*]
——————each, -aiche, *a.* Prone to strife or controversy.
iomarbhuidh, *s.f.* Hesitation, confusion about what to do, or how to proceed.
iomarbhas,** -ais, *s.m.* Sin. 2 Banishment. 3 Strife.
iomarcach, -aiche, *a.* Many, numerous. 2 Superfluous, redundant. 3 Excessive. 4 Oppressive. 5*In many straits, distressed. 6(CR) Trying, hard to bear, as cold, &c.—*Arran.* T' òigridh i., *thy numerous youth ;* á h-uisgibh i., *from many waters ;* gu h-i., *numerously.*
iomarcaidh, -e, *s.f.* Abundance, superfluity, excess, numerousness.
†iomarchur, -uire, *s. m.* Rowing or steering with oars, sculling. 2 Tumbling. 3 Wallowing. 4 Erring, straying. 5**Error.
iomardadh,** -aidh, *s.m.* Reproach.
iomarlach, see iomrallach.
ioma-ròl, *v.a.* Circumvolve.
————adh, *s.m.* Circumvolution.
iomarsgal,** -ail, *s. m.* Wrestling, struggling. Seachd là ag i., *seven days wrestling.*
iomarsgleo, see iomarsgal.
iomartach, -aiche, *a.* see iomairteach.
†iomartar, see iomaltar.
iomartas, -ais, *s. m.* Industry. 2 Motion. 3 Activity, bustling about. 4 Necessity. 5†† Sufficiency. 6††Competency.
iomasgaoil, see iomsgaoil.
————te, see iomsgaoilte.
————teachd, see iomsgaoileadh.
†iomasgrach,** -aich, *s.m.* Inn, lodging-house. 2 Lodgings.
ioma-sheòl, see iom-sheòl.
————adair, see iom-sheòladair.
————adh, -aidh, see iom-sheòladh.
ioma-shiollach, -aiche, *a.* Polysyllable.
ioma-shliosach, -aiche, *a.* Multilateral.
ioma-shluaghach, *a.* Many-peopled.
ioma-shruth, see iom-shruth.
——————ach, see iom-shruthach.
ioma-thaobhach, *a.* Multilateral.
ioma-theangach, *a.* Many-tongued.
ioma-tholltach, -aiche, *a.* Multicavous.
†iombath,** *s.m.* Adjoining sea. 3 Sea encompassing an island.
†————, *v.a.* Overwhelm. 2 Fall into a swoon.
†————adh, -aidh, *s. m.* Overwhelming. 2 Swoon. 3(AH) State of being half-drowned. Thàinig iad do 'n phort seo air iombathadh, *they landed in this port in a half-drowned state.*
iom-bathadh,(WC) *adv.* On purpose. Thàinig e air i. 'ga iarraidh, *he came purposely for it.*
iom-bhaidh, see ioma-bhaidh.
iom-bhuail, see ioma-bhuail.
iom-bhualadh, see ioma-bhualadh.
iomchaidh,(DC) *a.* Circumspect. Duine i., *a circumspect man—Uist.*
iomchain, *pr. pt.* ag iomchan, *v.a.* Bear, carry. 2(DMC) Find fault, blame.
iomchainich, see iomchain.
————te, *past pt.* of iomchainich.
iom-chainnteach,** *a.* Expressive. 2 Talkative. 3 Polyglot.
iomchainte, *past pt.* of iomchain. Borne, carried.
iomchair, see iomchoire.
iomchair, *pr.pt.* ag iomchar, *v.a.* Carry, bear. 2 Conduct, demean, behave. 3**Endure. 4 (CR) Accuse, blame—*Skye.*
iomchan, -ain, -an, *s.m.* Bearing, carrying, act of carrying. 2 Behaviour, comportment. Ag i—, *pr.pt.* of iomchain.
iomchaomhnas,** -ais, *s.m.* Question.
iomchar, -air, *s.m.* Bearing, act of carrying. 2 Behaviour. 3 Comportment, moving, gait. 4 **Bier. 5**Carriage. I. nam beus, *moral conduct ;* i. uallach, *stately gait ;* fear-iomchair airm, *an armour-bearer.* Ag i—, *pr. pt.* of iomchair. 6(CR) Accusing, blaming—*Skye.* Tha e ag i. air, *he is accusing* or *blaming him;* a dh' iomchar fios do 'n t-seann rìgh, *to carry word to the aged king.*
iom-charachd,(MS) *s.f.* Alternity.
iom-charag,** -aig, *s.f.* Female porter.
iomcharan, *s.m.* Bearing, carrying—*Dàin Iain Ghobha.*
iomchas,** *v.n.* Murmur, complain.
————aid,** *s.f.* Complaint.
iom-chathamh,** *s.m.* Whirling drift. Thig i., *a whirling drift shall come.*
iom-cheangail,‡‡ *v.a.* Oblige, make obligatory.
iomchein, see im-chian.
iom-cheist, see imcheist.
————each, see imcheisteach.
iom-cheumnachadh,-aidh, *s.m.* Perambulation, walking round.
iom-cheumnaich, *v.n.* Walk round, pace round, perambulate.
iom-chian, see im-chian.
iom-chlaidheamh,** -eimh, *s.m.* Sword-fighting, fencing.
——————air,** *s.m.* Sword-fighter, fencer.
iom-choimhead,** -id, *s.m.* Guarding, protecting.
iomchoire, -an, *s.m.* Reflection, blame, grudge, accusation. 2 Complement. A' cur i. orm, *reflecting on me.*
————ach, -eiche, *a.* Reflective, censurious, blaming, accusing. 2 Worthy of blame or reflection.
iomchoirich, *v.a.* Blame, reflect on. 2 Rebuke, chide, censure.
iom-choirneach, *a.* Having many corners.
iom-chomairich,** *s. f.* Petition, request, favour. 2 Farewell.
iom-chomarc,** -airc, *s.m.* Present, donation.
iom-chomhairle,** *s. f.* Perplexity, doubt, dilemma. 2 Jeopardy. Ann an i., *perplexed.*
——————ach,** *a.* Causing doubt or perplexity, perplexed.
——————achd, *s.f.* Unsettledness.
iomchombarc, see iomachagar.
iom-chòmhdaich,‡‡ *v.a.* Enwrap.
iom-chòmhradh, -aidh, -aidhean, *s.m.* Thesis, subject of disputation.
iomchorag, *Suth'd* for iomchoire.
iomchorc,‡ see iomachagar.
iom-chràbhach,‡‡ -aiche, *a.* Ascetic.
iom-chras,** -ais, *s.m.* Deportment, grace.
iomchruthach, -aiche, *a.* see ioma-chruthach.
iomchuairtich, *v.a.* Block, blockade.
iom-chuartachadh, -aidh,*s.m.* Blockade. Ag i— *pr.pt.* of iomchuairtich.
iom-chuirteach, *a.* Ambient, mazy.
iomchubhaidh, see iomchuidh.

iomchuidh, -e, *a.* Fit, meet, proper, decent. 2 Convenient. 3 Necessary, suitable, expedient. Is i. sin dhuit, *that is befitting your case;* mar chì thusa i., *as you see fit;* is i. dhuit dol dhachaidh, *it is proper that you should go home;* an àm i., *in good time.*
iomchuidheach, *a.* Applicable.
———d, *s.f.* Fitness, meetness, suitableness, applicability. 2 Propriety, decency. 3 Expediency, adequateness. 4 Convenience, advantageousness.
iomchuidhead, -id, *s.m.* Fitness, degree of fitness, propriety, convenience, suitableness, expediency.
iomchuinn, see iomchan.
†iom-dha, -ai, *s.m.* Anger. 2 Bed, couch. 3 Shoulder.
iomdhathach, see iomadhathach.
iomdhaithte, see iomadhaithte.
iom-dhealaichte,‡‡ *a.* Insulated.
iom-dhealbhach,‡‡ -aiche, *a.* Mosaic.
iom-dhearbh, *v.a.* Prove, demonstrate.
———adh, -aidh, *s.m.* Proof, demonstration. Bheir mi dhuit i. air, *I will give you a proof of it.*
iom-dhearbhail,** *a.* Demonstrative, capable of proof or demonstration.
iom-dhearbhta,** *past pt.* Proved, demonstrated.
†iom-dhearg,** *v.a.* Reprove, rebuke, reproach, dispraise.
†iom-dheargach, *a.* Prone to reprove or rebuke.
†iom-dheargta, *past pt.* Reviled, reproved, rebuked.
iom-dhìol,** *s.m.* Feast.
iom-dhòigheach,‡‡ -eiche, *a.* Diverse.
iomdhorus, -uis, -dhorsan, *s.m.* Lintel of a door. 2 Back door. 3 Porch.
iom-dhreachmhor, -oire, *a.* Changeable.
iomdhruid, *pr.pt.* ag iomdhruideadh, *v.a.* Enclose, surround, shut in. 2 Besiege.
———each,** *a.* Surrounding, encompassing, hemming in. 2 Besieging.
———eadh, -idh, *s.m.* Enclosing, act of enclosing, surrounding. 2 Enclosure. 3 Siege, besieging. Tha iad air i., *they are hemmed in on all sides.* Ag i—, *pr.pt.* of iomdhruid.
———te, *past pt.* of iomdhruid. Enclosed, surrounded.
iom-eagal, -ail, *s.m.* Terror, fright.
———ach, *a.* Fearful, terrible, frightful.
iom-eud, *s.f.* Jealousy, extreme suspicion.
———air, *s.m.* Jealous man, suspicious man.
———mhor, -mhoire, *a.* Jealous, suspicious.
iom-fhacal, -ail, *s.m.* Circumlocution.
iom-fheadan, *s.m.* Discomfiture.
iom-fhill,‡‡ *v.a.* Enwrap.
———teach,†† *a.* Many-folded.
———teachadh, -aidh, *s. m.* Act of folding frequently making manifold. Ag i—, *pr.pt.* of iom-fhilltich.
———tich, *v.a.* Fold often, make manifold.
———tichte, *past pt.* of iom-fhilltich. Often folded, made manifold.
†iom-fhorail, *s.f.* Superfluity, extravagance, excess.
†iom-fhorran, -ain, *s.m.* Skirmish. 2 Battle. 3 Comparison.
iom-fhuadan, *s.m.* Discomfiture.
iom-fhuasgail, *v.a.* Trade. 2 Relieve, loosen, slacken.
iom-fhuasgailteach, -eiche, *a.* Nimble.
iom-fhuasglach, -aiche, *a.* Giving immediate or temporary relief. 2 Apropos, seasonably useful. 3 Auxiliary.
iom-fhuasgladh, -aidh, -aidhean, *s. m.* Relief, release, convenience, assistance. 2* Traffic, trade. 3 Something to trade with. 4 Housekeeping. 5 Minor equipment, small conveniences, as those of the work-basket. Is tu sheall air t' i., *it is you that looked on your many-sided relief*—said when a person does a strange thing he might have done much better in another way.
iom-fhulang, -aing, -an, *s. m.* Patience, long-suffering, forbearance.
———ach, -aiche, *a.* Patient, forbearing.
iom ghabh, *v.a.* Take, conquer, reduce, capture. 2 Err, stray. 3 Avoid, shun. 4 Wander.
———ail, -ala, *s. m.* Taking, act of taking, reducing or conquering. 2 Erring, straying. 3 Shunning. Ag i—, *pr.pt.* of iom-ghabh.
iomghaoth, see iomaghaoth.
———ach, -aiche, see iomaghaothach.
†iom-ghnùis, *s.f.* Wonder.
iom-ghlainte, *past pt.* of iom-ghlan. Purified,
iom-ghlan, *v.a.* Cleanse, purify.
———adh, -aidh, *s.m.* Purifying, act of purifying. Ag i—, *pr.pt.* of iomghlan. cleaned.
iom-ghlòir, *s.f.* Noise of a multitude.
iom-ghnèitheach,** *a.* see ioma-ghnéitheach.
———d, *s.f.* see ioma-ghnéitheachd, (appendix.)
iom-ghointe, *past pt.* of iom-ghon. see ioma-ghointe, (appendix.)
iom-ghon, *v.a.* see ioma-ghon (appendix.)
———ach, -aiche, *a.* see ioma-ghonach.
———adh, -aidh, *s.m.* see ioma-ghonadh, (appendix.)
iom-ghuin,** *s.f.* see ioma-ghuin, (appendix.)
———each,** *a.* Painful. 2 Causing a variety of wounds. 3 Inflicting many wounds. Gu h-i., *painfully.*
iomhach,** *a.* Envious.
iomhadh,** -aidh, *s.m.* Envy.
iomhag, *s.f.* Ivory.
———ach, *a.* Ivory, pertaining to ivory.
ìomhaigh, -ean, *s. f.* Image, statue. 2 Likeness, similitude. 3 Countenance, expression of countenance. 4** Idiom, figure of speech. 'Na ì. féin, *in his own likeness;* ì. mhór, *a great image;* cha tuig thu a h-ì., *you will not understand its idioms.*
———each, -eiche, *a.* Full of images.
———eachd,** *s.f.* Imagery. 2‡‡Imagination.
iomharraichte,(MS) *a.* Peculiar.
†iomhas,** -ais, *s. m.* Knowledge, judgment, learning.
iom-itealaiche, *s.* Circumvolution.
iomla, see iomluath.
iomlach,§ *s.m.* The cup-shaped frond from which the long thongs spring in seaweed *hemanthalia lorea.*
iomlag, see imleag.
iomlagach, -aiche, *a.* see imleagach.
iomlaid, -ean, *s.f.* Exchange, barter. 2 Change. 3 Act of exchanging. 4* Course, duration. 5**Moving, gesture. Dean i., *exchange;* ann an i. da là, *in the course of two days;* i. chiomach, *an exchange of prisoners;* fear-i., *a broker;* luchd-i., *brokers;* am bheil i. nòt agad? *have you change for a £1 bank-note?* Ag i—, *pr.pt.* of iomlaid.
———, *v.a.* see iomlaidich.
———each, -eiche, *a.* Moving, fickle, prone to change. 2* Tossing, as a sick person, restless. 3††Fluctuating. 4** Exchanging, bartering. Side i., *changeable weather.*
———eachadh, -aidh, *s.m.* Changing, fluctuating. 2 Act of changing or exchanging. 3 Winding, rolling, turning. Ag i—, *pr.pt.* of iomlaidich.
———eachd, *s.f.ind.* Rolling, turning, wind-

ing, tumbling, unsteadiness, changeableness, fickleness, 2 Exchange, barter.
iomlaideadh, see iomlaideachadh.
iomlaidich, *pr.pt.* ag iomlaideachadh, *v.a.* Exchange, change, barter, commute.
iomlaidiche, *s.m.* Barterer, exchanger.
iomlaine, *s.f.* see iomlanachd. 1. cridhe, *integrity of heart.*
————, *comp.* of iomlan.
————achd, see iomlanachd.
iomlan, -aine, *a.* Full, complete, perfect. 2 Sound. 3 Absolute. 4 (DMC) Changeable. —*Harris.* Duine i., *a perfect man ;* fo i. blàth, *in full blossom ;* gu h-i. *completely.*
————, -ain, *s.m.* Whole, all. An t-i. dhiubh, *the whole of them.*
————achadh,** -aidh, *s.m.* Act of carrying to completion, completing.
————achd, *s.f.ind.* Perfection, fulness, maturity. 2 Integrity. 3**Completion, consummation, fulfilment, accomplishment.
————aich, *pr.pt.* ag iomlanachadh, *v.a.* Fulfil, complete, consummate.
————aichte, *past pt.* of iomlanaich. Consummated, perfected, completed.
————tachd, see iomlanachd.
iomlasgadh, see iomluasgadh.
iomlat,** -ait, *s.m.* Gesture.
iom-leabhar,** -air, -bhraichean, *s.m.* Volume.
iom-leag, see imleag.
————ach, see imleagach.
iom-loisg,** *v.a.* Parch.
————te, *a.* Adust.
iom-losgadh,** *s.m.* Adustion, parching.
†iomluadh, *s. m.* Talking much. 2** Great praise.
————,** *v.a. & n.* Speak often or too much. 2 Praise often or too much.
————,(MS) *a.* Maggotty.
†————ail, -e, *a.* Wandering, straying.
iom-luagach, *a.* Apt to stray, wandering, straggling.
iom-luagail,** *s.f.* Straying, wandering, straggling.
†iomluaiche, *s.* see iomluadh.
iom-luaidh,** *s.f.* Great praise.
iomluaineach, -eiche, *a.* Inconstant, unsteady.
————d, *s.f.ind.* Fickleness, inconstancy, unsteadiness, fidgeting.
iomluaineas,(MS) *s.m.* Humorousness.
iomluaisg, *v.a.* Confuse, disorder. 2*Toss, tumble. 3 Move often. 4** Move hither and thither.
————te, *past pt.* of iomluaisg. 2 Confused, disordered. 3 Rocked to and fro, moved hither and thither. 4 Moved often.
iomluas, see iomluathas.
iomluasg,** -aisg, *s.m.* Anxiety.
————ach, -aiche, *a.* Anxious, fidgeting, restless. 2 Moving to and fro. 3 Agitating, rocking, tossing to and fro. 4(MS) Giddy-headed. Gu h-i., *with a rocking motion.*
————adh, -aidh, *s. m.* Commotion, confusion. 2 Act of confusing, disordering or deranging. 3 Agitation, restlessness. 4 Moving, or rocking to and fro. Ag i—, *pr.pt.* of iomluaisg.
iomluath, -uaithe, *a.* Inconstant, wandering, giddy, arbitrary, wavering, fickle, changeable.
iomluathachas, see iomluathas.
iomluathas, -ais, *s.m.* Inconstancy, fickleness. 2**Lightness, freedom from weight or burden. 3**Velocity. 4 (MS) Solicitude. 5(MS) Giddiness. 6(MS) Humorousness.
iomnuach,(MS) *a.* Anxious. 2 Vigilant.
iomnaidh,** *s. f.* Care. 2 Diligence. 3 Anxiety, solicitude. 4 Haste.
————each,** *a.* Careful, intent. 2 Solicitous, anxious.
————eachd, *s.f.* Anxiety, solicitude.
iomnuachadh,** *s.m.* Polygamy.
iomnuachar,** -air, *s.m.* Polygamy.
iom-oisinneach, -eiche, *a.* Polygonous, multangular.
————d, *s.f.* Multangularness.
iomordadh,** -aidh, *s.m.* Reproach, expostulation.
iomorran,** -ain, *s.m.* Comparison.
iompachadh, -aidh, *s.m.* Conversion, turning, converting. 2 Act of converting. 3**Petitioning, beseeching. Tha e air i., *he is converted.* Ag i—, *pr. pt,* of iompaich.
iompachail,** *a.* Convertible.
iompachair,** -eau, *s.m.* Converter.
iompachan, -ain, *s.m.* Convert, proselyte. 2 **Penitentiary.
iompadh,(CR) *s.m.* Advice, counsel. Thug e i. air, *he advised him* ; Luchd-iompaidh, *the Cabinet. Skye.*
iompaich, *pr.pt.* ag iompachadh, *v. a.* Turn. reel. 2 Convert, persuade, constrain. 3 Beseech, pray.
————ear, *fut pass.* of iompaich.
————idh, *fut.aff.a.* of iompaich.
————te, *past pt.* of iompaich. Converted, persuaded.
iompaidh, see impidh & iompaichidh.
————,(MS) *s. & v.a.* Bias.
————each,** *a.* Intercessory, mediatory.
————each, *s.m.* Intercessor, petitioner. Converter.
iompair, *s.m.* see impire, (appendix.)
————eachd, *s.f.ind.* see impireachd.
————eil, *a.* see impireil.
iompoich, see iompaich.
iompoidh, see impidh.
iompoll,** -oill, *s.m.* Error.
iomrachadh, -aidh, *s.m. & pr.pt.* see imreachadh.
iomrachan, -ain, -an, *s.m.* Carriage, bier.
iomradh, *v.n.* Report, publish, divulge.
iomradh, -aidh, -aidhean, *s. m.* Fame, report, mention. 2 Reporting, mentioning, act of mentioning. 3 Rumour, saying. 4** Memory. 5**Abundance. 6 see iomramh. 7 (DMC) Consideration, thought. Tha 'n leithid sin de i. am measg dhaoine, *there is such a report among people :* duine gun i., *an obscure man ;* gu'n sgathadh e an i., *that he would cut off their memory.*
iomraich, see imrich.
————te, see imrichte.
iomraideach, -eiche, see iomraiteach.
†iomraidh, *pr. pt.* ag iomradh, *v. a.* Mention, publish, report, repeat.
iomraidh,(DMy) *s.* Anxiety. Tha i. agam air an son, *I am anxious about them.*
iomraidhteach, see iomraiteach.
iomraidich,(WC) *v.a.* Carry a burden. An i. thu sin ? *can you carry that ?*
iomraim, see iomramh.
iomraiteach, -eiche, *a.* Famous, famed, eminent, renowned, celebrated. Ni i., *a notorious thing ;* tha do chliù i., *your fame is well-known ;* dh' fhàs iad 'nan daoine i., *they became men of renown.*
————d,‡‡ *s.f.* Famousness.
iomrall, -aill, -an, *s.m.* Error, wandering, straying, aberration, departing. 2 Entanglement, entwining. Air i., *astray ;* chaidh làithean na seachduin i. orra, *they lost count of the days of the week.*
iomrallach, -aiche, *a.* Erroneous, wrong, straying, wandering, errant.

iomrallachd,‡‡ *s.f.* Preposterousness.
iomralladh, -aidh, *s. m.* Straying, wandering. Air i., *straying.*
iomrallaich,‡‡ *v.a.* Bewilder. 2 Blunder.
———e,‡‡ *s.m.* Blunderer. 2 Wanderer, straggler. 3 Vagabond.
iomram, see iomramh.
iomramh, *v.a.* see iomair.
iomramh, -aimh, *s.m.* Rowing, act of rowing, as a boat. Ag i—, *pr pt.* of iomair. Is e i. an droch là a ni là math gu i., *practise rowing in a rough sea and soon the rough sea will seem calm to you—lit.* 'tis the rowing of the bad day that makes the good day for rowing —a proverb that may be applied to matters of greater importance than the rowing of a boat.
iomramhaiche, -an, *s.m.* Rower.
iomrasgal,** -ail, *s.m.* Wrestling.
iom-reuson,** -oin, *s. m.* Verbal controversy, wrangle, dispute, argument.
———ach,** *a.* Controversial, inclined to wrangle.
———aiche,** *s.m.* Wrangler, controversialist, disputant.
iomridh, see feumaidh. 2 see iomraidh.
iomrol,** see iomrall.
———ach, see iomrallach.
iom-ruag, *v.a.* Disperse, rout, pursue. Invade. 3 Persecute. 4 Defeat.
iom-ruagach,** *a.* Scattering. 2 Persecuting. 3 Pursuing. 4 Scaring.
iom-ruagadh, -aidh, -aidhean, *s.m.* Persecuting. 2 Act of persecuting, persecution. 3 Dispersing, routing, rout, irregular scattered pursuit. 4 Invasion. 5 Defeat.
iom-ruagair, -ean, *s.m.* Persecutor. 2 Invader. 3 Pursuer.
iom-ruagte, *past pt.* of iom-ruag. Persecuted. 2 Dispersed, routed. 3 Invaded. 4**Scared.
iom-ruaig** see iom-ruag.
———, *s.f.* see iom-ruagadh.
———te, see iom-ruagte.
†iomruin, *v.a.* Assign, appoint.
†———eadh, *s.m.* Assigning, appointing. Ag i—, *pr.pt.* of iom-ruin.
iomruitheach, -eiche, *a.* Current, circulatory.
†iomsach, *a.* Revengeful, enraged, furious.
†iomsachan, -ain, *s.m.* Rage, fury.
iomsgair, *v. a.* Separate, disperse, rout. 2 Scare. 3 Excommunicate.
iom-sgaoil, *v.a.* Disperse, rout, scatter in various directions. 2 Scare. 3 Slack, loosen, untighten.
iom-sgaoileadh, -idh, *s.m.* Dispersing, routing. 2 Act of dispersing. 3 Scaring. 4 (MS) Currency.
iom-sgaoilte, *past pt.* of iom-sgaoil. Dispersed, routed, scattered.
iom-sgaoilteachd,* *s. f.* Slackness, looseness, freedom.
iom-sgaoiltear,** *s.m.* Disperser.
iom-sgapadh,(MS) *s.m.* Currency.
iomsgar, see iomsgair.
iom-sgarach,** *a.* Dispersing, separating, routing. 2 Scaring.
———d,** *s.f.* Separation, dispersement, scattering.
iom-sgarachduinn, see iomsgaradh.
iom-sgaradh, -aidh, *s.m.* Separation, dispersion. 2 Excommunication. 3 Act of separating or excommunicating.
iom-sgobadh, -aidh, -aidhean, *s.m.* Excessive anxiety. *prov.*
iom-sgoilt, *v.a.* Split into many pieces.
iom-sgoilte, *past pt.* of iom-sgoilt. Split into many pieces.
iom-sgoltadh, -aidh, *s.m.* Splitting. 2 Act of splitting into many pieces. 3‡‡Superfluity, excess.
iom-sheol, *v.a.* Circumnavigate.
———adair, *s.m.* Circumnavigator.
———adh, -aidh, *s.m.* Circumnavigation.
iom-shruth, *s.m.* Circumfluence.
———ach, *a* Circumfluent.
iom-shiolladh, -aidh, -aidhean, *s.m.* Polysyllable.
iom-shiubhail, *v.a.* Go round. 2 Surround. 3 Walk about, ramble.
iom-shiubhal, -ail, *s. m.* Walking about. 2 Ramble. Ag i—, *pr.pt.* of iom-shiubhail.
iom-shiubhlach, *a.* Erratic, wandering.
iom-shluaghach, -aiche, *a.* Many-peopled.
iom-shniomh,** *s. m.* Care, anxiety. 2 Restlessness. 3 Convolution. 4 Twisting. 5 Diligence.
———ach,** -aiche, *a.* Ghastly. 2 Restless, uneasy, anxious. 3 Twisting, convolving.
iomshruth,-uith, -uithean, *s.m.* Eddying stream or tide, cross-current.
iomshruthach, -aiche, *a.* Having counter-tides.
iom-shùileach,‡‡ *a.* Multocular.
iom-smuainich, *v.a.* Balance in the mind.
†iomtheachd, -an, see imeachd.
iom-theangach, -aiche, *a.* Of many tongues, polyglot.
†iom-thnùth, -a, -an, *s.m.* Zeal. 2 Envy.
†iom-thnùthair, -ean, *s.m.* Zealous lover.
†iom-thoineadh, -idh, -idhean, *s.f.* Digression. 2 Year.
iom-throm,** *a.* Very heavy.
†iom-thuathach, -aiche, *a.* Boundless, immoderate.
iom-thus,** *s. m.* Departure, migration. 2 Chance.
†iomthusa, *s.pl.* Adventures. 2 History.
iomuireadh,** -idh, *s.m.* Excess. 2 Exacting.
ion, -e, *a.* Fit, befitting, suitable, proper. [Used as a preposition in compounds to signify fitness.] Is i. dhuit teicheadh, *you have great reason to flee*; cha'n i. dhòmh-sa ach a bhi 'gad mholadh, *it is befitting indeed that I should praise you*; cha'n i. ni sam bith a dhiùltadh, *nothing is proper to be refused.*
ion-, *prefix,* Fitness. Ionmholta, *worthy to be praised.*
ion-,‡ *negative prefix* an before *d, f* or *g.*
ion, *adv. & prep.* Almost, all but. I. is iomlan, *almost perfect—Dàin I. Ghobha.*
†ion,** *prep.* In. Tuagh i. a làimh, *an axe in his hand.*
†ion, -a, -an, *s.m.* Image. 2**Sun. 3**Circle.
ion-acain, -e, *a.* Lamentable, deplorable.
iona-chasach, (WC) *s.m.* Seaweed black and very bushy on each stem found at low-water.
ionach,** -aich, *s.m.* Dirk.
ionad, -aid, -an, *s.m.* Place, room, abode, office. 2 Position. I. naomh, *a sanctuary*; i. aoraidh, *a place of worship*; i. tasgaidh, *storehouse, granary.*
†ionad, see annad
ionadach, -aich, *s.m* Enallage in *grammar,* inserting one word in place of another.
ionadach,** -aiche, *a* Local. 2 Representative, deputy. 3 Fond of one's place.
ionadachd, *s.f.ind.* Locality. 2 Deputation.
ionadal,(DMC) *a.* Friendly, hospitable. 2 Clannish.
ionadalachd, *s.f.* Kind disposition, fraternity.
ionadas,** -ais, *s.m.* Locality.
ionad-ciùil, *s.m.* Choir, part of a church.
ionadh, see ioghnadh.
ionadh, (e.g. c' iona ? *or* c' ion ?) Whither ?
ionaid,** *s.m.* Vicegerent.

ional, *v.a.* see ionnlaid.
ionailt,(MS) *s.f.* Feed, grazing. Ag i—, see (ag) ionaltradh.
ionailte, see ionailt.
†**ionair**,** *a.* Clothe.
——,** *s.m.* Pudenda.
†**ion-àirmhichte**, *a.* Numerable, that may be numbered.
ion-àiteachaidh,** *a.* Habitable.
ion-àiteachail, -e, *a.* Habitable.
ion-àitichte, *a.* Habitable. 2 Arable, fit for cultivation.
ionalach,(MS) *a.* Generative.
ionaltair, -ean, *s.f.* see ionaltradh.
——, *pres. part.* ag ionaltradh [and ag ionailt,] *v.a.* Pasture, feed, browse, graze, feed in rough ground, or in the fields after the removal of the crops. The word implies more of movement on the part of the animal than is required in an enclosed field of good grass. When used of animals in such a field, the word means that they are eating, not lying down or standing still. The word is also used of poultry wandering about in search of food.
ionaltrach,** *a.* Grazing.
ionaltradh, -aidh, *s.m.* Pasture. 2 Pasturing. feeding, grazing. 3 Act of pasturing. Ag i—, *pr.pt.* of ionaltair.
ionamhuil, *a.* Like, equal, the same, well-matched, seeming, comparable.
ionann, *a.* Equal, alike, similar, the same, "ditto," just so, all the same, in like manner, in a suitable manner. Is i. sin is mar a thachras dhuit, *just so shall happen you ;* is i. sin, *that is all the same* ; is i. iad, *they are all the same* or *identical* ; cha'n i. dhaibh, *they are not the same* ; cha'n i. a fhreagras dà là màrgaidh, *two market days do not correspond ;* cha 'n i. a thig an còta glas do na h-uile fear, *the grey coat does not become everyone equally well;* i. agus am fiaclan air chrith, *even their teeth chattering ;* tha i. an Donais ort, *you have the appearance of the Evil One ;* i. agus sinn, *equal to us ;* i. 's a bhi rùisgte, *the same as if naked;* uile i., *all the same, quite the same.*
ionnanach, *a.* Identical, equal, the same.
ionannachd, *s. f. ind.* Equality, equalization, identity, similarity, sameness.
ionannaich,‡‡ *v.a.* Compare, assimilate.
ionannas, -ais, *s.m.* Mediocrity. An i., *tolerable*
ionaol,** *v.a.* Whitewash. 2 Plaster.
ion-aoraidh, *a.* Adorable.
ionar,** -air, *s.m.* Kind of mantle. 2 The bowels. 3 Burden.
†**ionaradh**,** -aidh, *s. m.* Clothing. 2 (DMy) Tossing or moving violently with the feet.
ionarbhach,** -aich, *s. m.* Banisher. 2 Destroyer.
ionarbhadh,** -aidh, *s. m.* Banishing, banishment, expulsion.
†**ion-bhaidh**,** *s.f.* Time of a woman's bearing. 2 Parturition. 3 Time or hour.
ionbhar, -air, *s. m.* Confluence of waters. 2 Mouth of a river. 3 Cove or creek at the mouth of a river. 4*Angular piece of ground at the confluence of two waters. Often written *inbhir*, but its gender demands the termination *-ar*, and everyone says *ionbhar*.
ion-bholg,** *v.a.* Swell, bulge out, as a sail with wind.
————adh,** -aidh, *s.m.* Swelling, bulging out.
ion-bhreith,** *s.f.* Perfect birth.
ionbhruich, -ean, see eun-bhrigh & eanraich.
————each, -eiche, see eun-bhrigheach.
ionbhuadhach, -aiche, *a.* Victorious, triumphant.
ioncamas,** -ais, *s.m.* Gaelic spelling of *income*.
ion-cheadachas,(MS) *s.m.* Allowableness.
ion-cheannachach,** *a.* Purchasable.
ion-chliùiteach, -eiche, *a.* Admirable.
————d, *s.f.* Admirableness.
ion-choimeas, see ion-choimeasail.
ion-choimeasail,** *a.* Comparable. 2 Easily matched.
ion-choimheartaich,(MS) *v.n.* Allude.
ion-choimhead,** *a.* Conservable, easily preserved.
ion-choimheartas,(MS) *s.m.* Allusion.
ion-choimheartach (MS) *a.* Allusive.
ion-choluinneadh,** -idh, *s. m.* Incarnation, becoming incarnate.
ion-choimeas,** *a.* Comparable, easily matched.
ion-choireach, -eiche, *a.* Blameworthy.
————d, *s.f.* Blameworthiness.
ion-choluinnich,** *v.n.* Become incarnate.
————te,** *past pt.* Incarnated, become incarnate.
ion-chomharraichte, *a.* Remarkable, notable.
ion-chònspoideach, -eiche, *a.* Debatable.
ion-chosanta,** *a.* Defensible.
†**ion-chosg**, -choisg, *s.m.* Impediment, hinderance. 2 Desire. 3**Instruction.
†**ion-chosgair**,** *s.m.* Teacher.
†**ionchrasal**, -ail, *s.m.* Excrement.
ion-chruinn,** *a.* Homocentric.
ionchuinneach (MS) *a.* see eanchainneach.
ion-chuimhneachadh, -aidh, *a.* Memorable.
ion-dhealaiche,(MS) *s.* Separability.
ion-dhèanta, *a.* Feasible, practicable.
ion-dhìoladh,** *a.* Vendible.
ion-dhìtealta,** *a.* Indictable.
ion-dhìtidh, *a.* Indictable.
ion-dìolaiche,** *s.m.* One able to pay.
ion-duile,** *a.* Desirable.
ion-duthras,** -ais, *s.m.* Negligence.
ion-éirigh, *s.f.* Late sitting. Moch éirigh is i., *early rising and late sitting.*
ion-fhaicsinneach, -eiche, *a.* Worthy to be seen. 2 Notable.
ion-fhaileas, -eis, -an, *s.m.* Kind, sort, species.
ion-fhir,** *a.* Marriageable, fit for a husband.
ion-fhochaideach, -eiche, *a.* Mockable.
ion-fhorran,** -ain, *s.m.* Fight, skirmish.
ion-fhreagarrach, -aiche, *a.* Apt. 2 Fit.
ion-fhulang, *a.* Passable.
ionga, ingne, *pl.* ingnean [ionganan & inean,] *s. f.* Nail, claw, talon. 2 Hoof. 3 Cloven hoof. Inean a' ghrapa, *the prongs of the dung-fork ;* inean na cléithe, *the harrow's teeth ;* ionganan mar spuirean, *nails like claws;* chaidh am prìne 'san ionga, *the pin touched the quick;* i. eòin, *a bird's claw ;* i. eich, *a horse's hoof ;* is ann air 'ingnean a dh' aithnichear duin'-uasal, *the gentleman is known by his nails*—an old Hebridean rule for judging the rank of unknown bodies washed ashore by the sea. Neatly-pared nails were held to denote the gentleman, and insured for the corpse at least decent burial ; blanag nan ingnean, *the quick of the nails.*
iongach, -aiche, *a.* Having nails, clawed, hoofed. 2**Having long nails or claws. 3 Having strong hoofs. 4**Miserly, avaricious. An galar i., *agnail.*
iongadach, -aiche, *a.* see iongantach.
iongaideach, see iongantach.
iongain, *Suth'd* for ionga. Old oblique case used as nom.
iongannach, see iongach.
iongantach, -aiche, *a.* Wonderful, surprising, strange, extraordinary. 2 Droll. Fear i., *a droll fellow.*
————d,** *s. f.* Astonishment. 2 Marvellousness, miraculousness, strangeness. 3 Ad-

mirableness.
iongantaich, *v.a.* Astonish.
———e, *comp.* of iongantach.
iongantais, *gen.sing. & n. pl.* of iongantas.
iongantas, -ais, -an, *s.m.* Wonder, miracle, surprise, astonishment, marvellousness. 2 ** Curiosity, phenomenon. 3 Mark of admiration in *grammar* (!). Ghabh mi i., *I wondered;* tha thu 'cur i. orm, *you surprise me.*
iongantasachd,** *s.f.* Admirability.
iongar, *gen.* -air & iongarach, *pl.* -air, *s. m.* Matter, purulent matter, pus, corrupted humour.
———ach, -aiche, *a.* Purulent, abounding in purulent matter.
———achadh, -aidh, *s.m. & pr.pt.* see iongrachadh.
iongaraich, *v.n.* see iongraich.
†ion-ghabh, *v.a.* Manage, conduct, guide, lead. 2 Attack. 3 Subject, reduce.
†———ail, *s. f.* Management, reputation. 2 Conduct, gesture. 3 Circumspection.
ionghar,** -air, see iongar.
———ach, see iongarach.
ionghnadaireachd,(MS) *s.f.* Scratch.
ionghnadh, see iongnadh.
ion-ghnètheach,** *a.* Homogeneous.
ion-ghràidh,‡‡ -e, *a.* Worthy to be loved, lovely, becoming.
———achd, *s.f.* Charmingness.
ionglan,** *a.* Dirty, nasty, unclean.
iongmhas, see ionmhas.
———ach, see ionmhasach.
iongna, see ionga.
iongnach, -aiche, *a.* Pounced.
iongnadh, -aidh, -aidhean, *s.m.* Wonder, surprise, astonishment. Cha'n i. leam, *I am not at all surprised ;* gu m' i., *to my astonishment.*
———, *a.* [given as iunadh by **] *a.* Strange, wonderful, odd, curious.
iongneach, *a.* see iongach.
iongrach, see iongar.
———,†† *a.* Suppurating.
———adh, -aidh, *s.m.* Suppuration, act of suppurating. 2 Abscess. Ag i—, *pr. pt.* of iongraich.
———ail, see iongarach.
iongraich, *pr. pt.* ag iongrachadh, [& ag iongradh,] *v. a.* Suppurate. 2**Digest. Dh' i. a chas, *his foot suppurated.*
———te, *a. & past pt.* Suppurated.
iongraidh, -e, *a.* Worthy to be loved, dearly loved.
ionladh,** -aidh, *s.m.* Washing. 2 Thing acceptable.
ionlaid, see ionnlaid.
ionlairt, (ion+labhairt) *s.f.* Tautology, repeating the same word often.
ionlasda,** *a.* Inflammable.
ion-leighis, -e, *a.* Curable.
ion-leithsgeulach, -aiche, *a.* Excusable.
ionmail,(AF) *s.* Cattle.
ion-mhagaidh, -e, *a.* Ridiculous.
ionmhainn, see ionmhuinn.
ion-mhaith,** *a.* Ignoscible, pardonable.
———te, *a.* Pardonable.
ion-mhall,** *a.* Slow. 2 Fatigued.
———, *s.m.* Slowness. 2 Fatigue.
ionmhas, -ais, -an, *s.m.* Treasure, wealth, riches. Móran ionmhais, *or* ionmhas mór, *much treasure.*
ionmhasach, -aiche, *a.* Full of treasure. 2 Wealthy, rich.
ionmhasair, -ean, *s.m.* Treasurer.
———eachd,** *s.f.* Treasurership.
ionmhas-àite,** -achan, *s.m.* Treasury.
ion-mheadhonach,** *a.* Moderate, temperate.
ion-mheallta, *a.* Fallible, prone to err. 2 **Easily deceived.
ion-mheasail, -e, *a.* Estimable.
ion-mheasta, *a.* Reverend.
ion-mhiannachd, *s. f. ind.* Appetizement. 2 Desirability.
ion-mhiannaichte, *a.* Desirable.
ion-mholaidh, *a.* Adorable, praiseworthy.
ionmholta, *a.* Praiseworthy, laudable, deserving.
ionmholtachd,** *s. f.* Admirableness, praiseworthiness, meritoriousness.
ionmhothuichte, *a.* Perceptible.
ionmhùchta, *a.* Quenchable.
ionmhuinn, *comp.* -e, annsa & ionnsa, *a.* Dear, beloved. 2 Loving. 3 Kind, courteous. 4** Lovely. A mhac i., *his dearly beloved son ;* mar a b' i. leis, *as he greatly desired ;* is i. le gach neach a choslas, *every one is fond of his like.*
———,** *s.f.* Beloved person. I. bhàn, *a fair-haired beloved one.*
———each, -eiche, *a.* Beloved. 2 Lovely, lovable, desirable. 3 (DMC) Well-to-do, consequential. 4 Courteous, amiable. Duine i., *a man of position.*
———eachd, *s.f.* State of being beloved. 2 Endearment. 3 Amiability. 4 Kindness. 5 Courteousness.
———ich, *v.a.* Endear, make attached.
ion-mhuthachd,(MS) *s.f.* Alterableness.
ion-mhuthta,(MS) *a.* Alterable.
ionn-,‡ *prep. prefix* signifying Against, to. [Of same force as *frith* or *ri.*]
†ionn, *prep.* now written ann.
†ionn, -a, *s.f.* Upper part, head.
ionnach, see iomach.
†ionnad, see annad.
†ionnaibh, see annaibh.
ionnail, *v.a.* see ionnlaid.
ionnail,(AF) *s.* Cattle.
†ionnainn, see annainn.
ionnairidh, -ean, *s.f.* Watching at night. Luchd na h-ionnairidh, *the night watch.*
ionnal, see ionnlaid.
———adh, see ionnlad.
ionnaltoir, -ean, *s.f.* Bath. [** gives ionnaltair.]
†ionnam, see annam.
ionnan (gu h-), *adv.* Answerably.
†ionnar, -air, *s.m.* Gift.
†ionnarachd, *s.f.* Gift, donation, reward.
†ionnaradh, -aidh, *s.m.* see ionnarachd.
ionnas (gu h-) MS *adv.* Answerably.
ionnas, *conj.* (ionnas gu) Insomuch, so that. 2††Almost, nearly. C' ionnas ? *how ?*
———, -ais, *s.m.* see ionmhas.
†ionnchuir, *v.a.* Ingraft.
†———eadh, -idh, } *s.m.* Ingrafting. Ag i—,
ionnchur, -chuir, } *pr. pt.* of ionnchuir.
ionndag, see deanntag.
———ach, see deanntagach.
ionndraich, *v.a.* see ionndruinn.
———inn, see ionndruinn.
ionndrain, see ionndruinn.
ionndruich, see ionndruinn.
ionndruinn, *pr.pt.* ag ionndruinn, *v. n.* Miss, long for, feel the want of. Cò tha thu ag i. ? *who do you miss ?*
———, -ean, *s.m.* Missing, act of missing. 2 Want, feeling of want. 3 Straying, wandering. 4 The thing amissing. Am fac thu m' i. ? *did you see the thing I am missing ?*
ionnduras,** -ais, *s.m.* Purity, chastity.
ionndustaigh,(AC) *s.m.* Treasure-house.
ionnlach,** -aich, *s.m.* Fault, blemish. 2 Accusation.

ionnlad, -aid, *s.m.* Washing, act of washing, cleansing or bathing. Ag i—, *pr. pt.* of ionnlaid.
———ach, -aiche, *a.* Abluent.
ionnlaich,** *v.a.* Complain. 2 Accuse.
ionnlaid, *pr.pt.* ag ionnlad, *v.a.* Wash, bathe. 2 Cleanse, purify, purge.
———each,** *a.* Abluent. 2 Cleansing, purifying.
———eachd,** *s.f.* Bathing. 2 Cleansing, purification, state of being cleansed or purified.
ionnlaidte, *past pt.* of ionnlaid. Bathed, washed. 2 Cleansed.
ionnlaigh,** *s.f.* Accusation. 2 Fault, blemish.
ionnoir,** *s.pl.* Bowels, entrails.
†**ionnrac**, -aice, *a.* see ionraic.
ionnracan, -ain, see ionracan.
†**ionnracas**, see ionracas.
†**ionnrach**, -aich, see ionrach.
†**ionnradh**, see ionradh.
†———ach, -aiche, see ionradhach.
ionnraic, see ionraic.
ionnrain,** *v.a.* Count, reckon, calculate.
†**ionnramh**,** -aimh, *s.m.* Service, attendance.
ionnran,** -ain, *s.m.* Account, reckoning.
ionnrosg,** -oisg, *s.m.* Word.
ionnruith, -e, *a.* see ion-ruith.
ionnsa, see ionmhuinn.
ionnsach,** *a.* Sorrowful, fatal.
ionnsachadh, -aidh, *s.m.* Learning, information, scholarship. 2 Act of learning. 3 Teaching, art of teaching, training, instruction. Ag i—, *pr. pt.* of ionnsaich.
ionnsaich, *pr.pt.* ag ionnsachadh, *v. a.* Learn. 2 Teach, educate, instruct, train. 3** *rarely* Visit.
———te, *a.* & *past pt.* of ionnsaich. Learned, exercised, taught, trained, educated.
ionnsaigh, see ionnsuidh.
ionnsamhuil,** *a.* Comparable.
———,** *s.* Similitude.
ionnsramaid, Gaelic spelling of *instrument.*
ionnsuidh, -ean, *s. m.* Attempt. 2 Invasion. 3 Attack, assault, onset. 4* Rush, dash. Thug e i. orm, *he rushed at me.*
———, *prep.* (a dh' ionnsuidh) To, toward. Used substantively with possessive pronouns, do m' i., *to me;* do d' i., *to thee;* d' a i., *to him;* d' a h-i., *to her;* d' ar n-i., *to us;* do bhur n-i., *to you;* d' an i., *to them.*
†———, *v.a.* Attack, assault.
———each, -eiche, *a.* Irruptive, offensive. 2 Aggressive, apt to attack.
———each,** *s.m.* Aggressor. 2 Invader.
———ear,** *s. m.* Assailer, assailant, attacker.
ionnta, see annta.
†**ionntadh**, see tionndaidh.
ionntag, -aig, see deanntag.
———ach, -aich, *s.* see deanntag.
†———ach, -aiche, *a.* see deanntagach.
ionntas, -ais, -an, see ionmhas.
ionntlas, -ais, -an, *s.m.* Delight, bliss. 2 (WC) Pity—*Poolewe.* Chuir e i. orm, *I pitied him.*
——— ach, (WC) Pitiful. Nach i e? *is it not pitiful?*
ionntraich,‡ see ionndruinn.
ionnuil, *v.* see ionnlaid.
ionnus, see ionnas.
ion-ogha, see fionn-ogha.
ion-oibrichte, *a.* Malleable.
ion-òlta, *a.* Drinkable. 2 Palatable, as drink.
ion-pheanasda, *a.* Punishable.
ion-phòsaidh, see ion-phòsda.
ion-phòsda, *a.* Marriageable.
ionracan, -ain, -an, *s.m.* Upright or righteous man. 'Nuair a throideas na meairlich, thig an t-i. 'ga chuid, *when thieves cast out, the honest man gets his own.*
ionracas, -ais, -an, *s.m.* Righteousness, justness, innocence, integrity. Fear ionracais, *a righteous man;* fear na h-ionracais, *the righteous man;* luchd-ionracais, *righteous people;* luchd na h-ionracais, *the righteous people.*
†**ionrach**, -aich, *s.m.* Medical tent.
ionrachas, see ionracas.
ionradh,** -aidh, *s.m.* Plundering, laying waste, devastation.
ionradhach,** *a.* Devastating, laying waste, destroying.
———,** *s.m.* Plunderer. 2 Depopulator.
ionraic, -e, *a.* Righteous. 2 Just, faithful, honest. 3 Chaste. Duine i., *a just man.*
ionraice, *comp.* of ionraic. An ti a's ionraice, *the most upright person.*
ionranach, -aich, *s.m.* Accountant.
ion-roghnaichte, *a.* Preferable.
ion-roghnuidh, -e, *a.* Eligible. 2 Preferable.
ion-roghnuidheachd, *s.f.* Eligibility. 2 Preferableness.
ionruic, see ionraic.
ion-ruith,** *a.* Having a level, regular pace. 2 Running with equal speed. Each i., *a level-pa-ced horse.*
†**ion-samhuil**, *a.* Like, such like, just like, comparable.
ionsanach,** *a.* Tardy.
†**ion-sgamhach**,** -aich, *s.m.* Looseness of the skin.
ion-sgaraidh, (MS) *s.f.* Separability.
ion-shamhlachadh, (MS) *s.m.* Allusion.
ion-shamhlachaidh,‡‡ *a.* Imitable.
ion-shamhlaich, (MS) *v.n.* Allude.
ion-shamhlaichte,** *a.* Comparable.
ion-shamhuileach, *a.* Imitable.
ion-sheachnach, -eiche, *a.* Avoidable.
ion-shealgach, -aiche, *a.* Chaseable.
ion-shiubhal,** *a.* Passable.
ion-smachdachaidh, *a.* Punishable, torturable.
ion-smuaineach,** *a.* Imaginable, supposable.
†**iontadh**, -aidh, -aidhean, see tionndadh.
ion-thaitneach, -aiche, *a.* Cloyless.
ion-thollta,** *a.* Penetrable, easily bored.
ion-thruasach, -aiche, *a.* Pitiable.
———d, *s.f.* Pitiableness.
ionus, see ionnas.
iorailte,** *s.f.* Ingenuity.
———ach, *a.* Ingenious, inventive, well-contrived. Am feadan i., *the well-contrived flute.*
———achd, *s.f.* Ingenuity, inventiveness.
ioralt, -an, *s.m.* Trick. Ioraltan, *harmless tricks.*
ioralta, -ailte, *a.* Ingenious. 2 Distinct. 3 Artificial.
ioras, *adv.* Down, below.
ioraslaich, *v.a.* see irioslaich.
iorball, -aill, -an, see earball.
———ach, -aiche, *a.* see earballach.
iorbhail,‡ -ean, *s.f.* Infection, corruption, noxious taint. I. gach gaoid, *the taint of each blemish.*
iorcallach, -aich, *s.m.* Robust or strong man.
iorchadach, -aiche, *a.* Evil, pernicious.
ior-dhalta,** *a.* Certain, constant, continual.
———chd,** *s.f.* Certainty, constancy.
iorgail, see iargall.
iorgal, -ail, *s.m.* see iargall.
iorghuil, -ean, see iargall.
iorghuileach, -eiche, see iargallach.
†**iorghuis**,** *s.f.* Prayer, request.
iorgull, see iargall.
iorguilleach, see iargallach.
iorgull, see iargall.

iorlann,** *s.m.* Cellar, buttery, larder.
iomadh, *Lewis* for iomradh.
†iormailt, -ean, *s.f.* see iarmailt.
iornall,(DMK) *W. coast of Ross* for iomrall.
iorna, see iarna.
iornalais,* *s.f.* Lumber.
iornan, see iarnan.
†iorpais, -ean, *s.f.* Dropsy. 2 Restlessness, fidgeting. 3 Wrestling, striving.
iorpaiseach, *a.* Dropsical. 2 Restless.
iorrach, -aiche, *a.* Quiet, undisturbed.
iorrais,(DMC) *s.f.* Noisy, fidgety behaviour.
iorram, -aim, *s m.* Boat-song, rowing-song. 2 **Tedious rhyme. 3** Song sung during any kind of work, by way of lightening its burden. 4**Fidgeting. 5(DMC) Anything said repeatedly.
iorramach,†! *a.* Belonging to boat-songs, like a boat-song.
ios, *prep.* (a dh' fhios) To. A dh' fhios an àite, *to the place.*
ios,** *v.a.* Eat, dine.
†ios, *adv.* Down. 2**East.
ios ! *int.* Cry to incite a dog after any animal tame or wild. 2 (DMC) Cry to stop a horse.
iosad, see iasad.
†iosadh, -aidh, *s.m.* Eating, act of eating.
iosal, isle, *a.* Low, not high. 2 Low, humble, poor. 3 Low, mean, abject. 4**Downcast Os i., *secretly, privately.*
iosban, see isbean.
ioscaid, -ean, see iosgaid.
†iosda, -ais, *s.m.* House, dwelling.
†iosdail,** *a.* Convenient, commodious.
†iosdan,** -ain, *s.m.* Cottage.
iosdas,** -ais, *s.m.* Entertainment. 2 Accommodation, lodging.
iosgad, -aid, see iosgaid.
iosgaid, -ean, *s.f.* The hough, ham, thigh.
iosgaideach, -eiche, *a.* Belonging to houghs. 2 Having large thighs. 3 Having slender thighs.
iosgaideach,* *s.m.* Term of contempt for a tall slender person.
iosgann,** -ainn, *s.m.* Thigh, hip.
iosgannach, *a.* Having large thighs or hips. 2 Of, or belonging to the thigh.
iosgaidh ! *int.* Call to a dog to drive away cattle.
iosgas ! *int.* Call to a dog to drive away cattle.
iosg-thad ! *int.* Cry to a dog to drive away cattle.
ioslachadh, see isleachadh.
ioslaich, see islich.
ioslann, *s.m.* Pantry, storehouse, buttery.
iosop, -oip, *s.f.* Hyssop—*hyssopus officinalis.*
iosp, *s.m.* Clasp for a padlock on a door, meal-chest, &c 2 (WC) Tool used by tinkers for putting finishing touches on horn spoons.
iospainn, *s.* see isbean. 2 (DMy) Entrails.
iostal, *Suth'd* for iosal.
ios-thad ! *int.* Cry to incite a dog after any animal, tame or wild.
iosuid, *s.m.* Jesuit.
——each, *a.* Jesuitical.
iota, see iotadh.
iotach, -aiche, see iotmhor.
iotadh, -aich, *s.m.* Thirst. 2 Drought, parchedness.
iotail,** *a.* Thirsty.
iotan, see iotadh.
iotar, see iotmhor.
iotas, -ais, *s.m.* see iotadh.
†ioth, *s.m.* Corn.
ioth-chruinnich,** *v.a.* Purvey, forage.
ioth-ghaireach, *a.* Fertile, productive.
——————d, *s.f.* Fertility.
iothlann, see iodhlann.
ioth-losgadh, -aidh, *s.m.* Parching of corn. 2 Blasting of a standing crop.
iothros,§ *s.m.* Poppy, see meilbheag. 2 Corn cockle, see lus loibheach.
iotmhoire, *comp.* of iotmhor.
————achd, *s.f.* Thirstiness, droughtiness, parchedness.
iotmhor, -oire, *a.* Thirsty, dry. 2 Parched.
ir,(AF) *s.f.* Squirrel.
†ir, *s.f.* Gift
ir,(AC) Step. Treòraich o ìr gu ìr mi, *lead me from step to step.*
†ir, *s.f.* Anger. 2 Satire, lampoon.
irchiullach, -aich, *s.m.* Monster.
ircilt, *s.f.* Side-post of a door.
ìre, *s. f. ind.* Degree of growth, progress. 2 State, condition. 3††Maturity. An ì. seo, *this condition ;* gu h-ì., *about ;* cuir an ì., *upbraid, reproach ; 2 cause to believe ; 3 lay as an obligation upon ;* ni a thoirt gu h-ìre, *to effect or accomplish a thing ;* thàinig e gu ìre, *he is full-grown ;* tha mi an ìre maith leis, *I am well on with it.*
†ire, *s.f.* Ravage, plunder.
†ire, *s.f.* Ground, land, field, soil, earth.
†ireall,** *s.m.* Response, reply. 2 Salutation, greeting.
ireann, *s. f.* Patriarchal woman, mother of a race. 2 Dam. *Sàr-Obair.*
†ireas, -eis, *s.m.* Occursion, collision.
irich,* see éirich.
irimich, *Badenoch & Gairloch* for imrich.
irimidh, *Badenoch* for imiridh.
irinn, *Suth'd* for inghean (daughter.)
irinn, *Sàr-Obair* for ifrinn.
irionn, *s.m.* Field. 2 Land, ground.
iriosal, -aile, *a.* Humble, low. lowly, mean.
———, -ail, *s.m.* Lowly or humble person.
irioslachadh, -aidh, *s.m.* Humbling, act of humbling. 2*Debasement, degradation. 3 Condescension. Ag i—, *pr. pt.* of irioslaich.
irioslachd, *s.f.* Humility, lowliness. 2 Debasement, degradation. 3 Condescension.
irioslaich, *pr.pt.* ag irioslachadh, *v.a.* Humble, lower, degrade, humiliate. 2 Condescend.
————te, *a. & past pt.* of irioslaich Humbled.
†irire, -an, *s.f* Curse, malediction. 2 Anger. 3 Blame.
iris, -ean, *s.f* The handle of a basket. by which to carry it or sling it to a pack-saddle. 2 Hen-roost or perch 3 Crupper. 4* Braces. 5(WC) Small of the back. I. an droma, *the small of the back ;* dh' fheudadh gu'n toirinnsa air an i. agad, *I might strike you in the small of the back.*
†iris, -ean, *s.f.* Friend. lover. 2 Assignation. 3 Description. 4 Discovery. 5 Record, history 6 Law. 7 Faith, religion. 8 Epoch, era. 9 Brass.
iris-cleibh,(DU) *s.f.* Rope-band for carrying a creel.
iris-eallaich, *s.f.* Rope round a bundle, as of straw.
iriseileachadh, see irioslachadh.
iriseach, -eiche, *a.* Furnished with slings or handles. 2 Abounding in hen-roosts. †3 Just, judicious, equitable. 4**Lawful.
iriseal, -eile, *a.* see iriosal.
———ach, see iriosal.
iriseas,** -eis, *s.m.* Present.
iris-mhuineal, *s.f.* Shoulder-band of a creel.
irisleabhar, -air, *s.m.* Magazine. 2 Commonplace book. see aithris-leabhar.
irisleachadh, see irioslachadh.
irisleachd, see irioslachd.
irislich, see irioslaich.
†irr,** *s.f.* Tail, as of a fish. 2 End, conclusion.
irt,** *s.m.* Death.

is, (AF) *s.* Ox.

is, *conj.* And. [‡ Seemingly an idiomatic use of is, *is*—consider the idiom, ni e sin is mise an seo, *he will do it and I here (lit.* he will do it, I am here.) It is usually regarded as an abbreviation of *agus*, hence the forms *a's* and *'us*. *Is*, according to Windisch, is not an abbreviation of *agus*. *Et* was the word originally (from Latin) brought into use as a monosyllabic copulative for the use of the bards. The old monks wrote it *et*, and it gradually slipped into the form 7, still retained in printed Irish Gaelic. It is pronounced like English *iss*. See note under agus.]

is, *pres. ind. v. def. & irreg.* Thus conjugated: *Ind. pres.* is mi, *I am* ; is tu, *thou art* ; is e, *he is* ; is i, *she is* ; is sinn, *we are* ; is sibh, *you are* ; is iad, *they are*.

Ind. past, bu mhi, *it was I*, bu tu, *it was thou* ; *&c.* [Also used with a present meaning, see note [1] below.]

Subj. pres ma 's mi, *if it be I* ; ma' s tu, *if it be thou* ; *&c.* Ged is mi, *though it is I*, *&c.*

Subj. past, na'm bu mhi, *if it were I*, *&c.*

Interr. pres., am mi ? *is it I ?* , an tu ? *is it thou ?* an e, *is it he ?* *&c.* Nach mi ? *is it not I ?* *&c.*

Interr. past, am bu[1] mhi, *was it I ?* *&c.*
nach bu[1] mhi ? *was it not I ?* *&c.*

Negative pres. cha mhi, *it is not I* ; *&c.*
past, cha bu[1] mhi, *it was not I* ; *&c.*

It is remarkable that in the *pret. interr.* and *negative*, no part of the verb *is* is seen at all, the conjunctions *am*, *cha*, *nach*, *gur*, *mur*, *&c.* with the pronouns annexed to them, convey the sense as distinctly as if the verb were expressed. Nach e seo an t-each bàn ? (*is*) *not this the white horse ?* This omission of the verb *to be* occurs in the same way in Welsh, as, nid bara a brynwyd, (*it was*) *not bread that was bought.*

Is is used in describing the name, profession, identity, state or condition, under which objects definitely exist or did exist—Is mise Peadar, *I am Peter;* is tu mo bhràthair, *thou art my brother* ; is caiptean am fear ud, *yon fellow is a captain* ; is iarunn seo, *this is iron* ; bu chlachair e, *he was a mason* ; bu nàmhaid e, *he was a foe* ; cha bu robairean iad, *they were not robbers.* When the subject is pointedly and emphatically expressed or addressed, the verb *is* is used, as, is tus' an duine, *thou art the man*. In many cases *tha* cannot be used in place of *is*. We cannot say, tha thus' an duine, tha thu mo rùn, tha seo umha, *&c.*, we must say, is tus' an duine, is tu mo rùn, is umha seo, *&c.* When an adjective is in the predicate, either *bi* or *is* may be used, as tha a' chlach seo mór *or* is mór a' chlach i seo, *this stone is great* ; tha do cheum mall *or* is mall do cheum, *thy step is slow* ; but in all such cases when *is* is used the meaning is more emphatic. *Is* implies a more permanent state than *tha* ; contrast " is leam e " with " tha e agam " ; and " is i is màthair dhomh " with " tha i 'na màthair dhomh."

Is ann cha'n ann, *the fact is that it is not so* ; is math an airidh, *it is well deserved* ; is math an airidh e, *he well deserves it* ; ma's fìor dhuit e, *if it is the truth (as told) to you* ; c' àit' an tàmh dhuit ? *where is your abode ?* ; an slàn dhuit ? *are you well* , nach e seo an t-each bàn ? *is not this the white horse ?* ; cha bu gheamhna dhuinn air móran barrachd, *it would not be good enough for us even though much more were offered* (*lit.* for much more) ; na'm b' fhìor sin, *or* ma b' fhìor sin, *were it not a sham.*

Some idiomatic uses of is :—

is àbhaist dhomh, *I use, am wont.*
is àbhaist dha, *he is used or wont.*
b' àbhaist dhomh, *I used, was wont.*
is ag leam, *I doubt.*
is àill leam, *I wish, desire.*
is ait leam, *I rejoice, am glad.*
is aithne dhomh, *I know, am acquainted with.*
is aithreach leam, *I repent.*
is annsa leam, *I prefer.*
is àrd leam (e), *I think (it) high.*
is beag leam, *I think it too little.*
is beag orm, *I hate, dislike.*
is beò dhomh, *I live, am in life.*
is binn leam (e), *I like, think (it) melodious.*
is caomh leam. *I love, like.*
is còir dhomh, *I ought.*
is coma leam, *I care not, do not like* ; is coma leam dol 'na dhàil, *I don't like to have anything to do with him.*
is cruaidh leam, *I am sorry.*
is cuimhne leam, *I remember.*
is dàna leam, *it is presumptuous of me, I dare.* Usually used in the negative—cha bu d. leam, *I would not dare.*
is daor leam (e), *I think (it) dear.*
is deòin leam, *I am willing, wish.*
is dòcha leam, *I suppose, think, think it probable.*
is dŏcha leam, *I prefer.*
is dual dhomh, *it is natural to me.*
is duilich leam, *I regret, am sorry or vexed.*
is eagal leam, *I fear, am afraid.*
is éigin dhomh, *I must.*
is éis dhomh, *I delay, am detained.*
is eòl dhomh, *I know, am acquainted with.*
is fada leam, *I long.*
is fèarr dhomh, *it is better for me.*
is fèarr leam, *I am more glad, had rather, I rather wish, prefer.*
is fhiach leam, *I value, condescend.*
is fiach dhomh, *it is worth my while.*
is fuath leam *I hate, dislike.*
is gàbhaidh leam, *I wonder, am surprised.* [*it.*
is gann orm a chreidsinn, *I can hardly believe*
is gasda leam, *I delight.*
is gràin leam, *I abhor, disdain.*
is ion dhomh, *it becomes me.*
is leam, *I own, possess permanently.* Am fear leis an leis mi, *the man whose I am.*
is leas dhomh, *I ought.*
is léir dhomh, *I see, perceive.*
is leisg leam, *I am loath.*
is lugh' orm, *I hate more.*
is math leam (gu), *I am glad (that), wish, am willing.*
is miann leam, *I wish or desire.*
is mithich dhomh, *it is time for me.*
is mó leam, *I think more of.*
is mór leam, *I think it too much* ; is mór leam e. *I think much of it, or too much of it.*
is nàir leam, *I think it a shame.*
is nàrach dhomh, *I am ashamed.*
is neònach leam, *I wonder, am surprised.*

[1] *Bu*, is also used with a present meaning, as, cha bu tu mi, 's cha bu mhi 'n cù *you are not I and I am no cur*—a Celtic way of telling a man he is a hound ; cha bu tu bean a' mharsanta mhóir, *you are not as the big merchant's wife—you do not do as she does.* *Bu*, is, of course, an entirely different word to *is*, but as it is generally treated by grammarians as the past tense of *is*, examples of its use have been inserted here under that word, to enable readers to find them without difficulty.

is òg leam (e), *I think (it) young.*
is olc leam, *I regret.*
is tagh leam, see is toigh leam.
is taitneach leam (e), *(it) is pleasant to me.*
is toigh leam, *I prefer, like or love.*
is trom leam sin, *I think that heavy.*
is truagh leam, *I pity, am to be pitied.*
is ullamh le neach, *one is prone to, or ready.*

is beag nach, *adv.* Almost.

isbean, -ein, -an, *s.m.* Sausage.

isbeanach, -aiche, *a.* Of, or pertaining to sausages. 2 Full of sausages.

ise, *pers. pron.* emphatic of i. She herself.

iseag,‡‡ -eig, see uiseag.

iseal, isle, see iosal.

isean, -ein, -an, (*pl.* in *Suth'd* isean with the sound of final syllable lengthened.) *s. m* Chicken, the young of any bird or of the smaller quadrupeds. 2 Opprobrious term applied to an ill-mannered young person, or a dirty child, brat. 3 Puny person. 4 Gosling. 5‡‡ Term of endearment to an infant. 6 Mischievous child—*Argyll.* 7(AG) In *Suth'd* applied only to quadrupeds. I. ròin *the young of the seal—Uist;* i. eich, *the young of the horse—Lewis;* i. cait, *a kitten—Suth'd.*

iseanach, -aiche, *a.* Abounding in chickens, young of birds or resembling them 2 Pertaining to, or like an ill-brought-up child. 3 Dirty, as a child. 4 Like a gosling.

iseanachd, *s.f.* Mischief, as in children—*Argyll.*

isearan, *Arran* for eisearan.

isgeas,** -eis, *s.m.* Doubt.

is gann, *adv.* Scarcely.

†isin, for an sin.

isle, *s.f.ind.* Lowness. I. mara, *low tide*

isle, *comp.* of iosal. Lower, lowest. A' chuid a b' i. de 'n t-sluagh, *the lowest of the people.*

isleachadh, -aidh, *s.m.* Humbling, act of humbling, humiliation, condescension. 2 Abasement. 3 Subsiding. 4 Abjectness. Ag i—, *pr.pt.* of islich. Tha 'n abhainn air i., (*the water of*) *the river has subsided.*

isleachd, *s. f. ind.* Lowness, abjectness, littleness. 2 Lowliness, condescension.

islead, -id, *s.f.* Degree of lowness or abjectness. 2 Littleness.

islean, -ein, *s.m.* Low or humble person ; in *pl.* the common people, the lower classes.

isle còntraigh,(AH) *s.f.* Neap-tide.

isle mhara,(AH) *s.f.* Low water, low ebb.

islich, *pr.pt.* ag isleachadh, *v.a.* & *n.* Bring low, humble, abase. 2 Become low or humble, subside. 3 Condescend.

islichear, *fut. pass.* of islich. Shall be lowered.

islichte, *past pt.* of islich. Lowered, brought low, humbled, abased.

isneach, -ich, -ichean, *s.f.* Rifled gun, rifle.

isop,§ *s.* see iosop.

ist ! *int.* Hush ! hist ! whist !

ite, -an, *s. f.* Feather, quill. 2 Fin of a fish. 3 Artificial fishing fly. 4(AH) Blade of an oar. 5(CR) Adze—*Perthshire.* 6 (DMK) Blade of the propeller of a steamer—*W. coast of Ross.* 7**Down. 8**Wing. Itean éisg, *fins of fish* ; itean geòidh, *goose-quills* ; i. tombac, *a snuff-quill.*

iteach, -ich, *s.m.* Plumage, feathers, wings. I. éisg, *the fins of a fish.*

iteach, -eiche, *a.* Feathered, feathery, plumy, winged. 2 Finny, of many fins. Am bradan i., *the finny salmon.*

iteach, -ich, *s.m.* Art or act of fishing or angling with a fly. 2 Flight, flying, as of a bird or an arrow. Ag i—, *pr.pt.* of itich.

iteachan, -ain, -an, *s.m.* Weaver's bobbin, reel, or spool.

iteag, -eig, -an, *s.f., dim.* of ite. Feather, little feather, plume, quill. 2 Fin. 3 Flight of a bird.

iteagach, -aiche, *a.* Of many feathers, feathery, winged, feathery. 2 Finny.

iteagachadh, -aidh, *s.m.* Flying low, act of flying low. Ag i—, *pr.pt.* of iteagaich.

iteagaich, *pr. pt.* ag iteagachadh, [ag iteach in *Gairloch*] *v.n.* Fly low or near the ground.

iteagaich, *s.f.* see itealaich.

iteagh, *s.m.* see iteodha.

iteal, -il, *s.m.* Flight on wing, flying. 2 Fluttering of wings. Air i., *on wing.*

itealach, -aiche, *a.* Winged. 2 Flying. 3 Hovering, fluttering.

itealachadh, *s.m.* see itealaich.

itealachd, see itealaich.

itealaich, -ean, *s.f.* Flying, act of flying, avolation. 2* Fluttering. Ag i—, *pr. pt.* of itealaich.

itealaich, *pr.pt.* ag itealaich, *v.n.* Fly in the air. 2 Flutter.

itean-gàirdeanaich, *s.pl.* Primaries, see eun, 6, p. 98.

itean-sgéithe, see eun, 6, p. 398.

iteodha,§ &‡‡-oidhe, *s.* Hemlock. Cameron (§) suggests a derivation from *ite*, the idea being " feather-fledged."

ith, *pr.pt.* ag ith & ag itheadh, *v.a.* & *n.* Eat. 2 Gnaw, chew, devour. 3 Corrode. 4 Consume.

ith,** *s.f.* Eating. Ag i—, *pr.pt.* of ith.

†ith, see ioth.

ith,** *s.* Fat, tallow. 2 Corn.

†ithche, -an, *s.f.* see itheadh.

ith-dhias,** -dhéise, *s.f.* Ear of corn.

itheadh, -idh, *s.m.* Eating, act of eating, chewing, or gnawing. 2 Corroding, corrosion. Ag i—, *pr.pt.* of ith.

itheam, *1st. sing. imp.* of ith. Let me eat.

itheannaich, *s.f.ind.* Eating, feeding. 2* Damage done by cattle. 3 Something to eat.

ithear, *fut. pass.* of ith.

†ith-fheun, -a, -an, *s.m.* Corn-dray.

ithidh, *fut. aff. a.* of ith.

ithinnich, see itheannaich.

ith-iomradh, -aidh, *s.m.* Backbiting, slanderous report. 2 Murmuring.

†ith-iomradh, *v.a.* & *n.* Grumble. 2 Backbite.

ith-iomraiteach, *a.* Slanderous, backbiting, abusive. 2 Murmuring.

†ithir,** *s.f.* Corn-field. 2 Arable land, soil.

ithte, *past pt.* of ith. Eaten. 2 Consumed.

ith-teodha,(AC) *s.* Hemlock—*Lismore, & N. Argyll* see minmheur.

ithte, *past pt.* of ith. Eaten, consumed.

i-tiach, see de-tiach.

itich, *pr. pt.* ag iteach, *v.a.* Fish with a fly.

†i-tigheach, -ich, -ichean, *s.m.* Gullet

it-ioch, *s.* see de-tiach.

it-ros,** *s.m.* Headland, promontory.

†itu, *s.m.* Thirst, see iotadh.

iùbhaidh, see fiùbhaidh.

†iubhal, -ail, *s.m.* Time.

iubhar, -air, -an, *s.m.* Yew-tree—*taxus baccata.* Badge of the Frasers. 2 Bow. 3 Arrow. 4*Juniper. Cha dearg i. mi, *no arrow shall wound me.*

iubharach, -aiche, *a* Of, or abounding in, yew-trees. 2 Made of yew. 3 Like yew. 4 Abounding in, or armed with, bows. Na h-òighean i., *the daughters of the bow, huntresses.*

iubhar-beinne, *s.* Juniper—*Arran.*

iubhar-chreige,‡‡ *s.m* Juniper.

iubhar-sléibhe,‡‡ *s.m.* Ambrosia (plant.)

iubhar-thalmhainn,‡‡ *s.m.* Juniper.

iùbhrach, -aiche, *a* see iubharach.

iùbhrach, -aich, *s.f.* Yew-grove, group of yews.

2 Stately woman. 3**Active female. 4**Female archer. 5 Wherry, barge, skiff, cutter, see p. 78. 6 Vessel under sail. 7 Rod.
iùbhraich see fiodhraich (under bàta.)
iubhran,(AF) *s.m.* Castrated goat.
iùc, see niùc. Slit scallop, fissure. 2(AH) One of the two lower corners of a bag of potatoes, meal or grain. Earc iùc, *slit-eared cows*, ordinarily called torc-chluasach, *notch-eared*, or crodh-mara, *sea-cows.*
iuchair, -chrach, -chraichean, *s. f.* Key. 2 Screwed handle of a spinning-wheel to tighten driving cord. 3 Spawn or roe of female fish. [Roe in the immature or soft condition called "mealag"—*Lorn* (Fionn.) Applied only to herring and salmon in *W. of Ross*, where *bròg* is used of cod and other large sea-fish—CR. In *Gairloch* both "bròg truisg" and "iuchair truisg" are used—DU.] I. bodaich ruaidh, *cod's roe—Argyll.*
iuchaireach, -eiche, *a.* Furnished with keys. 2 Abounding in fish-spawn.
iuchaireag, -eig, -an, *s.f.*, *dim.* of iuchair. Little key. 2 Female fish, spawner. 3††Spawn.
iuchair-na-ciche, *s.f.* Key to adjust frame of flyers of spinning-wheel to tighten the cord.
iuchairneag,(AF) see iuchaireag.
Iuchar, -air, *s.m.* The dog-days, warm month, July. [Preceded by the art. *an t-.*]
iucharag, see iuchaireag.
iùchd, see iùc.
iuchrag, -an, see iuchaireag.
iuchraichean, *pl.* of iuchair.
iùdasach, -aiche, *a.* Treacherous, like the traitor Judas.
iùdasach, -aich, *s.m.* Traitor, infamous, treacherous or villainous fellow.
†iudh, -a, -an, *s.m.* Day,
†iudiceachd,** *s.f.* Judgment.
iudmhail, *s.m.* Fugitive. 2 Coward. 3 Low, feeble fellow.
iugh,‡ -a, *s.m.* The posture in which the dead are placed. 'Na luidh' air an iugha, *lying in the position of the dead.*
iughar, see iubhar.
iugharach, see iubharach & iùbhrach
†iùi, *s.f.* Arrow, (fiuthaidh.)
†Iùl, Iùil, *s.f.* Month of July.
iùl, iùil, iùilean, *s. m.* Guidance, direction. 2 Course, way. 3 Guide. 4 Land-mark at sea. 5 Knowledge, acquaintance. 6 Learning. 7 Art. 8 Judgment. 9 Chief, commander. 10 ‡‡Service, attendance. 11‡‡ Mariner's compass. Chaill e an t-i., *he lost the course ;* ni mise dhuibh i., *I will be your guide.*
iùlach,** *a.* Having knowledge. 2 Guiding, directing. 3 Rational.
iuladh, -aidh, see ioladh.
†iùlaigh, -ean, *s.m.* Leader.
iulainn, see iodhlann.
iùlag, -aig, -an, *s. f.* Small mariner's compass. 2††Small chart.
iulag,** see iullag.
iùlan riaghlaidh, *s.pl.* Politics.
iùlar, see iùlmhor.
iùlar, *Reay country* for ùrlar.
iùlarachd, see iùlmhorachd.
iùl-chairt, -ean, *s.f.* Mariner's compass. 2†† Chart.
iulla, *pr. pt.* ag iulla, *v. a.* Fish from a small boat with flies, usually for "sillocks." An robh thu 'g iulla an raoir ? Bha, agus fhuair mi leth-cheud saighean (or saoidhean), *were you fishing last night ? Yes, and I caught fifty saith—Lewis.*
iullag,(DU) *s.f.* Rock round which "sillocks" are plentiful, generally submerged.
iullag, -aig, -an, *s. f.* Sprightly, affected little female. 2* Skip, trip.
iullagach, -aiche, *a.* Light, airy, tripping lightly along. 2 Sprightly, cheerful, gay, frolicsome. 3 Giddy. 4 Making short steps. 5 Florid.
iullagachd,‡‡ *s.f.ind.* Jauntiness.
iullagaiche, *s f.* Lightness, airiness, sprightliness, cheerfulness.
————, *comp.* of iullagach. More or most light, airy, &c.
iulla-ghuanach, *s.* The name of MacTrein's banner.
iullanaiche, *s.f.ind.* Lightness, airiness, cheerfulness, sprightliness.
iullagaiche, *comp.* of iullagach. More or most light, airy, &c.
iùllar,(WC) *adv.* Down—*Perthshire.*
iùlmhor, -oire, *a.* Wise, learned, sagacious, sensible. 2(MS) Skilful. 3 Polite.
iùlmhorachd, *s.f.ind.* Wisdom, judgment, sagacity. 2 Politeness.
iùl-oidhche, *s.f.* Name of a star.
iumaidh, *s.f.* Level ground. 2 Open country.
iumaidh, *a.* Having level ground.
iumain, see iomain.
iumairt, see iomairt.
iùmhrach, -aich, -aichean, see iùrach.
iun,** *s.m.* Naughty creature.
iùnadh, see iongnadh.
iùnadh,** *a.* Strange, wonderful, odd, curious.
iumarach,** -aich, *s. m.* Change of place, removing.
iùnais, *s.f.* Want, deficiency. Tha i. iomadh ni orm, *I want many things.* More frequently used as a prep. phrase conjoined with the prep. *as*, as, as iùnais do chuideachaidh, *without thine aid* ; as t' iùnais, *without thee.*
iùnndrain, see ionndrainn.
iùnnrais, -ean, *s.f.* Stormy sky. 2 Storm, tempest.
iùnnraiseach, -eiche, *a.* Stormy, tempestuous.
iùnnras, -ais, see iùnnrais.
iunnsachadh, see ionnsachadh.
iunnsaich, see ionnsaich.
iunnsaichte, see ionnsaichte.
iùnntas, -ais, -an, see ionmhas.
iùnntasach, -aiche, *a.* Rich, opulent.
iuntas, see ionmhas.
iuntrain,(MS) *v.a.* Balk.
iur, see iubhar.
†iur, *s.m.* Plunder. 2 Bloodshed, slaughter.
iùrach, -aiche, -ean, see iùbhrach.
†iuramh, *adv.* Afterwards.
iùran, -ain, -an, see fiùran.
iùras,** *s.m.* Felon (whitlow.)
iurghuileach, *s.m.* see iargallach (appendix.)
iurpais, -ean, *s.f.* Restlessness, fidgeting. 2 Wrestling, struggling. 3**Dropsy.
iurpaiseach, -eiche, *a.* Restless. 2 Prone to strife or quarrelling. 3 Dropsical.
iurram, -aim, -an, see iorram.
————ach, see iorramach.
†iurrunn, -uinn, -uinnean, *s.f.* Want, defect.
iursach, -aiche, *a.* Dark, black. †2 Suspensory.
iursach,* -aiche, *s.f.* Girl.
iùsan,* -ain, *s.m.* Giddiness, levity. 2 Sudden whim.
iùsanach, *a.* Whimsical, giddy, light-headed.
iùthaidh, -ean, *s. f.* see fiuthaidh. 2 (DMy) Quality. I. mhath, said of a mast, oar, &c., that stands a heavy strain, or of boots or clothes that wear well.
iuthair, *gen. sing.* of iuthar.
iuthar, -air, -airean, see iubhar.
iutharach, see iubharach & iubhrach.
iutharn, -a, -airn, see ifrionn.
iutharnach, -aich, see ifrionnach.

L l

l, luis, *the quicken tree.* The tenth letter of the Gaelic alphabet now in use. When it is preceded by itself, or by any other consonant, and followed by *a*, *o*, or *u*, it has a broad lingual sound, to which there is none like in the English language ; as, làn, *full* ; lom, *bare* ; lus, *a herb.* When *l* is immediately followed by *e* or *i*, it is pronounced like the Italian *gl* in *gle* or *gli* ; as, litir, *a letter* ; linn, *an age.* In the case of nouns beginning with *l*, if the masc. poss. pron. go before, *l* is pronounced as in English ; as, a litir, *his letter* ; which differs essentially in sound from, a litir, *her letter.* With regard to verbs beginning with *l*, the preterite is pronounced as in English, and in most other situations it is pronounced as *ll.* The letter *l* when aspirated is not followed by *h* in writing, and the difference between the plain and aspirated sounds is generally only distinguishable to a keen ear, and is almost lost on most people, but when labhair, *speak*, which is plain, and labhair e, *he spoke*, which is aspirated, are correctly pronounced, the difference should be easily discernible.

là, *pl.* làithean & lathachan, *s. m.* Day, space from evening to evening. 2 Daylight. 3 On a certain day, one day.
An là a chì 's nach fhaic, *every day—present or absent*, one of the most frequently used of familiar sayings—generally added to a farewell as, " beannachd leat, an là a chì 's nach fhaic," *or* " a h-uile là " ; b' e sin an dà là, *what a change of days !* it is common to hear " 's ann air a thàinig an dà là " said of a person who has suffered a change of circumstances ; air là àraidh, *on a certain day* ; a h-uile là, *every day* ; a h-uile là riamh, *every single day* ; là mi-shealbhach, là còrr *or* là seachantach, *an unlucky day* ; là féille, *holy day, holiday, market day;* là breith, *a birthday;* là fliuch, *a wet day* ; là gailbheach, *a stormy day;* là breagh, *a fine day* ; là màth, *a good day* ; là seachduin, *a week-day* ; la Dòmhnuich, *a Sunday* ; là Luain, *a Monday*, also *a day that shall never arrive* or *one to which the moon gives light, Nevermas, the last day* ; là buan an lìn, *Nevermas;* a là *or* do là, *by day* , gu là, *till daylight.*
là na bliadhn' ùire, *New Year's day.*
là fhéill nan rìgh, *Epiphany*
là fhéill Brìghde nan coinnlean, *Candlemas.*
là cath choileach, *St. Bridget's day 14th. Feb. O. S.—2nd. Feb. N. S.* (*lit.* the day of cock-fighting.)
là fhéill Muire nan coinnlean, *Purification* [*Day.*
là Dhaibhidh, *St. David's Day.*
là Càisge, *Easter Day.*
là Muire, là na caillich, *Lady-day.*
là Bealltuinn, *May-day*
là na Crois Naoimhe, *Day of the Holy Cross.*
là aisig Rìgh Thearlaich a dhà, *Restoration Day.*
là fhéill Eòin Baiste, *St. John's Day* (*24 June.*)
là Lùnasd, *Lammas-day.*
là breith Muire, *Mary's Nativity.*
là fhéill Màrtuinn, *Martinmas.*
la fhéill Mìcheil, *Michaelmas.*
là nan uile Naoimhe, là Mairbh na cruinne gu coitchionn, **là Sàmhna,** an t-Samhuinn, *All-hallows, All-Saints'-day.*
là Nollaig, *Christmas Day.*
là fhéill Eòin, *St. John's Day.*
là fhéill Pàdruig Earraich, là nan trì seall-adh, *on St. Patrick's day in spring, three sights may be seen*—i.e. ploughing, sowing, and harrowing. Some versions mention seven sights. St. Patrick's day is also called " là nan seachd oibrichean fichead," *the day of the twenty-seven works*, meaning that twenty-seven different kinds of work are done on a farm on that day. Là sheachnaidh na bliadhna, *the day of the week on which 3rd. May falls* —on this day the Gael seldom began any work he wished to finish with expedition and success ; Nicolson says some apply the name to 2nd. May, and some to 5th. May—he does not say the days of the week on which these days fall, all through the year, which Armstrong's reference to 3rd. May seems to imply.

là,* *adv.* Once on a time.
là, *adv.* see làmh.
†la, *prep.* see le.
†lab, -a, -an, *s.m.* Lip.
làb,* -aib, *s.m.* Day's labour. 2 Mud, dirt, mire. 3**Puddle. 4 Swamp, bog.
làbail,** *a.* Dirty. 2 Puddly.
làbair,** *s.m.* Dustman, labourer.
làban, -ain, *s. m.* Mire, dirt. 2 Dirty work, drudgery. 3 Muddy place.
làbanach, -aiche, *a.* Miry, muddy. 2 Marshy. 3 Belaboured, laborious.
làbanach, -aich, *s. m.* Plebeian, day-labourer, drudge. 2 Dustman. 3 Smearer, dauber. 4 Slovenly fellow. 5 Draggler.
làbanachadh,** -aidh, *s.m.* Dirtying, smearing, draggling. 2(DMC) Drenching by rain.
làbanachd, *s.f.* Draggling, drenching. 2 Low dirty work. 3 Labour.
làbanaich, *v.a.* Puddle, moil. 2 Bedraggle. 3 Smear, daub.
làbanaich, *gen. sing. & n.pl.* of làbanach.
làbanaiche, -an, *s.m.* Drudge, draggler. 2 Labourer, plebeian. 3 One who works in clay or puddly ground. 4 Painstaking person.
làbanta,‡‡ -ainte, *a.* Plebeian, servile. 2 Draggling. 3 Vulgar. 4 Like a labourer.
labaonach,** *a.* Dissembling, pretending.
†labaonadh, -aidh, -aidhean, *s.m.* Dissimulation.
làbarach,(MS) *a.* Limous.
làbaranach,(MS) *a.* Limy.
labh, -aibh, *s.m.* Word 2 Lip.
làbhach, *s.m.* Mire, mud.
labhach, *a.* Miry, dirty. 2 Swampy. [** gives làbach.]
†labhachd, *s.f.* Matter
labhair, *pr.pt.* a' labhairt, *v.a.* Speak, say on. 2 Talk, commune. Labhair romhad, *say on.*
———each, see labhairteach.
labhairt, *s.f.* Speaking, act of speaking, speech. 2 Oration. 3 Conversation, discourse. 4 Language, utterance. 5 Voice, expression. A' l—, *pr.pt.* of labhair. Fear-l., *a speaker, interpreter* ; *2 spokesman* ; thar l., *beyond expression* ; droch l., *bad speaking* ; is math an l. a th' air, *what a good delivery he has !*
labhairte, *past pt.* of labhair. Said, spoken.
———ach, -eiche, *a.* Loquacious, inclined to speak. 2 Loud. 3 Utterable, expressible. 4 ‡‡Oral.
———achd, *s.f ind.* Loquacity, noisy boasting, talkativeness.
labhairtiche,** *s.m* Orator, spokesman. 2 Talkative fellow
la-bhallan,-ain, -an, *s.f* Shrew, water-shrew or mouse. 2 (AF) Weasel. 3 Mythical animal, supposed to be larger than a rat, and very noxious and to live in deep pools.
†labhar, -air, *s.m.* Gaelic spelling of *laver* (ewer.)
labhar, -aire [labhra & **labhara] *a.* Loud, loud ly sounding, noisy. 2 Boastful, clamorous. 3 Speaking loudly, loquacious. 4 Eloquent. 5

Audible. Is fearr cù luath na teanga l., *better is a nimble dog than a loud tongue;* cho l. ris a' ghaoith, *as noisy in speech as the storm;* cath labhar, *a war of words.*

labharra, see labhar.

labhra, *comp.* of labhar. More or most noisy or loquacious.

labhrach, -aiche, *a.* see labhar. Is laabrach na builg fhàs, *empty bags are loud-sounding.*

———d, *s.f.* Loudness. see labhairteachd.

labhrad, -aid, *s.m.* Loudness, degree of loudness. 2††Loquacity. 3* Noisy boasting.

labhradair, see labhraiche.

labhradh, *a.* labhar.

labhradh, -aidh, *s.m.* Speaking. 2 Speechifying. 3 Speech, discourse. B' e l. a mhill e, *speaking was his bane;* ùr-l., *utterance, elocution.*

labhraiche, *s.m.* Orator, speaker. L. pongail, *a distinct speaker.*

labhran,(AF) *s.m.* Young rabbit or hare.

labhras,§ -ais, -an, *s.m.* Laurel, bay-tree—*laurus nobilis,* (not the common garden laurel.) Badge of the MacLarens.

labhram, *1st. per. sing. imp.* of labhair. Let me speak.

†lac,(AF) *s.f.* Sweet milk.

lach, -a, *pl.* -an [-aidh, -ainn, lachaichean & lachainnean,] *s.f.* Wild duck—*anas boschas.* 2 *s. m.* Wild drake. 3*Widgeon.

lach, -a, -an, *s.m.* Reckoning, expense of entertainment at an inn, fare. 2* Reckoning at a penny wedding. 4 Contribution per head. 5 Horse laugh, loud burst of laughter. Tog an l., *raise* or *collect the reckoning.*

lach,(DU) *v.n.* Laugh loudly and for a long time.

405. Lach-a'-bhlàir.

lach-a'-bhlàir,¶ *s.f.* Bald coot, common coot—*fulica atra.*

lacha-ceann-ruadh, ‡‡ -an-ceann-ruadh, *s. m.* Celandine (plant.)

lachach, -aiche, *a.* Of, or belonging to, wild ducks. 2 Like a wild duck or drake.

lach-a'-chinn-uaine,¶ *s.f.* Golden eye—*fuligula clangula.* 2 (AC) Mallard or common wild duck.

lachadaich, see lachanaich.

lachadair,(AF) -ean, *s.m.* Diver (bird.)

lachadh,** -aidh, *s.m.* Act of diving like a wild duck.

lachag, -aig, -an, *s. f. dim.* of lach. Little or young wild duck. 2 Small reckoning.

———ach,†† *a.* Abounding in little ducks.

lachaidh, *n.pl.* of lach.

lach-Aigir,(AC) *s.m. & f.* Teal, elf-duck.

lachair, -ean, *s.m.* Diver.

lachaire, see lachadair.

lachan,‡ -ain, *s.m.* Loud laughter, *Scots* word.

lachan, -ain, *s.m.* Common reed.

———aich,* *s.f.* Loud continued laughter.

lachan-coille, *s.m.* see cuilc-fheur.

lachan-nan-damh,§ *s. m.* Jointed rush, wood small reed—*juncus articulatus.*

lach-an-sgumain,(AF) *s.* Tufted or crested duck.

lachan-gàire, *s.* Horse-laugh.

lach-Aoisgeir,¶ *s.f.* Eider-duck, see lach-Lochlannach. 2 (AF) Velvet scoter.

lachar, -air, *s.m.* Vulture. 2(AF) Any large bird of prey.

lachardaich, see lachanaich.

lach-bheag,(DMC) *s.f.* Teal.

lach-bhinn,¶ *s. f.* Long-tailed duck, see eunbuchainn.

lach-bhlàir,(DMC) *s.f.* White-headed coot.

lach-bhreac, ¶ *s. f.* Golden eye, see lach-a'-chinn-uaine. 2(AC) Mallard.

lach-ceann-molach,(AF) *s.f.* Tufted duck.

lach-ceann-ruadh, *s.f.* see ceann-ruadh.

lach-chinn-uaine, see lach-a'-chinn-uaine.

lach-Cholasaidh,¶ *s. f.* Eider-duck, see lach Lochlannach.

lach-crann,(AF) *s.* Teal.

†lachd, *s.m.* Family, see luchd. 2 see lac.

———ach,** *a.* Asphaltic.

lach-dhearg-cheannach,¶ *s.f.* Pochard, see lach-mhàsach.

lach-dhioladh,(MS) *s.m.* Amercement.

406. Lach dhubh.

lach-dhubh,¶ *s.f.* Velvet scoter—*oidemia fusca.*

†lachdmhor, see laemhor.

lachduinneachd, *s. f.* ‡‡Infuscation. 2 Swarthiness.

lachdunn, -uinne, *a.* Dun, tawny, swarthy, dingy, khaki, homespun grey. 2** Clumsy. Is coma leam a' bhriogais l., *I hate the grey breeks.*

lach-eigir, (AF) *s.f.* Little or dwarf duck.

lach-fhiacailleach,¶ *s. f.* Goosander—*mergus merganser.*

lach-ghlas,¶ *s.f.* Gadwall—*anas strepara.* 2 Mallard. 3 (AF) Widgeon.

lach-liath,(AC) *s.f.* Long-tailed duck.

lach-Lochlannach,¶ *s.f.* Eider-duck—*somateria mollissima.* (see illust. 407.)

lach-mhara,(AF) *s.f.* Sea-duck.

lach-mhàsach,¶ *s.f.* Pochard or dun bird—*fuliga ferina.* (see illust. 408.)

lach-Mhoire,(AC) *s.f.* (Mary's duck) Mallard.

†lachmhor, -oire, *a.* Comely.

lach mhór, *s.f.* *Harris* for lach Lochlannach. 2(AF) St. Cuthbert's duck. 3 (DMC) Eider-duck—*Uist.*

lach riabhach,(AC) *s.f.* Mallard.

lach ruadh,(AC) *s.f.* Mallard.

lach sgumanach,(AF) *s.f.* Tufted or crested duck.

lach-shìth,(AC) *s.f.* Teal, elphin duck.

407. *Lach-Lochlannach.*

408. *Lach-mhàsach.*

lach stiùireach,(AC) *s.f.* Long-tailed duck, rudder-duck, pintail.
lach stuadh,(AF) *s.f.* Wave-duck.
lach-uaine, *s.f.* Mallard.
†lacmhor, -oire, *a.* Giving much milk. 2 Abounding in milk. 3 Prolific.
làd, -àid, -an, *s.m.* [*f.* in *Badenoch.*] Load, burden, cargo, freight, lading. 2**Crowd. 3** Volley. Thoir a staigh làd uisge, *bring in two bucketfuls (a load) of water—Argyll;* thàinig dà làn oirnn, *our boat made two heavy seas —Lewis.* [Pronounced *lòd* in *Argyll, Poolewe, &c.*]
lad, -aid, -an, *s.m.* Water-course. 2 Mill-lead. 3 Puddle, stagnant water, foul pond. 4 Loud talk, clamorousness.
ladach, -aich, *s.m.* Volley.
làdach,†† *a.* Loaded, burdened.
làdach,(DMC) *s.m.* Burden of anything, armful.
làdail, *a.* Heavy laden, bulky, clumsy, cumbersome.
ladair, *gen.sing. & n. pl.* of ladar.
ladar, -air, *s.m.* Ladle, spoon, scoop. 2**Ladleful. 3 Church ladle. Gabh an l. no an taoman, *take the ladle* or *baling-dish.*
†làdar, -air, *s.m.* Thief, robber.
ladarach, -aiche, *a.* Of, or belonging to, ladles.
ladar-miot,†† *s.m.* Scrimmage, melée.
ladarna, -airne, *a.* Bold, daring, impudent, shameless. 2 Loquacious, clamorous. L. is faoin, *rash and vain ;* gu làmhach, l., *ready-handed and bold.*
———chd, *s.f.* see ladarnas
ladarnas, -ais, *s.m.* Boldness, impudence, audacity, impudent loquacity.
làdas,(CR) -ais, *s.m.* Loud talk—*Blair Athole & Loch Tay.* 2**Boldness in speech.
làdas,** *s.m.* Lordliness.
———ach, -aiche, *a.* Rich, lordly. 2 Having many loads, burdened. 3** Bold in speech, procacious.
———achd,†† *s.f.* Magisterialness.
ladh, -a, *s.m.* Sending, deputation, mission.
ladhadair, *s.m.* Plasm.
ladhaich, for laghaich, *dat.sing. fem.* of laghach.
ladhainn, -ean, see laghadair.
làdhan, see làgan.
ladhar, -air & -dhra, *pl.* -dhran, *s.m.* [*f.* in *Badenoch.*] Hoof. 2 Toe. 3 Claw. 4 Prong, fork. 5 Ludicrous name for a shanky leg. 6**Single hoof of a cloven-footed animal. Ladhar is toe (of a man) in *Arran & Islay,* where hoof is crodhan. Gach aon a sgoltas an l., *every one that has a cloven hoof ;* a' cur bruic á 'ladhran, *kicking badgers out of his toes*—said of one in a great rage ; teas na luaithreach 'nan ladhairean, *the heat of ashes in their feet—Arran ;* barail a' bhruic air a ladhran, *the badger's opinion of his own claws*—a poor opinion ; cho bìth ris an luch fo l. a' chait, *as quiet as a mouse under the cat's paw;* cha téid mo l., *not a bit of me will go ;* chaidh a' bhròg oirre 'nuair a bha bàrr nan l. gearrta dhi, *the shoe went on her (foot) when the tips of her toes were cut off.*
†ladharg, -airg, -an, *s.m.* Thigh.
†ladhna, *s.m.* Dumbness.
ladhrach, -aiche, *a.* Having hoofs, hoofed. 2 **Having large hoofs or claws. 3** Having large toes. 4 Forked, pronged. 5** Shanky. 6**Hasty. Tarbh l., *a bull with large hoofs ;* òrd l., *a claw-hammer.* làdhrach in *Gairloch.*
ladhrag,** -aig, *s. f.* Toe. 2 Hoof. 3 Fork, prong.
ladhran, see ladhran-tràghaid.
ladhran-tràghaid,(AF) *s.m.* Sandpiper, sandsnipe.
ladorna, see ladarna.
ladornachd, see ladarnachd.
ladornas, see ladarnas.
†ladran,-ain, *s.m.* Robber, thief. 2 Highwayman.
ladurna, see ladarna.
là-féill, *pl.* làithean-féill, *s.m.* Holiday.
lag, luig [& laig,] -an, *s.m.* [*f.* in *Badenoch, Poolewe, &c.*] Hollow, cavity. 2 Cave, den. 3 **Pit, dell. 4 **Feeble person. 5 (DMC) Hollow between two knolls. L. a shléisde, *the hollow of his thigh ;* lag a' mhionaich, *the abdomen ;* an cùis nan lag, *in the cause of the weak ;* lagan loisgeach, *burning pits.*
lag, laige, *a.* Weak, feeble, faint. Duine lag, *a weak man.*
lag, *v.n.* see lagaich. Tra lag m' anam, *when my soul fainted.*
lagach, -aich, *s.m.* Weakling, feeble person. 2 **Helpless person. Chaidh na lagaich o 'thaobh, *the feeble departed from him.*
———,** *a.* Full of dens, pits or hollows.
———adh, -aidh, *s.m.* Weakening, act of weakening. 2 Becoming weak. A' l—, *pr. pt.* of laganaich.
———ail,‡‡ -e, *a.* Infirmative.
lagadan cùl a' chinn,(DU) *s.m* Hollow at the back of the head where the neck begins.
lagadh, see lagachadh.
†———, -aidh, *s.m.* Praise, fame, honour.
lagadrag,** -aig, *s.f* Thigh.
lagaich, *pr.pt.* a' lagachadh, *v.a. & n.* Weaken, fatigue 2 Become weak. 3 Give up with fatigue. 4 Diminish. 5 Become fatigued.
lagaichte, *past pt.* of lagaich. Weakened, become weak, diminished, fatigued, debilitated.
lagair,(MS) *v.a* Slacken.
lagan, -ain, *s.m.* Flummery, sowens, a kind of food made from oatmeal by boiling the acid-

ulated juice to the consistency of a thick jelly.
lagan, *n.pl.* of lag.
——, -ain, -an, *s.m.*, *dim.* of lag. Little hollow or cavity. 2 Little pit or den. 3* Meal receiver in a mill. Lagan maise, *a dimple, as on the cheek*; l. uaigneach, *a lonely dell.*
——ach, -aiche, *a.* Full of dells or little hollows. 2 Like a dell.
làganach, -aiche, *a.* Of, belonging to, or like sowens or flummery.
lag-analach,** *s.m.* Asthma. 2 Gasp.
lagan-meath-ghair,** *s.m.* Dimple.
làgaraid,(MMcD) *s.f.* Flood, tidal wave, especially in a narrow estuary or loch of the sea
lagaranaich,(DMC) *s.f* The last throes of death.
lag-bheart, -eirt, -an, *s.f.* Weak instrument. 2 Silly performance.
————ach, -aiche, *a.* Weak. 2 Artless, silly.
————achd, *s. f.* Silliness. 2 Weakness, frailty.
lag-bhrigheach, -eiche, *a.* Of little substance or small value.
lag-chiall,‡‡ -chéille, *s.f.ind.* Indiscretion.
lag-chridhe, *s.f.* Faint heart, chicken heart. 2 Dejected heart.
————ach, -eiche, *a.* Faint-hearted, cowardly. 2 Feeble-minded. 3 Dejected in heart or spirit.
————achd, *s. f. ind.* Faint-heartedness, cowardliness, abjectness, dejectedness. 2 Frailty.
lag-chùiseach, -eiche, *a.* see lag-chridheach. 2 ** Unenterprising. 3 (DMC) Without help, friendless. 4 Weak. 5 (PJM) Wanting in pluck, mentally weak.
————d, *s.f.* see lag-chridheachd.
lagh, -a, *pl.* -anna & -annan, *s.m.* [*f.* in *Badenoch*] Law. 2 Order, method. 3 Act of Parliament. 4 Stretch or bend of a bow. L. na dùthcha, *the law of the land*; bogh' air l., *a bow on the stretch*; l. nan deas-ghnàth, *the ceremonial law*; l. a' chòir-cheartais, *the judicial law*; l. nam modhan (*or* modhannan), *the moral law*; l. na h-eaglais, *the canon law*; fo chasan an lagha, *under the feet of the law*—said of anyone who has committed a crime; air l., *trimmed, ready for action*; cha'n 'eil l. no binn agam dha, *I have neither law nor sentence for him*—I don't want to have anything to do with him, I despise him.
lagh,‡‡ *v.a.* see logh.
lagh,(DU) *v.a.* Mould to a certain shape, particularly applied to wood.
laghach, -aiche, *a.* Decent, tidy, neat. 2 Pretty. 3 Nice. 4 Kind. 5(DMC) Obliging. Duine l., *a kind man*; ni l., *a fine thing*; is l. a fhuaireadh e, *he did pretty well*; 2 *he did surprisingly*; is l. an duin' e, *what a nice man he is!* tha mi gu l., *I am well.*
làghach, *Gairloch* for laghach.
laghadair, -ean, *s. m.* Mould used in shaping horn spoons.
laghadh, see loghadh.
lagh-agartach,‡‡ -aiche, *a.* Litigious.
laghaich,** *v.a.* Permit, allow. Cha l. mi dhuit a dhèanamh, *I will not permit you to do it.*
lagh-aicheadh,(MS) *s.m.* Antinomy.
laghaig, see laghaich.
laghail, -e, *a.* Legal, legitimate, lawful, rightful. 2 Litigious. Ni l., *a lawful thing*; duine l., *a litigious person.*
——eachd, see laghalachd.
laghairt, -ean, *s.m. & f.* Lizard.
laghalachd, *s. f. ind.* Legality, lawfulness. 2* Litigiousness. 3** Allowableness, rightfulness. 4(DMC) Disputing, argumentation.
làghan, *Gairloch & Lewis* for làgan.
laghar, -ghra & -air, *pl.* -ghran, see ladhar.
——ach, see ladhrach.
laghard, *s.m.* Law-giving, moot-hill.
lagh-chleachdach, -eiche, *a.* Judicial.
laghdachadh, -aidh, see lughdachadh. 2** Alloy.
laghdaich, see lughdaich.
————te, see lughdaichte.
lagh-ghnàthach,‡‡ *a.* Judicial.
laghrag, -eig, see ladhrag.
lagh-stéidhichte, *a.* Legislative.
lagh-thabhairteach, -eiche, *a.* Legislative, lawgiving.
————————d,‡‡ *s.f.* Legislatorship.
lagh-thabhairtear,(MS) *s.m.* Lawgiver.
lagh-thartas, -ais, -an, *s.m.* Legislature, act of legislating.
lagh-thagairteach, -eiche, *a.* Litigant.
lagh-thagradair,‡-ean,*s.m.* Litigant, law-pleader.
lag-làmh, -làimh, *s. f.* Weak hand, pithless arm. 2 Weakliness, helplessness.
————ach, -aiche, *a.* Weak-handed, feeble-handed, helpless.
————achd, *s.f.* Weakness of hand.
lag na h-achlaise, *s.f.* Armpit.
†lagsaine, *s.f.* Freedom, liberty. 2 Remission.
lagsainn, see laigsinn.
lag-thaisde,** *s.f.* Abatement in a bargain.
lagus, -uis, *s.m.* Marl.
lài, Poetical abbreviation of làithe or làithean, *n. pl.* of là.
làib, -ean, *s.m.* Mire, clay. 2 Sediment. 3 Puddle. Cha 'n 'eil dorus gun l., *there is no door without a puddle.*
——each, -eiche, *a.* Abounding in mire, miry. 2 Clayey, full of clay. 3 Abounding in sediment.
laibeart, -eirt, -an, *s.m.* Tailor's sleeve-board.
làibeil, -eile, see làibeach.
laibh,** *s.f.* Clay, mire, dirt.
†laibhinn, *s.f.* Leaven.
†————each, *a.* Like dough or leaven. 2 Made of dough or leaven. 3 Raw, unfired as bread.
†————ich, *v.a.* Leaven.
laibhreach, *a.* Of, or belonging to laurel or bay.
laibhreach,** -ich, *s.f.* see lùireach.
laibhreal,** *s.* Bay tree.
laibhrichte, *a.* Laureate.
laibhreas, see labhras.
laibhrig, -ean, see laimhrig.
laichneas, -eis, *s.m.* Joy.
laidh, *v.n.* see luidh.
laidhe, see luidhe.
——achan, see luidheachan.
——agan, see luidheagan.
laidhm, see laom & laoim.
laidh-siùbhla, see luidhe-siùbhla.
Làidinn-nan-cèard, *s.* Tinker's language.
Làidinnear, -eir, *s.m.* Latin scholar.
Làidinnich, *v.a.* Latinize.
Làidinneach, -eiche, *a.* Latin.
Làidionnachadh, -aidh, *s.m.* Latinizing, act of translating into Latin. A' l—, *pr.pt. of* Làidionnaich.
Làidionnaich, *v. a.* Latinize, translate into Latin.
————————te, *past pt.* of Làidionnaich. Latinized, translated into Latin.
làidir, *a. 1st. comp.* làidire, *2nd. comp.* làidirid, *3rd. comp.* làidiread. [The forms treise, treasa, treasaid and treasad, given in Gaelic grammars as comparatives of làidir are not so. These are comparatives of treun.] Strong, stout, able-bodied, powerful. 2 Potent, intoxicating. 3 Fortified, secure from attack,

having great force or power. 4* Surprising, wonderful. 5‡‡ Hard of digestion, strong 6 ‡‡ Strong in smell. L. mar na daragaibh, *strong as the oaks*; duine l., *a strong man*; deoch l., *intoxicating liquor*, dùn l., *a well-secured fort*; 's ann is l. a gheibhear thu, *you act* or *behave surprisingly well*.
làidire, *comp.* of làidir.
———achd, *s.f.* Strength,fortitude,power,force. 2 Ableness. 3(MS) Raciness.
———ad, -eid, *s.f.* Strength, degree of strength Air a làidiread 'sam bheil e, *however strong he be*.
làidireas,** -eis, *s m* Strength, force.
laidirich, see làidrich.
làidreachadh, -aidh, *s m.* Strengthening, growing strong. A' l—, *pr.pt* of làidrich.
làidread, see làidiread
làidrich, *pr.pt.* a laidreachadh, *v a.* Strengthen. 2 Grow strong.
laig, *gen.sing.* of lag.
laige, *comp.* of lag. Weaker, weakest.
———, *s.f.* see laigse.
laigead, -id, *s.f.* Degree of weakness or langour. A' dol an l., *growing weaker*; air l. a neirt, *however weak his strength*.
laigh, see luidh.
laighe, -an, *s.f.* Spade, shovel.
laigheagan,†† -ain, *s.m.* Lying down, reclining.
laighean, -ein, *s.m.* Spear.
laigheur,** -eir, *s.m.* Verjuice.
laight,* *s. f.* Shape, mould. 2 Order, trim. 3(AH) Associates, company. Tha e 'san droch l., *he is mixed up with a bad set*, chuir thu m' ad as a l., *you put my hat out of its shape*; cuir 'na l. e, *put it in its natural order*; bogh' air l., *a bow on the stretch*.
laigse, -an, *s.f.* Weakness, debility, infirmity, feebleness. 2 Faint, langour, fatigue. Chaidh e an laigse, *he fainted*, do l., *your weakness*.
laigsinn, *s.f.* see laigse. 2 *rarely* Liberty, permission.
lail,§ *s.f.* Tulip—*hemerocalleæ*. Not the common tulip, but one which differs from it only in having the corolla and calyx joined together forming a long tube, and some of this variety have no bulb but tubers.
làilt,** *s.f.* Clay, mould.
——each, ** *a.* Clayish. 2 Having mould.
làimh, *gen.sing.* of làmh.
làimh,** *v.a. & n.* Attempt, accomplish,venture.
——— -bhasb,** *v.a.* Fence, practise the art of fencing.
——— -bhasbaireachd, *s.f.* Art of fencing.
——— -chèairde, see làimh-chèaird.
——— -chèard, -aird, *pl.* -an & -cheairde, *s. f.* Handicraft, mechanical trade. 2 Mechanic, artisan.
——— -chèardail,** *a.* Mechanical, like a mechanic. 2 Ingenious.
——— -chleas, -a, -an, *s.f.* Sleight of hand.
——— -chleasaiche, -an, *s.m.* Juggler, sleight-of-hand man.
làimhdeachas, -ais, *s.m.* Captivity, slavery.
†làimh dhia, -dhé, -dhiathan, *s. m.* Household god.
làimheach, *gen.sing.* of làmh in *Skye*.
làimh-fhoilead, ** -aid, *s.m.* Handkerchief.
làimh-ghleusach,‡‡ -aiche, *a.* Manual.
làimhich,** see làimhsich.
làimh-inneach,(AF) *s. m.* Octopus.
làimhreagadh,(DMK) *s.m.* Mixture of oatmeal and water added to the water in which meat had been boiled, thus making it into soup—*Caithness*.
làimh ri, *prep. phrase.* By, near, near to, at hand. L. rium, *near me*; laimh ris an tobar, *near the well*.
làimhrig, -ean, *s.f.* Landing-place, shore, natural landing-place on the shore. 2 Quay. 3 Harbour. 4 Ford. L. baintighearna, *an easy landing-place—lit.* a lady's landing-place.
làimhseach, *s.m.* see làimhseachadh.
———-—, -eiche, *a* Handling. 2 Prone to handle or meddle, apt to feel.
———-—adh, -aidh, *s. m.* Handling, act of handling. 2 Discussion, act of discussing or treating a subject. 3 Treatment of a person or thing. 4* Trade. 5 Management. 6†† Feeling with the fingers, fingering. 7 Wielding, as of a manual weapon. 8** Practising or exercising, as of an implement or tool. A' l—, *pr.pt.* of làimhsich. L. an ni sin, *the management of that affair*; am bheil l. 'sam bith aige? *has he any dealings among hands?* l. lann, *handling* or *wielding of swords*; l. goirt, *a severe handling*.
làimh-sgiath, -sgéithe, see làmh-sgiath.
làimhsich, *pr.pt.* a' làimhseachadh, *v.a.* Feel, handle, touch with the fingers, finger. 2 Handle or treat a person, thing or subject, manage, 3 Deal. 4 Exercise, wield an instrument.
————te, *past pt.* of làimhsich. Handled, fingered, felt. 2 Exercised, wielded. 3 Treated, discussed.
làimh-theann, -einne, } see làmh-theannach.
làimh-theannach, }
làimh-thionnach, see làmh-thionnach.
làimrig, see làimhrig.
làin-cheathairne, see làn-cheathairne.
làin-chéimnich, see làn-chéimnich.
làin-dèanta, see làn-dèanta.
làine, *s.f.* Fùlness, repletion. 2 Completeness. L. mara, *high water*.
làine, *comp.* of làn. Fuller, fullest.
laine,** *s.f.* Gladness, merriment, cheerfulness.
laineach, -eiche, see loinnear. 2**Glad, joyful, merry. Gu l., *joyfully*.
làineachd, see lànachd.
làinead, -id, *s.m.* Fulness, degree of fulness.
laingean,** *a.* Faithful. 2 Steady. 3 Steadfast.
lainn, *gen.sing. & n.pl.* of lann.
———, see loinn.
lainne, see laine.
lainneach, see laineach.
làinneach, -eiche, *a.* see lannach.
lainneil,** *a.* Buxom, handsome.
lainnir, -e, *s.f.* Good polish, brightness, brilliancy, beauty. 2 see lannair.
lainnireach, see loinnreach.
———-—d, see loinnearachd.
lainnirich, see loinnrich.
lainnreach, see loinnreach.
lainntear, see lanntair.
laipeid, *s.f.* Gaelic spelling of *lappet*.
laipheid, -ean, *s.f.* Instrument used in shaping horn spoons.
làir, -e & làrach, *pl.* -aichean, làiridhean & -idhnean, *s.f.* Mare. L.-asal, *a she-ass*.
lair, *s.f.* Offence. Cha ruig thu leas a leithid de l. a ghabhail as, *you need not pique yourself so much on that*.
làir, *gen. sing.* of làr.
lair,** *s.f.* Thigh, haunch.
làir-bhreabach, *s. f.* Rocking-horse. 2 See-saw—*Argyll*. 3 (WC) Turf-parer.
làirceach, -eiche, *a.* Stout and short-legged.
———-——, -aich, *s.m.* Man with thick short legs, fleshy, gross person.
làirceag, -eig, -an, *s.f.* Short fat woman.
làircean, -ein, -an, *s.m* Bulky, fleshy or fat boy or child.
làireach, -eiche, *a.* Having many mares, abound-

ing in mares.
làireach,(AF) *s.f.* Filly.
———, see làrach.
laireag, *s.f.* see learag. 2(AF) Lark.
lair-fligh, *s.* Pine grosbeak, see cnag. 2 Woodpecker.
†**làirge,** *s.f.* Thigh, haunch.
†**làiric,** see làirig.
làirich, see làirig.
làiridhean, *n.pl.* of làir.
làiridhnean, *n.pl.* of làir
†**làirig,** -ean, *s. f.* Moor, hill, sloping hill. 2 Way or pass between two mountains. 3** Burying-place.
lairigidh, see lair-fligh.
làir-mhaide(CR) *s.f.* See-saw—*W. of Ross.* 2 An làir-mhaide (the wooden mare,) an Uist game, generally played indoors, though sometimes outside also. A trapeze was made by means of two pieces of rope tied to a rafter and let down from the ceiling, with a pole tied to them at a distance of about three feet from the ground. On this pole the player had to balance himself, sitting astride. He held another pole in his hands. The object was to strike the ground on both sides with the pole without falling. Whenever one fell off, in addition to the severe shaking, one was out of the game. This game provided very beneficial exercise.—" Uist games " in *Celtic Review, No. 16.* Cuiridh mi air an làir-mhaide thu (I will put you on the wooden mare,) is used as a threat in *Argyll*, referring to the punishment of carrying a person astride on a pole resting on the shoulders of two others.—(AH)
lais,(DMy) *s.* Slap. L. 'san lethcheann, *a slap with the open palm on the cheek.*
†**lais,** see las. 2**Hand. 3 **Cry.
laisceanta,** *a.* Flaming. 2 Inflammable. 3 Passionate, furious. Gu l., *passionately.*
laisde, *a.* Easy, in good circumstances, comfortable.
laisde,** -an, *s.f.* Latchet.
———ach, *a.* Having latchets or thongs. 2 Full of latchets. 3 Like a latchet.
———achd, *s.f.* Easiness in circumstances, comfort.
†**laise,** -an, *s.f.* Flame of fire. 2 Flash.
laiseach,** *a.* Flashing. 2 Flaming. 3 Inflammable.
laisgeanta, -einte, *a.* Fierce, fiery.
————chd, *s.f.* Fierceness, fieriness.
laiste, *past pt.* of las. Kindled, lighted up. 2 Enraged. L. le boil chath, *kindled with ardour for battle.*
laistean, -ein, -an, *s.m.* Gold or silver lace.
laith,(AF) *s.f.* Sweet milk.
†**laith,**** *s.f.* Multitude. 2 Ale. 3 Feast. 4 Stomach.
laithe,(AF) *s.f.* Sweet milk.
laithe,** *s.pl.* Jeweller's scales.
làithe, / **laithean,** } *n.pl.* of là.
làithich,** *s.f.* see làthach.
laithigh, *s.m.* see làthach.
laithilt,** *s.m.* Weighing, as with scales.
làithir, -e, *s.f.* see làthair.
làithre,(AF) *s.f.* Cow. 2 see làir.
———ach, -ich, -ichean, see làrach
———achd, see làthaireachd.
laithrich,** *v.n.* Appear.
laitis,** *s.f.* Gaelic spelling of *lattice.*
†**lalach,** -aich, *s.m.* Giant, champion.
là-luain, *s.m.* Doom's day, the last day.
lamairean,(CR) *s.m.* Trifler, dawdler—*Arran.*
lamairig, see làimhrig. Eadar long is l., *between the ship and the pier—Arran.*

†**lamais,**** *s.* Poet.
lamalach,(AC) *a.* Corrupt.
lamanta,** *a.* Menstruous.
lamarag,†† -aig, -an, *s.m.* Awkward fellow. 2 Cowardly fellow.
———ach,†† -aiche, *a.* Awkward. 2 Cowardly.
lamaranta,(DMC) *a.* Soft. 2 In a half-boiled or half-baked condition.
lamban,‡ -ain, *s. m.* Milk curdled by rennet, see slaman.
———ach, -aiche, *a.* Abounding in or like curdled milk.
làmh, làimh (*gen.* làimheach in *Skye*), *pl.* -an, *s.f.* Hand. 2 Arm. 3 Handle of a tool or instrument. 4**Attempt, attack. 5* Hand, one of a crew. L. an uachdar, *the upper hand ;* thug e l. air, *he attacked him*, or *he attempted it ;* cuir do l. leinn, *lend us a hand ;* mo l. dhuit, (lit. *my hand to you*) *I can assure you;* làmh air làimh, *hand in hand ;* rug e air làimh oirre, *he shook hands with her ;* a' cumail làimh rithe, *paying his addresses to her, keeping her in hopes of marriage ;* tha e an làimh, *he is in custody*, or *he is in a strait ;* fo 'làimh, *under his hand, under his command ;* cum air do làimh, *stay thy hand ;* aig làimh, *at hand ;* mu'n làimh, *in hands, indifferently ;* cha'n 'eil ann ach rud mu'n làimh, *it is but an indifferent matter ;* as an làimh, *out of the hand, aside, off-hand ;* gabh os làimh, *undertake, engage in, assume ;* tha iad ag iomairt an làmhan a chéile, *they understand each other, there is a collusion between them ;* tha ceann mo lamhan air at, *my hands are swollen ;* cuir l. rithe, *sign, endorse.* For meanings of " an làmh ud thall," and " an làmh seo fhéin " see p. 77.
làmh,‡ *v.a. & n.* Dare.
làmh,‡*a.* Able.
làmhach, -aiche, *a.* Having hands or handles. 2*Dexterous, masterly, adroit. 3 Daring. 4 Presuming.
làmhach, -aich, *s.m.* Slinging, casting with the hand. 2 Firing, shooting, report of guns. 3 **Military manœuvres. 4†† Snappishness. 5 Haft. 6 Volley. Luchd-làmhaich, *artillerymen, bowmen, slingers.*
làmhach, -aich, *s.m.* Gleaning, act of gleaning. 2 The thing gleaned. A' l—, *pr. pt.* of làmhaich.
———adh, -aidh, *s.m.* Handling, act of handling, fingering, feeling, groping. A' l—, *pr.pt.* of làmhaich.
làmhachair, -e, see làmhchair.
————eachd, see làmhachaireachd.
làmhachas, -ais, *s.m.* Exercising of the hand or arm. 2 Dexterity. 3** Cannonading. 4** Grovelling. 5†† Snappishness. 6**Military evolutions. 7**Activity. 8**Management. 9 Groping, handling. 10††Taking, seizing, capture. 11††Readiness to finger. 12**Firing of guns. 13**Artillery. [†† gives *s. m.* for 11, and *s.f.* for 10.] Luchd-làmhachais, *artillerymen, archers ;* le l. làidir, *by force.*
làmhachas-làidir, *s.m.* Force, compulsion, undue exercise of power.
làmhachd, *s.f.* see làmhach.
làmhachdradh,†† -aidh, *s.m.* Needless handling. 2††Pawing.
làmhadair,* see làmhainnear.
làmhadh,(CR) -aidh, *s.m.* Axe—*Suth'd.* 2** Pawing, handling, groping.
làmhag,†† *s.f.* Small hand. 2 Axe. [This should be spelt làmhadh, but it is pronounced làmhag in *Gairloch, &c.* This peculiarity in the *Gairloch* dialect extends to most terminations

in -adh, e.g. padhag for padhadh, *thirst.*]
———an, -ain, -an, *s.m.* Handling, fingering. 2 Glove.
làmhaich, *pr.pt.* a' làmhach & a' làmhachadh, *v a.* Glean, as corn. 2 Handle. 3 Finger. 4 **Take in hand.
———te, *past pt.* of làmhaich. Gleaned. 2 Handled, felt with the hands
làmhaidh, *s.* Razorbill, see coltraiche. 2 (AF) Guillemot.
làmhainn, -ean, *s. f.* Glove, especially a kid glove. 2 Mitten. 3 Gauntlet.
làmhainn cat leacainn,§ *s.* Navel-wort, wall-pennywort—*cotyledon umbilicus.* Used as a poultice for scalds or pimples.
———each, -eiche, *a.* Having gloves, abounding in gloves.
———ear, -ir, -an, *s.m* Glover
———earachd, *s.f* Art or trade of glove-making.
———ich, *v. a.* Provide with gloves, put gloves on the hands.
———iche, see làmhainnear.
———ichte, *past pt.* of làmhainnich.
làmhair,** *s.m.* Gunner, shooter.
làmhairc,* *s.f.* Right hand stilt or handle of a plough. (The left one is called corrag.)
lamhairic, see làimhrig.
làmhairt,** *s.f.* Handling, fingering.
lamhalan, see labhallan.
làmhan,** -an, *s.m.* Glove, gauntlet.
làmh-anart, -airt, -an, *s.m.* Towel.
làmhan cat leacainn,** *s. m.* Common navel-wort, see làmhainn cat leacainn.
lamhannan,** -ain, *s.m.* Bladder.
lamhargan,(CR) *s.m.* Handle of a flail—*Arran.*
lamhas, -ais, *s.m.* Glove.
làmhchair, -e, *a.* Ready-handed, handy,clever, active, dexterous, adroit.
———eachd, *s.f.* Ready-handedness, dexterity, adroitness. 2 Sleight of hand. 3 Knack.
làmhchar, see làmhchair.
làmh-charach,(MS) *a.* see làmhchair.
———d,(MS) *s f.* see làmhchaireachd.
làmh-chèardail, -e, *a.* see làimh-chèardail.
làmh-cheird, see làimh-chèard.
———il, see làimh-chèardail.
làmh-chlag, -chluig, *s.m.* Hand-bell.
làmh-chleas, -an, see laimh-chleas.
———achd, see làimh-chleasachd.
———aiche, see làimh-chleasaiche.
làmh-chlì, *s.f.* The left hand.
làmh-choille, *s.f.* Cubit.
———ach, *a.* Cubital.
lamh-chomhart, -airt, *s. m.* Clapping of hands.
lamh-chòmhraig, *s.m.* Combatant
làmhchradh, (CR) *s.m.* Handling of sheep and cattle—*Skye.* 2 (Fionn) Pawing. 3 Needless handling.
làmhchran, see làmhrachan.
lamh-chrann, *s.f.* Handstaff of a flail. 2 Tree of a harp. 3 Handle of a plough.
làmh-chrathadh, *s.m.* Hand-shake.
làmh-dhèanadas, -ais, *s.m.* Handiwork.
lamh-dheanas, -ais, *s.m.* Restraint.
làmh-dhèanta, *a.* Manufactured, hand-made.
lamh-dhèantas, see làmh-dheanadas.
làmh-dheas, -an-deasa, *s. f.* The right hand. A dh'ionnsuidh na laimhe deise, *to the right hand.*
làmh-dhruidh, -ean, *s.m.* Chiromancer, palmist.
———eachd, *s. f.* Chiromancy, palmistry.
làmh-fhadach, -aiche, *a.* Longimanous.
làmh-fhàil, -ean, *s.f.* Bracelet.
———each,(MS) *a.* Armillary.
làmh-fhual, see famh-bhual.
lamhgar, *s.m.* Sunk ledge of rock covered with slippery seaware—*Lewis ;* e.g. sgeir lamhgair.
làmh-ghlais, *v.a.* Manacle, handcuff.
———te, *past pt.* of làmh-ghlais. Manacled, handcuffed.
làmh-ghlas, -ais, -an, *s. f.* Manacle, handcuff. (better glas-làmh.)
làmh-ghlasadh, -aidh, *s.m.* Manacling, act of manacling, handcuffing. A' l—, *pr. pt.* of lamh-ghlais.
làmh-ghleusach,(MS) *a.* Manual.
làmh-ghreim, *s.f.* Handle.
làmh-làidir, -àimh-, *s.m.* Force, oppression, violence. 2 Strong hand. Le l., *with a strong hand*—motto of the Mackays.
làmh-léigh, -ean, *s.m.* Surgeon.
———eachd, *s.f.* Surgery.
làmh-lorg, -luirg, -an, *s.f.* Handstaff of a flail.
làmh-mhuileann, -inn, -uilnean, *s. m.* Hand-mill.
†lamhnadh, -aidh, *s. m.* Bringing forth, nativity.
làmhnain, *s.f.* see lànan & lànann.
làmhnan, -ain, *s.m.* Bladder.
làmh-oibre, -an, *s.m.* Workman, labourer. 2 Good workman.
làmh-oibriche, see làmh-oibre.
làmhrachan, -ain, *s.m.* Handle, shaft. 2 (DMC) Big stick.
làmhrachdaich, *s. m.* Handling, act of handling awkwardly.
———,** *v. a.* Handle clumsily. 2 Grope.
làmhrachdas,** -ais, *s.m.* Groping, handling.
làmhrag, -aig, -an, *s.f.* Awkward, slovenly or indolent woman, slut. 2 Dowdy. 3**Silly woman.
làmhragan, -ain, *s.m.* Awkward handling or using of anything. 2 Groping. 3 Lazy or slovenly habit. 4(DMC) Slowness in doing a thing.
làmhraganach, -aiche, *a.* Of awkward, indolent or slovenly habits.
làmhraich, *pr.pt.* a' làmhrachadh, *v.a.* Handle awkwardly or unskilfully. 2 Grope.
làmhraig,(AF) *s.f.* Allen hawk.
làmh-ròd, -òid, *s.m.* By-road, footpath.
lamhsaich, see làimhsich.
lamhsaid, see langasaid.
làmh-sgiath, -sgéithe, -an, *s.f.* Target, shield.
làmh-sgrìobhadh, -aidh, *s.m* Handwriting. 2 Manuscript.
làmh-sgrìobhaidh,** *s.f.* see làmh-sgrìobhadh.
làmh-sgrìobhair, -ean, *s.m.* Clerk, amanuensis.
làmh-speic, -ean, *s.f.* Hand-spike.
———each, *a.* Abounding in hand-spikes.
lamh-stiùradh, -aidh, *s.m.* Manuduction.
lamh-threòrachadh, -aidh, *s.m.* Manuduction.
làmh-theann, -einne, *a.* see làmh-theannach.
———ach, -aiche, *a.* Close-fisted, gripping.
làmh-thionnach,** *a.* Desirous, eager. 2 Given to chiromancy.
lamh-thuagh, *s.f.* Axe.
lamh-uaireadair, *s.f.* Hand of a watch or clock.
làmhuinn, see làmhainn.
———each, see làmhainneach.
———ear, see làmhainnear.
———earachd, see làmhainnearachd.
———ich, see làmhainnich.
———ichte, see làmhainnichte.
làmh-uisge, *s.f* Sluice-handle.
lamna, *s.m.* Space of time.
†lamnad, *s.* Parturition.
lampa, *s.m.* Gaelic spelling of *lamp.*
lampar,(AF) -air, *s.m.* Small or unfledged bird.

†lamprag, -aig, *s. f.* Glow-worm, see cuileag-shnìomhain.
lamrag, -aig, -an, see lamhrag.
lamraig, see làimhrig.
lamraig,** *s.m.* Black bird with white spots, supposed to be an alien hawk.
làn, làine, *a.* Full. 2 Complete, perfect. 3 Filled, satiated, satisfied. Làn ùghdarras, *full authority ;* l. dhamh, *a full-grown stag or hart ;* l. chothrom, *ample justice, best opportunity ;* l. chumhachd, *discretionary power, full authority, carte-blanche ;* tha l. fhios agam air sin, *I know that quite well.*
làn, làin, *s.m.* Full, fulness, repletion. 2 The tide, flood tide. 3**Corpulence 4 *rarely* Church. 5 Lane. 6 **Swell, as of water. [MacAlpine gives " pique," which should be *lair.*] Rug an l. oirnn, *the tide overtook us ;* l. broinn, *a bellyful ;* l. beòil, *a mouthful ;* 's ann innte tha 'n l. ! *how corpulent she is !* l. dùirn, *a handful ;* 's ann 'san abhainn a tha 'n làn ! *what a swell there is in the river !* l. a chridhe, *enough, plenty ;* thug e l. a chridhe dha, *it gave him as much as he was fit for ;* thàinig l. orm, *my eyes suffused with tears.*
làn, *adv.* Completely, wholly, quite. Làn cheart, *quite right ;* l. fhiosrach, *fully certain ;* l. fhoghainteach, *fully equal to, fully competent.*
lànach, *a.* Fruitful. An grùnnd a b' fhèarr o shliabh gu tràigh, gu fasach, lànach, sultmhorra, *the best of land from hill to strand, productive, fruitful, fertile—Filidh, p, 22.*
lànachadh, -aidh, *s.m.* see lànachd.
lànachd, *s.f.* Fulness, abundance, repletion. 2 Completion, fulfilment.
lànadair, -ean, *s. m.* Smith's iron wedge or mould-piece, with which to shape the eye of an axe or hammer. 2 Funnel, filler.
lànag, *s.f.* Radius.
lanaig, (MMcD) *s.* Narrow path for cattle through the crofts in a township.
làn-aighear,†† *s.m.* Mirth, merry-making.
lànain,** -ain, -an, *s.f.* see lànan.
làn-amharc,‡‡ -airc, *s.m.* Perlustration.
†lànamhas, -ais, see lànanas.
lànamhnas, see lànanas.
lànanas, -ais, *s.m.* Congressus venereus.
lànamhainn, see lànan.
lànamhuin, see lànan.
lànan, -ain, -an, *s.m.* Couple, pair or brace. 2 Married couple. 3 Roof couple. Gu ma buan do 'n l. uasal ! *long may the noble couple live !* l. pòsda, *a married couple.*
lànann, see lànan.
làn-aois, *s.m.* Full age, advanced age.
làn-aosda, *a.* Full of age, of an advanced age.
làn-aosdachd, *s.f.* Fulness of age.
làn-bharail, *s.* Conviction.
làn-bheachd, -an, *s.f.* Full view. 2 Confidence, self-confidence.
làn-bheachdail, -e, *a.* Confident.
làn-bhuidheann, -bhuidhne, -dhnean, *s f.* Full band, gang, garrison, complement of men.
làn-cheathairne, -an, *s.m.* Guard, garrison.
†làn-chéimnich, *v.n.* Wander, ramble.
làn-chothrom, -oim, -an, *s.m.* Ample justice. 2 Full weight. 3**Good opportunity. Tha 'n l. agad, *you have a good opportunity.*
làn-chòthromach, -aiche, *a.* Affording ample justice. 2 Of full weight. 3**Quite convenient.
làn-chothromachadh, -aidh, *s.m.* Weighing, act of weighing thoroughly. A' l—, *pr.pt.* of làn-chothromaich.
làn-chothromaich, *v.a.* Weigh thoroughly.
làn-chothromaichte, *past pt.* Fully weighed.
làn-chrìochnachadh, -aidh, *s.m.* Finishing, accomplishing, act of completely finishing, completion, accomplishment. A' l—, *pr. pt* of làn-chrìochnaich.
làn-chrìochnaich, *pr.pt.* a' làn-chrìochnachadh, *v.a.* Complete, perfect, accomplish a work.
làn-chrìochnaichte, *past pt.* Accomplished, quite finished, brought to a final conclusion.
làn-chròdha, *a* Very brave or powerful.
làn-chruaidh,** *a.* Quite hard, well-tempered. Lannan l., *well-tempered swords.*
làn-chumhachd, -an, *s.m.* Full power, plenipotence
làn-chumhachdach, -aiche, *a.* Having full power plenipotent.
làn-chumhachdach, -aich, *s.m.* Plenipotentiary.
†land,‖ *s.* Scale.
làn-daingneachd, -an, *s.m.* Perfect hold or holding. 2 Perseverance, firmness of purpose.
làn-damh, -aimh, *s.m.* Full grown stag or hart, " royal."
làn-dèanta, *a.* Quite finished, perfectly formed. 2 Perfectly trained. L. ri airm, *well-trained to arms.*
làn-dearbh, *v a* Demonstrate, prove fully. 2 Try thoroughly
làn-dearbhachd, -an, *s.m.* Full proof, full conviction, assurance. Le l., *with full assurance.*
làn-dearbhadh, -aidh, *s.m.* Demonstrating, act of demonstrating, fully proving. 2 Full assurance, conviction. 3 Complete trial. L. air gach duine, *every man fully persuaded.*
làn-dearbhta, *a.* & *past pt.* of làn-dearbh. Fully proved, demonstrated, tried thoroughly, fully convinced.
làn-deimhinn, -ean, *s.m.* Certainty, full assurance or persuasion. Bha l. aige, *he was fully persuaded.*
làn-dhearbh, see làn-dearbh.
làn-dhearbhta, see làn-dearbhta.
làn-dhearcadh,‡‡ -aidh, *s.m.* Perlustration.
làn-dochas,‡‡ -ais, *s.m.* Assurance, certain expectation.
làn-dùirn,** *s.m.* Handful, maniple.
làn-dùbhlan, -ain, -an, *s. m.* Open challenge, open defiance. Bheirinn l. do d' naimh, *I would give an open challenge to thy foes.*
làn-fhios, -an, *s. f.* Full certainty, assurance, knowledge, conviction. Tha l. agad, *you know full well.*
làn-fhiosrach, -aiche, *a* Fully assured or certain. Tha mi l air, *I am quite certain of it.*
làn-fhiosrachadh, -aidh, *s.m* Making certain, act of making certain, assuring, convincing, conviction.
làn-fhiosrachd, see làn-fhios.
làn-fhiosraich, *pr.pt* a lan-fhiosrachadh, *v.a.* Make certain, convince. 2 Be assured or made certain.
làn-fhiosraichte, *past pt.* of lan-fhiosraich. Fully assured, made certain.
lang,** -aing, *s.m.* Feast.
†lang, *s.f.* Falsehood, treachery.
langa,†† *s.f.* Lank female.
langa, *s. f.* Ling (plant), see fraoch. 2 (AF) Ling (fish.) Is i an l. mart-fheòil na mara, *ling is the beef of the sea.*
langach, ¶ -aich, *s.m.* Common guillemot, see eun-dubh-an-sgadain.
langach, -aiche, *a.* Slim, slender. 2 *rarely* False, treacherous.
langach,** -aich, *s.m.* Ling.
langadal,(DMC) *s.* Slow female—*Harris.*
langadar, -air, *s.m.* The top of duidhean, a kind of seaware longer and smaller than tangles.
langaiche, *s.f.* Slimness, slenderness. 2 Falseness. 3 Slender, slim person.

langaid,* -ean, *s. f.* Horse-fetter—*Islay.* 2 ‡Guillemot—*Isles.*
langaideach, -eiche, *a.* Fettered, as a horse. 2 Of, or belonging to horse-fetters. 3 Like a horse-fetter.
langaidh,¶ *s.* Common guillemot, see eun-dubh-an-sgadain.
langaidich,(MS) *v.a.* Clog.
langain, *v.n.* Low, as a cow or deer.
———, *gen. sing.* of langan.
langair,** *s.m.* Seam. 2 Glutton.
langaire'(AH) *s.m.* Links and hook connecting muzzle iron of a plough and the big swingle-tree, commonly called the "bridle."
langais,(AH) *s.f.* Tow-rope.
langaiseachadh, *s.m.* Towing a boat by a rope from the shore. A' l—, *pr.pt.* of langaisich.
langaisich, *pr.pt.* a' langaiseachadh, *v.a.* Tow a boat along the shore.
langan, -ain, -an, *s.m.* Noise or bellowing of a deer, bray. 2 Noise, harangue. 3**Monotony of the human voice. 4**Cant. 5**Breast. 6 ** Shotten fish.
langanach, *a.* Continued bellowing or lowing, as a deer.
langanachd,** *s.f.* Diatribe.
langanaich, -e, *s.f.* Lowing, bellowing. 2 Monotonous sound. 3**Cant. 4(DMC) Yawning.
langanaich, *v.n.* Low, bellow, as a deer. 2 Make a monotonous sound.
langan-bràghaid, -ain-bh-, -an-b-, *s.m.* The weasand, windpipe.
langar, -air, -airean, *s. m.* Seam. 2 Fetter, chain. 3 Horse-fetter. 4 see langasaid.
langar-ìleach, -air-ìlich, -an-ìleach, *s.m.* Lamprey.
langasaid, -ean, *s.f.* Kind of sofa, couch or settee. 2**Courtesy. 3**Crouching
làn-ghealach,** -aich, *s.f.* Full moon. Solus na làn-ghealaich, *the full moon's light.*
làn-ghéilleach, -eiche, *a.* Non-resistant.
làn-ghuin, *s.f.* Period, full stop in *writing.*
langrach, *a.* Full of chains or fetters—*Sàr-Obair.*
làn-laghadh, -aidh, *s.m.* Plenary indulgence.
làn-luach, *s.m.* Full price. Air a l., *at its full price.*
làn-mara, -àin-mh-, *s.m.* Tide, full or high tide.
làn-mhath, *adv.* Full well.
lànmhor, -oire, *a.* Full, complete, plentiful.
lann, -a, -ainne, -ainn & -oinne, *pl.* -an, *s. f.* Blade of a sword or knife. 2 Sword. 3 Lancet. 4**Knife. 5 Weapon, any bladed instrument. 6 Disc. 7 Scale of a fish. 8 Scale or rove, round piece of metal on which nails are clinched inside a boat. 9 Film. Lannan is itean an éisg, *the scales and fins of the fish*; l. na sgéine, *the blade of the knife*; l. liomhaidh, *a polished sword*; l. thana, *a thin blade*; ma liùbhras mi mo chlaidheamh, is ann an aghaidh na lanna, *if I give up my sword, it shall be point first*—i.e. you must fight for it; tharruing iad an lann, *they drew their swords*; l. Spàinndeach, *a toledo*; l. a' bhàis air a shùilean, *the film of death on his eyes.*
lann,* *v.a.* Scale, take scales off fish. 2**Put to the sword. 3 Exercise or fence with the sword.
lann, lainn, -an & lanndaichean, *s.f.* Enclosure. 2 House. 3 Church. 4 Repository. 5 Stud, or boss, as on a shield. 6 Gridiron. 7 Scale (balance.) 8 *rarely* Land. 9 *rarely* Veil. 10 Corn-yard.
lannach, -aiche, *a.* Armed with swords. 2 Scaly, covered with scales. 3 Studded, bossy. 4** Gleaming, coruscant. 5 Bladed. Am bradan l., *the scaly salmon.*
lannachd, *s.f.* Scaliness.
lannadh, -aidh, *s.m.* Peeling. 2 Putting to the sword. 3 Sword exercise. 4 Scaling as of fish.
lannaibh, *dat. pl.* of lann.
lannair, *s.f.* Glitter, radiance, gleaming, reflection of rays from a polished surface. 2**Great flame. 3 Phosphoric glitter from fish scales in the dark, phosphorescence. 4(AF) Lanner, falcon, peregrine falcon. 5 (AF) Cow. 6 Splendour. 7(DMC) Calm or glitter caused by oil on water. Do shùil gun l., *thine eye without radiance.*
lannair, *a.* see lannaireach.
lannaireach, -eich, *a.* Gleaming, glittering, shining, radiant, phosphorescent, burnished, beaming. 2 Fond of sword exercise. Clogaidean l., *gleaming helmets.*
lannaireachd, *s.f.* Gleaming, shining, radiance. 2 Sword exercise. 3 Feats of arms. 4 see loinnearachd.
lannair-sheilge,(AF) *s.f.* Hunt-gleamer hawk.
lann-amharc,** *s.m.* Amphitheatre.
lannan, *n.pl.* of lann.
lannar,** *a.* Bright, gleaming, beaming, radiant. Bu l. a shnuadh, *bright was his aspect.*
lann-bheach,(MS) *s.f.* Apiary.
lann-bhuidhne,** *s.f.* Garrison, barracks.
lann-chuisle, *s.f.* Lancet.
lanndaichean, *n.pl.* of lann.
lanndair, see lanntair.
lann-gleidhte,** *s.m.* Enclosed place, enclosure. 2 Repository.
lann-ghorm, -ghuirme, *a.* Blue scaled, having blue scales.
lannrach, -aiche, see lannaireach.
†lannrach, -aich, -aichean, *s.f.* Vast flame, blaze, sudden conflagration.
lannrachadh, -aidh, *s.m.* Gleaming, glittering, glistening, flaming, shining.
lannraich, *v.n.* Gleam, glitter, shine, blaze, bespangle.
lannsa, *s.f.* Gaelic spelling of *lance.*
lannsach, *a.* Furnished with lances or lancets.
lannsaich, *v.a.* Bleed, let blood.
lannsaiche, *s.m.* Lancer, pikeman.
lannsaid,(CR) *s.f.* *Gairloch* for langasaid.
lannsair, *s.m.* Gaelic spelling of *lancer.*
làn-sgaoilte, *a.* Full-spread.
lann-smig, *s.f.* Razor.
lanntair, -ean, *s.m.* Gaelic spelling of *lantern.* 2 Pantry, partition. 3(CR) Inner part of old houses—*Arran.*
lanntair,* *s.m.* Landscape, beautiful side of a country, full of wood and arable land, facing the sea.
lanntaireach, *a.* Furnished with lanterns. 2 Safe.
làn-phunc, -uinc, *pl.* -an & -annan, *s.m.* Full stop, period in *writing.*
làn-sgrùd, *v.a.* Examine minutely. 2 Catechize. 3 Consider fully.
làn-sgrùdadh, -aidh, *s.m.* Minute examination or consideration.
làn-shealladh, -aidh, *s.m.* Perlustration.
làn-shoilleir, -e, *a.* Very clear, refulgent. 2 Evident, fully seen or understood. 3**Notorious.
làn-shoilleireachadh, -aidh, *s.m.* Making clear, act of making perfectly clear or intelligible. 2**Brightening. A' l—, *pr. pt.* of làn-shoilleirich.
làn-shoilleireachd, *s.f.* Full or complete light.
làn-shoilleirich, *pr. pt.* a' làn-shoilleireachadh, *v.a. & n.* Make quite clear. 2 Become quite clear or evident. 3**Become bright.
làn-shoilleirichte, *past pt.* Made quite clear. 2 Become quite clear.
làn-shoillse, *s.f.* Perfect or clear light. 2 Per-

fect day, broad daylight. L. na gealaich, *the light of the full moon ;* l. na gréine *the universal light of the sun.*
làn-shoillseach, -eiche, *a.* Giving perfect light. 2 Giving general light.
làn-shoillseachadh, -aidh, *s.m.* Giving of perfect light, act of dispensing perfect and general light, lighting wholly and completely. A' l—, *pr.pt.* of làn-shoillsich.
làn-shoillsich, *pr. pt.* a' làn-shoillseachadh. *v.a. & n.* Give perfect or complete light. 2 Make quite clear or evident.
làn-shoillsichte, *past pt.* Perfectly or completely lighted. 2 Made quite clear or evident.
làn-shùil, -shùla, -shùilean, *s.f* Full eye.
làn-shùileach, eiche, *a.* Full-eyed, having full eyes.
lànta,(MS) *a.* Abundant.
làntachd, *s.f.* Plethora, amplitude.
†**lantair**, see lanntair
làn-thlachd, *s. f.* Perfect liking, full contentment.
làn-thoil, *s.f.* Full satisfaction. 2 Concurrence. 3 Satiety.
làn-thoileach, *a.* Fully satisfied, quite contented. 2 Quite willing. Tha mi l., *I am quite contented.*
làn-thoileachadh, -aidh, *s.m.* Giving or act of giving complete satisfaction. A' l—, *pr.pt.* of làn-thoilich.
làn-thoilich, *v.a.* Give full or complete satisfaction. 2 Please to the utmost.
làn-thoilichte, *past pt.* Perfectly satisfied, well pleased, quite contented.
làn-tholl, -thuill, *s.m.* Perforation.
làn-th† holladh, -aidh, *s.m.* Perforation.
làn-thorach, *a.* Fully pregnant.
làn-ùghdarach, -aiche, *a.* Having full power, plenipotent.
làn-ùghdarach, -aich, *s.m.* Plenipotentiary.
làn-ùghdaras, ais, *s. m.* Full power, full authority.
laob,(AF) *s.m.* Cow.
laobh, *a.* Partial, prejudicial.
lao'cionn, see laoigh-cionn.
laoch, -aoich, *s.m.* Hero, champion, warrior. 2 Term familiarly used in applauding a youth.
laochail, -e, *a.* Heroic, brave, soldier-like. 2 Enterprising. 3 Chivalrous.
laochaileachd, *s.f.* Heroism, bravery.
laochalachd, see laochaileachd.
laochainn, *s.m.* Spiritless fellow—*Suth'd.*
laochan, -ain, *s.m., dim.* of laoch. Little hero. 2 Young champion. 3 Familiar term in addressing or applauding a man or a boy. 4 Would-be hero. Sin thu fhéin a laochain ! *that's your sort, my little hero,*—a boy is almost always addressed by this term.
laochar, see laochmhor.
laochmhor, -oire, *a.* Heroic, brave, soldier-like, chivalrous. Giùlan l., *heroic conduct;* gu l., *heroically.*
laochmhorachd, *s.f.* Heroism, bravery.
laochraidh, *s.m. & f.* [Not *pl.* as given by McL & D] Heroes, warriors. 2‡‡ Infantry. 3** Militia, 4* Corps of reserves for emergencies. Dh' eug an l. gharg, *the band of fierce warriors has perished.*
laochraidheach,(MS) *a.* Heroic.
laochraidheachd,(MS) *s.f.* Heroism.
laodag, see lùdag.
laodhan,‡ -ain, *s. m.* Heart of a tree. 2 Pith of wood. 3 Pulp, as of potatoes, wood, &c. 4**Marrow. 5 Remains of potato when seed slips are cut off (also glaothan & glaoghan.) 6 Glutinous substance. Brìgh á l. nam maoth-shlat, *juice from the pith of twigs.*
laodhanach, -aiche, *a.* Pithy, having pith, as wood. 2**Marrowy.
laogh, -aoigh, *pl.* laoigh & laoghan, *s.m.* Calf, the young of a cow or deer. 2 Term of endearment for a child. 3*Friend. Is binn guth laoigh á beinn, *pleasant is the voice of a fawn from the mountains ;* mo laogh geal ! *my dear soul—lit.* my white calf, which looks comical when translated—the English use 'ducky' in the same sense ; A laoigh mo chridhe ! *my darling !* Oidhche Shamhna theirear gamhna ris na laoigh, *at Hallow Eve calves are called stirks.*
laoidh, *s.f.* Pith of wood—*Islay.*
laoghach, -aiche, *a.* Abounding in fawns or calves. 2 see laghach.
laoghail, -e, *a.* Calf-like.
laoghain, *s.f.* see laodhan, 2.
laoghainn, *s.f.* Linen gauge—*Sgeulaiche-nan-caol.*
laogh alluidh, *s.m.* Fawn.
laoghan, *s.m., dim.* of laogh. Little calf. 2 see laodhan. 'S a l. 'ga leanntainn, *and her young (deer) following her—Beinn Dóran.*
laoghanach, -aiche, *a.* Abounding in little calves. see laodhanach.
laoghar, see ladhar.
laogh-bailceach,(AF) *s.m.* Fair, strong calf.
laogh-bailgfhionn,(AF) *s.m.* White-bellied calf.
laogh-balgain,(WC) *s.m.* Imitation calf, stuffed calf used to deceive the cow, her own calf's skin being used, tulchan-calf.
laogh-eilid,(AF) *s.m.* Fawn.
laogh-féidh,‡‡ *s.m.* Fawn.
laoghfheòil,** *s.f.* see feòil-laoigh.
laogh-gogain, *s.m.* Calf brought up by hand. 2 "Mammie's pet."
laogh-ligheach, *s.m.* Newly-calved cow.
laogh-lus, see lus-nan-laogh.
laogh-meadair,(WC) *s.m.* Calf brought up by hand.
†**laoi**, see là & làithean. 2 Hire. 3 Tail.
laoicionn, see laoighcionn.
laoidh, -ean, *s.m.* Verse. 2 Hymn, sacred song. 3 Poem or song in general. 4* Anthem.
laoidh, *a.* Exciting, animating.
†**laoidh**, *v. a.* Exhort, admonish. 2 Excite, animate.
laoidheach,** *a.* Hymnal. 2 Exhorting. 3 Admonishing. 4 Exciting
†**laoidheadh**, -idh, *s.m.* Exhorting. 2 Advice. 3 Hymn-singing. 4 Excitement.
laoidhean, -ein, *s.m.* Pith, pulp, marrow.
laoidheanach, *a.* Pithy, pulpy.
laoighcionn,‡ *s.m.* Tulchan-calf, calf-skin. L. laoigh, *calf-skin ;* l. searraich, *colt's skin.*
laoighfheoil, see feòil-laoigh.
†**laoi-leabhar**, -air, -bhraichean, *s.m.* Diary, day-book, journal.
laoim, *gen.sing.* of laom.
laoim,** *v.n.* Lodge or fall flat to the ground, as standing corn.
laoim,(DMK) *s.f.* Shift. Gheibh mise laoim mo chridhe ort, *I will be revenged on you to my heart's content—W. coast of Ross.*
laoimte, *past pt.* of laoim. Lodged, lying on the ground, as a corn crop.
laoineach, -eiche, *a.* Handsome, elegant, neat, shows, stately. 2** Foppish. Òg l., *an elegant youth.*
laoir, *v.a.* Drub most lustily.
laoireadh, -idh, *s.m.* Rolling in the dust or mire.
†**laoi-reult**, -a, -an, *s.f.* Morning star.
laoisg,(DMC) *s. f.* Number of little ones, litter, rabble.
laoisgean, see laoighcionn.

laom, -aoim, -an, *s.m.* Crowd. 2 Blaze of fire. 3 Sudden flame. 4 Gleaming. 5 Overgrowth without fruit.
laom, *pr.pt.* a' laomadh, *v.a. & n.* Lodge, fall to the ground, as corn from exuberant growth. 2 Cause to lodge or fall to the ground. 3 (CR) Go to shaw or tops (of potatoes.)—*Skye.*
laomach, -aiche, *a.* Glittering, gleaming, blazing. 2 Crooked, curved, as the shores of a lake.
———,(DU) *s.f.* Piece of land where corn falls flat from exuberant growth.
laomachd, *s.f.* Crookedness. 2 Winding, curvature. 3 Gleaming.
laomadh, -aich, *s.m.* Blazing. 2 Abundance, abounding. 3 Falling to the ground, lodging of corn.
laomaich,(WC) *s.f.* Lodged corn or grass. Cha robh ann ach l., *it was only lodged corn.*
laomaidh, *a.* Loamy.
laom-chrann,†† *s.m.* Main beam, rafter.
laomsgair, -e, *a.* Great, prodigious, vast. 2 Fierce, fiery, bold. 3**Abundant. Coire is laomsgaire bàrr, *a dell with most abundant crops*—i. e. a grassy dell.
laomsgaireachd, *s. f.* Vastness, greatness, prodigiousness. 2 Fierceness, furiousness, barbarity. 3 Abundance.
laomsgiorra, *a.* see laomsgair.
laomsgiorrachd, see laomsgaireachd.
laomta, *past pt.* Lodged, laid to the ground, as corn.
laomunn, -uinn, see leòmann.
laor, *s.m.* Toe, see ladhar.
laoran, -ain, -an, *s.m.* Person too fond of the fireside.
laos-boc, -uic, *s. m.* Castrated goat, wether goat.
laosg,(CR) *s.m.* Rabble.
lap,(WC) -an, *s. m.* Defective spot in colour painting or dyeing.
lapach, -aiche, *a.* Faltering, stammering. 2 Feeble, decrepit, impotent, spiritless. 3 Slim. 4 Frost-bitten, benumbed. 5 (MS) Lame.
làpach, -aiche, see làbanach.
làpach, -aich, *s.f.* Marsh, swamp, bog, puddle.
làpach, *a.* Skinny.
lapach, *a.* Benumbed. 2 Frost-bitten. 3 Inactive. 4 Awkward. Neo-l. 'sa chòmh-strì, *active in the combat.*
làpachadh, -aidh, *s.m.* Benumbing, state of becoming benumbed, feeble or spiritless. 2 Becoming swampy or marshy. Tha mo làmhan air l., *my hands have become benumbed.* A' l., *pr.pt.* of lapaich.
lapachas, -ais, *s. m.* Faltering or stammering habit. 2 Feebleness, impotence. 3 Sluggishness. 4 Pliability.
làpachas, -ais, *s.m.* Swampiness, bogginess. 2 Benumbedness. 3 Failing. 4 Mistake.
lapadan, -ain, *s.m.* Species of sea-fish.
lapadh, -aidh, *s.m.* Paw. 2 Claw. 3 Clumsy fist.
lapaich, *pr.pt.* a' lapachadh, *v.a & n.* Be benumbed or stupified, become feeble or spiritless. 2 Benumb, stupify. 3 Become frostbitten. 4* Flap. 5 Flag, lag. Fear nach l, clachain-meallain, *a man whom hailstones cannot benumb.*
lapaiche, *s.* Lameness. 2 Debility.
lapaichte *past pt.* Benumbed, stupified, enfeebled. 2 Frost-bitten.
lapan,(AH) -ain, *s.m.* Sound of footsteps with wet feet, noise made by water in boots.
lapan,(WC) *a.* Spotted, as in colours.
làpan, see làban.
làpanach, -aiche, see làbanach.
lapanach,(DU) *a.* Lame. 2 Feeble, physically unfit.
làpanach, -aich, *s.m.* Full-grown individual who is undersized although sinewy and muscular.
lapasdair,(MMcD) *s.m.* Clumsy, inactive, awkward fellow. L. duine, *a clumsy fellow.*
lapraich,(MS) *v.n.* Lap.
lapra naich,(MS) *v.n.* Lap.
làr, see làir.
làr, -àir & -a, *s. m.* The ground, earth. 2 Floor, ground floor. 3** Centre. 4 Low ground. 5 (CR) Applied to the floor of any room when formed of stone, clay or earth, in *W. of Ross.* Air l., *on the ground, on the floor* ; a' dol mu l., *going to nought* ; cuir mu làr e, *abrogate it*; mu l. *forgotten, neglected* ; *2 lost* ; *3 abolished* ; do thùineadh mu l., *thy dwelling underground;* nèamh is l., *heaven and earth.*
làr, *a.* see làn. Làr-bhurraidh, *a complete blockhead.*
làrach, -aich, -aichean, *s.f.* Site of a building, vestige. 2 Ruin. 3 Field of battle, scene of a battle. 4 Habitation, abode. 5 Farm. 6 see làireach. 7(DMC) Mark, scar. An l. nam bonn, *on the spot—lit.* in the print of the soles.
làrach, -aiche, *a.* see làireach.
làrag, *s.f.* Larch-tree.
làr-bhrat, -bhrait, *s.* Carpet.
làr-chaibe,(AH) *prov.* for caibe-làir.
làr-mhaide, see làir-mhaide.
†larum, -uim, Gaelic spelling of *alarm.*
larumach, *a.* Giving an alarm or warning.
las, *pr.pt.* a' lasadh, *v.a. & n.* Kindle, light. 2 Get into a passion, enrage. 3 Sparkle, flash, shine. 4 Burn, blaze, gleam, inflame. L. an teine, *kindle the fire* ; l. a' choinneal, *light the candle.*
las, *s.* Flame.
las, *a. W. of Ross.* for lasach.
lasach, -aiche, *a.* Slack, loose, loosened. 2 Fiery, inflammable. 3 Not firm.
lasachadh, -aidh, *s.m.* Slackening, loosening, act of slackening. 2 Remission, cessation, relaxation. 3 Relief. 4 Ease. A' l—, *pr.pt.* of lasaich. Tha na teudan air l., *the strings have become loosened* ; fhuair e l., *he got relief* ; beagan lasachaidh, *some relaxation.*
lasachail, *a.* Anodyne, antalgic.
lasachd, *s.f.* Looseness, slackness.
lasaiche, see lasachd.
lasadair, -ean, *s.m.* Inflamer.
lasadan, -ain, *s.m.* Match to set on fire with.
lasadh, -aidh, *s. m.* Lighting, act or state of lighting. 2 Blazing, shining. 3 Flame. 4 Flaming. 5 Flush, blush. 6(MS) Animosity. 7 Lust. 8 Lace. 9 Inflaming. L. na h-oidhche, *the flame of night* (*a beacon*); a' cur lasaidh 'na gruaidhibh, *giving a flush to her cheeks.* A' l—, *pr. pt.* of las.
lasag, -aig, -an, *s.f.* Little flame or blaze, scanty fire. 2 Fit of anger. 3 Faggot. 4 Passionate woman. 5 Combustible substance.
lasagach, -aiche, *a.* Burning in little flames. 2 Blazing. 3 Combustible. 4 Passionate.
lasaich, *pr.pt.* a' lasachadh, *v.a.* Slacken, loose. 2 Ease, relieve. 3 Remit. 4 Intermit. 5 Give over, cease. 6 Flag, lag. L. an còrd, *slacken the rope* ; nach l. thu ? *will you not give over ?*
lasaichear, *fut.pass.* of lasaich.
lasaichte, *past pt.* Slackened, loosened, eased, relieved.
lasail, -e, *a.* Fiery, inflammable.
lasair, -srach & -sair, *pl.* -sraichean, *s.f.* Flame, flash of fire. 2 Spark. 3 Flashy young fellow. L. feirg, *a flame of anger* ; o chumhachd na lasrach, *from the power of the flame.*

lasair-chéire, *s.f.* Waxlight, candle-light.
lasair-chlach, -chloiche, *pl.* -sair-chlachan, *s.f.* see clach-lasair.
lasair-choille, -srach-, -sraichean-coille, *s. f.* Goldfinch—*carduelis elegans.* 2**Woodpecker.

409. Lasair-choille (1) 410. Lasair-choille. (2)

lasair-choille,¶ *s.f.* Green woodpecker—*picus viridis.*
lasaireach, *a.* see lasrach.
lasair-lèana,§ *s.f.* Spearwort, see glas-leun.
lasan, -ain, -an, *s.m.* Anger, passion. 2 Fit of passion. 3 Flame of wrath. 4 Spark.
lasanta, -ainte, *a.* Fiery, passionate, subject to fits of anger. 2 Brave. 3 Hot.
lasantachd, *s.f.ind.* Fierceness, fieriness, passionateness. 2 Inflammableness. 3 Ardour.
lasarach, see lasrach.
lasarachail, see lasrachail.
lasarachd, see lasrachd.
lasarra, *a.* Combustible. 2(MS) Acrimonious 3(MS) Ardent. 4(MS) Hot.
lasartha, see lasradh.
lasd,** -aisd, *s.m.* Ballast. 2 Lading.
lasdach, -aiche, see lastanach.
lasdachd, *s.f.* Lordliness.
lasdadh, *s.m.* Lace.
làsdadh,(MS) *s.m.* Lastery.
làsdail, *a.* Lordy, imperious, saucy, boastful. Air tionndadh an diugh cho làsdail, *has become to-day so lordly—Duanaire. 166.*
lasdaire, see lasgaire.
làsdalachd, see lastan.
lasgaire, -an, *s.m.* Youth, young man, "spark," fop, beau, dandy. 2 Champion. 3**Macaroni.
lasgaireach, -eiche, *a.* Foppish, beauish.
lasgaireachd, *s.f.* Foppishness, beauishness.
lasgan,(AH) -ain, *s. m.* Slight outburst. L. gàire, *merry peal of laughter* ; l. gaoithe, *fresh breeze.*
lasganta, *a.* Ardent.
lasgar, -air, -ean, *s.m.* Sudden noise.
lasgarra, *a.* Active, brave, fiery. 2 see lasarra. 3 see lasgaireach.
lasrach, -aiche, *a.* Flaming, burning, emitting flames. 2 Combustible. 3 Passionate.
lasrach, *gen.* of lasair.
———, -aich, *s.m.* Flames, flashes of light.
lasrachail, *a.* Flaming, burning, gleaming. 2 Combustible.
lasrachd, *s. f.* Combustibleness, tendency to kindle or flame.
lasradh,** -aidh, *s.m.* Flaming, burning, gleaming.
làsradh, *s.m.* Lastery, red colour.
lasraich,* *s.f.* Conflagration.
last,** see lasd.
lastain, *s.f.* Hem, fringe, edge.
làstan, -ain, *s.m.* Pride, sauciness, lordliness, boasting for nothing.
làstanach, -aiche, *a.* Proud, lordly, saucy, imperious, overbearing.
làstanachd, *s.f.* see lastan.
lasuchadh, see lasachadh.
lasuich, see lasaich.
†lat, *s.m.* Foot.
†lath, -aith, *s.m.* Youth. 2 Champion. 3 Dog.
làth, *pr.pt.* a' làthadh, *v.a. & n.* Benumb, be benumbed. 2 Besmear.
latha, *pl.* -chan & làithean, see là.
làthach, -aich, *s. f.* Clay, mire. 2 Puddle, swampy place. 3††Soft clay on the sea-shore. 4 Mortar. 5 Sea-weed, sea-ware. 6 Stuff drifted to the shores of a sea or lake. Post an l., *tramp the mortar.*
làthachach,** *a.* Cloddy. 2 (DC) Muddy, boggy. 3 Clayey.
làthachail, -e, *a.* Religinous, limous. 2**Muddy, marshy, puddly. 3** Full of seaweed or seaware.
lathachan, *n.pl.* of là.
làthadh, -aidh, *s.m.* Besmearing. 2 Act of besmearing. A' l—, *pr.pt.* of làth.
làthaich, *s.* Moss, moor, peat-moss—*Suth'd.* 2 (DMK) also Mud—*W. coast of Ross.* 2 (DC) Clay, mud on shore.
lathaichean, *n.pl.* of là.
lathail, -e, *a.* Daily.
lathailt, -e, -ean, *s. f.* Knack, art, method. 2 Limit, bound. 3* Mould, shape. 4 see laithilt. Cuir an l., *arrange* ; fhuair mi an l. air, *I have got the knack of it.*
———each, -eiche, *a.* Having a knack or right method of doing anything, methodical. 2 Adequate. 3 Becoming. Gu l., *aptly.*
———eachd,** *s. f.* Method. 2 Methodicalness. 3 Adequateness. 4 Seemliness. 5 (DC) Bragging—*Argyll.*
làthair, -e, *s.f.* Presence, existence, company, sight. †2 Victory. Na tig an l., *do not present yourself* ; mach as mo làthair ! *out of my presence* ; an l. a chéile, *face to face, in the presence of each other* ; cum as an l., *keep out of sight.* (an làthair is not an *adv. & a.* as given by McL & D and Armstrong, but always a *s.*) An làthair, Present. 2 Near, at a small distance. 3 Alive, surviving, remaining. 4 Truly, indeed, verily. Am bheil e an l. ? *is he in existence ?* neas a bhios mi an l., *while I am present, while I live* ; am fear nach 'eil an l., *he that is no more,* or *he that is absent* ; an robh e an l. ? *was he present ?* gun chrioman an l., *without a morsel remaining ;* thoir an l., *produce, put down before me.*
lathaire,** *s. f.* Thigh. 2 (DC) Splay-foot—*Argyll.*
làthaireach,** *a.* Present.
———-—d, *s.f.ind.* Presence, company. A l., *his bodily presence.*
†lathar, -air, -ean, *s.m.* Acquisition. 2 Provision. 3 Hidden meaning, mystery. 4 Secret, private story. 5 Strength, vigour. 6 Knowledge. 7 Assembly. 8 Place of meeting. 9** Narrative.
làthar, *s.* see (an) làthair.
làth-leabhar, see leabhar-là.
lathrach, -aich, see làrach.
lathus, *s.m.* see spealt.
là-traisg, *pl.* làithean-t-, *s.m.* Fasting-day.
———aidh, *Gairloch &c.* for là-traisg.
le, *prep.* With, together with, in company with. 2 With, by, by means of. 3 In possession of. 4 In favour of, on one's side. 5 Along with, down with, down with the current. 6 In estimation of, with, in feeling or sentiment. Bhuail e i le cloich, *he struck her with a stone ;* tha e le 'r càirdean, *he is along with, in the in-*

terest of, or *he belongs to, our friends* ; b' fhada le Seumas an là, *James felt the day tedious* ; sìth le d' anam, *peace with thy soul* , le mnaoi, *by means of a woman* ; le seo, *by the way* , le d' chead, *by your leave* ; iad-san is le Criosd, *they who are Christ's* ; na dealbhan bu le a h-athair, *the pictures that were her father's* , le d' chead, *by your leave.*

Thus combined with the personal pronouns : leam, *with me* , leat, *with thee* ; leis, *with him* ; leatha, *with her* ; leinn, *with us* , leibh *with you* , leò, *with them.* *Emphatic forms* : Sing. 1 leam-sa, 2 leat-sa, 3 *m* leis-san, *f.* leatha-sa ; plur. 1 leinne, 2 leibh-se, 3 leò-san.

lea, see leatha.

lèab, -a, -an, *prov.* for leòb.

leaba, see leabaidh.

leabach, *gen. sing.* of leabaidh.

lèabach, -aiche, *a.* see leòbach. 2**Awry. 3** Awkward, staring.

leabachadh, -aidh, *s.m.* Imbedding. 2 Lodging. A' l—, *pr.pt.* of leapaich. Tha 'n t-uisge a' l. an seo, *the water is lodging here* ; a' l. 'nam fheòil, *imbedding in my flesh.*

leabachan, -ain, -an, *s.m.* Bedfellow.

leabachas, -ais, *s.m.* Lodgment.

leabadh, see leabaidh.

leabag, -aig, -an, *s.f.dim.* of leabaidh. 2 Little bed.

lèabag, -aig, -an, *s.f.* **Auricle. 2**Flap. 3 **Anything that hangs broad and loose. 4 **Leaf of a door.

lèabag, -aig, -an, *s.f.* Flounder.—*pleuronectus solea.* 2**Loch Lomond flounder—*pleuronectes Leviniœ.* 3 Sole (fish.)

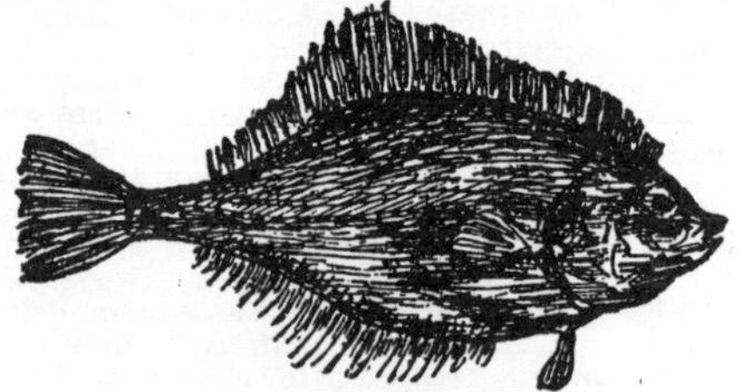

411. Lèabag (1.)

leabagach, -aiche, *a.* Abounding in little beds.

lèabagach, -aiche, *a.* **Flapped. 2 Hanging loose. 3 Folding, as a door. Dorus l., *a folding door.*

lèabagach, -aiche, *a.* Abounding in flounders.

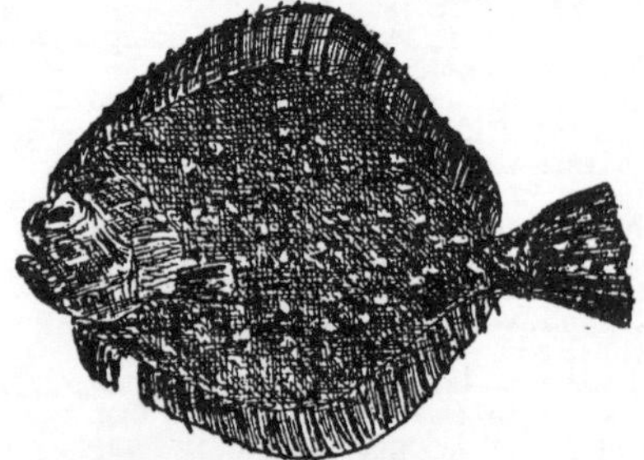

412. Lèabag-bhrathainne.

lèabag-bhrathainne,(AF) *s.f.* Turbot.

lèabag-bhreac, *s.f.* Plaice—*Lewis.*

lèabag-chèarr,(AF) *s.f.* Sole (fish.) ill. 413.

lèabag-chlogaide, *s.f.* Beaver (hat.)

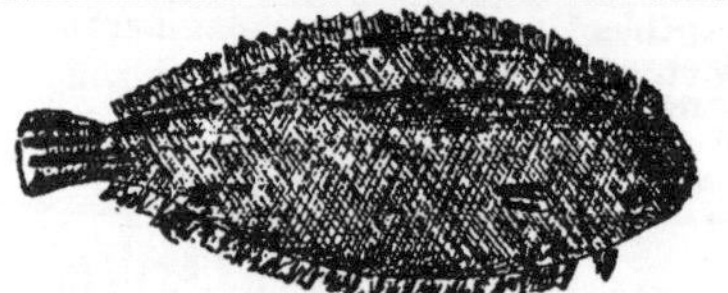

413 Lèabag-chèarr.

lèabag-ghlas, *s.f.* (*Lewis*) Flounder. 2 Sole.

lèabag-leathann, (DC) *s.f.* Halibut—*W. coast.*

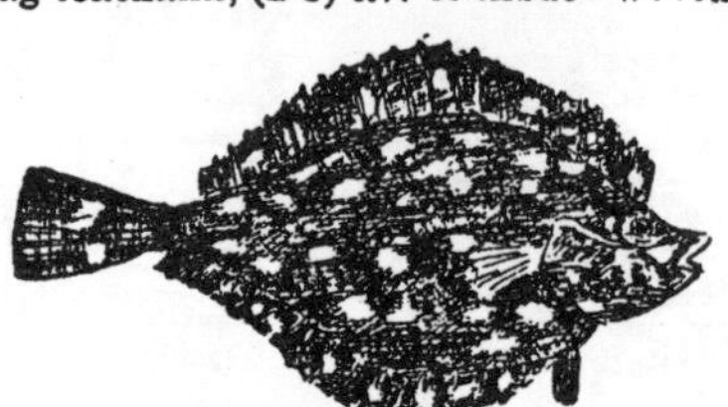

414. Lèabag-mhór.

lèabag-mhór, *s.f.* Plaice (fish.)

lèabag-uisge, *s.f.* Whitch

leabaich, *pr.pt.* a' leapachadh, *v.a.* Imbed. 2 Lodge, as water.

leabaichean, *n.pl.* of leabaidh.

leabaidh, *gen.* leapa & leapach, *pl.* leapaichean, *s.f.* Bed, couch. 2 Channel of a river. 'Na l., *in his bed* ; a l. dhoilleir, *its gloomy channel* ; l. lùthaidh, *or* l. thogalach, *a folding bed* ; l. chùl-béince, *a bed intended for the promiscuous repose of a family and of guests*—it was formed by the cottage wall on one side, and by the trunk of a tree or a plank on the other, with a sufficient quantity of heath, fern or straw and some blankets ; l. chlòimh *or* l. itean, *a feather-bed* ; l.-chònnlaich, *or* l.-fhodair, *a straw-bed* ; l.-fhraoich, *a heather-bed* ; l.-luachrach, *a bed of rushes* ; l.-mhuill, *a chaff-bed* ; l.-na-taoim, l.-thaoim, l.-na-taoma *or* l.-taomaidh, *place where the water gathers for the baling-dish.*

leabaidh-laoigh,(DU) *s.f.* Uterus (of the lower animals.

leabaidh-loisgte,(CR) *s.f.* Ricochet—*Gairloch.*

leabaidh-righe,(CR) *s.f.* Ricochet—*Lochbroom.*

———————, (DU) *s.f.* Bier or bed on which a dead body is straightened.

leabaidh-shiùbhladh, see luighe-siùbhladh.

lèabh, see leugh.

———adh, -aidh, see leughadh.

†**leabhadh,** -aidh, -aidhean, *s. f.* Race, generation.

leabhaireachd,(MS) *s.f.* Reading.

leabhar, -air, -bhraichean, *s.m.* [*f.* in *Badenoch*] Book, volume. Leabhar Eòin (given by MacAlpine, apparently for leabhar sheun), *a book full of receipts for witchcraft and incantation* ; l.-ùrnuigh, *a prayer-book* ; an l. dearg, *the Red Book, a MS. collection of ancient Gaelic poetry.*

leabhar, *a.* see leobhar.

leabhar-ceasnachaidh, } *s.m.* Catechism.
leabhar-ceasnaich, }

leabhar-cheangladair, see leabhar-cheanglair.

leabhar-cheangladh, -aidh, *s.m.* Bookbinding.

leabhar-cheanglair, -ean, *s.m.* Bookbinder.

leabhar-cheist, *s.m.* Catechism.

leabhar-chlàr, -àir, *s. m.* Pasteboard. 2 The "boards" of a book.

leabhar-choimhead, *s.* Book-keeping.

leabhar-chòir,** *s.f.* Copyright.

leabhar-chuimhneachain, *s.m.* Album. 2 Notebook.

leabhar-cùnntais, *s.m.* Account-book.

leabhar-fhiach, -air-, -bhraichean-fiacha, *s. m.* Ledger, account-book.
leabhar-là, *s. m.* Diary, journal. 2 Account-book.
leabhar-làimh, *s.m.* Manual.
leabhar-lann, -ainn, -an, *s.m.* Library.
———air,** *s.m.* Bookseller.
leabhar-poc, *s.m.* Pocket-book.
leabhar-reiceadair, *s.m.* Bookseller.
————eachd, *s.f.* Bookselling, business of bookselling.
leabhar-reicear, see leabhar-reiceadair.
leabhar-thràth-eachdraidh, -air-, -bhraichean-, *s.m.* Chronicle. 2**Minute-book.
leabhar-ùrnuigh, *s m.* Prayer-book.
leabhodach, see lethbhodach.
leabhrach, -aiche, *a.* Bookish, abounding in books.
leabhrach,** -aich, *s.f.* Library.
————an, -ain, -an, *s.m.* Pamphlet.
leabhrachan-cràbhaidh, *s.m.* Manual.
leabhradair,* -ean, *s. m.* Publisher, editor, author.
leabhradan, -ain, -an, *s.m.* Library.
leabhragan, -ain, -an, *s.m.* Library.
leabhraiche,* *s m.* Librarian. 2 Bookseller.
————an, *n.pl.* of leabhar.
leabhran, -ain, -an, *s.m.*, *dim.* of leabhar. Little book, manual, pamphlet.
————ach,†† *a.* Abounding in small books.
leabhrathair, see lethbhrathair.
leabhruadair, see lethbhruadair.
leabhruich, see lethbhruich.
leab-luidhe,** *s.f.* Confinement to bed. 2 Lying in bed.
————each,** *a.* Bed-ridden.
†leac,** *v.a.* Flay. 2 Destroy.
leac, lice [& **lic] *pl.* leacan, *s.f.* Flag, slab, flat stone. 2 Tomb-stone. 3 Plate, as of metal. 4 Slate to write on. 5 Declivity. 6 Cheek. 7‡‡*poetically* Hill, declivity, summit of a hill. 9 (DMy) Ledge of rock jutting out from the foot of a cliff on the foreshore, and covered by the sea at flood tides. 8 House. Taobh na lice, *at the side of the tomb-stone;* gu l. an rìgh, *to the king's house;* do 'n òg-mhnaoi a b' àillidh leac, *to the virgin of fairest cheeks;* l. an teallaich, *the hearth-stone;* l. an teintein, *the hearth;* l. eidhre, *a sheet of ice;* mhaolaich an leac a bhàrr, *the plate blunted its (the tool's) point.*
leacach, -aiche, *a.* Abounding in tomb-stones, flags, plates or slabs. 2‡‡Having large cheeks. 3**Slaty. 4 Flat. 5*Granite. 6 Having declivities. Sron l., *a flat nose.*
————, -aich, -ean, *s f.* The bare summit of a hill. 2** *s.m.* Side of a hill.
————adh, -aidh, *s.m.* Paving, act of paving or laying with flat stones. A' l—, *pr. pt.* of leacaich.
leac-a'-chealaich, *s.f.* Flue-stone of kiln, see under àth.
leacadan,** -ain, *s.m.* Chin-cloth, child's bib.
leacadair, *s.m.* Tiler.
leacadh,** -aidh, *s.m.* Destroying. 2 Laying with flags.
leacag, -aig, -an, *s.f.*, *dim.* of leac. Little flat stone or flag. 2**Slate.
————ach, -aiche, *a.* Abounding in small flat stones or slates.
leacaich, *pr.pt.* a' leacachadh, *v.a.* Pave or lay with flat stones. 2 Tile.
————te, *past pt.* of leacaich. Paved, laid with flat stones.
leacaid, -ean, *s.f.* Stroke on the cheek.
————each, -eiche, *a.* Placoid, plate-like.
leacainn, see leacann.
leacainneach, see leacannach.
leacainte, see leacanta.
leacan, -ain, -an, *s.m.* Navel-wort, wall-pennywort, penny-leaf, penny-pies,—*cotyledon umbilicus.* 2**Little flag.

415. Leacan.

leacanachadh, -aidh, *s.m.* Making flat. 2 Act of flattening or making flat. A' l—, *pr. pt.* of leacanaich.
leacanaich, *pr.pt.* a' leacanachadh & a' leacanaich, *v.a.* Flatten, make flat. 2 Get inseparably fond of, as a child of a nurse. 3 (DMy) Lay awake in bed. 4 Recline and idle away the time outside. A' leacanaich air a leabaidh, *lying lazily on his bed.*
————te, *past pt.* of leacanaich. Flattened, made flat.
leacann, -ainn, -an, *s. f.* The broad side of a hill, broad slope, steep shelving ground. 2** Steep green surface. 3** Shelvingness. 4** Downhill. 5 Side of the head, cheek, see lethcheann. Sruth na leacainn, *the stream of the mountain-side.*
————ach,** *a.* Having steep surfaces. 2** Hilly. 3 Having large cheeks.
leacanta, -ainte, *a.* Laid with flat stones. 2 Full of flat stones or flags. 3 Stiff, precise, rigid, exact, punctilious, formal. 4 Forward, impudent. 5 Ceremonious. 6 Starched. 7 Neat.
————chd, *s.f.* Stiffness, rigidness, precision, exactness, punctiliousness. 2 Ceremoniousness. 3 Impudence, forwardness. 4 Neatness.
leac-an-tealaich, *s. f.* Flue-stone of a kiln, see àth. 2 (DMK) also Hearth-stone of a dwelling house—*W. coast of Ross.*
leac-chrè, *s.f.* Tile.
leac-deighe, *s.f.* Flake of ice.
leachd, see leac.
————ach, see leacach.
————ann, see leacann.
leachdanntachd,(MS) *s.f.* Prolation.
leachlach, see lethchlach.
leachrun, see lethchrun.
†leacht, *s.f.* Lesson.
†————an, -ain, *s.m.* Lecture, lesson.
leac-iobairt,* *s.f.* Altar.
leaclach,* *s. f.* Granite.
leac-lighe, *s.f.* Grave-stone, tombstone, monumental slab.
leac-lithidh, see leac-lighe.

leac-oighre, see leac-eidhre.
leac-ruaidhe, *s.* The rose (disease) when it is hard and flat.
leac-ruiteach, -eiche, *a.* Ruddy-cheeked. Ribhinn l., *a rosy, ruddy-cheeked girl.*
leac-shuaine, *s.f.* Tile. 2 (DMy) Slate
leacta,** *past pt.* Flagged, paved with flags or slabs.
leac-thana, *s.f.* Lamina, very thin slab.
leac-theallaich, see leac-an-teallaich.
leac-uaighe, *s.f.* Grave-stone, tombstone.
leac-ùrlar, -air, *s.m.* Pavement, paved floor.
lèad, see leud.
lead,* see leadan. liodair in *Argyll*—DC.
leadain, *gen.sing. & n. pl.* of leadan.
leadair, *pr.pt.* a' leadairt, *v. a.* Mangle, rend, maim, bruise, torment. 2* Drub, lay hold of a person's hair in one hand and belabour him furiously with the other. 3 Abuse. 4**Massacre. 5††Trample on.
leadairt, *s.f* Tearing, mangling, maiming 2 Abusing. 3 Massacring, massacre. Air an l. le geur lainn, *they being mangled by sharp swords.* A' l—, *pr pt.* of leadair.
leadairt, *v.a.* see leadair.
———e,** *a.* Weary. 2 (DC) Draggled.
leadan, -ain, -an, *s.m.* Teazle—*dipsacus sylvestris.* 2 Notes in music. 3 Head of hair, long flowing hair, lock of hair, ringlet. [* gives Little pretty head of hair. 4 The Litany. 5 Barnacle goose, see cathan. 6††The Rosary L. bréige, *false hair.*

416. Leadan.

leadanach,** -aich, *s.m.* Cloth dresser.
———, -aiche, *a.* Musical, melodious. 2 Abounding in teazle. 3 Having long and fine hair. 4 Precise. 5 Belonging to the Litany.
leadan-an-fhùcadair,‖ *s.m.* Fuller's teazle—*dipsicus fullorum.*
leadan liosda,§ *s. m.* Burdock, see suirichean suirich.
leadarra, *a.* Harmonious, melodious, musical. 2 Elegant. 3 Sharp. 4 Mangling. 5 (AH) Fastidious in choice of words, (applied to children and others inclined to indulge in elegant and laboured platitudes.
———chd, *s.f.ind.* Harmoniousness, melodiousness. 2 Elegance. 2 (AH) Finicalness in conversational diction or choice of expressions.
leadhmann, see leòmann.
leadraigeadh,(DMy) *s.m.* Leathering, flogging.
leafhacal, see leth-fhacal.
leag, *pr. pt.* a' leagail & a' leagadh, *v. a. & n.* Throw down. 2 Demolish. 3 Lay, lay down. 4 Lay with, as paving. 5 Cool. 6††Fell. 7* Put down, as a wrestler.
Leagaidh mi thu, *I will knock you down;* l. do cheann far am faigh thu 'sa mhaduinn e, *lay your head where you will find it in the morning;* l. mi mo chas air an fhàradh, *I set my foot on the ladder;* l. mi mo chas a dh' ionnsuidh a' chaisteil, *I bent my steps towards the castle;* l. mi m' uchd (*or* carraig m' uchd) air an t-snàmh, *I set forth swimming, began to breast the wave;* cha do l. a lùdag air feadan piobaire a b' fheàrr, *no better piper ever laid his little finger on a chanter;* leagaidh tu do chùrsa a' cheart thaobh a ghabh iad, *you will set your course in the precise direction they have taken;* chaidh amharus a leagail air, *suspicion was laid upon him;* cìs a leag na Lochlannaich air Albainn, *a tribute which the Lochlanners laid on Scotland;* l. iad peanas oirnn, *they laid penalties upon us;* leagadh dleasdanas eudthromach orra, *heavy responsibilities were laid on them;* feumaidh iad a bhi leagta ris a' bhreith sin, *they must bow to, be satisfied with that judgment;* thog a' Ghréig a cùis a dh' ionnsuidh nan rìoghachdan móra, agus dh' aontaich i bhi leagta le 'm breith-san, *Greece appealed, and brought her case before the Great Powers, and agreed to abide by their decision;* leig bunait, *lay a foundation.*
leagach,** *a.* Dilatory. 2 Dowdy.
leagadh, -aidh, *s m.* see leagail. An Leagadh, *Adam's fall.*—††
leagaid, *s.m.* Legate. 2 Offering.
leagail, *gen.* leagalach, *s. f.* Fall. 2 Throwing down, act of throwing down or demolishing. 3 That part of a boat that is flattened out before building up the sides. 4 (DMC) Laying down. An àm togail na sithne agus a leagalach, *between descrying the game and bringing it down.*
——— -shaighdear, *s.m.* Uist game, see propataireachd.
leagair,** *s.m.* Idler. 2 Jogger (man.)
———eachd, *s.f.* Lagging.
leagait, see leagaid.
leagarra,†† *a.* Plausible, smug. 2 Insinuating. 2 Self-satisfied. *Argyll.*
†leagfadh, -aidh, see leagadh.
leagh, *pr.pt.* a' leaghadh, *v.a. & n.* Melt, cause to melt. 2 Melt, dissolve, become liquid. 3 Fuse. 4 Thaw. 5 Smelt. L. mo chridhe, *my heart melted.*
lèagh, see leugh.
leaghach, -aiche, *a.* Soluble, that can be melted, colliquent.
†leaghad, -aid, *s.m.* Bandage, band.
leaghadach, -aiche, *a.* see leaghach.
leaghadair, -ean, *s.m.* Melter, smelter, founder.
———eachd, *s.f.ind.* Melting, process of melting or smelting, foundry.
leaghadh, -aidh, -aidhean, *s.m.* Melting, act of melting, dissolving. 2 State of becoming liquid. A' l—, *pr.pt.* of leagh.
†leaghan, -ain, -an, *s.m.* Liquor, liquid.
leaghantachd, *s.f.ind.* Liquescency.
leaghta, *past pt.* of leagh. Melted, smelted, molten, dissolved, become liquid. An iomhaigh l., *the molten image.*
———ch, -aiche, *a.* see leaghach.
leaglaidh, *s. pl.* Rushes.
leaghtach, see leaghach.
leagta, *a.* & *past pt.* of leag. Thrown down, demolished. 2 Laid down. 3 Resolved, intent upon, bent on. 4 Let fall, overturned, thrown. 5 (DMK) In agreement with. 6 ** Felled. Tha mi leagta le sin, *I agree with that.*
lealamh, see lethlamh.
———ach, see lethlamhach.
lealg,** *pr.pt.* a' lealgadh, *v.a.* Lick.
lealgadh, -aidh, *s.m.* Licking. A' l—, *pr.pt.* of lealg.
leam, *prep.pron.* With me. 2 By me. 3 In my favour, on my side. 4 In my opinion or estimation. 5 Along with me. 6*By my means. 7 My property.

Is leamsa seo, *this is mine*; thalla (falbh) leamsa, *come along with me*; rinneadh sin leamsa, *that was made by me*; agus thubhairt e " cò is leamsa ? " *and he said " who is on my side ? "* is doirbh l. a chreidsinn, *I can hardly believe it*; is soirbh leam sin a chreidsinn, *I can easily believe that*; thar, dar, ar, leam, *I would suppose, I think*; leig l., *let me alone*; leig l. i, *let her accompany me*; is math l. sin, *that pleases me*; cò leis an cù ? tha e leamsa, *or* is leams' e, *whose is the dog ? it is mine*; shaoil l., *I thought*; théid l., *I will prosper*; l. fhéin, *alone, by myself*; ge b' oil l., *in spite of me*; bu mhithich l. sgeul fhaotainn, *it seemed to me time to get information*; leam leat, *fickle—lit.* with me and with you; ar leam gu'm bheil, *I think that it is so*; marbhar leam e, *he will be killed by me.* For many idiomatic compounds formed by *is* and *leam*, see under *is.*

lèamann, see leòmann.

leamh, -a, *a.* Importunate, troublesome. 2 Flattering, mealy-mouthed. 3 Silly, foolish, insipid, jejune. 4 Raw. 5 Pertinacious. 6 Officious. 7 Unmannerly, impertinent, saucy. 8 Barefaced, shameless. 9 Fastidious. 10 Vexing, galling. 11 Busy. 12 Greedy. 13 Sneering—*Arran.* Bu l. leam, *I thought it galling*; nis bha seo l., *now this was galling*; blas l., *an insipid taste.*

leamh,(CR) *a.* Annoyed, provoked—*Arran.* Is mi tha l. dhe, *how annoyed I am with him.*

leamh,(DMy) *s.* Disgust, annoyance.

†leamh, leimh, *s.m.* Rower. 2 Elm. 3 Oar.

leamhach, -aiche, *a.* Flattering. 2 Insipid, tasteless. see also leamh.

——adh,(MS) -aidh, *s. m.* Harassing, irritation, annoyance.

——as, -ais, *s. m.* Importunity. 2 Pertinacity. 3 Indiscreetness. 4 Impertinence, impudence, sauciness. 5 Fastidiousness. 6* Vexation. 7 Insipidness. 8 Greediness. 9 Foolishness, silliness. 10 Irksomeness. 11 (MS) Plague.

leamhachd, *s.f.* see leamhachas.

leamhad, -aid, *s.m.* Degree of importunity, pertinacity, impertinence, impudence, sauciness, or vapidness.

leamhadair,(MS) *s.m.* Molester.

leamhadas, *s.m.* see leamhachas.

leamhadh, -aidh,** *s. m.* Marsh mallows—*althœa officinalis.*

417. Leamhadh.

leamhadras, -ais, see leamhachas.

leamhaich,‡‡ *v.a.* Plague, tease, aggrieve, irk, harass, exasperate.

——ead, -eid, *s.m.* Degree of insipidity.

leamhan,** *s.m.* Inner rind of a tree. 2 Rower. 3 Moth (for leòmann.) 4 Night butterfly. 5‡‡Pith of wood. 6 (MMcD) Quern-wedge —*Lewis.*

leamhan, *gen.* -ain & leamhna, *s.m.* Elm, the elm-tree—*ulmus campestris.* 2 Wood of the elm-tree.

418. Leamhan.

leamhanach, -aiche, *a.* Of, or belonging to, elm-trees or elm-wood. 2‡‡Having much pith of wood.

leamhan-bog,§ *gen.* -ain-buig [McL & D. gives also leamhna-buig for the *gen. sing.*, which would imply that it is sometimes *f.*] *s. m.* Hornbeam—*carpinus betulus.*

leamhar, see leobhair.

leamhas, see lethmhas.

419. Leamhan-bog.

420. Leamhnach.

leamh-dhàn, -dhàine, *a.* Forward, insolent. 2 Foolhardy. 3 Importunate.

——achd, *s.f.* see leamh-dhànadas.

——adas, -ais, *s. m.* Forwardness, insolence. 2 Foolhardiness. 3 Importunity.

leamh-ghàire,** *s.* Smile.

leamh-lachd,** *s.f.* Sweet milk. 2 Insipid milk.

leamhnach,§ *s.(? f.)* Common tormentil, bloodroot, potentil—*potentilla tormentilla.* [** gives leamhnachd, Common tormentil, septfoil—*tormentilla erecta.*]

leamhnachadh, -aidh, *s.m.* Stopping. 2 Growing insipid.

leamhnachd, see leamh-lachd. 2 see leamhnachd.

leamhnad,‡ see leamhragan.

leamhnadan, see leamhragan.

leamh-nàire, *s.f.ind.* Bashfulness, foolish shame, coyness.

——ach, -eiche, *a.* Bashful, coy.

——achd, *s.f.* see leamh-nàire.

leamhnan, **——achd,** **leamhnanan,** } see leamhragan.

leamhragan, -ain, -an, *s.m.* Pimple on the eyelid, stye.

leamhran, see leamhragan.

leamhranan, see leamhragan.

leamlachd, see leamhnachd.
leam-leat, *a.* Double-faced, fickle, infirm of purpose. Teanga l., *a deceitful tongue ;* duine l., is fhèarr leat na leam, *the double-faced man, let him be your friend, not mine.*
———, *s.* Deceit, fickleness, irresolution. 2 Fickle person.
leamnacht,‡ see leamhnachd.
leamsa, *emphatic form* of *prep.pron.* leam.
lèan, léin, *s.m.* see lèana.
lean, *pr. pt.* a' leantuinn, [a' leanmhuinn, a' leanachd, a' leanail & a' leanailt,] *v. a. & n.* Follow. 2 Pursue, chase. 3**Trace. 4 Adhere, stick, cleave to. 5 Continue. 6 Persevere. 7**Imitate. L. sinn iad, *we followed them ;* lean e ri m' làmhan, *it adhered to my hands ;* leanadh mo theanga ri m' chìobhall, *let my tongue cleave to my jaw ;* ma leanas an uair tioram, *if the dry weather continues;* lean mar sin, *persevere thus ;* na l. orm na's fhaide, *don't importune me farther ;* lean mise, *follow me*—the Breadalbane Campbells' motto ; l. gu dlùth ri cliù do shinnsre, *follow close the fame of your forefathers,* supposed to be Ossianic, being said by Fingal to Oscar—a common motto for so-called Gaelic and Highland societies.
lean, *v.a.* see leun.
†lean, *s.m.* Sorrow, ruin.
lèana, -n, *s.m.* Meadow. 2 Swampy plain. 3 **Field of luxuriant grass, green.
leanaba (a l— !) *voc.pl.* of leanabh.
leanabach, see leanabanta.
leanabachas, see leanabachd.
leanabachd, *s.f.* Infancy, childhood. 2 Boyhood. 3 Childishness, pusillanimity. 4 Boyishness, boyism. 5**Dotage.
leanabaidh, -e, *a.* Childish, puerile, infantile. 2 Having many children. 3**Pusillanimous. 4 Boyish. 'Na aois l., *in his dotage.*
———, *s.dim.* of leanabh—*Suth'd.* =bairnie.
———eachd, see leanabachd.
leanabail, see leanabanta.
leanabainte, *a.* see leanabanta.
leanabalachd, see leanabachd.
leanaban, *n., gen. & dat.pl.* of leanabh.
———, -ain, -an, *s. m. dim.* of leanabh. Infant, little child. 2 *in derision,* Silly person. 3 Petted child, spoilt child. M' aon l., *my only child.*
———ach, -aiche, *a.* see leanabanta. 2** Spoiled or petted as a child.
———achd, see leanabachd.
leanabanta, *a.* see leanabaidh.
leanabantachd, see leanabachd.
leanabas, -ais, *s.m.* see leanabachd.
leanabh, leinibh, *s.m.* Infant, child. 2 *in derision,* Childish person.
Thus declined :—

Nom. Sing.	leanabh	*Plur.*	leanaban
Gen.	leinibh		leanaban
Dat.	leanabh		leanaban
Voc.	a leinibh !		a leanaba !

leanabh-altruim, *foster-child, nursling.*
——— -cìche, *a babe.*
——— -gille, *male child.*
——— -liùdhach, ——— -liùdhaig, } *puppet, doll.*
——— -mic, *male child.*
——— -nighinne, *a female child.*
leanabhan, see leanaban.
leanabh-luasgadh, -aidh, *s.m.* Rocking, as of a cradle.
leanabuidh, see leanabaidh.
———eachd, see leanabachd.
lèanach, -aiche, *a.* Swampy, marshy.
leanachadh, -aidh, *s.m.* Pressing out, making thin. A' l—, *pr.pt.* of leanaich.
leanachd, *prov.* for leantuinn.
leanadail,** *a.* Attendant.
†leanadar, *v.* They followed—*Irish form.*
lèanag, -aig, -an, *s.f.dim.* of lèan. Small meadow or lawn.
leanaich, (DMC) *pr. pt.* a' leanachadh, *v. a.* Make thin, flatten out, press out bread, as in the last process of kneading in making scones.
leanail, leanailt, } *prov.* for leantuinn, *pr. pt.*
leanailteach, -eiche, *a.* Adhesive, adherent. 2 Persevering. 3 Enduring. 4 Incessant. 5 Following. 6**Clammy. Uisge l., *incessant rain ;* l. air obair, *persevering at work.*
———,* -eich, *s.m.* Adherent.
———d, *s.f.ind.* Adhesiveness, adhesion. 2 Perseverance, continuance, incessantness.
leanamhain,** *s.* Goods, substance. 2 Spouse, sweetheart. 3 Pet. 4 Concubine.
lèanan, -ain, *s.m.* Haugh.
leanar, *fut.pass.* of lean. Shall be followed.
leanartach,§ -aich, *s.m.* see leamhnach.
lèan-ghobhrag,(AF) *s.* Snipe, see gobhar-athair.
leanmhuinn, *s. m.* Following, act of following, or pursuing. 2 Adhering, adherence. 3 Emulation. 4* Kindred, clanship, bond of connection, tie of kinship. 5**Tracing. 6** Imitation. 7**see leanamhain. A' l—, *pr.pt.* of lean.
Tha l. a thaobheiginn eatorra, *there is some bond of connection or clanship between them ;* tha iad a' l. air an teaghlach sin, *they have some claim on that family ;* tha e a' l. ormsa seo, *he claims this from me, he insinuates his claim to this from me ;* a luchd-leanmhuinn, *his followers, kindred, vassals, minions ;* 'gam l., *following me.*
leanmhuinneach,** *s.m.* Follower, adherer.
———, -eich, *a.* Following, pursuing. 2 Adherent, adhesive. 3 Importunate. 4 Emulative. 5* Having claims of kindred. 6** Tracing. 7**Clammy.
———d, *s.f* Adherence, adhesion. 2 Incessantness.
leanmhuinniche,** *s.* Adherent, adherer, follower.
leann, -a, *pl.* -tan & -taidhean, *s.m.* Ale, beer. 2 Liquor, drink. 3 *pl.*‡Humours of the body. 4 (AC) Pool (for linne.) 5 *rarely* Coarse cassock. 6 Coat of mail. 7**Sore, ulcer. Deoch leanna, *a drink of beer ;* taigh-leanna, *a beer-house ;* droch leanntan, *bad humours ;* l. caol, *small beer ;* l. làidir, *strong beer ;* eadar dhà leann, *'twixt sinking and swimming* (*lit.* between two liquids, i.e. the upper and lower water ; *2 water-logged, as a boat.*
leannach, -aiche, *a.* Abounding in ale.
———, -aich, see leannachadh.
———adh, -aidh, *s.m.* Suppurating, state of suppurating, suppuration. 2 Inflammation. 3 Ulcer, ulceration. 4 Boil. A' l—, *pr. pt.* of leannaich.
———ail,** *a.* Ulcerous, like an ulcer. 2 Suppurating, tending to suppurate. 3 Causing ulceration or suppuration.
leannaich, *pr.pt.* a' leannachadh, *v.a.* Suppurate. 2 Ulcerate.
———te, *past pt.* of leannaich. Suppurated.
leannain, *gen.sing. & n. pl.* of leannan.
leannair,** *s.m.* Brewer.
leannan, -ain, -an, *s.m. & f.* Spouse. 2 Lover, mistress, concubine. 3 Sweetheart, beloved person, pet, darling, gallant. L.-peacaidh, *darling sin;* l. òinsich, *an idiot's choice ;* l.-sìth, given in the Bible for *a familiar spirit,* but it really means *a fairy sweetheart.*

leannanach, -aiche, *a.* Amorous, gallant. having many sweethearts. 2 Intriguing. 3 Buxom. 4 Wanton.
leannanachd, *s.f.ind.* Courtship, gallantry of lovers, intriguing, blandishment, dalliance. 2 Flattery. 3 ‡‡Whoredom, fornication.
leannan-locraidh, -ain-locraidh, *s. m.* Level, spirit-level.
leann-caol, *s.m.* Small beer.
leanndan, see leanntan.
leann-dubh, -uibh, *s. m.* Sadness, melancholy, melancholia, tears, dejection. Bha 'n l. air, *he was dejected ;* tha e (mi) fo l., *he is (I am) dejected.*
——ach,** *a.* Melancholic, despondent, hypochondriac.
leann-geur, *s.* Alegar, sour ale.
leann-goile, *s.m.* Chyle.
leann-goirt, *s.m.* Alegar. sour ale.
leann-làidir, *s.m.* Strong beer.
leann-loisgte, *s.m.* Dregs from distilling whisky. 2 Dregs from which ale is brewed.
leann-luibh, *s.* Hop, see lus-an-leanna.
——each, *a.* Abounding in hops. 2 Of, or pertaining to, hops.
leann-meirbhidh, *s.m.* Chyle.
leannra, *s.m.* Sauce, condiment. 2 Soup. 3 Aleberry.
leann-ràcadail, *s.m.* Ginger beer.
leannradh, see leannra.
leann-ruadh, -aidh, *s.m.* Choler, anger.
——aidh, *s.m.* Choler.
leanntaidhean, *pl.* of leann.
leanntalach,(MS) *a.* Livelong.
leann-tàlaidh, *s.m.* Allurement, power of enticing by charms.
leann-tàth, -a, *s.m.* Cement. 2 Solder. 3 Humours of the body. Chaill sinn uil' ar l., *we have all lost our esprit-de-corps* (or *stamina*—AH.)
——, *v.a.* Cement. 2 Solder.
leann-tàthaidh, *s.m.* Callus fluid. 2 Cement. 3 ††Animal spirits in the body.
leanntan,* *s. m.* Anger. 2 *pl.* of leann. The passions, the humours, the vapours.
leanntras, -ais, *s.m.* The vapours, humours of the body.
leann-ubhall, *s.m.* Cider.
leantach, -aiche, see leanailteach.
——, -aiche, *a.* Subjunctive (in *grammar.*)
lèantach, -aich, *s.f.* Country of plains, place abounding in plains. 2*Extensive plain.
leantail, *a.* Sticking. 2 Following.
leantalach, (MS) *a.* Adherent, gummy 2 Importunate. 3 Persevering. 4 (DMC) Following. L. air 'obair, *persevering at his work ;* tha 'n glaodh l, *the glue is adhesive ;* l. air an uisge, *raining incessantly.*
——d,(MS) *s. f.* Adherence. 2 Pursuance. 3 Success. 4 Track. 5 Continuance.
leantalas, *s.m.* see leantalachd.
leantuinn, *s.m. & pr. pt.* Following, act of following, pursuing. 2 Adhering, state of adhering, cleaving, see leanmhuinn.
——each, -eiche, *a.* Successive.
——eachd, *s.f.* Adhesiveness.
leapach, *gen.sing.* of leabaidh.
leapachan, -ain, -an, see leabachan
——, *n.pl.* of leabaidh.
leapaich, see leabaich.
leapaichean, see leabaichean.
leaphunnd, see lethphunnd.
lear, *s.m.ind.* The sea, *poet.* 2 The surface of the sea. 3 see learg-mhadaidh. Bhuail i gu lear, *she made towards the sea.*
†lear, *a.* Clear, discernible.
learach, for leathrach.

learag,§ -aig, -an, *s.f.* Larch-tree—*pinus larix.* 2 Larch-wood.
——ach, -aiche, *a.* Abounding in larch-trees.
†lear-dhromain, *s.m* Ridge of a hill.
learg, -eirg, -an, *s.f.* Rain-goose. 2 (AF) Cormorant. 3 see learg-mhadaidh.
learg, leirg, -an, *s.f.* Plain, plain field. 2 Little eminence, small hill. 3 Beaten path. 4 Shore, sea-coast, beach. 5 ‡‡Sloping declivity of a hill. 6**Field of battle. 7** Surface of the sea. 8 The sea. 9* Sloping place exposed to sun and sea. 10**Sloping green, green slope.
learg ! (DU) *int.* Term of contempt—Slowcoach!

421. *Learga.*

learga,¶ *s.f.* Black-throated diver—*colymbus arcticus.*
——ch, -aiche, *a.* Steep, sloping. 2 Having many slopes. 3 Of, or connected with plains, or 4 with Rain-geese. 5‡‡Beachy. 6 (DU) Slow, inert.
learga-chaol,¶ *s. f.* Red-throated diver, see learga-mhór.
learga-dhubh,(AC) *s.f.* Black-throated diver.
learga-fairge,¶ *s. f.* Red-throated diver, see learga-mhór.
leargaidh,** *s.f.* Slope of a hill. 2 Side of any high eminence.
leargainneach,** *a.* Sloping. 2 Steep. 3 Having steep pasture-ground.
leargair,** *s.m.* Sluggard. 2 Sailor.
learga-mhór,¶ *s.f.* Red-throated diver—*colymbus septentrionalis,* see ill. 422. 2(AC) Black-throated diver.
learga-mhór chaol, see learga-mhór,
leargan, -ain, -an, *s.m.* Sloping green, side of a hill.
——ach, -aiche, *a.* Sloping. 2 Having sloping greens.
leargann,** -ainn, *s.f.* Small sloping green field. 2 Side of a green hill. 3 Steep pasture ground. 4 Slope of a country side.
learga-uisge,¶ *s.f.* Red-throated diver, see learga-mhór.
learg-choileach dhubh, see learg-choilearach

422. Learga-mhór.

dhubh.
learg-choilearach, (*lit.* ringed or collared diver) *s.f.* Black-throated diver.
learg-choilearach dhubh, *s.f.* Black-throated diver.
learg-mhadadh, -aidh,(AF) *s. m.* Dog-fish, sea-dog, sea-fox.
learguin, see leargainn.
learman,§ -ain, *s.m.* Wood-rush, see luachar-coille.
learthag, see laireag.
lear-thaod,** -aoid, *s.m.* Spring-tide.
lear-thoid,** *s.m.* Football. (for leath-throid)
lear-uinnean,§ *s. m.* Squill (*lit.* sea-onion.)—*scilla verna.*

423. Lear-uinnean.

leas, -a, *prefix.* Nick-, step-, additional.
leas,** *a.* Proper, fit. Cha leas cadal gu moch, *it is not fit to go to sleep early*—i. e. going to sleep early is no advantage.
lèas, -eòis, *prov.* for leus.
leas, leis, leasraidh, see leis, *s. f.*
leas, -is, *s.f. prov.* for lios.
leas, *s.m.ind.* Benefit, advantage, profit, good. 2**Improvement. 3**Reason, motive. 'S e a bh' air do leas, *it is he that had your interest in view ;* cha'n e mo leas a bh' air t' fhaire, *it was not my interest you had in view ;* na'm bitheadh e air do leas, *if he had your interest at heart ;* cha ruig mi leas, *I need not.*
——ach,* -aiche, *a.* Trifling. 2 Sheep-shanked.
——ach, -aich, *s.m.* Manure, see leasachadh.
——ach,** -aiche, *s.m.* Rennet. Baigean leas-aich, *a rennet-bag.*
lèasach, -aich, *prov.* for leusach.
leasachadh, -aidh, *s.m.* Improving, act or state of improving, amending, benefiting, repairing or correcting. 2 Improvement, reparation, amendment, correction. 3 Manuring. 4 Dung, manure. 5 Increasing. 6 Appendix. 7 Guerdon. A' l—, *pr. pt.* of leasaich. A' l. an fhearainn, *manuring the land ;* a' l. a' ghnothaich, *improving the thing ;* a' cur a mach an l., *carting dung, laying out manure ;* cha l. air sin an ni sin, *that is no reparation for that affair ;* chum leasachaidh, *for correction.*
leasachail, -e, *a.* Improvable, that may be put to rights, corrigible.
leasachail. -e, *a.* Escharotic, caustic, epispastic, producing a blister on the skin.
leasachair, *s.m.* Improver, reformer, repairer. 2 Amender.
leasaich, *pr. pt.* a' leasachadh, *v. a.* Rectify, correct, amend, repair. 2 Supply. 3 Fill, replenish, renew. 4 Improve. 5 Manure, cultivate. 6 (DU) Increase. L. an ni sin, *improve that thing;* l. am fearann, *manure the land ;* l. do bheusan, *correct your morals ;* l. an eibhle, *put fuel on the fire ;* a' bhean a l. an stòp, *the woman who filled the tankard.*
leasaiche, -an, *s.m.* see leasachair.
leasaichte, *past pt.* of leasaich. Rectified, corrected, amended, improved, repaired. 2 Supplied, filled, replenished. 3 Manured. 4 Advanced. 5**Renneted, as milk.
leas-ainm, -ean, *s.m.* Nick-name.
————each, *a.* Apt to give nick-names.
leasan, -ain, *s.m.* Gaelic spelling of *lesson.*
leas-athair, -ar, -athraichean, *s.m.* Step-father.
leas-bhrathair,** *s.m.* Step-brother.
leasdair, *s.m.* Lamp. 2 Light, effulgence. 3** Crack.
†leasg,** *s.f.* Hood. 2 Rod. 3 Spot of ground.
leasg, *a.* see leisg.
leasg,** -eisg, *s.f.* Rain-goose.
leasgach, -aiche, *a.* Lurkish.
leasgan,(MS) *s.m.* Drone.
————ach,†† -aich, *s.m.* Cripple, deformed person.
leas-inghean,** -inghinn, *s.f.* Step-daughter.
†leas-luan,** -ain, *s.m.* Step-son.
leas-leathann,‡‡ -ainn, *s.* Beaver.
leas-luidhe,** *s.f.* Reclining, leaning.
leas-mhac, -mhic, *s.m.* Step-son.
leas-mhàthair, -ar, -mhàthraichean, *s.f.* Step-mother.
leas-mhursaid,** *s.f.* Gallon.
leas-nighean, -nighinn, -nigheanan, *s. f.* Step-daughter.
leas-òifigeach, *s.m.* Non-commissioned officer.
leas-phiuthar, -pheathar, -pheathraichean, *s.f.* Step-sister.
†leasrach, -aich, *s.m.* Thigh. 2 Loins.
leasradh, see leasraidh.
leasraidh, *s. f. coll.* The loins.
————each, -eiche, *a.* Lumbar.
leas-righ, *s.m.* Regent.
leastair, -ean, *prov.* for fleisdear.
leastaireachd, see fleisdearachd.
leastar,** -air, *s m.* Small boat. 2 Cup, vessel. 3 Furniture of a house. 4 Vessels of a house. 5 Stale butter. 6(AF) Milk-dish.
leasuich, see leasaich.
leat, *prep.pron.* With thee. 2 By thee. 3 To thee. 4 Along with thee. 5 In thine opinion or estimation. 6 In thy favour. 7 You, yours. Bithidh mi leat, *I will be with you ;* ciod th' air leat ? *what think you?* an leat seo ? *is this yours ?* seo leat ! *here's to your health !* tha mo ghuidhe leat, *my desire is the same as yours ;* leig leat, *said by one who knows things are not as they have been related by the other ;* nach truagh mi leat ! said to a guest who does not take as much as is offered to him ; also used as an equivalent to *what a nuisance you are !* cha téid sin leat, *that will not succeed with you ;* coma leat e ! *never heed him !*

leatach,(CR) *a.* Remote, isolated—*Berthshire.*
leath, -an, *s.m. prov.* for leth.
leatha, *prep. pron.* With her. 2 By her. 3 Along with her. 4 In her opinion. 5 In her favour. 6 Hers.
leatha, *comp.* of leathann.
leathachas, -ais, *s. m.* Partiality, unfairness, injustice. Na dean l. sam bith air, *show him no partiality.*
leathad, -aid & leòthaid, *pl.* leoidean, *s.m.* Declivity, side of a hill, slope, half-ridge, broad slope, brae. A' dol le leathad, *declining, going downhill.*
———ach, *a.* Declivitous.
leathag,** *s.f.* Plaice. 2 Flounder.
———an,§ *s.* see liaghag & see stamh.
——— -bhàn,(AF) *s.f.* Sole.
——— -dhearg,(AF) *s. f.* Flounder, fluke.
——— -fìor-uisg',(AF) *s.f.* Flounder.
——— -mhara,(AF) *s.f.* Turbot, talbot.
leathamaid,* *s.f.* Idiot.
leathanach, *s.m.* Hoar-frost—*Arran.*
leathann, leithne & leatha, *a.* Broad. 2 Spacious. "Leathann ri leathann is caol ri caol," *broad to broad and narrow to narrow,* an important rule observed by most writers of Gaelic, and which prescribes that the vowels next before and next after any given consonant in any given word shall be either both broad or both narrow, unless divided by a hyphen. Many of the past pasticiples of verbs do not conform to this rule, but they are the only exception. [MacBain spells leathann *leathan.*]
———achd, *s.f.* Wideness.
leathar, *gen.* leathair, leathrach & leathraich, *s.m.* Leather. 2 Hide. L. fionnta an daimh òig, *the young ox's hairy hide;* brògan leathrach, *leather shoes.*
——— -sginnein, see leathar-sginneir.
——— -sginneir, *s.m.* Buff-leather.
leatha-sa, *prep.pron., emphatic form* of leatha.
leathnaich, *v.* Flatten. 2 Malleate.
leathoir, see leth-oir.
leathrach, *gen.sing.* of leathar. [* and McL & D. given *nom.* leathrach, *gen.* -aich.]
———ail,‡‡ *a.* Leathery.
leath-throid,** *s.m.* Football.
leathuillinn, see lethuilinn.
leathunnsa, see lethunnsa.
leatrath see lethtrath.
leatrom, -truim, *s. m.* Burden, weight. 2 Grievance. 3 Injury. 4 Injustice. 5 Pregnancy (of women only.) 6 Oppression. 7** Counterweight.
———ach, -aiche, *a.* Burdensome, weighty. 2 Grievous, oppressive, unjust. 3 Pregnant (of women only.) Dh' fhàs i l., *she became pregnant.*
———achd, *s.f.ind.* Pregnancy (of women only.) 2**Counterweight.
leatromas, see leatromachd.
leatruime, see leatrom.
Lebhitheach, *s.m.* Levite.
Lebhitheachail, *a.* Levitical.
le bruthach, *adv.* Downhill.
le chéile, *adv.* With each other, together. Mharbh e iad le chéile, *he killed them both.*
†leibeann,** -inn, *s.m.* Long stride. 2 Stretch.
leibh, *prep.pron.* With you. 2 In your favour, on your side. 3 By you. 4 In your opinion or estimation. 5 Along with you. 6 By your means. 7 Your property.
†leibheann,** -einn, *s.f* Deck of a ship. 2 Scaffold. 3 Gallery. 4 Side of a hill.
leibhidh,-ean, *s.f.* Race, generation. 2‡‡Swarm, multitude, levy.
leibhist,(DMy) *s.* Half idiot.
leibhliadhna, see lethbhliadhna.
leibhreac, see lethbhreac.
leibid, -ean, *s.m.* Trifle. 2 Trifling accident, mischance. 3 Term of contempt. 4††Dwarfish fellow. 5 ‡ Dirt. L. ort! *mischance befall you! fie! out upon you!*
leibid,* *s.f.* Paltry female. 2 Paltry consideration.
———each, -eiche, *a.* Trifling, mean, worthless, contemptible. 2 Accidental. 3 Awkward. 4 Avaricious. 5 Tawdry. 6 Shabby, vile. 7 Long-legged. 8 (DU) Annoying, vexatious. Is l. an taigh nach toill fear eile fhathast, *it's a poor house that won't hold another still*—a very hospitable sentiment; is l. saoghal na sùlach, *paltry is the part of the world seen by the eyes.*
———eachd, *s.f.* Avarice, meanness, scantiness, pettiness, paltriness. 2‡‡ Silliness. 3‡‡ Awkwardness. 4**Tawdriness, shabbiness. 5 Worthlessness.
leibidean, -ein, *s.m.* Contemptible fellow, trifler. 'Nuair a gheibh an l. a staigh, 'se fear an taigh an truaghan, *when trifler gets in, pity the goodman of the house.*
léic, -e, *s.f.* Neglect.
leiceanta, see leacanta.
———chd, see leacantachd.
leiceas, see leigis.
leiceid,(CR) *Loch Tay* for leacaid.
léich, -ean, *s.m.* Physician. N'am b' urrainn mi, dheanainn léich dhuit, *if I could, I would act as physician to thee—Duanaire, p. 16.* (see léigh & lighiche.)
leicheathnra, see letheheathramh.
leicheid, *Blair Athole* for leacaid.
leicis, see leigis.
leid, *s. f.* †Longing, desire. 2 (MMcD) Shakedown or bed made on the floor.
léideach, -eiche, *a.* Strong, robust. 2 Shaggy, bristly.
———adh, *s.m.* Convoy.
†léidich, *v.a.* Convoy for a short way.
†léidig, see léidich.
léidig, *Caithness* for léitig.
léidinn,** *s.m.* Conduct.
———,** *v.a.* Convoy.
leidir,* *v.a.* see leadair.
leidire,(AF) *s.m.* Wolf.
léidmheach, -eiche, *a.* see léideach.
léig, -ean, *s.m.* see leug.
leig, *pr. pt.* a' leigeil & a' leigeadh, *v. a. & n.* Permit, allow. 2 Slip, as dogs to the chase. 3 Let out, let go, let off. 4 Milk, as cows. 5 Rain, commence raining. 6‡‡Apply to, commence. 7‡‡Break off, as an imposthume. 8 ‡‡Lay, lay upon. 9‡‡Set out. 10**Overturn. 11**Place. 12**Lower. 13**Diminish. 14 * Broach. 15*.Fire. 16* Lance.

Leig (*or* ghabh) sinn oirnn, *we pretended, assumed;* leig ort a bhi tinn, *pretend to be sick;* cha do leig sinn dad oirnn riutha, *we disclosed nothing to them, we never made a sign to show them what we knew, we did not "let on" to them;* leig ris daibh, *explain to them;* duine ris an leiginn ris mo bhriathran, *one to whom I could unbosom myself.*

Leigidh mi an àth 'na teine, *I will set the kiln on fire;* leig aomadh anns a' phosta, *put the post in a slanting position;* leig as, *let go;* leig as na siùil, *unfurl the sails;* leig as an leac, *drop the flagstone;* leig as am ball langais, *let go the towing-rope;* leig mi e mu bharraibh nan tonn, *I dropped it into the waves, I confided it to the mercy of the sea.*

Leig na coin ann, *set the dogs at him* ; cum do chù ri a leigeil, *keep your dog till it is time to slip him* ; is tric a bha leigeadh fada aig fear gun chù, *a man without means* (*lit.* without a dog) *has often had a long slipping* (*i.e.* a long innings) ; leig chun a chéile iad, *let them at each other* ; leig air an adhart iad, *let them move forward* ; leig air, *begin, commence* ; leig iad ris na deagh ghadhair, *they let slip the good hounds at him* ; leig an t-saighead, an urchair ris, *let fly the arrow, the shot at him* ; leig an gunna, *fire the gun* ; leigidh mi peilear annad, *I will drive a bullet into you* ; a' cheud {dallanaich / thraightseal / làmhach} a leig iad, *the first volley, broadside, they fired* ; leigidh mi fios chugad, dhuit, *I will send you word* ; leig gu a luim féin e, *leave him to his own resources, devices.*

Leig iad e gu radh a' chlaidheimh, na searraig, *they referred it, appealed, to the sword, to the bottle* (they made the sword or the bottle arbitrator) ; feumaidh tu leigeadh leamsa sin a ràdh, ars am breitheamh, *you must leave that to me to say, said the judge* ; leig sin an urra riumsa, *entrust that to me* ; leigeamaid chum tuigse a' mhinisteir teagasg a thoirt, *let us leave to the minister's judgment the question of the giving of teaching.*

Leig e cead ruith leis an tòrr bhuntàta, *he allowed the pile of potatoes to slide (in all directions)* ; leig cead dha, *let him alone* ; leig an linne, *let the water out of the reservoir* ; leig ruith leis an uisge, *let the water run forth* ; leig am moll leis a' ghaoith, *let the chaff go with the wind* ; tha fear ann a leigeas a mhaidean le sruth, *there is one that lets his wood go with the stream* ; leig am buideal, *broach, tap the barrel* ; leig an crodh, *milk the cattle* ; leig fuil, *lance for blood* ; leig an lionnachadh, *lance the tumour* ; an là a' brath leigeil fodha, *the day threatening to rain* ; leig e, *it has begun to rain* ; leig t' anail, *take it easy, take a breath* ; leig fead, *whistle (thou)* ; leig e glaodh as, *he uttered a cry* ; leig beum leis an sgòd, *let the sail-sheet suddenly out* ; leig sìos, *diminish, lessen* ; *2 let down* ; leig cudthrom, *or* leig taic, *lean.*

Leig leinn e, *let him come with us* ; *let it go, so that we can take it with us* ; leig leinn, *let us alone, let us go on as we are* ; leig leat, *you may go on talking, acting as you are doing, if you wish, but I will be even with you later on* ; also said to one who is exaggerating ; leigidh mi sin leat, *I will make that concession to you, I will allow you that* ; leig iad leatha car treis, *they let her alone, let her go on for a while* ; leigidh sinn leis a' chùis an dràsd, *we will leave the matter alone just now* ; lagh a tha 'g òrdachadh leigeil leis a' ghiomach, *a law making a close time for lobsters compulsory* ; ruigidh na féidh aois mhór ma leigear leò, *deer reach a great age if left alone* ; cha leig mi leis an seo e, *I will not let the matter rest here* ; cha'n fhaigh thu leat e, *you shall not be allowed to carry it out, you shall not have your own way in the matter* ; cha leig iad leis a dhìth, *they will not allow him to perish* ; gu'n leigeadh Dia ! *God grant !* nar leigeadh Dia ! *God forbid !* cha leig i leis car a dheanamh, *she will not let him do a single hand's turn* ; cha leig an t-eagal leam, *fear will not permit me* ; cha leag an nàire leam, *shame will not permit me* ; leig mi leò faighinn as a' ghàbhadh a tharruing iad orra féin, *I let them get out of the difficulty which they had brought upon themselves.*

Leig dhomh an t-òran a chluinntinn, *let me hear the song* ; leig dha falbh, *let him go* ; leig iad siubhal a chas do 'n each iaruinn, *they let the iron horse start away* ; cha do leig e stad dh' a chois gus, &c., *he never halted until, &c.* ; leig dhuit, *go on your own silly way* ; leig da, *do not have any more to do with it* ; leig tàmh dha, *let it alone, give it rest* ; ma bha iad gu math, is math—'s mur robh, leigear dhaibh, *if they were good, all right—and if they were not, let them be* ; leigeamaid do 'n ghlaodh gus an cluinn sinn a rithisd e, *let the shouting be, let us take no notice of the shout, till we hear it again* ; na leig a dhìth a' Ghàidhlig, *let not the Gaelic language come to grief, die.*

Leig eadar sinn féin 's na biodagan, *leave us to fight it out with our dirks* ; na cuireadh sin dragh 'sam bith ort, leig eadar mise agus sin, *don't let that trouble you, I will manage that, leave it to me.*

Leig iad dhiubh a bhi 'gabhail cùraim, *they ceased taking precautions, they ceased to be concerned* ; leig iad dhiubh a' chlach-neart, *they ceased practising with the putting-stone* ; leig mi dhiom mo dhreuchd, *I resigned, relinquished my office* ; leig dhìot, *desist, cease* ; leig dhìot puinneag bheag de d' bhoile, *calm yourself a little.*

Leig e seachad a' chòmhrag, *he let the matter of the combat pass* ; leig seachad gus an ath àireamh e, *postpone it till next number* ; is i mo chomhairle-sa dhuit an oidhche 'nochd a leigeil le càch, *my advice to you is to do tonight as you have done on other nights* ; leigidh siad an eucoir thairis orra, *they will permit errors to pass*—said of book-critics.

leig, Often used for ruig in parts of *Argyll, Skye, &c.*, e.g. cha leig e leas, which is common for cha ruig e leas.

leig,** -e, *s.f.* Spade, mattock.

léig, *gen.sing.* of leug.

léig, *pl.* -ean, *s.f.* Marshy or miry pool.—*Lewis.* Name given by the Fingalian bards to a lake in Ireland.

leig-chritheach, *s.* Quagmire.

léige,(MS) *s.f.* League (3 miles.)

leigeadair, *s.m.* Spigot.

leigeadh, -idh, *s.m. & pr.pt.* Same meanings as leigeil.

léigeart,** *s.* Leaguer.

leigeas,** -eis, see leigis.

leigeil, *gen.* leigealach, *s.m.* Permitting, act of permitting, allowing or granting. 2 Milking, act of milking. 3 Letting go, letting out, letting off. 4 Setting on, urging, as of boys. 5‡‡ Applying. 6‡‡ Breaking, as of an imposthume. 7 Setting out. 8‡‡Raining, act of raining. 9‡‡ Throwing down. 10**Lowering. 11**Letting fall. 12** Overturning. A' l—, *pr.pt.* of leig.

leigeil, *s. m.* Letting go, the hand is lowered to let the spun thread run on to the reel of spinning-wheel.

léigh, -ean, *s.m.* Physician, surgeon.

léigh,* *s.f.* Medicine.

léigheadair, see léigh. 2**Pharmacopolist.

———————eachd, *s.f.* Pharmacy.

léigheagan, -ain, -an, *s.m.* Stone superstitiously supposed to possess medical virtue.

léighean, -ein, *s.m.* Instruction, erudition.

—————ta,** *a.* Proficient.

leigheas, -ghis, -an, *s. m.* Cure, remedy, medicine. 2 Healing, curing, act of curing. A' l—, *pr.pt.* of leighis. L. a dheanamh, *to wor*

a cure.
———ach, -aiche, *a.* Medicinal, curing, healing, remediable.
———achd, *s.f.* Curableness.
———adh, -aidh, see leigheas.
———aiche,** *s.m.* Physician.
———ail,(MS) *a.* Remediable.
——— -uisge, *s.m.* Hydropathy.
leigheil,‡‡ -e, *a.* Medical.
leighiche,(MS) *s.m.* Practitioner.
leighis, *pr.pt.* a' leigheas, *v.a.* Cure, heal, remedy.
———each, see leigheasach.
———eachd, see leigheasachd.
———te, *past pt.* of leighis. Cured, healed.
léigh-lann, -lainn, *s.m.* Dispensary.
léigh-loisg, *v.a.* Cauterize, burn with caustic.
léigh-losgadh, -aidh, *s. m.* Cautery, act of cauterizing. 2**Caustic. A' l—, *pr.pt.* of léigh-loisg.
leigis,§ *s.* Leek—*allium porrum.*
———each,** *a.* Abounding in leeks. 2 Like a leek.
leigiun,** -iuin, *s.m.* Gaelic spelling of *legion.*
leigte, *past pt.* of leig. Permitted, let out, let off. 2 Milked. 3‡‡ Set out. 4 Laid, laid upon. 5**Overturned. 6**Lowered,diminished. 7** Lanced.
léim, -ean & -eannan, see leum.
——, *v.a.* see leum.
leimhe, *comp.* of leamh.
———, *s.f.ind.* Sauciness, impudence. 2 Fastidiousness. 3**Simplicity, folly. 4**Importunity.
leine, for leithne, *comp.* of leathann.
léine, *pl.* léintean, *s.f.* Man's shift, shirt or smock. 2 Woman's chemise. 3 Shroud, winding sheet. 4††Jacket. Tha e as a l., *he has his coat off, nothing on but his shirt ;* gun chiste, gun léintean, *without coffins or shrouds;* léin'-iochdar, *under-shirt ;* léine-thuilinn, *shirt of twilled linen.*
léineag,†† -eig, -an, *s.m.* Little shirt.
———ach, *a.* Having little shirts.
léine-aifrionn, *s.f.* Surplice.
léine-bhàis, *s.f.* Shroud.
léine-bhàn,(AH) *s. f.* Distinctive smock, which transgessors of ecclesiastical law were at one time obliged to wear in church during public worship on one or more Sundays—also called "gùn odhar" and "gùn na h-eaglaise."
leine-bheag, (DU) *s. f.* Inner lining of an egg-shell.
léine-chaol, *s.f.* White linen shirt (i.e. the shirt that has fine threads used in weaving the material of which it is made.)
léine-chneis, Same as léine-chrios. Tha thu 'd dhalt aig a bhan-righinn, mar léine-chneis aig a bràthair, *you are the queen's foster-brother and the body-guard of her own brother—Filidh.*
léine-chrios, *s. m.* Confidant, intimate, attendant, valet.
léine-chròich,** *s.f.* Saffron shirt or mantle, so called from its being dyed with saffron. It was worn in former times, by people of rank among the Gael, especially in the Western Isles. It was an upper garment, and consisted of 24 ells, tied round the middle by a belt, and reaching below the knees.
léine-mhairbh,(DU) *s.f.* Shroud.
léine-sheacair,(MMcD) *s.f.* Narrow striped or pleated shirt.
leinibh, *gen.sing.* of leanabh.
——— -luasgadh,** -aidh,see leanabh-luasgadh.
leinn, *prep.pron.* With us. 2 By us. 3 To us. 4 In our favour, on our side, ours. 5 In our company. Leig leinn, *let us alone* ; thalla (falbh) leinn, *come along with us ;* bi leinn, *be on our side ;* cuir do làmh leinn *help us.*
leinne, *emphatic form* of leinn.
léinteach, *a.* Having shirts, shirted.
———, -eich, *s.f.* Shirting.
léinteag, -eig, -an, *s. f. dim.* of leine. Little shirt or shroud.
leiphiuthar, see lethphiuthar.
léir,** *a.* Visible. 2 That can see.
léir, *s.m.ind.* Sight, perception, power of seeing or being seen. 2(MS) Plague. Used with the *prep.prons.* dhomh, dhuit, &c., as, cha léir dhomh, *I do not see ;* an léir dhuit e ? *do you see it ?* is léir dhomh e, *I see it ;* cha l. dhomh sin, *I cannot see that ;* is l. a bhuil, *the result is obvious ;* mar is l. dhomh, *as far as I can see ;* is math is l. dhomh, *I can see well :* cha l. dhomh do dheireas, *I cannot perceive your deficiency.*
léir, *adv.* (i.e. gu léir) Altogether, wholly.
léir, *pr.pt.* a' léireadh, *v.a.* Pain, torment, distress, harass, suffer. 2 Wound. 3 Steal. 4 Trample. 5 Vex, oppress. 6 Pierce. 7 Thrill. 8 Aggrieve.
†léir, *s.m.* Aggregate.
†léir, -e, *a.* Conspicuous, open, plain, obvious, evident. 2 Destructive, terrible. 3 Wise, prudent. 4 Close, managing.
léir-chreach, *s.f.* Complete spoiling, utter devastation.
léir-chunntas, -ais, -an, *s. m.* Census, general numbering. 2**General calculation.
†leire, *s.m.* Austerity, piety.
léireadh, -idh, *s.m.* Paining, act of paining, tormenting, distressing. 2 Wounding. 3 Stealing. 4 Trampling. 5 Torment, oppression, harassing. A' l—, *pr. pt.* of léir. 'Gam l., *tormenting me, giving me the most acute pain ;* a' l. nan sléisnean, *paining the thighs.*
†léir-fholach, -aich, *s.m.* Canopy.
leirg, -e, -ean, *s.f.* see learg. 2†† see làirig.
†leirg, -e, -ean, *s.f.* Reason, motive. 2 Road.
léir-ghlac,** *s.* Engross.
leirin-sugach,§ *s.* Mushroom, see balg-losgainn.
leirist, -e, -ean, *s.m. & f.* Foolish senseless person. 2 Slovenly woman, slut. 3 Awkward person.
———each, -eiche, *a.* Senseless, stupid. 2 Sluttish.
léir-laghadh,** -aidh, *s.m.* Amnesty.
léir-mhillteach,** *a.* All-consuming.
léir-mheas,** s. *m.* General consideration. 2 Full or general estimate. 3 General view. 4 Census. 5 Balancing, weighing, pondering.
léirse,** *s.f.* see léirsinn.
léir-sgrios, -an, *s.m.* Utter destruction, complete ruin. 2**Carnage, massacre.
———, *v.a.* Destroy utterly.
———ach, -aiche, *a.* see léir-sgriosail.
———ail, -e, *a.* Destructive, utterly ruinous.
———ta, *past pt.* of léir-sgrios, Ruined, utterly destroyed. 2 Ravaged. 3 Defaced.
léirsinn, *s.f.* Vision, sight, seeing. 2 Intellect, understanding. 3 Insight, knowledge, perception. A' dalladh a l., *blinding his vision ;* snitheach gun l., *tearful and blind** ; 2 leaky and dark*—applied to a house with rain coming through the roof (DMC) ; am bheil thu a' léirsinn ? *do you see ?*
léirsinneach, -niche, *a.* Seeing, perceiving. 2 Intelligent, discerning, enlightened. 3 Visible. Gu l., *visibly.*
———d, *s. f.* Light, vision. 2 Intelligence, understanding, sagacity. 3 Visibility.
léir-smuain, *s.m.* Consideration, reflection.
léirte, *past pt.* of léir. Pained, distressed. 2

Wounded, pierced. 3 Stolen. 4 Trampled.
léirtneas, *s.m.* Two fourpenny lands (a measure of land.)
léir-thionail, *pr.pt.* a' léir-thional, *v.n.* Congregate, gather together, muster.
léir-thional, -ail, *s.m.* General assembly, general gathering, muster. A' l—, *pr. pt.* of léir-thionail. L. Eaglais na h-Alba, *the General Assembly of the Church of Scotland* ; l. chrodh, *a general gathering of cattle.*
leis, -e, -ean, *s.f.* Thigh. Sùil na leise, *the hip-joint.*
léis, *gen.sing.* of leus.
leis, *prep.pron.* With him or it. 2 In his company, along with him. 3 Being his property or right. 4 By means of, with what. 5 By, by reason of. 6 In favour of. 7 Belonging to. 8 Downhill. 9 Down the stream.

A' dol l., *going along with him* ; l. fhéin, *all alone, without assistance* ; l. an t-sruth, *down the stream* ; ciod leis a ghlanas an t-òganach 'uile shlighe féin ? *by what means shall the young man purify all his ways ?* cò l. thu ? *whose are you ?* tha mi leat-sa ma cheannaicheas tu mi, *I am yours if you bribe me well* ; is leis an duin' uasal seo mi, *I am the son* (or *daughter*, or *servant*) *of this gentleman;* ciod leis a ni thu e ? *by what means will you do it ?* co leis an téid thu ? *with whom will you go ?* leat-sa, *along with you* ; leis an dithis seo, *by means of these two* ; leis a' chabhaig, *on account of the hurry* ; is aithreach leis, *he regrets;* co leis a tha thu? *on whose side are you ?* leis a' ghaoith, *with the wind* ; leis a' bhruthach, *down the hill* ; leig e leis, *he fainted, fagged* ; *2 he permitted him* ; bha leis gu'm faodadh e a h-earbsadh riutha, *he thought he might trust her with* (to) *them;* cuiridh mi tuillidh neart leis a' chloich an ath uair a thilgeas mi i, *I will apply more strength to the stone the next time I throw it* ; an duine is leis iad (also, leis an leis iad *and* d' an leis iad,—bad idiom. MM) *the man to whom they belong.* [For other idiomatic uses of leis, see under *is*.]

In *Arran*, cuidich leat féin, *help yourself* ; cuidich leis leis an obair, *help him with the work* ;

In *Lochalsh*, thug mi leis e (*for* thug mi leam e), *I brought it with me* ; a' bhean leis an robh i, generally used to signify *the woman whose she was*, is in *Lochalsh* changed to, a' bhean a bha i leis. [DMK says that in Lochalsh such improper expressions, are only made use of by the younger people and that he has heard some of the older people express their disgust at them.]

leis,* *a.* Lee, leeward, larboard, (port) side of a vessel. Air an taobh leis, *on the larboard side;* am fearann leis, *the land to leeward* ; leig leis ! *slack sheet ! let go before the wind !* leis oirnn, *to leeward of us* ; cum leis oirnn, *keep to leeward of us* ; a' ruith leis, *running before the wind.*
leis-bheart, -eirt, -an, *s.f.* Armour for the thigh, cuish. 2 Trousers, breeches.
leis-bhrat, -ait, -an, *s.m.* Pair of trousers.
leiscioball,* -aill, *s.m.* Minion, vassal, creature.
leisdear, -ir, -an, see fleisdear.
leisdeireachd, *s.f.* see fleisdearachd.
leise,** *s.f.* Happiness.
——adh,** -aidh, *s.m.* Mocking.
leisg, -e, *a.* Lazy, indolent, slothful. 2 Loath, reluctant, unwilling. Duine l., *an indolent man;* is l. leam, *I am loath* ; is l. leam cur a mach air, *I feel reluctant to cast out with him* ; is l. leis sin a dheanamh, *he feels reluctant to do that* ; gnothach a' ghille l. 'san fhogharadh —théid e fada leis, 's bithidh e fada ris, *the lazy fellow's business in harvest-time, he goes far with it and takes long to do it.* [* and ‡‡ spell this word "leisg," McL & D and give "leasg" and "leisg" but both prefer "leasg," ** gives "leasg" only, MM says "leisg" is wrong and "leasg" right but that the error has got into literature. "Leisg" is certainly the usual pronunciation at present.]
leisg, -e, *s.f.* [*m.* in *Badenoch.*] Laziness, sloth, slothfulness, indolence. 'S e an l. a thug ort sin a dheanamh, *sheer indolence made you do that* ; cha dean làmh na leisge beairteas, *the lazy hand will not earn riches.*
leisge, *comp.* of leisg. More or most lazy.
leisgeachd,‡‡ *s.f.ind.* Laziness, dulness.
leisgean, -ein, -an, *s.m.* Sluggard, lazy person. 2 Sloven. Seall thusa dhomh-sa an l., agus seallaidh mise dhuit-se am mèirleach, *you show me the sluggard, and I will show you the thief.* Another version is, baobach air an leisg' a th' ann, bheir i a clann chum na croiche, (confound that laziness, it brings its children to the gallows.)
leisgeanachd, *s.f.* Slothfulness, indolence.
leisgeanta, *a.* Slothful, lazy, indolent.
leisgeantachd, see leisgeanachd.
leisgear, see leisgean.
leisgeil, -e, *a.* see leisgeanta.
——eachd, see leisgeanachd.
leisgeul, -eil, -an, *s. m.* Excuse, pretence. 2 Apology. 3 Defence (in law.) Gabh mo l., *excuse me* ; a l. sin doibh, *their own affair be it.*
leisgeulach, -aiche, *a.* Excusing. 2 Ready to make excuses. 3 Mediatory. 4 Excusable.
————, -aich, *s.m.* see leisgeulaiche.
leisgeulachadh, *s.m.* Defence.
leisgeulachd, *s.f.ind.* Habit of making excuses, evasiveness. 2‡‡Excusableness. 3 Advocacy.
leisgeulaich,‡‡ *v.a.* Excuse, colour.
leisgeulaiche, -an, *s. m.* Excuser. 2 Mediator. 3 Deprecator.
leis-san, *prep.pron.*, emphatic of leis. With himself.
leistear, -an, see fleisdear. 2**Table.
——achd, see fleisdearachd.
†leite, see lite.
leiteachas, (DMC) -ais, *s.m.* Partiality, preference.
leith, (MS) *s.f.* Nerve.
leith, see leth.
lèith, *gen. & voc.* of liath. A dhuine lèith ! *O grey-headed man !*
leith-bhreac, -ic, -an, *s.m. & f.* see leth-bhreac.
leith-bhruthach, (DU) *s.f.* Gentle declivity.
leithcheann, see lethcheann.
leithchinn, see lethcheann.
léithe *comp.* of liath. More or most grey.
léithe, *s.f.* Greyness, greyishness. 2 Mouldiness, staleness, as of bread.
leitheach, -eiche, *a.* By half, half, as half-full. 2 Half-way through, half-way on a journey. L. làn, *half-full* ; l. bhruich, *half-boiled* ; dhùineadh tu do chluasan mu'm bithinn l., *you would close your ears before I had half (finished.)*
leitheach, see leathag.
leitheach-slighe, (DU) Half-way.
léithead, -id, *s.f.* Greyness, degree of greyness.
leitheag, see leathag.
leithid, -e, -ean, *s.f.* The like, equal, compeer, fellow. Is ainneamh a l., *his match is seldom met with* ; leithidean a chéile, *the very patterns of each other.* [*Leithid* is generally preceded by a possesive prouonn and not by an

article, as, a leithid seo, *the (his) like of this;* cha'n fhaca mi a l. riamh, *I never saw his (not the) like before;* in some cases the article is used, as an leithid mu 'n robh mi 'bruidhinn. *the like of which I was speaking.*]
leithinn, see leathann.
léithne, *comp.* of leathann. Broader, broadest.
———,** *s.f.* Breadth, broadness. 2 Extension.
———achd,** *s.f.* Breadth, spaciousness. 2 Extension.
———ad,** -neid, *s.* Breadth.
leithneagan,(DMy) *s.m.* Kiln-dried grain which is not dry enough to grind, and so gets flattened out.
leithnich,** *v.a. & n.* Extend, enlarge. 2 Make broad. 3 Become broad. L. an aran, *roll out the bread.*
———te,** *past part.* Extended, enlarged.
leithreachas,** -ais, *s.m.* Unjust dealing. 2 Separation.
leithridheach,** *a.* Partial, unjust.
———d,** *s. f.* Partiality.
leithrinn,** *s.pl.* Chains, fetters.
leithrist, see leirist.
leithse, see leatha-sa.
leithsgeul, -éil, -an, *s.m.* see leisgeul.
———ach, see leisgeulach.
———achd, see leisgeulachd.
léitig,** *s.f.* Convoy. Thoir l. dha, *give him a convoy.*
———, *v.a.* Convoy.
leitir, -e & -treach, *pl.* -ean & -trichean, *s. f.* Side of a hill. 2†† Place on the sea-shore. 3 Broad slope. 4**Sloping shore. 5 Countryside.
le leathad, *adv.* Downhill.
le 'm, With their. Le 'm biodagaibh, *with their dirks.*
le m', With my. Le m' each, *with my horse.*
le 'n, With their.
leò, *prep.pron.* With them, in their company. 2 By them. 3 On their side. 4 In their favour. 5 In their opinion. 6 Theirs. Th' air leò, *they thought, they should think;* bha i brònach leò, *she was sorrowful in their company;* is bòidheach leò am fàs, *beautiful in their estimation is their growth.*
leòb, -òib & leòba, *pl.* leòban, *s.m.* Piece, fragment, slice, shred, as of skin or leather. 2 Hanging lip. 3 (DU) Big mouth. Bhur bois gun leòb chraicionn, *your palms without a shred of skin.*
leòb, *pr.pt.* a' leòbadh, *v. a.* Tear into shreds, mangle.
leoba,(DMy) *s.* Small rig. An do chuir thu 'n leoba? *did you sow the small rig?*
leòbach, -aiche, *a.* In shreds or membranes. 2 Hanging in awkward folds or plaits. 3 Ragged, tawdry. 4**Flabby. 5**Skinny. 6 (DMK)Having hanging lips. 7(DU)Large-mouthed.
leòbadh, -aidh, *s.m.* Tearing, act of tearing into shreds or fragments. A' l—, *pr.pt.* of leòb.
leòbag, -aig, -an, *s.f.dim.* of leòb. Little shred or fragment.
———, *prov.* for lèabag.
———ach, -aiche, *a.* Abounding in shreds or fragments. 2 see lèabagach.
leobhair, *a.* see leobhar.
leobhar, see leabhar.
leobhar, -aire & leoibhre, *a.* Unshapely, awkward, tawdry, clumsy, trailing, untidy, too long, not fitting, as an article of dress.
———achd, *s. f. ind.* Unshapeliness, awkwardness, clumsiness, untidiness.
leòbus, -uis, *s.m.* Hanging lip. 2 Ugly mouth. L. odhar, *a squalid ugly mouth.*

leòbusach, -aiche, *a.* Having an ugly mouth or hanging lips.
leòcach, -aiche, *a.* Sneaking, mean, low, pitiful.
leòcaireachd, *s.f.ind.* Meanness, habit of mean or despicable acting.
leòd,** -eòid, *s.* §. Cutting, mangling, maiming.
leòdag, -aig, -an, *s.f.* Slovenly untidy female. 2 Prude. 3 Flirt.
———ach, -aiche, *a.* Sluttish. 2 Flirtish.
leòdair,(MS) *v.a.* Curry.
leog, -eoig, -an, *s.m.* Idle talk. †2 Marsh. DC gives *s.f.* for No. 2.
leog,* *v.a.* Fag on the stomach.
leogach, -aiche, *a.* Hanging loosely or awkwardly. 2 Having long or hanging ears. 3 Slovenly, untidy. 4 Dull, slow, heavy. 5 Fawning, meanly flattering. 6* Marshy, swampy. 7 (DU) Broad and heavy. 8 Slow or deliberate of speech. 9 (AH) Insipid and unpleasant in taste.
leogair, -ean, *s.m.* Idle or foolish talker. 2 Slovenly, lazy fellow.
———eachd, *s.f.ind.* Foolish or idle talk. 2 Slovenliness. 3 Laziness.
leogan, -ain, *s.m.* Slovenly untidy fellow. 2 see leòmann. 3 (MMcD) Small stone, generally applied to a round pebble that is easily thrown with the hand.
———ach, -aich, -an, see leogan.
———ach, -eiche, *a.* Slovenly, untidy.
leogh, see leagh.
leoghan,** -ain, *s.m.* Trowel.
leòghann, -ainn, -an, see leòmhann.
———ach, see leòmhanta.
———ta, see leòmhanta.
———tachd, see leòmhantachd.
leogarach, ** -aiche, *a.* Conceited, haughty, proud.
leogaradh,** -aidh, *s.m.* Haughtiness.
leoghantachd, *s.f.* Inconstancy, see luaineachd & luaineas.
†leoghar, -air, *a.* Stout. 2 Brave.
leòid, *gen.sing.* of leud.
leòide,** *s.f.* Breadth.
———ag, -eig, *s. f.* Disrespectful term for a woman.
———an, *pl.* of leathad.
leoig,* *s.f.* Ditch. 2 Morass.
leòime,** *s.f.* Pride, self-conceit. 2 Foppishness, prudery, coquetry.
leòimean,** *s.m.* Fop.
leòin, *gen.sing.* of leòn.
leòinte, *past pt.* of leòn. Wounded, maimed.
———ach,†† *a.* Hurtful.
———achd,†† *s.f.* Hurtfulness.
leòir, *s.f.ind.* Sufficiency, enough, as of food. Fhuair mi mo l., *I have had enough.*
leòir, *a.* Enough, sufficient.
leòis, *gen.sing. & n.pl.* of leus.
leòlag,(MS) *s.f.* Babery.
leolaicheann,§ *s. m.* Globe flower, boits, golden ball—*troilus europæus.*
leom, see leam.
leòm, -eòim & -eòime, *s. f.* Pride, conceit, gaudiness, foppishness, vain-glory, prudery. 2* Drawling pronunciation. 3 (AH) Flattery. B' fhèarr furan a pòige na té 'gan l. a cuid cruidh, *better the salutation of her kiss, than she whose pride is her cattle.*
———ach, -aiche, *a.* Conceited, vain-glorious, affected, prudish, foppish, vain. 2 Hairy, shaggy, rough. 3**Big. 4 Prim. 5**Airy. 6**Flirting. 7* Drawling in talk. 8 (DMC) Well-dressed. Cho l. ris an aon fhaoileig a bh' air taobh Chaoil-Muile, *as conceited as the one sea-gull along the Sound of Mull*—Long ago, the Mull people were supposed to be un-

able to support more than one seagull, but that one seagull, petted and spoilt to its heart's content, was as conceited as all the other Hebridean seagulls put together ; cho l. ri dà-bhliadhnach cait, *as conceited as a two-year-old cat.*
——achas, -ais, *s.m.* Vanity, affectation, conceit. 2 Foppery, prudery.
——achd, *s.f.* see leòmachas. [2 Prude.
——ag, -aig, -an, *s.f.* Affected, conceited girl.
——aich,(MS) *v.a.* Coquet.
leòmainn, *gen.sing.* of leòmann.
leòmair, -ean, *s.m.* Fop, conceited fellow.
————eachd,** *s.f.* Conceitedness. 2 Foppery, behaviour of a fop.
leomais, *s.f.* Dilly-dallying—*Dàin I. Ghobha.*
leòmann, -ainn, *s.m.* Moth. 2(AF)Leech. 3 (AF) Weevil.
————ach, -aiche, *a.* Abounding in moths. 2 Moth-eaten.
———— -fiodha,(AF) *s.m.* Wood-bug.
leòmhann, -ainn, *pl.* [-an &] -ainn, *s. m.* Lion. 2 The sign Leo (♌) in the zodiac.
————ach, see leòmhanta.
leòmhanta, -ainte, *a.* Lion-like. 2 Brave, strong. 3 Applied to anyone strange in his behaviour.
————chd, *s.f.* Bravery. 2 Strength.
leòn, -eòin, -eòntan, *s.m.* Wound, hurt. 2 Grief, affliction, severe distress. 3** Sprain of the wrist or ankle. 4 Bruise. 5*Vexation.
leòn, *v.a.* Wound, hurt. 2 Grieve, afflict, gall. 3** Sprain the wrist or ankle. 4** Maim, bruise.
leòna, Bean-leòna, *a mid-wife.*
leònadh, -aidh, *s.m.* Wounding, act of wounding, hurting. 2 Grieving, afflicting. 3 Affliction. 4 Maiming. A' l—, *pr.pt.* of leòn.
leonagan,‖ see leamhragan.
leondrag,¶ *s.f.* Snipe, see gobhar-athair.
leòn-lorg,** *s.* Cicatrice.
leònta. *past pt,* of leòn. Wounded, hurt. 2 Afflicted, grieved. 3 Pained. 4 Sprained, maimed.
leòntach, -aiche, *a.* Wounding, hurting. 2 Afflicting.
————d, *s. f. ind.* Hurtfulness. 2 Afflictiveness. 3 Bravery, brave actions. 4**Laxation. 5**Keenness of morals.
leòr, *s.f.ind. & a.* see leòir.
leòrachd,(MS) *s.f.* Amplitude.
†leòr-ghnìomh, -a, *s. m.* Satisfaction. 2 Work of supererogation. 3 Abundant labours.
†leòs, -eòis, *s.m.* Light, see leus. 2 Disclosure. 3 Blush. 4**Reproof.
——ach,** *s.m.* Radius. 2 Ray.
leò-san, *emphat. form* of leò. With themselves. Is leò-san rìoghachd néimh, *theirs is the kingdom of heaven.*
leosmhang, *s.* Radius.
leotha, *comp.* of leathann. *prov.*
leothad, -aid, see leathad.
leothaid, *gen.* of leothad (leathad.)
le 'r, With our. 2 By our. 3 Belonging to our. 4 In favour of our. Le 'r cliù, *with our fame.*
le 'r, With your. 2 By your. 3 Belonging to your. 4 In favour of your.
le-san, see leis-san.
leth, *s.m.ind.* Half. 2 Side, share, interest. 3 Charge. 4 One of a pair. Leth mar leth, *share and share alike* ; chaidh e as mo l., *he sided with me, took my part* ; chuir iad sin as a l., *they laid that to his charge ;* air l., *apart, separately ;* largely compounded with names of weights and measures, as, lethphunnd, *half-a-pound ;* lethchlach, *half-a-stone* ; lethunnsa, *half-an-ounce ; &c..*—gu leth signifies " one half more " of any specified measure, as, troidh gu leth, *a foot-and-a-half ;* mile gu leth, *a mile-and-a-half ;*—leth slighe, *half-way, midway, half the voyage ;* an l. a's mó, *the majority, bulk, greater part ;* leth an t-Samhraidh, *midsummer* ; là leth an t-samhraidh, *Midsummer Day ;* leth a' Gheamhraidh, *midwinter ;* fa leth, *severally, individually* ; à leth, as leth, *on behalf of, for the sake of ;* cuir as a leth, *lay to his charge ;* tha mi 'leth los, *I have half a mind* ; leth ri (see below.)
leth-, *pref.* Semi-, somewhat-, by-. 2 Duplicate, one of two.
leth, *s.* Mule. Followed by name of animal to describe what species is signified.
lethachas, see leathachas.
leth-adhairc,(DMC) *a.* One-horned.
leth-ainm, -eannan & -ainmean, *s.m.* Nickname.
—————each, -eiche, *a.* Given to nicknaming.
lethallt,(DMK) *s.m.* Burn having a high bank on one side. 2 (Fionn) Sloping land on one side of a burn.
leth-a-mach,** *s.m.* Outside, exterior.
—————, *a.* External.
leth-amadan,** -ain, *s. m.* Ninny, half-witted fellow.
leth-a-muigh,** *s.m.* Outside, exterior. O 'n l., *from the outside.*
leth-anmoch,(MS) *adv.* Latish, rather late.
leth-an-taighe, Bu tu gille mór leth-an-tighe ! *what a great half-the-house lad you are !*—said to a man-servant assuming too much authority in the house—N.G.P.
leth-aodach,** *s.* Deshabille. 2**Sheet of linen.
leth-aon, -aoin, *pl.* -an & -aona, *s.m.* Twin-child. 2 Match, fellow. 3 One of a pair. Leth-aona 'na bolg, *twins in her womb.*
leth-aonan (na), The sign Gemini (♊) in the zodiac.
leth-asal, *s.f.* Mule.
leth-a-staigh,** *s. m.* Inside, interior, inward part.
leth-bhàir, *s.* " Hail " or goal in shinty. In *Morvern & Mull,* leth-bhair=1 hail ; bàire, 2 hails ; bàire gu leth, 3 hails ; see bàire.
leth-bhalach,(CR) *s.m.* Halflin, young ploughman—*Perthshire & Argyllshire.* 2 (DU) Young man before puberty, hobbledehoy.
leth-bhalla, *s.m.* Battlement.
leth-bhann, *adv.* In gear, said of a quern, see brà, No. 11, p. 112.
leth-bharaille, *s.m.* Anker, kilderkin.
lethbhliadhna, *s.f.* Half a year. An ceann l., *in six months' time.*
lethbhodach, -aich, *s. m.* Half a mutchkin, a liquid measure equal to half an imperial pint.
leth-bhonn, -bhuinn, *s.m.* Half-sole of a shoe.
leth-bhuinn, see leth-bhonn.
leth-bhòt, *s.f.* Buskin.
lethbhrathair, *s.m.* Half-brother.
leth-bhreac, -bhric, *s.m.* Fellow, partner, one of a pair, duplicate, copy, half marrow. Leth-bhreacan a chéile, *the exact models of each other ;* mo l. fhéin, *my own equal, my compeer ;* cha'n 'eil do l. ri fhaotainn, *your match is not to be found.*
—————as,** -ais, *s.m.* Co-equality.
leth-bhreath, see lèth-bhreith.
leth-bhreith, -e, *s.f.* Partial judgment, partiality, unfair decision. Gun l., *without partiality.*
—————each, -eiche, *a.* Partial, unfair, unequal.
—————eachd, *s.f.* Partiality.
leth-bhreth, see leth-bhreith.
leth-bhruadar, -air, *s.m.* Vision.

leth-bhruich, *a.* Parboiled. half-boiled.
————, *v.a.* Parboil, half-boil.
leth-bhruthach,** *adv.* Aslope, on the slope.
————,* *s. m.* Gentle slope, declivity, inclination.
leth-chadal, -ail, *s.m.* Slumber, doze.
————ach, -aiche, *a.* Dozing, slumbering, lethargic.
leth-chaillte,** *a.* Half-lost. 2 Half-concealed, half-hidden. L. 'an neul, *half-hidden in a cloud.*
leth-chairt,** *s.f.* One-eighth, as of a yard.
leth-chairteil,(DU) *s. m.* Half a quarter of a pound, two oz. e.g. Leth-chairteil tombaca, is always used for *two ounces of tobacco*—not " dà ùnnsa."
leth-chaoch,** *a.* Half-blind.
leth-char, (a leth char) *adv.* Somewhat, in some respects. L. acrach, *somewhat hungry.*
leth-chas, -oise, -an, *s.f.* One foot. 2**Left foot. 3 One leg. 4 One of the two " casan gaoisid " generally used on a hand fishing-line, see dorgh. " Air a leth-chois," is a certain stage in the drying of peats, see mòine ; seas air do leth-chois, *stand (thou) on one foot.* (see also leth-chois.)
lethcheann, -chinn, *s. m.* Side of the head, cheek, temple. Do lethcheann, *thy temples.* [*pronounced* lei'chyen.]
————ach, -aiche, *a.* Awkward, sheepish, bashful.
leth-chearcall, -aill, *pl.* -aill & -clan, *s.m.* Semicircle.
leth-chearclach, -aiche, *a.* Semi-circular.
leth-cheathramh,* *s.m.* Two ounces. 2 Half a flank of a beast.
leth-cheil,** *v.a.* Half-conceal, half-hide. 2 See in part.
————te,** *past pt.* Half-concealed, half-hidden. 2 Seen in part.
leth-chiallach,(DMK) *s.m.* Half-witted person.
leth-chiallaich,‡‡ *v.a.* Insinuate.
lethchlach, *s.f.* Half-a-stone (weight.) [Preferable to " seachd puinnd " for 7 pounds.]
leth-chliathach, -aich, *s.m.* One side of the body.
leth-chliathaich,‡‡ -ean, *s.f.* see leth-chliathach.
leth-chluasach,(DMC) *a.* One-eared.
leth-chluich, *s.* Hail in shinty. In *Eigg* leth-chluich means 1 hail, cluich, 2 hails ; cluich gu leth, 3 hails ; see leth-bhàir.
leth-chodal, see leth-chadal.
————ach, see leth-chadalach.
leth-choinean,(AF) *s.m.* Strange rabbit.
leth-chois, *s.* Peculiar kind of land tenure by which the possessor, generally impoverished or without facilities for working the land, often furnished the land and seed corn, and the tenant cultivated it, the produce being divided equally between them. There have been instances of it in our own day—*Clan Donald, iii.*
leth-chos, see leth-chas.
leth-chosmhuil, *a.* Somewhat like.
leth-chothrom, -oim, *s. m.* Weight, burden. 2 Injustice.
————ach, -aiche, *a.* Unjust.
leth-chruinn, -e, *a.* Oval. 2 Hemispherical.
leth-chruinne, *s.f.* Semi-circle. 2 Hemisphere.
lethchrun, -uin, *s.m.* Half-crown (2/6.)
leth-chù,(AF) *s.m.* Lurcher dog.
leth-chuairt, -ean, *s.f.* Semi-circle.
————each, *a.* Semi-circular.
leth-chuid, -chodach, -chodaichean, *s.f.* Half-share. 2 Partiality.
leth-dheamhan,** -ain, *s.m.* Demi-demon.
leth-dhèanta, *a.* Half-formed. 2 Half-performed or executed, half-made, half-done. L. de mhùig, *half-formed of mist.*
leth-dhearbhachd,‡‡ *s.f.ind.* Probability.
leth-dibheach,(MS) *s.* Gullet.
leth-ditheach, (MS) (for leth-de-tigheach) *s. f.* Antestomach.
letheach,(MS) *a.* Subduple.
lethein, *s.* see leth-aon.
leth-eòlach, -aiche, *a.* Half-acquainted. 2 Half-informed.
————, -aich, *s.m.* Novice.
leth-eudach,** see leth-aodach.
leth-fhacal, -ail, *pl.* -ail & -fhaclan, *s. m.* By-word, proverb, article.
leth-fhaclach, -aiche, *a.* Proverbial, like a proverb. 2 Fond of proverbs.
leth-fhad,** *adv.* Aslope, on the slope.
leth-fhaicte, *past pt.* Half-seen, partly seen.
leth-fhaide, *s.f.ind.* Oblongness.
leth-fhior, *a.* Somewhat true.
leth-fhoghair, -ean, *s.m.* Semi-vowel.
leth-gheamhradh, *s. m.* The Winter half of the year—1st. Nov. to 30th. April.
leth-gheur, *a.* Somewhat sour
†**leth-ghrabal**,** -ail, *s.m.* Halfpenny.
leth-ghuilbneach,¶ *s. m.* Whimbrel, see eun-Bhealltuinn.
leth-innis, -innse, -innsean, *s.f.* Peninsula.
leth-iomall, -aill, -an, *s.m.* Border.
————ach, *a.* Bordering, of a border.
leth-lag,** *a.* Half-tired, half-fatigued.
lethlàmh, -làimhe, -an, *s.f.* One hand, one arm. 2 Left hand, left arm. Air leth-làimh, *having but one hand or arm* ; claidheamh 'na leth-làimh, *a sword in one hand.*
————ach, -aiche, *a.* One-handed. 2 Awkward. 3 (DMC) Without support.
leth-leabaiche, -an, *s.m.* Bedfellow.
leth-leann, -a, *s.m.* Small beer.
leth-linn, *s.m.* Half-wit. Bha e 'na leth-linn, *he was a natural, a half-wit.*
leth-luighe, *s. m.* Reclining posture. 2 Act of reclining or leaning. Tha e 'na l., *he is reclining.*
leth mar leth, *adv.* Half and half, share and share alike.
lethmhas, -àis, -an, *s.m.* Buttock, thigh. 2 Hip.
leth-mhèinn, -e, *s.m.* Antimony.
leth-muigh, see leth-a-muigh.
leth-oinnseach,** -ich, *s.f.* Half-witted female.
leth-oir, -e, *s. f.* One side or edge. 2 (DMy) Diffidence.
————, *adv.* Sideways, edgeways, to a side.
————each, -eiche, *a.* Superficial, indifferent. 2 Partial. 3 Singular. 4*Remote, lonely, secluded. 5‡‡Marginal. 6 (DMy) Diffident.
leth-phairt, *s.m.* Partiality.
————each, -eiche, *a.* Partial.
leth-pheighinn, *s.* Halfpenny land.
lethphiuthar, *s.f.* Half-sister.
lethphunnd, -uinnd, -an, *s. m.* Half-a-pound (weight.)
leth-rann, -ainn, *s.m.* Half verse, hemistich.
————ach, -aiche, *a.* In half verses or hemistiches. 2 Partial.
leth-rathad, -aid, -aidean, *s. m.* By-path, by-road.
————ach, -aiche, *a.* Of, or belonging to by-paths.
leth ri, *adv.* Towards. 2 Since, since it was so. 3†† Close to. 4††In consideration of. Leth ri éirigh na gréine, *towards the east, eastward*; tha 'n còta leth ri m' chraicionn, *the coat is next my skin* ; tha iad a' cadal is na plaideachan leth riu, *they sleep with the blankets next them—i.e.* without any sheets.
leth-ròd, -ròid, -ròidean, see leth-rathad.
leth-rosg, -roisg, -an, *s. m.* One eye. 2**Pur-

blindness.
————ach, -aiche, *a.* Having but one eye. 2 ‡‡Purblind. 3**Blear-eyed.
leth-ruadh, -ruaidhe, *a.* Somewhat red, reddish, brown.
leth-sgoiltean, *s.m.* Semi-colon (;) in *writing.* 2 Plank. 3 Joist. 4 Half handkerchief. 5 (DMC) Half a ridge.
leth-shamhradh, *s.m.* The summer half of the year—1st. May to 31st. Oct.
leth-shean, *a.* Middle-aged. Bha leth-sheann té ann, *a middle-aged female was there.* [Before *d, t, l,* or *n,* "sheann" is used.]
leth-sheise,** *s.m. & f.* Partner, mate. 2 Spouse. 3 Beloved person. Mo l., *my beloved.*
leth-shùil, shùla, -shùilean, *s.f.* One eye.
————each, -eiche, *a.* Having but one eye, monocular. 2 Purblind.
leth-tadhal,(AH) *s.m.* Hail in shinty. Tadhal =2 hails, tadhal gu leth=3 hails, see leth-bhàir.
leth-taobh, -aoibh, *s.m.* Side, one side. 2** Flitch. 3** (with art. *an*) Hysterics. A leth-taobh, *aside;* thug e a leth-taobh e, *he took him aside;* cuir air a leth-taobh e, *put it on its side.*
————ach, -aiche, *a.* Sidelong, sideways. 2 Hysterical.
————aich,(MS) *v.a.* Accumb.
————ail,** *a.* Hysterical.
leth-thràth,(DMC) *a.* Little too early.
leth-titheach, -iche -ean, *s.f.* see leth-dìbheach.
leth-trà,(DMC) *s.* Half the day.
leththrath,* *s.m.* Half rations. 2 Half allowance. 3 Milking once a day.
leth-trom, see leatrom.
————ach, see leatromach.
————achd, see leatromachd.
leth-tromas, see leatromachd.
leth-truime, see leatrom.
leth-uan, *s. m.* Twin lamb. 2 (DU) Human twin—*Lochewe.*
leth-uidheam,** *s.* Dishabille.
lethuileann, -inn, -an, *s. m.* One elbow. 2 Half an angle. 3**Acute angle. 4**Posture of half sitting half reclining. Air a leth-uilinn, *declining, going downhill.*
————ach, -aiche, *a.* Having angles on one side.
lethunnsa,* *s.m.* Half-an-ounce.
leub, see leòb.
leubag, see leòbag.
lèubag mhór, see lèabag.
leubaideach see leibideach.
————d, see leibideacho
leubh, see leugh.
————adair, see leughadair.
————adh, see leughadh.
leud, leòid, -an, *s. m.* Breadth. 2 Degree of breadth. 3**Extension. 4**Space, spaciness. L. ròine, *a hair's breadth;* air fad 's air l., *in length and breadth* · còig troidhean air l., *five feet in breadth;* l. boise, *a handbreadth.*
——ach, *a.* Wide, ample, diffuse, spacious. 2 Spreading, extending. Cainnt l., *diffuse language.*
——achadh, -aidh, *s.m.* Broadening, act of making or becoming broad or broader. 2 Spreading, extending, widening. 3 Increasing. 4 Extension. 5 Increase in breadth. A' l—, *pr.pt.* of leudaich.
leudachair,** *s.m.* Amplifier.
leudachd, *s.f.* Ampleness.
leudaich, *pr.pt.* a' leudachadh, *v.a. & n.* Make broad or broader, enlarge, dilate, make spacious, bespread, diffuse, widen, extend. 2 Become broader or larger. 3 Enlarge upon. Cha do l. e air sin, *he did not enlarge upon that (matter.)*
————te, *past pt.* of leudaich. Enlarged, dilated, widened, extended, made spacious.
leud iochdair, *s.m.* Bilge-piece of boat, see F 8 p. 73.
leug, léig, -an, *s.f.* Precious stone, jewel, adamant. 2 Small stone or pebble to which healing virtues are ascribed. 3 Beautiful woman. 4* Lye or ashes and water for bleaching. 5*Meteor. 6**Beloved person. 7 Sloth, laziness. Òr no l., *gold or crystal;* mar l. theine, *like a meteor;* mo l. phriseil, *my precious jewel, my darling.*
——, *a.* see leugach.
——ach, -aiche, *a.* Slow, dull, sluggish. 2 Of, abounding in, or belonging to precious stones or jewels. 3**Crystalline. 4**Like a meteor. 5*Drawling.
——aich,‡‡ *v.a.* Bestud.
——an, -ain, -an, *s.m.* Lazy, inactive person. 2 Little jewel.
——anach, -aiche, *a.* Precious. 2 Beautiful.
——anta,** *a.* Adamantine.
——art,** -airt, *s.m.* Siege.
leugh, *pr. pt.* a' leughadh, *v.a. & n.* Read, peruse. 2 Read, perform the act of reading. 3 Lecture, explain. 4††Think. Cha'n 'eil math dhomh a bhi leughadh sin dhuit-sa, *it serves no end to explain that to you;* a' leughadh a chall 's a chunnart, *expatiating on his loss and danger.*
leughach,‡‡ *a.* Bookish, studious.
leughadair, -ean, *s.m.* Reader. Deagh l., *a good reader.*
————eachd, *s.f.ind.* Reading, act or office of reading.
leughadh, -aidh, *s.m.* Reading, act of reading. 2 Perusing. 3 Lecturing. 4*Expounding, explaining. A' l—, *pr.pt.* of leugh.
leughair, -ean, *s.m.* Reader.
————eachd, *s.f.ind.* Reading, habit or business of reading.
leughta, *past pt.* of leugh. Read, perused.
leug-reiceadair,‡‡ -ean, *s.m.* Lapidary.
leum, *pr. pt.* a' leum, a' leumadh, a' leumartaich & a' leumnaich, *v.a. & n.* Leap, bound. 2 Leap over or across. 3 Spring, skip, frisk, hop, jump. 4 Start. 5*Fight, quarrel. 6†† Shake. 7††Flaw. 8 (MS) Cover. 9 Pass, as time, or through space. 10 (DU) Squirt out. 11 Make a slip of the tongue. Leum mo theanga(dh) orm, *my tongue slipped,* "I put my foot in it"—said by one who unwittingly says a thing that he regrets and would rather not have said—*W. coast of Ross;* leum iad air a chéile, *they quarrelled;* 'nuair a leumas e an Fhéill-Brighde, cha'n earb an sionnach 'earball ris an deigh, *when Candlemas is past, the fox will not trust his tail to the ice;* l. air, *attack suddenly, seize greedily.* l. e air a' mheadhon-oidhche, *it passed midnight;* bho Chluaidh nan long gleusda gu'n leum e Port Phàdruig, *from Clyde of the trim ships till Port Patrick (in Islay) is reached.*
leum, léim *pl.* leuma, -an, & leumannan, *s.m.* [*f.* in *Badenoch.*] Leap, bound, spring, frisk, start, shake. 2 Leaping, act of leaping, jump. 3 Animal semen. 4 Emission. 5††Flaw. 6 (DU) Sudden rage, impulsive anger. 7 (AF) Milk. L. gàbhaidh, *a desperate leap;* thoir leum, *leap;* ghabh e seachd leumannan de 'n chaothach, *he became exceedingly enraged, frenzied.* A' l—, *pr.pt.* of leum.
leum a' bhradain,(DMC) *s.* The salmon leap.
leumach, see leumachan.
————an, -ain, -an, *s.m.* Frog.

leumachanach, -aiche, *a.* Froggy, pertaining to frogs.
———as,(MS) *s.f.m.* Dissilience, bursting or leaping asunder, starting asunder.
leum-a-chrann,§ *s. m.* Honeysuckle or woodbine—*Strathardle, &c.* see uilleann.
leumadaich, see leum & leumnaich.
leumadair, -ean, *s.m.* Jumper, leaper. 2 Dolphin. 3 Kind of small whale. 4*Salmon between the size of the grilse and a full-grown fish—*Islay*. 5 (AF) Skipjack, the blue fish, saurel, a fish resembling a lizard. 6 Busybody in other people's affairs. 7** Spark, or scale of iron.
———eachd, *s. f. ind.* Jumping, habit of jumping, continued jumping.
——— -feòir, *s. m.* **Grasshopper. 2(AF) Cricket.
——— -uaine,* *s.m.* Green grasshopper. 2 (AF) Cricket.
leumadh,-aidh, *s.m. & pr.pt.* of leum, see leum & leumnaich.
leumaidh, *fut.aff.a.* of leum. Shall or will start, leap, &c.
leum-àrd, *s.m.* High jump.
leumardaich, see leumartaich.
leumartaich, *s.f.* Leaping, springing, frisking, hopping, caper, capering. 2 Repeated leaping. A l—, *pr. pt.* of leum.
leum-droma, *s.m.* Lumbago.
leum-fada, *s.m.* Long jump.
leumhann, *s.m.* Meal-receiver.
leum-iochd, *s.m.* Balk. Is fhèarr l. a's t-Fhoghar na sguab a bharrachd, *a balk in autumn is better than a sheaf the more*—the leum-iochd or bailc (*Scots* bauk), is a strip of a corn-field left farrow. The fear of being left with the last sheaf of the harvest, called the "caill-each" or "gobhar bhacach," always led to an exciting competition among the reapers in the last field. The reaper who came on a leum-iochd would of course be glad to have so much the less to cut. Rev. Mr. Michie of Dinnet has heard the above saying used in a different sense in the Highlands of Aberdeenshire, viz. that in lands allotted on the run-rig system, the crofter who got a balk attached to his rig was considered luckier than his neighbour with a somewhat larger rig, but without the balk, the grass of which was of more than compensating value.—*N.G.P.*
leumnach, -aiche, *a.* Jumping, skipping, starting, bounding, hopping. 2 Dissilient, liable to start or burst asunder. Fuaim nan carbad l., *the noise of the bounding chariots.*
leumnach, -aich, *s.m.* Frog. 2 Any creature that moves by leaping, see leumadair.
——— -uaine, *s.m.* Grasshopper.
leumnaich, *s.m.* Jumping, act of jumping, leaping, bounding, springing or hopping, skipping, repeated leaping. A' l—, *pr. pt.* of leum. A' l. o neul gu neul, *bounding from cloud to cloud.*
———e,** *s.m.* Caperer.
leumrachan, see leumachan.
leumraich, see leumnaich.
leum-ruith,‡‡ -an-, *s.m.* Running leap.
leum-shneachd, *s.m.* Avalanche.
leum-uisge,* *s.m.* Waterfall.
leun, see leòn.
leun, léin, see lèana.
——ach, see lèanach.
——adh, see leònadh. Tha mo làmh air 'l., *my wrist is sprained.*
leursainn, see léirsinn.
leus, leòis, *s.m.* Blaze, flame. 2 Light, ray of light, glimmering light. 3** Fir-candle. 4 Torch used in fishing at night. 5 Blister. 6‡ Cataract on the eye, blemish or white spot on the eye. 7**Link. 8 Gall. 9 Bladder. 10‡‡ Lightning, flash of lightning. 11*Blink, glimmer. 12 Young man. An dreach mar leòis, *their appearance like torches*; cha'n 'eil leus soluis an seo, *there is not a ray of light here*; mil air do bheul ged robh leus air do theanga, *honey on your mouth though a blister on your tongue*; l. teine, *a flame of fire, blaze*; duine aig am bheil l., *a man who has a spot on his eye*; leòis air a basaibh, *blisters on her palms.*
leusach, -aiche, *a.* Emitting light or rays of light. 2 Blazing, flaming, flashing. 3 ** Combustible. 4 Blistering, blistered. 5 Having torches, abounding in torches. 6 Having a spot, spotted, marked. Sùil l., *a spotted or blemished eye.*
———adh, -aidh, *s.m.* Blistering, act of blistering, rising in blisters. 2 State of becoming blistered. 3**Flaming, blazing. A' l—, *pr.pt.* of leusaich.
———ail, -e, *a.* That raises blisters. 2 Blistered, having blisters. 3 Apt to blister. Làmhan l., *blistered hands* or *hands that are apt to blister.*
leusaich, *pr.pt.* a' leusachadh, *v.a. & n.* Blister, raise blisters. 2 Become blistered. 3 Make a flame.
———te, *a. & past pt.* of leusaich. Blistered. Làmhan l., *blistered hands.*
leusan,‡‡ -ain, -an, *s.m.* Small torch.
leus-chnuimh, -e, -ean, *s.f.* Glow-worm.
———each, -eiche, *a.* Of, or belonging to glow-worms. 2 Full of glow-worms.
leus-ghath, -a, -an, *s.m.* Ray of light. 2 Sultry beam.
leus-mara, *s.m.* Beacon.
leus-mùire, *s m.* Morphew.
leus-sùil, *s.f.* Pearl-eye.
leus-teine, leòis-theine, *pl.* -eòis-theine & leus-an-teine, *s.m.* Firebrand.
'l fhios am bheil, Is it so?—*Arran.*
lì, lithe, lithean, *s.f.* Paint, colour, tinge, hue. 2**Complexion. 3**Prosperity. 4** Happiness. 5**Festival. 6††Gloss. 7 (AC) Water (formerly fresh or salt, now fresh only.) †8 The sea. 9**Solemnity. 10**Pomp. 11** Jewel. [No. 1 is generally used in giving an unfavourable opinion—AH.]
lì, *a.* Coloured, tinged.
†li, see leatha.
†lia, see leò.
†lia, *a.* More. 2 Nimble, active. 3 see liath.
†lia, *s.f.* [& ***m.*] Stone, great stone. †2 Hunger. 3‡‡Flood. 4‡‡Welting. 5‡‡Hog, pig. 6 **Stream.
liab,(CR) *s.m.* Rag, tatter—*Perthshire. prov.* for lèab and leòb.
liabag, see lèabag.
liac,(DMC) *pr. pt.* a' liacadh, *v. a.* Besmear, spread anything soft.
liacadh,(DMC) *s.m.* Besmearing. A' l—, *pr.pt.* of liac.
liach, see liagh.
lia-chac,** *s.m.* Hog's dung.
liachd,** *s.f.* Multitude, great many.
liachlan,** -ain, *s.m.* Spoonful.
lia-chrò,** *s.m.* Pig-sty.
liad, see leud.
liadh, léidhe, -an, see liagh.
——ach, -aiche, see liaghach.
liadhag, -aig, -an, *s.f.* Tangle, sea-oak (kind of seaweed.) 2(MMcD) Root-part of the stem of serrated tangle-leaf, sometimes used as food—*Lewis.* [Different from stamh in *Gairloch.*]

liadhagach, -aiche, *a.* Abounding in tangle or seaweed.
liadhbhog, see lèabag.
†lia-fàil, -e, *s.f.* The stone on which the Scottish, and as some say the Irish kings used to be crowned, now in the coronation chair in Westminster Abbey, also called clach-na-cinneamhuinn.
liag, see leug.
——ach, see leugach.
liagair, *s.* Loveage (plant)—*Islay.*
liagan,** -ain, *s.m.* Obelisk, small stone.
liagh, léigh, *pl.* -an & léigh, *s.f.* Ladle. 2 Feather or blade of an oar. 3** Large spoon. 4 (DMC) Brave fellow. Làn léigh, *a ladleful; nach b' e an l. e? isn't he a brave fellow?*
liaghach, -aiche, *a.* Of, or connected with ladles. 2 Bladed, as an oar.
liaghag,§ Top or leaf of tangle or oar-weed—*W. of Ross,* see liadhag & stamh. 2†† Edible tangle.
liagh-dhealg,** *s.f.* Bodkin. 2 Clasp. 3 Button.
liaghra, *s.f.* Two sticks crossed together in the centre and set on a swivel-pin in a block of wood called the *stoc.* A pin of wood is fixed in each of the four extremities of the sticks, and round this a hank of thread is placed which is unravelled and made into a ball, as the operator spins the instrument round. Thread-winder. Also called "crann-tachrais"; na sgiathan in *Caithness,* crois-iarna in *Gairloch,* eachan (little horse) in *Argyll,* crois-lionraidh in *Lewis,* and bodach-sgiathan in *Suth'd.*

424. Liaghra.

liamh, -a, see liomh.
lian, -a, -an, *s.m.* Field, plain, meadow. 2 see lion.
lian, see lion, Cia lian?=cia lion?
——ach, -aiche, *a.* Of many fields, plains, or meadows.
——ach, -aich, *s. f.* Species of fucus, *prov.* 2 § Plants known as confervæ, such as *enteromorpha* and *cladophora.* 3**Sea-green plant, often applied by the Hebrideans to the temples and forehead to dry up the defluxions and also to draw up the tonsils, which among that people are apt to swell at certain seasons, see lionanach.
lianachan, -ain, *s.m.* Little meadow.
lianag, -aig, -an, *s. f. dim.* of lian. Small field or meadow.
———ach, -aiche, *a.* Abounding in small fields or meadows.
lianaich,** *s.f.* Sea-ware.
lianaraich, *s.* see lìonanach.
liaphutag,** -aig, *s.f.* Pig's pudding. 2 Sausage.
liaragaich, *s.f.* Kind of seaweed—*alga marina viridis.*
liaranaich, see liaragaich.
lias, léis, *s.f.* Thigh.
lias, leòis & léis, *pl.* -an, *prov.* for leus.
lias, leis, *s.m.* Hut for calves or lambs. 2 (AF) Lamb. 3(AF) Sheep-cot.
——ach, -aiche, see leusach.
——aich, see leusaich.
lias-mara, see leus-mara.

liatas,§ -ais, *s.m.* Lettuce—*lactuca sativa.*
———, -ais, *s.m.* Fustiness, mildew, blight, see liathtas.
——— -a'-bhalla, *s. m.* Wall-lettuce—*lactuca murialis.*

425. Liatas a'-bhalla.

liath, *s.* see liagh.
liath, léithe, *a.* Grey, grey-coloured. 2 Grey-headed, grey-haired. 3 Mouldy. 4** Lilac. 5**Pale. Falt l., *grey hair,* aran l., *mouldy bread.*
liath, *v.a. & n.* Make grey. 2 Become grey. 3 Mould, grow mouldy. 4 Make mouldy. 5 Grow pale. 6 Make grey-headed. Aran air liathadh, *bread become mouldy;* liath e, *he became grey-headed.*
liathach, -aiche, *a.* Greyish, somewhat grey. 2 Pale. 3 Blank.
————adh, -aidh, *s.m.* Making grey. 2 Growing or becoming grey. 3 Growing mouldy. A' l—, *pr. pt.* of liathaich.
————d,‡‡*s.f. ind.* Staleness. 2 Whitishness.
liathad, -aid,** *s.* Staleness, as of bread.
liathadh, -aidh, *s.m.* Act of making grey. 2 State of becoming grey or mouldy. 3** Grey tinge. A' l—, *pr.pt.* of liath.
liathag, -aig, -an, *s.f.* Salmon-trout, young fish of the salmon species, grilse.
————ach, *a.* Abounding in salmon-trout.
liathaich, *v.a. & n.* Make grey. 2 Become grey.
—————te, *past pt.* of liathaich. Made grey. 2 Become grey.
liathan,§ -ain, -an, *s.m.* Corn-marigold, see bile bhuidhe.
———ach,(CR) *s.m.* Hoar-frost—*Arran.*
———ach, -aich, *s.m.* Grey-headed man.
———achd,** *s.f.* Mouldiness. 2 Fustiness.
liath-bhàine, *s.f.* Paleness.
——————, *comp.* of liath-bhàn.
liath-bhàn, -bhàine, *a.* Pale.
liath-bhrochan, *s.m.* Thick gruel made of milk and meal, well boiled with a piece of butter in it—*Gael. Soc. of Inverness,* xiv, 149.
liath-bhuidhe,** *a.* Tawny.
liathchearc, -chirce, -an, *s. f.* Heath-hen, female of the black grouse or black-cock, see coileach-dubh. Liath-chearcan fraoich, *heath-hens.* Considered a bird of ill-omen. Am faca tu l. an raoir? *did you see a heath-hen last night?* is said to a person who looks pale and

worried.
liath-chluasach, -aiche, *a*. Grey-eared.
liathdras,** -ais, *s.m*. Mustiness, mouldiness.
liath-fàil, see lia-fail.
liath-fheasgar, -air, *s.m*. Evening twilight. 2** Grey evening.
liathgad-mara,(AF) *s.m*. Limpet. (bàirneach)
†**liath-ghath**, -ghaith, -an, *s.m*. Destructive dart. 2**Violent dart.
liath-ghlas, -aise, *a*. Light grey. 2 Hoary. 3 **Bleak.
liath ghorm, -ghuirme, *a*. Cerulean, azure. 2 Columbine (colour.) 3*Lilac.
liath-ghuirme, *s.f.ind*. Light-blue colour.
——————, *comp*. of liath-ghorm.
——————achd, *s.f.ind*. Bluishness.
liath-luidneach,** -ich, *s.f*. Banner of Diarmaid O' Duibhne.
liath-lus,§ -luis, -an, *s.m*. Mugwort—*artemesia vulgaris*.
————ach, -aiche, *a*. Abounding in mugwort. 2**Like mugwort
liath-lus-roid,§ *s. m*. Common cotton rose—*filago germanica*.

426. Liath-lus-roid.

liath-mhùig, -e, *s.f*. Grey mist. L. nan tonn, *the grey mist of the waves*.
liathnach,* *s.m*. Hoar-frost.
liath-phurpur, *s.m*. Mauve.
liathra, see liaghra.
liathradh,** *s. m*. Mustiness. 2**Sliding, rolling. 3**Sprinkling.
liath-reòdh, see liath-reothadh.
liath-reòth, see liath-reothadh
——————adh, -aidh, *s.m* Hoar-frost.
†**liathroid**,** *s. f*. Ball. 2**Roller. 3**Knob. 4**Chaff.
liathruisg, see liath-truisg
liath-ruisgean,(DMy) *s.m*. Name given to the months March and April when fodder is scarce.
liath-sgrath, *s.m*. Moss.
liath-taois, see liathtas.
liathtas, -ais, *s. m*. Greyness. 2 Blue mould. L.-sneachd, *sprinkling of snow sufficient to make the land grey*.
————ach, -aiche, *a*. Mouldy.
liath-troisg, } see liath-truisg.
liath-trosg, }
liath-trasg, see liath-truisg.
liath-truisg, *s.m*. Fieldfare—*turdus pilaris*. see ill. 427.
liathtus, see liatrus.
liatrus, -uis, see liathtas.
liatus, -uis, *s.m*. Lettuce, see liatas.
libeag, *dim*. of *lip*. 2 see lèabag.
———ach, *a*. see lèabagach.
†**libh**, see leibh.
libheadan, -ain, *s.m*. Leviathan. 2**Dowry.
libhearn,** *s. m*. Dowry. †2 Ship, galley. †3

427. Liath-truisg.

Habitation. †4 Cattle. Freothal mara ri taobh libheirn, *the eddy of the sea round a ship*.
libhirt, *s*. Heritage.
libhrig, *past pt*. lirt, *v. a*. Deliver—*Dàin Iain Ghobha*. L. na bheil agad, *stand and deliver —your money or your life !*
libinn, see lipinn.
lic, *gen.sing*. of leac.
liceag,** -eig, *s.f*. Little slab.
licheach, see ligheach.
lid, see lide.
lide, -an, *s.m*. Syllable, articulation. 2 Word, least part of a word. 3 Jot, tittle, particle, bit. 4**Article. 5*Letter. Cha tuit l., *nothing shall fall*. [** gives *s.f*.]
lideach, -eiche, *a*. Lisping, stammering.
————as, -ais, *s.m*. Stammering, lisping.
lideadh, -idh, -idhean, *s.m*. see lide.
lidh, *v.a*. see lì.
lì-dhealbh, *v.a*. Paint, colour.
——————adh, -aidh, *s.m*. Painting, art or act of painting.
——————adair, -ean, *s.m*. Painter.
——————ta, *a. & past pt*. of lì-dhealbh. Painted.
lidhte, *past pt*. of lì. Coloured.
lidiche, *s.m*. see lideachas.
lìgeach, -eiche, *a*. Sly, cunning.
———as, -ais, *s.m*. Slyness, cunning.
†**ligh**, *v.a*. Lick, pass over with the tongue.
ligh, *s.m*. see lì.
lighe, *pl*. -achan & -an, *s.f*. Flood, fulness or overflowing of a stream. 2**That part of a river where the water stagnates.
ligheach,** -ich, *s.f*. Cow.
ligheach, -eiche, *a*. Flooded, inundated.
————an, *n.pl*. of lighe.
lighich, *v.a. & n*. Doctor, lance, let blood.
lighiche, -an, *s.m*. Physician, surgeon. Nach leighis aon l. ? *cannot any physician heal ?*
lìgiche, *s.m.ind*. see lìgeachas.
†**lileadh**,** -idh, *s.m*. Sucking, licking.
lili, -dhean, *s.f*. Lily.
lili bhàn,§ *s*. White water lily, see duilleag-bhàite-bhàn.
lili-bhuidhe-'n-uisge, *s.f*. Yellow water-lily, see duilleag-bhàite-bhuidhe.
lilidheach, *a*. Abounding in lilies. 2 Like a lily. 3**Flexible.
liligh, see lili.
lili-ghugacach,§ *s. f*. Bluebell, wild hyacinth, see fuath-mhuc.
lili-nan-gleann, see lili-nan-lòn.
lili-nan-lòn, *s.m*. Lily of the valley—*convallaria majalis*.
†**lilleach**,** *a*. Pliant, flexible.
lìn, *gen.sing*. of lìon.
lìn,** *s.f*. Thread. 2 Line. 3 Series. 4 Score.
†**lind**, *s*. Drink.
†**lind**, *s.m*. Disease.
lìneachadh, -aidh, *s. m*. Delineating, delinea-

tion.
linealtas, -ais, s.m. Spruceness.
linean,§ -ein, s.m. Sea-moss, see coireall.
linear,** a. Rectilinear.
†ling, v.n. Skip. 2 Dart. 3 Go away.
lingeadh,** -idh, s.m. Skipping. 2 Flying off. 3 Flinging. 4 Darting.
lìnginneach,** a. Somewhat round.
linich,** v.a. Line. 2 Delineate, draw.
lìnig, -ean, s.m. Lining, facing, act of lining clothes. 2 Sheathing, as a vessel. Dram mar l. cléibh, *a dram as a lining for the chest.* [** gives s.f.]
lìnig, pr. part. a' lìnig & a' lìnigeadh, v. a. Line, as clothes. 2 Sheathe as a vessel. 3** Ceil.
——eadh, -eidh, -eidhean, see lìnig.
lìnigir, see lìnig.
lìnig-taighe,** s. m. Ceiling. 2Wooden lining round the walls of a room.
lìnigte, *past pt.* of lìnig. Lined, supplied with lining.
linn, -ean, te & -tean, s. m. Age. 2 Century. 3 Generation. 4 Race, offspring, family. 5 Ministration, incumbency or time in office. 6 Long, long ago. Ri l. do sheanmhar, *during the life of your grandmother ;* anns na linntean deireannach, *in the latter days ;* ri l. Mhaighstir Alasdair, *during the incumbency of Mr. Alexander ;* ri m' l., *in my day, while I was there ;* ri d' l.-sa, *during your incumbency ;* cogadh o l. gu l., *war from generation to generation ;* ri d' là 's ri d' l., *during your day and generation ;* l. Dhiarmaid an tuirc, *the family of Dermid of the boar (the Campbells);* gu l. nan linntean, *for many generations to come ;* ri l. dhuit dol dhachaidh, *when you go home ;* iomlan 'na l., *perfect in his generation ;* " eadar dà linn," given by * should be " eadar dhà leann," see leann.
linn,(AC) s.f. Brood hen. 2 Brood of twelve—over 12 is " linn mhór," and under 12 " linn bheag."
linn,** a. Wet.
linne, pl. -achan, linnteachan, linntichean, linnichean & linntean, s.f. Pool, pond, lake, linn, gulf. 2* Mill-dam, channel. 3‡‡ Cataract, waterfall. 4‡‡Sea. 5** Abyss. 6** Strait, sound. 7 **Entrance to a gulf. 8 Pool in a river. 9 Part of the sea near the shore. 10 Bay. Linne-lìn, *a lint-dam ;* air l. shéimh, *on a calm sea;* a' dol thar na linne, *crossing the channel.*
†linne, see leinne.
linneach,(AF) s.m. Wild duck.
linneachan, pl. of linne. 2 (MS) After-ages.
linnean,‡ -ein, -an, s.m. Shoemaker's thread. 2 Thread. 3 Little line.
———ach,** a. Thready, having threads. 2 Like a thread or line. 3 Like a shoemaker's thread. 4 Abounding in lines.
linnearach, s. Fucus, see lianach.
linne-lus,** s.m. Pondweed—*potamogeton.*
linngeineach, -eiche, a. Gently moving, or heaving, as the sea in a calm.
linngineach,** a. Roundish.
linnich,* v.a. see lìnig.
———, s.f. see lìnig.
———,* s.f.ind. Line, note. 2 Card. 3 Layer. 4 Brood of eggs. L.-phòsaidh, *marriage-line;* cuir l. g' a ionnsuidh, *drop him a card ;* l. mu seach, *alternate layers.*
linnig, see lìnig.
—— -te, *past pt.* of linnig, (for lìnig.)
linnseach, -ich, s.f. Linen cloth. 2 One clothed in linen. 3* Shrouds, canvas. L. thrusaidh, *packing cloth of linen.*
linnseag, -eig, -an, s.f. Shroud. 2 Covering of coarse linen or canvas worn by delinquents when doing penance before a congregation. 3 (DMC) Film, thin coating.
linnsgearadh,** -aidh, s.m. Genealogy.
linnte, pl. of linn. Gu l. céin, *to distant ages.*
linnteachan, n.pl. of linne.
linntean, n.pl. of linne.
linntean, n.pl. of linn.
linteach,** a. Lineal.
linntichean, pl. of linn.
liob, -a, -an, s.f. Lip. 2‡‡Part of a bagpipe.
——ach, -aiche, a. Lipped. 2 Having large lips.
liobair, -ean, s.m. Person with thick or hanging lips. 2 Slovenly or awkward person. [** gives liobar as *nom.*, and -air as *gen.*]
liobard,(AF) s.m. Leopard. [** gives liobart.]
liobarnach, -aiche, n. Slovenly, awkward.
————, -aich, s.m. Slovenly or awkward person. 2††Sluggard.
liobasda, -aisde, a. Slovenly, untidy. 2 Awkward, clumsy.
————chd, s. f. Slovenliness, untidiness. 2 Awkwardness, clownishness.
————ir, s.m. Sloven. 2 Awkward person, lob.
lìobh, see lìomh.
——,(AC) s. Love, attachment.
——,* s.f. Slimy substance like blood on the surface of water.
lìobhach, see lìomhach.
liobhadair,** s.m. Burnisher.
lìobhadh, see lìomhadh.
liobhag,§ s.f. Broad-leaved pondweed, see duileasg-na-h-aibhne. 2 Dutch rushes, shave grass, see a' bhiorag.
liobhagach, see liobhragach.
liobhair, see liubhair.
————t, see liubhairt.
lìobhan, -ain, -an, see lìomhan.
liobhan, see leamhan.
lìobhanach, see lìomhanach.
liobhar, s.m. White of wood or timber.
lìobhar, a. Polished, burnished—*Sàr-Obair,* see lìomharra.
lìobharachd, see lìomharrachd.
lìobharra, see lìomharra.
liobhgach,(AF) s. Cow with calf.
liobhghruag,** -aig, s.f. Wig.
liobhradh, -aidh, s.m. & pr. pt. for liubhradh, see liubhairt.
liobhragach,* -aich, s.f. Kind of seaweed or sea-lichen of a greenish colour. 2** Weed growing in standing water.
liobhruig, see liubhair.
liobhta, see lìomhta.
lìobhta, see lìomhta.
liobrach,** a. Thick-lipped.
liocadan,** -ain, s.m. Chin-cloth.
liocard, see liobard.
liod,* s.m. see liot.
——ach,* -aiche, a. see liotach.
——ach, -aidh, s.m. see liotaiche.
liodag, see liotag.
liodaiche, see liotaiche.
liodair, see leadair.
liodairt, see leadairt.
liodan, -ain, s.m. Dittany, see leadan. 2 Teazle, see leadan.
liodan,(MS) s.m. Rogation.
liodan-an-fhùcadair, s. m. Fuller's teazle, see liadan-an-fhùcadair.
liodar,(DMC) s. m. Clumsy fellow. 2 Muddy place.
liogadh,** -aidh, s. m. Whetting, sharpening.
†liogar,** -air, s.m. Tongue.

liogh,** *s.f.* see liagh.
†liogha, *a.* Brave. 2 Strong.
liughach,** *a.* Strong. 2 Fair. 3 Fine.
.———,** *s.m.* Superiority.
lioghais,** *s.f.* Bravery. 2 Strength. 3 Ability.
lioghan,** -ain, *s.m.* Trowel.
†liughar, -air, *s.m.*
liom, see leam.
liomaid, *s.f.* Lemon, see liomain.
liomain, *s. m.* Lemon.
lioman, see liomain.
liomh, -a, *s.f.* Polish, gloss. 2 Colour, see lì.
liomh, *v.a.* Polish, smooth, furbish. 2 Lubricate. 3‡‡Sharpen, grind.
liomha, see liamhaidh.
liomhach,** *a.* Smoothing, polishing, filing, burnishing. 2 Smooth, polished, burnished.
liomhachadh, (MS) *s.m.* Affriction.
liomhachas, -ais, *s.m.* see liomharrachd.
liomhachd, *s.f.ind.* Polish.
liomhadair,** *s. m.* Burnisher, polisher. 2 Filer. 3 Whetter.
liomhadh, -aidh, *s. m.* Polishing, act of polishing, furbishing, burnishing, smoothing. 2 Whetting, act of sharpening. Clach liomhaidh, *a grindstone.*
liomhaich, (MS) *v.a.* Burnish.
liomhaidh, -e, *a.* Polished, furbished, burnished. 2 Glittering, bright. 3 Beautifully smooth and fair. 4 **Sharpened, whetted. 5 Ladylike. Clach l., *a grindstone.*
liomhain, see liomhaidh.
liomhan, -ain, -an, *s. m.* File. 2 Burnisher. Clach liomhain, *a grindstone.*
———ach, *a.* Like a file. 2 see liomharra.
———aiche,** *s.m.* File-maker.
liomharra, *a.* Glossy, polished, bright. 2 Filed.
liomharrachd, *s.f.ind.* Brightness. 2 State of being polished, smoothed, sharpened or filed. 3 4 Polish, smoothness, sharpness.
liomhraidh, *s.m.* & *pr.pt.* see lionrath.
liomhta, *past pt.* of liomh. Polished. 2 Sharpened, whetted.
lion, -in, *pl.* liontan, [lìn—DMy] *s.m.* Lint, flax —*linum usitatissimum.* 2 Linen. 3 Net, fishing net. 4‡‡ Gin, snare. 5 Line, limit, boundary. 6 Proportionate quantity or complement. 7**Number, quantity. 8**Lining. 9** Parcel. 10 Fishing-line.
Là buan an lìn, *N-vernas* : linne lìn, *a lint dam* ; a' bualadh an lìn, *beetling the flax* ; l. làn éisg, *a net-ful of fish* ; biadh le a l. de anlainn, *food with its complement of condiment* ; a l. de 'n Fhéinn 's a bh' ann, *as many of the Féinn as were present* ; a l. fear is fear, *one by one*; a l. dithis is dithis, *two by two* ; a l. triùir is triùir, *three by three* ; a l. beagan is beagan, mar a dh' ith an cat an sgadan, *little by little, as the cat ate the herring*; lìn mhóra, *long (fishing) lines*; lìn bheaga, *short (fishing) lines.* l. an damhain-alluidh, *a cobweb* ; l. sgadanaich, *a herring-net* : l. fuilt, *a hair-net.*
l.-eisirean, *a dredge.*
l.-iadhaidh, *sweep-net, drag-net.*
l.-iasgaich, *a fishing-net.*
l.-obair, *network.*
lìon, *pr.pt.* a' lionadh, *v.a.* & *n.* Fill, replenish, satiate. 2 Become full. 3 Flow, as tide. 4 *Completely please or satisfy. L. an soitheach, *fill the vessel* ; cha'n 'eil seo 'gam lìonadh, *this does not entirely please me* ; tha e 'lìonadh, *it (the tide) is flowing.*
lìon, (cia lìon ? *adv.* How many ?)
lionach, *a.* Abounding in lint, flax, nets, &c.
lionachan, -ain, -an, *s.m.* Filler, funnel.
lionad,** -aid, *s.m.* Plenitude, fulness, repletion.
lionadair, -ean, *s.m.* Filler, funnel. 2 Syphon.
lìonadh, *past pass.* of lìon. Was or were filled.
lìonadh, -aidh, *s. m.* Filling, act of filling, replenishing. 2 State of being filled, approaching to fulness. 3 Fulness. 4 Rising, as the tide. L. na mara, *the flowing of the tide.*
——— -deiridh, *s.m.* Deadwood in stern of a boat, see O3, p. 73.
——— -toisich, *s. m.* Deadwood in bow of a boat, see N4, p. 73.
lìonan, (MS) *s.m.* Reticle. 2 Toil. 3(DU)Lady's hair-net.
——ach, *s. m.* Plumosa, a bright green alga in pools left on rocks by receding tide. 2 Seaweed of different sizes and different colours, kind of water fungus that grows on other seaweed, wood, &c., that has been long floating in the sea. Tha lìonanach mu d' cheann a' fàs, in *S.-nan-caol, p. viii.* refers to a board cast ashore among wreckage. The fact of the *lionanach* growing on it showed that it had been long afloat since first torn away from the ship of which it once formed a part—*J. MacFadyen.* 3 Green weed that grows on the boulders in a stream. 4 (MMcD) The scum that accumulates on stagnant water.
lìonanach, -aiche, *a.* Reticular, membraneous.
lion-anart, -airt, -an, *s.m.* Sheet (for a bed.)
lìon-aodach,** -aich, *s.m.* Sheet. 2 Linen. 3 (DMy) Shroud.
lionar, *fut. pass.* of lìon. Shall be filled. 2 *a.* see lìonmhor.
——achd, see lionmhorachd.
lionaraich, (MS) *v.a.* see lionmhoirich.
lionaraich, (MS) *s.* Sea-fennel, samphire.
lìon-bhrat,** -ait, *s. m.* Sheet. 2 Winding-sheet. Air 'fhilleadh 'san l., *wrapped in the winding-sheet.*
lioncaise,** *s.* Spaniel. 2 Tether. 3 Line fastened from the head to the fore foot, or from the fore to the hind foot of a beast.
lionchar,** *a.* Pleasing, delightful.
lìon-cinn, *s.m.* Hair-net.
lìon-eudach, see lìon-aodach.
lìon-ghlac, *v.a.* Ensnare.
lionmhoire, *comp.* of lionmhor. More or most plentiful.
———-—achd, see lionmhorachd.
lionmhor, -oire, *a.* Numerous, plentiful, copious, abounding. 2 Populous. Cainnt l., *copious language* ; l. an lón is dearg, *abounding in elks and red-deer.*
———achadh, -aidh, *s.m.* Multiplication, act of multiplying, making or becoming numerous or abundant. A' l—, *pr.pt.* of lionmhoraich.
lionmhorachd, *s. f. ind.* Multiplicity, plenty, abundance. 2 Multitude. L. dheth, *abundance of it.*
lionmhoraich, *v. a.* & *n.* Multiply, increase, cause to increase in number, become numerous.
——————te, *past pt.* Multiplied, increased in number.
lionn, see leann.
lionnach, see leannach.
lionnachadh, see leannachadh.
lionnadh, *Barra* for leannachadh.
lìon-na-h-aibhne,§ *s. m.* River-flax, pilewort, crowfoot, see fleann-uisge.
lionnaich, see leannaich.
lìon-nam-ban-sìth,§ *s.m.* Fairy flax—*linum catharticum,* see illust. 428.
lìon-na-mna-sìth, see lìon-nam-ban-sìth.
lionnan-locraidh, -ain-locraidh, see leannan-locraidh.
lionn-dubh, -uibhe, see leann-dubh.

428. Lìon-nam-ban-sìth.

lìonn-dubhach, see leann-dubhach.
lìonn-luibh, see leann-luibh.
——-——each, see leann-luibheach.
lìonn-ruadh, see leann-ruadh.
lìonn-ruadhaidh, see leann-ruadhaidh.
lìonnsag,** *s.f.* Shroud.
lìonnsgail,(MS) *v.n.* Lay.
lìonn-tàtha, see leann-tàthaidh.
lìon-obair, -oibre, *s.f.* Net-work. 2**Chequer-work.
lìon-oibriche, -an, *s.m.* Net-worker.
lìonor, see lìonmhor.
lìonradh, -aidh, -aidhean, *s.m.* Gravy, juice. 2 Sauce. 3 Thin, unsubstantial drink. 4 Insipid drink. †5 Web. 6††Washy fluid. 7** Aleberry. 8* for lìomhradh. Clach lìonraidh, *a grindstone.*
lìonraith, *a.* Sharpened by grinding.
lìonrath, *pr.pt.* a' lìonrath, *v.a.* Grind, sharpen by grinding.
lìonrath, -aith, *s.m.* Sharpening, act of sharpening by grinding. A' l—, *pr.pt.* of lìonrath. Clach lìonraith, *a grindstone.*
lìon-sgrìobaidh, *s.m.* Drag-net.
lìonta, *a. & past pt.* of lìon. Filled, full. 2 Fat, plump. 3 Abundant.
lìonta, *n.pl.* of lìon.
lìonta, see lìonte.
lìontach, -aiche, *a.* Filling, replenishing, satiating. 2 Full. Sùil l., *a full eye*; tìr chruach ach, sguabach, lìontach, *a land with plenty of stacks and sheaves—Filidh. 22.*
lìontachadh, -aidh, *s.m.* Filling, act of filling, replenishing. A' l—, *pr.pt.* of lìontaich.
lìontachail, -e, *a.* Fat, plump, sleek.
lìontachd, *s.f.ind.* Fulness, repletion, state of being full, satiety.
lìontaibh, *dat.pl.* of lìon.
lìontaich, *v.a.* Fill, replenish.
lìontaichte, *past pt.* of lìontaich. Filled, replenished.
lìontaidh, -e, *a.* Full, satiated, replenished. 2 2 Plump. 3 Meshy, full of meshes.
lìontaidheachd, *s.f.* Fulness, plumpness.
lìontan, *pl.* of lìon.
lìonte, *past pt.* of lìon.
lìon-uinneag, *s.f.* Lattice.
liop, -a, -an, see liob.
liopach, see liobach.
liopaire,†† *s.m.* Person with thick lips.
liopard, -aird, *s.m.* Leopard.
lioragaich, *Argyll* for lìonanach.
liorc, *s.* Shrivel, wrinkle.
liorc, *v.a. & n.* Pucker, shrivel, wrinkle.
liorcach, -aiche, *a.* Wrinkled.
liorcaich, *v.a. & n.* see liorc.
lios, lise, & -a, *pl.* -an, *s.f.* Garden. 2 Fuller's or printer's press. 3 Mangle. 4**Longing in pregnancy. †5 Dispute, debate, strife. †6 House, habitation. †7 Palace. †8 Fortified place. 9 Enclosure or stall for cattle. 10**Court. L. luibhean, *a garden for herbs*; l. àraich, *a nursery;* l. rìoghail, *a royal court* ; l. ìosal, *a low court* ; l.-olaidh, *an olive garden.* [** gives *s. m.* for Nos. 4, 5 & 9, and *f.* for the others WC gives *s.m.*]
liosach,†† *a.* Having gardens.
liosadair, -ean, *s.m.* Gardener. 2 Printer, pressman.
——-——eachd, *s.f.ind.* Gardening, act of gardening. 2 Printing.
liosadan, -ain, *s.m.* Little garden.
liosair, -ean, *s.m.* see liosadair. 2**Garden.
liosair,* *v.a.* Press, as cloth. 2 Print. 3 Mangle. 4 Drub most heartily.
liosairte, *past pt.* of liosair. Smoothed. 2 Printed. 3 Pressed.
lios-àraich,‡‡ *s.f.* Nursery (for plants.)
liosda, -isde, *a.* Slow, lingering, tedious. 2 Importunate. 3 Stiff. Gu l., gu luath, *now slow, now quick.*
liosdachd, *s. f. ind.* Slowness, tediousness. 2 Importunity. 3 Instance. 4**Stiffness. 5* Greed.
liosdair, -ean, *s.m.* Wrangler. 2 Barrister. 3 Pettifogger.
——-——eachd,** *s.f.* Wrangling. 2 Pettifogging.
lios-mheas, -an, *s.f.* Orchard.
lìosradh, see lìosraigeadh.
lìosraig, *v.a.* Smooth, dress or iron, as linen.
lìosraigeadh, -idh, *s.m.* Smoothing or ironing, as linen. A' l—, *pr.pt.* of lìosraig.
lìosraigte, *past pt.* of lìosraig. Smoothed, dressed, ironed.
liosta, see liosda.
liostair, see liosdair.
liot, *s.m.ind.* Stammer, lisp.
liotach, -eiche, *a.* Lisping, stammering.
liotachd, *s.f.ind.* Lisping, stammering, impediment of speech.
liotag,** -aig, *s.f.* Girl that lisps.
liotaiche, *s.m.* Stammerer, lisper. 2* Impediment of speech.
liotaiche, *comp.* of liotach.
liotan,** -ain, *s.m.* Litany.
†lìothadh, -aidh, *s.m.* Frightening, dismaying, dismay.
lìothra,** *s.m.* Hair.
lip, *s.f.* -e, -ean, see liob.
lipinn, -e, -ean, *s. f.* Quarter peck (measure of grain) "lippy." [also lipinn.] Still used in *Uist* for measuring whelks, &c—DC.
†lìr, *s.* Jaundice.
lìr, *s.* Litter, as of pigs, whelps, &c.
lìreagach,†† -aich, *s. f.* Green weed growing in stagnant water.
lìrean, -ein, *s.m.* Species of marine fungus—*N. Highds.* 2(DU) Applied to greenish fresh-water growth.
lìreanach, *Suth'd.* for lìonanach.
lìreanach, -aiche, *a.* Abounding in marine fungus.
lirt, *past pt.* of libhrig. Delivered—*Dàin Iain Ghobha.*
lis,** *s.f.* †Mischief, evil. 2 (DMy) The dark crust on the top of heads of young babies till it is removed by frequent applications of butter.
lisg,** *s.pl.* Feelers of a fly.
+lit, *s,* Activity. 2 Celerity.
lite, [*gen.sing.* litinn now in *Skye*, formerly also in *Badenoch.—Gael. Soc. Inv.* xxiii, 84.] *s.f.* Porridge, pottage. 2**Posset.

liteach, -eiche, *a.* Abounding in porridge. 2 Like porridge.
'lith,(CR) *s.f.* Grease for smearing—*Skye.* Tha 'n fheòil anns a' phoit gun an lith thairis, *the flesh is in the pot and the water not covering it (the flesh) completely*—from one of Campbell's Tales, in which, because the water in the pot did not cover the fish completely, a blister arose on the fish. Fingal, then a boy, put his wet finger on the blister with the well-known result that he ever after, upon sucking this finger, obtained any information he wished.
lith, -e, -ean, *s.f.* see li. 2**Pool, stagnant water. 3(MS) Greasiness. 4 (WC) Fat on top of soup or broth.
lithe, *s.f.* see lighe.
litheach, -eiche, *a.* Coloured. 2 Speckled. 3 Slimy, greasy.
litheadh, -idh, -idhean, see lighe.
litheadh,(AC) *s.* Bathing. Bi 'gad l., *be bathing thee.* [AC gives lithiu.]
lithear, -eir, *s.m.* Dyer.
litheas,** -eis, *s.m.* Solemnity, pomp.
litir, litreach, -trichean, *s.f.* Letter of the alphabet. 2 Letter, epistle. 3 The literal or expressed meaning. 4‡‡ Learning, education.
litir-chòmhraig,** *s.f.* Challenge.
litir-dhealachaidh, *s.f.* Bill of divorce.
litir-fhoghlum, -uim, *s.m.* Literary knowledge, erudition, lore.
litir-ghaoil, *s.f.* Love-letter.
litir-ghrinnich,** *s.f.* Challenge.
litir-leannanachd,** *s.f.* Love-letter.
litir-naidheachd, *s.f.* Newspaper, news-letter.
litreach,†† *a.* Lettered.
litreach, *gen.sing.* of litir.
litreachadh, -aidh, *s.m.* Orthography.
litrich, *v.a.* & *n.* Letter, print. 2 (MM)Spell.
litrichean, *n.pl.* of litir.
liùbh, *s.m.* Lythe, pollack, see liùgh.
liubhag, -aig, *s.f.* Moppet.
liubhair, *pr.pt.* a' liubhairt & a' liubhradh, *v. a.* Deliver, give up, surrender, resign. 2 Abandon. 3 Rescue. [‡ gives liubhar, ‡‡ liùbhar.]
liubhairt, *s. m.* Delivery, act of delivering, resignation, addiction, surrender, assignment. 2 Abandonment. 3 Rescue. A' l—, *pr. pt.* of liubhair.
liubhairte, *past pt.* Delivered, addicted, &c.
liubh-bhiast,(AF) see luibh-bhiast.
liùbhrach,** *a.* Flaggy.
liubhradh, -aidh, *s.m.* & *pr.pt.* see liubhairt.
liuc, *s.* Shout, noise.
liuch-bhlian, *North Gairloch* for dubh-chléin.
liudan, ** -ain, *s.m.* Lever crow. 2 Gaveloc.
liudanach,** *a.* Like a lever.
liùdh, see liùgh.
liùdhag, -aige, -an, *s.f.* Doll. 2 see liùgh.
liùg, -iùige, *s.f.* Lame hand or foot. 2 Bandy-leg. 3 Sneaking gait. 4‡‡Sneaking look. 5 **Creeping. 6††Twist in a shoe. [** gives *s.m.* and *gen.* liùig.]
liùg, *pr.pt.* a' liùgadh, *v.a.* & *n.* Creep, steal away. 2 Bend, bow. 3 Sneak.
liùgach, -aiche, *a.* Sneaking, abject. 2 Having a maimed limb. 3 Bandy-legged. 4 Crooked, as the law. 5 Of a mean personal appearance. 6**Shabby, sorry. 7**Creeping.
liùgach,** -aiche, *s.m. gen.* -aich, Sorry fellow.
———,* *s.f.* Unhandy woman. 2 Drab.
liùgachd, *s.f.* Deformity of bandy legs.
liùgadh, -aidh, *s.m.* Creeping, act of creeping, stealing away. 2 Bending, bowing. 3 Sneaking. A' l—, *pr.pt.* of liùg.
liùgag, *s.f.* Unhandy woman. 2 Drab. [given by * as liùgach.]
liugair,(AF) *s.m.* Newt (lurker.)
liùgair, -ean, *s. m.* Sneaking, abject fellow. 2 Helpless, lame fellow. 3 Cajoler. 4 Flatterer, parasite. 5*Unhandy fellow. 6*One with a lame hand.
liùgaireachd, *s.f.* Sneaking, abject habit. 2** Cajolery.
liùgh,†† -a, -achan, *s.f.* Lythe (fish.)
†liugh, *s.f.* Cry, shout.
liugha, see liuthad.
liughad, -aid, see liuthad.
liùghag,(DMC) *s.f.* Small lythe.
liughag,(MS) *s.f.* Poupeton.
liùil,(AC) *s.* Bath, bathing, washing, lustrating, purification.
lium, see leam.
liumh,** *s.m.* Cry.
†liun, *s.f.* Sloth, laziness, idleness.
†liun, *a.* Slothful, lazy.
†liunachas, -ais, *s.m.* Idleness, sloth, laziness.
liu nan lasa,(AC) *s.* Water of the flame, lustral fire.
Liùnasd, *s.f.* Lammas. 2 Month of August.
Liùnasdail, see Liùnasd.
Liùnastainn, see Liùnasd.
liunchlos,** *s.m.* Rest.
liunn, see leann.
liunn-dubh, see leann-dubh.
liunn-tàth, *v.* see leann-tàthaidh.
liunntras, -ais, see leanntras.
†liur, *s.m.* Noise, clamour, prating.
†liurach, *a.* Noisy, clamorous, prating.
liurc, *v.* & *s.* see liorc.
liurcach, see liorcach.
liurcaich, see liorcaich.
liùsb,(AH) *s.f.* Woman's tattered skirt. 2 Anything hanging in a loose and slovenly manner. 3 Sluttish, untidy woman.
liùsbach, *a.* Clumsy, untidy.
liùsbaid,(DMC) *s.f.* Untidy female.
liuth, see liùgh.
liuth, see liuthad.
liutha, see liuthad.
liuthad, *a.* & *adv.* Several, many. 2 So many. 3* Frequent.
Cia l. uair 'sa thàinig e? *how often did he come?* cia l. uair 'sa dh' innis mi sin dhuit? *how many times have I told you that?* liuthad laoch 's a thàinig, *when so many braves came.* Frequently used with the poss. pron. masc., as, is math a dh' fhimireadh an dàn a dheanadh, 's a liuthad fear-millidh a th' aige, *the poem would need to be well made, since it has so many spoilers*—bad reciters and carping critics—N.G.P.
liùthag, see liùbh & liùgh.
liuthail, see liuil.
liuthair, see liubhair.
liuthairte, see liubhairte.
liutharadh, -aidh, see liubhradh.
lò, *s.m.ind.* Poetical form of là.
†lo, *s.m.* Lock of wool. 2 Water.
lob, -oib, *s.m.* Puddle.
lobach,(AF) *s.m.* Lobworm.
lobair,* *pr. pt.* a' lobairt, *v.a.* Draggle in the mud, roll in the mire. 2 Paddle.
lobairt, *s.f.* Draggling. 2 Paddling. A' l—, *pr. pt.* of lobair.
lobais,** *s.f.* Craft, ingenuity.
lòban, -ain, -an, *s.m.* Creel for drying corn. 2 Wooden frame put inside corn-stacks to keep them dry. 3††Hurdle. 4 Kind of basket same shape as the rusgan (see illust. there) but of different size. 5 When peats are to be carted, the ordinary sides and ends of the cart in many districts are laid aside, and lighter ones (lòban) of spars or rods provided for the purpose. These had been evidently preceded

by sides and ends of wicker or wattle-work—CR. There was an ancient form of cart, called "cart-loban," which gave origin to the name Loban, see MacKenzie's Guide to Inverness, 1903.—DMK. [Also loban.]
loban, see lòban.
lòbanach, -aiche, *a.* Draggling, wallowing, dragged, wallowed.
lòbanachd, *s.f.* Draggling, frequent or continued wallowing. 2 Drenching. 3† Diverging, straggling, spreading.
lòbanadh, *s.m.* see lòbanachd.
lòbanaich, *s.f.* see lòbanachd.
lobanaich, *pr. pt.* a' lobanaich & a' lobanachd, *v.a.* Bedrench. 2 see làbanaich.
lobanaichte, *past pt.* Bedrenched.
lobar,(DC) *s.f.* Puddle, mud—*Argyll.*
lobarcan, -ain, *s.m.* Person drenched with wet, or daubed with mire. 2 Dwarf, diminutive person.
lobh, *pr.pt.* a' lobhadh, *v.a.* & *n.* Rot, putrefy. 2 Become or make putrid. 3**Stink.
lobh, *a.* see lobhach.
lobhach,** *a.* Rotten, stinking, fœtid.
lobhachas, -ais, *s.m.* Putridness.
lobhachd,** *s.f.* Rottenness, fœtidness.
lobhadas,** -ais, *s.m.* Rottenness, fœtidness.
lobhadh, -aidh, *s.m.* Rotting, putrefying. 2 Act or state of putrefying or becoming putrid, putrefaction. 3 Stinking. 4 Rottenness, fœtidness. 5 Disease of potatoes. A' l—, *pr.pt.* of lobh.
lobhaidh, *fut.aff.a.* of lobh. L. an abhainn, *the river shall stink.*
lobhair, *gen.sing.* & *n.pl.* of lobhar.
lobhaircean,** -ein, *s.m.* Dwarf.
lobhar, -air, *s.m.* Leper. 2 Disgusting wretch. 3 Term of much personal contempt. †4Work. †5 Day's work.
lobharach, -aiche, *a.* Leprous.
lobharachd, *s. f.* Rottenness. 2 Leprosy, see luibhre.
lobharan,(MS) -ain, *s.m.* Leper.
lobhar-leigheas, -is, *s.m.* Antiseptic.
lobhgach, (AF) -aich, *s.* Cow with calf.
lobhrach, see lobharach.
———d, see luibhre.
lòbhradh,** -aidh, *s.m.* Leprosy, state of becoming leprous.
lobhragan, see lobarcan.
lòbhran, *s.m.dim.* of lobhar.
lobht, -a, -achan, [lobhtaichean in *Gairloch*,] *s.m.* Loft, floor, gallery. 2 Highest floor. 3 Storey of a house or building. 4 Foot-board of a spinning-wheel, 5(CR)Any floor of wood, upstairs or down—*W. of Ross & Uist.* 6(DU) Deck of a boat. Le lobhtaibh iochdarach, *with lower stories* ; lobhta làir, *a ground floor.*
lobhta, *a.* & *past pt.* of lobh. Rotten, corrupt, putrid, putrifying. Creuchd l., *a putrefying sore.*
lobhtach, -aiche, *a.* Having many lofts, galleries or stories.
lobhtachd, *s.f.* Corruptness.
lobrachan, -ain, *s.m.* Draggletail.
lobrogan,* -ain, *s.m.* Drenched, smeared fellow.
†loc, *v.a.* Refuse. 2 Hinder.
†loc, *s.m.* Place.
locadh,** -aidh, *s.m.* Refusal. 2 Hinderance.
locair, *pr. pt.* a' locradh, *v. a.* Plane, smooth with a plane. 2 Polish.
locaireachd,‡‡ *s.f.* Art of planing.
locar, -air, *pl.* -an & locraichean, *s. m.* Carpenter's plane. [* and ‡ give locair, as *nom.* & *s.f.*]
-——ach, see locrach.
-——adh, see locradh.
locar-chraois, -craichean-c-, *s.m.* Razor.
locar-dlùthaidh, *s. m.* Plough-plane, rebate-plane.
locar-dùirn, *s.m.* Hand-plane.
locar-grobaidh, *s.m.* Plough-plane, rebate-plane.
locar-sgathaich, *s.pl.* Shavings, spills of wood.
locar-sguitsidh, *s.m.* Jack-plane.
loch, *gen.* -a, [luich, very seldom used.] *pl.* -an & -annan, *s.m.* [generally *fem.* in *Caithness, Suth'd* and most parts of *Ross* -DMu] Arm of the sea. 2 Lake. A fresh-water lake is "loch uisge." Miann lach—an l. air nach bi, *a duck's desire—the lake where she is not.*
†loch,* *a.* Dark, black. 2 Every, all.
lochach, -aiche, *a.* Of, or belonging to lakes. 2 Abounding in lakes.
lochadh,** -aidh, *s.m.* Fleece.
lochain,** *s.* Sea-grass, seaweed, sea-wrack.
lochair,** *s.* Chaff.
lochal,§ -ail, *s. m.* Brooklime—*veronica beccabunga.*

429. Lochal.

lochan, -ain, -an, *s.m.dim.* of loch. Little lake, pool or pond. †2 Chaff.
lochan, *n. pl.* of loch.
lochanach, -aiche, *a.* Abounding in little lakes or pools.
lochan-monaidh, (AH) *s.m.* Mountain-tarn.
lochan-nan-damh,§ see lachan-nan-damh.
lochan-tàimh,(CR) *s. m.* Loch having no outflow.
loch-àrmunn, -uinn, see luch-àrmunn.
lochasair,** *s.m.* Shower of rain.
loch-bhléin, *s. f.* The flank, region under the short ribs. (dubh-chléin)
loch-bhléineach, *a.* Inguinal, pertaining to a groin.
lochd, -a, -an, *s.m.* Evil, mischief. 2 Fault, crime, sin. 3 Want, defect. 4 Closing of the eyes in sleep. 5 Moment's sleep, nap, wink.
lochdach, -aiche, *a.* Faulty, having flaws. 2 Criminal. 3 Mischievous, hurtful. 4 Defective. 5 Blamable. 6 Obnoxious.
lochdachadh, -aidh, *s.m.* Injuring, act of injuring. 2 Censuring or blaming. 3(MS) Annoyance. A' l—, *pr.pt.* of lochdaich.
lochdachas,(MS) *s.m.* Reprehensibleness.
lochdachd, *s.f.* Mischievousness.
lochdaich, *pr.pt.* a' lochdachadh, *v. a.* Injure, impair. 2 Blame, censure.
lochdaichte, *past pt.* of lochdaich. Injured. 2 Blamed, censured.
lochdalachd, *s.f.ind.* Prejudicialness. 2 Blamableness.
lochdan, -ain, *s. m.* Little sleep, nap, wink of sleep.
lòchdan,(DC) *s.m.* Laver, kind of alga, either the green or purple—*Uist.* [Also slòchdan.]
lochdmhor, *a.* Malefic.
lochdninn,** *s.* Beggarliness.
lochlannach,* -aich, *s.f.* Widgeon.
loch-'léin, see loch-bhléin.

loch-mhaoim, *s.m.* see loch-thaomadh.
lòchradh,(CR) *pr. pt.* Soaking. Bha sinn a' l. le fallus, *we were soaking with perspiration—Skye.*
lochraidh,(AF) *s.* Cattle.
lòchran, -ain, *s.m.* Light. 2 Lamp, torch, lantern.
lòchranach, -aiche, *a.* Having lamps or torches. 2**Like a lamp or torch. 3** Lighted with lamps.
†**lò-chrann**, *s.m.* The sun.
loch-thaomadh, -aidh, -aidhean, *s. m.* Sudden bursting of water. 2 Bursting of water from a mountain.
loch-thaomaidhean, see loch-thaomadh.
loch-uisge, *s.m.* Fresh-water lake.
locrach, -aiche, *a.* Furnished with planes. 2 Of, or connected with planes. 3 Like a plane.
locradh, -aidh, *s.m.* Planing, act of planing. A' l—, *pr.pt.* of locair. Crann caol air dheagh l., *a slender pole well planed.*
locraich, *v.* see locair.
locusd,(AF) *s.m.* Locust.
lod, -uid, -an, *s.m.* Puddle, pool, marsh.
lòd, -òid, -an, *s.m.* Cavalcade. 2 Bulk. 3 see làd. 4* Broadside. Leig iad l., *they fired a volley*; l. shluaigh, *a cavalcade of people*; l.-luach, *freightage.*
lodach, -aiche, *a.* Abounding in pools or puddles.
lòdach, *a.* Collective. Cunntas l., *collective numerals.*
lodachadh, -aidh, *s.m.* Stagnating, state of becoming stagnant, marshy or boggy. A' l—, *pr.pt.* of lodaich.
lòdachadh, -aidh, *s.m.* Loading, freighting, act of loading. A' l—, *pr.pt.* of lòdaich.
lodaich, *pr.pt.* a' lodachadh, *v.a.* Stagnate, become marshy or boggy.
lòdaich, *pr. pt.* a' lòdachadh, *v.a. & n.* Lade, burden. 2 Become bulky or clumsy. 3 Clog.
lòdaichte, *past pt.* of lòdaich. Eiridneach l., *a patient burdener*—i.e. under the torment of his disease—*Dàin I. Ghobha.*
lòdail, -e, [& lòdala,††] *a.* Heavy, laden. 2 Bulky, clumsy, cumbersome. 3 Wealthy. 4 Proud, haughty.
lodain,** *s.* The privy parts. 2 Flank.
lodair,(DMC) *s.m.* Lad.
lòdalachd, *s.f.* Weightiness. 2 Bulkiness, unwieldiness. 3 Wealth. 4 Pride, haughtiness.
lodan, -ain, -an, *s. m. dim.* of lod. Little pool. 2 Water in one's shoe. 3 Bog, little marsh. 'S fhéarr sùgh 'mhogain na sùgh lodain—a common proverb, meaning that a leaky boot is better than none at all.
lodanach, -aiche, *a.* Abounding in little pools.
lodhainn, -e, -ean, *s.f.* Number, as a pack of dogs, " leash," see lomhainn.
lodhainn-chraos,(WC) *s.f.* Little insect found in ponds and pools.
lòdrach, -aich, *s.m.* Company, crowd, many.
lòdrach, *s.f.* Baggage, luggage.
lodragan, -ain, *s. m.* Plump, robust boy. 2 Clumsy, little old man.
lodraganach, -aiche, *a.* Bluff, clumsy.
lòdraich, see lòdrach, *s.f.*
lodraigeadh, *s.m.* Sousing.
log, see lag.
†**log**, -oig, *s.m.* Pit or ditch of water. 2 Dungeon. 3 Place.
logaiche,** *s.m.* Fool.
logaidh,(CR) *s. m.* Long hair on forehead of cattle. 2 Mane of a horse.—*Skye.*
logairt,** *s.f.* Bad treatment, abuse. 2 Wallowing.
logais, -ean, *s.m.* Awkward, unwieldy person. 2*Slipper, patched shoe, " bauchle "—*Argyll.* 3††Anything unwieldy. 4 (DC) Greedy boy. 5 (AH) Inordinate supply of liquid, sloppy food. Tog do l. ! *hurry up !*
logaiseach, -eiche, *a.* Shambling, walking awkwardly. 2††Wide, unwieldy. 3 (AH)Swashy, sloppy, applied to food.
logaist, see logais.
logaisteach, see logaiseach.
logan, see lagan. 2**Hollow of the hand. 3** Country. 4**Peace.
logar,(CR) *s. m.* Kind of reed. 2 (DMy) Motion of the waves after the storm is over.
logh, *pr.pt.* a' loghadh, *v.a.* Pardon, remit, forgive.
logh,** *s.* Renown. †2 see lagh.
loghadair,(MS) *s.m.* Pardoner.
loghadh, -aidh, *s.m.* Forgiving, act of forgiving or pardoning. 2 Forgiveness, pardon. 3††Indulgence.
loghaich, *v.* see logh.
loghaileachd, *s.f.* Foolishness, foolery.
loghan,** -ain, *s.m.* Indulgence, remission. 2 Jubilee.
loghmhoireachd, *s. f.* Excellence, celebrity, famousness. 2 Grandeur, splendour.
loghmhor, -oire, *a.* Excellent, famous. 2 Stately, majestic. 3 Bright, valuable.
log-thir,(AC) *s. f.* Lake-land.
loguid, -ean, *s.m. & f.* Varlet, rascal. 2 Soft, effeminate fellow. 3 Lean, starving cow. 4 Ghost. Gus an cuireadh mac-talla na h-oidhche maoim fo na loguidean, *till the nightly echo would frighten the timid fellows away—Gàidheal*, v, 50.
loguideach, -eiche, *a.* Rascally. 2 Effeminate. 3 Cowardly. 4 Abounding in starved cows. 5 Like a starved cow. 6††Ghostly.
loguideachd, *s.f.* Cowardly habit or disposition.
loibean, -ein, -an, *s.m.* Puddler, one who works in puddly earth. 2 One who works constantly in all kinds of weather. 3 One who works in marshes.
loibeanachd, *s.f.* Puddling. 2 Habit of working continually regardless of weather.
loibheach, -eiche, *a.* Fœtid, somewhat rotten. 2 Term of contempt. Tòchd l., *a fœtid smell.*
loibheachas, -ais, *s.m.* Fœtidness, degree of rottenness or putridness.
loic, *Lewis* for lochd 5.
loicealach, -aiche, see loiceil.
loicealachd, *s.f.* Foolish fondness. 2**Dotage.
loiceil, -e, *a.* Foolishly fond, doting.
†**lòich**, *s.f.* Slattern, trull. 2 Place.
loiche, see loichead.
loichead,** -eid, -an, *s.m.* Lamp, light, torch. 2 Lightning. 3 Splendour.
loicheadair,** *s.m.* Chandler.
loigear, -eir, -an, *s.m.* Untidy or ragged person. 2 Loiterer.
loigearach,** *a.* Awkward.
loigearachd, *s.f.* Untidiness of dress, raggedness. 2 Awkwardness. 3 Loitering.
loigeireachd, see loigearachd.
loilgeach, see lulgach.
loiliseag,(AF) *s.f.* Reed or sedge warbler.
loime, *comp.* of lom, for luime.
loime,** see luime.
loimic,** *s.f.* Plaster for taking off hair.
lòin, *gen.sing.* of lon.
†**lòin**, *s.f.* Little stream, rivulet.
loin,(AF) *s.m.* Swan.
lòine, -an, *s.f.* Lock or tuft of wool, flock. 2 Flake of snow. 3 (DMC) Fine flowing hair.
lòine, see lòinidh.
lòineag, *s.f. dim.* of lòine. Little tuft of wool. 2*Fleece of very fine wool. 3**Lock of wool, or any such substance. 4 (DU) Snowflake. 5

(DMy) Nap on the "right" or out-side of cloth. L. bhrèagh air taobh caoin an aodaich, *a nice nap on the right side of the cloth.*
lòineagach, -aiche, *a.* Abounding in tufts of wool, or in 2 Flakes of snow.
lòinean, -ein, -an, see lonan. 2(DMK) The fat covering of the kidneys of beef or mutton—*Caithness.*
lòinean, -in, -an, *s.m.* see lonan. 2 (CR) Easy, careless, fat, untidy fellow—*Arran.*
lòineanach,** *a.* Abounding in little meadows.
loinear,** -eir, *s.m.* see loinnear.
loinearach, see loinnreach.
loinearachd, see loinnearachd.
loineid, see loinid.
loineis, see loinneas.
loingbhriseach,** *a.* Causing shipwreck.
loingbhriseadh, *s.m.* Shipwreck.
loingeach, -eiche, *a.* Nautical.
loingear, -ir, *s.m.* Marine, sailor, pilot.
loingeas, -is, *s. m.* [*f.* in *Badenoch*] Ship. 2 Ships, shipping, navy, fleet. 3 Barge. 4 Exile. L. crannach, *a high masted ship* ; l. cogaidh, *a warship* ; l. marsantachd, *a merchant-ship* ; l. spuinnidh, *a privateer.*
loingeasach, -aiche, *a.* Of or belonging to, or abounding in ships or fleets, naval.
loingseach, -ich, *s.m.* Mariner.
loing-shaor, -shaoir, *s.m.* see long-shaor.
loingsich, *v.n.* Sail, set sail.
loinid, -e, -ean, *s. f.* Churn-staff. 2 Whisk. 3 Instrument like a churn-staff but of smaller size, and with a twisted rope of hair round the horizontal part of it, with which milk or whey is frothed, called also "loinid-omhain."
loinideach, -eiche, *a.* Of, or belonging to, or like, a churn-staff or frothing-stick.
lòinidh, *s.m.ind.* Rheumatism, sciatica. [With art. *an.*] Greim lòinidh, *a rheumatic twinge;* gu h-olc leis an lòinidh, *ill with the rheumatism.*
lòinidheach, -eiche, *a.* Rheumatic.
loinid-omhain, see loinid.
loinig, -ean, see loininn.
lòininn, -ean, *s.* Lane for cattle. *Scots,* loaning.
loinn, -e, *s.f.* Good condition, fatness. 2 Joy, gladness. 3 Beauty, elegance, comeliness, order 4 Esteem, regard. 5 Choice. 6 Badge of distinction, crest, arms. 7* Propriety, ornament. 8 (CR) Stack-yard—*Perthshire.* 9 (CR) Garden—*Strathbraan.* †10 Corn-field. †11 Corn-pen. †12 Barn-yard. †13 Court, enclosed ground, area. 14*Decorum. 15 Glade. 16**Fun, cheerfulness. Dean le l. e, *do it gracefully* ; cha bhi l. ach far am bi thu, *there is no decorum but where you are* ; is beag l. a bhitheas air do ghnothach, *your errand will scarcely be a graceful one* ; chuir thu bho l. e, *you have spoiled it* ; dh' fhalbh l. an taighe leis, *the elegance of the house went with him* ; cha mhór a l., *its consequence is not very promising* ; brògan a chur m' ar cinn cha dean l. d' ar casan, *to put shoes on our heads will not make our feet elegant.*
loinn, -ean, *s.m.* The locative case of lann, used in place-names—‡.
loinneach, -eiche, *a.* see loinnear.
lòinneach, -eiche, *a.* Abounding in tufts of wool or flakes of snow.
lòinneag, see lòineag.
lòinneagach, -aiche, *a.* see lòinneach.
loinnear, -eire, *a.* Beautiful, elegant, becoming. 2 Cheerful, joyful, bright, pleasant. 3 Shining. 4 Splendid, fine. 9** Proper, neat. Duine l., *a splendid, proper fellow* ; ceòl l., *fine music ;* taigh l., *an elegant house.*
loinnear,** -eir, *s. m.* Light, gleam of light, flash of light.
loinnearach, -aiche, *a.* see loinnreach.
loinnearachd, *s f.* Beauty. 2 Brightness, effulgence, gleaming, clarity. 3 Loudness, sonorousness.
loinneas, -eis, *s.f.* Wavering, act or habit of wavering, rambling. 2 Eagerness of desire. 3 Elegance, comeliness. 4 Cheerfulness. 5 Fast speaking. 6††Art, skill, dexterity. 7 Sprightliness. 8**Neatness, seemliness.
loinneil, -e, *a.* see loinnear.
loinnir, see laimnir.
loinnireachd, see loinnearachd.
loinnreach,** -eich, *s.m.* Blaze, gleam.
loinnreach, -eich, *a.* Bright clear, shining, glittering. 2 Loud, sounding, sonorous. 8 Changeable, variable, changing. 3 Burnished. 4**Splendid. 5**Brave. Claidheamh l., *a gleaming sword.*
loinnreachadh, -aidh, *s. m.* Shining, act of, or causing to shine. A' l—, *pr.pt.* of loinnrich.
loinnreachair,** *s.m.* Burnisher.
loinnreachas, -ais, *s.m.* Burnish.
loinnrich, *v. a.* Shine, brighten, cause to shine, bespangle, glitter, sparkle.
loinseach,** -ich, *s.m.* Exile.
lòintean, *n.pl.* of lòn.
loir,** *pr.pt.* a' loireadh, *v.* see loirc.
loirc. *v.a.* Wallow, roll in the mud. 2*Drub.
loirc, -e, -ean, *s.f.* Deformed leg, foot or shank. †2‡‡Gammon of bacon, thigh of a hog. 3(AC) Footmark.
loirceach,* *a.* Short-legged.
———,* *s. f.* Very short-legged woman.
loirceadh, -idh, *s.m.* Wallowing, act of wallowing in mud. A' l—, *pr.pt.* of loirc.
loirceag, -eig, -an, *s.f.* Woman having deformed legs. 2 Tawdry, diminutive girl. 3 (AC) Active female child.
loircean, -in, -an, *s.m.* Man with deformed legs. 2 Dwarfish boy. 3 Uncouth boy. 4 see laoigucionn. 5 (AC) Active male child. 6* Short-legged man whose body is almost on the ground.
loirceineach, -ich, see loircean.
loirceire,* see loircean.
loireach, (DMy) *a.* Soiled, as when a sheep's wool is bedaubed with mud. 2 State of not being dyed or barked brightly. Dath loireachain air an aodach (*no* air an t-seòl), *a dull colour on the cloth* (*or sail.*)
loireachan, *s.m.* Boggy or wet place.
loireadh, see laoireadh.
loireag, -eig, -an, *s.f.* Handsome, rough or shaggy cow. 2 Fat little girl. 3 Pan-cake. 4 (AF) Petrel. 5 (AC) Water-nymph, water-sprite, water-fairy. The loireag presided over the warping, weaving, waulking and washing of the web—AC.
Loiream, *s.m.* Trifler. Nuair a bhitheas càch air an eathar, bithidh siubhal nan taighean aig Loiream, *when the others are afloat, and working hard at the fishing, Trifler goes from house to house.*
loirean, (AF) *s.m.* Lamb late of weaning.
loireanach, -ich, *s m.* Male child just able to walk. 2*Bespattered, dirty little fellow.
loireanachd, *s.f.ind.* The first walking of an infant, first attempts at walking. 2 Plashing through mud.
loirgneadh, -idh, *s.m.* Stalk.
lois, see loch-bhléin.
lois, (AF) *s.* Fox.
loisceanta, see loisgeanta.
loisdean, *s.m* Primrose—*Arran.*
†loise, *a.* Inflamed.

†loise, *s.f.* Flame. 2 Clearness.
†loiseadh, *s.m.* Flame. 2 Clearness.
loisdin, *s.* **Home, (lodging.) 2(AF) Small kind of fish.
loisdineach, *s.* Guest.
loiseann, see loch-bhléin.
lòiseam, -eim, *s.m.* Show, pomp of appearance. 2 Showy assemblage of persons. 3** Company of gentry. B' uallach do l., *noble was thy company.*
lòiseamach, -aiche, *a.* Showy, of pompous appearance.
loisg, *pr.pt.* a' losgadh, *v.a. & n* Burn, inflame, cause to burn. 2 Consume, be wasted by fire. 3 Parch, singe, scorch, scald. 4 Fire, as a gun. L. iad e, *they burnt him in effigy.*
loisgeach, -eiche, *a.* Burning, flaming. 2 That burns or produces burning. 3 That can be burnt, inflammable. 4 Fiery. 5 Eager, keen. 6 Caustic, corroding.
———ail,(MS) *a.* Combustible.
loisgeadair, -ean, *s.m.* Incendiary. 2 Burner.
loisgean, -ein, -an, *s.m.* Pimpernel, poor man's weather-glass, burnet. 2 see falcair. 3 **Salamander.
loisgeann, see losgann.
———ach, see losgannach.
loisgeanta,* *a.* Very keen. 2 Fiery. 3 Inflammatory, inflammable, parching, scorching. 4 Blasting. 5**Keen.
———chd,* *s.f.ind.* Fieriness.
loisgearnach, -aiche, *a.* Swift, nimble.
loisgionn,** *s.m.* Locust.
loisgrean,** -ein, *s.m.* Burnt corn, corn burnt out of the ear instead of being threshed.
loisgte, *past pt.* of loisg. Burnt, scorched, scalded, parched, inflamed. Leann l., *dregs from which ale is brewed.*
loisid, -e, -ean, *s.f.* see losaid.
———each, -eiche, see losaideach.
loisidh, *s.f.* (AF) Fox. 2 **Flame.
loisneach, -eiche, *a.* Cunning, crafty. 2 Inconstant. 3 Unquiet, disturbed.
loist,** *s.f.* Pillion, pannel. 2 Sloven.
loisteach,** *s.m.* Trough.
loistean, -ein, -an, *s. m.* Lodging, tent, booth, dwelling-place.
†loisteil,** *a.* Slothful, inactive.
loistich-fuinidh,** *s.f.* Kneading-trough.
loit, *v.* see lot.
loit, *s.f.* **Whore. 2 see lot.
loite,** *past part.* Stung, bitten.
loiteach,(MS) *a.* see loibheach.
loiteachd, *s.f.ind.* } for loibheachd, see loibheachas.
loiteadh,(MS) *s.m.* }
loiteag,** -an, *s.f.* Nettle. 2 Whore.
loitheach, *a.* see loibheach.
loitheachd, see loibheachas.
loithreach, *a.* Tattered, ragged –*Dàin I.Ghobha.*
loit-shealgair,** *s.m.* Debauchee.
loithte,(MS) *a.* see lobhta.
———achd,(MS) *s.f.* see loibheachas.
lom, luim & luime, *a.* Bare, naked, without covering. 2 Threadbare. 3 Bleak, without verdure, open, exposed. 4 Lean. 5 Defenceless. 6 Stinted, miserly. 7 Cutting, satirical. 8 Smooth. Cho l. ri òigh, *as smooth as a virgin;* is l. an leac air nach buaineadh tu bàirneach, *it is a bare rock on which you will not be able to find a limpet*—said of a mean exacting person; lannan lom, *naked swords;* cha bhi sonas air bus lom, *a bare mouth will not be lucky*—i.e. politeness is better than bluntness; Iain L., *cutting John.*
lom, *pr.pt.* a' lomadh, *v.a.* Shear, clip, shave. make bare. 2 Pillage, plunder. 3**Strip. 4 **Fret. 5††Unhusk.
lom, luim & luime, *s.m.* Bare surface or plain, field.
lomadair, -ean, *s. m.* Shearer, shaver, barber, parer, one who shears, shaves, or makes bare. 2 Sheep-shearer. 3 Spoiler, plunderer.
———eachd,** *s. f. ind.* Sheep-shearing. 2 Shaving. 3 Plundering.
lomadh, -aidh, *s. m.* Shearing, act of shearing, shaving, or making bare. 2 Plundering, act of plundering, pillaging. 3 Desolation. 4* Utter devastation, ruination. 5(MS) Rasure. A' l—, *pr. pt.* of lom. 6 When the grain was hardened by the fire previous to being put into the quern to grind, it was placed in a tub and stamped with the bare feet to separate the hard inner shells of the corn; this operation was called "lomadh."—MMcD. DMK says *lomadh* was performed with the flail, and consisted in breaking the spikes of the barley after it was threshed. Also performed by driving a spade into a tub containing the grain, the clippings being afterwards removed by winnowing—DU.
lomag agus tiorlaman, *s.* Whisky and oatmeal—*Arran.*
lomaidh,(AF) *s.f.* Shorn sheep.
lomain,** *s.f.* Shield.
lomair, -ean, *s.m.* see lomadair. 2 Fleece.
lomair, *pr. pt.* a' lomairt & a' lomradh, *v.a.* Fleece, shear, as sheep. 2 (MS) Denude.
lomairt, -ean, *s.m.* Fleecing, act of fleecing or shearing of sheep. 2‡‡Fleece. 3 Peeling, 4 Shaving. A' l—, *pr.pt.* of lomair. [** gives *s.f.*]
†lomairteach, -eiche, *a.* Bare, shorn, bald.
†———,** -eich, *s.m.* Bald man.
loma-luath, *adv.* As soon as. Cho loma-luath 's a chì thu e, *the very instant you see him.*
loman, -ain, *s. m.* Bald man. 2 Poor naked man. 3 Miser, niggard. 4**Knot in timber. 5** Piece of timber stripped of its bark. 6** Knot in timber stripped of its bark. 7 Ensign, standard. 8** Shield. Gheibh an l. an lom-dhonas, *the niggard will receive his full share of misery.*
———ach, -aich, *s.m.* see loman. 2**Person of meagre form.
lomar, -air, *s.m.* Fleece.
lomar, *fut.pass.* of lom.
———ach,** *a.* Fleecy, woolly. Caoraich l., *fleecy sheep.*
lomardach, see lomartach.
†lomargain,** *s.f.* Devastation, ravaging, plundering. 2 Fleecing.
lomarta, *past pt.* of lomair. Shorn, fleeced. An treud l., *the shorn flock.*
lomartach, -aiche, *a.* Bare, naked, shaven, bald, uncovered.
———d,** *s.f.* Nakedness, bareness.
lomartair, -ean, *s.m.* see lomadair.
lombair, -e, see lompair.
lombar, see lompair.
lomchar, -air, -airean, *s.m.* Bare place. L. nam màlaidhean, *the space between the eyebrows.*
lom-chasach, -aiche, *a.* Bare-footed.
lom-chnàimheach, -eiche, *a.* Bare-boned.
lom-dhonas,** -ais, *s.m.* Misery, poverty.
lom-éiginn, -e, -ean, *s.f.* Absolute necessity.
lom-fhulangas, -ais, -an, *s.m.* Bare permission.
lomhainn, -e, -ean, *s.f.* Cord or thong to lead a dog, leash. 2*Pack of hounds. L. chon, *a leash of hounds.*
lomhair,** *s.f.* see lomhainn.
lomhair, -e, *a.* Brilliant, shining, gleaming, glittering, bright, effulgent. 2 Transparent. 3 Stately.
lomhar, see lomhair.

lom-làn, *a.* Quite full, brim-full.
lom-luath, see loma-luath.
lomna,** -aidh, *s.m.* Rope.
lomnachas, -ais, see lomnochdaidh.
†lomnair,** *s.m.* Harper.
lomnoch, *a.* see lomnochd.
lomnochd, *a.* Naked, uncovered, bare.
——, *s.f.* Nakedness.
——achd,** *s. f.* Nakedness, bareness, state of being uncovered, L. na tìre, *the nakedness (bareness) of the land.*
——adh, *s.m.* Denudation.
——aich, *v.a.* Denude.
——aiche, *s.f.* see lomnochdaidh.
——aidh, *s. f. ind.* Nakedness, bareness, baldness, state of being uncovered.
——uiche,** *s.f.* see lomnochdaidh.
——uidh, see lomnochdaidh.
lompair, *a.* Bare. 2 Unfertile.
——, -e, -ean, *s. f.* Bare plain. 2 Unfertile, sterile plain. 3**Field having a meagre crop of grass. 4* Common. 5**Bare surface.
lompais, *s.m.ind.* Niggardliness. 2 Straitened circumstances, poverty. [** gives s.*f.*]
lompas, -aide, *a.* Sparing, niggardly.
lompas,†† *s.m.* see lompais.
lomrach,* -aiche, *a.* Fleecy, woolly. 2 Fleecing, shearing. Caorach l., *a fleecy sheep.*
lomradh, -aidh, -aidhean, *s.m.* Fleecing, act of fleecing, shearing of sheep. 2 Fleece. 3** Effulgence. 4 Gorgeousness.
lomraisteach,** *a.* Naked.
lom-sgrìob, -an, *s.f.*Bare sweep,complete devastation, laying entirely waste. 2**Sweepstake. 3 Complete erasure.
——, *pr.pt.* a' lom-sgrìobadh, *v.a.* Erase. 2 Destroy utterly. 3 Lay waste.
——adh, -aidh, *s. m.* Destroying, act of destroying utterly. A' l—, *pr. pt.* of lom-sgrìob.
——ta, *past pt.* Utterly erased, destroyed, laid waste.
lomta, *past pt.* of lom. Shorn, made bare, peeled, clipped, fleeced, stripped, shaven, made naked.
lòn, -òin, *s.m.* Food, provision, diet, dinner, store. The Gael of old, like other ancient nations, had but one meal or diet daily—the lòn. The terms dinneir, biadh-nòin, &c. are modern introductions. Air bheag lòin, *on a scanty diet;* l. de luibhibh, a *dinner of herbs.*
lón, óin, -óintean, *s.m.* Meadow, lawn. 2 (CR) Small brook, especially with marshy banks—*Skye.* †3 Marsh, morass. †4 Pond, lakelet, water, mud.
lon, -oin, *s.m.* Elk. 2 (AF) Moose deer. 3 (AF) Bison, buffalo. 4 Blackbird, ouzel, see lon-dubh. Is binn guth loin, *sweet is the blackbird's note.*
lon, -oin, -an, *s.m.* Rope of raw hides, used by the inhabitants of St. Kilda, by which a man is lowered down a precipice in search of wild-fowl or their eggs. Lon làidir na feuma, *the strong rope of need.*
lon, -oin, *s. m.* Greed, voracity, hunger. 2 Prattle.
lonach, *s.m.* Avenue.
lònach,** -aich, *s.m.* Larder, pantry.
lonach, -aiche, *a.* Greedy, voracious, hungry. 2**Bewraying, prone to tell secrets. 3 Futile. 4 Talkative, forward, prattling. 5 Alert. 6 Abounding in elks, or 7 in blackbirds.
——,* *s.f.* Garrulous, voracious female.
lónach, -aiche, *a.* Full of marshes or meadows. 2 Abounding in food, alimental. An coire l., *the meadowy dell.*
lonachan,(AC) *s.m.* Rope in uprights of loom.
lonachd, *s.f.ind.* Greediness, voracity. 2 Talkativeness, habit of prattling or tale-telling.
lonach-shligneach, -ich, -achan, *s. m.* Crocodile.
lonach-shlionach, (AF) see lonach-shligneach.
lonadh, -aidh, *s.m.* Greed, voracity, see lon.
lonag, -aige, -an, *s.f.* Prattling female, tale-telling female. 2 Blackbird, see lon-dubh.
——ach, -aiche, *a.* Tattling, prattling like a female.
lonaiche, *s.f.* see lonachd.
——, *comp.* of lonach. More or most greedy.
lonaid, see loinid.
lònaid, (MS) *s.f.* Lane.
lonaig, *s.f.* Alley, lane for cattle.
lònail, *a.* Alimental.
lònailt,** *s.f.* Repository, storehouse, pantry.
lònainn,** *s.f.* Cord. 2 Lane or passage for cattle.
lonair,* -ean, *s.m.* Voracious man.
lonais, *s. f. ind.* Prattling, disposition to tell tales, prating. 2 Futility.
lonaiseach,‡‡ -eiche, *a.* Prating.
lonan, -ain, -an, *s.m.* Greedy person. 2 Forward prattler, tale-teller. 3 Prattling, vain talk, tale-telling. 4 Blackbird, see lon-dubh. 5 Nightingale. Nach sguir thu de d' lonan? *will you not cease your prattling?*
lonas, see lonachd.
lòn-cheannachd, *s.f.* Grocery, groceries.
lòn-cheannaiche, *s. m.* Grocer.
lon-cheilearach,(AF) *s.f.* Ring-ouzel.
lon-chraois, *s.m.* Bull-head. 2‖ Bulimia. 3 (AF) May-fly. 4 (AF) Water-spider, water-beetle, water-demon, water-glutton. 5 (AF) Angler-fish. 6 Canine appetite. 7(DMK) Inordinate desire or appetite.
lon-dubh, loin-duibh, *s. m.* Blackbird, ouzel—*turdus merula.* 2 Nightingale.

430 Lon-dubh.

431. Long.

long, *gen.* luing & luinge, *pl.* -an, *s.f.* Any kind of ship. 2 Three- or four-masted barge. For the names of parts of a ship, see under bàta. Tha iomadh tonn eadar an l. 's an tìr, *there*

is many a wave between the ship and land—said of what children will do, &c. when they grow up.
†long, -oing, *s.m.* Ling (fish.) 2 Cup. 3 Bed, hammock (this for langa.) 4 House, place. 5 Breast. 6 Enclosure. 7 Encampment.
†long, *v.a.* Destroy, devour. 2 Worry.
longach, -aiche, *a.* Naval, nautical.
longadan,** -ain, *s.m.* Swing-swong.
longadh,** -aidh, *s.m.* Casting, throwing. 2 Devouring. 3 Rocking. †4 Supper, meal, diet.
longair,** *s.f.* Ship's crew.
long-aisig, luinge-, longan-, *s.f.* Transport.
long-amar, -amrach, -amraichean, *s.m.* Dock.
longart, *s.m.* see long-phort.
longas, -ais, *s.m.* Shipping. 2 Banishment.
long-athair, *s.f.* Air-ship.
———— -teine, *s.f.* Fire-balloon.
long-bhàthadh, -aidh, *s.m.* Shipwreck.
†long-bhraine, *s.f.* Prow of a ship.
long-bhriseach, -eiche, *a.* Causing shipwreck.
long-bhriseadh, -idh, -idhean, *s.m.* Shipwreck.
long-cheannaiche, -an-, *s. f.* see long-mharsantachd.
long-chogaidh, luinge-,longan-, *s.f.* Man-of-war. 2 Privateer.
long-chreachaidh,(AH) *s.f.* Privateer.
long-dhìona, luinge-, longan-, *s. f.* Convoy, guardship.
long-dhìdein, *s.f.* Guardship.
long-Eireannach, *s. m.* Well-known Gaelic waulking-song, sung by the women when waulking cloth. The sweetheart of each girl present is named in turn by the singers as the song proceeds, the whole of the workers taking up the chorus. (*lit.* " the Irish ship.")
long-fhada,‡‡ luing-, *s.f.* Galley. 2 Yacht. 3 Lymphad, (as in the arms of Clanranald.)
long-lann,‡‡ *s.f.* Dock-yard.
long-lòdaidh, *s.f.* Ketch.
long-lòdail, see long-lòdaidh.
long-mharsantachd, *s.f.* Merchant-ship.
long-phort, -phuirt, -an, *s.m.* Harbour, haven. 2 Camp, garrison. 4 Palace, royal residence. 5 Tent. 6 Sheiling-hut.
long-phortach, -aiche, *a.* Abounding in harbours or camps. 2 Of, or belonging to, camps, harbours, or garrisons.
long-ràmhach, luing-, -an-, *s.f.* Galley, pinnace.
long-sgar, -air, -airean, *s.m.* Leak or chink in a ship.
————ach, -aiche, *a.* Causing rifts in a ship.
————adh, -aidh, -aidhean, see long-sgar.
long-shaor, -aoir, *s.m.* Ship-builder, ship's carpenter.
long-shuaicheantas,** -ais, *s.m.* Aplustre.
long-spuille, *s.f.* see long-spùinneadh.
long-spùilleadh, -idh, see long-spùinneadh.
long-spùinneadair, -ean, *s.m.* Pirate, sea-robber.
long-spùinneadh, -idh, -idhean, *s.m.* Piracy, act of plundering ships.
long-spùinnidh,‡‡ *s.f.* Privateer, pirate-ship.
long-thogail, *s.f.* Shipbuilding. 2 Art or trade of shipbuilding.
lonloingean,** -ein, *s.m.* Gullet, throat. 2 Any pipe.
lon-mhonaidh,(AF) *s.f.* Ring-ouzel.
lonn, -oinn, -an, *s.m.* [*s.f.* **] see lunn & lann.
lonn, -a & luinn, *s.m.* Anger, choler. 2 High swelling of the sea, surge. Air lonn a dhol dhachaidh, *on the point of going home.*
lonn, luinn & luinne, *a.* Strong, powerful. 2‡ Fierce.
lonnach, -aiche, *a.* High-swelling.
————adh,** -aidh, *s. m.* Abiding, dwelling, sojourning. 2 Continuance.
†lonnagan, -ain, *s. m.* Passionate young man.
lonnair,** *a.* Gorgeous.
†lonnrach, -aich, *s.* see loinnreach.
————, -aiche, *a.* see loinnreach.
lonnrachadh, -aidh, *s.m.* & *pr. pt.* see loinnreachadh.
lonnrachd, *s.* see loinnearachd.
lonnradh, -aidh, see loinnreachadh.
lonnraich, *pr.pt.* a' lonnrachadh, see loinnrich.
lonnraichead,** *s.* Brightness.
lonrach, *a.* Well-fed, satisfied—*Dàin Iain Ghobha.*
lònuinn,** *s.* Alley.
lon-uisge,¶ *s.* Common dipper, see gobha-uisge. 2 (AF) Water-craw.
lòpan,* -ain, *s.m.* Wain, see lòban.
lòpan, -ain, *Suth'd* for làban.
————ach, -aiche, see làbanach.
lorachadh,(DMK) *s.m.* Reviling, traducing.
loramach, -aiche, *a. Suth'd* for lomartach.
————d, *Suth'd* for lomnochd.
loramadh, *Suth'd* for lomradh, (fleece, fleecing.)
†lorc, *a.* Fierce, cruel.
†lorc, luirc, *s.f.* Foot.
lorc,* loirc, *s.m* see liorc. 2 Cramp –*Arran.* †3 Murder, parricide.
lorcach, -aiche, *a.* Lame, crawling.
lorc-chosgach,** *a.* Anti-spasmodic.
lorchair,(AF) *s.m.* Foal.
lor-daothain,** *s.* Sufficiency, enough. [leòir-doithinn—*Irish.*]
lorg, luirge, -an, *s.f.* Staff. 2 Crutch. 3 Haft of a spear. 4 Staff of a flail. 5 Straight stick with the bark on. 6 Shaft or tram of a cart. 7**Stalk of a plant. 8**Shaft of a banner. 9 Footstep, track, path, print. 10 Mark. 11 Sign. 12 Consequence. 13 Vestige. 14 Troop, band. 15 Progeny, offspring. 16 Leg, shank. shin. 17 Thigh. 18 Woman. Lean mi air an luirg aige,*I followed his track;* an l. a' ghnothaich seo, *as the consequence of this thing;* cù luirge, not necessarily *a terrier,* as given by **, but *any dog that tracks;* l. a dha shùla, *guiding himself by landmarks,* or *following the tracks with both his eyes.*
†lorg, *a.* Blind.
lorg, *pr.pt.* a' lorg & a' lorgadh, *v.a.* see lorgaich. A' l. lòin, *foraging provision.*
lorgach, -aiche, *a.* Having a staff or crutch. 2 Tracing, that tracks by scent or footprints. 3 Having many marks, abounding in marks or footprints. 4 Pursuing. 5 Searching.
————adh, -aidh, *s.m.* Tracing, act of tracing or tracking. 2 Pursuing. 3 Walking on crutches. A' l—, *pr.pt.* of lorgaich. A' l. lòin, *foraging provision.*
lorgadair, see lorgair.
lorgadh, -aidh, *s. m.* & *pr. pt.* of lorg. Same meanings as lorgachadh. Cù lorgaidh, *a dog that tracks, as a terrier, or pointer.*
lorgaich, *pr.pt.* a' lorgachadh, *v.a.* Trace, track, search, pursue, follow by scent or footprints. 2 Search for information. 3 Forage. 4 Investigate. 5**Walk on crutches.
lorgaichte, *past pt.* of lorgaich. Traced, tracked, found out by tracing, pursued. 2 Searched.
lorgair, -ean, *s.m.* One that traces or tracks. 2 Searcher. 3‡‡Imitator. 4 Dog that follows by scent, as a foxhound. 5 Slow-hound. 6 **Bloodhound. 7 (AF) Pointer. 8**Spy. 9 **Terrier.
————eachd, *s.f.ind.* Tracing, act or habit of tracing. 2**Inquisitiveness. 3**Espionage.
lorgan, see lorgair.
————ach,** -aich, *s.m.* Sluggard.
lorganach-shneachda,(CR) *s.m.* Sufficient snow to show a track
lorg-bheart,** *s.f.* Foot harness, covering for

the legs and feet. 2 Armour for the legs.
lorg-iomain, luirg-, *s.f.* Goad or stick for driving cattle, rod. [McL & D gives *s.m.*]
lorg-slighe, luirg-sh-, *s.m.* Genealogy. 2 Recital of one's genealogy or descent, formerly done on the death of a chieftain.
lormachd, *Suth'd* for lomnochd.
los,†† *adv. & prep.* About to. 2 In-order-to.
los, *s.m. ind.* Purpose, intention. 2 Sake, account. 3 Design. 4 Strength. 5 Virtue. 6 Control. 7**Effect, consequences. Tha làn an t-saoghail fo l. a' bhàis, *everyone is under the control of death*: tha mi a' dol air a l., *I am going in search* (*lit.* on account) *of it*; tha mi l. dol dhachaidh, *I have a mind to go home;* tha mi a' leth los, *I have half a mind*; air l., *for*; siod na bh' agam air l. mo thuruis, *that is all I got for my journey.*
†los, lois, *s.m.* Point, end of a thing. 2 Tail.
losaid, -e, -ean, *s.f.* Kneading-trough. 2 Sirloin of beef—*Lewis.* 3 Hip. Chaidh a' bhò as a losaid, *the hip of the cow went out of joint.*
——-each, -eiche, *a.* Abounding in kneading-troughs.
†losc,‖ *s.m.* Lame person.
losg,(AC) *s.* Leprosy.
†losg,** *a.* Cripple. 2 Blind. 3 Dumb.
——,** *s.m.* Lame person. 2 Blind person.
losgach, -aiche, *a.* see loisgeach.
losgadair, -ean, *s.m.* see loisgeadair.
losgadh, -aidh, -aidhean, *s. m.* Burning, act or state of burning, combustion. 2 Firing, as soldiers at a target, or an enemy. 3 Kindling, inflaming, singeing, scorching. 4 Scalding. 5 Parching. 6 Burn, scald. A' l—, *pr. pt.* of loisg. L. na gréine, *the scorching of the sun, especially on a person's skin*; l. dealanaich, *blasting by lightning*; L.-an-leanna, what the Highland smugglers call the process of distilling worts or beer, the product being low-wines or ceud-tharruing.
———— -braghaid,‖ *s.m.* Heart-burn. [Preceded by the art. *an.*]
———— -daighi,‖ Heart-burn.
losgan,** -ain, *s.m.* Childhood.
losgann, -ainn, -an, *s. m.* Toad. 2 Frog. 3 Wretch, contumelious appellation. 4***rarely* Childhood. 5(DU) Frog- or toad-spawn. 9 (DU) Jellyfish.
————, *s.f.* Sort of drag or sledge. [†† gives *s.m.*]
————ach, -aiche, *a.* Abounding in toads, frogs or sledges. 2 Like a toad, frog or sledge.
———— -buidhe, (AF) Toad. 2 Frog.
———— -dubh, [** gives l.-buidhe for *frog*,
———— -nimhe, and l.-dubh for *toad.*
losg-bhra-teine,** *s.* Ducking or throwing of stones obliquely against the water, so that they rebound several times from the surface.
losg-lann,** *s.m.* Fire-receptacle.
losgunn, see losgann.
lot, *gen.* -a & loit, *pl.* -an, *s.m.* Wound, hurt, stab, bruise. 2**Whore. 3**Wool. 4**Leg. 5**Washing. A' l—, *pr.pt.* of lot. L. urchair, *a gun-shot wound*; l.-claidheimh, *a sword-wound*; làn lot, *full of wounds.*
lot, *pr.pt.* a' lot & a' lotadh, *v.a.* Wound, pierce, hurt, stab, bruise. 2 Disease. 3 Take out a piece with the teeth. ***rarely* Commit fornication. L. i móran, *she has wounded many.*
lotach, -aiche, *a.* Wounding, piercing, stabbing, hurting, bruising, maiming. 2 Apt to wound or pierce. 3 Destructive. Lannan l., *destructive swords.*
lotadh, -aidh, *s.m.* Wounding, act of wounding stabbing, hurting, maiming. 2 Wound, bruise, stab. 3***rarely* Fornication. A' l—, *pr. pt.* of lot.
lotadh, *3rd. per. sing. & pl. imp.* of lot. L. e iad, *let him wound them.*
lotag,§ *s.f.* Nettle, see deanntag.
lotar,** -air, *s.m.* Ruining. 2 Mangling.
lotar, *a.* Sharp.
——, *fut. pass.* of lot. Shall be wounded.
lot-ghearradh, -aidh, -aidhean, *s.m.* Incision
†loth,** *s.m.* Beard. 2 Sweat.
loth, -a, -an, *s. f. & m.* Filly, foal, colt. 2 (DC) Colt up to a year old—*Uist.* 3**Meal, diet. 4 Marsh—*Suth'd.* L. asail, *an ass's colt.*
lothach, -aiche, *a.* Having many fillies, abounding in fillies. 2 see làthach.
lothad, see lòd.
lothag, -aig, -an, *s.f., dim.* of loth. Little filly, foal or colt. 2 Young filly, foal or colt.
lothagach, -aiche, *a.* Having many young fillies, abounding in little or young fillies.
lothail, -e, -ean, *s. f.* Brooklime—*veronica beccabunga.* 2 Lavender, see lus-na-tùise.
lothainn, see lomhainn.
lothair,** *s. m.* Lavender, see lus-na-tùise. Uisge an lothair, *lavender-water.*
——, *s.m*, see lothar.
lothal,** -ail, -an, see lothail.
†lothar, -air, *s.m.* Assembly. 2 Cauldron. 3 Trough. 4 Hound. 5 Cloth, raiment.
lothta,(MS) *a.* see lobhta.
†lu, *a.* Little.
†lua, *s.m.* Water. 2 Heap. 3 Oath. 4 Foot. 5 Kick. 6**Hand.
luach, *s.m.ind.* Value, worth. 2 Amends. 3 Wages. L. ciatach, *a good price*; l. saoithreach, *price of labour, wages*; cha deanainn air mhór luach e, *I would not do it on any consideration*; l.-peighinn, *a* (*Scots*) *pennyworth;* l.-saoraidh, *a ransom*; làn luach, *full price.*
luach, *pr.pt.* a' luachadh, *v.a.* Value, fix as the value. 2 Comprehend, understand.
——-ach, -aiche, *a.* see luachmhor.
luachadair,** *s.m.* Appraiser.
luachaid,** *s.f.* Frost.
luachail, ala, *a.* Rateable.
luachair, luachrach, *s.f.* Common rush—*juncus conglomeratus.* A single rush is called luaichirean. Leabaidh luachrach, *a bed of rushes.*
luachair,** *a.* Bright, resplendent.
————,** *s. f.* Splendour, brightness. 2 Tempest.
———— -bhog, *s.f.coll.* Bulrushes, the soft rush —*juncus effusus.*

432. *Luachair-bhog.*

luachair-bhogain, *s.f.* Lake-scirpus—*Colonsay.*
luachair-choille, *s.f.* Wood-rush—*luzula sylvatica.*
luachaireach, -aiche, *a.* see luachrach.
——————d,(MS) see luachmhoraichd.
luachair-ghòbhlach,§ *s.f.* Bulrush, lake-scirpus —*scirpus lacustris.*
luachairneach, -eich, *s.f.* Place where rushes grow.
luach-aisig,** *s.m.* Ferriage, water fare.
luachar, -air & -luachrach, *s.f.* Bulrush, rush, rushes.
luach-armunn, -uinn, see luch-armunn.
luacharn, see lòchran.
luach-giulain, *s.m.* Fare. 2 Freightage.
luachmhoire, *comp.* of luachmhor.
luachmhoireachd, *s. f. ind.* Valuableness, preciousness, meritoriousness, excellence, worthiness.
luachmhor, -oire, *a.* Valuable, precious, excellent.
————achd, see luachmhoireachd.
luach-peighinn, -e, *s.m.* Pennyworth, good bargain.
luachrach, *a.* Full of rushes, rushy. 2 Like a rush. 3 Made of rushes. An glacag l., *the rushy dell.*
————, *gen.* of luachair.
luachrach,**-aich, *s.m.* Place where rushes grow. 2 Crop of rushes. [** gives *s.f.*]
luach-saoithreach, -ich, *s.m.* Reward. 2 Hire, wages.
luach-saoraidh, *s.m.* Ransom. 2 Payment.
luad, luaid, *s.m.* Joint. 2 Little finger.
luadair,** *s.m.* Flax-wheel. 2 Flyer of a jack.
luadar,** -air, *s.m.* Motion. 2 Haste.
luadh, luaidh, *s.m.* Mention, conversation, rumour, talk. 2 Praise. 3 Hope. 4 Desire. 5 Panegyric. 6 *rarely* Motion. 7 see luadhadh. 9* Beloved object. Mo luaidh! *my dear!* gun l. air éirigh, *without word of rising;* mac mo luaidh, *the son of my praise;* a l. air sgeul mo ghràidh, *his talk concerning the tale of my love.* A' l—, *pr.pt.* of luaidh in *Gairloch & Lochbroom.*
luadh, *v.a.* see luaidh.
luadha, see luadhadh.
luadhach,** *a.* Fulling, milling, as of cloth. Muileann l., *a fulling-mill.*
luadhadair, -ean, *s.m.* Fuller of cloth.
luadhadaireachd, *s. f. ind.* Business or art of fulling.
luadhadh, -aidh, *s. m.* Fulling, act of fulling, process of fulling. 2 Charging, laying to one's charge. 3**Mentioning. 4**Praising. A' l—, *pr.pt.* of luaidh.

Where fulling-mills are at a distance, the waulking or fulling of cloth is performed by females in the following manner. Six or eight, or sometimes as many as fourteen, take their stations, at equal distances, on each side of a long frame of wattled work, or sometimes of a board ribbed longitudinally, and placed on the ground. Thereon is laid the wetted blanket or cloth which is to undergo the process of waulking. The women then kneel, and with their hands rub it firmly against the frame with all their strength, at the same time singing loudly some spirited melody. When their arms grow tired, they naturally have recourse to their legs; then sitting upon the ground, and tucking their petticoats up to their knees, the cloth is forthwith put under a course of more vigorous friction than before. As the work grows warm the song grows louder and louder. The song is known as *òran luadhaidh,* and the house or shed in which the work is performed, *an taigh luadhaidh.*

luadhairle,** *s.f.* Motion, exercise.
luadhar, *fut. pass.* of luadh. Shall be praised.
luadh-ghair, see luath-ghair.
luadhmhoire, *comp.* of luadhmhor.
——————achd, *s.f.ind.* Renown, state of being renowned.
luadhmhor, -oire, *a.* Famous, renowned. Gu l., *in a notable manner.*
luadhradh,** -aidh, *s.m.* Fame, report.
luadhraich,** *v.a.* Report. 2 Make renowned or notable.
luag,** -aig, *s.f.* Child's doll.
luagh, see luadh.
luaghainn, *s.* Wobbling. 2 (DMy) Paunch, stomach. Cha b'e rud beag a lìonadh a l., *a little would not fill his stomach.*
luaghair, see luath-ghair.
————each, see luath-ghaireach.
————eachd, see luath-ghaireachd.
luaghasachadh, see luathsachadh.
luagh-ghair, see luath-ghair.
——————each, see luath-ghaireach.
——————eachd, see luath-ghaireachd.
luaghlas,** -ais, *s.m.* Manacle, handcuff, fetter.
luaghsachd, see luathsachd.
luaghsaich, see luathsaich.
————te, see luathsaichte.
luaghuta,** *s.m.* Gout, gout in the fingers.
luaichirean, *s.f.* A single rush—*collect.* luachair.
luaidh, *pr.pt.* a' luaidh, *v.a. & n.* Mention, make mention. 2 Liken to. 3 Praise, celebrate, make noted. Na l. a leithid sin rium-sa, *do not lay such a thing to my charge;* na l. dée eile, *do not mention other gods.*
luaidh, *pr.pt.* a' luadhadh, *v.a.* Full, mill, or thicken cloth. L. an t-aodach, *full the cloth.* [For description of the process, see luadhadh.]
luaidh, *s.m.* Mentioning, act of mentioning, speaking. 2 Praising, act of praising. 3 Praise. Dean l., *make mention;* gun fhilidh gun luaidh, *without bard without praise.* A' l—, *pr.pt.* of luaidh.
luaidh, -e, -ean, *s.m. & f.* Beloved person, object or subject of praise. 2**Song or poem in praise of one. 3 Respect, esteem—*Dàin I. Ghobha.* A luaidh! *my dearest!* is glas mo l. *pale is my beloved.*
luaidh, -e, *s.m. & f.* Lead. 2 Plummet or lead of a sounding-line. 3 Any kind of shot made of lead. L. is stàilinn, *lead and steel;* l. dhubh, *black lead;* l. gheal, *white lead;* cothrom luaidhe, *a weight of lead;* l. ghorm, *blue lead;* l. chaol, *lead drops, small shot;* eitean luaidhe, *a lead drop.*
luaidh, *a.* Of lead, leaden.
luaidh air, (CR) Nearly—*Perthshire.* Cha'n 'eil e luaidh air bhi deas, *it is not nearly ready.*
luaidh-chèard, -chèird, *s.m.* Plumber.
luaidhe, *a.* see luaidh, *a.*
————, *gen.sing.* of luaidh.
————,** *s.f.* Coition, copulation.
luaidheach, -iche, *a.* Abounding in lead. 2 Leaden. 3 Praising, giving much praise, laudable.
——————d, *s.f.ind.* Praising, frequent praising, habit of praising. 2 Mention, frequent mention. 3 Reward, recompense, requital. 4 Love. 5**Renown.
luaidhreal, see laibhreal.
luaidh-shreang, -eing, -an, *s.f.* Plummet.
luaidhte, (AH) *past pt.* of luaidh. Fulled. 2 Mixed, combined, bemingled, intermingled, impregnated with, suffused, transfused.
luaidrean, -ein, *s.m.* Vagabond. 2 Vagary.

luaigh, see luaidh.
——,** *a.* Cheerful, pleasant.
——,** *s.f.* Buying. 2 Price.
——eachd, see luaidheachd.
luailleach,** -ich, *s.m.* Mimic. 2 Buffoon.
————, -aiche, *a.* Mimicking, full of gestures.
————, see luathailteach.
luailte, see luathailt.
————ach, *a.* see luathailteach.
————achd, see luathailteachd.
luailtich, see luathailtich.
luaim,* *s.f.* Restlessness. 2 Giddiness.
luaimear, -ir, -irean, *s.m.* One who speaks too much, prattler, prater. 2 Tell-tale.
————achd, *s.f.ind.* Prating, habit of prating, volubility. 2 Tale-telling.
luaimh,** *s.m.* Abbot.
————neach, see luaineach.
†luaimh-nighe,** *s.f.* Wave-offering.
luaimneach, see luaineach.
—————d, see luaineachd.
luain,* *s. f.* see luaineachd. 2** Loins. 3** Kidneys. 4 *gen. sing.* of luan, as, Di-luain, *Monday.*
luaineach, -eiche, *a.* Restless, changeable, inconstant, fickle, fleeting. 2 Ambulatory. 3 Uncertain, by fits and starts. 4 Frisking, hopping, jumping. 5 Moving, in motion, as a stream. 6**Mercurial. 7‡‡ Restless, volatile. Gu l., *restlessly;* leabaibh nan neul l., *a bed of restless clouds;* ceò l., *unsteady mist;* uisge l. an lòin, *the running stream of the meadow.*
————, -ich, *s.m.* Traveller, wanderer. 2 Volatile or fickle man.
luaineachas, -ais, see luaineachd.
luaineachd, *s.f.ind.* Changeableness, fickleness, inconstancy. 2*Giddiness. 3 Ambulatoriness. 4 Constancy of motion. 5 Motion as of a stream. 6 Restlessness, volatility, unsteadiness. 7 Propensity to frisk or skip, continued frisking or skipping, habit of frisking or skipping. 8 Humorousness. 9(MS) Vagrancy.
luaineas, -eis, *s.f.* see luaineachd.
luain-ghalar,** *s.m.* Lunacy. 2 Nephritic pains.
—————ach,** *a.* Lunatic. 2 Causing nephritic pains. 3 Affected with nephritic pains.
luaintean,** *a.* Nephritic.
luaireag,¶ -eig, -an, *s.f.* Storm petrel—*thalassidroma procellaria.* ("Mother Cary's chickens.")

433. Luaireag.

luaireagan, -ain, -an, *s. m.* Grovelling person. 2 Driveller. 3 Child that delights to sit at the fire.
————ach, -aiche, *a.* Grovelling, wallowing. Amadan l., *a grovelling idiot.*
————achd, *s.f.ind.* Habit of grovelling or wallowing.
luairean, *s.m.* Senseless lump. 2 (DMy) Giddiness. Tha l. 'nam cheann, *my head is giddy.*
luaireanta, see luaithreanta.
luaisd,** see sluaisd.
luaiseagan,¶ -ain, -an, *s.m.* Storm petrel, see luaireag.
luaisg, *pr. pt.* a' luasgadh, *v.a. & n.* Shake, cause to shake, toss, wave, bob, swing, shake, rock, jolt, brandish. 2** Drive away. 3** Float.
———each, -eiche, *a.* Shaking, rocking, swinging, floating, tossing.
———eachd,** *s.f.* Rocking motion, continued rocking, swinging, or tossing.
luaisgean, *s.m.* Giddiness.
—————ta, -einte, *a.* Movable.
luaisgte, *past pt.* of luaisg. Shaken, tossed, rocked, swung.
luaith, *gen.sing.* of luath.
luaithe, *comp.* of luath.
————, *adv.* Sooner, soonest.
————ad, -eid, *s.m.* Swiftness, celerity, degree of swiftness, quickness or despatch. Air l. 's gu'm bheil e, *however swift he be.*
————ad-phonc, *s.m.* Minim in *music.*
luaithir,* *v.a.* Toss in the ashes.
luaithneachas, *s.m.* Fiddle-faddle.
luaithre, *s.f.* Ashes, dust. Ann an l., *in ashes.*
————ach, -eiche, *a.* Ashy, dusty, covered with ashes, full of ashes. 2 Like ashes. 3 Early, as seed—*Islay.* Sìol l., *early seed;* foghara dh l., *an early harvest.*
————ach, *s.m.* Ashes, quantity of ashes, dust.
luaithreach,** *a.* Expeditious, active.
luaithreachadh, *s.m.* Calcination.
luaithreachd,* *s.f.* Earliness.
luaithreadh, -idh, *s.m.* Dust, quantity of dust. 2 Pulverisation, state of becoming dust or ashes. L. a chois, *the dust of his feet.*
luaithreadh,* *pr. pt.* of luaithir. Tossing in ashes.
luaithreagan, see luaireagan.
luaithrean, see luairean.
luaithreanta, -einte, *a.* Dusty, covered with dust or ashes. 2**Pulverized.
luaithrich, *v.a.* Calcine. 2* Hasten.
luaithsgean,(MS) *s.m.* Levity.
†luam,** -aim, *s.m.* Abbot. 2 Pilot.
luamaich, *s.f.* Lesser paunch.
luamair,** -ean, *s.m.* Astronomer. 2 Navigator, pilot.
†luaman,** -ain, *s.m.* Little hand. 2 Veil.
luamh,* *s.f.* The lesser paunch.
†luamh,** -aimh, *s. m.* Abbot. 2 Prior. 3 Sneaking person. 4 Corpse.
†luamhair,** -ean, *s.m.* Pilot.
†luamhnachd,** *s.f.ind.* Abbacy, abbotship. 2 Priory, priorship.
†luan, -ain, *s.m.* Greyhound. 2 Woman's breast.
Luan, -ain, *s.f.* The Moon. 2 Monday. 3*Paunch. Là luain, *a Monday; 2 a day lightened by the moon,* i. e. *a day that shall never come, Nevermas;* gu là luain, *never (future time only);* an luan mu dheireadh de 'n ràidh, *the last Monday of the quarter.*
†luan, -ain, *s. m.* **Loin. 2 **Kidney. 3** Champion, warrior. 4 (AF) Lamb.
†luanaisg,** *s.f.* Chains for the legs.
†luanasgach,** *a.* Chaining, fettering, binding. 2 Chained.
luan-ghalar,** *s.* Nephritic pains.
luan-lus,§ -luis, *s. m.* Moonwort—*botrychium lunaria.* Found but sparingly in Scottish Gaeldom. It is a small plant of the fern tribe, but very unlike the ordinary fern, a few inches in height with a frond of small fan-like leaves and a spike of dusty-coloured spores.
luarach,** -aich, *s.f.* Chain. 2 Milking fetter.

fetters. (buarach.)
luarach, -aiche, *a.* Vulgar, common.
luaran,‡ -ain, -an, *s.m.* Dizziness, faint. (luairean—DMy.)
luargan,** *s.m.* Grovelling person.
————ach,** *a.* Grovelling.
————aich,** *v.n.* Grovel.
————achd, *s.f.ind.* } Grovelling.
————as, -ais, *s.m.* }
luas, -ais, *s.m.* see luathas.
——achadh, -aidh, *s.m. & pr.pt.* of luasaich, see luathasachadh.
luasachail, see luathasachail.
luasaich, see luathsaich.
————te,. see luathsaichte.
luas-analach, -aich, see luathas-analach.
luasgach, -aiche, *a.* see luaisgeach.
————d, see luaisgeachd.
luasgadair, -ean, *s.m.* Swinger, rocker, tosser.
luasgadh, -aidh, *s.m.* Tossing, act of tossing or shaking. 2 State of being tossed, rocked or rolled. 3 Rolling, trembling, rocking. 4 **Floating. 5* Oscillation. A' l—, *pr.pt.* of luaisg.
luasgain,‡‡ *v.a.* Shake, vibrate.
luasgan, -ain, -an, *s.m.* Tottering. 2 Jolting or rocking a cradle. 3††Heaving, tossing. 4 Fear, dread. 5 Giddiness. 6 The spring of a cycle. 7 Swing. 8 Fidgeting. 9**Cradle. 10 **Childhood. Gaoth a chuireas l. air meòir a' phris, *a wind that shall make the branches of the bush to shake.*
luasganach, -aiche, *a.* Swinging, tossing, rocking. 2 Fickle, inconstant. 3 Restless, fidgety, unsteady. Tonn l., *a tossing wave ;* am breac l., *the restless trout.*
————d, *s.f.ind.* Rocking, tossing. 2 Inconstancy, fickleness. 3** Unsteadiness. 4 ** Amusement of swinging.
luasganaich, *s.f.* Tossing, rocking, jolting.
————e, -an, *s.m.* One who tosses, swings or rocks.
————e, *s.f.ind.* Rocking, jolting, tossing. 2**Swinging, tossing in a swing.
luath, *gen.* luaith, luatha & luathainn, *s. f.* Ashes, see luaithre. 2 see luadh.
luath, luaithe, *a.* Swift, fleet, nimble. 2 Quick, speedy. 3**Transient. Each l., *a swift horse;* darag a's luaithe fàs, *an oak of the quickest growth.*
——, *adv.* Soon, quickly. 2 Early. Is fhad' a bha thu, 's l. a thàinig thu ! *you are long of coming, and have come full soon ;* cho l., *so soon, so quickly.*
——, *v.a.* see luathaich. 2 see luaidh.
luatha, *gen. sing.* of luath.
luathach, -aiche, *a.* Ashy, abounding in ashes, like ashes. 2 see luadhach.
————adh, -aidh, *s.m.* Hastening, act of hastening, accelerating, act of accelerating. 2 see luadhadh. A' l—, *pr.pt.* of luathaich.
luathadh, *s.m. & pr. pt.* of luath. 2 see luadhadh.
luathaich, *pr.pt.* a' luathachadh, *v.a.& n.* Hasten, hurry, make haste, accelerate, speed, move. L. ort, *make haste.*
————te, *past pt.* of luathaich. Hastened, accelerated.
luathailt, -e, *s. f.* Swiftness, speed, despatch, rapidity, hastiness.
luathailteach, -eiche, *a.* Swift, quick, rapid, expeditious. 2 Nimble. 2 Full of gestures. 3 **Volatile.
————d, *s. f. ind.* Swiftness, hastiness, 2 Rapidity. 3 Volatility.
luathailtich, *v. a.* Accelerate, hasten, forward, despatch.

luath-air-a'-bheul,(AH) *s.* Indiscreet speaking, garrulity. Ged is luath-air-a'-bheul dhomh a ràdh, *although I say it who should not.*
luath-air-a'-theangaidh, see luath-air-a'-bheul.
luathaire,(MS) *s.* Expedition, haste.
luath-aireach, -eiche, *a.* Precocious, immature. 2 Apprehensive. 3 Quick-witted.
————ail, *a.* see luath-aireach.
————d, *s.f.* Precociousness, immatureness. 2 (MS) Acceleration.
luath-araich, see luath-ailtich.
luatharan,¶ -ain, -an, *s.f.*(***m.*) Sea-lark, sandlark, sandpiper—*totanus hypoleuca.*
luatharan-glas,¶ *s.m.* Sanderling—*calidris arenaria.* 2 (AF) Common sandpiper.

434. Luatharan-glas.

luathas, -ais, *s. m.* Speed, quickness, expedition, swiftness. 2 Agility. 3 Earliness. L. an fhoghair, *the earliness of the harvest ;* l. analach, *asthma ;* cha bhi l. agus grinneas, *there cannot be expedition and neatness.*
luathas-analach, *s.m.* Asthma. 2 Palpitation.
luath-bhar,** *a.* see luathmhor. Each liath l., *a swift grey horse.*
luath-bhàs,** -bhàis, *s. m.* Sudden death. 2 Untimely death.
luath-bhàta, *s.m.* Cutter. 2 Fly-boat, see p. 78.
luath-bheulach, -aiche, *a.* Talkative, prating, fond of gossiping stories, gabbling, talkative.
————d, *s.f.* Babble.
luath-bhileach, -eiche, *a.* Talkative, prating, gabbling.
luath-chainnt,** *s.f.* Babble.
luath-chainnteach, -eiche, *a.* Talkative, prating.
luath-cheumnach, -aiche, *a.* Swift, that walks swiftly, nimble.
luath-choragach,** *a.* Nimble-fingered, pilfering.
†luath-chridhe, *s.* Cardiacus.
luath-dhearg, *s.f.* Red ashes.
luath-ghàir, -ean, *s.m.* Joy. 2 Shout of joy. 3 Shout of triumph. 4 Loud rejoicing. 5***rarely* Reward. [** gives *s.f.*]
————each, -eiche, *a.* Glad, joyful, exultant.
————eachd,***s.f.* Continued joy, rejoicing.
luath-ghinteach, -eiche, *a.* Primogenial, first begotten.
luath-laimh, *s.f.* Combat.
luath-làmhach, -aiche, *a.* Clever, active, expert. 2 Thievish, pilfering. 3 Covetous. 4 Apt to strike. 5 Ready-handed, quick-handed.
————d, *s.f.ind.* Ready-handedness, dexterity. 2 Thievishness. 3 Covetousness. 4 Knack. 5**Legerdemain.
luath-long, -luinge, *s.f.* Cutter, see p. 78. 2 Any fast-sailing ship.

luath-mharc,** *s.m.* Racehorse. 2 Swift horse.
————achd,** *s.f.* Swift riding, riding express.
————air, -ean, *s.m.* Rapid rider. 2 Express.
luath-mhire,** *s.f.* Gasconading, vaunting.
luathrachadh, -aidh, *s.m. & pr. pt.* see luathachadh.
luathrachd,** *s.f.* Forwardness. 2 Quickness.
luathraich, *v.a.* see luathaich.
————te, see luathaichte.
luaths, luaiths,†† *s.m.* Swiftness, speed.
luathsach,** -aiche, *a.* Allowing, permitting, allowable, admissible.
————, -aich, *s.m* Allowance.
luathsachadh, -aidh, *s.m.* Allowing, permitting, act of allowing, permission. Na tha Dia a' l. dhomh, *what God allows me;* am bheil thu a' l. dhomhsa seo a dheanamh ? *do you allow, or advise, me to do this ?* A' l—, *pr. pt.* of luathsaich.
luathsachail,** *a.* That may be permitted.
luathsachd, -an, *s. f.* Permission, leave. 2 Admission. 3 Allowance.
luathsaich, *pr.pt.* a' luathsachadh, *v.a.* Permit, allow, give leave. 2 Confer. An l. thusa dhomhsa ? *do you permit me ?* l. Dia clann da, *God ordained that he should have offspring.*
luathsaichte, *past pt.* of luathsaich.
luath-shiùbhlach, -aiche, *a.* That goeth fast, swift, fleeting.
———— ————d, *s.f.ind.* Swiftness, fleetness.
lùb, lùib, -an, *s.f.* Bend, curvature. 2 Bending of the shore, creek. 3 Loop, noose. 4** Tache. 5 Eddying, as of wind. 6 Winding, meandering. 7 Maze. 8 Snare. 9 Deceit, guile. 10 Young man or woman. †11 (AF) Wolf. 12(AC)Beam. 13‡‡Plait, fold. 14‡‡Cunning,craft. 15**Flexibleness. 16**Inclination, tendency. 17**Bow. 18**Thong. 19 Iron loop at middle or end of swingle-tree, (No. 18, p. 263.) A lùb eibhinn ! *thou beauteous beam !* sop an lùib gach làimh, *a wisp grasped in every hand ;* is cruaidh fhortan gun fhios a chuir mis' an lùib do ghaoil, *it was bad luck unrecognized that involved me in the toils of your love—Carmina Gadelica* ; 'na lùib, *in its fold* ; an lùib an Domhnuich, *in contact with the Sabbath—Dàin I. Ghobha ;* an luib, *under the influence of ;* Caothan nan lùban uaine, *green-winding Caothan ;* tre lùbaibh cam, *through crooked windings.*
lùb, *pr.pt.* a' lùbadh, *v.a. & n.* Bend, incline. 2 Humble, subdue. 3 Yield, consent. 4 Stoop, bow. 5 Meander. 6**Assert. 7 Be deceived by. 8 Submit. L. an t-slat, *bend the switch;* lùb i leis, *she yielded to him ;* darag nach lùb, *an oak that will not bend ;* lùb Fillean a bhogha, *F. bent his bow.*
lud, -uid, -an, *s.* Pudding. Luba dudha, *black puddings.*
†lub, *s.* Roe—*Sàr-Obair.*
lub,†† -uib, *s.m.* Pool, dub.
luba,* *s.f.* Dub, marsh, pool.
lubach, *s.* see lobadh.
lùbach, -aiche, -aichean, *s.f.* Loop, noose. 2 Hinge. 3**Loop-hole. 4 Loop of iron on a swingle-tree, see No. 18, p. 263.
————, -aiche, *a.* Deceitful. 2*Meandering. 3 Eddying. 4††Twisted, tortuous. 5**Bending, bowing. 6** Flexible, pliant. 7 Crooked, winding. 8 Cringing. 9 Crafty. 10 Perverse. 11 Angular. L. 'na theangaidh, *perverse in his tongue ;* slatag l., *a pliant switch ;* gu l., *pliantly, craftily ;* l., carach mar bu dual, *deceitful and shifty as his nature was.*
————,* *a.* Marshy, full of pools.
lùbachas,(MS) *s.m.* Artifice.
lubachd, *s.f.ind.* Anfractiousness.
lùbadair,** *s.* see lùbair.
lùbadh, -aidh, *s.m.* Act or state of bending,bowing or inclining. 2 Winding, meandering. 3 Yielding, act of yielding, consenting. 4 Plaiting, folding. A' l—, *pr. pt.* of lùb. Tha 'n abhuinn a' l., *the river meanders ;* cha d' rinn mi leat l., *I did not yield to thee.*
lùbag, -aig, -an, *s. f. dim.* of lùb. Little bend, bow or curvature. 2 Little loop. 3 Curved stake used in constructing booths. 4 Hank of yarn. 5 Little twist or meander. 6 Eyelet, little loop-hole. 7** Tenter. 8 (DU) Iron staple. Lùbag cas-laoigh, *a half-hitch knot.*
————ach, -aiche, *a.* Abounding in small bends, curvatures or windings.
lùbaidh, *fut.aff.a.* of lùb.
lùbair, -ean, *s.m.* One who bends to every purpose, cunning, crafty fellow. 2**Bender. 3 **Cringer.
lubair, *pr.pt.* a' lubairt, see lobair.
lùbairneach, -ich, *s.m.* Clumsy, ill-formed man.
lubairt, *s.f. & pr.pt.* of lubair, see lobairt.
lùban, -ain, -an, *s.m. dim.* of lùb. Same meanings as lùbag.
lùban, *n.pl.* of lùb.
lùbarsaich,* *s.f.ind.* Contortion, serpentine motion, as of eels.
lùb-charach,(MS) *a.* Amusing.
lùb-cheangail, lùib-, -an-ceangail, *s. m.* Hinge. 2 Snare, trap.
lùb-chleasachd, *s.f.ind.* Legerdemain.
lùb-dhubh, *s.f.* Black pudding.
lubh,** *s.* Archangel.
†lubha,** *s.m.* Body, corpse. 2 Praise, fame.
†lubhan, -ain, *s.m.* Lamb.
†lubh-ghort, -ghoirt, *s.m.* Garden.
lubhra, *s.f.ind.* see luibhre.
————ch, -aiche, *a.* see lobhrach.
lùb-lìn,** *s.f.* Curved line.
————each,** *a.* Curvilinear.
lùb-mhurain, *s. f.* Rope of grass, plaited or woven in horse-collar.
lùb-ruith, -ùib-ruith, -an-ruith, *s.f.* Running noose or knot.
lùb-shruth, -a, -an, *s. m.* Winding or meandering stream.
————ach, -aiche, *a.* Abounding in meandering streams.
lùbta, *past.pt.* of lùb. Bent, made crooked,made to yield.
lucas,(CR) -ais, *s.m.* Lugworm, worm found in sand and used as bait for small lines—*W. of Ross-shire.*
luch, -a &-ainn, *pl.* -an & -aidh, *s. f.* Mouse. 2 *rarely* Prisoner. Peasair-nan-luch *or* peasair-luch, *vetches.* [** gives *s.m.*]
————ach, -aiche, *a.* see luchagach.
lucha fairge,¶ *s.f.* Storm petrel, see luaireag.
luchag, -aig, -an, *s.f.dim.* of luch. Mouse, little mouse.
————ach, -aiche, *a.* Abounding in mice.
———— -fheòir, *s.f.* Field mouse, harvest mouse.
luchaidh, *n. pl.* of luch. 2 (MM)*s.f. dim.* of luch.
———— -fhairge,** *s.coll.* Stormy petrels, *pl.* of luch-fairge.
luchainn, *n. pl.* of luch.
lùchair,** *s.f.* Glittering colour. 2 Brightness. 3 Gleaming, glistering.
luchaire,** *s.m.* Mouser.
lùchairt, -e, -ean, *s. f.* Palace. 2 Castle. 3** Court. 4**Fort. 5** Retinue. Ionad-lùchairte am measg nan Gàidheal, *the place of retinue among the Gael ;* mar chrannaibh lùchairte, *like the bars of a castle.*

lùchairteach, -eiche, *a.* Having palaces, courts, forts, or castles.
lùchar,** -air, *s.m.* Light.
lucharan,(MS) *s.m.* Pigmy.
———anach, see luch-àrmunnach.
luch-àrmunn, -uinn, -an, *s.m.* Pigmy, dwarf.
—————ach, *a.* Like, or pertaining to, a dwarf or pigmy.
†luchbrac, *s.m.* White head of hair.
luchd, -a, -an, *s.m.* [*f.* in *Badenoch.*] Burden, load. 2 Cargo, ship's cargo. 3***rarely* Kettle, cauldron. L. an t-soithich, *the cargo of the cargo-boat*; l.-luing, *a ship-load, cargo*; l.-cartach, *a cart-load.*
luchd, *s.* People, folks, company. Used instead of *fir*, when the reference may be to women as well as men.
l.-a'-chridhe-cheirt, *the just.*
l.-ainneirt, see l.-fòirneirt.
l.-àirde, *attendants, retinue.*
l.-aideachaidh, *professors, those that profess religion or devotion.*
l.-àiteachaidh, *inhabitants*; *2 husbandmen.*
l.-aithris, *talebearers.*
l.-aithris-sgeòil, see l.-aithris.
l.-àitich, see l.-àiteachaidh.
l.-amharc, *spectators, lookers-on.*
l.-amharc-thairis, *superintendents, overseers.*
l.-anacainnt, *evil speakers*; *2 backbiters*; *3 reproachful persons.*
l.-an-fhuar-chràbhaidh, *hypocrites*; *2 superstitious persons.*
l.-bleith, *grinders.*
l.-brath, *betrayers, spies, traitors.*
l.-brathaidh, see l.-brath.
l.-buain, *reapers.*
l.-buainidh, see l.-buain.
l.-buanaidh, see l.-buain.
l.-cagarsaich, *whisperers.*
l.-càineadh, see l.-càinidh.
l.-càinidh, *slanderers.*
l.-calcaidh, *caulkers.*
l.-casaid, *accusers, complainers.*
l.-ceannairc, *traitors, rebels.*
l.-ceart-dheuchainn, *jury.*
l.-cèirde, *artificers, craftsmen, mechanics.*
l.-coimheadachd, see l.-coimhideachd.
l.-coimhid, *keepers, watchmen, guard*; *2 observers. 3 attendants.*
l.-coimhideachd, *attendants, servants-in-waiting, retinue*; *2 overseers.*
l.-comhairle, *advisers, counsellors.*
l.-comh-pàirt, *partakers, sharers.*
l.-comh-thuruis, *fellow-travellers.*
l.-creachainn, *abactors.*
l.-creich, *abactors.*
l.-cumaidh, *formers, contrivers, devisers, projectors.*
l.-cumhaidh, *mourners.*
l.-cur-spioradan-fo-gheasaibh, *exorcists.*
l.-dàimh, *kindred.*
l.-dèanamh, *workers.*
l.-deuchainn, *jury.*
l.-dìon, *watchmen.*
l.-droch-bheart, *evil doers.*
l.-droch-bheus, *evil doers.*
l.-eagail, *timid* or *fearful persons.*
l.-ealadhain, see l.-ealain.
l.-ealaidh, *skilful persons*; *2 musicians*; *3 gay or merry persons.*
l.-èalaidh, *hunters, deerstalkers, sportsmen.*
l.-ealain, *carpenters*; *2 artisans*; *3 skilled persons of all kinds.*
l.-éisdeachd, *hearers.*
l.-eithich, *perjurers.*
l.-eòlais, *acquaintances.*
l.-eucoir, *unjust people*; *oppressors.*
l.-easaontais, *transgressors.*
l.-faire, *watchmen, the watch.*
l.-fairge, *seafaring men, mariners.*
l.-fàisneachd, *soothsayers, augurs.*
l.-feall-fholach, *ambuscade, liers in ambush* or *in wait.*
l.-fiach, *debtors.*
l.-fianuis, *witnesses.*
l.-fiosachd, *augurs, soothsayers, wizards.*
l.-foireigin, *extortioners, oppressors.*
l.-foireignidh, see l.-foireigin.
l.-fòirneirt, *oppressors.*
l.-freachd,(AC) *breakers.*
l.-frithealaidh, *attendants.*
l.-gaoil, *lovers*; *2 beloved persons*; *3 relations.*
l.-gearraidh, *hewers, cutters.* L. fiodha, *hewers of wood.*
l.-gleidhidh, *keepers.*
l.-iodhal-aoraidh, *idolaters.*
l.-iomain, *drivers, as of herds* or *flocks.*
l.-iomchair, *bearers.*
l.-làmhachais, *artillery*; *2 bowmen*; *3 slingers.*
l.-làstain, *impudent, petulant, proud* or *haughty people.*
l.-leanmhuinn, *followers*; *2 imitators, devotees*; *3 persecutors*; *4 pursuers.*
l.-loingeas, *sea-faring men, sailors.*
l.-malairt, *traders, merchants, exchangers, barterers.* L. an airgid, *money-changers.*
l.-millidh, *spoilers, destroyers, plunderers.*
l.-mi-ruin, *malicious persons, haters.*
l.-muinntir, *servants, the servants of an establishment* or *family.*
l.-munaidh, *teachers, instructors.*
l.-na-comh-fhéisde, *fellow guests*, (comh-luchd-na-féisde is better.)
l.-na-h-aingidheachd, *the wicked.*
l.-na-h-ainneirt, *violent persons.*
l.-ràiteachais, *boasters.*
l.-reubainn, *robbers.*
l.-riaghlaidh, *rulers, officers, overseers.*
l.-sanais, *scouts, spies, informers, watchers.*
l.-saobh-chreidimh, *sect, superstitious persons*; *2 heretics.*
l.-seinn, *singers.*
l.-sgeòil, *tale-tellers, raisers of false reports.*
l.-sgleò, *tattlers.*
l.-shaighead, *archers.*
l.-snaidhidh, *hewers of stone.*
l.-snathaidh, see l.-snaidhidh.
l.-stiùraidh, *leaders, directors.*
l.-tagraidh, *pleaders*; *2 accusers*; *3 creditors.*
l.-tàir, *reproachers.*
l.-taigheadais, *housekeepers.*
l.-taimhlis, *mockers.*
l.-tarcuis, *despiteful persons*; *2 despisers.*
l.-tiolpaidh, *cavillers*; *2 purloiners, pilferers.*
l.-togail, *builders*; *thieves, robbers*; *2 collectors, gatherers.* Luchd-togail na cìse, *tax-gatherers*; luchd-togail-sgeòil, *raisers of false reports.*
l.-triall, *travellers.*
l.-triallaidh, see luchd-triall.
l.-tuaileis, *slanderers, quarrelsome persons.*
l.-tuairgnidh, *faction.*
l.-turuis, *travellers.*
l.-urrais, *sureties.*
luchdach, -aiche, *a.* Heavy, ponderous, weighty. 2 Heavy laden. 3 Loading, that loads or makes heavy, burdening, freighting.
————adh, -aidh, *s.m.* Loading, lading, freighting, act of loading or burdening. A' l—, *pr. pt.* of luchdaich.
luchdaich, *pr. pt.* a' luchdachadh, *v. a.* Load, lade, burden. Dì-luchdaich, *discharge, as a cargo.*
————te, *past pt.* Laden, burdened, filled.

Luchdaichte le h-aingidheachd, *laden with iniquity.*
luchdail, -e, *a.* see luchdmhor.
luchdair,** *s.m.* Freighter.
luchdmhoire, *comp.* of luchdmhor.
——————achd, *s.f.ind.* Capaciousness.
luchdmhor, -oire, *a.* Capacious, capable of containing much. 2 Laden, heavily laden. 3 Full, bulky. 4 Burdening, burdensome.
luch-fhairge,‡‡ *s.f.* Storm petrel, see luaireag.
luch-fheòir,‡‡ *s.f.* Grass-mouse, common shrew.
luch-Fhrangach,(AF) *s.f.* Rat.
luch-Ghallda,(AF) *s.f.* Mole.
luch-lann, -lainn, *s.m.* Prison.
lù-chleas, -ais, *s.m.* see lùth-chleas.
————achd, see lùth-chleasachd.
luch-léin, see loch-bhléin
luch-mhór, (AF) *s.f* Seal. (AF gives luch-mór.)
luch-shìth, (AC) *s.f.* Fairy mouse, lesser shrew.
lùchuirt, -ean, see lùchairt.
†**lud**, *s.m.* Pond.
lùdach, -aich, *pl*, -aich & -aichean, *s.m.* Hinge.
lùdag, -aig, -an, *s.f.* The little finger. 2 Hinge. 3 Little hinge. 4 Joint. Màthair na lùdaig, *the ring-finger.*
——ach, -aiche, *a.* Supplied with little fingers or hinges.
——an, -ain, -an, *s.m.* Hinge, little hinge. 2 Pivot of a hinge. 3**The little finger. 4(MS) The little-finger joint.
lùdaichean, *n. pl.* of ludach.
ludair, *pr.pt.* a' ludairt, *v. a.* see luidir.
ludair, -ean, *s.m.* Slovenly person, trull. 2 One of an awkward gait. 3 Boor. 4**Fawning.
———eachd, *s.f.* see luidearachd
ludairt, *s. f.* Wallowing, &c. 2 Waddling in mire, as ducks. A' l—, *pr.pt.* of ludair.
lùdalann, see lùdan.
ludan, -ain, -an, *s.m.* Pool.
lùdan, -ain, -an, *s.m.* Hinge. 2** The little finger.
———ach, *a.* Having hinges. 2 Like a hinge. 3 Jointed.
ludar, *s.* see ludair.
ludar,(MS) *s.m.* Hind. 2 Lob.
———ach, *a.* see luidearach.
———achd, see luidearachd.
ludarnachd, *s.f.* see luidearachd.
ludarra,* *a.* see luidearra. 2‡‡Unwieldy.
ludarsaich,(MS) *s.f.* Clumsiness.
†**ludasach**,** *a.* Strong, powerful.
ludh, *s.m.* Way, manner. 2 Appearance. 3** Likeness. L. an spioraid, 'dol timchioll na drochaid, *the way of the ghost, going round the bridge.* MacIntosh's translation of this, given by Armstrong, is " go about the bridge as the ghost did." The superstition here referred to is illustrated in *Tam o' Shanter*, where the infernal pursuers have no power to go beyond the keystone of the bridge ; thachair ludh an uinnsinn fhiadhaich dha, cinnidh e gu math, ach millidh e a' chraobh a bhios an taice ris, *the way of the wild ash befel him, it grows well but kills the tree that's near it*— N.G.P.
lùdhaig, *pr.pt.* a' lùdhaig & a' lùdhaigeadh, *v.* Gaelic spelling of *allow.* 2‡‡Appoint. 3 *Loch Tay* for lùig.
——, *pr.pt.* of lùdhaig, see lùdhaigeadh.
lùdhaigeadh, *s. m.* Allowing, permitting. 2‡‡ Appointing. A' l—, *pr.pt.* of lùdhaig.
lùdhaigte, *past pt.* of lùdhaig. Allowed, permitted. 2 Appointed.
lùdhainn, *prov.* for lùdhaig.
lùdhainneachadh, -aidh, see lùdhaigeadh.
ludhainnich, *v a. prov.* for lùdhaig.
ludhar,** *a.* Awkward, clownish, slovenly.
lùdnan, see lùdan.
lùdnanach, *a.* see lùdanach.
ludradh, -aidh, *s.m.* & *pr.pt.* see ludraigeadh.
ludragan, -ain, -an, *s. m.* Slattern. 2 Shambling fellow, one who moves awkwardly. 3 Untidy person, sloven. 4 Heavy, dull person. 5 Groveller.
————ach, -aiche, *a.* Shambling, moving awkwardly. 2 Untidy, slovenly. 3 Grovelling.
ludraig, *pr.pt.* a' ludraigeadh, *v. a.* Bespatter with, dip or roll in foul water.
ludraigeadh, -eidh, *s. m.* Bespattering, act of bespattering with foul water. A' l—, *pr. pt.* of ludraig.
lùg, *s.m.* see liùg.
luga,* *s.f.ind.* Sea sandworm.
lugach, -aiche, see liùgach.
lùgachd, *s.* see liùgachd.
lugadh, -aidh, *s.m.* Thirst.
lugaidh, *s.f.* (DC)Lugworm—*Uist.* 2**Little ansated wooden dish. (" Luggie," so called from its ears or " lugs.")
lùgan, -ain, -an, *s.m.* Short, crooked, deformed imbecile person. 2 Sorry looking fellow. 3 Bow-legged man.
lùganach, -aiche, see liùgach.
lùganachd, *s.f.* see liùgachd.
lugas, -ais, *s.m.* Sandworm, lobworm—*Gairloch, Lochbroom, &c.*, see lucas.
lùg-chas, -ois, -an, *s.f.* Bandy leg.
—————ach,(MS) -aiche, *a.* Bandy-legged.
lùgh, lùigh, *s.m.* see lùth.
lùgh, *pr.pt.* a' lùghadh, *v.* Swear, blaspheme.
lùgha, see lùghadh.
lugha, *comp.* of beag. Less, least. 2 More or most disagreeable. 3 (DC) Used as the positive degree in *Uist*, as, tha e cho lugha-miobhaidh, *he it so well-behaved.* Is l. orm thu na sneachd, *you are more distasteful to me than snow* ; cha l. na amadan a ni sin, *no less than a fool will do that* ; bithidh fodar gann na 's l. na thig frasan matha, *fodder will be scarce, unless good showers come* ; cha'n urrainn da a faicinn, agus móran na's l. na sin, cha'n urrainn da a cluinntinn, *he cannot see her, much less can he hear her* ; air a' chuid a's l., *at the least* ; am fear a's l. de 'n triùir, *the least of the three.*
lughach, *a.* see laghach.
lùghachadh, -aidh, *s.m.* Swearing.
lùghachan, *n. pl.* of lughadh.
lughad, -aid, *s.f.* Littleness, degree of littleness. Air a l., *however little it may be.* [** gives *m.*]
lughadachd, *s.f.* Inferiority.
lughadaich, see lughdaich.
lùghadh, -aidh, *pl.* lùghachan, *s.m.* Swearing, blasphemy, act of swearing. Oath. 3**Want. 4**Thirst. A' l—, *pr. pt.* of lùgh. A' l. na Trianaid, *blaspheming the Trinity.*
lùghadh, see lùth.
lughadachadh, -aidh, *s.m.* Lessening, diminishing, act of lessening, assuaging. A' l—, *pr.pt.* of lughdaich.
lùghadair,* *s.m.* Blasphemer.
————eachd, *s.f.ind.* Blasphemy, especially taking the name of the Deity in vain. Ri l., *blaspheming.*
lughadrach,* -aiche, *a.* Blasphemous.
lughaich, see ludhaig.
lughaide,* *comp.* of beag. Cha l. e sin, *it is not the less for that* ; cha lughaide, *perhaps.*
lughaig, *v.a.* see ludhaig.
lughaigeadh, see ludhaigeadh.
lùghar, see lùthmhor.
lugharr, see lùthmhor.
————achd, see luthmhoireachd.
lughasachadh, see luathsachadh.

lughasaich, see luathsaich.
lughchleas, see lùth-chleas.
———**achd**, see lùth-chleasachd.
lughdachadh,** -aidh, *s.m.* Diminishing, abating, dimution, subtraction, decrease, abatement, decreasing. A' l—, *pr.pt.* of lughdaich.
lughdachail, -e, *a.* Diminishing.
lughdachd, *s.f.ind.* Minority.
lughdag, see lùdag.
———**an**, see lùdagan.
lughdaich, *pr. pt.* a' lughdachadh, *v. a. & n.* Lessen, diminish, abate, decrease, assuage, mitigate. 2 Allay. 3(MS) Abstract. 4*Subtract. 5*Undervalue.
———**e**, -an, *s.m.* Abater, one who lessens or diminishes.
———**te**, *past pt.* of lughdaich. Lessened, diminished, abated, assuaged.
lughdaireachd, *s.f.ind.* Diminishing, lessening, abatement. 2 Disparagement.
lughdalan,* see lùdagan.
lughdarna, } *a.* Heavy, clumsy, unwieldy. 2
lughdarra, } Stupid.
lughdarnachd,* *s.f.* Clumsiness. 2 Drawling, unseemly gait. 3 Untidiness.
lùghmhoire, *comp.* of lùghmhor.
lùghmhoireachd, *s.f.* see lùthmhoireachd.
lùghmhor, -oire, see lùthmhor.
lùghor, see lùthmhor.
lùib, -e, -ean, *s.f.* Fold, corner, angle, angular turning, winding or bend, as of a stream. 2 Eddy, as of wind. 3 Little glen. 4 Creek, bay, bending of the shore. 4 see lùb.
lùibeach, -eiche, *a.* Abounding in folds, angles, or turns, flexuous. 2 Full of little glens, or 3 of creeks. 4 see lùbach.
lùibean, -ein, -an, *s.m.* Crafty fellow, one who will bend to any purpose.
lùibeanachd,‡‡ *s.f.ind.* Craftiness, cunning.
luibh, -ean, *s.m.* & *f.* Herb, plant. 2 Weed. 3 Grass.
luibh-a'-chait,§ *s. m.* Cudweed, everlasting,—*gnaphalium dioicum & g. sylvaticum.*
luibh-a'-chneas, *s. m.* Queen-of-the-meadow—*Colonsay.*
luibh-an-ìthe, *s.* Lettuce, see liatas.
luibh-an-ladhair, *s.f.* Cleaver.
luibh-an-liùgair, -ean-, *s.m.* Common loveage—*ligusticum officinale.*
luibh-bheann,§ *s.* The hill plant, see machall-monaidh.
luibh-bhiast, -bhéist,-bhéistean,*s.m.*Caterpillar.
luibh-bhiastach, -aiche, *a.* Abounding in caterpillars.
luibh-Chaluim-Chille, *s.m.* Bog asphodel—*Colonsay.*
luibh-chridhe, *s.f.* Heart's ease. Is l. leam fhéin e, *it's heart's-ease to myself.*
luibh-chrudh-an-eich, *s.f.* Aurora.
luibh-do-labhairt,‡ *s.* Bitter-sweet,—*solanum dulcamara.*
luibhe,(MS) *s.* Bosvel.
luibheach, -eiche, *a.* Abounding in herbs, weeds or plants, herbal, botanical. Gàraidh luibheach, *a botanical garden* ; *a garden full of weeds.*
luibheadair,* *s.m.* Herbalist, botanist.
luibhean, -ein, -an, *s.m.dim* of luibh. Little herb or plant. 2 Blade of grass.
luibheanach, aiche, *a.* Full of little herbs or plants, herbal, botanic, vegetable.
luibheanach, -aich, -aichean, *s. m.* Herbalist, botanist. 2 Weeder. 3 Weeds, noxious weeds. 4 Herbage.
luibheanachd, *s.f.ind.* Botany, study of botany. 2 Herbage.
luibhean-diolan, *s.m.* Queen-of-the-meadow.
luibheannach, see luibheanach.
luibh-eòlach, -aiche, *a.* Skilled in botany. 2 Skilled in the virtues of herbs.
luibh-eòlas, -eòlais, *s.m.* Botany, knowledge of plants and herbs.
luibh-ghort,** *s. m.* Garden. 2 Green-garden, kitchen-garden.
luibh-leighis, *s.m.* Camomile, —*anthemis nobilis.*

435. *Luibh-leighis.*

luibh-na-cabhruich, *s.m.* Cleavers—*Colonsay.*
luibh-loibheach, -ich, see lus-loibheach.
luibh-na-luaithre,** *s.m.* Ash-weed.
luibh-na-maclan, *s.m.* Herb Robert—*Colonsay.*
luibh-na-macraidh,* *s.m.* Wild thyme.
luibh-nan-tri-bheann, *s.m.* Bog-bean—*Colonsay.* 2**Trefoil.
luibh-nan-tri-bhilean, *s.m.* Trefoil.
luibhne,** *s.f.* Dart, spear. 2 Shield. 3 The fingers. 4 The toes.
luibhneach, -eiche, *a.* see luibheach & luibheanach.
———,** -ich, *s.m.* Weed.
luibhre,‖ *s.f.ind.* Leprosy.
luibhreachd, *s.f.ind.* Leprousness.
luibh-reicear, -ir, -an, *s.m.* Seller of herbs.
luibh-sgàile, -ean-sgàile, *s.f.* Gourd.
lùibte, see lùbta.
luich, (*rarely*) *gen.* of loch.
luid, *gen.sing. & n.pl.* of lod.
luid, -e, -ean, *s.f.* Rag. 2 Drudge. 3 Slovenly or filthy person.
luideach, -eiche, *a.* Ragged. 2 Slovenly, untidy. 3 Filthy. 4 Having long shaggy hair (of animals.) 5 Bumpkinly.
luideag, -eig, -an, *s.f. dim.* of luid. Rag, little rag. 2 Slovenly woman, little slut, little slattern. 3 ** *in ridicule*, Bank-note.
luideagach, -aiche, *a.* Ragged, tattered. 2 Slovenly. Is mairg a bheireadh droch mheas air gille l. is air loth pheallagaich, *a ragged boy and a shaggy filly should never be despised*—the latter part of this proverb is often applied to a shabbily dressed young girl.
luideagan, *s.m.* Tailor's cabbage (not a plant,) refuse.
luidealach, -aich, *s.m.* Lazy fellow. 2 Slovenly lounger. 3 Bumpkin. 4 Dabbler. 5 Ploughman. 6 Ragged person. 7 Shaggy beast.
lùidean,** -ein, *s.m.* The little finger.
luidearach, -aiche, *a.* Slovenly. 2 Sluggish. 3 Wallowing, grovelling.
luidearachd, *s.f.ind.* Laziness, indolence. 2 Slovenliness. 3 Slovenly mode of walking.

luidearra, -eire, *a.* Sluggish, indolent. 2 Heavy. 3 Clumsy. 4 Boorish.
luidh, see luigh.
†**luidh**, ** *s.m.* Word of endearment. (luaidh.)
luidh, -e, -ean, *s.m. & f.* see luibh.
luidhean, -ein, *s.m.* Fetlock.
luidhear, -eir & -e, *pl.* -eirean, *s. m.* Chimney-vent, flue.
luidhearach, *a.* Chimneyed.
luidh-leabaidh, *s.m.* Lullaby. (for laoidh-leabaidh.)
luidich,(MS) *v.a.* Bemoil.
luidir, see luidreagan.
luidir, *pr.pt.* a' luidreadh, *v. a. & n.* Wallow, roll in mud or mire. 2 Paddle or wade through water or mud, dabble 3**Flounder, wallop. 4 Besmear. 5‡‡Lumber more heavily. 6 Bedraggle.
luidireach, see luidreach.
luidireachd,** *s.f.* Awkwardness.
luidneach, -eiche, *a.* Drenched, drooping or heavy, as flowers or herbage after rain.
luidreach,** *a.* Wallowing. 2 Walloping. 3 Paddling. 4 Guddling.
luidreach,* *s f.* Ragged garment. 2 Ragged clumsy person.
luidreadh, -eidh, *s.m.* Wallowing, act of wallowing. 2 Paddling, wading or walking clumsily through water or mud. 3 Floundering. 4 Guddling. 5*Besmearing. A' l—, *pr. pt.* of luidir.
luidreagan, -ain, *s.m.* Ragged fellow.
luidrich, *v.* see luidir.
luidrig, *v.* see luidir.
luidse, -an, *s.m.* Clumsy fellow. 2 Booby. 3 Churl. 4 Coward. 5*Dull, stupid person.
luidseach, -eiche,; *a.* Clumsy, awkward. 2 Boobyish, like a booby. 3 ††Cowardly. 4 Heavy-heeled.
luidseachd, *s. f. ind.* Clumsiness, awkwardness. 2 Silliness, sheepishness.
luidsear, -ir, -an, see luidse.
luidsearachd,†† *s.f.* Cowardliness.
lùig*(CR) *v.n.* Desire, long, wish—*Perthshire.* At *Loch Tay* " ludhaig air " is used in the sense of to wish to or on one.
luig, *gen.sing.* of lag. Chun an luig, *towards the hollow.*
lùigean, -ein, -an, *s. m.* Weakling. 2 Inactive fellow. 3**Untidy fellow. 4 Silly person.
lùigeanach, -aiche, *a.* Weakly, silly. 2 Inactive. 3 Untidy.
lùigeanachd, *s.f.ind.* Weakness, silliness. 2** Untidiness. 2**Inactivity.
luigh, -e, -ean, *s.* see luibh.
luigh, *pr. pt.* a' luighe, *v. n.* Lie, lie down, recline, couch. 2 Light, perch, settle, as a bird. 3 Subside, as the wind. 4 Set, as the sun. 5 Settle, lie upon, press upon, affect. 6 Urge, importune. Luigh chuige, *heave to* or *lie to, as a boat ;* l. mi teann air, *I lay near him ;* l. an iolair air bàrr an teach, *the eagle perched on the top of the dwelling ;* chaidh e a l., *he went to bed ;* l. an cù, *the dog couched ;* l. e air an làr, *he stretched himself on the ground ;* l. i leis oirnn, *she (the boat) stretched to leeward of us;* l. e orm gus an d' thug e orm a dheanamh, *he importuned me till he made me do it ;* l. a' ghrian, *the sun set ;* l. a' ghaoth, *the wind subsided.*
luighe, *s.m.& f.* Lying, act of lying, reclining. 2 Subsiding, as of wind. 3 Act of setting, as of the sun. 4 Act or state of settling upon. 5 **Situation. 6**Incubation. 7**Death. 8 Tack or stretch, as of a ship. 9 Perching, as a bird. A' l—, *pr. pt.* of luighe. A' ghrian air l., *the sunset* (luighe na grèine) ; tha e 'na l., *he is in bed.*
luigheach, -eiche, *a.* Lazy, indolent.
luigheachd, *s.f.* Gratification. 2 Gratuity.
luigheachan, -ain, *pl.* -an, [**-ain,] *s. m.* Ambush, ambuscade, snare.
luigheachanach,** -aich, *s.m.* One who lies in wait.
luigheag, see fuigheag.
luigheagan, -ain, -an, *s.m.* Lying down, reclining. 2 Couch.
luigheaganach, -aiche, *a.* Inclined to lie down.
luighe-siubhladh, -aidh, *s.m.* Child-bed, parturition.
luighinn, *1st. sing. past subj.* of luidh, I would lie.
luighse, (for luigh thusa) Lie thou.
luigh,** *v.a.* Tear. 2 Encourage, abet.
luighe, ** *s.f.* Proof. 2 Cauldron, kettle.
luigheachd, -an, *s.f.* Reward, recompense, requital. Thoir l., *reward, requite.*
luigheachdaich,** *v.a.* Requite, recompense.
luigheadair, see luibheadair.
luighean,** -ein, *s.m.* Nave. 2 Centre.
luighean,‡ *s. m.* Tendon. 2 Ankle. 3 Foot 4 Leg, as of a deer.
———**ach**, see luibheanach.
luighearnach, see luibheanach.
luigheasach, -aich, *s.m.* see luathsachadh. Allowance, permission.
luigheasach, -aiche, *a.* see luathsach. 2 Allowing, permitting, that permits.
luigheasachd, see luathsachd.
luigheasaich, *v.a.* see luathsaich. 2 Reward.
lùighich,(MS) *v.a.* Defray.
luighig, *v.* see luathsaich.
luighigeadh, -eidh, *s.m. & pr.pt.* see luathsachadh.
luighne,** *s.pl.* Javelins, spears.
luilgeach, *s.f.* Milch-cow.
luim, *gen.sing.* of lom.
luim, -ean, *s.m.* Shift, means, art, invention. 2 Remedy. Leig 'ga l. féin e, *leave him to his own resources.*
luim,(AF) -e, *s.f.* Milk.
†**luim-dheirg**,** *s.* Deep. 2 Deep water. Deep channel of a river. 4 Abyss. Bruach na l., *the verge of the deep.*
luime, *s.f.ind.* Barrenness, bleakness,bareness, nakedness. 2 Poverty. 3 Smoothness. 4** Bare or smooth part. Is i an luime a thug air a dheanamh, *sheer poverty forced him to do it;* l. a mhuineil, *the smooth part of his neck.*
luime, *comp.* of lom. More or most bare.
luimead, -eid, *s.m.* Bareness, baldness, nakedness, degree of nakedness or barrenness. Air a l. 's gu'm bheil e, *however bare it be.*
luimean, -ein, -an, *s.m.* Barren hillock. 2 Poor man. 3 Miser. 4 Lean man. 5 Target, shield.
luimeanach, -aiche, *a.* Bleak, bare. 2 Abounding in bleak parts or hillocks.
luimeil,†† *a.* Shifty, artful.
luimlinn, *s.f.* Stream of milk.
luimneach, -eiche, *a.* Active. 2 Brave. 3 Swift, rapid. 4 Bare. 5††Barren. 6 Torn.
luimneach,** *s.m.* Ensign, standard-bearer.
luimneachd, *s.f.ind.* Bareness. 2 Bravery. 3 Activity, swiftness. 4 Excitation. 5†† Swift. 6**Ensign-bearer.
luimrig,(MS) *s.f.* Beach.
†**luin**, see luinn.
luing, *gen. sing.* of long.
luing-bhris,** *v.a. & n.* Cause shipwreck. 2 Suffer shipwreck.
luing-bhriseach, *a.* Causing shipwreck.
luing-bhriseadh, *s.m.* Shipwreck, act of suffering shipwreck.

luingeanachd,(MS) see luingearachd.
luingearachd, *s.f.ind.* Seamanship, navigation. 2 Sailing, yachting, cruising.
luingeas, -eis, *s.f.* see loingeas.
———ach, see loingeasach.
luingis, see loingeas.
luin-iasg.(AF) see luinn-iasg.
luingeasach,‡‡ -aiche, *a.* Naval, of ships. 2 Abounding in ships.
luingios, see luingeas.
luinn, *gen. sing. & n. pl.* of lonn.
†luinn, -e, *s.f.* Sword, spear. 2 Blade of a weapon. 3 Fingal's sword.
luinne, *comp.* of lonn.
†luinne, *s.f.* Anger, passion. 2 Impetuosity. 3 Mirth. 4 Melody.
luinneach, -aiche, *a.* Armed with sword or spear. 2 Brave, warlike. 3** Angry. 4 Mirthful, jovial. 5 Melodious. Leòmhann guineach, calma, luinneach, *a keen lion, stout and brave.*
luinneag, -eig, -an, *s.f.* Song, ditty. 2 Chorus. 3 Burden of a song. 4 Gaelic song or catch. 5 Bob. 6*Mournful voice or sound. L. luaidh, *a poetical panegyric.*
luinneagach, -aiche, *a.* Having many songs or ditties. 2 Musical. 3 Like a ditty. Merrily inclined, jovial, cheerful. 5 Having Gaelic songs or ditties.
luinneanach, -aiche, *a.* Tossing, floundering. 2 Paddling. 3 Frisking. 4 Skipping.
luinneanachadh, -aidh, *a.* Tossing, floundering 2 Paddling.
luinneanachd,* *s. f. ind.* Paddling. 2 Sailing. for pleasure about quays.
luinneanaich, *v a.* Flounder, paddle. 2 Wallop
luinneanaiche, *s.f.ind.* Continued tossing, paddling, walloping or floundering. 2 Habit of skipping or frisking.
luinnearaich, see luinneanaich.
luinneas, -eis, *s.m.* see loingeas.
luinn-iasg,** *s.m.* Sword-fish.
luinnirich, see luinneanaich.
luinnireachd, see luinneanachd.
luinnse, *s.m. & f.* see luinnsear.
luinnseach, -eiche, *a.* Sluggish, lazy.
luinnseach, -eich, -idhean, *s. m.* Watch-coat, heavy great-coat. 2 Heavy, clumsy article. 3* Very tall, slim, bowed-down fellow. 4 †† Lazy man, sluggard.
luinnsear, -eir, -an, *s.m.* Lounger, sluggard. 2 Lazy vagrant. 3 Watchman.
lùir,* *pr.pt.* a' luireadh, *v.a.* Torment, torture, give most acute pain. 2 Drub most lustily.
luirceach,(MS) *a.* Lame.
luircneach,** *a.* Lame.
luircneachd,** *s.f.* Lameness, limping.
luireach, *a.* Pretty—*Arran.* (lurach.)
lùireach, -ich, -ichean, *s.f.* Large cloak, covering. 2**Coat or covering of mail, harness. 3 Tattered or patched garment or covering. 4 Cast garment. 5 ** Apron. 6 *figuratively* Cowardly, mean-spirited person. 7††Untidy female. Càireadh gach fear a l., *let each prepare his mail ;* eadar altaibh na lùirich, *between the joints of the harness* ; l. mhàilleach, *a coat of mail, habergeon ;* l. leathair, *a leather apron.*
lùireadh, *pr.pt.* of lùir. Torturing, tormenting. 'Gam l., *tormenting me.*
luireag, see loireag.
luirg, *gen.sing.* of lorg.
luirg, -e, *pl.* -gne, -gean & -gnean, *s.f.* Shaft or tram of a cart. 2 Stalk of a plant. 3 see lurgann. L. an fheòir, *stalk of the grass ;* luirgne cath, *spurs.*
luirg-bheairt, *s. f.* Armour for the legs. 2 Covering for the legs.
luirgeann, -inn, *s.f.* see lurgann.
Luirgeann luath, *s. m.* Certain character in Highland romance.
luirgne, *pl.* of luirg.
luirgneach, -eiche, *a.* Long-legged. 2 Having a long handle or stalk. 3 Nimble, swift. 4 Sheep-shanked. Lus l., *a long-stalked weed.*
luirgneach,¶ -eich, *s.* Black-winged stilt—*himpantopus melanopterus.* Now very rare in Scottish Gaeldom, though it was to be found in many districts not so long ago, e. g. Glen Clova, in Forfarshire, and Ben Lawers in Perthshire. It was a rare bird in Glensheil in 1836.

436. Luirgneach.

luirgnean, *n.pl.* of luirg.
luirg-ruisgeach, -aiche, see luirg-rùisgte.
luirg-rùisgte, *a.* Bare-legged.
lùiriste, -an, *s.m.* Tall, slender, slovenly, untidy person.
lùiristeach, -eiche, *a.* Slovenly, untidy. 2 Shabby. 3 Paltry. 4 Lazy.
lùiristeachd, *s.f.ind.* Slovenliness, untidiness.
luis, *gen.sing. & n.pl.* of lus.
——,(CR) *s.coll.* Multitude of small objects, especially crawling insects—*W. of Ross.*
——,§ *s. f.* Mountain-ash or rowan-tree—*pyrus aucuparia.* [Badge of the MacLachlans.] 2**Quicken-tree, letter *l* of the Gaelic alphabet. 3** *rarely* Hand. 4 Drink.

437. Luis.

——,(CR) *s.m.* Outrush of water—*Perthshire.*
†——, *v.n.* Dare. 2 Adventure.
luis-bhalgair,§ *s. pl.* *Lycopodium clavatum, annotinum,* and the rest of that family of plants.
luisd,** *s.f.* Slouch.

luisean, -ein, -an, *s.m.* see lusan, *dim.*
——ach, -aiche, *a.* see lusanach.
——achd,** *s.f.* Vegetable.
luisgich,** *v.a. & n.* Soak.
luis-meiligeagach,§ *s. coll.* The order of plants called *leguminiferæ* or pod-bearers.
†luisne,** *s.f.* Flame, flash. 2 Blush. 3 Kind of beaten flax.
luisreadh, -eidh, *s.m.* Plain abounding in herbs or plants. 2 Superabundance, exuberance, as of herbs.
luisreag, -eig, -an, *s.f.* Plant. 2 Little plant or herb. 3 Female skilled in herbs, who knows the virtues of plants, or works cures with them, female botanist.
——ach, -aiche, *a.* Abounding in herbs. 2 Dealing in herbs. 3**Botanical.
luisrigeadh, -eidh, see luisreadh.
luiste, *s. m.* Slouch. 2 Sluggard. 3 Clown. 4 Straw pannel.
luithe,** *s.f.* see luaithead.
——ach,** *a.* Joyous.
lùitheach,** *s.pl.* Veins, sinews.
lùithreach, -ich, -richean, *s.m* [*f.*] see lùireach.
luitig, *s. f.* Bilge-water in a boat—*Lewis.*
lulagan, see laoighcionn.
lulaic,(AF) *s. f.* Milk of newly-calved cow.
lulgach,(AF) -aich, Newly-calved cow.
lum, *s.m.* The part of an oar between the handle and blade.
lumadheirg,** *s.f.* The deep. 2 Deep water. 3 Deep channel of a river.
luman, -ain, -an, *s. m.* Covering, coarse covering. 2 Plaid. 3 Veil. 4 Sackcloth. 5 Large great-coat. 6 Beating, dressing. [** gives *pl.* -ain.]
lumanach, -aiche, *a.* Having a covering, having a coarse covering, like sackcloth.
lumar, see lomar.
lumhair,(AF) *s.m.* Diver (bird.)
lumha-làn, see lom-làn.
lumhan, see lubhan. 2 Lamb.
lumpat, see lupaid.
lun, see lon.
Lùnasd, -aisd, see Lùnasdal.
Lùnasdal, -ail, *s.f.* Month of August. 2 First day of August. 3 MM says "a certain epoch only—not the month of August."
Lùnasdainn, -e, see Lùnasdal.
Lùnasdain, *Arran* for Lùnasdal.
lunasg,(AF) Sword-fish, see iasg-a'-chlaidheimh.
lund, see lunn.
lundach, -aiche, *a.* see lunndach.
lundair, -ean, *s.m.* see lunndair.
lundrainn,** *s.* Thrashing, see lunndraigeadh.
lung, see long.
lungach,(AF) *s.m.* Sandworm.
lunn, *v.* Penetrate—*Sàr-Obair.*
lunn, -uinn & -a, *pl.* -an, *s.m.* Middle part of an oar-handle. 2 Staff. 3 Churn-staff. 4 Wave, roller, heaving billow, heaver that does not break. 5 Bier. 6 Spoke. 7 Lever. 8** Bar. 9††Launching roller. 10‡‡ Staff, bar, bearer or pole of a bier or litter. 11**Bond. 12(AH) Mid-part of a boat. 13 (AH) Rolling of the sea in a calm. 14 Vessel.
lunnach, -aiche, *a.* Having handles, as oars. 2 Furnished with staves, poles, bearers, launching rollers, levers, &c. 3 Like a bar, staff, &c. Ràmhan min l., *smooth-handled oars.*
lunnach,** *s.m.* Active youth.
lunnadh,** -aidh, *s.m.* Invading, invasion. 2 Pressing on, or forward.
lunnaid,(CR) *s. f.* Pin of a cow-fetter—*W. of Ross.*
lùunair,(MS) *s.m.* Idler, lazy fellow.
lunn-charach, *a.* Heaving, rolling, applied to waves of the sea.
lunn-chas, *s.m.* Stretcher, footwaling of a boat, see bàta, G9, p. 73.
lunndach, -aiche, *a.* Idle, lazy. 2 Sauntering, loitering, lounging. 3**Sluggish. 4 Musty.
——d,* *s.f.ind.* Extreme indolence or laziness, lounging.
lunndair, -ean, *s.m.* Lazy, indolent person, sluggard, idler, drone.
——each,** *a.* Dilatory, indiligent.
——eachd, *s.f.* Laziness, idleness, sluggishness, resupination.
lunndan, (CR) *s. m.* Green, meadow, marshy ground—*Perthshire.*
lunndrachadh, -aidh, *s.m.& pr.pt.* of lunndraich, see lunndraigeadh.
lunndraich, see lunndraig.
lunndraig, *pr.pt.* a' lunndraigeadh, *v.a.* Thump, beat, strike, punish by striking. 2 Box. 3 Kick.
lunndraigeadh, -eidh, *s.m.* Beating, act of beating, striking, punishing with blows. 2 Boxing. 3 kicking. A' l—, *pr.pt.* of lunndraig.
lunndrainn, -ean, *s.m. prov.* for lunndraigeadh. [** gives *s.f.*]
lunntair, *pr.pt.* a' lunntairt, *v.a.* see lunndraig.
lunntairt, *pr.pt.* of lunntair, see lunndraigeadh.
lupach, see lopach.
lupaid, *s.f.* Pig, swine.
lupat, see lupaid.
lur, -a & -uir, *pl.* -uir, *s.m.* Delight, pleasure. 2*Gem, jewel, treasure. 3** Lovely object. Tha a luir ! *yes, my treasure, my dear !*
lur,** *a.* Beloved, lively, pretty.
lurach, -aiche, *a.* Lovely, pretty. 2 Neat. 3 Airy, nimble, lively. 4**Beloved. 5* Gem-like, jewel-like. 6 (DU) Loving, lovable. T' fhalt l., *thy lovely brown locks.*
lurachan, -ain, -an, *s. m.* The flower of ramps (garlic,) see gairgean.
lurachas, -ais, *s.f.* Loveliness, prettiness, neatness. 2 Airiness, nimbleness, liveliness.
luradair, -ean, *s.m.* Jeweller.
lurag, -aig, -an, *s.f.* Pretty female. 2 Beloved female, term of endearment.
luragach,‡‡ -aiche, *a.* Pretty, 2 Engaging, like a female.
luraichead, -eid, *s.f.* Loveliness, degree of loveliness, prettiness, degree of prettiness, neatness. 2 Airiness, degree of airiness. 3 Nimbleness, liveliness.
luraicheas, see luraichead.
luramachd, *W. Ross & Suth'd* for lomnochd.
luramadh, *Badenoch* for lomradh.
luran, -ain, -an, *s.m.* Pretty youth or boy. 2 Beloved youth or boy, term of endearment. [** gives *n.pl.* lurain.]
——ach, -aiche, *a.* Comely, as a smart youth or boy. 2 Gallant. 3 Fond.
——ach, -aich, *s.m.* Gay, sprightly youth. 2 Lover, gallant.
lurc, -uirc, -an, *s.m.* Crease in cloth. 2††Lame foot.
lurcach, -aiche, *a.* Lame in the feet.
lurcach, -aich, *s. m.* Lameness, unsteadiness. 'S mòran lurcaich 'n ad' ghlùinibh, *and much lameness in thy knees—Donn. bàn.*
lurcaiche, *s.f.ind.* Lameness in the feet, limping.
lurcaire, see lurchaire.
lurchaire,(AF) *s.m.* Foal, colt.
lùrdan, -ain, -an, *s. m.* Cunning, sly fellow, knave, worthless person.
——ach, -aiche, *a.* Cunning, crafty, sly.
——achd, *s.f.ind.* Slyness, cunning, craftiness. 2 Practice of cunning or slyness.
lùrdanta, -ainte, *a.* Cunning, crafty.
lurg, see lurgann. 2‡‡Ridge of a hill extending

gradually into a plain. L. an fheóir, *the stem of the grass.*
lurgadh, see lurgann.
lurgag, -aig, -an, *s.f.* Small leg.
lurgainneach, see luirgneach.
lurgann, -ainn, *s. f.* Shaft, shin, leg. 2 Contemptuous term for an unshapely or slender leg. 3 Hind-leg of a horse. 4 Shaft. 6 Haft, handle. 6 see lurg. 7†† Ascent. 8 Stalk of a plant.
———ach, -aiche, *a.* see luirgneach.
———ach, *s.m.* Shaft.
lurg-bheairt,** *s.f.* see luirg-bheairt.
lurg-iomain, luirg-, -an-, *s.f.* see lorg.
lùs, *v.n.* Teem, abound.
lùs, -ùis, *s.m.* see lùths.
lus, -uis & -a, *pl.* -an, *s. m.* Herb, plant, weed, flower.

438. Lus-a'-bhainne. *439. Lus-a'-bhalla.*

lus-a'-bhainne,§ *s.m.* Milkwort, procession flower, rogation flower—*polygala vulgaris.*
———,§(2) *s.m.* Bog-violet, see mòthan.
lus-a'-bhalgair,§ *s. m.* Foxglove. see lus-nam-ban-sìth. 2§ Club-moss, see crotal-nam-madadh-ruadh.
lus-a'-bhalla, *s.m.* Wall pellitory, bartram—*parietaria officinalis.*

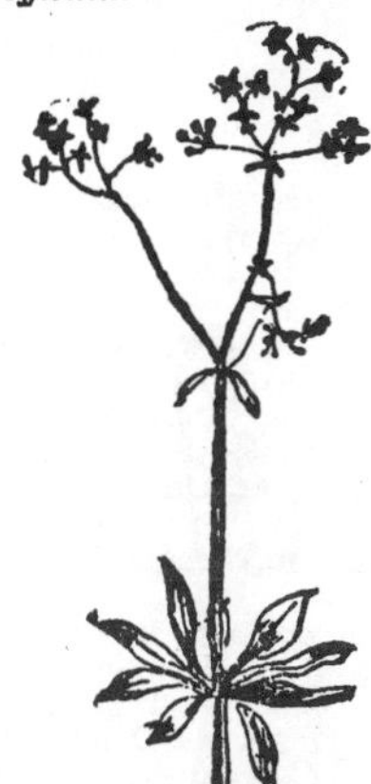

440. Lus-a'-chaitheimh.

lus-a'-chaitheimh,§ *s. m.* Sweet Woodruff—*asperula odorata.*
lusach, -aiche, *a.* Herby, abounding in plants. 2 Weedy. 3 Botanical. 4 Herbaceous. 5 (MS) Herbescent.
lus-a'-chadail, *s.m.* Poppy.
lus-a'-chalmain,§ *s. m.* Columbine—*aquilegia vulgaris.*

441. Lus-a'-chalmain.

lus-a'-choire, *s.m.* Coriander—*coriandrum sativum.*
lus-a'-chomain,** *s.m.* Welcome-to-our-house.
lus-a'-chorrain, *s.m.* Black spleenwort, see dubh-chasach. 2§Sneezewort, see cruaidh-lus.

442. Lus-a'-choire. *443. Lus-a'-chraois.*

lus-a'-chraois,§ *s.m.* Dwarf cornel—*cornus suecica.* [§ says, improperly used for honeysuckle which is uilleann.]
lus-a'-chridhe, *s.m.* Self-heal, see dubhan-ceann-

444. Lus-a'-chrom-chinn.

chòsach.

us-a'-chrom-chinn, *s. m.* Daffodil—*narcissus pseudo-narcissus* and *narcissus jonquilla.* [ill. on page 611.]

445. Lus-a'-chrùbain. *447. Lus-an-fhògair.*

lus-a'-chrùbain,‖ *s.m.* Field gentian—*gentiana campestris.*

lusadair, -ean, *s.m.* Botanist, herbalist.

———eachd,* *s.f.* Botany. 2 Study of botany.

lùsadh, *s.m.* Abounding, teeming, as with fish. A' l—, *pr.pt.* of lùs.

lus-a'-ghràidh, *s.m.* Amaranthe, love-lies-bleeding—*amaranthus caudatus.*

lusairneach, -eich, *s.f.* Place where weeds grow.

lusan, *n.pl.* of lus.

lusan, -ain, -an, *s.m.*, *dim.* of lus. Little herb, weed, or flower. 2 Young herb.

-——ach, -aiche, *a.* Of, or belonging to, herbs, plants or weeds. 2 Abounding in the same. 3 Producing the same. 4**Herbaceous, flowery.

lus-an-àirneig,§ *s. m.* Liverwort—*marchantia polymorpha.*

lusan-Albannach,§ *s. m.* Trailing azalea—*azalea procumbens.*

lusan-bileach,§ *s.coll.* The class of plants known as *labiatæ.*

lusan-ceann-oir-a'-sgadain,(DMu) *s.m.* Betony—*Suth'd.* [Sometimes used there as a substitute for tea.]

lus-an-eallain,§ *s.m.* The herb Robert, see righeal cuil.

446. Lus-an-easbuig.

lus-an-eàrnaich,§ *s. m.* Round-leaved sundew, see ròs-an-t-soluis.

lus-an-easbuig,§ *s. m.* Bishop's weed, goat-weed, gout-weed—*ægopodium podagraria.* 2§ Ox-eye—*chrysanthemum leucanthemum*, see an neòinean mór.

lus-an-fhògair,§ *s.m.* Water-pepper—*polygonum hydropiper.*

448. Lus-an-fhògraidh.

lus-an-fhògraidh,§ *s.m.* Chase-the-devil, love-in-a-mist, devil-in-the-bush, fennel-flower—*nigella damascena.* 2§ St. John's wort, see eala-bhuidhe.

lus-an-fhucadair, *s.m.* Teazle, fuller's teazle.

lusan-glùineach,§ *s.coll.* The class of plants *polygonaceæ.*

449. Lusan-grolla.

lusan-grolla,§ *s.m.* Dwarf red-rattle—*pendicularis sylvatica.*

450. Lus-an-leanna.

lus-an-leanna,§ *s.m.* Hop—*humulus lupulus.*

lus-an-leasaich,§ *s.m.* Yellow bedstraw, see ruin.

lus-an-leusaidh, *s.m.* (DM) Spurge—*euphorbia.*

lusan-lipeach, see lusan-bileach.

lus-an-liùgair, *s.m.* Lovage, see luibh-an-liùgair. [McL & D gives lus-an-liagaire.]

lus-an-lonaid,§ *s. m.* Wood-angelica, see lus-nam-buadha.

lus-an-righ,§ *s.m.* Basil thyme calamint. wild basil—*calamintha clinopodium.* 2 Common tansy, see lus-na-Fraing.

451. Lus-an-rìgh. *452. Lus-an-sìth-chainnt.*

lus-an-ròcais, *s.m.* Ranunculus.

lus-an-ròis, *s.m.* The herb Robert, so called on account of its being used as a charm to cure the disease, the rose.—DU. 2 Red campion —*Colonsay.*

lus-an-sìth-chainnt,§ *s.m.* Spiked lythrum, loosestrife—*lythrum salicaria.*

lus-an-torranain,(AC) *s. m.* Figwort, see lus-nan-cnapan.

lus-an-t-samhraidh,* *s. m.* Gilliflower, see lus-leth-an-t-samhraidh.

453. Lus-an-t-saoidh.

lus-an-t-saoidh, *s. m.* Fennel, (*lit.* hay-weed.)—*fœniculum vulgare.*

lus-an-t-seann-duine,§ *s.m.* Southernwood, see meath-challtainn.

lus-an-t-siabainn,§ *s.m.* Soapwort, bruisewort, bouncing bet—*saponaria officinalis.*

us-an-t-sicnich,§ *s. m.* Rupture-wort, burstwort—*herniaria glabra.*

lus-an-t-siùcair, *s. m.* Succory, chicory—*cichorium intybus.* [lus.

lus-an-t-slànuchaidh,§ *s.m.* Ribwort, see slàn-

454. Lus-an-t-siabuinn. *455. Lus-an-t-sicnich.*

456. Lus-an-t-siùcair.

lus-an-t-sleisneach,§ *s.m.* Yarrow, see lus-chosgadh-na-fola.

lus-a'-pheubair, *s.m.* Dittany, pepper-wort—*origanum dictamnus.*

lus-a'-phiobair, see lus-a'-pheubair.

lus-a'-phione,§ Peony—*pæonia officinalis,* see meacan easa.

lusarnach,* *s.f.* Weeds.

lus-bàchair, *s. m.* Lady's glove.

lusbardan, see luspardan.

457. Lus-Beathaig.

lus-Beathaig, *s.m.* Wood-betony, bishop's wort,

—stachys betonica.
lus-bhalgair, see **luis-bhalgair.**

458. *Lus-Bheinn-Labhair.* 459. *Lus-buidhe-mór.*

lus-Bheinn-Labhair,§ *s.m.* Ben Lawers' plant—*saxifraga cernua.*
lus-buidhe-Bealltainn, *s. m.* Marsh-marigold, see a' chorrach shod.
lus-buidhe-mór,§ *s.m.* Dyer's yellow weed, dyer's weed, dyer's rocket, weld—*reseda luteola.*
lus-caolach,§ *s.m.* Fairy-flax, see lion-nam-ban-sìth.
lus-Chaluim-Chille, *s.m.* St. John's wort, see eala-bhuidhe. 2 Wood-loosestrife, yellow pimpernel, see seamrag-Muire.
lus-chlòimh, *s.m.* Gossamer.
lus-chneas-Chuchulainn, *s. m.* Meadow-sweet, see crios Chuchulainn.
lus-chnuimh, -e, -ean, *s.f.* Caterpillar.

460. *Lus-chosgadh-na-fola.*

lus-chosgadh-na-fola, *s. m.* Yarrow—*achillea millefolium.* McL & D gives Milfoil.
lus-chrann-ceusaidh,§ *s.m.* Spotted persicaria, see glùineach-mór.
lus-chrùin, -ùin & -a, -ùintean, *s.m.* Garland of flowers.
lus-chuach, -aich, -an, *s.f.* Caterpillar.
lus-Chuchulainn, *s. m.* Yellow bedstraw, see ruin. 2 see crios-Chuchulainn.
lus-crè, *s.m.* Common speedwell, medicinal tea, fluellen, ground hele—*veronica officinale.* [McL & D gives Male speedwell.]
lus-curaidh, *s.m.* Jessamine.
lusdadh, -aidh, *s.m.* Flattery.
lus-deathach-thalmhuinn,§ *s.m.* Fumitory—*fumaria officinalis.*

461. *Lus-crè.*

462. *Lus-deathach-thalmhuinn.*

lus-eòlas,** *s.m.* Botany.
lus-eun,(AF) *s.m.* Mountain finch.
lus-feidhleagach, see luis-feidhleagach.
†**lusga,**** -ai, *s.m.* Space of five years. 2 Lustrum. 3 Infancy. 4 Cave.
†**lusgadh,** -aidh, *s.m.* Lurking, skulking.
lusgair,** -ean, *s.m.* Troglodyte, hermit.
——each,** *a.* Like a troglodyte or hermit. 2 Lurking.
——eachd,** *s.f.* Living retired in caves. 2 Solitariness.
lus-garbh, *s.m.* Goose-grass—††*gallium aparine.*
lus-ghàraidh, *s.m.* House-leek, see lus-nan-cluas.

463. *Lus-ghlinne.*

lus-ghlinne, *s. m.* Wood mercury—*mercurialis perennis.* [McL & D gives Dog's mercury.]
lus-Ghlinne bhracadail, (bracadh, *suppuration*) see lus-ghlinne.
lus-ghionaich,§*s.m.* Dog-lichen—*peltidea canina.*

lus-gnàth-ghorm,§ *s. m.* Cranebill, see crobh-priachain.
lus-gràidh, see lus-a'-ghràidh.
lus-gun-mhàthair-gun-athair, *s. m.* Duckweed, see mac-gun-athair.

464. Lus-leighis. 465. Lus-leth-an-t-samhraidh.

lus-leighis,§ *s.m.* Petty spurge,—*euphorbia peplus.*
lus-leth-an-t-samhraidh. *s.m.* Wallflower, gillyflower, July flower (*lit.* Midsummer plant)—*cheiranthus cheiri.* [McL & D gives this for Sweet-william in Eng.-Gael. part.]
lus leusaidh, *s.m.* Spurge, see lus-leighis.
lus-liath, *s.m.* Lavender, see lus-na tuise.

466. Lus-loibheach.

lus-loibheach, *s.m.* Corn-cockle.
lus-maireannach, *s. m.* Amaranth, see lus-a'-ghràidh.
lus-Màiri, *s.m.* Marigold, see lus-buidhe-Bealltuinn.
lus-Marsalaidh,§ *s.m.* Marjoram, see oragan.
lus-MhicBeathaig, see lus-Beathaig.
lus-mhic-Cuimein, *s.m.* Cumin—*cuminum cyminum.* Badge of the Cumins. 2§ Caraway, see carbhaidh.
lus-Mhic-Raonuill, *s. m.* Chase-the-devil, see lus-an-fhògraidh.
lus-mhic-righ-Bhreatuinn, *s. m.* Wild-thyme, brother-wort—*thymus serpyllum.*
lus-midhe,§ *s.m.* Marsh scorpion-grass, forget-me-not, see cotharach.
lus-midi,(AF) *s.* Scorpion.
lus-mòr, *s.m.* Spearwort. 2 Asparagus. 3 Foxglove. 4 Great white mullen.
lus-molach, *s.m.* Woodruff, see lus-a'-chaitheamh.
lus-Muire, *s.m.* Marsh marigold.
lus na banrighinn,§ *s. m.* Auricula,—*primula auricula.*
lus-na-feannaig, see lus-na-fionnaig.
lus-na-feàrna-guirme, see lus-na-feàrnaich.
lus-na-feàrnaich, *s.m.* Sundew—*drosera rotundifolia.* Very common in Scottish Gaeldom, has little red, spoon-like leaves with red hairs and always covered with dew-drops, see ròs-an-t-soluis.

467. Lus-mhic-rìgh-Bhreatuinn. 468. Lus-na-fionnaig.

lus-na-fionnaig, *s.m.* Crowberry, crakeberry—*empetrum nigrum.* §Badge of the Macleans, some say of the Camerons.

469. Lus-na-fola (2) 470. Lus-na-Fraing.

471. Lus-na-h-oidhche.

lus-na-fola,* *s.m.* Yarrow, milfoil, see lus-chosgadh-na-fola. 2 Shepherd's purse — *capsella bursa pastoris.* [ill. on p. 615.]
lus-na-Fraing, *s.m.* Common tansy, buttons,—*tanacetum vulgare.* [ill. on p. 615.]
lus-na-gaoithe, *s m* Windflower.
lus-na-géire-boireannach, see grainnseag.
lus-na-gineil-goraiche,§ *s.m.* Bluebell, wild hyacinth, see fuath-mhuic.
lus-na-h-oidhche,§ *s.m.* Deadly nightshade, belladonna, dwale, banewort,—*atropa belladona.* [ill. on p. 615.]
lus-na-h-òighe,‡ *s.m.* Enchantress' nightshade, see fuinnseach
lus-na-macraidh,* see lus-mhic-righ-Bhreatuinn.
lus-na-maighdinn,* *s.m.* Tassel.

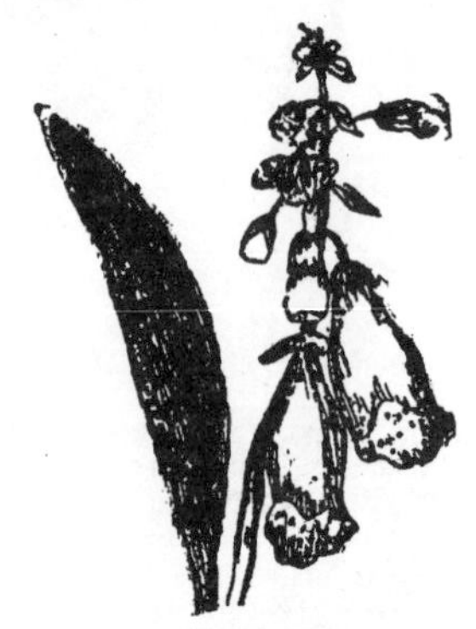
472. Lus-nam-bàn-sìth.

lus-nam-ban-sìth, *s.m.* Foxglove—*digitalis purpurea.*
lus-nam-biast,* *s.m.* Absinthium.

473. Lus-nam-braoileag. 474. Lus-nam-buadha.

lus-nam-braoileag,§ *s. m.* Red whortleberry, brawlins, cowberry, flowering box—*vaccinium vitis idœa.* Badge of some of the septs of Clan Chattan.
lus-nam-buadha,§ *s.m.* Wood angelica—*angelica sylvestris.*
lus-na-meala,‡ *s.m.* Honeysuckle, see uilleann. 2 Lousewort—*Colonsay.*
lus-nam-meall-mòra, *s.m.* Common mallow.
lus-nam-mial,** *s.m.* Mouse-ear, scorpion-grass, lousewort, red-rattle, see lus-riabhach. 2 Marsh scorpion-grass, forget-me-not, see cotharach.
lus-nam-mios,§ *s.m.* Moonwort.
lus-nam-muisean,§ *s.m.* Cowslip. 2 Primrose—McL & D.
lus-na-nathrach, *s.m.* Viper's bugloss—*echium vulgare.*

475. Lus-na-nathrach. 476. Lus-nan-cluas.

lus-na-nathrach,‡ (2) *s.m.* Adder's-tongue fern, see teanga-na-nathrach.
lus-nan-cam-bile,§ *s.m.* Common chamomile, see camomhail.
lus-nan-cluas,§ *s. m.* House-leek—*sempervivum tectorum.* 2 Saxifrage.
lus-nan-clugan, (AC) *s.m.* Figwort. see lus-nan-cnapan.
lus-nan-cnàmh, *s. m.* Samphire — *crithmum maritimum,* see saimbhir.

477. Lus-nan-cnapan.

lus-nan-cnapan, *s. m.* Fig-wort—*scrophularia nodosa.* [Great Figwort—McL & D.]

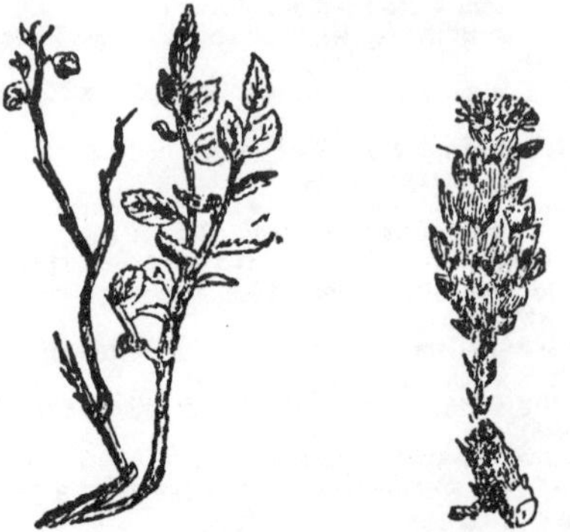
478. *Lus-nan-dearc.* 480. *Lus-nan-laoch.*

lus-nan-dearc,§ *s. m.* Whortleberry-plant, bilberry, blaeberry, blueberry—*vaccinium myr-*

tillus.

lus-nan-eidhreag, see lus-nan-oighreag.

lus-nan-gillean-òga,§ *s. m.* Meadow-sweet—*Argyll.* see crios-Chuchulainn.

lus-nan-gnàithseag,* *s.m.* Whortleberry-plant.

lus-nan-gorm-dhearc, *s.m.* Black- or blueberry plant.

479. *Lus-nan-gràn-dubh.*

lus-nan-gràn dubh, *s.m.* Alexanders *smyrnium olusatrum.* Not found north of Stirling in Scotland.

lus-nan-laoch, *s.m.* Roseroot—*sedum rhodiola.* Badge of the Gunns. [Not rose-wort, as given by McL & D.—ill. on p. 616.]

481. *Lus-nan-laogh.*

482. *Lus-nan-laogh (2.)*

lus-nan-laogh, *s.m.* Golden saxifrage—*chrysosplenium oppositifolium.* 2 § Orpine—*sedum telephium.*

lus-nan-leac, *s. m.* Eyebright—*euphrasia officinalis.*

lus-nan-oighreag, *s.m.* Cloudberry-bush—*rubus chamæmoris.*

lus-nan-saighdearan,§ *s.m.* Children's name for ribwort in *Perthshire and Argyllshire,* see slàn-lus.

lus-nan-sgor, *s. m.* Clown's all-heal, hedge-woundwort—*stachys sylvatica.*

lus-nan-tri-bilean,§ *s.m.* Valerian, see lus-bileach.

483. *Lus-nan-leac.*

484. *Lus-nan-sgor.*

485. *Lus-na-peighinn.*

lus-na-peighinn,§ *s.m.* Marsh pennywort—*hydrocotyle vulgaris.*

486. *Lus-na-purgaid.*

487. *Lus-na-seabhaig.*

lus-na-purgaid,§ *s.m.* Monk's rhubarb—*rumex alpinus.* 2§ Rue. [ill. on p. 617.]
lus-na-seabhaig,§ *s.m.* Hawkweed—*hieracium.* [ill. on p. 617 represents Mouse-ear hawkweed —*hieracium pilosella.*
lus-na-seilge, *s.m.* Black spleenwort, see **dubh-chasach.**
lus-na-siochaiant,§ see **lus-na-siothaimh.**

488. *Lus-na-siothaimh.*

lus-na-siothaimh, *s.m.* Common or yellow loosestrife—*lysimachia vulgaris.*

489. *Lus-na-smàileag.*

lus-na-smàileag, [-smaileag‡‡, -smalaig**,] *s.m.* Smallage, garden celery—*apium graveolens.*
lus-na-Spàinnd, *s.m.* Pellitory of Spain—*anthemis pyrethrum.*
lus-na-staoine, *s.m.* Gill.
lus-na-staoiaig,§ *s. m.* Crowberry, see **lus-na-fionnaig.**
lus-na-tùise,§ *s.m.* Common lavender—*lavendula spica.*
lùspaid,(DMC) *s.f.* Clumsy person.
lusparden, -ain, -an, *s. m.* Pigmy, dwarf. 2 Sprite. 3 Term applied to a dwarfish child or boy. 4 Contemptuous term for a puny man.
———ach, *a.* Dwarfed, dwarfish.
lus-Phara-léith,§ *s.m.* Groundsel, see **bualan.**
lusrach, -aiche, *a.* see lusach.
———, -aich, *s.m.* Herbage. 2* Place well supplied with herbs. Is maoth l. an t-sléibhe a' seargadh, *and the tender herbage of the hill withering.*
lusradh, -aidh, *s. m.* see lusrach, *s.* †2 Procession.
lusrag, -aig, -an, *s.f.* Charm made of herbs. 2 see luisreag.
———ach, -aiche, *a.* see lusach.
———an, ain, -an, *s.m.* Florist. 2 Botanist, one skilled in herbs. 3 Apothecary. 4 Perfumer. Seòltachd an lusragain, *the art of the herbalist* or *apothecary.*

490. *Lus-riabhach.*

lus-riabhach, *s.m.* Lousewort, marsh red-rattle —*pedicularis palustris.*
lus-righ,* see lus-mhic-righ-Bhreatuinn.
lus-ròs,§ *s.m.* The herb Robert, see **righeal-cuil.**

491. *Lus-taghta.* 492. *Lus-teang'-an-daimh.*

lus-taghte,§ *s. m.* Fragrant orchis—*gymnadenia conopsea.*
lustair,** -ean, *s.m.* Flatterer. 2 Low cunning fellow.
———each,** *a.* Flattering, cajoling, fawning.
lustradh,** -aidh, *s.m.* Flattering, flattery, cajoling, fawning.
lus-teang'-an-daimh,§ *s. m.* Small bugloss—*lycopsis arvensis.*
lùth, -a [& luith, *s.m.* Strength, power, vigour, activity 2**Power of motion. 3*Joint. 4**Pith. 5† Longing, desire. Os cionn an lùith, *above the joint*, sgian lùth, *a clasp-knife* ; tha a chas gun l., *his foot is powerless* ; chaill e l. a làimhe, *he lost the use of his hand* ; chaill e a l., *he lost his power of locomotion.*
lùth, *v.* see lùgh. 2 see luadh.
——ach, -aiche, *a.* see lùthmhor. 2 see luadhach. 3‡‡Weakly.
†——ach, aich, *s* The sinews, veins.
lùthachadh,‡‡ -aidh, *s.m.* Invigoration. A' l—, *pr pt.* of lùthaich.
†**lùthadh,** -aidh, *s.m. & pr. pt.* see lùghadh. 2 (MS) Conflexure. 3 see luadhach.
lùthaich,‡‡ *v.a.* Invigorate.
luthaig, *v.a.* see luathsaich.
-———eadh, -eidh, *s. m.* see luathsachadh. 2 (MS) Receivedness. 3 Fatality.
luthaigte, see ludhaigte.

lùthair, -e, *a.* see lùthmhor.
———eachd,(MS) *s.f.* Agility.
lùthar, *a.* see lùthmhor.
lùthas, -ais, *s.m.* see lùth.
luthasachadh,†† -aidh, *s. m.* see luathsachadh.
luthasaich,†† *pr.pt.* a' luathasachadh, *v. a.* see luathsaich.
lùth-chleas, -a, -an, *s. m.* Agility, activity. 2 Manly feat, brave deed. 3 Athletic exercises. 4 Gambolling, frisking about. 5 Sleight of hand, jugglery, activity of the hand, legerdemain. 6†† Valour, bravery. L. nan uan, *the frisking of lambs;* lùth-chleasan, *agile movements, feats in legerdemain.*
————ach, -aiche, *a.* Agile, active, nimble. 2 Manly, stout. 3 Frisking. 4 Merry. 5 Skilled in jugglery, dexterous. 6** Chivalrous.
————achd, *s.f.* Bravery, chivalry. 2 Legerdemain, activity of the hand. 3 Activity, nimbleness, agility, adroitness, dexterity.
————aiche,** *s.m.* Juggler, conjurer, adept in legerdemain. 2 Chivalrous person,
lùth-chùirt, -e, -ean, see lùchairt.
lùthdag, -aig, -an, see lùdag.
————ach, see lùdagach.
lùth-eun,¶ *s. m.* Mountain-finch, see bricein-caorainn.
lùth-fhalbhach, *a.* Giddy-paced.
lùthmhoire, *comp.* of lùthmhor.
lùthmhoireachd, *s.f.ind.* Strength, activity, agility.
lùthmhor, -oire, *a.* Strong, able. 2 Nimble, vegete, agile, supple, bending. 3 Sinewy, muscular. 4 Swift. 5 Jointed. 6 Voluble. Gu l., *vigorously.* Fear luath, lùthmhor, *a swift muscular man.*
lùthor, -oire *a.* see lùthmhor.
lùths, -ùiths, *s.m.* see lùth.
lutraig,(DU) *s.f.* Spaces betweed the ribs in the bottom of a boat. 2 Place to keep mussels from being washed about, formed by making a shallow dyke round the bed.

M m

m, muin, *the vine.* The eleventh letter of the Gaelic alphabet now in use. When *m* has its simple sound, it is articulated much the same as in other languages, as, mór, *great* ; caman, *a club ;* lom, *bare.* When *m* is aspirated, that is, when it is immediately followed by *h*, a new combination or letter is formed, somewhat like *v* in English, as, a mhuineal, *his neck ;* tàmh, *rest.* Dialectally, though never at the beginning of words, *mh* is often pronounced like a nasal *oo*, as, ràmh, *an oar ;* and sometimes *mh* is entirely mute in the middle and at the end of words,as, còmhnard, *level ;* domh, *to me ;* but nasality generally attaches to the vowel preceding the elision.
'm, *cont.* for am, *art.*, used after words ending with a vowel. Is tu 'm balach ! *you're the boy !*
'm, *cont.* for am, *in the.* Taobh na creige 'm blàthas na gréine,*beside the rock in the warmth of the sun.*
'm, *cont.* for am (ann mo,) *in my.*
'm, *cont.* for am, Whom. Mu 'm bi iad ag ràdh, *about whom they assert.*
'm ? *cont.* for am ? *interr. conj.* 'M faigh thu sin ? *will you get that ?*
'm, *cont.* for am, *poss. pron.* Their. (before labials.) Le 'm beul 's le 'm bilibh, *with their mouth and with their lips.*
m', *cont.* for mo, *poss.pron.* My. M' athair, *my father ;* m' anam, *my soul.*
m', for mu, *prep.* About.
m' a, for mu a. About his, about her (before vowels.) M' a cheann, *about his head* ; m' a casan, *about her feet.*
ma, *conj.* If. Ma 's àill le neach sam bith tighinn 'nam dhéidh-sa, *if any man will come after me* ; ma 's e gu'm bi, *if so be that it be ;* ma 's urrainn mi, *if I can.* [Aspirates the initial consonant of verb following, and is used with the *past aff.*, *fut. subj.*, and *pres.* and *past* of bi.]
†**ma**, *s.m.* Breach.
†**ma**, *prep.* for mu.
mab, -aib & -a, *pl.* -an, *s.m.* Stutter, lisp, stammer. 2 Tassel, fringe, (babag.)
màb, *pr.pt.* a' màbadh, *v. a.* Abuse,vilify, reproach in angry terms. 2 Affront, disgrace.
mabach, -aiche, *a.* Entangled, confused, ravelled. 2 Stammering, stuttering or lisping in speech. 3 Furnished with tassels or fringes (babagach.) An ciaran mabach, *the tawny stammerer*
————,* -aiche, *s.f.* Stuttering, stammering female.
————d,* *s.f.ind* Stammering.
mabadh, -aidh, -aidhean, *s. m.* Impediment or lisping in speech, stammering. 2 Entangling, perplexing, ravelling. Cha'n fhaigh fear mabaidh modh, *a stutterer is never respected.*
màbadh, -aidh, *s. m.* Abusing, act of abusing, vilifying, reproaching in angry terms. 2 Affronting, act of affronting. A' m—, *pr. pt.* of màb.
mabag, -aig, -an, see babag.
————ach, -aiche, see babagach.
mabaiche,‡‡ *s.f.ind.* Inarticulateness, lisp.
mabaid,(DMC) *s.f.* Gossiping female.
mabail,(MS) *v.a.* Hack. 2 Maim
mabair, -ean, *s.m.* Stammerer, stutterer.
màbair, -ean, *s.m.* Abusive person, one who uses abusive language. 2 One who affronts or causes disgrace.
————eachd, *s.f.ind.* Habit of using bad language.
mabaireachd, *s.f.ind.* Stammering, act of stammering or stuttering.
maban, see moibeal.
mabladh,(MS) *s.m.* Hacking. 2 Maiming.
mablàis,(DMC) *s. f.* Indistinct or unintelligible talk.
†**mac**, *a.* Clear, pure, clean.
†**mac**, *v.a.* Bear, carry.
mac, *gen. & pl.* mic, *dat. pl.* macaibh. *s.m.* Son. 2 The young of any animal. 3 *poetically* The male of any animal. [Aspirates a proper name following it, except when it commences with *c* or *g*, as MacPhàrlain, MacCriomain, MacGriogair, but when signifying the son of an individual, a name beginning with *c* or *g* is also aspirated after *mac.* Thus, Iain MacCoinneach means *John MacKenzie*, but Iain mac Choinnich, means *John the son of an individual called Kenneth.*] ** gives " mac-'san-lagh " for *son-in-law* (which is cliamhuinn) ; but a son-in-law is not a son in *law.*
†**maca**, *s.m.* Like, equal, emblem.
macabh, *s.m.ind.* Liberal, generous, accomplished man. 2 Fair youth. 3 Young hero. *pl.* Heroes, renowned persons.
†**macadh**, -aidh, *s.m.* Bearing, carrying.
macadhamhaich, *v.a.* Macadamize.
macadhamhachadh, *s.m.* Macadamizing.
macaibh, *dat.pl.* of mac. 2 see macabh.
Macaibh mór, *s.m.* Favourite character (giant)

in Gaelic tales, probably the macaobh (youth) of the older language.
macail, -e, *a.* Like a son, filial. 2**Affectionate.
†macail, *v.a.* Nurse, foster, rear.
macaimh, see macabh.
macaineachd, *s.f.ind.* Boyish play or games. 2 Heroism. 3 Ordering, directing. 4(MS) Gaiety.
macaladh, -aidh, *s.m.* Fostering, rearing a child after weaning.
mac-alla, see mac-talla.
macamh, see macabh.
maca-mnà, *s.f.* Young or fair woman. 2**Handsome young female.
macan, -ain, -an, *s.m.dim.* of mac. Little son. 2 Term of approbation or encouragement addressed to a boy or youth. 3 Hero. 4** Young son. 'S math thu,'mhacain ! *well done, my boy !*
mac-an-aba, *s.m.* Ring-finger.
mac-an-abair, see mac-an-aba,
macanachd,** see macaineachd.
macanadh,(CR) *s.m.* Sobbing—*Arran.*
macanas,** -ais, *s.m.* Bravery, heroism.
mac-an-dogha,§ s. Burdock, for meacan-dogha, see suirichean-suirich.
mac-an-luinn, *s.m.* Name of Fingal's sword.
mac-an-og,(MMcD) *s.m.* see meacan-og.
macanta, -ainte, *a.* Meek, gentle, mild. 2** Submissive. 3**Kind, filial. 4**Honest. 5** Modest. Na daoine m., *the meek.*
——chd, *s.f.* see macantas. Spiorad na m., *the spirit of meekness.*
——s, -ais, *s.m.* Meekness, mildness, urbanity. 2**Submissiveness. 3 Puerility. 4** Honesty. 5**Affectionateness.
mac-an-Toisich,(CR) *s.m.* Whisky—*W. of Ross.* (From association with Ferintosh.)
mac-balaich, *s.m.* Clown, rustic, rude fellow.
mac-bràthair-athar, *s.m.* First cousin, father's brother's son.
mac-bràthair-màthar, *s.m.* First cousin, mother's brother's son.
mac-bràthair-seanamhar, *s.m.* Maternal grand uncle's son, second cousin.
mac-bràthair-seanar, *s. m.* Paternal grand uncle's son, second cousin.
mac-bràthar, *s.m.* Nephew, brother's son.
mac-céile, mic-ch-, *s.m.* Step-son, husband's or wife's son.
MacCruslaig 's na mucan, *s. m.* MacCruslaig and the pigs. A favourite game among Uist children. Described in No. 16, *Celtic Review.*
mac-fraoir,(AF) *s. m.* Gannet. 2 Solan goose. 3 Voracious fowl or person—*Sàr-Obair.*
mac-fuirme,** *s.m.* Poet of the 2nd. order.

493. Mac-gun-athair.

mac-gun-athair,‡ *s.m.* Lesser duckweed—*lemna minor.*
mach, *adv.* (a mach) Out, without. Thugaibh a mach, *take (ye) out ;* a mach 's a mach, *wholly, thoroughly, altogether ;* bithibh cinnteach gu 'm faigh bhur peacadh a mach sibh, *be sure that your sins will find you out ;* thug an Tighearn a mach Clann Israeil á taigh na daorsa, *the Lord brought the children of Israel out of the house of bondage ;* m. air a chéile, *at variance ;* cuir a m. e, *put him out ;* thoir a mach ort *; get out !*
mach,(a) *int.* Out ! Get out !
mach,* *conj.* Except, but. Mach o h-aon, *but one, except one.*
macha,(AF) *s.* Royston crow.
macha-dhubh,(MMcD) *s.f.* Otter—*Lewis.*
machair, *gen.*-charach & -chrach, *pl.* machraichean, *s.f.* Extensive low-lying fertile plain. 2 Level country. 3 Name given by the Scottish Gael to the southern or low-lying parts of Scotland. 4 Extensive beach. 5(CR) Low and level part of a farm. 6(AC) *pl.* Long ranges of sandy plains fringing the Atlantic side of the Outer Hebrides. They are closely covered with short green grass, thickly studded with herbs of fragrant odours and plants of lovely hues. Luibh na macharach, *the herb of the field* ; air mh., *in the Lowlands ;* air feadh na macharach, *among the lowlands.* [* says seldom used in common speech for anything but *beach.*]
machaireach, -eich, *s.m.* Inhabitant or native of a low-lying country, especially the south of Scotland.
——, -eiche, *a.* Abounding in fields, level.

494. Machall-coille. *495. Machall-monaidh.*

machall-coille,§ *s.m.* Common avens, the herb burnet—*geum urbanum.*
machall-monaidh,§ *s. m.* White dryas, mountain avens—*dryas octopetala.* Little shrub-like plant with leaves somewhat like the oak, and eight large white petals on flower. Badge of the MacNeils, and Lamonts.

496. Machall-uisge.

machall-uisge,§ *s.m.* Water-avens—*geum rivale.*
macharach, *gen. sing.* of machair.
mach-bhaile, -bhailtean, *s.m.* Village in the

suburbs of a great town.
†machd, *s.m.* Wave.
†——nach, -aich, *s.m.* Observer.
†machdual, -uail, *s.m.* Sponge.
machlach,* see machlag.
machlag, -aig, -an, *s.f.* Matrix, womb. 2 Belly. 3 Mating.
——ach, *a.* Uterine. 2 Bellying.
machrach, *gen.sing.* of machair.
machraichean, *pl.* of machair.
mach-sheòmar,** *s.* Antechamber.
machtra ! *int.*
machuil, *s.f.* Spot, blemish.
mac-làmhaich, *s.m.* Sea-devil, cat-fish, angler, fishing-frog. 2 Wolf-fish.
mac-làthaich, see mac-làmhaich.
mac-leabhar,** mic-, *s. m.* Copy of a book, volume of a book.
mac-leisg, *s.m.* Lazy, indolent person, laziness personified, (*lit.* son of laziness.)
mac-mallachd,* *s.m.* The devil.
mac-meamna, see mac-meanmna.
————ch, see mac-meanmnach.
mac-meanmna, *s.m.* Fancy, imagination, conceit.
————ch, -aiche, *a.* Imaginative, fanciful.
————dh, -aidh, *s.m.* Imagination, fancy.
mac-mic,** *s.m.* Grandson.
†mac-mnà,** *s. f.* Handsome young female. 2 Young girl.
mac-muirigheach,(AF) *s.m.* see maighdeag.
mac-na-bracha, *s.m.* Whisky (*lit.* son of malt.)
mac-na-dearcaig, *s.m.* Wine.
mac-na-praisich,** *s.m.* Whisky.
macnas, -ais, *s.m.* Wantonness, lasciviousness. 2 Sport, mirth. 3 Fancy. 4**Festivity. 5** Kindness. 6**Prosperity. 7** Fondne[ss].
macnasach, -aiche, *a.* Wanton, lascivio[us]. 2 Licentious. 3 Sportive, merry, gay, mirt[hful], jovial, festive.
———d, *s.f.* see macnas. 2‡‡Buxomness.
mac-peathar, *s.m.* Sister's son, nephew.
mac-piuthair-athar, *s.m.* Father's siste[r's son], first cousin.
mac-piuthar-seanamhathar, *s.m.* Grandmother's sister's son, second cousin.
mac-piuthar-seanar, *s.m.* Grandfather's sister's son, second cousin.
macraidh,‡‡ *s.f.coll.* Band of young men, youths, male children. 2 Sons.
†macraidh,** *s.f.* Disease.
†macrail, *a.* Like, as.
macrail, *s.f.* Gaelic spelling of *mackerel.*
macras,** *s.m.* Sobbing, peevishness.
——ach,** *a.* Peevish, sobbing, sighing.
mac-ratha, *s.m.* Prosperous or fortunate person, (*lit.* son of prosperity.) Is tu mac-an-ratha, *what a lucky fellow you are !*
macruidh, see macraidh.
mac-samhladh,** -aidh, *s.m.* Equal. 2 Equivalent. 3 Fellow, match.
mac-samhlaidh, see mac-samhuil.
mac-samhuil, *s.m.* Likeness, sameness, similitude. 2 Emblem.
————,** *a.* Like as, such like, similar.
————t,** *s.m.* Equal, compeer. 2 Fellow, match. 3 Emblem. Do mh air misneach, *thine equal in courage.*
mac-sgal,* *s.m.* Echo. Bheireadh e m. á creagaibh, *he would make the very rocks re-echo.*
mac-stalladh,(DC) *Uist* for mac-talla.
mac-strodha, } ** *s. m.* Candlewaster. 2**
mac-struidhe, } Spendthrift.
mactach,** *a.* Pernicious. 2 Destructive.
†mactadh, -aidh, *s.m.* Killing, slaying, slaughter. 2**Surprise.
mac-talla, *s.m.* Echo. (*lit.* son of the rock,) also mac-talla-nan-creag.
mac-talladh, } see mac-talla.
mac-thallaidh, }
mac-thogail,** *s.f.* Adoption.
mac-tìre,(AC) *s.f.* [***m.*] Wolf.
†mad,** *s.m.* Hand.
mada, see madadh.
madach,** *a.* Canine.
——ail, -e, *a.* Doggish. 2 Fierce. 3 Surly.
mada-chuain,(AF) *s.m.* Grampus.
madadh, -aidh, -aidhean, *s. m.* Dog. 2 Mastiff. 3 Any wild animal of the dog species. 4 Wolf. 5 Fox. 6 Cock of a gun-lock (the part in which the flint used to be fixed.) 7**Butt-end of a gun. 8 The large mussel, like the bait-mussel and as large as the mùsgan. M. is the usual term in *Arran* for *a dog*, where cù is seldom heard.
m.-allaidh, *wolf.*
m.-all, see m.-allaidh.
m.-donn, -aidh-dhuinn, *otter. 2 brown mastiff.*
m.-gul, -aidh-ghuil, *wolf.*
m.-mór,(AC) *wolf.*
m.-ruadh, -aidh-ruaidh, *pl.* madaidh-ruadha, *fox ; 2 brown mastiff.*
m.-ulaith, see m.-allaidh.
m.-uisge, *otter ; 2 fresh-water pearl-mussel—W. of Ross & Lewis.*
madadhail, see madachail.
mada-galluidh, see madadh-allaidh.
madaidheach, see madachail.
[ma]dail, see madachail.
[ma]lag, see màdog.
[ma]ainn, see maduinn.

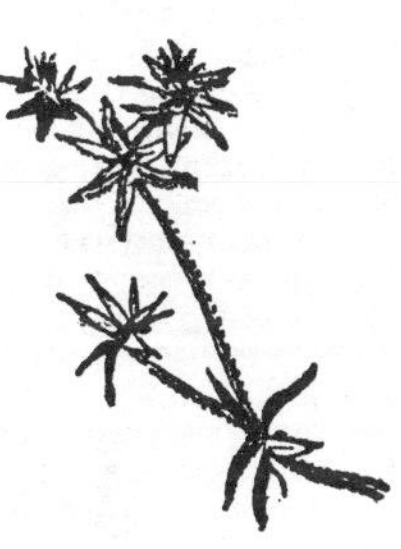

498. Màdar. *499. Màdar.*

màdar, -air, *s.m.* Wild madder—*rubia peregrina.* 2 The colour produced therefrom. Luchd-dheiseachan màdair, *the wearers of red coats.* [ill. 498 represents Wild madder—*rubia peregrina*, and 499 Field madder—*sherardia arvensis.*]

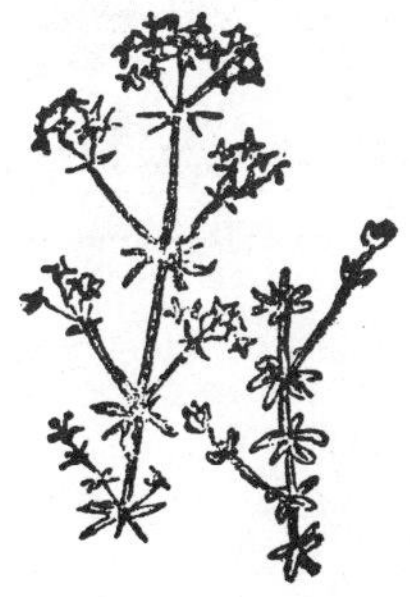

500. Màdar-fraoich.

màdar-fracich,§ *s.m.* Heath-bedstraw—*gallium saxatile*. [ill. on p. 621.]
—— -na-machrach, -air-, *s.m.* Field-madder—*sherardia arvensis*.
madh, -aidh, -an, see magh. †2 Ecstasy. M. beag, *a little, a small share.*
——, *conj.* see ma.
†**madha**, *a.* Unlawful, unjust.
madhanta, -ainte. *a.* Dexterous in arms, valiant. 2 Coy Siod am fear m., *yonder is the hero dexterous in arms*
——chd, *s.f.ind* Dexterity in the use of arms. 2**Valour 3**Coyness.
madhar, -air, *s.m* see maghar.
madh-fhiadh, see maigheach.
madhm, -a, -an, see màm.
†**Madhrail**,** *s.f.* July.
màdog, *s.m.* Mattock, kind of pick-axe, with broad instead of pointed ends. 2 Spade. 3 Hoe.
——ach,** *a.* Like a mattock, spade or hoe.
madrach, -aiche, *a.* Doggish, like a dog
—— -alluidh, *s.* Wolves.
madradh, see madadh.
madraidh, *s.f.collect.* Number of dogs. 2 The dog species.
madrail, -e, *a.* see madrach.
madralachd,** *s.f.* Doggishness.
madruich, see madraidh.
maduinn, maidne, -ean, *s. f.* The morning. Moch 'sa mhaduinn, *early in the morning.*
——each, -eiche, *a.* Early. 2 Auroral.
——eag, -eig, *s.f.* The morning star.
——eagach, *a.* Like the morning star. 2 Auroral.
——ean, *s.pl.* Morning devotions, matins.
——eil,‡‡ -e, *a.* Matin.
màg, -àig, -an, *s.f.* Paw. 2 Claw. 3 Ludicrous term for the hand. 4 Seal's paw—*Argyll.* 5 see màgach. 6* Soft, plump hand. Air a mhàgan, *on-all-fours* ; m. an leòmhainn, *the lion's paw* ; gu 'n gleidheadh Dia a' mhuirichinn 's a' mhàg-bhleòthainn, *may God keep the children and the milking hand*—a Perthshire wish when one gets a drink of milk.
màg, -àig, -an, *s.f.* Arable field, field that can be ploughed, arable land—*North.* 2 Very broad ridge of land—*West.* Chuir mi a' mh. liath ort, *I have finished my rig before you*—*Suth'd.*
mag, *pr.pt.* a' magadh, *v.a.* Scoff, deride, banter, ape. 2**Mock, jeer. [Followed by *air*, simple or compounded.] M. air, *mock at him.*
mag, -a, *s.m.* see magadh.
màg, *pr. pt.* a' màgadh & a' màgail, *v.n.* Creep, move on all fours.
——ach, -aich, *s.f.* Toad. 2 Frog.
——ach, -aiche, *a.* Having clumsy hands. 2 Having paws. 3 Creeping, crawling 4 Belonging to a paw. 5* Having short legs and broad, as a cow. 6*Having large, soft, plump hands.
——ach, -aiche, *a.* Abounding in arable fields.
magach, -aiche, *a.* Mocking, given to mocking or derision.
magadh, -aidh, *s.m.* Deriding, act of deriding, scoffing, mocking. 2 Mockery, derision, ridicule. 3 Burlesque. A' m—, *pr pt.* of mag.
magadh, *s m & pr.pt.* Creeping on all fours.
magadh-ulaidh, see madadh-alluidh.
màgag, see màgach *s.*
magaid,‡ *s.f.* Whim.
magail, *s.f. & pr.pt.* see magadh.
màgail, see màgach.
——, *v.* see màg.
magail,** *a.* Apish.
——eachd,** *s.f.* Apishness.
magair, -ean, *s.m.* Jester, scorner, mocker, derider.
màgair, *pr.pt.* a' màgairt, *v. a. & n.* Creep, crawl. 2 Paw, handle clumsily.
magair, *pr.pt.* a' magairt, *v.n.* **Ape.
——eachd, *s f.ind.* Habit of mocking or jesting. 2 Buffoonery.
——le, -an, *s.m.*[***f.*] Testicle, stone.
magairleach,** *a* Having testicles. 2 Having large testicles. 3 Like the testicles. 4 Of, or belonging to the testicles.
magairlean, *n.pl.* of magairle.
magairt, *s.f.* Pawing. 2 Creeping. A' m—, *pr. pt.* of màg.
màgan, -ain, -an, *s.m.* Little paw. 2 see màigean. [‡ Properly mial-mhàgain, *squat beast.*] 3 Clumsy little hand.
magar.** -air, *s.m.* Word, expression.
màgarain,** *v.n.* Creep. 2 Move on all fours. 3 Walk with a creeping gait.
màgaran, -ain, *s. m.* Creeping on all fours. 2 Crawling. 3 One who has a creeping gait. 4 Person of low habits. 5 (AF) Toad. 6(Fionn) Young child before it begins to walk.
——ach, -aiche, *a.* That creepeth on all fours.
——achd, *s.f.* see màgaran.
——aich, (MS) *v.n.* Grovel.
màgarlan, (MS) *s.m.* Cod. 2 *pl.* Posteriors.
màgarnach, (MS) *s.m.* Sneaking.
màgarsaich,** *s.f.* Creeping.
mag-dhealbh, *s m.* Caricature.
magh, -a & -aigh, -an, *s. m.* (*f.* in *Badenoch.*) Field. 2 Level country. 3 Field of battle. 4 surface. Buaidh air m., *victory on the field of battle.*
——ach, -aiche, *a.* Of many fields or plains. 2 Abounding in fields.
†**maghair**. *s.m.* Ploughed land.
ma-ghamhuinn, see math-ghamhuinn.
——each, see math-ghamhuinneach.
maghan, (AC) see math-ghamhuinn.
maghan, *s.m.* Stomach—*Suth'd.*
magh-aoraidh, *pl.* -a- & -an-, *s.f.* Field or plain of worship.
maghar, -air, -airean, *s.m.* Bait to fish with, artificial fly, fly for saith. [also ite-mhaghar.] 2 Spawn, young fishes. 3 Moving about when fishing, in contradistinction to "air chruaidh" (at anchor)—*Uist.* 4 Act of fishing for young saith, &c. with a fly—iasgach a' mhaghair.—(AH.)
†**maghar**, -air, -an, *s.m.* Word, expression.
magharach, -aiche, *a.* Having much fishing-bait, or 2 Spawn.
†**magh-fhal**, -ail, *s.m.* Field barrack.
magh-ghamhuinn, see math-ghamhuinn.
†**magh-lann**, -lainn, *pl.* -lainn & -lannan, *s.m.* Field-barrack.
magh-shluagh,**-shluaigh, *s.m.* People inhabiting low countries. 2 (DMy) Common people, the masses, in contradistinction to the classes.
magh-suinne, *s.f.* Slavery.
magh-uisge, -ean & -eachan, *s.f.* Winter lake.
màgranach, see màgaranach.
maibean, -ein, -an, *s.m.* Bunch, cluster. 2 Mop, tuft.
——ach, -aiche, *a*, Clustered, bunchy. 2 Growing in bunches. 3**Tufty, moppy.
†**maicne**, *s.pl.* Children, relations.
maide, -an & -achan, *s.m.*[***f.*] Wood, timber. 2 Stick. 3 Staff, cudgel. Cas mhaide, *a wooden leg or shaft* ; cha mh. balachain do shleagh, *thy spear is no boy's staff* ; ged bhiodh na trì gill 'san aon mhaide, *if I had engagements three, I would fly to succour thee*—(*lit.* were there three wagers on one stick)—in

allusion to the old style of keeping a score by nicks on a stick, by those who could not write ; tha 'n t-àm cur anns na maidean, *it is time to be starting* (*lit.* to put [motion] into the sticks, i.e. the oars.)

m.-a'-bhallain, *s.m. stick run through the handles of a tub when carrying it.*
m.-a'-bhuntàta, *stick for mashing potatoes.*
m.-briste, *broken stick ; 2 pair of tongs formed of a broken stick.*
m.-builg, *bilge-piece of boat, see bàta, F8, p.73.*
m.-buinn, *base* or *stock of a spinning-wheel.*
m.-ceangail, *piece of wood joining the two beams of the rafters of a house.*
m.-coire, *spirtle—Arran.*
m.-crois, *a crutch.*
m.-doichill, (*lit.* stick of inhospitality), *stick placed across a doorway instead of closing the door, when people were dining.* No one entered when they saw it up.
m.-droma, *roof-tree.*
m.-feannaig, (MMcD) *a projecting piece of wood* which appears above the thatch at each end of a "black" house.
m.-frasaidh, *stick used for separating the ears of corn from the sheaves.* A sheaf was held top downwards in the left hand, and the top struck smartly with a stick held in the right.
m.-leigidh, *weaver's turning-stick.*
m.-leisg, (DMK) *s.m.* Trial of strength performed by two men sitting on the ground with the soles of their feet pressing against each other. Thus seated, they held a stick between their toes which they pulled against each other till one of them was raised from the ground. [*Scots,* smeir-stick.]
m.-lunndaidh, *lever, handspike.*
m.-meatsg, *boy's top.*
m.-meidhe, *beam of a balance.*
m.-milis, *liquorice,* (siùcar dubh.)
m.-na-cudainne, (DMK) The cudainn differed from other tubs in having a stave on each side projecting above the others. These were perforated and the *maide* thrust through the perforations. The cudainn was thus suspended from *maide-na-cudainn,* which was borne by two persons on their shoulders, the cudainn being filled with water or other commodity.
m.-nigheadaireachd, *washing-stick.*
m.-poit, *thivel, pot-stick, spirtle.*
m.-reang, *stringer of a boat, see bàta, F 5, p.73 ; 2 ladder-step—Arran.*
m.-rongais, see m.-reang.
m.-singlidh, *single-stick.*
m.-siubhail, *connecting-rod of spinning-wheel.*
m.-slabhraidh, *beam from which the chain hangs over a fire in a black-house.*
m.-slachdaidh, *swingle-stick. 2 washing-stick.*
m.-sniomh, *distaff.*
m.-sniomhaidh, *distaff.*
m.-sreinge, *rubbing-piece in a boat, see E 6, p. 73.*
m.-starraig, see m.-feannaig.
m.-stiùraidh, *pot-stick ; 2 tiller of a rudder.*
m.-sùirn, *stick over the flue of a kiln.*
m.-ton-an-eich, *stick placed under the tail of a horse when rigged in the pack-saddle.*

maid'-a'-chrann-sparraidh, *s.m.* Stick in plough for holding mould-board, see p. 263.
maideachan -ain, -an, *s.m.* see maidean.
———, *n.pl.* of maide.
maideag, see maighdeag.
maideag, -eig, -an, *s.f.* Pivot. 2 see maighdeag.
maidealag,* *s.f.* Small shell—*Lewis.* 2 Part of a spinning-wheel.
maidean, -ein, -an, *s m. dim.* of maide. Little staff or stick. 2 Piece of timber. 3 Little piece of wood.
———, *pl.* of maide.
———ach, -aiche, *a.* Abounding in little sticks, or 2 Pieces of timber.
———nas, -ais, *s.m.* Morning dram.
maideog, *s.* Mussel—*Harris,* see maighdeag.
maidh, see maoidh.
———each, -ich, see maigheach.
———eag, -eig, -an, *s.f.* Midwife.
màidheau, -ein, -an, *s.m.* Delay, slowness. 2 Tediousness, irksomeness. 3**Laziness.
———ach, -aiche, *a.* Delaying, dilatory, slow. 2 Deliberate. 3 Late. 4 Tedious, irksome. 5 Remiss.
———achd, *s.f.* Tediousness, irksomeness. 2 Slowness, tardiness. 3** Laziness.
màidheanaiche, *s.m.* Protractor, procrastinator.
maidhm, -ean, *s.m.* see maoim.
———eadh, -eidh, see maoimeadh.
maidinn, see madainn.
maidne, *gen.sing.* of maduinn.
———ach, -eiche, see maduinneach. Dh' éirich mi maidneach, *I arose early.*
———achadh.** -aidh, *s.m.* Dawning, drawing towards morning.
———ag, -eig, -an, see maduinneag.
———agach, see maduinneagach.
———an, *s.pl.* for maduinnean.
maiduich,** *v.n.* Dawn.
màidse, -an, *s.f.* Uncouth or shapeless lump. 2 Applied in ridicule to persons. 3* Curd.
———ach, -eiche, *a.* Lumpish, clumsy, shapeless.
màidsear, -eir, -an, *s.m.* Major in the army.
———achd,** *s.f.* Majority in the army.
màig, *gen.sing.* of màg.
màig,** *s.f.* Affected attitude and disposition of the head.
maigeag, -eig, *s.f.* Midwife.
màigean, -ein, *s.m.* Fat little man. 2 Child beginning to walk. 3 Toad. 4 Frog. 5 Ludicrous term for a man with a creeping or sprawling gait, or moving on all fours.
———ach, -aiche, *a.* Creeping, crawling like a toad. 2 Fat and little. 3 Abounding in toads or frogs. 4 Like a frog. 5 Of, or pertaining to, a frog.
———achd, *s. f. ind.* Habit of creeping. 2 Creeping gait.
†maigh, -e, *a.* Pleasant, agreeable.
Màigh, -e, *s.f.* Month of May.
maighdeag, -ig, -an, *s. f.* Empty shell of the scallop fish—*concha veneris.* 2 (AF) cowrie. 3 Periwinkle. 4 Mussel—*Harris.* 5 Upright support of flyers of spinning-wheel.
maighdeag-thràghaid, *s.f.* see maighdeag.
maighdealag,* -aig, -an, *s. f.* Whelk. 2 see maighdeag.
maighdean, -ein, *pl.* [maighdinnean &] -an, *s.f.* Maid, maiden, virgin. 2 Any female servant. 3 Chambermaid. 4 Last handful of a crop of corn cut off the land. 5 Standard or bearer of driving-wheel (spinning-wheel.) 6 Upright support of flyers of spinning-wheel. 7 Beheading instrument. 8 The sign Virgo (♍) in the Zodiac. M. sheòmair, *a chambermaid ;* ma's fios do mhaighdinnibh rùn maighdein, *if maidens know a maiden's wish.*
maighdeanachd, *s.f.* Maidenliness.
maighdeanail, -e, *a.* Maidenly, modest, chaste.
maighdeanas, -ais, *s.m.* Virginity, maidenhead. Comharran maighdeanais, *tokens of virginity.*
maighdean-buaine, *s.f.* Last handful of corn cut off the land.

maighdean-chuain, *s.f.* Mermaid.
maighdean-coimhead, *s. f.* Waiting-woman, lady's maid.
maighdean-mhara, *s.f.* Mermaid.
maighdean-na-tuinne, see maighdean-mhara.
maighdean-phòsaidh, *s.f.* Bridesmaid.
maigheach, -iche, *s.f.* Hare. Cuilean maighiche, *a leveret.*
——————ail, -e, *a.* Leporine.
maigheach-gheal, *s. f.* White, blue, alpine or mountain hare.
màighean, -ein, see màidhean,
——————ach, see màidheanach.
——————achd, see màidheanachd.
maighisdreachd, see maighstireachd.
maighistir, see maighstir.
maighneas,** -eis, *s.m.* Field.
maighre,(AF) *s.m.* Salmon. 2 Salmon-trout. 3 Shoal of salmon.
——————adh.(AF) *s.m.* Shoal of salmon.
maighrealan,(AF) *s.m.* Salmon trout.
maighstir, -ean, *s. m.* Master. 2 Teacher. 3 Ruler.
—————— -dannsaidh, *s.m.* Dancing-master.
——————each, -eiche, *a.* Magisterial.
——————eachd, *s.f.ind.* Office of a master. 2 Superiority, mastery, rule. 3 Habit of assuming authority. 4*Officiousness. 5 Masterdom. 6 Superintendence.
——————eas, *s. m.* Same meanings as maighstireachd.
——————eil, -e, *a.* Masterly, lordly, authoritative, assuming authority, domineering, dogmatical, arbitrary. Gu m., *in a lordly manner.*
——————eileachd, *s.f.* see maighstireachd. 2 Assumption of undue authority.
—————— -sgoil, -ean-, *s.m.* Schoolmaster.
—————— -sgrìobhaidh, *s.m.* Writing-master.
maildheach, -eiche, see mailgheach.
màile, -an, see màille & màla.
——————ach, -eiche, *a.* see mailgheach & màilleach.
——————achan,* -ain, *s.m.* Elf.
——————an, see mailghean.
maileathan, see malaidhean.
màileid, -e, -ean, *s. f.* Bag, wallet, knapsack, budget, satchel, scrip. 2 *in derision,* The belly or stomach. 3 Clumsy, indolent person.
——————ich,(MS) *v.a.* Bag.
——————each, -aiche, *a.* Having bags or wallets. 2 Large-bellied. 3 Clumsy, indolent. 4** Like a wallet or knapsack.
†mailge, *s.f.* Funeral pile.
mailgeag, -eig, *s.f.* Midwife.
mailgheach, -eiche, *a.* Having large or shaggy eyebrows, beetle-browed.
mailghean, *pl.* of mala.
màilin, màilne, -ean, *s.f.* Eyebrow, see mala. 2 Space between the eyebrows, also called "maolchair na mailne."
mailios,** *s.f.* Cloak-bag, wallet.
†mailis, *s.f.* Ill-will *(malice.)*
†——————each, *a.* Malicious.
mailisidh,** *s.f.* Gaelic spelling of *militia.*
maille, *s.f.ind.* Delay, hinderance, impediment. 2 Slowness, tardiness. 3 Deficiency, want. A' cur m. air an léirsinn, *dazzling their eyes* (used e.g. of the sun or of anything gorgeous)—*Arran.*
maille, *comp.* of mall.
màille, *pl.* -an & -achan, *s. f.* Ring. 2 Armour, mail. 3 Helmet. 4 Heddle of a loom.
maille, (maille ri) *prep.* With, together with. M. ri sin, *together with that;* maille rium, *with me.*
màilleach, -eich, *s. f.* Armour, mail, coat of mail.
màilleach, -eiche, *a.* Furnished with rings. 2 Made of rings. 3 Mailed, armoured. Made of mail. Lùireach mh., *a coat of mail.*
mailleachadh, -aidh, *s.m.* Retarding, act of retarding or hindering, deferring, act of deferring, procrastinating. A' m—, *pr.pt.* of maillich.
màilleachan, -ain, *s.m.* Sprite, brownie.
——————, *n.pl.* of màille.
maillead, -eid, *s.m.* Slowness, degree of slowness.
màilleag, -eig, -an, *s.f.* Ear-ring.
maillich, *v.a. & n.* Retard, hinder, delay, procrastinate, defer, retard. 2 Suspend.
——————eadh, -eidh, -ean, *s.m.* Obstacle, hinderance, impediment. 2 Act of retarding or hindering. A' m—, *pr. pt.* of maillich.
maillig, *v.* see maillich.
mailmheas,** *s.m.* Malmsey.
——————ach, -aich, *s.m.* Malmsey.
maim, *s.f.* see màm & maoim.
maim,* *s.f.* Panic, horror.
maimseach, -ich, *s.m.* Bubonocele.
main, (a mhain) *adv.* Downwards.
màin, (a mhàin) *adv.* Alone, merely.
màin, *gen.sing.* of màn.
†main, -e, -ean, *s. f.* Hand. 2 Delay. 3 see maduinn. 4 Day.
†main, *s.f.* see man.
†màin, *v.n.* Remain, linger, stop. [chill.
†mainchill, -e, -ean, *s.f.*[***m.*] Sleeve, see muinimaindreach,** -ich, *s.m.* Hut, booth. 2 Fold.
màineachdail, *a.* Neglectful. 2 Lingering. 3 Undevout.
†màineag, -eig, -an, *s.f.* Little hand.
†màineag, -eig, -an, *s.f.* Glove.
†mainear, -eir, *s.m.* Gaelic spelling of *manor.*
maineil,(AC) *a.* Mindful.
†maineas, -eis, -an, *s.m.* Mistake, blunder.
màinidh,** *s.f.* Madness. 2 Rage. 3 Folly. see bàinidh.
mainistir, -ean, *s.m.* Monastery. [** gives *nom.* mainistear, *gen.* mainistir.]
maing, see minn.
maingeag, *s.f.* Pod.
mainne, -an, see mainneas.
——————as, -ais, -an, *s.f.* Delay, procrastination, hinderance, impediment, slowness, tardiness, sluggishness. 2 Deficiency, want. 3**Drawling. *prov.* for maille, s.
mainneasach, -aiche, *a.* Slow, tardy, procrastinating, sluggish.
mainnich,(MS) *v.a.* Relax.
mainnir, -ainnreach & -anrach, *pl.* -ean & mainnrichean, *s.f.* Fold for cattle, sheep or goats on the hill-side, pen. 2 Booth. 3 Prison. O 'n mh., *from the fold.*
mainnis, -e, see mainneas.
mainniseach, -eiche, *a.* see mainneasach.
mainnreach, *gen.sing.* of mainnir.
——————, *a.* Abounding in, or having folds or pens for cattle, sheep or goats. 2 Of, or belonging to, folds, pens or prisons. 3 Having prisons.
mainnreach, -rich, *s.m.* Hut, booth. 2 Fold. 3 Prison. [** gives *s.f.*]
mainnsear, -eir, -an, *s. m.* Gaelic spelling of *manger.* [** gives *s.f.*]
main-obair, -oibre, *s.m.* Handiwork.
†mainse, *s.f.* Maintenance, sustenance.
mair, *pr.pt.* a' maireann, a' mairsinn & a' maireachduinn, *v.n.* Live, exist. 2 Continue, last, endure. Am feadh 's a mhaireas an ruaig, *while the pursuit lasts*; cha mhair iad leth an là, *they shall not live half their days*; mairidh tròcair Dhé gu sìor, *God's mercy*

shall endure for ever ; am m.. e ? *is he alive ?* or *will he live ?* cha mh. e, *he is not alive,* or *he will not live.*
mairbh, *gen.sing. & nom.pl.* of marbh.
——e, see mairbhead.
——ead, -eid, *s.f.* Degree of deadness. 3 State of being dead or lifeless.
mairbh-ghreim, -e, *s. f.* Morphew, scurf on the face.
mairc,* *s. f.* Objection, subject of regret. Cò chuir m. ort ? *who objected to you ?* cha do chuir mise m. sam bith air, *I did not oppose him.* 2 see mairg.
màireach, *s.m.* The morrow, next day. An diugh 's am m., *to-day and to-morrow ;* air an là m., *on the morrow ;* an là an déidh am m., *the day after to-morrow.* [In the old Tales, and in common conversation both in Scotland and Ireland, "an la arn-a-mhàireach" is used for "to-morrow"—MM.]
maireachduinn, *s.f. & pr.pt.* see mairsinn
mairealach, -aiche, *a.* Benumbing.
mairealadh,** -aidh, *s. m.* Benumbing. 2 Numbness.
maiream, (for mairidh mi), I shall live.
maireann, *a. & pr.pt.* of mair. Lasting, durable, enduring, perpetual. 2 Surviving, alive, existing, remaining, living, in the land of the living. 3 *substantively,* Life-time. Ri d' mh., *during your life-time ;* cha mhaireann e, *he is not living* ; am fear nach m., *he that is no more* ; am m. da ? *is he alive ?* is m. a chliù, *lasting is his praise.*
——ach, -aiche, *a.* Everlasting, eternal, lasting, perpetual. 2 Long-lived. A' bheatha mh., *everlasting life* ; saoibhreas m., *durable riches.*
——achd, *s.f.ind.* Durability, long continuance. 2 Long life.
maireantas, see maireannachd.
maireasail,** *s.f.* Life.
maireulan, see maighreulan.
maireun, *s.m.* Small salmon.
mairg, *a.* Pitiable, deplorable. 2 Despicable, 3 Silly, foolish, simple. 4 Woeful, sorrowful. Sonn nach m., *a hero that is not to be pitied ;* is m. a loisgeadh a thiompan dhuit, *pity him who would burn his harp to (warm) you.*
mairg, *s.f.ind.* Pity, woe. 2 Subject of regret. 3**Folly. 4††Object of pity. Cha mh. té a fhuair e, *she is no object of regret that got him or it ;* is m. dhuit a rinn e, *it is a pity you did it ;* is m. dhuit nach tigeadh tu, *it is a pity you could not come* ; a mh. dhuit ! *woe to you !*
†mairge, -an, *s.f.* Groan, distress.
mairgeach, -eiche, *a.* Woeful, piteous, sorrowful, sad, mournful, sighing, groaning.
†mairgne, -an, *s.m.* Woe, sorrow. [** gives *f.* & no †.]
mairgneach, -eiche, see mairgeach.
†mairgnich, *v.n.* Groan, sob. 2 Bewail, deplore.
mairich, -ean, see maraich.
màirich, -ean, see màireach.
mairiche, see maraiche.
mairidh, *fut.aff.a.* of mair.
mairionn, ——ach, } *a.* see { maireann. ——ach.
mairiste, -an, *s.m.* Cohabitation, marriage. 2 Congressus venereus. 3**Match. 4**Husband. 5**Coupling. Fhuair i an deagh mh., *she made a good match ;* a' deanamh suas a' mh., *making up the match.*
——ach, -eiche, *a.* Of, or belonging to, cohabitation, conjugal, spousal. 2 Marriageable. 3 Fond of match-making. Tha i m. banail, *she is marriageable and modest.*
†màirl, *v.a.* Bruise, pound, crumble. 2 Maul.
†màirn, *v.a.* Betray.
——,** *s.f.* Spying. 2 Betraying.
——each,** -nich, *s.m.* Betrayer.
mairneach,(AF) *s.m.* Full salmon.
màirneal, -eil, -an, *s. m.* Delay, lingering, detention 2 Hinderance, obstacle. 3 Dalliance. 4 Backwardness. 5 Procrastination. Na dean m., *or* na cuir m., *do not delay.*
mairnealach, -aiche, *a.* Slow, dilatory, apt to delay. 2 Causing delay, hindering, procrastinating. 3 Drawling in manner, tedious. 4 Backward. 5 Slothful.
——, -aich, *s.m.* Mariner. 2 Pilot who fortells the state of the weather from the appearance of the sky, or from a certain arrangement or modification of clouds.
——d, *s.f.ind.* Delay, procrastination, habit of procrastinating. 2 Slothfulness. 3 Backwardness. 4 Slowness, tediousness, dilatoriness.
màirnealaich, *v.n.* Delay, procrastinate.
——e, *s.m.* Delayer.
mairneamh,** -nimh, *s.m.* Spy.
mairseal,(CR) *s.m.* Merchant—*Arran.*
mairseanta, see marsanta.
——chd, see marsantachd.
mairsinn, *s.m.* Lasting, state of lasting, continuing, abiding, remaining. 2 Continuance, duration. A' m—, *pr.pt.* of mair.
——eachd, see mairsinn.
mairt, *gen.sing.* of mart.
mairt,** *s.m.* Matter. 2 Consequence. 3 Harm. An deamhan m., *the devil may care.*
mairteach, -eiche, *a.* see martach.
mairt-fheoil, -fheòla, *s.f.* Beef.
mairt-fheolach, *a.* Beef, pertaining to beef. 2 Abounding in beef.
mairtheann, ——ach, } *a.* see { maireann. ——ach.
——achd, see maireannachd.
mairtir, -ean, *s.m.* see mairtireach.
——each, -eich, *s.m.* Martyr.
——eachd, *s. f. ind.* Martyrdom, fate of a martyr.
màis, *gen.sing.* of màs.
†mais, -e, -ean, *s.f.* Lump. 2 Heap. 3 Acorn.
†maise,** *s.f.* Food, victuals.
maise, *s.f.ind.* Beauty, comeliness, gracefulness, elegance, bloom. 2 Ornament, decoration. Chuireadh tu m. air baile, *you would prove an ornament to a town ;* m. nam ban, *the ornament of women ;* air son m., *for beauty ;* m. 'na dealbh, *handsome in her person or form.*
maiseach, -iche, *a.* Beautiful, handsome, fair, graceful. 2 Modest. 3 Of engaging manners. 4 Ornamental. 5** Having an imposing appearance. Is maisiche thu na clann nan daoine, *thou art fairer than the sons of men* ; nighean mh., *an elegant female.*
maiseachadh, aidh, *s. m.* Beautifying, act of beautifying, adorning, decking or decorating. A' m—, *pr. pt.* of maisich.
maiseachail, -e, *a.* see maiseach. 2 (MS) Cosmetic.
maiseachd, *s.f.ind.* Beauty, handsomeness, elegance, comeliness. 2* Superiority in beauty.
maiseag, -eig, -an, *s.f.* Pretty female. 2 Modest or engaging female.
maisealachd, *s.* see maiseachd. 2**Delightfulness.
maiseil, -e, *a.* see maiseach.
maise-mnà, -an-, *s.f.* Female beauty,
maisich,** *v.a.* Deck, decorate, beautify.
——e, *comp.* of maiseach.
maisleadh,** -idh, *s.m.* see masladh.
maislean, see mislean.
maislinn,** *s.* Mastlin.

maisteag,§ -eig, -an, *s.f.* The mastic tree—*pistacia lentiscus*. Much used for chewing in the East.
maistidh,(AF) *s.* Mastiff dog.
maistig, see maistidh.
maistir, *s.m.* Urine prepared for dyeing.
———,(AF) *s.f.* Churn.
———, *pr.pt.* a' maistireadh, *v.a.* see maistrich.
———eadh, *pr.pt.* of maistir.
———ich, see maistrich.
maistreachadh, -aidh, *s. m.* Churning, act of churning, making butter. 2 Mixing. 3 Agitating. 4* The quantity of butter taken off a churn. A' m—, *pr. pt.* of maistrich.
maistreadh, *s.m.* & *pr.pt.* see maistreachadh.
maistrich, *pr. pt.* a' maistreachadh, *v.a.* Churn. 2 Mix together. 3 Agitate.
————te, *past pt.* of maistrich. Churned. 2 Shaken together, mixed.
maiteach, see maithteach.
maith, -e, *a.* see math. Also pronounced *moith* in *Arran.*
———, *pr.pt.* a' mathadh, *v.a.* Forgive, pardon. 2 Suffer, allow, permit. 3 Abate. Cha mh. mi peighinn, *I will not abate a penny.*
maith, *s.* & *adv.* see math.
maithe', *s.pl.* for maithean.
maitheach, -eiche, *a.* Ready to forgive, relenting.
————, -eich, -eichean, *s.f.* see maigheach.
————as,** -ais, *s. m.* Forgiveness, pardon. 2 Abatement. 3 Manure.
maitheadh, -eidh, *s.m.* Forgiving, act of forgiving, pardoning, remitting. 2 Suffering, allowing. 3 Slackening. 4 Abatement, discount.
maithean, *s.pl.* Chieftains, nobles, rulers. 2 Heroes. 3*Magistrates, aldermen. 4 Best of any class of beings. M. an treud, *the principal of the flock ;* thàinig àrd-bhàillidh agus m. Bail'-ath-cliath a mach 'na choinneamh, *the Lord Mayor and magistrates of Dublin came out to meet him ;* m. na Féinne, *the nobles of the Feinne.*
————achd,‡‡ *s.f.* Nobleness.
maitheanas, -ais, *s.m.* Pardon, forgiveness, remission of a penalty. Tha mi ag iarraidh maitheanais, *I ask pardon ;* m. dhuit ! *may God forgive you !*
——————achd,(MS) *s.f.* Pardonableness.
maitheas, -eis, *s.m.* Goodness, kindness, mercy, bounty. 2 Virtue. 3 Druidism, sorcery.
————ach, -aiche, *a.* Good, benevolent, virtuous, forgiving, lenient, benign.
————achd, *s.f.* see maitheas.
maithich, *prov.* for mathaich.
maithreach,(AF) *s.f.* Mother cow or sheep.
——————adh,(MS) *s.m.* Matriculation.
màithrean,** -ein, *s.m.* Aunt on the mother's side.
maithrich,(MS) *v.a.* Matriculate.
maithteach, -eiche, *a.* Forgiving. 2 Forbearing, charitable.
——————as, -ais, *s.m.* Forgiveness. 2 Readiness to forgive. 3 Forbearance, indulgence.
†mal, -ail, -an, *s.m.* King. 2 Prince. 3 Champion, soldier. 4 Poet. Seachd cathan de mhal-shluagh, *seven companies of soldiers.*
màl, -àil, *s.m.* Rent, tribute, tax, subsidy. La a' mhàil, *rent-day ;* an àm togail màil, *in the time of collecting rents.*
mal, -ail, -an, *s.f.* see màl.
màla, -n, *s.f.* Bag, budget sack, satchel, scrip. Bag of a bag-pipe. 3**Husk, shell. Dà mh., *two bags.*
mala, *pl.* -ichean [mailghean & malaidhean,] *s.* Brow, eye-brow. 2 Brow of a hill. M. na sgòrr, *the brow of the rock ;* bha mise 'n Talla nan cruth saileathan, is chunna mi 'n crùn a' dol mu thrì malaidhean, *I have been to the hall of the engraved beams and seen the crown placed upon three brows—Sgeul.-nan-caol ;* m. cnoic, *the brow of a hill.*
màlabhar,** -air, *s.m.* Dwarf elder.
màlach, -aich, -aichean, see màla.
malach,** -aich, *s.m.* Load.
————, see mala.
————,* -aiche, *a.* Having large eyebrows. 2 Surly, sulky, forbidding.
màladair, -ean, *s.m.* One who pays rent, tenant. 2** Farmer of the customs. 3*Sub-tenant who pays rent in kind.
màladh, -aidh, -aidhean, see màla.
maladh, -aidh, -aidhean, see mala.
malaich,(DU) *Gairloch* for mala.
malaid, -ean, see màileid.
malaid,** -ean, *s.f.* Flail. 2 Scourge. 3 Thong.
malaidhean, *n. pl.* of mala.
màlaind, see malairt.
màlair, -ean, *s.m.* Merchant, barterer. 2 Renter. 3 Cottager holding of a farmer The màlair does not depend for his whole support on farm labour, but may derive his sustenance from any handicraft of which he is master, the farmer of whom he holds, however, expects his aid during harvest. Màlair is also applied to a cottager who builds his hut on a barren spot of ground, and digs and cultivates patches around it, for which he pays no rent for a certain number of years—**.
malairt, -ean, *s.f.* Exchange, barter. 2 Exchanging, act of exchanging. 3 Business. 4 Affair. 5*Space. A' m—, *pr. pt.* of malairtich. Thoir am m., *give in exchange ;* a' deanamh m., *exchanging.*
————,* *v.a.* Exchange, barter, traffic, trade.
————each, -eich, *s.m.* Exchanger, barterer. M.-airgid, *money-changer, banker.*
————each, -aiche, *a.* Exchanging, given to exchange or barter. 2 Exchangeable, fit to exchange. 3 Mutual, reciprocal.
malairteachadh, -aidh, *s. m.* } & *pr pt.* of mal-
malairteachd, *s.f.ind.* } airtich, see malairt.
malairtear,* see màlair.
malairtich, *pr.pt.* a' malairt, a' malairteachd & a' malairteachadh, *v.a.* Exchange, barter.
—————e, *s.* see malairteach, *s.*
—————te, *past pt.* of malairtich, Exchanged, bartered.
màlanach,†† *a.* Rented.
————, (DU) *s. m.* One who pays rent—*Gairloch.*
malart, see malairt.
malc, *pr.pt.* a' malcadh, *v.a.* & *n.* Rot, putrefy. 2 Become putrid. 3 Cause to rot. 4 Corrupt. 5** Carry, bear.
——ach, -aiche, *a.* Rotten, putrid. 2 Apt to rot. 3 Causing rottenness or putrefaction.
——achd, see malcaidheachd
——adh, -aidh, *s.m.* Rottenness, putrefaction. 2 State of becoming putrid 3 Act of causing to rot. 4**Carrying, bearing. A' m—, *pr.pt.* of malc.
malcaidh, -e, *a.* Rotten, putrid 2 Stinking.
————eachd, *s. f. ind.* Rottenness, putrescence
malcair,** *s.m.* Porter (of a burden.) 2 Salesman.
————eachd,** *s.f.ind.* Porterage 2 Selling, sale.
malcta, *past pt.* of malc. Rotten, putrid. 2 Become rotten or putrid 3 *a.* Cadaverous.
malcte, see malcta.
màlda, *a.* Mild, calm, gentle, modest, coy,

bashful.
màldachd, *s.f.ind.* Mildness, gentleness, modesty, diffidence.
màldag, -aig, -an, *s.f.* Mild, modest, quiet, gentle female.
———ach,** *a.* Mild or modest, as a female.
mal-ios,** *s.m.* Portmanteau.
†mall,** *a.* Bad.
mall, -aille, *a.* Slow, moving slowly. 2 Lazy. 3 Not forward. 4 Calm, placid. 5 Tardy, late. 6 Weak. pithless. 7 Dull, senseless. Bitheadh gach duine ealamh chum éisdeachd, m. chum labhairt 's m. chum feirge, *let every-one be ready to hear, slow to speak and slow to wrath* ; feasgar m. 's na h-eòin a' seinn, *a calm evening and the birds warbling* ; m. a chluinntinn, *dull of hearing* ; is m. a chas, *pithless is his leg.*
mall, *s.m.* see mathalt, 1.
mallachadh, -aidh, *s.m.* Cursing, act of cursing. 2 Swearing. 3 Curse, imprecation. 4**Oath. Luchd-mallachaidh, *swearers* ; bheir e m. orm, *he will bring a curse on me.* [Pronounced *mollachadh* in *Argyll.**]
mallachd, -an, *s.f.* Curse. 2 Oath, imprecation. M.-eaglais, *excommunication.*
màllachd,** *s. f.* Modesty, gentleness, softness, mildness. 2 Debility.
mallaich,** *v.n.* Grow mild, grow calm or composed.
———, *v.a. & n.* Curse. 2 Swear, imprecate. 3 Execrate. 4††Condemn.
———te, *a. & past pt.* of mallaich. Cursed, accursed. M. gu'n robh an corruich, *cursed be their wrath.*
mallan,(AF) -ain, *s.m.* Mole.
mall-bheurlach, -aiche, *a.* see mall-bhriathrach.
mall-bhriathrach, -aiche, *a.* Hesitating, slow of speech. 2 Drawling in speech. 2 Not fluent in language. 4 Having feeble language.
——— ———-as, -ais,*s.m.* Slowness of speech.
——— ———-d, *s.f.* Slowness of speech.
mall-cheumach, -aiche, *a.* Slow, that walks slowly, having a feeble gait. 2 ‡‡Gradual.
mall-cheumnaich,‡‡ *v.a.* Jog.
mall-chodach,** *s.m.* One who sups late.
mall-chreideach, -eiche, *a.* Incredulous.
mall-chreidimh, *s.m.* Incredulousness.
mall-dromach,** *a.* Saddle-backed.
mall-ghluasadach, -aiche, *a.* Slow.
mall-imich, see mall-cheumnaich.
mall-mhuir,** *s.f.* Neap-tide.
mall-phunc, *s.m.* Semi-breve, in *music.*
mall-shiùbhlach, *a.* Loitering.
mall-shluagh,* see mal-shluagh.
mall-smuainteadh, -eidh, -eidhean, *s.m.* Deep musing or study.
mall sneimh, *s.m.* Delay.
mall sniamh, *Arran* for mall sneimh.
mallta, see malda.
mall-thriallach, -aiche, *a.* Slow or feeble in travelling, slow, lazy, loitering.
malluchadh, -aidh, *s.m. & pr.pt.* see mallachadh.
malluich, *v.* see mallaich.
———te, see mallaichte.
maloimh, *s.pl.* Mallows (plants)—*malvæ.*
malpais, see craobh-mhalpais.
malraich,** *v.a.* Exchange, barter.
mal-shluagh, -uaigh, *s.m.* Host, army. 2 Commonalty.
malt, see mathalt, 1.
malta, see malda.
———chd, see maldachd.
màltag, see màldag.
———-ach, see màldagach.
màl-thosd, *s.m.* Hush-money.
maluidh, -ean, see mala.
†màm, -àim, -an, *s.f.* Hand, fist. 2 Might, power. 3 Gap, pass through mountains. 4 Mother. 5 Breast, pap. 6**Eruption, sally. 7 ***rarely* Battle. 8** *rarely* Breach.
màm, -àim, -an, *s.m.* Hill of a particular form, slowly rising and not pointed, large round hill. 2 Handful, as much of grain or of any such substance as can be taken up by holding the two hands together. M. air muin an t-saic, *a handful over and above the sack* ; m. nan gleann, *the hill of the valleys.*
màm, -àim, -an, *s.m.* Boil or ulcerous swelling in armpit, or palm of the hand. 2††Mole on the skin.
mamaidh, -ean, Gaelic spelling of *mammy.*
ma màr, ma màrsa, } ** *prov. expressions.* signifying On my word, by my troth. Ma màr fhéin, *by my troth.*
mamas,** -ais, *s.m.* Might, strength, power.
màm-léighin,‡‡ *s.m.* Kind of multure paid for sifting meal in a mill.
màm-sic,*s.m.* Rupture, swelling, hernia.
mamuin,** *s.m.* Instant.
màn, see màm.
†man, -ain, *s.m.* Hand.
m' an, *cont.* for mu+an. About the. 2 About their. Ag iadhadh m' an tòrr, *hovering about the hill* ; dubhradh m' an gruaidh, *gloom about their visage.*
†mana, *s.m.* Cause. 2 Condition.
manach, -aich, *s.m.* Monk. 2 Friar. 3 Foreteller. 4 Conventual. 5 Angel-fish. 6 (AF) Hooded skate.
———ail, -e, *a.* Monkish, recluse, monastic, conventual. 2 Predicting.
———an, -ain, -an, *s.m.* The groin.
———as, -ais,*s.m.* State of a monk, monkhood. 2 Monkishness. 3 Monkish or conventual practice or observance.
———d, *s.f.ind.* State of a monk, monkhood. 2 Monkishness. 3**Cloister, monastery.
———uinn, -ean, *s. f.* Convent, monastery. [‡ gives manachainn.]
mànadail,(MS) *a.* Auspicious.
manadaireachd, *s.f.ind.* Foreboding, predicting, foretelling.
manadh, -aidh, -aidhean, *s.m.* Chance, luck, fate, lot. 2 Incantation, enchantment. 3 Omen, sign. 4 Prediction. 5 Allegation, plea. 6** Trump at cards. 7 (AF) Owl. 8 Apparition. Chunnaic e m., *he saw on apparition* ; tha e 'cur air mh. dhomh, *he prophesies to me.* [** gives mànadh for Nos. 1, 3, and 4.]
manag, -aig, -an, *s.f.* Glove, mitten.
———ach,** *a.* Gloved, having gloves on.
managhise,** *s.f.* Spear.
manaich, *gen.sing. & n. pl.* of manach.
manaig, see manag.
manair, see mainnir. [grieve.
manaistear,** *s. f.* Monastery. 2(WC)Overseer,
manaran, *s.m.* Necromancer, conjurer. 2 see mànran.
mànas,** -ais, *s.m.* Strength, power.
mànas, -ais, -an, *s.m.* The portion of an estate cultivated by the proprietor, "mains," home-farm. 2 Farm. large or level farm. 3††Manse. 4**Farm-steading.
†manchàin, *s.* Tribute of the hand, gifts, presents given at wakes and funerals.
†man-chruimh, *s.f.* Cheese-mite, maggot.
ma'n cuairt, see mu'n cuairt.
mandal,** -ail, *s.m.* Anger. 2 Roughness.
mandrag, -aig, -an, *s. f.* Mandrake—*mandragora officinalis.*

mandragach, *a.* Abounding in mandrakes. 2 Like a mandrake. 3 Of or pertaining to, a màndrake.

mang, -aing, -an, *s.f.* Fawn. 2 Deer one-year old, brocket. 3**Young hart. 4**Craftiness, deceit. 5**Bag, budget. 6** Moroseness, sourness. Gleann 'san lionmhor mang, *a glen where harts abound.*

——ach, -aiche, *a.* Abounding in fawns or young harts. 2 Of, or belonging to, a fawn or hart. 3 Bounding. 4 Crafty. 5**Deceitful. 6 Morose, sour. Laoghach, m., maoisleach, *abounding in calves, deer and roes.*

——ach,(AF) *s.m.* Whiting (fish.)

——ail,** *a.* Deceitful, treacherous.

†**mangair**,** -ean, *s.m.* Inn-keeper, taverner. 2 Costermonger. 3 Pedlar.

——an, -ain, -an, see mathghamhuinn.

——anach, see mathghamhuinneach.

mann,§ *s.* Wheat, see cruithneachd.

†——, -ainn, *s.m.* Food. 2 Wedge. 3 Ounce. 4 Sin.

†——, *a.* Bad, naughty.

†**mannar**,** -air, *s.m.* Evil, loosening.

mannd,* *s.m.* Lisp, stammer.

mannda,** *a.* see manntach.

———ch, see manntach.

manndaich,(MS) *v.a.* Hack.

manndaiche,(MS) *s.f.* Inarticulateness, lisp.

manndaidh,** *a.* Gagged.

manndair, *s.m.* see manntair.

manndal, see mantal.

mannraichean, *pl.* of mainnir.

mannraichibh, *dat.pl.* of mainnir.

mannta, see manntach.

———ch, -aiche, *a.* Lisping, stammering, stuttering, tongue-tied. 2 Demure, modest, bashful.

———ch,** -aich, *s.m.* One who stutters or lisps.

———chd, *s. f.ind.* Stuttering, stammering, lisping 2 Bashfulness, demureness.

manntair, -ean, *s.m.* Stutterer, stammerer. 2 Demure person.

———eachd, see manntachd.

manntal,** -ail, see mantal.

manntan, -ain, *s.m.* Slight degree of stammering in speech. 2 Timidity, bashfulness, demureness. Crith manntain, *a bashful tremor.*

manoise, *s.f.* Spear.

manrach, -aich, -aichean, *s.f.* see mainnir. 2 Gift.

†———d,** *s.f.* Gift. 2 Happiness.

manradh, -aidh, *s.m.* Destruction.

màurain, *v.n.* Dander. M. thus' air t' aghaidh, *dander forward.*

màuran, -ain, -an, *s. m.* Tuneful sound, melody. 2 Humming of a song or tune, cooing. 3 Entertainment, feasting. 4 Blandishment. dalliance, amorous discourse. 5 Report, rumour, intelligence, news. 6 Murmur. 7** Love-song or sonnet. 8††Humming song. 9* Dandering. Le m. 's le mireadh, *with feasting and fun ;* cumhach air lag mhànrain, *disconsolate, with a faint voice ;* m. binn an òrain, *the sweet melody of song ;* ri m. ciùil, *singing a love-song.*

———ach, -aiche, *a.* That hums, humming, given to humming of songs or tunes. 2 Melodious, musical, tuneful. 3 Amorous, toying, skilled in love language. 4 Abounding in rumours. 5‡‡ Ready to raise or spread reports. 6‡‡Noisy. 7 Murmuring. 8**Hospitable, feasting, convivial. Òigh a' bheòil mhànranaich, *maid of the melodious voice.*

———achd, *s.f.ind.* Habit of humming tunes. 2 Melodiousness. 3 Blandishment, habit of dallying. 4 Amorousness. 5 Noisiness. 6** Musicalness.

———aich,(MS) *v.a.* Carol.

manras,** -ais, *s.m.* Motion. 2 Noise.

†**mantach**, -aich, *s.m.* Toothless person.

mantag,** -aig, *s. f.* Bridle-bit. 2 Gag. 3 Muzzle.

mantal, Gaelic spelling of *mantle.*

mao-bhlasda, see maoth-bhlasda.

maoch,** *s.m.* Bleaching-green.

maodal, -ail, -an, *s.f.* Stomach, maw, tripe, paunch. 2 *ludicrously* Large belly, gorbelly. 3**Bird's crop. Cho dorch ri m. a' mhairt dhuinn, *as dark as the brown cow's inside.* [** gives *m.*]

———ach, -aiche, *a.* Having a stomach, paunch, crop or maw. 2 Having a large stomach or paunch. 3 Like, or belonging to, the paunch, stomach or crop. 4 Fat, gorbellied, corpulent, clumsy.

———ach, -aich, *s.m.* & *f.* Paunches, tripe. 2 Big-bellied or corpulent person. 3 Greedy, voracious person. 4‡‡Young woman. 5(CR) Maid-servant who does more or less other work than house-work. 6*Clumsy or corpulent female.

maodh, -oidhe, *a.* see maoth.

———adh,** -aidh, *s.m.* Moistening. 2 Boasting. 3 Reproaching. 4 Proclaiming.

maodhaich, see maothaich.

maodhain, *gen.sing.* of maodhan.

maodhan, see maothan.

———ach, see maothanach.

———achd, see maothanachd.

maodhar, -air, -an, *s.m.* see maghar.

maodlach,(MS) *a.* Pot-bellied.

maodlach,** -aich, *s.m.* Servant.

maoidh, *pr.pt.* a' maoidheamh & a' maoidheadh, *v.a. & n.* Grudge, give unwillingly. 2 Reproach, upbraid. 3 Threaten, bully. 4 Cast up to one a favour bestowed on him. 5 Boast, vapour. 6** Envy. 7** Proclaim. Dia, a bheir do gach neach gu pailt agus nach m., *God, who giveth to all men liberally and upbraideth not ;* is fheàrr a mh. no dhìbir, *it is better obtained grudgingly than not at all ;* mh. sinn cath, *we proclaimed battle.*

maoidh,** *s.* Grudge.

———each, -eiche, *a.* Grudging, giving unwillingly. 2 Reproaching, upbraiding. 3 Threatening. 4 Boasting. 5 Proclaiming.

———eachas, -ais, *s.m.* Habit of grudging. 2 Upbraiding. 3 Threatening. 4 Proclaiming. 5 Objection. 6 Vain-glory, boasting.

———eadh, -eidh, *s.m.* Grudging, act of grudging or giving reluctantly. 2 Upraiding, act of upbraiding, reproaching. 3 Threatening, act of threatening, threat. 4 Proclaiming, proclamation. 5 Boasting, boast, bravado. 6* Casting up favours bestowed. A' m—, *pr.pt.* of maoidh. Tha e 'm. orm, *he is threatening me ;* tha e 'm. gu'n d' rinn e siod 'us seo dhomh, *he casts up that he did this and that for me ;* nach dean m., *who upbraideth not.*

———eamh, -eimh, *s.m.* & *pr.pt.* see maoidheadh.

———ean, -ein, -an, *s.m.* Interest, personal influence, favour. 2 Entreaty, supplication. 3 Good work. Deanaibh m. as mo leth, *or* air mo shon, *make supplication for me.*

———eanach, -aiche, *a.* Having personal interest or influence, favoured. 2 Entreating, supplicatory. 3(CR) Friendly—*Perthshire.*

———eanachd, *s.f.ind.* Entreating, supplicating.

———ear,** *s.m.* Bully.

maoidhm, see maoim.

maoidhseig, see maoiseag.

maoil, see maol.
maoile, *comp.* of maol. Balder, baldest.
———, *s.f.ind.* Baldness. 2 Bluntness of an edge or point. 3 (MS) Homeliness. 4 Heap. 5 see maol. An àite fuilt bithidh m., *instead of hair there shall be baldness ;* sgaoil do mh., *spread thy baldness ;* m. nan cruach, *the baldness of the rocks.*
———, -an, *s.f.* Brow of a hill. 2 Forehead. 3 Upper part of the forehead.
maoileachd,(MS) *s.f.* Thickness.
maoilead, -eid, *s.m.* Baldness, degree of baldness. 2 Bluntness, degree of bluntness Air mh. 's gu'm bheil e, *however bald he be* ; a' dol am m., *growing more and more bald.*
maoileag,(AC) *s,f* Stout little girl. 2 Filly. 3 Young female animal.
maoilean, -ein, *s.m* Bald person. 2 Stupid person. 3 Brow of a bleak hill. 4 Bleak eminence. 5**Summit. 6 Postern. 7** Sea-maw. Thar a' mhaoilein bhàrr-liath, *over the grey-coped postern.*
———ach, -aich, *s.m.* Youth who goes bare-headed. 2†† Bald or bare-headed man.
———ach, -aiche, *a.* Bald, like a bald person. 2 Abounding in bleak hills. 3 Having a bleak top, as a hill. 4**Ridgy, topped, as a hill. 5**Pinnacled. 6** Of, or belonging to, sea-maws. 7**Abounding in sea-maws.
maoileann, (AF) *s.m.* Mule.
maoilinn, -ean, see maoilean.
———each, see maoileanach.
maol-mhullaich, (DU) Common in *Gairloch* for maoile 1.
maoilseach, see maoisleach.
maoim, -e, -ean, *s.f.* Terror, alarm, consternation, fear. 2 Surprise, panic, flight. 3 Sudden burst, sally, eruption, as of water. 4 Onset, sudden attack. 5*Wild expression of countenance. 6*Expression of fear. 7**Impetuous onset. Bitheadh m. air do naimhdean, *let your enemies be panic-stricken ;* le m , *with terror ;* m. sléibhe, *a water-spout, a mountain torrent.*
———, *pr.pt.* a' maoimeadh,*v a.& n.* Be afraid, or terrified. 2 Hesitate, pause from doubt or fear. 3 Horrify, terrify.
———each, -eiche, *a.* Causing terror. 2 Bursting forth suddenly. 3 Impetuous, as a torrent. 4 Causing mountain torrents. 5** Boasting.
———eadh, *s. m.* State of being alarmed or terrified. 2 Hesitating from fear or doubt. 3 Pouring forth, bursting forth, as a stream. 4 Sallying, making an onset. 5 Terror, alarm. A' m—, *pr. pt.* of maoim.
——— -sleibhe,* *s. m.* Water-spout, sudden plump of rain.
maoin, -e, -ean,*s.f.* Substance, property,wealth, goods and gear. 2 Small quantity. 3 *rarely* Love, esteem. 4* Hoarded wealth, wealth worshipped. An spréidh agus am m., *their cattle and their substance* ; m. a mhaighstir, *the goods of his master.*
maoin-chunntas, -ais, *s.m.* Inventory.
maoineach, -eiche, *a.* Wealthy, substantial. 2 Fertile, productive. A' Bhealltuinn mh., *productive May.*
———ail, -e, *a.* see maoineach.
maoineas, -eis, *s.f.* Slowness, tardiness.
———ach, -aiche, *a.* Slow, tardy.
maoir, *gen.sing. & n.pl.* of maor.
——-each, -eich, *s.m. prov.* for maorach.
——-eachd, *s.f.* Stewardship—*Dàin I. Ghobha.*
maoirne, -an, *s.m.* Bait for a fishing-hook 2 Single bait. 3*Little one. 4 see maoirnean.
———ach, -eiche, *a.* Furnished with fishing-baits.
maoirneachd-eaglais,(MS) *s.f.* Sextonship.
maoirneag,* -eig, *s.f.* Spat.
maoirnean, -ein, -an, *s.m.* The least quantity of anything. 2 Small potato 3††Kind of cockle.
maoirseachd,** see maorsainneachd.
maois, -e, -ean, *s.f* Large basket or hamper, now used principally as a measure for herrings. 2 Certain number of fish, 500 herrings. 3 Quantity of seaweed collected and bound together, and floated to any desired place. 4 **Burden. 5**Carriage. 6**Gaelic spelling of *maize.* 7** Bag. M. sgadan, *a measure of 500 herrings.*
maoiseach, -eiche, *a* Of, or belonging to, large baskets or hampers, or to 2 heaps of seaweed. 3**Mosaic. 4 In measures of 500. 5 **Like maize. 6 Abounding in roes or deer. 7 Like a roe or deer.
————, -eich, -eichean, *s. f* Roe (female of the hart, a species of deer smaller than fallow-deer.) 2 Doe (female of fallow-deer or buck.) 3 Heifer. 4 see miseach.
maoiseag, -eig, -an, *s.f., dim* of maois. Little hamper, burden or pack. 2 Scolding female. 3 Stingy, niggardly female. 4**Heifer.
————ach, -aiche, *a.* Abounding in small baskets or hampers. 2 Like a basket or hamper. Abounding in does. 3 Like a scolding female. 4 Like a niggardly female. 5 Prone to scold.
maois-eisg,‡ *s.f.* Five hundred fish.
maoisgeag,†† -eig, -eigean, see maoiseag.
maoisleach, -eich, -eichean, *s.f* see maoiseach. Caraid na maoislich, *twin roes.*
————, -eiche, *a.* Abounding in roes or does. 2 Like a roe or doe. Maugach, m., *abounding in deer and roes ;* a' Bhealltuinn mh., *roe-producing May.*
maoith, see maoidh.
maoithe, *s.f.ind.* Softness, tenderness.
———, *comp.* of maoth.
———ach, -eiche, *a.* see maoidheach.
———achas, see maoidheachas.
maoithead, -eid, *s.m.* Softness, degree of softness or tenderness.
maoitheadh, -eidh, -eidhean, *s.m. & pr. pt.* see maoidheadh.
maol, -aoile, *a.* Bare. 2 Bald. 3 Hornless. 4 Blunt, edgeless, pointless. 5 Bare, without foliage. 6 Foolish, silly, easily deceived. 7 Barren, bleak. 8 (MS) Home-bred. Iarunn m.. *blunt iron ;* mullach m. liath, *a bleak grey eminence* ; maol,gun duilleach, *bare,without leaves.*
maol, -aoil, *s.m.* Brow of a rock. 2 Cape, promontory,mull. 3††Forehead. 4**Bald head. 5 **Shaved or shorn monk. 6*Holy man's servant. 7 Great bare rounded hill. 8 Hornless cow, see maolag. Mar chrainn ri maol carraig, *like trees on the brow of a rock.* [** gives *pl.* -ean.]
maol, *v.a. & n.* Make blunt, bald or bare. 2 Become so. see maolaich.
maolachadh, -aidh, *s.m.* Act of making bald, blunt or bare. 2 State of becoming bald, blunt or bare. 3* Laying down of the ears, as a horse. 4 Gibbosity, gibbousness. A' m—, *pr.pt.* of maolaich.
maolad, see maoilead.
maoladh, -aidh, *s.m. & pr. pt.* of maol. Same meanings as maolachadh.
maolag, -aig, -an, *s.f.* Hornless cow. 2 Stupid female. 3††Bald woman. 4 Footless stocking (mogan.) 5††Small tub without handles. 6* Dish for milk.
———ach, -aiche, *a.* Having footless stockings.
maolaich, *pr. pt.* a' maolachadh, *v.a. & n.*

Blunt. 2 Make bald or bare. 3 Become so. 4††Lower the ears, as a horse, hare or doe. 5** *rarely* Allay, calm. Mh. an leac a bhàrr, *the plate blunted its point*; cha mh. iad an cinn, *they will not make bald their heads*; mh. mo chlaidheamh, *my sword became blunt*; mh. an t-each a chluasan, *the horse drew back his ears.*

———te, *past pt.* of maolaich. Made or become blunt, bald or bare.

maol-aigeann,** -aigne, *s.f.* Dull comprehension, stupidity.

—————ach, -aiche, see maol-aigneach.

maol-aigeantach, see maol-aigneach.

maol-aigneach, -eiche, *a.* Stupid, dull of comprehension. 2**Blunt.

maolainn,** *s.f.* Mule.

maolan, -ain, *pl.* -ain & -an, *s. m.* Dull person. 2 Beacon 3(AF) Hornless animal. 4**Bleak eminence. 5**That part of a pile which is above the water in a fishing weir. 6††Bald man.

maolanach, -aich, *s.m.* Stake used in constructing wooden folds or pens. 2** Stake driven into the ground to support " flakes " (movable hurdles) for keeping cattle in a fold. 3 Blunderer. 4 see maoileanach & maolan.

————,** -aiche, *a.* Like a beacon. 2 Of, or belonging to, a beacon. 3 Abounding in beacons. 4 Bleak.

maol-aodainn,** *s.f.* Bald brow. 2 Bleak hill-side.

maol-aodainneach, -eiche, *a.* Noiseless. 2** Bald. 3**Bleak-sided, as a hill.

maol-aodainneachd,** *s.f.* Baldness. 2 Bleakness.

†maolas, -ais, *s.m.* Sandal.

maol-bhathais,** *s.m.* Bald forehead

maol-bhathaiseach, -eiche, *a.* Bald in the forehead. 2 **Having a bald forehead.

maolchar, -an, *s. m.* Space between the eyebrows. [Also called " maol-char nam malaidhean."]

maolchar,** *a.* Having a large space between the eyebrows.

maol-cheann,** -chinn, *s.m.* Bald head. 2 Stupid-head, dunder-head.

maol-cheannach, -aiche, *a.* Blunt. 2 Shy, bashful sheepish. 3 Bald-headed. 4 Stupid.

maol-chiaran, -ain, *s.m.* Forlorn person, child of grief. 2 Term of pity or reproach. 3 Hermit. 4 Melancholy—*Sàr-Obair.*

maol-chluas,** -chluaise, *s.f.* Blunt or deaf ear.

maol-chluasach, -aiche, *a.* Dull of hearing, somewhat deaf. 2**Tame, gentle. 3**Inactive. 4 *Blunt, dull. 5 Stupid.

maol-chluasaiche,* *s.f.* Stupidity, dulness, lifelessness.

maol-chnuac,** *s.f.* Bald forehead or brow.

—————ach, *a.* Having a bald forehead or brow.

maol-coinein, *s. m.* Rabbit. 2 Brown mole.

maol-dhearc,§ -an, *s.f.* Mulberry—*morus nigra.* Craobh mhaol-dhearc, *a mulberry-tree.*

—————ach, -aiche, *a.* Abounding in mulberries. 2 Like, of, or pertaining to, mulberries.

—————ag, -aig, -an, *s.f.* see maol-dhearc.

—————agach, -aiche, see maol-dhearcach.

maol-dobhrain,(AF) *s.m.* Otter. 2 Mole or spot on a person's skin.

†maol-dorn, -uirn, *s.m.* Sword-hilt.

maol-fhaobhar,** -air, *s.m.* Blunt edge.

—————ach, -aiche, *a.* Blunt-edged, as a bladed instrument.

maol-labhartas,‡‡ -ais, *s.m.* Meanness of writing. 2 Baldness.

maoloisean, see maol-oisinn.

maol-oisinn, -ean, *s.f.* Obtuse angle. 2 Rounded angle. 3 High temple.

—————each, -eiche, *a.* Having obtuse angles. 2 Having the hair far back upon the forehead. 3 Having large temples. 4††Bare in the temples, high-templed.

maol-ruainidh, *s.f.* Nickname for an idle female fond of places of amusement. Cha'n 'eil féill no faidhir air nach faighear m., *there is no fair or market where m. cannot be found.*

maol-snaotha, *s.m.* Mental vacancy, suspended perception.

maol-snèimh,(DU) *s.m.* Indifference.

maol-snèimhealas, -ais, *s. m.* Carelessness, indifference. 2 Tawdriness, slovenliness.

maol-snèimheil, -e, *a.* Careless, indifferent. 2 Tawdry, slovenly.

maoltan, *pl.* of maol, *prov.*

maoluich, see maolaich.

maoluin, see maolainn.

maom, *s. & v.* see maoim, *s. & v.*

maomach, -aiche, see maoimeach.

maomadh, -aidh, *s.m. & pr.pt.* see maoimeadh.

†maon,** *a.* Dumb, mute.

†maon,** -aoin, *s.m.* Hero.

maonag,** -aig, *s.f.* Bog-berry.

maon-chlar, *s.* Invoice.

maor,(AC) *s.m.* Field.

maor, -aoir, *s.m.* Officer of justice, bailiff, catch-poll, messenger. 2 Inferior officer in various capacities, constable. 3 Underling agent superintending part of a gentleman's property, steward. †4**Baron. 5 (WC) Church-officer. 6 (WC) Grave-digger. A ni a chuir na maoir a dh' ifrinn, farraid a ni a b' fheàrr a b' aithne dhaibh, *that which sent the officers to hell, asking what they knew full well*—the maor is a person inveterately disagreeable to the Celtic mind.—N.G.P.

maora, see maorach.

maorach, -aich, *s. m.* Shell-fish in general. 2 ‡‡Mussel. 3 (AF) Limpet. 4 Fishing-bait.—*North.* 5 Bait, allurement, enticement. 6** Place where shell-fish is found.

————, -aiche, *a.* Abounding in shell-fish, mussels, limpets, &c.

maorach-bàn,(AF) *s. m.* Shell-fish.

maorach-Muire,(AF) *s. m.* Kind of limpet—*Eriskay.*

maor-baile,* *s.m.* Under bailiff. 2 Town-officer.

maor-chladaich,(AF) *s.m.* Redshank.

maor-cìse,‡ *s.m.* Tax-gatherer, assessor.

maor-coille,* *s.m.* Wood-ranger.

maor-eaglais,** *s. m.* Beadle, church-officer, churchwarden.

maor-ghairm,** *s.m.* Herald. Chruinnich e na maoir-ghairm, *he summoned the heralds.*

maor-rìgh,* *s.m.* Messenger-at-arms. 2 King's messenger.

maor-rinndeil,* *s.m.* Ground-officer.

maorsachd, *s.f.* see maorsainneachd.

maorsainneachd, *s.f.* Stewardship. 2 Office of an under-bailiff or officer of justice. 3 The duties of such an officer. 4* Officiousness, meddling. 5**District, prefecture. 6**That part of a landed gentleman's property that is under the inspection of a bailiff or ground-officer. 7** Office or business of a constable. 8 * Office of a messenger.

maor-sàraidh, *s.m.* Bailiff.

maor-siorraimh,* *s.m.* Sheriff-officer.

maor-siteig,(Fionn) *s.m.* Sanitary officer or inspector. (siteag, *a dunghill.*)

maor-sìth, *s.m.* Policeman.

maor-striopaich, *s.m.* Pimp, pander.
maos,(AC) *s.m.* Goat. Air sgealbh mhaosa, *for luck of goats.*
maosganach, -aich, *s.m.* Unshapely, large lump. 2 Huge or shapeless trunk.
————, -aiche, *a.* Shapeless, clumsy, abounding in shapeless lumps.
maotag,(AF) *s.f.* Cabbage-worm.
maoth, maoithe, *a.* Soft, tender, delicate. 2 Young, of tender age. 3 Effeminate, of delicate constitution. 4 Soft, moistened. 5 Enervated. 6‡‡Gentle, calm, tranquil, quiet. 7 ** Tame. 8** Smooth. Muirichinn mh., *a large family slenderly provided for, of tender age* ; an osag mh., *the gentle breeze* ; tha a' chlann m., *the children are tender.*
maoth, *v.* see maothaich.
maothach, -aiche, *a.* Producing softness, emollient, softening, soothing, lenitive. 2 Tender, gentle. 3 Moistening. 4** Enervating.
————adh, -aidh, *s.m.* Softening, act of softening or soothing. 2 State of becoming soft or tender. 3**Smoothing. 4**Taming. 5** Becoming soft, tender, or smooth. 6 Becoming tame. 7 Moistening. 8 Irrigation. 9 Enervation. A' m—, *pr. pt.* of maothaich.
maothachail, -e, *a.* see maothach.
maothachd, see maothalachd.
maothag, -aig, -an, *s.f.* Premature or shell-less egg. 2 Delicate young female.
maothaich, *pr. pt.* a' maothachadh, *v. a. & n.* Soften, make soft. 2 Soften, alleviate, mitigate. 3 Moisten. 4 Become soft or less hardened. 5 Become delicate enervated or effeminate. 6 Become moist. 7**Tame. 8** Enervate. 9**Grow exorable, grow less hardened or less cruel. 10 (MS) Addulce.
————ear,** *fut. pass.* of maothaich.
————te, *past pt.* of maothaich. Softened, become soft. 2 Mitigated, alleviated. 3 Enervated. 4 Moistened. 5 Tamed.
maothail,* -e, *a.* see maothach.
maothain,* *s.* Abdomen. 2 Disease of young persons caused by lifting heavy burdens.
maothalach, -aiche, see maothach.
————d, *s.f.ind.* Softness, tenderness, delicacy. 2 Gentleness, calmness. 3 Pity. 4 **Brittleness. 5 Moistness. 6 Smoothness. 7 Tameness. 8 Lenitiveness. A thaobh mùirn agus m., *on account of tenderness and delicacy.*
maothan, -ain, -an, *s.m.* Twig. 2 Tendril. 3 Bud. 4 Osier, see fineamhuin. 5 The chest or breast. 6 Anything cartilaginous or soft. 7 The cartilage terminating the lower part of the sternum—*xiphoides.* 8 Young person, youngster. 9 Anything tender or soft. 10 The gristle in the *scrobiculum cordis.* 11 Cowardly fellow. Gun mh. ri 'taobh, *without a tendril by her side* ; gach m. snidheach, *every tender maid weeping* ; cha gearan i 'm., *she will not complain of her chest.*
————ach, -aiche, *a.* Abounding in twigs or osiers. 2 Like a twig, osier or tendril. 3 Of, or belonging to, the human chest. 4 Cartilaginous. 5**Slender in person.
————achd, *s.f.ind.* Gristliness, likeness to gristle or cartilage. 2 Tenderness, softness. 3 Cowardliness. 4**Slenderness. 5**Limberness.
maothar, -aire, *a.* see mòdhar.
maoth-bhlas, -ais, *s.m.* Mild taste. 2 Sweet taste or flavour.
————da, *a.* Sweet-tasted, mild-tasted, pleasant to the taste. Snothach m., *the sweet-tasted sap of trees.*
————dachd, *s. f. ind.* Pleasantness of taste or flavour.
maoth-bhlàth, -a, -an, *s.m.* Soft or tender blossom or twig.
————, -àithe, *a.* see meagh-bhlàth.
————an, see maoth-bhlàth.
————as, -ais, see meagh-bhlàthas.
maoth-bhos, -ois, -an, *s.f.* Soft or smooth palm of the hand. Do mh. a bu ghrinne, *thy soft palm that was the fairest.*
————ach, -aiche, *a.* Having soft or smooth palms.
maoth-bhuidhe, *a.* Softly or delicately yellow.
maoth-chaidreamh, *s.m.* Indulgence.
maoth-chlòimh, *s.f.* Soft down or wool. Leabaidh mh., *a bed of soft wool.*
maoth-chnàimh, *s.m.* Cartilage.
maoth-dhèanadach, -aiche, *a.* Lenitive.
maoth-lus, -luis, -an, *s.m.* Tender herb or flower. 2** Grass. Mar mh. fàsaidh tu, *like a tender herb thou shalt grow.*
maoth-lusach, -aiche, *a.* Abounding in soft or delicate herbs.
maoth-lusrach, see maoth-lusach.
maothran, -ain, *pl.* -an & -ain, *s.m.* Tender twig. 2 Tendril. 3 Infant, suckling. 4 Little boy or girl.
maothranach, -aiche, *a.* Puerile, tender, of tender age, infantile.
maoth-ròsach, -aiche, *a.* Soft and delicate as a rose, rosy.
maoth-rosg, -roisg, -an, *s.m.* Tender or soft eyelid. 2 Tender or delicate eye. 3 Mild eye, eye expressive of a mild temper. 4 Languid eye. 5 Languid look.
————ach, -aiche, *a.* Having soft or tender eye-lids or eyes. 2 Having a mild, gentle look. 3 Having a languid look.
maoth-shùil, -shùla, -shùilean, *s. f.* Soft eye, tender eye.
————each, -eiche, *a.* Tender-eyed, soft-eyed. 2 Ophthalmic.
————eachd, *s. f. ind.* Tenderness or softness of the eyes. 2 Wateriness of the eyes.
maothuich, see maothaich.
mapag,(DC) *s.f.* Moppet—*Uist.*
mapaid,(DC) *s.f.* Moppet—*Uist.*
mar, *conj.* As, even as, like, like as, in the same manner, in this or that manner.

Mar tha, *already* ; am bheil e air sgur mar tha ? *has he ceased already ?* mar seo, *in this manner, in this direction* ; mar sin, *in that manner, in that direction* ; mar sin fhéin, *so and so* ; mar seo chaith sinn an oidhche, *thus we spent the night* ; mar a's sine am boc, 's ann a's cruaidhe 'n adharc, *the older the buck, the harder the horn* ; mar siod, *in yon manner* ; mar a theicheas iad, *as they scamper* ; mar rinn mise, *just as I did* ; rinn e m. sin, *he did so, in like manner* ; mar bu mhiann leis, *just as he would wish* ; mar gu'm b' ann, *just as it were* ; mar siod agus, *so also* ; m. aon, *together* ; mar gu'n, *as if* ; na's mó mar àird a' chinn, *higher by a head* ; mar uisge balbh, *like still waters* ; cha robh e mar mhìle dhomh, *he was not within a mile of me* ; is e a's fhaisge mar dhà mhìle, *it is nearest by two miles* ; mar mhiltean dhomh, *within miles of me* ; tha e mar sin, *he* or *it is so* ; mar sin bha mi òg, *so was I in my youth* ; mar nach olc, *not at all badly* ; is ann mar seo a tha a' chùis, *the case stands thus* ; mar ...., *as* .... *so* ....; mar a thubhairt thu, mar sin thachair e, *as you said, so it happened* ; leth-mar-leth, *half-and-half.*

[Governs a noun definite in the *nom.*, but a noun indefinite in the *dat.* and aspirated. It does not aspirate a definite noun beginning with *d*, *s*, or *t.*]

mar, Compared with. [Not *over* as transla-

ted in *W. H. Tales*, in the sentence " mar reul air na riounagan mar mhuir mor air lodannan."]
màr fhéin,** *prov. expression*, On my word, on my troth.
mara, *gen.sing.* of muir.
màrach, see màireach.
màrach,‡ *s.m.* Big, ungainly woman—*Argyll.*
marachadh, -aidh, *s. m.* Anchoring, mooring. 2 Anchorage.
marachan, *Suth'd.* for manachan.
marachann, see marbhchann.
marachd,* see maraidheachd.
marag, -aig, -an, *s.f.* Blood-pudding. 2 *in ridicule*, Fat, shapeless person. 3 Mustard. M. dhubh, *a blood-pudding* ; m. gheal, *a pudding made of meal, &c.* Cha truagh leam cù is m. m' a amhaich, *I don't pity a dog having a pudding about its neck*—applied to anyone who was thought to have enough, and should be satisfied. [** gives sausage.]
———ach, -aiche, *a.* Abounding in puddings or sausages. 2 Like a pudding. 3 Corpulent, fat, shapeless, pot-bellied.
marag-bhuidhe,§ *s.f.* Cherlock, wild mustard—*sinapsis arvensis.*

501. *Marag-bhuidhe.*

502. *Maraiche.*

maraich,** *v.a. & n.* Moor, anchor. 2 Ride at anchor.
maraiche, -an, *s.m.* Sailor, mariner. 2 Scurvy-grass—*cochlearia officinalis.*
————adh, -idh, -idhean, *s.m.* Iron or wooden bolt, used to drive out another.
maraidheachd, *s.f.ind.* Seamanship, business of a mariner, navigation. Ri m., *following the sea.*
maraig, *gen. & dat. sing.* of marag.
màrain, *gen. sing.* of màran.
maraireachd, see maraidheachd.
maraiste, -an, see mairiste.
————ach, -aiche, *a.* see mairisteach.
màran, -ain, see mànran.
———ach, -aiche, see mànranach.
mar an ceudna, *adv.* Likewise, also, too, in like manner.
maranna, marannan, } *pl.* of muir.
maraon, *adv.* Together, in concert, (*lit.* as one.) Ghluais iad m., *they moved together.*
maras,** -ais, *s.m.* Myriad, ten thousand.
marasgail, *v.a.* see marasglaich.
marasgal, -ail, -an, *s. m.* Master, regulator, overseer. 2 Managing. 3 Subjection, servitude. 4 Marshal. M.-cogaidh, feachd-m. *or* m.-feachd *a field-marshal* ; cuir air droch mh., *set a bad master over him.*
marasgalach, see marasglach.
marasglach, -aiche, *a.* Ruling, bearing rule. 2 ‡‡ Magisterial. 3** Marshalling. 4** Like a marshal.
————————adh, -aidh, *s.m.* Ruling, act of ruling or bearing sway, exercising of mastery, management, superintendence, supervision. 2**Marshalling, regulating. 3* Traffic. A' m—, *pr.pt.* of marasglaich.
—————d, *s. f. ind.* Regulating, superintending, bearing rule. 2 Marshalling. 3 Office of marshal, marshalship. 4**Subjection. Fo 'mh.-san, *under his subjection.*
marasgladh, see marasglachadh.
marasglaich, *v.a.* Superintend, regulate, rule, guide, oversee. 2* Trade with.
marasglaiche,** *s.m.* Conductor.
marbh, mairbhe, *a.* Dead, lifeless. 2 Dull. 3 Benumbed, torpid. 4 Vapid, tasteless, as beer. 5 Spiritless. Duine m., *a dead man* ; corp m., *a dead body.*
marbh, *pr.pt.* a' marbhadh, *v.a.* Kill, slay, assassinate, murder, slaughter. 2 Subdue, mortify. 3 Benumb. 4 Make stale or flat.
marbh, -airbh, *s.m.* Dead person, *pl.* the dead. Am beò 's na mairbh, *the living and the dead.*
marbh, -airbh, *s.m.* Stillness, silence, repose. 2 State of quietness, absence of life or motion. M. na h-oidhche, *the dead of night* ; m. a' gheamhraidh, *the dead of winter.*
marbhach, -aiche, *a.* see marbhtach.
marbhachd,** *s.f.* Languor, languishment. 2‡‡ Slaughter. 3‡‡Havoc.
marbhadair, -ean, see marbhaiche.
marbhadairean, The Gael of old were of the opinion that the food in the stomach was digested by a number of living creatures, to which they gave the name of marbhadairean —DMy.
marbhadh, -aidh, *s.m.* Killing, slaying, act of killing, slaying or slaughtering. 2 Mortifying, act of mortifying or subduing. 3 Slaying, massacring. A' m—, *pr.pt.* of marbh. Chum a' mharbhaidh, *to the slaughter.*
marbhaiche, -an, *s.m.* Slayer, killer, murderer, assassin. 2 Sanguinary warrior.
marbhaibh, *dat. pl.* of marbh.
marbhaidh, *gen.sing.* of marbhadh.
marbhaidh, *fut. aff. a.* of marbh.
marbhain, *gen.sing.* of marbhan.
marbhaisg, -e, -ean, see marbh-phaisg.
marbhalachd, see marbhantachd.
marbham, *1st.per.sing. imp.* of marbh.
marbhan, -ain, -an, *s.m.* Dead body, corpse. 2 Carcase. 3**Margin of a book. Cha téid do mh., *thy carcase shall not go.*
marbhanach, -aiche, *a.* Like a dead body. 2 Abounding in dead bodies or carcases.
marbhanach,* -aich, *s.m.* Person almost dead, or pretending to be dead. 2(DU) Sluggish roller seen in calm weather, gentle undulation of the sea without any crest. 3 (DMy) Wool or fleece of a sheep killed at Hallowtide. (called " rusg " when shorn off in May.)
marbhan-leabhair, *s.m.* Margin of a book or page.
marbhanta, -ainte, *a.* Dull, inactive, not lively, 2 Benumbed. 3 Lukewarm. Gu m., *inactively, in a spiritless manner.*
marbhantachd, *s. f. ind.* Dulness, inactivity, stupor, deadness, torpidness. 2 Lukewarmness.
marbhantas, -ais, *s.m* see marbhantachd.
marbh-aodach, -aich, *s.m.* Dead-clothes, shroud.
marbh-aodaich,** *v.a.* Shroud, clothe or dress a dead body.
marbh-bhreith, *a.* Stillborn.
marbhchann, *s. m.* Morling, flayed skin of a

sheep. 2 Wool from a dead sheep. Olainn-mharbhchann, *or* clòimh-mharbhchrann, *wool from the dead skin.*
marbh-chras, -ais, -an, *s.m.* Carcase.
marbh-chu, (AF) *s.m.* Wolf.
marbh-dheoch, -a, -an, *s.f.* Deadly draught or drink, poison. 2 Dirge, funeral dirge.
marbh-dhraoidh, -ean, *s.m.* Necromancer.
marbh-dhraoidheach, *a.* Necromantic.
marbh-dhraoidheachd, *s.f.* Necromancy.
marbh-fhonn, -uinn, *s. m.* Death-song, dead march, dirge, funeral air.
mar bhi, *prov.* for mur bhi.
mar-bhith, (AC) *s.* Fault. Gun mh., *without fault.*
marbh-là,** *s.m.* Still, cloudy day, dull, heavy day.
marbh-lap,** *v.n.* Become benumbed or frost-bitten. 2 Become torpid.
marbh-lapach,** *a.* Benumbed, frost-bitten. 2 Causing torpor or paralysis.
marbh-lapachd, *s.f.* Numbness, torpor.
marbh-lapadh, *s.m.* Numbness, torpor.
marbhnach, ** -aich, *s.m.* Epitaph. 2 Elegy.
marbhphaisg, -e, -ean, *s. f.* Death shroud, grave-clothes. 2 Generally used as an imprecation—m. ort! (*lit.* a death-shroud upon thee!) fatal end, catastrophe, woe. 3 * says "Coffin used as hearses are now. It was very ingeniously constructed, having a slider in the bottom, and otherwise formed so as to prevent the body being seen till covered by the earth. Afterwards it was conveyed to the church, there to be kept till again required."
marbh-phaisg, *v.a.* Shroud, clothe with a shroud.
——————te, *past pt.* Shrouded.
marbh-phasgadh,** -aidh, *s.m.* Shrouding. Air là do mharbh-phasgaidh, *on the day of thy shrouding.*
marbhrann, -rainn, -an, *s.m.* Elegy. 2 Epitaph. 3 Funeral song.
——————ach, -aiche, *a.* Elegiac, funereal.
marbh-sgìtheachd,‡‡ *s. ind.* Lethargy.
marbh-sgìos, *s.m.* Lethargy.
marbh-shruth, -a, -an, *s.m.* Still stream. 2 The wake of a ship. 3††Tide at the turning-point. 4**That part of a river or stream the current of which is scarcely perceptible.
marbh-shruthach, -aiche, *a.* Abounding in still streams.
marbhtach, -aiche, *a.* Deadly, mortal. 2 Destructive. 3 Fierce. 4 Murderous, ready to kill. 5 Expert at killing or slaughtering. 6 Poisonous. 7 Baneful. 8 Sanguinary. 9 Cruel.
marbhtach, *s.m.* Wool from a dead sheep—*Skye.*
————d, *s.f.* Deadliness, destructiveness. 2 Banefulness. 3 Cruelty. 4 Bloodiness.
marbhuach,** *s.m.* see marbhnach.
†marbhuas, (AF) *s.m.* Many cows.
†marbraid, -ean, *s.f.* Fort.
†marbul, *s.m.* Playing marble.
marc, -airc, -an, *s.m.* Horse, charger, steed. M. uaibhreach, àrd-cheumach, *a proud, high-bounding steed*; m.-choimhliong, *a horse-race;* m. dubh, *a black horse.*
marcach, -aich, *s.m.* Horseman, rider, equestrian. 2 Knight. 3 Dragoon. 4 see marcachadh.
marcach, *s.m.* Standard or bearer of driving-(spinning-) wheel.
marcachadh, -aidh, *s.m. & pr. pt.* of marcaich. Same meanings as marcachd.
marcachd, *s.f.* Riding, art or act of riding, equestrianism, horsemanship. A' m—, *pr. pt.* of marcaich.
marcach-dàin, *s. m.* Rehearser of poetry. 2 Person who attended the poet.
marcachd-shìne, (WC) *s. f.* Wild and stormy shower.
marcachd-shìth, (AC) *s.f.* Kind of paralysis in the spine of sheep, cows and horses, attributed to fairies riding on them. 2 In some places, the perspiration, due to weakness which comes out on cattle. [Preceded by the art. *a'*.] Also called "na marcaich-shìth."
marcach-sìan, (DMy) *s.* Sea-drift in a storm at sea, when the wind sweeps along the tops of the waves.
marcaich, *pr.pt.* a' marcachd & a' marcachadh, *v a. & n.* Ride. 2 Sail. Marcaichidh e le greadhnas, *he will ride joyously.*
marcaich, see marcach.
marcaiche, see marcach.
marcaichean-sìon, *s. pl.* The storm-riders, see gath-dubh.
marcair, -ean, see marcach.
marcaireachd, *s.f.ind. prov.* for marcachd.
marcais, see marcuis.
————eachd, see marcuiseachd.
marcait, *s.f.* see margadh.
marcan, see marcachd.
marcan,** -ain, *s. m.* Horse.
marc-cheann, (AF) *s.m.* Leader among horses.
marchann, see marbhchann.
marclach, -aich, *s.f.* Provision, victuals.
marc-lann, -ainn, -an, *s.m.* Stable.
marc-raineach, § *s. f.* The male fern—*lastrea filix-mas.*

503. Marc-raineach.

marc-shluagh, -shluaigh, *s. sing.* Horsemen, riders. 2 Cavalry.
marcuis, *s.m.* Marquis.
————eachd, *s.f.ind.* Marquisate. 2 Riding, horsemanship.
màr fhein, *int.* On my word, by my troth; *prov.*
marg, -airg & -a, -an, *s. f.* Merk, Scots coin value 13⅓d. sterling. 2 Merk-land, i.e. land of the annual value of 13/4 Scots. Marg fhearainn, *a merk-land.*
margach,** *a.* In merks, of money. 2 Like a fair or market.
margad, -aid, *s.m.* see margadh.
margadail, -e, *a.* see margail.
margadalachd, see margalachd.
margadh, -aidh, -ean, *s.m. & f.* Market, fair. 2 Buying or selling, sale. An d' fhuair thu m. dha? *have you obtained a sale for it?* baile margaidh, *a market-town.*

m. an éisg, *the fish-market.*
m.-chaorach, *the sheep-market.*
m.-chlòimh, *the wool-market.*
m.-chruidh, *the cattle-market.*
m.-na-feòla, *the meat-market* or *shambles.*
m.-na-mine, *the meal-market.*
m.-nam-meas, *the fruit-market.*
m.-nan-luibhean, *the green* or *vegetable market.*
m.-nam-muc, *the hog-market.*

margaidh,* see margadh.

margail, -e, *a.* Marketable, saleable.

margalachd, *s.f.ind.* Saleableness, marketableness.

marghan, -ain, *s.m.* Gaelic spelling of *margin.*

marglaiche, *s.m.* Merchant.

ma' ri, for mar ri or maille ri.

màrla, *s.m.* Marl, kind of clay. [‡ says "The Gaelic has the sense of *marble* also, where it confuses this word and the English "marble" together."]

màrlach, -aiche, *a.* Marly, like marl. 2 Abounding in marble.

marmhor, see marmor.

marmhur, -uir, see marmor.

marmor, -oir, *s.m.* Marble. [A playing marble is marbul—‡.]

——ach, -aiche, *a.* Abounding in marble, marbly, marble.

marnialach,** -aich, *s.m.* see màirnealach.

màrr,* *v.a.* Obstruct, hinder.

——ach,* -aich, *s.m.* Thicket to catch cattle in. 2 Labyrinth. 3 Enchanted castle that kept one spell-bound.

marraisgeach,(MS) *s.* Virgin.

mar ri, *prep.* With, together with, in company with. Mar ri nàmhaid, *together with the enemy.* see maille & maille ri.
Mar ribh, *with you*; mar ruinn, *with us*; mar ris, *with him*; mar riu, *with them*; mar rium, *with me*; mar riut, *with thee*; mar rithe, *with her.*

màr-ròs,** *s.m.* Rosemary.

marrthaisgeach, see marraisgeach.

marruinn,(AC) Milk, cream, and their products.

——each, (AC) *a.* Productive of cream, milk, &c. Mart math m., *a good productive cow.*

marrum, see marruin.

màrsadh, -aidh, *s.m.* March, marching of troops.

màrsail, -e, *s.f.* see màrsadh.

marsainn,* *s.* Strength. 2 Strong constitution. 3 Durableness.

——each, *a.* Hardy, strong, 2 Durable, perpetual.

màrsal, -ail, *s.m.* Marching. 2 see marasgal.

marsal,** -ail, *s.m.* Merchant, shopkeeper.

marsalachd,** *s.f.* Business of shopkeeping.

màrsaladh,** -aidh, *s.m.* Marching. 2 Marshalling.

marsan, -ain, see marsanta.

marsannachd, see marsantachd.

marsanta, -an, *s.m.* Merchant, one who deals in wares.

——corc, -n-, *s.m.* Earwig. [So called from the "knife" in its tail.]

marsantach,‡‡ -aiche, *a.* Mercantile.

marsantachd, *s.f.ind.* Merchandise, wares. 2 Trade or business of a merchant, traffic, dealing.

mar seo, *adv.* In this manner, thus. 2 In this direction, towards this place.

mar sin, *adv.* Mar sin duit-se, *the same to you.*

mar siod, *adv.* see mar.

marsonta, see marsanta.

——chd, see marsantachd.

mar sud agus so, *likewise.*

Màrt, -àirt, *s.m.* Month of March. 2 Tuesday. 3 Time suitable for agricultural work. 4* Busiest time at anything. 5 Great haste. 6* Seed-time
There appears to be considerable confusion in Gaelic proverbs, &c., regarding the first three significations given above for Màrt, as is exemplified in the following notes from Nicolson's Gaelic Proverbs (NGP), Waifs & Strays (W), and Carmina Gadelica (AC.)
In the first-place the old "months" appear to have been moveable, and depended for the time of their commencement upon whether the suitable weather had already arrived. If the weather had not come, neither had the month, e g. Luath no mall g'an tig am Maigh, thig a' chubhag, *late or early as May comes,* (*i.e.* as May-weather comes), *so comes the cuckoo.* The names of several months, or rather periods, of various lengths occur twice, while Mart occurs no less than three times.
The comparatively modern Màrt O. S., which is still in vogue in some parts, (says AC in speaking of the months in general) being still used in an O.S. manner, does not commence until the orthodox calendar month is half gone. AC i. 245, ii. 263, & NGP 413, both make Màrt extend into April. Nicolson appears to have been puzzled, for his explanations are obscure. On p. 26 (NGP) he translates "an ciad Mhàrt." as *the first Tuesday,* while from a note explaining the same proverb, it is evident that he thought Màrt stood for March.
The first Tuesday of the sowing-time or times, would appear to be "An ciad Mhàrt de Mhàrt-na-curachd," in the same way as there was a Bealltuinn of the Bealltuinn and a Liùnasdal of Liùnasdal. AC gives "gaoth gheur nam Màrt" (*pl.*) NGP p. 26 speaks of three Màrts. W. iii. 218, 298, 299 speaks of three—Apl. 12 to May 1, Aug. 12, Sept. 12—(This triple occurrence of 12 is noteworthy.)
NGP says 1st. week of April is too soon to sow, so he would appear to prefer the 2nd. or 3rd. week. Is fhearr an sneachd na 'bhi gun sian, an déidh an siol a chur 'san talamh, *better snow than no rain-storm, when the seed is in the ground,* (p. 251) shows that sowing were better done when snow is out of season, i. e. late in April. AC says seed is winnowed by "gaoth gheur nam Màrt," before being sown, therefore the Màrt or Màrts must be nearly over, i.e. late in April, before the seed is in the ground. W. gives Apl. 12 to May 1, i.e. late in April. Another proverb, (NGP. 24) Am feur a thig a mach 'sa Mhàrt, théid e staigh 'sa Ghiblean, *the grass that comes out in March shrinks away in April,* implies that seed should not appear till Màrt be over, or else it will be killed by the weather.
On the other hand, NGP gives Is fhearr aon oidhche Mhàirt na tri là Foghair (for growth), so the seed, to judge by this, ought to be coming up in March, or else that sowing ought to be done earlier. [It is most likely that it is not growth which is referred to in this proverb, as Nicolson supposes, but the winnowing referred to by AC.] NGP says Tuesday for sowing, AC prefers Friday. There was also the "fìor," or suitable Màrt.

mart, -airt, *s.m.* Cow or steer fattened for killing. The common expression was m.-lamhaig, or m.-tuaighe, (*lit.* a hatchet cow—JM.) 2(WC) Milch-cow—*Gairloch.* M. geamhraidh, *a winter "mart."* [Mart in a general sense, is applied to cattle of any description. Gille dubh nam mart, *the black-haired drover—West coast of Ross.*

martach, -aiche, *a.* Having many cows. 2 Pertaining to cows.

Màrtain,** s.f. Martinmas.
martair, -ean, s. m. Cripple, lame person. 2 Mutilated person. 3 One who maims.
martanach, -aich, s.m. Cripple.
martarach, see mairtireach.
mart-bainne, pl. -airt-bh-, s.m. Milch-cow.
martfheoil, -fheola, s.m. see mairtfheoil.
mart-fheolach, see mairtfheolach
mart-geamhraidh, s m. Cow for winter food.
mar tha, Already.
mart-làmhadh, s m. Cow for killing.
mart-làmhaig see mart làmhadh
martlan,(AF) s m. Maw-worm belly-worm
martrachadh -aidh, s.m Laming act of making lame. 2 Maiming. A m—, *pr pt* of martraich.
martradh, -aidh, s.m & pr.pt. see màrtrachadh.
martraich, *pr.pt* a' martrachadh v a Lame, make lame. 2 Cripple, maim 3**Mutilate
————te, *past pt* of martraich Lamed. 2 Crippled, maimed.
mart-tuaighe see mart-làmhadh.
ma's, [ma, *conj.*+is v] If. Ma 's e, *if it be he or it*; ma 's e agus, *if it so be;* ma 's e agus gu, *if it so be that*; ma 's e nach, *if it so be that not*; ma 's fior e féin, *if he judges aright.*
màs, -àis, -an, s. m. Hip, buttock, breech. 2 Bottom of a vessel, as of a cask. 3 Bottom of a cart. 4 **Mace. 5** Thigh. Do mhàsan, *your buttocks*, m. na cuinneige, *the bottom of the pitcher*; m. a' chroinn, *the rear-piece of the plough*
mas, *conj*, for mu'n or mu'm.
†mas, a Excellent. 2 Handsome. 3 Round, heaped.
màsach, -aiche, a. Having large buttocks or hips, round-hipped, broad-hipped. 2 Of, or belonging to the hips. Laoch giocach, màsach, *a sturdy, stout-thighed person.*
màsach, -aiche, s.f. Large-hipped female.
masag, -aige, -an, s.f. Small red berry.
————ach, -aiche, a. Abounding in small red berries.
màsaglas, -ais, s.m. Species of red berry.
màsair,* -ean, s.m. Large-hipped man. 2 Mace-bearer.
màsan, -ain, s.m. Delay, slowness, dilatoriness. 2**Reproof.
màsan, n.pl. of màs.
————ach, -aiche, a. Slow, tedious, dilatory.
————achd, s.f.ind. Slowness, tardiness, habit of dilatoriness, delay.
masduidh,** -ean, s.m. Large dog, mastiff.
————each, a. Like a mastiff.
ma seach, see mu seach.
ma seadh, *conj.* If so, if it be so, then.
masg, *pr.pt.* a' masgadh, v. a. Compound, mix. 2 Infuse or steep, as malt or tea.
————achadh,(MS) s.m. Maceration.
masgadh, -aidh, s.m. Mixing, act of mixing. 2 Steeping, infusing, mashing. 3 Mash, infusion. A' m—, *pr.pt.* of masg Ionad masgaidh, *a place for steeping malt.*
masgair, -ean, s.m. Steeper, infuser. 2 Mashman. 3**Lump.
————eachd, †† s.f. Mixing. 2 Mashing.
masganach, -aiche, a. Mingled, mixed. 2 Confused.
ma sgaoil, see mu sgaoil.
masgta, *past pt.* Mixed. 2 Infused.
masgul, -uil, s.m. Flattery, sycophancy, cajoling
————ach, -aiche, a. Flattering, inclined to flatter, sycophantic. Gu m., *in a sycophantic manner.*
————achd, s.f.ind. Sycophancy, habit of flattering, disposition to flatter.
————aiche, -an, s.m. Flatterer, sycophant.
masla, see masladh.
maslach, -aiche, a. Disgraceful, ignominious, reproachful, shameful, slandering, reproaching, degrading. Iomchar m., *disgraceful conduct.*
————adh, -aidh, s.m. Reproaching, shaming, act of reproaching, mocking, affronting scandalizing, disgracing, degrading, affront, reproach, slander. A' m—, *pr pt.* of maslaich. Fhuair e m., *he was disgraced.*
————ail. a. Affronting. 2 Libellous.
————d ‡‡ s.f.ind Opprobriousness.
————air ** s.m. Affronter.
masladh -aidh, -ean, s.m. Reproach, disgrace, shame. 2 Affront, scandal. Cha mh. sìth ri laoch, *peace with a hero is no disgrace*; mo nàire 's mo mh. ! *shame and confusion !*
maslaich, *pr.pt.* a' maslachadh, v.a. Reproach, slander. 2 Disgrace, degrade. 3 Affront. 4 Taunt
————te, *past pt* of maslaich. Reproached, slandered. 2 Disgraced, degraded. 3 Affronted. 4 Shamed.
maslail,** a. Disgraceful.
maslain,** s.f. Mastlin, mong-corn.
masluchadh, see maslachadh.
masluich, see maslaich.
mastuidh, see maistidh.
mat,(AF) s.m. Pig. 2 Monster.
mata, see mat.
†mata, s.m. Mattress.
ma tà, *adv.* Really, truly, indeed. Ma ta gu dearbh, *verily, indeed*; ni mis' e ma ta, *I will do it then*; am bheil thu falbh ? ma tà, tha, *are you going ? yes I am, yes indeed.*
†mata, a. Great. 2 Dark, gloomy.
màtag, -aig, -an, see màdag.
————ach, see màdagach.
math, *pl.* -a, a. *1st. comp.* fèarr *or* feabha, *2nd. comp.* fèairrd *or* feabhaid, *3rd. comp.* feabhas. [‡ says fearr is a *comp.* from the *prep.* ver (= Gaelic far, for, *super.* Now *comp.* for math, but evidently once for fern, *good.* Stokes refers Old Irish ferr to vers, *raise.*]
Good, having the proper or desired qualities. 2 Proper, fit, expedient, convenient. 3 Useful, profitable. 4 Uncorrupted, undamaged. 5 Good to eat, pleasant to the taste. 6 Complete, full. 7 Favourable, favouring, kind. 8 Good, moral, virtuous, pious. 9 Charitable, compassionate. 10 Valid, legal. 11 Consolatory. 12 Considerable, not trifling. 13 Pleasant, agreeable. 14 Dexterous, skilful, skilled, expert. 15 Proper, becoming, befitting, seemly. 16 Powerful, able, strong, influential, having authority, mighty. 17 Healthy, in good health. 18**Happy, glad. 19 Correct, accurate. 20 Prosperous, successful. 21 Sound, not false. 22‡‡Ready, prepared. 23 Desirous, willing. 24 Just. 25 Fine, excellent.

Duine m., *a good man*; astar m. air falbh, *a considerable distance off*; ithibh na nithe 'tha m., *eat the things which are good*; is m. leam, *I am glad*; *2 I am willing*; *I wish*: is fhèarr leam, *I am more glad*, *2 I had rather*; *3 I rather wish, I wish more*; is fhèarr dhomh, *it is better for me*; is m. leam sin, *I am glad of that*; is m. dhuit, *it is happy for you*; am m. leat mis' a dheanamh seo ? *do you wish me to do this ?* bha e m. dhuinn, *he was kind to us*; is m. mo chòir air, *I have a good right to it*; ma's m. mo bheachd-sa, *if my opinion be correct*; fhuair sinn cuid mh. dheth, *we had a considerable portion of it*; is m. an salann, *salt is useful*; tha e m. aig a h-uile ni, *he is dexterous at everything*; làithean matha fhaicinn, *to see prosperous days*; cho m. 's a bha iad, *as prosperous as they were*; is m. an ni dhuit fhaicinn, *you can hardly see it*; là m. dhuit! *good day to you!* oidhche mh. dhuit! *good night to you!* tha e m. air dol dachaidh a nis, *he is desirous of going home now*; tha mi m. air a h-uile ni dhiubh seo a dhearbhadh, *I am prepared to prove all these things*; is m. leam e, *I am fond of it; I am glad of it*; tha 'n t-earrach ann 's gur m. leam e, *it is spring and I rejoice at it*; math thu fhéin! *well done!* m. an airidh, *well-deserving*; 2 *deservedly, rightly*; bu mh. an airidh sin a thachairt dha, *that has deservedly befallen him*; gu'n robh m. agad! *thank you!* gu'n robh móran m. agad! *thank you very much!*

math, *adv.* Well, pretty well, considerably, skilfully. Is math a labhair thu, *you spoke well*; is m. a chì thu, *you see well*; is m. a gheibhear thu, *you do well*; is m. a fhuair thu, *or* is m. a fhuaireadh thu, *you did well*; am m. thig e dhuit? *does it become thee? is it well for thee?* is m. a rinn thu siod, *you did yon well.*

math,†† *pl.* -a & maithean, *s.m.* Noble, hero.

math, -aith, *s.m.* Good, profit, advantage, benefit, prosperity. 2 Inclination, wish. 3 Amelioration. 4**Fruit. 5***rarely* Hand. 5 Purpose, end. 6* Kindness. Is ann air do mh. fhéin a tha mise, *it is your own interest I have in view*; m. an aghaidh uilc, *good for evil*; cha'n 'eil m. sam bith an sin dhuit, *that serves no end to you*; dé am m. a th' ort? *what good are you?* am m. leat sin? *do you wish that?* am m. 's an t-olc, *the good and bad.*

math, *v.a.* see maith.

mathachadh, -aidh, *s.m.* Manuring, act of manuring land. 2 Improvement, cultivation. 3 Anything to enrich land. A' m—, *pr.pt.* of mathaich. A' m. an fhearainn, *improving the land*; a' m. air, *to insist on his believing—lit.* making it good upon him.

mathadh, -aidh, *s.m.* & *pr.pt.* see maitheadh.

mathaich, *pr.pt.* a' mathachadh, *v.a.* Manure, cultivate, as land. 2**Ameliorate. 3(MS) Expostulate. 4**Improve, make good.

———te, *past pt.* of mathaich. Manured. 2 Cultivated. 3**Improved, made good.

mathaim, for mathaidh mi. I will forgive or abate.

mathain,** Mercy, disposal. 2 Good-nature.

†**mathair**, *s.f.* Gore, matter.

màthair, -ar, -thraichean, *dat.pl.* màthraichibh, *s.f.* Mother. 2 Dam of a beast. 3 Cause, source. Mo mh., *my mother*, cha bhruich thu meann 'am bainn' a mhàthar, *thou shalt not seethe a kid in its mother's milk*; m. aobhair, *a primary cause.* A Highlander when addressing his mother, sometimes says "a bhean," *woman*, like the Hebrews of old; but when writing to her, or in apostrophising, he uses "a mhàthair," not "a bhean."

màthair-altruim, *s.f.* Nurse.

màthair-an-duileisg,§ *s.* Irish moss, see cairgein.

màthair-aobhair, *s.* Primary cause.

màthair-bhaile, *s.m.* Metropolis.

màthair-bhaiste, **màthair-bhaistidh**, } *s.f.* Godmother.

màthair-chéile, *s.f.* Mother-in-law.

màthaireachd, *s.f.* Motherhood, right of a mother.

màthaireag, see mughairn.

màthairealachd, *s.f.* Motherliness, female tenderness, kindness.

mathaireas,* -eis, *s.m.* Motherhood.

màthaireil, -e, *a.* Motherly, like a mother, tender, kind. Mac m., *a son like his mother.*

———-eachd, *s.f.* Motherliness. 2 Female tenderness, kindness.

màthair-ghuir,* *s.f.* Cause of suppuration. 2 Queen of the hive.

màthair-iongair, see màthair-ghuir 1.

màthair-mhort,* see mort-màthar.

————-——adh, see mort-màthar.

————-——air, see mortair-màthar.

màthair-na-lùdaig, *s.f.* Third or ring-finger.

mathairne, **mathairneag**, } see mughairn.

màthair-òrn, see mort-màthar.

màthair-uisge,* *s.f.* Reservoir, conduit, source of a river, well, fountain-head, deduction.

mathalachd,** *s.f.* Allowance.

mathalt, *s.m.* (CR) Potato-basket. 2 Blunt sword, knife, or other weapon.—*Sàr-Obair.*

†**màthan**, -ain, *s.m.* Twig, sucker, see maothan.

mathan, -ain, -an, see math-ghamhuinn.

———ach, -aiche, *a.* Bearish.

mathanas, see maitheanas.

———-—ach, -aiche, see maitheasach.

matharail, see màthaireil.

mathas, -ais, see maitheas.

———ach, -aiche, see maitheasach.

———achd, see maitheas.

math-ghamhuinn, -mana, -ean, *s.m.* Bear. Dà mh. bhoirionn, *two she-bears.*

—————each, *a.* Bearish. 2 Like a bear. 3 Abounding in bears.

màthraichean, *n.pl.* of màthair.

màthrail, see màthaireil.

màthralachd, see màthaireileachd.

mathroinn,* *s.f.* Disposal, risk. Fàg air a mh. e, *leave it to his risk*; air mo mh.-sa, *at my disposal, at my risk.*

mathsadh,** -aidh, *s.m.* Doubt.

math-shlogh, -oigh, **math-shluagh**, -uaigh, } see mór-shluagh. 2 (DMy) Common people.

matruis,** Gaelic spelling of mattress.

mé, see méith.

mè, *a.* Tender, fat.

meaban,* -ain, *s.m.* Scovel. 2 (WC) Refuse of anything. M. daine. *an insignificant person.*

meabhadh,** -aidh, *s.m.* Defeat. 2 Bursting.

†**meabhal**,** *s.m.* Perfidy, shame, reproach. 2‡‡Fraud, deceit. 3‡‡Flattery.

†———ach,‡‡ *a.* Deceitful, treacherous, fraudulent. 2 Shameful.

meabhar, see meamhair.

meabhlach, *a.* see meabhalach.

†**meabhra**,** *s.m.* Fiction, lie.

†———ch, *a.* Cheerful, merry, pleasant.

†———ich,** *v.a.* see meamhraich.

†———ichte, *past pt.* see meamhraichte.

meacan, -ain, -an, *s.m.* Root of a tree or plant. 2 Bulb. 3 Birth, extraction, nativity. 4 Parsnip. 5(MS) Carrot. 6 Turnip. 7 Hire, reward. 8 Offspring. 9 Twig, shoot. 10 Small rod. 11 Plant. 12 (DMK) Individual. Is buan m. na folachd, *long lasts the rod whose root sprang from blood*; cha robh m. ann, *there was not an individual there.—Caithness.*

———ach, -aiche, *a.* Abounding in roots, having many or strong roots. 2 Like a root. 3 Like a parsnip, carrot, or turnip. 4 Abounding in, or belonging to, parsnips, carrots or turnips.

——— -a'-chruidh,§ *s.m.* Cow-parsnip, see odharan.

———aich, *s.f.* Sobbing.

meacan-an-rìgh,§ *s. m.* Parsnip—*pastinaca sativa.* [ill. see p. 637.]

meacan-an-tathabha,§*s.m.* Bulb of the white lily. 2 Parsnip, see meacan-an-rìgh.

meacan-buidhe, -ain-, -an-buidhe, *s.m.* Carrot.

504. *Meacan-an-righ.* 505. *Meacan-buidhe an t-sléibhe.*

meacan-buidhe-an-t-sléibhe,§ *s.m.* Mackinboy, one of the spurge family—*euphorbia hibernia.*

meacan-dogha, -ain-, -an-, *s.m.* Burdock, burr—*arctium lappa.*

meacan-dubh, *s. m.* Comfrey—*symphytum officinale.*

506. *Meacan-dubh.* 507. *Meacan-dubh-fiadhain.*

meacan-dubh-calgach, *s.m.* Prickly comfrey.

meacan-dubh-fiadhain,§ *s.m.* Bugle—*ajuga reptans.*

meacan-each, -ain-, -an-each, *s.m.* Horse-radish —*armoracia rusticana.*

508. *Meacan-each.* 509. *Meacan-easa.*

meacan-easa,§ *s.m.* Pæony—*pæonia.*

meacan-òg,(MMcD) *s.m.* Root with thorny prominencies slanting upwards, something like

510. *Meacan-dubh-calgach.*

the tines of an antler. It was hung up to the rafters, and used for banging balls or hanks of woollen thread on—*Lewis.*

meacan-racadal, *s.m.* Horse-radish, see meacan-each.

meacan-ragaim, *s.m.* Sneezewort, see cruaidh-lus.

meacan-raguim,‡ *s.m.* Horse-radish, see meacan-each.

meacan-raguim uisge,§ *s.m.* Sea-radish—*raphanus maritimus.* [McL & D gives water-radish.]

511. *Meacan-raguim-uisge.* 512. *Meacan-righ-fiadhain.*

meacan-raidigh, *s.m.* Garden radish. [** gives m.-raidich for Carrot.]

meacan-righ, -ain-, -an-, *s.m.*Parsnip, see meacan-an-righ.

meacan-righ-fiadhain,‡ *s.m.* Wild parsnip—*pastinaca sativum.* 2 Wood angelica, see lus-nam-buadha.

meacan-roibe, *s.m.* Sneezewort.

meacan-ruadh, -ain-ruaidh, -an-ruadha, *s. m.* Radish—*raphanus raphanistrum.*

513. *Meacan-ruadh.* 514. *Meacan-sléibhe.*

meacan-sléibhe, -ain- -an-, *s.m.* Stinking hellebore, great bastard black hellebore, bear's foot—*helleborus fœtidus.*

meacan-tobhach, -ain-, -an-, *s.m.* Great common burdock, bur, cloth-bur, see suiricheán-suirich.
meacan-tobhach-dubh,§ *s.m.* Burdock (*lit.* the black plant that seizes—tobhach, *wrestling, seizing,*) see suirichean-suirich.
meacan-uilleann, -ain-uilleinn, -an-uilleann, *s. m.* Elecampane, see aillean.
†meach, -a, *s.m.* Hospitality. [** gives *f.*]
†meach, *a.* Soft, tender. 2 Kind, hospitable.
meach,(AF) *s.* Bee. (for am beach—eclipsis.)
meach, *a.* Mild, modest.
meachainn,** *s.* Luck-penny, discount, abatement, as of rent. 2†† Softness. 3 Kindness, mercy.
meachainn, -e, *s.m.* Abatement, discount, deduction. 2 Power, discretionary power or will. 3 Mercy. 4 Lenity. 5*Partiality. Is mairg a rachadh fo d' mh., *I pity him that depends on your will.*
meachair, -e, *a.* Soft,tender,delicate. 2 Agreeable. 3 Mellow. 4 Pretty, beautiful, handsome. 5 Cheerful, sportive, talkative. 6* Having an uncommonly white countenance tinged with red. Gruaidhean m., *pretty cheeks, cheeks having red and white delicately mixed* ; m. mar mhaighdean, *pretty, as a maid.*
meachannas,* -ais, *s.m.* Lenity, indulgence. 2 Mitigation, partiality. Gun mh. do dhuine seach duine, *without partiality to anyone.*
meachar,†† -aire, *a.* Soft, tender, mild. 2 Kind.
———,†† *s.m.* see meacharachd.
meacharachd, *s. f.* Sweetness or delicacy of look. 2††Softness, tenderness. 3*Beautiful countenance, beautiful mixture of colours in the face.
meacharan, see meachran.
————ach, see meachranach.
meachdann, -ainn, -an, *s.m.* see meacan 9 & 10.
meachnasach,* -aiche, *a.* Indulgent, lenial. 2 Partial.
meachrainich,(MS) *v.a.* Meddle.
meachran, -ain, -an, *s.m.* Hospitable kind person. 2 Officious person. 3**Obliging person.
meachranach, -aiche, *a.* Kind, hospitable. 2 Obliging, ready to serve. 3 Busy. 4 Officious, meddling. Gu m., *officiously.*
—————d, *s.f.* Kindness,hospitality. 2 Officiousness, habit of meddling.
meachranaich,‡‡ *v.a.* Feel, try. 2 Meddle, interfere.
—————e,‡‡ -an, *s.m.* Meddler.
meachuinn, see meachainn.
meac-treabhaidh,(AF) *s. m.* Ox or horse next the plough.
meacuinn, -ean, see meacan.
mèad, see meud.
meadach,** -aich, *s.m.* Knife.
meadachadh, see meudachadh.
meadag,** -aig, *s.f.* Knife.
mèadaich, see meudaich.
meadan,(MS) *s.m.* Lay.
meadar, -air, *pl.* -an & -draichean, *s.m.* Small pail, or circular wooden vessel. 2(AF) Milk-pail. 3 Bicker. 4 Churn. 5 (AF)Measure. [The Irish meadar is of one piece, quadrangular, and hollowed with a chisel, the Scottish Gael's meadar is like the lowland "luggie," round, hooped and ansated.—**] M.-bleoghainn, *a milk-pail* ; m.-ime, *a butter-pail* ; m.-imideal, *a pail whose mouth is covered with a skin* (*for any liquid*) ; m.-fhuail,vessel, frequently fashioned out of a solid block of wood. It stood just outside the door of a dwelling-house and was used for storing urine in, which was used, when stale, for washing, on account of the ammonia it contained.—*W. coast of Ross.*
†meadar, meadrach, *s m.* Metre, verse.
meadarach,** *a.* Like, or pertaining to a bicker. 2 Ansated, as a bicker. 3 In verse or rhyme.
†meadarachd, *s.f.* Metre, verse.
meadaraich,** *v.n.* Versify, modulate.
meadaran, -ain, -an, *s.m.,dim.* of meadar. Little circular wooden dish.
mèad-bhronn, see meud-bhronn.
†meadh, *s.m.* Metheglin, mead.
meadh, *s.f.* see meidh.
†meadhach, -ich, *s.m.* Stallion.
————, *a.* Fuddled with mead. 2 Like mead. 3 Of, or belonging to, mead. 4 Abounding in mead.
meadhach,(AF) *s.* see meidh-each.
meadhachan,** -ain, *s.m.* Force.
meadhaich, *v.a.* see meidhich.
meadhail, -ean, *s.f.* Mirth, joy, ecstasy. 2 Company. 3** Carousal. 4 Uncommon and unaccountable burst of joy on the eve of getting some distressing news. 5**Memory. 6** Belly, paunch. Cha robh m. mhór riamh gun dubh-bhròn 'na déidh, *there never was an extravagant burst of joy without afflicting news in its train.*
meadhail,** see meaghalaich.
meadhaileach,** *a.* Carousing. 2 Prone to carouse.
meadhair, -e, -ean, see meaghar.
meadhal, see meaghal.
meadhar,‡‡ -air, *s.f.* Memory.
————ach,** *a.* Cheerful, lively, glad, festive. Brataichean m., *cheerful banners.*
meadharachd,** *s. f. ind.* Cheerfulness, liveliness, gladness, festiveness.
meadh-bhlàth, -bhlàithe, *a.* Lukewarm. Do bhrìgh gu 'm bheil thu m., *because you are lukewarm.*
meadh-bhlàthachadh,** -aidh, *s. m.* Warming, making lukewarm.
meadh-bhlàthaich, *pr. pt.* a' meadh-bhlàthachadh, *v.a.* Make lukewarm.
meadh-duach,§ *s.* Fever few—*matricaria parthenium.*

515. Meadh-duach.

meadhlachd, see meadhradh.
meadhlaich, see meaghalaich.
meadhon, -oin, -an, *s.m.* Middle, centre, midst. 2 The waist. 3 Mean, means. 4 Medium. 5 Average. Dean meadhonan, *strike an average* ; bitheadh mo chaomhaich ait am m. mo chàirdean,*let my loved ones be glad in the centre of my friends,* ; am m. nan tom, *in the midst of the hills* ; 's fhèarr iomall a' phailteis na teis-meadhon na gainne, *the border of plenty is better than the centre of want* ; mu d' mh., *about your waist* ; smuainticheadh e air

meadhonaibh, *let him devise means.*
meadhona, meadhonan, } *s.pl.* Means.
meadhonach, -aiche, *a.* Intermediate, central. 2 Indifferent, middling, tolerable. 3 Instrumental. Aite gu math m., *a pretty central situation* ; ciamar tha thu ? meadhonach, *how are you ? middling well, in a middling state.*
meadhonach, -aich, *s.m.* Middle state, in point of situation or health.
meadhonachd, *s.f.ind.* Mediocrity, intermediateness. 2 Instrumentality.
meadhonail, *a.* Internal.
meadhonaireachd, *s.f.ind.* Interposition, mediation.
meadhonan,* -ain, -an, *s. m.* Medium, average. 2 *n.pl.* of meadhon. Dean m., *strike a medium.*
meadhon-aoiseach, *a.* Mediæval.
meadhon-aomach,** -aiche, *a.* see m.-aomachdail.
meadhon-aomachdail, -e, *a.* Centripetal.
meadhon-aosda, *a.* Middle-aged.
meadhon-là, *s.m.* Mid-day, noon. Fad an déidh mh., *long past mid-day;* roimh mh., *in the forenoon.*
meadhon-làthach, -aiche, *a.* Meridian.
meadhon-oidhche, *s.m.* Midnight. Mu mh., *about midnight, at midnight.*
meadhon-sheachnach, -aiche, *a.* Centrifugal.
meadhrach, -aiche, *a.* Glad, joyful. 2 Festive, hospitable. 3 Pleasant, lively, cheerful. 4 *Lustful, merry.
meadhrachadh, -aidh, *s. m. & pr. pt.* see meòrachadh.
meadhrachas, -ais, *s.m.* Gladness, joyfulness, cheerfulness. 2* Lust.
meadhrachdail, see meadhrach.
meadhrachdas, see meadhrachas.
meadhradh, -aidh, -aidhean, *s.m.* Deceiving, deception, alluring. 2 Gladness, joy, ecstasy. 3 Sport, festivity. 4** Ravishment. 5* Lust. C' arson a bhios tu air do mh. ? *why wilt thou be ravished ?*
meadhraich, *v.n.* see meòraich.
meag, see meig.
†meag,** *s.m.* The earth.
mèag, -èig *or* -éig, see meòg.
mèagach, -aiche, see meogach.
meagad, see meig.
meagadan, (AF) *s.* Snipe, see gobhar-adhar.
meagail, see meig.
meagail, see meògach.
meaghail, (AC) *s.* Expression. M. a gnùis, *the expression of her countenance.*
meaghairn,** *s.* Joy.
meaghal, -ail, *s.m.* Barking of a dog. 2 Mewof a cat. 3(AC) Bleating of a lamb. 4 Alarm.
meaghalaich, *v.* Bleat.
————, *s.f.* Continued barking. 2 Mewing of a cat. 3 Bleating. Thòisich e air m., *he began to mew.*
meaghar, -air, *s.m.* Sport, mirth, festivity. 2 Speech, talk. 3**Cheerfulness. 4**Prettiness. 5**Pomp. 6 see meamhair.
meagh-bhlàth, -àithe, see meadh-bhlàth.
meagh-bhlàthachadh, *s. m.* see meadh-bhlàthachadh.
meagh-bhlàthaich, *v.a.* see meadh-bhlàthaich.
meaghlach, -aiche, *a.* Barking. 2 Mewing. 3 Alarming. 4 Glad, joyful.
meaghlachd, *s.f.ind.* Alarm, giving an alarm. 2 Barking. 3**Gladness, joyfulness.
meaghrach, see meadhrach.
meaghradh, -aidh, see meadhradh.
mèairle, see mèirle.
meal, *pr. pt.* a' mealtuinn & a' mealadh, *v. a.* Possess. 2 Enjoy. 3**Suffer, brook. Gu'm m. 's gu'n caith thu e ! *may you enjoy and wear it !*—said to a person who wears any new garment for the first time, and considered unlucky if first said to the wearer by a female; na 'n na mheal thu e ! *may you never enjoy it !*—*never live to wear it.* In *Arran*, meal do naidheachd, *I congratulate you,* is the set phrase for congratulating a bride and bridegroom on their home-coming : chuir e m.-a-naidheachd air, *he congratulated him* ; chuir e m.-an-naidheachd orra, *he congratulated them.*
meal, (DU) *Gairloch* for mil.
meala, *gen.sing.* of mil.
meala,** *s.m.* Reproach, grief.
mealach, *Suth'd. gen.sing.* of mil.
mealach, -aiche, *a.* Honied, sweet. 2 Abounding in honey. 3 Of, or like, honey. 4 Disposed to enjoy, brook or bear. Snothach m., *the sweet sap of trees ;* gu m. céireach, *abounding in honey and wax ;* do phog mhear mh., *thy wanton honied kiss*
mealadh, -aidh, *s.m. & pr.pt.* of meal, see mealtuinn.
mealag, *s.f.* Belly, protuberance.—*Sàr-Obair.*
————, see mealg.
————ach, -aiche, *a.* see mealgach.
————achadh, -aidh, see mealgachadh.
mealaich, *s.* Broom, see bealaidh.
mealaidh, *s.m.* Reaper.
mealaidh, *Skye* for bealaidh.
mealannan, *s.pl.* Sweetmeats.
mealasg, -aisg, -an, *s.m.* Flattery, fawning. 2 Great rejoicing. 3**Cajoling. 4 Clamorous joy.
————ach, -aiche, *a.* Flattering, fawning. Rejoicing greatly. 3**Cajoling.
mealbh, see mealbhag.
mealbhac,* -aic, see meal-bhuc.
mealbhag, -aig, -an, *s. f.* Corn-poppy, see meilbheag. 2**Satchel, knapsack, budget.
————ach, -aiche, see meilbheagach.
mealbhan, (CR) *s.m.* Stretch of sand dunes with sea-bent growing on them—*W. of Ross-shire.* Sea-bent—*Easter Ross & Suth'd.*
meal-bhuc, § -uic, -an, *s.f.* Melon—*cucumis melo.*
————ach, -aiche, -aiche, *a.* Abounding in melons. 2 Like, of, or belonging to, a melon.
meal-bhucag,** -aig, *s.f.* Little melon.
meal-bhucan, -ain, *s.f.* see meal-bhuc.
————ach, -aiche, see meal-bhucach.
mealcair, *s.f.* Hasty pudding.
mealg, meilg & -a, -an, *s.f.* Milt of a fish.
————ach, -aiche, *a.* Having much milt (of fish.) 2**Like milt. 3 Adipose. 4 Abounding in smelt.
————achadh, -aidh, *s.m.* Spawning.
meall, *pl.* -an & mill, *s. m.* Lump, mass of any matter. 2 Heap, as of earth, hill, eminence, great shapeless hill, mound. 3 Knob, boss. 4 Bunch, cluster. 5 (DC) Shower (properly meall-uisge)—*Uist.* 6(DMy) The croop. Am mullach nam m., *at the top of the heights, the height of passion ;* m. luaidhe, *a lump of lead ;* m. fhìgean, *a bunch of figs ;* m. a' chalpa, *the calf of the leg ;* ceathach mu na meallaibh, *mist around the hills.*
meall, *pr.pt.* a' mealladh, *v.a.* Deceive, beguile, defraud, cheat. 2 Entice. 3 Disappoint. Mur am m. thu 'nam bharail mi, *unless you deceive me in my opinion,* c' arson a mh. thu mi ? *why hast thou beguiled me ?* mh. thu mi, *you deceived me ;* mh. e staigh mi, *he enticed me into the house ;* mh. an nathair Eubh, *the serpent beguiled Eve ;* meallaidh gach neul a dhall-shùil, *every cloud deceives his dim eye.*

meallach, -aiche, *a.* Abounding in lumps, heaps, or clusters. 2 Knobby, bossy. 3 Hilly, abounding in hills or eminences. 4 Lumpish, roundish. 5** Soft. 6** Fat, rich. 7** Rank. 8 ** Alluring. 9 (DC) Showery—*Uist.* 10** Knotty.
mealladh, -aidh, *s.m.* Deceiving, act of deceiving, cheating, beguiling. 2 Enticing. 3 Disappointing. 4**Allurement, deceit, delusion. 5**Goods, riches. 6 Deception. A' m—, *pr. pt.* of meall. Mur 'eil mi air mo mh., *if I am not mistaken;* bithidh m. ann, *there will be disappointment.*
mealladh-dùil,(WC) *s.m.* Disappointment.
mealladh-naidheachd,(WC) *s.m.* Good wishes.
meallaidh, *fut. aff. a.* of meall.
meallain, *gen.sing. & n. pl.* of meallan.
————ich,(MS) *v.n.* Hail.
meallair, see mealltair.
meallan, -ain, -an, *s.m. dim.* of meall. Little lump, knob, knot, heap. 2 Knoll, little hill. 3 Bulb. 4 Cluster. Clachan meallain, *hailstones;* meallain-chruinne, *gourds.*
————ach, -aiche, *a.* Abounding in small lumps, heaps, knobs or clusters. 2 Knotty, knobby, lumpy. 3 In hillocks or eminences. 4 Of, or like hail. Sian mh., *a hail-storm.*
meallanaich,‡‡ *v.a.* Kern.
meallan-criona,(WC) *s.pl.* Chilblains.
meall-an-sgòrnain, *s.m.* Adam's apple.
meallan-tachais, *pl.* -ain-th-, *s.m.* Chilblain.
meallar, *fut. pass.* of meall. Shall be deceived, &c.
meall-reum,(CR) *s. m.* Pyrosis, water-brash—*Gairloch.*
meall-sgrìobhadh, *s.m.* Forgery.
meall-shuil, -ula, -uilean, *s.f.* Full, round eye. 2 Winning or alluring eye. 3 Goggle-eye. 4 Leering eye.
————each, -eiche, *a.* Having full round eyes. 2 Having winning or alluring eyes. 3 Leering. 4* Goggle-eyed. 5*Having a deceiving eye.
meallta, *a. & past pt.* of meall. Deceitful, fraudulent, false. 2 Deceived, cheated, beguiled. 3 Enticed. 4 Mistaken. Tha thu m., *you are mistaken;* gu m., *falsely.*
mealltach, -aiche, *a.* Fraudulent, deceitful, false, deceiving, deceptive. 2 Alluring. Meidhdhean m., *false weights;* gu m., *deceitfully.*
mealltachd, *s.f.ind.* Deceitfulness, imposition, imposture, fraud, swindling. 2 (MS) Attractiveness.
mealltair, -ean, *s.m.* Deceiver, cheat, swindler, fraudulent person, sharper, impostor. 2** Biter.
————eachd, *s.f.ind.* Fraudulence, deceitfulness, imposition, imposture. 2 Habit of deceiving or cheating. M. a' pheacaidh, *the deceitfulness of sin;* luchd-m., *deceivers, swindlers;* m. mnà, *the deceitfulness of woman.*
meal-maig,(AF) see mial-mhàg—*Badenoch.*
meal-mhàgain, see mial-mhàgain—*Badenoch.*
mealodach, *s.m.* Melitot.
mealtag,(AF) *s.f.* Bat. (ialtag.)
mealtuinn, *s.m.* Enjoying, act of enjoying, enjoyment, possessing. A' m—, *pr.pt.* of meal. Math a mh. 'na shaothair, *to enjoy good in his labour.*
†meam, *v.a. & s.m.* Kiss.
meamanach, -aiche, see meanmnach.
meambran, -ana, *s.m.* Parchment.
meamhair, -ean, *s.f.* Memory, remembrance, faculty of memory. 2 Memorandum. Faigh air do mheamhair, *get by rote;* gleus do mh., *excite your memory.*
meamhair, *v.a.* see meamhraich.
meamhlach, see meabhalach.
meamhrach, -aiche, *a.* Mindful, having a good memory. 2 Meditating, pensive. 3 Gentle
————,** -aich, *s.m.* Record, register.
meamhrachadh, -aidh, *s.m.* Meditating, act of meditating or pondering. 2 Recollecting, act of recollecting. 3 Study, remembrance. A' m—, *pr.pt.* of meamhraich.
meamhrachan, -ain, *s.m.* Memorandum, record, minutes. 2 Note-book.
meamhraich, *pr.pt.* a' meamhrachadh, *v.a.* Remember, recollect. 2 Consider, meditate, ponder, think. 3 Mention, put in mind. Scheme, plot. 5 Note, commit to memory.
————e, *s.m.* Recorder.
————te, *past pt.* Remembered. 2 Mentioned, considered of.
meamhran,** -ain, *s.m.* Membrane. 2 Register. 3 Memorandum.
————ach,** -aich, *s.m.* Memorandum, memorial. 2 Note-book. 3 Record. 4 Minutes.
meamna, see meanmna.
————ch, see meanmnach.
meamnachair, see meanbh-chrodh.
meamnachd, see meanmna.
meamnadh, see meanmna.
meamnag,‡‡ *s.f.* Amorous woman.
meamnaich, *v.a.* see meanmnaich.
meamra,** -ai, *s.m.* Shrine, tomb.
meamram,** *s.m.* Vellum, parchment.
mean, -a, *a.* see meanbh.
meanach, see mionach.
meanachair, *s.m.* see meanbh-chrodh. 2 (DMy) Smallness.
meanad, -aid, *s. f.* Smallness, minuteness, degree of smallness.
meanadh, -aidh, *s.m.* see manadh. 3 see minidh. Tha thu 'cur meanaidh orm, *you provoke me—Arran.*
mèanadh,** -aidh, *s.m.* Gaping, yawning.
meanaidh, see minidh.
meanaigean,** *s.pl.* Mittens, gloves.
meanalach, see mionalach.
mèanan, -ain, -an, *s.m.* Yawn, gape.
meanan, -ain, -an, *s.m.* Sawdust, dung of sheep, goats, deer or doves. 2††Anything quite small. M. còinnich, *a species of scented wild herb.*
†meanan, *a.* Plain, clear.
meananach, -aiche, *a.* Abounding in, or like saw-dust. 2 Of, or resembling the dung of sheep, goats or deer.
mèananach, -aiche, *a.* Yawning, gaping, given to yawning or gaping.
meananach, -aich, *s.m.* Manikin, dwarfish person.
mèananaich, -e, *s.f.* Ostitation, continued gaping. 'S ann ort tha a' mhèananaich! *how you do yawn!* thòisich e air mh., *he began to yawn.*
meanbh, -a, *a.* Little, small, diminutive. 2 Pulverized. 3 Pigmy. Lusan m., *little herbs;* a chogadh ris an iarmad mh., *to fight with the pigmy race.*
meanbhachd, *s.f.ind.* Smallness, minuteness.
meanbhachd,(MS) *s.f.* Tenuity.
meanbhad, *s.* Smallness.
meanbhaich,(MS) *v.a.* Bedwarf.
meanbhaidh,* *a.* see meanbh.
meanbh-bheathach, *s.m.* Animalcule.
meanbh-bheò, see meanbh-bheathach.
meanbh-bhiastag,(AF) *s.f.* Insect, vermin.
meanbh-bhith, -ean, *s.m.* see meanbh-bheathach.
meanbh-chrodh, -chruidh, *s.* Sheep or goats, (*lit.* small cattle.)
meanbh-chruimh, *s.* Mite, cheese-mite.
meanbh-chuileag, -eig, -an, *s.f.* Midge, gnat. M. shamhruidh, *the summer gnat.*

meanbh-chuileagach, -aiche, *a.* Abounding in midges or gnats.
meanbh-chùis, -ean, *s.f.* Trifling matter. 2 Parsimony, stinginess.
———————each, -eiche, *a.* Trifling, unimportant. 2 Curious, prying. 3 Parsimonious.
meanbh-eachdraidh, *s.pl.* Annals.
meanbh-fhraoch, *s.m.* Young growth after the old heather has been burnt.—*Colonsay.*
meanbh-ghàir, *s.m.* Ridicule, derision.
——————each, -eiche, *a.* Ridiculing, deriding.
meanbh-ghàirdean, *s.m.* Armlet.
meanbh-ghuireanach,(MS) *a.* Miliary.
meanbh-ghuireanan,(MS) *s.m.* Miliary fever.
meanbhlach, -aich, *s.f.coll.* Dross, refuse, fragments. 2* Small potatoes, or the refuse of such. 3††Herd of small beasts.
meanbh-pheasar, -srach & -air, *s.m.* Millet seed, millet plant—*Bible.*
meanbh-reic,** *v.* Retail.
——————eadair,** *s.m.* Retailer.
meanbh-righ,**§-rean, *s.m* Petty king.
meanbh-spréidh, -e, *s.* see meanbh-chrodh.
meandanach,** -aich, *s.m.* Mendicant.
meang, -a & -ing, -an, *s. f.* Craft, deceit, guile. 2 Blemish, want, fault. 3**Deformity. 4** Branch. 5††Knob. Gun mh., *faultless, without blemish* ; mo charaid gun mh., *my guileless friend.*
meang, -eing, *s.m. prov.* for mèag, Whey.
meang, *v.a.* Lop, or cut off branches.
meangach, -aiche, *a.* Branchy, of or belonging to a branch. 2 That lops off branches. 3 see meangail.
meangach,§ -aich, *s.f.* Common cinquefoil—*potentilla reptans.*
meangach,†† *s.m.* Branches lopped off.
meangadh, -aidh, *s.m.* Lopping, pruning or cutting off of branches. 2 Act of cutting or lopping off. A' m—, *pr.pt.* of meang.
meangail, -e, *a.* Crafty, deceitful, cunning. 2 Blemished, full of blemishes, faulty. Gu m., *deceitfully.*
meangalachd, *s.f.ind.* Deceitfulness. 2 Faultiness, blemishment. 3**Sprouting, budding.
meangan, -ain, *pl.* -an & -ain, *s.m.* Branch, twig, bough. 2‡‡Tooth or fork of a trident.
meanganach, -aiche, *a.* Branchy, having branches or boughs. 2 Of, or belonging to, a branch.
meanganaich, see meang, *v.*
meangan-Muire,§ *s.m.* Alpine lady's mantle, see trusgan.
meanglan, -ain, *pl.* -an, *s.m.* see meangan, 2 Creeper (bird), see snaigear.
meanglanach, -aiche, *a.* see meanganach.
meanglanachd, *s.f.ind.* Branchiness.
meanglanaich, *v.a.* Shorten. 2 Burgeon.
meanglanaiche,(MS) *s.m.* Brancher.
meangta, *past pt.* of meang. Lopped, cut off, as branches.
meamna, see meanmna.
————ch, see meanmnach.
meamnaich, see meanmnaich.
meanmainn, *Suth'd.* for meanmna.
meanmainneach, -eiche, *a.* see meanmnach.
meanmann, -ainn, see meanmna. 2 see meanmhuinn.
meanmarach,** -aiche, *a.* Spirited.
†meanmaradh, -aidh, *s.m.* Thought.
meanmhuinn, *s.* Titillation of the nose, an omen of a stranger's arrival, or of good news.
†meanmlaige,** *s.f.* Dulness. 2 Laziness. 3 Weakness.
meanmna, *s.m.ind.* Courage, magnanimity. 2 Spirit, pride, mettle. 3 Boldness, bravery. 4 Strength. 5 Joy, gladness. 6 Will, desire, wantonness. 7 Imagination, fancy. 8* Sensation about the lip or elbow, supposed to portend sudden death. 9 Mettlesomeness. 10 Whim. 11**Animal spirits. 12 Titillation of the nostril, which, when felt, is supposed to portend the arrival or sight of a relation or acquaintance. Lìon m. sinn uile, *proud joy filled us all.*
————ch, -aiche, *a.* Courageous, magnanimous. 2 High-spirited, proud. 3 Prancing, mettlesome, of a horse. 4 Bold, brave strong. 5 Joyful, glad. 6 Wanton, lustful. 7**Violent. A' beucaich gu m., *roaring violently* ; gu treun m., *strong and proud.*
—————chadh,** -aidh, *s.m.* Cheering, inspiriting. 2 Exhortation.
meanmnaich,** *v.a.* Cheer, inspirit, exhort. 2 Regale.
meanmuin,** *s.f.* Gladness, joy.
————neach, *a.* Joyful, glad.
meann, minn, *s.m.* Kid. 2 Young roe. 3 Goat. 4** *rarely* Rib. Dà dheagh mheann, *two good kids* ; ceann§a' mhinn, *the kid's head.*
meann,** *a.* Dumb. 2 Clear, manifest. 3 Famous.
meannach, -aiche, *a.* Abounding in kids or young roes. 2 Like a kid. A' Bhealltuinn mh., *kid-producing May.*
meannad,** -aid, *s.m.* Place, room.
meannan, -ain, *pl.* -ain & -an, *s.m.,dim.* Little kid. 2 Young kid. 3 Little goat. 4 *rarely* Rib. Ionaltair do mheannain, *feed thy kids.*
meannanach, -aiche, *a.* Of, or abounding in young kids. 2 Like a young kid. 3 Frisky.
meannanachd,** *s.f.* Friskiness.
meannan-athair, -ain-, -an-, *s.m.* Snipe, see gobhar-athair.
meannanaich,(AC) *s.* Bleating like a kid, applied to the snipe.
meann-bhoc, -bhuic, *s.m.* Year-old he-goat.
meann-chòinneach, *s.m.* Kid's moss.
meannd, see meannt.
meann-earba,(AF) *s.m.* Fawn.
meann-mhara,(AF) *s.m.* Whale.
meannrachd,** *s.f.* Happiness, bliss. 2 Good luck.
meannt, -a, *s.m.* Mint, cartal. 2 Spearmint.
meanntach, -aiche, *a.* Abounding in mint.
meannt-an-arbhair,§ *s.m.* Corn-mint—*mentha arvensis.*

516. Meannt-an-arbhair. 517. Meannt-eich.

meannt-an-uisge,‡‡ *s.m.* Water-mint.
meanntas,§ -ais, *s.m.* Garden-mint, see meannt-ghàraidh. 2**Spearmint.
meannt-choille,§ *s.m.* Horse-mint, see meannt-eich.
meannt-eich,§ *s.m.* Horse-mint—*mentha sylvestris.*
meannt-fiadhaich, } see meannt-eich.
meannt-fiadhain, }
meannt-ghàraidh,§ *s.m.* Garden-mint, spearmint

518. *Meannt-ghàraidh.* —*mentha viridis.*

meanntachd,** *s.f.* Happiness, bliss. 2 Good luck. [** gives meanntrachd.]
meantail,** *s.f.* Deceit.
meantairig, *v.* Gaelic form of *venture.*
meanntalach,** *a.* Deceitful.
meantalachd,** *s.f.* Perfidy.
meantan,** -ain, *s.m.* Snipe, see gobhar-athair.
meapaid,(WO) *s.f.* Mop for tarring.
mear, -a & meire, *a.* Merry, joyful. 2 Sportive, playful. 3 Wanton. 4 *poetically* Incited, keen, enraged. 5 Lustful. 6**Apish. 7** Buxom. 8‡‡Agitated, in quick motion. 9** Sudden or quick in motion. 10(MS) Airy. 11 (MS)Comical. 12 Very joyful, in high glee. Le sùilibh m., *with lustful eyes* ; éisteadh a' bhantrach mh., *let the wanton widow listen* ; bha sibh m., *ye were merry.*
méar, -eòir, *s.m.* see meur.
mearachadh, -aidh, *s.m.* Perishing from exposure. A' m—, *pr.pt.* of mearaich. Chaidh a mh. air a' mhonaidh, *he perished from exposure on the hill*—a common occurence in snowstorms—*Caithness.*
mearachas,†† -ais, *s.m.* Mirth.
mearachasach, see mearcasach.
mearachd, -an, *s.f.* Error, mistake, fault. 2 Wrong, injustice. 3 Aberration. 4 Oversight. 5 Merriness. Chaidh thu am m., *you have gone wrong* ; tha thu am m., *you are mistaken* ; mur 'eil mi am m., *if I am not mistaken* ; cò tha gun mh. ? *who is faultless ?* na h-abair mu choinneamh an aingil gu'm bu mh. e, *say not before the angel that it was an error;* m.-céill, *madness, an error of judgment* ; m. is laigsinn, *error and weakness.*
mearachdach, -aiche, *a.* Wrong, erroneous, incorrect. 2 Improper. 3 Culpable, faulty. 4 Wrong, unjust. 5 Misleading, false. Barail mh., *an erroneous opinion* ; a' deanamh na meidhe m., *falsifying the balances.*
mearachdachadh, -aidh, *s.m.* Mistaking, act of mistaking, erring or missing. A' m—, *pr. pt.* mearachdaich.
mearachdachd,* *s.f.ind.* Erroneousness, faultiness. 2 Culpability.
mearachdaich, *pr.pt.* a' mearachdachadh, *v. a.* Mistake. 2 Miss. 3 Err. 4 Go wrong. 5 Put wrong.
mearachdas, -ais, -an, *s.m.* Merriment, hilarity, mirth. 2 Error, mistake. 3 Liability to mistake. 4 Wantonness, indelicate romping, nearly wanton joy.
mearachdasach, -aiche, *a.* Wanton. 2 Fond of sport or amusement, merry.
†mearadh,** -aidh, *s.m.* Affliction.
mearadh-loisgeach, } *s.m.* Phosphorus—*Ar-*
mearadh-sionachain, } *ran.*
mearagan, -ain, -an, *s.m.* Puppet. 2 Automaton.
mèaragan, see meuragan.
mearaich, *pr. pt.* a' mearachadh, *v.* see mearachdaich. 2(DMK) Perish from exposure.
mearaiche, -an, *s m.* Merry-andrew, droll. 2** Merry fellow. 3**Mountebank. 4**Fool.
mearaichinn, -e, *s. f.* Madness, insanity. 2 Drunkenness. 3 Giddiness.
mear-aithne, *s.f.* Slight acquaintance of a person.
mearal, -ail, -an, *s.m. prov.* for mearachd. 2 **Disappointment. M. na h-aoise, *the dotage of old age.*
mearalachadh, *s. m.* Disappointment, disappointing, erring.
mearalachd,** *s.f.* Disappointment. 2 Error.
mearaladh, *s.m.* Disappointment.
mearalaich,** *v.* Disappoint. 2 Put wrong.
mearan, -ain, -an, *s. m.* Madness, delirium, brain-sickness. 2 Drunkenness. 3 Lasciviousness.
mèaran, -ain, -an, *s.m.* see meuran.
mearanach, *a.* Delirious, mad, insane, brainish, brain-sick. 2 Drunk. 3 Lascivious. 4 (MS)Hypochondriacal.
mearanachd, see mearan.
mearan-céille, *s.f.* Light-headedness.
mearanta, *a.* ††Mirthful. 2 see mearanach.
mearbh, *Reay co.* for meanbh.
mearbhadh, -aidh, *s.m.* Lie, fiction.
mearbhal,** -ail, *s.m.* Mistake. 2 Random.
†mearc,** -a, *s.f.* Merchandise, wares, goods.
mearcach, -aiche, *a.* Rash, confident, headstrong.
mearcachas, -ais, *s.m.* Rashness, confidence.
mear-caiteach, *a.* see mearganta. An tìr ro òrdail mh. far am bheil na daoine còire, *the orderly lively land, where the honest kind men are*—*Filidh, 21.*
mearcantas,‡‡ -ais, *s.m.* Sportiveness.
mearcasach, -aiche, *a.* Proud, elate, boastful. 2 Active,nimble,vigorous—*Sàr-Obair.* 3††Rash. 4††Wanton.
mearchall,(AC) *s.* Death-loss (of cattle, &c.)
mearchann, *s.* see mear-chinn.
mear-cheannach,** *a.* Insane. 2 Giddy, light-headed.
mear-chinn,** *s.m.* Insanity, delirium. 2 Giddiness.
mear-chunnt, *v. a.* Miscalculate. 2 Cheat by misreckoning.
mear-chunntadh, -aidh, *s.m.*see mear-chunntas.
mear-chunntas, -ais, *s. m.* Miscounting, miscalculation, misreckoning.
mear-dhàn, *a.* Foolhardy.
————achd, *s.f.* see mear-dhànadas.
mear-dhànadas, -ais, *s.m.* Fool-hardiness.
meardradh, *s.m.* Metre, crambo.—*Sàr-Obair.*
meargadaich, *v.n.* Be impatient.
mearganta, -ainte, *a.* Brisk, lively, sportive. 2 Obstinate. 3 Wanton. Mar réitheachan m., *like wanton rams.*
meargantachd, *s. f. ind.* Briskness, liveliness, sportiveness. 2**Obstinateness.
meargantas, -ais, *s.m.* Same meanings as meargantachd.
mear-ghràdh, -àidh, *s. m.* Fondness, excess of love, wanton fondness.
—————ach, -aiche, *a.* Fond, amorous, wanton. Gu m., *wantonly.*
mèarla, see mèirle.
mearlach, -aich, see mèirleach.
mearlag,§ -aige, *s.f.* Scale-fern.
mearmainn, see mearmna.
mear-macnusach, -aiche, *a.* Wanton, full of sport or pleasure.
mèars, *pr.pt.* a' mèarsadh, *v.a.* Gaelic form of *march.*
mèarsadh, -aidh, *s.m.* Marching. A' m—, *pr.pt.*

of mèars, see màrsadh.
mearsuinn, -e, *s.f.* Strength, constitution. 2** Durableness.
———each, -aiche, *a.* Hardy, strong. 2 Durable. 3**Perpetual.
mèarsail, *s.m.* see màrsadh.
———, *a.* Stately in gait.
mearsal, -ail, *s.m.* see màrsadh.
mear-shaillt,* *a.* Nitrous.
mear-shal, -ail, *s.m.* Brine.
mear-shalainneach, *a.* Nitrous.
mear-shalann,* -ainn, *s.m.* Nitre, saltpetre.
mear-shalann-gintinn, *s.m.* Nitrogen.
mearsuinn, see marsainn.
———each, *a.* see marsainneach.
†**meart**,** *s.m.* Garment.
meartuinn,(AH) *s.f.* Cold-resisting quality in a man.
meartuinneach,(AH) *a.* Enduring extreme cold without any ill-effects.
†**meas**,(AF) *s.m.* Fish, salmon.
†**meas**, *s.m.* Measure. 2 Rod to measure graves. 3 Weapon. 4 Point, edge. 5 Pair of shears. 6 Wind. 7 Foster-child.
meas, -a, -an, *s.m.* Fruit. 2 Acorn. M. nan craobh, *the fruit of the trees.*
meas, *s.m.ind.* Respect, regard, esteem. 2 Reputation, fame. 3 Opinion, judgment, valuing, estimate, appraisement. 4 Conceit, fancy. 5 Act of valuing or appraising. 6* Public notice. Le m. is miadh, *with respect and esteem*; thoir gu m., *bring to notice*; cha robh m. aig' air Cain, *he had no respect for Cain*; tha m. aig' air-fhéin (or dheth-fhéin) *he has a good conceit of himself*; cha d' thug mi m. freagairt air, *I did not give him the honour of a reply*; mu chall a mh., *about the loss of his fame, reputation*; a réir do mheas, *according to your reputation*; m. nan taighean, *the appraisement, valuation* or *estimate of the houses*; gun mh., gun mhiadh, mar Mhànus, *without respect or approbation, like Magnus*; is beag m. a bh' agad-sa air, *you lightly esteemed him.*
meas, *pr.pt.* a' measadh & a' meas, *v.a.& n.* Consider, think, judge, suppose. 2 Attribute, impute. 3 Value, appraise, estimate, reckon, weigh, calculate. 4 Esteem, deem, regard, respect. 5 Presume. 6**Lay a tax or rate on. Measar an t-amadan fhéin 'na dhuine ghlic nuair a bhios e 'na thosd, *even a fool may be reckoned a wise man while he holds his tongue*; mh. iad am bàrr 's na taighean, *they appraised*, or *valued the crop and steadings*; tha mi a' m., *I regard, esteem*; na measaibh, *do not think, do not suppose.*
measa, see miosa.
measach, -aiche, *a.* Fruitful, abounding in fruits. †2 Fishy.
measad, -aid, see miosad.
measadair, -ean, *s.m.* Appraiser, valuer, valuator.
measadaireachd, *s.f.ind.* Business of appraising or valuing, employment of an appraiser.
measadh, -aidh, *s.m.* Considering, act of considering, thinking. 2 Reckoning, judging, valuing. A' m—, *pr.pt.* of meas.
measag,** -aig, *s.f.* Acorn.
measaidh, *fut. aff. a.* of meas.
measail, -e, *a.* Respectable, worthy. 2 Estimable, esteemed, respected, valued. Duine m., *a respectable individual*; m. aig uaislibh is ìslibh, *respected by high and low*; gu m., *reputably.*
measain, *gen.sing.* of measan.
measair,(DMy) *pr.pt.* a' measradh, *v.a.* Churn. M. am bàrr, *churn the cream.*
measair, -rach, -raichean, *s.f.* Dish, measure (mias.) 2 Tub, measure. 3 Measure of a powder-flask or belt. 4 of meal. 5** Appraiser. 6 Weight or measure. 7(AF) Milk-dish. 8 Just weight or measure.
measairich,** *v.a.* Measure.
measalachd, *s.f.ind.* Respectability, merit, dignity. 2 State of being respected.
measan, -ain, *s. m.* Lap-dog. 2 Little dog. 3 Pert or forward person, "puppy."
measanach, -aiche, *a.* Puppyish, forward, pert.
measanachd, *s.f.* Forward or petulant conduct.
meas-an-tuirc-allta,§ *s. m.* Marsh St. John's wort (*lit.* wild hog's fruit—so called from its smell when bruised)—*hypericum elodes.*

519. Meas-an-tuirc-allta.

520. Meas-an-tuirc-coille.

meas-an-tuirc-coille,§ *s.m.* Common tutsan, or sweet amber—*hypericum androsæmum*—one of the most beautiful of the St. John's worts, growing from *Ross-shire* southwards and fairly frequent in *Argyll.*
measar, *fut.pass.* of meas.
measar, -air, *s.m.* see miosar.
measara, see measarra.
measarach, -aiche, *a.* Having measures. 2 Abounding in measures. (also miosarach.)
measarachd, see measarrachd.
measaradh, see measarra.
measardha, *a.* see measarra.
measarra, *a.* Temperate, sober, moderate, reasonable. 2 Frugal. 3 Modest. 4 Continent. Uime sin, bithibh m., *therefore be sober.*
measarrachd, *s. f. ind.* Temperance, sobriety, moderation, moderateness, frugality. 2 Continence. Am m., *in moderation.*
measarradh, see measarra.
meas-chaor,** -chaoir, *s.m.* Plummet. 2 Sounding-line.
meas-chraobh, -chraoibh, -chraobhan, *s.f.* Fruit-tree.
meas-chruimh,** *s.* Canker.
meas-chruinneachadh, -aidh, *s.m.* Gathering of fruit. 2 Gathering of acorns.
meas-chruinnich,** *pr. pt.* a' meas-chruinneachadh, *v.a.* Gather fruit. 2 Gather acorns. 3 Gather corn.
meas-chù, -choin, *s.m.* see measan.
meas-chuilean, -ein, -an, *s. m.* Young lap-dog, little lap-dog.
measg, (am measg) *s.* Among, amongst, in the midst. Am measg bheanntan fàsail, *among desert mountains*; am measg tamhaisg a shluaigh, *amidst the spectres of his people*; am measg na strì, *in the midst of the battle*; 'nar measg-ne, *among us*; 'nam measg, *among them*; 'nur measg-ne, *among you.*
measg, *v.a. pr. pt.* a' measgadh. Mingle, mix, stir about, move. Mharbh i a feòil, mheasg i a fuil, *she hath killed her beasts, she hath mingled her blood.*
measgach, see measg.
measgachadh, -aidh, *s.m. & pr.pt.* of measgaich. Same meanings as measgadh.
measgachd, *s.f.ind.* Miscellaneousness.

measgadh, -aidh, *s.m.* Mixing, act of mixing or mingling, stirring about. 2 Mixture. A' m –, *pr.pt.* of measg.
measgadh-litreach, *s.m.* Monogram.
measgaich, *v.a.* Same meanings as measg.
measgaichte, see measgta.
measgain,(AC) *s.* Miscellaneous articles.
measgan, -ain, -an, *s.m.* Dish used to hold butter, butter-crock. 2‡‡Mash. 3**Butterwort.
measgnachadh, see measgadh.
measgnadh, -aidh, see measgadh.
measgnaich, *v.a.* Same meanings as measg. 2 **Copulate.
measgnaichte, see measgta.
meas-ghort, -ghoirt, -an, *s. m.* Fruit-garden, orchard.
measgte, *past pt.* of measg. Mixed, mingled.
measra, see measarra.
measrach, *gen.sing.* of measair.
————adh, -aidh, *s. m.* Thinking, act of thinking, judging, supposing. 2 Thought, design. 3 Act of rendering temperate or moderate. 4 State of becoming moderate. 5(MS) Apprehension. 6 Conception. A' m—, *pr. pt.* of measraich.
measrachail,(MS) *a.* Apprehensible.
measradh, see measarra.
————,(DMy) -aidh, *s.m.* The quantity of cream or butter in the churn at any given time. A' m—, *pr.pt.* of measair. Am bheil m. agad an diugh ? *have you a churning to-day ?* tha i a' m., *she is churning.*
measraich, *pr.pt.* a' measrachadh, *v.a.* Think, judge, suppose. 2 Temper, moderate, sober. 3 Become sober, temperate or moderate. 4 Conceive.
————ean, *n.pl.* of measair.
————te, *past pt.* of measraich. Tempered, sobered, become temperate.
meas-tuirc-allta, see meas-an-tuirc-allta.
meas-tuirc-caol,‡ see meas-an-tuirc-coille.
meata, *a.* Feeble. 2 Soft, cowardly, timid, faint-hearted. 3** Distrustful. Siol m., *a timid race ;* cha bhuadhaich am m. gu bràth, *the chicken-hearted shall never conquer,* or *prosper.*
meatach, -aiche, *a.* see meata.
meatachadh, -aidh, *s.m.* Enfeebling, act of enfeebling, debilitating or terrifying. 2 State of becoming weak, faint, soft or cowardly, dispiriting, growing timid. 3* Benumbing, daunting, damping the spirits. 4*Starving with cold. A' m—, *pr.pt.* of meataich. Thug sin m. mór as, *that daunted him greatly.*
meatachd, *s.f.ind.* Cowardice, timidity, faintheartedness. 2 Feebleness. 3**Dismay. 4** Hinderance. 5*Delicacy of feeling or sentiment. Sheas Fionn air leirg gun mh., *F. stood on a declivity undauntedly.*
meatag, -aig, -an, see miotag.
————ach, -aiche, see miotagach.
————aich, see miotagaich.
————aichte, see miotagaichte.
meataich, *pr.pt.* a' meatachadh, *v.a. & n.* Enfeeble, terrify, make feeble. 2 Make spiritless. 3 Grow effeminate. 4 Become feeble, weak, effeminate or fearful. 5 Daunt, damp the spirits. 6†† Be afraid or terrified. 7 Starve with cold, benumb. Mh. siod gu mór e, *that daunted him greatly ;* na meataicheadh gart a' chuain sibh, *let not the threatening aspect of the sea terrify you.*
meatailt, see miotailt.
————each, see miotailteach.
meath, -a, *a.* Oily. 2 Fat, rich. Talamh m., *rich soil.*
meath, -a, *s.m.* Decay, failing, fading. 2 Consumption. 3**Effeminacy. A' m—, *pr. pt.* of meath. Na h-alltaichean a' fàs, agus na h-aibhnichean a' m., *the burns increasing and the rivers failing*—a proverb applied to the growth of new families and the decay of old ones ; a' toirt m. dhòmh-sa, *taunting me.*
meath, *pr.pt.* a' meath, *v.a. & n.* Move with pity, affect. 2 Discourage, dishearten. 3 Intimidate, make timid. 4 Decay, wither, fade. 5 Become weak, soft, effeminate or timid. 6 ** Die. 7 see meat- aich. Mh. a' chraobh, *the tree faded ;* mh. i gach cridhe, *she softened every heart,* or *she damped every spirit.*
meath, *a.* see meathach.
meathach, -aiche, *a.* Affecting, causing pity. 2 Discouraging, disheartening. 3 Decaying. 4 Perishable. 5 Causing decay or languor. 6 Mild, soft, tender. 7 Despondent. 8 Meek, soft-hearted. 9 Causing effeminacy.
meathach, -aich, *s.m.* Weakly, effeminate or disheartened person. 2 Degenerate person. 3 Despondent person. 4 Tender, excoriated part of the skin.
————adh, -aidh, *s.m. & pr.pt.* of meathaich, see meathadh.
meathachan, -ain, *s.m.* Effeminate or cowardly person. 2†† Decaying or fading man. 3** Glutton.
meathadh, -aidh, *s. m.* Affecting. 2 Causing of pity. 3 Discouraging, act of discouraging, of damping the spirits. 4 State of becoming timid or weak. 5 State of withering, decaying fading or failing. 6 Shrinking, degenerating, desponding, despondency. 7*Taunt, jeer, gibe. 8 Act of moving, as with fits. 2 Effeminacy. A' m –, *pres. part.* of meath. Cha ruig thu leas a bhi toirt meathaidh dhòmh-sa, *you need not taunt me.*
meathaich, *v.a. & n.* see meath.
————te, *past pt.* of meathaich. Affected, softened, moved with pity. 2 Discouraged, disheartened. 3 Withered, decayed. 4 Become weak or timid.
meathanas,** -ais, *s.m.* Consumption.
meathas,** -ais, *s.m.* Fat, fatness. 2 Effeminacy.
meath-challtuinn, *s.m.* Southernwood, old man —*artemisia abrotanum.* Sometimes used instead of hops in the preparation of malt liquors.
meath-chridhe, -chridheachan, *s.m.* Faintness of heart, cowardice, timidity. 2**Faint-heart.
meadh-chridheach, -eiche, *a.* Faint-hearted, cowardly, timid, effeminate. Tha sith 'gam fhàgail m., *peace renders me effeminate.*
meath-chridheachd, *s.f.* see meath-chridhe.
meath-chrith, -e, *s.f.* Trembling from fear or cowardice.
meath-chrom,** *v.* Crouch.
meath-ghàire, -an, *s.f.* Smile. [meath-gàire in *Gairloch*—CR.]
meath-ghalar, *s.* Disease. Is treasa deagh-àrach na m., *good nurture overcomes disease.*
meath-ionnsuidh, -e, -ean, *s. f.* Feeble attempt or attack, feeble onset. 2 Spiritless invasion. Thug e m. air, *he feebly attempted it.*
meathlachadh, -aidh, see meathadh.
meathlaich, see meathaich. 2††see meilich.
————te, see meathaichte.
meath leigheiseach, *a.* Antiseptic.
meath-oidheirp, -e, -ean, *s.f.* Feeble attempt.
meath-oidheirpeach, -eiche, *a.* Making a feeble attempt. 2 Irresolute. 3 Unenterprising.
meathras,** -ais, *s.m.* Fat, grease.
meath-shùil, -shùla, -ean, *s.f.* Blear-eye.
meath-shùileach, -aiche, *a.* Blear-eyed.
meath-thinneas, -eis, -an, *s. m.* Consumption.

wasting disease. 2**Debilitating sickness.
meath-thogar,** -air, *s.m.* Faint inclination. 2 Indifference.
meath-thograch, -aiche, *a.* Indifferent, having but a faint desire, lukewarm.
meath-thogradh, -aidh, -ean, *s.m.* Faint inclination or desire, indifference, lukewarmness.
meathusradh,(AF) *s.* Fatlings.
meatras, see meathras.
meiceinn, -ean, *s.m.* see meacan.
†meide, *s.f.* The neck.
†meideach, -eich, see meidh-each.
meideal, -eil, *s.m.* Gaelic spelling of *medal.*
†meidealach, -aich, *s.m.* Large knife. 2 Leather hinge of a flail.
meidh,(DU) *pr.pt.* a' meidheadh, *v. a.* Prune, clear of twigs.
meidh, -e, -ean, *s.f.* Balance, beam for weighing, scale. 2 Weight, measure. 3 Stem, stock, trunk. 4 The sign Libra (♎) in the zodiac. Is fhèarr guth na m., *a word is better than a balance*—a dubh-fhacal. The meaning probably is, that the voice of a powerful friend is of more value than strict impartiality. In his first edition, Macintosh gives the word *meithe;* and his translation is, *better speak than lose right*—N.G.P ; anns na meidhibh, *in the balances.*
meidh, *a.* see meath.
meidh-àile, *s.f.* Barometer. 2 Anemometer. 3 Thermometer. 4 Thermoscope.
meidh-allach, see meitheallach.
meidh-chothrom,** *s.f.* Balance.
†meidhe, see meidh 3.
meidh-each, -eich, *s.m.* Stallion.
meidheach, -eiche, *a.* Of, or belonging to, beams or balances. 2 Like a scale or balance. 3** Having scales, weights, measures or balances.
meidheach, -eiche, *a.* see meathach.
meidheachadh, -aidh, *s. m.* Weighing, act of weighing. A' m—, *pr.pt.* of meidhich.
meidheadair, -e, -ean, *s.m.* Weigher. 2 Steelyard, instrument for weighing. 3 Balancer.
meidheadh, -idh, see meidheachadh.
mèidhean, *s.m.* Favour, influence.
meidhich, *pr.pt.* a' meidheachadh, *v.a.* Weigh, balance, weigh with scales or balances.
meidhichean, see meidhinnean.
meidhichte, *past pt.* of meidhich. Weighed, balanced.
meidhin, see meadhon.
meidhinnean, *s. pl.* The hip-joints. 2 The back side of the hip below the small of the back. As na meidhinnean, *the hip-joint dislocated.*
meidhis,* *s. f.* Instalment. 2 Part, measure. Phàigh sinn air mheidhisean e, *we paid it by instalments;* a' cheud mh., *the first instalment;* 'na mheidhisean, *by instalments.*
meidhisich,* *v.n.* Graduate.
meidhlich, see meaghalaich.
meidil, -ean, *s.f.* Medlar-tree.
meidileach, -eiche, *a.* Of, or abounding in medlars. 2 Belonging to a medlar.
meig,* *s. f.* Protuberant chin. 2 Snout of a goat.
meig, *s.m.* Voice, cry. 2(CR) Sign of life. Cha'n 'eil m. ann, *he shows no sign of life—W. of Ross.*
mèig, -e, -ean, *prov.* of meidhinnean.
meigead, -eid, -an, *s.m.* The bleat of a goat or kid.
meigeadaich, *s.f.* Continued bleating of a goat or kid. Le m. fann, *with faint bleating.*
meigeadan,(AF) *s.m.* Goat. 2 Kid.
meigeall, *pr. pt.* a' meigeallaich, *v.n.* Bleat, as a goat or kid.
meigeall, *s.m.* Mewing, caterwauling.
meigeallach,** *a.* Bleating, as a goat.
meigeallaich, *s.f.* Bleating, as of a goat. A' m—, *pr.pt.* of meigeall.
mèigean, *prov.* for meidhinnean.
meigeardaich,* see meigeadaich.
meigeil,* see meigeall.
meigh, -ean, *s.f.* see meidh. 2 Part of a hand fishing-line, see under dorgh.
meigheach, -eiche, see meidheach.
meighich, see meidhich.
meighlich, see mèilich.
meil, *pr.pt.* a' mèilich, *v.n.* Bleat as sheep or lambs.
mèil, -ean, *s.f.* Bleating of sheep or lambs.
meil, *pr.pt.* a' meilich, *v.a.* Grind, as corn, pulverize. Meileadh mo bhean do neach eile, *let my wife grind to another* ; a' chailc air a meileadh, *the chalk pulverized.*
meilbheag, -eig, -an, *s.f.* Poppy—*papaver rhœus.*

620. *Meilise.* 521. *Meilbheag.*

meilbheagach, -aiche, *a.* Abounding in poppies.
meilc,(AC) *s.* Sweetness. M. a bhi 'nam aodann, *sweetness be in my face.*
meilcein, see milcein.
meilcheart, *s.f.* Chilblain—*Argyll.*
meildear, -ir, -an, see meiltear.
meildidh,(CR) see meildreach.
meildir, see meildreach.
meildreach, ich, -ean, *s.m.* Quantity of grain sent to be ground, grist, multure. 2 Food, provision—*Suth'd.*
meile, -an, *s.f.* The stick by which a quern is turned, mill-staff. 2 Quern, hand-mill. 3(AF) Sheep. 4**Jaw-bone. 5**Pestle.
meileach,** *a.* Of, or belonging to a quern. 2 Like a quern. 3 Apt to faint with cold.
meileach,(DC) *s.m.* Meal ground very fine. 2 Thin, spindle-shanked child.
meileachadh, -aidh, *s.m.* Fainting with cold. 2 Grinding with a quern. 3**Reproaching. A' m—, *pr.pt.* of meilich.
meileachd,* *s. f. ind.* Multure. 2 Reproach, abuse.
meileadair, see meiltear.
meileadh, -eidh, *s.m.* Grinding, act of grinding very fine, as corn. A' m—, *pr.pt.* of meil. In *Uist* ordinary meal is said to be "air a bhleith," fine meal, "air a mheileadh."
meileadaireachd, see meiltearachd.
mèileadh, *s.m.* Bleating, as of sheep.
meileag, see beileag.
meilean, -ein, -an, *s.m.* Hasty pudding.
meilearach,§ -aich, *s. m.* Sea-maram, sea-matweed, see muirineach.
meileartan,* *s.pl.* Flesh mites, generally under the toes. 2 *Arran* for meille-chartan.
†meilg, *s.m.* Death. 2 Pod. 3 Milk.
meilg,(DU) *s.f.* Milt of a fish. [In *Gairloch* both mealg and meilg are used as *nom.*]
meilgeag, see meiligeag.

mèilich, *s.f.ind.* Bleating, act of bleating, as sheep or lambs. 2*Querulousness. A' —, *pr. pt.* of mèil. M. nan caorabh, *the bleating of the sheep*; m. mhaoth, *soft bleating*.
méilich, *v.* Bleat, as sheep or goats. see mèil.
meilich, *v.a.* & *a.* Chill, benumb. 2 Become faint from cold, become chilled.
meilich, *s.* Hollow. Gun mheilichean) gun tòicean, *without hollows or howes—Beinn Doran.*
meiligeag, -eig, -an, *s.f.* The husk of pease, or of any leguminous vegetable.
meiligeagach, -aiche, *a* Having husks or pods. 2 Like husks or pods. A' pheasair mh., *the podded peas*.
meiligir, *s.* Mill.
meilinnich, see meile.
meilis, see milis.
meilise, *s. f.* Hedge-mustard, bank-cress—*sisymbrium officinale*. [illust. on p. 615.]
méill, -e, -ean, *s. f.* Cheek. 2 Mill-clapper. 3 Blubber-lip. 4**Idiot. [meill in *W. of Ross*—CR mèill in *Lochcarron*—DMK.]
méilleach, -eiche, *a.* Having large or swollen cheeks, pouch-mouthed. 2 Blubber-lipped. [‡‡ gives meilleach.]
méilleachadh,** *s.m.* Numbness.
méilleadh, -idh, *s.m.* Inciting, incitement. 2 Encouragement.
meilleag, -eig, *s. f.* Bridle-bit. 2 Blubber-lip. 3 Blubber-lipped female.
méilleag, -eig, -an, *s.f.* Outer rind of bark. 2 §Bark of the birch-tree.
méilleagach, -aiche,*a.* Blubber-lipped. 2 Of, or pertaining to, blubber lips. 3 Having pouting lips.
meillean,** -ein, *s.m.* Blame, reproach.
méillear, -ir, -an, *s.m.* Blubber-lipped person.
meille-chartan, -ain, *s. f.* Cailblain, itching in the sole of the foot.
meille-chraosach,(MS) *a.* Pouch-mouthed.
meillg,** *s.f.* Rind. 2 Pod.
†**meilliach**, *s.f.* The globe.
meilliceach, -eiche, *a.* see meilleagach.
meillicean, -ein, -an, *s.m.* Blubber-lipped person, one with pouting lips.
meillicir, see meillicean.
meillich,(MS) *v.a.* Pouch, pocket.
meilt,** -e, *s.f.* Grinding, mastication, chewing. 2 Hurling, casting. 3 Consuming. 4 Friction.
meilte, *past pt.* of meil. Ground, as grain. Gràn m., *ground grain*.
meiltear, -ir, *pl.* -teirean, *s. m.* Grinder, miller, hand-mill grinder.
meiltearachd,** *s.f.ind.* Grinding, business of a miller. 2 Handmill grinding.
meiltir, -treach -trichean, *s.f.* see meildreach.
meiltreach, -eiche, *a.* Smooth, level, plain.
meiltrichean, *pl.* of meiltir.
mein, -e- *s.f.* see mèinn, & mèinneach.
meineabhag, -aig, *s.f.* Fondling, caressing.
——————ach, -aiche, *a.* Fondling, caressing, given to fondling. 2 Affectionate.
——————aich, -e, see meineabhag.
mèineach, -eiche, *a.* see mèinneil.
mèinear, -eire, *a.* see mèinneil.
mèinear, *s.* mèinnear.
mèinealachd, see mèinnealachd.
mèineil, see mèinneil.
meinich, *Gairloch & Lochbroom* for meilich (become numb.)
meiniche, *comp.* of meinneach.
meinigeag, see meilig.ag.
meinigean, *s.pl.* Gloves, mittens.
meinn, *s.f.* see meannna.
meinneach, -eiche, *a.* see meanmnach.
meinmin, -e, see meaumna.

mèinn, -e, *s.f.* Ore. 2 Mine. 3 Vein of metal. 4 Mind, desire, inclination, disposition, whether good or bad. 5 Native quality or energy. 6 Love,fondness. 7 Discretion, clemency. 8* 9 Expression. 10**Air. 11 Mien. 12**Mercy. 13**Kindness. 14**Tenderness.
Is don' a' mh. a th' ort, *your expression of countenance does not betoken anything good*; cia mór a mh. ! *how majestic his countenance!* fàg 'na mh. féin e, *leave it to his own discretion*; duine air 'fhàgail g'a mh. fhéin, *a man left to his own prudence*; tha e 'nad mh. fhéin, *it is left to your own clemency*; am m. na gaoithe, *to the mercy of the wind*; talamh a bheir bàrr o a mh.fhéin,*land that produces crops of its own native energy*; to mh., *with the purpose of, having a mind to*; m. airgid, *silver ore*; 2 *a silver mine*; m. iarainn, *iron ore*; 2 *an iron mine.*
meinn-Æthiopach, *s.f.* Æthiop's metal.
mèinn-àite, -an, *s.m.* Mine.
meinne, see meann.
mèinneach, -eiche, *a.* see mèinneil. 2 Having a good mien. 3 Airy.
mèinneach, *s.m.* Mercy, pity. 2 Discreetness. 3 Fondness.
mèinneadair, -ean, *s. m.* Miner. 2 Mineralogist, student of ores.
————————eachd, *s. f.* Occupation of a miner, mining. 2 Mineralogy.
mèinnealachd, *s.f.ind.* Goodness of disposition, amiableness. 2 Kindness. 3 Discretion. 4 Tractability. 5 Flexibility, ductility, as of metal. 6**Tenderness. 7**Fondness. 8** Affableness. 9 Softness, as of leather, grass or tallow. 10*Productive quality.
mèinnear, -eir, *s.m.* Mineral. 2 Miner. 3 Mineralogist.
————ach,** -aiche, *a.* Mineralogical.
————ach, -aich, *s.m.* Mineralogist. 2 Miner.
mèinnearachd,** *s.f.* Mining. 2 Mineralogy.
mèinneil, -e, *a.* Mineral, abounding in ore or mines. 2 Substantial. 3 Sappy. 4 Flexible, ductile. 5 (MS) Placid. 6 Productive, prolific, as a female. 7 Native. 8 Valuable, desirable. 9‡‡Well-disposed. 10‡‡ Affable,kind. 11‡‡Discreet, prudent. 12 ‡‡Tractable. 13 **Tender, affectionate, merciful,pitiful, fond.
mèinnire, *s.m.* Mine-sieve.
mèinneachd, see mèinneadaireachd.
mèinneadair, -ean, *s.m.* Miner. 2 Mineralogist.
——————eachd, *s.f.ind.* Mineralogy, business of a mineralogist. 2 Occupation of a miner.
mèinn-eòlas, -ais, *s.m* Mineralogy.
mèinn-theagasg, see mèinn-eòlas.
†**meirbh**, -e, *s.f.* Sour or weak drink.
meirbh, -e, *a.* Slender, slim, delicate, slight. 2 Silly, feeble, spiritless. 3 **Slow, tedious.
meirbh, *pr.pt.* a' meirbheadh, *v.a.* & *n.* Digest, concoct in the stomach.
meirbhe, *s.f.ind.* Slenderness, delicacy of form. 2 Silliness, feebleness, weakness. 3**Dullness, slowness, tediousness. 4**Lie. 5 Spiritlessness.
meirbhe, *comp.* of meirbh.
meirbheal, -eid, *s. f.* Slenderness, degree of slenderness. 2 Silliness, degree of silliness. 3 Feebleness.
meirbheadh, -eidh, *s.m.* Digestion, process of digestion. A' m—, *pr.pt.* of meirbh.
meirbhean, (AC) -ein, *s.m.* Indigestion.
†**meirceann**,** -inn, *s.m.* Finger.
meirc, see milc.
meircean,(DU) *s.m.* Stem of various kinds of tangle. When pared, the stem is eaten by children, who consider it a delicacy.
†**meirdreach**, -eich, -ean, *s.f.* Concubine,courte-

zan, harlot.
————as, -ais, s.m. Concubinage, fornication.
meire, see mire.
meireal, (MS) s.m. Brine.
meirealach, (MS) a. Brackish, briny.
meirean, -ein & -e, see mearan.
————-nam-magh, s.m. Agrimony.
meirg, s.f. prov. for mairg.
meirg, -e, s.f. Rust.
meirg, v.a. & n. Rust, become rusty. 2 Cause to rust or corrode.
†meirge, see meirghe. 2 Sign, signal.
meirgeach, -eiche, a. Rusty, covered with rust. 2 Cadaverous, ill-tempered, as a person. 3 Having banners. 4 Of, or belonging to, a banner.
————adh, s.m. & pr.pt. see meirgeadh.
meirgeachd, (MS) s.f. Rust.
meirgeadh, -eidh, s.m. Rusting, state of becoming rusty. 2 Rust. 3 Act of causing to rust. A' m—, pr.pt. of meirg.
meirgeal,** -eil, s. m. Cadaverous person. 2 Part of crann-nan-gad, No. 20, p. 263.
meirgeall,** -ill, s.m. Roughness, ruggedness.
meirghe, -an, s. f. Banner, standard, flag, pennon. 2 Band, troop, company. 3**Pair of colours or flags.
meirgheach, -eiche, a. Having banners or flags. 2 Like a banner or flag. 3 In companies or troops. 4 Having many troops.
meirgich, see meirg.
meirgichte, see meirgte.
meirgneach, -eiche, a. see meirgeach.
meirgneachadh, -aidh, s.m. & pr. pt. of meirgnich, see meirgeadh.
meirgnich, v. see meirg & meirgich.
————te, see meirgte.
meirgte, past pt. of meirg. Rusted, covered with rust. Claidheamh m., a rusted sword.
meirin, see mearan.
————each, see mearanach.
mèirle, s.f.ind. Theft. 2 Thieving, act or habit of stealing. 3 Thing stolen.
mèirleach, -ich, s.m. Thief, robber. 2**Rogue. 3**Rebel.
————-as, -ais, s.m. see mèirle. 2**Treason rebellion.
————-d, see mèirle.
mèirleadh, s.m. see mèirle.
méirneal, -eil, -an, s.m. Merlin—falco æsalon. 2(AF) Falcon.

523. *Méirneal.*

meirse,** s.f. Smallage, fine.
†meirtneach,** a. Feeble. 2 Fatigued.
†meis, a. Bad, wicked.
mèis, gen.sing. of mias.
†meis-cheòl, -chiùil, s.m. Singing, modulation, music.
meisd.** s.f. Rust.
meisd, -e, comp. of olc. see misde.
meisde,**s.f. Deterioration. A' dol am m., *growing worse and worse.*
mèise, gen sing. of mias.
méisean,** -ein, s.m. Little plate.
meisg, -e, s.f. see misg.
————each, see misgeach.
————ear, -eir, -eirean, see misgear.
————eireachd, see misgearachd.
meisimean, (for misimean dearg) s.m. Bog-mint, see cairteal.
meislean,** -ein, s.m. Mastlin.
meisneach, see misneach.
meisnich, see misnich.
meite, (DMC) a. Weak, frail. 2 Imbecile.
meiteal, (DMC) a. Proud, boasting (moiteil.)
meiteal, -eil, s.m. Metal. 2 Mettle, hardness, strength of body or mind. 3 Courage, stuff.
————ach, see meitealtach.
————achd, (MS) s.f. Dwarfishness. 2(DMC) Weakness. 3 (DMC) Imbecility.
————tach, -aiche, a. Metallic. 2 Mettled, hardy, spirited, enduring, strong. 3**Keen, smart, made of good stuff.
meith, v.a. & n. see meath.
mèith, -e, a. Fat, greasy, oily. 2 Fat, corpulent. 3 Sappy, rich, as soil. 4**Soft, timid. Mias mh. an t-sagairt, *the priest's fat mess.*
mèitheachd,** s.f. Fatness. 2 Softness. 3 Timidity.
mèithealach, -aich, s.m. Fatling. 2 Nursling.
————d, s.f.ind. Oiliness. 2 Fatness, corpulency. 3 Sappiness, richness, as of soil.
mèitheallach, (AF) s.m. Fat cattle.
meithean,§ -ein, s.m. Sea-rush—*juncus maritimus & acutus.*

524. *Meithean.* 525. *Meòir Moire.*

mèitheas, -eis, see mèithealachd.
mèitheil, -e, a. see mèith.
†meithle, s.pl. Reapers. 2 Crowds, concourse.
meithleachadh, (MS) s.m. Algor.
meithlich, v. see meilich.
meithreas,** s.m. Kitchen stuff. 2 Fatness.
†melg, s. Death.
————, see meilg.
melis, (DMu) a. *Suth'd* for milis.
meò-bhlàth, -àithe, a. see meadh-bhlàth.
————achadh, see meadh-bhlàthachadh.
————aich, see meadh-bhlathaich.
meòdar, s.m. Luxuriant pasture.
meòg, -eòig & -eig, s.m Whey. [meang in some parts—DMC. *Gen. sing.* in *N. Argyll* is mig—AH.]
meògach, -aiche, a. Of whey, like whey, serous.
————d, (MS) s.f. Serosity.

meògail, -e, *a.* see meògach.
meoghail, -e, *s.f.* Mirth, joy, jollity. 2 Medley, mixture. 3 Company, mixed company.
meoghair, -e, *s.f.* see meamhair. 2 see meaghail.
meoghlach,** *a.* Mixed, confused, in a medley
meoghrach, -aiche, *a.* see meadhrach.
meoinn,(AF) *s.* Cat.
meòir, *gen sing.* & *n.pl.* of meur.
meòir Moire,§ *s.m.* Kidney vetch, lady's fingers —*anthyllis vulneria.* [ill. 525 on p. 647.]
meomhair, see meamhair.
————-each, -eiche, *a.* see meamhrach.
————-eachadh, -aidh, see meamhrachadh.
meomhairich, see meamhraich.
meòmhrachadh, -aidh, see meamhrachadh.
meòmhrachan, see meamhrachan.
meòmhraich, see meamhraich.
meòrach, -aiche, *a.* see meamhrach.
————-adh, -aidh, *s. m.* & *pr. pt.* see meamhrachadh.
meòrachan, see meamhrachan.
meòragan, see meuran.
meòraich, *v.* see meamhraich.
meòran, see meuran.
meòranach, -aich, see meamhranach.
meothal,** -ail, *s.m.* Help.
†mer,‖ *s.m.* Madman.
mere, merg, } (AF) Blackbird, see lon-dubh.
mersgirra (AF) *s.* Angler-fish—*Caithness.*
meuchd, *s.f.* Mixture, mass or compound formed by mixing—*Dàin I. Ghobha.*
meud, *s.m.ind.* Greatness, largeness, degree of greatness or largeness, dimension, extent, quantity, stature, size, bulk. 2 Degree, measure, extent. 3 *coll.* As many as, magnitude, number, quantity.
M. an taighe, *the size of the house*; air mh. 's gu 'm bheil e, *let him* (or *it*) *be ever so great*; mu 'n mh. ud, *about yon size*; m. do ghàirdean, *the greatness of thy arm*; m. a bhròin, *the magnitude of his grief*; ciod e a mh.? *what is his stature* (or *its size*)? ; m. a' ghoirtein, *the size of the field*: co mh. a th' ann? *how many are there?* agus a' mh. 's a bhean ris, leighis e iad, *and as many as touched him, he healed them*; a mh. 's a tha làthair, *as many as are present, as many as are alive, or surviving*; a mh. agus gu 'n d' rinn thu sin, *inasmuch as you have done that*; co m. a fhuair thu? *what quantity did you get?* a' dol am m., *growing in size, stature or extent.*
meudachadh, -aidh, *s.m.* Increasing, act of increasing, enlarging, or making larger. 2 State of becoming larger or greater. 3 Increase, augmentation, adding, addition. 4* Growth. A' m—, *pr.pt.* of meudaich.
meudachail, -e, *a.* Intensitive. 2 Metric.
meudachd, *s.f.ind.* Bulk, size, magnitude, greatness, dimension. 2 Stature. 3 Increase. Is ionghnadh leam a mh., *I am surprised at its dimensions*; duine de mh. mhoir, *a man of great size or stature*; agus thainig Iosa air aghaidh am m., *and Jesus increased in stature.*
meudaich, *pr pt.* a meudachadh, *v.a.* & *n.* Increase, multiply, cause to increase. 2 Enlarge, become larger, grow in size, improve. 3 Abound. 4 Add to, augment. Meudaichidh mi do dhoilgheas, *I will multiply thy sorrow*; meudaichidh tu a luach, *thou shalt increase its price*; am fear nach m. an càrn, gu 'm meudaich e a' chroich, *he that will not add (a stone) to the cairn, may he add to the dignity of the gallows*; far an do mh. am peacadh gu ro mhó a mh. gràs, *where sin abounded grace did much more abound.*
meudaicheam, *1st. sing. imp.* of meudaich. Let me increase.
meudaichear, *fut.pass.* of meudaich.
meudaichte, *past pt.* of meudaich. Increased, augmented, enlarged. 2**Advanced.
meud-bhronn, *s.f.* The dropsy. [Preceded by the art. a'.] 2**Pregnancy. Theasd e leis a' mh., *he died of the dropsy.*
————————ach, -aiche, *a.* Dropsical. 2 Swag-bellied.
meudmhor,** *a.* Ample.
meudrach, *a.* Metrical.
meudradh, *s.m.* Metre.
meug, see meòg, mèig & mìge.
meugach, see meògach.
meugail, see meògach.
meugar,** *s.m.* Serous.
meunan, see mèanan.
————ach, see mèananach.
————aich, see mèananaich.
meunaich, see meanaich.
meunanda, see meuranda.
meur, -eòir, *pl.* -eòir, *s.m.* Finger. 2 Toe. 3 Branch, bough. 4 Branch of a family, kindred, clan. 5 Branch of a river. 6 Prong. 7* Knot in wood. 8 Slight degree. Thum an sagart a mh., *the priest dipped his finger*; na casan agus am meòir, *the feet and their toes*; meur a' ghràpa, *the prong of the fork*; m. de 'n teaghlach sin, *a branch of that family*; tha meòir 's an fhiodh, *the wood is knotty*; m. de 'n chaitheimh, *a slight degree of consumption*; m. a' ghiomaich, *the lobster's claw*; ged nach rachadh clach ceann a' mheòir an aghaidh na gaoithe, *though one could not send a stone a nail's breadth against the wind*; am m. meadhoin, *the middle finger.*
meurach, -aiche, *a.* Fingered. 2 Branchy. 3 Pronged. 4*Knotty, full of knots or bumps. 5**Nimble-fingered.
————adh, -aidh, *s. m.* Act of fingering. 2 Growing into branches, putting forth of branches. 3** Pawing. A' m—, *pr. pt.* of meuraich.
meurachd *prov* for mèarachd.
meuradan,* -ain, *s. m.* Delicate, slender, weak person.
——————ach, -aiche, *a* Delicate.
——————achd,* *s.f.* Conduct of a delicate person. 2 Eating or dealing with gently.
meurag, -aig, -an, *s. f. dim.* of meur. Small finger. 2 Small clew or ball of yarn. 3 Tuft of wool, *prov.* 4‡‡Small pebble.
————ach, -aiche, *a.* Abounding in small clews or tufts of wool. 2 Abounding in small pebbles.
————aich, *v.a.* see meuraich.
————an, ain, *pl.* -ain & -an, *s. m.* Fingering, handling 2 Little thimble.
————anaich, see meuraich.
meuraibh, *dat.pl.* of meur.
meuraich, *pr pt.* a' meurachadh, *v.a.* Handle, finger. 2*Fidget. 3**Branch.
——————te, *past pt.* of meuraich. Fingered, handled. 2 Branched.
meuran, -ain, *pl.* -ain & -an, *s. m.* Thimble 2 Little branch. 3 Small finger. 4 (DMC) Piece of cloth sewn in the form of the finger of a glove and worn as such.
meuran-a'-bhàis,(DMK) *s. m.* Foxglove—*West coast of Ross.*
————ach, -aiche, *a.* Of, or belonging to, thimbles. 2 Like a thimble. 3 Full of thimbles. 4 Branchy.
————da, -ainde, *a.* Weakly, delicate, tender, 2 **Tiny.
————dachd, *s.f.ind.* Weakliness, delicateness

tenderness. 2 Silliness of person.
meuran-na-mnà-sìth, see lus-nam-ban-sìth.
——— -nan-cailleachan-marbha, *s. m.* Fox-glove, see lus-nam-ban-sìth.
——— -nan-daoine-marbha,§ *s. m.* Fox-glove, see lus-nam-ban-sìth.
——— -sìth,§ *s.m.* Fox-glove, see lus-nam-ban-sìth.
meuranta,* *a.* Delicate.
———chd,** *s.f.* Delicacy of constitution. 2 Silliness of person.
meurlag,¶ *s.f.* Polypody, see clach-raineach.
mh, For words beginning with mh, see under *m.*
mhàin, (for a mhàin) *adv.* Only, alone. Is tus' a mhàin Iehobhah, *thou alone art Jehovah ;* cha'n e sin a mhàin, *that is not all.*
mhàn, see a bhàn.
mheud (for a mheud) *adv.* Inasmuch, forasmuch.
Mhoire ! *int.* By Mary ! common form of asseveration. Air Moire ! *by Mary !*
†mi, *s.f.* Month.
mi, *pref. neg.* Indicating the opposite of, or the want of, the quality expressed by the word to which it is prefixed, equivalent to the English, *in-*, *un-*, as ciall, *reason* ; mi-chiall, *folly.* *Sometimes it signifies Evil, the worst.
mi, *pers. pron.* I, me. *Emphatic,* mise, mi-fhéin (*prov.* mi-fhìn) *myself.* Is mi, *it is I ;* bithidh mi, *I shall be.* [Always aspirated when used immediately after *bu* and *cha*, as cha mhi, *it is not I.*]
mi-abairt, -ean, *s.f.* Mis-saying.
miabhadh, -aidh, *s.m.* Chagrin.
miabhail, -e, *a.* see mi-bhàigheil.
miabhalachd, *s.f.* see mi-bhàighealachd.
miabhalas, -ais, *s.m.* see mi-bhàighealachd.
miabhan,** -ain, *s.m.* Megrim.
miach,** *s.* Budget. 2**Measure. 3 Bag, satchel.
———air,** *a.* Kind, loving, affable. Gu m., *kindly, affably.*
miad, see meud & miadan.
miadaich, *v.* see meudaich.
miadan, -ain, *pl.* -an & -ain, *s.m.* Meadow, plain, grassy plain.
———ach, -aiche, *a.* Abounding in meadows or grassy plains.
miadar, -air, -an, see miadan.
miad-fheur, -fheòir, *s.m.* Meadow grass.
————ach, *a.* Abounding in meadow grass, grassy. 2**Having long grass.
mi-àdh, -àidh, *s.m.* Bad fortune, evil luck, misfortune, unlucky event.
miadh, *s.m.ind.* Honour, esteem, respect. 2* Demand, call. 3 (DMC) Love, desire for. Cha'n 'eil m. sam bith air crodh, *there is no demand for cattle ;* meas agus m., *respect and approbation ;* gun m. gun bhàigh, *without honour or affection ;* Fionn a chuir m. oirnn, *Fionn who honoured us.*
miadh,** *s.m.* Misfortune, mishap, bad luck.
———ach, -aiche, *a.* Precious. 2 see miadhail.
mi-àdhach, -aiche, *a.* Unfortunate, unlucky.
miadhail, -e, *a.* Honourable, noble. 2 Esteemed, respected. 3 Famous. 4 Desirable. 5 In great demand, precious, valuable. 6 *Fond of. Tha 'm buntàta m., *potatoes are in great demand ;* m. mu 'chloinn, *dotingly fond of his children ;* gnothach m., *a precious thing.*
miadhalachd, *s. f. ind.* State of being held in great respect or esteem. 2 Preciousness. 3 Rareness. 4(DMC) Attachment, fondness. 5 Degree of demand.
miadhar, -aire, *a.* see mi-àdhmhor.
mi-adhartach, -aiche, *a.* Backward, hesitating. 2‡‡Unprogressive.
———————d, *s.f.ind.* Backwardness, hesitation. 2 State of being backward in any work.
mi-àdhmhor,** *a.* Unfortunate, unlucky, untoward. 2 Awkward.
———————achd, *s.f.ind.* Unfortunateness.
miaduigh,(AF) *s.f.* Hog, sow.
miag, see meigead.
miag, *s.* see miog. 2* Mew. (DC) see mèag—*Perth.*
miag,* *v.* Mew, as a cat.
miagach, see miogach.
miagail, see meigeall. 2 Mewing, as a cat.
mi-agh,** *s.m.* Disrespect, dishonour, disrepute.
miagh, see miadh.
———ach, see miadhach.
miaghar, see miaghail.
mi-àghmhor, see mi-àdhmhor.
——————achd, see mi-àdhmhorachd.
mi-àigh, see mi-adh.
———-ail, see miadhail.
miag-shùil, -shùla, -shùilean, see miog-shùil.
—————each, -eiche, *a.* see miog-shùileach.
mi-aithris, *v.a.* Miscite.
mial, -a, -an, *s.f.* Louse. 2 (AF) Barbel, see breac-feusagach. †3 Any animal.
mialach, -aiche, *a.* Lousy, pedicular. An galar m., *phthyriasis, the lousy disease.*
————as, -aich, *s.m.* Lousiness.
————d, *s.f.ind.* Lousiness.
mialag, -aig, -an, *s.f.dim.* of mial. Little louse.
————ach, -aiche, *a.* Abounding in small lice.
mialaich, ‡‡ *v.a.* Louse.
mialaint,(DMC) *s. f.* Misfortune, trouble. M. ort ! *bother you !*
————each, (DMC) *a.* Troublesome, annoying.
mialair, *s.m.* Bearer of a quern (stick on which the upper stone rests.)
————eachd, *s.f.* Lousiness.
mial-bhalla,(AF) *s.f.* Wall-insect or louse.
mial-bhuidhe,‡‡ *s.f.* Hare.
mial-bhùirn,(AF) *s.f.* Whale.
mial-chaorach, *s.f.* Sheep-tick. 2 Sheep-ked—*melophagus ovinus.*

526. *Mial-chaorach.*

527. *Mial-nan-each.*

mial-bhuidhe,(AF) *s.f.* Hare.
mial-choille,(AF) *s.f.* Wood or tree-louse.
mial-chon** *s.f.* Dog-louse, dog-tick.
mial-chòsach,(AF) *s.m.* Centipede.
mial-chrion, *s.f.* Moth. 2 Wood-louse.
mial-chù, -choin, *s.m.* Greyhound.
miala-crìona, *s.pl.* Tineæ acari. 2(DMC) Ring-worm. 3 (DU) Frequently applied to chilblains.
mial-fhiodha, *s.f.* Bug.
mial-gaileach,(AF) *s.* Barbel, see breac-feusagach.
mial-goile,** *s.f.* Belly-worm.
mial-iognach, *s.f.* Crab-louse.
mial-mhàg, see muile-mhàg.
————ach, see màgach.

mial-mhàgain, *s.f.* Toad, squat beast.
mial-mhaigheach,(AF) *s.* Hare.
mial-mhara, *s.f.* Whale. 2 Sea-monster. 3 Sea-louse.
mial-mhonaidh,(AF) *s.f.* Water-louse, flea, water-spider.
mial-mhór, *s.f.* Whale.
mial-mhór-a'-chuain, *s.f.* Sea-serpent.
mial-mhór-mhara,(AF) *s.f.* Sea-monster. Seachd ròin sath mial-mhór-mhara, *seven seals make a meal for the sea-monster.* This cannot represent the whale, as it is generally translated, for whales could not swallow seals.
mial-mòine,* *s.f.* Peat-louse.
mial-nan-each, *s. f.* Horse-louse—*trichodectes equi.* [illust. 527 on p. 649.]
mial-nam-muchd, *s.f.* Sow-louse—*hæmatopinus suis.*

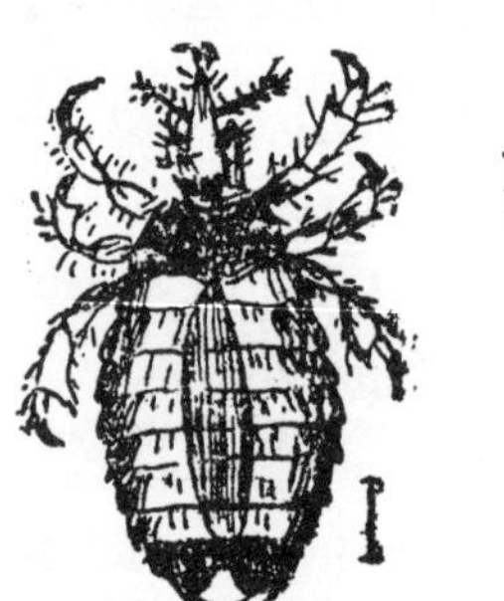

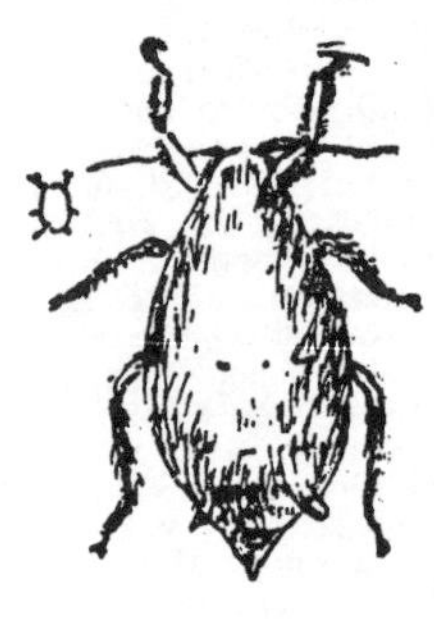

528. Mial-nam-muchd. *529. Mial-phònair.*

mial-phònair, *s.f.* Bean-plant louse—*aphis fabæ.* The wingless female is shown in illust. 529, and the winged male in 530.

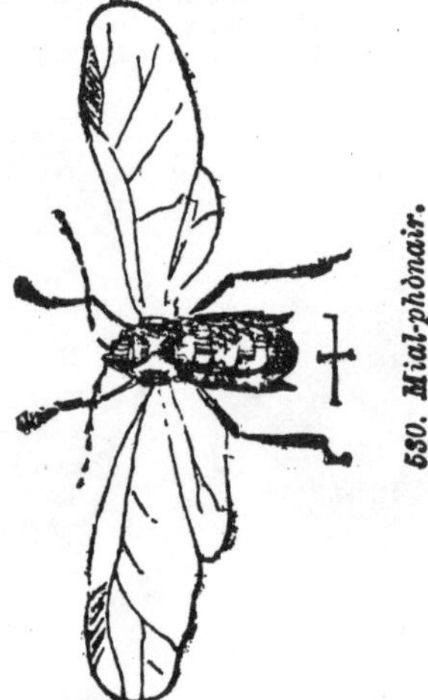

530. Mial-phònair.

mial-ròn, *s.f.* Seal.
mial-spàgach,* *s.f.* Crab-louse.
mialta, *a.* Of a soft, pleasant or sweet countenance, *prov.* for màlda.
mialtachd, *s. f. ind.* Softness, pleasantness, sweetness of look.
mialtag, *s.f.* see ialtag. 2 (AF) Fly, gnat.
——— -leathair, see ialtag.
mial-thràghad,(WC) *s.f.* Seashore-flea.
mi-altrum, -uim, *s. m.* Bad nursing or careless rearing. Cinnidh mac o mh., ach cha chinn e o 'n aog, *a son may grow in spite of bad nursing, but he cannot escape the grave.*
miamh, (AC) *s.* Substance.
———, *a.* Fat. sweet, rich, as milk. Le guth màlda m. *in a voice low and sweet.*
miamh,‡‡ *v.a* Mew.
miamhail, -e, *s.f.* Mewing, as of a cat.
mian, see mèinn.
mianach,** *a.* Abounding in ore, (mèinneil.)
mianan, -ain, -an, *prov.* for mèanan.
mian-fhaoilidh,** *s.* Yawn.
miann, -an, -tan, *s.m. & f.* Desire, will, purpose, intention. 2 Appetite, hunger. 3 Desire, love, lust. 4 The thing desired or loved. 5 Longing peculiar to a woman with child. 6 Mole on the child, due to that desire not being satisfied. 7 Complete satisfaction. 8 **Delight.
'Dé tha a' mh. ort a dheanamh ? *what do you intend to do ?* am m. leat blàr ? *is your intention battle ?* an sàsaich thu miann an leòmhainn òig ? *wilt thou satisfy the appetite of the young lion ?* a shluaigh gun chiall, a thug miann do 'n òr, *ye senseless people that bestowed your affections on gold ;* tha a' mh. sin orm, *I purpose to do that ;* tha a' mh. air teicheadh, *he means to desert, to decamp ;* m. nan aingidh, *the desire of the wicked ;* bàs mo naimhdean cha mhiann leam, *I do not desire the death of my foes ;* ma tha a' mh. ort dol dhachaidh, *if you intend going home ;* cha'n 'eil am m.-san sàsaichte, *their appetite is not appeased ;* am m. leat sìth ? *do you wish for peace ?* rinn e e g' ad mh., *he did it to your entire satisfaction ;* tha m. air 'aodann, *there is a mole on his face ;* bu mh. leis triall, *he chose to go* m. mo shùl, *the delight of my eyes ;* m. a' chait 'san tràigh 'us cha toir e fhéin as e, *a proverbial saying referring to the cat's fondness for fish, which he cannot catch himself.* In *Arran*, tha e a mh.=*he wishes to*, as,tha e a mh. a dheanamh, *he wishes to do it.*
miannach, -aiche, *a.* Desirous, wishful, longing. 2 Hungry, having a keen appetite. 3 Desirable, longed for, loved. 4 Covetous, greedy. 5**Pleasant.
———adh, -aidh, *s.m.* Desiring, act or circumstance of desiring, longing, wishing for. 2 *Coveting. A' m—, *pr. pt.* of miannaich. A' m. cuid dhaoin' eile, *coveting the property of others ;* a' m. gu mór 'fhaicinn, *longing to see him.*
———as, -ais, *s.m.* Appetite, desire, longing. 2**Greed. 3**Flavour.
———asach, *a.* Desirous.
———d, see miann.
miannag,** -aig, -an, *s.f.* Covetous female. 2 Greedy girl.
———ach, -aiche, *a.* Fond of dainties. 2 Desirous of trifles.
miannaich, *pr.pt.* a' miannachadh,*v.a. & n.* Desire, wish for, long for. 2 Covet. 3 Lust after, fix one's heart on. Na m. a sgèimh, *do not lust after her beauty.*
———te. *past pt.* Desired, longed for, wished. 2 Coveted.
miann-amhairc,(MS) *v.n.* Leer.
miannar, -aire, *a.* (for miannmhor) see miannach.
miannas, see miann.
———ach, -aiche, *a.* Covetous, greedy. 2 Lustful, longing, desirous.
———achd, *s.f.ind.* Covetousness, greediness, lustfulness.
miann-fion, *s.m.* Kind of mole, known as "port-wine mark."
†**mianngħas**, -ais, see ana-miann.
miannmhor, see miannach.

miannmhorachd, see miann.
miann-Muire,§ *s.* The plant Alpine lady's mantle—*alchemilla alpina*, see trusgan.
†**miannuich**, see miannaich.
mi-aogas, -ais, *s.m.* Bad or uncomely appearance, unseemliness. 2 Unlikelihood.
———ach, -aiche, *a.* Unseemly, unbecoming, of a bad appearance. 2 Unlikely. 3 Indecorous.
mi-aoidh, -e, *s.f.* Disfavour.
mi-aontachd, *s. f. ind.* Inconformity, nonconformity.
miapachd, see mi-thapachd.
miapadh, -aidh, *s. m.* Disgracefulness. 2 Surprise, scare. 3 Cowardice. 4 see mi-thapadh.
miapaidh, -e, *a.* see mi-thapaidh. 2**Disgraceful. 3**Sad. 4(DMC) Frightful, easily scared. 5* Cowardly.
miar, -eóir, -an, see meur.
——achd,(CR) *s.f. Skye* for **mèarachd**.
miarag, see meurag.
miaran, see meuran.
miaran, *Skye &c.* for **mèanan**.
miarbhail, see mìorbhuil.
———each, see mìorbhuileach.
mias, -èise, -an, *s.f.* Plate, dish, platter. 2 Plate of meat. 3 (DU) Basin. 4** *rarely* Altar. Geal-mhias mhór, *a large white plate*; ceann Eòin Baistidh air mèis, *the head of John the Baptist on a dish.*
miasach, -aiche, *a.* Abounding in plates or dishes. 2 Like a plate or dish.
miasdadh,(DC) *s.m.* Mischief done by cows and horses that have broken loose in corn, &c.—*Uist.*
miath, -a, *a.* see mèith.
———achd, see mèitheachd.
miathlachd, *s.f.* Huff—*Dàin I. Ghobha*, for mìothlachd (=mi-thlachd.) 2 (DU) Unpleasantness (particularly applicable to a person in a social capacity.) Cha'n 'eil m. sam bith ann, *he is quite a pleasant fellow (socially.)*
miathluimich, (MS) *v.a.* Agrease.
mi-bhàigh, -e, *s.f.* Unkindness, want of compassion. 2* Unfriendliness. Fear na m., *the merciless man.*
———each, -eiche, *a.* see mi-bhàigheil.
mi-bhàigheil, -e, *a.* Unkind, unmerciful, cruel, merciless, unfeeling. 2**Unfriendly. Gu m., *cruelly.*
mi-bhàighealachd, *s.f.* see mi-bhàigh.
mi-bhail, -e, *s.f.* Profusion, extravagance, unthriftiness.
mi-bhail, *a. MacMhaighstir Alasdair* for mìomhail.
mi-bhaileach, -eiche, *a.* Extravagant, profuse, unthrifty. Gu m., *unthriftily.*
———adh, -aidh, *s.m. & pr. pt.* see mi-bhuileachadh.
mi-bhailich, *v.* see mi-bhuilich.
mi-bhanail, -e, *a.* Immodest, unwomanly. Gu m., *immodestly.*
mi-bhanalachd, *s.f.ind.* Immodesty, indelicacy.
mi-bhanalas, -ais, *s.m.* see mi-bhanalachd.
mi-bheus, -a, -an, *s.m.* Bad-breeding, bad-manners. 2 Immorality, vice. 3 Immodesty. 4 Indecency. Éirig nam m. a rinneadh, *a recompense for the mis-deeds committed.*
———ach, -aiche, *a.* Unpolite, ungenteel. 2 Immoral, indecent. 3 Immodest. 4 Ill-bred. Gu m., *immodestly.*
mi-bheusachd, *s.f.ind.* Unpoliteness, rudeness, bad-breeding. 2 Want of principle. 3 Immodesty. 4* Immorality.
mi-bhlasda, -bhlaisde, *a.* Ill-tasted. 2 Insipid, tasteless. Do phògan mosach m., *thy nasty tasteless kisses*; biadh m., *unsavoury food.*
———chd,* *s.f.* Insipidity.
mi-bhòidheach, -eiche, *a.* Unhandsome, ugly. 2 Unseemly. 3 Unbecoming. Iomchar m., *unseemly conduct.*
mi-bhreith, -e, -ean, *s. f.* Wrong judgment or decision.
———neachadh, -aidh, *s.m.* Misconceiving, misconception, misapprehension. 2 Misinterpretation. A' m—, *pr. pt.* of mi-bhreithnich.
———nich, *pr. pt.* a' mi-bhreithneachadh, *v.a.* Misconceive, misapprehend. 2 Misinterpret.
———nichte, *past pt.* of mi-bhreithnich. Misconceived, misunderstood. 2 Misinterpreted.
mi-bhuaidh, -e & -bhuadhach, *pl.* -ean, *s.f.* Unsuccessfulness, bad luck, unluckiness. 2 Calamity, disaster. 3 Defeat.
———each,** *a.* Unsuccessful in fighting. 2 Unlucky.
mi-bhuaireas, -eis, *s.m.* Placidity of temper. 2 Quietness, tranquility. 3 Harmlessness.
———ach, -aiche, *a.* Quiet, not quarrelsome, good-tempered. Gu m., *quietly.*
mi-bhuidheach, -hiche, *a.* Unthankful, ungrateful. 2 Dissatisfied, displeased, discontented. 3 Greedy. Do bhag m., *thy greedy guts.*
mi-bhuidheachas, -ais, *s.m.* Unthankfulness, ingratitude. 2 Discontent, dissatisfaction.
mi-bhuil, *s.m.* Misapplication, abuse. 2 Misimprovement. 3* see mi-bhail. 4 Profusion. Rinn thu m. dheth, *you misapplied it, wasted it.*
———eachadh, -aidh, *s. m.* Misapplying, abusing, abuse, extravagance, squandering, neglecting to improve. A' m—, *pr. pt.* of mi-bhuilich.
mi-bhuilich, *pr. pt.* a' mi-bhuileachadh, *v. a.* Misapply, abuse, misimprove, squander. Mh. thu t' uine, *you wasted your time.*
———te, *past pt.* of mi-bhuilich. Misapplied, abused, misimproved.
mi-bhuineadh,** -eidh, *s. m.* Despair. 2 Distrust.
mi-bhunailteach, see mi-bhunaiteach.
———d, see mi-bhunaiteachd.
mi-bhunaiteach, -eiche, *a.* Unsteady, insecure. 2 Not well founded. 3 Unsettled, changeable.
———d,** *s.f.ind.* Unsteadiness. 2 Changeableness. 3 Want of foundation.
mic, *gen.sing. & n.pl.* of mac.
†**michadas**,** -ais, *s.m.* Affront. 2 Ingratitude.
mi-chaidreach, -eiche, *a.* Unfriendly, unkind, not affectionate. 2 Unsociable. 3*Disaffected.
———ail, -e, *a.* see mi-chaidreach.
mi-chaidreamh, -eimh, *s. m.* Bad fellowship, want of fellowship. 2 Want of familiarity. 3 Unfriendliness. 4 Shyness. 5 Unsociableness.
mi-chaidreas,** -eis, *s. m.* Unfriendliness. 2 Unsociableness. 3 Shyness.
mi-chàil,(MS) *s.* Grossness.
mi-chàileil,(DMC) *a.* Unpalatable, distasteful.
mi-chàirdeach, -eiche, *a.* Unfriendly. 2 Unkind.
———as, -ais, *s.m.* Unfriendliness. 2 Unkindness.
mi-chàirdealachd, *s.f.* see mi-chàirdeachas.
mi-chàirdealas, see mi-chàirdeachas.
mi-chàirdeas, -eis, *s.m.* Want of friendship, unkindness.
mi-chàirdeil, -e, *a.* see mi-chàirdeach. Gu m., *unkindly.*
mi-chàirich, *v.a.* Abuse, mismanage.
mi-chalma, *a.* Feeble, weak. 2**Not stout, of

a slender form. 3 Cowardly. 4 (DMC) Unable to stand cold or fatigue.
mi-chalmachd, *s.f.ind.* Feebleness, weakness, 2 Cowardliness.
mi-chalmarra, *a.* see mi-chalma.
mi-chaoimhinn, *v.a.* see mi-chaomhainn.
mi-chaoimhne, *s.f.* Unkindness. 2 Unfriendliness.
——————**alas**, -ais, *s.m.* see mi-chaomhalachd.
mi-chaoimhneas, -eis, *s.m.* Unkindness. 2 Unfriendliness.
mi-chaoimhneil, *a.* Unkind. 2 Unfriendly. Gu m., *in an unfriendly manner.*
mi-chaomhainn, *v.a.* Mis-spend, squander. Is baileach a mhi-chaomhainn thu do mh., *you have completely squandered your substance.*
mi-chaomhalachd, *s. f.* Unkindness. 2 Unfriendliness.
mi-chaomhnach, -aiche, *a.* Prodigal, squandering.
mi-chaomhnadh, -aidh, *s. m.* Mis-spending, squandering, prodigality. A' m—, *pr. pt.* of mi-chaomhainn.
mi-chean, -a, *s.m.* see mi-chion.
————**ail**, -e, *a.* Surly, sulky.
mi-cheanalta, -ailte, *a.* Ungenteel. 2 Unhandsome. 3 Unclean. 4 Unkind, unamiable. 5 Untidy, unbecoming, unseemly.
mi-cheannsa,** *a.* Impudent.
mi-chearmanta,** *a.* Untidy, slovenly. Gu m., *untidily.*
mi-cheart, -eirte, *a.* Wrong, unjust, evil, not right, not proper.
————**ach**, -aiche, *a.* Wrong, unjust.
————**achadh**, -aidh, *s. m.* Disarranging, setting out of order. A' m—, *pr. pt.* of mi-cheartaich.
mi-cheartaich, *pr. pt.* a' mi-cheartachadh, *v. a.* Confuse, put out of order, misadjust.
————**te**, *past pt.* of mi-cheartaich. Discomposed, put out of order.
mi-cheartas, -ais, *s.m.* Injustice. 2 Impropriety.
mi-chéill, -e, see mi-chiall.
mi-chéillidh, -e, *a.* Unwise, foolish. 2 Insane. 3**Unconjugal. 4(MS) Absonant.
mi-chiall, -chéille, *s. f.* Folly, imprudence. 2 Madness, insanity. 3**Want of meaning. Tha thu air mhi-chéill, *thou art mad.*
————**ach**, -aiche, *a.* Unwise, imprudent. 2 Insane. 3 Without meaning. Gu m., *foolishly.*
————**achd**,‡‡ *s.f.* Irrationality.
mi-chiat,** *s.m.* Poor opinion. 2* Dislike. Is mór mo mh. dheth, *I have a very poor opinion of him.* [Is beag mo mh. dheth, in *W. coast of Ross.*]
mi-chiata, see mi-chiatadh.
mi-chiatach, -aiche, *a.* Unseemly, unbecoming, improper, ungainly. Urra m., *an ungainly person;* giùlan m., *unseemly conduct.*
mi-chiatadh, -aidh, *s.m.* Disapprobation, dislike.
mi-chiatfach, see mi-chiatach.
mi-chiatfadh, see mi-chiatadh.
mi-chineamhuinn, *s. f.* Misadventure, mishap, mischance.
——————**each**, *a.* Misadventurous, misfortunate.
mi-chinnte, *s.f.ind.* Uncertainty, doubt.
mi-chinnteach, -eiche, *a.* Uncertain, doubtful.
————**as**, -ais, *s.m.* see mi-chinnte.
mi-chinnteachd, *s.f.ind.* Uncertainty.
mi-chion, -chin, *s.f.* Aversion, displeasure, dislike.
mi-chiùin, -e, *a.* Boisterous, troubled, stormy, fierce, not mild, not calm. Gu m., *boisterously.*
mi-chiùineas, -eis, *s.m.* Storminess, boisterousness, disquiet.
mi-chleachd, *v.a.* Abrogate, disuse, render obsolete.
mi-chleachdalach, -aiche, *a.* Unusual, unwonted. 2 Of bad habits, immoral.
mi-chleas, -a, -an, *s.m.* Low, dishonest deed, trick.
mi-chleasach, -aiche, *a.* Full of tricks, dishonest.
mi-chlis, -e, *a.* Inactive, lazy, awkward, not clever, inexpert.
mi-chliù, *s.m.* Infamy, bad fame, disgrace, reproach, dishonour, defamation. Lot agus m., *a wound and dishonour.*
mi-chliùiteach, -eiche, *a.* Infamous, dishonourable, reproachful, disgraceful. 2 Not renowned, obscure. Gu m., *infamously.*
mi-chliùitich,** *v.a.* Defame, disparage, bring into disrepute.
mi-chliùthaich,** *v.a.* Defame.
mi-chneasta, -eiste, *a.* Uncharitable, uncivil. 2 Cruel, inhuman, barbarous. 3 Perilous, ominous. [also mi-chneasda] Gu m., *inhumanly.*
mi-chneastachd, *s.f.ind.* Uncharitableness. 2 Incivility. 3 Cruelty, inhumanity, barbarity. 4 Ominousness, perilousness. 5 Atheisticalness. [also mi-chneasdachd.]
mi-choidhis,** *a.* Not indifferent. 2 Nice or fastidious in appetite.
mi-choingheall, -eill, -an, *s.m.* Disobliging action. 2 Inconvenience. 3 Deceit, treachery.
mi-choingheallach, -aiche, *a.* Disobliging. 2 Treacherous. 3‡‡Inconvenient. 4**Unwilling to lend.
mi-choisrig,‡‡ *v.a.* Desecrate.
mi-choltach, -aiche, *a.* see mi-choslach. 2(DU) Improper, wrong. Gnothach m., *an improper, unseemly deed.*
mi-choltachd, *s.f.* see mi-choslas.
mi-choltas, -ais, see mi-choslas.
mi-chomhairlich,‡‡ *v.a.* Miscounsel.
mi-chòmhnard, -airde, *a.* Uneven, not level.
mi-chompanta, -ainte, *a.* Unsociable, morose, reserved, distant.
mi-chompantach, -aiche, *a.* see mi-chompanta.
mi-chompantachd, *s.f.ind.* Unsociableness, reservedness, moroseness, distant manner.
mi-chompantas,** -ais, *s.m.* State of being without a companion.
mi-chòrd, *pr.pt.* a' mi-chòrdadh, *v.a.* Disagree, dissent.
mi-chòrdadh, -aidh, -aidhean, *s.m.* Disagreeing, dissenting, disagreement. A' m—, *pr. pt.* of mi-chòrd.
mi-chorrach, -aiche, *a.* Not steep, easy of ascent or descent. 2 Steady, not giddy.
mi-choslach, -aiche, *a.* Unlikely. 2 Dissimilar, unlike.
mi-choslas, -ais, *s.m.* Improbability, dissimilarity, unlikeliness.
mi-chosmhuileachd, *s.m.* Dislikeness.
mi-chosmhuileas, *s.m.* Dislikeness.
mi-chothrom, -oim, -an, *s.m.* Injustice, unfairness. 2 Disadvantage.
mi-chothromach, -aiche, *a.* Disadvantageous, unfair, unjust. 2* Rugged, uneven. 3 Disproportionate, inconvenient. 4(DU) Poverty-stricken.
mi-chràbhachd,‡‡ *s.f.ind.* Indevotion.
mi-chreasda, see mi-chneasta.
mi-chreasdachd, see mi-chneastachd.
mi-chreid,* *v.n.* Disbelieve.
mi-chreideach, -eiche, *a.* see mi-chreidmheach.
mi-chreideamh, -imh, *s.m.* Heresy, unbelief. 2 Want of faith, scepticism. 3**Infidelity. Air son am m., *for their unbelief;* luchd-m., *sceptics.*

mi-chreideas, -eis, s.m. Distrust, want of confidence, unbelief, incredulity, want of credit.
mi-chreideasach, -aiche, a. Distrustful, unconfiding. 2 Discreditable, unworthy of confidence. 3*Disrespectful. Gu m., *uncreditably*.
mi-chreidimh, see mi-chreidheamh.
mi-chreidmheach, -eiche, a Sceptical, unbelieving, distrustful.
mi-chreidmheach, -ich, s. m. Infidel, heretic, unbeliever, sceptic.
mi-chreidmhiche,** s.m. Same meanings as mi-chreidmheach.
mi-chridhealachd, s.f. see mi-chridhealas.
mi-chridhealas, -ais, s.m. Dejection, dulness, lowness of spirits. 2**Heartlessness.
mi-chridheil. -e, a. Dull, dejected, disheartened. 2 Heartless. Gu m., *dejectedly*.
mi-chruinnealas, -eis s.m. Slovenliness, want of neatness, carelessness, untidiness. 2 Profusion.
mi-chruinneil, -e, a Slovenly, untidy, careless. 2 Profuse, uneconomical. 3 Heartless. Gu m., *untidily*.
mi-chù, (AF) s.m. Fox.
mi-chuileag, see mion-chuileag.
mi-chuimhne, s f. Thoughtlessness, carelessness, heedlessness, forgetfulness.
mi-chuimhneach, -eiche, a. Careless, thoughtless, forgetful, unmindful. Gu m., *carelessly*.
mi-chuimhneachail, -e, a. Forgetful, unmindful. 2 Careless. Gu m., *forgetfully*.
mi-chuimse, s.f. Misproportion.
————-—ach, a. Disproportionate, unproportioned. 2 Aimless.
mi-chuineas,** -eis, s.m Donation.
mi-chuis, -e, -ean, s.f. Misfortune 2 Unworthy deed 3*Jilting. 4*Smirking.
mi-chùiseach, -eiche, a. Unfortunate 2 Of, or belonging to, unworthy deeds. 3 Coquettish, flirting. 4**Modest, unassuming 5** Attractive, bewitching. 6**Unenterprising.
mi-chùiseach, -ich, s.m. Coquette, flirt.
mi-chùiseachd,* s f. Flirtation, coquetry. 2 Assumed indifference.
mi-chumachd, s.f. see mi-chumadh.
mi-chumachdail, -e, a Unshapely, unhandsome, not proportioned. 2 Clumsy. Gu m., *clumsily*.
mi-chumadail, -e, a. see mi-chumachdail. Do chasan m., *thy shapeless legs*.
mi-chumadh, -aidh, s.m. Shapelessness, want of shape or form. 2 Clumsiness
mi-chunnadail, see mi-chumachdail.
mi-chunntas,‡‡ -ais, s.m. Miscomputation.
mi-chùram, -aim, s.m. Carelessness, negligence, remissness.
mi-chùramach, -aiche, a. Careless, negligent, inattentive. 2 (DMC) Irreligious. Gu m., *carelessly*.
——————d,‡‡ s.f. Carelessness.
mi-dhàichealachd, s.f.ind. Awkwardness, unhandsomeness, ungracefulness. 2 Absurdity.
mi-dhàichealas, -ais, s.m. see mi-dhàichealachd.
mi-dhàicheil, -e, a. Awkward, ungraceful, unhandsome, ungenteel. 2 Unstately, undignified. 3*Absurd, nonsensical. Fear m., *an awkward man*.
mi-dhaonnachd,‡‡ s.f. Inhumanity.
mi-dheabhaltach, see mi-dhealbhtach.
mi-dhealbh, v.a. Deform, mis-shape. 2 Take a bad likeness.
mi-dhealbh, -a, s. m. Inconsistency, unseemliness. 2 Unshapeliness. 2 Mismanagement. 3* Absurdity.
——————ach, -aiche, a. Unshapely, unhandsome. 2 Improbable, unlikely. 3 Inconsistent. 4**Unmatched. 5* Absurd. 6** Unseemly.
mi-dhealbhachadh,‡‡ -aidh, s.m. Deformity.
mi-dhealbhaich,‡‡ v.a. Deform, distort.
mi-dhealbhaltach, see mi-dhealbhtach.
mi-dhealbhtach, a. Frugal.
mi-dhealbhte, past pt. Deformed.
†mi-dheamhnas,** -ais, s.m Honour, exaltation.
mi-dheanadach,(DMC) a. Inactive, not industrious.
mi-dhèanadair, s.m. Misdoer.
mi-dhearcach, -aiche, a. Absent.
mi-dhearcadh,(MS) s.m. Absence.
mi-dheas, -dheise, a. Awkward, unskilful, inexpert. 2 Wrong, unprepared. 3 Unhandsome. 4**Unstately in gait.
mi-dhéirceil, -e, a Uncharitable.
mi-dheòin,* s.f. Reluctance.
mi-dheònach, -aiche, a. Reluctant.
mi-dhiadhachd, s.f.ind. Irreligion, ungodliness, unholiness, profanity.
mi-dhiadhaidh, -e, a. Irreligious, ungodly, profane.
mi-dhiadhaidheachd, s.f. ind. see mi-dhiadhachd.
mi-dhileas, -dhilse. a. Treacherous, unfaithful, dishonest. Gu m., *faithlessly*.
mi-dhilseachd, s.f.ind. Faithlessness, treachery, disloyalty.
mi-dhilsead, -eid, s.f. Faithlessness, degree of unfaithfulness.
mi-dhiongalta, see mi-dhiongmhalta.
mi-dhiongmhalta, -ailte, a. Imperfect, ineffectual, insufficient. 2 Improper. 3 Not firm. 4 Not tight.
——————chd, s.f.ind. Insufficiency, imperfection, inefficacy, unmeetness, want of firmness
mi-dhirichead, -id, s.m Disingenuity.
mi-dhiugh, (DMC) s. Carelessness, disinterestedness.
——————ail. a. Careless, negligent.
mi-dhiùthaich, v.a. Scorn.
mi-dhleasannach, -aiche, see mi-dhleasnach.
mi-dhleasnach, -aiche, a. Disloyal, undutiful, unfaithful, unfriendly. Gu m., *undutifully*.
mi-dhleasnas, -ais, s.m Undutifulness.
mi-dhleasdanas, see mi-dhleasnas.
mi-dhlighe, -an, s. f. Undutifulness, unlawfulness
mi-dhligheach, -eiche, a Not due, undutiful, unlawful 2 Not according to its kind. Gu m., *unlawfully*.
mi-dhligheadh, see mi-dhlighe.
mi-dhligheil, -e, see mi-dhligheach.
mi-dhluigheil,** a. Careless, inattentive.
mi-dhlùthaich,‡‡ v.a. Misjoin.
mi-dhochas, -ais, s.m. Despondency, despair. 2 **Want of conceit.
————--ach, -aiche, a. Despondent, despairing. 2*Diffident, unpretending, retiring, not conceited.
mi-dhòigh, -e, s.f. Want of method. 2 Awkwardness. 3* Absurdity. 4**Want of condition, want of health.
mi-dhòighealachd,‡‡ s.f.ind. Immethodicalness.
mi-dhòigheil, -e, a. Awkward, immethodical. 2 Ill-tempered. 3* Absurd. 4 (DMC) Disorganized. Gu m., *unmethodically*.
mi-dhreach, -a, -an, s m. Deformity, disfiguration. 2 Bad look, unpleasant appearance, unpleasant exterior.
mi-dhreachadh,** s.m. Disfiguring.
mi-dhreachaich,(MS) v.a. Besmirch, deflower. 2 Deform.
mi-dhreachail, -e, a. Deformed. 2 Disfiguring. 3 Not pleasant to look at, ugly. 4 Botchy. 5**Disfigured.

mi-dhreachmhor, -oire, *a.* see mì-dhreachail.
mi-dhualach, *a.* Degenerate.
mi-dhualchas,(MS) -ais, *s. m.* Degeneracy, degenerateness.
mi-dhuineil, *a.* Unfriendly, unsociable. 2 Unmanly.
mi-dhùrachd, -an, *s.f.* Negligence. 2*Insincerity. 3 Ill-will. 4 Inattention.
——ach, -aiche, *a.* Negligent, indifferent, careless. 2 Insincere. 3 Inattentive.
mi-eagnaidh, -e, *a.* Indiscreet, unwise.
——eachd, *s.f.ind.* Indiscretion, imprudence.
mi-earbsa, *s.m.* Distrust, suspicion.
——ch, -aiche, *a.* Distrustful, suspicious. 2 Despondent, despairing.
mi-éifeachd, *s.f.ind.* Inefficiency, insufficiency, ineffectualness.
——ach, -aiche, *a.* Ineffectual, inefficacious, useless, vain. Gu m., *ineffectually.*
mi-eireachdail, -e, *a.* Unhandsome, unseemly. ugly. Giùlan m., *unseemly conduct ;* gu m., *ungenteelly.*
mi-eireachdas, -ais, *s. m.* Deformity, unseemliness of appearance. 2 Rudeness of behaviour, ungenteelness.
mi-eudmhor, -aire, *a.* Unsuspicious. 2 Not jealous. 3 Disloyal. 4**Not zealous.
mi-fhàbhar, -air, -an, *s.m.* Disfavour.
——ach,** *a.* Adverse.
mi-fhaiceallach, -aiche, *a.* Inattentive, not watchful, unobservant. 2 Incautious. 3 Inconsiderate. Gu m., *inattentively.*
——d,‡‡ *s.f.ind.* Inattention.
mi-fhaicill, -e, *s.f.* Inattention, carelessness. 2 Incautiousness, unguardedness. 3 Want of observation.
mi-fhaighidinn, see mi-fhoighidinn.
mi-fhaighidneach, see mi-fhoighidneach.
mi-fhallan, -aine, *a.* Unwholesome, unsound, unhealthy. 2**Rotten. Gu m., *unsoundly.*
——eachd, *s.f.ind.* Unwholesomeness, unsoundness, unhealthiness. 2**Rottenness.
mi-fharasda, -aisde, *a.* Inquiet, turbulent, ungentle, not mild. 2 see mi-fhurasda.
mi-fhasgach,** *a.* Unshelterable. 2 Affording no shelter, unsheltering.
mi-fhearail, -e, *a.* Soft, effeminate, cowardly, unmanly. Gu m., *in an unmanly manner.*
mi-fhearalachd, *s.f.* see mi-fhearalas.
mi-fhearalas, -ais, *s. m.* Softness, effeminacy, cowardice, unmanliness.
mi-fhearantas,** *s.m.* Emasculation.
mi-fheargach, -aiche, *a.* Not angry. 2 Not easily provoked. 3 Not causing provocation, unirritative.
mi-fhéin, *emphatic form* of mi. Myself.
mi-fheum, -a, *s.m.* Bad use, misapplication. 2 Uselessness.
——alachd, *s.f.* see mi-fheum.
mi-fhialachd, *s.f.ind.* Churlishness, niggardliness, unsociableness, inhospitableness.
mi-fhialaidh, -e, *a.* Churlish, inhospitable, niggardly, unsociable.
——eachd, *s.f.* see mi-fhialachd.
mi-fhianuis,‡‡ -ean, *s. m.* Misallegation. [‡‡ gives *s.f.* and *gen.sing.* -e.]
mi-fhios,‡‡ -a, -an, *s.m.* Misinformation.
mi-fhiù, *a.* Worthless, useless.
mi-fhiùghachd,** *s.f.* Worthlessness, demerit.
mi-fhiùghaireach,** *a.* Spiritless, dull. Gu m., *spiritlessly.*
——d, *s.f.* Spiritlessness, dulness.
mi-fhiùghantach, -aiche, *a.* Illiberal, niggardly. 2 Cowardly. Gu m., *illiberally.*
——d, *s.f. ind.* Illiberality, niggardliness. 2 Cowardice.
mi-fhiùghar,** *a.* Spiritless, dull.
mi-fhlathail, -e, *a.* Mean, of mean appearance, ungenteel, ignoble.
mi-fhoighidinn, *s.f.ind.* Impatience, restlessness. 2* Greed. 3* Keenness.
mi-fhoighidneach, -eiche, *a.* Impatient, restless. Gu m., *impatiently.*
mi-fhoisdinneach,‡‡ -eiche, *a.* Careful.
mi-fhoisneach,** *a.* Anxious.
——d ** *s.f.* Aching.
mi-fhonn,** *s.m.* Indifference, lowness of spirits.
mi-fhonnmhor,‡‡ *a.* Absonant, indifferent, low in spirits.
mi-fhortan, -ain, -an, *s.m.* Misfortune, mishap, bad luck.
——ach, -aiche, *a.* Disastrous, unlucky, unfortunate. Gu m., *unluckily.*
mi-fhreagarrach, -aiche, *a.* Unsuitable, unfit, unanswerable, unanswering.
——d, *s.f.ind.* Unsuitableness, unfitness.
mi-fhreasdal,(DMC) *s.m.* Misfortune.
mi-fhreasdalach, -aiche, *a.* Improvident, heedless. 2 Unfavourable. 3 Inattentive. 4 Unassisting. Gu m., *improvidently.*
mi-fhurachail,* -e, *a.* see mi-fhurachair.
mi-fhurachair, -e, *a.* Inattentive, careless, unguarded, unobservant. Gu m., *carelessly.*
mi-fhurachras, -ais, *s.m.* Inattention, carelessness, unwatchfulness.
mi-fhuran, -ain, *s.m.* Churlishness, unsociableness. 2 ‡‡Sadness, dulness. 3**Disinclination to welcome or congratulate. 4**Joylessness.
——ach, -aiche, *a.* Churlish, inhospitable. 2‡‡Dull, sad. 3** Backward to welcome or congratulate. Gu m., *churlishly.*
mi-fhuras, -aise, *a.* see mi-fhurasda.
mi-fhurasach, -aiche, *a.* Impatient, restless. Gu m., *impatiently.*
mi-fhurasda,* *a.* Hard, difficult to accomplish.
migead, -id, -an, see meigead.
migeadaich, see meigeadaich.
migeanaich, see meigeadaich.
mi-ghean, -a, *s.m.* Dissatisfaction, displeasure, discontent, disgust, discord. 2 Sadness, melancholy. 3 Grudge. Fògraidh tu m., *thou shalt banish disgust.*
mi-gheanach,** *a.* Angry.
mi-gheanmnaidh, -e, *a.* Incontinent, lewd, unchaste. Gu m., *incontinently.*
——eachd, *s.f.ind.* Carnality, unchasteness, incontinence, lewdness. 2**Dishonesty.
mi-gheimnidh, see mi-gheanmnaidh.
mi-ghéire,‡‡ *s.f.ind.* Dulness.
mi-gheur,** *a.* Blunt. 2 Stupid.
——aich, *v.a.* Blunt.
mi-ghiùlan, -ain, *s.m.* Misconduct.
mi-ghleidh,** *s. f.* Abuse, mismanagement, want of frugality.
mi-ghlic, -e, *a.* Foolish, unwise, silly, rash, inexperienced. Gu m., *unwisely.*
mi-ghliocas, -ais, *s.m.* Folly, imprudence.
mi-ghloine, *s.f.ind.* Filthiness, uncleanness.
mi-ghnàthach, -aiche, *a.* Abusive. 2 Misapplying. 3**Mischievous. 4 Rare, not customary, unusual.
——adh, -aidh, *s.m.* Abusing, act of abusing or misapplying. 2* Misconduct. A' m—, *pr.pt.* of mi-ghnàthaich.
mi-ghnàthachd, *s.f.ind.* Misapplication, bad usage. 2 Rareness. 3‡‡Strangeness.
mi-ghnàthaich, *pr.pt.* a' mi-ghnàthachadh, *v.a.* Abuse, misapply, put to an improper use. Mh. iad i, *they abused her.*
mi-ghnàthaichte, *past pt.* Abused, misapplied.

2 Rare, uncommon, unusual.
mi-ghnèithealachd, -*s.f.ind.* Badness of temper or disposition. 2 Ungratefulness, unthankfulness. 3 Ill-favouredness.
mi-ghnèitheil, -e, *a.* Ill-tempered, ill-disposed. 2 Ungrateful. 3 Ill-looking, having a bad complexion. 4**Having a forbidding look.
mi-ghniomh, -a, -ara, *s.m.* Bad action or deed, mischief. 2 Lewdness. Luchd-m., *evil doers.*
mi-ghniomhach, -aiche, *a.* Idle, lazy, deedless, indolent. 2 Mischievous, misdoing. 3 Profligate.
mi-ghoireas, -eis, *s.m.* Inconvenience. 2 Insufficiency.
mi-ghoireasach, -aiche, *a.* Inconvenient. 2 Insufficient. 3 **Immoderate.
mi-ghramail, -e, *a.* Insufficient, unfirm, unsteady, unstable. 2 Slim, slender. 3**Infirm, not muscular.
mi-ghramalachd, *s.f.ind.* Insufficiency, unfirmness. 2 Slimness. 3 Want of resolution or mental decision. 4 Instability.
mi-ghramalas, -ais, *s.m.* see mi-ghramalachd.
mi-ghràs, -àis, *s. m.* Gracelessness, want of grace.
mi-ghràsail, -e, *a.* Graceless, abandoned, reprobate.
mi-ghreann, -a, *s m.* Disdain, loathing, disgust.
mi-ghrunnd, -a, *s.m.* see mi-ghrunndas.
mi-ghrunndail, -e,*a.* Profuse, prodigal, careless, unfrugal. 2 Not industrious.
mi-ghrunndas, -ais, *s. m.* Want of economy, carelessness, indifference.
migiall, see meigeall.
migiallach, see meigeallach.
migiallaich, see meigeallaich.
mi-inncalta,** *a.* Inelegant, ungenteel, clumsy, unseemly, ungraceful.
mi-innealtachd, *s.f.ind.* Awkwardness, ungracefulness.
mi-iomairt, -e, *s.f.* Bad usage, abuse.
mi-iomchuidh, -e, *a.* Improper, indecent, unfit. 2**Inconvenient.
mi-iomchuidheachd, *s.f.ind.* Impropriety, unfitness, indecency.
mi-iomradh, -aidh, -aidhean, *s. m.* Evil repute, bad name, slander, obloquy, evil report.
mi-ionracas,** *s.m.* Disingenuity.
mi-ionraic, -e, *a.* Dishonest,unjust, unrighteous.
mil,(AC) *a.* Mild. A Mhicheil mhil ! *O mild Michael !*
mil, *gen.* meala [mealach in *Suth'd.*], *dat.* mil, *voc.* a mhil ! *pl.* mealan, *s.f.* Honey. Do phòg air blas na meala, *your kiss with the taste of honey.*
mi-labhrach, -aiche, *a.* Speaking wrongously, impudent, forward, pert. 2*Taciturn, sullen.
mi-laghachadh,** *s. m.* Abrogation. 2 Abolition.
mi-laghachair, *s.m.* Abolisher.
mi-laghaich,** *v.a.* Abrogate. 2 Abolish or repeal a statute.
mi-laghail, -e, *a.* Illegal, unlawful, illicit, prohibited.
mi-laghaileachd, *s. f. ind.* Illegality, unlawfulness.
†**milbhir**, *s.m.* Mead, metheglin.
mil-bhriathrach, -aiche, *a.* Of sweet words, speaking pleasant words.
milc,(AC) *a.* Sweet.
milc,(AC) *s.* Sweetness.
milcein,(AC) *s.* Solid warm white whey.
mil-cheò,* *s.m.* see mill-cheò.
†**mil-chnuimheag**, -eig, -an, *s.f.* see mill-cheò.
mil-chuileag, *Arran & Kintyre* for meanbhchuileag.
mil-dheoch, -a, *s.m.* Mead.
mil-dheòghladh, -aidh,*s.m.* Extraction of honey, sucking honey, as from flowers.
mile,(DU) -achan, *s.m.* Sweet.
mile, -lte & -ltean, *a.* Thousand. Làn mh., *a full thousand.* [Commonly used in the *sing.* with numerals otherwise followed by the *pl.* and generally followed by the *sing.*, as deich mile,*ten thousand;* mile fear, *a thousand men ;* dà mh. bliadhna, *two thousand years ;* but, mile miltean, *a thousand miles.*]
mile, -ltean, *s.f.ind.* Mile. Dà mh., *two miles ;* deich m., *ten miles;* m. shlighe, *a mile of road, a mile in length ;* clach-mhile, *a milestone.*
mil-each, -eich, *s.m.* Blood-horse, war-horse.
mileach, -eiche, see meallach.
mileachadh, -aidh, *s. m.* Benumbing, starving with cold. A' m—, *pr. pt.* of milich. see meileachadh.
mileachd,(MS) *s.f.* Mellification.
mileadh, -idh, -idhean, *s.m.* see milidh.
mileag, -eig, -an, *s.f.* Melon, see meal-bhuc. & mealbhag.
mileag,(CR) *s.f.* Mean woman—*Arran.*
mileagach,†† *a.* Abounding in melons. 2 see mealbhagach.
mileamh, *a.* Thousandth. Am m. bliadhna, *the thousandth year.*
milean,(CR) *s.m.* Fawning—*Perthshire.*
mileanach,(DC) *s. m.* Marine grass — *zostera marina.*
mileanta, -einte, *a.* Soldier-like, heroic, brave 2 Elegant, stately. 3 Pompous. An ceannsgalach m.,*the brave commander—MacVuirich.*
mileanta,* -einte, *a.* Sweet-lipped.
mileantachd, *s.f.ind.* Bravery, heroism. 2 Handsomeness. 3 Genteelness. 4‡‡Feats of valour. 5**Stateliness.
milearach,§ *s.m.* Sweet tangle, see smeartan. 2 (AC) Sea grass, sweet grass—*alva marina.*
mile-ghath, -a, -an, *s.m.* Anxiety. 2 Hurry.
mileid,§ *s.f.* Millet-grass—*millium effusum.*

531. *Mileid.* 532. *Mil-mheacan.*

milich,* *v.a.* Benumb, see meilich.
milidh, -ean, *s.m.* Soldier, champion, hero. 2 Renowned person. Cathan mhilidh, *the battles of heroes.*
milidheach,‡‡ -eiche, *a.* Military.
mi-liosda, *a.* Unimportunate, unsolicitous, unobtrusive.
mil-itheach,** *a.* Mellivorous. 2 Pale, wan.
milis, milse, *a.* Sweet, savoury. 2 Melodious, musical. 3**Flattering. Cainnt mh., *fair or flattering speech* ; aran m., *any sweet kind of bread, especially ginger-bread.*
mill, *pr.pt.* a' milleadh, *v.a.* Spoil, mar, injure, hurt, destroy. 2 Lay waste. 3**Abuse, make useless. 4 Ruin, violate. 5* Benumb with cold. (meil) 6* Disarrange. Mhill thu e, *you spoiled it ;* mh. mo bhròg mo chas, *my shoe has blistered my foot.*

mill, *pl.* of meall.
mill-cheò, *s.m.* Mildew, blight, blast.
milleach,* -eich, see millteach.
milleadair,‡‡ -e, -ean, *s.m.* Destroyer. 3 Waster, spendthrift.
milleadh, -eidh, *s.m.* Spoiling, act of spoiling, marring, injuring, damaging. 2 Destroying, destruction. 3 Laying waste. 4 Starving with cold. 5 Defacing. 6**Bane. A' m—, *pr.pt.* of mill.
milleadh-maighiche, *s.m.* Harelip.
milleadh-maitheis,(WC) *s.m.* Despoiler. 'S e m. a th' ann, *he is a despoiler.*
millean,** -ein, *s.m.* Tax.
milleantach, (DC) *a.* Showery—*Uist.*
milliudh, *s.m.* Blasting eye. 2 Fascinating look.
millneach, *a.* Brave, gallant.
millneachd,** *s.f.* Bravery.
millse, see milse.
millseachd, see milseachd.
millsead, -eid, see milsead.
millsean,** -ein, *s.m.* Milt.
millseanach, -aich, see milseanach.
millte, *past pt.* of mill. Spoiled, destroyed. 2 Laid waste. 3‡‡Starved with cold. 4 Made useless, violated.
millteach, -eiche, *a.* Ruinous, destructive 2 Prodigal. 3 Abusive. 4 Grassy. 5 Verdant. 6 Wasting. 7(MS) Baneful. 8**Deadly. Mar uisge m., *like destructive waters* ; maghanan m., *verdant meadows.*
millteach, -ich, *s.m.* Good grass, tufts of grass, mountain grass. 2‡‡Destructive person. 3‡‡ Prodigal. 4**Wicked man. 5‡‡see milleadh. Barr a' mhilltich, *the top of the grassy tufts* ; gleann a' mhilltich, *the grassy glen.*
millteachd, *s.f.ind.* Destructiveness. 2 Destruction. 3 Prodigality, profusion. 4 Injury. 5 Abuse. 6 Balefulness.
millteachd-rathaid, *s.f.* Highway robbery.
millteachd-uisge,§ *s.m.* Sweet floating grass,see milsean-uisge.
millteag, -eig, *s.f.* Bottle of thatch.
milltean,** -ein, *s.m.* Prodigal.
millteanas, -ais, *s.m.* Blunder. 2 Injury.
milltear, -eir, -an, *s.m.* Destroyer, spoiler. 2 Oppressor. 3 Waster, spendthrift. Is bràthair e do 'n mh. mhór, *he is a brother to the great waster ;* o shannt a' mhillteir, *from the greed of the destroyer.*
milltear, *fut.pass.* of mill. 2 *imp. pass.* of mill.
milltearachd, see millteachd.
milltich, *s.pl.* Tufts of good grass.
milltineachd,** *s.f.* Bravery, gallantry. (millneachd.)
mil-mheacan, -ain, *pl.* -an & -ain, *s.m.* Mallows —*malvæ.* (illust. 532 on p. 655.)
milneach, -ich, *s.m.* Thorn. 2 Bodkin.
mi-loinn, -e, *s. f.* Awkwardness, untidiness, want of order. 2 Irregularity. 3 Impropriety. 4 Inelegance, ungracefulness.
mi-loinnealas, -ais, *s.m.* Want of order. 2 Irregularity. 3 Impropriety.
mi-loinneil, -e, *a.* Awkward,disordered, untidy. 2 Irregular. 3 Disfigured. 4 Improper. Gu m., *without order.*
milse, *s.f.ind.* Sweetness.
milse, *comp.* of milis. More or most sweet. Ciod is m. na mil ? *what is sweeter than honey?*
milseach, -eiche, *a.* Sweet. 2 Enticing,alluring.
milseachadh, -aidh, *s. m.* Sweetening, act of sweetening. 2 Growing sweet. A' m—, *pr. pt.* of milsich.
milseachd, *s.f.* Mellification. 2 Sweetness, savouriness, lusciousness. 3 Fragrance. 4 Flattery. 5(MS) Mellowness.
milsead, *s.m.* Degree of sweetness. Air mh. 's guim bheil e, *however sweet it be ;* is m. an deoch an siùcar, *drink is the sweeter for sugar ;* mar mhil air mh., *like honey for sweetness.*
milsean, -ein, -an, *s. m.* Anything sweet, as sweetmeats. 2 Flatterer. 3 Eel-grass.
milseanach, -aich, -an, *s.m.* see milearach. 2 see milsean.
milseanach, -aiche, *a.* Desirous of sweets or sweetmeats.
milseanach,** -aich, *s. m.* Confectioner. 2 Sweet-lipped person.
milseanachd,** *s.f.* Confectionery.
milseanaiche, *s.m.* Confectioner.
milsean-crom-luis,** *s.m.* Syrup of poppies.
milsean-mara, -ein, -an, *s.m.* Sea-pink—*caryophyllum.* 2 Edible sea-weed.
milsean-measan, *s.m.* Jam.
milsean-monaidh,§ *s. m.* Red-rattle, see lusriabhach.
milseanta, -einte. *a.* Sweet,sweetish,sweetened.
milsean-uisge,§ *s.m.* Floating sweet grass—*glyceria fuitans.* 
mil-shliosnach,** -aich, *s. m.* Chiliadron.
mi-shruthachd, *s.f.ind.* Mellifluence.
milsich, *pr.pt.* a' milseachadh, *v.a.* Sweeten, make sweet, addulce. 2 Make savoury. 3 Make fragrant.
——te, *past part* of milsich. Sweetened. made sweet. 2 Made fragrant. Fion m., *mulled wine.*
milte, *pl.* of mile. Mìlte de mhuillionaibh, *thousands of millions* [many.
milteach,‡‡ *a.* Numerous,very 533. *Musan-uisge.*
milteamh, *a.* Millesimal.
miltean, *pl.* of mile.
mi-luchdmhor, -oire. *a.* Incapacious.
——————achd, *s.f.ind.* Incapaciousness.
mi-mhacanta. -ainte, *a.* Disobedient. 2 Not meek. ungentle. 3**Unfilial. 4**Dishonest.
——————chd, *s.f* see mi-mhacantas.
mi-mhacantas, -ais, *s.m.* Want of meekness or gentleness. 2**Dishonesty.
mi-mhaighdeanail, -e, *a.* Immodest, unmaidenly, unwomanly.
mi-mhail, see miomhail.
mi-mhaise, *s.f.* Deformity, unseemliness, unhandsomeness.
mi-mhaiseach, -eiche, *a.* Deformed. unhandsome, uncomely. Gu m., *unhandsomely.*
mi-mhaiseil, -e, see mi-mhaiseach.
mi-mhaisich, *v.a.* Deflower.
mi-mhalda, *a.* Immodest, indelicate. 2 Not mild. 3 Unkind. 4**Not lenient.
——————chd, *s.f.ind.* Immodesty. indelicacy. 2 Want of mildness, gentleness. or kindness.
mi-mhar, see miomhar.
mi-mheadhonach, -aiche. *a.* Immoderate, disproportionate. 2 Eccentric, not centrical.
——————d, *s.f.ind.* Eccentricity.
mi-mheas, -a, *s m.* Contempt. disrespect, affront 2 Indifference, abjection. Cuir air m., *show disrespect.*
——————, *v.a.* Disrespect, disesteem, despise, undervalue.
——————ail, -e, *a.* Contemptible. 2 Disrespected. 3 Disrespectful. Gu m., *disrespectfully.*
mi-mheasarra, *a.* Intemperate, immoderate. 2 Dissolute, incontinent.
——————ch, see mi-mheasarra.
——————chd, *s.f.ind.* Intemperance, im-

moderateness.
mi-mheasta, *past pt.* of mi-mheas. Disrespected, despised. 2 Vile, mean, ignoble.
mi-mhèinn, -e, *s.f.* Indisposition. 2(DM) Misdisposition.
————eil,(DMC) *a.* Unfeeling, ungracious.
mi-mhìneachadh, -aidh, *s.m.* Misinterpretation, act of misinterpreting. A' m—. *pr. pt.* of mi-mhìnich.
mi-mhìnich, *pr. pt.* a' mi-mhìneachadh, *v. a.* Misinterpret, misconstrue.
————te, *past pt.* Misinterpreted, misconstrued.
mi-mhisneach, -ich, *s.m. & f.* Want of courage, discouragement, fear, irresolution, cowardice, shyness, diffidence, damp. Cuir air m., *discourage, dispirit.*
mi-mhisneachadh, -aidh, *s.m. & pr. pt.* Discouraging.
mi-mhisneachail, -e, *a.* Faint-hearted, uncourageous, cowardly. 2 Discouraging, disheartening. 3* Backward. 4** Dispirited, desponding, irresolute. 5 Dastardly.
mi-mhisnich, *pr. pt.* a' mi-mhisneachadh, *v. a.* Discourage, dishearten. 2* Dismay, damp the spirits, blunt. 3 Terrify.
mi-mhodh, -a, -an, *s. m.* Bad manners, disrespect, rudeness, impertinence. 2 Immodesty. 3**Improper habit. Dad de mh., *aught of incivility ;* àird' a' mhi-mhodha, *the height of impertinence.*
mi-mhodh, *v.n.* Act unpolitely towards one. 2 Reproach, revile, profane.
mi-mhodhail, see mìomhail.
mi-mhodhalachd, see mìomhalachd.
mi-mhodhar, see mìomhar.
mi-mhoil, see mìomhail.
mi-mhol, *v.a.* Dispraise. 2 Disparage.
mi-mholadh, -aidh, *s.m.* Dispraising, act of dispraising. 2 Disparagement. A' m—, *pr. pt.* of mi-mhol.
mi-mhuinighinn, -e, *s.f.* Distrust, diffidence.
————each, -eiche, *a.* Diffident, distrustful.
mi-mhurrach,‡‡ -aiche, *a.* Incapable.
mi-mhurrachas, -ais, *s.m.* Disqualification.
mìn, -e, *a.* Soft, delicate, tender. 2 Smooth, not rough. 3 Level, of even surface. 4 Mild, meek, gentle. 5 Pleasant, melodious, harmonious, sweet, tender (of sound.) 6 Calm, unruffled (as water.) 7 Small, reduced to powder, pulverized, ground. 8 Soft, woolly, fine, like wool, of fine fabric. 9 Acute. 10 In *Arran*, Soft, gentle, where "a dhuine mh." is used as "a dhuine chòir" elsewhere, and "pàisdean m." is an expression of endearment. 11**Polished, plain. Bruthaidh tu ro mhìn, *thou wilt bruise very small ;* mìn bhasan bàna, *delicate white hands ;* aodach m., *smooth cloth ;* clachan mìne an t-sruith, (*or* srùtha) *smooth stones from the stream ;* an gille m., *the gentle inoffensive lad ;* an nighean mh., *the gentle maid ;* min mh. *fine meal ;* buntàta m., *small potatoes ;* buin gu m., *deal softly* or *gently.*
min, -e, *s.f.* Meal. 2 Any comminuted or pulverized substance. M. iaruinn, *iron filings ;* soitheach mine, *a vessel of meal.*
m.-choirce, *oatmeal.*
m.-chruithneachd, *wheat meal.*
m.-eararaidh, *meal from parched corn.*
m.-eòrna, *barley-meal.*
m.-ghradain, *meal made from parched corn.*
m.-pheasrach, *pease-meal.*
m.-phonair, *bean-meal.*
m,-sheagaill, *rye-meal.*
m.-uraraidh, see min-eararaidh.

mìn, *s.m.* Plain field.
min-, see mìon-.
mi-nàdur, -uir, *s.m.* Ill-nature. 2 Inhumanity.
————ra, *a,* Preternatural, unnatural. 2 Void of natural affection, cruel, inhuman. 3 Ill-natured. Neo-ghloine mh., *unnatural impurity.*
mi-nàdurrach, -aiche, see mi-nàdurra.
mi-nàdurrachd, *s.f.ind.* Monstrousness.
mi-nàdurrail, -e, *a.* see mi-nàdurra.
mi-nàire, *s.f.* Shamelessness, impudence, effrontery, immodesty.
mi-nàireach, -eiche, *a.* Shameless, impudent.
————d, *s. f. ind.* Shamelessness, impudence.
minean, -ain, *s.m.* Dross.
min-aois, see mion-aois.
mi-naomha, -naoimhe, *a.* Profane, unholy, irreligious, unsanctified.
mi-naomhachadh, -aidh, *s.m.* Profaning, act of making unholy, profanation. A' m—, *pr. pt.* of mi-naomhaich.
mi-naomhachd, *s.f.ind.* Profanity, unholiness.
mi-naomhaich, *pr pt.* a' mi-naomhachadh, *v.a.* Profane, unhallow, deprave, deprive of holiness. A mh. an t-sàbaid, *that profaned the sabbath.*
mi-naomhaichte, *past pt.* of mi-naomhaich. Profaned.
mi-nàrach, see mi-nàireach.
mìn-bhailtean, see mion-bhailtean.
mìn-bhallach, see mion-bhallach
mìn-bhàrr,§ -a, -an, *s. m.* Hemlock, see min-mheur.
mìn-bhean,** *s.f.* Tender name for a wife.
mìn-bheulach, -aiche, *a.* Soft-mouthed, flattering, of smooth speech.
mìn-bheulachd, *s.f.* Soft words.
mìn-bhileach, -eiche, see mìn-bheulach.
mìn-bhriathar, -air, -thran, *s.m.* Soft expression, gentle word, flattering word or expression.
mìn-bhriathrach, -aiche, *a.* Of mild words. 2 Flattering, fawning, smooth-worded.
mìn-bhris, *v.a. & a.* Pound, pulverize. 2 Fall in pieces, crumble.
mìn-bhriseach, *a.* Pulverizing, crumbling. 2 Apt to pulverize or crumble.
mìn-bhriseadh, -idh, *s. m.* Pounding, act of pounding, pulverizing. 2 State of crumbling or falling in pieces. A' m—, *pr. pt.* of mìn-bhris.
mìn-bhriste, *past pt.* of mìn-bhris. Broken or crumbled into small pieces, powdered, pulverized.
mìn-bhruich, *v.a.* Boil.
mìn-bhrùth, *v.a.* Pound, pulverize, mince.
min'chadh, for mìneachadh.
mìn-chagainn, *v.a.* Masticate, chew into small pieces, munch.
mìn-chagainnte, *past part.* of mìn-chagainn. Chewed, masticated.
mìn-chagnadh, -aidh, *s.m.* Mastication, munching. A' m—, *pr.pt.* of mìn-chagainn.
mìn-chlach, -chloich, -chlachan, *s. f.* Smooth stone. 2 Pumice-stone.
————ach, -aiche, *a.* Abounding in smooth stones, or pumice-stone.
mìn-chlòimh, *s.f.* Down.
mìn-chruth, -a, -an, *s.f.* Delicate form or figure. 2 Delicate person. 3 Smooth-skinned person.
————ach, -aiche, *a.* Of a delicate form or figure. 2 Soft-featured. 3 Smooth-skinned. 4**Soft-complexioned.
†minde, *s.f.* Stammering.
mìn-chùiseach, see mion-chùiseach.
mìn-dhuine, see mion-dhuine.
mìn-dhus, *s.m.* Powder. 2 Fine sand. 3 Dust.

mìne, *s.f.ind.* Smoothness, polish. 2 Softness, delicacy. 3 Minuteness, smallness. 4 Comminution. 5 Pusillanimity.
mìne, *comp.* of mìn. Aiuuir bu mh. gnè, *a virgin of the softest temper ;* na's m. na oladh, *smoother than oil.*
mìneach, -eiche, *a.* Mealy, abounding in meal, like meal.
mìneach,(CR) *s.m.* Tender grass.
———adh, -aidh, *s.m.* Expounding, act of expounding, explaining. 2 Explanation, illustration, account, exposition. 3 Polishing, act of polishing. 4**Taming. 5**Pulverizing. 6 Smoothing. A' m—, *pr.pt.* of mìnich. A' m. na h-earrainn seo, *explaining this passage ;* m. a' Bhiobuill, *an exposition of the Bible.*
mìneachail, -e, *a.* Illustrative, explanatory.
mìneachd, see mìne.
mìnead, -eid, *s. m.* Degree of smoothness. A' dol an m., *growing smoother.*
mìneadach, -aiche, see mionaideach.
mìneadair, *s.m.* Glosser, glossator.
mìneadair, *s.m.* Mealman.
mìneag, -eig, -an, *s.f.* Gentle, meek or mild woman. 2**Smooth-skinned girl.
———ach, *a.* Gentle-tempered, as a female.
mìnean,** -ein, *s.m.* Dross, the small or dust of coals. 2 Any drossy substance.
mìnean, -in, *s.m.* see mèanan.
-———ach, see mèananach.
mìneanach, -aich, *s.m.* see mionanach.
mìnear, -eire, *a.* see mìneach.
mìn-earghnas,** -ais, *s.m.* Ignorance.
mìneideach, -eiche, *a.* see mionaideach.
mìneil, -e, *a.* Mealy, like meal.
mìneit, see mionaid.
———each, see mionaideach.
mìn-eòlach, see mion-eòlach.
mìn-eòlas, see mion-eòlas.
mìneag,(WC) *s. f.* Very endearing term of address, commonly used in *Gairloch, &c.*, e. g. mineag nach toir thu dhomh pòg ? Always used to children by their mothers.
mìn-eun,(WC) *s.m.* see mion-eun.
mìneurach, see mìlearach.
mìn-fhalt, *s.f.* Down. 2 Soft, smooth or fine hair.
mìn-fheur, -fheòir,*s.m.* Soft or smooth grass, especially sheep's fescue grass. 2 Meadow. 3 Flag, bulrush, see luachair. 4**Closely-shaven grass.
mìn-fheurach,†† *a.* Abounding in soft or smooth grass.
mìn-fheur-chaorach, *s.m.* Soft sheep-grass.
mìn'g, see minic.
mìn-ghadachd, } see mion-ghaduidheachd.
mìn-ghaduidheachd }
mìn-gheal, -ghile, *a.* Soft and fair. Mo chaileag bhuidhe mh., *my yellow-haired maid with skin so soft and fair.*
mìn-ghob,(AF) *s.* Avocet.
mìn-ghoideachd,** *s.f.* see mion-ghaduidheachd.
mìn-iasg, see mion-iasg.
mìn-iarruinn, *s.m.* Iron-filings. (also smùr- or smùrach-iarruinn.)
minic, see minig.
miniceag,(CR) *s.f.* Kid-skin.
mìnich, *pr.pt.* a' mìneachadh,[mìn'ceadh—*Dàin I. Ghobha,*] *v.a.* Explain, expound, illustrate, interpret. 2 Polish, smoothe. 3 Make small, pulverize. 4**Tame. M. seo dhomh, *explain this to me ;* mh. iad slighe Dhé na bu choimhlionta, *they expounded the way of God more perfectly.*
mìniche, -an, *s.m.* Interpreter, expounder.
mìnichear, *fut.pass.* of mìnich.
mìnichte, *past pt.* of mìnich. Explained, interpreted, expounded. 2 **Smoothed, polished. 3 Abstracted.
minicionn, -inn, -an, *s.m.* Kid-skin.
———-laoigh,(DMy) *s.m.* Calf-skin.
minicneag,(JM) *s.f.* Skin. 2 (DMC) Piece of lamb-skin with wool on, put under saddle. M. uain, *skin of a newly-born lamb.*
minid, *N. Argyll, Glenlyon, &c.* for binid.
minidh, -e, -ean, *s.m.* Shoemaker's awl. 2 (AF) Owl. (meanaidh is a better form.—MM)
———-teallaich,†† *s.m.* Hot iron for burning holes in wood. (deigh in *Argyll*—Fionn.)
———-teine, *Suth'd.* for minidh-teallaich.
minig, *a.* Frequent, often, frequently. Ni m., *a common thing ;* t' anmhuinneachd mh., *thy frequent infirmity.*
minig (i. e. gu minic) *a.* Frequently. Is m. uair 's is tric, *many a time and oft ;* is m. a thachras a leithid sin, *the like of that frequently happens.*
minigeach,(MS) *a.* Accustomed.
minigeachd, *s.f.* Frequency.
minis,* *s. f.* Degree, set portion. Ni sinn air minisibh e, *we shall do it by degrees* or *allotted portions ;* a' cheud mh. dheth, *the first portion of it.*
minisdreachd, see ministrealachd.
ministear, -eir, -an, *s.m.* Clergyman. 2 Minister. 3**Servant. Ionnus gu'm bithinn 'nam mh. aig Iosa Criosd, *so that I might be a minister of Jesus Christ ;* b' annsa leam ministear-maide na madadh-ministir, *I prefer a wooden minister to a ministerial hound*—said by a ploughman who had served under two ministers. One was a " Moderate " and a gentleman, the other an Evangelical and a tyrant. To a friend, who asked his opinion of the respective merits of the " ministear-maide " and the " ministear-diadhaidh," the ploughman replied as above. Cròg ministeir agus spòg iolaire, *a minister's " paw " and an eagle's claw*—a saying attributed to " Dall Mór," a North Uist bard and catechist.
ministeir, see ministear.
ministeireach, see ministreil.
ministeireachd, *s.f.* see ministrealachd.
ministrealachd, *s.f.ind.* Ministry, the clerical function, office of a clergyman, ministration, act of discharging the duty of a clergyman. 2* Incumbency. M. an Fhacail, *the ministration of the Word.*
ministreil, -e, *a.* Ministerial, connected with the clerical profession.
mìn-ite, *s.f.* Smooth feather.
mìn-lach,§ *s.* Field chamomile—*anthemis arvensis.* 2**Finest of grass. 3**Dross.

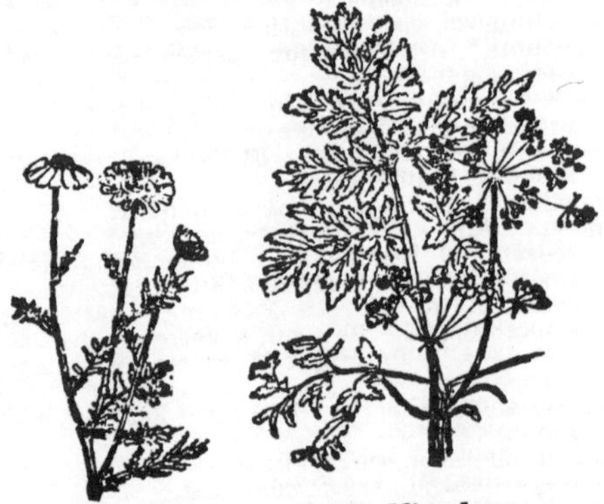

534. Mìn-lach. 535. Minmheur.

min-lamh, *s.f.* Soft hand. 2 Soft arm.
min-lear,** *s.f.* Calm sea. Clos na m. uaine, *the repose of the calm green sea.*
minmheur,§ -ir, *s.m.* Hemlock—*conium maculatum.* (ill. 535 on p. 658.)
minn, *gen.sing.* & *n.pl.* of meann.
minneacu,** -ich, *s.m.* Mill-mountain (plant.) 2 **Purging flax. 3**Lie.
minnean, -ein, -an, *s.m.*, *dim.* of meann. Little kid. 2 Little fawn or young male of the roe. 3(WC) see mineun. Na minneanan laghach, *the pretty young kids.*
——-ach, -aiche, *a.* Abounding in kids or fawns.
minnein, see minnean.
———each, see minneanach.
minniceag,-eig, -an, see miniceag.
minnicean, see minicionn.
minnseach, see minnseag.
minnseag, -eig, -an, *s.f.* Yearling she-goat. 2 Doe in its first year, kid.
———ach, *a.* Abounding in yearling she-goats or does.
mi-nòs, -òis, -an, *s.m.* Bad custom or habit. 2 Immorality, misbehaviour, unchasteness.
——ach, -aiche, *a.* Given to bad habits, misbehaving, unchaste, immodest. 2**Crabbed, morose.
——mhor, -oire, *a.* see mi-nòsach.
min-phroinnte, *past pt.* of min-phronn. Pounded, pulverized, bruised.
min-phronn,*pr.pt.*a' min-phronnadh,*v.a.* Pound, bruise, pulverize, granulate.
————, *a.* Pounded, pulverized.
————adh, -aidh, *s. m.* Pounding, fact of pounding, bruising, pulverizing. A' m—, *pr. pt.* of min-phronn.
min-rann, -rainn, *s.f.* Smooth verse.
min-rosg, -roisg, -an, *s.m.* Soft, meek, mild or gentle eye-lid. 2††Soft eye.
———ach, -aiche, *a.* Meek-eyed, having a meek or gentle look.
minseach, see minnseach & minnseag.
min-shùil, -shùla, -ean, *s.f.* Mild-eye, soft eye. 2 Pink eye.
————each, -eiche, *a.* Mild-eyed. 2 Pink-eyed.
minsich, see minnseag.
min-uchd,** *s.f.* Soft breast. 2 Smooth breast. O 'm. bàn, *from her soft fair breast.*
————ach, *a.* Having a soft or smooth breast, soft or smooth breasted.
mio-, *prefix*, see mi-.
mìobhadh, *s.m.* Ill-usage, as by weather.
mìobhail, -e, *a.* see miomhail.
————eachd, see miomhalachd.
mioch,** s. Bushel.
miochuineas, *s.m.* Donation.
miochuis,* *s.f.* Flirtation, pretended indifference, coquetry.
—————each,* *a.* Coquettish, flirting as a prude, leering with the eye.
—————eachd,* *s.f.* Flirtation, coquetry, assumed indifference.
miodair,** *gen.sing.* & *n pl.* of miodar.
miodal, -ail, *s.m.* Flattery, fawning. 2 Fair speech. 3 Insinuation. Le m. tlàth, *with smooth flattery* ; luchd-miodail, *flatterers.*
miodalach, -aiche, *a.* Fawning, flattering, smooth-lipped. Beul m., *a flattering mouth.*
————d,** *s.f.* Habit or practice of flattery, sycophancy.
miodalaiche,** *s. m.* Fawner, flatterer. 2 Amuser.
miodalair, -ean, see miodalaiche.
————eachd, see miodalachd.
miodalan,(DMC) *s.m.* Flatterer.
miodar, -air, *pl.* -air & -an, *prov.* for meadar. 2 Pasture-ground, meadow, good pasture.
miodarach, -aich, *s.m.* Ansated wooden dish.
————, -aiche, *a.* see meadarach. 2 Having good pastures, abounding in pasture. 3 (MS) Ansated. 4 Full of wooden dishes.
miodaran, -ain, *s.m.* Noggin. (meadaran.)
mìodhòigh, *s.* Anarchy.
miodhoir, -e, *a.* Niggardly, penurious, paltry, mean, contemptible, avaricious. 2 Coarse, sordid. Gu m., *penuriously.*
miodhoir, -e, -ean, *s.m.* Churl, niggard, paltry, mean, contemptible person. 2 Miser. 3 Churlishness.
———eachd, *s.f.ind.* Churlishness, niggardliness, paltriness, meanness, baseness, avarice, penuriousness, sordidness. 2 Abjectness, poverty. 3 Dirtiness.
mìodhuil, *s.* Dislike, aversion.
miog, -a, -an, *s.f* Smile, smirk, sly or wanton look. (‡‡miog)
——ach, -aiche, *a.* Smiling,smirking,sly-looking. 2**Sparkling. A bhanarach mh.! *thou dainty smiling dairymaid !* sùil mh. bhòidheach, *a sly pretty eye.*
miogadaich, *s.f.* see meigeadaich.
mìoghlachadh,(CR) *s.m.* State of suspense,fearing or anticipating evil.
mioghnathaichte,(MS) *a.* Odd.
mi-oileanach,(MS) *a.* Home-bred.
mìog-shuil, -shùla, -ean, *s.f.* Smiling or laughing eye, sly look, inviting eye, leering eye.
mìog-shuileach, -eiche, *a.* Smiling, smirking, having a laughing eye, sly-looking, leering. 2 Pink-eyed. 3**Having an inviting eye.
mi-oidhirpeach, -eiche, *a.* Slothful, lazy, unindustrious. 2 Not endeavouring, unenterprising.
mi-oileanaich,‡ *v.a.* Misteach.
miol, -a, -an, see mial.
——ach, -aiche, *a.* see mialach.
miolag,** *s.f.* Melon. 2 Any small thing.
miolainn ort ! (CR) *int.* (mi-loinn) Bad condition to you ! (an imprecation.)
miolairtich, *pr. pt.* a' miolairtich, *v.a.* Fawning. 'S e (an cù) m. gu sodanach, *and it (the dog) fawning joyfully—Donn. Bàn.*
miolan,** -ain, *s.m.* Lie.
miolaran, -ain, *s.m.* The low barking howling or whining of a dog when fawning, whimper. 2 Lament, soft, wailing voice. Rinn e m., *he howled.*
————ach, -aiche, *a.* Barking,howling or whining with a low voice. 2 Lamenting.
————aich, -e, *s.f.* Continued barking with a low voice, howling or whining, whimpering. 2**Wailing voice. 3**Loud lament.
————aich,(MS) *v.n* Fawn.
miolasg, -aisg, *s.f.* Flattery, fawning, as of a dog. 2 Keen desire. 3 Skittishness of a horse.
————ach, -aiche, *a.* Flattering, fawning. 2 Keenly desirous. 3 Skittish, restive. 4 Cajoling. Gu m., *in a flattering manner.*
————achd, *s.f.ind.* see miolasg.
————air, -ean,*s.m.* Flatterer, fawning fellow.
†miolc, s. Whey.
miolc, *v.a.* Soothe, cajole. 2 Flatter.
———ach,** *s.m.* Churl, clown.
———ach, *a.* Flattering, prone to flatter. 2 Clownish.
———adh, -aidh, Flattering. 2 Cajoling, soothing. A' m—, *pr.pt.* of miolc.
———air, *s.m.* Cajoler.
———aireachd, *s.f.* Flattery, practice of flattery.
———ais,(CR) *s.f.* Caressing, foudling—*West of Ross-shire.*

mìol-choille,** *s.m.* Woodlouse.
mìol-chù, -choin. see mial-chù.
mìol-mhàg, see muile-mhàg.
mìol-mhàgag,(MS) *s.f.* see muile-mhàg.
mìol-fhiodha, see mial-fhiodha.
mìol-mhór, *s. m.* see mial-mhór.
mìoltag, -aig, -an, see ialtag.
mìoltag-leathair, *s.f.* see ialtag.
†mìomasg,** -aisg, *s.m.* Lance, spear, javelin.
†mìomhadh, -aidh, -aidhean, see mi-mhodh.
†mìomhaich, see mi-mhodh.
mìomhail, -e, *a.* Disrespectful, ill-bred, unmannerly.
mìomhalachd, *s. f. ind.* Rudeness, impertinence, unpoliteness. 2 Immodesty. 3 Disrespectfulness.
mìomhar, *a.* Ill-bred, uncivil, impertinent. 2 Of unbecoming habits.
mìomnalachd, see mi-mhodhalachd.
mìon, *s.m.* Diadem.
mion, -a, *a. & pref.* Small. 2 Punctual, exact. 3 Distinct. 4 Mean.
†mionach, -aich, *s.m.* Metal.
mionach, -aich, -ean, *s.m.* Bowels, entrails, intestines, guts. 2 Fairy-flax, see lìon-nam-ban-sìth. 3(DU) *metaphorically*, The works in a watch or mechanism. Nighidh tu a mh.,*thou wilt wash its entrails.*
———ail,‡‡ -e, *a.* Intestinal.
mionachd,‡‡ *s.f.ind.* Minuteness.
mionachas, see mion-acras.
mion-acrach, -aiche, *a.* Hungry, voracious, ravenous. 2**Having a false appetite. 3*Eating but little at a time, as an invalid.
mion-acras, -ais, *s.m.* Extreme hunger, voraciousness, ravenousness, craving for food. 2 False appetite.
————ach, -aiche, *a.* see mion-acrach.
mìonad, -aid, *s. m.* Degree of minuteness or fineness. Is m. a' chlach gach buille, *the stone becomes more powdered at every blow.*
mìonag,‡ -aige, -aigean, *s. f.* Cranberry, see muileag. 2(WC) see mineag.
mionaich,†† see mionach.
mionaid, -e, -ean, *s. f.* Minute, moment of time. 2**Minute of proceedings. Air a' mh., *this minute, this instant* ; mionaidean comuinn, *a society's proceedings* ; m. no dhà, *a minute or two* ; m. gu leth, *a minute and a half.* [McL & D gives *s.m.*]
———each, -eiche, *a.* Constant, perpetual, in quick succession. 2 Punctual, precise, particular. 3*Minute. 4 Circumstantial. Iarr gu m., *search minutely.*
———eachadh,** -aidh, *s.m.* Inculcating, explaining, minute explanation. 2 Act of taking down minutes.
———ich,** *pr. pt.* a' mionaideachadh, *v. a.* Inculcate, explain minutely. 2 Take down minutes.
mionaigir,** *s.f.* Vinegar.
mionaire,(MS) *s.* Barefacedness, brass.
mionalach,(MS) *a.* Grail.
mionalaich,(MS) *v.n.* Garble.
mionan, -ain, see meanan.
———ach, *s.m.* Mannikin.
mion-aois, -e, *s.f.* Minority, state of being under full age.
————each'‡‡ *a.* Minor.
mionarach,(MS) *a.* Audacious, bare-faced.
mionbhaich,‡‡ *v.a.* Bedwarf.
mion-bhailtean,*, *s.pl.* Suburbs.
mion-bhallach, *a.* Having small spots, spotted, speckled. Laoigh mh., *spotted calves.*
mion-bhradach, *a.* Light-fingered, prone to petty theft.
mion-bhraide,** *s.f.* Petty larceny.
mion-cheasnachadh,** -aidh, *s.m.* Scrutinizing cross-examination,close questioning. A' m— *pr.pt.* of mion-cheasnaich.
mion-cheasnaich, *pr. pt.* a' mion-cheasnachadh *v.a.* Scrutinize, examine minutely or strictly cross-examine.
mion-chlach, *s.f.* Gravel.
————ach, *a.* Gravelly.
mion-chorrach,** *a.* Very steep, precipitous.
mion-chruth, -a, -an, *s.m.* Abridgment.
mion-chuileag, -eig,-an,*s.f.* see meanbh-chuileag.
mion-chùiseach, -eiche, *a.* Punctilious, particular about trifles. 2**Mean. 3**Strictly punctual.
mion-chunntas, -ais, -an, *s.m.* Short, or particularly strict account or reckoning, detailed account.
miondan, -ain, *s.m.* Long-tailed titmouse.
mion-dearbhadh, *s.m.* Account. 2 Detailed proof or evidence.
mion-dhealbh, *s.m.* Miniature (picture.) 2 Little image.
mion-dhuine, *pl.* -dhaoine, *s.m.*Dwarf,mannikin, diminutive fellow.
mion-dreach, *s.m.* Little image.
†mion-eallach, (AF) -aich, *s. m.* Small cattle (sheep and goats.)
mion-eòlach, -aiche, *a.* Intimately or thoroughly acquainted.
mion-eòlas, -ais, *s. m.* Intimate or thorough acquaintance.
mioneun,(DU) *s.m.* Meadow-pipit.
mion-fhacal, -ail, *s.m.* Article. 2 Minute word.
mion-fhiosrach,‡‡ -aiche, *a.* Well-acquainted.
mion-fhliuch,‡‡ *v.a.* Bedew.
mion-fhraoch, see fraoch-Frangach.
miong, *Suth'd.* for mèag.
miongach,(AC) *a.* Sour-faced.
mion-ghadachd, see mion-ghaduidheachd.
mion-ghaduidheachd, *s.f.ind.* Petty theft, pilfering, larceny.
mion-ghèarr, *v. a.* Cut into small pieces, hash, mince.
————adh, -aidh, *s. m.* Mincing, act of mincing or cutting into small pieces. A' m—, *pr.pt.* of mion-ghèarr.
————ta, *past pt.* of mìn-ghèarr. Cut into small pieces, minced.
mion-ghrinneas,(MS) *s.m.* Refinement.
miongradh, -aidh, *s.m.* Gnawing.
mion-iasg, -éisg, *pl.* -an & -éisg, *s.m.* Small fish or fishes. 2 Minnow. 3 Shoal of fish.
mion-ite, *s.f.* Small feather.
mion-léirsinn,(MS) *s.f.* Penetration.
mion-mhèirle, *s.f.* Larceny.
mion-mhothachail,‡‡ -e, *a.* Nervous.
mionn, -a, -an, *s.m. & f.* Oath, imprecation. 2 Vow. 3 Curse. 4**Bell. †5 Crown of the head. †6 Skull. †7 Crown, diadem. 8* Declaration on oath. Saor o m' mhionnaibh, *free from my oath* ; m. nach còir a dheanamh cha chòir a ghleidheil, *an oath that ought not to be made ought not to be kept*—a great deal could be said both for and against the morality of this proverb. If one ventures in a company of Gaels to disapprove of it, the retort usually is, "then you think Herod acted rightly in beheading John the Baptist,"—which silences orthodox folk. Thoir mionnan, *swear, give oath;* gabh mionnan, *administer an oath* ; ceangal nam mionn, *the obligation of oaths* ; mionnan-eithich, *a false oath.* [*nom. sing.* in *Gairloch* is mionna.]
mionn, *s.* Particle, jot, atom. Cha'n 'eil m. de m' rùn dhiot, *thou hast not a particle of my affection.*
mionn, *v.a. & n.* see mionnaich.

mionn, see meannt.
mionnach, -aiche, *a.* Prone to swear. 2 Cursing, swearing. 3 Votive.
————adh, -aidh, *s. m.* Swearing, act of swearing or making oath. 2 Cursing, act of using imprecations. 3 Vow, imprecation. A' m—, *pr.pt.* of mionnaich.
mionnachail, -e, *a.* Juratory.
mionnadh, *s.m.* see mionn.
mionnaibh,** *2nd. per.pl. imp.* of mionn. Swear ye.
mionnaich, *pr. pt.* a' mionnachadh, *v.a. & n.* Swear, make oath, vow, avow. 2 Administer an oath. 3 Swear, imprecate, curse. M. dhòmh-sa air Dia, *swear to me by God.*
————te, *past pt.* of mionnaich. Sworn, bound by oath. 2**Cursed, accursed. Tha e m. ris gu'n cuir e as dhuit, *he is bound by an oath to finish your days.*
mionnan, -ain, *s.m.* Small mound.
mionnan, *n.pl.* of mionn. 2 *dim.* of mionn.
mionnaran, see miontan.
mionnt, -a, *s.m.* Mint, spearmint, peppermint.
———ainn,(AH) *s.f.* Water-mint—*N.Argyll.*
———air, *s.m.* Swearer.
———an, see mionnain & miondan.
mionntan,** -ain, *s.m.* Wren. 2 Tom-tit.
mionntas, -ais, *s.m.* see meannt.
mionntuinn, *s.m.* see meannt.
mion-ocrach, see mion-acrach.
mi-onoir, *s.m.* Dishonour, disgrace. 2 Dishonesty, fraud.
mi-onoireach, -eiche, *a.* Dishonourable, disgraceful. 2 Dishonest, fraudulent.
————adh, -aidh, *s. m.* Dishonouring, act of dishonouring. A' —m, *pr.pt.* of mi-onoirich.
mi-onoirich, *v.a.* Dishonour.
mion-rann, -rainn, *s.f.* Short verse, short poem.
mion-rannsaich, *v.a.* Search thoroughly. An do mhion-rannsaich thu e ? *did you search it minutely ?*
†mionsa, *s.f.* Month, now mìos.
mion-sgrudadh, -aidh, *s.m.* Criticism.'
mion-shùileach,‡‡ -eiche, *a.* see min-shuileach.
miontan, -ain, -an, *s.f.* Long-tailed titmouse, see cìochan. (also mionntan.)
mion-theagasg, -aisg, *s.m.* Instillation.
miorailt, -e, *s.f* see miorbhuil.
————each,* -eiche, see miorbhuileach.
————eachd, *s.f.* see miorbhuileachd.
†miorbhadh, -aidh, *s.m.* Killing, destroying.
miorbhuil, -e, -ean, *s.f.* Miracle, wonder. 2 Prodigy, phenomenon. [†† gives *m. & f.*]
————each, -eiche, *a.* Miraculous, marvellous, wonderful, amazing.
————eachd, *s.f. ind.* Wonderfulness, miraculousness, marvellousness.
mi-ordail, -e, *a.* Disorderly.
miortail, see miortalach.
miortal, -ail, -an, *s.f.* Myrtle—*myrtus communis.*
————ach,** *a.* Abounding in, or like myrtle.
————ach,** -aich, *s.m.* Myrtle shrubbery or thicket. 2 Place where myrtles grow. [** gives *s.f.*]
miortalnach,** -aich, *s.f.* see miortalach.
miorun, -uin, see mi-rùn.
————ach, -aiche, *a.* see mi-rùnach.
————achd, *s.f.* see mi-rùnachd.
mìos, -a, -an, *s.m.* Month. 2 *rarely* Moon. O mh. a dh' aois, *from a month old* ; fuil mìos, *flowers, menstrual courses.* [McL & D gives *m. & f.*]
mìos, -éis, -an, see mias.
mios, see meas.
miosa, *comp.* of olc. Worse, worst. [Used as positive degree in *Uist, W. of Ross. &c.*, as, tha i cho miosa, *she is so bad.*] Riut-sa na's miosa na riù-san, *with thee worse than with them ;* am fear a's m., *the devil.*
miosach, -aiche, *a.* Monthly, menstrual. An galar m., *menstrual courses.*
————, -aich, *s.f.* Fairy-flax, see lìon-nam-ban-sìth. [Purging-flax, mill-mountain—McL & D]
————an, -ain, *pl.* -an & -ain, *s.m.* Calendar, almanac. 2 (MM) Monthly magazine.
miosad, -aid, *s.f.* Degree of badness.
mìosadair, *s.m.* see miosachan.
miosail, -e, *a.* see measail.
miosail, -e, *a.* see miosach.
miosar, -air, -airean, see measair & meadar.
————ach, -aiche, *a.* see measarach.
————achd, *t.f.* Measurement. 2 Mensuration.
miosairich, see measairich.
mios bochuin,(*lit.* month of swelling—AC) *s.m.* May.
mios buidhe, (am), *s.m.* July.
mioscuisich,(MS) *v.a.* Lessen. 2 Prejudice.
mìos-dhortach,** *a.* Menstrual, flowing monthly.
mios-dhortadh, -aidh, *s.m.* Menstrual courses.
mìos dubh, (am) *s.m.* November.
miosg, see measg.
miosgainn, -e, *s.f.* see miosguinn.
miosgais, -e, *s.f.* see miosguinn.
————each, see miosguinneach.
miosgan, -ain, *pl.* -an & -ain, *s.m.* Kit, wooden vessel for holding butter. 2 Cheese-vat. see measgan.
————ach, -aiche, *a.* Of, or belonging to, kits or cheese-vats. 2‡‡Having much butter. 3** Butter-making. A Bhealltuinn mh., *butter-making May.*
miosguinn, -e, -ean, *s.f.* Malice, spite, hate. 2 Grudge. 3 Poorness. Luchd do mh., *people who have a grudge against you ;* le m. garg, *with bitter spite.*
miosguinneach, -eiche, *a.* Spiteful, malevolent. 2 Envious, grudging.
miosguinneachd, *s.f.* see miosguinn.
mios marbh, (am) *s.m.* December. 2 February in *N. Argyll*—(AH.)
mìos mhadrail, *s.m.* July.
miosneach, -ich, see misneach.
————ail, *a.* see misneachail.
miosraich,(CR) *v.n.* Think, suppose, conjecture. —*W. of Ross-shire.* (measraich)
mios-shruth,** *s.* Courses.
miosta, see miostadh.
miostadh,** -aidh, *s.m.* Mischief. 2 Loss. 'S ge b' aobhar strì e, gu'm fuilginn miostadh, *and although it should be a cause of strife, I would suffer* or *forego loss* ; 'g a ghleidheadh o mhiosta, *preserving him from harm or loss*—*Duanaire.*
miotag, -aig, -an, *s.f.* Mitten, worsted glove. 2 Any glove.
†miotag, -aig, -an, *s.f.* Fright, terror. Cha ghabh thu fuathas no m., *thou shalt not be afraid.* (meatag)
———ach, -aiche, *a.* Wearing mittens, having mittens, like a mitten. 2 Full of gloves or mittens. 3 Gloved.
———achadh, -aidh, *s.m.* Putting on of mittens or worsted gloves, gloving. A' m—, *pr. pt.* of miotagaich.
miotagaich, *pr.pt.* a' miotagachadh, *v.a.* Put on worsted gloves.
————te, *past pt.* Furnished with mittens. 2 Gloved.
miotag-bhuidhe,§ *s. f.* Bitter-sweet, woody nightshade, see searbhag-mhilis.
miotailt, *s.f.* see meiteal.
————each, see meitealtach.
miotair,(MMcD) *s.f.* Drinking-cup, called also

" noigean."
†miothag, -aig, -an, see spitheag.
——aich, see spitheagaich.
—— -bhuidhe, *s. f.* Woody nightshade—*solanum dulcamara.*
miothair,(MS) *a.* Beggarly
miothaird,* *s.f.* State of not being looked after, unprotection. (mi-aird)
miothaireachd,(MS) *s f* Scantiness.
miothapadh,(MS) *s m* see miapadh.
miothar, -aire, *a.* see miodhoir.
——achd, *s.f* see miodhoireachd.
miothlachd, *s.f.ind* Offence. displeasure, resentment 2‡‡Unhandsomeness, unpleasantness. 3**Contempt, disrespect. 4 Listless. 5 Discontent disgust. 6 Discord. A' toilltinn m. duine sam bith, *incurring the resentment of any person*, smachd air luchd-m., *sway over the discontented*
mi-phàirteach, -eiche, *a.* Niggardly not willing to communicate or share.
——ail, -e, *a.* see mi-phairteach.
mi-phiseach,(MS) *s.m.* Loss.
mi-phongaich,‡‡ *v.a.* Mispoint.
mir, *s.f.* Mow, built up pile of hay, corn, straw peats, &c. 2 Section of a mow. [** gives mire.]
mir,(AC) *s.* Wort.
mir, *pr.pt.* a' mireadh, *v.a.* Sport, play, frisk, wont. 2 Flirt.
mir, -e, *pl.* -ean & -eannan *s. m.* Bit, part or piece of anything, as of bread, &c. 2 Luncheon. Cha'n 'eil m. agam, *I haven't a particle;* na h-uile m., *every bit*; mir mòna, *a subdivision of a peat-stack*; m. fearainn, *a patch of ground*; criomag mire, *a small bit of bread*; gearraidh tu e 'na mhiribh, *thou shalt cut him in pieces*; m.-cuthaige, see greim-cuthaige.
†mir, -ean, *s.m.* Top, summit. [** gives *s.f.*]
mircean,§ -ein, *s.* Badderlocks, hen-ware—*alaria esculenta.*
mircean, *s. m.** Certain part of seaweed called " badderlock." It consists of the kind of leaf-like growths,called " earball-sàile " from their bitter or salt taste. On each side of the mircean is the " rùsg " or peel, and between it and the short bare stem (close to the rock) called " cas dhubh," are the " duilleach," several short leaves or sprouts.
mir-còrr, see mir-mór.
mire, *s.f.ind.* Play, pastime. 2 Mirth, sportiveness, merriment, levity, giddiness. 3 Buxomness. 4 Flirting, wantoning. 5 Transport, rapture, ecstasy. 6 Transport of rage, fury, ardour, vehemence. 7 *poetical,* Madness. 8** Quickness. 9**Dissoluteness. 10 see mir. Ri m. ghoraich, *indulging in foolish mirth*; air mh., *in a transport, in an excess of mirth*; tha e air mh., *he is stark mad*; cuir air mh., *transport with joy* dh' éirich iad suas gu mire, *they rose up to play*; m -chatha, *rage of battle*; m.-chuthaich, *madness, quickness* or *violence of motion*; m.-shruth, *a rapid, raging stream.*
mire, *comp.* of mear.
miread, -id, *s. f.* Merriment, degree of merriment, sportiveness, hilarity
mireadh, -idh, *s.m.* Playing, sporting, diversion, frolic, mirth. 2 Pastime. A' m—, *pr. pt.* of mir. Dh' éirich iad gu m., *they rose to play*; air mh., *going to excess in mirth, transported with joy*; a' m., *flirting, sporting, merry-making*; a' m. ri, *flirting with.*
mireag, -eig, -an, *s.f. dim.* of mire. Sporting, playing, frisking. 2 Pastime. 3** Playful, wanton girl. Is tric rinn mi m. riut, *oft have I sported with you*; spréidh ri mireig, *cattle sporting.*
mireagach, -aiche, *a.* Playful, sportive, frolicsome. 2 Wanton. Sùilean m., *wanton eyes*; gu m., *playfully.*
mireagachd, *s.f.ind.* Playfulness, sportiveness, jocoseness. 2 Wantonness.
mireag-nan-cruach, *s.f.* Uist game—a more advanced form of the game " tig," which is played in harvest-time round the hay- and corn-stacks, the passages among which give splendid opportunities of hiding. When the signal is given, the chaser comes round the stacks after the other players, and as each one is found, he is out of the game till they are all discovered. when the first to be caught is made hunter for the next round. The signal for this game to begin is the shout of " Mhalaic nan cruach " This is a combination of "hide and seek and "tig " for the players hide round the stacks, but it is not enough for the searcher to see them, as in " hide and seek," he must touch them as in " tig." On the other hand, those caught are out of the game till all are caught, when the first caught becomes the chaser—*Uist Games* in *Celtic Review.* No 16. [Called " cur nan sgiobag" in *Lewis*—DMy]
mirean,** -ein, *s. m.* Frolicsomeness playfulness, sportiveness. Gille mirein, *a whirligig.*
mirean, § *s.m.* Agrimony, see mur-dhroighinn.
mirean, -ein, -an, *s. m., dim.* of mir. Little piece, portion, fragment. 2 Grig. 3 " Piece."
mireanach, -aiche, *a.* Merry, playful, causing merriment. Fonn m., *a lively strain.*
mireanach, -aiche, *a.* Abounding in small pieces, portions or fragments.
mireanach, -aich, *s.m* Bridle-bit.
mireanachd. *s.f.* Sportiveness, playfulness. 2 **Liveliness, merriness.
mireanaich, *v.a.* Shatter. 2 Portion, share, piece.
mireann, see mirean.
——ach, *a* see mireanach.
mireanaichte,** *past pt.*Shattered, 2 Portioned.
mireannach, *s.m.* Bit.
mireannan, *n.pl.* of mir.
mire-chatha,** *s.f* Battle-frenzy, extreme individual fury in battle. Bithibh air mh., *rage ye for battle*; a' sgathadh cheann le m., *hewing heads in the fury of battle.*
mire-chuthaich,** *s.f.* Madness, frenzy, transport of madness, raging madness.
mire-meala,(AC) *s.* Honey in the comb.
mire-mhulan, *s.f.* Children's game among the corn-stacks, something like " mireag-nan-cruach."
mire-reothairt, *s.f.* Fury of spring-tide. 2 Violent spring-tide.
mire-shruth, *s. m.* Rapid stream, boiling, impetuous current.
mi-reusan, -ain, *s.m.* Repartee.
mi-reusanta, *a.* Irrational, unreasonable, not right, absurd. Gu m., *unreasonably.*
mi-reusantachd, *s.f.* Unreasonableness, unconscionableness.
mirfhionnach,(DC) *s.m.* Bit for a horse's mouth —*Uist.* (also mireanach)
mir-guailne,** *s.f.* Shoulder-piece.
mi-riaghailt, -e, -ean, *s.f.* Misrule, disorder,confusion, irregularity 2 Anarchy, uproar, riot, tumult, quarrel, rebelliousness, dissoluteness, informality, unruliness.
mi-riaghailteach, -eiche, *a.* Disorderly,confused, irregular. 2 Turbulent, rebellious, quarrelsome, riotous, unruly intractable. 3 Informal. 4 Dissolute. 5 Eccentric.
mi-riaghailteachd, *s.f.* see mi-riaghailt.

mi-riaghailtich, *v.a.* Confuse, confound, disarrange.

mi-riaghladaireachd, *s.f.* Mis-government, maladministration.

mi-riaghladh, -aidh, *s.m.* Anarchy. 2 Confusion. 3 Mis-managing, mis-management, maladministration.

mi-rian -a, -an, *s.m.* Disorder, turbulence, confusion. 2 Want of humour.

mi-rianail, -e, *a.* Disorderly, disordered, confused. 2 Indiscreet. Tha mo chàirdean m., *my friends are indiscreet.*

mi-rianalas, -ais, *s.m.* Disorder, confusion. 2 Indiscretion.

mi-riasanta, see mi-reusanta.

————chd, see mi-reusantachd.

mìr-còrr, see mìr-mór.

mi-rìoghachd,** *s.f.* Anarchy. 2 Republicanism.

mi-rìoghail, -e, *a.* Unkingly, unbecoming a king, *unprincely. 2 Disloyal.

mi-rìoghail,* *v.a.* Misrule.

mi-rìoghailt, *s.f.* see mi-riaghailt.

mi-rìoghalachd, *s.f.ind.* Disloyalty, republicanism.

†mirle,** *s.f.* Ball, globe.

mìr-mór, *s.m.* Mess composed of chopped collops and herb seeds.

mirr, -e, *s.m.* Myrrh—*myrrhis odorata.* 2§ Sweet cicely or great chervil—*Braemar*—see cos-uisge.

536. Mirr.

mìr-uchd, *s.m.* Brisket. [carran-uchd in *Lewis* —DMy.]

mi-rùn, -rùin, *s.m.* Malice, ill-will, spite, malevolence. Luchd mo mhi-rùin, *those who hate me.*

mi-rùnach, -aiche, *a.* Malicious, spiteful, malevolent. Seachainn a' mhuinntir mh., *avoid malicious people*; gu m., *maliciously.*

mi-rùnachd, *s.f.* Same meaning as mi-rùn.

mis, see mìseach.

mis, see mìos.

mis' an diugh ! *int.* Alas ! (*lit.* me the day.)

misd', see misde.

misde, *comp.* of olc. Worse, worst. Cha mh. thu sud, *you are not a bit the worse for yon*; 'dé is m. thu e? *what are you the worse for it?*

misdeachd,* *s.f.ind.* Inferiority, deterioration. 2 Tear.

mi-sdiùir, see mi-stiùir.

mise,(AC) *s.* see mìseach.

mise, *pers. pron. 1st. pers. ind., emphat.* of mi. Myself. Cò a rinn e? mise, *who did it? I did.*

mìseach, -ich, -ichean, *s.f. W. Ross-shire and Suth'd.* for minnseach or minnseag. Gobhair, mìsich is òisgean, *goats, kids and ewes.*

misean, *Suth'd.* form of mise.

misg, -e, *s.f.* Drunkenness, intoxication. 2 Debauch, inebriation. Le geòcaireachd agus le' m., *with surfeiting and drunkenness*; air mh. *drunk*; uair air mh. is uair air uisge, *one day drunk and another drinking water.*

misgeach, -eiche, *a.* Drunken, addicted to drinking. 2 Drunk, intoxicated. Cha dean (duine) m. breug, *a drunkard never lies*; fear m., *a drunkard.*

————d, *s.f.* see misgearachd.

mi-sgeadaich,** *v.a.* Dismantle.

misgealachd, see misgearachd.

misgear, -eir, -an, *s.m.* Drunkard, tippler. Am m. agus an geòcair, *the drunkard and the glutton.*

————achd, *s.f* Drunkenness, habit of drunkenness. 2*Potations. Ri m., *at potations.*

misgeil, -e, *a.* see misgeach.

mi-sgeilm,(DMy) *s.f* Untidiness.

————ar, *a* Untidy

mi-sgeinm, -e, *s.f.* Slovenliness.tawdriness, untidiness 2* Indecorum. indecency

mi-sgeinmeil, -e, *a.* Slovenly, untidy, tawdry. Gu m., *untidily.*

misgeir, see misgear.

mi-sgeul, -éil, -eòil, *s.m.* Bad or false report or tale, calumny. Tog m., *raise a false report.*

mi-sgiamhach, *a.* Homely, inelegant.

misgich,‡‡ *v.a.* Inebriate.

mi-sgileil, *a.* Unskilled.

mi-sgiobalta, -ailte, *a.* Inactive, lazy. 2 Slovenly, untidy, sluttish. 3 Awkward in dress or gait, not smart, clumsy. Gu m., *untidily.*

mi-sgiobaltachd, *s.f.ind.* Inactivity, laziness. 2 Slovenliness, sluttishness. 3 Awkwardness in dress or gait. 4* Untidiness.

misgiort, *s.f.* Indecent behaviour—*Suth'd.*

mi-sgoinn, -e, *s.f.* Inactivity, want of energy. 2 Blameableness. 3 Indecency. 4 Carelessness, negligence, inattention, indifference, want of method.

mi-sgoinneil, -e, *a.* Inactive, wanting energy. 2 Silly, awkward. 3 Careless,inattentive,causing indifference or disdain. 4(MS) Incorrect. Gu m., *carelessly.*

mi-shamh,** *a.* Rough, rugged. 2 Hard.

mi-sheadh. -a, *s.m.* Want of sense, stupidity, absurdity, nonsense. 2 Heedlessness, indifference, inattention, carelessness. 3 Worthlessness. 4 Indolence.

mi-sheadhach, -aiche, *a.* Illogical. 2 Nonsensical.

mi-sheadhail, -e, *a.* Senseless, stupid, absurd, nonsensical. 2 Heedless, indifferent. 3 Indolent. 4 Weak. 5(DMC) Worthless.

mi-sheadhar,** *a.* Heedless, inattentive. 2 Senseless. 3 Weak.

mi-shealbh, -a, -an, *s.m.* Misfortune, disappointment, ill-luck.

mi-shealbhach, -aiche, *a.* Disastrous, unfortunate, unlucky.

mi-shealbhachd, *s.f.* Disastrousness, unsuccessfulness.

mi-shealbhar,** *a.* Adverse, see mi-shealbhach. Gu m., *unluckily.*

†mi-sheamhas, -ais, *s.m.* Bad luck, mishap.

†mi-sheamhsar, -aire, *a.* Unlucky, unfortunate. 2 Ominous.

mi-sheirc, -e, *s.f.* Want of charity or benevolence, unkindness, uncharitableness. 2 Disaffection, dislike.

mi-sheircealachd, *s.f.* see mi-sheirc.

mi-sheirceil, -e, *a.* Uncharitable. 2 Surly, unaffectionate.

mi-sheòl, *v.a.* Mislead, misguide, misdirect.

————adh, -aidh, *s.m.* Misleading, act of misleading or misguiding. A' m—, *pr. pt.* of mi-sheòl.

mi-sheòlta, *a.* Wanting ingenuity, unskilful,inexpert, unhandy Gu m., *inexpertly.*

mi-sheòltachd, *s.f.ind.* Want of ingenuity, dexterity or skill, inexpertness, ignorance, un-

skilfulness.
mi-sheun, -a, *s.m.* Ill-luck, misfortune, mishap.
mi-shiobhaltsachd, see mi-shiobhaltachd.
mi-shiobhalta, -ailte, *a.* Rude, uncivil, unpolite. 2 Turbulent, troublesome, unquiet. 3 Impertinent.
————chd, *s.f.ind.* Turbulence, unquietness. Incivility, unpoliteness, rudeness, impertinence.
mi-shnas,‡‡ -ais, -an, *s.m.* Inelegance.
mi-shnasaich,(MS) *v.a.* Botch.
mi-shnasail, *a.* Homely, uncomely, inelegant.
mi-shnasalachd,(MS) *s.f.* Bungle. 2 Rusticity.
mi-shnuadh,(DMC) *s.m.* Palefacedness, sickly look.
————ail, (DMC) *a.* Palefaced, poorly looking.
mi-shocair, -e, -ean, *s.f.* Discomfort, uneasiness. 2 Disquietude, uncomfortableness, unsettled state.
mi-shocair,* see mi-shocrach.
mi-shocrach, -aiche, *a.* Troubled, disturbed, uneasy, uncomfortable. 2 Not firmly situated, unsettled, unstaid. Gu m., *uncomfortably.*
mi-shoilleireachd, *s.f.ind.* Inevidence.
mi-shona, *a.* Unhappy, unfortunate, unblest. Gu m., *unhappily.*
mi-shonas, -ais, *s.m.* Misfortune, mishap, unhappiness. 2 Bad luck.
mi-shuaimhneach, -eiche, *a.* Restless, uncomfortable, disquieted, disturbed, annoyed, distressed. 2 In confusion. 3 Causing trouble or confusion.
mi-shuaimhneachd, *s.f.* Same meanings as mi-shuaimhneas.
mi-shuaimhneas, -eis, *s.m.* Disquietude, trouble, vexation. 2 Agitation. 3 Discontentment.
mi-shuairc, -e, *a.* Inhumane. 2 Uncivil, unpolite. 3 Ungenerous. Gu m., *uncivilly.*
mi-shuairceas, -eis, *s. m.* Want of generosity, ungenerousness, illiberality. 2 Incivility, churlishness. 3 Inhumanity.
mi-shubhailceach, *a.* Unvirtuous.
mi-shùghar, -aire, *a.* Sapless, unsubstantial, pithless. 2 Indiscreet, imprudent. 3 Uncivil, unpolite.
mi-shuim, *s.m.* Heedlessness, indifference, carelessness, neglect, inattention. Cuir air m., *neglect, regard with indifference.*
mi-shuimeil, -e, *a.* Heedless, indifferent, careless. Gu m., *heedlessly.*
mi-shunnd,(WC) *s.m.* Spiritlessness, dulness.
————ach,(DMC) *a.* Spiritless, cheerless.
mi-shùrd, -ùird, *s.m.* Indolence, inactivity, laziness, lowness of spirits, dulness, want of industry.
————ail, -e, *a.* Indolent, inactive, lazy. 2 Melancholy, dull, sad.
————alachd, *s.f.ind.* Indolence, habit of laziness or inactivity.
mi-simean-dearg, -ein-deirg, *s.m.* Bog-mint, see cairteal.
mi-shomairt,** *s.f.* Foul or unfair play.
mi-sleach, *s. m.* see minnseag. 2 Sweetness—*Dàin I. Ghobha* for milseachd.
misleach i,(MS) *s.f.* Smoothness.
mislean,(AH) -ein, *s.m.* Very small potato.
mislean, -ein, *s. m.* Sweet meadow grass—*anthroxanthum odoratum.* 2 see beitean.
————ach, -aiche, *a.* Abounding in sweet mountain grass. 2 Springing up as grass, vegetative. Glacag m., *a grassy dell.*
mis eanach, *s.* see milearach.
mislein, see mislean.
mislich, *v.a.* see milsich.
misneach, -nich, *s.f.* [& *m.*] Courage, spirit, fortitude. 2 Alacrity. 3 Manliness. 4 Cheer. 5 Encouragement. Biodh deagh mh. agaibh, *be of good cheer;* glac m., *or* gabh m., *pluck up courage;* le dìth misnich, *for want of courage;* is beag m. tha sin a' toirt dhòmhsa, *that affords but slender encouragement to me;* cum suas do mh., *keep up your spirits;* thoir m. math dha, *keep him in good spirits;* cum am m. mhath e, *keep him in good hopes;* fear na misnich, *the brave man;* chaill e a mh., *he is quite disheartened;* cha'n 'eil a' mh. agad, *you have not the courage;* do mhac-samhuilt am m., *thy equal in courage.*

537. *Mislean.*

misneachadh, -aidh, *s.m.* Exhorting, act of exhorting or encouraging, abetting, encouragement. A' m—, *pr.pt.* of misnich.
misneachail, -e, *a.* Courageous, spirited, intrepid, brave, manly, undaunted. M. treubhach, *courageous and heroic;* gu m., *courageously.*
misneachair, *s.m.* Encourager, exhorter.
misneachas, -ais, *s.m.* see misneach.
misneachd, *s.f. prov.* for misneach.
misneachdail, -e, *prov.* for misneachail.
misnealachd, *s.f.* Courageousness.
misneil, -e, *a.* see misneachail. Gu m., *courageously.*
misnich, *pr.pt.* a' misneachadh, *v.a. & n.* Exhort, encourage, inspire, enliven, refresh, cherish. 2 Be encouraged, become spirited. 3 Venture. Am fear nach m. cha bhuannaich, *who won't venture shall not win—N.G.P.*
misreadh, see measradh.
mi-stàth, *s. m. ind.* Mischief, harm, evil. 2 Vanity, idleness. 3‡‡ *s.f.* Inutility.
miste, see misde.
mistear, -ir, -irean, *s. m.* Cunning, designing person, under-dealer.
mi-stéidhealachd, *s.f.ind.* Instability, unsteadiness, fickleness, giddiness, tottering condition.
mi-stéidheil, -e, *a.* Wavering, unsteady, not having a good foundation.
mi-steòrn, *v.a.* Mis-spend.
mi-stiùir, *pr. pt.* a' mi-stiùradh, *v. n.* Mislead, misguide, misadvise. 2 Steer in a wrong course.
mi-stiùireachd, *s.f.* Misconduct.
mi-stiùireadair,** *s.m.* Misleader, misguider. 2 Bad steersman.
————eachd,** *s.f.* Misguiding. 2 Missteering.
mi-stiùireadh, -idh, *s.m.* Misleading, act of misleading or misguiding, mismanagement. 2 Bad steering. 3 Anarchy. 4* Seducing, seduction. 5* Unmanageableness.
mi-stiùireach, -aiche, *a.* Misleading, misguiding. 2 Mis-steering.
mi-stiùrach, see mi-stiùireach.
mi-stiùradh, *pr. pt.* of mi-stiùir.
mi-stiùrannan, *s.pl.* Misdeeds, bad courses. 2 Bad intentions. 2 (DMC) Bad instruction, evil counsels.

mi-stuama, *a.* Immodest, immoral, unchaste. 2 Immoderate, intemperate. 3 Unguarded. Gu m., *immodestly.*

mi-stuamachd, *s.f.ind.* Immodesty. 2 Intemperance, immoderateness. 3 Unguardedness.

miteag, -eig, -an, see miotag.

miteagach, *a.* see miotagach.

mith, -e, -ean, *s.m.* Obscure or humble person, one of the common people. *pl* The common people Gach m. agus maith, *each peasant and noble.*

mi-thàbhachd, *s.f.ind.* Inefficiency. 2 Silliness, weakness. 3** Meanness. 4** Uncomeliness. 5 (DMC) Undaring.

mi-thàbhachdach, -aiche, *a.* Inefficient, unsubstantial. 2 Weak, silly, feeble. 3 Uncomely. 4**Mean. 5 (DMC) Unventuresome.

mi-thàbhachdas, -as, see mi-thàbhachd.

mi-thaicealachd, *s.f.ind.* Feebleness, infirmity. 2 Unsubstantialness.

mi-thaiceil,** *a.* Feeble, infirm, not stout, unable to give support. 2 Unsubstantial.

mi-thaing, -e, *s.f.* Thanklessness, ingratitude, ungratefulness.

mi-thaingealachd, Same meanings as mi-thaing.

mi-thaingeil, -e, *a.* Unthankful, ungrateful, not easily satisfied or pleased. Gu m., *unthankfully.*

mi-thairbhe, *s.f.ind.* Disprofit. 2 Damage. 3 Inefficacy. 4 Disadvantage.

mi-thaitinn, *v.n.* Dissatisfy, displease, offend. 2 Disagree with. Mh. e ris an Tighearn. *it displeased the Lord.*

mi-thaitneach, -eiche, *a.* Disagreeable unpleasant, offensive, unsatisfactory. Gu m., *unsatisfactorily.*

mi-thaitneadh, -eidh, *s.m.* Displeasing, act or displeasing or dissatisfying. 2 State of becoming displeasing or disagreeable. 3 Disagreeing with. 4 Disagreeableness. A' m—, *pr.pt.* of mi-thaitinn.

mi-thaitneas, -eis, *s.m.* Offence.

mi-thaitnich, *v.n.* Same meanings as mi-thaitinn.

mi-thapachd, *s.f.ind.* Inactivity, slowness, sluggishness, slowness, unalertness. 2 Inexpertness. 3* Cowardice.

mi-thapadh, -aidh, -aidhean, *s.m.* Misfortune, mishap. 2 Same meanings as mi-thapachd.

mi-thapaidh, -e, *a.* Inactive, sluggish, dull. 2 Not stout, infirm. 3(DMC) Unforward. Duine m., *a grumbler—Arran*; is mi-thapaidh (*pron.* miapaidh), *'tis pity—Arran.*

mi-tharbhach, -aiche, *a.* Unsubstantial, unprofitable, unfruitful, unproductive, fruitless. Tha iad uile m., *they are all nnprofitable.*

mi-tharbhachd. *s. f. ind.* Unprofitableness, unproductiveness, unfruitfulness.

mithean, *n.pl.* of mith.

mithear, -eire, *a.* Weak, infirm, crazy. Gu m., *crazily.*

mi-theist, -e, -ean, *s.f.* Calumny, reproach.

mi-theisteas,* -eis, *s. f.* Ill-repute, misallegation.

mi-theisteil, -e, *a.* Reproachful, disgraceful, disreputable.

mi-theistneas, see mi-theisteas.

mi-theòma,** *a.* Artless, unacquainted.

mi-theòmachd, *s.f.* Artlessness. 2 Sluggishness.

mithich, *a.* Timeous, opportune.

mithich, *s.f.ind.* Time, proper or fit time or season. Is m.dhuinn falbh, *it is time we should be off*; is m. dhuibh éirigh, *it is time you should rise*; cha'n uair roimh a' mh. e, *it is not an hour before the proper time*; air mh. a' dol dhachaidh, *on the eve of going home*; is mithidh a bhi 'bogadh nan gad, (see under gad); rug i leanabh roimh 'n mhithich, *she was delivered before the time.*

mi-thlachd, -an, *s.f.* see miothlachd.

mi-thlachdar, see mi-thlachdmhor.

mi-thlachdmhor, -oire, *a.* Ill-favoured, unhandsome. 2 Disagreeable, unpleasant, disgusting, contemptible. 3 Unsatisfactory. 4 Impersonable. 5**Choleric, angry. 6* Vexing, galling.

mithlean, -ein, *s.m* Sport, diversion, amusement. 2 Trick, crafty deed. 3†† Bad manners.

———ach, -aiche, *a.* Sportive, playful. 2 Cunning, crafty. 3 Mischievous. 4 Having bad manners.

mi-thlus, -uis, *s.m.* Hard-heartedness, want of tenderness or compassion, want of affection or feeling.

mi-thlusail, -aile, *a.* see mi-thlusar.

mi-thlusar, -aire, *a.* Hard-hearted, cruel, unfeeling, devoid of tenderness, compassion, feeling, or affection. 2 Cold, as clothes next the skin, uncomfortable.

mi-thlusarachd, *s. f. ind.* Harshness, cruelty, unkindness. 2 Coldness of manner. 3 Uncomfortableness, as of clothes.

mi-thogarrach, -aiche, *a.* Averse, unwilling, uninclined, backward. Gu m., *unwillingly.*

mi-thogradh, -aidh, -ean, *s.m.* Aversion, unwillingness. 2 Evil propensity. 3 Lust.

mi-thoil, -e, *s.f.* Want of will, unwillingness, reluctance, backwardness. 2 Ill-will.

mi-thoileach, -aiche, *a.* Averse, unwilling. 2 ‡‡Discontented, dissatisfied, displeased. Gu m., *unwillingly.*

——— ———adh, -aidh, *s.m.* Displeasing, act of displeasing or dissatisfying. 2 Dissatisfaction. A' m—, *pr.pt.* of mi-thoilich.

mi-thoileachas,‡‡ -ais, *s.m.* Discontentedness.

mi-thoilich, *v.a.* Displease, dissatisfy.

———te, *a.* & *past pt.* of mi-thoilich.

mi-thoillteannach,‡‡ *a.* Undeserving.

mi-thoillteannas,‡‡ -ais, *s.m.* Undeservedness.

mi-thràthaich, *v.a.* Mistime.

mi-threòrach, *a.* Weak.

mi-thròcair, -e, *s. f.* Cruelty. 2 Inclemency. [McL & D gives *s.m.*]

———each, -eiche, *a.* Cruel, merciless. Gu m., *cruelly.*

mi-thorachas,‡‡ -ais, *s.m.* Infertility.

mi-thruacanta, -ainte, *a.* Hard-hearted, unfeeling.

——— ———chd *s.f.* see mi-thruacantas.

——— ———s, -ais, *s.m.* Inclemency, uncompassionateness.

mi-thuarail,(DC) *a.* Ill-looking—*Uist.*

mi-thuig, *pr.pt.* a' mi-thuigsinn, *v.n.* Misunderstand, misconceive.

———se, *s.f.ind.* Misunderstanding, stupidity, want of comprehension, senselessness.

———seach, -eiche, *a.* Senseless, stupid, unintelligent. 2* Absurd.

———sinn, -e, *s.f.* Misunderstanding, act of misunderstanding, misconception. A' m—, *pr.pt.* of mi-thuig.

mithur,** see miodhoir.

mi-uaibhreach, -eiche, *a.* Condescending, humble, not proud. Gu m., *condescendingly.*

mi-uaigneach,** *a.* Not solitary, not secret. Gu m., *publicly.*

mi-uaill, -e, *s.f.* Humility, condescension, want of pride, ignobleness.

mi-uallach, -aiche, *a.* Dull, spiritless. 2 Humble, not proud.

mi-uasal, -uaisle [& -uasaile] *a.* Ignoble, mean, ungenteel. 2 Condescending.

mi-uaisle, *s.f.* Meanness.

miùg, see meòg.
miùghair, -e, -ean, see miodhoir.
——, -e, *a.* see miodhoir.
———each, -eiche, *a.* see miodhoir.
———eachd, *s.f.* see miodhoireachd.
miùinte, *a.* Lady-like.
mi-ùmhail, -aile, *a.* Disobedient, rebellious, contumacious, unsubmissive, insubordinate.
mi-ùmhlachd, *s.f.ind.* Disobedience, rebelliousness, disloyalty, insubordination.
miun, *s.m.* see miann.
miùran, -ain, -an, *s. m.* Carrot, parsnip. M. geala, *a parsnip.*
———ach, -aiche, *a.* Abounding in, or like, carrots or parsnips.
mi-urram, -aim, *s. m.* Dishonour, disrespect, disgrace.
———ach, -aiche, *a.* Dishonouring, disrespectful. 2 Dishonourable.
———achadh, -aidh, *s.m.* Dishonouring, act of dishonouring or disobeying. A' m—, *pr. pt.* of mi-urramaich.
mi-urramaich, *v. a.* Dishonour, disrespect, disobey. 2 Disgrace, degrade.
miùthair, -e, see miodhoir.
———eachd, *s.f.* see miodhoireachd.
miùthara,** see miodhoir.
mnà, (for mnatha) *gen.sing.* of bean.
mnai, *n. pl.* of bean (see mnathan.)
mnaibh, (for mnathaibh) *dat.pl.* of bean.
mnai'ealachd, see mnathalachd.
mnaoi, *dat. sing.* of bean. Thug e dha a nighean 'na mnaoi, *he gave him his daughter to wife ;* mar mhnaoi, *as a wife.*
mnaoidh, *dat. sing.* of bean.
mnaoidheil, -e, *a.* see mnathail.
mnatha, *gen.sing.* of bean.
mnathaibh, *dat.pl.* of bean.
mnathail, -e, a. Womanish, like a woman, effeminate. 2 Modest. Gu m., *modestly.*
mnathaileachd, see mnathalachd.
mnathalachd, *s.f.ind.* Womanliness, modesty.
mnathan, *n.pl.* of bean. Women. 2 Wives.
mo, *poss.pron.* My, mine. Mo cheum, *my footstep ;* mo nighean, *my daughter.* [Aspirates its noun.]
mò, *comp.* of mór. Larger, largest. 2 Greater, greatest. Is esan a's m., *he is the greatest ;* cha mh. orm thu 's an cù, *I do not value you more than a dog ;* dé is mò orms' thu ? *what do I care for you ;* cha mho a ni mi e, *neither will I do it ;* is mò e na sin, *it is greater than that ;* cha mhò leam dé a their thu is beagan, *I care miserably little for what you say ;* o 'n aon a's lugha gus an aon a's mò, *from the least to the greatest ;* is mò e na gach aon, *he is greater than all ;* cha mho orm, *I don't like ; I care not ;* gu ma mò a ni sibh, *may you do more ;* cha mhò na thu féin a gheibheadh e, *none but a friend like yourself would get it ;* na 's mo agus na 's mò, *or* ni bu mho 's ni bu mhò, *greater and greater ;* na 's mo na mise, *taller than I ; (2) any more than me.* In *Arran,* is mo tha 's nach 'eil, is a common formula of reply to questions answered with yes or no, and has the force of a modified or qualified assent, e.g. in reply to Are you tired ? it means a "little," the phrase 'S mo seadh 's no nach eadh, is similarly used.
†mo. *s.m.* see †modh.
mòan, see mòthan.
mob,** *s.f.* Mob. 2 Tumult. 3 Mop, tuft.
mobach,** *a.* Bushy, shaggy. 2 Moppy. 3 **Tufty.
mobag, -aig, -an, *s.f. prov.* see mabag. 2 Young girl with moppy hair.
———ach, -aiche, *a. prov.* for mabagach.
mobainn, *pr.pt.* a' mobainn & a' mobainneadh *v.a.* Maltreat, abuse, tug, handle roughly.
———, *s.m. & pr.pt.* see mobainneadh. Fhuair e a mh., *he got himself roughly handled.*
mobainneadh, -eidh, *s.m.* Maltreating, act of abusing. 2 Tugging, rough handling. A' m—, *pr.pt.* of mobainn.
moc, *v.a.* Move, yield, give way.
moch, moich [& muiche,] *a.* Early. O dhùsgadh na maidne moich, *from the awakening of early dawn.*
moch, *adv.* Early, betimes, soon. Éirich m., *rise early ;* moch an dé, *early yesterday ;* is m. a dh' éirich thu ! *how early you rose !* m. is anmoch, *early and late ;* m. am màireach, *early to-morrow ;* gu moch, *early.*
moch, *s.m.* Dawn, morn. O mhoch gu dubh, *from dawn till dusk ;* anns a' mh., *in early dawn.*
moch-abachd,** *s.f.* Early ripeness, prematurity.
moch-abaich,** *a.* Soon ripe, premature, precocious.
mochaireach,(MS) *a.* Early.
———d,(MS) *s.f.* Earliness.
†mochd, *s.f.* Promotion, advancement.
moch-eirigh, *s.f.* Early rising. Is tu a rinn a' mh. ! *how early you are a-foot !* rinn iad m., *they rose early ;* dean m., *rise early.* [*pron.* moch'erĭ.]
moch-éirigh, *a.* Rising early. M. agus ion-éirigh, *rising early and sitting late ;* bi subhach, sùgrach, m., *be cheerful, temperate and an early riser*—advice to those who do not wish to shorten their days.
mo chràdh ! *int.* My torment !
mo chreach ! *int.* Alas ! (my plundering.)
mo chreachadh ! see mo creach !
moch-ghlaodh, *s.m.* Early cry. Chual na creagan a mh., *the rocks heard his early cry.*
mochthrath, *s. f.* The morning, dawn. 2 (DU) "Morning" i. e. morning dram. 'S a mh., *in the dawn, early in the morning.*
mochthrath, *adv.* Very early. Bha e seo m., *he was here very early.*
———ach, -aiche, *a.* Early.
mòd, -òid, -an, *s.m.* Court, court of justice. 2 Assembly, meeting. 3 Petty court. 4 Baron baillie court. 5 Court at which presides the agent of landed proprietors, to adjust differences among tenants, and to take cognizance of all abuses of any portion of his employées' property. 6 Annual competition held in Gaelic literature and music, &c., under the auspices of An Comunn Gàidhealach. 7 Discontent. A' dol do 'n mh., *going to the court.*
mòdach, -aiche, *a.* Holding courts or meetings 2** Of, or belonging to, a court. 3 Fond of meetings, forensic.
†modh, *s.m.* Man. 2 Male of any creature. 3 Servant. 4 Work.
modh, -a, -an & -annan, *s. f.* Manner, mode, fashion, method. 2 Manners, good breeding. 3 Respect, honour. 4 Mood in *gram.* 5 Address. 6 *pl.* Morals, good morals. Duine gun mh., *an ill-bred man ;* air a' mhodh seo, *in this manner ;* air mh. àraidh *in a particular way.*
modh, *pr.pt.* a' modhadh, *v.a.* Train, tame, as a horse.
modhadh, -aidh, *s.m.* Taming, act of taming or training. A' m—, *pr. pt.* of modh.
modhail,** *a.* Mannerly, well-bred, courteous. 2 Moral, well-principled. 3 Delicate, mild. 4 Fashionable, modish.
modhalachd, *s.f.ind.* Mannerliness, good breeding, politeness, courteousness. 2 Morality, modesty, delicateness. 3 Mildness. 4**Ad-

dress.

modhalan-buidhe,§ -ain, *s.m.* Yellow rattle or cock's-comb, pennygrass—*rhinanthus crista-galli.* [** gives Red-rattle.]

538. Modhalan-buidhe.

modhalan-dearg,§ *s. m* Lousewort, red-rattle, see lus-riabhach.

modhan, -ain, *s. m.* The sound of a bagpipe or other musical instrument. †2 Childbirth, travail.

modhanach, -aiche, *a.* see modhail. 2 Ceremonial, customary.

modhanaiche, *comp.* of modhanach.

modhanail, -e, *a.* Ethical, moral. 2 Ceremonial, (see modhail.)

modhannan, *s.pl.* Ethics, means, modes, ceremonies, principles. Lagh nam m., *the moral law.*

mòdhar, -aire, *a.* Soft, mild, tender. 2 Quiet, calm, still. 3 Silly. 4 Gentle. 5 Limber, mannerly. 6 Precise. 7 Moving calmly. 8 Mettlesome. An gleann m. nan sruthan lùbach, *in the still vale of the meandering streamlets* ; oidhche mh., *a calm night.*

mòdharachd,** *s.f.* Mildness, composedness, sedateness, calmness.

modh-dhamh, -dhaimh,(AF) *s.m.* Plough-ox.

†modh-lann, -lainn, *s.m.* Tabernacle, tent.

†modh-mhargadh, -aidh, *s.m.* Slave market.

modh-oide,‡‡ -an, *s.m.* Moralizer.

mo dhòruinn ! *int.* My anguish !

modh-saine,** *s.m.* Slavery.

modh-sanntachd, *s f.* Slavery.

modh-searrach, (AF) Filly or colt of a cart-horse.

modh-sgéil,‡‡ -e, *s.* Apologue.

modh-siolaich, *s. m.* Remnant of seed left to produce more. 2 Manner of breeding.

mo dhuilichinn ! *int.* Alas ! (my sorrow.)

mòg, -òig, -an, *s.f.* see màg.

mogach, -aiche, *a.* see màgach.

mogach,‡‡ -aich, *s. m.* Raw youth. 2**Shaggy fellow. 3**Shaggy creature.

mogach, -aiche, *a.* Shaggy, hairy, rough. M. ladhrach, *shaggy and long-toed.*

mogaiche,‡‡ *s. f. ind.* Shagginess, hairiness, roughness.

mogaiche, *comp.* of mogach.

mògaiche, *comp.* of mògach.

mogain, *gen.sing. & n.pl.* of mogan.

mogais,(AC) Ancient form of anchor, formed of a cylinder made of heather ropes, bound strongly together, closed at one end and filled with stones. 2 see mogan.

mogal, -ail, -an, see mogul.

———ach, see mogulach.

mogan, -ain, -an, *s.m.* Stocking worn without the part to cover the feet. 2 Old stocking. 3 Boot-hose, sock. 4 Loose sleeve worn over another. 5 Blouse. 6 Leg of a pair of trousers or drawers. 7 (AC) Spirits distilled from oats—*Uist.* 8** Defect in a thread. A' dol 'nam mogan, *putting on their foot-gear—Arran* ; m. briogais, *the leg of trousers ;* dùthaich nam m. *the name given to Duirinish, Dunvegan by the inhabitants of Trotternish.*

†mogan, -ain, *s.m.* Young hero.

moganach, -aiche, *a.* Of, or belonging to, old stockings, or 2 boot-hose, or 3 whisky made from oats. Am Fearann m., (or mogaiseach), *the name given to Duirinish, Dunvegan, by the inhabitants of Trotternish.*

mogarra,‡‡ *a.* Robust, brawny.

†mogh, see modh.

mòghar, -aire, *a.* see mòdhar.

mogh-saine, see modh-saine.

mogh-sanntachd, see modh-sanntachd.

moghul, see mogul.

moghna, (AF) *s.m.* Salmon.

moghan, -uin, see modhan.

moglach, see mogulach.

moglachadh, -aidh, *s.m.* Husking, act of husking, or taking off husks. 2 (AH) The act, on the part of fish, of going into the meshes of a drift-net. A' m—, *pr. pt.* of moglaich.

moglaich, *pr. pt.* a' moglachadh, *v. a.* Husk, take off the husks, unhusk. 2 Knit. 2(AH) Get involved in the meshes of a drift-net.

———te, *past pt.* of moglaich. Husked, stripped of the husks.

moglaidh, *a.* Soft.

moglan-garbh, (CR) *s.m.* Sea-urchin—*Gairloch.*

mogul, -uil, -an, *s.m.* Husk, as of nuts. 2 Mesh, interstice of a net. 3 Shell, as of fruit. 5** Branch. 6**Skin of a boiled unpeeled potato. 7**Glebe. 8 Mesh, heddle-eye in loom. 9 Cluster, as of nuts. 10 (WC) Entanglement made by a conger eel in a herring-net. M. nan sùl, *the apple of the eye, the eye-lid ;* bha e 'sa mhogul, *he was hesitating, undecided —Glenlyon.*

mogulach, -aiche,*a.*Husky,abounding in husks. 2 Reticular, formed in meshes, as a net. 3 Like net-work. 4 Shelled, husked. 5 Plenteous. 6 Branchy.

mogulan-tràghad, (WC) *s.m.* Sea-urchin—*Poolewe.*

mogul-lìn, *s.m.* Mesh.

mogunn, -uinn, see mogul.

mogur, -uire, *a.* Bulky, clumsy, corpulent.

moibeal, -eil, -an, *s.m.* Broom, besom, mop.

———ach, -aiche, *a.* Of, or abounding in, brooms or mops. 2 Like a broom.

moibean, -ein, -an, see moibeal.

———ach,** *a.* In tufts, moppy.

———achadh, -aidh, *s. m.* Act of rubbing, scrubbing or washing with a mop. A' m—, *pr.pt.* of moibeanaich.

moibeanaich, *v.a.* Rub, mop, wash with a mop.

———te, *past pt.* of moibeanaich. Rubbed or washed with a mop.

moibill,* *pr. pt.* a' moibleadh, *v.a. & n.* Gnaw, half-chew. 2 Mumble, mutter.

moibleach,** *a.* Gnawing, chewing. 2 Half-chewing, nibbling.

moibleadh, -eidh, *s.m.* Gnawing, half-chewing, "making a mop of." 2** Nibbling. 3 Mumbling, muttering.

moibleas, *s.m.* see moibleadh.

moiblich,†† *pr.pt.* a' moibleadh, *v.a. & n.*Gnaw, half-chew. 2 Mumble.

moiche, *comp.* of moch.

moiche, *s.f.* Earliness, as of the day, dawn.

moichead, -id, *s.m.* Degree of earliness. A' dol am m., *growing earlier.*

mòid, *adv.* More, the more.

mòid, *comp.* of mór.

mòid, -e, *s.f.* Greatness, degree of greatness.

2 Height, size, bulk, dimensions.
Cha mh. gu'n tig e, *perhaps he will not come;* uime§sin bu mh. a dh' iarr na h-Iudhaich a mharbhadh, *in consequence of that, the Jews desired still more to kill him;* m. meanmnaidh, *the height of courage* ; bu mh. a ghlaodh e, *the more he cried ;* cha mh. e sin, *it is nothing the greater for that.*
mòid, *gen. sing.* of mòd.
mòid, -e, -ean, *s.* see bóid. 2 *v.* see bóid.
——each,** *s. & a.* see bóideach.
——eachadh, -aidh, *s.m. & pr.pt.* see bóideachadh.
mòideadh, see bóideadh.
moidheach, see maigheach.
mòidich, see bóidich.
———te, see bóidichte.
moidireadh, *a.* Out of sorts. 2 Heedless from sickness.
moidreag, see moighreag.
mòidte, see bóidte.
moigean, -ein, -an, see mogan. 2†† Dumpy little fellow. [mòigean in *W. of Ross.*]
moigeanach, -aiche, *a.* see moganach. 2 Fat, squat, plump, chubbed. 3 Jolly.
moigh, see muigh,
———each, see maigheach.
moigheanar,** *a.* Happy, festive.
moighre, *a.* Stout, robust. 2 Handsome. 3 Bouncing.
moighre, -an, *s.m.* Stout or handsome man. 2 *s.f.* Bouncing female.
moighreag, *s.f.* Plump girl, fat, plump, good-natured female child.
moil, -e, *s.f.* Hair matted together. 2 Heap cast up. 3 Kind of black worm. 4 see maille. 5‡‡ Swelling caused by hammering on the handle or head of a tool. [†† gives moile for No. 5.]
moilcheann, (CR) *Suth'd.* for muinichill.
moile, *s.m.* Impatience—*N. Argyll.* (boile.) [M. is due to eclipsis.]
moileadair,** *s.m.* Molester.
moilean, -ain, -an, *s.m.* Plump, fat child. 2** Bulb. 3 Little lump or heap. 4(AC) Kind of cake made on the palm of the hand. 5**Diminutive, rotund person. 6* Plump man. 7 Stout, young male animal.
moileanach, -aiche, *a.* Plump, fat and of low stature. 2 Bulby. 3 Having the hair matted together.
moileanach,* *s.m.* Plump young man.
moille, *prov.* for maille.
———ach,** *a.* Dilatory, tardy. 2 Pampering.
moilt,** see muilt.
moilteag, -eig, -an, *s.f.* Woman of low stature and stout ; term of ridicule. 2**Lusty little girl. 3**Comely little girl.
moiltean,** *s.m.* Hoggrel.
moim, -e, -ean, see maoim.
mòine, *gen.* mòna [& mòine,] §*s. f. ind.* Moss, mossy place, morass, bog. 2 Peat, turf. Cruach mòna, *a peat-stack ;* poll mòna, *a peat-moss* ; fòid mòna, *a peat ;* ris a' mhòine, *making peats.*

NAMES OF PARTS OF A PEAT-BANK, (bac-mòine, poll-mòna, ♉ poll-mòineach *or* ♉ poll-monach.) Names supplied by D. Murray, Aberdeen, are distinguished by a ♉.

bàrr-fhad, *top tier of sedgy marsh when cutting peats.* (barrfhad—♉.)
broinn a' phuill, ♉ *front of peat-bank.* (DMC) iochdar a' phuill.
caoran (an), ♉ *lowest tier in peat-bank.*
carcair, ♉ *portion of peat-bank stripped of the top turf from end to end.*
ceann a' phuill, ♉ *upper end of bank.*
druim a' phuill, ♉ *back of peat-bank.*
earball a' phuill, *lower end of bank.*
fàd a' ghàraidh, ♉ *second tier, if it is three deep.—prov.* for fòd a' ghàraidh.
fàd a' chaorain, *or* an caoran, ♉ *lowest tier in a peat-bank.*
resg, riasg, *or* rùsg, ♉ *top turf above moss, the sedgy marsh or moss of which the peats are composed.*
rudhan (an), ♉ *the small heap in which peats are built to dry, after being cut for a month, consisting of three peats and one on top.*
sgeir, (AH) *a peat-bank with an adjoining piece of heath-land on which the cast peats are spread to dry.*

When 12 peats are placed in a circle to dry, they are called *teinnteanan ;* 12 placed crosswise are *bocsaichean ;* peats placed diagonally (generally in long lines) are *air a chois bhig* ; set two and two diagonally in rows they are said to be *dà fhòid air aon.*
mòineach, see mòinteachail.
————ail, see mòinteachail.
moineag,** -eig, *s.f.* Bogberry.
———ag, -aig, -an, *s.f.* Pea- or bean-pod.
moineas, (AF) -eis, *s.* Female seal. 2 see moineiseachd.
————ach, see moineiseach.
mòine-chaibe, (DMK) *s. m.* Kind of peats cut with a common spade, without the surface of the ground having been previously pared—*Caithness.*
moineil,(AC) *a.* Slow.
moineis, *s.m.* False delicacy. 2 †† Slowness, laziness, see mainneas. 3(AC) *s.f.* Female of the grey seal.
moineiseach, -eiche, *a.* Low. 2 Diffident. 3 Dilatory, sedate, mild, dull, inactive, see mainneasach. 4 Fastidious. 5 (AC) Delicate, backward.
moineiseachd, *s.f.* Tardiness, dilatoriness, dulness, inactivity, sedateness, mildness.
mòine-sluasaid,(DMK) *s.f.* Kind of peats having the same breadth and thickness. They are cut by the operator standing in the face of the bank, and pushing the spade forward horizontally—*Caithness.*
mòin-fheur,§ -fheòir, *s.* Waved hair-grass, mountain grass, coarse meadow-grass — *aira flexuosa.* 2 Meadow.
moingeasach, see moineiseach.
†moingreult, *s.f.* Comet.
moinig, -e, *s.f.* Vanity, boasting, confidence. 2 Boasting of favours conferred. 3 Fastidiousness.
moinig,** *a.* Vain, boasting. 2 Trusting to.

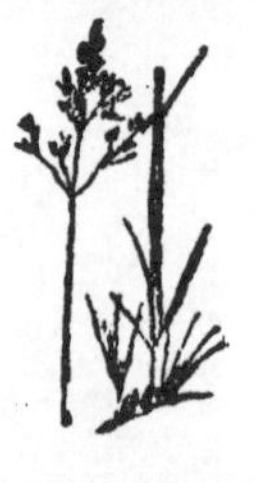

539. Mòin-fheur.

moinigeag, see meiligeag.
moinigeil,* -e, *a.* Fastidious, assuming indifference, making nice.
moinse, -an, *s.f.* Great pit. 2 Peat moss.
moinseach,** *a.* Abounding in large pits.
mòinteach, -eich, *s.f.* Mossy place, moss, peat-moss. 2 Moorland. M. liath, *grey moss ;* a' siubhal mòintich, *travelling the moors* or *moss.*
mòinteach, -eiche, *a.* see mòinteachail.
mòinteachail, -e, *a.* Mossy, boggy, marshy, fenny.
mòinteach liath,§ *s.f.* Bog-moss—*sphagnum.*
mòintean, *pl.* of mòine.
mòintich, -e, *a.* Moorish.
mòintidh, -e, *a.* Mossy, boggy, marshy, moorish.
mòintidheachd, *s.f.ind.* Bogginess, marshiness.
moipeal, -eil, -an, see moibeal.
moipean, -ein, -an, see moibean.

móir, *gen.sing.masc.* of mór.
moirb,** -ean, *s.f.* Emmet, ant.
moirbh, see moirb
móircheart, -eirt, *s.m.* Justice. 2**Mercy.
moircheas,**-eis, *s.m.* Falling sickness,epilepsy.
Moire ! see Mhoire !
móire, *gen.sing.fem.* of mór.
moireachd, see moraireachd.
móiread, -eid, see meud.
moireag, -eig, -an, *s.f.* Borer, toredo. 2‡‡Small shell—*testudo exigua.*
moireagad, *s.f.* see moirigeachd.
moireagan, *dim.* of moireag
moireal, -eil, -an, *s. m.* Boring iron, wimble, auger. 2 see moireag (deigh.)
moirealach, -aiche, *a.* Furnished with augers. 2 Like an augur 3 Boring like an auger.
moireamas,** *int.* †Marry *prov.* corruption of Moire (the Virgin Mary) or perhaps mispronunication of moramas, m' oram,or air m' urram, *on my honour*
moirear, -ir, -an, see morair
moirearachd, *s f.* see moraireachd.
moireas, -eis, *s m* Haughtiness pride. 2** Epilepsy.
moireasach, -aiche, *a* Haughty, proud. 2** Epileptic.
moireasadh,** -aidh, *s.m.* Epilepsy.
moirfhear, -ir, -an, *s.m.* see morair.
————achd, see moraireachd.
moirgean,(CR) *s.m.* Fat little person—*West of Ross-shire.*
moirneag,(AF) *s.f.* Small shell-fish. 2 Shell.
mòirneas, -eis, *s.m.* Great cascade or waterfall. 2 Volcano. 3 Melted metal. Mar mh. de theine theintich, *as a stream of lava.*
moirneasach,** *a.* Streamy, streaming.
moirt,** *s.f.* Dregs, lees.
moirteach,** *a.* Dirty, having dregs.
moirteal,** -eil, *s.m.* Cripple. 2**Rafter. 3** Mortar, plaster.
moirtear,** -eir, -an, *s.m.* Mortar.
moirteis,** *s.f.* Mortice. [Tenon, as given by ** is wrong.]
†mois, *s.* Custom, manner. Mois-leabhar, *a book on ethics.*
moiseach, *a.* Snouty, sullen, surly.
moisean, -ein, -an, see muisean.
moiseanach, -aiche, see muiseanach.
————d, see muiseanachd.
moislich,(CR) *v.n.* Stir (out of sleep)—*Strathtay.* Smoislich in *N. Argyll*—(AH) (mosglaich.)
moit, -e, *s.f.* Sulkiness, sullenness, moroseness. 2 Pride. 3 Short neck, as of a bird cresting up. 4 see moitealachd. 5* Pretended indifference about a thing one is very keen for, nicety about a thing one is fond of. Goic m., *a cocking up of the head with a short neck;* bean gun mh., *a wife without sulkiness.*
moitealach, -aiche, *a.* see moiteil.
moitealachd, *s.f.ind.* Fastidiousness, nicety, shyness, daintiness, pettishness, prudery, assuming airs of importance. 2 (MS) Toss.
moiteil, -e, *a.* Sullen, sulky morose. 2 Pettish. 3 Proud, gallant. 4 Airy, assuming airs, dainty, fastidious. 5 Shy. 6 Prudish. 7 Affectioned. 8* Pretending indifference. 9 Boasting. Maighdean mh., *a sulky maid, a prude.*
mol, *pr.pt,* a' moladh, *v.a.* Praise, extol. 2 Recommend, advise. 3*Exalt, magnify. Moladh m' anam Dia, *let my soul praise God ;* mholainn dhuit dol dachaidh. *I would recommend you to go home ;* mholainn dhuit na buinn a thoirt leat (*or* a thoirt as,) *I would recommend you to take to your heels.*
mol, -oil & -a, -an, *s.f.* Shingly beach. 2(DU) Shingle. 3(AF) Flock of birds.
†mol, -oile, *a.* Loud, clamorous.
†mol, -a, *s.m.* Number. 2 Flock. 3 Assembly, gathering. 4 Ball. 5 Heap. 6 Beam.
molach, *s. m.* (MS) Shough. 2 Rough-haired dog, poodle.
molach, -aiche, *a.* Hairy, rough. 2 Stormy. 3 Hoarse. Cas mh. Bhrain, *Bran's rough leg ,* a' mhuir mh., *the stormy sea ;* mar fhalluinn mholaich, *like a hairy garment.*
molachan,** -ain, *s.m.* Tuft of hair. 2 Hairy place. 3 Slough, bog. 4 Vessel.
molachas, -ais *s.m.* Roughness, hairiness. 2 Hoarseness.
moladair,** *s.m.* Applauder, approver.
moladh, -aidh, *s. m.* Praising, eulogising, applauding. 2 Act of praising or commending. Recommending, advising. 3 Act of recommending or advising. 4 Praise, applause. A' m—, *pr.pt.* of mol. M. na h-ainnir, *the virgin's praise ;* tha e air a dheagh mh., *he is well praised ;* cha mh. do mh., *your eulogy is no praise.*
molam,** *1st.sing.imp.* of mol.
molan, -ain, -an, Small temporary stack of corn, see mulan.
molanach, -aiche, see mulanach.
mo laochan ! *int.* Well done ! (my hero)
molar, *fut.pass.* of mol.
molcha,(AF) *s.* Horned owl, see comhachag-adharcaiche.
mòldair,(MS) *s.m.* see mòlltair.
moldair-ime, *s.m.* Butter-print.
mo léireadh ! *int.* Alas !
mo leòn ! *int.* Woe's me ! alas !
moll, muill, *s.m.* Chaff, dust. 2**Refuse. 3** Station. 4**Frame. Mar mh. air 'fhuadachadh le gaoith, *as chaff driven by the wind ;* leaba mhuill, *a chaff-bed.*
molla,(AF) *s.* Sheep.
mollach, -aiche, *a.* see mollmhor.
mollachd, *s.f.ind.* *Northern* form of mallachd.
mollaich, *Northern* form of mallaich.
mollar, see mollmhor.
molldair, *s.m.* Plasm.
mollmhor, -oire, *a.* Chaffy, abounding in chaff.
mollsgaid,(MS) *s.f.* Negligence.
————each, *a.* Negligent.
mòlltair, -ean, *s. m.* Mould or frame, for casting iron or other substance in a molten state. 2**Plasm. 3 Model.
molltair, -ean, *s.m.* Mill dues, multure, miller's toll.
mollte, *past pt.* Praised, lauded.
molluich, see mallaich.
mol mhògag, *W. of Ross* for muile-mhàg.
mol-mhuilinn,** *s. m.* Beam which turns round in a mill, and sets the whole in motion.
mol-olla,** *s.m.* Ball of wool.
†molrach,** -aich *s.m.* Giant.
molt, *gen.* moilte & muilt, *s.m.* see mult.
molta, *past pt.* of mol. Praised, extolled.
moltach, -aiche, *a.* Praising, laudatory, given to praising or commending. 2 Praiseworthy, commendable. 3 Ready to praise
moltachail, -e, *a.* Laudatory.
moltainneach -eiche, *a.* Recommendatory. 2 Panegyrical.
moltair, -ean, see molltair.
————,(CR) *s m.* Grist, grain to be ground—*Skye.* Mar mh. an opar *like grain in a hopper.*
molt-fhear,(MS) *s.m.* Applauder.
moluach,** -aich, *s.m.* Marsh.
momha, see mò.
momhaide,* see mòid.
momhar, see momharach.

momharach,** *a.* Stately, noble, pompous.
mo mhasladh ! *int.* Alas ! (*lit.* my disgrace !)
mo 'n, see mu 'n.
†mon, -oin, *s.m.* Truck.
mòna, *gen.sing.* of mòine.
monabhan, *s.m.* see monmhar.
mona-bhuachaill, see muna-bhuachaill.
monach, -aiche, *a.* see monadail. 2**Wily, cunning.
monachan, *s.pl.* Hills, mountains. 2 Moors. (better monaidhean.)
monadail, *a.* Mountainous, moorish, hilly. 2 Desert.
monadalachd,‡‡ *s.f.* Mountainousness.
monadh, -aidh, -aidhean, *s.m.* Mountain, moor, range. 2 Heath, heathy expanse, desert. 3 Tolerably level hill-ground. 4(AH) Any hill-pasture as distinguished from meadow and arable land. †5**Money. Air feadh mhonaidh, *through the moor* ; 's a' mhonadh, *on* (lit. *in*) *the hill* ; mullach a' mhonaidh, *the highest part of the moor.*
monag, see monog.
——an, (DC) *s. m.* Little child at the stage when he or she goes on all fours.
monaghair, -e, -ean, *s.f.* see monmhar.
————each, -eiche, *a.* see monmharach.
monaghar, see monmhar.
monaidh, *gen.sing.* of monadh.
monair, *gen. sing.* of monar.
mo nàire ! *int.* Alas ! (*lit.* my shame.) Mo nàire ort fhéin ! *fie upon you !*
mo nàire 's mo leaghadh, *int.* Alas ! alas ! (*lit.* my shame and my melting.)
mo nàire 's mo mhasladh ! *int.* O for shame !
monais, -e, *s.f.* Slowness, dulness. 2 Inattention, negligence. 3**Sedateness. 4** Gentleness. 5 (DMu) Sense, coherent talk, said of a patient. 6(AH) Clumsiness or awkwardness in any manual work. Am bheil m. aige ? *does he talk coherently ?—Black Isle.*
——each, -eiche, *a.* Slow, dull. 2 Inattentive, negligent. 3**Gentle. 4**Sedate.
——eachd, *s.f.ind.* see monais.
monaistir,** *s.f.* see mainistir.
monar, -air, -airean, *s.m.* Dwarf, diminutive person or thing. 2 Small matter, trifle. 3* Refuse. 4 Contemptible person or object. 5** Murmur. 6 Purling noise. 7†† Uproar. †8 Work. Tha, 's cha b' e m. e, *yes, and it is not the refuse—he is a great man or person.*
monaran, -ain, -an, *s.m.* Mote. 2**Dogberry.
monasg, -aisg, *s. f.* Chaff. 2 Dross, refuse. 3 Particle—*Arran.*
monasgach, -aiche, *a.* Abounding in chaff, dross, or refuse.
mong, muing, *s.m.* see muing. †2 Edge, border.
mongach,** *a.* Fiery. 2 Red.
mongach-mheur, *pl.* -aich-mheura, *s.f.* Hemlock, see minmheur.
mongaineach, -eiche, *a.* Maned.
mongair,** *s.m.* Shaver, trimmer, clipper.
mongar,** -air, *s.m.* Roaring.
mong-steudach, (AF) *s.m.* Fine-crested steed.
monlach,** *a.* Hairy, rough, shaggy. 2 Brushy.
monmhar, -air, -an, *s.m.* Murmur, uproar. 2 Detraction. 3 Complaint, grumbling. 4 Moaning. Is binn m. thonn do 'n ròn, *sweet is the moaning of waves to the seal.* [Sometimes monmhur.]
————ach, -aiche, *a.* Murmuring, complaining, grumbling. 2**Noisy.
monog,§ *s. f.* Bog- or peat-berry. 2 Cranberry. see muileag.
mo nuar ! ** *int.* Alas ! alack-a-day ! woe is the day !
monusg, see monasg.
mop,** moip, see mob.
mopach, -aiche, *a,* see mabach. 2 see mobach.
mopag, see mobag.
mór, *1st. comp.* mò. *2nd. comp.* mòid, *3rd. comp.* muthad, *a.* Great, large, of great size. 2 Great, many, of great number. 3 Great in extent, extensive. 4 Important. 5 Chief, principal. 6 Noble, of high rank. 7 Tall, of high stature. 8 Proud. 9 Lofty. 10 Familiar, much acquainted. 11 Valued, esteemed. 12 Hard, difficult of accomplishment. 13 Spacious, capacious. 14 Much, in great degree. 15 Abundant, copious. 16 Mighty, powerful. 17 Haughty. 18**Heavy. 19**Wide. 20 Corpulent, bulky. 21 Vivid, of lightning. 22 (DC) Notorious for evil qualities, or such as are not to one's credit—*Argyll.*
Duine m., *a great man* ; sluagh m., *a great* or *numerous people* ; an sluagh m., *the nobility;* ni m., *an important affair* ; cho m. as féin ris a' mhac-mhollachd, *as self-important as Lucifer* ; tha iad m. aig a chéile, *they are great chums* ; tha iad cho m. aig a chéile 's is urrainn iad, *they are as familiar as possible* ; tha e m. ort a dheanamh, *it is hard for thee to do it* ; tha e m. leat 'ga dheanamh, *you don't want to be bothered with it* ; bu mh. aca féin e, *they thought much of it themselves* ; is m. a dh' fhulaingeas cridhe ceart mu'm bris e, *a well-regulated heart will suffer much ere it break* ; bha 'n dealan m., *the lightning was vivid* ; thachair a bhràthair m. ris, *he has met one stronger than himself* ; eadar bheag is mhór, *both small and great* ; mór-uisge a' taomadh, *a great torrent pouring* ; gille m. mhic Eòghain, *the notorious son of Hugh—Argyll.*
mór, *adv.* Much, many. Is m. leam, *I think it too much* ; is m. leam sin a dheanamh, *I think it too much to go that length* ; is m. a dh'fhuiling mi, *greatly did I suffer* ; tha e ro mh., *it is too big* ; *2 it is too much* ; cha mh. a chì e, *few shall see it* ; cha mh. math a th' air, *it is not worth much* ; am m. leat na dh' itheas e ? *do you grudge what he eats ?* cha mh., *almost* ; cha mh. nach do bhuail e mi, *he almost struck me* ; cha mh. nach e, *'tis not quite that* ; is mór aig' e, an ironical expression meaning *little does he think of it,* or *he makes little of it—W. coast of Ross.*
mór, -a, *s.m. poet.* Renowned, famous or mighty person. 2 Chivalrous person. Co tha coltach ri m. nan cliù ? *who is like the mighty of renown ?* am beag is am m., *both great and small* ; cha mh. nach, *almost.* [Generally mòr in poetry.]
mòr, see mór. Mòr is the spelling adopted by all Gaelic grammars and dictionaries except MacBain's and MacEachan's. MacBain's orthography has been adopted here.
morabanas,(WC) -ais, *s.m.* Murmuring.
————ach, *a.* Complaining.
mòrach,** *a.* August.
mòrachadh, -aidh, *s.m.* Enlarging, act of enlarging. 2 Exalting, act of exalting of dignifying. 3 Aggrandizement. A' m—, *pr.pt.* of mòraich.
mòrachd, *s.f.* Greatness, majesty, dignity, rank. 2 Excellency. 3* Mightiness. Do mh. rìoghail, *your royal highness.*
moradh,** -aidh, *s.m.* Augmentation.
moragan,(WC) -ain, *s.m.* Lump-sucker (fish)—*Poolewe.*
moraghanach, -aiche, *a.* Calculous.
mòraich, *pr.pt.* a' mòrachadh, *v. a.* Enlarge, make greater. Exalt, dignify, ennoble, magnify. Mòraichear t' ainm, *thy name shall be exalted.*
——te, *past pt.* of mòraich. Enlarged, 2

Exalted, dignified, advanced.
mór-aigeannach, -eiche, *a.* see mór-aigneach.
mór-aigeantach, see mór-aigneach.
neo-aigeantachd, *s. f. ind.* Magnanimity. 2 Highmindedness. 3** Ambition.
mòr-aigne, *s.* Magnanimity. 2** Ambition.
———ach, -eiche, *a.* Magnanimous. 2** Ambitious. 3** High-minded.
———adh, -aidh, *s.m.* see mòr-aigne.
mòrail, -e, *a.* Majestic, magnificent. 2 Great. 3** Proud, pompous. 4** Powerful. 5** Vain-glorious.
mòrail,** -e, *s.f.* Triumph.
mòrainn,(DMK) *s.* The day before yesterday—*Skye.* [Used with the article.]
morair, -ean, *s.m.* Lord. 2 Earl. 3 Nobleman.
——— dearg, *s.m.* Judicial lord, law lord.
———eachd, *s.f.ind.* Lordship, title, dignity. 2 **Earldom.
mòralach, -aiche, *a.* see mòrail.
———d, *s.f.* Greatness, dignity, majesty, magnificence. 2 Excellence. M. rìoghail, *royal majesty* ; m. 'na shùil, *majesty in his aspect* ; cainnt na m., *excellent speech.*
moralta, *a.* Moral.
———chd, *s.f.ind.* Morality.
———iche, *s.m.* Moralizer.
moram,** (air m' urram) On my word, on my honour.
moramas,** Marry, a sort of oath, see moireamas.
móran, -ain, *s.m.coll.* Great number, multitude, many. 2 Much, great quantity. Tha m. aca ag ràdh, *many of them assert* ; m. eile, *many more* ; m. nithean, *many things* ; m. chuideachd, *much company* ; m. éisg, *a great quantity of fish* ; m. nighean, *a great number of daughters* ; tha 'm beagan air fàs 'na mh., *the few have increased into a multitude.*
móran, *adv.* By a great deal. M. na's fhaisge, *a great deal nearer.*

540. Moran.

moran,§ -ain, *s. m.* Meadow saxifrage, fair maids of France, first of May—*saxifraga granulata.* 2§ Heath-rush, stool-bent, see bru-chorcan.
mór-aoibhneas,** -eis, *s.m.* Great joy.
mór-aonach,** -aich, *s.m.* Great assembly. 2 Market-place. 3** Great heath or moor.
morarail, -e, *a.* Lord-like.
mòr-beam,§ *s.* Mulberry—*morus.*
morbhach,‡ -aich, *s.f.* Land liable to sea-flooding.
mór-bhaile, -bhailtean, *s.m.* see baile-mór.
morbhan, -ain, see borbhan.
mór-bhan-diùc,(MS) *s.f.* Arch-duchess.
mór-bhileach, -eiche, *a.* Broad-brimmed.
mór-bhruidhneachas, -ais, *s.m.* Magniloquence.
mór-bhuadhach, -aiche, *a.* Having great or noble qualities. 2 Heroic, conquering.
mór-bhuaidh, -e, -bhuadhan, *s.f.* Heroism, bravery. 2 Great conquest. 3 Heroic achievement.
†morc, *s.* see torc. 2 (AF) Sow.
†morc, *a.* Great, huge.
morcaich,** *v.a. & n.* Corrupt, rot, (also morgaich.)
———, *a.* Corrupt.
morcaidheachd,** *s.f.* Corruption.
morcas, -ais, *s.m.* Corruption, rottenness.
morchadh, see morbhach.
mór-chiontach, -aiche, *a.* Capital (criminally.)
morchlais,** *s.f.* Magnificence.
mór-chliabhach, -aiche, *a.* Broad-breasted.
mór-chliùiteach, -eiche, *a.* Greatly renowned.
mór-chnàmhach, -aiche, *a.* Big-boned.
mór-choinnde,** *s.f.* Fleet.
mór-choinneal, -choinnle, *s.f.* Flambeau, torch.
mór-cholàinneach, -eiche, *a.* Large or thick bodied, corpulent, bulky.
mór-chridhe, ** *s. m.* Great heart, generous heart. 2 Brave heart. 3 High or noble mind.
———ach, -eiche, *a.* Great-hearted, generous, magnanimous.
mór-chuairt, -e, -ean, *s.f.* Great circuit, grand tour. 2 Justiciary circuit.
mór-chuan, -ain, -antan, *s.m.* Great ocean.
mórchuis, -e, *s.f.* Pride, pomp, magnificence, splendour. 2 Boasting, vain-glory, ambition, state, pride, glory. 2 Exploit. Gu'n till thu le m., *that you may return with glory* ; crìonaidh do mh., *thy grandeur shall fade.*
———each, -eiche, *a.* Proud, pompous, magnificent, splendid. 2 Ambitious, high-minded, haughty, vain-glorious. 3 Powerful. 4 Heroic. Bu mh. a cheum, *proud was his pace.*
———eachd, *s.f.ind.* see mórchuis.
mór-chuisle,** -an, *s.f.* Artery, great artery.
mór-chuisleach, *a.* Having great arteries, arterial.
†morcroid, *s.m.* The highway. (marc-rod, *horse-road.*)
mordha,(AH) *s.* see morghath.
mòrdha, *a.* see mòr, mòrach, & mòrail.
———chd, *s.f.* see mòrachd.
mòr-dhàil, -ean, *s.m.* Great assembly, diet, congress, parliament. M. Bhreatuinn, *the British Parliament* ; m. na Gearmailt, *the Germanic Diet* ; m. shagart, *a conclave.*
mòrdhalach, ** *a.* Magnificent. 2 Proud, pompous. 3 Powerful. 4 Brave.
mòrdhalaich,(MS) *v.a.* Aggrandize.
mór-dhamh,(AF) *s.m.* Leader among cattle.
mór-dhéidh, *s. f.* Aspiration, ardent desire, great fondness.
mór-dhòchas, -ais, *s.m.* Sanguineness.
mór-dhuilleagach, -aiche, *a.* Broad-leaved.
mor'ear, -eir, see morair.
———achd, see moraireachd.
mór-earballach, -aiche, *a.* Broad-tailed.
mór-earrann, *s.m.* Great division, see roinn-ruith.
mo réire, *int.* Certainly.
mor-fhach, } see morbhach.
mor-fhaich, }
morfhaich, see morbhach.
mór-fhairge, -an, *s.m.* Great sea, ocean, high-sea.
mór-fhàs,** *s.m.* Train oil. 2 Great growth.
mór-fhear, see morair.
———achd, see moraireachd.
mór-fhearrann, *s.* Great land, see roinn-ruith.
mór-fhlaithe, *pl.* of mór-fhlath.

mór-fhlath, -aith, *pl.* -aithe & -aithean, *s. m.* Great chief. 2 Grandee, one of the nobility.
mór-fhleadh,** *s.f.* Great feast, epulation.

541. *Mór-fhliodh.*

mór-fhliodh, -a, *s.m.* Great masterwort—*peucedanum ostruithium.*
†morgach,** -aiche, *a.* Rotten, corrupt.
morgachadh, see morgadh.
morgadh, -aidh, *s.m.* Rottenness, corruption.
morgaich,** *v.a, & n.* Corrupt, rot, (also morcaich.)
morgan,(AF) *s.m.* Dog-fish.
†morgantach, -aiche, *a.* Magnificent.
———————d, *s.f.ind.* Magnificence.
morgha, *a.* see mór.
morghadair, *s.m.* Smelt.
mòrghaileach,** *a.* Boastful.
mór-ghairdeachas,** -ais, *s.m.* Rapture.
morghan,(CR) *s.m.* Gravel, shingle. 2 Bank of gravel or shingle. 3 Pebbly beach.—*West of Ross-shire.*
mór-ghaisge, *s.f.ind.* Heroism, prowess.
———————il, -e, *a.* Heroic, of great prowess.
morghath,‡ *s. m.* Fishing-spear, trident. 2 Large spear, javelin.
———————ach, *a.* Armed with fishing-spears or tridents.
mór-ghlonn, -ghluinn, *s.m.* Heroism, prowess.
mór-ghlonnach, -aiche, *a.* Heroic, of great prowess.
mór-ghnìomh, -a, -ara, *s.m.* Great deed, exploit.
———————ach, -aiche, *a.* Of great deeds, performing great deeds. 2 Magnificent.
mór-ghràin,** *s.f.* Abomination, detestation.
mór-inntinn, -e, -ean, *s.f.* Great or noble mind.
———————each, -eiche, *a.* Noble-minded. 2 High-minded, ambitious.
———————eachd, *s.f.ind.* Greatness of mind, magnanimity. 2**High-mindedness, ambition.
mór-ionghnadh, -aidh, -aidhean, *s.m.* Astonishment, amazement. M. air gach neach, *everyone amazed.*
mòrlanachd, *s.f.ind.* Labour performed by tenants for their landlord. 2**Duty. (bòrlanachd is a better form. The *m* is due to eclipsis—am b—.)
mór-lannachd,** *s.f.* Feat in swordsmanship. 2 Carnage.
mór-lannair,** *s.m.* Powerful swordsman.
mór-laoch,** -laoich, *s.m.* Hero, champion.
mór-leththromach, -aiche, *a.* Far advanced in pregnancy (also mór-leatromach.)
mór-leththromachd,** *s. f.* Advanced state of pregnancy.
morlo,(AF) *s.m.* Seal.
mór-luach, -a, *s. m.* Great value, great price. Cha deanainn air mh e, *I would not do it for a great reward.*
†mormanta, *s.m.* Wormwood.
mor-manta,§ *s.* Mugwort, see liath-lus.
mór-mhadadh, *s.m.* (AF) Wolf. 2 (AF) Pike.
mór-mhaor, -mhaoir, *s.m.* Lord-mayor 2 High-steward. 3 High constable. 4 see morair.
mór-mheanmnach, -aiche, *a.* High-minded, aspiring. 2 High-spirited. 3 Magnanimous.
mór-mheanmnachd, *s.f.ind.* High-mindedness, pride. 2 Magnanimity.
mór-mheanmnadh, see mór-mheanmnachd.
mór-mheas, -a, *s.m.* High esteem, admiration. Am m., *in high esteem.*
————,** *v.a.* Esteem greatly, value highly, respect.
mór-mhial,(AF) *s.f.* Whale.
mór-mhiann,** *s.* Aspiration.
mór-mhuinntir, -e, *s.f.* Great multitude. 2 Numerous household.
mór-mhùirne,** *s.f.* High spirit, mettle. 2 Gladness.
mòr-mhùirneach,** *a.* High-spirited, mettlesome. 2 Cheerful. Each m., *a mettlesome horse.*
mornaich, -e, *s. f.* Considerable quantity or number.
mòrnan, -ain, -an, *s.m.* Small timber dish.
moroich, see morbhach.
mor'-oich, see morbhach.
mór-righ, -righrean,‡‡ *s.m.* Emperor.
morran,§ *s m.* Seakale or cabbage, see praiseach bhuidhe.
mór-rath,** *s. m.* Great luck. 2 Continued luck 3 Prosperity.
mór-roinn, -e, -ean, *s.f.* Province (*lit.* Great division.)
—————each, -eiche, *a.* Provincial, of or belonging to, a province.
mor-sgoil, *s.f.* Academy.
mór-shàr, -àir, *s. m.* Hero, mighty hero. 2 Great distress or trial. Lann a' mhór-shàir, *the sword of the mighty hero.*
mòr-sheisear, *s.f.* Seven persons.
mór-shluagh, -shluaigh, *s.m.* Multitude, host. 2 Congregation. 3 Army.
———————ach,(MS) *a.* Legionary. 2 Many peopled.
———————achd, *s.f.* Populousness.
mór-shoillse,** *s.f.* Splendour.
mort, -oirt, & muirt, *s.m.* Murder, manslaughter. 2 Massacre. M. Ghlinne-Comhainn, *the massacre of Glencoe.* A' m—, *pr. pt.* of mort.
mort, *pr. pt.* a' mortadh [& a' mort] *v.a.* Murder, massacre, slay. (also murt.)
———ach, -aiche, *a.* Murderous. 2 Murdering, massacring.
———achail, -e, *a.* Murderous, sanguinary.
———adh, -aidh, *s.m.* Murdering, act of murdering, slaughter. A' m—, *pr.pt.* of mort. Na dean m., *do not kill ;* farmad is m., *envy and murder.*
———ail, -e, *a.* see mortach.
———air, -ean, *s.m.* Murderer, assassin. 2 Mortar.
———aireach, -eiche, *a.* Murderous, like a murderer.
———aireachd, *s.f.ind.* Murdering, massacring. 2 Murderousness.
mortal,** -ail, *s.m.* Mortar. 2 Lime.
mortar, -air, *s.m.* Mortar. 2 Lime.
mort-fhear, see mortair.
mór-thional,** *s.* Diet (meeting.)
mór-thir, -e, -ean, *s.f.* The mainland. 2 Continent. 3**Great shore. Mar neart tuinne gu m., *like a billow rolling in its strength to the main shore.* [** gives " Fàilt' ort-féin a mh. bhòidhich ! *hail, thou beauteous mainland !* " but this saying refers to the Morar district, incorrectly written Mór-thir' in Gaelic.]
———————each, -eiche, *a.* Continental, of, or pertaining to a continent.
———————each, -eich, *s.m.* Mainlander, native or inhabitant of the mainland.
mór-thorach, -aiche, *a.* Very fruitful.
mór-thorach, -aiche, *a.* Far advanced in preg-

nancy.
mór-thriath, -a, -an, *s.m.* Great prince or chief.
mór-thuil,** *s.m.* Deluge.
†moruach, -uaich, *s.f.* Mermaid, sea-monster.
mór-uachdaran, -ain, -an, *s.m.* High governor, viceroy, regent.
mór-uaisle, *s.f.ind.* High nobility or rank.
———-an, *s.pl.* The nobility, nobles.
mór-uasal,** *a.* Noble in birth. 2 Most noble, of the highest rank in nobility.
mór-urranta, -ainte, *a.* Very bold, daring, dauntless. 2**Self-confident. Gu m., *boldly.*
————chd, *s.f.ind.* Great boldness, intrepidity.
mór-ùthach, -aiche, *a.* Big-uddered.
†mos, *s.m.* Manner, fashion.
mò's, *adv.* Too. Tha a' chomain mò's mòr, *the compliment is too great.* [The s stands for *is* as in "tuille's mòr."]
†mosach, *a.* Of, or belonging to, fashion or manner.
mosach, -aiche, *a.* Nasty. 2 Filthy. 3 Worthless. 4 Insignificant. 5 Sordid, mean, avaricious, niggardly. 6* Inhospitable. 7 Rough, bristly. 8**Of dirty habits. Ni m., *a filthy thing* ; is tu tha m. ! *how inhospitable you are !*
mosag, -aig, -an, *s.f.* Tawdry, drabbish woman, 2 Worthless woman. 3 Mean, parsimonious or avaricious woman.
mosaiche, *comp.* of mosach.
————, *s.f.ind.* Nastiness. 2 Filthiness, smuttiness, scrubbiness, dirtiness. 3 Worthlessness, insignificance. 4 Avarice, parsimony.
————-ad, -eid, *s.m.* Hoggishness.
mosaidh, see musaidh.
mosan, -ain, -an, *s.m.* Nasty fellow. 2 Sloven. 3 Worthless fellow. 4 Avaricious fellow.
mosan, -ain, *s.m.* Chaff. 2 Refuse.
mosg,** see mosgan.
mosgaid,(DC) *s. m.* Sumph, "a chiel to whom Providence has denied gifts, without making him an indisputable idiot"—*James Hogg.*
mosgaid,†† *s.f.* Sloth, negligence.
————each, *a.* Sumphish, clownish.
————each, -eiche, *a.* Dull, heavy, slow, spiritless.
mosgail, *pr. pt.* a' mosgladh, *v.a. & n.* Waken, rouse. 2 Awake, arise from sleep. Mosglaidh iad o 'n eug, *they shall awake from death.*
mosgain, -e, *a.* Rotten, musty, carious, mouldy, worm-eaten, moth-eaten. Fiaclan m., *rotten teeth.*
————each, see mosguineach.
————eachd, see mosgain.
mosgal,(DU) -ail, *s.m.* Refuse, leavings.
mosgalach, -aiche, *a.* Watchful, vigilant, attentive. 2 Active. 3 (WC) Trashy, dirty.
————d, *s.f.ind.* Watchfulness, vigilance, wakefulness, observance.
mosgaltach, see mosgalach.
————d, see mosgalachd.
mosgan,‡ -ain, *s.m.* Mustiness, rottenness, cariousness. 2* Dry-rot. 3††Rotten tree.
————ach,†† *a.* Abounding in, or pertaining to, rotten trees. 2††Full of rotten trees. 3 Musty, rotten, carious, mouldy, grey. 4 Worm- or moth-eaten 5 Troubled. 6‡‡Rheumy.
mosganachd, *s. f* Rheuminess. 2 Mustiness, mouldiness.
mo sgaradh ! *int.* Alas ! woe's me !
mosgladh, -aidh, *s.m.* Act of wakening, causing to awake 2 Act of awaking rising from sleep. 3**Excitation. A' m—, *pr.pt.* of mosgail.
mosglaidh, *fut.aff.a.* of mosgail.
mosguineach, -eiche, *a.* Religiously inclined, devout.
mosguineachd, *s.f.ind.* Devoutness.
mosrach, -aiche, *a.* Caressing coarsely, using indecent freedoms.
mosradh, -aidh, *s.m.* Coarse dalliance, maudlin civilities, indecent freedoms. 2 Brutality, brutal licentiousness.
mosraiche,* *s.f.* see mosaiche.
†mota, *s.m.* Mount. 2 Mote.
†moth, *s.m.* Male of any creature.
moth,** *s.m.* Sex.
moth, "air a' mhoth 'n dé," *Arran* for "air bhò 'n dé," *the day before yesterday.*
motha,(CR) Too (good, soon, &c.) Tha e motha 's tràth, *it is too early—Arran* for, tha e tuilleadh 's tràth—CR.
†mothach, -aiche, *a.* Fertile, fruitful. 2 Pregnant.
mothachadh, -aidh, *s.m.* Act of feeling, perceiving. 2 Sense of feeling, sensibility. 3 Attending. A' m—, *pr.pt.* of mothaich. Chaill e a mh.. *he lost his sense of feeling* ; muinntir air dhaibh am m. a chall, *people who being past feeling* ; duine gun mh., *a senseless man.*
mothachail, -e, *a.* Sensible, observant, perceptive. 2 Feeling, kind, considerate.
mothaich, *pr. pt.* a' mothachadh, *v.a.* Perceive, observe. 2 Feel, know, understand. M. seo, *feel this* ; mh. sinn a ghuth 'ga thréigsinn, *we noticed his voice failing* ; mh. sinn gun làth a mheòir, *we noticed his fingers without feeling, becoming feeble* ; an do mhothaich thu e 'dol seachad ? *did you observe him passing ?* ; mh. iad do 'n righ, *they observed the king—W.& S. 2.22* ; mh. an sgioba do dh'fhearann, *the crew observed land—McD. 166.1* ; mh. an rìgh dhuinn a' toirt a chlaidheimh a mach, *the king felt us taking his sword away—W.H. 1.14.*
————eadh, see mothachadh.
————te, *a.* Discreet.
mòthail, *s.f.* Loud lowing. 2 Repeated or continued lowing—*Perthshire.* see mòdhar.
mothaileachd,** *s.f.* Apprehensiveness.
mothal, -ail,(DMK) *s.m.* Refuse, particularly of fish. M. iasg, *refuse of fish—W. coast of Ross.*
mothalachd,‡‡ *s.f.ind.* Feeling, perception.

542. Mòthan.

mòthan,§ *s.m.* Bog-violet—*pinguicula vulgaris.* 2 (AF) Steep grass, earning grass. On cows' milk it acts like rennet. 3 (AC) Love-philtre. The woman who gives it goes upon her left knee and plucks nine roots of the plant (bog-violet,) and knots them together, forming them into a "cuach" or ring. It is placed on the mouth of a girl to make the man who kisses her her bond-man, under parturient women to ensure safe delivery, and is carried by wayfarers to safeguard them on their journeys. If a man makes a miraculous escape, it is said of him, Dh'òl e bainne na bó bà a dh'ith am m., *he drank the milk of the guileless cow that ate the* mothan.
†mothar, -air, -airean [& -thraichean,] *s.m.* Bunch, cluster. 2 Clump of trees. 3 Tuft of grass. 4 Green grass. 5 Park, enclosure.

mòthar, -air, *s.m.* Loud or great noise. 2 Murmur. 3 High or swelling sea. 4 Deep toned sound, as of a person in a cave. 5††Echo. 6 Melodious sound. Thug e m. as, *he gave a most appalling cry;* chuala sinn m., *we heard a most unearthly sound.*
mothar, -aire, *a.* see mòdhar.
——ach, -aiche, *a.* High-sounding, loud.
motharachd, see modharachd.
moth-chat, -ait, (AF) *s.m.* Tom-cat.
mothrach, -aich, *s.m.* Damp woody place.
mo thruaighe ! *int.* Alas ! (*lit.* my misery.) Mo thruaigh mi ! *woe's me !*
mothuchail, see mothachail.
mothuich, see mothaich.

543. *Moth-ùrach.*

moth-ùrach,§ *s.* Early orchis—*orchis mascula.*
mra, see mnatha.
mrathan, see mnathan.
mu, *prep.* About, around. 2 Of, concerning. 3 On account of, for. Mu'n cuairt, *about, round about;* mu thimchioll, *about, around;* 2 *concerning;* mu choinneamh, *opposite;* mu dheich mìle, *about ten thousand;* bha iad a' bruidhinn mu d' dhéidhinn, *they were speaking about you;* a' taomadh mu a chliabh, *pouring about his breast*, leig leo dol mu chùl a' ghnothaich, *let them take a back seat:* ciod mu 'm bheil thu ? *what are you about ?* òigh mu 'm bheil mo bhròn, *a maid for whom is my grief;* m' a càirdean, *about her friends.* In *the South-west* mu is used for gu, as, chaidh e mu thuath, *he went to the north;* tha e mu thuath, *he is in the north;* 'nuair a bhitheas an sgadan mu thuath, *when the herring is in the north;* an tìr mu thuath, *the north country.* [One cannot say "tha e gu tuath," although "chaidh e gu tuath" is quite correct.] Chuairtich e mu h-aon agus mu dhà, *he went round it once and twice—W.S.2.98;* thàinig an té mu dheireadh a mach, *the last (female) one came out.*
Thus combined with the personal pronouns: umam, *about me;* umad, *about thee;* uime, *about him;* uimpe, *about her;* umainn, *about us;* umaibh, *about you;* umpa, *about them.* [Aspirates a noun sing., definite or indefinite, and governs the dative case.]
mù, for mò, *comp.* of mór.
mu, *conj.* see mu'n.
muabhraighe,** *s.f.* Platform.
†**muadh**, *v.a.* Form, shape.
muadh,** -aidh, *s.m.* Form, shape, image. 2 Cloud.
——,** *a.* Soft, moist.
——air,** *s.m.* Rogue.
muadh-bhràighe, see muabhraighe.
muaidh,** *a.* Shapely, well-formed. 2 Noble, good. 3 Soft, tender. 4 Middle. Loingeas mh., *a well-formed ship.*
muaidh,** *s.f.* Sound. 2 Cloud.
mual, -ail, *s.m.* Top of a hill.
mualach,** -aich, *s. m.* Way, passage. 2 Cowdung.
mualaich, **mualan**, } *s.m.* (DMC) Bellowing—*Uist.*
muasgan, (AF) *s.m.* Shellfish, said to open like a boot—*Arran.*
——,(CR)*pl-* -ain & -anag, *s. m.* Shellfish like the fresh-water pearl-mussel, about the same length—3 to 4 inches—but broader and thicker; its shell is not so dark as that of the *madadh*, and both are smaller than the *eachan.* (brallach in *Lewis.*)
muasgan-caol, *s.m.* Prawn.
mubran,** -ain, *s.m.* Corn heated in the mow.
——ach,** *a.* Heated, as corn in the mow.
muc, muic, -an, *s.f.* Sow, pig. 2 Perch. 3 The heap raised over the mouth of a vessel in measuring. 4††Large hay-rick. 5* Large ball of snow.
†**muc**, muic, -an, *s. f.* Instrument of war, by which besiegers were protected when approaching a wall. It was covered with twigs, hair-cloth and raw hides, and moved on three wheels.
muc-abhainn, (AF) *s.m.* Bear.
mucach, -aiche, *a.* Swinish, piggish. 2 Abounding in swine. 3 Heaped up, as a measuring vessel. 4* Dirty. 5 Surly. 6 Stupid. 7 †† Abounding in hay-ricks. A' ghràisg mh., *the swinish mob.*
——an,** -ain, *s.m.* Clown. 2 Piggish fellow.
——d,** *s.f.* Swinishness, hoggishness. 2 Moroseness. 3 Grimness.
mucag, -aig, -an, *s.f.* Hip, fruit of the dog-rose. 2 Little sow or pig. 3 *rarely* Cup. Mucagan is sgeachagan, *hips and haws;* m. fhailm, *a hip of the dog-rose—Colonsay.*
mucagach, *a.* Abounding in hips, or 2 in little sows or pigs.
mucag-fhiacal,(DMC) *s.f.* Gumboil, boil on the neck.
mucaibh, *dat. pl.* of muc.
mucail, -e, *a.* see mucach.
muc-ainidhe,(AF) *s.f.* Sow with young.
mucair, -ean, *s.m.* Swine-herd. 2 Swine-dealer. 3**Hoggish fellow.
——eachd, *s.f.ind.* Herding of swine. 2 Dealing in swine.
mucalachd, *s.f.ind.* Swinishness, hoggishness.
mucanta,** *a.* see mucach.
muc-bhiorach, -aich, -an-biorach, *s.f.* The long-beaked porpoise. 2 Bottle-nosed dolphin. 3 Beaked whale.
muc-bhlonag, -aig, *s. f.* Hogs' lard, swine's grease.
muc-bhuachaill, -ean, *s.m.* Swine-herd.
muc-bhuachailleachd,** *s.f.* Swine-herding.
muc-creige, *s.f.* The fish lump-sucker—*cyclopterus lumpus.* 2 Ballan wrasse, see muc-ruadh.
muc-disgearnach,(AF) *s.f.* Fierce boar.
muc-fàileag, -an-fàileag, see mucag.
muc-failm,* *s.f.* see mucag.
muc-fhinn,(AF) *s.f.* Milk pig, brood sow.
muc-forais,(AF) *s.f.* House-fed pig.
muc-ghaineamh, -eimh, *s. f.* Sandbank. 2 Quicksand.
muc-glasach,(AF) *s.f.* Fatted pig.
much,(AC) see moch.
mùch, *v. a.* Quench, extinguish. 2 Smother, suffocate. 3 Press upon, squeeze together.

4 Quell, pacify. 5 Mutter, hum, sing in a low tone or voice. Na mùchaibh an spiorad, *do not quench the spirit*; m. fonn, *utter an air.*

†much, -a, *s.m.* Grief, affliction. 2 Smoke.

†mucha,(AF) *s.* Long-eared owl, see mulchan.

mùchach, -aiche, *a.* Extinguishing, that extinguishes or quenches. 2 Suffocating. 3 Pressing or squeezing together. 4 Muttering, humming.

mùchadair, -ean, *s.m.* Extinguisher.

mùchadh, -aidh, *s.m.* Act of quenching or extinguishing. 2 Smothering, suffocating, act of suffocating. 3 Act of pressing upon or squeezing together. 4 Act of quelling or pacifying. 5 Act of muttering, humming or singing in a suppressed voice. 6 Extinction, suffocation. 7 (DU) Asthma, [with art.] A' m—, *pr.pt.* of mùch.

muchag,** -aig, *s.f.* Broom-rape.

muchais,(DMK) *s.pl.* Moths—*Caithness*

muchag,§ *s.f.* The class of plants known as *orobanchaceæ.*

mùchan, -ain, *pl.* -an [& -ain,] *s. m* Vent or chimney. *prov.*

————ach, (CR) *a. Blair Atholl* for mùganach.

———— -teine, (DMC) *s. m.* Half-extinguished fire.

mucheirigh, see mocheirigh.

mu choinneamh, *prep. phrase.* Opposite, over against. Bha dorus mu choinneamh a h-uile là anns a' bhliadhna air an taigh, *there was a door for every day of the year in the house*; tha airgiod agam mu choinneamh a' mhàil, *I have money to meet the rent.*

mùchta, see mùchte.

mùchte, *past pt.* of mùch. Extinguished, quenched. 2 Suffocated. 3 Pressed upon, squeezed together. 4 Quelled. 5 Muttered, hummed. M. fo bhròn, *suffocated* or *oppressed with grief.*

muchthrath, see mochthrath.

muclach, -aich, *s.m.* **Herd of swine. 2†† *s.f.* Piggery.

muclanag, *s.f.* Lard. (muc-bhlonag.)

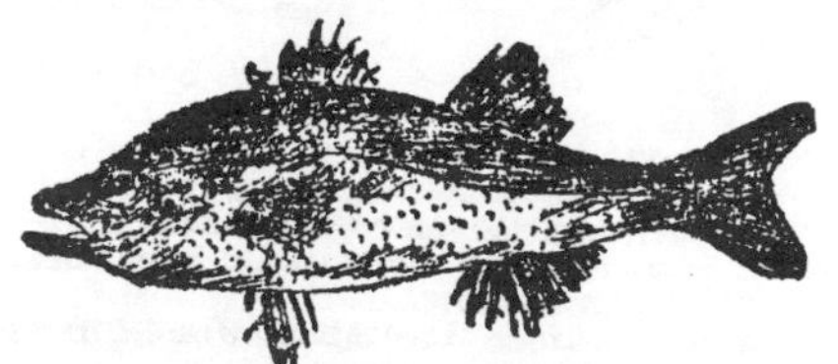

544. Muc-locha.

muc-locha, -uic-, -an-, *s.m.* The common perch.

muc-lochaidh, see muc-locha.

muc-mhara, -uic-, -an-mara, *s.f.* Whale. 2(AF) Sea-hog, seal. 3 (AF) Porpoise.

mucnach,** *a.* Hoggish, swinish, morose.

————d,** *s. f.* Hoggishness, swinishness, moroseness.

mucraidh, *s. pl.* Herd or sounder of swine. 2 Gammon of bacon. 3**Far.

545. Muc-ruadh.

muc-ruadh,- uic-, -an-ruadha, *s.f.* The fish ballan wrasse—*labrus maculatus.* (muc-creige.)

muc-sgideil,†† see muc-bhiorach.

muc-sheilche,(WC) *s. f.* Fresh-water monster, said to have been often seen in Loch Maree and neighbouring lochs by anglers and others. The late Mr. Bankes of Letterewe tried, at great expense, to drain Loch-na-béiste, near Aultbea, to prove the identity of one seen there, but failed. It is thought to be a huge eel.

muc-shneachda,-uic-,-an-, *s.f.* see muc-sneachdaidh.

————————idh, -uic-, -an-, *s.f.* Monster snowball.

muc-steallain,* *s.f.* Porpoise.

mucuin, (muc-fhinn) (AF) *s.f.* Snouted pig or other animal.

mucusg,** *s.m.* Swine's grease.

mùd, see mòd.

mu d', for mu do.

mudach,** *a* Gross.

546. Mùdag.

mùdag,(MMcD) *s.f* Wool-basket, about 3 ft. in height made of straw. The top part called *a' ghuite*, is used for holding the carded wool (peurdan), when spinning, the uncarded wool being placed in the bottom part—*W. of Ross & Lewis.* (mùrlag in *Argyll*—Fionn.)

mudag,(AF) *s.f.* Maw-worm.

mudaidh,** *a.* Dun-coloured.

mùdan, -ain, -an, *s.m.* Cover, covering. 2 Covering, as of skin or leather for a gun.

mùdan-croicne,** *s.m.* Bit of skin to cover the lock of a gun.

†mudharn, -airn, -an, *s.m.* Ankle.

mu dhéibhinn, see mu dhéidhinn.

mu dhéidhinn, *prep.* Of, about, concerning. Mu dhéidhinn seo, *concerning this*; mu m' dh,, *concerning me*; mu d' dh., *about thee;* m' a dh., *concerning him*; m' a déidhinn, *concerning her;* m' ar d., *concerning us*; m' ur d., *concerning you*; m' an d., *concerning them.*

mu dheireadh, *adv.* At last, at length.

mu dheireadh thall, *adv.* After all.

mùg, -ùig, -an, *s.f.* see mùig. 2* Snuffle through the nose.

mug,** -uig, -an, *s.f.* Mug.

——ach, -aiche,*a.* Snuffling. 2 Speaking through the nose. 3 Gloomy, cloudy. 4 Of a gloomy countenance. 5 Sullen, surly, morose. 6 Guttural. 7 Murky, misty. O chùl nan sliabh m., *from behind the misty mountains.*

mùgach,* -aich, *s.f.* see mùgag.

mùgag, -aig, -an, *s.f* Surly, morose woman. 2 Snuffling woman.

mùgaich, -e, *s.f.* Snuffling voice. 2 Snuffle. 3 Surliness, moroseness. 4 Cloudiness, gloom.

mugaid, *s.f.* Contents of a dyeing-vat. 2 Dyeing-vat.

mùgair, -ean, *s.m.* Gloomy, surly or morose fellow. 2 Snuffling fellow, snuffler.

————eachd, *s.f.ind.* Inhospitality. 2 Snuffling.

mugairle, *s.* Bunch of nuts—*Glenmoriston.*

mùgalach, see mùigeanach.

mùgan, -ain, -an, see mùgair. 2 *pl.* for mùigean, *pl.* of mùig.
mugan,** -ain, *s.m.* Mug.
mùganach,(CR) *a.* Damp and misty (of weather)—*Perthshire.* (muggy.)
†mugart,** -airt, *s.f.* Hog. 2 Hogs' flesh.
mùgh, *v. a.* Kill, destroy, see mùth.
mugha, see muthadh.
———ch, *a.* Gloomy—*Suth'd.*
mughadh, see mùthadh.
mughairn, see mugharn.
mughairneach,* *a.* Having large ankles.
mughard,§ -aird, *s.m.* Mug-wort, see liath-lus.
mugharn,* *s.m.* Ankle.
mùghtach, -aiche, *a.* see mùiteach.
———d, see mùiteachd.
mugna. see moghna.
muic, *gen. sing.* of muc.
muiceanach, -aich, *s.m.* Mean person, plebeian.
muiceil, -e, *s.f.* see muic-fheòil.
muic-fheoil, -fheòla, *s.f.* Pork.
mùiche,** *s.f.ind.* Earliness. 2 Dawn.
mùiche,* *s f* Dulness, sadness. 2 Mistiness, darkness, gloom.
muiche, *comp.* of moch, *prov.* for moiche.
———ad, -id, see moichead.
muicnis,** *s.f.* The rope which ties a basket on a porter's back.
mùidh, -ean, see muing.
muidh,(DMC) *v.* see muigh.
muidhe, *pl.* -an & -achan, *s.m.* Churn. Thoir a mh., *churn (lit.* bring to churn—*Lochcarron, Gairloch & Torridon.* 2(CR) Paddle-churn—*Lochbroom.*
———ach, -eiche, *a.* Of, or belonging to, churns.
mùidheach, -eiche, *a.* see muingeach.
muidheachan, -ain, -an, *s.m.*, *dim.* of muidhe. Little churn.
mùidheadh, see mùigheadh.
mùidhean, -ein, -an, see màidhean.
muidhe-buana,(CR)*s.m.*Harvest-home—*Arran.*
muidhe-làgain, *s m* Sowens-tub.
muidse, -an & -achan. *s. f.* [*m.* in *Badenoch.*] Woman's common head-dress, mutch, linen cap. [*m.* in *Gairloch* where it is muisde.]
mùig, -ean, *s.m* Cloudiness, darkness, gloom, 2 Frown. 3 Gloominess, surliness, discontented expression of countenance. 4 Melancholy, sadness, sorrow. 5 Snot, snivelling nose. 6** Mistiness, smoke. 7 Gloomy sky. Cuir m. ort, *frown* ; torra fo mh., *mist-covered hills* ; sheall e orm fo na mùgan (mùigean), *he looked at me from under his scowling eyebrows.* [†ᵀ gives *s.f.* ; McL & D gives *s.m.* but *gen. sing.* -e.]
mùig, *v.a. & n.* Quench, smother, suffocate. 2 Suppress, quash. 3 Become gloomy, misty or dark.
mùige, *s.f.* see mùigeachd.
———ach, -eiche, *a.* Misty, gloomy, dark. 2 Surly, frowning. 3 Cold, reserved, shy. O chùl nan sliabh m., *from behind the misty mountains.*
———achd, *s.f.ind.* Mistiness, gloominess, darkness. 2 Surliness. gloominess. 3 Smokiness.
———adh, -idh, *s.m* Act of quenching or suffocating. 2 State of becoming dark or gloomy. A' m—, *pr.pt.* of mùig.
mùigean, -ein, -an, *s.m* see mùgair. 2**Mist.
———ach, -aiche, *a* Surly, churlish. 2 Gloomy. 3 Misty. 4 Shy.
———achd, *s.f.ind.* see mùigeachd.
mùigeas, -eis, -an, *s.m.* Sour, gloomy or downcast look. 2 Surliness. 3 Snuffling.
———ach, -aiche, *a.* Sour, gloomy, downcast.
mùigeil, -e, *a.* see mùigeach. 2‡‡Misty, dark, obscure.
muigh, *adv.* Out, without, outside. 2 Superficially. A m., *on the outside ;* a chum am m. is am mach, *that, by all means ;* abair ris a bhi an seo am màireach muigh 's a mach, *tell him to be here, by all means, to-morrow.*
mùigh,** *v.a.* Fail, falter. 2 Fall. 3 Be defeated. 4 Decay. 5 (DMC) Threaten.
muigh-buan, *s.m.* see muidhe-buana.
muighe, -an, -achan, see muidhe.
muigheach,‡ -eiche, *a.* see muidheach.
———,(MS) *a.* Dareful, daring. 2 Huffish.
———d, see mùigheadh.
mùigheadh, (MS)*s.m.* Bravado. 2 Menace, commination, threat.
muighear, (MS) *s. m.* Bully, threatener. (for maoidhear.)
muighte,** *past pt.* Changed, altered. (mùthte.)
———ach, see mùiteach.
muigire,* *s.m.* see mùgair.
mùig-mhonadh,** -aidh, *s.m.* Misty mountain, misty hill.
muil, -e, -idhean,*s.m. & f.* see muileid maol & maoile.

547. Muilceann. *548. Muileag.*

muilceann, -inn, *s.m.* The plant spignel or baldmoney—*meum athamanticum.* 2 Fellwort—*swertia perennis,*is given by some dictionaries, but it is a different plant, and is not now found in Britain—§.
muilceannach, -aiche, *a.* Abounding in, or belonging to, spignel or baldmoney.
muilcheeann,(CR) *W. of Ross-shire* for muinichill.
muilchear,(CR) *E. Perthshire* for muinichill.
muilchill, see muinichill.
muilchinn, -ean, see muinichill.
muilchir, *Perth* for muinichill.
muilcionn, see muinichill.
muileach, -aiche, *a.* Dear, valued, beloved.
muileacha-mhàg, *s.pl.* of muile-mhàg.
muileag,§ -eig, -an, *s.f* Cranberry (*lit.* the frogberry)—*vaccinium oxycoccos.* 2**Frog.
———,‡‡, -eig, -an, *s.f.* Dear or beloved female.
———ach, -aiche, *a.* Abounding in cranberries, or 2 in little frogs.
muileann, -inn, *pl.* -an, & muilnean, *s.m.* Mill.
m.-bleith, *a grinding-mill.*
m.-brachaidh, *a malt-mill.*
m.-bràdha, *a quern.* (see below.)
m.-bualaidh, *a threshing-mill.*
m.-calcaidh, *a fulling-mill.*
m.-cardaidh, *a carding-mill.*

m.-deilbh, *a warping-mill.*
m.-gaoithe, *a wind-mill.*
m.-làimhe, *a handmill, quern.*
m.-lìn, *a lint-mill.*
m.-luaidh, see m.-luadhaidh.
m.-luadhaidh, *a fulling-mill.*
m.-mine, *a meal-mill.*
m.-sàbhaidh, *a saw-mill.*
m.-snaoisein, *a snuff-mill, snuff-box.*
m.-tòine-ri-làir, (DMK) *s. m.* The old turbine mill, with the horizontal water-wheel. The axle passed vertically through the nether millstone and, there being no gearing, the upper stone made only one revolution for each turn of the water-wheel. Three of these mills were at work in Assynt about 1860-5, but they were superseded soon after by a modern mill.
m.-uisge, *a water-mill.* (see below.)
Air cùl a' mhuilinn, *behind the mill.*

muileannach, -aiche, *a.* Of, or belonging to, a mill.

muilleannachd, *s.f.* Occupation of a miller. 2 Grinding.

muileann-brà, *s.m.* Quern. (for illustrations and names of parts see brà.) The quern was formerly the only mill for corn-grinding used in the Gàidhealtachd. It is still in use in many parts of northern Europe and in Asia, and the " two women grinding at the mill " (quern) may be seen to-day in Nazareth exactly as they were in the days of Christ. The implement consists of two stones, the lower being about two feet in diameter, and commonly hollowed to the depth of about six inches. This hollow is of equal depth and diameter. Within this is placed horizontally, a smooth round flag about four inches thick, and so fitted to the cavity that it can just revolve with ease. Through the centre of this revolving flag there is bored a hole for conveying the grain. In the lower stone, in the centre of its cavity, there is fixed a wooden pin on which the upper stone is placed in such exact equiponderance, that, though there be some friction from their contact, a little force applied will make the upper stone revolve for several times, when there is no grain underneath. On the surface of the upper stone, and near the edge, are two or three holes, just deep enough to hold in its place the stick by which it is turned round. The working of the quern is left to the women, two of whom, when the grain is properly dried, sit squatting on the ground, with the quern between them and singing loudly an appropriate song, perform their work, one turning round the stone with the handle placed in one of the holes, and the other dropping the corn in through the large hole. The law of Scotland attempted in vain to discourage the use of the quern. In the year 1248 it was enacted "that no man shall presume to grind quheit, maisloch or rye, with hand mylnes, except he be compelled by storm, and be in lack of mylnes quhilk should grind the samen ; and in this case, if a man grinds at hand-mylnes, he shall give the threttein measure as multer ; and gif any man contraveins this our prohibition, he shall tyne his hand-mylnes perpetuallie."

muileann-uisge, *s.m.* Water-mill.

Parts of a Water-mill (DMy) :—
1 Loch a' mhuilinn, *mill-pond.*
2 Eas a' mhuilinn, *mill-race, stream of water that turns the mill-wheel.*
3 Roth mór a' mhuilinn, *the mill-wheel which drives the mill.*
4 Drabhailt, *mill-hopper, into which the grain is put to feed the mill.*
5 Clagan, *mill-clapper with three ridges, striking the spout of hopper to cause the grain to fall into the eye of the mill.*
6 Sùil a' mhuilinn, *eye of mill.*
7 Fiacaill a' mhuilinn, *nether side of upper stone and upper side of nether stone.*
8 Aotroman, *screw for increasing or decreasing pressure of stones on the grain and thus making meal fine or coarse.*
9 Rothan a' mhuilinn, *mill-wheels.*
10 Cnoguisean, *no* fiaclan nan rothan, *cogs on mill-wheels.*
11 An Criathar mór, *mill-sieve, with two or three sheets, and worked by water power instead of by hand.*

muilear, see muillear.

muileid, -e, -ean, *s.m. & f.* Mule. 2 Mullet (fish.)

———each, -eiche, *a.* Mulish. 2 Abounding in mules. 3 Abounding in mullets.

———eachd, *s.f.* Mulishness. 2 Bad smell.

muile-mhàg, -àig, *pl.* -acha-màg, *s.f.* Toad. 2** Frog. Cha b' ann air muileacha-màg a chaidh m' àrach-sa, *it was not on toads that I was reared*—a saying current at the time of the Napoleonic wars and indicating the absurd contempt that then prevailed towards the French.

muilichdeann, *neighbourhood of L. Ewe for* muinichill.

muilicheann, -an, *s.m.* see muinichill.

———ach, -aiche, *a.* see muinichilleach.

muilichinn, -ean, see muinichill.

———each, see muinichilleach.

muilichinnean, *s.pl.* see muirlinn.

muilionn, -inn, -ean, see muileann & builionn.

muill, *gen. sing.* of moll. 2 *Arran* for muinichill.

muill, *v.a.* Prepare, get ready.

muille, *s.f.* see muileid.

muille, *Arran* for muinichill.

———ach,** -ich, *s.m.* Puddle.

———an, -ein, -an, *s.m.* Husk, particle of chaff. 2 Truss of thrashed hay or straw. [DU has heard a precocious youth describe the puffs out of a smoker's mouth as " muilleanan."] 3 Little bell.

———anach, -aiche, *a.* Husky, chaffy. 2 Abounding in bundles or trusses of straw.

muillear, -eir, -an, *s. m.* Miller.
m.-càrdaidh, *a carding-miller.*
m.-lìn, *a flax-miller.*
m.-luadhaidh, *a fuller of cloth.*
m.-mine, *a meal-miller.*

———achd, *s. f.* Business of a miller. 2 Grinding.

muil-leathann,** *a.* Flat-headed.

muilleid, see muileid.

muillion, -an, *s. m.* Million. [Followed by a noun in the *gen. pl.* unaspirated.] Muillionan de shluagh an fheòir, *millions of the tenants of the grass.*

muillnean, -ein, -an, see muillean.

muilneach,†† *a.* Of, or pertaining to, a mill.

muilnear, see muillear.

muilt, *gen.sing. & n. pl.* of mult.

———eag, -eig, *prov.* for muileag.

———ean, -ein, -an, *s.m. dim.* of mult. Little wether or ram.

muilteanach,†† *a.* Abounding in little wethers or rams.

muiltein, (car a mh—,) *s.m.* Somersault.

muilt-fheoil, -fheòla, *s.f.* Mutton.

muilt-fheolach,†† *a.* Abounding in mutton.

muime, -achan, *s.f.ind.* Nurse. 2 Step-mother.

3 Godmother. 4 Midwife. Fhuair i m., *she got a nurse.*
·———ach, -eiche, *a.* Novercal.
·——— -chiche, *s.f.* Wet-nurse.
·——— -altrum,** *s.f.* Dry-nurse.
mùin, *gen.sing.* of mùn.
mùin, *s.m.ind.* Making water.
muin, *v.a.* Teach, instruct, educate. 2 Show, point out. 3 Rear. 4* Instruct in lesson of politeness or good-breeding.
muin, *s.f.ind.* The back, back part of the neck. 2 Fat adhering to the entrails of an animal. 3**Mountain. †4 The vine, see crann-fìona. 5 Gaelic name of the letter M. †6 Thorn, bramble. Thog e air a mh. an laoch, *he raised the hero on his back* ; air m. a chéile, *on each other's backs, upon each other* ; air m. a' mhonaidh, *on the top of the hill* ; chaidh e air a m., *he had carnal connection with her.*
mùin, *v.a.* Micturate, make water.
muince,** *s.f.* Collar.
muincheall, see muinichill.
————ach, see muinichilleach.
muinchill, -ean, see muinichill.
muinchille, see muinichill.
————ach, -eiche, *a.* see muinichilleach.
muinchinn,** *s.m.* Headland. 2 Sea-coast.
muine, *W. of Ross* for muinne.
†muine, *s.f.* Whore. 2 Mountain. 3 Thorn. 4 Bramble. 5 The redding.
muineach,†† *a.* Learned, educated, taught. 2 Of, or belonging to, the neck, necked. 3** Strong-necked. 4**Thorny. A mharc ghlas-mh., *his grey strong-necked horse*—so given by **, but ghlas-mhuingeach, *grey-maned*, is no doubt what is meant.
muineach, -eiche, *a.* see muingeach.
————adh,** -aidh, *s.m.* Taking possession. 2 Possession.
muinead, -eid, *s.m.* Collar. 2 Necklace.
muineadh, -eidh, see munadh.
muineal, -eil, -an, *s. m.* The neck of a person, (amhach, of a beast.) 2 The breast. 3**Jaws. M. na làimhe, *the wrist*—given by ** is a jocular expression.
muinealach, -aiche, *a.* Necked. 2 Long-necked. 3 Having large jaws.
muinean-Muire,§ Parsley, see pearsal.
muinear, -eir, -an, *s.m.* Teacher, instructor.
muineil, *gen.sing.* of muineal.
muing, -e, -ean, *s.f.* Mane of a horse.
muinge,** *s.* Carcanet. 2 Collar.
———ach, -eiche, *a.* Maned. 2 Of, or belonging to a mane. 3 Having a long or thick mane.
muinghiall, -a, -an, *s.f.* Headstall of a halter or bridle.
————ach, -aiche, *a.* Having a headstall, as a bridle or halter.
muinghin, -e, -ean, see muinighin.
————each, -eiche, *a.* see muinighineach.
muinicheall, -ean, see muinichill.
—————ach, see muinichilleach.
muinichill, -ean, *s.m.* Sleeve.
————each, *a.* Sleeved. 2** Having long sleeves.
muinighin, -e, -ean, *s.f.* Hope, trust, confidence. 2 Assurance. 3 Stay, dependence. 4 Security. 5*Fort, fortress. 6**Reliance. Am m. a chosnaidh, *depending on his daily labour* ; is tu mo mh. threun, *thou art my chief confidence* ; m. 'na ainm-san, *trust in his name.*
——————each, -eiche, *a.* Hoping, trusting, confident, relying. 2 Hopeful, sanguine. 3 Secure.
—————eachd,** *s.f.* Confidence. 2 Hopefulness, sanguineness.
muininn, *s.f.* see muinighin.
muinle, (CR) see muinichill.
muinmheur, -ir, *s.m.* see minmhear.
muin-na-mnà-mìne,§ *s. f.* Cloudberry, (*lit.* the gentlewoman's vine,) see oighreag.
muinn, see muin.
muinne, -achan, *s.f.* Tallow tripe. 2††Stomach —*Argyll.*
muinnidh, -e, -ean, *s.f. prov.* for muing.
muinninn, see muinighin.
muinnlear, -ir, -an, *s.m.* see muillear.
muinnte, *a.* see muinte.
mùinnteachd, *s.f.* Disposition, *prov.*
muinntearach, *pl.* -aich, simply a genitive of muinntir, although given in dictionaries as a nominative, see muinntireach.
——————, *a.* see muinntireach.
——————d, see muinntireachd.
muinntearas, see muinntireas.
muinntir, -e & -treach, *s.f.coll. & sing.* People, men. 2 Inhabitants. 3 Parents. 4 Relation. 5 Family, household. 6 Tribe, clan. 7 Servants. 8 Farm-hands. Cha do ghabh a mh. féin ris, *his own [relations] did not receive him;* m. a' bhaile seo, *the people of this town* ; m. an taighe seo, *the inhabitants of this house* ; do mh., *your people, your relations* ; do mh. chéile, *your spouse's people* ; 'sann de mh. Uidhist a tha e, *he is a native of Uist*, or *his relations are Uist people* ; m. do dhùthcha, *thy countrymen.* In some places they say " a' mh. bheag is a' mh. mhór " for an fheadhainn bheag is an fheadhainn mhòr," *the big ones and the little ones.* [These nouns are not *pl.* so the adjectives must be *sing.*, but the pronouns would be *pl.*]
muinntireach, -eiche, *a.* Having a numerous household. 2 Of, or belonging to, a household. 3**Kind, friendly.
——————, -eich, *s.m.* Servant, hireling. 2* Acquaintance. 3 Follower. 4**Establishment of servants, household. Rùn a muinntireach, *the love of her household* ; sean mh., *an old acquaintance.*
——————d,* *s.f.ind.* Acquaintance, dealings, correspondence. Sean mh., *old acquaintance.*
muinntireas, -ais, *s.f.* Service, servitude, office of a servant. 2* Correspondence, dealing, communication. 3(AC) Covenant. 4††Indentureship. 5**Kindness.
muinntir Fhionnlaidh, *s.pl.* The fairies—*Lewis.*
muin-sheud, *s.m.* Carcanet, onch.
muinte, *past pt.* of muin. Taught, instructed, educated. 2 Polite, well-bred. 3 Beauteous.
muinteachd, *s.f.* Disposition.
muintear -eir, -an, see muinear.
muin-theud, *s.m.* Collar.
muir, -e, *s.f. prov.* for mùire.
muir, *gen.* mara, *dat.* muir, *voc.* a mhuir ! *pl.* marannan, *s.m. & f.* The sea. 2 Sea, ocean. 3 Wave. 4 *pl.* Large billows. [*fem.* in *Badenoch.* In *Lewis* the *nom.* is *f.*, and the *gen.* is *m.*—A' mhuir, ceann a' mhara.] Lean mi thar m. thu, *I followed thee over the sea* ; air muir 's air tìr, *by sea and by land* ; a' mh. mhór, *the ocean* ; a' Mh. Dhubh, *the Black Sea* ; a' Mh. Bhuidhe, *the Yellow Sea* ; M.-na-meadhon-tìre, *the Mediterranean Sea* ; airm mara, *a navy.*
muir, (AH) *s. f.* Worry, discomposure, mental suffering. Nach ann air a tha a' mhuir an diugh ! *how troubled he is to-day* ! tha m. ort an diugh, a Dhomhnuill, *you are in the dolours to-day, Donald.*
muirbhleachadh, -aidh, *s.m.* Amazement.
muirbhleasg,** *s.m.* Stupidity. 2 Amazement.
muirbhrinn, *s.pl.* Scarecrows. 2 Termagants.

muir-bhrùchd, -an, *s. m.* High tide. 2 (MM) Sea-ware on a large scale.
muir-bhuachaill,¶ *s.m.* Great northern diver—*colymbus glacialis*. 2 Red-throated diver, see learga mhór.
muir-chabhlach,** -aich, *s.f.* Squadron, fleet.
muircheartach,** *s.m.* Expert.
†muir-chreach,** *s.f.* Wave. 2 Piracy, sea-plunder.
muircinn,(CR) *s.f.* Ankle—*Suth'd.* [Oblique case the correct *nom.* is muirceann.]
muir-dhealbhadh, see muir-eòlas.
muir-dhealbhair, *s.m.* Hydrographer.

549. *Muir-dhroighinn.*

muir-dhroighinn, *s.m.* Agrimony—*agrimonia europœa.*
mùire, *s.f.* Leprosy. 2* Hurry. 3**Earth. 4 Mortar. 5 Dry scab. 6 Scurvy.
†mùireach, -eiche, *a.* Leprous.
†————, -eich, *s.m.* Leper.
muireach,** -eich, *s. m.* Sovereign. 2 Sailor mariner, marine. [** says †.]
mùireach, *a.* Scabious.
muireach, -eiche, *a.* Marine.
muireachan, -ain, *s.m.* Bulwark.
mùireadh, -eidh, see mùire.
muireadh, see muirgheadh.
†muirean,** -ein, *s.m.* Woman. 2 Young woman. [** gives *f.*]
muireann,** -inn, -an, *s.m.* Fish-spear. 2 Spear, dart.
muireannach, *a.* Like a spear or dart.
muireardach, *s.f.* Female fighter or champion. 2 Undaunted female—*Sàr-Obair.*
muireil, *a.* Naval, maritime. 2 Like a sea.
muir-eòlas, -ais, *s.m.* Hydrography.
muir-fheachd,** *s.f.* Fleet, squadron.
muir-ghobhal,** -ail, *s.m.* Arm of the sea.
muirgeag,** -eig, *s.f.* Firth, narrow sea.
muirgheadh, -eidh, *pl.* -an & -ghean, *s. f.* Trident, fish-spear.
muir-gheadh, -gheòidh, *s.m.* Bean-goose—*anser segetum.* [** gives *anas anser.*]
†muir-gheilt, *s.f.* Mermaid.
muir-gheòidh, *pl.* of muir-gheadh.
muirghin-muire, see maighdean-mhara.
muirghin-na-tuinne, see maighdean-mhara.
muirghineach, -eiche, *a.* Dull, stupid.
——————d, *s.f.ind.* Dulness, stupidity.
muir-ghinneach, see muirighinneach.
muirgineas,** -eis, *s.m.* Dulness, stupidity.
muirghe, see muirgheadh.
muirgrim, *s.f.* Naval engagement.
muirichinn, see muirighinn.
muirichinn, *s.pl.* Children, family. 2 Burden, care. 3* Hurry-burry. 4 Inmates or occupants of one house—*Sàr-Obair.* 5* Young throng, ill-provided for family. Màthair na muirichinn, *the mother of the family.*
muirichinneach, -eiche, *a.* Having a numerous offspring. 2 Burdensome, bringing much care. 3*Hurried. 4* Hard-pressed.
muirichlinn,* see muirlinn.
muirighean,(MS) *s.m.* Generation. 2 After ages.
muirighinn,** *s. f.* Noise. 2 Burden, heavy charge. 3 Family.
————each,** *a.* Burdensome. 2 Having a heavy charge. 3 Poor. 4 Numerous, as a family.
muirineach,§ *s.m.* Sea-maram, sea-matweed—*ammophila arenaria & psamma arenaria.* see muran.
muirirean,§ *s.* Badderlocks, hen-ware, see mircean.
muir-làn, -àin, *s.m.* High-tide, high-water.
muirlinn,* *s.f.* Birses, kind of edible sea-weed.
muir-mhaighistir,¶ *s.m.* Large white gull, glaucous, see faoileag mhór.
mùirn, -e, *s. f.* Cheerfulness, joy. 2 Delicateness, tenderness, nicety. 3 Natural affection, love, fondness, regard. 4 Respect. 5 Hospitatity. 6**Caressing, caress. 7††Grandeur, pomp. 8††Politeness. 9** Troop, company. 10* Entertainment with excessive tenderness or fondling, as of children.
'S ann rompa a bha a mh.,*how hospitably they were received* ; le furbhailt is m., *with complacency and hospitality ;* taigh na mùirne, *the home of hospitality ;* a thaobh m. , *by reason of hospitality* ; le m., *on account of delicacy.*
mùirneach, -eiche, *a.* Cheerful, joyful. 2 Delicate, tender. 3 Dear, beloved, fond. 4 (AC) Precious, endearing, prepossessing. 5 Respectful, showing respect, polite. 6* Hospitable. 7 Spoilt, as a child. 8††Grand, pompous. 9**Spirited. 10 **Pleasant, exhilarating. Mac m., *a dearly-beloved son ;* m. uime, *caressing him ;* an dùrdail mh., *the pleasant murmur ;* each mór-mh., *a high-spirited horse.*
mùirneachd, *s.f.* Daintiness.
mùirneadh, -aidh, *s. m.* Fondling, caressing, dandling.
mùirneag, -eig, -an, *s. f.* Cheerful woman or girl. 2 Tender or delicate woman. 3 Darling, beloved woman. 4††Civil or polite female. 5 Affectionate girl.
————ach,** *a.* Cheerful. 2 Fond, affectionate, as a girl.
mùirnealachd, *s.f.ind.* Nicety.
†mùirneamh,** -imh, *s.m.* Overseer.
mùirnean, -ein, -an, *s.m.* Dearly-beloved person, darling. 2 Petulant person. 3 Minion. 4†† Polite man. 5††Pompous man. 6**Cheerful young person. 7**Affectionate young person.
————ach,** *a.* Affectionate. 2 Cheerful. 3 Beloved, fond. 4 Caressing.
mùirnear, (MS) *s.m.* Cheerer.
mùirnich, *v. a.* ** Burden, load. 2 Caress, fondle, dandle. 3 (MS) Joy.
mùirnin, *v.a.* Caress, fondle, dandle.
muir-reubann, -ainn, *s.m.* Piracy.
muir-seilche,(AF) *s.f.* Tortoise. 2 Turtle.
muir-sgian, -sgein & -iain, *pl.* -an, *s. m.* Spout-fish, razor-fish.
——————ach, -aiche, *a.* Abounding in spout-fish. 2 Like a spout-fish.
muir-sgrìobhadh, -aidh, *s.m.* Hydrography.
muir-spùinne,** *s.f.* Piracy.
——————adair, see muir-spùinnear.
muir-spùinneadh, -eidh, -eidhean, *s. m.* Piracy.
muir-spùinnear, -eir, -an, *s. m.* Pirate, sea-robber.
——————achd, *s.f.ind.* Piracy, sea-robbery.

†muirt, *s.f.* Riches.
muirteachd, *s. m.* General term for the genus *medusa* of naturalists, vulgarly called "sea-blubber." 2 Unnavigable sea. [muirtèachd —*W. coast of Ross.*]
muir-thàcar, -air, -an, *s. m.* Sea-spoil, whatever goods are found on the sea-shore. 2 Sea-chance. (also tàcar-mara.)
muir-theud, -éid, -an, *s.m.* Cable.
muir-thoradh,** -aidh, *s.m.* Product of the sea.
muir-thuil, -tean, *s.m.* High tide. 2 Inundation by the sea.
muirtis,** Gaelic spelling of *mortice.*
muir-titheachd,* see muirteachd.
muir-tiughachd, see muirteachd.
muir-tràigh, *s.f.* Low-water.
muisde, *Gairloch* for muidse.
mùiseach,** *a*, Surly.
mùiseadh, -eidh, -eidhean, *s.m.* see mùiseag.
mùiseag, -eig, -an, *s.f.* Threat, threatening. 2†† Fear, terror. 3 **Severe treatment. Fo mhùiseig, *disquieted* (*lit.* under threatening.)
———ach, -aiche, *a.* Threatening. 2 Fearful, terrified. 3**Prone to threaten.
———adh,**-aidh, *s.m.* Threatening. 2 Threat.
muiseal,-eil, -an, *s. m.* Muzzle, curb, check. 2 Muzzle of a plough.
———ach, -aiche, *a.* Having a muzzle or curb. 2 Like a muzzle or curb.
muisean, -ein, -an, *s.m.* Mean or sordid fellow. 2 Ramscallion. 3 The devil.

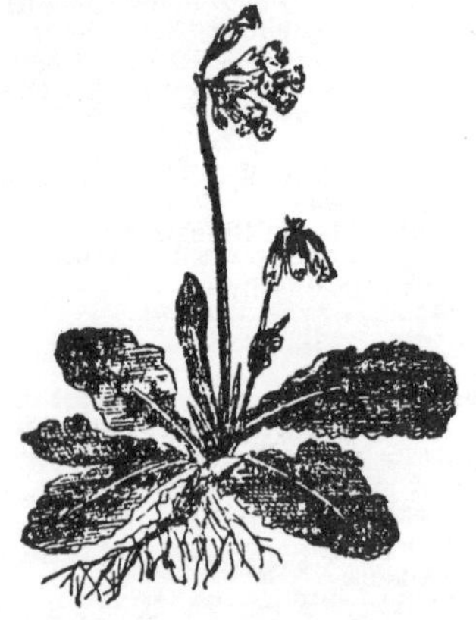

550. *Mùisean.*

mùisean,§ -ein, -an, *s.m.* Cowslip, palsywort—*primula veris.* 2 Primrose.
———ach, -aiche, *a.* Abounding in cowslips or primroses. 2 Like a cowslip or primrose.
muiseanach, -aiche, *a.* Low, sordid, mean, dirty, rascally.
muiseanachd, *s.f.* Meanness.
muisgean, *s.m.* Spout-fish—*Arran.*
muisginn, -e, -ean, *s.f.* Gaelic spelling of *mutchkin (pint,)* see bodach.
muisigich, *v.a.* Snub.
†muite, *a.* Dumb, mute.
mùiteach, -eiche, *a.* Changeable, changing, irresolute, fickle, unsteady, giddy, volatile, variable. 2 Feverish.
———d, *s.f.ind.* Changeableness, fickleness, variableness, inconstancy.
mùithteach, see mùiteach.
muitse, Gaelic spelling of *mutch* (headdress.) see muidse.
mul, -uil, -an, *s.m.* Conical heap, mound. 2 Bank or heap of sand. 3 Pebbly or shingly beach. 4 Axle-tree. 5 Axis. 6**Multitude.
mul.(MS) *s.m.* The pole.
mulabhar,§ -air, *s.m.* Dwarf elder, see fiodh-a'-bhalla.
mulach, -aich, *s. m.* see mullach. 2 (AF) see mulachag.
mulach,** -aich, *s.m.* Puddle, water, dirt. 2 Owl.
mulachag, -aig, -an, *s.f.* A cheese, the lump, a kebbuck. Giùlain a' mhulachaig, *carry the cheese.*
———ach, -aiche, *a.* Abounding in cheeses. 2 Shaped like cheeses.
mulachan, -ain, *pl.* -an [& -ain**,] *s.m.* see mulachag.
mulad, -aid, -an, *s. m.* Sadness, melancholy, grief, dejection. Thig math à m., *good comes out of sadness.*
muladach, -aiche, *a.* Sad, sorrowful, melancholy, enduring sadness, grievous. M. a ghnàth, *for ever sad*; is m. an gnothach e, *it is a melancholy business*; naidheachd mh., *distressing news.*
muladachd,** *s.f.* Afflictedness. 2 Pensiveness. 3 Piteousness. 4**Distressing nature or circumstances of a case.
muladaich,‡‡ *v.a.* Aggrieve, vex.
mulag,** -aig, *s.f.* see mullag. 2 see muileid. 3 Little heap, knoll.
———ach,** *a.* Hilly, knolly.
mulaid, *gen.sing.* of mulad.
mulaideach,* see muladach.
mu-làimh, *adv.* Indifferently.
mulan, -ain, -an, *s. m.* Small stack or rick of corn. 2 Little hill, hillock, knoll. 3 Conical hillock. 4 Large conical wave or billow. 5 Little field. 6(MS) Knob. M. tomailteach, *bulky stacks of corn.* [* says " never applied to hay ;" but it is in Argyllshire.]
mulanach, -aiche, *a.* Abounding in small ricks or stacks, full of stacks. 2 Full of lumps. 3 Hilly, abounding in hillocks, knolly.
mulard,** -aird, *s.m.* see malard (appendix.)
mulart,§ -airt, -an, *s.m.* Dwarf-elder, see fiodh-a'-bhalla.
mulbhach,(AF) *s.m.* Sea-calf, seal. 2 Porpoise.
mulc, *pr.pt.* a' mulcadh, *v.a.* Push, butt with the head, as a calf or ram. 2 Dig with the snout, as a pig. 3*Dive, duck.
mulc,* muilc, -an, *s.m.* Lump, shapeless lump. 2 Duck, dive.
mulcach, -aiche, *a.* Pushing with the horns or head, butting. 2 Digging with the snout. 3 Jostling. 4**Apt to push or butt.
mulcadh, -aidh, *s.m.* Butting, act of butting. 2 Digging, act of digging with the snout. 3†† Stuff, ram down. 4 Shoving, jostling. 5 Push, shove, jostle. A' m—, *pr. pt.* of mulc.
mulcan, see mulchan.
mulcha, see mulbhach.
mulchan,** *s.m.* Long-eared owl, see comhachag-adharcach.
mul-cheann, -inn, *s.m.* The pole.
mul-chù, *s.m.* The pole.
mul-dhorn,** *s.* Fist.
mulghart,** -airt, *s.* The pole.
mull, see maol.
mullach, -aich, -aichean, *s.m.* The top, summit, or upper extremity of anything. 2 Height, hill, eminence. 3 Height. 4 Roof. 5 Apex, ridge. 6*Essence. 7 Puddle, water. 8 Owl. 9 see mulbhach. 10 see mulchan. 11 Main dorsal, portion of plough-beam. M. na beinne, *the ridge of the hill*; air mullach an taighe, *on the roof of the house*; m. an t-slaoightire, *a most complete rogue*; m. liath, lom, *a grey, bleak eminence*; na m., *in her top*; m. nan

rionnag, *the height of the stars.*
mullachail, -e, *a.* Coronal.
mullach-dubh,§ -aich-dhuibh, -ean-dubha, *s.m.* Knapweed—*centaurea nigra*, see cnapan-dubh.
mullachd, -an, *Suth'd* for mallachd,
mulla-chlach, *s.f.* Pebble. Mu mhulla-chlachan a' chaolaich, *about the water-worn stones of the beach—Sgeulaiche-nan-caol, p. 106.*
mulladh, -aidh, -aidhean, *s.m.* Mould for casting.
mullag, -aig, -an, *s.f.* Cover of a chalice,patine.
mullaid, see muileid.
mullait, *a.* Wicked.
mullan,** -ain, *s.m.* Mole. 2 Kind of milking vessel.
mullard,(AF) *s.m.* see malard (appendix.)
mulldair, -ean, see molltair.
mul-mhàgan,** -ain, *s.m.* Kind of large toad, (*var.* of muile-mhàg.)
mul-mhògag, *s.f.* *W. of Ross* for muile-mhàg.
mulp,** -a, *s.m.* Lump. 2 Knot. 3 Hump.
-——ach,** *a.* Lumpy. 2 Knotty. 3 Gnarled, knaggy.
-——an,** -ain, *s.m.* Little lump. 2 Little knot. 3 Knag.
-——anach,** *a.* Full of little knots.
-——anachd,†† *s.f.ind.* Knobbiness.
mul-sneamh, ** *s.m.* see maol-snèimh.
——————ach,** }
——————ail,** } *a.* see maol-snèimheil.
mult, -uilt, *s.m.* Wether (sheep.)
mult-cró, *s.m.* Harvest-home after potatoes have been secured—*Arran.*
mult-réithe, *s.m.* Tup.
mu 'm, mu 'n, *prep.* conjoined with *art., poss.* or *rel. pron., &c* About the, their, my, whom, which. 2 Concerning the, their, my, whom, which. ‡‡3 *adv.* Lest. 4 Before, ere.
mum, *conj. & adv.* see mu' m.
mu 'n, *conj. & adv.* see mu 'm.
Mu 'n d' thubhairt iad, *of whom they asserted.* [also used instead of " mar a thubhairt iad," *as they said.*]
mun, *conj. & adv.* see mu 'm.
mùn, *v.* see mùin.
mun,* *v.* see muin.
mùn, -ùin, *s.m.* Urine. Galar mùin, *the gravel.*
muna-bhuachaill,(AF) *s.m.* Allan-hawk. 2 Cormorant. 3 Diver.
mùnach,**½*a.* Incontinent of urine.
munachas, (AC) *s.m.* Prosperity.
mùnadh, -aidh, *s.m.* Act of making water. A' m—, *pr.pt.* of mùin.
munadh, -aidh, *s. m.* see monadh. 2**Education, instruction. 3 Admonition, discipline. Deiseachd munaidh, *the ornament of education.*
munadh, -aidh, *s.m.* Teaching, instruction. 2 Act of teaching or instructing. 3 Act of showing or pointing out. 4**Affability. 5 Good behaviour. 6 Education. A' m—, *pr. pt.* of muin.
munar, -air, -an, *s.m.* Trifle. 2 Trifling person. 3 Fact, deed.
munaran,** *a.* Insignificant, trifling.
-————, *s.m., dim.* of munar.
†munata, *s.m.* Champion.
mu'n cuairt, *prep.* Around, about. Mu'n cuairt domh, *about me, around me* ; mu m' chuairt, *around me* ; mu d' chuairt, *around thee* ; mu 'chuairt, *around him* ; mu'n cuairt da, *around him* ; m' ar cuairt, *around us* ; mu'n cuairt duinn, *around us* ; m' ur cuairt, *around you;* mu'n cuairt duibh, *around you* ; m' an cuairt, *around them* ; mu'n cuairt daibh, *around them.*

mung, -a, -an, see muing.
mungach,(AC) *a.* Shuffling.
mungach-mear,(AC) *s.m.* Hemlock—*Lochaber.*
munganach,(AH) *s. m.* Blustering, noisy, overbearing fellow.
munganachd, *s.f.ind.* Bullying.
mùn-gonain,(DU) *s.m.* Small painful tumour.
mùnlaichte,** *a.* Be-pissed, be-mired.
mùnloch, -oich, -an, *s. m.* Puddle, foul water, mire.
munmhur, -uir, -an, see monmhar.
munmhor, see monmhar.
munnta, see muinte.
mun-aidh, *s.f.* Pam, knave of clubs at loo.
mu'n seach, see mu seach.
mur, *conj.* If not, except, unless. M. dean thu, *except you do* ; m. dean sibhse aithreachas *except ye repent* ; m. bhitheadh gu'n do thog e a chùis, *were it not that he had appealed* ; m. bhith, *unless.*
mur, for mar.
mùr, -ùir, *pl.* -ùir & -ùirean. *s. m.* Wall. 2 Bulwark, rampart. 3 Fortified place. 4 House. 5 Hill. 6 Palace. 7 Countless number, as of insects. 8 see mùire. A' caoidh 'sa mhùr, *wailing in the hall* ; gach gregh bha 'n ar m., *every dog in our house* ; m.-ollamh, *an academy.*
mùr, *v.a.* Wall in. 2 Fortify.
mura-bhith,* *s. f.* Excuse, pretence, exception. Gun mh. sam bith, *without any exception.*
mura-bhuachaill,* see muir-bhuachaill.
mùrach,* -aich, -aichean, *s.m.* Down, sand-hill on the sea-shore. 3 (DMC) Digging, see mulcadh. Feadh nam mùraichean, *among the downs.*
mùrach,** *a.* Walled.
murachan (AC) *s.m.* Wealth. M. na mara, *the wealth of the sea.*
mùrach dubh,** *s.m.* Blackmoor.
muradh,** *s.m.* Bent.
————ach,** *s.m.* Siren.
murag,(AF) *s.f.* Murex, purple-fish. 2(DC)Anything cast ashore by the sea—*Uist.*
———an, see moireag.
muran, -ain, *s. m,* Sea-maram, sea mat-weed, sea-bent, see muirineach. 2§ Carrot, see curran. 3 Sea-reed—*Colonsay.* 4 Rope of grass, plaited or woven in horse-collar. 5** Rents.
———ach, -aiche, *a.* Abounding in sea-bent. 2 Like sea-bent.
murasg,** -aisg, *s. m.* Sea-shore. 2 Marsh. 3 Sea-marsh. 4 Quicksand.
mur-bhuachaill,** -ean, *s.m.* see muir-bhuachaill.
mur biodh,** *v. cond. neg.* Were it not, had it not been. 2 Were it not, had it not that.
murcach, -aiche, *a.* Sad, sorrowful. 2††Dark, muddy. 3 Gloomy.
murcan, ain, -an, *s.m.* Lump-fish.
murcas, -ais, *s.m.* Sadness, sorrow. 2 Gloominess. 3††Muddiness.
murdachan,(AF) *s.m.* Mermaid.
mur-dhroighinn, see muir-dhroighinn.
mùrla, -ùirle, -an, *s.m.* Coat-of-mail. 2 Conical creel.
mùrlach, -aich, -aichean, *s. m.* The bird kingfisher. 2 Woman having an ugly head of hair. —*Islay.* 3**Dog-fish. 4(AF) Halcyon. 6 see mùrlag.
mùrlag, -aig & -aige, -aigean, *s.f.* Canoe-shaped basket to hold the uncombed wool for the comber—the creel holds the *rolagan* of combed wool. The basket is sometimes egg-shaped, with a hole at the top to admit the hand, and is also called " ciarachan."

murlaich,(CR) see murthail.
murlainn, see mùrlag. (*Scots*, merlin.)
murlan,* -ain, *s.m.* Ugly or rough head of hair. 2 Dirty, matted hair. 3**Rough head or top.
murlaoch, (AF) *s.* Dog-fish, see mùrlach.
murloch, (AF) *s.m.* Dog-fish, see mùrlach.
mùrluinn, see mùrlag.
mùrn,(AC) *s.m.* Darling. 2 Maiden,damsel,girl.
murrach, -aich, *a.* Able, capable. 2 Efficacious. 3‡ Rich. 4 Adequate. Tha mi m. air a dheanamh, *I am able to do it* ; ciod an ni a's murraiche ? *what is more able ?*
murrachail,(MS) *a.* Adequate. Gu m., *adequately.*
murrachas, -ais, *s. m.* Ability, capability. 2 cogency, adequateness. 3 Superiority, sufficiency.
murrachd,* *s.f.* (MS) Solvency. 2 see murrachas.
†mur-radhach, -aich, *s.m.* Orator. 2 Babbler.
murraichd,* *s.f.* Handsome present. 2 Spoil on the sea-shore.
murraiche, *comp.* of murrach. More or most capable.
murraiche,** *s.f.* Ability, capability, power, sufficiency.
mursaig,(AF) *s.f.* Razor-fish.
†mursanach, -aich, *s.m.* Subject.
mursanta,** *a.* Servile.
————chd, *s.f.ind.* Subjection.
murt, see mort.
——achail,** *a.* Murderous, massacring.
murtachd, *s.f. ind.* Sultry heat, sultriness. 2 Weariness or dulness produced by heat.
murtadh, -aidh, see mortadh.
murtaidh, -e, *a.* Sultry, suffocating. 2 Languid or weary from excessive heat. 3 Murderous, cruel.
murtair, -ean, see mortair.
————eachd. see mortaireachd.
murthail,(CR) *s.f.* Grumbling—*Perthshire.*
†murtill,** *a.* Dull.
murusg, -uisg, *s.m.* Sea-shore. 2 Sea-marsh.
mùs, (mò 's *or* motha 's) *a.* Too much, exceeding. 2 Exhorbitant. M. làn, *too full.*
mus, *conj.* (i.e. mus an) see mu'm, mu'n. Ere, before. Mus fhaillinneadh aran, *ere bread should fail—Suth'd.* ; mus tàinig an dìl' o nèamh, *before the deluge came from heaven*—R. 3, 5.
†mus, *a.* Pleasant, agreeable. 2 Handsome.
musach, -aiche, *a.* see mosach.
musag, see mosag.
musaiche, *s.f.* see mosaiche.
————, *prov. comp.* of mosach.
musaidh, -ean, *s.m.* Dirty or nasty fellow. 2 Mean, vile fellow.
musal,(CR) *s.m.* Evil threat.
muscata, *s.m.* Nutmeg.
mu seach, *adv.* Alternately, by turns. 2 Laid by. 3** In return. 4**To and fro. Uair mu seach, *time about* ; deanaibh mu seach e, *do (ye) it alternately* ; an uachdar mu seach, *alternately up and down* ; fear mu seach, *one by one* ; tha 'obair dol mu seach air, *his work accumulates on his hands* ; airgiod mu seach, *money laid by.*
musg, -uisg, -an, *s.f.* Musket.
musg,** *v.n.* Grow mouldy or musty.
mùsg, -ùisg, -an, *s.m.* Eye-rheum. 2 Ugly eye. 3 Gore of the eyes.
——ach, -aiche, *a.* Rheumy. 2 Mouldy, musty. 3 Rheum-eyed.
musgach, -aiche, *a.* Armed with muskets. 2 Of, or belonging to, muskets. 3 Like a musket. 4 Full of muskets.
mùsgachd, *s.f.ind.* Blearedness.
musgadair,** *s.m.* Musketeer.
musgaid, *s.f.* see musg.
musgail, see mosgail.
musgain, see mosgain.
musgalach, see mosgalach.
mùsgaltach, see mosgalach.
————d,** *s.f.* see mosgalachd.
musgan, -ain, *s.m.* see mosgan.
mùsgan, -ain, -an, *s.m.* Hose-fish, gaper. 2(AF) Mussel. 3 (AF) Large razor-fish. 4 see mosgain.
————ach, -aiche, *a.* Abounding in hose-fish.
musganach, -aiche, *a.* see mosganach.
musganachd, see mosganachd.
mu sgaoil, *adv.* Abroad, at large. Chaidh a leigeil mu sgaoil, *he was set free.*
musgladh, -aidh, see mosgladh.
mustar,** -air, *s.m.* Self-sufficiency. 2 Muster.
mustar-mhaighstir,** *s.m.* Muster-master.
mùsuinn, -e, -ean, *s.f.* Confusion, tumult, hurly-burly. [** gives †.]
mut,** *s.m.* Any short thing.
mutach, -aiche, *a.* Short, thick and blunt.
mùtach,** *a.* Mouldy, musty.
mutag, see miotag.
mutaiche, *s.f.* Mouldiness, mustiness.
mùtaire,(AH) *s.m.* Fellow who likes to act on the sly. 2 Smuggler.
————achd, *s.f.* Concealed or hidden deeds. 2 Smuggling.
mùtain, *gen. sing. & n.pl.* of mùtan.
mùtan, -ain, -an, *s.m.* Muff (article of dress.) 2 Thick glove. 3 Old rag or anything worn by time or disease. 4 Fingerless glove. 5†† Small leather covering. 6**Cover for a gun. 7* Stump of a finger. 8 see mùdan.
mùth, *v.a. & n.* Change, alter. 2 Begin to rot, decay, deteriorate. 3 Kill, destroy. 4**Give in exchange. 5** Shift, turn. 6 Diversify. Mh. e mo thuarasdal, *he changed my wages.*
mùth, *s. m.* Change, alteration, difference. Vicissitude. 3 Novelty. 4 Decaying. 5 Small money in exchange for larger pieces.
mùtha, see mùthadh.
mùthach, *v.* see mùch.
muthach, -aich, -aichean, *s.m.* Herd, herdsman. 2 Cowherd. 3††Milk contractor. Caillear bò an droch mhuthaich seachd bliadhna roimh am mithich, *the bad herdsman's cow is lost seven years before the time.*
mùthach, *a.* Changing, changeable.
mùthachadh, -aidh, see mùthadh.
muthachd,(MS) *s. f.* Fustiness.
mùthadh, -aidh, *s.m.* Changing, act of changing, shifting or altering. 2 Alteration, change, difference, vicissitude, transition. 3 Novelty. 4 Change in money. 5 Killing, act of killing or destroying. 6 Destruction, perdition. 7** Decaying. A' m—, *pr. pt.* of mùth. Tha m. air, *he is changed* ; thoir dhomh m. crùin, *give me change for a crown (five shillings)* ; théid a dhreach am m., *its fashion shall perish* ; a' dol am m., *perishing, decaying* ; do bhràthair lag a' m., *thy weak brother perishing* ; air mh. dòigh, *in a different manner.*
muthaidh,(MS) *a.* Fusty.
mùthaidh, *fut. aff. a.* of mùth.
muthairn, -e, -ean, *prov.* for mughairn. 2 (AC) Little mother, dear little mother.
————each, -eiche, *a.* see mughairneach.
muthalach, -aiche, *a.* see mùiteach.
————d, *s.* see mùiteachd.
muthan,** -ain, *s.m.* see maothan.
mùthar, *fut.pass.* of mùth. Shall be changed.
mu thimchioll, *prep.* About, around, concerning. Mu m' thiomchioll, *about me* ; mu d' th., *about thee* ; mu 'th., *about him* ; m' a.t.,

about her; m' ar t., *about us*; m' ur t., *about us*; m' an t., *about them.*
mu theinn, *adv.* Busy—*Arran.* A phrase in constant use, e.g. tha thu mu theinn, *you are busy*; tha na madaidh mu theinn, *the dogs are busy (barking.)*
mùth-ionadach, -aiche, *a.* Inverse.
mùthtach, -aiche, see mùiteach.
————d, *s.* see mùiteachd.
muthteachas, see mùiteachd.
mu thuaiream, *prep.* About (in estimate.) Mu thuaiream fichead là, *about twenty days*; dh' fhàg mi mu thuaiream seo e, *I left it hereabouts.*

N n

n, nuin, *the ash-tree*; the twelfth letter of the Gaelic alphabet at present in use. N, when immediately preceded by *i*, sounds like *n* in English *win*; *nn*, when immediately preceded by *i*, sounds like *gn* in French *guigne*, or *ng* in English *sing.* When preceded and followed by broad vowels, *nn* has a particularly deep and broad sound, which has no equivalent in English. The monosyllable *an*, when the next word begins with *c* or *g*, sounds like *ang*, as, an cù, *the dog.* The letter *n* when aspirated is not followed by *h* in writing, and a distinction between the plain and aspirated sounds is not generally made in Northern Gaelic, although there is an appreciable difference between the *n* in, nigh do chasan, *wash your feet*, which is plain, and that in, nigh e a chasan, *he washed his feet*, which is aspirated, when they are correctly pronounced.
'n, *cont.* for an, *art.* Dh' òl iad de 'n fhìon, *they drank of the wine.*
'n, *cont.* for an, *rel.pron.* Mu 'n d'thubhairt iad, *of whom they asserted.*
'n, *cont.* for an, *poss.pron.* Le 'n làmhan 's le 'n casan, *with their hands and feet.*
'n, *cont.* for an. 'N taigh, *in a house.*
'n, *cont.* for an ? *interr. particle.* 'N d' fhàg thu mi ? *have you left me ?*
'n, *cont.* for an, *particle.* A chionn gu 'n robh eagal orra, *because they were afraid.*
n-, is placed between the possessive pronouns ar, *our*, and bhur, *your*, and the noun following when it begins with a vowel. Mar sin rinn bhur n-aithrichean, *so did your forefathers.*
na, *gen.sing.fem.* of *art.* an. Fo ghruaim na h-oidhche, *under the gloom of the night.*
na, *nom.& dat. pl.* of *art.* an. Air na beanntaibh, *on the mountains.*
na, *conj.* Than. Na's fhearr na sin, *better than that.*
na, *pron.* fulfilling the function of an antecedent and relative in English (=an do, contracted.) That which, what, those who, those which. Mu na thubhairt 's na rinn thu, *concerning what thou hast said and done*; na thàinig, *those that came*; na 's urrainn mi, *that which I can*; na dh' fhanas, *those that remain, that which remains.*
na, *adv.* Not, let not. Na tig an seo, *do not come here.*
na, *prov.* for do 'n. Chaidh e na bhaile, *he went to (into) the town—Badenoch, &c.*
†na, *conj.* for no.
na, *particle*, Used before preterites of verbs (i.e. an do.) Far na thiodhlaic sinn an triùir, *where we have buried the three.*
'n a, *cont.* for an a. Fanaibh gach duine 'n a àite féin, *abide ye every man in his own place*; 'na choigreach, *he being a stranger.*
'na, before a *poss. pron.* for an & ann, *prep.* Am bheil tha 'nad shlàinte ? *are you in health ?* tha iad 'nam fianuisibh 'nan aghaidh féin, *they are witnesses against themselves.*
na, *adv.* (i.e. o'n a) Since that, whereas, forasmuch as.
nàbachail, -e, *a.* Neighbourly.
nàbachas, -ais, *s.m.* Neighbourhood, vicinity. 2 Neighbourliness.
nàbachd, *prov.* for nàbaidheachd.
nàbaidh, -ean, *s. m.* Neighbour. [* says "a neighbour" in the *North*, and "a North Highlander" in the *West.*]
————eachas, see nàbaidheachd.
————eachd, *s.f.ind.* Neighbourhood, vicinity. 2 Neighbourliness.
nàbuidh, see nàbaidh.
nach, *pron. ind.* Who not, which not, whom not, that not. An t-aon nach tig, *the one that will not come*; suinn nach beò, *heroes that are not living.*
nach, *adv. & conj.* That not, not. A chionn n. 'eil an rìgh a' toirt fògaraich air an ais, *because the king does not restore fugitives,*
nach ? *neg.interr.particle.* Nach 'eil fhios agad fhathast ? *knowest thou not yet ?* n. truagh mi leat ? *am I not to be pitied with you ?* n. math e ? *is it not good ?* n. tig thu ? *will you not come ?*
nad,** *s.m.* The posteriors.
'n ad, *cont.* for an ad (an do.) 'Nad chridhe, *in thy heart.*
†nada, *s.* Nothing.
nàdar, -air, -airean, see nàdur.
————rach, -aiche, see nàdurra.
nàdmhorrach, *a.* see nàdurra.
nàdur, -uir, -uirean, *s.m.* Nature, constitution of the material world. 2 Constitution of any particular thing. 3 Disposition, temper, mind. 4 Nature, constitution or fitness of things. 5 Sinful or depraved nature of man, in a spiritual sense. 6 Bent, inclination, instinct, naturalness. Obair nàduir, *the work of nature*; do dhroch n., *your bad temper.*
————ra, *a.* Natural, according to nature. 2 Good-natured, of a good natural disposition. 3 Affectionate. 4 In a state of nature, unrenewed by divine grace. 5**Humane. Nighean n., *an affectionate daughter*; deagh-n., or math-n., *good-tempered.*
————rach, -aiche, *a.* see nàdurra.
————rachd,* *s.f.ind.* see nàdur.
————rail, -e, *a., prov.* for nàdurra.
nagair,** *a.* Comely, handsome.
†naibh,** *s.f.* Ship.
†————eag,** -eig, *s.f.* Little ship.
naid, -e, -ean, *s.f.* Lamprey. 2**Husband.
naidheachd, *s.f.ind.* News, tidings. Dé do n.? *what news have you ?* droch n. dhuit-se, *bad intelligence for you.*
†nail,** *a.* Another.
naill-bheul,** bheòil, *s.m.* Bridle-bit. (an aill-bheul.)
nàile, *int.* Indeed, truly. *Emphatically*, nàile féin ! a common form of asseveration. N. féin théid mi dhachaidh, *by my sooth I shall go home.*
†naim,** *s.f.* Bargain, covenant.
nàimh, *gen.sing. & n.pl.* of nàmh.
nàimhde, *pl.* of nàmhaid.
nàimhdeach, -eiche, *a.* see nàimhdeil.
nàimhdealach, see nàimhdeil.
————————d, *s.f.* see nàimhdeas.
nàimhdealas, -ais, see nàimhdeas.

nàimhdean, *pl.* of nàmhaid.
———as, see nàimhdeas.
nàimhdeas, -eis, *s.m.* (*s.f.* in *Badenoch*.) Enmity, hostility, malice. 2**Viciousness, rancour. 3 Keenness, eagerness, vehemence. 4* Vindictiveness, resentment.
†**naindean**,** -ein, *s. m.* Valour, chivalry. 2 Hero.
†———ach, *a.* Valorous, chivalrous.
†———ach,** *s.m.* Valorous person.
nàimhdeil, -e, *a.* Hostile, warlike, like an enemy. 2 Malicious. 3**Rancorous, vicious. 4 Keen, vehement, eager.
†**naing**,** *s.f.* Mother.
†——— -mhór, -mhóir, *s.f.* Grandmother.
nàir, -e, see nàire.
'n àird, *adv.* Aloft, up, upward. 2 From below. 3 On high. Chaidh e 'n àird, *he went aloft.*
†**naire**,** *a.* Clean, neat, trim, tidy.
nàire, *s.f.ind.* Shame, disgrace, ignominy. 2 The feeling of shame. 3 Bashfulness, modesty. Mo n. ! *for shame ! fy !* gabh n., *feel ashamed;* gun n. gun athadh, *without shame or confusion of face* ; fo n., *ashamed* ; air bheag n., *shameless.*
†**naireach**,** *a.* Brave. 2 Generous.
nàireach, -eiche, *a.* Shameful, disgraceful. 2 Bashful, modest, shamefaced, sheepish. 3* Easily abashed. Ni n., *an ignominious thing* ; tha 'n duine n., *the man is bashful.*
nàireachadh, -aidh, *s. m.* Ashaming, act of ashaming or causing shame. 2*Abashing, disgracing. A' n—, *pr. pt.* of nàirich. Tha mi air mo n., *I am ashamed.*
nàireachd, *s.f.* see naire.
nàirich, *v.a.* Shame, affront, make ashamed, browbeat, insult.
———ear, *fut.pass.* of nàirich.
———idh, *fut.aff. a.* of nàirich.
———te, *past pt.* of nàirich. Ashamed, made ashamed, affronted.
nairne,** *s.f.* Purity, chastity, modesty.
nais,** *s.f.* Furnace. 2 Fire-hearth in a forge.
nàisein,(AH) *s.f.* Old inhabitants of a country.
naisg, *pr.pt.* a' nasgadh, *v.a.* Bind, make fast, 2 Seal. 3 *Deposit, money, pledge. Naisgeadh càch le càirdeas, *let the rest be bound by friendship.*
†**naisg**, -e, -ean, *s.f.* Ring, seal.
naisgear, -eir, *s.m.* Conjunction in *grammar.*
———,** *fut.pass.* of naisg. Shall be bound.
naisgidh, *fut.aff.a.* of naisg.
naisgte, *past pt.* of naisg. Bound, made fast, secured. 2 Sealed.
naisich, *v.a.* Embellish.
nàisinn,* see nàistinn. [* gives, Deep and over-delicate sense of duty, excessive sense of gratitude, particularly in matters of hospitality that puts to inconvenience.]
†**naisir**,** *s.* Old inhabitants of a country.
nàisneach, -eiche, *a.* see nàistinneach.
nàisneachadh,** *s.m.* Decoration.
nàisneachd, see nàistinneachd.
naisnich,** *v.a.* Decorate, embellish.
nàistinn, -e, *s.f.* Care, wariness, attention, vigilance. 2** Circumspection, modesty. 3 Native. 4 (AH) Sense of duty, as in a servant towards his master's interests. 5 (DMC) Nation, tribe. Na bitheadh n. sam bith ort air mo shon-sa, *don't put yourself to any inconvenience on my account* ; is beag n. a th' orm air a shon sin, *I do not feel any excessive sense of propriety to return that favour;* n. an àite, *a native of the place* ; làn nàistinn, *full of circumspection.*
nàistinneach, -eiche, *a.* Careful, wary, attentive. vigilant. 2 Modest, shamefaced. 3‡‡Native. Continent, sober, temperate. 4**Cosmetic. 5* Feeling a deep sense of obligation. 6*Perseveringly at work from a sense of duty (to a fault.) 7 Showing excessive hospitality and decency to a stranger from a delicate sense of the laws of such.
nàistinneachd, *s. f. ind.* Modesty, shamefacedness. 2**Continence,soberness,temperateness. 3* Deep sense of duty or propriety of the observance of hospitality. 4* Too much keenness at work from the same feeling.
Le n. agus stuaim,*with shamefacedness and sobriety* ; 'gan sgeadachadh féin le n., *adorning themselves with shamefacedness.*
naitheas, -eis, -an, *s.m.* Harm, injury, mischief, hurt.
———ach, -aiche, *a.* Harmful, mischievous, injurious.
†**nall**, *s.m.* Bridle.
nall, (i.e. a nall) *adv.* To this side, hither, towards us, from the other side. A nunn 's a nall, *thither and hither* ; thigeadh e a nall, *let him come over.*
†**nallod**, see allod.
†**nallus**, see fallus.
na 'm (i. e. na+am, *particle*) *conj.* If. Na 'm bitheadh, *if it were ;* na 'm bitheadh mo chliù-sa cho maireann, *were my praise so lasting.* [Used before verbs beginning with a labial.]
nam, *gen.pl.* of *art.* an. Glac nam beann, *the gorge of the hills.* [Used before a labial.]
'nam, *cont.* for an am, *in their.* 'Nam meadhon, *in their midst.*
'nam, *cont.* for an mo, *in my.* 'Nam fhearann, *in my land.* [Followed by aspirate.]
nàmh, -àimh, see nàmhaid.
nàmhach, -aich, *s.m.* see nàmhaid. Mar dhà n., *like two enemies.*
———, -aiche, *a.* see nàimhdeil.
———ail, -e, *a.* see nàimhdeil.
———as, -ais, *s.m.* see nàimhdeas.
nàmhad, *gen.sing.* of nàmhaid.
nàmhadach, -aiche, *a.* see nàimhdeil.
nàmhadas,** -ais, *s.m.* Fierceness, 2 Enmity.
nàmhaid, *gen.sing.* nàmhad, *pl.* nàimhdean [& nàmhaidean] *s.m.* Enemy. 2 Antagonist.
———each, -eiche, *a.* see nàimhdeil.
nàmhaidealachd, *s.f.ind.* see nàimhdeas.
nàmhaideas, -eis, see nàimhdeas.
nàmhaideil, -e, *a.* see nàimhdeil.
nan, *gen.pl.* of an.
na'n, *conj.* If. [Used before verbs beginning with a vowel or lingual.]
'nan, *cont.* for an an, *in their.*
'n ann, ? *cont.* for an ann ? *is it ?* 'N ann mar sin a tha e ? *is it like that ?* 'n ann mar sin a dh' àithn mi dhuit ? *is it so that I commanded you ?*
†**naochad**, *a.* Ninety.
†**naochadamh**, *a.* Ninetieth.
naodh, see naoi.
†**naodhamh**, *a.* Ninth. (naothamh)
naodhan,** -ain, *s.m.* Well, fountain.
naogad,** *a.* Ninety. N. fear, *ninety men.*
———amh,** *a.* Ninetieth.
†**naoi**, *s.f.* Hip. 2 Man, person.
naoi, *a.* Nine. An ceann n. mìosan, *at the expiration of nine months.*
naoi-bhaisteach, -ich, *s.m.* Pædobaptist.
naoi-deug, *a.* Nineteen. N. fir dheug, *nineteen men ;* naoi fir dheug thar fhichead, *thirty-nine men.* [These words are really *numerals* and neither *nouns* nor *adjectives*, although genetermed one or the other.]
———, *s. m.* Nineteen. Seo naoi-deug, *here are nineteen.*

naoidh, see naoi.
naoidhe, see naoidhean.
naoidheach,** *a.* Infantile, like a babe or suckling.
—————ail, -e, *a.* Infantile.
—————an, -ain, -an, *s.m.* Infant, babe. 2 Young child.
†—————dach, -aich, *a.* Chief, principal.
naoidhean, -ein, -an, *s. m.* Infant, babe, suckling. 2 Bantling, urchin. 3** Bravery.
—————ach, -aiche, *a.* see naoidheanta.
—————achd, see naoidheantachd.
—————ta, *a.* Childish, child-like, infantile.
—————tachd, *s.f.ind.* Infancy, childhood. 2 **Childishness.
—————tas, -ais, *s.m.* see naoidheantachd.
naoidh-mhort, -a, *s.m.* Infanticide.
—————air, *s.m.* Slayer of infants.
naoimh, *gen.sing. & n.pl.* of naomh, *s.*
naoimhios,** *s.m.* November.
†—————dadh, -aidh, *s.m.* Sanctuary.
†naoineal, -il, *s.m.* Prowess, chivalry.
naoinear, *s.m.coll.* Nine persons. [Followed by genitive pl.]
naoisg, see naosga.
naoitheamh,* see naothamh.
naomh, -aoimh, *s.m.* Saint. Na naoimh, *the saints.* Air son nan naomh, *on account of the saints.*
naomh, -aoimhe, *pl.* naomha, *a.* Holy, pious. 2 Divine. 3 Sacred, consecrated.
—————a, *a.* see naomh.
naomhachadh, -aidh, *s.m.* Sanctifying, act of sanctifying or consecrating, sanctification, consecration. A' n—, *pr.pt.* of naomhaich.
naomhachail,** -e, *a.* Sanctificatory, adorable.
naomhachd, *s. f. ind.* Holiness, sanctity. 2 Sanctification.
naomhadh,** -aidh, *s.m.* Sanctifying. 2 Sanctification.
naomhag,** -aig, *s.f.* Coble, see p. 78.
naomhaich, *pr.pt.* a' naomhachadh, *v.a.* Hallow, sanctify, consecrate. 2 Canonize. Gu'n naomhaichear t' ainm, *thy name be hallowed* ; n. e, *he sanctified.*
—————te, *past pt.* of naomhaich. Sanctified, consecrated.
naomh-aithis, -e, -ean, *s.f.* Blasphemy. 2 Blasphemy against saints, or 3, against holy things.
—————, *v.a.* Blaspheme.
—————each, -eiche, *a.* Blasphemous.
naomh-cheannachd, *s.f.ind.* Simony, purchasing of holy things with money.
naomh-chiste,** *s.f.* Sacristy.
naomh-chleachdas, -ais, *s.m.* Pious habit.
naomh-choisrig, *v.a.* see coisrig.
—————eadh, -idh, *s.* see coisrigeadh.
—————te, see coisrigte.
naomh-dhean,** *v.a.* Canonize, deify, sanctify.
—————amh, -aimh, *s.m.* Canonizing, deifying, canonization.
naomh-dhéirc, -e, -ean, *s.f.* Pious gift, deodand. 2 Collection made for the poor at church.
naomh-dhion, -a, -an *s.m.* Sanctuary, asylum.
naomh-dhion,** *v.a.* Give refuge in a sanctuary. 2**Take refuge in a sanctuary.
—————achd, *s. f.* Protection afforded by a sanctuary.
naomh-dhionta, *past pt.* Protected in a sanctuary.
naomh-dhiontach,** *a.* Affording an asylum. 2 Having the privilege of protecting, as a sanctuary.
naomh-ghnàths, -àis, *s.m.* Habitual piety.
naomh-ghoid, -e, *s.f.* Sacrilege. Am bheil thu ri n.? *dost thou commit sacrilege !*
—————each, -eiche, *a.* Sacrilegious.
naomh-ghoidiche,** *s.m.* Sacrilegious person.
naomh-mhallachadh, -aidh, *s.m.* Blasphemy. 2 Blaspheming, profane swearing. 3 Excommunication, anathema. A' n—, *pr. pt.* of naomh-mhallaich.
naomh-mhallachair, -ean, *s.m.* Blasphemer, profane swearer.
naomh-mhallachd, -an, *s.f.ind.* Blasphemy. 2 Excommunication, anathema.
naomh-mhallaich, *v.a.* Blaspheme. 2 Excommunicate, anathematize.
—————te, *past pt.* Excommunicated.
naomh-òigh,** *s.f.* The Virgin Mary. 2 Nun.
naomh-òran, -ain, *pl.* -an & -ain, *s.m.* Anthem, hymn, psalm.
naomh-reachd, -an, *s. m.* The holy or divine law, the canon law.
naomh-riaghailt,** *s.f.* The canon.
naomh-shluagh, -uaigh, *s. f. coll.* Holy people, saints.
naomh-shònrachadh, -aidh, *s.m.* Ordination.
naomh-thaisg,** *s.f.* Sacristy, vestry.
naomh-thréig, *pr. pt.* a' naomh-thréigsinn, *v.a.* Apostatize.
—————each, -eiche, *a.* Apostate, apostatizing.
—————each, -eich, *s.m.* Backslider.
naomh-thréigiche, -an, *s.m.* Apostate, renegade.
naomh-thréigire,* see naomh-thréigiche.
naomh-thréigsinn, -e, *s.f.* Apostacy, secession. 2 Act of apostatizing. 3* Hypocrisy. 4* Infidelity. A' n—, *pr.pt.* of naomh-thréig.
naomh-thuisleachadh,** *s.m.* Apostacy.
naomh-thuisleachair,** *s.m.* Apostate.
†naon, *a.* Certain, assured.
naonar, -air, see naoinear.
naontach,* -aich, *s.f.* Ninety.
naosg, -aoisg, *s.m.* Snipe.
naosga, *s.m.* Snipe, see gobhar-athair.
naosgach,** -aich, *s.m.* Snipe.
naosgach, -aiche, *a.* Abounding in snipes. 2 Like a snipe. Coire n., *a dell abounding in snipes.*
naosgair,** -ean, *s.m.* Inconstant man.
—————eachd,** *s.f.* Fickleness, inconstancy.
naosgamh, -aimh, *s.m.* see naosga.
naoth, see naoi.
naothadh, see naothamh.
naothamh, *a.* The ninth. An naothamh bliadhna, *the ninth year.*
naothamh-deug, *a.* The nineteenth. An naothamh fear deug, *the nineteenth man.*
nar, *adv.* Not, may not, let not. Nar leigeadh Dia ! *God forbid !*
'nar, *cont.* for an ar, *in our.* 'Nar cadal, *in our sleep* ; 'nar meadhon, *in the midst of us ;* tha sinn 'nar luighe, *we are in bed.*
'nar, *adv., prov.* for 'nuair.
'nar, (an bhur) see 'nur.
nàr, -àir, *s.f.* see nàir.
nàr,** -àire, *a.* Ashamed. 2 Shameful, disgraceful. 3 Feeling affronted. Is n. an gnothach e, *it is a shameful business.*
†nar,** *a.* Good. 2 Happy.
nàrach, -aiche, *a.* see nàireach.
nàrachadh, -aidh, see nàireachadh.
nàrachair,** *s.m.* Affronter.
nàrachd,‡‡ *s.f.* Bashfulness.
nàraich, *v.a.* see nàirich.
—————ear, see nàirichear.
nàraichidh, see nàirichidh.
nàraichte, see nàirichte.
nard,** *s.m.* Science, skill, knowledge.
narrach,** *a.* Cross, ill-tempered.
†nas, -ais, *s.m.* Anniversary. 2 Band, tie (nasg.) 3 Death. 4 Assembly.
na's, *comparative particle.* Than. Cha b' ur-

rainn da na's fhearr a dheanamh, *he could not do better*; tha Dòmhnall na's àirde na Seumas, *Donald is taller than James*.
†nas, -ais, -an, *s.f.* see neas. 2 (AC) Worth.
nàsach, see nòsach.
nasach, see neasach.
†nasach, *a.* Noble. 2 Famous, noted.
†nasadh, -aidh, -aidhean, *s.m.* Fair. 2 Assembly. 3 Fame, reputation, report.
nàsag, -aig, -an, *s.f.* Empty shell.
nasc,(AF) *s.m.* Chained dog, see nasg.
nasg, *v.a.* see naisg.
nasg, naisg, -an, *s. m.* [*s. f.* in *Badenoch.*] Tie-band, wooden collar for a cow, formerly made of plaited or twisted birch or other twigs. 2 Seal. 3 Deposit, pledge. 4 Store, provision. 5 Chain. 6 Ring. 7 (AF) Chained dog. 8 (MS) Air. 9 (DMC) Wooden ring of a sieve or fan. 10 (DMC) Film. Tha 'n t-airgiod an n., *the money is left in pledge, is deposited as security.*
nasgach, -aiche, *a.* Having collars. 2 Like collars or tie-bands. 3 Binding, that binds. 4 Obligatory. 5 **Chained. 6 **Full of rings.
nasgadh, -aidh, *s.m.* Binding, as with a collar. 2 Collar. 3 Chaining. 4 Covenant, treaty. 5 Tie, bond. 6**Obliging, obligation. 7**Sealing. 8* Pledging, depositing. A' n—, *pr. pt.* of naisg. Còir ort le n. a' chléir, *a right to thee by the binding af a clergyman—wedlock.*
nasgaich,* see nasgaidh.
nasgaidh, (i.e. a nasgaidh) *adv. phrase*, Freely, without price, gratis, as a pledge, deposit, or gift. Fhuair mi a n. e, *I received it free*; a n. fhuair sibh, a n. thugaibh bhuaibh, *freely ye have received, freely give;* thug e dhomh a n. e, *he gave it to me as a gratuity.*
nasgaidh,** *s.f.* Treasure, gift.
————eachd,* *s.f.ind.* Freeness, unconditional freeness, gratuity, gratuitousness.
nasgair,** *s.m.* Surety.
nasgar,** -air, *s.m.* Surety. 2 Defence, fortification.
nasg-chu,(AF) *s.m.* Chained dog.
natar, -air, *s.m.* Nitre.
†nath, *s.m.* Science, knowledge.
†nathach, *a.* Learned. 2 Dark, grey, gloomy.
nathair, nathrach, -thraichean, *s.f.* Serpent, viper, snake, adder. Mheall an n. mi, *the serpent beguiled me*; n. challtuinn, *a harmless snake.*
nathaireach, see nathaireil.
nathaireag, -eig, -an, *s.f.* Little serpent.
nathaireil, -e, *a.* Viperine.
nathair-ghainmheach,(WC) *s. f.* Sand-serpent, found in the sand on sea-shore.
nathair-gun-phuinnsean, (AF) *s.f.* Snake.
nathair-lus,§ *s.m.* Ground-ivy, see iadh-shlat-thalmhainn.
nathair-mhara,(DMC) *s.f.* Sea-serpent.
nathair-nimhe, *s.f.* Cockatrice. 2 Poisonous serpent, adder, asp.
nathair-thràghad,(AF) *s. f.* Small sand-fish or eel. 2 Shore- or sea-serpent.
nathair-sgiathach, (AF) *s.f.* Dragon.
uathair-umha, *s.f.* Brazen serpent.
nathair-uisge,(AF) *s.f.* Hydrus.
†nathan, *a.* Noble. 2 Famous.
nathrach, *gen.sing.* of nathair.
nathraichean, *n.pl.* of nathair.
-ne, *emphat. particle.* A certain emphatic adjection to the *poss.pron.* ar, *our*; placed after the noun with which the *poss. pron.* is associated. Ar n-athair-ne (*better*, an t-athair againne) *our own father.*
'n déidh, *adv.* After, behind.
'n è ? *cont.* for an e ? Is it ? is it he ? Cha 'n e, *no, not he.*
†neabhaidh,** *s.m.* Enemy.
neabhan,(AF) *s.m.* Royston crow, raven.
neacadair,** -ean, *s.m.* Nectarine. Crann n., *a nectarine tree.*
————each,** *a.* Abounding in nectarines. 2 Like a nectarine.
neach, *s. m. ind.* Person, any person, one, someone. 2**Apparition. N. sam bith, n. air bith, *anyone*; n. eile, *another person*; gach n., *every one*; n. éigin, *someone*; n. no n. éigin, *someone or other.*
†neachd,** *s.f.* Tribe, family. 2 Pledge.
†neachdachd,** *s.f.* Neutrality.
neachdair,§ *s.m.* Nectarine (kind of peach)—*amygdalus persica nectarina.*
†neachdar, *adv.* Neither. 2 Outwardly, without.
†neachdarach,** *a.* Neutral.
nead, nid, *s.m.* [*f.* in *Argyllshire.*] Nest. 2 Circular hollow.
neadach, -aiche, *a.* Abounding in nests.
————adh, -aidh, *s.m.* Nestling, act of nestling. 2 Act of making or building a nest. 3 (DU) *metaphorically*, Settling down, making at home. A' n—, *pr. pt.* of neadaich. A' n. 'nam fheòil, *imbedding in my flesh.*
neadaich, *pr. pt.* a' neadachadh, *v. a.* Nestle, house, lie, as in a nest. 2 Build or make a nest. 3* Bed, imbed.
————te, *past pt.* of neadaich. Housed or lodged, as in a nest, nestled.
neadan, -ain, -an, *s. m., dim.* of nead. Little nest. A n. creachta, *her little nest plundered.*
————ach, -aiche, *a.* Abounding in little nests.
'n eadh ? *v.* Is it ?
nead-thogalach,‡‡ *a.* Building nests.
neag, see eag.
——ach, see eagach.
——aich, see eagaich.
——aid,* *s.f.* Little sob or sigh oft repeated, as a person before or after weeping. 2 Suppressed sighing or sobbing.
†neal, *a.* Noble.
neal,(DMu) *s.m.* & *f.* Term of endearment. An gabh thu seo, neal ? *will you take this, my dear !—Suth'd.*
neal, see neul.
neallair,** -ean, *s.m.* Rogue, ramscallion.
————eachd,** *s.f.* Roguery, rascality.
neal-mhàgag,(CR) *s.f.* Frog—*Skye.*
nèamh, nèimh & nèimhe, *pl.* -an, *s.m.* Heaven, firmament, the skies. 2 The abode of bliss. Driùchd nèimh, *the dew of heaven.*
neamh, see neimh. †2 see neo.
nèamhach, *a.* see nèamhaidh.
nèamhach, -aich, *s.m.* Heavenly being, angel.
————d, *s.f.* Heavenliness, heavenly mindedness, holiness, solemnity, blessedness, angelicalness.
nèamhaich,** *v.a.* Deify, glorify.
nèamhaidh, -e, *a.* Heavenly, divine. 2**Celestial.
————each,** -ich, see nèamhach.
————eachd, see nèamhachd.
nèamhail, see neimheil. 2** Angelic.
neamhain, -mhna, -ean, *s. f.* see neamhnuid. 2**Impetuosity, violence. 3 Activity. A cheann-bheart clochara neamhain, *his headpiece set with stones and pearls.*
————,** *a.* Made of pearl.
————each, -eiche, *a.* see neamhnuideach.
neamhaird,** *s.f.* Remissness.
neamhalachd, see neimheileachd.
nèamhalachd,** *s.f.* Angelicalness.
neamhan,** -ain, *s.m.* Raven, crow.
neamhann,(MS) *s.* Margarite.

ncamhnad, see sleamh'ian.
neamhnagan,†† -ain, *s.f.* Stye on the eye.
neamhnaid, see neamhnuid.
neamhnuid, -e, -ean, *s.f.* Pearl. N. nan iomadaidh bua lh, *a pearl of many virtues.*
neamhnuideach, -eiche, *a.* Pearly, abounding in pearls. 2 Like a pearl.
nèamhuidh, -e, see nèamhaidh.
†**nean**,** *s.m.* Inch. 2 Span. 3 Wave.
neanaidh, *s.f.* Fond name for a grandmother.
neanntag, -aig, see deanntag.
neanntagach, -aich, *s.* see deanntag.
nèapaicin, -e, -ean *s.f.* Napkin, handkerchief. N. pòca, *a pocket handkerchief*; n. amhaich, *a neckerchief.*
neapaigin, see nèapaicin.
near,** *a.* Boorish.
†**near**,** *s.m.* Wild boar. 2 Water, river.
'near, *cont.* for an ear.
nèarach, *a.* Happy, fortunate. 2 Prosperous. Is n. an duine a smachdaicheas Dia, *fortunate is the man whom God correcteth.*
nèarachd,†† *s.f.ind.* Luck. 2 Happiness. 3 Prosperity.
nèarachd,** *a.* see nèarach.
nearag, -aig, -an, *s.f.* Daughter.
near-àite,***s.m.* Place frequented by wild boars.
'nearar, *cont.* for an earar.
nearc,(AC) *s.* Means. Beannaich dhomh mo n. 's mo nì, *bless to me my means and my cattle.*
†**nearnadh**,** -aidh, *s.m.* Likening, comparing. 2 Likeness, comparison.
neart, neirt, *s. m.* Strength, power, might, energy, pith, force, vigour. 2 Plenty, abundance, many, number. 3**The greater part of anything. 4** Valour. 4***rarely* Miracle. Le t' uile n., *with all your might*; cuir do n. ris, *apply to it your whole vigour*; n. airgid, *a vast quantity of money*; n. buntàta, *a great quantity of potatoes*; n. éisg, *an abundance of fish*; cha'n 'eil n. aige air son sin, *he has not strength enough to do that*; bha neart dhiubh marbh, *the greater part of them were dead*; neart a' chuim, *the valour of his breast*; n. nan dàn, *the strength of song.*
neartachadh, -aidh, *s.m.* Strengthening, act of strengthening. 2 Confirming, ratifying. A' n—, *pr.pt.* of neartaich.
neartaich, *pr.pt.* a' neartachadh, *v.a.* Strengthen, fortify, invigorate. 2**Actuate. 3**Confirm, ratify, establish.
neartaichear, *fut.pass.* of neartaich.
neartaichte, *past pt.* of neartaich. Strengthened, fortified, re-inforced. 2**Actuated. 3** Confirmed. 4 Animated.
neartail, -e, *a.* Emphatic in *gram.* 2 see neartmhor.
neartalachd,* see neartmhorachd.
neartar,** see neartmhor.
neartmhor, -oire, *a.* Strong, powerful, able. 2 Robust, vigorous.
neartmhorachd, *s. f. ind.* Strength, might, powerfulness. 2 Pithiness, energy of character, vigorousness.
neartor,** see neartmhor.
†**neas**,** *a.* Noble, generous, magnanimous.
neas, nise, *s.f.* Weasel. 2 Stoat. 3**Ferret. 4 **Hurt, wound. 5**Fortified hill. [†† gives *gen.sing.* neasa.]
neas, *adv.* While, whilst. Neas is beò mi, *while I live.* n. a bha e air falbh, *while he was away*; n. a chì mi, *while I see.* [for an fheadh 's.]
†**neas**, *s.m.* Isthmus. 2 Promontory, headland.
neas,** *s.m.* Tool for making earthen pots.
neas-abhag,** -aig, -an, *s.m.* Ferret.
neasachd,** *s.f.* Proximity, nearness.
neasadair,** *s.* Ferreter.
†**neasan**, -ain, *s.m.* Next or nearest place.
neas-bheag, *s.f.* Stoat.
neasg, -a & neisg, -an, see neasgaid. 2**Tie, bond. 3**Snail.
neasgaid, -e, -ean, *s.f.* Boil, ulcerous sore, pustulous sore. 2 Carbuncle.
neasgaid-chloich, *s.f.* Stone bile.
———each, -eiche, *a.* Full of boils, ulcerous 2 Causing boils or ulcers.
neasgaid-fhola,§ *s.f.* Hæmorrhoid.
neasgaid-ghobhail,‖ *s.f.* Hæmorrhoid.
neas-gheal,(AF)*s.f.* Stoat, ermine, white weasel.
neas-mhór, *s.f.* Weasel.
neas-nam-fuar-thirean,(AF) *s.f.* Ermine, Armenian rat.
†**neasta**,** *a.* Just, honest.
neath,** *s.m.* Wound.
†**neatha**, *a.* Wounding, inflicting wounds.
†**neathas**, -ais, *s.m.* Manslaughter.
neich,** *a.* Good, noble, excellent.
neid,** *s.* Battle. 2 Wound received in battle.
néil, *gen.sing.* of neul. [generally neòil.]
néilean, -ain, -an, *dim.*of neul. *s.m.* Little cloud.
nèimh, *gen.sing.* of nèamh.
neimh, -e, *s.m.* Poison. 2 Bitterness, malice, animosity. [generally nimh.]
——,** -e, *s.f.* Brightness, splendour. 2 Stain.
neimh,** *v.a.* & *n.* Corrupt, soil.
neimheach,** *a.* Glittering, shining, splendid, bright.
neimheacha-'n-iar, (AH) *adv.* In a confused hurry, tumultuously, helter-skelter.
neimhead,**, -eid, *s. m.* Consecrated ground. 2 Glebe land.
†**neimheadh**, -idh, *s.m.* Poem. 2 Science.
neimhealachd, see neimheileachd.
neimheil, -ala, *a.* Poisonous, baneful, viperous, venomous, malicious, bitter, malignant. 2 Passionate. 3* Venomously cold. 4*Keenly wicked.
neimheileachd,** *s.f.* Painfulness, sourness, malignity, venomousness. 2 Passionateness. 3 *Greediness in wickedness. 4* Piercing coldness.
†**neimhi**, *s.pl.* Ants' eggs.
neimhich, *v.a.* Poison. [generally nimhich.]
†**neimhidh**, *s.* Church-land.
neimhneach, -eiche, *a.* see neimheil. 2** Sore, painful.
neimhneachan, -ain, *s.m.* Rheumatism.
neimhneachas, -ais, *s. m.* Soreness. 2 Venomousness. 3 Passionateness.
neimhneachd, *s.f.ind.* Poisonousness, virulence, banefulness. 2 Animosity, bitterness.
†**neimneime**,(AF) *s.* Non-exempt cattle.
nèip, *pl.* -ean & -eis, *s.m.* Turnip—*brassica rapa.*
——each, -eiche, *a.* Abounding in turnips. 2 Like a turnip.
neirt, *gen.sing.* of neart.
nèip-fiadhain,§ *s.m.* Wild navew—*brassica campestris.* (illust. on p. 688.)
†**neith**, *s.* Fight, engagement.
neo, *cont.* of neimhidh, occuring in place-names.
neo-, *priv. prefix.* Prefix implying the negation or absence of the quality expressed by the adjective or word itself. Glic, *wise*; neo-ghlic, *unwise.*
neo,†† *adv.* Otherwise, else. N. is truagh mo chàradh, *else poor is my condition*; air n., *otherwise*, or *else*; n. teichidh mi, *otherwise I will decamp*; n. théid mi dhachaidh, *otherwise I will go home.*
neo-àbhaist, *s.f.* Rare occurrence.
————each, *a.* Unusual.
neo-abuich, -e, *a.* Unripe, premature, abortive.
neo-adhartach, *a.* Idle.
neo-àdhmhor, -oire, *a.* Unsuccessful, unfortun-

551. *Nèip-fiadhain.*

ate, hapless. 2**Inglorious. 3**Joyless.

——————achd,** *s.f.* Unsuccessfulness. 2 Ingloriousness.

neo-àghmhor, see neo-àdhmhor.

neo-aimsireil, -e, *a.* Unseasonable.

neo-ainmeach,** *a.* Anonymous.

neo-ainmneach, see neo-ainmeach.

neo-ainmichte, *a.* Anonymous.

neo-air-chàs, *s.m.* Carelessness.

neo-aire, *s.f.ind.* Heedlessness, inattention, inadvertence, unguardedness. 2 Absence of mind. 3(MS) Aspernation.

neo-aireach, -eiche, *a.* Heedless, inattentive, careless, forgetful. 2 Inadvertent. 3 Absent in mind.

neo-aireachail, -e, *a.* see neo-aireach. 2 (DMC) Unsympathetic, unfeeling, callous.

neo-aireil, -ala, *a.* see neo-aireach.

neo-aireileachd, *s.f.ind.* Inconsiderateness.

neo-àireamhach,(MS) *a.* Innumerable.

neo-àireamhchail,(MS) Innumerable.

neo-airidh, -e, *a.* Unworthy, undeserving, worthless. N. air peanas, *unworthy of punishment.*

neo-airidheach, -eiche, *a.* Indign.

neo-air-thoirt,(WC) *s.m.* Carelessness, indifference.

neo-airtnealach, -aiche, *a.* Not sorrowful, cheerful, joyful. Ag éirigh dhuinn n., *when we rose joyful.*

neo-aithnichte, *a.* Unknown, undiscovered. 2 Unrecognized. Rìoghachdan n., *unknown kingdoms.*

neo-aithreach, -eiche, *a.* Impenitent, not contrite, obdurate. 2**Not curious.

neo-aithreachail, -e, *a.* Impenitent, obdurate.

neo-aithreachas, -ais, *s.m.* Impenitence, obduracy, hardness of heart.

neo-altmhor,(MS) *a.* Home-bred.

neo-àluinn, -e, *a.* Ordinary.

neo-àluinneachd, *s.f.* Inelegance.

neo-amaisgeal,(WC) *a.* Elusive.

neo-amhalach,* -aiche, *a.* Slily and without drawing attention. Gu n., *unawares, slily*; thàinig e a stigh gu n., *he came in unawares.*

neo-amharus, -uis, *s.m.* Unsuspiciousness, want of suspicion.

neo-amharusach, -aiche, *a.* Unsuspicious, indubitable, unquestionable.

neo-amharusachd,** *s.f.* Unsuspiciousness, indubitableness.

neo-amhluidh, -e, *a.* Unlike, dissimilar.

neo-amhluidheachd, *s.f.ind.* Unlikeness.

neo-aobharach, *a.* Uncaused, unprovoked.

neo-aobharachd,(MS) *s.f.* Groundlessness.

neo-aogasach, -aiche, *a.* Unseemly. 2 Of a forbidding appearance, unbecoming.

neo-aogasachd, *s.f.ind.* Unseemliness. 2 Bad or forbidding appearance.

neo-aoibheil,* *a.* Cheerless.

neo-aoibhinn, -e, see neo-aoibhneach.

neo-aoibhneach, -eiche, *a.* Not joyful, sorrowful, sad, joyless, downcast, cheerless, surly.

neo-aoibhneas, -eis, *s.m.* Sadness, sorrow, gloom.

neo-aoidhealachd, *s. f. ind.* Unpleasantness of appearance. 2 Churlishness.

neo-aoidheil, -e, *a.* Unpleasant, having a sour look. 2 Churlish.

neo-aonachd, *s.f.* Opposition.

neo-aon-fhlaitheach,** *a.* Anti-monarchical.

neo-aon-fhlaitheachail, *a.* Anti-monarchical.

neo-aon-fhlaitheachd,** *s. f.* Anti-monarchicalness.

neo-aontachadh,** -aidh, *s.m.* Disagreeing, disunion, dissentience. 2 Act of disagreeing.

neo-aontachail, -e, *a.* Adverse, averse, disinclined. 2 Disagreeing, discordant, dissentient, disunited.

neo-aontachas, -ais, *s.m.* Incongruity.

neo-aontachd, *s.f.* Incongruity.

neo-arta,** *a.* Untilled.

neo-ar-thaing, *a.* Independent. N. cho dona rium, *every bit as bad as I am.*

neo-ar-thaingeil,(WC) *a.* Unthankful.

neo-ascaoin, -e, *a.* Friendly. 2 Humane.

neo-aslaichte,(MS) *a.* Inexorable.

neo-athach,(DMC) *a.* Daring, desperate.

neo-athachd, *s.f.* Desperateness.

neo-atharrachail, -e, *a.* Indeclinable.

neo-atruasach,(MS) *a.* Hard-hearted.

neo-bhacta, *a.* Arbitrary.

neo-bhàigheach, -eiche, see neo-bhàigheil.

neo-bhàighealachd, *s.f.ind.* Unkindness, harshness, cruelty, inclemency.

neo-bhàigheil, -e, *a.* Unkind, harsh, merciless, cruel, not sparing, unfeeling. Gu m., *mercilessly.*

neo-bhallsgail,** *a.* Home-bred.

neo-bhaodhalach, *a.* Unprecarious.

neo-bhàsmhoire, *comp.* of neo-bhàsmhor.

neo-bhàsmhoireachd, see neo-bhàsmhorachd.

neo-bhàsmhor, -aire, *a.* Immortal.

neo-bhàsmhorachd,** *s.f.* Immortality.

neo-bheachdmhor, *a.* Unobservant.

neo-bheachdmhorachd, *s.f.ind.* Inconsiderableness.

neo-bheairteach, see neo-bheartach.

neo-bheartach, -aiche, *a.* Not rich.

neo-bheartaichte,** *past pt.* Unharnessed, unyoked.

neo-bheathachail, -e, *a.* Inalimental.

neo-bheathail, -e, *a.* Lifeless, spiritless, inanimate.

neo-bheathalachd, *s. f. ind.* Lifelessness, want of spirit or animation.

neo-bheothail, -e, *a.* Lifeless, spiritless, inanimate.

neo-bheudar, -aire, *a.* Harmless. 2 Inoffensive.

neo-bheus,†† *s.m.* Immodesty, indecency. 2 Immorality.

neo-bheusach,** *a.* Immodest, indecent. 2 Immoral.

neo-bhinn, *a.* Absonant.

neo-bhith, -e, *s. f.* Non-existence. 2 Non-entity.

neo-bhlasda, -aisde, *a.* Tasteless, insipid. 2 Unsavoury.

——————chd, *s.f.ind.* Tastelessness, insipidity. 2 Unsavouriness.

neo-bhloigheach, *a.* Indivisible.

neo-bhog, -bhuige, *a.* Hard, firm. 2 Hardy. 3 Courageous, not soft, not effeminate.

neo-bhogaichte, *a.* Infusible.
neo-bhòidheach, -eiche, *a.* Not pretty, unhandsome, unseemly.
neo-bhràtharail, -e, see neo-bhràthaireil.
neo-bhràthairealachd, *s.f.ind.* Unbrotherliness.
neo-bhràthaireil, -e, *a.* Unbrotherly. Giulan n., *unbrotherly conduct.*
neo-bhràthrail, -e, see neo-bhràthaireil.
neo-bhrìgh, -e, *s. f.* Insignificance, unimportance. 2 Contempt. 3 Inefficacy. 4 Want of substance. Chuir sibh an n. aithne Dhé, *you have made the command of God of no effect.*
neo-bhrìgheach, -eiche, *a.* Insipid.
neo-bhrìghichte,** *a.* Cancelled.
neo-bhrìghmhor, *a.* Unsubstantial. 2 Unnutricious.
neo-bhruailleanach, *a.* Gentle.
——————d,(MS) *s.f.* Rest.
neo-bhuaireasach, -aiche, *a.* Inoffensive.
neo-bhuairte, *a.* Undisturbed, untroubled. 2** Untempted, unprovoked.
neo-bhuan, -uaine, *a.* Not lasting, not durable, transitory, evanescent.
neo-bhuanach, *a.* Gainless, unprofitable.
neo-bhuanachd,** *s.f.* Transitoriness, momentariness, evanescence. 2 Gainlessness.
——————dail, -e, *a.* Fruitless.
neo-bhuidheach, -eiche, *a.* Unthankful, discontented.
neo-bhuileachaidh, *a.* Inalienable.
neo-bhunailteach, see neo-bhunaiteach.
——————d, see neo-bhunaiteachd.
neo-bhunailteas, see neo-bhunaiteas.
neo-bhunaiteach, -eiche, *a.* Unsteady, unfixed, changeable. 2 Groundless. 3 Not well founded.
——————d,** *s.f.* Unsteadiness. 2 Want of sure foundation.
neo-bhunaiteas, -eis, *s.m.* Want of steadiness, instability.
neo-bhuinnigeach, *a.* Gainless.
neo-bhuinnigeachd, *s.f.* Gainlessness.
neo-bhuntuinneach,** *a.* Disinterested.
neo-bhuintinneach,(MS) *a.* Impalpable.
neo-chadalach, -aiche, *a.* Sleepless.
neo-chàil, -e, *s.* Inappetence.
neo-chàirdeach,(MS) *a.* Alien.
neo-chairdealachd, *s.f.ind.* Coolness.
neo-chàirdeil, -e, *a.* Unfriendly. Gu n., *in an unfriendly manner.*
neo-chaldachail, *a.* Untameable.
neo-chaochlaideach, -eiche, *a.* Unchangeable.
neo-chaochlaideachd, *s. f.* Unchangeableness, immutability.
neo-chaochlaidheach, -eiche, see neo-chaochlaideach.
neo-chaochlaidheachd, see neo-chaochlaideachd.
neo-chaochluidheach, see neo-chaochlaideach.
neo-chaomhantach, -aiche, *a.* Unthrifty.
neo-charach, -aiche, *a.* Designless.
neo-charachadh,(MS) *s.m.* Indolence.
neo-chàramh, *s.m.* State of not being put up, as hair—*Wm. Ross.*
neo-charas, -ais, *s.m.* Impassibility.
neo-charaichte, *a.* Unmoved, unstirred.
neo-charaidheach, -eiche, *a.* Immovable, fixed, steady.
neo-charaidheachd, *s.f.ind.* Immobility, steadiness, fixedness.
neo-charraideach, -eiche, *a.* Not quarrelsome, peaceful, peaceable, quiet, without toil.
neo-charuichte, see neo-charaichte.
neo-charthannach, -aich, *a.* Uncharitable, unfriendly.
neo-charthannachd, *s.f.ind.* Uncharitableness, unfriendliness.
neo-charthannas, -ais, *s.m.* see neo-charthannachd.
neochdair,§ see neachdair.
neo-cheadaich,* *v.a.* Prohibit.
neo-cheadaichte, *a.* Illicit, unlawful, illegal, prohibited, not permitted.
neo-chealgach, -aiche, *a.* Sincere,undesigning, upright, unfeigned, candid, not cunning.
neo-chealgachd, *s.f.ind.* Sincerity, uprightness, unfeignedness, candour, fairness, unaffectedness.
neo-cheanalta, -ailte, *a.* Unhandsome, unbecoming, inelegant. 2 Indelicate.
neo-cheanaltachd, *s.f.* Unhandsomeness, unbecomingness.
neo-cheangail,* *v.a.* Untie.
neo-cheangailte, *a.* Unbound, disengaged, free, at liberty. 2 Absolute. 3(MS) Incoherent.
neo-cheangailteachd,** *s.f.* Absoluteness. (MS) Incoherence.
neo-cheangaltachd, see neo-cheangailteachd.
neo-cheangaltas, -ais, *s. m.* Freedom, liberty unconstraint. 2(MS) Absoluteness.
neo-cheannsachaidh, *a.* Bateless.
neo-cheannsaichte, *a.*Untamed, unconquerable unrestrained, unquelled, unappeased, unsubdued. 2 Absolute. 3 Dissolute.
neo-chearbach, -aiche, *a.* Tidy, neat, trim. Accurate, exact. 3*Efficient.
neo-chearbaiche, *s.f.ind.* Tidiness, neatness.
neo-chearmanta,** *a.* Botchy.
——————chd,** *s.f.* Clumsiness.
neo-cheart, -eirte, *a.* Not true, not right unfair, ill-founded. 2 Unhandsome, unjust.
neo-cheartachd, *s.f.* Incorrectness.
neo-cheartaichte, *a.* Uncorrected, unadjusted.
neo-cheòlmhor, -oire, *a.* Tuneless.
neo-chiallach, -aiche, *a.* Foolish, imprudent, 2 Mad. 3 Unmeaning.
neo-chinnte, *s.f.* Same meanings as neo-chinnteachd.
neo-chinnteach, -eiche, *a.* Uncertain, doubtful, fickle, indecisive, precarious, equivocal, problematical. 2 Precarious.
neo-chinnteachd, *s.f.* Uncertainty, whimsicality, fickleness, incertitude, indecisiveness.
neo-chinntealas,** -ais, *s.m.* Apocryphalness.
neo-chionnsaichte, see neo-cheannsaichte.
neo-chiont, see neo-chiontachd.
neo-chionta, *s.m.* see neo-chiontachd.
neo-chiontach, -aiche, *a.* Innocent,unblameable, harmless, spotless, simple.
neo-chiontach,** -eich, *s.m.* Innocent person.
neo-chiontachd, *s.f.ind.* Innocence, integrity, harmlessness, guiltlessness, uprightness, spotlessness.
neo-chiontas, -ais, *s.m.* Harmlessness, spotlessness.
neo-chiosnaichte,** *past pt.* Untamed, unquelled, unconquered, unappeased.
neo-chìrte,** *past pt.* Uncombed.
neo-chlaimhsinich, (MS) *v.a.* Unlatch.
neo-chlaon, -aoine, *a.* Straight, not awry, not squinting. 2 Upright, impartial, just.
neo-chlaonachd, *s.f.ind.* Impartiality.
neo-chlaon-bhreitheach, -eiche, *a.* Judging impartially.
neo-chlaon-bhreitheachd, *s. f.* Impartiality of judgment.
neo-chleachd,** *v.a.* Abrogate, discontinue the practice of.
neo-chleachdach, -aiche, *a.* Unusual, unwont.
neo-chleachdainn,* *s.f.* Abrogation, discontinuing the practice of.
neo-chleachdta, *a.* Unaccustomed, not inured, unpractised, unhabituated.
neo-chléir,** *s.f.* The laity.

neo-chléireach,** -ich, *s.m.* Layman.
neo-chli, *a.* Not awkward, expert, dexterous. 2 Not weak, active.
neo-chnuasachd,** *s.f.* Indigestion.
neo-chnuasaichte, *a.* Undigested, unchewed.
neo chogach, -aiche, *a.* Immartial.
neo-choguiseach, -eiche, *a.* Inconscionable.
neo-choigealtach, -aiche, *a.* Unthrifty, profuse.
neo-choigilt, *a.* see neo-choigilteach.
————each,** *a.* Unthrifty, profuse.
neo-choigreach.(MS) *a.* Home-born.
neo-choigreachail, *a.* Domestic.
neo-choimeasach,** *a.* Incomparable.
neo-choimeasachd, *s.f.* Peerlessness.
neo-choimeasgach, -aiche, *a.* Immiscible.
neo-choimeasgta, *a.* Unmixed.
neo-choimheach, -eiche, *a.* Kind, affectionate. 2 Affable, not surly, not stingy, free, not shy, not strange, easy of access, frank, generous. 3(MS) Home-born.
————as, see neo-choimhicheas.
neo-choimheartach. *a.* Incomparable.
neo-choimhicheas,-eis, *s.m.* Kindness, affection. 2 Affability, condescension. 3 Freedom. 4 Complacency, want of shyness. 5* Making oneself at home.
neo-choimhlionta, *a.* Incomplete. 2 Half-strained.
neo-choimhliontachd, *s.f.* Incompleteness.
neo-choingheallach, -aiche, *a.* Ill-natured, unaccommodating, disobliging. 2 Perfidious.
neo-choireach, -eiche, *a.* Blameless, not blamable, innocent, inculpable.
neo-choireachd,* *s.f.* Blamelessness, innocence, guiltlessness.
neo-choisrigte, *a.* Unhallowed, not consecrated. 2 Not dedicated.
neo-choitcheannachd, *s.f.* Anomalousness.
neo-chomarach,(MS) *a.* Aidless.
neo-chomaraich, *s.f.* The state of being free from obligation or favour, non-protection.
neo-chomas, -ais, *s. m.* Inability, impotence. 2 **Debility.
neo-chomasach, -aiche, *a.* Unable, impotent. 2 Impossible.
neo-chomasachd, *s. f. ind.* Incapability. 2 Impossibility.
neo-chomhairle, *s.f.ind.* Irresolution.
neo-chomhairlichte, *a.* Unadvised. 2**Unresolved.
neo-chomharraichte, *a.* Undistinguished. 2 Indefinite in *grammar.*
neo-chòmhnard,** *a.* Uneven on the surface, not level, not plain.
neo-chòmhnuidheach, -eiche, *a.* Non-resident.
neo-chòmhnardachd, *s.f.ind.* Asperity.
neo-chompanta, -ainte, *a.* Unsociable, uncompanionable.
neo-chompantas,* -ais, *s. m.* Unsociableness, unamiableness.
neo-chomraich, *s.f.* see neo-chomaraich.
neo-chomunnach, -aiche, *a.* Uncommunicating, incommunicable.
neo-chòrdach,** *a.* Discordant.
neo-chòrdachd, *s.f.ind.* Inconstancy.
neo-chòrdadh,** -aidh, *s.m.* Disagreement, discordance, dissonance.
neo-chorporra, *a.* Spiritual.
neo-chorporrachd, *s.f.ind.* Immateriality
neo-choslach, -aiche, see neo-chosmhuil.
neo-choslachd, see neo-chosmhuileachd.
neo-chosmhail, see neo-chosmhuil.
neo-chosmhalachd, see neo-chosmhuileachd.
neo-chosmhuil, -e, *a.* Unlike, dissimilar. 2 Unlikely, improbable.
neo-chosmhuileachd, *s.f.ind.* Unlikelihood. 2 Dissimilarity. 3 Improbability.

neo-chosach, -aiche, *a.* Imporous.
neo-chothrom, -oim, *s.m.* Disadvantage, want of opportunity. 2 Unfairness, injustice. 3 Disproportion.
neo-chothromach, -aiche, *a.* Disadvantageous. 2 Unfair, unjust. 3 Uneven, rough. 4 Inconvenient, not opportune. 5 (DMC) Improvident.
neo-chràbhach, -aiche, *a.*Irreligious. 2 Profane. 3 Impious. 4 Not hypocritical. 5* Not austere in religious matters.
neo-chrathaidh, *a.* Inconcussible.
neo-chreideach, -aiche, *a.* see neo-chreidmheach.
————d, see neo-chreidmheachd.
neo-chreidimh, *s.f.ind.* Incredibility. 2 Incredulity.
neo-chreidmheach, -eich, *s.m.* Unbeliever, infidel, see tic.
neo-chreidmheach, -eiche, *a.* Unbelieving, infidel, unholy, atheistical.
neo-chreidmheachd, *s.f.ind.* Atheisticalness, infidelity, scepticism.
neo-chreidsinneach, -eiche, *a.* Improbable.
neo-chriathairte, *a.* Unsifted.
neo-chriochnach, -aiche, *a.* Endless, infinite, everlasting, unlimited.
neo-chriochnachaidh, *a.* Illimitable.
neo-chriochnachail, -e, *a.* Illimitable.
neo-chriochnachas, *s.m.* Illimitedness, indefinitude.
neo-chriochnachd,** *s.f.ind.* Boundlessness.
neo-chriochnaichte, *a.* Unfinished, unlimited, endless, undone, incomplete.
neo-chriochnuidheach, -eiche, see neo-chriochnach.
neo-chriochnuidheachd, *s.f.* Infinitude, endlessness.
neo-chrion, -a, *a.* Generous, liberal, magnanimous.
neo-chrionna, *a.* Injudicious.
neo-chrionndachd, *s.f.* Imprudence.
neo-chronail, -e, *a.* Harmless.
neo-chruadal, -ail, *s.m.* Impatience.
neo-chruadalach, -aiche, *a.* Not hardy. 2 Wanting energy, impatient of fatigue or hardship, soft, effeminate. 3* Lubberly. 4 Not cruel, not hard-hearted.
neo-chruinn,** *a.* Not round. 2 Not sane.
neo-chruinneil,** *a.* Awkward.
neo-chruinnichte, *a.* Uncollected, scattered, ungathered, unassembled.
neo-chruthaichte, *a.* Uncreated, unformed.
neo-chubhaidh, -e, *a.* Unseemly, unmeet, improper, unbecoming, unfit. 2 Unmerited. 3 Not hereditary.
neo-chubhaidheachd, *s.f.* Inexpedience.
neo-chùbhraidheachd, *s.f.* Unsavouriness.
neo-chuid,** *s.f.* Poverty.
neo-chuideach,** *a.* Poor, indigent. 2 Improvident.
neo-chuideamach, *a.* Immaterial.
neo-chuimhne, *s. f.* Forgetfulness, negligence. 2 Carelessness, heedlessness.
neo-chuimhneach, -aiche, *a.* see neo-chuimhneachail.
neo-chuimhneachail, -e, *a.* Forgetful 2 Heedless, careless.
neo-chuimir,** *a.* Awkward.
neo-chuimseach, -eiche, *a.* Not aiming well. 2 Excessive, immoderate, intemperate, exhorbitant. 3 Infinite. 4 Unsuitable. 5 Disproportionate.
neo-chuimseachd, *s. f.* Disproportion. 2 Immoderation.
neo-chuimsich, *v.a.* Disproportion.
neo-chùirteil, -e, *a.* Uncourtly, uncourteous.
neo-chulach, -aiche, *a.* Lean. 2 Silly

neo-chumachd, *s.f.ind.* Informity.
————ail, -e, *a.* Informous
neo-chumadail, *a.* Unshapely, untidy.
neo-chumadh,(MS) *s.m.* Asymmetry.
neo-chumaireachd,* *s.f.* Deformity.
neo-chumaltach, -aiche, *a.* Irretentive.
neo-chumanta, -ainte, *a.* Uncommon, unusual.
————chd, *s.f.ind.* Uncommonness, rareness, novelty.
neo-chùmhnantach, -aiche, *a.* Unconditional, admitting of no conditions.
neo-chunbhalach, -aiche, *a.* Capricious, changeable, inconstant, deciduous, variable.
————,(MS) *s.m.* Fugitive.
————d, *s.f.* Capriciousness.
neo-chunbhalas, *s.m.* Inconstancy.
neo-churaidh,** *a.* Gentle,
neo-churam, -aim, *s.m.* Negligence, carelessness, neglect, indifference, inattentiveness. 2 ** Security.
————ach, -aiche, *a.* Negligent, inattentive, inadvertent, indifferent, careless. 2 Prodigal. 3 (DMC) Irreligious.
————achd, *s. f. ind.* Inconsiderateness. 2 Desperateness.
neo-churanta, -ainte, *a.* Unwarlike.
neo-dhàichealachd, *s.f.ind.* Unhandsomeness, want of gentility. 2 Improbability, unlikelihood, absurdity.
neo-dhàicheil, -e, *a.* Unhandsome, ungenteel. 2 Improbable, absurd, unlikely.
neo-dhàimh, -e, *s.f.* Inconnexion.
neo-dhàimheach,(MS) *a.* Alien.
neo-dhàimheil, *a.* Alien.
neo-dhaingneachd, *s.f.ind.* Laxness.
neo-dhaingnichte, *a.* Unbound, unfixed. 2 Unratified, unconfirmed. 3‡‡Disengaged, unengaged. 4 Unsatisfied.
neo-dhaonnach, -aiche, *a.* Inhuman, unkind. 2 **Inhospitable.
neo-dhaonnachd, *s.f.* Inhumanity, unkindness.
neo-dhealbh, -eilbh, *s.m.* Informity.
neo-dhealachaidh, *a.* Inalienable.
neo-dhean,** *v.n.* Annul, undo.
neo-dhearbhachd, *s.f.ind.* Inconsequence.
neo-dhearcach, -aiche, *a.* Inattentive.
————d, *s.f.* Inattentiveness.
neo-dhearbha,(MS) *a.* Precarious, unreliable.
neo-dheas,** *a.* Not active. 2 Not neat.
————achd, *s.f.* Inconcoction.
neo-dheisealachd, *s.f.* Disaccommodation.
neo-dheithichte, *a.* Unsmoked.
neo-dheothasach,** *a.* Cool.
neo-dhiadhaidh, -e, *a.* Ungodly, impious, unholy, profane, irreligious.
neo-dhiadhaidheachd, *s. f.* Ungodliness, irreligion, impiety, atheism.
neo-dhiadhuidh, see neo-dhiadhaidh.
neo-dhibireach, *a.* Accurate.
neo-dhìleas, -dhìlse, *a.* Faithless, unfaithful, disloyal, undutiful. 2**Unrelated.
neo-dhìlse, see neo-dhìlseachd.
neo-dhìlseachd, *s.f.ind.* Faithlessness, unfaithfulness, disloyalty, unfriendliness. 2** Non-relationship.
neo-dhioclaideach,(MS) *a.* Indeclinable.
neo-dhioghaltachd,(MS) *s.f.* Pardonableness.
neo-dhioghaltas, -ais, *s.m.* Impunity.
neo-dhìolta,** *past pt.* Unpaid, unrewarded. 2 Unrequited, unrevenged.
neo-dhiongmhalta, -ailte, *a.* Insufficient. 2 Not firm. 3 Not firmly bound or fixed. 4* Precarious, uncertain.
————chd, *s. f.* Insufficiency. 2 Want of firmness, insecurity, uncertainty. 3 Not bound or fixed. 4 Want of mental firmness.
neo-dhiongmhaltas, *s.m.* Insufficiency.
neo-dhleasdanach, -aiche, see neo-dhleasnach.
neo-dhleasnach, -aiche, *a.* Disobedient to parents, undutiful, irreverent.
neo-dhleasnas, -ais,*s.m.*Disobedience to parents, undutifulness, irreverentness.
neo-dhligheach, -eiche, *a.* Undutiful. 2 Lawless, unlawful, illegitimate. 3 Not hereditary. 4 ‡‡Unnatural. 5* Undue. Do dhaoine n., *to lawless men.*
neo-dhligheachas, -ais, *s.m.* Illegality.‡
neo-dhòigheil, -e, *a.* Disorderly.
neo-dhreachmhor, -oire, *a.* Implausible.
neo-dhuine, *pl.* -dhaoine, *s.m.* Insignificant or unmanly fellow, ninny, a nobody. 2*Decrepid person, useless person.
neo-dhuinealachd, *s.f.* see neo-dhuinealas.
neo-dhuinealas, -ais, *s.m.* Unmanliness, softness, effeminateness, effeminacy, cowardice.
neo-dhuineil, -e, *a.* Cowardly, unmanly, effeminate.
neo-dhùrachd, *s.f.* Negligence, heedlessness. 2 Insincerity. 3 Irresoluteness.
————ach, -eiche, *a.* Negligent, careless. 2 Insincere. 3 Irresolute. Gu n., *negligently.*
neo-eagalach, -aiche, *a.* Fearless, bold, not fearful, unappalled. 2 Causing no fear. 3** Not skittish.
neo-eagnaidh, -e, *a.* Inexact, inaccurate. 2 Ignorant, unlearned. 3 Foolish, imprudent.
neo-eagnaidheachd, *s.f.ind.* Folly, imprudence. 2 Ignorance. 3 Indistinction.
neo-ealanta, -ainte, *a.* Unartificial. 2 Artless, unlearned, unskilful, inexpert. 3 Inelegant. 4 (MS) Homely. Gu n., *inartificially.*
neo-ealantachd, *s.f.* Inexpertness, unskilfulness. 2 Unlearnedness. 3*Awkwardness.
neo-éid, *v.a.* Disarray, unclothe, strip.
neo-éifeachd, *s.f.* Inefficacy, inefficiency, insufficiency. 2 Incapacity.
neo-éifeachdach, -aiche, *a.* Inefficacious, ineffectual, inefficient, incapable. Gu n., *ineffectually.*
neo-eignuidheachd, *s.f.* see neo-eagnaidheachd.
neo-eiseamealachd, *s.f.* Indifference. 2 (DMC) Outspokenness.
neo-eisimealach, (MS) *a.* Hardy. 2 Plain, outspoken.
neo-éisleanach, -aiche, *a.* Healthy, sound. 2 **Spirited.
neo-éisleanachd, *s. f.* Healthiness, soundness, freedom from disease. 2 Spiritedness.
neo-éithichte, (MS) *a.* Unperjured.
neo-eòlach, -aiche, *a.* Ignorant, unacquainted. 2 Not expert, not cunning.
neo-eugasach, -aiche, *a.* Unpromising, (also neo-aogasach.)
neo-fhàbharach, -aiche, *a.* Unfavourable. 2 Unkind, not favouring. 3 Not fair, unfair, averse, as wind. Gu n., *unfavourably.*
neo-fhaicinneach see neo-fhaicsinneach.
————d, see neo-fhaicsinneachd.
neo-fhaicsinneach, -eiche, *a.* Invisible.
neo-fhaicsinneachd, *s.f.* Invisibleness.
neo-fhàilneach, -eiche, *a.* Indefatigable.
neo-fhàilneachd, *s.f.* Indefatigability.
neo-fhalamhaichte, *a.* Inexhausted.
neo-fhallaineachd, *s.f.* Unsoundness, unhealthiness. 2 Unwholesomeness.
neo-fhallan, -aine, *a.* Unsound, unhealthy, not in good health. 2 Not healthful, unwholesome. Biadh n., *unwholesome food.*
neo-fhallsa, *a.* Not false, sincere, fair, real, unfeigned, candid.
neo-fhallsall, -e, *a.* see neo-fhallsa.
neo-fhaoilidh,** *a.* Cold (indifferent.)
neo-fhaoinsmuaineach, *a.* Unspeculative.]

neo-fhasanta, -ainte, *a.* Unfashionable, uncommon, old-fashioned. Gu n., *unfashionably*.
neo-fhasantachd, *s. f.* Oddness, unfashionableness, rareness.
neo-fhearantas,** *s.m.* Enervation.
neo-fhéin-chuiseach,** *a.* Disinterested.
neo-fhéinealachd, *s.f.* Disinterestedness.
neo-fhéineil, -e, *a.* Disinterested, unselfish.
neo-fheumail, -e, *a.* Needless, unnecessary, superfluous. 2 Unavailing, useless. Is n. sgrìobhadh, *it is superfluous to write*.
neo-fhiachail,** *a.* Valueless. 2 Trifling.
neo-fhiachalachd,** *s.f.* Baseness.
neo-fhinealtachd,** *s.f.* Coarseness.
neo-fhìor, -a, *a.* Untrue, false.
neo-fhios, -a, *s. m.* Ignorance. 2**Want of information.
neo-fhiosrach, -aiche, *a.* Ignorant. 2 Unconscious, not aware, unacquainted. 3 Not intelligent. Gu n., *unconsciously*.
neo-fhìreannach, see neo-fhìreantach.
————————d, see neo-fhìreantachd.
neo-fhìreantach, -aiche, *a.* Unrighteous, unjust, wicked, not faithful. 2 Disingenuous.
neo-fhìreantachd, *s.f.* Wickedness, unrighteousness, sinfulness. 2 Insincerity, faithlessness. 3 Disingenuousness. An n., *in unrighteousness*.
neo-fhìrinneach, -aiche, *a.* see neo-fhìreantach.
neo-fhìrinneachd, see neo-fhìreantachd.
neo-fhiùghail, *a.* Unworthy.
neo-fhiùghalachd, *s.f.* Base-mindedness.
neo-fhlathaileachd, *s.f.* Illiberality.
neo-fhoghainteach, -eiche, *a.* Infirm, not stout, not strong. 2*Ineffectual, inefficacious. 3* Cowardly.
neo-fhoghluimte, *a.* Ignorant, unlearned, rude, untaught. N. an cainnt, *rude in speech*.
neo-fhoghluimteachd, *s.f.* Illiteracy.
neo-fhoghlumachd, *s.f.* see neo-fhoghluimteachd.
neo-fhoighidinn, -e, *s.f.* Impatience.
neo-fhoillealachd, (MS) *s.f.* Plainness.
neo-fhoillsichte, *a.* Unrevealed, undiscovered.
neo-fhoirbhidh, *a.* see neo-fhoirfe. 2* In nonage.
neo-fhoirfe, *a.* Imperfect, incomplete, insufficient.
neo-fhoirfeachd, *s.f.* Imperfection, incompleteness, insufficiency.
neo-fhoirfidh, see neo-fhoirfe.
neo-fhoirfidheachd, see neo-fhoirfeachd.
neo-fhoiseil, see neo-fhoisneach.
neo-fhoisneach, -eiche, *a.* Restless, impatient, fidgety. 2 Turbulent. 3 Disturbed, uncomfortable, uneasy, unquiet.
neo-fhoisneachd, *s. f.* Restlessness, uneasiness, impatience. 2**Turbulence. 3 Uncomfortableness. 4* Disquietude, disturbance.
neo-fhonn, -fhuinn, *s.f.* Discord of sound.
neo-fhonnmhor, -oire, *a.* Not tuneful, unharmonious, discordant, unmusical. 2 Dejected, not in humour.
neo-fhonnmhorachd, *s.f.* Discordance, want of harmony, dissonance. 2 Dejectedness.
neo-fhortanach,** *a.* Unfortunate, unlucky.
neo-fhreagarrach, -aiche, *a.* Inapplicable, unfit, unsuitable, unanswerable, not fitting, not corresponding.
neo-fhreagarrachd, *s. f.* Unfitness, unsuitableness, unanswerableness. 2 Contrariety.
neo-fhreasdalach, -aiche, *a.* Improvident, unfavourable, difficult. 2* Inattentive, careless. Gu n., *improvidently*.
neo-fhreasdalachd, *s.f.ind.* Improvidence, carelessness. 2 **Unfavourableness.
neo-fhuaighealaich, *v.a.* Unstitch.
neo-fhulangas, -ais, *s.m.* Impassibility.

neo-fhuras, -ais, *s.m.* Impatience. 2 Difficult.
————, *a.* see neo-fhurasda.
neo-fhurasach, -aiche, *a.* Impatient, uneasy.
neo-fhurasda, -aisde, *a.* Difficult, hard, not easy. 2**Not patient.
neo-ghaisgeanta, -einte, *a.* Immartial.
neo-ghaothar, (MS) *a.* Windless.
neo-gharail, -e, *a.* Incommodious, inconvenient.
neo-ghealtach, -aiche, *a.* Not timid, bold, unappalled, intrepid, fearless.
neo-ghealtachd, *s.f.* Boldness, intrepidity, fearlessness.
neo-gheamanta, *a.* Single-minded.
neo-gheanmnaidh, -e, *a.* Incontinent, unchaste. 2 Intemperate. Luchd n., *intemperate people*.
neo-gheanmnaidheachd, *s.f.* Incontinence, unchasteness. 2**Intemperance.
neo-ghean, -a, *s. m.* Disaffection, bad humour, hatred, dislike, enmity.
neo-gheanail, -e, *a.* Out of humour, peevish, morose, infestive.
neo-gheanalachd, *s.f.* Infestivity.
neo-gheanmath,** -aith, *s. m.* Dissatisfaction, disapprobation. 2 Disaffection.
neo-ghéillear, *a.* Unyielding.
neo-gheimnidh, see neo-gheanmnaidh.
neo-gheimnidheachd, *s.f.* see neo-gheanmnaidheachd.
neo-gheur, -a, *a.* Blunt on edge or point. 2 Dull, stupid, simple, blunt in comprehension. 3 (MS) Anti-acid. 4* Not sour.
neo-gheuraichte, *a.* Not sharpened. 2 Unfermented, unleavened. 3 Not soured. Aran n., *unleavened bread*.
neo-ghleadhrach, *a.* Hushed.
neo-ghlaine, *comp.* of neo-ghlan.
neo-ghlaine, *s.f.* Abominableness, uncleanness, filthiness, impurity. 2 Pollution.
neo-ghlainte, *a.* Not sublimated by heat.
neo-ghlan, -aine, *a.* Impure, abominable, unclean. 2 Polluted. Cairbh spréidh neo-ghlain, *the carcase of unclean cattle*.
neo-ghlic, -e, *a.* Foolish, unwise, witless, thoughtless. Anamain chrìne nan gnìomh n., *thou little soul of unwise deeds!*
neo-ghliocas, -ais, *s.m.* Insipiency.
neo-ghloicealachd, *s.f.* Wisdom, prudence.
neo-ghloiceil, -e, *a.* Wise, prudent.
neo-ghloidhcealachd, see neo-ghloicealachd.
neo-ghloidhceil, see neo-ghloiceil.
neo-ghloine, *s.f.* see neo-ghlaine.
neo-ghluaisneach, *a.* Hush.
neo-ghluaisneachd, (MS) *s. f.* Rest. 2 see neo-ghluasadachd.
neo-ghluaiste, *a.* Unmoved, unagitated, unruffled.
neo-ghluasadach, -aiche, *a.* Immovable, undisturbed, unruffled. Gu m., *immovably*.
neo-ghluasadachd, *s. f.* Immovableness. 2 Stagnation.
neo-ghlutail, -e, *a.* Abstemious.
neo-ghnaithte,* *a.* Unaccustomed, unpractised, abrogated, unusual.
neo-ghnàthach, -aiche, *a.* Not customary, unusual, strange, extraordinary. 2**Idle.
neo-ghnàthachaidh,** *a.* Impracticable.
neo-ghnàthaichte, *a.* Unattempted, unpractised, unperformed. 2 Extraordinary, uncommon.
neo-ghnìomhach, -aiche, *a.* Idle, negligent, indolent.
neo-ghnìomhachas, -ais, *s.m.* Inactivity.
neo-ghoireasach, -aiche, *a.* Inconvenient, unfit. 2 Unfavourable. 3 Immoderate, excessive, intemperate. 4* Unnecessary.
neo-ghoireasachd, *s.f.* Inconvenience. 2 Immoderateness, excess.
neo-ghoirt, *a.* Not sour. 2 Not sore. 3 (MS)

Antacid.
neo-ghoirteachadh,** -aidh, s. m. Process of taking away the acid from any substance. 2 Not fermenting. 3 Not souring, sweetening.
neo-ghoirtich,** v.a. Take off sourness, sweeten. 2 Unacidulate.
neo-ghoirtichte, a. Unfermented, unleavened. 2 Unacidulated. 3 Sweetened.
neo-ghrad, -aide, a. Not quick, not sudden, slow, sluggish, dilatory, unapt. Is n. e, *he is slow, sluggish.*
neo-ghrad-charach, -aiche, a. Lazy, sluggish, indolent.
neo-ghramail, -e, a. Flabby.
neo-ghràsmhor, -oire, a. Unmerciful, ungracious. 2 Graceless, without grace. Gu n., *ungraciously.*
neo-ghràsmhorachd, s. f. Unmercifulness, ungraciousness. 2 Gracelessness.
neo-ghreanntachd, s.f. Clumsiness.
neo-ghrinn, -e, a. Inelegant, untidy, awkward. 2 Not showy. 3*Coarse, unmannerly. 4*Unkind.
neo-ghrinneas, -is, s.m. Inelegance, untidiness, awkwardness. 2* Unkindness. 3**Lack of finery.
†neoid,** a. Strong. 2 Stout, thick. 3 Penurious, scanty. 4 Wicked.
neoid,** s.f. Wound.
neòil, *gen.sing. & n. pl.* of neul.
neo-inbh,* -e, a. see neo-inbheach.
neo-inbheach, -eiche, a. Abortive, unripe, not come to maturity, premature. 2 ‡‡Inferior. 3* Under age. Torraichead n., *a premature conception* ; tha e n., *he is not of age, he is a minor.*
neo-inbheachd,* s.f. Prematurity, abortiveness, non-age.
neo-inbheach,** a. Unripe, untimely, not come to maturity, not come to full growth. Gin n., *an untimely birth.*

552. *Neòinean.*

neòinean, -ein, -an, s.m. Daisy—*bellis perennis.*
neòineanach, -aiche, a. Abounding in daisies, daisied. 2 Of or like a daisy.
neòinean-cladaich,§ s.m. Thrift, sea-pink, see tonn-a'-chladaich.
neòinean-gréine, s.m. Sunflower.
neòinean-mór,§ s. m. Ox-eye—*chrysanthemum leucanthemum.*
neòinean-puinnsein, s.m. Sun-spurge—*Colonsay.*
neo-ìnnleachd,** s. f. Want of ingenuity, uninventiveness, non-contrivance.
neo-ìnnleachdach, -aiche, a. Not ingenious, uninventive, not contrivant, artless, unskilled, inexpert.
neo-inntinneach, -eiche, a. Insipid.
neo-ìnntleachd, see neo-ìnnleachd.
neo-ìnntleachdach, see neo-ìnnleachdach.
neo-ìochdmhoire, *comp.* of neo-iochdmhor.
neo-iochdmhor, -oire, a. Pitiless, cruel, unfeeling, inhuman, merciless.
——————achd, s.f.ind. Cruelty, unfeelingness, inhumanity, mercilessness, pitilessness.
neo-ìochdranach, -aiche, a. Disobedient, disloyal, unbecoming a subject, insubordinate.
——————d, s.f.ind. Disobedience, insubordination, disloyalty.
neo-ìogarra, a. Haughty, arrogant. Gu n., *haughtily.*
——————chd, s.f.ind. Haughtiness, arrogance.
neo-iomaguineach, -eiche, a. Careless, heedless.
neo-iomallach, -aiche, a. Interminable.
neo-iomchuidh, -e, a. Improper, unmeet, unfit, unbecoming, inconvenient, unqualified, not commodious.
——————eachd, s.f.ind. Impropriety, unmeetness, unfitness, unbecomingness.
neo-iomlan, -aine, a. Imperfect, incomplete, unfurnished.
——————achd, s.f.ind. Imperfection, incompleteness, incompletion.
neo-iompaichte, a. Unconverted, unchanged.
neo-iompaidhteach, a. Inconvertible.
neo-iomrallach, a. Inerrable, accurate.
——————d, s.f. Inerrability, inerrancy.
neo-ionann, a. Dissimilar, unequal, unlike, differing. Is m. dhuit e, *he is unlike you.*
——————achd, s.f.ind. Inequality, dissimilarity. 2* Unlikelihood.
——————as, -ais, -ais, s.m. see neo-ionannachd.
neo-ionmhuinn, -e, a. Unbeloved. 2 Unlovely, unamiable, morose.
neo-ionmhuinneachd, s.f.ind. The state of not being beloved. 2 Moroseness, unloveliness.
neo-ionnsuichte, a. Illiterate, ignorant, unlearned, untaught, rude, untrained, unskilful, inexpert.
neo-iotmhorachd, s.f.ind. Insitiency.
neo-iteagach, -aiche, a. Displumed.
neo-iùlmhor, -oire, a. Ignorant, unskilful, untaught.
neo-laghail, -e, a. Illegitimate, unlawful. Gniomh n., *an illegitimate action.*
neo-laghalachd, s.f.ind. Illegality, unlawfulness, illegitimacy, illegitimateness.
neo-làmhach, -aiche, a. see neo-làmhchair.
——————d, s.f.ind. Inability.
neo-làmhchair, -e, a. Awkward, unskilful, inexpert, clumsy-handed. 2 Handless.
——————eachd,**s.f.see neo-làmhcharachd.
neo-làmhcharachd, s.f. Awkwardness, unskilfulness, inexpertness, clumsiness. 2**Handlessness.
neo-làn, a. Lank.
neo-lapach, a. Unbenumbed. 2 Unenfeebled, 3 Unfaltering. Gur neo-lapach do dhreach 'us d' fhonn, *unfaltering are thy appearance and habits* (or *mood.*)—*Duanaire, 101.*
neo-lasanta, -ainte, a. Incombustible.
neo-lasta,** a. Uninflamed. 2 Unlighted.
neo-làthaireach, s.m. Absentee.
neo-làthaireach, -eiche, a. Absent, invisible. 2 Apt to be absent.
——————d, s.f.ind. Absence of person. 2 Invisibility. 3 Contrariety.
neo-leabhrach, -aiche, a. Bookless.
neo-leanabaidh, -e, a. Not childish, manly.
——————eachd, s.f. Manliness.
neo-leasaichte, a. Uncorrected, unimproved. 2 Unmanured, undunged. 3 Unamended.
neo-leigheasach, -aiche, a Immedicable, incurable.
neo-leithbhreitheachd, s.f.ind. Impartiality.
neo-lìomhta, a. Unpolished. 2(DMC) Blunt.

neo-liotach, -aiche, *a.* Not stammering, having no stammer. 2 Easily pronounced, of easy accent.
neo-lochdach, -aiche, *a.* Harmless, inoffensive. 2 Blameless, unblemished, spotless, unspotted, faultless, sinless, uncontaminaned. Naomh agus n., *holy and unblemished.*
neo-loinneil, -e, *a.* Deformed.
neo-loisgeach, -eiche, *a.* Incombustible, not burning, uncaustical, asbestive. 2 Not hasty, keen or passionate. 3**Not corrosive.
——d, *s.f.* Incombustibility.
neo-loisgeantach, *a.* Deformed. 3 Uninflammable, incombustible.
neo-loisgear, *s.m.* Asbestos.
neo-lom. *a.* Gnarled.
neo-luachmhorachd, *s.f.* Worthlessness.
neo-luaineach, -eiche, *a.* Steady, constant. 2 Sedate.
——as, -ais, *s.m.* Steadiness, constancy.
neo-lùbadh, -aidh, *s. m.* Inconformity, unbendingness, unyieldingness.
neo-lùchdaich, *v.a.* Disburden, unload, unship, lighten.
——te, *past pt.* of neo-luchdaich. Disburdened, unloaded, lightened.
neo-luchdmhoireachd, *s.f.* Incapaciousness.
neo-lughdachaidh, *a.* Bateless.
neo-lùthach, -aiche, *a.* Nerveless.
neo-mhairsinneachd, *s.f.* Discontinuance.
neo-mhaitheach, -eiche, *a.* Unforgiving, unrelenting. 2 (DU) Indifferent to public or other opinion, unconventional. 2(AH) Straightforward, outspoken, downright, blunt, unflattering.
neo-mhaitheanasach,(MS) *a.* Unpardoning.
neo-mhaithteach, see neo-mhaitheach.
neo-mharbhach, see neo-mharbhtach.
——d, see neo-mharbhtachd.
neo-mharbhtach, -aiche, *a.* Not killing, not deadly, not mortal, immortal. 2 Not sanguinary.
——d,** *s.f.* Immortality.
neo-mheadhonach, -aiche, *a.* Immediate, without intermediate cause. 2* Not central, out of place, eccentric. 3* Awkward in point of situation.
——d, *s.f.* Immediateness. 2 Eccentricity.
neo-mheadhonaireachd, *s.f.* Immediacy.
neo-mhealltach, -aiche, *a.* Not deceiving, honest, sincere, candid, undisguised, undissembling, fair.
neo-mheangail, -e, *a.* Unblemished, sound, healthy, whole.
neo-mhearachdach, -aiche, *a.* Unerring, infallible, true. 2* Wise.
neo-mhearachdail, see neo-mhearachdach.
neo-mhearachdalachd, *s.f.* Inerrability.
neo-mheas, -a, *s.m.* Disrespect, contempt.
——ail, -e, *a.* Disrespected. 2 Contemptible, aweless. 3* Disrespectful.
neo-mheasarra, *a.* Intemperate, immoderate, debauched. 2 Excessive, beyond measure. Gràdh n., *intemperate love, whoredom.*
——chd, *s.f.* Intemperance, immoderation, debauchery, excess, glut. 2 Immenseness.
neo-mheasgach,** *a.* Incommiscible.
neo-mheasgta, *a.* Unmixed, unmingled, uncompounded.
neo-mheata, *a.* Bold, daring, fearless. 2 Stout.
——chd, *s.f.ind.* Boldness, daring, fearlessness. 2 Resoluteness.
neo-mhiann, -a, *s.m.* Inappetence.
neo-mhin,** *a.* Rough-grained, unsmooth.
neo-mhìnichte, *a.* Unpolished.
neo-mhiosail,** see neo-mheasail.
neo-mhisgeach, -eiche, *a.* Sober, not addicted to drunkenness or tippling.
neo-mhisgealachd,* *s.f.* Sobriety.
neo-mhisgeil,* *a.* see neo-mhisgeach.
neo-mhodhail, -e, *a.* Rude, uncultured.
neo-mhodhalachd, *s.f.* Insensibility.
neo-mhothachadh, -aidh, *s.m.* Insensibility, unfeelingness, apathy, stupor, callousness. 2 Stupidity.
neo-mhothachail, -e, *a.* Insensible, unfeeling, callous, torpid, unfeeling. 2 Stupid. 3(AH) Unmannerly, impolite.
neo-mhothachalachd,* *s.f.* see neo-mhothachadh.
neo-mhothuchadh, see neo-mhothachadh.
neo-mhùchalach, *a.* Unquenchable.
——d, *s.f.* Unquenchableness.
neo-mhùigheach,(MS) *a.* Indulgent.
neo-mhurrachas, -ais, *s.m.* Incompetency.
neo-mhùthach, -aiche, *a.* Certain, unchangeable.
neònach, -aiche, *a.* Curious, surprising, droll, eccentric, amusing, strange, whimsical, novel, rare, capricious, unusual. 3†† Trifling. Ni n., *a novel* or *curious thing* ; duine n., *a droll fellow* ; is n. leam, *I am surprised* ; is n. leis, *he thinks it strange.*
——as, -ais, *s.m.* Curiosity, surprisingness, drollness, eccentricity, strangeness, whimsicalness, surprise, wonder. 2**Droll person. N. an ni seo, *the strangeness of this thing* ; tha n. orm, *I am surprised.*
neònachd,** *s.f.* Admirableness. 2‡‡Oddity.
neonad, see sleamhnan & neamhnagan.
neònagan, -ain, *s.m.* Stye on the eye, see sleamhnan & neamhnagan. [In *Gairloch* leònad—DU.]
neònaiche, *comp.* of neònach.
neònaid, see neamhnuid.
neònan, see neòinean.
——ach, see neòineanach.
neònasachd,** *s.f.* Admirability.
neo-neach,** *s.m.* Insignificant person, a nobody. 2 (DC) Imbecile—*Skye.*
neo-neart,** -neirt, *s.m.* Pithlessness, feebleness.
——ar, see neo-neartmhor.
——mhor, -oire, *a.* Not forcible, feeble, infirm. 2 Unwarlike.
neo-neulach, -aiche, *a.* Cloudless.
neoni, *s.f.ind.* Nothing, nonentity. 2 Chaos. 3 Trifle. 4* Ninny. Thig iad gu neoni, *they shall come to nothing* ; 'nuair a chuala neoni guth a bheòil, *when chaos heard the voice of his mouth.*
neoinich,** *v. a.* Annihilate, annul, neutralize, bring to nothing. see neonithich.
neonitheach, -eiche, *a.* Trifling, insignificant, valueless, inconsiderable. 2 Abortive.
——adh, *s.m.* Annulment, annulling.
——d, *s f.* Triflingness, nothingness, insignificance, inconsiderableness. 2 **Abortiveness. 3 Nothing.
neonithich, (MS) *v.a.* Abolish blank, annihilate.
neo-oileanach,(MS) *a.* Bumpkinly, presumptuous.
neo-oileanaichte, *a.* Untaught, illiterate, unmannerly, impatient, ill-bred.
neo-oireamhnach, *a.* Incompatible, unbecoming, inadequate, improper.
——d, *s.f.* Impropriety.
neo-omhailleach, see neo-umhailleach.
neo-onoireach, see neo-onorach.
neo-onorach, -aiche, *a.* Dishonest, thievish. 2 Ignoble, mean.

neo-phàirteachd, *s.f.* Neutrality.
neo-phàirtidheachd, *s.f.* Incommunicability.
neo-pheacach, -aiche, *a.* Impeccable.
neo-phearsanta, see neo-phearsantail.
neo-phearsantachd, *s.f.* Impersonality.
neo-phearsantail, -e, *a.* Impersonal.
neo-phòitearachd, *s.f.* Abstemiousness in drinking or diet, sobriety, temperance.
neo-phòiteil, -e, *a.* Sober, abstemious, temperate, not given to excess in eating or drinking.
neo-phrìs, -e, *s.f.* Want of value, uselessness. 2 Disrespect, contemptibleness, contempt. Na cuir an n., *do not despise.*
———eil, *a.* Abject.
neo-phronntach, -aiche, *a.* Immalleable.
neo-phurpail,** *a.* Inaccurate. 2 (DMy) Nonsensical.
neo-rag, -raige, *a.* Flaccid, docile.
neo-rann-phàirteach, -aiche, *a.* Incommunicable.
———————d, *s.f.* Incommunicableness.
neo-ranntach, -aiche, *a.* Blank.
neor-eisiomail, *s.f.* Independence, not being in one's reverence.
neo-réiteach, -eiche, *a.* Irreconcilable.
————as, -ais, *s.m.* Irreconciliation.
neo-reusanta, *a.* Unreasonable.
neo-riaghailt, -e, -ean, *s.f.* Incongruity.
—————each, -eiche, *a.* Irregular, anomalous. 2 Turbulent, quarrelsome, heteroclite.
—————eachd,* *s.f.* Irregularity, anomaly. 2 Turbulence.
neo-rianail, *a.* Unruly, disorderly.
neo-rianalachd,** *s.f.* Contrariety.
neo-riantanach,(DMC) *a.* Needless, uncalled for.
neo-riatanach, (MS) *a.* Needless.
neo-riochdail, -e, *a.* Inelegant.
neo-roinnteach, *a.* Indivisible.
neo-roinntealachd, s.f. Indivisibility.
neorra-tha, *phrase,* Indeed it is—*Arran.*
neorra-thaing, see neo-ar-thaing.
neo-sgàilich, *v.a.* Unveil.
neo-sgairte, *a.* Inseparable, not to be divided or parted.
————il, -e, *a.* Dull, spiritless, inactive.
neo-sgarail, -e, *a.* see neo-sgairte.
neo-sgàthach, -aiche, *a.* Fearless, undaunted, unappalled, not timid.
neo-sgàthachas, *s.m.* Fearlessness.
neo-sgeadaich, *v.a.* Undress, disrobe, disarray, divest, unadorn.
——————te, *past pt.* of neo-sgeadaich. Undressed, disrobed, stripped, unadorned.
neo-sgiobalta, *a.* Awkward, clumsy.
neo-sgìth, *a.* Unwearied, unfatigued, willing.
————eil, *a.* Unwearied.
————ichte, *a.* Unwearied, unfatigued, untired. 2 Ceaseless.
neo-sgoinnealachd, *s.f.* Frivolousness. 2 (DMC) Sluggishness.
neo-sgoinnear, -a, *a.* Heedless, inattentive.
neo-sgoinneil, -e, *a.* Flimsy. 2 Drabbish. 3 Idle. 4 (DU) Lacking in bodily vigour. 5 (DMC) Sluggish.
neo-sgonnar, see neo-sgoinnear.
neo-sgrubach,(DMK) *a.* Unscrupulous, not hesitating, not niggardly.
neo-shaidealta, *a.* Unshamed.
——————chd, *s.f.* Boldness.
neo-shaillte, *a.* Unsalted, unseasoned. 2**Insipid.
neo-shalach, -aiche, *a.* Undefiled, unpolluted, clean, cleanly. An leabaidh n., *the bed undefiled.*
neo-shaltraichte, *a.* Untravelled, untrampled.
neo-shamhluidheachd, *s.f.* Matchlessness. 2 Disconformity.
neoshannt, -a, *s.m.* Want of desire, indifference. 2**Lack of ambition. 3 Loathing, squeamishness.
neoshanntach, -aiche, *a.* Not covetous, unselfish. 2 Unambitious, indifferent. 3 Loathing.
neo-shanntaich,(MS) *v.a.* Blunt the desire, appetite or craving.
neo-shaothrach, *a.* Idle.
neo-shàrachaidh, -e, *a.* Unconquerable, indefatigable, keen.
neo-shàrachail,* -e, *a.* see neo-shàrachaidh.
neo-shàraichte, *a.* Unoppressed, unconquered. 2 Unfatigued, unharassed.
neo-sheachach, -aiche, *a.* Imarcinable.
neo-sheachanta, -ainte, *a.* Indispensable.
—————chd, *s.f.* Indispensability.
neo-sheachnach, -aiche, *a.* Avoidless, unavoidable.
neo-sheachranach,(MS) *a.* Inerrable, infallible.
neo-sheadhachail, -e, *a.* Insignificative.
neo-sheadhail,(DMC) *a.* Insignificant.
—————eachd, *s.f.* Insignificance.
neo-sheadhair,** *a.* Cold (indifferent.)
neo-shealbhach, -aiche, *a.* Ill-starred, unlucky. 2 Averse.
neo-shealbharra, see neo-shealbhach.
neo-sheamhsar, -a, *a.* Hapless.
neo-sheannsail, *a.* see neo-sheannsar.
neo-sheannsar,** *a.* Unlucky, ominous. 'S neosheannsar a' chulaidh," (speaking of the new objectionable trousers imposed on the Gael) *ominous is the article of apparel—Donn. Bàn, p. 128.*
—————achd,** *s. f.* Unluckiness, ominousness.
neo-sheargach,** *a.* Unblasting, unscorching. 2 That does not wither, unwithering, undecaying.
neo-sheargach, (MS) *a.* Asbestine.
neo-sheargaichte, see neo-sheargta.
neo-sheargaidheachd,(MS) *s.f.* Incorruptibility.
neo-sheargta, *a.* Unwithered, undecayed, unscorched, unblasted.
neo-sheasach,* -aiche, see neo-sheasmhach.
neo-sheasmhach, -aiche, *a.* Unsteady, unstable, fleeting, not durable, inconstant. 2(MS) Incoherent. 3 (DMC) Unreliable. N. mar uisge, *unstable as water.*
——————d, *s. f.* Instability, unsteadiness, fleetingness, want of durability, unquietness, restlessness, uncomfortableness, state of not being firmly placed. 2 Transientness. 3 (MS) Repugnance.
neo-sheasmhuidheachd, *s. f.* Levity, discongruity.
neo-sheircealachd, *s.f.* Intoleration.
neo-sheòlta, (MS) *a.* Artless.
neo-sheòltachd, *s.f.* Immethodicalness.
neo-shìolmhorachd, *s.f.* Fruitlessness, infertility.
neo-shìthealachd,(MS) *s.f.* Intranquility.
neo-shlàinteil,** *a.* Bad in health, unhealthy, fitful.
neo-shlamanach,(MS) *a.* Incoagulable.
neo-shlannach, -aiche, *a.* Antacid.
neo-shnasmhor, -oire,*a.* Ill-finished, incompact, inelegant, untidy, unpolished.
neo-shocair, -e, *a.* Uneasy, unsettled, restless.
—————, *s.* Uneasiness, unsettledness, restlessness.
neo-shocrach, -aiche, *a.* Restless, unquiet, uneasy, uncomfortable. 2 Hard, difficult. 3 Not firmly placed, unsteady.
neo-shocrachd,* *s.f.* see neo-shocair.
neo-shoilleir, -e, *a.* Indistinct, not clear, not

transparent, not bright, dark, gloomy, unintelligible.
neo-shoilleireachd,** *s. f.* Indistinctness, absence of light, unintelligibleness, state of being dark or not bright.
neo-shoirbheachadh, -aidh, *s.m.* Unsuccessfulness, state of not succeeding or prospering.
neo-shoirbheachail, -e, *a.* Unsuccessful, unprosperous, unfortunate.
neo-shoirbheachalachd,* *s. f.* see neo-shoirbheachadh.
neo-sholarach, -riche, *a.* Improvident, shiftless. Gu n., *improvidently.*
neo-sholarach,** -aich, *s. m.* Improvident person.
neo-shòlasach, -aiche, *a.* Joyless, mournful,sad, uncomfortable, delightless.
neo-shona, *a.* Luckless, unlucky, hapless, unhappy. An tìr n. seo, *this unlucky land.*
neo-shònruichte, *a.* Indefinite, undetermined, unresolved. 2 Not remarkable.
neo-shrianach, -aiche, *a.* Bitless, unbridled, uncurbed, unrestrained, uncontrolled. 2 (DMy) stripeless, without stripes.
neo-shuaimhneach, -eiche, *a.* Restless.
neo-shuarach, -aiche, *a.* Not insignificant, not valueless.
neo-shubhach, -aiche, *a.* Joyless, comfortless. 2 (DC) Unsatisfied. Gun charaid, n., *without a friend, joyless.*
neo-shudhar,(MS) *a.* Unessential.
neo-shùghar, see neo-shùghmhor.
neo-shùghmhor, *a.* Juiceless, sapless, arid. 2 (DMy) Without strength.
neo-shuidhichte, *a.* Unsettled, unsteady, discomposed, unplanted.
neo-shuidhichteachd, *s.f.* Levity.
neo-shuigeartach, *a.* Heavy.
neo-shuilbhir, -e, *a.* Morose, not merry or cheerful, peevish, gloomy, cheerless, unobliging.
neo-shuime,** *s. f.* Carelessness, indifference, negligenhe. Na cuir an n. *despise not.*
neo-shuimealachd, *s.f.* Inattention, negligence, indifference.
neo-shuimeil, -e, *a.* Negligent, indifferent, inattentive.
neo-shulchair,** *a.* Distant.
neo-shunnd,(DMC) *s.m.* Dulness, spiritlessness.
neo-shunndach, -aiche, *a.* Dispirited, dejected, melancholy, spiritless, morose. 2 In bad health. 3 Backward. 4*Drowsy. Gu n., *dejectedly.*
neo-shusbainteach, *a.* Frivolous, unsubstantial, without substance, inefficient.
neo-smiorail, -e, *a.* Spiritless, dull. Daoine n., *spiritless men.*
neo-smioralachd, *s.f.* Spiritlessness, dulness.
neo-smuaintealachd, *s.f.* Inconsiderateness.
neo-sparragach, -aiche, see neo-shrianach.
neo-spéiseach,(MS) *a.* Favourless.
neo-spéiseil, -e, *a.* Underrating, undervaluing. 2 Heedless, careless, inattentive. 3*Unloving.
neo-speisichte, *a.* Unregarded.
neo-shioradachd,(MS) *s.f.* Corporeity.
neo-spioradail, *a.* Abject. 2 (DMy) Unspiritual.
neo-spòrsail, -e, *a.* Not merry, not inclined to merriment. 2 Humble, not proud, not scornful. 3 Not prone to deride.
neo-spraiceil,* see neo-smiorail.
neo-stàthach, -aiche, *a.* Null, bootless.
neo-stóidheachd, *s.f.* Indetermination.
neo-stòlda, *a.* Incomposed, restless.
————chd,(DMC) *s.f.* Restlessness.
neo-stràicealachd, *s.f.* Want of pride or conceit, modesty.
neo-stràiceil, -e, *a.* Not conceited, unassuming, modest, not forward.
neo-striochdail,** *a.* Disobedient. 2 (DMK) Unyielding.
neo-struidheil, -e, *a.* Not extravagant, frugal.
neòtair, *a.* Neuter.
neo-thàbhach, ** *a.* Futile, pithless, weak, impotent, unimportant, immaterial, ineffectual, unprofitable, unavailable.
————-——d, *s.f.* Insufficiency, futility, pithlessness, weakness, unimportance, impotence, ineffectualness.
————-——dach, -aiche, *a.* Ineffectual, futile, pithless, unsubstantial,impotent, immaterial, unprofitable.
————-——dachd,‡‡ *s.f.* Imbecility.
neo-thabhairteach, -eiche, *a.* Stingy, niggardly, not inclined to give.
neo-thacmhor,(MS) *a.* Aidless.
neo-thagairte, *a.* Uncontroverted, unclaimed, unpleaded.
neo-thairbhe, *s.f.ind.* Unprofitableness, unproductiveness,unfruitfulness,unsubstantialness, unserviceableness.
neo-thaise,(MS) *s.* Apathy.
neo-thaisichte, *a.* Infusible.
neo-thaitinn, *v.n.* Displease, dissatisfy, disagree with, disapprove. N. i ris, *she did not satisfy him.*
neo-thaitneach, -eiche, *a.* Disagreeable, unacceptable, unwelcome, displeasing, unsatisfactory, unpleasant.
neo-thàmhaiche, -e, *s.m. & f.* Non-resident.
neo-thapaidheachd, *s.f.* Inability.
neo-tharbhach, -aiche, *a.* Unfruitful,unproductive, unprofitable, unsubstantial, gainless, abortive, unfruitful, unavailable, unserviceable. Fearaun n., *unproductive land ;* ri oibribh n., *with fruitless works.*
neo-tharbhachas, see neo-thairbhe.
neo-tharbhachd, see neo-thairbhe.
neo-tharbhachdach,(MS) *a.* Slight.
neo-tharbhaiche, *s.f.* see neo-thairbhe.
————————, *comp.* of neo-tharbhach. More or most unproductive or unsubstantial.
neo-theagaisgte, *a.* Untaught, unlearned.
neo-theagamhach,(MS) *a.* Assured, undoubted, unperplexed.
neo-theagamhachd, *s.f.* Assuredness.
neo-theagmhaidheachd,(MS) *s.f.* Assurance.
neo-theanntachd, *s.f.* Laxness.
neo-thearbach, *a.* Inseparable.
neo-thearbaidheachd, *s.f.* Inseparability.
neo-thèaruinte, *a.* Insecure, unsafe, unprotected, unsaved.
neo-thèaruinteach, see neo-thèaruinte.
————————d, *s. f.* Insecurity, want of safety, unprotectedness. 2* Incautiousness.
neo-theòma, *a.* Unskilful, inexpert, ignorant. 2 Infirm, weakly. 3 Awkward.
neo-theòmadh, see neo-theòma.
neo-theth,** *a.* Not hot, cool, not zealous.
neo-thimchioll-ghearr, *v.a.* Uncircumcise.
neo-thimchioll-ghearradh, -aidh, *s. m.* Uncircumcision.
neo-thimchioll-gheàrrta, *a.* Uncircumcised.
neo-thimeil, -e, *a.* Abortive, untimely.
neo-thlusail, -e, *a.* Incompassionate.
neo-thlusalachd, *s.f.* Incompassionateness.
neo-thogarrach, -aiche, *a.* Disinclined, averse, passionless, amort. 2 Reluctant, as a person. 3 Uninviting, as weather.
neo-thoil, -e, *s.f.* Disinclination, aversion, unwillingness, backwardness, reluctance, nolition.
neo-thoileach,-eiche, *a.* Disinclined, unwilling, averse, backward, reluctant.
neo-thoileachadh, -aidh, *s.m.* Dissatisfying, act

of dissatisfying or displeasing. A' n—, *pr. pt*· of neo-thoilich.

neo-thoileachas-inntinn, *s. m.* Dissatisfaction, discontent.

neo-thoileachd,** *s.f.* Stubbornness,reluctance. perverseness, disinclination. 2 Disgust.

neo-thoilealachd, *s. f.* Stubbornness, aversion, reluctance, disgust.

neo-thoileil,** *a.* Stubborn, reluctant, perverse.

neo-thoilich, *v.n.* Dissatisfy, displease.

——— ———te, *past pt.* of neo-thoilich. Dissatisfied, displeased, discontented, averse. Iochdaran n., *a malcontent.*

neo-thoillteannas, -ais, *s.m.* Unworthiness, demerit, bad desert, undeservedness.

neo-thoilteanach, see neo-thoilltinneach.

neo-thoilltinneach, -eiche, *a.* Undeserving, unworthy, unmeriting.

neo-thoinisgeach, -eiche, *a.* see neo-thoinisgeil.

neo-thoinisgeil, -e, *a.* Foolish, senseless, stupid, unintelligent. 2 (DMC) Inconsiderate.

neo-thoirt, -e, *s.f.* Indifference, negligence, disinclination. 2 Contempt.

neo-thoirtealachd,** *s.f.* Negligence, indifference, carelessness. 2 Harmlessness.

neo-thoirteil, -e, *a.* Indifferent, negligent, careless, inattentive. 2 Causing no harm or loss.

neo-tholltach, -aiche, *a.* Imperforated.

neo-thoirt-fainear,** *s.* Inattentiveness.

neo-thomhaiseach,(MS) *a.* Fathomless.

neo-thorach, -aiche, *a.* Unfruitful, unproductive, barren. 2 Not pregnant (of women only.) 3 Past child-bearing. Ris a' mhnaoi neo-thoraich, *to the barren woman.*

neo-thorachas, -ais, *s.m.* see neo-thoraichead.

neo-thorachd, * *s.f.* see neo-thoraichead.

neo-thoraiche, *comp.* of neo-thorach.

———————, *s.f.* Unfruitfulness, unproductiveness, barrenness. M. do chuim, *the barrenness of thy womb.*

neo-thoraichead, *s.f.* Degree of unfruitfulness, barrenness, abortiveness, or infecundity. 2 Female barrenness.

neo-thoraicheas, *s.m.* see neo-thoraichead.

neo-thràigheach, -eiche, *a.* Inexhaustible, infinite, that cannot be drained.

neo-thràighte, *a.* Unexhausted, undrained.

neo-thraoighte, see neo-thràighte.

neo-thràthail, -e, *a.* Late. 2 Unseasonable, untimely.

neo-thràthalachd, *s.f.* Unseasonableness.

neo-thréigsinneach, -eiche, *a.* Indefectible.

neo-threòrach, -aiche *a.* Invalid, week, aidless.

neo-threòraichte, *a.* Undirected, unguided, not led.

neo-thròcaireach, -eiche, *a.* Pitiless, unmerciful, cruel, relentless, callous.

———————d, *s.f.* Cruelty, relentlessness, pitilessness.

neo-thruacanta, -ainte, *a.* Pitiless, unfeeling, uncompassionate, unmerciful, cruel. Is n. a ghnùis, *pitiless is his aspect.*

———·———chd, *s.f.* Unfeelingness, uncompassionateness, unmercifulness.

neo-thruacantas, see neo-thlusalachd.

neo-thruaillichte, *a.* Unadulterated, undefiled, uncorrupted, unsoiled, unmarred, unviolated.

neo-thruaillidh, -e, *a.* Incorruptible, liberal, uncorrupted, undefiled, unadulterated.

——————eachd, *s.f.* Incorruption, undefiledness. 2**Incorruptible purity.

neo-thruasail, -e, see neo-thlusail.

neo-thruasaichte,(MS) *a.* Unpitied.

neo-thruasalachd, see neo-thlusalachd.

neo-thuairpeach, *a.* Hurtless. 2(MS) Placid. 3 Peaceable, not pugnacious.

neo-thuairpeachd, *s.f.* Iudisturbance.

neo-thuasaideach, -eiche, *a.* Not quarrelsome.

neo-thuigse, *s.f.ind.* Want of sense, stupidity, fatuity, senselessness, absurdity, lack of judgment.

——·——ach, -eiche, *a.* Senseless, foolish, stupid, unintelligent, irrational. Cinneach n., *a foolish nation.*

neo-thuigsinneachd,(MS) *s.f.* Incomprehensibility.

neo-thùirseach, -eiche, *a.* Not sad, not mournful. 2**Not causing sadness.

neo-thuisleach, -eiche, *a.* Infallible, stable, established, not liable to stumble.

neo-thuisleachd, *s. f.* Infallibility, stability, firmness.

neo-thuiteamach, -aiche, *a.* Infallible,unerring, indeciduous, unstumbling, steady, sure.

——— ———d, *s.f.ind.* Infallibleness, firmness, infallibility.

neo-thùrail, -e, *a.* Injudicious. 2 (DMK) Uninventive, unintelligent. 3 (DMC) Senseless.

neo-uaisle, *s.f.ind.* Illiberality.

neo-uallach, -aiche, *a.* Humble, not vain, not conceited, not proud, unambitious.

neo-uasal, -uaisle, *a.* Ignoble, mean, unassertive of rank, not proud.

neo-uidheam, -eim, *s.f.* Dishabille, undress. 2 Want of preparation, unpreparedness.

———·——aichte, *a.* Unprepared, undressed, not ready.

neo-uireasach, see neo-uireasbhuidheach.

neo-uireasbhuidh, -ean, *s. m.* Independence, easiness of circumstances,absence of poverty.

neo-uireasbhuidheach, -eiche, *a.* Independent, easy in circumstances, not poor, not needy, not destitute. 2 (MS) Accurate.

neo-uisgidh,(CR) *a.* Hardy, capable of bearing exposure to wet—*W. of Ross-shire.* 2 (DU) Potentially bold, applied to one who would "take the bull by the horns."

neo-ullamh, -aimhe, *a.* Unprepared, not ready, not done. Gu'm faigh iad sibh n., *that they shall find you unprepared.*

neo-ullamhachd, *s.f.* Unpreparedness, unreadiness.

neo-umhailleach, -eiche, *a.* Heedless, careless, listless, inconsiderate, inattentive, secure, guardless, without care or thought. Gu n., *heedlessly.*

neo-ùraireachd, *s.f.* Brackishness.

neo-urchaideach, -eiche, *a.* Quiet, inoffensive, harmless. 2 Safe, comfortable. 3**Not troublesome. 4 Innocent. 5**Tame.

neo-urrainneach, -eiche, *a.* Incapable. 2 Ineffectual.

neo-urrainneachd, *s.f.* Incapability.

neo-urramach,** *a.* Aweless. 2 Abject.

neo-ururach, -aiche, *a.* Oscitant.

neul, *gen.* neòil, *pl.* neòil, neulta & neulan, *s.m.* Cloud. 2 Hue, complexion. 3 Swoon, fainting-fit. 4 ‖Trance. 5 Star. 6 Blemish, stigma. 7 Nap or wink of sleep. 8 Sight. 9 Glimpse of light.

Mar a' ghrian agus n. 'ga sgàileadh, *as the sun and a cloud overshadowing it ;* cha d'fhuair mi n. cadail, *I did not get a wink of sleep ;* neul bainne, *a slight tinge of the colour of milk* ; tha n. deoch air, *he has a slight appearance of drink ;* chaidh e an n., *he went into a trance, he fainted ;* a' mùthadh nan n., *changing in colour of the complexion ;* cha d'fhuair mi na chuireadh neul bhàrr cait, *I did not get as much as would relieve a cat's faintness*—said after a visit to an inhospitable house ; neòil dhubha na Càisge, *the dark clouds of Easter*—the name for a period a week before Easter : thàinig neul 'nam cheann, *I grew giddy*—

Caithness ; mar neul rùiteach, *like a ruddy cloud* ; air chùl neòil, *behind a cloud.*
neulach, -aiche, *a.* Cloudy, dark, obscure. 2 Ghostly, pale. 3 Coloured.
neulachas, -ais, *s.m.* Mistiness.
neulachd, *s.f.* Mistiness.
neuladair, -e, -ean, *s.m.* Meteorologist. 2 Astrologer.
neuladaireachd, *s.f.* Meteorology. 2 Astrology. 3 Astronomy. 4**Sneaking and gazing about.
neulaich, *v.a.* & *n.* Obscure, darken, cover as with a cloud. 2 Become cloudy. 3 Become pallid. 4**Colour, gloss. 5** Assume a colour. N. pàircean agus miodair gu bàs, *parks and meadows took on the hue of decay.*
neular, -aire, *a.* Well-coloured, having a good colour, well-complexioned, well-favoured.
neul-dubh, see under neul.
*neul-fhurtadh,** -aidh, *s.m.* Slumbering.
neulmhor, -oire, *a.* Cloudy, cloud-bearing.
neul-sùla, *s.m.* Cataract (of the eye.)
neulta, *pl.* of neul.
neultach, -aiche, *a.* Cloudy, misty, dark. Là n., *a cloudy day.*
———d, *s.f.* Cloudiness, mistiness. 2 Gloominess.
neup, -a, -an, see nèip. Neupais, *turnips*—**.
neupach, -aiche, *a.* see nèipeach.
ni, *adv.* Not. Ni h-eadh, *no, it is not.* Also used for *cha.* Ni 'n guth mi o neul, *I am not the voice from a cloud.*
ni, *pl.* nithe,nithean & nitheana, *s.m.ind.* Thing, circumstance, affair,business, deed, fact,substance. Ni sam bith (*or* ni air bith), *anything;* ni eigin, *something* ; beag nithe, *a small quantity* ; air bheag nithe,*almost,to a small degree* ; an Ni Math, *God* ; air ghaol Ni Math, *for the love of God.*
nì, *s. pl. ind.* Cattle, neat, nowt. Applied to flocks and herds of all kinds. 2††Goods.
ni, *fut.aff.a.* of dean. Shall or will do. Ni e 'n gnothach, *it will do.*
'n i ? (for an i ?) Is it she ? Cha'n i, *it is not she.*
†nia,** *s.m.* Sister's son.
†niach, -a, -an, *s.m.* Champion, hero.
niadh,** *a.* Strong.
———,** *s.m.* Honour,veneration. †2 Champion.
niadhachd, *s.f.* Bravery, chivalry.
†niadhas, -ais, *s.m.* Valour, bravery.
niadh-chus, see niadhas.
niag,* *s.f.* Squint-eye.
niagach,* -aiche, *a.* Surly. 2 Squint-eyed.
nial, -a & neòil, see neul.
†nial, *s.* Letter.
nialach, -aiche, *a.* see neulach.
nialadair, -ean, see neuladair.
nial-eide,** *s.f.* Mantle of clouds. Tràigh nan nial-eide, *the cloud-covered shore.*
nial-mhàgain, *Suth'd* for mial-mhàgain (toad.)
niamh,** *s.m.* Brightness. 2 Colour or appearance of anything.
niamh,** *a.* Beautiful.
niamh,** *v.a.* Gild, cover over, gloss.
niamhachd,** *s.f.* Brightness. 2 Pleasantness.
niamhail,** *a.* Bright. 2 Pleasant.
niamh-ghàire,** *s.f.* Smile.
niamh-ghlas,** *a.* Greenish.
'niar, *s.f.*, *cont.* for (an) iar.
niar,** *a.* Boarish.
niarach, (AC) Envy. Mo niarach neach aig am bi thu, *I envy whosoever has thee.* [Dialectic form of nèarachd.]
niarachd, *a.* Happy—*Dàin I. Ghobha.* 2 Lucky. Am foinne mu'n iath a' ghlaic, is n. mac air am bi e, *wart on palm is luck to lad.*
niauradh,(CR) *a.* Grinding. Clach n., *a grinding-stone.*
nias, see neas.
†niat,** see niata.
niata, *a.* Brave, courageous. 2††Fierce. 3 (DC) Inexorable—*Uist.*
———chd, *s.f.* Bravery, valour.
niatal, -ail, -an, *s.m.* Reed.
ni b' fhaide, *adv.* Longer, farther. (for na b' fhaide.)
ni-bheil, Not, no. The Irish and past literary form of *pres. neg.* of the *v.* bi.
nic, *contr.* of nighean. Used with female patronymics, as, Iain MacDhòmhnuill *or* Domhnullach, but Sìne NicDhòmhnuill *or* Dhomhnullach, which literally translated are *John Donaldson* and *Jane Donaldsdaughter.* The Gaelic *nic* really "grand-daughter," stands for *inghean mhic* or *ní mhic.* We have recorded in 1566, Nc VcKenze (McLeod Charters)—‡.
nic-cridhe ! *int.* Term of endearment to a female. My dear lassie (*lit.* daughter of my heart.)
nichean,(CR) *pl.* nicheanan.*s.m.* Used often in emphasis for *ni.* The -*an* has not the sound of the diminutive -*an* ; so it may represent nitheann—*Perthshire* Prouounced nichinn in *Gairloch*—DU.
†nid, *s.f.* Manslaughter.
ni 'd, (for ni iad) They shall do.
nid, *gen.sing.* & *n.pl.* of nead.
†nidhe, *s.* Time.
†nigh, -e, *s.f.* Daughter. 2 Niece.
nigh, *pr. pt.* a' nigheadh, *v.a.* Wash, cleanse, purify. 2 Bathe. N. do chasan,*wash your feet.*
nigh-àite,** *s.f.* Bathing-place, bath.
nigheachan, -ain, -an, *s. m.* Washing of linen. Bean nigheachain, *a laundress* ; taigh nigheachain, *a laundry.*
nigheadair, -ean, *s.m.* Washer, one who washes, cleanser.
nigheadaireachd, *s.f.ind.* Washing, business or process of washing linen. 2 Bathing. 3* Cleansing.
nigheadh, -eidh, *s.m.* Washing, act of washing, cleansing, purifying or bathing. A' n—, *pr. pt.* of nigh.
nighean, *gen.def.* na h-ighne, (& nighinne) *dat.* nighinn, *pl.* nigheannan, *s.f.* Daughter. 2 Damsel, maiden. 3 (CR)Unmarried woman. Applied to an unmarried woman all her life in *W. of Ross-shire.* [Corruption of *inghean* —‡.]
nigheanag, -aig, -an, *s.f.*, *dim.* of nighean. Little daughter. 2 Little girl, young girl. 3 Little washer. N. bheag a' bhròin, *the sorrowful little washer*—this is the naiad or water-nymph who presides over those about to die, and washes their shrouds on the edge of a lake, &c.
nighean-céile,** *s.f.* Daughter-in-law.
nighean-Iomhair, *s.f.* (*lit.* Ivor's daughter) Serpent, probably an error for "an nimhir "(AC)
nighinne,** *gen.sing.* of nighean.
nighneag, see nigheanag.
nighte, *past pt.* of nigh. Washed, cleansed, purified. 2 Bathed. A gruaidh n. le deòir, *her cheek washed by tears.*
———ach, -eiche, *a.* Abluent.
†nightean, -ein, *s.m.* Soap. 2 Mixture of dung and urine for washing linen.
nighidh, *s.f.* Robin, see brù-dhearg.
ni 'gin, (for ni eigian) Something.
nigir,** *a.* Sore. 2 Sick. 3 Bitter.
ni h-ann, No, not, nay, not so, it is not so. Ni h-ann mar tre aon duine, *not as through one man.*
ni h-è, No, not, it is not so. Beubaibh bhus

cridhe agus ni h-è bhur n-aodach, *rend your hearts and not your garments.*
ni h-eadh, Nay,not, not so, it is not so.
ni 'm, (for ni mi) I will do or make. 2 (for ni am) Not. Ni 'm faigh mi, *I will not get.*
nimh, -e, *s.m.* see neimh.
nimh, *s.f.* Drop.
nimhe, (AF) *s.* Exempt cattle.
†nimheach, see neimhneach.
nimhnealachd, see neimhneachd.
nimheil, -e, *a.* see neimheil.
nimh-fhògrach,** *a.* Alexipharmic.
nimhich, see neimhich.
nimhir,(AC) *s.* Venom. 2 Serpent.
nimhneach, -eiche, *a.* see neimheil. Tha a shùil n., *his eye is baneful.*
nimhneachan, -ain, see neimhneachan.
nimhneachd, see neimhneachd.
ni'nn, for nighinne.
ninneach,** *a.* Pleasant.
†niogharach,** *a.* Constant.
nioghnag, see nigheanag.
niomhach,** *a.* Bright, shining.
niomhas,** -ais, *s. m.* Brightness, clearness, transparency.
niomsa, (for ni mise) I shall or will do.
†nion,** *s.m.* Wave. 2 Letter.
nionach,** *a.* Pleasant. 2 Speckled. 3 Forked. 4 Catching.
†nionadh, -aidh, *s.m.* Prey, booty, plunder.
nionadh,** -aidh, *s.m.* Child-bearing.
nionag, see nigheanag.
niopag, -aig, *s. f.* Gaelic spelling of *nippock*, diminutive of *nip.*
nior, *adv.* Not, never. Nior chualas, *I have not heard* ; 'anam nior thog, *who never lifted his soul.* [Used with past tense only.]
nìos, *adv.* (a nìos) From below, up (towards the speaker.) Thoir a nìos, *bring up* ; a sìos agus a nìos, *to the bottom and to the top, down and up* ; thig a nìos, *come up* (but falbh *suas, go* up.)
nios, see neas.
nios,* *s.m.* Top, summit.
niosgaid, -e, -ean, *s.f.* see neasgaid.
————each, see neasgaideach.
ni's, (for na is *or* nì is.) Usually precedes an adj. to express the *comp.* degree. (see na's.)
nis, *adv.* (a nis) Now, at this time. 2 Now, therefore. A nis, bha seo mar sin, *now, this was that way* ; thig a nis, *come along now* ; a nis 's a rithis, *now and again* ; nis, 's fheudar dhomh innseadh dhuit, *now I must plainly tell you.*
ni's, *cont.* for ni, *s.*, & is, *v.*,—(i.e, ni 's.)
nise, *gen.sing.* of neas.
nisean, *Suth'd* for nis, *now.*
niste, *Moidart & other parts of W. coast* for nis, *now.*
nitear, see nitnear.
nìth, see nì. 'Nuair 'thiginn dachaidh o 'n nìth, *when I would come home from the cattle—Duanaire*, 145.
†nith, *s.f.* Slaughter, battle. 2 Manslaughter.
nithe, *n.pl.* of ni, *a thing.*
†nitheach,** *a.* Warlike.
nitheannan, *n.pl.* of ni, *a thing.*
nithear, *fut pass.* of dean.
niùc, -a, -an, *s.f.* Gaelic spelling of *neuk.*
niùcach, -aiche, *a.* Abounding in nooks.
niugh, *corruption* of an diugh by eclipsis.
niula,[?] (AC) *s.f.* Dawn.
nò, see nòdh.
no, *conj.* Or. 2 Nor, neither. 3 Otherwise, else, if not. Cha tog sinn taigh no taigh, *we will not build a house at all* (*lit.* a house nor a house.)
nobha, see nuadh.
†nobhaidh, *s.f.* Time, season.
noch, see nach.
nochd, *a.* see nochdaidh.
nochd, *s.f.ind.* Nakedness. Chòmhdaich iad n. an athar, *they covered their father's nakedness* ; mo n. is mo nàire ! *my nakedness and my shame !*
nochd, [*pl.* na nuichd—*Isles*—not good Gaelic] *s.* Naked person.
nochd, *adv.* (an nochd) To-night, this night. An tig e an nochd ? *will he come to-night ?* In the Bible *an nochd* (this night,) is applied to what is now called in English *last* night, as in 1 Sam. xv. 16. " what the Lord said unto me this night." This is like the custom in Hebrew — " and the evening and the morning were the first day," the evening before being counted as belonging to the day, and not the evening after, as is the present English usage.
nochd, *v.a.* Show, reveal, disclose, discover. 3 Present, offer. 3 Strip, make naked. 4 Peel. N. an t-airgiod, *show the money* ; nochdaidh mi dhuit, *I will show you* ; ni math cò a nochdas dhuinn a nis ? *who will now show us any good thing ?*
nochdach, -aiche, *a.* see nochhdaidh.
————-adh, see nochdadh.
————-d, see nochdaidheachd.
nochdadh, -aidh, *s.m.* Showing, act of showing, revealing, disclosing, discovering. 2 Presenting, act of presenting or offering. 3 Stripping, making bare. 4††Exemplification. 5†† Manifesto. 6 (DMC) View. A' n—, *pr. pt.* of nochd.
nochdaich, *pr. pt.* a' nochdachadh, see nochd.
nochdaichidh, *fut. aff. a.* of nochd.
nochdaichte, *past part.* of nochdaich, see nochdte.
nochdaidh, -e, *a.* Naked, bare, exposed. 2 Desolate, bleak. 3 Revealing. 4 Stripping. 5 (DMC) Visible, apparent.
————-, *fut.aff.a.* of nochd.
————-, *gen.sing.* of nochdadh.
————-eachd,** *s.f.* Nakedness.
nochdam, *1st. sing.imp.* of nochd. Let me disclose. 2 for nochdaidh mi, I shall disclose.
nochdar, *fut.pass.* of nochd. Shall be disclosed.
nochd-larach,** -aich, *s.m.* Laying waste, desolation. 2 Place that is laid waste. Chum an deanamh 'nan n.,*to make them a desolation.*
nochdte, *past. pt.* of nochd. Shown, revealed,disclosed, discovered. 2 Presented, offered. 3 Bare. 4 Shabby, ill-dressed. 5 (DMC) Easily seen.
nochduidh, see nochdaidh.
†nod, *s.m.* Abbreviation. 2 Difficulty. 3 Emergency, need.
nòd, -oid, *s.m.* Note. 2 see nòdh.
†nod, *v.a.* Understand.
nodachadh,** *s.m.* Grafting. A' n—, *pr.pt.* of nòdaich.
nòdachair,** *s.m.* Grafter.
nodadh, -aidh, -aidhean, *s.m.* Suggestion,wink, nod. 2 see nòdh. 3 (DU) Bodily growth. Cha d' thàinig n. air, *he hasn't grown an inch.*
nòdaich,** *pr.pt.* a' nòdachadh, *v. a.* Graft. 2 Knot.
————-te, *past pt.* Grafted. 2 Knotted.
nòdair,** -ean, *s.m.* Grafter. 2 Abridger. 3 see nòtair.
————eachd,** *s.f.* Circumstances of abridging. 2 Use of abbreviations. 3 see nòtaireachd.
nodan,* -ain, *s.m.* Short sleep.
nòdh,(AC) *s.* Knowledge, intelligence, information. Cha'n 'eil nòdh agam air, *I have no knowledge of him.*

nodh,** *a.* Noble, excellent.
nodha, see **nuadh.** **Ùr nodha,** *quite new.*
nogan, see **noigean.**
noibhiseach,** -ich, *s. m.* Gaelic spelling of *novice.*
noig, -e, -ean, *s.f.* The anus. 2* Old-fashioned face. 3 Nock (*Scots* for clock.)
noigean, -ein, -an, *s.m.* Cup. 2 Wooden cup. 3 Noggin (measure of ¼ pint.) 4 (DMC) Short, stout fellow.
noigeanach, *a.* Snuffy.
noigean-creadha, -ein-, -an-, *s.m.* Earthenware jug.
noigeasach,* -aiche, *a.* Snuffy.
nòin, *s.m.ind.* Noon, mid-day. **Is èasgaidhe n. na maduinn,** *noon is more lively than morning.* [Most people are more lively after dinner than before.] In Welsh it is applied to noon, but in Manx to evening. "**Trath nòine bhreagha,** *a fine evening,*" is quite a customary salutation in Ireland. **Biadh n.,** *dinner* ; **trà n.,** *noontide.*
nòin-dhorchadh,** -aidh, *s.m.* Eclipse of the sun.
nòinean, -ein, -an, *s.m.* see **neòinean.**
———**ach,** -aiche, *a.* see **neòineanach.**
†**nòin reult,**** *s.m.* Evening star.
noir, *s.m.ind.* see **ear.**
†**nois,**** *a.* Excellent. 2 Noble.
nois,** -e, *adv.* see **nis.** (Irish.)
nòis,** *gen.sing.* of **nòs.**
nòisean, Gaelic form of *notions. s.pl.* Trifles, bagatelles—*Dàin I. Ghobha.*
†**noit,** *s.* Church. 2 Congregation.
†**noitheach,** *a.* Noble.
nolla,(?) (AC) *s.* Greatness.
Nollaig, -e, -ean, *s.f.* Christmas. **Là Nollaig,** *Christmas Day.*
Nollaig bheag, -e-bige, -ean-beaga, *s. f.* New Year's Day.
Nollaig mhór, -e-móire, -ean-móra, *s.f.* Christmas.
nomha, see **nuadh.**
nonn, see **nunn.**
norra,‡ *s.m.* Wink of sleep, nap.
norradaich,(MS) *s.f.* Sleepiness, dozing.
norradh, } see **norra.**
norrag, }
norp,** *s.m.* House-leek.
nòs, -òis, -an, *s.m.* Custom, manner, habit. **Cha bu n. do Dhiarmad eagal,** *D. was not wont to fear.*
nos,** -ois, *s.m.* Knowledge.
nòs, -ùis, *s. m.* Cow's first milk after calving, chyle, beastings. 2 First of anything. **Bheir e nòs a mhàthar as a shròn,** *he will make the chyle drop from his nose* ; **bainne nùis,** *beasty milk—Argyll.*
†**nos,** *a.* White, milk-white. 2 Pure.
nòsach, -aiche, *a.* Usual, customary. 2 Ceremonious, adhering to customs, habitual, fashionable.
nòsachd, *s. f. ind.* Customariness, adhering to custom, habitude.
nòsadh, -aidh, *s.m.* Liking, approving.
nòsaich,** *v.a.* Enact. 2 Approve. 3 Practice, make customary.
nòsail, -e, *a.* see **nòsach.**
nòsalachd,** *s.f.* Formality.
nòsar, -aire, *a.* Juicy, sappy. 2 White. 3 see **nòsach.**
nòsara, see **nòsar,**
nòsarachd,** *s.f.* Custom, modishness.
nòsda,(AC) *n.pl.* of **nòs.** Laws.
nòs-luinge,(AH) } *s.m.* Ship-dock.
nòs-luingeis,** }
nòsmhor,** *a.* Modish.
———**achd,**** *s.f.* Modishness.

nòt,** *s.m.* Gaelic spelling of (bank-)*note.*
nòtachan, *s.pl.* Notes.
nòtair, -ean, *s.m.* Notary.
———**eachd,** *s.f.* Business of a notary.
nothaist, -e, -ean, *s. m. & f.* Foolish person, idiot, half-witted peason.
———**each,** -eiche, *a.* Foolish, idiotical.
———**eachd,** *s.f.* Idiotism.
nothaistealachd, see **nothaisteachd.**
nuachallachd,** *s.f.* Astonishment.
†**nuachar,** -air, -ean, *s.m. & f.* Companion. 2 Bridegroom. 3 Bride.
nuadarra, *a.* Surly, angry, gloomy, sulky.
nuadarrach, see **nuadarra.**
————**d,** *s.f.* Surliness, gloominess, sulkiness, angriness.
nuadh, -uaidhe, *a.* New, fresh, recent, modern, unfamiliar.
———**achadh,** -aidh, *s.m.* Renewing, act of renewing renovating. 2 Renovation. **A' n—,** *pr.pt.* of **nuadhaich.**
nuadhachd, *s.f.* Newness, freshness, recentness, modernness, novelty, renovation.
nuadhaich, *v.a.* Renew, renovate.
————**te,** *past pt.* of **nuadhaich.** Renewed, renovated.
nuadhalachd,(MS) *s.f,* Recentness.
nuadharra, see **nuadarra.**
————**chd,** see **nuadarrachd.**
nuadhas,** -ais, *s. m.* see **nòs.**
nuadh-bheath,** *s. f.* Reformed life, new life, amended life.
nuadh-bhreith, *s.m.* Regeneration, new birth.
nuadh-bhrìgh, *s.m.* Transubstantiation.
————**eachadh,** -aidh, *s.m.* Act of transubstantiating. **A' n—,** *pr.pt.* of **nuadh-bhrìghich.**
nuadh-bhrìghich, *v.a.* Transubstantiate.
nuadh-bhrìogh, see **nuadh-bhrìgh.**
nuadh-chreidmheach, -eich, *s.m.* Novice, young convert, proselyte.
nuadh-mhilidh, -ean, *s. m.* Recruit, untrained soldier.
nuadh-theanngnair,** *s.m.* Innovator.
————————**eachd,**** *s.f.* Innovation.
nuadh-thionnsgantair,** *s.m.* Innovator.
nuadh-thionnsgnach, *a.* Innovating, fond of innovation.
nuadh-thionnsgnadh,** -aidh, *s.m.* Innovation.
nuag,* -aige, -an, *s.f.* Sunk eye.
nuagach,* -aiche, *a.* Sunk-eyed. 2 Surly.
nuaidhe, *comp.* of **nuadh.**
nuaidheachd, see **naidheachd.** 2** Tidiness. **Droch n. ort !** *woe betide you* ; **fear-n.,** *a newsmonger* ; **paipear-n.,** *a newspaper.*
†**nuail,** -ean, see **nuall & nuallan.**
†**nuail,** *v.a.* Roar, howl.
nuaimhneach,** *a.* Fearful.
'nuair, *adv.* (an uair) When, at the time, seeing that, (*lit.* the hour.)
nuall, -a, -an, *s.m.* Lamentation. 2 Roaring, howling. 3 Lowing of cattle. 4 Loud and soft sound. 5**Murmur. 6 Shriek. 7 Screech of the owl. 8 Opinion. 9 Freak. 10(AC) Incantation, hail. 11 Loud drawling howl, as of a lion or wild cat. **N. Nollaig,** *a Christmas hail* ; **n. gun ghaoid,** *a true saying.*
nuall, -aill, *s.m.* Praise.
nuall,** *a.* Noble. 2 Famous.
nuallach, -aiche, *a.* Howling, roaring. 2 Lowing. 3 Making a loud and soft sound. 4** Wailing. 5**Shrill. 6**Freakish.
nuallach,§ -aich, *s. m.* Germander speedwell, angels' eyes, birds' eyes, God's eye—*veronica chamædrys.* A small trailing plant with a bright blue flower scarcely ½ inch in diameter. (illust. 553 on p. 701.)

553 Nuallach

nualladh, -aidh, *s.m.* Howling, wailing, roaring.

nuallaich,** *s.f.* Howling, yelling, howl, bellowing, yell. A' n—, *pr.pt.* of nuallaich.

———, *pr.pt.* a' nuallaich, *v.n.* Howl, roar, yell.

nuallan, -ain, -an, *s.m.* see nuall. N. thonn, *the murmur of waves ;* n. na pioba, *the sound of the bagpipes.*

————ach, see nuallach. Pìob n., *a loud-sounding pipe.*

nuallanaich *s.f.* Continued howling, roaring, lowing or shrieking. N. spréidhe, *the lowing of cattle.*

nuallair, (AC) -ean, *s.m.* (*lit.* rejoicers) Waits or carol-singers who went about singing at Christmas, New Year, &c.

nuallartach, *a.* Howling, roaring. 2 Lowing. 3 Shrieking, wailing loudly.

nuallartaich, *s.f.* An exaggerated howling, see nuallanaich.

nuall-ghuth, -a, -an, *s. m.* Howling or loud voice. 2 Roar, howl.

————ach, -aiche, *a.* Howling, roaring, lowing.

nuallsan,** *a.* Noble, generous.

nualraich,** *s.f.* Howling, roaring.

nuamhanair,** *s.* Embroidery.

†nuar, *int.* Alas ! woe 's me.

nuar, -air, *s.m.* Woe, gloom. 2 Frown.

'nuar ! *int.* Alas ! alack-a-day ! Mo nuar ! *alas !*

nuarranta, -ainte, *a.* Woeful, sad 2 Sour, surly. 3 Wild. A mhios nuarranta, garbh-fhrasach ! *O tempestuous heavy-rainy month !—Oran a' Gheamhraidh, v. 18.*

——————d, *s.f.* Woefulness, sadness 2 Sourness, surliness, gloominess. 3†† Wildness.

nuas, *adv.* (a nuas.) Down, downward (towards the speaker.) Thig a nuas, *come down* (but falbh *sìos*, *go* down.)

nuas,* *s.f.* Bottom, ground.

†nuathaigh, *s.* Heaven.

nuathar, -air, *s.m.* Wedding.

nuatharra,†† *a.* Surly, gloomy. 2 Fierce.

nuichd, *gen. sing. & n.pl.* of nochd, (naked person.)—*Isles.*

nùidh, *v.n.* Acquiesce. [With *prep.* le.] 2 (DMC) Move. N. a dh' ionnsuidh, *propend.*

nùidheadh, (MS) *s.m.* Acquiescence. 2 Declination, inclination. 3 Bias. 4 (DMC) Motion, movement.

nùidheil (gu). *adv.* (MS) Accessorily.

nuig, *prep. & adv.* (gu nuig is the correct form, but gu ruig the usual one.) To, unto, as far as. 2 Till, until.

nuimhir, -e, -ean, *s.* Number.

————each,** *a.* Numerous. 2 Numerical.

————each,** -eich, *s.m.* Accountant, arithmetician, calculator.

nuimhreachadh,** -aidh, *s.m.* Calculation. 2** Numbering, computing.

nuimhreachail,** *a.* Arithmetical.

nuimhrich,** *v.* Calculate. 2 Number, compute.

†nuin, *s.f.* The ash-tree. 2 Old Gaelic name of the letter N.

†nuinean,** -ein, *s.m.* Dwarf.

'n uiridh, *adv.* (an uiridh) see uiridh.

null, *adv.* (a null) see a nunn.

nuallach, (AF) *s.m.* Germander goose, (*lit.* roarer or howler.)

nuna,** *s.m.* Hunger.

nunn, *adv.* (a nunn) Thither, to the other side, beyond, over. Theirig a nunn, *go over ;* a nunn 'a nall, *hither and thither ;* dh' eubh e oirre a nunn ri 'thaobh, *he called her over to his side.* Nunn is the correct word, null is merely the northern erroneous dialectic form analagous to nall.

'nur, *adv.* see 'nuair.

'nur, *contr.* for ann bhur.

'nuraidh, 'nuruidh, } for an uiridh, see uiridh.

nùs, -ùis, *s.m.* see nòs.

O o

O, onn, *gorse*, the 13th. letter of the Gaelic alphabet now in use.

Ò, with a grave accent sounds long and open, like *o* in *lord* : as còrr, *excellent ;* òr, *gold ;* tòc, *a smell ;* and short, like *o* in for, as, cor, *condition.* It also has a sound like *o* in *cold ;* long, as, mór, *great ;* and short, as sodan, *gladness.* O, followed by *gh*, has a sound, to which there is none similar in the English language ; short as, roghainn, *choice ;* long as, roghnaich, *choose.*

O ! *int.* O ! oh ! Alas ! An exclamation of varied signification. 2‡‡ Expression of wish or desire, as, O gu'n tigeadh e a mach ! *O that he would come forth !*

o, *adv.* Since, from that time. O thàinig e as a' bholg, *since he was born.*

o, *prep.* From. O làimh mo bhràthar, o làimh Esau, *from my brother's hand, from the hand of Esau.* Combined with the personal pronouns thus :— uam, *from me ;* uat, *from thee;* uaidh, *from him ;* uaipe, *from her ;* uainn, *from us ;* uaibh, *from you ;* uapa, *from them.* [Aspirates consonants following it, except *l*, *n* and *r*, and these are affected in pronunciation.]

o, *conj.* Because, seeing that, for.

†o, *s.* Ear.

ob, (AC) *gen.* oib & oibe, *pl.* ob, *s.* Spell, charm, incantation. Bios i ris na h-ob, *she practises spells ;* tha na h-ob a' dol as, *spells are going out of use.*

òb, -a, -an, *s.m.* Bay, creek, harbour. 2(DU) Shallow pool.

†ob, *s.m.* Hop-plant. 2 Fruit of the hop.

ob, *pr.pt.* ag obadh, *v.a. & n.* Refuse, deny, reject. 2 Shun, avoid. 3 Fail, faint, give over. 4 Abnegate. 5 Except. Na ith 's na ob cuid an leinibh bhig, *neither eat nor reject the child's food ;* am bodach ruadh nach obadh dubhan, *the codling that ne'er refuses hook*—the codling and cod are, as a rule, keen on any bait, even stones being often found in their stomachs.

oba, see ob, (spell.)

obach,‡‡ -aiche, *a.* Negative. 2** Denying. 3 **Refusing, rejecting. 4**Shunning.

———,** -aich, *s.m.* One who refuses or shuns.

obadh, -aidh, *s. m.* Refusing, act of refusing, denying, rejecting. 2 Refusal, denial, rejection. 3 Shunning, act of shunning, avoiding.

4 State of failing, fainting or giving over. 5 **Provocation. 6**Force. Ag o—, *pr. pt.* of ob,
obag, -aig, -an, *s.f.* Hurry. 2 Abruptness. 3 Confusion. 4 see gormag. 5 (DU) In *pl.* = Convulsions. Anns na h-obagan deireannach, *suffering the final convulsions.*
obag,(AF) -an, *s.f.* Witch. 2 *dim.* of ob, *spell.* 3 (AF) Hobby falcon.
obagach, -aiche,*a.* Hurried, abrupt. 2 Confused. 3 Causing hurry.
òbagag, *dim.* of òbag.
obagaich,** *s.f.* Flurry, confused anxiety. 2 Abruptness.
obagan, (*pl.* of obag.) Witchcraft, charms, spells.
obaidh, see ubag.
obaig,(MS) *a.* Abrupt.
obaig,** *s.f.* Hurry, flurry, confusion. 2 Abruptness.
obaigeachd, *s.f.* Suddenness, rashness.
obain, -e, *a.* see obann.
òbain, *gen.sing.* & *n.pl.* of òban.
obainn,** *a.* see obann.
obainne, *s.f.ind.* Suddenness, hastiness, quickness, rashness. 2 Frowardness. 3 Nimbleness.
obainne, *comp.* of obann.
———achd, see obannachd.
———ad, see obainne.
obair, oibre, *pl.* obraichean & oibrichean, *s.f.* Work, labour, process of working. 2 Work, work performed. 3 Intermeddling. 4 Workmanship. 5 Fuss. †6 Confluence. O. do mheuran fhéin, *the work of your own hands;* a dh' aon o., *purposely, intentionally, chaffing;* car o., *a turn of work, performance;* obair is ath o., *idle repetition of labour,* (doing work so carelessly that it has to be done over again.)
o.-chèardach, *smithy-work.*
o.-chèardail, *engine, machinery, work done by machinery.*
o.-chreadha,** *porcelain, china-work, earthenware, delf, pottery.*
o.-chumta, *a task.*
o.-dhìon,* *a rampart, bulwark.*
o.-ghloine, *glass-work.*
o.-ghréis, *arras, embroidery.*
o.-iaruinn, *foundry.*
o.-inntinn, *a theory.*
o.-la, *day's work; 2 a name in* Skye *for a pothanger and chain.*
o.-làimhe, *handiwork; 2 work done by hand in contradistinction to that done by machinery.*
o.-lionain, *network, chequer-work.*
o.-lin, *network, chequer-work.*
o.-shlabhruidh, *chain-work.*
o.-shnaidhte, *hewn work.*
o.-shnàthaid, *needlework, embroidery.*
o.-tharsuinn, *network.*
o.-theine, *firework; 2 steam-engine.*
o.-thrailleil, *servile work.*
o.-uaireadair, *clockwork.*
o.-uchd, *breast-plate; 2 parapet,breastwork.*
o.-uisge, *waterwork; 2 jet.*
òbairt,(AH) *s.f.* Retching, involuntary act of trying to vomit. Generally used with "diobhairt" or "cur o mach," as, ò. diobhairt.
obam, *1st.sing. imp.* of ob. Let me refuse.
oban,(AC) *pl.* obann, *s.m.* Wizard.
òban, *s.m. dim.* of òb. Creek, little bay.
———ach, *a.* Abounding in bays or harbours.
obann, -ainne, *a.* Sudden, unexpected. 2 Quick, nimble, agile. 3 Rash, hasty. 4* Pert, meddling. Eagal o., *sudden fear;* o. le 'bheul, *rash with his mouth;* gu h-o., *suddenly, quickly.*
obannachd, *s.f.* Suddenness, unexpectedness. 2 Quickness, nimbleness. 3 Rashness, fieriness. 4 Abruptness. 5**Hastiness of temper. 6* Pertness, impertinence. 7* Readiness concerning things not your own.
obar,** -air, *s.m.* Refusal, denial.
obar, *fut.pass.* of ob. Shall be refused or denied. Cha'n o. leis an gàbhadh, *he shall not reject the situation of danger.*
†obh, see abh.
obhan, -ain, *s.m.* see omhan.
†obhainn, see abhainn.
obhanach, -aiche, see omhanach.
†obhann,** -ainn, see uamhann.
o bhàrr, *prep.* Off, from the top.
obhnaig,(CR) *v.a.* Touch, meddle with—*Perthshire.* (*Scots,* own.)
obh obh! *int.* Expression of wonder, derision, pain or grief. Och ay!
ob-obagail,* *s.f.* Flutter.
obhraig,(CR) *s.f.* Church collection—*Perthshire.* Gaelic spelling of *offering.*
obi, see ob (spell.)
obraichean, *n.pl.* of obair.
obta, *past pt.* & *a.* Unaccepted.
obuig,** *a.* Abrupt, sudden. 2 Rash.
obuinn, -e, *a.* see obann.
———e,** *s.f.* Rashness. 2 Suddenness.
obuinneachd, see obannachd.
obunn, see obann.
†oc, *s.m.* Poet.
†ocad, -aid, *s.m.* Permission, pleasure, will. 2 Occasion, business.
†ocaid, *s.* see ocad.
ocaideach,(DMy) *a.* Duine o., *a good-for-nothing fellow, a "wont-work."*
ocairear, -an, *s.m.* see ocarair.
ocairiche, -ean, *s.m.* Lender of money.
ocar, -air, *s.m.* Interest on money. 2 Usury, extortion. Airgiod air o., *money lent on usury.*
ocarach,** *a.* Usurious, extortive in money matters. 2 Of, or belonging to, usury.
ocarach,** -aich, *s.m.* see ocarair.
ocarachd,** *s.f.* Usuriousness, practice of usury.
ocarair, -ean, *s.m.* Usurer, extortioner.
ocaras, -ais, *s.m.* see acras. 2 Practice of usury.
———ach, see ocarach.
ocar-fhear, *s.m.* see ocarair.
ocas,** -ais, *s.m.* Interest, usury. 2 Annual rent.
och! *int.* Alas! ah! Och is och eile! *my conscience thrice over!*
och, -an, *s.m.* Sigh.
o chàch,** *adv.* Apart.
ochain! see ochan!
ochain nan och! *int.* Alas! and alack-a-day.
ochal,** -ail, *s.m.* Moan, howl, wail. 2 Moaning, howling, wailing.
ochan! *int.* Alas!
ochan, -ain, *s.m.* Sigh. 2 Lamentation.
ochanaich, -e, *s.f.* Sighing, sobbing.
ochan-i! *int.* Woe 's me!—*Arran.*
†ochas,** -ais, *s.m.* Itch, see tachas.
ochas,** -ais, *s.m.* Mallows.
ochd, -an, *s.m.* see uchd.
ochd, *a.* Eight.
ochdlach,** -aich, *s. m.* Good key of voice. 2 Octave.
ochdad,* *a.* Eighty. O. fhear, *eighty men.*
ochdail (gu h-o—) Eighthly.
ochdamh, *a.* Eighth. Air an o. bliadhna, *on the eighth year.*
ochdamh, -aimh, *s. m.* Four pennylands, an eighth of a davoch—a measure of land.
———ach,* -aiche, *a.* Octangular.
———ach,* -aich, *s. m.* Octagon, figure of eight sides.

ochd-bhallach,(AF) s.m. Octopus.
ochd-bhliadhnach,‡‡ a. Octennial.
ochd-bhileach,‡‡ a. Octopetalous.
ochd-chearnach,‡‡ -aich, s.m. Octagon.
ochd-deug, a. Eighteen. Ochd bliadhna deug a dh' aois, *eighteen years of age.*
ochd-dhuilleach,‡‡ see ochd-bhileach.
ochdmhad, s. Eightieth.
†ochd-mhios, -a, s.m. October (*lit.* 8th. month.)
ochdnar, s. Eight (of persons only.) [Followed by the *gen.pl.*]
ochd-ràmhach, s.m. Eight-oared galley.
ochd-roinneach, s.m. Gyrony-of-eight.
ochd-oisneach, -eiche. a. Octangular.
ochd-oisneag, -eig, s.f. Octagon.
ochd-shlisneach, -eiche, a. Octagonal, having eight sides.
ochd-shlisneach, -eich, s.m. Gun having an octagonal barrel.
ochd-shlisneag,‡‡ s.f. Octagon.
ochd-shùileach, a. Octonocular.
o cheann, adv. Some time ago, long ago, since. [Always followed by a noun of time.]
o cheann treis, adv. A while ago.
o chian, adv. Of old.
o chian nan cian, adv. From time immemorial.
o chionn, adv. see o cheann.
o chionn treis, see o cheann treis.
och is ochain nan och éire ! Interjection of deep grief.
och nan ochain ! int. Alas ! woe of woes !
ochòin ! int. Oh ! alas !
ochòin fhéin ! int. Ah me ! woe 's me !
†ochra, s.pl. Shoes.
ochras, -ais, s.m. Gill of a fish.
ochthon, see ochòin !
òcrach, *Gairloch* for òtrach.
ocrach, -aiche, a. see acrach.
ocras, -ais, s.m. Gill of a fish. 2 *rarely* Bosom. 3 see acras.
———ach, -aiche, a. see acrach.
ocrasan, -ain, -an, see acrasan.
od ! int. Tut ! no ! ay !
od, s. see oda.
od, see ud.
o d' (*contr.* for o+do.) From thy. O d' cheann, *from thy head ;* o d' sheanair, *from your grandfather.*
oda,(AC) s. Race. 2 Racecourse. These great annual race-meetings were once very popular. The last one was held in Barra in 1828, in S. Uist in 1820, in Benbecula in 1830, in N. Uist in 1866, and in Harris in 1818.
odaidh, see oda.
odan, *Lewis* for rùdan, *knuckle.*
†odh,** oidh, s.m. Music. 2 Point of a spear. 3 Sharp end of anything.
odha, -ichean, s.m. see ogha.
odhail,(DMy) s.f. Bustle. Ciod an o. a th' ort? *why do you bustle so?*
†odhall,** a. Deaf.
odhan, -ain, see omhan.
———ach, -aiche, see omhanach.
———achd, see omhanachd.
odhann, -ainn, see aghann.
odhar, -air & uidhre, a. Dun, dun-coloured, pale, sallow, drab, dapple, yellowish.
———ach-mhullach,§ odharaich-mhullaich, [s. m. in McL & D., f. in **.] Devil's bit scabious, see ura-bhallach.
———ag, s.f. see òrag. 2 Young of the cormorant.
———aich, a. see odhraich.
———aidh,(AH) a. Dark, swarthy.
———an, -ain, -an, s. m. Cow-parsnip—*heracleum spondylium.*
odhar-bhàn,** a. Sallow. 2 Of a darkish white colour.

554. Odharan.

odhar-chù,(AF) s.m. Otter—*Suth'd.* 2 Wolf.
odhar-liath, a. Dapple-coloured.
odh-mheas,** s.m. Homage, great respect.
odh-mheasach,** a. Respectful, dutiful.
odh-mheasail,** a. Respectable,much respected.
odhraich, v.a. & n. Make dun, pale or sallow. 2 Become dun, pale or sallow.
———te, *past pt.* of odhraich. Made dun, pale or sallow.
odhra-sgàirneach, s. m. Young chat or cormorant.
†oe,(AF) s.f. Sheep.
ofhaich, (CR) s. f. Use, worth—*Blair Athole.* Am bheil o. ann ? *is it of any use or value ?*
ofhaich,(CR) Bustle, fuss. Ciod e an o. a th' ort ? *what are you in such a bustle about ?—W. of Ross-shire.*
ofhaichear,(CR) s.m. Officer.
ofraideach,** -aich, s. m. Offerer, as of a sacrifice. 2 Druidical priest.
ofrail, -e, -ean, s.f. Offering, sacrifice.
ofrail,‡‡ pr. pt. ag ofraladh, v. a. Offer, sacrifice.
òg, òig, -an, s.m. Youth, young man. 2 Young child.
òg, òige, a. Young, youthful. Bean òg, *a young wife;* mar sin bha mi òg, *so was I when yonng.*
ògachd, see ògalachd.
ògail, -e, a. Youthful, young. 2 Of youthful appearance. 3 (MS) Tiny.
ògain, *gen.sing.* of ògan.
ògair, -ean, see òigear.
ògalachd, s.f. Youthfulness, youth. 2 Conduct of youth. 3 Season of youth.
ogan,(CR) *Suth'd* for sogan.
ògan, -ain, -an, see òganach. 2 Young branch. 3 Twig, tendril. 4 Seedling. 5 (MS) Germ. Bàrr an ògain, *the top of the branch ;* ceud òg-an aobhach, *a hundred joyous young men.*
òganach, -aich, s. m. Young man, youth. 2 Stripling. 3 Minor. 4 Bough, branch, twig. Marbhar an òganaich, *their youths shall be slain.*
òganachd, see ògalachd.
òg-aoiseach,‡‡ a. Non-aged.
òg-bhean,**,-mhna, (&c. as bean) s. m. Young woman. 2 Young wife, newly-married woman.
òg-bhó, (-bhoin &c. as bó) s. f. Young cow, heifer.
òg-chullach,** -aich, s.m. Young boar, grice.
og-fhaillean,(MS) s.m. Layer.
òg-fhionn, -fhuinn, see òg-ghnàths.
òg-ghnàths, s.f. Juvenility.

ogh, One of the names of the letter *o.*
†ogh,** -a, *s.f.* Virgin.
†ogh, *a.* Pure. 2 Sincere. 3 Whole, entire.
ogha, *pl.* -chan & -ichean, *s.m.* Grandchild. 2 Nephew. Is iad oghachan peathar is bràthar, *they are second cousins.*
òghachd,** *s.f.* Virginity.
oghan, see omhan.
———ach, see omhanach.
oghar, see odhar.
†oghum, -uim, *s.m.* The occult manner of writing used by the ancient Gael; polygraphy. The ogham alphabet was formed on a proto-telegraphic system by so many strokes for each letter, above, through or below a stem line, which was often formed by the angle of a stone monument thus :—

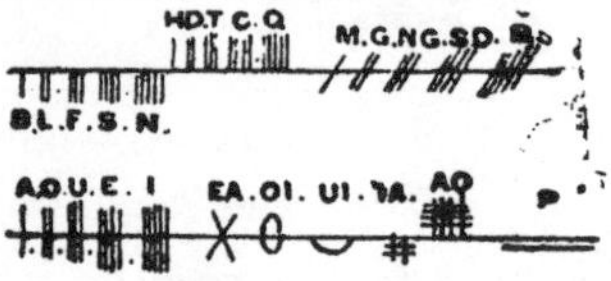

2* Occult sciences.
òglach, -aich, *s. m.* Lad, youth, stripling. 2 Man-servant. 3 Soldier. 4**Vassal. 5 Young hero. Ban-òglach, *a handmaid, maid-servant.*
———as, -ais, *s.m.* Farm-service. 2 Servitude, slavery, vassalage. 3** Fourth stage of human life, from 34 to 54 years of age.
oglachas,** -ais, *s.m.* Kind of Gaelic verse.
òg-losgann, -ainn, -an, *s. m.* Tadpole, young frog, little frog.
ogluichd, see ogluidheachd.
ogluidh, -e, *a.* Awful, gloomy, dismal. 2 Afraid, awe-struck. 3 Bashful. 4 Peevish. 5††Wild. 6(DMy) Unsteady. Tha 'm bàta o., *the boat is unsteady.*
———eachd, *s.f.ind.* Fear, dread, terror. 2 Gloom. 3 Fearfulness, awfulness. 4 Bashfulness. 5 Wildness. 6 Peevishness. 7(DMy) Squeamishness, as when a person is ready to vomit with sea- or other sickness. Làn o., *full of gloom ;* là o., *a day of gloominess.*
òg-mhaduinn, òg-mhaidne, *s.f.* Early morn, the dawn.
——————each, *a.* Early in the morning.
òg-mhaise,** *s.f.* Youthful beauty. 2 Youthfulness. 3 Handsomeness. Có seo 'na o. ? *who is this in his youthful beauty ?*
òg-mhart, -mhairt, *s.m.* Young cow.
òg-mheur,** -mheòir, *s.m.* Young branch. 2 *by a figure of speech,* Young person. Air bàrr nan o. samhraidh, *on the top of the young summer branches.*
Òg-mhios, -a, *s.m.* June. [Preceded by the article *an t-.*]
òg-mhnaoi, *dat.sing.* of òg-bhean. [Erroneously given by ** as an alternative form of the *nom.*]
òg-mhoirear, *s.m.* Young lord, son of a chief.
òg-narach,** *a.* Bashful, as youth.
ògraidh, see òigridh.
òg-thighearna, -n, *s.m.* Young lord, son of a chief.
†oi, see ai.
oibeag, -an, *s.f. dim.* of ob, (a spell.) see ubag.
†oibid, *s.f.* Submission, obedience.
oibne, *s.f.* Quickness, suddenness, (syncopated obainne.)
———ach,** -aiche, *a.* Sudden, quick.
oibre, *gen.sing.* of obair.
oibreach, *a.* Industrious.
———adh, -aidh, *s. m.* Working, act of working. 2 Labour. 3 Fermenting, state of fermenting, fermentation. 4 Mixing up, act of mixing together. 5 Agitation. Ag o—, *pr. pt.* of oibrich. An caochan ag o., *the wash fermenting ;* 'ga o., *mixing it ;* is goirt a tha air 'o. ! *how hard he is worked !*
oibreachail,** *a.* Effective, effectual, operative. 2‡‡Mechanical. 3‡‡Laborious. 4 Industrious.
oibrich, *pr.pt.* ag oibreachadh, *v.a. & n.* Work, operate, labour. 2 Mix, work to a consistency, as lime or clay. 3 Ferment. 4 Effect by labour.
———e, -an, *s.m.* Worker, workman, labourer. O. ealanta, *an ingenious workman.*
———te, *past pt.* of oibrich. Wrought, accomplished, effected. 2 Operated. 3 Mixed or wrought into a certain consistency. 4 Fermented. O. le obair ghréis, *wrought with needlework.*
oich ! *int.* Expression of bodily pain.
oich,** *s.* Post in the army. see oifhich.
oiche, see oidhche.
oiche,** -an, *s.m.* Counting-house.
oich ! oich ! *int.* Expression of bodily pain.
oid'-altruim, *s.m.* Foster-father.
oide, -an, *s.m.* Foster-father. 2 Stepfather. 3 Godfather. 4 Teacher. 5 *rarely* Grandfather.
——achadh, -aidh, *s.m.* Instructing.
oideachas, -ais, see oideachd.
——achd, *s.f.ind.* Instruction, counsel, tuition. 2* Instruction from evil or familiar spirits, occult science.
†oideadh, *s.m.* Massacre, death.
oideag,-an, *s.f.* Fillet.
oidean,** -ein, *s.m.* Degree of nobility. 2 Love, tenderness. 3 Generosity.
oideas, -eis, *s.m.* see oideachd. Beul-oideas, *oral instruction.*
oide-baistidh, *s.m.* Godfather.
oide-ciùil, *s.m.* Music-master.
oide-dannsaidh, *s.m.* Dancing-master.
oide-foghluim, *s.m.* Instructor, preceptor. Ar n-o., *our schoolmaster.*
oide-muinte, *s.m.* Instructor, preceptor.
oide-sgoile, *s.m.* Schoolmaster.
oidhche, -annan, -an & -achan, *s.f.* Night, evening. 2 Darkness. Beul na h-oidhche, *the evening ;* an o. nochd (*generally* an nochd), *to-night ;* 'san o. dhuibh dhuirch, *in the pitch-dark night ;* ré na h-oidhche, *all night ;* a là 's a dh' o., *by day and night ;* air feadh na h-o.,*during the night ;* meadhon-o., *midnight ;* meadhon na h-o., *the middle of the night ;* marbh na h-o., *the dead of midnight ;* o. mhath dhuit, *good night to thee.*
oidhcheach, -eiche, *a.* Nightly.
oidhcheil, -e, *a.* Nightly.
oidhche-mhèirleach,** *s.m.* Night-thief, night-robber.
oidhche-nam-bannag,(MMcD) *s.f.* Christmas-eve —*Lewis.*
†oidhe, see aoidh.
oidheachd, see aoidheachd.
†oidheadh, -eidh, *s.m.* Tragical death.
oidheam, -eim, -ean, *s.m.* Book. 2 Secret meaning, inference, idea. 3 Slight degree of knowledge. 4 Hint. 5‡‡Sensation, feeling. 'Nuair a dh'fhosgail e an t-oidheam, *when he expounded the meaning ;* is e sin an t-o. a thug mise as, *that is the inference I drew from it ;* gnothach gun o., *a thing without meaning ;* cò is urrainn o. sam bith a thoirt as ? *who can make any sense of it ?*
———ach, -aiche, *a.* Tractable. 2 Ideal. 3 ††Sensitive.
oidhearp, see oidheirp.
———ach, -aiche, see oidheirpeach.
oidheas,** -eis,*s.m.*Instruction, counsel. 2 Freestone.

oidheirp, -e, -ean, *s. f.* Attempt, endeavour, undertaking, trial. Dean o., or thoir o.,*make an attempt*; thug e o. air, *he tried it.*
———each, -eiche, *a.* Endeavouring, attempting. 2 Industrious, diligent, persevering.
———eachadh, -aidh, *s.m.* Attempting, act of attempting, endeavouring. Ag o—, *pr. pt.* of oidheirpich.
———ich, *pr. pt.* ag oidheirpeachadh, *v.a.* Attempt, endeavour.
———iche, -an, *s.m.* Attempter.
oidhirp, see oidheirp.
-———eachadh, see oidheirpeachadh.
oidhre, *s.f.* see eighre.
oidhre, -achan, *s.m.* see oighre.
oidhreachd, see oighreachd.
oidich,(MS) *v.a.* Rear.
oid-ionnsachaidh,* *s. m.* Familiar spirit. 2 Instructor in occult sciences.
oid'-ionnsaich,** *s.m.* Instructor. 2 Guide. O. a h-òige, *the guide of her youth.*
oifhich, -e, *s.f.* Office. 2 Post in the army.
†oifhiche, *s.f.* Water.
oifig, -e, -ean, *s. f.* Office, situation, post, employment. Glacadh neach 'oifig, *let one seize his office.*
——each, -ich, *s.m.* Officer, official.
——each,** *a.* Official, pertaining to office. 2 Fond of office.
——eil,** *a.* Official.
oifrionn, -inn, see aifrionn.
òig, *gen.sing.* of òg.
†oig,** *s.m.* Champion.
†oige, *s.f.* see eige.
òige, *s.f.ind.* Youth, season of youth. 2 Youthfulness. Cha tuig o. aimbeart, *youth thinks not of want.*
òige, *comp.* of òg. Younger, youngest.
——ach, -eich, *s. m.* Stallion, young horse or colt.
òigead, -eid, *s.m.* Degree of youth.
òigealachd,* *s.f.* see òige.
òigean, -ein, -an, *s.m.* Lad.
òigeil,* -e, *a.* see ògail.
òigear, -eir, *s. m.* Youth, young man. Roghadh òigeir, *a choice young man.*
òig-fhear, see òigear.
oigh, see aigh.
òigh, -e, -ean, *s.f.* Virgin, maiden. 2 Young woman. 3 *rarely* Stag.
òigh-cheòl, -chiùil, *s.m.* The musical voice of a virgin. 2 Virginal. Na's ceòlmhoire na ò., *more musical than a virginal.*
†oighe, *s.f.* Fulness, entireness.
oighe, see eighe.
òigheach,** *a.* Like a virgin. 2 Modest, bashful.
————d,*s.f.ind.* Virginity. 2 Virgin modesty. A' caoidh air son m' o., *bewailing my virginity.*
oigheam, -eim, *s.m.* Obedience, homage.
òighean, *n.pl.* of òigh.
oigheann,** oighne, see aghann.
-————ach, -aich, *s.f.* Thistle.
òigheil, -e, *a.* Maiden-like, modest.
oighidh,** *s.m.* Guest.
oighionnach, -aich, *s.f.* see oigheannach.
òigh-mhara, *s.f.* Mermaid, sea-nymph, nereid.
òigh-nàir,** *s.f.* Virgin modesty, virgin bashfulness.
òigh-nàrach, -aiche, *a.* see òigheil.
oighneach,** *a.* Liberal, generous.
òigh-nighean, -ighne, -an, *s.f.* Virgin-daughter, unmarried daughter.
oighre, *s.f.* see deigh (ice.)
oighre, -achan, *s.m.* Heir, heiress. Beiridh bean mac, ach 's e Dia a ni o., *a woman may bear a son, but it is God that makes the heir.*

oighreachail, -e, *a.* Inheritable, hereditary.
oighreachd, -an, *s.f.* Heirship. 2 Inheritance. 3 Possession, freehold estate, landed property. 4 (MS) Barony. Am bheil o. againn? *have we an inheritance?*
oighreag, -eig, -an. *s. f.* Cloudberry, mountain-strawberry—*rubus chamœmorus.*
————ach, -aiche, *a.* Abounding in, of, or belonging to cloudberries.

556. *Oighreag.*

oigimh,** *s.m.* Stranger.
oig're, see oigridh.
òigridh, *s.f.coll.* Children, youth, young folks. 2 Body of young men. Tha 'n o. a' crathadh an sleagh, *the youth are brandishing their spears.*
òil, see òl.
oil, *v.a.* Rear, educate, nurse, instruct in politeness. Mar a dh' oil i a clann, *as she reared her children.*
oil, *s. f. ind.* Vexation, grief, pain. 2 Offence, annoyance, regret. 3 Spite. Ge b' oil leis, (leithe, leinn, leibh, leò) *in spite of him (her, us, you, them)*; cha'n o. leam ged a bhitheadh tu air do chrochadh, *it were no offence to me though you were hanged*; 'dé a chuir gu 'm b' oil leam-sa? *why should it offend me?* ma's o. leat sin, na dean a rithis e, *if that be an offence to you,don't do it again*; tha siod agamsa ge b' oil leis na madaidh aig am bheil am fodar, *I possess that in spite of the dogs that have the straw—Skye*; mharbh thu mo thri nigheanan,mharbh ma 's o. leat,*you have killed my three daughters, even though you do not like it.*
oil, see saoil.
oil,** *s.f.* Learning, education, tuition. Oilthaigh, *a schoolhouse.*
†oil, -e, -ean, *s.f.* Stone. 2 Rock. 3 Reproach, infamy. 4 Offence. 5 Stumbling-block. 6** Frightful precipice.
oil-athair,** -athar, -athraichean, *s.m.* Foster-father.
oilbheum, -eim, -an, *s. m.* Offence, stumbling-block, reproach, scandal. 2 Disobligation. 3 Stumble. 4††Blasphemy. Carraig oilbheim, *a rock of offence.*
-————ach, -aiche, *a.* Reproachful, offensive. 2 Causing reproach or offence. 3 Shameful, disgraceful, scandalous.
-————achd, *s.f.ind.* Reproachfulness. 2 Scandalizing, scandalousness. 3††Blasphemy.
oilbheumaich,‡‡ *v.a.* Offend. 2 Blame.
oilbheumaiche, *comp.* of oilbheumach.
oilbhiast, see uile-bheisd.
†oilbhreo, *s.m.* Funeral fire.
†oilcheas, -chis, *s.m.* Doubt, hesitation.
†————ach, *a.* Doubtful, hesitating. 2 Scrupulous.
†oile, see eile.
oileabhan,(AF) *s.m.* Elephant.
oileadair,* -ean, *s.m.* Professor.
oileag,(DMy) -an, *s.f.* Flat stone, larger than a pebble, for throwing at horses, cattle, &c.
oileamhach, *s.f.* University.
oileamhaid,* *s.f.* University.
oileamhain, -e, *s.f.* see oilean.
oileamhnach, -aich, -ean, see oileanach.
oileamhnaich, *v.* see oileanaich.
oilean, -ein, -nan, *s.m.* see eilean.
oilean, -ein, -an, *s.m.* Education, instruction. 2 Household instruction, breeding. 3 Nurture, food. 4** Aisle of a church. 5** Honeysuckle. Droch oilean, *bad breeding*; gu bràth cha dealaich o. riut, *breeding shall never*

forsake thee.

oileanach, -aiche, *a.* Educating, training, instructing. 2 Nourishing. 3 Well-bred. 4 Educated, trained, polite, civil. 5 see eileanach.

oileanach, -aich, *pl.* -aich & -aichean, *s.m.* Student, pupil, scholar, academician.

————adh, -aidh, *s.m.* Instructing, act of instructing or teaching. Ag o—, *pr.pt.* of oileanaich.

————d,** *s.f.* Doctrine, teaching. 2†† Curing. 3††Drilling.

oileanaich,* *s.m.* Scholar, student, pupil.

oileanaich, *v.a.* Instruct, teach. 2 Rear. 3†† Cure, remedy. 4††Drill.

————te, *past pt.* of oileanaich. Reared, brought up, nourished. 2 Instructed, taught. 3 Well-bred, polite.

oileanda, -ainde, see oileanaichte.

oileanta, -ainte, see oileanaichte.

oileantachd, (MS) *s.f.* Scholarship.

oilear, -eir, -ean, for eilthire.

——ach, -aich, see eilthireach. 2 Nursery.

——adh, -aidh, *s.m.* see eilthireachd.

oileas,** -ais, *s.m.* Custom, use, habit, usage.

†-——ach, *a.* Frequent, usual, customary.

oileid,* *s.f.* College.

oilich,** *v.a.* Frighten.

oilire,* *s.m.* Professor.

oillbhastair,** *s.m.* Alabaster.

oillbheint,** *s.* Elephant.

oilleabhaint,** *s.* Elephant.

oillmheidh,** -ean, *s.f.* Balance, weight.

oillt, -e, -ean, *s.f.* Terror, dread, horror, detestation, disgust. Dlùth-chrith air gach cnàimh le h-o., *every bone shaking with horror.*

oillt-chrith, -e, *s.f.* Trembling from fear or terror. 2 Horror.

————each, -eiche, *a.* Trembling from fear. 2 Causing to tremble from fear.

oillteachadh, -aidh, *s.m.* Trembling, act of trembling. 2 Dreading, detestation, horror. Ag o—, *pr.pt.* of oilltich. Tha mi air m' o. ris, *I am shocked at him.*

oilltealachd, *s.f.ind.* Terribleness, horribleness, dreadfulness. 2 Ugliness. 3**Detestableness.

oillteil, -e, *a.* Terrific, dreadful, terrible, horrible. 2 Ugly, disgusting in the highest degree. 3**Fearful.

oillthaigh, see oil-thaigh.

oilltheud,** -théid, -an, *s.m.* see oil-theud.

oilltich, *v.a. & n.* Frighten, terrify. 2 Be afraid, be horrified. 3 Tremble from fear. 4 Regard with horror, shudder with horror, detest. Dh' o. mi ris, *I detest him, I am horrified at him.*

-——te, *past pt.* Afraid.

oilltioil, -e, *a.* see oillteil.

oilphaint,** *s.* Behemoth.

oil! oil! *int.* Form of address to an infant. 2 Expression of derision at finery.

oil-thaigh, -ean, *s.m.* School, seminary, college, academy.

————each, see oil-thaigheil.

————eil,** *a.* Academical.

oiltheireachd, see eilthireachd.

†oil-theud,** -théid, *s.m.* Cable, rope.

oil-thire, *s.f.* see eilthir.

———ach, -eiche, *a.* see eilthireach, *a.*

oil-thireach, -ich, *s.* see eilthireach, *s.*

————d, see eilthireachd.

oil-threubhach,** *a.* Valiant, truly brave.

————d, *s.f.* Transcendant valour.

†oin, -e, -ean, *s.f.* Loan. 2 The thing lent.

oin,* *s.f.* Death-agony.

oineach, -ich, *s. m.* Liberality, generosity. 2 Clemency. 3‡‡Truce. 4**Merciful person. 5 **Liberal person.

oineach, -eiche, *a.* Merciful, compassionate. 2 Liberal, bountiful.

———d,** *s.f.* Mercy, mercifulness. 2 Liberality

oingeal, -eil, -an, *s.f.* see aingeal.

òinich,(JM) *W. Isles* for àinich. Panting, especially when struggling hard with an enemy, or to get out of a difficulty.

òinid, -e, -ean, *s.f.* Fool, idiot. 2 Foolish woman, silly person, stupid person.

-——each, -eiche, *a.* Foolish, idiotical, of, or pertaining to an idiot. 2 Absurd.

-——eachd, *s.f.* Foolishness, folly, simpleness.

oinidh,** -e, *a.* Generous, liberal, magnanimous.

oinigh,** *s.f.* Prostitute. Air gràdh na h-o. na tog trod, *do not raise a quarrel for a harlot's sake.*

———each,** *a.* Whorish, like a harlot.

———eachd,** *s.f.ind.* Whorishness, prostitution.

oinmhid, -e, -ean, *s.f.* òinid.

oinmhidh,** see òinid.

oinmhideach, *a.* see òinideach.

————d, see òinideachd.

oinnean, -in, -an, *s.m.* see uinnean. 2**Pebble.

———ach, see uinneanach.

òinseach, -ich, -ichean, *s.f.* Foolish woman. 2 Harlot. 3**Idiot. 4 Bagpipe. Cha leannan òinsich e, *he is not a fool's choice.*

òinseachail, -e, *a.* Foolish, idiotical. 2 Like a foolish woman. 3**Whorish. Gu h-o., *foolishly.*

òinseachas, see òinsealachd.

òinseachd,** *s.f.* Whoredom.

òinsealachd, *s.f.ind.* Foolishness, stupidity.

oinseann, for craobh-uinnsinn.

oir, *conj.* For, because that. Oir chuimhnich iad, *for they remembered*; oir is fhèarr leam, *because that I prefer.* Oir a b' annas an leithid 'san fhonn, *for their like were scarce in the land—Rob Donn.*

†oir, *prep.* see air.

oir, *v.* Befit, become.

†oir, *a.* Fit, becoming, proper.

oir, -e, -ean, *s. m.* Border, edge, margin, hem, selvidge, boundary, limit, coast. Oir an aodaich, *the hem of the cloth*; oir an t-sruthain, *the margin of the brook*; gun o., *without a border*; air leth oir, *sideways.*

†oir, -e, -ean, *s.f.* Furze, whins, gorse. 2 Old Gaelic name for the letter O.

oir, *s.m.ind*, see ear.

òir, *gen.sing.* of òr.

557. Oir.

oir,§ *s.f.* The spindle-tree—*euonymus europæus.*

oirbh, *prep. pron.* On you. 2 Owed by you. 3 The matter with you. 4 You under the necessity. Bheir mi o., *I will force you*; beiridh mi oirbh, *I will catch you*; cuiribh o. e, *put it on you*; tha e o. a dheanamh, *you are obliged to do it*; ciod a tha 'cuir oirbh? *what ails you?*

am bheil dad aig' oirbh? *has he any claim on you? do you owe him anything?* na gabhaibh oirbh e, *take it not on you, take no heed of him (or it.)* [emphatic, oirbh-se.] see air.
oirbheart, -eirt, -an. *s m.* **Good deed or action, exploit.** Bu o dhuit a dheanamh, *it were an act of charity in you to do it;* cha'n o. sam bith dhuit a leithid a dheanamh, *it would be no act of charity in you to do the like.*
———ach, -aiche, *a.* **Performing good deeds or actions. 2 Charitable. 3 Great, noble. 4 Gracious.**
oirbheirteach, see oirbheartach.
oirbhidinn,** *s.f.* **Honour, respect, veneration.**
oirbheas.* see oirbheart.
oirbhidneach,** *a.* **Honoured, respected, venerated.**
oirbhir,** *s f* **Reproach. 2 Curse. 3 Armful.**
oirbh-se, *emphatic* of oirbh.
†oirc,‡‡ *s.* **Lapdog. 2 Lapwing, see adharcan-luachrach.**
oirceadal, -ail. *s.m.* **Instruction. 2 Doctrine.**
oircean,(CR) *s.m.* **Horizon, heavens, only used in "tha stoirm air an oircean," said when a storm or squall is seen approaching**—*Arran.*
oircean, -ein, -an, see uircean.
oirceart,** -eirt, *s.m.* **Hurt, bruise, wound.**
oirceas, -eis, *s.m.* **Mess.**
òir-cheard, -eird, -an, see òr-cheard.
oircheas, -eis, -an, *s.m.* **Pity, mercy, clemency. 2 Kindness. 3 Act of charity. 4 Fitness, propriety.**
———ach, -aiche, *a.* **Pitying, merciful. 2 Charitable, benevolent. 3 Kind, generous. 4 Needy, in want. 5 Fit, proper.**
———achd, *s.f.ind.* **Charitableness. 2 Need, necessity, poverty, want. 3 Fitness, propriety. 4 see oircheas. 5**** *rarely* **Mess.**
———aich,(MS) *v.a.* **Aid.**
òir-chiabh, -a, -an, *s.m.* **Yellow or golden lock or ringlet.**
———ach, -aiche, *a.* **Having yellow or golden locks or ringlets.**
†oirchill, -e, -ean, *s.f.* **Provision reserved for the absent. 2 Reward. 3 Concealment, ambush.**
†oirchill, *v.a.* **Carry, bear.**
oirchilleach,** *v.* **Bearing, carrying.**
oirchind,** *s.f.* **Providence.**
oirchios,** -chise, *a.* **Proper, meet.**
oirchios, -a & -ise, see oircheas.
———ach, -aiche, *a.* see oircheasach.
———achd, see oircheasachd.
†òir-chisd, for òr-chist.
†———ear, -eir, -an, *s.m.* **Treasurer.**
òir-chisdearachd, *s.f.* **Bursary.**
òir-chisdear-àrdsgoil, *s.m.* **Bursar.**
oir-chneas, -eis, -an, *s.m.* **The foreskin.**
oir-chriadh,** *s.* **China.**
òir-chrios, -a, -an, *s.m.* **Studded belt. 2 Ornament, such as a necklace. 3**Gold necklace.**
oircne, see oirc.
òirde, *pl.* -an [& **òirdnean,] *s.f.* **Piece or lump of anything. 2**Splinter. 3** Order. 4** Improvement.** O. fhiodha, *a log of wood.*
òirdhearc, *v.n.* **Flourish. 2 Be famous.**
òirdheirc, -e, *a.* **Famous, illustrious, noble, excellent, honourable, superb, worthy, glorious.**
òirdheirceas, -eis, *s. m.* **Excellency, nobleness, honourableness, worthiness. 2 Splendour, brightness, superbness, lustre. 3††Renown. 4* Pre-eminence.** Ò. cumhachd, *the excellence of power;* ò. an eòlais, *the excellence of knowledge.*
oirdneadh,** -idh, *s.m.* **Ordination.**
oirdnean, *s.pl.* **Splinters.**
oireach,‡‡ -eiche, *a.* **Marginal.**
———as, -ais, *s.m.* **Pre-eminence, superiority.**

†oireachdan, *s.pl.* **Statutes, ordinances.**
oireachdas, -ais, see eireachdas. **2**Assembly.**
†oiread, -eid, see uiread.
oireadh, -idh, *s.m.* **Befitting, becoming.**
oireag,§ see oighreag.
†oireagail, *s,f.* **Habitation. 2 Waste house, deserted house.**
oireamhan,** -an, *s. m.* **Concord, agreement, union.**
oireamhnach,** -aiche, *a.* **Genuine. 2 Meet, proper, expedient. 3 Accommodated.**
———d, *s.f.* **Genuineness.**
oireamhuin,** *s.* **Pertinence. 2 Influence. 3 Fitness.**
———each,** *a.* **Pertinent.**
oirean, *s.m.* **Selvidge, (borders.)**
oirear,** *a.* **Pleasant, agreeable. 2 Comely, becoming.**
oireil,** *a.* **Meet, proper, becoming, seemly, comely, handsome.**
oirfeid, -ean, *s.m.* **Music, melody.** Na uile o. na Crìosdachd, *than the whole melody of Christendom;* o. eagarach, *well-arranged music.*
———each, -eich, *s.m.* **Musician.**
———each, -eiche, *a.* **Musical, melodious, harmonious. 2 Unanimous.**
———eachd, *s.f.ind.* **Harmony, melody, music, musicalness.**
oir-fheadhnach,** *a.* **Having excellent leaders, as an army.**
oirfideachd,‡‡ see oirfeideachd.
oirgheadh,** -eidh, *s.m.* **Destroying.**
oirghean,** -ein, *s.m.* **Destruction.**
oirghios,** *s.* **Cheer. 2 Mess.**
oir-ghreus, -ghréis, *s.m.* **Embroidery, tapestry, needlework, tambouring, ornament.**
oir-ghreusach,** *a.* **Embroidered.**
oir-ghreusaiche,** *s.m.* **Embroiderer.**
oiridh,** see àiridh.
òiridh,** *s.pl.* **Devices wrought in gold.**
†oirior, *s. m.* **Day-after-to-morrow. (see earar, ear-thrath.)**
oiris, *s.f.* **Chronicle. 2 Delay, hinderance.**
†òirle, -an, *s.f.* **Piece, fragment.**
òirleach, -ich, *s.f.* **Inch. 2**Slaughter, massacre.** Is treasa aon ò. de'n ghille na dà ò. de 'n nighinn, *one inch of the boy is stronger than two inches of the girl* (*i.e.* when growing.)
òirleachail,‡‡ -e, *a.* **Inched.**
oirligh,(AF) *s.* **Eagle, see iolair.**
oirlioch,** *s.* **Havoc.**
oir-lìon,** *v.a.* **Increase.**
òirlis, *Kintyre* for òrrais.
òir-mhiann,** *s.m.* **Avarice, covetousness.**
———ach,** *a.* **Avaricious, covetous.**
oirmhid** *s.f.* **Decency. 2 Credit, respect.**
†oirn, *v.a.* **Appoint, constitute, set, ordain, put in authority.**
†oirneadh, -idh, *s.m.* **Appointing, constituting, ordaining, ordination.** Ag o—, *pr. pt.* of oirn.
oirnealta,** *a.* **Elegant, neat, ornamental, beautiful. 2 Having an imposing exterior.**
———chd,** *s.f.* **Elegance, neatness, handsomeness, ornament.**
òirneimh,** *v.a.* **Shine with gold.**
oirneis, see airneis.
oirnn, *prep.pron.* **On us, upon us. 2 Owed by us. 3 Matter with us.** Bheir e o. a dheanamh, *he will make us do it,* tha e o. a dheanamh, *we must do it, it is our duty to do it;* togamaid o., *let us bestir ourselves, let us be moving;* na gabhamaid o. e, *let us not heed him, let us take no notice of him;* thairis o., *over us;* a Thighearna seall oirnn, *Lord look upon us.*
oirnne, *emphatic form* of oirnn.

oirp, see oidheirp.
oirp,§ *s.* House-leek, see **lus-nan-cluas.**
oirpe, -an, see oidheirp.
oirre, *prep.pron.* On her, upon her. 2 Owed by her. 3 Matter with her. 4 Over her. 'Dé a th' oirre ? *what is the matter with her ?* tha e o. a dheanamh, *she is bound* or *obliged to do it* ; 'dé tha 'cur o. ? *what ails her ?* 'de a th' agad oirre ? *how much does she owe you ?* cha 'n 'eil eagal oirre, *she is not afraid ;* moran uachdaran o., *many rulers over her ;* chaidh e o., *he had carnal connection with her ;* dh' éirich e o., *he belaboured her* ; togadh i o., *let her bestir herself, let her be off.*
oirsceart,** s. The East.
oirthir, -e, -ean, *s. f.* Coast, shore, beach. 2 Border, frontier. 3 see ear (east.) 4 The Eastern world. O. ghaineimh, *a sandy shore, a sandbank ;* bàthadh mór aig o., *wrecks are frequent near a shore.*
———each, -eiche, *a.* Of, or belonging to, a coast, border or frontier. 2 Maritime, bordering on shore. 3 Terminal. 4 Eastern, oriental.
oisbheas,** -an, *s.m.* Epicycle.
———ach,** *a.* Like an epicycle. 2 Of, or belonging to, an epicycle.
†oisbhreug,** -an, *s.* Hyperbole.
ois-cheum,** *s.m.* Eminence, superiority.
ois-chreideamh,** -imh, *s.f.* Superstition.
†ois-chreideimh, -e, *s.f.* Superstition.
òiseach, -ich, -ichean, *s.f.* see òinseach.
- ———ail, -e, *a.* see òinseachail.
òisealachd, see òinsealachd.
oiseann, see oisinn. [** gives *gen.* oisinn.]
òisg, -e, -ean, *s.f.* see othaisg. 2 see oisinn.
oisgealachd, see othaisgealachd.
òisgean, for othaisgean, *n.pl.* of othaisg.
oisneach, *s.* Rifle—*Sàr-Obair.* (isneach.)
òisgeil, see othaisgeil.
oisin,** *v.a.* Lie with the face upwards,
oisinn, oisne, oisnean, *s.f.* Corner, angle. 2 Nook. 3 Bevel. Na h-oisnean, *the temples ;* o. an taighe, *the corner of the house.*
———each, -eiche, *a.* Cornered, angled, angular. Roth o., *a bevel wheel ;* oibreach o., *bevel-gearing.*
———eachd, *s.f.* Angularity.
———eag, -eig, -an, *s. f. dim.* of oisinn. Little corner, angle, or nook. 2 Angular figure. Tri-o., *a triangle ;* ceithir-o., *a quadrangle.*
oisinneagach, -aiche, *a.* Having little corners or angles.
oisinnich, *v.a.* Bevel.
†oisionair,** *s.m.* Tabard, habit formerly worn over a gown.
oisir, -e, -ean, *s.f.* see eisir.
oislin,** *s.pl.* Charms.
ois-sgrìobhadh,** -aidh, *s.m.* Superscription.
oistein, *s.f.* see eisir.
†oistir, *s.m.* Door. see Clann-an-oistir.
oistric, -e, -ean, *s.f.* Gaelic spelling of *ostrich.*
oit ! oit ! *int.* Exclamation used to express a sudden sense of heat or burning. Oit mo chròig, *alas my hand !*
oiteag, -eig, -an, *s.f.* Breeze of wind, light squall or blast. 2‡‡Zephyr.
———ach, -aiche, *a.* Breezy, squally, windy. Gaoth o., *a wind that comes in gusts or squalls.*
oitir, -e, -ean, *s.f.* Bank or ridge in the sea. 2 Shoal, shallow. 3 Low promontory jutting into the sea, rock projecting into the sea. 4* Links. 5 Headland. O. ghaineimh, *a sandbank.*
oitreach, *a.* Innavigable.
òl, *pr.pt.* ag òl, *v.a. & n.* Drink, perform the act of drinking. 2 Sup. 3 Absorb. Dh'òladh tu 's cha phàigheadh tu, *you would drink and not pay ;* ag òl brochain, *supping porridge.*
òl, òil, *s.m.* Drinking, act of drinking. 2 Habit of drinking intoxicating liquors. 3 Drunkenness, inebriation. 2 Supping. 3 Absorbing. Ag ò—, *pr.pt.* of òl. Tha e trom air an òl, *he is a hard drinker* ; 's e ant-òl a chuir an dunaidh ort, *it is drink that played the mischief with you* ; an t-òl, *drinking diabetes.*
†ol, *v.def.* Quoth, said. Dh' ol Fionn, *F. said.*
ola, *s. f.-ind.* Oil. 2 Ointment. 3**Olive. [* says never *lamp-oil,* which is ùilleadh, but *ola* is always used in *Gairloch, Lewis, &c.* for lamp-oil, and ** gives ola chum soluis, *oil for light.*]
ola-bais, *s.f.* Extreme unction.
olabhar,** -air, *s.m.* Great army.
olach, *s.* Rank grass growing near steadings where manure abounds, see fòghlach.
olach, -aiche, *a.* Oily. 2 Greasy. 3 Balsamic.
òlach, -aiche, *a.* Hospitable. 2 see òlar.
òlach, -aich, *s.m.* Hospitable person, one liberal of his own. 2 Beautiful person. 3 Term familiarly used in addressing or speaking of a person of low rank. 4 Eunuch. 5 Fumbler—*Sàr-Obair.* 6* Odd fellow. 7* One castrated for committing adultery. 8 (DMy) Champion, hero, giant. Có dhiubh a th' annad, o. a tha 'g iarraidh gleachd no còmhraig, no ò. a tha 'g iarraidh maighstir ? *which are you, a lad that wants to wrestle or fight or a lad that wants a master* ; ò. tapaidh, *a kind and brave man, a commendable man ;* nach b' e an t-ò. e ! *what a hero he is !* mar a dh' iobras ólach, *as a hero gives way.*
òlachan,** -ain, *s.m.* Immoderate drinking. 2 Drinking-match. 3 Carousal.
òlachas, -ais, *s.m.* Hospitality, kindness, bounty.
òlachd, *s.f.* see òlachas. 2* Castration for adultery.
ola-chroinn-ola, *s.f.* Olive-oil.
oladh, -aidh, *s.f.* see ola. Corn olaidh, *a cruse of oil ;* measgte le h-oladh, *mixed with oil.*
oladh-céireach,** *s.f.* Cerate.
oladh-ungaidh, *s.f.* Anointing-oil.
ola-fhrois-lìn, *s.f.* Linseed-oil.
ola-ghuail, *s.f.* Paraffin.
olaidh, *gen.sing.* of oladh.
olainn, see olann.
———each,** *a.* see olla, *a.*
òlair, -ean, *s.m.* Imbiber.
ola-leighis, *s.f.* Balsam.
ola-mhilis, *s.f.* Sweet oil.
ola-nan-creag, *s. f.* "Rock-oil," an ointment made from a thin film obtained on rocks by the sea, and used as a relief for burns and scalds.
ola-nan-trosg, *s.f.* Cod-liver oil.
olann, -ainn, *s.f.* Wool.
olann-mharbhchainn, *s. f.* Wool from a dead [sheep.
òlar, *fut.pass.* of òl. Shall be drunk.
——, -aire, *a.* Given to drunkenness, drunken, sottish, bibulous. 2**Absorbent.
——achd, *s.f.ind.* Habitual drunkenness.
ola-ròin, *s.f.* Seal-oil.
olart,** -airt, -an, *s.m.* Hone.
——ach,** *a.* Pertaining to the office of a hone. 2 Like a hone.
†olartar,** -air, *s.m.* Bad smell.
olastair,** -ean, *s.* Carbine. 2 Holster.
———iche,** *s.m.* Carbineer.
olc, uilc, *s.m.* Mischief, evil, wickedness. 2 Apparition. 3‡‡ Hurt, loss, damage, harm. Chaidh e chun an uilc, *he went to the mischief;* seachain an t-olc agus seachnaidh an t-olc thu, *avoid evil and evil will avoid you ;* olc na

cùis gu deireadh, *put off the evil part to the last*; 's fheàrr an t-olc eòlach na 'n t-olc aineolach, *the known evil is better than the unknown evil*—one is better prepared to meet it; cha bhi olc an aona bhliadhna fada 'dol seachad, *one year's grievance will soon pass away*.

olc, *adv.* (gu h-olc) Ill, badly, wickedly. Is o. a fhuaradh tu, *you behaved very badly*; is olc an airidh e, *it is a pity*; is tric fhuair "olc-an-airidh" car, *often "'tis a pity" has been crossed*.

olc, *gen.sing.* uilc, *a.* Bad, evil, wicked. 2 Evil, untoward, unfortunate. 3 Bad, incomplete, not good of its kind. 4**Mischievous. Duine olc, *an evil man*; béisd olc, *a wicked beast, a wicked person*; leann olc, *bad ale*; olc air mhath le càch e, *whether the others like it or not*; gu h-olc, *sick, very badly*.

1st. comp. miosa, *2nd. comp.* misde, *3rd.comp.* miosad.

olcad, -aid, *s.f.* Degree of badness.

olcadan, (AF) *s.m.* Owl.

olcas, -ais, *s. m.* Naughtiness, wickedness. 2 Badness. 3 Sickness. 4**Mischief. Air o. 'sam bheil e, *let him be ever so bad*; chual thu 'olcas, *you have heard its mischief*.

olc-dheanadach, -aiche, *a.* Maleficent.

olchobhair,** *s.f.* Pleasure. 2 Avarice.

o leth mo chùil, *phrase*, Coming towards me from behind my back.

†oll, -a, *a.* Great, grand, high.

olla, *a.* Woollen, made of wool. Aodach olla, *woollen garments*.

olla, -idhean, see ollamh. 2 see olann.

olla, *a.* Woollen. [Though called and translated as an adj. by some, this word, which is for *olna* or *ollna*, like *uillne* from *uileann* (elbow,) is *gen.* of olann.]

ollabhar, -air, *s.m.* Great army, great host.

ollach, -aiche, *a.* Woolly, fleecy.

———ail,** *a.* Rabbinical. 2 Lettered, literary.

olladh, *a.* see olla.

olladh, -aidh, -aidhean, see ollamh.

———aich, *v.* see ollamhaich.

olladhaichte, see ollamhaichte.

ollag, -aig, -an, *s.f.* Offal, refuse. 2 see ullag.

ollaidh, *gen.sing.* of olladh.

Ollaig, *Badenoch* for Nollaig.

ollain, for olainn.

ollamh, -aimh, -an, *s.m.* Doctor, physician. 2 Apothecary. 3 Learned man. 4 Chief bard.
ollamh-diadhachd, *a doctor of divinity*.
ollamh Iùdhach, *a Rabbi*.
ollamh lagha, *a doctor of laws*.
ollamh leighis, *a doctor of medicine*.
ollamh arsaidheachd, *Antiquary*.

ollamh, -aimhe, *a.* see ullamh.

ollamhachd, *s.f.ind.* Doctorship.

ollamhaich,** *v.n.* Graduate. 2 Take the degree of doctor. 3 Teach.

ollamhaichte, *past pt.* Graduated.

ollamhain, *s.pl.* The learned.

————, -e, *s.f.* Instruction.

————, *gen.sing. & nom.pl.* of ollamhan.

ollamhan,** -ain, *s.m.* Doctor, medical man. 2 Learned man. 3 Bard of the first order. O. ri diadhachd, *a doctor of divinity (D.D.)*; o. ri lagha, *a doctor of laws (LL.D.)*; o. ri leighis, *a doctor of medicine (M.D.)*

————ta, -ainte, *a.* Learned.

————tas, -ais, *s.m.* Professorship. 2 Doctorship. 3 Superiority.

ollamhnachadh, -aidh, *s. m.* Instructing, act of instructing, instruction. Ag o—, *pr.pt.* of ollamhnaich.

ollamhnachd, *s.f.* Superiority. 2 Preparation.

ollamhnaich, *v.a.* Instruct, teach. 2 Solemnize.

————te, *past pt.* of ollamhnaich. Instructed, taught.

ollamhrachd, *s.f.ind.* Professorship. 2 Superiority.

ollanach, -aiche, *a.* Lanigerous.

ollanachadh, -aidh, *s.m.* Preparing, act of the preparing of the dead. 2 Burial. 3 see oileanachadh.

ollanachd, *s.f.ind.* Preparing of the dead for interment. 2 Burial, funeral. 3 oileanachd.

ollanaich, *v.a.* Prepare, make ready for burial. 2 Bury, entomb. 3 Solemnize. 4 see oileanaich. A Dhia, o. féin mi, *God, teach thou me thyself*.

————te, *past pt.* of ollanaich. Prepared, made ready. 2 Buried. 3 Solemnized. 4 se oileanaichte.

ollaodach,* -aich, *s.m.* Woollen cloth.

ollas,** -ais, *s.m.* Boast.

oll-drag, see oll-dreag.

oll-dreag, -eig, -an, *s.f.* Funeral pile. 2**Bonfire. 3**Ignis fatuus.

oll-ghaireach, -ich, *s.m.* Dane.

†oll-ghlòr, -òir & -òire, *s.m.* Bombast, fustian language.

†oll-mhaitheas, -eis, *s.m.* Great riches.

oll-thuath,** -thuaidh, *s. f.* Large axe. 2 Battle-axe.

òlmhor, -oire, *a.* see òlar.

————achd, *s.* see òlarachd.

†olom,** *a.* Crop-eared.

oludh,(AF) *s.* Sucking ewe.

†oluidh,** *s.f.* Cow.

oluinn, *gen.sing.* of olunn.

olunn, -uinn, see olann.

o m', for o and mo.

òmar, -air, *s.m.* Amber. 2 see amar.

——ach, *a.* Amber, made of amber.

——aich, *v.a.* Amber.

ombra, *s.m.* see òmar.

†omh, *a.* Lonesome, unfrequented, solitary.

omhail, -e, *s.f.* see umhail. 2 Act of saying "omh," to express a doubt or disagreement, or to indicate discomfort. 'Dé an o. a th' ort? *what are you grunting about?*

omhaill, *s.f.* Heed, attention. 2 Care. Gabh o., *pay attention*; ciod an o. a th' ann? *what matters it?* ciod an o. a th' agad? *what do you care?*

omhailleach,** *a.* Heedful, attentive. 2 Careful.

†omhan, -ain, *s.m.* Fear.

omhan, -ain, *s.m.* Froth of milk or whey, especially the thicker whey pressed out of curds. [* gives omhar.]

———ach, -aiche, *a.* Frothy, abounding in froth of milk or whey.

———achd,** *s.f.* Frothiness, foaminess.

†omhnach, *a.* Terrible. 2 Frothy.

†omhnear, -eir, *s.m.* Embryo.

†omna, *s.m.* Oak. 2 Lance. 3 Spear.

†omoid, *v.a.* Obey.

omoideach, *a.* Obedient.

omrann, -ainn, *s.f.* Share, division.

o 'n, *conj.* see o.

o 'n, (o+an) O 'n taigh, *from home, abroad*; is fhada o 'n là, *it is long sincet he day broke*; is fhada o 'n dà là sin, *it is long since we met before*; o 'n aithrichibh, *from their fathers*.

†on, oin, *s.m.* Advantage, profit. 2 Loan. 3 Thing lent. 4 Cause, reason. 5 Blemish, stain, blot, fault. 6 Reproach. 7 Sloth, laziness. 8 Anger, rage.

†on, -a, *a.* Excellent, noble, good. 2 Advantageous.

onadh, see onfhadh.

onagaid,‡ *s.f.* Confusion, row, disturbance.

onaid, see oinid.
onaideachd,(MS) see oinideachd.
onair, see onoir.
onairich, see onoraich.
———te, see onoraichte.
ònar, see aonar.
——aich, see onoraich.
——an, see aonaran.
on-chù,(AF) Wolf. 2 Otter.
oncs, *s.m.* Stenlock—*Arran.*
onda,** *a.* Simple, silly.
ondhreag, -eig, *s. f.* Meteor. O. uamharra, *a terrible meteor.*
onfha, see onfhadh.
onfhadh, -fhaidh, -fhaidhean, *s.m.* Blast, storm. 2 Raging of the sea. 3** Furious billow. 4 Rage, fury. 5††Noise of the waves. 6**Storm at sea. 7 (DU) Raging hunger.
———ach, -aiche, *a.* Stormy, tempestuous. Cuan o., *a stormy sea.*
ong, *v.a.* see ung.
†ong, *s.m.* Tribulation. 2 Chastisement. 3 Disease. 4 Restraint.
†ong, *s.m.* Sorrow. 2 Sigh, groan. 3 Healing. 4 Fire. 5 Hearth.
†ong, *a.* Clean. 2 Clear, bright.
ongadh, -aidh, see ungadh.
†ongalar, see ong, *s.*
onial,** *s.* Corner.
†onn, -a, -an, *s.m.* Stone. 2 Entire horse, stallion. 3 Furze, gorse. 4 Name of the letter O [** gives *oinn* as *gen.sing.* of 1 & 2]
onnchon, -oin, -an, *s.m.* Ensign, standard.
onnchu,(AF) *s.m.* Leopard.
onoid,(MS) *s.f.* Sot.
onoir, -e, -ean, *s.f.* Honour, magnanimity. 2 Respect, esteem, reverence. 3 Fame, renown. 4 High rank or place, dignity. 5 Honesty, integrity. Na bitheadh m' o.-sa air a h-aonadh, *let not mine honour be united ;* gun o., *without honour.*
onoirich, *v.* see onoraich.
———te, see onoraichte.
onorach, -aiche, *a.* Honourable, honest. 2 Distinguished, exalted, famed. 3**Honorary. Ball o., *an honorary member ;* duine o., *an honest man ;* gu h-o., *honourably.*
———adh, -aidh, *s.m.* Honouring, act of honouring or reverencing. Ag o—, *pr. pt.* of onoraich.
onoraich, *pr. pt.* ag onorachadh, *v.a.* Honour, reverence, respect, revere.
———te, *past pt.* of onoraich. Honoured, respected.
ònrac, *Arran* for aonrachd (solitude.)
ònrachd, see aonrachd.
———ach, see aonrach.
———an, see aonrachdan.
———anach, see aonrachdanach.
op,** *s.* Hop, see lus-an-leanna.
òpar,(CR) Gaelic spelling of *hopper* (of a mill.)
òpar, (MMcL) *s.m.* Mark of travel. Tha ò. air, *he is travel-stained.*
òr, -òir, *s.m.* Gold.
òr, *pr.pt.* ag òradh, *v.a.* Bedeck.
òr, *v.a.* Gild.
or, *s.f.* see orra.
or, ora, *pl.* ora, orthachan, orrachan & orthannan, (AC) *s.* Prayer, rhymed prayer, hymn, supplication, petition, incantation. Domhnall beag nan o., *little Donald of the supplications.* Or and ob are now used indiscriminately.
or bhàis, *death-spell.*
or bhalbh, *charm to silence an opponent.*
or ghlas ghuib, *spell to lock an enemy's mouth.*
or ghonaidh, *wounding incantation.*
or ghrùdlaireachd, *spell to spoil another's brewing.*
or na h-Aona, *the Friday spell.*
or sheamlachais, *charm to induce one cow to take to the calf of another.*
or stoirm, *spell to raise a storm to drown a foe.*
†or, *s.m.* see oir. 2 Mouth. 3 Voice. 4 Sound.
ora, see or & òrag.
ora, *a.* see òrach & òrail.
orabhar,** *a.* Bushy, as hair.
orach,†† *s.m.* Enchantment.
òrach, -aich, *a.* Abounding in gold, golden, auriferous.
———an, -ain, *pl.* -an & òraichean, *s. m.* Jewel, ornament.
———d,* *s.f.ind.* Fictitious ornament, fantasies, fantastic dress. 2* Hoarding gold. Tuilldh 's a chòir de òrachdan, *too many fantastic ornaments* or *assumed airs.*
oracuil. *s.f.* Gaelic spelling of *oracle.*
òradair,(MS) *s.m.* Gilder.
òradh, -aidh, *s.m.* Gilding, act of gilding. 2 Burnishing. 3 Reflection of the sun's rays. Ag ò—, *pr.pt.* of òr.
oradh, -aidh, *s.m.* Chanting incantations. 2 Spell.

558. Orafoirt. *559. Oragan.*

orafoirt,§ *s.* White horehound—*marrubium vulgare.*
òrag, -aig, -an, *s.f.* Sheaf of corn set up to dry. 2 Young of birds in the downy stage, especially the swan, shag and cormorant.
——an, -ain, -an, *s.m.* Marjoram, organy—*origanum marjorana & origanum vulgare.* [ill. 559 represents o. vulgare.]
oragan, -ain, -an, *s.m.* see orgain.
òraganach, -aiche, *a.* Abounding in, or like, marjoram or organy.
òraid, -e, -ean, *s.f.* Speech, harangue, oration, essay, prayer. Rinn e ò., *he made a speech.*
——each, -eiche, *a.* Of, or belonging to, speeches or harangues, oratorial.
——each, -eich, *s.m.* Speaker, orator, declaimer.
——ear, -ir, *s.m.* Orator, declaimer.
——ich, *v.n.* Declaim, harangue, speechify.
——iche, *s.m.* Haranguer, orator, declaimer.
òrail, -e, *a.* Gold, golden. 2 Gilt.
òrain, *gen.sing. & n.pl.* of òran.
òran, -ain, -an, *s.m.* Song. 2 Poem. Cha dean sinn ò. dheth, *we will not make a song of it.*
ò.-buachaill,** Eclogue.
ò.-luadhaidh,** *s.m.* Catch, waulking-song.
ò.-neamhaidh, *s.m.* Hallelujah.
——ach, -aiche, *a.* Of songs. 2 Fond of singing songs, tuneful.
——achadh, -aidh, *s.m.* Cantation.
——aich, *v.a.* Berhyme.
——aiche, -an, *s.m.* Singer, songster. 2 Ballad singer. 3 Blue-throated warbler, see ceileiriche. Deagh ò., *a good singer.*

orair, -ean, *s.m.* Porch.
òrais, -e, -ean, *s.f.* Tumultuous noise.
òraisd, -ean, *s.f.* Orange.
——each, *a.* Full of oranges. 2 Like an orange.
òraisg, *v.n.* Vomit—*Arran.*
oran-nan-car, *s.m.* Cantata.
orban,** -ain, *s.m.* Patrimony.
orbhaire,** *s.f.* Mercy, goodness.
òr-bhann, -ainn & -oinn, -an, *s.m.* Gold lace. 2 Hinge or band of gold.
————ach, -aiche, *a.* Having gold lace. 2 Having gold hinges or bands.
òr-bhàrr, *a.* Having yellow hair 2 Having a yellow top, tipped with gold. Falt o., *golden hair.*
òr-bheart, -eirt, -an, *s.f.* Noble deed, feat.
————ach, -aiche, *a.* Performing illustrious or noble deeds. 2 Magnanimous.
òr-bhonn, -bhuinn, *s.m.* Gold piece or coin.
òr-bhuadhach, -aiche, *a.* Noble, illustrious. 2 Victorious, triumphant.
òr-bhuidhe, *a.* Yellow, of a golden colour, auburn. Nighean ò., *a golden-haired girl.*
òr-bhuidheach,** -ich, *s. m.* Or *or* topaz in *heraldry.* 2 The pure yellow in arms of an earl or lord, or sol in that of a king or prince.
orc,* see uircean.
orc (an), see forc.
†orc, oirc, -an, *s.m.* Collop. 2 Calf of the leg. 3 Death. 4 Little hound. 5 Hen's egg. 6 Salmon. 7 Whale. 8 Pig. 9 Cramp, numbness. 10 Prince. 11 Hero. 12 Prince's son. 13** Beagle.
†orc, *v.a.* Kill, murder, destroy.
orca, } see orc.
oreab, }
orcadh,** -aidh, *s.m.* Killing, massacring. 2 Destroying, destruction.
†orcain, *s.f.* Murder, killing.
orcan, see uircean & orc.
——ach, see uirceanach.
òr-chainnt, *s.f.* Rhetoric.
orchan,** -ain, *s.m.* Incantation.
òr-chasach, *a.* Gold-hilted.
òr-cheannach, *a.* Gold-headed.
òr-cheàrd, -chèird, *s.m.* Goldsmith. 2 Jeweller.
òr-chiabh, -a, -an, *s.m.* Golden lock. 2 Golden-coloured hair.
————ach, -aiche, *a.* Yellow-haired.
òr-chleac, -a, -an, *s.f.* see òr-chùl.
or-choilear, -eir, *s.m.* Golden collar. 2 Golden necklace.
òr-chradh, -aidh, *s.m.* Grief, sorrow.
òr-chùl, -chùil, -an, *s.m.* Yellow or golden lock.
orc-iasg, *s.m.* Torpedo (fish.) 2**Cramp-fish.
òr-ghruag, -uaig, -an, see òr-chùl.
òrd, òird, òirdean,†† *s.m.* Log of wood, piece.
òrd, ùird, *s.m.* Mountain of a round form and steep. †2 Death, manslaughter.
†òrd,** *a.* Bold, valiant.
òrd, ùird, *pl.* òrdan & ùird, [ùird in *Gairloch, &c.*] *s.m.* Hammer. 2 Dog-head of a gun, the part of a gun-lock from which the flint strikes fire. 3 Piece, fragment, junk. 4 Stub. 5 Mallet, mall. 6(MS) Cut, cutting. 7*Sledge-hammer. Mar fhuaim ùird, *like the noise of a hammer ;* òrd éisg, *a cut* or *slice of fish.*
†òrd, -a, -an, *s.m.* Order, series.
òrda, see òrd.
òrdachadh, see òrduchadh.
òrdag, -aig, -an, *s.f.* Thumb. 2 Great toe. Air òrdaig an làimhe deise, *on the thumb of their right hand* ; air òrdaig an coise deise, *on the great toe of their right foot ;* an ò. an aghaidh na glaic, *the thumb against the palm, the thumb at strife with the palm ;* ò.-an-t-suic, see crann-nan-gad (p. 263) ; thug ò. a choise sanas do bhun a chluaise, *the toe of his foot gave a hint* or *whisper to (struck) the root of his ear,* a graphic picture of the violence of the throw —he was not only thrown on his back, but his feet flew up in the air, and his head so far rebounded that toe and ear met ; òrdag, sgolbag, fionna-fada, Mac-an-aba, cuibhteag (the names of the fingers or toes among children, beginning at the thumb or great toe.) Another rhyme of these names in *Arran* is "ò., calagag, fionna-fad, mac-an-ab is cuisteag," another, "ò., corrag, meur-meadhon, màthair an lùdain(*or* na lùdaig,)"&c. also, "seo an té a leagan sabhal, seo an té a ghoid an sìl (*not* sìol), seo an té a sheas ag amharc, seo an té a ruith;air falbh, seo an té bheag a b' fheudar dhith a phàigheadh air fad," the last being apparently only a Gaelic translation of the Scottish rhyme, *this is the man that broke the barn, this is the man that stole the the corn, this is the man that stood and saw, this is the man that ran awa', and wee peeriwinkie paid for a'.*
òrdagach, -aiche, *a.* Having large thumbs or great toes. 2 Digital.
òrdagh, -aigh, -aighean, see òrdugh.
òrdaich, see òrduich.
òrdail, -e, *a.* Orderly, decent, regular. 2 Ordinal.
òrdair,** *s.m.* Hammerer.
òrdan, -ain, -an, *s.m.,dim.* of òrd. Little hammer or mallet. 2 Small piece, fragment. 3 *Skye* for òrdugh.
òrdan,** -ain, *s.m.* Generosity. 2 Dignity. 3 Solemnity. 4 Degree, gradation. 5 Music.
òrd-bhàirnich, *s.m.* Limpet-chisel.
òrdha, *a.* Saturnian. 2 Golden. 3 Shining like gold, golden. 4 Excellent, precious—*Sàr-Obair.*
òr-dhearg, *s.m.* Redness of gold.
òrd-ladhrach, *s.m.* Claw-hammer.
òrd-laoch,** -laoich, *s.m.* Hero.
òr-dhuilleag, -eig, -an, *s.f.* Gold-leaf.
ordon,** see òrdugh.
òrduchadh, -aidh, *s. m.* Ordering, act of ordering, ordaining, decreeing, commanding. 2 Institution, decree, command. 3 Appointment, ordination. 4 Arranging, arrangement. A' *pr.pt.* of òrduich.
òrdugh, -uigh, -uighean, *s. m.* Order, decree, command. 2 Order, arrangement, array. 3 Ordinance, rite, observance commanded. 4 The Eucharist or Lord's Supper, celebration of that feast. [The *pl.* "na h-òrduighean," is very often used in the *West of Ross* to denote not only the dispensation of the Lord's Supper, but the accompanying services held on Thursday, Friday, Saturday and Monday.]
Ò. o 'n Taigh-chuspainn, *a decree from the Custom House ;* cuir an ò., *put in order ;* gun ò., *without instruction* or *direction;* an ò.-catha, *in battle-array;* ò.-blàir, *battle-array.*
——ail,** *a.* see òrdail.
òrduich, *v.a.* Order, ordain, appoint, decree, prescribe, assign, command. 2 Arrange, set in array. 3 Give instructions, issue orders. Dh' ò. Dia, *God ordained.*
————ear, *fut.pass.* of òrduich.
————te, *past pt.* of òrduich. Ordained, appointed, decreed, assigned. 2 Arranged, set in order. 3 Ordered, commanded, prescribed.
òrensin, *Moladh Mòrag, 100.* for "orange-an," *oranges,* in "Phoebus 'dath nan tonn air flamh òrensin."
orgaid,** *s.f.* Organ.
——iche,** *s.m.* Organist.
orgain,** *s.f.* Slaughter. 2 Organ.

organ, see oragan.
organaiche,(MS) *s.m.* Organist.
òr-ghruag, -aig, -an, see òr-chùl.
————ach, -aich, *s.f.* Yellow-haired maid.
————ach, *a.* Yellow-haired.
†orgun, *s.m.* Death.
orlachadh, -aidh, *s. m.* Bespewing.
òr-lasta, -laiste, *a.* Shining or burnished like gold.
————il, -e, *a.* see òr-lasta.
or-leathair,** *s.m.* Paternal uncle.
òr-loinneach, -eiche, *a.* Highly elegant, beautiful, becoming.
——————d, *s.f.* Extreme elegance.
orm, *prep.pron.* (air+mi) On me, upon me. 2 Owed by me. 3 Wrong with me. 4 In my possession. 'Dé a th' aig' orm ? *what do I owe him ?* 'dé a th' orm ? *what is wrong with me ?* a' cur orm, *dressing myself ;* tha e orm a dheanamh, *I am obliged to do it ;* théid aig' orm, *he will get the better of me* ; fuirich orm, socair orm, *softly, leisurely !*
òr-mhaduinn, -mhaidne, -ean, *s.f.* The break of day, morning.
òr-mheas, *s.m.* Orange.
òr-mhèinn, -e, -ean, *s. f.* Gold ore. 2 Gold mine.
——————each, -eiche, *a.* Abounding in, or having gold ore.
orm·sa, *emphatic* of orm.*
†orn, -a, *s.f.* [*m.***] Slaughter.
òrna, see eòrna.
ornaich, *v.a.* Adorn.
ornaid,** *s.f.* Ornament.
———each, *a.* Ornamental.
ornail,** *s.f.* Upper part of a door-case.
òrnaileis, *s.f.* Tissue.
ornais, *s.f.* Nauseousness, qualm.
orp,§ *s.m.* Orpine, house-leek—*sedum telephium.*
orr, *s.* see orra.
orra, *prep. pron.* (air+iad) On them, upon them. 2 Owed by them. 3 Wrong with them. 4** In their possession. Cuir o. e, *put it on them ;* cha'n 'eil ni agam orra, *they owe me nothing;* cha'n 'eil sgillinn o., *they have not one penny in their possession ;* bheir mise orra a dheanamh, *I will make them do it ;* ciod a th' orra ? *what is wrong with them ? 2 how much do they owe ? 3 how are they dressed ?*

560. *Orp.*

orra,* -chan, *s.f.* Amulet, enchantment, charm, incantation. O.-an-donais, *an amulet to send one to the mischief ;* orra-bhalbh, *one to prevent one's agent making a defence in court ;* o.-chomais, *one to deprive a man of his virility, especially on the marriage-night ;* o.-ghràidh, *one to provoke unlawful love ;* o.-sheamlachais, *one to make one cow allow another's calf to suck her;* chuir thu an o.-sheamlachais orm, *you have duped me*—hence imposture of any kind ; o. na h-aoine, *an amulet to drown a foe;* o. an donais, *one to send one's foe to the mischief.* see also or.
òrrachdan, -ain, -an, see aonrachdan.
orradh, -aidh, -aidhean, *s.m.* Shift. 2†† Exertion, endeavour. 3** Superstitious charm. Leagh an cridhe 'am chliabh le 'cuid orrachan, *my heart melted within me through her spells ;* tha mi air m' o. an dràsd, *I am bewitched at present.*
———, *prep. pron.* see orra.
orraidheachd,** *s.f.* Superstitious ceremonies, charms, enchantments.
orrais, -e, -ean, *s.f.* Squeamishness, nausea. 2 Water-brash. Chuireadh tu ò. air mathghamhuinn, *your conduct would make a bear squeamish ;* tha 'n ò. ri m' fhiacail fad an là, *water-brash annoying me the live-long day.* see òraisg.
———each, -eiche, *a.* Squeamish, qualmish. 2 Fastidious.
———eachd, see òrrais.
——— -thilgidh, see òrrais.
orrar, see orair.
orra-san, *emphatic* form of orra.
orrlain, see eòrlain.
†orrtha, *s.m.* Music, melody. 2 Melodious voice. 3 Bewitchery.
orrthannan,(MS) *pl.* of or. Enchantment.
òrruidh, -e, *a.* see òrbhuidhe.
òr-sgiathach, -aiche, *a.* Having golden wings. 2 Having golden shields. Dream ò., *a golden-shielded people.*
òr-sheud, -a, -an, *s.m.* Jewel of gold.
ort, *prep. pron.* (air+thu) On thee, upon thee. 2 Owed by thee. 3 Wrong with thee. 'Dé a th' aig' ort ? *how much do you owe him ?* ro mhath an airidh càch ort, *others well deserve you—R. 66 ;* cuir o. e, *put it on thee* ; nach cluinn mi o. ? *shall I not hear of thee ?* ciod tha 'cur ort ? *what ails thee ?* tha e ort a dheanamh, *you are bound to do it.*
†ort, *s.* Killing, death.
òrta,* *a.* see òrdha.
ortha, see or (prayer.)
òr-thaigh,* -ean, *s.m.* Treasury.
ort-sa, *emphatic* form of ort.
òr-ubhal,§ -ail, -bhlan, *s.m.* Orange—*citrus auranthium.*
oruin,§ *s.* Beech—*O'Reilly*, see craobh fhaidhbhile. 2 Ash—*Bible*, see uinnsean.
os, *prep.* Above, over. Os do cheann, *superior to thee (lit.* above thy head) ; os (as) do sheasamh, *on the spot* (*lit.* on thy standing)—*Dàin I. Ghobha.*
os, -a & ois, *pl.* -an, *s.m.* & *f.* Elk, deer, stag. Lean thus' an os bhallach, *follow thou the spotted stag.*
os, -a, -an, *s.m.* Mouth or outlet of a river, *prov.* 2 Bar or sandbank in a harbour.
os, *v.def.* see arsa.
osadh, -aidh, -aidhean, *s.m.* see fosadh.
osag, -aig, -an, *s.f.* Blast, breeze, gust, wind. O. a' bhàis, *the blast of death.*
——ach, -aiche, *a.* Breezy, squally, gusty.
——an, *n.pl.* of osag.
os-aird, *adv.* Openly, publicly. 2 Loudly.
os-alluidh,(AF) *s.m.* Elk, deer, stag.
osan, -ain, *pl.* -ain & -an, *s.m.* Hose, stocking, the leg of trousers. 2 (DMy) Headless stocking.
osanach, -aiche, *a.* Wearing hose, of hose. Gu brògach, o., *having shoes and stockings on.*
————d,** *s.f.* Hosiery.
osanaiche, -an, *s.m.* Hosier.
osann, -ainn, *s.m.* Deep sigh or sob. [In *Gairloch*, osna—DU.]
————aich,* *s.f.* Continuous sighing or sobbing. 2 Heavy blasts or gusts of wind.
osan preasach,** *s.m.* Very long plaited stocking, once worn by the women in Breadalbane when in full dress.
†osar, *a.* Younger.
osar,** -air, *s.m.* Burden, pack. 2 Preferment. exaltation.
——aiche,** *s.m.* Porter, carrier.
os bàrr, Besides, moreover, over and above.
oscach, -aiche, *a.* Eminent, superior, excellent.
oscar,** -air, *s.m.* Leap, bound. 2 Guest, traveller. 3 Ruinous fall. 4 Champion. 5 Mo-

tion of the bands in swimming.
oscarach, -aiche, *a.* Bold, intrepid, energetic. 2 Renowned, famous. 3 Loud. 4*Fierce. 5 Masculine, as a female. 6* Indelicate. 7** Emphatical.
oscarachd, *s.f.ind.* Boldness, intrepidity. 2 Loudness. 3 Emphasis. 4 Fierceness. 5* Masculineness, as in a female. 6*Indelicacy. 7**Energy.
oscaradh, -aidh, see oscarach.
oscardha, oscartha, } see oscarach.
———chd, see oscarachd.
oscarra, see oscarach.
oscarra-lann,** -lainn, *s.m.* Hospital.
os ceann, *adv.* Over, above.
os-cheumachadh,** -aidh, *s.m.* Superiority, pre-eminence, excelling.
os-cheumnaich, *v.a.* Excel, exceed.
os-chràbhach,** *a.* Superstitious. 2 Hypocritical.
os-chràbhadh,** -aidh, *s.m.* Superstition. 2 Hypocrisy.
os cionn, see os ceann.
†os-cràbhadh, -aidh, *s.m.* Superstition.
òsd, see òsda.
òsda, -n, (taigh-òsda) *s. m.* Inn, ale-house. 2 (DU)Right to sell excisable liquors. A' bhean-òsda, *the "lady" of the inn.*
òsda,†† *a.* Pertaining to an inn.
òsdair, -ean, *s.m.* Innkeeper, host. also fear-òsd.
———eachd, *s.f.ind.* Office or occupation of an innkeeper.
òsdadh, see òsda.
òsdag, -aig, -an, *s.f.* Hostess, female innkeeper.
òsd-fhear, see òsdair.
òsd-thaigh, see taigh-òsda.
†osgail, see fosgail.
†———te, see fosgailte.
osgalan, see fosgalan.
òsgan, -ain, *s.m.* see othaisgean.
osgarach,** *a.* Frail. 2 Brittle.
osgarra,** *a.* Audible, distinct. 2 Emphatic. 3 see oscarach.
———chd,** *s.f.* Audibleness. 2 Augustness. 3 Emphasis.
osgriobhan,** *s.m.* see os-sgrìobhadh.
os ìosal, Softly, privately, quietly, underhand, secretly, covertly.
oslabhairt, *s.f.ind.* Hyperbole.
osmag, -aig, *s.f.* Sigh, sob, see ospag.
———ach,** *a.* Sighing, sobbing. 2 Panting. see ospagach.
———ail,** *s. f.* Sigh, sighing. 2 Anhelation, panting. see ospagail.
osna, -ai, *s.f.* Sigh, sob, groan. 2 Breeze, blast.
osnach, -aiche, *a.* Sighing, groaning. 2 Blustering, as wind. 3 Blubbering, as a person. 4 Troubled.
†———, -aich, *s.f.* Carrion. 2 (MS) Blore, violent gust of wind.
———ail, -e, *a.* Sighing, groaning. 2 Troubled, sad.
osnadh, -aidh, -aidhean, *s.m.* Sigh, sob. 2 Blast, breeze. 3**Hair of the head. 4**Groan.
osnaich, -e, -ean, *s.f.* Sighing, act of sighing or groaning, continued sobbing or blubbering. 2 *pl.* Sighs, groans. 3 *pl.* Blasts of wind.
osnaich, *pr. pt.* ag osnachadh, *v.a.* Sigh, moan.
osnaichean, *n.pl.* of osnaich.
osnaigh, for osnaidh, *n.pl.* of osnadh.
os n-ìosal, see os ìosal.
osp,* *v.* see ospag.
ospag, -aig, -an, *s.f.* Sigh, sob, gasp. quick deep sob. 2 Pang, throe. Ospagan a' bhàis, *the pangs of death*; an o. dheireannach, *the last gasp.*
———, *v.a.* Gasp, sob quickly.
———ach, -aiche, *a.* Sighing, sobbing. 2 Hysterical, prone to sob.
———aich, -e, *s.f.* see ospagail.
———ail, -e, *s.f.* Sighing, act of sighing or sobbing. 2 Apt to sigh or sob.
ospairn, see ospag. 2**Struggle.
———ich, see ospagail & osnaich.
†os-sgrìobhadh, -aidh, -aidhean, *s.m.* Epigram. 2 Superscription.
†osrau, -ain, *s.m.* Peace.
òsta, see òsda.
òstag, see òsdag.
òstair, see òsdair.
ostal, -ail, see abstol.
osunn, -uinn, -an, *s.f.* see osnadh, osann & osag.
otar,** -air, *s.m.* Labour.
oth,* *s.m.* Water, large body of water.
othag,‡‡ -aig -an, *s.f.* Afflatus.
othail, -e, -ean, *s.f.* Hurry. 2 Confusion, hubbub, tumult. 3 Delight.
othainn,* *s.f.* River, see abhainn. [* says *o.* is used to denote the largest kind of rivers, and *abhainn* a secondary river.]
othaisg, -e, -ean, *s. f.* Sheep, one-year-old ewe, dry ewe, ewe teg. 2** *in derision,* Bashful person, simpleton. 3* Soft, lubberly person.
———each,** *a.* Like a sheep or hog, abounding in hogs. 2 Bashful, sheepish.
———ealachd,** *s. f.* Sheepishness, foolishness.
———eil,** *a.* Sheepish, silly.
othan, -ain, *s.m.* see omhan.
———ach, -aiche, *a.* see omhanach.
othar, -air, -an, *s.m.* Abscess, ulcer, intumescence. 2 Ailment.
†othar, -air, -an, *s.m.* Wages, reward. 2 Labour.
†———, -aire, *a.* Sick. 2 Wounded, mutilated. 3 Maimed. 4 Weak.
———ach, -aiche, *a.* Ulcerous. 2 Wounded.
othasg, see othaisg.
othraich, (MS) *v.a.* Exulcerate.
†othras, -ais, -an, *s.m.* Disease, disorder, ailment. 2 Ulcer. 3 Wound.
†othrasach, -aiche, *a.* Sick, diseased. 2 Wounded. 3 see otharach.
———,** -aich, *s.m.* Hospital, infirmary.
òtrach, -aich, -aichean, *s.m.* Dunghill. 2 Dirt, filth, dung. 3 Drabbish, very fat female—*Islay.* 4 Term of contempt. [òtrach in *Gairloch, &c.*]
———ail, -e, *a.* Filthy, dirty, fœtid. 2 Drabbish. 3††Full of dunghills.
òtraich, *gen.sing.* of òtrach.
———ibh, *dat. pl.* of òtrach.

P p

P, the 14th. letter of the Gaelic alphabet now in use, called beith bhog (i.e. soft *b.*) It sounds like *p* in English, and when aspirated, that is, when immediately followed by *h*, it sounds like *f* in *fool*, or *ph* in *pharmacy.*
pà, *s.m.ind. & int.* Papa.
pab, -aib, -an, *s.m.* Shag, rough woolly hair. 2 Refuse of flax, oakum. 2 see babag.
pab, *v.a.* Become shaggy. 2 Become matted or twisted together. 3††Buffet.
pabach, -aiche, *a.* Shaggy. 2 Full of the refuse of flax. 3 Nasty. 4 see babagach.
pabadh, -aidh, -aidhean, *s.m.* Shagginess, state of becoming shaggy. 2 Becoming matted,

tangled or twisted together. 3 Overgrowth, luxuriance, as of grass. 4†† Buffetting. A' p—, *pr.pt.* of pab.
pabag,* see babag.
———ach,* -aiche, *a.* see babagach.
pàbar,* -air, *s.m.* Crew.
pab-cheann, -chinn, *s.m.* Shaggy head.
————ach,‡‡ *a.* Shaggy-headed.
pàbhail,* *s.f.* see pail-chlach.
pac, *pr.pt.* a' pacadh, *v.a.* Pack up. 3 Get out of the house.
pac,(CR) *s.m.* The sheep that a shepherd is allowed to keep as a part of his remuneration —*W. of Ross-shire.*
paca, -nnan, *s. m.* Pack, wallet, knapsack. 2 Budget. 3 Mob. A phaca ! *ye vile crew !* dh' ìobair e am paca, *he sacrificed the pack.*
p.-chairtean, *a pack of playing-cards.*
p.-clòimhe, *a pack of wool.*
p.-chon, *a pack of hounds.*
p.-mhèirleach, *a gang of thieves.*
p.-mosach, *a vile crew.*
pacach, -aiche, *a.* Having packs.
———adh, -aidh, *s.m. & pr. pt.* of pacaich. see pacadh.
——— cèarr,(AF) *s.* Turbot, halibut, flounder.
pacadh, -aidh, *s. m.* Packing, act of packing. A' p—, *pr.pt.* of pac.
pacaich, *v.a.* see pac. *v.*
pacaid, -e, -ean, *s. f.* Packet. 2 Packet-boat. 3* Female tell-tale or tattler. P. litrichean, *a packet of letters.*
———each, -eiche, *a.* Of, or connected with, packets.
pacaig, *v.a.* see pac, *v.*
pacaigeadh, see pacadh.
pacainn,** *pr. pt.* a' pacainn, *v.a.* Pack up. 2 Load. 3 Heap up.
———, *s.f.* Packing. 2 Loading. 3 Heaping up. A' p—, *pr.pt.* of pacainn.
pacair, -ean, *s. m.* Packer, one that packs. 2 Pedlar, packman. 3 Churl.
———eachd, *s.f.ind.* Pedling, business of a pedlar, hawking.
pacharan-chapuill, *s.m.* Marsh trefoil, see pònair-chapuill.
pacarras, -ais, *s.m.* Mass of confusion.
pachd, -a, -an & -annan, see pac.
———aich, see pacaich.
———air, see pacair.
paclach, -aich, -aichean, *s. m.* Armful, packed burden, the fill of both arms of hay, straw,&c.
pacraidhe,** *s.f.* Baggage, luggage.
padhach, -aiche, *a.* Thirsty.
padhadh, -aidh, *s.m.* Thirst. Tha p. orm, *I am thirsty* ; am bheil p. ort ? *are you thirsty ?*
padhal, -ail, *s.m.* Ewer. 2 Pail.
pàg, -àig, -an, *s.f.* see pòg—*Rob Donn.*
pàgach, -aiche, *a.* see pògach.
pàganach, -aiche, *a.* Heathen, pagan. 2** Gentile.
————, -aich, *s.m.* Heathen, pagan.
————d, *s. f. ind.* Heathenism, paganism. 2**Gentilism.
pàganta, *a.* Heathenish.
————chd, see pàganachd.
paghadh, see padhadh.
†paghuilleun, see pailliunn.
paibhil,** *s.* Flooring.
paid,* see paidir.
paideag,** -eig, *s. f.* Torch, made of tallow lapped upon linen.
paideal,(AF) *s.* Peacock.
paidearan, *s.m.* Clustering body, as of berries or nuts, garlands. " 'Na paidearan lìonmhor, cùirneanach, gu brìoghmhor, sùghmhor, sòlasach, *in numerous clusters, dewy, substantial, juicy, soothing.*
paideirean, see paidirean.
paidgheal, see paideal.
pàidh, *pr.pt.* a' pàidheadh, *v.a.* Pay. 2 Remunerate. 3 Suffer for, atone, make amends, require. Pàidhidh tu sin fhathast, *you shall suffer for that yet.*
pàidh, -ean, *s.m.* Same meanings as pàidheadh.
pàidheadh, -idh, *s.m.* Pay, payment. 2 Paying, act of paying wages. 3 Remuneration, requital.
pàidhear, -ir, -irean, *s.m.* Payer, sufferer.
paidhir,** *v.a.* Pair, couple.
paidhir, -dhreach, -dhrichean, *s.f.* Pair, couple, brace.
pàidh-mhaighstir,** *s.m.* Paymaster.
————-————eachd, *s.f.* Paymastership.
pàidhneachadh,** -aidh, *s.m.* Punishing,fining, punishment, fine. 2 Bail, bailing, security. 3 Insurance A' p—. *pr.pt.* of pàidhnich.
pàidhneachas, -ais, *s.m.* Penalty. 2 Bail, security, pledge. 3 Insurance. Ann am p. fichead punnd Sasunnach, *under the penalty of £20.*
pàidhnich, *pr. pt.* a' pàidhneachadh,*v.a.* Punish, fine. 2 Bail. 3 Insure.
pàidhnichte, *past pt.* of pàidhnich. Punished, fined. 2 Bailed. 3 Insured.
paidhreach, *gen. sing.* of paidhir.
————-adh, -aidh, *s.m.* Pairing, act of pairing or coupling. A' p—, *pr. pt.* of paidhrich.
paidhrich, *pr.pt.* a' paidhreachadh, *v.a.* Pair, couple, as birds, &c.
————ean, *pl.* of paidhir.
————te, *past pt.* Paired.
pàidhte, *past pt.* Paid. 2 Remunerated, requited.
paidir, -e, -drichean, *s.f.* The Lord's prayer. 2 Rosary, string of beads used by Roman Catholics. Tha tuilleadh 's a ph. aige, *he knows more than his beads.*
paidirean, -in, -inean, *s.m.* String of beads, rosary, necklace. 2 Bracelet. 3 Chaplet. 4 Garland of flowers. 5 Children's name for a string or " sop " of daisy-heads. 6 Cluster. 7 Dangling bunch. 8 (DC) Daisy. 9 (AH)Corn-marigold—*Argyll.*
paidireanach, -aiche, *a.* Wearing a rosary or necklace. 2 Dangling in clusters. 3 Full of beads.
paidreag, -eig, -an, *s.f.* Patch, clout.
paidrean, see paidirean.
paidrich,* *v.a.* String together.
paidrichean, *pl.* of paidir.
pàigh, see pàidh.
pàigheadh, see pàidheadh.
pàighte, see pàidhte.
pàighteach, see pàiteach.
pàighteachd, see pàiteachd.
pail, see pabhail.
pail-chlach, -chloiche, -chlachan, *s. f.* Stone-pavement, causeway. 2**Paving-stone.
†pailin, -ean, *s.m.* Shroud, winding-sheet.
paillios,* *s.f.* Gaelic spelling of *palace.*
pailleart, -irt, -eartan, *s.m.* Box on the ear. 2 Blow on the head. 3** Slap with the palm of the hand. 4* In *Irish*, a tune or air on the bagpipes.
pailleartach, -aiche, *a.* Apt to strike with the hand, striking with the hand, ready to strike with the hand.
pailleartaich,** *v.a.* Slap with the palm of the hand.
pàilliun, -iuin, -an *s.m.* Tent, tabernacle, pavilion. 2 Dwelling. 3 Booth, hut. 4**Palace. Dèanamaid trì pàilliunan, *let us make three tabernacles.*
pàilliunach, -aiche, *a.* Abounding in tents or

tabernacles.
pailm, -e, -ean, *s.f.* Palm-tree (craobh-phailm.)
pailm-chnuimh, *s.f.* Palmer-worm.
pailmeach, -eiche, *a.* Palmy.
pailm-sgath, -àith, -an, *s.m* Gourd.
pailt, -e, *a.* Plentiful, abundant, full. 2 Capacious. 4 Copious. 4 Numerous, abounding. Tùr p. le céill, *a mind abounding in knowledge;* beannaich sinn gu pailt, *bless us abundantly*, tha e pailt cho àrd rium-sa, *he is fully as tall as I am.*
pailteachd, see pailteas.
pailteas, -eis, *s.m.* Plenty, enough, abundance, amplitude. Tha 'm p. agam, *I have enough;* làn ph., *quite enough.*
pailteasach, -aiche, *a.* Plenteous.
paimhleid,** *s.f.* Gaelic spelling of *pamphlet.*
paimhleidiche, *s.m.* Pamphleteer.
†pain, *s.f.* Bread, cake.
paind,* see paindeag.
paindeag,* *s.f.* Pebble.
paindeal, -il, -an, *s.m.* Panther.
paindealach, -aich, *s.m.* Person laced up like a dandy. 2 Article of dress too tight.
pàineachadh, see pàidhneachadh.
pàineachas, -ais, *s.m.* see pàidhneachas.
paineal, see painneal.
pàinich,* *v.a.* see pàidhnich.
———te, see pàidhnichte.
painneal, -il, *s.m.* Panel, pieces of wood.
painnse, -achan, *s.f.* Paunch. 2*Tripe.
painnseachan,(MS) *s.m.* Tripe.
painnsean,(MS) *s.m.* Tripe.
painnidh,** *a.* Strong, furious.
painnteal,** -eil, *s.m.* Snare, trap, gin. 2(DMy) Snare for catching cats, &c., formed by a cord made fast at one end to some fixed object while the other end terminates in a running noose which is adjusted at the aperture through which the animal to be caught is expected to pass. * Panther.
painntear, -ir, *pl.* -an & -irean, *s.m.* Gin, snare. 2**Panther.
painntearach, -aiche, *a.* see painntireach.
painntearachd, see painntireachd.
painntin,** *s.f.* Patten.
painntir, see painntear.
painntireach, -eiche, *a.* Wily, ensnaring, full of snares.
painntireach, -ich, *s. m.* Ensnarer, insidious person, beguiler.
painntireachd, *s.f.* Ensnaring, entanglement.
painntireadh, -idh, see painntreadh.
painntirich, see painntrich.
painntirichte, see painntrichte.
painntreadh, -eidh, *s.m.* Ensnaring, act of ensnaring, inveigling. A' p—, *pr. pt.* of painntrich.
painntrich, *v.a.* Ensnare, inveigle, trap, beguile.
painntrichte, *past pt.* of painntrich. Ensnared, entangled, inveigled.
painte,** *s.f.* Lace. 2 String to lace clothes. [*Eng.* point.]
pàintidh,(DMK) *s.f.* The clay of which crockery is manufactured. 2 Fragments of broken pottery—*Caithness.*
paintir, *s.* see painntear.
paipean bàn,‡‡ *s.m.* White garden poppy—*papaver album sativum.*
paipean dubh,§ *s.m.* Black poppy—*papaver nigrum sativum.*
paipean ruadh,§ *s.m.* Common red poppy, see meilbheag.
pàipear, -eir, -ean, *s. m.* Paper, a paper. 2* Advertisement. [McL & D., ‡, ‡‡, and †† give paipeir.
p.-craicinn, *parchment.*
p.-donn, *brown paper.*
p.-glas, *brown paper, grey paper.*
p.-naidheachd, *a newspaper.*
p.-sgrìobhaidh, *writing-paper.*
p.-sùghaidh, *blotting-paper.*
pàipearach, -eiche, *a.* Paper, papered.
pàipearachadh, -aidh, *s.m.* Papering, act of covering with paper. A' p—, *pr.pt.* of pàipearaich.
pàipearachd,†† *s.f.* Papering.
paipearachd, *s.f.* Stationery.
paipearaiche, *s.m.* Stationer.§
pàipearaich, *pr. pt.* a' pàipearachadh, *v. a.* Paper, cover with paper.
paipin, -ean, *s.m.* Poppy, see meilbheag.
pàirc, *v.* see pàircich.
pàirc, -e, -ean, *s. f.* Park, enclosure, enclosed field.
pàirceach, -eiche, *a.* Abounding in parks. 2 Enclosed, as a park.
pàirceachadh, -aidh, *s.m.* Enclosing round, act of enclosing, making into a park. 2 Confining, act of confining in a park. 3** Forming into parks. A' p—, *pr.pt.* of pàircich.
pàircich, *pr.pt.* a' pàirceachadh, *v. a.* Enclose with a wall. 2 Park, form into parks. 3 Confine in a park.
pàircichte, *past pt.* of pàircich. Enclosed, formed into parks. 2 Confined in a park. 3 Walled round.
pairilis, *s.f.ind.* Palsy, paralysis.
pairinn, -ean,** *s.m.* Paring of moss-turf.
pairisleach, -eiche, *a.* Palsied.
pairseil,(MS) *s.f.* Parsley.
pàirt, -e, -ean, *s.f.* Part, share, portion. 2 Connection, interest. 3 Relation, kindred, relationship. 4**Confederacy. P. dheth, *some of it;* ghabh e a ph., *he took his part;* cha bhi cuid no p. agam dheth, *I will have no connection with it whatever.* Pàirt, with the possessive pronouns, corresponds in *Arran* to English mine, ours, &c., e.g. am bheil do làmhan-sa tioram ? tha mo phàirt-sa fliuch, *are your hands dry ? mine are wet.*
pàirt-dhathach, -aiche, *a.* Parti-coloured.
pàirteach, -eiche, *a.* Sharing, having a share. 2 Communicating. 3 Generous, liberal. 4 Divided into parts or shares. 5 Ready to share. 6‡‡Related.
pàirteach, *s.* see pàirtiche.
pàirteachadh, -aidh, *s.m.* Partnership. 2 Sharing, act of sharing, dividing, act of dividing. 3 Communication, act of communicating. A' p—, *pr.pt.* of pàirtich.
pàirteachail, -e, *a.* Divisible. 2 Sharing, ready to share, communicating, portionable.
pàirteachas, -ais, *s.m.* Participation, partnership.
pàirteachd, *s.f.ind.* Bountifulness.
pairteag, Gaelic spelling of *partridge.*
pàirtean, *pl.* of pàirt. 2 *vulgarly,* Abilities, powers.
pàirtear,** -eir, -an, *s.m.* Sharer, partner, one who possesses or receives a part. 2 Participle in *grammar.*
pàirteil, -e, *a.* Favouring, kind. 3** Partial. 3††Participating. Iriosal p., *humble and kind.*
pàirt-fhear, -fhir, *s.m.* see pàirtear.
pàirtich, *v.a.* Share, divide. 2 Communicate, impart, bestow. 2 Partake.
pàirtiche, -an, *s. m.* Partner. 2 Abettor. 3 Distributer, sharer. 4 Accomplice. 5 Partaker. 6 Associate.
pàirtidh, -ean, *s.* Gaelic spelling of *party.*
pais, *s. f.* Slap, blow with the open hand. 2 Box on the ear—*Sàr-Obair.*
†pais, -e, *s.f.* Passion, suffering.
pàisd, -e, -ean, *s. m. & f.* [*m.* in *Badenoch*] Child, infant, babe. 2 In *W. of Ross-shire*

this word is restricted to a female child, although the term "pàisd nighinn" may be heard there—(CR)
pàisdeachas,(MS) -ais, *s.m.* Boyhood, boyism.
pàisdealachd, *s.f.ind.* Childishness, puerility, babyism.
pàisdean, *n.pl.* of pàisd.
pàisdean, -in, -an, *s.m., dim.* of pàisd. Infant.
pàisdeanach,†† *a.* Childish.
pàisdeil, -e, *a.* Childish, puerile, babyish.
paisean, -ein, -ean, *s. m.* Fainting fit, swoon. Cuiridh mi p. ort, *I will knock you senseless ;* p. bàis, *a dead faint.*
paiseanach, -aiche, *a.* Swooning, subject to swoons or fainting fits.
paiseanadh, see paisean.
paisein, see paisean.
paisg, -e, *pl.* -ean & -eachan, *s.f.* Web or parcel of cloth. 2 Anything folded up. 3 Faggot. 4 Bunch, as of keys. P. iuchraichean, *a bunch of keys ;* p. shlat, *a faggot of twigs.* also pasg.
†paisg,** *s.f.* Severe cold.
paisg, *v.a.* Wrap, involve, fold in. 2 Wrap up, fold, roll together. 3 Imply. 4** Swathe, swaddle, shroud. 5** Benumb with cold. 6 Dismount anything. P. do shlat, *take down and tie up your fishing rod ;* p. do ghunna, *dismount your gun ;* ph. si i féin, *she wrapped herself ;* p. an t-aodach, *fold up the cloth.*
paisgeach, -eiche, *a.* Of, or belonging to, parcels, as of folded cloth.
paisgean,** -ein, *s.m.* Bundle, pack. 2 Sindon, wrapper.
paisgearra,** *s.f.* Midwife.
paisgte, *past pt.* of paisg. Wrapped, wrapt up, swathed. 2 Folded. 3 Rolled together, shrouded, swaddled.
pàist, see pàisd.
——ean, see pàisdean.
pait, -e, *pl.* -ean & -eachan, see poit.
pait, -e, -ean, *s.f.* Hump, lump, swelling. 2 Thump. 3 Smart blow on the head. 5 (CR) Stepping-stones—*W. of Ross-shire.* 4 Ford. 5 Protuberance. 6(AF) Hare. 7(AF) Young of any animal.
pàiteach, -eiche, *a.* Thirsty. 2 Parched, droughty.
paiteach, -eiche, *a.* Humpy, hunchy, having a hump or bunch. 2 *humorously,* Phrenological. 3 Having protuberances.
paiteachd, *s.f.ind.* Thirstiness.
paiteag, -eig, -an, *s.f.* Butter. 2 Small lump of butter. 3 Periwinkle (shell-fish.) 4 (AF) see pait 6 & 7.
paitean, -ein, *s.m.* Gaelic spelling of *patten.*
paitir,* -ean, *s.m. humorously* Phrenologist.
——eachd,* *s.f.ind.* Phrenology. 2 Thumping.
paitrisg, *s.f.* Gaelic spelling of *partridge.*
pàl,(DU) *s.m.* Old fish or one in poor condition. P. truisg, *a poor cod.*
pàlas, *s.* Gaelic spelling of *palace.*
palltag,** -aig, *s.f.* Thump, blow.
palmadair, see falmadair.
palmair, -ean, *s.m.* ‡Rudder. 2 see falmadair.
pànair, see pònair.
pànaireach, see pònaireach.
panna, Gaelic spelling of *pan.*
pannag,** -aig, see bannag & bonnag.
pannagan,** -ain, *s.m.* Pancake.
pannal, see bannal.
pannan, see bannal.
pantair, see pantraidh.
pantraidh, Gaelic spelling of *pantry.*
paoic, (CR) *s.f.* Piece, lump, as of butter.
paoiteag, see boiteag.
Pàpa, -n & -chan, *s.m.* Pope.
pàpach, -aiche, *a.* Pontifical.
pàpachd, *s.f.ind.* Popedom, papacy, papal dignity.
pàpanach, -aiche, *a.* Popish.
————, -aich, *s.m.* Papist, Roman Catholic. Ban ph., *a female Roman Catholic.*
————as, -ais, *s.m.* Popery. 2 Popedom.
————d, *s.f.* Popery. 2 Popedom.
pàpanas, -ais, *s.m.* see pàpanachas.
pàpar, *Badenoch, Glenurquhart, &c.* for pàipear.
parabal, -ail, *s.m.* Gaelic spelling of *parable.*
paracait,** *s.f.* Paroquet. 2 Parrot.
paracas, -ais, *s.m.* Rhapsody.
paradh, -aidh, *s.m.* Pushing, act of pushing, 2 Brandishing.
Paraidh, (variation of Para, *Patrick,* often erroneously used for *Peter) s.* Stormy-petrel. —*Lewis.* So called from its being always on the water, and the fact that St. Peter walked on the water. also Peadaireach.
paralais, see pairilis.
paralus,** -uis, *s.m.* Parlour, room to entertain.
para-nan-cearc, *s.* Kite, gled.
pàrant, *s.m.* Parent.
para-riabhach,¶ *s.* Honey-buzzard, see clamhan riabhach.
para-riabhach-nan-cearc,** *s.m.* Kite, gled.
paras,** -ais, see parras.
pardag, -aig, -an, *s.f.* Pannier, hamper used in mountainous places for carrying things on both sides of horses or mules.
parladh,** *s.m.* Parley.
Pàrlamaid, -e, -ean, *s.f.* Parliament.
————each, -eiche, *a.* Parliamentary.
†parn,** *s.m.* Whale.
parr, see parra. 2 see para-riabhach.
parra,(AF) *s.* Jay. 2 Woodpecker. 3 Jackdaw.
parracait, *s.f.* see paracait.
parrachan, *s.m.* Jackdaw.
parraist, -ean, *s.m.* Gaelic spelling of *parish.*
————each, -eiche, *a.* Parochial.
————each, -ich, *s.m.* Parishioner.
Pàrras, -ais, *s.m.* Paradise, heaven. A chuid de Ph. dha ! *may he be enjoying his share of Paradise !*—a common termination to obituary notices.
pàrrasail,** *a.* Elysian.
pàrtach, -aiche, *a.* see pàirteach.
partan, -ain, -an, *s.m.* Small edible sea-crab of a black colour and 3 or 4 in. long and 2 or 3 in. broad. 2 (CR) Crab smaller than crùbag, with a dark shell reddish underneath and not used for food—*W. of Ross-shire.* 3 (AF) Crab-louse. 4 The sign Cancer (♋) in the zodiac. 'S fheàrr am p.-tuathal na bhi gun fheartaighe, *better the unnatural crab than to be without a husband*—a sarcastic phrase used when a woman consents to marry a diminutive man—the partan always moves northwise, or against the sun's course. [But partan-tuathal is applied to the hermit-crab in some parts, which would suggest a rich wife and a husband who was poor, and who, like the hermit-crab, occupies a house which is another's.] N.G.P. explains the saying as follows : two women lived together, one of whom stole the other's meal out of her bag, the sufferer then put a live lobster (crab) in her bag, and the next time the thief put her hand in she was caught ; she cried out "tha 'n Donas 'nad phoca-sa," (the devil 's in your bag,), "tha," said the other, "'nuair 'tha thus' ann," (yes, when you are there.)
partanach, -aiche, *a.* Abounding in, or like, crabs or crab-lice. 2**Greedy, rapacious.
————d,** *s.f.ind.* Rapaciousness, extreme greed.

partan-tuathal,(DC) Hermit-crab.
pascart, see bascaid.
pasg,** -aisg, *s. f.* Wrapper. 2 Covering. 3 Swaddling-cloth. see paisg
pasg, *v*, *& s.f.* see paisg
pasgach, -aiche, *a* Wrapping, folding up, covering, swaddling, swathing
———,* *s.f.* Wrapper.
pasgadh, -aidh, *s. m.* Wrapping, act of wrapping, covering, or folding up 2 Envelope. 3 Swathing, swaddling, binding up. A' p—, *pr. pt* of paisg. Beagan pasgaidh nan làmh, *a little folding of the hands.*
pasgairt, see pasgart.
pasgan, -ain, -an, *s. m.* Bundle 2 Wallet. 3 Little group or flock. 4 Volume of a book.
pasganach, -aiche, *a.* In bundles. 2 In little groups or flocks.
pasgar, *fut. pass.* of pasg.
pasgart, -airt, -an, *s.m.* Basket, pannier.
pasmunn, -uinn, -an, *s.m.* Expiring pang.
pastaghadh,(AF) *s.* Diver (bird.)
pat,(MS) *v.a.* Bethump.
pata,(AF) *s.* see poit. 2** Leveret.
pataidh,(CR) Anything big of its kind—*Arran.*
patan, -ain, *s.m.* see pait. 2**Leveret. 3 Cloth tied round the cheeks as for toothache—CR.
patantachd,** *s.f* Thickness.
pàtaran, *s.m.* Gaelic spelling of *pattern.*
path, *s.m.* see padhadh.
pàthach, see pàiteach.
pathadh, see padhadh.
†patnide,‡ "Leporinus."
patraigeadh, (DMC) *s.m.* Batter.
pàtran,** -ain, *s.m.* Patron.
peabar, -brach, -aichean, *s.f. & m.* Pepper. 2 Spicery.
peabarach, -aiche, *a.* Peppered.
peabar-uisge, see lus-an-fhògair.
peabh-chearc,** -chirc, -chearcan, see peucag.
peabh-choileach, see peubh-choileach.
peabh-eun, see peubh-eun.
peabrach,†† *a.* Peppery.
peabrach, *gen.sing.* of peabar.
peabrachadh, -aidh, *s.m.* Act of seasoning with pepper or spices. 2‡‡ State of receiving or acquiring taste for spice, pepper, &c. 3 (DMC) Exciting, irritating. A' p—, *pr.pt.* of peabraich.
peabraich, *v.a.* Season with pepper or spice.
peabraichean, *pl.* of peabar.
peabraichte, *past pt.* of peabraich. Peppered. 2 Spiced.
peabh-eun, -eòin, *s. m.& f.* see peucag & peubh-choileach. A' giùlan pheubh-eun, *carrying peafowl.*
peac, see peacadh.
†peac, -eic, -ean, *s.f.* Any long, sharp, pointed thing. 2 Germ of a vegetable. 3 see peuc.
peacach, -aiche, *a.* Sinful.
pèacach, see peucach.
peacach, -aich, *s.m.* Sinner.
peacachadh, -aidh, *s.m.* Sinning, act of sinning, erring. 2 Transgression. A' p—, *pr. pt.* of peacaich.
peacadh, -aidh, -aidhean, *s.m.* Sin. Ris a' ph., *sinning.*
p.-bàis, *mortal sin.*
p.-beag, *a peccadillo.*
p.-collaidh, *incest.*
p.-gine, *original sin.*
p.-gniomha, *actual sin.*
p.-leanainn, *habitual sin.*
p.-sola, *a venial sin.*
p.-so-laghadh, *a venial sin.*
peacag, see peucag.
peacaich, *pr.pt.* a' peacachadh, *v.a.* Sin, transgress, offend.
peacaidheachd, see peacaireachd.
peacail, -e, *a.* see peacach.
peacair, -ean, *s.m.* Sinner.
———eachd, *s.f.ind.* Sinfulness. 2††Sinning.
peacalachd, see peacaireachd.
peacarach,(AF) *s.m.* Noxious animal (sinner.)
peachdaidheachd, see peacaireachd.
pea-chearc, see peucag.
pea-choileach, see peubh-choileach.
pea-choileach, see peubh-choileach.
peadaireach,(AC) -ich, *s.m.* Stormy petrel.
pealag, -aig, -an, *s.f.* Pelican.
pealaid, -e, -ean, *s.f.* see peallaid.
pealarach,(AF) *s.m.* Stormy petrel.
peall, pill, *pl.* -an & pillean, *s. m.* Hairy skin, hide. 2 Couch, pallet. 3 Veil, covering, coverlet. 4 Bunch of matted hair. 5 Mat. †6 Horse. 7(MMcL) Tarpaulin—*Lewis.*
peall, *v.a.* Cover. 2 Pull asunder, pluck, tear in pieces. 3 Clot, mat, as wool. 4 Teaze.
peallach, -aiche, *a.* Shaggy, having rough or matted hair. 2 Having couches or pallets. 3 Matted. 4 Covered with mats. 5* Paltry, trifling. 6 Teazing. 7 Slatternly. 8 Having ragged harness. A shine pheallaich! *thou shaggy old age!*
peallach,(AF) *s.m.* Porpoise.
pealladh, -aidh, *s.m.* Covering, act of covering. 2 Pulling, act of pulling or tearing asunder. 3 Clotting, matting. A' p—, *pr. pt.* of peall. Tha 'ghruag air pealladh, *his hair is matted.*
peallag, -aig, -an, *s.f.dim.* of peall. Shaggy hide or skin. 2 Little bunch of hair. 3 Clout. 4 Little couch or pallet. 5 Little covering. 6 Trollop, ill-dressed or ragged woman. 7†† Little mat or rug. 8 Hassock. 9 Umbrella. 10 Coarse harness, primitive or ill-kept harness. 11 Cart-harness. 12 Inferior wool—*Skye.* 13* Mat of straw. 14* Bass. 15* Sort of under pack-saddle. 16**Coarse blanket.
peallagach, -eiche, *a.* see peallach. Na toir droch mheas air loth ph., *do not despise a shaggy filly.*
peallaid, -e, -ean, *s.f.* Sheep-skin stripped of its wool or hair. 2 Little ball, pellet. 3 Fillip. 4* Paltry female.
peallaideach, -eiche, *a.* Dressed in skins or hides. 2 Abounding in sheep-skins.
peallan,†† -ain, *s.m.* Tar-mop.
peallastair, -ean, *s.m.* see peilistear. 2 (DMC) Impertinent or cheeky fellow.
pealltag, -aig, -an, *s.f.* Patched cloak. 2 Pall.
pealtag,** -aig, *s.f.* Clod.
pean, see peann.
peana, (DU) *pl.* peanachan, *Gairloch* form of peann.
peanachas, -ais, -an, see peanas.
†peanaid, see peanas.
peanaideach, see peanasach.
peanaisd, -ean, see peanas.
peanaisdeachadh, -aidh, *s.m. & pr.pt.* of peanaisdich, see peanasachadh.
peanaisdich, *v.* see peanasaich.
peanaiste, *past pt.* Punished.
peanaisteachadh, (MS) *s.m.* Tantalism.
peanaistich,(MS) *v.a.* Avenge.
peanar, -air, see peannar.
peanas, -ais, -an, *s.m.* Punishment. 2 Penance, chastisement, correction.
peanasach, -aich, *a.* Punishing. 2 Penal. 3 Prone to punish. 4 Annoying. 5 Vengeful. 6 Of, or relating to, punishment.
peanasachadh, -aidh, *s. m.* Punishing, act of punishing, punishment. A' p—, *pr. pt.* of peanasaich.
peanasachail, -e, *a.* see peanasail.

peanasaich, *pr.pt.* a' peanasachadh, *v.a.* Punish. 2 Torture. 3 *Annoy. 4 Avenge. 5** Chastise, correct.
peanasaiche, -an, *s.m.* Punisher, chastiser. 2 Executioner.
peanasaichte, *past pt.* of peanasaich. Punished, chastised, corrected.
peanasail, -e, *a.* Actionable. 2 Penal, punishable. 3‡‡ Inflictive. 4** Deserving punishment.
peanas-cuirp, *s.m.* Corporal punishment.
peanasda,** *a.* Penal.
peanas-eaglais, *s.m.* Ecclesiastical punishment.
peang, -aing, -an, *s.f.* Tenon in *joinery*.
peann, -a, -tan, *s.m.* Pen. P. iaruinn, *an iron pen.*
peannagan, -ain, -an, *s.m.* Pen-case. 2** Penner.
peannaid,** *s.f.* Pain.
peannair, -ean, *s.m.* Penman. 2 Good writer. 3**Pen-case.
peannaireachd, *s.f.* Penmanship.
peannar, -air, see peannair.
peann-ite, *s.m.* Quill-pen.
peann-leac, *s.m.* Slate-pencil.
peann-luaidhe, *s.m.* Lead-pencil.
peannsair,** *s.m.* Fencer. 2 Pair of pincers.
peannsal,** -ail, -an, *s. m.* Gaelic spelling of *pencil.*
peanntach,†† *a.* Of, or belonging to pens.
peanntair, *v.a.* Scribble, scrawl.
———**eachd**,* *s.f.ind.* Scribbling, scrawling.
peanntan, *pl.* of peann.
peapag, -aig, -an, *s.f.* Squash, pompion.
peapog, see peapag.
pèarla,** *s.m.* Gem, precious stone. 2 Gaelic spelling of *pearl.*
pèarlach,** *a.* Abounding in gems or pearls. 2 2 Like a pearl. 3 Plaited, corrugated.
pèarlaich, *v.a.* Bedeck with pearls or gems. 2 Plait, corrugate.
pèarluinn, -e, -ean, *s. f.* Fine linen, muslin, cambric, gauze.
pèarluinneach, -each, *a.* Of, or abounding in, fine linen, muslin, cambric or gauze. 2 Like fine linen, &c. 3 Made of fine linen, &c.
†**pears**, see pearsa, 3.
pearsa, -chan & -nnan, *s. m. & f.* Person, any one. 2 Person, bodily shape or appearance. †3 Gaelic spelling of purse. Do ph. dheas, ghrinn, *thine active elegant form*; mile p., *a thousand persons.*
pearsachadh, -aidh, *s.m.* Personification, act of personifying. A' p—, *pr.pt.* of pearsaich.
pearsachan, *pl.* of pearsa.
pearsaich, *v.a.* Personify, represent.
pearsail, -e, *a.* Personal.

561. *Pearsal.*

562. *Peasair-an-arbhair.*

pearsal, -ail, *s. m.* Parsley—*petroselinum sativum.*
pearsal mór, *s.m.* Smallage, wild celery, see lus-na-smalaig.
pearsalach,** *a.* Abounding in, or like, parsley. 2 Of parsley.
†**pearsan**, -ain see pearsa.
pearsannan, *pl.* of pearsa.
pearsanta, -ainte, *a.* Personal, personable, of good appearance, handsome, portly.
pearsanta,* *adv.* (gu p—) Personally.
pearsantachd, *s.f.ind.* Handsomeness, portliness. 2 Personality.
pearsantail, -e, *a.* Personal.
pearsluibh,** *s.f.* Parsley.
pears-eaglais, -an-, *s.m.* Clergyman.
peartog, see cearc-thomain.
peas,** *s.m.* Purse. P. ghadaiche, *a cutpurse.*
peasair, peasrach, peasraichean, *s. f.* Pease, pulse. Eitean peasrach, *a grain of pease.*
peasair-a'-mhadaidh-ruaidh, *s.f.* Bird's-foot trefoil—*lotus corniculatus.*
——— **-an-arbhair**,§ *s. f.* Hairy vetch, common tare—*vicia hirsuta.*

563. *Peasair-bhuidhe.* 564. *Peasair-nam-preas.*

——— **-bhuidhe**,§ *s.f.* Yellow vetchling—*lathyrus pratensis.*
——— **-chapuill**,§ *s.f.* Vetch, see flatghal.
peasair-each, *s.f.* Bush-vetch.
peasair-fiadhain,§ *s.f.* Vetch, see flatghal.
peasair-gheal, *s.f.* White pease.
peasair-luchag, *s.f.* Tufted vetch.
peasair-nam-preas,§ *s.f.* Bush vetch,—*vicia sebium.*
peasair-nan-each, see peasair-each.

565. *Peasair-nan-luch.*

peasair-nan-luch,§ *s.f.* Tufted vetch—*vicia cracca.* 2 Lentil, chick-pease.
peasair-radain, see peasair-nan-luch.
peasair-tuilbh,§ *s.f.* Heath-pease, see cairmeal.
peasan, -ain, *pl.* -an [& -ain**], *s.m.* Petulant or impudent person, varlet. 2 Sorry little fellow. 3**Imp, brat, puppy. 4**Purse.
———**ach**, -aiche, *a.* Petulant, impudent, pert, troublesome. 2 Sorry, mean, little. 3 Impish, barefaced. Gu p., *impudently.*
———**achd**, *s. f. ind.* Petulance, impudence, pertness, barefacedness, impishness.
peasan-leannain,‡‡ *s.m.* Amatorculist.
———**ta**,* see peasanach.
———**tachd**, see peasanachd.

pesar, see peasair.

peasg, peisg, -an, *s.f.* Gash, notch, kibe, cranny 2 Chap on the skin, incision, bursting of the skin, as with cold. 3 Crevice, as in wood

peasg, *pr. pt.* a' peasgadh, *v.a.* & *n* Notch, gash, slash. 2 Become gashed or notched. think. 3 Chap, as the hands, burst, as the skin with cold. 4†† Irritate, the skin as with salt water.

peasgach, -aiche, *a.* Gashed, cut. 2 Abounding in gashes or notches. 3 Chapped, burst, as the skin with cold. 4 Causing gashes or notches. 5 Causing the skin to burst with cold.

peas-ghadaiche, -ean, *s. m.* Pick-pocket, cutpurse.

peasgadh, -aidh, *s.m.* Gashing, cutting, act of gashing, cutting or notching. 2 State of becoming gashed or notched. 3**Slight incision. 4 Bursting of the skin. A' p—, *pr.pt.* of peasg.

peasgta, *a.* Chapped.

peasrach,* *gen.sing.* of peasair.

———,†† *a.* Pertaining to pulse or pease.

peasraichean, *pl.* of peasair. Kinds of pease, fields of pease.

peata, *pl.* -n & -chan, *s.m.* Pet, tame animal. 2* Spoiled child.

peatach,†† *a.* Petted.

peatadh, -aidh, -aidhean, *s.m.* see peata.

peatag,(AF) *s.f.* Plover—*Dean of Lismore.*

peata-odhar,(AF) *s.m.* Cormorant—*Dean of Lismore.*

peatarnachd,* *s.f.ind.* Fondling.

peata-ruadh,¶ *s.m.* Puffin.

peathair, -e, -ean, *s.m.* see peithear & peithir.

peathar,* *gen. sing.* of piuthar.

peathrachas, -ais, *s.m.* Sisterhood.

peathraiche, (a ph— !) *voc.pl.* of piuthar.

———an, *n.pl.* of piuthar.

peath-shaileach,(AF) *s.* Pea-hen, see peucag.

pecoc, see peucag.

peghinn, see peighinn.

peic, -e, -eannan, *s. m.* Peck (measure of two gallons. 2 The vessel used for this measure.

péic,** *s.f.* Long tail. (see peuc.)

peiceag, -eig, -an, *s.f.dim.* of peic. Little peck. Cha'n fhaigh sinn p. bracha thogail, *we cannot brew a peck of malt.*

péiceallach,** *a.* Having a long tail.

peicein, *s.m.* see peiceag.

peich, *v.a.* Sniff with anger.

peichil,** *s.f.* Sniffing with anger. 2 One twentieth part of a davoch—AH. see note under dabhach.

peighinn, -e, -ean, *s.f.* Penny Scots, one twelfth of a penny sterling. 2* Denomination of land, equal to a *còta-bàn*, groat-land. 3 Round bit, like a coin. Cha'n 'eil p. agam, *I have not a penny*; na h-uile p., *every coin*; 'ga ghearradh 'na pheighinnean, *cutting it into round bits*; p. ruadh, *a penny sterling.*

The following note is from D.C.

The system of land measure which prevailed in the Western Isles and then took root in Argyllshire, was neither Pictish nor Irish, but Norse. The unit was the "ounce-" land, i.e. the extent of land which paid the rent of an ounce of silver. The word was borrowed by Gaelic, and appears as *unnsa*. The land term was *unga* (e.g. Unganab in North Uist and in Tiree.) It appears in old charters as, *teroung*, *teiroung*, &c. This extent was divided into 20 parts—sometimes into only 18—such parts being called *peighinn*; hence many place-names (e.g. Pennymore, Peighinnchornach, &c.) In some places the pennyland was subdivided. On Lochfyneside we meet with Lephinmore, Lephincorrach, (the big half pennyland, and the rough half pennyland); also an Fheòirling, (the farthingland.) A conventional use of the term *peighinn* is met with in Skye—the crofting township of Elgol is separated by a march dyke from the deer-forest; each crofter is responsible for the upkeep of a specified length of the dyke, and it is called the *peighinn* of his croft: similarly the part of the shore allotted to each croft for seaware is called the *peighinn* of that croft. The full fractional division of land was carried out in Islay thus:—

1 oz. land	=20d. sterling	=12 markland	=133s. 4d. Scots	=	Tirunga
½ ,,	=10d. ,,	= 5 ,,	=66s 8d.	=	Leth pheighinn.
¼ ,,	= 5d. ,,	= 2½ ,,	=33s 4d.	=	{ Ceathramh, quarterland.
⅛ ,,	= 2½d. ,,	= 1¼ ,,	=16s. 8d.	=	Ochdamh.
1-16th ,,	= 1¼d. ,,	= ⅝ ,,	= 8s 4d.	=	Leothras.
1-32nd ,,	= ⅝d. ,,	= 5-16ths,,	= 4s. 2d.	=	{ Còta bàn or groat land.
1-64th ,,	= 5-16d. ,,	= 5-32nds,,	= 2s. 1d.	=	Dà sgillinn.

Lands in Islay were valued in 1541 in quarters, half quarters and eighths; in 1562 these began to be given as equivalents of multiples and fractions of 10 marks, which sum was taken as amounting in value to an ounce of silver.

peighinneach, -eich, *a.* Full of pence, rich.

peighinneach, -eiche, *a.* Spotted, dappled as a horse, pock-marked.

peighinnich,* *v.a.* Make round bits, as coins.

peighinn-rìoghail,§-e-, *s.f.* Pennyroyal—*mentha pulegium.*

peigidh, *s.f.* Herpes, shingles.

peilc,(CR) *s.* Large stomach, as of a cow that has eaten its fill—*Arran.*

peileag,** -eig, *s.f.* see péilig. 2 Felt. 3 Any coarse cloth.

———ach,** *a.* Coarse, as cloth. 2 Like felt. 3 Made of felt.

peileagach, -aiche, *a.* Given to chattering.

566. *Peighinn-rìoghail.*

peilear, -an, *s.m.* Ball, bullet, p.-beithreach, *thunderbolt*, p.-lann, *cartouch*; *a place where balls are piled.*

up.
p.-mullaich, *balloon, in architecture.*
p.-tàirnich, *thunderbolt.*
p.-tàirneanaich, *a thunderbolt.*
peileasach, -aiche, *a.* Frivolous. 2 Troublesome.
peileastair, *s.m.* Quoit. 2††Small flag (stone.) see peilistear.
peileid, -e, -ean, *s.f.* Cod, husk. 2 Bag. 3 Mangled sheep-skin. 4 Blow, slap on the cheek. 5* see péilig.
——each, -eiche, *a.* Covered with a cod or husk. 2 Furnished with bags. 3 Like a bag.
peileir, see peilear.
——each, -eiche, *a.* Abounding in balls or bullets. 2 Like a ball or bullet.
peil-ghuin,** *s.f.* Pang, torment.
———each, -eiche, *a.* That tormenteth or giveth pain.
péilig, -e, -ean, *s. f.* Porpoise, sea-hog.
peiliocan,** -ain, *s.m.* Pelican.
peilistear, -eir, -eirean, *s.m.* Small flat stone used in place of a quoit. 2 Game of quoits.
peilleag,** *s.f.* Felt.
peillic, -e, -ean, *s.f.* Hut or booth built of earth and branches and roofed with skins. 2 Felt. 3 Any very thick or coarse cloth. 4 Covering made of skins or coarse cloth. 5*Pit. 6(CR) Basket of untanned hide.
———each, -eiche, *a.* Clumsy. 2 Thick, coarse. 3 Like felt. 4 Made of felt.
peillichd, see peillic.
peilp,** *s.* Futility, gabble. 2 Insolence.
——each,** *a.* Futile.
——eanta,** *a.* Communicating, gabbling. 2 Huffish. 3 Insolent.
péin, *gen.sing.* of pian.
péin, -e, *s.f.* Pain, punishment, torment, (pian.)
péin-dlighe, -an, *s.m.* Penal law.
péinealtach,†† *a.* Tyrannical. 2 Painful.
————d,†† *s.f.* Tyranny. 2 Pain.
péineil,†† *a.* Painful.
———teachd,†† *s.f.* Tyranny.
péingilteach, -eiche, *a.* Rigorous, bare. 2 Tyrannical.
—————d, *s.f.* Rigour. 2 Tyranny, cruelty.
†peinn, -e, -ean, *s.f.* see beinn.
peinneag,* *s.f.* Chip of stone for filling crevices in a wall.
peinnt,* see peinnteag.
peinnteag,* -eig, -an, *s.f.* Small pretty shell or pebble.
peinnteal, -eil, -an, *s.m.* Snare. 2 Straitening, confinement. 3* Mare.
———ach, -aiche, *a.* Of, or pertaining to, snares, snaring. 2 Straitening, compressing. 3 Penurious.
———ach, -aich, *s.m.* Slender, tightly-laced, dandified person. 2 Strait article of dress, as coat, trousers, &c.
———achd,** *s.f.* Penuriousness.
peinntealadh, -aidh, *s.m.* Cooping, compressing, straitening, cramping.
peinntealta, -eilte, *a.* Straitened, compressed, 2 Punctual, precise, *prov.* 3 (MS) Stiff.
peintealtachd,(MS) *s.f.* Rigour.
peinntealtaich, (MS) *v.a.* Refine.
peintear,(MS) *s.m.* Mouse-trap.
peirceall, -ill & -cle, *pl.* -an & -clean, *s.m.* Jaw. 2 The jaw-bone. 3 Lower part of the face. 4 Corner, nook, angle. 5 Abdomen. 6* Lantern jaw, lean, large, lank jaw.
———ach, -aiche, *a.* Lank-jawed, lean. 2 Having large jaws. 3 Angled, cornered. 4 **Chapless. 5 Thin-faced. 6 Mandibular.
———ach,*s.m.* Lean, lank, or lantern-jawed person.
peircle, *gen.sing.* of peirceall.
peircleach, -eiche, see peirceallach.
peirclean, *pl.* of peirceall.
péire, *gen.*, & *pl.* of peur. 2 The buttocks.
peireadh,** -idh, *s.m.* Rage, fury.
†peireagal, -ail, *s.m.* see peirigill.
peirealais, (for pairilis, *paralysis*) Distraction, bewilderment. A' cheann a chur gu p. ag eilid Beinne-dorain, *his head bewildered through the hind of Ben Doran.—Donn. Bàn, p. 97.*
péirean, *s.pl.* The buttocks. 2 *pl.* of peur.
peireid,* *s.f.* Ferret.
peirigill, -e & -gle, *pl.* -ean & -glean, *s.f.* Danger, peril. 2 Urgent necessity, *prov.* 3 Awkward predicament. 4* Agonies of death. 5* Excruciating mental tortures or torment.
peirigle, *gen. & pl.* of peirigill.
———adh, see peirigill. 2 (DMC) Swoon. 3 (DMC) Severe pain.
———an, *pl.* of peirigill.
peirigleach, *a.* Periculous, in an awkward predicament. 2 Perilous, dangerous.
peiriglich,* *v.a.* Torture, torment.
péiris,‡ *s.* Testiculi.
péirlin, *s.m.* see pèarluinn.
†péirse, -an, *s.f.* Row, rank. 2 Perch in length.
——ach, -eiche, *a.* Formed into ranks, well ordered. 2 Divided, into perches, as land.
peirseal,** *s.* Smallage.
peirsill,** *s.f.* Parsley.
—— -mhór, *s.f.* Smallage.
peirteag,** -eig, -an, *s.f.* Partridge.
——— -dhearg-chasach,(AF) *s.f.* Red-legged partridge.
peirtealach,** *a.* Pert, impudent.
————d,** *s. f. ind.* Pertness, impudence, effrontery. 2 Huffishness.
peirteil,** *a.* Pert, impudent. 2 Huffish.
peisd,** *s. f.* Plague. 2 Loss. 3 Ailment. 4 Pest.
péisd, see béist.
peisg, *s.* see peasg.
peislear,* -ean, *s.m.* Trifling person.
peisteal,** -eil, *s.m.* Pestle.
peit,** *s.m.* Musician.
†peiteach, -ich, *s.m.* Music.
peiteadh,** -idh, *s.m.* Music.
peiteag, -eig, -an, *s.f.* Waistcoat, short jacket. 2 Doublet. 3 Woollen shirt.
——ach, -aiche, *a.* Wearing a jacket or waistcoat. 2 Of, or belonging to, a vest.
—— -mhuinicheallach, *s.f.* Jacket.
peitean, -ein, -an, *s.m.* see peiteag. [Peitean is used in *Gairloch.*]
———ach, -aich, *a.* see peiteagach.
peitearlach,** -aich, *s.m.* The Old Law or Testament. 2 Sacred history.
peitearlaichte,** *a.* Versed in sacred history.
†peith-bhog, *s.f.* Gaelic name of the letter P.
peithireachd,* *s.f.* Running of messages.
peithear,(MS) *s.m.* Parker.
peithir, -ean, *s. m.* Forester. 2 Gamekeeper. 3 Hunter. 4 Message-boy. 5‡‡Thunderbolt.
peitirich,(AC) *s.pl.* see peadaireach.
peitseag, -eig, *s.f.* Peach—*amydalus persica.*
———ach, -aiche, *a.* Abounding in peaches. 2 Like a peach. 3 Of a peach.
peòdar, -air, *s.m.* see feòdar. 2** *in ridicule,* Harum-scarum.
peòdarach, see feòdarach.
peòdarair, *s.m.* see feòdarair.
peothair, see peithir.
peubar, *v. & s.* Gaelic spelling of *pepper.*
———ach,** *a.* Peppery.
peubh-chearc, -chirc, -an, *s.f.* see peucag.
peubh-choileach, -ich, *s.m.* Peacock.
peubh-eun,** -eòin, *s.m.* Pea-fowl.

peuc, see peucag.
peuc,** *s.* Long tail. 2 Any sharp-pointed thing. 3 Sprouting germ of any vegetable.
peucach, -aiche, *a.* Gaudy, showy. 2‡‡Long-tailed.
peucag, -aig, -an, *s.f.* Peahen. 2 Peacock. 3 Beautiful woman.
——ach, -aiche, *a.* Beautiful, as a peacock. 2 Abounding in pea-hens.
peucail,* -e, *a.* Trim, neat, cleanly.
peuc-choileach, *s.m.* see peubh-choileach.
peuchdag, see peucag.
————ach, see peucagach.
peula,* *s.m.* Milk-pail. Gaelic spelling of *pail.*
peur, -éire & -a, *pl.* -an & -éirean, *s.f.* Pear. 2 Buttock—*Skye.*
——ach, -aiche, *a.* Full of pears. 2 Like a pear.
peurd, *v.a.* First card in carding wool.
peurda, -an, *s.m* Tuft of wool off the cards in the first carding 2 Roll of carded wool.
peurdag, -aig, -an, *s.f.* Partridge. 2 see peurda, 3.
————ach,†† *a.* Abounding in partridges.
peurlach,** *a.* Corrugant,corrugated,wrinkled.
peurladh,** -aidh, *s.m.* Corrugation, wrinkle.
peurlaich,** *v.* Corrugate
peurlag,(AF) *s.f.* Partridge.
peur-lann, *s.m.* Perry.
peurs,* *v* F—t drawlingly.
peursa,(DMC) *s.m.* Signal pole.
peurtag,¶ *s.f.* Partridge, see cearc-thomain.
———— -dhearg-chasach,¶ see cearc-thomain dhearg-chasach.
peurtanan,(CR) *Strathspey* for feursann.

ph, For words beginning with ph, see under *p.*

Phairiseach, -eiche, *a.* Pharisaical.
————, -ich, *s.m.* Pharisee.
————ail, -e, *a.* see Phairiseach, *a.*
Phairisneach, see Phairiseach.
Pharasach,†† *a.* Pharisaical.
piaid, *s.f.* see pioghaid.
——each, see pioghaideach.
pian, péin, -tan, *s.f.* Pain, pang, torture, torment, anguish,trouble,sorrow. 2 Punishment. [** gives piantaidh also for *pl.*]
pian, *pr.pt.* a' pianadh, *v.a.* Torment, torture, pain. 2 Distress, annoy. 3 Punish. Ph. e mi, *he tortured me.*
pianadair, -ean, *s. m.* Tormenter, afflicter. 2 Punisher.
pianadh, -aidh, *s.m.* Tormenting,act of tormenting. 2 Torment, pain, affliction. 3 Annoying. 4 Punishment. A' p—, *pr.pt.* of pian.
pianail, -e, *a.* Painful, causing pain or torment.
pianalachd, *s.f.ind.* Painfulness.
pianas, see peanas.
piannta,(DU) Gaelic spelling of *pint.*
pianta, *pl.* of pian.
piantach, -aiche, *a.* Tormenting,painful, excruciating. 2**Annoying, vexatious.
————adh, -aidh, -aidh, see pianadh.
————ail,* see piantach.
————air,** -ean, *s. m.* Tormenter. 2 Punisher.
piantaich, -ean, *s.m.* Pitiable object, overwrought, ill-used or distressed person.
————, *v.a.* see pian.
————te, *past pt.* of piantaich. Pained, tormented, afflicted. 2 Annoyed. 3 Punished.
piantaidh, *s.pl.* Pains, pangs, punishment.
piantail, see pianail.
piantair, see pianadair.
piantalachd, *s.f.ind.* Soreness.
piantan, *n.pl.* of pian.
piartag, see cearc-thomain.
piasgach,** *a.* Rough, shaggy, hairy.
piast, -an, see biast.
piastag, -aig, -an, see biastag.
piastaga, *s.m.* Vermicelli.
piata,(DU) *s.m.* Poor eater. Nach b' e tu am p. !—said to a person who is not supposed to be taking an ordinary quantity of food.
pib, -e, -ean, *s f.* see piob.
pìbhinn, -e, -ean, *s.f* Lapwing, see adharcan-luachrach.
————each, -eiche, *a.* Abounding in lapwings. 2 Like a lapwing.
†pic, -e, *s.f* Disorder in the tongue and throat of fowls.
pìc, -e, -ean, *s.f.* Pike (weapon.) 2 Pick-axe. 3 *Niggardliness, churlishness.
pic, -e, -ean, *s.f.* Pitch. Còmhdaichidh tu a staigh 's a muigh le pic, *thou shalt cover it within and without with pitch.*
pic, *pr pt.* a' piceadh, *v.a.* Pitch, cover or daub with pitch.
pic-catha, *s.f* Battle-axe, halberd.
piceach, -eiche, *a.* Armed with pikes. 2 High-peaked, as a ship. 3 Furnished with pick-axes. 4 Like a pick-axe.
piceach, -eiche, *a.* Abounding in pitch, pitchy. 2 Like pitch. 4 Asphaltic.
————adh, *s.m.* Same meanings as piceadh.
piceadh, -idh, *s.m.* Pitching, act of covering, laying or daubing with pitch. 2 see piocadh. A' p—, *pr.pt.* of pic.
pic-chlach,** *s.f.* Asphalt.
piceal, -il, -an, *s.f.* Gaelic spelling of *pickle.*
picear, -eir, *s. m.* Rogue, mean fellow. 2 Pilferer. 5 Avaricious person, niggard, churl.
picear, -eir, -an, *s.m.* One armed with a pike. 2 Pick-axe man.
————achd, *s.f.ind.* Digging with a pick-axe.
picearachd, *s.f.ind.* Roguery, villany. 2 Pilfering. 3 Avarice, avaricious practices.
pichd, *s. & v.* see pic.
picich, *pr.pt.* a' piceachadh, see pic, *v.*
picil, -e, *s.f.* see piceal.
——, *v.a.* Pickle.
picillich, see picil.
picleach,†† *a.* Pickled. 2 Abounding in pickles.
picleadh, -idh, *s.m.* Pickling, act of pickling A' p—, *pr.pt.* of picil.
picilte, *past pt.* of picil. Pickled.
piclig, *v.a.* see picil.
————eadh, see picleadh.
————te, see picilte.
pic-mheallach, *s.f.* Lochaber-axe.
pic-thalmhuinn, *s.f.* Asphalt. 2**Mortar.
pige, -achan, *s.m.* see pigeadh.
——ach, *a.* Pertaining to earthenware jars or pitchers.
——adair, -ean, *s.m.* Potter.
——adaireachd,†† *s.f.* Pottery (business.)
pigeadh, -idh, -idhean, *s. m.* Earthenware jar, pitcher or pot.
pigean, -ein, -ean, *s. m.*, *dim.* of pige. Little earthen jar, pitcher or pot. 2 Small pail. 3 Fragment of earthenware. 4 Gorbelly, little gorbellied person.
pigein, see pigean.
pighe, see pigheann.
pigheann, *s.m.* Pie, pastry
————ach, -aiche, *a.* Abounding in pies.
————air,** *s.m.* Pastrycook.
pighein, -e, -ean, see pioghaid.
————each, -eiche, *a.* see pioghaideach.
pighinn,* see pigheann.
pigidh, -ean, *s.m.* Robin, robin red-breast. 2 Sometimes used for pigeadh & pigean.
pileagach, -aiche, *a.* Smart-tongued.
†pilear, -eir, -an, *s.m.* Gaelic spelling of *pillar.*
pileistreadh,(MS) *s.m.* Rancidness.
pilig, *v.a.* Gaelic form of *peeling*, used to express

peel.

pill, -e, -ean, *s.f.* Cloth or skin on which corn is winnowed. 2 (DC) Clump or patch of heather. An nead am p. fraoich, *the nest in a patch of heather;* pill-bràthainn, *quern-cloth*, pill-fhasgnaidh, *winnowing-cover.*

pill, *pr.pt.* a' pilltinn & a' pilleadh, *v. a. & n.* Turn, cause to turn or return. 2**Turn aside 3 Turn, return, go back, come back. Phill ris, *he has got a relapse.*

pill-chur, *s.f.* Sheet holding seed-corn when sowing.

pilleadh, -idh, *s.m.* Turning, act of turning or returning, return. A' p—, *pr.pt.* of pill.

——-—, *3rd. sing. & pl. imp.* of pill

pilleadh-facail, *s.m.* Contradiction.

pilleag, *s.f.* see pillean & peallag.

pilleam,** *1st. per. sing. imp.* of pill. Let me return. 2 (for pillidh mi) I will return.

pillean, -ein, -an, *s.m.* Pack-saddle. 2 Cloth put under a pannel, cushion, pad. 3 Hassock. 4 *pl.* of peall. 'S mi 'm pillein cùbhraidh cùl-ghorm fraoich, *and I resting in a patch of heather, sweet-scented, purple.—Ross*, p. 11.

pilleanach, -aiche, *a.* Of, or pertaining to, a pack-saddle.

pillear,** *fut. pass.* of pill.

pillin, -ean, see pillean.

pillsear,** -eir, *s.m.* Pilchard.

pillteach,** *a.* Inclined to return. 2 Returning frequently.

pilltinn, -e, *s.f.* Returning, act of returning. 2 Return, retrogression. A' p—, *pr. pt.* of pill.

pincean,** *s.m.* Gillyflower.

pin-chrann,§ -chroinn, *s. m.* Pine—*pinus.* 2 Also applied to all the *coniferæ.*

pincin,§ *s.* Stock, "queen stock" of the garden—*matthiola incana.* 2 Wallflower, leaved stock, gillyflower.

pinn, *pr.pt.* a' pinneadh, *v.a* see pinnich.

pinn, *gen. sing. & n. pl.* of peann.

pinne, *pl.* pinneachan & pinneacha, *s. m.* Pin, peg, spigot. 2 (DU) Steady flow of water from a small pipe or any circular orifice.

pinneach,†† *a.* Abounding in pegs.

567. *Pincin.*

pinneachadh, -aidh, *s.m.* Fastening, act of fastening with pegs or pins. A' p—, *pr.pt.* of pinnich.

pinneadh, -aidh, *s.m.* Same meanings as pinneachadh. 2 Piercing—*Beinn Doran.* A' p—, *pr.pt.* of pinn.

pinnear,** -eir, *s.m.* Ink-horn. 2 Pen-case.

pinne-cluaisein, *s.m.* Drag-pin of a cart.

pinne-na-h-aisil, *s.m.* Axle-pin of a cart.

pinne-na-garmain, *s.m.* The pin of the beam.

pinnich, *v.a.* Pin, fasten with pins. 2††Pierce.

————te, *past pt.* of pinnich. Pinned, fastened with pins.

pinnt, -ean, *s.m.* Pint, imperial liquid measure, ½ pint Scots. Stòp pinnt, *a quart pot;* tri cheathrannan pinnt, *three-quarters of a pint.*

———e, see pinnichte.

pinnteachadh, (DMC) -aidh, *s.m.* see binndeachadh.

pinntich, see binndich.

pinteal,** *v.a.* Paint.

-———ta,** *past pt.* Painted.

piob, -a, *pl.* -an & -achan, *s.f.* Pipe, bagpipe. 2 Pipe, tube, syphon. 3 *figuratively*, Smoke.

PARTS OF A BAGPIPE:—

1 Altan-gleusaidh, *tuning-slides.*

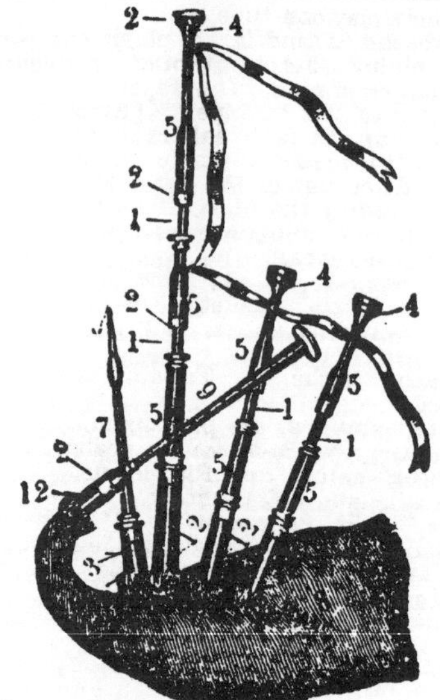

568. *A' Phìob-mhor.*

2 Bann, *ferrule.*
3 Clochag, *valve.*
4 Cupan, *cup inside ferrule at top of drones.*
5 Dos, *pl.* -an, *drone.*
6 Feadan, Seannsair, *chanter.*
7 Gaothaiche, *mouth-piece.*
8 Màla, *bag.*
9 Ribheid, *reed.*
10 Sumair, *drone.*
11 Sionnach, *bellows in an Irish bagpipe.*
12 Stoc, *stock, that part of each of the five pipes to which the bag is tied.* Stoc an fheadain, *the chanter-stock;* stoc an dos mhóir, *the big drone-stock*, &c.
13 Bonn an fheadain, *sole of chanter.*

The bagpipes are spoken of in Gaelic in the singular—a' phìob.

The use of the bagpipe can be traced to the most remote antiquity, although it seems, if not comparatively modern in connection with the Highlands, at least to have held a second place in comparison with the harp in the estimation of the bulk of the people, until during the last few centuries. The Greek word sumphōnía, which appears as an Aramic loan-word in Daniel, iii, 5, is translated "bagpipe" by every competent translator. There is no doubt that the verse relating the arrival of the prodigal son's brother in the New Testament, should be rendered "now his elder son was in the field, and as he came and drew nigh to the house, he heard bagpipes and dancing."—*Expository Times, Jan. 1905.*

piob, *v.a. & n.* Pipe, play on the pipes. 2 Squeak.

piobach, -aiche, *a.* Having pipes. 2 Like a pipe. 3 Tubulous, tubular, fluted.

————an, *pl.* of piob.

piobadair, -ean, *s. m.* Pipe-maker. 2 Bagpipe-maker.

-————eachd,** *s.f.* Pipe-making. 2 Bagpipe-making.

piobadh, -aidh, *s.m.* Piping, act of piping. 2 Squeaking. A' p—, *pr. pt.* of piob.

piobag, -aig, -an, *s.f., dim.* of piob. Small pipe.

piobagach,†† *a.* Abounding in small pipes.

piobair, -ean, *s.m.* Piper, bagpiper. P. an aona phuirt, *an indifferent piper* (*lit.* a piper who

can only play one tune.)
piobaireachd, *s.f.ind.* Art of playing on the bag-pipe, piping. 2 Act of piping. 3 Business or occupation of a piper. 4 Pipe-tune. 5 Music peculiar to the bagpipe. [Erroneously applied by non-Gaelic speakers to mean *ceòl mòr* only, but it means any pipe-music.] For a detailed account of the articulate music formerly used by the MacCrimmons and others in the pipers' colleges, see canntaireachd.
Pìoball, see Bìoball.
pìoban, -ain, -an, *s. m.*, *dim.* of piob. Small pipe. 2 Little flageolet. 3 Reed. 4 Small tube. 5 Throat, gullet. 6 Pip in fowls.
——, *n.pl.* of piob.
pìobanach, -aiche, *a.* Tubular, tubulous. 2 Fluted.
pìobanta, -ainte, *a.* see pìobanach.
pìobar, -air, *s.m.* *Badenoch* for peabar.
pìob-cheol, -chiùil, *s.m.* Pipe-music.
pìob-fhuail, -an-, *s.f.* Catheter.
pìobhar,** *s. m.* Searce, sieve. 2**Honeycomb.
pìob-leigidh, *pl.* -an-, *s.f.* Cock of a barrel.
pìob-mhàla, *pl.* -an-màla, *s.f.* Bagpipe. [McL & D. gives pìob-mhàlaidh.]
pìob-mhor, *s.f.* The great Highland bagpipe.
pìob-mùin,** *s.f.* Catheter.
pìob-na-comb-sheirm, *s.f.* The union pipes.
pìobraich,(MS) *v.a.* Enchafe. 2 Pepper.
pìob-shionnaich, *pl.* -an-sionnaich, *s.f.* Bellows-pipe, Irish bagpipe.
pìob-thaosgaidh, *pl.* -an-taosgaidh, *s.f.* Pump.
pìob-theannaich, *pl.* -an-teannaich, *s.f.* see pìob-shionnaich.
pìob-thombac, *s.f.* Tobacco-pipe.
pìob-uisge, *pl.* -an-uisge, *s.f.* Water-pipe, conduit-pipe.
Pìobull, see Bìoball.
pioc, *pr.pt.* a' piocadh, *v.a.* Pick, nip, nibble. 2 Pinch. 3 Dig with a pickaxe. P. an coimheach, *pinch the stranger* ; p. taingeadh, *pick a thank.*
pioc, -a, -an, *s.m.* Crumb, small portion. 2 Nip, pinch with the nails or teeth. 3**Pickaxe.
piocach, -aiche, *a.* Pinching. 2 Nibbling. 3 Pungent. 4**Taunting.
piocach, -aich, *s.m.* The coal-fish in its third and fourth years—*Argyll.* 2 (DU) *metaphorically*, Small fellow.
piocachadh, -aidh, *s.m.* Digging, act of digging or working with a pick-axe or mattock. A' p—, *pr.pt.* of piocaich.
piocadair, -ean, *s. m.* Picker, nibbler, carper. pecker.
piocadh, -aidh, *s. m.* Picking, act of picking, pinching, nibbling or nipping. 2 Digging with a mattock. 3 (DU) Pecking as a bird. A' p—, *pr.pt.* of pioc.
piocag, -aig, -an, *s.f.*, *dim.* of pioc. Little crumb. 2 Slight pinch. 3 Pair of nippers or pincers. 4 Small mattock. 5 Taunting female.
piocagach, -aiche, *a.* In small crumbs. 2 Pinching lightly. 3 Nibbling.
piocaich, *pr.pt.* a' piocachadh, *v.a.* Work or dig with pick-axe or mattock.
piocaid, -e, -ean, *s.f.* Pick-axe. 2 Mattock. 3 Pincers.
-——each,†† *a.* Having picks, mattocks or pincers.
piocaidh, *fut.aff.a.* of pioc.
piocair, -ean, *s.m.* One who works with a pick-axe or mattock. 2 Nibbler. 3 Pincher.
pìocair,** -ean, *s.m.* Pikeman. 2**Pioneer.
piocaireachd, *s.f.* Working with a pick-axe, digging with a mattock. 2 Nibbling. 3 Pinching.
piocaireachd, *s. f.* Business of a pikeman, or 2 of a pioneer.
piocairean,(MS) *s.pl.* Nippers.
piocais,(MS) *s.* Nippers.
piocas, -ais, *s.m.* Scabies, the itch [with art.*am*] 2*Herpes, shingles—*Skye.* 3 Magpie.
pìoch,* *v.a.* Wheeze.
pìoch, *s.m.* Croup [with art. *am.*]
pìochair,* *v.a.* Line, as cats. 2**Caterwaul.
pìochan, -ain, *s.m.* Wheezing in the throat. 2 One who wheezes in the throat.
piochanach, -aiche, *a.* Wheezing, breathing with a noise in the throat, or with difficulty.
piochanaich, -e, *s. f.* Wheezing in the throat Ciod a' ph. a th' ort ? *why do you wheeze so ?*
piochdach,** -aich, *s.m.* Plunderer.
————,** *a.* Given to plundering.
pìochradh,* -aidh, *s.m.* Lining, as cats. A' p—, *pr.pt.* of pìochair.
pioghaid, -e, -ean, *s.f.* Magpie. 2(AF) Jackdaw. 3(DU) Useless, talkative young woman. 4 (D MC) Parrot.
pioghaideach, -eiche, *a.* Abounding in magpies. 2 Like a magpie. 3 Garrulous, talkative. 4 **Piebald, pied.

569. *Pioghaid ghas.*

pioghaid ghlas,¶ -e-glaise, -an-g-, *s.f.* The great shrike or butcher-bird, called *buidsear* by MacMhaighstir Alasdair—*lanius excubitor.*
pioghaid thruisg,(AF) *s.f.* Partridge.
piol, *v.* see spiol.
piolachadh, -aidh, see spiolachadh.
piolachair, see spiolachair.
piolachan,** see spiolachan.
piolaich, *v.* see spiolaich.
piolaid, -e, -ean, *s.f.* Pillory. 2 Palace, prince's palace.
piolair,** *s.* Gaelic spelling of *pillar.*
piollach, -aiche, *a.* Fretful. 2 Curious-looking. 3 Neat, trim, tidy. 4** Hairy. see peallach.
piollachas, -ais, *s. m.* Neatness, trimness, tidiness. 2 Hairiness.
piollachd, see piollachas.
piollag, see peallag.
piollair,** *s.m.* Pill.
piollaiste, -an, *s.m.* Trouble, vexation, annoyance.
piollaisteach, -eiche, *a.* Troublesome, vexatious, vexing, annoying, teazing.
pion, Gaelic spelling of *pine.*
pionach,* *a.* Pineal.
pionail, ** *a.* Pineal. An fhàireag ph., *the pineal gland.*
pionamhuil, see pionail.
pionar, *s.* Pionafore. A' faidhmeadh bhann is phionar an àm chur grinnis air ghrèis, *hemming straps and pinafores when doing ornatal sewn work—Filidh, p. 4.*
pionas, see peanas.
pion-chrann, see pin-chrann.
†pionnsarach, ** *a.* Wily, cunning.
†pionnsarachd, *s.f.* Wiliness.

pionsa,** -ai, *s.m.* Artifice, wile.
pioradh,(AH) *s.m.* Fierce gust of wind.
piora-ghruag, -aig, -an, see piorbhuic.
pioraid, -e, -ean, see biorraid. 2**Gaelic spelling of *pirate*. 3**Parrot.
pioraideach, -eiche, *a.* see biorraideach. 2** Piratical. 3**Like a parrot.
pioraruig,†† see piorbhuic.
———each, see piorbhuiceach.
piorbhuic, -e, -ean, *s.f.* Periwig, wig.
piorbhuiceach, -eiche, *a.* Wearing a periwig or wig.
piorr, *pr.pt.* a' piorradh, *v. a.* Scrape, dig. 2 Make a dash at. 3 Pierce. 4 Purr.
piorrabhag, *Uist* for piorbhuic.
piorrabhuic, see piorbhuic.
piorradh, -aidh, *s.m.* Scraping, act of scraping or digging. 2 Dashing at. 3 Stabbing quickly. 4 Piercing. A' p—, *pr. pt.* of piorr.
piorradh, -aidh, -aidhean, *s.m.* Squall, blast. 2 **Pear.
piorraid, *s.f.* Parrot.
pios, -a, -an, *s.m.* Gaelic spelling of *piece*. Piece, morsel, fragment. 2 Patch, bit of cloth. 3 Coin, piece of money.
pios,*v.a.*Gaelic spelling of *piece*. Cut into shreds, tear, lacerate. 2 Patch.
pios, -a, -an, *s.f.* Silver cup. 2**Fowling-piece. 3 (DC) *humorously*, Wag—*Argyll*.
piosach, -aiche, *a.* In pieces, morsels or fragments. 2 In patches, patched. 3 Having silver cups. 4**Splintering.
piosach, -aich, see piseach.
piosadh, -aidh, *s.m.* Patching, act of patching or sewing together 2 Tearing. 3 (DU)Pinching A' p—, *pr pt.* of pios.
piosag, -aig, -an, *s f.* Small bit.
†**piosaga,** *s.f.* Witchcraft.
piosagach, -aiche, *a* Abounding in small bits.
piosan, -ain, -an, *dim* of pios. Small piece or patch. 2 Small coin.
piosanach, -aiche, *a.* In small pieces, abounding in small pieces, fragments or small patches.
piosarnach,** -aich, *s.m.* Whispering.
piosarnachd, *s.f.* Whispering.
†**piosarnaich,** -e, *s.f.* Whispering.
piostal, -ail, -an, *s.m.* Gaelic spelling of ***pistol***.
piostalach, *a.* Having pistols.
piothaid, see pioghaid.
piothann, see pigheann.
piothannach, -aiche, *a.* see pigheannach.
pìreas,(CR) *s.m.* Appearance. Cha robh p. ann, —said of a worthless thing—*W. of Ross*; brad p. bàrr, *a good appearance of crop*; p. de chreutair, *a poor, puny creature, or mere appearance of a creature—Suth'd & W. of Ross.* [The Eng. word (*ap*)*pearance*.]
piridh, -ean, *s.f.* Boy's top. 2 Whirligig. *Scots*, peerie.
pischan, Given in Eng. part of McD & Dewar under *whenever*, evidently meant for piochan.
piseach, -ich, *s. m.* Increase. 2 Good fortune, prosperity, success. 3 Fate. 4 Blessing. 5 Issue, progeny. 6**Avail. 7 (MS) Improvement. 8 (MS) Augmentation. [** gives *s.f.*]
P. air do ph. agus p. ann ad bhroinn! *may you see your offspring's offspring and have a young progeny yourself!* p. ort! *success to you!* am bi p. orra? *will they prosper?* le p. a bhilean sàsuichear e, *by the increase of his lips he shall be filled*; dh' òladh e a pheighinn ph., *he would drink his last penny*; buaidh is p. leat! *success and prosperity be with you!* p. math ort! *I wish you good luck, I wish you a good match!* cha do shaltair neach air a ph., *no one ever prevented his fate.*

piseachail, -e, *a.* Fortunate, prosperous. 2 Prolific.
piseachd, *s f.* Same meanings as piseach.
piseag, -eig, -an, *s.f.*, *dim.* of pios. Patch, clout, rag, fragment of cloth, old or new. P. air toll is e sin an tairbhe, ach p. air piseig 's e sin an lùireach, *a patch on a hole is saving, but a patch upon patch makes a ragged cloak.*
piseag, -eig, -eigean, *s.f.* Kitten, young cat. 2 Sorcery, witchcraft, divination.
piseagach, -aiche, *a.* Having kittens. 2 Like a kitten. 3 Superstitious, like a wizard or sorcerer.
piseagach,** *a.* In rags, in pieces, as cloth. 2 Ragged.
piseagaiche,** *s.m.* Enchanter, wizard. 2 Superstitious person.
pisean,** -ein, *pl.* -ein & -an, *s.m.* Tom-kitten.
†**pisearlach,** -aiche, *a.* Juggling, conjuring. 2 Superstition.
pisearnach, see piosarnach.
pisich,(MS) *v.a.* Increase.
†**pisreag,** -eig, -an, *s.f.* Sorcery. 2 Superstition.
†———ach, *a.* Superstitious.
pit, -e, -ean, *s.f.* Hollow, pit. 2 Prefix in farm and townland names in Pictland, meaning a farm or portion.
piteag, -eig, *s.f.* Effeminate person. 2 (MS) Henpecked man.
piteanta,** *a.* Effeminate. 2 Lascivious, lewd.
———chd,** *s.f.* Effeminacy. 2 Lasciviousness, lewdness.
pithe, see pigheann.
pithean, see pigheann.
pitheannan, *pl.* of pithean (for pigheannan.)
piùg, -iùig, -an, *s.f.* Plaintive note, querulous voice. 2 Sorry, mean appearance.
piùgach, -aiche, *a.* Having a querulous voice. 2 Having a mean or sorry look.
piùirn,(CR)*s.m.* Bobbin, Gaelic spelling of *pirn*.
piùirneach,** *a.* Full of pirns. 2 Of, or relating to a pirn.
piuthair, *dat. & voc.sing.* of piuthar.
piuthar, *gen. s.* peathar, *dat.* piuthair, *voc.* a phiuthair! *pl.* peathraichean, *voc.pl.* a pheathraiche! *s.f.* Sister. 'S i mo ph. i, *she is my sister*; clann do pheathar, *thy sister's children*; ogha peathar is bràthar, *second cousins.*
piuthaireil, see piutharail.
piutharag, see piùthrag.
piutharail, -e, *a.* Sisterly.
piutharalachd, *s.f.* Sisterliness.
piuthar-altrum, peathar-a, peathraichean-a, *s. f.* Foster-sister.
piuthar-athar, peathar-a-, peathraichean-a-, *s.f.* Father's sister, paternal aunt. Piuthar m' athar, *my paternal aunt.*
piuthar-chèile, peathar-ch-, peathraichean-c-, [not -*ch* in *pl.*] *s.f.* Sister-in-law. Mo phiuthar-chèile, *my sister-in-law.*
piuthar-màthar, peathar-m., peathraichean-m., *s.f.* Mother's sister, maternal aunt. Piuthar mo mhàthar, *my maternal aunt.*
piuthar-seanamhar, peathar-s-, peathraicheans-, *s.f.* Grandmother's sister, grand aunt. Piuthar mo sheanamhar, *my grandmother's sister.*
piuthar-seanar, peathar-s-, peathraichean-s-, *s. f.* Grandfather's sister, grand aunt. Piuthar mo sheanar, *my grandfather's sister.*
piùthrag, -aig, -an. *s.f.*, *dim* of piuthar. Little sister. 2 Confidential friend or gossip.
piùthragach,* -aich, *s.m.* Gossiping.
plab, *v.n.* see plub.
plab, -a, -aidhean, *s.m.* see plub. 2 Smut. 3 Fillip. 4 Spot.
——ach, -aiche, *a.* see plubach.
——adaich, see plabartaich.

plabadh,-aidh,-aidhean,*s.m.& pr.pt.*see plubadh.
plabair,** *s m.* Babbler.
plabaireachd, *s.f.* Babbling.
plabardaich, -e, *s.f.* Soft noise, as that caused by the motion of the wings of a bird, flapping.
plabartaich, -e, *s.f.* Continued soft sound, as of water gently beating the shore. 2 Unintelligible talk, rumbling noise in speech. see plubbartaich.
plabraich, -e, *s. f.* Flapping or fluttering noise. Ri p. mu chrann-brataich, *flapping about a flag-staff.*
†plac,** -aic, *s m.* Mouthful.
placaid, -e, -ean, *s.f.* Wooden dish. 2 Close timber vessel. 3* Fat, broad, good-natured female.
placair,** *s.m.* Chubby-faced fellow. 2 Glutton.
placantach,** *a.* Coarse, rough. Gu p., *roughly.*
————d,** *s.f.* Coarseness, roughness.
plàdar,(CR) *s.m.* Circular dish made of plaited straw, used for corn—*Tiree.* 2 Platter.
pladh, -a, see plath.
———ach, -aiche, *a.* see plathach.
———adh, -aidh, see plath.
plagh, see plath.
plaghadh, see plath.
plaibean, -ein, -an, *s.m.* Lump of raw flesh. 2 Fat, plump boy.
†plaic, -e, -ean, *s.f.* Fine, amercement.
plaichead,** *s.* Flagon.
†plaichid, -e, -ead, *s.f.* see plaichead.
plaid, (MS) Await.
plaid, -e, -ean, *s.f.* see plaid-luighe.
plaid,* *v.a.* Drill potatoes. 2 Lay out ground in plots. 3 Plant, as greens or colewort.
plaid,(CR) *s. f,* Said of a person falling his whole length on the ground. Fhuair e p., *and* nach d' fhuair e p.!—*Arran.* [splaid in *Lorn.*]
plaide, *pl.* -an & -achan, *s.f.* Blanket. 2 Plaid, (not tartan-plaid.) 3 Coarse flannel. 4*Plot of ground. Còta plaide, *an under-petticoat of coarse flannel.*
———ach, -eiche, *a.* Having blankets or plaids.
———achan, *pl.* of plaide.
plaideag, -eig, -an, *s.f.* Little blanket or shawl.
————ach, -aiche, *a.* Having small blankets or plaids.
plaide-luighe, *s.f.* Lying in ambush. 2 Ambuscade. Deanamaid plaide-luighe, *let us lie in wait.*
——————ach,** *a.* Lying in wait. 2 Like an ambush. 3 Fond of lying in wait. 4 Skulking, treacherous.
plaidse, see splaidse.
———ach, *a.* see splaidseach.
———adh, see splaidseadh.
plàigh, -e, -ean, *s.f.* Plague, pestilence. 2 Epidemic fever. 3 Troublesome person.
plàigh-choisgeach,** *a.* Antipestilential.
plàigheach, -eiche, *a.* Plaguy, pestiferous, pestilential.
plàighealachd, *s.f.* Plaguiness, contagiousness.
plàigheil, -e, *a.* Pestiferous, pestilential. 2 Contagious. 3 Infectious.
plaigh-sgaoilteach, *s.f.* Spreading plague.
plàigh-shlat,(AF) *s.* Blind *or* slow-worm.
plàigh-uaine,** *s.f.* The yellow fever [With the art. a' ph—.]
plais, *pr.pt.* a' plaiseadh, *v.a.* Splash. 2 Daub with dirt or mire.
plaiseadh, -eidh, *s.m.* Splashing, act of splashing or daubing with mire or dirt.
†plaitean, -ein, *s.m.* Skull. 2 Little head.
plaitse, see splaidse.
plaidseach, see splaidseach.
plam,* *a.* Curdled.
——, -aim, -an, *s.m.* Anything curdled or clotted. 2 Fat blubber cheek.
plamacaidh, *a.* see plamcaidh.
plamach, -aiche, *a.* Curdled, thick. 2 Slimy. 3 Of a dull or pale colour. 4* Fat-cheeked, fair-haired and pale-faced.
plamaic,* *v.a.* Fumble, mix, handle awkwardly.
plamcaidh, -e, *a.* Doughy, flabby.
plamrachadh, -aidh, *s.m.* Warming of milk for curdling. 2 Grumousness. A' p—, *pr. pt.* of plamraich.
plamraich, *pr.pt.* a' plamrachadh, *v. a.* Warm or prepare milk for curdling. 2††Make a soft noise.
planaid, -ean, *s.f.* Gaelic spelling of *planet.*
plancaich,** *v.* Contabulate.
plancaid, -e, -ean, *s.f.* Gaelic spelling of *blanket.*
————each, *a.* Having blankets.
plang, -aing, -an & -annan, *s.m.* Plack (Scots coin) value ⅓d. (2 bodles.) 2**Gaelic spelling of plank. 3 (DMC) Any small coin. also planca.
plangach,** *a.* Having planks. 2 Like a plank. 3 Made of planks.
plangaich,** *v.a.* Provide with planks.
plangaid, -e, -ean, *s.f.* Blanket.
———— -bhàn, *s.f.* White plaiding.
———— -ghorm, *s.f.* Blue plaiding.
plangaidich, (MS) *v.a.* Blanket.
planuda, -n & -ichean, see plannta.
————chadh, see planntachadh.
plannt, see planntaich.
plannt,-a & plainnt, -aichean, *s.m.* Plant.
planntachadh, -aidh, *s. m.* Planting, act of planting. 2 Plantation. A' p—, *pr. pt.* of planntaich.
planntachair,** -ean, *s.m.* Planter.
planntaich, *pr.pt.* a' planntachadh, *v.a.* Plant. Settle or establish a colony.
————te, *past pt.* Planted.
planntaig, see planntaich.
————eadh, see planntachadh.
planntair, -ean, *s.m.* Planter.
————eachd, *s.f.* Occupation of planting. 2 Business of a planter.
planntan, *s.m.* Set.
planntar,* -air, *s.m.* Choice corn for seed. 2 Choice quality of oats.
plaoisg, *v.a.* see plaosg. 2**Appear.
————ean, -ein, -an, *s.m. dim.* of plaosg. Small or thin husk.
————eanach, -aiche, *a.* Having a thin husk.
plaosg, *pr.pt.* a' plaosgadh, *v.a. & n.* Peel, skin. 2 Awake, open the eyes. 4 Open, burst, uncover, disclose. 2 Burst, as from the husk. 5 Make a noise or sound.
plaosg, -aoisg, -an, *s.m.* Husk, shell. 2 Outer peel or skin of a vegetable. 3 Shell of an egg. 4 Glimmer, glimpse. 5 Opening of the eyes from sleep. 6 Sound, sudden noise. Cnòthan a's taine p., *the thinnest shelled nuts;* gus am p., *to the husk;* p.-buntàta, *a potato skin.*
———ach, -aiche, *a.* Husky, shelly. 2 Peeling, that peels or skins. 3 Having a rind. 4 Uncovering. 5 Glimmering. 6 Making a noise or sudden sound, noisy. 7* Capsular.
———achd, *s.f.* Crustiness.
plaosgadh, -aidh, *s.m.* Peeling, act of peeling or skinning, taking off the husk or shell. 2 Awaking, act of awaking or opening the eyes. 3 Bursting, act of bursting, as from the husk. 4 Act of making a noise. 5 Sudden noise. 6 Glimmering light, flash, blaze. 7** Appearing, discovering of one's self. A' p—, *pr. pt.* of plaosg.
plaosgaid,* -e, -ean, *s.f.* Soft, stupid woman.
plaosgair,*-ean, *s.m.* Soft, stupid fellow, dullard.
plap, (DMC) *s.m.* Flapping of the wings of a

bird. 2 Sudden " leap " of the heart through fright.
plap(DMC) *pr. pt.* a' plapail, *v.* Flutter with the wings.
——ail, -e, *s.f.* Fluttering with the wings. A' p—, *pr.pt.* of plap.
plapadh,(MS) *s.m.* Anhelation.
plapraich, -e, see plabraich.
plàsd, -a, *pl.* -an & -aidhean, *s.m.* Plaster. 2 Daub. 3* Poultice.
plàsd, *v.a.* Plaster, daub, cover with lime or other substance. 2* Spread awkwardly.
†plàsda,** *a.* Feigned.
plàsdach, -aiche, *a.* Plastering, that plasters. 2 Having plasters. 3 Using plasters. 4 Like a plaster. 5 Daubing.
————,** *s.m.* Plaster.
————adh, -aidh, *s.m. & pr.pt.* see plàsdaich.
————d,** *s.f.* Plastering, daubing or smearing, covering with lime or clay.
plàsdadh, -aidh, *s.m.* Plastering, act of plastering, smearing or daubing. A' p—, *pr. pt.* of plàsd.
plàsdaich, *v.a.* see plàsd.
————te, *past pt.* Plastered, daubed.
plàsdaidhean, *pl.* of plàsd.
plàsdair, -ean, *s.m.* Plasterer.
————eachd, *s.f.* Business or occupation of a plasterer. 2 Work performed by a plasterer. 3**Smearing, daubing.
plàsdrachadh, -aidh, *s.m. & pr.pt.* see plàsdadh.
plàsdradh, see plàsdadh.
plàsdraich, *v.a.* see plàsd.
plàsdraichte, see plàsdaichte.
plàsdrail,** *s.f.* Plastering, besmearing.
plàt,(CR) *s m.* Corn bag made of plaits of straw.
plàt, -a, *pl.* -an, -achan & -aichean, *s. m.* Kind of cloth made of straw or rushes. 2(MS) Sack. 3 Plaid of straw or rushes. 4 (DMy) Mat on which sheep are killed. 5 (MMcL) Any heavy covering. Tilg a' ph. sin thairis air, *throw that covering over him* ; p.-eich, *straw-cloth of a pack-saddle* ; p.-fhasgnaidh, *straw-cloth on which corn is winnowed.*
†plàt, -a, *s.m.* Gaelic spelling of *plate.*
plàt,* *v.a.* Thrust in, clap upon. Ph. e a làmh air, *he clapped his hand on it.*
plàtach,(CR) *s.m.* Mat of plaited straw for putting on a horse's back under the crook saddle—*W. of Ross-shire.*
plàtaichean, *pl.* of plàt.
plàtan, -ain, -an, see plàt.
plath, -a, -an, see plathadh.
plath, * *v.a.* Puff, blow upon. 2 Flash. 3(DC) Momentary glance.
——ach, -aiche, *a.* Glancing, twinkling, momentary, transient. 2 Flashing, shining suddenly. 3 In clouds or volumes, as smoke. 4 Gusty, in gusts or squalls, as wind.
plathadh, -aidh, *s.m.* Glance, twinkling of the eye. 2 Instant of time, moment. 3 Beam of light, flash. 4 Volume as of smoke. 5 Gust of wind. 6 Swoon. 7** Momentary appearance of anything, as of lightning. 8 Meteor. 9* Puff of wind. 10**Sudden gloom. 11†† Volume of flame or wind.
A' p—,*pr. pt.* of plath. Thàinig p. oirnn,*a puff came on us* ; am p., *in a moment* ; fhuair sinn p. dheth, *we had a glimpse of it* ; a' p. m' ar n-aodann, *puffing about our faces* ; a' ghrian fo ph., *the sun under a sudden gloom* ; mar ph. dealanaich, *like a flash of lightning.*
plathag,(MS) *s.f.* Squall of wind.
plathaich,(MS) *v.a.* Glance.
plathaigeach, *a.* Windy.
pleachd,(CR) *s.f.* Roll of wool ready for spinning—*W. of Ross-shire.*
pleadh,** -a, *s.m.* Digging, dibbling, spudding.
——ach, *a.* Digging or dibbling. 2 Made for digging or dibbling.
————ag, -aig, -an, *s.f.* Dibble, paddle.
————agach, -aiche, *a.* Working with, or using a paddle or dibble. 2 Of, or belonging to, paddles or dibbles. 3 Like a paddle or dibble.
———agachadh, see pleadhagaich.
pleadhagaich, *s.f.* Act of using a paddle or dibble, paddling, dibbling. A' p—, *pr. pt.* of pleadhagaich.
pleadhagaich, *v.a.*Dig or work with a paddle or dibble.
pleadhagaichte, *pr.pt.* of pleadhagaich.
pleadhaich, see pleadhagaich.
————te, see pleadhagaichte.
pleadhain, *gen.sing. & n.pl.* of pleadhan.
pleadhair, -ean, *s.m.* Dibbler, one who uses a dibble.
pleadhairt,* -e, -ean, *s.f.* Importunate petition.
pleadhan,†† *a.* Paddling. 2 Trifling.
————, -ain, -an, *s.m.* Little oar, scull. 2** Paddle, dibble. 3††Small leg. 4 (CR) Spattle for turning bread—*W. of Ross-shire.*
pleadhanach, -aiche, *a.* Having a little oar, oars, or paddles. 2 Trifling. 3 Given to trifling pursuits. 4 see pleadhagach.
————d, *s. f. ind.* Paddling or sculling with a little oar. 2**Digging, dibbling. 3 Trifling, pursuing of silly or trifling things.
pleadhan-teannachaidh,* *s.m.* Busk.
pleadhart, -airt, -an, *s.m.* Buffet, blow or slap on the cheek.
pleadhartach, -aiche, *a.* Buffeting, dealing blows.
pleaghag, see pleadhag.
pleaghan, -ain, -an, see pleadhan.
pleanais,** *s.f.* Species of coarse linen.
pleasg, -a, -an, *s.m.* Noise, crack. 2 Loud blow. 3 String of beads. [*gen.s. & n.pl.* plisg—DU.]
pleasg, *s.a.* Crack, burst, break.
pleasgach, -aiche, *a.* Cracking, noisy, making a noise, thumping, crashing. 2 Ready to crack, burst or break.
pleasgadh, -aidh, *s.m.* Cracking, act of cracking, bursting. 2 Crashing noise. A' p—, *pr. pt.* of pleasg.
pleasganach, -aiche, *a.* That cracketh or breaketh. 2 That striketh. 3 Noisy, striking, crashing, bursting.
pleat, Gaelic spelling of *plait.*
pleat,* *v.a.* Plait, fold. 2 Patch, mend. 3** Wreathe, braid. 4 Seam. 5 Tress.
pleata,* *s. m.* Patch ,piece.
pleatach,(AC) *a.* Flat, broad, even. 2 Wreathed. 3 Plaited, folded, doubled. Casan p., *broad feet, flat feet, as in a flat-footed person* ; falt p., *braided hair.*
pleatadh,(DMC) *s.m.* Folding. 2 Seaming.
pleath, *pr.pt.* a' pleathainn, *v. n.* Beg a thing to be paid for.
pleathainn, *s.f.* Act of begging a thing you are to pay for. A' p—, *pr.pt.* of pleath.
pleid, see bleid.
pleidear, see bleidir. 2 (DMC) Beggar.
pleideil, see bleideil.
pleideir,* *v.n.* Plead, beg importunately or incessantly.
pleigh,‡ *s.f.* Quarrel, fight.
————,(CR) *v.a.* Fight—*Perthshire.*
pleisg,**v.a.* Revile or abuse with all your might.
pleisgeadh,* *s.m.* Reviling. 2 Scolding in a cold sarcastic manner. A' p—, *pr.pt.* of pleisg.
pleiste,** *s.* Testicle.
pleod,* *v.a.* Warm slightly, as milk.
pleodag,* -aig, -an, *s.f.* Soft, simple female. 2 Snow-flake—*Uist.*

pleòdar,** *s.m.* Harum-scarum. 2 Soft, spiritless fellow. 3 see feòdar.
———ach, see feòdarach.
———air, see feòdarair.
pleodhaisg, see pleòisg.
pleòisg, -e, -ean, *s. m. & f.* Simpleton, booby, bumpkin.
pleòisgeach, -eiche, *a.* Booby-like, silly, foolish.
pleòisgeag, -eig, -an, *s. f.* Foolish, silly, stupid woman.
pleòisgealachd, *s.f.ind.* Stupidity, silliness
pleòisgean, -ein, *s.m.* Doltish, stupid boy.
pleòisgeil, -e, *a.* Doltish, sottish, stupid.
pliacais,(DJM) *s.* Edible dog-fish.
pliad, -a, -an, *s.m.* Plot of ground. *prov.*
pliadach,(AC) *a.* see pleatach.
pliadan, -ain, -an, *s. m., dim.* of pliad. Little plot of ground.
pliadanach, -aiche, *a.* Abounding in little plots of ground.
pliadh, -a, -an, *s.f.* Splay-foot. 2 Bandy-leg.
pliadh,** *v.n.* Swagger.
pliadhach, -aiche, *a.* Splay-footed. 2 Bandy-legged—*Sàr-Obair.*
———,* -aiche, *s.f.* Splay-footed female.
pliadhaiche, *s.f.ind.* Splay-footedness.
pliadhair,* -ean, *s.m.* Splay-footed or bandy-legged man.
pliarain, -aim, *s.m.* Babbling. *prov.*
pliaramach, -aiche, *a.* Babbling. *prov.*
pliath-rod,** -roid, *s.m.* Slipper.
pliathroid, see pliath-rod.
plibean,** -ein, *s.m.* Plover.
pliobair, *s.m.* Flunkey, worthless fellow. 2(DC) Mean fellow—*Lismore.* Gille pliobair, *an underling.*
pliodair,* *v.* see pliotair.
plioghtaire, see pliotair.
plionas, -ais, *s.m.* Hypocritical smile—*Argyll.*
pliotair, -ean, *s.m.* Fawner, sycophant, mean cringing fellow, cajoler, flunkey.
pliotair, *pr.pt.* a' pliotairt, *v.n.* Cajole, seduce by flattery.
pliotaireachd, *s.f.* Cringing, mean flattery.
pliotairt,* *s.f.* Cajoling, caressing, as a child. A' p—, *pr.pt.* of pliotair.
pliut, -a, -an, *s.m.* Clumsy foot or paw. 2 (D MC) *in derision,* Hand or foot.
pliutach, -aiche, *a.* Clumsy-footed, broad-pawed. 2 (AH) Clumsy and benumbed through exposure to cold—applied to the fingers.
———,* *s.f.* Clumsy-footed or splay-footed female.
pliutach, -aich, *s.m.* Seal, sea-calf. *prov.*
pliutaiche, *s.f.ind.* Baker-foot.
pliutair, -ean, *s.m.* Clumsy-footed person.
pliutaireachd, *s.f.ind.* Clumsiness of feet. 2 Clumsy walking.
plobht,(CR) *s.m.* Plump of rain. 2 Sound of anything falling into water—*Perthshire. Scots,* plout. 3 (DC) Shoal of herring. B' e 'n seaÌladh e, 's cha b' e plobht dubh an sgadain! *that was the sight and not the mean shoal of herring!*
ploc, pluic, -an, *s.m.* Any round mass. 2 Piece of earth, large turf, large clod. 3 Club or bludgeon with a round or large head. 4 Head of a pin. 5 Block of wood. 6 Short stump of a tree. 7 Bung, stopper. 8 Block, pulley. 9 Round head. 10 Hump, hunch. 11 Chump. 12 Cheek. 13 Potato-masher. 14 Lumpish promontory. 15**Blockhead. 16 Block-headed stick. 17 Block-headed instrument.
P.-chul-teallaich, *a block of wood placed at the back of the fire.*
ploc, *v.a.* Strike with a club, block, clod or pestle. 2 Strike on the head. 3 Bruise, pound. 4 Ram against. 5 Mash, as potatoes, greens, &c.
plocach,* *s.m.* Boy, lad.
plocach, -aiche, *a.* Abounding in pieces of earth, turf or clods. 2 Abounding in blocks of wood. 3 Like a block. 4 Having a large head or end like a club or bludgeon. 5 Having clubs or bludgeons. 6 Having blocks or pulleys. 7 Humped. 8 Sturdy, stout. 9 Having large or swollen cheeks. 10 **Turgid. 11**Full-faced. An galar p., *the quinsy, mumps.*
plocadh, -aidh, *s.m.* Striking. 2 Act of striking with a block or pestle. 3 Striking on the head. 4 Bruising, act of bruising, pounding or mashing. A' p—, *pr.pt.* of ploc. A' p. a' bhuntàta, *mashing the potatoes.*
plocag, -aig, -an, *s.f.* Corpulent little woman. *prov.*
plocagach, *a.* Thick-set.
plocaich,** *v.a.* Bung.
plocaidh, *fut.aff.a.* of ploc. Shall or will bruise, &c.
plocaidh, *gen.sing.* of plocadh.
plocair,** *s.m.* Haggler.
plocaireachd,** *s.f.* Haggling.
ploc-a'-mhàis, *s.m.* Buttock.
plocan, -ain, -an, *s.m., dim.* of ploc. Wooden hammer, mallet. 2 Little clod or block. 3 see blocan. 4 Potato-masher. 5 Policeman's baton. P. a' bhàis, *the hammer of death;* p. a' bhuntàta, *the potato-masher—West coast of Ross.*
plocanach, -aiche, *a.* Abounding in small clods. 2 Furnished with mallets or wooden hammers. 3 Furnished with small blocks or pulleys.
plocan-bhuntàta, *s.m.* Potato-masher.
plocanta, -ainte, *a.* Stout, sturdy. 2 Having full or swollen cheeks. 3 Lumpish. 4 Round-headed. 5 Full-faced. 6 Blockish.
plocantachd, *s.f.ind.* Stoutness, sturdiness. 2 Swelling of the cheek. 3 Fullness of visage. 4 Lumpishness, blockishness, doltishness.
ploc-cheannach, *a.* Beetle-headed.
ploc-dubh, see dòrdalan.
ploc-lomaidh,‡‡ *s.v.* Block of wood, hollowed out and furnished with a ponderous wooden pestle, having a handle inserted towards its upper extremity, at right angles, which is used for hulling barley, or pounding bark for tanning.
ploc-mhalach,** *a.* Beetle-browed.
ploc-mhaildheach,** see ploc-mhalach.
plod, -a & -uid, *pl.* -an, *s.m.* Clod. 2 Pool, standing water. 3 Carnage. 4 Damage. 5 Fleet of shipping, especially herring-boats. P. mór loingeis, *a large fleet of vessels;* is iad a rinn am p.! *what carnage they have made!* [** gives both 2 & 5 as †, with *gen.sing.* -oid,]
plod, *v.a.* Pelt or strike with a clod or clods. 2 Scald, parboil. 3 (CR) Remove clods from turnip-land. †4 Float, cause to float. A' plodadh na muice, *scalding the pig.*
plodach, -aich, -aichean, *s.m.* Puddle, mire. 2 ††Lair for burial.
plodach, -aich, *a.* Abounding in clods.
plodach, -aiche, *a.* Lukewarm. 2 Parboiling, that parboils. 3 Parboiled. 4 Scalding. 5 Buoyant, floating, like, or belonging to, a float. Uisge p., *lukewarm water.*
plodachadh,** *s.m.* Floating, buoyancy.
plodachd,** *s.f.ind.* Lukewarmness.
plodadh, -aidh, *s.m.* Striking, act of striking or pelting with clods. 2 Act of parboiling. 3 Scalding, scald. 4 **Buoyancy. 5 **Float. 6 Removing clods from turnip-land.—*Skye.* 7**Fleet. 8 (AH) Jettisoning. A' p—, *pr. pt.* of plod.

plodag, -aig, -an, *s.f.* Water gruel, warm posset. Deoch phlodaig, *a drink of gruel.*
plodaich, *v.a.* see plod.
plodaiche, *s.f.ind.* Lukewarmness. 2 State of being parboiled.
plodaireachd,** *s.f.ind.* Buoyancy.
plodan, -ain, -an, *s. m.*, *dim.* of plod. Small clod. 2 Small pool. 3**Small float. 4 Small boat of a smack, see p. 78.
plodanach, -aiche, *a.* Abounding in little clods, or 2 in little pools.
plodanachd, *s.f.ind.* Paddling in water. 2 Floating. 3 **Guddling.
plodanaiche,** *s.m.* Dabbler.
plodar, see plodmhor.
plod-fhèath,(AH) *s.* Dead calm. [fèath-gheal.]
plodh,* *s.m.ind.* Anything put temporarily together. 2 Sick person that dies on getting the least cold or injury. 3 Man or anything hardly hanging together.
plodhaisg, see pleòisg.
plodhaisgeach, see pleòisgeach.
plodhaisgeachd, see pleòisgealachd.
plodhaisgeag, see pleòisgeag.
plodhaisgean, see pleòisgean.
plodhaman,* see pleòisg.
plodmhor,** *a.* Buoyant, floating.
plodraich, -e, *s.f.* State of becoming stagnant. 2*Carnage. 3 Havoc. 4* State of lying here and there uncared for.
ploic,‡ -e, -ean, *s.f.* The mumps [with the art. a' ph—.]
ploiceach, -eiche, *a.* Having the mumps. 2 Plump-cheeked.
ploiceag, -eig, -an, *s.f.* Plump-cheeked woman.
ploicean, -ein, -an, *s.m.* Plump-cheeked boy.
ploiceanach, -aiche,†† *a.* Plump-cheeked.
ploiceanach, -aich, *s.m.* see ploicean.
ploichd, see ploic.
ploichdeach, see ploiceach.
ploide, see plaide.
ploideag, *s.f.* Good-natured female. 2* Shawl.
ploidhisg, see pleòisg.
ploidhisgeach, see pleòisgeach.
ploidhisgeag, see pleòisgeag.
ploidhisgean, see pleòisgean.
plòiseach,(DMK) *s. m.* Portion of anything, as of a piece of cloth—*Caithness.*
ploisg, see plosg.
plòigh, Gaelic spelling of *Scots* ploy.
†**ploisg**, -e, *a.* Spongy. 2 Elastic. 3**Inflammable. 4 Quick. 5**Dry.
ploiteach,* -eiche, *a.* Downy.
ploiteag, (DC) *s.f.* Earthworm—*Uist.*
plòitean,(MMcL) *s.m.* Downy peat.
plosg,** *a.* Quick.
plosg, *pr.pt.* a' plosgadh, a' plosgail & a' plosgartaich, *v.n.* Palpitate, throb, start, pant, gasp. 2 Sigh, sob. A chridh' a' plosgail, *his heart palpitating.*
plosg, -oisg, -an, see plosgadh. Gun ph. air dèile, *lifeless on the bier.*
plosgach,** *a.* Panting, throbbing, gasping. 2 Causing to pant or throb. 3 Like a pant or sob. 4 Quick. 5 Bold.
plosgadh, -aidh, -aidhean, *s. m.* Palpitation, quick motion of the heart. 2 Start, throb, throbbing of the heart. 3 Sigh. 4 Loud sound or noise. 5 Life, breath. 6 Aspiration. A' *pr.pt.* of plosg. Gun ph. air dèile, *without a gasp on the stretching board.*
plosgail, *s.f. & pr.pt.* of plosg, see plosgadh.
plosgarnach,** *a.* Quick, bold. 2 Panting.
plosgarnaich,** *s.f.* Panting.
plosgair,(MS) *v.* Blow.
plosgartach, -aiche, *a.* Breathless, panting. 2 Throbbing. 3 Quick. 4 Bold. 5 Open.
plosgartachd,** *s.f.* Panting, gasping, throbbing.
plosgartaich,** *v.n.* see plosg.
plosgartaich, *pr. pt.* of plosg & **plosgartaich, see plosgadh.
plosgat,§ -ait, *s. m.* Corn-marigold, see bile-bhuidhe.
plot, see plod.
plotadh, see plotadh & plutadh.
plub, *pr.pt.* a' plubadh & a' plubairt, *v.n.* Plump, fall suddenly into water. 2 Emit a noise, as of liquor in a cask, or of porridge boiling. 3 Speak inarticulately and rapidly.
plub, -uib & -a, -an, *s.m.* Any great and soft unwieldy lump. 2 Sudden plunge. 3 Sound as of a stone falling into water. 4 Noise of liquor when moved in a cask not quite full. 5 Noise of porridge boiling. 6 Clumsy, lubberly person 7**Round-head, jolt-head. 8** Brain-pan. P. chadail, *a moment's sleep.*
plubach, -aiche, *a.* Sounding as liquor moved in a half-filled cask. 2 Sounding as a stone falling into water. 3 Speaking indistinctly and rapidly 4* Soft and clumsy. 5††Plunging. 7 **Round headed, jolt headed.
plubach,* -aiche, *s.f.* Soft, lubberly female.
plubadh, -aidh, *s.m.* Act of falling suddenly into water. 2 Act of sounding, as agitated liquor in a half-filled cask. 3 Act of speaking indistinctly and rapidly. A' p—, *pr. pt.* of plub.
plubadaich, -e, *s.f.* see plubadh.
plubaiche, *s.f.ind.* Lumpishness, clumsiness 2 Habit of speaking indistinctly and rapidly.
plubair, -ean, *s.m.* Booby. 2 One who speaks indistinctly and rapidly. 3 Lubber 4**Jolt-headed fellow. 5 Chubby-faced fellow.
———**eachd**, *s.f.ind.* see plubraich.
———**neach**, -ich, see plubair.
———**sin**, -ean, *s.m.* Marsh-marigold.
plubairt, *s.f. & pr.pt.* see plubadh
plubais,** *s.f.* Paddling. 2 Paddling noise. 3 Gurgling noise.
plubartaich, see plubraich.
plub-cheann, -chinn, *s.m.* Lumpish head.
———**ach**, -aiche, *a.* Lump-headed. 2 Dull, stupid.
plubrach, -aiche, *a.* Making a plumping noise. 2 Gurgling, guggling 3 Paddling or playing in the water. 4 Floundering.
plubraich, -e, *s.f.* Continued noise as of stones falling into water. 2 Paddling in water 3 Continued noise of agitated water. 4 Gurgling, guggling. 5 Speaking indistinctly, 6 Plunging, floundering P. nan tonn, *the gurgling of the waves;* na bric ri p., *the trout floundering.*
pluc, -uic & -a, -an, *s.m.* Lump. 2 Knot. 3 Bunch. 4 Tumour. 5 Pimple. 6 Bung. 7 The rot in sheep. 8 Head of a pin. 9 see a' phloic. 10**Hunch P.-mhaildeach, *beetle-browed.*
pluc, *pr.pt.* a' plucadh, *v.a.* Blow, puff out. 2 Stop with a bung. 3 Knot. 4 Make bunchy.
plùc, *pr.pt.* a' plùcadh, *v.a. & n.* Beat, thump. 2 Pelt. 3* Jumble. 4††Pluck.
plucach, -aiche, *a.* Lumpy, knotty. 2 Bunchy. 3 Full of tumours or pimples. 4 Having the mumps. 5 Having the rot, as sheep. 6*Jumbling. 7**Chubby. 8**Hunchy. Sròn ph., *a pimply nose;* an galar p., *the quinsy, 2 rot in sheep.*
plucadh, -aidh, *s.m.* Blowing of the cheeks. 2 State of becoming knotty or bunchy. 3 Act of bunging, or stopping with a bung. A' p—, *pr.pt.* of pluc.
plùcadh, -aidh, *s.m.* Beating, act of beating or thumping. 2 Pelting. A' p—, *pr.pt.* of plùc.

plucaich, *v.a.* Plug.
————e, *s.f.ind.* Lumpishness, bunchiness. 2 Knottiness.
plucair, -ean, *s.m.* Person having a swollen or pimpled face. 2††Beater, thumper. 3 Chubby faced fellow.
————eachd,** *s f.* Chubbiness. 2 Impertinence.
plucais,** *s.f.* Flux.
plucan, *n.pl.* of pluc.
———, -ain, [*pl*- -ain & -an,] *s.m.*, *dim.* of pluc. Little lump 2 Little knot or bunch. 3 Little tumour or pimple. 4 Small bung. 5* Little jumble of sea.
———ach, -aiche, *a.* Abounding in little lumps, knots or bunches. 2 Abounding in little tumours or pimples. 3* With a little jumbling of sea.
pluc-aodach,** *s.* Baize
plucas, -ais, *s.m.* Diarrhœa.
———ach -aiche, *a.* Affected with diarrhœa. 2 Causing diarrhœa.
plùch, *v.a.* Press, squeeze slowly and tightly, compress. 2 Smother. 3**Throng. 4**Mouth when eating. 5**Constringe.
plùchadh -aidh. *s.m.* Squeezing, act of squeezing, compressing. *squeezing slowly and lastly tightly. 2 Smothering. 3**Thronging. 4 **Mouthing in time of eating. A' p—, *pr.pt.* of plùch. [plùchdadh in *Gairloch*—DU.]
pluc-mhailgheach, -eiche, *a* Beetle-browed.
pluic, -e, -ean, *s.f* The cheek. 2 Blub-cheek. 3 *pl.* of ploc. 4 Beard. Loisg iad air a chéile leis na pluic, *they fought (fired on) each other with turfs* ; tha a' bhreug 'nad ph., *thou liest —lit.* the lie is in thy cheek ; do phluicean mar na caoran; *thy cheeks like the rowan-berry.*
———each, -eiche, *a.* Blub-cheeked, chubby-cheeked, having large cheeks.
———each, -eich, *s.m.* Blub-cheeked person.
———each, -ich, *s.f.* The toothache. [With the art. *a' ph*—.]
pluicean, -ein, -an, *s.m.*, *dim.* of pluic. Little round cheek. 2 (AF) Chub (fish.)
————ach, -aiche. *a* Having little round cheeks.
————ach. -aich, *s.m.* Blub-cheeked person.
pluideach, -eiche, *a.* Club-footed, splay-footed.
pluideiche, *s.f.ind.* Distortion of the feet.
pluidse,* *s.m.* Big lumpish man or beast.
————ach,* -eiche, *s.f.* Clumsy, awkward female, lumpish female.
pluinnse. *s.f.* Swash. Gaelic spelling of *plunge.*
————ach,** *a.* Plunging.
————ag,(DMy) *s f* Large coarse apron.
pluirean. -ein -an. *s.m.* Flower
————ach, -aiche, *a.* Flowery.
pluit,* *s.f.* Claw.
plùm, -ùim, *s.m.* One who sits stock-still. 2* Dead calm. 3†† Anything that stands stock still. 4* Hum-drum.
plum, *pr.pt.* a' plumadh, *v.n.* Plunge, sink under water, as lead.
pluma. *s.m* Plummet
plumach,(DU) *a.* Black and deep. Lochan p. MhicLeoid.—the name of a small deep lake on the south side of Loch Ewe.
plumadh, -aidh, *s.m.* Act of falling or plunging into water. 2 Plunge, dash. A' p—, *pr pt.* of plum.
plumag, *s.f.* see pluma. 2 (DU) Little deep pool.
plumaich,* *v. n.* Coagulate without yeast, as milk. 2 Stagnate.
—————te, *a.* Curdled. Bainne p., *curdled milk.*
plumaid,(CR) *s.f.* Gaelic spelling of *plummet.*
2 Plump female. Nach b' e a' ph. i ! *how plump she is !*
plumanaich, -e, *s. f.* Continued noise, as of stones falling into water. 2 Dashing. Noise of waves. 4**Plunging. 5 (DU) Darkening. Anns a' ph., *in the darkening or late twilight.*
plumastair,(AH) *s.m.* Dull, sullen, dour man.
plumb, -a, -an, *s.m.* Plunge. 2 Noise of any substance falling into water.
plumb, *v.* see plum.
——,* *s.f.* Heavy shower.
plumba, -idhean, *s.m.* Plummet.
plumbach, -aiche, *a.* Making a noise in the water.
plumbadh, -aidh, *s.m.* & *pr.pt.* see plumadh.
plumbais, -e, -ean, *s.f.* Plum. P. sheargta, *a prune.*
———— -fhiadhain,§ *s.f.* Wild plum—*prunus domesticus.*
————each, -eiche, *a.* Full of plums.
———— -sheargta, *s.f.* Prune.
plumbas, see plumbais.
————ach, see plumbaiseach.
plundrainn, -e, -ean, *s.f.* Pillage, spoil. Gaelic spelling of *plundering.*
—————, *v.a.* Plunder, pillage, spoil.
plùr, -ùir, *s.m.* see flùr. 2**Nosegay. 3 Flour.
plùrach, -aiche, see flùrach.
plùran, see flùran.
———ach, see flùranach.
———achd, see flùranachd.
plùranaiche, see flùranaiche.
plùran-cluigeanach, see flùran-cluigeanach (in appendix.)
plùr-an-lochain, see flùr-an-lochain (appendix.)
plùran-seangain, see flùran-seangain (appendix.)
plùr-na-cubhaig, see flùr-na-cubhaig (appendix.)
plùr-na-gaoithe, see flùr-na-gaoithe (appendix.)
plùr-na-gréine, see flùr-na-gréine (appendix.)
plutadh, -aidh, -aidhean, *s.m.* Breaking down. 2‡ Falling down, as of rain.
pnàmh, see pràmh.
pobal, [** for pubull] see gallan-mór.
†pobhlar, -air, -an, *s.m.* Poplar-tree.
pobhnaidh, see pònaidh. Gaelic spelling of Scots *pownie.*
pobhuilleach,** *a.* Abounding in, or belonging to, poplar.
†pobhull, -uill, -an, *s.m.* see pobhlar.
pobull, -uill, -an, *s.m.* People. 2 Tribe. 3 Congregation. 4 Nation.
———ach, -aiche, *a.* Laical. 2 Populous. 3 Of, or belonging to, the people. Dùthaich ph., *a populous country.*
———achd,** *s.f.ind.* Populousness.
poc,‖ *s.m.* The mumps. [With the art. *am.*] 2 (DMK) Disease in cattle—*Caithness.*
poc, *pr.pt.* a' pocadh, *v.a.* & *n.* Put into a bag or sack. 2 Become like a bag or sack. also pocaich
pòc, *pr.pt.* a' pòcadh, *v.a.* & *n.* Put into a pocket. 2 Furnish with pockets. also pòcaich.
poca, -n & -nnan, *s.m.* Bag, little sack, satchel. 2 (DMy)Blister. P.-saic, *a large sack thrown across a horse's back, and large enough to contain a load* ; air a' ph., *begging.*
pòca, -n, -nnan, *s. m.* Pocket. 2 Small bag. Leabhar-pòca, *a pocket-book*; airgiod pòca, *pocket-money.*
poca-buidhe,(CR) *s.m.* Deer's stomach—*West of Ross-shire & Suth'd.*
pòcach, -aiche, *a.* Having pockets. 2 Like a pocket. 3 Having large pockets or pouches.
pocach, -aiche, *a.* Having bags. 2 Abounding in bags. 3 Like a bag. 4 Bagged.
pocachadh, -aidh, *s. m.* Act of putting into a

bag. 2 State of becoming like a bag, bagging· A' p—, *pr.pt.* of pocaich.
pòcachadh, -aidh, *s.m.* Pocketing, act of pocketing. 2 Act of furnishing with pockets. A' p—, *pr.pt.* of pòcaich.
pòcachan, -ain, -an, *s.m.*, *dim.* of pòca. Little pocket.
pocaich, *pr.pt.* a' pocachadh, *v.a. & n.* Put into a bag or sack.
pòcaich, *pr.pt.* a' pòcachadh, *v.a. & n.* Put into a pocket. 2 Furnish with pockets. Ith do leòir 's na p. mìr, *eat as much as you like but pocket nothing*—said to boys going to a party.
pòcaid, -e, -ean, *s.f.* see pòca.
———**each**, -eiche, *a.* see pòcach.
———**ich**, *v.a.* Pocket.
pocain, *gen.sing. & n.pl.* of pocan.
pòcair,** *s.m.* Beggar.
pòcait, see pòcaid.
pocan, -ain, -an, *s.m.*, *dim.* of poc. Little bag or sack. 2* Little squat fellow. 3 *in derision*, Impudent little fellow.
pòcan,†† -ain, -an, *s. m.*, *dim.* of pòca. Little pocket.
———**ach**,†† -aiche, *a.* Abounding in little pockets.
pocanach, -aiche, *a.* Having little bags. 2 Like a little bag. 3 Impudent, ill-bred. 4**Squat, diminutive in person. Is fhèarr màthair ph. na athair claidheamhach, *better is a mother with a bag (full of victuals) than a father with a sword by his side.*
pocanan, *pl.* of pocan.
pòcanan, *pl.* of pòcan.
pocan-garbh,(CR) *s.m.* Sea-urchin—*Gairloch.*
pocan-na-buidseachd, (DMK) *s. m.* Small bag containing odds and ends used by witches in the practice of their vocation.
poca-puinsein, *s.m.* Spider.—*Ballachulish, Benderloch, &c.*
pocanta, -ainte, *a.* Like a bag or little bag. 2 Squat, thick and short in stature, stumpy, diminutive.
pocantachd, *s.f.ind.* Squatness, thickness and shortness of stature, stumpiness.
poca-salainn,(CR) *s.m.* Large grey spider found in the open air. It has white legs which are shorter than those of the "damhan-alluidh." In some places every kind of spider is called *poca-salainn*, the term *damhan-alluidh* being considered quite bookish.
pochd, see poc.
pòg, -òig, -an, *s.f.* Kiss.
pòg, *pr.pt.* a' pògadh, *v.a.* Kiss. P. mi, *kiss me.*
pògach, -aiche, *a.* Kissing. 2 Given to kissing.
———,* *s.f.* Blandishing female. 2 Offerer of kisses.
pògadh, -aidh, *s.m.* Kissing, act of kissing, kiss. A' p—, *pr.pt.* of pòg.
pògaidh, *fut.aff.a.* of pòg. Shall kiss.
pògair, -ean, *s.m.* Kisser, one who kisses. 2 Gallant.
———**eachd**, *s.f.ind.* Kissing, frequent kissing, continual kissing.
pògan, see pòigean.
pòganta, -ainte, *a.* see pògach. 2 Fond of kissing.
———**chd**, see pògaireachd.
pògarsaich,** *s.* Kissing.
pògh-lìn,(MS) (am) *s.m.* Gaelic spelling of *bowline.*
pògta, see pògte.
pògte, *past pt.* Kissed.
poibleach, -ich & -a, -an, *s.m.* Tribe, people, nation. 2 The common people, mob, populace. 3 Plebeian. 4* Commonwealth.
———**—**, *pl.* of pobull.
poibleach, -eiche, *a.* Popular. 2**Plebeian, of the populace. 3 Like a rabble.
poibleachas,** -ais, *s.m.* Popularity.
†**poibleag**, *s.f.* Poplar-tree.
poiblidh,†† -e, *s.f.* Public manifest.
———,* *gen.* of pobull.
†**poibligheachd**, *s.f.* Commonwealth.
poicean, -ein, -an, *s.m.* Short, squat fellow, see pocan.
———**ach**, *a.* Thick, short, squat.
poichean, -ein, *s.m.* Pithless, diminutive fellow. 2 Little impudent fellow. 3 Little pig.
poichean ! *int.* Call to a little pig—*E. Perthsh.*
poichidh, *s.f.* Young pig. Am fac thu na poichidhean ? *have you seen the young pigs ?—East Perthshire.*
poichidh ! } (CR) *int.* Calls to young pigs—
poich ! poich ! } *E. Perthshire.*
pòigean, -ein, -an, *s.m.*, *dim.* of pòg. Little kiss, smack. Thoir p. dhomh, *kiss me.*
———**ach**, -aiche, *a.* Kissing. 2 Fond of kissing.
pòil, Gaelic spelling of *pole.*
pòilich, see bòilich.
poilleadh,** -idh, *s.m.* Boring, piercing
poineach, see ponach.
pòinidh, -ean, *s.m.* see pònaidh.
pòinireach, see pònaireach.
pòir, -ean, *s.m.* Pore.
poircean,(AF) *s.m.* Little pig. 2 Porpoise
poirse, Gaelic spelling of *porch.*
pois,** *v.a.* Haul, drag, lug.
pòisde, } see pòsde.
pòiste, }
poit, -e, *pl.* -ean & -eachan, *s.f.* Pot, cauldron.
pòit, *v.* Drink deeply or to excess, carouse.
——, *s.f.* see pòite.
poit-chamag,** *s.f.* Pot-hook.
poit-chreadha,** *s. f.* Earthen pot. 2 Potter's clay. If the accent be on *chreadha* the meaning is "an earthenware pot," but if on *poit* it signifies "potter's clay."
poit-dhubh (a' ph—,) *s.f.* The "sma'" still.

We are indebted to DMK for the following names of its parts, and a drawing from which the annexed sketch was made.

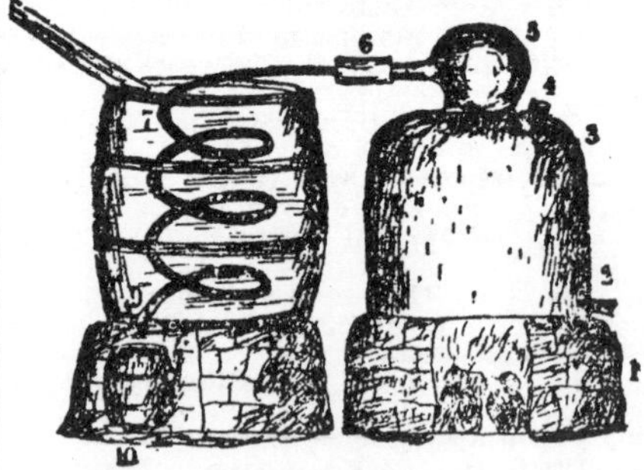

570. A' phoit-dhubh.

1 An Leid, *the fire-place—Ross-shire;* an Sorchan—,(AH) *N. Argyll* ; an Teallaich—*Lorn.*
2 Bod-an-leanna, *the discharge cock.*
3 Am Bràghad, *the shoulder.*
4 An Lionadair, *the charger.*
5 An Ceann, *the still-head.*
6 An Gearradan, *the connecting piece.*
7 A' Chliath, *the worm.* A' chaora chrom—Bainne aig na caoraich uile 's galan aig a' chaora chruim, *all sheep have milk, but the*

still-worm (*lit.* the crooked sheep) *has a gallon—Old Port-a-beul—(Fionn.)*
8 An stann cléith, *the worm-tub.*
9 Am Feadan, *the spout.*
10 An Glacadan, *the spirit-receiver.*
11 An Spùdan, an spùdan fuar, (*Fionn*) Feadan,(DM) *the chute for supplying the worm-tub with cold water for condensing the vapour that passes from the still to the worm.*

poite, see poit.
pòite, *s.f.* Drinking,tippling, drinking to excess. [** says excess in eating or drinking. McL & D, ‡, & * give pòit.]
pòiteach, -eiche, *a.* Drunken, addicted to drink.
poiteach, -eiche, *a.* Having pots. 2 Using pots.
pòiteadh, -idh, *s.m.* Tippling.
poiteag, -eig, -an, *s.f.*, *dim.* of poit. Little pot.
———ach, *a.* Having or using small pots.
poiteal,** -eil, -ealan, *s.m.* Pottle (=four imperial pints.)
poitean, see boitean & poiteag.
———ach, see boiteanach & poiteagach.
pòitear, -eir, -an, *s.m.* Drinker, bottle companion. 2 Drunkard, gourmand.
poitear,** -eir, *s.m.* Potter, pot-maker.
pòitearach, -aiche, *a.* Tippling, addicted to drinking, drunken.
————d, *s.f.ind.* Drinking, drinking to excess, carousing, banqueting. 2 Habit of tippling or drunkenness. 3** Gormandizing.
poitearachd,** *s.f.* Pot-making.
poit-fheòla,* *s.f.* Flesh-pot.
—— -fhuail, *s.f.* Chamber-pot—*W. coast of Ross.*
—— -fhlùran, *s.f.* Flower-pot.
—— -ghlanaidh, *s.f.* Fining-pot.
poitidh ! (CR) *int.* Call to a pig.
poitigir,(MS) *s.m.* Pharmacopist.
poit-leabach, *s.f.* Chamber-pot.
—— -luibh, -e, -ean *s.f.* Pot-herb.
—— -luibhean,** *s.f.* Flower-pot.
—— -mùin, *s.f.* Chamber-pot, jordan.
poit na h-adhairc, *s. f.* Ludicrous name for a tea-pot.
poit-phronnaidh, *s.f.* Mortar.
poit-ruadh,* *s.f.* Still.
poit-sheòmair, *s.f.* Chamber-pot.
poit-thogalach,** *s.f.* Still.
pòl,** -òil, *s.m.* Pall.
pola,(DMy) *s.* Bowl. P. bainne, *a bowl of milk.*
polachan,(MMcD) *s.m.* Small clay jar about 15 to 18 inches high, used in Lewis for holding cream.
polar,** *s. m.* Sign. [** gives it for pollair.]
polaradh,(AH) -aidh, *s. m.* The groove along which the nail-holes are pierced on a horse-shoe.
poll,** *s.m.* Pole of land, containing 30¼ square yards.
——,** *v.a.* Hole, bore.
poll, puill, *pl.* -uill & -an, *s. m.* Hole, pit. 2 Mire, mud. 3 Bog. 4 Pond, pool. 5 Deep stagnant water. 6 Dark and deep part of any stream. 7 Wet, miry meadow. 8 Nostril. Am pollaibh a shròine, *in his nostrils.*
p.-acaireachd, p.-acarsaid, p.-acraiche, } *a bay to anchor ships.*
p.-bùiridh, *rutting-place of deer.*
p.-creadha, *a clay-pit.*
p.-damhair, *a rutting-place for deer.*
p.-domhain, *a deep pool.*
p.-éisg, p.-iasgaich, } *a fish-pond, 2 a pool where fish lie. 3* a fishing-station.*
p.-làimhrig, *a landing-place.*
p.-leathair, *a tanner's pool.*
p.-marcachd, *a road for ships.*
p.-mòine *or* p.-mòna, *a peat-moss, peat-bank, peat-hag.*
p.-nan-tunnag, *the duck-pond.*
p.-salainn, *a salt-pit.*
pollach,(CR) *s. m.* Cod—*Suth'd & Easter Ross.* 2 Half-sized cod—*Farr.*
pollach, -aiche, *a.* Lumpish, stupid, *prov.* 2 Holed, hollowed. 3 Fungous. 4 Porous. 5 (MS) Thick.
————as, -ais, *s. m.* Lumpishness, stupidity, *prov.*

571. Pollag (3.)

pollag, -aig, -an, *s.f.*, *dim.* of poll. Little pool, hole, pit or pond. 2 Dimple. 3 Gwiniad, fresh-water herring, found in lakes in Wales and Cumberland. 4 Pollock, lythe. 5 Whiting. 6 Pollan, powan, vendace. 7 (AC) Corn-mortar,—a primitive form of hand-mill consisting of a hollowed-out stone. The grain was placed in the hollow and pounded into meal with a stone pestle. Meal thus prepared was called " min-phronntaidh " (bruised meal.) The pollag, which is a more primitive form of mill than the quern, was in use in the Outer Hebrides in comparatively recent times. 8 (Fionn) Nostril—*Lorn.* 9 (AH) Potato-pit left out on the field during winter and spring. 10 see pollair.
———ach, *a.* Of, belonging to, or abounding in, little holes, pits, ponds, dimples, &c.
——— -chnotaidh, *Argyll* for clach-chnotainn.
——— -seirce, see pollag.
polla-ghuirean,** *s.* Ozœna.
pollair, -ean, *s.m.* Nostril. 2 Searcher of holes and corners.
pollaireachd,* *s.f.* Searching of holes and corners.
pollairean, see pollaran.
pollan, -ain, -an, *s.m.* Plash. 2 (MS) Nostril. 3 (AF) see pollag. P. na sròine, *nostril.*
pollaran, *s.m.* The dunlin—*pelidna alpina*, also called Bird-of-the-mud-pits—*Tringa variabilis.* Also pollairean in summer, and gille-feadaig in winter.
poll-cheannach, -aiche, *a.* Lump-headed, jolt-headed, stupid.
poll-cheannan, -ain, -an, *s.m.* Tadpole.
polldach, -aich, -aichean, *s.f.* Marshy ground.
poll-iasgaich,* *s.m.* Fish-pond. 2 Pool where fish lie.
poll-mhògag, (CR) *s.f.* Toad—*W. of Ross-shire.*
poll-mòna,* *s.m.* Peat-pit. 2†† Peat-hag.
poll-suathaidh,(AF) *s.m.* Rubbing-pool of kiln, see àth (in appendix.)
pollta, *past pt.* of poll. Bored.
ponlltach,†† *a.* Full of holes.
pòloich, see bòilich.
polt,** *s.* Nostril.
ponach,‡ -aich, *s.m.* Boy, lad. 2 (CR) Child up to 2 or 3 years—*Perthshire.* [poineach in *Argyll—(Fionn.)*
pònaidh, -ean, *s.m.* Pony, small horse. 2 ** Docked horse.
pònair, *gen.* pònarach, *s.f.coll.* Beans—*faba vulgaris.*
——— -àirneach,§ *s.f.coll.* Kidney beans.
——— -chapull,§ *s. f. coll.* Bog-beans, buck-beans, marsh-trefoil—*menyanthes trifoliata.* (ill. 572.)

572. Pònair-chapull.

pònair-churaich, see pònair-chapuill.
——each, -eiche, *a.* Full of beans, like beans, of beans. Aran p., *bean-bread.*
—— -Fhrangach, *s.f.coll.* French beans.
—— -nan-each, *s.f.coll.* Horse-beans.
pònarach, see pònaireach.
ponc, -uinc, -an & -uincean, see punc. 2 (AF) Goat.
poncaich, see puncaich.
poncachas, see puncachas.
poncaireachd, see puncaireachd.
pong, -uing, -an & -ean, see punc.
——ach, -aiche, see puncach
——aid, see puncaid.
——aideach, see puncaideach.
——ail, -e, see puncail.
——aileachd, see puncalachd.
pongalachd, see puncalachd.
pongan, *pl.* of pong, see punc.
pongannan, *pl.* of pong, see punc.
pong-labhairt, see punc-labhairt.
pong-labhraiche, see punc-labhraiche.
ponnan,(MS) *s.m.* Bunch, cluster, group, herd, parcel.
——aich, *v.a.* Herd.
†**pont**, *a.* Fierce, vehement. 2 Cruel.
pòr, -òir, -an, *s. m.* Seed. 2 Grain, corn. 3 Crops generally (corn, potatoes, turnips, &c.) Ciamar tha 'm p. agaidh ? *how are your crops progressing ?* Race, clan, progeny. 4 Pore of the skin. Am p. dubh, *the wicked race* ; droch ph., *bad seed*; mo phòran dùinte, *my pores stopped* ; p. nan gearr-mheann,*the race of young kids* ; p. Dhiarmaid, *the race of Dermid—the Campbells* ; p.-cochuill, p.-cochullach, *pulse.*
pòrach, -aiche, *a.* Full of seeds, grain or corn. 2 Seminal. 3 Porous.
†**poraiste**,** *s.f.* Parish.
———ach, -ich, *s.m.* Parishioner.
porc,** -an, *s.m.* Sow, pig. 3 Gaelic spelling of *pork.*
——an,(AF) *s.m.* Little sow, young pig.
porcanta,** *a.* Piggish, swinish. 2 Porky.
pòr-cochullach, -aiche, *a.* Leguminous as plants. see luis meiligeagach.
porc-thriath,(AF) *s.m.* Stall-fed hog.
porfaor, *s.m.* Porphyry.
pòr-neimhneach, -eiche, *a.* Venomous, poisonous, radically venomous.
pòrsan, -ain, -an, *s.m.* Gaelic spelling of *portion.*
——ach,†† *a.* Partial.
——aich,*v.a.* Portion, give a marriage portion.
†**port**,** *a.* Fierce, vehement. 2 Cruel. 3 Severe.
port, -uirt, *pl.* -uirt & -an, *s.m.* Port, harbour. 2 Ferry, passage. 3 Strait, firth. 4**Gate. †5 **Fort. †6**Garrison. †7**Bank. †8**Area of a place. †9** House. †10**Common food. †11 **Door. 12(AH) Bay. Rì port, *storm-stayed;* baile-puirt, *a seaport town.*
port, -uirt, *pl.* -uirt & -an, *s.m.* Tune, tune sung or played on a musical instrument. 2*Favourable opportunity. Gabh port air, *watch your opportutunity* ; gabh port, *play a tune* ; port-a-beul, *a mouth-tune, "diddling"*—an accompaniment to a dance used when a musical instrument is not available.
portach,‡‡ -aiche, *a.* Full of havens.
portair, -ean, *s.m.* Porter, bearer. 2 Janitor. 3 Ferryman. 4 Porter (beer.)
———eachd, *s.f.ind.* Business of a porter, doorkeeper, janitor or ferryman. 2 ** Porterage, ferriage.
portan, -ain, -an, see partan.
portan,(AH) *s. pl.* Corners of a person's mouth. Bha 'n deoch a' tilleadh a mach aig p. a bheòil, *the drink was flowing back at the corners of his mouth*—an expression often applied to a sick or dying person.
portan-tuathal, see partan-tuathal.
portas,* -ais, -an, *s.m.* Mass-book.
port-gunna,** *s.m.* Loop-hole.
pòs, *pr.pt.* a' pòsadh, *v.a.* Marry, perform the marriage ceremony. 2 Become a married person.
pòsach,** *a.* Bridal.
——ail, -e, *a.* Marriageable.
pòsadh, -aidh, -aidhean, *s.m.* Marriage, wedlock. 2 Marrying, ceremony of marriage. 3 Wedding. A' p—, *pr. pt.* of pòsadh. Tha 'm p. coltach ris an t-seillean, tha mil ann 's tha gath ann, *marriage is like a bee, there's honey in it and there's a sting in it* ; toileach air do ph., *willing to marry you* ; là a' phòsaidh, *the wedding-day.*
posaid,(MS) *s.f.* Posset.
pòsaidh,** *a.* Bridal.
posaidich,(MS) *v.a.* Posset.
pòsam, *1st. pers.sing.imp.* of pòs. Let me marry. 2 (for pòsaidh mi) *fut.aff.a.* I will marry.
pòsda, *a. & past pt.* of pòs. Married, wedded, see pòste.
posda, see posta.
pòsde, *past pt.* of pòs. Married, wedded. Fear nuadh-phòste, *a newly-married man.*
pòs-gheall,* *v.n.* Betrothe.
———-adh,* -aidh, *s.m.* Betrothing, betrothal. 2 Promise of marriage. A' p—, *pr.pt.* of pòs-gheall.
poslach,** -aich, *s.m.* Bunch, tuft. 2 Group.
post, *pr.pt.* a' postadh, *v.a.* Tramp, tread with the feet. P. an làthach, *tread the clay.*
post, puist, *pl.* -an, -achan & -aichean, *s. m.* Pillar. 2 Beam, rafter. 3 Post, office. 4 **Post in the army. 5†† Leaden slug.
posta, -chan, *s.m.* Letter-carrier, postman. [* *pl.* postaichean.]
postachd, *s.f.ind.* Business of the post-office. 2 Postage. 3 Letter-carrying. Cairt-ph., *a post-card.*
postadh, -aidh, *s.m.* Trampling with the feet, act of treading or trampling. A' p—, *pr.pt.* of post. In scouring woollen clothes, blankets or coarse linen, when strength of arms and manual friction are found insufficient, Highland women put them into a tub with a proper quantity of water, then, with petticoats tucked up, they commence the operation of "posting," which they continue till every part of the clothes receives an effectual cleansing. When three women are employed, one commonly tramps in the middle, and the other two tramp round her.
postaichean, *pl.* of post.
postail, *a.* Post-like.
postan, -ain, -an, *s.m.,dim.* Little pillar or beam. 2**Little post. 3 (DMy) Little narrow trough to feed lambs from during wintering, also call-

ed " p.-nan-uan."
postanach, -aiche, *a.* Having stout legs or supporters.
————,* -aich, *s.m.* Thick-set child just beginning to walk. 2** Person with stout legs. 2 That which has props.
pòste, *past pt.* see pòsde.
†pota, -an, *s. f.* see poit. 2 (CR) Hole from which peats have been cut—*Skye.*
†potadair, see poitear.
potair, see poitear. 2 (DMy) Man who makes himself a nuisance by always remaining indoors and so hindering the domestic duties of a house.
†———eachd, see poitearachd. 2 (DMy) Habit or act of hindering domestic duties by one's constant presence in the house.
†poth, -a, *s.m.* Bachelor.
prab, *pr.pt.* a' prabadh, *v.a.* Disorder, discompose, put into disorder. 2 Spoil. 3 Ravel. 4 Entangle. 5 Hamper, cumber, perplex.
prab,* *v.* Unfit.
prab, -aib, -an, *s.m.* Rheum in the eyes.
†prab, *a.* Quick, active, " clever."
pràbach, -aiche, *a.* Disorderly, confused, out of order. 2 Shaggy. 3 Dishevelled, ravelled, not neat.
prabach, -aiche, *a.* Blear-eyed, rheum-eyed. 2 *Contemptible.
————,* *s.f.* Contemptible female.
pràbadh, -aidh, *s.m.* Confusing, act of confusing, disordering, disarranging. 2 Botching, bungling, spoiling. 3 Ravelling, tangling, entanglement. A' p—, *pr.pt.* of pràb.
prabag-linn,(DU) *s.f.* Old torn net.
prabaiche,‡‡ *s.f.ind.* Lippitude.
prabair, -ean, *s.m.* Worthless fellow, one of the rabble, untidy fellow,ramscallion, contemptible fellow.
pràbal see pràbar.
praban, *s m.* Shebeen—*Skye.* 'Nuair a bha mi a' cumail p. an Cornal, *when I kept a shebeen in Cornal.*
pràbanach,** -aich, *s m.* Comely young boy or lad.
prabar, *s.m.* Refuse of grain or seed—*Sàr-Obair.*
pràbar, *fut.pass.* of pràb. Shall be entangled, as thread.
prabar, -air, -an, *s.m.* The rabble, the mob. 2* Little people. Am p. porcanta, *the swinish multitude.*
———ach, -aiche, *a.* Of, or belonging to, the rabble.
———daich,* *s. f.* Smattering, slight knowledge. P. leughaidh, *a smattering of reading;* p. chùnntais, *a smattering of arithmetic.*
pràbarsaich, see pràbardaich.
prabht,(CR) *s.* Trick. From Scots *prat—Perthshire.*
———ach,(AH) *a.* Flat-footed. 2 Splay-footed.
pràblach,§ -aich, *s. m.* Sea-ware, tangle, see propach. 2** Thread or hair entangled. 3** Anything much entangled.
prabladh,(DMy) *s. m.* Grasping suddenly, attempting to seize.
prab-shùil, -shùla, -ean,-*s.f.* Blear-eye, rheum-eye.
————each, -eiche, *a.* Blear-eyed, having rheumy eyes.
pràbta, see pràbte.
pràbte, *past pt.* of pràb. Entangled.
prac, *s.m.ind.* Teinds, tax. A term peculiar to some of the northern districts and isles of Scotland for the vicarage dues or small tithe, being a tenth of the yearly increase of live stock, and under local usages,of certain other articles of produce, paid in kind, prior to valuation, and distinct from the large, or corn tithe. [**gen. praic.]
pracadair, -ean, *s.m.* Collector of tithes.
————eachd, *s.f.ind.* Collection of tithes.
pràcais, -e, -ean, *s.f.* Idle talk, irrelevant language.
pracas, -ais, *s.m.* Gallimaufry, hotch-potch. 2* Dispute not easily settled. 3* Nonsensical difference.
pradhainn,* *s.f.* Press of business, urgent business, hurry, flurry. 2 Affliction.
————each,* -eiche, *a.*Pressed for time, hurried, flurried. 2**Earnest.
————eachd,** *s. f.* Earnestness, state of being in a hurry or great haste.
praghain, *s.f.* see pradhainn.
pràib, -e, *s.f.* Rabble. 2 Filth, ordure. *prov.*
praicleis, (AH) *s.f.* Lumber, rubbish, litter,odds and ends.
†praidhean, -ein, see pradhainn.
†praidhinn, -e, -ean, *s.f.* see pradhainn.
†praidhlinneach, -eiche, *a.* see pradhainneach. 2 Afflicting.
praidseach, -eich, see proitseach.
praimh, *gen.sing.* of pramh.
praingealas,* -ais, see pracas. [* gives -ais as the *nom.*, and *s.f.*]
prainn, *gen.sing.* of prann (for pronn.)
prainnseag, -eig, -an, *s. f.* Mince collops. 2 Haggis (taigeis.)
prais, -e, *s.f.* Pot of a creel.
pràis, -e, *s.f.* Brass. 2 Pot-metal. 3 (CR) Cast-iron pot—*W. of Ross-shire.* 4 Still. 5 see praiseach.
pràisbhallach, -aiche, *a.* Strong or brazen-limbed. 2**Well-fortified, as with brazen walls. 3 Strong, as a fortification.
praiseach, -eich, -eichean, *s.f.* Pot. 2 Crucible. 3 Broth. 4 Pottage, gruel. 5 see prasach. Cas na praiseich a' tighinn an uachdar, *the stump of the pot coming to the surface*—said by the landsman on seeing a porpoise tumbling! mac-na-praiseich, *whisky.*
pràiseach, -ich, *s.f.* Brass, impudence. 2 Bold or lewd woman, bawd. 3 Slut. 4 Crib, manger, see prasach. Ath-ph., *a harridan, an old whore.*
pràiseach, *a.* Brassy, made of brass. 2 Brazen-faced.
praiseach,§ -eich, -ean, *s.f.* Cabbage—*brassica.*

573.Praiseach-a'-bhalla. 574.Praiseach-bhaidhe.

———— -a'-bhalla, *s.f.* Wall-kale, wall-goose-foot—*chenopodium murale.*
———— -bhaidhe,§ *s.f.* Sea-kale or cabbage—*brassica oleracea.*
———— -bràthar,§ *s.f.* Good King Henry, wild spinach, English mercury, mercury goose-foot—*chenopodium Bonus Henricus.* (ill. 575.)
———— -féidh,§ *s.f.* Penny-cress, bastard mustard, boor's or mithridate mustard—*thlaspi*

575. Praiseach-bràthar. arvense. *576. Praiseach-féidh.*

praiseach-fhiadhain,§ *s. f.* White goose-foot—*chenopodium album.*

577. Praiseach-fhiadhain. 578. Praiseach-gharbh.

praiseach-gharbh,§ *s.f.* Charlock, wild mustard—*sinapsis arvensis.*

——— -ghlas,§ *s. f.* White goosefoot, see p.-fhiadhain. [** gives fig-leaved goose-foot.]

579. Praiseach-mhin. 580. Praiseach-na-mara, 1.

praiseach-mhin,§ *s.f.* Common orache—*atriplex hastata & patula.*

——— -na-mara,§ *s.f.* Sea-side goose-grass—*suæda maritima.* 2 Glass-wort, crab-grass—*salicornia herbacea.* § says the Gaelic name is used for both these plants indiscriminately.

581. Praiseach-na-mara 2. *582. Praiseach-na-tràgha.*

praiseach-tràgha,§ *s. f.* Seakale—*cramba maritima.*

pràiseachd, *s.f.ind.* Brazenness.

praiseag,** -eig, -an, *s.f.* Little pot.

pràisealachd,(MS) *s.f.* Brassiness.

praisg,** -e, *s.f.* Pottage.

prais-ghnùiseach, -eiche, *a.* Impudent.

pràisiche, -an, *s.m.* Brazier.

pràl, *v.n.* Beseech.

——ach,** *a.* Beseeching, craving.

——adh ,** -aidh, *s.m.* Beseeching.

pràmh, -àimh, *s. m.* Slumber, nap, slight sleep. 2 Heaviness, drowsiness. 3 Grief, sorrow, dejection. 4*Melancholic dullness. [Properly *blear-eyedness* hence slumber, applied to a dozing condition, as, p. a' chadail, also to dimness, as, a' cur reultan fo phràmh.] Fo phràmh, *sleeping, slumbering* ; a' gabhail pràimh, *taking a nap* ; p. chadail, *a nap.*

pràmhach, -aiche, *a.* Sleepy, narcotic, lethargic, drowsy, slumbering, dozing. 2 Sad, sorrowful. 3**Disheartening.

————d, *s.f.ind.* Somnolency, drowsiness, lethargy, sleepiness. 2 Dejection, disheartenedness. 3 Sorrowfulness.

pràmhail, -e, see pràmhach.

————eachd, see pràmhachd.

pràmhalachd, see pràmhachd.

pràmhan, -ain, *s.m., dim.* of pràmh. Slumber. 2 Gloom, melancholy.

pràmh-chadal,(MM) *s.m.* Doze, slumber.

pràmh-cheò, *s.f.ind.* Slumber, sleepiness, inclination to sleep. 2 Stupidity. 3 Forgetfulness.

pramhtach, *a.* see prabhtach.

pramsgal, (DMy) *s.m.* Worthless talk. 2 Refuse of grain, &c.

†prann,** -ainn, *s.m.* Wave.

prann, see pronn.

prannasg, *s.f.* see pronnasg.

prantair, -ean, *s.m.* see pronnadair 5.

————,* *v.a.* Scribble. 2 Mutter.

prantair, see pronnadair 5.

praonan, see braonan.

prap, -a, *a.* Quick, speedy, ready, sudden, *prov.*

——adh, -aidh, *s.m.* Quickness, *prov.*

prapag,(CR) *s.f.* Hay-cock of the smallest size, about 18 in. in height.—*Argyll.*

pràpanach, *s.m.* Child, boy. Gu 'm b' i siod an t-sùil àluinn bh' aig mo ph. bòidheach, *yon was the lovely eye that my beautiful (lively) child had—Fiidh, p. 75.* (propairneach.)

prap-shùileachd, *s. f. ind.* Blearedness of the eyes.

pras,* *s.m.* Brass.

prasach, -aich, *s.f.* Manger, crib, stall. 2(AF) *s.m.* Fox. P.-each, *a horse-stall.*

prasair,* *s.m.* see pràisiche.

prasgan, -ain, -an, *s. m.* Little herd, flock, bunch or group. 2 Group of people, gang. 3 Mob, rabble, populace. P. ghabhar, *a flock of goats.*

————ach, -aiche, *a.* In little flocks. 2 Like a flock. 3††Full of bundles or groups. 4 Like a gang or mob.

prat, -an, *s.m.ind.* Trick, artifice, prank. 2 (CR) Tantrum—*Arran.*

——ach,** *a.* Arch. 2 Pranky, tricky, mischievous.

——achd,** *s.f.* Archness.

——ail, -e, *a.* Tricky, pranky.

prathaig,(MS) *s.f.* Heap. 2 Crowd, rabble. 3 Varletry.

†preab, see breab.

†preabach, see breabach.
†preabadair, see breabadair.
preabag, see breabag.
preabail, see breabail.
preabair, see breabair & breabadair. 2**Brave man.
——eachd, see breabadaireachd. 2**Acting bravely, gallantry.
preaban,** *s.m.* Circus. 2 see breaban. 3**Wincing horse. 4**Courtyard.
——ach, *a.* see breabanach.
——achd, see breabanachd (appx.)
——aiche, see breabanaiche.
preach,** *v.* Crucify. †2 Hold. †3 Stand,stay. †4**Grasp. †5 Punish.
preach,* *s.f.* Bog, marsh, morass. 2**Grasp, hold. 3* Little fen—*Argyll.* Chaidh a' bhò 'sa phreach, *the cow stuck in the bog.*
preach,*v.a.Speak as with the voice of a bittern.
——ach,** *a.* Grasping, greedy, ravenous. Gu p., *greedily.*
——air,* -ean, *s.m.* Croaking preacher, miserable orator. Am p. grannda bodaich, *the ugly old croaking orator.*
——ag,(DMy) *s.f.* Any substance that, owing to its consistency, spreads when poured on the ground, as porridge, &c. When a woman falls in a heap, it is said, Thuit i 'na preachaig air an talamh.
preachain,** *s.f.* Bones taken out of pork when making bacon.
preachan, -ain, *s.m.* Mean orator.
preachan, -ain, -an, *s.m.* Crow. 2 Raven. 3 Kite. 4 Moor-bittern. 5 Little fen—*Argyll.* 6 (AF) Jackdaw. 7 (AF) Vulture. 8 Any ravenous bird.
——ach, *s.m.* see preachan.
——ach, -aiche, *a.* Ravenous, vulturine, grasping, greedy, like a kite or other ravenous bird. 2 Querulous, croaking. 3 Full of little pits, kites or ravenous birds.
——achd, *s.f.ind.* Ravenousness, voracity, greediness.
—— -ceannann, (ceann-fhionn) Osprey.
—— -ceirteach, Kite.
—— -cnàimheach, Raven.
—— -cnaimhlithgheach, see p.-cnàimheach.
—— -craosach, Vulture.
—— -gearr, Buzzard.
—— -ingneach, Vulture, see fang.
—— -nan-cearc, Ring-tailed kite.
prealaid,** *s.m.* Bishop. Gaelic spelling of *prelate.*
preamh, *Blair Athole* for pràmh (slumber.)
†preamh,** *s.m.* Root, stock. 2 Tribe. (freumh)
preas, *pr.pt.* a' preasadh, *v.a. & n.* Plait, fold, corrugate. 2 Braid. 3 Become wrinkled or corrugated. 4 Squeeze, crush by weight or force.
preas, pris, *pl.* -an & pris, *s.m.* Bush, shrub. 2 Thicket. 3 Brier. 4 Gaelic spelling of *press,* (cupboard,case.) Thilg i an leanabh fo aon de na preasan, *she threw the child under one of the shrubs;* am p.,*in a thicket;* cha deach car do theadhair mu phreas, *your tether has not gone round the bush*—said of a person who looks well. *Preas* is not used in *Arran* where they say *craobh* for a garden bush and *tom* for a wild bush.
p.-chrabhsag, *a gooseberry-bush.*
p.-dhearc, p.-dhearcag, p.-nan-dearc, } *a berry bush.*
p.-dris, *a bramble-bush.*
p.-droighinn, *a thorn-bush.*
p.-fhiontag, *a cloudberry bush.*
p.-nan-ròs, *a rosebush.*
p.-nam-flontag, *a crowberry bush.*
preas, -a, -an, *s.m.* Wrinkle, crease. 2 Plait,fold. 3 Corrugation. Tha preasan 'na aodann, *his face is wrinkled;* gun ph., gun smal, *without wrinkle or spot.*
——ach, -aiche, *a.* Furrowed, wrinkled, corrugated. 2 Striped. 3 Plaited. 4 Abounding in bushes. 5 Abounding in presses or cases. 5 Like a wrinkle. 6 Like a bush. Aghaidh ph., *a wrinkled face.*
——achail, -e, *a.* Corrugant.
——achd, *s.f.* Crispiness.
preasadh, -aidh, *s.m.* Plaiting, act of plaiting, or folding. 2 Braiding. 3 State of becoming wrinkled or corrugated. 4 Wrinkle. Gun smal gun ph., *without spot or wrinkle.* A' p—, *pr.pt.* of preas.
preasag, -aig, -an, *s.f.*, *dim.* of preas. Wrinkle, plait. 2 Little bush, little thicket. Làn ph., *full of wrinkles.*
——ach, -aiche, *a.* Wrinkled, plaited, full of wrinkles.
preasaich, *v.* see preas.
preasan, -ain, -an, *s.m.dim.* of preas. Little bush. 2 Free-will offering, 3 Wedding boon.
preasan, *n.pl.* of preas.
preasant, Gaelic spelling of *present.* [* "preasantan" hens' eggs given to landlords by tenants as a part of the rent—in *Irish,* a wedding-present. "preasanta," a hen so given.]
preasarlach,(MS) *s.m.* Coppice.
preasarnach, -aich, *s.f.* Shrubbery, arbour,place full of shrubs or thickets.
——d, *s.f.* Bushiness.
preas-deilgneach,§ *s.m.* Barberry, see barbrag.
preas-droighinn,** *s.m.* Thorn-bush. Mar phreas droighinn, *like a thorn-bush.*
preas-àarnag, see àirne.

583. Preas groiseid.

preas-groiseid,§ *s. m.* Gooseberry bush—*ribes grossularia.*
preaslach,(MS) *s.m.* Undergrowth.
preas-mhucag,* see ròs-nan-con.
preas-mìneachaidh, *s.m.* Mangle.
preas-nam-mucag,§ *s.m.* Dog-rose, see ròs-nan-con.
preas-nan-àirneag,§ *s. m.* Blackthorn, sloe—*prunus spinosa.*
preas-nan-geur-dhearc,§ *s.m.* Barberry, see bàrbrag.
preas-nan-gorm-dhearc,§ *s. m.* Blue bramble, dewberry bush—*rubus cæsius.* Badge of the MacNabs. (ill. 584.)
preas-nan-sgeachag,§*s.m.*Whitethorn,hawthorn, see sgitheach geal.
preas-nan-smeur,** *s.m.* Bramble.
preas-nan-spiontag,** *s.m.* Currant-bush.
preas-shùidheag,§ *s. m.* Raspberry, see preas-sùbh-chraobh.
preas-sùbh-chraobh,§ *s. m.* Raspberry—*rubus*

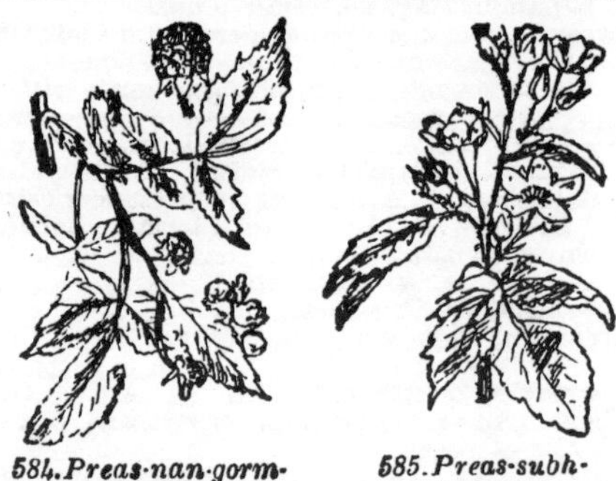

584. *Preas-nan-gorm-dhearc.* 585. *Preas-subh-chraobh.*

idæus.

preastaidh,** *a.* Unable to bear cold. 2 Timid.
preathal,** -ail, -an, *s.m.* Dizziness. see breithеal.
preathalach, *a.* Dizzy, confounded. see breithealach.
——-——adh, see breithealachadh. (appx.)
preathalaich, see breithealaich.
préisgeadh, *s.m.* Preaching.
priacail,** *s.f.* Danger.
priam, see pràmh.
prib, see priob.
pribhleid, Gaelic spelling of *privelege.*
pribleach,** *a.*, *contr.* of priob-shuileach.
pric,** *v.* Gaelic spelling of *prick.*
priceadh, *s m.* Pricking. 2 Stinging.
prigear,(MS) *s.m.* Higgler. (*Scots*, prigger.)
prigeireachd,** *s. f.* Chaffery. 2 Higgling. (*Scots*, prigging.)
prighig, *v.a.* Fry.
———eadh, -idh, *s.m.* Frying, act of frying. A' p—, *pr. pt.* of prighig.
priginn,** *s.f.* Haggling (*Scots*, prigging.)
primideach, *a.* Primitive, ancient, original, radical, not derived. Facal p., *a primitive word.*
———-——d,** *s. f.* Primitiveness, originality, radicalness.
†primidil, *s.f.* Firstlings, first produce or offerings.
prine, -achan, *s.m.* Pin, as used in fastening clothes. P. reamhar, *a blanket-pin*; p.-iaruinn, *an iron pin.*
——ach, *a.* Abounding in pins.
——achadh, -aidh, *s.m.* Act of pinning, securing with pins. A' p—, *pr. pt.* of prinich.
prineachan, -ain, -an, *s.m.*, *dim.* of prine. Little pin. 2 Pin-case. 3 Pin-cushion. 4 *pl.* of prìne.
prìnich, *pr.pt.* a' prìneachadh, *v. a.* Tuck, pin, secure with pins.
-———te, *past pt.* of prinich. Pinned, fastened or secured with pins.
priob, *pr.pt.* a' priobadh, *v. a.* Wink, twinkle, as the eye. Cha do ph. mo shuil, *I did not sleep a wink.*
priob,** *s.m.* Wink, twinkle of the eye.
———ach,** *a.* Winking. 2 Having a habit of winking, twinkling.
priobadh, -aidh, -ean, *s.m.* Winking, act of winking, act of winking or twinkling. 2 Twinkle, wink. 3 Moment. 4 Glimpse. Bi an seo am priobadh, *be here in a twinkling*; p. cadail, *a wink of sleep.*
priobaiche,** *s.m.* Blinkard.
priobaid, -e, -ean, *s f.* Trifle. 2 Evergreen privet, see ras-chrann-sìor-uaine.
priobair, -ean, *s.m.* Worthless fellow, blinkard. 2 Miser.
———eachd, *s.f.* Meanness of spirit. 2 Avarice.
priobairneach, -ich, *s.m.* Rousing, any sudden excitement.
priobairtich, *s.f.* see priobaireachd.
†priobarach, -aiche, *a.* Brave, heroic. 2 Quick.
†———-——d, *s. f.* Bravery, heroism, gallant conduct.
priobarsaich, *s.f.* see priobaireachd.
priobhaid, *s.f.* Secret. 2 Secrecy, privacy.
priob-losgadh, -aidh, -ean, *s.m.* Sudden burning or sense of heat. 2 Twinkling. 3 Sparkle, blaze.
priob-luasgach,(MS) *a.* Frisky.
priob-luasgadh,(MS) *s.m.* Anxiety, ecstasy.
priob-shùil, *s.f.* Twinkling eye.
priob-shuileach,** *a.* Winking. 2 Having the habit of winking or twinkling.
†prioc, *v.a.* Prick, sting.
———adh, -aidh, *s.m.* Pricking. 2 Stinging. 3 Puncture.
†priodal, -ail, see briodal.
prioga-breac,(AF) *s.m.* Sturgeon.
prioghainn,* *s.f.* Sauce or seasoning in viands. 2 Choice food.
———-——ich, *v.a.* Season, as viands. 2 Feed with choice food.
prìomh, *a. & prefix.* Prime, chief, principal, first.
——— -abhainn, *s.f.* Large river.
———ach,** *a.* Principal, chief. 2 Supreme. 3 Fond of superiority.
———ach,** *s.m.* Favourite.
———achd, *s.f.* Source. 2**Supremacy. 3** Principality.
———adh,** -aidh, *s.m.* Primate.
——— -aimsireach,** *a.* Antediluvian.
prìomhair, -ean, *s.m.* Premier, prime-minister. 2 Chief man, noble, chief.
prìomh-arcal,** -ail, *s.m.* Main beam.
prìomh-athair, -athar, -athraichean, *s.m.* Patriarch, progenitor, ancestor.
prìomh-athaireach,** *a.* Patriarchal.
——————as, *s.m.* Patriarchate.
prìomh-athaireil, *a.* Patriarchal.
prìomh-bhaile, -bhailtean, *s.m.* Chief town, metropolis, capital.
prìomh-bhailteach, *a.* Metropolitan.
prìomh-bhan-diùc,** *s.m.* Arch-duchess.
prìomh-bhàrd, *s.m.* Chief bard or poet, poet laureate.
prìomh-chathair, -chathrach, -chathraichean, *s.f.* Chief town, metropolis.
prìomh-cheann, -chinn, *s.m.* Supreme head.
prìomh-chiall, -chéille, *s.f.* Great understanding, supreme or superior wisdom. 2 Primary sense, as of a word.
prìomh-chlachair, -ean, *s.m.* Architect.
——————eachd,** *s.f.* Architecture.
prìomh-chlàr, -àir, -an, *s.m.* Autograph, original writing.
———-———ach,** *a.* Autographical.
prìomh-chléireach, -ich, *s. m.* Prime notary, proto-notary, chief secretary, chief clerk.
prìomh-chléirsinneachd,** *s.f.* Employment or office of chief clerk.
prìomh-choltas, -ais, -an, *s.m.* Archetype.
prìomh-choslach,** *a.* Archetypal.
prìomh-choslas, -ais, -an, see prìomh-choltas.
prìomh-chrann, -chroinn *pl.* -chroinn [& -chrannan] *s. m.* Main-mast.
prìomh-dhiadhair, -ean, *s.m.* Chief divine.
prìomh-dhiùc, -an, *s.m.* Archduke.
prìomh-dhraoidh, -ean, *s.m.* Arch-druid.
prìomh-dhuine, -dhaoine, *s. m.* Noble, chief, grandee.
prìomh dìon-sgéith, Greater wing coverts, see No. 5, p. 328.
prìomh-eaglais, -ean, *s.f.* The primitive church.

2 Cathedral. 3 Established church. 4 High church.
prìomhear, -ir, *s.m.* see prìomhair.
prìomh-easbachd,** see prìomh-easbuigeachd.
prìomh-easbuig, -ean, *s.m.* Metropolitan, archbishop.
——————each, *a.* Archepiscopal.
——————eachd, *s.f.* Archbishopric. 2 Dignity of an archbishop.
prìomh-fhàidh, -ean, *s.m.* Ancient prophet, chief prophet. 2 Primate. 3 Archbishop.
prìomh-ghineadas,** -ais, *s.m.* Primogeniture. A thaobh còir prìomh-ghineadais, *by right of primogeniture.*
prìomh-ghleus, -a, -an, *s.m.* Beginning, foundation.
prìomhlaid,* -ean, *s.m.* Prebendary. Gaelic spelling of *prelate.*
—————each, *a.* Prelatical.
—————eachd, *s.f.* Prelacy.
prìomh-laoch, -laoich, *s.m.* Great hero, hero of the first order.
prìomh-long, -luing, -an, *s.f.* First-rate ship. 2 Admiral's-ship.
prìomh-long-phort,** -phuirt, *s. m.* Royal residence. 2 Principal sea-port or fort. 3 Principal camp.
prìomh-luingeas, -eis, -an, *s.f.* see prìomh-long.
prìomh-mhuinntir, *s.coll.* Aborigines.
prìomh-phrionnsa, -an & -achan, *s. m.* Prince-royal.
prìomh-shamhlachail, *a.* Archetypal.
prìomh-shamhladh, *s.m.* Archetype.
prìomh-sheòl, -shiùil, *s.m.* Main-sail. Thog iad am p., *they hoisted the main-sail.*
prìomh-shona,** *a.* Supremely happy, supremely blessed.
prìomh-shonas, -ais, *s.m.* Supreme or chief happiness. 'Se am p. a bhi 'creachadh, *their chief happiness is to plunder.*
prìomh-shluagh, -shluaigh, *s.m.* Aboriginal inhabitants of any country.
prìomh-thùs, -ùis, *s.m.* Beginning, origin. 2 Foundation. 3 Principle. 4 Element.
prìomh-uachdaran, -ain, *pl.* -ain & -an, *s. m.* Chief ruler.
————————achd, *s. f.* Supremacy, supreme rule or authority.
prìomh-ùghdair, -ean, *s.m.* Original author, inventor.
†prìomh-ùrlamh, -aimhe, *a.* Ready-handed. 2 First engaging.
priompallan, -ain, *s.m.* Beetle. 2 Noise like that of a beetle.
—————ach, *a.* Like a beetle. 2 Making a noise like a beetle.
prionnsa, *pl.* prionnsan, prionnsaidh & prionnsachan, *s.m.* Prince.
prionnsach, -aiche, *a.* see prionnsail.
prionnsachail, -e, *a.* see prionnsail.
prionnsachan, *n.pl.* of prionnsa.
prionnsachd, *s.f.* see prionnsalachd.
prionnsadh, see prionnsa.
prionnsaidh, *n.pl.* of prionnsa.
prionnsail, -e, *a.* Princely, like a prince, royal, authoritative, influential, commanding respect.
—————eachd, see prionnsalachd.
prionnsalach,‡‡ -aiche, *a.* Princely. 2 Authoritative, commanding respect, influential.
prionnsalachd, *s. f.* Principality. 2 Princeliness.
prionnsan, *n.pl.* of prionnsa.
prionnt, Gaelic spelling of *print.*
————air, Gaelic spelling of *printer.*
————aireachd, *s.f.* Printer's work, printing.
prìosan, -ain, -an, *s.m.* Prison, gaol. Am p., *in prison.*
prìosanach, -aich, *s.m.* Prisoner, captive.
——————, -aiche, *a.* Very confined, within narrow bounds.
——————adh, -aidh, *s.m.* Imprisoning, act of imprisoning, imprisonment. keeping in bondage. A' p—, *pr.pt.* of prìosanaich.
——————d, *s.f.* Imprisonment, captivity.
prìosanaich, *pr.pt.* a' prìosanachadh, *v. a.* Imprison, incarcerate. 2 Take captive.
——————, *gen.sing. & n.pl.* of prìosanach.
——————te, *past pt.* Imprisoned, incarcerated.
prìosantachd,** *s.f.* Arctation.
priosun, -uin, see prìosan.
pris, *gen.sing. & n.pl.* of preas.
prìs, -e, -ean, *s.f.* Price, value, rate, worth. 2 Respect, esteem. Ciod a' ph. da? *what is its price?* 'ga chur am p., *raising it in estimation:* tha e am p., *it is in high estimation;* p. na circe, *the value of the hen;* p. a' phrìne, *the value of the pin.*
prìseachadh, -aidh, *s.m.* Estimating, act of estimating or valuing, valuation. A' *pr. pt.* of prìsich.
prìseadh, -eidh, *s.m.* Valuing, valuation.
prìsealachd, *s.f.ind.* Value, preciousness, dearness.
prisean, -ein, -an, *s. m., dim.* of preas. Little bush. 2 Little thicket.
prisean, *n.pl.* of prìs.
prìseil, -e, *a.* Precious, valuable, dear.
prìsich, *v.a.* Estimate, fix the price, price, value. 2 Prize.
pri-taoil,(CR) *s.f.* Clatter—*Perthshire.* Na leig a mhàin e le p., *do not let it down with a clatter* or *suddenly;* thàinig e staigh le p., *he came rushing in.*
prò,(DMy) *a.* Croaky, harsh. 2 Stentorian, deep, as a bass voice. 3 The opposite of *binn.*
†probhadh,** -aidh, *s.m.* Proof.
probhaid, -e, -ean, *s.f.* Profit.
—————each, *a.* Profitable.
—————eil, -e, *a.* Advantageous, profitable.
—————ich, *v.* Profit, advantage.
probhaist, -ean, *s. m.* Provost. 2 *in derision,* Corpulent or clumsy fellow.
—————each, -eiche, *a.* Of, or belonging to, a provost. 2 Corpulent, clumsy.
†probhal, -ail, *s.m.* Consul.
—————ach, *a.* Consular.
—————achd, *s.f.* Consulate.
procach, see progach.
procadair, -ean, *s.m.* Advocate, procurator. 2 Man of business. P. rìgh, *a king's advocate.*
—————eachd, *s.f.* Procuratorship. 2 Business of a proctor. 3 Pleading. 4 Importunity.
procaid,(DU) *s.f.* Conversation carried on in low tones for the sake of secrecy.
prochdair, Gaelic spelling of *proctor.*
—————eachd, *s.f.* Proctorship.
prog! (CR) *int.* Call for a horse—*Perthshire, Badenoch & N. Argyll.*
progach,(AF)*s.m.* One-year-old stag.—*Suth'd.*
progaidh! *int.* see prog.
proghain, *s.f.* Care.
—————each, *a.* In care or anxiety.
proghan, -ain, *s.m.* Dregs, lees, sediment, refuse. 2(DU) Mixture of the remains of different foods used to feed calves.
—————ach, *a.* Full of dregs, sediment or lees. 2 In care or anxiety.
proidhid, see probhaid.
—————eil, see probhaideil.
—————ich, see probhaidich.
proidseach, see proitseach.
proimbeallan,** see proimsheillean.
proimhidh, -e, *a.* Fat, *prov.*
proimsheillean, -ein, *s. m.* Drone bee. 2 Beetle.

proinistear, *Perth* for pronnasg.
proinn, -e, -ean, *s.f.* Dinner. 2 Meal. 3 Voracity. 4 *gen.* of pronn.
proinne, *comp.* of pronn.
———ach,(AH) *s.f.* Fish of a good size. Bha 'n sgadan a dh' iasgaich sinn an raoir p. laghach, *the herring we caught last night were of a fair size.* (also broinneag.)
———achadh, -aidh, *s.m.* Dieting. 2 Diet. 3 Dinner 4 Dining.
proinnich, *pr.pt.* a' proinneachadh, *v.n.* Dine. 2 Take a meal.
proinnistean, see pronnasg.
proinn-lann, -a, -ainn, -an, *s.m.* Refectory, dining room, eating-room.
proinn-lios,** see proinn-lann.
proinnte, *a. & past pt.* of proinn. Pounded, mashed, pulverized, mauled, bruised.
proinnteach, -eich, -eichean, *s.f.* Same meanings as proinn-lann.
———d, *s.f.* Grittiness.
proinstear, *Perth* for pronnusg.
pròis, -e, *s.f.* Pride, haughtiness. 2 Flattery. 3 Humouring, cajoling. 4 Ceremony. 5 Neat, punctilious little female, prude. 6 (DU)Conceit. 7**Niceness. Bean gun ph., *a wife without pride.*
pròis,** *v.a.* Tiddle. 2 (CR) Beseech, entreat, urge—*Perthshire.* 3**Flatter, cajole, put in good humour.
proisdeal, -eil, -an, *s.m.* Bottle.
pròiseach,** *a.* Apt to flatter. 2 Ready to humour. 3 Requiring flattery or humour.
pròiseadh,** -idh, *s.m.* Flattering. 2 Humouring, cajoling.
pròiseag, -eig, -an, *s.f.* Prude, coquette.
pròiseal,** *a.* see proiseil.
———achd, *s.f.ind.* Pride, haughtiness. 2 Punctiliousness, niceness, ceremoniousness. 2 Humouring flattering. 3 Punctilious prudery or neatness.
pròisean, -ein, -an, *s.m.* Proud or haughty person. 2 Puppy, conceited person. 3**One who flatters or humours. 4 One who requires to be flattered or humoured.
pròiseil, -e, *a.* Proud, haughty. 2 Ceremonious, nice, punctilious. 3 Gallant. 4** Requiring flattery or cajoling. 5 Conceited, foppish. 6 *Uppish, as a prude. 7*Neat, little and punctilious.
proitseach, -ich, *s.m.* Boy, stripling. 2* Good lump of a boy.
pronaistear, *W. Perthshire* for pronnasg.
pronastal, see pronnasg.
pronastan,(CR) *Sleat & Lewis* for pronnasg.
pronn, -oinn & -uinn, *s.m.* The coarsest part of oatmeal with the seeds left in sifting. 2 (AF) Pollard (fish.) 3 Food. 4 Dinner. 5(DMy) Ground oats for sowens, (also p.-coirce.) Ghabh iad p. agus deoch, *they took food and drink.*
pronn, *pr.pt.* a' pronnadh, *v. a.* Pound, bray, mash, bruise. 2** Grind, pulverize, mince. 3 Maul. 4 *Mutter. †5 Give, bestow, distribute. Ged ph. thu amadan, *though thou bray a fool* ; thug e là air pronnadh òir, *he spent a day in distributing gold* ; le phuirt thrileanta shiubhlach, 'phronnar luthmhor le dion, *with quavering, brisk tunes played quickly with keenness—MacMh. Alasdair, Oran an t.-S 9* ; crunluath lomara 'ga phronnadh, *a "crunluath" being pounded or broken—i-e.* the continuous sound of the pipe-tune being broken into small fragments or short notes. *—Mol. an Leòmh., 10. 13.*
pronn, pruinne, *a.* Pounded, brayed, mashed. 2 ** In fragments. 3 Crisp, brittle, friable. 4**Smooth. Siùcar p., *moist sugar.*
pronnach, -aiche, *a.* That pounds or breaks into fragments, pulverizing, dividing, distributing. 2 Generous. 3 " Drossy."
———, -aich, *s.f.* Anything pounded or broken in small fragments, " dross."
pronnadair, -ean, *s.m.* One who mashes or pounds. 2 Mortar. 3 Pestle. 4 Grinder, bruiser. 5**Hammer.
———eachd, *s.f.* Pounding, braying, breaking into fragments, bruising.
pronnadh, -aidh, *s.m.* Pounding, act of pounding, braying, breaking or mashing. 2 Bruise, bruising. 3 Splintering, grinding, mincing. 4 see pronndal. A' p—, *pr.pt.* of pronn.
†pronnadh, -aidh, *s.m.* Distributing, giving, bestowing. 2 Generosity. 3 Destruction.
pronnag, -aig, -an, *s.f.* Small crumb. 2 "Dross." 3 Anything minced or pulverized.
———ach, -aiche, *a.* In fragments, pulverized. 2**" Drossy."
pronnaich,(MS) *v.a.* Grind .
pronnal, -ail, *s.m.* see pronndal.
———ach, -aich, see pronndalach.
———aich, -e, see pronndalaich.
pronnan. *s. pl.* Bits, fragments. P. arain, *bread crumbs.*
pronnan, -ain, *pl.* -an & -ain, *s. m.* Fragment, bit, splinter. 2 One who divides. 3 Generous person.
———ach, -aiche, see pronnagach.
pronnar, see pronnmhor.
pronnas,(DU) *s.m.* Leavings of food, fragments of any sort, detritus.
pronnasg, -aisg, *s.m.* Brimstone, sulphur.
———ach, -aiche, *a.* Sulphureous, brimstony. 2 Asphaltic.
pronnasgail,** *a.* Sulphureous, sulphury.
pronnasdail, *Badenoch* for pronnasg.
pronnastair, *Arran* for pronnasg.
pronnasgachd,(MS) *s.f.* Sulphureousness.
pronn-bhiadh, -bhidh, *s.m.* Fragments of victuals. 2**Minced meat. 3 Fragments of nuts.
pronnastail, *Strathspey* for pronnasg.
pronnastal, *Edinbane (Skye)* for pronnasg.
pronn-chainnt, -e, *s.f.* Small talk.
———each, -eiche, *a.* Loquacious. 2 Trifling in conversation.
pronndach,** *a.* Pulverizing, bruising. 2 Splintering.
pronndal, -ail, *s. m.* Muttering, murmuring, grumbling, growl, undertone. 2 Low noise or note. 'Dé am p. a th' ort ? *what are you muttering about ?*
pronndalach, -aiche, *a.* Muttering, murmuring, making a low noise, grumbling.
pronndalaich, -e, *s.f.* Murmur, continued muttering or low sound, growling, grumbling.
pronn-ghlòir, -e, *s. f.* Small talk, loquacity, tattle. 2 Whispering.
———each, -eiche, *a.* Loquacious, tattling. 2 Whispering.
pronn-ghlòrach, see pronn-ghlòireach.
pronn-lios, see proinn-lann.
pronnmhor, -oire, *a.* Ground, minced, pulverized, in fragments.
pronnt, see pronntach.
pronnta, *a. & past pt.* of pronn. Pounded, brayed, mashed, bruised, pulverized.
pronntach, *s. m.* Meal obtained by pounding grain in a stone mortar—still used in some parts.
pronntachd,(AC) *s.f.* Prosperity.
†pronntain, -e, *s.f.* Provender.
pronntair, -ean, see pronnadair.
pronnte, see pronnta.
pronnusg, -uisg, see pronnasg.

pronnusgach, see pronnasgach.
prop, -a & -uip, -achan, *s.m.* Prop, support, pillar, undersetter, post.
prop, *pr.pt.* a' propadh, *v.a.* Prop, support, back, uphold.
propach, -aich, -aichean, *s.m.* Seaware, kelpware, black tangle, lady-wrack—*fucus versiculosus*. 2 Smart boy, *prov.* for propairneach.
propach, *a.* Propping.
propadh, -aidh, *s.m.* Propping, act of propping, supporting or sustaining. 2 Support, prop. A' p—, *pr. pt.* of prop.
propaidh, *fut. aff. a.* of prop.
propainn, *v.a.* see prop.
———te, *past pt.* of propainn.
propairneach, -ich, *s.m.* Stripling, stout sturdy lad.
propanach, *Argyll* for propairneach. 2* Well-built boy beginning to run about. Am p. àluinn, *the handsome stripling.*
propataireachd, *s.f.* There are two games in Uist called by this name.

1. A game like quoits or pitchers. Two large stones or props are set up on end at a distance from each other of about 20 yards. The number of players varies from two to six. If more than two play, they may do so singly or in picked sides. The only articles needed are the props and two flat pieces of stone, as nearly balanced as possible, wherewith to toss. The game goes by points, a certain number, usually 21, being agreed on as game. The pointing or scoring, which is not reckoned in the same way anywhere else, is as follows in Uist. Three points if you knock the prop down fairly, one point if that pitcher lies nearer the prop than any other, one point if your other pitcher lies nearer than any of your opponent's. Thus, if your two quoits be nearer the prop than your opponent's two, you have two points ; if only one is nearer then you have only one point. In the case of two players, both stand at the same prop and toss at the opposite prop endeavouring to hit it or lie as near to it as possible. In the case of sides (say, two on each side) one member of each side takes the stones, while the other two stand at the opposite prop, and toss each his two quoits to the best of his ability. These are then in turn tossed towards them again by those at the other end, the game counting, as usual, in points.

propataireachd(2),or leagail shaighdear (felling the soldier.) Game played on the same principle as skittles. There are two equal sides of any number, usually about seven, and each player has a prop, which he sticks in the ground just enough to make it stand. Each player is provided with two stones for throwing at the props. The side which wins the toss then starts to knock as many as possible of their opponents' props down in this way. The first man in the row throws his two quoits trying to knock as many down as he can ; his neighbour follows, and so on, till all the row have thrown their quoits. If they knock down all the opposing props, the game is theirs ; if not, their opponents start in exactly the same way to knock theirs down. If they succeed, they win the game ; if not, the props are set up again and play recommences.—" Uist Games " in *Celtic Review, No. 16.*
propta, *past pt.* Propped, sustained, supported, upheld.
propte, see propta.
prosda,** *a.* Strong, firm, stout.
prosnach, *a.* see brosnachail.
prosnachadh, see brosnachadh.
prosnachail, see brosnachail.
prosnaich, see brosnaich.
———te, see brosnaichte.
prosnan, -ain, *pl.* -ain & -an, *s. m.* Company, band, group.
———ach, -aiche, *a.* In companies, bands or groups.
prosnuchadh, see brosnachadh.
prosnuich, see brosnaich.
protaig,‡ *s.f.* Trick—*Badenoch.*
pròtail,‡ *a.* Proud—*Arran*, see bròtail.
prothaid, see probhaid.
prothaist, see probhaist.
———each, see probhaisteach.
†**pruchlais**, -e, -ean, *s.f.* Den, cave.
pruidh ! *int.* Call to cattle—*Perth, N. Argyll. Mull.* 2 Call to a cow or calf—*W. of Ross.* 3 Call to a calf—*Arran.*
pruidh-dhé ! *int.* Call to a cow—*Badenoch. & N. Argyll.*
pruidh-dhé bheag ! *int.* Call to a calf—*N. Argyll.*
pruidh-é ! *int.* Call to a calf—*Perth & Suth'd.* 2 (MM) Call to a cow near at hand—*Argyll.*
pruidh-seo ! *int.* Call to a calf—*Mull.*
pruigean ! *int.* Call to a cow or calf—*W. of Ross.*
pruinn, *gen.* of pronn.
pruinne, *comp.* of pronn.
pruinnean, *s.m.* Chastisement.
pruinneasdan,(MS) *s.m.* Sulphur.
pruip, *gen. sing. & n. pl.* of prop.
pruis ! *int.* Call to a cow—*Arran.*
pruisidh ! *int.* Call to a cow—*Arran.*
pruis-o ! *int.* see pruidh-seo !
prunaistean, *Glendale* for pronnusg.
prunnan,** *s.m.* Fardel.
prui-seog ! (AH) *int.* Call to a horse—*N. Argyll.*
pru-siuch ! *int.* Call to a horse—*W. of Ross.*
pùbaid, see cùbaid.
pùbal,** -ail, see pubull 4.
pùbull, -uill, -an, *s.m.* Tent, booth, pavilion, marquee. 2 Alcove. 3 Covering. 4§Butter-bur or pestilence - wort, see gallan mór. Shuidhich iad am pùbuill, *they pitched their tents.*
pùbullach, -aiche, *a.* Tented, full of tents or booths. 2 Of, or like tents or booths. Magh p., *a tented field.*
pùbull-beannach, *s.m.* Butter-bur, see gallan mór.
pùc, *pr.pt.* a' pùcadh, *v.a.* Push, jostle, shove. 2* Fumble, ram, cram.
pùcadh, -aidh, *s.m.* Jostling, act of jostling, pushing, shoving. A' p—, *pr. pt.* of pùc.
pucaid, -e, -ean, *s.f.* Pimple, blotch. 2 Scab, itch. 3 see bucaid.
———each, -aiche, *a.* Pimpled, blotched. 2 Having the itch. 3 Scabbed 4 see bucaideach.
———eachd,** *s.f.* Scabbiness. 2 Itch.
pùcail, -e, *s.f.* see pùcadh. 'S ann ort 'tha a' ph. ! *how you do push !*
†**pucan**, see pocan.
puc-tholl, *s.m.* Plug-hole of a boat.
pùda,* *s.* Poult.
pùdach,(DU) *s.m.* Young of any bird, except of domestic fowl (whose young is *eòin.*) F.-tunnaig, *a duckling* ; p.-faoileag, *a young gull.*
pùdar, -air, *s.m.* see fùdar.
pùdarach, see fùdarach.
pùdaraich, see fùdaraich.
———te, see fùdaraichte.
pùdhair,** Gaelic form of Scots pronunciation of *power.*
pudhar, -air, -an, *s.m* Mishap, loss, damage, harm, injury. 2(CR) Hurt, sore, ulcer, sup-

purating sore—*W. of Ross.*
pudharach, *a.* Hurtful, harmful, injurious. 2 Ulcerous, having ulcers.
———adh, -aidh, *s.m.* Suppuration.
pudharaich,(MM) *v.* Suppurate.
pudharan,(DC) *s.m.* Black stalk of corn found occasionally in a field of growing oats—*Uist.*
puibleachadh,** -aidh, *s. m.* Publishing.
†puibligh, -e, *a.* Public.
†puiblich, *v.a.* Publish, proclaim.
pùic, -e, -ean, *s.f.* Bribe. Fhuair e p., *he has been bribed*; cha d' thug e p. dheth, *he made nothing of him.* Also used for pùc.
pùic, *v.a.* Bribe.
pùiceach, -eiche, *a.* Bribing, giving bribes. 2 Receiving bribes. 3 Easily bribed. 4**Like a bribe.
pùiceach,* -eich, *s.f.* Female briber.
puicean, -ein, -an, *s.m.* Veil or covering over the eyes. 2 Game of blind-man's-buff. 3 bribe.
pùicear, -eir, -an, *s.m.* Briber.
———achd, *s.f.* Bribery.
puichean, -ein, -an, *s.m.* Little impudent fellow. 2 Pithless, sickly, diminutive fellow.
puicneadh,** -aidh, *s.m.* Blindfolding. 2 Imposition.
puicne-sgreabhal,** *s.* Spangle.
pùidse, -an, *s. f.* Pocket. Gaelic spelling of Scots pronunciation of *pouch.* P. uaireadair, *a fob*; p. briogais, *a trousers pocket.*
pùidseach, *a.* Having pockets or pouches.
puilgean,(CR) *s.m.* Little fat person—*W. of Ross,* see builgean.
puinc, -e, -ean, see punc.
†puincearn, -uirn, -an, see puingearn.
puing, see punc.
puingean,** -ein, *s.m.* Roll of butter.
puingearn,** -eirn, *s.m.* Beam for measuring or weighing goods, the graduated beam. (pungiarunn.)
puinnd, *gen. & pl.* of punnd.
puinne, *s.* Drop, spout, stream, see buinne. 'Dol le puinne 'na chuaich,—*Rob Donn.*
puinneag,§ -eig, -an, *s.m.* Common sorrel, see buinneag.
————ach, -aiche, *a.* Abounding in sorrel. 2 Of, or pertaining to, sorrel.
puinneagan, -ain, *s.m.* Sorrel.
puinneanach, -aich, *s. m.* Same meanings as puinneanachadh. 2**Bruiser, pugilist.
puinneanachadh, -aidh, *s. m.* Beating, act of beating or thumping, thrashing, belabouring. A' p—, *pr.pt.* of puinneanaich.
puinneanaich, *pr. pt.* a' puinneanachadh, *v. a.* Beat, thump, belabour, bruise.
puinng, see punc.
puinse, Gaelic form of *punch*, toddy. Am p. milis, guanach, *the sweet heady punch.*
puinseach, *a.* Abounding in punch. 2 Of, or belonging to, punch.
puinsean, -in, -an, *s. m.* Poison, venom. 2** Term of contempt or disgust. A phuinsein a tha thu ann! *reptile that thou art!* [*puinnsean* is nearer the usual pronunciation, but as the best Gaelic Dictionaries give *puinsean*, that spelling has been followed here. McL & D gives *puinsean* in the Gael.-Eng. part, and and *puinnsean* in the Eng.-Gael. part.]
———ach, -aiche, *a.* Poisonous, venomous. 2**Baneful.
puinseanachadh, -aidh, *s. m.* Poisoning, act of killing by means of poison. A' p—, *pr.pt.* of puinseanaich.
puinseanaich, *pr.pt.* a' pùinnseanachadh, *v. a.* Poison, take off or kill by poison.
puinseanaichte, *past pt.* of puinseanaich. Poisoned, killed by poison.
puinseanta, *a.* Poisonous, venemous.
puinseantachd, *s.f.* Same meanings as puinseantas.
puinseantas,* -ais, *s.m.* Poisonousness, venomousness. 2 Vindictiveness, resentment.
puinsion, -in, -ean, see puinsean.
———ach, see puinseanach.
puinsionachadh, see puinseanachadh.
puinsionaich, see puinseanaich.
puinsionaichte, see puinseanaichte.
puinsionta, see puinseanta.
puintealta,** *a.* Precise. 2 Punctual.
puip,(DMu) *a.* Worthless, untidy. Am fear p. sin, *that worthless fellow—Suth'd.*
pùirleag, -eig, -an, *s.f.* Crest, tuft.
pùirleagach, -aiche, *a.* Crested, tufted.
puirneach,** -ich, *s.m.* Hunter.
puirt, *gen. & pl.* of port.
puirtean, -ein, -an, *s. m., dim.* of port. Sonnet. 2 Little harbour or haven. 3 Little turret.
puis, -ean, *s.m.* Puss, kitten, little cat.
puiseag,(DU) *s.f.* Kitten.
†puisg,** *v.a.* Beat, whip, lash.
puisidh, Gaelic spelling of *pussy.*
puision, see puinsean.
puist, *gen.sing. & n.pl.* of post.
†puitric, *s.* Bottle.
pulag, -aig, -an, *s. f.* Round stone. 2 Ball. 3 Pedestal. 4 Footstool of a pillar. 5**Porpoise. 6* Large round stone.
pulagach, -aiche, *a.* Abounding in round stones. 2 Like a round stone or ball.
pulaidh,(CR) -nean, *s.f.* Turkey. Coileach p., *a turkey-cock*; cearc-ph., *a turkey-hen—W. of Ross-shire.* 2 (DMy) Champion, hero, especially in strenth and boxing. 'S Niall MacAoidh 'na ph. orra, *and Neil MacKay a turkey-cock over them.*
pùlais, *S. Suth'd* for bùlas.
pula-mhullach,** pulaichean-m-, *s. m.* Dome, cupola.
pùlas, see bùlas.
pulbhag,** -aig, -an, *s.f.* Round stone, sizeable round stone.
pulbhag,** *s.f.* Pollock (fish.)
pullag, -aig, -an, *s.f.* †Pantry. 2 (AF) Pollack. lythe (fish.)
pulpaid, Gaelic spelling of *pulpit.*
pumpaid,(CR) *Arran* for cùbaid (pulpit.)
pumpais, (MMcD) *s.f.* Pimples on the face or skin—*Lewis.*
pumpais,(MS) *s.f.* Pump.
punan,** -ain, *s.m.* see punnan.
punc, -uinc, -an, *s. m.* Point, tittle. 2 Point, stop. 3 Article. 4 Note in music. 5 Quirk. 6 Quibble at law. 7 Aspiring. 8 (MS) Position. 9††Tone. 10 Point in a debate. Chuir thu as mo phunc mi, *you defeated my intention*; tha e làn phuncan, *he is full of quirks*; air a' ph. sin, *on that point.*
puncach,** *a.* Pointed, having points.
puncachadh, -aidh, *s.m.* Punctuation.
puncachas, *s.m.* Position.
puncaich, *v.a.* Point.
puncaid,* -e, -ean, *s.f.* Quirk, stratagem. Làn de phuncaidean, *full of quirks.*
puncaideach,* -eiche, *a.* Full of quirks or tricks, stratagetical.
puncail,(MS) *v.a.* Adjust.
puncail, -e, *a.* Distinct, articulate. 2 Exact, accurate. 3 Pointed. 4 Punctual. 5 Tidy. 6* Business-like in everything.
puncaireachd, *s.f.* Punctuation.
puncalachd, *s.f.* Distinctness, articulateness. 2 Exactness, correctness, accuracy. 3 Pointedness. 4 Punctuality. 5 Tidiness. 6* Great

attention.
puncalas, see puncalachd.
puncan-dearbhaidh, s. Quotation points (" ".) 2 (DMy) Proofs, tests.
puncar, -ais, s.m. Article in *grammar*.
puncglas, -ais, s.m. Species of purple grass.
punc-labhair,** v.a. Articulate.
punc-labhairt, puinc-, s.m. Articulation. 2 Accent, accentuation.
punc-labhraiche,** s.m. Distinct articulator.
pund, see punnd.
pundglas, -ais, see puncglas.
pung, -uing, -an, see punc.
pungach, see puncach.
pungachadh, -aidh, see puncachadh.
pungaid, see puncaid. 2 (DMy) Stiff, inactive female.
pungaideach, see puncaideach.
pungail, -e, see puncail.
pungalachd, see puncalachd.
punnag,‡‡ -aig, -an, s.f. Baloon in *architecture*.
punnan, -ain, -an, s.m. Sheaf of corn. 2 Bundle of hay or straw. 3**Burden. 4**Fardel. 5** Blast, as of a horn. 6**Bittern.
punnd, -uinnd, s.m. Pound weight.(1 ℔) 2 Fold to confine cattle that trespass. 3 £1 sterling. Punnd Sasunnach, *£1 sterling*.
punnd, *pr.pt.* a' punndadh, v.a. Pound cattle.
punnnainn, see funntainn. [* says, Bad usage in being confined in a damp place. 2 State of being confined in a cold place.]
punndair, -ean, s.m. One who confines straying cattle, pounder. 2 (DU) Shepherd paid by a district to herd sheep during summer.
———eachd, s.f. Confining of straying cattle, pounding. 2 Herding sheep. Tha e ris a' ph., *he is engaged as a district shepherd*.
punnt, s.m. Couch-grass.
punntainn,‡ s.f. Benumbment (also funntainn.)
punt, -uint. see punnd.
puntain, -e, see funntainn.
pùpaid, Gaelic form of Scots *poopit*.
purgadair, -ean, s. m. Purgatory. 2 Purifier. 3 Tormenter. 4* The greatest anxiety to get freedom, or to shift quarters.
purgadaireach, -ich, s.m. One undergoing the changes and pains of purgatory.
purgadaireach, -aiche, a. Purgatorial.
purgadaireachd, s.f. Purification. 2 State of purgatory. 3**Changes of purgatory. 4** Doctrine of purgatory.
purgadaireadh, -eidh, s.m. Purgatory.
purgadoir, see purgadair.
purgaid, -e, -ean, s.f. Purge, purgative, aperient medicine. P. duine, *a dour man*—(DMy)
purgaideach, -eiche, a. Purgative, cathartic cleansing, vomitory.
purgaideachadh, -aidh, s.m. Medication.
purgaideachd,** s.f. Laxativeness, frequent purging.
purgaidich, v.a. Purge.
pùrlag, -aig, -an, s.f. Tatter. 2 Fragment of anything, *prov.*
pùrlagach, -aiche, a. Ragged, tattered.
purp,* -uirp, s.m. The faculties of the mind. 2 Full possession of mental powers. Chaill e a ph., *he lost his faculties* ; an fheadh 's a bhitheas mo ph. agam, *while I possess my faculties* ; gun ph., *uncollected*.
purpaidh,§ s.f. Purslane-like orache—*atriplex portulacoides* 2§ Poppy. 3**Purslane.
purpaidh,‡‡ -e, a. Purple—*Suth'd & N.Argyll*.
purpail,* -e, a. Collected, in one's senses. 2 Sound in mind. 3 Punctual. 4 Accurate. 5 Pointed. 6**Courageous. 7**Active.
purpaileachd,** s.f. Courage. 2 Activity.
purpais, see purp.
purpalachd,* s.f. Collectiveness, full possession of faculties. 2 Punctuality.
purpur, -uir, s.m. Purple colour.
purr, *pr. pt.* a' purradh, v.a. Push, thrust, drive, urge. 2 Jerk. 3 Butt, strike with the head. 4 Poke. 5 Jostle. 9 Dash at, as a bull.
purrach,** a. Apt to push or shove, pushing, shoving. 2 Jostling.
purradair, -ean, s.m. Putter.
purradh, -aidh, -aidhean, s.m. Pushing, act of pushing, thrusting, shoving or driving. 2 Jerking, jerk. 3 Butt, act of butting with the head. 4 Jostling. 5 Push, thrust. A' p—, *pr.pt.* of purr. A' p. le 'adharcaibh, *butting with his horns* ; an reithe a' p., *the ram butting*.

586. Purpaidh.

purraghlas, -ais, s.m. Cat.
purt, puirt, see port.
pus, -uis, -ean, Gaelic form of *puss*.
pus, -uis, -an, see bus.
pùs, see pòs.
pusach, see busach.
pusachag, -aig, -an, s.f. Whining girl.
pusachan, -ain, -an, s.m. Whining boy.
pùsadh, see pòsadh.
pusag, -aig, -an, s.f., dim. of pus. 2††see busag.
pusaidh, see puisidh.
pùsda, see pòsda.
pùst', see pòsda.
put, -a, -an, s.m. The cheek.
put, *pr.pt.* a' putadh, v.a. Push, thrust. 2 Jostle. 3 Put with the head.
put, s.m. Push, shove.
pùt, -a, -an, s.m. Young of moorfowl, young grouse (pout.) 2 Large buoy, generally of sheepskin, inflated. 3 Corpulent person. 4 Any bulging thing.—*Suth'd*. [2 is *put* in *Harris* and not *pùt*.] P. meadhon, *a middle buoy* ; p. suab, *the buoy on end of cable* ; p. sais, *the buoy placed just below the surface to prevent the ceann-mara (cable) lying on the bottom*. [** gives *pùit* as *gen.* of No. 1.]
put,(CR) s.m. Bruised swelling caused by a blow, as in fighting. 2 Spadeful of the caschrom. [1 & 2 *Ross-shire*.] Thug mi p. air, *I marked him* ; am p. fuaraidh, an ceap fuaraidh, *the first turned sod of a furrow*.
puta, see pait.
puta,* s.m. Trout—*North*. 2 see pùt 1.
pùtach, -aiche, a. Abounding in young grouse. 2 Of, or belonging to, buoys, like a buoy. 3 Producing young moorfowl. (bùtach.)
putach,** a. Pushing, shoving, jostling.
putadh, *3rd. sing. & pl.imp.* of put.
putadh, -aidh, -ean, s.m. Pushing, shoving, act of pushing, jostling. 2*Butting. 3 Piece of soil turned over at one time with a spade. 4 ‡‡Check. 5 ‡‡Quick turn.
puta-fuaraidh,(CR) s. First sod or spadeful of a furrow in delving.—*W. of Ross-shire*.
putag, -aig, -an, s.f. Oar-pin, rowlock, thole. 2 Bodkin. 3 Pudding. 4 Small ridge of land. 5 Haft or handle of a scythe.
putagach, -aiche, a. Of, having or pertaining to, thole-pins. 2 puddings, or 3 small ridges of land. 4**Having thole-pins, as a boat.
putagaich, v.a. Provide or furnish with thole-pins, as a boat.
putagaichte, *past pt.* of putagaich.
putagan,** -ain, s.m. Pudding, pock-pudding.
putain, *gen.sing. & n.pl.* of putan.

putair, -ean, *s.m.* One who pushes or impels. 2 Dibble.
putaireachd, *s.f.* Pushing. 2 Dibbling.
pùtan, -ain, -an, *s.m.,dim.* of pùt. Young grouse, little poult. 2 (AF) Young animal. 3** Young hare.
putan, -ain, -an, *s.m.* Button. 2 Sny or toggle, see bàta, No. 1, p. 76. P.-duirn, *a sleeve button.*
putan, see pait.
putanach, -aiche, *a.* Buttoned. 2 Abounding in buttons. 3 Like a button.
putanachadh, -aidh, *s.m.* Buttoning.
putanachd, *s.f.* Button-making.
putanaich, *v.a.* Button.
putanaichte, *past pt.* Buttoned.
putan gorm,‡ *s.m.* Sheep-bit, see dubhan-nan-caora.
pùtanta,** *a.* Shy, as young moor-fowl, coy.
pùtantachd,** *s.f.* Shyness, coyness.
putar, *fut.pass.* of put.
puth, *s.m.* Snort. 2 Puff. 3 Sound of a shot. 4 Syllable. A' cur puthan as a shròin, *snorting with his nose.*
puthag, -aig, -an, *s.f.,dim.* of puth. Little puff or explosion. 2 Porpoise, grampus.
puthaid, (Fionn) *s.f.* Recess in the wall for holding small articles. 2 Ventilator in a byre wall, so called because it resembles the recess in a house wall.
puthaig,¶ *s.f.* Marsh-harrier, see clamhan-lòin.
puthar, -air, -an, *s.m.* Harm, hurt. 2 Wound, scar. 3 Sore, cause of sorrow. 4 Suppurating sore. Gaelic spelling of Scots pronunciation of *power.*
'S tha 'eunlaith fo phuthar 'an dubhar a chruachan—*Cruachan Beann, Filidh, p. 60.*
putharachadh, -aidh, see pudharachadh.
putog,(MS) *s.f.* Puddock.
†putrall -aill, -an, *s.m.* Lock of hair.

R r

r, (ruis, *elder-tree,*) the fifteenth letter of the Gaelic alphabet. It generally sounds like *r* in *raw, more;* as rach, *go;* mór, *great.* If in the same syllable *r* be preceded or followed by a small vowel (*e* or *i*, or both,) it has a sound to which there is none quite similar in English, but it resembles that of the French *r* in prairie, *a meadow;* as in airidh, *worthy;* fir, *men.*
'r, *cont.* for ar, Our.
'r, *cont.* for bhur or 'ur, Your.
r', *cont.* for ri, *prep.*
rà, *cont.* for ràdh.
rà, -than, *s.m.* see ràth.
ra, *adv.* see ro.
rà. *s.m.* Going, moving, *prov.*
ràbach, -aiche, *a.* Litigious, quarrelsome. 2** Plentiful, fruitful.
ràbachas, -ais, *s.m.* Litigiousness, quarrelsomeness. 2** Plentifulness, fruitfulness. Fear ràbachais, *a litigious fellow.*
rabaid, Gaelic spelling of *rabbit.* Cuilean r., *a young rabbit.*
——**each,** *a.* Abounding in rabbits. 2 Like a rabbit.
ràbair, -ean, *s.m.* Litigious, troublesome, tiresome person. 2††Roarer. 3 Wrangler. Cha'n 'eil ann ach r. òglaich, *he is but a wrangler of a fellow.*
——**each,** *a.* see ràbach.
——**eachd,** *s.f.* see ràbachas. 2†† Roaring 3 Wrangling.
ràbal,** **-ail,** *s.m.* Noise, bustle.
——**ach,** *a.* Noisy, bustling.
——**achd,** *s.f.* Noisiness, continued noise, continued bustle.
rabh,* *v.a.* Warn, guard.
rabh, see robh.
rabhacair,* -ean, *s.m.* Nonsensical rhapsodist. 2 Haranguer, proser. see rabhdair.
rabhacaireachd,* *s.f.* Rhapsody, prosing, haranguing, talking nonsense. see rabhdaireachd.
rabhach, -aiche, *a.* see rabhachail.
rabhachail, -e, *a.* Warning, admonitory, giving a caution or hint, hinting.
rabhach,** *a.* Admonitory.
rabhachan, -ain, -an, *s.m.* Warning. 2 Beacon. 3 Advertiser.
†rabhad, -aid, *s.m.* Precedent, example.
rabhadair,* -ean, *s.m.* Spy, scout. 2 see rabhachan. 3‡‡Citer. †4 see robh.
rabhadh, -aidh, *s.m.* Warning, alarm, hue and cry. 2** Advice, instruction. 3 Advertisement. 4 Example, precedent. 5 Caution, hint. 6 (MS) Memento. Thoir r. dha, *inform him, give him a hint;* rabhadh eaglais, *an ecclesiastical edict;* a' faghail rabhaidh, *receiving instruction.*
ràbhag,(DU) *s.f.* Person full of fun, or fond of practical joking.
rabhagach,‡ **-aich,** *s.f.* White water-lily, see duilleag-bhàite-bhàn. 2††Weeds growing at the bottom of water.
rabhaic, *Arran & Islay* for raoic.
rabhaidh,* *v.a.* Advertize.
rabhail,* -e, *s.f.* Rhapsody delivered in a drawling manner. 2 Mad saying. 3 Drawling manner or gait.
rabhail,** *a.* Admonitory.
rabhairt,* *s.f.* see reothart.
rabhan, *Arran* for ràbhan.
ràbhan, -ain, -an, *s.m.* Rhapsody, long and tedious repetition, rigmarole.
†rabhan, -ain, -an, *s.m.* Spade.
rabhan, (CR) *s.m.* Kind of grass that grows in still water, which sheep often wade in to eat and are drowned. It is sometimes cut for fodder. rabhann in *W. of Ross.* Pronounced *rafan* in *Reay Country & heights of Kildonan.*
rabhan, *s.m.* Remains of spate or tide on the shore—*Suth'd.*
ràbhanach, -aiche, *a.* Rhapsodical, tedious. 2 **Haranguing.
ràbhanach, -aich, *s.m.* Rhapsodist, tedious story teller. 2**Haranguer.
ràbhanachd, *s.f.* Rhapsody, harangue.
rabhanaiche,** *s.m.* see rabhanair.
rabhanair,** **-ean,** *s.m.* Rhapsodist. 2 Haranguer. 3 Proser.
rabhann,(CR) *s.m.* Grass or reed that grows in pools and is cut for fodder. It has many large joints which burst when dry, and white roots —*Strathconan.* 2 Water-lily—*W. of Ross-shire.* 3 Plant with leaves branching alternately on each side of the leaf-stem and floating on the water—*W. of Ross-shire.*
rabhart,** **-airt,** *s.m.* Upbraiding. 2 Senseless talk.
ràbhart, -airt, *s.m.* (AH) Fun, pleasantry. 2 see rabhd.
——**ach, -aiche,** *a.* see rabhanach.
†rabhartha, *a.* Overrunning.
rabhd, -a, -an, *s. m.* Idle or nonsensical talk. 2 Coarse, tiresome language, vapouring, tedious harangue, boast. 3 Idle talker. 4 Rant.
rabhdach, -aiche, *a.* Talking idly, given to idle talk, haranguing. 2 Using coarse or unbecom-

ing language.
rabhdadh, see rabhd.
rabhdair, -ean, *s.m.* Idle, tiresome talker, boaster, gossip, prater, rhapsodist, vapourer. 2** Bully. 3 One who uses coarse or unbecoming language. 4††Fabulist. 5 Ranter.
———eachd, *s.f.ind.* Habit of talking idly, coarsely or tiresomely, rhapsody, prosing, haranguing, verbosity, vapouring, gossiping
rabhdal, -ail, *s.m.* Coarse jesting, *prov.* 2 Prosing.
———ach, -aiche, *a.* Coarsely or vulgarly sportive.
rabhdarach, -aiche, see rabhdalach.
rabhladh, -aidh, *s.m.* see rabhdal. 2 Boasting.
rabhoil, see rabhail.
ràc, -aic, -an, *s.m.* Rake. 2 Ring keeping the yard to the mast, traveller, see bàta, 24, p. 76 [‡ gives *rac* for No. 2.]
ràc, -àic, -an, *s. m.* Drake.—**North.* 2 Discordant, disgusting music—**West.*
ràc, *s m.* Crash, prolonged crash. 2 Prattling. 3 Gushing 4 Shedding, as tears. 5 Croaking noise, as of crows.
†rac, *s.m.* King, prince. 2**Bag, pouch.
rac, *v a. & n., & s.* see srac.
rac, *pr pt.* a' racadh. *v a. & n* Rake, harrow. 2 Quack, as ducks or geese. 3 Make a crashing noise. 4 Croak 5 Rehearse, repeat.
ràcach, aiche, *a.* see ràcanach. 2 Crashing noisy. 3 Abounding in or belonging to, drakes.
ràcadal, -ail, *s.m.* Horse-radish. 2**Wild radish. [‡ gives racadal.]
———ach, -aiche, *a.* Abounding in horse-radish.
ràcadh, -aidh, -aidh, *s.m.* Raking, harrowing, act of raking or harrowing. 2 Quacking of ducks or geese. 3 Crashing noise. 4 Noise made by the tearing of cloth. (sracadh.) A' r—, *pr.pt.* of ràc.
racadh, -aidh, *s.m.* see sracadh. A' r—, *pr. pt.* of rac.
racaid, -e, -ean, *s.f.* Noise, disturbance. 2 Continual crashing noise. 3 Discordant voice, croaking. 4 Racket. 5*Drawling female. 6 Strong blow. Thug mi r. dha 'sa chluais, *I gave him a hard box on the ear.*
racaideach,†† -aiche, *a.* Bustling, noisy.
ràcail, *s.f.* Quacking, as of ducks or geese. 2 Continued crashing noise. 3 Discordant voice.
ràcain, *gen.sing. & n.pl.* of ràcan.
ràcair, -ean, *s.m.* Lying, talkative fellow, romancer. 2 Impertinent prattler. 3 Rehearser. 4 Raker. 5 One having a harsh or discordant voice. 6* Drawling, croaking orator or piper. 7* Croaker of a preacher. 8 Loud talker. 9 Talkative, lying person.
———eachd, *s. f.* Habit of lying, romance. 2 Impertinent loquacity, verbiage, rehearsing. 3 Discordance of voice, oratory or music, croaking. 4 Raking.
ràcan, -ain, -an, *s.m.* Rake. 2 Instrument for breaking clods and used as a harrow. In the *W. Isles*, it consists of a block of wood with a few teeth, and is used in such places as will not admit of the use of a harrow. It is commonly tied to the horse's tail, but not unfrequently it is dragged along the surface by women and boys. In *W. Ross-shire* it is applied to a short heavy rake with a head over 2 in. in thickness and a handle under 4 ft. in length. With it the seed is covered, clods are broken, and potato ground, before the tops come through, is raked or harrowed to keep down weeds—CR. 3 Noise, croaking noise. 4 Crash. 5 Bandy or crooked stick. 6 Mischief, evil, wickedness. 7 Bowling 8 Riot, noise. 9 Provincial denomination of arable land (ceann-ràcain.) Nach ann annad ' tha 'n r. ! *how mischievous you are !—Arran.* [*racan* not *ràcan* in *Arran.*]
ràcan, *pl.* of ràc. Rakes, harrows.
———ach, -aich, *s.m.* Mischievous person.
———ach, -aiche, *a.* Of, belonging to or furnished with rakes or hand-harrows. 2 Crashing. 3**Croaking. 4**Prating. 5**Dissonant.
racan-arbhair,(Fionn) *s.m.* Corn-craik.
rac-an-fheoir,(CR) *s m.* Corn-craik.
ràcanta,** *a.* Clashing, noisy. 2 Croaking. 3 Loquacious.
racas, -ais, *s.m* Sail-hoop. *prov.*
rach, for rachadh (would go.)
rach, *def. v.* Go, proceed, move, travel, walk.
Active Voice—
IND. *past*, chaidh mi, &c., *I, &c. went.*
,, *fut.* théid mi, &c., *I, &c will go.*
[Although commonly given by grammars as the future tense of rach, *théid* is quite a different word.]
INTERROG. & NEG. *past*, (an ? nach ? cha) deach *or* deachaidh mi, &c.
,, ,, ,, *fut.* (an ? nach ? cha) téid mi, &c.
SUBJUNCT. *past*, (ged) rachainn, (*though*) *I would go* ; (ged) rachadh tu, e, i, (*though*) *thou wouldest go, he, she would go*; (ged) rachamaid, (*though*) *we would go* ; (ged) rachadh sibh, iad, (*though*) *you, they, would go.*
,, *fut.* (ma) théid mi, &c., (*if*) *I, &c. shall go.*
IMPER. *1st. per.sing.* racham, *let me go.*
INFIN. a dhol, *to go.*
PRES. PART. a' dol, *going.*
Used Impersonally thus—
IMPER. rachar, theirigear, na rachar.
IND. *past*, deachas, chaidheas, an deachas ? cha deachas.
,, *fut* téidear, théidear, an téidear ? cha téidear.
Am fear a théid lideag am mearachd, *the man who goes a syllable, letter, least bit, wrong;* chaidh làithean na seachduin iomrall orra, *they got confused about (lost count of) the days of the week* ; chaidh a' chùis 'sa mhuileann orm, *I became hopelessly puzzled over the matter* ; chaidh thu gu Dun-bheagain orm, *you went to the extreme with me*—lit. *to Dunvegan,* a Lochaber saying—N.G.P. ; chaidh mi 'nam cheò, 'nam bhreislich, *I became mystified, muddled* ; chaidh mi bho obair, bho rath, bho fheum, *I have become very useless* ; chaidh mo thoirt as mo ghabhail, *I have been disappointed of my original intention* ; chaidh mi thar mo shiubhail, thar mo sgeòil, *I have deviated from, lost, my road, my story* ; chaidh sinn thar a chéile, *we quarrelled, fell foul of each other* ; chaidh mi am feirg choimhich, *I became transported with rage* ; chaidh iad gu bròn 's gu briseadh-cridhe, *they gave way to mourning and heart-grieving* ; chaidh mi a rìs gu m' smuaintean, *I reconsidered things, reviewed matters again* ; chaidh e gu mór bho 'aire féin, *he was so distraught as to be hardly himself* ; chaidh am bàta air chrith, *the boat began to quiver;* cha deach sin gu math dhaibh, *that did not suit them at all, it upset them* ; ciamar a chaidh dhuit ? *how did you manage, get on, how did things turn out for you* ; rach air t' aghaidh, *or* rach air aghart, *proceed* ; ma 's tu a th' ann, is tu chaidh as, *if that be you, you have sadly altered, you are merely the shadow of your former self* ; chaidh e as orm, *he*

escaped from me, evaded me ; chaidh an teine as orm *the fire I kindled* (or *was tending*) *went out* ; chaidh as daibh, *they died, were killed, their influence ceased* , cha téid anam á mac bodaich le mùiseig, *threats will not kill a churl's son* ; is mairg a rachadh to do mheachannas, *pity him who would trust to your discretion or mercies* ; chaidh Righ Lochlainn am meinn na Féinne, *the king of Lochlann begged the clemency of the Fingalians* ; chaidh mi an dail, an ceann, an seilbh *no* an tarruing na h-oibre, *or* chaidh mi an sàs anns an obair, *I set about the work* ; chaidh agam air, *I managed it, accomplished it* ; or *I prevailed over him* , cha téid gad air gealladh, *you cannot bind a promise with a withy* ; cha téid fiach air beul duinte, *a closed mouth does not run into debt* ; cha téid plàsd air bagairt, *a threat needs no plaster* ; chaidh a' bhròg oirre mu a cois, *the shoe fitted her foot, slipped on to it* ; chaidh na geinneagan air a' chòta, *the buttons were attached to the coat* ; chaidh eòin an geall caithream, *the birds began chorusing* ; na h-igheanan is bòidhche 'théid air ùrlar, *the lasses who dance most elegantly* ; an nighean a's deise 'théid to 'n éideadh, *the girl who dresses most tastefully* ; an là théid clò ùr air faiche, *the day the new cloth or dress is sported in public* ; théid iad air faoigh, *they will go on a genteel begging expedition* ; théid iad air a' bhannaig, *they will go on a bannock-begging Christmas round* ; théid iad air an déirc, *they will go begging for alms* ; théid iad air chéilidh chuige, *they will go on a visit to him* ; théid iad 'nan deannaibh, *they will go, running furiously* ; rachaibh dhachaidh, *go (ye) home* ; théid sinn dhachaidh, *we will go home*; na téirig dhachaidh, *don't go home* ; chaidh sinn dhachaidh, *we went home* ; an deachaidh e dhachaidh ? *did he go home ?*

rachadh, *past subj.* of rach. Would go. 2 *2nd. & 3rd. per. sing. & pl. imp.* of rach. R. e, *let him go.*

†rachail, *s.f.* Winding-sheet.

rachainn, *1st. per. sing. past subj.* of rach. I would go.

†rachall, -aill, *s.m.* Winding-sheet.

racham, *1st. per. sing. imp.* of rach. Let me go.

rachamaid, *1st. per. pl. past subj.* of rach. We would go. 2 *1st. per. pl.* of rach. Let us go.

rachar, *used impersonally.* Rachar suas leo, *they ascended.*

rachd, *s.f.ind.* see reachd. [‡ gives *rachd.*]

ràchd, *s.m. & v.* see ràc.

rachd, -an, see reachd.

ràchdadh, see ràcadh.

rachdaid, see racaid.

ràchdail, see ràcail.

ràchdair, see ràcair.

ràchdan, see ràcan.

rachdan, -ain, -an, *s.m.* Tartan plaid worn in the shape of a mantle or cloak.

rachdmhor, -oire, *a.* see reachdmhor.

————achd, see reachdmhorachd.

rache,(AF) (? raitche) *s.* Scent-hound.

†racholl, -oill, -an, *s.m.* Winding-sheet.

rac-mhara,(AF) *s.* Salmon.

rac-mhaighreadh,(AF) *s.* Salmon.

racuis, -e, -ean, *s.f.* Rack. 2 Toasting apparatus.

ràd, -àid, -an, see ròd.

†rad, -a, *a.* Ready, furnished.

radaidh, *a.* Dark, sallow. Duine r., dorcha, *a sallow-complexioned man.* (also rodaidh)

radaireal,** -eil, *s.m.* see rodaireal.

radan, -ain, -an, *s.m.* Rat. 2 Cunning person. R. Armeniach, *an ermine.*

ràdan, *n.pl.* of ràd

radanach, -aiche, *a.* Abounding in rats. 2 Like a rat.

ràdanach, -aiche, *a.* Not affectionate, distant. 2 Dissembling, uncandid.

radan-dubh, *s.m.* Black rat.

radan-ùir, (AF) *s.m.* Mole.

radan-uisge, *s.m.* Craber, water-rat.

ràdh, *s.m.* Saying, act of saying, affirming, or expressing. 2 Word, saying, adage, proverb 3 Noise. 4* Assertion. 5 Speech. Ag r—, *pr. pt.* of abair. Tha 'n r. ud fìor, *that saying is true* ; tha mi 'g r., *I say.*

radh, *s.* Settled intention—*Suth'd.* Tha mi air r. seo a dheanamh, *I intend doing this.*

†ràdh, *past aff.* of abair. Do r. e gach uair, *he said each time.*

radhad, -aid, -an, see rathad.

radhadh, -aidh, -aidhean, see rabhadh & roghainn.

ràdhainn, *prov.* for ràdh.

radhaircin, see raghaircin.

radhar, see raghar.

radharc, -airc, *s.m.* Sight, power of vision. 2 View, prospect. 3 Pupil of the eye—*Lewis.* R. mo dhà rosg, *the sight of my two eyes.* [also fradharc.]

————ach, -aiche, *a.* Seeing, having the faculty of sight. 2 Commanding a good or extensive prospect. 3**Observant. 4** Conferring the faculty of sight.

radmuinn,(AF) *s.* Fox.

rafan, see rabhan.

rag, -aige, *a.* Stiff, rigid, not pliable. 2 Stiff, benumbed. 3 Obstinate, pertinacious. 4 Inflexible, inexorable. 5 Unwilling, disinclined. 6**Tight, as a rope. 7**Tough. 8**Dim. 9 Asinine.

rag, *pr.pt.* a' ragadh, *v.a.* Become stiff or distended to stiffness. 2 Be benumbed.

rag, -a, -achan, *s.m.* Starch. 2 Wrinkle. 3 see luideag. 4 Term of personal contempt. 5 Shabby fellow.

ragach, -aiche, *a.* Wrinkled. 2** Tough, stiff, obstinate. 3 see luideagach.

ragachadh, -aidh, *s.m.* Act of stiffening or making stiff. 2 State of becoming stiff or rigid. 3 Toughening, tightening as a rope. 4** Wrinkling.

ragachail, -e, *a.* Inclining to stiffness, having a tendency to, or causing stiffness, toughness or tightness.

ragadair, -ean, *s.m.* Stretcher. 2 (DMy) Ragman.

ragadh, -aidh, *s.m.* Growing or becoming stiff.

ragaich, *pr.pt.* a' ragachadh, *v.a. & n.* Stiffen, make stiff. 2 Become stiff or rigid. 3 Curdle, congeal. 3 Toughen, tighten, or stretch, as a rope. 4 Become tight, as a rope. 5 Condensate.

————te, *past pt.* of ragaich. Stiffened, become stiff, tightened, stretched, toughened.

ragaim, *s.f.* Sneezewort (meacan ragaim.)

ragair, -ean, *s.m.* Extortioner. 2 Violent man. 3 Villain, rogue, deceiver. 4**Instrument for tightening a rope. 5** Person with a wrinkled face.

ragaireach, -eiche, *a.* Violent, using violence, oppressive. 2 Roguish, villainous. 3 Deceiving, deceitful. 4** Extortive.

ragaireachd, *s.f.ind.* Violence, practice of violence. 2 Extortion, oppression. 3 Roguery, villainy. 4 Deceit, deceitfulness. 5 Clamminess.

rag-bhalach, ‡‡ -aich, *s.m.* Lubber.

rag-bharalach, ‡‡ -aiche, *a.* Opinionative.

————————d, ‡‡ *s.f.* Positiveness.

rag-bheart, -bheirt, -an, *s m.* Obstinacy. 2 Villainous, mischievous or wicked deed. 3 Forced work.
————ach, -aiche, *a.* Obstinate, perverse, headstrong. 2 Committing mischievous or villainous deeds.
————achd, *s.f ind.* Perverseness,obstinacy. 2 Mischief. 3 Wickedness.
————as, -ais, -ais, *s.m.* Same meanings as rag-bheartachd.
ràgh,* *s.m.* Row, rank. (*Scots*, raw=row,rank.) 2 Raft of wood. R. shaighdearan, *a rank of soldiers.*
ragha, see roghainn.
raghadh, -aidh, see roghainn.
raghaidh,(CR) *s.* Warning—*W. of Ross* for raghadh. (*pron.* răo'i.)
raghain, see roghainn.
raghaircin, *s m.* Eyebright (plant.)
raghan, -ain, -an, *s.m.* Churchyard.
raghar, -air, -an, *s.m.* Arable land not in tillage 2 *sometimes* Grazing ground enclosed between the arable land and the open moor *Perthshire.*
rag-bheirteach,(MS) *a.* Mad-brained.
rag-mheirleach, -ich, *s.m.* Arrant thief.
rag-mhuinealach, -aiche, *a.* Stiff-necked, stubborn, headstrong, perverse.
————————d, *s.f ind.* Contumacy,stiff-neckedness, obstinacy,stubbornness, perverseness. 2 Depravity.
rag-mhuinealas, -ais, *s. m.* see rag-mhuinealachd.
rag-roth,** *s.m.* Torturing-wheel.
rag-sheallach, -aiche, *a.* Stiff-looking, awkward, unbecoming.
rag-shùil, -shùla, -shùilean, *s.f.* Dim eye.
————each,** *a.* Dim-eyed.
†raib, *s.f.* Turnip. 2 Rope.
raibeach,** *a.* Loose.
†raibh, see robh. (Irish form.)

587. Raibhe.

raibhe,§ *s.f.* Radish.—*raphanus.*
raibheic,* see raoic.
————eil, *s.f.* see raoiceadh.
raibleachan,** -ain, *s.m.* Scullion.
ràic, -e, *s. f.* Impertinence, impudence. 2 Idle prattling. 3 Gibberish. 4 Boastfulness.
——ealachd, *s.f.ind.* Habit of talking idly. 2 see raic.
——eil, -e, *a.* Impertinent. 2 Troublesome. 3 Given to idle talk.
ràichd, -e, see raic.
†raicneach, -ich, *s.f.* Queen.
ràid, *gen.sing.* of ràd.
ràide,** *s.f.* Cunning, slyness. Luchd ràide, *cunning people.*
ràideachas,** -ais, *s.m.* Boastful speech, arrogant language, arrogance, pride. 2 Saying. 3 Report. 4 Trial of skill.
raideag,** -eig, *s f.* Myrtle.
ràidealach,** *a* Cunning, sly, insidious.
†ràidealachd, *s.f.ind.* Invention, readiness in devising plans. 2 Cunning, slyness, artfulness.
ràideil, -e, *a.* Inventive. 2 Sagacious. 3 Cunning, crafty, sly.
†ràidh, *v.a.* Threaten, menace. 2 Appeal,look.
†raidh, *s.f.* Radius.
ràidh, -e, -ean, *s.f.* Arbitration. 2 Decision. 3 Appeal, entreaty. 4 Threat, threatening. 5 Umpire. 6 Good will. 7 Competition. Leig gu ràdh nan daoine seo e, *submit it to the arbitration of these men*; tha mise, a dhaoin' uaisle,a' leigeil a' ghnothaich seo g' 'ur raidhse, *I appeal to you gentlemen, in this matter*; fear-ràidhe, *an arbitrator*; a' raidh air a chéile, *competing with each other*; thoir r., *threaten.* [** gives *s.m.* for Nos. 1. 2 & 3.]
ràidh,** *s.m,* Judge.
ràidh, -ean, *s.m.* Rank, as of soldiers (ragh.) 2 Speech. 3 Entreaty. 4 Intercession. 5 see ràith.
ràidh,(CR) *s.f.* Boasting, brag, vain-glory Tha pailteas r. ann, *he is much given to boasting—W. of Ross-shire.*
ràidh, -e, -ean, *s.f.* [McL & D gives *m.*] Quarter (of a year.)
ràidhe, *s.f.ind.* Umpirage, arbitration. 2**Arbiter.
———ach,** *a.* Prone to threat, threatful. 2 Appealing.
———achd,** *s.f.ind.* Habit of threatening, minaciousness. 2 Circumstance of appealing.
raidhean,** -ein, *s.m.* Crowd, rabble.
ràidhean, -ein, *s.m.* Quarterly, as a paper or magazine.
ràidheil,* -e, *a.* Challenging, fond of challenging. 2 Boasting.
ràidheil, -e, *a.* Quarterly.
raidhir, see raoir.
raidhm, *s.* Rheum.
†raidhmheas, -eis, -an, *s.m.* Dream. 2 Romance. 3**Cubit.
†————ach, -aiche, *a.* Romantic,fabulous, gasconading.
†raidhreach, -eich, -ean, *s.m.* Prayer, petition, request.
ràidhteach, -eiche, *a.* see ràiteach.
raidse, -an, *s.m.* Prating fellow, idle talker. 2 **Verbiage.
———ach, -aiche, *a.* Prattling, garrulous, prating, verbose. *prov.*
———ach,* -eich, *s.f.* Chief witch.
———achas, -ais, *s. m.* Habit of prating, idle talk, verbiage. 2 Witchery, enchantment.
raidis,** -ean, *s.f.* Gaelic spelling of *radish.*
raige, *s.f.ind.* Stiffness. 2 Obstinacy.
raige, *comp.* of *a.* rag.
raigead, -eid, *s.m.* Degree of stiffness or obstinacy. 2 Tightness, toughness, tenseness. Is r. an còrd an tarruing sin, *that pull has made the cord tighter.*
raigealachd,** *s.f.* Impetuosity.
raigealtach, (CR) *s. m.* Rascal. 2 Rollicking fellow—*Perthshire.*
raigeann,(DC) *s.m.* Obstinacy, stiffneckedness. —*Uist.* 2(MS) Slowness. 3 Harshness.
†raigh, *s.f.* Frenzy.
raighe, *s.f.* see ruighe. 2 Rank or file of soldiers (ragh.)
raigheil,** *a.* Frantic.
raigionn,(DC) see raigeann.
raigle, *s.f.* see réilig.
———ar,** -eir, *s.m.* Ragged, untidy person.
raigneachadh,* -aidh, *s.m.* Stiffening, benumb-

ed. A' r—, *pr.pt.* of raignich. Tha mo làmhan air raigneachadh, *my hands are benumbed.*
raignich,* *v.a.* Stiffen. 2 Benumb.
rail,§ *s.* Oak, see darach.
railidh,§ *s.* Oak, see darach.
railig, see réilig.
railleach,(AF) *s.* Redshank.
raillidh,** *s. f.* Fight, fray *(rally.)* 2 (AH) Boisterous fun or sport.
ràimh, *gen. sing.* & *n.pl.* of ràmh.
†raimh, *s.f.* Brimstone.
raimhdeas,** -eis, *s.m.* Fatness, greasiness.
raimhe, see reamhra.
raimhead,* see reamhrad.
raimhre, see reamhra.
raimigil, -e, *s.f.* Confusion, *prov.*
raimisg,* *s.f.* Coarse, vulgar person.
ràin, *gen.sing.* of ràn.
ràin, see ràn. 2 *contr.* of ràinig.
rainche,(AF) *s.m.* Fox.
raineach, -nich, *s.f.* Fern, brake—*filix fœmina vulgaris.* Goisean rainich, *a tuft of fern.*
———ail, -e, *a.* Abounding in fern, ferny. 2 Like fern.
——— -an-fhàile,§ *s.f.* Sweet mountain fern, see crim-raineach.

588. *Raineach-Beinn-Ghobhrdaidh.*

——— Bheinn Ghobhrdaidh,§ *s.f.* Mountain bladder-fern—*cystopteris montana.* [Found wild only on Ben Gourdie.—§]

589. *Raineach chruaidh.*

——— chruaidh,§ *s. f.* The hard fern—*blechnum spicant.* [Preceded by the art. *an.*]
——— -chuilinn, -ich-c-, *s.f.* Holly fern—*poly-*

590. *Raineach -chuilionn.* 591. *Raineach-Muire.*

stichum lonchitis.—*Lern, &c.* [colg-raineach in *Breadalbane.*]
raineach-mhara,§-ich-m-, *s.f.* The sea-fern (kind of sea-weed.)—*halydris siliquosa*—*Skye.*
——— -mhór,§ -ich-móire, *s.f.* Common brake fern—*pteris aquilina.* [Preceded by the art. *an.*]
——— -Muire,§ -ich-M-, *s.f.* The lady-fern—*athyrium filix fœmina.* [** gives Common male fern—*filix major vulgaris.*
——— -na-mara,‖ *s.f.* Sea-fern—*asplenium marinum.*
——— -nan-creag,§ *s.f.* Polypody, see clach-raineach.

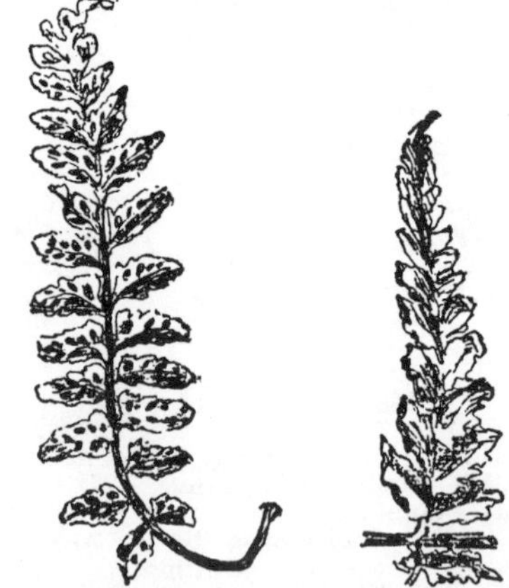

592. *Raineach-na-mara.* 593. *Raineach-nan-radan.*

raineach-nan-radan,§ -ich-, *s.f.* *lastrea spinulosa* and the allied species *dilatata* and *fœnisecii.* (ill. 593 is fœnisecii.)
——— -reangach,-ich-,*s.f.* see r.-rìoghail, (called " reangach " from its wand-like stalks.)
——— -rìoghail,§ -ich-, *s.f.* The royal fern—*osmunda regalis.* (ill. 595.)
——— -uaine,§ -ich-, *s.f.* The green fern—*asplenium adiantum nigrum.* (ill. 596.)
raineas,** -eis, *s.m.* Romance, fable.
ràineas, see ràinig. R. tìr nam fìonan trom, *I reached the land of vines heavy (with grapes.)*

[An inflection preserved chiefly in the *North.*]

594. Raineach-nan-radan (dilatata.)

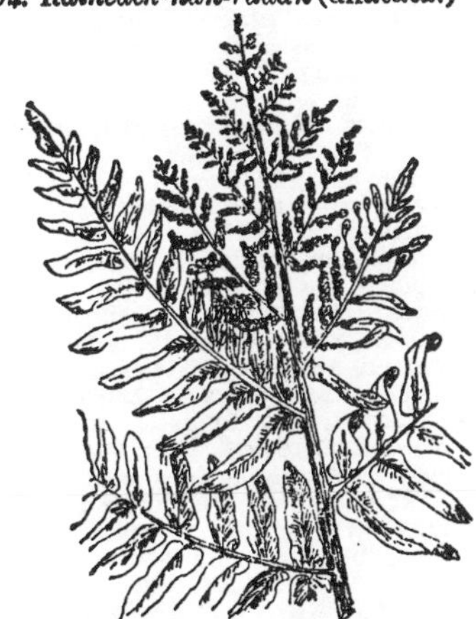

595. Raineach-rìoghail.

596. Raineach-uaine.

raing,(DMK) *s. f.* Ring of meal that forms around the edge of the upper mill-stone when the mill is grinding—*Caithness.* [*reached.*
ràinig, *past ind.* of ruig. R. sinn, *we arrived,*
ràinigeadh, *past. ind. pass.* of ruig. R e., *it was reached.*
rainn, *gen. & pl.* of rann. 2 see roinn.
rainn-an-uisge,** *s.m.* Eyebright.
†**rainne-ruisg,** *s.f.* Eyebright.
rainn-mhill,** *v.a.* Abolish, abrogate.
rainnsich,** *v.a.* Arrange, put in rows or ranks.
———**ean,** *s.pl.* Ranges, rows, ranks.
———**te,** *past pt.* of rainnsich. Arranged.
rainnt, Gaelic form of *rent.—Suth'd.*
rainnte,** *a.* Articulate.
rain-sgrios,** *v.a.* Abolish.
raip, -e, *s.f.* Filth. 2 Foul mouth. *prov.* 3* Debauchery.
raipeach,†† *a.* Filthy. 2 Foul-mouthed.
raipeas, -eis, see raip.
raipleach, -eich, -an, *s.f.* Filthy or slovenly woman.
raipleachag, -aig, -ag, *s.f.,dim.* of raipleach. Little squalid woman.
raipleachan,** -ain, *s.m.* Scullion.
rair, see (an) raoir.
†**rais,** *s. f.* Path, way. 2 (DMy) Play. R. a' chuilein ris an t-seann chù, *the puppy's play with the old dog.*
raisean, -ein, -an, *s.m.* Goat's tail, *prov.* 2 (AF) Goat. 3 (AF) Tousy-headed child. [*gives raisinn for No. 1.]
rais-mhaol, see ras.
raitche,(AF) *s.f.* Bitch, female dog.
ràite, -an, *s.f.* Saying, word. 2 Aphorism, proverb, adage. 3**Idle conversation, gibberish, verbiage. 4 Arrogant language,boasting. 5 One who talks idly.
ràiteach, -eiche, *a.* Verbose, sententious. 2 Boasting. 3**Fluent. Mór r., *babbling* ; beag r., *taciturn, quiet.*
ràiteach, -ich, *s.m.* Desultory prater.
———**ail,** -e, *a.* Boasting, vain-glorious, arrogant, challenging. Daoine r., *boasters.*
———**as,** -ais, *s.m.* Boasting, vain-glory, ostentation, pride, arrogance, bluster. 2 Saying, speech. 3 Competition, contest, emulation. 4 Lie, report, idle surmise. 5*Trial of strength. A' r. air a chéile, *competing, emulating each other* ; a ràiteachais, *his lies.*
———**d,** *s. f.* Same meanings as ràiteachas. Luchd-r., *idle talkers.*
ràitealachd,(MS) *s.f.* Arrogation.
ràitean,** -ein, *s.m.* Pleasure.
ràiteanas, -ais, see ràiteachas.
ràith, see ràidh.
ràith, *v.* Threaten. 2 (CR) Scold—*Perth-shire.* R. e air, *he scolded him.*
raith,§ -e, -ean, *s. f.* Common brake, see an raineach mhór.
ràith-dorch,*s.m.* see ràth-dorcha.
ràithe, see ràidhe.
———**ach,** see ràidheach.
———**achd,** see ràidheachd.
ràitheil, -e, *a.* see ràidheil.
raithne, *s.f.* see raineach.
raithneach, -ich, see raineach.
ràitinn, see ràdh.
ràitse,** *s.f.* Idle conversation, boasting. 2 Desultory prater.
raitseach,(CR) *s.f.* Strong and lazy young woman—*W. of Ross-shire.*
ralls,* *v.a.* see ràc.
rallsa,* *s.m.* see ràcan.
rallsadh,* -aidh, -aidh, see ràcadh.
ramachdair, -ean, *s.m.* Coarse, vulgar fellow. 2 Romping, noisy fellow.
———**eachd,** *s.f.ind.*Coarse play,romping.
ramachdas, -ais, *s.m.* Coarseness.
ramair,* -ean, *s.m.* Romp. 2 Blockhead. 3* Vulgar coarse fellow.
———**eachd,*** see ramachdaireachd.
ramaisceil,(CR) *a.* Romping, noisy—*Arran.*
ramalair, -ean, *s.m.* ‡Rambler. 2 see ramachdair.
ramallag,* -aig, -an, *s.f.* Puddle.
ramas,** *s.m.* Rhyme. 2 Romance.
———**ach,**** *a.* Romantic, fabulous.
ramasg, -aisg, *s.m.* Sea-oak, a kind of seaweed. *Scots,* tangle.
ràmh, -àimh, -an, *s. m.* Oar. 2**Tree. 3** Branch. 4**Wood. Talamh nan r., *the country of woods.*

PARTS OF AN OAR :—

1 Cnotan, *box,* placed on the oar to protect it from wear. Clàdan—(AH) *cleat.*
2 Dorn, *handle* or *grip.* Doirneag, dorn-chur.
3 Lunn, part between the handle and box,

4 Seasgadh, part between the box and feather. 5 Liagh, *feather, blade.*

ramh,§ *s.* The family of plants known as *rhamnaceæ*—individually *rhamnus.*

ràmh,** *v.a.* Row a boat.

ràmhach, -aiche, *a.* Oared. 2 Woody. 3 Branchy.

ràmhach, -aich, *s.m.* Raft. 2 Boat propelled by oars. 3 Galley. 4 Set of oars. 5**Rowing. 6 ** Rowing-match. Sè-ràmhach, *a six-oared boat.*

ràmhachadh, -aidh, *s.m.* Rowing, act of rowing. 2 Furnishing with oars. 3 Branching. A' r—, *pr.pt.* of ràmhaich.

ràmhachd, *s.f.ind.* Rowing, pulling. 2 Branching. 3**Oar-making.

ràmhadair, -ean, *s.m.* Oar-maker. 2 Rower. 3 *rarely* Traveller.

ràmhadaireachd,** *s.f.* Oar-making. 2 Rowing.

ràmhadh, -aidh, *s.m.* Rowing. Air a r., *rowed.*

ràmhag,(CR) *s.f.* Root. Cha'n 'eil sion ach an r. ann, *it is all but dead*—used of animals but not of human beings—*W. of Ross.* [Used of persons also in *Gairloch*—DU.] (frèamhag)

ràmhaich, *v.a.* Row (iomair.) 2**Supply with oars. 3**Man with oars.

ràmhaiche, -an, *s.m.* Rower, oarsman.

ràmhaichte, *a. & past pt.* of ràmhaich. Furnished with oars. 2 Impelled by oars, rowed.

ràmhair, -ean, *s.m.* Rower.

———eachd, *s.f.ind.* Rowing, employment of rowing. 2 Oar-making.

ràmhan, *n.pl.* of ràmh.

ramhan, *Perthshire* for ràbhan.

ramhar, -mhra, see reamhar.

ràmh-bràghad,(AH) *s.f.* Forward, or pilot oar.

ràmh-deiridh, *s.m.* Stroke-oar.

597. *Ràmh-dhroighionn.*

ràmh-dhroighionn,§ -inn, *s. m.* Prickly buckthorn—*rhamnus catharticus.*

ràmh-gualainn, *s.m.* Stroke-oar. 2 (DMy)One of the foremost oars, or oars nearest the bows.

ràmh h-amar,(DMy) *s.m.* One of the oars nearest the stern.

ramhlair, -ean, *s.m.* Humourist. 2 Noisy fellow. 3**Rambler. [** gives ramlair.]

———eachd, *s.f.ind.* Play, sport. 2 Noisiness. 3 Rambling.

ràmh-long, -luing, -an, *s.f.* Galley, boat or vessel fitted for rowing, (long-ràmhach, see p.78.)

ramhraich,* *v.* see reamhraich. 2 Come to high-water as spring-tide. 3 Beat till one's body swells.

†rampair, -ean, *s.m.* Rampart.

ràn, -àin, *s.m.* Roar, loud cry, shriek, bellow. 2 *Melancholy cry. 3* Drawling, dissonant roar or cry. Thoir r., *cry out;* thug e r. as, *he cried out.*

ràn, *pr.pt.* a' rànaich, a' rànach & a' rànail, *v.n.* Roar, shriek, bellow, cry out, make a noise. 2 **Crash loudly. Ged rànadh sléibhtean, *though hills should roar.*

†ran, *s.m.* Frog.

ran,** -ain, *s.m.* Crumb, morsel. 2 Truth.

†ran,** *a.* Clear, evident. 2 Nimble. 3 Noble.

ranach,* -aich, *s.m.* Cave that gives an echo. 2 Large ill-furnished house.

rànach,(CR) *a.* Hoarse—*Arran.*

rànaich, *s.f.* Roaring, act of roaring, shrieking aloud, as with pain, bellowing. 2* Drawling crying. A' r—, *pr.pt.* of ràn.

rànail, *s.m. & pr.pt.* Same meanings as rànaich.

rànaiche,‡‡ *s.m.* Bellower, roarer.

rànan, -ain, -an, *s.m. dim.* of ràn. Roar of a stag. 2 Shriek, cry, bellow.

randach,** -aich, *s.m.* Partisan. (*Scots*, randy.)

randonaich,** *v.a.* Abrogate, abolish.

rang, -aing, -an, *s.* Category. 2 Column. 3 Rank, row, order, range. 4 Bank of a river. 5 Stream. 6 Wrinkle.

rangach, -aiche, *a.* In ranks, ranges or rows. 2 Wrinkled.

rangachail,** *a.* Tactical.

rangachadh,** -aidh, *s. m.* Tactics. 2 Putting in rows, arranging, arrangement.

rangaich,** *v.a.* Put in ranks or rows, arrange.

rangaichte,** *past pt.* Put in order, arranged.

rangair, -ean, *s.m.* Wrangler, *prov.*

rangan, see rong.

rangan,** -ain, *s.m.* Sloth.

rangan,** *n.pl.* of rang. Ranks, rows.

rang-eòlas,** *s.m.* Tactics.

rang-oilean, *s.m.* Tactics.

rann, -ainn, -an & ranntaichean, *s.f.* Part, portion, division, section. 2 Verse, stanza, distich, catch, canto, section. 3 Epigram, song, poem. 4 Quatrain, stave. 5 Genealogy, pedigree, ancestry. 6 Relationship. 7** Bond, tie. 8**Promontory. 9 Verse of a chapter. 10 see reang. 11* Oration, in poetry.

ranna, see roinne, *gen.sing.* of roinn.

rannach, -aich, *s.m.* Songster. 2 Rhymer, bard. 3 Story-teller, reciter.

rannach,* *a.* Belonging to a peninsula.

rannach,‡‡ -aiche, *a.* Distributed in parts or portions. 2 Metrical, in verses. 3 Versifying.

rannachadh, -aidh, *s.m.* Act or art of versifying, prosody. A' r—, *pr.pt.* of rannaich.

rannachd, *s.f.* Rhyme, metre, versifying, versification. 2 Tale, story. 3 Satire.

rannadh, -aidh, -aidhean, *s. m.* Division. 2 Bringing to a point, sharpening. 3**Beginning. 4(AH) Continent. Còig rannaidhean ruadha 'n domhain, *the five great continents of the globe.*

rannadhail,* -e, *s.f.* Rhapsody, rant, ranting.

———each,* -eiche, *a.* Rhapsodical. 2*Nonsensical in oratory.

rannag, -an, see reannag.

rannaich, *v. a.* Compose verses, versify, rhyme. 2 Bring to a point.

rannaiche, -an, *s. m.* Versifier, songster, poet, bard.

rannaicheachd, see rannachd.

rannaichte, *past pt.* of rannaich. Made into verses, versified. 2 Pointed.

rannaidheachd, *s.f.ind.* Prosody, versification, metre.

rannair, -ean, *s.m.* Divider, distributor, divisor. 2 Versifier, poet. 2 Orator, rhapsodist.

rannan,** -ain, *s.m.* Lowing of deer. 2 (DMy) Slime of fish.

———, *pl.* of rann.

ranndachd, *s.f.* Versification, metre, poetry. 2 *Extent of territory.

ranndadh,** *s.m.* Rondeau.

ranndaichean, *pl.* of rann.

ranndar, -air, *s. m.* Murmuring, complaining, discontented language. *prov.*

rannghall,(CR) *s. m.* Inferior poetry, doggerel, —*W. of Ross-shire, Inverness & Argyll.*

rann-leabhar,* -air, *s.m.* Anthology.
rann-mheas, -a, *s.m.* Scanning of verse.
rann-phàirt, -e, *s.f.* Participation. 2 Participle. 3**Portion.
rann-phàirteach, -eiche *a.* Partaking, sharing, apt to share. 2 Communicating.
rann-phàirteachadh,-aidh, *s.m.* Sharing,communicating. A' r—, *pr.pt.* of rann-phàirtich.
rann-phàirteachail, -e, *a.* see rann-phàirteach. 2 Portionable.
rann-phàirtich, *v.a.* Partake, share. 2 Distribute. 3 Communicate, impart.
rann-phàirtiche, -an, *s.m.* Partaker, sharer. 2 Distributor.
rann-phàirtichte, *past pt.* Shared, imparted. 2 Communicated. 3 Divided into shares or sections.
rannsachadh, -aidh, *s.m.* Searching, enquiring into,scrutinizing, review, reviewing, searching minutely. 2 Rummaging. 3* Search, scrutiny. A' r—, *pr.pt.* of rannsaich.
rannsachail,‡‡ -e, *a.* Inquisitive.
rannsachair, -ean, *s.m.* Searcher, explorer, examiner, inspector, reviewer.
rannsaich, *pr.pt.* a' rannsachadh, *v.a.* Search, scrutinize, examine minutely, explore, review, rummage.
rannsaiche, -an, *s.m.* Searcher.
rannsaichidh, *fut.aff.a.* of rannsaich.
rannsaichte, *past pt.* of rannsaich. Searched, explored, examined, inspected, scrutinized.
rannsuchadh, see rannsachadh.
rannsuich, see rannsaich.
————te, see rannsaichte.
rannta, *past pt.* Shared, divided.
ranntach,*a. & s.* see rannach.
———d, see rannachd.
———d,* *s.f.ind.* Extent of territory, jurisdiction, sphere.
ranntair,‡‡ -ean, *s.m.* Poet, songster.
ranntair,* *s.f.* Range, extent of territory, "division." Tha 'n r. ioma-chumhann, *the range is limited;* a' tighinn a staigh air an r. againn, *encroaching on our territory.* (rann-tìr.)
ranntannan, *s.pl.* Title-deeds, deeds of conveyance. 2 Chattels. *Sàr-Obair.*
ranntar-buth, *s.m.* Confused dance without system.—*Sàr-Obair.*
ranntrach,* -aiche, *a.* Extensive.
rannuidheachd, see rannachd.
rant,** -a, *s.m.* Rant. 2 Noise. 3 Confused dance.
rantair,** Gaelic spelling of *ranter.*
rantaireachd,** *s.f.* Noisiness, ranting. Is ann ort tha 'n r.; *how noisy you are!*
raob,** *v a.* see reub. 2 Prop.
——ach,** *a.* see reubach.
raobachd,** *s.f.ind.* see reubachd. 2 Excess. 3 Gluttony.
raochd, see raoic.
raod, -aoid, -an, see rud.
raod, see reudan.
raodach,(CR) *a.* Kindly—*Arran.*
raodan, -ain, see reudan.
raodhair, raodhraichean, *s. m.* see raghar. 2 Hope.
raog, -aoig, -an, *s.m.* Rushing, *prov.*
raogag, -aig, -an, *s.f.* Woman of an impetuous temper.
raogha, see rogha.
raoghnaich, see roghnaich.
raoic, *v.n.* Roar, bellow. 2 Belch. Mar a raoiceas leòmhan, *as a lion roars.*
raoic,** *s.f.* Bellow, roar. 2 Voice of a deer. 3 Belching noise. 4 Sound made by cattle when fighting. 5*The roar that a cow gives when gored by another.
raoiceach, -eiche, *a.* Roaring, bellowing. 2 Flatulent, making a belching noise. 3 Making a hoarse noise.
raoiceadh, -idh, *s.m.* Roaring, act of roaring, bellowing. 2 Belching. A' r—, *pr.pt.* of raoic.
raoiceil, see raoiceadh.
raoichdeil, see raoiceadh.
raoichdich, see raoiceadh.
raoichd, see raoic.
raoichdeach, see raoiceach.
raoid,(AC) *s.f.* Sheaf of corn consisting of 24 handfuls, each bound with three stalks of corn. 2(DC) Sufficient quantity of corn,hay, straw, &c. for a meal for a horse or cow—*Uist.*
raoimeach,** *a.* Plundering.
raoimeadh,**-idh, *s.m.* Depredation, plundering.
raoin, *gen.sing.* of raon.
raoine,‡ *s.f.* Young cow that has had a calf, or even two, but is barren and has the calf's share of milk on her thighs.
raoineadh,** -idh, *s.m.* Triumph, victory.
raointeach, -eiche, *a.* Full of plains or fields, meadowy, agrarian.
raointean, *pl.* of raon.
raoir, (an raoir) *adv.* Last night.
raoit, -e, -ean, *s.f.* Indecent mirth. 2 Rakish female. 3††Drunkenness.
raoitealachd, *s.f.* Prodigality. 2 see raoit.
raoiteach,†† *a.* Drunken.
raoiteil, -e, *a.* Indecently merry. 2 Prodigal.
raoiteir, ean, *s.m.* Drunkard.
————eachd, *s.f.* Drunkenness.
raomadh,** -aidh, *s.m.* Phlegm.
†**raon,** *v.a.* Turn, change. 2 Tear, break.
raon, -aoin, *pl.* -tan, -aichean & raointean, *s. f.* Field, plain. 2 Mossy plain. 3 Green. 4 Road, way. 5 Hope. 6 Upland field, down.
raonach,* -aich, *s.m.* Plain country.
raonach, -aiche, see raointeach.
raonadh,** -aidh, *s.m.* Way, road. 2 Haunt. 3 Breaking, tearing. 4 Changing.
raonaichean, *pl.* of raon.

598. Raosar dearg. *599. Raosar dubh.*

raosar dearg,§ *s.m.* Red currant—*ribes rubrum.*
raosar dubh,§ *s.m.* Black currant—*ribes nigrum.*
raosar geal,§ *s.m.* White currant—*ribes album.*
†**rap,** -a, *a.* Sudden, quick.
†**rap,**(AF) -a, -an, *s.m.* Any creature that digs for its food, or draws its food towards it, as cows. 2**Noise.
rap,* *s.m.* Bad halfpenny. 2 see rop.
rapach, -aiche, *a.* Nasty, filthy. 2 Slovenly. 3 Drivelling. 4 Foul-mouthed. 5(CR) Stormy, dirty, of weather—*W. of Ross-shire, Inverness & Argyll.*

ràpach, -aiche, *a.* Noisy.
rapail,(MS) *a.* Sumptuous.
ràpair, -ean, *s. m.* Frothy, noisy fellow. 2** Slovenly fellow. 3*Worthless fellow. 4* Drawling fellow.
ràpaireachd, *s.f.* Noisiness, habit of noisiness. 2††Foolish, idle talk.
rapaireachd,** *s.f.ind.* Slovenliness.
rapais, -e, *s.f.* Filth, nastiness, slovenliness. 2 Drab, careless female.
ràpal, -ail, *s.m.* Noise, bustle.
rapal,* *s.f.* Nonsensical talk.
ràpalach, -aiche, *a.* Noisy, bustling.
rapas, -ais, see rapais.
r' ar, (for ri ar) By or beside our, to our. R' ar taobh, *to our side.*
ràs, -àis, *s.* Fury, rage—*Dàin I. Ghobha.*
ras, -ais, *s.m.* Shrub, underwood. 2 (AF) Seal, sea-calf.
rasach, -aiche, *a.* Shrubby, boughy, branchy.
rasach,(MMcD) *s.f.* Grating placed against the wall, in which grass, &c. is placed for feeding young sheep wintered in the house—*Lewis.* (prasach.)
rasachd,** *s.f.* Shrubbery, shrubbiness.
rasaiche,** *s.f.* Gipsy, hussy, rambler, rambling woman. Generally used to denote a roving lewd woman.
rasair,** *s.m.* Rambler.
rasaireachd,** *s.f.* Rambling.
ràsal, -ail, -an, *s.m.* see ràsdal.
ràsan, -ain, -an, *s. m.* Harsh, grating discordant noise, bickering. 2 Loquacity, constant speaking. 3 Tedious highway. 4 Smell. 5 **Unpleasant monotony. 6** Monotonous speaker.
rasan, -ain, -an, *s.m.* Brushwood, underwood, copse, shrubbery. 2 Rivulet.
ràsàn, *pl.* of ràs.
rasanach, -aiche, *a.* Abounding in brushwood or underwood, or 2 rivulets.
ràsanach,** *a.* Tedious, long-winded, loquacious. 2 Discordant. 3 Monotonous.
ràsanach,** -aich, *s.m.* Dull, prosy speaker.
ràsanachd,** *s.f.* Cant, diatribe. 2 Monotony. 3 Tedious verbiage.
ràsanaich,** *v.* Cant.
ràsar, -air, Gaelic form of *razor.*
ras-chrann, -ainn, *s.m.* Shrub.
ras-chrannach,** -aich, *s.m.* Shrubbery.
ras-chrannach, -aiche, *a.* Abounding in shrubs. 2 Made of shrubs.

600. Ras-chrann-sìor-uaine.

ras-chrann-sìor-uaine,‖ *s.m.* Evergreen privet—*ligustrum vulgare.*
rasdach,** -aiche, *a.* Churlish, unpolite.
rasdach,** -aich, *s.m.* Churl.
ràsdail, *v.a.* Rake, harrow.
ràsdail, *gen.sing.* of ràsdal.
rasdair,** *s.f.* Great satiety.
ràsdal, -ail, -an, *s.m.* Rake. 2 Hand-harrow. 3 Harrow. 4**Barebone. 5 Frizzling sound, as of flesh being fried.
ràsdal-ghead, *s.m.* Hand-harrow.
ràsdalach,†† *s.m.* Harrowing. 2 Of, or belonging to, rakes. 3 That can be raked. 4 Like a rake.
ràsdaladh, -aidh, *s.m.* Raking, act of raking together, as hay. 2 Gathering. A' r—, *pr. pt.* of ràsdail.
ràsdalaiche,** *s.m.* One who works with a rake. 2 Raker of hay.
rasg, -aisg, -an, see rosg.
rasgach, -aiche, *a.* see rosgach & reasgach.
rasgair,** *s.m.* Idle talker.
rasgaireachd,** *s.f.* Idle talk.
rasgan, *Lewis* for rosgan.
rasmhaol,** -mhaoil, *s.m.* Sea calf.
rastach, -aich, *s.m.* see rasdach.
rastach,** *a.* Country.
rastair, see rasdair.
ràsuidheach,** *a.* Rambling.
ràsuidheachd,** *s.f.* Rambling.
†rat, *s.* Motion.
†ràth, *s.m.* Fortress. 2 Artificial mound or barrow. 3 Village, town. 4 Royal seat. 5 Fern. 6 Plain, cleared spot. 7‡‡Residence.
rath, -a, *s.m.* Prosperity, fortune, success, increase, profit, advantage, good luck. 2 (AF) Shoal. 3 Surety. 4 Character. 5 Wages. Is beag r. a bhitheas ort, *your success will be very precarious* ; is beag r. a rinn e dhòmh-sa, *it did very little good to me* ; chaidh e bho r., *he went to pigs and whistles* ; mac-rath, *a lucky, fortunate person* ; r. éisg, *a shoal of fish* ; is duilich r. a chur air neach a dh'aindeoin, *you can't make a man lucky against his will*—in spite of the strong general belief in fate and luck, there are several Gaelic proverbs to the effect that a man makes his own fate or luck, or that one who makes no effort himself cannot have good luck.
ràth, see ràgh.
ràth, -a, *s.m.* Circle. 2 Raft. 3 see ràthan.
ràthach, -aiche, *a.* Of, or belonging to, circles, or 2 rafts. 3 Abounding in circles, or 4 rafts.
rathach, -aiche, *a.* see rathail & rathmhor.
†rathach, -aich, *s.m.* Hough.
rathachadh, -aidh, *s.m.* Prospering, succeeding. 2 Act of making prosperous. 3 Prosperity, success. A' r—, *pr.pt.* of rathaich.
rathachas,†† -ais, *s.m.* Success, fortune.
rathad, -aid, *pl.* -an & -aidean, *s.m.* Road, way, highway. 2 Path, track. 3* Method. R. mór an rìgh, *the public road, the king's highway* ; as an rathad, *out of the way, aside* ; air an rathad, *on the way, coming; 2 pregnant (of women only)* ; gabh do r.! *begone!* luchd-gabhail an rathaid, *wayfarers* ; rè an rathaid, *the whole way.*
rathadach,†† *a.* Pushful, diligent.
rathad-dìridh, *s.m.* Ascent.
rathad-iaruinn, *s.m.* Railway, railroad.
rathaich, *v.a.* Make prosperous. 2 Bless.
rathaich,(AC) *s.* Passion.
rathail, -e, *a.* Prosperous. 2 Astute. 3 Fortunate. 4 Famed, well spoken of. Dream r., *a prosperous people.*
rathamhnas, -ais, *s.m.* Prosperity. 2 Happiness.
rathan, ain, *s.m.* Bunch. 2 Bundle. 3 Strumpet.
rathan, -ain, -an, *s.m.* see rothan. 2 Sheave of the flyers of a spinning-wheel, the grooved drum that receives the driving-cord.

ràthan, -ain, -an, *s.m.* Surety, security. Chaidh e an r. air, *he became surety for him*; théid mis' an r. ort, *I can assure you* (*North*); théid mi am bannaibh dhuit, *or* théid mi an urras ort, *or* bàirnidh mis' thu (*Islay*.)
rathanach, *a.* Having pulleys. (rothanach)
ràthanas, -ais, *s.m.* see ràthan.
rath-dorcha, *s.m.ind.* The moon in the wane.
rathmhoire, *comp.* of rathmhor.
rathmhor, -oire, *a.* Prosperous, successful, fortunate. 2 Noted. 3 Happy.
rath-sholus, -uis, *s.m.* The space between the front and back doors of a house.
rath-soluis, *s.m.* The time of moonlight at night.
rath-thiodhlaicidh, (CR) *s.m.* Lair, grave-plot—*W. of Ross-shire.*
rati, *s. f.* Ludicrous appellation applied to whisky—*Sàr-Obair.*
ratreut, *s.m.* Retreat.
ré, *s.f.ind.* [** gives *m.*] The moon. 2 Time, season, duration, space of time. 3 Life, existence, life-time. 4**Planet. Ré nuadh, *the new moon*, (*generally*, an solus ùr); fad mo ré 's mo là, *during my day and generation.*
rè, *adv. & prep.* During. Rè an là, *during the day*; rè na bliadhna, *all the year, during the whole year*; rè an rathaid, *all the way* [Governs the genitive case.]
re see righ & ri.
rèab, see reub.
rèabach, see reubach.
rèabail, see reubail.
reaban, *s.m.* (MS)Minnow. 2(DMy)The fringe of whiskers men were formerly in the habit of leaving when shaving from ear to ear.
†reabh,‡ *s.m.* Wile, trick, cunning.
†reabhach, -aiche, *a.* Subtle, crafty, cunning. 2 **Joyful.
reabhach,** -aich, *s.m.* Mountebank, one who plays tricks, hence a wicked fellow, a devil. 2 The Devil. An r. thu, *devil take you.*
reabhag,(AF) *s.f.* Linnet, titling.
——— -mhonaidh,(AF) *s.f.* Mountain linnet, meadow pipit, heather lintie.
——— -fhraoich,(AF) see reabhag-mhonaidh.
reabhair, -ean, *s.m.* Crafty, subtle fellow.
rèabhair,(CR) *s.m.* One fond of running about —*Perthshire.*
rèabhaireachd,(CR) *s.f.* Running about—*Perthshire.*
reabhaireachd, *s.f.ind.* Craftiness
reabhart, -airt, -an, *s.m.* see reothart.
reabhdan, see reudan.
†reabhlangar,** *a.* Skipping, playing, sporting.
reabhradh, - aidh, *s.m.* Disporting, as of boys—*Badenoch.* 2**Skipping.
reabunn, -uinn, see reubainn.
†reac, *s.f.* Woman, damsel
reacar,** *a.* Swift. 2 Growing quick. 3 Hot. 4 Strong.
reach, *prov.* for rach.
reachadh, see rachadh.
reachd, *s.m.* Law, statute, ordinance. 2 Right, due 3 Toll. 4 Command, power, authority. 5 Keen sorrow. 6 see reachdmhoireachd. Dream gun aireamh fo d' r., *people without number under thy command*
reachd, *s.f.ind.* Great vexation, keen sorrow. 2**†Loud sob or sigh. 3 Emotion, tears, shedding of tears from vexation or a feeling of insult. 4 (AC) Strength, toughness 5 (AC) Emulation. Bhris r. air, *he gave expression to his sorrows;* thainig r. 'am mhuineal, *a lump* (or *choking sensation*) *came in my throat*; thàinig r. orm, *emotion came upon me*; bhris air mo r., *my strength broke down.*
reachdach, -aiche, *a.* Of, or belonging to, a law. 2 Right, lawful. 3 Imperative, giving law. 4 Authoritative. 5 Strong. 6 Vexatious, annoying. 7 Haughty. 8 Prone to take offence. 9 Causing deep sorrow. 10 Strong, stout, powerful. 11**Enactive, legislative.
reachdachadh, -aidh, *s.m.* Enacting, act of enacting or legislating. A' r—, *pr. pt.* of reachdaich.
reachdachd,** *s.f.* Legislation, enaction.
reachdadair, -ean, *s.m.* Lawgiver, legislator. 2 **Ruler, rector.
reachdadh,** *s.m.* Legislation.
reachdaireachd, *s.f.ind.* Legislation, enaction, decreeing. 2 Rectorship.
reachdaich, *pr.pt.* a' reachdachadh, *v.a.* Enact, legislate, ordain, decree, appoint.
reachdaichte, *past pt.* Enacted, prescribed by law, ordained.
reachdail, *a.* Legal, lawful. 2 Regular. see reachdach.
reachdair, *s. m.* see reachdadair. 2** *rarely* Dairyman.
reachd-airm,** *s.f.* Court of Judicature.
reachdar, see reachdmhor.
reachd-cheangail, *v.a.* Bind by a law or decree. 2 Stipulate. 3 Article, articulate.
reachd-cheangailte, *past pt.* of reachd-cheangail. Bound by law or decree. 2 Stipulated.
reachd-cheangal, -ail, *s.m.* Binding by a law or decree. 2 Stipulating, act of stipulating. 3 Fixing by law. A' r—, *pr. pt.* of reachd-cheangail.
reachd-dhaingneach, -eich, -an, *s.m.* Decree, statute.
reachd - dhaingneachadh, -aidh, see reachd-cheangal.
reachd-dhaingnich, see reachd-cheangail.
reachd-dhaingnichte, see reachd-cheangailte.
reachd-mhathair,** -mhathar, *s.f.* Mother-in-law.
reachd-mhòd, -òid, -an, *s.m.* Court of law, court of justice.
reachdmhoire, *comp.* of reachdmhor.
———-achd, *s.f.ind.* Validity. 2 Stoutness. 3 Rankness. 4 Productiveness, as of corn. 5 Substantialness, pithiness. 6 Sorrowfulness. 7 Spiritedness.
reachdmhor, -oire, *a.* Stout, energetic, strong, robust. 2 Valid. 3 Rank, luxuriant full of substance, substantial, pithy. 4 Spirited. 5 Sorrowful, tearful. 6 Commanding. 7 Imperative. 8 Legislative. 9 Vexatious, tormenting. 10 Easily offended. 11 Handsome, fair. 12* Productive, as corn. Seachd diasan r. agus math, *seven ears of corn, rank and good.*
———achd, *s.f.ind.* Vexatiousness. 2 Readiness to take offence.
reachd-shaoirseach, see reachd-shaor.
reachd-shaor, -shaoire, *a.* Licensed, authorized.
reachd-thabhairteach, -eiche, *a.* Legislative, lawgiving. 2 Fond of, or pertaining to legislation.
reachd-thabhairtear, -ir, -an, *s. m.* Legislator, lawgiver.
†reacht, -an, *s.m.* Man. 2 see reachd.
rèadan, -ain, -an, *s.m.* see reudan.
†readan, -ain, -an, *s.m.* Reed, pipe, tube.
rèadanach, see reudanach.
read-chord, -chuird, *s.m.* Rein of a bridle.
†———-an, *pl.* of read-chord.
readh, see readhag.
readh, see rachadh.
readh,** *a.* Tough, hard. Chagnadh e sleagh r., *he would chew a tough spear.*
rèadh, see riadh.
readhag,(AF) *s.* Mad bull or ox.

†readh-sgaoileadh,** -idh, s.m. **Flux.**
reafog, -oig, -an, s.f. Linnet.
†reag,** -eig, s.f. Night.
reag-dhall,** a. Purblind.
reaghlorach,** a. **Resounding.**
rèal, see reul.
rèall, see reul.
reallag,(AF) s.f. Linnet.
rèalt, see reul.
reamaid, see rachamaid.
reamain, s.f. Beginning.
reamalair, *Perthshire* for ramalair & ramachdair.
†reamh, see roimhe.
reamha, see reamhra.
reamhad,** -aid, s.m. **Bulk, fatness.**
reamhag, see riabhag.
reamhain,** s.f. Foretelling, prognostication.
reamhair,** -ean, s.m. Traveller, wayfaring man, vagabond.
reamhar, -mhra, a. Fat, plump, fleshy. 2 Fat, greasy, oily. 3 Big, great. 4 Thick, gross, of great circumference. 5**Coarse. An sneachd nach tig mu Shamhuinn, thig gu r. mu Fhéill-Brighde, *the snow that comes not at Hallowmas will come thickly at Candlemas* ; r. am feòil, *fat-fleshed.*
†reamh-cheuman, s.pl. Ancestors, forefathers.
reamhra, *comp.* of reamhar.
reamhrach, -aiche, a. Coagulative, thickening. 2 Fattening.
——adh, -aidh, s.m. Fattening, act of fattening or making fat. 2 State of becoming fat, gross, thick or large. 3 Grossness, fatness. 4 Coagulation. A' r—, *pr. pt* of reamhraich.
——ail, -e, a. Fattening, having a tendency to fatten, or make fat.
——d, s.f.ind. Fatness, grossness. 2 Suet. 3* High-water, full spring-tide—*Islay*. R. a' bheathaich, *the fatness of the beast* ; r. 'sa phoite, *suet in the pot* ; r. muic-mara, *blubber* ; r. na talmhainn, *the fatness of the earth.*
reamhrad, -aid, s.m. Fatness, degree of fatness or grossness.
reamhraich, v.a, & n. Fatten, make fat. 2 Become fat, thick or gross. 3 Concrete, coagulate, clot
——te, *past pt.* of reamhraich. Fattened, fed, made fat.
rean,** s.f. Span.
reang, v.a. & n. Kill, starve or subdue with hunger. 2 Become emaciated or lean.
reang, reing, -an, s.f. Rib, see bàta, E 3, p. 73 ; see rong. 2 Joggled frame in a boat, see bàta, C p. 73. 3 Wrinkle in the face. 4(AC) Bar. 5 (AC) Stalk. 6 (AC)Rod, pole, wand. 7 (AF) Hare.
reang, -a, -an, s.m. Rank, row, series. 2 Rein. 3 Kidney. Reanga, *reins.*
reangach, -aiche, a. Lean, starved, cadaverous. 2 see rongach. 3* Full of wrinkles, wrinkled. 4 Full of strings or fibres. 5 Delaying, lingering. 6††Ranked, ranged. 7 Like a rein. 8 Like a kidney. 9**Having reins or kidneys. 10 Ribbed, as a boat or ship.
reangachadh, -aidh, s.m. Starving, act of starving with hunger. 2 State of becoming lean or emaciated. 3 Putting in ranks or rows. A' r—, *pr.pt.* of reangaich.
reangadh, see reangachadh.
reangaich, v. see reang.
reangaichte, *past pt.* of reangaich. Starved with hunger. 2 Lean, cadaverous.
reangair, -ean, s.m. Loiterer, lingerer. 2 Wrangler.
——eachd, s.f. ind. Indolence, lingering, sloth.
reangan, see rong.
reangas, s.m. Stringer of boat, see bàta, F5, p. 73.
reann, see reang.
†reann, -a, pl. -an, [& rinn**,] s. m. Star. 2 Land, soil. 3 Country.
reanna, s.pl. Stars.
reannach, -aiche, a. Spotted, striped.

601. Reannach.

reannach, -aich, s.m. Mackerel. 2 Mackerel-sky. 3**Strong, robust man.
reannach uaine, s.m. Blue mackerel.
reannag, -aig, -an, s.f. Star. 2 Starlet. 3 Shooting star. R. earballach, *a comet.*
reannagach, -aiche, a. Starry, studded with stars, spangled. 2 Like a star.
†reannair, -ean, s.m. Astrologer, astronomer.
reannan, -ain, s.m., *dim.* of reann. Little star, starlet.
reann-ghlan,** a. Starbright. Na rosgan r.,*the starbright eyes.*
reann-raineach, s.f. Royal fern, see raineach rìoghail.
rèap,(CR) s. m. Untidy person—*Suth'd.* [In *Gairloch* riap—DU.]
rèapach, *Suth'd* for riapach.
rear, (AF) s. Blackbird.
†rear, s.m. Provision.
rearg,(AF) s. Blackbird.
reas, reis, s.m. Rice.
reas,* s.m. Head of dry curled hair.
reasach, -aiche, a. Prattling, talkative. 2 Having dry curled hair.
reasan, see reas.
rèasan, see reusan.
——aich, see reusanaich.
†reasart, -airt, s.m. Preservation. 2 Health.
reasbait,** s.m. Beggar's brat.
reasgach, -aiche, a. Stubborn, froward, perverse. 2 Restive, impatient. 3 Irascible. 4††Rough. 5 Skittish. Each r., *a restive horse.*
reasgachd, s.f.ind. Stubbornness, perverseness, frowardness. 2 Irascibility. 3 Restiveness, impatience. 4** Contumacy. 5††Roughness. 6 Skittishness. 7**Aching.
reasgaiche, see reasgachd.
reasgaicheachd, see reasgachd.
reasgaichead, -eid, s.m. Stubbornness, degree of stubbornness. 2 Contumacy. 3 Irascibility. 4 Impatience, restiveness. Is r. an t-each an spor, *the spur makes the horse more restive.*
rèasg-shuil, -shùla, -shùilean, s.f. Blear-eye.
——each, -eiche, a. Blear-eyed.
rèasonta, see reusonta.
reasuall,(AF) s. Whale.
†reatair, s.m. Clergyman, clerk.
†reatas, -ais, s.m. Enmity, hatred.
rèath, a. see reidh.
reath, -a, -an, s.m. see reithe.
reatha, s. see reith.
reathach, a. see reitheach.
reathachas, -ais, see reitheachas.
reathadh, *Northern form* of rachadh.
reathadh, -aidh, s.m. see reitheachas.
rèathlan,** -ain, s.m. see reidhlean.
†reathream,** s.m. Climate.
ré-chearcall, -aill, -an, s.m. Halo.
†redhream, s.m. Climate.
réibean,(MS) s.m. Moustache. 2 Stickleback, see reaban.

†reibh, see ribh.
reic, *s.m.* Sale, auction, selling, act of selling. A' r—, *pr.pt.* of reic.
reic, *pr.pt.* a' reic, *v.a.* Sell, vend.
réic, *pr.pt.* a' réiceil, *v.n.* Roar, howl.
reic-chead,** *s.m.* License or permission to sell publicly.
————ach,** *a.* Licensed, authorized to sell.
reiceach, -eiche, *a.* Selling, fond of selling, trucking. 2 Saleable.
réiceach, -eiche, *a.* Roaring, howling.
reiceadair, -ean, *s.m.* Seller, salesman, broker. 2 Auctioneer.
————eachd, *s.f.ind.* Selling, business of selling. 2‡‡Merchandize. 3 Auctioneering.
reiceadh, -idh, *s.m. & pr.pt.* of reic, see reic.
réiceadh, -idh, *s.m.* Roaring, act of roaring or howling. A' r—, *pr.pt.* of réic.
reicealachd,(MS) *s.f.* Vendibleness.
reicear, *fut.pass.* of reic. Shall be sold.
——, *s.m.* Seller, auctioneer.
réiceil, -e, *s.f.* Roaring, act of roaring, howling. A' r—, *pr.pt.* of réic.
reiceireachd, see reiceadaireachd.
reic-fhollaiseach,(MS) *s.f.* Auction.
reicidh, *fut.aff.a.* of reic.
reicte, *past pt.* of reic. Sold.
réide, see réite.
réideach, see réiteach.
————adh, see réiteachadh.
réideachair, see réiteachair.
reideadh, *s.m.* Reaping. A' r—, *pr. pt.* of reidich.
†reidh, *s.m.* Rope. 2 Withe.
réidh, -ean, *s.m.* Plain, meadow, level ground.
réidh, -e, *a.* Plain, level, smooth. 2 Polished. 3 Straight, uninterrupted, clear of obstruction. 4 Free, exempt. 5 Reconciled, at peace, appeased, conciliated. 6 Safe, not dangerous. 7 Ready, prepared. 8 Disentangled. 9 Unravelled. 10 Harmonious, clear, melodious. 11 Ordered, arranged, disposed, in order. 12** Allied. 13** Regular. Àite r., *a plain* or *cleared place* ; tha mi r. dheth, *I have done with it* ; tha iad r. a nis, *they are at peace now* ; r. ri Dia, *at peace with God* ; am bheil thu r.? *are you prepared?* gu h-òrdail, r., *well-ordered and harmoniously* ; gu r., *at leisure* ; fiodh r., *smooth wood* ; gabh r. a' bhlàir, *betake yourself to the plain* ; fhuair e réidh 's e, réidh 's a' chùis, *he got clear* or *rid of it, rid of the business—Arran* ; ni mi r. e, *I will appease him.*
réidh, *gen. sing.* of riadh.
réidh-bheart, bheirt & -e, *pl.* -ean. *s.f.* Concord, harmony.
——————ach, -aiche, *a.* Harmonious, agreeing.
réidh-charbadair,‡‡ *s. m.* Hackney-coachman, cabman.
rèidheachd, *s.f.ind.* Plainness, state of being plain or level, smoothness. 2 Polish. 3 Uninterruptedness, straightness. 4 State of being free or exempt. 5 State of being reconciled or at peace. 6 Safety 7 Readiness, state of being prepared. 8 State of being disentangled or unravelled. 9 Harmony, melody. 10 State of being arranged or regularly disposed. 11 Ready service, officiousness.
†réidheadh, -idh, *s.m.* Agreement, assent.
réidhealachd,(MS) *s.f.* Accommodation.
réidheas,* -eis, *s.f.* Peace. Faigh le r. e, *get it in peace, without disturbance.*
réidh-fhiodh, -a, *s.m.* Plane-tree.
reidhir, see raoir.
réidh-labhart, -airt, *s.m.* Eloquence, smoothness of speech or utterance.
réidh-labhrach, -aiche, *a.* Eloquent, speaking smoothly.
réidhleach,* -eich, *s.m.* Down.
réidhlean, -ein, -an, *s.m.* Green, level plain, meadow. 2**Bowling-green. 3 (AH) Scope, range, latitude, elbow-room. Air an r., *on the plain* ; chun an r., *to the plain.*
reidhlean, -ein, -an, *s.m.* Wheel of a pulley, see ùlag, 6, p. 78.
réidhleanach, -aiche, *a.* Abounding in plains or meadows, meadowy. 2 Plain, level. 3 (AH) Unconstrained, unconfined, unrestrained.
réidhlic, see réilig.
reidhneach,(AF) *s.m.* Barren cow—*Suth'd.*
reidhne-mairt,(CR) *s.m.* Cow that does not give milk and is not with calf—*W. of Ross-shire.*
réidh-raineach,§ *s.* Polypody, see clach-raineach.
réidh-shnasaich, *v.a.* Anatomize.
réidhte, see réite.
————ach, see réiteach.
reidich,(DMy) *v.a.* Cut oats or barley with a sickle.
réidich, *v.a.* Reconcile, conciliate, appease. 2 Clear away, disentangle, adjust. (see réitich.)
————te, *past pt.* of réidich. Reconciled, conciliated, propitiated. 2 Cleared of obstruction, disentangled, adjusted.
reige, *s.f.* Ridgling.
†reighlios, *s.* Church, shrine, sanctuary.
réil, *gen.sing.* of reul.
†reil,** *a.* Clear, manifest.
réile, -an, *s.f.* Pebble.
réileag, see réilig.
————ach, see réiligeach.
réilig, -e, -ean, *s.f.* Grave, burying-place. 2** Church. 3* Crypt or burying place under a church. 4* Stone chest where bones dug out of graves are placed. Bithidh dùil ri fear fairge ach cha bhi ri fear-réilige, *there may be hope of a man at sea, but none of one in the grave.*
rèilige, see réilig.
réiligeach, *a.* Like a churchyard. 2 Having a churchyard. 3 Belonging to a churchyard.
réilteag, -ig, *s. f., dim.* of reul. see reultag. 2 Herb robert, see righeal-cùil.
————ach, *a.* see reultagach.
réiltean, -an, [**pl. -tein,] *s.m., dim.* of reul. Asterisk. 2 Little star. 3**Astrolabe.
reim, Gaelic spelling of *rheum.*
reim,(CR) *s.f.* Wheel of a spinning-wheel. 2 Grooved rim of a spinning-wheel. 3 Rim of driving-wheel.
réim, -e, -ean, *s.f.* Power, authority, dominion, sway. 2 Way. 3 Progress, order. 4 An order. 5 Calling out. 6 Troop, band. 7 Evenness of temper 8 Course of life, career. 9** Consistence. 10(CR) Self-command, self-control.—*W. of Ross-shire.* 11**Series. 12 (MS) Pituate.
†réim-bhriathar, -thran, *s.m.* Adverb.
réimealachd, *s.f.ind.* Sway, authority. 2 Constancy.
réimeas,** *s.m.* Rhyme.
réimeil, -e, *a.* Authoritative, bearing sway. 2 Persevering. 3 Even-tempered, constant, even-minded. 4**Progressive. 5 (MS) Rheumatic. 6 (MS) Pituitous. 7 Phlegmatic. 8** Rampant. Steòrnadh r., *steady steering.*
reimhe, *s.f.ind.* Fatness, thickness, grossness. 2 Pride.
reimheach, -eiche, *a.* Arrogant, proud, petulant, conceited.
reimheachd,** *s.f ind.* Arrogance, forwardness, petulance, conceitedness.
reimse, -an, *s.m.* Club, staff.
reimseach, -eiche, *a.* Heroic.

reimseach, -ich, -an, *s.m.* Coarse, sturdy woman.
reing, -e, -ean, see reang & rong.
reing-an-ruisg,§ see lus-nan-leac.
reingeach,** -ich, *s.m.* Ship-timber.
————, -eiche, *a.* Abounding in, of, or like ship-timbers.
†**réir**, see raoir.
réir, *gen. & dat.sing.* of riar.
réir, (a réir & do réir) *phrase.* According to, as, like as. Na'm bithinn 'nad r., *if I were of the same opinion as you;* iomadh gille òg am r., *many a youth fond of me* ; tha sinn a r. a chéile, *we are pleased with each other, on the best of terms ;* fleadh do m' r., *a feast worthy of me ;* a r. cuimhne dhomhsa, *to the best of my recollection.* M' a réir, is often used for "free,"as,leig iad m'a réir e,*they set him free.*
reirceire,(AF) s. Plover.
reir-chearc,(AF) *s.f.* Grouse. 2 Heather-hen.
réis, -e, -ean, *s.f.* Race, chase. 2 Span (9 in.) 3 Running course. Ruith e 'r., *he ran his race*, r. d' a theangaidh, *a span of his tongue.*
réisde, Therefore, then. Is beag an t-ioghnadh a r. ged robh teangaidh do bheòil-sa 'seinn gu binn cliù éibhinn t' fhir pòsd', *it is little wonder,therefore, that your tongue should sing sweetly your husband's glad praise.—Dàin I. Ghobha.*
réisg, *gen. sing.* of riasg. Le 'n sròin ag iarraidh nan aighean riabhach feadh shliabhchnoc réisg, *seeking with their noses the brindled hinds among the mountain grass.*
réisg, *v.a.* Arrest. 2 Seek.
reisghiobhar,** -air, *s.f.* Prostitute.
reisiche,** *s.m.* Rehearser. 2 Romancer.
réisimeid, -e, -ean, *s.f.* Regiment.
————each, -eiche, *a.* Regimental.
†**reismeirdreach**,** -ich, *s.f.* Harlot, street prostitute.
reisgeadh, *s.m.* Hanging of fish or flesh up to dry —*Suth'd.*
réit, see réite.
réite, -ean, *s.f.* Concord, agreement, harmony, reconciliation. 2 Expiation, atonement. 3 Agreement, contract, settlement, adjustment. 4 Marriage espousals or contract. 5**Disentanglement. Dean r. *be reconciled ;* a dh' fheuchainn an dean mi r. air son bhur peacaidh, *to try if I shall make atonement for your sins.*
réiteach, -ich, -ichean, *s.m.* see réite. 2**Plain, any level place.
———— -ich, see réiteachadh. Leannbh réitich, *an illegitimate child—Lewis.*
————, *a.* see réiteachail.
réiteachadh, -aidh, *s.m.* Act of reconciling, settling, agreeing. 2 Act of clearing, unravelling or disentangling, disentanglement, adjustment. 3* Putting in order. 4* Smattering. 5**Harmony. 6**Union. 7**Covenant. A' r—, *pr.pt.* of réitich. R. pòsaidh, *a betrothment, marriage-contract.*
réiteachail, -e, *a.* Reconciling, that reconciles or conciliates. 2 Ready to be reconciled, fond of reconciling. 3 Fond of clearing away obstructions or entanglements. 4 Appeasable, arbitrable. 5 That unravels or disentangles.
réiteachair,** *s.m.* Appeaser, reconciler, conciliator, mediator, one who clears away obstructions.
réiteachd, *s.f.ind.* Reconciliation, agreement, state of being reconciled. 2 Disentanglement, state of being disentangled. 3 Peace, concord.
réitealachd,(MS) *s.f* Appeasableness.
réitear, (MS) *s.m.* Peace-maker, reconciler, appeaser.
réith, -e, see réidh.
reith, *v.a.* see réitich.
réith-bheart, see réidh-bheart.
————ach, see réidh-bheartach.
reithe, -achan, *s. m.* Ram. 2 Dimmont tup. 3 The sign Aries (♈) in the zodiac.
reitheach, -eiche, *a.* Rammish, like a ram. 2 Ruttish.
reitheachadh, -aidh, *s.m.* Lining, rutting, as a ram. A' r—, *pr.pt.* of reithich.
reitheachan, *pl.* of reithe.
reitheachas, -ais, *s. m.* Rammishness, tuppishness. 2 Ramming. 3 Rutting of sheep.
reitheachd, *s.f.* see reitheachas.
reitheadh, -idh, *s. m.* see reitheachadh. A' r—, *pr. pt.* of reith
reithean, *s.m.*, *dim.* of reithe. Young or little ram.
reithe-cogaidh, *pl.* -achan-cogaidh, *s.m.* Battering-ram.
reithe-slachdaidh, *pl.* -achan-slachdaidh, *s. m.* see reithe-cogaidh.
†**reithe-raobhta**, *s.m.* Battering-ram.
reithe-séisdidh, *s.m.* Battering-ram.
reithich, *v.a.* Line, rut, as a ram,
réithleach, -ich, -an, see réidhlean.
réithlean, see réidhlean.
réitich, *v.a. & n.* Reconcile, conciliate. 2 Agree upon, ratify. 3 Adjust, determine, regulate, set in order, disentangle. 4 Prepare. 5 Adjust or settle the terms of marriage, be betrothed. 6 Articulate. 7 Appease. 8 Clear away, clear. R. an taigh, *put the house in order ;* réitichear a' cheist, *the question shall be determined ;* r. thu àite fa chomhair, *thou hast prepared a place for him ;* r. an snàth, *disentangle the thread ;* r. an rathad, *clear the way.*
réitichte, *past pt.* of réitich. Reconciled. 2 Agreed upon, ratified. 3 Adjusted, determined, set in order, regulated. 4 Prepared, set in order. 5 Betrothed. 6 Appeased. 7 Disentangled, disencumbered.
re na h-ùine seo, Meanwhile.
reò, see reòdh & reòthadh.
reobhart, see reothart.
reódh, *v.a. & n.* Freeze, cause to freeze. 2 Become frozen.
reòdhadh, -aidh, *s.m.* Act of freezing or causing to freeze. 2 State of freezing or becoming congealed. 3 Frost. [Used for ice as well as frost in *Arran.*] A' r—, *pr.pt.* of reòdh.
reòdh-leac,** -lic, *s.f.* Sheet of ice.
————,** *v.n.* Congeal.
reòdhta, *a. & past pt.* Frozen. 2 Cold, frosty.
reòdhtach, *a.* Freezing, frosty.
reòdhtachail,* -e, *a.* Congealable.
reòdhtachd, *s.f.ind.* Algidity.
reòdhtadh, -aidh, *s. m.* Freezing, congealing. 2 Frost. Taigh reòdhtaidh, *an ice-house ;* oidhche reòdhtaidh, *a frosty night.*
reòidhte, see reòdhta.
reolaist,* *s.f.* Doggerel.
reò-leac, -ic, -an, *s.f. & v.* see reòdh-leac.
reomhad, see romhad.
reòn,** -òin, *s.m.* Span.
reò-shruth,** *s.m.* Frozen stream.
reòta,(CR) s. Frost. Fuachd an reòta, *the cold of the frost.*
reòta, see reòdhta.
reòtach, see reòdhtach.
reòtadh, see reòdhtadh.
reòtaidh, *Strathtay* for reòdhta. Oidhche r., *a frosty night.*
reòtanach, -aiche, *a.* Stinging.
————d, *s.f.* Stingingness.
reòtanda, *a.* Stinging.

reòth, see reòdh.
reòtha, see reòdhadh.
reòthadh, see reòdhadh.
reothart, -airt, -an, *s.m.* Spring-tide. 2 The time of spring-tide. [An r., *spring-tide ;* àirde-reothairt, *height of spring-tide ;* r. an dingh agus còntraigh am màireach, *up to-day and down to-morrow*—expressive of too much and too little; r. nan eun, *the spring-tide of the birds*—also called "r. mór na Féill-Pàdruig," *the high spring-tide of St. Patrick's day.* At that time of the year the spring-tides are usually very high, and large quantities of sea-ware are cast ashore, which is occupied later on as a nestling-ground for large numbers of birds. [*fem.* in *Argyll-shire.*]
reòthta, see reòdhta.
rè 'r, (rè+ar & rè+'ur) During our. 2 During your. Rè 'r là, *during our day.*
rè seal, *adv.* For a time.
reub, *v.a.* Tear, rend, pull asunder. 2 Wound, mangle. 3 Abuse. 4*Gore, as a bull. 5 Lacerate, pain intensely 6* Tear as with a shearing hook or any jagged instrument. Reub e 'aodach, *he rent his clothes.*
reub, -a, -an, *s.m.* see reubadh.
reubach, -aiche, *a.* Rending, tearing. 2 Wounding, lacerating, bruising.
reubachd, *s.f.ind.* Tearing.
reubadh, -aidh, *s.m.* Rending, act of rending, tearing or lacerating. 2 Rent or fissure produced by tearing. 3 Avulsion. 4 Wound. 5* Goring. A' r—, *pr.pt.* of reub.
reubaidh, *fut. aff. a.* of reub. Shall tear.
reubail,†† *pr pt.* a' reubladh, *v.* Tear, mangle. [†† gives rèabail.]
reubainn, *s.f.* Robbery, plundering, freebooting, rapine.
————**each**, -eiche, *a.* Plundering, robbing, piratical.
————**eachd**, *s.f.ind.* Robbery, practice of robbery, plundering or freebooting.
————**ear**, -an, Same meanings as reubair.
reubair, -ean, *s.m.* Robber. 2 Violent person. 3 Render, tearer, bruiser.
reubaireachd,** *s.f.* Robbery, plunder. 2 Tearing, lacerating.
reubal, -ail, *s.m.* Rebel.
———**ach**, -aiche, *a.* Rebellious.
———**ach**, -aich, *s.m.* Rebel.
———**achd**, *s.f. ind.* Rebellion.
reubaltach, -aiche, *a.* see reubalach.
————, -aich, *s.* see reubalach.
————**d**, see reubalachd.
reubam, *1st. sing. imp.* of reub. Let me tear 2 *fut.aff.a.* of reub (for reubaidh mi) I shall tear.
reuban, see reubainn.
reubanair, see reubainnear.
reubar, *fut.pass.* of reub. Shall be torn.
reubhag, -an, see riabhag.
reubta, *past pt.* of reub. Torn, rent, pulled asunder. 2 Wounded, mangled, maimed. R. le dealan, *wounded by lightning.*
reuchdal, -ail, -an, *s.m.* Tediousness, wearisome ceremony, dilatoriness.
reuchdalach, -eiche, *a.* Tedious, wearisome, ceremonious.
reud, see reudan.
reudan, -ain, -an, *s.m.* Moth, timber-worm. 2* Dry-rot in wood. 3(AF) Weevil. 4** Wood-louse. 5 Pedicular insect that eats through timber and paper. 6**Pipe. 7**Reed.
reudan, *pl.* of reud.
reudanach, -aiche, *a.* Abounding in moths or woodlice. 2 Moth-eaten. 3*Dry-rotten. 4 Reedy.
reudanaich,* *v.a.* Dry-rot.
————**te**, *a.* & *past pt.* Moth-eaten. 2 Dry-rotten.
reul, **réil**, **reultan**, *s.f.* Star. 2 Belle. R.-chomhaideachd, *satellite, planet ;* r. na madra, *the dog-star ;* r. seachrain, *a comet ;* r. seachranach, *a planet ;* r. seasmhach, *a fixed star;* solus nan reultan, *starlight.*
reulach, -aiche, *a.* see reultach.
reuladair, -ean, *s.m.* Astronomer. 2 Astrologer, star-gazer.
————**eachd**, *s.f.ind.* Astronomy. 2 Astrology, star-gazing.
reuladh,** -aidh, *s.m.* Declaration.
reulag, -aig, *s.f., dim.* of reul. Little star, boss. 2 Asterisk. 3 Star—*Arran.*
———**ach**, -aiche, *a.* Glittering with little stars. 2 Starry, astral. 3 Studded.
reul-airgiodach,** *a.* Studded with silver. Claidheamh r., *a silver-studded sword.*
reulanach,(MS) *a.* Astriferous.
reul-an-iuchair, *s.f.* The dog-star.
reul-bhad, *s.m.* Constellation.
reul-bhuidheann, see reul-bhad.
reul-chearbach, -tan-, *s.f* Comet.
reul-chuairt, -ean, *s.f.* Orbit.
reul-dhealrach, -aiche, *a* Star-blazing.
reul-dhiadhaireachd, *s.f.ind.* Astro-theology.
reul-dhruidh, -ean, *s.m.* Astrologer.
————**each**, *a.* Astrological.
————**eachd**, *s.f.ind.* Astrology.
reul-eòlach, -aiche, *a.* Skilled in astronomy or astrology. Gu r., *astrologically.*
reul-eòlas, -ais, *s.m.* Science of astronomy or astrology.
reul-fheasgair, *s.f.* Evening star.
reul-ghrigleach,** *a.* Sideral, astral. 2 Thick-set with constellations.
reul-ghrigleachan, -ein -an, *s.m.* Constellation, cluster or group of stars, as Pleiades.
reul-ghriglean, -ein, -an, *s.m.* Constellation.
reul-grigleanach,** *a.* see reul-ghrigleach.
reul-iùil, *s.f.* Pole-star.
reul-na-maidne, *s.f.* Aurora (plant.) 2 The morning-star.
reul-sholus, -uis, *s.m.* Star-light.
reult, -a, *pl.* -an & reilte, see reul.
reulta, *pl.* of reul.
reultach, -aiche, *a.* Starry, astral. 2 Starred. Oidhche r., *a starry night.*
reultag,** -aig, -an, *s.f.* Starlet. 2 Asterisk. 3 Stud. 4 Astrolabe.
reultagach, *a.* Starry, abounding in little stars. 2 Studded.
reultaich,** *v.a.* Stud.
reultaichte, *past pt.* Studded.
reultair, see reuladair.
————**eachd**, see reuladaireachd.
reultanach, -aiche, *a.* see reulach.
reultan, *pl.* of reul. 2 *dim.* of reul.
reult-bhuidheann, see reul-bhuidheann.
reult-chosgair,** -ean, *s.m.* Astronomer. 2 Astrologer, star-gazer.
reult-chuirt,** *s.f.* The star-chamber.
reult-iasg,(AF) *s.* Star-fish. 2**Fish with shining teeth.
reum, -a, (AH) *s. m.* Viscuous saliva, rheum secreted in abnormal profusion. 2(DU) Sense, consistency. Cha'n 'eil r. 'nad chainnt, *your talk is senseless.*
reumach,** *a.* Phlegmy. 2 Afflicted with catarrh. 3 Rheumatic.
reumalachd,** *s.f.* Constancy, perseverance, steadiness. 2 Phlegmatic temperament.
reumail,‡ -e, *a.* see réimeil.
reumhach, *Skye* for freumhach.
reumhair,**-ean, *s.m.* Traveller wayfaring man,

rover, vagabond.
reumhaireachd,** *s.f.* Travelling, wayfaring, roving, roaming.
reusan, -ain, -ain, -an, *s.m.* Reason, cause, motive, argument.
reusanach, -aiche, *a.* see reusanta. 2 Argumentative.
reusanachadh, -aidh, *s.m.* Reasoning, act of reasoning or arguing, ratiocination, argument, expostulation. A' r—, *pr. pt.* of reusonaich.
reusanachd, *s. f. ind.* Rationality, reasonableness, reasoning, argument, justness, just grounds, conscionableness.
reusanaich, *v.a.* Reason, argue, ratiocinate, expostulate, think.
reusanaiche, -an, *s.m.* Reasoner.
reusanta, *a.* Endowed with reason, rational. 2 Reasonable, just.
reusontachd, see reusanachd.
reusantas,** -ais, *s.m.* Ratiocination.
reusbaid, (CR) *s.f.* Groove or bed in the keel of a boat to receive the edge of the *fliuch-bhord* or *eàirlinn*, that is, of the first strake or plank. 2 Rascal, beggar's brat, term of contempt—*Arran.*
reusbanadh, (CR) s.m. Mal-treatment, ill-usage. Is tu a rinn an r. air, *how badly you have beaten him*, or *used it—Suth'd.*
reuson, see reusan.
reusonta, see reusanta.
ri, *prep.* To, implying similarity or likeness. 2 To, denoting equality of one object with another. 3 To, implying adhesion. 4 To, towards. 5 Denoting attention or earnestness. 6 To, in the direction of. 7 To, unto. 8 To, implying exposure. 9 To, to be, implying possibility. When placed before present participles it changes them into the future passive—an absurd grammatical statement that passes current. 10 Against, in opposition to. 11 At, near to. 12 During, whilst. 13 For, implying expectation or hope. 14 In, denoting employment or occupation. 15 Of, concerning. 16 Up, upwards. 17**With. 18 As, like as. 19* In contact with.

Cho mìn ri minicionn, *as soft as kid-skin*; ri d' chluas, *to your ear*; ri gréin' *(exposed) to the sun*; ri bruthach, *ascending the acclivity*; a' cogadh ri gaisgeach, *fighting with a hero*; bhuail e a chas ri cloich, *he dashed his foot against a stone*; ri saorsainneachd, *employed as a carpenter*; ri 'làimh, *at his hand*; ri linn Thèarlaich, *in the days of Prince Charles*; ri là gaoithe, *on a windy day*; mar dhuilleig ri doinionn, *like a leaf in the blast*; na caomhaich ri sìth, *the friends at peace*; gun dùil ri pilleadh, *without hope of returning*; an raineach ri turram 'sa ghaoithe, *the fern whistling in the wind*; cho ciùin ri aiteal, *as mild as a breath of wind*; bha 'n righ òg ri móran àbhachd, *the young king was at much pleasure—W.H. 1.12*; cha'n 'eil againn ri dol na's fhaide, *we have not to go any further—W.H. 1.14*; thàinig e gu aoise dol ri ceaird, *he came of age to learn a trade*; thàinig e ri a bheatha féin, *he took his own life, committed suicide*; uibhir ri càch, *as much as the rest*; beul ri trì miosan, *nearly three months*; bha e ri tighinn, *he was to come. Ri in Lewis* often takes the place of *ag*, as, tha e ri bualadh, *he is striking.*

Compounded thus with the personal pronouns :—
Rium, *to me*; riut, *to thee*; ris, *to him*; rithe, *to her*; ruinn, *to us*; ruibh, *to you*; riu, *to them.*

r ! *int.* see righ !
ria, see rithe.
riab, *prov.* for reub.
riabadh, *prov.* for reubadh.
riabh, see riamh.
riabhach, -aich, *s.f.* Common lousewort.
riabhach, -aich, *s. m.* Grey or grizzled person. An riabhach mór, *the devil.*
riabhach, -aiche, *a.* Brindled, greyish, grizzled. 2 Brown, drab. 3 Yellow-grey—*Arran.* Bò r., *a grizzled cow*; sleagh r., *a brown spear.*
riabhag, -aig, -an, *s.f.* Lark. 2††Hedge-sparrow.
riabhagach,†† *a.* Abounding in larks or hedge-sparrows.
riabhag-choille,¶ *s.f.* Wood-lark, see uiseag-choille. 2 Tree-pipit—*anthus arboreus.*
riabhag-fhraoich,¶ *s. f.* Mountain linnet see riabhag-mhonaidh.
riabhag-mhonaidh,¶ *s.f.* Tit-lark, see snathadag. 2 Mountain linnet—*linota montium.* [** gives *alauda pratensis.*]
riabhaiche, *s.f.ind.* Greyishness.
riabhaichead, -eid, *s.f.* Degree of greyness, brindledness, greyishness or brownness.
riabhan, -ain, -an, *s.m.* see riadhan. 2**Handsome young stripling. 3 Dappled, speckled place. 4 (DMu) Chain of doctrines.
riabhanach,** *a.* Handsome, like a stripling.
riach, see riabhach.
riach, *pr.pt.* a' riachadh, *v.a.* Cut the surface, graze or plough along the surface. 2* Cut, as when flaying a beast. 3 (DU) Rule, as a slate or paper. R. e air mo chraicionn, *it grazed my skin.*
riachadh, -aidh, *s.m.* Act of cutting the surface, slightly cutting, grazing or scratching the skin, slight cut or scratch. 2 (DU) Ruling, as a slate or paper. A' r—, *pr.pt.* of riach.
riachaid, -e, -ean, *s. f.* Distributing, dividing, partition. 2**Controller.
†riachan, *s.m.* Anything grey.
riachdail,** *a.* see riochdail.
riachdaileachd,** *s.f.* see riochdalachd.
riachdailleas,** -eis, *s.m.* Necessity, want.
riachdalas,** -ais, *s.m.* Clearness, manifestness.
riachdanach, -aiche, *a.* Necessary. 2 Immoral, impure. 3 Fond of sexual intercourse. 5 Needy, necessitous, needful. 6 Dutiful, incumbent. 7 Given to uncleanness.
†riachdanas, -ais, *s.m.* Necessity, want, indigence, misery. 2 Indispensable duty. 3**Fornication, uncleanness. 4 Necessaries. 5 Force.
riad, (CR) *s.* Crack, split in wood—*Blair Athole.*
riadh, réidh, *s.m.* Interest of money. 2 Usury, rent, hire. R. agus calpa, *interest and principal*; taigh-réidh, *a bank*; airgiod air r., *money invested for interest.*
riadh,** *s.m.* Correction. 2 Racing. 3 Taming. 4 Grief. 5 Kind of capital punishment among the Irish Gael.
riadh, -a, -an, *s.f.* Snare. 2**Rib.
riadh, *Badenoch* for riamh & ruith.
†riadh, *v.a.* Hang. 2**Crucify.
riadh, see riagh.
riadh, *s.m.* Row, drill, as of potatoes—*Badenoch.*
riadhach, -aiche, *a.* Usurious. 2**Hired.
riadhadair, -ean, *s.m.* Usurer.
†riadhadh, -aidh, *s.m.* Hanging. A' r—, *pr.pt.* of riadh.
†riadhadh, *s.m.* Gallows.
riadhan, (DMy) *s. m.* Trail, as when grain or meal is escaping from a bag while carrying it. 2 Raking of hay, anything continued in a long line. 4 Streak. 5 Temporary passage for water to run in.
riadhan, (CR) *s.m.* Swathe of hay that has been turned with the rake—*W. of Ross-shire.* 2 see riaghan.

riadh-lann,** -lainn, *s.m.* House of correction.
riadh-mhortair,** *s.m.* Hired assassin, bravo.
riadranach,** -aich, *s.f.* Old maid. 2 Cast-off mistress.
†riagh, *a.* Religious.
riagh, see riadh.
†riagh, -a [& reigh**,]*pl.* -an, *s.f.* Cross, gallows.
riaghail, *pr.pt.* a' riaghladh, *v.a.* Rule, govern, reign, regulate, order, settle, direct, arrange. Riaghlaidh làmh an dichiollaich, *the hand of the diligent shall govern.*
riaghail, -e, -ean, *s.f.* see riaghailt.
riaghailt, -e, -ean, *s.f.* Weaver's rule. 2 Rule, regulation. 3 Law directory. 4 Mariner's compass. 5††Foot-rule. 6 Sense, judgment. 7**Ascertainment. 8 Government, direction. Is math an r. sin,*that is a good law ;* chaidh e as a r., *he lost his senses* ; r. eaglais, *a law of the church ;* dean r., *apportion ;* dean r. air an annlan, *apportion the sauce carefully.*
——— -chèarnach,(DM) *a.* Square, rectangular.
riaghailt-chlaonaidh, *s.f.* Joiner's bevel.
riaghailteach, -eiche, *a.* Regular, according to rule. 2 Peaceable, orderly. 3 Accurate. 4 Moderate, sober.
riaghailteachadh, *s.m.* Adjustment.
riaghailteachd, *s.f.ind.* Orderliness, regularity. 2 Sobriety, sedateness. 3 Peacefulness. 4** Religiousness.
riaghailtear,* *s.m.* Regulator.
riaghailtearachd,** *s.f.ind.* Administration.
riaghailtich, *v.a.* Arrange, adjust by rule, regulate, put in order, govern, apportion.
————e, *comp.* of riaghailteach.
————te, *past pt.* Adjusted, arranged by rule, governed.
†riaghaire, -an, *s. m.* Hangman. 2** Scapegallows, rogue.
riaghal-cuil, see righeal-cùil.
riaghalta, *past pt.*of riaghail. 2***rarely*; Devout.
————chd, see riaghailteachd.
riaghaltair, see riaghladair.
riaghan, -ain, -an, *s.m.* Swing. 2 Exercise of swinging. 3††Drill. 4††Gibbet. 5(MS) Sling.
riaghanach,†† *a.* Abounding in swings, drills or gibbets.
riaghlach, -aiche, *a.* Regular.
†riaghlach, -aich, *s.f.* Old woman.
riaghlachadh, -aidh, see riaghladh.
riaghladair, -ean, *s.m.* Ruler, governor, regulator.
riaghladaireachd, *s.f.ind.* Ruling, governing. 2 Office or practice of ruling, governorship, management, administration.
riaghladh, -aidh, *s.m.* Ruling, administration, direction, management. 2 Mustering. A' r—, *pr.pt.* of riaghail. R. air slòigh, *the mustering of hosts.*
riaghlaich,** *v.* Same meanings as riaghail.
riaghlaichte, *past pt.* of riaghlaich.
riaghlair, -ean, see riaghladair.
riaghlaireachd, see riaghladaireachd.
riaiche, *comp.* of riach (for riabhach.)
rialls,* *v.a.* Handle roughly or unseemly, as a female.
riallsadh,* -aidh,*s.m.* Rough or unseemly handling. A' r—, *pr.pt.* of rialls.
riamh, -a, -an, *s.m.* Series, number. 2 Drill, as of potatoes, turnips, &c., *prov.* 3* Duration.
riamh,* *v.a.* Drill, as turnips, potatoes, &c.—*Skye.*
riamh, *adv.* Ever, at any time before. 2 Always, (or with the negative—never.) [Used only of past time.] An robh r. ? *was there ever ?* bha e r. mar sin, *he was always so* ; mar nach robh riamh a leithid ann, *such as never was the like* ; r. is roimhe, *still and before, abidingly ;* na h-uile duine riamh agaibh,*every man of you.*
†riamh, -a, *s.m.* Beauty, elegance.
riamhach, -aiche, see riomhach.
riamhadh, -aidh, -aidhean, *s.m.* see riomhadh.
riamhag, -aig, -an, *s.f.* Small root or thread, (or friamhag, for freumhag.)
riamhagaich, -e, *s.f.* Filaments appearing in a wound, *prov.* (for freumhagaich.)
riamlach, *a.* see driamlach.
rian,(MS) *s.m.* Appointment.
rian, -an, *s.m.* Mode, method, manner, fashion, form. 2 Order, management, arrangement, adjustment. 3 Regularity. 4 Economy. 5 Sobriety. 6 Good or peaceable disposition. 7 **Span. 8**Carriage. 9**Sea. †10 Road, way, path, footstep. 11 System.
rianachadh, -aidh, *s.m.* Adjusting, act of adjusting, arranging, distributing, act of distributing. A' r—, *pr.pt.* of rianaich.
rianadair, -ean, *s. m.* Governor, arranger, supercargo, representative, director, steward.
rianaich, *v.a.* Adjust, arrange. 2 Divide, distribute.
rianaiche,** *s.m.* Wanderer, traveller. 2 Slow, lazy, shiftless man.
rianaichte, *past pt.* Arranged, adjusted. 2 Distributed, divided.
rianail, -e, *a.* Methodical, in just or due order. 2 Economical. 3 Well-disposed, of a mild or peaceable disposition. 4**Consistent. 5** Well-formed or fashioned. 6**Good-tempered. [ness.
rianalachd, *s.f.ind.* see rian. 2 Aristocraticalness.
rian-atharrachadh, -aidh, *s.m.* Inversion.
rian-grèine, *s.m.* The solar system.
rian-roighe, *s.m.* The Herb Robert, see righeal-cùil.
riapach,(CR) *a.* Untidy, slovenly.
riapail, *v.a.* Mangle. 2 Bungle, botch, manage clumsily.
riapaladh, -aidh, *s.m.* Mangling, act of mangling. 2 Bungling, act of bungling or botching. A' r—, *pr.pt.* of riapail.
riapailte, *past pt.* of riapail. Mangled. 2 Bungled, botched.
riar, réir, *s.m.* Pleasure, will, inclination, dictate, desire. 2*Approbation, satisfaction. 3 Word of honour. 4(MS) Allotment. 5**Judgment, decree. Agus ni thu mo r., *and thou shalt do my will ;* dean mo riar-sa, *act up to my approbation* ; mo r. fhéin ! *upon my word of honour !* ma ni thus' a riar, *if you act up to his approbation* ; dean thusa mo r.-sa, *study to please me* ; mo r.-sa nach tig e 'n nochd, *forsooth, he will not come to-night* ; mo r.-sa nach 'eil ! *upon my word it is not so !* cha'n 'eil e soirbh a r. a dheanamh, *it is not easy to please him ;* mo r.-sa, *my desire.*
riar, *v.* see riaraich.
†riarach, -aiche, *a.* Submissive. 2**Ready to please, obliging. 3 Contented, pleased. 4 Ready to participate, ready to share, dispensing.
riarach,** -aich, *s.m.* Servitor.
riarachadh, -aidh, *s.m.* Pleasing, satisfying, act of satisfying. 2 Satisfaction. 3 Sufficiency. 4 Distributing, sharing. 5 Act of distributing, or dividing. 6* Attending at table. 7 Distribution of elements at a sacrament. A' r—, *pr.pt.* of riaraich. R.-inntinn, *satisfaction of mind ;* air a r., *distributed.*
riarachair,** *s.m.* Portioner.
riarachas, -ais, *s.m.* Same meanings as riarachadh.
riarachd, *s.f.ind,* Same meanings as riarachadh. R.-inntinn, *contentment.*

riaraich, *pr.pt*, a' riarachadh, *v.a.* Please, satisfy. 2 Divide, distribute. 3 Dispense the sacrament. 4**Carve. 5**Dish. R. orra e, *distribute it among them.*
riaraiche,‡‡ -an, *s. m.* Steward, dispenser of food. 2 Economist. 3 Sharer.
riaraichte, *past pt.* of riaraich. Pleased, satisfied. 2 Shared, served, distributed, supplied.
riarainniche,(MS) *s.m.* Administrator.
riaraiste,** *s.pl.* Arrears.
riarta,** *past pt.** Shared, served out, distributed. 2 Content.
riasail,*v.a.* Tear flesh asunder, mangle,"tousle."
———te, *past pt.* of riasail, see riaslaichte.
riasan, -ain, see reusan.
riasant, see reusanta.
riasg, réisg, *s. m.* Moor, fen, marsh. 2 Ley ground. 3 Coarse mountain-grass (beitean.) 4 Sedge or dirk-grass. 5 Place in which this grass grows. 6 (DMy) Peat-moss. 7* Land that cannot be ploughed or dug on account of the dirk-grass it contains, or so hidden with it that it cannot be cultivated. 8*Indocility, stubbornness. 2 (DU) Bog-cotton plant (not the flower.)
riasgach, -aich, *s.m.* see riasg.
———, -aiche, *a.* see riasgail. 2* Turbulent.
riasgachd, (MS) Sterility.
riasgaidheachd,(MS) *s.f.* Harshness.
riasgail, -e, *a.** Moorish, marshy. 2 Heathy. 3 Uncultivated, untractable, wild. 4 Haggard. 5 (MS) Sgraggy. 6 Indocile. 7**Stiff.
riasgalachd, *s.f.ind.* Indocility. 2 Turbulence. 3 Untractableness.
riasglach, -aich, -aichean, *s. f.* Mangled carcase. 2†† Sedgy morass. 3 (CR) Land that cannot be cultivated.
riasg-shùil, see rèasg-shùil.
———-each, see rèasg-shùileach.
riaslach, -aiche, *a.* Tearing, mangling. 2 Apt to tear or mangle. 3 Criticizing.
riaslachadh, -aidh, see riasladh.
riasladh, -aidh, *s.m.* Tearing asunder. 2 Act of tearing or mangling. 3 Criticizing. 4 Caressing. 5 Murdering—*Dàin I. Ghobha.* A' r—, *pr.pt.* of riasail. Òganaich 'gan r. fo eachaibh, *young men mangled under horses.*
riaslaich, *v.a.* see riasail.
———e, see riaslair.
riaslair,** *s.m.* Tearer, mangler.
riason, see reusan.
———ach, see reusanta.
———achadh, see reusanachadh.
riasonta, see reusanta.
———chd, see reusanachd.
riaspach, -aiche, *a.* Confused, disordered, disorderly.
riaspaiche, *s.f.ind.* Coarseness. 2 Confusion.
riaspan, *s.m.* Slowness.
———ach, *a.* Slow, taking unnecessary time.
riasplach, see riaspach.
riasplaiche, see riaspaiche.
riasp-shùil, -shùla, -shùilean, *s. f.* Blear-eye. *prov.* see rèasg-shùil.
———-each, -eiche, *a.* Blear-eyed, *prov.* see rèasg-shùileach.
riastadh,** -aidh, *s.m.* Welt.
riastaidheachd,* *s.f.* Fornication—*North.* 2 Wantonness—*Mac Mhaigh. Alasdair.*
riastair, *v.a. & n.* Become turbulent or disorderly. 2 Confuse, disturb, put into disorder, entangle. 3 Wander hither and thither.
riastar,** -air, *s.m.* Insult. 2 Drawing, hauling.
riastradh, -aidh, -aidhean, *s. m.* Turbulence, disorder, disorderly conduct. 2 State of becoming turbulent or disorderly in conduct. 3 Act of confusing, disturbing, putting into disorder or breeding strife. 4 Act or habit of wandering hither and thither. 5 Outbreaking, immorality, eruption—*Sàr-Obair.* A' r—, *pr.pt.* of riastair.
riastraidh, *fut. aff.a.* of riastair.
riastran,** -ain, *s.m.* Outrage, insult.
———ach, -aiche, *a.* Turbulent, disorderly. 2 Of dissolute habits. 3**Insulting, outraging, outrageous.
———achd, *s.f.ind.* Turbulence, disorderliness. 2 Dissoluteness of manners. 3 Outrageousness, outrages.
riatach, -aiche, *a.* Wanton, immodest. 2 Illegitimate. 3 Foreign.
riatachas, -ais, *s.m.* see riatachd.
riatachd, *s.f.ind.* Wantonness, immodesty, immodest mirth. 2**Illegitimacy. 3**Outlandishness, state of being foreign.
riataich, *a.* Illegitimate—*Sàr-Obair.*
riataiche, *s.f.ind.* Illegitimacy, state of being born in fornication, bastardy. Leanabh r., *a bastard child.*
riataidheachd, see riatachd, riastaidheachd & riataiche.
riatanach, -aiche, *a.* Necessary, indispensable. *prov.*
riatanas, -ais, *s. m.* Necessity, indispensableness. *prov.*
riathach, see riabhach.
rib, *pr.pt.* a' ribeadh, *v. a.* Ensnare, entangle. 2 Separate seed from flax. 3 Involve. 4*Try to take away a person who is the guest of another.
ribe, -achan, *s. m.* Hair. 2 Rag, clout, tatter. 3 Gin, snare. 4**Impediment. 5(MS)Cobweb. 6*Snare to catch fish. 7* Double rope to keep a mad bull. 2* Shag. 9†† Blade. 10 ** Ambuscade.
Ribeachan nan cuinneana, *the hairs of the nostrils.*
ribeach, -eiche, *a.* Rough, hairy. 2 Entangling, ensnaring. 3 Ragged, torn. 4* Cold. Reithe r., *a rough ram.*
———ail, -e, *a.* Ensnaring, ready to ensnare.
———an,** -ain, *s. m.* Denticulated piece of wood, used for separating flax from the seed.
ribeachan, *n.pl.* of ribe.
ribeachas, -ais, *s.m.* Tendency or readiness to ensnare. 2 Ensnaring, entanglement. 3 State of being ensnared.
ribeachd, *s.f.* see ribeachas. 2 Hairiness, roughness.
ribeadh, -idh, *s. m.* Ensnaring. 2 Act of ensnaring or entangling. 3 Process of separating its seed from flax, by pulling it in handfuls through a denticulated piece of wood. A' r—, *pr.pt.* of rib.
———, *past pass.* of rib. Was ensnared. 2 *3rd. pers. sing. & pl. imp.* of rib.
ribeag, -eig, -an, *s.f.*, *dim.* of ribe. Hair, little hair. 2 Small rag or tatter. 3 Tassel, fringe. 4 Bunch of anything hairy. 5 Handful of flax. 6 Dossil or pledget of lint. 7**Whisker. 8 One hair—*Arran.* 9 (AF) In *St.Kilda*, a hair-rope once used for rock climbing, or rather lowering. Now it is made of hide-thongs, three-ply, covered with sheep-skin or some similar material to prevent chafing. This is a very valuable and scarce possession, and has been known to form the dowry of a bride.
ribeagach, -aiche, *a.* Ragged, clouted, tattered. 2 Tasselled, fringed. 3 Abounding in hairy bunches, dossils or pledgets. 4*Hairy.
ribeag-bhròin, *s.f.* Weeper, white cufflet formerly worn at funerals.
ribean, -ein, -an, *s.m.* Ribbon, fillet. 2 Sash

worn by females.
ribeanach, -aiche,*a.* Of, or belonging to,ribbons.
ribear, -eir, -an, *s.m.* Ensnarer, sharper.
——, *fut.pass.* of rib. Shall be entangled.
ribh, *prep.pron.* (ri+sibh) To you, against you. 2 With you. 3* Molesting you. 4* Mastering you. A' bruidhinn r., *speaking to you ;* a' gleachd r., *sparring with you ;* cò tha r.?, *who is molesting you ?* a' cur r., *mastering you, "sorting" you ;* cuirear seo r., *this shall be added to you ;* thig e r., *he will please you ;* cha tig dad ribh, *no harm will happen to you.*
ribheag, see riobhag.
———aichte, see riobhagaichte.
richeannaich,(DMy) *s.pl.* Ragged skin at the base of the nails.
ribheid, -e, -ean, *s.f.* Reed. 2 Reed of a wind-instrument. 3 Music. 4 Musical note or voice. 5* Barb of a hook. 6 (CR) Cord attaching a buoy to a herring-net. 7**Pipe. 8**Oaten pipe. 9**Chanter.
———each, -eiche, *a.* Furnished with reeds, as a wind-instrument. 2 Musical, melodious. 3 **Fistulous.
ribheideachd,** *s.f.ind.* Canorousness. 2 Melody.
ribhid, see ribheid.
———each, see ribheideach.
rìbhinn, -e, -ean, *s.f.* Nymph, maid. 2 Beautiful female. 3 (AF) Serpent. ‡4 Young lady. 5‡ Queen. 6††Quean. R.-shìth, *a fairy ;* a r. ùr.! *thou blooming maid !* [Professor MacKinnon holds that it is a mistake for rìghinn, which is suggested by righbhean in Irish. In Neil MacLeod's poems he has made *rìbhinn* "rìghinn."
ribhinn-chrò, (AF) *s.f.* Barren ewe.
rìbhinneach, -eiche, *a.* Beautiful, maiden-like. 2 Lady-like.
ribich, *v.a.* Hook.
ribin, see ribean.
-——each, see ribeanach.
ribleach, -ich, -an, *s.m.* Long string or line. 2 Anything entangled. 3**Entanglement. 4** Knottiness. 5* Fringe. 6 Man in rags. 7†† Anything in tatters. 8 Shagginess. Tha 'n cord 'na r., *the rope is quite entangled.*
ribleach,** *a.* Entangled. 2 Ragged, torn.
———adh,** -aidh, *s.m.* Entangling,entanglement.
———d,** *s. f.* Entanglement. 2 Anything much entangled. 3**Knottiness.
riblich,* *v.a.* Fringe. 2 Make hairy or 3 Entangled.
ribliche, -ean,‡*s.m.* Man in rags.
ribte, *past pt.* of rib.
ribteach, ** *a.* Entangling, ensnaring. 2 Involving. 3 Apt to entangle or ensnare.
†richasan,‖ *s.m.* "Carbunculus."
†richead, -eid, -an, *s.f.* Kingdom.
†riclean, -ein, -an, *s.m.* Dwarf.
ricus,** *s. m.* One of the Gaelic names of the letter R.
rideag,§ -eig, -an, *s.f.* Bog-myrtle, sweet myrtle, sweet gale, see roid.
rideal, see rideil.
ridealach,** see ridealach.
ridealadh, see ridleadh.
ridealair,** *s.m.* Sifter, winnower.
ridealach,** *a.* Like a riddle or sieve.
ridealadh, -aidh, *s.m.* Riddling. 2 Act of riddling or separating by a coarse sieve, sifting.
rideil, *v.a.* Riddle, sift, winnow.
——, *s.m.* Riddle, sieve. Cho tollach ri r., *as full of holes as a sieve.*
A' r—, *pr.pt.* of rideil.
rideilich,* *v. a.* Riddle, sift, winnow.
rideilichte, *past pt.* of rideilich. Riddled, sifted.
ridein, (AC) *s.f.* Queen. 2 Handsome maiden, beautiful girl.
ridgileanach, see cam-ghlas.
ridghuileanach,¶ -aich, *s.m.* see cam-ghlas.
ridhe, -an & -achan, see righe
ridhe, see righe. 2‡‡Wrist.
ridheach, -eiche, *a.* see righeach.
ridhil, *pr. pt.* a' ridhleadh, *v. a. & n.* Twine yarn upon a reel. 2**Twirl, hurl, roll. 3 see righil.
ridhil, -e & -dhle,*pl.*-ean -dhleachan & -dhlean, *s. m.* Reel on which yarn is wound. 2**Hurl. 3 see righil.
ridhle, *gen. sing.* of ridhil.
ridhleach, -eiche, *a.* Having reels. 2 Like a reel.
ridhleadh, -eidh, *s.m.* Winding. 2 Act of winding yarn upon a reel. 3 Hurling,rolling. A' r—, *pr.pt.* of ridhil.
ridhlean, -ein, -an,‡ *s. m.* Small reel. 2**Little wheel. 2 Wheel of any vehicle. 3 Sheave of a pulley, see ulag, 6, p. 78.
ridhlichean, -ein, *s.m.* Small reel.
ridhreadhachd, *s.f.* Verity.
ridil, see rideilich.
ridil, see rideil.
ridir, -ean, *s.m.* Knight.
r. beò-shlàinte, *a knight-bachelor.*
r. òighreachd, *a knight-baronet.*
r. spleadhach, r. nan sleagh *or* r. claidheimh, *a knight-errant.*
R. a' Chluarain, *Knight of the Thistle* (K.T.)
R. Phàdruig, *Knight of St. Patrick* (K.P.)
R. a' Ghartain, *Knight of the Garter* (K.G.)
R. a' Chroinn mhóir, *Knight of the Grand Cross* (K.G.C.)
R. Feadhnach, *Knight Commander of the Bath* (K.C.B.)
R. Deòrsa, *Knight of St. George* (KG)—a Russian order.
R. Uilleim, *Knight of King William* (K.W.)—a Flemish order.
R. Anna, *Knight of St. Ann*(K.A.)—a Russian order.
R. Ainndreis, *Knight of St. Andrew* (K.A.)—a Russian order.
R. na Gealaich ùire, *Knight of the Crescent* (K. C.)—a Turkish order.
R. na Rionnaige Tuathaich, *Knight of the N. Star*—a Swedish order.
R. na h-Iolaire Ruaidhe, *Knight of the Red Eagle*—a Prussian order.
R. na h-Iolaire Gile, *Knight of the White Eagle*—a Polish order.
R. na h-Iolaire Duibhe, *Knight of the Black Eagle*—a Russian order.
R. an Leòmhainn 's na Gréine, *Knight of the Lion and Sun*—a Persian order.
R. an Lomairt Òir, *Knight of the Golden Fleece*—a Spanish order.
R. an Dùin 's a' Chlaidheimh, *Knight of the Tower and Sword*—a Portuguese order.
R. Iolair nam Beann, *Knight of the Mountain Eagle*—an order it was intended to establish had the Chevalier St. George succeeded in gaining the British throne.
[** gives the above Gaelic names of foreign orders.]
ridireach, -eiche, *a.* Knightly. 2 Chivalrous.
-———d, *s.f.* Knighthood. 2**Knightliness, chivalry.
ridireil, see ridireach.
ridirich, *v.a.* Knight.
ridleadh, -eidh, *s.m.* & *pr.pt.* see ridleadh.
rief, *s.* Brimstone.

rif, see riof.
rifeid, see ribheid.
———each, see ribheideach.
rig, see ruig.
†rig, *s.* Spy.
rige,(AF) *s.* Ram. 2 Semi-castrated ram—*Skye & Argyllshire.*
rigean, see ridean.
rigear, *fut.pass.* of rig.
righ, *v.* Lay out or stretch a body. 2* Dress or shroud as a corpse. A righ, nach robh thu air do righeadh ! *I wish to God you were shrouded !*
rìgh, *pl.* -rean & righre, *s.m.* King. An ceud r. Teàrlach, *King Charles I.*; bàs R. Seumas, *the death of King James*; r. nan dùl, *the governor of the elements*; r. nan gràs, *the disposer of sovereign grace*; A Rìgh glèidh sinn ! *O Lord preserve us !* r. nan uamhann, *the king of terrors.*
rìgh ! *int.* Strange !
righbhinn, see ribhinn.
————each, see ribhinneach.
rìgh-bhùth,** *s.m.* Royal residence. 2 Royal pavilion.
rìgh-chathair, -chathrach, -chathraichean, *s. f.* Throne. 2 Metropolis (from the supposition that it contains the king's residence,)
rìgh-chiste, -an, *s.f.* Royal treasury.
rìgh-cholbh, -chuilbh, -an, *s.m.* Sceptre.
rìgh-choron, -oin, -an, *s.m.* Royal crown.
rìgh-chrùn, -ùin, *s.m.* Royal crown.
rìgh-damhna,** *s.m.* King's heir.
rìgh-dhail, -e, -ean, *s.f.* Assembly, parliament. 2**Congress of sovereigns.
righdir, see ridir.
righe,(CR) *a.* Stretched, tight, tense. Tha 'n còrd righe, *the cord is tense—W. of Ross-shire.*
righe, *s.m.* Field. 2 Bottom of a valley.
righe, -an, *s. m.* Wrist. 2 Arm. 3 The fore-arm. 4 Outstretched part or base of a mountain. 5 Slope. 6 Summer residence for herdsmen and cattle, sheiling. 7 Reproof. Bac na righe, *the hollow or bend of the arm.* [McL & D gives also for *pl.* righeachan & righeannan. ** gives *s.f.*]
rìgheach,(MS) *a.* see rìoghail.
righeach, -ich, -ichean, *s.f.* †Thong, pinion. 2 **Arm. 3 (DMy) Sinew, muscle.
————, -eiche, *a.* Having strong arms. 2 Having handsome arms. 3†† Pertaining to, or abounding in, sheiling huts.
rìgheachadh, see rìoghachadh.
righeachan, (for ridheachan & righean,) *pl.* of righe.
righeachas,†† -ais, *s. m.* Wrestling at arms' length.
righeachd, see ruigheachd.
rìgheachd, see rìoghachd.
righeadh, *s.m.* Stretching out. 2 Act of stretching. A' r—, *pr.pt.* of righ. Corp a r., *to shroud a corpse.*
righealadair, see riaghlair.
righealair, see riaghlair.
righeal cùil,§ *s.m.* The herb Robert, stinking crane's bill,—*geranium Robertianum.*
righeal-rìgh, *s.m.* The herb Robert, see righeal-cùil.
righean, see ridhean & ruighean, *pl.* of righe.
righeannan, for ridhean or ruighean, *pl.* of righe.
righe-mheas, *s.m.* Cubit.
righeil, see riaghail.
rìgh-fhalluing,** *s.* Pall.
rìgh-fheadhnach,** -aich, *s.m.* Generalissimo.
rìgh-fheall, *s.f.* Treason.
rìgh-fhéinneach, *s.m.* see rìgh-fheadhnach.

602. *Righeal-cùil.*

rìgh-fhéinnidh, see rìgh-fheadhnach.
rìgh-ghuileanach,(AF) *s.m.* Redshank, see camghlas.
rìghich, *v.* see rìoghaich. Rìghichidh an Tighearn gu saoghal nan saoghal, *the Lord shall reign for ever and ever.*
————, *s.f.* Handcuffs—*Skye.*
righidir, see ridir.
righil, righle, rìghleachan, *s.m.* Reel, a Scottish dance. 2‡‡ Yarn-reel. [Righle is also used as *nom.*] Righle Thulaichean, *the Reel of Tulloch,*—a form of reel from which females are generally excluded.]
righil, *v.a.* Dance a reel.
righinn, righne, *a.* Tough. 2 Adhesive. 3 Elastic, supple, pliant, flexible. 4 Sluggish, drowsy, dilatory, slow. 5**Lasting, durable, made of good stuff. 6**Clammy. 7 Viscid, stiff. 8** Rigid, contumacious. 9‡Tenacious. Chaidh sleaghan r. a bhearnadh, *tough spears were hacked.*
rìghinn,** *s.* Snake. 2 see ribhinn. 3*Princess.
righinneachd, *s.f.* Clot.
rìgh-lann, -ainn, -an, *s. m.* Palace, royal residence. 2**King's court.
rìgh-laoch, -laoich, *s.m.* Princely warrior. 2** Respectable man. 3**Good fellow.
rìghle, -achan, *s.m.* see righil.
rìghleadh, -eidh, *s.m.* Reeling, dancing reels. 2*Floundering. A' r—, *pr.pt.* of righil.
rìgh-mhilidh, -ean, *s.m.* Heroic chief.
rìgh-mhort, *s.m.* Regicide.
rìgh-mhortadh, -aidh, *s.m.* Regicide (act.)
rìgh-mhortair, -ean, *s.m.* Regicide (person.)
rìgh-na-coille,§ *s.m.* The oak, see darach.
rìgh-nan-iasg,(AF) *s.m.* Salmon.
rìgh-nathair, -thrach, -thraichean, *s.f.* Cockatrice. 2 Large serpent, basilisk.
righne, *comp.* of righinn.
rìghneadh, see rìghnead.
————adh, -aidh, *s.m.* Act of making tough, adhesive or clammy. 2 Growing tough. 3 State of growing tough, adhesive or clammy. 4 Act of delaying, procrastinating or prolonging. A' r—, *pr.pt.* of rìghnich.
————as, -ais, *s.m.* Toughness. 2 Sluggishness, laziness, drowsiness. 3 Stiffness. 4 Delay. 5 Clamminess.
————d, *s.f.ind.* see rìghneachas. 2** Gift. 3**Favour.
righnead, -eid, *s.m.* Degree of toughness or 2 Glutinousness.
rìghneas, -eis, see righneachas. 2 Tenacity.
rìghnich, *pr.pt.* a' righneachadh, *v.a.&n.* Toughen, make adhesive or clammy. 2 Become tough, adhesive, viscid or clammy, clot. 3 Delay, procrastinate, prolong the time. 4 Make stiff. 5 Grow stiff.
————te, *past pt.* of rìghnich. Toughened, adhesive or clammy. 2 Procrastinated. 3

Stiffened.
rìgh-phàilliun, -iuin, -iuinean, *s.m.* King's pavilion. 2**Tabernacle.
rìgh-phubull, -uill, -an, *s.m.* see rìgh-phàilliun.
rìgh-raineach,‡ *s.f.* Royal fern, see raineach reangach.
rìgh-rath, -a, -an, *s.m.* Royal fortress or seat.
righre & rìghrean, *pl.* of rìgh.
rìgh-seisg, -e, *s.m.* Greater bur-reed, branched bur-reed, see seisg-rìgh.
rìgh-shlat, -ait & -a, *pl.* -an, *s.f.* Sceptre, see slat-rìoghail.
rìgh-theach, -an, *s.m.* King's house or palace.
†rìghtheach, -eich, -an, *s.m.* see rìgheach.
rìgh-theachdair, -ean & -theachdraichean, *s.m.* Envoy, ambassador, plenipotentiary, embassy. (teachdair-rìgh.)
rìgh-uilleanach, see cam-ghlas.
rìgleachan,** *s.m.* Castrated ram.
ri h-ùine, *adv.* By-and-by.
rill,** *v.a.* Riddle. 2 Winnow.
rilleadh,** -idh, *s. m.* Riddling, winnowing, sifting.
rillean,** -ein, *s.m.* Riddle, coarse sieve.
†rimh, -e, -ean, *s.f.* Number.
†rimh, *v.a.* Reckon, compute, number.
rimheach, *a.* see rìomhach.
rimheadh,** -idh, *s.* see rìomhadh.
†rimhiadh, -idh, *s.m.* Pride.
rimhinn, see ribhinn.
———each, see ribhinneach.
rinc,** *v.a. & n.* see ring.
rinceach, see ringeach.
rinche,(AF) *s.* Kitten.
rineach, *s.m.* *Arran &c.* for reannach.
ring,** *v.a. & n.* Tear. 2 Pull. 3 Dance, hop.
ringeach,** -eiche, *a.* Tearing. 2 Pulling. 3 Parting. 4 Dancing.
ringeadh,** -eidh, *s. m.* Tearing. 2 Hanging. 3 Dancing, dance.
ringeal,* *s.* Circle, sphere—*Mainland.*
ringear,** -eir, *s.m.* Dancer.
ringheall,** -ill, *s.m.* Promise.
ringheimhlean,** *s.pl.* Chains.
†ringtheach, -eiche. *a.* see ringeach.
rinn, *prep.pron.* (ri+sinn) To us. 2 Against us. 3 Meddling with us. Thubhairt e r., *he said to us*; maille r., *with us, together with us*; na bi r., *do not meddle with us*; cuiridh iad r., *they will ply us, they will try our mettle, they will add to us*; an Spiorad a' cur r., *the Spirit applying to us*; cha tig e r., *it will not please or satisfy us*; cha tig ni r., *no harm will befal us.*
rinn, -e, -ean, *s.f.* Acumen, acumination. 2 Promontory, point. 3 Planet (reann.) 4**Music. 5 **Barb. 6**Nib, 7 **Foot. 8**Tail. 9(MS) Apex. 10††Edge. 11(DU) Point of a pin. 12 **see roinn. An iochdar na Rinne, *in the farthest off parts of the rhinns or peninsula*; Rìgh na rinne, *King of the planets*; r. snathaid, *the point of a needle*; dh' fhalbh an r. di, *its point is off.*
rinn, *past ind.* of dean. Rin iad sinn, *they did that.* Is olc a r. thu! *how badly you acquitted yourself!* dh' aon rud 's gu 'n d' rinn e, *despite of all he could do.*
rinn-an-ruisg, -ean-nan-rosg, *s.f.* Apple or pupil of the eye. 2 Eyebright, see lus-nan-leac.
†rinn-bhearthag, -aig, -an, *s.f.* Surgeon's knife.
rinn-bhior, -a, -an, *s.m.* Sharp stake.
———ach, -aiche, *a.* Sharp-pointed.
rinndeal,* -eil, *s. m.* Sphere, extent, limits, boundaries, territory. Tha 'n r. iomachumhann, *the boundaries are limited*; leabhar an rinndeil, *the rental- or stent-book*; de an r. fearainn a th' agad? *what extent of land do you possess?* a' cheart r., *the very extent or sphere.*
†rinne, -an, *s.f.* The understanding.
rinne, *emphat. form* of rinn, *prep. pron.*
rìnneach,(CR) *s.* Loose shreds of skin at the base of the finger-nails—*Arran.*
rinneach, -eiche, *a.* Cuspated, pointed, having a sharp point. 2 Abounding in promontories or headlands.
———adh, -aidh, *s.m.* Sharpening, forming into a point, 2 Act of forming into a point. A' r—, *pr.pt.* of rinnich.
rinneadair,** *s.m.* Carper, spyfault.
†rinneadar, *v.* They did.
rinneadh, *past.pass.* of dean.
rinneamh,** -eimh, *s.m.* The constellations.
rinn-gheur, -e, *a.* Sharp-pointed, acute.
rinn-gheuraich,(MS) *v.a.* Barb.
rinnich, *v.a.* Sharpen into a point.
———e, -an, *s.m.* Graving tool.
———te, *past pt.* of rinnich. Sharpened into a point.
†rinnreim,** *s.* Constellation.
riob,* *v. & s.* see rib.
rioba,* see ribe.
———ch,* see ribeach.
———chan, *pl.* of riob.
———chd,* see ribeachd.
———dh, -aidh, *s.m. & pr.pt.* see ribeadh.
riobag,* see ribeag.
———ach,* see ribeagach.
riobaich, *v.a.* see ribich.
riobaid, -ean, *s. m.* Spendthrift.
———each,** *a.* Extravagant, prodigal.
———eachd,** *s.f.* Extravagance.
riobain, see ribean.
riobalach,* *s.m.* Hairy, curious-looking, ragged person.
rioban, see ribean.
———aich,** *v.a.* Deck with ribbons.
riobhag,** *s.f.* Barb, as of a hook.
———ach, -aiche, *a.* Barbed, barbated.
———aich, *v.a.* Barb.
———aichte, *past pt.* Barbed.
riobhaid,** see ribheid.
———each, see ribheideach.
†riobhar, -air, -an, *s.m.* Sieve. 2 Honeycomb.
†riobh-chlàr, -chlàir, -an, *s.m.* Catalogue.
†riobhlach, -aich, *s.m.* Rival.
rioblach, *a. & s.* see ribleach.
———adh, see ribleachadh.
———d, see ribleachd.
rioblaich, see riblich.
riobta, see ribte.
riobte, see ribte.
riobtach, see ribteach.
rioch,* *v.a.* see riach.
riochd, -a, -an, *s.m.* Likeness, form, appearance. 2 State, condition. 3 Stead, place. 4 Ghost, spirit. 5 Person of wan appearance. 6 Relative size, proportion. 7* Interpretation, exposition. 8 Hue. 9 (MS) Air. Chaidh i an r. gearraidh, *she assumed the shape of a hare*; 'dè is r. dè m' aisling? *what is the interpretation of my dream?* an r. mairbhe, *having the appearance of a dead man*; a réir r. gach aon dhiubh, *according to the proportion of each.*
riochdachadh, -aidh, *s.m.* Personating. 2 Act of personating or representing. 3 Substitution. A' r—, *pr.pt.* of riochdaich.
riochdaich, *v.a.* Personate. 2 Represent, pourtray.
———te, *past pt.* of riochdaich.
riochdail, -e, *a.* Actual, real, positive. 2 Handsome, stately. 3 True. 4 Manifest. Gu r., glan, *actually and really so*; dh' innis e dhòmhsa e gu r., glan, *he told it me as a positive fact.*

riochdail,* *s.* Skeleton, poor-looking person.
riochd-ainm,-e, -eannan, *s.m.* see riochdair.
————each, *a.* see riochdarail.
riochdair, *s.m.* Representative, substitute. 2* Delegate. 3 Plenipotentiary.
riochdair, -an, *s.m.* Pronoun in *grammar.*
———eil, -e, *a.* Pronominal.
riochdalachd, *s.f.ind.* Reality. 2 Comeliness of shape or dress. 3‡‡Portliness. 4 Manifestness.
riochdall, -aill, -an, *s.m.* Dwarf. 2 Fairy.
riochd-bhriathar, -air, -thran, *s.m.* Metaphor.
riochd-bhriathrach, -aiche, *a.* Metaphorical.
riochd-dhealbhach, -aiche, *a.* Mosaic.
riochd-fhacal, -ail, -an, *s.m.* Pronoun.
riochd-fhear,** *s.m.* Agent.
riochdmhor,** -oire, *a.* Shapely, proportioned.
†riochos, *s.m.* King. 2 Rule.
†riodh, *s.m.* Ray or beam of light.
riof, *pl.* -a, -annan & -achan, *s.m.* Reef of a sail. 2‡‡Sunken rock.
riogh, see rìgh.
rìoghach,* *s.f.* Pinion, string to tie the arms of a prisoner. An r. air an òlach, *may the fellow be pinioned!—deuce take the fellow!*
rìoghachadh, -aidh, *s.m.* Reigning. 2 Act of reigning. 3 Reign. 4 Governing, governance. A' r—, *pr.pt.* of rioghaich.
rìoghachd, -an, *s.f.* Kingdom, realm, empire. 2 Dominion, sway, government. Is farsuing do r. 's gur fial, *extensive and hospitable is thy dominion.*
————ail, -e, *a.* National.
rìoghaich, *v.a.* & *n.* Reign, rule, govern. 2*Pinion, tie. R. e dà bhliadhna dheug, *he reigned twelve years.*
rìoghail, -e, *a.* Royal, kingly. 2** Princely. 3 Loyal. Lios r., *a royal court*; taigh r., *a palace.*
rioghainn, (CR) *pr.pt.* a' rioghainn, *v.n.* Reach to, arrive at. An r. thu air? *can you reach it?—Perthshire.*
rìoghair,* -ean, *s.m.* Royalist.
rìoghalach, -aich, *s.m.* Loyal subject.
————d, *s.f.ind.* Royalty. 2 Loyalty. 3 Dignity of port and character. 4 Regal pomp. 5 Princeliness. 6 Majesty.
rìoghann, see rìbhinn.
†rioghthach,* -aich, *s.f.* Fellee of a wheel.
rioghlach,** -aich, *s.f.* Old hag.
rioglachan,(AF) *s.m.* Wild duck.
rìogh-bhuth, see rìgh-bhuth.
rìogh-lann, see rìgh-lann.
rìogh-laoch, see rìgh-laoch.
rìogh-nathair, see rìgh-nathair.
rìogh-phubull, see rìgh-phàilliun.
rioluinn, -e, -ean, *s.f.* Cloud. 2 (AH) Fantastically dressed woman. (†† riolainn.)
————each,†† *a.* Cloudy.
riomb,* *s.m.* Wheel.
riomba,* *s.m.* Semi-circular bay or beach.
riomball,* -aill, *s.m.* Circle, halo. R. mu 'n ghealaich, *a halo round the moon*; gearr r., *draw or describe a circle.*
————ach,* -aiche, *a.* Circular, circuitous, like a circle.
————achd,* *s.f.ind.* Circularity, roundness, circuitousness.
rìomh,* *s.m.* Costly jewel.
rìomh, see riamh.
†riomh, *s.m.* Reckoning, numbering, computation. see rimh.
†———, *v.a.* Number, compute. see rimh.
rìomhach, -aich, *s.m.* Beau, dandy.
————, -aiche, *a.* Fine, elegant, handsome, beautiful. 2 Precious, valuable, costly. 3 Gaudy, conceited. 4 Gorgeous, superb. 5* Fond of. 6 Stately. 7 Regal. De chulaidhean r., *of gorgeous apparel.*
rìomhachas, -ais, *s. m.* Fineness, elegance, handsomeness, beauty, superbness. 2 Costliness, preciousness, valuableness. 3 Gaudiness. 4 Conceitedness. 5 Gorgeousness. 6 Regality.
rìomhachd, *s.f.* see rìomhachas.
rìomhadh, -aidh, *s. m.* see rìomhachas. 2** Fondness. 3 Habiliment. 4 Enumeration.
riomhaich,‡‡ *v.a.* Grace, set off.
riomhainn, -e, -ean, see ribhinn.
————each, -eiche, *a.* see rìbhinneach.
riomhair, -ean, *s.m.* see rìomhach. 2 Counter, reckoner, arithmetician. 3 Calculation.
———,** *v.* Calculate.
riomhaireachd, *s.f.* Calculation, arithmetic.
riom-sa, see rium-sa.
riomsachan,** -ain, *s.m.* Searcher.
rìon, *s.m.* *see rian. †2 Way, road, track.
rionachas, see rionnachas.
†rionadair,* see rianadair.
rionaich,** *v.a.* Carve, engrave.
rionaiche,** -an, *s.m.* Carver, engraver.
rionaidheas,** *s.m.* see rionachas.
rionluas,** -ais, *s.m.* Career.
rionnach, -aiche, *a.* see reannach.
rionnach, -aich, *s.m.* see reannach.
†rionnachas,** -ais, *s.m.* Engraving. 2 Sculpture. 3 Graven work.
rionnachd,** *s.f.* Burial, interment.
rionnach-uaine, see reannach-uaine.
rionnadh,** -aidh, *s.m.* Redness.
rionnag, see reannag.
————ach, see reannagach.
rionnaidh,** *s.m.* Satirist.
rionnal,** -ail, *s.m.* Graving, sculpture.
rionnalaiche,** *s.* Graver.
rionntaidh, see rionnaidh.
riopail, *v.* see riapail.
riopladh, -aidh, *s. m.* & *pr. pt.* of riopail. see riapaladh.
riostal,* -ail, see risteal.
rìreadh, (i. e. da rireadh *or* a rìreadh.) [Always da riribh at *Poolewe.*] Truly, actually, indeed, seriously, verily, of a truth, certainly. An ann da rireadh a tha thu? *are you serious?* tha e cheart r., *he is in real earnest.*
rìreamh,** *s.* Good.
ris, Form of the *prep.* ri used before the article, e.g. What is now written "ris an duine" should be "ri san duine," the *s* belonging to the article. 2††Exposed to view. 3 In the practice of, in the habit of. 4 Employed at, engaged in. Tha e ris, *it is exposed to view*; casan ris, *barefooted*; leig ris, *expose, divulge, reveal your mind to*; ris an tombaca, *using tobacco*; ris an t-snaoisean, *using snuff*; 'dè tha thu 'cur ris? *how are you employed? what are you engaged in?* ris a' chlachaireachd, *employed as a mason, engaged at mason-work*; ris an àm seo, *during this weather.*
ris, *prep. pron.* (ri+e) To him; with him; against him or it; equal to him or it. Cum ris, *do not yield to him* or *it*; is math a tha thu a' cumail ris, *you match him well,* or *how you persevere at it!* or *you wear your years well*—look younger than one would expect you to at your age; na bi ris, *do not molest him, do not use* or *practice*; abair ris, *say to him*; theirig ris, *fight him, try him*; sìn ris, *be seduced by him*; 'dè do ghnothach ris? *what is your business with him?* thig mi ris, *I will do for him, I will finish him, 2 I will please him*; cuir r., *master him, 2 add to it, 3 exert yourself*; tha dòchas, (*or* dùil, *or* sùil) agam ris, *I expect him*; feuch ris, *try it.*

rìs, *adv.* (i. e. a rìs) see rithis.
rìs, *s.m.ind.* Rice.
†**ris**, *s.f.* History. 2 Knowledge. 3 Cause, party.
†**ris**, -ean, *s.m.* King.
risd, see rithis.
risdich, *Suth'd* for rithis.
†**riseach**, -ich, *s.m.* Romance. 2 Story-teller.
risean,** -ein, *s.m.* Historian.
———, see ris-san.
riseil,(CR) *v.n.* Rustle—*Perthshire.*
risgeanach, -aich, *s.m.* Brave soldier.
risic, *s.f.* Affix.
†**rision**, -an, *s.m.* Historian.
†———, see ris-san.
risleadh, *v.a.* Rustle. 2 Move things about—*Perth.* A' r—, *pr.pt.* of riseil.
ris-san, *emphat.* of ris.
rist, see rithis.
risteal, -eil, -an, *s.m.* see crann-ruslaidh.
rith, see ruith.
†**rith**, -e, -ean, see righe.
rithe, *prep.pron.* (ri+i) Against her. 2 Molesting her. 3 To her. Na bi r., *do not molest her* ; na h-abair r., *do not say to her* ; cuir r., *master her.*
†**ritheadh**, -idh, *s.m.* Grove.
rìthinn, *a.* see righinn.
rithis, *adv.* (i. e. a rithis.) Again, second time. Cha mhallaich mi a rithis an talamh, *I will not again curse the earth* ; an dràsd 's a rithis, *now and again* ; a choigrich, guil a rithis ! *stranger, weep again !*
rithisd, see rithis.
rithist, see rithis.
rithistich, *Badenoch* for a rithis. Thoir gaol do d' bhean (mhnaoi) rithistich, *love thy wife again.*
rithinneachd, see righneachd.
rith-learg,** *s.* Extemporaneous rhyme.
rìthneas,** -eis, *s.m.* see righneas.
rithnich, see rìghnich.
riù, (ri+iad) *prep.pron.* To them, unto them. 2 Against them. 3 Towards them. 4 With them. Cuir riu, *manage them, add to them;* cum r., *keep up to them, supply them, do not yield to them* ; na bi riù, *do not molest them, do not annoy them* ; thig e riù, *he or it will please them* ; cha tig dad riù, *no harm will befall them.*
†**riubh**, *s.m.* Brimstone.
riugha, see rudha, rudh & rudhadh.
riùdean, see rùdan & reudan.
————ach, -aiche, see reudanach.
————aich, see reudanaich.
rium, (ri+mi) *prep. pron.* To me. 2 Against me. 3 Towards me. 4 With me. Thubhairt e r., *he said to me*; cum rium, *keep up to me, supply me as I want, hold up to me, do not yield to me;* thig e rium, *it will please me, it will become me* ; na bi rium, *do not molest me, do not meddle with me* ; abair r., *say to me* ; còmhla r., *along with me* ; an robh fiughair agad r.? *did you expect me ?* cha tig dad rium, *no harm will befall me* ; rium-riut, *a false person ;* maille r., *together with me.*
rium-sa, *emphat.* of rium.
riù-san, *emphat.* of riù.
riut, *prep.pron.* (ri+thu) To thee. 2 Against thee. 3 Towards thee. 4 With thee. An tig e riut ? *will it please thee ?* maille r., *or* comhla r., *along with thee ;* thachair e r., *he settled you, gave you a "proper dressing"* ; fear riumriut, *a false, double-dealing person ;* à iomall na talmhainn éibhidh mi riut, *from the ends of the earth I will cry unto thee* ; có a bha r. *who was meddling with you ?* cha tig dad r. *nothing will harm you.*
riutha-san, *emphat.* of riù.
riut-sa, *emphat.* of riut.
ro, *adv.* Very much, exceedingly. Used as a prefix to adjectives, and supplying the place of a superlative. Math, *good* ; ro mhath, *very good.* The initial consonant of the adjective following is always aspirated, except *s* when followed by any consonant but *l, n* or *r.* 2 Too much. Tha e ro fhuar, *it is too cold.* 3 Used as an intensive particle. Aire, *attention ;* ro aire, *great attention.*
Ro mhór, *too large, too great ;* is tu an Dia ro mhór, *thou art the very great God* ; cha'n 'eil mi ro chinnteach, *I am not very sure ;* tha e ro bhochd, *he is very sick* (or *poor*); cha'n 'eil e ro thogarrach, *he is not excessively willing* ; ro sgairteil, *very active ;* ro shleamhainn, *very slippery ;* bu ro chaomh leam tighinn, *I should very much like to come*—a common idiom in Gaelic for expressing *very much.*
rò,* *s.m.* Romance, gasconading. Tha e cho làn r. 'sa thachdas e, *he is as full of romancing as he can hold*—he "draws a long bow."
ro, (AC) *s.* Path.
ro', see roimh.
ro' see troimh.
ro-aire, *s.f.ind.* Great attention, care or diligence. Thoir an r. air, *take great care of him.*
ro-amaideach, *a.* Ridiculous.
ro-aoibhneas, -eis, -an, *s.m.* Great joy or gladness.
ròb, -òib, *s.m.* Coarse hair. 2 Shag. 3 Hairiness, shagginess. 4 Slovenliness. 5 Filthiness. 6**see ‡ràp. 7‡Gaelic form of *robe.* R.-bhrat, *a shaggy mantle.*
rob, see rop.
ròbach, -aiche, *a.* Rough, hairy. 2 Slovenly. 3 Filthy. 4 Not clear-sighted. 5* Shaggy. 6 ††Wet, as weather.
ròbag, -aig, -an, *s.f.* Coarse, slovenly, sluttish woman, slut, drab.
robag,(DC) *s.f.* Pet name for a little girl—*Uist.* 2(DU) Small, clever child. 3 (WC) Anything small. R. paisde, *a clever little child* ; r. balaich, *a clever little boy ;* r. eitheir, *a little boat.*
ròbaiche, *s.f.ind.* Slovenliness.
robaidh-raoighde,(WC) *s.m.* Robin.
robail,** *s.f.* Robbery.
robain, *s.pl.* Towering waves, swelling, roaring billows. 3 Heavy rains. *Sàr-Obair.*
robainn,** *v.a.* Rob.
———, *s.f.* Robbery, plundering. 2 see ropainn.
robair, -ean, *s.m.* Gaelic form of *robber.*
———eachd, *s.f.ind.* Robbery.
———neach,‡‡ -ich, *s.m.* Smart or clever boy.
roban, (DC) *s.m.* Pet name for a little boy—*Uist.*
robann, -ainn, see reubainn.
roban-roid, *s.m.* Robin, see brù-dhearg.
†**robar-fola**,‖ *s.m.* Fluxus sanguinis.
robh, *past* form of bi, used with *interr. & neg.* particles. An robh thu ? *were you ?* c' àit' an r. thu ? *where were you ?* cha robh mi ? *I was not.*
robh,** -a, -achan, *s.m.* Roll of bread.
robhadh, -aidh, -aidhean, see rabhadh.
ro-bhàigh,** *s.m.* Great mercy.
robhainn,** *v.a.* Roll, roll together. 2 Wallow.
robhair, see rothair.
robhairt, see reothart.
†**robhar**, *a.* Red.
robhar, -air,** *s.m.* Sieve.
ro-bhàs, -àis, *s.m.* Violent death.
robhas, -ais, -an, *s.m.* see rabhas, (appx.)

ro-bheagan, -ain, *s.m.* Very small quantity.
robh'd, *s.* Lump, bit—*Badenoch.*
ro-bheus,** *s.m.* Good breeding.
rob-ruadh,(AF) *s.m.* Robin-redbreast.
robuist,** *s.f.* Custody.
robunn, -uinn, *s.m.* see reubainn.
roc, -oic, -an, *s.m.* Gaelic form of *rock.*
roc, ruic, *s.f.* Anything that tangles a fishing-hook. 2 Entanglement. 3 Curl, wrinkle, plait or corrugation, particularly in cloth-waulking, caused by drawing threads too tight in weaving. 4(AH) Tangle, species of seaweed. 5** The tops of seaweed that appear above water. 6 (AF) Skate, thornback (fish.) 7 Fold, plait. 8 AH) Sunken, tangle-grown rock. 9 (AH) Hollow, impotent or gurgling cough as that emitted by a man with with a bone or a cow with a turnip stuck in its throat. Cuiridh tu do cheann an r., *you will entangle yourself;* roc aodannach, *having a wrinkled face.* [McL & D gives *gen.* -a, *pl.* -an.]
roc, *v.n.* Wrinkle, become wrinkled.
ròc, -a, -an. *s.m.* Hoarse voice or cry. 2 Hoarse sound. 3 Haw. 4††Rook. 5 Cough, retching, *prov.* [** gives *gen.* roic.]
ròc, *pr.pl.* a' ròcadh, *v.n.* Cry hoarsely, utter a hoarse sound.
Rocabarra, *s.* Imaginary rock in the mythical lore of the Hebrides. Like the fairy-flag of Dunvegan, it has already appeared twice, and when it appears the third time the destruction of the world may be expected. 'N uair a thig Rocabarra ris, is dual gu'n téid an saoghal sgrios, *when Rocabarra appears again, the world is doomed to destruction.*
ròcach, -aiche, *a.* Hoarse, having a hoarse voice. 2 Uttering a hoarse sound or cry.
rocach, -aiche, *a.* Wrinkled. 2 Curly. 3** Crisp. 4**Rocky. 5**Plaited. 6 Dishevelled, as hair.
ròcadaich, -e, *s.f.* Retching, coughing. 2 Hoarse screaming, as of birds of prey.
ròcadh, -aidh, *s.m.* Act of crying hoarsely or uttering a hoarse sound. A'r—, *pr. pt.* of ròc.
rocadh, -aidh, *s.m.* Becoming wrinkled. A' r—, *pr.pt.* of roc.
ròcaideach,* *s.m.* see ròcas.—*Islay.*
ròcail, *pr.pt.* a' ròcladh, *v.a. & n.* Tear, mangle. 2 Corrugate. 3 Become corrugated. 4 †† Croak, roar hoarsely.
ròcail, -e, *s.f.* Roaring or crying with a hoarse voice, croaking, hawing.
ròcair, -ean, *s.m.* Man with a hoarse voice.
rocair,** -ean, *s. m.* Customer. 2 Common guest, one who haunts or often visits a place.
ròcaireachd, *s.f.ind.* Hoarseness of voice. 2 Habit of speaking hoarsely.
ròcais, *n.pl.* of ròcas.
rocal, -aīl, -an, *s.m.* Coarse clothing.
ròcaladh, -aidh, *s.m. & pr.pt.* see ròcladh.
rocall, see rocal.
rocan, -ain, *s. m., dim.* of roc. Plait, fold. 2 Intricacy. 3 Wrinkle. 4**Stumbling-block.
†rocan, -ain, -an, *s.m.* Little cottage, hut. 2 Hood, mantle, cloak, surtout. 3 Thicket. 4 Fray.
ròcan, -ain, -an, *s. m.* Hoarseness. 2 Hoarse voice. 3** Person with a hoarse or rough voice. 4††Wooden clip for seaweed.
rocanach, -aiche, *a.* Crisp. 2 Wrinkled. 3 Plaited, folded, in folds. 4 Mantled, hooded. 5 Of, or like a cot or hut.
ròcanach, -aiche, *a.* Hoarse, having a hoarse or rough voice. 2 Hawing.
ròcanachd, *s. f. ind.* Hoarseness, continued hoarse sound.
ròcanaich,* *s.f.* Hawing, hemming.
roc-aodann, *s.* Wrinkled face.
————-ach, -aiche, *a.* Having a wrinkled face.
ròcas, -ais, -an, *s.f.* [*m.* in *Badenoch.*] Rook—*corvus frugilegus.* 2‡ Crow. [*pl.* -ais in *Ross.*]
roc-eudainneach, see roc-aodannach.
roc-eudann, see roc-aodann.
————-ach, see roc-aodannach.
ròcas-dhearg-chasach, (AF) *s.f.* Chough—*Skye.* The chough which is characteristic of the arms of so many Cornish families, is now almost extinct in Cornwall. The author remembers his father shooting one near Countisbury, Devon, about 1874, and the keeper then remarking on its rarity.
rochaid, see rochnaid.
rochall, -aill, *s. m.* Coverlet. *2 Stumbling-block. †3 Fray.
rochaill,* *s.f.* Blustering female.
rochair,** *v.a.* Slaughter.
†rochar, *s.m.* Slaughter.
rochcaidh,(AF) *s.* Whale.
ròchd, -a, -an, *s.m.* see ròc.
rochd, see roc.
rochdach, see rocach.
ròchdadaich, see ròcadaich.
ròchdail, see ròcail.
rochdair see rocair.
†rochdan,** -ain, *s.m.* Thicket.
rochduin,** *s.f.* Ascent. 2 Arriving at, reaching.
ro' chéile, for troimh chéile. 2 for roimh-chéile, *one in a hurry-burry.*
ro-chriontachd, *s.f.ind.* Oversaving.
ro-choill, -e, *pl.* -an & -ltean, *s.f.* Thick wood.
————-each, -eiche, *a.* Of, or belonging to, thick woods.
ro-chrann, -oinn, *pl.* -an & -oinn, *s.m.* Stately or lofty tree. 'S biodh do gharrain de ro-chrannaibh ! 'gan comhdachadh le h-uaill—*W. Ross, p. 4.* Air meangan àrd nan ro-chrannaibh *on a high branch of the stately trees.* —*Ross, p. 9.*
————-ach, -aiche, *a.* Abounding in stately or lofty trees.
rochuaid,** -ean, *s.* Lamprey.
†rochuaidh, -ean, *s.f.* see rochuaid. 2 Plague.
rochuaideach,** *a.* Full of little lampreys. 2 Like a lamprey.
rochuilleach,** *a.* Terrible. 2 Very dangerous.
ro-chùram, -aim, -an, *s. m.* Great anxiety, excessive care. 2**Vigilance.
————-ach, -aiche, *a.* Over careful.
ròcladh, -aidh, *s.m.* Mangling, act of mangling or tearing. 2†† Croaking or roaring hoarsely. A' r—, *pr.pt.* of ròcail.
rocus, -uis, see ròcas.
ròd, -òid, *pl.* ròdan & ròidean, *s. m.* Way, road, path, track. 2 Ditch. 3 Perch of land. 4 **Method. 5* Reed of mason-work. 6 (AH) Measure of six lineal yards. Ròd mór, *a highway;* r. mór an righ, *the king's highway;* r. réidh, *a plain road;* ré an ròid, *all the way* taobh an ròid, *the roadside;* r. cartach, *a cart-road.*
ròd, -òid, -an, *s.m.* Quantity of seaware cast on the shore. 2**Cast, shot. 3 (CR) Row or drill of potatoes—*Skye.*
ròd, -òid, -an, *s.m.* Foaming sea beating against the shore. 2*Foam.
ròd,* *pr. pt.* a' ròdadh, *v. a.* Scarify. 2 Blade, come through the ground. R. do chas, *scarify your foot.*
rodachd,** *s.f.* Covering. 2 Fence.
ròdadh, -aidh, s.m. Scarifying, 2 Blading, coming through the ground—*Skye.* Tha 'm bun

tàta a' r., *the potatoes are coming through the ground.*
rodaidh, -e, *a.* Coarse-featured. 2* Ruddy. 3 Darkish, *prov.* 4**Rotten. 5**Having a rotten smell. 6**Shrunken. 7 Rough, forward.
——eachd, *s.f.ind.* Coarseness of features. 2* Ruddiness. *prov.*
ròdail,** *a.* Prosperous. 2**Lancing, scarifying.
ròdair,** *s.m.* Wayfaring man.
——eil,** -eil, *s.m.* Strolling. 2 Wandering.
ròdan, *n.pl.* of ròd.
rodan, see radan.
rodh,* -a, *s.m.* Water-edge. 2 Water-mark.
rodha,** see roladh.
ro-dhéidh, -e, -ean, *s.f.* Great desire, striving.
————eil,†† *a* Very desirous.
ro-dhoineanta, -einte, *a.* Very stormy.
ro-dhoinionn, -inn, -an, *s.m.* Severe tempest.
ro-dhùil, -e, -ean, *s.f.* Eager or earnest expectation. 2**Jealousy. 3 Earnest hope.
†**ro-dhuine**, *pl.* -aoine, *s.m.* Nobleman. 2** Excellent man. 3**Commoner. 4**Rogue.
ro-dhùrachd, -an, *s. f.* Great care or diligence. 2 Strong desire or inclination.
†**rodmuin**, *s.m.* Fox.
ro-earail,** *s.f.* Importunity. 2 Earnest desire. Rinn e r., *he urged.*
ro-earbsa, *s.f.* Entire confidence.
ro-eòlas, -ais, *s.m.* Familiarity, intimate acquaintance.
ro-fhonn,** *s.m.* Earnest longing, keen desire.
ro-fhuachd, *s.m.ind.* Great cold.
ròg, -òig, -an, *s.m.* Gaelic form of *rogue.* 2 Roguery, slyness. 3 Theft.
rogainn,** *v. a.* Pluck. 2 Tease. 3 Handle roughly.
——,** *s.f.* Rough handling. Fhuair e r., *he got a rough handling.*
rogair,§-ean, *s.m.* see ragair.
——each, see ragaireach.
——eachd, see ragaireachd.
rogh,** *s.m.* Order. 2 Custom. 3 Wreath. 4 see roghainn.
†**rogh**, *v.a.* Choose.
rogha, see roghainn. Rogha chéile, *the best of husbands* or *wives.*
roghadh, -aidh, *s.m.* see roghainn. R. is taghadh, *the best and choicest.*
ròghail, -e, *a.* Fond of romancing.
roghainn, -ean, *s.m.* Choice, option, preference, selection, choosing. 2 Best of anything. 3 Eligibleness. Theirig do roghainn bhealach, *go where you will ;* r. de sheudar, *the best of cedar* ; tharruing i sreang le r. beachd, *she drew a string with her best aim ;* r. nam ban, *the best of women ;* tha sin 's a r. a bhi dha, *that may be as it pleases—W.& S.2. 4;* tha sin 's a r. agad, *be that as you pleases—W. H. 1.45 ;* tha diugh is r. ann, *there is pick and choice among them ;* r. an t-sealgair, *the best of marksmen ;* an r. air sin. *in preference to that;* dean do r. ris, "*make a kirk or a mill of it.*"
roghainneach, -eiche, *a.* see roghnach.
roghainnich, *v.* see roghnaich.
ròghalachd,* *s.f. ind.* Romancing disposition, gasconading inclination.
roghanachadh, *Suth'd.* for roghnachadh.
roghann, see roghainn.
roghannachd, see roghainn.
roghlach,** -aich, *s.m.* Choosing or selection of soldiers. 2 Body of picked soldiers.
†**roghlach**, *a.* Angry, enraged.
†**roghmhal**, -ail, *s.m.* Election of a prince.
†**roghmhar**,** *a.* Valiant. 2 Very dangerous.
†————, -air, *s.m.* see ruathar & ruamhar.
roghnach, -aiche, *a.* Eligible to be chosen or desired. 2 Optionable. 3 Preferable. 4 Choosing, picking, selecting. An roghnaiche leat seo ? *do you prefer this ?* is roghnaiche, *yes ;* 's e seo a's roghnaiche leam, *I think this is preferable* ; cò a 's roghnaiche leat, *whoever you may choose.*
roghnachadh, -aidh, *s.m.* Choosing. 2 Act of choosing or selecting. 3‡‡Preferring. 4 Selection, election.
roghnaich, *v. a.* Choose, select, pick out. 2‡‡ Prefer, like.
————e, *comp.* of roghnach.
————ear, *fut.pass.* of roghnaich.
————te, *past pt.* of roghnaich. Chosen, selected, elected. 2 Preferred.
roghnuchadh, see roghnachadh.
roghuuich, see roghnaich.
·————e, *comp* of roghnach.
·————te, see roghnaichte.
roghuinn, see roghainn.
————each, see roghnach.
rogh-ràdh,** *s.m.* Apophthegm.
roi', *cont.* for roimh & troimh.
roi'-ainmichte, see roimh-ainmichte.
roi'-aithne, see roimh-aithne.
roi'-aithnich, see roimh-aithnich.
ròib, -e, *s.f.* Filth. 2 Slovenliness. 3 Filth about the mouth. 4 Overgrown or squalid beard. 5 Circle of hair. 6 Pubes.
ròibeach, -eiche, *a.* Filthy. 2 Slovenly. 3 Having filth round the mouth. 4 Having an overgrown or squalid beard.
ròibeadh, *s.m.* Ear-mark on sheep, see comharradh-eluais.
ròibeag, -eig, -an, *s.f.* Moustache.
ròibean, -ein, -an, *s.m.*, *dim.* of ròib. Filthiness. 2 Filth around the mouth. 3 Squalid little beard. 4**Bushy beard. 5 Moustache, whisker. 6**Small rope or cord. 7**Mop. 8 Wick. Cha b' i pòg an ròibein duibh i, *it was not the kiss of the squalid little black beard—Gill. 140.*
————ach, -aiche, *a.* see ròibeach. 2 Having a moustache or whiskers. 3 Bushy, as a beard. 4 Ropy. 5 Moppy.
————achd, *s.f.ind.* see ròib. 2 Bushiness, as of a beard. 3 Moppiness.
ròib-fheusagach, -aiche, *a.* Having a squalid beard.
roibhe,§ *s.m.* Sneezewort, see cruaidh-lus.
†**roibne**,* -an, *s.m.* Dart, lance.
roibneach,** *a.* Sharp. 2 Pointed. 3 Like a lance or dart. 3 Armed with a lance or dart.
ròic, *v.a.* Tear.
——, -ean, *s.m.* Banquet, sumptuous but unrefined feast. 2 Luxury of the table. 3 Fondness for good eating. 4 Eating greedily, gluttony. 5* Superabundance of the good things of life without any of the refined manners of good society. [**ròice.]
roic, see raoic.
ròic-chuilm, *s.* Carnival.
roiceach,** -eiche, *a.* Bellowing, roaring. 2 Rifting. 3 Belching. An eas r., *the roaring cascade.*
ròiceach, -eiche, *a.* see ròiceil.
ròicealachd, *s.f.ind.* Luxury, luxuriousness. 2 Epicurism, sort of brutish luxury or gluttony.
roiceil, -e, *a.* Roaring, bellowing. 2 Rifting. 3 Belching.
ròiceil, -e, *a.* Luxurious. 2 Gluttonous, eating voraciously. 3 Fond of fat meats, epicurean.
roichd, see raoic.
†**roid**, *v.* Run fast.
ròid, Gaelic form of *road.* 2 *gen.sing.* of ròd.

roid, -e, *s.f.* Bog-myrtle, sweet-myrtle, sweet-gale—*myrica gale.* [Badge of certain septs of the Campbells.]
roid, -e, -ean, *s. f.* Short race, bounce, race before a leap. 2 Gale. 3 Force produced by motion. Thug e r. a staigh, *he bounced in* or *rushed in;* a' dol r. do 'n bhail' ud thall, *going for a little while to yon town;* leum r., *a running leap, a running long leap.* (cruinn-leum, *a bound.*)
roid-chinn, *s.* Head-stretch—*Dàin I. Ghobha.*

603. *Roid.*

roide,§ *s.f.* Wormwood, see burmaid.
roidean,** -ein, *s.m.* Wildfire.
roideas, -eis, *s.f.* Running about, frisking, *prov.* (also ruideas.)
roid-ghuilbneadh,¶ *s.m.* Bar-tailed godwit—*limosa rufa.*
roidhleag-urchrach, *s.f.* Cartridge.
roidhse,** -an & -achan, *s.f.* see roinnse.
———ach, see roinnseach.
———achd, see roinnseachd.
roidhsich, see roinnsich.
†roididh, -e, *a.* Rotten. 2 Shrunken.
ròig, *s.* Den, cave—*Rob Donn.*
roighchd, see raoic.
roighne, see roghainn.
roighneach, see roghnach.
————adh, see roghnachadh.
roighnich, see roghnaich.
————te, see roghnaichte.
ròil, *gen. sing.* of ròl.
ròil, (DMy) *s.* Slaver.
ròileach, *a.* Slavering.
roilbh,** -e, *s.f.* Mountain.
———each,** *a.* Hilly.
†roile, for ri chéile.
roileag,** -eig, *s.f.* Church. 2 Burying-ground. (réilig.)
roilean, -ein, *s.m.* ‡Snout of a sow. 2 (WC) Round piece. R. ìme, *a "print" of butter.*
roilean, see roithlean. Ròileinean, *rollers of a spinning-wheel.*
roileanach,** *a.* Having a snout like a sow's.
roileasg, -eisg, -an, *s.m.* Confused joy or person. *prov.* 2 Confused haste.
———ach,†† *a.* Confused. 2 Hasty. 3 Frisky. 4 Confused with joy.
roileiseach, (MS) *a.* Remiss.
roilig, -ean, *s.* see réilig. 2 Frolicsome person.
——each,* -eiche, *a.* Frolicsome.
roille, *s.f.* Fawning or too cordial reception. 2 Tare. 3§ Darnel, rye-grass, see breoillean.
——ach,** *a.* Abounding in, or like darnel.
roilleachan,** -ain, *s.m.* Rolling stone.
roillean, -ein, -an, *s.m.* Corn-fan. 2 (WC) Fat, thick person.
roille-chraos, -aois, -an, *s.m.* Slavering mouth, *prov.*
————ach, -aiche, *a.* Having a slavering mouth, *prov.*
roilleamas, -ais, *s.m.* Coarse play, *prov.*
————ach, -aiche, *a.* Given to coarse play.
roilleun, see roillean.
roimh, *prep.* see troimh & troimhe.
roimh, *prep.* Before, in respect of situation or place. 2 Before, in respect of time. 3 Above, in preference to. R. na h-uile ni, *in preference to everything;* cò roimhe a bhitheadh eagal orm? *of whom should I be afraid?* r. ghin, *in preference to any;* r. do ghnùis, *before thy face;* cuir r., *put before, prompt, dictate;* an là roimhe, *the day before the other day;* r. sgrios théid uabhar, *pride goeth before a fall;* r. an àm, *before the time.*

Combined thus with the personal pronouns: romham, *before me;* romhad, *before thee;* roimhe, *before him;* roimpe, *before her;* romhainn, *before us;* romhaibh, *before you;* rompa, *before them.* Imich romhad, *or* gabh romhad, *go forward; 2 go about your business;* cuir romhad, *determine, resolve, intend;* tha thu 'cur romhad cur as da, *you are determined to finish him;* chuir mi romham dol dachaidh, *I was determined to go home;* am bheil romhad dol dachaidh? *do you intend to go home?* tha 'n gnothach gu math romhad, *your work is cut out, (the business is well before you.)* [Aspirates a consonant following, and governs the dative.]
roimh, -e, *s.f.* Earth, soil. 2 Family burying-ground.
roimh-abuich,‡‡ -e, *a.* Precocious.
————ead, -eid, *s.m.* Precociousness.
roimh-a-chéile, *adv.* Prematurely, too hastily.
roimh-ainmich, *v.a.* Prenominate.
———— ———te, *a.* Forementioned, forecited, above-cited.
roimh-aisneis, -e, -ean, *s.f.* Foretelling.
roimh-àithn,** *v.a.* Command, foreordain.
roimh-aithne, *s.f.ind.* Foreknowledge, precognition.
roimh-àithne,** *s. f.* Previous commandment, former injunction.
roimh-aithneachadh, -aidh, *s.m.* Foreknowing. 2 Act of foreknowing, anticipation. A' r—, *pr.pt.* of roimh-aithnich.
roimh-aithnich, *v.a.* Foreknow, anticipate, foresee.
roimh-aithnichte, *a.* & *past pt.* Foreknown.
roimh-aithris, -e, -ean, *v.a.* Previously rehearse. 2 Forebode, foretell.
roimh-aithris, -e, -ean, *s.f.* Previous rehearsal. 2 Foreboding, foretelling.
————each, -eiche, *a.* Predictive.
roimh-aom,‡‡ *v.a.* Predispose.
————adh, -aidh, *s.m.* Predisposing, predisposition. A' r—, *pr. pt.* of roimh-aom.
roimh-bhacail, -e, *a.* Preclusive.
roimh-bharail, -e, *s.f.* Anticipation, presentiment, preconception.
roimh-bhàsaich,‡‡ *v.a.* Predecease.
roimh-bheachd, -an, *s.m.* Preconception, foreknowledge, presentiment, anticipation.
———— ————ach, -aiche, *a.* Preconceiving, foreknowing, looking forward, anticipating. 2 Giving a presentiment.
roimh-bheachdachadh, -aidh, *s.m.* Preconceiving. 2 Act or circumstance of preconceiving or preconsidering, precognition, anticipation, foreknowledge. A' r—, *pr. pt.* of roimh-bheachdaich.
roimh-bheachdaich, *v.a.* Preconceive, foreknow. 2 Consider beforehand.
roimh-bheachdail, -e, *a.* Provident, cautious, foresightful, prescient.
roimh-bheatha, *s.f.* Pre-existence.
roimh-bheathachadh, (MS) *s.m.* Antepast.
roimh-bhith, -e, *s.f.* Pre-existence.
roimh-bhlais, *pr.pt.* e' roimh-bhlasad, *v.a.* Foretaste. 2 Ante-date, anticipate.
roimh-bhlas, -ais, -an, *s. m.* Foretaste, anticipation.
roimh-bhlasad, -aid, -an, *s.m.* Foretasting. 2 Act of foretasting. A' r—, *pr. pt.* of roimh-bhlais.
roimh-bhlasdachd,** *s.f.* Anticipation.
roimh-bhreith, -e, -ean, *s.f.* Pre-judgment.
roimh-bhriathar, -air, -thran, *s.m.* Adverb. 2 Preposition. 3** Preface, preamble.

roimh-bhriathrach,** *a.* Adverbial. 2 Prefatory.
roimh-chaochail, *v.* Pre-decease.
roimh-charadh, -aidh, *s.m.* Predisposition.
roimh-chéile, see troimh-chéile.
roimh-cheum,** *s.m.* Precedence. 2 Generation before or past.
roimh-chiallachadh, -aidh, *s. m.* Presignification. A' r—, *pr.pt.* of roimh-chiallaich.
roimh-chiallaich, *v.a* Presignify.
roimh-chluich, -e, -ean, *s.f.* Prelude.
roimh-chnuasachadh, -aidh, *s.m.* Premeditation.
roimh-chomhairleachadh,** *s.m.* Premonition.
roimh-chomhairleachail,** *a.* Premonitory.
roimh-chomhairlich, *v.a.* Preadvise.
roimh-chraicionn, -inn, -cnean, *s.m.* Foreskin.
roimh-chreid, *v.a.* Presume.
roimh-chuir, *v.a.* Precede.
roimh-chùis, -e, -ean, *s.f.* Prelude.
roimh-chùmhnant, -aint, -an, *s.m.* Precontract.
——————ach, -aiche, *a.* Precontracted.
roimh-chunnuil, -e, -ean, *s.f.* Premonition.
roimh-dhealbh, -dheilbh, -an, *s.m.* Preform.
roimh-dhìlinneach, -eiche, *a.* Antediluvian.
——————, -eich, *s.m.* Antediluvian.
roimhe, *prep.pron.* (roimh+e) Before him or it. 2 In front of him. 3 In preference to him. Am fear nach seall roimhe, *he who will not look before him* ; ghabh e eagal r., *he was afraid of him.* 4 *Roimhe* before *it*, the indefinable *it* in it is a good day. Before, formerly, previously. Chunnaic mi r. thu, *I saw you before;* an la r., *the other day, the former day.*
roimheach, *a.* Relative.
roimh-eadradh, -aidh, -aidhean, *s.m.* Forenoon.
roimhear, -eir, -eirean, *s. m.* Antecedent, relative. 2 Preposition.
roimhe-chéile, see troimh-chéile.
roimh-eòlas, -ais, *s.m.* Foreknowledge, anticipation, precognition, preconception.
roimh-fheuch, *v.a.* Precaution.
——————ainn, -ean, *s.m.* Foreseeing, taking precaution. 2 Foretaste. 3 Forecast.
roimh-fheumail, -e, *a.* Perquisite.
roimh-fhidreachadh,(MS) *s.m.* Precognition.
roimh-fhios, -a, *s.m.* see roimh-eòlas.
——————rachadh, *s.m.* Anticipation.
——————rachd, *s.f.ind.* Presension.
roimh-fhìrinnean, *s.pl.* Premises.
roimh-ghabh, *v.a.* Anticipate.
——————ail, *s.m.* Anticipation. 2 Antepast. A' r—, *pr. pt.* of roimh-ghabh.
roimh-gheall,** *v.a.* Promise beforehand, preengage.
——————adh, -aidh, *s.m.* Pre-engagement.
——————tainn, -ean, *s.m.* Promising beforehand, pre-engagement. A' r—, *pr.pt.*of roimh-gheall.
roimh-ghlac, *v.a.* Anticipate.
roimh-ghoile, *s.f.* Ante-stomach.
roimh-ghoireas, -eis, *s.m.* Prerequisite.
roimh-iarr, *v.a.* Pre-require.
roimhibh, see romhaibh.
roimhid,* *adv.* see roimhe.
romhid-a-chéile, *prov.* for troimh-chéile.
roimh-imeachd, *s.f.ind.* Precedence. A' r—, *pr. pt.* of roimh-imich.
roimh-imich, *pr. pt.* a' roimh-imeachd, *v. n.* Precede.
roimh-innis, *v. a.* Foretell, predict, tell beforehand.
——————each, -eiche, *a.* see roimh-innseach.
——————eadh, -eidh, see roimh-innseadh.
——————ear, see roimh-innsear.
roimh-innseach, -eiche, *a.* Predictive.
roimh-innseadh, -eidh, *s.m.* Foretelling, predicting. 2**Divination. A' r—, *pr. pt.* of roimh-innis.
roimh-innsear, -eir, -an, *s.m.* Predicter.
roimh-ionnsuich, *v.a.* Pre-instruct.
roimh-làimh, *adv.* Beforehand, previously.
roimh-làimh, *a.* see roimh-làimheach.
——————each, *a.* Prelusive.
——————ich,(MS) *v.a.* Ante-date.
roimh-làn, *a.* Pluperfect in *grammar.*
roimh-làthaich,(MS) *v.a.* Ante-date.
roimh-lòn, -lòin, -an, *s. m.* Provision for a journey, viaticum.
roimh-luaidhte, *a.* Above-cited.
roimh-mheadhon-là,** *s.m.* Forenoon.
roimh-mhealtuinn,** *s.m.* Anticipation.
roimh-mheasrachadh, *s.m.* Preconception.
roimh-mheasraich, *v.a.* Preconceive.
roimh-mheirbheadh, -idh, *s.m.* Predigestion.
roimh-mhìnich, *v.a.* Premise, preface.
roimh-nithe, *s.pl.* Premises.
roimh-oidhirpich, *v.a.* Pre-occupy.
roimh-òrduchadh, -aidh, *s.m.* Ordering beforehand. 2 Act of ordering beforehand. 3 Foreordaining, predestinating. 4 Act of predestinating. A' r—, *pr.pt.* of roimh-òrduich.
roimh-òrduich, *v.a.* Order beforehand or previously. 2 Fore-ordain, predestinate.
——————te, *past pt.* of roimh-òrduich. Ordained beforehand or previously. 2 Fore-ordained, predestinated.
roimhpe, see roimpe.
roimh-ràdh, -àidh, -an, *s.m.* Preface, preamble, prologue.
——————ach, -aiche, *a.* Prefatory.
roimh-ruitheach, -eiche, *a.* Precursory.
roimh-ruithear, -eir, -an, *s.m.* Fore-runner.
roimh-ruith-fhear, see roimh-ruithear.
roimhse,** *s.f.* Sin, iniquity.
roimh-sgrìobh, *v.a.* Ante-date.
roimh-shamhlachail, -e, *a.* Prefigurative.
roimh-shamhlaich, *v.a.* Presignify.
roimh-shealbhadair, -ean, *s.m.* Prepossessor.
roimh-sheall, *v.a.* Look forward. 2 Provide against.
roimh-sheallach, -aiche, *a.* Looking forward, foreseeing, cautious, prospicient.
roimh-shealladh, -aidh, -aidhean, *s.m.*Foresight. 2 Previous look or sight. 3 Front view. 4 Prospectus. 5 Caution, prospicience.
roimh-shealltainn, *s.m.* Looking forward, 2 Act of looking forward. 3 Act of providing against. 4 Foresight, precaution. A' r—,*pr.pt.*of roimh-sheall.
roimh-sheòmar, -air, -sheòmraichean, *s.m.* Antichamber.
roimh-shocrachadh, -aidh, *s. m.* Pre-establishment.
roimh-shocraich, *v.a.* Pre-establish.
roimh-smaoin, -e, -tean, *s.f.* see roimh-smuain.
roimh-smaoineachadh, -aidh, see roimh-smuaineachadh.
roimh-smaoineachail, see roimh-smuaineachail.
roimh-smaoinich, *v.* see roimh-smuainich.
roimh-smuain, -e, -tean, *s.f.* Forethought, previous reflection.
——————eachadh, -aidh, *s. m.* Act of preconsidering or anticipating, forethought. A' r—, *pr.pt.* of roimh-smuainich.
roimh-smuainich, *v.a. & n.* Think beforehand, preconsider.
roimh-smuaineachail, -e, *a.* Thinking beforehand, provident, cautious.
roimh-stallair,** -ean, *s.m.* Forestaller.
——————eachd, *s.f.* Forestalling.
roimh-stéidhich, *v.a.* Premise.
roimh-thagh, *v.a.* Fore-choose, pre-elect.
——————adh, -aidh, *s.m.* Fore-choosing. 2

Act of fore-choosing or pre-electing. 3 Predestination, pre-selection, pre-election.
roimh-thaghta, *past pt* of roimh-thagh. Fore-chosen, pre-elected, predestinated.
roimh-thaisbean, *v.n.* Prelude.
roimh-theachdair, -ean & -chdraichean, *s. m.* Forerunner.
roimh-theagaisg, *v.a.* Pre-instruct.
roimh-thionnsgainn, *v.a. & n.* Premeditate.
———————each, -eiche, *a.* Premeditated.
roimh-thionnsgnadh, -aidh, *s.m.* Premeditation. A' r—, *pr.pt.* of roimh-thionnsgainn.
roimh-thràthail, -e, *a.* Premature,
roimh-thuilteach, *a.* & *s.* Antediluvian.
roimh-thùradh, *a.* Afore-named, aforesaid.
roimh-uidheamaich, *v.a.* Pre-dispose.
roimpe, *prep.pron.* (roimh+i) Before her. 2 In front of her. 3 In preference to her. Gabh r., *go before her, stop her progress ;* cuir r., *prompt her, dictate to her.*
roimpe-se, *emphat.* of roimpe.
roimse,** -an, *s.f.* Pole, stake.
roimseach,** *a.* Like a pole or stake. 2 Of poles. 3 Inactive.
————,** -eich, *s.m.* Inactive person.
ròin, *gen.sing. & n. pl.* of ròn.
ròin, -e, -ean, *s.f.* A single hair. 2 One hair of a horse's tail or mane. 3 Small quantity of wool or of any hairy substance. 4** Crest or tail of any beast. 5 Hair-cloth. Leud ròine, *a hair's breadth ;* saic-aodach ròine, *sackcloth of hair.*
ròin-aodach,** -aich, *s.m.* Hair-cloth.
roineach, see raineach.
ròineach, -eiche, *a.* Hairy, full of hairs, as meat. 2 Made of hair.
————,** -ich, *s.m.* Hair, horsehair.
————adh, -aidh, *s.m.* Stuffing with hair. 2 Fitting or dressing with hair, as fish-hooks. A' r—, *pr.pt.* of ròinich.
————d, *s.f.* Hairiness. 2 Roughness.
ròineag, -eig, -an, *s.f.* Single small hair. 2 Small quantity of wool or any hairy substance.
————ach, -aiche, *a.* Hairy. 2 Rough. 3 Having small quantities of wool or any hairy substance.
ròine-chlòimh,(WC) *s.f.* Bunch of wool pulled from the shorn fleece and given to the poor women who frequent the sheep-fold at shearing time.
ròinich, *v.a.* Stuff with hair. 2 Provide with hair. 3 Dress with hair, as a fish-hook.
roinn, *gen.sing.* of rann.
roinn, -e, -ean, *s.f.* Share, portion. 2 Division, dividing, class, distribution, proportion. 3 Sect, division, schism. 4 Section in writing (§.) 5 Pair of compasses. 6 Part of a sword distinct from the point. 7 see rinn. Mo r. fhéin, *my own share ;* an r. a rinn e orra, *the division he made of them ;* r. mhic is athar, *share and share alike, equal distribution ;* a' togail roinnean, *raising divisions or sects ;* r. dà leth, *a bipartition.*
roinn, *s.m.ind.* Dividing. 2 Act of dividing. A' r—, *pr.pt.* of roinn. A' r. orra, *distributing among them.*
roinn, *pr.pt.* a' roinn, *v.a.* Divide, impart, distribute. 2 Deal, as cards. R. orra e, *distribute or divide it among them ;* roinneadh esan aig am bheil dà chòta, *let him that has two coats divide.*
roinn, *v.* see roinnich.
ròinn, -e, -ean, see ròin.
roinn-bhearrag,** *s.* Bistoury.
roinn-cuairt,‡‡ -e, -ean, *s.f.* Arch.
ròinne, see ròin.
————ach, see ròineach.
roinneach, -eiche, *a.* Distributive. 2 see rinneach.
————adh, -aidh, *s.m. & pr.pt.* of roinnich, see rinneachadh.
ròinneachadh, see ròineachadh.
ròinneachd, see ròineachd.
roinneadair, -ean, *s.m.* Divider, divisor.
roinneadh, see roinn.
roinneag, see ròineag.
roinneagach, see ròineagach.
roinnear, *fut.pass.* of roinn.
roinne-bhaidhe,** *s.f.* Hair-cloth.
roinn-gheur, -a & -eòra, *a.* see rinn-gheur.
ròinnich, see ròinich.
roinnich, *v.a.* see rinnich & roinn.
————te, *past pt.* of roinnich, see rinnichte.
roinnidh, *fut.aff.a.* of roinn.
ròinnidh, -e, *a.* Hairy. 2 Long-haired. 3 Thick-haired.
ròinn-léine, -léintean, *s.f.* Hair-shirt.
roinn-phàirteach, -eiche, *a.* Sharing, dividing. 2 Imparting. 3 Divisible.
roinn-phàirteachadh, -aidh, *s.m.* Distributing. 2 Act of distributing, imparting or sharing. A' r—, *pr.pt.* of roinn-phàirtich.
roinn-phàirtich, *v.a.* Share, divide, distribute. 2 Impart. 3 Partake.
roinn-phàrtach, see roinn-phàirteach.
roinn-phàrtachadh, see roinn-phàirteachadh.
roinn-ruithe, *s.f.* Run-rig, division or common run. This system of occupying land is often spoken of as *mór-earrann,* (great division) or *mór-fhearann,* (great land.) It prevailed, of old, all over the British Islands and the continent of Europe,and was common in Ireland. It is now extinct in England, and obsolete in Scotland,except in parts of the Western Isles.
roinnse, -achan, *s.f.* Rinse.
————ach,** *a.* Rinsing, scouring. 2 Acting as a rinse, like a rinse.
————achadh,** -aidh, *s. m.* Rinsing, scouring, scrubbing. A' r—, *pr.pt.* of rinnsich.
————ar, *s.m.* Rinser.
roinnsich,** *v.a.* Rinse, scour, scrub.
————te, *past pt.* Rinsed. scoured,scrubbed.
roinn-slachdan, see slachdan.
roinnte, *a. & past pt.* of roinn. Divided,shared, distributed. 2 Disagreeing, dissentient.
roinnteachadh, *s.m.* Separation.
roinntealachd,(MS) *s.f.* Partibility.
roipe, see roimpe.
roipeach,** *a.* Extravagant. 2 Drunken.
roipear,** *s.m.* Rapier. 2 Tuck.
rois, see ros.
rois, *gen.sing.* of ros.
ròis, *gen.sing.* of ròs.
rois, *pr.pt.* a' roiseadh, see frois.
roisceal,** *s.* see roisgeul.
ròisd, see ròsd.
roiseachan,** -ain, *s.m.* Instrument for bolling flax.
ròisead, see ròiseid.
roiseadh, -eidh, *s.m. & pr.pt.* of rois, see rosadh.
roiseag,(WC) *s.f.* The pith of the rush used for wicks.
roiseagan,(CR) *s.pl.* Very small and numerous potatoes—*W. of Ross-shire.*
ròiseal, -eil, -an, *s. m.* High-swelling wave or surge. 2††Surge of a wave. 3 Assault, attack. 4 Gasconade. 5 Boast, boasting. *6 Pomp. 7 Force or rapidity of a vessel in motion, weigh, impetus. 8**Novel. 9 Lowest or basest rabble—*Sàr-Obair.* 10 *Display of ability. 11 Pretensious fuss. Le r., *with an ostentatious display ;* r. teine, *a big, blazing fire ;* r. soluis, *a fine bright light* or *display of light.*

ròiseal, -eile, *a*. The lowest, most base.
——,* *v.a.* Display, make a pompous display.
——ach, -aiche, *a*. Abounding in high waves or surges. 2 Making an attack or assault. 3 Boastful, boasting. 4 Sailing swiftly. 5* Pompous, ostentatious. 6* Fond of displaying one's feats or ability.
——achd,* *s.f.ind.* Boasting. 2 Pomposity, ostentation
roisean,(DC) *s.m.* Flail, the striker of which is made of strong thick rope, used for taking the grain from corn, but not so completely as an ordinary flail. The process of using a *roisean* is called *roiseadh*, and sometimes *tapadh—Uist.*
roisean,(CR) *s.m.* Tail or train of a skirt—*W. of Ross-shire.* 2 (DU) Wet or mud on the train of a skirt. 3 Wet or muddy train. 3 (DMu) Tail of a cow. 4 (WC) Tail of a deer.
ròiseid, *s.f.ind.* Resin. R.-fìdhle, *violin-resin.*
——each, -eiche, *a*. Resinous. 2 Covered with resin.
roisg, *gen. & pl.* of rosg, see ruisg.
roisg,** *a*. Callow. 3 Unfledged.
roisgeach,** *a*. Wise.
ròisgeul, -eil, -ad, *s.m.* Romance, romantic tale. 2 Boasting, swelling words. 2 Sentence, verdict, decree. [**roisgeòil.]
——ach, -aiche, *a*. Telling romantic or marvellous tales. 2 Boastful.
——achd,** *s.f.* Same meanings as ròisgeul.
roisg-mhèairleach,** *s.m.* Tory. 2 Burglar.
ròis-iarunn, -uinn, -an, *s.m.* Roasting spit.
roisire,** *s.f.* Anger, choler. 2 High spirits, exhilaration.
ròist, *pr.pt.* a' ròstadh, *v.a.* Roast, toast. 2 Parch, scorch.
roiste,** *s.f.* Roach.
ròiste, *past pt.* of ròist. Roasted, toasted, scorched, parched.
roisteach, -ich, -ichean, *s.f.* Roach. 2 Bream,

604. Roisteach.

roistean,** -ein, *s.m.* Gridiron. 2 Frying-pan.
roit, Wormwood, see roid.
roit, -e, -ean, *s.f.* see roid.
†roith, -e, -ean, *s.f.* see roth.
†roithean, see roithlean.
roithleach, -eiche, *a*. Rolling, tossing, unsteady. 2 Wheely, having wheels. 3** In rolls.
†roithleachan, -ain, -an *s.m.* Circle. 2 Wheel.
roithleagan,** -ain, *s.m.* Twirl. 2 Little roll. 3 Circle. 4 Little wheel. 5 Pulley of flyers in a spinning-wheel, the grooved drum that receives the driving-cord.
roithlean, -ein, -an, *s.m.* Little wheel. 2 Rim of a wheel. 3 Grooved wheel of a pulley, see ulag, p. 78. 4 Knee-pan. 5 Wormwood, gall. 6 Trucks of a boat, see H3, p. 73. 7(MS) Fly. 8 Pulley of flyers in a spinning-wheel, the grooved drum that receives the driving-cord.
roithleanach, -aiche, *a*. Having small wheels.
——adh,(MS) *s.m.* Twirl.
roithlear, -ir, -an, *s.m.* Wheelwright, cartwright. 2* see rolair.
roithlearachd, *s. f. ind.* Business of a wheelwright or cartwright. 2**Rolling.
roithleas, see roileasg.
roithleis, see roileasg.
roithleiseach, see roileasgach.
†roithleun, -ein, -an, *s.m.* see roithlean.
roithlich, -e, *s.f.* Noise of the shrouds of a ship in a storm.
roithre,** *s.m.* Prater, babbler.
——achd, *s.f.* Prating, babbling, loquacity.
rol, see rola.
rol, *v.a.* Roll, make into rolls, as hay, roll together.
ròl,(CR) *s.m.* Long-continued noise—*Skye.*
rola, -oil & -a, -an, *s.m.* Volume. 2 Roll, as of tobacco. 3** Swathe or roll of hay or grass. 4** List.
rolach, (MS) *s.m.* Sally.
rolach, -aiche, *a*. In volumes or rolls.
roladh, -aidh, *s.m.* Rolling. 2 Act of rolling, or making into rolls. 3 Roll, swathe. 4 Volume. A' r—, *pr.pt.* of rol. A' r. na criathair, *shaking the sieve*—to separate the husks from the corn.
ròlag, -aig, -an, *s.f., dim.* of rola. Little roll. 2 Anything small rolled together. 2 Swathe of grass, line of cut grass as left by the scythe. 4 Rowans, the long roll of wool as it leaves the cards for the spinning-wheel. 5 Little volume. R fheòir, *a roll* or *swathe of hay or grass.*
rolagach, -aiche, *a*. Rolled. 2 In rolls, like carded wool or hay.
rolagan,(DU) -ain, -annan, *s.m.* Half-sized cod.
—— -truisg, *s.m.* Half-sized cod.
ròlaich,(CR) *s.f.* Long-continued noise—*Skye.* R. òrain, *an interminable song;* nach ann orra tha 'n r. ! *what a noise they are making !*—said of cattle when making a great lowing.
rolaig,(DC) -ean, *s.f.* (variant of réilig) One single grave.
rolair, -ean, *s.m.* Roller. 2 Ruler. 3**Cylinder. 4**One who rolls ground.
rolaireachd,** *s.f.* Rolling. 2 Ruling. 3 Employment of rolling ground.
rolais,(DMy) *s.* Slip-shod way of working.
rolaiseach,(DMy) *a*. Slip-shod. Buain r., *slipshod reaping.*
rolaist, -ean, *s.m.* Romance. 2 Declamation. 3 Exaggeration. 4††Rigmarole.
ròlaisteach, -eiche, *a*. Fabulous. 2 Given to exaggeration or declamation. 3 Restless (of children)—*Suth'd.*
rolan, -ain,** *s.m.* Roll, volume. 2 Roller which turns flyer of spinning-wheel.
roltach,(MS) *s.m.* Run.
ròm,* *s.f.* Pubes. 2 Shag.
ròmach, -aiche, *a*. Hairy, rough with hair. 2** Bearded, shaggy. Am fear r., *the hairy caterpillar.*
ròmach,(AF) *s.m.* Hairy caterpillar.

ròmachad, see ròmaichead.
ròmag, -aig, -an, *s.f.* Athole brose—drink of oatmeal, honey and whisky. 2 Drink of oatmeal and whisky,—*Suth'd.* 3 ** Female with a beard. 4** Pudenda of a female.
ròmagach,** -aiche, *a.* Having a beard, as a female. 2 Hairy, rough, shaggy.
ròmaiche, *comp.* of ròmach.
——, *s.f.* see ròmaichead.
ròmaichead, *s.f.ind.* Hairiness, roughness, shagginess.
ròmas, -ais, -an, *s.m.* Hairiness.
ròmasach, see ròmach.
romh,* see roimh.
romhad, *prep.pron.* roimh+thu) Before thee or you. 2 Previous to you. 3 In your contemplation or intention. 4 At you. 5 Of you. 6 With you. 7 In opposition to you. 8 In preference to you. Bithidh mise r. fhathast, *I will be upsides with you yet*—you have done me an ill turn, but I will pay you off yet; is beag eagal a th' aige romhad, *little does he dread you*; 'dé a tha thu 'cur r.? *what do you intend to do?* tha mi 'cur romham sin a dheanamh, *I am determined to do that*; gabh r., ! *go about your business, begone!* abair r., *or* labhair r., *say on*; am bheil r. thu fhéin a mhilleadh *? do you mean to ruin yourself?*
romhad-sa, *emphat.* of romhad.
romhaibh, *prep.pron.* (roimh+sibh) Before you. 2 In front of you. 3 In preference to you. 4 In opposition to you. 5 Before your presence. Tha r., *you are determined*; gabhaibh r.! *begone, go your way!*
romhaibh-se, *emphatic* of romhaibh.
romhainn,** *v.a. & n.* Roll. 2 Wallow.
romhainn, *prep.pron.* (roimh+sinn) Before us. 2 In front of us. 3 In preference to us. 4 In opposition to us. Sheas iad r., *they stood before us*; gabhaidh e r., *he will oppose us*; cuir r., *prompt us, dictate to us.*
romhainne, *emphat.* of romhainn.
romhair,** -ean, *s.m.* Roller or cylinder for levelling ground. 2 Cylindrical rule. 3 One who rolls ground.
——eachd,** *s.f.* Rolling, levelling ground.
romham, *prep.pron.* (roimh+mi) Before me. 2 Prior to me. 3 In front of me. 4 In preference to me. 5 In opposition to me. Tha mi 'cur r., *I propose*; théid mi r., *I will go my way*; 's iomadh linn a chuir mi r., *many a generation have I put past me.*
romham-sa, *emphat.* of romham.
ròmhan, -ain, -an, *s.m.* Groan. 2§Wheat, brank, see cruithneachd. 3 (CR) Wild talk, raving, rigmarole, *prov.*
ròmhanaich, -e, *s.f.* Groaning, uttering of hollow groans. 2 Irrational talk. 3§Wild exclamation, raving—*Dàin I. Ghobha.*
ro-mhar,** *s.f.* Spring-tide. 2 Full sea.
romhas, -ais, -an, *s.m.* see robhas.
ro-mheud, *s.m.* Excessive greatness.
ro-mhiann, -a, -an, *s.m.* Excessive or great desire.
ro-mhiannach, *a.* Excessively desirous.
ro-mhòid, -e, *s.f.* Excessive greatness.
†romhradh, -aidh, *s.m.* Sight.
romhuibh, see romhaibh.
romnacois,** *a.* Yellow and grey.
rompa, *prep.pron.* (roimh+iad) Before them. 2 In front of them. 3 Prior to them. 4 In preference to them. 5 In opposition to them. Dh' imich iad r., *they went their way*; cuir r., *oppose them, prompt them, dictate to them.*
rompa-san, *emphat.* of rompa.
ròn, -òin, *s.m.* Seal, sea-calf. 2*Fetters for the fore feet of a horse—*Inverary.* 3 (AF) Milk-whipper or frother. 4* Rim of hair on same. 5 see ròin. Is toigh leinn an ròn, ach cha toigh leinn naidheachd an ròin, *we like the seal, but not the seal's news*—which is, that bad weather is at hand; ròn lonaid, *a circle of hair round the frothing-stick*; ionad falaich nan r. slapach, *the hiding-place of the splashing seals.*
†ròn, *a.* Strong-bodied.
ronach, -aich, *s.m.* Seal-hunt. 2 Seal-hunting.
rònach, -aiche, *a.* Abounding in seals. 2 Shaggy, hairy, like a seal.
rònachan, -ain, *s.m.* Fellow resembling a sea-calf.
ròndh, -aidh, *s.m.* Club, stake.
ro-nàdurra, *a.* Very natural.
rònan, -ain, -an, *s.m.*, *dim.* of ròn. Little seal or sea-calf.
roncais, see rongais.
rong, -a & -oinge, *pl.* -an, *s.f.* Joining spar. 2 Rung. 3 Any piece of wood by which others are joined. 4 Rib or timber of a boat. 5 Staff, bludgeon. 6 Lean, cadaverous-looking person. 7 Idle or lounging person. 8 Dronish person. 9* Bandy. 10**Hoop.
rong, -oing, *s.m.* The vital spark, life. Cha'n 'eil r. ann, *he is lifeless.*
rongach, -aiche, *a.* Of, or belonging to, spars, 2 bludgeons or staves. 3 Ribbed, as a boat. 4 Lean, cadaverous. 5 Lazy, idle, droning, lounging. 6 Tedious, lingering, delaying. 7†† Languishing. 8**Having rungs or spars.
rongachadh, -aidh, *s.m.* State of becoming lean or meagre. 2 Act of lingering or delaying. A' r—, *pr.pt.* of rongaich.
rongaich, *v. n.* Become lean, bony, meagre or cadaverous. 2 Linger, delay, lounge. 3†† Languish.
rongaiche, *s.f.ind.* Leanness, meagreness. 2 Idleness, laziness. 3 Lounging.
rongair, -ean, *s.m.* Loiterer, lingerer. 2 Indolent, idle or listless fellow. 3 Lean, meagre or cadaverous person. 4 Lounge, lounger. 5**Hoop-driver. 6 Ugly, big-boned animal or person. 7 Languishing person.
rongaireachd, *s.f.ind.* Loitering, lingering, delay. 2 Laziness, idleness. 3 Leanness, meagreness. 4* Tedious, drawling, lounging manner, sluggishness, dronishness. 5**Hoop-driving.
rongais, -ean, *s.m.* see rongas.
rongas, -ais, *pl.* -an & -ais, *s. m.* Joining-spar, rung. 2 Timbers or ribs of a boat, see bàta. E3, p. 73. 3 Staff, bludgeon. 4 Bat, bandy. 5 Baluster. 6**Hoop. 7***in derision*, Dronish person.
ròn-mara, (AF) *s.m.* Seal.
ròn-mulbhach, (AF) *s.m.* Sea-calf.
ròn-mullach, see ròn-mulbhach.
†ronn, -a, -an, *s.m.* Chain. 2 Bond, tie.
ronn, -oinn, -an, *s. m.* Slaver, spittle. 2 Any drop of liquid of a ropy consistency. 3 Rheum. Piobair nan ronn,—a nickname for a slovenly piper.
ronnach, -aiche, *a.* Abounding in spittle or saliva. 2 Ropy, viscous, glutinous, (of liquors.) 3 Slavering. 4 Causing salivation. 5 (WC) see reannach. Rinn e balgam r. dheth, *he made it a theme of slavering scoff.*
ronnach,* -aich, *s.f.* Slavering, dirty female.
——, -aich, *s.m.* see rannach.
ronnachadh, -aidh, *s.m.* Act or state of slavering or emitting saliva. 2 State of becoming ropy. 3 Act of rendering viscous or ropy. 4 Salivation, slaver. A' r—, *pr.pt.* of ronnaich.
ronnadh,** -aidh, *s.m.* Club, staff.
ronnag, -aig, -an, see reannag.

ronnagach, -aiche, *a.* see reannagach.
ronnaich, *v.a. & n.* Spit, emit saliva. 2 Become ropy or viscid. 3 Make ropy or viscid.
ronnair, -ean, *s.m.* Slavering person, driveller, slabberer.
———eachd, *s.f.* Discharging of spittle or sailva. 2 Habit of slavering or spitting.
ronnaireachd, *s.f.* When the notes of the bagpipes seem to be played with spittle in the chanter—*MacMhaigh. Alasdair.*
ronnan, -ain, -an, *s.m.* see ronn.
ronn-chraos, -aois, -an, *s.m.* Slavering or slabbering mouth.
—————ach, -aiche, *a.* Emitting slaver or spittle.
ronngan, *s.m.* Slaver. Séididh Uisdean piob an ronngain, *Hugh will blow the slavering pipe —Donn. Bàn p. 189.*
ronn-ghalar,§ -air, *s.m.* Rheumatism. 2 Salivation. 3 Catarrh.
ronnsachadh, see rannsachadh.
ro-oirdheirceas,** -eis, *s.m.* Excellency. Air son ro-oirdheirceas eòlais, *for the excellency of knowledge.*
†ro-òlach, *s,* Crapitalatus vino.
ròp, *pr.pt.* a' ròpadh, *v.a.* Fasten with ropes. 2 Entangle, ravel. 3* Sell by auction. 4††Rivet. [†† gives ropa for No. 3.]
rop,* *v.a.* Gore. 2 Tear open a bag with a knife. 3 Let out the viscera with a knife.
ròp, -a, -an, *s.m.* Rope. 2 Tow. 3 Collection of seaweed floated along for convenience of landing. 3* Auction. 4 (AF) Any creature that digs for its food, or that draws its food towards it, as a cow, (also rap.) Cas ròpa, *a hair-rope used as a stirrup.* [†† gives *pl.* ròpaichean. ** gives *gen. sing.* ròip.]
ròpach, -aiche. *a.* Of, or belonging to, ropes. 2 Like a rope. 3 Furnished with ropes. 4 Made of ropes. 5 Abounding in heaps of seaweed. 6 Slovenly, squalid, unmethodical, (of a person.) 7 Ravelled. 8 Moppy 9 Entangled. 10 (DU) Slow. 11* see ronnach.
ropach, *a.* Viscous, glutinous.
ròpadair, -ean, *s.m.* Rope-maker, cordwainer. 2**see ròpainnear.
———eachd, *s.f.* Rope-making, cordwaining.
ròpadh, -aidh, *s.m.* Fastening, act of fastening with ropes. 2 Act of entangling or 3 Ravelling. A 'r—, *pr.pt.* of ròp.
ròpag, -aig, -an, *s.f.* Slut, slovenly woman.
ròpaiche, *s.f.ind.* Slovenliness. 2 Sluttishness.
ròpainn,** *s.* Sale by auction. 2 see reubainn.
———ear, *s.m.* Auctioneer.
ropair,** *s.m.* Rapier. 2 Treacherous person. 3 Robber (robair.)
ròpair, -ean, *s.m.* Sloven. 2 Fabulist. 3 Auctioneer. 4 (DU) Unmethodical person.
———eachd, *s.f.ind.* Slovenliness. 2 Tedious rehearsal, nonsensical tales.
ròpal, -ail, *s.m.* Rhapsody, vain idle talk, vapouring, vaunting.
——ach,†† *a.* Rhapsodical.
ròpan, -ain, *pl.* -an & -ain, *s. m., dim.* of ròp. Little cord, small rope.
ròpanach, -aiche, *a.* Abounding in little cords.
ròp-barraich,(DMK) *s.* Rope made of twigs of birch twisted together—*W. coast of Ross.*
ro-phris, *s.f.* Great price, great value.
———ealachd,** *s.f.* Excellence, great worth, preciousness, transcendent value.
ròram,* -aim, *s. m.* Liberality with much ostentation, dealing out extensively among a family, as provisions. 2 Hospitality. 3 Ability to stand fatigue.
roramach,* -aiche, *a.* Liberal. 2 Lasting long, and being capable of dividing well in a family, as provisions, profusely hospitable.
ròramachd,* *s.f.ind.* Liberality. 2 Extensive usefulness in a family.
rorcual,(AF) *s.* Whale.
rort,** -oirt, *s.m.* Run, race.
rortadh,** -aidh, *s.m.* Flowing over.
rorual, see rorcual.
ròs, -òis, -an, *s. m.* Rose. 2 Red or rose-like colour. 3 Erysipelas [with the article *an.*] [††gives *gen. sing.* -a.]
ros, -ois, -an, *s.m.* Seed. 2**Linseed. 3 Promontory. 4 Isthmus. 5 Peninsula. †6 *rarely,* Science, knowledge. 7**Arable land. R.-lin, *linseed.* Cha'n 'eil r. agam, *I have no knowledge*; cha d' fhuair mi r. air, *I did not get knowledge of him*; an r. Muileach, *the peninsula* or *promontory of Mull.*
ros, *pr.pt.* a' rosadh, *v. a. & n.* Shake off seed or grain from its stalk, as by wind in autumn. 2 Be stripped of seed or grain. 3 Defeat, miscarry, disappoint. †4 Create, make. R. e orm, *I have been disappointed in it*; r. an làr bracha seo, *this floor of malt miscarried,* or *went wrong.*
ròs,†† -a, -achan, *s.* see ròst.
†ros, *a.* Pleasant, pretty, delightful.
ròsach, -aiche, *a.* Rosy, red, as a rose. 2 Abounding in roses.
rosach, -aiche, *a.* Seedy, full of seed. 2 Shaking off seed or grain from the stalk. 3*Disappointing, defeating.
ròsachd,** *s.f.* Enchantment. 2 Charm. 2 Witchcraft.
rosad, -aid, -an, *s.m.* Mischief, mischance, misfortune. 2 Low, mean, despicable person. 3 **Fatuity. 4 Enchantment, evil spell. 5 Charm. 6 Witchcraft. 7* Disappointment. 8††Worthless person. 'Dè an r. a rug ort? *what the mischief came over you?*
rosadach, -aiche, *a.*Mischievous, hurtful. 2 Unfortunate, untoward.
rosadh, -aidh, *s.m.* Shaking, act of shaking seeds of corn from the stalk, as by wind. 2 State of being denuded of seed. †3 Creating. 4* see rosad. A' r—, *pr.pt.* of ros.
ròsag,** -aig, *s.f.* Rose-tree.
ròsaich,** *v.a.* Cover or bedeck with roses.
ròsaid, see ròiseid.
———each, see ròiseideach.
ròsail, see ròsach.
†rosal, -ail, *s.m.* Judgment.
rosal,(AC) *s.m.* School, college.
rosan,** -ain, *s.m.* Shrub.
ròsan,** *s.m.* Sing-song.
ros-an-ceòl, *s.m.* Nightingale, see spideag.
ròsann,** -ainn, *s.m.* Roasting.
ròs-an-t-soluis,§ *s. m.* Round-leaved sundew—*drosera rotundiflora,* (ill. 605.)
ròsarnach, -aich, -ean, *s.m.* Place where roses grow, rose-garden.
ròsbach,** *a.* Bleared.
ròsbachd, *s.f.* Blearedness.
ròsbaich,** *v.* Blear.
rosbhan,** -ain, *s.m.* Apple of the eye.
ròs-bheul, -éil & -eòil, *pl.* -an, *s.m.* Rosy mouth, rosy lips.
—————ach, *a.* Rosy-mouthed. 2 Rosy-lipped.
rosblach,** *a.* Dim-sighted, sand-blind.
ròsblachd,** *s.f.* Dimness.
ròsb-shuileach,** *a.* Blear-eyed.
ròs-chrann, -ainn, *s.m.* Rose-bush or tree. R.-gàraidh, *a garden rose-tree.*
ròs-chrannach, -aiche, *a.* Abounding in rose-bushes.
ròs-chraobh, *s.f.* Rhododendron.
ròsd, see ròist.
ròsdadh, see ròstadh.

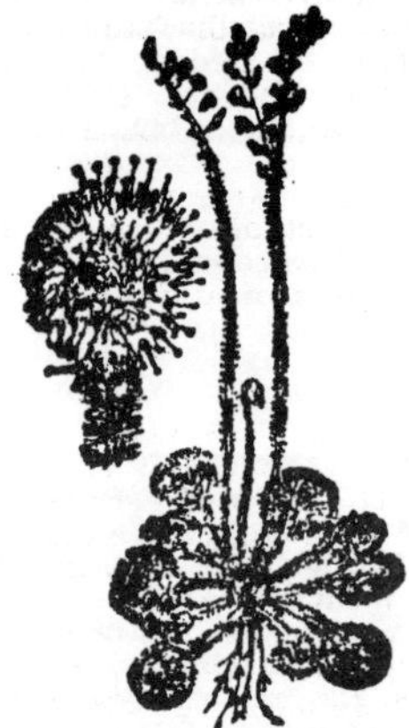

605. *Ròs-an-t-soluis.*

rosdadh, see rostadh.

ro-sheòl, *s.m.* Highest of a ship's sails, top-gallants. 2 Full sails—*Sàr-Obair.*

ròs-dhearg, -dheirge, *a.* Blushing as the rose.

rosg, roisg & ruisg, *pl.* -an & ruisg, *s.m.* Eyelid. 2 Eye-lash. 3 The eye. 4 Eyesight. 5 Dawn, understanding. 6 Incitement to battle, war-ode. 7 Prose, prose writing. Is lom an t-sùil gun an r., *naked is the eye that wants an eyelash.*

rosgach, -aiche, *a.* Having large or full eyes. 2 Having handsome eyes. 3 Having large or long eye-lashes. 4 Angry. 5**Wise, knowing. 6 Of, or belonging to, eyes or eye-lids. 7** Dawning. 8**Clear-sighted.

rosgadh,** -aidh, *s.m.* Eyesight. 2 Eye-lid. 3 Eye-lash. 4 Eye. 5 Looking. 6 Observation. 7 Dawn. 8 Dilution.

rosgail, -e, *a.* Clear-sighted.

rosgal,** -ail, *s.m.* Joy, pleasure. Dh' éirich r. 'nad chridhe, *joy rose in thy heart.*

†rosg-catha, *s.m.* Speech to an army, incitement to battle.

†rosg-dhalladh, *s.m.* Error, mistake. 2 Blindness.

rosg-fhradharc,** -airc, *s.m.* Sharp sight, clear sight. 2 Vision.

rosg-fhradharcach, -aiche, *a.* Sharp-sighted, clear-sighted.

ròs-ghàraidh,§ *s.m.* Cultivated rose.

rosglach,** -aiche, *a.* Joyful, glad, merry,

———,** -aiche, *a.* Sharp-sighted, quick-sighted, clear-sighted.

ro-sheòl, *s.m.* Highest sails of a ship, top-gallants. 2 Full-sail—*Sàr-Obair.*

rosg-shùileach,* *a.* Sharp-sighted. 2 Having long eye-lashes.

rosg-troghad, *s.* Soft rolling eyes. 2 Full-orbed eyes—*Sàr-Obair.*

ròs-lachan, *s.* Duckweed, see mac-gun-athair.

ròsladh,** -aidh, *s.m.* Assation.

ros-lìn, *s.m.* Flax seed.

ròs-Màiri,§ *s.m.* Common rosemary, old man—*rosmarinus officinalis.*

ròs-Màiri-fiadhaich,§ *s.m.* Marsh andromeda [*lit.* wild rosemary)—*andromeda polifolia.* [The plant rosemary belongs to a different order—*labiatæ.*] Badge of Clan Rose.

ròs-mall,§ *s.m.* Hollyhock—*althæa rosea.*

ròs-Muire, see ròs-Màiri.

ròs-nan-con,§ *s.m.* Dog-rose—*rosa canina.*

ròs òr,§ *s.m.* Wood loose-strife or yellow pimpernel (ròs+òr) see seamrag-Muire.

606. *Ròs-Màiri-fiadhaich.* 607. *Ròs-nan-con.*

rosp,* *s.f.* Blear eye.

rosp-shùileach, -eiche, *a.* see rèasg-shùileach.

ròs-sìor-gheal,** *s.m.* Rosemary.

ròst, -a, -achan, *s.m.* Roast, piece of roast meat.

ròst, *v.a.* see ròist.

ròsta, see ròiste.

ròstach,** *a.* Roasting, toasting.

rostadh,** -aidh, *s.m.* Mishap.

ròstadh, -aidh, *s.m.* Roasting, as of meat. 2 Roast. Feòil air a r., *flesh roasted.* A' r—, *pr.pt.* of ròist.

rot,(CR) *s. m.* Anything thick. R. maide, *a thick stick*; r. caillich, *a corpulent woman*—*W. of Ross-shire.*

rot, -oit, -an. *s.m.* Belch, belching. 2 Bursting, as of waves. *prov.* 3 (DMy) Driving, chasing, as of cattle in the corn or preserved pasture. R. air a' chladach, *waves breaking on the shore.*

rot,(DU) *s.m.* Lumpish person.

rotacal, -ail, *s.m.* see racadal.

rotach, -aich, *s.f.* Rush at starting, running, bound. 2 The flux. 3 Circle of mud gathered by a female's dress off a muddy road. 4 Hand-rattle, used to frighten cattle from corn or grass. 5 Storm—*Suth'd.*

rotach,(DU) *a.* Medium-sized, stumpy, lumpish.

ròtadh, -aidh, *s.m.* see reòdhtach.

rotadh, -aidh, -aidhean, *s.m.* Cutting out, dividing. *prov.*

rotag,(CR) *s.f.* Stone not greater than that two could be lifted by a man—*W. of Ross.* R. cloiche, *a small stone.*

rotaiche, *s.f.ind.* Bursting of waves.

ròtaidh, see reòdhta.

ròtair, -ean, *s.m.* Clumsy, awkward fellow. 2* Slaver. 3* Sloven. 4††Lazy fellow.

———eachd, *s.f.* Clumsiness, awkwardness. 2 Coarseness.

rotal, -ail, *s.m.* The wake of a ship under sail.

†rotan, -ain, *s.m.* Redness.

rotanach,(DU) *s.m.* Anything of middling size. R. balaich, *a well-grown boy.*

roth, -a, -an, *s.m.* Wheel. 2**Rim of a wheel. 3 Halo. Tha r. mu'n ghealaich, *there is a halo round the moon;* r. a' mhuilinn, *the mill-wheel*; r.-cartach, *a cart-wheel*; r. mòr, *the driving-wheel of spinning-wheel*; eadar na rothan, *between the wheels.*

PARTS OF A WHEEL :—

1 Aiseal, *axle,*
2 Bachall, *hoop, tyre (iron ring on wheel.)* Crudha. Cearcall.
3 Bannan-ciche, *nave-bands.*
4 Bas, *spoke.* Clàr. ‡‡Spòg. Tarsnan-rotha, (*pl.*) *spokes.*
5 Cairt-cheap, *nave.* Ceap-chartach. Crùb. ‡‡Crubh. (MS) Imleag-rotha. Cloch na

cuidhle.
6 Crann-aisil, *axle-tree.*
7 Cuairsgean, *felloe.* Foileas. Roth, *the felloes together.* Reim. (WC)Cuairtlean.
8 Gramaiche, *trigger*—a catch to hold the wheel when driving on steep ground.
9 Ream, *rim.* Roithlean. Ruithlean.
10 Tarunn-aisil, *lynch-pin* — pin that keeps the wheel on axle. Tarrung-cuibhle.
11 Slios, *flange.*
roth, *v.a.* Wheel, coil. also rothaig.
rotha, -n, *s.m.* Screw. 2 Vice. 3 see rola.
rothach, -aiche, *a.* Furnished with wheels. 2 **Rimmed, as a wheel. 3**Rotular.
rothachadh, -aidh, *s.m.* Swathing. 2 Act of swathing, wrapping up or shrouding. A' r—, *pr.pt.* of rothaich.
rothach-tràgha, see praiseach-tràgha.
rothadair, -ean, *s.m.* Wheelwright.
———-eachd,†† *s.f.* Business of a wheelwright.
rothadh, -aidh, *s.m.* Wheeling. 2 Coiling. A' r—, *pr.pt.* of roth.
ròthadh, *Arran* for reòthadh. Uisgeanan ròdhadh, *icicles.*
rothaich, *pr.pt.* a' rothachadh, *v. a.* Twine, roll, swathe, wrap up, shroud.
———eadh, -eidh, see rothachadh.
———te, *past pt.* of rothaich. Swathed, wrapped up, shrouded.
rothaidhe, -an, *s.m.* Cyclist.
———achd, *s.f.ind.* Cycling.
rothaig, *v.a.* see rothaich.
———eadh, -eidh, *s.m. & pr.pt.* of rothaig, see rothachadh.
———te, *past pt.* of rothaig. see rothaichte.
rothair, -ean, *s.m.* Cylinder. 2 Roller.
rothaireachd, *s.f.ind.* Wheeling. 2 Spinning.
rothan, -ain, *pl.* -an, [& -ain] *s.m., dim.* of roth. Little wheel. 2 Little rim.
———ach, -aiche, *a.* Having little wheels.
rothar, *s.* Bagpipe-chanter—*Rob Donn.*
rothar, -air, -an, *s.m.* Cycle.
rothar-dà-chuidhleach, *s.m.* Bicycle.
rothar-trì-rothan, *s.m.* Tricycle.
rothas,(WC) -ais, *s. m.* Knowledge, acquaintance. Cha'n 'eil r. agam air, *I am not acquainted with him.*
rothas, see ros.
roth-fiaclach, *s.m.* Cog-wheel.
rothlag, see ròlag.
rothlair, -ean, *s.m.* see rothair.
rothlas, -ais, *s.m.* Evolution.
ro-thoil, -e, *s.f.* Great desire. 2 Great willingness. Bha r. agam *I was greatly desirous,*
———each, *a.* Very desirous.
rù, *s.m.* Rue. 2§ Plants resembling rue.
†rù, see rùn.
ruadh, -aidhe, *a.* Reddish, of a reddish colour, ruddy. 2 Red in general. 3 Red-haired. 4 Dried, scorched. 5**Brown. An tuil r., *or* an dìle r., *the general deluge ;* sgillinn r., *a penny ;* Seumas r., *red-haired James.*
ruadh,* -aidh, *s.m.* Reddish colour, redness.
ruadh, -aidh, *s.f.* Deer, hind, roe. 2 Red-deer. 3**Strength, virtue. 4(MS) St. Anthony's fire, erysipelas.
ruadh, -a, *a.* Strong, valiant.
ruadhachadh, -aidh, *s.m.* Reddening, act of making red. 2 State of becoming red. A' r—, *pr.pt.* of ruadhaich.
ruadhadh, -aidh, *s.m.* Making red or brown. 2 Becoming red, brown or tanned. 3 Rusting. 4 Blushing. Mar ghàd air r., *like a rusted bar.*
ruadhag, -aig, -an, *s.f. dim.* of ruadh. Young deer, hind or roe. 2 Robin, see brù-dhearg. 3 (AF) Crab. 4**Goat. An r. a' spìoladh air t' uaigh, *the young roe browsing on thy grave.*
ruadhagail,‡ -e, *s.f.* Thrift.
ruadhaich, *pr.pt.* a' ruadhachadh, *v.a. & n.* Redden, make red. 2 Redden, become red. 3 Embrown, become brown. 4(DMy) Expose or point out a person. R. e mach mi, *he exposed me*, or *pointed me out.*
———e, (MS) *s.* Carrotiness.
———te, *past pt.* of ruadhaich. Reddened, made red. 2 Become red.
ruadhaig,** *gen.sing.* of ruadhag.
ruadhain,** *a.* Fusty.
———eachd,** *s.f.* Fustiness.
ruadhair, see ruamhair.
ruadhan, -ain, *s.m.* Mineral scurf that collects on the surface of wells and other waters. 2 Sediments mixing with agitated waters. 3 Any kind of meat overdone in cooking. 4 Ruddle, any substance that dyes brown. 5 Reddishness, brownness, reddish or brown tinge. Tha 'n t-iasg 'na r., tha 'n t-aran 'na r., tha na h-uighean 'nan r., *the fish, bread, eggs are overcooked ;* bùrn glan gun r., *clear water without a brown tinge.*
ruadhan,(AF) *s.m.* Robin.
——— -aille,(AF) *s.m.* Sparrow-hawk.
ruadhar, see ruamhair.
ruadharach, see ruamharach & ruatharach.
ruadharadh,** -aidh, see ruamhar & ruathar.
ruadh-bhàrr, *s.m.* Rhubarb.
ruadh-bhiast, -an, *s.m.* Moor-fowl, *prov.*
ruadh-bhoc, -bhuic, *pl.* -an & -bhuic, *s.m.* Roebuck.
ruadh-bhoinne, see ruadh-bhuinne.
ruadh-bhòrd, *s.m.* The plank next to the garb in a boat.
ruadh-bhuidhe, *a.* Of a reddish-yellow colour, auburn.
ruadh-bhuinne, *s. f.* Mountain torrent. 2 Torrent embrowned by being impregnated with peat. 3**Flood-water.
ruadh-chailc, -e, *s.f.* Ochre, ruddle.
———each, *a.* Ochreous. 2 Asphaltic.
ruadh-chrèadh, -a, *s.f.* Red clay, ruddle.
ruadh-chrèadhach,†† *a.* Pertaining to red clay.
ruadh-chù,(AF) *s.m.* Wolf.
ruadh-laith, *s.f.* Choler.
———each,** *a.* Choleric.
ruadh-thuil, -e, -ean, *s.f.* Great flood, hill torrent reddened by the peat in mossy grounds through which it passes. 2 The deluge.
ruag, *pr.pt.* a' ruagadh, *v. a.* Pursue, course, chase. 2 Put to flight. 3 Persecute, harass.
ruagach, -aiche, *a.* Pursuing, that pursues or puts to flight. 2 Persecuting, harassing. 3 Scaring, dispersing, banishing, like a pursuit or flight.
ruagadh, -aidh, *s.m.* Pursuing. 2 Act of pursuing or putting to flight, pursuit, flight, dispersion. 3 Persecuting, harassing. A' r—, *pr.pt.* of ruag.
ruagair, -ean, *s.m.* Pursuer, chaser, hunter. 2 Any dislodging instrument. 3 Wedge. 4 Latch of a door. 5 Small bullet, swan-shot, slug. 6**Fugitive, outlaw, wanderer. 7 Persecutor. 8**Bar, bolt. 9 Any instrument used for scaring birds or other creatures. 10** Hunter.
———eachd, *s.f.ind.* Pursuing, hunting, chasing. 2 Persecution.
ruagalaiche,** *s.m.* Fugitive. 2 Gipsy.
ruaghag, see ruadhag.
ruaghan, see ruadhan.
ruaichill,** *v.a.* Buy, purchase.
———te, *past pt.* of ruaichill.
ruaidh, *gen. & voc. sing.* of ruadh.
ruaidh,** *v.a.* Redden, embrown.
ruaidhe, *s. f. ind.* Redness, ruddiness. 2 Defect

in fir timber. 3 Erysipelas [with the art. *an.*] 4 Nettle-rash—*Arran.* 5 (AF)Rash in cattle. 5*Herpes, shingles.
ruaidhe, *comp.* of ruadh.
ruaidhle,** *s.m.* Poor worn-down creature.
ruaidhmre,** *s.* Cochineal.
†ruaidhneach, -ich, *s.f.* Hair.
ruaidh-rinn,** *s.pl.* Red points or edges.
ruaig, (CR) *s.f.* Shower of rain—*Perthshire.*
ruaig, -e, -ean, *s.f.* Pursuit, hunt, chase. 2 Flight, defeat, precipitate retreat. 3 Persecution. 4 Scaring away, dispersion, banishment. Thog iad an r., *they took up the pursuit;* chuir sinn an r. orra, *we put them to flight;* gabh iad an ruaig, *they took to flight;* r. an tuirc, *the boar-hunt;* ruaig sionnaich, *a fox-chase.*
ruaig, see ruag.
ruaigidh, *fut.aff.a.* of ruaig.
ruaille, -an, *s.f.* Poor, wretched female.
rù ailpeach,§ *s.m.* Alpine rue.
ruaim, -e, -ean, *s.f.* Flush of anger on the face. 2††Red scum. 3 Fishing-line. 4 Line.
†ruaim, -ean, *s.f.* Alder-tree.
ruaimeanach,** -ich, *s.m.* Marsh.
ruaimhseanta,* *a.* Jolly, hearty though very old.—*Islay.*
——————chd,* *s.f.ind.* Heartiness of an old person, vigour.
ruaimill,* *v.a.* Rumble, agitate, as water.
ruaimle, -an, *s. f.* Red muddy water, dirty pool, standing water impregnated with clay. 2 see ruaim.
ruaimleach, -eiche, *a.* Muddy, as water, turbid, agitating. Conadh r., *dark rage—Moladh an Leòmhainn.* Gu r., *muddily.*
——————,†† *s.m.* Red, muddy water or mire.
ruaimleachadh, -aidh, *s.m.* Agitating. 2 Act of agitating water. 3* Muddiness of water. A' r—, *pr.pt.* of ruaimlich.
ruaimleachd,** *s.f.* Muddiness.
ruaimleadh,* *s.m.* see ruaimleachadh. 2 Water-lily—*Colonsay.*
ruaimleachd, *s.f.ind.* Muddiness, turbidness.
ruaimlich, *pr.pt.* a' ruaimleachadh, *v. a.* Agitate as fluid. 2††Make muddy.
————te, *past pt.* of ruaimlich.
ruaimneach, -eiche, *a.* Strong, active, robust.
ruaimneachd, *s.f.ind.*Strength, activity, robustness.
ruain,** *s.f.* Kind of weed which gives a reddish colour.
ruaineach, -eiche, *a.* Fierce. 2 Froward. 3 Strong.
ruaineachd,** *s.f.* Fierceness.
ruainidh,** -e, *a.* Reddish. 2 Strong, able. 3 Charitable.
————,** *s.m.* Strong, boisterous fellow. Maol-r., see maol-ruainidh.
ruainn, ** *s.f.* Water in which dye stuff is boiled.
ruainne, *s.f.* see ròin.
ruais,* *s.f.* Rhapsody. 2 Rhapsodist.
——,** -ean. *s. m.* Clown, sluggish, stupid fellow. 2 Noisy fellow.
ruaisealachd,** *s.f.* Clownishness. 2 Disorderliness.
ruaiseil,* -e, *a.* Rhapsodical. 2 **Clownish, disorderly.
†ruaithne, *a.* Reddish green, grey.
ruam,* -aim, *s.m.* Kind of plant used in dyeing red.
†ruamh,* -aimh, -an, *s.f.* Spade. 2§Yellow bed-straw, see ruin.
ruamhair, *pr.pt.* a' ruamhar & a' ruamhradh,*v.a.* Delve, dig with a spade. 2 see ruathair.
ruamhar, -air, *s.m.* Delving. 2 Act of delving or digging with a spade. 3 Stirring up. 4 see ruathar. A' r—, *pr.pt.* of ruamhair.
ruamharach, ** *a.* Digging, delving. 2 Stirring.
ruamharaiche,‡‡ *s.m.* Delver.
ruamhradh, -aidh, see ruamhar.
ruamhraidh, *fut.aff.a.* of ruamhair.
ruamnach,** *a.* Indignant, angry.
ruamnadh,** -aidh,*s.m.* Reproof. 2 Reprehension.
ruanach, *a.* Firm, steadfast, stony. 2 Fierce, —*Sàr-Obair.*
ruanachd, *s.f.* Fiction, novel, romance. 2 Harangue.
ruanaiche,** *s.m.* Romancer. 2 Haranguer.
ruanaidh,** *a.* Red, reddish. 2 Strong, able. 3 Charitable.
ruanaidh,** *s.f.* Anger. 2 Darkness. 3**Strong boisterous fellow.

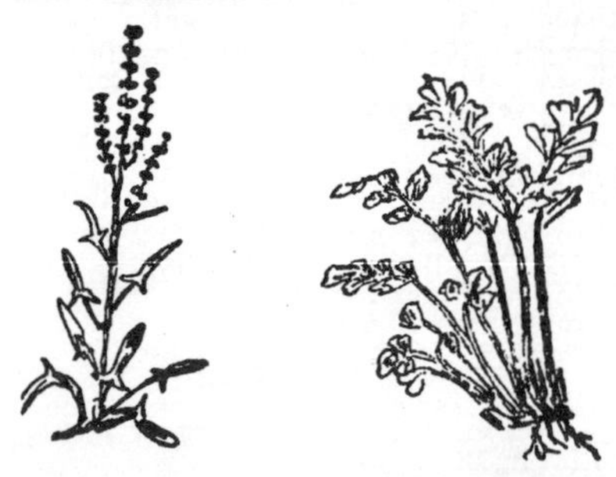

608. *Ruanaidh.* 609. *Rù-bhallaidh.*

ruanaidh,§ *s.* Sheep's sorrel—*rumex acetosella.* The seed-bearing part is called *samh.*
ruanail,** *a.* Lying, false, untrue, fictitious.
ruapais,* -ean, *s.f.* Rigmarole.
ruar, (DMu) Used in the phrase, Mo ruar, *my miserable one—Suth'd.*
ruar, -air, see ruamhar & ruathar.
ruaracan,** -ain, *s.m.* Floundering. 2 Groveller.
ruarach, see ruatharach.
————,** *s.m.* Liar, romancer.
ruaradh, -aidh, *s.m.* see ruatharadh.
ruashual,(AF) *s.m.* Lamprey.
ruathag, see ruadhag.
ruathair, *v.a.* Rummage. 2 Make sudden onset, fight. 3 see ruamhair. 4 (DMy)Epidemic. Tha r. 'san teaghlach —said when one after another would fall ill and the cause was not definitely known.
ruathar, -air, -an, *s.m.* Violent onset, fierce attack,rush. 2 Force, violence. 3 Force produced by motion. 4 Expedition. 5 Skirmish. 6 Misfortune, sudden unexpected calamity. 7 Hurried exertion. 8 Invasion. 9 Pillage. 10 Incursion. 11 Heat.
ruatharach, -aiche, *a.* Making a sudden or violent onset or attack. 2 Having much force or velocity. 3 Unfortunate, bringing a sudden or unexpected calamity. 4 Struggling. 5 Skirmishing. 6 Rushing. 7 see ruamharach.
ruatharachadh,** -aidh, *s.m.* Digging, delving, stirring up. 2 Rushing, making an onset.
ruatharaiche,** *s.m.* Attacker.
ruathradh, -aidh, -aidhean, *s.m.* see ruamhar, ruathar & ruamhradh.
rub, *pr.pt.* a' rubadh, *v.a.* Rub.
ruba, *s.* Small quantity of wool—*Skye.*
rubach,** *a.* Rubbing. 2 Prone to rub.
rubadh, -aidh, *s.m.* Rubbing. 2 Act of rubbing, friction. A' r—, *pr.pt.* of rub.
rubaig, see rub.
———eadh, see rubadh.

rubaigte, see rubta.
rùbail,* s. f. Tumult. 2 Rumbling. 3 (AH) Rumbling noise in the intestines.
rubair, -ean, s.m. Rubber, one who rubs. 2 Any instrument with which one rubs or scrapes.
†ruban, -ain, -an, s.m. Barrel, anker. 2 Rubber.
rùban, -ain, -an, s.m. Ruby. 2(DMy) Ribbon.
rù beag,§ s. m. Lesser meadow rue—*thalictrum minus.*
rù bhallaidh,§ s. m. Rue fern—*asplenium ruta muraria.*
rubhadh, -aidh, s.m. see rughadh.
rubhag,** -aig, s.f. Thong of hemp or flax. 2 Shoemaker's wax-end. 3**Pulling, snatching violently.
rubta, *past pt.* of rub. Rubbed.
ruc, -uic, -an & -annan, s. m. Rick of hay or corn. 2 Heaped measure. 3 (AF) Sow, pig. (also rùc.)
ruc,* v.a. Make ricks. 2 Build peats into small stacks.
rucach,** a. Abounding in ricks.. 2 Like a rick.
rùcail, s.f. see ròcail & rùchail. 2(WC)Noise in the bowels.
rucan, -ain, -an, s.m., *dim* of ruc. Small round hill. 2 Small rick of corn or hay. [also rùcan.]
rùcan, see rùchan & ruc.
rùcanach, see rùcharnach.
rucanach,** a. Abounding in stacks of corn.
rucas, -ais, s.m. Fondness, keen desire, foolish tenderness. 2 Arrogance, pride, forwardness, sauciness. 3 Fawning, fondling. 4* Jostling kind of fondness. 5**Frisk. Le r. bhi 'g ad fhòirneadh, *with arrogance intruding thyself.*
rucasach, -aiche, a. Fond, foolishly fond of any-one. 2 Arrogant. 3 Fawning, fondling. 4 Frisking. 5 Forward, pert, saucy.
———d, s.f.ind. see rucas. 2‡‡Habit of fondling. 3 Fawning. 4 Fondness, foolish fondness, keen desire. 5 Arrogance. 6†† Foolish mirth.
rùchail,** s.f. Hoarse voice, hoarseness. 2 Any hollow, hoarse sound. 3 Croaking. 4 Rumbling. 5 Grunting. 6 Tearing, rending.
rùchail,(CR) v.a. Rummage—*Arran.*
ruchall,** -aill, s.m. Fetter.
rùchan, -ain -an, s.m. The throat. 2**Windpipe. 3 Wheezing or rattling in the throat. 4 Hoarse noise.
———ach, -aiche, a. Wheezing.
rùchd, -a, -an, s.m. Grunt. 2 Belch. 3 Retching. 4 Rumbling noise. 5** Mask. 6**Sow, pig. 7**Entrails. 8 Lamentation. 9 see ruc.
ruchd, see ruc.
rùchd, *pr.pt.* a' rùchdail, v.a. Grunt as a sow. 2 Retch groaningly. 3 Belch. 4 Make a hoarse noise, shout, croak. 5 Make a rumbling noise, roar.
†ruchd, see riochd.
ruchd,** a. Vehement.
ruchdach, see rucach.
rùchdach, -aiche, a. Grunting. 2 Belching. 3 Retching. 4 Croaking hoarsely. 5 Making a rumbling noise.
rùchdadh, -aidh, s.m. & *pr. pt.* of rùchd, see rùchdail.
rùchdail, -e, s.f. Grunting, as of a sow. 2 Belching. 3 Retching. 4 Rumbling noise. 5 Hoarse noise. 6 Hoarseness of the voice. 7 Croaking. 8 (DMy) Choking with cough, strangling. A'r—, *pr. pt.* of rùchd.
rùchdan,** -ain, s.m. Throat. 2 Hoarse noise in the throat.
ruchdan, see rucan.
rud, -uid, -an, s.m. Thing, matter, affair, business, circumstance. 2 Small quantity of anything. 3 Term of contempt. 4 Membrum virile. Ciod an r. a tha thu 'g ràdh? *what are you saying?* r. mhosaich! *you nasty thing!* agus r. eile dheth, *and another thing;* an r. nach buin duit na buin da, *do not meddle with what does not concern you;* rud air chor-eiginn, *something or other.*
rùda, see rùta. 2 Aged tup or three-shear ram in *Lewis*, where a young ram is *reithe.*
rudach, -aiche, a. Concerned in many things, busy. 2 Officious, meddling. 3 Trifling. 4 (CR) Kindly attentive. 5 Affectionate—*Perthshire.* 6‡ Hospitable. 7** Particular about small matters.
rudadh, (AC) a. Obstinate.
rùdail,(DMK) s.f. Rumbling noise in the bowels—*Caithness.*
rudainnte,* see rudanach. 2 a. Particular, somewhat odd. 3 Done.
rudan, -ain, -an, s.m., *dim.* of rud. Little thing, trifle.
rùdan, -ain, *pl.* -an [& -ain**,] s.m. Knuckle. 2 Pastern—the part of a horse's foot between ankle and hoof. 3 Tendon.
rudan, *n.pl.* of rud. Things.
rudan,** -ain, s.m. Little thing. 2 Pudenda juvenis.
———ach, -aiche, a. Odd, queer, comical. 2 Trifling. 3 Abounding in trifles. 4 Particular.
rùdanach, -aiche, a. Knuckled. 2 Having large or strong knuckles. 3 Of, or belonging to, a knuckle. 4 Sinewy, strong, robust.
rùdanachadh,(AH) s.m. Fisticuffs.
rudanachd, s.f.ind. Pragmaticalness.
rudanaich,* v.a. Dress. 2(AH) Engage in fisticuffs.
rùdas,(AH) s.m. "Push," enterprise.
———ach,(AH) a. Unduly enterprising—*Argyll.*
rùdh, rùidh, s.m. see rù.
rudh, see rugh.
rudha, s.m. Point of land, promontory. 2††see rudhadh. Feuch am fuar thu 'n rudha, *see if you can weather the point;* cuiridh seo rudha seachad, *this will serve for our turn;* mar a' chuan air ruadh r., *like the sea on a brown promontory.*
rùdh-Ailpeach,§ s.m. Alpine meadow rue—*thalictrum alpinum.*
rudhach, -aiche, a. Abounding in points of land or promontories. 2 Blushing. 3 Causing blushes. 4 Blooming, rosy, ruddy-cheeked.
rudhadh, -aidh, s.m. Blush, erythema. 2** Hanging. Ni mò bha r. air an gruaidh, *neither was there a blush on their countenance.*
rùdhag, -aig, -an, s.f. Crab.
———ach, -aiche, a. Abounding in crabs.
rudhagail,* s.f. Thrift, shift. Tha e gu math r., *he is pretty thrifty;* g' a r. féin, *to his own thrift.*
ruadhaglach, a. Thrifty.
rudhain,** a. Musty. Bruchd rudhain, *the acid return from the stomach.*
rudhan, -ain, -an, s. m., *dim.* of rudha. Little headland or promontory.
rùdhan, -ain, -an, s.m. see rùghan.
———ach, see rùghanach.
rudhar, see ruamhar.
rùdh-beag,§ s.m. see rù-beag.
rùdh-bhallaidh,§ s. m. see rù-bhallaidh.
rùdh-gharaidh, see rù-gharaidh.
rùdhlach, *Kintyre* for rùdhrach.
rùdhrach,** a. Searching, groping. 2 Scrambling. 3 Long, straight.
rùdhrach, -aich, s. m. see rùdhrachadh. 2 **Tenant, sojourner. 3 Darkening, darkness.

4**Gloomy countenance.
rùdhrachadh, -aidh, *s. m.* Searching. 2 Act of searching or groping. 3 Act of confusing things in searching. A' r—, *pr. pt.* of rùdhraich.
rùdhrachas,** -ais, *s.m.* Length. 2 Obscurity.
rùdhraich, *pr.pt.* a' rùdhrach & a' rùdhrachadh, *v.a.* Search for, grope. 2 Confuse things in searching.
———te, *past pt.* of rùdhraich. Searched. 2 Confused or disordered by searching.
rug, -a & -uig, *pl.* -annan, *s.m.* Wrinkle. 2 Plait. 3 Old man. 4 One having a wrinkled face.
rug, (given by grammars as *past.ind.* of *v.* beir, but it is a different word.) Bare. 2 (with *preposition* air, either simple or compounded) ** Caught, overtook, seized. R. iad clann, *they bare children*; r. i uan, *she yeaned*; r. i meann, *she kidded*; r. i cuileanan, *she whelped* or *cubbed*; r. i searrach, *she foaled*; r. i ugh, *she laid an egg*; r. i uirceanan, *she farrowed;* r. sinn oirre, *we overtook her*; r. e air bhuam, *he laid hold of it out of my hands*; r. a' bhan-righ air an ugh, *the queen seized the egg—W.H. 1. 19.*
ruga,* *s.f.* Rough cloth or female.
rugach, -aiche, *a.* Wrinkled. 2 Plaited. Agh-aidh r., *a wrinkled face.*
———, -aich, *s.m.* Old man.
rugadh, (given by grammars as *past pass. v.* beir, but it is a different word.) Was born. 2 (with the *prep.* air) Was caught or undertaken. R. air, *he was caught*; o 'n r. mi, *since I was born.*
rugadh, -aidh, *s. m.* Greedy grasping of anything. 2**Rush towards any common property. 3**Cheap purchase, good bargain.
rugadh, -aidh, *s.m.* Old person, person with a wrinkled face.
rugaid, -e, -ean, *s.f.* Long neck. 2 Old cow. 3 Worthless female.
———each, -eiche, *a.* Having a long neck.
rugair, -ean, *s. m.* Drunkard, tippler. 2 see ruagair.
———eachd, *s.f. ind.* Tippling, frequenting of taverns. *prov.*
ruganta, -ainte, *a.* Strong, stout, able, muscular. 2**Tough. 3**Made of good metal.
———chd, *s.f.ind.* Stoutness. 2 Strength. 3 Toughness.
rugh, see rù.
rùgh, *s.m.* Small stack of peats—*Suth'd.*
rugha, see rudha, rudhadh, rudh & ruadhadh.
rughach, -aiche, *a.* see rudhach.
rughadh, see ruadhach & rudhadh.
rughaich, see ruadhaich.
rùghan, -ain, -an, *s. m.* Small stack of hay, corn or peats.
rùghanach, -aiche, *a.* Abounding in small stacks of hay, corn or peat.
rù-ghàraidh,§ *s. m.* Common rue, countryman's treacle herb of grace—*ruta graveolens.*
rùghteach, *a.* see rùdhach.
ruibe, see ribe.
———ach, see riobach.
ruibeag, see ribeag.
ruibealtaich, *s.m.* Lounger.
ruibean, see rioban.
———ach, see riobanach.
———aich, see riobainich.
†**ruibh**, -e, *s.f.* Sulphur.
ruibh, see ruith & ribh.
†**ruibhne**, -achan & -an, *s. f.* Lance, spear. 2 Lancet.
†———ach, -aichne, *a.* Armed with a lance or spear. 2 Of, or belonging to, a lance or spear. 3 Strongly guarded.
†**ruibhneach**, ** -ich, *s.m.* Spear-man, lancer.
ruic,** *s.f.* Fleece. 2 (DU) Fussy fawning, making much of one in a demonstrative fashion, the fuss or demonstration arising out of sincere pleasure. 'S ann ort tha 'n r.! *what a fuss you are making!*
ruice,** *s.f.* Reproach, rebuke. 2 Defeat. 3 Red shade. 4 Blush occasioned by shame. Nach ann air tha 'n r.? *is he not ignorantly proud;*
ruiceach, *a.* Reproaching. 2 Rebuking, reproving. 3**Exalting, lifting up.
ruicean, -ein, -an, *s.m.* Pustule, red pimple, acne. 2 Pimply-faced person. *prov.*
ruichealt,** -eilt, *s.* Close concealment.
ruideach,** *a.* Glib, flowing.
ruideag,¶ -eig, *s.f.* Kittiwake, see seagair.
ruideaga,§ *s.* Stone-bramble, see caora-bad miann.
ruideal, *s. & v.* see rideil.
ruideal,‡ -eil, *s.m.* The herb robert, see righeal-cùil.
ruidealach, see ridealach.
ruidealadh,** *s.m.* see ridealadh.
ruidealaich, see rideilich.
———te, see rideilichte.
ruidealair, see ridealair.
ruidean, *pl.* of rùdan.
ruideas, -eis, *s.f.* Sportive mood, frisking, capering, leaping.
———ach, -aiche, *a.* Sportive, playful, frisky, gambolling. Bu r. gamhainn is laoigh, *playful were the stirks and calves.*
ruideis, *s.f.* see ruideas.
ruid-ghuilbneach, (AF) *s.* Bar-tailed godwit. 2 Stunted curlew. (rid-ghuileanach) see camghlas.)
ruidh, see ruith.
ruidhe,** *s.* Dairy. 2 Sheiling.
†**ruidheadh**,** -idh, *s. f.* Reproof, censure. 2 Ray.
ruidheadh, -eidh, see rughadh.
ruidhteach,* see ruiteach.
ruidhil, see ridhil.
———each, -eiche, see ridhleach
———eadh, see ridhleadh.
ruidhleach, see ridhleach.
ruidhlean, see ridhlean.
ruidhleas,** *a.* Very faithful.
ruidhlichean, see ridhleachan.
ruidhte, see ruite.
ruidhtear, see ruitear.
ruidhtearach, see ruitearach.
———d,** *s.f.* see ruitearachd.
ruidhtearaich, see ruitearaich.
ruidhtire, see ruidhtear.
ruididh, -e, *a.* Merry, glad, frisky, cheerful.
ruididheachd,** *s. f.* Gladness, cheerfulness, merriness.
ruidil, see rideil.
ruidir, see ridir.
ruig, *v. irreg.* Reach, extend to. 2 Reach, arrive at. 3 Attain to. 4**Hold forth, stretch out. 5 Border. 6 (with *leas*) Need, must, needs.

Active Voice.
IND. *past*, ràinig mi, &c., *I, &c. reached.*
„ *fut.* ruigidh mi, &c., *I, &c. shall reach.*
INTERROG. & NEG. *past.* (an ? nach ? cha) d' ràinig mi, &c., *did I, &c. (not) reach? I, &c. did not reach.*
„ *fut.* (an ? nach ? cha) ruig mi, &c., *shall I, &c. (not) reach, I &c. shall not reach.*
SUBJ. *past.* (ged) ruiginn, *(though) I would reach*; (ged) ruigeamaid, *(though) we would reach*; (ged) ruigeadh tu, e, i, sibh, iad, *(though) thou wouldst, he, she, you, they*

would reach.
„ *fut.* (ma) ruigeas mi, &c., (*if*) *I, &c. reach.*
IMP. *1st. per. sing.* ruigeam, *let me reach.*
INFIN. a ruigheachd & a ruigsinn, *to reach.*
PRES. PART. a' ruigheachd & a' ruigsinn, *reaching.*
Passive Voice.
IND. *past,* ràinigeadh mi, &c., *I, &c. was reached.*
„ *fut.* ruigear mi, &c., *I, &c. shall be reached.*
INT. & NEG. *past,* (an ? nach ? cha) d' ràinigeadh mi, &c., *was I, &c. (not) reached ? I, &c. was not reached.*
„ *fut.* (an ? nach ? cha) ruigear mi, &c., *shall I &c. (not) be reached ? I &c. shall not be reached.*
SUBJ. *past,* (ged) ruigteadh mi, &c., (*though*) *I, &c. should be reached.*
„ *fut.* (ma) ruigear mi, &c., *if I, &c. shall be reached.*
PAST PART. ruigte, *reached.*
R. an seo, *reach here, extend your hand to this ;* ràinig mi air, *I reached at it ;* an ruig e an nochd ? *will he arrive to-night ?* cia fhad' a ruigeas tu ? *how far will you go ?* cha ruig mi air, *I cannot attain to it ;* cha ruig thu leas a bhi aig do dhragh, *you need not trouble yourself ;* 's nach ruigeamaid leas a bhi 'feitheamh, *and that we did not require to wait ;* ruig Tormad Dòmhnullach, *go to Norman MacDonald;* cha ruig greim de 'n fheòil sin sinn, *a bit of that flesh will not suffice us ;* gach ni air an ruigeadh iad, *everything that they could seize.*
ruig, *prep.* (gu ruig, properly gu nuig) To, until. 2 As far as. Gu ruig seo, *to this place ;* gu r. an taigh, *as far as the house.*
ruig,-eachan, *s.m.* Half-castrated ram (ridgling) or other animal.
ruige, see ruig.
ruigeachd,** *s.f.* Castration. 2 State of being castrated. 3 see ruigheachd.
ruigeam, *1st. per. sing. imp.* of ruig. Let me reach.
———aid, *1st. per. pl. past subj.* of ruig. We would reach.
ruigear, *fut. subj. pass.* of ruig. (Ma) r. e, *if it be reached.*
ruigeas, *fut. subj. act.* of ruig. (Ma) r. mi, (*if*) *I reach.*
ruigh, see righe.
———e, *s.f.* see righe.
———each, see righeach.
ruigheachas, see righeachas.
ruigheachd, *s.f.ind.* Reaching. 2 Act of reaching. 3 Extending to, arriving at. 4 Attaining to. 5*Arrival. 6 Mental trial. A' r—, *pr.pt.* of ruig. Air dhuinn r., *on our arrival;* a' ruigheachd air, *stretching (his hand) towards it.*
ruigheachdail, -e, *a.* Pertinent. 2 Accessible.
ruighean, -ein, *s.m.* Wool-roll ready to spin.
ruigheanas,** -ais, *s.m.* Brightness.
ruighe-mheas, *s.m.* see righe-mheas.
ruighinn, *s.f. & pr.pt.* of ruig, see ruigheachd.
ruighinn, see righinn.
ruighneachd, (MS) *s.f.* see righneachd.
ruighteach,** *a.* Blank.
ruigidh, *fut. aff. a.* of ruig. Shall reach.
ruiginn, *1st. per. sing. past subj.* of ruig. I would reach.
ruighteach,** *a.* see ruiteach.
ruighich, (CR) *s.f.* see righich.
ruigleachan,** *s.m.* Castrated ram.
ruiglean,** -ein, *s. m.* Ridgling, half-castrated goat.
———ach,** *a.* Of, like, or belonging to, ridglings. 3 Castrated.

ruigsinn, *s.f.* Arriving, reaching. 2 Attaining. 3 Arrival. A' r—, *pr.pt.* of ruig.
———each, *a.* Accessible, attainable.
ruigte, *past pt.* of ruig. Reached.
ruigteadh, *past subj. pass.* of ruig. (Ged) r. e, (*though*) *it should be reached.*
ruileag, -eig, -an, *s.f.* Roll. 2 Polite term for a falsehood.
ruim, *gen. sing.* of rum.
ruimhe,** *s.f.* Reproof. 2 Reproach.
ruimneach,** -ich, *s.m.* Marsh.
ruin,§ *s.* Yellow bedstraw—*galium verum.*
rùin, *gen. sing. & n. pl.* of rùn.
rùine, *pl.* rùintean, *s.f.ind.* Secrecy, mystery. 2 Private intimation.
rùinean, -ein, -an, *s.m.* Darling.
†**rùinidh,** *s.pl.* Secrets.
ruinigil,** *s.f.* Dangerous navigation.
ruinigin, see ruinigil.
ruinn, *prep. pron.* see rinn.
ruinn, -e, -ean, *s.f.* see roinn.
ruinn-bhior, -a, -an, *s.m.* see rinn-bhior.
———ach, -aiche, *a.* see rinn-bhiorach.
rùinne, see ròin.
ruinneach, -eiche, *a.* see rinneach.
†**ruinneach,** -eich, *s.f.* Grass.
ruinneadh,** -idh, *s.m.* Consumption. 2 Detersion, cleansing.
ruinn-gheur, -éire, *a.* see rinn-gheur.
ruinnich,†† *pr.pt.* a' ruinneachadh, *v.a.* Point, sharpen.
ruinnleachadh, (MS) *s.m. & pr.pt.* of ruinnlich. Rumple.
ruinnlich, *v.a.* Rumple.
ruinn-ruise,§ *s.m.* Male pimpernel, poor man's weather-glass, see falcair.
ruinns, *v.a.* Gaelic spelling of *rinse.*
ruinnse, -an, *s.f.* Long stick or stake. 2 Tail of an animal. 3 Rump, the part immediately above the tail. 4 Scourge, whip. 5‡‡ see roinnsear. 6*Anything long. 7††Draggled skirt.
ruinnseach, -eich, -eichean, see ruinnse.
———, -ich, -ichean, *s.f.* Base or worthless woman, a term of contempt. 3††Tall vulgar female.
———, -iche, *a.* Having long sticks or stakes. 2 Having a draggled skirt.
———adh, -aidh, *s.m.* see roinnseachadh.
ruinnsear,** Gaelic spelling of *rinser.* 2 Searcher. 3‡‡ Gauger. 4 Base or worthless fellow.
ruinnsich, *v.a.* Rinse, scour. 2 Whip, scourge.
———te, *past pt.* of ruinnsich. see roinnsichte.
ruinnsinn,** Gaelic form of *rinsing.* see roinnseachadh.
ruinnte, see roinnte.
ruintealas,§ *s. m.* Darnel- or rye-grass, see breoillean.
rùintean, *n. pl.* of rùn.
ruipleachan,** -ain, *s.m.* Gorbellied fellow.
rui-rai, *Argyllshire* for rù-rà.
ruire,** *s.m.* Knight, champion. 2 Lord.
——ach,** -aich, *s. m.* Champion, knight. 2 Exile.
——ach,** *a.* Famous.
——achail,** *a.* Championlike, knightly. 2 Famous.
——achas,** -ais, *s.m.* Lordship, dominion. 2 Renown. 3 Bravery.
†**ruis,** -e, -ean, *s.f.* Way, road.
ruiseadh, *s.m.* Dash forward, (rush.)
ruis,§ -e, -ean, *s. f.* Common elder—*sambucus nigra.* †2 Name for the the letter R. 3‡ Rash.
†**ruisceanta,** see ruisgeanta.
ruisealachd,** *s.f.* Hastiness, rashness. 2 Disorder.
†**ruisean,**** -ein, *s.m.* Luncheon.

610. *Ruis.*

ruiseanta,** *a.* Hasty, rash. 2 Disorderly.
ruiseil,** *a.* Rash, hasty, precipitate. 2 Disorderly.
rùisg, *pr.pt.* a' rùsgadh, *v. a. & n.* Strip, peel, make bare. 2 Fleece, shear sheep. 3 Chafe the skin, as by friction. 4 Disclose, reveal, discover, expose. 5 Undress, excoriate. 6* Gall, denude, unsheathe. 7 Shave. 8** Tear, rend. 9 Clip, strip.
R. am buntàta, *peel the potatoes;* r. a' chraobh, *strip the tree;* r. do chlaidheamh, *unsheath thy sword;* r. e a ghàirdean, *he made bare his arm;* na r. do dhearas do d' nàmhaid, *do not reveal your defects to your enemy;* rùisgidh brù bràghad, *the belly will strip the neck.*
ruisg, *gen.sing. & n.pl.* of rosg.
rùisg, -e, *a.* see rùisgte.
†rùisg, -e, -ean, *s.f.* Vessel made of bark. 2 *n.pl.* of rùsg. Peelings.
ruisg, *s.f.* Fray, skirmish.
†ruisg, *v.a.* Smite, strike, pelt.
rùisg-chòmhdach, -aich, *s.m.* Incrustation.
rùisg-chòmhdaich, *v.a.* Incrust.
rùisgeach,** *a.* Caustic, escharotic.
ruisgean,(DMy) *pl.* of ruisg.
rùisgean, -ein, *s.m.* Vessel made with the bark of trees.
ruisgeanta,** *a.* Fond of fighting or frays, quarrelsome.
ruisg-eòrna,(DMy) *s.* Twelve sheaves of barley in a semi-circle instead of six pairs of sheaves of oats in a straight line—*Lewis.* WC says ten sheaves of barley.
rùisgidh, *fut.aff.a.* of rùisg.
ruisg-shùileach, see rosg-shùileach.
ruisg-shùl, *s.pl.* Hair of the eye-lids, eye-lashes.
rùisgte, *a. & past pt.* of rùisg. Naked, bare, exposed. 2 Stripped, peeled, made bare. 3 Fleeced, shorn. 4 Chafed. 5 Disclosed, revealed, discovered. 6 Shelled, unsheathed. R. agus lomnochd, *stripped and naked.*
rùisgteachd, *s.f.ind.* Obnoxiousness.
ruit,* -e, -ean, *s.f.* Rakish female. 2 Javelin.
ruite, *s.f.ind.* Gluttony. 2 Revelry, rioting.
ruiteach, -eiche, *a.* Ruddy, florid, rosy-cheeked. 2 Flushing, blushing. 3 Apt to blush. 4 Floriferous. 5 Bloomy. 6 see ruitheach. Bha e r. *he was ruddy.*
——d,** *s.f.* Ruddiness, floridness.
ruiteachan, -ain, *pl.* -ain & -an, *s.m.* Ruby.
ruiteachas, -ais, *s.m.* Ruddiness.
ruiteachd,** *s.f.* Ruddiness, floridness. 2 Freshness.
ruiteag, -eig, -an, *s.f.* Roe-buck berry. 2 Blush. 3 Redness, slight tinge of red.
ruiteagach, -aiche, *a.* Blushing. 2 Ruddy.
ruiteau,** Fetlock. 2 Pastern. 3 Ankle-bone. 4 Dirt-grovelling child.
ruitear,* -ean, *s. m.* Rake, abandoned man, drunkard. 2 Glutton. 3 Riotous liver, carouser, reveller.
ruitearach, -aiche, *a.* Gluttonous. 2 Revelrous. 3 Drunken.
ruitearachd, *s. f. ind.* Gluttony. 2 Revelry, riot, carouse, drunkenness.
ruidhtearaich, *v.* Carouse.
ruith, *pr.pt.* a' ruith, *v.n.* Run, race, rush. 2 *Melt, as lead or suet. 3 Flow, as a stream. 4 *Speak fast. 5 *Chase. 6 *Distil. 7 Retreat. 8 *Run over, look over.
R. e, *he ran;* r. an fhuil, *the blood flowed;* r. e as mo dhéidh, *he chased me;* a' r. ceud tharruing; *distilling low wines;* r. orra, *run superficially over them;* r. e mach, *it was exhausted or expended;* is math a r. sibh! *how well you ran!*
ruith, -e, *s.f.* Running, act of running. 2 Race, rushing, chase. 3 Flowing, act of flowing as a stream. 4 Pursuit, flight, as of an army. 5 *Fast speaking or talking. 6* Treatment. 7 Slight arrangement. 8*In line with, parallel. 9‖ The diarrhœa, flux [with the article *an.*] 10**Army. 11**Troop. 12 Rate, full speed. 13 Dysentery. 14††Average, ratio. 15 Course. A' r—, *pr.pt.* of ruith.
Esan 'na r., *he at full speed;* air an r. cheudna, *at the same rate;* air a' cheart r., *at precisely the same rate;* thoir an aon r. dhaibh, *give them the same treatment;* air r. an taigh seo, *parallel with this house;* thoir r. cladaich dhith, *run her aground;* r. na teanga, *a complete scold;* leig r. dha, *let it run, let it flow;* gille-r., *a footman, runner, forerunner;* r na cubhaige, *an April fool's errand;* r. air theas, *running to and fro, as cattle in hot weather;* thoir r. orra (or dhaibh), *give them a slight adjustment, make the numbers run;* is iomadh uair a thug mi air ruith, *many an hour I spent on running;* is iomadh uair a thug mi ruith air, *many a time I made him run;* is iomadh uair a thug mi air a ruith, *many an hour I spent chasing him;* ruith air falbh, *or* ruith leis, *running before the wind.*
ruith-analach, -aich, *s.m.* Breathlessness.
ruith-chladaich,(WC) *s.f.* Running ashore of a vessel. Thàinig r. oirnn, *we had to run aground;* r. ort! *bad luck to you!*
ruith-chuim,(WC) *s.f.* Diarrhœa. [With the art. *an.*]
ruithe, *s.f.* Dairy.
ruitheach, -eiche, *a.* Running. 2 Flowing, fluent. 3 Moving, on the march. 4 Running. 5 Slippery, as shot. Uisge r., *flowing water.*
————, -eich, *s.f.* Hand-cuff.
ruitheachd,(MS) *s.f.* Currency.
ruithean,** *a.* Red-hot. 2 Blazing.
————, -ein, *s.m.* Delight, pleasure.
————as,** -ais, *s.m.* Brightness, splendour, glitter.
ruitheanna, *s.pl.* The "runs" or quasi-rhymes of the old folk-tales.
ruith-fhual,‖ *s.f.* Diabetes [with the art. *an.*]
ruith-fola, *s.m.* Hæmorrhoids, piles.
ruith-gu-cladach,‖ *s.f.* Diarrhœa [with art. *an.*]
ruithiche,(MS) *s.m.* Poster (man.)
ruithil, -thle, -thlean, *s.m.* see righil.
ruith-iongrach, -aich, *s.m.* Ichor.
ruithleach, -eiche, *a.* Flowing.
ruithleadh,** *s.m.* Advolution.
ruithlean, -ein, -an, *s.m.* see roithlean.
————ach,** *a.* Having wheels or rims. 2 Having little wheels or rims.
ruith-leumnach,-aiche, *a.* Running and leaping. 2 Rampant, in *heraldry.*
ruith-mara,(WC) *s f.* Heavy wave. 2 Heavy sea.
ruithneadh,** -idh, *s.m.* Flame.
ruithteil, -e, *a.* Lickerous.

ruith-sgiùrsadh,** -aidh, *s.m.* Running the gauntlet.
ruithteach, see ruitheach & ruiteach.
———-d, see ruiteachd.
†**ruitin,**** *s.* Hucklebone. 2 Ankle. 3 Pastern.
ruladh,** -aidh, *s.m.* Slaughtering, massacre.
rùm, -ùim *pl.* -an, -aichean, & -annan, *s. m.* Room, place, space. 2 Room, chamber. 3** Floor. R. beòil, *a front room*; dean r., *make room*.
rumach, -aich, -aichean, *s.f.* Marsh, quagmire, puddle, slough.
rùmachadh, -aich, *s.m.* Act of making room or enlarging a space. A' r—, *pr. pt.* of rùmaich.
rumachail, -e, *a.* Marshy, boggy.
rumaich, -aichean, *s.f.* see rumach.
rùmaich, *pr.pt.* a' rùmachadh, *v.n.* Make room, enlarge a space, give place, stand aside.
rumail,** Convulsion. 2 Rumbling noise.
rùmail, -e, *a.* Roomy, spacious. 2 Trunked.
rùmalachd,* *s.f.* Spaciousness, roominess.
rùmball, -aill, -an, *s.m.* Tail. 2 Rump. 3 Docked tail.
———ach, -aiche, *a.* Having a large rump. 2 Pertaining to a rump.
rumhar,** -air, *s.m.* Mine.
rump,* see rumball.
rùmpull, -uill, -an, see rùmball.
rùn, -ùin, *pl.* [-ùntan, -ùinte[&] -ùintean, *s.m.* Secret, mystery, secrecy. 2 Inclination, bent, disposition. 3 Regard, love, fondness, desire, affection. 4 Object beloved. 5 Person beloved. 6 Intention, purpose, design, determination. 7 Wish. 8**Accord.
Tha r. an Tighearn aig an dream d' an eagal e, *the purpose of the Lord is with them that fearhim*; 'dè tha 'n ad r.? *what do you mean?* 'dè an r. am bheil e dhuit? *how is he disposed towards you?* tha e an r. nan tuagh dhomh, *he would wish to cut me down*; an r. nam biodag d' a chéile, *at daggers' drawing*; na innis do r. do nàmhaid ghlic no do charaid ghorach, *do not reveal your business to a wise enemy nor to a foolish friend*; tha, a rùin! *yes, my love!* mo r. a' tighinn, *my love coming*; cha'n 'eil a' bheag de m' r. dhuit, *you have nought of my love*; tìr mo rùin, *the land of my affection*; a dh' aon r., *of one mind, unanimous*; ma ni thu r. orm agus gu'm faigh mis' e, *if you will privately arrange with me so that I can get it*; tha r. orm, *I suppose* or *intend*.
rùnach, -aiche, *a.* Beloved. 2 Lovely, partial, fond. 3 Confident, trusty, trustworthy. 4 Dark, mysterious, mystical, secret. 5 Purposing.
rùnach, -aich, *s.m.* Beloved person. 2 Confidant. 3**Mistress. 4 Secret code of writing, cipher.
———adh, -aidh, *s.m.* Inclining. 2 Act of inclining or wishing. 3 Act of designing, purposing, intending or determining. 4 Loving. A' r—, *pr.pt.* of rùnaich.
rùnag, -aig, -an, *s.f.* Beloved woman. 2 Little sweetheart.
rùnaich, *pr.pt.* a' rùnachadh, *v.a. & n.* Incline, wish, desire. 2 Resolve, purpose, design, intend, determine. 3 Propose.
———, -ean, *s.m.* see rùnach.
———e,** *s.m.* Confidant. 2 Discreet person. 3 Beloved person.
———te, *past pt.* of rùnaich. Desired, wished. 2 Resolved, fixed upon, designed, definitive.
rùn-aimhleis, *s.m.* Intrigue.
rùnair, -ean, *s.m.* Secretary.
———eachd, *s. f. ind.* Secretaryship, office of secretary.
†**rùn-airm**, *s.m.* Council chamber.
†**rùn-bhocan,**** -ain, *s.m.* Pretence.
rùn-chléireach, -ich, *s.m.* Secretary. 2 Private secretary.
————d, *s.f.ind.* Business of a secretary.
rùn-chléirsneachd,** *s.f.ind.* Secretaryship. 2 Private secretaryship.
rùn-diomhair, -ùin-, *pl.* -ùin-, -ùintean & -ùntan-dìomhair, *s.m.* Secret purpose or intention. 2 Mystery. 3 Secret. 4 Private intention.
————each,** *a.* Mysterious, mystical. 2 Plotting.
rùn-falaich, -ùin-fhalaich, *s.m.* Secret love.
rungas, see rongas.
runna, see reannag.
runnach, see rumach.
runnag, see reannag.
runnsa, *s.* see ruinnse.
rùnnsan, (MS) *s.m.* Rump.
rùn-phàirteach, -eiche, *a.* Communicative, ready to communicate, communicable. 2 Apt to reveal secrets.
————, -ich, *s.m.* Partaker of a secret or mystery.
rùn-phàirteachadh, -aidh, *s.m.* Communicating 2 Act of communicating secrets. 3 Consulting. 4 Act of consulting together. 5 Partaking of a secret. A' r—, *pr.pt.* of rùn-phàirtich.
rùn-phàirtich, *pr.pt.* a' rùn-phàirteachadh, *v.a.* Communicate or disclose secrets. 2 Deliberate, consult together. 3 Partake of a secret.
rùn-phàirtichte, *a. & past pt.* of rùn-phàirtich. Communicated, disclosed. 2 Communicable.
rùnrach,* *s.m.* see rùdhbhach.
rùnraich,* *v.a.* see rudhraich.
rùn-ràite, -ùin, *pl.*-ùin- & -ùntan-ràite, *s.f.* Resolution, solemn vow, *prov.*
rùn-sheòmar, -air, -sheòmraichean, *s.m.* Council chamber.
rùntan, one of the *pls.* of rùn.
rupail,** *s.f.* Rumbling sound, continued rumbling.
ruparachadh, *s.m.* Scandalizing—*Suth'd.*
rù-rà, (CR) *adv.* Jumbled, confused, mixed up —*W. of Ross-shire.* 2 Topsy-turvy—*Arran.*
rùrach,†† *a.* see rùdhrach.
rùrachadh,†† -aidh, *s.m.* see rùdhrachadh.
rùraich, see rùdhraich.
rùraich, see rùdhrach.
rurgaid, *s.f.* Rhubarb. 2 *prov.* for purgaid.
rurgaideach,**a.* Abounding in, or like, rhubarb.
†**rus**, -uis, *s.m.* Knowledge. 2 Skill. 3 Wood.
rùsail,†† *v.* see rùsal.
rùsal, *pr. pt.* a' rùsladh, *v. a.* Search, turn over things. 2 Scratch, scrape.
rusar, see raosar.
rusg,** *v.a.* Beat, strike, pelt.
rùsg, -ùisg, -an, *s.m.* External covering, rind, skin, husk. 2 Bark of a tree. 3 Fleece of wool. 4 Shell. Neòil 'nan rùsgaibh bàna, *clouds in white fleeces.*
rùsgach, -aiche, *a.* Having a covering, as a rind, skin or husk. 2 Fleecy. 3 Fleecing, that fleeces, peels, or takes off the covering or husk, stripping. 4 Having many rinds, as an onion. 5**Crustaceous. Reithe garbh-rùsgach, *a thick-fleeced ram.*
rùsgadh, -aidh, *s.m.* Peeling. 2 Act of peeling, fleecing, or taking off the bark or any covering. 3 Discovering. 4 Act of discovering, disclosing or revealing. 5 Driving thatch off. 6 Shelling. 7 Fleece. 8 Husk. 9 Stripping. undressing, making bare or naked. 10 Unsheathing. A' r—, *pr.pt.* of rùisg.
rùsgadh, -aidh, *s.m.* Chafing (also fuithein.) R. cléibh, *hoarseness*; r. air basaibh, *excoriations*

on the palms.
rùsgail,** a. Epispastic.
rùsgair, -ean, s.m. Strong clumsy fellow, prov.
rùsgaireachd, s.f.ind. Clumsy strength, prov.

611. Rùsgan 6.

rùsgan, -ain, -an, s.m., dim. of rùsg. Any little or thin covering, as a rind or husk. 2 Piece of skin peeled off. 3 Little fleece. 4 Circular dish made of roots, used to measure meal, &c. 5 Small boat made of bark. 6 Kind of basket (ill. by M. McD.)
rùslach,** a. Scratching, excoriating.
rùsladh, -aidh, s.m. Searching. 2 Act of searching or overturning things in searching. 3 Scraping. 4 Act of scraping or scratching. A' r—, pr.pt. of rùsal.
†rustach, a. Rude, clownish, Gaelic form of rustic.
†rustach, -aich, -aichean, s.m. Boor, churl. Gaelic form of rustic.
rustag,** -aig, s.m. Bear.
rustan, -ain, -an, s.m. Lump. 2 Hillock, heap.
rut,* v.a. Rust, corrode—Arran.
rùta, rùtan, -chan & rùtaichean, s.m. Ram, 2 Ridgling, tup. see ruig.
ruta,** } s.m. Herd, rout. 2 Tribe of
rutadh, -aidh, } people.
rùtach, a. Abounding in rams.
rùtachd, s.f.ind. Rutting.
rutaidh, a. Surly, butting, bumping, bumptious, ram-like.
rùtan, -ain, -an, s.m.dim. of rùta. Little ram or ridgling. 2 Horn of a roe-buck.
rùtas, s.m. Greed.
ruth,(AC) s. Desire, genesis, generation, procreation. 2 Prosperity. Car. Gad. 2. 164.
ruth,** s.m. Chain. 2 Link. 3 (AF) Skate, thornback. 4**Salary, wages, hire.
rutha, -chan, s.m. see rudha.
rùtha, -chan, s.m. (AF) Hedgehog. 2 see sornan.
ruthach, -aiche, a. see rudhach.
ruthadh, -aidh, -aidhean, s.m. see rudhadh.
rùthag, -aig, -an, s.f. see rùdhag.
rùthan, -ain, see rùghan.
rutharach, -aiche, a. Quarrelsome, fighting.
rutharachd, s.f.ind. Quarrelsomeness. 2 Continued or frequent fighting.

S s

s, (Suil, willow-tree) the 16th. letter of the Gaelic alphabet now in use. It has two sounds—1st., small like sh, in sheet, when, in the same syllable, it is preceded or followed by e or i, as, bris, break; séimh, quiet; sniomh, twine; stéidh, foundation. 2nd. broad, like s in sun, this, in all other situations. Exceptions—is, am, (pron. iss); so, this, (pron, sho, and accordingly spelt seo in this work); sud, yon, (pron. shoot, and accordingly spelt siod in this work.) S, when aspirated, is like h in him, as, shuidh, sat (pron, hooie); shrann, snorted (hrawn.—aw as ow in brown.) Before l and n, sh is almost, if not altogether silent, as, shlanuich, healed; shniomh, twisted. S, followed by a mute consonant is never aspirated. S, when preceded by the letter t with a hyphen is silent, as an t-sluaigh, of the people (pron. an tlooay.) 'S in expressions such as "'s e seo an duine," is sounded as sh.

The slender sound of s is heard in Arran in iseal (ìosal, low,) and treise (treasa, stronger), esan, (pron. eisean) piseir (pease,) uirsinn (door-post,) deis (ready,) dìlis (faithful,) faileis (shadow.) There is no s sound in Arran and Kintyre in the combinations rd and rt, as, bòrd, mart, cairt, &c. In rtl, neither s nor t is heard as, ceirtle, fairtlich. An seo, an sin, an siod, are sometimes pronounced an t-seo, an t-sin, an t-siod, and sometimes ann a seo, ann a sin, ann a siod; and ann an seo, ann an sin, ann an siod. Initial sr has no inserted t, as, srath, sruth (not strath, struth), except strac (to tear) stràc, (to stroke) and strub (a spout.) Some dialects, on the contrary, have strath, stròn, &c., but srac and srub. Before l, followed by a slender vowel, as, slighe, sleamhuinn, s has its sh sound, and not, as in some districts, its broad sound.

's, cont. for agus. 'S their thu, and thou shalt say; là de na làithean 's am famhair bho 'n bhaile, one day when the giant was from home.
's, cont. for is, v. 'S i' it is she; 's e, it is he; 's esan, it is he himself; 's mór t' fhacal, ostentatious is thy word.
's, contr. for anns. 'Sa cheò, in the mist, in amazement.
s', cont. for seo.
-s', cont. for -sa, -san and -se. Thus' for thusa; iad-s' for iad-san.
-sa, Emphatic adjection used in connection with possessive pronouns and adjoined to the noun following them. If the noun is followed by an adjective, the syllable -sa is placed after the adjective, thus, do làmh-sa, thine own hand; do làmh gheal-sa, thine own white hand. It becomes -ne when used in connection with ar, our, as, ar n-athair-ne, our own father; and -san when in connection with an, am, their, as, an taigh-san, their own house.
sa, Emphatic syllable used in combination with the personal pronouns. It becomes se after a small vowel (ne in the 1st. per. pl.) and san in the 3rd. per. sing. & pl. Mi, mise; thu, thusa; e, esan; i, ise; sinn, sinne; sibh, sibhse; iad, iadsan.
'sa, cont. for anns an. In the. 'Sa cheò, in the mist, in amazement. 2 cont. for anns, prep., and a, pers.pron.
sa, prov. for seo. (Used as a suffix.)
†sab, a. Strong, able,
†sab, s.m. Death. 2 Bolt, bar.
sabadh,** -aidh, s.m. see sabaid.
Sàbaid, -e, -ean, s.f. The Sabbath.
sabaid, -e, -ean, s.f. Brawl, quarrel, fight, fray, row.
——each, -eiche, a. Brawling, quarrelsome, given to fighting or strife.
sàbaideach, -eiche, a. Sabbatical, of, or belonging to the Sabbath.
———d, s.f. Sabbatism.
sabaideachd,* s.f.ind. Quarrelsomeness.
sabaidiche, s. Brawler.
sabail,** s.f. see sabhal.
Sàbailt, s.f. see Sàbaid.
Sàbainnd, see Sàbaid.
sabh, s.m. see samh.
sàbh, -àibh, -an, s.m. Ointment, salve. 2**Spittle. 3**Bolt, bar of a gate. [‡sabh.]
sàbh, -àibh, pl. -àibh & -an, s.m. Saw. S.-làimh, or s.-sgrìob, a hand-saw; s.-duirn, a whip-saw, hand-saw; s.-mór, two-handled saw for

use in a saw-pit.
sabh, -aibh, -an, *s.f.* see samh.
sàbh, *pr.pt.* a' sàbhadh, *v.a.* Saw, cut with a saw.
sàbhach, -aiche, *a.* Of, or belonging to, saws. 2 Cutting, as a saw. 3 Of, or belonging to, ointment or salves. 4 Having healing ointments. 5 Like a healing ointment.
sabhach, -aiche, *a.* see samhach. 2**Quarrelsome.
sabhadair,* see sabhdair.
sàbhadair, -ean, *s.m.* Sawyer.
————eachd, *s.f.ind.* Occupation of a sawyer. 2 Process of sawing.
sàbhadh, -aidh, *s.m.* Sawing. 2 Act of sawing. A' s—, *pr.pt.* of sàbh. Air a sh., *sawn;* muileann sàbhaidh, *a saw-mill;* sloc-sàbhaidh, *a saw-pit.*
sabhadh, -aidh, *s.m.* see samh. 2 Quarrel.
sàbhaig, *v.* see sàbh.
————eadh, *s.m.* see sàbhadh.
————te, see sàbhta.
sàbhail, *pr.pt.* a' sàbhaladh, *v.a.* Save, rescue. 2 Spare. 3 Protect, defend. 4 Preserve, use frugally.
sabhail,** *v.a.* Store up in a barn.
sabhail, *gen. sing.* of sabhail.
sàbhail,** *s.f.* Saving, protecting, sparing. 2 Protection, 3 Frugality.
————each,** *a.* see sàbhailteach.
————eachd, see sàbhailteachd.
sàbhailich, see sàbhail.
sàbhailich, -ean, *s.m.* Preserver, one who save or rescues. 2 Economist, frugal persons.
sàbhailiche,** *s.m.* Frugal man, economist. 2 Preserver.
sàbhailt, -e, *a.* Safe. 2 Saved, rescued. 3 Spared. 4 Protected, defended.
————e, *past pt.* of sàbhailt.
————each, -eiche, *a.* Saving, rescuing. 2 Sparing. 3 Protecting, defending. 4 Frugal, economical.
————eachd, *s.f.* Security, safety, safe state or condition. 2 Saving disposition.
sàbhair, see sàbhadair.
————eachd, see sàbhadaireachd.
sabhairle,** Mastiff, cur.
————an,(AF) *s.m.* Mastiff.
sabhal, -ail,*pl.* -an & saibhlean,*s.m.* Barn, granary.
————ach, -aiche, *a.* Of, or belonging to barns. 2 Like a barn.
sàbhalach, see sàbhailteach.
sàbhalachd, see sàbhailteachd.
sàbhaladh, -aidh, *s.m.* Saving. 2 Act of saving, rescuing or sparing, salvation. 3 Protecting, defending. 4 Preserving. 5 Retrenchment. 6 Preservation. 7 Frugality. A' s—, *pr.pt.* of sàbhail. Is mór an s. sin, *that is a great retrenchment.*
sàbhalaich, see sàbhailiche.
————e,** *s.m.* Frugal person. 2 Protector, preserver, saviour.
sàbhaltachd, *s.f.ind.* } see sàbhailteachd. 2
sàbhaltas, -ais, *s.m.* } **Parsimony, frugality, economy.
sabhan, see samhan. 2|(AF) Mastiff, cur. 3** Cub.
sàbhan, -ain, *pl.* -an & -ain, *s.m., dim.* of sàbh. Little saw.
sàbhan, *n.pl.* of sàbh.
sàbhanach,* *a.* Pertaining to a little saw. 2 Like a little saw.
†sabhas, -ais, see sabhs.
†sabhasair, -ean, see sabhsair.
sabhd, -a, -an, *s.m.* Lie, fable, *prov.*
sabhd, *a.* Straying. Cù s., *a stray dog;* chaidh e air s., *he strayed away.*
sabhdach, -aiche, *a.* Lying, fabulous, *prov.*
sabhdag, -aig, -an, *s.f.ind., dim.* of sabhd. Little lie, fib, *prov.*
sabhdagach, -aiche, *a.* Telling little lies.
sabhdair, -ean, *s.m.* Liar, fabulist, foolish talker. 2 Stroller, lounger.
sabhdaireachd, *s.f.* Habit of lying. 2 Lies, foolish talk. 3 Strolling, lounging.
sàbh-duirn, *s.m.* Whip-saw. 2* Hand-saw.
sàbhlach,** *a.* Healing, like a salve, unctuous.
sàbhlach,** -aich, *s.m.* Spittle.
sàbhladh,** -aidh,*s.m.* Salve, healing ointment. 2 Stirring up. as of corn in a barn.
sàbh-mór,* *s.m.* Whip-saw.
sabhs, saibhse, -an, *s.m.* Sauce of any kind. 2 *Gravy. 3 (DU) Water in which fish has been boiled. S. éisg, *fish-sauce.*
sabhsach, -aiche, *a.* Of, or belonging to sauce. 2 Like sauce. 3 Abounding in fish-soup.
sabhsachadh, -aidh, *s.m.* Seasoning. 2 Act of seasoning with sauce. A' s—, *pr.pt.* of sabhsaich.
sabhsaich, *v.a.* Season with sauce.
————te, *past pt.* of sabhsaich. Seasoned with sauce.
sabhsair, -ean, *s.m.* Sausage. 2**One who makes sauce.
sabhsaireachd,** *s.f.* Sauce-making. 2 Sausage-making.
sàbh-shùil, -aibh-, -an-, *s.m.* Eye-salve.
sabhstair, see sabhsair.
sabhuil, see sabhal.
Sàboinn, } *Lewis* for Sàbaid.
Sàboinnd, }
sac, -aic, *pl.* -aic, & -an, *s.m.* Sack, bag. 2 Burden, load. 3 Horse-load, cart-load. 4 (DC) Asthma—*Uist.* 5 Measure of corn (5 bushels.) 6**Measure of coals (3 bushels.) 7 *in derision,* Short, fat fellow. Tha s. air, *he has asthma;* s. mine, *a sack of meal;* s.-mine, *a meal-sack;* s. droma, *a back-load, a man's load;* s. imrich, *a load of furniture at a flitting;* s. uisge-beatha,*a pack-saddle with a cask of whisky on each side;* s.-shrathair, *a pack-saddle.*
sac, *v.a.* see sacaich.
sacach, -aiche, *a.* Having sacks or bags. 2 Having many sacks. 3 Like a sack or bag. 4 Carrying a load or burden. 5‡‡That burdens or loads. 6**Short and corpulent.
sacachadh, -aidh, *s.m.* Loading. 2 Act of laying on of a burden. 3 Act of pressing into a bag. 4 Putting up in a bag or sack. A' s—, *pr.pt.* of sacaich.
sacadh, *s.m.* & *pr.pt.* of sac. Same meanings as sacachadh.
sacaich, *v.a.* Load, lay on a burden, as on a horse. 2 Press or put into a bag or sack 3** Fill to satiety.
sacaichte, *past pt.* of sacaich. Loaded. 2 Pressed into a bag, as grain. 3 Filled to satiety.
sacaid,** -ean, *s.f.* Little bag or sack.
sacail, -e, *a.* Like a sack or bag. 2 That loads or presses by weight. 3 Heavy, burdensome.
sacail, *s.f.* see sacachadh.
†sacair,** *s.m.* Priest.
sacan, -ain, -an, *s.m., dim.* of sac. Little sack or bag. 2 Little load or burden. 3 Trifling fellow. 4 Unmannnerly or impudent fellow. 5**Short, corpulent fellow.
sacanta, -ainte, *a.* Like a bag or sack. 2 Corpulent, squat. 3 Trifling. 4 Impudent.
sacantachd, *s.f.* Corpulency, squatness. 2 Impudence.
sac-aodach, -aich, *s.m.* see aodach-saic.
sacarbhuig,** *s.f.* A confession.

sacbut, Gaelic spelling of *sackbut*.
†sach, *v.a.* Sack, besiege.
sàchair, -e, *s.f.* see sàmhchair.
sachasan, -ain, -an, *s.m.* Sand-eel, lesser launce.
sachasanach, -aiche, *a.* Of, or belonging to, sand-eels. 2 Abounding in sand-eels.
sachc, sachd, } see sac.
sachdachadh, see sacachadh.
sachdadh, see sacachadh.
sachdaich, see sacaich.
saclan,** *s.m.* Standard.
sacraidh, *s.f.coll.* Baggage, luggage.
sacraigh, see sacraidh.
sacrail,** *s.f.* Sacrifice.
sàcramaid, -ean, *s.f.* Sacrament.
sàcramaideach, -eiche, *a.* Sacramental.
sàcramaind, see sàcramaid.
sac-shrathair, -thrach & -e, *pl.* -ean, *s.f.* Pack-saddle.
sad, -aid, *s. m.* Small dust shaken out of anything by striking or beating. 2 Smart blow, thud, dump. 3 Dislike, aversion. 4 (JM) 5 see dad. 6 Seed—*Lewis*. 7 (DU) Water splashed about, froth of waves. 8 The sea breaking over anything. 9 Meal-dust. Ghabh e s. dheth, *he conceived a dislike to it.*
sad, *pr.pt.* a' sadadh, *v. a.* Shake or brush off dust. 2 Beat, thump, fustigate. 3(DC) Throw, as peats or stones—*Uist*. 4 *Dash upon, as dust.
sadach, -aich, *s.f.* Meal-dust. 2 Mill-dust. 3 Saw-dust. 4 Dust of any description. 5 Small drizzling rain.
sadach, -aiche, *a.* Of, or belonging to, small dust. 2 That shakes out, or shakes off dust. 3 Causing dislike, aversion or nausea.
sadachadh, -aidh, *s.m.* & *pr.pt.* of sadaich. Same meanings as sadadh.
sadach-shàbhaidh, *s.f.* Saw-dust.
sadadh, -aidh, *s.m.* Brushing. 2 Act of brushing off dust by striking. 3 Beating. 4 Act of beating or thumping. 5**Whisk. 6 Sowing of seed.—*W. of Ross-shire.* A' s—, *pr.pt.* of sad. 'Ga sh. 'nam shùilean, *dusting it in my eyes.*
sadaibh, (i. e. an sadaibh) *adv.* In haste.
sadaich, -e, -ean, *s.f.* Brush. 2 Anything to strike or beat off dust, whisk.
———, *v.a.* Dust. 2 Beat dust out of cloth.
———te, *past pt.* of sadaich. Dusted. 2 Brushed.
sadanach, -aiche, *a.* see soideanach.
sad-bhuille, -an, *s.f.* Smart stroke, thump.
sad-bhuilleach, -eiche, *a.* Giving smart blows or thumps.
sadhail,** *a.* Pleasant.
sadhail,** *s.f.* Neglect. 2 Delight. 3 Good house.
sadhal,**-ail, -an, *s.m.* Saddle.
sàdhalachd, see sòdhalachd.
sadharcan, (AF) *s.m.* Lapwing, see adharcan-luachrach. 2 Grey plover.
saduich, see sadaich.
†saeth, *s.* Labour, tribulation, disease.
saf, (MS) *s.* Zaffer.
†sàgan, -ain, -an, *s.m.* Roundel, circle. 2 Fold of a serpent. 3 Spire.
sagart, -airt, -an & -airtean, *s.m.* Priest. 2** Churchman. Ciod is fhiach s. gun chlèireach? *of what use is a priest without a clerk?* cha bhi dùthchas aig mnaoi no aig sagart, *neither a woman nor a priest may have any local ties—they must go where the necessities of husband or church demand.*
sagart, *s.m.* Ram with one of its testicles wanting—*Lewis.*
sagartach, -aiche, *a.* see sagartail.
sagartachd, *s.f.ind.* Priesthood.
sagartail, -e, *a.* Priestly, priestlike, clerical. 2 *rarely* Pious, holy.
sagartalachd, *s.f.ind.* Priestliness.
†sàgh, sàigh, *s.f.* Bitch.
†sàgh, *v.a.* Drink, suck, guzzle.
sàgh, see sàth.
sàghach, see sàthach.
saghaidh, -e, -ean, see saobhaidh.
saghail,** *s.f.* Attack.
†saghain, see samhan. 2 see saigh.
saghal,** *a.* Nice, tender.
saghalachd,** *s.f.* Delight, content. 2 Voluptuousness.
sagharlachd,** *s.f.* Delight, satisfaction, content.
sagh'ic-tìre, (AF) Wolf.
†saghmhair, *s.m.* Sink, kennel.
sàibh, *gen.sing.* of sàbh.
saibhin, see samhan.
saibhir, see saoibhir, *a.* & saoibhrich, *v.* 2(MS) *a.* Able.
saibhir, (MS) *a.* Lascivious.
saibhir, -ean, *s.f.* Watercourse below a road for a stream to run through, covered with stone lintels, as a sewer, conduit.
saibhire, *comp.* of saibhir.
saibhireach, see saoibhreach.
saibhireachd, see saoibhreas.
saibhleach,†† *a.* see sabhalach.
saibhlean, *n.pl.* of sabhal.
saibhlich, (MS) *v.a.* Garner.
sàibhreach, (MS) *a.* Auspicious.
saibhreachadh, see saoibhreachadh.
saibhreachd, see saoibhreas.
saibhreas, see saoibhreas.
sàibhreas, (MS) Auspiciousness.
saibhrich, see saoibhrich.
saibhrichte, see saoibhrichte.
saic, *gen.sing.* & *n.pl.* of sac.
saic-dhìollaid,** *s.f.* Pack-saddle.
saicean, -ein, -an, *s.m.* see sacan.
saic-éideadh, -idh, see aodach-saic.
saic-eudach, see aodach-saic.
†saich, *s.m.* Plenty, enough. 2 Bellyful.
sàich,** *a.* Sated. (sàthach)
saich, (CR) *a.* Ill, bad in health—*Perthshire.*
†saide, *s.f.* Seat, couch.
saidealach, see soidealtach, *s.* & soidealta, *a.*
saidealachd, see soidealtachd.
saidealta, -eilte, see soidealta.
saidealtach, see soidealtach.
saidealtachd, see soidealtachd.
saidealtas, -ais, see soidealtas.
saidh, -e, -ean, *s.f.* Any upright beam, post. 2 Prow of a ship or boat. 3 Handle of any instrument. 4 The part of any blade that is inserted in the handle. 5 Chevron in *heraldry*. 6 **Bitch. 7**Mildness. 8**Treasury. 9 Edge. 10 Brach. 11 see saoidhean.
612. Saidh, 5.
saidhbhir, see saoibhir.
saidh-dheireadh,* *s.f.* Stern-post of a boat, see O 1, p. 73.
saidhe, *s.m.ind.* Hay. Feur-saidhe, *grass kept for hay; 2 hay.*
saidheadair, -ean, *s.m.* Mower, hay-cutter.
saidhean, -ein, *s.m.* Coal-fish in 2nd. and 3rd. years, saith. see saoidhean.
saidhean, *s.pl.* see saidh-dheireadh & saidh-thoisich.
†saidhiste, *s.f.* Seat.
saidhlich, (MS) *v.a.* Garner.
saidh-thoisich, *s.f.* Stem-post of a boat, see N 1, p. 73.
†saidir, -e, see làidir.

saidse, -an, *s.f.* Sound of a falling body. 2 Crash.
saidse,(DMK) *s.* Hurry, haste. Cuir s. ris an teine, *blow up the fire and add fuel to it;* chuir iad s. ris a' bhuain, *they expedited the reaping.*
saidse,§ *s.f.* Chives, see feuran.
saidseach, -eich, *a.* Making a noise, as a falling body, crashing.
saidseach, -ich, *s.f.* Beggar's mantle, *prov.* 2** Wallet.
saidsear,* *s.m.* Heavy, clumsy man.
saifear, -eir, *s.m.* Gaelic form of *sapphire.*
saifearach, *a.* Abounding in, or like, sapphires.
saigean, -ein, -an, *s.m.* Corpulent, little man.
saigeanach, -aiche, *a.* see saigeanta.
saigeanach, -aich, *s.m.* see saigean.
saigeanna,** see saigeanta.
saigeanta, -einte, *a.* Short and corpulent.
saigeantach, *a.* Short and corpulent. Duine s., *a short, corpulent man.*
saigeantachd, *s.f.* Corpulency and shortness of stature.
saigh, -e, -ean, *s.f.* Bitch, female dog. †2 Sharp edge, sharp point. 3 see saoidhean. Cuimhnich an t-saigh earblach dhonn, *remember the brown bitch with the big tail—L. na F. 199.3, 200 a 2.*
saigh-chulanach, see saigh.
saighd,* *v.* see saighead.
saighde, *gen.sing.* of saighead.
saighdeach, -eiche, *a.* Arrowy, like an arrow. 2 Furnished with arrows. 3 Pointed. 4*Piercing.
saighdeadh, -eidh, *s.m.* Darting, act of darting forward, as an arrow. 2* Popping or dashing forward. A' s—, *pr.pt.* of saighead.
saighdean, *n.pl.* of saighead.
saighdear, -eir, -an, *s.m.* Soldier. 2 Brave man. 3 Active, mettlesome fellow. 4 The sign Sagittarius (♐) in the zodiac.
s.-coise, *infantryman, foot-soldier.*
s.-eachraidh, *cavalryman, dragoon.*
s.-fairge, *a marine.*
s.-mara, *a marine.*
s.-tochlaidh, *a pioneer.*
Saighdearan dearga, *red-coats,* a name given to the government soldiers in the risings of 1715 and 1745, in contra-distinction to the supporters of the Stuart cause, who were generally known as " saighdearan dubha."
saighdearach, -aiche, *a.* Of, or belonging to soldiers. 2 Military, martial.
saighdearachd, *s.f.* Soldiership, soldiering, the profession of a soldier, the army. 2 Bravery, heroism. 3 Agility, activity.
saighdearachd, *s.f.* Archery.
saighdeireil, -e, *a.* Soldier-like, brave, warlike, martial. 2* Regimental.
saighead, saighde, -ghdean, *s.f.* Arrow, dart. 2 Stitch. S. neimhe, *a poisoned arrow.*
saighead, *v.n.* Dart forward, as an arrow. 2 Move swiftly.
saigheadach, -aiche, *a.* see saighdeach.
saigheadair, *s.m.* Arrow-maker. 2 Archer. 3 see saighdear.
————-each. *a.* Of, or belonging to, arrow-makers, or 2 archers.
saighead-shìth, *s.f.* Fairy-arrow—the popular name for the flint arrow-heads so much prized by antiquaries.
saigheas, -eis, *s.m.* Age, old age. 2 Antiquity, oldness.
saigheil, -e, *a.* see sòghail.
saighein, see saoidhean.
saighnean,** -ein, *s.m.* Lightning. 2 Hurricane.
sàignteach, *a.* Piercing, cutting.
sail, -e, -ean & sailthean, *s.f.* Beam, joist, log of wood. Crùth sailthean, *beams with engraved figures.—Sgeulaiche-nan-caol.*
†sail, -e, -ean, *s.f.* Willow-tree. 2 The letter S.
sàil,* *s.m.ind.* see sàl.
sail, see taileadh.
†sail, *v.a.* Salute.
sàil, -e, **sàl & sàlach, *pl.* -ean & -ltean, *s.f.* Heel. S. beinne, *the foot of a hill.*
sàil, *v.a.* Provide with heels, as shoes.
†sàil, *s.f.* Guard, custody.
sail-bhreaghadh, -aidh, *s.m.* Rejoicing.
sàil-bhroillich, *s.f.* Front cross-beam of a cart—*Isles.*
sàil-bhrùth, see sàil-bhrùthadh.
sàil-bhrùthadh, -aidh, *s.m.* Bruise on the heel.
sail-bhuinn, -e, -ean-b-, *s.f.* The sole. 2 Lower beam of a partition. 3 Lower cross-bar of "crann-deilbhe."
sàil-bhuinn,§ -e, -ean-b-, *s.f.* Groundsel, see bualan.
sailche, *comp.* of salach.
sailchead, -eid, *s.m.* Dirt, degree of dirtiness. 2 ‡‡Drossiness. 3 Defilement.
sailcheas, -is, *s.m.* Bad taste. 2 Musty smell.
sail-chuach, -aich, -an, *s.f.* Dog-violet, see dail-chuach. 2**Pansy. Coille is guirme s., *a wood where the violet is bluest.*
sail-chuachach,†† *a.* Abounding in dog-violets. 2 Pertaining to dog-violets.
sàil-chuachag, -aig, *s.f.* Young dog-violet, little dog-violet.
sail-dheiridh, *s.f.* Hind cross-beam of a cart—*Isles.* 2 Box of a cart.
†saile, *s.f.* Saliva.
sàile, see sàl.
sàileach, -eiche, *a.* Pertaining to a heel. 2 see salach.
saileadh, see taileadh.
sàileag, -eig, -an, *s.f.,dim.* of sàil. Little heel. 2 Heel-step. 3 Heel-piece.
saileag, -eig, -an, *s.f. dim.* of sail. Little beam. 2 Little willow, young willow.
sàileagach, -aiche, *a.* Abounding in creeks, bays or inlets of the sea.
sailean, -ein, -an, *s.m.* Willow—*Arran.*
sàilean, -ein, -an, *s.m.* Little inlet or arm of the sea, deep bay.
sàileanach, *a.* Abounding in little creeks or inlets. 2 Like, or of a bay or firth.
sàileanta, *a.* Brinish.
†sàilear, -eir, -an, *s.m.* Cavern, grotto.
sàilear,(MS) *s.m.* Sailor.
sàileas, -ais, *s.m.* Salt water. 2 The sea.
saileid, *s.f.* Gaelic form of *salad.*
sailetheach, (AF) *s.* Hind.
sàil-ghille, -an, *s.m.* Footman, page.
sàilich,(MS) *v.a.* Heel, as shoes.
sailinn, *pl.* -tean, see sàilean.
saill, -e, *s.f.* Fatness. 2 Fat, blubber. 3*¦Suet, grease. 4 Pickle, brine. Saill nan dubhan, *the fat of the kidneys;* fillean saille, *collops of fat.*
saill, *pr.pt.* a' sailleadh, *v.a.* Salt, season, cure or pickle with salt.
sailleach, -eiche, *a.* Having fat. 2 Fat, corpulent. 3 Greasy. 4* Full of suet.
sailleach, -ich, *s.* see seileach.
sailleachan, -ain, -an, *s. m.* Salting-tub. 2‡‡ Beef-stand.
sailleachd,** *s.f.* Fatness, fat. 2 Greasiness. 3 Corpulence.
sailleadair, -ean, *s.m.* Salter. 2 Fish-curer.
————-eachd, *s.f.ind.* Process of salting or curing with salt.
sailleadh, -idh, *s.m.* Salting, act of salting. 2 Pickling. 3 Salt, saltness. A' s—, *pr. pt.* of saill.

sailleann, -inn, *s. m.* Weaver's paste, used to smoothe the thread.
saillear, -ir, -an, *s.m.* Salt-cellar, tub or cask. 2 Cellar for storing salted fish. 3†† Salter, fish-curer.
———, *a*, see sailleir.
———, *fut.pass.* of saill. Shall be salted.
———ach,** *a.* Of, or belonging to, a salter or pickler.
———achd,** *s.f.ind.* Business of a salter or pickler.
sailleil,** *a.* Unctuous.
sailleir,†† *a.* Fat, fed. 2 Greasy. 3 Corpulent. 4 Lusty.
saillmhor, -oire, *a.* Fatted, fat and full. 2 Greasy. 3 Pickled.
sàil-lom,‖ *s.f.* Flat foot.
saillte, *a, & past pt.* of saill. Salted, seasoned, pickled. 2 Salt, tasting of salt, briny. Bùrn s., *salt-water.*
saillteach, see saillte.
———d, *s.f.ind.* Saltness. 2(MS) Brine. S. t' uisgeachan, *the saltness of thy waters.*
sailm, -e, -ean, *s.f.* Decoction. 2‡ Oak-bark decoction to staunch blood. 3‡ Consumptive pectoral. S. uchd, *a pectoral given in a case of consumption, made of rose leaves and sugar-candy.*
———, *gen.sing. & n.pl.* of salm.
——— -dharaich,** *s.m.* Decoction of oak-bark.
———eachd,** *s.f.* Psalmody.
——— -uchd,** *s.m.* Ointment of which fresh butter and healing herbs are the principal ingredients.
sail-mhullaich, *s.f.* Upper cross-bar of crann-deilbhe.
sail-spiorad,** -aid, *s.m.* Guardian spirit.
sàilteachadh,** *s.m.* Tracing or following footsteps.
sailteachd, see saillteachd.
sàiltean, *n.pl.* of sàil. Heels. 2 Steps, footsteps. 3 Vestiges.
sailteart, -eirt, see saltairt.
sàiltheach,†† *a.* see sàileach.
sailtheach, -ich, -ichean, *s.f.* Big, fat or lusty housewife.
sailtheach,** *a.* Beamed, joisted. 2 Like a beam or joist.
sailthean, *pl.* of sail. S. a sheòmra, *the beams of his chambers.*
sàilthean-màis, } *s.pl.* Stots of a cart, see p.
——— -ùrlair, } 152.
sailtich,** *v.a.* Provide with beams or joists.
sàiltich,** *v.a.* Follow by tracing the footsteps.
sailtichean, *s.pl.* Hatches of a ship. 2 Steps.
sailtichte,** *past pt.* Provided with beams or joists.
sàiltichte,** *past pt.* Heeled, provided with heels, as shoes.

612. Saimbhir.

sail-ùrlair, *s. f.* Summer, the central beam of a floor that receives the joists.
†saim, *a.* Rich.
saimbhir,‡ *s.* Samphire—*crithmum maritimum.*
sàimh, -e, *s.f.* Luxury, pleasure, delight, ease. 2 Sensuality. 3 Peace, peacefulness, quietness, stillness. 4**Joy. 5 Quiet spot. An lear an s. shuaine, *the sea in profound repose.*
saimh,** *a.* Quiet, still. 2 Mild, pleasant. 3 Sweet. Ri oidhche s., *on a quiet night.*
†saimh, *s.pl.* Twins, pair, brace, couple.
saimh, *gen.sing.* of samh.
——— -bhreitheach,** *a.* Twin-producing.
sàimh-bhriathar, -air, -thran, *s. m.* Flattering word or speech. 2 Smooth language.
sàimh-bhriathrach, -aiche, *a.* Flattering, cajoling.
———————as,** -ais, *s.m.* Cajoling language.
sàimhche, *comp.* of sàmhach.
———ad, -eid, *s.m.* Degree of tranquility.
sàimh-chealg, -cheilg, *s.f.* Hypocrisy. [McL & D gives sàimh-cheilg as *nom.*]
sàimh-chealgach, -aiche, *a.* Hypocritical.
saimhe,‡ *s.f.* Luxury. 2 Sensuality.
———ach,** *a.* Luxurious. 2 Fond of ease or pleasure.
†saimheach, -eiche, *a.* Pleasant.
saimheachas,** -ais, *s.m.* Luxury. 2 Fondness of ease or pleasure.
sàimheachd, *s.f.ind.* Love of pleasure. 2 State of luxury or pleasure. 3 Luxurious habit.
sàimhear, -ean, *s.m.* Sensualist.
saimh-ghrìos,** *v.a.* Allure, entice.
———ach,** *a.* Alluring, enticing.
saimh-ghrìosadh,** *s. m.* Enticement, allurement.
saimhiche,** *s.m.* Votary of pleasure.
sàimhiche, *comp.* of sàmhach.
sàimhich,(MS) *v.* Allay.
†saimhin, -ean, *s.m.* Bait, allurement.
saimhneachadh,** *s.m.* Yoking, coupling.
saimhnich,** *v.a.* Yoke, couple.
———te, *past pt.* Yoked, coupled.
†saimhrighe, *s.pl.* Lovers of pleasure.
saimhrigheach,** *a.* Easy, satisfied, content. 2 Quiet.
———d,** *s. f.* Ease, satisfaction. 2 Quiet.
saimhsealair,** -ean, *s.m.* Counsellor.
saimir, *s.f.* Trefoil clover.
sain,** *a.* Sound, healthy.
†sain, *v.a.* Vary, alter, change.
†sain-chreach,** *a.* Healed, sound.
saindrean,** *s.m.* Seat. 2 Society.
saineas,** *s.m.* Diversity, variety. 2††Sedition.
†saine, *s.f.* Variety, variation. 2 Soundness. 3 Sedition. 4 Discord.
saineil,** *a.* Graceful, beautiful, handsome. 2 Various.
sain-fhios, -a, -an, see sanas.
sainis,†† -e, -ean, see sanas.
———each, -eiche, see sanasach.
sainn,(AC) *s.* Coveting.
sainnseal, -eil, -an, *s. m.* New year's gift. 2 Handsel.
———ach, -aiche, *a.* Belonging to a handsel, or New year's gift. 2 Sending New year's gifts.
———aich,†† *pr. pt.* a' sainnsealachadh, *v. a.* Give a New year's gift.
———aiche, -an, *s.m.* Giver of a New year's gift.
saiunt, see sannt.
sainntreabh, see saintreabh.
sainre,** *s.f.* Reddish purple, sanguine colour.

2 Flesh colour.
saintreabh,** *s.* Family, house.
saipeid,(AH) *s.f.* Full meal.
saiphir, see sàpair.
saipleis,(MS) *s.* Suds.
sàir, *gen.sing. & n.pl.* of sàr.
sairse,** *s.f.* Sieve.
sàirbhrigh, -e, -ean, *s. f.* Attribute. [also sàr-bhrigh.]
sàir-chiall, -chéille, *s.f.* Good sense.
sàirdeal, -eil, -an, see sàrdail.
——ach, see sàrdaileach.
sàir-eòlas, -ais, *s.m.* Great skill.
sàir-fhios, see sàr-fhios.
sàir-ghnìomh, -a, -ara, *s.m.* Noble action.
sàisde,§ *s.m.*(*f.***) Garden sage, see athair-liath.
sàisdeach,** *a.* Of, like, or abounding in, sage.
sàisde bheag,** *s.f.* Small garden sage—*salvia hortensis major vulgaris.*
sàisde chnuic,§ *s.m.* Mountain-sage—*salvia alpina.*
sàisde-coille,§ *s.m.* Wood-sage—*teucrium scorodonia.* [** gives *salvia agrestis.*]

613. Saisde-coille. *614. Samh.*

sàisde-fiadhain,§ see sàisde-coille.
sàiteach, see sàthach.
saith, -ean, *s.m.* The backbone. 2 Joint of the neck or backbone. 3**Multitude. 4**Piercing. 5**Space. 6**Haft. 7**Treasure, abundance of money. 8 see sàth. 9 (AF) see saigh. 10 *pl.* Stakes. 11 Swarm of bees.
saith,** *a.* Vulgar, vile. 2 Cheap.
sàith,* *s.f.* Bellyful, satiety—*Islay.*
sàitheach, -eiche, *a.* see sàthach.
sàitheachd, *s.f.ind.* Satiety, repletion, gormandizing, frequent stuffing.
saithean, ‡‡ -in, -an, *s.m.* Stake or pole driven into the ground.
saitheas, -eis, *s.m.* Vileness, badness. 2 Cheapness.
sàithich, see sàthaich.
——te, see sàthaichte.
sàithte, see sàthta. An sleaghan sàithte 'san leirg, *their spears thrust in the plain.*
saitse, see saisde. 2 (AH) *s.f.* Hatch of a ship. 'San loingeas daraich a' crìonadh, dh' òilte fìon air an saitse, *and their oaken ships decaying, wine was drunk on their hatches—Ian Lom p. 56.*
sàl, *gen.* sàil & sàile, *s.m.* The sea. 2 Sea- or salt-water. A' leum thar an t-sàl, *bounding over the sea.*
sal, sail, *s.m.* Filth, impurity. 2 Mud. 3 Dross, refuse of anything. 4 Dust. 5 Spot, blemish. 6 Scum. 7 Coom of a wheel. 8 Wax of the ear. 9 Willow, see seileach. 10 (AF) Eggs of the moth. 11*Slimy dirt. Air s. an raoin, *on the dust of the plain.*
salach, -aiche & sailche, *a.* Foul, dirty, filthy, nasty, unclean, polluted. 2 Troubled, agitated, as a fluid. Cuan s. nan garbh-thonn, *the troubled billowy ocean ;* fuil sh., *polluted* or *foul blood.*
salachadh, -aidh, *s.m.* Defiling, act of defiling, polluting, rendering unclean, sullying, soiling. 2 Filth, defilement. 3 Adulteration. A' s—, *pr.pt.* of salaich.
salachar, -air, -an, *s.m.* Filth, filthiness, grossness, nastiness, impurity, corruption, dross. 2 Dirt, dung, excrement.
——achd, *s.f.ind.* see salachar.
sàlag,** -aig, -an, *s.f.* Heel-piece.
——an,(CR) *s.m.* Pyrosis, water-brash—*Lochbroom & Lewis.*
salaich, *pr.pt.* a' salachadh, *v.a.* Defile, pollute, sully, contaminate, spoil, soil, make dirty. Sh. thu am paipear, *you soiled the paper.*
——te, *past pt.* of salaich. Defiled, polluted, soiled, contaminated, spoiled.
salaid, Gaelic form of *salad.*
salainn, *gen.sing.* of salann.
——each, -eiche, *a.* Abounding in salt, salting. 2 Communicating a salt taste. 3 Brinish.
——eachadh, -aidh, *s.m.* Salting, act of salting, pickling, seasoning. A' s—, *pr. pt.* of salainnich.
——ich, *pr.pt.* a' salainneachadh, *v.a.* Salt, cure or season with salt, pickle.
——ichte, *past pt.* of salainnich. Cured or seasoned with salt.
salann, -ainn, *s.m.* Salt. An Fhairge Shalainn, *the Salt Sea ;* poll-salainn, *a salt-pit.*
——ach, see salainneach.
——an, -ain, -an, *s.m.* Salt-pit or -pool. 2†† Vault.
salann-fuail, *s.m.* Sal-ammoniac.
salann-na-groide, *s.m.* Alkali.
salann-tàthaidh, *s.m.* Borax.
sal-bhodach, *s.m.* Dustman.
salchadh, -aich, see salachadh.
salchar,** see salachar.
sàl-cluaise,** *s.m.* Cerumen, ear-wax.
sàl-chuach, see sàil-chuach.
sal-fàchd,(AH) *s.m.* Distasteful and offensive memento. Dh'fhàg e sal-fàchd glan aig a charaid, *he gave his friend a fine memento at parting (ironically.)*
†sall,** -aill, *s. m.* Bitterness. 2 Satire. 3 Invective, lampoon.
†sallan, -ain, *s.m.* Singing. 2 Harmony.
salldair, -e, -draichean, *s.f.* Chalder, Scots measure of 16 bolls. 2 Chaldron, imperial measure of 36 bushels.
salm, sailm, *s.f.* Psalm. 2* Anthem.
salmach, -aiche, *a.* Singing psalms. 2 Abounding in psalms or psalm-tunes. 3 Like a psalm.
salmadair, -ean, *s.m.* Psalm-book, psalter. 2†† Psalmist. 3‡‡Songster, chorister. S. chraoibh dhlùth-dhuillich, *the songster of the leafy tree.*
——eachd, *s.f.ind.* Psalm-singing. 2 The office or business of a clerk or precentor.
salmair, -ean, *s.m.* Psalmist, songster, precentor, clerk, chorister.
——eachd, see salmadaireachd.
†salt, -ailt, -an, *s.m.* see sult. 2**Colour.
†saltair, -ean, *s. m.* Psalter. 2 Psaltery. 3 Chronicle. 4 Salt-monger. 5** The title of certain Irish traditional records, as, S. na Teamhrach.
saltair, *pr.pt.* a' saltairt & a' saltradh, *v.a. & n.* Tread, trample. 2 Tread, walk.
saltairt, *s.f.* Treading, act of treading or trampling. 2 Act of treading or walking. A' s—, *pr. pt.* of saltair.
saltrachadh, -aidh, *s.m.* see saltairt.

saltrachd, (MS) *s.f.* Insult.
saltraich,** *s.f.* Treading, trampling. 2 Continued trampling. 3 Tramp, tread.
saltraich, *v.* see saltair.
———te, *past pt.* of saltraich. Trodden under foot.
saltraidh, *fut.aff. a.* of saltair.
†sàm, s. Rest, ease.
†sam, *s.m.* Sun.
saman,§ *s. m.* Wood-loosestrife,yellow pimpernel, see seamrag-Muire.—*Mid Highlands.*
sàmgaich,** *v.a.* Sprawl.
samh,§ -aimh, -an, *s.m.* Common sorrel—*rumex acetosa.* 2§ That part of the sheep's sorrel (*rumex acetosella*) that bears seed. 3 see seamrag. (ill. on p. 785.)
samh, -aimh, -an, *s.m.* Stink. 2 The suffocating smell occasioned by excessive heat or closeness of air in a room.‡ 3 Clownish or rustic person. 4 Savage. 5 (AC) Flock, fold,herd. 6(AC) Fish. 7 Giant, strong person, a god. 8 *rarely*, The sun. 9 The sea—*Suth'd.* 10 (A F) Pig. S. éisg, *fish odour* ; s. trom éisg, *a strong smell as from a large body of fish at sea.*
samh,(AC) *a.* Fat, rich, productive.
samh, *s.m.* Surge, agitation of waves on the sea-beach. 2 Crest of whitened billows—*Sàr-Obair.*
sàmh, -àimh, see sàimh.
sàmh, see sàbh.
samhach, -aiche, *a.* Abounding in sorrel. 2 Rustic, clownish.
sàmhach, -aiche, *a.* Quiet, still, calm, serene. 2 Peaceful, undisturbed, at rest, easy. 3 Silent. 4 Mild, pleasant. 5 Peaceable, peaceably disposed. Feasgar s., *a calm still evening* ; bithibh s., *be still* ; fan s., *keep quiet.*
samhach, -aich, -aichean, *s.f.* Wooden haft or handle of any instrument, as an axe or hammer. 2**Shaft. 3**Edge of a weapon. 4* Axe, hatchet. Chaidh an tuagh bhàrr a s., *the axe went off its handle* ; s. sgéin, *the haft of a knife.*
sàmhachair, see sàmhchair.
samhachan,** -ain, *s.m.* Soft, quiet person.
samhadh, -aidh, *s.m.* Wood-sorrel, see seamrag.
samhadh, -aidh,*s.m.* Edge, as of a hatchet.
†samhadh,** -aidh, *s.m.* Congregation.
samhadh-caora,§ *s.m.* Sheep's sorrel, see ruanaidh.
samhaich,(MS) *v.a.* Helve, furnish with a handle, as an axe.
samhaicheadas,(MS) -ais, *s.m.* Quiet.
samhail, *a.* see samhuil & sàmhach.
samhailt, see samhuilt.
samhain, see sàimh.
Samhainn, see Samhuinn.
samhaircean, -ein, -an, *s.m.* Primrose.
samhaisg,(AF) *s.* Heifer.
samhaltan, -ain, -an, *s.m.* Emblem, hieroglyphic.
———ach,-aiche, *s.m.* Emblematical,having emblems or hieroglyphics.
samhan, -ain, *s.m.* Savin—*juniperus sabina.* 2 (AC) Female dog, bitch. 3 Little giant. 4(A F) Horse. 5 Large river trout—*Fàilte na Morair.*
samhanach,* -aich, *s.m.* Savage, giant, monster. Chuireadh tu eagal air na samhanaich, *you would frighten the very savages*—an Islay saying ; mharbhadh e na samhanaich, *it would kill the savages*—said of something very overpowering or unwholesome—N.G.P.
samh-an-aithreach, -eich, *s.m.* Punishment. 2 Sore produced by rubbing off the skin in one's sleep. 3* Cause of regret. 4* Object of regret.
samharcan,** -ain, *s.m.* see samhaircean.
†samhas, -ais, -an, *s.m.* Delight, pleasure, satisfaction. 2 Ease.
†———ach,** *a.* Causing delight or pleasure. 2 Agreeable. 3 Causing satisfaction. 4 Undisturbed, at ease.
†———aiche,** *s.m.* Suttler.
sàmhchair, -e, *s.f.* Quietness, tranquility, rest, repose, ease, ataraxy, calmness, composure.
———each, -eiche, *a.* Quiet, tranquil,peaceful, undisturbed.
———eachd, *s.f.* see sàmhchair.
samhla, see samhladh.
samhlach, -aiche, *a.* Likening, comparing. 2 Emblematical, typical. 3 Ghostly, spectral. 4 Allegorical. Dath s., *copying ink* ; fàsgadh s., *a copying press.*
———adh, -aidh, *s.m.* Comparing, act of comparing or likening. 2 Comparison, simile, image, type, analogy, emblem. 3* Laying something bad to one's charge. A' s—, *pr. pt.* of samhlaich.
———ail, -e, *a.* see samhlach.
———an, see samhladh.
———as, see samhladh.
samhlachd, *s.f.ind.* Comparability, state of being comparable. 2 Affinity. 3(MS)Draught.
samhladair, -ean, *s.m.* Imitator.
samhladh, -aidh, -aidhean, *s. m.* Appearance, shape, form, resemblance, likeness. 2 Pattern, sample, copy, antitype. 3 Apparition, spectre, ghost. 4 Proverb, by-word. 5 Example. 6 Allegory. 7 Act of "evening." 8 Resembling, comparing, comparison, analogy, similitude. 9 Slender person. S. na h-altarach, *the pattern of the altar* ; s. nam briathar fallain, *the form of sound words* ; baoth-sh. nam marbh, *the dread apparition of the dead* ; is trian suiridhe s., *to be evened,* or *coupled in conversation as a likely match, is a third of courtship.*
samhlaich, *pr.pt.* a' samhlachadh, *v.a.* Compare, liken. 2 Allegorize. 3 Assimilate, resemble. 4 *v.n.* Lay to one's charge. Na s. an leithid sin riumsa,*do not lay such things to my charge.*
———te, *past pt.* of samhlaich. Likened, compared.
samhluchadh, see samhlachadh.
samhluich, see samhlaich.
———te, see samhlaichte.
samhluth,** *a.* Brisk, active.
Samhna, *gen.sing.* of Samhuinn.
samhnach,* *s.f.* see samhnag. 2 Deer-park, winter park.
samhnachan,(AF) *s.m.* Large river trout.
Samhnadh, see Samhuinn.
samhnag, -aig, -an, *s.f.* Bon-fire or torch kindled on Hallow-eve. 2 (AF) see samhnachan.
———ach, -aiche, *a.* Having many bon-fires or blazing with bon-fires on Hallow-eve.
samhnaich,* *v.a.* Winter.
samhnan, -ain, -an, *s.m.* Large river-trout,*prov.* for samhnachan.
samhnas,** -ais, *s.m.* Anger.
samhra, see samhradh.
samhrach, -aiche, see samhrachail.
———ail, -e,*a.* Summer-like, of,or belonging to, summer. 2 Bringing summer.
samhradh, -aidh, -aidhean, *s.m.* Summer. Seòmar samhraidh, *a summer parlour* ; taigh-samhraidh, *a summer-house* ; toiseach an t-samhraidh, *the beginning of summer* ; *2 the month of May.*
†samhrag, -aig, -an, *s.f.* Clover, trefoil, shamrock.
———ach,** *a.* Abounding in trefoil or shamrock.

samhraidh, *gen.sing.* of samhradh.
samhrail, -e, *a.* see samhrachail.
samhsa, see samhsadh.
samhsach,** *a.* Abounding in, of, or like sorrel.
†samhsadh, *s.m.* Sorrel seed.
samht,(CR) *s.m.* Thud. 2 · Very stout person.
samhthach, see samhach.
samhuil, -mhla, -ean, *s.m.* Likeness, image, copy, resemblance, match, representation.
samhuil,** *a.* Like, as, such.
samhuilt, -e, -ean, *s.f.* (i.e. mac-samhuilt, *son of the image.*) Precise resemblance, image, apparition. 2** Slender person. S. aithne ormsa, *unrecognized by me*—you have the advantage of me. Bha s. aithne aige air an duine, *or* bha e 'deanamh s. air an duine, (he knew that he ought to know the man, but could not recall who he was)—*Arran.*
Samhuinn, *gen.sing.* Samhna, *s.f.* Hallow-tide, the feast of All-souls, 1st. Nov. 2 The month of November. [Preceded by the art. *an t-*.] O Bhealltainn gu S., *from May-day to Hallow-tide ;* siubhal na Samhna dha, *may he never return !*—i. e. may he pass as Hallowmass passed ; coltas na Samhuinn, *like about Hallowtide*—a deprecative kind of remark applied to the weather in summer when cold and wet.
samman,§ -ain, *s.m.* see seamrag-Muire.
sampiair, -ean, *s.m.* Copy, pattern. 2 Example.
sampull, -uill, -an, *s.m.* Example. Ball sampuill, *an object* or *example.*
samrag, see seamrag.
's an, *contr.* for anns an. 'S an taigh, *in the house ;* tha e 'staigh, *it is indoors.*
's an, And the.
-san, *emphatic adjection*, see note under -sa. A chuid-san, *his own property ;* 'eich-san, *his own horses.*
†san, *a.* Holy.
†sàn, *v.a.* Release, dissolve.
†sanadh, -aidh, *s.m.* Releasing, dissolving.
sanarc,** -airc, *s.m.* Red orpiment.
sanas, -ais, -an, *s.m.* Whisper. 2 Advice, suggestion, warning, hint, alarm. 3 Secret. 4 Greeting, salutation, salute. 5 Knowledge science. 6 Etymology. 7 Notice, placard, advertisement. 8 Mark, proof. 9 Low sound. 10 Peace. 11 Augury. 12 Glossary. 13** Private sign. Bheir e sanas le 'chois, *he will give a hint with his foot ;* mar sh. do gach tir, *as a warning to every country.*
†sanas, -ais, -an, *s.m.* Dictionary.
sanasach, -aiche, *a.* Warning, giving hints or cautions, hinting, whispering. 2 Allusive. 3 Greeting, saluting.
sanasaich,** *v.a.* Allude.
————e, *s.m.* Etymologist.
sanasail, -e, *a.* see sanasach.
sanasair, -ean, *s.m.* Suggester. 2 Monitor. 3** Advertiser.
sanasan,** -ain, *s.m.* Glossary. 2 Etymology. 3 Private hint, low whisper, warning.
————aiche,** *s.m.* Etymologist.
†sanct, Gaelic form of Latin *sanctus.*
†sanctair,** *s.m.* Sanctuary.
sandan, see sàrdail.
sannadh,** -aidh, *s.m.* Loosening, looseness. 2 Separating.
sanndag, see sachasan.
sannt, -ainnt & -a, *s.m.* Inclination, desire. 2 Covetousness, avarice, greed. 2 Ambition. 4 *Lust. Tha s. orm, *I intend ;* s, gnìomh, *inclination to work ;* s. gun sonas éiridh an donas dha, *hopeless greed ill betides ;* esan e dh' fhuathaicheas s., *he that hates covetousness ;* ma tha s. sin air, *if he has a desire for that ;* o sh. a' mhillteir, *from the ambition of the destroyer.*
sanntach, -aiche, *a.* Desirous, keenly desirous. 2 Covetous, greedy, avaricious. 3 Lustful. 4 **Ambitious. Duine s., *a covetous man ;* s. air buannachd, *greedy of gain.*
————,** -aich, *s.m.* Covetous man.
————adh, -aidh, *s. m.* Coveting, covetousness. 2 Act of coveting. 3 Lusting. 4 Lust, desire. Air s.dha, *after he coveted.* A' s—, *pr.pt.* of sanntaich.
sanntachd, *s.f.ind.* Covetousness, greediness. 2 Ambition. 3 Lustfulness.
sanntaich, *pr. pt.* a' sanntachadh, *v.a.* Covet, desire, long for. 2 Lust after. 3*Incline. Ma sh. thu, *if you inclined* or *coveted ;* sanntaichidh e gu mór, *he will covet greedily.*
————te, *past pt.* of sanntaich. Coveted, desired. 2 Lusted after.
sanntair,* -ean, *s.m.* Covetous man.
sanntalachd,(MS) *s.f.* Avariciousness.
sanntuich, see sanntaich.
sant, *s.m.* Squelch.
santair,** *s.m.* Stroller. lounger.
———eachd, *s.f.* Strolling, lounging.
sanuis,(DC) *s.f. Uist* for sanas, *s.m.* Thig an t-s. os cionn bùird, *the whisper gets above board.*
sanus, see sanas.
———air, see sanasair.
saoban,** -ain, *s.m.* Swing. 2 Swinging or waving to and fro.
———ach,** *a.* Swinging. 2 Like a swing.
———achadh,** -aidh, *s.m.* Swinging, as on a rope.
———achd,** *s.f.ind.* Jactation, swinging, as on a rope.
———aich,** *v.a.* Dandle. 2 Swing.
———aich,** *s.f.* Swinging, as on a rope.
———aichte, *past pt.* of saobanaich.
saobh, -aoibh, *s.m.* Dissimulation, hypocrisy.
saobh, -a & -aoibhe, *a.* Silly, foolish. 2 Mad, deranged. 3 Wrong, erroneous. 4 Unfortunate. 5 Dim, blind. 6‡ Apt to err. 7*Eddying. S.-shruth, *an eddy-tide.*
saobh, *pr.pt.* a' saobhadh, *v. a.* Turn aside or away, mislead, lead astray. 2 Infatuate, charm, amuse. 3 Go aside, go wrong, err. 4 Dissemble. 5 Prevaricate. 6(MS) Imprecate. Sh. iad, *they erred.*
saobhach,†† *a.* Dissimulating.
saobhadh, -aidh, *s. m.* Turning aside, act of turning aside or misleading. 2 Infatuation, act of infatuating. 3 State of becoming silly. 4 Act of going wrong. 5 Dissembling, act of dissembling or prevaricating. 6 Imprecation. 7 Foolishness. 8 Error. 9 Amusement. 10 Asservation. A' s—, *pr.pt.* of saobh.
saobhaidh, -ean, *s.f.* The den of a wild beast. 2 Litter and den of a fox.
saobhail, *a.* Erroneous—*Dàin I. Ghobha.*
saobhal, *Suth'd.* for saoghal.
saobh-aoradh,** -aidh, *s.m.* Superstition.
saobh-chainnt, -e, -ean, *s.f.* Foolish or impertinent talk. 2 Prattle, gabble.
————————each, -eiche, *a.* Prattling, gabbling, talking foolishly. 2 Fond of idle or foolish talk.
saobh-char, -chuir, see saobh-ghnothach.
saobh-chiall, -chéill, *s.f.* Nonsense. 2 Folly, stupidity.
————————ach,** -aiche, *a.* Foolish, nonsensical, stupid.
saobh-choire, -an & -achan [**-choirichean,] *s.m.* Whirlpool.
————————ach, *a.* Having whirlpools.
saobh-chòmhradh, see saobh-chainnt.
saobh-chòmhraideach, -eiche, see saobh-chainnt-

each.
saobh-chràbhach,†† -aich, *s.m.* Hypocrite.
saobh-chràbhach, -aiche, *a.* Superstitious. 2 Insincere, false-hearted, hypocritical.
saobh-chràbhadh, -aidh, -aidhean, *s.m.* Superstition. 2 False devotion, hypocrisy.
saobh-chràbhair,** *s.m.* Hypocrite.
saobh-chreideach, see saobh-chreidmheach.
saobh-chreidiche,** *s.m.* Superstitious or credulous person. 2 Heretic.
saobh-chreidimh, *s.m.* Superstition. 2 Heterodoxy, heresy. 3**Wild opinion.
saobh-chreidmheach, -eiche, *a.* Superstitious. 2 Heterodox, heretical.
——————, -eich, *s. m.* Superstitious person. 2 Holder of heterodoxy or heresy, heretic.
saobh-chreidmheachd, *s.f.* see saobh-chreidimh.
saobh-fhàidh, -ean, *s.m.* False prophet.
————eachd, *s.f.* False prophecy.
saobh-ghlòr, -òir, *s.m.* Vain-glory. 2‡‡see saobh-chainnt.
————ach, -aiche, *a.* Vain-glorious. 2 see saobh-chainnteach.
saobh-ghnothach,‡‡ -aich, -aichean, *s.m.* Job.
saobh-lèigh, *s.m.* Quack.
saobh-mhiann, -a, -an, *s.m.* Foolish or vain desire. 2 Dishonest or iniquitous wish. 3 False appetite. 4 Punctiliousness. 5 Idle ambition.
saobh-mhiannach, -aiche, *a.* Desiring vain things. 2 Having iniquitous wishes or desires. 3 Having a false appetite. 4 Punctilious. 5**Foolishly ambitious.
saobh-nòs, -òis, -an, *s. m.* Bad habit. 2 Bad breeding. 3 Anger, indignation. 4 Foolish habit.
saobh-nòsach, -aiche, *a.* Having bad or vicious habits. 2 Unmannerly, ill-bred. 3 Angry. 4 Morose, peevish.
saobh-sgeul, -sgeòil, *s.f.* Idle talk. 2 Romance, fiction. 3**Improbable fiction.
saobh-sgeulach,-aiche,*a.* Telling tales or romances.
saobh-sgeulachd, -an, *s.f.* Idle tale, fiction. 2 Telling of tales.
saobh-sgeulaiche, -an, *s. m.* Teller of fictitious tales, romancer, novelist.
saobh-sgrìobhadh, -aidh, -aidhean, *s. m.* Bad writing. 2 Libel, libellous composition.
saobh-sgrìobhair, -ean, *s.m.* Libeller.
saobh-sheadh, see saobh-sheagh.
————ach, see saobh-sheaghach.
saobh-sheagh, -a, -an, *s.m.* Equivocation.
saobh-sheaghach, -aiche, *a.* Equivocal.
saobh-shruth, -a, -an, *s.m.* Eddy, eddying tide. 2 Contrary current.
saobh-shruthach, -aiche, *a.* Abounding in eddying tides.
saobh-smaoin, see saobh-smuain.
saobh-smuain, -tean, *s. m.* Vain or foolish thought. 2 Wicked or dishonest thought. 3 Whim. 4 False conception, idea or conceit. 5 ††Distraction.
saobh-smuaineadh, see saobh-smuain.
saod, -aoid, *s.m.* Care, attention. 2 State,trim, condition. 3*Prosperous condition. 4 Hope, expectation. 5 Track, journey. 6 Good humour. 7 Expedient. 8††Activity. 9‡ Intention.

Cuir s. air. *put it in a likely* or *prosperous condition.*; 'dè 'n s. a th' ort ? *how do you do ?* gun s. air dol as, *without an expedient to escape;* feumaidh sinn s. a chuir air, *we must devise an expedient to accomplish it,* or *we must put him in good humour.*

saodach, -aiche, *a.* Careful, attentive. 2 In good condition. 3 In good health, strong. 4** Driving, as cattle.
saodachadh, -aidh, *s.m.* Driving. 2 Act of driving cattle to pasture, or to a resting-place for the night, 3 Conducting,guiding,tending. 4 **Taking care of. A' s—, *pr. pt.* of saodaich.
saodaich, *pr.pt.* a' saodachadh, *v.a.* Drive cattle or flocks to pasture, or to a resting-place for the night. 2 Conduct. 3 Tend, take care of. 4 (MS) Run. 5* Coax away in good humour. [‡ gives saodaidh for No. 1.]
saodaichear, *fut.pass.* of saodaich.
saodaichte, *past part.* of saodaich. Driven to pasture, or to a resting-place for the night, as cattle or flocks. 2 Tended, taken care of.
saodail,†† *a.* Active, careful.
saodar, see saodmhor.
saodhan, *s.m.* see saoidhean.
†saodh, *s.* Pain.
saodmhor, -oire, *a.* In good condition. 2 Well, in good health. 3 Prosperous, successful. 4 Attentive. 5* On good terms. 6* Well-planned.
saodmhoireachd,** *s.f.* Prosperity. 2 Good condition of health or fortune.
saoduchadh, see saodachadh.
saoduich, see saodaich.
saoghal, -ail, -an, *s.m.* The world, a world. 2 Age, generation. 3 Life, lifetime. 4 Means, wealth, substance, riches. 5 Business of life, occupation, pursuits. 6 Subsistence, living.

Feadh an t-s., *throughout the world ;* fad do shaoghail, *during your life-time ;* s. fada dhuit! *long life to you !* droch sh., *bad times ;* mo chuid de 'n t-s. ! *my dearest dear !* (lit. my all) ; ma gheibh mi s., *if I live ;* ma bhitheas s. agam, *or* ma gheibh mi s., *if I live ;* gu s. nan s., *henceforth and for ever ;* an saoghal salach, *the deceitful world ;* air son an t-saoghail, *for the whole universe ;* c' àit' air an t-saoghal am bheil e ? *where in the world is he ?* cha bu sh. dhaibh am beatha tuilleadh, *their life was life to them no more ;* cha mhath an s. an t-sealg, *hunting is a poor living ;* cùram an t-saoghail, *worldly care ;* air fad an t-saoghail, *or* air feadh an t-saoghail, *throughout the world.* It is said of anyone who is prospering in the world, Tha 'n s. aige air sheot, *he has the world by the tail*—DMK.

saoghalach, -aiche, *a.* see saoghaltach.
saoghalachd, see saoghaltachd.
saoghalan, -ain, *s.m.* Old man.
saoghalta, -ailte, *a.* Worldly, of the world. 2 Devoted to the world, covetous. 3 Impious, ungodly. 4 Secular. 5 Terrestrial. 6 Long-lived. Foghlum s., *worldly wisdom.*
saoghaltach, -aiche, *a.* see saoghalta.
saoghaltachd, *s.f.* Love of worldly things, conformity to the ways of the world, worldliness. 2 Longevity.
saoi, see saoidh.
saoibh, -e, *a.* Foolish, senseless. 2 Peevish, morose. 3**Mad.
saoibh-chleasachd, -an, *s.f.* Buffoonery.
saoibhir, -e & -bhre, *a.* Rich, wealthy, opulent. 2*Plentiful, pretty full. Còta s., *a pretty-full coat, an easy coat ;* bliadhna sh., *a plentiful year ;* duine s., *a rich man.*
saoibhneach, -eiche, *a.* see saoibh. 2**Joyless.
saoibhneas, -eis, *s.m.* Dulness, heaviness, peevishness, sorrow, moroseness, joylessness.
saoibhneasach, -aich, *a.* Causing dulness, heaviness, sorrow, moroseness or joylessness.
saoibhreach, see saoibhir. 2 Enriching, fertile.
saoibhreachadh, -aidh, *s. m.* Enriching, act of making rich. 2 Prospering, state of prospering, prosperity. A' s—, *pr.pt.* of saoibhrich.
saoibhreas, -eis, *s.m.* Wealth,opulence, affluence.

2 Prosperity,success. 3 Plenty. 4(MS) Blissfulness.
saoibhreasach, see saoibhir.
saoibhreasaich,(MS) *v.a.* Elate.
saoibhrich, *pr.pt.* a' saoibhreachadh, *v.a.* & *n.* Enrich, make rich. 2 see soirbhich.
————te, *past pt.* of saoibhrich. Enriched, made rich.
saoibhsgeul,** -sgeòil, *s.m.* Fable. [also saobhsgeul—with hyphen.]
saoidh, -ean,*s.m.* Good,worthy or deserving person. 2 Righteous man. 3 Generous, brave or magnanimous man. 4 Warrior, hero. 5 Learned man, man of letters. 6 Tutor, preceptor. 7 (AF) Mare. 8**Nobleman. 9 see saoidhean. 10**Worthy. Saoidhean Mhanuis, *Manus' warriors.*
saoidh, -e, *a.* Good, worthy, deserving. 2 Generous, brave, magnanimous. 3 Godly, pious. 4 Heroic.
saoidh,(CR) *s.m.* Tub—*Arran.*
saoidh,** *s.f.* Hay. S. lòin, *meadow-hay;* muinntir na saoidh, *the hay-makers.* Feur-saoidhe, *natural hay that grows on alluvial soil*—not *meadow-hay*—(DMK.)
saoidh-dàna, *s.m.* Poet.
saoidh-dhearg, *s.f.* Sainfoin (plant.)
saoidheadair,** -ean, *s.m.* Hay-cutter. 2 Haymaker.
——————eachd,** *s.f.* Hay-cutting. 2 Haymaking.
saoidhealachd,** *s.f.* Generosity.

615. *Saoidhean.*

saoidhean, -ein, -an, *s. m.* The coal-fish, saithe. Named according to its age as follows :—
1st year, Siol or siolagan.
2nd. year, Cudaig, cudainn or saoidhean.
3rd. year, Smalag, cuideanach or saoidhean.
4th. year, Saoidhean or piocach.
5th. year, Saoidhean dubh or saoidhean mór.
6th. year, Ucsa or ugsa.
[1st. year, Cudaig ; 2nd. year, Smalag ; 3rd. year, Saoidhean ; 4th. year, Saoidhean mór ; after 4th. year, Ucas—*Lewis,* (DMy.)]
Bu mhath a' chudaig far nach faight' an saoidhean, *the cuddy is good when no saithe can be got.* The young saithe is called *cuddy* in some parts of Scotland, and *podly* in others. It is *sillock* in Shetland. Raasay people are nicknamed " na saoitheanan."
saoidhean, *n.pl.* of saoidh.
saoidheanach, -aiche, *a.* Abounding in coal-fish or saithe.
saoidhean-dubh,(AF) *s. m.* Coal-fish in its 5th. year, in some places erroneously called lythe.
saoidhean-mór, see saoidhean-dubh.
saoidhear,** *s.m.* Hay-maker.
saoil, -e, -ean, *s.f.* Seal, see seula.
saoil, *pr.pt.* a' saoileadh, *v.a.* see seulaich.
saoil, *pr.pt.* a' saoilsinn, a' saoiltinn, & a' saoileachdainn, *v. n.* Think, suppose, imagine. 2* Seem. Sh. mi, *I thought or imagined ;* an s. thu ? *do you think ?* sh. e gur e nàmhaid a bh' ann, *he thought he was an enemy;* nach s.thu ? *do you not think ?* shaoileadh duine, *one would suppose ;* ma shaoileas tu,*if you think* or *judge;* c' àit' an deach e, saoil thu ? *where do you think he has gone ?*
saoileachdainn, -ean, *s.m.* Supposition. 2 Thinking, thought, reflection. *Prov.* A' s—, *pr.pt.* of saoil.
saoileadh, -aidh, *s.m.* & *pr.pt.* of saoil, see seuladh.
saoileam, *v.* " Methinks." 2 *1st. per. sing. imp.* of saoil. Let me think.
saoilear,** *fut.pass.* of saoil.
saoilidh,** *fut.aff.a.* of saoil.
saoilneas, -eis, -an, *s.m.* Opinion, supposition.
saoilseanach, see saoilsinneach.
saoilsinn, -e, *s.f.* Thinking, act of thinking,supposing, imagining or judging. A' s—, *pr. pt.* of saoil.
saoilsinneach,** *a.* Deducible. 2 Imaginant.
saoilsinneas,** *s.m.* Deducement.
saoilte, see seulta.
saoiltinn, -e, see saoilsinn.
saoiltinneas, -eis, see saoilneas.
saoimeach,** *a.* see soimeach.
————d, see soimeachd.
saoineil, *a.* Well-seasoned—*Dàin I. Ghobha.*
saoi-oileanta, -einte, *a.* Well-trained, educated. 2 Well-bred. Each s. sith-fhada, *a well-trained, bounding steed.*
saoir, *gen sing.* of saor.
saoire,* *s.f.* Cheapness.
saoire, *comp.* of saor. Na 's s., *cheaper.*
saoire,** *s.pl.* Festivals, holidays.
saoiread, -eid, *s.m.* Degree of cheapness. A' dol an s., *getting cheaper and cheaper.*
saoirreal,* -eil, *s.m.* Freestone.
saoirghean,(MS) *s.m.* Liberality.
saoirse, *s.f.* see saorsa.
————ach,** -aich, *s.m.* Freeman.
————ach, -aiche, see saorsachail.
————achd, see saorsachd.
saoirsinn, see saorsainn.
saoirsinneachd, see saorsainneachd.
saoirsne,(MS) *s.* Allowance.
saoirsneachd, see saorsainneachd.
saoith,** see saoidh.
saoith, see sùith.
saoitheag, see sùbhag.
saoithealachd, see saoidhealachd.
saoitheil,** *a.* Expert. 2 Generous (saoidh). 3 Skilful, 4 Learned.
saoithreach, *a.* see saothrachail.
saoithreach, *s.* see saothraiche.
saoith'reach, in Mackintosh's G. Proverbs is for sòradh, *grudging.*
saoithreachadh, see saothrachadh.
saoithreachail, see saothrachail.
saoithrich, see saothraich.
————e, see saothraiche.
saonas,†† -ais, *s.f.* Vexation. 2(WC) Offence. Ghabh e s., *he took offence.*
————ach,** *a.* Peevish.
————achd, *s.f.* Peevishness.
saor, -aoire, *a.* Free, at liberty, not enslaved. 2 Uncompelled, unrestrained, free from engagements of any kind. 3 Permitted, allowed. 4 Freed, set at liberty, delivered. 5 Exempt, clear. 6 Free, gratuitous, not purchased. 7 Free, liberal, frank, not parsimonious. 8 Free, unrestrained, unrestricted. 9 Cheap. 10 Free, familiar, unreserved. 11 Free, without obstructions or impediments. 12 Easily split or broken, as wood or stone. 13*Absolute. 14 15 Ransomed.
Sometimes used before its noun, as, saorthabhartas, *a free offering.* Buntàta s., *cheap potatoes ;* clann na mnà saoire, *the children of the free woman ;* s o 'n mhionnan, *free from the oath ;* s. o 'n alladh sin, *free of that aspersion ;* bheir mis' a mach saor thu, *I shall take you out free of expense ;* bheir mi dha gu s.,

I shall give him freely; clach sh., *free-stone;* ùine sh., *vacation, holidays;* saor chairtealan, *free lodgings.*

saor, *pr.pt.* a' saoradh, *v.a.* Free, deliver, rescue, liberate. 2 Save, redeem. 3 Except. 4 Acquit. 5 Set at liberty, disentangle. 6 Cheapen, make cheaper. 7 Absolve. 8*Purge. 9 (AH) "Ship," as an oar. 10* Free of aspersion or calumny. S. am boireannach seo, *clear this woman (from scandal);* cha sh. mi thu, *I will not acquit you;* s. do ràimh, *"ship," or take in your oars.*

saor, *gen. & pl.* -aoir, *dat. pl.* saoir, *s.m.* Carpenter, joiner. Tuagh an làimh an t-saoir, *an axe in the carpenter's hand.*
s.-bhàtaichean, *a boat-builder. 2 a ship's carpenter.*
s.-chairtean, *a cartwright.*
s.-charbad, *a coach-builder.*
s.-chlach, *a stone-mason, stone-hewer and polisher.*
s.-chuidhlean, *a wheelwright.*
s.-fheuna, *a cartwright.*
s.-luinge, *a ship-builder. 2 a ship's carpenter.*
s.-mhuilnean, *a millwright.*

†saor, -aoire, *a.* Noble.

saor, *conj.* Except, save. Saor o dhithis, *except two, persons, save two persons;* s. o na dh' ith na h-òganaich, *except that which the young men have eaten.*

saorach, -aiche, *a.* see saothrach. 2**Freeing, ransoming. 3 Exempting. 4 Cheapening.

saorachadh, -aidh, *s. m.* Cheapening, act of cheapening or making cheaper. 2**Freeing, setting at liberty, ransoming. 3 Acquittal. A' s—, *pr.pt.* of saoraich.

saorachd, *s.f.* Freedom, state of being free, acquittance. 2 Cheapness.

saoradair, -ean, *s.m.* Liberator.

saoradh, -aidh, *s.m.* Freeing, act of freeing, delivering, rescuing, liberating, liberation, freedom. 2 Deliverance, rescue. 3 Saving, act of saving, redeeming, redemption. 4 Acquitting, act of acquitting or absolving. 5 Act of disentangling or setting at liberty, emancipation. 6 Cheapness. 7 Discharge of a soldier. 8 Ransoming. 9*Exemption. 10* Absolution. 11 (D Mu) Oath, imprecation. Fhreagair e leis na saoraidhean bu mhó, *he answered with the strongest imprecations—Suth'd.* A' s—, *pr.pt.* of saor.

saoragan, see sadharcan.

saoraich, *pr.pt.* a' saorachadh, *v. a.* Cheapen, make cheaper. 2 Rescue. 3 Acquit, set at liberty. 4 Affranchise. 5** Ransom. [†† gives s. for saothraich.]
———e,†† see saothraiche.
———te, *past pt.* of saoraich. Cheapened, made cheaper.

saoranach,** -aich, *s.m.* Free man, freed man, independant man, burgess, citizen, denizen.

saoranachadh, *s.m.* Denization.

saoranachd,** *s.f.* State of being free, condition of a freed man or burgess.

saoradh,†† -aidh, *s.m.* Freeing. 2 Cheapening. 3 (MS) Answer.

saoranaich,** see saoraich, 4.

saor-bhàtaichean, *s.m.* Boat-builder, shipwright. 2 Ship's carpenter.

saor-chairtean, *s.m.* Cartwright.

saor-chlach, *s.m.* Mason.

saor-chlann, *s.f.* Freemen.

saor-chomas, -ais, *s.m.* Unrestrained liberty, free will.

saor-chridheach, -eiche, *a.* Free-hearted, candid. 2 Unbetrothed.

saor-chriddeachd, *s.f.* Candour, ingenuousness, candidness.

saor-chuairt, -e, -ean, *s.f.* Circulation, free circulation. S. na fola, *the circulation of the blood.*

saor-chuidhlean, *s.m.* Wheelwright.

saor-dhail,** *s.f.* Acquittance. 2 Cheapness. 3 Freedom.

saor-dhàlach,** *a.* Cheap. 2 Free.

saor-dhìouadair, -ean, *s.m.* Volunteer (soldier.)

saor-dhuais, *s.* Premium (in commerce.)

saor-fheuna, *s.m.* Cartwright.

saorgan, *s.m.* Peewit—*Arran.*

saor-inntinneach, -eiche, *a.* Having an easy mind. 2 Having freedom of thought or liberty of conscience.
————d, *s.f.* Ease or quietness of mind, 2 Liberty of thought or of conscience.

saor-inntinniche,** *s.m.* Free-thinker.

saor-loingeis,* *s.m.* Ship-builder.

saor-luinge, *s.m.* Ship-builder. 2 Ship's carpenter.

saor-mhuilnean, *s.m.* Mill-wright. [saor-mhuilinn.]

saorsa, *s.f.* Liberty, freedom. 2 Deliverance. 3 Redemption. 4*Cheapness. 5* Abatement. S. o 'n olc, *freedom from evil;* s. an ni seo, *the cheapness of this thing;* is mór an t-suim air an do cheannaich mi an t-s. seo, *great is the sum with which I purchased this freedom.*

saorsach, -aiche, see saorsachail.
———adh,** -aidh, *s.m.* Cheapening.
———ail, -e, *a.* Free, unrestrained. 2 Giving freedom.
———d, see saorsa. 2 see saorsainneachd.

saorsadh, -aidh, see saorsa.

saorsaich,** *v.a.* Affranchise. 2 Cheapen.

saorsainn, see saorsadh.
———eachd, *s.f.* Carpentry, joinery. 2 Office of a deliverer or redeemer. 3 State of being redeemed or saved.
Some terms used in Joinery :—
Fiacal, *dove-tail.*
Fiodh grobte, *grooved timber.*
Glaodhadh, *glueing.*
Grobadh, *grooving.*
Ite, *feather.*
Locradh, *planing.*
Peang, *tenon.*
Tarr-pheang, *mortice.*
Tàthadh, *splicing.*
Truain, *screw.*

saorsanach, -aich, *s.m.* Helper at work. 2 Free labourer, unhired worker. 3†† Free man.

saor-shealbhadair, see saor-sheilbheadair.

saor-sheilbh, -ean, *s.f.* Freehold possession.
————eadair, -ean, *s.m.* Freeholder, one having a freehold possession.

saor-thabhairt,** *s. f.* Giving freely or voluntarily.
————ear, -ir, -an, *s. m.* One who gives freely, voluntarily, liberally or gratuitously.

saor-thabhartas, -ais, -an, *s. m.* Free gift, free-will offering.

saor-thiodhlac, -ean, see saor-thabhartas.

saor-thoil, -e, *s.f.* Free-will.

saor-thoileach, -ich, *s.m.* Volunteer.

saor-thoirbheartas, -ais, *s.m.* Free gift.

saor-thoirt, see saor-thabhairt.

saor-thùis, -e, -ean, *s.f.* Frankincense.

†saoth, -aoith, *s.f.* Labour. 2 Tribulation. 3 Punishment. 4 Disorder, disease, evil. 5 Prince. 6 Life, existence.

†saoth, *v.a.* Castigate, punish.

saothach, see soitheach.

saothach, *a.* Castigatory.

saothachan,** -ain, see soitheachan.

saothadh, -aidh, *s.m.* Castigation, exculpating, exculpation.

saothail,** -e, *a.* Laborious, toilsome. 2 Painstaking.

saothair, *gin.* -thrach [saoithreach,**] -thraichean, *s.f.* Labour, toil,work. 2 Travail, pains of child-bed. 3 ** Ado. 4** Service ,work, drudgery. Is s. leis, *he thinks it a hard matter ;* s. chloinne, *travail, labour of child-bed ;* Le moran s., *with much toil ;* deanaibh s., *labour, toil ;* gabh s., *bestow pains, toil for it ;* luach saothrach, *what it is worth one's while or pains ;* cha'n fhiach dhuit do sh., *it is not worth your while ;* air bheagan s., *without much trouble ;* tàileamh mo shaothrach, *the result of my toil ;* an s., *in great travail, labour of child-bed ;* a dh' aindeoin do shaothrach, *in spite of all your labour.*

saothair, [saobh-thìr] *s. m.* False-land, side-land, low promontory covered at high-water, the similar bank between an *Eilean Tioram* and the mainland.

saothair,** *s. m.* Punisher, torturer. 2 Diseased man.

saothair-dhamh,(AF) *s.m.* Labouring ox.

saothaireach, *a.* see saotharach. 2 (MS) Adventurous.

saothaireachail,** see saothrach.

saotharach, -aiche, *a.* see saothrach.

saotharcan,** *s.m.* see sadharcan.

saothargan, see sadharcan.

saothmhor,** *a.* Toilsome,laborious, grudging. 2 Difficult.

————achd,** *s.f.* Toilsomeness.

saoth-phort,** -phuirt, *s.m.* Imposthume.

saothrach,-aiche,*a.*Laborious,taking great pains, bestowing much labour. 2 Difficult. 3 That costs much pains or labour, toilsome. 4 Servile.

saothrach, *s.m.* Labour, fatigue, work. 2 *gen.* of saothair.

saothrachadh, -aidh, *s.m.* Labouring, act of labouring, bestowing pains or care. 2 Working, plodding. 3 Toil, tillage. A' s—, *pr. pt.* of saothraich.

saothrachail, *a.* see saothrach.

saothraich, *v.a.& n.* Labour,work, bestow pains. 2 Plod. 3 Labour, till ground, dress, as soil. 4(MS) Manufacture. An ni a shaothraich mi air a shon, *what I toiled for ;* sh. mi a nuas, *I put myself to the trouble of coming down ;* thug thu orm saothrachadh, *you put me to the trouble of coming ;* s. am fearann, *labour the ground.*

————e, -an, *s. m.* Labourer, workman, working-man. 2 One who takes much pains, plodder. 3 Churl. [McL & D gives *nom.* saothraich, *gen.* -e, *s.m.*]

saothruich, see saothraich.

sàpair, *s.* Gaelic form of *sapphire.*

———each,** *a.* Pertaining to, or abounding in, sapphires.

sàpheir, -ean, *s.m.* see sàpair.

sàr, An augmentative prefix, expressing a great degree of any quality. S. chothrom, *an excellent opportunity ;* s. ghaisgeach, *a complete hero ;* s. chù, *a dog, every inch of him ;* s. shlaodair, *a most abandoned villain ;* " Sàr Obair nam bàrd Gàidhealach " *the Beauties of Gaelic Poetry*—a well-known collection of G. poems. [Always placed before its nouns, and aspirates a all aspirable consonants, i.e. all except *s,* followed by any consonant except *l, n, r.*]

sar, *a.* Excellent, matchless. 2 Noble, brnve.

sàr,** *v.a.* Apprehend.

sàr, -àir & -a, *s.m.* Hero, brave warrior. 2 Worthy, excellent man. Cha robh eagal air sàr riamh, *a true hero never knew fear ;* chualas le s. a ghuth, *a hero heard his voice ;* a shàr ! *O hero !*

sàr, -àir, *s.m.* Oppression, violence. 2 Distress, difficulty. 3 see sàradh. 4 Stoppage,hinderance, prevention. Cuir s. 'san obair, *put a stop to the work.*

sar, -air, -an, *s.f.* Tick, sheep-louse.

sàra, see sàr.

sàr-ab,* *s.m.* Chief abbot.

sàr-abuich,** *a.* Quite ripe.

sarach,(AF) *s.* Salmon.

sarach, -aiche, *a.*Abounding in sheep-lice,lousy.

sàrach, *s.m.* see sàrachadh. 2 Opposing, putting a stop to.

sàrachadh, -aidh, *s.m.* Oppressing, act of oppressing, distressing or doing violence to anyone. 2 Harassing, wearying, fatiguing. 3 Wronging, act of wronging or injuring. 4 Act of rescuing violently or illegally. 5 Oppression, violence. 6 Strait. 7 Fatigue. 8 Infringement. 9 Perplexing. 10 Conquest, victory. 11 Extortion. A' s—, *pr.pt.* of sàraich. 'G am sh., *oppressing* or *harrassing me.*

sàrachail, -e, *a.* Oppressing, using violence. 2 Harassing, fatiguing, wearying, wearisome, burdensome, oppressive, tiresome. 3 Wronging, injuring, that injures. 4 Onerous, requiring pains or trouble.

sàrachair,** *s.m.* Oppressor, harasser. 2 Conqueror. 3 Extortioner. 4 Infringer. 5 One who rescues violently or illegally.

sàradh, -aidh,-aidhean,*s.m.*Arrestment for debt, distraining. 2 Obstacle, opposition, impediment. 3††Consumption. 4 Broaching—*Sàr-Obair.*

sarag, -aig, -an, *s.f. dim.* of sar. Little louse.

sarag,** -aig, *s.f.* Gloss.

saragach,** *a.* Lousy.

sàraich, *pr.pt.* a' sàrachadh, *v.a.* Oppress, distress, use violence. 2 Harass, weary, fatigue, vex, trouble. 3 Wrong, injure, deal unjustly with one. 4 Rescue violently or illegally. 5 **Conquer. 6 Put to trouble. 7* Burden. 8* Overcome.

sàraiche, -an, s.m. Oppressor. 2 One who harasses, wearies, fatigues or troubles. 3 One who wrongs or injures. 4 One who rescues violently or illegally.

sàraichte, *past pt.* of sàraich. Oppressed. 2 Wronged, injured. 3 Harassed, wearied, fatigued, vexed, troubled. 4 Rescued violently or illegally. 5**Conquered. 6 Perplexed. 7 *Exhausted. 8* Beaten.

sàr-bhan,** *s.f.* Excellent woman.

sàr-bheachd,** *s.f.* Good thought, deep thought.

sàr-bhuille,** *s.f.* Heavy blow.

sàr-bhuilleach,** *a.* Heavy-handed. 2 Giving heavy blows.

sàr-chliù,(MS) *s.m.* Acclamation.

sàr-chumpach, *a,* Well-shaped. Na laoigh òga sliosrach, dìreach, sàr-chumpach, *the young glossy,well-set,shapely calves.—Donn. Bàn,* p.60.

sàrdail, -ean, *s.f.* Sprat. 2 (AF) Sardine.

sàrdaileach,** *a.* Abounding in, or pertaining to, sprats.

sàr-dhochar, -air, -an, *s.m.* Excessive hurt.

sàr-dhuine, *pl.* -dhaoine, *s.m.* Excellent man. [For the difference in meaning between *duine* and *fear,* see duine.]

sàr-fhear, -fhir, *s. m.* Excellent individual, worthy.

sàr-fhios, -a, *s.m.* Certain knowledge. Tha s. agam, *I know quite well.*

————rach, -aiche, *a.* Having complete or perfect knowledge.

sàr-ghoileach, -eiche, *a.* Insatiable.

————————d, *s.f.ind.* Insatiableness.

sàr-laoch,** -laoich, *s.m.* Great hero.

sar leat, for soraidh leat.
sàr-lìon, *v.a.* Increase.
sàr-mhaise, *s.f.* Great beauty or handsomeness.
——-——ach, -eiche, *a.* Exceedingly beautiful.
sàr-mhaith, *a.* Exceedingly good, excellent.
sàr-ògau,** -aiu, *s.m.* Excellent young woman.
sàr-righ,** *s.m.* Czar.
sàruchadh, -aidh, see sàrachadh.
sàruchail, see sàrachail.
sàruich, see sàraich.
———te, see sàraichte.
sàr-ùmhal, -aile, *a.* Very obedient, very submissive.
sàs, -àis, *s.m.* Straits, difficulties, adversity. 2 Confinement, bondage, restraint, custody, durance. 3 Hold, grasp, grapple. 4**Distress, trouble. Tha e 'n s., *he is in custody;* air dha bhi an s., *having happened to be in durance;* is math an s. thu fhéin an sin; *you yourself are well equal to that;* tha thu daonnan an s. an rud-eigin, *you are always busy at something;* an s. teann, *in sore trouble;* tha na balaich an s., *the boys are fighting* or *wrestling;* tha 'n crodh an s. a chéile, *the cattle are pushing each other.*
sàs,** *a.* Fast, laid hold of. 2 Straitened. 3 Distressed. 4 *rarely*, Capable. Tha 'n casan an s., *their feet are fast (ensnared);* chaidh an snàthad an sàs 'nam chois, *the needle pierced my foot;* chaidh e 'n sàs (in *Suth'd* cha' 'sàs) *he stuck fast.*
sàs, -ais, -an, *s.m.* Instrument, engine. 2 Means. 3 Cause. 4**Arms.
sàs, *v.a.* Lay hold of, sieze upon. 2 Fix upon, adhere to. 3** Grasp, grapple.
sàsach, -aiche, *a.* Apt to grasp, lay hold of or fasten upon. 2 Satiating, satisfying or glutting. 3 Satiated, glutted. 4**Of a grasping disposition.
sàsachadh, -aidh, *s.m.* Satiating, act of satiating, filling or cloying. 2**Greediness. A' s—, *pr. pt.* of sàsaich. A' s. na feòla, *satisfying the lusts of the flesh.*
sàsachd, *s.f.ind.* Readiness to grasp or lay hold of. 2 Abundance, satiety, cloyment, sufficiency, repletion, saturation. 3 Greediness. 4 †† Bonds, fetters, restraint.
sàsadh,** -aidh, *s.m.* Satisfaction, comfort. 2 Content. 3 Sufficiency, fulness.
sasag, -aig, -an, *s.f.* Straw-chair, a rude chair made of twisted straw. 2 Vessel, see brà. No. 12, p. 112. [DMy says s. is the large basket into which the meal goes through the hand-sieve, the coarse or bran left in the sieve being emptied into the rusgan.] 3 (WC)Cushion made of straw.
sasag, *s.f.* Kind of basket same shape as the *rusgan* (which see) but of a different size—*Lewis.*
sasagach, -aiche, *a.* Having straw-chairs. 2 Of, or belonging to, straw-chairs. 3 Clumsy awkward. 4 Corpulent, thick-set.
sàsaich, *pr.pt.* a' sàsachadh, *v.a.* Satisfy, fill, satiate, cloy, glut, gorge. 2(MS) Bestick. 3** Saturate. 4*Improperly used for sàs, as sh. e orm, *he attacked me tooth and nail.*
———te, *past pt.* of sàsaich. Satisfied, filled, satiated, sated, cloyed.
sàsamh,** *s. m.* Pleasure, satisfaction. 2 Amends.
sàsda, sàisde, *a.* Easy, comfortable, satisfied, having peace of mind. 2* Saucy, contemptuous, 3**Grateful. 4**At leisure. 5**Easy-minded.
sàsdach, -aiche, see sàsda.
———d, *s.f.ind.* Easiness of circumstances, comfort, peace of mind, contentment. 2*Sauciness, pride. 3**Indolence.
sàsdadh, see sàsdachd.
sàsdadh, see sàsda.
sàsdas, -ais, see sàsdachd.
sàs-mhort, -mhoirt, *s.m.* **Massacre, revengeful murder.**
————ach,** *a.* **Massacring, murdering from revenge.**
————adh,** -aidh, *s.m.* **Massacre, revengeful murder.**
————air,** *s.m.* **Murderer, revengeful murderer.**
sàsta, *past pt.* of sàs. Fixed, fixed upon.
sasta, *a.* Neat, handsome, elegant.
sàsuchadh, see sàsachadh.
sàsuich, see sàsaich.
sath,(AF) *s.m.* Cattle, drove.
sàth, -àith, *s.m.* Plenty, great abundance, enough, as of meat or drink, surfeit, fill, satiety. Cha'n ith a sh. ach an cù, *none but a dog eats his fill;* teann-sàth, *full-fed;* is mòr s. a' choin ghortaichte, *great is the gorge of a famished dog.*
Seachd sgadain, sàth bradain;
seachd bradain, s. ròin;
seachd ròin, s. muice mara bhig;
seachd mucan-mara beaga, s. cionnain crò;
seachd cionnain crò, s. mìol-mhóir a' chuain;
seven herrings, a full meal for a salmon;
seven salmon, a full meal for a seal:
seven seals a full meal for a small whale;
seven small whales a full meal for a large whale;
seven large whales, a full meal for a bull whale;
seven bull whales, a full meal for the Leviathan of the sea. [This proverb can only apply figuratively to the comparative amount of food required to satisfy different sized fishes, for no whale could swallow anything nearly so large as a seal.
sàth,** *s.m.* Stab, thrust. 2 Push. Fear toireadh nan s. 's gearradh nan cnàmh, *a man to give thrusts with his sword and cut bones through with it—Chaidh na fir a dh' òl* (old pìobaireachd.)
sath,(CR) *s.m.* Ill, in the phrase "cha d' thubhairt e math no s., *he said neither good nor ill—Arran.*
sàth, *pr.pt.* a' sàthadh, *v.a.* Thrust. 2 Transfix. 3 Push, squeeze. 4** Stab, pierce. Sh. e 'dhubhain annam, *he transfixed his clutches in me;* sh. e ann e, *he thrust it into him* or *it;* sàthar sleagh troimhe, *he shall be pierced through with a spear;* s. a staigh e, *push it in.*
sàthach, -aiche, *a.* Filling, satiating. 2 Causing satiety, eating to satiety. 3 Satiated, filled, satisfied, as with food or drink. 4††Corpulent. 5 Thrusting, giving thrusts, stabbing, piercing. S. agus acrach, *full and hungry;* s. builleanach, *giving thrusts and blows.*
sathach, see soitheach.
sàthachadh, see sàsachadh.
sàthadh, -aidh, *s.m.* Thrust. 2 Push. 3 Stab. 4 Pierce. 5 Act of thrusting, pushing or stabbing. 6 Piercing. 7 (DU) Thrust with a caschrom, spade or peat-knife. A' s—, *pr.pt.* of sàth. Thug e s., *he gave a thrust.*
sàthaich, see sàsaich.
————te, see sàsaichte.
†sàthail, -e, *a.* see sàthach.
sàthar, see sàth.
sàth-oide,** *s.m.* Preceptor.
Sathuirn, -e, *s.f.* (i.e. Di-sathuirn,) Saturday.
Sathuirn, see Sathairn.

sb

For words beginning with *sb*, see under *sp*.
sc, For words beginning with *sc*, see under *sg*.
Scot-bheurla,** *s.* Broad Scots. [Not a good word.]
sd, For words beginning with *sd*, see under *st*.
's e, (for is e, *he* or *it is.*) Used in answer to

questions, as, An e seo e? 's e, *is this he? yes.*
se, *pers.pron.* He.
-se, *emphat. particle,* see -sa.
sè, *a.* Six. Sè taighean, *six houses.*
sèa, *a.* see sè.
sèab,(DU) *s.m.* (monosyllable) Great quantity of food taken at one meal. 2 The repletion or surfeit resulting therefrom.
sèab, *v.a.* & *n.* see siab. 2 see sèap.
——ach, see sèapach.
sèabadh, see sèapadh.
sèabair, see sèapair.
———eachd,** see sèapaireachd.
seabh,* *v.n.* Stray.
——,** *s.m.* Quid of tobacco.
——ach, -aiche, *a.* Neat, trim, *prov.*
——achas, -ais, *s.m.* Trimness, neatness, *prov.*

616. Seabhag.

seabhag, -aig, -an, *s. f.* Peregrine falcon—*falco peregrinus.* Cearc-sheabhaig, a fowl paid of old to the falconer of the lord of the soil as a yearly tax. Is duilich s. a dheanamh de 'n chlamhan, *the carrion kite will make a bad hawk.*
seabhag, aig, -an, *s.f.* +The spleen.
———ach, -aiche, *a.* Abounding in hawks or falcons. 2 Like, or pertaining to, a hawk or falcon.
———ail, -e, *a.* Falcon-like, hawk-like, fierce.
———air, -ean, *s.m.* Falconer.
———aireachd, *s.f.ind.* Falconry, business of a falconer.
———an,** -ain, *s.m.* Call of a hawk. 2 Place where hawks are kept.
seabhag-dhearg-chasach,¶ *s. f.* Red-footed falcon—*falco rufipes.*
seabhag-fheasgair,¶ *s. f.* Hawk-owl, see seabhag-oidhche.
seabhag-ghèarr,*s.f.*Ger-falcon, see gèarr-sheabhag.
seabhag-ghorm,¶ *s. f.* Peregrine falcon, see seabhag.
seabhag-ghorm-an-fhraoich,¶ *s.f.* Merlin hawk, see meirneal.
seabhag-Lochlannach,¶*s.f.*Iceland falcon—*falco islandicus.*
seabhag-mhór,¶ see glas-sheabhag. 2 see gèarr-sheabhag.
seabhag-mhór-bhàn,¶ see seabhag - mhór - na-seilge.
seabhag-mhór-ghorm,¶ see seabhag. 3 see seabhag-Lochlannach.
seabhag-mhór-na-seilge,¶ *s.f.* Ger falcon—*falco greenlandicus.*
seabhag-nan-uiseag,¶ *s.f.* Hobby falcon, see gormag.
seabhag-na-seilge,¶ *s. f.* Peregrine falcon, see seabhag.
seabhag-oidhche,¶ *s.f.* Night-hawk, see sgraicheag-oidhche. 2 Hawk-owl—*surnia funerea.*

seabhag-riabhach,¶ *s. f.* Goshawk, see glas-sheabhag.
seabhag-sealgair, see seabhag.
seabhaid, -e, -ean, *s. f.* Error. 2 Wandering, going astray. 3**Range. Air s., *astray.*
seabhaid, *v.a.* Wander, go astray. 2 Run hither and thither.
———each, -eiche, *a.* Wandering, excursive. 2 Apt to wander or go astray, straying. 3 Errant, erratic.
———eachd, *s.f.ind.* Habit of wandering. 2 Aptness to wander or go astray. 3 State of being astray.
seabhaidich, see seabhaid.
————e, -an, *s.m.* Wanderer.
seabhais, see seabhas.
seabhaiseach, see seabhasach.
————d, see seabhasachd.
seabhaltrach,* *s.m.* Straggler.
seabhas, -ais, -an, *s.m.* Wandering. 2 Fatigue, weariness. 3**Labour. 4**Strolling, stroll.
sèabhas,(CR) *s.m.* Meaningless talk, nonsense.
——-ach, *a.* Meaningless.
seabhasach, -aiche, *a.* Wandering, straying. 2 Weary, fatigued. 3**Laborious. 4**Discursive. 5**Meaningless.
seabhasachd, *s.f.ind.* Wandering. 2 Aptness to go astray. 3 Weariness, fatigue. 4** Laboriousness. 5**State of being astray. Tha mi sgith le s., *I am tired of wandering.*
†seabhrach, *a.* Certain, sure, true.
seac, *pr.pt.* a' seacadh, *v.a.* & *n.* Wither, cause to wither or fade. 2 Scorch, dry, parch. 3 Wither, become withered, fade, decay, waste, blast. Tha e air searcadh, *it is withered.*
seac, -a, *a.* Withered, decayed, shrivelled. 2 Blighted, scorched, dried, parched. 3 Sapless, without substance. Meanglan s.. *withered branches.*
seac, *s.* Blight.
seacach, -aiche, *a.* Withering, causing to wither. 2 Apt to wither. 3 Withering, fading. 4 Parched.
seacachadh, -aidh, see seacadh.
seacachd, *s.f. ind.* State of being withered, dried up, scorched or parched. 2 Dryness.
seacadh, -aidh, *s.m.* Withering, act of withering or causing to wither. 2 State of withering or fading. 3 Scorching, act or state of scorching, drying up or parching. 4 Wasting, state of wasting or decaying. 5**Scorching heat. 6** Scorched or withered part. A' s—, *pr. pt.* of seac. Air s. nan raon, *on the withered surface of the upland fields*; air s., *withered.*
seacaich, *v.* see seac.
seacaichear, *fut.pass.* of seacaich.
seacaichte, *past pt.* of seacaich, see seacta.
seacaidh,(DU) *a.* Withered. Buntàta s., *a withered potato.*
seacaireachd,(MS) *s.f.* Dryness.
†seacamh, -aimh, -an, *s.m.* Helmet, headpiece.
seacanta, -ainte, *a.* see seacach & seacta.
seacantachd, *s. f.* see seacachd. 2 Aptness to wither.
seacd, see seachd & seac.
seacdach, see seacach.
seacdadh, see seacadh.
seacdaich, see seacaich.
seacdaichte, see seacaichte.
seach, -a, -an, *s.m.* Turn, alternation. Fa s., or mu s., *alternately*; gach aon mu seach, *each one alternately.*
seach, *adv.* Past, gone by. 2 Away, aside. 3 In comparison of. 4 In preference to. Chaidh e mu seach orm, *I missed it*; *it did not occur to me*; tha mise los sin uile a thoirt leam, s. a bhi 'fàgail pàirt dheth 'nar déidh, *I intend*

to take all this with me, rather than leave part behind us ; deò-gréine a chaidh s., *a sunbeam that has gone by.*

seach,** *v.a.* Shun, pass by.

seach, *prep.* Past, beyond, **farther than.** 2 More than, rather than.

S an dorus, *past the door ;* cha téid e s. seo, *he will not pass this,* or *here ;* s. aon eile, *rather than anyone else ;* s. leigeil da dol seachad, *rather than he should pass by ;* do aon s. aon, *to one more than to another ;* s. a chéile, *one from another , 2 one past the other ;* fear s. fear, *one man more than another;* cha'n aithne dhomh aon seach a chéile, *I do not know one from the other;* s. innseadh air, *rather than inform against him ;* cha téid e s. am baile seo, *he will not go beyond this villcge;* s. e fhéin a mhilleadh, *rather than spoil himself ;* tha sinne gu math dheth s. sluagh bochd nan Innsean, *we are well off in comparison to the poor people of the Indies ;* fear mu s., *man by man, one by one, each in rotation ;* uair mu s., *time about ;* grathuinn mu s., *while about ;* a là, *still alive ;* am bheil e seach là fhathast ? *is he still alive ?—Suth'd.* *Seach* is used as a *prep.* in two ways,as Seach gu'n iarradh iad i, *seeing that they would look for her ;* and, s. iad 'ga h-iarraidh, *rather than that they should look for her—Celtic Review, xii. 357.* [Followed by the *nom.* case.]

seachad, *adv.* By, along, on, onward, forward. 2 Aside. 3 Out of the way. 4 Past. 5 Beyond, more. 6 Gone by.

A' dol s., *passing by* or *along ;* a' dol s. air t' ais 's air t' aghaidh, *not calling, passing and repassing;* an là a' dol s., *the day passing ;* a' cur s. na h-ùine, *passing the time ;* cuir s. seo, *put this by ;* s. oirnn, *past us ;* na cuir s. orm e, *do not put it by me, 2 give me the option (of refusing it) ;* cha chuireadh e olc seachad orm, *he would always charge me with wrong-doing ;* thig e s. orm-sa, *he will come past me ;* leigidh sinn sin s., *we will let that pass ;* cuir s. airgiod, *hoard money ;* theirig s., *pass by ;* cha'n 'eil s. air fichead ann, *there are not more than twenty in it;* s. air mile, *more than a thousand, more than a mile ;* tha e deich bliadhna agus s., *he is more than ten years of age ;* is math s. e, *it is as well to be done with it ; it is well to have it laid by ;* tha e deich bliadhna agus s., *he is more than ten years of age ;* labhair 's an dol s., *speak inpassing.*

seachad ! *int.* By with you ! away with you !

seachad, *pr.pt.* a' seachadadh, *v. a.* Hoard, lay by. †2 Deliver, surrender.

seachadach, -aiche, *a.* Hoarding, laying by, frugal, parsimonious. 2**Traditionary.

seachadachd, *s.f.ind.* Hoarding, laying by. 2 Disposition to hoard or lay by. 3 Frugality, parsimony. 4 Tradition.

seachadadh, -aidh, *s. m.* Hoarding. 2 Act of hoarding or laying by. †3 Tradition. A' s—, *pr.pt.* of seachad.

seachadaich,** *v. a.* Put aside. 2 Avoid. 3 Hoard.

seachadail, -e, *a.* Past.

seachadas,** -ais, *s.m.* Tradition. 2 (MS) Preteriteness. S. dhaoine, *the traditions of men.*

seachaid,** *pr.pt.* a' seachaideadh, *v.a.* Lay by, store, hoard. 2 Deliver, surrender.

———each,** *a.* Laying up, storing. 2 Frugal. 3 Delivering, surrendering.

———eachd,** *s.f.* Disposition to hoard. 2 Frugality. 3 Hoarding.

seachain, *pr.pt.* a' seachnadh, *v.a.* Avoid, shun. 2 Spare, dispense with. 3 Want. 4 Lend. 5 Abstain. 6 Stay, *prov.* 7*Keep at a distance from. S. an t-olc, *avoid evil ;* an s. thu seo ? *can you spare* or *dispense with this ?* mholainn dhuit mis' a sheachnadh, *I would advise you to keep me at arms' length.*

seachain,** *s.pl.* Idle tales. 3 Allegory.

seachainte, *a. & past pt.* of seachain. Shunned, avoided. 2 see seachanta.

————, *comp.* of seachanta.

————ach, -eiche, *a.* see seachanta.

†seacham, *prep.pron.* Beyond me, past me. *Emphatic,* seacham-sa.

seachamh-inntinn,(CR) *s.* Gratification, satisfaction. Thug siod s. gu leòir dha, *that satisfied him fully.*

seachanta, -ainte, *a.* Shunning, avoiding. 2 To be shunned or avoided. 3 Shunned, avoided. 4 Unlucky. 5 Allegorical. 6 Dismal, ominous. 7 Evitable. 8 Wandering, straying. 9* Avoidable, guarded aghinst. Là s. na bliadhna, *Childermas day ;* là s. na seachduin, *Friday.*

seachantach, -aiche, *a.* see seachanta. S. air òl, *guarded against drunkenness.*

seachantachd, *s.f.ind.* Shunning, avoiding. 2 *Avoidableness. 3 Unluckiness, unpropitiousness. 4 Tendency to wander. 5* Continued precaution to avoid.

seacharan, -ain, -an, see seachran.

seachbho, see seachlach.

seach-bhriathar,** *s.m.* Allegorical saying.

seachd, *v. & a.* see seac.

seachd, *a.* Seven. Rè sh. bliadhna, *during seven years ;* gabhaidh tu nan seachdaibh iad, *thou shalt take them in sevens ;* seachd fir fhichead, *twenty-seven men ;* s. sgìth, *completely tired.*

seachdach, -aiche, *a.* see seacach.

seachdachadh, see seacachadh.

seachdadh, see seacadh.

seachdaich, *v.a.* see seacaich. 2 Arrange in sevens, septimate, septuplicate.

seachdaichear, *fut. pass.* of seachdaich.

seachdaichte, *past pt.* of seachdaich.

seachdain, see seachduin.

————each, see seachduineach.

seachdadaireachd, see seacaireachd,

seachdamh, *a.* The seventh. [7mh.] 2 *s.* The seventh part. An s. là, *the seventh day.*

seachdamh-deug, *a.* The seventeenth. [17mh.] 2 *s.* The seventeenth part. An seachdamh-taigh-deug, *the seventeenth house.*

seachdaran,(MS) *s.m.* The bear (constellation.)

seachdarran,(MS) *s.m.* Pleiades.

seachd-deug, *a.* Seventeen. Seachd craobhan deug, *seventeen trees.*

seachd-dùbailt,** *a.* Septuple, sevenfold.

seachd-fillte, *a.* Seven-fold.

seachd-fillteach, *a.* see seachd-fillte.

seachd-mhìos, -a, *s. m.* The seventh month, July. [* gives "September," but the seventh month is always understood to mean July now in spite of the literal meaning of the name.]

seachd-mhìosach, -aich, *s.m.* Child born in the seventh month of pregnancy.

————, *a.* Born in the seventh month of pregnancy. Leanabh s., *a seventh-month child.*

seachdnar, *s. coll.* Seven (applied to persons only. Followed by the *gen.pl.*)

seachdran,†† -ain, *s.m.* The Pleiades.

seachd-reultach, (an t-) *s.* see seachd-reultan.

seachd-reultan, (na) *s.pl.* The Pleiades.

seachd-rinn, see seachd-reultan.

seachd-searbh, *a.* Nauseating, utterly disagreeable.

seachd-shlisneach, *a.* Heptagonal.

————, -eich, -ean, *s.f.* Heptagon.

seachd-shlisneag, -eig, -an, *s.f.* Heptagon.
seachd-siona,(AC) The seven elements (fire,air, earth, water, ice, wind and lightning.)
seachd-thaobhach,* see seachd-shlisneach.
seachduan,** -ain, *s.m.* Fold.
seachduin, -e, -ean, *s.f.* Week, seven days. S. bhogadh-nad-gad, *rogation week;* s. bho 'n diugh, *this day se'ennight (forwards)*; s. gus an dé, *yesterday se'ennight (past time)*; uair 's an t-s., *once a week*; s. mu seach, *week about, a week in rotation*; gach dara s., *every alternate week*; s. na luaithre, *ember week*; eadar seo agus ceann seachduin, *in a week's time.*
seachduineach, -eiche, *a.* Weekly. 2**Hebdomadal.
seach-labhair,*v.n.* Allegorize, speak allegorically.
seach-labhairt, -e, *s.f.* Speaking allegorically. 2 Act of speaking allegorically, allegorizing. 3 Allegory. A' s—, *pr.pt.* of seach-labhair.
seach-labhrach, -aiche, *a.* Allegorical. 2 Speaking allegorically. 3 Prone to speak allegorically.
seach-labhradh, -aidh, -aidhean, *s.m.* Allegory, allegorical speaking.
seachlach, -aich, *s.f.* Cow that has been two years without a calf. 2 Heifer that continues barren when of the age to have a calf.
seachlag,** *s.f,* Park.
seachlaimh, -a, *a.* Remaining, " bydand,"—the motto of the Gordon Highlanders. 2*In store.
———, -e, *s.f.* That which has been preserved or saved, savings.
seachlan, -ain, *s.m.* Any insignificant worthless thing. 2 Warren.
seach-laoghach, -aich, -aichean,*s.* see seachlach.
seach-luidh,** *v.n.* Lie apart, lie aside.
———e,** *s.m.* Lying apart.
†seachmhal,-ail, -an, *s.m.* Forgetfulness, oblivion. 2 Digression. 3 Partiality.
†seachmhalla, see seachmhallach.
seachmhallach, -aiche, *a.* Forgetful, oblivious. 2 Digressive.
seach-mhallachd,** *s. f.* Oblivion, forgetfulness.
seachmh-inntinn,(CR) *s.m.* Gratification, satisfaction—*Suth'd.* (seachdamh-inntinn)
†seachn-ab, -a, *s.m.* Prior.
seachnach, -aiche, *a.* Avoiding, shunning. 2 Avoidable.
†seachnach, -aich, see seicneach.
———adh, Same meanings as seachnadh. A' s—, *pr. pt.* of seachnaich.
seachnadh, -aidh, *s. m.* Avoiding. 2 Act of avoiding or shunning. 3 Lending. 4 Act of lending. 5 Wanting, missing. 6*Sparing. 7* Act of sparing. A' s—, *pr. pt.* of seachain.
seachnaich,** *pr. pt.* a' seachnachadh, *v. a.* Avoid, shun. 2 Miss. 3 Escape.
seachnaichte, *past pt.* of seachnaich. Avoided, shunned, 2 Lent.
seachnair,** *s.m.* Avoider.
†seachrach,** *a.* Dirty.
seachrain, *v.n.* Err, go astray, wander.
———, *gen.sing.* of seachran.
seachran, -ain, -an, *s.m.* Wandering, going astray. 2 Transgression, error. Air s., *astray, out of one's course*; s. a' mhiann, *the wandering of desire*; mo sh., *my error.*
seachran, -ain, *s.m.* Wandering. 2 Act of wandering, going astray or erring. 3‡‡Transgression. A' s—, *pt.pt.* of seachrain.
seachranach, -aiche, *a.* Straying, going astray, wandering. 2 Apt to wander or go astray. 3 Misleading, causing to wander or stray. 4 Erring, sinning. 5 Apt to err or sin. 6 Causing to err or sin. 7 Wrong, erroneous. 8 Private, unfrequented. Rathad s., *a by-road*; dh' imich an luchd-turuis air rathadaibh s., *the travellers walked through by-ways*; reulta s. *wandering stars*; *comets.*
seachranach,†† -aich, *s.m.* Wanderer.
seachranachadh,(MS) *s.m.* Bearing in hand.
seachranachd, *s.f.ind.* State of being astray. 2 Aptness to stray. 3 Error, proneness to error or sin.
seachranaich, -ean, *s. m.* Wanderer, one who strays or is strayed. 2 One apt to go astray. 3 Sinner, one that errs.
seachranaich, *v.a.* Bewilder.
seach-rathad, -aid, -an, *s.m.* By-way.
————ach, -aiche, *a.* Abounding in byways.
seach-ròd, -òid, see seach-rathad.
seach-ròdach, see seach-rathadach.
†seacht, see seachd.
†seachtar, see seachduar.
seach-theinn, see seac-thinn.
seac-mharbh,(DU) *a.* Completely dead, in a condition of *rigor mortis.*
——— ———,* *v.a.* Kill outright. S. e i, *he killed her outright.*
seac-thinn, -e, -ean, *s.f.* Severe illness, disease, mortal sickness. 2 Consumption.
————, *a,* Mortally sick. 2 Severely indisposed.
seac-thinneach, -eiche, *a.* Severely ill. 2 Labouring under a chronic illness. 2 Consumptive. 3 Causing a severe or wasting sickness. 4 Mortally sick.
seac-thinneas,** -eis, *s.m.* Severe illness, mortal sickness.
seachuin, see seachain.
seacta, *past pt.* of seac. Withered, dried up, shrivelled, parched. 2 Wasted, decayed.
séad, -a, -an, see seud, seòd & séada.
†sead, *s.m.* Likeness of a thing. 2 Seat.
séad, *s.m.* Way, road.
seada,(AF) *s.m.* Deer.
seadair,** *s.m.* Dolt. 2 Sneaking fellow.
seadaireach, *a.* Sneaking.
seadaireachd,** *s.f.* Sneaking.
†seadal, -ail, *s.m.* Short space of time.
†sead-gabhla, *s.m.* Increase.
seadh, *int.* Yes, it is, just so, just as you say. 2 Yes, indeed, truly, furthermore. S., a Thighearna; *yes,Lord!* s. gu dearbh,*yes, just so*; seadh, seadh; *just so! truly! really!* ma seadh, *if so, if it be so, likewise*: Moire s., *yes, indeed, by Mary it is so.*
seadh, -a, -an, *s.m.* see seagh.
†seadh, -a, *a.* Strong, stout, able.
†seadh, -a, *s.m.* Strength.
†seadh,** *v.a.* Esteem, prize, value. 2 Saw. 3 Plane.
seadhach, -aiche, *a.* see seaghach.
seadhachadh, see seaghachadh.
seadhachail, see seaghachail.
seadhachas, see seaghachas.
seadhaich, see seaghaich.
seadhail, see seaghach.
seadhalachd, see seaghachas.
seadhan,* -ain, *s.m.* Rogation. 2 (DMy) Puffing with exertion. Thug siod s. ort! *that made you puff!*
seadhar, see seaghach.
————arachd, see seaghachas.
seadhmhor, see seaghach.
seadh-suiridh, see seagh-suiridh.
seafaid,(AF) *s.* Heifer.
seagad,** *a.* Sixty.
seagaid, see seachlach.
seagair,¶ *s. m.* Kittiwake—*larus tridactylus.*
seagal, -ail, *s.m.* Rye—*secale cereale.*
seagalach, -aiche, *a.* Abounding in rye. 2 Per-

taining to rye.
seagh, -a, -an, *s.m.* Meaning, sense, purport, import 2 Discourse, dialogue. 3 Sense, understanding. 4 Cause, reason, purpose. 5 Esteem, value, respect. 6 Crop of a bird. Dè is s. dha ? *what is the purport of it ?* s. na lice seo a dh'fheòraich, *to enquire into the import of this tombstone ;* gabh s., *pay attention.*
[*Seadh* is the form used in the Bible and in the dictionaries, but *seagh* is better.]
seagha,** *a.* Curious, ingenious.
seaghach, -aiche, *a.* Discreet, sensible, prudent. 2 Weighty, important, having much meaning. 3 Sagacious. 4 Fit, proper. 5 Courteous, respectful, of gentle manners. 6** Attentive, heedful.
seaghachadh, -aidh, *s.m.* Act or state of signifying. 2 Holding forth, showing, importing, meaning. A' s—, *pr.pt.* of seaghaich.
seaghach,(AF) *s.m.* He-goat.
seaghachail, -e, *a.* Implicative.
seaghachas, -ais, *s.m.* Sense, intellect, understanding. 2 Sagacity, acuteness, penetration. 3 Courtesy, gentleness. 4 Attentiveness.
seaghaich, *v.a.* Signify, import, imply.
seaghail, -e, *a.* see seaghach.
seaghalachd, *s.f.* see seaghachas.
seaghar, -aire, see seaghach.
seaghas, see seaghachas.
seaghas,** -ais, *s.m.* Wood.
seaghlan,** *s.* Column, post. 2 King.
seaghlan,** *s.m.* Old man. 2 Infirm person. 3 Pithless person.
seaghlanach,** *a.* Infirm, stiff. 2 Columnal.
seaghmhor, -mhoire, see seaghach.
seaghmhorachd, *s.f.* see seaghachas.
seagh-suiridh, -a-, -an-suiridh, *s.f.* Love-token.
seagsaid, see seasaich.
seaguil,* see seagal.
seal, -a, -an, *s.m.* While, space of time, season 2** Glimpse. 3 Course, turn. 4 Spot. 5 see seul. 6 (MS) Mean. Car s., *or* rè s., *for a while.*
sealach, -aiche, *a.* Momentary, of short continuance, transitory.
sealacha,(CR) *s.pl.* Seals.
†**sealadach**, -aiche, *a.* Alternate, by turns. 2 Transitory.
sealaidheach,** *a.* Transitory.
sealaidheachd,** *s.f.* Transitoriness, alternation. 2 Vicissitude, change.
sealan, -ain, -an, *s.m., dim.* of seal. Little while. 2 Halter or rope for execution.
sèalan, -ain, -an, *s.m.* Sheep-louse, tick.
sèalanach, -aiche, *a.* Abounding in sheep-lice or ticks.
sealanach,** -aich, *s.m.* Executioner. 2 Villain. 3 Meagre man or beast.
sealanach,†† *a.* Of short duration.
sealanta,** *a.* Rigid.
sealantas, -ais, *s.m.* Rigidness.
sealastair,(DC) *s.f.* *Uist* for seilisteir.
sealbh, seilbh, -an & -ean, *s.m.* Possession. 2 Inheritance. 3 Cattle, drove, stock. 4 Field. 5 Luck, good luck. 6 (AC) Corn. 7 *rarely,* Pretence, colour. Gach s. a th' agam, *every living creature I possess ;* fhuair e s. *he got possession ;* fad-sealbh, *infeoffment ;* thoir fad-sealbh. *infeoff ;* gu 'n gléidh an S. mi ! *fortune preserve me !* s. chaorach, *a stock of sheep ;* s. chrodh, *a possession of black cattle.*
sealbhach, -aiche, *a.* Fortunate, lucky. 2 Prosperous. 3 Possessive.
sealbhachadh, -aidh, *s. m.* Possessing, act of possessing, enjoying. 2 Act of acquiring or winning property, inheriting. A' s—, *pr. pt.* of sealbhaich.
sealbhachail, -e, *a.* Inheritable.
sealbhachas, -ais, *s.m.* Luckiness, state of being lucky, fortunate or prosperous. 2††Stock.
sealbhachd, *s.f.* see sealbhachas.
sealbhadair, -ean, *s. m.* Possessor, owner, proprietor. 2 Occupant.
————eachd, *s.f.* Ownership, possession.
sealbhadh,** -aidh, *s.m.* Possessing, inheriting. 2 Possession.
sealbhag,§ -aig, -an, *s. f.* Common sorrel, see samh.
sealbhagach, -aiche, *a.* Abounding in sorrel. 2 Of, or like sorrel.
sealbhag-na-fiodha,§ *s.f.* Wood-sorrel, see seamrag.

617. Sealbhag-nam-fiadh.

sealbhag-nam-fiadh,§ *s.f.* Mountain sorrel—*oxyria reniformis.*
sealbhag-nan-caorach, *s.f.* Sheep-sorrel.
sealbhaich, *pr.pt.* a' sealbhachadh, *v.a.* Possess, inherit. 2 Enjoy, own. 3 Gain, acquire, win.
sealbhaiche, -an, *s.m.* see sealbhadair.
sealbhaichear, *fut.pass.* of sealbhaich.
sealbhaichte, *past pt.* of sealbhaich. Possessed. 2 Won, acquired.
sealbhaidh,** *s.f.* Encounter, encountering.
sealbhan, -ain, -an, *s.m.* Herd, drove, number of cattle, or of small cattle (sheep, goats, &c.) 2 Multitude, company. 3 The throat, throttle. 4(AF) Tocher, possession of cattle. 5 Little possession, little inheritance. An s. a' chéile air uchd an t-srutha, *at each other's throats on the breast of the stream ;* bha e s. uairean an seo, *he was here several times.*
sealbhanachadh, -aidh, *s. m.* Act of seizing by the throat, throttling. A' s—, *pr.pt.* of sealbhanaich.
sealbhanaich, *pr.pt.* a' sealbhanachadh, *v.a.* Seize by the throat, throttle.
————te, *past pt.* of sealbhanaich. Seized by the throat, throttled.
sealbhar, -aire, *a.* see sealbhmhor.
sealbharach,** *s.m.* Prosperousness, propitiousness, good luck. 2 Possession of property.
sealbharachd, see sealbhmhorachd.
sealbh-dhlighe, *s.f.* Inheritance.
sealbh-ghlacadair, -ean, *s.m.* Impropriator.
sealbh-ghlacadh, -aidh, *s.m.* Occupancy.
sealbhmhor, -oire, *a.* Having many or great possessions, rich. 2 Prosperous, enjoying prosperity. 3 Lucky, propitious. Ged a bhithinn cho s. ris, *though I were possessed of as much property as he.*
sealbhmhorachd, *s.f.ind.* State of being wealthy or rich. 2 Wealth, riches. 3 Prosperity, state of being prosperous. 4 Fortune, good luck, propitiousness. 5 State of being lucky or fortunate. 6**Possession of property.
seal-coise, *s.m.* Foot-board or treadle of spin-

ning-wheel.
sealg, *pr.pt.* a' sealg,*v.a.* & *n.* Hunt, chase,fowl, hawk. 2 Lay snares for, lie in wait. 3* Watch narrowly. S. dhomh sithionn, *hunt venison for me.*
sealg, -eilg, *pl.* -a & -an, *s. f.* Hunt, hunting, fowling, hawking, the chase. 2*Milt of swine. 3 Spleen of man or beast. 4 Bellyache. Is aoibhinn an obair an s., *the chase is a joyous occupation.*
sealgach, -aiche, *a*, Hunting. 2 Hawking. 3 Fond of hunting or fowling. 4** Having spleen, splenetic.
sealgadh, -aidh, *s.m.* Same meanings as sealg. A' s—, *pr.pt.* of sealg.
sealgag,§ *s.f.* Common sorrel, see samh.
sealgair, -ean, *s.m.* Hunter, huntsman. 2** Fowler, falconer. 3 Sportsman. 4 Gamekeeper. 5 Forester. 6 Falcon, see seabhag. 7* Sneaker. S. a theab, *an unsuccessful hunter.*
sealgaireach,** *a.*Like, or pertaining to, a hunter or huntsman.
sealgaireachd, *s.f.ind.* Hunting, hawking, fowling. 2 Business of a huntsman, gamekeeper, hawker or fowler 3* Watching narrowly.
sealgair mór, (an), *s.m.* The constellation Orion. The crios (Orion's belt) is made up of three stars of a good second magnitude. A' bhiodag, (the dirk), is slung from two of these ; it shows as three small stars with a larger one at the end of the sheath. An sporan, is suspended from the other, and Am breacanguailne is blowing awav on the breeze to the left.
sealg-bhata, -aite, -aichean, *s. m.* Hunting pole.
sealghag, *Lewis* for sealgag.
seal-iomairt, -e, -ean, *s.f.* Temporary convenience.
seal-iomairteach, -eiche, *a.* Affording temporary convenience.
seall, *pr.pt.* a' sealltainn, *v.a.* See, look,behold. 2 (CR) Show—*W. of Ross.* Seallaidh mi dhuit e, *I will show it to you* ; seall orm,, *look at me;* Dia s. oirnn ! *God have mercy on us !* am fear nach s. roimhe, seallaidh e as a dhéidh, *he who will not look before him must look after him.*
seall ! *int.* Look ! see ! behold ! S. an gaisgeach treun a' teachd, *see the conquering hero comes!*
seallach,†† *a.* Seeing, viewing.
sealladh, -aidh, -aidhean, *s.m.* Sight, spectacle, view. 2 Compass of vision, extent to which one can see. 3 Sight, eye-sight, power of vision. 4 Look, cast of the eyes. 5 Sight,glance. 6 Vision, dream. 7**Supernatural sight. 8** Short while. †9 Cell. 10(MS) Air. Fearseallaidh,*a seer;* s. cùil, *a back-look;* s.-taoibh, *a side-look,side-glance* ; le s.-taoibh bu mhór an aire, *with side looks they watched attentively* ; s. annasach, *or* s. nòsach, *a raree-show* ; s. gobhlach, *a squint* ; a' dol as an t-sealladh, *going out of sight* ; as mo sh., *out of my sight* ; s. nan sùl, *eyesight* ; a réir an t-seallaidh seo uile, *according to all this vision* ; s.-cùil, *a back look, looking behind* ; chaill e a sh., *he lost his eye-sight* ; fad mo shealladh, *the extent of my view.*
seallagan, -ain, -an, *s. m., dim.* of sealladh. Peep, glance, glimpse, view.
seallam, *1st.per.sing.imp.* of seall. Let me see.
seall-fhios,** *s.m.* Ocular proof, certainty. Tha s. agam air, *I am quite certain of it.*
seallan, see sealain.
seal-mara, *s.* Space from which the tide has receded. 2(DMy) The period of about six hours of flowing to ebb and *vice versa.* A' dol do 'n t-seal-mara, *going to look for whelks, seaware, &c.*
sealltach,** *a.* Looking, gazing, staring. 2 Cautious, circumspect.
sealltainn, *s.m.*Looking, act of looking, seeing, viewing. 2 Observation, view.
———each,†† *a.* Careful.
sealtuidh,** *s.m.* Sheltie, Highland pony.
†**sealtuir**,** *s.m.* Sword.
†**sealuidheachd**, *s.f.ind.* Course of time.
sèam, -a, -an & -annan, *s. m.* Hook, peg, pin 2 Mote.
sèam, *pr. pt.* a' sèamadh, *v.a.* Forbid, prohibit. 2 Enjoin, warn, caution, bodge.
sèam, *s.f.* Entreaty, earnest petition, request. Is iomadh s. a thug mis' air, *many an earnest request I made.*
seam,** *s.m.* Mote, atom. 2 Any small object
sèamach,** *a.* Warning, hinting, winking.
seamadair,* -ean, *s.m.* Petitioner.
sèamadh,** -aidh, *s.m.* Caution, warning,winking. 2 Act of warning or cautioning. 3 Forbidding. 3 Act of forbidding or prohibiting. A' s—, *pr. pt.* of sèam. Tha mi a' s. dhuit, *I give you warning* ; thug mi s. dhuit, *I gave you warning.*
seama-guad,* *s.m.* Shuffle, quibble.
seamaide,§ *s.* Blades of grass.
seamair,* *s,f.* see seamrag.
seamair Muire,§ see seamrag Muire.
sèaman, -ain, -an, *s.m.* Little stout person. 2 Small nail riveted. 3** Pin. 4**Nail. [also seaman.]
———ach, -aiche, *a.* Stout. 2 Jolly, cheer-3**Rivetted, as a nail.
———ach, *s.m.* One sturdily indifferent to the rights of others. S. balaich, *a rough, churlish bullying character.*
seamanach,(AF) *s.m.* Wasp.
sèamanachd, *s. f. ind.* Stoutness. 2 Jollity, cheerfulness. 3††Inattentiveness.
seamann,(AF) *s.* Small snail.
seamar, see seòmar & seamrag.
seamasan,* -ain, see seamsan.
————ach,* -aiche, *a.* see seamsanach.
————achd,* see seamsanachd.
————achadh, see seamsanachadh.
————aich,* see seamsanaich.
sèamh, -a & sèimhe,*a.* Peaceful, quiet, tranquil, calm. 2 Mild, modest, gentle. 3 Small,slim, slender, tender. 4* Enchantment to make one's friends prosper. [**seamh.]
sèamhach, -aiche, *a.* see sèamh.
———d, *s.f.ind.* Peacefulness, tranquility, quietness, mildness,modesty,gentleness,calmness. 2 Smallness, thinness, slimness, tenderness. 3 **Comeliness.
sèamhaich,†† *pr. pt.* a' sèamhachadh, *v. n.* Be quiet. 2 Calm, tranquillize.
sèamhaidh, -e, *a.* Discreet, prudent. 2‡‡Slender. 3**Subtle. 4 see sèamh.
————eachd, *s.f.* see sèamhachd.
sèamhail, -e, *a.* see sèamhaidh & sèamh.
sèamhalachd, see sèamhachd.
sèamhas, -ais, *s.m.* Good luck, chance, prosperity.
———ach, -aiche, *a.* Fortunate, lucky, prosperous.
———achd,** *s.f.* Luck. 2 Continued good luck.
———air,** *s.m.* Lucky or fortunate man.
———ar,** *a.* Lucky, fortunate. 2 Bringing good luck. 3 Boding good luck. Gu s., *luckily.*
seamh-mheas,** *s.m.* Mellow fruit.
seamhrag,** -aig, *s.f.* Small nail. 2 Small peg. 3 see seamrag.
sèamhsail, -e, *a.* see sèamhasach.

seamhsail,* -e, *a.* Fortunate, lucky.
sèamhsalachd,** *s.* Fortunateness, luckiness.
seamhsar, -aire, *a.* see sèamhasach.
seamlach, -aich, -aichean, *s. f.* Cow that gives milk without her calf beside her. 2* Cow that allows another cow's calf to suck her. 3 Impudent,troublesome fellow. 4 Silly person,one easily imposed upon.
seamlachas,* -ais, *s.m.* Imposture. Chuir thu an orra-sheamlachais orm, *you duped me.*
seamlachadh,* -aidh, *s. m.* Duping, imposing upon. A' s—, *pr.pt.* of seamlaich. 'Gam sh., *duping me.*
seamlaich,* *v.a. & n.* Dupe, impose upon.

618. Seamrag (2.) *619. Seamrag bhàn.*

seamrag, -aig, -an, *s.f.* Shamrock, trefoil, clover. Breac le seamragan is neòineanan, *studded with clover and daisies.* 2§ Wood-sorrel—*oxalis acetosella.*
———ach, *a.* Abounding in shamrock. 2 Pertaining to shamrock.
seamrag-an-deocadain, see seamrag-an-deocain.
seamrag-an-deocain, (AC) *s.f.* Four-leaved or five-leaved shamrock,see seamrag-nam-buadh.
seamrag bhàn,§ *s. f.* White or Dutch clover—*trifolium repens.* [This name is never applied to wood-sorrel.]

620. Seamrag bhuidhe.

seamrag bhuidhe,§ *s. f.* Yellow clover or hop trefoil—*trifolium porcumbens.*
seamrag chapuill,§ *s. f.* Red clover, purple trefoil—*trifolium pratense.*
seamrag còig-bhileach, see còig mheòir Muire.
seamrag chré,§ *s. f.* Common speedwell, see lus chré.
seamrag dhearg, *s.f.* Purple clover—*Colonsay.*
seamrag gheal, *s.f.* White clover—*Colonsay.*
seamrag Muire, *s.f.* Wood loose-strife or yellow pimpernel—*lysimachia nemorum.*
seamrag-nam-buadh, *s.f.* Four-leaved clover. 2 (AC) Five-leaved clover.

621. Seamrag chapuill. *625. Seamrag Muire.*

seamrag-nan-each, *s.f.* (AC) Four- or five-leaved clover, see seamrag-nam-buadh. 2 Knapweed, hard-heads—*Colonsay.*
seamrag-nan-searrach,(AC) see seamrag-nan-each.
seamsag,** -aig, *s.f.* Small nail or peg. 2 Wood-sorrel—*oxalis acetosella.*
seamsan, -ain, -an, *s.m.* Hesitation. 2 Delay. 3 Sham. 4 Quibble, to gain good time or ends, quirk, stupid evasion. 5 Laziness, indolence.
———ach, -aiche, *a.* Hesitating. 2 Delaying. 3 Lazy, indolent. 4 Evasive, tricking. 5* Absurd in the extreme.
———achadh, -aidh, *s.m.* Tricking, deceiving. A' s—, *pr.pt.* of seamsanaich. 'Gam sh. air an dòigh sin, *tricking me like that.*
seamsanachd,* *s.f.ind.* Evasiveness, quibbling, quirking. 2 Shamming habits.
seamsanaich,* *v.a. & n.* Sham. 2 Shuffle, evade. 3 Coax one out of his right.
———, -e, *s. f.* Hesitation. 2 Delay. 3 Laziness, indolence.
sean, *1st. comp.* sine, *2nd. comp.*sinid, *3rd.comp.* sinead. Old, aged, ancient. C' ar son a dh' fhàsas iad s.? *why do they become old?* an s. sruthan sin, *that ancient stream* ; o sh., *anciently, of old* ; fhuair e bàs 'na sheann duine, *he died an old man ;* cha sean do m' shean agus cha 'n òg do m' òg thu, *you are neither old with my old nor young with my young*—i.e. as you are not related to me I will have nothing to do with you. [*Sean* does not aspirate a word following if if begins with *d*, *s* or *t*. It is pronounced and spelt *seann* when preceding a noun beginning with *d*, *s*, *t*, *l*, *n*, or *r*, but spelt *sean* and pronounced *seann* when placed before a noun beginning with any of the other letters.]
†**sean**, -a, *s.m.* Supper.
†**sèan**, *s.m.* Prosperity. 2 Happiness. Cuir a sh., *squander.*
sèan, -a, -an, *s.m.* see seun.
——, *v.a.* see seun.
seanacach, -aiche, *a.* Sagacious. 2 Knowing, crafty, wily.
seanacaidheachd, *s.f.* Sagacity. 2 Craftiness, wiliness.
seanacar, -air, *a.* Sagacious. 2 Old-looking, old-fashioned. 3**Prospective.
———achd, *s.f.ind.* Sagacity. 2 Oldness of appearance.
seanacas, see seanachas.
seanach,** *a.* Crafty. 2 Lucky.
seanachadh, *s. m.* State of becoming old. A' s—, *pr.pt.* of seanaich.
seanachaidh, -ean, *s.m.* Reciter of tales or stor-

ies. 2 Antiquarian, one skilled in ancient or remote history. 3 Historian. 4 Recorder. keeper of records. 5 Genealogist. Bha e 'na sh., *he was a recorder.*

————each, -eiche, *a.* Versed in tales, history or antiquities. 2 Fond of, or reciting, tales or antiquities. 3 Like a reciter of tales or stories. 4 Skilled in genealogy.

seanachar, see seanacar.

————achd, see seanacaracbd.

seanachas, -ais, -an, *s.m* Tale, story, narration. 2 Conversation, discourse, talk. 3 Speech, language. 4 Tradition, chronicle, history. 5 A history. 6 Antiquities. 7 Genealogy. 8* Biography. 9* Talk about old stories. Tha droch sh. aige, *he uses bad language;* cron seanachais, *an anachronism.*

seanachasach, -aiche, *a.* Abounding in conversation, talkative, having many tales, narrative. 2 Of, or belonging to, speech. 3 Conversable. 4 Skilled in history, genealogy or antiquities. 5 Fond of reciting tales, stories or genealogies. 6 Traditionary.

seanachasail, see seanachasach.

seana-cheann, -chinn, *s.m.* Wise or experienced person. 2 Ludicrously applied to extraordinary intelligence or sagacity in early youth. 2 Precocious person.

————ach, -aiche, *a.* Wise, sagacious. 2 Experienced. 3 Precocious. [ness.

seanachd, *s.f.ind.* Antiquity, ancientness, old-

sèanachd, see seunachd.

seanachrionta,* *a.* Long-headed, wise, sagacious. 2 Experienced. 3 Precocious, old-fashioned, too wise for one's years.

seanadair, see seunadair.

————eachd, see seunadaireachd.

sèanadh, see seunadh.

seanadh, -aidh, -aidhean, *s.m.* Senate, synod.

seanagar,(CR) *a.* see seanacar.

seanagarra, -aire, *a.* Old, old-like. 2††Sagacious, wise.

————chd, *s.f.ind.* Old appearance or look. 2††Sagacity.

seana-ghille, -an, *s.m.* Old bachelor. 2 Youth arrived at the age of puberty.

————achd, *s.f.ind.* Bachelorship.

seanaich, *pr. pt.* a' seanachadh, *v. n.* Become old.

seanaiche,** *s. m.* Senator, member of parliament. 2 Member of a synod. 3 Antiquarian.

seanaid,** *s.f.* Synod. 2 Senate.

————each, *a.* Senatal. 2 Synodal.

sèanail, see seunail.

seanailtireas, -eis, *s.m.* Decree.

sean-aimsir,** *s.f.* Olden time.

————eil,** *a.* Old-fashioned. 2 Antique.

seanair, -ean, *s. m.* Grandfather. 2 Elder. 3 **Ancestor. 4 Presbyter. 5 Member of Parliament, senator. 6 (MS) Alderman. 7 Ancient bard. 8** Druid. S. an t-seanair, *a great great grandfather.*

seanaireach,** -eich, *s.m.* Presbyterian.

————, -eiche, *a.* Senatorial. 2 Presbyterian.

————d, *s.f.* Presbytery. 2 Presbyerianism. 3 5th. stage of human life, from 54 to 84 years of age. 4**Bird-catching. 5**Ancestry. 6 (MS) Primogeniture.

seanait,** see seanaid.

seanalair,* -ean, *s.m.* General.

seanamhair, *s.m.* see seanmhair.

sèanan, see seunan.

seanan,(AF) *s.m.* Kite.

seananach,** -aich, *s.m.* Wasp.

sean-aois, -e, *s.f.* Old age. 'Na s., *in her old age.*

sean-aosach,(MS) *a.* Antic.

sean-ar,** *s.m.* Old land.

sèanar, *s. m.* Six. [Applied only to persons and is followed by the *gen. pl.*] S. mhac, *six sons.*

seanarasg,** -aisg, *s.m.* Proverb, old saying.

seanas, -ais, *s.m.* Cicely.

sèanas, see seun.

seanas,** -ais, *s.m.* Shortness of sight.

——ach,** *a.* Genealogical. 2 Skilled in genealogy.

seanasan,** -ain, *s.m.* Etymology.

sean-athair, -athar, -athraichean, *s.m.* see seanair.

————eachd, see seanaireachd.

sean-bhean, -mhnà, *dat.* -mhnaoi, *n.pl.* -mhnathan, *s.f.* Old woman. 2 Often applied to the oldest woman in a village. An t-sean-bhean bhochd, *poetical name for Ireland ; 2 name of a patriotic Irish song.*

sean-bheanachd,** *s.f.* Anility.

seanchaidh, -ean, see seanachaidh.

seanchar, -aire, see seanachar.

seanchas, -ais, -an, see seanachas.

————ach, see seanachasach.

sean-cheann, see seana-cheann.

————ach, see seana-cheannach.

sean-chomharra,** *s.m.* Old token. 2 Monument. [** gives sean-chomhar, *gen.* -air.]

sean-chuimhne, *s.f.* Tradition. 2 Genealogy.

sean-chuimhneach,** *a.* Traditional. 2 Genealogical. 3 Having old acquaintanceship.

seanda, see seanndaidh.

seandachd, *s.f.ind.* see seanndachd.

seandaidh,* *a.* see seanndaidh.

seandaidheachd. see seanndachd.

seanfhacal, -ail, -an, *s.m.* Old saying, proverb, by-word, adage.

seanfhaclach, -aiche, *a.* Of, or belonging to, proverbs, proverbial. 2 Fond of proverbs.

sean-fhasanta, *a.* Old-fashioned.

sean-fhasantachd,(MS) *s.f.* Antiqueness.

sean-fhear,** -fhir, *s.m.* Old man. 2 Elder. 3 Presbyter. 4 Dotard.

————achd,** *s.f.* Presbyterianism. 2 Dotage. 3 Senility.

seang,(AC) *s.* Roebuck, deer.

seang,** *v.a. & n.* Make or grow slender or slim.

seang, -a, *a.* Slender, lank, slender-waisted, slim. 2 Hungry. 3 Lean, hungry-looking, gaunt. 4** Small-bellied. 5**Nimble, agile. A choin sh., *his lean dogs ;* a s. chorp, *her slender body ;* each s., séiteach, *a small-bellied, snorting steed ;* cha tuig an sàthach an s., *the well-fed do not understand the feelings of the famished.*

seangach,** *a.* Slender in body. 2 Slim. 3 Causing bodily slenderness.

seangachadh, -aidh, *s.m.* Act of making slender or attenuating. 2 State of becoming slender. 3**Reducing in shape. A' s—, *pr.pt.* of seangaich.

seangachd, *s.f.ind.* Slenderness. 2 Leanness. 3 Hungry look.

seangaich, *pr.pt.* a' seangachadh, *v.a. & n.* Make slender or slim. 2 Reduce in bodily bulk. 3 Become slender, grow gaunt.

seangaichte, *past pt.* of seangaich. Made slender, attenuated.

†seangal, *a.* Wise, prudent. 2 Shrewd.

seangan, -ain, *pl.*-an & -ain, *s.m.* Ant, pismire. 2 Mean fellow. 3 Cross fellow. 4 Cloven stick placed on the tail of a dog suffering from rabies. 5 *in derision,* Slender person. 6 ‡ Small yellow clover—*trifolium minus.* Imich chum an t-seangan, *go to the ant.*

seanganach, -aiche, *a.* Abounding in ants or in

2 Small yellow clover. 3 Like an ant. 4 Of ants.
seangalachd,(MS) *s.f.* Slenderness.
†**seangan-mhàthair**, *s.f.* Great-grandfather's or or great-grandmother's mother.
seangant, *a.* Wily.
seangarra, -airre, *a.* Old-like, having an old appearance. 2 Becoming old. 3 Sagacious. 4*Withered in person.
seangarrachd, *s.f.ind.* Oldishness, old appearance. 2 State of becoming old. 3 Sagacity.
seang-bhoc,(AC) *s.m.* Roebuck.
seang-fhiadh,(AC) *s.m.* Roebuck.
†**seanghain**, *s. m.* Conception, child near the time of its birth.
sean-ghàll,(DU) *s.m.* Wiseacre.
sean-ghille,* see seana-ghille.
————achd, see seana-ghilleachd.
sean-ghnàthach,(MS) *a.* Antique.
sean-sgeulach,(MS) *a.* Antique.
sean-ghin, *s.m. & f.* Child begotten in old age.
sean-lith, *s.* Happiness.
seanmhair, -ar, -airean, *s.f.* Grandmother. 2 2 Aged mother. 3 In some places applied to a brood sow. Am fear a dh' itheas a sheanmhair, faodaidh e a h-eanraich òl, *he that eats his grandmother may sup her broth.* When Farquhar the leech had tasted the "bree" of the serpent, his master, who knew that his apprentice now had his eyes opened to see the secrets of nature, and his ears to understand the language of birds, threw the pan at him in wrath, crying, "Ma dh' òl thu an sùgh, ith an fheòil," *if you have suppedthe juice, eat the flesh*—N.G.P.
seanmhàthair, -arach & -ean, *s. f.* see seanmhair.
sèanmhor, see seunmhor.
seann, *a.* Old, aged, ancient, antique. [Always precedes its noun, see note under sean.]
seannach, -aich, *s.m.* see sionnach. Cha mhair an s. ri shìor ruith, *the fox cannot hold out a chase for ever.*
seannachaich,** *v.* Play the fox.
seannachail, -e, *a.* see sionnachail. 2**Meagre.
seannachan,** -ain, *s. m.* Wily fellow, term of personal contempt. 2(AF) Young or little fox.
seannail,** *a.* Sweepy.
seannda, *a.* see seanndaidh.
seanndachd,** *s.f.* Antiquity. 2††Seniority. 3* Aged appearance or look, oldness.
seanndaidh,** *a.* Old, antique, old-fashioned. 2 Oldish.
————eachd, see seanndachd.
seann-duine,** *s.m.* Old man. 2 The oldest man in a village. Na seann-daoine, *the old men ; 2 men of old ;* tha e 'na sheann duine, *he is an old man.*
seann-nòs,***s.m.*Old custom, old habit or usage.
seann-nòsach, -aiche, *a.* Old-fashioned, fond of old customs, retaining old habits.
seann-radh,** *pl.* seann-ràite, *s. m.* Old saying, adage, proverb.
seann-ràite,*s.pl.* Old sayings. 2 The Book of Proverbs.
seann-ràiteach, *a.* Proverbial.
seanns, see seamhas.
seannsa,** *s.m.* Luck.
seann sail, -e, *a.* see seamhasach.
seannsar,** *a.* Lucky, prosperous.
seannsair, *s. m.* Chanter. 2** Drone of a bagpipe. 3 Pipe. A' gleusadh 'sheannsairean, *tuning his pipes—Donn. Bàn.*
seannsaireach, *a.* Supplied with chanters.
————d,** *s.f.ind.* Chanting.
seannsalair,** *s.m.* Chancellor.
————eachd,** *s.f.* Chancellorship.
seann-sgeul,** -sgeòil,*s.m.* Old tale, legend.
seann-sgeulach, -aiche, *a.* Legendary. 2 Archæological. 2 Of, or belonging to, old tales or legends. 4 Skilled in old tales. 5 Fond of reciting old tales or legends.
seann-sgeulachd,** *s.f.ind.* Old tale, tradition legend. 2 Archæology.
seann-sgeulaiche,** *s.m.* Archæologist.
seanntachd, see seanndachd.
seann-talamh, -aimh & talamhainn, *s.m.* Fallow field, land long unploughed, "old lea."
Seann-Tiomnadh, -aidh,*s.m.*The Old Testament.
seann-turach, -aiche, *a.* Well acquainted. 2 Frequenting a particular place.
sèanta, see seunta.
seantaidh, *a.* Senile. 2**Primeval. 3**Primitive.
————eachd,** *s.f.* Primitiveness.
seanntur, -uir, -an, *s.m.* Old acquaintance. 2 Old acquaintance or familiarity. 3 Frequenter of a place.
seap,(MMcD) *s.m.* Gaelic spelling of *shape.*
sèap, *v.a. & n.* Flinch. 2 Sneak, slink. 3 Drag or draw off privately. 4** Pursue closely. 5 **Crouch. Sh. e air falbh, *he slunk away.*
sèap, -a, -an, *s.m.* Long tail. 2 Animal's tail hanging down, as a dog's when cowed. 3* Stealthy, skulking. 4 (DU) Slow person. 5* Skulking or slinking out of battle. Nach b' e tu an s. ! *what a slowcoach you are !* [‡seap.]
sèapach, -aiche, *a.* Having a long or hanging tail. 2 Tawdry, slovenly. 3 Sneaking, slinking. 4 Sly. 5 Clandestine. 6**Crouching. 7**Flinching. 8 (DU) Slow.
sèapach,* -aich, *s.f.* Sly, slinking female. 2 *s.m.* Sly, slinking fellow.
sèapachas, -ais, *s.m. & f.* Tawdriness, slovenliness in dress. 2 Habit of sneaking or slinking.
sèapachd, *s.f.* see sèapachas.
sèapadh, -aidh, *s.m.* Flinching, act of flinching. 2 Act of sneaking or slinking. 3 Act of dragging away by stealth. 4**Crouching. A' s—, *pr.pt.* of sèap.
seapail, Gaelic spelling of *chapel.*
sèapair, -ean, *s.m.* Sneaking, slinking fellow. 2 Mean, sheepish fellow. 3 Crouching fellow 4*Poltroon, de e ter. A sh ! *thou slinking fellow !* cha'n fhuirich ach s., *none but a slinking fellow will stay.*
sèapaireachd,*s.f.ind.*Habit of sneaking or slinking. 2 Meanness.
sèapaiche, *s.f.* see sèapachas.
seapan, see seipeinn.
sear, *s.m.* see ear.
searach,†† -aich, *s.m.* Six-months old beast.
searadair, -ean, *s.m.* Towel. 2 Hand-napkin. 3* Drudge. A' brath s. a dheanamh dhiom, *meaning to make me his drudge.*
sea-ràmhach, see sè-ràmhach.
†**searb**, seirb, *s.m.* Theft, larceny.
†**searbaid**,* *s.f.* Boat-thwart.
searbh, *v.a. & n.* Sour, embitter, acidulate. 2 Grow sour.
searbh, -a & -eirbhe, *a.* Bitter. 2 Disagreeable, intolerable. 3 Grievous, distressful. 4 Sour, pungent, acrid, tart. 5 Disgusted. 6 Sharp, severe, harsh. 7 Sarcastic. Measan searbha, *bitter fruits ;* tha e s., *it is pungent or acrid ;* gnothach s., *a disagreeable business ;* tha mi s, dheth, *I am disgusted with it;* 'nuair a bu sh. leam éisdeachd ris, *when I found it intolerable to listen to him.*
searbhach,** *a.* Causing sourness or bitterness.

2 Sharp, severe.
searbhachadh,** -aidh, s.m. Act of making bitter. 2 State of becoming bitter. 3 Act of making or growing sharp or severe. A' s—, *pr.pt.* of searbhaich.
searbhachd, *s.f.ind.* Bitterness, acidness, sourness. 2 Harshness, severity. 3(MS) Gall.
searbhad, -aid, *s.m.* Degree of bitterness, sourness, harshness or severity. A' dol an s., *growing more and more sour.*
searbhadh, -aidh, *s.m.* see searbhachadh.
searbhadair, -ean, see searadair.
searbhadas,(MS) -ais, *s.m.* Gall.
searbhadas, -ais, *s.m.* Bitterness, sourness. 2* Disgust, dislike, displeasure. 3 Severity, sharpness. 4 Harshness of taste or sound. Pìob ri s., *a pipe making a harsh sound.*
searbhàg,(CR) *s.f.* Small-pale-green, sorrel-tasting trefoil growing in cool, shady places—*W. of Ross-shire.*
searbhag, -aig, -an, *s.f.* Bitter draught. 2 Refuse of liquids. 3 Acid. 4* Pickle. 5**Bitter, sarcastic female. 6 (AH) Toil, travail, struggle, difficulty, tough job, perplexity.

*623. *Searbhag mhilis.*

searbhag mhilis,§*s.f.* Woody nightshade, bittersweet—*solanum dulcemona.*
searbhaich, *pr. pt.* a' searbhachadh, *v.a.* & *n.* Make bitter, embitter. 2**Acidulate. 3 Become bitter. 4*Disgust. 5 *Tease. Sh. e mi, *he disgusted me, teased me or embittered my life.*
searbhaichte, *past pt.* of searbhaich. Embittered, made bitter, become bitter. 2*Teased.
searbhain muc,§ *s.* Endive, see eanach-ghàraidh.
searbhalachd, see searbhachd.
searbhan,** *s.pl.* Oats. 2 (WC) Disgust. Chuir e s. orm, *he disgusted me.*
searbhan, -ain, *s.m.* Tribute. 2(DU) see searbhachd.
searbhan-muice, see eanach-ghàraidh.
searbhanta, -n, *s.f.* Servant. 2 Maid-servant, indoor or outdoor. S. Mhic Dhòmhnuill Dhuibh, (Lochiel's servant)—a name applied to those dry easterly winds which often prevail in September, and are such a god-send to the farmer whose harvest is late. The origin of the connection with Lochiel is not clear.
————chd,* *s.f.ind.* Service. 2 Office of a maid servant. 3** Handiwork of a female servant.
searbhas, see searbhachd.
searbhasachd,** *s.f.* Sourness, bitterness, asperity. 2 Harshness, severity.
searbh-bhriathar,** -air, *s.m.* Bitter saying. 2 Sarcasm.
searbh-bhriathrach,** *a.* Bitter in language. 2 Sarcastic.
searbh-chainnteach, -eiche, *a.* Maledicent.
————d,** *s.f.* Malediceney.
searbhdaich,* *v.* see searbhaich.
————te, see searbhaichte.
searbh-dharach, -aich, *s.m.* Cerrus.
searbh-ghlòir, -e, *s.f.* Vain-boasting, vain-glory. 2 Raillery, sarcastic language, cacophony.
————eachd, *s.f.ind.* Habit of boasting.
searbh-ghlòrach, -aiche, *a.* Boasting, vain-glorious.
searbh-ghuthach, -aiche, *a.* Absonous.
searbhlachd, *s.f.* see searbhachd.
searbh-luibh,§ *s. f.* Wormwood, see burmaid. Formerly used instead of hops to increase the intoxicating quality of malt liquors. Chuir e air mhisg mi le searbh-luibhean, *he made me drunken with wormwood.*
searbhòs,** -òis, *s.m.* Deer, roe, stag.
searbh-radh,** *pl.* -raite, *s. m.* Bitter saying, sarcasm, cacophony.
searbh-ràiteach,** *a.* Bitter in language. 2 Sarcastic.
searbhta, *past pt.* of searbh. Soured, embittered, acidulated. 2 Pickled.
searbhtach,** *a.* Causing sourness, embittering, acidulating,
searbh-ubhal,** -ubhlan, *s.m.* Tart apple, crab-apple, coloquintida.
searbòs, see searbhòs.
searc, -eirc, see seirc.
†searc, *v.a.* Love.
searcadh, -aidh, see seargadh.
searcag, -aig, -an, *s.f.* see seirceag.
searcail, see seirceil.
searcall, -aill, *s.m.* Flesh. 2 Delicate meat, best part of flesh-meat.
searcan, -ain, -an. *s.m.* see seircean. 2(AC) see seircean-mór.
searcoll,(AF) *s.m.* Flesh of the woodcock.
seardair, see searadair.
†searg, *s.* Consumption.
searg,* *a.* Dry, withered, shrivelled.
searg, -eirg & -a, *pl.* -an, *s.m.* Trifling, insignificant or puny man or beast. 2 Person or beast shrivelled with age or infirmity. 3*Shrivelled or decayed person. 4 (DU) (an t-searg) Disease common to sheep.
searg, *pr.pt.* a' seargadh, *v.a.* & *n.* Dry, wither, fade, scorch, cause to dry, wither or fade. blast with heat, drought or cold, decay, shrivel. 2 Fade, wither, pine away. Sh. na lusan, *the herbs withered.*
seargach, -aiche, *a.* Fading. 2 Causing to fade or wither, blasting, scorching, withering. 3 Apt to fade wither or become blasted. 4†† Withered.
seargachadh, -aidh, *s.m.* & *pr. pt.* of seargaich, see seargadh.
seargadair, -ean, *s.m.* Languisher.
seargadh, -aidh, *s.m.* Withering, act of withering or causing to wither, fade, decay or pine away. 2 Blasting, as of corn. 3 Scorching. 4* Fading, pining. A' s—, *pr. pt.* of searg. Air s., *withered ;* tha 'n duine sin a' s. air falbh , *that man is pining away.*
seargaich, *pr.pt.* a' seargachadh, *v.a.* & *n.* Same meanings as searg.
————ear, *fut.pass.* of seargaich.
————te, *past pt.* of seargaich.
seargair,* -ean, *s. m.* Pining person, withered or puny person.
seargan, *s.m.* see searg.
searganach, -aiche, *a.* Withered, dried up. 2 Causing to wither, that withers.
searganach, -aich, *s.m.* Person of shrivelled appearance.
searganta,†† *a.* see searganach.

seargte, *past pt.* of searg. Dried up, withered, faded, consumed, blasted, shrivelled. Fraoch s., *withered heath.*
searmag, *W. of Ross* for seamrag.
searmaid, see searmon.
searmon, -oin, -an, *s.f.* Sermon, discourse, lecture, pleading. Cionnas a ni iad s. ? *how can they preach ?*
searmonach,†† *a.* Abounding in sermons.
searmonachadh, -aidh, *s.m.* Preaching, act or business of preaching. A' s—, *pr. pt.* of searmonaich.
searmonaich, *pr.pt.* a' searmonachadh, *v.a.&n.* Preach, perform the act or office of preaching, lecture. disconrse. 2 Harmonize.
searmonaiche, -an, *s.m.* Preacher.
searmonaichte, *past pt.* of searmonaich.Preached.
searn,** *v.a.* Loose, untie.
——,** *s.m.* Youth, stripling.
†**searnach,**** *a.* Dissolvent, 2 Separable.
†**searnadh,**** -aidh, *s.m.* Dissolution,separation, loosening. 2 Yawning,stretching of the limbs, extension.
searpan,** -ain, *s.m.* Order. 2 Custom. 3 Swan.
searr, -a, -an *s.f.* Sickle, reaping-hook. 2 Scythe. 3 Saw. 4**Phial. [** gives *s.m.*]
seàrr, *pr. pt.* a' seàrradh, *v. a.* Cut, hack, as with a knife. 2 Reap,mow,shear. 3 Slaughter, kill, make havoc, massacre. 4**Yawn. 5** Stretch the limbs.
searr, (AF) *s.m.* see searrach.
searrach, -aich, *s. m.* Foal, colt. 2 (DC) Colt till housed—*Uist.* 3 Filly. [A Gael considers it a bad omen to have a back view of the first foal or young of any grazing quadruped of that season he sees in any year.] Deich searraich, *ten foals ;* càmhail le 'n searraich, *camels with their foals ;* chunnaic mi s. 's a chulaibh rium, *I saw a foal with its back to me.*
searrach,** *a.* Edged, pointed,sharp, like a hook or scythe.
searrach-ruadh,(AF) *s.* Buzzard.
searrachach, -aiche, *a.* Abounding in foals,colts or fillies. Coire s. uanach, *a dell where foals and lambs abound.*
searrachail, -e, *a.* Like a foal. 2 Slim, small. 3 Slender-footed, as a foal. 4 Abounding in foals.
seàrradh, -aidh, *s.m.* Cutting, act of cutting or hacking, as with a knife. 2 Reaping, act of reaping or mowing. 3 Slaughtering, act of slaughtering. 4 (DMy) (searradh) Stretch of the leg. A' s—, *pr. pt.* of seàrr. Fichead troidh searradh an fhéidh is troidh thar fhichead s. a' mhial-choin, *twenty feet the deer's bound and twenty-one the greyhound's.*
searrag, -aig, -an, *s.f.* Bottle,flask, phial, stoup. 2 Leathern bottle. 3**Cup. 4 Bundle of hay. This is simply a translation of the English phrase "a bottle of hay." (ceannag fheòir.)
searragach, -aiche, *a.* Of, or belonging to, bottles or phials. 2 Like a bottle or phial. 3 Full of bottles or phials.
searragaich, *s.f.* Pilewort, *cole-wort—*ranunculus ficaria.*
searragaich,** *v.a.* Bottle, lay up in bottles.
————te, *past pt.* Bottled, laid up in bottles.
searrag-phòcaid,* *s.f.* Flask.
seàrr-fhiacall, -aill, -an & fhiaclan, *s. f.* Sharp tooth.
seàrr-fhiaclach, -aiche, *a.* Having sharp teeth. 2**Having teeth like a sickle.
seàrr-shuil, -shula, -ean, *s.f.* Squint-eye.
seàrr-shuileach, -eiche, *a.* Squint-eyed.

sèars,‡ *v.a.* Gaelic form of *charge.* 2*Brandish
sèarsadh,** -aidh, *s.m.* Charge, as of a gun.
sèarsainn,** *v.a.* Charge or load a gun.
searsa-mach,(CR) *s.m.* Notice to quit—*Perthshire.*
searsanach,‡ -aich, *s.m.* Sheriff-officer.
searthonn,** -uinn, *s.m.* Chief poet. 2 Prince. 3 Art. 4 Knowledge.
seas,** *s.m.* Plank for stepping into a boat. 2 Bench made on a hay-rick by cutting off part of the hay.
seas, *pr.pt.* a' seasamh,*v.a.* & *n.* Stand. 2 Maintain, support, defend. 3 Continue, endure. 4 Profit, avail. 5*Stop. 6**Lust. 7**Stand by. 8††Cause to stand. An s. thu 'nam fhianuis ? *will you stand in my presence;* cò a sheasas tu ? *who will support you ?* s. an còir, *maintain their rights ;* a dh' aindeoin có a sheasadh tu, *in defiance of all that will take your part ;* cha'n urrainn mi seo a sheasamh, *I cannot endure this ;* seasaidh mis' thu an còir 's an eucòir, *I will support you, right or wrong.*
seasach,* -aiche, *a.* see seasmhach.
seasachail,** *a.* Ascititious.
seasachas,** *s.m.* Truce. 2 Sitting. 3 Standing-room.
seasadh, -aidh, see seasamh.
seasaich,(AF) *s.* Barren cow, barren cattle.
seasaidh, *fut.aff.a.* of seas.
seasaidh, (AF) see seasaich.
seasaimh, see seasamh.
seasaireachd,* *s.f.ind.* Penance in church.
seasam, *1st.pers.sing.imp.* of seas. Let me stand. 2 *1st.sing.fut.aff.* of seas. I will stand.
seasamain,** Gaelic form of *jessamine.*
seasamh,** *v.* Stand. 2 Rise up. 3 Stop, endure, last.
seasamh, -aimh, *s.m.* Standing, act or posture of standing. 2 State of enduring or continuing. 3 Maintaining, act of maintaining, sustaining, defending. 4 Stability, firmness. 5 Station. 6**Footing. 7**Cessation. 8 Lasting. A' s—, *pr.pt.* of seas. 'Na sh., *he standing ;* 'na s., *she standing ;* cha bhi s. an drochbheart, *there is no stability in mischief ;* s, chlaidheimh, *standing on one's head ;* dean s., *stand up ;* air droch sh. chas, *on uncertain footing.*
seasamhach, see seasmhach.
seasamhachd, see seasmhachd.
seasaothar,** -air, *s.m.* Seat in a boat.
seasamh-claidheamh,(AH) *s.m.* Act of standing on one's head.
seasda,** *s.m.* Defence.
———r,** -air, *s.m.* Defence. 2 Peace, rest, repose, comfort. 3 Pallet, pillow, place whereon to rest.—*Sàr-Obair.*
seasdan,** -ain, *s.m.* Shout. 2 Hunter's cry.
seas-dubh, -duibh, -an-dubha, *s. m.* Ink-stand.
seasg, -a & seisge, *a.* Barren, unprolific. 2 Yielding no milk, dry, not giving suck. 3 Addle. Ni sam bith s. 'nad thìr, *anything barren in thy land ;* cìocha seasga, *dry breasts ;* ni mó bhios e s., *neither will he be barren ;* crodh s., *barren cattle, cattle that yield no milk.*
seasg,* *s.m.* Barrenness.
seasg,* *s.m.* Sedge,water-sedge. 2 Burr-reed. A' buain s., *cutting sedge.* [** & †† *gen.* seisg.]
seasgach, -aiche, *a.* Causing barrenness. 2 Barren, see seasg. Beinn sh. nam fuaran, *the barren mountain of springs.*
seasgach, -aich, *s.m.coll.* Cows giving no milk, farrow cattle, barren cattle. 2 Reedy place. 3 (DMK) Bachelor. 4** Dry cow. 5 (DU) (an seasgach, *s.coll.*) Young cattle kept on the hill all summer.

seasgachas, -ais, see seasgaiche.
seasgachd, *s.f.* Barrenness. 2 Herd of barren cattle.
seasgad, -aid, *s.m.* Degree of sterility.
seasgadh,(MMcD) *s. m.* The part of an oar between the box and feather.
seasgaich,** *s.f.* Barren cow.
seasgaiche, *s.f.ind.* Barrenness, sterility, state of being barren.
seasgaiche, *comp.* of seasgach.
seasgair, -e, *a.* At ease, in easy circumstances, quiet, comfortable, snug, warm, dry and soft. 2 Sheltered, protected. 3 Effeminate. 4* Settled, still, as calm weather. Bi s., *be quiet;* fan s., *keep quiet.*
seasgair, -ean, *s.m.* One in comfortable circumstances, cosy person. 2 Lazy person. 3 Effeminate person. 4**Shelter 5**One who threshes corn by the bulk. Is s. thu ri fuachd, *thou art a shelter in the cold.*
seasgaireach, -eiche, *a.* see seasgair. Gu s.,*comfortably, snugly.*
seasgaireachd, *s. f. ind.* Comfort, ease, quietness, snugness, tranquillity, peace, warmth, cosiness. An s., *at ease* ; luchd na s., *people in easy circumstances.*

624. *Seasgan (6.)*

625. *Seic. (ill. by MMcD.)*

seasgan, -ain & -a, -an, *s.m.* Shock or handful of gleaned corn. 2** Gleanings of corn. 3 Truss of gleaned corn. 4 Moorish ground, fenny country 5**Land that has been gleaned. 6§ Reed-grass—*arundo phragmites.*
seasganach, -aiche, *a.* In handfuls or shocks, as gleaned corn. 2 Abounding in gleaned corn.
————, aich, *s.m.* Bachelor.
————d,** *s.f.* Celibacy.
seasgann, see seasgan
———ach,** *a.* Marshy.
seasgar,** -aire, *a.* Soft, effeminate. 2 Still, calm. 3 Comfortable. 4 Dry and warm,snug. [also seasgair.]
seasg-bhò, -bhoin, *s.f.* Barren cow, heifer.
seasg-chorp,** -chuirp, *s. m.* Barren body. 2 Constitutional barrenness.
seasg-chorpach, -aiche, *a.* Barren, farrow, unprolific.
seasg-chrodh, *s.f.* see crodh-seisg.
seasglach,** -aich, *s.m.* Barren cattle.
seasglaich,(AF) s. see seasglach.
seas-ghrian, -ghréine, *s. m.* The solstice. 2 Equinoctial line—*Sàr-Obair.*
seasgrach, see seasgach.
seasgta, *a.* Juiceless.
seasmhach, -aiche, *a.* Firm, steadfast. 2 Fixed, established, firm, constant, durable, persevering, enduring, steady, settled. 3 (MS)Agreeable. 4 Positive, in *grammar.* 5 (DU) Reliable. Duine s., *a man of his word*, àite-còmhnuidh s., *a fixed abode* ; bithidh gach facal s., *every word shall be established.*
seasmhachd, *s.f.ind.* Firmness, steadiness, stability, steadfastness, constancy, durableness. 2 Settled state, as of weather.
seasrach,** -aich, *s.m.* Lad, youth.
seasunta,** *a.* Prosperous.
seasuntachd,** *s.f.* Prosperity.
seat,** -a, *s. m.* Satiety of food, bellyful. 2 Quean. (seid.)
seathadair,** -ean, *s.m.* Skinner.
sèathadh, see sèathamh.
†**seathadh**,** -aidh, *s.m.* Skin, hide.
seathaid, *s.f.* Sucking ewe.
sèathamh, (6mh.) *a.* The sixth
sèathamh-deug, *a* The sixteenth. The substantive is placed between the component parts, as, an t-sèathamh chearc deug, *the sixteenth hen.*
seathan,(CR) *s.m* Panting, hard breathing. Tha s. air, *he is panting, he is out of breath.—W. of Ross-shire*
†**seathar**, *a.* Strong, able. 2 Good.
†**seathar**, -air, *s.m.* Library, study.
————ach, *a.* Divine.
sèath-bhaist, -e, -ean. *s.f.* see sèabhaist.
sèath-bhaisteach, -eiche, *a.* see sèabhaisteach.
sèathnar, see sèanar.
seath-bhog,§ -bhuig, *s.f.* Marjoram, see oragan.
†**secc**, *a.* now seac.
secel, -eil, Gaelic spelling of *shekel.*
sè-chasach, *a.* Six-footed.
sè-chearnach,** *a.* Hexangular.
sè-chèarnag,** -aig, *s.f.* Hexangle, hexangular figure.
†**sed**,(AF) Standard of cows or cattle by which prices &c. were determined, i.e. one milch cow Sed bò dile, *a standard made up of different kinds of live stock.*
†**segh**,(AF) *s.* Wild ox, buffalo. 2 Moose, elk. 3**Milk.
seib,§ *s.* Buck-bean, see pònair-chapuill.
seic,(MMcD) *s.f.* Bag of eight pecks for holding grain or meal, made wholly of reeds or *sioman luachair.* A rope was rove through the handles when full and the mouth brought close together. It was like a 2-boll bag of meal in shape—*Lewis.* (ill. 625.
seic, -ean, *s.m.* Flier of a spinning-wheel, the part armed with teeth by which the thread is conducted to the reel. (also teic.)
seic, -ean, *s.m* Rack of a stable, manger.
seic, -e, -ean, *s.f.* see seiche. 2 Bag made of hide or skin 3 The peritonium. 4 The exterior or interior membrane surrounding the brain. 5**Sack-wine. 5**Bone. Màm-seic, *a rupture.* In *Argyllshire*, peritonium is *sic*, and rupture *màm-sic.* S. an tairbh, *the skin of the bull ;* a dh' aindeoin do sh., *in spite of your skin*
seiceach,** *a.* Having a thick skin or hide. 2 Of a skin or hide.
seiceal, -eil, -cle &-clean, *s.m.* Heckle for dressing flax.
seicean,** *s.m.* Membrane that covers the intestines. 2 Pellicle. 3 Film. 4 The skull. 5 The pellicle of the brain.
seiceanach,** *a.* Filmy, having a pellicle.
seich, see seiche.
†**seich**, *s.m.* Combat. 2 Adventurer.
seiche,(AF) *s.* Selling cattle.
seiche, -an, -eannan [& -eachan,†† e.g. *Gairloch*—DU] *s.f.* Hide, skin. S. eich, *a horse's skin*; s. mairt, *a cow's skin.*
seicheach, -eiche, *a.* Of, or belonging to, hides.

or skins. 2 Like a hide or skin.
seicheadair, -ean, *s.m.* Skinner, currier.
seicheadaireachd,†† *s.f.* Skinning.
seichearnach,* -aich, *s.f.* Tan-work. 2 Cube.
seichim,** *s.m.* Shechem-wood.
seicil, *s.* **Brake. 2††Heckle for flax, flaxcomb.
seicil, *pr. pt.* a' seicleadh, *v.a.* Dress or comb flax. 2* Beat or scold lustily.
seicilte, *past pt.* of seicil. Heckled.
seicle, *s.* Flier of a spinning-wheel. (also séicle)
seicleadh, -eidh, *s.m.* Dressing, act of dressing flax. A' s—, *pr .pt.* of seicil. Lìon air a dheagh sh., *flax well dressed.*
seiclear, -ir, *pl.* -an & -eirean, *s.m.* Flax-dresser. hackler.
———, *fut. pass.* of seicil. Shall be combed or dressed, as flax.
———achd, *s.f.ind.* Flax-dressing, hackling.
seicilte, *past pt.* of seicil. Dressed (of flax.)
seicne, -an, *s.f.* see seic.
seicneach, -eich, *s. m.* Stout or corpulent man. 2 Stomachful, full meal.
seid, -e, -ean [& -eachan**] *s.f.* Tympany, swelling of the body from flatulence. 2* Swelling in a person from luxurious living and deep potations. 3 Full meal. 4 Bellyful, surfeit. 5 Bed spread on the floor, pallet, shakedown. 6 Truss of hay, grass or straw. 7 Bench or form to sit on, made of grass or heath. 8** Voluptuousness. 9 Load. [WC gives séid for Nos. 5, 6 & 7.] Nach ann a tha 'n t-seid! *how the fellow is puffed up!* fhuair e a sh., *he got his fill*; 'na luidhe air s., *sleeping on a pallet*; s. luachrach, *a bed of rushes*; sop as gach s., *a wisp from every truss.*
séid, *pr.pt.* a' séideadh, *v.a. & n.* Blow, as the wind. 2 Breathe, breathe upon or into. 3 Blow, drive away by blowing. 4 Pant, puff. 5 Flatter, swell by flattery. 6 Inflate. 7*Instigate, prompt to evil. Sh. e is sh. e, *it blew and it blew*; *it blew into a hurricane*; is tus' a tha 'ga shéideadh, *it is you that instigate him*; sh. e an cuinneinibh a shròine anail na beatha, *he breathed into his nostrils the breath of life*; s. suas a' phìob, *play the pipes.*
séid, -ean, *s.m.* Blowing, puff.
seideach, -eiche, *a.* Swollen by tympany. 2 Fat, corpulent. 3 Having trusses of grass, hay or straw. 4 Like a truss. 5 Having beds spread on the ground. 6 Having benches or forms of grass or heath. 7 Lazy, indolent. [WC gives séideach for Nos. 3, 4, 5 & 6.]
séid each, *s.m.* Snorting.
séideach, -eiche, *a.* Blowing, that blows. 2 Boisterous, stormy, windy, blustering. 3 Flattering, blowing up by flattery. 4 Inflating. 5 Puffing. 6(MS) Fustian.
séideadh, -idh, *s.m.* Blowing, act of blowing. 2 Act of breathing upon or into. 3 Act of blowing away, or driving away by blowing. 4 Act of panting for breath. 5 Breathing. 6 Act of flattering or swelling by flattery, 7 Inflating, act of inflating. 8 Storm, blast, wind. 9** Puffing. A' s—, *pr. pt.* of séid.
seideag, -eig, -an, *s.f. dim.* of seid. Little bed spread on the floor. 2 Small bench or form made of grass or heather. 3 Small truss of grass, hay, or straw.
séideag, -eig, -an, *s. f.* Light breeze, gentle blowing. 2 see seudag.
seideagach, -eiche, *a.* Having small beds spread on the ground. 2 Having small forms or benches of grass or heather 3 Having small trusses of grass, hay or straw.
séideagach,** *a.* Blowing gently.
séidean, -ein, *s. m.* Blowpipe. 2**Blowing. 3 Blow, puff, panting, anhelation.

†seidean, -ein, *s.m.* Quicksand.
séideil, see séideadh.
seideir,** *s.f.* Cider.
———each,** *a.* Abounding in cider. 2 Of cider.
seidhir, *pl.* -dhrichean, *s.f.* Gaelic form of *chair.* 2**Chaise. S. reidh, *a hired chaise*; s. dà-làimh, *an arm-chair.*
seidhre, *gen. & pl.* of seidhir.
seidhreach, *s.m.* Settee.
seidhrichean, *pl.* of seidhir.
séidich, *v.a. & n.* Aspirate.
séidich,** *s.f.* Blowing, panting.
séididh, *fut.aff.a.* of séid.
seidir, -ean, *s.m.* Lumpish fellow, corpulent or clumsy fellow. 2 Lazy, inactive fellow.
séidir, -ean, *s. m.* Swell, puffed up fellow.
seidireachd, *s.f.ind.* Lumpishness, stupidity. 2 Corpulency, clumsiness. 3 Laziness, inactivity.
seidirneach, -eich, *s.m.* see seidir.
————d, see seidireachd.
seidrich, *v.n.* Snort.
séidrich,* *s.f.* Hissing of serpents.
seidrich, *s.f.* Snorting of a horse. 2 Blowing. breathing hard, panting, anhelation. 3**Blustering, as of wind.
séidrich,** *a.* Asthmatical.
séidte, *past pt.* of séid. Blown. 2 Blown away. 3 Puffed up by flattery. 4 Inflated. 5 **Blown up.
†seigh, -ean, *s.f.* Hawk.
†seigheann,-inn, *s.m.* Champion, warrior.
†seighear, -eir, -an, *s.m.* Falconer.
†seighnean, -ein, *s.m.* Hurricane, tempest. 2 Lightning.
seilbh,(CR) *s. f.* Herd of cattle at grass, (not used of a drove in *W. of Ross-shire.*)
seilbh, -e, -ean, *s.f.* Possession, property. 2 Herd or drove of cattle. 3 Farm-stock. 4 Propinquity, nearness. 5 see sealbh. Gabh s., *take possession*; rach 'na sh., *take him* or *it in hand.*
seilbheach, -eiche, see sealbhach.
seilbheachadh, -aidh, see sealbhachadh.
seilbheachail, -e, *a.* Possessive.
seilbheadair, *s.m.* Abider.
seilbh-ghabhail, see sealbh-ghabhail.
seilbhich, *v.* see sealbhaich.
———te, see sealbhaichte.
seilche,(AF) *s.* Tortoise. 2 Turtle.
seilche, *comp.* of salach, see sailche.
seilcheag, -eig, -an, *s.f.* Snail. 2 Slug. 3 *in derision*, Inactive person.
———ach, -aiche, *a.* Abounding in snails. 2 Like a snail, snailish.
————an,** *n.pl.* of seilcheag.
seilcheag-chlaiseach,(AF) *s.f.* Striated snail.
seile, -an, *s.m.ind.* [***f.*] see sile. 2(AC) Placenta, after-birth of a hind.
seileach, ** see sileach.
seileach, -ich, -ean, *s.m.* Willow—*salix.* 2 Willow copse. 3 Place where willows grow. Slat seilich, *a willow switch.* (ill. 626 is *salix alba*—white willow.)
seileachan,§ -ain, *s.m.* Mountain willow—*epilobium montanum.* The older name *eilig* was retained as well as *seileachan* in *Glenlyon* and elsewhere, one of the hills in that glen being called Creag-eilig from the plant. (ill. 627.)
seileach-an-t-sruth,§ *s.m.* Babyloinan willow—*salix babylonica.*
seileachan-buidhe,§ *s.m.* see lus-na-siothaimh.
seileachan-Frangach,§ *s.m.* Rosebay—*epilobium augustifolium.* (ill. 628.)
seileach-Frangach,‡‡ *s.m.* French willow—*salix*

aquatica.

626. *Seileach.* 627. *Seileachan.*

628. *Seileachan-Frangach.* 629. *Seimhean.*

seileachd,(MS) *s.f.* Defluxion.
seileach-geal, *s.m.* Sallow.
seileach-uisge, *s.m.* Osier—*Colonsay.*
seileadach, -aich, see sileadach.
seileadach, -aich, *s.m.* Pocket-handkerchief.
seileadan,** see seileadach. 2 Spitting-box.
seileag, -eig, -an, *s.f.* see sileag.
———ach, see sileagach.
sèileann, -inn, -an, see sèalan.
————ach, -aich, see sèalanach.
seilear, -ir, -an, *s.m.* Cellar. [** gives seileir as *nom.*]
———ach, -aiche, *a.* Cellared. 2 Cellular.
seilear-bidh,†† *s.m.* Pantry.
seilear-dibhe,* *s.m.*Spirit cellar. 2 Public house
seilear-iochdrach,‡‡ *s.m.* Under cellar.
seilear-làir,* *s.m.* Vault.
seileicheag, see seilcheag.
seileid,** *s.f.* Bellyful, surfeit. 2 Big belly.
seileir, see seilear.
———each, see seilearach.
seilg,* -e, *s. f.* Hunt, chase, hunting. 2 Venison. 3 What is hunted. Iùran na seilge, *the huntsman.*
——, *gen.sing.* of sealg.
seilich, see silich.
seilicheag, see seilcheag.
—————ach, see seilcheagach.
seilide,** *s.f.* Snail.
seilidh, see seilcheag.
seilisdeir, -ean, *s.m.* Yellow iris, sedge, yellow water-flag, see bog-uisge.
seilisdeir-nan-gobhar, *s. m.* Great wood-rush—*Colonsay.*
seilisdeireach, -eiche, *a.* Abounding in yellow iris, yellow water-flag or sedge.
seillean, -ein, -an, *s.m.* Bee. heath or field-bee. 2 Teasing request or repetition.
s.-achaidh, *a field bee.*
s.-diomhain, *a drone* or *idle bee.*
s.-lunndach, *a drone bee.*
s.-mòr, *a bumble bee.*
s.-nimh, *a hornet.*
s.-seimhid, *a snail.*
seilleanach, -aiche, *a.* Full of bees. 2 Teasing, importunate. 3 Capricious, flighty.
seilleanachd, *s.f.ind.* Caprice.
seilleann,(AF) *s.* Ked, sheep-louse, tick, see sèalan.
————ach, see sèalanach
seilliunn,** -uinn, *s.m.* see sèalan.
seilmiger,(AF) *s m.* Imperfect ram. 2 *contemptuously,* Useless man.
seilt,** *s.f.* Dropping. 2 Drivelling, slavering, mucous salivation.
seilteach,** *a.* Slavering, causing salivation,mucous.
seilteachd,** *s.f.* Infirmity of slavering, course of salivation. 2 Ooziness
seilticbean, *s.pl.* Scrofulous sores.
seil-uisge, *s.* Leech.
sèim, -e, *s.f.* Squint. 2 Squinting. S. shuileach, *squint-eyed.*
†seim, -e, *s.f.* Publishing.
seirmeachd, *s.f. ind.* Sonorousness.
sèimh, -e, *a.* Mild, tranquil, placid, smooth. 2 Affable, gentle, soft, kind. 3 Delicate. 4** Comely. 5** *rarely* Little. 6**Single. 7** Quiet. 'San fhairge shèimh, *in the calm sea;* s. gu'n robh do thàmh, *soft be thy repose;* gu s., *quietly, softly;* na's sèimhe, *more mild.* (also sèamh.)
sèimhe, *s.f.ind.* Mildness, gentleness,quietness. calmness, smoothness. 2 Kindness. 3** Softness. 4**Peacefulness.
sèimheach, -eiche, *a.* Making calm, producing calmness. 2 Quiet, calm, mild. 3 see sèimh.
sèimheachadh, -aidh,*s.m.* Calming, act of calming, quieting or soothing. A' s—, *pr. pt.* of sèimhich.
sèimheachd, *s.f.* see sèimhe.
sèimhealachd,(MS) *s.f.* Dispassion, coolness. 2 Delicacy.
seimhean,§ -ein, *s.m.* Bog-rush—*schœnus nigricans.*
seimheanachd,* *s.f ind.* Indulgence in ease. 2 Chambering. 3 Effeminate conduct.
sèimhich, *v.a. & n.* Calm, make calm or placid, smoothe. 2 Become calm. 3 Adorn. 4 Soothe. 5 Grow kind, soft or gentle.
————te, *past pt.* of sèimhich. Calmed, stilled.
seimhide, -an, *s.f.* Snail.
sèimhidh,(AF) *s.f.* Snail, slug.
sèimhidh, *a* Subtile.
seimh-mheas,** *s.m.* Mellow fruit.
seimilear, -eir, -an, *s.m* see similear.
———ach, -aiche, *a.* see similearach.
————aich, *v.a.* see simileariaich.
————aichte,*past pt.* of seimilearaich, see similearaichte.
seine, see sine.
seineach,* *s.m.* Pad, donkey. Cha mhò orm thu na's mò air s. a mhàthair, *I care as little for you as a donkey cares for his mother.*
seing, see seang.
seiniolach,(AF) *s.m.* Nightingale.
seinn, *pr.pt.* a' seinn, *v.a. & n.* Sing, chant,carol. 2 Play on an instrument. 3 Ring as a bell. 4 Report, promulgate, proclaim. Na h-eòin a' seinn, *the birds warbling;* sh. e an fhiodhall, *he played upon the violin;* air a' chlàrsach, *on the harp;* s. an clag, *ring the bell—Inverness*

[gliong an clag—*Argyll*] ; air a sh. feadh na dùthcha, *reported through the country ;* droch sh., *bad melody, bad church music.*
seinn, -e, *s.f.* Singing, act of singing. 2 Act of playing upon a musical instrument. 3 Ringing, act of ringing, as a bell. 4 Reporting, act of reporting, spreading a report. 5 Warbling. Là s. do chluig, *the day of thy bell-ringing (funeral.)* A' s—, *pr.pt.* of seinn. [** gives s.m.]
seinneadair, Irish inflection of seinn.
seinneam, *1st. sing. imp.* of seinn. Let me sing.
seinnear,** *fut. pass.* of seinn. Shall be sung.
seinnibh, *2nd. per.pl.imp.* of seinn.
seinnim, (for seinnidh mi) I will sing.
seinnlean, (CR) *Kincardine-on-Oykel & Creich, Suth'd* for seillean.
seinnlear,(CR) *Rogart* for seillean.
seinnsearachd, see sinnsearachd.
seinntig, *v.* Gaelic form of *change.*
seinse, *s.* Gaelic form of *change.* Taigh seinse, *a change-house.*
séip, *v.a. & n.* see sèap.
seipealach,** *a.* Having chapels. 2 Of, or relating to, a chapel.
seipear, see sèapair.
seipeil,‡ *s.f.* Gaelic form of *chapel.* 2**Sepulchre.
seipeinn, -ean, *s.m.* Choppin, quart (liquid measure.) [** seipinn.]
seipeinneach,** *a.* In chopins. 2 Containing a chopin. [** seipinneach.]
seipeireachd, see sèapaireachd.
seipinn, see seipeinn.
seirbh, see searbh.
seirbhe, *comp.* of searbh. 2 see searbhachd.
seirbheachd, see searbhachd.
seirbhead, see searbhad.
————as, see searbhadas.
seirbhe-ciùil,** *s.* Dissonance.
seirbhis, -e, -ean, *s.f.* Service, work, labour. 2 Advantage, profit. 3 Use. S. chruaidh, *hard or grievous service.*
seirbhiseach, -ich, *s. m.* Servant, employée. 2 Domestic.
seirbhiseach, -eiche, *a.* Performing work. 2 Useful, profitable, advantageous.
seirbhiseachadh, -aidh, *s.m.* Serving, act of serving or acting as a servant. 3 Working, act of working. A' s—, *pr. pt.* of seirbhisich.
seirbhiseachd, *s.f.ind.* State or condition of a servant. 2 Business of a servant.
seirbhisich, *pr.pt.* a' seirbhiseachadh, *v.a.* Serve, attend upon, as a servant. 2 Work, perform work.
seirc, -e, *s.f.* Love, affection. 2 Benevolence, charity, the Christian virtue. 3†† Beauty. Ball seirc, *a beauty spot.*
seirceach, -eiche, see seirceil.
seircealachd, *s.f.ind.* Lovingness, charitableness, amiableness, benevolence, kindliness.
seirceag, -eig, -an, *s.f.* Beloved female. 2 Benevolent female. 3 Mistress, sweetheart.
seircean, -ein, -an, *s.m.* Beloved person. 2 Benevolent person. 3**Jerkin. A s.-se a rug i, *the beloved (choice) one of her who bore her.—Song of Solomon.*
seircean-mòr,§ *s. m.* Burdock, see suiricheansuirich.
seircean-suirich,§ *s.m.* Burdock, see suiricheansuirich. 2 Cleavers—*Colonsay.*
seircear, see seircean.
seirceil, -e. *a.* Affectionate, loving, fond. 2 Benevolent, charitable. 3 Dutiful. Gu s., *charitably.*
†seircin, -e, -ean, *s.f.* Gaelic form of *jerkin.*
seirdean,** -ein, *s.m.* Pilchard. 2 Sardine.
seirdin, see seirdean.
†seire,** *s.f.* Food.
seireacan,(AF) *s.m.* Silkworm.
†seireach,** *a.* Liberal of food.
seirdeanach,***a.*Abounding in pilchards. 2 Like a pilchard.
seirean, -ein, -an, *s.m.* Shank, leg, particularly a spare or slender leg. 2 One having spare or slender legs. 3(CR) Ankle—*Strathtay & Loch Tay.* 4(MS) Pastern.
séirean,(AH) *s. m.* Wheezing noise made in breathing by an asthmatical person, or by a person running hard.
seireanach, -aiche, *a.* Having small or slender legs.
seirg, *gen.sing.* of searg.
†seirg, *s.* Red clover, see seamrag-chapuill.
seirge, *comp.* of searg
seirge, *s.f.* see seirgeachd.
seirgeachd, *s.f.* Witheredness, dryness.
seirgean, -ein, -an, *s.m.* Withered or shrivelled person. 2 Sickly or consumptive person. 3** Shrunken form. 4**Jerkin
seirgleach, *s.m.* see seirgean.
seirglidh, -e, *a.* Withered, wasted.
——-——,** *s.m.* Withered person.
seirglidheachd, *s.f.ind.* State of being withered or wasted.
seirgne, see seirgneach.
seirgne,** *a.* Sickly
seirgneach, -ich, -ichean, *s.m.* Sickly person, one worn down to a skeleton. 2 Skeleton. 3 **Consumptive person.
seirgniche, see seirgneach.
seiric,** *a.* Strong, able.
seiric, -e, *s.f.* Silk, superfine silk.
seiriceach,** *a.* Silken, silky.
†seiricean,** -ein, -an, *s.m.* Silk-worm.
seirgniche, see seirgneach.
seirm, -e, *s.f.* Noise, musical noise, noise of music. 2 Music, melody. 3 Skill, dexterity, art. 4 Manner, appearance, attitude. 5*Tune, tone, *trim. 6**Peal of bells. Cuir air s., *attune, tune, trim ;* am bheil an clàrsach air s. ? *is the harp in tune ?*
seirm,‡ *v.* Ring, as a bell.
seirm,(AC) *v.* Follow. Bitheadh e soilleir no doilleir ri seirm, *let it be bright or dark (for us) to follow.*
seirmeach, -eiche, *a.* Making a musical noise. 2 Musical, melodious, sweet. 3 Skilful, skilled.
seirmeadair,* -ean, *s.m.* Precentor 2 Tuner.
seirmeil, -e, *a.* see seirmeach. 2* In trim, tuned, attuned. 3* In a business-like manner.
séirs,* see seurs.
séirsealach, -aiche, *a.* Strong, robust. [‡seirsealach.]
————-—, -aich, *s.m.* Strong, robust man.
————-——d, *s.f.ind.* Strength, vigour, robustness.
séirsean, -ein, -an, *s.m.* see séirsealach.
————ach, -aich, *s. m.* see searsanach. 2** Auxiliary, unhired workman.
seirt,** -e, *s.f.* Strength, power.
seirteil,** *a.* Strong.
seis, -ean, *s.m.* Anything grateful or pleasant to the feelings or senses 2 Sufficiency, enough. 3 One's match or equal. 4 Friend, companion. 5** Satisfaction. 6** Treat, entertainment. 7**Company 8**Anything that agrees ill or well with one. 9†† Pleasure, delight. Cha d' fhuair Fionn a sheis riamh, *F. never met his match ;* tha do sh. an taic riut, *your match is in contact with you ;* barrachd s a sh., *more than his match.*
séis, -ean, *s.m.* Tune, musical air. 2 Noise, tumult, bustle. 3(AC) Dirge. Séis-bhàis, *death-*

dirge.

séis,(CR) *s.m.* Hum or buzz made by wild bees in their nest when disturbed—*W.of Ross-shire.* 2(WC) Any hissing sound.

†**seis**, -e, -ean, *s.f.* Skill, knowledge.

seis,(MMcD) *s.* Kind of chest, see ciste-chaol.

séis, *v. W. of Ross* for séist.

séisd, -ean, *s.m.* [*s.f.***] Siege. 2 see séist. Cuir s., *besiege ;* fo sh., *under a siege.*

séisd, *pr.pt.* a' séisdeadh, *v.a.* Besiege, invest. 2 Straiten, reduce to difficulties.

séisd, -e, -ean, *s.f.* see séid.

séisdeach, -eiche, *a.* Besieging, investing. 2 Straitening, reducing to straits or difficulties.

———d,** *s.f.*State of being besieged, siege. 2 Act of reducing to straits or difficulties. 3 Act of surrounding or besetting. 4**Frequent or continued besieging. A' s—, *pr. pt.* of séisd.

séisdeadh, -idh, *s.m.* Besieging, siege. 2 Act of reducing to straits or difficulties. 3 Act of surrounding or besetting. A' s—, *pr pt.* of séisd.

séisdear,** *s.m.* Besieger.

seisdeil, *a.* Mild.

séisdeil,‡‡ -e, *a.* Of, or belonging to, a siege.

seisdich,(MS) *v.a.* Beleaguer.

seise,* see seis.

séiseach, -eich, -ean, *s.m.* Timber couch or oblong wooden chair to lean upon, sofa.

seiseach, -eiche, *a.* Pleasurable, agreeable. 2 Satisfying. 3 Cheerful, delightful. 4 Libidinous.

séiseach,** -eiche, *a.* Noisy, tumultuous.

seiseachadh, -aidh, *s. m.* Act of satisfying, as with food. 2 Act of entertaining or treating. 3 Matching,act of matching or being suitable. A' s—, *pr.pt.* of seisich.

seiseachd, *s. f.* Sufficiency, 2 Entertainment, treat. 3** Pleasure, delight. 4**Sensuality.

séiseachd,** *s.f.* Noisiness.

†**seiseadh**, *a.* The sixth.

seisean, -ein, -an, *s. m.* Kirk-session, a petty court in the kirk, consisting of the minister who presides, the parish schoolmaster who acts as clerk, and the elders, the lowest ecclesiastical court. 2 Court assizes. 3 Session of a college. Cuir air an t-seisean, *summon before a kirk-session.*

———ach, *a.* Pertaining to sessions or assizes.

seisear, *s.coll.* Six persons, see seathnar. Éireadh s. ghleusta, *let six active men rise—Mac Mhaigh. Alasdair.*

seiseil,** *a.* Pleasant. 2 Humane. 3 Mild.

†**seiseilbh**, *s.f.* Talk, discourse.

seisg,§ *s.f.* Sedge, bog-reed—*carex.* 2 (AC) see seis.

seisge, *s.f.* Dryness.

seisgeach,** *a.* Sedge, abounding in bog-reeds.

seisgeach, see seasaich.

seisgead,** -eid, *s.m.* Barrenness.

seisgeann,** -einn, *s.m.* Fenny country. 2 Extended marsh. 3 Bog-reed.

seisg-madaidh,§ *s.f.* Upright bur-reed—*sparganium simplex.* [**Great bur-reed—*sperganium erectum.*]

seisg-mheirg,§ see seisg-rìgh.

seisg-rìgh,§ *s.f.* Branched bur-reed, bede-sedge —*sparganium ramosum.*

seisich, *pr.pt.* a' seiseachadh, *v.a. & n.* Satisfy, as with food. 2 Entertain, treat well. 3 Match, cause to fit. 4 Match, suit.

seisichte, *past pt.* of seisich. Satisfied, as with food. 2 Entertained, well treated. 3 Matched, fitted- 4 Matching, fitting.

seisir, see seisear.

seis-madraidh, see seisg-madaidh.

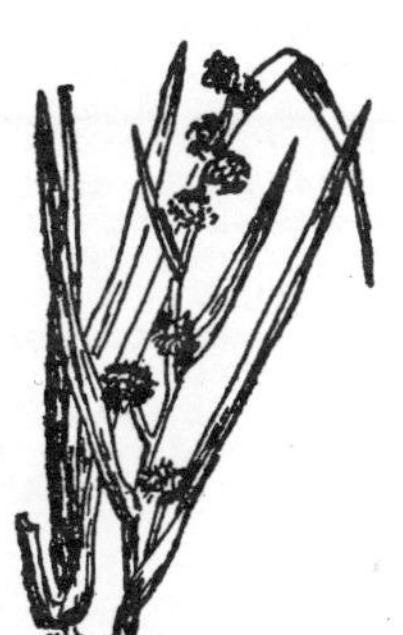

630.Seisg-madaidh.

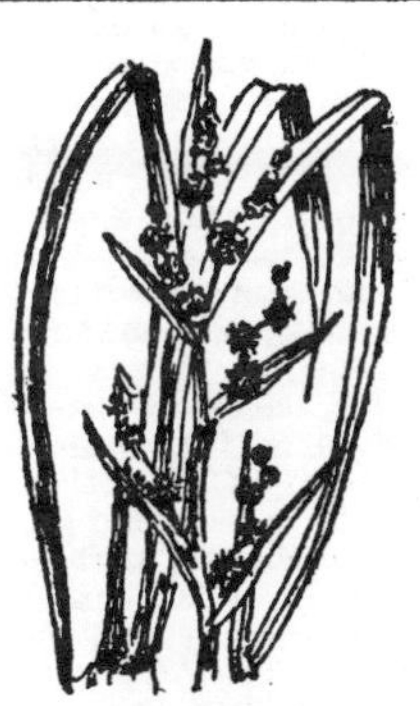

631.Sessg-rìgh.

seisreach, -ich, -ichean, *s. f.* Plough with six horses. 2 Team of horses. The team was reduced successively from six to four, and then to two, and the word keeping pace with the reduction is now applied e.g. in *Arran, W. of Ross,Lorn,&c.*to a pair of horses. The six-horse plough was in use in Ireland about 1000 A.D. and was employed in Scotland till a comparatively recent date. It was also in use in England in the lifetime of persons now living. The wooden plough continued in use well within living memory, but that was probably of an improved type. The horses were yoked abreast in the same manner as in the four-horse ploughs used in Sutherland and Caithness in the middle of the 12th. century. The elder-wood was considered superior to all other kinds for making the working parts of a wooden plough. S. fearainn, *a ploughland.*

seisreach,(AF) *s.* Allowance of milk for six persons—one gallon.

seisreadh, see seisreach.

seisreinn,(CR) *s. f.* Carucate, plough-land, as much land as can be tilled with one plough in a year.

séist, -ean, *s.m.* Melody of a tune. 2 Chorus or refrain of a song. 3 Tune, ditty, 4 Sneer. Òran air an t-séist cheudna, *a song set to the same tune.*

seist, -ean,** *s.m.* Bed, couch. S. luachrach, *a bed of rushes.*

séisteach, -eiche,*a.* Melodious, sweet, as a tune. 2 Having many tunes or ditties. 3 Fond of singing tunes or ditties. 4 Sneering.

séit, see séid.

séiteach, see séideach.

seiteach,** -eiche, *s.f.* Wife.

seiteicean,(AF) *s.m.* Silkworm.

seithe, see seiche.

seithir, -thre, -thrichean, *s.f.* see seidhir.

séitrich, -e, *s.f.* see séidrich.

†**seo**, *s.m.* Substance.

seo, *dem. adj.* This, these. An duine s., *this man ;* an nighean s., *this girl ;* na daoine s., *these men.* [Generally spelt *so*, but as *seo* represents the modern pronunciation and is the old form, it is used in this work.]

seo, *pron. & int.* Here,see here, take it, used in handing or offering anything to another, also used in addressing one when a thing is about to be done or attempted. [Generally spelt *so*, but as *seo* represents the modern pronunciation, and is the old form it is used in this work.]

Seo, seo, falbhamaid, *come, come let us go ;* rinn mi mar seo, *I acted thus ;* c' ar son seo? *why so ?* mar seo, *in this manner ;* an seo,*here;*

gluais as an seo ! *leave this place, be off !* ; mar seo is mar siod, *in this way and that way;* gus an seo, *till now* ; gus an seo bu treun e, *till now he was valiant* ; o 'n àm seo, *henceforward, hence* ; seo agad e ! *here you have him* (or *it*) ; thoir á seo e, *take him hence* (or *away*); seo mar a ni thu, *thus will you do* ; an seo 's an siod, *here and there*.
seobhag, see seabhag.
seòbhgan, for seabhagan—*Òran nam fineachan*.
seòc, -eòic, -an, see seòcan.
seocach,** *a*. Plumed, plumy, as a helmet.
seocail, -e, *a*. Active. 2 Portly and tall. 3 Having a proud gait. 4 Precocious. S. air mo chasan, *active on my feet*.
seocair,* -ean, *s.m.* Portly fellow.
seòcair,(MS) *s.m.* Falconer.
seocalachd,* *s.f.ind.* Portliness and tallness.
seòcan, -ain, -an, *s.m.* Plume of a helmet. 2 Helmet. S. air 'aghaidh, *a plume* (or *veil) on his face*.
seoc-da-leig,** *s*. Kind of clasp-knife. A corruption of the name John de Liege its inventor.
seochaidh,(WC) *a*. Lazy and canny.
seochlan,-ain,-an, *s.m.* Feeble person, one who performs any service feebly or awkwardly. 2 Pithless fellow. 3 Old man. 4††Staggering person.
———ach, -aiche, *a*. Feeble, pithless. 2 Performing any service feebly or awkwardly. 3†† Staggering.
———achd, *s.f.ind.* Feebleness. 2 Performing of any service feebly or awkwardly. 3 Pithlessness. 4††Staggering.
seòd, -òid, *s. m.* Jewel. 2 *often figuratively*, Hero, valiant man, chief, warrior. †3 (AF) Cow as property. 4 Cow with calf. 5 (AF) Deer.
seòd, see seud.
seòd-ghabhta,(AF) *s.m.* Cow with calf.
seòg,(AF) *s.f.* Little falcon. 2 Merlin.
seòg, *pr.pt.* a' seògadh,*v.a.* Swing to and fro. 2 Dandle. 3 Jog. 4** Shake laterally. 5**Hobble. 6 (CR) Fly—*Arran*.
——ach, -aiche, *a*. Swinging anything to and fro. 2 Dandling. 3 Pendulous. 4 Shaking. 5 Vibrating.
——adh, -aidh, *s.m.* Swinging, act of swinging to and fro. 2 Dandling, act of dandling. A' s—, *pr.pt.* of seòg.
seògain, see seòg.
seogal, -ail, see seagal.
seògan, -ain, *s.m.* Swinging or pendulous motion. 2 Hobbling.
seòganach, see seògach.
———d, *s.f.* Same meanings as seògan.
seòganaich, -e, *s.f.* Same meanings as seògan.
†seòid,** *a*. Strong.
seòid, *gen.sing.* & *n.pl.* of seòd. [** gives it as *nom.* too.]
seòighn, *a*. Rare, superior, out of the common order, eccentric—*Sàr-Obair*.
seòin, *s*. Feast—*Suth'd*.
seòl, -òil, -an, *s. m.* Method, mode or way of doing a thing. 2 Way, means, opportunity. 3 Aim. 4 Direction, instruction, guidance. 5 Expedient. 6**Shawl. Air s. eile, *by another method* ; gun s. air dol as, *having no way of escape* ; an s. ceart, *the proper method;* s. labhairt, *a manner of speech, an idiom* ; air an t-seòl seo, *in this manner* ; cuir s. air, *arrange, make preparation, set in order* , thoir s. dha, *direct him;* s.teichidh, *a way to escape;* cha'n 'eil s. air biadh fhaotainn, *there is no way of getting food—W.H., 1. 17*.
seòl, siùil, siùil, *s.m.* Sail. 2**Ship. Bràigh-sh., *a top-sail* ; chunnaic sinn s., *we saw a sail* ; s.-mullaich, *top-gallant* ; s. spreòid, *a jib* ; s. beag toisich, *a jib* ; prìomh-sh. *or* s. mór, *a mainsail* ; s. toisich, *a foresail* ; siùil dhalla, *topsail and jib* ; s. uachdrach, *topsail* ; s. meadhonach, *a mainsail* ; m' anam mar sh. 'san doinionn,*my soul like a sail in the storm* ; crann-siùil, *a mast* ; thog iad an siùil, *they hoisted their sails* ; s. cinn, *jib*.

Names of Parts of a Sail :—
[Gaelic names not marked are from DMy.]
1 Am pic, an coise. *gaff*.
2 Lubach. Cainb-a'-mheurain,(AH) *cringle*.
3 Sgòd thoisich, *clew*.
4 Bonn, *foot*.
5 Ceann, *head*.
6 Taom, *luff*.
7 Ceanglaichean, *reef-points*.
8 Crann-sgòide. Slat-bhuinn,(AH) *boom*.
9 Ball toisich. Cluas an t-siùil,(AH) *tack*.
10 Ball deiridh. Leud deiridh(AH)*afterleech*.
11 Sgòd dheiridh, *clew-piece*.
12 (MMcD) Corse, the part between upper reef-points and yard—*Lewis*.
13 (MMcD)During very bad weather when the end of the yard is tied to the foot of the mast and the point of the yard hoisted, it is called *a' chrois—Lewis*.

seòl, *pr.pt.* a' seòladh, *v.a.* Sail. 2 Navigate, guide a vessel. 3 Float. 4 Direct, guide, conduct. 5 Instruct. 6 Point out, show. S. an rathad dha, *show him the way* ; sh. sinn, *we sailed*.
†seòl, -oil, -an, *s.m.* Weaver's loom. 2 Bed. 3 Pasture.
seòlach, -aiche, *a*. Having many sails. 2 see seòlta.
seòlach,‡‡ -aiche, *a*. Guiding, directing. 2 Willing to guide. 3 Having many expedients, ingenious, shifty.
seòladair, -ean, *s.m.* Sailor. 2 Steersman,navigator.
———each, -eiche, *a*. Nautical.
———eachd, *s.f.ind.* Sailing, act or process of sailing. 2 Seafaring life. 3 Art or business of a sailor. 4 Navigation, steering, sailing. Bha s. cunnartach, *sailing was dangerous*.
seòladh, -aidh, *s.m.* Sailing, act of sailing. 2 Act of guiding or navigating a ship. 3 Directing. 4 Act of directing,teaching, pointing or showing. 5 Instruction, direction. 6**First semimetre of a verse. 7 Floating. A' s—, *pr.pt.* of seòl. 'Gam sh., *directing me* ; air s.,*afloat*.
seòlaid, *s. f.* Pier, haven. 2 Passage for vessels—*Dàin I. Ghobha*. 3 Anchorage, harbour —*Sàr-Obair*. 4(DC)Fairway in the sea—*Uist*.
seòlaireachd, Same meanings as seòladaireachd.
seòlam, *1st. sing. imp.* of seòl. Let me sail.
seòlaim, *Irish* form of *fut. aff. a.* (for seòlaidh mi) I will sail.
seolas, (DMy) *s. m.* Passage for boats cleaned of stones.
seòl-bhacadh,** *s.m.* Embargo.
seòl-bhàt,** -aichean, *s.m.* Pilot-boat.
seòl-bhat,** -aichean, *s.m.* Goad, staff for driving cattle.
seòl-chrann, -chroinn, *s.m.* Mast.
seòl-chrannach, -aiche, *a*. Masted, having a mast or masts. 2 Having high masts.
seòl-chois, *s*. Footboard or treadle of spinning wheel.
seòldair, see seòladair.
seòllairt, *s.m.* Phrase in *gram*.
seòl-mara, -ùil-, *dl*. siùil-mh *or* -an-m-,*s.m.* Side current. 2**Tide. 3(WC) Ebb tide. 4(WC) Full tide. Fad an t-siùil-mara, *the whole time of the tide*.

seòl-meadhon, *s.m.* Mainsail.
——————ach, see seòl-meadhon.
seòlta, *a. & past pt.* of seòl. Instructed, directed, taught, guided. 2 Methodical, set in order, arranged. 3 Ingenious, having expedients. 4 Prudent, wise, cautious. 5 Cunning, crafty, artful, wily. 6 Skilful. Gu s., *wisely, prudently* ; buineamaid gu s., *let us deal wisely.*
seòltachd, *s.f.ind.* Method, arrangement. 2 Ingenuity. 3 Prudence,caution. 4 Craftiness, wiliness. 5 Skilfulness, skill.
seòltaiche,(AC) *s.m.* Cunning man.
seòltair,(MS) *s.m.* Lagger.
seòlt-charach, -aiche, *a.* Insinuative.
seoma-guad, see seama-guad.
seòmair, *gen.sing.* of seòmar.
————eachd, see seòmadaireachd.
seomalta, *a.* see somalta.
seòmar, -air [& -mrach—not a good form,] *pl.* -mraicheau, *s.m.* The apartment or division of a house among the poorer Highlanders considered the principal one, "the room." 2 Chamber, room.
——— -aghaidh, *s.m.* Front room. 2 Ante-chamber.
——— -aoidheachd,‡‡ *s.m.* Dining-room, banquet-room.
——— -aodachaidh,** *s.m.* Vestry, robing-room.
——— -àraich, *s.m.* Nursery for children.
——— -biadhtachd,* *s.m.* Dining-room.
——— -beòil, *s.m.* Front room.
——— -bìdh, *s.m.* Larder.
——— -cadail,* *s.m.* Bedroom.
——— -cloinne, *s.m.* Nursery.
——— -cuideachd,* *s.m.* Drawing-room.
——— -cùil,* *s.m.* Back room.
——— -culaidh, *s.m.* Vestry.
——— -dìomhair, *s.m.* Consulting room.
——— -éididh, *s.m.* Dressing-room.
——— -feòla, *s.m.* Larder.
——— -gnothaich, *s.m.* Business-room, office.
——— -leabhraichean, *s.m.* Library.
——— -leapach, *s.f.* Bedroom.
——— -luidhe, *s.m.* Bedroom.
——— -marsantachd, *s.m.* Shop, ware-room.
——— -mòid, *s.m.* Court-room, court of justice.
——— -mullaich, *s.m.* Upper room, garret.
——— -samhraidh, *s.m.* Summer parlour.
——— -stuidearachd, *s.m.* Study.
——— -suidhe, *s.m.* Sitting-room.
——— -taobh, *s.m.* Ante-chamber.
——— -toisich, see seòmar-taobh.
seòmarach, -aiche, *a.* Having many rooms or chambers. 2 Cellular, vascular.
————d, *s.f.ind.* see seòmradaireachd.
seòmrach, see seòmarach.
seòmradair, -ean. *s.m.* Chamberlain, treasurer. 2 Intriguer, rake, chamberer.
——————eachd, *s.f.* Office of chamberlain or treasurer. 2 Chambering, rakishness.
seòmraichean, *pl.* of seòmar.
seonadh,** -aidh, *s. m.* Augury, sorcery. 2 Druidism. Martin says that *Seonaidh* is the name of a water-spirit which the inhabitants of Lewis used to propitiate by a cup of ale in the following manner. They came to the church of St. Mulway, each man carrying his own provisions. Every family gave a pock of malt, and the whole was brewed into ale. One of their number was chosen to wade into the sea up to his waist, carrying in his hand a cup filled with ale. When he reached a proper depth, he stood and cried aloud "Seonaidh, I give thee this cup of ale, hoping that thou wilt be so good as to send us plenty of seaware for enriching our ground during the coming year." He then threw the ale into the sea. This ceremony was performed in the night-time. On his coming to land, they all repaired to church, where there was a candle burning on the altar. There they stood still for a time, when,on a signal given, the candle was put out, and straightway they adjourned to the fields where the night was spent mirthfully over the ale. Next morning they returned to their respective homes, in the belief that they had insured a plentiful crop for the next season.
seona-saobha, see seonadh.
seorast, s Prop.
seorbh, see searbh.
seorpan,(MS) *s.m.* Politician.
seòrsa, -chan, *s.m.* Sort, kind, genus, species.
seòrsach,†† *a.* Abounding in sorts.
————adh, -aidh, *s.m.* Arranging, act of arranging or classifying. A' s—, *pr.pt.* of seòrsaich.

632. Seòrsa còinnich.

seòrsa còinnich,§ *s.* Mossy cyphel—*cherleria sedoides.* [Plentiful on Ben Lawers.]
seòrsaich, *pr. pt.* a' seòrsachadh, *v. a.* Arrange, classify, sort.
————te, *past pt.* of seòrsaich. Arranged, classified.
seòrsda, see seòrsa.
seot, -a, *pl.* -aichean & -achan, *s.m.* Short tail, stump of a tail that remains after docking. 2 Encumbrance, impediment. 3 Lean beast, "shot," rejected animal, the worst beast. 4†† Refuse of sheep.
seot, *v.a. & n.* Sprout, as greens. 2 Pick the best. Sh. an càl, *the greens sprouted.*
seotach, -aiche, *a.* Having a short or docked tail. 2 Embarrassed, encumbered. 3 Untidy, slovenly. 4 Lazy, indolent. 5 Dull.
seotaiche, *s.f.ind.* Untidiness, slovenliness. 2 Laziness, indolence. sloth.
seotair, -ean, *s.m.* Slovenly or untidy fellow. 2 Lazy fellow, drone. 3 Lounger.
————eachd, *s.f.ind.* Slovenliness, untidiness. 2 Laziness, indolence.
seotal, *s.m.* Small receptacle in stock of spinning-wheel in which the first filled pirn is kept till the other is ready for being reeled with it. It is also used for other purposes. (*shuttle.*) 3 (DU) Small box-shaped compartment with a lid, in one end of a trunk or chest, for keeping papers, &c.
seotanachd, Same meanings as seotaiche.
seotanta, -ainte, *a.* see seotach.
————chd, see seotaiche.
seothag, -aig, -an, *s.f.* see seabhag.
seothan,(CR) *Arran* for seathan.
sè-ràitheach,(CR) *s.m.* Gimmer, six-quarter-old sheep—*W. of Ross-shire.*
sè-ràmhach,* -aiche, *a.* Six-oared.
——————,* -aich, *s. m.* Six-oared galley, felucca.
†serg, see searg.
séseau, *s.m.* Dawn. Bha mi air mo chois an s.

na maidne, *I was up at dawn—Lewis.*
sè-shlisneach, *a.* Hexagonal.
————,** *s.m.* Hexagon, cube.
sé-shlisneag, -eig, -an, *s.f.* Hexagon, hexagonal figure.
seth, (*i.e.* gu seth) *adv.* Severally. 2 Moreover, also, likewise. 3 (with a negative preceding) Neither.
seth,(MS) *s.* Purport.
sè-thaobhach, *s.m.* Cube, hexagon.
————, *a.* Hexagonal.
seubh, see seabh.
seubhas,* -ais, *s.m.* Wandering, as beasts.
seuchd, -a, -an, *s.m.* Mantle, covering, tunic.
seud, *pl.* -an & seòid, *s.m.* Jewel, precious stone, 2 Darling. 3 Reward. 4*Thing, nothing. 5 Hero. 6** Instrument. 7**Way, path. Cha 'n 'eil s. math air, *it is not worth anything;* gach s. a th' agam, *everything I have;* cha bhi s. ort, *nothing will be wrong with you;* s.-suiridh, *a love-token;* mar sh. ghointe, *like a destructive instrument;* seudan òir is seudan airgid, *jewels of gold and jewels of silver.*
seudach, -aiche, *a.* Abounding in jewels, jewelled. 2 Like a jewel or precious stone.
————adh, -aidh, *s.m.* Adorning, act of adorning with jewels. A' s—, *pr. pt.* of seudaich.
————an, -ain, -an, *s.m.* Jeweller. 2 Jewel-box. 3 Jewel-house, museum.
seudag, -aig, -an, *s.f.* Little jewel, charm. 2 Excellence.
————ach, -aiche, *a.* Abounding in little jewels. 2 Like a little jewel.
seudaich, *pr.pt.* a' seudachadh, *v.a.* Adorn with jewels, garnish, bestud.
————te, *past pt.* of seudaich. Adorned with jewels.
seudail,†† *a.* Abounding in jewels. 2 Pertaining to jewels.
seudair, -ean, *s.m.* Jeweller, 2 Cedar-tree.
————eachd, *s.f.ind.* Setting of jewels. 2 Making of jewels, occupation of a jeweller.
seud-Chaluim-Chille, *s.m.* St. John's wort, see eala-bhuidhe.
seud-ghlasaidh, -an-g-, *s.f.* Locket.
seud-lann, -ainn, -an, *s.m.* Jeweller's shop. 2 Casket. 3 Jewel-house, museum.
seudraidh, *s.f.coll.* Jewels. 2 Collection of jewels.
†seughal, -ail, see seula.
seul, see seula.
seul, *pr.pt.* a' seuladh, see seulaich.
seula, -n & -chan, *s.m.* Seal, stamp. 2 Impression of a seal. 3 Any mark or impression. 4 Resemblance, likeness.
seulach, -aiche, *a.* Sealing. 2 Having seals. 3 Like a seal. 4 Of seals. 5 Sealed.
————adh, -aidh, *s.m.* Sealing, act of sealing. A' s—, *pr.pt.* of seulaich.
seulaich, *pr. pt.* a' seulachadh, *v.a.* Seal, mark with a seal. 2 Mark, bestow a mark.
————ear, *fut.pass.* of seulaich. Shall be sealed.
————te, *past pt.* of seulaich. Sealed.
seulta, *past pt.* of seul. Sealed.
seum,* see sèam.
seumadair,* see sèamadair.
seumaich,* see sèam, *v.*
seumalair, see seumarlan.
seumar, see seòmar.
seumarlan, *s. m.* Factor, Gaelic spelling of *chamberlain.*
————achd, *s.f.* Factorship.
Seumasach,** *s.m.* Jacobite.
seumas ruadh,¶ *s. m.* Puffin—*Barra.* 2 (AF) Coulterneb.
seun, *v.a.* Defend by enchantment. 2 Avoid, shun. 3 Forbear, refrain. 4 Refuse, deny. 5 Cross, make the sign of the cross. 6 Bless. 7 Make sacred. 8 Conceal. 9 (MS) Admonish. 10**Defend from the power of enchantment. 11(MS) Recant. Sh. na h-òighean, *the maid ens forbore;* sh. 'a' ghealach i féin fa neulaibh, *the moon concealed herself under a cloud.*
seun, -a, *pl.* -an & -tan, *s.m.* Charm for protection, spell, charm, amulet. 2 Protection. 3 Denial. 4 Sign of the cross. 5**Prosperity, good luck.
seunach, -aiche, *a.* Of, or belonging to charms or enchantments. 2 Like a charm or amulet. 3 Having magical power or virtue. 4 Defending by enchantment, or 5 from enchantment. 6 Concealing. 7 Apt to conceal one's self. 8 Denying, apt to deny or refuse. 9 Avoiding anything as if enchanted. 10 Forbearing. 11 Conjuring.
————d, *s.f.ind.* The power of charms or enchantment. 2 Defence by enchantment. 3 Defence from enchantment. 4 State of being defended by enchantment. 5 Refusal, denial. 6**Forbearance.
seunadair, -ean. *s.m.* Charmer, one using charms or enchantments. 2 Conjurer. 3**One who refuses. 4 Defender from enchantment.
————eachd, *s.f.ind.* Using of incantations, conjuring, enchantment, charming.
seunadh, -aidh, -aidhean, *s.m.* Act of defending by charms or enchantment. 2 Defending from enchantment, charming, augury, druidism. 3 Act of avoiding anything as if defended by incantations. 4 Denial, refusal. 5 Act of denying or refusing. 6 Hiding. 7 Act of concealing. 8 Sense, intellect. 9 Meaning. 10 Blessing. 11 Forbearing. A' s—, *pr.pt.* of seun. Tha mi 'gam sh., *I am crossing myself;* cha ghabh mi s. no àicheadh, *I will be neither refused nor denied.*
seunail, -e, *a.* Happy, prosperous, fortunate. 2 Like a charm or incantation. 3 Happy, prosperous. [or lucky.
seunalachd, *s.f.ind.* State of being prosperous
seunan,(*i.e.* breac-sheunain) *s.pl.* Freckles.
seunas,* -ais, *s.m.* Beauty-teeth.
seun-bholadh,** -aidh, *s.m.* Stench.
seun-Chaluim-Chille,(AC) *s.m.* St. John's wort. (St. Columba's charm.)
seunmhoire,** *comp.* of seunmhor.
seunmhor, -oire, *a.* Enchanted. 2 Having magical or enchanting power. 3 Using charms or enchantment.
————achd, *s.f.ind.* Magical power. 2 State of being enchanted.
seunsail,(DC) *a.* Risky, open to the influence of enchantment.—*Uist.*
seunta, *a. & past pt.* of seun. Enchanted defended by enchantments or charms, charmed, bewitched. 2 Defended from enchantment. 3 Avoided as being enchanted. 4 Blessed, sacred. 5 Concealed, hidden. 6 Denied. 7 Fortunate, lucky. 8 Auspicious, in a superstitious sense.
seuntachd,‡‡ *s.f.ind.* Inviolability.
seuntas, -ais, *s. m.* Charm, enchantment. 2 Magical power. 3 State of being defended by charms or enchantment. 4 Propitiousness, in a superstitious sense. 5** Denial, concealment. 6**Stench.
seup, *v.* see sèap.
seurs, *v.* see sears.
seusar,* -air, *s.m.* Acme, perfection, height or utmost point. An s. a' chluich, *in the heart or middle of the thing.*
seusrach,* -aiche, *a.* Mettlesome, in high condition, as a horse.

's fheudar, *v. impers. & def. past.* It behoveth, it must be, it must be so. See also éigin.
sgà, see sgàth.
sgab, Gaelic form of *scab.*
sgab, see sgap.
sgabach, -aiche, *a.* Scabby, scabbed.
†sgabadh, -aidh, see sgapadh.
sgabag, -aig, -an, *s.f.* Cow killed for winter provision. 2 Beef. *prov*
———an, *n.pl.* of sgabag. Beeves.
sgabaiste, -an, *s.m.* Anything pounded, macerated or hashed. 2**Robbery, felony, rapine. [** *s.f.*]
———ach, -eiche, *a.* Pounded, bruised, hashed. 2**Committing robbery or rapine, felonious. Gu s., *feloniously.*
———achadh, -aidh, *s. m.* Pounding, act of pounding, beating down, mashing. A' s—, *pr. pt.* of sgabaistich.
sgabaistich, *pr. pt.* a' sgabaisteachadh, *v. a.* Beat down, pound, mash.
———te, *past pt.* of sgabaistich. Beaten down, pounded, mashed.
sgaball, -aill, -an, *s. m.* Helmet, head-piece, hood. 2**Guard for the shoulder used by the ancient Caledonians. 3**Scapular. 4**Cauldron. [* gives *s.f.* for No. 1.]
———ach, -aiche, *a.* Wearing a helmet hood or headpiece. 2 Like a helmet.
———ach,** -aich, *s.m.* Wardrobe keeper.
sgabar,** *a.* Thin.
sgàbard, -aird, -an,*s.m.* Gaelic form of *scabbard.* (truaill.)
———ach, -aiche, *a.* Having a sheath. 2 Like a sheath
sgabh, -aibh, *s.m.* Saw-dust.
———ach, *a.* Abounding in saw-dust.
sgabhaiste, *s.f.* Good. †2 Advantage.
sgăbhal,** -ail, -an, *s.m.* Scaffold. 2 Booth,hut, shop. 3 Screen covering the entrance to a door.
sgàbhal,** -ail, -an, *s. m.* Cauldron, kettle. 2 Baking-trough. 3 Large bowl.
sgabhrach, -aich, *s.m.* Club-footed man.
———, -aiche, *a.* Club-footed. 2 Splay-footed.
———d, *s.f.*Infirmity of a club-foot or splay-foot.
sgabhrag, -aig, -an, *s.f.* Splay-footed woman. 2 Club-footed woman.
sgabhraiche, *s.f.ind.* Club-footedness.
sgabull, -uill, see sgaball.
sgabullach, see sgaballach.
's gach, And each, and every.
's gach, In each, in every. 'S gach àm, *always, at every time.*
sgad, -aid, -an, *s. m.* Loss, mischance, misfortune, grief, woe, ruin. 2 see sgat. Mo s, ! *woe's me! my ruin!*
sgadadh, -aidh, *s.m.* Scissure.
sgadan, -ain, *s m.* Herring—*clupea harengus.*
s. bleac, *pale or shotten herring.*
s. blia, see s. bleac.
s. garbh, *large herring, " alewife."*
s. gèarr, *sprat.*
s. goile, *gut-pock herring.*
s. mhòrlannach, *pilchard,* see seirdean.
s. sligeach, *pilchard.*
sgadanach, -aiche, *a.* Abounding in herrings. 2 Like a herring.
sgadarlach, -aich, *s.m.* Set of low persons. 2* Anything scattered. [sgadartach—‡.]
sgaf,** Gaelic form of *skiff.* Cock-boat.
sgafair, -ean, *s.m.* Courageous, stout or brave man. 2 Handsome man. 3 Scolding man. 4††Bold hearted man.
sgafal,** Gaelic form of *scaffald.*
sgafald,** -aild, Gaelic form of *scaffold.*
sgafaldach, *a.* Scaffolded, having scaffolds.
sgafaldaich, *v.a.* Erect scaffolds.
sgafall,** -aill, *s.m.* Gaelic form of *scaffold.* 2 Booth, hut, shop.
———ach,** *a.* Scaffolded, full of scaffolds.
———achadh,** -aidh, *s.m.* Act of erecting a scaffold.
———achd,** *s.f.* Scaffolding.
———aich,** *v.a.* Erect a scaffold.
sgafalt,** Gaelic form of *scaffold.*
sgafanta, -ainte, see sgafarra
———chd, see sgafarrachd.
———s,** -ais, *s.m.* Boldness. 2 State of being in good spirits.
sgafarra, -airre, *a.* Spirited, manly, brave. 2 Handsome. 3**Hearty. 4**Active, alert. 5 *Vehement in speech. 5*Venomous in scolding 7*Emphatically speaking. 8** In good spirits.
———chd, *s.f.ind.* Manliness. 2 Spiritedness. 3 Handsomeness. 4*Vehemence of speech. 5 *Quality of scolding keenly.
sgafart,* *s.f.* Scolding female.
sgag, *pr.pt.* a' sgagadh, *v.a. & n.* Split, cause to split or crack, as from heat. 2 Crack, shrink. 3**Chap. 4 Filter, strain. 5 Winnow. 6 Become lean or starved. 7 Burst. 8 Cleanse. 9* Chop.
———ach, -aiche, *a.* Full of splits, chinks or cracks. 2 Full of chaps. 3 Apt to split or crack, as the surface of anything. 4 Causing to split or crack. 5* Chinked, cracked. 6 Filtering, straining. 7 Winnowing. 8 Lean, emaciated. 9**Cleansing. Teas s. samhraidh, *the cracking heat of summer.*
sgagadh, -aidh, *s.m.* Act of splitting or cracking. 2 State of cracking, chinking or bursting. 3 Act of filtering or straining. 4 Act of winnowing. 5 State of becoming lean or emaciated. 6 Split, as on the surface of anything, chink, cranny or crack. 7**Cleansing. 8**Filtering. 9**Filter. 10**Winnow. A' s—, *pr.pt.* of sgag.
sgagaid, -e, -ean, *s.f.* Split, crack, as on the surface of deal, cleft, fissure.
———each, -eiche, *a.* Abounding in splits, cracks, clefts or fissures. 2 Causing splits, cracks or clefts.
sgagaidh,(DMy) *a.* Insipid. Iasg s,, *a tasteless fish—one neither fresh nor stale.*
sgagaidh, *fut.aff.a.* of sgag. Shall split, &c.
sgagair,* *s.m.* Poltroon, coward, one that chinks at appearance of danger.
———eachd,* *s. f. ind.* Cowardice, unfounded fear.
sgagait,** see sgagaid. [*s.m.***]
———e,** *a.* Split, cracked, burst. 2 Cleansed. 3 Filtered. 4 Winnowed.
sgagaiteach, see sgagaideach.
sgagta, *past pt.* of sgag. Split, cracked. 2 Filtered, strained. 3 Winnowed. 4 Become lean or emaciated.
sgaifean, -ein, -an, see sgaipean.
———ach, -aiche, *a.* see sgaipeanach.
———achd, see sgaipeanachd.
†sgaifir,** *s.f.* Stern of a ship.
sgaift,* *v.n.* Burst through eating too much.
———,* *s f.* Notorious bellyful.
sgaighnean,** -ein, *s.m.* Hand-winnow, winnowing-fan.
sgaigte, see sgagta.
sgail, -e & -each, *pl* -ean & -eachan, *s.f* Shade, shadow. 2 Veil, curtain, covering, mask. 3 Example, pattern. 4 Ghost, spectre. 5 Pretence. 6 Bower. Fo s. do sgéithe, *under the shadow of thy wing* ; an sgàileachan, *their cur-*

tains ; s. a' bhàis, *the shadow of death.*
——, *pr.pt.* a' sgàileadh,*v.a.* Shade, overshade, darken, cover, as with a cloud. 2*Sprinkle. 3**Eclipse. 3* Approach. Cha s. seo air, *this will not come near the thing* ; cha dèan e s. air, *it will not go near it.*
†sgail, -e, *s.f.* Splendour, brightness. 2 Flash. flame.
sgàil-bhothan, -ain, -an, *s.m.* Arbour.
sgàil-bréige,-ean-, *s.f.* Mask, visor.
sgailc, -e, -ean, *s. f.* Smart knock or blow. 2 Sound of a blow, report of a shot. 3 Good full draught of any liquid. 4 Bumper of any spirituous liquor taken before breakfast, dram, "morning," see under friochd. 5 Baldness of the head. 6 Pate—*Dain I. Ghobha.* 7**Loud momentary noise, smart report. Tarruing s. air, *give him a smart blow.*
sgailc,* *v.a.* Pelt. 2 Beat in a masterly manner.
sgailceach, -eiche, *a.* Bald 2 Giving smart blows. 3 Making a loud and sudden report. 4 Drinking full draughts or bumpers.
————d, *s.f.ind.* Sleekness, smoothness.
sgailceag, -eig, -an, *s. f. dim.* of sgailc. Slight knock. 2 Low sudden sound. 3 Small bumper or draught.
sgailceanta, -einte, *a.* Giving smart blows. 2 Making a loud and sudden report. 3 Smart, active. 4 Passionate. 5††Elastic. 6**Explosive.
————chd, *s.f ind.* Smartness, agility. 2 Passionateness. 3††Elasticity
sgailcear,** -ean, *s.m.* Bald-headed man. [sgailcire—*]
sgailcearra, *a.* see sgailceanta.
————chd, see sgailceantachd.
sgailc-mhullaich,* *s.f.* Dandruff.
sgailc-sheide, *s. f.* Dram taken in bed before rising in the morning—*Sar-Obair.*
sgaile, -ach, *pl.* -an & -achan, *s.m.* see sgàil.
sgaile,** *s.f.* Printing type.
sgaileach, -eiche, *a* Shadowy. 2 Affording a shade, shading. 3 Veiled, covered. 4 Ghostlike, unsubstantial, spectral. 5†† Full of ghosts. 6**Masked.
sgàileach,* -eich, *s.m.* Veil, curtain.
————adh, -aidh, see sgaileadh.
————ail,(MS) *a.* Subtile.
sgaileachd, *s.f ind.* Shadiness, darkness. 2 State of being veiled or masked. 3* Sprinkling.
sgàileadair, -ean, *s.m.* Any object that shades, masker, shader. 2 Masquerader.
sgàileadaireachd,†† *s.f.* Shading.
sgaileadan, -ain, -an, *s.m.* Bower.
sgaileadh, -eidh, *s.m.* Covering, act of covering, shading or obscuring. 2* Sprinkling. 3 Shading, shadowing, veiling, masking. 4(MS) Air. A s—, *pr. pt.* of sgàil. An s. a' lugha, *the least sprinkling* or *shade* ; neul 'ga s., *a cloud veiling it.*
sgàileag, -eig, -an, *s. f. dim.* of sgàil. Little shade or shadow. 2 Thin shade, veil. 3 Parasol, umbrella. 4 Arbour. 5 Cottage, booth. 6 Awning. 7**Fan. 8**Little dish. 9**Plate. 10(CR) Passing shower—*W. of Ross-shire.*
————an, -ain, -an, *s m.* Fan. 2‡‡Umbrella.
sgàilean, -ein, *s.m.* Same meanings as sgàileag.
————ach, -aiche, *a.* Shady, veiling, like a shade or veil. 2 Like an umbrella, or parasol. 3 Full of arbours. 4 Like an arbour. 5 Abounding in cottages or booths. 6 Like a cottage or booth. 7** Filmy. 8†† Full of fans. 9** Like a fan. 10†† Full of umbrellas or shades.
————achd,** *s.f.* Shadiness. 2 Shadowiness. 3 Filminess.
sgàileanta, -einte, *a.* Vain.
sgàilean-uisge, *s.m.* Umbrella
sgàilear, -eir, -an, see sgàileadair.
sgàile-bhothan,** *s.m.* Arbour.
sgàile-gréine, *s.f.* Sunshade, parasol.
sgàilich, *v.* see sgàil.
————te, *past pt.* of sgàilich. Veiled, masked, shaded, covered, obscured.
sgàil-ionad, -aid, -an, *s m.* Bower.
sgaill,(DU) s. Bald patch.
sgailleag, -eig, -an, *s. f.* Smart blow, slap. 2 Quick and loud sound. 3* Smart slap on the cheek. 4**Slap with the palm of the hand.
sgailleagach, -aiche, *a.* Giving smart slaps or blows. 2 Making a loud and sudden sound. 3** Striking with the palm of the hand, slapping
sgailleas, -eis, *s.m.* Disdain.
————ach, -aiche, *a.* Disdainful. Gu s., *disdainfully.*
————achd,** *s.f.* Disdainfulness.
†sgailp,** -ean, *s.f.* Den, cave.
————each,** *a.* Abounding in dens or caves.
sgailt, *v.* see sgald.
————e, *past pt.* Scalded.
————each,** *a.* Scalding.
————ean, see sgoiltean.
sgailltei1,** *a.* Calid.
sgàil-thaigh, *s.m.* Porch, grotto.
sgàil-uisge, *s.f.* Umbrella
sgàin, *pr.pt.* a' sgàineadh, *v.a. & n.* Burst, burst asunder, cleave, rive, rend. 2 Cause to burst or rend asunder. S. e, *it burst asunder.*
sgàin,* *s.* Complete bellyful, surfeit.
sgaindear,** -eir, *s.m.* Division, dissension.
sgàine, *s.m.* see sgàineadh.
sgàineach, -eiche, see sgàinteach. 2††Rending.
sgàineadh, -idh, *s.m.* Bursting, act of bursting or causing to burst. 2 State of bursting or bursting asunder. 3 Rending, act or state of rending asunder. 4 Rent, cleft. 5 Splitting, cleaving. 6 Burst, split. 7**Sally, attack. 8**Flaw. 9 Laceration. A' s—, *pr. pt.* of sgàin.
sgàineadh, *3rd. per.sing. & pl.imp.* of sgàin. S. e, *let it burst.*
sgàinne, -an, *s.m.* see sgàineadh.
sgainne,** *s. f.* Sudden irruption or sally. 2 Attack. 3 Flaw.
sgainneal, -eil, -an, *s.m.* Scandal, reproach, calumny. 2 Slander, false reproach. 3 Disgrace, matter or cause of reproach. Thog thu oirnn s., *thou hast calumniated us.*
————ach, -aiche, *a.* Calumnious, raising calumnies or false reproaches. 2 Disgraceful, shameful, reproachful, slanderous.
————achadh, -aidh, *s.m.* Calumniating, act of calumniating or raising scandal against one, slandering, reproaching. A' s—, *pr. pt.* of sgainnealaich.
————achd,** *s.f.* Abusiveness.
sgainnealaich, *pr. pt.* a' sgainnealachadh, *v. a.* Slander, calumniate, raise false reproaches against one, scandalize, reproach.
———— ————te, *past pt.* of sgainnealaich. Calumniated, accused of anything scandalous, scandalized, reproached.
sgainnearach, -aiche, *a.* Scattering, dispersing. 2 Having faults or blemishes. 3** Scaring, persecuting. 4 see sgainnir.
———— ————d, *s.f.* Abusiveness.
sgainnearadh, -aidh, *s. m.* Scattering, act of scattering or dispersing. 2 Scaring. 3 Persecuting, persecution. 4**Sudden dispersion. A' s—, *pr. pt.* of sgainnir.
sgainneart, -eirt, -an, *s.f.* Dispersion, scattering. 2 Contest, engagement. 3**Swing. 4 Persecution. 5 Trial of strength. Faiceamaid

a. glan, *let us see a fair trial of strength.*
sgainneartach, -aiche, *a.* Scattering, dispersing. 2 Contending, struggling. 3**Persecuting. 4 **Powerful.
sgainnir, *v.a. & n.* Scatter, disperse. 2*Stroll. 3**Persecute. 4(MS) Abuse. S. sibh iad, *you dispersed them.*
sgainnir, -e, -ean, *s.f.* Blemish, fault. 2 Scattering, dispersion. 3(MS) Shame. 4 Persecution. 5(MS) Prate. 6 see sgainneal.
————each, -eiche, see sgainnearach.
————ich, *v.a.* Vilify, abuse.
————te,: *past pt.* of sgainnir. Scattered, dispersed.
sgàinnteach, -ich, -ichean, *s.f.* Corroding pain. 2 Pain occasioned by excessive fatigue, as in walking. 3* Rheumatism.
——————ail,* *a.* Rheumatic.
sgàinte, *past pt.* of sgàin. Burst, burst asunder. 2 Rent, rent asunder. S. o chéile, *burst asunder.*
————ach, -eiche, *a.* Causing to burst, rend or split. 2 Apt to burst, rend or split. 3 Chinky. 4 Bursting, splitting, cleaving, tearing asunder, riving.
sgaip, see sgap.
——ean, -ein, -an, *s.m.* Dwarf, ninny, term of personal contempt.
——eanach, -aiche, *a.* Dwarfish, ninnyish.
——eanachd, *s.f.* Dwarfishness, ninnyism, futility, trifling talk.
sgaipte, *past pt.* of sgap, see sgapta.
————ach, *a.* Generous, lavish. 2(MS) Rife.
————achd, *s.f.* Diffusiveness. 2(MS) Rifeness. 3(MS)Revery.
sgair, see sgar.
sgair, *s.f.* Any place where a thing is laid to [dry.
sgair,* -e, -ean, *s.f.* Stitch. 2 Seam. 3 Splice. 4 Nails, see tairngnean-sgair, p. 77.
sgàird, -e, *s.f.* Flux, looseness, diarrhœa. [with the art. *an.*] 2**Loose stool. 3**Skit. 4** *rarely,* Smock. 5(DMK) Scree, shingly slope —*Gairloch.*
————each, -eiche, *a.* Affected with flux, diarrhœa or dysentery. 2**Habitually loose in the bowels. 3 Squirting, pouring, sprinkling. 4 (DU) *metaphorically,* Worthless, contemptible person. Peasan s., *a worthless wretch;* is minig a bha laogh math aig boin sgairdeich, *a skittering cow has often had a good calf.*
————eachd, *s. f. ind.* State of being affected with flux, diarrhœa or dysentery.
sgàirdeadh, -idh, *s. m.* Squirting, syringing, pouring, sprinkling.
sgàirdean, -ein, -an, *s.m.* Trifling or nasty person, a term of contempt.
sgàirdear,** *s.m.* One afflicted with weakness of the bowels. 2 Squirt, syringe, water-gun.
sgaireab,** *s.* Lavishness.
sgàireach, see appendix.
sgaireach, -eiche, *a.* Prodigal 2 Cold and windy, threatening rain, as weather.
————, -eich, *s.m.* Prodigal.
†————d, *s.f.* Crying, shrieking. 2 Creaking.
sgàireag,(CR) *s.f.* Passing shower—*W. of Ross-shire.*
sgaireag, *s.f.* see sgarbh. 2 see seagair. 3 Young scart, one-year-old gull. [sgàireag—‡.]
sgaireag,¶ -eig, -an, *s. f.* Lesser black-headed gull—*larus fuscus.*
sgaiream,(CR) *s.m.* Idle talk—*Skye.*
sgàireanaich,(AC) *s.f.* Sound of the flapping of wings. An sgiathan a' s., *their wings flapping.*
sgaireap, -a, *s.f.* Lavishness, profusion, prodigality. 2 Weather with whistling wind, threatening rain. 3 Sudden skirl, as of bagpipes. 4 Extravagance.
————ach, -eiche, *a.* Lavish, profuse, extravagant. Gu s., *lavishly.*
sgaireapail,* -e, *a.* Whistling, gusty and threatening rain.
sgairg,(AF) *s.f.* Scorpion, see sgairp.
sgairg,** *s.f.* Stony, gravelly bottom.
sgairiop, see sgaireap.
sgairn, -ean, *s.m.* Howling of dogs or wolves. 2 Loud murmuring noise. 3 Noise of stones 4 **Shriek. 5 see sgairt. B' fhad chluinnte an s., *their howling was heard afar off.*
sgàirneach, -eiche, *a.* Crying aloud, shouting. 2 Shrieking. 3 Howling, as dogs or wolves. 4 Making a loud murmuring noise. 5 ††Rumbling noise.
————-—, -ich, *s.m.* Continuous heap of loose stones covering a hill-side 2 The sound of such stones falling along a steep and rocky hill-side. 3 Continued howling. 4*Deserted quarry. 5 Great number of stones, like a deserted quarry, on a hill. 6†† Large heap of stones. [Nos. 4 & 5, *s.f.*—*]
————-—, -eiche, *a.* Abounding in heaps of loose stones. 2 Like a rocky hill-side covered with loose stones.
sgàirneil, -e, *s.f.* Shrieking, crying out. 2††see sgàirneach.
†sgàirnigh, -e, *s.f.* Separation. 2 Broken pieces.
sgairp, -e, -ean, *s.f.* Scorpion. 2 The sign Scorpio (♏), in the zodiac.
sgairpeach, ** *a.* Like a scorpion. 2 Full of scorpions. 3 Of scorpions.
sgàirt, *s.f* Flux—*Dàin I. Ghobha.*
sgairt, *v.* see sgairtich.
sgairt, -e, -ean, *s.f.* Loud cry, roar or shout. 2 Shriek. 3 Strength, vigour, activity, bustle. 4 The midriff [with the *art.*] 5 Diaphragm or caul covering any of the intestines or viscera. 6 Energy, business. 7 Appearance. 8 Authority. 9*Smart breeze. 10 War. 11** Tuft of trees, shrubs, branches or bushes. 12**Bush. Dèan do ghnothach le s., *do your business with energy;* le s. de ghaoith tuath, *with a smart breeze of northerly wind;* s. an cridhe, *the caul of their hearts;* thàinig e le s., *he came with a bustle.*
————each, -eiche, *a.* That bawls aloud, shouting. 2 Shrieking. 3 Acrimonious. 4 Roaring, clamorous. 5 Active, bustling. 6 Having a caul. 7 Like, of, or belonging to, a caul. 8** Having a large caul.
————eachadh, -aidh, *s.m.* Shouting, act of shouting or crying. 2 Shrieking, act of shrieking or roaring. 3 Bustling motion. A' s—, *pr.pt.* of sgairtich.
————eachd, *s.f* Same meanings as sgairteachadh. Na tannais a' s., *the spectres shrieking;* s. gheur, *a piercing shriek or cry.*
————eadh,** -eidh, *s. m* Shouting, roaring, bawling, shrieking. 2 Bustling noise. 3 ** Bustling motion.
sgairte falaich, see sgarta falaich.
sgairtealachd, *s.f.ind.* Vigour, liveliness, activity. 2* Half stormy weather. 3 Boldness of manner. 4 Vigorousness. 5** Bustling manner.
sgairtear, -ir, -an, *s.m.* Crier, one who cries or bawls.
————achd,†† *s.f.* Business of a crier.
sgairteil, -e, *a.* Brisk, vivacious, lively, vigorous. 2 Loud, shrill, sharp. 3 Bustling, active, energetic. 4 Bold in manner. 5* Breezy. Duine s., *an energetic person,* an là s., *the half-stormy* or *blowy day.*
sgairtich, *pr. pt.* a' sgairteachd & a' sgairteachadh, *v.a.* Shout, cry aloud, utter a loud and piercing cry, shriek.

†sgaiste, *s.m.* Robbery, rapine.
sgait, *s.f.* see sgat.
sgaite, see sgaithte.
sgaite, -an, *s.f.* see sgaiteachd.
sgait,‡ *s.* Pickle.
sgaite,** *s.f.* Short angry rebuke. 2 Cut. 3 Snarl. 4 *in derision*, Short-tempered person. Thug e s orm, *he rebuked me angrily, he snarled at me.*
sgaiteach, -eiche, *pl* -a, *a.* Sharp, having a keen edge. 2 Cutting, that cuts. 3 Keen, piercing. 4 Satirical, using cutting words or bitter language, cynical. 5 Stormy, boisterous. 6 Destructive 7 Active, lively. 8 Abounding in skate (fish.) 9 Like a skate. 10 Biting, as a dog. 11** Shabby 12 (DMK) Penetrating. 13**Energetic. 14**Angry Gunna s., *a penetrating gun* ; mar chlaidheamh s., *like a sharp sword* ; gu s.. *sharply, cuttingly* ; gaoth s., *a piercing wind* ; cainnt s., *cutting language* ; iathaidh bilean dearg daithte, teangaidh s., lom, ghèarrta, *red lips may surround a bitter, cutting tongue.*—R.61.
sgaiteachas, -ais, *s.m.* Same meanings as sgaiteachd.
sgaiteachd, *s.f.ind.* Sharpness, keenness of edge. 2 Sharpness, keenness, as of cold. 3 Bitterness of speech. 4 Raillery. 5 Storminess, boisterousness. 6 Liveliness, activity. 7 Asperity.
sgaiteag, -eig, -an, *s.f.* Little skate.
sgaitear, -eir, -an, *s.m.* Cynic.
sgaitean, *s.m.*, *dim.* of sgat.
sgaith, *s.f.* (AC) Roof-tree.
†sgaith, *s.f.* Flower.
sgàithean, -ein, -an, *s.m.*, *dim* of sgàth. Small shadow. 2 Small shade, parasol.
sgaithleach, see sgaiteach.
sgaithte, *past pt.* of sgath. Lopped off, cut off, pruned. 2 Bitten. 3 Stung. 4 Destroyed.
sgaitichead,** *s.* Acrimony.
†sgal, *s.m.* Man, hero, champion. 2 Scorching.
sgal, -a, -an, *s. m.* Shriek, yell, loud shrill cry. 2 Blast, sound of high wind. 3 Appearance of the sea in a squall. 4 Howl of a dog when hurt ; or when hunting. †5 (AF) Calf. 6** Skirl of the bagpipes. 7 see sgàladh. 8(DU) Outburst of speech, crying, &c. 9(DU) Spell of any form of activity. 10* Sudden, quick cry S. a chuilein, *the howl of his dog* ; s. gaoithe, *a squall of wind* ; s. air càineadh, air iomradh, air itheadh, &c., *a spell of scolding, rowing, eating, &c.*—*Gairloch.* [**Tray.
sgàl, -ail, *s.m.* Meal-trough. 2 Baking-trough. 3
sgal, *pr. pt.* a' sgaladh, a' sgalart & a' sgalartaich, *v.n.* Howl,give a shrill cry,squall,shriek. 2 Shriek or squeal suddenly.
sgala, -n, *s.m.* Ill-shaped hood or tunic.
sgalach, -aiche, *a.* Loud, shrill, sonorous 2 Shrieking, yelling, howling. 3* Shrill and sharp. 4**Apt to shriek, howl, yell or squall.
sgàladh,** -aidh, *s.m.* Meal-trough, kneading-trough. 2**Large bowl, kettle, cauldron.
sgalag, -aig, -an, *s.f.* Workman, farm-servant. 2 Ploughman. 3**Slave. 4†† Rustic. [*s.m* —McL & D.]
———ach, -aiche, *a.* Having many male farm-servants. 2 Of, or belonging to, a male farm-servant. 3††Rustic.
———achas, -ais, *s.f.* The occupation of a male farm-servant.
———achd,** *s.f.* Slavishness.
sgalaiche, *s.m.* Man ready to raise a hue and cry against his neighbour.—*Sar-Obair.*
sgàlaichean, Gaelic form of *scales*
sgalaid,§ -e, -ean, *s.f.* Shallot—*allium ascalonicum.* 2**Noise.

sgàlain, *s.pl.* Scales for weighing. 2**Weights.
sgalair, -ean, *s.m.* Squaller.
sgalais,* *s. f.* Jeering, gibing, continuous jeering.
sgalan, -ain, -an, *s.m.* Stage, scaffold. 2 Hut. 3 Rostrum 4 see sgàilean
sgalan,** -ain, *s m.* Goblet 2 Knee-pan.
sgàlanach, *a* Abounding in stages, scaffolds,&c.
sgalanta, -ainte, *a* Loud, shrill sounding, sonorous Piob s., *a loud-sounding pipe*
———chd, *s.f ind* Loudness, shrillness of sound, sonorousness.
sgalar,(AF) *s.m.* Hounds' cry when hunting.
sgalart, see sgalartaich
———aich, -e, -ean, *s.f* Shrieking, act of shrieking or yelling. 2 Howling, act of howling. 3 Howl. 4 Yell. A' s—, *pr pt.* of sgal.
sgalartaiche, -an, *s.m.* Bellower.
sgalb, see sgolb.
sgalbhail,(CR) *s.f.* Continued barking of a dog —*Suth'd.*
sgalcairneach, -eich, *s.m.* see sgailc.
sgald, *v.a.* Scald, burn with hot water. 2 Wash with hot water. 3 Pain, torment, torture.
———ach, -aiche, *a.* Scalding, that scalds or burns. Painful, tormenting, causing torment.
†sgaldach, -aich, *s.m* Stubble.
sgaldadh, -aidh, *s.m.* Act of scalding or burning with hot water. 2 Act of washing with hot water. 3 Act of tormenting or torturing. 4 Anguish, torment. A' s—, *pr. pt.* of sgald.
sgaldruth,** *s.m.* Fornicator.
sgaldta, *past pt.* of sgald. Scalded, burnt with hot water 2 Washed with hot water. 3 Afflicted, tormented.
sgal-fhar, see sgal-fhart.
sgal-fhart, -airt, -an, *s.m.* Howl, loud barking, see sgalartaich.
———aich, -e, *s.f.* see sgalartaich.
sgall, -aill, -an, *s. m.* Baldness. 2 Scall, scab. 3 Bald head—*Dain I. Ghobha.*
sgall,** *v.a.* Scald. 2 Trouble, disturb
sgalla,* *s. f* Old hat. 2 Large wooden dish cut out of a tree.
sgallach, -aiche, *a.* Bald. 2 Troublesome. 3 Impertinent.
———an, -ain, *s.m* Bald-headed person. 2 Unfledged bird. *Scots*, scaldie.
———d, *s.f.ind.* Baldness. 2**Troublesomeness. 3**Disturbance.
sgalladh, -aidh, *s.m.* & *pr.pt.* of sgall.[see sgaldadh.
†sgallagach, -aich, *s.m.* Bird-seed.
sgallaid, -e, -ean, *s.f* see sgallais.
sgallais, -e, -ean, *s.f.* Insult, contempt, derision, mockery, ridicule. 2 Flattery. Ri s., *deriding.*
sgallaiseach, -eiche, *a.* Insulting, showing contempt, deriding, mocking, ridiculing, opprobrious. 2 Given to mockery. 3 Flattering.
———adh, -aidh, *s. m.* Deriding, act of deriding, ridiculing or insulting. A' s—, *pr. pt.* of sgallaisich.
———d,** *s.f.* Practice of ridicule.
sgallaisich, *pr. pt* a' sgallaiseachadh, *v.a.* Deride, ridicule, insult.
———te, *past pt.* of sgallaisich.Derided, ridiculed, insulted.
sgalld, see sgald.
———achan, see sgallachan.
———adh, -aidh, see sgaldadh.
sgalldair,(MS) *s.m.* Brawler.
———eachd, *s f.* Bad language.
sgallt, see sgald.
———a, *a.* Bald, bare. 2 see sgaldta.
———ach, see sgaldach.
sgalpan,(CR) *s.m.* Chaff—*Lewis.* DMy. says s.

comes off oats only—calgan is the barley beard.

sgàm, -àim, *s.m.* Spot. 2 Spot on linen. 3 Iron-mould.

sgamal, -ail, *s.f.* Scale.

——, -ail, -an, *s. m.* Exhalation. effluvia. 2 Phlegm. 3**Scum.

——ach, -aiche, *a.* Scaly. 2 Abounding in phlegm.

sgamh, -aimh, *s.m.* Lobe of the lungs, lights. [*s.f.*—*] S.-eighe, *file-dust, filings.*

sgamh,** *s.m.* Wry mouth.

——ach,** *a.* Having good lungs. 2 Of lungs, pulmonary.

——ag,** -aig, *s.f.* Wry mouth.

——ainn, *pr pt.* a' sgamhnadh, *v.a.* Build up corn or hay in a barn.—*Gairloch, &c.*

sgamhan, -ain, -an,*s.m.* The lungs, the lights. 2 Liver. 3 Dolt, blockhead. 4 Refuse. dross. 5 Appellation of extreme contempt. 6 Villainous person. 7 Corn or hay built up in a barn. s.-coirce, *oats built up in a barn.*
s.-eorna, *barley* ,, ,,
s.-fheòir, *hay* ,, ,,

sgamhanach, -aiche, *a.* Having large or strong lungs. 2 Pulmonary, of, or belonging to lungs or lights; or 3 liver. 4 Roan, drab, of the colour of lights. Aodach, s., *roan-coloured cloth.*

sgamhanach, (DMy) *s. m.* Feeble man whose breath shortens at a little exertion.

sgamhanaich,* see sgarthanaich.

sgamhar, -air, *s.m.* Saw-dust.

sgamh-chnuimh, -e, *s.f.* see sgamh-ghalar.

sgamh-chridhe,* *s.m.* Caul.

sgamh-ghalar, -air, *s. m.* Consumption in the lungs.

†sgamh-ghlonn, *s. m.* Vile prank, vicious deed, shabby action.

sgamhnadh, -aidh, *s.m.* Building up of corn or hay in a barn. A' s—, *pr.pt.* of sgamhainn.

sgamhnaidh, *fut. aff.a.* of sgamhainn.

sgann, -ainne, *s.m.* Multitude. 2 Herd, drove. 3††Swarm of bees. 4**Parcel. S. fhiadh, *a herd of deer.*

sgann, -ainn, -an, *s.m.* Membrane. 2* Hand. 3 Multitude, swarm. [*s.f.*—*]

——ach,** *a.* Membranous. 2 Filmy. 3 Swarming, in swarms or multitudes.

sgannal, -ail, -an, *s.m.* see sgainneal.

——ach, *a.* see sgainnealach.

sgannairt,(AH) *s.f.* Wreck, ravages, devastation—*Argyll.*

sgannan, -ain, -an, *s.m., dim.* of sgann. Little herd or drove. 2 Thin membrane, caul or film, pellicle. 3 Gristle. 4 Reticle. 5**Group of people. 6**Little parcel. S. saille, *a caul.*

——ach,** *a.* Membraneous. 2 Reticular.

sgann-sgriod,(AF) *s.m.* Herd of cattle.

sgànrach, ** *a.* Dispersing, scattering, scaring, routing, terrifying. 2 Like a dispersion rout or persecution. 3 Persecuting.

sgànradh, -aidh, *s. m.* Surprise, fright. 2 Dispersion from fright or terror. 3 Act of dispersing or terrifying into dispersion, scaring, routing, scattering, dispelling. 4 Rout, confusion. 5**Frightening of cattle. 6**Persecution. A' s—, *pr pt.* of sgànraich. A' s. doinionn, *dispelling the storm.*

sgànraich, *v. a.* Scare, affright. 2 Disperse through fear, rout, scatter. 3**Persecute.

——te, *past pt.* of sgànraich. Scared, affrighted. 2 Scattered or dispersed through fear, routed.

sgànraidh, for sgànraichidh, *fut. aff. a.* of sgànraich.

——,** *s.f.* Dispersement through fear or astonishment. 2**Defamation. 3 Sudden dispersion. 4 Astonishment.

sgaog, -aoig, -an, *s.m. & f.* Foolish, fickle or giddy young woman. 2 Giddy or unsteady person generally.

——ach, -aiche, *a.* Giddy, inconstant, volatile, flighty.

——achas, -ais, *s.m.* see sgaogachd.

sgaogachd, *s.f.ind.* Giddiness, levity, volatility, inconstancy.

sgaogag, -aig, -an, *s. f., dim.* of sgaog. Giddy girl.

sgaogaiche, *s.f.ind.* see sgaogachd.

sgaogan, -ain, -an, *s. m. dim.* of sgaog. Giddy youth.

——achd, see sgaogachd.

sgaoil, *pr.pt.* a' sgaoileadh, *v.a. & n.* Stretch out, extend. 2 Scatter, disperse, spread. 3 Enlarge, dilate, expand. 4 Dismiss, send away, give leave of departure. 5 Divulge, publish. 6 Loose, dissolve, untie. 7 Unsew. 8 Be unsewed. 9 Unfold. 10 Be unfolded. 11 Destroy. 12†† Fray. 13**Dishevel. S. e a làmhan, *he extended his hands*; s. iad feadh an t-saoghail, *they dispersed throughout the world*; s. e an sgoil, *he dismissed the school*; s. an t-sreang, *untie the cord*; s. e an naidheachd, *he divulged the news*; cuir fa sgaoil, *release*; s. an eaglais, *the congregation dispersed.*

sgaoil,* *s.m.* Liberty, freedom. Mu s., *at liberty*; cuir mu s., *set sail, weigh anchor.*

sgaoile, see sgaoileadh. 2**Scattered state. 3 **Looseness.

——ach,** *a.* Causing to spread or scatter. 2 Diffusing. 3 Dishevelling, loosening, unfolding. 4 Divulging. 5 Diffuse.

sgaoileadh, -idh, *s.m.* Spreading, act of spreading, stretching out, extending. 2 Scattering, act of scattering or dispersing. 3 Dispersion. diffusion. 4 Dishevelling. 5 Enlarging, act of enlarging, dilating or expanding. 6 Dismissing, act of dismissing, sending away or giving leave of departure. 7 Act of divulging, revealing, promulgating or publishing. 8 Loosing, act of loosing. 9 Dissolving. 10 Untying. 11 Unsewing, act of unsewing. 12 State of being unsewed. 13 Rent in cloth or leather. 14 State of being unfolded. 15 Laceration. 16††Fraying. 17**Destroying. A' s—, *pr. pt.* of sgaoil. Theab e s., *he nearly burst (with laughter)*; bu chian ar s., *far apart were we dispersed.*

sgaoilear, *fut.pass.* of sgaoil. Shall be spread.

sgaoilidh, *fut. aff.a.* of sgaoil.

sgaoilte, *past pt.* of sgaoil. Spread, stretched, extended, expanded. 2 Dispersed, scattered. 3 Dismissed. 4 Divulged. 5 Loosened. 6 Dissolved. 7 Untied. 8 Unsewed. 9 Dishevelled. 10(DU) Loose-witted. Cuirm s., *a banquet spread.*

sgaoilteach, -eiche, *a.* Spreading, that spreads, scattering, that scatters. 2 Divulging, spreading abroad. 3 Diffuse, liberal, profuse, bountiful. 4 Scattered, in a scattered state, wide, spread. 5*Unguarded, imprudent. 6 Apt to loosen or dislodge. 7††Fraying. 8**Apt to spread or scatter. 9**Apt to divulge. Cainnt s., *unguarded expressions; diffuse language*; fear b' fhad s. cliù, *a man of widely-spread fame*; duine s., *a lecherous man.*

——, -eich, -ean, *s.f.* Ground on which to spread anything to dry, e.g. peats or nets.

——ail, -e, *a.* see sgaoilteach.

——d, *s.f. ind.* State of being spread or scattered. 2 Tendency to spread or scatter. 3 Readiness to divulge or publish abroad. 4 State of being divulged. 5 Diffuseness, liber-

ality, bountifulness, profuseness.
sgaoilteag,** -eig, *s.f.* Sheet. 2 Winding-sheet.
sgaoim, -e, *pl.* -ean & -annan, *s.f.* Fright, sudden terror, alarm. 2 Starting or sudden movement from fear or terror. 3*Skittishness, as of a horse or beast. 4* Terror from false alarm.
sgaoimeach, -eiche, *a.* Apt to be frightened. 2 Restless, unquiet. 3 Terrified, timid, skittish. 5 Causing to start.
———d, *s.f.ind.* Aptness or readiness to be terrified. 2 Timidity, skittishness. 3 Restlessness.
sgaoimealachd,* see sgaoimearachd.
sgaoimear,** *a.* Timid. 2 Skittish.
sgaoimear, -eir, -an, *s.m.* Coward, timid fellow. 2 Restless fellow. 3 Any shy creature.
———achd, *s.f.ind.* Cowardice, timidity. 2 Shyness. 3 Restlessness.
sgaoimeil, see sgaoimeach. 2* Skittish.
sgaoimeiche, see sgaoimeachd.
sgaolar,** *a.* Coy.
———achd,** *s.f.* Coyness.
sgaoll, -aoill, *s.m.* see sgaoim.
———air, -ean, *s.m.* see sgaoimear.
———air, -e, *a.* see sgaoimeach.
———aireachd, see sgaoimeachd.
———mhor, -oire, *a.* see sgaoimeach.
———mhorachd,** *s.f.* Timidity, shyness.
sgaoman uisge,(CR) *s.m.* Light shower—*Lochbroom.*
sgaoth, -a, -an, *s.m.* Swarm, great number, multitude. 2 Flight of birds. 3††Flock. [*gen.* cgaoith—**]
———ach, -aiche, *a.* In swarms or multitudes.
———aich, *v.a. & n.* Crowd.
sgaothan,** -ain, *s.m.* Chamber-pot.
sgap, *pr.pt.* a' sgapadh, *v. a.* Scatter, spread, disperse. 2 Squander. 3 Afflict. 4*Hack, hash. 5* Distribute profusely.
sgapach, -aiche, *a.* That scatters or disperses, scattering, spreading, squandering, diffuse. 2 **Apt to scatter, spread or squander.
sgapadair, -ean, *s.m.* Scatterer, one who scatters, disperser, disseminator. 2* Hasher.
sgapadh, -aidh, *s.m.* Scattering, act of scattering,dispersing, spreading or routing, dispersion. 2* Hacking, hashing. A' s—, *pr. pt.* of sgap. A' s. càise, *hacking down cheese.*
———, *3rd. pers. sing. & pl. imp.* of sgap. S. e, *let it scatter ;* s. iad, *let them scatter.*
———, *past pass.* of sgap. Was scattered or dispersed.
sgapaidh, *fut.aff.a.* of sgap.
sgapair, -ean, see sgapadair.
———eachd,** *s.f.* Scattering,dispersion,routing. 2 Extravagance.
sgap-litir, *s.f.* Handbill.
sgapta, *past pt.* of sgap. Scattered, dispersed, routed. 2 Squandered.
sgaptach, *a.* see sgaipteach.
sgar, *pr.pt.* a' sgaradh & a' sgarachdainn, *v.a.* Separate, disjoin, sever, disunite. 2 Tear asunder, pull asunder, split. 3 Torment,afflict, harass, gall. 4 Divorce, part. 5*Secern. 6** Unfold for drying. 7**Wound.
sgar, -air, -an, *s.m.* Knot on the surface of wood. 2 Fissure in wood. 3 Seam or joint, as in a boat. Tàirnean sgair, *seaming nails ;* s. an droma, *or* s. an leigeil, *rebate,* see bàta, A 3, p. 73.
sgara, see sgaradh.
sgarach, -aiche, *a.* Knotty, having knots or asperities on the surface. 2 Having fissures (of wood.) 3 Separating, disjointing, severing, disuniting, schismatic. 4 Tearing asunder. 5 Tormenting, harassing, galling, afflicting. 6 Distinguishable—*Dàin I. Ghobha.* 7**Wounding
sgarachduinn, *s.m.* Separating, act of separating, disjoining, severing, disuniting. 2 Act of tearing or pulling asunder. 3 Wounding. 4 Harassing. 5* Separation by force. 6**Dissension, division, faction, schism. Tha s. 'nur measg. *there are divisions among you.* A' s— *pr. pt.* of sgar. [*s.f.***]
sgaradair,** *s.m.* Separator. 2 Tearer asunder. 3 Harasser, tormentor.
———eachd,** *s.f.* Separation, schism, separability.
sgaradh, -aidh, *s.m.* Same meanings as sgarachduinn. 2 Faction, divison. 3 Shed of the warp in weaving. 4 Mark, as of a blow. 5 Torment, woe. 6* Ruin. A' s—, *pr. pt.* of sgar.
———,(MS) -aidh, *s.m.* Aperture.
——— !*int.* Imprecation, expression of ill-will.
sgarag,(AF) see sgabag.
sgarail,** *a.* Separable.
sgarait,** *s.f.* Table-cloth.
sgarar, *fut.pass.* of sgar.
sgarbh, -airbh, *pl.* -an & -airbh, *s. m.* Cormorant, shag—*phalacrocorax carbo.* 2**Bittern, see corra-ghrian. 3**Heron. 4** Shallow water, ford. Trod nam ban mu'n s. 's an s. air an loch, *the women disputing who shall have the scart, and the scart out on the loch*—i.e. disposing of the hare before it is caught.
sgarbh,** *v.a.* Wade. 2 Cross a river by a ford.
sgarbh-a'-bhothain, see sgarbh-an-sgumain.
sgarbhach,-aiche, *a.* Abounding in cormorants. 2 Like a cormorant. 3 Of a cormorant.
sgarbhan,** -ain, *s. m.* Little cormorant. 2 Young cormorant.
sgarbh-an-sgumain,¶ -airbh-, *s.m.* Shag, green cormorant—*phalacrocorax crisbantus.* 2(AF) Crested scart.
sgarbh-an-uchd-ghil, see sgarbh-an-sgumain.
sgarbh-buill, see sgarbh.
sgar-bhoc,** *s.m.* Scurvy.
———ach,** *a.* Scurvied. 2 Like a scurvy.
sgàrd,** *v.* Squirt, pour, sprinkle.
sgàrd, see sgàird.
———ach, see sgàirdeach.
———adh, see sgàirdeadh.
sgàrdach, -aich, *s.m.* Bunch of furze or thorns placed before the tap in a mash keeve. 2 Vomiting. 3 Squirt.
sgàrdair, see sgàirdear.
sgàrdan, (CR) *s. m.* Scree, continuous run of stones on a hill-side—*W. of Ross.*
sgàrlaid, -e, *s.f.* Scarlet colour.
———, *a.* Scarlet.
———each, *a.* Scarlet.
sgarmaich, *s. f.* Flux of stones on a hill-side —*Badenoch.* (sgàirneach.)
sgàrnal, -ail, see sgàirneil.
sgarrag,(AF) *s.f.* Skate, ray-fish.
sgarrthach, -aich, *s.f.* Temporary shower, flying blast of foul weather.
sgart, see sgairt.
sgarta, *past pt.* of sgart. Separated, disjoined, disunited. 2 Pulled or torn asunder. 3 Afflicted, tormented. 4 Galled, harassed.
sgarta falaich, (AC) *s.* Rift, rent, cleft, cave, recess in a rock in which to hide or shelter.
sgarthanaich, -e, *s.f.* Dawn,twilight, day-spring. Bha e an seo 'san s., *he was here at dawn.*
sgat, -ait, -an, *s.f.* Skate (fish.) [*s.m.***]
Tha a' mheòir an déidh na sgait, *his fingers are after the skate*—said of a bad piper. The saying originated with a young piper, who was being instructed at the piper's college at Boreraig in Skye. Having had skate to dinner one day, which he did not approve of,

and playing afterwards indifferently, he was asked what was wrong with him. "The skate sticks to my fingers," was his reply. Ma cheannaicheas tu iasg ceannaich iasg sgait, *if you buy fish, buy skate.* The Highland prejudices against certain meat and fish are sometimes very absurd. The skate is most unjustly undervalued by the natives of the western coasts of Scotland—N.G.P.

sgata, see sgat.

-——ch, *a.* Abounding in skates.

sgat ghlas, *s.f.* Large soft grey skate—*Lewis.*

sgàth, -a, -an, *s.m.* Shadow, shade. 2 Pretence. 3 Disgust. 4 Fright, fear, dread, apprehension. 5 Sake, account. 6 Nearness, propinquity. 7 Bashfulness, timidity. 8 (AG) see sgoth. 9*Shelter, protection. 10**Veil, covering. Tha mi fo s., *I am afraid;* tha thu 'cur s. orm, *you make me feel squeamish;* s. Dhé, *the fear of God;* s. an taigh, *the shelter of the house;* fo s. do sgéith, *under the covert of thy wing;* air s. sgoinne, *for decency's sake;* na dh' fhuiling e air mo sgàth-sa, *what he suffered on my account;* gun s., *without dread;* air s., *for the sake of; on pretence of;* a' gabhail s., *taking fright.*

sgàth, -a, -an, *s.f.* Hurdle. 2 Door secured by a hurdle. *Prov.* 3 Threshed or scutched flax. 4 Wattled door, large bundle of rods tied closely together and used as a door.

sgath, *pr.pt.* a' sgath & a' sgathadh, *v.a.* Lop off, prune, cut off. 2 Destroy. 3 Bite, sting. 4 Injure, hurt, do harm. 5**Curdle. S. an ceann dheth, *chop off his head;* s. na meanglain, *chop off the twigs.*

sgath, -a, *s.m.* Consuming, destruction, waste, havoc. 2 Damage by cattle. 3 Tow, thirds, the short part of lint called brairds.

sgàth, see sgàthadh.

sgathach, -aiche, *a.* Pruning, cutting, lopping off. 2 Biting, that bites or stings. 3 That injures or hurts. 4 Destructive, destroying. 5 Wasteful. 6 Pernicious. 7 Doubtful. 8** Skirmishing.

sgàthach, -aiche, *a.* Shady, shadowy. 2 Covering, sheltering. 3 Timid, fearful, afraid. 4 Bashful. 6* Skittish. 7 Aghast. 7(MS)Backward. 8** Causing fear. Tha 'n t-each a bhuailear 'sa cheann s., *the horse struck in the head will be timid.*

sgathach,** -aich, -aichean, *s.m.* Fence made of loppings. 2††Branches lopped off. 3 (CR) Loppings of any wood except birch—*W. of Ross-shire.* 4* Hurdle or great bundle of twigs to serve as a portable porch at a Highlander's door. [*s.f.***]

———, -aich, *s.m.* Drink of water and milk in equal proportions and the sour thick milk under the cream that was kept for butter, churned into a froth—*Gael.Soc.Inv. xiv. 148.*

———an, *s. m.* Tail. Feumaidh fear na b-aona bhà car d' a h-earball, no a s. m' a dhorn, *the man who has only one cow must twist her tail round his fist*—i.e. look well after her.

———as, -ais, *s.m.* see sgàth.

sgàthachd, *s.f.ind.* Timidity.

sgathadair, -ean, *s.m.* Cutter, lopper off. 2‡‡ Blacksmith's chisel for cutting iron.

sgathadh,(CR) *s. m.* Drawing straw for thatching. 2(DMy) Cutting the roots off the barley sheaves for thatching purposes—*Lewis.*

———, -aidh, *s.m.* Lopping off, severing, act of lopping off or pruning. 2 Biting, act of biting. 3 Hurting, act of hurting or injuring. 4 Segment, shred. 5 Incision, puncture. 6** Destruction. 7**Loss. 8**Skirmishing. 9** Bickering. 10 (AH) "Shipping" or taking in (of oars.) Air s. gun iochd, *cut down without pity;* nach robh s. de thalamh 'san fhradhrac, *that there was no trace of land in sight;* s. ràimh, *shipping of oars;* cha d' fhuair s. nach d' fhuiling nàir, *they never met with loss who did not suffer blame.* A' s—, *pr. pt.* of sgath.

sgàthag,(CR) *s.f.* Fright—*Skye.*

sgathag, -aig, -an, *s.f.* Trefoil in flower.

———ach,** *a.* Full of trefoil in flower.

sgathag fhiadhain,§*s.f.* Cotton-sedge, see canach.

sgàthaich, *v.a.* Discourage. 2(MS) Awe. 3(MS) Bescreen.

sgathair, -ean, *s.m.* Spruce fellow, beau. 2 see sgathadair.

———eachd, *s.f.ind.* Cutting down, lopping off, as of branches.

sgàthaireachd,†† *s.f.* Timidity, fear.

sgàthalachd, *s.f.* Umbrosity.

sgàthan, -ain, -an, *s.m.* Mirror, looking-glass. 2 **Gazing-stock. Is math an s. sùil caraid, *a friend's eye is a good mirror;* a réidh-ghorm lith mar s., *her smooth blue pools like mirrors.*
s. balgach, *a convex mirror.*
s.-còmhnard, *a plain mirror.*
s. tolgach, *a concave mirror.*

———ach, *a.* Abounding in mirrors.

sgatharra, *a.* Hewing, lopping, pruning, cutting down.

sgath-bhàrd, -àird, *s.m.* Satirist, lampooner.

———achd, *s.f.* Satire, ribaldry, lampooning. An s. a bu chruaidhe gu léir, *the keenest satire of all.*

sgàth-fhras,(CR) *s. f.* Passing shower—*W. of Ross-shire & Argyllshire.*

sgàth-lann, -lainn, -an, *s. f.* Booth, cover, tent, shed, shop, penthouse.

sgàth-thaigh, -ean, *s.m.* Porch.

sgàthmhor, -oire, *a.* see sgàthach.

sgathmhor, see sgathach.

sgathta, *past pt.* of sgath. Pruned, lopped off. 2 Bitten, stung. 3 Injured, hurt.

sgé, *poetic* for sgiath. 2* see sgeith.

sgeach, -eich, -an, *s. m.* see sgeachag. 2 see sgitheach. 3**Bush. 4**Bust.
s.chaor, *whitethorn.*
s.-chùbhraidh, *sweet-briar.*
s.-mhadraidh, *dog-rose.*
s.-spionnain, (*gen.* -ain,) *gooseberry-bush.*

sgeachag, -aig, -an, *s.f.* Hawthorn-berry.

sgeachagach, -aiche, *a.* Abounding in hawthorn berries. 2 Like a haw. 3 Pertaining to haws. Mios s., *the month of hawthorn berries.*

sgeachagan, *n. pl.* of sgeachag. Haws.

sgeachag Muire,§ *s.f.* Bur-marigold—*bidens cernua.*

633. Sgeachag Muire.

sgeachanach,** *a.* Bushy, brambly.
sgeach·ach, -aiche, *a.* Full of bushes or thorns. 2 Prickly. 3 Of briars or brambles.
sgeachradh, -aidh, -aidhean, *s m* Prickle. 2 **Briar, bramble.
sgeach-spionnan,** -ain, *s m.* Gooseberry-bush.
sgead.** *s.m.* Speck, white spot 2 Ornament.
——ach,** *a* Fond of dress. 2 Speckled. 3 Sky-coloured. 4 Cirrocumulated. Neul s., *a cirrocumulus cloud.*
sgeadach.* -aich, *s m* see sgeadas. [*s.f.**]
——-adh, -aidh, *s.m.* Clothing, act of clothing 2 Dress, clothes. 3 Adorning, bedecking, ornamenting. 4 Ornament 5 Dressing. 6 Dress, clothes. A' s—, *pr pt* of sgeadaich. S. gu leòir, *enough of ornament.*
sgeadachail,** *a* Ornamental. 2 Beautifying. 3 Fond of ornament, fond of dress. 4 Gallant.
sgeadachair,** *s.m.* One who adorns or beautifies, garnisher, decker.
sgeadachd, *s.f.* Drapery 2(MS) Honour.
sgeadaich, *pr. pt.* a' sgeadachadh, *v. a.* Dress, clothe. 2 Dress, garnish, adorn with dress. 3 Conjugate 4**Accomplish. 5(MS)Blazon. 6(MS) Prank. S. an teine, *make up the fire ;* s. an lampa, *trim the lamp.*
————ear, *fut.pass.* of sgeadaich. S. na lòin, *the meadows shall be adorned.*
————te, *past pt* of sgeadaich. Clothed, dressed. 2 Adorned, ornamented with dress. 3 Conjugated. 4 Accomplished.
sgeadas, -ais, -an, *s m.* Ornament, gayness of dress. 2 Decoration. 3 Spottedness,speckledness.
————ach, -aiche, *a.* Having a gay dress. 2 Fond of gay dress. 3**Ornamental. 4**Spotted, speckled.
————achd, *s.f.ind.* Dress, gaudiness of dress. 2 Fondness or gay dress.
sgeafag,** *s.f.* Filip. 2(DMy) Slight bite of a dog, or little cut by a knife on a person.
sgeafard, see sgeafag.
sgeal, see sgeul.
——achd, see sgeulachd.
sgealag,** -aig, see sgeallag.
————ach,** *a.* see sgeallagach.
sgealan, see sgeallag.
sgealanach, see sgeallagach.
skealb, -eilb, -an, *s.f.* Splinter, broken fragment of wood, stone or any hard substance. 2**Cliff. 3**Sherd. Air sgeilb creige, *on the fragment of a rock ;* chaidh am bàta 'na sgealbaibh, *the boat went to splinters.*
sgealb, *pr.pt.* a' sgealbadh, *v. a. & n.* Split. 2 Dash into pieces or fragments, splinter. 3 Become pieces or fragments. 4 Fritter. 5 Tear. 6**Snatch.
——ach, -aiche, *a.* In pieces, fragments or splinters. 2 That breaks into pieces. 3 Having a tendency to break or disunite into fragments or splinters,splintering,smashing,cleaving, rending, snatching. 4**Smashed.
——adh, -aidh, *s.m.* Act of splitting or dashing into fragments or pieces. 2 State of falling into fragments. 3 Splintering, smashing, cleaving. 4 Plucking, snatching. 5 Fragment, rent, splinter. A' s—, *pr pt.* of sgealb.
sgealbag, -aig, -an, *s.f.*, *dim.* of sgealb. Small piece or fragment. 2**Little rock. 3**Pinch
————ach, -aiche, *a.* Abounding in small fragments 2 Breaking into splinters.
sgealbagaidh,(DMK) *s. f.* The forefinger—*Lochbroom.*
sgealbair, -ean, *s.m.* Splitter, one that splits or breaks anything into pieces. 2 Stout young fellow.
————eachd, *s.f.ind.* Act of splitting or dashing into pieces
sgealb-chreag, -chreige, an, *s.f.* Splintered or shelvy rock or cliff Àirde nan s., *the pinnacles of the splintered cliffs.* [*s.m.*—McL & D.]
————————ach, -aiche, *a* Abounding in rugged or shelvy rocks or cliffs. 2 Full of splintered rocks or cliffs.
sgealbta, *past pt* of sgealb. Dashed in pieces.
sgeallag,§ -aig, *s.f.* Wild mustard,charlock—*sinapsis arvensis.* [*s.m.*—McL & D.]
————ach, -aich, *s.m.* see sgeallag. 2 Quantity of wild mustard.
————ach, *a.* Abounding in wild mustard. Having a kernel.
sgeallag meilte, *s. f.* Mustard-seed.,
sgeallan,§ -ain, *s.m* see sgeallag. 2**Kernel.
————ach, see sgeallagach.
sgeallag-bhuachair,(DC) *s.f.* Mushroom—*Uist*, see balg-bhuachaill.
sgealp, -a & -eilp, -an, *s.f.* Slap with the palm of the hand. 2 Sound of a blow so given. 3 Quick, sudden sound 4 (DMK)Sharp report, as of a pistol—*Caithness.* 4 see sgealp. [*s.m.*—**]
——,* *s.m.* Tall, lively man.
——,* *s m.* Shelf
——, *v.a.* Strike with the palm of the hand.
——ach, -aiche, *a.* see sgealbach. 2**Striking or slapping with the palm of the hand
——adh, -aidh, Striking, act of striking with the palm of the hand. *Scots*, skelp. A' s—, *pr.pt.* of sgealp.
——arra, *a.* Loud and shrill. 2 Emitting a loud and shrill sound. 3 Forcible. 4††Elastic. 5**Smart, as a report. 6††Agile. Piob s. MhicCruimein, *MacCrimmon's loud-sounding pipes;* braidhe s., *a smart report;* cainnt s., *loud and articulate utterance.*
————arrachd, *s.f.ind.* Loudness and shrillness of sound. 2**Elasticity. 3**Smartness as of a report. 4††Shrill sound.
sgeamalain,(AH) *s.f.* Harum-scarum, loquacity. 2 Loquacious person.
sgeamh, -a, *s. m.* Severe or cutting language, abusive words. 2 Disgust, antipathy. 3†† Scolding. 4 Speck on the eye. 5* Thin skin, membrane. 6* in *Irish*, Polypody. 7 see sgiamh.
sgeamh,** *v.a.* Reproach.
sgeamh, -a & -eimh, *s.f.* Polypody.
————ag,* *s.f.* Small slice.
————ail, -e, *a.* Satirical. 2 Disgusting. 3 Comely. 4 Using severe or cutting words. 5 see sgreamhail.
sgeamhair, -ean, *s.m.* Satirist. 2 One who uses cutting words.
————eachd, *s.f. ind.* Satire. 2 Troublesome talk. 3 Habit of using cutting words.
sgeamhaltrach,* -aich,*s.m.*Person that does anything furiously.
sgèamhanach,* -aich, *s.m.* Macaroni.
sgeamh-dharaich,§-a-, *s.f.* Oak-fern—*polypodium dryopteris.*
sgeamhla, see sgeamhladh.
sgeamhladh, -aidh, -ean, *s.m.* Sudden fright, alarm. 2 Skirmish. 3 Keen appetite.
sgeamnaidh,** *a.* Concinnous.
————————eachd,** *s.f.ind.* Concinnity.
sgeamh-nan-clach,§ *s. f.* Polypody, see clachraineach.
sgèan, -a, *s.m.* see sgeun & sgian.
sgean, -a, *s.m.* Cleanliness, neatness. 2 Polish.
†**sgèana**, *gen.sing & n.pl.* of sgian.
sgèanach, see sgeunach & sgianach.
sgeanach,* -aich, *s.m.* Chop.
sgeanachail, -e, *a.* see sgeanail.
sgèanachas, -ais, *s.m.* see sgeunachas.

sgèanadh, -aidh, see sgeunadh
sgeanag,†† -aig, -an, *s. f.* Species of edible sea-weed.
sgèanag, see sgeunag & sgianag.
sgèanaich, see sgeunaich.
sgeanail, -e, *a.* Clean, neat. tidy. 2 Brisk, lively—*Dàin I. Ghobha.*
sgeanalachd, *s.f.ind.* Neatness, cleanliness.
sgeanamhail, *a.* see sgeanail. Biodag direach, tana, glé s., *a straight dirk, thin and well polished*,—*Donn. Bàn*, 5th ed. p. 75.
†**sgèanan**, *pl.* of sgian.
sgeann, -a, -an, *s. m.* Stare, gazing upon anything, glaring.
sgeann,* *s.f.* Cleanliness.
——, *v.n.* Stare,gaze upon anything, glare. S. e orm, *he stared at me;* s. a shuilean 'na cheann, *his eyes glared in his head.*
——ach, -aiche, *a.* Staring, gazing, glaring. 2 Bull-eyed.
——adh, -aidh, *s.m.* Staring, act of staring or gazing, gaze, glare. A' *pr.pt.* of sgeann.
sgeannag,** -aig, *s.f.* Staring female.
sgeannail,* *a.* Neatly clean.
sgeannair, -ean, *s.m.* Starer, gazer.
sgeap, -ip, *pl.* -an & -aichean, *s.f.* Beehive, skep. 2 (MMcD) Straw basket for holding grain when sowing, always slung round the shoulder by a straw rope—*Lewis.* 3 Hand-winnower. S. sheillean, *a straw beehive.* [*gen.* sgeapa —**]
sgeap,* *v.a.* Gaelic form of *skip.* *Pass over.
sgeapach, -aiche, *a.* Abounding in beehives. 2 Like a beehive. 3 Of, or like, a basket. 4 Abounding in baskets.
sgeap fhriaisg,(DMy) *s.f.* Small basket made of stalks or "cuiseagan," for taking home limpets to bait the small lines.
sgeap mhór,(DMy) *s.f.* Large basket made of the same materials as sgeap fhriasg, but with a stouter cord attached, for carrying fish from the rocks, potatoes, &c.—*Ness, Lewis.*
sgeapaichean, *n.pl.* sgeap.
sgearach,** *a.* Happy.
sgearach,* -aich, *s.m.* Anything scattered. 2** Square.
sgearadh,** -aidh, *s.m.* Stage-play.
sgearaich,* *v.a.* Scatter.
sgearail,** *a.* Happy.
————eachd,** *s.f.* Happiness.
sgeath, see sgeith.
——ach,** see sgeitheach.
sgeath-chosg, see sgeith-chosg.
sgeathrach, see sgeitheach.
sgeathraich, see sgeithrich.
sgéi', *poetical contr.* of sgéithe, *gen. sing.* of sgiath.
sgeig, -e, *s.f.* Mockery, derision, jeering, scorn, ridicule 2 Taunt. 3 Buffoonery, waggery. S.-fhiacaill, *a hissing.*
sgeig, *pr.pt.* a' sgeigeadh, *v.a.* Mock,ridicule,deride, taunt, scorn.
sgeigeach, -eiche, *a.* Mocking, deriding, ridiculing. 2 Taunting, scorning. 3 Having a prominent chin, or 4 a beard of strong straight hair—*Suth'd.* 5 Prone to mock or ridicule, scornful, taunting. 6 Waggish.
————, -ich, *s.m.* Mocker, derider, buffoon, zany, wag. 2 Irony. 3 Taunter, scorner.
sgeigealachd, *s.f.ind.* Mockery, taunting,satire,
sgeigear, -ean, *s.m.* Mocker, wag, buffoon,lampooner, banterer. 2¶ Gander, see gànradh.
sgeigearachd, *s. f. ind.* Mockery, derision, buffoonery, waggery, waggishness. 2 Habit of mocking or deriding.
sgeigeas, -is, *s.f.* Waggery, buffoonery. [* gives sgeigeis as *nom.*]
sgeigeasach, -aiche, *a.* see sgeigeil.
sgeigeil, -e, *a.* Reproachful, scornful, mocking. given to mockery or derision, jeering, jibing, taunting, scorning, burlesque.
sgeigeir. see sgeigear.
sgeigeireachd, see sgeigearachd.
sgeigidh, *fut.aff.a.* of sgeig. Shall or will mock.
sgeigire,* see sgeigear.
sgeil,(CR) *s.f.* Loud and rapid utterance, gabble. Nach ann tha 'n s. air do theangaidh! *what a gabble you are making.*
sgéil, *gen.sing. & n. pl.* of sgeul. [also sgeòil.]
sgéil,** -e, *s.f.* Misery, pity, calamity, disaster. Mo s.! *alas!*
sgeil, *s.f.* Gaelic form of *skill*, see sgil. 2** Shelling grain. Fear gun s., *a man without skill.*
sgeilb,* see gilb.
sgeilc,** *v. n.* Crack, make a crackling sound—*Perthshire.*
——,(CR) *s.f.* Crackling sound. 2**Smart explosion. 3**Loud report.
sgeilcearra, *a.* Supple, elastic. 2 Active, lively, sudden, quick. 3 Giving hard blows. 4** Smart or loud, as a report or explosion.
————chd, *s.f.ind.* Suppleness, elasticity. 2 Activity, quickness, liveliness. 3 Suddenness.
sgeilceil,(CR) *s.f.* Crackling. 2**Knacking.
sgéile, *s.f.ind.* Misery, pity, calamity. [** gives [sgéil, -e.]
sgéileach, -eiche, *a.* Calamitous, ruinous. 2 Pitiable, pitiful. 3 Painful.
sgéileadh, -idh, see sgéile.
sgeileas, -eis, -an, *s.m.* Bill, beak. 2 Thin face. 3 Talkativeness, garrulity, *prov.*
sgeileasach,-aiche,*a.* Thin-faced. 2 Loquacious, garrulous, *prov.*
————, -aich, *s.f.* Loquacious, garrulous woman.
sgeileid, -e, -ean, *s.f.* Skillet, small boiler,"goblet," saucepan.
sgeileil, see sgileil.
sgeileit, see sgeileid.
sgeilm, -e, *s.f.* Boasting, vain-glory. 2 Prattling, vain or idle talk. 3 Neatness of dress,spruceness. 4 Razor- or thin-lipped mouth. 5 Taste. 6 Decency, propriety. 7 Countenance indicating a scolding, prating, impertinent disposition. 8**Chatterer. 9 Brightness. 10 †† Mouth made for scolding. 11* Prater's mouth. 12**Tale-telling. 13**Tell-tale. 14**Impertinent prater. 15 Loquacious, forward girl. 16 Forward or impertinent talk.
sgeilm, *s. f.* Joiner's chisel—*Suth'd.*
sgeilmeach, -eiche, *a.* see sgeilmeil.
sgeilmeach,* -eich, *s.f.* Prating, vain, silly woman.
sgeilmeag,†† -eig, -an, *s.f.* Chattering woman.
sgeilmear, -eir, -eirean, *s.m.* Foolish boaster. 2 Prattling fellow. 3 Neatly-dressed person.
sgeilmearra, *a.* see sgeilmeil.
————chd, *s.f.* see sgeilmeileachd.
sgeilmeil. -e, *a.* Boasting, vain-glorious. 2 Prating, given to idle language. 3 Neat, tidy, trim in dress. 4 Piquant. 5 Tattling, impudently garrulous. 6 Quick, nimble. 7 Bright. 8 (MS) Cavalier. 9 Beauish. 10* Having a pert, prating, officious mouth or expression of countenance. 11 Baubling. 12 Addicted to forward or impertinent talk.
sgeilmeileachd, *s.f.ind.* Habit of boasting. 2 Habit of prating. 3 Neatness or tidiness of dress. 4 (MS) Plausibleness. 5 Garrulousness, talkativeness.
sgeilmich, *v.a.* Bedizen.
sgilmireachd,* *s.f.* Impertinent prattle or garrulity.

sgeilmrich,** *s.* Chatter.
sgeilmse, *s. f. ind.* Surprise, sudden attack. Thàinig iad oirnn 'nan sgeilmse, *they attacked us unawares.*
———ach, -eiche, *a.* Attacking or coming upon one unawares.
sgeilmsich,(MS) *v.a.* Bicker.
sgeilp, *s. & v.* see sgealp.
sgeilp, -e, *pl.* -ean & -eachan, *s.f.* Shelf or cliff of a rock. 2 Shelf in a keeping place.
sgeilpeach, -eiche, *a.* Shelvy, furnished with shelves. 2 Abounding in cliffs or rocks.
———an, *pl.* of sgeilp.
sgéil-theachdair, -ean, *s.m.* see sgeul-theachdair.
sgeim,** *s.f.* Foam.
sgèimh, -e, *s.f.* Comeliness, beauty. 2 Personal elegance. 3 Ornament, handsomeness. 4 Scheme. 5 Draught, schedule. 6(MS) Honour. Sheas iad 'nan s., *they stood in their beauty*; s. an naomhachd, *the beauty of their holiness*; s. àrd, *high bloom, good plight* or *habit of body.*
sgèimh,** *v.a.* Adorn, beautify. 2 Make a draught or scheme. 3 Skim, scum.
———each, -eiche, *a.* Handsome, graceful, elegant, blooming, ornamental, beautiful, fair, lovely. 2 Like a scheme or draught. Maise s. an caoin-shruth, *the exquisite beauty of their fair forms*; s. mar a' ghealaich, *fair as the moon.*
———eachadh, -aidh, *s. m.* Adorning, act of adorning, ornamenting or beautifying.
———eachd, *s.f.ind.* Beauty, comeliness, gracefulness, ornament, elegance. 2 State of being adorned.
———ealach, -aiche, *a.* Handsome, fair, graceful. 2 Well-dressed, ornamented, adorned.
———ealachadh, *s.m.* Garnishment.
———ealachd, *s.f.ind.* Handsomeness, neatness. 2 Accomplishment.
sgèimheiche, *comp.* of sgèimheach.
sgèimheil, -e, *a.* see sgèimheach.
sgèimhich, *pr.pt.* a' sgèimheachadh, *v.a.* Adorn, ornament. 2 Beautify, make fair, bedeck. 3 Blazon.
———ead, -eid, *s.m.* Beauty, handsomeness, degree of beauty.
sgèimhichte, *past pt.* of sgèimhich. Adorned, ornamented. 2 Made fair, beautified.
sgeimhle, *s.m.* see sgeimhleadh. 2 (CR) Swagger—*Perthshire.*
sgeimhleadh, -eidh, *s.m.* Skirmish, fight. 2 Act of skirmishing. 3 Surprise. 4 Bitterness of speech, biting words, bickering. 5 Act of using bitter language. 6 Alarm. A' s—, *pr. pt.* of sgeimhlich.
sgeimhlear, -eir, -an, *s.m.* Fighter, disputer. 2 One who uses bitter words.
———achd, *s.f.ind.* Habit of bickering or quarrelling.
sgeimhlich, *pr.pt.* a' sgeimhleadh, *v.a. & n.* Surprise, alarm. 2 Skirmish. 3 Bicker, use bitter words.
sgèimhnidh,** *a.* Clean. 2 Fierce.
sgeimineach,(AC) *a.* Dignified.
sgèin, see sgeun.
sgéin, *dat sing.* of sgian.
sgein,** *s.m.* Hiding-place.
sgéine, *gen.sing.* of sgian.
sgèineach, see sgeunach.
sgèineil, see sgeunach.
sgeineil,** *a.* see sgeanail.
sgeing,** *s.f.* Bounce, start.
———each,** *a.* Bouncing, starting.
sgeinm,* *s.f.* see sgeilm. 2**Tidy person.
———each, see sgeilmeil.
sgeinmeachd,** *s.f.* Garrulousness. 2 Tidiness, smartness. 2 Nimbleness.
sgeinmeil, see sgeilmeil.
sgeinn, see sgeinnidh. 2†† see sgeilm.
sgeinne,** *s.f.* Funicle.
sgéinne, *s.f.* Pack-thread.
sgeinneadh,** *s.m.* Eruption. 2 Gushing forth. 3 Bouncing. 4 Sliding, sally.
sgéineadh,** -idh, *s.m.* Pack-thread.
sgeinnich, *v.a.* Tie, cord.
sgeinnidh, *s. m.* Flax, hemp. 2 Thread, small twine. 3 Skein. 4†† Fishing-line. Sgiùrsair de s. chaol, *a scourge of small cords.*
sgeir, -e, -ean, *s. f.* Rock in the sea nearly or quite covered by neap-tides and quite covered by spring-tides. 2*Peat-bank. 3**Cliff. 4 Sharp, flinty rock. 5(CR) Covering, top-layer, as on cold porridge, or of fat, soup, &c.—*Arran.*
sgeireach,-eiche, *a.* Rocky, full of rocks. 2 Cliffy. 3 Flinty. 4 Unnavigable.
sgeireag, -eig, -an, *s.f. dim.* of sgeir. Little rock in the sea. 2**Chip of stone, &c. 3** Sharp rock. 4**Sharp splinter of a rock.
sgeireagach, -eiche, *a.* Full of little sea-rocks. 2**Full of splinters of stones. 3**Apt to break into splinters.
sgeirean,(CR) *s.pl.* Drops of food, as on clothes, &c.—*Arran.*
sgeir-liamhraidh,(DC) *s.f.* Yarn-winder. [Called eachan in *Argyll.*]
sgeirmeis,** Gaelic spelling of *skirmish.*
———each,** *a.* Skirmishing. 2 Like or of skirmishes.
———eachd,** *s. f.* Continued or frequent skirmishing.
sgeirmeil,(CR) *a* Clean, tidy—*Arran.*
sgeirmse,* *s.f.* Panic. 2 Skirmish.
sgeir-thonn, -ean-thonna, *s.f.* Breaker.
sgeith, *s.m.* Vomit, food thrown up from the stomach. 2 Vomiting, act of vomiting. 3** Spawn. 4 Fraying of cloth. A' s—, *pr. pt.* of sgeith.
sgeith,*pr. pt.* a' sgeith & a' sgeitheadh, *v.n.* Vomit. [confined to cats and dogs in *Perthshire.*] 2**Spawn. 3**Avoid. 4* Overflow, as a river. 5 Spread, as water. Am an treabhaidh, 'nuair thòisicheas an talamh ri s. na h-ùrach, *the time for ploughing, when the ground begins to cast up earth*—after hard frost.
sgèith, *pr. pt.* a' sgèitheadh, *v. a.* Cut out, reduce to a shape, as cloth. 2 Cut off. 3 Fit, suit.
sgèith,(CR) *s.* Shape—*Perthshire.*
sgeith-an-ròin,†† *s.m.* Kind of small jelly-fish.
sgeith-chosg,** *s.m.* Anti-emetic.
sgeitheach, -eiche, *a.* Nauseous, causing to vomit, emetic, anacathartic. 2 Ready to vomit. 3**Spawning.
sgeitheadh, -idh, *s.m.* see sgeith.
sgèitheadh, -idh, *s. m.* Cutting out. 2 Act of cutting out or reducing to a shape or form, fitting, A' s—, *pr.pt.* of sgèith.
sgeitheadh-fèithe, *s.m.* Rupture of a blood-vessel. 2††Varicose vein. [also sgeith-fèith.]
sgeith-na-muice-mara,(AF) *s.m.* Kind of large jelly-fish.
sgeith-nan-reultag,‡‡ *s. m.* Glutinous substance vulgularly supposed to fall from the stars.
sgeithreach, *s.* see sgeitheadh.
sgeithreach, *a.* see sgeitheach.
sgeithrich, -e, *s.f.* Vomiting. 2**Vomit.
sgeithrich, *v.n.* Vomit.
sgeith-rionnaig,(DC) *s.f.* Meteor. 2 sgeith-nan-reultag.
sgeith-ròin,†† *s.m.* See-blubber, jelly-fish.
sgèithte, *past pt.* of sgèith. Cut out, reduced in shape or form. Obair s., *a task.*
sgeithte, *past pt.* of sgeith. Vomited, cast up.

sgeo,(AC) *gen*. sgiach, *s.m.* Haze, fog, vapour. 2 Dimness—*Dàin I. Ghobha.*

†sgeò, *s.m.* Understanding.

sgeòb,* *s.m.* Aperture. 2 Wide mouth.

sgeòblach,(CR) *s.m.* Untidy person or dress—*Arran.*

sgeòc, -eòic, -an, *s.m.* Long neck. 2 Neck of a bottle or phial. 3††Tallness.

sgeòcach, -aiche, *a.* Long-necked, as a bottle or phial.

sgeòcag, -aig, -an, *s.f.* Long-necked female.

sgeòcan, -ain, -an, *s. m.* Long-necked youth or boy. 2 *in derision,* Long neck. 3**Neck of a bottle.

sgeòd, -eòid, -an, see sgòd.

sgeòdach, see sgòdach.

sgeòdag, see sgòdag.

sgeòg, see sgeòp.

sgeogair, -ean, *s.m.* Foolish talker. 2* Silly fellow.

sgeogaireachd, *s.f.ind.* Foolish talk.

sgeòil, *gen.sing. & n.pl.* of sgeul.

sgeòlach, *s.m.* The name of one of Fionn's cups.

sgeoldair,(CR) *s.m.* Jelly-fish—*Farr.*

sgeòp, -òip, *s.m.* Torrent of foolish words. 2 ††Loud tattling. 3 Aperture. 4 Wry mouth.

sgeòpair, -ean, *s.m.* Tattler.

sgeòpaireachd, *s.f.ind.* Tattling, prattle.

sgeòpraich. see sgeòpaireachd.

sgeot,** -eoit, *s.m.* Shield, target.

sgeuban, *Strath, Suth'd* for geuban.

sgeudach, see sgeadach.

sgeudachadh, -aidh, see sgeadachadh.

sgeudaich, *v.a.* see sgeadaich.

sgeudaichte, see sgeadaichte.

sgeugach, *a.* Having a physical peculiarity, applied only to the meaning of having a projecting chin, or one that has a beard of a peculiarly strong straight hair—*Suth'd.*

sgeugh, *s. & v.* Shape.

sgeul, -éil, -éile & -eòil, *pl.* -eòil & -an, *s. m.* [*f.* in *Badenoch.*] Narrative, relation, narration. 2 Tale, fable, story. 3 False or malicious report, falsehood. 4 News, information, tidings. Innis s.,*tell a tale,relate a story;* sgeul thairis ! *change the subject !—Arran* ; air aon s., *of one opinion ;* dè do s. ? *what is your news ?* s. mu'n Fhéinn, *a tale about the Féinne ;* droch s., *bad intelligence ;* bi air s., *be in pursuit of information ;* am bheil e air s. ? *is he* (or *it*) *to be found ?* a dh' innseadh sgeòil, *to tell the result;* eadar dà s., *by the way ;* a' deanamh sgéile, *making a tale, telling a tale or falsehood; narrating, uttering a speech ;* choigrich na sgéile truaighe ! *stranger of the mournful tale !* air s., *found.*

sgeula, see sgeul.

sgeulach, -aiche, *a.* Having many tales. 2 Fond of reciting tales or stories. 3 Like a tale. 4 Tale-telling. 5 News-mongering. 6*Running from house to house with reports.

sgeulachd, -an, *s.f.* Tale, fable, fiction, romance. 2 Tradition. 3 Telling or reciting of tales, fables or traditions. 4 Legend, history. 5 Archæology. 5* Vague reports. Sgeulachdan shean bhan, *old wives' tales ;* gun aire thoirt do sgeulachdaibh, *without heeding fables.*

sgeulaich,‡‡ *v.a.* Narrate.

sgeulaiche, -an, *s.m.* Relater of tales, fictions or fables. 2 Newsmonger. 3 Promulgator of false reports. 4**Historian. 5**Archæologist. Cha robh s. nach robh breugach, *there never was a tale-bearer that did not tell some falsehoods.*

sgeultach,* -aich, *s.f.* Female gossip.

sgeultach,* *a.* see sgeulach.

sgeultachd,* *s.f.ind.* Tradition, legendary lore. S. mu'n Fhéinn, *tradition about the Féinn,* s. nan seanar, *the tradition of the elders.*

sgeultair,* *s.m.* see sgeulaiche.

sgeul-rùin, *s. m.* Secret. Cha s. e, 's fios aig triùir air, *it's no secret if three know it.*

sgeul-theachdair, -ean, *s.m.* Tale-bearer.

sgeumh, -a, see sgèimh.

sgeun, -éin, *s.m.* Shyness, wildness, readiness to be frightened. 2 Sudden fright or dread, causing to start or fly away suddenly. 3 Look expressive of fear, dread or terror. 4*Squint. 5**Mad look,terror, astonishment. 6‡ Dread. Dh' fhalbh an t-each air s., *the horse bolted.*

sgeun,* *v.n.* Squint.

sgeun, see sgian.

sgeunach, -aiche, *a.* Shy, skittish, easily frightened, wild, mettled, apt to run off in fright, as a horse. 2 Suddenly frightened, flying off in fear. 3 Having a look of fear or terror. 4 Timid.

sgeunachadh, -aidh, *s.m.* Scaring,act of scaring, affrighting or chasing away for fear. A' s—, *pr.pt.* of sgeunaich.

sgeunachas, -ais, *s.m.* see sgeun.

sgeunadh, -aidh, *s.m.* see sgeun.

sgeunaich, *pr.pt.* a' sgeunachadh, *v.a.* Terrify, scare, chase away for fear.

———te, *past pt.* of sgeanaich. Terrified, scared, chased away by fear.

sgeunail, -e, *a.* Neat, in good order. 2 Pruned. 3 see sgeunach.

sgia. see sgiath.

sgiab, -a, -an, *s.f.* Quick or sudden movement, start. 2 Snatch or pull at anything.

sgiab, *v.a. & n.* Start or move suddenly. 2 Pull or snatch at anything. 3**Skim. 4(AH)Open widely, as the legs of a compass,straddle one's legs. 5(AH) Gape, yawn—*Argyll.* S. do chasan, *straddle your legs.*

sgiabach, -aiche, *a.* Moving quickly or suddenly. 2 Snatching or pulling at anything. 3 (AH) Yawning. 4(Fionn) Blustering. Là s., *a blustering day.*

sgiabadh, -aidh, *s.m.* Moving. 2 Act of moving suddenly or quickly. 3 Act of snatching or pulling at anything. 4 see sgiab. 5 Straddling. A' s—, *pr.pt.* of sgiab. Thoir tuilleadh sgiabaidh do 'n fhàradh, *give more slant to the ladder.*

sgiabag, -aig, -an, *s. m.* Slap given in play. 2 Hasty touch or snatch.

sgiabair, -ean, *s.m.* Snatcher, one who snatches or pulls at anything.

sgiadh, see sgiath.

sgial, see sgeul.

sgialachd, see sgeulachd.

sgiamh, -éimh, *s.f,* see sgèimh.

sgiamh, -a, *s.m.* Shriek, yell. 2 Caterwauling of a cat. 3 see sgèimh. 4 Yelp. 5 Squeal. 6* Wild expression of countenance. [*s.f.**]

sgiamh, *v.n.* Shriek, yell. 2 Mew, caterwaul. 3 Squeal, as a pig. 4 see sgeamh.

———ach, -aiche, *a.* see sgèimheach.

———ach, -aiche, *a.* Yelling, shrieking. 2 Mewing, caterwauling.

sgiamhachadh. -aidh, *s.m. & pr. pt.* of sgiamhaich, see sgèimheachadh.

sgiamhachair,** *s.m.* Decorator.

sgiamhachd, see sgèimheachd.

sgiamhadh, -aidh, *s. m.* Shrieking. 2 Act of shrieking or yelling. 3 Mewing. 4 Act of mewing or caterwauling. 5* Squealing. A' s—, *pr. pt.* of sgiamh.

sgiamhaich, *v.a.* see sgèimhich.

————e, see sgèimhiche.

————ead,** -eid, see sgèimhichead.

sgiamhaichte, *past pt.* see sgèimhichte.

sgiamhail,** *pr.pt.* a' sgiamhail, *v.n.* Shriek, yell, mew, caterwaul. 2 Squeal, as a pig.
sgiamhail, -e, *s.f. & pr.pt.* of sgiamh. [McL & D gives *s.m.*] see sgiamhadh.
sgiamhail,** *a.* Squally. 2 Squeaking 3 Mewing, as a cat. 4* Seemly, decent.
sgiamh-àrd,** -àird, *s.m.* High bloom.
sgiamh-òradh,** -aidh, *s.m.* Gilding.
sgiamhas, -ais, *s.m.* Trimming (of dress.)
sgiamhlaich, *v.* see sgiamhail.
sgiamhuilich,(MS) *v.n.* Grunt, as a pig.
sgian, -ine & -éine, *dat.* sgithinn, *pl.* sgianan, sgianan, sginichean, sgèanan & sgéinichean, *s.f.* Knife. Air son na sgéine, *for the knife.*
sgian, see sgeun.
sgianach, -eiche, *a.* Furnished with knives, having knives. 2 Like a knife. 3 see sgeunach.
sgian-achlais,** *s. f.* Large pocket-knife, once much used by the Gael and put to various uses,—it was particularly serviceable in close fight.
sgianadair,** *s.m.* Cutler.
sgian-adhairceach,** *s. m.* Sheep with sharp horns.
——————————, -eiche, *a.* Sharp-horned, as sheep.
sgianag, -aig, -an, *s.f.,dim.* of sgian. Little knife.
sgianagach, -aiche, *a.* Having little knives.
sgianaich, see sgeunaich.
sgian-bharrain, *s.f.* Hedge-knife, pruning-hook.
sgian-bhèarraidh,‡‡ *s.f.* Razor.
sgian-bhùird, *s.f.* Table-knife.
sgian-cheann, -chinn, *s.m.* Witless head.
sgian-cheannach, -aiche, *a.* Addle-headed, foolish, witless.
sgian-chollag,‡‡ *s.f.* Chopping-knife.
sgian-corrain,(MMcD) *s.f.* Knife made from the blade of an old sickle—*Lewis.*
sgian-fola, *s.f.* Lancet.
sgian-lùthaidh,* *s.f.* Clasp-knife.
sgian-pheann, *s.f.* Pen-knife.
sgian-phinn, see sgian-pheann.
sgian-phòca, *s.f.* Pocket-knife.
sgian-phronnaidh, *s.f.* Chopping-knife.
sgiansgar, -air, *s.m.* Side starting, as of a horse. 2 Sudden fear.
————ach, -aiche, *a.* Skittish, apt to shy. 2 Easily frightened.
sgian-sgathaidh, *s.f.* Bill.
sgiap,** *s.m.* see siab.
sgiap, Gaelic form of *scoop.* 2**Skip.
sgiapach, see siabach. 2**Skipping.
sgiarnag,(AF) *s.f.* Hare.
sgiatan,** -ain, *s.m.* Dart.
sgiath, -éith & -éithe, *pl.* -an, *s.f.* Wing, pinion. 2 Wing of a house or army. 3 Portion of land jutting into the sea. 4 Shelter, protection. 5 Shield, buckler, target. 6 Bilge-piece in boat, see bàta, F 8, p. 73. 7 Furrow-board of a plough. 8 Top-sides or floats of a cart. 9 *pl.* (na sgiathan) *Caithness* for liaghra, which see. 10 Side-wing of a boat, see p. 77. S.-mhuilinn-gaoithe, *fan of a windmill*—small circular apparatus at back to keep the sails to the wind; s. faochaig, *the disc which forms the door of a whelk;* fo d' sgéith, *under thy wing*; le 'sgiath 's le 'chlogaid, *with his shield and his helmet;* feadh bholg a sgéith, *around the boss of his shield.*
sgiathach, -aiche, *a.* Winged. 2 Shielded, having a shield or shields. 3 Affording shelter or protection. 4 Winged, as a house. 5 (AF) White-streaked. 6* White-sided.
————,(AF) -aich, *s.m.* White-streaked cow.
sgiathadaich, -e, *s. f.* Fluttering about upon wing.
sgiathadair,** *s.m.* Shield-bearer.
sgiathag, -aig, -an, *s. f., dim.* of sgiath. Little wing. 2 Little shield or buckler.
————ach, -aiche, *a.* Having little wings.
sgiathaibh, *dat.pl.* of sgiath. Air s. na gaoithe, *on the wings of the wind.*
sgiathair, -ean, *s.m.* Flutterer. 2 Idler.
sgiathaireachd, *s.f.ind.* Fluttering idly about
sgiathalachadh, -aidh, *s.m.* Act of fluttering or plying of the wings. A' s—, *pr.pt.* of sgiathalaich.
sgiathalachd, *s.f.* Fluttering.
sgiathalaich, *pr.pt.* a' sgiathalachadh, *v.n.* Flutter, ply the wings.
——————,* *s.f.* Fluttering.
sgiathan, -ain, -an, *s.m., dim.* of sgiath. Little wing. 2 Twig partition. 3 Portion. 4**Fan. see also sgiathag.
sgiathan, *n.pl.* of sgiath.
sgiathanach, -aiche, *a.* Winged. 2 Jutting out into promontories.
sgiath-chatha,** *s.f.* Battle-shield.
sgiath-chòmhraig, *s.f.* Aegis.
sgiath-dheargan,¶ *s.m.* Redwing—*jardus iliacus.*
sgiath mhealltach, *s.f.* Bastard wing of a bird, see No. 3, p. 398.
sgiath-mheurach, *s.m.* Pterodactyle.
sgiath-shùileach, -eiche, *a.* Wall-eyed.
sgiath-theaghlaich, *s.f.* Escutcheon.
†sgib, *s.f.* Hand, fist.
†sgib, -e, -ean, *s.f.* Ship, skiff.
sgibeach, -eiche, *a.* Neat, tidy, spruce, trim. Gu sgrideil, s., *lively and spruce.*
————as, -ais, *s.m.* Neatness, tidiness.
sgibear, -eir, -an, *s.m.* see sgiobair.
————nag,** -eig, *s.f.* Hare.
†sgibheal, -eil, *s.m.* Eaves of a roof.
sgibid,** *s. m.* Slap given by children to one another at play. 2 The game "tig."
sgibidh, see sgibeach.
sgid, *s.m.* Little excrement.
sgidean,* -ein, *s.m.* Contemptible little man.
sgidealach,†† *a.* Pertaining to a plash of water
sgideil, *s. m.* Plash of water. Muc sgideil, *a small whale.*
sgig, see sgeig.
sgil, *pr.pt.* a' sgileadh, *v.a.* Unhusk, shell grain. 2*Loosen, as the pile of a beast.
sgil, *s. m.* Skill, knowledge. 2**Address. 3 Skilfulness. 4 Learning. 5††Loquacity, gabbling. 6**Process of shelling grain. 7*Expertness, dexterity.
sgilbheag, *s.f.* Chip of slate—*Argyll.* 2(AH) Chip of stone, cloth or leather.
sgildaimhne,** see sgioldaimhne.
sgileadh, -idh, *s.m.* Shelling. 2 Act of shelling or preparing corn by grinding off the husks. 3 Corn after the husks are ground off. 4*Baring.
sgileam,** *s.m.* Busy-body.
sgilear, -eire, *a.* Skilful.
sgilig, *s.* Shelled grain.
sgilig, *v.a. & n.* Pop.
sgileil, -e, *a.* Skilful, knowing, intelligent, dexterous.
†sgille, *s.f.* Fright, terror.
sgilleag, -eig, *s.f.* Small pebibe.
sgillean, *s.pl.* Scales of a fish.
sgillinn, -e, -ean, *s.f.* English penny. 2 12 Scots pence. 3 Shilling-land. S. meant *a shilling* in Scots money when this system of denominating land was instituted, but when English money came into use in Scotland, it was found that the English penny was of the same value as the Scots shilling, and so *sgillinn* came in modern Gaelic to mean a penny ster-

ling. The old meaning is still retained in land denomination. S. Shasunnach, *an English shilling*; s. Albannach, *a Scots shilling*; dà s. is bonn-a-sè, *twopence-halfpenny*; gun uiread is s., *without so much as a penny*. [Used in the *sing*. with numerals requiring plural nouns.]

sgilm, see sgeilm.

sgilm,†† *s. m.* Mouth made for scolding. 2 Gabbling. 3* Razor-lipped mouth. 4 Expression of countenance indicating a scolding, pert, prating, impertinent disposition.

sgilmeil, see sgeilmeil.

———eachd, see sgeilmeileachd.

sgilp, see sgeilp.

sgilte, *past pt.* of sgil. Unhusked, hulled (of grain.)

sgimeach,(MS) *a.* Mucilaginous.

sgimheal,** -eil, *s.m.* Pent-house.

sgimilear, -eir, -an, *s.m.* Vagrant parasite. 2 Gossip, intruder, moucher. 3†† Instrument for skimming. 4*Mean person that steals out of pots.

———ach, -aiche, *a.* Obtrusive, impudent.

———achd, *s. f.* Obtrusiveness, impudence, intrusion. 2*Mean habit of popping in upon people at meals, living and doing nothing about gentlemen's kitchens.

sgine, *gen.sing.* of sgian.

sgineach, -ichean,(DMy) *s.m.* Cutlet. S. feòla, *a meat-cutlet*; s. éisg, *a fish-cutlet*.

sgineadh,** -idh, *s.m.* Leap, skip.

sgineag,** -eig, *s.f.* Flight.

sgineal,** -eil, *s.m.* Leap, skip, start.

———ach,** *a.* Leaping, skipping, starting.

sging, *Badenoch, Argyll & W. of Ross* for sginn, *s.* S. e troimh, *he squeezed through*.

sgineideach,** *a.* Skittish.

sginichd,** *s.f.* Squeezing, pressing, hugging with force.

sginichd,** *v.a.* Squeeze, press, hug with force.

sginmeil, see sgeilmeil.

sginn, *s.f.* Spring, force. 2 see sgeinnidh. Cha chuir s. a mach e, *force will not put it (the pump) out of order*.

sginn, *pr.pt.* a' sginneadh, *v.a. & n.* Protrude. 2 Spring or gush out, as water. 3 Squeeze or force out of its skin or socket.

sginn, *s.* Squeeze. 2 Hardship.

sginneachadh, -aidh, *s. m. & pr. pt.* see sginneadh.

sginneadh, -idh, *s. m.* Protruding. 2 State of being protruded. 3 Gushing out. 4 State or act of gushing out. 5 Act of squeezing or forcing out. A' s—, *pr.pt.* of sginn.

sginneag,* *s.f.* Crack (noise.)

sginnear,(MS) *s. m.* Furrier. Gaelic form of *skinner*.

sginnich, *v.* see sginn & sgeinnich.

———,* *s.f.* see sgeinnidh.

sginnichd,* *v.* see sginn.

sginnichte, *past pt.* of sginnich. Squeezed, forced out.

sgiob,* *s. f.* Dutch-built boat. 2 Scoop. 3 see sgiab.

sgiob,* *v.a.* Man, as a boat. 2 see sgiab. Air a sgiabadh le gillean sgairteil, *manned with smart fellows*.

sgioba, -n, *s.m. & f.* Ship's or boat's crew. 2 Any party or company associated for any purpose. Fo làn s., *having a full complement of crew*.

sgiobach, see sgiabach.

sgiobach,** *a.* Like a ship or boat. 2 Having ships or boats. 3 Of ships or boats. 4 Tidy, spruce, trim.

sgiobadh, see sgioba.

sgiobag, -aig, -an, *s.f.* see sgiabag & sgiobait.

sgiobaidh.** *a.* Tidy, neat, spruce. 2 Trim fit person.

sgiobailt,* *s.f.* Touch. 2 The game "touch and be gone," (*Scots*, "tig.")

sgiobair, -ean, *s.m.* Skipper, master or captain of a boat. 2 Pilot. 3 Helmsman.

———eachd, *s.f.ind.* Office or business of a shipmaster, skipper, pilot, or helmsman. 2 Navigation, art of navigating a ship. 3*Command of a ship.

sgiobal, -ail, -an, *s.m.* Barn, granary.

———ach,* -aiche, *a.* Having barns or granaries.

sgioball, -aill, -an, *s.m.* The loose folds or skirts of a garment. 2 Mantle. 3 Garment. Cuir 'nad s. e, *put it in the fold of your coat*; air s. na gaoithe, *on the skirts of the wind*. [*s.f.**]

———ach, -aiche, *a.* Mantled, robed, having flowing garments. 2 Skirted, as a garment.

———an,** -ain, *s.m.* Brush for sweeping cattle with.

sgiobalta, -ailte, *a.* Quick, active, clever, agile, 2 Tidy, neat. 3 Portable. Gu s., *tidily*.

———achd, *s.f.ind.* Activity, quickness, alacrity, agility. 2 Neatness, tidiness, trimness, spruceness, tightness. 3* Portability. 4* Snugness.

sgiobarnag,(AF) -aig, *s.f.* see sgibearnag.

sgioblachadh, -aidh, *s.m.* Act of adjusting one's dress, or adjusting one's self for work. A' s—, *pr.pt.* of sgioblaich.

sgioblaich,* *pr. pt.* a' sgioblachadh, *v. a. & n.* Tuck up or adjust one's dress, truss. 2 Make tidy, neat or trim. 3 (CR) Clear away, take away—*Skye*.

sgioblaichte, *past pt.* of sgioblaich. Adjusted. 2 Having one's clothes tucked up or made neat. 3 Having the dress adjusted for any work.

sgioblan,(CR) *s.m.* Lapful—*Arran*.

sgiobul, see sgiobal.

sgiod, *v.* see sgud.

sgiodair,(AF) *s.m.* Medusæ (fish.)

sgiodar, -air, *s. m.* Plashing through bogs or mire. 2††Diarrhœa.

———laich, see sgiodar.

sgiogair, -ean, *s.m.* Jackanapes, impertinent fellow.

———eachd, *s.f.ind.* Impertinence, behaviour of a jackanapes.

sgiol, *pr.pt.* a' sgioladh, see sgil.

sgioladh, -aidh, *s.m. & pr.pt.* see sgileadh.

sgiolaid, see sgeileid.

sgiolam, -aim, *s.m. & f.* see sgeilm.

———ach, -aiche, see sgeilmeil.

sgiolamail, see sgeilmeil.

sgiolan, ain, *s.m.* Oats or barley with the husks taken off, groats.

sgiolc, *v.a. & n.* Slip in or out with a sudden or unexpected motion. 2 Push in or out suddenly. 3††Skulk. Sgiolcaidh am buntàta Sgiathanach as an rùsg gu bàrr a' chroinn, *the Skye potato will jerk out of its jacket to the top of the mast*—a sailor's saying. The Skye potatoes are wet until the end of the season. The idea is, that by taking a potato and squeezing one part, the jacket rips and the tuber is so wet that it bounds away.

———adh, -aidh, *s.m.* Act of slipping in or out with a sudden motion. 2 Act of pushing in or out suddenly. A' s—, *pr.pt.* of sgiolc.

———anta, -ainte, *a.* That glides in or out with a sudden motion. 2 That pushes in or out with a sudden motion. 3 Elastic. 4 Agile, quick.

———antachd, *s.f.ind.* Sudden motion or act of

sliding in or out. 2 Elasticity. 3 Agility, quickness.
sgiolcarra, see sgiolcanta.
sgiolcarrachd, see sgiolcantachd.
sgioldaimhne,** s. Minnow.
sgioll,** v.a. see sgil.
sgiolladh,** -aidh, s.m. Decidence.
sgiollag,(AF) s. f. Minnow. 2 Small fish. 3 Sand-eel.
sgiolmhor,** -oire, a. Talkative.
sgiolta, a. Tidy, trim, neat. 2 Active, nimble, quick. 3 Small, slender. 4 see sgilte. 5†† Eloquent. 6**Bald. Am buicean s., *the light young buck.*
sgioltachd, s.f.ind. Tidiness, trimness, neatness. 2 Activity,quickness,lightness. 3 Smallness, slenderness. 4††Eloquence.
sgiom,* s.m. Fat sticking to dishes. 2 Scum on the surface of water.
sgiomalair,* -ean, s.m. Skimmer, instrument to take suet, &c. off a pot. 2 see sgimilear.
————eachd, see sgimilearachd.
sgionabhagan, s.pl. Smithereens—*Argyll.*
sgionnadh,‡ -aidh, s.m. Starting. 2 Eyes starting with fear.
sgionn-shùil, -shùla, -ean, s.f. Squint-eye.
————each, -eiche, a. Squint-eyed.
sgiop, Gaelic form of *scoop.*
sgiopaidh, -e, a. see sgibeach.
sgiorbha,** s.m. Gall.
sgiord, pr.pt. a' sgiordadh, v.a. & n. Squirt. 2 2 Purge, cleanse. 3**Spit.
sgiord, s.m. Squirt, spurt. 2 Purge. 3 Lift.
sgiordach, -aiche, a. Squirting. 2 Purging.
sgiordadh, -aidh, s. m. Act of squirting. 2 Purging, act of purging. A' s—, pr.pt. of sgiord.
sgiordan, -ain, -an, s.m. Syringe, water-gun. 2 Purgative.
sgiordte, *past pt.* of sgiord.
sgiorlaich, (CR) v.a. Crush, squash, as an orange—*Perthshire.*
sgiorr, pr.pt. a' sgiorradh, v.n. Slip, slide, stumble. 2 Run a risk. 3* Happen.
sgiorr,(AF) s. Black spaul, disease of cattle.
sgiorrach, -aiche, a. Apt to slip, slide or stumble. 2 Running a risk, foolhardy.
sgiorradh, -aidh, s.m. Act of slipping, sliding or stumbling. 2 Act of running a risk, risking. 3 Accident, adventure, mischance. 4 Sudden danger. 5 Mischief, harm. A' s—, pr.pt. of sgiorr. Gun s. gun tubaist, *without slip or mishap.*
————-facail, see sgiorr-fhacal.
sgiorrag,** -aig, s.m. Flatus.
sgiorradail, -e, a. Accidental. 2 Hurtful in consequence of an accident. 3 Risking. 4 Calamitous, mischievous, disastrous.
sgiorrail, see sgiorradail.
sgiorralachd,** s.f. Accidentalness.
sgiorran, -ain, -an, s. m. Stumbler, one who slips or stumbles. 2 One who runs a risk. 3 dim. of sgiorradh. 4 Slight accident, mischance. 5**Slip.
sgiorr-fhacal, -ail, -an, s.m. Random expression, hasty word. 2 Mistake in speaking. 3 3**Ill-timed expression.
sgiorr-fhaclach, -aiche, a. Using random expressions. 2 Committing errors of speech.
sgiorrta,** a. Slipped, fallen.
————chd,** s.f.ind. Frequent risking, foolhardiness. 3 Liability to accidents.
sgort, -a, -an, s.m. Edge or folds of a garment. 2 Skirt, edge, border. 3 Riding-skirt.
sgiort, v. see sgiord.
————ach, -aiche, a. Skirted, having skirts. 2 Like a skirt. 3 Bordered.
sgiortachadh, -aidh, s. m. Skirting, bordering, furnishing with a skirt or border. A' s—, pr. pt. of sgiortaich.
sgiortadh, -aidh, s.m. & pr.pt. see sgiortachadh. 2**Skirt, border.
sgiortaich, pr.pt. a' sgiortachadh, v. a. Skirt, furnish with skirts. 2**Border.
————te, *past pt.* of sgiortaich. Furnished with a skirt or border.
sgiort-cuim,** s.m. Clyster.
sgios, s.f.ind. Weariness, fatigue. 2 Toil,labour. Leig do s., *rest yourself;* ag obair gun s.,*working indefatigably* ; cia mór an s. e ? *what a weariness it is!* a chlann na s. ! *ye sons of toil :* le s., *on account of toil* ; is e s. a' chosnaich a bhi 'na thàmh, *it fatigues the good worker to be idle.* [s.m.**]
sgiosachadh, -aidh, s.m. & pr.pt. see sgitheachadh.
sgiosaich, pr.pt. a' sgiosachadh, see sgithich.
————te, see sgithichte.
sgiot, pr.pt. a' sgiotadh, v.a. Disperse,scatter. 2 Fling or throw about.
†sgiot, -a, -an, s.m. Dart, arrow
sgiotach, -aiche, a. Scattering, that scatters or disperses. 2 Flinging, that flings or throws about. 3 Scattered, straying.
sgiotadh, -aidh, s.m. Scattering. 2 Act of scattering or dispersing. 3 Act of flinging or throwing about. A' s—, pr.pt. of sgiot.
sgioth,** s. Partition of wattled work.
†sgioth, see sgith.
†sgiothas, see sgios.
sgiothlaich,** s.f. Haunch.
sgipidh, a. Neat, active.
sgipiteach,‡*Uist* form of sgiobag, sgiobagaich or sgiobatan.
sgirbh,** Rocky ford. 2 Stony bottom.
sgire, -an, see sgireachd.
sgireachd, -an, s.f. Parish. Cruinneachadh s., *the gathering of a parish.*
————ail, -e, a. Parochial, of or belonging to a parish.
sgireachdair,** -ean, s.m. Parishioner.
sgireil,(MS) a. Parochial.
sgirt, see sgiord.
sgirtean, s.m. Disease in cattle, called in Scotland " the black spaul " or " quarter-ill."
sgistear,** -an, s. m. Droll, prater, talkative fellow.
————achd,** s.f. Prating, drollery.
sgite, see sgith.
sgite,** s.f. Maiden-ray (fish.)
sgiteal, -eil, -an, see sgideil.
sgìth, -e, a. Weary, fatigued, tired. 2 Fatiguing, wearying, that wearies or fatigues, laborious, oppressive. Seac s., *quite tired, utterly fatigued.*
sgith,(AF) s. Maiden-ray (fish.)
sgitheach,†† a. see sgith.
sgitheach, -eich, s. m. Whitethorn, hawthorn—*cratægus oxacantha.* 2 Thicket of hawthorn. Preas sgitheich, *a hawthorn bush ;* s. an fhàsaich,‡*the thorn of the wilderness.* (ill. 634.)
sgitheach dubh,§ s.m. Blackthorn.
sgitheach geal,§ see sgitheach. Badge of Clan Ogilvie. [Also called bàn-sgitheach.]
sgitheachadh, -aidh, s.m. Growing weary or tired. 2 Wearying. 2 Act of wearying or fatiguing. Air s., *fatigued.* A' s—, pr. pt. of sgithich.
sgitheachail, a. see sgitheil.
sgitheag, -eig, -an, s.f. Stalk or prickle of hawthorn. 2 see sgeach. 3 Diminutive hawthorn tree.
sgithealachd, s.f.ind. Irksomeness. 2 Prolixity. 3 Tiredness.

634. Sgitheach.

sgìtheas, see sgios.

sgìtheil, *a.* Wearisome, tiresome, tedious. 2‡‡ Importune.

sgìthich, *pr. pt.* a' sgìtheachadh, *v.a. & n.* Weary, fatigue, tire. 2 Grow tired or fatigued. Na s. d' a smachdachadh, *do not weary of his correction* or *reproof.*

———te, *past pt.* of sgìthich. Wearied, tired, fatigued.

†**sgìthiol**, *s.m.* Sheiling-hut.

sgiùcan, -ain, *s.m.* The cackling plaintive notes of a moor-hen or female grouse.

sgiuch,* *s.f.* Activity, cleverness.

sgiucha,(AC) *s.* Bursting, see sgoch. Eòlas s. feithe, *a charm for a bursting vein.*

sgiùchail,* -e, *a.* Active. 2 Clever.

sgiùchan, see sgiùcan.

sgiùgan, -ain, *s.m.* Whimper, whimpering. 2 Habit of whimpering. 3**Snubbing.

———ach, -aiche, *a.* Whimpering. 2 Apt to whimper.

———aich, -e, *s.f.* Same meanings as sgiùgan. Thòisich e air s., *he began to whimper.*

sgiùird,* *s.f.* The flux. 2 see sgiort.

———ire,* see sgiordan.

sgiùirleach,(CR) *s.m.* Lapful—*S. end of Arran.*

sgiùirt see sgiort.

sgiùlt,* *a.* Smug.

———a, see sgiolta.

———achd,* see sgioltachd.

sgiùnach, -aich, -aichean, *s.f.* Bold, forward, impudent or shameless woman. 2* Charm for getting all the fish about a boat or headland into one's own boat amidst the amazement of the neighbours. 3* Amulet to excel in anything.

sgiùr,** *v.a.* Scour, purge, cleanse, see sgùr.

sgiùrdan, see sgiordan.

†**sgiùrlong**.** -oing, *s.m.* Fugitive, deserter.

sgiùrrte, see sgiùrte.

sgiùrs, *pr.pt.* a' sgiùrsadh, *v.a.* Scourge, whip. 2 Afflict, persecute. 3 Chase, drive away, pursue. 4**Scare or scatter suddenly. Sgiùrsaidh iad sibh, *they shall scourge you.*

sgiùrs, -a, -an, *s.m.* Scourge, whip. 2 Scaring. 3 Scattering. 4 Woe, affliction. 5 Persecution.

sgiùrsa, see sgiùrsadh.

sgiùrsach, -aiche, *a.* Scourging, whipping. 2 * Afflicting. 3 Like a scourge or lash. 4 Chasing, driving away, scattering. 5 Inclined to whip or persecute, persecuting. 6**Like a persecution. 7 Of a scourge, lash or persecution.

———,* see siùrsach.

———as, see siùrsachd.

sgiùrsadair, see sgiùrsair.

sgiùrsadh, -aidh, -aidhean, *s.m.* Scourge, whip. 2 Scourging, act of scourging. 3 Driving away, chasing, act of driving away. 4 Whipping. 5 Afflicting, lashing, persecuting. 6* Pain. 7*Persecution. A' s—, *pr.pt.* of sgiùrs. Ruith sgiùrsadh, *running the gauntlet* ; s. na teangaidh, *the scourge of the tongue.*

sgiùrsaidh, *past pass.* of sgiùrs. Was scourged. 2 *3rd. sing. & pl. imp.* of sgiùrs. S. e, *let him scourge.*

sgiùrsag, -aig, -an, *s.f.* Scourge, whip.

———ach, *a.* Having scourges or whips.

sgiùrsair, -ean, *s.m.* Scourge, whip. 2 Scourger, one who scourges. 3 One who chases or drives away. 4††Lumbering lout. 5*Whoremonger. 6 (AH) Undutiful, wilful incorrigible maid.

sgiùrsaireachd, *s.f.ind.* Scourging, act of scourging. 2 Chasing or driving away. 3††Lumbering. 4 (AH) Acting like an ill-conducted, misguided maid.

sgiùrste, *past pt.* of sgiùrs.

sgiurt, see sgiort.

sgiut,* *v.n.* Dart or dash forward. 2 Slip by. 3 (CR) *Perthshire* for sgiot.

sgiut,** *v.a.* Scatter.

sgiùthadh, -aidh, -aidhean, *s.m.* Lash, strike with a goad or whip, " cut." 2 Flourish. *Prov.* 3††Flourish with a whip.

sgiùthanta,-ainte, *a.* Smarting, as a lash. *Prov.*

sgiuts, see sgiùrs.

sglàbh, -àibh, *s.m.* Slave.

———achd,** *s.f.* Slavery, bondage.

———adh,** -aidh, *s.m.* Slave, bondsman.

sglàbhaiche,** -an, *s.m.* Slave.

sglàbhaidheachd,** *s.f.* Slavery, bondage, servitude.

sglabhair, -e, -ean, *s. m. & f.* Foul-mouthed man or woman. 2 Scold.

sglabhaireachd, *s.f.* Scolding. 2 Abusive language.

sglabhart, -airt, -an, *s.m.* Blow on the side of the head.

sglabhartach, -aiche, *a.* Giving blows.

sglàib,* *s.* Plaster.

sglàib-deoch, *s.f.* Drink for nothing, drink got through ostentation.

sglàibeadair,* -ean, *s.m.* Plasterer.

sglaigean,** *s.m.* Beam of a cart, draught-tree.

sglaim,* *s. f.* Questionably acquired wealth, booty.

sglaim,* *v.a.* Usurp wealth or property, monopolize. 2** Seize violently or greedily. 3** Grasp. 4**Snatch. 5**Clutch.

sglaimheach, -ich, *s. m.* Glutton. 2 Hungry mastiff.

sglaimir,* -ean, *s.m.* Usurper.

sglaimsear,* see sglaimir.

sglamadh, -aidh,*s.m.* Snapping, seizing quickly.

sglamh,* *v.n.* Eat voraciously, glut. 2 Scold. 3 **Seize greedily, snatch. 4 Grasp. 5 Wrangle. 6 Usurp. 7* Eat as a hungry dog. 8 Scold suddenly or furiously.

sglamhach, see sglaimheach.

sglamhach,-aiche, *a.* That snatches away greedily. 2 Greedy, snatching, grasping, clutching.

sglàmhach,** *a.* Abusive, scolding, wrangling. 2 Foul-mouthed.

sglamhachadh,** *s.m.* Engrossment.

sglàmhachd,** *s.f.* Abusiveness, habit of scolding or wrangling, abusive language.

sglamhachd, *s.f.* see sglamhadh.

sglàmhadh, -aidh, *s. m.* Scolding, abusing, wrangling. 2 Scold, abuse, wrangle. 3 Sudden scolding. 4 Greedy seizing. 5 Eating voraciously.

sglamhadh, -aidh, *s. m.* Seizing greedily upon anything. 2 Snatching of anything by force, clutching. 3 Usurpation. 4 **Greedy grasp

or snatch, clutch.
sglamhaich,** *v.a.* Engross to one's self, monopolize.
sglamhaiche,** *s.m.* Curmudgeon, engrosser.
sglamhaid,** *s.m.* Glutton.
sglàmhair, -ean, *s.m.* Scolder. 2 Abusive, foul-mouthed fellow. 3††Harsh scolder.
sglamhair, -ean, *s.m.* One that snatcheth away or seizeth greedily. 2 Usurper. 3 *Glutton. greedy fellow. 4†† Snapper. 5* Voracious fellow.
sglamhaireachd, *s.f.* Seizing violently. 2 Greediness. 3 Usurpation. 4††Snapping. 2*Voracity, glut, monopoly.
sglàmhaireachd, *s. f.* Abusiveness, scolding, wrangling. 2 Bad language.
sglàmhrach, -aiche, *a.* Contumelious, scolding, abusive, wrangling.
sglàmhradh, -aidh, *s.m.* see sglàmhruinn.
sglamhradh, -aidh, *s.m.* Clawing, scratching of the skin, itch.
sglàmhruig,(MS) *s.f.* Squabble.
sglàmhruinn, -e, -ean, *s. f.* Scolding, abusive words. 2‡‡Asperity. 3 Wrangle, reprimand. 4 Ribaldry. 5 Scold, one given to scolding. 6 Raillery.
sglàmhruinn,** *v.* Abuse.
sglàmhruinneach, -eiche, *a.* Scolding. 2 Scurrilous. 3 Apt to scold. 4 Abusive.
sglàmhruinneachd, *s.f.ind.* Habit of scolding. 2 Aptness to scold.
sglàmhruinnte, *past pt.* Abused.
sglànrachd, see sglàmhruinneachd.
sglànradh, see sglàmhruinn.
sglànruinn, see sglàmhruinn.
sglàruinn, see sglàmhruinn.
sglèad, see sglèat. Taigh s., *a slated house.*
sglèadach, see sglèatach.
sglèadair, see sglèatair.
————-eachd, see sglèataireachd.
sgleafart,** *s.* Knock, slap or blow with the open hand.
sgleafartaich,** *v.a.* Strike with the open hand.
sgleamacair,* -ean, *s.m.* Dauber. 2 Mean, low, worthless fellow. 3(DU) Bore.
sgleamacaireachd,(DU) *s.f.* Boring talk, act of boring.
sgleamaic,* *pr. pt.* a' sgleamacadh, *v.a.* Plaster or flatten outwardly. 2 Daub filthily.
sgleamaid,* *s.f.* Horrid snotter.
sgleamhas, -ais, *s. m.* Meanness, sordidness, vileness. 2** Scroyle, term of extreme personal contempt.
sgleamhasach, -aiche, *a.* Mean, sordid, vile, ignoble. 2 Scroylish.
sgleamhraidh, -ean, *s.m.* Stupid, senseless person. 2 Awkward, untidy fellow. 3 Mean or ignorant fellow. 4 Bumpkin.
sgleamhraidheachd, *s.f.* Stupidity, senselessness. 2 Awkwardness, untidiness. 3 Meanness. 4 Ignorance.
sgleamhsa,** *s.m.* Mean fellow.
sgléap,(CR) *s.m.* Scolding, rating. Thug e s. dha, *he gave him a scolding—Suth'd.*
sgléap, (CR) *s.f.* Torrent of speech—*W. of Ross-shire.*
sglèap, -èip, *s.f.* Ostentation. 2 Meanness under a plausible appearance. 3 Awkwardness. 4* Low meanness under the guise of liberality. Deoch sglèip, *a drink at others' expense.*
sglèap,* *v.a. & n.* Flatten, spoil the shape of. 2 Draw down your under lip. 3 Wag your head. 4 Flatter. 5 Stare open-mouthed at one.
————ach, -aiche, *a.* Ostentatious, vain-glorious, vaunting. 2 Mean-spirited. 3**Awkward Gu s., *ostentatiously.*
sglèapaid,* *s.f.* Female who stares open mouthed at one.
sglèapair, -ean, *s. m.* Vain, vaunting fellow. 2 Mean-spirited fellow. 3* Foolish, boorish starer, applied to children who are backward through being brought up in remote corners, where they have seldom seen strangers. 4 Ostentatious fellow. 5 Awkward, sprawling fellow.
sglèapaireachd, *s.f.* Habit of silly boasting. 2 Meanness of spirit. 3* Unmannerly staring. 4 Ostentatiousness. 5 Awkwardness.
sglèat, -a, -an, *s.m.* Slate. Creag sglèata, *a slate-quarry.*
sglèat, *v.a* Slate, cover with slates.
sglèatach, -aiche, *a.* Of, or belonging to, slates. 2 Like a slate.
————-,* *s.f.* Slate-quarry. 2 Granite (?)
sglèatadh, -aidh, *s.m.* Slating. 2 Act of covering with slates. A' s—, *pr. pt.* of sglèat.
sglèatair, -ean, *s m.* Slater. 2** Milliped. 3 "Sgletter," (not cheslip, as given in the dictionaries—MM.)
sgleataireachd, *s.f.* Business of a slater, or 2 of a slate-quarrier. 3 Employment of house-slating. 4 Slate-quarry. 5 Slate-work.
sgleatar,** *a.* Slaty. 2 Laminar.
sgleimce,(CR) [*pron.* sgleimichde—*m* long] *s.* Cajolery, wheedling—*W. of Ross-shire.*
sgleinnseard, -an, *s.m.* Kind of scone.
sgleò,** *s.m.* Vapour, mist. 2 Shade, darkness. 3 Idle talk, rodomontade, romance, verbiage, falsehood. 4 High-puffing, fustian. 5 Spectre. 6 Struggle. 7 Misery. 8 Compassion. 9††Dimness of the eyes. 10* Disease of the eyes, glare about the eyes. 11* Amazement. 12* Misapprehension. 13*Romancing of one who sees imperfectly and consequently misrepresents facts. Iomar sgleò, *a contest maintained with varying success.*
sgleòbach, -aiche, *a.* Sluttish, slovenly.
sgleòbag, -aig, -an, *s.f.* Slovenly woman.
sgleòbaid, see sgleòbag.
sgleòbaideach, -eiche, see sgleòideach.
sgleòcach, -aiche, *a.* Having bad-sighted large eyes.
sgleòcair, -ean, *s.m.* Foolish starer.
sgleòcaireachd, *s.f.* Foolish staring or gaping.
sgleòchaid, -ean, *s.f.* Foolish, staring woman.
sgleòchdair, -e, -ean, *s.m.* see sgleòcair.
————-eachd, see sgleòcaireachd.
sgleodhach, -aiche, *a.* Shadowy, filmy, ill-coloured. 2 Affected.
sgleòdhair,(MS) *s.m.* Quack.
sgleò-dhan, *s.m.* Boasting, puffing, bombast. 2 Shade, film. 3 Vapour, mist. 4 Dimness of the eyes, produced by looking at anything luminous. 5 Ghost, spectre. 6 Fable, romance. 7 Misery. 8 Pity. 9 Carcase.
sgleò-éiligheachd,(MS) *s.f.* Libel.
sgleog, -oig, -an, *s. f.* Saliva, snot, phlegm. 2 Knock, sudden collision. 3††Sound. 4(CR) Slap—*Suth'd & Farr.* 5 Drivel.
sgleogach, -aiche, *a.* Falling like snot or saliva, drivelling. 2 Striking suddenly against each other. 3 (DU) Easy-going, imperturbable.
sgleogair, -ean, *s. m.* Troublesome prattler. 2 Lying, flattering fellow. 3 Driveller.
————-eachd, *s.f.* Silly prattling talk.
sgleò-ghlòir, -e, *s.f.* Loud cry, huzza.
sgleoiceach,(DMy) *a.* Cearc s., *a hen with a lump on each side of its head.*
sgleòid, -e, -ean, *s.m. & f.* Silly man or woman, one easily imposed upon. 2 Slovenly man or woman, drab, slut. 3 One who indulges in idle talk. 4* Heavy, clumsy, lifeless female. 5**Filth.

sgleòideach, -eiche, *a.* Silly, senseless. 2 Slovenly, filthy, drabbish. 3 Gawky. Gu s., *drabbishly.*
gleòideil, -e, *a.* see sgleòideach.
sgleoit. see sgleòid.
sgleop,(CR) *v.* Slap.
sgleothach,* -aiche, see sgleòdhach.
sgleòthail,* -e, *a.* Romancing.
sgleòthair,* -ean, *s.m.* Romancer. 2 Swaggerer.
sgliamach, -aiche, *a.* Slippery-faced.
sgliamair, -ean, *s.m.* One having a slippery face.
sgliamhach, -aiche, see sgliamach.
sgliamhair, see sgliamair.
sgliap, see sglèap.
———aireachd, see sglèapaireachd.
sgliat, see sglèat.
sgliatach, see sglèatach.
sgliatadh, see sglèatadh.
sgliatair, see sglèatair.
———eachd, see sglèataireachd.
sgliatar, see sglèatar.
sgligean,** -ein, *s.m.* Speckled or spotted creature.
sgligeanach,** *a.* Speckled, spotted.
sglìmeach, -eiche, *a.* Troublesome, as an unwelcome guest.
sglìmeachas, -ais, *s.m.* Troublesomeness.
sglìmear, -ir, -an, *s.m.* Troublesome guest.
sglimsear, -ir, -an, *s.m.* Flattering fellow. 2 Parasite.
sglimsearachd, *s.f.* Sordid, parasitical flattery.
sgliobhag, *s.f.* Light blow.
sgliofag,(CR) *s.f.* Light blow—*W. of Ross.*
sgliog,(MS) *s.* Box.
sgliogaist,(CR)*s.f.* Large spit, distinguished from *sglongaid* by absence of colouring matter—*Perthshire.*
sgliomair,* see sgimilear. [*loch.*]
sglioungaid, (MS) *s.f.* Mucus. [splaingeid—*Gair-*
sgliughaisg,* *s.f.* Dowdy.
sgliùireach, see sgliùrach.
sgliùisgeach, -eiche, *a.* Dowdy.
sgliùrach, -aich, -aichean, *s.f.* Slut, slattern. 2 Gossip, female tattler. 3 Whore. 4 Clumsy person. 5‡‡Young sea-gull. 6*Newly-fledged crow or sea-gull.
sgliùrachd, *s.f.* Sluttishness. 2 Gossipping, tattling. 3 Whorishness.
sglog-bhàrdachd, *s.f.* Bathos.
sglòid, -e, *s.f.* Filth, dirt. 2 see sgleòid.
sglòideach, -eiche, *a.* Filthy, dirty, *prov.*
sgloidhseach,(CR) *s. f.* Anything broad and flaccid. S. mhór arain, *a broad thin piece of bread—W. of Ross-shire.*
sgoige,** *s.f.* Throat.
sgloigeach,** *a.* Guttural.
sgloing,** *s.f.* Snot.
sgloingean, see sglongaid.
sgloingeanach, -aiche, *a.* see sglongaideach.
sgloingeanachd, see sglongaideachd.
sglong, see sglongaid. 2* *s.f.* Horrid snotter.
sglongach, -aiche, see sglongaideach. 2*Dirtily viscous.
sglongachd, see sglongaideachd.
sglongaid, -e, -ean, *s.f.* Snot, saliva, spit, mucus. 2**Term of personal contempt.
sglongaideach, -eiche, *a.* Snotty, mucuous, snivelling.
sglongaideachd, *s. f.* Snottiness, mucousness. 2 Habit of snivelling.
sglongair,†† *s.m.* Snotty fellow.
————eachd,†† *s.f.* Snottiness.
sglorach, *s.m.* Big slattern—*Islay.*
sgluait,(CR) *s.f.* Slattern—*Arran.*
sgnog, *s. & v.* see sgrog.
sgnoganach, *Mull, &c.* for sgroganach.
sgo, *s.* Stray cloud—*Eigg & Skye.*

sgob, *v.a.* Snatch, pluck, pull. 2 Sting, bite. 3 Scoop out. 4* Nibble lightly. 5(DU) Peck, as a bird.
sgobach, -aiche, *a.* That snatches plucks or pulls. 2 Stinging, that stings or bites. 3 Scooping. 4 Apt to pluck.
sgobadh, -aidh, *s.m.* Snatch, act of snatching, plucking or pulling. 2 Act of stinging or biting., 3 Twitch, wound. 4* 'Short while. 5** Pluck, tug, pull. 6* Nibbling. 7 (DU) Act of pecking. S. bho 'n bhaile, *a little while from home ;* s. dheth, *a little while of it.* [*pl.* -aichean—††.] A' s—, *pr.pt.* of sgob.
sgobag, -aig, -an, *s.f.* Little twitch or wound. 2 Small dram, small quantity of any liquor to drink. 3(DU) Spoonful of porridge, gruel, pudding, &c.
———ach, -aiche, *a.* Twitching or wounding lightly.
sgobair,** *s.m.* Biter.
sgoballach, -aich, *s.m.* Piece or morsel to eat.
scobanta, -ainte, *a.* Eager, voracious. 2††Snatching.
————chd, *s.f. ind.* Eagerness, voraciousness. 2†† Snatching.
sgobhachan, *s.pl.* Pieces—*Badenoch.*
sgobhrag,** *s.f.* Fairy.
sgoch, *pr.pt.* a' sgochadh, *v. a.* Gash, scarify, hack, notch. 2(DMy) Sprain. S. mi mo chas, *I sprained my foot.*
sgoch,* *s.m.* Gash, incision, notch, cut, slit. 2 (AC) Bursting. 3 First shot from a still—*Perthshire.*
sgocha, see sgoch.
sgochach,** *a.* Full of cuts, slits or incisions. 2 Causing cuts or slits.
sgochadair,** *s.m.* Scarificator.
sgocha-feithe, (DU) *s.f.* Sprain. Eòlas s., *the charm by which sprains were healed.*
sgochraich,* *s.* Liver.
sgòd, -òid, -an, *s.m.* Corner of a cloth or garment, lappet. 2 Sheet of a sail (rope.) 3 Corner of a sail. Error, defect, blemish. 4 Conceit, affectation, pride, airiness, coquetry, foppery, vanity. 5 Command, lordliness, rule. 6** Disposal. S. an t-siùil mheadhoin, *the mainsheet ;* s. an t-siùil thoisich, *the foresail-sheet ;* s. an t-siùil chinn, *the jib-sheet ;* ainnir gun s., *a maid without conceit ;* fuidh d' s., *under thy rule ;* crann-sgòid, *ship-boom ;* cainnt gun s., *language without affectation.*
sgòdach, -aiche, *a.* Having corners or lappets. 2 Furnished with sheets (ropes.) 3 Defective, blemished. 4 Trailing, dragging. 5 (CR) Ragged—*Skye.* [sgeòdach in *Gairloch.*] 6 Awkward. 7 Conceited, affected, pedantic, beauish, proud, haughty, airy, flashy, foppish. 8 Lordly, having command.
sgòdag, -aig, -an, *s.f.* Slovenly, awkward woman. 2 Conceited, vain girl, coquette, airy or affected female.
sgòdaich,(MS) *v.a.* Eke.
sgòdail,** *a.* Big. 2 see sgòdach.
sgòdan, -ain, -an, *s.m. dim.* of sgòd. Little corner or lappet. 2 Small defect or blemish. 3 Sheet of a sail. 4 (MS) Patch.
sgog, -oig, -an, *s.m.* Fool, idler.
sgog,* *v.n.* Hesitate, waver.
sgogach, -aiche, *a.* Foolish, senseless. 2 Idle.
sgogarsaich,* *s.f.* Hesitation.
sgòid, *prov.* see sgòd. 2 *s.f.* **Neck. 3 *gen.sing.* of sgòd. 4**Shirt.
sgòideach, -eiche, see sgòdach.
sgòideag, -eig, -an, see sgòdag.
————ach,** *a.* Vain, airy, as a girl, coquettish, showy.
sgoideas, -eis, *s.f.* Pageantry, vain show, osten-

tation, pride, airiness, coquetry, flirting, vanity. [* gives sgoideis for *nom.*]

———ach, -aiche, *a.* Showy, foppish, proud, airy, coquettish, flirting, formal, fond of pageantry, vain, conceited.

sgòideil,** -e, *a.* Vain, airy, conceited, foppish, flirting, showy, formal, fond of show or pageantry.

sgoideiseach, see sgoideasach.

sgoige,** *s.f.* The throat.

———ach,** *a.* Gutteral.

sgoignean, -ein, *s.m.* Fan.

sgoil,* *v.a.* School, teach.

sgoil, -e, -ean, *s.f.* School. 2 Education, learning, knowledge, 3 Science, literature. Am bheil s. aige? *is he educated?* a' dol do 'n s., *going to school*; cha'n 'eil s. agam air, *I know nothing of it*; taigh na sgoile, *the school-house.*
s.-na-cruinne, *doctrine of the sphere.*
s.-àitean, *topography.*
s.-bhalbhan, *deaf-mute schooling.*
s.-bhasbaireachd, *fencing.*
s.-bhùird, *boarding-school.*
s.-chlaidheamh, *sword-exercise.*
s.-chogaidh, *military academy.*
s.-chreige, *geology.*
s.-chèaird, *mechanics.*
s.-chruinne, *geography.*
s.-dannsaidh, *dancing-school.*
s.-diadhaireachd, *theology.*
s.-dìomhair, *private school.*
s.-dorn, *boxing.*
s.-dreag, *meteorology.*
s.-dreagaireachd, see sgoil-dreag.
s.-dubh, *the black art.*
s.-eachdraidh, *historiography.*
s.-eun, *ornithology.*
s.-fhacal, *etymology.*
s.-fhairge, *navigation.*
s.-fhearainn, *agriculture; 2* land-surveying.*
s.-fhreumhachd, see s.-fhacal.
s.-fhuaigheil, *sewing-class.*
s.-leughaidh, *reading-school.*
s.-lusan, *botany.*
s.-mhara, *navigation.*
s.-mharcachd, *riding-school.*
s.-mharsantachd, *book-keeping.*
s.-mhiotailt, *mineralogy.*
s.-oide, *schoolmaster, usher.*
s.-oidhche, *a school taught at night-time.*
s.-nàduir, *physiology.*
s.-nan-reult, *astronomy.*
s.-nan-sian, *meteorology.*
s.-na-fairge, *navigation.*
s.-reul, *astronomy.*
s.-sgrìobhaidh, *writing-school.*
s.-sheinn, *singing-school* or *class.*
s.-speur, *astronomy.*
s.-uisge, *hydrostatics.*
s.-uisgearachd, see sgoil-uisge.

The following given by * are undesirable or incorrect, and should not be used. S.-fhollaiseach, *a public school*; s.-inntinn, *philosophy*; s.-mhulcach, *phrenology*; s.-riomball, *spherics*—riomball is a *circle*, not a *sphere*; s.-na-cumasg, *chemistry*; s.-na h-inntinn, *intellectual knowledge*—knowledge is *eòlas*, not *sgoil.*

sgoildha,** *a.* Scholastic.

sgoileach,†† *a.* Pertaining to a school.

sgoileag, -eig, -an, *s.f., dim.* of sgoil. Little school.

———ach,†† *a.* Pertaining to a little school.

sgoileam, -eim, *s.m.* Loquacity, garrulity, prattle. 2**Impertinent garrulity.

———ach, -aiche, *a.* Loquacious, prattling, garrulous. 2 Scolding. 2* Venomous in scolding. 4**Impertinently garrulous.

———ach,* -aich, *s.f.* Shrew, scold, scolding female.

sgoileamachd, *s.f. ind.* Habit of loquacity or prattle.

sgoilear, -eir, -an, *s.m.* Scholar, school-boy, student. 2 Scholar, man of learning. Deagh s., *a good scholar.*

———ach, -aiche, *a.* Scholastic, learned, like a scholar, academical.

———achd, *s.f.ind.* Scholarship, learning, erudition, education, intelligence.

———an, *n.pl.* of sgoilear.

———ra, *a.* Schooled, scholastic.

sgoileil,** *a.* Academical. 2 Scholastic.

sgoileisdeach,** *a.* Academical.

———,** *s.m.* Academician.

sgoileisteach, see sgoileisdeach.

sgoilm,‡ *s.* see sgoileam. 2 Razor-bill. 3*Mouth or face expressive of a scolding disposition. *High key in scolding.

———each,** *a.* see sgoileamach.

sgoilmeis,* *s.f.* Biting severe cold. 2 Garrulity.

———eachd,** *s.f.* Garrulity.

sgoilmrich,** *v.* Chatter, prate.

———,** *s.f.* Chatter, prating.

sgoilt, *pr.pt.* a' sgoltadh, *v.a. & n.* Split, cleave, burst asunder, break, crack. 2 Gut fish. Sgoiltidh sùil a' chlach, *an (evil) eye will split a stone*; an ti a sgoltas fiodh, *he who cleaves wood.*

sgoilte, *past pt.* of sgoilt. Cleft, splintered, riven, burst, cracked. 2 **Abrupt. 3 (DU) Bifurcate.

———ach, -eiche, *a.* Splitting, cleaving, cracking. 2 That splits or cleaves. 3 Causing to split, cleave or burst. 4 Apt to split or cleave. 5**Bursting.

sgoilteadh, *3rd.sing. & pl.* of sgoilt.

sgoiltean, -ein, -an, *s.m.* Splinter, slice. 2 Cleft. 3 Colon in *gram.* 4 Half of a square neckerchief. 5 Billet of wood. 6 Slit stick, used by children for throwing pebbles. 7 Seed-slip of a potato. 8* Half. 9(DMy) Parting of the hair of the head.

———ach, -aiche, *a.* Abounding in splinters.

sgoiltear, -eir, -an, *s. m.* see *coltair. 2 see sgoltair.

———, *fut. pass.* of sgoilt.

sgoim, -e, *s.f.* Wandering or ranging about. 2 see sgaoim.

sgoineadh, -idh, -idhean, *s.m.* Keen attack. 2 Eager longing. S. acrais, *a vehement attack of hunger.*

sgoinn, -e, *s.f.* Care, attention, carefulness, moment. 2 Heed. 3 Efficacy, power, effect, good effect or purpose. 4 Neatness, trimness. 5 Decency, taste, propriety. 6 Affection. 7 (CR) Small pool in the rocky bed of a stream, in which salmon get imprisoned and caught when the tide is low.—*W. of Ross-shire.* 8 (DU) Potential or active energy, force, activity. Tha s. air, *he is active*; dèan le s. e, *do it tastefully*; rinn e air sgàth sgoinne, *I did it for decency's sake*; is beag s. a bhitheas air do ghnothach, *your business will be done with little propriety;* cha'n 'eil s. air an làimh, *they are wasteful* or *extravagant.*

sgoinn, (DMy) *s.f.* Hurry. C' àit' am bheil thu dol leis an s. seo? *where are you going in such haste?*

sgoinn,* *v.a.* Check, reprove, scold bitterly.

sgoinneach,* -eiche, *a.* Bitter in scolding.

———,* -eiche, *s.f.* Bitter scolding female.

sgoinnear,** *a.* Heedful, see sgoinneil.

sgoinneil, -e, *a.* Careful, heedful. 2 Attentive. 3 Efficacious, producing a good effect. 4 Neat, trim, tidy. 5 *Decent, tasteful. 6 (DMy) Energetic, active, bustling. Duine s., *an active brisk man.*

sgoirm, -e, -ean, *s.f.* The throat. 2 The lower parts of a hill or heap. 3*Brow of a hill. An droighean gorm air s. nan càrn, *the green thorn on the brow of the cairns.*
†**sgoit**,** *s.f.* Shield, target.
sgoiteach, -eiche, *a.* Quack.
———d, *s.f.ind.* Quackery.
†**sgoith**, *v.* see sgath.
sgoithean,** *s. m.* The best or prime of any-thing.
sgoitich, -ean, *s.m.* Quack, mountebank.
sgoitidheachd, *s.f.* see sgoiteachd.
sgol, *pr.pt.* a' sgoladh, *v.a.* Rinse, wash, make clean. 2 Drench. 3††Scull.
†**sgol**, -oil, *s.m.* Skull. 2 Loud laughter.
sgòl,(AH) *s.m.* Viscous matter usually exuding from and covering an ill-dressed wound.
sgoladh, -aidh, *s.m.* Rinsing, cleaning, washing. 2 Act of washing. 3 Draught. 4††Waddling. 5††Sculling. A' s—, *pr.pt.* of sgol.
sgolag, -aig, *s.f.* Olive-tree. 2 see sgalag.
sgolagag,(DC) *s. f.* Forefinger—coigag or sgolabag in *Argyll.*
sgolaisd, see colaisd.
sgolaisdeach, see sgoileisdeach.
sgolap, Gaelic form of *scollop.*
sgolb, -uilb, -an, *s.m.* Splinter. 2 Prickle, thorn. 3 Wooden pin or wattle, used for fixing thatch on a roof. 4 Single floorings (nails.) 5**Skirmish or fight with knives or dirks. 6**Doubt. 7 Split.
sgolbach, -aiche, *a.* Prickly, thorny. 2 Splinttered, splintering.
———,** *s.m.* Spray or wattle, used in thatching houses.
———d,(MS) *s.f.* Prickliness.
sgolbaich,(MS) *v.a.* Split.
sgolbanach, -aich, *s.m.* Stripling, youth.
sgolbanta, -ainte, *a.* Thin, slender. 2 Apt to break into splinters. 3 *Sharp, prickly.
———chd, *s.f.ind.* Thinness, slenderness. 2 Tallness. 3 Aptness to break into splinters.
sgolgair,** -ean, *s.m.* Scold.
†**sgol-ghàire**,** *s.f.* Loud laughter, horse laugh.
sgoll,* *v.a.* Scull, as a boat. 2 see sgol. 3** Deplume. 4 Scold in a high key.
sgoll,* *s.m.* Scum, as on proud flesh.
sgollachan,* -ain, *s.m.* Unfledged bird.
sgollag, -aig, *s.f.* Dingey, see p. 78.
sgolt,** -oilt, -an, *s.m.* Split, slit, cleft, rent.
sgoltach, -aiche, *a.* Splitting, cleaving, slitting, riving. 2 Bursting, breaking. 3 Apt to split or cleave. 4 Apt to burst or break.
sgoltadh, -aidh, -aidhean, *s. m.* Split, chink, cleft, crack, slit. 2 Splitting, act of splitting, slitting, cleaving, rending or riving. 3 Bursting, act of bursting or breaking asunder. 4 Ear-mark on sheep, see under comharradh-cluaise. 5 Laceration. 6**Burst. A' s—, *pr. pt.* of sgolt. A s. cheann, *to cleave heads.*
sgoltair,** *s.m.* Cleaver, splitter of wood.
sgoltan,¶ -ain, *s.m.* Nut-hatch—*sitta europæa.*
sgomhal-sgarach,** *a.* Astride, astraddle.
sgonasach,** *a.* Eager, greedy.
sgonn, sguinn & sgoinn, *pl.* -an, *s. m.* Short block of wood. 2 Shapeless mass. 3 Dolt, blockhead, dunce, rude, uncultivated person. 4 Bull-calf. 5 Trifler, prater. 6 Shapeless hill. 7 Base of a couple imbedded in the wall of a house, balk. 8* Large mouthful, gulp, glut. 9* Huge, unshapely person. 10 (DU) Large slice, as of bread, meat, &c. S. labhair, *prate, blab foolishly* ; s. cabair, *a block of wood*; s. cloiche, *a block of stone* ; s. gille, *a heavy-headed fellow* ; s. arain, *a block of bread.*
sgonn,* *v.n.* Gulp, glut, eat in large mouthfuls.
sgonna-bhard,(JM) *s.m.* Poetaster.
sgonnach, -aiche, *a.* Lumpish, coarse, shapeless. 2 Stupid, senseless. 3 Rude, unpolished.
sgonnadh, -aidh, *s.m.* Gulping. A' s—, *pr. pt.* of sgonn. 'Ga s. air, *gulping it up.*
sgonnag, *s.f.dim.* of sgonn. Crack (noise.) Clach mhór bhun sgonnaig, *the upright flagstone at the base of the couple as a partition, to prevent cows injuring one another—Scots,* buisting-stanes,—*buist* is the space between, holding two cows.
sgonnag, -aig, *s.f.* Hasty word. 2 Flatus.
sgonnair, -ean, *s.m.* Lumpish fellow. 2 Dunce. 3 Boor, rustic, trifler, whiffler, rascallion. 4* Gulper.
sgonnaireachd, *s.f.ind.* Stupidity, senselessness. 2 Boorishness, rusticity. 3** Behaviour of a dunce. 4 Whiffling, prating, trifling.
sgonnan, -ain, -an, *s.m., dim.* of sgonn. Short, thick piece of wood, little block. 2 The peg of a cas-chrom on which the right foot is placed. 3 The wind-pipe, as distinguished from *an slugan,* the gullet. 4 Handle of a quern by which it is turned.
sgonnasach,** *a.* Trifling, whiffling, prating.
sgonnasachd,** *s.f.ind.* Habit of trifling, whiffling or prating.
sgonn-bhalach, -aich, *s. m.* Lumpish boor. 2 Dunce. 3 Trifler, rascallion.
sgonn-chu, -choin, *s.m.* Surly or vicious dog.
sgonn-labhairt, *v.a.* Prate, blab foolishly.
sgonn-labhairt,** *s.f.* Prating, blabbing.
sgonnsa,** *s.m.* Fort, sconce.
sgop, *s.m.* Foam, froth.
sgopraich, *a.* Senseless.
sgor, -oir, -an, *s.m.* (AF) Stud of horses. 2 (CR)Slice of bread—*W. of Ross-shire.* 3(DU) Slice of fish, fillet. 4 (CR) Swathe or sweep of the scythe—*Suth'd.* 5†† Cut, notch,*gash.
sgòr, -òir, -an, *s.m.* Sharp, steep hill rising by itself, or a little, steep, precipitous height on another hill or mountain. 2 Peak, pinnacle. 3 Tail of a bank in the sea, concealed rock jutting into the sea. 4 Asperity.
sgor, -oir, -an, *s.m.* Mark, notch or cut, made by any sharp instrument. S. creige, *a cleft in a rock.*
sgor,* *s.f.* Fork. Sgian agus s., *a knife and fork.*
sgor, *pr.pt.* a' sgoradh, *v.a.* Cut, hack, gash, scarify, lance, cut in pieces. 2 Erase. 3 Fork peats or hay. 4 Lay out peats to dry.
sgoraban,(CR) *s.m.* Little pointed rock—*W. of Ross-shire.*
sgòrach, -aiche, *a.* Rocky, full of pointed rocks. 2 Peaked. 3 Pronged. 4 *Cliffy. 5*Conical. 6 Rugged. [stòrach—DU]
sgorach, -aiche, *a.* Cutting, hacking, scarifying. 2 Abounding in cuts or notches. 3**Erasing. 4 Having a buck-tooth.
sgora-cùil,(AC) *s.* Leaning-rod. Gun s., *without a leaning-rod.*
sgoradh, -aidh, *s.m.* Cutting, act of cutting, hacking, gashing or scarifying. 2 Scoring, scratching, erasing, erasure, scratch, score. 3*Forking. 4 Laying out of peats. 5††Piercing. A' s—, *pr. pt.* of sgor. Dheanadh tu tora 'dheanadh an toll is sgoradh 'na bhonn gu shàil, *thou wouldst make an augur that would bore the holes and cut into his sole to his heel—Duanaire, p. 37.*
sgorag, -aig, -an, *s.f.* Piece of turf. 2 Roasted limpet. 3 Scollop, waving edge. 4††Small bit of stone.
———ach,‡‡ -aiche, *a.* Full of small pieces of stone or turf. 2††Scalloped.
sgoragaich, *v.a.* Scollop, cut the edge of cloth, &c. in a wavy line.
sgoranach, -aich, *s.m.* Youth, stripling.
sgòr-bheannach,** *a.* Rocky, hilly.

sgòr-bheinn, -e, *pl.* bheannta & -eanntan, *s. f.* Rocky, conical mountain. 2 Mountain cliff. 3 Projecting cliff. 4 Blasted cliff. 5 Cliffy rock.
†**sgor-chailbhe**, see sgorn-chailbhe.
sgor-éild,** *s.m.* Hill frequented by roe-deer. 2 Upland rock.
sgor-fhiacail, -cla, *pl.* -clan, *s.m.* Buck-tooth.
sgor-fhiaclach, -aiche, *a.* Buck-toothed.
sgòrn, -òirn, -an, *s.m.* Throat, windpipe, gullet.
sgòrnach, -aich, see sgòrnan.
sgòrnan, -ain, -an, *s.m.* The throat, neck, throttle, gullet. 2* Windpipe. Tha 'n s. fosgailte mar uaigh, *their throat is an open sepulchre.*
sgòrnan, *n.pl.* of sgòrn.
———**ach**, -aiche, *a.* Wide-throated. 2 Bronchial. 3(MS) Guttural.
———**achas**, -ais, *s.m.* Gutturalness.
———**aich**, *v.a.* Gorge.
sgòrn-chailbhe, -an, *s.f.* The epiglottis.
sgòrr, -a, -an, see sgòr.
sgorr,(DMy) *v.* Secure a boat with two or more sticks to hold it on an even keel.
sgòrrach, see sgòrach.
sgorrach,(AF) *s.m.* Perch (fish.)
sgorradh,(DU) -aidh, *s.m.* Act of propping up a boat on even keel. 2 The props taken collectively. (Sgorraidhean, the props taken individually.)
sgorrag,(DMK) *s.f.* Small bannock of oatmeal with a hole in the centre, made for children —*Caithness.*
sgòrr-bheinn, see sgòr-bheinn.
sgor-shuil, -shula, -shuilean, *s.f.* Blink-eye.
sgor-shuileach, -eiche, *a.* Blink-eyed,
sgor-shruth,** -ach, *s.m.* Rocky stream.
sgorthanach, see sgoranach.
sgot, -oit, -an, *s.m.* Small farm. 2 Piece of land cut off another. 3 Small flock. 4* Small village.
sgòt, see sgòd.
†**sgot**, -oit, *s.m.* Shot, reckoning. 2 Part or portion of a reckoning. Tha s. agam ort, *I have capped your witticism—Lewis.*
sgotan, -ain, *s.m* Small farm. 2 Small flock. 3 Small group of persons. 4 Small blemish.
sgot-bhaile,* *s.m.* Village.
sgoth,** *v.a.* Pull.
sgoth, -a, -an, *s.f.* Boat, skiff, large winter fishing-boat, yacht. †2 Flower. 3 (AC) Shade, shelter, hut for concealing sportsmen. 4**Son. 5**Choice part of anything. 6**Disease. 7 (DU)Boat with stem and stern vertical—sgòth in *Gairloch.* Imich 'nad s., *depart in thy skiff.*
sgoth, -achan, *s.f.* (AC) Steep rock, abrupt hill. 2 (AC) Bank of cloud, overhanging haze. 3 (CR) The shade caused by a cloud obscuring the sun.—*W. of Ross-shire.* 4 (CR) Dimness on glass caused by breath—*Strathspey.*
sgothadh, -aidh, *s.m.* Pull. 2 Gash, slash, cut.
sgothag, -aig, -an, *s.f.dim.* of sgoth. Little skiff, small yacht, cutter.
sgothaich,(MS) *v.a.* Overcloud.
sgothan, see sgot.
sgoth-long, -luinge, -an, *s.f.* Yacht, ship's flyboat, see p. 78.
sgoth-luath, *s.f.* Cutter (boat) see p. 78.
sgrab,** *v.a.* Erase. 2 Scratch. 3 Write.
sgrab,¶ *s.* Great shearwater, see sgriab. 2 Razor-bill—*Barra*, see coltraiche.
sgrabach, -aiche, *a.* Rough, rugged, shaggy. 2 Rare, scarce.
sgrabachan, -ain, *s.m.* Roughness.
sgrabachas, -ais, *s.m.* Roughness, shagginess, ruggedness.
sgrabadh, see sgrobadh.
sgrabail,¶ *St. Kilda* for sgriab.
sgrabair, -ean, *s.m.* Greenland dove, see **sgriab.**
sgraban, -ain, *s.m.* Currycomb.
sgrabanach, -aiche, see sgrabach.
sgrabanachd, see sgrabachas.
sgragall, *s.m.* Gold-foil, tin-foil, gold-leaf, spangle.
sgragallach, -aiche, *a.* Spangled. 2 Like tin-foil gold-leaf or gold-foil.
sgraibhseadh, -idh, -idhean, *s. m.* Hand-saw. [*sgraibhse, *s.f.*]
sgraicheag,¶ -aig, -an, *s.f.* Jay—*garrulus glandarius.* 2(AF) Redwing, see sgiath-dheargan, & sgreuchag.
———— **-ghlas**,¶ *s.f.* Missel-thrush. 2 Redwing, see sgiath-dheargan.
———— **-oidhche**,¶ *s.f.* Night-jar, goat-sucker.

635. Sgraicheag-oidhche.

sgràid, *s.f.* Old hag. 2 Old mare or cow.
———**each**, -eiche, *a.* Shrivelled and ugly.
sgràideach,** *a.* Diminutive. 2 Of a shabby exterior.
sgràideag, -eig, -an, *s.f.* Small morsel. 2 Small or ugly female. 3*Small potato. 4*Any small thing.
———**ach**,** *a.* Diminutive, puny. 2 Shabby. 3 Ugly.
sgràidean, -ein, -an, *s.m.* Diminutive, dwarfish man. 2 Shabby-looking fellow. 3 Ugly little fellow.
sgràideanach,†† -eiche, *a.* Diminutive and ugly. 2 Shabby. 3 Having an ugly diminutive person. 4**Puny.
sgraidht, -ean, *s.f.* Shrivelled and ugly old woman.
———**each**, see sgràideach.
sgraid-shàbh, *s.f.* Hand-saw.
sgraig, *v. a.* Strike, hit one a blow.
sgraigeadh, -idh, *s. m.* Striking, act of striking a blow. A' s—, *pr.pt.* of sgraig.
sgraigte, *past pt.* of sgraig. Struck.
sgrail,¶ *s.f.* Manx-shearwater—*puffinus anglorum.*
sgràill, *v.a.* Rail at, revile, satirize, abuse with words, scold harshly. [‡‡sgraill.]
sgràilleadh, -idh, *s.m.* Railing, act of railing at one, satirizing, abusing with words, reviling. 2**Offensive language, greatest abuse. A' s—, *pr.pt.* of sgràill.
sgràilleag, -eig, -an, *s.f.* Sand-piper.
sgraillig,(AF) *s.f.* Dunlin.
sgraing, -e, -ean, *s.f.* Angry look, frown, scowl, gloomy, contracted countenance. 2 Forbidding aspect. 3 Niggardliness. 4**Gloom.
sgraingeach, -eiche, *a.* see sgraingeal.
sgraingeag, -eig, -an, *s.f.* Surly, sullen-looking woman. 2 Niggardly woman.
sgraingealachd, *s.f.ind.* Sullenness, gloominess of aspect. 2 Forbidding look. 3 Niggardliness. 4* Surly morosity.
sgraingeil, -e, *a.* Gloomy, sullen, frowning, scowling. 2 Of a forbidding aspect. 3 Niggardly. 4**Having a frowning or forbidding visage.
sgraingean, -ein, -an, *s.m.* Surly-looking fellow. one with a frowning or gloomy visage. 2 Nig-

gardly fellow.
sgraingear,* -eir, -an, *s.m.* Scowler, curmudgeon.
sgràist, -ean, *s.m.* Sluggard, slothful person. 2 Sluggishness.
———each,** *a.* Sluggish, indolent, slothful. 2 Slovenly.
———each, *s.m.* Sluggard, sloven.
———eachd, *s.f.ind.* Laziness, sluggishness. 2 Slovenliness.
sgràisteag, -eig, -an, *s.f.* Lazy, indolent woman, 2 Sloven. 3**Slothful young female.
sgràistealachd, see sgràisteachd.
sgràisteil, -e, *a.* Slothful, lazy, sluggish. 2 Slovenly. Gu s., *sluggishly.*
sgrait, -e, *pl.* -ean & -eachan, *s.f.* Shred, rag.
sgraiteach, -eiche, *a.* Shredded, ragged, shabby. Gu s., *raggedly.*
sgraiteachd,** *s.f.* Raggedness, shabbiness.
sgraiteag, -eig, -an, *s.f.* Ragged female, shabbily dressed female.
sgraitean, -ein, -an, *s.m.* Ragged fellow, shabbily dressed fellow.
sgraith, see sgrath.
sgraithte, *past pt.* of sgrath.
sgràl, *s.m.* Host, large number, applied to minute insects. [In other cases *sgròd* is used.]—*Dàin I. Ghobha.* S. a' bhaile, *the children of the township gathered together.*
sgram,** *s.m.* Scratch. 2 Snap.
sgram,** *v.a.* Wipe off.
sgramain,** *s.m.* Extortioner.
sgràmail, Gaelic form of *scramble.*
sgràmalaich, *v.a.* Scramble.
sgràmalair,** *s.m.* Sprawler.
sgràmalanach,** *a.* Sprawling.
sgràmalanaich,** *s.f.* Sprawling.
sgrath, -a, -an, *s. f.* Outer skin or rind of anything, husk, peel. 2 Bark of a tree. 3 Coat of an onion. 4 Turf, green sod, divot, as used for covering roofs of houses. 5†† Horror, dread. 6 Rust. 7 Scale. 8** Rough handling. 9**Long rhyme. 10 Pull, tug. 11* What covers the kiln of grain. 12** Greensward.
sgrath, *v.a.* Peel, take off the rind or skin. 2** Excoriate, pare, as a surface. 3 Thatch with turfs. 4**Tug, pull or handle roughly.
sgrathach, -aiche, *a.* Having a rind or skin of any kind. 2 Peeling, that peels or takes off the rind or skin. 3 Abounding in sods, divots or green turfs. 4**Skinny, having a thick or strong rind. 5** Having many rinds, as an onion. 6 Filmy. 7 Scaly, crusty, of a broken skin.
sgrathachadh, -aidh, *s.m. & pr. pt.* of sgrathaich, see sgrathadh.
sgrathadh, -aidh, *s.m.* Peeling, act of peeling, taking off the peel, rind or skin. 2 Thatching, act of thatching with turf. 3**Pull, tug. 4 Scouring. A' s—, *pr. pt.* of sgrath.
sgrathag, -aig, -an, *s.f.dim.* of sgrath. Thin covering, peel or rind of any kind. 2 Small turf.
sgrathagach, -aiche, *a.* Having a thin rind or skin of any kind. 2†† Full of small peelings. 3 Abounding in little sods.
sgrathaich, *v.* see sgrath.
sgrathaichte, *past pt.* of sgrathaich. Peeled, skinned. 2 Pared, as a surface. 3 Thatched with turf.
sgrathail, -e, *a.* Destructive, tearing, destroying. 2 Pernicious. 3 Terrible. 4**Peeling, paring.
sgrathair,* -ean, *s.m.* Skeleton.
sgrathal, *s.coll.* Small ones of anything. 2 Refuse, rubbish. [*sgrathall.]
sgreab, -a, -an, *s.f.* Scab, blotch. 2 Mange. 3 **The itch. 4 Scurf. 5(MS) Anthrax. 6‡ *Crust. 7 (DU) Thin layer or film of dirt, &c
sgreabach, -aiche, *a.* Scabbed, blotched, mangy. 2 Itchy. 3**Affected with mange or itch.
sgreabachd,(MS) *s.f.* Scabbiness. 2 Scurfiness.
sgreabair,* -ean, *s.m.* Mean fellow.
sgreab-chinn, *s.f.* Dandruff.
sgreabhag, -aig, -an, *s. m.* Omelet. 2 Crust. 3 Harl. 4(MS) Husk. 5**Scab.
sgreabhal,** -ail, *s. m.* Favour given by a newly-married couple. 2 Annual tribute of 3d. paid at the command of the monarch by the petty princes of Ireland to St. Patrick.
sgrèach, -a, -an, *s.f.* see sgreuch.
———ach, see sgreuchach.
———adh, see sgreuchadh.
———ag, see sgreuchag.
———agach, see sgreuchagach.
———an, -ain, see sgreuchan.
sgread, -a, -an, *s.m.* Screech, shriek, cry. 2 Squall, bawling. 3 Any shrill jarring noise. creaking noise, crushing noise, grating sound. * Gnash. 5** Clashing or crashing noise.
sgread, *pr. pt.* a' sgreadail & a' sgreadadh, *v.a.* Shriek, cry, screech, scream. 2 Make a harsh sound, creak. 3 Clash. 4 *Squall.
sgreadadh,** -aidh, *s.m.* Shrieking, screeching, creaking, squalling, squall, shriek, screech. 2 Creak, grating. 3 Clashing.
sgreadach, -aiche, *a.* That shrieks, shrieking, squalling. 2 Creaking, making a grating noise. 3* Argute. 4 Crashing. 5 Clashing.
sgreadachan,** -ain, *s.m.* Little squaller, shrieking child.
sgreadag, -aig, -an, *s. f. dim.* of sgread. Little shriek. 2 Sharp, sour drink. 3* Acid. 4** Shrieking female, shrill-voiced female. 5* Anything sour.
sgreadaich, *v.a.* Howl.
sgreadail, -e, *s.f.* Screeching, act of screeching, screaming or crying. 2 Continued shrieking. 3 Grating, shrill or clashing noise. 4* Gnashing. 5**Loud creaking. A' s—, *pr.pt.* of sgread.
sgreadair, -ean, *s.m.* Bawler, shrieker, screecher, brayer, crier. 2 One with a shrill voice.
sgreadalach,** *a.* Shrieking, screaming, bawling. crying. 2 Creaking, grating, clashing.
sgreadan, -ain, *s. m.* Disagreeable sound. 2 Noise of anything tearing asunder. 3 Creaking or grating noise. 4 Scream, shriek. 5 Bawler, shrill-voiced fellow. Cruaidh a' sgreadan air cruaidh, *steel grating on steel.*
———ach, -aiche, *a.* Making a disagreeable or grating sound. 2 Creaking, clashing. 3 Screaming.
sgreadhadh,* -aidh, *s.m.* Scissure, parchedness.
sgreadhail,* -e, -dhlaichean, *s.f.* Trowel. 2 (DU) Wooden trowel used for digging up spout-fish. 3 *pl.* used in the sense of Broken boards. Chaidh i 'na sgreadhlaichean, *she was smashed into fragments.*
sgreag, *pr.pt.* a' sgreagadh, *v.a. & n.* Dry, parch, shrivel, cause to shrivel. 2 Become dry, parched or shrivelled. 3* Dry the outside hurriedly without entering into the inner part.
sgreagach, -aiche, *a.* Dry, hard, shrivelled. 2 Rocky, parched (of soil.) 3 Stingy, penurious, mean.
sgreagadh, -aidh, *s.m.* Drying, parching. A' s—, *pr.pt.* of sgreag.
sgreagag, -aig, -an, *s.f.* Shrivelled old woman. 2 Penurious, stingy woman.
sgreagair, -ean, *s. m.* Shrivelled old man. 2 Close-fisted, stingy man.
sgreagan, -ain, -an, *s.m.* Anything dry, shrunk or shrivelled. 2** Hard, rocky ground. 3 (DMy) Cord placed about a span between the half hitches on the tops of fishing-rods. Talamh s.

hard, rocky ground.
————ach, -eiche, *a.* see sgreagach.
————ta, -ainte, *a.* see sgreagach.
sgreagar,** *a.* Rocky.
sgreamh, -eimhe, & -a, *s.m.* Loathing, abhorrence, disgust, nausea. 2** Disgusting sight. 3*Thin scum, rind or ugly skin. 4**Disgusting object. S. no sgaoim, *disgust or fear.—L. na Féinne, 208/3.* 5.(=fiamh no sgàth); ghabh e s., *he was disgusted.*
————ach, -aiche, see sgreamhail.
————achadh, -aidh, *s.m.* Nauseating, act of nauseating. A' s—, *pr.pt.* of sgreamhaich.
————aich, *v.a. & n.* Loathe, turn the stomach, disgust, abhor.
————aichte, *past pt.* of sgreamhaich. Disgusted, shocked.
————ail, -e, *a.* Loathsome, abominable, nasty, abhorrent, fearful, dreadful horrifying, disgusting, horrible. 2 Apt to take disgust.
————aileachd, see sgreamhalachd.
————alach,†† *a.* Disgusting.
————alachd, *s.f.ind.* Disgustfuluess, abominableness, loathing. 2 Fearfulness, dreadfulness. 3 Readiness to be shocked or disgusted.
————ladh,* *s.f.* Thick wettish rash through the skin.
sgrèanach,†† -aiche, *a.* Inclement, rough, stormy.
sgreang, -a, -an, *s. f.* ‡‡Wrinkle. 2 Wrinkled woman.
sgreangail, -e, *a.* Wrinkled, corrugated.
sgreann, *s.m.* Scowl—*Dàin I. Ghobha.*
†sgreapal,** -ail, *s.m.* Scruple (weight.)
†————ach,** *a.* In scruples (of weight.)
†sgreastadh,** -aidh, *s.m.* Destruction.
sgreat, *s.m.* Disgust, abhorrence, abomination.
sgreatachd, *s.f.* Same meanings as sgreamhalachd.
sgreataich,* *pr. pt.* a' sgreadachadh, *v.a. & n.* Horrify, highly disgust. 2 Loathe, abhor.
sgreataidh, -e, *a.* Same meanings as sgreamhail
————eachd, *s.f.* Same meanings as sgreamhalachd.
sgreatas, -ais, *s.m.* Queasiness.
sgreath,* see sgreubh, sgreag & sgreumh.
————ail, see sgreamhail.
sgreig,** *s.f.* Rocky ground.
sgreig,** *v.a.* Fry.
————eadh,** *s.m.* Frying.
sgrèiteachd, see sgreamhalachd.
sgreitheil,** *a.* see sgreamhail.
sgrèitidh, see sgreamhail.
sgrèitidheachd,** see sgreamhalachd.
sgreòd,(CR) *s.m.* Group, crowd—*W. of Ross-sh.*
sgreoth,* *v.a.* see sgreubh.
sgreothainn,** *s.f.* Straw used in the place of hair-cloth on a kiln. 2 Drawn straw.
sgreubh, *v.n.* Dry up, crack by drought, parch.
————ach,†† *a.* Drying, as by heat.
————adh, -aidh, *s. m.* State of drying up or cracking from drought. A' s—, *pr. pt.* of sgreubh.
sgreuch, *pr. pt.* a' sgreuchail, *v. n.* Scream, screech in a croaking and drawling manner. 2 Whoop. 3 Cry with a shrill and loud voice.
sgreuch, -a, -an, *s.m.* Scream, screech, shrill cry.
sgreuchach, -aiche, *a.* Screeching, screaming.
sgreuchadh, -aidh, see sgreuchail.
sgreuchag, -aig, -an, *s. f.* Jay. 2 Night-jar, screech-owl. 3 Shrill-voiced female.
————ach, -aiche, *a.* Abounding in jays. 2 Like a jay. 3 Shrill-voiced.
sgreuchag-choille,** *s.f.* Jay. 2 Screech-owl.
sgreuchag-oidhche,** *s.f.* Screech-owl.
sgreuchag-reilge,** *s.f.* Owl.
sgreuchail, -e, *s.f.* Shrieking, screeching, act of screeching or screaming. 2* Continuous screeching. 3 Whooping. [* gives *s. m.* for No. 2.] A' s—, *pr. pt.* of sgreuch.
sgreuchair,* -ean, *s.m.* Screecher, squaller.
sgreuchan, -ain, -an, *s.m.* One who screeches or screams. 2**Person with a shrill voice. 3** Vulture.
sgreuchan-coille,* *s.m.* Jay.
sgreuchan-craosach, *s.m.* Vulture, see fang.
sgreuchan-ıongach,(AF) *s.m* Vulture.
sgreubach, *a.* Wet, gusty, stormy, windy—*Argyll.*
sgreunach,‡ -aich, *s.m.* Shivering—*Arran.*
sgreuth,(CR) *v.a.* Shrivel, shrink with drought, as a tub—*Skye.* [sgrèidh in *Gairloch*—DU.]
sgriab,¶ *s.* Greater shearwater—*puffinus major.*
sgriach, -a, -an, *prov.* for sgreuch. 2 *s.m.* Score, scratch, streak.
sgriachag, -eig, -an, *prov.* for sgreuchag.
sgriachail, see sgreuchail.
sgriachan-criosach, see sgreuchan-craosach.
sgrib, -e, -ean, see sgriob.
sgribeag, -eig, *s.f.* Small griddle.
sgribh, *v.* see sgriobh.
sgribhinn, -e, -ean, *s.f.* Rugged, rocky side of a hill. 2**Rugged, sloping shore.
————each, -eiche, *a.* Rocky, having rugged sides(of hills.) 2 Having rugged, sloping shores.
————eachd,** *s.f.* Rockiness, ruggedness.
sgribhisg,** *s.f.* Notes, comments.
sgribhte, see sgriobhta.
sgrid,(AC) *v.* Scrape. 2* Breathe your last in consequence of laughing or weeping.
sgrid,(AH) *s.f.* Any small, stunted living thing. S. phaisde, s. laoigh, &c.
sgrid, -e, -ean, *s.f.* Breath. 2 The least breath of life or air. 3** Voice. 4* Gasp. Cha'n 'eil s. ann, *there is not a breath in him, he is quite dead.*
——ealachd, *s.f.* Life, vigour, liveliness. 2 (MS) Mettle.
——eil, -e, *a.* Lively, vigorous, active, sprightly.
sgrilleag,(AF) *s.f.* Sanderling, sandpiper.
sgrin,** -e, *s.f.* Shrine.
——each,** *a.* Having a shrine. 2 Like a shrine.
sgriob, *pr.pt.* a' sgriobadh, *v.a. & n.* Scrape, rub off the surface. 2 Scratch, tear, mark with slight incisions. 3** Carve, engrave. 4 Draw lines or strokes on any surface, draw scratches. 5 Make a furrow. 6 Scribble, scrape, write. 7 Sweep off, make bare by rubbing. 8 Carry off, take away. 9 Comb or curry as a horse. 10 Snatch. 11 Lay waste, make desolate by a calamity. 12*Drag or dredge for fish or oysters. S. leat e, *snatch* or *sweep it away with you;* a' sgriobadh 'sa phort, *dredging in the harbour;* a' sgriobadh buntàta, *scraping potatoes.*
sgriob, -a, -an, *s.f.* Scratch, track, mark, line. scrape. 2 Furrow, as of a plough. 3 Cart-rut. 4 Trip, journey, excursion. 5 Calamity, bereavement. 6 Itching of the lip, superstitiously supposed to portend, a kiss (s.-pòige), or s.-dibhe (*or* s.-drama), a dram. 7 Curry-comb. 8 Stroke of a whip-saw. 9†† Hurt. S. do 'n Ghalltachd, *a trip to the Lowlands;* thoir s. mu 'n cuairt, *take a turn round, make a circuit;* s. an t-sàibh mhóir, *a stroke of the whip-saw;* s.-croinn, *the furrow of a plough;* s. bhuntàta, *a drill of potatoes.*
sgriobach,‖ -aich, *s.f.* The itch, mange, scurvy. 2* Scotch or Highland fiddle.
sgriobach, -aiche, *a.* Scratching, scraping. 2 Prone to scratch or scrape. 3††Itching. 4 Furrowing. 5 Curry-combing.
sgriobachan,** -ain, *s.m.* Scraper. 2 Wooden instrument for raking ashes, wooden rake without teeth. S. na luaithre, *the wooden fire-shovel.*
sgriobadair, -ean, *s.m.* Scraper. 2 Nutmeg-grat-

er.
sgrìobadaireachd,†† *s.f.* Scraping.
sgrìobadan, -ain, -an, *s.m.* see sgrìobadair.
sgrìobadh, -aidh, *s.m.* Scraping, act of scraping or scratching. 2 Act of scribbling, drawing lines or furrows. 3 Act of carrying off or taking away. 4 Laying waste, act of laying waste. A' s—, *pr.pt.* of sgrìob.
sgrìobachan, -ain, -an, *s.m.* see sgrìobadair.
sgrìobag, -aig, -an, *s. f. dim.* of sgrìob. Slight scratch.
sgriobag,(AF) *s.f.* Cockle, see creachag.
sgrìobagach,†† *a.* Abounding in scratches.
sgrìobaidh, *fut.aff.a.* of sgrìob.
sgrìobair, -ean, *s.m.* Graving tool. 2 Scraper, scratcher. 3 Grater. 4* Dredge. 5*Curry-comb. 6 see sgrìoban.
sgrìobaireachd,** *s.f.ind.* Continued scraping or scratching. 2 Working with a graving tool.
sgrìoban, -ain, -an, *s.m.* Any kind of hoe, rake or scraper. 2 Wool-card. 3 Curry-comb. 4 Hand fishing-line. 5 Scraping. Dorghadh leis an sgrìoban, *fishing with the hand-line;* earba bheag an sgrìobain, *the scraping young roe—Donn.Bàn, p. 54.*—they have a habit of scraping with their fore-feet; gheibh cearc an sgrìobain rud-eigin, *the scratching hen will find something.*
sgrìobanach, -aiche, *a.* Abounding in rakes, &c. 2 Like a scraper, or curry-comb.
sgrìoban-dorobhaich, (DJM) *s. m.* Hand-line, used in bottom fishing for cod.
sgrìobar,** *fut. pass.* of sgrìob.
sgrìobh, *v.a.* Write, perform the act of writing. 2 Compose a book or writing. 3 Record. 4 **Engrave. S. d' a ionnsuidh, *write to him;* a' sgrìobhadh leabhair, *writing a book.*
sgrìobh, *s.m.* see sgrìobhadh.
sgriobha, *s.* & *v.* see sgrobha.
sgrìobhach, -aich, -aichean, *s.m.* Writer, scribe, clerk. 2 **Notary.
sgrìobhach, -aiche, *a.* Writing, that writes, composes or records. 2 Fond of writing, composing or recording.
sgrìobhadair, -ean, *s. m.* Writer, scribe, clerk. penman. 2 Notary. 3 Attorney.
sgrìobhadaireachd, *s.f.ind.* Writing, business of a writer, clerk or notary. 2 Attorneyship. 3 Penmanship.
sgrìobhadh, -aidh, -ean, *s.m.* Writing, penmanship. 2 Act of writing. 3 Composing, act of composing. 4 Recording, act of recording or committing to writing. 5* Handwriting. 6 Engraving. A' s—, *pr. pt.* of sgrìobh. Fath-sgrìobhaidh, *an appendix.*
sgrìobhadh, *past pass.* of sgrìobh.
sgrìobhaiche, see sgrìobhadair.
sgrìobhaichean,** *s.pl.* Writings. 2 Writers.
sgrìobhainnear,** -eir, *s.m.* Writer, clerk, scribe. 2 Notary. 3 Scrivener.
sgrìobhainn,** *s.f.* Bill, writ, evidence.
sgrìobhair, -ean, *s.m.* Writer, scribe, clerk, agent, penman. 2 Notary. 3 Attorney.
sgrìobhaireachd, see sgrìobhadaireachd.
sgrìobham, *1st. sing. imp.* of sgrìobh. Let me write. 2 *1st. fut.aff.a.* I will write.
sgrìobhar, *fut. pass.* of sgrìobh. Shall be written.
sgrìobh-lochd, -an, *s.m.* Fault or error in writing, erratum.
sgrìobh-thaigh,* *s.m.* Writer's office.
sgrìobhtach,** *a.* Writing. 2 Fond of writing. 3 Writing frequently.
sgrìobhta, *past pt.* of sgrìobh. Written, recorded, registered, composed.
sgriobtuir, -ean, *s.m.* Scripture.
————each, -eiche, *a.* Scriptural.
————eil,* *a.* Scriptural.
sgrìobhuinn,** -ean, *s.f.* Bill or evidence. 2 Writings.
sgrìoch,** *s.m.* Scratch, score, line, furrow.
sgrìoch,** *v.a.* Dash. 2 Scratch, score, notch, draw a line or furrow.
sgriodadh, -aidh, *s.m.* Shingle.
sgrìodan, -ain, -an, *s. m.* Stony ravine on a mountain side. 2 Track of a mountain torrent. 3 Continuous heap of small stones on a mountain side.
sgrìodanach, -aiche, *a.* Cleft by ravines. 2 Abounding in continuous heaps of small stones. 3 Like a mountain torrent. 4**Full of channels. 5* Like a mountain. 6**Of torrents.
sgriodanaich,(MS) *v.a.* Streak.
sgriogalach, *s.f.* Bare mountain top beyond the line of vegetation. Anns an sgriogalaich seo, *in this barren wilderness.*
sgrios, *pr.pt.* a' sgrios & a' sgriosadh, *v.a.* & *n.* Destroy, ruin, annihilate, consume. 2**Abolish. 3 Stumble, slip. 4* Scrape or sweep off the surface. 5*Ruin. Sgrìosaidh mi an duine, *I will destroy man;* a' sgriosadh an leathrach, *scraping the rind off the leather;* s. mo chas, *my foot slipped.*
sgrios, -a, -an, *s.m.* Destruction, ruin, annihilation. 2* Sweeping off a surface, scraping rind. 3*Stumbling, slip. Mo s., *my ruin!* bheir thu s. oirnn, *you will annihilate us.* [*s.f.]
sgriosach, -aiche, see sgriosail.
sgriosadair, -ean, *s.m.* Destroyer, pillager, one who lays waste.
sgriosadaireachd, *s.f.ind.* Destroying, sweeping away, annihilation, continued pillaging or wasting.
sgriosadh, -aidh, -aidhean, *s.m.* Destroying, act of destroying, or ruining. 2 Abolition, pillaging, destruction, waste, pillage. 3 Act of stumbling or slipping the foot. 4 Cutting or peeling off the skin by accident. 5 Act of opening an ulcer by paring off its surface with any sharp instrument. 6**Slip, tumble. A' s—, *pr.pt.* of sgrios.
sgriosag, -aig, -an, *s.f.* Wreath of yarn on a clew. 2 (DU) Small ball of yarn.
sgriosagach, -aiche, *a.* Made up in clews.
sgriosail, -e, *a.* Destructive, ruinous, pernicious. 2**Wasteful. 3** Slippery. 4**Apt to stumble.
sgriosalach,(AC) *s.m.* Cloud. 'Nan sgriosalaich móra, *in great clouds.*
sgriosalachd,** s. f. Balefulness, banefulness.
sgriosan, *s.m.* Trousseau—*Arran.* 2 (AH) Torrent of vituperation. Chuir e 'na s. dheth, *he lectured in very offensive language.*
sgriosar, *fut.pass.* of sgrios. Shall or will be destroyed.
sgrios-na-beithire, (AC) *s. m.* Destruction by lightning.
sgriosta, *past pt.* of sgrios. Destroyed, ruined.
sgriot,(DMu) *v.a.* *Suth'd.* for sgrùd (examine.)
sgriot,(DU) *s.f.* Tale of distress.
sgriotachan, -ain, *s. m.* Squalling creature, infant. 2* Child that is likely to die.
sgriotal, *s.m.* *Suth'd* for sgriothail.
sgrioth,‡ *s.m.* Gravel.
sgriothail,‡ *s. pl.* Lot of small items, as small potatoes—*Badenoch.* Chuir e sgriotal (sgriothail) dheth, *he spoke a great many words with little substance in them.* 2††Crowd of young creatures.
sgriothal,††-ail, *s.m.* Crowd of young creatures or small things.
sgriobh, see sgrobha.
sgrisleach, -eich, *s.m.* Tartar.
sgròb, *v.a.* Scratch, scrape with the nails. 2**

Scrawl.
sgròb, -a, -an, *s.f.* Scratch, scrape, line, scrawl.
sgròbach, -aiche, *a.* That scratches or scrapes, scrawling, scratching, inclined to scrape.
sgròbadair, -ean, *s.m.* Scratcher, scraper.
sgròbadaireachd, *s.f.* Scratching.
sgròbadh, -aidh, *s.m.* Scratching, act of scraping or scratching with talons or nails, scrawling, scratch, scrawl. A' s—, *pr.pt.* of sgròb.
sgròbag, -aig, -an, *s.f.* Slight scratch.
sgròbagach,†† *a.* Scratching.
sgròbaich, see sgròb.
sgròbair, -ean, see sgròbadair.
sgròbaireachd, *s.f.* Unskilful writing, scrawling.
sgròban, -ain, -an, *s.m.* Scraping or scratching with the nails or talons. 2 Crop of a bird. 3 Dewlap. 4**Gizzard.
sgròbanach, -aiche, *a.* Scratching. 2 That scratches with nails or talons. 3 Of, or belonging to, a bird's crop or gizzard. 4 Having a crop or gizzard. 5 Having a large crop or gizzard. 6 Hanging down, as a dewlap.
sgrobha, -a, -achan, *s.m.* Screw. 2**Vice. 3 see sgrath. 4**Corkscrew.
sgrobha, *v.a.* Screw.
sgrobhach, -aiche, *a.* Twisted, like a screw, spiral. 2 Having screws.
sgròb-bhèarnach, *a.* Do dheud s., *your scratched and distorted teeth—Donn. bàn, p. 183.*
sgroch, see sgròb.
———ail,* *v.a.* Scrawl, scribble.
———ladh, -aidh, *s. m.* Scrawling, scribbling. 2 Scrawl, scribble. A' s—, *pr.pt.* of sgrochail.
sgròd, *s.m.* Host, large number. S. chloinne, *a host of children* ; s. bhuntàta beaga, *a quantity of small potatoes—Dàin I. Ghobha.*—not good grammar,
sgrodha, see sgrobha.
sgrodhach, see sgrobhach.
sgrog, -oig, -an, *s.m.* The head, side of the head, *in ridicule.* 2 The neck, *in ridicule.* 3 Hat, bonnet. 4 Bite, mouthful. 5** Skull-cap. 6 ††Biting word. 7 see sgrogag. A sgrog, *his nob*—an expression used in playing cribbage.
——,(AF) *s.f.* Old cow or ewe. 2††Shrivelled person.
sgrog, *v.a.* Put on the bonnet firmly, pull on, as a helmet. 2 Doff. 3 Cock. 4 Compress, shrivel. 5 Become shrivelled. 6 Do away with. 7 *Bite, as a horse. 8††Nag. S. e mi, *he bit me* ; s. do bhoineid ort, *tighten your bonnet on your head* ; s. e am balach, *he killed the fellow.*
sgrogach, -aiche, *a.* Shrivelled. 2 Impotent. 3 Mean, contemptible. 4 Having a hat or bonnet.
sgrogadh, -aidh, *s.m.* Act of putting on a hat or bonnet. 2 Shrivelling, act of shrivelling. 3 State of becoming shrivelled. 4 Act of doing away with, finishing. A' s—, *pr.pt.* of sgrog.
sgrogag, -aig, -an, *s.f.* Anything shrivelled and contemptible. 2 Little old woman. 3 Useless old timber. 4 Stunted growing timber. 5** Oath. 6(AF) Old cow or ewe. 7††Little horn. 8(CR) Crumpled horn—*W. of Ross-shire.* 9(CR) Mythical aquatic animal—*Skye.* 10 (DU) Drinking-horn. Làn na sgrogaig, *a hornful (of liquor)*; bèist na sgrogaig, *the unicorn in armorial bearings.*
sgrogaid,* *s.f.* Old hat or cap.
sgrogair,-ean, *s.m.* Shrivelled old fellow. 2 Biter. carper.
sgrogan,** -ain, *s. m.* Skull-cap. 2 (DU) Little man, dwarfish person.
sgroganach, *s.m.* Short-necked man. S. de bhodach còir, *a thick-set, sturdy, elderly kind little man.—Sgeul.-nan-caol, p. 294.*
sgroid,(AC) *v.a.* Search.
sgroidhseach,(CR) *s.f.* Hag, cormorant—*W. of Ross-shire.*
sgroig,†† -e, -ean, *s.f.* see sgroigean.
sgroig, *gen.sing* of sgrog. [*nom.* in *Gairloch*—DU.]
sgroigean, -ein, -an, *s.m.* see sgruigean.
sgròill, -ean, *s.f.* Peeling, paring, anything torn off.
sgròill, *v.a.* Peel, pare, excoriate.
sgròille,** *s.f.* Peeling, paring. 2 Any part that is torn off a skinned or coated surface.
sgròilleach, -eiche, *a.* Peeling, excoriating, that peels or pares. 2 In peels or parings. 3**Apt to peel or pare.
sgròilleachadh,** *s.m.* Scarification.
sgròilleag, -eig, -an, *s.f. dim.* of sgròill. Little peeling or paring. 2**Scale. 3 Any part torn from a coated surface.
sgròilleagach, -aiche, *a.* see sgròilleach.
sgròillich, see sgròill.
sgroingean,** *s.m.* Barebone, curmudgeon.
sgroingeanach,** *a.* Close-handed, illiberal.
sgròingeanachd,** *s.f.* Illiberality.
sgroinneach, *a.* Ragged—*Arran.*
sgroitheach, -eiche, *a.* see sgrathach.
sgroithean, *n.pl.* of sgroth.
sgròl,(CR) *s.m.* Multitude, crowd, great number. S. chloinne, *a crowd of children—W. of Ross-shire.*
†sgroll,* *s.m.* Large wide piece.
sgroth, -oith, -oithean, *s.m.* see sgrath.
sgrothach, -aiche, see sgrathach.
sgrothach,§ -aich, *s.m.* Sea furbelows, bulbous-rooted tangle—*laminaria bulbosa.*
sgrothachd,(MS) *s.m.* Scaliness.
sgrothadh, see sgrathadh.
sgrothaiche,(MS) *s.m.* Epidermis, morphew.
sgrub, *s.m.* Hesitation, scruple.
sgrub, *v.a.* & *n.* Hesitate, delay. 2 Be niggardly, act in a niggardly manner.
sgrubadh, -aidh, *s.m.* Delaying, act of hesitating or delaying. 2 Act of playing the niggard. 3 Scrubbishness. 4 Draught (liquid.) A' s—, *pr.pt.* of sgrub.
sgrubail, -e, *a.* Hesitating, dallying. 2 Scrupulous. 3 Niggardly, parsimonious.
sgrubair, -ean, *s.m.* Churl, niggard, miser, scrub.
sgrubaireachd, *s.f.ind.* Churlishness, scrubbishness.
sgrubal, -ail, -an, *s.m.* Scruple. 2 Doubt.
sgrubalach,†† *a.* In scruples. 2** Hesitating, scrupulous.
sgrubanta,* see sgrubail.
sgrùd, *v. a.* Search, scrutinize, pry, examine. 2**Question.
sgrùdach,** *a.* Examining, catechising, questioning, prying, searching, inquisitive, investigating.
sgrùdachadh, -aidh, *s.m.* & *pr.pt.* of sgrùdaich, see sgrùdadh.
sgrùdadh, -aidh, *s.m.* Searching, act of searching, scrutinizing, prying, examining, questioning, investigation. 2 Search. 3 Inquisitiveness, curiosity. 4 Audit (of accounts.) Utmost scraping of anything in a dish. A's—, *pr. pt.* of sgrùd. A' s. gach ionaid, *searching every place.*
sgrùdaich, *v.a.* see sgrùd.
sgrùdaichte, *past pt.* of sgrùdaich. Tried, examined, searched.
sgrùdair, -ean, *s.m.* Searcher, investigator, scrutinizer.
sgrùdaireachd, *s.f.* Searching.
sgrugaill,(CR) *s.f.* Neck of a bottle. 2 Neck of a hen—*Suth'd.*
sgruibleach, -ich, *s.f.* Refuse, rubbish.
sgruibleachan,** -ain, -an, *s.m.* Scribbler.

sgrùidte, *past pt.* of sgrùd, see sgrùdaichte.

sgruigean,‡-ein,-an,*s.m.* Neck of a bottle, or anything shaped for the hand. 2 The neck, *in ridicule.* 3**Short neck, *in ridicule.* 4**Short-necked person, *in ridicule.* 5 Hat, bonnet. Rug i air an s. air, *she grasped him by the neck.*

sgruigeanach,** *a.* Short-necked.

sgruig dheiridh, *s.f.* Parts of stern-post about the gunwale.

sgruig thoisich, *s.f.* Parts of stem-post about the gunwale.

sgruimbean, -ein, -an, *s m.* Scrub.

sgruimbeanach, *a.* Scrubbed.

sgruinge,** *s.f.* Ensign.

sgruit, -ean, s. *m.* Old, shrivelled person. 2 Thin, meagre person. 3**Old man. 4**Niggard. 5(AF) Lean, hard cow. 6**Harangue. 7* Old decayed person. 8**Old hard-featured person.

sgruiteach, -eiche, *a.* Old, withered, wrinkled. 2 Meagre, thin. 3**Niggardly.

sgrum, *s. m.* Shell of the same shape and colour as a mussel, but smaller. They are used when ground small to entice coal-fish into the bag which catches them.

sgrung,(DMK) *s.* Ill-conditioned animal, one having a hard, skinny, bony appearance—*Rob Donn.*

sgrut, see sgruit.

sgrutach,** -aich, *s.m.* Itch.

sgrutach, see sgruiteach.

sgruthan, -ain, *s. m.* Shock of corn—*Assynt.* [sgru'an.]

sguab, -aib, *s.m.* Besom, broom, brush. 2 Sheaf of corn. 3 The plant bealaidh (from which brushes are made.) 4**Sweepings, refuse. S. choirce, *a sheaf of oats* ; mar leus air an s., *like a flame on the sheaf*; s.-aodaich, *clothes'-brush* ; s.-làir, s-ùrlair, *floor-brush* ; s.-deannaich, *whisk.*

sguab, *pr.pt.* a' sguabadh, *v. a.* Sweep, sweep away, brush. 2**Bind into sheaves. 3**Move quickly or with a sweep. 4†† Clean with a broom or besom.

sguab, *s.m.* Extinguisher, hollow, conical shaped apparatus for putting out a candle without smell or spilling of grease.

sguabach, -aiche, *a.* Abounding in sheaves. 2 Sweeping, that sweeps, brushing. 3 Cleanly, cleansing. 4 Moving with a sweep.

sguabach, -aich, -aichean,*s.f.* Besom, floor-brush

sguabachan, -ain, -an, *s.m. dim.* of sguabach, see sguabag.

sguabachail, *a.* Sweepy.

sguabadair, -ean, see sguabair.

sguabadh, -aidh, *s.m.* Sweeping, act of sweeping, brushing or cleaning. 2 Sweeping motion. 3** Sweepings, refuse. A' s—, *pr. pt.* of sguab. Meòir a' s. na cruit, *fingers sweeping nimbly along theharp-strings.*

sguabag, -aig, -an, *s.f. dim.* of sguab. Little besom, whisk. 2 Small sheaf of corn. 3 Smart breeze of wind. 4**Female that moves with a sweeping gait. 5†† Gusty wind. Tri là Sguabag, *three days, the 7th., 8th., and 9th. of April.*

sguabaichean,***n.pl.* of sguabach.

sguabair, -ean, *s.m.* Sweeper.

sguabaireachd, *s.f.* Sweeping.

sguabair-luidheir, *s.m.* Chimney-sweep.

sguaban aodaich, *s.m.* Clothes'-brush.

sguaban-stòthaidh, *s.m.* Resource. Is mairg do 'n s. bò mhaol odhar MhicGhill'Eoinidh, *pity him whose resource is MacGillony's hornless dun cow.* Macintosh says that MacGillony was a famous hunter in the Grampians, and several vestiges of his temporary huts were still to be seen in 1785, in the mountains of Atholl. His " dun cow " was the wild mountain doe. Macintosh gives *staghail* (an unknown word) for *stòthaidh*, which makes the proverb meaningless. S. means the cutting of corn short, as would be done for a hasty supply. The MacGillonies belonged to the Clan Cameron, but were originally allied to the Macleans.—NGP.

sguabanta, *a.* Portable, trim.

sguab-ghàbhaidh** (an), *s.f.* The banner of Oscar, son of Ossian.

sguabhair,** -bhrean, *s.f.* Square.

sguab-lìon, *s.f.* Trawl or sweep-net, drag-net.

sguabta, *past pt.* of sguab. Swept, brushed.

sguaib, -e, -ean, *s.f.* see sguab.

sguaibte, see sguabta.

sguaigeis, -e, *s.f.* Coquetry, flirtation.

sguain, -e, *s.f.* Train of dress, tail. 2 Crowd, swarm. Gille-sguain, *a train-bearer.*

sguainseach *s. f.* Hussey, hoyden—*Argyll.*

sguair,** Gaelic form of *square* or *squire.*

sguan,(AC) *s.m.* Slur, slander, gossip.

sguasaichean,(DMK)*s.pl.* Long narrow and thin strips of wood laid across the thatch of a house to keep it in position—*Lochbroom.*

sguch, *v.a.* Sprain or strain a joint.

sguch,(CR) *v.n.* Move, stir. Na sguchaibh,*don't move, sit still—Suth'd & Farr.*

sguchadh, -aidh, -aidhean, *s.m.* Sprain, strain. 2 Spraining, act of spraining a limb A' s—, *pr.pt.* of sgruch.

sguchta, *past pt.* of sguch. Sprained.

sgùd, -ùid, -an, *s.m.* Scout, spy. 2 Cluster. †3 Ship. 4 Ketch (boat)—*Hebrides.*

sgud, *pr.pt.* a' sgudadh, *v.a.* Lop. prune, cut off at one stroke,hew down. 2 Curtail. 3 Snatch. 4 Abscond. 5**Walk quickly.

sgùd, -a, -an, *s.m.* Dirty water, foul drops.

sgudach,** -aiche *a.* Walking quickly, or with a sweeping gait. 2 Lopping off, hewing down at a blow. 3 Absconding.

sgùdach,** *a.* Spying, apt to spy. 2 Abounding in dirty water or foul drops.

sgùdachd,** *s.f.* Espionage, habit of spying. 2 Frequent spying or scouting.

sgudachd,** *s.f.* Continued cutting. 2 Sweeping gait. 3 Nimble motion.

sgudadh, -aidh, *s.m.* Lopping off cleverly, hewing down at a blow. 2**Sweeping gait. A' s—, *pr.pt.* of sgud.

sgudag,** -aig,*s.f.* Female with a sweeping gait. 2 Active, tidy girl.

sgudal, -ail, -an, *s.m.* Fish guts, offal, filth. 2 *Trash, refuse of anything.

sgudalach,†† -aiche, *a.* Abounding in offal or filth.

sgudalair, see sguidilear.

sguga, -n & -chan, *s.m. & f.* Coarse clumsy person. 2††Person in a crouching posture.

sgugach, -aiche, *a.* Coarse, clumsy. 2 (DU)Shy and awkward.

sgugach,* -aich, *s.m.* Soft, boorish fellow.

sgugairneach,(AF) *s. m.* Useless or worthless bird. 2 see sgug. S. de dh' ian deireadh Foghair, 's mairg a dh' fheith ri d' bhreith 's a' Mhàrt, *useless bird at harvest-end, pity those who waited for your birth in March*—applied to clumsy workers, more in the way than useful.—NGP.

sguibhir,** *s.m.* Squire, esquire.

sguiblich,** *v.a.* Tuck up.

sguich,(AH) *s.f.* Booty, spoil, plunder—*Argyll.*

sguideireachd, see sguidilearachd.

sguidilear, -eir, -an, *s.m. & f.* Dirty drudge, scullion.

sguidilearachd, *s.f.ind.* Foul drudgery, sluttishness.
sguids, *v.a.* Thrash, switch, lash. 2 Drive. 3 Dress flax. (*Scots*, skutch.)
sguidseach, -ich,-ichean, *s.m.* & *f.* Stripling,*prov.* 2*Very tall, slender young man. 3 Prostitute, *prov.* 4††Lank young girl.
sguidseadh, -idh, *s.m.* Switching, act of switching, thrashing or lashing. 2 Act of dressing flax. A' s—,*pr.pt.* of sguids. Deireadh mo sgéil mo s., *the end of my tale will be whipping.*—*i.e.* confess and be hanged.
sguidsear,** -eir, *s.m.* Beetle, thresher, dresser of flax.
sguidseineach, -ich, *s.m.* see sguidseach.
sguidsich,** see sguids.
sguilbneach, see guilbneach.
sguil,* *s.* Tray.
sgùile, see sgùlan.
sguileach,** -ich. *s.m.* Rubbish, refuse.
sgùilean, -ein, -an, see sgùlan.
sguilear,(CR) *s.m.* Mean, contemptible fellow—*south end of Arran.*
sguille,** *s. m.* Kitchen-boy. 2 Scullery.
sguilleir,** *s.m* Scullery.
sguir, *pr.pt.* a' sgur & a' sgurachd, *v.a.* & *n.*Stop cease, leave off, terminate, desist, settle. 2 ††Cause to stop. S. dheth, *desist, be done with it; mu'n do s. sinn, before we stopped;* nach s. thu? *will you not stop?*
sguirb,** *s.f.* Cessation.
sguirbeadh,** -idh, *s.m.* Condemning, condemnation.
sgùird, -e, -ean, *s.f.* The lap. 2 Lapful. 3 Shift, smock. 4 Apron. 5 Skirt.
sgiùrd, *v.* see sgiord.
———each,†† -eiche, *a.* In lapfuls.
sgùird-shoirbheis,(MS) *s.f.* Mackerel-gale.
sguiridh, *fut.aff.a.* of sguir.
sgùirt, -e, -an, see sgiord.
———e, see sgiordte.
sguit, -e, *pl.* -ean & -ichean, *s.f.* Board on the bottom of an open boat, fore and aft, on which passengers place their feet, foot-board. 2 Stern-seat in a boat. 3 *s.pl.* *Skates. 4(DM K) Basket used for holding wool, something of the shape of a beehive and made of straw or twigs—*Lochbroom.*
sguit, -ean, *s.m.* Wanderer.
sguit, *locative* of sgot. Piece of land cut off another.
sguit-dheiridh, } see bàta, p. 77.
sguit-thoisich, }
sguiteal, Gaelic spelling of *scuttle.*
sguithe,(AF) *s.* Pig.
sguitlear,** -eir, *s.m.* Low, menial drudge.
———achd,** *s.f.* Menial drudgery, scullery.
sguits, see sguids.
sguitseach, see sguidseach.
sguitseadh, see sguidseadh.
sguitsear, see sguidsear.
sgula, *s.m.* see sgulag.
sgulag, *s.f.* Little person.
sgulag, -aig, -an, *s.f.* Basket for holding the linen—*Suth'd.* 2 see sgalag. 2 Basket for fishing-lines.
sgulair, -ean, *s. m.* Large old hat.
sgùirteach,** *s.* Skirted. 2 Having a shirt or smock.
sgùlan, -ain, -an, *s.m.* Wicker basket for fishing-lines. 2 Potato-basket. [*u* short in *Arran*—CR.] 3 Large coarse basket made of willow twigs, hamper. 4 Creel.
sgulan, -ain, -an, *s. m.* Little old man. 2 Old man.
———ach,(AC) *a.* Flippant.
———ach,(AC) -aich, *s. m.* Flippancy. 2 Evil-speaking. Shallow person.
sgùlan-làimhe, *s.m.* Maund.
sgùm, *s.m.* Foam, scum. 2‡‡Refuse. S. an t-saoghail, *the refuse of mankind.*
's gu 'm, And so that. Tog brigh do chluiche 's gu 'm faighinn a bhi 'g imeachd, *take the stake of your game, so that I may get away*—*W.H.1.12.*
sgùmach,** *a.* Scummy, frothy.
sgùmadair, -ean, *s.m.* Scummer.
———eachd,** *s.f.* Business of scumming. 2 Continued scumming.
sgùman, -ain, -an, *s.m.* Bag formed by temporarily gathering up the four corners of a square of cloth, and often used as a strainer. 2 Skirt, train tucked up. 3 Tawdry head-dress. 4 ‡Sack of corn. 5 Lock of hair on the forehead, especially of sheep. 6 Baling-dish for a boat. 7**Skimming-dish. 8 Stack of corn—McL & D.
sgùmag,(AH)*s.m.*see sgùman. 2 Untidy person. [dowdy, *prov.*
sgumhan,(AC) -ain, *s.m.* Lobe.
sgumhara,** *a.* Fat.
sgumrag, -aig, -an, *s.f.* Fire-shovel. 2 Slattern,
sgumragach, -aiche, *a.* Slovenly. 2**Slatternly.
sgùr, *pr.pt.* a' sgùradh, *v.a.* Scour, wash, clean, rub up, purge. 2 Purify. 3 Burnish. A' sgùradh nan iarunn, *polishing the fire-irons.*
sgur, *s.m.* Desisting, ceasing, leaving off,giving over, cessation, stopping. 2** Termination, conclusion. A' s—, *pr.pt.* of sguir. Buidheachas gun s., *thanks without ceasing;* gun s., *unceasingly.*
sgùrach,** *a.* Aperient. 2 Scouring, burnishing, cleansing, purging, purifying.
sgurachd, *s.f.* & *pr.pt.* of sguir, see sgur.
sgurachdainn,* see sgur.
sgùradair,** *s.m.* Burnisher, cleanser.
sgùradh, -aidh, *s.m.*Cleansing, act of cleansing, scouring, burnishing, purging, purifying. A' s—, *pr.pt.* of sgùr.
sgùrainn, *s.f.* Washing-water, scourings, ley, toplash. 2**Water in which much soap has been dissolved in the course of clothes-washing, called in Broad Scots, *sapple.* 3††Seeds. 4* Any trash of liquor, *in contempt.*
sgur-éild,** see sgòr-éild.
sgùrr, -a, -an, *s.m.* High, sharp-pointed hill. 2 Large conical hill (sgor.)
sgùrrach, *a.* Rugged.
sgurt,* see sgiut.
sgut, see sgud.
sgùt, -ùit, see sgùd.
sgùtach, see sgudach.
sgutach,** see sgudach.
sgùtachd, see sgùdachd.
sgutachd, see sgudachd.
sguth, *s.* Sprain.

sh,

For all words beginning with *sh*, see under *s.*

shios, *adv.* Down, in position.
si, *pers.pron.* She, see i. *S.* is never used to denote the object after the verb like *i.* Phòs e i, *he married her.*
's i, *contr.* for is, *v.*+i, *pers.pron.* It is she. 'S i rogha nam ban òg, *she is the choice of damsels.*
's i, *contr.* for is, *conj*+i, *pers.pron.* And she. 2 As she. 3 Whilst she.
sia, *a.* see sè.
siab, *pr.pt.* a' siabadh & a' siabail, *v.a.* & *n.*Rub, wipe, cleanse by rubbing. 2 Drift, as snow. 3 Sweep along, pass by with quick motion. 4 Skim. 5 Snatch, snatch away, 6 Breathe away dust. 7 Fish, angle. 8(CR) Cast a line in angling, " whip " a steam. 9(DC)Blow away, as thatch off a house in a storm—*Uist.*

A' cur 's a' siabadh, *snowing and drifting.*
siab,** *s.m.* Wipe, rub. 2 Cleansing. 3 Flinching. Thug e s. dha, *he gave it a rub.*
——ach, -aiche, *a.* Wiping, rubbing, cleansing by rubbing. 2 Passing along with a quick continuous motion. 3 Snatching, that snatcheth. 4 Flinching. 5 Sarcastic, cutting.
——adh, -aidh, *s.m.* Wiping, act of wiping or rubbing. 2 Cleansing by rubbing. 3 Act of passing along with quick continuous motion. 4 Snatching, act of snatching away. 5 Breathing away. 6††Sweeping. 7††Plying a fishing rod. 8 Drifting—*Arran.* A' s—, *pr.pt.* of siab.
siabail,** *a.* Abstergent.
siabail (a'), *pr.pt.* of siab. Angling—*W. of Ross-shire.*
siabair, -ean, *s.m.* Wiper, one who wipes or rubs. 2 Snatcher, one who snatches. 3 Awkward fellow. 4 Cleanser. 5 **Sarcastic fellow.
siabaireachd, *s.f.* Wiping, rubbing. 2 Awkwardness.
siaban, -ain, *s.m.* Sand-drift, *prov.* 2 Sea-spray. 3 ††Slight shower. The dry sand in which the muran (sea-maram) always grows is called s. when it drifts in a storm. The breaking of sea waves in a storm drifts in the same manner, and is called " s. nan tonn móra."
siabh, -a, -an, *s.m.* Dish of stewed periwinkles. —*Hebrides.* 2††Broth of grouse.
siabh,‡ *v.* see siab.
———ach, see siabach.
siabhadh, see siabadh.
siabhair,* *v.a.* Tease, weary out.
———eachd,†† *s.f.* Skimming about like a swallow.
siabhrach,‡ -aich, -aichean, *s. m.* Fairy. 2†† Ghost. [also siabhraich, *s.f.*]
siabhas, -ais, -an, *s.m.* Idle ceremony.
siabhasach, -aiche, *a.* Idly ceremonious.
siabuinn, *gen.sing.* of siabunn.
siabunn, -uinn, *s.m.* Soap.
siabunnach, -aiche, *a.* Soapy.
siabunn-nam-ban-sìth, *s.m.* Milkwort—*Colonsay.*
siacair, see siachair.
siach, *v. a.* Sprain or strain a joint. 2 (CR) Avoid—*Strathtay.* 3**Filter.
siachadh, -aidh, *s.m.* Sprain, spraining, act of spraining. 2 Scratch on the skin. 3**Filtering. A' s—, *pr.pt.* of siach.
siachair, -ean, *s.m.* Pithless wretch.
siachaireach, -eiche, *a.* Pithless, contemptible.
siachaireachd, *s.f.ind.* Pithlessness, want of spirit.
siachaireil, -e, *a.* Selfish.
sia-chasach, *a.* see sè-chasach.
sia-chearnach, *a.* sè-chearnach.
sia-chearnag, see sè-chearnag.
siach-inntinn, see seacha-inntinn.
's iad, *contr.* for is, *v.*+iad, *pers.pron.* It is they. 2 They were the persons. [they.
's iad, *contr.* for is, *conj.*+iad, *pers. pron.* And
siad, *pers.pron.* This pronoun is another form of *iad*, but it is not, like *iad*, employed to denote an object after an active verb. *S.* is used in such expressions as, Mharbh s. iad, *they killed them.* [The Gael never say, mharbh iad siad.]
siad, see seòd.
siad,* *v. n.* Sheer, go obliquely. 2**Sneak, skulk.
siad, -a, -an, *s.m.* Stink. 2 Laziness, sloth. 3 ‡‡Filthiness. 4 Fusty smell.
siadach,†† -aiche, *a.* Having a fusty smell.
siadair, -ean, *s.m.* Stinkard. 2 Filthy person. 3 Lazy fellow, shuffler. 4 Sneaking fellow. 5 Buzzard. 6* Sly, skulking fellow. 7**Booby. numskull.
siadair,* *v.n.* Stink.
siadaireachd, *s. f.* Filthiness. 2 Laziness. 3 Slinking, shuffling, sly conduct, sneaking. 4 Meanness. 5 Stupidity.
sia-deug, see sè-deug.
siadha, (AC) Testicle. S. coin-ghèarr, *the testicle of the wolf.*
siadhail,** *s.f.* Sloth, sluggishness.
siadhan, -ain, *s.m.* State of confusion.
siadhan,** *a.* Confused, topsy-turvy.
sialach, *a.* Harum-scarum—*Arran.*
siaman, see sìoman.
siamarlan,** -ain, *s.m.* Gaelic spelling of *chamberlain.* 2 Factor. 2 Land-agent.
sian, -ine, -tan, *s. m.* Shriek, scream, roar. 2 *Squeal. 3**Voice. 4 (AC) Soft, sorrowful music, generally applied to the music heard in a fairy knoll. 5* Drawling scream. 6(DC) Appearance. S. fala mu d' shùilean, *an appearance of blood about your eyes.*
sian, -a, -tan, see seun.
——, *v.a.* see seun.
sian, *pr.pt.* a' sianail, *v. n.* Scream, cry, shriek. 2*Squeal. 3 Yell, bellow. 4 Scream tediously, raising one's voice gradually.
sian, -ine, -an, *s. m.* Pile of grass. 2 Beard of barley.
sian, *s.m.ind.* see sìon.
sian, -ine, *pl.* siantan, siantaidh & siantaidhean, *s.f.* Any storm, as wind, snow or rain. 2 Season. 3 *in pl.* The elements. An dèidh tàirneanaich a' gheamhraidh thig aon chuid sìde ro mhath no sìde nan seachd siantan, *after winter thunder, comes either very good weather or the weather of the seven elements*—that is, the roughest weather that could possibly come—a mixture of wind and rain, snow and frost, thunder and lightning, and hailstone. 4** Blast. 5 (DC) Age, period. Gu sian-saoghail, *to the world's end.*
sianach,** *a.* Screaming, shrieking, yelling, roaring. 2 Stormy, showery. 3 see seunach.
sianach, (AF) *s.m.* Monster.
sianachd,** *s.f.ind.* Screaming, shrieking, yelling. 2 Storminess, continued showers or blasts.
sianadh, -aidh, *s.m. & pr.pt. Prov.* for seunadh.
sianaiche,** *s. m.* One who shrieks, screams, roars or yells. 2 (DC) Changeling, fairy-child.
sianail, -e, *s.f.* Screaming, crying, shrieking, squealing, yelling. 2 Act of squealing or yelling. 3* Drawling, squealing. A' s—, *pr. pt.* of sian.
——,** *a.* Screaming, shrieking, yelling. 2 Stormy. 3 Showery.
sianan, see seunan.
sia'nar, see sèathnar.
sianar,** *a.* Stormy. 2 Showery.
sianas,** -ais, *s.m.* Hate, hating.
———ach,** *a.* Harmonious, melodious, pleasant. 2 Doleful.
sian-steud,** *s.m.* Driving blast. A' casgadh sian-steuda nan speur, *calming the driving blasts of the sky.*
sian-bhuailte, *past pt.* Weather-beaten.
———-——ach,** *a.* Exposed to the weather.
sian-bhualadh,** -aidh, *s.m.* Beating of wind or weather.
siann, *a.* see sionn.
siannt, *a.* see sionn.
sianntan, see siantan.
siansadh,** -aidh, *s.m.* Harmony, melody. 2 Pleasantness.
siansan,** *s.* Hum.
siant, (*poetical*) *n.pl.* of sian.
siantach,** *a.* Stormy, rainy, showery, snowy.
———d,** *s.f.* Storminess. 2 Showiness.

siantaidh, *n.pl.* of sian.
————, -ean, *s.m.* Hardy man, hero.
siantan, *pl.* of sian.
siap,* *v.n.* see sèap & siab.
siapach, see siabach.
siapadh, see siabadh.
siapunn, see siabunn.
siar, *a.* The west, westward. 2 Back, backward, behind. 3 Sideways, aside. 4** Onwards. Gu tràigh s., *to a western shore ;* ruith e s. le tartar, *he rushed onwards with a noise;* siar ort, *to the westward of you.*
——,†† *a.* Oblique.
siar, *pr.pt.* a' siaradh, *v.a. & n.* Cast awry, move or throw obliquely or awkwardly. 2* Lurch. 3††Waste. 4 Decay. 5 (CR) Sprain—*Skye.* Sh. mi mo chas, *I sprained my ankle.*
siarachd, *s.f.* Melancholy.
siaradh, -aidh, -aidhean, *s.m.* Casting. 2 Act of casting obliquely. 3††Oblique line. 4†† Decaying. 5 (MS) Caracole. 6 (DU)Obliquity of vision—*Gairloch.* A' s—, *pr.pt.* of siar. Tha leann dubh air mo sh., *melancholy is wasting me.*—R. 71.
siaraich, *v.* see siar.
siaraidhean,(CR) *s.pl.* Rheumatism, (*lit.* contortions)—*Suth'd.*
siarainnich, *pr.pt.* a' siarainneachadh, *v.n.* Languish, pine away. 2††Turn, become sour, as milk.
sia-ràmhach, see sè-ràmhach.
siaranachadh, -aidh, *s.m.* Languishing. 2 State of languishing or pining away. A' s—, *pr.pt.* of siaranaich.
siaranaich, *pr.pt.* a' siaranachadh, *v.n.* Languish, pine away.
siar-shùil, -shùla, -shùilean, *s.f.* Squint-eye. 2 **Oblique or side look.
————each, -eiche, *a.* Looking awry. 2 Squint-eyed.
sias, (for sìos.) Cha bhi slat a sìas (sìos) o chrùn deth, miann gach sùl e anns an fhaidhir, *not a yard of it will be less than a crown, 'twill be sought by everyone at the market—Donn. Bàn. p. 155.*
†siasar, -air, *s.m.* Session, sitting of a court assizes.
sia-shlisneach, see sè-shlisneach.
sia-shlisneag, see sè-shlisneag.
siasnadh, *s.m.* Wasting, decaying, fading away, —*Rob Donn.*
siat,** *s.m.* Tumour, swelling, puffing up.
——,** *v.n.* Swell, puff up.
siataidh ! *int.* Puss ! (call to a cat.)
siatag, *s.f.* Sciatica, rheumatism.
siathamh, see sèathamh.
sibean, see sioban. 'Nuair a chuir iad sinn air tìr am measg sìbein (siabain) is murain, *when they landed us 'mid sand-drift and sea-bent—Duanaire,71 ;* thog bàrr-ghucag fairge gu sibean (siaban), *the foam of the sea rose to spindrift—Sgeulaiche-nan-caol, p. 101.*
sibh, *pers. pron. 2nd. pers. pl.* Ye, you. [Used instead of *thu*, when addressing a person older or of higher social rank than the speaker, also when speaking to more than one person collectively of any age or rank. In *Arran*, the use of *thu* and *sibh* is determined solely by number, and never by age or rank, except that old people say *sibh* to a minister—CR.] *Emphatic forms*, sibh-se, sibh-féin, *yourself, yourselves.* 'Dé a nì sibh ? *what will ye do ?*
sibheag,(DC) *s.f.* Wick of a lamp—*Uist.*
sìbhealta, -eilte, *a.* see sìobhalta.
————chd, see sìobhaltachd.
sìbheilt, see sìobhalt.
————eachd, see sìobhaltachd.

sibhin,§ s. Bulrush, see luachair-ghobhlach.
sìbhreach,* -eich, -an, *s.m.* Fairy, spectre, apparition.
sìbhreachail,* -e, *a.* Fairy-like.
sibhreag,(CR) *s.f.* Fairy.
sibh-se, *emphatic form* of sibh.
sibht,* Gaelic spelling of *shift.* Plan, contrivance, subterfuge.
sibhteach,** *a.* Full of shifts, schemes or plans, contrivant.
sibhtealachd, *s.f.* Providentness. 2**Contrivance. 3 Cunning, craftiness.
sibhteil, -e, *a.* Shifty, inventive. 2 Provident, thrifty.
sic, -e, -ean, *s.f.* The prominence of the belly. 2 Peritonium. 3 The inner skin which is next the viscera in animals. 4 (AC) see sicean. Bhris an t-sic, *the inner skin broke ;* màm-sic, *rupture, hernia.* 5 see seic.
sic,(CR) -e, -ean, *s. f.* Snatch. 2 Attempt. 3 Sudden effort to take hold of one. 4** Sudden personal onset, swoop. 5** Firmness, strength. 6**Inside of the skull. Rug e le s., *he grasped suddenly ;* thug an cù s. air, *the dog snapped at him ;* thug e s. as a dhéidh, *he made a snap after him. All from Perthshire.*
sic, *v.n.* Dash to, lay hold of.
†sic, *a.* Dry, parched, droughty.
sice,§ *s.f.* see craobh-shice.
sicean,(AC) *s.m.* Particle, grain, infinitessimal quantity. S. sil, *a small grain of seed.*
sichd, -e, -ean, *s.f.* see sic.
sichd,* *v.n.* see sic.
siciamin,§ *s.* Mulberry, (sycamine in Bible), see maol-dhearc.
sicir, -e, *a.* Shrewd, sagacious, wise. 2**Acute. 3 Prudent, steady, firm, sure. 4 Accurate. 5 **Advisable. 6**Advised. 7**Not easily imposed upon.
——eachd, *s.f.ind.* Accuracy, acuteness. 2 Management. 3 Considerateness. 4 Advisableness. 5 Prudence, sagaciousness.
sid,‡ see siod.
sìd, -e, *s. f.* Weather, good or bad. 2 Abatement of a storm. 3 Abatement of rage, pacification, cessation. 4** see sioda. 5* Mood, humour. [McL & D gives *s.m.*] 'Nuair a nì e sìd, *when the storm abates ;* dé an sìd a th' ort ? *in what humour are you ?* am bheil s. air a nis ? *is his rage abated?* sìd mhath, *good weather ;* droch shid, *bad weather.*
sid,** *s.m.* Lair, as of a bear.
sideach,** *a.* see siodach.
————d,** *s.f.* see siodachd.
†sìdeadh, -idh, -idhean, *s.m.* Blast, as of wind.
sìdeil,* -e & sìdeiliche, *a.* More moderate, as wind. 2 In good humour, in good temper, as a person.
sidhe,** *s.f.* see sìdheadh.
————ach,(AF) *s.m.* Wolf.
sidheadh,** -idh, *s.m.* Blast.
†sidheang, *s.m.* Infamy.
†sidhich, *v.a.* Prove. (suidhich.)
sid-naich, (an), *emphat. form* of sid—*Badenoch & Glen Urquhart,* (siodanaich.)
sifheag,(CR) *W. of Ross* for siobhag, (wick.)
sifinn,(DU) *s.f.* see sithfean.
sifir, sifire, sifreach, } (AC) *s.m.* Male fairy. (sibhreach.)
sigeach,* -eiche, *a.* Slim. 2 Slimy. 3 (DC) Sly.
sigean, -ain, -an, *s. m.* Diminutive creature. 2 Silly person or thing. 3 (*sigeann) Pleasant countenance.
————ta, -einte, *a.* Diminutive. 2 Silly. 3 Delightful, pleasant. 4* Cheerful.
————tachd, *s.f.ind.* Diminutiveness. 2 Silli-

ness. 3 Delightfulness. 4* Cheerfulness. 5 Affability, complacency.
sigh,* *v.n.* Glide, skip, dash forth, dart. A' sigheadh air mullach nam beann, *skipping on the top of the hills* ; sh. i seachad, *she glided by.*
sigh, see sìth.
sigheach, see sidheach.
sigheadh,* -eidh, *s.m.* Gliding, vanishing, skipping. see sitheadh. A' s—, *pr. pt.* of sigh. Thug e an s. ud, *he made such a bolt.*
sigheann, see sithionn.
sighear,** -eir, *s.m.* Mountaineer.
sighich, *s.m. & f.* see sìthich.
sighideach,* -eich, *s. m.* Spectre. 2 Fairy. 3 Person taken away by the fairies. [**s.f.*]
†sighin, Gaelic spelling of *sign.*
——ich, *v.a.* Sign, mark.
†sigir, *s.f.* Silk.
sigirean,(AF) *s.f.* Silk-worm.
†sigle, *s.f.* Seal.
†signead, -eid, Gaelic sgelling of *signet.*
sil, *pr. pt.* a' sileadh, *v.a. & n.* Drop, distil. 2 Drop, drip, shed, let fall in drops. 3 Cause to drop. 4 Rain. 5 Shower. Shil e, *it rained* ; a' sileadh o 'n taigh, *dripping from the house* ; mu 'n s. e, *ere it rain* ; a' sileadh nan deur, *shedding tears* ; tha e a' sileadh, *it is raining*; silidh an là, *it will rain.*
sil, -e, -ean, *s.m.* Drop, see sile. S. nan sùl, *a tear*—a dropping of the eye.
sil,** -e, *s.f.* Shower, heavy rain.
sil, *gen.sing.* of sìol.
silc,(AC) see sicean.
silcean,(AC) see sicean.
sile,(AC) *s.f.* Nectar. 2(AF) Milk. Blas na s. 'nam bhile, *the taste of nectar on my lips.*
sile, -an, *s.m.* Spittle, saliva. 2 (AC) Salve. 3 **Issue.
sileach, -eiche, *a.* Spitting, that spits. 2 see silteach.
sileach,** *a.* Rainy, showery. Aimsir sh., *showery weather.*
sileachadh, -aidh, *s.m.* Spitting, act of spitting or slavering. A' s—, *pr.pt.* of silich.
sileadach, -aich, -ean, *s.m.* Handkerchief.
sileadan, -ain, -an, *s.m.* Spittoon.
sileadh,(AC) -lidh, *s.m.* Stem-platform in a boat.
sileadh, -idh, -ean, *s.m.* Dropping, act or state of dropping, distilling. 2 Raining, dripping of rain through a roof during a shower. 3 *Dispensation, economy. 4 Shedding. 5 Issue, issuing. 6 Drop, drip. A' s—, *pr.pt.* of sil.
Mar shìor-shileadh uisge tha aimhreitean mnà, *as the continual dropping of waters are the contentions of a woman;* fo sh. an t-soisgeil, *under the gospel dispensation* ; fo sh. an t-Seann Tiomnaidh, *under the Mosaic dispensation* ; gach s., *every drop* ; s. na h-oidhche, *dew* ; s. nan speur, *rain* ; s. nan sul, *tears* ; a sùil a' s., *her tears falling—lit.* her eyes shedding.
sileadh, *3rd.pers.sing. & pl.imp.* of sil.
——-sùith,(DMK) *s. m.* Rain percolating through the sooty thatch of a house and falling in large black drops indelibly staining everything it comes in contact with—*Caithness.*
sileag, -eig, -an, *s.f.,dim.* of sil. Little drop.
——ach, -aiche, *a.* Falling in small drops, dripping.
silean,(AC) see sicean.
silean, -ein, -an, *s.m.,dim.* of sìol. Small single grain. 2 The worst part of grain. 3 Stunted grain.
——ach, *a.* Abounding in small grain.
sile-reum, see sile-ronn.
sile-ronn,* *s.m.* Salivation.
silich, *pr.pt.* a' sileachadh, *v.n.* Spit, slaver.
siliche, -an, *s.m.* Spare, meagre, lean, pithless creature.
sìlidh,** *s.* Breed, pedigree, genealogy, lineage, race.
silidh, *fut.aff.a* of sil. Shall or will drop.
silimeag, *W. of Ross* for seamrag.
silin,§ see craobh-shiris.
silmeag,(CR) *s.f. W. of Ross* for seamrag.
sil-shùil, *s.f.* Watery eye.
——each, -eiche, *a.* Fearful. 2 Watery-eyed, blear-eyed.
silt, -e, -ean, *s.f.* Drop. 2 Spittle. 3 Issue. [** gives silte for *nom.*]
silte, *past pt.* of sil. Dropped, distilled.
——ach, -eiche, *a.* Dropping, that drops, dripping, oozing, moist. 2 Issuing, as matter from a sore, running, as an ulcer. 3 Scrofulous. 4 Tearful. 5**Thin, fading. 6* Often raining. 7* Discharge. Sùil sh., *a tearful eye* ; uair sh., *showery weather* ; cneadh s., *a scrofulous issue.*
——ach, -ich, -ichean, *s.f.* Issue, discharge. 2 *pl.* Scrofula. 3**Flowers. 4**Person afflicted with scrofulous sores. Ma dhùinear a suas 'fheòil o 'shilteach, *if his flesh be stopped from his issue* ; làithean a siltich, *the days of her menstruation* ; air son a shiltich, *on account of his issue.*
silteachail, -e, *a.* Ichorous.
silteachan,** -ain, *s.m.* Still. 2 Distiller.
silteachd, *s.f.ind.* Constant dropping. 2 Ulcerous habit. 3*Raininess.
siltichean, *s. pl.* Scrofula.
simeacha-guaid,(AH) *s.f.* Falseness, fraud, deceit, guile.
simear,(DMK) *s. m.* Long rafter of a kiln—*Caithness.*
simid, -e, -ean, *s.m.* Mallet, beetle, batlet. 2 **Rammer. 3 Rolling-pin. 4 (AF) Beetle (insect.)? 5 (DMy) Potato-masher. 6(DMy) Tail-half of fishes. Ceann-simid, *a tadpole* ; s. an truisg, *the tail-half of the cod* ; s. na bioraich, *the tail-half of the dog-fish.* [** gives *nom.* simide & *s.f.*]
simideach, -eiche, *a.* Formed like a mallet or beetle, or rolling-pin. 2 Of a hammer or rammer.
simidean,* *s.m.* see simid. 2††Tadpole.
simileach,†† -ich, -ichean, *s.m.* Coward.
——d,†† *s.f.* Cowardice.
similear, -eir, -an, *s.m.* Chimney, vent. Gaelic form of *chimney.* Ceann simileir, *a chimney-stalk* ; troimh an t-simileir, *through the vent.*
similearach, -aiche, *a.* Of, or belonging to, chimneys.
similearaich, *v.a.* Put a chimney on.
——te, *past pt.* Chimneyed.
similidh, -e, *a.* Cowardly, dastardly. 2 Feeble, silly.
simisd,(CR) *s.f.* Beam, of which there were three, laid across a corn-kiln to support the " sticlean beaga," see sticil.—*W.of Ross-shire.*
simleag, -eig, -an, *s.f.* Silly woman.
sìmonach,** *a.* Simoniacal.
——d,** *s.f.* Simony.
sìmonaiche,** *s.m.* Man guilty of simony.
simplich,** *v.a.* Simplify.
simplidh, *a.* Simple, single-hearted, artless. 2 Silly. 3**Plain, meek, mean. 4**Unalert.
——eachd, *s.f.ind.* Simpleness or singleness of heart, plainness, honesty. 2 Silliness. 3 Unaffectedness, meekness. 4 Unalertness. 5 **Meanness. Na biodh s. oirbh, *let there be no unalertness in you.*
sin, *demons.pron.* That, those. Na daoine sin, *those men* ; an duine sin, *that man* ; an t-àm sin, *that time* ; mar sin, *in that manner* ; 'se sin ri ràdh, *that is to say* ; an sin, *then, on*

that occasion ; there,in that place ; an sin fhéin, *at that very time ; in that very place ;* sin mar a thàinig e, *it was in that manner he came ;* mar sin sìos, *and so on ;* o sin, *since.*

sin ! *int.* There ! Well done ! Sin ! sin ! *enough ! enough ! ;* sin thu, a laochain ! *well done, my good fellow !* as an sin thu ! *be off with you ;* sin agad sin ! *there it is for you !* sin thu-fhéin ! *well done yourself !*

sìn, *pr.pt.* a' sìneadh, *v.a.* Stretch. 2 Increase in length, stretch out. 3 Hand, reach anything to another. 4 **Prolong. 5* Pursue, chase. 6**Grow in stature. 7* Lean or lounge on a bed. 8 Lie at full length. 9††Extend. 10 (DU) Begin, commence.
S. dhomh sin, *hand me that ;* s. do làmh, *stretch out your hand ;* s. do làmh dha, *extend your hand to him ; drub him ;* tha e a' sìneadh, *he is growing ;* ma shìneas Dia mo làithean, *if God prolong my days ;* sh. sinn orra, *we pursued them with all our might;* an déidh sìnidh, *having commenced ;* sh. i ris, *she was seduced by him ;* s. air, *chase him ;* tha e 'na sh., *he is leaning or lounging on the bed ;* sh. e as, *he hurried off—W.S. 2. 216 ;* shìninn mo làmh, *I would stretch my hand ;* sìnidh e a làithean, *he will prolong his days.*

sìn, *pr.pt.* a' sìneadh, *v.* see tòisich.

sìn, -e, siantan, *s.f.* see sian.

sindeagaich, *v.a.* Pace.

sine,** *s.f* Age, oldness. A' shine chas-aodainneach, *wrinkled age.*

sine,* -an & -achan, *s. f.* Teat, dug, nipple. 2 (AF) Udder.

sine, *comp.* of sean. Older, elder. 2 Oldest, eldest. Cò dhiubh a's sine ? *who of them is the elder,* or *eldest ?*

sìne, *gen.* of sian & sìon. 2 *gen.* of sìthionn.

sìne, *s.f.* Blast, stormy weather, see sian.

sineach, -eiche, *a.* Having large dugs.

sineachan, *pl.* of sine.

sineachd,(MS) *s.f.* Seniority.

sineachdainn, (an sineachdainn) *adv. emphat.* form of sin—*Badenoch & Gairloch.*

sinead, -eid, *s.m.* Seniority, degree of seniority. Air a sh., *let him be ever so old ;* an s. 's an donad,mar a bha cuilean a' mhadaidh ruaidh, *the older the worse, like the fox's whelp.*

sìneadair, *s.m.* Stretcher, see bàta, No. 38, p.76.

sìneadh, -idh, *s.m.* Stretching, act of stretching or extending. 2 Increasing in length, act of stretching out. 3 Act of reaching anything to another. 4 Lying at full length. 5 Prolonging, act of prolonging, prolongation. 6 Length, stretch, pursuit. 7 Pursuing. 8 Holding at full length, as of wool when it is being spun. 9 Reclining. 10 Delaying. 11 (DU) Beginning, commencing. A' s—, *pr. pt.* of sìn. S. làithean, *length of days ;* 'na shìneadh dlùth dhith, *stretched beside her.*

sineag, *s.f.* (AC) Handful of corn cut at one stroke of the reaping-hook. 2 Wick made from a rush by peeling off the green covering. 3 (DC) Wick of a lamp—*Uist.* 4(CR) Rush—*Dornoch, Creich.* 5 (DU) Teat of a child's feeding-bottle.

sineal,§ -eil, *s.m.* Stinking mayweed—*anthemis colula.* [Not found in the Highlands, but common in Ireland.] illust. 636.

sinean, see spealt.

sine-bhog,(AF) *s.f.* Soft crab.

singil,** *s.* Bastinade.

singil,** *v.a.* Dress flax, prepare flax for the hatchel (seicil.) 2 Belabour, give a thrashing.

singil,** *v.* Swinge.

sìngil, *a.* see simplidh.

singilear,** -eir, -an, *s.m.* One who prepares flax for the hatchel.

singilearachd,** *s.f.* Preparation of flax for the hatchel.

singilte,** *a.* Single, alone, not double. 2 Having one pleat. 3 Not mixed.

——,** *past pt.* of singil. Dressed or prepared for the hatchel, as flax.

singleadh, -idh, *s.m.* Preparing of flax for the hatchel (seicleadh.) 2 Belabouring,thrashing.

singlidh, *fut.aff.a.* of singil.

sìnidh, *fut. aff.a.* of sìn.

sinn, *pers.pron.* We, us. *Emphatic forms,* sinne, sinn-féin. Rinn sinn e, *we did it, we made it;* their sinn, *we shall say ;* sinn-fhìn is sinn-fhìn, Cloinn Cholla (*locally,* Cl. Tolla) Ghlasdruim, dh' fhalbh am prabar ud,*ourselves and ourselves, the MacColls of Glasdrum, that rabble has gone*—a saying current in the Appin district, and often used to point out specially noticeable clannishness ; it is also used as a rallying-shout when playing games ; bhuail e sinn, *he struck us.*

sinne, *emphat. form* of sinn.

sinne, see sine.

——ach, see sineach.

sinneach,** -ich, *s.f.* Wen.

sinneach, *a.* Mammal.

sinnean,** -ein, *s.m.* Little dug, teat or udder.

sinn-seanair, -ean, *s.m.* Great-grandfather.

sinn-seanmhathair, -thar, -thraichean, *s.f.* Great grandmother.

sinnseanach, (seann sionnach)(AF) *s.m.* Fox.

sinn-seachad-sinn-seanair,* *s. m.* Great-great-great-grandfather.

sinn-seachad-sinn-seanamhathair,* *s. f.* Great-great-great-grandmother.

sinnsear, -ir, -irean, *s.m.coll.* see sinnsir.

——, -ir, -an, *s.m.* Elder, the eldest.

——achd, see sinnsireachd.

sinn-sinn-seanair, *s.m.* Great-great-grandfather.

sinn-sinn-seanamhathair,**s.f.*Great-great-grandmother.

sinnsir, -sre & -e, -ean & -srean, *s.* [*sing.* in number, *coll.* in meaning.] Ancestors, fathers.

sinnsireach, -eiche, *a.* Patrimonial.

——d, *s.f.* Right of succession. 2 Ancestry. 3 Genealogy, account of families. 4 Customs of ancestors. 5 see sinnsir. 6**Seniority, eldership. 7**Descent. 8**Progeny. Mo sh., *my ancestry, my fathers;* gun s., *without descent.*

sinnsireil, -e, *a.* Ancestral.

sinnsre, see sinnsir.

——adh, see sinnsir.

sinridean,(AF) *s.pl.* Pieces of wood in kiln, laid across the *slugan.*

sìnte, *past pt.* of sìn. Stretched. 2 Increased in length. 3 Prolonged, extended. 4* Reached. 5 Grown in stature. 6 Couchant, in *heraldry.* 7*Fetched. S. r' a thaobh, *stretched*

636. *Sineal.*

by his side.

sinte, -an, *s.m.* Traces by which a horse draws a plough.

sinteach, -ich, -ichean, *s.f.* see sinte.

———, -eiche, *a.* Straight, long, extending far, extended, tall. 2*Prostrate. 3 Stretching. 4 With long steps. 5**Growing fast in stature.

sinteag, -eig, -an, *s.f.* Skip, bound, hop. 2 Pace, stride. 3**Straight line. 4 Stepping-stone. 5 ††Stroke in swimming. Cha ghabh mi na sinteagan, *I will not go the way of the stepping-stones.*

———ach, -aiche, *a.* Skipping, bounding. 2 Striding, making long strides or paces. 3 Bouncing.

sinteagaich,** *v.* Pace.

sinteag-féidh, *s.f.* (stag's leap.) Old Highland linear measure equal to 30 English feet.

sintean (for siantan) *n.pl.* of sian.

sintealachd,(MS) *s.f.* Tractibility.

siob,* *v.* see siab.

siobadh, -aidh, *s.m.* see siabadh.

siobag, -aig, -an, *s.f.* Blast of the mouth, whiff, puff.

siobaid,** *s.f.* Scallion, onion, see uinnean. 2 The plant cibol.

———each,** *a.* Abounding in scallions, onions or cibols.

siobail,* *v.* see siab.

sioban, see siabunn.

sioban,(AH) -ain, *s.m.* Spindrift, see siaban.

siobann,§ *s.* Onion, see uinnean. 2**Cibol.

siobhach,§ *s.* Darnel rye-grass, see breòillean.

siobhag, -aig, -an, *s.f.* Straw. 2* Pile of rye-grass. 3 Wick of a lamp or candle.

———ach,** *a.* Abounding in, or like straws.

siobhaide, *a.* Blighting. Le saighdean s. siubhlach 'gam leòn, *wounding me with blighting swift arrows—Dàin I. Ghobha.*

siobhailt, see siobhalta.

siobhailteachd, see siobhaltachd.

siobhalta, -ailte, *a.* Civil, courteous. 2 Peaceful, mild, placid. 3 Obliging, kind, urbane. (also siobhalt.)

———chd, *s.f.ind.* Civility, courtesy, peacefulness.

———s, -ais, *s.m.* see siobhaltachd.

siobhas, -ais, *s.m.* Rage, madness, fury.

———ach, -aiche, *a.* Furious, frantic, mad.

siobhrag,** *s.f.* Elf.

†**siobhraich**, -e, -ean, *s.f.* Fairy work, magic, enchantment.

sioblach,* -aich, *s.m.* Streamer. 2 Long person. 3††see siobladh. 4 (DU) "Cast" of a fishing-line or tackle.

siobladh, -aidh, *s.m.* Fishing with the boat under weigh. 2 Time of tide suitable for fishing. 3††Result of one's rod-fishing. A' s—, *pr. pt.* of siobail. 4 (DU) Fishing by trailing the flies on the surface of the water.

sioc ! *int.* Call to a goat—*W. of Ross.*

†**sioc**, *s.m.* Frost. 2 The umbilical region.

†**sioc**, *v.a.* Freeze. 2 Dry up, grow hard.

†——aichte, *past pt.* Frozen. 2 Dried up, grown hard. 3 Obdurate.

siocair,** *s.m.* Motive, reason. 2 Natural. 3 Opportunity.

sioch,* *v.* see siach.

sìoch,* *s.f.* Peace, quiet, repose, comfort.

siochadh,* -aidh, see siachadh.

sìochaich,** *v.a.* Assuage, compose, settle, calm. 2 Grow composed or calm.

sìochadh,(CR) *s.m.* Peace—*Perthshire.*

sìochail,* -e, *a.* Peaceful, quiet. 2 Causing peace or quietness. 3 Prosperous. Gu s., *peacefully.*

sìochaiche,** *s.m.* Peace-maker.

sìochaileachd, see sìochalachd.

sìochaint, -e, *s. f.* Peace, peacefulness, quiet, repose. 2 Assuagement.

———each, -eiche, *a.* Peaceful, tranquil. 2 Silent. 3**Silencing. 4*Undisturbed, unmolested.

———eachd,* *s.f.ind.* Peacefulness, quietude. 2 Appeasableness. 3 Happy repose and peace.

sìochair, -e, -ean, *s. m.* Dwarf. 2 Fairy-like person. 3 Contemptible fellow, trifling person, brat.

sìochainteil,(MS) *a.* Appeasable.

sìochaintiche, *s.m.* Peace-maker.

sìochaireach, -eiche, *a.* Dwarfish. 2 Mean, contemptible.

sìochaireachd, *s.f.ind.* Dwarfishness. 2 Contemptible habits. 3 Personal insignificance. 4 Pusillanimousness. 5* Trifling conduct, quantity or consideration.

sìochaire-baic,(AH) *s.m.* Boy who, when peats are being cut, lifts on to the bank any that may accidentally fall off the peat-spade.

sìochalachd,* *s. f.* Peacefulness, quietude. 2 Peaceableness. 3 Peace-making.

sìocharra,(AC) *s.pl.* Fairy darts.

sìothchath,** *s.f.* Peace, tranquility, abstainment from war. 2 Silence.

siod, *demons. pron.* Yon, that, there. An siod, *yonder, there ;* s. an duine, *yonder is the man ;* an siod 's an seo, *there and here ;* s. e, *yonder he is ;* siod agad siod, *there is your match ;* s. fhéin, *for every reason, because I thought it proper ;* mar s. 's mar seo, *that way and this way ;* s. an t-àite, *yonder is the place ;* 'dé bha 'n s. ? *what was that ? ;* c' ar son s. ? *why yon way ?* an téid thu an s. ? *will you go yonder ?* chaidh e an s., *he went yonder ;* s. mar a dh' iomchair e 'chluiche, *yon is the way he played his cards ;* an deach thu an s. ? *did you go yonder, to yon place ? ;* s. an làmh a thogas an t-sleagh, *there is the hand that can play vengeance with the spear ;* s. mar a chìteadh an Greugach, *thus was the Grecian seen ;* s. mar a thachair dhuinn, *so it happened to us.*

sìoda, -chan, *s.m.* Silk. Trusgan de shìoda, *a garment of silk.*

——,* *a.* Silken, of silk.

——ch, -aiche, *a.* Silky, silken.

——chail,** *a.* Silken.

——chan, *emphat.* of siod.

——chd,** *s.f.ind.* Silkiness.

——il, -e, *a.* Silky, like silk.

siodail,††*pr.pt.* a' siodal, *v.a.* Milk the last drop. 2 (DC) Nag, importune—*Argyll.*

sìoda-lus,§*s.m.* Ragged robin—*lychnis flos-cuculi.*

sìoda-monaidh, *s.m.* Cotton-grass, mountain silk—*eriophorum.*

sìod-chruimh, -e, -ean, *s.f.* Silk-worm, see cruimh-shìoda.

sìodha,(AC) *s.* Fay, fairy.

sìodhach,(AC) *s.m.* Fay, fairy.

siog,* *s. f.* Cadaverous appearance.

sioga,* *s.m.* Weakling.

sioga, *s.m.* Streak. 2 Rick.

siogach, -aiche, *a.* Pale, ill-looking, ill-coloured.

siogach, -aiche, *a.* Inactive, lazy. 2 Greasy, slimy. 3** Streaked. 4 ** Ill-shaped. Eòrna s., *barley not well-filled in the grain,* or *reaped before it was ripe.*

637. Sìoda-monaidh.

siogach,(AF) *s.m.* Wolf.

siogada-sinn-seanaireach,(AC)*a.* Sly, old-fashioned. Cho siogada-sinn-seanarach ri sionnach

na Maoile (Maol Chinntìre), *as great-great-great-grandfatherish as the fox of the Mull (of Kintyre.)*
siogaid, -ean, *s.m.* Lean, dwarfish, weakly fellow. 2 Starveling.
———each, -eich, *s.m.* see siogaid.
———each, -eiche, *a.* Lean, cadaverous, famished looking. 2 Dwarfish, bony, ill-made—*Sàr-Obair.*
sìogaidh,** -ean, *s.m.* Fairy. 2 Pigmy.
sìogaidh, *a.* Twining—applied to the motions of a serpent, and hence to music, which twines and coils round the heart. It is translated *calming* in *W. H. Tales.*
†siogail,** *a.* Streaky, striped.
siogaisdeach,** *a.* Shapeless and long in person. 2 Having long limbs. 3 Tough.
————d,** *s.f.* Shapelessness of person. 2 Toughness.
siogan,** -ain, *s.m.* Gizzard.
sioglachadh, -aidh, *s.m.* Milking or sucking to the last drop—*Sleat.*
siogladh, -aidh, *s.m.* Sucking an udder to the last drop.
siogar, Gaelic form of *cigar.*
siogaran, *s.m.* Cigarette.
sìol, sìl, *s.m.* Seed of any kind. 2 Progeny, descendants. 3** Ancestry. 4 Tribe, clan. 5 Spawn or roe of fish. 6**Corn. 7**Oats. A shìl nam fonn ! *O children of song !*—i.e. bards. [Generally aspirates a proper name following it, except one commencing with *T.*] Sìol Dhiarmaid—*also* Sìol Diarmaid (na Duibhnich,) *the Campbells ;* Sìol Torcuil, *the MacLeods of Lewis ;* s. gruinnd, *seed for sowing.*
sìol ! * *int.* Mode of calling geese.
siol, s.m. Sprat (fish)—*clupea sprattus.*
sìol,** *v.a. & n.* Sow. 2 Drop, spill, drivel.
siola, -chan, *s.m.* [*f.* in *Badenoch*]. Gill, gill measure. 2 *pl.* Wooden hames for plough-horses. 3**Prow of a boat. 4 Syllable, see sioladh. 5 (DMy) Milt of male fishes, in herring termed *mealg.* [** gives *nom.* siol for Nos. 1, 3 & 4.]
sìolach,* -aich, *s.m.* Breed, brood, offspring, particularly applied to cattle, birds, &c. 2 Descendant. S. àluinn nan speur, *the beautiful offspring of the skies.*
——, *a.* Having progeny, prolific. 2 Having seed, spermatic.
sìolach, see sìolaidh.
sìolachadh, -aidh, *s. m.* Propagating, propagation, breeding, generating. 2 Increasing in number, multiplying. 3 State of being multiplied. 4 Filtering, clarifying. 5 Clarification, colation. A' s—, *pr.pt.* of sìolaich.
sìolachan, -ain, -an, *s.m.* Filter, strainer, colander.
————, *pl.* of siola.
sìoladair,** -ean, *s.m.* Sower. 2 Seedsman.
————eachd,** *s.f.* Employment of sowing seed. 2 Business of a seedsman.
sìoladh, -aidh, *s.m.* Subsiding. 2 State of subsiding. 3 Straining. 4 Act of straining or filtering. 5 Sinking. 6 State of sinking. 7 Propagation. 8 Dropping. 9**Breeding, generating, sowing. 10**Race, offspring. A' s—, *pr. pt.* of sìolaidh. A' s. a' bhainne, *straining the milk ;* tha a' ghaoth a' s., *the wind is subsiding ;* tha 'n t-uisge a' s., *the water is filtering, the sediments in the water are subsiding ;* a' s. as, *passing quietly away.*
sìoladh, see sìolaidh.
sioladh,* -aidh, -aidhean, *s.m.* Syllable. 2 Gill. 3 Prow of a ship.
————ach, -aiche, *a.* Syllabic.
sìolag, -aig, -an, *s. f, dim.* of sìol. Seedling. 2 Small or stunted grain of corn or potato. 3 Breeding-sow—*Perthshire & Sutherland.* 4 Young pig—*E. Ross.*
sìolag,** -aig, -an, *s. f.* Strainer. 2 Gill (measure.)
siolag,(DC) -aig, -an, *s.f.* Viper-fish. Supposed to be the male of the sand-eel or launce—*ammodytes lanceolatus.* This little reptile comes to the shallow fords of Uist in myriads, and is largely used as food.
sìolagach, -aiche, *a.* Abounding in seedlings.
siolagach,** *a.* Abounding in gills. 2 Fond of drams, tippling.
siolagag, see sìolag.
siolagaig, see siolag.
sìolaich, *v.a. & n.* Propagate, breed, multiply, engender, beget, be fruitful. 2 Spring from, as seed. 3 Abound. Sh. iad, *they increased* or *multiplied ;* sìolaichibh is fàsaibh lìonmhor, *increase and multiply ;* o Dhiarmad sh. clann nach gann, *from Dermid sprung a numerous progeny.*
sìolaich, -ean, *s.m.* Propagator. 2††Stallion.
sìolaichidh, *fut.aff.a.* of sìolaich.
sìolaidh, *pr. pt.* a' sìoladh, *v.a. & n.* Subside, compose. settle down, strain, filter, cause to subside, cleanse, as a fluid. 2 Sink, lower. 3 Grow less. 4 Become composed. 5(MS) Reside. Sh. an soirbheas, *the wind subsided* ; sh. confhadh lot gu sìth, *the rage for wounds subsided into peace ;* sìoladh m' anam o strì, *let my soul subside from struggle;* s. am bainne, *strain the milk ;* leig leis sìoladh, *let it subside.*
sìolaidh, *fut.aff.a.* of sioladh.
sìolaidh, *gen.sing.* of sìoladh.
sìolaidh,(MS) *v.a. & n.* Avail.
sìolaidh,** *s.f.* Race, offspring. 3 Stallion.
siolaigh,(CR) *s.m.* Stallion—*Arran.*
sìolan,** -ain, -an, *s. m.* Strainer, filter. 2 see sìolag.
sìolar,** *a.* Abounding in seed. 2 Prolific, productive, generative, fruitful.
siolarnach,** *a.* Snoring, snorting.
siolastar,§ *s.m.* Yellow flag, see bog-uisge. (seilistear.)
siolc, *v.a.* Snatch, seize upon. 2 Pilfer. 3 Wink. 4††Slip, bound. 5* Seek.
——ach, -aiche, *a.* Snatching, seizing upon. 2 Pilfering. 3 Winking.
——adh, -aidh, *s.m.* Snatching. 2 Act of snatching or seizing upon. 3 Pilfering. 4 Twinkling. 5 Act of twinkling. 6†† Quick motion, bound, skip. A' s—, *pr.pt.* of siolc.
siolcair, -ean, *s.m.* Rogue, light-fingered fellow. 2††One that skips off.
————eachd, *s.f.* Petty theft.
sìol-chonnlach, -aich, *s.f.* Unthreshed straw, given as fodder.
sìol-chuir, *pr.pt.* a' sìol-chur, *v.a.* Sow seed.
————te, *past pt.* Sown.
sìol-chur, -a, *s.m.* Sowing seed. 2 Act of sowing seed. A' s—, *pr.pt.* of sìol-chuir. [***gen.* s-chuir.]
siol-coise, *s. m.* Footboard on the treadle of a spinning-wheel, No. 17, p. 290.
sìol-cuir, *s.m.* Sowing-seed, seed to sow.
sìol-cura, see siol-cuir.
siolgach, -aiche, *a.* Lazy, spiritless, sorry, pitiful, dwarfish.
siolgair, -ean, *s.m.* Spiritless, mean sluggard.
————eachd, *s.f.ind.* Inactivity, tardiness, laziness. 2 Meanness.
siol-ghobach, -aich, *s.f.* Sand-eel. 2(DJM)Pipe-fish.
sìol-ghinidh,** sìl-, *s.m.* Seed of copulation.
sioll,* *s.m.* Turn, rotation. S. mu seach, *time about, in rotation, alternately ;* 's e seo mo sh.-sa, *this is my turn ;* an d' thàinig do sh.-sa a

staigh fhathast? *has your turn come round yet?*
siolla, see siola.
siolladh, -aidh, -aidhean, *s. m.* Syllable, see sioladh.
siollaimeach,(MS) *s.m* Prevaricator.
siollan,** -ain, *s.m.* Skinny, meagre creature.
siol-lann,** *s.m.* Granary.
siolman, -ain, -an, *s.m.* Seedling. 2 Refuse of corn. Cha'n 'eil ann na's miosa na s., *there is no refuse worse than that of the corn-pickle*—said of mean gentry.
sìolmheinn, see sìolmhuinn.
sìolmhoire, *comp.* of sìolmhor.
————achd, see sìolmhorachd.
sìol-mhór,(CR) *s.f.* Eel resembling the sand-eel, but growing to a length of two feet, usually found in the company of the gurnet—*West of Ross-shire.*
sìolmhor, -oire, *a.* Prolific, fertile, generative, fruitful. 2 Abounding in seed. 3 Productive, substantial, as corn.
————achd, *s.f.* Fertility, fecundity, productiveness. 2 Impregnation.
sìolmhuinn, *s. f.* Progeny, stock, race. 2 Fecundating substance—*Dàin I. Ghobha.*
siol-oladh, *s.m.* Spermaceti.
siolp,(CR)*v.n.* Slip in or out unperceived, skulk. —*Skye.* 2 (DU) Pilfer. 'Dé tha thu a' siolpadh ? *what are you sneaking off ?*
——adh,(CR) *s.m.* Pilfering.
——air,(CR) *s.m.* Pilferer.
——an,(DMK) *s.m.* Constable's baton—*W. coast of Ross.*
sìolradh, -aidh, *s.m.* Breed, race, offspring.
sìolraich, *v.a.* Breed, generate, propagate.
sìol-reicear, -ir, -an, *s.m.* Corn-chandler.
siol-roinn,** *s.* Diæresis.
siolruin, see siol-roinn.
sìolta, *pl.* sìoltaidhean, *s.f.* Teal, small wild duck, see crann-lach.
——— -bheag,¶ see lach-fiacailleach.
sioltach, see seamlach.
sioltachan, -ain, -an, see sìolachan.
sìoltachd, *s.f.ind.* Propagation, the multiplying of a stock.
sìolta dhearg,¶ *s.f.* Red-breasted merganser—*mercus serrator.*
sìoltaich, -ean, *s. m.* Red-breasted merganser, see sìolta dhearg. 2 see sìolaich. 3 see lach-fiacailleach. 4* Stallion. 5*Propagator. [* gives sìoltaiche for Nos. 4 & 5.]
———— breac,¶ *s.m.* Smew—*mergus albellus.*
sìoltan,¶ -ain, *s. m.* Red-breasted merganser, see sìolta dhearg & lach fiacailleach.
——— bàn,¶ *s.m.* Smew, see sìoltaich breac.
——— breac,¶ *s.m.* see sìoltaich breac.
sìol-treubh** -treibh, *s.m.* Family. [*sìol-triabh.]
†siolt-shuileas,** -eis, *s.m.* Running of the eyes.
sioma,(AF) *s.m.* Whale.
siomaguad, *s.m.* Shuffle, evasion, subterfuge.
—————ach,** *a.* Evasive, shuffling, equivocating.
—————achd,** *s.f.* Habit of evading or shuffling.
siomaid, see simid.
————each,** see simideach.
siomaidean,* see simid.
sìomain, see sìoman.
siomal, -ail, *s.m.* Ceiling.
siomaltach,(MS) *a.* Merry.
sìoman, -ain, -an, *s.m.* Rope of twisted straw or hay. 2 Rope of twisted heather—*Skye.* 3** Rope, cord. 4 *in derision,* Tall, shapeless fellow. Corr-shìomain, *bent stick, used for making straw-ropes ;* cho mear ri ceann-sìomain, *as merry as a rope's end.* (*Scots,* thraw-crook.)
————ach,** *a.* Like a rope of straw, hay or heather. 2 Having ropes of straw, hay or heather, as a rick.
————aiche,** *s.m.* One who makes ropes of hay, straw or heather.
———— -barraich, (DU) *s. m.* Rope of twigs, withes.
sìoman-òrdaig,(DMK) *s.m.* Rope made of straw or hay twisted with the thumb—*Caithness, Argyll, &c.*
siomlach, -aich, -aichean, *s.* see seamlach.
————d,* *s.f.* Chicken-heartedness, sheepishness, cowardice.
siomlag,* -aig, -an, *s.m.* Great coward.
siomlaidh, -e, *a.* Chicken-hearted, sheepish, spiritless, heartless.
siomlainn, see similear.
siomlair,* see similear.
siomrag, see seamrag.
sìon, -tan, *s.m.* Something, anything. 2 *with a negative,* Nothing. 3(MS) Atom. 4*Climate. 5 Element. 6 Air, blast. 7 Drift. Cha'n 'eil s. agam *I have nothing ;* gach s. a th' agam, *every particle I possess ;* cha'n 'eil s. math air, *it is worth nothing ;* a' dol an aghaidh an t-s., *going against the blast ;* an s. 'na chùlaibh, *the drift of the rain at his back ;* tha na sìontan air atharrachadh, *the climate has changed;* fo m' shìontan dùthchasach, *under my native climate, in my native atmosphere ;* mar chrith-each 'san t-s., *like the aspen in the blast ;* tamhasg air èideadh le sìontaibh, *a spectre shrouded with the elements.* [** *s.f. & gen.* sìne.
†sion, sine, -e, *s.f.* Chain, bond. 2 see sionn & sian.
sion,** s.m. Whisper. 2 Phenomenon. 3 Brightness. 4 Warning.
sion,(AF) *s.m.* Craw-fish, cray-fish.
†siona, *s.m.* Delay.
sionadh, -aidh, -aidhean, *s. m.* Lord, noble, chief, prince. [** *nom.* sionaidh.]
sìonail,** see sianail.
sìon-bhuailte, see sian-bhuailte.
sìon-bhuailteach, see sian-bhuailteach.
sìon-bhualadh, see sian-bhualadh.
†siongailte, see singilte.
sion-giomach,(AF) *s.m.* Craw-fish, cray-fish.
†sionn, *adv.* In this place, here.
sionn, *s.m.* Foxglove, see lus-nam-ban-sìth. 2 (AC) Light, brightness, lurid light. 3 (AC) Region of lurid light.
sionn,(AC) *a.* Mysterious. 2 Phosphorescent. 3 Lustrous.
sionn, *s.m.* Phosphorous—*Dàin I. Ghobha.*
sionnach, -aich, *s.m.* Fox. 2 Bagpipe-reed. 3 Wind-valve of a bagpipe. 4 Wind-valve of smith's bellows. †5 Tub, keeve.
————air,** -ean, *s.m.* Fox-hunter.
————an, -ain, *s.m.* Will-o'-the-wisp. 2(DU) Phosphorus. Teine sionnachain, *phosphorus ;* tha s. 'sa mhuir, *the sea is phosphorescent.*
————as,** -ais, *s.m.* Craftiness, low cunning.
sionnachla,(AF) *s.* Weather gaw, seagull.
sionnadh,** -aidh, *s.m.* Reproof, rebuke, scoff.
sionnaich, (AC) *a.* Bright. Domhnach s., *a bright Sunday.*
sionusa, see sionnsar.
sionnsair, see sionnsar.
sionnsar, -air, -an, *s.m.* Chanter. 2 Gaelic spelling of *censer.* [** *nom.* sionnsair.] *Prov.* for seannsar.
————ach, -aiche, *a.* Having a chanter. 2 Like a chanter. 3 Furnished with censers. 4 Like a censer. [seannsaireach is best form.]
————achd, see seannsaireachd.
sionradhach,** *a.* Single.
†sionsa, *s.m.* Censer.

sion-steud, see sian-steud.
siontach, see siantach.
———d, see siantachd.
siontaibh, *dat. pl.* of sion.
siontan, *n.pl.* of sion.
siop. Cuir an siop, *despise, turn tail on—Dàin I. Ghobha.*
siopunn, see siabunn.
———ach, -aiche, *a.* see siabunnach.
sior, *a.* Continual, long, perpetual. 2 Persevering. [Always placed before the noun or verb qualified.] A' s.-amharc orm, *eternally staring at me* ; a' s.-mhagadh air, *perpetually gibing him.*
——,* *s.m.* Time, circuit of time. Gu s., *for ever* ; thuit mo ghrian gu s., *my sun has set for ever.*
siorachd, *a.* Melodious, plaintive.
sior-atharrach, -aiche, *a.* Variable, inconstant.
—————adh, -aidh, *s.m.* Variableness, continual variation or shifting.
—————ail, -e, see sior-atharrach.
siorbhai,** *s.m.* Theft.
sior-bheò,** *a.* Everlasting, eternal. 2**Evergreen.
sior-bhraighlich,** *s. f.* Continued loud noise, constant rattling or clattering.
sior-bhualadh, -aidh, *s.m.* Continual striking, beating or thumping.
sior-bhuain,***v.a.* Cut, shear or mow frequently.
sior-bhuan,** *a.* Everlasting, eternal.
————as, -ais, *s.m.* Perseverance.
————tachd,** *s.f.* Eternity of being, eternity of existence.
————tas,** -ais, *s.m.* Durableness.
siorcall,** -aill, -an, *s.m.* Gaelic form of *circle.*
———ach,** *a.* Circular, circled.
———aich, *v.a.* Circle, encircle.
———aichte, *past pt.* Circled, encircled, surrounded.
sior-chainnt,** *s.f.* Garrulity, constant prating.
—————each, -eiche, *a.* Prating, garrulous, continually talking.
—————each, -eich, *s.m.* Babbler, constant talker.
sior-chas,** *v.n.* Turn to and again.
————ach, *a.* Running to and fro. 2 Walking frequently.
sior-cheangaltachd, *s.f.ind.* Indissolubility.
sior-chleachd,** *v.a.* Exercise often, train to.
—————adh,-aidh, -aidhean, *s.m.* Constant habit, regular practice.
siorda,** -ai, *s.m.* Great favour or present.
siordan,** -ain, *s.m.* Rattling noise, rustling noise.
———ach,** *v.* Making a rattling noise. 2 Rustling.
sior-éighe,** *s.f.* Continued crying, shouting or shrieking.
————ach,** *a.* Continually crying, shouting or shrieking.
sior-euchd, *s.f.* Softness—R. 8.
sior-ghàir,** *s.f.* Continued laughter, noise or clamour.
sior-ghlac,** *v. a.* Grip. 2 Handle roughly. 3 Grasp frequently.
————,** -aic, *s.m.* Grip. 2 Rough handling. 3 Frequent grasping.
sior-ghnàth, *s.m.* Continual use, constant habit.
—————ach, *a.* Habitual, having a continual habit.
—————achd, *s.f.ind.* Perpetuity.
—————aich, *v.a.* Practice much or often. 2 Use frequently.
sior-ghnothachair, *s.m.* Amateur.
sior-ghuidhe, *v.* Desire.
sior-iarr, *v.a.* Importune.
sior-iarraidh, *s. f.* Importunity, constant or urgent petitioning.
—————each,** *a.* Importunate, troublesome by means of frequent requests or petitions.
————tach, -aiche, *a.* Importunate.
sior-imrich,** *s.f.* Transmigration.
sior-làmhach,** *a.* Long-handed.
sior-loisg,** *v.a.* Burn perpetually or eternally.
sior-losgach,** *a.* Burning perpetually or eternally.
sior-losgadh,** -aidh, *s.m.* Continual burning. 2 Eternal fire.
siormag, *N. Argyll* for seamrag.
sior-mhaireannach,** *a.* Everlasting, eternal. 2 Immortal. 3 Durable.
——————d, *s.f.ind.*Perpetuity,durableness. 2 Immortality, state of being everlasting or eternal.
sior-òl,** *s.m.*Hard drinking, frequent drinking.
sior-osd,** *v.n.* Gape or yawn frequently.
sior-phlucas, -ais, *s.m.* Lientery.
siorr,* *v.n.* Scud, slip in or out.
siorra, see siorram.
siorrachd, see siorramachd.
siorradh, -aidh, -aidhean, *s.m.* Deviation, excursion. 2 Onset, attack. 3 Darting. 4 Dart. 5 see siorram.
siorraimh, -ean, see siorram.
siorralach,§*s.m.*Broom-rape—*orobanchacæ major & o. minor.*

638. Siorralach.

siorram, -aim, -an, *s.m.* Sheriff.
———achd,*s.f.*Sheriffdom, county. 2 Office of sheriff.
siorruich,** *v.a.* Eternize, immortalize, perpetuate.
siorruidh, *a.* Eternal, everlasting. Gu s., *for ever.* Gu suthain siorruidh, *for ever and ever.*
siorruidheachd, *s.f.ind.* Eternity. 2 Immortality. 3 Perpetuity.
siorsan,** -ain, *s.m.* Pleasant or good news.
————ach,** *a.* Slow, tedious.
————ach,** -aich, *s.m.* Slow, tedious person.
sior-sheasmhachd, *s.f.* Immovableness.
sior-shileach,** *a.* Dropping or dripping continually.
sior-shileadh,** -eidh, *s.m.* Continual dropping.
sior-shiolaidheach, -aiche, *a.* Insensible.
†siort, *v.a.* Strike.
†siortair, -ean, *s.m.* Executioner.
sior-thoireas,** -eis, *s.m.* Request.
sior-uaine, *a.* Evergreen.
————, *s.m.* Evergreen.
sior-uisge,** *s.m.* Running stream. 2 Perennial fountain. 3 Constant rain.
—————ach,***a.*Abounding in running streams or perennial fountains. 2 Raining continuously.
sios, *adv.* Down, downwards (from one)—down

towards one is *nuas*. 2 (shìos) Resting below.

In *W. of Ross* shìos and sìos naturally mean west and westward respectively, that is, down the course of the streams and valleys, and shuas and suas, east and eastward. Yet, shìos rathad Chataibh, *down the way of Sutherland*, is the usual way of speaking of the part of Sutherland on the Moray Firth. These meanings of *sìos* and *suas* are now perpetuated in a curious way in the east of Ross-shire when speaking English; *e.g.* "go east to the kitchen," "go west to the byre," &c., expressions that strike anyone as very comical till he understands how they originated and that they have no connection with *ear* and *iar*. This does not apply exclusively to Ross-shire.

In *Gairloch*, shìos and shuas mean practically north and south. South Earradale, for example, in the south of the parish, is called Eàrradal shuas and Eàrradal a deas, and North Earradale is Eàrradal shìos and Eàrradal a tuath. Am baile shuas and Am baile shìos at Red Point, furnish another instance —CR. in *Gael. Soc. of Inverness, xxiv, 369.*

In *Perthshire*, East, eastward. 2**Future.

S. ud [*or* s. an siod], *down yonder*; a' dol s., *going down, setting, as the sun*; o shiùbhal s. agus suas, *from going down and up*; s. agus suas, *eastwards and westwards*; "*but and ben*" *of a house*; falbh suas do 'n t-seòmar, *go "ben the hoose"* (in some places, *go west to the room*); cluinnidh aimsir sìos ar cliù, *future times shall hear our praise*; cuir s., *send eastward* or *downward—Perthshire.*

In *Sutherland*, it is invariably "tha a' ghaoth à shuas," for westerly wind, and "a' ghaoth à shìos" for easterly wind.

In *all parts*, the use of sìos and suas is regulated by the direction in which the water flows, thus, it is customary to say, "a' dol suas gu ceann an loch," *or* "suas do 'n eaglais," if in a contrary direction to the general flow of the surrounding streams, even although the journey may be dowhill all the way from where the speaker stands.

†siosa, *s.m.* Court, parliament.

siosacot, *s.m.* Doublet.

siosar, -air, -an, *s.m.* Pair of scissors or shears.

——ach, -aiche, *a.* Of, or belonging to scissors or shears. 2 Abounding in scissors or shears. 3 Like scissors or shears.

siosarnaich,** *s.f.* Hissing.

siosdan,** -ain, *s.m.* Hunter's cry.

siosma, *s.* Gaelic form of *schism*. 2 Private conference, whisper.

——ch,** *a.* Schismatic. 2 Conferring privately, whispering.

siosmair,** -ean, *s. m.* Seceder, schismatic. 2 Whisperer.

——eachd,** *s.f.ind.* Schismatising, seceding. 2 Whispering.

siostacota,* *s.m.* see siosacot.

siostair,** *s.m.* Barrator.

siota,‡ *s.* Blackguard. 2 Pet. 3 Ill-bred or spoilt child. 4 (AF) see seota.

siotach,** *a.* Ill-bred, as a petted child. 2 Pampered.

——,** *s.m.* Ill-bred person, pampered person.

siotaidh,** *s.f.* Trifle, jot.

sioth, see sìth.

siothach, see sìtheach.

siothach, see sìth.

siothachadh,(MS) Appeasement.

sìothachair, *s.m.* Pacificator.

sìothadair, *s.m.* Pacificator.

siothadh, -aidh, *s.m.* see sìth.

siothaich, see sìthich.

siothaimh,(MS) *s.* Ataraxy.

siothalachd, *s.f.ind.* Peacefulness.

siothamh, -aimh, *s. f.* Peace, rest. Seallaidh sìothaimh, *sights of peace.*

siothann, see sìthionn.

sìothchaich,** *v.* see sìthich.

sìothchail, see sìtheil. 2 Prosperous.

sìothchaileachd, see sìochalachd.

sìothchaimh, see sìothaimh.

sìothchainnt, see sìochaint.

sìoth-chainnt, see sìthchaint.

sìoth-chainnteach, also sìochainnteach.

sìothchainnteach, see sìthchainnteach.

sìoth-chainntiche, also sìochainntiche.

sìothchath, see sìochath.

sìoth-choimheadaiche, see sìth-choimheadaiche.

siothlachan,(DC) see sìolachan.

siothladh,** *s.m.* Clarification.

siothlag,** *s.f.* Filter.

siothlaich, *v.a.* Drain.

siothlaidh, see sìolaich.

siothlaidh, *v.* see sìothlaich.

siothlan,** *s.m.* Strainer. 2 Sack.

sìoth-shaimh, ——each, ——eachd, see sìth-thàmh, &c.

sìoth-thaimh, see sìth-thàmh.

——each, see sìth-thàmhach.

——eachd, see sìth-thàmhachd.

sir, *pr. pt.* a' sireadh & a' sireachd, *v.a.* Seek, search. 2 Seek, ask, request. 3 Want. S. e, *seek it*; dé tha thu a' sireadh? *what do you want? what are you seeking?* esan a shireas, *he that seeks*; s. air, *ask of him*; sh. i oirbhse, a fhlatha, *she asked of you, ye nobles.*

sìr,** *a.* see sìor.

sìr-bhuain, see sìor-bhuain.

sìr-bhualadh, see sìor-bhualadh.

sìr-chaint, see sìor-chainnt.

——each, see sìor-chainnteach.

sìr-chleachd, see sìor-chleachd.

sìreach,** *a.* Seeking, searching, prying, scrutinous. 2 Lean, poor.

sireachd, *s.f.* & *pr.pt.* Same meanings as sireadh.

siread,** -eid, *s.m.* Ferret.

——ach,** *a.* Like, or abounding in, ferrets.

sireadair, -ean, *s.m.* Questant, inquirer.

sireadan,** -ain, *s.m.* Sound, probe, in *surgery.*

sireadh, -idh, *s.m.* Searching, act of searching. 2 Seeking, act of seeking. 3 Asking, requesting, demanding, begging. A' s—, *pr. pt.* of sir.

sireamh, -eimh, *s.m.* Disease.

siris, -ean, *s.f.* Cherry, see craobh-shiris.

——each, -eiche, *a.* Of, or belonging to, cherries.

sirist, see siris.

——each, *a. prov.* for siriseach.

——each,* *s.m.* Shelty, pony.

sìrnearan,(AF) *s.pl.* see sìnridean.

sìr-shileadh, see sìor-shileadh.

†sist, *s.* Time, while.

sisteal,** *s.m.* Cistern. 2 Flaxcomb.

sistealach,** -aich, *s.m.* Flax-dresser. 2 Woolcomber.

sistealach,** *a.* Having cisterns or flaxcombs. 2 Like a cistern or flaxcomb.

——d,** *s.f.ind.* Flax-dressing. 2 Woolcombing or carding.

sistealair,** *s.m.* Flax-dresser. 2 Wool-comber.

site, -achan, *s.f.* Gaelic form of *sheet*. S. phaipeir, *a sheet of paper.*

——ach, *a.* Sheeted, in sheets. 2 Like a sheet.

siteag, -eig, -an, *s.f.* Dunghill. Originally applied to the dung that was allowed to accumulate in a byre for twelve months, and cleaned out in the spring time. The custom still obtains in *Lewis.*—DMK. 2 Nice young fe-

male. 3 (DU) In *Gairloch*, applied to outside generally. Cuir chun na siteig e, *turn him out.*
———ach, *a.* Abounding in dunghills. 2**Nice, as a young female. 3**Effeminate.
sitealachd,** *s.f.* see sibhtealachd.
†sitearn, -eirn, *s.m.* Harp. [*s.f.]
siteil, *a.* Cunning, crafty, designing.
sith, -ean, Hill, mount. 2 Prefix in the names of many hills.
sith, -ean, *s.m. & f.* Fairy.
sith, -e, -ean, *s.f.* Peace, quietness, tranquility. 2 Rest from war. 3 Reconciliation. 4 Truce. Cogadh no s., *war or peace;* an s., *in quietness.*
sith, *s. f.* Mark in which to fix anything—*Rob Donn.*
sith *a.* Spiritual. Daoine s., *fairies ;* bean-sh., *a familiar spirit.* [Leannan-s. is given in the Bible for the *power of bringing the spirit of a dead person into one's presence,* or *witchcraft ;* its colloquial meaning is, *a fairy sweetheart.*]
sith, -ean, *s.m.* Stride, long quick pace. 2 Onset, dart to. 3 Shock. 4 Gnash. 5 Sudden attempt to grasp or bite. 6 Span, squint—*Sàr Obair.* 7 Determined position in standing. S. giomaich, s. rionnaich. s. ròin—trì sithean na muire móire, *rush of lobster, rush of mackerel, rush of seal—the three rushes of the ocean ;* s. nan còp corn-dhubh, *the shock of round black bosses.* [**s.f.]
sith-aigean,** -aigne, *s. f.* Mind disposed to peace, tranquil mind.
——————tach,** *a.* Disposed to peace, peaceable, tranquil in mind.
——————achd, *s.f.* Placability.
sith-aigneach, -eiche, *a.* Peaceable, conciliatory.
sithain,** see sìthean.
sithamh,** see sith-thàmh.
sith-bheath,** *s.f.* Immortality.
sith-bheò,** *a.* Eternal, immortal. 2 Perennial, Plùran s., *a perennial flower.*
sith-bhollsair,** -ean, *s.m.* Herald, one who proclaims peace.
———————eachd,** *s.f.* Proclaiming of peace, office of a herald of peace.
sith-bhreitheamh, -eimh, -an, *s.m.* Justice of the peace.
sith-bhriseach, -ich, -ichean, *s.m.* Rebel.
sith-bhriseach,** *a.* Peace-breaking, riotous, rebellious.
sith-bhriseadh,** -idh, *s.m.* Disturbance, rebellion.
sith-bhrog, see sìth-bhrugh.
sith-bhrugh, -a, -uighean & -ughan, *s.m.* Fairy hill or mansion.
—————ach, *a.* Abounding in fairy-hills.
sith-bhruth, see sìth-bhrugh.
sith-bhruthach, see sìth-bhrugh.
sìth-bhuan,** *a.* Eternal, immortal. 2 Perpetual, perennial.
——————tachd, *s.f.* Eternity, immortality.
sithchail, see sìtheil.
sith-chainnt,** *s.f.* Salutation. 2 Words of peace, peaceful language.
——————each, *a.* Saluting. 2 Speaking peacefully.
sithche, -an, *s.m.* see sìthich.
———an, *pl.* of sìthich.
sith-cheangail,** *v.a.* Join in a confederacy. 2 Bind over to keep the peace.
sith-cheanglach,** *a.* Confederative. 2 Binding over to keep the peace.
sith-cheangladh,** -aidh, *s.m.* Confederation. 2 Binding over to keep the peace.
sith-cheanglaiche,** -an, *s.m.* One of a confederacy. 2 One who binds over to keep the peace.
sith-choimheadaiche,** *s.m.* Constable, one who keeps the peace.
sith-dheanadach, -aiche, *a.* Pacific.
sìth-dhuine, *pl.* -dhaoine, *s.m.* Fairy.
sith-dhùn,** *s.m.* Fairy knoll.
sìtheach,* -eich, *s.m.* Male fairy—*Argyll.*
sitheach, -eiche, *a.* Making long and quick strides or paces. 2 Rushing impetuously. 3 Making a sudden assault.
sitheach, *a.* see sìtheil.
sitheachadh, -aidh, *s.m.* Pacifying, act of pacifying. A' s—, *pr.pt.* of sìthich.
sìtheadair. -ean, *s.m.* Pacifier.
sitheadh, -idh, -idhean, *s.m.* Force, impetuosity. 2 Violent attack or onset. 3 Rush or shoot of fish. 4**Bending, sloping, declining. 5†† Stride.
sìtheag, *s.f.* Female fairy.
sitheag, (DMK) *s.f.* Core of rushes used as a wick in a cruisgean—*W. Highlands.*
sitheal,** -an, *s. m.* Trowel. 2 Drinking-cup. 3 Body.
sìthealachd, *s.f.ind.* Peacefulness, amity.
sìthean, -ein, -an, *s.m.* Little hill or knoll. 2 Fairy hill. 3 *rarely,* Big rounded hill. S. mullach a' chinn, *the crown* or *very top of the head where the hair parts.*
—————ach, -aiche, *a.* Abounding in little hills or knolls. 2 Fairy. 3 see sìthionnach.
sìthean-as-nach-cinn, *s.m.* First year's growth of the foxglove—*Colonsay.*
sìtheann, see sìthionn.
——————ach, see sìthionnach.
sìtheil, -e, *a.* Peaceful, tranquil, silent. 2(AH) Charmed, fairy-like. Tha falbh s. aig tiodhlacadh daonnan, *a funeral always has a weird or fairy-like mode of progression.* S. in this connection does not mean *peaceful* in the ordinary sense but rather *enchanted*—AH.
sithfean, (DMK) *s.m.* Infinitessimal quantity. 2 (DU) Thing of little value. Cha chuir mi s. a dhiubhras eatorra, *I cannot see a particle of difference between them—West coast of Ross.*
sith-fhad,** *a.* Long-limbed. 2 Striding. 3 Bounding. 4 Prancing.
——————,** *s.m.* Long stride. 2 Bound. 3 Prance. 4 Name of one of Cuchullin's chariot horses. [sith-fhada.]
sith-fhear,** -fhir, *s.m.* Strong man.
sith-ghaoth, -ghaoithe, *s.f.* Whirlwind.
sith-ghlic,** *a.* Politic, cunning.
sith-ghliocas,** -ais, *s.m.* Policy, cunning, artfulness.
sìthich, *pr.pt.* a' sìtheachadh, *v. a.* Pacify becalm, quiet, allay, agree, reconcile. 2 Grow calm, grow pacified, grow reconciled.
sìthich,** -ean, *s.m.* Fairy, elf.

The sìthich is the most active sprite of Highland mythology. It is a dexterous child-stealer and is particularly intrusive on women in travail. At births many covert and cunning ceremonies are still used to baffle the fairies' power; otherwise, the new-born infant would be taken off to fairy-land, and a withered brat laid in its stead. They are wantonly mischievous, and have weapons peculiar to themselves, which operate no good to those at whom they are shot. A clergyman of the kirk, who wrote concerning fairyland about the end of the 17th. century, says of these weapons that "they are solid earthy bodies, nothing of iron, but much of stone, like to a yellow soft flint spur, shaped like a barbed arrow-head, but flung like a dart with great force—**.

sìthiche,†† -an, *s.m.* Fairy.
———ach,†† *a.* Fairy-like.
sìthichte, *past pt.* of sìthich. Pacified, reconciled.

quieted. 2 Pleased—*Caithness.*
sithionn, -inn & ìthne, *s.f.* Venison. 2 Flesh of rabbits, hares or poultry.
————ach, -aiche, *a.* Abounding in venison. 2 Like venison.
sìth-mhaor, -mhaoir, -an, *s.m.* Herald. 2 Constable, policeman. 2**Watch.
————sainneachd,** *s.f.ind.* Jurisdiction of a constable.
sìthne, *gen.sing.* of sithionn & sitheann.
sìthneachan, *n.pl.* of sìthne.
sithnne, see sìne.
————ach, see sìneach.
————an, *n.pl.* of sìthnne.
sìth-shaimh, -e, *s.f.* Peace, peacefulness, quiet, tranquility.
————each, -eiche, *a.* Tranquil, peaceful.
sìth-sheirc,** *s.f.* Constant affection.
————eil,** *a.* Constantly affectionate.
sìthte, *a.* Glad, pleased, contented. Tha mi ro sh. dheth sin, *I am very glad of that—Suth'd.*
sìth-thàmh,†† -e, *s.f.* Tranquility, peaceful rest. 2 Supineness.
————ach,†† *a.* Tranquil.
————achd,** *s.f.* Enjoyment of peaceful rest or sound repose.
sitig, -e, -ean, *s.f.* Rafter laid across the part of a kiln on which corn is kiln-dried. 2**Dunghill. Saighdear-sitig, *a dunghill soldier, a fireside warrior*—a term applied contemptuously to holiday soldiers.
sitin, see siteag.
——-each, see siteagach.
sitinn, -e, -ean, see sitig.
sitir, -e, *s.f.* Bray, neighing of a horse.
sitir,* *v.n.* Neigh, as a horse.
sitireach, see sitreach.
sitireun, see sigirean.
sitirich, see sitrich.
sitreach, -eiche, *a.* Neighing.
sitrich, *v.n.* Bray, neigh, as a horse. 2 Sneeze.
———, *s.f.ind.* Neighing of a horse, continuous neighing. 2 Act of neighing. 3 Sneezing. 4 Tittering.
sit-sit ! *int.* Hush !
———e, -an, *s.m.* Brayer.
sitta,§ *s.* Shittah tree—*acacia seyal.*
siu, see seo.
siubhad,(DU) *v.* Equivalent to *imp.* of siubhal. The only part in use—*Gairloch.*
siubhail, *pr.pt.* a' siubhal, *v. a. & n.* Go, move, walk, stroll. 2 Depart, set off. 3 Fly, vanish. 4 Die. 5 Pass over, traverse. 6*Search. 7 March. Siùbhlaidh sinn 'le 'n anam do 'n àraich, *we shall accompany their souls to the battlefield;* sh. mi am baile, *I traversed the whole town;* siùbhlaidh sinn gu léir, *we shall all die;* siùbhlaidh an t-saighead, *the arrow shall fly.*
siubhal, -ail, *pl.* siùbhlaichean, *s. m.* Moving, act of moving or walking. 2 Departing, act of departing. 3 Dying, act or state of dying. 4 Traversing, act of traversing or travelling. 5 Motion, progress. 6 March, journey. 7 Turn, course. 8 Certain part of a tune, see *ceòl mór*, in appendix. 9 Ruin, extinction, destruction. 10 Dysentry, diarrhœa. 11*Searching. 12 Driving, as a cart. 13 Flight. 14** Swiftness. 15 Travail. A' s—, *pr.pt.* of siubhail.

A' siubhal a' bhaile, *traversing the town;* tha e a' siubhal, *he is dying;* seo mo sh.-sa, *this is my turn;* marsantan-siubhail, *travellers;* tha i air sh., *she is salacious;* air an t-s. seo, *at this time*; s. eile, *at another time;* bithidh fios do sheud 's do shiubhail agam-sa, *I will know the object of your journey;* s. a chaidh mi do 'n Ghalltachd, *a journey I took to the Lowlands;* an dubh-shiùbhlach, *the street-walker;* air gach s., *at every trip;* bean-siùbhla, *a woman in child-bed;* luidhe-shiùbhladh, *confinement at or before child-bed;* tha s. sìth aig bàta-tòrraidh, *a funeral-barge aye gets a quiet sea*—as in many other matters, so here, the exception may be said to prove the rule, for there have been plenty of instances where funeral-barges have been overturned by the elements, and the corpses of mourned and mourners have been recovered together. S.-fola, *a bloody-flux;* biadh-siubhail, *provision for a journey;* tha e a' siubhal gu dian, *he driveth furiously.*

siubhalach, see siùbhlach.
siubhalaiche,** *s.m.* Traveller, wayfaring man. 2 Pedestrian. 3 Stroller.
siubhaltair, *s.m.* Perambulator.
†siubhas, *adv.* Before.
siùbhla, see luighe-siùbhla.
siubhlach, -aich, -aichean, *s.m. & f.* Vagrant man or woman.
†siubhios, *adv.* Before.
siùbhlach, -aiche, *a.* Swift, speedy. 2 Nimble. 3 Fleeting, speeding, passing away. 4 Wandering, fond of wandering, ambulatory. 5 Restless, transient. 6 Fluent. 7 Traversing. 8 Travelling, moving. 9 Migrating, flitting. 10 Departing. Aighean s., *restless deer.*
siùbhlachadh,(MS) *s.m.* Acceleration.
siùbhlachail, -e, *a.* Locomotive.
siùbhlachan, -ain, -an, *s.m.* Traveller, one fond of travelling or wandering. 2 Stream, rivulet.
siùbhlachas, -ais, *s. m.* Swiftness, speediness, speed. 2 Nimbleness. 3 Habit of travelling or wandering. 4 Pedestrianism. 5 Fluency.
siùbhlachd, *s.f.ind.* see siùbhlachas. 2 Continued travelling, moving or flitting. 3 Restlessness. 4 Transientness.
siùbhladh, -aidh, *s.m.* Ambulation, travelling, departure, motion. 2 Death. 3 Looseness of the bowels.
siùbhlaiche, see siubhalaiche.
siùbhlaichean, *pl.* of siubhal.
siùbhlaideach, -eiche, *a.* see siùbhlach.
————d, *s.f.* see siùbhlachas.
siuc ! *int.* Word by which horses are called. 2 Away, begone, disperse—*Sàr-Obair.*
siuc, -a, *a.* Dry, parched. 2 Scorched. (for sioc.)
siucain,(MMcD) see surcain.
siùcar, -air, *s.m.* Sugar. S. pronn, *moist sugar;* s. candaidh, *candied sugar;* s. dubh, *liquorice;* s. geal, *white sugar.*
———ach, -aiche, *a.* Abounding in sugar. 2 Like sugar, sugary, saccharine, sweet.
siuch,* *s.m.* Drain, sewer.
siuchag,(AH) *s.f.* Small patch of smooth green sward amid rough heathery ground.
siùd, *pr.pt.* a' siùdadh, *v.a.* Swing, rock to sleep, dandle. 2 Fondle. 3*Fall to.
siùdadh, -aidh, *s.m.* Swinging, act of swinging, vibrating or rocking. A' *pr.pt.* of siùd.
siudadh,* *s.m.* Commencement.
siùdagain, *v.a.* see siùd.
siùdagan, *s.m. & pr.pt.* see siùdan.
————ach, -aiche, *a.* see siùdanach.
siùdain, *pr.pt.* a' siùdan, *v.a.* Same meanings as siùd.
————, *gen.sing.* of siùdan.
siùdan, -ain, -an, *s.m.* Swinging, rocking, vibrating. 2 Swing. 3 Oscillation. 4**Any instrument for swinging or rocking on. A' s—, *pr. pt.* of siùdain. A' s. a nunn 's a nall, *oscillating this way and that way;* ri s. *vibrating, swinging;* slat shiùdain, *a pendulum.*
siùdanach, -aiche, *a.* Swinging, rocking, oscil-

lating, vibrating, dandling. 2 Fond of swinging, tossing or dandling.
siùdanachadh,** -aidh, *s. m.* Swinging, tossing, dandling, rocking.
siùdanachd,** *s.f.* Jactitation, nustling, rocking, swinging, dandling, amusement of swinging.
siùdanadh,(DU) *s.m.* Act of swinging or rocking to sleep—*Gairloch.*
siùdanaich, see siùdain.
siug! *int.* Mode of calling hens. 2‡ Call to drive away hens. 3 (AH) In *N. Argyll*, mode of driving away hens, *diug* being the *int.* used to call them towards one.
siùil, *gen.sing.* & *n.pl.* of seòl (sail.)
†siuir, *s.f.* Sister.
siulmhor, see suilbhear.
siulpan, *s.m.* Short stout stick. 2 Policeman's baton—*Suth'd.* (siolpan.) 3 (DU) Short thick stick used for threshing corn. 4 (DU) The part of a flail that strikes the corn.
siumrag, see seamrag.
siunan,** -ain, *s.m.* Vessel made of straw to hold meal.
siunas, -ais, see sunais.
siunn, see sionn.
siunnachan, see sionnachan.
siunnailt, *s. f.* Likeness, comparison, resemblance—*Sàr-Obair.*
†siunnsa, *s.m.* Sense.
siunnsaireachd,** *s.f.* see seannsaireachd.
siunnsar, -air, -ean, *s.m.* see seannsair.
————ach, -aiche, *a.* see seannsaireach.
siùp, -a, -an, *s.m.* Tail, appendage.
siupach, -aiche, *a.* Having a foolish tail or appendage.
siurdan,** *v.n.* Rattle, rustle, make a noise.
siurdan,** -ain, *s.m.* Tattle. 2 Rattling noise. 3 Rustling noise.
siurdanach,** *a.* Rattling. 2 Noisy. 3 Rustling.
————-——d,** *s.f.* Continued rattling or rustling.
siurdanadh,** -aidh, *s. m.* Rattling, rustling, rattling or rustling noise.
siùrra feamainn, *s.* Wrack along the water-mark, mistranslated "seaweed seekers" in *W. H. Tales.*
siurran,** -ain, *s. m.* Giddiness. 2 Drunkenness. 3 Watery mist.
siùrsach, -aich, -aichean, *s. f.* Whore, strumpet.
siùrsachail, -e, *a.* Unchaste, whorish.
siùrsachalachd, *s.f.ind.* Unchasteness.
siùrsachd, *s.f.ind.* Whoredom, prostitution.
siùrsaich, *gen.sing.* of siùrsach.
siùrsaiche,(MS) *s.m.* Belswagger, debauchee.
siùrsaichean, *n.pl.* of siùrsach.
siùrsaidheachd, see siùrsachd.
siùrsair,* -ean, *s.m.* Whoremonger.
siùrtach, -aich, -aichean, *s.f.* see siùrsach.
siùrtachail,** *a.* Whorish.
siùrtachd,** see siùrsachd.
siùrtaich, *gen.sing.* of siùrtach.
siùrtaichean, *n.pl.* of siùrtach.
siùrtag,** -aig, see sùrdag.
siùrtagach, see sùrdagach.
siùsan,** -ain, *s.m,* Humming noise. 2 Buzz, buzzing. 3 Whisper.
siùsanach,** *a.* Humming. 2 Whispering.
siùsanadh,** -aidh, *s.m.* Humming, hum. 2 Whispering, whisper.
siùsarnadh, -aidh, see siùsanadh.
siùsarnaich, *s.f.* Whispering.
siutach,(DMy) *a.* Thievish.
siutair,(DMy) *s.m.* Thief.
siuthad, *v. def.* Say away, begin, go on, help yourself. *Pl.* siuthadaibh, only used in *2nd. pers. pl. imp.*
siuthadadh,* -aidh, *s.m.* Commencement.
siuthadaibh, *v. def.* Say ye.
slàbag,** -aig, -an, *s.f.* Slut, slattern.
slàbair,** -ean, *s.m.* Sloven, draggler. 2 One who works among mire.
slàbaireachd,** *s. f.* Slovenliness. 2 Working amongst mud or mire. 3 Miriness.
slàban,** -ain, *s.m.* Sloven, draggler.
———ach,** *a.* Slovenly, dirty. 2 Miry.
slabhacan, see slabhagan.
slabhag, -aig, -an, *s.f.* Horn-pith. 2 Socket of horn. 3 Tenderling, deer's first horn.
slabhagan, -ain, *s.m.* Kind of reddish seaweed, an article of food formerly cooked till it dissolved, when it was eaten with bread and butter. see slòcan. [McL & D gives slabhgan.]
slabhaig, see slaoic.
slabhaigeadh,(CR) *s.m.* Beaten eggs spread on oatcake before it is turned in firing. This is done when the cake is to be used as provision on a journey, and prevents it from crumbling—*W. of Ross-shire* The cake thus treated is "aran slabhaigidh," *(Gairloch)* but is applied to cakes that have not been spread over with egg—DU.
slabhar,** *a.* Narrow.
slabhartaich, *v.a.* Slap.
slabhcar,‡ -air, *s.m.* Slouching fellow. 2 Taunter. 3 Spiritless fellow—*Suth'd.*
slabhraich, *v.a.* Shackle.
slabhradair,* -ean, *s.m.* Chair-maker.
slabhraidh, -e [& slaibhre]. -aidhean, *s.f.* Chain. 2 Pot-hanger. 3(AF) Cattle, herds. Tinne na slabhraidh, *a link of the chain ;* s. òir *a gold chain ;* bas na slabhraidh, *the pot-hook.*
slabhraidheach, -eiche, *a.* Furnished with chains. 2 Of chains.
slabhruidh, see slabhraidh.
slac, *v. a.* Thrash, beat with a mallet. 2 Dash against. 3 Cane, drub. 4 Bang. 5 Bruise. 6 Strike with a batlet. 7 Maul.
slac, *s.m.* Mallet.
slachdach,** *a.* Prone or inclined to beat, thrash, maul or bruise.
slacadaich,(DU) *s.f.* Sound made by beating with a heavy body.
slacadh, -aidh, *s.m.* Thrashing, act of thrashing or beating, as with a mallet. 2 Dashing, act of dashing against. 3 Bruising. 4 Slaughtering, act of slaughtering. A' s—, *pr. pt.* of slac.
slacaich, *v.a.* see slac.
slacainn,** *v.n.* Beat, maul, bruise, thrash.
slacainn, *v.a.* see slac.
————, s. see slacadh.
slacainn, *s. f.* Beating, thrashing, mauling, bruising. Fhuair e s., *he received a thrashing;* thoir a dheagh sh. dha, *give him a good thrashing.*
slacair,** *v.a.* see slacainn.
slacair, -ean, *s. m.* Thrasher, one that beats with a mallet or beetle. 2 Slaughterer. 3 Bruiser.
slacaireachd, *s. f. ind.* Thrashing, beating, noise of hard labour. 2 Constant dashing of one thing against another. 3 Slaughtering. 4**Business of slaughtering. 5 Bruising. 6 Buffeting. 7 Striking with a batlet.
slacairt,** *s. f.* Beating, thrashing, bruising, mauling.
slacan, -ain, -an, *s.m.* Beetle, mallet for washing clothes or fulling cloth. 2 Impediment, drawback. 3 Brake of a cycle. 4 Block of wood, or any weight tied to an animal to prevent its escape. 5 Bat, as for cricket, rounders, &c. 7†† Club. S.-druidheachd, *a*

magic wand.
slacan, *s.m.* Circular depression, like a kiln.
slacanaich, *v.a.* see slac. 2 *s.* see slacaireachd.
slacan-bàta, *s.pl.* Davits of a boat. (No 16, p.76.)
slacan-craigeir, *s.m.* Cricket-bat.
slacarsaich, *s.f.* Battery. 2 Beating, thrashing, mauling, buffeting. 3 Continued beating or thrashing. 4 Beating with a batlet.
slachd, see slac.
slachdach, see slacach.
slachdaich, *v.* see slac.
slachdair, see slacair.
slachdairt, see slacairt.
slachdan, see slacan.
slachdanaich, see slacanaich.
slachdraich, see slacraich.
slachduinn, see slacainn.
slacran, -ain, *s.m.* Battering-ram.
slacraich, -e, *s.f.* Maul. 2††Beating, thrashing. 3††Noise of beating, or ponderous hammering. 4 Buffeting. Bhiodh laoich churranta slacraich bhàis 'nuair 'bu trod 'bu bheus doibh. *stout heroes would give death-dealing blows when scolding was their frame of mind—Duanaire, 193.*
slacta, *past pt.* of slac. Beaten with a mallet or beetle. 2 Dashed against. 3 Slaughtered.
slacuinn, see slacainn.
slad, -aid, *s.m.* Theft, robbery. 2 Plunder, booty. 3* Havoc, carnage. 'S iad a rinn an s.! *what havoc they have made!* 's ann an sin a bha an s.; *that was the awful place for carnage!* ceal-shlad, *sacrilege.*
slad, *v.a.* Steal, rob, plunder. 2 Fag, cause to fag, deprive of strength. 3‡‡ Pommel. Sh. sinn seachad iad, *that made them fag, it palled on their stomach;* sh. e mo chlì bhuam, *it deprived me of my strength.*
sladach, -aiche, *a.* Robbing, plundering, thievish.
sladachd, *s.f.ind.* Theft, robbery, plunder, thievishness. Gun dad s., *without any theft.*
sladadh, -aidh, *s.m.* Stealing, act of stealing, robbery, pillaging, theft. A' s—, *pr. pt.* of slad.
sladaiche, -an, *s.m.* Robber, plunderer, thief.
sladaidheachd, see sladachd.
slàdaig, (air) (CR) *v.n.* Working hard at, going at it—*Perthshire.*
sladair, -ean, *s.m.* see sladaiche.
sladaireachd, *s.f.* Thievishness, robbery, plundering. Ceal-sh., *sacreligiousness.*
sladhag, -aig, -an, *s.f.* Sheaf of straw prepared for thatching, sheaf of drawn straw. 2‡‡Sheaf of corn ready to be threshed. 3 (DC) Keratin, outer sheath of the horn of an ox, sheep, &c.
slad-mharbh, see slat-mhort.
slad-mharbhadh, -aidh, *s.m.* see slad-mhortadh.
sladmhoireachd,** *s.f.* Thievishness, robbery.
†slad-mhort, *v. a.* Rob and murder on the highway. 2 Murder in order to conceal a robbery.
slad-mhortadh,** -aidh, *s. m.* Robbery and murder.
slad-mhortair, -ean, *s.m.* Robber and murderer, one who commits murder to effect or conceal a robbery.
slad-mhurt, see slad-mhort.
slad-mhurtadh, see slad-mhortadh.
slad-mhurtair, see slad-mhortair.
sladta, *past pt.* of slad. Robbed, stolen, plundered. see slaidte.
slafaist, *s.* Loosely-built person.
slag,** -aig, *s.f.* Spoonful of any inspissated substance, as porridge. 2 Flummery.
slagan, (CR) -ain, *s.m.* see slaman. 2 Cup-shaped interior of a kiln.
slagan cùl a' chinn, (DMy) *s.m.* Hollow at the back of one's head—*Lewis, Gairloch, &c.* for lagan cùl a' chinn.
slàib, -e, *s.f.* Mire, sediment of water, filth, dirt. 2 Mire by the side of a stream.
slàibeach, -eiche, *a.* Miry, filthy, dirty. 2 Puddling in mire, draggling.
slàibear,** -eir, *s.m.* Dirty fellow, draggler. 2 One who works in mire or mud.
slàibearachd,** *s.f.* Draggling.
slàibeil, -e, *a.* see slàibeach.
slaibhre, see slabhraidh. †2 *s.f.* Purchase.
slaibhreas,** -eis, *s. m.* Chains. 2 Servitude, bondage. 3 State of being in chains.
slaic, *v.* see slac.
slaicinn,* *v.* see slac.
slaid, -e, -ean, *s.f.* Munificent gift or present. 2 Booty. 3 Theft, robbery.
slaid, see slad.
slaideach, see sladach.
slaideadh, *s.m.* Depredation.
slaidear, -ir, -an, *s.m.* Robber, thief, plunderer, defrauder.
slaidearachd, see sladachd.
slaidse,** Gaelic spelling of *slash.*
——ach,** *a.* Slashing, lashing, whipping.
——anta,** *a.* Stout, robust.
——arachd,** *s.f.* Lashing, whipping.
slaidte, *past pt.* of slaid. Stolen, robbed, plundered.
slaighdean,** -ein, *s.m.* Cold, cough.
slaighre,** -richean, *s.f.* Sword, scimitar.
slaight, -e, *s.f.* Roguery, villainy, knavery.
slaight,* *v.n.* Sneak or steal by. Sh. e seachad, *he sneaked by.*
slaightear, -ir, -an, *s.m.* Rogue, rascal, knave, blackguard.
——ach, -aiche, *a.* Knavish, roguish.
——achd, *s. f. ind.* Roguery, dishonesty, thievery, faithlessness, villainy, sneaking.
slaighteil,* -e, *a.* Roguish, knavish, sneakish.
slaim, -e, *pl.* -ean & -eannan, *s.f.* Great booty, plunder, much booty. 2 Heap. 3‡ Riches.
slaimeach, *a.* Having prey or booty. 2 Of prey or booty. 3 In heaps.
slaimean,** -ein, *s.m.* Dirty person.
slàine, *comp.* of slàn. More or most healthy.
——, *s.f.* Wholeness, entireness. 2 Convalescence.
——ad,** -eid, *s.m.* see slàine, *s.f.*
slàinnte, see slàinte.
slàinte, *s.f.ind.* Health. 2 Salvation. 3 Toast, health. 4**Healing virtue. Agus 'nan s. do na cnàmhan, *and health to the bones;* chionn gu'n do dhì-chuimhnich thu Dìa, do shlàinte, *because thou hast forgotten God thy salvation;* thoir dhuinn s., *give us a toast;* dh' òl sinn do dheoch-s., *we drank your health;* air do sh., *to your good health;* s. agad-sa, *thank you, the same to you;* s. leat, (*usually* slàn leat) *farewell;* thig mi thaobh mo sh., *I will come if I be well, if my health permit.* [††*pl.* -eachan.]
——ach, -eiche, see slàinteil.
——achail, *a.* Healthsome.
——alachd, *s.f.* Healthiness. 2 Benignity.
——il, -e, *a.* Healthy, in good health. 2 Healthy, bringing health. 3 Benign. 4 see tàth.
slais, *v.a.* Gaelic form of *lash.* 2††Splice, as a rope.
slais,* -e, -ean & -eachan, *s.f.* Great quantity or number. S. éisg, *a great quantity of fish;* fhuair iad s., *they got a great quantity;* s. airgid, *a quantity of money.*
slaiseadh, -idh, *s.m.* Lashing, act of lashing, whipping. 2 Splicing, act of splicing. A' s—, *pr.pt.* of slais.
slaisich, see slaisnich.
——te, see slaiste.

slaisneach,(MS) *s.m.* Lath.
slaisnich,(MS) *v.a.* Lash, lath.
slaiste, *past pt.* of slais.
slait,** *a.* Strong, robust.
slam,** *v.a.* Teaze, pluck or card wool.
slam, -aim, -an, *s. m.* Lock of hair or wool, (in *N. Argyll*, tlàm—AH.) 2 Slime. 3 Curds.
slamach, -aiche, *a.* see slamanach. 2**Teazing, plucking, as wool. 3 Carding. 4 In locks, as hair. 5 In flocks, as wool.
———adh,** -aidh, *s.m.* Coalescence. 2 Teazing wool (in *N. Argyll*, tlàmadh—AH.)
slamadh,(DU) *s.m.* Lull in a gale—*Gairloch.*
slamag, -aig, -an, *s. f.* Little lock of hair. 2 Small flock of wool. 3 see slaman.
———ach, -aiche, *a.* Curled. 2 In small locks, as hair. 3 In little flocks, as wool. 4 see slamanach.
slamagan, *s. pl.* Tresses—*MacMhaighstir Alasdair.*
slamaich,** *v.* Clot, curdle.
———te, *past pt.* Clotted.
slamair,** *s.m.* One who eats voraciously.
slaman, -ain, *s.m.* Curdled milk. 2 Any flabby substance.
———ach, -aiche, *a.* Flabby. 2 Abounding in or like curdled milk. 3 Lentous, mucous, clotty. 4 Producing curds.
slamanachd,** *s.f.* State of being curdled. 2 Coagulation. 3 Tendency to coagulate.
———aich, *v.a.* Curdle.
——— -ceathaich,** *s.m.* Light dry mist. 2 Stratus cloud, fall cloud.
——— milis, *s.m.* Jelly.
——— -tàth, *s.m.* Glue.
slamb,* see slaman-milis.
slamban,* -ain, *s.m.* see slaman.
———ach, see slamanach.
———achd,** see slamanachd.
slamhach,** -aich, *s.f.* Frothstick, instrument for frothing cream.
slamhagan, see slabhagan.
slamhagan,** *s.pl.* Locks of hair or wool.
slamhan,§ *s.m.* Elm, see leamhann.
———, -ain, *s.m.* Mucilage.
———ach, -aiche, *a.* Mucilaginous. 2 see slamanach. 3 Abounding in elms. 4 Made of elm.
———achd, *s.f.* Mucilaginousness.
slan, *s.m.* Defence, protection. 2 Garrison. *Sàr-Obair.*
slàn, -àine, *a.* Healthy, in good health. 2 Healed. 3 Sound. 4 Uninjured, unhurt. 5 Unbroken, whole.

Am bheil thu s.? *are you in good health?* thoir dhomh s. e, *give it me whole;* s. leat! *farewell!* gu ma s. gu'n till thu, *may you be well till you return;* an s. dhuit? *art thou well?;* tha i gu s. fallain, *she is perfectly well;* òighean bhòidheach, s. leibh! *ye pretty maids, farewell!;* nighean nan òr-chleachd, an s. dhuit? *maiden of the golden locks, art thou well?;* gu ma s. a chì mi thu, *may I see you well;* gu s. fallain, *safe and sound, in perfect health.*

†slan,** -ain, *s.m.* Defiance, challenge.
†——ach, *a.* Defying, challenging. 2 Ready to defy or challenge. 3 Of a defiance or challenge.
slànach,* -aiche, *a.* Convalescent. 2**Healing, curing, having a healing virtue, salubrious, salutary.
slànachadh,** -aidh, *s.m.* A' s—, *pr. pt.* of slànaich. see slanuchadh.
slànachail, -e, *a.* Curative.
slànadh, -aidh, *s.m.* Healing, saving, salvation, security.
slànaich, see slànuich.
slànaichear, see slànuichear.
slànaichidh, see slànuichidh.
slànaichte, see slànuichte.
slanaighear, see slanuighear.
slan-ic, see ic.

639. Slàn-lus.

slàn-lus, -luis, -an, *s.m.* Rib-wort—*plantago lanceolata.* 2**Any medicinal herb. 3§ Self-heal, see dubhan ceann-chòsach. 4§ Garden-sage, see athair-liath.
———ach, *a.* Abounding in rib-wort, or 2 in Medicinal herbs, or 3 in Self-heal, or 4 in Garden-sage.
slànphairteach, *a.* Aliquot.
slàn-reic, *s.* Wholesale.
slàntachd,(MS) *s.f.* Solidity.
slànuchadh, -aidh, *s.m.* Healing, act of healing, curing or remedying. 2 Saving, act of saving (in a spiritual sense.) 3 Repairing, mending. 4 Growing whole. A' s—. *pr. pt.* of slànuich.
slànuich, *pr. pt.* a' slànuchadh, *v. a.* Heal. 2 Save (in a spiritual sense.) 3 Cure, remedy, make whole. 4 Grow whole. 5 Mend, repair.
———ear, *fut. pass.* of slànuich. Shall be healed.
———idh, *fut.aff.a.* of slànuich. Shall or will heal.
———te, *past pt.* of slànuich. Healed, cured. 2 Saved (in a spiritual sense.) 3 Mended.
slànuighear, -ir, *s.m.* Healer. 2 Saviour (in a spiritual sense.) An Slànuighear, *the Saviour.*
slaobach,** *a.* Dowdy.
slaod, *pr.pt.* a' slaodadh, *v.a.* Drag, haul, trail along the ground, draw. 2**Walk with a trailing gait.
slaod, -aoid, -an, *s.m.* Raft, float. 2 Sledge. 3 Trail, trailing burden. 4 Act of dragging along. 5 Clumsy, lazy person. 6**Solution. 7**Murder, slaughter. 8 Pulley, crane. 9†† Lounge. 10††Large quantity.
slaodach,(MMcD) *s.f.* Seaweed—*Lewis*, see feamainn dubh.
———, -aiche, *a.* Trailing, dragging, drawing, pulling. 2** Like a drag. 3 Like a raft or float. 4 Clumsy. 5 Lazy. 6 Ill-dressed, slovenly, untidy. 7 Awkward. 8 Having a sluggish gait. 9* Lounging.
———d,** *s.f.* Awkwardness. 2‡‡Drowsiness.
slaodadh, -aidh, *s.m.* Dragging, act of dragging, trailing or hauling along. 2 Trailing burden, 3 Sledge, drag. 4 Sluggish gait. 4 Raft, float. A' s—, *pr. pt.* of slaod.
slaodag, -aig, -an, *s.f.* Slut, slovenly woman. (DU) Sledge.
slaodaiche, *s.f.ind.* Drawing, trailing, dragging. 2 Slovenliness.
slaodail, -e, *a.* see slaodach.
———,** *s.f.* Continued dragging, trailing or pulling. 2 Like a raft. 3 Like a drag.
slaodair, -ean, *s.m.* Lazy, awkward, slovenly

fellow, untidy fellow, sluggard, lounger.
———eachd, s.f.ind. Awkwardness, slovenliness, untidiness. 2 Laziness, sluggishness. 3 (MS) Backwardness. 4(MS) Restiveness.
slaodalachd, see slaodaireachd.
slaodan, -ain, -an, s.m. Track or rut of a cart-wheel or sledge. 2 **Cold, cough. 3**Little raft, little float. 4**Little trailing burden.
———, n.pl. of slaod.
slaodanach,*-aich, s.m. Heavy fellow. 2 Slouching fellow.
slaod-mheurach, -aiche, a. Clumsy-fingered.
slaod-mheuraiche, s.f.ind. Clumsiness in fingering, as of a musical instrument.
slaodrach, -aich, -aichean, s.f. Hinge. 2**Foundation.
slaodraich, -e, -ean, s.f. Continual trailing. 2 Mass of lumber or luggage. 3* Great haul of fish.
slaod-theine,** s.m. Wasting or consuming fire. 2 Great fire in which many persons were consumed.
slaod-uisge,(AH) s.m. Raft.
slaoic,(CR) s.f. Large slice, as of bread—*Perthshire*. 2 Large piece. 3 (DC) Buttocks. Air a sh., *prone on the ground.*
———,** a. Inverted. 2 Lying. 3 (AH) Uneven, crooked, unmatched, slouching to one side. Mart s., *a cow having one horn extending in a different direction to the other ;* tha s. air an fhear ud, *that man has a slouching gait.*
slaoichd, see slaoic.
slaoid, see slaod. 2 *gen.sing.* of slaod.
slaoighte, see slaight.
———il, see slaighteil.
slaoightir,* see slaightear.
————eachd, see slaightearachd.
slaoit, -e, s.f. †Dross, refuse of metal. 2**Dirt, filth.
slaonasadh,** -aidh, s.m. Tragedy.
slaonasair,** s.m. Tragedian.
slaop, *pr.pt.* a' slaopadh, v. a. Parboil, simmer, boil slowly, as shell-fish for bait.
slaop, -aoip, s.m. Slovenliness, sluggishness.
slaopach, -aiche, a. Parboiled. 2 Trailing, drawling. 3 Lazy. 4 Awkward. 5 Slovenly, sluggish, tawdry, untidy. 6 Unclean. 7†† Dragging lazily.
————d, s.f. Awkwardness. 2 Slovenliness, untidiness, tawdriness. 3 Uncleanness.
slaopadh, -aidh, *pr. pt.* Act of parboiling or simmering. A' s—, *pr.pt.* of slaop.
slaopaidh, a. see slaopach.
slaopair, -ean, s.m. Drawler. 2 Trailer. 3 Sloven, sluggard, awkward, untidy fellow.
————eachd, s.f.ind. Trailing. 2 Drawling. 3 Slovenliness. 4 Awkwardness. 5 Sluggishness.
slaot,** -aoit, s.m. Dirt, dross. 2 see slaod.
slaotan, -ain, see slaodan.
slap,* s.m. Flap, flapping.
slap, *pr.pt.* a' slapail & a' slapadh, v.a. Flap, fling. A' slapail mu m' chluasan, *flapping about my ears.*
slapach, a. Lukewarm. 2 Slovenly, sluttish.
slàpach, see slapach.
slapag, -aig, -an, s.f. Slut, drab, slattern.
———ach,** a. Sluttish, drabbish.
slapaich,* v.n. Get flappish, get soft and pliant, as greens heated.
slapail,* -e, s.f. Flapping. A' s—, *pr.pt.* of slap.
slapair, -ean, s.m. Slovenly fellow. 2 Dangler. 3 Sluggard. 4**One who works in mud.
————eachd, s.f.ind. Slovenliness.
†slapar,** s.m. Skirt, train of a long robe.
†———ach, a. Having a long skirt or train, as a robe.
†———aich, s.f. Din.
slap-chàl,* s.m. Spinach, see blòinigean-gàraidh.
slapraich, -e, s.f. Din, noise. 2 Sound of tramp-ling, as of men or horses.
slasdach,** a. Envying, invidious. 2 Having a grudge.
————d,** s.f. Envy, grudge.
slat, -ait, -an, s.f. Any rod or twig. 2 Switch, wand. 3 Yard in length. 4 Yard to measure with. 5 Handle-bar of a cycle. 6 Stay of a plough. 7** Penis. Thog e an t-slat, *he lifted the rod* ; s. air fad, *a yard long ;* s. ghlas de 'n chritheach, *a green rod of aspen ;* eadar an t-sùgh 's an t-slat, *between the bark and the tree.*
slatach, -aiche, a. Abounding in rods or twigs. 2 Like a rod. 3 Straight, erect. 4 Stately, tall. 5 Branchy, branching, sprouting. 6 Pliant, as a switch. 7 In rods or wands. 8 In switches. Na fiùrain sh., *the pliant tendrils.*
slatag, -aig, -an, s.f., dim. of slat. Small rod, twig, wand or switch. 2 Chat (of brushwood.)
———ach, -aiche, a. Abounding in small rods, twigs, tendrils, wands or switches. 2 Like a small rod.
slatail,** a. Amorous. 2** Goatish. 3 Tall, stately, straight, upright. 4 Limber.
———eachd,** s. f. Amorousness. 2 Uprightness, tallness, stateliness.
slatair,* -ean, s.m. Debauchee. 2**Amorist.
slatan,** -ain, s.m. Little rod, little wand.
———, n.pl. of slat.
———ta,** a. Flexible.
slatarra,** a. Straight, tall, upright.
slat-bheòil,* s.f. Gunwale, see bàta, E 7, p. 73.
slat-bhrodaidh, s.f. Goad.
slat-bhrogaidh,** s.f. Goad.
slat-bhuilg, s.f. Bilge-piece, see bàta, F 8, p. 73.
slat-draoidheachd,* s.f. Mace, rod of office. 2 The magic wand of the folk-tales.
slat-ghorm,§ s.f. Woody-nightshade, bitter-sweet, see searbhag-mhilis.
slat-ghreasaid,‡‡ s.f. Whip, goad.
slat-gunna,‡‡ s.f. Ram-rod of a gun.
slathag,(AC) s.f. Handful of corn cut at one stroke of the reaping-hook.
slat-iasgaich,**s.f. Fishing-rod.
slat-iomain,* s.f. Goad.
slat-ladhrach, s.f. Gaff, see bàta, H, p. 73.
slat-leòid, s.f. Temple, stretcher, in *weaving.*
slat-mhara, -ait- & -aite-, pl. slatan-mara, s.f. Sea-oak, oar-weed, tangles, see stamh. 2†† Large grey tangle.
slat-mharcachd,* s.f. Rider's whip or switch.
slat-òir, (an t-s—,) s.f. Golden-rod—*Colonsay.*
slat-réil, s.f. Astrolabe.
slat-rìoghail,* s.f. Sceptre.
slat-sgiùrsaidh,* -an-, s.f. Lash, scourge, cat-o'-nine-tails. [These names in English are applied only to instruments of hemp or leather, but *slat* is essentially one of wood.]
slat-sgòid,(AH) s.f. Boom of a ship.
slat-shiùil, s.f. Sail-yard, gaff, see bàta, H, p.73.
slat-shuaicheantais, s.f. Sceptre, mace. 2 Flag-staff, banner-staff.
slat-thomhais, s.f. Wand, yard-measure, ell-measure. 2 ** Any rod used for making lineal measurements. 3 Pole. 4 The three brilliant stars popularly known as "Orion's belt," [preced by the article *an t-*.] 5 (DU) Centipede, *prov.*
slaucar,‡ -air, -an, s.m. see slabhcar.
sleac, *Badenoch* for leac.
sleachd, see sleuchd.
†sleachd,** v.a. Cut, dissect, lance, scarify.
†———adh,** -aidh, s.m. Cutting, dissecting, lancing, scarifying. 2(MS) Obeisance.
sleag,(AH) s.f. State of listing very much to one side as a sailing-boat in a stiff breeze. Tha

s. brèagh orra, *she has a fine list.*
sleag, *v.a.* Sneak, drawl.
——ach,** *a.* Sneaking, drawling.
——adh,** -aidh, *s.m.* Sneaking, drawling.
sleabhag,(AC) -aig, -an, *s.f.* Kind of mattock for digging up carrots and roots of plants used in tanning and dyeing.
sleagair,** -ean,*s.m.* Sneaking fellow. 2 Drawler.
———eachd,** *s.f.* Habit of sneaking. 2 Behaviour of a sneaking fellow. 3 Drawling.
sleagan,** -ain, *s.m.* A shell.
sleagh, -a [& slèigh**] *pl.* -an [& sléigh,] *s. f.* Spear, lance, javelin. Bhitheadh ur sleaghan mar theachdairean a' bhàis, *let your spears be as the messengers of death ;* thog sinn sleaghan, *we lifted spears.*
——ach, -aiche, *a.* Of,or resembling a spear or lance. 2 Armed with a spear, lance or dart.
sleaghadair, see sleaghair.
————eachd, *s.f.ind.* Tournament.
sleaghair,* -ean, *s.m.* Spearman, lancer. 2(DC) Lazy busybody, one given to frequenting houses.
———eachd,** *s.f.* Shooting with a spear, spearing. 2 Fighting with spears.
sleaghag,(MMcL) *s.f.* The stick used for stirring the grain when in a large pot before the fire after having been cleaned from the husks, before being sifted previous to grinding in the *brà.—Lewis.* 2(DMy) Pointed instrument for digging. 3 Little spear. 4 (DMy) Pot-stick to stir potatoes, also for planting potatoes in newly reclaimed soil.
sleaghaich,(MS) *v.a.* Indart.
sleaghan, -ain, *s.m.* Kind of turf-spade, spaddle, instrument for digging. 2 Little spear.
sleaghan, *n.pl.* of sleagh.
sleamachd, see sliomachd.
sleamcaire,(MS) *s.m.* Dangler.
sleamhain, -mhna, see sleamhuinn.
sleamhan,** -ain, see leamhan.
———ach, see leamhanach.
sleamhna, *comp.* of sleamhuinn.
sleamhnachadh, -aidh, *s.m.* Slipping, act of slipping, sliding. 2 Slipperiness. 3 Gliding. 4* Retrograding, getting worse. A' s—,*pr. pt.* of sleamhnaich. Cùl-s., *backsliding.*
sleamhnachd, *s.f.* Slipperiness. 2 Smoothness.
sleamhnad, -aid, *s.m.* Degree of slipperiness. 2 Degree of smoothness.
sleamhnagan, see sleamhnan.
sleamhnaich, *pr.pt.* a' sleamhnachadh,*v.n.* Slip, slide. 2 Make slippery. 3 Make smooth. 4 Glide, move imperceptibly.
sleamhnan, -ain, -an, *s. m.* Any slippery substance. 2 Sneaking fellow. 3 Piece of ice on which to slide. 4 Mucus, saliva. 5 Stye, inflammation of the eyes, *prov.*
sleamhanachd,(AC) *s.f.* Exorcism of a stye.
sleamhuuchadh, see sleamhnachadh.
sleamhnuich, see sleamhnaich.
sleamhragan, see sleamhnan.
sleamhran, see sleamhnan.
sleamhuinn, sleamhna, *a.* Slippery. 2 Smooth.
sleant,** *s.m.* Tile.
sleantach,** *s.m.* Flake. 2 Slice.
†sleas, sleis, *s.m.* Mark, sign. 2 Ridge. 3 see slios.
sleasd,** *v.a.* Smear, bedaub, bespawl.
sleasdach,** *a.* Smeary, dirty.
sleasdaich,** *v.a.* Smear, bedaub, bespawl.
sleasdair, see sleastair.
————eachd, see sleastaireachd.
sleasg,** *v.a. & n.* Split, crack.
———ach, *a.* Cracking, splitting.
sleasgadh,** -aidh, *s. m.* Cracking, splitting, crack, split.
sleastair,‡ *v.a.* Bedaub—*Badenoch.*
————eachd, *s.f.* Smearing, bedaubing, bespawling.
sléibhe,* *gen.sing.* of sliabh.
sleibheag, see sleabhag.
sléibhte, *pl.* of sliabh.
sléibhteach, -eiche, *a.* Mountainous, hilly. 2 Dwelling among mountains. 3 Of mountains.
—————, -eich, *s.m.* Mountaineer.
—————d, *s.f.* Mountainousness.
sléibhtean, *n.pl.* of sliabh.
sléibhtrich,†† *s.f.* Wreckage, things strewn.
†sleidm, *s.* "Saniem."
sléigeil,‡ -eala, *a.* Dilatory. 2††Drawling,slow. 3††Sly.
sleimhne, *comp.* of sleamhuinn.
sleimhne, *s.f.ind.* see sleamhnachd.
sleimhneach,** *a.* Slipping, slippery. 2 Smooth.
——————d,** *s.f.* Slipperiness. 2 Smoothness.
sleimhneag,†† -aig, -an, *s.f.* Slide.
sléis, *gen.sing.* of slias.
sléisde, *gen.sing.* of sliasaid.
sléisdeach,†† -aiche, *a.* Large-thighed.
sléisdean, *pl.* of sliasaid.
sléisne, see sléisde & sléisdean.
sléisneach, -eich, *a.* Large-thighed.
sléisneadh, *s.m.* Back-sliding—*Dàin I. Ghobha.*
sléisnean, see sléisde & sléisdean.
sleithe,** *s.f.* Section, division, cutting.
sleog,* *v.a.* Pall on the stomach.
sleogach, -aiche, *a.* Qualmish, queasy. 2*Slimy. 3* Apt to pall on the stomach.
sleogadh, -aidh, *s.m.* Qualm, qualmishness, queasiness.
sleuchd, *pr.pt.* a' sleuchdadh, *v.n.* Kneel, prostrate, bow down reverently,worship. 2 Yield, submit, surrender.
sleuchdach, -aiche, *a.* Bowing down reverently, prostrating. 2 Yielding, submitting, submissive.
sleuchdadh, -aidh, *s.m.* Prostrating, act of prostrating or bowing down reverently, worshipping, prostration. 2 Yielding, submitting. A' s—, *pr.pt.* of sleuchd.
sleuchdamaid, *ist. pers. pl. imp.* of sleuchd. Let us kneel.
sleuchdair,(MS) *v.a.* see sliachdair.
sleug,* *v.a.* Sneak, drawl.
sleugach,* -aich, *s.f.* Sneaking, sly, drawling female.
sleugach,* -aiche, *a.* Sly and slow. 2 Dilatory.
sleugair* -ean, *s.m.* Sly, drawling, sneaking fellow, sneaker, drawler.
sliabadh, see sliobadh.
sliabh, sléibhe, *pl.* sléibhte & sléibhtean, *s. m.* Mountain of the first magnitude. 2 Extended heath, alpine plain,moorish ground. 2 Extensive tract of dry moorland. 3 Mountain grass, moor bent grass. 5 Face of a hill. Seann s.,*withered bent, gathered for bedding in spring —W. of Ross-shire ;* sléibhtean creagach, coillteach, *rocky, wooded mountains.*
sliabh, (AF) *s.m.* Soup made from periwinkles. (called *siabh* in *W. Highlands* generally. 2 Juice of leeches.
sliabhach, -aiche, *a.* Mountainous. 2 Abounding in extensive heaths. 3 Abounding in mountain-grass.
sliabhair, -ean, *s.m.* Mountaineer.
sliachdair, *v.a.* Extend or spread any soft substance by trampling. 2 Plaster or daub over.
sliachdrachadh, see sliachdradh.
sliachdradh, -aidh, *s.m.* Spreading out, act of spreading out any soft substance by trampling. 2 Act of plastering or daubing over. A' *pr.pt.* of sliachdair.

sliachdraich, see sliachdair.
sliachdraichte, *past pt.* of sliachdraich. Spread out by trampling. 2 Plastered, daubed.
sliadh, see sliabh.
sliaisd, see sliasaid.
slias,** sléis, -an, *s.f.* Thigh. 2 Coarse part of a thread.
sliasach,** *a.* Having large thighs. 2 Of, or belonging to, the thigh.
sliasad, see sliasaid.
sliasaid, sléisde & sléisne, *pl.* sléisdean & sléisnean, *s.f.* The thigh. 2 The part of a ship's side towards the stern. 3 Strand of rope or thread. 4**Coarse part of a thread. 5††Gigot, leg of meat. Lag a shléiste, *the hollow of his thigh.*
sliasaideach,(MS) *a.* Crural.
sliasb,** *v.* Draggle.
sliasbair,** *v.* Draggle.
sliasd, *s.m.* Ledge in a loom.
sliasdan, -ain, *s.m.* Ledge in a loom.
sliast, see sliasd.
sliaspair,** *v.a.* Draggle, daggle.
sliaspair,** *s.m.* Draggler.
sliaspairt,** *s.f.* Draggling, covering or besmearing with mud. A' s—, *pr.pt.* of sliaspair.
sliast, see sliasd.
——an, see sliasdan.
slib, see sliob.
slibist, -ean, *s.m.* Sloven, paltry or sorry fellow.
——,* *a.* Clumsy, unhandy.
slibisteach, -eiche, *a.* Slovenly, mean, abject.
slige, *pl.* -an & -achan, *s.f.* Shell. 2 Scale of a balance. 3 *Hull of a vessel. 4†† Coin, *in ridicule.* 5 Bent timber in a boat, see bàta, D, p. 73. 6 Skin of a boat, see bàta, E 4, p. 73. 7**Drinking-shell. 8** Splinter of earthenware. 9 Scallop-shell. 10**Bomb. Chaidh e 'na shligeachan, *it broke in splinters.*
sligeach,* *s.f.* Wreck. 2 Crustaceous surface.
sligeach, -eiche, *a.* Shelly, having a shell. 2 Abounding in shells. 3 Like a scale. 4 Of, or like a bomb. Bradan s., *a sturgeon.*
sligeachan, *n.pl.* of slige.
sligeachd, *s.f.ind.* Crustiness.
sligeadachd,** *s.f.* Conchology.
sligeadair, -ean, *s.m.* ** says Conchologist, but it means rather " a maker of shells."
sligeadh, -idh, *s.m.* **Fomentation. 2 Dividing with shells. 3 Drinking from shells. Shells and horns were the chief drinking-vessels of old. Fìon 'ga shligeadh beòir 'ga h-òl ac', *they had wine from shells and plenty of beer to drink—Duanaire, p.* 143.
sligeag, -eig, -an, *s.f., dim.* of slige. Little shell.
sligeagach, -aiche, *a.* Abounding in small shells.
sligean,** -ein, *s.m., dim.* of slige. Little shell. 2 Little scale or balance. 3 Little splinter of earthenware.
sligeanach,** -aiche, *a.* Spotted. 2 Sky-coloured. 3 Green. 4 Cirrocumulated. 5 Scaled, scaly. 6 see sligeach. Nathair bhreac, sh., *a spotted green serpent.*
sligeanach, -aich, *s. m.* Tortoise. 2 Chelonian. 3 (AF) Turtle.
sligear,* -ir, -an, *s.m.* Conchologist.
——achd,* see sligeadachd.
sligearnach, -aiche, *a.* Made of shells. 2 Full of shells.
sligearnach, -aich, *s.m.* Place abounding in shells.
sligeart, -eirt, -an, *s.m.* Pumice-stone.
sligeas, -eis, -an, *s.m.* The chin, *in ridicule.*
slige-bhloighdeach, *s.f.* Bomb-shell. Fadadh na slige-bloighdich, *the fusee.*
slige-chabon,(MMcD) *s.f.* Large cockle scalloped shell—*Lewis.*

640.Slige-chreachainn. *641.Slige-chabon.*

slige-chreach, *s.f.* Scallop-shell.
slige-chreachainn, *s.f.* Scallop-shell, clam.
slige-chreadha, -an-creadha, *s.f.* Potsherd.
slige-neamhnuid, -e, -ean, *s.f.* Mother-of-pearl.
slige-neamhnuinn,(AF) *s. f.* Pearl-oyster shell. 2 Mother-of-pearl.
slige-neamhuinn, see slige-neamhnuid.
slige-thomhais, -ean-tomhais, *s.f.* Balance scale.
slighe, -an & -achan, *s.f.* Way, path, road, passage, inlet. 2 Journey. 3 Manner, conduct. 4* Craft. 5**Approach. 6**Track. Dh'fhalbh e air s. na fìrinn, *he has gone on the way of truth*—said of one who is dead.
sligheach, -eiche, *a.* Artful, sly, crafty, wily, cunning, full of stratagems, deceitful.
sligheachas, -ais, *s.m.* Slyness.
sligheadair, -ean, *s.m.* One who lives by fraud. 2 Artful, scheming fellow.
sligheadaireachd, *s.f.ind.* Craftiness, cunning, artfulness, deceitfulness, slyness, practice of stratagems.
slighearachd, see sligheadaireachd.
slighearra, -eire, *a.* see sligheach.
slighreach, -eiche, *s.m.coll.* Shreds, shards,*prov.*
sligich, *v.a.* Crust.
sligir,* see sligear.
——eachd, see sligeadachd.
sligheach, -eich, *s.f.* Icicles. 2 Scales of a fish.
——, -eiche, *a.* see sligeach & sligeanach.
slìm, -e, *a.* see slìom.
slimseag, -eig, -an, *s.f.* Silly, tawdry woman. 2 Whore.
slimseagach, -aiche, *a.* Silly, tawdry. 2 Whorish.
——d, *s.f.ind.* Silliness, tawdriness. 2 Whorishness.
slinn, -eachan, *s.m.* Weaver's sleay or reed, see beart-fhigheadaireachd. 2**Flat stone. 3** Tile. 4**Flag. [***s.f.*]
slinn-chrann,** -chrainn, *s.m.* Flag-staff.
slinneag,†† -eig, -an, *s.f.* Shoulder-blade. A' chuid nach 'eil air an t-slinneag tha e air a' chliathaich, *what is not on the shoulder may cover the ribs.*
slinnean, -ein, slinneinean, *s. m.* Shoulder, shoulder-blade. 2††Fore-quarter of mutton.
——ach, -aiche, *a.* Shouldered, broad-shouldered. 2 Of a shoulder. Fear s. leathann, *a large, broad-shouldered man.*
——ach,** -aich, *s.m.*Broad-shouldered man.
——achd, *s.f. ind.* Species of augury, performed by inspecting the shoulder-blade of an animal, by eating the flesh without touching the bone with tooth or nail.
——aich, *s.pl.*Scapulars, see eun, No.2, p.398.
slinnteach,** -ich, *s.f.* House-tiles, quantity of house-tiles.
slìob,** *s.m.* Polish, gloss.
slìob, *v.a.* Stroke, rub gently with the hand. 2 Polish, gloss, varnish. 3 Lick. 4* Cajole. 5 Anoint. 6**Lubricate. 7 Smear, daub, spatter, cover. 8**Cherish. 9**Japan. 10††Steep. S. bodach is sgròbaidh e thu, *stroke a churl and he will scratch you.*
——ach, -aiche, *a.* Clumsy, awkward.
——ach,** *a.* Smoothing, polishing. 2 Besmear-

ing. daubing, spattering.
——achadh,** -aidh, *s.m.* Smoothing, polishing, glossing. 2 Besmearing, daubing, spattering.
——achd, *s.f.* Sleekness.
——adh, ** *3rd.sing. & pl. imp.* of sliob.
——adh, -aidh, *s.m.* Stroking, act of rubbing gently with the hand. 2 Act of licking. 3 Act of polishing, smoothing or glossing. 4** Besmearing, daubing, spattering. 5** Varnish, gloss, polish. 6††Steeping. A' s—, *pr. pt.* of slìob.
——aich, *v.a.* see slìob.
——aichte, *past pt.* Smoothed, polished, glossed, varnished. 2 Besmeared, daubed.
slìobair, -ean, *s.m.* Clumsy, awkward fellow. 2 *Cajoler. 3**Japanner.
———eachd, *s.f.ind.* Clumsiness, awkwardness.
sliobaist, -ean, see slibist.
———each, -eiche, *a.* see slibisteach & sliobasta.
sliobasta,* *a.* Clumsy.
sliobastachd,* *s.f.* Clumsiness.
slìob-cheannach,***a.* Having smooth hair, glossy-haired. Anna chìoch-chorrach, shlìob-cheannach, *round-breasted, glossy-haired Anna.*
sliobhag,(AC) *s.f.* Small, 3-pronged mattock, used by the inhabitants of the Isles to assist in lifting carrots on *Domhnach Curran* (carrot Sunday.) 2(DC) Dibble for planting potatoes in the "lazy-beds,"—*Uist.* [pleadhag in *Argyll.*]
sliob-oladh, *s.m.* Varnish.
slìobradh, -aidh, *s.m.* Glossiness. 2 Draught.
slìobta, *past pt.* Stroked, gently rubbed. 2 Licked. 3 Polished, varnished, glossed, smoothed. 4**Anointed.
sliochd, -a, -an, *s.m. coll.* Seed, offspring, progeny, descendants, posterity. 2 Tribe, clan. 3 Troop. 4* Track, print, rut. 5 Multitude. S. nan rothan, *the track of the wheels* ; s. a mheur, *the print of his fingers ;* s. Dhiarmaid, *the offspring of Dermid (the Campbells.)*
sliochdach, -aiche, *a.* see sliochdmhor. 2** Having tracks.
sliochdachadh,(MS) *s.m.* Generation, prolification.
sliochdar, see sliochdmhor.
sliochdmhor, -oire, *a.* Prolific, having many descendants. 2 Populous.
sliochdmhorachd, *s.f.ind.* Fertility, procreativeness.
†slìocht, see sliochd.
sliodach,** -aiche, *a.* Cunning, artful. Gu s., *cunningly.*
slìog,** *s.m.* Polish, gloss.
slìog, *v.a.* see slìob. 2 *v.n.* Peak.
slìog,(AF) *s.f.* Cray-fish. 2 Scallop. 3 see slige.
slìogach, -aiche, *a.* Sly, subtle. 2 Sleek, slim. 3 Sneaking. 4 Caressing, stroking. 5 Lubricated. 6 Glossy, smooth. 7 Silky. 8 Fawning. 9 Testaceous.
slìogadh, see slìobadh. A' s. an ula, *stroking their beards.* A' s—, *pr.pt.* of slìog.
slìogaich, *s.pl.* Feelers.
slìogair, -ean,*s.m.* Sneaking,sly fellow. 2*Stroker, cajoler.
sliogan, *dim.* of slìog, *s.m.* Shell, bomb. 2 Cup. 3 Hulk. 4 Scale.
slioganach,** *a.* Dappled.
sliogard,** -aird, *s.m.* Crust. 2 Pumice-stone.
sliogardach, ** *a.* Crusty. 2 Hard.
sliogarnach,** *v.* Made of shells, shelly.
slìogarra,** *a.* Smooth, glossy, sleek. 2 Silky. 3 Lubricated.
slìogarrachd,** *s.f.* Smoothness, sleekness,glossiness.
slìogta, *past pt.* Stroked, smoothed, caressed. 2 Glossed. 3 Lubricated. 4** Silky. 5 Fawned. 6 see slìobta.
slìogte, see slìogta.
sliom,(AC) *s.* Buttercup, see cearban.
slìom, -a, *a.* Sleek, smooth, glossy. 2 Slippery. 3 Inert, dull, inactive. 4 Slim, slender. 5 Insincere, deceitful. 6 Lubricated. Na bric sh., *the sleek trout.*
slìom, *v.* see slìob.
slìomacaireachd,(MS) *s.f.* Adulation, mealy-mouthedness.
slìomach,-aiche, *a.* Cringing, flattering. 2 Mean. 3 Deceitful, plausible. 4 Slim. 5 Sleek, smooth, glossy. 6 see slìom.
slìomachd,** *s.f.* Sleekness. 2 Lubricity. 3 Smoothness. 4 Glossiness. 5 Slipperiness. 6 Slimness.
slìomachd, *pr.pt.* a' slìomachdadh, *v. a.* Fawn, sponge in a mean fashion. 2 Daub.
slìomachdair,†† -an, *s.m.* Mean parasite,spongy, lazy, inactive person, adulator.
————eachd, see slìomaireachd.
slìomadair, see slìomair.
slìomadaireachd, see slìomaireachd.
slìomaich,(MS) *v.a.* Agrease.
slìomaich,(MS) *v.a.* Coax.
slìomaich,** *v.a.* Make sleek, smooth or glossy. 2 Lubricate. 3 Fawn, flatter.
slìomair, -ean, *s. m.* Meanly flattering fellow, flatterer, deceitful and fair-speaking person, fawning fellow. 2 Lazy, inactive person. 3 Weakling. 4 Craven. 5 Thief, filcher.
slìomaireachd, *s.f.ind.* Mean flattery. 2 Deceitful and fair talk. 3 Laziness, inactivity. 4 Filching.
slìomcair, -ean, *s.m.* see slìomair.
slìomcaireachd, see slìomaireachd.
slìomchaireachd,(MS) *s.f.* Assentation.
slìomchrathach,(MS) *a.* Pinguid.
slìomhaireachd, see slìomaireachd.
slìom-shligneach, *s.m.* Ganoid.
slionc,** *v.a.* Beat.
sliop, -a, -an, *s.f.* Lip, blubber-lip.
sliopach, -aiche, *a.* Lipped. 2 Blubber-lipped.
sliopag,(AC) -aig, -an, *s.f.* see sliobhag. 2** Thick-lipped young female.
sliopair, -ean, *s.m.* Blubber-lipped-person. 2* Sulky, surly fellow.
sliopaireachd, *s.f.* Blubbering.
sliop-chraos, -aois, -an, *s.m.* Fat, thick, slavery lips.
slios, -a, -an, *s.m.* Side. 2 Side of a man or beast, flank. 3 Side of a country. 4 Extending,sloping declivity. 5 Coast, border, edge. 6 Drag-rope, trace, see No. 19, p. 263. 7(DC) Slap on the side of the head.
An stoirm èitidh ri s. carraig, *the dreadful tempest beating against the side of a rock* ; s. nan liath-bheann, *the side of the grey hills* ; s. a sgéith, *the edge of his shield.*
sliosach, -aiche, *a.* Having sloping sides. 2 Having many sides. 3 Having a border.
sliosag, see sliseag.
sliosan, *s.pl.* Plates of a loom. 2 Drag-ropes or traces, see under crann-nan-gad.
sliosda,** *a.* Fair. 2 Courteous. 3 Flattering, fawning.
sliosdachd,** *s. f.* Fairness. 3 Courteousness. 3 Flattery.
sliosmhor,** *a.* Glossy, polished. 2 Extensive, as a country side.
sliosnach,** *a.* Having sides, lateral, multilateral. 2 Angular.
sliosrach,(AC) *s.* Slope, declivity.
sliosraig,‡ *Badenoch* for liosraig.
slis, -e, -ean, *s. f.* Chip, slice, shave. 2 Lath, thin board. 3 Spill.

slis,** *v.a.* Slice, chip, shave, as wood.
slis-cheumnach,** *a.* Apt to make a digression.
slis-cheumnaich,** *v.a.* Make a digression.
sliseag, -eig, -an, *s.f.dim.* of slis. Spill or shaving of wood. 2 Thin slice of anything. 3** Temple, upper part of the head.
sliseagach, -aiche, *a.* Sliced, in shavings, cut into thin slices. 2 Of, or belonging to, shavings. 3 Abounding in shavings, slips or spills.
sliseagachadh, -aidh, *s.m.* Chipping, act of chipping or planing of wood. 2 Cutting, slicing, act of cutting into slices. A' s—, *pr. pt.* of sliseagaich.
sliseagaich, *pr. pt.* a' sliseagachadh, *v.a.* Chip, plane, cut into slices.
sliseagaichte, *past pt.* of sliseagaich. Cut into slices, planed, chipped.
sliseagan, *n.pl.* of sliseag. Wood-shavings,chips.
sliseag-uchd,*s.f.*Breast-beam of loom—*Hebrides.*
slisinn, *s.* Ear-mark on sheep, see under comharradh-cluais.
slisneach, -ich, *s.f.coll.* Chips, shavings, spills. 2**Scales.
slisneach, -eiche, *a.* Having many sides.
slisneach,(AC) *s. m.* Plant like the heal-wort (slàn-lus.)
sliucanach,** *a.* Horned.
slob,** -uib, *s.m.* Dam, pond. 2 Splash, puddle. ——ach,** *a.* Splashy. 2 Puddly.
sloban, -ain, *s.m.* Puddle, little pool.
sloc, -uic, -an, *s.m.* Pit. 2 Den. 3 Hollow, cavity, dell, hold, hole. 4 Grave. 5 Dungeon. 6 Pool, gutter, ditch. 7 Marsh. 8 Plough. S.-guail, *a coal-pit;* s.-sàbhaidh, *a saw-pit.*
slocach, -aiche, *a.* Full of pits, dens, hollows, cavities, dungeons ditches or marshes. 2 Like or pertaining to any of these.
slocachadh, -aidh, *s.m.* Hollowing, act of hollowing out or excavating. 2 Digging,act of digging or making a pit or ditch,den or dungeon. A' s—, *pr.pt.* of slocaich.
slocaich, *pr.pt.* a' slocachadh, *v.a.* Hollow or excavate anything. 2 Dig or make a ditch or pit, draw a ditch.
slocaichte, *past pt.* of slocaich. Hollowed out, excavated. 2 Dug, made into a pit or ditch.
slòcan, -ain, -an, *s.m.* Sloke (seaweed)—*porphyra laciniata.*
slocan, -ain, -an, *s. m., dim.* of sloc. Little pit, ditch, hollow, dell or den. 2**Little pool. 3 (MS) Socket.
slòcan, see lòchdan.
slocanach, -aiche, *a.* Full of little pits, ditches, hollows, dens, caves or dells.
sloc-buntàta, *s.m.* Potato-pit. The potato-pits in Sutherlandshire before the clearances were made about 3 ft. square and nearly 3 ft. deep. In a shelving bank that greatly resembles an old beach, above the shepherd's house at Learable in Kildonan, may be seen in a row some twenty or thirty such pits, now partly filled up by the falling in of the sides. In olden times, when a blacksmith's customers had to bring him their own fuel, an empty potato-pit was used to convert the necessary quantity of peat into charcoal. This kind of pit is still used for potatoes in the county—CR.
It was, of old and till recently, the custom in *Uist* to dig a hole in the floor near the hearthstone, and now and again take a live peat from the fire, dip it in water and put it into this hole. The charcoal thus accumulated was for use in the smithy, as everyone who needed the smith's services had to provide the necessary charcoal.—DC.
sloc-chartach, see crotag.
slochd, see sloc.
†sloch-sine, *s.f.* Flake of snow.
sloc-sàbhaidh,** *s.m.* Saw-pit. [**s.-shabhaidh,]
slod, -oid & -uid, *pl.* -an, see lod.
slodach,** *a.* Full of little pools or puddles.
slodan,** -ain, *s.m.* Little pool or puddle. [for lodan.]
slodanach, *a.* Full of little pools or puddles.
slodhag, -aig, -an, *s.m.* **Lining of a horn. 2 see sladhag & slabhag.
slodhagach, *a.* Lined, as a horn.
slogag,(DU) *s.f.* Dell.
slogair, *s.m.* Gulf.
slogan, see sluagh-ghairm.
slògh, -òigh, *s.coll.* People. 2 *gen. pl.* of sluagh.
slògha, (a sh— !) *voc.pl.* of sluagh.
sloidhe, *s.f.* Section, division.
slòigh, *n. & dat. pl.* of sluagh.
slòigh, *gen. & pl.* of sluagh.
slòighre, *s.f.* Sword, scimitar.
sloighte, see slaight. 2 *past pt.* Beaten. 3**Run dross from the ore of metal. Obair sh., *beaten work.*
sloightear, -ir, -an, see slaightear.
sloightearachd, see slaightearachd.
sloightearachd, see slaodaireachd.
sloighteil, *a.* see slaodach.
sloighteil, see slaighteil.
sloinn, *v.a.* Surname, bestow a surname. 2 Trace one's pedigree. Cò uaith a shloinneadh i ? *from whom was she surnamed ?* sloinnidh se e féin, *he will surname himself.*
sloinne, *s.f.* see sloinneadh.
sloinneach, *a.* Clannish. 2 Fond of genealogy.
sloinneachail,** *a.* Genealogical.
sloinneadh, -idh, -idhean, *s. m.* Surname, patronymic. 2 Surnaming, act of surnaming. 3 Act or mode of tracing one's pedigree. A' s—, *pr.pt.* of sloinn.
sloinneadh, *3rd.pers.sing.* & *pl. imp.* of sloinn.
sloinnear, *fut.pass.* of sloinn.
sloinnich, *v.a.* Surname, give a surname.
sloinnte, *past pt.* of sloinn. Surnamed. 2 Having one's genealogy traced.
sloinnte,** *s.f.* Genealogy. Nuair a dh'airmheadh an s., *when their genealogy was reckoned.*
sloinntear, -eir, -an, *s.m.* Genealogist.
————,(DMy) *s m.* Dishonest person—*Lewis.*
sloinntearach,** *a.* Genealogical.
sloinntearachd, *s.f.* Act or habit of tracing genealogies. 2 Genealogy. 3 Extraction. S. neo-chriochnaich, *endless genealogies.*
sloinnteil, -e, *a.* Genealogical. 2 Arranged genealogically. 3 Skilled in or fond of genealogy
sloisir, *pr. pt.* a' sloisreadh, *v. a.* Dash, beat against, as the sea against the shore. 2 Wash by working backwards and forwards in water 3 Mix soft substances together. 4 Daub, daub over.
sloisreach, -eiche, *a.* Dashing, rumbling, as the surge beating against the shore. 2 Washing. 3 Mixing soft substances together, 4 Daubing, daubing over.
sloisreadh, -idh, *s.m.* Dashing, as of the waves against a rock. 2 Act of washing by working anything in water. 3 Act of mixing soft substances together. 4 Daubing, act of daubing over. A' s—, *pr.pt.* of sloisir.
sloisridh, *fut. aff.a.* of sloisir.
sloitir, see slaightear.
slonnadh,** -aidh, *s.m.* Cattle, flocks.
sluagh, *gen.*sluaigh, *dat.*sluagh, *voc.* a shluaigh ! *n.pl.* slòigh, *gen.* slògh, *dat.* slòigh, *voc.* a shlògha ! *s.m.* People, folk. 2 Multitude. 3 Host, army. 4(AC)The hosts,the spirit-world. O shluagh !—an exclamation having much the same import as *O dear !*—a calling for succour to the fairies.

sluaghach, -aiche, *a.* Populous, thickly inhabited.
sluaghail, -e, *a.* see sluaghach.
sluaghar, see sluaghmhor.
sluagh-chunntas, -ais, *s.m.* Census.
sluagh-ghabhaltachd,‡‡ *s.f.* Popularity.
sluagh-ghairm, -e, -ean, *s.f.* Signal for a gathering among the Highland clans. Every clan and many districts had their own distinctive war-cry, e.g. Càrn na cuimhne ! (Braemar) ; Creag Ealachaidh ! (Grants) ; Fraoch ! (MacDonalds) ; Loch Slòigh ! (MacFarlanes) ; Àrd Chaillich ! (MacGregors) ; Tulach àrd ! (MacKenzies) ; Creag dhubh ! (MacPhersons.) The war-cries &c. of most of the clans will be found in *Am Feillire, 1900.*
sluagh-ioghnadh, -aidh, *s.m.* Popularity.
sluagh-iùl, *s.m.* Politics.
s. aghartach, *liberal politics.*
s. ais-cheumach, *reactionary politics.*
s. athaiseach, *conservative politics.*
s. aonachdach, *unionist politics.*
s. pàirteach, *socialist politics.*
sluagh-iùlach, *a.* Political.
sluaghmhoire, *comp.* of sluaghmhor.
sluaghmhoireachd,(MS) *s.f.* Publicity. 2**Populousness.
sluaghmhor, -oire, *a.* Same meanings as sluaghach.
sluagh-mhortadh, -aidh, *s.m.* Massacre.
sluagh-rùn, *s.m.* Policy.
s. coimheach, *foreign policy.*
s. na dùthcha, *national policy.*
s. na h-impireachd, *imperial policy.*
sluagh-thaitneachd, *s.f.ind.* Popularity.
sluaigh, *gen.sing.* of sluagh.
sluaigheach,* -eich, *s.f.* Expedition.
†sluaigheachd, -an, *s.f.* Expedition. 2**Population.
sluaisd, see sluaisdir & sluasaid.
sluaisde, -an, *gen.* of sluasaid.
sluaisdeach,** *a.* Shovelling. 2 Shoving.
sluaisdeachadh, see sluaisreadh.
sluaisdeachd, *s.f.* & *pres.pt.* of sluaisd.
sluaisdean, *pl.* of sluasaid.
sluaisdich,** see sluaisdir.
sluaisdichte, *past pt.* of sluaisdich.
sluaisdir, *pr. pt.* a' sluaisreadh, *v.a.* Shovel, clean or work with a shovel. 2 Mix or work together, as lime. 3 Shove aside as with a spade or shovel. 4*Draggle. 5*Poke.
sluaisir, see sluaisdir.
sluaisne, *gen.* of sluasaid.
sluaisnean, *pl.* of sluasaid.
sluaisreadh, -eidh, *s.m.* Mixing, act of mixing or beating together lime, &c., with a shovel. 2 Cleaning, shoving or cleansing with a shovel. 3††Slubbering. A' s—, *pr. pt.* of sluaisir.
sluasaid, *v.n.* see sluaisdir.
sluasaid, -e, -ean, *s.f.* Shovel, spade. S.-ghrìosaich, *a fire-shovel.*
sluasaideach, *a.* Abounding in shovels or spades.
†sluch,** *v.a.* Quench, extinguish, stifle. 2 Overwhelm.
sludrach,** -aich, *s.m.* Foundation.
†sludhach,** -aich, *s.f.* Horn.
sludhagan,** -ain, *s.m.* Horn. 2 Lining of a horn.
sludraiche, see sludrach.
slug, *v.* see sluig.
slug,* -uige, -an, *s.f.* Miry puddle.
slug, -uig, *s.m.* Gulp.
slugach, -aiche, *a.* That swalloweth, gulping. 2 Apt to swallow or gulp.
slugadh, -aidh, *s.m.* Swallowing, act of swallowing or gulping. 2 Absorbing, act of absorbing. 3 Engulphing,act of engulphing or overwhelming. 4 Devouring, act of devouring. A' s—, *pr.pt.* of sluig. Craos-shlugadh, *a voracious swallowing, gluttony.*
slugag,†† -aig, -an, *s.f.* Small pool.
slugaid, -e, -ean, *s f.* Slough, deep miry place. 2 Quicksand. 3 Throat, gullet.
slugaideach, -eiche, *a.* Abounding in sloughs or quagmires. 2 Like a quagmire. 3 Having a large throat. 4 Voracious.
slugaideachd, see slugaireachd.
slugair, -ean, *s.m.* Glutton, devourer. 2 Spendthrift. 3 Hard drinker.
slugaireachd, *s.f.ind.* Voracious gulping or swallowing. 2 Gluttony. 3 Extravagance.
slugaite,** -an, *s. m.* Quicksand. 2 Slough, muddy place.
slugan, -ain, -an, *s. m.* Orifice of the gullet—windpipe is sgonnan. 2 Neck of a bottle. 3 Whirlpool. 4 Gulf. 5(AF) Opening of a kiln, whereon the corn to be dried is laid. 6 Sheaf-swallow of a pulley, see Ulag 5, p.78. 7**Little deep pool, deep pool in a stream. 8**Gorge. 9††Pit. Bha 'leum dlù aig s. carraig, *he sprang quickly into the pool of the rock*; bha mo chridhe 'nam sh., *my heart was in my mouth (with terror.)*
sluganach, -aiche, *a.* Voracious, gluttonous. 2 Having a large throat. 3 Swallowing, gulping. 4 Gulfy, abounding in gulfs. 5††Pertaining to a pit. 6 Abounding in deep pools.
sluganachd,** *s.f.* Gluttony, greediness. 2(DC) Bronchitis.
slug-ghaineamh,** -eimh, *s.m.* Quicksand.
slug-pholl, -phuill, *s.m.* Whirlpool.
sluic, *gen.sing.* & *n.pl.* of sloc.
sluichd, see sluic.
sluig, *pr.pt.* a' slugadh, *v. a.* Swallow. 2 Absorb. 3 Engulph,overwhelm. 4 Devour. Shluig e daoine, *it devoured men.*
sluigean,* -ein, *s.m.* ‡‡Glutton. see slugan.
sluigear, *fut.pass.* of sluig. Shall be swallowed.
sluigidh, *fut.aff.a.* of sluig. Shall swallow.
sluigte, *past pt.* of sluig. Swallowed. 2 Absorbed. 3 Engulphed. 4 Devoured. 5 Engorged.
sluinn,** *s.f.* Telling, declaring.
sluinnse,(DMK) *v.* Lash, thrash—*Caithness.*
sluisich, -e, *s.f.* Wash, the food of pigs.
sluisin, *v.* see sluaisir.
sluisneadh, *s.m.* & *pr.pt.* see sluaiseadh.
†slus, *v.a.* Dissemble. 2 Counterfeit.
smachd, *s.m.ind.* Authority, control, rule, discipline, subjection, command. 2 Awe. 3 Reproof, correction. Fo d' s.-sa, *under your control ;* cum s. air, *or* cuir s.air, *correct him, discipline him;* s. airme, *military discipline ;* cuir fo s., *bring into subjection.*
———,(CR) Syllable—*Suth'd.*
———,** *v.a.* Chastise. 2 Correct, reprove. 2 Correct. 3 Rule, keep under subjection, keep in awe, discipline.
smachdach, -aiche, *a.* Having or using control, authoritative. 2 Correcting, chastising, reproving. 3 Prone to chastise or correct, ruling, lording, keeping in subjection or awe.
————adh, -aidh, *s.m.* Reproving, act of reproving or correcting. 2 Chastising. 3 Correction. 4 Proof. 5 Rule, awe, subjection. A' s—, *pr.pt.* of smachdaich.
smachdachd, *s.f.ind.* Austereness, severity.
smachdaich, *pr.pt.* a' smachdachadh, *v. a.* Reprove,correct,check. 2 Chastise. 3 Discipline, rule, command. 4 Reprove severely.
smachdaichte, *past pt.* of smachdaich. Reproved, corrected. 2 Chastised. 3 Brought under subjection.
smachdail, -e, *a.* Authoritative, commanding,

disciplinary, lordly, overbearing. 2 Austere.
smachdair,** -ean, *s.m.* Disciplinarian, authoritative person.
smachdaire,(DC) *s.m.* Ptarmigan, see tàrmachan.
smachdalachd, *s.f.ind.* Authority,keeping under awe or control. 2*Firmness of character.
smachdan,(DC) *s.m.* Ptarmigan, see tàrmachan.
smachd-bhann,** -ainn, *s.m.* Penal law, code of criminal law.
smachd-lann, -ainn, -an, *s.m.* House of correction.
smachduchadh, see smachdachadh.
smachduich, see smachdaich.
smàd, *v.a.* Threaten, use threatening words. 2 Intimidate, scare. 3 Beat away. 4 Abuse, revile terribly. 5**Boast.
smad, *s.m.ind.* Particle, jot, the smallest particle of anything. 2 Spot, stain. 3** Smut, soot.
smadach,** *a.* Sooty, smutty.
smàdach,** *a.* Prone to boast. 2 Prone to beat off. 3 Intimidating, scaring.
smàdadh,** -aidh, *s. m.* Threatening, act of threatening or using threatening words. 2 Intimidating, act of intimidating. 3 Act of beating away. 4 Abusing, abuse. 5**Boasting. 6††Scolding. A' s—, *pr.pt.* of smàd.
smàdail, -e, *a.* Threatening, scaring, that threatens. 2 Intimidating. 3 Beating away. 4* Abusive. 5‡‡Knocking down at a blow. 6** Boastful.
smadan, -ain, *s.m.* Soot, smut. 2 ||Particle of smut or soot. 3 Jot, particle.
smadanach,** *a.* Smutted, sooted. 2 Dusty.
smàg, -àig, -an, *s.f.* Paw. 2 *in derision*, Clumsy paw, clumsy foot. 3 Large hand. 4 see smàig. 5 see smàigean. Air smàgan, *on all fours.* (for màg.)
smàg, *v.a. & n.* see smàgaich.
smàgach, -aiche, *a.* Pawed, as a beast. 2 Having large paws. 3 Clumsy-footed. 4 Pawing, groping.
smàgach, -aich, -aichean, *s.m.* see smàigean.
————adh, -aidh, *s.m.* Act of creeping along. 2 Moving on all fours. 3**Pawing. 4 Groping. A' s—, *pr. pt.* of smàgaich.
smàgaich, *v.a.* Creep along. 2 Move on all fours. 3 Grope. 4 Sprawl.
smàgail, *s.f.ind.* see smàgaireachd.
smàgair, -ean, *s.m.* One that creeps along, or moves on all fours. 2 Lazy fellow. 3**Clumsy-footed fellow. 4**Clumsy-fisted fellow. 5 Sprawler. 6 Groper.
smàgaireachd, *s.f.ind.* Creeping along, creeping on all fours. 2 Groping. 3 Pawing.
smàgairneach,** *s.m.* Any creature with large paws. 2 Large-boned person. 3* Large-pawed squat fellow or beast.
smàgairneach, *a.* Having large paws. 2 Large-boned.
smàgarsaich,** *s.f.* Pawing. 2 Groping. 3 Creeping. 4 Moving on all fours.
smàgarsanaich, (a') *pr.pt.* Moving on all fours.
smaichd, see smachd.
smàidse, see màidse.
smaidseart,** -eirt, *s.m.* Active young man.
smàig,* *s.f.* Tyranny, the upper hand, ascendant, despotism. Fo d' s., *under your sway* or *despotism.*
smàig, *gen.sing.* of smàg.
smàigealachd, *s.f.* Extreme despotism, great degree of tyranny.
smàigean, -ein, *pl.* -an & -geinean, *s.m.* Toad. 2 Frog. Cluich nan smàigean, *leap-frog.*
————ach, -aiche, *a.* Of, or belonging to, toads or frogs. 2 Full of frogs. 3 Like a frog. 4 Creeping. 5 Groping.
smàigeanachd, see smàgaireachd.
smàigeil, -e, *a.* Despotic, arbitrary.
smàigir,* -ean, *s.m.* Tyrant, despot.
————eachd,* see smàigealachd.
smàil, *gen. & voc. sing.* of smàl.
smàil, *pr.pt.* a' smàladh, *v.a.* Snuff, top, as a candle. 2 Extinguish. 3 Knock down, dash to the ground. 4(DU) "Rest" a peat-fire by covering half-burnt peats with ashes to retard combustion. In the morning these live peats are blown into flame to rekindle a fire. S. e as a chéile iad, *he dashed them to pieces;* s. as an teine, *extinguish the fire.*
smaile,** *s.f.* Blow, buffet.
smaiteard, see smaidseart.
smàl, *gen.* -àil [smeòil—*W. of Ross-shire,*] *pl.* -an, *s.m.* Snuff of a candle. 2 Vapour, cloud,gloom. 3 Cinders, embers. Gleann smeòil, *glen of mist* —*Sàr-Obair.* Fo s., *extinguished.*
smàl, *v.a.* see smàil.
smal, -ail, *s.m.* Dust, dust covering anything. 2 Obscurity, dimness. 3 Stain, blemish, spot. 4 Sorrow, vexation. 5**Infirm or sickly person. 6**Blot, blemish. Thàinig s. air an òir, *the gold became dim;* a' chòisridh nach fhanadh gnè s. air an inntinn, *the company on whose minds no gloom would stay—Beinn Doran,l.89.*
smalach,†† *a.* Dusty, stained, spotted.
smàladair, -ean, *s.m.* Pair of snuffers. 2**Extinguisher.
smàladaireachd, *s.f.* Business of a candle-snuffer. 2 Act of candle-snuffing.
smàladan, -ain, -an, see smàladair.
smàladh, -aidh, *s.m.* Snuffing, act of snuffing a candle. 2 Blowing out, act of blowing out extinguishing or quenching a flame. 3** Quenching. 4** Knocking down. 5 Smashing, dashing to pieces. 6(DU) Act of resting a peat-fire. A' s—, *pr.pt.* of smàil. A' s. an t-eanchainn asda, *dashing out their brains;* cnap-smàlaidh, *a gathering coal, to keep the fire alive overnight.*
smàlag, -aig, -an, *s.f.* Fillip, jerk of the finger.
smalag, -aig, -an, *s.m.* Saith, cuddy, coal-fish going into its second year. 2(AF) Smelt. 3 *Smacking kiss.
smalan, -ain, *s.m. dim.* of smal. Gloom, melancholy, grief, sorrow. 2**Dust, particle of dust.
smalan,** -ain, *s. m.* Hillock. 2 Little blow, fillip.
smalanach, -aiche, *a.* Sorrowful, dejected, grieved, vexatious. 2**Full of hillocks.
smalanachd, *s.f. ind.* Sorrowfulness, grievousness, gloominess.
smàl-shoitheach, -ich, -ichean, *s.m.* Extinguisher.
smaogal,** -ail, *s.m.* Husk, hull. S. chnò, *the husk of a nut.*
smaogalach, *a.* Husky, having a husk or hull.
smaoin, -e, -tean, *s.f.* see smuain.
smaoineachadh, see smuaineachadh.
smaoinich, *pr. pt.* a' smaoineachadh, *v.* see smuainich.
smaointe, see smuain.
smaointeach, see smuaineach.
————adh, see smuaineachadh.
smaointeachail, see smuaineachail.
smaointean, see smuainean.
smaointich, see smuainich.
smaointinn, see smuaineachadh.
————each, -eiche, see smuaineach.
smaolach,** -aich, *s.m.* Thrush, ouzle.
smaosdrach, ** -aich, *s.m.* Cartilage, gristle.
smaosrach, -aich, see smaosdrach.
smarach, -aich, *s.m.* Lad, growing youth—*Badenoch.* 2* Large louse.

smàrag, -aig, -an, *s.f.* Emerald.
smàragach, *a.* Abounding in emeralds. 2 Of emeralds. 3 Like an emerald.
smat,** *s.* Gobbet.
smeac,** *s.m.* Smack. 2 Kiss. 3 Fillip with the finger.
smeacadh, -aidh, *s.m.* Palpitation, panting. 2 Smacking with the lips.
smeach,* *v.n.* Make a fillip with the fingers.
smeach,* -a, *s.m.* Smart, quick blow, fillip. 2 see smeachan.
smeachach,** *a.* Chinned. 2 Having a peaked chin. 3 Having a long neck.
smeachan, -ain, -an, *s.m.* The chin. 2††Band-age round the chin. 3 Band under the jaw of a horse, chin-bit or cheek-band of a bridle. 4 4 Person with a peaked chin. 5(MS) Nozzle. 6 Little chin. 7 (DMy) ['s an toirsgein] the step on the peat-spade on which the person cutting places his right foot every time he cuts.
smeachanach, -aiche, *a.* Chinned. 2 Having a prominent or peaked chin.
smeacharan,* -ain, *s.m.* see smeacharanachd.
smeacharanachd, *s.f.ind.* Taking too great a liberty with people or with edged tools, e.g. taking a person by the chin, bandying civilities with your betters, officious interference. 2* Tampering.
smeacharra, *a.* Lively, brisk.
smeacharrachd, *s.f.ind.* Liveliness.
smeachranachd, see smeacharanachd.
smeadairneach, -eich, *s.f.* Slumber, slight sleep.
smeag,(MMcD) *s.f.* Neck-rope for a cow, tied to the *dornan—Lewis.*
smealach, -aich, -aichean, *s.f.* Offal. 2 Remains of goods, provisions or money. 3 Dainties, sweets.
smealach,* -aiche, *a.* Having a beautiful eye or engaging countenance.
smeal-ghobach, -aiche, *a.* Fond of dainties.
smealas, -ais, *s.m.* Relish for sweet things.
smeallach, see smealach.
smèar, *v.* see smeur.
smear, -a, *s.m. prov.* for smior.
smearach, -aiche, *a.* see smiorach & smeurach.
smearachadh, see smeurachadh.
smearachan, -ain, *s.m.* Kitchen brat, lick-plate.
smèarachd, see smeurachd.
smèaradair, see smeuradair.
smèaradh, -aidh, see smeuradh.
smearag, see smeurag.
smearaich, see smeuraich.
smearaiche,** *s.f.* Second swarming of a hive.
smearail,** *a.* see smiorail.
smèarain, *s.pl.* Brambles—*Arran.* (smeuran.)
smearalachd, see smioralachd.
smearalas, -ais, *s.m.* see smioralas.
smèaran, *pl.* of smèar (for smeur.)
smearoid,** *s.f.* Coal, burning coal, hot ember.
smearsnachadh,(AH) *s.m.* Fainting from exposure to inclement weather—*Argyll.*
smeartan,§ -ain, -an, *s.m.* Sweet tangle, sea-belt —*laminaria saccharina.*
smearta, see smeurta.
smeat,** -a, *s.m.* Simper, smile.
smeatach, -aiche, *a.* see smiotach. 2 Snouty. 3 3 Short-snouted. 4**Simpering.
smeatadh,** -aidh, *s.m.* Simpering. 2 Simper. 3 Snout.
smeatag,** *s.f.* Simpering young female. 2 Flat-nosed young female.
smeataiche, *s.f.* see smiotaiche.
smèid, *v.a. & n.* Nod, wink. 2 Beckon. 3 Take aim, *prov.* 4 Hiss. S. i air e thighinn na bu dlùithe dhith, *she beckoned to him to come nearer her—W.H. 1, 41* ; s. air, *wave to him, beckon to him.*
smèid,** *s.f.* Nod, wink. 2 Beckoning.
smèideach, -eiche, *a.* That beckons or nods. 2 Nodding, beckoning, making private signs. 3 Hissing.
smèideach, -eich, *s.m.* One who nods, beckons, or makes private signs.
smèideadh, -idh, *s.m.* Winking, act of winking or nodding. 2 Wink, nod. 3 Beckoning. 4 Beckon. 5 Hissing. 6 Hiss. 7 Act of aiming or taking aim, *prov.* 8 Slight tinge or degree. 9* Waving. A' s—, *pr.pt.* of smèid. Cuir s. mar seo e, *put it a slight degree this way* ; s. eile, *another touch* ; s. air, *wave to him, beckon to him.*
smèideadh, *3rd. pers. & pl. imp.* of smèid.
smèideag, -eig, -an, *s. f.* Little nod or wink, slight beckoning.
smèideagach,†† *a.* Pertaining to little winks or nods.
smèideagan, -an, *s.m.* Wooden bar on a loom, see beart-fhigheadaireachd.
smeig, -e, -ean, see smig.
smeigeach, see smigeach.
smeigead, see smigead.
smeil,** *s.f.* Pale look, ghastly look.
smeileach, -eiche, *a.* Pale, ghastly, puny.
smeileag, -eig, -an, *s.f.* Pale, puny female.
smeilean, -ein, -an, *s.m.* Puny, pale creature.
smeirne, *s.f.* Spit. 2 Brooch.
smeirseach,(AH) *s. f.* Stiff cuach of stingo. Fhuair e deagh s., *he got a good strong glass of spirits.*
smeòirn, -ean, *s.m.* The end of an arrow next the bow-string. 2**Point of a dart, spear or arrow. 3 The notch at the end of the arrow which required delicate adjustment in order to fit the string. Bogh an iuthair nach dìobair, air 'm bu ro-mhath cur sìoda, agus fleisdear an Lìbhinn 'cur s. air, *a yew-bow that never disappoints, on which is a first-rate service of silk and the fletcher of Leven fitting the arrow-notch to it*—an ideal equipment ; cho cinnteach ri èarr na smeòirn, *as certain as the end of the arrow-head* (*arrow-notch*—CR.) [** gives *nom.* smeòirne, & *s.f.*]
smeòirneach, ** *a.* Sharp. 2 Pointed, as a dart or spear. 3 Like a spear's point.
smeòla, see smeòrach.
smeòlach, see smeòrach.
smeòr, *s.f.* see smeòrach.
smeòr, *v.a.* see smeur.
smeòrach, -aich, -aichean, *s.f.* Thrush, mavis—*turdus musicus.* 2** Linnet. 3 Dog's name. 4 Ear-mark on sheep, see comharradh-cluais.
smeòrach, see smeurach.
smeòrachadh, see smeurachadh.
smeòrach an t-sneachda,¶ *s.f.* Redwing, see sgiath-dheargan.
smeòrach bhuidhe,¶ see smeòrach.
smeòrach ghlas,¶ *s.f.* Missel-thrush, see smeòrach mhòr.
smeòrach mhór,¶ *s.f.* Missel-thrush—*turdus viscivorous.*
smeòradair, see smeuradair.
smeòradaireachd, see smeuradaireachd.
smeòradh, see smeuradh.
smeòraich, see smeuraich.
smeòraichte, see smeuraichte.
smeur, *v.a.* Anoint, smear, as sheep.
smeur, -a, -an, *s.f.* Blackberry, brambleberry. 2 Mulberry. 3 Any fruit resembling a blackberry. Craobh-nan-smeur, *a mulberry-tree—Bible.*
smeurach, -aiche, *a.* Full of bramble-berries. 2 Pawing, groping, fingering, handling clumsily.
smeurachadh, -aidh, *s.m.* Groping, act of groping, fingering awkwardly, pawing, fumbling. A' s—, *pr.pt.* of smeuraich.

smeurachan,**-ain, *s.m.* Kitchen-brat, lick-plate, bone-picker.
smeurachd, *s.f.* Continual groping. 2 Habit of groping or fumbling. 3 Greasing, smearing. 4§ Common bramble, see dris.
smeuradair, -ean, *s.m.* Smearer, one who smears or anoints sheep.
smeuradaireachd, *s.f.ind.* Smearing, employment of smearing sheep.
smeuradh, -aidh, *s.m.* Smearing, act of smearing or anointing sheep. A' s—, *pr.pt.* of smeur.
smeurag,§ -an, *s.f.* Fruit of the common bramble.
smeuragach, *a.* Full of bramble-berries. 2 Of, or belonging to, bramble-berries.
smeuraich, *v.n.* Grope, search by feeling in the dark. 2**Grease, smear. 3*Grope for vermin.
smeuraichidh, *fut.aff.a.* of smeuraich.
smeuraichte, *past pt.* of smeuraich.
smeuran, *n.pl.* of smeur.
smeur dhearg, *s.f.* Wineberry—*rubus phœnicolasius.*
smeur-dhubh, -a-duibhe, -an-dubha, see smeur.
smeur Loganach, *s.f.* Logan-berry.
smeur-phreas, § -an, *s.m.* Common bramble, see dris.
smeur-phreasach, *a.* Abounding in brambles. 2 Of brambles.
smeurta, *past pt.* of smeur. Smeared.
smiach,(CR) *s.* Syllable, sound. Cha d' thubhairt e s., *he did not utter a syllable—W. of Ross-shire.*
smiar, *v. & s.* see smeur.
smid, -e, -ean, *s.f.* Syllable, word. 2 Opening of the mouth. Na h-abair s., *mum, hush! do not open your lips;* gun s., *mute;* gun s. tha ceann an eòlais, *silent is the head of knowledge.*
smid, *v.* see smèid.
smideach, see smèideach.
smideacail, -e, *a.* Syllabic.
smideam,(CR) *s. m.* Pith, mettle—*Perthshire.* (*Scots*, smeddum.)
smig, -ean & -eachan, *s.m.* The chin. 2**Smile. 3**Mirth. [**, ††, & * *s.f.*]
smig-bhrat, *s.m.* Bib.
smigeach, -eiche, *a.* Chinned, having a prominent chin. 2**Smiling. 3**Mirthful.
smigead, -eid, -an, *s.m.* Chin.
smigeadach, -aiche, see smigeach.
———, -aich, *s.m.* Chin-cloth, bib.
smigeadh, -idh, -ean, *s.m.* Smile. 2**Mirth.
smigeal,* *s.f.* Smirking, smiling.
smigean, -ein, -an, *s.m. dim.* Little chin. 2** Mirth. 3**Smile.
smigeanach,†† *a.* Having a little chin.
smigeil,* -e, *a.* Smirking, smiling.
sminigleadh,(AH) *s. m.* Eating grain, hay or straw without zest and in a fastidious manner, (applied solely to cattle and sheep.)
smileach, -eich, *pl.*-eich & -ichean, *s.m.* Philomel. 2**Nightingale.
smileag, see smileach.
smiodam, -aim, *s.m.* Spirit, pluck. 2 Animal spirits. 3 Smartness. 4 Stamina. Cha'n 'eil s. annad, *you have no pluck.*
smiodamach, *a.* Having spirit or pluck. 2 Having animal spirits. 3 Having stamina.
smiol, -a, *s.f.* Nightingale.
smiolach,** *a.* Abounding in nightingales. 2 Of nightingales. 3 Sweet, as the nightingale's voice.
smiolach, -aich, *s.m.* Nightingale.
smioladh, -aidh, see smeoradh.
smiolag, -aig, -an, *s.f.* Nightingale, young nightingale.
smiolamas,* see smolamas.
smior, -ir & a, *s.m.* Marrow, pith. 2 *fig.* Strength, power, vigour. 3 Courage, spirit, mettle. 4* Hero. 5 Vivacity. 6 Best part of anything. S. an t-sìl, *the best of the seed;* duine gun s., *a man without energy;* smior-chailleach, *the spinal-marrow;* briseadh a' chnàimh agam-sa 's an s. aig càch, *the breaking of the bone for me, the marrow for the rest.*
smìor, see smeur.
smiorach, see smeurach.
smiorach, -aiche, *a.* Abounding in marrow. 2 Of marrow. 3 Pithy.
smiorach,* -aich, *s.m.* Lively louse.
————an, -ain, *s.m.* Kitchen-brat, lick-plate, bone-picker.
smioradh, see smeuradh.
smiorail, -e, [*comp.* smiorala—MM] *a.* Strong, courageous, vigorous, doughty. 2 Lively, active, agile, brisk, alert. 3 Hardy, enduring. 4 Manly. 5 Having marrow, pith or pluck. 6 Like marrow.
smioralachd, *s.f.ind.* Habitual manliness. 2 Activity, briskness, liveliness. 3 Spiritedness. 4 Hardiness.
smioralas, -ais, *s.m.* Strength, courage, vigour, pluck. 2 Liveliness, activity, briskness, agility, alacrity, alertness. 3 Hardiness. 4 Manliness.
smiorcadh, -aidh, *s.m.* Mettle, courage. 2(DMK) Sense—*Caithness.* Cha'n 'eil s. (de chiall)aige, *he has no "fight" in him—Suth'd;* cha'n 'eil s. céill' aige, *he has not a spark of sense.*
smior-chailleach, -eich, *s. m.* Spinal marrow. 2 Spine—*Lewis.*
smiorsnachadh, *s.m.* State of being frost-bitten.
†smiot, -a, -an, *s.m.* Ear, small ear. 2 Particle, small portion of anything.
smiot, *v.a.* Throw in the air with one hand and strike with the other.
smiot, *s.m.* Box, smart blow.
smiotach, -aiche, *a.* Short-eared. 2 Of, or belonging to the ear. 3 (CR) Pug-nosed—*W. of Ross-shire.*
smiotag, -aig, *s.f.* Hand or glove without fingers, mitten. (miotag.)
smiotan, -ain, *s.m.* Fillip. 2 Small ear.
smist,** *v.a.* Smite.
smiste,** *s.f.* Pestle. 2 Mallet.
smisteadh, -idh, *s.m.* Smiting, pounding.
smistean,** -ein, *s.m.* Short thick stick, cudgel. 2 Pestle.
smiùr, *v.a.* see smeur.
smiùrach, see smeurach.
smiùradair, see smeuradair.
————-eachd, see smeuradaireachd.
smiùradh, see smeuradh.
smiùirte, see smeurta.
smòcan,§ -ain, *s. m.* Name given to *callithamnion plocamium*, and various small red seaweeds seen in ladies' albums.
smod, *s.m.ind. prov.* for smad. 2 Dirt, filth. 3 Grain of dust. 4 Drizzling rain, moist haziness, creeping mist. 5††Particle. 6 Smut.
smodach, -aiche, *a.* Dirty, filthy. 2 Dusty, covered with dust. 3 Smutty. 4 Drizzling, hazy, misty.
smodadh, -aidh, see smod.
smodal, -ail, -an, *s.m.* Sweepings, crumbs, fragments of food. 2*Smattering. 3 (DC) Gleanings of corn, &c.—*Uist.* 4††Trash.
smodalach, *a.* see smodanach. 2††Trashy.
smodan, -ain, *s.m.*, *dim.* of smod. Little spot or blemish. 2 Small dust, smut. 3 see smod.
smodan, -ain, *s.m.* Drizzling rain, moistness, haze, haziness.
smodanach, -aiche, *a.* Spotted, soiled, dirty. 2 Abounding in small dust. 3 Drizzling, moist, hazy, misty.
smodanachd, *s.f.ind.* Drizzliness, haziness.

smòg, -òig, -an, *s. & v.* see smàg.
smògach, see smàgach.
————-adh, see smàgachadh.
smògadh, see smàgadh.
smògaich, see smàgaich.
smògair, see smàgair.
————neach, *s. & a.* see smàgairneach.
smògarsaich,** *s.f.* Pawing, awkward groping.
————, *v.n.* Sprawl.
smògraich, *v.a.* Grope, feel. 2 Sprawl.
smògran,(CR) *s.m.* Crawling—*W. of Ross.*
smoidseach,(CR) *s.f.* Lug-worm—*Argyll.*
smoigleach,** *a.* Smutted, soiled, dirty.
smoigleadh, -aidh, *s.m.* Smut, dirt.
smoislich, (CR) *W. of Ross, Argyllshire and Perthshire* for smuaislich.
smoit, -e, *s.f.* Sulkiness, sulky fit.
smoiteach, *a.* Sulky. 2 see moiteil.
————d, *s.f.* Habitual sulkiness.
smòl, see smàl.
smòlach, -aich, *s.m.* Ember. 2 Thrush.
smòladair, see smàladair.
smòladan, see smàladan.
smolamas, -ais, *s.m.* Trash. 2 Fragments of victuals.
smolasg,** -aisg, *s.m.* Dross, refuse, sweepings.
smoldach, see smoltach.
smòltach,(AF) *s.* Nightingale. 2 Thrush.
smot,** *v.n.* Snuffle.
smot,** *s.m.* Mouthful. 2 Pluck.
smotach, *a.* Snuffling.
smotail, *s.m.* Snuffling. 2 Snorting of a horse. Ciod an s. a th' ort ? *why do you snuffle so ?*
smotan, -ain, *s.m.* Block, log, stock. 2 Mouthful. 3 Pluck.
smuaich, *pr. pt.* a' smuachadh, *v.a.* Break into bits.
smuain, *v.* see smuainich.
smuain, -e, -tean, *s. f.* Thought, notion, fancy, reflection, imagination. 2 Prudence. 3 Presence of mind.
smuain-dhitheach,(MS) *a.* Absent-minded.
smuaineach, -eiche, *a.* Thoughtful, reflecting, prudent, pensive, prone to reflect, cogitative. 2 Fanciful.
smuaineachadh, -aidh, *s. m.* Thinking, act of thinking, considering, reflecting, fancying. 2 Imagitation. 3 Meditation. A' s—, *pr.pt.* of smuainich.
smuaineachail, *a.* Thoughtful, studious, contemplative. 2 Sedate. 3 Considerate, cautious.
smuaineachair,** *s.m.* Apprehender.
smuaineachdainn, *pr.pt.* of smuainich—*West of Ross-shire.*
smuaineachd,‡‡ -an, *s.f.* Conjecture. 2(MS) Conceit. 3 Apprehensiveness. 4 Pensiveness.
smuaineadh, -idh, -idhean, *s.m.* see smuain.
smuainean, *pl.* of smuain.
smuainich, *pr. pt.* a' smuainteachadh & a' smuaineachdainn, *v. n.* Think, reflect suppose, consider. 2 Imagine, ponder, meditate. 3 Devise, purpose, intend.
smuain-sheachranach, -aiche, *a.* Absent-mindedness.
smuainte, -an, see smuain.
smuainteach, -eiche, *a.* Thoughtful.
smuainteachadh, -aidh, see smuaineachadh.
smuainteachair. see smuaineachair.
smuainteachd,(MS) *s.f.* see smuaineachd.
smuainteachail, see smuaineachail.
smuainteadh, see smuain.
smuaintean, *pl.* of smuain.
————ach,(MS) *a.* see smuaineach.
————achd,(MS) *s.f.* see smuaineachd.
smuaintich, *pr.pt.* a' smuainteachdainn, *v.n.* see smuainich.

smuairean, -ein, *s.m.* Grief, dejection, sorrow anxiety, vexation, melancholy. 2 Slight offence. Cha chuir e s. orm, *it will not vex me in the least.*
————ach, -aiche, *a.* Grieved, dejected, low-spirited. 2 Apt to be sorrowful or dejected. 3 Causing dejection or vexation. 4*Somewhat melancholy.
————-achd, *s.f.ind.* Dejection, sorrow, vexation. 2 State of being sorrowful or dejected. 3**Pensiveness.
smuais, -e, *s.f.* Juice of the bones, fatness, marrow, grease intermixed in the bone. 2 Pith, strength, vigour. 3**Sweat. 4**Sap. 5**Gristle of the nose. 6** Shivers, splinters. 7 Smashing. Chaidh e 'na s., *it went into shivers.*
smuais, *v.a.* Break into pieces, splinter, smash.
smuaiseach, -eiche, *a.* Juicy, greasy, fat, full of marrow. 2 Sweating. 3 Stirring up, exciting, moving. 4 Having marrow or pith. 5 Breaking in pieces, smashing, shivering, splintering.
smuaiseachadh, -aidh, see smuaiseadh.
smuaiseadh, -idh, *s. m.* Act of breaking into pieces, smashing. A' s—, *pr.pt.* of smuais.
smuaisich, *v.* see smuais.
————te, *past pt.* of smuaisich, see smuaiste.
smuaislich,(CR) *v.n.* Stir (out of sleep)—*Lewis.*
smuaisrich, -e, *s.f. & coll.* Breaking into pieces, smashing. 2 Fragments, splinters.
smuaiste, *past pt.* of smuais. Broken, smashed.
smuanoirt, *s.m.* Proposition.
smùc, -ùic, *s.m.* Nasal sound, snore. 2 Snivel.
smùcach, -aiche, *a.* Snivelling. 2 Making a nasal sound, snoring.
smùcaiche, *s.f.* see smùc.
smùcail, -e, *a.* Act of speaking through the nose. 2 Snivelling. 3 Snoring, snore. 4*Purring through the nose.
smùcair, -ean, *s.m.* One that snivels.
————eachd, *s.f.ind.* Snuffling, speaking nasally.
smucan,‡ -ain, *s.m.* Smoke, drizzle.
smucanach, *a.* Smoky, smoking.
smucanaich, *s.f.* Snivelling. 2 Snoring. 3 Nasal utterance.
smùch, *s.f.* Nasal sound.
smùch, *pr.pt.* a' smùchail & a' smùchadh, *v. a* Sneeze. 2††Snivel. 3 Purr. 4 see mùch. 5 see smùch.
smùchadh, -aidh, *s.m.* Sneezing. 2 Snivelling. 3 see mùchadh. A' s—, *pr.pt.* of smùch.
smuchail,* see smucail.
smùchair,†† -ean, *s.m.* Sniveller.
————eachd, *s.f.* Snivelling.
smuchan, -ain, *s.m.* Half-smothered fire.
smùchan,** -ain, *s.m.* Smoke.
————ach, *a.* Smoky.
smùd, see smùid & smùdan.
smudal, -ail, *s.m.* see smodal.
smùdan, -ain, -an, *s.m.* Musical note of any singing-bird. 2¶ The rock-dove—*columba livida.* 3 Wood-pigeon, see calman fiadhaich. 4 Turtle.
smùdan, -ain, -an, *s.m.* Small block of wood. 2 Kiln. 3 Smoke. 4 Smoke raised as a signal. 5 Particle of dust. 6†† Smoky fire. 7 Mote. Soot, smut. Tha a s. féin á ceann gach fòid, *every peat has its own smoke.*
smùdanach, *a.* Abounding in ring-doves or wood-pigeons. 2 Of wood-pigeons. 3 Smoking, smoky.
smug, -uig, -an, *s.m.* Snot, spittle, phlegm. 2 Nasal cartilage. 3 (CR) Muggy weather, mist and rain—*W. of Ross-shire* ; s. na cubhaig, see under smugaid.
smug, *v.a. & n.* Spit, snot.

smugach, -aiche, *a.* Phlegmatic, mucous, full of spittle. 2 Having a habit of spitting. 3 Snotty. 4 (DU) Muggy, applied to weather. Tha e s., *it is muggy and drizzling.*
smugachd,‡‡ *s.f.* Mucousness.
smugadair,** *s.m.* Pocket-handkerchief. 2 Bespawler.
smugadanaich, *s.f.* Spitting.
smugadh, -aidh, *s.m.* Spitting.
smugaid, -e, -ean, *s.f.* Spittle. Tilg s., *spit;* s. na cubhaig, *the froth or scum on certain growing herbs in summer, woodsare (iphis fly.)*
smugaideach, -eiche, *a.* Discharging spittle. 2 Like spittle. 3 Phlegmatic, salival.
————d,** *s.f.* Salivation. 2 Habit of spitting.
smugaidean, *n.pl.* of smugaid.
smugaidich,(MS) *v.a.* Bespawl.
smugail,** *s.f.* Mucus, snot.
smugarsaich, *v.* Bespawl.
smugair,(DU) *v.a.* Suck.
smugradh,(CR) *s.m.* Sucking, as a child sucking his fingers—*W. of Ross.*
smug-shileadh, -idh, *s.m.* Running at the nose. 2 Phlegm, snot, catarrh.
smug-shùileach, -eiche, *a.* Rheum-eyed.
smùid, -ean, *s.m.* Smoke, vapour. 2 Blaze, signal-fire. 3**Fume. 4**Mist. 5* Column of smoke. A' cur smùid, *smoking as a peat-fire before it blazes.* [***s.f.*]
smùid, *v.n.* Smoke. 2 Blow of a whale. 3 Dash to pieces, smash. 4* Curse. 5 Explode. 6**Fume. 7 Exhale. S. e as a chéil' e, *he dashed it in pieces.*
smùideach, -eiche, *a.* Smoking, vapoury. 2 Effluvious. 3 Fuming. 4 Exhaling.
smùideadh, -idh, *s.m.* Smoking, act or state of smoking, emitting smoke. 2 Dashing, smashing. 3*Cursing, swearing terribly. A' s—, *pr. pt.* of smùid.
smùidean, -ein, -an, *s.m.* Particle of dust, mote.
smùideanach, -aiche, *a.* Dusty, abounding in particles of dust.
smùideil, -e, *a.* see smùideach.
smùidich, *v.n.* Exhale.
smùidir, *v.* see smùid.
smùidre,** *s.pl.* Clouds, as of smoke or dust. 2 Exhalation. 3 Mist.
smùidreach,** *a.* Smoking, smoky.
smùidreach,* -ich, *s.f.* Bolt of smoke.
smùidreadh, -eidh, *s. m.* Smoking. 2 Cloud of smoke, smoke driven by the wind. A' s—, *pr. pt.* of smùidir.
smùidrich, *pr.pt.* a' smùidrich, see smùid.
————, -e, *s.f.* see smùidreadh. A' s—, *pr.pt.* of smùidrich. Le s. ghlas, *with grey smoke.*
smuig, -e, -ean, *s.f.* Snout. 2 Face, *in ridicule.* 3**Snot, phlegm. 4**Dirt, filth.
smuig-aodach, -aich, -ean, *s. m.* Handkerchief.
smuigeach, *a.* Having a snout or nose. 2 Snotty, phlegmy, mucous. 3**Dirty, filthy.
smuigeadach,**-aich, *s.m.* Pocket-handkerchief.
smuilc, -e, -ean, *s.f.* Curled nose. 2††Huff, the sulks, glumness, dejection.
smuilceach,* -eiche, *a.* Curl-nosed. 2†† Huffy, sulky.
smuilceag,(DC) *s.f.* Pert girl—*Argyll.*
smuilcean,(DC) *s.m.* Pert boy—*Argyll.*
smuinteachadh, see smuaineachadh.
smùintich, see smuainich.
smùir, *s.m.* Dust, particle of dust, spot, blot, blemish. 2 Earth. 3 Ashes. Fo s., *under dust.*
smuir,** *s.f.* Beak, snout.
smùirich,(MS) *v.a.* Bedust.
smùireadh, see smeuradh.
smùirneach, -eiche, *a.*Dusty, full of dust, atomy, drossy.
smùirneag, see smùirnean.
smùirnean, -ein, -an, *s.m.dim.* of smùir. Mote, atom, particle of dust. 2 Ace. 3 Peppercorn.
smùirneanach, -aiche, *a.* Full of motes. 2** Dusty.
————————d,** *s f.* Dustiness.
smùis, -e, *s.f.* see smuais.
———each, -eiche, *a.* Juicy.
smuisean,** -ein, *s.m.* Term of much personal contempt.
smùiseirnich, -e, *s.f.* The crashing noise made by the breaking of bones.
smùisreadh, -idh, *s.m.* Breaking of bones.
smuisich, *v.a.* Suck, extract the juice from—*Rob Donn.*
smùislich, *Loch Ness side* for smuaislich.
smuit,** *s.f.* Nose, bill, beak, snout.
smulag,** -aig, *s.f.* Fillip with the fingers.
smulan,** -ain, *s.m.* Lump of wood.
smulc,** *s.m.* Snout. 2 Surly look.
———ach,** *a.* Snouty. 2 Surly. 3 Having a surly look.
———air,** *s.m.* Person having a surly look. 2 Boxer.
———anta,** *a.* Snouty. 2 Having a surly look.
smùr, ùir & -ùire, *s. m.* see smùrach. Gun s. gun smodan, *without spot or blemish.*
smùr, *v.a.* see smeur.
———ach,** *a.* Drossy, dusty. 2 Having blots, spots or blemishes.
smùrach, -aich, *s.m.* Dross, dust. 2 Rubbish, fragments. 3 Ashes. 4 Blot, blemish. 5 Groping. 6*Groping among dust with the hands. A' s—, *pr.pt.* of smùraich. S. móine, *peat dross.*
smùrach-eighe, *s.m.* Filings.
smùrachd, *s.f.ind.* Drossiness.
smùraich,* *pr.pt.* a' smùrach, *v.n.* Grope in dust.
smùranach, -aiche, *a.* Drossy.
smùsach, *a.* Sucking, extracting the juice from—*Rob Donn.*
smut, -uit, -an, *s.m.* Bill, beak, snout, flat nose, pug-nose. 2 Peaked chin. 3 Stump. 4 Short log.
smut,* *pr.pt.* a' smutail, *v.n.* Sniff.
smutach, -aiche, *a.* Short-snouted, billed, beaked, snouty, saddle-nosed, pug-nosed. 2 Having a peaked chin. 3 Having a long snout.
smutag,¶ -aige, -an, *s.f.* Cole titmouse, black-cap, "snorter." 2 Flat-nosed or saddle-nosed female.
smutan, -ain, -an, *s.m.* Block, log. 2 *dim.* of smut.
sna, for 'sna.
snàd,** -àid, *s.f.* see snàthad.
snadb,** *s.m.* Sup.
snàdh, -a, see snàth.
snadhach,** *a.* Sappy, juicy.
snadhadh,** -aidh, *s.m.* Protection, defence. 2 Guardian angel.
snàdhainn, see snàthainn.
—————each, see snàthainneach.
snadh-ghairm,** *s.f.* Appellation, naming. 2 Appeal.
snadhm, see snaidhm.
snàg, *v.a.* see snàig.
snàg, -àig, *s.m.* One with a creeping gait, one whose motions are slow. 2*Creeping, sneaking.
snag, -aig, -an, *s. f.* Little audible knock. †2 Hiccough.
snag,¶ -aig, -an, *s.m.* Wood-pecker, see snagandaraich.
snàgach, -aiche, see snàigeach.
snagach, -aiche, *a.* Like a woodpecker. 2 Of a woodpecker.
snagadaich, -e, *s.f.* see snagardaich & snagaireachd.
snàgadh, -aidh, *s.m.* Creeping, crawling, sneaking. A' s—, *pr.pt.* of snàig.

snàgail,(DU) *v.a.* Whip a hook on a line.
snàgail, -e, *s.f.* Creeping, slow motion.
snàgair, -ean, *s.m.* One who creeps along,creeper. 2 Lazy fellow. 3 Sneaking fellow. 4** Snarler. 5 Reptile.
snagair, *v.a.* Carve or reduce a piece of wood to a shape with a knife.
snagair-daraich, see snagan-daraich.
snàgaireachd, *s.f.* Creeping along, crawling, sneaking. 2 Habit of creeping, crawling or sneaking.
snagaireachd, *s.f.* Cutting or carving of wood with a knife, whittling. A' s—, *pr.pt.* of snagair.
snagairt, *Arran* for snagaireachd.
snàgaladh,(DU) *s.m.* Thread wound round a fishing-hook to attach it to the hair-line. [In *Argyll*, snòdaladh—AH.]
snagan, -ain, -an, *s.m.* Little tinkling or clinking. 2 Comma, in *writing*. 3 Deep drink. 4 Short drink or draught.
snàgan, -ain, *s.m.* Creeping or slow motion. 2 Crawler, one with a creeping gait. 3* Sly creeping.
snàgan, *dim.* of snàg.
snaganach, -aiche, *a.* Tinkling, clinking.
snàganaich,** *s.f.* Creeping, crawling.
snagan-allt,¶ *s.m.* Water-rail—*rallus aquaticus.*
snagan-daraich,¶ *s.m.* Great spotted woodpecker—*picus major.*
snagan-dubh,¶ *s.m.* Water-rail, see snagan-allt.
snagardach,** -aich, *s.m.* Woodpecker.
snagardaich,** *s.f.* Gnashing, grating. 2 (DC) Chattering of the teeth with cold. S.-fhiacal, *gnashing of teeth.*
snàgardaich,** *s.f.* Creeping, crawling.
snagarra, *a.* Active, alert, lively, smart. Gu s., *alertly.*
————chd, *s.f.* Activity, alertness, liveliness, smartness.
snagarsaich, see snagardaich.
snagartaich, *s.f.* see snagardaich.
snag-labhair, *v.n.* Stammer in speaking.
snag-labhairt, -e, *s.f.* Stammering, act of stammering, hesitating in speech. A' s—, *pr.pt.* of snag-labhair.
snag-labhairteach, -eich, *s.m.* Stammerer.
snag-labhairtiche, see snag-labhairteach.
snaidh, *v. a.* Hew, cut down, slash. 2 Reduce wood or stone to a certain form. 3 Whet, sharpen. 4 Consume, waste, pine away. 5 Lop. 6 Defalcate. 7 Pine away. 8 Protect, patronize. 9 Slice. 10(MS)Inscribe. 11 Whittle. 12 Carve.
snaidh,** -e, *s.f.* Slice, lopping, chip.
snaidheach, -eiche, *a.* Hewing, hewing down, lopping, reducing to form. 2 Whetting, sharpening. 3 Carving,slicing. 4 Consuming,wasting. 5 Defalcating.
snaidheadair, -ean, *s.m.* Hewer, one who cuts down, or reduces to form by hewing, one who lops. 2 Whetter, one who whets or sharpens. 3 Defalcator. 4 (DU) One who whittles or carves.
————eachd, *s. f.* Hewing, business of a hewer, carving, cutting in chips.
snaidheadh, -idh, *s.m.* Hewing, act of hewing down, or reducing to form by hewing. 2 Whetting, act of whetting or sharpening. 3 Consuming, act of consuming. 4 Blocking. 5 Defalcation. 6 Slicing, lopping.* 7 Pining away. 8 Carving. 9 Whittling. A' s—, *pr. pt.* of snaidh. A' s. as, *pining away ;* s. fiodha, *a carving of wood ;* s. chlacha, *a hewing of stone.*
snaidhearachd, *s.f.* Hewing of stone, carving, cutting in chips.
snaidhm, see snaim.
snaidhte, *past pt.* of snaidh. Hewn, cut down, reduced to form by hewing, carved, lopped off. 2 Sharpened, whetted. 3 Consumed. 4 Defalcated. 5 Polished. 6 Dressed as a stick. 7 (DU) Wasted with ill-health. 8(DU) Whittled. 9 (DU) Carved. Clachan s., *hewn stones.*
snàig, *pr. pt.* a' snàgadh, *v. n.* Creep, crawl, sneak, steal softly, grabble.
snaig, -eachan, *s.f.* Latch of a door. Cuir an t-s. air an dorus, *latch the door.*
snaig,** *v.a.* Latch as a door.
snàigeach, -eiche, *a.* Creeping, crawling, sneaking. 2 Having a creeping gait.
snàigeach,(AF) *s.m.* Reptile.
snaigeachan, *n.pl.* of snaig.
snàigeadh, -idh, *s.m.* see snàgadh.
snàigean, -an, *s.m.* Reptile. 2 Creeping thing. 3 One with a creeping gait.
snàigeanach, *a.* Creeping, having a creeping gait.
————d, *s.f.* Creeping, creeping gait.

642. Snàigear.

snàigear,¶ -eir, -an, *s.m.* Creeper—*certhia familiaris.*
snaigh, see snaidh.
snaigheach, see snaidheach.
snàigheach, see snàigeach.
snaigheadh, see snaidheadh.
snaigheadair, -ean, *s.m.* see snaidheadair.
————eachd, see snaidheadaireachd.
snaighte, see snaidhte.
snaim, -ean & -eannan, *s.m.* Knot, tie. 2 Difficulty, puzzle. 3 Bunch. Daoine a dh'fhuasgladh gach s., *men who would solve every difficulty.*
1 lùbag cas-laoigh, *a half-hitch knot.*
2 lùb ruith, *a running-knot.*
3 snaim a' bhanna, *a reef-knot,a square knot.*
4 s. a' bhreabadair, *the weaver's knot.*
5 s. a' bhuailtein, *the clove-hitch.*
6 s. an fhigheadair, *the weaver's knot.*
7 s. an t-seòladair, *the reef-knot.*
8 s. calpa an dubhan, *the knot put on fishing-hooks' shanks.*
9 s. calpa an dul, *half hitch on the loop.*
10 s. casa caorach, *sheep-shank knot.*
11 s. chaillich, *granny's knot.*
12 s. chruaidh, *a hard knot.*
13 s. do sheanmhar, *your granny's knot.*
14 s. gartain, *knot used when garters were fastened outside the stocking.* It is illustrated in Logan's "Scottish Gael," 2nd. ed., vol. 1, p. 265. Cladaich, Lochawe, was a famous place for knitting garters.
15 s. na banaraich, *the milkmaid's knot*—the way she fastens her dress at the back after lifting it.
16 s. ruith, *a slip knot, running knot.*
17 s. snota, *the knot put on the snoods of horse-hair.*

[Names of knots, Nos. 4, 6, 8, 9, 10, 13, 15, 16 & 17 from DMy; 4, 7 & 11 from AH; and 14 from "Fionn."]

snaim, *pr. pt.* a' snaimeadh, *v. a.* Knot. tie a knot, tie with a knot. 2 Bind, fetter.

——each, -eiche, *a.* Knotty, abounding in knots or ties. 2 Difficult. 3 Jointed.

snaimeadh, -idh, -idhean, *s.m.* Knotting, act of knotting or tying with a knot. A' s—, *pr. pt.* of snaim.

snaimean, -ein, -an, *s.m. dim.* of snaim. Little knot.

————ach, -aiche, *a.* Knotty, full of little knots.

————achd, *s.f.* Knotting, tying, knottiness.

————an, *pl.* of snaim.

†snaimeas, -eis, -an, *s.m.* Rout, multitude.

snaime-gaoisid, *s.m.* Part of a hand fishing-line, see dorgh.

snaimh,* see snaoth and snaidh.

snaimneach, see snaimeach.

snaimte, *past pt.* of snaim. Knotted, bound with a knot, tied.

snàith, see snàth.

snaith, *v. a.* Rebate. 2 Thread a hook—*Suth'd.* 3** see snaidh.

snaithe bathta,§ *s.m.* Water-milfoil — *myriophyllum spicatum & alterniflorum.*

snaitheadair, -ean, *s.m.* see snaidheadair.

————eachd, *s.f.* see snaidheadaireachd.

snaitheadh, *s. m.* see snaidheadh.

643- Snaithe bàthta.

snaithean, see snàthainnean.

snàithne, -an, see snàthainn.

snàithneach, see snàthainneach.

snàithnean, -ein, *s.m.* Small thread. 2 String. 3 Skein.

————ach, *a.* Abounding in small threads.

snàithne-tomhais, *s.f.* Measuring-line.

snàmh, *pr.pt.* a' snàmh, *v.a.* Swim, perform the act of swimming. 2 Bathe. 3 Swim, be afloat. 4 Float. 5 Soak, deluge. Air s., *swimming, afloat;* tha m' anam a' s. an ceò, *my soul swims in mist;* a' cur an taigh air s., *deluging the house;* cuirear an tìr air s., *the land shall be deluged.*

snàmh, -àimh, *s.m.* Swimming, act of swimming or floating. 2 Soaking, deluging. A' s—, *pr. pt.* of snàmh. Math air an t-s., *good at swimming.*

snamh, -aimh, *s.m.* Slimy track of a snail.

————, *3rd.sing.& pl.imp.* S. e, *let him swim.*

snàmhach, -aiche, *a.* Floating, swimming. 2 That floats or swims naturally. 3 Fond of swimming. 4 Prone by nature to swim, as fish. 5 Buoyant. A' bhileag sh., *a long weed that lies on the surface of water.*

————, -aich, *s.m.* Swimming, floating, slow sailing, slow swimming.

————an, -ain, -an [& -ain,] *s.m.* Raft, float, anything that swims.

snàmhadair, see snàmhair.

snàmhadh, -aidh, *s.m. & pr.pt.* see snàmh.

snàmhaiche, *pl.* -an & -ain, *s.m.* see snàmhair. Chaill mi s. a' chaolais, *I have lost the swimmer of the strait.*

snàmhaidh, *fut. aff. a.* of snàmh, *v.* 2 *gen. sing.* of snàmh, *s.*

snàmhair, -ean, *s.m.* Swimmer. Deagh sh., *an expert swimmer.*

snàmhag,(DMK) *s. f. euphemism* for a Louse. Tha snàmhagan air, *there are lice on him—W. coast of Ross.*

snàmhan, -ain, *s.m.* see snàmhach.

snàmh luath, *a.* Swift in swimming, swift-swimming.

snaodaire,(AF) *s. m.* "Leader" of a flock of animals. 2(DC) Bell-wether. 3(DC) Bull.

snaodh, see snaoth.

snaogh, see snaoth.

snaoic,(CR) *s.f.* Gaelic spelling of *snack.*

snaoidh,* see snaoth & snaidh.

†snaoidh,** *a.* Flowing, running.

snaoimh,* see snaoth.

snaois, -e, -ean, *s.f.* Slice, piece of anything. 2 *Boat's prow. 3 Spit of dried fish—*Sàr-Obair.* S. arain, *a slice of bread.*

————each, -eiche, *a.* In slices. 2 Of, or belonging to, a boat-prow.

————eachadh, -aidh, *s. m.* Slicing, cutting in slices. A' s—, *pr.pt.* of snaoisich.

snaoisean, -ein, *s.m.* Snuff. 2 Pinch of snuff. 3 **Powder. 4*Huff.

————ach, -aiche, *a.* Snuffy, of, or belonging to, snuff. 2 Abounding in snuff. 3 Fond of taking snuff. 4**Pulverized, powdered. 5 Snuffing.

————achd, *s.f.* Habit of taking snuff, snuffing. 2 Calcination.

————adh, -aidh, *s.m.* Calcination.

snaoisein, *v.a.* Calcine, pulverize.

snaoisich, *v.a.* Slice, cut in slices.

————te, *past pt.* Sliced.

snaomanach, -aich, *s f.* Strong, robust fellow. 2 Jolly fellow.

snaomanach, -aiche, *a.* Robust, stout. 2 Jolly.

snaoth, -aoith, -an, *s.m.& f.* Bier, *prov.* Air an t-snaoith, *on the bier.*

snaoth,(AC) *s.m.* Leader, chief, king. Ceann s. nan iasg, *the head chief of the fish;* ceann snaoth na nì, *the head chief of the nowt.*

snaoth,* *v.n.* Jerk, twitch.

snaothadh,* -aidh, *s.m.* Jerking. 2 Jerk. A' s—, *pr.pt.* of snaoth.

snap, -aip, -an, *s.m.* Trigger of a gun. 2 Morsel.

snap, *pr.pt.* a' snapadh, *v.a.* Pull the trigger. 2 Miss fire.

snapach, -aiche, *a.* Having a trigger. 2 That misses fire. 3** That fireth. 4 That strikes fast.

snapadh, -aidh, *s.m.* Act of pulling the trigger. 2 Act of missing fire. A' s—, *pr. pt.* of snap.

snapaireachd, *s.f.* Snapping, snapping sound, as that caused by pulling the trigger of a gun.

snas, -ais, *s.m.* Regularity, order, perfectness. 2 Good or becoming appearance. 3 Elegance, gloss, ornament, polish. 4 Decency. 5 Proportion. 6 Colour, aspect. 7 Analysis, analyzing. 8 (DU) Trimness, tightness. Dean le s. e, *do it decently;* gnothach gun s., *an absurd thing, business without any degree of propriety;* cha'n 'eil s. air, *it is not tight* or *well-fitting.*

snàs, -ais, *s.m.* Slimy track of a snail. (snamhas.)

snas,* *v.a.* see snasaich.

snasach, -aiche, *a.* see snasmhor.

snasachadh, -aidh, Act of reducing to order or regularity. 2 Act of polishing, ornamenting or making elegant. 3 Carving. 4 Analysis in *gram.* A' s—, *pr. pt.* of snasaich.

snasachd, *s.f.* Neatness, elegance, trimness, spruceness. 2 Trimming, making neat. 3 Criticism. 4 Lopping, cutting down.

snasadair, *s.m.* Dissector, trimmer, pruner. 2 Critic. 3 Analyzer.

snasadaireachd, *s. f.* Dissecting. 2 Analyzing
snasadh, -aidh, *s.m. & pr. pt.* of snas, see snasachadh. 2**Amputation.
snasaich, *pr.pt.* a' snasachadh, *v.a.* Reduce into order or regularity. 2 Polish, ornament, make elegant. 3 Prune. 4 Analyze. 5 Criticize. 6 Trim, cut, dissect, amputate.
snasaichear, *fut. pass.* of snasaich.
snasaichidh, *fut.aff.a.* of snasaich.
snasaichte, *past pt.* of snasaich. Reduced to order or good appearance. 2 Polished, ornamented, made elegant. 3 Trimmed, lopped, pruned. 4 Fixed—R.13. 5 (DU) Trim, tight, taut.
snasail, *a.* Accomplished. 2 see snasmhor.
snasaireachd, see snasmhorachd.
snasar, see snasmhor.
snas-bhriathrach, -aiche, *a.* Oratorical, rhetorical, eloquent.
snas-bhriathraich, *v.a.* Embellish words.
snas-chainnt, -e, *s.f.* Rhetoric. 2 Philology.
snas-chlachaireachd, *s.f.* Finely-finished masonry.
snas-chopan, -ain, -an, *s.m.* Cross.
snasda, *s.m.* Colour.
snasda, *a.* see snasta.
snas-labhair, *v.a.* Modulate in speaking.
snas-labhairt, *s.* Modulation, accent.
snas-mhineachadh, *s.m.* Analysis.
snasmhoire, *comp.* of snasmhor.
snasmhor, -mhoire, *a.* Neat, elegant. 2 Polished, ornamented. 3**Decent. 4 Accurate. 5 Trimmed, lopped. 6 Brave. Cainnt sh., *accurate or elegant language.*
snasmhorachd, *s.f.* Neatness, polish, ornament, elegance. 2 Accuracy. 3(MS)Composition. 4 ††Perfectness.
snasta, *a. & past pt.* of snas. Orderly, regular, neat. 2 Ornamented. 3 Jointed. 4 Brave, gallant. 5 see snasaichte. Deud geal s., *an elegant white tooth.*
snastach, *a.* Trimming, lopping, pruning. 2 Criticizing.
snàth, -àith & -a, *pl.* snàithean, *s.m.* Thread in general. 2 Quantity of thread, yarn. 3 Line. Snàth-fuaidhle, *sewing-thread* ; snàth-clòimhe, *or* snàth-olla, *woollen thread, yarn, worsted ;* snàth-galadh, [snàth-reilidh in *Lewis*—DMy], *the thread which binds a fishing-hook to the line* ; snàth-moineis, *soft thick twine used for lacing fishing-nets together* ; snàth-cuir, *waft* ; snàth-riaghailt, *basting-thread* ; snàth-sìoda, *a silk-thread* ; snàth-dlùthaidh, *abb* ; snàth-lìn, *linen thread, linen yarn.* [††*pl.* snàthan.]
snàth, *v.a.* Thread, string.
snath, *v.a.* see snadh.
†snatha, *s.m.* Easing or riddance from pain. 2 Grief, trouble.
snàthach, -aiche, *a.* Full of thread or yarn.
snàthaclachadh, (DMK) *s. m.* Act of rigging hooks to a fishing-line—*West coast of Ross.* [" Reileadh-dhubhan " in *Lewis*—DMy.]
snàthad, -aid, -an, *s.f.* Needle. 2 Ear-mark on sheep, see comharradh-cluais. 3 (CR) Hook to hold the blade of a scythe at the proper angle. (Also called snàthad-fheòir—AH.) Crò snàthaid, *the eye of a needle.*
snàthadach, -aiche, *a.* Furnished with needles. 2 Like a needle.
snàthadachan, -ain, -an, see snàthadan.
snàthadag,(CR) *s.f.* Titlark—*Suth'd.*, *W. of Ross & Perth.*
snàthadan, -ain, -an, *s.m.* Needle-case.
snathad an t-seic, *s.f.* Spindle or axle of flyers of spinning-wheel, see No. 23, p. 290.
snàthad-mhara,(AF) *s.f.* Needle-fish.
snàthadair, -ean, *s.m.* Needle-maker.
snathag,¶ -aig, -an, *s.f.* Meadow-pipit, heather lintie—*anthus pratensis.*
snàthainn, -e & snàithne, *pl.* -ean & snàithnean, *s.m.* Thread, single thread. 2 String. 3 Skein. 4 Line. S. ascaird, *a thread of tow.*
snathainn,(DMK) *s.f.* Colon or lower bowel of an animal.
snathainn-bhàthaidh,§ *s. f.* Water-milfoil—*myriophyllum spicatum & alterniflorum.*
snàthainnean, -ain, -an, *s.m.*, *dim.* of snàthainn. Little thread.
snàthainneanach, -eiche, *a.* Abounding in small threads. 2 Ropy. 3 Fibrous.
snàth-cuir,* *s.m.* Waft.
snàthdag,(DU)*s.f.* Small glass of whisky, "nip." 2(DC) Meadow-pipit.
snàthlainn, *Uist* for snàthainn.
snathteag, see snàthdag.
sneabhartaich, *s.f.* Sneezing—*Arran.* (sreabhartaich.)
sneachd, -a, *s.m.* Snow. Ris an t-sneachd, *snowing* ; fliuch shneachd, *sleet* ; cloch shneachd, *hail;* crann shneachd, *dry snow;* ball sneachda, *a snowball* ; muc sneachd, *or* muc aitidh, *a large heap of snow made by rolling in time of thaw.*
sneachda, see sneachd.
sneachdach, -aiche, *a.* see sneachdail
sneachdadh, -aidh, *s.m.* see sneachd. An uisge sneachdaidh, *in snow-water* ; là sneachdaidh, *a snowy day* ; muc sneachdaidh, *a huge snowball.*
sneachdag,(AF) *s.f.* Common ptarmigan.
sneachdail, -e, *a.* Snowy, abounding in snow. 2 Like snow. 3 White like snow.
sneachdaire,(DC) *s.m.* Ptarmigan, see tàrmachan.
sneachdan,(DC) *s.m.* Ptarmigan, see tàrmachan.
sneachdar, *a.* Snowy. 2 Like snow.
sneachd-gheal, -ghile, *a.* Snow-white.
sneadh, -a, -an, *s.f.* Nit. 2 Egg of pediculus.
sneadhach, -aiche, *a.* Nitty, full of nits. 2 Like nits.
sneadhanach, see sneadhach.
sneadh na miol chaorach, *s.m.* Nit of the sheep-bot fly—*œstrus ovis.*
sneag, *v.a.* Notch, nick, dent, cut.
sneag, *s.* Notch, see eag.
sneagach, see eagach.
sneagachadh, -aidh, see eagachadh.
sneagaich, see sneag.
snèagair, *s.m.* Crawler, see snàigear.
sneagaireachd, *s.f.* Hacking. 2 Notching, indentation.
sneagh, see sneadh.
sneaghach, see sneadhach.
sneaghan, -ein, *Arran*, *E. Perth*, *W. of Ross and Kintyre* for seangan.
sneaghanach, see seanganach.
sneamh, -eimh, see sneadh.
sneamhabh, see sneadhach.
†sneidh, see sneigh.
sneidhe, see snidhe.
†sneigh, *a.* Straight, direct. 2 Little.
snèip, *s.* Turnip—*Suthd.*
sneomh, see sneadh.
sniagair,(MS) *v.n.* Hover.
sniamh, *v.* see snìomh.
sniamhair, see snìomhair.
snichd, *s.m.* see snichdean.
snichdean, -ein, -an, *s.m.* Stitch of a needle. 2 Stitch of clothing. Gach s. a th' agam, *every stitch I have* ; cha robh s. air, *he was naked.*
snidh, see snigh. [McL & D gives *snidh*, and MacBain *snigh.*]
snig, *s.f.* Nit.
snigh, *v.n.* Drop, let fall in drops. 2 Leak, let in water. 3 Ooze through in drops. 4*Shed

tears. Bheireadh do ghnàthachadh air na clachaibh snigheadh, *your conduct would make the very stones shed tears.*

snigh, *s.m.* see snighe.

snighe, *s.m. ind.* Rain coming through the roof of a house. 2 Drop. 3 Tear. 4 Sorrow, vexation.

——ach, -eiche, *a.* That droppeth rain. 2 That admits drops of rain. 3 Oozing, as rain through a roof. 4 Tearful, in tears, moist with tears, weeping, sad. Taigh s., *a house whose roof lets the rain through* ; s. gun lèirsinn, *tearful and blind.*

snigheadh, -idh, *s.m.* Dropping, act of falling in drops. 2 Oozing through in drops. 3 Shedding of tears. 4 Sadness. A' s—, *pr. pt.* of snigh.

snimhean, Bha s. nan riombalaibh buidhe, (*the falling leaves) were twirling in circles in the whirlwind.—Sgeul.-nan-caol, p. 102.*

snioghag, (*pron.* sniû-ag) *Suth'd* for seangan.

snioghan, *S. Inverness-shire* for seangan.

sniom, *s.* Distress.

sniomh, *pr.pt.* a' sniomh, *v.a. & n.* Twist,twine. 2 Spin. 3 Wind. 4 Wind yarn. 5 Curl. 6 Wrench. 7**Wring. Sh. na muathan, *the women spun* ; sh. e à m' làimh e, *he wrenched it out of my hand* ; sh. e an ceann dheth, *he wrung its head off* ; ar cridheachan air an s., *our hearts wrung.*

sniomh, -a, *s.m.* Sadness, heaviness. 2††Great pain. Tha s. air mo chridhe, *my heart is sad.*

sniomh, -a, *s.m.* Spinning. 2 Twist, twine. 3 Twist in yarn. 4 Curl of hair, ringlet. 5 Sprain. 6 Wrench. 7 see sniomhadh. Deagh sh., *good spinning* ; math air an t-sniomh, *good at spinning* ; a shealgair a's àillidh s., *O,huntsman of the comeliest locks.* A' s—, *pr.pt.* of sniomh.

sniomhach, -aiche, *a.* Sad, declivous.

————,†† -aich, *s.m.* see sniomhachas.

————, -aiche, *a.* Twisting, twining, that twists or twines. 2 Winding, that winds. 3 Spinning, employed in spinning. 4 In ringlets or curls, curling. 5 Spiral. 6 Twisted,twined, helical. 7 Tending to twist or twine. 8 Spun. Falt s., *hair in ringlets.*

sniomhachan, -ain, *s.m.* Spinner.

sniomhachas, -ais, *s.m.* Employment of a spinner, spinning. 2 Anything spun. 3 Curling, as of the hair. 4 Tendency to form into curls. 5** Spun yarn. [wainer.

sniomhadair,** -ean, *s. m.* Spinner. 2 Cord-

sniomhadh, -aidh,*s.m.* Spinning, act of spinning. 2 Twisting,twining,act of twisting or twining. 3 Winding, act of winding. A' s—, *pr. pt.* of sniomh.

sniomhaiche, -an, *s.m.* Spinner. 2 see sniomhair. Ban-sh., *spinster, spinstress.* [of sniomh.

sniomhaidh, *gen.sing.* of sniomhadh. 2 *fut.aff.a.*

sniomhain, -e, *a.* see sniomhach. Cùl s., *curled hair* ; air staidhrichibh s., *on winding stairs.*

————each,** *a.* see sniomhach. Falt s., *finely-twisted lock of hair.*

sniomhair, -ean, *s.m.* Wimble, borer, auger. 2 **Spinner. 3**Cordwainer.

————eachd,** *s.f.ind.* Business of a spinner. 2 Business of a cordwainer.

sniomhan, see sniomhach.

————, *s.* see sniomh.

sniomhanach, *s.* see sniomh.

sniomhanach, -aiche, *a.* see sniomhach. Ciabh s., *a plaited ringlet* ; falt s., *hair in ringlets.*

————d,(MS) *s.f.* Limberness.

sniomhta, *past pt.* of sniomh. Spun. 2 Twisted, twined. Wound.

sniouga, see sneadh.

snisean, -ein, *s.m.* see snaoisean.

snith, see snigh.

snithe, see snigh.

——ach, -eiche, *a.* see snigheach.

†**sno**, *s. m.* Visage. 2 Appearance. 3 Colour. (snuadh,)

snòd, *pr. pt.* of snòdadh, *v.a.* Fix a fishing-hook to a line. 2 Dress a hook.

snòd, -òid [& ††-a,] *pl.*-an & -aichean, *s.m.* Twisted hairs which are fastened to a fishing-hook, "snood." 2 The part of a fishing-line to which the hook is fastened. 3 Tippet.

snod,* *s.f.* Fishing-line.

snòdach,** *a.* Snooded, as a fishing-line.

snòdadh, -aidh, *s.m.* Act of preparing a hook for fishing, snooding as a fishing-hook. A' s—, *pr.pt* of snòd. [In parts of *Argyll*, this is called "a' tapadh dhubhan." It is also called stalcadh dhubhan—*Fionn.*] [&c.

snodail,(DC) *v.* Snuff the wind, as deer, dogs,

snòdan, -ain, -an, *s.m. dim.* of snòd.

snodan, -ain, *s.m.* The rapid motion of a boat. *prov.*

snòdanach,†† *a.* Abounding in little tippets.

snodha, -n, *s.m.* (i.e. snodha gàire) Smile on the countenance. (snuadh.)

snodhach, -aich, *s.m.* Sap or juice of a tree, particularly of the birch. 2*Foliage, verdure. 3 ††Pertaining to hooks or fishing-lines. 4 (MS) Bloom, efflorescence. 5 (JMcF) Bud. Is geal gach nodha gu ruig s. an fhearna, *everything new is white, even to the bark of the alder*—the alder when newly-peeled is white, but turns red in a short time ; a' choill' a' snodhachadh, *the woodlands budding.*

snodhach an leamhain, *s. m.* Sap of the elm, used of old as a hair-restorer.

snoghach,** *a.* Beautiful. (snuadhach.)

snòid,* *v.a.* see snod.

snòidean, see snòitean.

snoidh, see snaidh.

snoig,* *s.f.* Expression of countenance of a testy or snuffy person.

snoigeas, -eis, -an, *s. m.* Testiness, peevishness. 2 Testy, peevish look.

snoigeasach, -aiche, *a.* Testy, peevish. 2 Having a testy or peevish look.

snoileun,¶ *s.m.* Grey or blue titmouse, blackcap, see cailleachag cheann-ghorm.

snòitean, -ein, *s.m.* Snuff. 2 Pinch of snuff. 3 One who snuffs, in ridicule.

snomhach,(MS) *s.m.* Blowth. see snodhach.

snot, *pr.pt.* a' snotadh & a' snotail, *v.a.* Smell, snuff the wind. 2 Turn up the nose in smelling. 3 Suspect, have a suspicion. 4 Snuffle.

snotach, -aiche, *a.* Smelling, that smells. 2 Suspecting, suspicious. 3**Snuffling, snorting.

snotadh, -aidh, *s.m.* Smelling, act of smelling. 2 Snuffing up the wind. 3 Suspecting, act of suspecting, suspicion. 4 Snorting. A' s—, *pr. pt.* of snot. A' s. bhileagan, *smelling leaves*—R. 46.

snotaich, see snot. [In *Gairloch*, snòtaich, *pr-pt.* a' snòtach, Smell, snuff—DU.]

snotail, -e, *pr.pt.* & *s.f.* see snotadh.

snothach, see snodhach.

snòthd, *s.* Part of a hand-line, see under dorgh.

snotraich, -e, *s.f.* see snotadh.

†**snuadh**,** *v.* Flow as a stream.

snuadh, -aidh, *s.m.* Hue, colour, appearance, complexion. 2 Beauty. †3**River, brook. 4 **Blood. 5**Hair of the head. 6*Aspect. Air tréigsinn a shnuaidh,*having changed its colour*; bheir thu air a sh. caitheadh mar leomann, *thou shalt make his beauty to consume as a moth.*

——ach, -aiche, *a.* Good-looking, having a

good complexion or colour. 2 Comely, elegant. 3 Having an imposing appearance. 4 Bloomy. S. treun, *good-looking and valiant*; duine s., *a comely person*.

snuadhachadh, -aidh, *s.m.* Act of giving a good appearance or colour to anything. A' s—, *pr pt.* of snuadhaich.

snuadhaich, *pr.pt.* a' snuadhachadh, *v.a.* Give a good colour or appearance to anything, adorn. 2 Imbue. 3 Bloom.

——te, *past pt* of snuadhaich. Well-coloured, adorned, bedecked.

snuadhar, -aire, *a.* see snuadhach. S. treun, *personable and strong*; A shòbhraibh! is s. do ghnùis, *O, primrose, pleasant is thy appearance*.

†snuadh-chlais, -ean, *s.f.* Channel of a river.

snuadhmhor, -oire, *a.* see snuadhach. Duine s., *a comely person*.

snuim,** *s.* Bunch.

snuim, see snaim.

snuisean, see snaoisean.

——ach, see snaoiseanach.

——achd, see snaoiseanachd.

so, *dem.pron.*, *adv.* & *int.* see seo.

so-, Initial particle prefixed to adjectives and substantives, implying facility, aptness, fitness, ease, equality, and sometimes goodness. It is similar to the termination *-ble* in English, and *-bilis* in Latin. Dèanta, *made*, or *done*; so-dhèanta, *easily done*. [The reverse of *do-*.]

†so, *a.* Young.

†soadh, *s.* Bed, couch. 2 Turning, return. 3 Eclipse.

so-aideachaidh, *a.* Avowable.

so-aimsir,** *s.f.* Calm weather, fair weather, pleasant weather. 2 Season of pleasure.

so-àireamh, -e, *a.* Numerable, computable, easily numbered.

so-àiteachaidh, *a.* Arable. 2 Inhabitable.

so-aithneach,** *a.* Easily known or recognised. 2 Conspicuous.

so-aithneachadh, *a.* Easily recognised.

so-aitreabhach, -aiche, *a.* Inhabitable.

so-aithriseach, -eiche, *a.* Allegable.

so-aithriseil, -e, *a.* Allegable.

†so-alt, *s.* Good leap.

so-aomaidh, -e, *a.* Flexible, exorable, easily persuaded, easily bent.

so-aslachadh, *a.* Exorable.

so-atharrach, -aiche, *a.* Alterable, easily moved.

——adh, *a.* see so-atharrach.

so-atharraichte, *a.* see so-atharrach.

sobh,§ s. Common sorrel, see samh. **Sobhatalmhainn, *strawberries*.

sobhaidh, *v.a.* & *n.* Turn, prevent. [‡sòbhaidh.]

sobhal, see sabhal.

sobhaladh, see so-bholadh.

sobhdan, see sodan.

——ach,** *a.* Equanimous.

so-bheanailteach, -eiche, *a.* Tangible.

——d, *s.f.ind.* Palpability.

so-bheantuinneachd, *s.f.* Tactility.

so-bheus, -an, *s.m.* Good breeding. So-bheusan, *good manners*.

——ach, *a.* Well-bred.

so-bhinntichte, ** *a.* Coagulable, easily curdled.

so-bhlasda, -bhlaisde, *a.* Savoury, tasty.

so-bhogachaidh,** *a.* Moveable. 2 Pliant. 3 Easily softened.

so-bholadh, -aidh, -aidhean, *s. m.* Fragrance, sweet smell.

so-bholtanachd, see so-bholadh.

so-bholtrach, -aiche, *a.* Sweet-smelling.

sòbhrach, -aich, -aichean, *s.f.* see sòbhrag. 2* Kind of clover.

sòbhrach, *a.* see sòbhragach.

——an, -ain, *s.m.* Young primrose. 2 Primrose—*Colonsay*

sòbhrag, -aig, -an, *s. f.* Primrose—*primula vulgaris*.

644. Sòbhrag.

sòbhragach, -aiche, *a.* Abounding in primroses. 2 Like a primrose.

sòbhrag chluasach,§ *s.f.* Auricula, see lus-nam-ban-righ.

sòbhrag-gheamhraidh,§ *s. f.* Winter primrose—*primula polyanthus*.

sobhraide,** *s.f.* Sobriety. 2 Mildness, gentleness.

so-bhreith, *a.* Arbitrable.

so-bhrisidh, *a.* Frangible.

so-bhriste, *a.* Frangible, brittle.

——achd, ** *s.f.* Brittleness, frangibility. 2 Weakness.

so-bhròn,** -òin, *s. m.* Pleasant sorrow, melancholy pleasure.

so-bhruidhneach, -eiche, *a.* Accostable.

so-bhuailteach, -eiche, *a.* Easily hit or struck, assailable.

so-bhualta, -ailte, *a.* see so-bhuailteach.

soc, suic, *s.m.* Forepart or end of anything. 2 The beak, snout. 3 Chin. 4 Plough-sock. 5 **Coulter, 6 Socket. 7**Point. 8 *Ploughshare. S. croinn, *the sock of a plough*; a' geurachadh 'shuic, *sharpening his sock*; claidhean s. ri s., *swords point to point*.

soc,** *v.a.* Fit a plough with a sock (** says coulter.) 2 Provide with a socket. 3 Point. 4 Fit a plough with a sock.

soc,** *s.m.* Silence.

—ach,** *s.m.* Soccage, tenure of lands by service fixed and determined in quality. 2 Certain extent of arable land. 3 Point of land jutting out between two rivers. 4 see soc. [As a place-name, *Succoth* in English. *gen. sing.* socaich.]

socach,* *s.f.* Pert female.

——, -aiche, *a.* Snouted, beaked. 2 Coultered or socked, as a plough. 3 Having a peaked chin. 4 Pointed. 5 Like a coulter. 6 Like a beak or snout.

socadh, -aidh, -aidhean, *s.m.* Act of fastening the coulter to a plough. 2 see soc.

†socaiche, *s.f.* Army, host, multitude.

socaid, -e, *s.f.* Socket.

†socail, *s.f.* Ease, rest, tranquility. 2 Mildness.

socail,** *a.* Easy, mild, gentle.

socain, *gen.sing.* of socan.

socair, -e & socrach, *s.f.* Ease, rest, tranquility. 2 Comfort. 3 Mildness. 4 Prop, pillar, rest. 5 Assuagement. 6* Leisure. 7 Peace. Opposite of docair. Gabh s., *take ease*; am bheil thu air do sh.? *are you at leisure?* a' cheud s. a thig, *the first*

abatement of the storm ; gun s. oidhche no là, *without peace night or day ;* s. a dhuine, *take it easy, my dear sir !*
socair, -e, *a.* Easy, quiet, at ease, tranquil. 2 Pleasant. 3 Mild, gentle, comfortable, safe. 4 Slow. Tha mi s., *I am at peace;* tha 'm feasgar s., *the evening is mild.*
socair ! *int.* Avast ! avast !
socait,** -ean, *s.f.* Socket.
——each,** *a.* Socketted. 2 Like a socket.
socal,** -ail, *s.m.* see socail.
socalach,** -aiche, *a.* Easy, mild. 2 At rest.
socamhlach, -aiche, *a.* see socalach.
socan, -ain, -an, *s.m.dim.* of soc Little snout or beak. 2 Little coulter. 3 Big-bellied man. 4 Little sock. 5 Little rest or prop. 6**Fieldfare. 7 Little ploughshare.
socanach, -aiche, *a.* Pertaining to little snouts, socks, coulters, &c.
socarach, see socrach.
†sochaidh,** *s.f.* Army, host, multitude.
sochair, -e, -ean, *s.f.* Benefit, profit, emolument. 2 Immunity, privilege. 3 Comfort, ease. 4 (AC) Right. 5††Gift. 6 Favour. Cha s. sam bith sin dhomh-sa, *that is no advantage to me ;* sochairean chlann Dhé, *the privileges of God's children.*
so-chàirdeach,** *a.* Nearly related. 2 Intimately acquainted.
so-chairdean, *s.pl.* Friends, intimate friends.
so-chairdeas,** *s.m.* Friendship, intimate friendship.
sochaireach, -eiche, *a.* Yielding profit, beneficial, advantageous. 2 Holding or enjoying privileges or immunities. 3 Obliging. 4 Lucrative. 5 Easy-minded. 6 Right.
————d,** *s.f.* Blessedness. 2 Obligingness. 3 Lucrativeness. 4 Easy-mindedness.
sochairean, *s.pl.* Benefits, blessings.
sochairich,** *v.* Bless.
so-chaitheamh,** *a.* Consumable.
so-chamadh,** *a.* Flexible.
so-chaochlaideach, -eiche, *a.* Easily changed, changeable, transmutable, convertible.
so-chaochlaideachd, *s.f.ind.* Mutability, facility of being changed.
so-chaochlaidh, -e, *a* see so-chaochlaideach.
sochar, -air, *s.f.* Silliness, weakness, instability of purpose, yielding or too compliant disposition, simplicity. 2 Indulgence. 3 Immunity. 4(MS)Interest. 5 (MS) Present, donation. 6 see sochair. 7 (DMy) Bashfulness, shyness. Is i an t-s. a thug orm a dheanamh, *pure simplicity made me do it ;* is miosa an t-s. na 'mhèirle, *simplicity is worse than theft.*
——ach, -aiche, *a.* Silly, of a too yielding disposition. 2 Boyish. 3**Obliging, ready to favour. 4**Lucrative. 5** Easy-minded. 6** Right. 7‡ Simple, compliant. 8* Easily imposed upon. Duine s., *a weak* or *simple person*, bho 'n a bha mi cho s., *since I was so simple ;* c' ar son a bha thu cho s. ? *why were you so soft ?*
so-charachaidh,** *a.* Agitable.
socharachd,* *s.f.ind.* Gullibility
socharaich,* see sochar.
so-charaichte,** *a.* Agitable.
so-charnaidh, *a.* Congestible.
so-chasta,** *a.* Handy, manageable.
so-cheannsachaidh, *a.* Exuperable.
so-cheannsachd, *s.f.* Manageableness.
so-cheannsaichte, *a.* Conquerable.
so-cheannsaidheachd, *s.f.ind.* Manageableness
sochd,‡ *s.m.* Silence 2 Peace, quietness. 3 see soc.
so-cheangladh,** *a.* Associable.
so-chdach, -aich, -an, see socach.
sochdair, see socair.
so-chinealta,** *a.* High-born.
————chd, *s.f.* High birth, nobility.
————s, *s.m.* High birth, nobility.
so-chiùineachadh,**a. Easily appeased, placable, exorable.
so-chiùinichte, *a.* Easily appeased.
sochladh,** *a.* Sensible.
sochladh, -aidh, *s m.* Fame, character.
so-chlaistinn, *a.* see so-chlaistinneach.
——————, *s.* Audibleness.
——————each, -eiche, *a.* Audible.
so-chlaoidhte,** *a.* Easily conquered.
so-chlaonadh, -aidh, *s.m.* Aptness to bend. flexibility. 2 Aptness to go astray, towardness.
so-chloiste,** *a.* Audible.
so-chloistinn,** *s.f.* Audibleness.
so-chluinntinn, -e, *a.* Audible, easily heard.
————,** *s.* Audibleness.
sochmadh,** *a.* Abstemious.
sochmhor,** *a.* Abstemious.
so-chnàimhteachd, *s.f.ind.* Corrodibility.
so-chnàimhte, *a.* see so-chnàmhta.
so-chnàmh,** *a.* Easy of digestion, digestible.
so-chnàmhach, see so-chnàmhadh.
so-chnàmhadh,** *a.* Digestible.
so-chnàmhaiche,** *s.m.* One who has a good digestion.
so-chnàmhta,** *a.* Easy of digestion, digestible.
so-chobhaiste,** *a.* Conformable.
so-choimeasgta, *a.* Compoundable.
so-choimheid, *a.* Preservable.
sochoire,(MS) *s.* Flexibility.
so-choireachaidh, *a.* Impeachable.
so-chois,** *s.m.* Learned man.
so-choisinnteachd, *s.f.ind.* Maintainableness.
so-choisneadh,** *a.* Attainable.
so-chomhairleach, -eiche, *a.* Easily advised or entreated. 2 Versatile.
——————d, *s.f.ind.* Persuasiveness. 2 Versatility.
so-chomhairlich, -e, *a.* see so-chomhairleach.
so-chomharraichte,** *a.* Easily distinguished, observable, conspicuous.
so-chòmhdachaidh, *a.* Maintainable.
so-chòmhradhach,** *a.*Conversable, affable, complaisant.
so-chòmhraideach, -eiche, *a.* Affable, conversable, complacent. 2 (MS—chòmhraiteach) Familiar.
——————d, *s.f.* Affability.
so-chompanta,** *a.* Associable.
so-chonradh, -aidh, *s.m.* Cheapness.
so-chordach, *a.* Agreeable.
so-chosmhuil, -e, *a.* Conformable.
sochrach,(MS) *a.* Available. [MM.]
sochraid,** *s.f* Multitude of people. [Irish—
so-chràimhte, see so-chnàmhta.
so-chràmhta, see so-chnàmhta.
so-chreidimh, -e, *s.f.* Credulity.
so-chreidmheach, -eiche, *a.* Credulous.
——————,** -eich, *s.m.* Credulous person.
so-chreidsinn, -e, *a.* Credible.
so-chridheach, -eiche, *a.* Kind, good-hearted, tender-natured.
——————d, *s.f.ind.* Good nature, cordiality, kindness.
so-chrionadh,** *a.* Adustible.
so-chrùbadh, *a.* Contractible.
so-chuimte, *a.* Mouldable, easily shaped.
so-chumta. see so-chuimte.
so-chunntach, -aiche, *a* Countable.
socrach, -aiche, *a.* Easy, quiet, comfortable, at rest. 2 Affording ease or comfort. 3 Not easily moved or excited. 4 Slow, sedate, not easily hurried. 5** Firmly-footed, fixed, steady, established. 6* *Smooth, plain, equal. 7*

Moderate. Feachd bu sh. ceum, *a host of the steadiest step*, or *marching in line;* gu s., *leisurely, coolly, softly;* gabhaidh mi an t-slighe gu s., *I will lead the way at leisure.*
socrachadh, -aidh, *s.m.* Establishing, act of establishing, fixing, ordering, arranging, appointing, adjusting, making steady or tranquilizing. 2 Tranquility. 3 Comfort. A' s—, *pr. pt.* of socraich.
socrachd,** *s.f.* Steadiness, undisturbedness.
socradh,** *s.m.* Ease, leisure. 2 Tranquility, calmness, smoothness.
socraich, *pr.pt.* a' socrachadh, *v.a. & n.* Establish, fix, make firm or steady. 2 Determine, appoint, decree. 3 Authorize. 4 Arrange, dispose, settle. 5 Appease, quiet, compose, assuage. 6 Stand firm. 7 Stop or cease any motion. 8* Level, make even. 9 Fix or place on a firm footing or foundation. 10 Stand at ease. 11(MS) Ballast. 12(MS) Becalm.
Sh. iad uile air an lòn, *they all stood firm on the plain;* sh. am feasgar, *the evening settled;* sh. e fichead punnd Sasunnach oirre 'sa bhliadhna, *he settled £20 per annum on her;* sh. e a chridhe air sin, *he set his heart on that;* sh. 'fhearg, *his rage subsided;* sh. e an gnothach sin, *he arranged that business;* s. an t-àite seo, *level this place;* socraichidh mi mo smuaintean, *I will fix my thoughts.*
socraichear, *fut.pass.* of socraich.
socraichidh, *fut.aff.a.* of socraich.
socraichte, *past pt.* of socraich. Established, fixed. 2 Determined, appointed. 3 Arranged, disposed, settled. 4 Appeased, assuaged. 5* Made level, levelled. A chridhe s. air peacadh, *his heart bent on sin;* tha 'n t-àite sin s., *that place is levelled.*
socras,** -ais, *s.m.* Ease, tranquility.
socul, see socal.
sod, -a, *s.m.* Noise of boiling water. 2 Steam of water in which meat is boiled. 3 Boiled meat. 4**Noise of water when meat is boiling in it.
sod, -oid, -an, *s.m.* Sod. 2 Clumsy or awkward person. 3**Stout, corpulent person.
sodach, -aiche, *a.* Clumsy, awkward. 2 Untidy. 3 Sodish. 4**Stout.
——, -aich, *s.m.* Stout, robust or clumsy man. Is tric a chinn an cneadach 's a dh'fhalbh an s., *often does the puny grow and the stout decay.*
——as, -ais, *s.m.* Clumsiness, awkwardness.
sodag, -aig, -an, *s.f.* Clout, pillion, pannel. 2 Mat made of woven straw and placed under a burden. *Prov.* 3††Turf.
sodagach, -aiche, *a.* Ragged, clouted. 2 Turfed.
sodail, *gen.sing.* of sodal.
sodair,** *v.a. & n.* Trot.
——, -ean, *s. m.* Strong-built man. 2 Strong-built or clumsy animal. 3**Clumsy, awkward fellow. 4** Trotting horse. 5 Trotter.
——eachd, *s.f.* Clumsiness, stoutness of form or make.
sodal, -ail, *s.m.* Flattery. 2 Pride, vain-glory. 3 Fawning, adulation. 4** Arrogance.
——,** *a.* Flattering, fawning. 2 Proud, arrogant.
——ach, -aiche, *a.* Flattering, fawning. 2 Proud, arrogant. 3 Luxurious, epicurean. Gu s., *fawningly.*
——ach, -aich, *s.m.* Flatterer, adulator, parasite, charlatan, cajoler.
——achd, ‡‡*s.f.ind* Habit or practice of flattery. 2 Pride. 3**Luxury, epicurism.
——aich,** *v.a.* Flatter, fawn, cajole. 2 Soothe.
——aich, -e, *s.f.* Habit of flattery, continued or frequent flattery, fawning or cajoling.
sodalaiche, *s.*, see sodalach, *s.*
sodalair,** *s.m.* Adulator, coaxer.
sodalanach, -aiche, *a.* Parasitic.
sodaltach, -aiche, *a.* Parasitic.
sodan, -ain, *s.m.* Joy, blithesomeness. 2 Appearance or expression of joy or gladness at meeting. 3 Joyous reception. 4 Caressing. 5*Fawning. 6* Complaisance. Air son sodain riut-sa, *out of sheer complaisance to you;* rinn an cù s. ris, *the dog fawned upon him.*
sodanach, -aiche, *a.* Joyful, glad, cheerful, complaisant.
sodanaich,(MS) *v.a.* Cocker.
sòdar, -air, *s.m.* Solder.
sodar, -air, *s.m.* Trotting. 2 Trotting horse.
——ach,** *a.* Trotting.
sodaran,(MS) *s.m.* Jogger.
sodar-bhrochan,* -ain, *s.m.* Thick gruel.
sodarnach, -aiche, *a.* Able-bodied, strong, robust, strong and sound for marching. 2** Clumsy. 3 Able to trot. 4 **Trotting.
sodarnach, -aich, -aichean, *s.m.* see sodair.
sòdh, -a, see sògh.
†sodh,** *s.m.* Turning, winding, changing. 2 Eclipse.
†sodh,** *v.a.* Turn.
so-dhaingneach,** *a.* Affirmable.
sodhan, see saoidhean.
†sodhan,** *a.* Prosperous.
so-dhealbhach, see so-dhealbhaidh.
so-dhealbhaidh, *a.* Contrivable. 2 Figurable, well-formed, handsome.
so-dheanamh, see so-dheanta.
so-dhèanta, *a.* Practicable, possible. 2 Easily done.
so-dhèantachd, *s.f.* Possibility, practicability.
so-dhearbhaidh, *a.* Probable.
so-dhearbhta, *a.* Easily proved, evincible.
so-dhianta, see so-dheanta.
so-dhionaidh, *a.* Fortifiable. 2 Justifiable.
————eachd, *s.f.* Justifiableness.
so-dhionta, *a.* Defensible, easily defended.
so-dhochanta, -ainte, *a.* Damageable, easily hurt.
so-dhòirte,†† *a.* Apt to pour out. 2 Fluent in speech.
so-dhrùighidh, *a.* Permeable.
so-dhrùighteachail, -e, *a.* Impressive.
so-dhruidte, *a.* Easily shut.
sodrach, -aiche, *a.* Trotting, that trots.
————, -aich, *s.m.* Trotting pace.
sodradh, -aidh, *s.m.* Quick or rapid motion. 2 Trotting, galloping. 3 Quick decay of anything. 4 Lewdness.
sodraich, see sod.
sodsag** -aig, *s.f.* Pillion.
so-earalachd, *s.f.* see so-chomhairleachd.
†soeth,‖ s. see saeth.
so-fhadaidh,‡‡ *a.* Inflammable.
so-fhadaidheachd,‡‡ *s.f.* Inflammability.
so-fhaghail,** *a.* Attainable, easily got.
so-fhaicinn, see so-fhaicsinn.
so-fhaicinneach, see so-fhaicsinneach.
so-fhaicseanta, *a.* see so-fhaicsinneach.
so-fhaicsinn, *a.* Easily seen, apparent, evident, conspicuous.
so-fhaicsinneach, *a.* Visible, apparent, easily seen, conspicuous, aspectable.
so-fhaicsinneachd, *s.f.* Conspicuity.
so-fhaithreachd, *s.f* Facility.
so-fhalamhachadh,** *a* Voidable.
so-fhaotainn, -e, *a.* Acquirable, easily found, attainable.
so-fhireanachaidh, *a.* Justifiable.
so-fhireantachd, *s.f ind.* Justifiableness.
so-fholach, -aiche, *a.* Concealable, easily hidden.

so-fhuasglaidh, *a.* Redeemable.
sog, *s.m.ind.* see sogan.
sogach, see sogail.
sogail, -e, *a.* Merry, joyous, festive.
sogan, -ain, *s.m.* Mirth, joy, delight, hilarity. 2* Good humour. 3‡ Tipsiness. Nam bitheadh s. air, *were he in good humour.*
sogan, see sugan.
soganach, -aiche, *a.* Merry, joyful. 2 Festive, maudlin.
sogh,(AF) *s.m.* Greyhound.
sògh, -òigh, *s.m.* Pleasure, joy, luxury, delicious fare, luxurious ease. 2 Riot, riotous living. 3 Dainties, delicacies. 4 Satiety. 5 Sumptuousness. 6 Prosperity. 7 (AF) Juice, sap. Sògh-nan-òigh, *the joy of maidens ;* s. rìoghail, *royal dainties.*
so-ghabhaltach, *a.* Impressive.
sòghach, -aiche, *a.* see sòghail.
sòghail, -e, *a.* Luxurious, sumptuous. 2 Fond of delicacies. 3 Cheerful. 4 Prosperous. 5 Juicy, sappy. 6 Delicious. Biadh s., *delicious food.*
sogh-aimsir, see so-aimsir.
soghainn,* *s.* Batter.
sòghainn, *a.* Pleasant, agreeable, cheerful.
———,** *s.f.* Kind of paste used by weavers to smooth their threads, treisgein, technically called " dressing."
sòghair,** *s.m.* Votary of pleasure. 2 Epicure. 2 Epicurean.
———eachd,** *s.f.* Luxuriousness, sumptuousness. 2 Epicurism. 3 Epicureanism.
sòghalachd, *s.f.ind.* Luxury, daintiness, sumptuousness. 2 Deliciousness. 3 Surfeit, overflowing. 4 Abundance of juice and fatness or sap.
sòghan,** *a.* see sòghainn, *a.*
so-ghaolach,(MS) *a.* Amiable.
sòghar, -aire, *a.* see sòghail.
sògharachd, *s.f.* see sòghair.
sogh-chu,** -choin, *s.m.* Greyhound, hound bitch.
so-gheanalachd,(MS) *s.f.* Amicableness.
so-ghéillidh, *a.* Flexible.
so-ghiùlainteachd, *s.f* Portableness.
so-ghiùlan, -aine, *a.* Portable. 2 Easily borne. 3 Easily suffered.
so-ghlacaidh, -e, *a.* Easily caught or taken, apprehensible.
so-ghlacta,** *a.* Easily caught or taken.
so-ghleidhidh, *a.* Preservable.
so-ghluaiseach, -eiche, *a.* see so-ghluasad.
so-ghluaiste, see so-ghluasad.
so-ghluasad, *a.* Movable. 2 Wavering, easily affected or impressed. 3 Agitable, easily put in motion.
sòghmhar, see sòghail.
sòghmhor, -oire, *a.* see sòghail.
———achd, see sòghalachd.
so-ghnaidh,** *a.* Fair, comely, handsome.
so-ghnìomh, -a, -ara, *s.m.* Good deed.
so-ghnìomhach, -aiche, *a.* Doing a good deed, beneficent.
so-ghnùis, -e, -ean, *s.f.* Fair face or countenance, comely face.
———each, -eiche, *a.* Fair, comely.
so-ghnùiseas, -eis, *s.m.* Comeliness, beauty.
so-ghointe, *a.* Vulnerable, easily hurt or bruised.
so-ghuidhe,** *a.* Exorable.
so-ghràdh, -àidh, *s.m.* Sincere love or fondness. Luchd mo sho-ghràidh, *the people I sincerely love.*
so-ghràdhach, -aiche, *a.* Acceptable, amiable, lovely. 2 Affectionate. 3 Very dear, much loved. Le cridhe s., *with an affectionate heart.*
so-ghràdhaich, *v.a.* Love exceedingly or tenderly.
———te, *past pt.* Tenderly beloved.
†soghsur,** -uir, *s.m.* Fatness.
so-iarrta,(MS) *a.* Accessible.
so-iarrtach,(MS) *a.* Appetible.
so-iarrtas,(MS) *s.m.* Appetibility.
†soib,** *s.f.* Hand.
soibh-, *particle* sometimes used in place of so-.
soibheus, see so-bheus.
———ach, see so-bheusach.
soibhriste, see so-bhriste
soibhristeachd, see so-bhristeachd.
soibhsgeul, see soisgeul.
soicead, -eid, *s.m.* Gaelic form of *socket.*
soich,(AF) see soigh
soicheal,** -eil, *s. m.* Joy, mirth Opposite of doicheall.
———ach, *a.* Joyful, mirthful, gay. 2 Causing joy or mirth.
———achd, *s. f.* Joyfulness, mirthfulness, gaiety. Luchd na s., *the gay.*
soichinealta, see so-chinealta.
———chd, see so-chinealtachd.
———s, see so-chinealtas.
†soichle, *s.f.* Joy, mirth, pleasure, gaiety.
soideal, -eil, *s. m.* Rudeness, vulgarity, ignorance. 2 Timidity arising from ignorance
soidealach, -aich, *s.m.* Rude, ignorant fellow 2 Awkwardly bashful person. 3 Silly, sheepish fellow. 4 Lazy, indolent person.
soidealach, -aiche, *a.* see soidealta.
———d, *s.f.* see soidealtas.
soidealta, *a.* Rude, ignorant. 2 Awkwardly bashful, timid, silly, sheepish. 3 Indolent, lazy. 4 Simple, easily imposed upon.
soidealtachd, *s.f.* Same meanings as soidealtas.
soidealtas, -ais, *s.m. ind.* Rudeness, rusticity, ignorance. 2 Bashfulness or timidity from ignorance, coyness, sheepishness, silliness. 3 Indolence, laziness. 4 (MS) Shame.
soidean, -ein, -an, *s.m.* Jolly and stout-looking person.
———ach, -aich, *s.m.* see soidean.
———ach, -aiche, *a.* Jolly and stout-looking.
soideirneach,†† see sodair, s.
soidheach, -aich, -aichean, *s.m.* see soitheach.
soidhineach,** *a.* Liberal. Gu s., *liberally.*
soidseag,(DC) *s.f.* Fetter for horses or cows. (dileum in *Barra*, langaid in *Islay.*)
†soi-fillte, *a.* Supple, easily folded or unfolded.
soigh,(AF) *s.f.* Bitch.
soighdear, see saighdear.
———achd, see saighdearachd.
†soighead, -ghde, -ghdean, see saighead.
soigheam,** -eim, *s.m.* Precious stone or gem.
soighidh, *s.f.* Attack.
soighlear, -eir, *s.m.* Jailer.
soighme,** *s.f.* Thunderbolt. 2 Flash of lightning.
soighne, *a.* Pleasant—R. 44.
soighne, *s.* see soighneas.
soighneadh,(MS) *s.m.* Condiment.
soighnean,** -ein, *s. m.* Puff of wind. 2 Thunderbolt. 3 Flash of lightning.
soighneas, -eis, *s.m.* Pleasure, delight.
———ach, -aiche, *a.* Delightful, pleasant. 2 Rejoicing, glad.
soighniomh, see so-ghnìomh.
———ach, see so-ghnìomhach.
†soil, *s.* The sun.
soil ! *int.* Cry to drive away a pig—*Glenlyon.* (sail in *Argyll*—DC.)
soil-bheachd,** *s.* Jest.
soil-bheum,** *s.m.* Flash of lightning. 2 Thunderbolt.
soilbhir, see suilbhear.
———e, see suilbhire.
soileach, see seileach.
soi-leaghta, see so-leaghta.

soileas, -eis, *s.m.* Officiousness. 2 Partiality. 3 Flattery, adulation.
soileasach, -aiche, *a.* Officious. 2 Partial. 3 Flattering, given to flattery.
———d, *s.f.* see soileas.
†**soilfeachd**, *s.f.* Charm.
soilgheas, -eis, *s.m.* Wind. 2 Fair wind.
———ach, -aiche, *a.* Windy, blowing a fresh and fair wind.
soilleadh,(DC) *v.* Roast, fry—*Skye.*
soilleag, -eig, -an, *s.f.* Willow, sallow.
———ach, *a.* Abounding in willows or sallows. 2 Of or like a willow or sallow.
soilleir, -e, *a.* Clear, not dark. 2 Bright, luminous, shining. 3 Transparent, limpid. 4 Evident, manifest, apparent. 5 Intelligible, perspicuous. 6 Pure, clean. 7 Visible, discernible. 8 Sensible, intelligent. 9* Shrewd, clear-sighted. 10* Conspicuous. Tha sin s., *that is obvious ;* là s., *a clear day ;* s. mar chriostal, *clear as crystal ;* sruth s., *a limpid stream ;* a' deanamh a' ghnothaich s., *making the business clear.*
soilleir-dhonn, *s.m.* Light brown (colour.)
soilleire, *comp.* of soilleir.
soilleireachadh, -aidh, *s.m.* Enlightening, act of enlightening. 2 Illustrating, act of illustrating 3 Explaining or making manifest. 4 Explanation. 5 Clearing up. 6 Incipient light. 7 Brightening, cleaning 8 Making intelligible, ascertainment. 9 (MS) Air. 10 * Dawn. A' s—, *pr.pt.* of soilleirich. A' s. a' ghnothaich seo dhomh, *making this affair evident to me ;* s. an là, *the dawn :* anns an t-s., *about the dawn.*
soilleireachd, *s.f.ind.* Brightness, clearness, perspicuity, intelligibleness. 2 The dawn. 3 Transparentness, limpidness. 4*Conspicuousness. 5*Accuracy.
soilleirich, *pr. pt.* a' soilleireachadh, *v.a. & n.* Clear up, manifest, make manifest. 2 Become clear or bright. 3 Explain, illustrate. 4 Point out, show, make clear or bright, elucidate, enlighten. 4††Brighten. Sh. an là, *the day brightened up.*
———te, *past pt.* of soilleirich. Cleared up, manifested, made manifest. 2 Explained, illustrated, shown, pointed out.
soilleirse,** *s.f.* Axiom.
soilleirsinneachd,(MS) *s.f.* see so-léirsinneachd.
soillse, *s.m.ind.* Light. 2 The light of the sun. 3 Ray of light. 4 Clearness, brightness, effulgence. 5* Luminary. 6 Elucidation. 7* Light from heaven.
soillseach, -eiche, *a.* Bright, clear, not dark. 2 Clear, transparent, pellucid. 3 Shining, effulgent. 4 That makes bright or clear. 5 Causing to brighten up. 6 Causing light.
soillseach,* *s.* Eyebright.
soillseachadh, -aidh, *s.m.* Enlightening, act of enlightening. 2 State of becoming clear. 3 Act or state of shining. 4 Brightening. 5 Illuminating. 6 Elucidation, explanation. 7* Gleaming. A' s—, *pr.pt.* of soillsich.
soillseachan, *s.m.* Phosphorus.
soillseachd, *s.f.* Brightness, clearness, effulgence. 2 Transparentness.
soillseachd-nan-sùl,§ *s.f.* Eyebright, see lus-nan-leac. [McL & D & ** give soillse-nan-sùl, *s. m.*]
soillseadh, see soillseachadh.
soillsean, *s.m.* Tinsel. 2 Taper.
soillsear,* -eir, -an, *s.m.* Lantern.
soillse-nan-sùl, see soillseachd-nan-sùl.
soillsich, *pr.pt.* a' soillseachadh & a' soillseadh, *v.a. & n.* Enlighten, brighten. 2 Shine, glitter. 3 Become clear. 4 Show forth, illustrate explain, elucidate. 5 Gleam, flash. 6*Dawn. Sh. an là, *the day cleared up ;* nach s. tuilleadh do chlaidheamh, *that thy sword shall gleam no more,*
soillsichear, *s.m.* Lucifer match.
———, *fut.pass.* of soillsich.
soillsichidh, *fut.aff.a.* of soillsich.
soillsichte, *past pt.* of soillsich. Enlightened, brightened. 2 Illuminated.
soimeach, -eiche, *a.* Good-natured, of an easy disposition or manner, quiet, tranquil, peaceable. 2 Comfortable, in easy circumstances. 3 Idle, inactive. 4 Harmless. 5 Agreeable. Is s. fear-fearainn, ach is sona fear-cèirde, *the landed man is at ease, but the tradesman is happy*—like many popular sayings, sometimes true, sometimes not. Constant financial embarrassment effectually dispels both ease and happiness where it exists.
———d, *s.f. ind.* Comfortableness, exemption from toil. 2††Good nature, goodness of temper. 3††Idleness.
———an, -ain, -an, *s. m.* Good-natured, soft person. 2 One in easy circumstances. 3 Idler.
———as, -ais, *s.m.* Good natnre. 2 Comfort. 3 Idleness, freedom from labour
soimh,** *a.* Quiet, peaceable, good-natured. 2 Comely. 3 Tame.
soimhe, see saimhe.
soimheach, see soimeach.
soimheachan, see soimeachan.
soimheachd,‡‡ *s.f.* Softness, gentleness.
soimheagan, see soimeachan.
soimhneach,** *a.* Peaceable, agreeable, quiet.
soimhneas,** -eis, *s.m.* Fretting. 2 Reconciliation.
soin,** *v.a.* Sound, make a noise.
soin, -e, *s. f.* Esteem. 2 Comeliness. 3 Sound, noise.
so-in, (an so-in & an so-in-ich) Slang form of seo—*Badenoch.*
soinchearb,** *s.* Synalæpha, contraction by suppressing a final vowel or diphthong before another vowel or diphthong, so that the final syllable of one word runs or melts into the first syllable of the next.
soineach,** *a.* Noisy.
soineachas,** -ais, *s.m.* Noisiness, noise.
soinealachd, *s.f.ind.* Comeliness, handsomeness. 2**Decency.
soineann, see soinnionn.
———ach, -aiche, *a.* see soinnionnach.
soineanta, see soinnionta.
———chd, see soinniontachd.
soineas, ** -eis, *s.m.* Sulkiness.
soineil, -e, *a.* Comely, handsome. 2 Esteemed, estimable.
†**soinmheach**,** *a.* Happy, fortunate.
soinne, Air sgàth s., *for the sake of peace—Sgeul-nan-caol, p. 89.* (sgoinne)
soinneach, -eich, *s.m.* Racehorse.
soinneachd, *s.f.* Starting.
soinnionn, -inn, *s.f.* Fair or calm weather, sunshine. 2 Cheerfulness, gaiety. 3 Mildness. pleasantness. 4 Blast.
soinnionnach,** *a.* Calm, as weather. 2 Shining. 3 Pleasant, gay, cheerful.
soinnionta, -inte, *a.* Calm, fair. 2 Well-sheltered. 3 Good-tempered, meek, pleasant. 4 Cheerful, gay. 5 Gentle. 6 Serene, as weather.
———chd, *s. f. ind.* Calmness, stillness of weather. 2 State of being well sheltered. 3 Meekness, pleasantness of temper 4††Gentleness. 5**Comeliness.
so-innseadh, *a.* Easily told, effable, expressible.
so-innsidh, see so-innseadh.

so-iomchaire, *comp.* of so-iomchair.
so-iomairteachd, *s.f.ind.* Manageableness.
so-iomchair, -e, *a.* Tolerable, easily borne, portable.
so-iomchaire, *comp.* of so-iomchair.
so-iomcharachd, *s.f.* see so-ghiùlainteachd.
so-iompach,** *a.* Easily converted, convertible.
so-iompachaidh, *a.* Convertible.
so-iompaichte, *a.* Convertible, easily converted.
so-ionnsachaidh, *a.* Docile.
soipean, -ein, -an, *s.m. dim.* of sop. Little wisp or handful of hay or straw.
———**ach**, -aiche, *a.* Abounding in small wisps or bunches, as hay or straw. 2 Scattered in small quantities, as hay or straw.
soir, see ear. Sheòil am bàta soir, *the boat sailed eastward.*
soir, -e, -ean, *s.m.* Sack, bag. 2 Vessel, vase, bottle. 3 Womb. 4††Dish. S. na cloinne, *the womb.*
soirbh, -e, *a.* Easy, easily accomplished. 2 Calm, quiet, gentle. 3 Affable, courteous, kind. 4 Pliant, pliable. 5* Tractable, docile. 6 Prosperous. 7 Languid. 8 Apt. Duine s., *a tractable person ;* ni s., *an easy thing ;* righ math s., *a good quiet king.*
soirbhe, *s.f.* see soirbheachd.
soirbhe, *comp.* of soirbh.
soirbheach, -eiche, *a.* see soirbh.
———**adh**, -aidh, *s.m.* Act or state of prospering, succeeding or favouring. 2 Success, prosperity. 3 Growing affable, calm or quiet. A' s—, *pr.pt.* of soirbhich. S. math leat ! *success to you !*
soirbheachd, *s.f.ind.* Easiness, facility, possibility. 2 Calmness, quietness, gentleness. 3 Affability, courteousness, kindness. 4 Pliableness, flexibility. 5 Prosperity, success. 6 Languidness. 7 Addibility. 8 (MS) Readiness.
soirbheas, -eis, *s.m* Prosperity, success. 2 Gentleness, docility. 3 Fair wind on the sea—*Skye.* 4 Wind, flatulence—*Argyll.* 5* Easiness, quietness. Saoghal fada is soirbheas ! *long life and prosperity !* là an t-soirbheis, *the day of prosperity ;* s. math leat ! *good speed to you !* cha 'n éirich s. leis, *he will not prosper ;* tha 'n s. air caochladh, *the fair wind is changed.* Opposite of doirbheas.
———**ach**, -aiche, *a.* Prosperous, successful, thriving. 2**Fair, as wind. 3 Breezy. 4 Favourable. Gaoth sh., *a favourable wind ;* turus s., *a prosperous journey.*
soirbhich, *pr.pt.* a' soirbheachadh, *v.n.* Prosper, succeed, thrive. 2**Speed. Ciamar a sh. leat ? *how did you succeed ?* soirbhichidh leis gach ni a ni e, *everything he does shall prosper.*
———**idh**, *fut.aff.a.* of soirbhich.
soirbhriste,** *a.* Ductile.
soirch,** *a.* Clear, bright. 2 Light. 3 Conspicuous.
soirche, *comp.* of sorcha.
soirche,** *s.f.* Clearness, brightness, light. 2 Conspicuousness. 3 Joy.
soircheachd,** *s.f.* Clearness, brightness.
soirchead,** -eid, *s.m.* Clearness, brightness.
soire, see soir, *s.m.*
soireach, *a.* Abounding in sacks, bags, vessels, &c.
soireadh, see soir.
soireag, -eig, -an, *s.f.dim.* of soire. Little vessel, bottle or sack.
soireagach, -aiche, *a.* Pertaining to little vessels, bottles or sacks.
soireanach, -aich, *s.m.* Jolly, fat person.
soireanach,** *a.* see soinnionta.
soireann, -inn, see soinnionn.
soireanta, -einte, *a.* see sainnionta.
soireit, -e, *s.f.* Easiness of temper, accommodating, conciliatory disposition. (so-réite)
soireiteach, -eiche, *a.* Conciliatory, accommodating. (so-réiteach)
soiridh,** *a.* Convenient. 2 Agreeable.
soiridh,** *s.* see soirigh.
soirigh,** *s.* Primrose.
soirionn, -inn, *s.f.* see soinnionn.
soirionta, see soinnionta.
soirmeil, *a.* Harmoniously. Gu fonnmhorach, soirmeil, *melodiously, harmoniously—Donn. Bàn, p. 35.*
soirn-liadh,** -leidh, *s.f.* Baker's peel.
soirthe, -an, *s.f.* see soire.
sois,* -e, *a.* Fond of ease, snug.
soise,** *s.f.* Alteration, change.
soise,* *s.f.* Bolis or ball of fire moving majestically in the heavens, often near the earth supposed to presage the death of some personage or the fall of some nation. These are very common in the Highlands. (soillse)
soisealach,** *a.* Airy. 2 Hearty. 3 Proud.
soisealta,* *a.* Fond of ease, effeminate, unmanly.
———**chd**,* *s.f.ind.* Indulgence in ease, effeminacy.
soisgean, (CR) *s.m.* Primrose—*S. end of Arran.*
soisgeul, -eil, *s.m.* The Gospel. 2 Glad tidings.
———**ach**, -aiche, *a.* Evangelical. 2 Bringing good news or tidings.
———**ach**, -aich, *s.m.* see soisgeulaiche.
soisgeulachd,** *s. f.* Evangelism, evangelical teaching. 2 Tale or tidings of joy.
soisgeulaich,** *v.n.* Bring or bear good news. 2 Preach the Gospel.
————**e**, -an, *s.m.* Evangelist. 2 Bringer of good news.
soisgeulta,** *a.* Evangelical.
soi-shinte, see so-shinte.
soishion,** *s.* Freedom, privilege. (so-shìon)
soisich,* see soillsich.
soisil,** *a.* Proud, haughty.
soisinn,* *s.f.* Taste, decency. 2††Complacency, snugness, ease.
———**each**, *a.* Tasteful. 2 Snug.
†**soisior**,** *a.* Younger.
soisie, *s.f* Brightness.
soislean,** -ein, *s.m.* Firm or bold standing.
soislean, *s.pl.* The white feathery ventral fins by which the salmon balances itself.
†**soistean**, -ein, *s.m.* Good habitation, residence. 2 Sense, meaning.
soithchean, (for soithichean) *pl.* of soitheach.
so-ithe, *a.* Eatable, edible. 2 Palatable.
soitheach, -ich, -ichean, *s.m.* Vessel of any kind in which meat, liquors, or anything is placed. 2 Ship of any size. 3 Wooden dish, pitcher. Clùd nan soithichean, *the dish-cloth.*
s. creadha, *an earthenware vessel.*
s.-fuarachaidh, *cooler, refrigerator.*
s.-fuail, *a chamber-pot.*
s.-ionnlaid, *a basin.*
s.-teine, *pot, pan.*
s.-tùis, *censer.*
s.-uisge, *ewer, bucket.*
soitheachan, -ain, *s.m.* Small dish or plate.
soitheagan,** -ain, *s.m.* Soft, good-natured person.
soitheamh, -eimhe, *a.* Gentle, mild, affable, modest. 2 Comely, fair. 3 Tractable, docile, easily prevailed upon, good-natured, tame. 4 Easily done. 5††Peaceable. Duine s., *a docile or tractable person ;* mo laochan s., sìobhalta, *my good-natured, civil lad.*
soitheamhachd, *s.f.ind.* Ductility, tractability, docility. 2‡‡Placidness.
soitheamhaich, (MS) *v.a.* Placate.
soithibh,* see soitheamh.
———**eachd**,* see soitheamhachd.

soithich, (gu)** *adv.* Badly.
soithichean, *n.pl.* of soitheach.
soithleag,** -eig, *s.f.* Circle.
-———an,** -ain, *s.f.* Little circle.
soithmheannach,** *a.* Covetous. (so-mhiannach)
soithneach,** *a.* Desirous.
soithnich, *v.a.* Allure, entice. 2 Desire.
-————te,** *past pt.* Allured.
soithsheamhach,(MS) *a.* Pacific. (so-shèimheach)
so-ithte, see so-ithe.
†**sol**, *s.m.* The sun.
sol, *adv.* Ere, before that—*Ross.*
sòl,* *s.m.* Delight.
sola, see soladh. 2†† see so-lughadh.
sòla,(DU) *s.m.* Bottom thwart containing mast-step of a boat.
so-labhairt, -e, *a.* Expressible, easily spoken or pronounced. Opposite of do-labhairt.
so-labharra,** *a.* Exorable.
so-labhrach, -aiche, *a.* Speaking with ease and fluency, affable.
so-labhrachd,** *s.f.* Eloquence, affability.
so-labhradh,** *a.* see so-labhrach.
sòlach,* -aiche, *a.* Highly delighted, jolly.
soladh,(AC) -aidh, *s. m.* Broken food—whelks, cockles, limpets, mussels and other shellfish, broken and thrown into the sea to attract fish. Tuill solaidh, *bait holes*—hollows in the rocks prepared to hold shellfish and prepare bait. They resemble cup cuttings, for which antiquaries have mistaken them.
soladh,** -aidh, *s.m.* Profit.
so-laghach,** *a.* Venial, pardonable. (so-lughach)
-————d,** *s.f* Venialness, pardonableness.
solaidh, *s.* Advantage, good profit—*Rob Donn.*
sòlaimte,** *a.* Solemn. Gu s., *solemnly.*
-———achd,** *s.f.* Solemnity.
solair, *pr.pt.* a' solar & a' solaradh, *v. a.* see solaraich.
-———each, see solarach.
-———eachd, see solarachd.
solaitheach,** *a.* Venial.
sòlamanta,** *a.* Solemn, solemnized.
-————chd,** *s.f.* Solemnity, solemnization.
solamh,** *a.* Quick, ready, dexterous.
sòlamuin, *s.f.* Solemnity.
solar, -air, -an, *s.m.* Providing, preparing, purveying of useful things 2 Things provided or furnished, provision. 3 Getting, providing, procuring, catering. 4**Forage. 5(MS)Gain. 6**Shifting for. A' s—, *pr.pt.* of solair.
solar, *cont.* for solaradh.
solarach, -aiche, *a.* Provident, making provision, catering, purveying. 2 Industrious. 3 Frugal. Fear s., *a provident man.*
-————adh, -aidh, *s.m.* Providing, act of providing, procuring or furnishing necessaries, catering. A' s—, *pr.pt.* of solaraich.
solarachd, *s.f.* Providence. 2 Business of a caterer, purveying.
solaradh, -aidh, *s.m.& pr.pt* of solair, see solarachadh. 2 Provisions provided.
solaraich, *pr.pt.* a' solarachadh, *v. a.* Provide, gather, prepare, procure, cater, purvey, provide accommodation. 2 Get, gain, acquire. 3**Shift for. Sh. i nead dhith fhéin, *she provided a nest for herself ;* a' solarachadh lòin, *purveying* or *catering provisions.* [*pr.pt. a' solar.]
solaraiche,** *s.m.* Provider, caterer, purveyor, forager.
solaraichidh, *fut.aff.a.* of solaraich.
solaraichte, *past pt.* of solaraich. Provided, procured, furnished, purveyed.
solar-itheannaich, *s.m.* Ménu.
solas, see solus.
†**solas**,** -ais, *s.m.* Round ball thrown into the air.
sòlas, -ais, *s.m.* Comfort, consolation, solace. 2 Intellectual pleasure or gratification. 3 Cheerfulness, contentment. 4 Joy, rejoicing, delight, calm luscious pleasure.
-——ach, -aiche, *a.* Comforting, comfortable giving comfort, pleasure or consolation. 2 Comfortable, enjoying comfort or ease. 3 Cheerful, content. 4 Joyful, causing joy or happiness. 5 Rejoicing, glad. 6 Pleasant to the mind, highly gratifying.
solasach, see solusach.
sòlasachadh, -aidh, *s.m.* Comforting, act of comforting, consoling, making glad, consolation. A' s—, *pr.pt.* of sòlasaich.
sòlasachd, *s.f.* Delectableness.
sòlasaich, *pr.pt.* a' sòlasachadh, *v. a.* Comfort, console, make happy or glad.
-————idh, *fut.aff.a.* of sòlasaich.
-————te, *past pt.* of sòlasaich. Comforted, consoled, made glad or happy, given continued soothing joy.
so-lasarach,‡‡ -aiche, *a.* Inflammable.
solasda, see solusach.
-———chd, see solusachd.
solastar,(AF) *s.m.* Starfish.
so-leaghachd,‡‡ *s.f.ind.* Liquation.
so-leaghadh,** see so-leaghta.
so-leaghta, *a.* Fusible, easily melted. 2 Soluble.
-————ch, -aiche, *a.* see so-leaghta.
so-leigheas, *a.* Medicable, that may be cured.
so-leirseanta,(MS) *a.* Aspectable.
so-léirsinn,* *a.* Very visible.
so-léirsinneachd, *s.f.* Obviousness.
so-leisgealachd,‡‡ *s.f.ind.* Pardonableness.
so-leòinte, see so-leònta.
so-leònadh, see so-leònta.
so-leònta, *a.* Vulnerable.
so-leudachaidh, *a.* Extensible.
so-leughachd,‡‡ *s.f.ind.* Legibility.
so-leughadh, *a.* Legible.
so-leughta, *a.* so-leughadh.
soll,** *s.m.* Bait for fish.
sollach,** *a.* Jolly, stout. 2 Comely, handsome, personable.
-———d,** *s.f.* Jollyness, stoutness. 2 Comeliness, personableness, handsomeness.
sollain, -e, -ean, *s.f.* Welcome. 2 Rejoicing. 3 **Carnival. 4 Gladness, mirth. Là s., *a day of rejoicing, mirth* or *feasting*—said of a day like Christmas Day or New Year's Day.
sol mu'n, *adv.* Before, ere.
so-loisgeach,‡‡ -eiche, *a.* see so-lasarach.
-————d, *s.f.* Combustibility.
so-loisgte,** *a.* Adustible.
solt, *prov.* for sult.
solta, *a.* see sultmhor. 2 Demulcent, mollient. 3 Tender. 4 (DMy) Meek, quiet, harmless—*Lewis.* Tha e cho s. ris an uan, *he is as meek as a lamb.*
soltanas, -ais, *s.m.* Jollity, mirth.
so-lùbachd, *s. f. ind.* Flexibility, elasticity. 2 Exorableness.
so-lùbadh, *a.* Flexible, elastic.
so-lùbaidh, *a.* Flexible. 2 Exorable.
so-lughadh, *a.* Venial, pardonable.
so-lughta, see so-lughadh.
so-lughtachd,†† *s.f.* Pardonableness, slightness.
solumas,(CR) -ais, *s.m.* Abundance.
sòlumta,‡‡ *a.* Solemn, see sòlaimte & sòlamanta.
solus, -uis, -an, *s.m.* Light. 2 Light, as a lamp or candle. 3 Knowledge, information. 4 Phase of the moon. 5 *rarely*, Quoit. 6 Round ball thrown into the air. An s. ùr, *the new moon ;* an s. seo chaidh, *the last moon ;* atharrachadh (*or* mùthadh) an t-soluis, *a change* or *phase of the moon ;* s. Shathuirn a's t-fhoghar, bidh e aona chuid 'na rìgh air seachd no gabh-

aidh e an cuthach seachd uairean, *the harvest moon which comes in on a Saturday will either be king of seven or go mad seven times*—i.e it will bring in its train either very good or very bad weather S. is used adjectively in *Arran*, as, uisge solus, *clear water ;* aodach solus, *white* or *light-coloured clothing*. [** gives 7 The moon, and 8 Heavenly body.]
solusach, -aiche, *a.* Full of light, luminous,shining. (soillseach is better.)
———adh, -aidh, *s. m.* Lighting, shining, kindling.
———d, *s.f.ind.* Luminousness. (soillseachd is better.)
solusda, see solusach.
———ch, -aiche, *a.* see solusach.
solus-gràbhaltach, *a.* Photographic.
solusmhor, -oire, see solusach.
solus-sionn, *s.m.* Electric light—*Dàin I.Ghobha.*
solus-tharruing, *v.a.* Photograph.
———, *s.f.* Photograph.
soma,** *s.f.* Flock of swans. 2 Learning.
somachan,** -ain, *s.m.* Soft, good-natured, innocent person.
somailtean,(MS) *s.m.* Pith.
somain,** *s.f.* Wealth.
———each,** *a.* Rich, wealthy.
somalta, -ailte, *a.* Bulky, large. 2 Gentle, mild, placid. 3 Liberal, generous. 4 Imprudent. 5 Personable, comely. 6 Negligent. 7††Dull, heavy.
somalta,** *a.* Aspirate.
somaltach, *a.* Decidiose.
somaltachd, *s.f.ind.* Bulk, bulkiness, stoutness, largeness. 2 Gentleness, mildness, placidity. 3 Liberality, generosity, generousness. 4 Carelessness, indifference, negligence. 5 Laziness. 6 Easiness. 7 Comeliness. 8 Abundance. 9 Imprudence.
somaltas, *s.m.* see somaltachd.
somar,(AF) *s.m.* Wild sheep, chamois.
somha,(AC) *v.a. & n.* Convert, convince. 2 Controvert, overturn, upset, render of no avail.
so-mhagaidh,‡‡ *a.* Mockable.
sòmhail, -e, *a.* see sùmhail.
so-mhaithleachd, *s.f.* see so-leisgealachd.
so-mhaithte,‡‡ *a.* Ignoscible.
so-mhaithteachail,‡‡ *a.* Ignoscible.
so-mharbhachd,** *s.f.* Mortality.
so-mharbhta,** *a.* Mortal. 2 Easily killed.
so-mheallta, *a.* Deceptive.
so-mhealltachd, *s.f.* Deceptibility.
so-mheasraichte,(MS) *a.* Comprehensible.
so-mheirbhidh, *a.* Digestible.
so-mheudachas, -ais, *s.m.* Addibility.
so-mhiannach,** *a.* Desirable.
so-mhineachaidh, *a.* Explicable.
sòmhlach, see sùmhlach.
———adh, -aidh, *s. m. & pr.pt.* of sòmhlaich, see sùmhlachadh.
sòmhlachd, see sùmhlachd.
sòmhlaich, see sùmhlaich.
———ear, see sùmhlaichear.
———idh, see sùmhlaichidh.
———te, see sùmhlaichte.
somhlan, -aine, *a.* Safe and sound, unhurt.
sòmhlanachd,** *s.f.* Safeness, secureness, soundness.
so-mhothachaidh, *a.* Mollifiable.
sòmhrach,(MS) *s.m.* Horsefoot.
so-mhuinte,‡‡ *a.* Tractable, docile. 2 Careless, indifferent. 3 Lazy.
so-mhùthadh,** *a.* Commutable.
so-mhùthtachd, *s.f.ind.* Changeableness.
somolta, see somalta.
somuiltean,(CR) *s.pl.* Senses, wits—*Skye.* Bu tu an creutair gun s., *or* nach tu a chaill do s., (said to a stupid or careless person)
somult see somalta.
somultachd, see somaltachd.
son, *s.m* Sake, cause, account. 2 Good, profit, advantage, stead.
Air mo sh.-sa, *on my account, for my sake ;* air an s.-san, *for their sake, in preparation for them ;* dh'fhalbh e air mo sh.-sa, *he went on my account, in my place* or *stead*, air mo sh. fhéin, *for myself, for my own part, as for me ;* air na h-uile son [air na h-uile c'ar son—MM], *for every reason ;* air a sh. sin, *nevertheless ;* air a son-se, *on her account ;* air an son-san, *on their account.*
son, *prep.impr. & adv.*(air son) *adv.* For,because of, on account of. 2 For the purpose of. 3 Because, because that.
Air son‖ mo chodach-sa dheth, *for my part of it;* air son tighinn dhachaidh, *for the purpose of coming home ;* air son‖ dithis, *as for two, in the matter of two ;* air son‖ teicheadh, *for the purpose of decamping, as a reward* or *penalty for deserting ;* air son dithis no triùir is coma leam cò aca, *as for two or three I don't care as to which of them ;* air son‖ sin dheth,*as for that matter ;* c' arson ? *why ? wherefore ? on what account ?* air son siod fhéin, *because I judged it right ;* air son falbh, *as a reward for going, in order to go ;* c'ar son seo ? *why so ? on whose account is this ?* air son sgillinn, *as to a penny, for a penny.* [*Son*, where marked ‖ above,—from * are mostly bad idiom influenced by *for* in English—MM.]
†sòn, -òin, *s.m.* Sound, voice. 2 Word. 3 Good, advantage. 4 Stake, beam.
†son,** *a.* Tall.
sona, *a.* Lucky, fortunate. 2 Happy, in a state of happiness, blessed. Is fèarr a bhith s. na éirigh moch, *luck is better than early rising(?);* s. bithidh tu is éiridh gu math dhuit, *happy shalt thou be and it shall be well with thee ;* is s. a bhithinn-sa, *happy would I be ;* gu s. sòlasach, *happy and quite contented ;* cha toir muir no monadh a chuid o dhuine sona, *neither seas nor mountains can bar the lucky.*
sonachas,(AC) -ais, *s.m.* Blissfulness.
sonadh, see sona.
sonairte, *s.f.* Strength, courage.
sonann, -ainn, *s.m.* Fertile land, good soil.
sònas, -ais, -an, *s.m.* Vexation, grief. 2 Passion, fit of passion, pet. Cuir s., *vex, disoblige.*
sonas, -ais, -an, *s.m.* Good fortune, prosperity, luck. 2 Success. 3 Happiness, felicity, bliss. Sonas is àgh ort, *success and prosperity to you;* mo sh. féin, *my own happiness ;* sonas no donas, *success or misfortune ;* s. an lorg an caitheimh, *good luck follows the liberal ;* sannt gun s., éiridh an donas dha, *hapless greed will not succeed.*
sonasach, -aiche, *a.* Happy. 2 Prosperous, lucky.
sònasach, -aiche, *a.* Vexatious, grievous. 2 Easily vexed. 3 Passionate, pettish.
sonasan,(CR) Young frog in the tadpole stage —*Skye & W. of Ross.*
sonn, -uinn, *s.m.* Stout man. 2 Hero,champion. 3*Courier—*Islay.* Uamh an t-suinn, *the hero's cave.*
sonn, -uinn, *s.m.* Bait for fish. 2 Club, staff, cudgel, stake, beam. 3 Tree.
sonn, *v.a.* Pierce, thrust. 2 Hew down. 3 Press. 4 Oppress.
sonnach, -aich, *s.m.* Palisade. 2 Peg, thick peg. 3 Stout, ill-shaped person. 4 Castle, fortress. 5 Wall. Dail nan s., *the plain of palisades.*
sonnadh, -aidh, *s.m.* Piercing, thrusting, act of piercing or thrusting. 2 Act of hewing down.

3 Act of pressing upon or oppressing. 4 Contention, strife. A' s—, *pr.pt.* of sonn.
sonnadh,** -aidh, *s.m.* Fort, garrison.
sonnag,(DC) *s.f.* Beehive chair, made of twisted straw or sea-bent—*Uist.* [sùthag in *Mull.*]
sonnalta,* *r.* Liberal, handsome, very generous.
———chd,* *s.f.ind.* Liberality.
sonn-bhrochan, *s.m.* Gruel.
sonn-mharcach, -aich, -aichean, *s.m.* Courier on horseback, post, messenger. 2 Aide-de-camp.
sonnta, *a.* Heroic, courageous. 2**Confident. 3 **Merry.
sonnta, *past pt.* of sonn.
sonntach, see sonnta.
sonntachd, *s.f.ind.* Boldness, heroism, courage. 2**Confidence. 3**Mirth.
so-nochdadh,** *a.* Avowable.
sònrach, -aiche, *a.* see sònraichte.
sònrachadh, -aidh, *s.m.* Appointing, act of appointing, choosing or ordaining. 2 Act of specifying, individualizing or particularizing. 3 Intending, act of intending. 4 Arbitration. 5 Noting, remarking. 6 Determination. 7†† Marking. 8††Ordering. 9 Pointing out. 10 Appointment. A' s—, *pr.pt.* of sònraich. 'G am sh., *individualizing me.*
sònrachair,** *s.m.* Assigner, establisher.
†sonraic, *a.* Righteous.
sònraich, *pr. pt.* a' sònrachadh, *v.a. & n.* Appoint, ordain, fore-ordain, authorize. 2 Choose, specify, particularize, individualize. 3 Intend. 4 Note, remark. 5*Make a butt or tool of. 6 Determine. Neach a sh. Dia 'na ìobairt-réitich, *one whom God set forth as a propitiation.*
sònraicheam, *1st.sing. imp.* of sònraich. Let me specify, &c. 2 Irish form of sònraichidh mi, *fut.aff.a.* I will specify, &c.
sònraichear, *fut.pass.* of sònraich.
sònraichidh, *fut.aff.a.* of sònraich.
sònraichte, *a. & past pt.* of sònraich. Specific, special, notable, particular, novel. 2 Appointed, specified, particularized, determined, ordained, fore-ordained, marked out. 3 Remarked. 4 Noted. Gu s., *particularly*; gnothach s., *a particular business*; air an là s., *on the appointed day*; sluagh s., *a peculiar people*; duine s., *a certain* or *notorious man*; bha adharc sh. aige, *he had a notable horn*; gu s. an duine seo, *particularly this man.*
sònraichteachd,(MS) *s.f.ind.* Remarkableness.
sònruich, see sònraich.
———te, see sònraichte.
sontach, *a.* see sonnta.
sonuige,** *a.* Lucky, propitious.
so-oibrichte, *a.* Easily wrought, figurable.
so-òilte, *a.* Drinkable.
so-òlta, see so-òilte.
sop, -uip, *pl.* -an & -uip, *s.m.* Wisp, loose bundle of straw or hay. 2 Loose or useless bunch of anything. 3 Useless or cowardly fellow. 4** Top or crest of a hen or other bird. S. fodair, *a wisp of straw*; s. as gach seid, *a wisp from every truss,*—said of those who have nothing but what they borrow; [* said of those who court every one]; s. reic, *a tavern-* or *shop-sign.*
sopach, -aiche, *a.* Abounding in wisps of hay or straw. 2 Abounding in scattered straw or hay. 3 Cowardly, silly.
sopachan,(DMK) *s.m.* Handful of fine heather, tied tightly together and used for scrubbing dishes, particularly milk-dishes—*Caithness, Suth'd., Gairloch, &c.* 2(DU) Small wisp of straw in which the ends of knitting-needles are stuck. It is tied to the knitter's belt or pinned to her dress—*Gairloch.*
sopag,** -aig, *s.f.* Small bundle of straw. 2 One drawn and combed out for thatching—*Uist.* 3**Well.
sopan, -ain, -an, *s. m., dim.* of sop. Little wisp, little handful of hay or straw. S. saidhe, *a wisp of hay.*
sopanach, -aiche, *a.* see sopach.
†sopar, *prov.* for tobar.
sop-cheann,†† *s.m.* Bushy or uncombed head.
sop-cheannach, -aiche, *a.* Having a bushy or uncombed head of hair.
so-phroinnte, *a.* see so-phronnaidh.
so-phronnaidh, *a.* Friable, easily pulverized.
so-phronnta, *a.* see so-phronnaidh.
soplach, -aiche, *a.* see sopach. 2 Useless. 3 Insignificant.
soplach, -aich, -aichean, *s.m.* Refuse of straw or provender.
soplachan,(AC) -ain, *s. m.* Wisp, tuft. 2 Sustenance. 3 Handful of corn in ear given to a weak animal.
soplas, *s.m.* Soap-suds.
so-phòsaidh, *a.* Marriageable.
so-phronntachd,(MS) *s.f.* Friability.
sop-reic, *s.m.* Sign of a tavern or inn. 2 Sign of a shop.
sop-seilbhe, -an-seilbhe, *s.m.* Infeftment in house and land by the delivery of a wisp of straw to the entrant.
sop-suiridhe,(DMy) *s.m.* Love or courting wisp, thrown at a person to attract his attentions.
sòr, *pr.pt.* a' sòradh, *v.a.* Hesitate, pause, delay. 2 Grudge, give unwillingly. 3 Shun, avoid. 4 Spare. 5 Refuse. 6**Scruple. Cha sh. e do mharbhadh, *he will not hesitate to kill you.*
sòr, *s.m.* Stop, hesitation.
†sor,(AF) *s.m.* Louse.
sòrach,** *a.* Hesitating, scrupulous.
sorachadh,** -aidh, *s.m.* Act of acervating, accumulation.
sorachag,(AF) *s.f.* Jackdaw, jay.
sorachan, see sorchan.
sorachar, see sorchar.
sorachda, see sorachta.
sorachta,** *a.* Acervated, accumulated, heaped.
sòradh, -aidh, *s.m.* Hesitating, act of hesitating, delaying, pausing. 2 Grudging, act of grudging. 3 Shunning, act of shunning. 4 Sparing, act of sparing. 5 Hesitation, delay. 6 Scrupulousness. A' s—, *pr.pt.* of sòr.
sòradh,(MS) *s.m.* Demur.
soraich,** *v.a.* Accumulate, heap up.
soraideadh,** -idh, *s.m.* Salutation.
soraidh, *s.f.* Farewell, blessing, compliments. 2 Success, health, happiness. 3 Salutation. S. slàn do 'n Gàidheal ghasda, *success and health to the handsome Gael*; s. leat, a ghràidh! *farewell, my beloved!* thoir mo sh. le dùrachd, *give my best respects, my sincere blessings.*
soraidh,** *a.* Happy, successful.
†sorb, *v.a.* Contaminate, pollute.
†sorb, -oirbe, *a.* Foul, dirty.
†——, -oirb, *s.m.* Fault, blemish.
sorbach,** *a.* Foul, polluted, dirty. 2 Faulty.
———adh,** -aidh, *s.m.* Polluting.
sorbaich,** *v.a.* Pollute.
sorb-aoireadas,** -ais, *s.m.* Satire, lampoon.
sorb-chàineadh,** -aidh, *s.m.* Satire, lampoon.
†sorb-chàrn,** -chàirn, *s.m.* Dunghill.
sorc,** *s.m.* Delight, pleasure.
sorcair,** -ean, *s.m.* Cylinder.
sorcaireach,** *a.* Cylindrical.
sorch,* *s. m.* Pedestal, gantry. 2 Eminence, heap.
sorcha, soirche, *a.* Light, bright, clear, conspicuous, manifest. Opposite of dorch.
sorchaich, *v.a.* Enlighten, make clear, light or

manifest. 2 Heap up. Opposite of dorchaich.
sorchaichidh, *fut.aff.a.* of sorchaich.
sorchaichte, *past pt.* of sorchaich. Enlightened, made clear, light or manifest 2 Heaped up,
sorchàin,** *s. f.* Satire, lampoon, scurrilous rhyme, slander.
sorchan, -ain, *pl.* -an & -ain, *s.m.* Rest, support, that on which anything leans or rests. 2 Stool, footstool, trestle. 3 Light-stand, peerman. 4 ††Place of rest. 5 Little eminence, hillock. 6 *Bracket. 7 Bolster of a cart 8(MS) Horse-block. 9 Fireplace of a still (see p. 730.) 10 Little one. 11 Place for ball or cricket. S.-leigidh, *a trestle* or *gantry*.
sorchanach, -aiche, *a.* Having rests or supports. 2 Like a stool or trestle. 3 Having little eminences or hillocks.
sorchan-cuigeil, *s.m.* Stand of a distaff.
sorchar,(AC) *s. m.* Brightness. 2 Clear man. 3 Lightener. S. nan reul, ***lightener of the stars.***
sord, see sùrd.
sordail, see sùrdail.
sordan,(AF) *s.m.* Animal.
so-reamhrachadh,*a.* Coagulable, easily fattened.
so-reamhraichte,*a.* Coagulable, easily thickened or fattened.
so-réite, *s.f.* Propitiation, expiation.
so-réiteach, *a.* see so-réitichte.
so-réitichte, *a.* Easily arranged or adjusted. 2 Easily reconciled, reconcilable. 3 Easily disentangled, as a string.
so-riaghladair,** *s. m.* Mild governor, lenient ruler. 2 One who rules with facility.
so-riaghladh, *a.* Easily governed, easily managed, governable, manageable.
so-riaghlaichte, see so-riaghlaidh.
so-riaghlaidh, *a.* Governable, manageable.
so-riaghailtichte, see so-riaghlaidh.
so-riaghluichte, see so-riaghlaidh.
sorn,(AF) *s.* Eagle.
sòrn, -ùirn, *s.m.* Snout. 2 Flue of a kiln or oven. 3 Concavity. 4(DC)Kiln for drying corn—*Uist.* 5**Disagreeable visage. 6 Hearth—*Sàr-Obair.* 7 Fireplace of an oven or kiln. S.-rac, *an oven-rake* or *baker's peel* ; damh-sùirn, *a kiln-joist, lantern of a kiln.* [*gen.* sòirn.**]
sòrnach, -aiche, *a.* Long-chinned. 2 Having a snout. 3 Pettish, ill-natured. 4 Having a flue or chimney.
sòrnach,(JMcF) *s.f.* Great heap of boulders at the foot of a precipice. Is iomadh linn o 'n a thuit an t-sòrnach seo gu léir *it is many generations since the whole of this heap of boulders fell—Sgeul.-nan-caol, p.125.*
sornag, -aig, -an, *s.f., dim.* of sòrn. Little kiln. 2 (DC) Shagreen ray (fish.)
sòrnair,** *s.m.* Baker. 2 Long-chinned person. 3 Peevish fellow.
sòrnaireachd,** *s.f.* Business of a baker.
sòrnairean, *n.pl.* of sòrnair.
sòrnan, -ain, -an, *s.m.* Thornback (fish.) 2 Small skate. 3†† Little flux. 4 (DC) Ray, shagreen ray—*Uist.* 5 Little flue. 6 Little snout. 7 Little chin. 8 Hillock. 9* Young skate.
sornanach,** *a.* Abounding in skate (fish.) 2 Of, or like skate. 3 Having little hillocks.
sòrnan biorach, *s.m.* Sharp-snouted white skate—*Lewis.*
sòrnan busach, *s.m.* White round skate—*Lewis.*
sòrnan sgreabach,(DMy) *s.m.* Rooker (fish.)
sòrn-aoil, *s m.* Lime-kiln. [McL & D gives *s.f.*]
so-roghnuichte, see so-roghnuidh.
so-roghnuidh, *a.* Eligible, preferable, excellent.
so-roinneadh,** *a.* Divisible.
so-roinnte, *a.* Divisible, easily divided.
sorsa, see seòrsa.
sòrt, -òirt, *s.m.* Sort, kind, species.

sortan,** -ain, *s.m.* Shout. 2 Praise, glory.
sorthan,** -ain, *s.m.* Reproof. 2 Prosperity.
soruidh, see soraidh.
so-ruigheachd,** *a.* Approachable, attainable, easily reached.
so-ruigsinn,** *a.* Attainable, approachable.
so-ruitheadh, *a.* Glib.
sos, -ois, *s.m.* Any unseemly mixture of food. 2 Coarse mess. 3†† Large bellyful of food. 4 Food for dogs—*W. of Ross.*
sos,** *s. m.* Cessation, giving over. 2 Knowledge.
sosadh,** -aidh, *s.m.* Dwelling, abode.
sosar,** *a.* Younger, youngest.
so-sgaoileadh,‡‡ *a.* Expansible.
so-sgaoilte, *a.* Dissoluble.
so-sgaradh, *a.* Refrangible.
so-sgìtheachaidh, *a.* Fatiguable.
so-sgoilte, *a.* Fissible.
so-sgoltadh, see so-sgoltaidh.
so-sgoltaidh, *a.* Fissible.
so-sgriosadh,** *a.* Consumable.
so-shàilleadh, *a.* Conditive.
so-shamhlachadh,** *a.* Comparable, applicable, easily matched.
so-shamhlachaidh,** *a.* Applicable. 2 Coagulable.
so-shamhlachail,(MS) *a.* Comparative.
so-shamhlachd, *s.f.ind.* Imitability.
so-shamhluichte, *a.* Applicable.
so-shaoilsinn, *a.* Conceivable.
so-shaoraidh, *a.* see so-fhuasglaidh.
so-shàruchaidh,‡‡ see so-sgìtheachaidh.
so-shàruichte,*a.* Conquerable. 2 Easily fatigued. 3 Easily oppressed.
so-sheachanta, *a.* Avoidable, easily shunned.
————chd,** *s.f.* Avoidableness.
so-sheachnach,** see so-sheachanta.
so-sheachnadh, see so-sheachanta.
so-sheachnaidh, see so-sheachanta.
so-sheargta,** *a.* Adustible.
so-sheasamh,‡‡ *a.* Maintainable.
so-sheilbhichte,(MS) *a.* Appropriable.
so-sheòlaidheachd,‡‡ *s.f.ind.* Navigableness.
so-sheòlta, *a.* Navigable, easily directed or guided.
so-shìneadh,** *a.* Easily stretched.
so-shìnte,** *a.* Ductile, as wire, easily stretched.
————achd,** *s.f.ind.* Ductility.
sosmaid,(DC) *s. m.* Hash of meat, mixture of fragments of food—*Argyll.*
so-smuaineachaidh,‡‡ see so-shaoilsinn.
so-smuainteachadh, *a.* Conceivable.
————————, -aidh, *s.m.* Conceivableness.
sosraich,(CR) *s.* Food for cattle—*Gairloch.*
†sosta,** *s.m.* Abode, dwelling-house.
sostan, -ain, *s.m.* Noise. 2 Cry.
———ach,** *a.* Noisy, clamorous.
———achd,** *s.f.* Noisiness, clamorousness.
so-stiùraidh, -e, *a.* Governable, manageable.
so-streapaidh,†† *a.* Mountable.
sot,** *v.a.* Boil anything overmuch.
sotail,* *v.a.* & *n.* see dean sodal.
sotal, -ail, *s.m.* see sodal.
——ach, -aiche, *a.* see sodalach.
——achd,* *s.f.* see sodal.
——aich, see sodalaich.
sòth, see sògh.
so-thagraidheachd,‡‡ *s.f.ind.* Justifiableness.
sòthail, see sòghail.
so-thaiseachaidh,‡‡ *a.* Mollifiable.
sothaisgean, see soisgean.
sothan,** *s.m.* Spruce fellow.
so-thaomadh,* *a.* Exhaustible.
so-thaosga, *a.* Exhaustible, that may be drained.
so-thaosgadh, see so-thaosgaidh.
so-thaosgaidh, *a.* Exhaustible, that may be

drained.
so-tharruing, see so-tharruingte.
so-tharruingte, *a.* Easily drawn.
so-thàth,** *a.* Associable.
so-theagaisgte, *a.* Docile, teachable
so-theagasg,** *a.* Easily taught, docile.
so-theanndadh,** *a.* Easily turned.
so-thionndach,‡‡ see so-iompachaidh.
so-thionnsgalach,‡‡ -aiche, *a.* Contrivable.
so-tholladh,** *a.* Perforable, easily bored.
so-thollaidh, *a.* ‡‡Permeable. 2 Boreable, perforable.
so-thollta, *a.* Boreable.
so-thomhaiseachd,‡‡ *s.f.* Measurableness.
so-thomhasachd,‡‡ *s.f.* Measurableness
so-threabhach, -aiche, *a.* Arable.
so-threabhaidh, -e, *a.* Arable.
so-threòruichte, *a.* Easily led or directed.
so-thruaillidh, -e, *a.* Corruptable, easily corrupted.
so-thruaillidheachd, *s.f.ind.* Corruptibleness.
so-thuigse, *s.f.ind.* Quickness of comprehension or understanding.
so-thuigseach,(MS) *a.* Comprehensible.
so-thuigseachd, *s.f.ind.* Perspicuity.
so-thuigsinn, *a.* Intelligible, easily understood, apprehensible.
so-thuigsinneachd, *s.f.ind.* Perspicuity.
sotlaidh,** *s.f.* Harm, damage.
———,** *a.* Bad, naughty.
sotsach,** *a.* Plump, fat, chubby.
sotsag,** -aig, *s.f.* Plump young girl. 2 Pillion.
so-uisgeach, *a.* Waterish, that may be moistened, moist, watery, apt to be moist, easily watered.
so-uisgichte, see so-uisgeach.
so-uisgidh, *a.* see so-uisgeach.
so-ùrachaidh, *a.* Renewable.
spac,** -a, *s.m.* Sudden exertion, as in wrestling. S. cleachdaidh, *wrestling, a wrestling-match;* tha iad a' cur s. cleachdaidh, *they are wrestling.*
spacadh,(CR) -aidh, *s.m.* Wrestling—*Perthshire.* Tha iad ri s., *or* tha iad a' cur spacaidh, *they are wrestling.*
spachadh,** -aidh, *s.m.* Plucking by the roots.
spad, *pr. pt.* a' spadadh, *v.a.* Kill, knock down at a blow, fell. 2 Flatten, strike flat to the ground.
spad,* -aid, *s.m.* Gaelic spelling of *spade.* [***s.f.*]
†spad, -a, -an, *s.m.* Clod, lump, sod.
spad, *a.* Flat. 2 Dead. 3 Lumpish. 4 Flapping, hanging down.
†spadach, -aiche, *a.* Full of clods. 2 Sluggish. 3 Stupid.
spadach,** *a.* Like, or full of, clods or turf. 2 Like a spade, of a spade. 3 Felling, knocking down. 4 Flattening. 5 Prone or ready to bruise. 6 Ready to strike or fell to the ground.
spadadh, -aidh, *s.m.* Killing, knocking down, felling. 2 Flattening, act of flattening, making flat. 3 Bruising. 4 Digging with a spade. A' s—, *pr.pt.* of spad.
spadag, -aig, -an, *s. f.* Filip. 2 Quick blow, knock-down blow. 3 Oath 4 Quarter of a limb of an animal cut off. 5††Ham. 6**Kind of play. 7††Light blow.
spadag, *s.f.* Limb. Cha'n 'eil aig' ach a cheithir spadagan fhéin, *he has only his own four limbs* —said of a man without encumberance—*West coast of Ross.*
spadagach,†† *a.* Abounding in light blows, or 2 in quarters of animals, &c. 3**Filliping. 4** Knocking down.
spadaiche,** -an, *s.m.* Feller. 2 Bruiser, pugilist.
spadaidh, *fut.aff.a.* of spad. Shall knock down.
spadail, -e, *a.* see spaideil.
———, *gen.sing.* of spadal.
spadair, -ean, *s.m.* Fop. 2 Braggart. 3††Killer. 4††Dull person. 5**Bruiser pugilist. 6 ††Dandy. 7 Feller. 8 [* spadaire] Terrible swearer.
———eachd, *s.f.ind.* Foppery. 2 Boasting, habit of boasting gasconade. 3 Killing, slaughtering. 4 Bruising, pugilism. 5 Frequent or continued felling, knocking down.
spadal, -ail, -an, *s.m.* Paddle. 2 Plough-staff. for removing adhering earth
———ach, *a.* Pertaining to a paddle or plough-staff.
spadalachd,(MS) *s.f.* Airiness
spadanach,** -aich, *s.m.* Sluggard.
———,** -aiche, *a.* Slow sluggish.
spadanta,‡‡ -ainte, *a.* Mean, niggardly 2 Sluggish. slow 3 Benumbed. 4††Dull, heavy
spadantachd,‡‡ *s.f* Meanness niggardliness. 2 Sluggishness, laziness, slowness
spadar,** *fut. pass.* of spad.
spad-chas,* *s.f.* Splay-foot. 2 Flat foot, plain sole.
———ach, -aiche, *a.* Splay-footed. 2 Clumsy. 3 Plain-soled.
———ach, -aich, *s.m* Splay-footed person.
spad-chluas, -aise, -an, *s.f.* Dull ear. 2 Flapping, hanging ear, flat ear.
spad-chluasach, -aiche, *a.* Flat-eared. 2 Dull of hearing.
———, -aich, *s.m.* Flat-eared person. 2 Deaf person.
spad-choisbheart,** *s.* Gaiters.
spad-chos, see spad-chas.
spad-fhacal, -ail, *s.m.* Vaunting expression, boast, rhodomontade.
spad-fhaclach, -aiche, *a.* Vaunting, boasting, gasconading. 2 Ostentatious.
spad-fhaclair, *s.m.* Gasconader, braggadocio.
spad-fhèath,(DC) *s.m.* Flat calm—*Argyll.*
spadh,* *v.a.* Jerk, twitch.
spadh, -a, -an, *s.m.* Swathe of mown grass.
spadhach,** *a.* In swathes, as mown grass. 2 Having a good swathe.
spadhadh, -aidh, *pl.* -an & -annan, *s.m.* Strong and quick pull when rowing or mowing. 2 The utmost extent of the arms when stretched out. 3 What grass is cut by one stroke of a scythe, layer of mown grass, swathe of grass. 4††Space from which a swathe of grass is cut.—*Perthshire, W. of Ross-shire, &c.* 4 Bout or course by which a swathe is cut. 5 Elasticity. 6†† Pith. 7* Jerking, twitching, twitch.
spad-phluic, *s.f.* Blub cheek, chubby face.
———each, -eiche, *a.* Blub-cheeked, chubby faced.
———each, -eich, *s.m.* Blub-faced person, chubby-cheeked person.
spadrach, *s.m.* Attention to dress—*Suth'd.*
spad-shròin, -shròna, *s.f.* Flat nose.
———each, see spad-shrònach.
spad-shrònach, -aiche, *a.* Flat-nosed.
———, *s.m.* Flat-nosed person.
spadta, *past pt* of spad. Killed, knocked down at a blow, felled. 2 Flattened, laid flat.
spadte, see spadte.
spad-thalamh, -thalmhainn, *s.m.* Unproductive ground, fallow ground.
spad-thinn,** *a.* Apoplectic.
spad-thinneas, -eis, *s.m.* Lethargy. 2 Apoplexy. 3 Epilepsy (falling sickness.)
———ach, -aiche, *a.* Apoplectic.
spàg,** *s.f.* Fold of the leaf of a book, caused by improper usage. 2 Distortion of a shoe occasioned by walking awry.
spàg, -aig, -an, *s.f.* Claw. 2 Paw. 3 Club-foot. 4 Limb of an animal. 5**Foot of a cloven-footed quadruped. 6** Long flat foot, plain

sole. 7** *in derision*, Clumsy foot. 8 Stilt of a plough. 9 Ham. Os cionn a spàgan, *above her feet* ; s.-cùirn, *the beam of a sledge or waggon* ; spagan dubha, *hams dried in smoke.*
spàg, *v.a.* Make awry, distort anything. 2 Fold up the leaves of a book. 3 Distort a shoe.
spàgach, -aiche, *a.* Uttering words indistinctly. 2††Having a long chin. 3**Folded up, as the leaves of a book by improper usage. 4** Distorted, as a shoe.
spàgach, -aiche, *a.* Clawed, having claws. 2 Pawed, having paws. 3 Walking awkwardly. 4 Having awkward legs or feet. 5 Distorted, turned awry. 6 Club-footed. 7 Broad-footed. 8 Out-toed. 9 Like or pertaining to hams.
spàgach,* -aich, *s.f.* Club-footed female.
spagada-gliog,** *s.* Balderdash, ostentation, gasconade. S. Chloinn Dòmhnuill, *the MacDonald swagger.*
spàgadh, -aidh, -ean,*s.m.*Obliquity of the mouth.
spàgadh, -aidh, *s.m.* Distorting, act of distorting. A' s—, *pr.pt.* of spàg.
spàgair, -e, -ean, *s.m.* An awkward-footed fellow. 2 One who walks awkwardly. 3 Flat-footed person. 4 Club-footed person. 5†† Clumsy-footed fellow. [*nom. -e.]
——**eachd**,** *s.f.* Awkward, sprawling gait.
spàgaire-tuinne, *s. m.* Little grebe, see spàg-ri-tòn.
spagh, see spadhadh.
spaghadh, see spadh & spadhadh.
spagluinn, -e, *s.f.* Ostentation, show, conceit, bombast. 2* Attitude of having the arms a-kimbo and the foot stretched out. 3* Fool's pride. [*spagloinn]
——**each**, -eiche, *a.* Ostentatious, showy, conceited, bombastic.
——**each**,** *s.m.* Ostentatious, conceited person.
——**eachd**, *s.f.* see spagluinn.
spàg-nam-mionaidean, *s. f.* Minute-hand of a timepiece—*W. coast of Ross.*
spàg-ri-tòn,¶ *s.f.* Little grebe, dabchick—*podiceps minor.* [***colymbus auritus*]

645. Spàg-ri-tòn.

spaid, -e, *pl.* -eachan, Gaelic spelling of *spade*, see spad. 2**Clod.
——, *gen.sing.* of spad.
†——, *s.f.* Drug. 2 Sluggard. 3 Eunuch. 4 Carrion. [fruitful.
†**spàid**, *a.* Dull, heavy. 2 Dead, insipid. 3 Un-
spaide,** *s.f.* Show, ostentation. 2 Foppery. 3 Sluggishness.
spaideal, -eil, *s.m.* Spatula. 2**Slice. 3 Spaddle. 4 Plough-staff.
——**ach**, -aich, *s.m.* Baw-cock, spark, gay young man.
——**achd**, *s.f.ind.* Conceitedness, showiness, foppishness, gaudiness. 2**Sluggishness.
spaideantachd,** *s.f.* Obtuseness.
spaideil, -e, *a.* Well-dressed, conceited, beauish, foppish, gaudy, showy, proud. 2**Sluggish.
spaid-fhìon,** -fhìona, *s.m.* Flat or dead wine.
spaidhe, *s.* Slide.
spaidheilearachd, see speileireachd.
spaidhir,* -e & -dhreach, *pl.* -ean, *s.f.* Pocket-hole of a petticoat, placket. 2 Flap of trousers. 3**Petticoat.
spaidhleireachd,†† *s.f.* Unnecessary climbing, fidgetting.
spaidir,* *v.a.* Scatter carelessly.
spaidreach,* -eich, *s.f.* The thing scattered, the state of lying here and there.
spaidsear, see spaisdear.
spaidsireachd, see spaisdearachd.
spaidsirich, see spaisdirich.
spaid-thalamh,** -thalmhainn, *s.m.* Unproductive ground.
spaig, -e, -ean, *s.f.* Wry mouth. 2 Long chin.
spàig,** *s.f.* Lame leg.
spàil, *v.a.* Swaddle, swathe, wrap up. (spaoil.)
spàilleach, see spaoileach.
——**adh**, see spaoileachadh.
spailleachdalachd, *s.f.ind.* see spailleichd.
spailleadh,** -idh, *s.m.* Check. 2 Abuse. 3 Fall.
spàilleadh, see spaoileadh.
spailleichd, -e, *s.f.* Vain-glory, boasting, ostentation, conceitedness, foppery.
spailleichdeach,** *a.* see spailleichdeil.
spailleichdear,** *s.m.* Coxcomb.
spailleichdear, -ir, -ean, *s.m.* Boaster, vain-fellow, fop, ostentatious man, vaunter, egotist.
——**ach**, -aiche, *a.* Coxcomb-like.
spailleichdeil, -e, *a.* Vain-glorious, ostentatious, conceited, foppish.
spàillich, see spaoil.
spaillichdealachd,** *s. f.* Vain-gloriousness, ostentation, conceitedness, foppery.
spailp, -ean, *s.m.* Pride, spirit, courage, boldness. 2 Conceit, self-conceit. 3 Foppish young man, beau. 4* Airs of importance. 5** Armour, belt. 6**Kiss. 7 Lie. [**spealp.] 8** Attitude of the foot stretched out, as of a self-important fellow. [** gives *s.f.* & *gen.* -e.] Cha ruig thu leas a bhith 'cur s. ort rium-sa, *you need not assume such airs in my presence ;* shiubhail mi cian leat air m'eòlais, agus spailp de 'n stròic air m' aineol, *I have travelled far with you in parts known to me, and a creditable length of the journey where I was not acquainted.—Agus ho Mhòrag.*
spailp,** *a.* Notable.
spailp, *v.n.* Strut, walk proudly or affectedly. 2 Stamp authoritatively with the foot in commanding,
spailpair,* see spailpean.
spailpe, *s.f.* see spailpeis.
spailpeach, -eiche, *a.* see spailpeil.
spailpeachd,†† *s.f.* Ostentation.
spailpeadh, -idh, *s.m.* Strutting, act of strutting or walking proudly. 2|Act of stamping authoritatively. A' s—, *pr.pt.* of spailp.
spailpean, -ein, -an, *s.m.* Fop, beau. 2 Mean insignificant fellow. 3 Conceited fellow, spalpeen. 4**Intruder. 5**Rascal.
spailpeanach, -aiche, *a.* Beauish, foppish. 2 Insignificant from vanity or conceit.
——**d**, *s.f.ind.* Foppishness, beauishness. 2 Silly vanity.
spailpeanta, *a.* see spailpeil.
spailpear,** -eir, -an, *s. m.* Beau, fop, spruce fellow. 2 Intruder.
spailpearra, *a.* see spailpeil.
——, *s.m.* see spailpean.
——**chd**, *s.f.ind.* Conceitedness, foppishness. 2 Habit of silly boasting or vain-glorious talk.
spailpeas, -eis, *s.m.* Stateliness.
spailpeil, -e, *a.* Conceited, foppish, beauish, spruce. 2 Boasting, vain-glorious, silly. 3 Walking proudly, strutting. 4 Notable.
spailpeir, -ean, see spailpean. [*-air]
spailpeis, *s.f.* Self-conceit.
spailpire,* see spailpean.

spailpireachd,* *s.f.* Self-importance. 2 Important airs of a silly person.
spàin, -e, *pl.* -ean & -eachan, *s. f.* Spoon. Làn-spàine, *spoonful.*
spàin-aoil,** *s.f.* Trowel.
spàin-bhròg, *s.f.* Shoe-lift, shoe-horn.
spàineach, -eiche, *a.* Of or belonging to spoons. 2 Like a spoon.
spàineachan, *n.pl.* of spàin.
spàineag, -eig, -an, *s. f., dim.* of spàin. Little spoon. 2‡‡Spoonful.
——ach, *a.* Of, or belonging to, little spoons.
spàinean, *n.pl.* of spàin.
spàinneach, see spàinteach.
spàinteach, -ich, *s.m. & f.* Spaniard, long kind of fowling-piece understood to have been made in Spain. 2 Spanish sword, toledo. 3 Spoonful. Is lìonmhor s. air taobh cli aca, *many a sword hangs by their side* ; s. ime, *a spoonful of butter* ; lann Spàinteach (*a.*), *a toledo.*
spairis,* *s.f.* Conceitedness, foppishness, conduct or attitude of having the hands in the trousers' pockets.
spairiseach, -eiche, *a.* see spairisteach.
——d, see spairisteachd.
spàinn,** *v.n.* Strive, struggle, wrestle.
spàirn, -e, *s.f.* Effort, hard struggle, violent exertion. 2 Striving, contest, conflict. 3 Emulation, rivalry. 4 Pain, agony. 5 Difficulty. 6 Stress, violence, force. 7**Log of wood. 8** Wrestle. Cha s. sin orm, *that is no hard task to me* ; ni mi sin gun s., *I can manage that without an effort* ; s. a' bhàis, *the death-agony;* s. nan laoch, *the struggle of the heroes.*
spàirneach,** *a.* Emulous, causing emulation. 2 Struggling, striving, making an effort. 3 Rivalry, 4 Wrestling. [also spàirneil]
spàirneachd, *s.f.* see spàirnealachd.
spàirneadh,** -eidh, *s.m.* Wrestling. 2 Contest. exertion.
spairneag,** -an, *s.f.* Conch.
——ach, -aiche, *a.* Shelly.
spairneag-bàirneach,* *s.* Limpet.
spàirnealachd, *s.f.ind.* Struggling, wrestling, continued and hard struggle. 2 Difficulty. 3 Uneasiness. 4**Emulation, rivalry.
spairisteach, -eiche, *a.* Beauish, foppish, gaudy. 2 Arrogant, conceited, strutting, showy.
——, -eich, *s.m.* Beau.
——d, *s.f.ind.* Foppishness, gaudiness. 2 Arrogance, conceitedness, strutting gait.
spairneag, *s.f.* Shell.
——ach, *a.* Shelly.
spàirneil, -e, *a.* Making great efforts, struggling, emulous, striving, contending. 2 Enduring agony. 3 Causing agony. 4 Laying stress upon anything. 5 Using strength or force. 6 Difficult, arduous, troublesome. 7 Requiring struggles or efforts.
spàirniche, *s.m.* Striver.
spàirnidh, *fut.aff.a.* of spàirn.
spairt,** *a.* Thick.
spairt, -e, -ean, *s.f.* Turf, clod. 2 Splash of water. 3 Drop, least drop of any liquid. 4** Violent knocking down. 5**Smash, smashing. 6**Daub, daubing. 7††Plaster. 8**Inspissated fluid. Le spairtibh ùire, *with clods of dust.*
spairt, *pr. pt.* a' spairteadh, *v.a.* Plaster, daub over, as with lime or clay. 2 Splash with water. 3 Spatter, bespatter. 4 Pelt. 5**Knock down, throw to the ground with violence. 6‡ Brain. 7**Smash.
spàirte, *past pt.* of spàrr. Fastened, fixed, wedged in, bolted, thrust, jammed.
spairteach,* -eiche, *a.* Thick, as cream. 2‡‡ Daubing. 3‡‡ Splashing. 4‡‡ Abounding in clods. 5‡‡In large drops. 6**Smashing.
spairteachd, *s.f.* Frequent splashing, daubing or smearing. 2**Smashing.
spairteadh, -idh, *s.m.* Daubing, act of daubing. 2 Splashing, act of splashing. A' s—, *pr. pt.* of spairt. [see spultadh.]
spairtidh,†† -e, *a.* Tart, acid, alum-like.
†spaisd,* *v.n.* see spaisdirich.
spaisdear, -ir, -an, *s. m.* Saunterer, stroller rambler.
spaisdearach, -aiche, *a.* Sauntering, strolling, walking, parading, rambling.
——,* *s.m.* Walk in a garden, promenade.
——d, *s. f.* Walking, act of walking, strolling, sauntering, promenading, parading for pleasure. 2**Airing. 3 Kind of tune in ceòl-mór. A' s—, *pr.pt.* of spaisdirich. Tha mi dol a ghabhail ceum s., *I am going for a stroll* ; àite-s., *a promenade.*
spaisdir,* see spaisdirich.
——ich, *pr. pt.* a' spaisdireachd & a' spaisdearachd, *v.n.* Walk, saunter, strut along, walk proudly, ramble, walk for pleasure.
spaisdreach,* *s.m.* see spaisdearach.
——d, see spaisdearachd.
spaisdrich, see spaisdirich.
spaisean,** -ein, *s.m.* Term of contempt for a boy.
spàl, -àil, -an, *s,m.* Weaver's shuttle.
spàl, -a, -an, *s.m.* see spathalt.
spàlach, -aiche, -aiche, *a.* Of, or belonging to shuttles. 2 Like a shuttle.
spàladair, -ean, *s.m.* Shuttle-maker.
spàlag, -aig, -an, *s.f.* Cod or husk of any leguminous vegetable, as a pea or bean. 2 Stroke of an oar in rowing. 3 Piece of dried bark. 4 ‡‡Small spoon.
spàlagach,** *a.* Podded, having a large pod or husk. 2 Pertaining to pods or husks.
spàlagan, *s.m.* Oar-stroke.
spàlan, -ain, *s.m.* see spàlag.
†spall,** *v.a.* Beat, strike.
spalla,** *s.* Wedge, fragment of stone used in building. 2 Pinning in building.
spalladh, see spalla.
spallair,** -ean, *s.m.* Espalier.
spalp, see spailp.
——adh, see spailpeadh.
spalpair,* see spailpear.
spang, -aing & -a, *pl.* -an, *s.f.* Any small thin plate of metal. 2 Anything shining or sparkling. 3**Span. 4††Drop. 5‡ Spangle.
——ach, -aiche, *a.* Abounding in thin plates of metal. 2 Like a plate of metal. 3 Shining, sparkling.
spangachadh,** -aidh, *s.m.* Spanning.
spangaich,** *v.a.* Span.
spangan, (*pl.* of spang.) Spangles, glittering toys, decorations, embellishments—*Sàr-Obair.*
spann, -an, *s.* Hinge. 2 Hasp. see bann.
spann, -adh, *v. a.* Sever, cut asunder, divide, splinter. 2 Dash. 3 Wean, as a child. 4†† Kill with one stroke, despatch.
spannach,* -aich, *s.f.* Splinter. S. iorgaill, *a bone of contention.*
——adh,†† *s. m.* Knocking down flat. 2 Killing with one stroke, despatching. A' s—, *pr.pt.* of spannaich.
spannadh, -aidh, *s.m.* Severing, act of severing, cutting asunder, dividing. A' s—, *pr. pt.* of spann. Tha mi an dòchas nach faigh thu mise fo d' s., *I hope you will not get me into your power—Lewis.*
spannaich, *pr.pt.* a' spannachadh, *v.a.* see spann.
spaoil, *v.a.* Wrap up, swathe, swaddle. (‡spaoill.]
spaoile,* *s.m* Spindle of yarn.
spaoileach,** *a.* Swaddling, swathing, wrapping

up.
spaoileadh, -idh, *s.m.* Wrapping, act of wrapping up, swathing or swaddling. 2 (CR)Staring, gaping, looking in alarm—*Suth'd.* A' s—, *pr.pt.* of spaoil. Brat spaoilidh, *a swaddling band.*
spaoileadair,** *s.m.* Swaddler, swather.
spaoilear, *fut. pass.* of spaoil.
spaoilidh, *fut. aff. a.* of spaoil. 2 *gen. sing.* of spaoileadh.
spaoilte, *past pt.* of spaoil. Swathed, swaddled.
spar, see spor—*Arran.* Spar a' choilich *for* spor a' choilich.
spàr, -a, -an, see spàrr.
spàrach, see spàrrach.
spàrag,(CR) *s.f.* Boasting, boastfulness.
sparan, see sparran.
sparasach, -aiche, *a.* see spairiseach.
————d, see spairiseachd.
spàrd,* see spàrdan.
spàrdan, -ain, -an, *s.m.* Roost, hen-roost. 2 Little eminence or hill, flat at top. 3(CR)Short, steep acclivity.—*West of Ross-shire.* 4 Level shelf on a hill-side, where one would naturally rest.
spàrdanach, -aiche,*a.* Having roosts. 2 Abounding in roosts. 3 Like a roost. 4 Roosted, perched as a roost.
sparn, see spàirn.
sparnag,** *s.f.* see spairneag.
spàrr, *pr.pt.* a' spàrradh, *v.a.* Drive, as a nail or a wedge. 2 Induce by force. 3 Fix, rivet, nail. 4 Thrust. 5 Enforce by argument,inculcate. 6**Dash, dash forward. S. e a làmh ann (*no* innte) ; *he thrust his hand into it ;* s. air e, *clap it on it ;* a' crannadh 's a' spàrradh an doruis *bolting and wedging the door ;* a' spàrradh an ni seo oirnn, *inculcating this thing on us.*
spàrr, -a, -an, *s.m.* [*f.* in *Badenoch & Gairloch*] Joist, beam, spar of wood. 2 Cross-beam of a roof, purlin, see under taigh. 3 Roost, hen-roost. 4 Large nail. Am mac air an s. 's an t-athair gun bhreith, *the son on the roost and the father unborn*—i.e. the smoke of a fire not kindled, said of things loudly proclaimed before they exist—N.G.P.
sparraban,(AG) *Reay country* for bannanan.
spàrrach,***a.*Having a roost. 2 Like a roost. 3 Roosted, perched, as on a roost. 4 Joisted.
sparrach,** *a.* Driving, shoving. 2 Dashing. 3 Nailing, riveting. 4 Inculcating, enforcing.
sparrach,* -aich, *s.f.* Sheath.
spàrradh, -aidh, *s.m.* Driving, act of driving, as a nail or wedge. 2 Act of inducing by force. 3 Fixing, act of fixing, riveting or nailing. 4 Thrusting, act of thrusting or shoving. 5 Enforcing, act of enforcing by argument, urging, inculcating. 6 Injunction, charge. 7**Nail, rivet. 8**Dashing. A' s—, *pr. pt.* of spàrr. Thug e s. dhaibh, *he gave them a charge ;* a'cur s. orra, *charging them ;* teann s., *a strict injunction ; firm nailing or riveting.*
sparrag, -aig, -an, *s.f.* Bridle-bit. 2 Intricacy, difficulty. 3 Undue vehemence in enforcing an argument. 4 Positiveness, petulance. 5 Rivet, nail.
————ach, -aiche, *a.* Having a bit, as a bridle. 2 Difficult, intricate. 3 Obstinate. 4 Vehement, petulant. 5**Nailed, riveted.
sparragaich,** *v.a.* Drive. 2 Nail, rivet. 3 Inculcate. 4 Charge strictly. 5 Bridle, curb.
————,** *a.* Having a bit, as a bridle. 2 Nailed, riveted.
————te, *past pt.* of sparragaich.
sparraich,* *s.pl.* Household furniture—*Islay.*
sparrall,** *a.* Peremptory.

spàrran, -ain, -an, *s. m., dim.* of spàrr. Bolt or bat. 2 Crisping-pin. S.-doruis, *a door-bolt.*
sparranan,* *s.pl.* Spasms.
sparrasach, see spairiseach.
————d, see spaisiseachd.
spàrr-buinn, *s.* Part of dealbh, p. 317.
spàrr-ealaig,(DC) *s.m.* Pin projecting above the roof at each end of house to which to fasten the ropes for holding the thatch in its place—*Uist.*
spàrr-gaoithe,(DC) *s.m.* Cross-joist near ridge of a house strengthening the couples—*Uist.*
spàrr-mullaich, *s.m.* Part of dealbh, p. 317.
sparrta, *past pt.* Adacted.
spàrsan, -ain, -an, *s.m.* Dew-lap of a beast. 2†† Gizzard of a bird. 3 **Diminution. 4 Diminutive person. 5**Dry stalk. 6** *in contempt,* Flaccid, hanging lip.
————ach, -aiche, *a.* Dew-lapt, having a dew-lap. 2 Having a flaccid lip. 3††Having a gizzard.
spart,* -airt, *s. m.* Essence, quintessence. 2 see spairt. 3 Clod. S. an uachdair, *the essence of cream, best of cream ;* s. càbhruich,*the farina of sowens without the liquid part.*
†spart,** *a.* Heavy, dull, dense.
spàt,(DMK) *s. m.* Heavy shower of rain. S.-uisge, *a heavy fall of rain—Caithness.*
spat,** *s.m.* Flap.
spathalt, -ailt, -an, *s. f.* Limb. 2 Large and clumsy limb. 3**Joint of meat.
————ach, -aiche, *a.* Limbed. 2 Having large and clumsy limbs.
speac,** *s.m.* Spoke, bar.
————ach, *a.* Having spokes or bars, as a wheel or gate.
speacaich,** *v.a.* Provide with spokes or bars.
speach, -a, -an, *s.f.*[& *m.***] Wasp. 2 Any venomous little creature. 3 Bite or sting of any venomous creature.
speach,(AC) *s.* Stone, doorstep, flat stone in a byre floor 2 Certain stone in a byre drain. S. na bàthcha, *the doorstep of the byre.*
speach, -a, *pl.* -an & -annan, *s.m.* Blow. 2 Kick. 3 Thrust. 4**Froth. 5**Game called "fillip." 6 Stitch in the side. 7 Dart—*Sàr-Obair.* 8 (DC) Cuts on face, hands, *&c.* 9* Smart, clever blow
speach,(AC) *s.* Claw, hoof. 2 Animal.
speach,* *v.a.* Bite, strike smartly. 2(DC) Mark as by cuts. Tha 'aodann air a s., *his face is marked by cuts.*
speachach, -aiche, *a.* Abounding in wasps. 2 Like a wasp. 3 Venomous, stinging.
speachag, *Uist* for spitheag. Tilg s. air a' bhoin, *throw a stone at the cow.*
speachadh,(MS) *s.m.* Gap.
speachair, -ean, *s.m.* One who strikes, beats or kicks. 2 Waspish, peevish fellow. 3 Little, trifling fellow.
speachannach, -aiche, see speachanta.
speachanta, -ainte, *a.* Waspish,peevish, vicious. 2 Quick, nimble. 3**Dealing blows.
speachantachd, *s.f.* see speachantas.
speachantas, -ais, *s.m.* Peevishness,waspishness. viciousness. 2 Quickness, nimbleness. 3** Crossness.
speacharra, see speachanta.
————chd, see speachantas.
speaclairean, see speuclairean.
spead,* -a, -an, *s.f.* Very small foot or leg. 2 Cow's or sheep's kick—*Badenoch.*
speadach,* -aiche, *a.* Sheep-shanked. 2 Kicking—*Badenoch.*
————,* *s.f.* Sheep-shanked female.
speadair,* -ean, *s.m.* Sheep-shanked man.
speal, -a, -an, *s.f.* Scythe. 2 Sword. 3 Touch.

4 Scythe-blade. 5**Mowing hook. 6**Short spell at any kind of work. 8**Short spell of vigorous exertion. Thoir s. air an obair, *bestow a short while at the work.* [In *Gairlodh*, Nos. 1 & 7 are represented by different Gaelic words, No. 1 being speall with the diphthong short and the *ll* short, and No. 7 speall, the *e* only being sounded—DU.]

NAMES OF THE PARTS OF A SCYTHE:—

Bann, *ring* securing heel of blade to the handle.

Cearcall-buana, (AH) *hoop* arranged on the shaft to help in laying the corn evenly for binding. The ellipse formed by the hoop is sometimes covered with thin canvas or cotton.

Crann, crann-speala, dorn, putag, *handle-haft, shaft.*

Geinn, *wedge* tightening the ring.

Iarunn, *blade.*

Snàthad, Snàthad-feòir(AH), *hook* which holds the blade at the proper angle.

speal, *pr.pt.* a' spealadh, *v.a.* Mow, cut down. 2 Scythe, cut with a scythe. 3 Use cutting words.

spealach, -eiche, *a.* Of, or belonging to, a scythe. 2 Like a scythe or hook. 3 Mowing. 4 Using cutting words.

spealadair, -ean, *s. m.* Mower, scytheman. 2 Scythe.

——eachd, *s.f.ind.* Mowing.

spealadh, -aidh, *s.m.* Mowing, act of mowing or cutting down. 2 Act of using cutting words. 3 Scolding, scold. 4**Shelling, (for spioladh.) A' s—, *pr.pt.* of speal.

spealain,** *s.pl.* Shavings.

spealair, -ean, *s. m.* Mower, one that cuts or mows fast. 2 Satirist, one who uses cutting words.

——eachd, see spealadaireachd.

spealan, -ain, *s.m.* Scythe.

spealanta, -ainte, *a.* Acute, cutting, that cuts. 2 Quick, ready. 3 Sharp, satirical, using cutting words. 4‡‡Clever, active. 5 Ready-spoken.

——chd, *s.f.ind.* Acuteness. 2 Quickness, readiness. 3 Sharpness of language. 4††Cleverness, activity, acuteness.

speal-bheòil,(DMK) *s.f.* Razor—*Gairloch.*

speal-chraois,(Fionn) *s.f.* Razor.

spealg, *v.a. & n.* Break with violence, make splinters of, split. 2 Chip, cleave. 3 Fritter. 4 Fall into splinters or pieces.

spealg, -eilg, -an, *s.f.* Splinter, fragment.

——ach, -aiche, *a.* Splintered. 2 That splits or splinters. 3 Full of splinters or fragments. 4 Smashing, splitting.

——ach,‡‡ -aich, *s.f.* Quantity of splinters, fragments or chips. 2* Splinter.

spealgadh, -aidh, *s.m.* Breaking, act of breaking with violence, smashing, splintering, splitting. 2 Cleaving, chipping. 3 Splinter, chip. 4 State of falling into pieces or fragments. A' s—, *pr.pt.* of spealg.

spealgair, -ean, *s.m.* One who splinters or breaks into fragments or splinters, cleaver.

——eachd,†† *s.f.* Splintering.

spealgan, *n.pl.* of spealg.

spealgarra, *a.* Splintering.

spealgta, *past pt.* of spealg. Splintered, broken into fragments.

spealp, -eilp, *s.m.* see spailp.

——air, see spailpear.

——aireachd, see spailpearachd.

——arra,** *a.* Beauish, spruce.

——arrachd, see spailpearachd.

spealt, -a, -an, *s.f.* Splinter. 2 Lath. 3 Dash in *writing* (—.) 4* Tall person. 5 (DMy) Splint to keep a broken limb in place.

spealt, *pr.pt.* a' spealtadh, *v.a* Cleave, split, break with force, smash. 2 Strike with violence. 3**Clash.

——ach, -aiche, *a.* Splintered. 2 Splitting, that splits. 3 Abounding in splinters or chips. 4 Chipping, smashing 5 Clashing

——achd, *s.f.ind.* Cleaving, splitting, shivering, chipping.

——adh, -aidh, *s.m.* Splitting, act of splitting, cleaving A' s—, *pr.pt.* of spealt.

spealtag, -aig, -an, *s. f.*, *dim.* of spealt. Small splinter.

——ach, -aiche, *a.* Abounding in small splinters.

spealtair, -ean, *s.m.* One who splits or cleaves. 2 Any instrument to split or cleave with, cleaver.

——eachd, *s.f.ind.* Continued cleaving or splitting. 2 Violent striking. 3 Clashing. Lainn ri s., *swords hacking*

spealtan, -ain' *pl.* -an & -ain, *s.m.dim.* of spealt. Fragment, splinter, shiver, chip. 2 *pl.* of spealt.

——ach, -aiche, *a.* Same meanings as spealtagach.

spealt-chleas,** *s. m.* Mutual violence, giving blow for blow.

——achd,** *s.f.* Mutual violence.

speansa,** *s.m.* Cellar, parlour.

spearag,** -aig, *s.f.* see speireag.

spearl,** *v.a.* Spoil.

——ach,** *a.* Spoiling.

——adh,** -aidh, *s.m.* Spoiliation.

spearrach, see speireach.

spearrach, -aich, -aichean, *s.f.* Cow-fetter. 2 (CR) Goat-fetter. 3 Fetter placed on one of the fore-feet and one of the hind-feet of an animal to prevent its climbing or jumping over dykes. 4**Ham-string. 5 (DMK) String tied tightly round the hamstring of an animal with the object of impeding its locomotion. 6 6* Cross-fetters for sheep. Cuir s., *hamstring.*

——adh,** -aidh, *s.m.* Ham-stringing.

spearraich, *v.a.* Fetter feet of cattle. 2 Hamstring.

——,** *gen.sing.* of spearrach.

spearraichear, *fut. pass.* of spearraich.

spearraichte, *past pt.* of spearraich.

spearralach,* -aich, *s.f.* Ham-string.

spearralaich,* *v.a.* Ham-string.

spéic, -e, -ean, *s.f.* Spike. 2 Bar, spar, spoke. 3 **Long nail. 4 Prop. 5 Blow, stroke. S. cuibhle, *the spoke of a wheel;* s.-làimhe, *the spoke* or *bearer of a bier.*

spéic, *pr. pt.* a' spéiceadh, *v. a.* Spike, fasten with spikes. 2 Prop, support. 3 Strike. 4 Spar.

——each, -eiche, *a.* Spiked. 2 Of, or belonging to, spikes, nails, bars, spars or props. 3 Fixing with spikes, bars, &c. 4 Like a spike, &c. 5 Furnished with spikes, &c. 6 Furnished with props, propped. 7 Like a prop. 8 Propping. 9 Sparred. 10 Striking blows. 11 Apt to strike blows. 12**Nailing. 13 Sustaining.

——eadh, -idh, *s.m.* Spiking, act of spiking or fixing with spikes. 2 Propping, act of propping. 3**Striking, act of striking. 4**Nailing. A' s—, *pr.pt.* of spéic.

speicean, *s.pl.* Tram or shaft of a cart.

spéid,* -e, *s.f.* see spid.

speid,** *s.f.* Spate, sudden flood, as in a stream after heavy rain.

——each,** *a.* Like, or pertaining to, a spate.

spéideach, see spìdeil.
spéideil, -e, *a.* see spìdeil.
speidhil, *v.a.* see spéil.
speidhleachan, -ain, *s.m.* see spéileachan.
speidhleadh, -eidh, *s.m.* see spéileadh.
spéidhleireachd,** see spéileireachd.
spéidich, *v.a.* see spìdich.
speil, -e, -ean, *s.f.* Cattle, herd. 2 Drove, particularly of swine. (also speil-mhuc.)
spéil, *v.a.* & *n.* Slip, slide, skate. 2* Climb—*Islay.*
spéileach, -eiche, *a.* Apt to slip or slide.
speileachan, -ain, *s.m.* Skate.
speileadaireachd, *s.f.* Climbing. 2 Sliding.
spéileadh, -idh, *s.m.* Sliding, act of sliding, slipping, skating. 2 Stumbling. A' s—, *pr. pt.* of spéil.
spéileag,†† see béilleag.
speilean, *s.m.* Uist game corresponding to the game of "cat and bat." The necessaries for the game are the Speil or Cat, the Driver or Bat, and the Ball of worsted or hair. Two sides of equal numbers are picked, one side taking the first of the batting and the other of the fielding, as they win or lose the toss.
A hole is made in the ground with the heel, and one end of the Speil (a small piece of wood) is put into it. The ball rests in the hole on the inner end of the speil. The first batter strikes the end which protrudes with the driver, thus sending the ball into the air. While the ball is in the air, he smites it with all his power, the object being to drive it as far as possible from the hole. If any of the opposing side catch it before it touches the ground the striker is out, but if no catch is made the first fielder to reach the ball gives a bowl (faireag) to the batsman. The latter again drives the ball as far as possible, and if a catch be made he is out. If, however, no catch be made, the first player of the opposing side to reach the ball, throws the ball into, or as near as he can, the hole. This is called "pìceadh." If it goes into the hole the player is out. If not, he measures the length of the ball from the hole by means of the bat. If it is not one bat's length he is out, if it is one or more, he plays on until he is out, when another member of his side comes in in his place. This continues till one side counts 100, or is all out, when the opposite side comes in. If neither side reaches the set number of points, whichever scores the highest is said to be the winner. This game is fairly popular still and is one of the healthiest and best of Uist games —*Celtic Review, Vol. IV, p. 362.*
spéilean, -ein, -an, *s.m.* Slippery place, place to slide on.
———achd,‡‡ *s.f.* Sliding, slipping. 2 Amusement of sliding or skating.
speileanta,* -einte, *a.* Eloquent.
————chd,* *s.f.ind.* Eloquence.
spéilearachd, see spéileireachd.
speile-cheann,(AF) *s.m.* Leader among pigs.
spéileireachd, *s.f.* Amusement of sliding or skating. 2 Frequent slipping or stumbling, A' s—, *pr. pt.* of spéilich.
spéileirich,‡‡ *pr.pt.* a' spéileireachd, *v.a.* Slide, skate.
speilg,* *s.f.* Sheep-shank.
speilgeach,* -eiche, *a.* Sheep-shanked.
————,* -eich, *s.f.* Sheep-shanked female.
speilgeir,* -ean, *s. m.* Sheep-shanked man. 2 Trifling-looking fellow.
speiligein,†† -ean, *s.m.* Spindle-shank, weakling.
————each, *a.* Having spindle-shanks.
speill, *v.* see spaoil.
speilleach, *a.* see spaoileach.
speilleadair, see spaoileadair.
speilleadh, see spaoileadh.
spéilleag †† -eig, -an, *s.f.* Curled bark.
————ach, -aiche, *a.* Pertaining to curled barks.
speillear, see spaoilear.
spéillidh, see spaoilidh.
spéillte, see spaoilte.
speilp,** *s.f.* Armour. 2 Belt. 3 Pride, foppery, conceit. (spailp)
speilteir,** *s.m.* Zinc.
speinnse,** *s.* Partition.
speir, -e, *pl.* -ean -eachan, *s.f.* Ham or hough of a beast. 2 Hoof, claw, talon. 3 Ankle and thereabouts of the human leg. 4***in derision,* Sparrow-hawk. 5** Spades. 6 Clutch. 7 Hamstring of a horse. Cha'n fhàgar s. dhiubh, *not a hoof of them shall be left.*
spéir *gen.* of speur.
speirbh,* *s.f.* Very slender leg or foot.
speirbheis,* -e, -ean, *s.f.* Sheep-shanked female.
spéird, *s.f.* Energy, force,—*Dàin I. Ghobha.*
speireach, -ich, -ichean, *s.f.* see spearrach.
speireach, -eiche, *a.* Slender-limbed. 2 Hoofed. 3 Clawed. 4 Cloven-footed. 5 Shanky. 6 Like a hawk. 7 Having houghs or hams.
spéiread, -eid, *s.m.* Strength, force, vigour. 2 Courage, bravery. 3 see spiorad.
spéireadail, -e, *a.* Spirited, bold, brave, courageous.
speireag, -eig, -an, *s. f.* Sparrow-hawk—*accipiter nisus.* (also speir-sheabhag.) 2**Slender-limbed girl. 3** Any slender-limbed creature of the feminine gender. 4**Shank.
speireagach, -aiche, *a.* Of, or belonging to sparrow-hawks. 2**Slender-limbed. 3**Shanked. 4**Having claws.
speirean,** -ein, *s.m.* Spindle-shank.
————ach, *a.* Spindle-shanked.
speirge, see speireag.
speirid,* *s.f.* Energy. 2 Speed, expedition.
speirideil,* -e, *a.* Active, expeditious.
spéirleag, -eig, -an, *s.f.* Spurling.
speir-sheabhag, -aig, -an, see speireag.
speir-sheog, -oig, -an, *s.f.* see speireag.
spéis, -e, *s.f.*Liking, regard, attachment, endearment, affection, fondness, esteem. Thoir s., *bestow regard* or *affection* ; ma bheir mi s. do dh' aingidheachd, *if I regard iniquity* ; tha s. aige dhith, *he is attached to her* ; féin-s., *self-conceit.*
spéiseal, see spéiseil.
spéisealachd, *s.f ind.* Fondness, attachment. 2 Pride. 3 Esteem.
speisealta, -eilte, *a.* Clean, neat, tidy, cleanly, as a cook or housewife. 2 Well-arranged, regular. 3 Acceptable. 4 Tight. 5**Becoming, comely, having a good appearance. 6* Neatly-dressed, tasteful. Gu s., *becomingly, handsomely.*
————chd, *s.f.ind.* Cleanness, neatness. 2 Regularity, order, arrangement, comeliness, seemliness, handsomeness. 3 Tightness. 4 Fondness, attachment, state of being esteemed. 5 Tastefulness.
spéisear,** *s.m.* Admirer.
spéiseil, -e, *a.* Fond, attached, loving. 2 Loved, esteemed. 3 Estimable. 4 Acceptable. 5 Cleanly, tight, tidy. 6 Proud, having self-esteem. Tha thu agam ro s., *I esteem you very much.*
spéiseileachd, see speisealtachd.
spéis-thabhairteach, -eiche, *a.* Observant.
speubhaidh,(CR) *s.f.* Spavin—*Suth'd.*
speuc, *pr. pt.* a' speucadh, *v.a.* & *n.* Diverge, divaricate. 2 Cause to diverge. 3 Tear asunder.

speuc, see spéic.
speucach, -aiche, *a.* Diverging, divaricated. 2 Causing to diverge or divaricate. 3 Tearing asunder. 4(MS) Ansated.
speucadh, -aidh, *s.m.* Diverging, act or state of diverging. 2 Tearing, act of tearing asunder. 3 Rent. A' s—, *pr.pt.* of speuc.
speuclair, -ean, *s.m.* Pair of spectacles. 2**Spy-glass. 3**Optician. 4* Object of surprise or wonder. S.-lùghainn, *temple-spectacles.*
————each, -eiche, *a.* Spectacled, wearing spectacles.
————each, -eich, *s.m.* Optician.
————eachd, *s. f. ind.* Optician's trade. 2 Speculation. 3 Surprise.
————ean, *n.pl.* of speuclair.
speuclairiche, *s.m.* Optician.
speuclan,(DU) *s.m.* Spectacles. [In *Gairloch* spiaclan.]
speur,* -a, *s.m.* [*f.* in *Badenoch*] The sky, firmament, heavens, heights. 2 Star. 3 Climate. 4 (DU) The buttoned opening in trousers, &c. Nèamh nan speur, *the firmament ;* mar theine-speur, *like star-light, the fire-ball* ; nochdaidh na speura gnìomh a làimhe, *the firmament sheweth forth his handiwork;* a' cur speura mo chinn troimh a chéile, *muddling* or *confuseng the skies of my head—a brown study.* [*gen.* spéir.**]
speur, *v.a.* Blaspheme, swear by the heavens—*Islay & Gairloch.*
speurach, -aiche, *a.* Heavenly, celestial. 2 Ethereal, atmospheric.
speurad, -aid, see spéiread.
————ach, -aiche, *a.* see spéireadail.
speuradair, -ean, *s.m.* Star-gazer, astrologer. 2 Astronomer. 3 Meteorologist. 4 Blasphemer.
————eachd, *s.f.ind.* Star-gazing, astrology. 2 Astronomy. 3 Meteorology. 4 *Oaths. 5 Aeroscopy.
speuradh,* -aidh, *s.m.* Blasphemy, an oath by heaven—*Argyll.*
speuraibh, *dat.pl.* of speur.
speuraidhean, *s. pl.* of speuradh. Curses, imprecations. Used in *Gairloch*, where the occurrence of the *sing.* is rare. Thug e speuraidhean air, *he cursed and swore at him.*
speuran, *n.pl.* of speur.
speuranta, -ainte, *a.* Ethereal.
speur-bhodaich,(DU) *s.m.* Old form of buttoning usually seen in old men's garments.
speur-choimhead,* -id, *s.m.* Aeroscopy.
speur-dhealrach, -aiche, *a.* Sky-glittering.
speur-eòlach, *a.* Versed in astronomy or astrology.
speur-eòlas, -ais, *s.m.* Astronomy, astrology.
speur-ghlan, -ghlaine, *a.* Clear-skied, cloudless, serene.
speur-ghlan, *s.f.* Clear sky.
speur-ghorm, -ghuirme, *a.* Blue-skied. 2 Azure.
spiac, see speuc.
spiacach, -aiche, see speucach.
spiacair, -ean, *s.m.* see spiocair.
spiacaireachd, see spiocaireachd.
spiaclan, *Gairloch* for speuclan.
spial, see spiol.
spian, see spion.
spiantag,* -aig, -an, *s.f.* Maggot.
————ach, -aiche, *a.* Maggotty.
†spìc, -e, -ean, see spéic.
†spice,(DMK) *s.f.* Pinnacle, conical peak, anything pointed—*Caithness.*
spìceach, see spéiceach.
spiceach, see spiocach.
spìd, *s.m.* Spite, malice. 2 Reproach, shame. 3 Censure. 4 Contempt. 5 Speed, expedition. 6 Activity, quickness. 7 Preparation, order. 8*Tyranny. 9 Infamy. Cuir s. ort, *bestir yourself ;* cuir s. air siod no seo, *prepare this or that quickly ;* a' caitheadh s. orm, *using me contemptuously ;* fo d' s., *under your tyranny* or *contemptuous sway ;* duine gun s., *an inactive, weakly man.* [***s.f. & gen.* -e.]
spìdeach,** -eiche, *a.* Spiteful, malicious. 2 Shameful. 3 Reproachful. 4 Contemptible. Gu s., *spitefully.*
spìdeachas,** -ais, *s.m.* Spitefulness.

646. Spìdeag.

spideag, -eig, -an, *s. f.* Nightingale—*philomela luscinia.* 2 (AF) Robin. 3 (AF) Any delicately formed creature. 4 Any slender creature. 5 Spiteful young female. 6 Taunt, affront. 7 ††Little blow [**spìdeag.]
————ach, -aiche, *a.* Taunting, apt to taunt. 2 Spiteful, as a female. 3** Abounding in nightingales. 4 Like a nightingale. 5**Melodious.
spìdeag-Muire,(AF) *s.f.* Robin.
spideal, -eil, -an, *s.m.* Spital, hospital.
spidealach, -aich, *s.m.* Meagre, sickly creature.
spidealachd, *s.f.ind.* Contempt. 2 Reproachfulness, reproach. 3 Malicious disposition, desire of reproaching. 4 Malicious and malignant conduct. 5 Spitefulness. 6 Shamefulness.
spidean, *s.m.* Game which resembles closely the common game of "pitch and toss," the difference being that buttons are always used in place of coins. A small stick is set up as a "spid," and a line drawn at a distance of about 10 feet. At this line the players take their stand. The game is open to any number of players—in fact, the more players the better the game. Each player tosses his button at the *spid*, his object being to come as near it as possible. He whose button lies nearest the *spid* gathers the other buttons in his hands, shakes them, and finally tosses them in the air. All which fall face downwards he gathers and keeps ; the remainder are lifted by the player whose button lay second, and thrown by him, those falling face upwards being in turn claimed by him. This continues till the buttons have all been gained, the first man often getting a second throw if the buttons last so long. The players all take their stand again on the line, the last tosser of the former time being the first to play this time, and continue throwing till they have lost all their buttons, or are otherwise forced to desist.

Should the *spid* be hit fairly by any man except the first, all buttons, no matter how near, must be lifted and re-tossed. The advantages in being first man consist in the following. The first player may, if he choose, reclaim his toss by saying, "Cha luigh mi" (I shall not lie,) but if his toss be good enough, he says "Luighidh mi," (I will lie,) thus compelling all who follow to "lie," no matter how poor their attempt may be. If, however, the first player says "Cha luigh mi," those following can all say the same, till such time as someone remarks " Luighidh mi," after which they are all forced to " lie." Another advantage the first man has is, that though he strike the *spid* fair he can yet "lie." Still popular, this was one of the most cherished games of the young Gael of former times, and many were the severe thrashings meted out to them for its sake. A boy departed to school with perhaps 30 buttons on a string and returned home with none, yea, without one on his clothes, which were held in place by pieces of wood or string—*Uist Games in Celtic Review, Vol. IV.* [Called an " Uist " game in above, but it is in reality as much an English as an Uist one.]

spideig, *gen. sing.* of spideag.

spideil, -e, *a.* Reproaching, reproachful. 2 Contemptuous. 3 Censuring. 4 Clever, hasteful, business-like, making speed, making progress, quick. 5‡‡Healthy. 6 Spiteful. 7 Infamous. 8 Despicable. 9 Shameful.

spideileachd, see spidealachd.

spidich, *v.a. & n.* Speed, cause to make speed.

spid-shuileach, -eiche, *a.* Purblind.

spig,** *v.a.* Mock, scoff.

spigeil,** *a.* Mocking, scoffing.

spile,** see spalla.

spilgein, see spiligean.

spiligean, -ein, -an, *s.m.* Small grain, as of corn. 2 Thin, light grain—*W. of Ross-shire.* 3 Seedling. 4 *in derision*, Dwarfish person. 5 Single grain of oats, barley, &c. S. mullaich, *the top pickle on an ear of corn;* s. arbhair, *a grain of corn.*

——ach, -aiche, *a.* Abounding in small grains, or 2 in seedlings. 3 Like a seedling. 4 Dwarfish.

spille,** *s.f.* Measure of yarn.

†spin, *s.* Thorn.

†spineil,** *a.* Thorny.

spinn, -e, -tean, *s.f.* Measure of yarn.

spinnle, see spinn.

spìoc, -a, *s. f.* Dastardliness, cowardice. 2 Meanness, insignificancy. 3 Niggardliness.

spìocach, -aiche, *a.* Dastardly, mean-spirited, cowardly. 2 Mean, insignificant. 3 Niggardly, miserly, avaricious.

spiocadh, -aidh, *s.m.* see spioc.

spiocaiche, *s.f.* Niggardliness, stinginess, parsimony. 2 see spioc.

spiocaicheachd,** *s.f.* Avarice.

spiocaid, -e, -ean, *s.f.* Spigot, tap 2(MS)Rowel.

spiocair, -ean, *s.m.* Dastardly, mean-spirited fellow 2 Niggard, churl. 3 Insignificant fellow, dwarf, ninny.

——eachd, *s.f.ind.* Dastardliness, pusillanimity. 2 Meanness, insignificance. 3 Niggardliness, parsimony, churlishness, shabbiness

spiochag,** -aig, *s.f.* Purse, bag.

——ach, *a.* Like a purse. 2 Of a purse.

spiochan, -ain, *s.m.* Wheezing in the throat. 2 **Person who has a wheezing in the throat. 3**Purse, bag (piochan.)

——ach, -aiche, *s. f.* Having a hoarse or wheezing voice. 2 Like a purse or bag

——aich, -e, *s.f.* Continued wheezing in the throat.

spiocnard, -aird, *s.* Spikenard—*valeriana nardostachys.*

spiod, see spid.

spiod, -a, -an, see bioda.

spiod,* *v.a.* Tug, pull tightly—*Islay.*

†spiodach, -aiche, *a.* see biodach.

spiodadh,* -aidh, *s.m.* Tugging, quick pull or tug. 2 Hint. A' s—, *pr.pt.* of spiod.

spiol, *s.m.* Wool from a dead sheep, pluck. A skin of this sort (marbhchann) is often washed first in the strong lye in which clothes have been steeped for the wash. It is washed in each lather as the clothes are taken out, and after rinsing, hung on a pailing to drip and nearly dry When a skin is sufficiently dry to be plucked, it is placed on the back of a chair near the fire—the warmth makes the plucking easier—with a clean creel underneath into which the tufts of wool fall as they are plucked. The cutch, or coarse wool, remains on the skin, if the fingers are deft enough. The wool is then either teazed for carding, or dyed should it be needed for mixtures. This kind of wool is not generally considered so excellent as that shorn from the sheep, but serves admirably for tweeds, or for dyeing and mixing with the better quality of wool in common use—*K.W.G. in Mòd prize paper.*

spiol, *pr.pt.* a' spioladh, *v.a.* Pluck, pull, snatch. 2 Nibble, bite at. 3 Peel. 4 Unshell, as an egg. 5 Tease, carp. 6 Grasp. 7 Browse, as cattle. 8* Pick in a childish way.

spiolach, -aiche, *a.* Plucking, snatching, that plucks or snatches, tugging. 2 Nibbling, biting at. 3 Grasping. 4 Browsing.

——adh, -aidh, see spioladh.

spiolachair, -ean, *s. m.* see spiolachan. 2 One who digs out of the earth.

——eachd, see spioladaireachd.

spiolachan, -ain, -an, *s.m.* One that nibbles or bites at anything. 2 Dwarfish person. 3** Spaddle. 4 Instrument to pluck or dig with.

spioladair, -ean, *s.m.* One that plucks, or tugs, plucker, snatcher. 2 Pair of pincers, forceps, or nippers. 3 Teaser, carper.

spioladaireachd, *s.f.ind.* Continual plucking or snatching. 2 Tugging. 3 Constant nibbling at anything.

spioladh, -aidh, *s.m.* Plucking, act of plucking or snatching. 2 Nibbling, act of nibbling or biting at anything. 3 Carping. 4 Grasping. 5 Browsing. 6 Snatch, tug, pluck. 7 Tugging, picking. A' s—, *pr.pt.* of spiol.

spiolag, -aig, -an, *s.f.* Snatch, slight bite, small crumb, as of bread. 2 Little mouthful of anything. S. tombaca, *a chew of tobacco.*

——ach, -aiche, *a.* Plucking or biting slightly. 2 Abounding in small crumbs.

——an, (DMK) *s. m.* Grain, as of oats, hand-shelled for eating. 2 Hand-shelling of grain and eating the kernel.

spiolaich, *v.* see spiol.

——te, *past pt.* of spiolaich.

spiol-bhòt,** *s.m.* Boot-jack.

spiolg, *pr pt.* a' spiolgadh, *v.a.* Unhusk, unshell.

——ach, -aiche, *a.* Shelling, that shells or unhusks.

——adh, -aidh, *s.m.* Unhusking, act of unhusking or shelling. A' s—, *pr.pt.* of spiolg. A' s. nam faochag, *shelling the winkles.*

——air, -ean, *s.m.* One who unhusks or shells, husker 2 Lightly-formed person.

——aireachd, *s.f.ind.* Continued unhusking or shelling. 2 Slenderness or slightness of form.

spiolgan,** -ain, *s.m.* Plucking, tugging 2 Nippers.

spiolgta, *past pt.* of spiolg. Unhusked, shelled.

spiolta, *past pt* of spiol. Plucked, snatched. 2 Nibbled at, slightly bitten.

spìon, *pr.pt.* a' spìonadh, *v.a.* Pull, pluck up, tear. 2 Snatch. 3 Drag, tear or take away by force or violence. 3 Root. 4 Peel—*Arran.* 5††Eradicate. Na s. o m' ghaol mi, *do not tear me away from my love;* s. as a bhun e, *eradicate it, root it out;* s. an cnap, *peel*

the potato—Arran.
——ach, -aiche, *a.* Pulling, that pulls or plucks, plucking, dragging, tearing, apt to drag, pull, tug or tear.
——ach,†† -aich, -aichean, *s.f.* Plucked or emaciated creature.
†spionad, -aid, *s.m.* Sinew.
†——ach, *a.* Sinewy.
spionadair, -ean, *s.m.* One who plucks, pulls, tears, drags, or snatches away. 2**Nippers.
spionadh, -aidh, *s.m.* Plucking, act of plucking or pulling. 2 Act of snatching or taking suddenly away. 3**Motion, action. 4 Pull, pluck, tear. 3(AH)Drizzle. A' s—, *pr. pt.* of spion. S. uisge, *a slight drizzle of rain*
spionadh, -aidh, *s.m.* Plucking sheep instead of clipping—*Gairloch*,(called *rooing* in *Shetland.*) 2(DMK) Plucking feathers off birds. A' s. na circe, *plucking the hen.*
——, *3rd. pers. sing. & pl. imp.* of spion. 2 *past pass.* of spìon.
spionag,(DC) *s.f.* Poorly-nourished girl 2 Feckless person. 3 Poorly-grown tree, bush, &c.—*Argyll.*
spionaidh, *fut.aff.a.* of spion.
spionan,** -ain, *s.m.* Gooseberry-bush.
spionar, *fut.pass.* of spion.
spionn, see spionnadh.
spionna, see spionnadh.
spionnadach, -aiche, *a.* Strong, vigorous.
spionnadail,(MS) *a.* Robust.
spionnadar, -aire, *a.* see spionnadach.
spionnadh, -aidh, *s.m.* Strength, might, force, pith, power.
spionnadh-iasaid, *s. m.* Loan-strength. Gheibh cobhartach s., *a helper will get loan-strength.*
spionnag,(CR) *s.f.* Bandage round the forehead as for a headache—*Suth'd.*
spionnar,** *a.* Strong, powerful, pithy.
spionndach,* -aiche, *a.* see spionnadach.
spiontachas, see spionnadh.
spionntail,(CR) *a.* Strong—*W. of Ross.*
spionta, *past pt.* of spìon. Pulled, plucked. 2 Snatched, torn away. [chann.)
spiontach,* *s.f.* Skin-wool—*Perthshire.* (marbh-
——an,* -ain, *s.m.* Person like a plucked fowl. 2**Searcher.
spiontag, -aig, -an, *s.f.* Currant. 2 Gooseberry. 3 Particle in the throat that causes coughing. 4 Kind of maggot. 5 Small drop of rain or flake of snow preceding a shower.
——ach,** *a.* Abounding in, or pertaining to currants, &c.
spiorad, -aid, -an, *s.m.* Spirit (ghost.) 2 Spirit, mind, vigour, heart, animal spirits. 3* Spirituous liquors. S. briste, *a broken spirit* or *heart*; an S. Naomh, *the Holy Spirit*; droch s., *an evil spirit*; s. beò, *a lively spirit*; s. buidhe, *spirits of salts* (*lit.* yellow spirits.)
spioradail, -e, *a.* Spiritual. 2 Devoted to spiritual things. 3 Like a spirit. 4 Lively, spirited, courageous. Gliocas s., *spiritual understanding.*
——t, see spioradail.
spioradalachd, *s.f.ind.* Spirituality, immateriality. 2 Vigour, liveliness. 3(MS) Raciness. 4 Spiritedness.
spioradan, -ain, -an, *s.m.,dim.* of spiorad. Trifling dwarf. 2 Ghost. 3 Fairy.
spiorad-buidhe, *s.m.* Spirits of salts.
spiorad-lodain, *s.m.* Ignis-fatuus.
spiorag, see speireag.
spiorsag,** *s.f.* see speireag.
spios, -a, -an, *s.m.* see spìosradh.
——, *v.a.* Spice.
spiosach, see spìosrach.
——adh, see spìosrachadh.
spiosachan,** -ain, *s.m* Spice-box. 2 Embalmer
spiosadach,** *a.* Spicy, spiced
spiosaich, *v.a.* Spice. 2 Embalm.
spiosrach,* *s.m.* Spicery
spiosrach, -aiche, *a* Abounding in spice or spices. spiced. 2 Spicy. 3 Aromatic, perfuming.
——adh, -aidh. *s.m.* Seasoning, act of seasoning with spices. 2 Process of perfuming or embalming. A' s—, *pr.pt.* of spiosraich
——an, **-ain, *s.m.* Embalmer.
spiosrachd,** *s.f.* Embalming 2 Perfuming. 3 Spicery, perfumery. 4 State of being embalmed or perfumed.
spiosradh, -aidh, *s.m.* Spice, spicery.
——ach, -aiche, see spiosrach.
spiosraich, *pr. pt.* a' spiosrachadh *v. a.* Spice, season with spice or spices. 2 Aromatize, perfume. 3 Embalm.
——e,** *s.m.* Embalmer. 2 Perfumer.
——ear, *fut.pass.* of spiosraich.
——idh, *fut. aff. a* of spiosraich.
——te, *past pt.* of spiosraich. Aromatized. 2 Embalmed.
spiosraidh, *s.f.* Spices, spiceries.
spiothag, -aig, -an, *s.f* see spitheag.
——ach, see spitheagach.
spiothair,** *s.m.* Spy, scout.
——eachd,** *s.f.* Spying, frequent spying.
spire,(AC) *s.f.* Welkin. Mac na spire, *son of the welkin.*
spiric,-*s.* Steeple, spire. 2 Pinnacle. 3 Acme.
spiriceach,** *a.* Apeak. 2 Pertaining to, or like, a spire or steeple.
spiricean,** -ein, *s.m.* Acme. 2 Little spire or steeple.
——ach,** *a.* Having spires or steeples.
spiris, -e, -ean, *s.f.* Hen-roost, cock-loft. 2 Hammock. 3* Spire.
spiriseach,-eiche,*a.* Having roosts or hammocks. 2 Like a roost or hammock. 3**Conical.
spirlinn,** s. Fall. 2 Chance.
spirseag,** -an, *s.f.* Sparrow-hawk.
——ach,** *a.* Like a sparrow-hawk. 2 Abounding in sparrow-hawks.
spisneachail, *s.f.* Aromatization.
spisnich, see spiosraich.
spisniche,(AC)*s.m.* Prop, pillar, column,support.
spisreadh, -idh, -idhean, *s.m.* see spiosradh.
spiteal, -il, *s.f.* Spittal.
spitheag, -eig, -an, *s. f.* Small bit of wood. 2 Small stone to throw with the hand, pebble. 3 Bite, nip, pinch. 4**Flake
——ach, -aiche, *a.* Full of small pieces of wood. 2 Full of small stones or pebbles, pebbled. 3 That nips or pinches.
spitheagaich, *v.a.* Bite, pinch.
——, *s.f.* Pinching, nipping.
spithear,** *s.m.* Emissary, scout.
spiul, see spiol.
spiulgan, -ain, *s.m.* see spiolgan.
spiuthair,(MS) s.*m*, Filcher, robber, depredator.
spiuthaireachd, *s.f.* Depredation.
splad, -aid, *s m* Squash. 2 Fall, tumble, falling flatly on the ground. 3**Noise, as of a door shutting. 4 Bang
splad,** *v.a. & n.* Fall. 2 Bang. 3 Slam, shut as a door with violence.
splaid, *s m.* Thud. Thuit e le s. air an ùrlar, *he fell with a thud on the floor*—as when a child falls flat in running, or a door is suddenly shut by the wind, &c. [McL & D gives *souse* in Eng.-Gael. part.]
splaid,* *v.* see splad.
splaidse, *s.f.* Squelch, squash.
——ach, *a.* Squashing.
——adh, *s.m.* Squash.
splaidseil,(DU) *a.* Falling with a thud. 2 Bang-

ing, as a door with the draught.
†splang,* s.f. Sparkle, flash, blaze.
†———,* v.n. Sparkle, flash.
splang,(DC) s.m. Share, lot, as of fish, &c. 2 (DMy) The belly from the ribs to the thighs of a person or animal. The region of the fat on the *maodal* of sheep or cattle.
———ach,** s.m. Nill. 2**Ashes of a smithy.
———adh,** -aidh, s.m. Sparkling, blazing, flashing
splangaid, -ean, s.m. Snot, mucus, phlegm.
———each, -eiche, a. Snotty, mucous, phlegmatic.
———eachd, s.f ind. Snottiness, phlegminess.
spleacan,(AC) see sleabhag.
splèachd, pr.pt a' spleachdadh, see spleuchd.
spleachdair, see spleuchdair.
spleadh,* v. Fall with a crash.
spleadh, -a, -an, s.m. Romance, fiction, tale. 2 Ostentation, boasting, vain-glory, hyperbole. 3 Falsehoods told with a view to flatter. 4** Flattery. 5 Dependance. 6 Exploits. 7 Splay-foot. 8* Enormous splay-foot. Cum a staigh do spleadhan, *keep in your ugly feet*, or *toes*.
———ach, -aiche, a. Fabulous, fictitious, romantic. 2 Given to fiction. 3 Ostentatious, boasting, gasconading. 4 Flattering by falsehoods, dependence, hyperbole. 5††Splay-footed. 6*Having enormous feet, having ugly feet.
———achas, -ais, s.m. see spleadhaireachd.
———adair, -ean, s.m. Teller of tales or romances. 2 One fond of the marvellous. 3 Boaster, vain-glorious person. 4 One who flatters by telling falsehoods.
———adh,* s.m. Fall, crash, falling.
spleadhaich,(MS) v.n. Amplify.
spleadhair, -ean, s.m. see spleadhadair. 2 (AF) Bully, despotic man.
spleadhaireachd, s.f.ind. Romance, fictitiousness. 2 Disposition to deal in fictions or romances. 3 Disposition to flatter by retailing falsehoods. 4 Amplification. 5**Errantry. 6 *Wonder, surprising nature or quality of anything.
spleadhan, -ain, -an, s.m. Wooden paddle, used in digging for shell-fish and sand-eels.
spleadhas, see spleadhaireachd.
spleadhnach,** a. Gorgeous.
spleadhnas,†† -ais, s.m. Fiction.
spleadhnasach,†† a. Fictitious.
spleadhrach,* -aiche, a. Romantic. 2 Incredible. 3 Enormous. 4 Gasconading, romancing.
spleadhraich, s.f. see spleadhaireachd.
splèamas,†† -ais, s.m. Affected surprise, vulgar show.
spleangaid,** s.f. Snot, mucus, phlegm.
———ach,** a. Snotty, phlegmy.
spleicean, s.m. see sleabhag.
spleoid,** s.m. Satan.
spleuchd, v.a. & n. Stare, gaze. 2 Squint. 3 Spread out by trampling. 4†† Plaster awkwardly. 5*Flatten awkwardly. 6*Open one's mouth and eyes and stare like a fool.
spleuchd, -a, -an, s.m. Squintness of the eyes, squint. 2 Gaze, stare. 'S ann ort a tha 'n s., *how you do stare!*
spleuchdach, -aiche, a. Squinting, having squint eyes. 2 Staring, gazing, apt to stare or gaze 3 That spreads out by trampling. 4 Spread out by trampling. 5* Flat, ugly as stamped cloth or print. (*spleucach.)
spleuchdadh, -aidh, s.m. Squinting, act of squinting. 2 Staring, act of staring. 3 Gaze, stare. 4 Act of spreading out by trampling. A' s—, *pr.pt.* of spleuchd.
spleuchdag, -aig, -an, s.f. Squint-eyed female.
spleucdaid,* s.f. Foolish starer. (*spleucaid)
spleuchdair, -ean, s.m. Squint-eyed person, one who squints. 2 Starer, gazer. 3**Eye-glass. (*spleucair)
———eachd, s.f.ind. Staring, continued staring or gazing, 2 Squinting, habit of squinting. 3 Spreading out of anything by trampling. 4††Plastering awkwardly.
———ean, n.pl. of spleuchdair.
spleuchdan, -ain, -an, s.m. Pair of spectacles, *prov.* 2 Tobacco pouch—*Arran.*
spleuchdlan, see spleuchdan.
spliachd, see, spleuchd.
splionach,** -aich, s.m. Ill-thriven animal.
spliongag,(AH), s.f. Sharp sound produced by drawing the bulb of the middle finger quickly and firmly across the bulb of the thumb.
spliot,** v.a. Dash or throw carelessly aside.
spliùc,* s.f. Fluke of an anchor.
spliucan, see spliùchan.
———ach, see spliùchanach.
spliùchan, -ain, -an, s.m. Tobacco pouch. 2** Leather purse. 3**Bladder. (also splinchan in *Gairloch*—DU.]
spliùchanach, -aiche, a. Of, or belonging to, tobacco-pouches. 2 Like a tobacco-pouch.
spliùdrach,** -aich, s.m. Bad beer, swipes.
spliug, -a, -an. s.m. Snot. 2 Icicle. 3 Anything hanging down. S. a' choilich Fhrangaich, *the turkey cock's proboscis.*
spliug,†† -iùig, -an, s. f. Discontented look, hanging lip. 2**Wry mouth (such as is occasioned by crying. 3* Blubber-lipped person's mouth.
spliùgach, -aiche, a. Splay-footed.
spliugach, -aiche, a. Snotty. 2 Snivelling. 3 Drivelling, stupid. 4†† Discontented. 5†† Having a hanging lip.
spliugaid,* s.f. Blubbering female.
spliùgair, -ean, s.m. Splay-footed person.
spliugair, -ean, s.m. Snotty person. 2 Sniveller. 3 Driveller, idiot. 4††Blubbering fellow. 5†† Slovenly fellow.
spliùgan, -ain, s.m. Splay-footed person.
spliùig, -e, -ean, s.f. Discontented and disagreeable countenance.
spliùigeach, -eiche, a. Discontented, having a discontented and disagreeable look.
spliùigear, -ir, -an, s.m. One who has a discontented and disagreeable look. 2††Slovenly fellow.
spliut, -a, -an, s.m. Lame hand or foot. 2* Splay-foot [pliut, *a cat's paw.*]
spliut, v.a. Slop, splash. 2 Flounce. 3 Circumfuse. 4 Dash. 5††Gush out. 6* Gash.
spliutach, -aiche, a. Lame of a hand or foot. 2 ‡‡Gushing out suddenly, as any liquid, owing to the vessel containing it being broken.
spliutadh, -aidh, s.m. Gushing, act of gushing out suddenly, as liquor from a broken vessel. A' s—, *pr.pt.* of spliut.
spliutaiche, s.f. Lameness of one hand. 2 Any liquor that has been spilt by the breaking of the vessel containing it. 3 Bad or stale beer.
spliutaire,* s.m. Splay-footed man. 2 Splay-footed female.
spliutradh, -aidh, s. m. Mean and parasitical flattery. 2 Going from house to house for parasitical ends.
spòc, -a, -an, s.m. Spoke of a wheel.
spòcach, -aiche, a. Having spokes.
spoch, v.a. Address one angrily and quickly. 2 Intimidate by speaking hastily or angrily. 3 Provoke. 4 Affront. 5 Rob, spoil, despoil. 6 *Attack angrily.
spoch,(DC) s.m. Bite, blow, and especially the marks resulting—*Lochaber, Kintail,* &c. 'S

gun dìol gach rìgh 'bheir spoch aisde, (a bhoineid), *and every king who clips it will regret (his act.)—Filidh, p. 33.* 2*Sudden attack or assault, as of a cat.
spochadh, -aidh, *s.m.* Act of addressing one hurriedly or angrily. 2 Provoking, act of provoking, provocation. 3 Depredation. A' s—, *pr. pt.* of spoch.
spochanach,* *a.* Fond of picking quarrels.
————d,* *s.f.* Picking quarrels, as a feeble-natured person.
spodh, see spoth.
spodha, see spothadh.
spodhadair, see spothadair.
spodhadaireachd, see spothadaireachd.
spodhadh, see spothadh.
spog, -òig, -an, *s.f.* Claw, talon, paw. 2 *in ridicule*, the foot or hand. 3 Fluke of an anchor. 4**Spoke of a wheel. 5 Tram or shaft of a cart or barrow. 6**Clumsy leg. 7* Flat foot.
spog, *pr.pt.* a' spògadh, *v.a.* Seize upon with the claw or talon.
spogach, -aiche, *a.* Clawed, pawed, armed with talons. 2**Clumsy-footed. (spàgach.)
spògadh, -aidh, *s.m.* Act of seizing upon with the paws or talons. A' s—, *pr.pt.* of spòg.
spòg an uaireadair,(DMK) *s.f.* Hand of a timepiece—*W. coast of Ross.* S. nan uairean, *the hour-hand ;* s. nan mionaidean, *the minute-hand.*
spòg bheag,(DU) *s.f.* Hour-hand of a time-piece.
spòg mhór,(DU) *s.f.* Minute-hand of a timepiece.
spòg-na-cubhaig,§ *s.f.* Heart's ease, pansy, see bròg-na-cubhaig.
spòg-snnàmha, *s.f.* Web-foot.
spoid,** *s.f.* Hasty word.
spoidear,** -eir, *s.m.* Hasty person.
spòilinn,** *s.f.* Small joint of meat.
spoineadh,** *s.m.* Bite.
spoingeach,** see spongach.
spoinnich,* *v.* Bristle against.
spòirneach, see spàirneach.
spoithte, *a.* & *past pt.* of spoth, see spothta.
spòl, -òil, *s.m.* see spathalt.
spòld,** *s.m.* Piece of a joint of meat. S. laoigh, *a joint of veal.*
spòlda, see spathalt.
spòldaich,** *s.pl.* Slain bodies, carcases.
spoll,* -a, *s.f.* Quarter, leg or joint, as of a sheep or fowl.
spoll, *v.* see spolt.
spolla, *s.m.* spathalt. Spòlla laoigh, *a joint of veal.*
spollachdach, -aiche, *a.* Sottish, sluggish. 2 Stupid.
spollachdair, -ean, *s. m.* Stupid person, blockhead.
spolladach,* *a.* see spollachdach.
spollaidh, *s.f.* Shape of the head. Dh' aithnich mi thu air do s., *I knew you by the shape of your head.*
spollan,(DC) *s.m.* Senseless blockhead, sumph.
spòlt, *pr. pt.* a' spòltadh, *v. a.* Tear, mangle, 2 Quarter. 3 Hew down, slaughter, as in battle. 4** Abuse.
spolt, *v a.* Sprinkle, bespatter. 2 Splash, sprinkling.
spòlt, *s.m.* Piece or joint of meat.
spolta, see spòlt.
spoltach, -aiche, *a.* That hacks or hews down in battle. 2**Tearing, mangling. 3 Apt to tear, mangle or devour. 4 Abusing. 5 Devouring.
spoltach, -aiche, *a.* Sprinkling.
spòltadh, -aidh, *s.m.* Hacking, hewing down, slaying, slashing, massacring 2 Mangling, tearing. 3 Abusing. A' s—, *pr.pt.* of spòlt.
spoltadh,(CR) -aidh, *s.m.* Scattering drops of water &c. from a vessel, sprinkling—*Perthshire.* 2 Bespattering.
spoltair, *s.m.* see spultair.
spòltaidh, *fut. aff. a.* of spòlt.
spoltan,(CR) *s.pl.* Drops of water, &c. scattered from a vessel—*Perthshire.*
spòn, see spàin.
spònag,** -aig, *s.f.* Spoon, little spoon.
spong, -uing, -an, *s. m.* Sponge. 2 Tinder, pith, touchwood. 3 *in contempt*, Niggard. 4 (DMK) Excrescence that grows on the roots of birch-trees—*W. coast of Ross.* 5*Meanness.
spongach, -aiche, *a.* Spongy. 2 Niggardly, parsimonious 3 Fungous.
spongail, -e, *a.* see spongach.
spongair, -ean, *s.m.* Niggard, churl, moucher.
spongaireachd, *s.f.ind.* Niggardliness, churlishness, mean disposition.
spongairean, *n pl.* of spongair.
spongalach,** *a.* Parsimonious, niggardly, churlish.
spongalachd, see spongaireachd.
spor, -uir, *pl.* -an & -uirean, *s. m* Riding-spur. 2 Claw, talon. 3**Dew-claw. 4 Gun-flint. 5 Incitement. 6‡ Flint. 7(DU) Piece of quartz or quartzite used in lieu of flint for making a light—*Gairloch.* 8‡ Tinder. 9** Spur of a cock. 10 Goad. Spuir air a spògan, *spurs on his legs.* [* *s.f.*]
spor, *pr.pt.* a' sporadh, *v.a.* Incite, spur, push on, instigate, goad.
spor,(CR) *v. a.* Search by scratching, groping or fumbling—*Perthshire.*
sporach, -aiche, *a.* Spurred, as a horseman, having spurs. 2 Having talons or claws. 3 Having flints. 4 Like a flint. 5 That spurs or instigates. 6**Tenacious. 7**Apt to grasp, of a grasping disposition.
sporadair,** *s.m.* Spurrier, spur-maker. 2 Flint-cutter.
————eachd,** *s.f.* Spur-making. 2 Flint-cutting. 3 Greediness.
sporadh, *3rd. pers. sing. imp.* of spor. S. e, *let him spur.*
sporadh -aidh, *s.m.* Inciting, act of inciting, spurring on, instigating, goading. 2 Search, grope, fumble. A' s—, *pr. pt.* of spor.
sporag,¶ *s.f.* House-sparrow, see gealbhonn. 2 Hedge-sparrow, see gealbhonn-nam-preas.
sporaidh, *fut.aff.a.* of spor.
sporail, see sporthail.
sporalaich, see sporthalaich.
sporan, *n.pl.* of spor.
sporan, -ain, -an, *s.m.* Purse. 2 Dewlap. The sporan molach of the Gael is a purse made of badger-skin, goat-skin, &c It is fastened by a leathern belt round the waist and hangs down in front, often having tassels dangling from it.
sporan,§ (an), *s.m.* Shepherd's purse (plant), see lus-na-fola.
sporanach, -aiche, *a.* Of, or belonging to, purses. 2 Like a purse.
sporan cas feannaig, see sporan feannaig.
sporan feannaig,(DC) *s. m.* Mermaid's purse—egg of the skate or dogfish. It is enclosed in a tough, square-shaped sac, which, on development, the ovum can open from the inside. The sac has stringers for attaching itself to seaware, stones, &c.
spor-an-teintein, see losg-bra-teine.
sporas,(DU) *s.m.* see sporag.
spordhail, see sporthail.
sporg,* *v.* Ruzzle, struggle without effect.
sporgail,* *s.f.* Ruzzling noise, struggling without effect, ruzzle. A' s—, *pr.pt.* of spor.
sporraich,* *v.n.* Bristle. S. e rium, *he bristled up to me.*

spòrs, -a, *s.f.* [*m.* in *Badenoch.*] Sport, play, diversion, fun. 2 Derision, mockery, scorn. 3 Pride. Gheibh sinn s., *we shall get some fun;* 's i an s. a thug ort sin a dheanamh, *sheer pride made you do that;* luchd na s., *scorners.*
spòrsach,** -aiche, *a.* Sporting, fond of sport. 2 Playful, funny. 3 Causing sport or diversion. 4 Prone to deride or scorn.
spòrsail, -e, *a.* Sportful, jocose, merry. 2 Scornful, proud, disdainful, haughty. 3 Foppish, beauish, gallant. 4**Jeering, deriding. 5** Funny.
———**eachd**, see spòrsalachd.
spòrsair,(MS) *s.m.* Amuser.
spòrsalachd, *s.f.ind.* Sportiveness, playfulness. 2 Fastidiousness. 3 Pride, foppery. 4 Sportfulness. 5**Habit of jeering or deriding. 6** Conceitedness, haughtiness, disda nfulness. 7 (MS) Air. Fear s., *a fop.*
sporthail, *s.f.* Noise of scratching on boards. 2 (AH) Subdued rattling noise, such as is made by a stone wall about to fall, rats, mice, &c. in a hole, box, &c.
sporthail,(CR) *v.n.* Make a rustling noise in searching for anything.—*W. of Ross-shire.*
sporthalaich, *s.f.* Rustling. Crubagan a' s. 'nam faiche, *crabs making a clawing* or *rustling noise in their burrows.* A' s—, *pr. pt.* of sporthail.
spot,** *v. a.* Spot.
spot, -oit, -an, *s.m.* [*f.* in *Badenoch.*] Spot, stain, blemish. 2 Plot of ground. Air an s., *immediately.*
spotach, -aiche, *a.* Spotted, speckled. 2 Stained.
spotag, *s.f.dim.* of spot. Little speckle, blemish.
spotagach, -aiche, *a.* Spotted, blemished.
spotaich,** *v.a.* Spot, speckle, blemish.
spotaichear, *fut.pass.* of spotaich.
spotaichte, *past pt.* of spotaich.
spoth, *pr.pt.* a' spoth & a' spothadh, *v. a.* Geld, castrate, spay. 2* Prepare straw for thatch. S. an t-sìl, *separate the grain from the straw and beard after the threshing is over*—DMy.
spoth, *s.m.* see spothadh.
spothadair, -ean, *s.m.* Gelder.
spothadaireachd, *s.f.ind.* Operation or business of gelding or castrating.
spothadh, -aidh, *s.m.* Gelding, castrating, spaying. 2 Castration. A' s—, *pr.pt.* of spoth.
spothaidh, *fut. aff.a.* of spoth.
spothar, *fut.pass.* of spoth.
spothta, *past pt.* Gelded, castrated. 2*Prepared for thatch, as straw. 3* Very bare, as a measure.
†**sprac**,** -a, *s.m.* Spark. 2 Life. 3 Motion.
spracach,** *a.* Strong, vigorous.
spracadh, -aidh, *s.m.*Strength, vigour, exertion, sprightliness, boldness, courage.
spracail, -e, *a.* Strong, active, powerful. 2 Commanding
spracalachd, *s.f.ind.* Strength, activity, exertion.
spraic, -e, -ean, *s.f.* Reprimand, severe or harsh reproof. 2 Frown. 3 Imperious mandate. 4 Vigour. 5 Exertion, effort. 6**Sprightliness. 7* Augury. 8 Authoritative tone of voice and attitude. 9* Cleverness.
spraiceach, -eiche, *a.* see spraiceil.
spraicealachd, *s.f.ind.* Habit of reproving with harshness or severity. 2 Habit of frowning or threatening by looks. 3 Imperiousness in ordering. 4 Habit of perseverance. 5††Severe censoriousness. 6**Arbitrariness. 7**Vigorousness. 8**Much exertion, frequent exertion. 9**Frequent scolding.
spraiceil, -e, *a.* Reprimanding severely or harshly, scolding. 2 Inclined to reprove severely or harshly. 3 Frowning. 4 Imperious, uplifted, proud. 5 Harsh, severe. 6 Vigorous, strong, powerful, lively, active, energetic. 7 Persevering. 8**Passionate. 9 **Sprightly. 10 Arbitrary. 11 Authoritative, commanding.
spraid,** *s.f.* Blast, puff. 2 Report of a gun.
spraidh, -ean, *s. m.* Loud blast. 2 Shot, report of a gun. 3 Any loud and sudden sound. 4 **Crack. 5**Jerk. 9 Explosion.
spraidheach, -eiche, *a.* see spraidheil.
spraidheil, -e, *a.* Loud, as a blast. 2 Squally. 3 Causing any loud or sudden sound. 3 Sounding, as the report of a gun. 4 Blustering.
spraigh, *v.n.* see spreadh.
spraigheadh,* -eidh, *s. m. & pr. pt.* of spraigh, see spreadhadh.
spreadh, *pr.pt.* a' spreadhadh, *v. a. & n.* Burst. 2 Emit a loud sound in bursting. 2 Kill, despatch, finish. 4 Scatter, dismiss, disband. 5 ††Explode. 6(DMy) Spray.
spreadh,** *s.m.* Crack. 2 Stirring up, provocation. 3 Rude onset, sudden onset, as of two fowls fighting, sudden shock. 4 (DMy) Spraying. 5(DU) Explosion.
spreadh,(DC) -an, *s.m.* Sherds, fragments.
spreadhadair,* -ean, *s.m.* Cartridge.
spreadhadh, -aidh, *s.m.* Bursting, act of bursting. 2 Act of emitting a sound in bursting. 3 Killing, act of killing, finishing or despatching one. 4 Sudden and hard blow. 5 Loud, sudden sound, noise. 6 Scattering, dismissing, disbanding. 7 Activity. 8††Life. A' s—, *pr. pt.* of spreadh.
spreadhan, -ain, *s.m.* Potsherd.
spreadhan, *s.m.* Pot for melting cod-liver. or for roasting or frying, frying-pan. 2(DMK)Vessel to hold oil for anointing wool—*Lochbroom.* 2 see spreighean.
spreadhta, *past pt.* of spreadh. Burst suddenly. 2 Scattered, disbanded.
spreag, see spreig.
spreagach, -aiche, see spreigeil.
spreagachadh, -aidh,*s.m.& pr.pt.* of spreagaich, see spreigeadh.
spreagadh, -aidh, *s.m. & pr.pt.* see spreigeadh.
spreagaich, for spreigich, see spreig.
spreagail,** *a.* Bold, active, smart.
spreagair, -ean, *s. m.* Reprover. 2 Inciter, provoker.
spreagaireachd, see spreigealachd.
spreagan‡‡ -ain, -an, see spreangan.
spreamb,** *v.a.*Tighten one's clothes about one, confine oneself with tight clothes.
spreambach,** *a.* Drawing one's clothes tightly about one.
spreangan, -ain, -an, *s.m.* Cloven stick used to close the wound when cattle are bled.
spréid,(AF) *s.f.* Flock of sheep.
spréid, *v.* Gaelic spelling of *spread.—Perthshire.*
spréideach, *a.* Spreading, apt to spread or diffuse.
spréidh, -e, *s.f.coll.* Cattle of any kind. 2 (AF) Sheep. 3 Live-stock. 4 (AF) Marriage portion of cattle.
spreidh, see spreadh.
spréidh,(AF) *s.f.* Shoal of fish.
spréidheach, -eiche, *a.* Abounding in cattle. 2 Having many cattle.
spréidte, *past pt.* of spréid. Spread out.
spreig, *pr.pt.* a' spreigeadh, *v.a.* Blame, chide, reprove, scold, accuse. 2 Prompt, incite, stir up, instigate. 3 Enforce, press. 4 Divulge anything you are enjoined to keep secret. 5 (MS) Pronounce. 6 Govern, in *grammar.* 7 ††Enforce with words.
spreige,** *s.f.*Disparagement. 2‡‡Reproof, scold, accusation. 3(DU) *pl.* spreigeachan, Sparable

for a boot.
spreigeach, -eiche, *a.* Inclined to scold, blame or accuse. 2 Enforcing. 3 Expressive. 4 Forcible. 5 Active, in *grammar.*
spreigeadh, -idh, -ean, *s. m.* Blaming, accusation, act of blaming, reproving, chiding or scolding. 2 Inciting, act of inciting, prompting, instigating or stirring up. 3 Enforcing. pressing, act of enforcing. 4 Reproof, scold. 5*Pith, energy. 6* Divulging a secret. A' s—, *pr.pt.* of spreig. Mòine gun s., *pithless peats.*
spreigealachd, *s.f.ind.* Habit of reproving, reprimanding, chiding or scolding. 2 Tendency or readiness to reprove, reprimand, chide or scold. 3 Proud language, insolence of speech. 4 Boldness, audacity, undauntedness. 5 Activity. 6 Authoritativeness, imperiousness. 7 Provoking, provocation.
spreigeanta, -einte, *a.* see spreigeil.
————chd, see spreigealachd.
spreigear, *fut. pass.* of spreig.
spreigearra,** *a.* Scolding. 2 Smart in speech, expressive, forcible. Beurla s., *expressive English ; expressive language.*
spreigearrachd, *s.f.* Scolding 2 Smartness of language, expressiveness of speech.
spreigeil, -e, *a.* Reproving, censuring, blaming. 2 Prone to reprove, censure or blame. 3 Scolding, prone to scold. 4 Authoritative, imperious. 5 Bold, undaunted. 6 Active, lively, smart, energetic. 7 Vehement.
spreigeileachd, see spreigealachd.
spreigh, *v.* see spreadh.
spréigh, *s.f.* see spréidh.
spréigh, *s.* Velocity. 2 Gallant movement. 3 Gliding. *Sàr-Obair.*
spreigheadh, -idh, *s.m. & pr. pt.* of spreigh, see spreadhadh.
spreighean,(DMK) *s.m.* see spreadhan.
spreighich, -e, *s.f.* see spreadhadh.
spreighte, *past pt.* of spreigh, see spreadhta.
spreigich,** *v.a.* Reprove. 2 Provoke.
spreigich, *v.a.* see spreig.
spreigichidh, *fut.aff.a.* of spreigich.
spreigidh, *gen.sing.* of spreigeadh. Cha bu tu fhéin crìoch t' aobhar spreigidh air sluagh ach teicheadh gu 'n tearamunn, *you were not yourself the aim of your inciting of the people, but they to flee to their protector—Dàin Iain Ghobha.*
spreigidh, *fut.aff.a* of spreig.
spreill, -e, -ean, *s.f.* Blubber-lip. 2 The tongue hanging out in contempt, or from discontent.
spreilleach, -eiche, *a.* Blubber-lipped.
spreilleachd,***s.f.*The deformity of blubber-lips.
spreilleag,** -eig, *s.f.* Blubber-lipped female.
spreillear, -eir, *pl.* -a & -an, *s.m.* Blubber-lipped fellow.
spreilleasachadh,(MS) *s.m.* Distortion.
spreòcainn, *s.m.* Sick person, valetudinarian. 2 Any fragile or tender thing—*Skye.*
spreochainn,(MS) *s.f.* Strength.
spreòchan, -ain, *s. f.* Weakness, pithlessness, langour. 2 Weakling, weakly, decayed or decrepit person, infirm old person (most frequently applied to a female.) 3††Weak exertions. 4* Person or thing hardly hanging together. [*spreochainn.] S. truagh caillich, *an infirm old woman.*
spreòchanach, -aiche, *a.* Languid, decayed, decrepit from age, infirm, weak. 2** Imbecile. Gu s., *feebly.*
spreòchanachd, *s.f.* Weakness, infirmity, debility. 2**Imbecility. 3††Weak efforts.
spreòchanta, -ainte, *a.* see spreòchanach. 2** Piping.
spreòchantachd, see spreòchanachd.
spreòchdainn, *s.m.* see spreòcainn.
spreòd, *pr.pt.* a' spreòdadh, *v.a* Incite, set on. excite, provoke, goad on. 2 Abuse by words. 3 Enforce.
spreòd, -eòid, -an, *s.m.* Projecting beam. 2†† Bowsprit. Crann spreòid, *the bowprit of a ship.* (also spreod.)
spreòd,(CR) *v.a.* Spread (peats to dry, &c.)—*Arran.*
spreòdach,†† *a.* Exciting.
spreòdadh, -aidh, *s.m.* Exciting, act of exciting or inciting. 2 Provoking, act of provoking. 3 Abusing, act of abusing by words. 4 Cavilling. 5 Censuring. A' s—, *pr.pt.* of spreòd.
spreòdaich,(MS) *v.a.* Animate. 2 Tempt.
spreòid,** *v.a.* Cavil, censure.
spreòid, see spreòd & spreòit.
spreòit,** *s.m.* Useless thing. 2 Idler, drone. 3 Fragment. 4 see spreòd.
spreòtadh, see spreòdadh.
sprineag,** -eig, -an, *s.f.* Pebble.
sprineagach, *a.* Pebbly
spriollag,(MS) *s. f.* Boutefeu, incendiary. 2 Quarreler. 3 Baffler. 4 Wag.
spriollagach, *a.* Waggish.
spriong,** *v.a.* Wrinkle, corrugate.
spriong,** *s.m.* Wrinkle, corrugation.
spriongach,** *a.* Wrinkling, corrugating.
spriongadh,** *s.m.* Corrugation, wrinkling.
sprios,** -a, *s.m.* Twig, wicker. 2 Bramble.
spriosach,** *a.* Abounding in, of, or pertaining to, twigs or wicker.
spriosan,** -ain, *s.m.* Small twig or wicker. 2 Bramble. 3 Poor, diminutive creature. 4 *n. pl.* of sprios.
spriosanach,** *a.* Like a twig. 2 Diminutive. 3 Slender.
spriuchar,** -air, *s.m.* Sting.
spriudhan,(DC) -ain, *s. m.* Thin, undeveloped arms, legs, &c. 2 Stunted bushes, &c.
spriumhachan,** *s.m.* Budget.
spriunan,§ -ain, *s.m.* Red or white currant, see raosar dearg & raosar geal.
spriùnanach,** -aiche, *a.* Abounding in, of, or like, currants.
spriùtan,** -ain, *s.m.* Finger-end. 2 *in ridicule,* Finger, hard finger.
spriùtanach,** *a.* Hard-fingered.
sproch,** -a, *s.m.* Robbery.
sprochadh,** -aidh, *s.m.* Robbing.
sprochaill, see sprogaill.
sprochailleach, see sprogailleach.
sprochair, -ean, *s.m.* Robber.
————eachd,** *s.f.* Robbery. 2 Commission of robbery.
sprochd, *s.m.* Sadness, dejection, lowness of spirits, melancholy. 2 Bitterness. 3 Lament. Tog s. an laoich, *raise the hero's lament ;* a chuir m' anam fo s., *that brought sadness on my soul.*
sprochdach, -aiche, *a.* see sprochdail.
sprochdail, -e, *a.* Sad, dejected, in low spirits. 2 Causing sorrow or dejection. 3 Melancholy, mournful.
sprochdaileachd, see sprochdalachd.
sprochdalachd, *s.f.* Dejection of spirits or mind, mournfulness.
sprodh,** -a, -an, *s.m.* Sprat.
sprodhach, *a.* Abounding in, or of sprats. 2 Like a sprat.
sprodhan,** -ain, *s.m.* Young sprat.
spròg(CR) *s.*Sturdy, a disease of sheep—*Arran.*
spròg,* *s.* Dewlap.
sprogail, *Suth'd* for brogail.
sprogaill, -e, -ean, *s.f.* Crop of a bird. 2 Dewlap of cattle. 3 Double chin. 4**Cock's comb or

or st. [In *N. Argyll* dewlap and double chin are sprogan—AH.]
sprogailleach, -eiche, *a.* Having a large crop, dewlap or double chin. 2 Like a crop or dewlap. 3 Hanging down, as a dewlap or bird's crop.
sprogan, -ain, -an, *s.f.* see sgròban & sprogaill. 2(DC) Small tuft of hair under the chin of a deer. extended in use to a goat and a ram. Greim air s. a' Bhlàir, *hold of Blair's whisker—Fionn an Taigh a' Bhlàir bhuidhe*
sproganach, -aiche, *a.* see sgròbanach.
spronnag,** *s.f.* see spronnan.
spronnan,‡ -ain, *s. m.* Crumb. 2 *pl.* Crumbs, fragments. 3 Refuse.
spronnanach, -aiche, *a.* Abounding in small crumbs or fragments.
sproth, see sprodh.
spruacach,** *a.* Pettish.
spruacanach,** *a.* Pettish.
spruacanachd,** *s.f.* Pettishness.
spruan, -ain, -an, *s.m.* Brushwood, firewood. 2 *Shortbread. 3††Crumbs.
spruanach, -aiche, *a.* Abounding in brushwood or firewood.
spruanach, -aich, *s. m.* Quantity of brushwood.
spruchag,(CR) *s.f.* Hoard, savings—*S. end of Arran.*
sprùdan,‡ *s.pl.* Fingers, sprouts.
sprudhan, * *s.m.* see spruileach.
sprùidhean,** -ein, -an, *s.m.* Claw, paw, clutch. 2 *in derision*, The fingers.
sprùidheanach, *a.* Clawed, pawed, having hard fingers.
sprùidheanachd, *s.f.* Pawing or fingering clumsily.
spruidhleach, -eiche, see spruileach.
spruileach, -eiche, *s. m.* Fragments, crumbs, refuse.
offals.
spruileach, *v.a.* Distinguish.
spruille,** *s.f.* Crumbs, fragments, dross, refuse.
spruilleag, -eig, -an,*s.m.*Small crumb, fragment, offal.
spruilleagach, -aiche, *a.* Full of small crumbs or fragments. 2(MS) Roguish.
spruis,** *s.f.* Spruce (tree.)
spruisealachd, *s. f. ind.* Neatness. spruceness, trimness.
spruiseil, -e, *a.* Spruce, neat, well-dressed. Gu s., *tidily.*
sprunnan, see spronnan.
————-ach, see spronnanach.
spruthan, see spruan.
spuac,(MS) *v.a*, Strike. 2 Swaddle. (spuaic.
spuacach,** *a.* Pettish. 2 (DU) Shy and awkward, diffident.
spuacachadh, *pr.pt.* of spuacaich.
spuacadh, -aidh, *s.m.* Breaking, act of breaking or splintering. 2 Act of thumping or knocking on the head. 3 Act of blistering or raising blisters or pustules on the skin. 4 State of becoming blistered. 5 Daubing or plastering awkwardly. A' s—, *pr.pt.* of spuaic.
spuacaich, *pr.pt.* a' spuacachadh, *v.a.* Dint.
spuaic, *pr. pt.* a' spuacadh, *v.a. & n.* Break or splinter 2 Thump, knock on the head. 3 Blister, raise blisters or pustules on the skin. 4 Become blistered or covered with blisters or pustules. 5* Plaster awkwardly with all your might. 6 ††Smudge. 7 Bruise, maul.
spuaic, -e, -ean, *s.f.* The crown of the head. 2 Pinnacle of a tower. 3 Callosity, kind of swelling. 4 Blister, pustule. 5 Scab. 6††Speck. 7 Smudge. 8** Blue mark. 9 (CR) Mole or spot on the face—*Suth'd.* 10**Pettishness. 11 ††Wound. 12* Bruise, maul. 13* Tumour on the side of the head. S. theanga, *a disease in cattle.*
spuaiceach, -eiche, *a.* Breaking, that breaks or splinters. 2 Thumping, that thumps or knocks. 3 Blistered, having blisters or pustules. 4 Causing blisters. 5‡‡ Scabbed. 6**Bruising, mauling. 7**Pinnacled.
spuaicearra, *a.* see spuaiceach. 2**Pettish.
spuaichdeach, see spuaiceach.
spuaiche,** *s.f.* Pet, pettishness.
spuaicheach, *a.* Pettish.
spucaid,* -e, *s.f.* Wheal. 2.(DU) Pustule.
spuch, *pr pt.* a' spuchadh, *v.a.* Strike with the paw, as a cat.
spùd,** *s.m.* Balderdash.
spudan, *s.m.* Chute of a still (p. 731.)
spuidreach,** -ich, *s.m.* Slip-slop.
spuidsear, *s.m.* Baling-dish for a boat. 2 Bucket with a wooden handle to lift water from the sea—*Arran.* 3(AH) Watering-can.
spùill, -e, -ean, *s.f.* see spùinn.
spùill, *pr.pt.* a' spùilleadh, see spùinn.
spùille, see spùinn.
spùilleach, see spùinneach.
spùilleadair, see spùinneadair.
spùilleadaireachd, see spùinneadaireachd.
spuilleadh, see spùinneadh.
spùillean, -e, -ean, see spùinn.
spùillear, see spùinneadair.
————, *fut.pass.* of spùill.
spùillearachd, see spùinneadaireachd,
spùillearan, *n.pl.* of spùillear.
spùille-chogadh, see spùinne-chogadh.
spuillinn, see spùinne.
spuillir(e)-buidhe,(AF) *s.m.* Marsh harrier.
spuing,§ -ean, *s.f.* Cork-like fungus growing on trees—*polyporus.* 2 Sponge. 3 Tinder, touchwood. 4 *in derision,* Niggard.
spuing, *gen.sing.* of spong.
spuingealachd,** *s.f.* Sponginess. 2 Parsimoniousness, niggardliness.
spuingeil,** *a.* Spongy. 2 Parsimonious, niggardly.
spuinn, -e, -ean, *s.f.* Spoil, booty, plunder. 2 Capture. 3 Burglary, robbery. [** gives *nom.* spùinne.]
spùinn, *pr.pt.* a' spùinneadh, *v.a.*Spoil, plunder, rob. 2 Deprive of anything. An s. duine Dia? *shall a man rob God?*
spùinneach, -eiche, *a.* Spoiling, robbing, plundering 2 Having much spoil or plunder.
spùinneadair, -ean,*s.m.* Robber, plunderer, spoiler. 2 Brigand.
spùinneadaireachd, *s.f* Robbing, spoiling, plundering, robbery, practice of robbery.
spùinne-chogadh,** -aidh, *s.m.* Predatory warfare.
spuinneadairean, *n.pl.* of spùinneadair.
spùinneadh, -aidh, *s.m.* Plundering, act of plundering, robbing or spoiling. 2 Depriving, act of depriving or taking away 3 Spoil, booty, robbery. A' s—, *pr.pt.* of spùinn.
spùinnear, -ir, -an, see spùinneadair. 2 *fut.pass.* of spùinn.
spùinnear, *s.m.* Tarry rope—*Arran.*
spùinnearach, *a.* Piratical.
spùinnearachd, see spùinneadaireachd.
spùinnearan, *n.pl.* of spùinnear.
spuir,* *gen.sing. & n.pl.* of spor.
spuir, see spor. S. na h-iolaire, *the eagle's claw.*
spuirean, *n.pl.* of spor.
spuirse, *s.f.ind.* Spurge, milkweed—*euphorbia exigua & e. helioscopia.*
spuirseach, -eiche, *a.* Abounding in spurge. 2 Like spurge or milkweed.
spuis, -e, -ean, *s.f.* Pocket.
spulgan,(DU) *s.m.* Kiln-dried corn. 2 Small

quantity taken and eaten after husking with the teeth. Used collectively, see spiolgan.
spull,* s.f. Nail of a cat. 2 Clutch. 3††Cat's claw.
spullach,* -aiche, a. Nailed. 2 Greedy.
spullach,* -aich, s.m. Greedy, monopolizing female. [*s.f.]
spullair,* -ean, s.m. Greedy man.
spult, v.a. Spatter, bedabble, sprinkle. 2 Splash. sprinkle. 3 Tear, mangle. (also spolt.)
spult,** s.m. Splash, sprinkling. (also spolt.)
spultach, a. Splashing, bespattering, sprinkling. 2 Tearing, mangling. 3 Devouring. (also spoltach.)
spultadh, -aidh, s.m. Respersion. 2 Splashing. sprinkling. 3**Aspersion. 4 Tearing, mangling. A' s—, pr.pt. of spult. (also spoltadh.)
spultaidh, fut.aff.a. of spult.
spultair,** s.m. Dabbler, one who splashes or bespatters. 2 Tearer. mangler. (also spoltair.)
spultaireachd,** s.f. Splashing, bespattering, sprinkling. 2 Tearing, mangling.
spultairean, n.pl. of spultair.
spultar, a. Apt to splash or bespatter.
spultar, fut.pass. of spult.
spungail,** a. Niggardly, churlish. (spongach.)
spungair,** -ean, s.m. Niggard, churl.
spungaireachd, s.f. Niggardliness, churlishness.
spungairean, n.pl. of spungair.
spungalachd, s.f. Niggardliness.
spuran, see sporan.
spursan, -ain, -an, see spàrsan.
spursanach, see spàrsanach.
spurt, see spòrs.
sput,** s.m. Eunuch.
spùt,(DMK) s. The smallest particle. Cha'n 'eil s. céille aige, *he has not the smallest particle of sense—W. coast of Ross.*
spùt, -a, -an, s.m. Spout, spout of water. 2 Pour of rain. 3 Flux. 4 Cascade. 5 *in contempt*, Bad drink. 6(DMy) Disease in cattle, diarrhœa in cattle or sheep. Bò s., uan s., *a cow with diarrhœa, a lamb with diarrhœa*; tobraichean 'nan spùtaibh dian, *fountains in impetuous torrents*; gunna-spùt, *a syringe*. [** gives *gen.* spùit.]
spùt, pr.pt. a' spùtadh, v.a. & n. Spout, pour out, squirt.
spùtach, -aiche, a. Spouting, squirting, that spouts or squirts. 2 Sloppy, miry or vapid (of drink.) 3**Pouring. 3 (DU) Worthless, contemptible.
spùtachan, -ain, -an, s.m. Syringe, squirt. Gunna spùtachain, *a syringe.*
spùtadh, -aidh, s.m. Spouting, act of spouting or squirting. 2 Pour of water. 3 Torrent, cascade. A' s—, pr.pt. of spùt.
spùtaidh, fut.aff.a. of spùt.
sputair,* -ean, s.m. Bird. 2 Syringe.
spùtan, -ain, -an, s.m., dim. of spùt. Small spout or squirt. 2 Small cascade, jet or rill. 3 Syringe.
spùtanach, -aiche, a. Full of little spouts, squirts or cascades. 2 Like a syringe.
spùtar, fut.pass. of spùt.
spùtarsaich,** s.f. Slip-slop.
sputhuinn, (CR) s. Straw not threshed but seedless—*Argyll.* 2 (DC) Straw drawn and combed for thatch.
srabag,(AF) s.f. Cockle.
srabadh,** s.m. Abstertion.
sràbh, -àibh, -an, s.m. Straw. 2††Straw fuse for blasting. 3**Plenty. 4 Falling water. A' trusadh nan s. agus a' leigeil nam boitean leis an abhainn, *gathering straws and allowing the trusses to go with the stream*; s. uisge, *water pouring, as from the roof of a house.* [*pl.* in *Gairloch* sràibhean—DU.]
sràbh,* v.a. Scatter here and there.
srabhach, -aiche, a. Strawy, full of straws. 2 Like a straw. 3* Scattered. 4**Plentiful. 5 Squandering.
sràbhadh,** s.m Diffusion.
sràbhag, -aig, -an, s.f. dim. of sràbh. Little straw. 2 Straw laid on wood in a kiln under the grain.
sràbhagach, -aiche, a. Full of little straws.
†srabhan, -ain, s m Superfluity.
sràbhan, -ain, -an, s.m. Little straw. 2 *pl.* of of sràbh. 3 (DU) Broken straw mixed with kiln-dried corn.
sràbhanach, -aiche, a Full of little straws.
sràbhard, s.m. Quarrel, dispute, riot—*Rob Donn.*
srac,(DU) v.a. Stroke with a tawse, &c
srac, pr.pt. a' sracadh, v.a. & n. Tear, rend, cut asunder. 2 Rob, spoil, plunder.
srac, sraic, s m. Noise of cloth in the act of tearing 2 Noise made by a scythe in the process of mowing. 3 Prattling.
sràc,(DU) s.m. Stroke given with a tawse or rod. 2 Strickle for sharpening a scythe. S. spealain, *scythe-strickle.*
sracach, -aiche, a. Tearing, that tears or rends. 2 Full of rents. 3**Apt to tear.
sracadair, see sracair.
————eachd, see sracaireachd.
sracadh, -aidh, s.m. Tearing, act or state of tearing or rending, rent, tearing, cutting asunder, fissure. 2 Robbing, act of robbing or plundering. 3 Twig, shoot, sprout. 4**Pulling. 5** Fissure, tear, rent. 6 Robbery, spoil, extortion. A' s—, pr. pt. of srac.
sracadh,(DU) s.m. Act of striknig with a tawse or rod.
sracair, -ean, s. m. Tearer, render, one who tears or rends. 2 Spoiler, robber. 3 Champion. 4 Extortioner.
sràcair,** s.m. Gossip.
sracaireach, -eiche, a. Tearing, rending. 2 Given to extortion. 3 Given to fighting.
sracaireachd, s.f. Tearing, continued tearing or rending. 2 Habit of tearing. 3 Extortion, 4 Hard fighting. 5 Oppression.
sràcaireachd,** s.f. Gossiping.
sracanta,* -ainte, a. Turbulent. 2 Oppressive, apt to extort. 3 Vigorous, stout. 4 Tearing. (see sracaireach.)
sracantachd, see sracaireachd.
srachd, see srac.
———ach, see sracach.
———air, see sracair
———aireach, see sracaireach.
———aireachd, see sracaireachd.
srachdta, see sracta.
sracta, past pt. of srac. Torn. 2 Spoiled, robbed.
srad, pr.pt. a' sradadh, v.n. Sparkle, emit sparks, strike fire. 2††Run swiftly.
srad, -aid & -a, pl, -an, s. f. Spark of fire. 2 *Quick temper. 3**Drop.
srada-bianain, s.f.pl. Ignis-fatuus.
sradach, -aiche, a. Emitting sparks. 2 Full of sparks.
sradadh, -aidh, s.m. Sparkling, act of sparkling or emitting sparks. A' s—, pr.pt. of srad.
sradag, -aig, -an, s.f.dim. of srad. Little spark. 2 Nettle—*Hebrides*, see deanntag. Beum nan sradagan, *the stroke that causes sparks.*
sradagach, -aiche, a. Emitting sparks. 2 Full of sparks.
sradaich,(MS) v.n. Glisten.
sradanta,* -ainte, a. Quick-tempered.
sradrach,* -aich, s.f. Sparkle. 2 Half inebriety

sràibhlean, -ein, -an, *s.m.* Little straw. 2 Single straw.
———ach, -aiche, *a.* Abounding in little straws.
sràid, -e, -ean, *s.f.* Street, lane. 2 Walk, promenade, saunter, act of walking, as for exercise. 3 Row, rank. S.-leth-taoibh, *a by-street ;* mar pholl nan sràidean, *like the mire of the streets;* gabh s., *take a walk.*
sràid,* *v.n.* Walk, pace. 2* Walk the streets.
——each, -eiche, *a.* Full of streets. 2 Having many or fine streets. 3 Like a street. 4‡‡ Walking, fond of walking.
——,* *s.m.* Lane.
sràideachan, -ain, *s.m.* Saunterer. 2 Vagabond.
sràideachd, *s.f.* Habit of walking or sauntering. 2 Act of walking or sauntering, promenading.
sràideag, -eig, -an, *s f., dim.* of sràid. Little street or lane. 2 Skip, leap, long pace. 3 Short walk. 4 Street walker, whore. 5**Mat.
sràideamachd,* *s.f.ind.* Walking for pleasure or exercise. 2 Pacing.
sràideamaich,* *v.a.* Walk for pleasure or exercise.
†**sraidean**, -ein, -an, *s. m.* Shepherd's purse (plant.)
sràidean, -ein, -an, *s.m.* Little street. 2 Village. 3 *n pl.* of sràid.
sràidear, -ir, -an, *s.m.* Saunterer, lounger.
————achd, *s.f.ind.* Lounging, sauntering about, promenading, promenade.
sràideas, -eis, *s.m.* see sràidearachd.
sràideasachd,** *s.f.* Airing.
sràideisich, *v.a.* Stroll, walk.
sraidheag, -eig, *s.f.* Cake.
sràidich, *v.a.* Jaunt.
sràid-imeachd, *s.f.ind.* Walking about at ease, promenading, lounging, sauntering.
sràid-sheòmar, *s.m.* Gallery.
sraigh,* -e, *s.f.* The cartilage of the nose. Cuiridh mi car an sraigh do shròine, *I will twist the cartilage of your nose.*
sraigh, *pr.pt.* a' sraigh, *v.a.* see sreoth.
—— eartaich,* *s.f.* see sreothartaich.
sraing, *s.f.* Lace, embroidery-work—*Dàin Iain Ghobha.*
†**srait**, * *s.f.* Tax, fine.
sraith, see sreath.
sram,** *s.m.* Matter running from the eyes.
——ach, *a.* Bleareyed.
sramh, -aimh, *s.m.* Jet of milk running from a cow's udder. †2 Matter running from the eyes. 3(DMy) Jet of beer or whisky that comes through the hole in the cask.
srang,** -aing, *s.m.* Frown.
srann, -ainn & -a, *pl.* -an, *s.f.* Snore, snorting. 2 Whizzing or whistling sound. 3 Whistling of the wind, as in the cordage of a ship. 4 Loud noise of a bagpipe. 5 Hum. 6 Any aërial sound produced by quick motion. 7 ** Twanging noise. 8** Noise of a bowstring. 9 Impetus of one walking fast. 10 Drink as deep as one's breath will permit. Pìob a's beachdaile s., *a pipe of the cheeriest strain*; tha s. aice, *she is snoring ;* s. na sìne, *the noise of the blast.*
srann, *pr.pt.* a' srannail, *v.n.* Snore. 2 Snort, 3 Make a humming or whistling noise. 4†† Buzz. 5**Twang. 6††Hum. 7* Drink deep.
srannach, -aiche, *a.* Snoring, snorting. 2 Humming, making a humming sound. 3 Making a whistling or whizzing sound. 4 (DMK) Speaking through the nose—*Caithness.*
————an, -ain, -an, *s. m., dim.* of srann, see srannan.
srannadh, -aidh, *s.m. & pr.pt.* Same meanings as srannail. 2* Great offence.
srannaich. see srannail.
sranna-ghaoth, -ghaoithe, *s. f.* Loud-sounding wind.
srannail, *s.f.* Snoring, act of snoring or snorting. 2 Humming, act of making a humming sound. 3 Act of making a whistling or whizzing sound. 4*Great offence. 5 Neighing. 6 Loud hoarse noise. 7††Buzzing. 8**Continued whizzing. A' s—, *pr.pt.* of srann. S. a chuid each, *the snorting of his horses.* [Not *neighing*—MM.]
————,** *a.* Humming loudly. 2 Snoring, snorting. 3 Neighing. 4 Whizzing.
srannair, -ean, *s.m.* Snorer.
srannan, -ain, -an, *s. m. dim.* of srann. Rattle (child's plaything.) 2 Grasshopper. 3 Humming noise. 4 Whizzing noise. 5 Great hoarseness. 6 Rattling in the throat. 7†† Buzzing toy. S. séididh, *a kind of whirligig.* (see srannchan.)
————ach, see srannach.
————aich,(MS) *v.a.* Hum, as bees. 2 Hiss.
srannartach, -aiche, *a.* Snorting. 2 Timid. 3 Skittish (of horses.)
srannartaich, -e, *s.f.* see srannail. Thòisich e air s., *he began to snort.*
srannchan,** -ain, *s.m.* Humming-board, thin notched piece of wood attached at one end to a string, and making a loud humming noise when moved with a swift vertical motion. [Srannan in *Argyll.*]
sranndanaich, see srannanaich.
srannrach, see srannach.
srannraich, -e, *s.f.* see srannail. Beachan gheug ri s.. *the bees of the branches humming.*
†**sraodh**, -a, *s.m.* Sneeze.
sraoidhleagan, -ain, *s.m.* Battledore.
†**sraoil**, *v.a.* Push. 2 Scatter. 3 Tear.
sraoileach, *a.* Apt to tear, given to tearing. 2 Easily torn.
sraoileadh, see fraoileadh.
sraoileagach, *a.* Queanish, sluttish. 2 Sparkling, as fire.
sraoilleag, *s.f.* Scullion, dirty hussy. 2 Spark of fire. 3 Species of berry.
sraoilleanach, *s.m.* Scullion.
sraoin, -e, *s.f.* Huff, pet. [pride.
———eis, *s.f.* Huff, pet, swell of petulance or
———eiseach, *a.* Huffish, petulant, pert, querulous.
sraon, -aoin, *s.m.* see sraonadh. 2(DU) Shove to a floating body Cuir s. fodha, *shove it off.*
sraon, *pr.pt.* a' sraonadh, *v.a.* Make a false step, fall sideways. 2 Stumble, slide. 3 Rush forward with violence. 4 Stray. †5 Turn. †6 Scatter. 7(DU) Shove.
sraonadh, -aidh, *s.m.* Act of making a false step, or falling sideways. 2 Stumbling, act of stumbling 3 Act of rushing forward with violence. 4 Great offence. 5††Digression, slip. 6 Huff. 7 Impetus of one walking fast. 8 ††Rush. 9 **Quick motion. A' s—, *pr. pt.* of sraon. Guiniche sraonadh, *keenest speed—B. Doran, l. 50.*
sraonag, *s.f.* Vessel with a strong forward motion.—*Dàin I. Ghobha.*
sraonais, -ean, *s.m.* Huff, swell of sudden anger or arrogance. 2* Great snuffiness.
sraonaiseach, -eiche, *a.* Huffish, snuffy. 2 Arrogant. 3 Querulous, petulant.
sraonaiseachd, *s.f.* Pettishness, querulousness, huffishness. 2 Arrogance. 3 Pertness.
srath, -a, -an, *s.m.* Valley through which a river runs. 2 Low-lying or flat part of a valley district or farm. 3 Any low-lying country along a river, strath. 4 *Meadow. 5 The low, inhabi-

ted part of a country, in contra-distinction to its hilly ground. 6 Dell. 7 *rarely*, Marshy ground. 8 Plain beside a river. Eas a's àille srath, *a waterfall in the prettiest dell* ; luchd-àiteachaidh an t-srath, *the inhabitants of the valley.*

†srath, -aith, -an, *s.m.* Tax, fine, amercement.

srathach, -aiche, *a.* Full of straths or valleys. 2 Dwelling in valleys.

———adh, -aidh, *s.m.* Act or circumstance of imposing a general fine. 2 Taxing, taxation.

†srathaich, *v.a.* Impose a general fine, tax.

srathair, -ean, *s.m.* Stroller, lounger.

srathair, -e & -thrach, *pl.* -thraichean, *s.f.* Cart-saddle. 2 Pack-saddle. 3 Straddle. Bithidh na caidearan a' tighinn air na srathaichean, *the cadgers will be talking of pannier-saddles.*—i. e. every one to his trade.

srathan, -ain, -an, *s m. dim.* of srath. Little strath or valley.

srathanach,-aiche,*a.* Abounding in little valleys.

srathanach, -aich, *s.m.* Inhabitant of a little valley.

sreabh, see sramh.

†sreabhan, -ain, *s.m.* Cake.

sread, *s.* see sreath.

sread, see sreadan.

†sréad, -a, -an, *s.m.* Herd, flock. 2 Troop. 3 Row, rank.

sreadach, see sreathail.

sreadachadh, see sreathachadh.

sreadaich, see sreathaich.

sreadaichte, see sreathaichte.

sreadan,†† *s.m.* Tirade, torrent of words.

sreadh, see sreath.

sreafan, see streafon.

sream, -a, -an, *s.m.* see sreamadh.

sream, *pr.pt.* a' sreamadh, *v.a. & n.* Wrinkle, become wrinkled or corrugated. 2 Corrugate, contract into furrows or wrinkles. 3 Grin, as an angry dog. 4*Rheum.

sramach, -eiche, *a.* Wrinkled, corrugated. 2 Corrugating, causing wrinkles. 3 Grinning, as an angry dog. 5 Blear-eyed.

sreamadh, -aidh, *s.m.* State of becoming wrinkled. 2 Act of corrugating, or causing wrinkles. 3 Grinning, act of grinning, as an angry dog. 4 Wrinkle. 5 Distortion of the face. 6 ‡ Curbing or checking by the nose. 7 †† Rheum.

sreamaid,* -e, -ean, *s.f.* String of slaver or snot.

†sreamh, *v.n.* Stream, flow

†sreamh, -eimh, *s.m.* Stream, spring.

sreamhaich, *v.* Blear.

sreamh-shùil, -shùl, *s.f.* Blear-eye.

sreamh-shuileach, -eiche, *a.* Blear-eyed. 2 Having wrinkled eyes or eye-lids.

sream-shuileach,‡‡ -eiche, *a.* Having wrinkled eyes or eye-lids.

†srean, *s.m.* Wheezing.

sreang, *v.a.* Extend. 2 Draw out into threads. 3 Tear.

sreang, -einge, -an, *s. f.* String, line, cord. 2 Rope. 3 Charm to prevent harm from an evil eye. 4 Ridge. 5 The part of a hand fishing-line held in the hand. 6 In *pl.* applied to fishing-lines.—DU. Iasgach shreangan, *line-fishing* ; tharruing i an t-sreang le rogha beachd, *she drew the string with the best aim.*

sreangach, -aiche, *a.* Stringed, furnished with strings. 2 Stringy. 3 Composed of strings. 4 Capillary. 5 Dilute. 6 Lineal. 7 Strung, threaded. 8* Like a string or thread.

sreangachadh, -aidh, *s. m.* Stringing, act of stringing or fitting with strings. 2 Act of attenuating or making slender. A' s—, *pr.pt.* of sreangaich.

sreangag, -aig, -an, *s.f.* Small string, thread, cord.

sreangagach, -aiche, *a.* Full of little threads or strings, stringy.

sreangaich, *pr.pt.* a' sreangachadh, *v.a.* String, cord, fit with strings or cords. 2 Draw out into strings. 3 Attenuate, make slender. 4 Make subtle. 5**Bend with strings. 6*Get capillary.

sreangaichte, *past pt.* of sreangaich. Fitted with strings or cords. 2 Attenuated, made slender. 3 Tied. 4 Capillary.

sreangair,** *s.m.* Sneaking, half-starved fellow.

sreangan, -ain, -an, *s.m.* Small string. 2 Thread with which shoes are sewn. 3 Little rope or line.

sreaganach, -aiche, *a.* see sreangagach.

sreanganan, (DC) *s.m.* Reef-points of a sail—*Skye.*

sreang-art,** -airt, *s.f.* see sreang-tart.

sreangartach,** -aich, *s.m.* Tall raw-boned man, *in derision.*

————, *a.* Like a loadstone, magnetic.

sreang-bogha,§ *s.f.* Rest-harrow—*ononis arvensis.*

647. *Sreang-bogha.*

sreang-chumail, *s.f.* Awe-band.

sreang-lion,** -liontan, *s.f.* Casting-line, casting-net.

sreang-riaghailt,** *s.f.* Plumb-line, plummet, ruling-line, mason's parallel line.

sreang-stiùiridh,** *s.f.* Stern-rope.

sreang-tart,** *s.f.* Loadstone.

sreang-thomhais,** *s.f.* Measuring-line. 2 Surveyor's line or chain.

sreang-thrian, see sreang-bogha.

sreann,* see srann.

sreannartaich,* see srannartaich.

sreann-chor,* *s.f.* Whirlwind—*Islay.*

sreap, see streap.

sreat, *s.m.* see sreatan.

sreatan,* -ain, *s.m.* Screech. S. lughadaireachd, *a screech of blasphemies.*

sreath, -a, -an, *s. m.* Series, class, order, row, rank, stratum, layer, 2 Issue. 3 Round, circle. 4 (AH) Reef in a sail. 5 (AF) Herd, troop, flock. 6**Swathe, as of grass. 7 Drill or row of potatoes. 8** Long line. 9 (DU) Line of printing, print. 10(DU) Furrow. Tha e 'cur feamainn 'san t-s., *he puts seaware in the furrow* ; s. aghaidh, or sreath beòil, *the van* or *front rank of an army* ; s. meadhon, *centre rank* ; s. chùl, *the rear rank* ; an dà sh., *in two rows* ; le sreathaibh, *with rows (of jewels.)* On stated occasions of carousal it was customary among the Gael of old to sit in a circle, which they called *sreath.* The cup-bearer filled the cup to the brim at every round, and however potent the liquor might

be, it was cleared off at a draught. These scenes of intemperance often lasted for three days, and it was deemed effeminate in anyone to retire sober. At such drinking matches it was usual for two men to be in attendance at the door with a litter, to carry off to bed every individual as he fell senseless from his chair. —** [s.f.*]
sreathach, -aiche, *a.* see sreathail.
————adh, -aidh, *s m.* Arrangement. 2 Act of setting or arranging in ranks or rows. 3 Drawing up in lines. 4 Rolling into swathes, as grass. A' s—, *pr.pt.* of sreathaich.
sreathadh, *s.m.* Sneezing.
sreathaich, *pr.pt.* a' sreathachadh, *v.a.* Place or set in ranks or rows, draw up in ranks.
————te, *past pt.* of sreathaich. Placed in ranks or rows, drawn up in lines.
sreathail, -e, *a.* Ranked, in ranks or rows. 2 In classes. 3 Lineal. 4 Full of ranks or rows. 5**Full of rolls or swathes, as grass.
sreathainn, -e, *s.f.* Straw on which corn is laid in a kiln. 2 Kiln-straw. 3 Materials of a bed, i.e. drawn straw.
sreathal,** -ail, *a.* That is in rows.
sreathan, *n.pl.* of sreath. 2 *s.m.* Little row or rank. 3 see sreothan.
sreathan,** *s.m.* Vellum. 2 Filmy skin which covers an unborn calf. 3 Film. Cho tana ri s., *as thin as a film.*
sreathart, *v.* see sreothart.
————aich, *s.f.* see sreothartaich.
sreathnaich,** *v.a.* Wet, moisten. 2 Spread out, extend.
————te, *past pt.* Wetted, moistened. 2 Spread out.
sréine, *gen.* of srian.
sreing, -e, -ean, see sreang.
sreinge, *gen.sing.* of sreang.
sreinglean,* *s.f.* see sringlean. [*sringlein.]
sréip, *gen.* of sreup.
sreòdadh, (MS) *s. m.* Inciting, encouraging, giving advice.
sreoth, *v.n.* Sneeze.
sreoth, *s.m.* see sreothart.
sreothan, -ain, -an, *s.m.* Caul. 2 Semen. 3 Film. Sreothan òig-aoin, *after-birth.*
sreothart, -airt, -an, *s.m.* Sneeze.
————ach, -aiche, *a.* Sneezing. 2 Causing to sneeze.
————aich, -e, *s.f.* Sneezing, frequent sneezing. Thòisich e air s., *he began to sneeze.*
sreud, -a, -an, *s.m.* see sreath & treud.
sreud,(CR) *s.m. W. of Ross* for sreath.
——ach, see sreathach.
sreup, see streup.
——ach, -aiche, *a.* see streupach.
srian, -éine, *pl.* -ean & -tan, *s. f.* Bridle, curb, bridle and reins. 2 Restraint. 3 Stripe, streak.
srian, *pr. pt.* a' srianadh, *v.a.* Bridle. 2 Curb, restrain. 3 Control.
srianach, -aiche, *a.* Bridled, like a bridle, of a bridle. 2 Curbing, that curbs or restrains. 3 Cockled. 4*Streaked. Each s., ceumnach, *a bridled, prancing horse ;* an seillean s., *the ring-streaked bee.*
srianach, see strianach.
————d, *s.f.* Brindle. 2 State of being ring-streaked. 3 Ruling or managing by means of a bridle.
srianadair,(MS) *s.m.* Lorimer.
srianadh, -aidh, *s.m.* Bridling, act of putting in a bridle. 2 Bridling, act of curbing or restraining. 3 Reining. 4**Pulling down the power of an enemy. A' s—, *pr.pt.* of srian.
srianaich, *v.a.* Bit, bridle, as a horse. 2 (MS) Hold. 3* Marble.
srian-bhuidhe, *a.* Streaked with yellow.
srian-chlais, -e, -ean, *s.f.* Furrow in a column.
————each, -eiche, *a.* Furrowed, as a column or pillar.
srianta, *past pt.* of srian. Bridled. 2 Restrained, checked, curbed, reined. [*sriante]
srid, *v.n.* Dribble.
srideach, -eiche, *a.* White, streaked with dark colour.
srideag, -eig, -an, *s.f.* Drop. 2 Spark.
srideagach, -aiche, *a.* Falling in small drops. 2 Tabby.
srideagaich, *v.a.* Besprinkle.
sringlean, -ein, *s.m.* The strangles, a disease in horses.
sriod, see srad.
sriod, *pr pt.* a' sriodadh, *v.a.* Run swiftly, run like wild fire.
sriodag, see srideag.
————aich,* *v.* see srideagaich.
sriut, -iuit, *s.m.* Torrent of quick sounds, tirade. 2 Rote. 3**Long tedious rhyme. 4**Quick rehearsal, as of rhyme. 5**Speech rapidly delivered.
sriutach, -aiche, *a.* Rapid in rehearsing. 2 Rehearsing rapidly.
sriutach, -aich, *s.m.* Rapid rehearsal. 2 Rhyming. 3 Long and rapid rhyme, tedious rhyme.
sriutaiche, -an, *s.m.* One who repeats or recites rapidly. 2 Rhymer. [sriutaich—McL & D]
sriutan,** -ain, *s.m.* Long and quick repetition of news or poetry. 2(DU) Quick, jerky walk. S. ghuidheachan, *a torrent of oaths or swearing.*
srobach,** *a.* Apt to push, thrust or shove.
srobadh, -aidh, -ean, *s. m.* Push, thrust. 2 Pushing, thrusting, shoving. 3 Small quantity of liquor.
†sroghall,† -aill, *s.m.* Whip, lash.
sròil, *gen.sing.* of sròl.
sròin, *v.a.* Deviate, turn aside.
sròin,* *s.f.* Huff. Tha s. air, *he is huffed* or *offended.*
sròin-adharcach, *s.m.* Unicorn.
sròin-aodach,** -aich, *s.m.* Pocket-handkerchief.
sròine, *gen.sing. & n.pl.* of sròn.
sròineach,** *a.* Projecting, as a rock. 2**Large-nosed. 3 Sharp-nosed. 4 Apt to smell, snuff or snuffle. 5 Sharp-scented. 6 Nasal, like a nose. 7 Like a headland. 8 Projecting, as a headland. 9**Having headlands or promontories.
sròineachadh, -aidh, *s.m.* Breathing. 2 Smelling. 3 Snorting. 4 Snuffing, snuffling.
sròineadach,†† -aich, -aichean, *s. m.* Handkerchief.
sròineadh, *gen.sing.* of sròn—*Skye.*
sròineag, *s.f.* Projecting rock. 2 see srònag.
————ach, *a.* Having numerous promontories or jutting points.
sròineagaich, see srònagaich.
sròineall, *s.f.* Musrol, nose-thong of a horse's bridle.
sròinean, *s.m.* see sròineall. 2(DU) *dim.* of sròn. Toe of a stocking.
sròineann, *a.* (sròin + fhionn) White-nosed.
sròinean, *n.pl.* of sròn.
sròineil,** *a.* Nasal.
sròineis, -e, *s.f.* Snorting. 2 Snuffling. 3 Smelling. 4 Puffing, blowing from shortness of breath. 5* Huffiness.
sròineiseach, -eiche, *a.* Smelling, snuffling. 2 Snorting. 3 Apt to smell, snuff or snort. 4* see sraonaiseach.
sròineiseachd,** *s.f.* Habit of smelling, snuffling or snorting.

sròineisich,†† *pr. pt.* a' sròineiseachadh, *v. a.* Smelling. 2 Rubbing noses.
sròin-eudach,** -aich, *s.m.* Pocket-handkerchief.
sròin-fhionn,** *a.* White-nosed, as a quadruped.
sròin-iall, see sròineall.
sròinich, *pr.pt.* a' sròineachadh, *v. a.* Breathe through the nostrils. 2 Smell, apply the nose to anything. 3 Snort. 4 Trace with the scent, as a dog, scent. 5 Snuffle. 6 Pant.
sròinich, *s.* see sròineis.
sroinnionn, *a.* (for sròin-fhionn) Na laoigh òga sroinnionn guailleach, *the young, white-nosed, well-set-up calves—Donn.Bàn, p. 60.*
sròin-sréine, see sròineall.
sròintean, *n.pl.* of sròn.
sròl, -òil, *pl.* -an & -tan, *s. m.* Banner, ensign, flag. 2 Silk, satin, gauze, lace, crape. 3 Any flowing or fine part of a lady's dress. 4** Flowing ribbon, streamer, sash. Le 'n sioda,'s le 'n sròltaibh, *with their silks and their sashes.*
sròlach, -aiche, *a.* Having banners or ensigns. 2 Like a banner. 3 Abounding in, or like, silk, satin, crape or gauze. 4 Flowing, as the delicate parts of a lady's dress, ribbons or sashes. 5* Dressed with crape.
sròl-bhratach, -aich, -aichean, *s.f.* Silken banner, pennon or flag.
————, -aiche, *a.* Silk-flagged, having silk pennons, flags or banners.
sròn, -òine & -a, [sròineadh—*Skye*] *pl.*-an, -e** & sròintean, *s.f.* Nose. 2 Promontory, headland running from a mountain to a "strath." 3 Ridge of a hill. 4 Point of a plough. 5** Nostril. 6††Prow. 7(DU) Toe of a stocking. Ghabh e sin anns an t-sròin, *he took offence at that—lit. he look that in the nose ;* tha s. air, *he is huffed, he is offended* ; bràigh na sròine, *the bridge of the nose ;* s. chrom, *aquiline nose ;* s. dhìreach, *Grecian nose ;* s. smutach, *a pug nose.* [sròin—*Gairloch & Lochbroom*—DU.]
srònach, -aiche, *a.* Nosed, nasal. 2 Having a remarkable nose. 3 Abounding in promontories or headlands. 3** Sharp-scented. 5** Apt to smell or snuff. 6(DU) Ready to take offence.
srònach,* *s.f.* Nose-string.
srònachaidh,(AF) *s.* Sea-stickleback.
sròn-adharcach,* -aich, *s.m.* Rhinoceros.
srònag, -aig, -an, *s.f., dim.* of sròn. Small nose. 2 Small promontory. 3 Hillock. 4**Any prominent or projecting part of a rock or hill. Feadh nan s., *among the jutting rocks.*
———-ach, -aiche, *a.* Abounding in small promontories. 2* Having numerous headlands or promontories. 3 Jutting, as rocks. 4 Abounding in hillocks.
———-aich, -e, *s.f.* Smelling. 2 Tracing by scent, as a dog. 3**Snuffing, snuffling.
———-raich,** *s.f.* Smelling. 2 Snuffling. 3 Snorting.
srònail, -e, *a.* see srònach.
srònaiseach, -eiche, *a.* Affectioned. 2 Apt to smell, smelling. 3 Snuffing. 4 Snorting. 5 (DC) Petted. 6(DC) Supercilious.
————-d,** *s.f.* Habit of smelling, snuffling or snorting. Ciod an t-s. a th' ort ? *why do you snuffle so ?*
srònaisich, see srònagaich.
————, *v.* Scent, smell, nose.
srònamh,§ *s.m.* Onion, see uinnean.
sròn-an-laoigh,§ *s.f.* Snap-dragon—*antirrhinum orontium.* Known only in gardens in Scotland, and rare in Ireland as a wild flower, but it is found wild in various parts of the south of England. (ill. 648.)
srònan, -ain, *s.m.* see sròineall.
sròn-fhionn, -a, *a.* see sròin-fhionn.

648. Sròn-an-laoigh.

sròn-ghaothach, -aiche, *a.* Following the chase by scent or smell.
sròn-teud,** *s.* Bow-line, cable.
†**sroth,** -a, -an, *s.m.* Foam of water. 2 Stream. 3 Whirlpool.
srothan, see sruthan.
sruab, *v. a. & n.* Drink up any liquid with a noise of the lips. 2 Sweep off with eagerness. 3 Pull anything hastily out of the water. 4‡‡ Make a paddling noise in water.
———ach, -aiche, *a.* Making a disagreeable noise in drinking liquids. 2 Sweeping anything off with violence or avidity. 3 Pulling anything hastily out of water. 4‡‡ Making a paddling noise in water.
sruabadh, -aidh, *s.m.* Act of drinking water with a noise of the lips. 2 Act of sweeping anything away hastily or eagerly. 3 Act of pulling anything hastily out of water. 4 Noise of the lips in drinking. 5 Sudden or eager pull at anything. 6††Paddling in water. A' s—, *pr.pt.* of sruab. [sruabladh in *Poolewe*—WC.]
sruabair, -e, -ean, *s.m.* One who makes a noise with the mouth in drinking. 2 One who sweeps away anything greedily or eagerly. 3 Coarse, awkward fellow. 4‡‡One who paddles in water.
————eachd, *s.f.ind.* Drinking of liquids with a noise. 2 Snatching of anything with eagerness. 3 Coarseness and awkwardness of manner. 4‡‡Paddling in water.
sruabta, *past pt.* of sruab. Swallowed with a noise of the mouth. 2 Swept away eagerly or hastily. 3 Pulled hastily out of water.
sruaic,** *s.f.* Pustule.
sruall,(AF) *s.* Ruall (bird)—*Dean of Lismore.*
sruamach,** *a.* Streamy. 2 Powerful in armies, having great armies.
———,** -aich, *s.m.* Meeting of streams.
sruan,* -ain, *s.m.* Shortbread cake having five corners—*Islay.* 2**Triangular frame on which bread is set to bake before the fire.
srub, -uib, -an, *s.m.* Spout, as of a pump or kettle. 2‡‡Piece of timber, hollowed and placed in a falling stream for the convenience of filling vessels with water.
srùb, *pr.pt.* a' srùbadh, *v.a. & n.* Suck in or drink any liquid with the teeth set. 2 Suck, draw in, imbibe. 3 Inhale. 4 Drink with a noise of the lips. 5†† Pull anything hastily out of water. 6* Drink as long as your breath will permit.
——ach, -aiche, *a.* Sucking in. 2 Apt to suck or inhale. 3 Snuffing.
srubach, -aiche, *a.* Furnished with a spout. 2 Like a spout.

srùbadh, -aidh, *s.m.* Sucking in of liquor, act of sucking or drawing in. 2 Large mouthful of liquid, draught. 3 Inhaling. 4 Imbibing. 5††Drinking noisily. 6†† Snatching hastily. A' s—, *pr.pt.* of srùb.

srubag, -aig, -an, *s.f.* Little spout or pipe at the mouth of a vessel.

srùbag, -aig, -an, *s.f.* Small draught, gulp or mouthful of any liquid. 2 (AF) Cockle. Tha s. aige, *he has a fair amount of whisky (bit of a spree.)*

——ach, -aiche, *a.* In little draughts, gulps or mouthfuls. 2 Drinking by small draughts.

srubagach,-aiche,*a.*Furnished with small spouts.

srùbail,†† see srùb, *v.*

srùbair, -ean, *s. m.* Sucker, one who sucks in drink. 2 One who gulps or drinks greedily. 3 Sucker of a pump. 4 Inhaler 5(AF)Cockle

——eachd, *s.f. ind.* Noisy sucking in of liquors. 2 Frequent sucking. 3 Gulping, drinking greedily.

srùban, -ain, -an, *s. m. dim.* of srùb. Drawing or sucking in. 2(AF) Cockle. Tha s. air, *he has had a drop*—i.e. *he is the worse of drink—Arran.*

——ach, -aiche, *a.* Abounding in cockles. 2 see srùbagach.

srubh,** -a, *s.m.* Snout.

——ag,** -aig, *s.f.* Cake baked before the fire.

srubh an laoigh,§ *s.m.* Snap-dragon, see sròn an laoigh.

srubhan na muice,§ *s.m.*Wall hawkweed—*hieracium pilosella.*

649. Srubhan na muice.

†srudhar,** *a.* In small pieces.

sruil,* see sruthail.

sruit, *s.* see sriut.

sruith,** *s.f.* Harangue. †2 Knowledge, discerning.

sruithean, *pl.* of sruth.

srulach, -aiche, *a.* see sruthach.

srulachan,(DMy) *s.m.* Loop on point of the flap which covers the foot of the headless stocking. Also called "srulachan an osain."

sruladh, -aidh, see sruthladh.

srulag, see sruthlag.

——ach, see sruthlagach.

srùlamas, -ais, *s.m.* Person that speaks as if his mouth were filled with liquid.

sruth, *pr.pt.* a' sruthadh, *v.n.* Flow, run on, as a stream. 2 Melt, become liquid. 3 Shed, drip. 4 Stream, pour. 5 Derive. Sruthaidh na beanntan, *the hills shall melt.*

sruth, -a -uith, *pl.* -anna, -an, -uithean & -aidh, *s.m.* River, stream, torrent, brook, running water. 2 Stream, current, tide. 3 Fountain. 4 Motion of running water, or of any liquid flowing. 5 see struth.

Tha 'n s. 'nar n-aghaidh, *the stream is against us , the current is running right ahead;* saobh-sh., *an eddy-tide ;* am marbh-sh., *slack water ;* coileach an t-sruith, *the ripple of the current ; 2* (WC) *the middle of the stream ;* le s. agus soirbheas, *having a favourable tide and fair wind ;* tha 'n s. leinn, *the current is favourable (to us);* sruthan na beatha,*the fountains of life ;* onfhadh an t-sruith, *the rage of the torrent ;* bhris faire air monadh nan sruth, *dawn broke on the hill of streams ;* a' dol leis an t-s., *going with the stream ; going downhill.*

†sruth,(AF) *s.m.* Man of letters. 2 Ecclesiastic. 3 Astronomer

——ach, -aiche, *a.* Streaming, streamy, flowing. 2 Abounding in streams or currents. 3 Like a stream. 4 Dropping, as a liquid.

sruthadh, -aidh, *s.m* Streaming, act or state of streaming or flowing. 2 Dropping, shedding. 3 Spending, as corn in the shock. A' s—, *pr. pt.* of sruth. A' s. dheur, *shedding tears ;* a' s. a nuas, *dropping down.*

sruthag, see sruthlag.

——ach, see sruthlagach.

sruthaibh, *dat.pl.* of sruth.

——, *2nd. pl. imp* of sruth. Stream ye.

sruthaidh, *fut.aff.a.* of sruth.

sruthail, -e, *a.* see sruthach.

——, *pr.pt.* a' sruthladh, *v. a.* Rinse with water, cleanse, scour. 2*Gulp, drink. S. ort e, *gulp it up.* (*sruil.)

sruthain, *gen.sing. & nom.pl.* of sruthan.

sruthan,(AF) *s. m.* Man of letters. 2 Ecclesiastic. 3 Astronomer.

——, *n.pl.* of sruth S. ànradhach na h-aoise, *the mournful streams (tears) of age.*

——, -ain, *pl.* -ain & -an, *s.m.,dim.* of sruth. Streamlet, brook, rill, rivulet. Tharta tha na sruthain a' breabail, *over them the streams gurgle.*

——ach, -aiche, *a.* Full of streamlets or rills. 2**Purling, gurgling.

sruth-chlais, -e, -ean, *s. f.* Water-channel, conduit, canal. 2 Bed of a river or stream.

——each,** *a.* Like a conduit or canal. 2 Full of channels.

sruth-chlaon, *v.* Derive.

sruth-fhacal, *s.m.* Alliteration. 2**Derivative.

sruthlach, -aiche, *a.* Washing, rinsing, scouring, scrubbing. 2 That has the quality of cleansing or scouring. 3*Coming in streams.

sruthlach,‡‡ -aich, see sruthladh.

sruthladh, -aidh, *s. m.* Rinsing, act of rinsing. 2 Cleansing, scouring, scrubbing. 3 Violent motion of waves advancing upon and receding from the shore. 4* Half-washing. 5** Dirty streamlet. 6 Gulping. 7 (*sruladh) Suction of air. An s. a tha bho 'n dorus, *the suction* or *stream of air that comes from the door.* A' s—, *pr.pt* of sruthail.

sruthlag, -aig, -an, *s.f.* Small brook, rill. 2 Water conducted through a pipe. 3 Small spout of water falling from a pipe. 4* Discharge of a water-mill.

——ach, -aiche, *a.* Abounding in, or like, small brooks or rills.

sruth-lionaidh, *s.m.* Flowing tide.

sruth-mhillseachd, *s.f.ind.* Mellifluence.

sruth-tràghaidh, *s.m.* Ebbing tide.

†sta, *v.* see stad.

stà, *s.m.ind.* Use, profit, advantage, adhibition, service, serviceableness, avail, utility. Gun s., *useless ;* rud gun s., *a useless thing.*

stabh, -a, *s.m.* Iron vessel chained to a well by the way-side.

stabh, *v.a.* Gaelic form of *stave.*
stàbhach,** *a.* Straddle. 2 Striding. 3 Wide-forked. 4 Asunder.
stabhach, -aiche, *a.* Wide asunder, divaricated, straddling, badger-legged. Bò s., *a cow with wide-forked horns* ; caora s., *a sheep with hrrns turned outwards.*
stàbhachadh, -aidh, *s.m.* Straddling,act of straddling. A' s—, *pr.pt.* of stàbhaich.
stabhaic,* -e, -ean, *s.f.* Wry neck. 2 Sullen or boorish attitude of the head. [pron. staoi'c, staghaic, in *Argyll.*]
stàbhaich, *v. n.* Straddle, walk with a straddling gait.
stàblair,* -ean, *s.m.* Stabler.
stàbull, -uill, -an, *s.m.* Stable, stall. Gille stàbuill, *a stable-boy.*
NAMES OF THE PARTS OF A STABLE :—
Each-lann, march-lann, *stable.*
Each-chliath, *horse-rack, manger.*
Mainnsear, *manger—W. Ross-shire & Perthsh.*
Prasach, *manger.*
Seic, *rack.*
stàbullach, -aiche, *a.* Of, or belonging to a stable. 2‡‡Like a stable.
stac, -a & -aic, *pl.* -an & -annan, *s.m.* Precipice, steep, high cliff or hill. 2 Projecting rock. 3 Conical hill. 4 *Dullness of hearing. 5 (CR) Thick-set little man—*Perthshire.* A' leumnaich o s. gu s., *bounding from rock to rock.*
stac,** *v.a.* Deafen. 2 Drive stakes into the ground. 3 Make a false step.
stac,***s.m.*Stake or post driven into the ground. 2 Pillar, column. 3 Little eminence. 4 False step, hobbling step. 5 Halt. 6 Stack. 7 Thorn. Tha s. chrùbaich ann, *he has a halt in his gait.*
stacach,** *s.m.* Halter, lame man.
stacach, -aiche, *a.* Abounding in cliffs or precipices. 2 Rugged, uneven, peaky, rocky. 3 Dull of hearing, deaf. 4** Halt, lame, hobbling. 5* Uninflammable, very unready to take fire. 6**Pillared, columned. 7**Full of impediments. 8**Full of little eminences. 9 **Causing deafness. 10 Full of heaps. 11** Full of stakes. 12**Thorny. 13 Coacervated.
——adh,** -aidh, *s.m.* Heaping up, coacervation.
——d,* *s.f.* Deafness. 2 Uninflammability.
stacadh,** -aidh, *s.m.* Deafening. 2 Driving stakes into the ground. 3 Pillar. 4 False step. 5 Hobbling step. 6 Stack.
stacaiche,* *s.f.* Degree of deafness.
stacaich,** *v.a.* Heap up, coacervate.
stacag,(DC) *s.f.* Stubborn woman—*Harris.*
stacan, -ain, -an, *s.m.dim.* of stac. Little precipice or steep hillock. 2 Hinderance. 3** Little stake or post. 4 Pillar. 5 False step. 6**Little halt. 7**Little stack. 8**Knoll. 9 (DC) Stubborn man—*Harris.*
——ach, -aiche, *a.* Abounding in little precipices. 2 Founded. 3**Knolled. 4**Rugged. 5** Full of impediments. Na clachan s., *the founded stones;* cnocanach s., *knolled and rocky.*
stacarsaich,** *s.f.* Tramping or walking awkwardly.
stachaill,* *s.m.* Bar, barrier.
stad, -a, -an, *s. m.* Stop, cessation, pause. 2 Interruption, hinderance, impediment. 3 Period. 4 Abode. Tha s. 'na chainnt, *there is an impediment in his speech ;* cuir s. air, *put a stop to him* or *it ;* gun s. *incessantly ;* dean s., *wait, stop, pause ;* s. a h-aon, *a comma ;* s. dhà, *a semi-colon ;* s. trì, *a colon ;* s. ceithir, *a period ;* stad ceist, *a note of interrogation ;* s. iongantais, *a note of exclamation*—DMy.
stad, *pr.pt.* a' stadadh & a' stad, *v.a. & n.* Stop, cease to go forward, pause. 2 Stop, cause to stop, hinder, impede. 3 Stay, stand, wait for. 4 Rest. 5 Cease, desist.
stad, *s.m.ind.* Stopping, act,of stopping or ceasing. 2 Act of hindering or causing to stop. A' s—, *pr.pt.* of stad.
——ach, -aiche, *a.* Stopping, ceasing. 2 Hesitating. 3 Apt to stop. 4 Stammering, lisping. 5‡‡Impedimental, obstructive.
——achd, *s.f.ind.* Tendency or proneness to stop or cease. 2 Hesitation delay, delaying, hinderance, abiding, detention, pausing. 3 Impediment, obstruction. Ciod an s. a th' ort? *why do you pause* or *delay?*
——adh,** -aidh, *s. m.* Stopping, pausing, delaying, waiting for. 2 Stop, pause, delay, obstruction, impediment. A' s—, *pr. pt.* of stad.
stadadh, *past subj.* of stad. Would stop.
stadag, *s.f.* Stagger. Is e 'ga cur 'na stadagan, *and he sent her staggering.*
stadaich, -e, *s.f.* Stopping, hesitating. 2 Obstacle. 3 Impediment of speech. Duine aig an robh s. 'na chainnt, *a man who had an impediment in his speech.*
stadaidh, *fut.aff.a.* of stad. 2 *gen. sing.* of stadadh.
stadail, -e, *s.f.* see stad.
stàdail, -e, *s.f.* see stàideil.
stadar, *fut.pass.* of stad. Shall be stopped.
stad-chur, -uir, *s.m.* Inhibition.
stadh, *pr.pt.* a' stadhadh, *v.a.* Stretch, rax, extend, jog.
stadh, -a, *pl.*-an & -annan, *s.m.* see stagh.
stadh,** -a, *s.m.* Use, utility, service. 2 Work, working. 3(CR)*s.m.*Swathe of cut corn or hay —*Skye, &c.* 4 see stagh. Cha'n 'eil s. ann, *he is of no use ;* gun s., *useless.*
stadhach,†† *a.* Raxing, jogging.
stadhadh, -aidh, -aidhean, *s.m.* Sudden bending to a side, lurch. 2 Erect position. 3 Raxing, jogging. 4(WC) Bend backwards or curve in anything. Tha s. ann, *there it a bend in it.*
stadhar,** *a.* Useful, serviceable, good at working, industrious.
staduit,** -ean, *s.f.* Gaelic form of *statute.*
——each,** *a.* Pertaining to a statute.
staga boireannaich,(DMy) *s.* Stout, immodest woman.
stagarsaich,* *s. f.* Gaelic form of *staggering.* 2 Stammering.
stagh, -a, *pl.* -an & -annan, *s.m.* Stay, certain rope in the rigging of a ship. Ar s. 's ar tarruing cum fallain, *preserve our stays and our halyards.*
staghannan,(AH) *s.pl.* Stays of a ship.
stàid, -e, -ean, *s.f.* Estate. 2 Proprietorship. 3 Furlong. 4**Rank. 5††Situation. 6**Craft, wile. Is truagh mo s., *sad is my condition*
staid, -e, -ean, *s.f.* State, condition. An droch staid, *in a bad state.*
stàidealachd, *s.f.ind.* Stateliness. 2 Portliness. 3 Sedateness. 4 Pompousness of manner, self-importance.
stàideil, -e, *a.* Stately. 2 Portly, self-important, having a portly gait. 3 Sedate. 4**Airy. Is s. sìos is suas a cheum, *stately is his pace to and fro.*
stàideileachd, see stàidealachd.
staidhineach,** *a.* Having stays.
staidhinnean, *s.pl.* Stays of a female.
staidhir, -dhreach, -richean, *s.f.* Stair, pair of steps. An àird an staidhir, *up-stairs ;* mullach na staidhreach, *the top of the stair ;* s. shnìomhach, (*or* shnìomhain),*a winding stair.*
staidhre, see staidhir.
——ach, -eiche, *a.* Having stairs or many

stairs. 2 Like a stair. 3**Storied.
staidhreach, *gen.sing.* of staidhir or staidhre.
staidhrichean,* *n.pl.* of staidhir.
staid-radh, *s.m.* Statistics.
staifeid, see taifeid.
staigean, *s.m.* Punch (not whisky.) 2**Stout little fellow.
staigeanach,** *a.* Having a stout and squat person.
——————,** *s.m.* Squat fellow.
——————d,** *s.f.* Squatness of person. 2 Gait of a stout, squat person.
'staigh, (anns an taigh) *adv.* Within, in. 2 Within. [" To within," given as one of the meanings by McL & D, should be *steach*—MM.] Generally spelt *'stigh.* Tha iad a staigh air a chéile, *they are reconciled.* [See note under steach.]
staigheir, -ghreach, see staidhir.
staighineach,** *a.* Having stays. 2 Like stays.
staighinean, *s.pl.* Stays.
stàigh-sheàlladh, -aidh, *s.m.* Introspection.
†**stail,** *s.f.* Throw.
stail, -e, -ean, *s.f.* Bandage, strap. 2 Still. 3†† Whisky-pot. [stal—*Gairloch & Lochbroom.*] Taigh stail, *a distillery, a smuggling bothy.*
stailc, *pr.pt.* a' stalc & a' stailccadh, *v. a. & n.* Drive, press forward. 2 Butt. 3 Strike, knock against. 4 Stamp, put down the foot suddenly. 5 Lash against. 6** Cram. 7** Prick. 8†† Busk a fishing-hook. 9(DC)Stiffen oneself.
stailc, -e, -ean, *s.f.* Stop. 2 Stubbornness. 3 Thump. 4†† Pride. 5††Stump. 6** Driving, pressing or pushing forward. 7**Prick, thorn.
stailceach, -eiche, *a.* Driving, that drives or pushes forward. 2 Striking, that strikes against. 3 Stamping, striking with the foot 4 Stubborn, obstinate. 5‡‡ Beset with impediments. 6 **Prickly, thorny.
stailceadh, -idh, *s.m.* Driving, act of driving or pushing forward. 2 Striking, act of striking against. 3 Stamping, act of stamping. A' s—, *pr.pt.* of stailc.
stailcidh, *fut.aff.a.* of stailc.
stailcneach, -ich, *s. f.* Stubble. 2** Standing roots of burnt heath.
staileach, *a.* Of, or pertaining to, a still, 2 a whisky-pot, or 3 a bandage.
stàiliun, *s.f.ind.* Steel.
————each, -eiche, *a.* Abounding in steel. 2 of steel. 3 Like steel. 4 Chalybeate. 5* Adamantine.
————ich,** *v.a.* Harden, as iron. 2 Convert into steel.
————ichte, *past pt.* of stàilinnich.
staillinn, see stàilinn.
stailmrich, *s.f.ind.* Noise, tumult.
stàin,** *s.f.* Tin.
staing, -e, -ean, *s. f.* Ditch, moat, trench. 2†† Peg, cloak-pin. 3††Prickle. 4 Small, pointed rock. 5 Firm, well-built person or beast. 6* Insurmountable bar or barrier. 7(AC) Site, stance, situation. 8(AC) Stronghold, impregnable position. 9 (AC) Sacred enclosure, sacred ring. 10(AC) Gap in a wall, rock or mountain. 11(AC) Distress, difficulty. 12 *pl.* (staingean) Ribs of a creel. 13* Object not easily got rid of. S. dhomhain, *a deep ditch.*
staingeach, -eiche, *a.* Abounding in ditches or trenches. 2 Furnished with pins or pegs. 3 Abounding in small pointed rocks. 4* Difficult.
staingeachadh, -aidh, *s.m.* Digging, act of digging a ditch. 2 Act of sticking in, or falling into, a ditch. A' s—, *pr.pt.* of staingich.
staingean, *s.m.* Obstinate, boorish person.
staingich, *v.a. & n.* Dig a ditch or ditches. 2 Fall into, or stick in, a ditch.
————te, *past pt.* of staingich. Dug into ditches. 2 Fallen into, or stuck in, a ditch. 3 Ditched, trenched. Talamh s., *trenched ground.*
staipeal, -il, -an, *s.f.* (CR) Handful of drawn straw, tied at one end for thatching—*Arran.* 2 see stapull & stoipeal.
†**stair,** -e, *s.f.* History. 2 Tumult, strife. 3 Noise, confusion. Euchdach an s., *deadly in strife.*
stair, -e, -ean, *s.f.* Stepping stones in a river. 2 Path made over a bog. 3* Temporary bridge for cattle—*Skye,&c.* S. chasa-chaorach, *temporary bridge suitable for sheep.*
stairbheanach, *s.m.* Athletic, well-built person —*Sàr-Obair.* [starbhanach—*Argyll.*]
†**stairceach,**** *a.* Light.
staireach, -eiche, *a.* Laid with stepping-stones.
stairean,(DMy) *s.m.* Path for man and beast between a house and the main road.
staireanach, -aiche, *a.* see staireach.
staireanachd, *s.f.ind.* Stepping on stones.
stairirich, -e, *s.f.* see dairirich. Clachan meallain le s., *hailstones with a rattling noise.*
stairleag,(AF) *s.f.* Sea-maw, black-headed gull —*Badenoch.*
stairmeil,(CR) *a.* Sturdy, plucky.
stairn,(CR) *s.f.* Particle, small quantity. Am bheil s. ann ? *is there anything in it ?*
stairn, -e, *s.f.* Noise as the tread of horses' feet. 2 Violent push or throw. 3††Brain-swimming from liquor. 4**Loud noise, clamour, confusion. 5 Tramping. 6††Rumbling, as of stones. 7(WC) Pride, haughtiness. 8 (DC) Rank thick grass growing in fresh-water lochs.
stàirneach, -eiche, *a.* Making a loud noise, noisy, clamorous. 2 Pushing violently.
————, *s.m.* see stàirn.
stàirneal, see stearnal.
stàirneil, -e, *a.* Foppish, conceited, forward, ostentatious. 2**Obstreperous.
stàirneil,(MS) *s.f.* Fuss, noise.
stairneineach,†† -ich, *s.m.* Robustious fellow.
stairseach, see stairsneach.
stairsneach, -nich, -nichean, *s. f.* Threshold. 2 Bar, barrier. 3(AC) Stone step. 4 Obstacle, impediment. 5(MS) Rub. 'Na s. (*starrsach) an siod, *as a barrier yonder.*
stairt,* *s.f.* Trip, considerable distance.
———eadh,(DMy) *s.m.* Going to a place and returning without delay, as a hasty call at a house on one's way.
stàit,* -ean, *s.m.* Magistrate, great man of a place or city. Stàitean na tìre, *the great men of the country ;* stàitean a' bhaile, *the magistrates or chief men of the town.*
stàiteal,* *a.* Magisterial, portly.
————achd,* *s.f.* Magisterial conduct or gait, stateliness.
stal,** -ail, *s.m.* Stallion.
stalac, see stalc.
———ach, see stalcach.
stalag,(DMy) *s.f.* Drink as long as one's breath will allow. Stalagan, *drinks between breaths.*
stalan, -ain, -an, *s.m.* Stallion, entire horse.
———ach,†† *a.* Abounding in stallions.
stalc, *v.a. & n.* Stiffen, make stiff. 2 Become stiff. 3 Tie or dress a fishing-hook. 4 Walk with a halting gait. 5 Starch. 6* Tap. 7* Gaze, stare. 8* Dash your foot against—*Islay.* 9‡‡Stalk, as in hunting deer. 10*Thump.
stalc,(CR) *s.m.* Stout burly man.
——,** -ailc, *s.m.* Starch. 2 Stare. 3(DC)Thick food, as soup or porridge. S. lite, *a plate of thick porridge.*

stalc,(AF) *a.* Falcon. 2 Starling.
stalcach, -aiche, *a.* Stiffening, making stiff. 2 Hobbling, walking awkwardly. 3‡‡Stalking. 4††Gazing, staring. 5**Starching.
stalcadair, -ean, *s.m.* see stalcair. 2‡‡Starch.
stalcadh, -aidh, *s.m.* Stiffening, act of stiffening or making stiff. 2 State of becoming stiff. 3 Act of tying or hooding a fishing-hook. 4 Hobbling, act of walking awkwardly. 5 Dashing, thumping. 6 Starching. 7‡‡Stalking. 8 ‡‡Gazing,staring. 9 Fowling. A' s—, *pr.pt.* of stalc.
stalcaich, *v.a.* see stalc.
stalcair, -ean, *s.m.* One that hobbles or walks awkwardly. 2 Dresser of hooks. 3 Starch. 4 Blockhead. 5‡‡ Hunter, fowler, deer-stalker. 6‡‡ Gazer, starer. 7** Arrow-maker. 8**Pacing-horse. 9 Bully. 10 Robust fellow.
stalcaireachd, *s.f.ind.* Stupidity. 2 Occupation of a fowler. 3 Deer-stalking. 4 Habit of staring. 5 Frequent staring or gazing. 6 Business of dressing fishing-hooks. 7 see stalcadh.
stalcanta, -ainte, *a.* Firm, thick, stout, stiff. 2 Rigid. 3 Starched. 4‡ Strong.
———-chd, *s.f.ind.* Firmness, stoutness, robustness, thickness. 2 Stiffness.
stalda,** *a.* Stale.
stall,(CR) *s. m.* Bandage or swathe over the crown of the head and under the chin—*W. of Ross.* 2(DMy) Edge of the floor next the byre in old thatched houses.
stall,‡ *s.m.* Peat-bank.
stàll, *s.m.* Bearing, trim, proper state. Cha'n urrainn mi a thoirt gu s., *I cannot bring it into proper trim.*
stall, *v.a.* Dash violently against.
stalla, -chan, *s.m.* Overhanging rock, lofty precipice, craggy steep. 2††Sea-rock. 3(DMy) Ledge on the face of a rock.
stalla, *a.* Craggy, steep.
stallacaire, -an, *s.m.* Blockhead. (stalcair)
———-achd, see stalcaireachd.
stallach,†† *a.* Abounding in sea-rocks.
stallachdach, *a.* Stupidly deaf. 2 Careless. *Argyll.* 3††Foolish.
stalladh, -aidh, *s.m.* Dashing, thumping, dash thump. 2(DC) Solid rock underground—*Uist.*
stallag,(CR) *s.f.* Bandage over the cheeks, as for toothache—*Suth'd.*
stallan, *s.m.* Gaelic form of *stallion.*
stamac, see stamag.
stamag, -aig, -an, *s.f.* The stomach. 2 Appetite.
stamb, see stàmp.
———adh, see stàmpadh.
———te, see stàmpte.
stamh,§ -aimh, *s.m.* Sea-girdles, tangle—*laminaria digitata.* Bàrr-staimh & bragair are the broad leaves on the top. 2(DC) Stalks of the oar-weed—*Uist.* 3* Bull's —— dried for the purpose of lashing horses.
stamha,** *s.m.* Vase.
stamh, *pr.pt.* a' stamhadh, *v.a.* Subdue, train, tame, subject, reduce to order. 2 Break a young horse. 3 Drub lustily. 4* Press down, compress.
———adh, -aidh, *s.m.*Taming, training or breaking, as of a young horse. 2* Subjection.
stamhnadh,** -aidh, *s.m.* Managing. 2 Taming or breaking, as of a young horse. 2 Making pliable.
stamhnaich, *pr. pt.* a' stamhnachadh, *v.* see stamh.
stamhnaidh, -e, *a.* Manageable. 2 Pliable. 3 Tame.
stàmhor, -oire, *a.* Useful. [stàthail]
stàmp, *pr.pt.* a' stampadh. Gaelic form of *stamp.* 2 Trample.
stàmpadh, -aidh, *s.m.* Stamping, act of stamping. 2 Trampling, act of trampling. 3"Tramping" blankets. A cure for leum-droma (lumbago ?) was for a person of different sex to kneel on the patient's back and walk over him on all fours. This was called stàmpadh —DU. A' s—, *pr.pt.* of stàmp.
stàmpta, *past pt.* of stàmp. Stamped. 2 Trampled.
stàmpte, see stàmpta.
stàn, (i.e. a stàn) *adv.* Thig a stàn, *come down* —*Suth'd.* 2 Down, downwards—*Rob Donn.* [Down, below, *form of* a bhàn—‡]
stàn, -àin, *s.m.* see staoin & stàin.
stàn, *pr.pt.* a' stànadh, *v.a.* Make awry, bend,
stànadair, *s.m.* Tin-smith, tinker.
stanard,** -aird, -an, *s.m.* Stint. 2 Yard-wand. 3 Yard. 4 Upright piece of wood to which is affixed the rock of a spinning-wheel. Gun s., *without stint.*
stang, -aing, -an, *s.m.* Pool, standing water. 2 Ditch, trench. 3‡‡Sting. 4**Peg, pin. 5* Tank.
stang, *v.a.* Sting as a bee.
-——ach, -aiche, *a.* In pools. 2 Full of pegs. 3 Pettish. 4 Having upright horns. 5 Full of ditches or trenches. 6 Drained, trenched, as land. Gabhair nan adhaircean s., *the upright-horned goats.*
stangach.(AF) *s.m.* Beast with upright horns.
stangaich,** *v.a.* Dig a ditch or trench.
stangail, *v.a.* Fit a hook to a fishing-line, *prov.*
stangan, -ain, -an, *s.m.*, *dim.* of stang. Little pool or ditch.
stanganach, -aiche, *a.* Abounding in little pools or ditches.
stangar,†† -air, *s.m.* Stickleback.
stangaram, -aim, *s. m.* Stickleback, stinger—*Dàin I. Ghobha.*
stangarra,(AF) see stangar.
stann, -a, -an, *s. m.* Tub, vat. 2 Meal-tub. 3 Stall, stand, stance, as at a market. [stanna —McL & D.]
stannach,†† *a.* Abounding in large vats.
stanna-cléithe, -n- *s. f.* Worm-stand. 2 Tub, vat, worm-tub. (p. 731.)
stannadh, *Hebrides* for stamhnadh.
stannair(e),(AF) *s.m.* Buzzard.
stannart, -airt, -an, *s.m.* Stint, limit, bound. 2 Yard in measure. 3 Measuring-wand. 3 Affected shyness, coyness. 4††Gauge. 5 Gaelic form of *standard.* see stanard.
————ach, -aiche, *a.* Affected, coy, shy. 2 Pertaining to standards or gauges.
————achd, *s.f.* see stannart.
stannd, *s.m.* see stanna.
stannt, see stanna.
staof,** *a.* Gaelic form of *stiff.*
staofainn,** *s.f*, Starch. Gaelic form of *stiffing.*
staoig, -e, -ean, *s.f.* Collop, steak, piece of flesh, cutlet. 2(DC) Senseless woman—*Uist.* 3 Tax. S.-rathaid, *blackmail—Perthsh.*, (cis-mheachainn in *Argyll.*)
staoig,* *v.a.* Cut into clumsy steaks or lumps.
staoigeach, -eiche, *a* Abounding in collops. 2 Like a collop or steak.
staoigich,(MS) *v.a.* Hack.
staoile, see staoileadh.
staoileadh, *s. m.* Title, style. Staoileadh Eirinn, stéidh na creidimh, *Ireland's title, Faith's defender—Donn. Bàn, p. 30.* 'Se Gleann Urchaidh do staoile(adh), "*Glenorchy" is your style or title—Donn. Bàn, p. 36.*
staoin, *a.* Awry, oblique, bending, crooked. 2 Shallow. 3 (DU) "Soft," silly, applied to a person lacking in perspicacity. Truinnsear s., *a shallow tin plate—Dàin I. Ghobha.*

taoin, -e, *s.f.* Pewter. 2 Tin. 3 *in derision,* Soft, inactive fellow. 4 Laziness.
staoin,§ -e, *s.f.* Juniper, see aitionn. 2 see eidheann thalmhainn. Caoruinn staoine, *juniper berries.*
staoineach, -eiche, *a.* Abounding in pewter. 2 Like pewter. 3 Like tin. 4 Lazy, inactive.
————d, *s.f.ind.* Laziness, inactivity.
staoineag, -eig, -an, *s.f.* Juniper-berry. 2 Silly or foolish woman.
staon, -a, *a.* Awry, askew, oblique, inclined, crooked, bent.
staon, *v.a.* see staonaich.
staonach, *a.* Crooked, wily—*Dàin I. Ghobha.* 2 **Apt to bend or turn. 3 Oblique. 2 see staon.
staonachadh, -aidh, *s.m.* Bending, act of bending or making awry. 2 Curbing, act of curbing or restraining. 3 Bending, obliquity. 4 Bias, inclination. A' s—, *pr.pt.* of staonaich.
staonadh, -aidh, *s.m.* & *pr.pt.* see staonachadh.
staonag,* -aig, -an, *s.f.* Slaver, spittle, snot.
————ach,* -aiche, *a.* Catarrhal, abounding in spittle, snotty.
staonaich, *v. a.* Bend, incline, make awry. 2 Curb, restrain.
————te, *past pt.* of staonaich. Bent, made awry, inclined. 2 Restrained, curbed.
staonard,** -aird, *s.m.* Crick in the neck.
staonta, *past pt.* of staon, see staonaichte.
staorum, -uim, *s.m.* Bending of the body to one side.
stap,** -a, -an, *s.m.* Step, as of a stair. 2 Step of a dance. 3 Step, pace.
stapach,** *a.* Having steps. 2 Stepping, pacing.
stapag, -aig,-an, *s.f.* Mixture of meal and cream, milk or cold water, crowdie.
stapagach, *a.* "Dùthaich nan stapag," or "am fearann stapagach," is the name given to Trotternish, (Skye) by the MacLeods. The compiler has lively recollections of partaking of stapag uachdair in Trotternish over 20 years ago.
stapal, -ail, *s.m.* **Lamp. 2 see stapull.
staplaich, -e, *s.f.* Loud noise. 2 One of the noises of the sea.
staplainneach, -eiche, *a.* Noisy.
staplan, -ain, *s.m.* Noise of the sea.
stapull, -uill, *s.m.* Bar, bolt, staple. 2**Link. 3 Torch. 4 see stabull. S. nan spéilearan, *runner-staple of a cart.*
stapullach, -aiche, *a.* Of, or belonging to, bolts, bars or staples. 2 Like a bolt, bar or staple.
starach,(CR) *a.* Sagacious, wily, cunning, artful—*Suth'd.*
————d,* *s.f.ind,* Romping, blustering.
staraidheachd, *s.f.ind.* Chicane.
stararaich, see dairirich.
starbanach,* *s.m.* Stout fellow.
starbhan,** -ain, *s.m.* Noise. 2 Rustling noise.
————ach, -aich, *s.m.* Strong, robust fellow. Dithis s., *two robust men.*
————ach, -aiche, *a.* Firm, steady. 2 Robust. 3 Noisy, rustling.
starbhanachd,** *s.f.ind.* Stoutness, robustness. 2 Steadiness, firmness.
starbhanaich,** *s.f.* Continued noise. 2 Continued rustling noise.
starcach, -aiche, *a.* Firm.
starcaiche, *s.f.ind.* Firmness.
stard,* *s.f.* Moon-eye.
stard-shuileach,* -eiche, *a.* see starr-shuileach.
starn,* -airn, -airnean, *s.m.* Upstart.
——,(DU) *s.f.* Pride, haughtiness, conceit.
starnach,** *a.* Like an upstart.
starr,* *v. n.* Shove violently, dash. 2 Propel, push with a jerk. (sparr)
starr,* *s.m.* Sort of grass.—*Lewis.* [seasg in *Argyll.*]
starrach,** *a.* Propelling, pushing. 2(DMK)see starach.
starrachd, *s. f.* Roaming—*Skye.* 2 Taking a walk—*Skye.*
starradh, -aidh, -aidhean, *s.m.* Sudden and violent motion. 2 Whim, freak, odd fancy. 3 Failing, imperfection. 4 Fit of anger, passion. 5 Tramping. 6‡‡Leap, start. 7‡ Pushing violently,dashing against. 8 (DMy) Twist of the head and neck to one side. Cuap-starradh, *a stumbling-block, obstruction ; ball on the end of a spear.*
starrag,¶ *s.f.* see feannag ghlas. Hooded crow —*Harris.*
starrag,†† -aig, -an,*s.f.* Wry-neck, twist.
————ach, *a.* Having a wry-neck, twisted.
starraich,* *s.f.* Complete intoxication.
starrair,** *s.m.* Historian.
starram,†† -aim, *s.m.* Noise, din, tramping.
starran, *s. m.* Place for crossing a river or soft ground on stones, stepping-stones—*Lewis.*
starran, -ain, -an, *s.m.* Old dwarf.
starr-chosail, -e, *s.f.* Staggering.
starr-fhiacail, -cla, -an, *s.m.* Tusk, gag-tooth.
starr-fhiaclach, -aiche, *a.* Having gag-teeth.
starrs,* *s.m.* Gaelic form of *starch.*
starrsach,* *s.f.* see stairsneach.
starrsaich,* *v.a.* Starch, stiffen.
starr-shuileach, -eiche, *a.* Having the eyes distorted, squint-eyed, moon-eyed.
starr-shuilich,(MS) *v.a.* Stare.
starsach,(AC) see stairsneach.
stàt, -àit, *s.m.* Pride, haughtiness.
stàta, *s.m.* State, government.
stàtail, -e, *a.* Stately, proud, self-sufficient.
statalachd, *s.f.ind.* Stateliness, air of importance.
stàth,* *s.m.* Good purpose or end. 2 Use, benefit. Gnothach air bheag s., *a thing worth little ;* cha'n 'eil s. an sin dhuit, *that serves no end to you ;* cha'n 'eil s. a bhi 'tighinn air sin, *to speak of that serves no good purpose ;* cha 'n 'eil s. air seo, *this is useless ;* cha'n 'eil fios air s. an tobair gus an traigh e, *the value of the well is not realized till it dries—Arran ;* tha do mhathair fo dhùbhròn agus t' athair gun sùnnd air ri stàth ! *your mother is in deep sorrow and your father takes no pleasure in doing anything useful—Duanaire, p 13.*
stath,(DC) *a.* Supporting.
stathail, -e, *a.* Useful, profitable, advantageous, serviceable.
stàthalachd, *s.f.ind.* Usefulness, advantageousness.
stàthmhor, -oire, *a.* see stàthail.
stathrum,** *s.* Clash, see starram.
statuid, see stàtuinn.
statuin, see stàtuinn.
stàtuinn, -ean, *s.f.* Act,decree,statute. 2 Short distance. S. o 'n taigh, *a short distance from the house—W.H. 1. 13.*
stàtuis, see stàtuinn.
steabhag, -aig, *s. f.* Switch. 2** Staff, stick, club. Gille-steabhaig, was a foot-messenger or letter-carrier who ran from place to place with a long staff in his hand—**.]
steach, (i.e. a steach) *adv.* In, to within, into. 2 In the house, into the house. *Steach* is used with verbs of motion See note under *staigh.* Nuair a thàinig iad a s., *when they came in ;* cuir a steach e, *put him in ;* [am bheil e a staigh ? *is he in ?*] *is he in the house ?* A mach 's a steach, *out and in,* implies motion to and from a place, but, a muigh 's a staigh means rest in a place.
†steach, *v.n.* Enter.

steadhainn,* *s. f.* Firm or punctual mode in speech.
———, *a.* see steadhainneach.
———each,* -eiche *a.* Firm or punctual in speech. 2 Making a slight pause after every word in speaking or reading.
steafag, -aig, -an, *s. f.* Little staff, cane, stick, crutch or club.
———ach,†† *a.* Having canes or small staves.
steafaineachd, *s.f.ind.* Idle sauntering.
steair, see stear.
———dean,(CR) *s.m.* Sea-swallow, tern—*Skye.*
steaireadh,(AC) *s.m.* see stearadh.
steairn,(CR) *s.* Roaring fire—*Perthshire.* Tha s. air, *he is tipsy.*
stealdrach,* *s.f.* Torrent, state of being a good deal intoxicated.
steall, *pr.pt.* a' stealladh, *v. a. & n.* Spout, as from a squirt or pipe, squirt, gush, pour out irregularly, plash. 2 Cause to spout.
steall, -eill & still, *s.f.* Spout of any liquid, as if from a squirt. 2 Squirt. 3 Cataract. 4 Heavy shower of rain. 5 Considerable quantity of any liquid. 6 Diarrhœa. 7 Torrent, gush, plash. Mar steall aonaich, *like a mountain torrent.*
steallach, -aiche, *a.* That squirts or spouts, spouting, squirting. 2 That causes to spout or squirt. 3 Gushing suddenly, as water. 4 Showery.
stealladair, -ean, *s.m.* Squirt, syringe. 2 Squirter. 3(AF) Spout-fish, razor-fish.
———eachd, *s.f.ind.* Squirting of any liquid as through a syringe, syringing.
stealladh, -aidh.*s.m.*Squirting, act of squirting or spouting. 2 Gushing, plashing. 3 Spout, sudden gush of water from a pipe or squirt. 4**Heavy sudden shower. 5**Pissing. A' s—, *pr.pt.*of steall. A' s. bainne an cuachan, *spouting milk into a pail.*
steallag, -aig, -an, *s. f. dim.* of steall. Little spout, small quantity of liquid. 2 (DU) Wild mustard—*Gairloch & Lochbroom.*
———ach, -aiche, *a.* Abounding in small spouts squirting.
steallaich, *v.a.* Engrail.
steallair, -ean, *s.m.* Syringe, squirt. 2 Squirter, one who squirts. 3 Cascade. cataract. 4 Tap. 5 Clyster. 6 Piston. 7**Faucet. 8*Watering-can.
———eachd, see stealladaireachd.
steallairich,(CR) *s.f.* Sloppy food, thin drink—*W. of Ross.*
stealit, see steall.
steamadh,(WC) -aidh, *s.m.* Ramming the shot of powder in blasting a stone.
steapach,¶ *s.m.* see snàigear.
steapag,(DMK) *s.f.* see stopag-fhraoich.
stèapan,(DMK) *s.m.* Candle-wick. A Skyeman who was eating a penny dip is alleged to have said, An ith mi an s.? *shall I eat the wick?*
stear,** *v.* Cudgel, knock.
stear,(AC) *s.m.* Pole like the butt of a salmon-rod, used for stunning birds. 2**Rude blow.
stearadh,(AC) -aidh *s. m.* The operation of stunning birds with a rod as they fly overhead, the pole-man sitting on the edge of a cliff.
stearair,(AC) (stear) *s.m.* Pole-man, one who sits on the edge of a cliff, and strikes the birds with a pole (stear) as they fly overhead, causing them to fall stunned to the ground.
steàrdal, see steàrnal.
steàrnag, *Suth'd.* for steàrnal.
steàrnal, -ail, -an, *s.m.* Inn-keeper's sign. 2 Arctic tern—*sterna arctica.* 3**Bittern. 4** Butterbump. S. taigh-osda, *an innkeeper's sign.*
steàrnal beag, *s. m.* Lesser tern—*sterna minut*
——— **dubh,**¶ *s.m.* Black tern—*sterna nigra*

650. Steàrnal dubh.

steàrnall,¶ -aill, *s.m.* see corra-ghràin.
steàrnan,¶ -ain, -an, *s. m.* Common tern, sea swallow—*sterna hirundo.*

651. Steàrnan.

stearr, see stear.
stéibh,* *Suth'd.* for stéidh.
stéibheach,(MS) *s.m.* Base, basis.
stéibhich, see stéidhich.
steic,* *s.f.* Cow's stake or stall.
stèic,(CR) *s.m.* *W. of Ross* form of Eng. *stick.* Nach b' e 'n droch s. e! *what a bad boy he is!* 2 (with *t* sounded broad) Severe blow—*Gairloch.*
steic-bhràghad, -aid, -ean-bràghaid, *s. f.* The wind-pipe, weasand.
stéidh, -e, -ean, *s. f.* Foundation, basis. 2** Ground. 3**Piling of peats. 'S i mo làmh a leag s. na talmhainn, *it is my hand that has laid the foundation of the earth.*
stéidh,* *v.a.* see stéidhich.
stéidh-dhaingnich,** *s. f.* Foundation, basis, ground. S. na fìrinn, *the ground of truth.*
stéidheach, -eiche, *a.* Having ground for a foundation. 2 Having a strong foundation. 3 Solid in judgment, judicious, sensible.
stéidheachadh, -aidh, *s.m.* Act of laying a foundation, grounding, establishing. 2* Piling peats. A' s—, *pr. pt.* of stéidhich. Air dhuibh bhi air bhur s., *you being grounded.*
stéidheadh, *s. m.* Stay, support—*Dàin Iain Ghobha.* 2 (MS) Erection. 3 (DU) Upper built-up part of a peat-stack.
stéidhealachd, *s. f. ind.* Steadiness, solidity, stability, punctuality, firmness.
stéidheil, -e, *a.* Steady, well-grounded, well-founded. 2 Solid in judgment, judicious, sensible. 3* Decisive in character, firm. 4* Punctual.
stéidhich, *pr.pt.* a' stéidheachadh, *v.a.* Establish, found, settle, lay a foundation. 2* Pile peats.
———te, *a. & past pt.* of stéidhich. Firm, founded, established, settled, grounded, steady. An Eaglais stéidhichte, *the Established Church.*
stéidh-theagaisg, *s.f.* Text, as of a sermon.
stéig, -éige, Gaelic form of *steak.*
———each, *a.* In steaks or collops.
stéigh,‡ see stéidh.
stéigheil, see stéidheil.
stéighich, see stéidhich.
———te, see stéidhichte.
stéigich, *v.a.* Cut into steaks or collops.
stéileag,†† see stinleag.

stéill, *s.f.* Peg or pin on which to hang things, bracket. 2 Long fellow. 3(AC)Shelf. Thoir an gunna thar na stéill, *take the gun off the bracket*, cuir an cuman air an s., *put the pail upon the shelf.*
stéill, *gen.sing.* of steall.
stéille,** *s.f.* Lustiness, stoutness. 2 Ruddiness. 3 Laziness. 4 Laxativeness, looseness.
stéilleach, -eiche, *a.* Lusty, robust, stout. 2** Ruddy. 3**Lazy. 4**Loose, laxative. [also steilleach.]
steillean,** -ein, -an, *s.m.* Gantry, trestle.
steillear, -eir, -an, *s.m.* Strong and lazy fellow.
———adh, -aidh, -aidhean, *s.m.* see steillear.
steimhleag,* *s.f.* Hasp of a lock.
stéineadh, *pr. pt.* Tha iomadh cànain ann a' s. anns na Leabhar-lann—*Sgeul.-nan-caol, p. 3.* see stéinneadh, 5.
steing,(DC) *s.f.* Hook for hanging things.
†steinle,|| *s.f.ind.* Itch, mange. 2**Ulcer. Tha 'n s. ort, *you have the itch.*
———ach, -eiche, *a.* Itchy, mangy. 2 Purulent. 3 Ulcerated.
steinleachadh, -aidh, *s.m.* Exulcerating, state of exulcerating,exulceration. 2 Becoming mangy. 3**Itch. A' s—, *pr.pt.* of steinlich.
steinleachd,** *s.f.* State of being affected with itch, mange or ulcer.
steinlich, *v.n.* Ulcerate.
———te, *past pt.* Exulcerated.
steinloch,(AF) *s.m.* Coal-fish full grown. 2 Sten-lock.
steinn,* *pr.pt.* a' steinneadh, *v.n.* Disappoint. 2 Fade in colour. 3 (DMy) Explain, rehearse. S. e 'nam chluais e, *he rehearsed it minutely in my ears*; s. e orm, *he disappointed me, defeated my purpose.*
steinn, *v.* Gaelic form of *stain.*
———eadh,* -eidh, *s.m.* Disappointing. 2 Disappointment. 3 Staining. 4 Stain. 5(JMcF) Fading. 6 (WC) Piece of string fastening a buoy to disc.
———eil,** *a.* Keen, ardent, eager, emulous, endeavouring.
stèir, see stèic.
steirneal, see stearnal.
steòc, -a, *s.m.* Any person or thing that stands upright. 2 Attendant. body-servant. 3 Idler. 4 Bayard. 5** *s.f.* Idle female, one who is fond of staring idly at persons.
steòc, *v.n.* Walk, strut.
———ach, -aich, *s.m.* see steòc.
———ach, -aiche, *a.* Standing erect. 2 Idle. 3 Standing idly.
steòcair, -ean, *s.m.* see steòc.
———eachd, *s.f.ind.*Habit of standing or sauntering in idleness.
steoll, see steall.
steòrn, *pr.pt.* a' steòrnadh, *v.a.* Guide, direct. 2 Manage prudently, regulate, govern. 3* Guide by the stars. 4 (DC) Strut, swagger in walking—*Argyll.*
†steòrn,* *s. m.* Star.
steòrnach, -aiche, *a.* Guiding,directing. 2 Managing prudently, governing. 3 Starry.
steòrnadh, -aidh, *s.m.* Directing, act of directing or guiding by the stars. 2 Managing, act of managing prudently or economically, governing. A' s—, *pr pt.* of steòrn. Fear-steòrnaidh, *steersman, ruler*; luchd-steòrnaidh nan crìoch, *rulers of the land.*
steòrnaidh, *fut.aff.a.* of steòrn. 2 *gen. sing.* of steòrnadh.
steòrnail, -e, *a.* see steòrnach.
steothag,* *s.f.* see steabhag & steafag.
steothaireachd,* *s.f.* Sauntering with a switch in your hand.

steud. -a, -an, *s.f.* Race. 2 Horse, steed. 3 War-horse. 4 Wave, billow, surge. 5*Stride. 6* Fine young mare. 7**Charger.
Fonn nan s. 's nan rìbhinn òigh, *land of steeds and virgins fair;* sgaoth eunlaith air steuda sàil, *a flight of birds on the briny billows;* thoir s., *take a run,* or *race*; chuir siod 'nan s. iad, *that set them running.*
steud, *pr.pt.* a' steudadh, *v.n.* Run, run a race. Bu luaithe steudadh e na gaoth, *he could run faster than the wind.*
steudach, -aiche, *a.* Running, that runs or races. 2 Abounding in horses. 3 Managing horses. 4 Billowy, stormy. 5**Speedy,swift.
steudadh, -aidh, *s.m.* Race, running, act of running, racing or darting forward. 2 Wave, billow, surge. A' s—, *pr.pt.* of steud.
steudag, -aig, -an, *s.f.* Tidy girl.
———ach, -aiche, *a.* Tidy, neat, trim.
steud-each,** -eich, *s.m.* Swift horse. 2 Race-horse. 3 War-horse.
steud-shruth,†† -a, -an, *s.m.* Rapid stream.
———ach, *a.* Abounding in rapid streams.
steur,** *s.* Bang.
stiall, *pr.pt.* a' stialladh, *v.a.* Streak, stripe, mark with streaks or stripes. 2 Tear away in stripes or slices. 3 Scourge, beat, bestow stripes.
stiall, stéill, -an, *s.f.* Streak, strip, stripe. 2 Stripe, lash. 3 Ray of light. 4 Slice, piece taken off, as of leather or cloth. 5 (MMcD) Head-post in a byre—*Lewis.* Mar stiallan soluis, *like streams of light.* [***s.m.*]
stiallach,** -aich, *s.m.* Stripe, streak. 2 Split of a plank. 3 Chop taken from anything. An s. tana, *thin streaky cut of bacon.*
———, -aiche, *a.* Striped, streaked, brindled. 2 That scourges or inflicts lashes. 3 Tearing in shreds, pulling asunder. Sprèidh s., *streaked cattle.*
———d, *s.f.* see srianachd.
stialladh, -aidh, *s.m.* Streaking, colouring with stripes of various colours. 2 Scourging, flogging, act of scourging. 3 Act of tearing away in strips or slices. 4**Streak, stripe. A' s—, *pr.pt.* of stiall.
stiallag, -aig, -an, *s.f.dim.* of stiall. Small slip, streak or stripe.
———ach, -aiche,*a.* Marked with small stripes or streaks, pied. 2 Abounding in small strips or pieces.
stiallaich, *v. a.* Diaper. 2 ** Streak, stripe. 3 Rend in pieces or in strips. 4(MS) Flog. 5 (MS) Interweave.
stiallaichte, *past pt.* of stiallaich. Listed. 2 Streaked, striped.
stiallair, -ean, *s. m.* Anything large. 2(AF) Badger. 3†† Big man. 4*Long, ugly fellow. 5 Drawling f——.
stiall-chu, see stiallair 2.
stiall-cotain, *s.f.* Tape.
stic, see stèic.
stic, -ean, *s. m.* Fault, blemish. 2 Defect. 3 Pain, uneasiness of mind or body. 4 Blackguard. 5**Kiln-rafter. 6(AC) Imp, demon. 7 *in derision,* Long-legged person. 8* Stake.
Droch s., *evil imp*; s. an donais, *imp of the devil*; s. an deamhain mhòir, *imp of the great demon*; s. taighe, *house-imp*; s. stairsnich, *a doorstep-imp*—generally applied to a quarrelsome woman, occasionally to a quarrelsome man.
stic, *s.* Inclination, leaning, peculiarity.—*Rob Donn.*
stic,** *s.f.* Stitch in sewing. 2 Slice. 3 Staff, stick, pole. 4** *in derision,* Long-legged person. Cuir s., *sew a stitch.*

stic, *v.n.* Gaelic spelling of *stick*.
sticeach,†† *a.* Painful. 2 Clammy, adhesive, glutinous.
sticeadair, *s.m.* Sticker.
sticeadh,** *s.m.* Agglutination, sticking, cleaving, adherence.
sticean,** -ein, *s.m.* Little stitch in sewing. 2 Little slice. 3 Little staff. 4(DU) Small piece put on the sole of a boot.
sticeanta,** *a.* Adhesive.
sticeartach, -aich, *s.m.* Long person. 2*Apparition that stalks aside houses.
sticil,†† *pr.pt.* -cleadh, *v.a.* Cram, stuff.
sticil mhòr,(CR) *s.f.* One of the beams, of which there were three, laid across a corn-kiln to support the *sticlean beaga*. The latter were laid across the *sticlean móra* or *simidean* to support a layer of drawn straw upon which the grain was spread.—*W. of Ross-shire.*
sticleadh, -idh, *s.m.* Cramming, stuffing, *prov.*
stid,‡ *v.n.* Peep.
stideag,(DU) -eig, -an, *s.f.* Drop formed by splashing water or other liquid, e.g. drops off a revolving grindstone or a cycle-wheel.
stìdean, -ein, *s. m.* Cat. 2 *int.* Call for a cat. [‡stidean.]
stididh, *Badenoch* for stìdean.
stifinn, *Perthshire* for stuthaig (starch.)
stig, -ean, *s.m.* Skulking or meanly-abject look. 2††Sneaking fellow.
stigeach, -eiche, *a.* Skulking, mean, sorry, abject.
stigear, -ir, -an, *s.m.* Skulking, mean, sorry, abject fellow.
———achd, *s.f.ind.* Mean, sorry skulking or abject manner. 2††Sneaking.
stigh, see staigh.
stigleagan, see stiligean.
stil,(CR) -ean, *s.* Strain, trait, trick. [Generally used in the *pl.*] Tha droch stilean ann, *he has bad traits or tricks*,—said e.g. of an evil-disposed person, or of a refractory horse—*W. of Ross.*
stiligean, *s.m.* Small pieces of wood in kiln laid across the simidean.
still,** *s.f.* Swift motion. 2 Violent and sudden exertion. Earb 'na s. air astar, *the roe bounding swiftly afar.*
still, see steall. 2**Speed in water—*Dàin Iain Ghobha.*
still,** *v.a.* Divide. 2 Move swiftly. 3 Push suddenly and violently.
stim, -e, *pl.* -ean & -eanan, see stìom.
stinle,** *s.* Scab, see steinle.
stinleag, -eig, -an, *s.f.* Hinge of a trunk. 2 Hasp of a lock. 3 Hank of yarn. 4 Staple.
———ach, -aiche, *a.* Hinged, of or belonging to hinges, hasps, or hanks of yarn. 2**Salient. 3**Having staples.
stiob, *v.a.* Gaelic form of *steep*.
——adh,* *s.m.* Steeping, soaking. A' s—, *pr.pt.* of stiob.
stiobhard, see stiùbhard.
stìobull, -uill, -an, *s.m.* Steeple.
———ach, -aiche, *a.* Having a steeple or steeples.
stiocach, -aiche, *a.* Crippled, limping. 2††Weak.
stiocaiche, see stiocaireachd.
stiocail,(MS) *s.* Halt.
stiocair, -ean, *s.m.* One who limps in walking, cripple. 2††Feeble man.
———eachd, *s.f.* Halting, limping.
stiocall,* -aill, *s.m.* Buttress—*Islay.*
stiocanta,* -ainte, *a.* Adhesive.
stioda,* see stìdean.
stiodach, see stìdean.
stiog,* *s.f.* Stripe in cloth, &c.
stìog, *pr.pt.* a' stìogadh, *v.n.* Crouch, skulk, lie close to the ground.
stiog,** *s.m.* Steak, piece of meat.
stiog,(DU) *s.f.* Crouching attitude.
stìogach,* -aiche, *a.* Striped, streaked. 2 Sorry
———,* -aich, *s.f.* Slim, sleeky female.
stìogadh, -aidh, *s.m.* Crouching, act of crouching, skulking or lying close to the ground.
stiol,** *s.m.* Thread, string.
stiolan,** *s.m.* Latch, little thread, little string. 2(DC) Thin dress, as a woman's.
——ach, -aiche, *a.* Stringy.
stiolpan,* -ain, *s.m.* Truncheon.
stìom, -a, *pl.* -an & -annan,*s.f.* Head-band, bandlet, narrow white band of silk, satin, linen or wool worn round the head of maidens, snood. 2 Hair-fillet, hair-lace. 3 Ringlet, wreath. 4 Tape, ribbon. 5 Ferret (kind of tape.) 6†† Coarse ribbon. 7 Streak, stripe, line in any texture or device. 8**Belt. 9** Brace. Stìoman dh' obair shlabhraidh, *wreaths of chainwork.*
stìomach, -aiche, *a.* Having a head-band or hair-fillet. 2 Curling, in curls. 3 Ribbed. 4**Like a ribbon. 5**Like a belt. 6 Streaken,striped.
stìomadh, see stìom.
stiomag,(AF) *s.f.* Caddis-worm.
stìomag, *dim.* of stìom. *s.f.* Small head-band or hair-fillet. 2 Small curl. 3 Maiden in contradistinction to breideag (wife.)
———ach, -aiche, *a.* Having small hair-fillets. 2 In small curls. 3 Having small curls.
stiomaire, see stiom-éisg.
stìom-amhaich, *s.f.* Scarf.
stìom-bhràghaid, *pl.* -an-br-, *s.f.* Neckband.
stìon-cheangail, *pl.* -an-c-, *s.f.* Bandage.
stiom-éisg,(AF) *s.m.* Ribbon-fish.
stìom-oire,* *s.f.* Moulding. 2 Brace.
stiopall, see stìobull.
stiopan, see stipean.
stiopas, -ais, *s.m.* Drowsiness.
stìoradh, see tìoradh.
stiorap, -aip, -an, *s.m.* Gaelic form of *stirrup*.
———ach,-aiche, *a.* Of, or belonging to,stirrups. 2 Like a stirrup.
stiorc, *v.* Stretch (at death)—*Argyll.*
stìorlach,* *s.f.* Sorry, long female.
stìorlag, -aig, -an, *s. f.* Thin, worn-out rag. 2 Slender or emaciated woman.
———ach, -aiche, *a.* Abounding in rags.
stìorlan, -ain, -an, *s.m.* Tall, slender person. 2* Any ugly long thing.
———ach, -aiche, *a.* Slender, thin,emaciated.
stiornach,* -aich, *s.m.* see stirean.
stiorrach, *s.m.* Short and curly wool.
stipean, -ein, -an, *s.m.* Gaelic from of *stipend.*
stipeanair,* -ean, *s.m.* Stipendiary.
stirean, -ein,*-an, *s. m.* Small, slender tail. 2 Sturgeon (fish.) 3** *in derision*, Insignificant person.
stipinn, see stipean.
———ear, see stipeanair.
stireanach,** *a.* Like a sturgeon. 2 Abounding in, or pertaining to sturgeon.
stiùbhard, -aird, -an, *s.m.* Steward, overseer.
———achd, *s.f.ind.* Stewardship, bailiwick.
stiubhart, see stiùbhard.
———ach, see stiùbhard.
———achd, see stiùbhartachd.
stiug, *s.f.* Sleet—*Uist.*
stiùidheag,(WC) -an, *s.f.* Trick in an animal or man.
stiùir, *pr.pt.* a' stiùireadh & a' stiùradh, *v.a.* Direct, steer,lead,conduct,guide. 2 Superintend, rule, manage. 3 Bridle. S. am bàta, *steer the boat ;* s. dhachaidh e, *guide him home.*
stiùir, *gen.* -e & -each, *pl.* -ean & -ichean, *s. f.*

Helm, rudder, stern. 2 Rule. 3 Tail. 4 Cock's tail. 5 Lobster's tail. 6 Guide. Fear na stiùireach, *the helmsman ;* cha tig e an uisge na stiùireach dha, *he won't appear in his rudder's water—wouldn't hold a candle to him;* air an s., *at the stern;* iarunn s., *helm-hinge, pivot.*
stiùireach, -eiche, *a.* Steering, guiding, directing. 2 Having a rudder. 3 Like a rudder. 4 Tailed, having a tail. 5**Having a stern.
————, *gen.sing.*,of stiùir.
stiùireadair, see stiùradair.
——————eachd, see stiùradaireachd.
stiùireadh, see stiùradh.
————–, *3rd pers.sing. & pl.imp.* of stiùir. S. e, *let him steer.*
stiùireag,‡ *s.f.* Gruel, see stiùrag.
stiup, -a, -an, *s.m.* Long tail, train. 2 Foolish person.
——ach, -aiche, *a.* Long-tailed or trained. 2 Stupid.
stiupaiche, *s.f.ind.* Awkwardness of dress.
stiùr, see stiùir.
stiùradair, -ean, *s.m.* Steersman, helmsman, one who steers a vessel. 2 Quartermaster of a boat. 3**Pilot. 4**Director.
————eachd, *s.f.ind.* Steering, helmsman's occupation, steerage, piloting.
stiùradh, -aidh, *s.m.* Steering, act of steering, guiding or directing. 2 Managing, act of managing or superintending. 3 Management,guidance, direction. 4††Steering,piloting. A' s—, *pr.pt.* of stiùir.
stiùrag, *s.f.* Gruel,hot oatmeal drink-*—Badenoch.*
stò,(AC) *s.m.* Pail. S. bleoghainn, *milking pail.*
stob, *v.a.* Push. 2 Stab, thrust. 3 Fix in the ground, as a stake. 4 Mark off with stakes. 5 Prick, set, as potatoes, &c., by first making a hole.
stòb, see stòp.
stob, -uib, -an, *s.m.* Stake. 2 Any pointed iron stick. 3 Prickle, thorn. 4 Remaining stump of anything broken or cut. 5 Stab, thrust. 6 Puncture. 7 Instrument used by shoemakers for perforating leather in which tacks are to be fixed. 8**Any sharp-pointed stick.
stobach, -aiche, *a.* Abounding in stumps. 2 Like a stump. 3 That pushes or thrusts. 4 Prickly, thorny. 5(DU) Crusty, short of temper, applied to a person over ready to take offence.
stobadh, -aidh, *s.m.* Pushing, act of pushing. 2 Stabbing, act of stabbing or thrusting. 3 Act of driving stakes into the ground. 4 Act of marking off with stakes. 5 Push or thrust, as with a pointed weapon. 6 Planting potatoes by first making holes. 7 Pricking. 8 Stab, lunge. A' s—, *pr.pt.* of stob.
stòban, see stòpan.
stuban, -ain, -an, *s.m.dim.*of stob. Little stump, stick or prickle.
————ach, -aiche,*a.* Abounding in small stumps, sticks or thorns. 2 Like a stump, short and thick.
————ach, -aich, *s.m.* Stout boy.
stòbh, -òibh, -an, *s.m.* Stove.
stobh, *v.a.* Stow. 2 Stick to, as a person. 3 Feel affection for.
stòbh, *pr. pt.* a' stòbhadh, *v.a.* Stove, stew. 2 Crop. 3 Cut.
stobhach,†† *a.* Abounding in stoves. 2**Stewing. 3**Cropping. 4**Cutting.
stòbhadh, -aidh, *s.m.* Stewing, act of stewing. 2 Cropping. 3 Cutting. 4**Stew. A' s—, *pr.pt.* of stòbh.
stòbhta, *past pt.* of stòbh. Stewed. 2 Cropped. 3 Cut. [stòbhte]
stoc, -uic,*s.m.*Stock, trunk, root, stump. 2 Post, pillar. 3 Sounding horn, trumpet. 4 Family, race, progenitors. 5 Wealth, store, cattle, capital. 6* Pack of cards. 7* Cravat. 8 Cravat stiffener. 9 Stock of a rudder, see rudder 3, p. 78. 10 Principal part of any wooden structure. 11 Base of a spinning-wheel. 12 Stock of a bagpipe, p. 722. S. luinge, *the deck or gunwale of a ship ;* s. bàta, *gunwale of a boat ;* s. leabaidh, *bedstead* or *the sides of a bedstead ;* ged a bhàsaicheadh an stoc, *though the trunk should perish.*
stoc,* *v.n.* Object, cast up. Tha e a' stocadh siod agus seo rium, *he objects this and that ;* cha ruig thu leas a bhi a' stocadh sin rium, *you need not cast that up to me.*
†stoca, -n, *s.m.* Wallet-boy. 2 Rider's foot-boy, page. 3**Stocking.
stocach, -aich, -aichean, *s. m.* Kitchen-idler, lounger.
stocach, -aiche, *a.* Having a trunk, as a tree. 2 Like a stock. 3 Having posts or pillars. 4 Having sounding horns or trumpets. 5 Like a sounding horn or trumpet. 6 Wealthy, rich, having much stock or cattle. 7††Sounding.
stocachadh, -aidh, *s.m.* Stocking, act of stocking or furnishing with stock, as of cattle. 2 State of becoming cold, stiff or benumbed. A' s—, *pr.pt.* of stocaich.
stocadair, *s.m.* Stockbroker. 2 Stock-jobber.
————eachd, *s.f.* Stockbroking.
stocadh, -aidh, *s.m.* The flourishing or sound of a trumpet or signal-horn. 2** Benumbing, growing stiff. S. nam buadh, *the flourish of victories.*
stocadh, -aidh, *s.m.* Stocking. 2 Foot-boy, wallet-boy. Stocaidh gheal' air do chalpa, *white stockings on thy legs.*
stocaich,* *s.f.* see stocainn.
stocaich, *pr.pt.* a' stocachadh, *v.a. & n.* Stock a farm. 2 Grow stiff or numb. 3††Become rich.
————te, *past pt.* of stocaich. Stocked.
stocaidh, -e, -ean, *s.f.* see stocain.
————, *gen.sing. & n. pl.* of stocadh.
stocail, *a.* Radical, in *gram.*
stocainn, -ean, *s. f.* Stocking, hose. Dealg-stocainn,*stocking-wire, knitting-needle.* Figheadair s., *a stocking-weaver.*
stocainneach,†† *a.* Having stockings. 2 Like a stocking. 3**Wearing stockings. Brògach, s., *wearing shoes and stockings.*
stocainnean, *n.pl.* of stocainn.
stocainnich,* *v.a.* Season, as a cask. 2 Provide with stockings. 3 Put on stockings.
stocainnis,** *s.pl.* Stockings.—*Perthshire.*
stocainnte,** *a.* Stiff or numbed, as the legs after sitting a long while.
stocair, -ean, *s.m.* Trumpeter. 2** One who sounds a horn.
————eachd, *s.f.ind.* Continued blowing of a trumpet or horn. 2 The business or office of a trumpeter.
stoc-cuidhle, *s. m.* The stock [of] a spinning-wheel.
stoc-cuimhne, *s.m.* Memorandum.
stochd, see stoc.
stoc-leabach,** *s.m.* Bedstock, front board of a bed. 2 Bed-post.
stocnaich, see, stocainnich.
stocnais, see stocainnis.
stoc-steibhinn, *s.m.* Huge log formerly procured the day after Christmas and burned for eight days. 2 Person always in the way.
stod,* stoid, *s.m.* Huff, pet, sudden fit of peevishness. Ghabh e 'n s., *he was quite huffed at it.*
stodach,* -aiche, *a.* Huffy, pettish, peevish. 2

**Restive.
stodach,* -aich, s.f. Pet, huff.
stodag,** -aig, -an, s.f. Pettish or peevish young female.
stodair,* -ean, s.m. Pettish fellow.
stodan,** s. m. Huffish person. 2 Sulky child. 3(WC) Thick-built person. 4(WC)Stammerer.
——ach, s.m. see stodan.
——ach, -aiche, a. Sulky, pettish, peevish.
——achd,** s.f. Huffiness, sulkiness, peevishness.
stòibhte, *past pt.* of stòbh, see stòbhta.
sto-foil ! *int.* Cry to drive away a pig—*E.Perth.* ("foil" in *Argyllshire*—AH.]
†stoic, -e, -ean, s.f. String of beads.
stoich,** s.f. Stink.
†stoid, -e, s.f. Pet, fit of passion. 2** Peevishness. 3 Restiveness.
stoideag,** -eig, -an, s.f. Pettish or peevish girl.
stoidhil, Gaelic form of *style.* 2 Title. An s. ùr, an seann s., *bad forms for* an cunntas ùr, an seann chunntas.
stoilean,** -ein, s.m. Membrum mas.
——ach,** a. Wanton, lewd, lecherous, bawdy.
——achd,** s.f. Wantonness.
stoim,‡ s. Particle, whit, faintest glimpse of anything.
stoipeal, -eil, -an, s.m. Bung, stopple, plug.
stoipealach,** a. Like a stopple, having a stopple.
stoipealaich,** v. Bung. 2 Provide with a stopple.
†stoir, see †stoid.
stoir, see stair.
stoirean,** -ein, s.m. Sour, sulky fellow.
——ach,** a. Sulky, boorish.
stòiridh, -ean, Gaelic spelling of *story*—applied both to a tale and the story of a house.
stoirm, -e & -uirm, *pl.* -ean & -eannau, s.f. Tempest, storm. 2* Tingling or ringing sensation in the ear.
stoirmeach, see stoirmeil.
stoirmeachd, s.f. Storminess. 2 Stormy weather.
stoirmealachd, s.f.ind. Storminess, tempestuousness. 2**Manliness.
stoirmeil, -e, a. Stormy, blowy, keen, tempestuous. 2**Manly. Gaoth s., *a stormy wind.*
stoirmich, (MS) v.a. Bluster.
stòite, a. Prominent. 2 Projecting. A cìochan s., *her prominent breasts ;* a cìochan geal criostail, na'm faiceadh tu s. iad, *her crystal-white breasts, if you saw them projecting—Mol. Móraig, 86.*
stòl, -a & -òil, -an, s.m. Stool, seat, settle. 2** Stool of repentance. S.-coise, *a footstool ;* air an s., *on the stool of repentance, doing penance, undergoing church discipline ;* s.-posaidh, *or* s.-pòsda, *where the bride and bridegroom stood in olden times when being married by the minister or priest.* [*gen.sing.* & *n.pl.* in *Gairloch* is stuil.]
stòl, *pr.pt.* a' stòladh, v.a. & n. Settle, become calm, tranquil or sedate. 2 Settle, calm, quell, as a disturbance or tumult.
stòladh, -aidh, s.m. State of settling, or becoming calm or tranquil. A' s—, *pr.pt.* of stòl.
stòlda, stòilde, a. & *past pt.* of stòl. Steady, composed, sedate, staid. 2 Settled, quelled. 3 Tame. 4 Slow, at leisure. S. 'na chleachdaibh, *composed in his demeanour ;* thusa bu stòilde 'nad bheus, *thou who wast staid in thy manners.*
stòldachadh, -aidh, s. m. Contemperation. 2 Becalming. A' s—, *pr. pt.* of stòldaich.
stòldachd, s.f.ind. Steadiness, sedateness, staidness, quietness. 2 Tameness. 3 Slowness.
stòldaich, *pr.pt.* a' stòldachadh, v.a. Contemper. 2 Becalm.
stòl-lùthaidh, -an-l-, s.m. Joint-stool.
stòlta, see stòlda.
——chd, see stòldachd.
stonta,** s. Tub, vat.
stòp, -òip & -uip, -an, s.m. Wooden vessel used for bringing home the milk from the sheilings or for carrying water. The mouth is covered with a piece of sheepskin called *an imideal.* The stòp is narrower at the mouth than the bottom and about 18 in. in height. 2 Measure for liquors, stoup, wooden vessel like a flagon. Leasaich an s., *replenish the stoup* : s. siolaig, *a gill pot ;* s. muisginn, *a mutchkin.*
stop, *pr. pt.* a' stopadh, v.a. Stop, close up. 2* Prevent from running, bung.
stòpach, -aiche, a. Having flagons. 2 Like a flagon. 3 Of, or belonging to, measures for liquids. 4 Like a measure for liquids.
stopadh, -aidh, s.m. Stopping, act of stopping or bunging. A' s—, *pr.pt.* of stop.
stopag-fhraoich, (DMD) s.f. Single stalk of heather with the root attached—*Caithness.* [steapag—DMK.]
stopainn,** v.a. Stop, restrain.
stòpan, -ain, -an, s. f. *dim.* of stòp. Little flagon. 2 Small measure of liquids.
stopan, -ain, -an, s.m. see stoban & streaban.
stòpanach,†† a. see stòpach.
stopanach, s.m. Four-year-old stag.
stòp-bodaich,* s.m. Half-quart measure.
stòp-ceathramh,* s.m. Gill measure.
stòp-leth-bhodaich,* s.m. Half-pint measure.
stòp-pinnt,* s.m. Half-quart measure.
stòp-seipeinn,* s.m. Quart measure.
stopta, *past pt.* of stop. Stopped, bunged.
stòr, -òir, s.m. Store, ammunition. 2 Treasure. 3 Hoard. 4 Quantity of goods. 5 Magazine. 6 Store-house. Taigh-stòir, *a store-house.*
stòr, -òir, s.m. Steep, high cliff. 2 Broken or decayed tooth.
stòr ! *int.* Cry used to incite a bull towards a cow. 2 Cry to call a bull towards one—*Perthshire.* [toraidh ! toraidh ! in *Islay.*]
stòr,** v.a. Store, treasure, hoard up, lay by. 2 Furnish. 3 Replenish.
stòrach, -aiche, a. Having broken teeth. 2 Treasuring, hoarding, saving. 2 Having treasure or hoard. 4 Rich. 5 Having good manners. 6** Having goods or ammunition. 7 (WC) Having irregular or too many teeth.
stòrail, see stòrasach.
stòras, -ais, s.m. Store, wealth, riches, treasure, money, plenty, abundance. S.-cogaidh, *ammunition.*
——ach, -aiche, a. Wealthy, rich, full of stores, hoarding, treasuring, having goods or ammunition.
storb, (DC) v.n. Be filled with, as with food, be stiffened.
storbadh, s.m. Filling, stiffening. A' s—, *pr. pt.* of storb. Gu dàna, colgail, làn air s., 's àrda stoirm an t-seòrs' ud, *bold, fierce, forward, stiffened, high-reaches the fury of such—Donn. Bàn,—Òran nam Fineachan, p. 134.*
stòr-fhiacaill, -ean, s.f. Broken or distorted tooth. 2(DMy) Buck-tooth.
stòr-fhiaclach, -aiche, a. Broken-toothed.
storr,†† *pr.pt.* a' storradh, v.a. Overfeed, surfeit, cloy.
storr-fhiacaill, see stòr-fhiacaill.
stot,** v.a. & n. Rebound, as a ball from the ground.
——ail,** s.f. Rebounding from the ground.
stoth,* -a, s.m. Steam, hot stream, vapour. 2 Stench. An s. a thàinig as a' choire, *the*

steam that came out of the kettle.
stoth,*pr.pt.*a' stothadh, *v.a.* Lop off branches. 2 Cut corn high and irregularly.
stothadh, -aidh. *s m.* Lopping, act of lopping or cutting off branches. 2 Cutting of corn leaving long stubble. A' s—, *pr.pt.* of stoth.
stoth-bhàta,* *s.f.* Steamboat.
strabaid, -e, -ean, *s. f.* Strumpet, prostitute. 2 Low drab.
———**each**, -eiche, *a.* Whorish, like a strumpet. 2 Drabbish.
———**eachd**, *s.f.* Whorishness 2 Drabbishness
strabair,* -ean, *s.m.* Whoremonger.
stràbh, see sràbh.
strabhaig, *v.a.* Lay straw on a kiln, on which to dry corn.
stràbhag, *s.f.* see sràbhag.
————**eadh**, *s.m.* Straw laid on a kiln. 2 Act of laying straw on a kiln to dry corn. A' s—, *pr.pt.* of strabhaig.
stràbhan, see sràbhan.
stra-bhuille,†† *s.m.* Staggering blow.
strac, see srac.
stràc, *pr pt.* a' stràcadh, *v. a.* Strike, thrust, beat violently, thrash. 2 Strike corn level with the top of a measure, by applying a rule diametrically along the brim. 3 Fill to the brim without heaping. 4**Aim at.
stràc, -àic, -an, *s. m.* Ruler to measure grain, meal or salt in a vessel, by drawing it along the brim. 2 Mower's whetstone. 3 Blow, thrust or stroke. 4 Stroke of the scythe, strike or strickle. 5 Loud crashing sound. 6††Strake or plank of a boat. 7†† Copious eruption. 8†† **Strickle. 9††Stripe. 10** Crashing sound. 11 Thrash. 12 (DU) The fill of any vessel. Fhuair mi s. na meise, *I got the basin full, flush with the top.*
stràc, -àice, -an, *s. f.* Accent. S. gheur, *or* s. bhrisg, *acute accent ;* s. mhall, *grave accent.*
stràc,(CR) *s. m.* Quantity—*Loch Tay side.* S. math shneachdaidh, *a heavy fall of snow.*
stracach, see sracach.
stràcach,** *a.* Striking, thumping, thrashing. 2 **Prone to thump or thrash. 3 Like, or pertaining to, a strickle.
stràcadair,* *s.m.* Strickle.
stràcadh, -aidh, *s.m.* Striking, act of beating, thrashing or striking. 2 Act of adjusting a measure by drawing a rule across the brim. 3 Act of filling a vessel to the brim. 4 Aiming at. A' s. oirre, *aiming at her, bent on getting her.* A' s—, *pr.pt.* of stràc.
stracadh, see sracadh.
stràcair, -ean, *s.m.* Troublesome fellow. 2 Wandering or gossiping fellow. 3(CR) Vagabond. 4**Thrasher, bruiser.
———**each**, -eiche, *a.* Troublesome. 2 Wandering. 3 Gossiping. 4** Inclined to gossip or tattle. 5 Inclined to beat, thump, bruise or thrash.
———**eachd**, *s.f.* Troublesomeness. 2 Habit of gossiping, tattling. 3 Giving of blows. 4** Visiting.
stràcaireachd, *s.f.* Continued beating, frequent thrashing. 2 Hard fighting. Sùrd le sunnd air s.,—*Filidh, p. 64.* see sracaireachd.
stràcan,(CR) *s.m.* Tour, excursion—*Skye.*
strac-beòil, *s.m.* Saxboard of a boat, (E8, p. 73.)
stràc gheur, *s.m.* Acute accent (ó.)
strach,** *s.m.* Arch, vault.
strachd, see srac.
stràchd, see stràc.
———**ach**, see stràcach.
strachdach, see sracach.
stràchdair, see stràcair.
stràc mhall, *s.m.* Grave accent (ò.)
stradadh,(MS) *s.m.* Aspersion. 2 Conspersion.
stradagaich, *v.a.* Speckle.
stradhag, *s.f. E.Ross.* for sràbhaig.
stradhaigeadh, *Caithness* for stràbhaigeadh.
stragh,** -aigh, -aighean, *s.m.* Arch, vault.
stràic, -e, *s.f.* Pride, self-conceit. 2 Swell of anger or passion. 3 see stràc (roller, &c.) Mar sin a bhitheas luchd na stràice, *so shall fare the proud ;* gun s., *without being proud of wealth.*
straiceach, -eiche, *a.* see stràiceil.
stràicealachd, *s.f.* see stràic.
stràicean,** -ein, *s.m.* Truncheon, baton. 2 Conceited fellow.
stràiceil, -e, *a.* Proud, haughty, conceited. 2 Huffish, pettish. 3 Arrogant, insolent. 4* Purse-proud.
straidhear, see struidhear.
stràid-imeachd, see sràid-imeachd.
†**straif**, *s.* Sloe-bush, see preas-nan-àirneag.
straighil,* *v.a.* Thump noisily.
straighleach, -ich, *s.f.* Fit of intoxication.
straighleadh,* *s.m.* Thumping noisily. 2 Noisy, almost harmless blow. A' s—, *pr. pt.* of straighil.
straighlear,(CR) *s.m.* Noisy fellow.—*Perthshire.*
straighlich, -e, *s.f.* Great noise, bustle. 2 Rattling. 3 (**straoilich) Rattling noise, as of metal. 4 Sparkles, flashes.
straill,** *s.* Harlot.
†**straill** *v.a.* Pluck, tear in pieces. 2 Thump.
stràille, -an, *s.m.* Carpet, mat, rug. 2**Delay, neglect.
stràilleach,(CR) *s.m.* Sea-ware, seaweed—*Suth'd & Easter Ross.* 2 Seaweed left by the tide—*Moray Firth.*
strailleadh, -idh, -idhean, *s. m.* Loud stroke, Thump, knock.
strainnsear, *s. m.* Guest—*Rob Donn.* Gaelic form of *stranger.*
straipealair, *s.m.* Worn-out race-horse.
stramp,(CR) *v.n.* Tramp, trample, stand on, stamp with the foot. 2 Impact.
———**ach**, *a.* Tramping, trampling, stamping with the foot, prone to tread, tramp or trample.
strampail,** *s.f.* Tramping, trampling, treading, stamping with the feet.
———**adh**,** *s.m.* Impression.
strampair, *s.m.* Tramper.
strangach,** *a.* Plucky. 2 Twitching. 3 Quarrelsome. 4 Confused. 5 Lazy.
strangadh,** -aidh, *s.m.* Pluck, plucking. 2 Twitch, twitching. 3 Quarrel, quarrelling. 4 Confusion. 4 Laziness.
strangair, -ean, *s. m.* Lazy or quarrelsome fellow.
†**strangaireach**, -eiche, *a.* Wrangling, quarrelsome.
strangaireachd,** *s.f.* Laziness. 2 Contentiousness, quarrelsomeness.
strangal,‡‡ -ail, *s.m.* Brawl.
strangalach, -aiche, *a.* Wrangling, quarrelsome. 2 Perverse. Gu s., *contentiously.*
————**d**, *s.f.ind.* Contention, strife, contest, skirmish. 2 Quarrelsomeness. 3**Frequent skirmishing or fighting.
strann, see srann.
———**achan**, (for srannachan) see srannan.
strannan,(MS) *s.m.* Gig, whirligig.
strannraich,** *s.f.* Whizzing noise. 2 Snorting. 3 Loud, hoarse sound. S. nan speur, *the loud noise of the heavens.*
straoi, see strì.
straoidheach, -eiche, see struigheach & strothail.
straoidhear, see struidhear.
straoidhil,** *a.* Bastinade.

straoidhil, *v.* Bang.
straoidhle, *s.f.* see straoile.
straoidhleadh, *s.m.* Bastinading.
straoidhleagan,** *s.m.* Battledoor.
straoidhlear,** *s.m.* Hammerer.
straoile,** -an & -annan, *s.f.* Rude, heavy blow, thump, buffet.
——ach,** *a.* Striking rudely or heavily. 2 "Half-seas-over."
straoileach,(MS) *s.m.* Inebriation.
straoileadh, see straoile.
straoileag,** *s.f.* Slattern, slovenly female.
straoilearachd, *s.f.ind.* Verberation.
straoileid, see straoileag.
straoilich, -e, *s.f.* see straighlich.
straon, see sraon.
straon,** *v.n.* Stumble, tumble. 2 Slip, slide. 3 Go awry.
——ach,** *a.* Prone to tumble. 2 Causing to tumble. 3 Awry, oblique.
——adh, -aidh, *s.m.* Tumbling, slipping. 2 Turning.
straothag,(DC) *s. f.* Bed of straw in a kiln on which to lay corn when being dried—*Uist.*
strapadh,** -aidh. *s.m.* Strap, latchet.
strapaid, see strabaid.
strapainn,** *v.a.* Strap.
straplaich,** *s.* Clash, din.
strath, see srath.
strath,** *s.m.* Stay between topmast and foremast, by which it is supported.
streabhon(AC) -oin, *s.m.* see streafon.
streachail,***pr.pt.*a' streachladh, *v.a.* Lacerate.
streachladh,** -aidh, *s.m.* Laceration. A' s—, *pr.pt.* of streachail.
streachlan,** -ain, *s.m.* Band, garter.
streafon,(AC) -oin, *s.m.* Fringe, frill, fragment, beard, thin beard. 2 Tallow, thin tallow. 3 Pellicle, filament, film. 4 Film that covers the bone. 5 Membrane. 6 Membrane covering the calf and other animals in the womb. 7 (WC) Thin skin or membrane on tallow. 8 Carpet. S. stiallach a' ghille ruaidh, *the ragged beard of the red fellow ;* s. glas na caora duibhe, *the watery tallow of the black sheep ;* s. sìoda fo 'dà bhonn, *a carpet of silk beneath her two soles.*
streangachadh,(MS) -aidh, *s.m.* Question.
streangaich,(MS) *v.a.* Rack.
streap, *pr.pt.* a' streap & a' streapadh, *v.a. & n.* Climb, scale. 2 Labour with difficulty, strive against obstacles, struggle. 3 Scramble, clamber, mount with difficulty. 4†† Aspire vainly. Thar ròs-chrann gàraidh cha s. iad, *they shall not climb the rose-tree of the garden.*
streap, *s.m. & pr.pt.* see streapadh.
streapach,** *a.* Fond of climbing, scrambling, clambering.
streapachas,(MS) *s.m.* Arduousness.
streapadair, -ean, *s.m.* Climber. 2* Ladder.
streapadh, -aidh, *s.m.* Climbing, act of climbing or scaling. 2 Labouring, act of labouring with difficulty, or of striving against obstacles, struggle, strife, struggling. 3 Scrambling upwards. A' s—, *pr. pt.* of streap. Leinn dearbhar s. nan lann, *we shall try the strife of swords.*
streapag,** *s.f.* Confusion. 2 Passionate female. 3 see streupag.
——ach,** *a.* see streupagach.
strèapaid, *s.f.* Broil.
streapaid, see streupaid.
streapaideach,** *a.* Quarrelsome. [streupaideach.]
————d, *s.f.* Quarrelsomeness, [streupaideachd.]
streapaidh, *fut.aff.a.* of streap.
streapan, -ain, -an, *s.m.* Tuft or single stalk, as of heath or fern.
streapanach, -aiche, *a.* Full of tufts or stalks, as heather or fern.
streaphon, see streafon.
streathaig, *Lewis* for sràbhag.
streathainn,(MMcD) *s.f.* Membrane—*Lewis.*
streathan, see streafon.
streathladh, -aidh, *s.m.* Laceration. A' s—, *pr. pt.* of streachail.
streathart, -airt, -an, see sreothart.
streòdag,(CR) *s.f.* Small quantity of liquor—*Skye.*
streothart, see sreothart.
streup, -éipe, *s.f.* Strife, contention. 2 Quarrel. 3 Skirmish. 4 Insurrection. 5 (DU) Rough play, horse-play. [also streupaid.]
streupach, -aiche, *a.* Contentious, quarrelsome.
————,(AF) *s. m.* Creeper (bird.) 2 Bark-speeler.
streupag, -aig, -an, *s.f.* see streupaid.
————ach,** *a.* Fond of squabbling. 2 Of, or belonging to, a squabble.
streupaid, *s. f.* Squabble, skirmish, conflict, row, fray. 2**Passionate female.
————each, -eiche, *a.* Quarrelsome, prone to squabble. 2 Litigious.
————eachd, *s.f.* Quarrelsomeness, contentiousness.
strì, *s.f.ind.* Strife, contention. 2 Striving, endeavouring, earnest exertion. 3**Rivalry, contest. 4**Battle. Dèan s., *endeavour, attempt ;* s. nam fonn, *the contest of strains, musical competition ;* strìth àrda, *loud-sounding battles ;* is coma leam s,, *I dislike strife ;* cuir s., *strive.*
strì,** *v.n.* Strive, struggle. 2 Contend, emulate.
striall,** *s.m.* Strip, as of cloth. 2 Shred.
——,** *v.a.* Cut or tear into strips or shreds, as cloth.
striall, *s.f.* see stiall.
——ach,** *a.* In strips or shreds.
striam,* *s.m.* Long shred. [strian—MM.]
striamalach,* -aich, *s. f.* Anything long and ugly. 2 Tall, ugly person. 3†† Long trailing appendage. [strianalach—MM. *s.m.* in *Argyll*—DC.]
strianach,(CR) *s.m.* Beam or ray as is sometimes seen radiating from the sun amongst clouds near the horizon—*Suth'd.* [from srian.]
strianachas,(MS) *s.m.* Brindle.
strianach, -aich, -aichean, *s.m.* Badger. 2‡ Badge.
————, -aiche, *a.* see srianach.
strianagach, *a.* Brindled.
strianaich, see srianaich.
strìdeach *a.* Brindled.
stridich, *v.a.* Chamblet.
strigh, see strì.
strighmhor,** *a.* Emulative, contentious.
strì-gill, *s.f.* Emulation.
strilinn,** *s.f.* Garter.
strillean,** -ein, *s.m.* Mop.
stringlein, see sringlean.
stringleir, see sringlean.
striobh,* *v.n.* Gaelic form of *strive.*
strìobh, *s.f.* Gaelic form of *strife.*
strìobhail, -e, *a.* Emulous.
strioc,** *s.* see strìoch.
——ach, see strìochach.
strìoch, *pr.pt.* a' strìochadh, *v. a.* Delineate, draw lines.
strìoch, *a.* Brindled.
——, -a, -an, *s.f.* Streak, line.
——ach, -aiche, *a.* Streaky, brindled.
——adh, -aidh, *s.m.* Delineating, act of de-

lineatingor drawing lines. A' s—, *pr. pt.* of strìoch.
strìochd, *v.n.* Yield, submit. 2 Surrender. 3 **Bow, cringe. 4 Strike. Cha strìochdainn do dhuine, *I would not yield to anyone;* b' fheudar dhaibh strìochdadh, *they were compelled to yield* or *surrender;* an gaisgeach nach s., *the hero who will not yield.*
strìochd,** *s.m.* Yielding, submission. 2 Obeisance, bow. Dèan s., *yield.*
strìochdach, *a.* Submissive, submitting. 2 Causing to submit or yield. 3 Prone to yield.
strìochdadh, -aidh, *s. m.* Surrendering, act of surrendering. 2 Submitting, yielding, submission. 3 Obedience. 4 Concession. A' s—, *pr. pt.* of strìochd.
strìochdail, -e, *a.* Submissive, yielding.
strìochdalachd, *s.f.ind.* Buxomness. 2 Lowness.
strìochdar,** *a.* Submissive. 2 Under submission.
strìochdta, *a.* & *past part.* Yielded, submissive, compliant. [strìochdte.]
strìochlan, -ain, *s.m.* Rag. 2 Any valueless thing.
striodag, -aig, -an, *s.f.* Speckle. 2 Meretriciousness.
striodaich, *v.a.* Speckle. 2 Besprinkle.
strioll,* *s.f.* Girth, girdle. [**striolla.]
striop,(DMy) *s.* The same kind of cloth as stuth (11), except that it had red stripes in it, and was used for Sundays, market-days and other occasions when the best clothes were worn.
striop,* *s.f.* see strìopachas.
———ach, -aich, -aichean, *s.f.* Prostitute, strumpet, harlot, whore. Mar ri s., *as with a harlot.*
strìopachail, -e, *a.* Whorish. Le mnaoi s., *by means of a whorish woman.*
strìopachalachd, *s.f.* Meretriciousness.
strìopachas, -ais, *s.f.* Fornication, whoredom, prostitution. Torrach le s., *with child by whoredom;* fear-strìopachais, *a whoremonger.*
strìopaich, *gen.sing.* of strìopach.
strìopair, -ean, *s.m.* Whoremonger.
strìopais,** *s.* Trifle.
strioplach, -aiche, *a.* Dirty, foul. 2 Mixed, confused.
striteach,(MS) *a.* Brocaded, brindled.
strìth, see strì.
strìtheil, -e, *a.* Contentious, quarrelsome, causing disturbance. 2 Exerting oneself earnestly, striving, emulous.
strìthmhor, see strìghmhor & strìtheil.
strìub, see srub.
striutan,(DC) *s.pl.* "Kinks" of whooping-cough —*Benbecula.* 2 see striutan.
————,(WC) *s.m.* Hurried run. Ghabh e s., *he ran quickly.*
————ach, *a.* Running quickly or hurriedly, always out of breath.
†strò, *s.m.* see stròdh.
strobaid, -ean, *s.f.* Strumpet.
————eachd, *s.f.* Whoredom, whoring.
†stroda,** *s.* Strand, shore.
stròdh, -òidh, *s.m.* Prodigality, dissoluteness, extravagance.
stròdhach, see struidheil.
stròdhail, -e, *a.* see struidheil.
stròdhalachd, *s.f.* see struidhealachd.
strògh, see stròdh.
stròghail, -e, *a.* see struidheil.
stròghair, see struidhear.
stròghalachd, see struidhealachd.
stròghas, see struidheas.
stròic, *s.f.* Tatter, long rag. 2 Ragged person. 3 Long piece torn out of anything.
stròic, *v.n.* Tear asunder. 2*Lacerate. [**stroic] (srac)
stròiceach, -eiche, *a.* Abounding in rags, shivers or fragments. 2 Cutting into rags or fragments.
stròiceadh, -idh, *s.m.* Act of tearing into rags or fragments, teasing asunder. A' s—, *pr. pt.* of stròic.
stròiceil, see stràiceil.
stroid,(CR) *South end of Arran* for rotach.
stroidh, see struidh.
stroidheal, see struidheil.
stroidhle, *s.* see straighleadh.
stroidhleagan, -ain, *s.m.* Battledoor.
stroighean, -ein, *s.m.* Mud and straw mixed for a wall.
stroill, *s.f.* Delay.
stròl, see sròl.
stropach, -aiche, *a.* Wrinkled.
stropaiche, *s.f.ind.*State of being wrinkled or becoming wrinkled.
stròth, see stròdh.
strothaich,(MS) *v.a.* Palter.
strothail, -e, *a.* see struidheil.
strothalachd, *s.f.* see struidhealachd.
stròn, see sròn.
struabanach, *s.m.* Fish that lashes the water. S. math bric, *a good-sized trout,* as the trout of Loch Struaban.
strùan,(AC) *s. m.* Cake made on St. Michael's Eve of all the cereals grown on the farm, and eaten on St. Michael's Day.
struban,(DC) *s.m.* Cockle—*Uist.*
strubladh, *s.m.* Wetting, hard experience. 'S e fhuair an s., said of one who has been out in wind and rain—*Arran.*
strubhladh, -aidh, *s.m.* see sruthladh.
strudhan, see strùan.
struidh, *pr.pt.* a' struidh & a' struidheadh, *v.a.* Squander, spend lavishly, dissipate, waste, abuse.
struidh, *s.m.* & *pr. pt.* of struidh, see struidheadh.
struidhe,** *s.f.* Extravagance, waste, profusion, Luchd-s., *extravagant people.*
struidheach, -eiche, see struidheil.
—————d, see struidhealachd.
struidheadh, -idh, *s. m.* Squandering, act of squandering, wasting,dissipating, dissipation. A' s—, *pr.pt.* of struidh.
struidhealachd, *s.f.* Prodigality, dissoluteness, extravagance, squandering, profusion, wastefulness. 2 Chargeableness.
struidhear, -ir, -an, *s.m.* Prodigal, spendthrift, abuser.
————achd, see struidhealachd.
struidheas, -eis, *s.m.* see struidhealachd.
————ach, -aiche, *a.* see struidheil.
————achd,* *s.f.* see struidhealachd.
struidheil, -e. *a.* Profuse, lavish, squandering, consumptive, dissolute, extravagant. 2 Abusive. Gu s., *extravagantly.*
————eachd, see struidhealachd.
struidhleach,(DU) *s.f.* Wicked woman, one who acts from evil motives.
struighe, see struidhe.
————il, see struidheil.
struileag, *s.f.* An imaginary boat used in a contest of wit or singing at a marriage or other gathering. When one has sung or otherwise contributed to the amusement of the party, he says "cuiream s. seachad orm gu ——," naming some other person, who makes the same remark when he has finished his share of entertaining.
struill, -ean, *s.m.* Baton, cudgel, club.
———eadh, -eidh, *s.m.* see struill.
struladh,(AC) *s.m.* Rattle. 'Nuair a sguireas an

anail d' a s., *when the breath shall cease to rattle.*
strump,* *s.m.* Spout of a kettle.
strumpaid, -ean, *s.f.* Gaelic form of *strumpet.*
strup,* *s.m.* Spout, as of a kettle or teapot.
strupag, *s.f.* Little drop of spirits—*Arran.*
struth, -a, -an, *s.m. & f.* Ostrich.
——ach,** *a.* Like, of, or belonging to, an ostrich. 2 Abounding in ostriches.
——aich,(MS) *v.a.* Run.
——an, see sruan.
struth-chamhal, *s.m.* Ostrich.
stuacach,* -aiche, *a.* Stupid, boorish, churlish, gruff.
——d,* *s.f.ind.* Stupidity.
stuacair,* -ean, *s.m.* Blockhead.
——eachd,* *s.f.ind.* Stupidity.
stuach, *a.* Short-tailed. An cù s., *the short-tailed,* or *tailless dog—Lewis.*
stuadh, -uaidh, *n. pl.* -an, -annan, stuaidhean & stuaidh, *dat. pl.* stuadhaibh, *s.f.* Wave, billow. 2 Summit of a mountain. 3 Pinnacle. 4 Pillar, column. 5 Gable of a house. [Gable of a house built of stone and lime, see note under binneag—JM.] 6 Wall of a house. 7 Sheet of paper. 8 Scroll. 9 Flush on the face from anger. 10** Undulation. 11** *rarely,* Street. 12(DU) Weal formed by the lash. An stuadhaibh deataich, *in pillars of smoke ;* s. osaig air an fheur, *the grass undulating with the breeze ;* iomall nan stuadh, *the shore ;* o stuaidh an t-sàil, *from the briny billow;* casan 'nan stuadhan dearga, *legs covered with red weals.*
stuadh, *v.* see stuaidh.
stuadhach, -aiche, *a.* Billowy, surgy. 2 Having huge waves. 3 Peaked, having peaks or cliffs. 4 Pinnacled. 5 Having pillars. 6 Having thick walls or gables. 7**Tempestuous. Ruith sinn o 'n chuan s., *we sailed before the tempestuous sea.*
stuadhadh,* -aidh, *s.m.* Approaching, approximating. 2 Coming near in excellence. A' s—, *pr.pt.* of stuadh.
stuadh-bheannach, -aiche, *a.* Abounding in lofty or peaked hills.
stuadh-bheinn, -bheanntan, *s.f.* Lofty and peaked mountain. 2**Stormy hill. Mullach nan stuadh-bheann, *the top of the stormy hills.*
stuagh-bhraighaideach,** *a.* Stiff-necked.
stuadh-chorrach, *a.* Having mountain-like waves *Òran nam fineachan.*
stuadh-ghlas, -aise, *a.* Having azure, or green waves, as the sea. 2 Having grey walls. A' mhuir s., *the green-waved sea.*
stuadh-ghreannach, -aiche, *a.* Wave-furrowed. 2**Tempestuous, as the sea.
stuadhmhor, -oire, *a.* Broad-chested (of horses.) 2* Proud, high-spirited. 3 see stuadhach. Each s., *a high-spirited horse.*
stuagh, -aigh, see stuadh.
stuaghar, see stuadhmhor.
stuaic,(CR) *s.f.* Glum or sullen look—*Suth'd.* 2 Wry neck—*Arran.* see stùic.
stuaic, -e, -ean, *s. f.* Little hill, projecting crag, cliff or hillock, small round promontory. [‡‡stuaichd.]
†**stuaidh,*** *s.f.* see stuadh. 2 (AF) Flock or herd of animals. Dà uan as an s. mhóir, *two lambs from the great flock.*
stuaidh,* *v. n.* Come near, approximate. Cha stuaidh thu air, *you will not come near him ; this will not approximate it ;* cha stuaidh seo air a lìonadh, *this will not nearly fill it.*
stuaidh, *gen.sing.* of stuadh.
stuaidh-bheannach,a.* High-spirited. 2 Quick-paced. Each s., *a quick-paced horse.*

stuaigh, see stuaidh.
stuaim,-e & stuama, *s.f.* Temperance, moderation. 2 Modesty, bashfulness. 3 Guardedness. 4 Continence. 5 *rarely,* Air, mien. A' reusonachadh mu fhìreantachd, s. agus breitheanas, *reasoning about righteousness, temperance and judgment ;* s. agus macantas, *meekness and modesty ;* geal làmh na stuama, *the fair, prudent (cautious) hand ;* a' teagasg sutama, *teaching us to spend our lives soberly.*
stuama, -aime, *a.* Temperate, moderate, abstemious, sober. 2 Continent. 3 Modest, bashful.
stuamach, -aiche, *a.* see stuama.
——d, *s.f.ind.* Temperance, sobriety, moderation. 2 Continence. 3 Modesty.
stuamag, -aig, -an, *s.f.* Modest woman.
stubh,** -a, *s.m.* see stuth.
stubhach, see stuach.
stubhachd,(MS) *s.f.* Substantiality.
stùc, -ùic, *pl.* -an & -annan. 2**Baluster.
stùc, -ùic, *pl.* -an & -annan, *s.f.* Little hill jutting out from a greater, steep on one side and rounded on the other. 2 Cliff. 3 Pinnacle of a roof. 4 Horn. 5††Scowl. 6 Rock. 7*Lump. 8 see stùic. 9* Conical steep rock. 10*Precipice. Aig bun na stùic, *at the foot of the rock ;* an sealgair air na stùcaibh, *the hunter on the rocks.*
——ach, -aiche, *a.* Abounding in small projecting hills. 2 Abounding in cliffs or rocky pinnacles. 3**Craggy. 4†† Scowling, surly, morose. 5 Looking sideways. 6**Stiff, rigid. 7**Horned. 8 Hilly, rocky, rugged. 9**Prominent. 10* Full of bare rocks. 11††Jutting.
stucach,* *a.* Not inflammable.
——air, -ean, *s.m.* One that looks sideways. 2 Stiff, formal person. 3 Conceited fellow. 4 Churl, surly fellow.
——aireachd, *s.f.* Stiffness, coldness. 2 Looking askance. 3 Scowling. 4 Surliness.
——an, -ain, -an, *s.m.,dim.* of stùc. Little jutting hill. 2 Conical hill. 3 Rick or shock of corn.
——anach, -aiche, *a.* Abounding in projecting cliffs, hillocks or rocks. 2 Abounding in ricks or shocks of corn. 3 Having little hills.
stucanach, *a.* Established.
stùchd, -ùichd, see stùc.
——ach, see stùcach & stùiceach.
——air, see stùcair.
——an, see stùcan.
stùc-bheinn,** *gen.pl.* -bheann, *s.f.* Rocky mountain. 2 Precipitous hill. A' siubhal nan s.-bheann, *travelling over rocky mountains.*
stùc-shread,** *s.* Balustrade.
stughaig,* *v.a.* Starch.
stuib, *gen.sing. & n.pl.* of stob.
stuic, *gen.sing.& n.pl.* of stoc.
stùic, -e, -ean, *s.f.* see stuaic. 2 Angry gloomy look. 3 Surliness, lowering expression. 4** Scowling side-look of a bull or any quadruped. 4* Scowling side-look of a morose person. 6 Wry neck and sullen countenance. 7 Extreme boorishness. [* gives stuaic for 6.]
——each, -eiche, *a.* Surly, morose.
——eag, -eig, -an, *s.f.* Surly or angry-looking woman.
stùicear, see stùcair.
stùichd, see stùic.
stuidear, -an, *s.m.* Student. 2 Study.
——ra,* *a.* Contemplative, studious. 2 Composed, steady. 3††Morose.
——rach, *a.* Studious, see stuidearra.
†——rach, -aich, *s.m.* Student.
——rachd,* *s.f.ind.* Study, meditation, studiousness. 2 Composure. 3††Moroseness.

stuig, *pr.pt.* **a' stuigeadh**, *v.a.* **Incite, spur on, as dogs. 2* Instigate,**
stùig,(CR) *a.* **Projecting, jutting out.**—*Perthshire.*
stuig,* see stic, *s.*
stuigeadh, -idh, *s.m.* **Inciting, act of inciting or spurring on, as of dogs. A' s—,** *pr.pt.* **of stuig.**
stuirc,(DMy) see stùic 4.
stuirc(hd), *s.pl.* Storks—*Dàin Iain Ghobha.*
stùird, -ean, *s.m.* Vertigo. 2 Sturdy, a disease in sheep caused by water in the head. 3 Drunkenness.
stùirdean, -ein, *s.m.* see **stùird.**
stuirichd,** *s.f.* Pinnacle.
stuirt, -e, *s.f.* Huffiness, sulkiness. 2 Pride. 3 (MS) Prudery. 4 *Resolution, firmness of mind. 5 Gravity, sedateness, assumed gravity. 6††Anger.
stuirtealachd, *s.f.* Sulkiness, sullenness, moroseness. 2 Intractableness, see **stuirt.**
stuirteil, -e, *a.* Sullen, supercillious. 2 Resolute. 3 Steady, grave, sedate. 4 Dignified and morose but insignificant. 5††Angry. 6 (MS) Prudish. 7(DU) Sulky, huffy.
stnlcach, -aiche, *a.* Stubbed.
stulp,(CR) *s.m.* Knob, as of a chair or bed—*Perthshire.* 2(AH) Dour, taciturn, inaffable person, more often applied to a woman than a man.
stumpach,** *a.* Stumpy.
stùr, *v.a.* Cover or obscure with dust.
stùr, -ùir, *s.m.* Dust motes. 2 see **stòr.** Lur gun s., *an unsullied diamond ;* daoimean nach gabh s., *a diamond that catches no dust ;* cuir s. riu, *disperse them, scatter them as dust.*
stùrach, -aiche, *a.* Full of dust. 2 Of, or belonging to dust, dusty.
———**d,** *s.f.ind.* Dustiness.
stùradh, -aidh, *s.m.* Act of covering or obscuring with dirt or dust. A' s—, *pr.pt.* of **stùr.**
stùrd, see **stùird** & **sturdan.**
stùrdaidh, see **stùird.**
stùrdail,** *a.* Surly.
sturdan,* -ain, *s.m.* The plant darnel. 2 see **stùird.**
stùrr, -a, -an, *s.m.* The rugged point of a rock or hill. 2 Surliness.
stùrrach, -aiche, *a.* Rough, rugged, uneven. 2 Rough, surly in temper. 3††Rocky.
sturrag, -aig, -an, *s.f.* Turret. 2 Pinnacle. 3** Butting cliff. 4††Little hill.
———**ach,** -aiche, *a.* Pinnacled. 2 Turreted. 3 Like a turret or pinnacle.
sturraic, -e, -ean, *s.f.* ††Head or cap turned to one side. 2 see **stùrr.**
———**each,** -eiche, *a.* see **stùrrach.**
sturraicean, -ein, -an, *s.m.* Undress for a woman's head. *prov.*
sturrail, -e, *a.* Gross, thick.
sturranta, -ainte, *a.* Gross, thick, fat.
stùrt, see **stùirt** & **stùird.**
———**ail,** see **stùirteil.**
———**aileachd,** see **stùirtealachd.**
stuth, -uith & -uithe, *pl* -an & -uithean, *s. m.* Metal. 2 Any stuff, substance, matter or body. 3 Eatables, anything eatable. 4 Strong drink of any kind. 5 Camlet, kind of cloth made of wool and goat's hair. 6**Serge. 7‡‡Corn. 8 Strength. 9**Mettle. 10*Particle. 11(DMy) Kind of cloth made in olden times for petticoats and jackets for women (còta stuth, seacaid stuth.) The worsted or thread used was spun on the distaff and the thread required to be very even and was pressed, the process being termed *lisreagadh*, and the press employed, *am "press" lisreagaidh.* Gach s. a th' agam, *everything I possess ;* droch s., *bad stuff;* cha bhi s. ort, *nothing will be wrong with you ;* s. na Toiseachd, *the stuff of Ferintosh,* i.e. *whisky* ; deagh s., *good stuff.*
stuthadh,(MS) *s.m.* Afflux.
stuthaidh,(DMK) *s.f.* Large buoy usually made of the skin of a dog, and used to mark the off end of a drift of nets or long fishing-line—*W. coast of Ross, Argyllsh. & Inverness-sh.*
stuthaig, *s.f.* Starch.
stuthaig, *pr.pt.* a' stuthaigeadh, *v. a.* Stiffen, dress with starch.
———**eadh,** -idh, *s. m.* Starch, starching, act of starching.
———**te,** *past pt.* of **stuthaig.** Starched, dressed with starch.
stuthail,** *a.* High-mettled. 2 Of good stuff. 3 Tough, pithy, hardy. 4 Infinitive in *gram.*
suab, *s.m.* When fishing-lines are set, suab is the portion over and above the depth of the sea. Pùt suab, see under **pùt.**
stuth-cbridhe,* *s.m.* Cordial.
stuth-cùrainn, *s.m.* Tammy.
†suabus, -uis, *s.m.* Disease in horses by which their gums grow over their teeth.
†suabh,** *a.* Mild, gentle, mannerly.
†———**as,**** *s.m.* Mildness, mannerliness.
suabharaich,(AC) *v.a.* Illumine, explain. S. oirnn e, *explain it to us.*
suacan, -ain, -an, *s.m.* Earthen pot, earthen furnace, crucible. 2 Croslet. 3††Awkward mixture, anything wrought together awkwardly, as clay. 4 Basket containing wood, hung in the chimney to dry ; s. crè, *an earthen furnace.*
suacan-leaghaidh, *s.m.* Fining-pot.
suadh, *v.* see **suath.**
———**,*** see **suaidh.**
———**,**** *a.* Prudent, discreet.
†suadh, -aidh, *s.m.* Advice, counsel. 2 Learned man.
suadhadh, -aidh, *s.m.* Rubbing, friction.
suag,** -aig, *s.f.* Rope, cable.
———**air,**** *s.m.* Rope-maker.
suaib, see **suaip.**
suaib-chuthaich, *s.f.* Touch of madness. Is tric a bha s. air leanabh bodaich, *an old man's child has often had a touch of madness.*
suaibe,* *s.f.* Oar.
suaibhreach,** *a.* Gentle, quiet. 2 Not proud. 3 Easy.
suaicean, -ein, -an, *s.m.* Bundle of straw or hay twisted together. 2 Deformed person. 3 see **sùicean.** 4(AF) Pet calf or lamb.
suaicheanta, -einte, *a.* Remarkable, notable, signal. 2 Easily known by reason of dress or badge, banner or armorial bearings. 3 Emblematic. 4††Conspicuous. 3††Rare. 6 New, novel. Eididh s., *a notable dress, conspicuous dress.*
suaicheanteach, -aiche, *a.* Armorial, heraldic.
———**d,** *s.f.* Blazonry, heraldry.
suaicheantaich, *v.a.* Emblazon.
———**e,** *s.m.*** Herald, standard-bearer.
suaicheantas, -ais, *s.m.* Flag, streamer, ensign, standard, flag of a boat having crest or design on it, as that of a yacht-club, &c. 2 Escutcheon. 3 Any distinguishing mark. 4 Badge, crest. 5 Novelty, curiosity, rarity. 6 Portent. 7 Cockade. 8††Decoration. Cha s. còrr air cladach, *a heron on the shore is no novelty*—no sign of anything wonderful about to happen ; dha 'm bu s. giubhas, *whose badge was the pine ;* slat-shuaicheantais, *a sceptre.*
suaichneas, see **suaicheantas.**
suaidh,* *v.a.* see **suath.**
———**te,*** see **suathta.**
suaigh,** *a.* Prosperous.

suail, -e, *a.* Small, inconsiderable, moderate, insignificant, mean.
suaile,** *a.* Weak. 2 Weary. 3 Pale. 4 Dejected.
suaill,** *s.f.* Small quantity.
——-,** *a.* see suail.
suailmheasta,** *a.* Homely, ordinary.
suaim,** *s.f.* Sound, tone, note, accent.
suaimh,* *s.m.* Luxurious kind of rest.
suaimhne, see suaimhneas.
suaimhneach, -eiche, *a.* Quiet, calm, secure, safe, composed, gentle, tranquil. 2‡ Genial. 3*Enjoying a kind of luxury in ease and quiet, as after great danger or fatigue. Gu e., *composedly.*
suaimhneas, -eis, -an, *s.m.* Rest, quietness, security, calmness, peace, repose. 2 Luxury of ease and rest. 3* Great tranquility or quiet. Bheir mise s. dhuibh, *I will give you rest ;* greim tioram is s. leis, *a dry morsel in peace.*
————ach, see suaimhneach. Is s. an rìbhinn òg, *sedate is the young maiden.*
suaimhnich,** *v.n.* Take rest, be at rest, take ease.
suain,(CR) *s.f.* Cord fastening the skin of a buoy round the edge of the wooden disc—*W. of Ross-shire.*
suain, -e, *s.f.* Sleep, deep sleep. O sh. an éig, *from the sleep of death.*
suain, *v. a.* Wreathe round, envelope or twist a cord or rope round anything. [††suaineadh.]
suain-airm,** *s.m.* Dormitory.
suaineach, -eiche, *a.* Sleepy. 2 Causing sleep, narcotic. 3 Plaid. 4 Lethargic. 5* In a sound sleep.
suaineach,(DC) *s.m.* Sleepy person. 2 (DU) *s.f.* Narcotic. Is mis' a ghabh an t-s. á làimh mhic Ghillanndrais, *it was I who took the narcotic from the hand of Gillanders' son.*
suaineach, (DMy) *s. m.* Swede (i. e. a Swedish turnip.)
suaineachan, -ain, *s.m.* Sofa.
suaineachd,(MS) *s.f.* Sleepiness.
suaineadh, -idh, *s.m.* Twisting, act of twisting a rope round anything, wreathing, entwining. 2 The rope used for twisting round anything. 3 Roof of a house. A' s—, *pr.pt.* of suain.
suaineadh-muineil, *s.m.* Cravat.
suaineag,(DC) *s.f.* Girl up to three months of of age, during which period she sleeps most of her time.
suaineamh,** -eimh, *s.m.* Confluence of rivers.
suainean,(DC) *s.m.* Boy up to three months of age, during which period he sleeps most of his time.
————, -ein, -an, *s.m.* Thong, string. 2 Envelope. 3 (MS) Nap of sleep.
————ach,†† *a.* Abounding in thongs or envelopes.
suaineartach, -aiche, *a.* Sound asleep, narcotic, that sleeps soundly.
suaineas, -ais, *s. m.* Twist. Càradh suaineis gruag do chinn, *the twisted arrangement of the hair of your head—W.Ross, p. 38.*
suain-ghalar, -air, -an, *s.m.* Lethargy, habitual drowsiness.
suainich, *v.a.* see suain.
suainig,(MS) *v.a.* Swaddle. [suainich.]
suain-lann, *s.* Dormitory.
suainmhor, see suaineach.
————achd, *s.f.ind.* Sleepiness.
suaint,(DMK) *adv.* High degree of excellence. Tha e s. maith, *it is exceedingly good—Caithness.*
suainte,(AH) *a.* Quiet, peaceable. 2 Circumspect. *Easter Ross.*
suaip, -e, -ean, *s. f.* Likeness, faint resemblance. 2 Exchange of commodities, bartering. Tha s. eatorra, *they somewhat resemble one another ,* rinn iad s., *they have bartered commodities.* ha s. mhór aige ris, *he has a great resemblance to him.*
suaip, *v.a.* Exchange or barter commodities, swap. Sh. iad na h-eich, *they exchanged the horses.*
———each, -eiche, *a.* Exchanging, bartering. 2 Fond of bartering.
suaipeachail,(MS) *a.* Sweepy.
suaipeadh,-idh, *s.m.* Exchanging, act of exchanging commodities. A' s—, *pr.pt.* of suaip.
suairc, -e, *a.* Civil, kind, affable, polite. 2 Meek, gentle. 3 Urbane. 4 Courtly. 5 Generous. 6 Accostable. 7**Amicable. Le giùlan s., *with generous conduct;* s. siobhalta, *affable and civil.*
suairceachd,* *s.f.* see suairceád.
suaircead, -eid, *s.m.* Civility, degree of civility, kindness or affability.
suaircealachd, *s.f.* Gentleness. 2 Mannerliness.
suaircean,(AC) *s.m.* Bird. 2 (DMu) Term of endearment, applied to a meek and lovable man—*Black Isle.*
suairceas, -eis, *s. m.* Urbanity, affability. 2 Kindness, gentleness. 3** Amicableness. 4 Civility, complaisance. 5*Politeness. Gun s. ri damhaich, *unkind to strangers—MacCodrum.*
suaite, see suaithte.
suaiteachan, -ain, *s.m.* Shrugging of the shoulders. 2 Rubbing the body against the clothes. 3**Mixer. 4**Kneader.
suaiteachanach, -aiche, *a.* That shrugs the shoulders and rubs the body against the clothes.
†suaiteachd, *s.f.ind.* Fatigue, labour. 2 Tempering. 3 Mixing together. [Seeming.
suaitheantas, *s. m.* see suaicheantas. 2 (MS)
suaithte, *past pt.* of suath. Rubbed. 2 Kneaded. 3 Mixed. 4 Much broken, fatigued. 5** Stirred about, as posset.
sual,** -aile, *a.* Famous, renowned. [This and following word are spelt *suall* by ** in his appendix.]
——,** -ail, *s.m.* Wonder. 2 Tumours—*Sàr-Obair.*
sualach,** *a.* Famous, admirable.
suamhnas, see suaimhneas.
suan, -uain, see suain.
suanach, -aiche, -aichean, *s. f.* Hide, skin. 2 Plough-rein. 3 Covering or coarse garment. 4 Fleece. 5**Pall. 6 Plaid. 7* Mantle. Gun s., *without covering.*
suanaich, *s.pl.* Tha 'mhacraidh 'nan s. fo stéidh nam ballachan, *the race* (lit. *sons*) *are sleeping lower than the foundations of the walls—Filidh, p. 60.*
suanaran,** -ain, *s.m.* Sleeper.
suantach,** *a.* Lethargic, drowsy. 2 Narcotic.
suarach, -aiche, *a.* Insignificant, trifling, of little worth, valueless, not valuable, paltry, abject, mean. 2 Despised, contemned, of no repute. 3 Trifling. 4 Contemptible, silly. 5* Indifferent. Dealbh s., *a despised idol ;* na cuir s., *do not despise ;* tha mi s. uime, *I am indifferent about it;* duine no ni suarach, *a paltry person or thing;* bu shuarach dhuit ged a dheanadh tu sin, *it were a light matter though you should do that ;* gnothach s., *a paltry or shabby thing ;* cuir s., *despise.*
suarach,‡ *a.* Careless.
suarachan,(WC) *s.m.* Worthless person.
suarachas, -ais, *s.m.* Neglect, abjectness, indifference. 2 Insignificance. 3 Contempt. 4* Nought, trifling nature or quality. S. an ni seo, *the contemptible nature of this thing;* na cuir an s. an ni seo, *do not set this thing at nought,* do not make light of it.
suaraich, *v.a.* Derogate.
suaraiche, *s.f.* see suarachas. 2 *comp.* of *a.* suar-

ach.

suaraichead, -eid, *s.f.* Meanness, degree of meanness or insignificance. 2* Contemptibleness. 3**Diminution in value. 4* Degree of indifference. A' dol an s. uime, *getting more indifferent about it.*

suaraicheas, see suarachas.

suarcas,** -ais, *s. m.* Wit, drollery.

suarrach, -aiche, see suarach.

suarrachas, see suarachas.

suarrachd,(MS) *s.f.* Baldness.

suas, (i.e. a suas) *adv.* Up, upward, (away from one.) 2 Westwards. Shuas, *above, above there, above yonder* ; o seo s., *henceforth* ; thoir s. ort! *up with you!* chaidh e s., *he went up* ; chaidh e suas air beinn, *he went up into (on) a mountain* ; cha'n 'eil a suas air fichead ann, *there are not more than twenty* (lit. *in it*) ; sìos is s., *eastward and westward* (on the E. coast); tog s., *rear, educate* ; dean s., *make up, constitute.* *Suas* also conveys the idea of *resting* when completion of movement upwards is meant, as, tha e s., *he* or *it is above* ; suas leis a' Ghàidhlig ! *up with the Gaelic !*

†suas, -ais, *s.m.* Urbanity.

suasaid, see tuasaid.

†suas-mhol, *v.a.* Magnify, extol, flatter, exalt, puff up.

suath, *pr.pt.* a' suathadh, *v. a.* Rub, wipe. 2 Mix any soft substances together. 3 Stir, or move about, as porridge or any inspissated substance. 4 Mash, as potatoes. 5 Knead. 6 Thrash out barley by rubbing it with the feet. 7**Claw. 8**Temper. 9 Foment. 10 Fray. 11 Chafe.

suathach,†† *a.* Rubbing. 2 Afflicted.

suathadair, -ean, *s.m.* Rubber.

——————eachd,†† *s.f.* Rubbing.

suathadh, -aidh, *s.m.* Rubbing, act of rubbing or wiping, friction. 2 Act of mixing any soft substances together. 3 Act of stirring or moving anything about. 4 Mode of thrashing barley by rubbing it with the feet. 5 Kneading. 6 Affliction. 7†† Wringing of the hands. Is fèarr s. ri crois na fuaigheal ri crois, *better rub against a pest than be bound to a pest* ; aol-tàthaidh gun s., *untempered mortar.* A' s—, *pr.pt.* of suath.

suathaid,(DMy) *a.* Notable.

————eas,(DMy) *s.m.* Mark or cut caused by a blow. Is tu a chuir an s. orm, *how you have marked me !*

suathan-innseanaich, *s.m.* India-rubber.

suathran,** *s.m.* Vertigo.

suathta, *past pt.* of suath. Rubbed. 2*Mashed.

sùbag,** *s.f.* Hood, kerchief. Currac sùbaig, *a sow-backed mutch.*

sùbailte, *a.* Supple, flexible, pliant, agile, nimble, elastic. Spiorad s., *a flexible mind.*

————achd, *s. f.* Suppleness, flexibility, nimbleness, elasticity.

subaiste,** *s.f.* Mouth.

subas,** -ais, *s.m.* Mishmash, mess of wild berries and milk.

sùbh, -ùibh, -an, *s.m.* Berry. 2(AH) see sùdh. 3††Fruit generally. 4(AH)Plait, series of plaits or an excision in a garment to tighten it—the opposite of gore.

sùbh, *s.m.* Raspberry. [also subh.]

subh, *s. m.* Raspberry. 2 Fruit generally—*Argyll.*

†sùbh, see sùgh.

†subh, -a, *s.m.* Pleasure, delight, joy, mirth.

subhach, -aiche, *a.* Merry, happy, cheerful. Bha iad s., *they were merry.*

————as, -ais, *s.m.* Mirth, happiness, cheerfulness, gladness, merriness, pleasure, joy. Is mairg a dheanadh s. ri dubhachas fir eile, *pity him who rejoices in another's woe* ; deireadh an t-subhachais sin, *the end if that (mirth) laughter.*

subhag, -aig, -an, *s.f.* Raspberry. 2 Strawberry, see sùbh-thalmhainn. [‡also sùbhag.]

————ach, -aiche, *a.* Abounding in raspberries or strawberries.

sùbhag-làir, *s.f.* Strawberry.

subhaich,(MS) *v.a.* Rejoice.

subhaiche, *s.f.ind.* Happiness, state of being happy or joyful.

subhailc, -e, -ean, *s.f.* Virtue, moral goodness, moral excellence. Bean na s., *a virtuous woman.*

subhailceach, -eiche, *a.* Virtuous, of or pertaining to virtue, moral. Cò a gheibh bean sh., *who can find a virtuous woman ?*

subhailceachd, *s. f.* Virtuousness, quality of possessing virtue.

subhailcead,†† *s.* Degree of virtue.

†subhallach,** *a.* Religious.

†subhaltach, -aiche, *a.* see subhach.

†subhaltas, -ais, *s.m.* see subhachas.

subhan,** -ain, *s.m.* Juice, sap. 2 Water impregnated with the juice of corn-seeds, of which a coagulated kind of food, called sowens, is made. [sùbhan—*Gairloch.*]

sùbhan-làir, see sùbh-làir.

subhar, *a.* see sùghmhor.

sùbh-chraobh, sùibh-ch-, sùbhan-ch-, *s.m.* Raspberry-bush. 2 Any bush that yields wild berries.

sùbh-craobh, sùibh-c-, -an-c-, *s. m.* Raspberry. 2**Dewberry.

sùbh-chraoibh, see sùbh-chraobh.

subhlach,** -aich, *s. m.* Juice pressed out of apples or other fruit. 2 Liquor.

sùbh-làir, -ùibh-, -an-, *s. m.* Wood-strawberry, see sùbh-thalmhainn.

subhmhor, see sùghmhor.

sùbh-nam-ban-mìn, *s. m.* Stonebramble, see caora-bad-miann. 2 Bogberry.

sùbh-nam-ban-sìthe,§ Stonebramble, see caora-bad-miann.

sùbh-thalmhainn,§ *s.m.* Wood-strawberry.

sùblachadh, -aidh, *s.m.* Act of making supple or flexible. A' —s, *pr.pt.* of sùblaich.

sùblaich, *pr.pt.* a' sùblachadh, *v.a. & n.* Make supple or flexible. 2 Grow supple. 3 (DC) Recede, become less in bulk, as a swelling.

sùblaichte, *past pt.* of sùblaich. Made flexible or supple. 2 Grown flexible.

sùcan, -ain, *s. m.* Earthen pot. 2 Anything wrought awkwardly together, as clay.

sùcar, see siùcar.

sùcarach, see siùcarach.

†such, *v.a.* Suck, imbibe. 2 Saturate, fill.

such, *s.m.* Whispering noise.

suchadh, -aidh, *s.m.* †Imbibing. †2Filling, saturating. †3 Wave. 4 Suction, evaporation. A' s—, *pr.pt.* of such.

suchan, -ain, *s.m.* Sucker.

sùchd, *s.m.* Sake, account. Air s. mhaitheis, *for goodness' sake* ; air s. Chriosda, *for Christ's sake* ; air s. nan achd, *for the sake of these objections.*

sùchdar, see siùcar.

sùchta, *past pt.* of such, see sùghta.

†sucraidh, *a.* Easy.

suc ! suc ! (repeated several times) *int.* Call to sheep—*Islay.*

sud, see siod.

sudag,** -aig, *s.f.* Cake.

sudar, *s.m.* Currier.

sùdh, -ùidh, -an, *s.m.* Overlap in planks of a boat, see bàta, B, p. 73.

†**sudh**, *a.* Secure.
sùdh, see sùgh.
sùdhair, see sùghmhor.
sùdhar, *a.* see sùghmhor. 2 (MS) Alimental.
sudral,** -ail, *s.m.* Light. 2 Candle.
sùg, -a, *s.m.* Cheerfulness, hilarity, mirth, happiness.
sùg, *pr.pt.* a' sùgadh, *v.a.* Suck, imbibe. 2** Soak. 3**Attract.
sùg,* *s.m.* Lamb. 2 *int.* Mode of calling a lamb —*Argyll.*
sùgach, -aiche, *a.* Merry, cheerful, pleasant, festive. 2 (MS) Humorous, comical. 3(MS)Attractive.
sùgach, -aiche, *a.* Sucking, that sucks.
sùgachas, -ais, *s.m.* Jocularity, mirth.
sùgadh, -aidh, *s.m.* Sucking, act of sucking or imbibing, suction. 2**Attraction. A' *pr. pt.* of sùg.
sùgag, -aig, -an, *s.f.* Little drink or suck.
——,§ -aig, *s.f.* Red clover, see seamrag-chapuill. 2**Bloom of clover, so called from its containing a honeyed juice.
sugag,(G) *s.f.* Sheep—*Islay.*
sùgaich,(MS) *v.a.* Joy.
sùgaiche, *s.f.ind.* Cheerfulness, merriness, hilarity.
sùgaidheachd,** *s.f.* Joyousness.
sùgair, -ean, *s.m.* Droll or merry fellow, merry-andrew. 2 Sucker. 3 Mountebank.
sùgair,* *v.n.* Make merry, sport.
——eachd, *s.f.* Drollery, buffoonery.
sùgan, -ain, -an, *s. m.* Rope of twisted straw. 2 Rope of twisted heath. 3(DC)Thatch-rope—*Uist.* 4 Horse's collar—*Mull & Islay.* 5** Straw collar for cattle. Corra-shùgan, *a twist-handle.*
sugan, -ain, -an, *s.m.* Pet lamb.
sùgan, *s.m.* (i. e. corra-shugain) The reflection of the rays of light on the walls or roof of a house, from any luminous body in motion.
sùganach, -aiche, *a.* Abounding in straw-ropes. 2 Like a straw-rope.
sugar,** *s.m.* Band for the neck.
sùgh, -a & -ùigh, *pl.* -an, *s.m.* Juice, sap, moisture. 2 Sense, meaning. 3 Wave, billow. 4 Substance. 5**Berry. 6‡‡ Juice of meat, broth. 7‡‡Motion of the waves. 8* Huge receding wave. 9* Dearest object, darling. A shùgh mo chridhe! *my dearest! my darling!* s. feòla, *soup;* tha 'n s. fuar, *the moisture on the earth is cold;* gnothach gun s., *a senseless or sapless affair;* s. nan ubbal, *the sap of the apples;* s. nan gràn-ubhall, *the juice of the pomegranates;* s. am poit, *broth in a pot;* druim nan s., *the backs of the waves;* a ceann ris na sùghaibh, *her head against the billows.* [*pl.* sùghaichean in *Sgeul.nan caol, p. 101*—Na sùghaichean lùn-corrach, sìnteach a' gleannadh gu Cinn Inbhir-Àir, *the billows and their troughs rolling towards the Heads of Ayr.*]
sùgh, *v.a. & n.* Drain, dry, dry up, drink up. 2 Become dry, dry up. 3 Suck in, imbibe, swallow as if by suction. 4 Absorb. 5 Evaporate. 6 Season, shrink, as wood. 7 Extract. 8(DMy) Drip.
Sh. e 'm fallus, *it absorbed the perspiration;* sh. am fiodh, *the wood seasoned;* sh. an t-ombar an dùradan á m' shùil, *the amber extracted the mote from my eye;* sh. an còs an t-uisge, *the sponge absorbed the water;* s. ort e, *suck it in;* sh. a' phoit, *the pot dried up;* sh. a h-uile deur, *every drop evaporated.*
sùghach, -aiche, *a.* Attractive. 2‡‡Juicy. 3** Abounding in berries.
sùghachan, *s.m.* Syphon.
sùghadair,(MS) *s.m.* Attracter.
sùghadh, -aidh, *s. m.* Draining, act of draining, drying up or drinking up. 2 State of becoming dry. 3 Sucking, act of sucking or swallowing. 4**Absorption. 5 Seasoning, as wood 6 Motion of the waves. 7 Leakage—*Dàin I. Ghobha.* 8*Extracting the juice. A' s—, *pr. pt.* of sùgh. S. nan tonn, *the flux and reflux of the waves;* tha 'm fiodh air s., *the wood is seasoned;* a' s. an smior as, *extracting the very marrow from it;* thug an s. leis e, *the receding waves carried it away.*
sùghag, see sùbhag.
sùghail, -e, *a.* see sùghmhor.
†**sùghainte**, -an, *s.f.* Whirlpool, gulf.
sùghair, see sùghmhor.
sùghaireachd,* *s.f.* see sùghmhorachd.
sùghalachd,(MS) *s.f.* Alimentariness.
sùghan, -ain, *s.m.* Juice of sowens, or liquid from which they are made by boiling. (sùbhan.)
sùghanach, see sùghmhor.
sùgh an daraich,§ *s.m.* Mistletoe, see uil'-ìoc.
sùghar, see sùghmhor.
sùgh-bhrìgh, see sùgh-bruich.
sugh-bhrìgheach, *a.* Juicy.
sùgh-bhrìghear, see sùgh-bhrioghmhor.
sùgh bhrioghmhor, *a.* Juicy.
sùgh-bruich, *s.m.* Decoction, juice.
sùgh-cadail,‡‡ *s.m.* Opium.
sùgh-chraobh, see sùbh-chraobh.
sùgh-dharaich,** *s.m.* Mistletoe, see uil'-ìoc.
sùgh-làr, see sùbh-làir.
sùghmhor, -oire, *a.* Juicy, sappy, moist. 2 Substantial, having much substance or solidity, solid, strong. 3 Sensible, intelligent. 4 Inventive. 5**Billowy. 6* Pithy. 7*Succulent.
sùghmhorachd, *s.f.ind.* Juiciness, succulency, sappiness. 2 Substantiality, solidity, strength. 3 Understanding, intelligence, acuteness of mind.
sùgh-pheuran, *s.m.* Perry.
sùghta, *past pt.* of sùgh. Absorbed, dried up, evaporated. 2 Saturated, filled, tightened. 3 Seasoned, as wood. 4 Boiled in. 5 Sucked. Fiodh s., *seasoned wood.* (sùghte.)
sùgh-ubhall, *s.m.* Cider.
sùgrach, -aiche, *a.* Mirthful, sportful.
————ail, -e, see sùgrach.
sùgradh, -aidh, *s.m.* Mirth, diversion, sport, play, sporting, joke. Cha'n 'eil thu 'nad sh., *it is no joke to deal with you;* cha'n e an s. a chur ris, *it is no joke to manage,* or *master him;* dh'éirich iad suas gu s., *they rose up to play;* ri s., *in sport;* nigheann donn an t-sùgraidh, *the brown-haired sportive maiden;* a' s. ri 'mhnaoi, *sporting with his wife;* mu sh. *about mirth.*
sùgradh-baoth,(MS) *s.m.* Apishness.
suibbeag, -eig, -an, *s.f.* see sùbhag.
————ach, see sùbhagach.
suibhealas,** -ais, *s.m.* Sponging, sharking.
suibheallan,** -ain, *s.m.* Parasite.
suic, *gen.sing. & n.pl.* of soc.
sùicean, -ein, -an, *s.m.* Gag to prevent a calf from sucking.
suidh, *pr. pt.* a' suidhe, *v.a.* Sit down. 2 Incubate, sit on eggs.
suidh, ** *s.m.* Hero, champion. (saoidh.)
sùidh, see sùith.
sùidh, *v.* see sùgh.
suidhe, *pl.* -an & -achan, *s.m.* Beam or supporter of a house. 2 Seat. 3 Sitting. 4 Séjant, in *heraldry.* 5 Sederunt, session. 6‡‡Incubation. 7 Level shelf on a hill-side, where one would naturally rest. 8 see sùithe. 9* Act or state of sitting. A' s—, *pr. pt.* of suidh. Maide-

suidhe, *couple of a house; the spar to which is attached the chain or crook on which to hang pots over a fire in the middle of the floor*, also called maide-slabhraidh ; dean s., *sit, be seated; 'na sh., he sitting; 'na s., she sitting*; s. bìdh, *a meal.*

suidheachadh, -aidh, *s.m.* Settling, arbitration, act of settling, appointing, arranging, planning. 2 Planting, act of planting. 3 Letting, act of letting for rent. 4 Setting the pattern for tartan or other cloth to be woven, formed by placing threads on a small piece of wood, according to the design proposed and kept as a key to the number of threads of each colour and the positions of the various colours in the pattern. 5‡‡ Specimen, pattern. 6 Set or pattern, as of tartan. 7 Order, arrangement, disposition. 8* Laying foundation, making framework. 9* Planting, colonizing, establishing. 10* Situation, posture. 11 Betrothing, arranging terms of marriage. 12 *Plan, model. A' s—, *pr.pt.* of suidhich. Air a' cheart sh., *on the same plan or pattern, as cloth*; s. fearainn, *a letting of lands for rent*; s. inntinn, *gravity.*

suidheach ail, -e, *a.* see suidhchte.

suidheachan, -ain, -an, *s.m.* Seat, chair, stool, pew, bench to sit on, settle. 2**Rustic seat. 3 Cushion. 4 Stern-seat in a boat. 5 (DC) Stook of corn (6 or 8 sheaves)—*Uist.* 6* Turf-sofa.

suidheachas, *s.m.* see suidhichteachd.

sùidheag, see sùbhag.

————ach, see sùbhagach.

————an, *dim.* of sùidheag.

suidheagan, see suidheachan.

suidhealachd,** *s.f.* Gravity.

sùidhean, *s.m.* Seam joining divided planks in a boat (see p. 77.) (sùdh.)

suidheann,** -einn, *s.m.* Ship's cable.

sùidhe-bhalach, see sùith-bhalach.

suidhe-bìdh, *s.m.* Meal, diet.

sùidhe-làir,* see sùbh-làir. 2* *s.m.* Framework, groundwork.

suidhich, *pr.pt.* a' suidheachadh, *v.a.* Settle, appoint, order, plan, arrange. 2 Place, plant, set. 3 Set, let for rent. 4* Betrothe, settle terms of marriage. 5 Win. 6**Pitch. 7** Repose. 8††Lease. 9**Make an appointment, agree. Sh. e an taigh (*no* am baile) *he let the house* (or *the farm*); sh. e a nigheann air, *he betrothed his daughter to him*; s. àite far an tachair sinn, *appoint a place where we shall meet*; sh. iad an stéidh, *they laid the foundation*; sh. Fionn an t-seilg, *F. arranged the hunt*; agus sh. an Tighearna gàradh, *and the Lord planted a garden*; sh. e beosnlaint oirre, *he settled an annuity on her*; sh. e a bhùth, *he pitched his tent*; sh. iad faire, *they set a watch.*

suidhichdeachd, see suidhichteachd.

suidhichear, *fut.pass.* of suidhich.

suidhichte, *a. & past pt.* of suidhich. Planned, settled, arranged, appointed, determined, fixed. 2 Placed, planted, set. 3 Let, let for rent. 4 Sedate, grave, steady. 5 Pitched, as a tent. 6 Established. 7 Composed. 8* Laid, as a foundation. 9* Pointed out. 10**Stationary. 12(DC) Married or deforis familiated (applied to the daughters of a family)—*Arggll.* Tha 'n t-àite s., *the place is appointed or determined, the property is let*; tha mi suidhichte air sin a dheanamh, *I am determined to do that*; duine s., *a sedate person*; air an là s., *on the appointed day*; is còir do na mnathaibh 'bhi s., *wives ought to be grave.*

suidhichteachd, *s.f.ind.* Steadiness, equanimity. 2 Consideration.

sùidhte, see sùithte.

sui'eag, see sùbhag.

suig.(AF) *s.* Pig.

sùig, *v.a. & n.* see sùg.

suigean,‡‡ -ein, *s.m.* Place made of straw-ropes to contain grain in a barn. The grain placed in a heap on the floor is confined from spreading by straw-ropes set round the margin. 2 Crupper.

suigeanta,(MS) *a.* Alacrious.

súigeart, -eirt, -an, *s.m.* Gladness, cheerfulness, joy, frisking of an animal for joy. 2(MS) Pith. 3* Blustering kind of expression of joy. Òlamaid slàinte Thearlaich le s., *let us drink Charlie's health with gladness*; a' dol le s. do 'n choille, *going frisking to the wood.*

suigeartach, -aiche, *a.* Frisking for joy, glad-cheerful, blythe.

suigeartachd,** *s.f.* Blythesomeness.

sùigh, see sùith.

sùigh, *v.a. & n.* see sùgh.

sùigheach,** *a.* Absorbent.

suighean, (for suidhean) *pl.* of suidhe.

sùighte, see sughta.

sùighteach,(MS) *a.* Attractive.

suigionnach, -aiche, *a.* see suigeartach.

suigleadh,** -idh, *s.m.* Snot.

sùil, *gen.sing.* sùl & sùla, *dat.* sùil, *voc.* a shùil ! *n.pl.* sùilean, *gen.pl.* sùl, *dat.pl.* sùilean & sùilibh, *voc.pl.* a shùla, *s.f.* Eye, the eye. 2 Look, glance, cast of the eye in any direction, sight. 3 Hope, expectation. 4 Care, oversight, superintendence. 5 Orifice, opening. 6 Willow, see seileach. 7 Eye of a quern. 8**Regard, respect. 9**Loop-hole. 10** *rarely*, Tackle. 11 Eye through which the wool passes to spinning-wheel. 13 Thimble of a boat. 14**The letter S. 15(DC) Small cluster of herring in the water, less than a shoal—*Lochfyne.* 16 (AH) Hole in which the shaft of a tool like a pick-axe is fixed.

Bha mo cheud s., *my first glance or sight was*; thog e a sh., *he raised his eye*; gun s. r' a theachd, *not expecting his coming*; tha s. againn ris, *we expect him*; na bitheadh s. no dùil agad ris, *neither have expectation nor hope of him*; bitheadh s. agad orra, *watch or keep your eye on them*; an cuir tobar a mach as an aon sh. uisge milis is searbh ? *will a fountain send forth from the same opening sweet and bitter water ?* tha 'sh. ri teachd, *he expects to come*; dh' fhalbh na sùilean geala, *the blindness has gone*; nach ann agam bha na sùilean geala ! *how stupid I was !* fliuch do sh., *wet your eye*, (or, fliuch do sh. mu'n lean e rithe, *wet your eye lest it sticks to it*) i.e. in case you have the evil eye, and the thing referred to becomes yours or dwindles away. The remark is usually made when relating something of an auspicious nature about a person in the hearing, who in turn would say " fliuch do shùil," meaning that the narrator was not to be envious of the prosperity of the other. The remark may be used in reference to one's property, as well as to his fame, &c. Cha'n i mo sh. is eagal duit, *there is nothing for you to fear from my eye* (another saying of the same nature as the last, only it comes from the party who has made the favourable remark about anyone, and adding, " Cha'n e mo sh. a's eagal duit;"); 's mò làn do sh. na làn do bhronn, *the full of your eye is more than the full of your belly*; s. mo thruaighe, *the eye that deserves pity*—the equivalent of a woe begone look ; tha 'n s. ri lear, *their eye is towards the sea*; mòralachd 'na sh., *majesty in his aspect*; tha s. chrom aige, is said of one who looks from the outer corner of his eye in a furtive manner ; s. mu 'n t-sròn, *to his cheek*—used in this way, chaidh innseadh dha s. mu 'n t-s., *it was told him to his cheek.* Beul mu 'n fhiacail, has the same meaning, only the mouth and teeth are mentioned instead of the eye and nose; s. na bràthan, *the eye of the quern ;* s. rag, *a dim eye ;* s. gheur, *a sharp eye.*

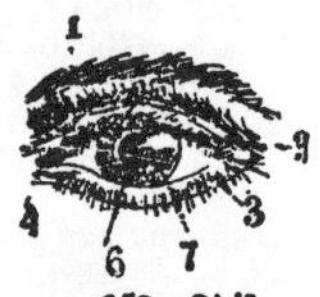

652. *Sùil.*

PARTS OF AN EYE—
1 Malaidhean, *eyebrows.*
3 Rosgan na sùla, fabhraidhean, *eyelashes.*
4 Toiseach na sùla, *end next to nose.*
5 Deireadh na sùla, *end farthest from nose.*
6 An dubhagan, fradharc na sùla, dubh na na sùla, *pupil.*
7 Cearcall na sùla, *iris.*
8 Ball na sùla, *eyelid.*
9 Clach na sùla, rinn an ruisg, ubhal, *eyeball.*
10 Geal na sùla, gealagan na sùla, *the white.*

†suil, *conj.* Before that, ere. see seal & sol. (sul.)
sùil-an-tòin,(AF) *s.* Cuttle-fish.
†suilbh, -e, *s.f.* Cheer, hospitality, geniality.
suil-bhalair, see suil-mhalair.
suilbhear, -a, *a.* see suilbhir.
———achd, *s.f.* see suilbhireachd.
sùil-bheum, -a, -an & -annan, *s.m.* Hurtful influence of the evil eye.
sùil-bheumach, -aiche, *a.* Having an evil eye. 2 Blasting with the eye.
suilbhir, -e, *a.* Cheerful, merry, joyful, hearty, pleasant. 2 *originally* Eloquent. Laoich nan gorm-shùil s., *hero of the cheerful blue eyes.*
suilbhire, *comp.* of suilbhir.
suilbhireach, -eiche, *a.* see suilbhir.
suilbhireachd, *s.f.ind.* Cheerfulness, joyfulness, gaiety, hilarity. 2 Alacrity. 3††Civility. 4 Frankness. 5 Merriness.
suilbhirich,** *v.* Animate.
sùil-charbh,(AF) *s,f.* Silver haddock.
sùil-chrìch, *Arran* for sùil-chritheach.
sùil-chrith, see sùil-chritheach.
sùil-chritheach, -ich, *s.f.* Quagmire, deep bog.
sùil-chruthaich, -e, see sùil-chritheach.
sùileach, -eiche, *a.* Having good eyes, sharp, quick-sighted. 2* Knowing. 3**Ocular. 4 Like an eye. 5 Eyed, having many eyes. 6 Of, or belonging to, the eye.
sùileachan,(CR) *s.m.* Warning, lesson, eye-opener. Bheir siod s. dha, *that will be a warning or lesson to him—W. of Ross.*
sùileachd,(AC) *s.f.* Influence of the evil eye.
sùileag, -eig, -an, *s.f.dim.* of sùil. Little eye. 2 Small orifice. 3 Small bubble, bell on liquor. 4 Little circular wooden vessel. 5**Pore. 6 (MMcD) Small vessel made of clay containing one Scots pint, and used for keeping milk —*Lewis.* 7(DC) Girl after three months of age, when see opens her eyes and looks about her. 8§ Common sallow (plant)—*salix caprea & s. aquatica.* 9 Earmark on sheep, see under comharradh-cluais. 10*Spot in cloth. 11 Little loop.
———ach, -aiche, *a.* Having little eyes. 2 Full of little eyes. 3 Full of small orifices. 4 Full of small bubbles. 5* Spotted. 6 Full of loop-holes.
sùilean, *n.pl.* of sùil.
sùilean,(DC) *s.m.* Boy child after three months of age when he opens his eyes and looks about him.
suileasg,** -eisg, *s.f.* Osier.
sùil-fhrasachd, *s.f.* Lachrymation.
suilleach,(CR) *a.* Clear, bright—*Suth'd.*
suilleag,** -eig, -an, *s.f.* Bell, bubble.
———ach, *a.* Full of bells or bubbles.
sùil-léigh, -ean, *s.m.* Oculist.
sùil-leìgheas,** -eis, *s.m.* Eye-salve.
sùil-leusach,** *s.f.* Wall-eye.
sùil-lighiche,* see sùil-léigh.
sùil-lionnach, -aiche, *a.* Watery-eyed.
sùil-mhalair, *s.m.* Cockatrice.
sùil-mhala-righ, see sùil-mhalair.
sùil-mhargach,** *a.* Forestaller.
sùil-mhargaidh, -ean, *s.m.* Forestaller on the market.
suil mu'n, *adv.* Ere, before.
sùil-radharc,*, *s.* Fascination. 2 Foresight. 3 Sense of sight, vision. 4 Fate.
———ach,** *a.* Fascinating. 2 Having the sense of sight.
sùilteach, -aiche, *a.* see sùileach.
suim, *v.a.* Sum, compute.
suim, -e, -eannan, *s.f.* Sum, amount. 2 Consideration, respect, regard, care, attention. 3 (AH) Number of cattle, sheep and horses assigned to a certain holding as that which the tenant is entitled to keep, see sum. Cha bhi s. aige dh' éiric, *he shall not regard a ransom ;* cha'n 'eil s. ann dhomh-sa, *it makes no difference to me ;* gabh s, *pay attention ;* mur dìol sinn an s. cheart, *if we do not pay the right sum;* cha 'n 'eil s. sam bith aige do d' ghnothach, *he pays no attention whatever to your business.*
suim-bhliadhnail, *s.f.* Annuity.
suimeachadh,(AH) *s.m.* The periodical counting and adjusting of stock by tenants holding grazing in common.
suimealachd, *s.f.ind.* Respect, regard. 2 Importance. 3 Attentiveness, care, considerateness.
†suimear, -ir, -an, *s.m.* Shin, shank.
suimeil, -e, *a.* Attentive, regardful. 2 Momentous, important, considerable. 3 Considerate. 4 Respectful. Gu s., *regardfully.*
———eachd, see suimealachd.
suinn, *gen.sing. & n.pl.* of sonn.
suineann,** *s.m.* Stammering.
suip, *gen.sing. & n.pl.* of sop.
suipean, see sopan.
suipear, -ach, -an, see suipeir.
suipeir, -e & -each, *pl.* -an, *s. f.* Supper. S. an Tighearna, *the Lord's Supper, Eucharist ;* an déigh na suipeireach, *after supper.* [*suipear.]
suipeireach, -eiche, *a.* Cenatory,
———, *gen. sing.* of suipeir.
suirbhe, see suiridhe.
suirbheach, -ich, *s.m.* see suiridheach.
suire, *s.f.* Maid, nymph, mermaid, syren, fairy, nereids. Also used in a *pl.* sense.—**
suireach,* -eiche, *a,* see suiridheach.
———,* -eich, *s.m.* see suiridheach.
suireadh, -idh, -idhean, *s.m.* see suire.
suireadh, see suiridhe.
suirghe,†† *s.f.* see suiridhe.
suirgheach, see suiridheach.
suirich, see suiridhe.
suiriche, *s.m.* Wooer. 2 Fool.
suirichean-suirich,§ *s, m.* Burdock (*lit.* foolish wooer)—*arctium lappa.* (ill. 653.)
suiridhche, see suiridheach.
suiridhe, *s.f.ind.* Courting, address, wooing, making love.
———ach, -ich, -ichean, *s.m.* Lover, wooer. 2

Shuffler. [‡ says better suirtheach & suireach, but he retains suiridhe & suiridheach as the principal spellings.]

653. *Suiricheán-suirich.*

suiridheach, -eiche, *a.* Courting, wooing, that courts or wooes. 2 Ready to court or woo.
————ail, -e, *a.* Gallant.
suirighe, see suiridhe.
suirim, -ean, *s.m.* see surram.
suirtheach, see suiridheach.
————adh, see suiridhe.
suirtheadh, see suiridhe.
suirthiche, -an, *s.m.* Suitor, lover.
suisdealadh,* -aidh, *s.m.* Drubbing. 2 Hard work, working by night and day.
sùist, -e, -ean, *s.f.* Flail. 2 Battle-flail, an implement of warfare much used in ancient times.
Parts of a Flail—
Buailtean, *swiple*, the part that threshes the corn.
Lorg, *staff, handle.* Lamhargan—*Arran.*
Sail shùiste, iall, iall shùiste, *the thong of sheepskin* which attaches the staff to the buailtean.
sùist, *v.a.* Thresh. 2 Beat, thump.
sùisteach, *a.* Pertaining to a flail. 2 Like a flail.
sùisteachadh,** -aidh, *s. m.* Threshing with a flail.
sùisteachd, *s. f.* Threshing, employment of a thresher.
sùisteadh, -idh, *s.m.* Threshing, act of threshing, 2 Thumping or beating, act of thumping or beating. A' s—, *pr.pt.* of sùist.
sùistear, -ir, -an, *s.m.* Thresher, one who threshes.
————achd, *s. f.* Process of threshing. 2 †† Business of threshing.
sùith, *s.m.* Soot. Neul an t-sùith, *the colour of soot.* [sùthaidh in *Gairloch.* ** gives *sùithe* as *nom.*]
sùith,** *v a.* Soot, cover with soot. 2 Season or dry in smoke.
sùith-bhalach, *s. m.* Chimney-sweep. [sùithebhalach.]
sùith dubh, *s.m.* The black sooty drops that fall from the inside of a thatched roof after a rainstorm.
suithe,** s. Balk, beam. (suidhe.)
sùitheach, -eiche, *a.* Sooty, of, or belonging to, soot. 2 Full of soot.
sùitheachd,(MS) *s.f.* Sootiness.
sùithte. *past pt.* of sùith.
†sul,(MM) *conj.* Ere, before.
sùl, *gen.pl.* of sùil. 2 see sùla. 3 see sult.
†sul, -uil, *s.m.* The sun.

sùla, *gen.sing.* of sùil.
sùla, (a sh— !) *voc.pl.* of sùil.
sulag.(MMcD) *s.f* see sùileag.
sùlaiche,(AF) see sùlair.
sùlair, -ean, *s.m.* Gannet, solan goose—*sula bassana* 2(AF) Any voracious bird. 3 Voracious person. [sulair—AH.]

654. *Sùlair.*

sùlaireach, -eiche, *a.* Of, or belonging to gannets. 2 Like a gannet. 3††Sharp-eyed.
sûlas, see sòlas.
sulas,* -ais, *s.m.* Complaisance, over-joy showing itself by gestures and expression of countenance. Air son sulais riut-sa, *out of sheer complacency to you ;* 's e a rinn an s. ! *how overjoyed he was !*
——ach,* -aiche, *a.* Over-joyed, complaisant—*Islay.*
sùl-bheachd, -an, *s.m.* Attention. 2 Watchful, diligent observation. 3 Eyesight. Air gach taobh tha s., *on every side there is watchfulness.*
————ail, -e, *a.* Attentive. 2 Observant.
sulchair, -e, *a.* Cheerful. 2 Affable. 3 Hospitable. 4 Jocular. 5* Overjoyed. Gu s., *heartily.* [‡sulchar.]
————e, see sulchaireachd.
————eachd, *s.f.ind.* Cheerfulness. 2 Affability, frankness, heartiness. 3 Hospitality. 4 Jocularity.
sùlmhor, -oire, *a.* Quick-sighted.
————achd, *s.f.* Quick-sightedness.
sul mu'n,(MM) *adv.* Ere, before.
sùl-radharc, -airc, *s.m.* Eye-sight. 2 Foresight. 3 Fate. 4 Fascination.
————ach,** *a.* Provident, foresighted, foreseeing. 2 Fascinating. 3 Sharp-sighted.
————achd, *s.f.* Providence. 2 Sharp-sightedness.
sùl-sgàilich,(MS) *v.a.* Blindfold.
sult, -uilt, *s.m.* Fat, plumpness, fatness. 2 Comeliness, beauty. 3 Mirth, joy, jest. 4(AF)Fat herring. 5††Blubber. De sh. na talmhainn, *of the fatness of the earth;* s. is ìgh, *fatness and plenty.*
sultach,** *a.* Fat. 2(MS)Flabby.
sultag,(AC) -aig, *s.f.* Fat little girl or female beast.
sultaireachd,* see sultmhorachd.
sultan,(AC) -ain, *s.m.* Fat little boy or male beast. Mios sultain, *the month of fatness* (*October.*)
sultar, see sultmhor.
sultmhor, -oire, *a.* Fat, plump, in good condition, corpulent, lusty. 7 Fertile. 3 Fair, comely. 4 Merry, joyful, jolly. 5 Jesting, pleasant, jocose.
————achd, *s.f.ind.* Fat, fatness, plumpness, corpulence. 2 Comeliness, beauty. 3 Mirth, joy, jest. [**sultmhoireachd.]
Sultuine, *s.m.* September. [Preceded by the art. *an.* DC says second half of October and first half of November.]
sum, -uim, *s.m.* Sum. 2 As much ground as will

suffice four sheep (*soume.*)
sumach, -aich, *s.m.* Plaid.
sumag, -aig, -an, *s.f.* Cloth below a pack-saddle, saddle-cloth. 2 Rug on the back below a burden. 3 Anything ragged. 4 Footcloth, galligaskins. 5 Panel. 6**Pad. 7**Pack-saddle.
——ach, -aiche, *a.* Ragged. 2 Patched. 3 Like, of, or belonging to, a pack-saddle.
sumaich,* *v.n.* Give the due number, as of cattle for joint pasture.
sùmaid, -e, -ean, *s.f.* Billow, surge, large wave. 2**Ridge. 3 The external senses. [‡sumaid.]
———each, -eiche, *a.* Wavy, billowy. 2 Boisterous. 3**Ridgy.
sumaidean, *s.pl.* *W.of Ross* for somuiltean.
sumain, *pr.pt.* a' sumanadh, *v.a.* Summon, cite, prosecute.
sumain,‡*s.f.* see sumanadh.
sùmainn, -e,-ean, *s.f.* Billow, surge, great wave. Cha siùil na sùmainnean glasa, *the blue billows are not sails.* [**sumain.]
————each, -eiche, *a.* Billowy, stormy. 2** Flowing. 3**Causing great waves.
sumair, -ean, *s.m.* Gulf. 2 Whirlpool 3 Sucker. 4 Swallower. 5 Drinker. 6 Glutton. 7 Sucker of a pump. 8 Drone of a bagpipe. (p. 722.) †9 Generation.
sumaire, *s.m.* Coarse cudgel, lethal weapon,beetle—*Sàr-Obair.*
sumaire,(AF) *s.m.* Leech. 2 Serpent. 3 Reptile.
suman,** *s.m.* Cital. †2**Interpellation.
——adh, -aidh, *s.m.* Summons. 2 Act of summoning. A' s—, *pr.pt.* of sumain.
sumanaich, *v.a.* Billow.
sumbaid, -e, -ean, *s.f.* see sumaid.
sumgadh,** -aidh, *s.m.* Aporrhœa.
sùmhail, -e, *a.* Close-packed, unbulky. 2 Tidy. 3 Quiet, peaceable, tame. 4** Strait-laced. 5* Humble, obedient, obsequious, as a person. 6††Smoothed. Opposite of dùmhail. Gu s., *tightly.* [pron. sùil in *Arran.*]
sumhaileachd,** *s.f.* Tightness.
sùmhlach,** *a.* Crowding, pressing together, abridging.
sùmhlachadh, -aidh, *s.m.* Packing closer, act of packing closer. 2 Taming, act of taming. 3 State of becoming tame or peaceable. 4 Abstract, abridgment, diminishing. 5 Bending tightly. 6 Bending together. 7* Creeping in, sitting or lying closer and closer. 8* Lessening or abridgment of bulk. A' s—, *pr.pt.* of sùmhlaich.
sùmhlachadh, -aidh, *s.m.* Syllabus.
sùmhlachair,** *s.m.* Abridger.
sùmhlachd, *s.f.ind.* State of being closely packed. 2 Condensation. 3 Peaceableness, quietness. 4 Tameness. 5* Obsequiousness. 6 Abjectness. 7* Littleness of bulk. 8 Tightness.
sùmhlaich, *pr.pt.*a' sùmhlachadh,*v.a.* Pack closer together, diminish in bulk, abridge, lessen, make less bulky. 2 Get less bulky. 3 Tame, make tame. 4 Become quiet or peaceable. 5 Bend tightly, tighten. 5*Lie closer together.
————ear, *fut.pass.* of sùmhlaich.
————idh, *fut.aff.a.* of sùmhlaich.
————te, *past pt.* of sùmhlaich.Packed close. 2 Tamed, made tame, &c.
sùmhlas, -ais, *s.m.* see sùmhlachd.
sunais, -e, -ean, *s.f.* Loveage—*ligusticum scoticum.* (ill. 655.)
sunn,** *s.m.* Puff, blast. 2 Push. 3 Fortification. 4**Wall.
——ach,** -aich, *s.m.* Strong fort. 2 Milking-place. 3 Summit.
sunnag, -aig, -an, *s.f.* Easy chair made of twisted straw.

655. Sunvis.

sunnailt, -e, -ean, *s.f.* Likeness, comparison, resemblance, match. S. t' eugais, *the likeness of thy face.*
sunnanadh,* -aidh, see sumanadh.
sunnanaich,* *v.a.* see sumain, *v.*
sunnara,(DC) *a.* Fixed, secure, as the foundation of a house.
sunnd, *s.m.ind.* Joy, cheerfulness, hilarity, good humour. 2 Good state of health. 3 Good appetite. 'Dé 'n s. a th' ort ? *how do you do ?*
——ach, -aiche, *a.* Merry, cheerful, lively,joyous, joyful, in good spirits. 2 Good-humoured. 3 Enjoying good health. 4 Having a good appetite. Gu s., *good-humouredly.*
——achail, *a.* see sunndach.
——achas, -ais, *s.m.* see sunnd.
——achd, *s.f.ind.* Alacrity, see sunnd.
sunndaich,(MS) *v.a.* Exhilarate.
sunndaichead, -aid, *s.m.* see sunnd.
sunndan,** *s.m.* Delight, short fit of gladness, sudden emotion of joy.
sunn-ghaoth,** -ghaoith,*s.f.*High wind. 2 Boast, gasconade.
————ar, *a.* Boastful, vain, blustering.
sunnt, see sunnd.
——ach, see sunndach.
sunrach.** *a.* Particular, special.
sùnrachadh, see sònrachadh.
sùnraich, see sònraich.
———te, see sònraichte.
suntaidh, *a.* Quick.
sùpail,* -e, *a.* see sùbailte.
sùpailte, see sùbailte.
sùpailteachd, see subailteachd.
sùpalachd,* *s.f.* see sùbailteachd.
sur,(AC) *s.m.* Flaw. Gun sal, gun sur, *without smear or flaw.*
sùr, *a.* Gaelic form of Scots pronunciation of *sour.*
surabhan,** -ain, *s.m.* Southernwood.
sùrag,§ -aig, -an, *s.f.* Wood-sorrel, see seamrag.
sùragach,** *a.* Abounding in or like, wood-sorrel.
surcain, (MMcD) *s. m.* Piece of skin or wood with sharp peg placed in it point upwards for attaching to a calf's snout to prevent its sucking its mother.
sùrd, -ùird, *s.m.* Alacrity, eager and willing exertion. 2 Industry. 3 Speed, "cleverness." 4 Preparation or bestirring for business. 5‡ Cheerfulness. 6* Hilarity. 7*Successful train or mode. Cuir s. ort, *bestir yourself for business.*
sùrdag, -aig, -an, *s.f.* Leap, skip, jump, spring, bound, cutting, caper, bounce. 2*Stride. A' gearradh sh., *bounding, cutting capers* ; a' teachd le s., *coming with a bound.*
———ach, -aiche, *a.* Bounding, leaping, bounc-

ing, apt to bound, leap or bounce. 2 Striding. An eilid sh., *the bounding roe.*
sùrdagaich, *v. n.* Leap, skip, spring, bound, bounce. 2 Stride.
———, *s.f.* Leap, skip, spring.
sùrdail, -e, *a.* Eager, prompt, active, diligent. 2 *Business-like. 3 Industrious, clever, pushing, shifty. 4* Full of spirits.
sùrdalachd, *s.f.ind.* Alacrity, diligence. 2 Fervour. 3 Industriousness. 4 Alertness. 5 Cheerfulness. 6††Activity.
surrag, -aig, -an, *s.f.* Vent of a kiln, the oblong space over which the wood, straw and grain are placed.
surram -aim, (i.e. surram suain) Sound sleep. 2 Snoring, noise as of one sleeping.
sùrtag, see sùrdag.
suntaidh,** *a.* Quick.
susbailteach, see susbainteach.
susbaint, -e, -ean, *s.f.* Substance, pith, strength. 2 Efficacy. 3 Import.
———each, -eiche, *a.* Substantial. 2(MS)Cardinal. 3 Sane, sound in judgment.
susbuin, see susbaint.
susbuinneach,** *a.* †Alible.
sùsdal, -ail, *s.m.* Bustling, much ado about trifles. 2 Affectedness. 3 Shyness, coyness. 4 ††Fuss. [‡sùsdal.]
sùsdalach, -aiche, *a.* Bustling, noisy, making much ado about trifles. 2 Affectedly shy, coy. 3 Prudish.
————d,** *s.f.* Prudery, prudishness, coyness.
sùsdan,(CR) -ain, *pl.* sùsdana, *s.m.* Thousand—*Caithness.*
sùstan, see sùsdan.
suspainn, see susbaint.
sutair,** *s.m.* Tanner.
———eachd, *s.f.* Tannery.
sùth, -ùith, -an, see sùgh.
suth,‡ *s.m.* Anything.
sùthag, *s.f.* see sùbhag. 2(DC) Bee-hive chair made of twisted straw or sea-bent.—*Uist.*
sùthaidh, *s.* see sùith.
suthainn, *a.* Eternal, continual, everlasting. 2 Infinite. 3 *rarely,* Prosperous. Gu s. is gu sìorruidh, *eternally and for ever.*
————eachd, *s.f.* Eternity. A thùs na s., *from all eternity.*
sùthair, see sùghmhor.
sûthan,** -ain, *s.m.* Booby, dunce, 2 Small beer.
———ach,(DC) *s.m.* Quicksand—*Uist.*
suthann, see suthainn.
sùthar,(DMK) *a.* Civil, affable, polite, gentle—*Caithness.*
sùth-bhrìgh, -e, *s.f.* see sùgh bruich & sùgh-bhrìgh.
—————each, see sùgh-bhrìgheach.
—————ear, see sùgh-bhrìoghmhor.
—————mhor, see sùgh-bhrìoghmhor.
sùthmhor, see sùghmhor.
————achd, see sùghmhorachd.
†suthuinn, -e, *a.* Prosperous.

T t

t, teine, the 17th. letter of the Gaelic alphabet now in use.

T, not aspirated has two sounds. (1)Nearly like *t* in *town,*exactly like *t* in Italian *tocco,*or in French *toucher.* (2) Like *ch* in *cheek,* as, tighinn, *coming ;* sailte, *salted.* When aspirated, it sounds like *h* in *him,* as thàinig e, *he came. Th* is silent in the middle of words, in the end of long syllables, in some tenses of certain irregular verbs, and in *thu, thusa;* as maitheas, *goodness* (pron. *my-yes*) ; maoth, *gentle (meu)* ; an d' thàinig thu ? *art thou come ? T,* is sometimes used before *fh* followed by a vowel in the Western Isles, as, an t-fhardach, *the household. T',* is used before vowels instead of do, *thy.*

t-, so-called euphonic,(once part of the article) is used (1) between the article and a masculine noun beginning with a vowel, in the nominative case singular, as, an t-each, *the horse.* (2) between the article and a masculine noun beginning with s followed by a vowel or *l, n,* or *r* in the genitive and dative cases singular, as, anns an t-solus, *in the light ;* glac cinn-fheadhna an t-sluaigh uile, *seize all the heads of the people.* (3) between the article and a feminine noun beginning with *s* followed by a vowel, or *l, n,* or *r,* in the nominative and dative cases singular, as, an t-slighe, *the road;* cha toir an t-saighead air teicheadh, *the arrow doth not cause him to flee ;* anns an t-sùil, *in the eye.*
t', (for ta) *v.* Is, am, are.
t', (for do before a vowel) *poss. pron.* Thy. Dr. Stewart does not approve of *t'* instead of *d',* but it is correct according to pronunciation and usage.
†ta, *s.m.* Water.
†tab, *s.m.* Start.
tabaid, -ean, see sabaid.
———each, see sabaideach.
———eachd, see sabaideachd.
tabaidiche, see sabaidiche.
tàbailt,(CR) *a.* Strong, vigorous.
taban, see tuban.
tàbar, -air, -an, *s.m.* Tabor. 2 Timbrel.
———ach, *a.* Abounding in tabors or timbrels.
tabh, -aibh, *s.m.* The ocean, the sea. Fuaim an taibh, *the sound of the main.*
tàbh, -àibh, -an, *s.m.* Spoon-net, fishing-net. T. chudaigean, *a hand-net for cuddies* ; t.-breac aich, *a hand-net for trout* (when catchin trout in burns.) (DC) *s.m. & f.* Frame net for fishing beside a rock for small saithe, or from a boat anchored in a tide-way. The fish are first attracted to the side by means of bruised shell-fish. The frame net fixed on a long pole is let down gently and brings up quite a quantity.
tàbh, *pr.pt.* a' tàbhach, *v.a.* Fish with hand-net on burns,
tabhach, -aich, *s.m.* Sudden eruption. 2 Forcing, pull, pressing.
tàbhach, (JM) *s.* Fishing with hand-net on burns. A' t—, *pr. pt.* of tàbh.
tabhach,** *a.* Marine.
tàbhach, *a.* Strong, lusty.
tàbhachd, *s.f.ind.* Substantiality, solidity, firmness, substance, stoutness. 2 Good profit, good effect, benefit, efficacy, effectiveness, advantage. 3 Number. 4 Valour. 5**Comeliness. Cha'n 'eil t. sam bith ann dhomhsa, *it is no profit* or *benefit to me ;* dé 'n t. a th'

ann? *what quantity is there of it?* mu 'n t. sin, *about that quantity;* taisbeinibh ur t., *show your valour.*

tàbhachdach, -aiche, *a.* Efficient, effectual, effective, valid, profitable, beneficial, advantageous. 2* Solid, substantial. 3**Stout, comely. 4(MS) Great. Buaillean tàbhachdach, *effectual blows;* ni t., *a profitable thing.*

tàbhachdach,(MS) *a.* Personable.

tàbhaidh,(AC) *a.* Strong. Iomachadh t., *a strong band.*

tabhail, *s.f.* Method, manner.

tabhaill.(CR) *s.f.* Sense, judgment, understanding, wits. Char e dheth a th., *he lost his wits, acted stupidly;* tha e dheth a th., *he is in his dotage;* duine gun t., *a man without sense—W. of Ross.*

tabhailt,(DC) *s.m.* Table-cloth—*Uist.* (tubhailt)

tabhainn, *pr.pt.* a' tabhainnich, *v.n.* Bay, bark, as a dog.

tabhair, *v.irreg.* Give, bestow, grant, see thoir. 2 Take away. Thabhair and Thoir are interchangeable. See under thoir for conjugation and examples.

tabhaiream, *1st.sing.imp.* of tabhair. Let me give.

tàbhairn, *s.* Feast, entertainment, conviviality. —*Rob Donn.*

tàbhairn, -ean, *s.m.* Gaelic form of *tavern.* 2** Sea.

tabhairt, *s.f.* Giving, act of giving or bestowing. 2 Presentment, gift, grant, bestowal. 3 Taking, act of taking. A' t—, *pr.pt.* of tabhair. A' t. an 'geall, *mort-gaging, pledging.*

tabhairteach, -eiche, *a.* Giving, that gives, generous, ready to give, bounteous, charitable, liberal. 2 Dative, in *grammar.* Duine t., *a liberal man;* gu t., *liberally.*

tabhairteach, -ich, *s.m.* Giver, one who gives or bestows. 2 Liberal person.

————d, *s.f.* Readiness to give or bestow, liberality, munificence, generosity.

tabhairtear,** -ean, *s.m.* Giver, donor.

tabhairteas, see tabhartas.

tabhal, -ail, -an, *s.m.* Sling to cast stones. †2** Plank, board. 2***rarely,* Chief. Crann tabhail, *the shaft of a sling.*

tabhann, -ainn, *s.m.* Bark, yelp, as of a dog. 2 Barking, constant barking or baying of dogs.

————ach, -aiche, *a.* Barking. 2 Ready to bark. 3 Noisy, as barking dogs.

————aich, *pr.pt.* a' tabhannaich, *v. a.* Bark, yelp.

————aich, -e, *s.f.* Barking or baying of dogs, continuous barking. 2(CR) Barking at some object—*West of Ross.* (*Comhartaich,* is barking at nothing.)

————aiche, *s.m.* Barker.

tàbhar, *s.m.* see tàbar.

tabh-ard,(AF) *s.m.* Flying beetle.

tàbharnadh, -aidh, *s. m.* State of being haunted. 2 Apparition. Bha t. air an taigh, *the house was haunted.*

tabhartach, -aiche, see tabhairteach.

tabhartair,* -ean, *s.m.* Bestower, giver.

tabhartan,** -ain, *s.m.* Leader, general.

tabhartas, -ais, *s. m.* Gift, offering, tribute. 2 Dedication. 3 Remittance. 4** Boon. 5 Present. T.-luaisgte, *a wave-offering;* t.-togta, *a heave offering;* t.-dighe, *a drink-offering.*

tàbhastal, -ail, *s.m.* Tedious nonsense, *prov.*

tabh-bhéisd,(AF) s. Large seal.

tabhram,** *1st. sing. imp.* of tabhair. Let me give.

tabhs,(AF) s. Gannet.

tabhuan,** *a.* Persevering.

————,** s.m. Perseverance. 2(AF) Sea-calf or lamb. seal.

tabhuanachd, *s.f.* Perseverance.

tabhuich,‡* *v.n.* Profit. 2 Exact.

tabhuil,** *a.* In order.

tabhuin, see tabhain.

tabhul,** -uil, *s.m.* Horse-fly, breeze, brize-fly.

tabhull, -uill, -uillean, *s.m.* see tabhal.

tabhun, see tabhan.

————aich, see tabhannaich.

tac,(CR) *s.m.* Prop, support, dependance, (taic) —*Suth'd.*

tac,* *s.f.* Space, time, season, Mu 'n t. seo an uiridh, *about this time last year;* ceithir bliadhna na taic seo, *this time four years.*

tac,‡ -a & -aic, *pl.* -aichean, *s.f.* Tack, lease of limited duration.

tac, see tachd.

taca, see tac. *Arran.* 2 (DMy) Tack of a boat. Gaoth nan seachd tacanan—said of the south-west wind, coming from Rona to the Butt of Lewis.

taca, *s.* see taice.

†taca, -n, *s.m.* Prop. 2 Surety. 3**Peg. 4 see tacaid.

tacachadh,(MS) *s.m.* Sustentation.

tacadh,** -aidh, *s.m.* Prosperity.

tacadh-froise,(DC) *s.m.* (*lit.* shower-choke) Darkness preceding a shower of rain—*Uist.*

tacaich, *v.a.* see taicich.

tacaid, -e, -ean, *s.f.* Tack, small nail. 2 Hob-nail. 3 Peg. 4 Pain, stitch. 5 Stab, wound, 6**Large-headed nail for ornament. 7**Stud, knob. Le tacaidibh airgid, *with silver studs;* bhuail t. mi, *a pain seized me.*

tacaideach, -eiche, *a.* Tacketed, nailed. 2 Causing pain. 3 Agonizing. 4 Wounding. Bròg-an t., *hob-nailed shoes or boots.*

tacaidich, *v.a.* Stick full of tacks. 2 Fasten with tacks.

tacail,** *a.* Strong, solid, able.

tacain, see tacan.

tacan, -ain, -an, *s.m. dim.* of tac. Short time, while. Eadar seo agus ceann tacain, *in a little time hence.*

tacar, -air, -an, *s.m.* Provision, plenty, heap, quantity. 2**Gleaning. 3**Fish. 4††Produce. Àite gun t., *a barren region;* fhuair mi t. éisg, *I got a heap of fish;* fhuair mi t. eun, *I got a quantity of birds.*

†tacar, -aire, *a.* Good, agreeable.

tàcarach, -aiche, *a.* Well-provisioned, fertile, plentiful. 2 Relating to provisions. 3(MS) Wealthy. (tacarach—AH.)

tacas, see tacsa. [AH.)

tàcar-mara, see muir-thàchdar. (tacar-mara—

tach,** *s.m.* Value, estimation.

tachailleag,(CR) *s.f.* Black and white wagtail, pied wagtail—*Suth'd.*

tachair, *pr. pt.* a' tachairt, *v.a. & n.* Happen, come to pass, meet with, meet, light upon, find. Tachraidh sinn fhathast, *we shall meet yet;* tachraidh sin fhathast, *that will happen yet;* an do th. thu air? *did you light upon it?* th. e gu math dhuit, *it has happened well to you;* agus thachair gu 'n deach e seachad, *and it happened that he passed by;* an uair a thachaireas an dà iarunn cho cruaidh, is dual dhaibh dealachadh, *when the two irons are equally hard, rebound they must*—applied to two persons equally quarrelsome and disagreeable; tachraidh an droch shìde ri neach a muigh ged nach toireadh e leis o 'n taigh i, *you will meet the bad weather outside—you needn't carry it from home with you*—excellent advice to people who are inclined to worry themselves over troubles which are far off, and which, after all, may never come any nearer

tàchair, *s.m.* Sea-weed—*algæ*.
tachairt, *s.f.* Happening, act of happening, coming to pass. 2 Meeting, act of meeting. 3 Opposition, act of opposing. A' t—, *pr. pt.* of tachair.
tachais, *pr.pt.* a' tachas, *v. a.* Scratch, scrape the surface of the skin, claw.
———te, *past pt.* of tachais. Scratched, clawed.
tachan, see taghan.
tàchar, see tàcar.
†**tachar**,** -air, *s.m.* Fight, skirmish, squabble.
tàchar, *s.m.* Dense volume of smoke—*Argyll.*
tachara,* see tàcharan.
tacharaidh, see tachraidh.
tàcharan, -ain, -an, *s.m.* Sprite, ghost. 2 Weak, helpless being. 3 Orphan. 4 Cowardly, feeble person. 5 Yelling of ghosts. 6(WC)Child left by the fairies.
————ach, -aiche, *a.* Full of ghosts or spirits. 2 Like a ghost. 3 Weak, helpless. 4 Like an orphan. 5 Cowardly. 6 Feeble.
tacharan-cubhaig, *s.m.* (*lit.* page of the cuckoo.) Meadow pipit, see snathadag.
tacharas, *Suth'd* for tachras.
tacharra,(MS) *s.* Changeling. 2 Pigmy.
tachartach,‡‡ -aiche, *a.* Eventful, contingent, 2 Ambulatory.
tachartas,†† -ais, -an, *s.m.* Event, occurrence, incident.
tachas, -ais, *s.m.* Itching, itchiness. 2 The itch. 3 Leprosy. 4‡ Scratching. T. tioram, *scurvy.*
tachas, -ais, *s.m.* Clawing, act of clawing, scraping or scratching. A' t—, *pr.pt.* of tachais.
———ach, -aiche, *a.* Itchy, having the itch. 2 Clawing, scratching. 3 Itching, causing an itching sensation. 4 Having a longing desire. 5 Acrimonious. Cluasan t., *itching ears.*
tachas-tioram,‖ -ais, *s.m.* Scurvy.
tachd, *pr.pt.* a' tachdadh, *v.a.* Choke, strangle. 2 Choke, stop up, prevent.
———ach, -aiche, *a.* Choking, that chokes, strangles or obstructs, suffocating.
tachdadair, -ean, *s.m.* Choker.
tachdadh, -aidh, *s. m.* Choking, act of choking, strangling or obstructing, suffocating. 2 *rarely,* Promise, security. A' t—, *pr. pt.* of tachd.
tachdaidh, *fut.aff.a.* of tachd.
tachdan, see tacan.
tachdar, *s.m.* **Chase, prize. 2 Produce—*B. Doran.* Cha bu diùbhail gin de 'n tachdar, *'twere no loss in the provision (deer) to anyone —Duanaire, p. 13.* [tacar—MM.]
tachdar, *fut. pass.* of tachd.
tàchdar, see tacar.
tachdmhor,(MS) *a.* Alimental, serviceable.
tachdrach, see tàcarach.
tachdta, *past pt.* of tachd. Strangled, choked. 2 Obstructed, as in growing.
tachlag, *s.f.* Wagtail (bird.)
tachradh, *s.m.* Weak, helpless person—J.G.C., W. 124.
tachraidh, *fut.aff. a.* of tachair.
tachrais, *pr.pt.* a' tachras, *v.a.* Wind yarn.
————te, *past pt.* of tachrais. Wound up.
tachran, see tacharan.
tachras, -ais, *s.m.* Winding, act of winding yarn. A' t—, *pr.pt.* of tachrais.
————ach,* -aich, *s.m.* see tachrasan.
tachrasan, -ain, *s.m.* Windlass. 2 Horizontal yarn-reel.
tachuil,(MS) *v.a.* Pierce.
tàclach,(WC) Purse or any receptacle. 2 Good quantity of anything.
tacmhor, see tachdmhor.
tacsa, *s.m.ind.* Support, substance, solidity. 2 Buttress. 3(MS) Comfort. Dèan t. dhomh, *support me.*
tacsa,(MS) *a.* Backed.
tacsaich,(MS) *v.a.* Nourish.
ta 'd, (for tha iad) They are. Ta 'd 'nan éire, *they are a burden.*
†**tad**, *s.m.* Lowness of spirits. 2 Thief.
tadaidh, see tàlaidh.
tàdh, -a, -achan, *s.m.* Ledge, layer.
†**tadhach**, *a.* Unsavoury.
tadhach,** -aich, -a, *s. m.* Ledge. Eadar na tadhacha, *between the ledges.*
tadhail, *pr.pt.* a' tadhal, *v.n.* Call, visit, haunt. Dh' iarr a' mhuir a bhi 'g a tadhal, *the sea wished to be resorted to*—a poetical idea suggested by the daily return of the tide, which seems to invite acquaintance—NGP.
tadhal, -ail, -aichean, *s.m.* Calling, visiting. 2 ‡‡Sense of feeling, touching. 3‡‡ Resort. 4‡ Frequenting, visiting. 5†† Goal or hail at shinty or football. Bha sibhse a' bualadh gun teagamh, ach chuir sinne t. air, *you were striking no doubt, but we sent it between the posts, made a goal of it.*
†**tadhal**, -ail, -an, *s.m.* Flesh-hook.
tadhalach, -aiche, *a.* Frequenting, resorting to, visiting, calling for one. 2 Fond of visiting. 3 Abounding in resorts.
tadhasg, -aisg, *s.m.* News, information.
†**tadhg**, -aidhg, -an, *s.m.* Poet.
tadhgan,(AF) *s.m.* Fox, see taghan.
tadhlach,** -aich, *s.m.* Swelling or pain in the wrist.
tafach,** *a.* Craving.
———,** -aich, *s.m.* Exhortation.
tafaid,* -e, -ean, see taifeid.
†**tafan**, -ain, see tabhann.
tag,* *s.m.* see tagan.
tàg,** *s.m.* Blow on the cheek.
tag,** *v.a.* Deliver.
tagach, *a.* see tacaideach.
tagair, *pr.pt.* a' tagairt & a' tagradh, *v.a. & n.* Plead, prosecute, plead a cause, crave. 2 Claim as a right. 3 Reason, argue, debate, dispute. 4 Accuse. Tha e 'tagairt orm, *he pleads of me, claims of me* ; tagair mo chùis a Dhé ! *plead my cause O God !*
tagaireach,* -eiche, *a.* Litigious.
—————, -eich, *s.m.* Pleader, counsel, advocate. 2 Creditor. 3 Appellant.
tagairteachd,(MS) *s.f.* Quarrel.
tagairt, -e, *s.f.* Pleading, act of pleading, craving. 2 Claiming as a right. 3 Reasoning, debating. 4 Plea, allegation. A' t—, *pr. pt.* of tagair.
tagan, -ain, *s.m.* Pocket, little bag, 2 Private or hidden purse, as of a wife. Tha t. math aice, *she has a good purse.*
taganach, -aiche, *a.* Baggy.
tagar,** -air, *s.m.* Order, course.
tagarach,** -aich, *s.m.* Pretender, claimer.
————,* Litigious, fond of pleading or debating.
————d,†† *s.f.* Pleading.
tagaradh, see tagradh.
tagarair,** *s.m.* Barrister. 2 Pleader, disputant, claimant.
tagarrach, see tagaireach.
tagartach, *a.* ††Claiming. 2(MS) Controversial.
tagartair,* *s.m.* Pleader, agent.
tagartas, -ais, -an, *s.m.* Pleading, claim, dispute. 2* Prosecution, law-plea.
tagh, *pr.pt.* a' taghadh, *v. a.* Choose, elect, select, pick. T. a' chuid a's fhèarr, *choose the best.*
tagh,* *a.* see toigh.
tagha, see taghadh.
taghach, -aiche, *a.* Choosing, that chooses. 2 Elective. see toigheach.

taghadair, -ean, *s.m.* Chooser, one who chooses or selects. 2‡‡ One who has the care of another's cattle. 3 Elector, voter.
taghadaireachd, *s.f.* The office of an elector or chooser. 2 Electioneering. 3 The office of taking care of another's cattle. 4*Electorate.
taghadh, -aidh, *s.m.* Choosing, act of choosing, electing or selecting. 2 Choosing, election. 3 Anything, person or persons chosen. 4 The best of anything, choice, selection, election. T. a' mhèirlich, *a choice thief*; t. coitchionn, *a general election*; t. air leth, *a by-election*; roghadh is t., *pick and choice*; luchd-taghaidh, *electors*; *2 the bodyguard of a Highland regiment* —a band of chosen men of the same clan, who fared at the same table with the chieftain, and each enjoyed his hospitality according to his deserts; dà ni ro dhuilich ri 'n t., bean is claidheamh, *two things very difficult to choose, a wife and a sword.*
taghadraidh,** *s.f.* Electorate.
taghadroinn,** *s.* Electorate.
taghaich, (for rathaich) Gheibht' an taghaich gu lìonmhor, do mhaithean na rìoghachd, *there would be found numerous callers of the nobles of the land—Donn. Bàn, p. 35.*
taghaidh, *fut.aff.a.* of tagh.
taghail, *v.* see tadhail.
taghaire, -an, *s.m.* Augur.
taghaireachd, *s.f.* Augury.
taghairm, -e, -ean, *s.f.* Echo. 2 Gathering summons. 3 Ancient mode of divination, said to be one of the most effectual means of raising the devil, and getting unlawful wishes gratified. The performance consisted in roasting cats alive, one after another, for some days, without tasting food; which if duly persisted in, summoned a legion of devils, in the guise of black cats, with their master at their head, all screeching in a way terrifying to any person of ordinary nerves.—NGP. "The divination by the t. was once a noted superstition among the Gael, and in the northern parts of the Lowlands of Scotland. When any important question concerning futurity arose, and of which a solution was, by all means, desirable, some shrewder person than his neighbours was pitched upon, to perform the part of a prophet. This person was wrapped in the warm smoking hide of a newly-slain ox or cow, commonly an ox, and laid at full length in the wildest recess of some lonely waterfall. The question was then put to him, and the oracle was left in solitude to consider it. Here he lay for some hours with his cloak of knowledge around him, and over his head, no doubt, to see the better into futurity; deafened by the incessant roaring of the torrent; every sense assailed; his body steaming; his fancy in a ferment; and whatever notion had found its way into his mind from so many sources of prophecy, it was firmly believed to have been communicated by invisible beings who were supposed to haunt such solitudes."—**
taghairmeach, -aiche, *a.* Echoing, responsive, oracular.
taghal, see tadhal.
taghald, *Suth'd* for tadhal.
taghall, see tadhal.
taghan, -ain, -an, *s.m.* Marten, pole-cat, stinkard. 2(MS) Foumart. 3(AF) Badger. 4(WC) Quarrelsome person.
taghanach, -aiche, *a.* Abounding in martens. 2 Cross, cankered.
taghan-tartaidh,(AF) *s.* Foumart.
taghan-tutaidh, see taghan-tartaidh.
taghar, -air, *s.m.* Distant noise.
tagh-ghairm, see taghairm.
tagh-ghuth,** *s.* Vote, voice at an election.
taghta, *a. & past pt.* of tagh. Chosen, elected, elect, select, selected. 2 Excellent, choice. Daoine t., *the elect, chosen men*; òr t., *choice gold.* [taghte.]
tagluinn, -e, *s.f.* Opposition. 2 Contest, squabble. 3**Animosity. Luchd t., *quarrelsome persons.*
tagluinneach, -eiche, *a.* Contestable. 2 Contumacious, quarrelsome, squabbling.
tagluinneachd, *s.f.ind.* Contumacy.
tagluinnich,** *v.* Chaffer.
tagluinniche,** *s.* Barrator.
tagrach, -aiche, *a.* Argumentative, using arguments. 2 Pleading, that pleads. 3 Fond of pleading. 4 Craving, soliciting. 5 Apt to crave, importunate, assertive. 6 Claiming.
tagrachd,** *s.f.* see tagradh.
tagradair,** *s.m.* Alleger. 2 Pleader, disputant, advocate, claimant. 3* Agent. also tagaireach.
tagradaireachd,** *s.f.* Business of a pleader or advocate.
tagradh, -aidh, -aidhean, *s.m.* Pleading, act of pleading, plea, craving, act of craving or 2 Claiming as a right. 3 Reasoning, act of reasoning. 4 Advocating. 5 Apology. A' t—, *pr.pt.* of tagair.
tagraidh, *fut.aff.a.* of tagair.
tagrair, see tagradair.
taibean, -ein, *s.m.* Tabby.
taibh,* see taibhean & tabh. Fada mach 's an taibh, *far out on the ocean—Iorram, MacD.*
taibhean,* -ein, *s.m.* Substance.
taibheanach,* -aiche, *a.* Substantial.
taibheart,** *s.f.* Disparagement.
tàibhearn, see tàbharn.
taibheid, see taifeid.
taibheirt,** *s.f.* see taibheart.
†**taibhle**, *s.pl.* Tables.
taibhleach,** *s.f.* Smart blow, box, box sideways.
taibhleas, -eis, *s.m.* Backgammon table. 2 Game of backgammon.
taibhleas beag, *s.m.* Game of draughts.
taibhleis, *s.f.* see taibhleas.
†**taibhliosg**, -isg, see tàileasg.
taibhreadh, -idh, *s.m.* Dream.
taibhreal,** -eil, *s.m.* Laurel, see laibhreas.
——ach, *a.* Abounding in, of, or belonging to, laurel.
taibhs, see taibhse.
taibhse, -an *s.f.* The shade of a departed person. 2 Vision, apparition, ghost, spirit. 3 Vision of the second-sight. 4(AF) Guillemot.
taibhseach, -eiche, *a.* Shadowy, ghost-like, spectral. 2 Superstitious, silly. †3 Proud. Is t. iad adharca nam bò thar lear, *showy or visionary are the horns of the cows beyond the sea.*
†**taibhseachan**,** -ain, *s. m.* Proud person. 2 Coquette.
†**taibhseachd**,** *s. f.* Pride. 2 Coquetry, 3 2††Eloquence.
taibhsean, *n.pl.* of taibhse.
taibhsdear, see taibhsear.
——achd, see taibhsearachd.
taibhsear, -eir, -an, *s.m.* Visionary, one who possesses the faculty of second-sight.
——achd, *s.f.ind.* Second-sight. 2*Bewildered conduct.
[The following is from Armstrong.]
At the sight of a vision of this kind, Dr. Martin observes, the eyelids of the gifted persons were erected, and the eyes continued staring till the vision disappeared. If an ob-

ject is seen in the morning, it will be accomplished in the afternoon; if at noon, on that very day; if in the evening, that very night; and if after candles are lit, on that night for certain. If a shroud is seen about a person, it foretells approaching death; and the time of it is more or less distant, according to the height at which the shroud is observed on the body. If it be seen about the middle, death is not expected within a twelvemonth; if as high as the head, it is not many hours distant. To see a spark of fire falling on one's arm, foretells that a dead child shall be seen in the arms of that person. To see a chair empty at at the time a person sits in it, is a sure sign of approaching death to that person. Seers did not observe supernatural appearances at the same time, though they might happen to be in the same apartment; but when one of them who saw a vision, touched any number of his brethren, they all saw it as well as the first.

The following are three instances recorded by an English nobleman in the 17th. century, who, previous to his going to the Highlands, was one of the sturdiest unbelievers in the second-sight.

1. "In the year 1652 I was travelling in the Highlands, and a good number of servants with me, as is usual there. One of them going a little before me, entering into a house where I was to stay all night, and going hastily to the door, he suddenly stepped back with a screech, and did fall by a stone which hit his foot. I asked what was the matter, for he seemed to be very much frighted. He told me very seriously that I should not lodge in that house, because shortly a dead body in a coffin would be carried out of it, for many were carrying it when he was heard to cry. I neglecting his words, and staying there, he said to the other servants he was sorry for it, and that what he saw would surely come to pass. Though no sick person was then there, yet the landlord died of an apoplectic fit before I left the house."

2 "In Jannary, 1652, Lieut.-Col. Alexander Munro, and I, were in the house of one Wm. MacLeod, of Ferinlea, in the county of Ross. He, the landlord, and I, were sitting on three chairs near the fire; and in the corner of the great chimney were two islanders, who were that *very night* come to the house, and were related to the landlord. While one of them was talking to Munro, I noticed the other looking oddly towards me. From his look, and his being an islander, I supposed him to be a seer, and asked him what he stared at. He answered me by desiriug me to rise from the chair, for it was an unlucky one. I asked him why. He answered me, because there was a dead man in the chair next to me. Well, said I, if he be in the chair next to me, I may keep my own. But what is the likeness of the man? He said he was a tall man with a long grey coat, booted, and one of his legs hanging over the arm of the chair, and his head hanging dead on the other side, and his arm backward, as if it were broken. There were some English troops then quartered near that place, and there being at that time a great frost after a thaw, the country was covered all over with ice. Four or five of the English riding by this house some two hours after the vision, while we were sitting by the fire, we heard a great noise, which proved to be those troopers, with the help of other servants, carrying in one of their number, who had had a very bad fall, and had his arm broken; and falling frequently into fits, they brought him into the hall, and set him on the very chair, and in the very posture that the seer prophesied. The man did not die, though he recovered with great difficulty."

3 "Among the accounts given me by Sir Norman MacLeod, there was one worthy of special notice—There was a gentleman in the Isle of Harris, who was always seen by the seers with an arrow in his thigh. Such in the isle who thought these prognostications infallible, did not doubt but he would be shot in the thigh before he died. Sir Norman told me that he heard it the subject of their discourse for many years. At last he died without any such accident. Sir Norman was at his burial at St. Clement's Church in Harris. At the same time the corpse of another gentleman was brought to be buried in the very same church. The friends on either side came to debate who should first enter the church, and in a trice from words they came to blows. One of the number, who was armed with a bow and arrows, let one fly among them. (Now every family in that isle have their burial place in the church in stone chests, and the bodies are carried in open biers to the burial-place.) Sir Norman having appeased the tumult, one of the arrows was found shot in the dead man's thigh. To this Sir Norman was a witness."—*Succinct accompt of my Lord Tarbolt's Relations, in a Letter to the Hon. Robert Boyle, Esquire, of the Predictions made by seers, whereof himself was Ear and Eye-witness.*

By pretension to second sight, no profit was ever sought or gained. It is an involuntary affection, in which neither hope nor fear are known to have any part. Those who profess to feel it do not boast of it as a privilege, nor are considered by others to be advantageously distinguished, They have no temptation to feign and their hearers have no motives to encourage an imposture.

Armstrong concludes his account with a lengthy description of the theories of Dr, Beattie of Aberdeen and the celebrated Dr, Samuel Johnson, but as they are only theories they have been omitted here.

taibhseil, see taibhseach.

†taibhsich, *v.n.* Reveal. 2 Appear, seem.

taibid, see teabaid.

——each, see teabaideach.

taib'-ionnsachadh, -aidh, *s.m.* Grammar.

taibreadh,(DC) *s.m.* Snatching.

taibse, *s.f.ind.* Propriety of speech. Leabhar-taibse, *a grammar.*

——ach, -eiche, *a.* Accurate in speech, grammatical.

taic, -e, *s.f.* Prop, support. 2 Strength, vigour. 3 Dependance, leaning. 4* Preparation. 6 *Fulcrum. 7* Contact, collision.

Cuir t. ri seo, *prop this;* cuir t. ris a' gheamhlaig, *put a fulcrum to the lever;* thàinig e an t. na cartach, *he came in contact with the cart;* t. ri bliadhna, *near a year;* cum t. rium, *support me; patronize me;* an t., *leaning;* shuidh iad ri t., *they sat leaning backwards;* an t, an Dòmhnuich, *in preparation for the Sabbath;* na leig do th. ris a sin, *do not depend too much to that;* an t- a' bhalla, *leaning on the wall;* cha ruig mi leas mo th. a leigeil riut-sa, *I need not depend much on your patronage* or *support;* laoich ri sleaghan an t., *heroes leaning on their spears;* a bhith an taice Lochaidh nam bradan, *to be in the*

proximity of Lochy of the salmon—Filidh, p. 21; an taic a chéile, *in collusion with each other* [—* says *in collision with each other.*]
taic, *pr.pt.* a' taiceadh, *v.a.* Support, patronize. 2*Buttress, sustain, bolster.
taiceachd, *s.f.ind.* One's utmost exertions. 2** Reliance.
taiceadh, -idh, *s.m.* Supporting, act of supporting. 2 Recommending, patronizing. 3 Depending. 4 Dependence. A' t—, *pr.pt.* of taic.
taicealachd, *s.f.ind.* Strength, solidity, firmness. 2 Portliness. 3 Alimentariness.
taicear, *s.m.* Auxiliary.
taiceil, -e, *a.* Substantial, solid, firm, strong, stout. 2 Auxiliary. 3(MS) Athletic.
taicich,* *v.a.* Buttress. 2 Help. see taic.
taid, -e, *s.m.* see taididh.
'tàid, *cont.* for ataid (tà iad or tha iad.)
taidhe, *s.f.ind.* Attention, heed, watchfulness, care. [Thoir taidhe (thoir do aidhe), take thy heed—a phrase to which the word is practically restricted, and which accounts for the short vowel of the Scottish Gaelic and Irish, the sentence accent being on the verb—‡.]
taidheach, -eiche, *a.* see toigheach.
taidheam, -eim, *s.f.* Meaning, import. Cha d' thug mi t. as a chainnt, *I did not comprehend his meaning.*
taidhean,** -ein, *s. m.* Troop. 2 Multitude, cavalcade. 3**Mill-pond.
taidhleach,** -liche, *a.* Splendid, delightful, pleasant.
———d,** *s.f.ind.* Complacency. 2 Pleasantness. 3 Splendidness.
taididh, *s.m. & int.* Father. Children's form of "Daddy." *Welsh* word.
†tàif,** *s.m.* Sea, see tabh. An t. fo bhruailean, *the sea (in agitation) in a storm.*
taifean, see tabhuan.
taifeid, -ean, *s.m.* Bow-string. 2 Taffety. T. 'san osaig a fuaim, *a bowstring sounding in the wind.*
———each, -eiche, *a.* Well-strung (of bows.)
†taifnichte, *past pt.* Driven away by force.
taig, -e, *s.f.* Attachment or devotion to a person or place. †2 Habit, custom.
tàigeanach,(CR) *s.m.* Squat person—*W.of Ross.*
taigeis, -e, -ean, *s.f.* Haggis, kind of meat-pudding. 2 Big-bellied person. 3 The scrotum.
———each, -eiche,*a.* Haggis-like. 2 Big-bellied.
taigh,-e, -ean, *s.m.* House. 'S'e 'ainm aoibhneach taigh na féile, *its joyful name is the house of hospitality ;* aig an taigh, *at home ;* o 'n taigh, *from home, abroad ;* mullach an taighe, *the top of the house ;* ceann taighe, *the head of a house or family ; head of the branch of a family ;* sìth ann ad chriadh-thaigh caol, *peace in thy cold mansion of clay ;* as an t., *out of the house ;* ann am thaigh, *in my house ;* ann ad th., *in thy house ;* 'na th. màile féin, *in his own hired house ;* an t. a' chomhagail, [an taigh comha =eadar-dhà-chomhairle—*Argyll*—AH.] *in a state of uncertainty ;* t. is aodach, *a tent.* [The *gen.sing.* in old Gaelic was *tige.*]

NAMES OF PARTS OF A "BLACK" HOUSE:—

1 Na Ceangail, [na Ceangail Ghàidhealach—(WC.) Lànan, *pl.* lànain & lànanan. Saidheachan—AH. Cas-choirbeil††.] *couples.* Fastened to the corner-poles with wooden pins. The couples are connected immediately below the ridge-pole by a piece of wood (an ad), and lower down by a cross-beam (an spàrr—No. 5.) Cascheangal, is one of the legs of a couple—*Lewis*—(DMy.)

2 Am bun-cheangal. [a' Chrùp, Bun baca.] The lower end of couple sunk in the wall and reaching the groin. [Crùp,(AH) (*pl.* crùpan, Upright beam built into wall and intended to support the couples.]

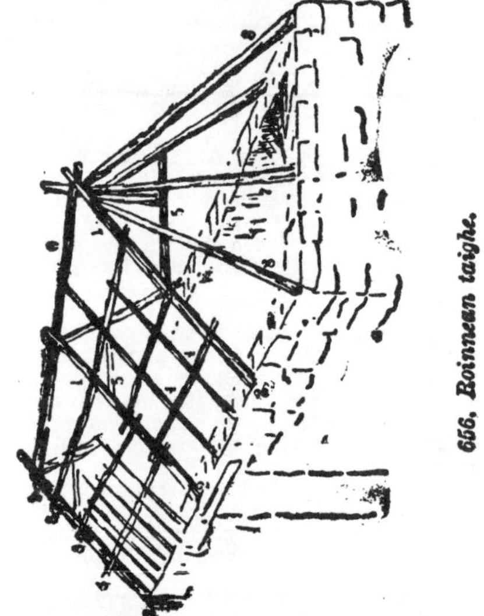
656. *Boinnean taighe.*

3 Pieces of timber laid across, and binding the couples together, called "na cléithean" in Skye, and " na taobhain " in Lewis. In *Lewis*, "an taobhan àrd " is placed about half-way between the ridge and wall, and "an taobhan ìosal" is about 14 inches below it and 18 in. from the top of the wall. —DMy. " Na clèithean " is the name applied in Lewis to the pieces of wood laid across the " taobhain " (No. 3) and running from wall to ridge to prevent the straw going through roof—DMy.

4 Na Cabair, *the side-rafters,* are placed over the cléithean (No. 3 in Skye), running from wall to ridge.

5 An spàrr, Small cross stick near the angle of couple to strengthen them. Spàrrghaoithe—(DC).

6 Am maide-droma, [Cabar-droma, Sgaith, ††Laom-chrann. Taobhan-mullaich—AH] *ridge-pole* or *roof-tree,* The beam along the ridge of the roof.

7 A' Chòrr,—so pronounced in *Skye & Argyll* at least, but dictionaries mark *còrr* as masculine. A thick stick like a couple, reaching from the middle of end wall (there are no gables of course) to top of nearest couple. Corr-thulchann are generally bent and meet at end of ridge-pole, where they are fastened to one another by a wooden pin called *crann-tarruing.*

8 An Roinn-oisinn [*or* -oisne,] Cabar-oisinn [*or* -oisne,](*pl.* na cabair-oisinn) [*or* -oisne] *corner-stick.* Strong sticks placed from each corner of wall to nearest couple.

9 Am Maide feannaig,[Maide starraig] stick running up through the thatch from the sparr at either end, and used as a peg round which to pass the Sìomain fraoich, " ach," continued my informant, " tha daoine a nis a' fàs cho Gallda nach foghainn daibh ach an nett-wire (*sic*) no na ròpan feòir as a' bhùthaidh !" (*people are becoming so anti-Gaelic now that nothing*

less than wire-netting or coir yarn ropes from the shop can satisfy them.) [Sparr-ealaig—*Uist*—DC]

10 An Similear crochaidh, made of thin wood or canvas to confine the smoke, generally, but not always, exists when the fire is at the end of the house.

11 An Luidhear, *the vent* to allow the smoke to escape through the thatch.

Acair, (*pl.* acraichean), Stones fixed in loops of heather-ropes, used as weights to keep the thatch in its place—*Lewis.*
Anainn, *top of wall inside.* [The corresponding position outside—AH.]
Bairceau, see dictionary.
Balla tarsuinn, see talan.]
Bonn, *found.*
Bonnacha-bac, *position above eaves* where the weights are set.
Bràigh, *summit.*
Buabhall-an-eich, *horse-stall—Lewis.*
Buabhall-na-bà, *cow-stall—Lewis.*
Bunntair, *foundation.*
Cabar-droma, *ridge-board.*
Cabar-fraighe,‡‡ *eave-beam.*
Calpa, *walls*, as distinct from roof—AH.
Casan-ceangail, *joists.*
Cas an teannachaidh, see dictionary.
Ceann-an-taighe, *upper end—Lewis.*
Ceann-shuas-an-taighe, see Ceann-an-taighe.
Cèarn, *kitchen* or "but" of a Highland house—DMK.
Clàidhean, *wooden door-latch, "sneck."* [Claidh-eamhan,(MMcL.) Clòidhean,(DU.)]
Cléithean-buinn, strips of wood running upwards from top of wall, and resting on the taobhain iosal—*Lewis*—(DMy.)
Cléithean mullaich, strips of wood fixed to the ridge at top and resting on top rafters (or taobhain àrda—(DMy.)
Cotan-nan-uan, kind of *pen* or enclosure to *confine the lambs by themselves* in the house in winter—*Lewis.*
Crann-tairngnean, *pins* or wooden nails used in fastening the various sets of beams.
Cuaille, *rafter.* [house—DMK.
Cùil, *private room* or "ben" of a Highland
Cùlaisd, *store, store-room.* Tha c. math aige, was said when the c. was full of potatoes, meal, &c. to tide over winter and spring—*Lewis.* [In *Uist*, the inner room of the house and which had access only through the common room. It is the room assigned to the use of the girls of a family—DC.] "Ben"—WC.
Dragh, straw-rope laid round the thatch 3 ft. from the top of wall and round which the loops of heather are bound before the weights (acraichean) are put in.
Dromanaich, *ridge-ropes*, ropes for fastening on thatch. 2 (WC) Bifurcated twigs for holding *lathus* in place on thatch.
Dronn, *ridge.*
Druim an taighe, *ridge.*
Duibheid, *turf for top of house. divot.*
Eadar-dhà-bhith, *space* between the outer door and the kitchen-door.
Faradh, *loft made of sticks covered with divots.*
Foid-buinn, *door-step.*
Foid fàil, *sods of turf laid along the top of the wall.*
Fraigh, *wall.*
Frioghan, see dictionary.
Gath-droma, *ridge-pole—Lewis.*
Glularan, glutaranadh, *packing* between outer and inner walls—MMcL.
Lathus, (WC) pieces of wood laid lengthwise on thatch.
Maide-aide, (*lit.* hat-stick) cross-piece joining the two door-posts at the top. So called from its coming into contact with hats of people who were not accustomed to bow down on entering a house. The common saying when anyone struck his hat in this way was, "cromaidh an coileach circe 'cheann fo 'n àrd-dorus."—*Lewis.*—(DMy)
Maide-slabhruidh, *cross-stick* laid on two upper rafters (taobhain) from which to hang chain and hook over fire.—*Lewis.*
Màs an taighe, *lower end—Lewis.*
Màthair-shìomain, *heather-rope* laid say three feet above eaves (outside,) and round which the loops are bound before weights are put on. 2 Stretch of heather-rope extended horizontally below the row of weights. (AH)
Sgolb, *pin* or *wattle for fixing thatch.*
Sgonn, *balk.*
Sgrathan, *divots for covering roof.*
Sìomain-fraoich, heather-ropes used for keeping thatch on house—(WC.)
Sparr-ealaig, see dictionary,
Sparr-gaoithe, see dictionary.
Spiris, *hen-roost.*
Stagh, *stay.* [houses.
Stall, *space* between door and fire in black
Talan, partition wall of stall, about 3 ft. or 4 ft. high.
Tràigh, *basement.*
Trannsa, *lobby.*
Tughadh, *thatch.* Frequently made of *bun dubh*—the black stem of a certain species of fern, which is very lasting. Bun dubh, stem of barley plucked by the roots—MMcL.

Various Kinds of Houses :—

t.-aifrinn, mass-house.
t.-aire, *or* t.-air, lykewake, a watch-house, house where vigils are held over a corpse. [Pronounced t.-àir in *E. of Ross*, and t-àir in *W. of Ross*—WC.]
t.-àisdigheachd, play-house.
t.-aisig, ferry-house.
t. an àir, slaughter-house.
t.-aolaich, necessary.
t.-aolaidh (fhoghluidh), college.
t-arm, armoury, depôt.
t.-bainne, dairy, milk-house.
t.-bainnse, house of a wedding.
t.-bàta, boathouse.
t.-beag, privy, convenience.
t.-buaile, fold-hut.
t.-cadail, sleeping-house.
t.-càine, toll-house.
t.-cànach, toll-house, custom-house.
t.-caol, narrow house, grave.
t.-carbaid, coach-house.
t.-cèaird, factory.
t.-chalman, dove-cot, ducket.
t.-chaorach, sheep-cot.
t.-chearc, hen-house.
t.-chon, dog-kennel.
t.-cìse, custom-house.
t.-cluiche, theatre, amphitheatre.
t.-cluig, belfry.
t.-cuspainn, custom-house.
t.-còmhnuidh, dwelling-house.
t.-cùil, back-house.
t.-cùinnidh, mint.
t.-cùirt, court-house.
t.-cuthaich, madhouse, lunatic-asylum.
t.-déirce, almshouse.
t.-deiridh, ship's cabin, stern-room.
t.-dìomhaireachd, jakes, privy.
t. dubh, thatched house whose walls are dry-

built without cement and double, the intervening space being filled with earth. The fire in such houses is generally situated in the middle of the floor.
t. dubh,(DMK) illicit distillery concealed among the hills—*W. coast of Ross.*
t.-eighe, ice-house.
t.-éiginn, privy.
t.-eiridinn, infirmary,hospital ; **poorhouse.
t.-fàil, turf-house—*Suth'd.*
t.-failcidh, bagnio. 2 Baths.
t.-faire, a watch-house.
t.-fairir, *Suth'd* for t.-air.
t.-fasdaidh, house where people are hired.
t.-feachd, barrack.
t.-fiodha, wood-house.
t.-foghluim, academy.
t.-fuinidh, bakehouse.
t.-fuirich, dwelling-house.
t.-geal,thatched house whose walls have their stones cemented together. In many parts such houses are now slated.
t.-ghèadh, goose-house.
t.-gléidhidh, museum.
t.-grùide, brewery.
t.-guail, coal-house.
t.-iaruinn, iron house.
t.-iongantais, museum.
t.-ionnsaiche, academy.
t.-itheannaich, ordinary.
t.-lagha, justice, court-house.
t.-leabhraichean, library.
t.-leanna, beerhouse, alehouse, inn.
t.-lionn, alehouse.
t.-litrichean, post-office.
t.-màile, hired house.
t.-malairt,exchange, bank.
t.-mach, see t.-muigh.
t.-marbhaidh, slaughter-house.
t.-marsantachd, shop, ware-room.
t.-mhanach, abbey, monastery, convent.
t.-mòid, court-house, court of justice.
t.-mór, mansion-house.
t.-muigh, out-house.
t.-mullaich, garret.
t.-mùnaidh, an academy.
t. na h-ùige, inn, dram-shop—*W. coast of Ross.*
t.-nam-fleadh, house of feasting.
t.-nam-bhochd, poorhouse, almshouse.
t.-nighe, wash-house.
t.-nigheachain, laundry.
t.-nigheadaireachd, wash-house.
t.-oibre, workhouse.
t.-oighreachd, mansion-house, the laird's house.
t.-òil, inn, tavern.
t.-oilein, academy.
t.-oircheis, bede-house.
t.-òsda, inn, alehouse.
t.-pòitearachd, alehouse.
t.-réidh, bank ; rented house.
t.-rìgh, royal palace.
t.-rìoghail, palace.
t.-saillidh, house in which fish is cured.
t.-salainn, salt-store.
t.-samhraidh, villa, summer-house.
t.-seinnse, inn, (changehouse) see t.-òsda.
t.-sgoile, schoolhouse.
t.-sheillean, bee-hive.
t.-siùrsachd, bagnio.
t.-siùrsaich, bagnio.
t.-slachdaidh, slaughter-house.
t.-smachdachaidh,house of correction; asylum.
t.-soluis, lighthouse.
t.-staoige, chop-house.
t.-stòr, pantry; depôt, warehouse,store ; granary.
t.-stòrais, a magazine.
t.-strìop, bawdy-house.
t.-strìopachais, bagnio, bawdy-house.
t.-suidhe, a privy.
t.-tàimh, inn.
t.-tainn,* inn.
t.-tàirn (tàbhairn,) beer-house.
t.-taisg, bin ; pantry, store-room ; treasury.
t.-tasgaidh, storehouse.
t.-teas, hothouse.
t.-teine, dwelling-house.
t.-teth, hothouse.
t.-tobhta, house built of turfs.
t.-togalach, brewery, brewing-house.
t.-toisich, forecastle of a ship.
taighdireachd, see taoitearachd.
taigheach,** *a.* Domestic.
taigheadas, -ais, *s.m.* Household. 2 Housekeeping. 3**Residence. 4**Husbandry. 6 (DU) Economy. Air a thaigh 's air a th., *he having a house and household.*
———ach, *a.* Diligent, careful, busy about housekeeping. 2 Hospitable.
taigheasach, *a.* Domestic. 2 Fond of, or belonging to, housekeeping.
taigheil,** *a.* Domestic.
taighlich,†† *s.f.* Chattels, paraphernalia.
taigh-spùinneadair,** *s.m.* Robber, burglar.
———eachd, *s.f.* Robbery,burglary.
taightirich, see taoitirich.
tail, -e, -ean, *s.f.* Substance, product. 2 Lump, *prov.* 3 Solidity. 4**Wages. 5 Matter,means. 6 see taileadh.
tail,** *a.* Solid, substantial.
tailbeart, see ailebeart.
———ach, see ailebeartach.
tailbhein, see tairbhein.
tailce,** *s.f.* Strength, force, vigour. 2 Courage. 3 (††tailc) Firmness, substantiality.
———ach, -eiche, *a.* Firm, sturdy, solid, well-formed, stately. 2**Prancing.
———anach, -aiche, see tailceach. 2††Stout.
———anach, -aich, *s. m.* Firm, strongly-built man. 2††Stout man.
tailcearra, *a.* Dogged, see tailceach. Gu foirmeil, tailcearra, *purpose-like and dogged.—Oran an t-Samhraidh.*
tailceas, -eis, *s.m.* Contempt, scorn, reproach, disdain. 2 Fastidiousness. 3** Spite. 4‡‡ Provocation. C' uim' an dean iad t. ort ? *why do they reproach thee ?*
———ach, -aiche, *a.* Scorning, disdaining, disdainful, despising,reproachful, contemptuous. 2 Contemptible,mean. 3**Spiteful. 4 Dainty, fastidious, as of kinds of food. Gu t., *contemptuously.*
tailceasachd,** *s.f.* Contemptuousness. 2 Reproachfulness. 3 Spitefulness.
tailceil, see tailceach.
tailcionta, -inte, *a.* see tailceach.
taile,** *s.f.* see tail.
taileabart, -airt, -an, *s.m.* Halbert. [‡tailebart.]
———ach, *a.* Armed with halberts.
taileadh,(AC) *s.m.* Cause, sake of, on account of. Fhuair mise trod an t. do ghnothaich, *I got a scolding on account of your business* ; tha mi air t. mo ghnothaich fhéin, *I am after my own business.*
tailealachd, *s.f.ind.* Solidity, substance.
taileas, -eis, *s.m.* Wages, hire.
tàileasg, -eisg, -an, *s.m.* Backgammon. 2 Chess. 3**Draughts. 4‡‡Sport, game, mirth. 5 (DU) Ghost. Gun t. gun cheòl, *without mirth or music* ; a' cluich aig t., *playing at chess* ; gun t., *without solidity.*
———ach, -aiche, *a.* Fond of backgammon or chess.
———an,** *s.m.* The game of draughts.

taileil, -e, *a.* Solid, substantial.
taileileachd, see tailealachd.
†**tailgean**, -ein, *s.m.* Holy offspring. 2 Religious soldier of God.
tailgneachd, see targradh.
tailisg,** *s.f.* War instrument.
†**taille**, *s.f.* Wages. 2 Tax, tribute. 3 Apprentice fee.
taile, see taileadh.
tàilleabh,**s.m.* Apprentice fee, premium, 2 Consequence, result. An do phàigh thu do th., ? *have you paid your premium ?* air t. a' ghnothaich sin, *in consequence of that affair ;* gheibh no meallaidh mi nis t.mo shaoithreach, *I will now enjoy the fruits of my labour.*
———ach, -aiche, *a.* Consequent,as the result.
———ach,* -aich, *s.m.* Apprentice.
———achd,* *s.f.* Apprenticeship. 2 Substantiality.
tàillear, -eir, -an, *s.m.* Tailor.
———achd, *s.f.* Tailor's trade, sewing.
taillse, *s.m.* Spectre, apparition.
tailm, -e, -ean, *s.f.* Tool, utensil, instrument. 2 Gin, snare. 3 Stroke. 4 Catapult. 5††Sling, noose.
tailmrich, *s.f.ind.* Noise, bustle, confusion,noise of footsteps.
tailmsich,** for tailmrich.
tailp, -e, -ean, *s.f.* Bundle, bunch, parcel,piece.
tailpeach, -eiche, *a.* Bunchy, lumpish.
taim, *poetical* for ataim (tha mi,) I am.
†**taim**, *s.f.* Town.
tàimh, -e, *s.f.* Death. 2 Mortality. 3 Silence. 4 Fainting.
———, *gen.sing.* of tàmh.
tàimheach, -eich, *s.m.* Residence.
tàimhidh,(CR) *a.* Gentle, still—*Skye.*
tàimh-leac, -lic, *s.f.* Tombstone. 2** Heap of stones collected on a spot where a person has been killed or buried.
tàimhleasg,** see tàileasg.
†**taimhliosg**, *s.m.* see tàileasg.
taimhlisg,(AC) *v.n.* Traduce, contemn. Is tu 'n t., might mean, a traducing person, or one worthy of being traduced.
taimh-neul,** *v.n.* Slumber, fall into a sleep or swoon.
———, -neòil, -an, *s.m.* Slumber. 2 Swoon. 3 Trance, ecstasy. Thuit e an t., *he fell into a swoon.*
———ach, -aiche, *a.* Slumbering, like a slumber, trance or swoon.
taimhslich,(WC)*s.f.* Sounds heard before a party comes to occupy a house. Bha iad a' cluinntinn t. an seo, *they heard mysterious sounds here*—said of a haunted house.
tàimhteachd, *s.f. ind.* Home, abode, dwelling—*Rob Donn.*
†**taimne**, *s.* Torpor.
†**taimthiu**, *s.* Bed-death.
tàin, -e, -tean, *s.f.* Cattle, herd or drove of cattle. 2 Spoil, plunder. 3 Mental endowments. 4††Goods. 5* Wealth in flocks.
†**tain**, -e, *s.f.* Water. Folach-tain, *water-parsnip.*
†**tàin**, *s.m.* Land, country. [*s.f. gen.* -e.—††]
tainceil,(MS) *a.* see taingeil.
taine, *s.f.ind.* Thinness, slenderness, leanness.
taine, *comp.* of tana, More or most thin.
tàineach, *a.* Abounding in cattle or goods.
tainead, -eid, *s.m.* Thinness, degree of thinness. 2 **Tenacity. A' dol an t., *growing thinner and thinner.*
taineamh, *s.* Thaw—*Arran.*
†**taineantach**, *a.* Darting a double ray, corruscating.
taing, -e, *s.f.* Thanks, gratitude, obligation. 2 Acknowledgement. Gun t. dhuit, *in defiance of you ;* ni mi sin gun t. dhuit, *I will do that in spite of you ;* a' nochdadh do th., *showing your sense of gratitude ;* t. is buidheachas dhuit, *many thanks to you ;* chuireadh e annainn gu'n t. gun, *he would insist that (it was so) ;* neo-ar-thaing dhuit, *no thanks to you.*
taingealachd, *s.f.ind.* Thankfulness, gratitude.
taingealas, -ais, *s.m.* see taingealachd.
taingeil, -e, *a.* Thankful, grateful, acknowledging. Is t. is còir dhuit a bhi, *you ought to be very thankful;* bi t. nach 'eil seo na's miosa, *be thankful this is not worse ;* gu t., *thankfully.*
taingich, *v.a.* Thank, give thanks.
†**tàinig**, see thàinig.
tàinisteach, -ich, *s.m.* see tànaiste.
tainistear, see tànaiste.
———achd, see tànaistearachd.
tàinisteas,** *s.m.* Domination.
tàinistre, see tànaistre.
tainneachadh,(MS) *s.m.* Stain.
tainneadh, *Arran* for tainneamh.
tainneamh,‡ *v.n.* Thaw.
tainnleag,(CR) *Helmsdale & Kildonan* for seillean.
tainntean,** -ein, *s.m.* Thread.
———ach,** *a.* Thready, filmy, viscous.
tainte,(AF) *s.f.* Cattle taken as booty or spoil, booty.
tàintean, *n.pl.* of tàin.
———,* *s.pl.* Talents, faculties, accomplishments. Is mór na t. a bhuilich Dia ort, *great are the talents God has bestowed on you ;* bithidh do sgoil 'na t. dhuit ri d' bheò, *your education will prove an accomplishment to you for life.*
taip, -e, -ean, *s.f.* Lump, mass. 2 Clumsy person. 3**Rock. 4*Great wealth without any of the refined manners of genteel society.
taipeach,†† *a.* Lumpy.
tàir,(CR) -àire, *a.* Bad, mean, base, ill. Cha'n 'eil mi cho t. ri sin, *I am not so bad* or *base as that ;* cha'n 'eil mi na's tàire, *I am not worse* (in health)—*W. coast of Ross ;* cha robh am beannachadh na bu tàire na bha e roimhe aig an dithis ri chéile, *their salutation to each other was no worse than formerly*—W.H. 1. 13; cha bu tàir e, *he was not bad*—i.e. he was very good.
†**tair**, see thar.
tàir, -e, -ean, *s.f.* Contempt, reproach,disgrace, Fo th., *despised ;* gun taise gun t., *without effeminacy or reproach.* [*s.m.***]
tàir, -e, *a.* see tàireil.
tàir, *pr.pt.* a' tàireadh [& a' tàir,*] *v.a. & n.* Get, obtain,acquire. 2 Come. 3‡‡Be able. 4 Move off, go. T. as, *flee, escape;* cha t. mi dol ann, *I cannot go ;* a' tàir orm, *despising me, looking down on me.*
tairbealach, see tairbhealach.
tairbeart, -eirt, -an, *s.f.* Isthmus. 2* Superabundance. 3 (McL & D) Peninsula.
———ach, *a.* Having isthmuses, peninsular.
———ach,(MS) *a.* Open-handed. 2* Superabundant, very abundant, almost superfluous, for tairbheartach.
tairbeartas, see tairbheartas.
tairbh, *gen.sing. & n.pl.* of tarbh.
tairbhe, *s.f.ind.* Profit, advantage, usefulness, avail, benefit. 2††Efficiency. Nithe gun t., *things without profit ;* t. eucorach, *unjust gain;* t. cha dean t' òr-chul réidh, *thy well-ordered golden hair cannot avail ;* an t-ainm gun an t., *the name or credit of anything without the profit or benefit of it*—*W. coast of Ross.*
———ach, *a.* see tarbhach.
tàirbhealach, -aich, -aichean, *s. m.* Defile, pass.

narrow mountain valley. 2 Ferry, passage.
tairbhealachd,(MS) *s.f.* Availment.
tairbhean,(AF) *s.m.* Colic. 2 Bull-calf.
tairbheann,(AF) *s.* Parasite, insect, cattle-insect.
tairbheart, -bheirt, *pl.* -an & -bheirt, see tairbheartas. 2**Liberal action.
——ach, -aiche, *a.* Profitable, beneficial, abundant, bountiful. 2 Gracious. 3**Fruitful. 4**Liberal. Cho tairbheartach 's a tha iad, *so abundant are they.*
——achd, *s.f.* Ampleness.
tairbheartas, -ais, *s.m.* Bounty, free gift, benefit. 2 Usefulness, profit, advantage. 3*Superabundance. 4* Overflowing goodness Tairbheartas a làimhe, *the superabundance of his goodness.*
tairbhein,(AC) Surfeit. 2 Bloody flux in cattle.
tairbheirt,** *s.f.* Turpentine.
tairbhich,(MS) *v.a.* Accrue.
tàir-chainnt, -e, *s.f.* Reproachful speech, vituperation.
——each, -eiche, *a.* Reproachful, vituperative, using contemptuous expressions. 2 ‡‡Libellous. Gu t., *reproachfully.*
taircheadal,** -ail, *s.m.* Prophecy.
taircheall,** -ill, *s.m.* Act, action.
tàir-chomharradh, *s.* Brand.
tair-chreich,** *s.f.* Desert, merit.
tàire, *comp.* of tàir.
tàireach,** *a.* see tàireil.
——d, *s.f.* see tàirealachd.
tàiread,** -eid, *s.m.* Degree of vileness or contempt. A' dol an t., *growing more and more contemptible.*
taireag,** -eig, *s.f.* Provision. 2 Preparation.
tàirealachd, *s.f.ind.* Contemptibility, baseness, vileness, reproachfulness, abjectness, disgracefulness, contemptuousness. 2**Long life.
tàiream,** -eim, *s.m.* Dispraise, disparagement
——ach,** *a.* Disparaging.
tàirean,** -ein, *a.* Descent.
taireasg, see tuireasg & toirsgian.
—— -luaithre, *s.* Sawdust, see tuireasg-l—.
tàireil, -e, *a.* Mean, base, contemptible, low, despised, disgraced, vile, disgraceful. 2 Degrading. 3 Reproachful, insulting, disdainful, contemptuous. A chainnt t., *his contemptible speech*; gach ni bha t., *everything that was vile.*
taireis,** *adv.* After, afterwards, afterhand. T. mo chur 's an uaigh, *after I am in the grave.*
tairg, *pr.pt.* a' tairgse, a' tairgseadh & a' tairgsinn, *v.n.* Offer, propose, proffer, bid. 2* see tairng. Th. e airgiod dhomh, *he offered me money*; t. air seo, *bid for this*—as at a sale by auction.
tairg,(CR) *s.f.* Cionnas a tha thu ? tha tairg agam, *how do you do ? I am fairly well.* Tha mi an tairg mhath, *and* tha tairg orm, which are heard in some parts are considered bad idiom in others—*Suth'd.*
†**tairgeadh**, -idh, *s.m.* Collecting. 2 Collection. 3** Endeavour. 4** Going, passing. 5 see tàirngneadh. Cha b' olc an tairge dha sin, *that was a most courageous attempt*—(WC.)
tairgeam,**(for tairgidh mi) I shall or will offer.
——, *1st.per.sing.imp.* of tairg. Let me offer.
tairgear, *fut.pass.* of tairg. T. uan geal dhuit-se a ghrian ! *a white lamb shall be offered to thee, O sun !*
——,** *s.m.* Bidder.
tairgeil, see tairgheal.
tairgeug,** -geuga, *s.m.* Graft.
taírgheag,** -eig, *s.f.* Imp, brat.
tairgheal, -eil, *s.m.* Offering, oblation.
†**tairgineach**, -eiche, *a.* Prophesying.
tairgir,* *v.* see targair, *v.*
tairgir(e),* *s.m.* Offerer, bidder.
tairgire, see targradh.
tairgireadh, -idh, *s.m.* & *pr.pt.* Prophesying. 2 Prophecy.
——an, *pl.* of tarrang.
tairgne, *pl.* of tarrang.
tairgneach, -eiche, *a.* Full of nails.
——d, *s.f.ind.* see targradh.
tairgre,** *s.f.* Prophecy.
tairgreach,** *a.* Prophetic, soothsaying. 2 Rhyming.
——d, *s.f.* Prophesying. 2 Proverb.
†**tairgreadh**, -idh, *s.m.* & *pr.pt.* Prophesying. 2 Prophecy.
tairgse, -achan, *s.f.* & *pr.pt.* of tairg, see tairgseadh. Thoir t., *make an offer.*
tairgse, *a.* Able. 2 (WC) Attempting. Tha mi tairgse bhi ag gluasad, *I am able to move about*—*W. of Ross.*
——ach,* *s.* see tairgseadh.
——ach,* *a.* Inviting, offering.
——adh, -idh, *s. m.* Offering, act of offering. 2 Inviting. 3 Offer, proposal. A' t—, *pr. pt.* of tairg.
tairgsear,** *s.m.* Bidder.
tairgsinn, *s.f.* & *pr.pt.* of tairg, see tairgseadh.
tairiosg, -isg, -an, see tuireasg.
tairirich, see dairirich.
tairis ! *int.* The dairymaid's cry to calm an unruly cow at milking.
tairis, -e, *a.* Kind, sincere, loving. 2 Compassionate, tender-hearted, soft, tender, kindly, urbane. 3 Confidential. 4**Trusty, faithful, loyal. 5**Acceptable. Cha t. leam ur fàilte, *your invitation is not acceptable to me* ; guth t. nam bàrd, *the mild voice of the bards.*
tairis,** *v.a.* & *n.* Love. 2 Come. 3 Stay, remain.
tairise, see tairiseachd.
tairiseach, -eiche, *a.* Loyal, faithful. 2 Ready. Earnest. 3 (DU) Loving, kind.
——d, *s.f.ind.* Lovingness, affection, friendship, attachment. 2 Faithfulness. 3 Compassion, tender-heartedness. 4 Fidelity. 5 Truth. 6††Fealty.
tairisean,** -ein, -an, *s.m.* Cross band, tie.
tairisgein, *s.f.* see toirsgian.
tairisgil, *s.f.* see toirsgian.
tairisiomh,***a.* Dear, intimate, friendly. 2 Trusty.
tairisneach, -eiche, *a.* see tairiseach.
——d, *s.f.* see tairiseachd.
tairiste, see tairis.
——ach, -eiche, see tairiseach.
——achd, see tairiseachd.
tairleach,** *s.m.* Moisture.
tair-learach, -aiche, *a.* Transmarine.
tairleas,(CR) *s.m.* Cupboard—*Perthshire.*
tairm, -e, *s.f.* see taghairm.
tairmcheall,** -ill, *s.m.* Circuit.
tàirmeas,* *s.m.* Disdain, contempt.
——ail,* *a.* Disdainful.
tairn,* *s.f.* see taghairm.
tairn, *v.* see tarruing & tàirng.
tairne, *gen.sing.* of tarrunn.
tàirneach,** *a.* Thundering. Mar thannasg air slèibhte t., *like a ghost on thundering mountains.*
tàirneach, -aiche, *a.* Attractive, enticing. 2 Pulling, drawing, extractive. Le briathraibh t., *with enticing words.*
tàirneach, -eich, *s.m.* see tàirneanach.
tairneag,** *s.f.* Drawer (in chest of drawers.)
tàirneanach, -aich, *s.m.* Thunder. 2 Thundering noise. Peilear tàirneanaich, *a thunderbolt.*
tàirneanachd, *s.f.* Fulmination.
tàirneanaich, *v.a.* Detonize.
tàirneanaiche,* *s.m.* Thunderer.
tàirng, -e, -ean, *s.f.* Nail, pin, peg. Bior-thàirng,

a coffin-nail.
tàirng, *pr. pt.* a' tàirngeadh, [a' tàirngich & a' tàirngeachadh,] *v.a.* Nail, fasten with nails. Tha t' fhardach air a thàirngeadh, *thy dwelling (coffin) is nailed.*
tàirnge, *s.pl.* Nails, pegs.
tàirngeach, -iche, *a.* Drawing, pulling. 2†† Abounding in nails.
tàirngeachadh,(a'), *pr.pt.* of tàirngich.
tàirngeadh, -idh, *s.m.* Fixing, nailing, act of fixing with nails.
tàirngich, *pr.pt.* a' tàirngeachadh,*v.a.* see tairng.
tàirngidh, *fut.aff.a.* of tarruing.
tairngire,** *s.f.* Promise.
tairn-na-ceusda, *s.f.* Pile-nail, passion-nail in *heraldry.* [Generally used in threes.]
tàirngnean-barraidh, *s. pl.* Rivet-nails in a boat—*Skye.*
tàirngnean-calpa, *s.pl.* Nails for joining planks together in a boat, see p. 77.
657. *Tàirng-na-ceusda.*
tàirngnean-daraich, *s.pl.* Boat-nails, see p. 77.
tàirngnean-fruillichd, *s.pl.* Roves.
tàirngnean-fuaigheil, *s.pl.* Nails for sewing together planks in a boat.
tairngnean-rang, see tàirnean-daraich.
tàirngnean-sgair, *s.pl.* Small nails, see sùidhean, under bàta.
tàirngte, *past pt.* of tàirng. Nailed, fixed with nails. 2 see tarruingte.
tàirnich,** *v. n.* Thunder, make a thundering noise.
tàirnnich,* (for tairngich) *v.a.* see tairng.
tàirnsinn,* see tairsinn.
tàirn-thoirm, -e, *s.f.* Thundering noise.
tairp,** *s.m.* Clod, (see tarp.)
-——each, *a.* Strong. 2 Grand, pompous. 3 Cloddy.
tairseach,**,-ich, *s.m.* Hinge of a door. 2 Threshold.
tairsgian, see toirsgian.
tair-shliabhach,** *a.* Transmontane.
tàirsinn, -e, *s.f.* Obtaining, act of obtaining or acquiring. A' t—, *pr.pt.* of tàir. Tàirsinn as, *flying, act of flying, escaping, or running away.*
tairsnean, see tarsannan.
tais, -e, *a.* Moist, damp, dank. 2 Soft, not tempered, as metal. 3 Faint-hearted, timid, not hardy. 4 Cold, spiritless. 5**Pitiful. 6 Remiss. 7 Relaxed. 8††Blunt. T. agus fiamh, *softness and fear.*
taisbean, *v. a.* Reveal, show, make manifest, table, present. 2 Bespeak. T. an t-airgiod, *table the money* ; t. do thròcair dhuinn, *reveal thy loving-kindness to us.*
———, -ein, -an, *s.m.* Vision, revelation. 2 Apparition. 3 Appearance, figure.
———ach, -aiche, *a.* Revealing, that reveals, discovering. 2 Manifest. 3 Of, or belonging to a vision or apparition, apocalyptical. 4 Indicative, in *grammar.*
———adh, -aidh, *s.m.* Revealing,act of revealing,revelation,showing or disclosing. 2 Show, pageant. 3 Epiphany, Twelfth day. 4††Advertisement. 5 Manifesto. 6 Demonstration, demonstrating, celebration. 7 Apparition. 8 Appearance, appearing, see taisbean. Leabhbar an taisbeanaidh, *the Book of Revelation.* A' t—, *pr.pt.* of taisbean.
taisbeanar,** *fut.pass.* of taisbean.
taisbeanta, *a. & past pt.* of taisbean. Revealed, discovered, shown, made evident, presented. Aran t., *shewbread.*
taisbein, see taisbean.
taisbeinte, see taisbeanta.
taisbinn,(AC) for taisbeam, *1st. per. sing. imp.* of taisbean. 2 *Irish 1st.sing.indic.* of taisbean.
taisc, see taisg.
-——ealach, see taisgealach.
-——ealadh, see taisgealadh.
tais-chridheach, -eiche, *a.* Tender-hearted. 2 Faint-hearted, soft-hearted. 3 Irresolute.
———— ————d, *s.f.ind.*Tender-heartedness. 2 Faint-heartedness. 3 Irresolution.
taisdeal, -eil, -an, *s.m.* Journey, voyage, journeying, voyaging, pilgrimage, travel, march. Gu t. nan tonn gàireach, *to travelling of the foamy waves—Òran nam fineachan,* G 3, 4.
taisdealach, -aich, *s. m* Pilgrim, passenger, traveller. 2 Wanderer, saunterer. 3 Person that scuds or vanishes by. 4 Ghost. 5 Vagabond, itinerant. 6 Contemptible person.
—— ————, *a.* Itinerant, journeying, travelling, of, or belonging to a journey or traveller. 2 Like a traveller. 3 Like a wanderer or vagabond.
taisdealachd, *s.f.ind,* Pilgrimage, journey. 2 Wandering, sauntering, lounging. 3**Pedestrianism, travelling.
taisdealaiche,** *s.m.* Traveller, pedestrian. 2 Pilgrim. 3 Saunterer, lounger.
taise,* *comp.* of tais. More or most soft or spiritless.
taise, see taisg.
—,** *s.pl.* Dead bodies. 2 Relics of saints.
—, *s.f.* see taiseachd.
taiseach, *a.* see taoiseach.
————adh, -aidh, *s.m.* Softening. 2 State of becoming soft, moist or damp. 3 Growing effeminate, act of softening or moistening. 4 Making effeminate. 5 Effeminacy. 6 Softness. A' t—, *pr.pt.* of taisich.
————ail, -e, *a.* Lenient, lenitive.
————d, *s.f.ind.* Moistness,softness,dampness. 2 Effeminacy. 3 Timidity. 4 Weakness. 5* Extreme cowardice.
taisead, -eid, *s.m.* Degree of softness. 2 Weakness. 3 Cowardice, or 4 Moisture. 5 Effeminacy. 6 Timidity. 7* Extreme degree of cowardice or moistness. A' dol an t., *getting softer or more timid.*
————ach,* -aich, *s.m.* Shroud, winding sheet. Ciste is t., *coffin and winding-sheet.*
taiseag,** -eig, *s.f.* Restitution.
tàiseal,(AH) *s.m.* Ghost. 2 Any mysterious object with a noiseless, irresistible motion—*Argyll.*
taisealach,(DMy) *s.m.* Any quantity in a heap or vessel of more bulk than was expected.
taisealachd, *s.f.* see taiseachd.
taisealadh, -aidh, *s.m.* Bulk, quantity, product. *prov.*
tàisealaich,‡‡ -e, *s.f.* Coming unperceived, like a ghost.
taisealan,‡‡ -ain, *s.m.* Reliquary, keepsake.
taisealbh,‡‡ *v.a.* Personate, represent.
————adh, -aidh, *s.m.* Act of personating. 2 Likeness. 3**Exhibition. 4**Representation. A' t—, *pr. pt.* of taisealbh.
taiseallach, see taisgealach.
taisealladh, see taisgealadh.
taisear, see taibhsear.
-————achd,(WC) *s.f.* Capers, fun.
taiseil,** -e, *a.* Dampish, see tais.
taisg, *pr. pt.* a' taisgeadh & a' tasgadh, *v. a.* Deposit, lay up, hoard, treasure. 2 Bury. Taisgeargach claidheamh 'na thruaill, *every sword shall be put up into its sheath* ; t. m' àitheantan, *lay up my commandments* ; 'ga thasgadh, seachad, *hoarding it up.*
taisg, -e, -ean, *s.f.* Pledge, stake 2 Treasure. 3

††Anything laid by, deposit. 4**Reconnoitring, spying. 5* Saving. Ni sam bith a tha 'n taisg, *anything treasured up.*
taisg-airm, -ean-airm, *s.f.* Armoury.
taisg-aodach, -aich, -ean. *s.m.* Winding-sheet.
taisg-aodaich, *s.m.* Wardrobe.
taisgeach, -eiche, *a.* That hoards or lays up, saving, frugal, hoarding. 2 Inclined to hoard or lay up.
taisgeach,* -eich, *s.m.* Store, store-house. 2 Saving, pose. 3 Thing given in charge, treasure, hoard. 4**Budget. An t. math sin, *that good thing.*
taisgeachan,** -ain, *s.m.* Store-keeper. 2(WC) Keepsake.
taisgeadach,* see taisg-aodaich.
——————, -aiche, see taisgeach.
taisgeadan, -ain, -an, *s.m. & f.* Storehouse, treasury. 2 Store accumulated for future supply.
taisgeadh,** -idh, *s.m.* Store, wealth.
taisgeal, -eil, -an, *s.m.* Finding of anything that was lost. 2* Reward for returning it. 3 (MMcL) Enchantment. 4*News. 'S ann air a thàinig na taisgealan 'nuair a rinn e sin! *what enchantment came over him when he did that!*
taisgealach, -aich, *s. m.* Spy, betrayer. 2 Reporter, discoverer. 3 Traveller, pilgrim. 4 Passenger.
——————d,** *s.f.* Pilgrimage.
taisgealadh, -aidh, *s.m.* Report, news. 2 Discovery. 3 Prognostication.
taisg-eide, see taisg-aodach.
taisg-eudach, see taisg-aodach.
taisg-eudaich, see taisg-aodaich.
taisgear, *fut.pass.* of taisg.
taisg-ghuthachd,‡‡ *s.f.ind.* Mellowness of voice.
taisgidh,** *s.f.* Trunk. 2 Hoarding, laying up.
taisg-inntinn,** *s.f.* Reservedness. 2 Equivocation, mental reservation.
taisg-ionad, -aid, -an, *s.m.* Storehouse, treasury.
taisgte, *past pt.* of taisg. Hoarded, laid up. 2 Buried.
taisg-thaigh, see taigh-stòir.
taisich, *pr.pt.* a' taiseachadh, *v.a. & n.* Moisten, soften. 2 Dabble. 3 Bedrench. 4 Daunt. 5 Make effeminate. 6**Shrink with fear. 7 Blandish. 'Nuair thaisicheas bròn iad, *when grief softens them ;* cridhe nach t. roimh fhuathas, *a heart that will not shrink before anything fearful.*
——————te, *past pt.* of taisich. Softened, made soft. 2 Made effeminate. 3 Become soft or moist.
taisill,** *s.f.* Trespass. 2 Damage, injury. 3 Injustice.
taisleachadh, -aidh, *s. m.* Softening, wetting, making damp. 2** Bathing. 3** Making effeminate.
taisleachd, see taiseachd.
taislear, -ir, -an, *s.m.* see taibhsear.
taislich, (DMy) *s.* Soft, ghostly sound or movement in the dark.
taislich, ** *v.a.* Bathe. 2 see taisich.
——————te, *past pt.* Bathed. 2 see taisichte.
taist,** *s.f.* Tache, button. 2 Loop. 3 Catch.
taisteag, -eig, *s.f.* Moment.
taisteal, see taisdeal.
——————ach, see taisdealach.
taistearachd, see taibhsearachd.
†**tait**,** *s.m.* Pleasure. 2**Mercury.
taite, -an, *s.f.* **Beginning, commencement. 2 †† Glimpse, peep.
taiteach,** -ich, *s.m.* Abuse, reproach.
taiteadh, -idh, *s.m.* Pleasure, delight.
taiteadh,** *v.a.* Domify, tame, reconcile to a new home—*Perthshire & Argyll.*

658. Taithean.

taiteag, -eig, -an, *s.f.* Moment.
taithean,§ *s.m.* Lyme grass—*elymus arenarius.*
taitheasg, -eisg, *s.m.* Repartee.
taithigh, -e, *s.f.* see tathaich.
——————each, -eiche, *a.* Usual, frequenting, coming often.
taithireach, *a.* Fond of. Chionn i bhi taithireach air fir, *because she is fond of men—Rob Donn.*
taithleach,** *s.m.* Peace, quietness.
taithleach,** *a.* Quiet, peaceable. 2 Bright. 3 Pleasant, handsome.
taithleach,** -ich, *s.m.* Excuse.
taithleachas, -ais, *s.m.* Excusation.
taith-léigh,** *s.m.* Surgeon.
taithneadh,** -idh, *s.m.* Splendour, brightness.
taithris, see tairis.
taitinn,** *s.f.* Pleasure, satisfaction.
taitinn, *pr. pt.* a' taitneadh, ††a' taitneachdainn & a' taitinn, *v.a.&n.* Please, satisfy, give delight to. 2(MS) Approve. 3**Be acceptable. Ciamar a th. e riut? *how did it please you?*
taitneach, -eiche, *a.* Pleasant, delightful, fascinating, agreeable, acceptable. 2**Grateful. 3**Satisfactory. 4**Becoming. Is t. an ni e, *it is a pleasant thing ;* t. do 'n t-sealladh, *pleasant to the sight ;* is t. leam t' fhaicinn, *I am happy to see you ;* seud t., *a precious jewel ;* toil th. Dhé, *the acceptable will of God ;* ma s' e 's taitniche leat, *if it be more agreeable (seem better) to thee.*
taitneachadh, *s.m.* Approving, approval.
taitneachail, (MS) *a.* Acceptable.
taitneachas, -ais, see taitneas.
taitneachd, *s.f.ind.* Amenity. 2 *Taste. 3 Pleasantness, agreeableness, attractiveness, delight, satisfaction, delightfulness. 4 Approval, approbation, acceptability. Ann ad th., *in thy delights.*
taitneachduinn, -e, *s.f. & pr.pt.* see taitneadh.
taitneadh, -idh, *s.m.* Pleasing, act of pleasing, delighting, pleasure. 2** Approval, satisfaction, approbation. A' t—, *pr.pt.* of taitinn. Tionndaidh e gu do th., *it will turn to your satisfaction.*
taitneas, -eis -an, *s.m.* Quality of exciting pleasure or delight. 2 Pleasure, delight, satisfaction. 3* Pleasing to the taste.
taitnich, *v.* see taitinn. 2(MS) Addulce.
taitniche, *comp.* of taitneach.
taitnidh, *gen.sing.* of taitneadh. 2 *fut. aff.a.* of taitinn.

tal,** s.f. Dropping.
tàl, -àil, -an, s.m. Cooper's adze, addice.
tàl-deis, s.m. Cooper's plane used for the right side.
tàl-cùil, s.m. Cooper's plane for the left side.
tàl-fuinn, s.m. Hoe.
tàlach,†† a. Having adzes.
talach, -aich, s.m. Complaint, murmur. 2 Dispraise. 3 Cause of reproach. Cha'n 'eil reusan talaidh agam, *I have no reason to complain.* 4 (DMy) Discontent, dissatisfaction.
talach,** -aiche, a. Complaining, murmuring, 2 Prone to reproach. 3 Apt to grudge.
talach, -aich, s.m. & pr. pt. of talaich, see talachadh.
talachadh, -aidh, s.m. Complaining, murmuring, act of complaining or murmuring. 2 Murmur, complaint. 3 Cause of complaint. 4 Repining. 5 Disparagement. A' t—, pr. pt of talaich. Cha'n ion dhuit a bhith talachadh, *you have no reason to complain* or *grumble.*
talachair,†† -ean, s.m. Complainer.
talachar, -aire, a. Complaining, murmuring. 2 Apt to complain.
tàladair,(MS) s.m. Attracter.
tàladh, -aidh, s.m. Enticing, act of enticing or alluring. 2 Act of taming, caressing or soothing, domesticating. 3 Hushing, act of hushing or rocking to rest, caressing. 4 Lullaby, cradle-song. 5* Getting attached to a person or house, as animals. 6**Making attached. 7**Elegy. A' t—, pr.pt. of tàlaidh.
tàladhach,** a. Attractive.
talag,(AF) -aig, s.f. Roach.
tàlag,†† -aig, -an, s.f. Little edge.
talaich, pr.pt. a' talach & a' talachadh, v.a.&n. Complain, murmur. 2 Be dissatisfied.
tàlaideach,(MS) a. Amusing, attractive.
tàlaideachd,(MS) s.f. Attraction.
tàlaidh, pr.pt. a' tàladh, v.a. Entice, allure. 2 Tame, caress, soothe, cajole, domesticate. 3 Hush to rest, as a cradled infant. 4 Get attached to a person or house, as an animal. Ma thàlaidheas peacaich thu, *if sinners entice thee.*
tàlaidhdair,(MS) s.m. Amuser.
tàlaidheach, -eiche, a. Abstractive.
tàlaidhte, past pt. of tàlaidh.
talainte,* s. m. Partition, division wall. [In *Gairloch*, nom. talaint, gen. -e, n.pl. -ean. Partition, generally made of wood—DU.]
talamh, gen. sing. -aimh & talmhainn, pl. -an, -nan & -anta,†† m. in the nom.sing. & f. in the gen. The earth. 2 Earth, land, soil. 3** Country. T. glas, *unploughed land* ; t. dubh, *black land* ; 2 figuratively, *open weather*, i. e. absence of snow in winter ; t. dearg, *ploughed land* ; t. fliuch, *moist* or *wet land* ; t. tioram, *dry land* ; t. treabhaidh, *arable land* ; t. tilgte, *soil removed from one place to another* ; aghaidh na talmhainn, *the face of the earth* ; na talmhannan, *the lands* or *cultivated lots of a crofting township* ; thugadh mi d' an t., *I was taken to their country.* [pl. also talmhainnean.]
talamhaidh, -e, a. see talmhaidh.
talamh-eòlaiche, s.m. Geologist.
talamh-eòlas, s.m. Geology.
talamh-eòlasach, a. Geological.
talamh gaothaidh, *Lismore* for purrag. (appx.)
talamh-toll,‡‡ s.m. Cave. 2(CR) Opening over a burn running underground—*Skye & Argyll.* 3 (WC) Quagmire, unsafe ground. An old Gaelic prayer ran " Gun gléidheadh tu sinn o thalamh-toll, o mhointichean 's o shaighdearan dearga 'n righ," *save us from quagmires, from peat-mosses and from the king's red soldiers.*
talan, see talainte. 2 (MMcL) Partition in black houses about 3ft. high, for separating the portion occupied by the cattle.
tàlan, -ain, pl--an & -tan, s.m. Chivalry, feats of arms.
tàlann, -ainn, pl. -an, -ainn, **-tan & -ainnean, s.m. Talent of money or mind.
talban,** -ain, s.m. Partition.
talca, -ailce, see tailce.
talcais,** s.f. Contempt.
talcanta, -ainte, a. see tailceach.
talcantas,** -ais, s.m. Sturdiness.
talcarra, a. see tailceach.
talchar, -air, s.m. Obstinacy.
talcharach,** a. Obstinate.
talcuis, s.f. see tarcuis.
-——each, a. see tarcuiseach.
-——eachd, see tarcuiseachd.
tal-fhradharc,** -airc, s. Caution, foresight, wariness.
——————ach,** a. Cautious, wary.
tàl-fuinn, -ean, s.m. Hoe.
talgadh,** -aidh, s.m. Quieting, pacifying, pacification.
talganta, see talcanta.
†tall, see thall.
tall, v. Cut.
†tall, -a, s.m. Theft.
talla, -chan, s.m. Hall. 2 **House. 3**Court. 4**Rock. 5**Cleft of a rock. 6**Tower. T. nan sian, *the hall of storms* ; mac talla, *or* mac talla nan creag, *the echo* ; t. a' chiùil, *the music-hall.* [** gen. -ai.]
tallach, -aiche, a. Of, or belonging to, halls, courts, &c. 2 Having halls, courts, &c.
talladh,** -aidh, s.m. Cutting off, lopping.
tallaid, s.f. see callaid. 2 Partition—*Badenoch.*
†tallair,** s.m. Thief, robber.
tallan,(AF) s. Hind.
talm,(AC) v.a. Obey, honour.
tàlmag,(CR) s.f. "Long-nosed mouse-like animal frequenting old walls," apparently the shrew —*Suth'd.*
talmaich,(AC) s. Honour, obeisance.
talmhaidh, -e, a. Earthly, terrestrial. 2 Temporal, worldly. 3 Irreligious 4 Powerful, strong, robust. 5 Weighty, substantial. 6 Sallow-complexioned, death-like. 7** Earthy. Nithean t., *earthly things* ; inntinn th., *a worldly mind* ; min th., *substantial meal* ; an cruinne t., *the terrestrial globe.*
talmhaidheachd, s.f.ind. Worldliness, earthliness, devotedness to worldly objects. 2 Paleness of look, sallowness. 3* Weightiness, substantiality.
talmhainn, gen.sing. of talamh.
talmhanach, a. Agrarian.
talmhanta, -ainte, -an, s.m. Mineral.
——————ch,** a. Mineralogical.
——————chadh,* -aidh, s.m. Growing or sticking together, as sods of earth. A' t—, pr. pt. of talmhantaich.
——————chd,** s.f. Mineralogy.
talmhantaich,* v.n. Grow, as earth. 2 Stick together, as sods.
talmhionach, -aich, s.m. Minerals.
talmhuidh, see talmhaidh.
——————eachd, s.f. Earthliness.
talmhuinn, see talmhainn.
talmraich, see tailmrich.
talog, see talag.
†tàl-radharc, see tàl-fhradharc.
——————ach, see tàl-fhradharcach.
ta 'm, (for ta mi) I am.
†tám,‖ s. Rest, repose. 2 Plague. 3 Death.
†tamach,** a. Dull, slow.

tàmadh,(CR) *s.m.* Onset, attack. 2 Grasping—*Dàin I. Ghobha.* Thug an cù t. air, *the dog tried to bite him*, or *tried to catch it.—W. of Ross-shire.*
tamaidh,** *s.m.* Slothful person.
tamail,(CR) *s.f.* Sense, judgment, wits. Chaill e a th., *he has lost his senses, he has lost his wits—W. of Ross.*
tàmailt, -e, -ean, *s. f.* Disparagement. 2 Disgrace, reproach, insult, scandal, shame, degradation. 3 Offence, indignity, affront, feeling of insult. 4 (MMcL) Chagrin. Thoir t., *disgrace*; dean t., *disparage*; osunn thàmailte nan laoch, *the heroes' sigh at their disgrace*; ball tamailte, *an object of disgrace.*
tàmailteach, -eiche, *a.* Humiliating, disparaging. 2 Reproachful, disgraceful, degrading, 3 Taunting, insulting. 4 Indignant, inflamed with resentment at an insult, indignant. 5 Ready to take offence, impatient of insult. [*comp.* -tiche,] Gnàth-fhacal t., *a taunting proverb.*
tàmailteachadh, *s.m.* Degradation, debasement, disgrace. 2 Disdain. 3 (MS) Aspersion. 4 Disgracing, degrading.
tàmailtear,* -eir, -an, *s.m.* Taunter, vilifier.
tàmailtich,** *v.a.* Degrade, disgrace. 2 Affront, reproach.
tamall,†† see tamull.
tamaluadh, *s.m.* Process of softening wool by putting butter on it.
taman,** -ain, *s.m.* Trunk or body of anything.
tàmh, *pr.pt.* a' tàmh, *v.n.* Rest, stay, remain, repose. 2 Settle. 3 Dwell, inhabit. 4 Cease, desist, give over. T. de d' sgeig, *give over your jeering*; tàmh ! tamh ! mo leanaibh, *sleep ! sleep ! my child*; ag obair gun t., *working incessantly*; 'san àm bu chòir dhomh tàmh, *when I ought to repose.*
tàmh, -àimh, *s.m.* Rest, quiet, ease, quietness. 2 Delay. 3 Sleep. 4 Dwelling, abode, act or state of dwelling. 5* Idleness, inactivity. 6 Staying, act of staying or remaining. 7 ** Ocean. 8**Plague. 9**Ecstasy.

Àite-tàimh, *place of rest, refuge*; c' àit' an t. dhuit ? *where is your place of abode ?* a' t. 'san àite seo, *dwelling here*; tha i 'na t., *she is idle*; tha e 'na th., *he is idle*; cha t. dhuit-sa, *you do not pass your time in idleness*; leig t. dhomh, *let me alone*; nach leig thu t. dhomh ? *will you not let me alone*; am fear a bhios 'na th. cuiridh e 'n cat 'san teine, *an idle man will put the cat on the fire*—the English equivalent is, *the devil always finds something for idle hands to do;* am bheil thu 'nad th. ? *are you at leisure ?* is olc a' mhuir a ghluaiseas á tàmh, *it's a bad sea that rises suddenly*; na féidh 'nan t. air sgur-eild, *the deer at rest on their rocks.*

tamh, -aimh, see tabh.
tàmhach, -aich, *s.m.* see tàmhaiche & tàmhachadh.
tàmhach, -aiche, *a.* Dull, heavy, drowsy. 2 Causing ease or rest. 3 Fond of rest, supine, indolent, sluggish. 4††Dwelling.
tàmhachadh, -aidh, *s.m.* State of resting, reposing or becoming tranquil, quieting, settling. 2**Acquiescence. A' t—, *pr.pt.* of tàmhaich.
tàmhachd, *s.f.ind.* Dulness, heaviness, sluggishness. 2** Rest, repose, tranquility, settled state. 3 Abode. Bhi t. am buuait, *dwelling in security—B.Doran, l. 97.*
tàmhadair, -ean, see tàmhaiche.
tàmhadh, -aidh, *s.m. & pr.pt.* see tàmh.
tàmhaich, *pr.pt.* a' tàmhachadh, *v.n.* Rest, repose, become tranquil. 2 Tranquillize, settle. 3**Acquiesce. 4††Dwell.
tàmhaiche, -an *s.m.* Dweller, inhabitant, resident, lodger. 2 Indolent, procrastinating person. 3**Dolt. 4††Lethargic person. Tàmhaiche baile mòir, *a citizen.*
tàmhaiche, *s.f.ind.* see tàmhachd.
tàmhaidh,(AF) *s.f.* Cow that stands gentle.
tàmhaim, (for tamhaidh mi) I will rest.
tàmh-airneis,** *s.f.* Fixtures, furniture that is immoveable.
tàmh-àite, -an, *s. m.* Habitation, abode. 2** Place of rest. 3 see tàbh.
†tamhan, -ain, -an, *s.m.* Trunk, body, block, stock. 2 Dolt.
tamhan,** -ain, *s.m.* The spleen.
tamhanach, -aiche, *a.* Vapourish, doltish, sluggish, splenetic.
tamhanach, -aich, *s.m.* Dolt, blockhead. 2 Inactive fellow.
tamhanachd,** *s.f.* Stupidity, doltishness. 2 Inactivity. 3 Sluggishness. 4††Idleness.
tàmhanta, -ainte, *a.* Doltish, sluggish, slow.
tàmhantachd, *s.f.ind.* Doltishness, sluggishness, slowness.
†tàmhantas -ais, *s.m.* see tàmhantachd.
tàmharach, see tàmhanach.
tamh-ard, see tabh-ard.
tamhasg, -aisg, -an, *s.m.* Blockhead, fool, senseless person. 2 Dwarf, pigmy. 3* Ghost, spectre, apparition. 4 Shade or double of a living person.—J.C.G.,W., 123. 5(DC) Snipe. 6†† Brownie. B' e do th. a bh' ann, *it was your double.*
tamhasgach, -aiche, *a.* Foolish, doltish, stupid, senseless. 2 Dwarfish. 3 Ghostly, spectre-like. 4 Abounding in brownies.
tamhasgail,* -e, *a.* see tamhasgach.
tàmh-leac, -lic, *s.f.* see taimh-leac.
tamhsan, see amhsan.
tàmh-shuain, -e, *s.f.* Trance, ecstasy. 2 Profound sleep.
tamull, -uill, -an, *s.m.* Space of time, length of time. 2 Space, distance, T. dhi 'na tosd, *she being a short while silent*; an ceann tamuill, *in a short while*; rè tamuill, *for a little while;* car tamuill bhig, *for a short while*; t. as, is a thaic ri 'shleagh, *a short distance away, leaning on his spear.*
†tàn, -àin, *s.m.* Country, region, territory. 2 Ground, land, earth.
†tàn, -àin, *s.m.* Time, season. An tàn, *when, at the time.* [tan.‡]
tàn,* -àin, *s.m,* see tàin.
tan,** *a.* Shelvy.
tana, taine, *a.* Thin, not thick. 2 Thin, not close together, not numerous. 3 Thin, as liquid. 4 Thin, slender, slim, lean, attenuated. 5 Shallow, as water. 6**Liquid. T. o là gu là, *thin from day to day*; ni t., *a thin thing*; duine t., *a lean person;* àite t., *a shallow place* (in water), *a shoal*; brochan tana, *gruel*; a' teachd le 'lainn th., *coming with his thin sword.*
tàna, *gen.* of tàn.
tànach, *gen.* of tàn.
tanachadh, -aidh, *s.m.* Thinning, act of making thin, slender or liquid. 2 Rarifying, diluting, dilution. 3 State of becoming thin. A' t—, *pr.pt.* of tanaich.
tanachail,** *a.* Attenuant.
tanachd, *s.f.ind.* Thinness.
tanad, -aid, *s.m.* see tainead.
tanadh, *a.* see tana.
tanaich, *pr.pt.* a' tanachadh, *v.a. & n.* Become thin. 2 Make thin, shallow, slender or lean, rarify, attenuate, grow thin, slender or lean, grow rarified. 3† Get shallow, shoal. 4(DU) Thin out turnips.
tanaichear, *fut.pass.* of tanaich.

tanaichte, *past pt.* of tanaich. Thinned, attenuated, made thin. 2 Diluted, rarified.

†**tanais,**** *s.f.* Parable.

tànaiste, -an, *s.m.* Anything parallel or second to another. 2 Next heir to an estate. 3 Lord, peer, governor. 4 Regent, tainist. 5** The third name of dignity among the ancient Caledonians. 6 The ring-finger. 7**Second son. 8**Thane, prince. 9 **Trustee. 10**Tutor. An t-oighre agus an t., *the heir and next son* or *heir presumptive.*

tànaisteach, -eiche, *a.* Swaying, governing, act of governing as a thane or lord. 2 Surveying. 3 Dynastic.

tànaisteachd, *s.f.ind.* Office of a governor or lord. 2 Dominion. 3 Regency. 4 Dynasty. 5‡‡Parallel, state of being parallel. 6 Thanistry. 7* Trusteeship.

The regulative law of Celtic succession. It embraced certain main features, one of which was that the succession was always continued in the family of the chief within three degrees of relationship to the main line. Brothers succeeded preferably to sons to provide the tribe with a leader in all enterprises, while the succession was always obliged to be carried on with the approval of the clan—*Clan Donald, iii.*

Form of government under which the eldest of the family was entitled to succeed to the sovereignty or lordship on the death of the ruling prince or lord, during whose lifetime the t. was commander-in-chief.—**

tànaistear, -an, *s.m.* see tànaiste.

——————achd, see tànaisteachd.

tànaisteas, -eis, *s.m.* see tànaisteachd.

tanaistre,** *s.pl.* Ancient laws or regulations.

tanalach, -aich, *s. m.* Shallow, shoal, shallow water. 2* Thin part of a hide. Thàinig am bàta o 'n doimhneachd gus an t., *the boat came from deep water to a shoal ;* t. na seiche, *the thin part of the hide.*

——————,** *a.* Short-winded.

tanas, see tannasg.

tànas, -ais, *s.m.* Dominion, lordship.

tanasg, see tannasg.

tanasgach, see tannasgach.

tancard, Gaelic spelling of *tankard.*

†**tangabhair,** *past* of thig, see thàinig.

†**tangadar,** *past* of thig, see thàinig.

†**tangamar,** *past* of thig, see thàinig.

tangaidich(MS) *v.n.* Restrain.

tàngnach,** *a.* Malicious, treacherous.

tàngnachd, *s.f.* Fraud, malice, grudge.

tàngnadh,** *s.m.* Treachery, deceit.

†**taun,** *s.m.* Prince.

t' ann, (for ta ann) Exists, Appears, Is present. 'S e a's àirde a t' ann, *he is the highest that exists.*

tannaidh, (DMK) *s f.* Inside fat of a bullock or sheep—*Suth'd.*

tannalach,** *a.* Bellowing. 2 Extremely painful.

——————, *s.m.* see tanalach.

tannaladh,** -aidh, *s.m.* Bellowing. 2 Agony.

tannas, -ais, *s.m.* see tannasg. Tannais fhuar' a' sgreadail, *grizzly spectres shrieking ;* feuch tannas dorch air creig, *lo, a dark spectre on the rock.*

tannasach, -aiche, *a.* see tannasgash.

tannasg, -aisg, *s.m.* Apparition, spectre, ghost, spectre of a dead person. Is toilinnuinn leam t. g' a langan a chluinntinn, *and delightful to me to hear her clear delicate lowing—Beinn Doran, l. 61.*

——————ach, -aiche, *a.* Abounding in spectres or ghosts. 2 Like a ghost, ghostly.

taobh, -aoibh, -an, *s.m.* Side, flank. 2 Course, way, direction. 3 Liking, kindness, friendship. 4 Partiality, favour, injustice. 5 Patronage, support, countenance, aid. 6 Cause, account. 7 Place, quarter. 8 Side-board of a cart. An t. a muigh, *the outside, exterior;* an t. a staigh, *the inside, interior;* an t. cùil, *or* an t. air chùil, *the hinder part ;* an t. beòil, *the front side ;* dé 'n t. a chaidh e ? *in what direction has he gone ? ;* cò 'n t. ? *which side ?* ri m' thaobh, *beside me ;* a thaobh, *aside, astray ; 2 by reason of ;* cha'n 'eil fhios agam 'dé is t. dha, *I do not know what has become of him, in which direction he went ;* thug e a thaobh i, *he seduced her ;* a thaobh sin, *about that, because of that, on that account ;* a th. sin dheth, *on that very account ;* do m' th.-sa, *as for me, for my part ;* cuir gu t., cuir a th., *put aside ;* t. ri t., *side by side ;* t. na mara, *the sea-side ;* t. tìr, *ashore, the water's edge ;* as an t. thall, *from the other side ;* th. 'ur cùil is 'ur beòil, *behind and before you—Mort na Ceapach ;* cum t. ris, *favour or countenance him.*

taobh, *pr. pt.* a' taobhadh, *v.n.* Side with anyone, favour, be partial. 2 Come nigh to, approach. Cha do th. e 'm baile, *he did not come near the town ;* cha th. e sinne, *he will not come near us ;* na t. mise, *do not come near me, keep at arm's length.*

taobhach, -aiche, *a.* Lateral, having sides. 2 Partial, favouring one party. 3 Inclined to be partial. 4 Friendly, kind.

——————d, *s.f.ind.* Partiality, injustice. 2** Faction. 3**Presumption.

——————adh, -aidh, *s.m.* Act of drawing another's kindness to oneself. 2 Leaning to a side or party, partiality. 3 Countenancing. A' t—, *pr. pt.* of taobhaich.

taobhadh, -aidh, *s.m.* Siding, act of siding with anyone. 2 Act of approaching. 3 Commission. 4**Trusting, relying. A' t—, *pr.pt.* of taobh.

taobhag, -aig, -an, *s.f.* Patch, clout.

taobhaich, *pr.pt.* a' taobhachadh, *v.a. & n.* Draw or secure another's kindness. 2 see taobh.

——————e, -an, *s.m. & f.* Partisan.

——————te, *past pt.* of taobhaich.

taobhaidheachd,(MS) *s.f.* Adjacency.

taobhail,‡‡ -e, *a.* Lateral.

taobhair,** *s.m.* Partisan. 2 Apostate.

taobhaisd, -ean, *s.* Hole in the side of a creel.

taobhalachd,‡‡ *s.f.ind.* Laterality.

taobh a mach, *s.m.* The outside.

taobh a muigh,** *s.m.* The outside. 2 Without. 3 Outward.

taobhan, -ain, -an, *s.m.* Rafter. 2 Rib or small beam, laid on the rafters in buildings. 3** Patch on the side of a shoe. 4 Stringer of a boat, see bàta, F5, p. 73. 5 ‡(MM) Purlin in *joinery.*

——————ach, -aiche, *a.* Having beams or rafters. 2 Like a beam or rafter.

——————aichte,** *a.* Raftered.

taobh-an-fhasgaidh, Lee-side.

taobh an fhuaraidh, Windward-side, weather-side (of a boat, &c.)

taobh a steach,** *s.m.* The inner-side.

taobh a staigh,** *s.m.* The inner side. 2 Within. 3 Inward.

taobh-bhreith, -ean, *s.m.* Partiality. 2 Partial or unjust decision. [Given by ** as a contraction of taobh-bhreitheamh.]

————————each, -eiche, *a.* Partial. 2 Unjust in deciding.

————————eamh, -eimh, *s.m.* Unjust judge. [** gives taobh-bhreith.]

taobh-cheum, -chéim, -an, *s.m.* Digression. 2‡‡ Side-step.

taobh-cheumach, -aiche, *a.* Apt to digress, digressing.
————nach,** *a.* see taobh-cheumach.
taobh-duilleig, -an, *s.m.* Page of a book.
taobh-ghabhail,** *s.f.* Secret fondness, hankering attachment, partiality.
taobh-gheal,** *a.* White-sided.
taobh-ghlas,** *a.* Grey-sided. O charraig thaoibh-ghlais, *from a grey-sided rock.*
taobh-ghorm,** *a.* Green-sided. 2 Blue-sided. Coire t., *a green-sided dell.*
taobh-ghreim, -e, *pl.* -ean & -eannan, *s.m.* Stitch in the side. 2 Pleuritic affection.
————each, *a.* Pleuritic.
taobh-leis, *s.m.* Lee-side.
taobh-leisg,(DC) *s.m.* (*lit.* a lazy side) Applied to the side of a boat when it bulges more than the opposite side.
taobh ri taobh, *a.* Accosted in *heraldry.*
taobh-shlat, *s.* Gunwale, see bàta, E7, p. 73. 2 Inside wale under the gunwale—*Argyll.*
taobh-shlatan, *s m.* Stringers, on which ends of rowers' benches rest in a boat.
taobh-shlighe, -an & -achan, *s.f.* By-way, footpath leading parallel to a highway.
————ach, -eiche, *a.* Having by-ways. 2 Fond of going in by-ways.
taobh-shruth,* *s.m.* Eddy-tide. 2 Back-water.
————ach, -aiche, *a.* Abounding in eddying tides.
taobh-thoir, -ean, *s. m.* Creditor. 2**Commissary.
taobh-throm, -uime, *a.* Pregnant.
————achd, *s.f.ind.* Pregnancy.
taobh-thruime, *s.f.ind.* Pregnancy.
taobh-tìre, -an-tìre, *s.m.* District. 2 The shore. 3 Edge of the shore.
taod, -aoid, *s.m.* Halter, head-rope. 2 Hair-rope. 3 Chain, binding. 4 Cable. 5 (CR) Rope for leading or tying. 6* Reins. Ar crainn 's ar taodan, *our masts and our cables ;* bò air t., *a cow being lead.*
taodach, -aiche, *a.* Of, or belonging to, halters, ropes or cables, haltered. 2 Furnished with ropes, &c. 3**Stubborn.
taodachan,** -ain, *s.m.* Stubborn creature.
taodan, -ain, -an, *s.m., dim.* of taod. Little halter, rope or cable.
———ach, *a.* Having, or pertaining to, little halters, ropes or cables.
taod-aoire, -an, *s.m.* Sheet (rope.)
taod-frithir,(AH) *s.m.* Halyard.
taodh,** *s.m.* Woollen yarn.
———al, see tadhal.
taodhair, -ean, *s.m.* Apostate.
————each, -eiche, *a.* Apostatical, that has apostatized.
————eachd, *s.f.ind.* Apostacy.
taog, -oig, see taoig.
taoghail, see tadhail.
taoghal, see tadhal.
————ach, see tadhalach.
taoghall, see tadhal.
taoghan, see taghan.
————ach, see taghanach.
taoghanta,** *a.* Shy.
taoghar,(MS) *s.m.* Occursion.
taoghas, -ais, -an, *s.m.* Grave.
taoghlaim, (for taodhlaidh mi,) I shall frequent.
†taoi, *a.* Ready. 2 Silent. 3 Mild.
†taoi, *s.f.* Birth. 2 Trope. 3 Turning.
taoibheumach, *a.* see toibheumach.
taoibhleach,†† -ich, *s.f.* Rough shove to a side.
taoig, -e, -ean, *s.f.* Fit of passion, frenzy.
———each, -eiche, *a.* Passionate. 2 Impassioned, angry, enraged, frantic.
†taoighin, *s.f.* Mill-pond.

taoim, -e, *s.f.* Bilge-water in a ship or boat. 2 **Dash of water.
taoimeach, -eiche, *a.* Having bilge-water. 2 Leaky, as a ship or boat.
taoinneadh,** -idh, *s.m.* Crispation.
taois, -e & taosa, *s.f.* Dough, leaven. T. ghoirt, *leaven.*
taois-cailc,* *s.f.* Putty.
taoiseach, -eiche, *a.* Of, or belonging to, dough, leaven or paste. 2 Abounding in dough. 3 Like dough, doughy. 4 Raw, ill-baked.
†taoiseach, -eich, *s.m.* Hero, chieftain, general, leader, commander, see toiseach. Bu lìonmhor t. 'na luighe, *many a hero was laid low.*
taoiseadair, -ean, *s.m.* Baker.
————eachd, *s.f.* Baking, bakery, business of a baker.
taoiseil,** *a.* Doughy.
taoisg,* *v.n.* see taosg.
taois-ghlaodh, -aidh, *s.f.* Paste.
taoisinn, *pr.pt.* a' taoisneadh, a' taoisnich & a' taoisneachadh, *v.a.* Knead, 2 Leaven. T. trì miosairean, *knead three measures.*
taoismhor,** *a.* Doughy.
taoisneach,** *a.* Like leaven or dough. 2 Of leaven.
taoisneachadh, -aidh, *s. m.* Kneading, act of kneading. 2 Leavening. A' t—, *pr. pt.* of taoisnich.
taoisneadh, -idh, Same meanings as taoisneachadh.
taoisnich, *pr.pt.* a' taoisneachadh, *v.a.* Knead. 2 Leaven. see taoisinn.
———te, *past pt.* of taoisnich. Kneaded. Leavened.
taoisnidh, *fut.aff.a.* of taoisinn.
taoitear, -ir, -ean, *s.m.* Tutor, oversman, curator. 3 Trustee—*Suth'd.*
————achd, *s.f.ind.* Office of tutor, or curator, tutorage. 2 Tuition.
taois-tàthaidh, *s.f.* Putty.
taoitirich, *v.a.* Tutor.
taolamach,** -aich, *s.m.* Parricide.
taom, -a, *pl.* -an & -annan, *s.m.* Plash of water or any fluid. 2 Jet,torrent. 3 Overflow. 4 Sudden illness. 5 Fit of anger or passion, frenzy. 6**Water that leaks through a vessel. Thàinig uisge 'na thaomaibh, *rain came in torrents.*
taom, *s.m.* Luff of a sail.
taom, *v.a. & n.* Pour out, bale, as water from a vessel. 2 Empty. 3 Overflow. 4 Shed. 5 Throw water out of any vessel. T. am bàta, *bale the boat ;* t. air e, *pour it on it ;* t. a' chairt, *empty the cart* (by tipping it) ; tràth thaom na filidhean an ceòl, *when the bards poured forth their strains.*
taomach, -aiche, *a.* That empties or pours out, emptying. 2 Overflowing, apt to overflow. 3 By fits and starts. 4 Subject to fits.
————adh, -aidh, *s.m. & pr. pt.* of taomaich. Same meanings as taomadh.
taomadh, -aidh, *s.m.* Pouring, act of pouring. 2 Emptying, act of emptying. 3 Overflowing, act or state of overflowing, flood. 4 Effusion. 5 Fit of sickness. A' t—, *pr.pt.* of taom. 6 (DMy) Turning the borders of ridges on the top, the practice of making "lazy-beds,"—*Lewis.* Fo th. dheòir, *under a fit of tears.*
taomaich, *v.a.* see taom, *v.*
taomaichte, *past pt.* of taomaich, see taomta.
taomair, -ean, *s. m.* Pump. 2 One who works with a pump.
————eachd, *s.f.ind.* Pumping.
taoman, -ain, -an, *s. m.* Vessel by which bilgewater is thrown out of a boat, baler. 2 Vessel to lave with. 3 Purlin, in *joinery.* Gabh

an ladar no 'n t., *take the ladle or baler.*
taom-boile, -ean, *s.m.* Fit of madness or frenzy, raging passion.
————ach, -eiche, *a.* Frantic, furious, raging with anger or passion. 2 Uncertain. Is t. an t-iasg, is teugmhaileach an t-sealg, *fishing is uncertain and hunting risky* (*as means of livelihood compared with agriculture.*)
taom-fheachd, Full muster band. 2 (MMcL) Down-pouring host, on-settling host. Tagaibh leibh gun airc, gun eusbhuidh, taom-fheachd seasmhach cunnbhalach, *raise a full-muster band, lacking nothing, without stint, trusty, competently arranged—Filidh, p. 63.*
taomta, *past pt.* Poured out, overflowed, emptied. [taomte.]
taosa, *gen.* of taois.
taosainn, *v.a.* see taoisinn.
taosdadh,(WC) -aidh, *s.m.* Cuddling or squeezing a girl. Dé an t. a th' ort ? *why do you cuddle so ?*
taosg, -a, -an, *s.m.* Precise full of a liquid measure. 2 Pour, jet, rush of any fluid. 3 Fit. 4††Good quantity of water in a vessel. 5* Near the full of a dish,cask, pitcher, cart, &c.
taosg, *pr.pt.* a' taosgadh, *v.a.* Pour out. 2 Pump. 3 Drain, empty. 4 Circumfuse, effuse.
taosgach, -aiche, *a.* Full to the brim. 2 Pouring, rushing. 3 Irregular, in fits, fickle, uncertain. 4 Apt to overflow. 5 Overflowing. Duine t., *a fickle man ;* ni t., *a precarious thing.*
taosgadh, -aidh, *s. m.* Pouring, act of pouring. 2 Pumping, act of pumping. 3 Draining, act of draining. 4 Overflowing, overflow. A' t—, *pr.pt.* of taosg. A' t. a duibh-neòil air na gleanntan, *pouring her dark clouds on the valleys.*
taosgaiche,** *s.m.* One who works at a pump.
taosgaid,* -e, -ean, *s.f.* Fickle female.
taosgair, -ean, *s.m.* One that pumps. 2 One who acts unsteadily or by fits and starts, fickle person.
————eachd, *s.f.ind.* Pumping, labouring at a pump. 2 Draining. 3 Unsteadiness. 4 Profusion. 5 Folly.
taosgan, -ain, *s.m.* Pump.
taosgta, *past pt.* of taosg. Poured out, emptied. 2 Pumped. 3 Drained. [taosgte.]
taosnadh, see taoisneachadh.
taosnadh, *s.m.* Horse-play, playing rantipole—*Rob Donn.*
taothal, -ail, -an, see tadhal.
tap, -aip & -a, *pl.* -an & -achan, *s. m.* Tuft of wool or flax wreathed on a distaff. 2 Forelock, forelocks.
tap, *pr. pt.* a' tapadh, *v.a.* Hood or thread a fishing hook—*Islay.* [stalcadh elsewhere.]
tapach, -aiche, *a.* Bushy, having thick forelocks.
tapachd, *s.f.* Quickness, activity, alacrity, cleverness. 2 Manliness, boldness, heroism.
tapadh, -aidh, *s.m.* Clever feat or action. 2 Activity, alertness, cleverness. 3‡‡Good luck, lucky event, success. 3 Activity, manliness, manhood. 4(DC) The process of thrashing with the froisean. 5* Heroic feat, achievement. 6* Thanks. Cuimhnicheadh gach aon a th., *let each remember his manhood ;* leabhar dearg Iain, 'gan tiopadh 's gan tapadh, *Mitchell's "Red Book" snapping and checking them (the witches)—Duanaire, p. 41 ;* t. leat, *thank you.*
tapag, -aig, -an, *s.f.* Accident, casualty. 2 Blunder in speech, slip of the tongue. 3 Fall. 4 (DC) Exclamation.
tapagach, -aiche, *a.* Accidental, casual. 2 Blundering in speech. 3 Apt to blunder in speech.
tapagail,* *s.f.* Blunder.
tapaidh, -e, *a.* Clever, quick, active. 2 Manly, bold, heroic, brave. 3 Successful in business. Bi t., *be brave ;* 2 *be smart, be quick ;* clann t. feardha, *a manly, active clan.*
————eachd, see tapachd.
tapais,** Gaelic form of French *tapis*, carpet.
tapan,* -ain, *s.m.* Little lock of wool or flax on a distaff. 2 Tuft of flax added to a larger quantity to make up a deficiency in weight.
tapanach,†† *a.* Like tow or flax on a distaff.
tapanta, -ainte, *a.* Quick, see tapaidh. Gu t., *quickly.*
————chd, *s.f.* see tapachd.
————s, -ais, *s.m.* see tapachd.
tapar,** -air, *s.m.* Gaelic form of *taper.*
tapas, -ais, -an, *s.m.* Hit.
tap-bheist, see tar-bheisd.
taplach, -aich, -aichean, *s.m.* Wallet, repository for small things.
taplaich,** *s. f.* Wallet, repository for small things.
taponta, see tapanta.
tar,* *s.m.* see tàrr.
tàr, *pr.pt.* a' tàrsainn, *v.a.* Evoke. 2**Go. 3** Send. 4**Come. 5**Descend. 6**Befall. 7 **Prepare. 8 Get time. 9 (DU) Be able. T. as, *evade ;* 2 *"bolt" ;* th. e mach, *he escaped out, he went out ;* gus an t. dhomh bàs is uaigh, *till death and the grave be my lot ;* chà do th. mi, *I was not able ;* an t. thu ? *will you be able ?*
tar, *prep.* see thar.
tàr, *pr.pt.* a' tàradh, *v.* see tàir.
tàr, -àire, *a.* see tàir, *a.*
tar,** *a.* Active, quick, clever.
tarabal, (a' t—,) *pr.pt.* Undulating.
taracadair,* -ean, *s.m.* Necromancer.
————eachd, *s.f,* Necromancy. Dé an t. a th' ort à *what necromancy are you practising ?*
taracantachd,**s.f. ind.* Necromancy. Bha sin air a chur 'san t. dha, (bu dàn dha sin), *that was put in his lot—WC.*
tarachair,‡ *v.n.* Gimlet, auger. 2 Seer. [for torachair.]
tarachd,** *s.f.* Activity.
tàrachd,** *s.f.* Going. 2 Coming.
tara-dalag,(MMcD) *s.m.* see tarbh-dallaig.
taradh, *s.m.* Noise at night (premonitory.)
tarag,* -aig, -an, *s.f.* Stud.
taragachd,(MS) *s.f.* Bodement.
taragaich, *v.a.* Presage.
taragair,** *v.* Bode.
taragaraich,(MS) *v.n.* Vaticinate. 2 Reason.
taragarachd, see taragachd.
taraghail,** *s.* see targradh.
taragrach, -aiche, *a.* Portentous.
taragradh,** *s.m.* Bodement, portentation.
taraid, *s.f.* Truncheon, staff of authority—*Dàin I. Ghobha.*
tàraidh, *fut.aff.a.* of tàr.
tarail,** *s.f.* Visit.
taran,‡‡ -ain, *pl.* -an & -ain, *s.m.* Ghost of an unbaptized child.
taranach,** *a.* Spectral.
tarang, *pl.* -aingean, see tarrang.
tarar, see tora.
tarbh, -airbh, *s.m.* Bull. 2 The sign Taurus (♉) in the zodiac. An tarbh, *a surfeit ;* móran tharbh, *many bulls ;* craicionn tairbh, *a bull's hide.*
tarbhach, *a.* Infinitive in *grammar.*
tarbhach, -aiche, *a.* Abounding in bulls. 2 Like a bull.
————, -aiche, *a.* Profitable, beneficial, gainful. 2 Substantial. 3 Important, of consequence. 4**Effectual. 5 Fertile, productive.

Bàrr t., *a substantial crop*; bualadh (*or* buille) t., *an effectual (decisive) blow*, or *pull in rowing*; cainnt th., *pithy language*; t. do dhuine, *profitable to man.*
tarbhachadh, -aidh, *s.m.* State of increasing in wealth or substance. 2 Act of gaining or of profiting. A' t—, *pr.pt.* of tarbhaich.
tar bhachas, -ais, *s.m.* see tarbhachd.
tarbhachd, *s.f.ind.* Gain, profit, advantage. 2 Substantiality. 3 Importance, consequence. 4 Fertility, productiveness, fruitfulness. 5 Availableness.
tarbhaich, *pr.pt.* a' tarbhachadh, *v.a. & n.* Increase in wealth or substance. 2 Gain, profit, grow gainful, grow fruitful. 3** Reap gain, profit, or advantage.
tarbhaichead, -eid, *s.m.* Degree of profitableness. 2 Degree of importance or substantiality. 3 Degree of fertility or fruitfulness. A' dol an t., *growing more and more fruitful.*
†tarbhaidh,** *s.f.* Hinderance, impediment. 2 Misfortune.
tarbhail, -e, *a.* Bull-like, brutish. 2 Bull-faced.
tarbh-alluidh,* *s.m.* Buffalo.
tarbhan, -ain, -an, *s.m.*, *dim.* of tarbh. Little bull. 2 Young bull.
tarbhanach,†† *a.* Abounding in little bulls. 2 Like a little bull.
tarbhanta, -ainte, *a.* Grim, stern, bull-faced. 2 Boorish. 3 Like a bull, fierce.
———chd,‡‡ *s.f.ind.* Grimness, sternness, bull-facedness.
tarbh-aoidhre, (DMK) *Northern counties* for tarbh-boidhre.
tarbharnach, *a.* Noisy, garrulous—*Sàr-Obair.*
tarbhas,** -ais, *s.m.* Surfeit.
tarbh-boidhre,(AC) *s. m.* Monster, demon. 2 God capable of changing himself into many form,—a man, a horse, a bull, &c., with supernatural powers.
tarbh-chù,* *s.m.* Bull-dog.
tarbh-coille, *s.m.* Dark cloud which when seen on New Year's Day portends a stormy season. 2 (AF) Fabulous monster.
tarbh-dallaig, *s.m.* Blue shark. It is the shape of a dog-fish, but of great size. I saw one of them in my own boat and its liver filled a barrel. Its head was hanging over the gunwale on one side and its tail over the gunwale on the other side, the total length being about 14 feet. When we took out its liver it never moved—(DMy.) The oil taken from the liver of this fish is greatly prized for medicinal purposes in the Western Isles.
tar-bheir,** *v.a.* Transfer, carry over.
tarbh-mhadadh, -aidh, -aidhean, *s.m.* Bull-dog.
tarbh-nathrach, *pl.* -airbh-nathraichean, *s. m.* Dragon-fly—*libella—Arran.* 2 (AF) Moth.
tarbh-réidh,* *s.m.* Farm-bull.
tarbh-ruagadh, -aidh, *s.m.* Bull-baiting.
tarbh-shiolag,((AF) *s.m.* Weever or viper fish.
tarbh-tàna, -airbh-thàna, *s.m.* Parish-, district-, or herd-bull, bull which is the property of a district. [*tarbh-taine.]
tàrbh-truid, *s.m.* Furious bull. [truid is the *gen. of* trod (fight), in modern Gael.scolding.]
tar-bhuileachadh,** -aidh, *s.m.* Consignment, conveyance, conveyancing.
tar-bhuilichte,** *past pt.* Consigned.
tarbh-uisge, -airbh-uisge, *s.m.* Water-bull, sea-bull or -cow, (fabulous.)
†tarcheau, *adv.* (i.e. thar cheann) Moreover, then, also, notwithstanding, although.
†tar-chonair,** *s.f.* Ferry.
tarcuis, -e, -ean, *s.f.* Contempt, despite, reproach, scorn. 2 Dispute. Dean t., *reproach, despise*; luchd t., *spiteful people.*
———each, -eiche. *a.* Contemptuous, despiteful. 2 Contemptible, contumelious, despicable, reproachful, scornful. 3(MS) Deplorable. 4(MS) Poor. Gu t., *reproachfully.*
———eachadh, -aidh, *s.m.* Despising, act of despising, reviling, showing contempt. A' t—, *pr.pt.* of tarcuisich.
———eachd, *s.f.* Despite, reproach. 2 Aptness to scold, contumeliousness.
tarcuisich, *pr.pt.* a' tarcuiseachadh, *v.a.* Despise, revile, contemn, scorn, affront.
————te, *past pt.* of tarcuisich. Despised, contemned, reviled.
tarcuisneach, see tarcuiseach.
tar-dearg, *s.m.* see tàrr 4.
tar éis, *prep.* After.
tar-fhradharc,‡‡ -airc,-an,*s.m.* Squint, squinting look, leer, ogle.
————ach, -aiche, *a.* Squinting, having a squint. 2 Goggle-eyed. 3 Looking askance, leering, ogling.
targach, *s.m.* Char (fish.)
targadh, -aidh, *s.m.* Governing, ruling. 2 Government, rule. 3 Assembly.
targaid, -e, -ean, *s.f.* Target, shield. 2 Rooker. 3 Skate (fish)—*Lewis.* The target of the Gael was orbed and made of light wood with a single covering of tough leather, or if thin, of several folds, studded with brass, iron or silver, according to the means of the owner.
———each, -eiche, *a.* Shielded, armed with a shield. 2 Like, or of a shield.
targair, *pr.pt.* a' targradh, *v.a.* Foretell, prophesy, divine.
targairich,(MS) *v.a.* Foreshow.
targanach, *s.m.* Prognostication, prophesying—*Sàr-Obair.*
targhail,** *v.* Forebode.
targhan,** -ain, *s.m.* Noise.
targrach,** *a.* Foretelling, prophetic.
targradh, -aidh, *s.m.* Foretelling, act of foretelling, prophecy, divination, predicting, prediction. A' t—, *pr.pt.* of targair.
targraich, see targair.
targraiche, -an, *s.m.* Foreboder.
targraidh, *fut.aff.a.* of targair.
tàrladh, *3rd. pers. sing. & pl. imp.* of *def. v.* tàrladh & tarlaidh. Happen, befall, meet. 2 *past subj.* of tàrlaidh. T. e, i, iad, *let him (it), her (it), them happen*; 'nuair a th. sibh euideachd, *when you met together.*
tarladh,* -aidh, *s.m.* Great demand or tearing from each other, as a scarce commodity. 2** Draught. 3**Leading in of corn or hay.
tàrlaid, -e (*f.*), -ean, *s.m. & f.* Slave, thrall. 2 Contemptible person. 3 Hackney. 4 Hulk of a ship. 5**Female drudge or slave.
tàrlaideach, -eiche, *a.* Slavish, drudging, drudgelike.
——————,(AF) -eich, *s.m.* Working horse.
——————d, *s.f.ind.* Drudgery.
tàrlaidh, *fut.* of *def. v.* tàrladh and tàrlaidh. Will happen, befall or meet.
tarlaidh,* *v.a.* Tear or drag away.
tarlaid-luinge, *s.f.* Hulk.
tàrlas, *fut.* of *def.v.* tàrladh, see tàrlaidh.
tarm,(AF) see torm.
tarmach,(AF) see tarmachan-dé.
tàrmach,* -aich, *s.m.* Source of disease. 2 see tàrmachan.
tàrmachadh, -aidh, *s.m.* Source, origin. 2 Act of originating or beginning. 3 Gathering, act of gathering or collecting, as a tumour. 4 Dwelling, circumstance of dwelling. 5 Producing, act of producing. 6 Extract. 7* Congregating. 8* Settling. A' t—, *pr. pt.* of tàrmaich.

tàrmachag,(DC) *s.f.* see tàrmachan.
tàrmachail, -e, *a.* Originary, constitutive.
tàrmachair, -ean, *s.m.* Propagator, incubator, breeder.

659. Tàrmachan.

tàrmachan, -ain, -an, *s. m.* Ptarmigan (bird)—*lagopus vulgaris.*T. breac na beinne, *the spotted ptarmigan of the mountain.* This is a rare species of moorfowl, seen on the tops of the highest Highland hills. The size of the ptarmigan is nearly that of the grouse, and its colour light grey, but in winter it is perfectly white. It is a very shy and timid bird ; but when the sportsman comes upon it by surprise, it is daunted even to stupidity, and has not always the courage even to fly from danger.—**
——— -beinne,(AF) *s.m.* Mountain ptarmigan.
——— -dé,(AC) *s.m.* The white butterfly. 2 *rarely,* The black and white butterfly, see dearbadan-dé.
——— -tràghad,(AF) *s.m.* Dunlin, shore-ptarmigan.
tàrmach-dé, see tàrmachan-dé.
tarmadh,** -aidh, *s.m.* Dwelling.
tarmagan, see tàrmachan.
tàrmaich, *v.a. & n.* Originate, be the source of. 2 Derive. 3 Gather, collect. 4 Settle. 5 Reside, dwell, lodge. 6 Produce, beget. 7 Begin—*Duanaire:* Ceann anns an do th. gliocas, *a head where wisdom dwelt* ; ann am àirnibh th. mo neasgaid, *in my reins my ulcer resides.*
———te, *past pt.* of tàrmaich. Gathered, collected. 2 Produced, begotten. 3‡‡Fermented.
tarman, see torman.
tàrmanach,¶ *s.m.* see tàrmachan.
tarman-dé, *W. of Ross* for dearbadan-dé.
tarmas,(MS) -ais, *s.m.* Affront.
———aich,(MS) *v.a.* Villainize.
tarmun,** -uin, *s.m.* Sanctuary, asylum. (tèarmunn.)
tarmunach,** *a.* Affording sanctuary or asylum. (tèarmunnach.)
tàrmus, -uis, *s. m.* Dislike of food, loathing of meat. (*tarmas.)
———ach, -aiche, *a.* Disliked or loathed, as one's food.
tarnach,* *s.f.*Thunder-clap. 2‡‡Any loud sound. 3‡‡Blow.
tàrnadair, -ean,* *s.m.* Inn-keeper, (*lit.* one who draws.)
———eachd, *s.f.ind.* Office of an inn-keeper.
tarnaid,** *s.f.* Tavern.
tàrnaidh, *fut.aff.a.* of tarruing.
tarnochd,** *s.f.* Nakedness. 2 The secret parts.
———,** *a.* Naked.
tarp, -a, -an, *s.m.* Clod, lump of earth or clay.
———ach, -aiche,*a.* Full of clumps or clods, cloddy. 2**Bulky. 3**Weighty.
tarpachd,** *s.f.ind.* Bulkiness.
tarpan,* -ain, *s.m.* Cluster. 2 Crab, see partan. 3 *dim.* of tarp. Little clod.
tarpanach,** *a.* Cloddy.
tàrr, -a, -an, *s.m.* Lower part of the belly. 2 Tail. 3 Breast. 4**Extremity. 5 (AF) Char (fish.) 6(DC) Ability, capability. Cùl cinn (druim—WC) an sgadain is tàrr a' bhradain, *the back of a herring's head and a salmon's breast*—the best parts ; breac tàrr-gheal, *a white-bellied trout.*
tàrr, for tarruing—*Dàin I. Ghobha.* 2 for tàr or tàir. Cha tàrr (tàir) mi an seinn—*Duanaire, p. 102.*
tàrr as, *v.* Betake.
tàrr,(MS) *v.a.* Befall.
tàrrach, -aich, *s.f.* Girth of a pack-saddle. 2 Belly-thong. 3**Crupper.
tarrach,** *a.* Fearful, timid. 2 Horrible.
tarrach,(AF) *s.m.* Kittiwake.
tarrachan,** -ain, -an, *s.m.* Glutton.
tarradh, -aidh, *s.* see tarragh.
tàrradh, Gach fear ag obair mar a thàrradh, *everyone doing his best—Duanaire p, 131.*
tarradh,(CR) *s.m.* see tarragh.
tar-radharc, see tar-fhradharc.
———ach, see tar-fhradharcach.
tarrag,** *s.f.* see tarrang.
tarrag(*for* tarrang)-a'-chroinn-sparraidh, see under crann-nan-gad.
tarrag (*for* tarrang)-maide-a'-chroinn-sparraidh, see under crann-nan-gad.
tarragach, see tairgneach.
tarragan, -ain, *s.m.* Char (fish.)
tarragh,** -aigh, *s.m.*see tarradh. Conveying of corn to the barn or yard. 2 Drawing, leading. 3 Frequent going to and from a place. Fèisd an tarraigh, *feast of the in-gathering.*
tarragh,** *v.a.* Convey corn from the field to the yard.
tarraghail,** *s.* Auspice.
tarra-gheal, -ghile, *a.* see tarr-gheal.
tarragheal, *s.m.* Alpine char—*salmo alpinus.*
tarraid, see earraid.
tarraigheal, see tàrr-gheal.
tarrail, *s.* Subsidy.
tarraire,(MS) *s.m.* Pavilion.
tarraisgein, *s.f.* see toirsgian.
tarranach, -aiche, *a.* Loud.
tarraig, *gen.sing.* of tarrag (for tarrang.)
tarran,(DC) *s.m.* Frame of network to hold grain over a slow fire for drying. 2(DMy) The straw which was below the grain on the kiln, and of no use. When it was put on the kiln it was called *streaghaig* and after the " tioradh " is finished it is *tarran.*
tarrang, -aing, & -airnge *pl.* -àirnge -àirnnean, -airngean & **tarraingean,*s.f.* Nail, boss,stud. T. 'na lethcheann, *a nail in his temple ;* t.-chuidhle, *or* t.-aisil, *lynch-pin of a cart.* [also tàirng.]
tarrannach, see tairngeach.
tarrangaich, *v.a.* Nail, peg.
tarrang-aisil, *s.f.* Lynch-pin of a cart.
tarrang-art, -airt, *s.f.* Loadstone. 2 Magnet. 3 Compass-needle.
tarrann, see tarrang.
tàrr-fhionn, -a, *a.* Having white buttocks. 2 White-bellied. 3 White-tailed.
tàrr-gheal, -ghile, *a.* White-bellied. 2 White-tailed.
———,* *s.f.* White-bellied cow.
tarroch, see tarrach.
tarruigeadh, *a.* Abluent.
tarr-pheang, -aing, -an, *s.m.* Mortice in *joinery.*
tarrsanan, see tarsanan.
tarrsuinn, see tarsuinn.
———eachd, see tarsuinneachd.
tarruing, *pr.pt.* a' tarruing, *v.a. & n.*Draw,pull. 2 Draw, attract, allure, lead. 3 Take the li-

quor from a cask. 4 Haul, pull along. 5 Draw near, approach, advance. 6 Extract, distil, as strong drink. 7 Aim. 8**Teaze.

Bi t. ! *off with you, away !—Perthshire* ; an t. thu mach lebhiathan le dubhan ? *can't thou draw leviathan with a hook ?* th. e 'n t-iongar, *it extracted the matter from the tumour* ; th. mi air, *I assaulted him;* le d' chlarsaich dlùth, *draw near with thy harp* ; tha 'n laoch a' tarruing a bhuille, *the hero aims his blow* ; tairngidh mi e, *I will draw it.*

t. air t' ais, draw back.

t. a mach, protract, lengthen.

t. am fagus, draw near.

t. as a chéile, pull asunder.

t. claidheamh, draw a sword.

t. dealbh, draw a picture.

t. fodar, draw straw for thatching. The ends of threshed straw are drawn asunder and placed in one hand, and the process is repeated until all the broken straw is dropped and what remains is long, smooth and even. Drawn straw in some districts was used only for placing under the corn on the kiln when the grain was hardened at home, and in consequence, some of the terms for it are defined as though they applied only when it was used for this purpose. Other materials, as rushes, a species of grass, &c., were used for thatch—CR.

t. fuil, draw blood, let blood.

t. gu crìch, draw to a conclusion.

t. suas, draw up.

t. suas ris, address, speak to him, cultivate his acquaintance.

t. t' anail, draw your breath.

tarruing, -e & tàirgne *pl.* -ean & tairgnean, *s.f.* Drawing, act of drawing or pulling, act of dragging or hauling along. 2**Draught, pull, drag. 3 Act of attracting. 4 Alluring or enticing. 5 Distilling, act of distilling. 6 Act of drawing liquor from a cask. 7 Act of drawing, painting or delineating. 8 Taking a photograph. 9 Drawing near. 10 Any weight or bulk that is drawn. 11 Extracting plaster. 12 *Demand. 13 Halyard. 14(MMcN) Peak-halyard-sheets, No. 2, p. 75. 15 Carriage-trace. —*W. of Ross.* 16‡‡Season of time, while, turn. 17 (DU) Low, distant thunder (*pl.* tarruingean. [††*pl.* tàirngean.]

Cuir t. air, *put an extracting plaster on it* ; a dh' aon t., *at once, at one time* ; t. chailleach, *drawing in a slovenly manner* (t. chailleach is to take load No. 1 say, a quarter-of-a-mile, turn back for load No. 2 and drop it with No. 1 ; then take up the latter and advance with it another quarter-of-a-mile ; then go back for No. 2, and so on till both are at destination; thus a person may fetch two loads simultaneously, (although there is no saving in time or labour, with the additional disadvantage of one load being left unguarded by the roadside most of the time) ; air a' cheud t., *at the first time, at once* ; t. éisg, *a draught of fishes* ; t. dùbailt, *double-distilled liquor* ; 's e seo mo th.-sa, *this is my turn.* A' t—, *pr.pt.* of tarruing.

tarruing-air-éiginn, s. *f.* Heath-rush—*Colonsay.*

tarruing-an-uisge-bheatha,(DMK) *s.f.* Distilling of low wines, the product being whisky—*W. of Ross.*

tarruing-art, see tarrang-art.

tarruing as, *v.a.* Chaff. Bha e 'tarruing asda, *he was chaffing them.*

tarruing-dhealain, *s.* Electro-magnetism.

tarruingeach, -eiche, *a.* Drawing, that draws. 2 Alluring, attractive.

tarruingeachd, *s.f.* Tractability.

tarruingeach-dealain, *a.* Electro-magnetic.

tarruingeadair, -ean, *s.m.* Artist.

tarruing-gun-taing, *s.f.* Heath-rush—*Colonsay.*

tarruing mhòr,(MMcN) Main halyard, see bàta, H4, p. 73.

tarruingte, *past pt.* of tarruing. Drawn. 2 Pulled. 3 Enticed. 4 Extracted. 5 Distilled.

tarruing-uisge,(AH) s. Draw water (on an oar.) 2 (DU) Draught of a boat or ship. 3(DU).Act of micturition.

tarrunaich, see tarrangaich.

tarruun, see tarrang.

tarsainn,†† -e, *a.* see tarsuinn.

tarsananachd, see tarsuinneachd, [& G2, p. 73.

tarsann, s. Breast-hook of a boat, see bàta, E5

tarsannain, *s.pl.* Cross-bars of a plough.

tarsannan, -ain, -an, *s.m.* Any beam extending across, cross-beam. 2 Transom of a boat. 3 Cross-bar. 4**Diameter. 5 Spoke of a wheel. 6 (MMcL) Rung of a ladder.

tar-sgrìobh,** *v.* Post.

tarsnain, *gen.sing. & n.pl.* of tarsnan.

tar-shoilleir,** *a.* Transparent.

tar-shoillseach, ** *a.* Transparent.

tar-shoillsean,** *s.m.* Transparency.

tar-sholus,** -uis, *s.m.* Transparentness.

tarsnan, -ain, see tarsannan.

tarsnan-iomall, *s.m.* Tangent-spoke.

tarspurlanaiche, (tarspullach) Fear-tarspurlanaiche, *a witling.*

tarsuing, -e, *a.* see tarsuinn.

tarsuinn, -e, *a.* Transverse, that crosses. 2 Oblique, lateral. 3 Cross, perverse, ill-humoured.

tarsuinn, *adv. & prep.* Across, transversely, obliquely. 2 Over, from side to side. Cuir t e, *put it obliquely* ; dhìrich sinn am bruthach air a th., *we ascended the hill obliquely.* In some parts *bruthach is fem.* which would give "dhìrich sinn a' bhruaich air a t.," *or* "air a fiaradh."

tarsuinneach, *s.f.ind.*Transverseness, obliquity. 2 Crossness, peevishness.

———d, *s. f.* Crossness, peevishness. 2 Trasverseness, obliquity.

tarsuinnich, *v.a.* Cut. 2‡‡Cross.

tarsunnanachd, *s.f.ind.* Species of poetry, lampooning, sarcastic language, satirizing. 2* Bickering.

†**tart** *prep.pron.* (tar + thu) see tharta.

tart, -airt, *s.m.* Thirst. 2 Drought, parchedness, want of rain. 3 (AH) Costiveness in cattle. Trid fearainn tairt, *through a thirsty land* ; tha t. orm, *I am thirsty.*

tartach, -aiche, *a.* Thirsty. 2 Causing thirst. 3 Droughty, dry.

†**tartan**,** -ain, *s.m.* Tartan. 2 Hillock. 3 Clod.

†———ach,** *a.* Hilly. 2 Cloddy. 3 Of tartan.

tartar, see tartmhor.

tartar, -air, -an, *s.m.* Noise, any great swelling sound. 2 Clamour. 3 Hurry, bustle, confusion. 4* Noise of tramping. A th. mar thuinn a' slachdadh sgeire, *his noise like waves buffeting a rock.*

——ach, -aiche,*a.* Noisy, making a great noise. 2 Clamorous, vociferous, loud, having a swelling sound. 3 Hurried, bustling, creating confusion. 4 Magnanimous, forward. 5*Noisy in stamping. Da 'm bu t. pìob, *whose pipe sounded loudly.*

——achd, see tartaraich.

——aich, *s.f.ind.* Noisiness. 2 Noise of footsteps, tramping. 3 Bustle, confusion. 4 Forwardness. 5 Magnanimity.

tar-thabhairt,** s. Conveyancing.

tar-thabhairtear,** *s.m.* Conveyancer.

tarthail,** *s.f.* Help, assistance.

tar-thoir,** *v.* Alienate. 2 Convey.
tar-thoirt,** *s.* Alienation. 2*Conveyance.
tar-tholl,** *s.* & *v.* Countermine, conveyance.
tartmhor, -oire, *a.* Thirsty. 2 Droughty, dry, parched. Ma bhios e t., *if he be thirsty.*
——**achd,** *s.f.ind.* Thirst. 2 Drought, parchedness, droughtiness. 3*Great drought. 4* Dry or droughty weather.
tar-uinneag, -an. see **far-uinneag.**
tarung, see **tarrang.**
tarunn, see **tarrang.**
tàs,** *s.m.* Cat-o'-nine tails, taws.
tàsan, -ain, -an, *s.m.* Slow, tedious, plaintive discourse, plaintive harangue, whining sermon. 2 Person who speaks in a drawling manner. 3* Bickering, scolding, fretting, discontented person. 4††Wrangling, grumbling, discontent. 5 Sloven. 6** Plaintive or tedious haranguer.
——**ach,** -aiche, *a.* Slow, tedious. 2 Plaintive. querulous, grumbling, discontented, bickering. 3 Slow or tedious in speaking, monotonous.
——**achd,** *s.f.ind.* Habit of slow wrangling, bickering, fretfulness, fretful disposition, fault-finding. 2 Slowness or tediousness in discourse, monotony. 3**Presbyterian cant.
tàsanaich, see **tàsanachd.**
tàsanaiche,** *s.f.* Tedious whining orator, *in ridicule.*
tasart,** -airt, *s.m.* Reproach, rebuke, calumny. Fo th., *under reproach.*
tasd,(AF) *s.* Reindeer.
tasdail,** *s.f.* Trial.
tasdan, -ain, -an, *s.m.* Shilling. 2**Groat.
——**ach,** -aiche, *a.* Having many shillings.
†**tasg,** -aisg, -an, *s.m.* Report, rumour, news, knowledge. 2 Character. 3 Gaelic spelling of *task.* Ann an taisg, *in store.*
tàsg, -àisg, -an, *s.m.* Ghost, apparition—*W. of Ross, Inverness-shire & Argyll.* [*pl.* tàisg in *Gairloch.*—DU.]
tasg, -aisg, -an, *s.m.* Larva of insects.
tàsgadh, (a') *pr pt.* of taisg.
tasgaidh,-e, -ean,*s.f.* Depository, thing laid by or preserved, store, treasure, hoard. 2 Treasurer. 3 Laying up, act of laying up. 4‡‡Darling. 5 Hoarding bureau. Tha, a thasgaidh ! *yes, darling !* A' t—, *pr.pt.* of taisg.
†**tasgail,**** *a.* Renowned.
tasgair,** *s.m.* One who assigns a job or task, taskmaster. 2**Slave.
tasgal, -ail,*s.m.* Money offered for the discovery of cattle lifted by Highland freebooters. There have often been instances of vassals, and even clans, taking an oath on the dirk never to receive such money and to put to death every person that should receive it. They took this oath in a solemn manner over a drawn dirk which they kissed, saying, "if we break this our oath, may we perish by this weapon or any other."
tasgal,** -ail, *s m.* Great wave.
tasgalachd,** *s.f.ind.* Rolling of the sea.
tasgar,** -air, *s.m.* Cavalcade.
tasg-thaigh,‡‡ *s.m.* Storehouse.
taslach, *s. m.* Supernatural premonition and ghost of living person—JGC., W.
tasp,* *s.m.* Severe sarcasm.
taspair(e),* -ean, *s.m.* Satirist.
taspannach,* -aiche, see **taspullach.**
taspullach, -aiche, *a.* Witty. 2 Sarcastic. 3 Petulant.
——**d,**** *s.f.* Wit, witticism. 2 Sarcasm.
taspurladh,(MS) *s.m.* Invective, retort.
†**tast,**** *s.m.* see **tasd.**
tastar, for tartar—*Rob Donn.*
tatadh,(MS) *s.m.* Caress.
tatag, -aig, -an, *s.f.* Clash.
tàtag,(MMcL) *s.f.* Stab. Also used metaphorically, as, thug e t. dha, *he gave him a stab (in speech.)*
tataidh,* *v.a.* see **tàlaidh.** 2(MS) Account.
tatar, *W. of Ross* for tartar.
tàth, *s.m.* Rebate in *joinery.* 2 Pitch. 3 Cement. 4 Strength. Leann tàth, *pith ;* duine gun t., *a man devoid of energy and spirit.*
tàth, *pr.pt.* a' tàthadh,*v.a.* Cement, join together, glue, solder, weld.
†**tath,** *s.m.* Lord. 2 Ruler. 3 Anger.
tath,(AF) *s.m.* Unpressed cheese made of sour milk curds.
tath,** *s.m.* Slaughter. 2 Bail, security.
tathabal,(AH) *a.* In possession of one's faculties, of sound mind. Am bheil e t. ? *is he all there ?* tha e t. gu leòir, *he is sane enough.*
tàthach,**-aiche, *a.* Cementing, that cements or solders, having the quality of soldering.
tathach, -aich, *s. m.* Guest, visitor, stranger. Bu tric tathaich o Thuath, *visitors from the North were frequent ;* m' aoidheachd ag iarraidh tathaich, *my hospitality in quest of a guest.*
†**tathad,** for tha iad, (they are.)
tàthadair,** *s.m.* Cementer. 2‡‡Adjunctive.
tàthadh, -aidh, *s.m.* Joining, cementing, act of joining or soldering. 2 Welding. 3 Leading. 4 Splicing, in *joinery.* 5* Joint, seam. A' t—, *pr.pt.* of tàth.
tathag, *s.f.* Small in-field—*Gairloch.*
tathaich, -e, *s.f.* Frequenting, act of frequenting or often visiting. 2 Resort. 3 Craving. 4 **Claim. 5 Investing. 6 Tendency to vomit or come back again. 7 Inclination to nausea which follows on intoxication. 8 (MMcL) *s.f. & s.m.* Ghost, apparition. 9 see **tighich.** A' t—, *pr.pt.* of tathaich. T. na daoraich, *cravers of intoxication—Dàin I. Ghobha.*
tathaich,(DC) *s.m.* Supernatural knowledge of the absent.
——, *gen.sing. & n.pl.* of tathach.
——, *pr.pt.* a' tathaich,*v.a.* Visit often, resort to. 2**Claim. 3 Dun. 4 Invest. 5 Crave, exact. 6 Profit. Is tric a th. thu i, *often did you resort to her ;* a' t. bhailtean, *visiting cities.*
——**e,** -an, *s.m.* One who visits often. 2 Acquaintance. 3 Guest.
——**each,** -eiche, *a.* Conversant, acquainted with, frequently visiting.
——**eadh,** -eidh, *s. m.* Frequently visiting. 2 Craving.
——**ear,**** *s.m.* Craver. 2 Dun.
tataidh,‡ *pr.pt.* a' tatadh, *v.a.* Attract, attach to one's self.
tàthaidh, *fut.aff.a.* of tàth.
tàthair,** *s.m.*Cementer, joiner. 2 Sluggish fellow.
tàthan, -ain, *s.m.* Hyphen (-).
tathasg,(MS) *s.f.* Shade, spirit. Is dlùth t. na màthar d' a dìlleachdain, *near is the mother's spirit to her orphans.* There was a beautiful idea among the Gael that orphan children are specially protected by the spirit of their departed mother, and many of the most pathetic Gaelic lullabies are said to have been composed by such spirits while watching over some little cot or cradle. 2(MS) Demon.
tath-bheum, -bhéim, -annan, *s.m.* Mortal blow. 2 Casting of darts or stones from the crann-tabhuill.
tath-bhuille, *s.m.* Mortal blow.
†**tathfann,** -ainn, *s.m.* see **tabhunn.**
tathlach, see **talach.**
tathlan,** -ain, *s.m.* Reproach, calumny.

tàthta, *past pt.* of tàth. Soldered, cemented, joined. [tàthte.]
tàth-thaois, *s.f.* Putty.
tathuich, see tathaich.
tathuinn, see tathainn.
tathunn, see tabhann.
———ach, -aiche, *a.* Latrant.
———aich, see tabhannaich.
———aiche, see tabhannaiche.
té, *s.f.ind.* Woman, female one. 2 Used of any object or thing of the feminine gender. An té seo, *this one*—said of any object of the feminine gender; an té a b' òige, *the youngest woman.*
†**te**, see teth.
tè, *a.* Insipid, slightly fermented. When fish, milk, preserves, &c. take the bitter or sharp taste caused by fermentation, they are said to be *tè.*
tè,(CR) *a.* Thick, as soup, gruel, &c—*Arran.*
†**tea**, see teth.
teab, *s.* Flippant person's mouth.
teabad, -aid, *s.m.* Stammerer. 2‡‡Accident. 3 *Stammer.
teabadach, -aiche, *a.* Stammering. 2 Accidental.
teabadaich, *a.* Lisping, faltering. 2 ‡‡Hesitation, delay.
———, *s.f.* Demur.
teabaid,‡ *s.f.* Taunt, repartee.
teabais,* *s.f.* Flippancy of speech.
———each,* -eiche, *a.* Flippant.
teabanta,* -ainte, *a.* Carping, captious.
———chd,* *s.f.* Captiousness, flippancy of speech, captious notice. 2‡‡Habit of carping.
teabarsnaich, -e, see teabadaich.
teabh,** *s.* Quid of tobacco.
teabhach,** -aiche, *a.* Renowned, brave. Gu t., *bravely.*
———d,** *s.f.* Fame, glory, exploit. 2 Bravery. Can anns an dàn an t., *sing their bravery in song.*
teabhachd, see tàbhachd.
teacair, see teachdair.
teach, *s.m.ind.* House, dwelling-place, also taigh. 'Na t. diamhair, *in her lonely dwelling.*
teach, *pr.pt.* see teachd. 2(CR) *s.m.* Pass, event, issue, occurence. Cha d' thàinig e teach, *it did not come to pass;* tighinn gu teach, *happening;* thàinig e fo theach, *it came to pass*—*Lewis & W. of Ross*, but, thàinig e mu'n teach, in *Arran & Perthshire.*
teachd, *s.m.ind.* Accession. 2 Arrival, coming, act of coming, approach, approaching. A' t—, *pr.pt.* of thig. Air dha t., *he having arrived;* t. mu'n cuairt na bliadhna, *expiration of the year;* air t., *come;* a' t., *coming;* tha 'n raineach uaine air t. thairis oirre, *the green fern has grown over her.*
teachd,(DU) *v.a.* Dry up. Th. mi leis a' phathadh, *I dried up with thirst.*
teachd, *v.n.* Fit in to, have space or room for. Cha t. e 'n seo, *it has not sufficient room here;* an t. mi ann? *can it contain me?* an t. e 'san leapa? *has he room in the bed?* an t. e anns an t-seòmar seo? *can this room contain it?*
teachd, *a.* Legal, lawful, right, just. 2 Belonging to. 3††Fitting.
tèachd,†† *s.f.* Silly boasting.
teachdadh,** -aidh, *s.m.* Closing.
teachdaiche,** *s.m.* Customer.
teachdail, -e, *a.* Future, in *grammar.*
teachdair(e), -ean, *s.m.* Messenger, courier, ambassador, anyone bearing, or that is sent, or that comes with a message, envoy, delegate, missionary. 2 Despatch, intelligence, news. Bhuail t. a' bhàis thu, *death's messenger has struck you;* t.-coise, *foot messenger.*
teachdaireach, -eiche, *a.* Of, or belonging to, a messenger, courier, or ambassador. 2 Like a messenger, courier, or ambassador.
———eachd, *s.f.ind.* Message, embassy, legation. 2 Tidings, news, intelligence. 3 Commission, errand, deputation. Air th., *on an embassy;* t. a chuir mòran gu truaighe, *information that caused sorrow to many.*
——— -litrichean, *s.m.* Letter-carrier.
teachd-a-mach, *s.m.ind.* Product, increase. 2 Expenditure. 3 Coming out, egress.
teachd-a-staigh, see teachd-a-steach.
teachd-a-steach,** *s. m.* Income, revenue. 2 Coming in.
teachd-an-tìr, *s.m.ind.* Subsistence, livelihood. 2 Diet. 3 Food. Gun t. gun bhiadh, *without diet or food;* a theachd-an-tìr, *his food.*
teachd-fodha,(DMK) *s.m.* Water oozing through the wall of a house at the foundation in wet weather—*W. coast of Ross.* [tighinn-fodha in *Argyll.*]
teachmhail,** *s.f.* Affliction, sickness.
tead, see teud.
teadalach, -aiche, *a.* Slow, inactive, dilatory. 2 Sickly.
———d, *s.f.ind.* Slowness, inactivity, dilatoriness. 2 Sickliness.
teadaltas, -ais, *s.m.* see teadalachd.
teadarnach,** *a.* Revengeful.
teadh, *a.* High-tasted.
teadhair, -dhrach, -dhraichean, *s.f.* Tether. 2 ††Rope. 3(DMK) Rope stretched across the kitchen having the ends attached to the couple, and used for hanging articles of clothing on to dry, also as a repository for such articles—*Caithness & Suth'd.* 4**Cart-rope. Dheanadh e t. de roinnean, *he would make a tether with a hair.*
teadhair, *v.a* see teadhraich.
teadh-bhais,** *a.* Phantasm, see taibhs.
teadharadh, *s. m.* Drawing out, spinning out. A' t—, *pr.pt.* of teadhair. Tha e a' t. na sìde, *he is spinning out the time.*
teadhrachadh, -aidh, *s.m.* Tethering, act of tethering or confining by a tether. A' t—, *pr. pt.* of teadhraich.
teadhraich, *pr.pt.* a' teadhrachadh, *v.a.* Tether, confine by a tether, tie.
teadhraichean, *n.pl.* of teadhair.
teadhraichte, *past pt.* of teadhraich. Tethered.
teadhran,(DC) *s.m.* Royal stag. This word was used by a forester who had spent his life in the Blackmount.
teagail,** *s.f.* House, habitation.
teagair, *pr. pt.* a' teagar, [a' teagaradh—*W. of Ross,*] *v.a.* Collect, provide, furnish, supply. 2 Thatch, cover. 3 Shelter, protect. 4 Economise, gather milk for butter by stinting the allowance of the family.
teagaisg, *pr.pt.* a' teagasg, *v.a.* Teach, instruct, educate by lecturing, teach by precepts.
———, *gen.sing.* of teagasg.
———each,** *a.* Didactic, instructive.
———ear, *fut.pass.* of teagaisg.
———te, *past pt.* of teagaisg. Taught, lectured.
teagaisgteach, -eiche, *a.* Docile, teachable.
teagamh, -aimh, -an, *s.m.* Doubt, uncertainty, hesitation. 2 Suspense, perplexity. 3 Doubtful case. 4 Difficulty. Fear-réitich gach teagaimh, *the solver of all difficulties;* th., *perhaps;* gun t., *without doubt;* an t., *in doubt.*
———ach, -aiche, *a.* Doubtful. 2 Doubting. 3 Uncertain. 4 Causing a doubt. 5 In suspense. 6 Suspicious, distrustful, sceptical. 7 **Perplexed.
———achd, *s.f.* Contingentness, doubtfulness,

doubt, uncertainty. 2 Scepticism.
teagamhaich, *v.a.* Mistrust.
teagamhaiche,** *s.m.* Doubter, sceptic.
———, *comp.* of teagamhach.
teagar, -air, *s.m.* Provision. 2**Purchase. 3** Warmth. A' t—, *pr.pt.* of teagair.
teagarach, -aich, *s.m.* Purchase.
———, -aiche, *a.* Warm, snug.
teagasg, -aisg, *s.m.* Teaching, instruction, act of teaching, instructing. 2 Doctrine. 3* Teaching by lectures, lecturing. 5 Preaching, text. 4** Druidism, sorcery. A' t—, *pr. pt.* of teagaisg. Le gach uile ghaoth teagaisg, *with every wind of doctrine*; fear-teagaisg (*pl.* luchd-teagaisg), *a lecturer*.
teagasgach,** *a.* Admonitory, instructive.
teagasgachd, *s.f.* Instructiveness.
teagasgail,** *a.* Admonitory. 2 Doctrinal.
teagasgair, -ean, *s. m.* Teacher, admonisher, preacher.
———eachd,** *s.f.ind.* Employment of a teacher.
teagasg-druidheachd, *s.m.* Sorcery, druidism.
†teagh, see taigh.
———as,** -ais, *s.m.* Small room, closet.
teaghlach, -aich, -aichean, *s.m.* Family, household, house in genealogy. 2†† House, dwelling. 3** Clan, tribe, race, progeny. Uile theaghlaichean na talmhainn, *all the families of the earth*.
teaghlachail, -e, *a.* Of, or belonging to a family, domestic.
teaghlachan,** -ain, *s.m.* Domestic.
teaglach,* -aiche, *a.* see teagamhach.
———d,* *s.f.* see teagamh.
teagmhach, -aiche, *a.* Conditional in *grammar*. 2**Apocryphal. 3**Ambiguous.
———d,***s.f.* Ambiguity. 2 Apocryphalness.
teagmhaiche, *s.m.* Boggler.. 2 Sceptic.
teagmhail, -e, -ean, *s.f.* Occurrence, recounter, contingency. 2 Meddling, interference, expostulation. 3 Strife, battle. 4 Revenge, retribution. 5 Fall. 6**Meeting.
††teagmhaileach, *a.* Contentious, striving, contending.
teagmhaileachd,** *s.f.* State of being liable to chance or accident.
teagmhais, -e, -ean, *s.f.* Accident, guess, venture, anything done at venture or random. 2 **Contingency. 3**Fall.
teagmhaiseach,** *a.* Adventurous, accidental, at a venture, at random, liable to chance or accident.
teagmhaladh, *s.m.* Meddling. Air chumha gun ghnè th., *without any kind of meddling*—R.21.
teagmhas, see teagmhais.
———air, *s.m.* Adventurer.
teagmhuil, see teagmhail.
teagmhus, see teagmhais.
teagnach,** -aiche, *a.* Using force or violence. 2 Making an exertion. 3 Difficult.
teagnadh, -aidh, -ean, *s.m.* Squeezing of anything through another. 2**Acquest. 3** Striving. 4**Forcing. 5 Violent exertion. 6 Tenesmus, applied particularly to a hen, and sometimes to persons. [* says *properly* teagmhail.]
teagradh, -aidh, *s.m.* Providing, act of providing, collecting. 2 Acquisition. 3 Defending, act of defending. 4 Gathering of milk economically. 5 Milk or butter so gathered. A' t., *pr.pt.* of teagair.
teagradh, *3rd. p. sing. & pl. imp.* of teagair.
teagraidh, *fut.aff.a.* of teagair.
teagram, *1st.sing.imp.* of teagair.
teaguisg, see teagaisg.
teairt,(CR) *s.f.* Grazing before morning milking—*W. of Ross.* Tha 'n crodh air an t., *the cows go out before being milked*; sguir iad de 'n t., *they have ceased to go out before being milked.* 2 (DMK) Morning milking-time, [also tràth teairt.] Tha tìm teairt ann, *it is time to take the cows in to milk them*—about 11 .a.m in summer—*Northern Counties.*
tealbh,(AC) *s.m.* Corn. Gach tàn is tealbh, *all flocks and corn.*
teall,‡ *s.m.* Sudden attack.
†tealla, *s.m.* The earth.
teallach, -aich, -aichean, *s.m.*Hearth, fire-place. 2 Smith's forge. 3**Anvil. 4**Furnace. Leac an teallaich, *the hearth-stone*; clach ceann an teallaich, is the large flag which stands behind a fire in Highland cottages; de luaith theallaich,*of the ashes of a furnace;*air cruaidh th., *on a hard anvil.* [*s.f.* in *Poolewe*—WC.]
teallachag, -aig, -an, *s.f.* Concubine. 2**Master's favourite servant maid.
teallaich, *gen.sing.* of teallach.
teallaid, -e, -ean, *s.f.* Lusty or bunchy woman. 2**Drab.
teallaideach,** *a.* Drabbish, sluttish.
teallrach,** *a.* Profuse.
teallsan,** -ain, *s.m.* Philosophy, erudition. 2 Philosopher, learned man.
teallsanach,* -aich, *s.m.* Sceptic. 2 Philosopher, sage, learned man. 3 Astronomer—*Sàr-Obair.* Cha'n 'eil cràbhach, t., no sagart ann, *there is neither hypocrite, philosopher nor priest (in it) there.*
———ail,** *a.* Philosophical, erudite.
———d,* *s. f.* Scepticism. 2 Philosophy, erudition.
teallsanair,** -ean, *s. m.* Learned man, philosopher.
tealrachd,** *s.f.ind.* Profusion, extravagance.
tealtachd,** *s.f.ind.* Simplicity.
tealtaidh, *a.* Silly, cowardly.
tèamhachd, *s. f.* Pleasantness, delightfulness, quietness.
tèamhaidh, -e, *a.* Pleasant, agreeable, delightful, quiet.
teamhair, -e, *a.* see tèamhaidh.
———, *s.f.* Time, season, in season—*Suth'd & N. Coast.* 2**Covered or shaded walk on a hill. Teamhair fhuar, *cold weather.*
———eachd, see teamhachd.
teamhall,* -aill, *s.m.* Slight swoon or stun.
teamharra,* *a.* Pertly eloquent, eloquent and flippant, as a young person.
teamhra,(MS) *s.m.* Hall.
teamhrachail,(MS) *a.* Palatial.
teamhrachd,* *s.f.* Flippancy, impertinent prattle of a young person.
teampull, -uill, *s.m.* Temple, church.
———ach, -aich, *s.m.* Church-officer, churchman, templar.
———ach, -aiche, *a.* Of, or belonging to, a temple or church. 2 Like a temple or church.
teanacadh, *s.m.* Deliverance, succour.
teanacaiste, see teanacas.
teanacas,* *s.* Healing, remedy, mercy, deliverance, salvation, saving power, coming to one's assistance—*W. Isles—Dàin I. Ghobha.* 2 Defence. Cò is urrainn t.? *who can be a defence?*
teanachair, see teanchair. 'S gu'm faigh iad gu bunailteach ri t. gharg an leòmhainn—*Filidh. p. 68*; t. a' ghobhainn, *smith's tongs.*
teanachd,* *v. a.* Save, avert, ward away. T. gorta, *avert famine*; t. dosgainn, *ward away misfortune from cattle*, protect from danger, distress or difficulty.
teanachdadh, -aidh, *s.m.* Saving, act of saving, protecting or recovering from instant peril. A' t—, *pr.pt.* of teanachd.

teanachdas, see teanacas.
teanachdsa,* -ais, see teanacas.
teanacsa,(AC) see teanacas.
teanacsadh, see teannacas.
teanail, *v.* see tionail.
teanal, *s.* see tional.
teanalach, see tionalach.
teanaladh,** *s.m.* Treasuring.
teanalaiche, see tionalaiche.
teancas, see teanacas.
teanchair, -ean, *s.m.* Pincers, tongs. 2 Smith's vice or tongs.
teanga, *gen. & dat.* teangaidh, *pl.* -n & -nnan, *s.f.* Tongue, 2 Speech, dialect. 3* Hold of a buckle. 4(AC)Oratory. T. Chaluim Chille, *the oratory of St. Columba* ; bun na teangaidh, *the root of the tongue* ; bàrr na teangaidh, *the tip of the tongue.*
teangach, -aiche, *a.* Loquacious. 2 Speaking many languages. 3 Langued, *in heraldry.* 4 *Having many tongues. Gu t., *loquaciously.*
teangachd, see teangaireachd.
teang'-a' choin,‡ *s.f.* Hound's tongue (plant)—*cynoglossum officinale.*

660. *Teang'-a'-choin.*

teangadh, -aidh, *pl.* -aidh, -aidhean & teangan, nan, *s.f.* see teanga.
teangaiche, -an, *s.m.* Linguist.
teangaidh, -e, -ean, *s.f.* see teanga.
teangair, -ean, *s.m.* Linguist. 2 Interpreter. 3 Orator. 4 Philologist. 5(WC) Smith's tongs.
———eachd, *s.f.ind.* Office of a linguist. 2 Interpreting,interpretation,skill in languages. 3 Philology. 4 Oratory. 5 Loquaciousness.

661. *Teanga-mhìn.* 662. *Teanga-na nathrach.*

teanga-mhin,§ *s.f.* White dead-nettle,archangel. —*lamium album.* 2§ White goose-foot, see praiseach fhiadhain.
teangan,** *s.m.* Tongue. 2 Language.
teanga-na-nathrach,§ *s.f.*Adder's tongue fern—*ophiglossum vulgatum.*
teang'-an-fhéidh, *s.f.* Hart's-tongue fern, burnt weed, Christ's hair—*scolopendrium vulgare.* [illust. under creamh-na-muice-fiadhaich.]
teangas,** -ais, *s.m.* Pair of pincers.
teann, teinne, *a.* Strait, tense, tight. 2 Rigid, stiff, firm. 3 Fixed, firmly fixed. 4 Closely packed. 5 (t. air) Near to. 6 Narrow,miserly. 7 Eager, keen. 8 In straitened circumstances. 9 Pumped tight. 10**Strict. 11**Besieged. 12* Severe. Tha 'n t-sreang t., *the string is tight* ; t. air mìos, *nearly a month* ; duine t., *a severe person* ; sheas ainnir teann air, *a virgin stood near him* ; gu t., *tightly, straitly, closely, stiffly, miserly, firmly.*
teann, *pr.pt.* a' teannadh, *v.a. & n.* Move, stir, proceed, go, approach, come. 2 Fall to,begin. 3 Approximate. 4**Tighten, straiten. 5**Press together. 6 see teannaich. T. as a sin,*away with you* ; th. iad ri falbh, *they began to move off* ; t. as mo rathad, *get out of my way* ; t. a nios, *come hither* ; teannaibh r' a chéile, *sit close* ; th. iad ri treabhadh, *they commenced ploughing* ; th. i ri lasadh a' chrùisgein, *she proceeded to light the lamp* ; th. i an lomradh, *she pressed the fleece together.*
t. a bhos, come near.
t. a mach, turn out.
t. a nall, come hither.
t. a nunn, get away from me, go over hither.
t. ris, begin it.
t. suas, go up, proceed westward.
t. uam, get from me.
teann ! teann ! *int.* Hold ! hold !
teanna,** *s.m.* Enough, sufficiency. 2 Abounding. 3 Surfeit. Tha mo th. agam, *I have enough* ; is mairg a rachadh air bhannaig is a th. aige fhéin, *it is pitiful to ask when one has enough of his own.* [teannan in *Poolewe*—Òl do theannan, *drink your fill*—WC.]
teann-abaich, 'S e 'm fùdar tioram teann-abaich air chùl an asgairt ghreannaich, *it is the hard, dry powder below the rough tow*—*Beinn Doran.*
teannacas, see teannachadh.
teannach,** -aich, *s.m.* Guiltless person.
teannachadh, -aidh, *s. m.* Straitening, act of straitening. 2 Squeezing, act of squeezing or crushing. 3 Oppressing, act of oppressing. 4 Clasping, act of clasping or embracing. 5 Besieging, act of besieging, siege. 6 Strait, difficulty. 7 Energy, force. 8 Screwing. 9 Constipation. 10 Tightening by pumping into. 11 Crowding, act of crowding. 12†† Rescuing. 13**Binding. 14**Tightening. A' t—,*pr. pt.* of teannaich. [†† gives teannachdadh.]
teannachail,†† -e, *a.* Constringent.
teannachair,** -ean, *s. m.* Binder. 2 Pair of pincers. 3 Tongs. 4 Vice.
teannachan,** -ain, *s.m.* Press. 2 Pair of pincers. 3 Vice.
teannachdadh,†† see teannachadh.
teannadach, -aiche, *a.* Ricketty.
teannadair,(MS) *s.m.* Girder.
teannadan, -ain, *s.m.* Bracer, brace.
teannadh, -aidh, *s.m.* Moving, act of moving, stirring, going or coming. 2 Tightening, straitening, pressing. 3 Stiffness, rigidity. 4 Proceeding towards anything. 5 Sufficiency, enough. see teannachadh. A' t—, *pr.pt.* of teann.
teannaich, *pr.pt.* a' teannachadh, *v.a.* Straiten, tighten. 2 Squeeze, crush. 3 Crowd, crowd together. 4 Oppress, besiege. 5 Tighten by

pumping. 6 Clasp, embrace. 7 Bind, clench. 8**Afflict. 9**Grasp. 10**Confine. Th. iad e, *they besieged it ;* cha teannaichear do cheumanna, *thy steps shall not be straitened.*
——te, *past pt.* of teannaich. Straitened, tightened. 2 Squeezed. 3 Crowded together. 4 Oppressed. 5 Besieged. 6 Clasped. 7 Adacted.
teannaidh,** *a.* Astringent.
teannair, -ean, *s.m.* Squeezer, any instrument to squeeze with. 2 Air-pump. 3 The noise of the sea in a cave. 4**Tightener, oppressor.
teannal,(AC) *s.m.* Keeping, protection. Biodh a shìth air do th. féin, *be its peace in thine own keeping.*
teannan, *Poolewe* for teanna.
teannas, -ais, *s.m.* Austerity.
teannasach, -aiche, *a.* Austere, severe. 2 Aluminous.
teannath, see teanna & teann-shàth.
teann-bhreitheach, -eiche, *a.* Critical.
teannchair, see teanchair.
teanndach, -aiche, *a.* Pressing, that presses. 2 Oppressive. 3 Afflictive. 4 (MS) Astrictive.
teanndachadh, see teannachadh.
teanndachan, -ain, *s.m.* Woman's stays.
teanndachd, see teanntachd.
teanndaich, see teannaich.
——te, see teannaichte.
teann-dheoch,‡‡ *s.f.* Fill-draught, large drink.
teann-dhruid,** *v.n.* Grasp, clench, hold fast. 2 Confine closely. 3 Besiege.
teann-fhàisg,** *v.a.* Squeeze hard, wring.
teann-fhàsgadh, -aidh, -ean, *s.m.* Hard squeeze, hard wringing.
teann-ghlac, *v.a.* Clench, grasp, hold fast.
teann-ghlacach,** *a.* Grasping firmly.
teann-ghlacadh,** -aidh, *s.m.* Grasping firmly. 2 Powerful grasp.
teann-ghlacta, *past pt.* of teann-ghlac.
teann-ghreim, *s.m.* Grasp.
teann-làmh,** -làimh, *s.m.* Tinder-box. 2 (MM) Hard fist. 3 Fire.
teann-làmhach, -aiche, *a.* Hard-fisted.
teannradh,** -aidh, *s.m.* Showing, manifestation. 2 Discovery.
teann-ri-teann,(AH) At close quarters, engaged in hand-to-hand struggle. An uair a thàinig a' chùis teann-ri-teann, *when the affair assumed a serious aspect.*
teann-shàth, -àith, *s.m.* Full meal, great abundance. 2 Impregnation. 3**Sufficiency. Òlaidh mi mo th., *I will drink my fill ;* tha a th. aige, *he has quite enough.* also teanna-shàth.
teann-shuil,(AF) *s.* Insect.
teannta, *a.* & *past pt.* Joined together, close, compact, tight, pressed together.
teanntach, see teanndach.
teanntach, see teannasach.
teanntachail, *a.* see teanntach.
teanntachd, *s.f.ind.* Strait, difficulty. 2 Adversity, trouble, distress. 3‡‡ Oppression, hardship. 4‡‡Frost. 5‡‡Constipation. 6 Scantiness. An àm t., *in time of trouble.*
teanntaich, see teannaich.
teanntaichte, see teannaichte.
teanntalachd, *s.f.ind.* Stickiness.
teanntan, -ain, -ain, *s.m.* Press, squeezer, winepress. 2‡‡Bruising.
tearadh,** -aidh, *s.m.* Contention.
tearainn, see teirinn.
tearb, *pr.pt.* a' tearbadh, *v.a.* Separate, as cattle, part, divide. 2 Wean.
tearb,** *s.m.* see tearbadh.
tearbach,** *a.* Divisible, separable. 2 Apt to divide or separate.
——d,** *s.f.* Divisibleness.

tearbadh, -aidh, *s.m.* Separating, act of separating, dividing or parting. 2 Division, separation. 3 Weaning. A' t—, *pr. pt.* of tearb. Ghabh mi t. o 'n treud sin, *I separated from that flock.*
tearbaidh, see tearb. Thearbaidh e na h-uain, *he separated the lambs.*
tearbaidhte,(MS) *a.* Loose, separate.
tearbain, see tearb.
tearbhadh, see tearbadh.
tearbta, *past pt.* of tearb. Separated. 2 Weaned.
†**tearc,**** *s.m.* Cow. see earc.
tearc, teirce, *a.* Rare, unusual, scarce, few. 2†† Bare. Bu th. a ràite, *few were his words ;* cha t. sinn mar laoich na Féinne, *we are not few like the heroes of the Fiann.*
tearcachd, *s.f.* Rareness, scarceness, fewness.
tearcad -aid, *s. m.* see teircead.
tearcadh,** -aidh, *s.m.* Fewness, scarceness.
tearc-eun, -eòin, *s.m.* Phœnix (*lit.* a rare bird.—*rara avis.*)
tearm, *s.m.* Noise made by trampling.
tèarmad, see tèarmann.
tearmadair, see tearnadair.
tearmaid,(MS) *v.a.* Bescreen.
tèarmainn, *v.a.* Protect, defend, bescreen.
tèarmainnte,†† *a.* Protecting.
tèarmann,-ainn, *s.m.* Protection, refuge, defence, safety. 2 Sanctuary. 3 Patron. Mo th. thu, *thou art my refuge ;* thoir t., *defend, protect ;* a' chion t., *for want of protection.*
†**tearmann,** -ainn, *s.m.* Limit, boundary.
tèarmannach, -aiche, *a.* Protecting, defendable. 2 Belonging to a sanctuary.
tèarmannachd, see tèarmann.
tèarmannaich, *v.a.* Protect, defend.
tèarmannaichte, *past pt.* of tèarmannaich.
tèarmannair, -ean, *s.m.* Protector, defender. 2 Defendant. 3 Patron.
————eachd,** *s.f.* Protection.
tearmasg, see tiormasg.
tèarmuid, -ean, *s.f.* see tèarmann.
tèarmuinn, see tèarmunnaich.
tèarmunn, see tèarmann.
tèarn, *v.a.* see tèaruinn.
tèarnach,** *a.* Condescending. 2 Descending, apt to descend. 3 see tèaruinteach.
tearnachd,** see tearuinteachd.
tearnadair, *s.m.* Fender.
tearnadair-o-theine, *s.m.* Fire-escape.
tèarnadh, -aidh, *s. m.* Escaping, act of escaping or evading. 2 Rescuing, saving. 3 Descent, descending, coming or going down, sinking. 4 Declension in *gram.* 5 Deliverance, protection, safety. 6*Preserving. 7* After-birth. A' t—, *pr.pt.* of tèaruinn & teirinn. Cha b' urrainn dhuit t., *you could not escape ;* Dia 'gar t. ! *may God protect us !* is ionghnadh do th., *thy deliverance is wonderful ;* an curach a' dìreadh 's a' t., *the bark rising and sinking;* bu t. dhuinn toiseach an t-sluaigh, *our safety was at the head of the host—Filidh, p. 16.*
tèarnar, *fut.pass.* of tèaruinn. Shall be saved.
tèarnta, *past pt.* of tèarn.
teàrr, -a, *s.f.* Tar, pitch.
teàrr, *pr.pt.* a' teàrradh, *v. a.* Tar, run over, smear or mark with tar, as sheep.
tearrach,** -aich, *s.m.* Crupper.
tearrachd,*s.f.ind.* Keen sarcasm, bitter remark.
——aich,** *v.* Animadvert.
——ail, -e, *a.* Censorious, satirical, sarcastic.
——air,** *s.m.* Animadverter.
teàrradh, -aidh, *s.m.* Daubing, act of daubing or marking with tar. 2 Tar. 3 Tar-mark on wool or sheep. 3 Pitching. A' t—, *pr. pt.* of teàrr. [** gives tearradh, also gath-tearradh,

a whitlow or *felon.*]
tearraid, see earraid.
——each, see earraideach.
——eachd, see earraideachd (appx.)
tearrain, *v.n.* Return.
†**tearran**,** -ain, *s.m.* Anger, vexation.
teart,(WC) see teairt.
tèaruinn, *pr.pt.* a' tèarnadh,*v.a.* & *n.* Escape, evade. 2 Rescue, save. 3 Protect, defend. 4 Descend. 5**Preserve.
——ean, see teàruinn.
tèaruinte, *a.* & *past pt.* of tèaruinn. Safe, saved, rescued. 2 Preserved, protected, secure, guarded. 3* Cautious.
——ach, -eiche, *a.* Secure. 2 Confident of security. 3 Saving. 4 Protecting, preserving.
——achd, *s.f.ind.* Security, safety, salvation. 2* Precaution, caution. An t., *in security.*
tèaruntachd, see tèaruinteachd.
teas, *s.m.ind.* [*f.* in *Badenoch.*] Heat, warmth. 2 Superabundance, too much of the good things of life. T. an là, *the heat of the day ;* ruith air th., *running to and fro*, as cattle on a hot day ; bha teas an teine 'na luirgnean, *the heat of the fire was in his shanks*—said of one well off and who does not appreciate it. Mothers often use this phrase to their youngsters on a wet day or night when they don't value their home comforts, but go abroad to their own discomfort.
†**teas**, *s.m.* Sound. 2 Message.
teasach, -aich, -aichean, *s.f.* Fever, restlessness on account of heat, cattle running from excessive heat. 2 Moult. 3 Warm water in milk. 4 Early stage of fever—*Arran.* Àirde teasaich, *the height of a fever ;* an t. bhuidhe, *the yellow fever.*
——adh, -aidh, *s.m.* Heating, act of heating. 2 State of becoming hot. A' t—, *pr. pt.* of teasaich.
—— -sgàrlaid,*s.f.* Scarlet fever.(With *art.*an.)
teasaich, *pr.pt.* a' teasachadh, *v.a.* & *n.* Heat, warm. 2 Become hot or warm. 3 Bake. [** says " this verb is not much in use."]
——te, *past pt.* of teasaich, Heated,warmed.
teasaigheachd,** *s.f.* Heat.
teasair,** *s.m.* Messenger.
teasairg, *pr.pt.* a' teasairginn, *v.a.* Save, rescue, deliver, defend, protect, relieve, interpose for the purpose of rescuing.
——each,** *a.* Saving, protecting, rescuing.
——inn, *s. f. ind.* Rescuing, act of rescuing, saving from danger, deliverance, rescue relief, preservation, salvation. A' t—, *pr. pt.* of teasairg. Chum ar t., *for our deliverance.*
teasairgte, *past pt.* of teasairg. Saved, rescued, delivered, safe.
teasbhach, -aiche, *a.* Sultry, warm.
——, -aich, *s.m.* Sultriness, warmth.
teas-bhat,** *s.m.* Hot bath.
——ach, *a.* Abounding in, of, or belonging to, hot baths.
teas-bhuala, *s.f.* Hot baths.
teasd,‡ *pr.pt.* a' teasd, *v.n.* Die, fail, expire, depart. Th. e, *he died.*
†**teasd**,** *s.m.* Report. 2 Witness.
——ail,** *s.f.* Want, defect.
teasdaim, *v.* I help, assist.
teasdam,(AC) *v.* I preserve, secure, keep.
teas-fhailce,** *s.f.* Hot bath.
teas-fheallsanach,** *s.m.* Chemist.
——d,** *s.f.* Chemistry.
†**teasg**,‡ *v.a.* Cut, wound. 2 Prune, lop off. Is iomadh ceann a theasgadh leis, *many a head was cut off by him.*
†**teasgach**, -aiche, *a.* Piercing, cutting.
teasgadh,** -aidh, *s.m.* Cutting down.
†**teasgair**, *v.* Cut. 2 Mangle, tear.
teasgal, -ail, -an,*s.m.* Boisterous wind, storm. **Scorching blasting wind. 3 Wave.
teas-ghaoth, -ghaoithe, -an, *s.f.* Parching wind
teas-ghràdh, -ghràidh, *s.m.* Ardour. 2 Fervent love, ardent affection.
——ach, -aiche, *a.* Ardent. 2 Cherishing a fervent love,loving ardently or affectionately.
teas-ghràdhaich,***v.a.*Love ardently or tenderly
——te, *past pt.* Ardently loved.
teas-ghuirean,** -ein, *s.m.* Pimple.
†**teasgon**,** *s.* Moon.
teas-is-fuachd, *s.f.* " Hot and cold shivers."
teas-loisgeach, *s.m.* Fervid or burning heat.
teas-mheidh,** *s.* Thermometer.
teasraig, *v.a.* see teasairg.
——inn, see teasairginn.
——te, see teasairgte.
teastail, see teasdail.
teastas,** -ais, *s.m.* Report.
teas-thoimhsear,(DM) *s.m.* Thermometer, thermoscope.
teas-thumait,** *s.f.* Hot bath.
teasuidheachd, *s.f.*Heat,warmth,moderate heat.
teath, see teth.
teathair, see teadhair.
teathar,** -air, *s.m.* Guiltless person.
teathra,(AF) Raven, royston crow.
†**teib**, see theab.
teibeid, *s.f.* Taunt, cut—*Badenoch.* see teabaid.
teibid, -ean, *s.m.* Physician.
teibideach, -eiche, *a.* Irresolute, halting,falling.
téibh,(MMcL) -ean, *s.m.* Root of bent-grass, used in making cisein, &c.
†**teibidh'**, *pl.* of teibid.
†**teibidh**,‡‡ -e, *a.* Smart, cutting, pedantic.
teic,* *a.* Due, lawful, legal. Cha t. na th' ann, *all there are, are too much ;* cha t. dhuit, *that is more than is due* or *lawful ;* an t. a h-aon, *is not one more than enough ?* bheir mise dhuit gus an abair thu " cha teic," *I will give you till you say "it is more than enough" ;* cha teic fhad 's 'thug mi 'm ùine cho stoirmt', *the time I continued so dull was not trifling.* A common *Argyllshire* phrase in the face of an evil is, " cha teic olcas," *its ill is not trifling* —DC.
teic, *s.m.* Flier of spinning-wheel, see seic.
teich, *pr.pt.* a' teicheadh, *v. n.* Flee, scamper, run away. 2 Desert, as a soldier. 3**Retreat. 4**Keep off or aside. O ghuth a' bhuaireis theich na sluaigh,*at the noise of the tumult the people fled ;* th. e, *he fled ; deserted the army.*
teicheach,* *a.* Fleeing, fleeting,
teicheachd,** *s.f.* Running away, flight. 2 Retreating. 3**Desertion. 4 Overthrow.
teicheadh,-idh, *s.m.*Fleeing, act of fleeing,flight, scampering, running away, taking to one's heels. 2 Desertion. 3 Retreating, retreat. A' t—, *pr. pt.* of teich. Cuir air t., *put to flight.*
teichmheach, -eiche, *a.* Fleeting.
téid, *fut. int.*& *neg.* of *irr.v.* Rach or theirig. An téid thu maille rium ? *will you go with me ?* nach téid thu mach ? *will you not go out ?*
teidheadh,(AC) *v.* (téideadh) Would go. Nach t. a' bhliadhna liom (leam),*that the year would not go well with me.* [*Lewis & Ireland* for rachadh.—MM]
teidhm, -e, -ean, *s.f.* Death.
teidhinn, (CR) Would go—*Suth'd, Lewis & Ireland* for *subj.* of rach.
teididh, -e, *a.* Wild, fierce.
——,* *s.f.* Wild fire.

†teidm, *s.* Pestilence.
†teidm leanamnachu,‖ *s.* Contagious or infectious disease.
teigeil,(MS) *a.* Oozy.
teighiollas,(AF) *s.m.* Salamander.
†teil,** *s.f.* Fertile ground.
teilbhein, see tairbhein.
teile, *s.f.* Lime or linden-tree.
teileach,** *s.m.* Lime or linden-tree. 2 Place where lime-trees grow.
———, -eiche, *a.* Abounding in limes or lindens.
teileag, -eig, -an, *s.f.* Little lime-tree. 2 Young lime-tree.
———ach,** *a.* Abounding in little limes.
teilg, -e, -ean, *s.f.* Fishing-line, cast. 2 (AC) String of a lyre, harp or other string-instrument.
teilg, see tilg.
teilgeach,-eiche,*a.*Furnished with a fishing-line.
teilich,** *v.a.* Refuse, deny, conceal.
teilig, see teilg.
teilin,(AC) *s.* Musical instrument, stringed instrument. Gaelic form of Welsh,telyn,(a harp.)
teilinn, see teillin.
teilis,** *s.f.* House.
teilleach, -aich, *s.m.* Blub-cheeked fellow, *prov.*
———,** -eiche, *a.* Blub-cheeked.
teilleag, *s.f.* see seillean.
teillim,(AC) *v.* I will harp.
teillean, *E. Perthsh. & Lewis* for seillean.
teinn,** *s.f.* Dart, arrow.
†teilm, *s.f.* Great terror.
teim, -ean, see teum.
†teimeal,** *s.* Dross.
teimh,** *s.* Death, curtain, cover.
teimhe,** *s.* see teim.
teimhealachd,***s.f.* Darkness, gloom,obscurity.
teimheil,** *a.* Dark, gloomy, obscure.
tein'-aighir, *s.m.* Bonfire.
tein'-aoibhneis, *s.m.* Bonfire.
tein'-athair, *s.m.* Lightning. †2**Thunderbolt. 3**Fire-ball. 4**Any luminous meteor.
†teind,‖ *s.* Sore.
teindear,* *s.m.* Fire-grate. [*teindire.]
teindreach,** -eich, *s.f.* Watch-chain.
teine, *pl.* teintean, *s.m.* [*f.* in *Colonsay.*] Fire, flame. 2 Conflagration. Chunnacas t. a' bhàis, *the flame of death was seen;* taobh an teine, *the fire-side;* cuir ri theine, *set on fire;* teine math, *a good fire.* [*dat.* teinidh.]
teine,§ *s. m.* Furze, see conasg. 2 Old Gaelic name of the letter T.
teineachan, -ain, -an, *s.m.,dim.* of teine. Small fire.
teineasach,** *a.* Fiery, hot. 2 Impetuous, hasty.
———d, *s.f.* Fieriness, impetuousness, hastiness.
teine-bhuth,** *s.* Fire-office.
teine-bràight,* see teine-dreallsach.
teine-braightseal,* see teine-dreallsach.
teine-chiarag,(AF) *s.f.* Cricket (insect.)
teine-chrios,** *s.m.* Iron for striking fire from a flint. [acfhuinn-theine—*Argyll.*]
teine-creasadh,(AF) *s.* Ferret.
teine-dé, *s.m.* Erysipelas. 2 Ring-worm. 3 St. Anthony's fire. 4* Herpes. 5 Tetter—JGC. W. 95. 6* see dearbadan-dé.
teine-dealan,(AF) *s.m.* Salamander.
teine-dhealan, see teine-ghealan.
teine-dreallsach,* *s. m.* Wild fire, phosphoric light from decayed wood or fish.
teine-éibhinn, see tein'-aoibhneis.
teine-éibhneis, see tein'-aoibhneis.
tein'-éigin, *s.m.* Fire by friction, forced fire or fire of necessity.

The tein'-éigin was considered an antidote against the plague and murrain and all infectious diseases among cattle. Dr. Martin says all the fires in the parish were extinguished and 81 married men, being deemed the proper number for effecting this purpose,took two planks of wood and nine of them were employed by turns, who by their repeated efforts, rubbed the planks against each other, till the heat thereof produced fire, and from this forced fire each family was supplied with a new fire. No sooner was the fire kindled than a pot filled with water was put thereon, which was afterwards sprinkled on people who had the plague,or on cattle that had the murrain, and this process was said to be followed invariably by success.—**

A term applied to fire produced by friction—in olden times a means employed to check evils arising from being bewitched. If a household suffered loss such as indicated being under evil influence, all fires in the district between two running streams were extinguished on a set day. Then a spinning-wheel was put in motion, and kept going furiously until the spindle became heated. Tinder or tow was applied to the hot spindle, fire was thus procured and distributed to all households affected by evil influences. Within the memory of persons still living, fire was thus procured to check witchcraft in a township in Uist where some sickness, supposed to be evil eye, carried off some cows and sheep. It is odd that neither cow nor sheep died after, possibly the epidemic had exhausted itself.—DC.

Last made in N. Uist about 1829, in Arran about 1820, in Helmsdale about 1818, and in Reay about 1830—AC.

teine-ghealan, *s.* Phosphoric light emitted from putrid fish or decayed wood in the dark.
teineil,** *a.* Fiery, hot. 2 Ardent, passionate. Ro th. an strì, *very fierce in battle.*
teine-rabhaidh, *s.m.* Beacon.
teine-sgeitheach,‡‡ -eiche, *a.* Ignivomous.
teine-shruthach,‡‡ -aiche, *a.* Ignifluous.
teine-sionnachain, *s. m.* Ignis-fatuus. 2 Phosphorescence, luminous appearance on the sea, 3 Will-o'-the-wisp, Jack-o'-lantern. 4 The rainbow-like brightness seen in spindrift on a clear sunny day. 5‡‡Whirlwind.
teine-sithe,‡‡ *s.m.* Wild fire.
teine-thar, *s.m.* Cross-fire.
teine-thionnachain, see teine-sionnachain.
teinghidh, -ean, *s.m.* Meteor.
teinidh, -e, *a.* see teinntidh.
———, *dat.* of teine. 'Cur ri theinidh, *setting on fire—Arran, Mull, &c.*
teinidh-dé, see teine-dealan & dearbadan-dé.
teinis,** *s.f.* Gaelic form of *tennis.*
——— -chùirt,** *s.f.* Gaelic form of *tennis-court.*
teinn, -e, *a.* see tinn.
teinn, -e, *s.f.* Sickness. 2 Distress, misery, calamity, predicament, strait. 3 Perplexity, jeopardy. 4 Haste, hurry. 5** Trouble, difficulty, hardship. Nach e bha 'na th.! *what a predicament he was in!* an aimsir carraid agus teinne, *in time of strife and distress;* t. mo chridhe, *my heart's grief;* ghlaodh iad 'nan t., *they cried in their trouble.*
teinnbhealach,** *a.* Perverse, obstinate, contumacious.
teinn-chràdh, *s.m.* Agony.
teinndeachd,* *s.f.* see teinnteachd.
teinne, *s.f.* Tension, rigidity, severity. 2 see tinne.
———, *comp.* of teann.

teinnead, -eid, *s.f.* Degree of lightness.
teinnsineach,(MS) *a.* Hot.
teinnteach, -ich, *s.m.* Lightning. 2 see teanntachd.
———, *a.* Hot, fiery, fierce. 2**Inflammatory, combustible. 2**Impetuousness of temper. Mar àmhuinn theinntich, *like a fiery furnace.*
———d, *s. f.* Fieriness, fierceness. 2**Inflammatoriness, combustibleness. 3(MS) Astringency.
teinntean, -ein, *s.m.* Hearth, fire-place. 2** Forge. 3**Furnace. 4††Peats laid out on the moss to dry. 5(CR) Fire-back, a stone placed as a back to the fire on the hearth in the middle of the floor—*W. of Ross.* Leac an teinntein, *the hearth-flag.* [†† gives teintein as *nom.*]
teinnteanach,** *a.* Having a fireplace, forge or furnace. 2 Of, or belonging to a fireplace, forge, furnace or hearth.
teinnteanach, -aiche, *a.* Of, or belonging to, a fireplace or hearth. 2 Having a fireplace or hearth.
teinntein, see teinntean.
teinntidh, *a.* Fiery, hot. 2 Inflammatory. 3 Combustible. 4 Keen. 5 Hot-tempered, impetuous. Mar chaoiribh t. o 'n chladach, *like fiery gleams from the beach.*
———eachd, see teinnteachd.
teinntineach,(MS) *a.* Hot.
teinntreach, -ich, *s.f. & coll.* Flashes of lightning. 2 Sparks of fire.
teinntreach,** *a.* Fiery, combustible. 2 Hot-tempered.
tein'-oidhche, see tein'-athair.
tein'-thara, *s. m.* Will-o'-the-wisp—*Dàin Iain Ghobha.*
teintidh,(AF) *s.* Dragon.
†teir, *fut.* of *v.* abair, see their.
teirbeadh, see tearbadh.
teirbeirt,** *s.f.* Bestowing, distributing. 2 Sending forth. 3 Scattering—*W. of Ross.* 4 Increase, growth. Air th. teine nan neul, *when clouds send forth their lightning.*
teirbheartaich,* *v.a.* Harass, weary. 2 Distribute.—*Islay.*
———te, *past pt.* Wearied, fatigued.
teirbhein, see tairbhean.
teirbheirt, *pr.pt.* a' teirbheart, *v.a.* Harass, stir on, cause to move. Cha bhi coin 'gan teirbheart ann, *there shall be no dogs to stir them on—Dàin I. Ghobha.*
teirbheirt,‡‡ -e, -ean, *s.f.* Fatigue.
———each, *a.* Fatigued. 2 Causing fatigue.
teirbheirteachadh, -aidh, *s.m.* Fatiguing, act of fatiguing. A' t—, *pr.pt.* of teirbheartaich.
teirc, Cha teirc iad-san nach dearc air sin, *not few are they who will not gaze on that.*
teirc, *a.* see tearc.
teirce, *s.f.ind.* Fewness, rareness, scarceness. 2 Poverty.
teirce, *comp.* of tearc. Scarcer, scarcest.
teirceachd,* *s.f.* Fewness, rareness.
teirceas,** -eis, *s.m.* Fewness, scarceness.
†teirc-fheòlach, -aiche, *a.* Lean, meagre.
teircead, -eid, *s.m.* Degree of scarcity, rareness, fewness or poverty. A réir teircead nam bliadhna, *according to the fewness of the years* ; a' dol an t., *getting scarcer and scarcer.*
teireachduinn, *s.m.* Decaying, state of decaying or wasting. A' t—, *pr.pt.* of teirig.
teireadh,** -idh, *s.m.* Recommendation.
teiric,(AC) s. Hake, herring-hake, herring eke or eek, (triangular frame with spikes on which herrings are hung up to dry.
teiridneach, *a.* Medicinal, having the power to cure—*Sàr-Obair.* [eiridneach.]
teirig, *pr.pt.* a' teireachduinn, *v.a. & n.* Fail, be spent, be exhausted. 2 Wear out, spend, exhaust. 3 Go, repair to. Th. orm, *all mine is run out* ; 'nuair a theirigeas gual teirigidh obair, *when coals run out (smith-)work is at an end* ; th. iad, *they are done, consumed* ; t. ris, *fight him, try him* ; cha'n e am bòrd a th. dhuit, ach am beagan fearainn, *it was not the mould-board of the plough that would not work enough, but you had not enough land to plough* ; th. an sgeul, *the tale was finished*—an idiomatic way of finishing a tale ; t. a steach d' a h-ionnsuidh, *go in to her* ; t. mu'n cuairt, *go round about* ; theirigear air a ghlùinean aig bonn na crannaige, *he knelt at the foot of the pulpit;* na t. a mach 'san oidhche, *do not walk out at night* ; gus an t. an là, *till the day comes to an end.*
teirigidh, *fut.aff.a.* of teirig.
teirigsinn,(MS) *s.* End.
teirgte, *past pt.* of teirig.
teirinn, *pr.pt.* a' tèarnadh, *v.a.* Come or go down, descend. 2 Alight, dismount. 3(MS)Pitch.
teiris,** *v.a. & n.* Tame, quiet, as unruly cattle. 2 Stop. 3 Be at peace.
teiris ! *int.* see tairis ! [teiris ! in *Poolewe.*)
teirisd ! *ind.* see tairis !
teirisi ! ‡ see tairis !
teirm,* -ean, *s.f.* Thumb. 2**Term. 3 Condition. 4 Season, while. Air na teirmean sin, *on those terms* ; teirmean a' chùirt, *law-terms.*
teirmeasg, -isg, *s.m.* Mistake, mishap, misfortune. T. ort ! *a plague on thee !*
teirmeasg,** *v.* Disappoint.
———ach, -aiche, *a.* Unfortunate.
teirm-ghéill,** *s.* Capitulation.
teirm-strìochd,** *s.* Capitulation.
teirt,** *s.f.* Sunrise.
téis, -e, -ean, *s.f.* Musical air, air to which any song or poem is sung. 2 Sound. 3 Diligence. Bu ghrinn thu 'thogail na téise, *you were good at raising a strain.*
teisbeirt,** (suppt.) see teirbeirt.
teisdeas, see teisteas.
teismeid, -e, -ean, *s.f.* see tiomnadh. Dèan do th., *make your will.*
teis-meadhon, -ein, *s.m.* Exact middle.
———ach, -aiche, *a.* Central, centrical, 2 Of, or belonging to, a centre.
teisreadh,(AC) *s.m.* Protecting. T. taighe, *house protecting*—an invocation.
teist, -e, -ean, *s.f.* Testimony, proof. 2 Character, reputation, esteem, respectability. Nach leig a th. air chall, *who will not suffer his fame to be bandied with.*
†teist,** *s.m.* Witness. 2 Drop.
——eachadh,(MS) *s. m.* Approbation, attestation, recommendation.
——eadh,** -idh, *s.m.* Defection. 2 Falling off.
——ealachd, *s.f.* State of holding a good reputation. 2 Fame, reputation, esteem. 3 Authority. 4* Respectability.
——eanas, -ais, -an, *s.m.* Certificate, witness, report, attestation, testimonial, evidence, reputation, testimony.
——eas, -eis, *s.m.* Testimony. T. Dhé, *the testimony of God.*
teisteil, -e, *a.* Respectable, esteemed. 2 Reputable, unblemished. 3 Chaste, pure, having a good character. Gu t., *chastely.*
teistich,(MS) *v.a.* Attest.
teith, see teth.
†teith, *v.n.* see teich.
teithneas,** -ais, *s.m.* Haste.
———ach, *a.* Hasty, in haste.
teò, *pr.pt.* a' teòdhadh & a' teòsainn, *v.a.* Warm,

make warm. 2 Simmer. 3 Air. 4 Glow with delight or affection. Cha do th. mi riamh ri-the, *I never had any affection for her.*
teò-chridheach, -eiche, *a.* Warm-hearted, affectionate, compassionate.
———d, *s.f.* Affectionateness. 2 Kindness, clemency.
teòdh, *v.* see teò.
teòdhadh, -aidh, *s.m.* Warming, act of making warm. 2* Simmering. 3*Glowing with love, feeling affection for. 4 Chafing. A' t—, *pr. pt.* of teò.
teòdhaich, *v.a.* see teò.
teòdhaichte, *past pt. & a.* Warmed.
teòghadh, see teòdhadh.
teò-ghràdhach, -aiche, *a.* see teò-chridheach.
teòidh, *v.* see teò.
———te, *past pt.* of teò. Warmed. 2*Simmered.
teòigh,(MS) *v.a.* Bake.
teòilteach,** *a.* Warm-hearted.
teòiteachan,** *s.m.* Chafing-dish, warming-pan.
teoithe, *comp.* of teth, see teotha.
———ad, -id, *s.m.* Degree of heat, see teothad.
Teòiridh, s. Trinity.
†teol, *s.m.* Plenty. 2 Substance. 3 Thief.
teòltachd, *s.f.* Cowardice—*Sar-Obair.*
teòm,(AC) *s.* Dole. T. eigir, *a small dole*; t. éisg, *a dole of fish*; t. an t-sionnaich, *bribe of the fox*; cho toinnte ri t. an t-sionnaich, *as twisted as the fox's gift.*
teòm, *v.* see teum.
teòma, *a.* Skilful, expert, adept, active, dexterous. 2 Apt, ready, quick. 3 Correct, performing anything correctly. 4 Shrewd. 5**Clever. T. an cogadh, *expert in war.*
teòmach,** *a.* see teòma.
———d, *s.f.* Expertness, skilfulness, activity, dexterity or proficiency in anything. 2 Aptness, readiness. 3 Shrewdness. 4 Manhood. 5 Address. 6**Cleverness. An gaisge is an t., *in valour and in manhood.*
teòmadh, -aidh, -aidhean, see teumadh. 2(DC) *s.m.* Splice of a rope, stick, &c.
teòm-chridheach,** *a.* Tender-hearted, compassionate, affectionate.
———d,** *s.f.* Tender-heartedness, compassionateness. 2 Affectionateness.
teòr, -eòir, *s.m.* Mark, limit. 2 Sign, token. see tiur.
teòra,(MS) *a.* Coarse. 2 *s.m.* Bourn. 3(MMcL) Three. An Teòra Bheannaichte, *the Blessed Trinity*; t. pòg, *three kisses.*
teòradh,** *s.m.* Stint.
teoran,** *s.m.* Mark.
teorchan,** -ain, *s.m.* The space of three hours.
teoranta,** *a.* Definite.
teorr, see tiur.
teòsainn, *s.f.* & *pr.pt.* of teòdh, Same meanings as teòdhadh.
teoth, see teò.
teotha, *comp.* of teth. Hotter, hottest.
teòthachadh, see teòdhadh.
teòthachan, -ain, -an, *s.m.* Warming-pan, chafing-dish.
teothad, -aid. *s.m.* Degree of heat.
teòthadh, -aidh, see teòdhadh.
teòthaich, see teò.
———te, *past pt.* of teòthaich. Same meanings as teòidhte.
teothaid, *2nd. comp.* of teth.
teothair, *v.* see teadhraich.
———, *s.* see teadhair.
teoth-chridheach, see teò-chridheach.
†teth, *a.* Fine, smooth, soft.
teth, *a.* *1st. comp.* teotha [& teoithe,**] *2nd.* teothaid, *3rd.* teothad. Hot, warm, sultry. 2 Keen. 3 Scalding. 4* Impetuous, angry. 5* Rancid, insipid, tasteless. 6** *rarely* Smooth, fine. Gu tinn, t., *feverishly hot.*
teth-loisgeach,** *a.* Burning-hot, scalding-hot.
teuchd, *v.n.* Congeal, be congealed. 2 Be parched, as with drought or thirst. 3††Wither, dry up.
†teuchd,** -an, *s.m.* Feat, exploit, heroism. 2 (CR) *s.f.* Brag, boast—*W. of Ross.* Duine a dheanadh t., *a man who could perform an exploit*; tha e a' deanamh t., *he is bragging*; tha e a' deanamh t. dheth, *he makes out what he has done to be a feat.* see euchd.
———, *v.* see teachd.
———ach,** *a.* Supremely valiant, heroic.
———adh, -aidh, *s.m.* Congealing, act of being congealed. 2 State of being parched. 3†† Parching, withering. A' t—, *pr.pt.* of teuchd.
teud, *v.a.* Supply with strings, as an instrument of music.
teud, -a & -éid, *pl.* -an *s. m.* [*f.* in *Badenoch.*] String, cord, rope. 2 String of a musical instrument. 3‡‡Music in general. 4**Harp. 5 **Any stringed instrument. Feadh thorman gach teuda, *through the music of every string*; mairidh e 'm fonn nan teud, *he will live in the music of the harp*; clàrsach gun t., *a stringless harp*; inneal binn nan teudan deich, *a melodious ten-stringed instrument.* [††*s.f.*]
teudach, -aiche, *a.* Stringed. 2 Having many strings.
teudach, -aich, *s.f.* Strings of any musical instrument, especially of a harp. 2 Assortment of musical strings. 3 Quantity of strings.
teudag,‡‡ -aig, -an, *s. f. dim.* of teud. Little string, cord or rope. 2 Small withe.
———ach, -aiche, *a.* Strong.
teudaiche,** -an,‡*s.m.* Harper.
teudan, -ain, *s. m. dim.* of teud. Little musical string. 2 *n.pl.* of teud.
teud-aoire, -an-aoire, *s.m.* see taod-aoire.
teud-bhràghad,** s. Collar.
teud-cheòl, -chiùil, *s.m.* Music of a stringed instrument. Bu bhinne na t. a guth, *her voice was sweeter than harp-music.*
teud-chleas,** *s.m.* Feat in rope-dancing.
———achd,** *s.f.* Rope-dancing.
———aiche,** -an, *s.m.* Rope-dancer.
teud-ghàradh,(WC) *s.m.* Wire-fence.
teud-shiubhlaidh, -e, -ean, *s.m. & f.* Rope-dancer.
teugair, see teagair.
teug-bhoil, -e, -ean, *s.f.* see teugmhail.
———each, -eiche, *a.* see teugmhaileach.
teugmhail, -mhala, -ean, *s.f.* Battle, contest. 2 Disease. 3 Danger. 4 Agony. 5**Severe affliction. 6* Agonies of death. Is minig a thàinig eagal gu teugmhail, *fear often begets danger*; tùs na teugmhàla [teug-bhoil**], *the front of battle.*
teugmhaileach, -eiche, *a.* Warlike, keen for battle. 2 Of, or belonging to, a battle. 3 Very dangerous. 4 Causing disease. 5 Diseased. 6 In torment or agony. 7 Agonizing, causing agony, afflictive. 8**Contentious.
teugmhais, -e, -ean, *s.f.* Hap, accident.
teugradh,* -aidh, see teagradh.
†teul,** *s.m.* Subterranean passage.
†teum, *a.* see teoma.
teum, *pr.pt.* a' teumadh, *v.a.* Bite, wound, sting. 2 Snatch suddenly at anything. 3 Tempt, beguile, draw aside—*Argyll.* 4 Cut, taunt. Th. nathair mi, *a serpent bit me*, [in *Argyll*, it would signify *a serpent beguiled*, or *enticed me*, and lot nathair mi, *a serpent bit me.*] 5(CR) Join, unite, splice. 6 (CR) Repair by bights or loops, as in wire-fencing. [Nos. 5 & 6—

W. of Ross-shire.] 7 (DU) Hook a fish, as when fishing with a hand-line, by a sharp pull on the line. Th. e iasg, *he hooked a fish* ; teumadh do bhò, *your cow is bitten* or *stung* —MacLagan's *Evil Eye, 17.*

teum, -a, -an, *s.m.* [*s.f.* in *Badenoch.*] Sudden snatch at anything. 2 Temptation, whim, caprice—*Argyll.* 3* Bite, morsel, mouthful. 4 5**Taunt, sarcasm. 6 Fit. T. arain, *a morsel of bread.*

teumach,†† -aiche, *a.* Snatching. 2 Biting, prone to bite. 3 (CR) Attentive, careful, diligent, anxious to do well—*W. of Ross.*

teumadh, -aidh, *s. m.* Biting, act of biting, wounding or stinging. 2 Snatching, act of snatching at anything. 3* Tempting, beguiling. 4 Bite. A' t—, *pr.pt.* of teum.

teumaidh, *fut.aff.a.* of teum.

teum éisg, (CR) *s.m.* One fish. Tha teum éisg aige, *he has one fish* ; bha dà theum éisg aige, *he had two fish*—*W. of Ross.* [Not used of greater numbers.]

teumnach,* -aiche, *a.* Whimsical, capricious. 2 Enticing, inviting, tempting. 3 Tart. Cha'n 'eil ann ach duine t., *he is but a whimsical man* ; cha'n 'eil e 'na ni t., *it is not an enticing affair.*

———d,* *s.f.* Capriciousness. 2 Tempting nature or quality.

teurmnasg,* -aisg, *s.m.* Bandage on the thumbs and great toes of a dead person, to prevent his ghost hurting foes.

teumta, *past pt.* of teum. Bitten, wounded, stung. 2 Snatched suddenly.

teurnadh, see tèarnadh.

teurnaidh, *fut.aff.a.* of teirinn.

teuthachd,* *s.f.* Rancidness.

th, For words commencing with *th*, and not given below, see under *t*.

tha, *pres.ind.* of *irr. v.* bi. Am, art, is, are.

thabhair, see thoir.

thabhairt, (a) *inf.* of tabhair.

thaim, (for taim) *poetic form* of tha mi.

thàin, for thàinig—*Perths. & Skye.*

thàine, for thàinig —*Perths.*

thàineas, *past part.* of thig. Was come.

thàini, for thàinig—*Arran, Kintyre. &c.*

thàinig, *past ind.* of thig. Came.

thair, see thar.

thairis. *adv.* Over, across, abroad. 2* Beyond, exceeding the bounds. 3 Remaining, as a surplus. 4 Athwart, to the farther side. 5 At an end. Chaidh e thairis, *he went abroad* (left the kingdom) ; a' dol th., *going to another country*, or *over the channel, strait or ferry;* cupan a' cur th., *a cup running over;* chaidh e th. air sin, *he went beyond that;* or, *it is beyond that* ; th. air moran, *beyond many* ; thug e th., *he overfatigued himself* ; thoir th., *give over, be done with it* ; chuir iad th. i, *they capsized her* (the boat); cha mhisd iad (na sgeulachdan) mise a thoirt sgrìob th. orra, *they will be none the worse of my relating them* ; thug e th. e air seachd beanntan, *he took him over seven hills*—*W.H., 1.39.* ; cha do chuir a ghualainn nach do chuir tuar thairis, *none did his best but turned (the obstacle) clean over* ; gach ni a bhios th., *everything that remains;* chaidh mi th. orra, *I went beyond*, or *excelled them.*

thairte, *prep.pron.* (thar+i) Over or beyond her or it. An abhainn a' cur th., *the river overflowing.*

thall,** *a.* Adjacent.

thall. *adv.* On the other side, yonder, beyond. 2 Abroad. 3*Over against. Thall 's a bhos, *hither and thither, here and there, on all sides;* am bail' ud thall, *yonder town.*

thall. *prep.* Beyond.

thalla, *v.def.* Come (thou) along. Th. leamsa, *come along with me.* [Used only in the *2nd.p. sing. & pl.* (thallaibh) *imp.*]

thallaid, (thall+ud) *adv.* Yon, yonder, see thall.

thallaibh, *v.def.* Come (ye) along.

thalla ! thalla !* *int.* Well ! well ! ay ! ay !

th' ann, (tha ann) That is, is in that place, exists. Cia meud a th' ann ? *how many are there ?* ciod a th' ann ? *what is it ? what is in that place ?* guth Dheirg is e 'th' ann, *it is the voice of Dargo.*

thanua, *Jura* for chunnaic.

thaobh, (a) *prep.* Concerning, touching. 2 By reason of, on account of, as for. 3 Aside. 4 Astray. A th. tuairmeis, *at a venture* ; dol a th., *going aside* or *astray, apostatizing.*

thar, *prep.* Over, across. 2* More than. 3 Beyond. Thus combined with the personal pronouns—tharum, over me ; tharad, over thee ; thairis air, over him ; thairis oirre, (**thairte,) over her ; tharainn, over us ; tharaibh, over you; tharta, over them. Deich thar fhichead, *thirty* (*lit.* ten beyond a score ; chuir thu th. a chéil' iad, *you set them by the ears* ; th. na còrach, *beyond what is proper* ; reubadh an luingeas th. (for bhàrr) an acraichean, *the fleet was torn from its anchors* ; tha 'n teagasg th. cheann chum math an t-sluaigh, *the teaching taken altogether is for the people's good* ; tharcheann, *average.* In *Arran*, tha 'n t-àm againn falbh thar a chéile, means, it is time for us both (or all) to go.

thàr, *Suth'd prov.* form of tàir. Get, obtain, come. After *conj.* nach, fhar & fhàr.

thar a chéile, At variance. 2 In disorder, in confusion. 3 Stirred about, agitated. 4**Deranged, crazed. Ri 'n gabhail thar-a-chéile, *to be taken together* ; cuir thar-a-chéile, *disarrange, confuse, drive mad.*

thar-a-chòir, Superfluous, too much.

tharad, *prep.pron.* (thar+thu) Over thee, across thee, beyond thee.

thàradh, see thàr.

tharaibh, *prep. pron.* (thar+sibh) Across you, over you.

tharainn, *prep.pron.* (thar+sinn) Across us, over us.

tharam, *prep. pron.* (thar+mi) Across me, over me, beyond me. Chaidh i th., *she capsized over me* ; seachd gealaich chaidh th., *I passed seven months* (*lit.* seven moons went over me.)

thàras, see thàr.

thàrladh, *past* of *def. v.* thàrlaidh. It happened, had happened, might happen, might have happened.

thàrlas, *fut.* of *def. v.* thàrlaidh. May happen, Shall happen, shall have happened, or met. [Used only in the *past & future.*]

thar leam, see ar leam.

thar leis, for ar leis, Thar leis gun do ghabh an gruagach boch, *he thought the wizard was delighted*—W.H.1.13.

tharta, *prep.pron.* (thar+iad) Across them, over them, beyond them. Chaidh am bàta th., *the boat capsized over them* ; cuir th. e, *put it over them.*

tharuibh, see tharaibh.

tharuinn, see tharainn.

theab, *def.v.* Miss. Th. mi tuiteam, *I missed falling.* The only parts used are—Theab mi, I had almost, (impersonally) theabadh, theabas ; INTERR. an do theab mi ? had I almost ? (impersonally) an do theabadh ? theabas ? ; NEGATIVE, cha do theab mi, I had not almost, (impersonally, cha do theabadh

theabas.) These forms are used in all the persons. Th. thu mo mharbhadh, *you had almost killed me*; chaidh "theab" le creig 's theab nach deachaidh, 's bhàthadh "shaoil leam" ged nach do shaoil cuid e, ach na'm biodh "b' fhearr leam" beò cha bhiodh ceann air coluinn, "*almost*" *fell over a rock, but it almost didn't*, "*I thought*" *was drowned though some thought not, but if* "*I had rather*" *were still alive no one else could then survive*; theab iad, *they had almost.*

theabadh, see theab.

theag, see theagamh.

theagamh, *adv.* Perhaps. mayhap. Th. gu'm bheil, *perhaps, perhaps it is so.*

théid, *fut.aff.a.* of rach. Will go. Th. mis' an urras gur e do bheatha, *I will warrant you that you are welcome*—W. H. 1.39.

theidheadh, *Suth'd.* form of *past subj.* of rach. An taigh gus an téidheadh tu, *the house to which you would go.* [*Lewis* also—MM.]

their, *fut.aff.a.* of abair. Will say. Th. cuid, *some will say*; their thu, *thou wilt say.* Th. leam, see ar leam.

theireadh, *2nd. & 3rd. pers. sing. & pl.* of abair. Would say. A dh' aindeoin cò theireadh e! *in spite of whoever would say it*; a dh' aindeoin na th. e, *in spite of what he would say.*

theiream, (for their mi) I will say, see abair.

theireamaid, *1st. per.pl. past subj.* of abair. We would say.

theirear, *fut.subj. pass.* of abair. Ma th. e, *if it be said.*

theirig, another form of rach, which see. Go.

———, *asp. form* of teirig.

theirinn. *1st.per.sing.past.subj.* of abair.

theirteadh, *past subj.pass.* of abair. Would be said. (Rinn e obair a bhitheas 'na carragh-cuimhneachain air,) an uair nach bi iomradh air feadhainn a bu luaithe theirteadh na e, *when those more likely to do it are not to be heard of.*

thibh, *Arran* for chì.

thibhear, *Arran* for chìthear.

thibhinn, *Arran* for chìthinn.

thig, *irr. v.* Come. 2 (with *prep.* do) Become, suit, fit, befit. 3 (with *prep.* ris) Agree with, please, be acceptable to. 4 (with *preps.* o, *or* de) Recover, escape, get the better of. 5 (with *prep.* air) Speak of, reflect upon, speculate about. 6 (with *prep.* eadar) Disagree, quarrel.

Conjugated thus:—

ACTIVE VOICE.

IND. *past*, thàinig mi, &c., *I, &c. came.*

,, *fut.* thig mi, &c., *I, &c., shall come.*

INTERROG. & NEG. *past.* (an ? nach ? cha) d' thàinig mi, &c., *did I &c., (not) come ? I, &c. did not come.*

,, *fut.* (an ? nach ? cha) tig mi, &c. *shall I, &c. (not) come ? I, &c. shall not come.*

SUBJ. *past*, (ged) thiginn, (*though*) *I would come.* (ged) thigeadh tu, e, i, sibh, iad, (*though*) *thou wouldst, he, she, you, they would come.* (ged) thigeamaid, (*though*) *we would come.*

,, *fut.* (ma) thig mi, &c, (*if*) *I, &c. shall come.*

IMP. *1st.pers.sing.* thigeam, *let me come.*

,, *2nd.* ,, ,, thig, *come thou.*

INFIN. a thighinn, *to come.*

PRES. PT. a' tighinn, *coming.*

PASSIVE VOICE— None.

Thig thusa leamsa, *you come with me*; thig sinn leibh, *we will come with you*; cha tig sinn leibh, *we will not come with you*; cha d' thàinig iad, *they did not come*; is math a thig an cota dhuit, *the coat becomes you well*; ciamar tha e 'tighinn dhomh ? *how does it become me?* ciamar a thig sin riut-sa ? *how will that please you?* cha tig sin gu math ris, *that will not please him well*; thig e uaith, *he will recover*; thig iad ort gu farsuing, fial, *they shall speak of you far and wide, everywhere and liberally*; bithidh iad a' tighinn oirnn, *they will speak of us, our conduct will be a matter of reflection*; thig air, *talk about it*; b' ann air gaol bha i 'tighinn, *it was love she was speaking of*—*R.14. 17*; cha'n 'eil stàth tighinn air sin, *there is no use in speaking of that*; thàinig againn air labhairt uime, *we chanced to speak about him*: thàinig iad am briathran seanachais air a' chéile, *they spoke concerning old times to each other* (*lit.* they came into the words of old-time talk on each other); dé tha tighinn ris ? *what ails him?* dé thigeadh r' a nàdur, *what would suit his nature ?*—*W.H.1. 12.*; thàinig eadar iad, *they have quarrelled*; thàinig orm falbh, *I was obliged to go*; cha tig snàth do mhnà-sa ri snàth mo mhnà-sa, *your wife's spinning will not compare with my wife's*; cha tigear o 'n ghàbhadh thric, *one would not come safely out of frequent danger*; thig orm, *I must*; thig ort, *you must. &c.*; thig orm falbh, *I must go.*

In *Arran*, thig means *go*, not *come*. Thalla a steach, (*pl.* thallaibh a steach) *come in*; thig a steach, *go in*; thig air falbh, *go away*; thig a dh' Irt, *go to St. Kilda*—the equivalent of "go to Jericho."

thig. *fut.aff.a.* of thig. Shall or will come.

thigeadh, *past subj.* of thig (except 1st. pers. sing. & pl.) Th. e n'am faodadh e, *he would come if allowed*; th dhuit a dheanamh, *you ought to do it*—it would become you to do it.

———, *3rd. sing. & pl. imp.* of thig. Let.... come.

thigeam, *1st. sing.imp.* of thig. Let me come.

thigeamaid, *1st.p.pl.past subj.* of thig. We would come.

thiginn, *1st. p. sing. past subj.* of thig. I would come.

thimchioll, see timchioll.

thirim,** for tioram.

thirr ! } *int.* Cry to incite a dog when it is
thirr thad ! } driving away cattle.

thisd ! *int.* Hush !

thoir, *irr. v.* Give, grant, deliver, bestow on. 2 Take. 3 (with prep. *air*) Persuade, compel. 4 (with prep. *as*) Take away. 5 (with prep. *air* and noun intervening governed by the verb) Betake thyself to.

Active Voice—

IND. *past*, thug mi, &c., *I, &c. gave.*

,, *fut.* bheir mi, &c., *I, &c. shall give.*

INTERR. & NEG. *past.* (an ? nach ? cha) d' thug mi, &c., *did I &c. (not) give ? I did not give.*

,, *fut.* (an ? nach ? cha) tabhair *or* toir mi, &c., *shall I, &c. (not) give ? I, &c. shall not give.*

SUBJ. *past*, (ged) bheirinn, *though I would give*; (ged) bheireadh tu, e, i, sibh, iad, (*though*) *thou wouldst, he, she, you, they, would give*; (ged) bheireamaid, (*though*) *we would give.*

,, *fut.* (ma) bheir mi, &c., (*if*) *I, &c. shall give.*

IMPER. *1st.per.sing.* thugam, *let me give.*

,, *2nd.* ,, thoir *or* thabhair, *give thou.*

INFIN. a thabhairt, a thoirt, *to give.*

PRES. PART. a' tabhairt, a' toirt, *giving.*

Passive Voice—

IND. *past* thugadh mi, &c., *I, &c. was given.*

,, *fut.* bheirear mi, &c., *I &c. shall be given.*

INTERR. & NEG. *past*, (an ? nach ? cha) d' thugadh mi, &c., *was I, &c. (not) given ? I,*

was (not) given.
,, *fut.* (an ? nach ? cha) toirear mi, &c. *shall I, &c (not) be given ? I, &c. shall not be given.*
SUBJ. *past*, (ged) bheirteadh mi, &c., (*though*) *I, &c. should be given.*
,, *fut.* (ma) bheirear mi, &c., (*if*) *I, &c. should be given.*
PAST PART. tugta, *given.*

This verb has two other forms for the past subjunctive, which are used after interrogative and negative particles. They are, (an ? nach ?) toirinn, *would I (not) give;* cha toirinn, *I would not give;* and (na'n) tugainn, (*if*) *I would give.* These two forms are conjugated as bheirinn, in the various persons —(*sing.* 1st. -inn, 2nd. -eadh, 3rd. -eadh ; *pl.* 1st. -eamaid, 2nd. -eadh, 3rd. -eadh.)

The past subj. passive, bheirteadh, is impersonal, and requires a prepositional pronoun after it to distinguish it from the same tense of *beir*. Bheirteadh mi, *I was born;* bheirteadh dhomh, (*it*) *was given to me.* The passive voice has parallel impersonal forms, as an toirteadh, *would (it) be given*, and an tugtadh, ma theirteadh, *if it would be said*, but, na'n abairteadh ; o 'n chiteadh, *since it would be seen ;* but, nach faicteadh, *would it not be seen ;* ged gheibhteadh, *though it should be got ;* but, mur faighteadh e, *if it should not be got.*

The word *thabhair* may be substituted for *thoir* in the following, or any similar sentences.

Thabhair (*or* thoir) air falbh, *take away, carry off;* thabhair (*or* thoir) leat e, *carry it with you;* tabhair a mach, *win ;* thugadh a mach a' cheud duais leis, *he won the first prize ;* bheir iad a mach nithean àrda, *they will do (win) great things ;* thug mi { siorradh / sgiutadh / saighde } asam, *I made a dart* (or *bound*) ; thug e mo char agus mo leth-char asam, *he cheated me all round ;* th. seo d' a ionnsuidh, *take this to him ;* th. d' an ionnsuidh, *take to them ;* thugaibh am monadh oirbh, *betake yourselves to the mountain.*

th. a bhos, reach, fetch me here.
th. aichmheil, avenge.
th. air, compel, force, persuade (him.)
th. air ais, withdraw.
th. aire, attend, observe.
th. air falbh, take away.
th. a mach, take out ; descry, spy.
th. an aghaidh, advance.
th. an aire, take care, beware.
th, an dorus ort, go to the door.
th. an geall, bet, pawn, pledge, mortgage.
th. as, take away, flee, escape.
th. as a chéile, disjoin, tear asunder.
th. as e, swig it off, gulp it up ; take it out of it.
th. as thu-féin, flee, deliver thyself.
th. a staigh, bring in ; tame ; cultivate as new ground.
th. a staigh ort, get in with you, get into the house.
th. breith, judge, decide ; give the sense.
th. bhuaidh, bring from, deprive(him) of it.
th. buidheachas, give thanks.
th. car as, cheat him.
th. ceum, step, make a step.
th. comas (do), enable, give, afford an opportunity.
th. comhairle (do), advise.
th. cuideachd, bring together.
th. dhomh, give me ; bring.
th. do chasan leat, take yourself off ; clear out !—*W. of Ross-shire.*
th. do leabaidh ort, go to bed.
th. dùbhlan, challenge.
th. duibh-leum, bound.
th. éighe, cry.
th. éisdeachd, listen.
th. fainear, attend, consider.
th. feum as, use it, apply it to use.
th. fianuis, witness.
th. fios (do), acquaint, inform ; warn ; invite.
th. fo ghéill, subdue.
th. freagradh (do), answer.
th. géill, yield, submit, obey, surrender, admit, concede. Na toir géill dha, pay no attention to anything he says.
th. gu buil, bring to a successful termination.
th. ionnsuidh (air), attempt, make an attempt (to do it) ; make an attack (on him.)
th. leat, carry, carry away, bring or take.
th. leum, jump.
th. luadh (air), (*or* dèan luadh), mention, make mention.
th. luigheachd (do), pardon.
th. mathanas (do), pardon, forgive.
th. mionnan, swear.
th. muidhe, churn, make butter—*W. of Ross.*
th. na buinn as, take to your heels.
th. na buinn asad, take to your heels.
th. na casan asad, take to your heels.
th. oidhirp, attempt, make an attack.
th. orm, prevail with me.
th. orra, compel them.
th. saighde asad, make a dart or dash at anything.
th. seachad, relinquish, deliver, give up.
th. sgal, scream, shriek.
th. sgoil (do), educate.
th. sgiutadh, dart, bolt.
th. sgread, scream, shriek.
th. siorradh, dart, bolt.
th. sìos, lower, take down.
th. smachd, chastise, rebuke.
th. suas (e), yield, cede, surrender, abdicate, give up, resign (it.)
th. tàmailt (do), offend, insult.
th. thairis (do), cease, give over ; give over from fatigue ; resign, abdicate, surrender.
th. thairis e, bring him over; overfatigue him. Thug e thairis, he knocked himself up.
th. thu-féin as ! begone !
th. tuairmeas, guess.
th. urram, pay respect, reverence.

thoir as ! *int.* Begone !

thonnai, *Knapdale* for chunnaic.

thu, *pers.pron. 2nd. pers. sing.* Thou. 2**Thee. *Emphatic*, thusa, *thyself ;* thu-féin, *thine own self.*

Tu, when nominative to a verb is always aspirated (thu), except with *is*, and in the future indicative, and the two tenses of the subjunctive active. The unaspirated form is never used with the passive forms of the verb. The accusative form is always *thu.* A tendency to use *tu* instead of *thu* after verbs ending in s must be carefully guarded against. 'S e chrùnas tu le coron gràidh, given in some editions of the Scriptures (some are correct) as the equivalent of *it is he who will crown thee*, in Ps. ciii, really means " it is he whom thou wilt crown." In the same manner *tu* is erroneously used in, an Tighearn a slànuichthu, ma ta e ann a fhreagaireas thu, co a bhrathas thu ? &c. " Thusa " ach sibh-se dar bhios sibh ann 'ur taigh féin, "*thou,*" *but* "*you*" *when you have a house of your own—*

example of the peculiar idiomatic use of *thu* and *sibh—Badenoch.*
thubhairt, *past ind.* of abair. Said.
thuca, see chuca.
thud ! thud ! *int.* Expression of disparagement or contempt.
thug, *past ind.* of tabhair. Gave. 2‡Brought. Th. e dhomh e, *he gave it to me;* thug e 'm monadh air, *he went to the hill—W.H. 1. 42* ; thug mac an rìgh an rathad air, *the prince took to the road—W.H.1.40* ; thug Iain a sheòmar féin air *John went to his own room;* a mach th. am, molt, *off went the wether* ; thug e amhadh air a cheann, *he turned his head—W.H.1, 15* ; cò thug coinneamh dha ? *who met him ?—W.H.1, 39* ; thug mac an rìgh a chùl air an oganach, *the prince turned his back on the youth* ; ciod a thug ort a' chlach a chuir mar sin ? *what induced you to put the stone like that ?*
thugad, *prep.pron.* see chugad.
——— ! *int.* Out of the way ! Often said to those whom we wish to warn of immediate personal danger (*lit.* let to yourself, look to yourself.)
thugaibh, *2nd.pers.pl.imp.* of tabhair. Give ye. see chugaibh.
——— ! *int.* Leave (ye) that !
thugainn, see chugainn.
thugam, *1st. per. sing. imp.* of tabhair. Let me give.
thugar, used impersonally. Was brought.
thugam, see chugam.
thugas, for thugadh.
thugtar, *imp. pass.* of thoir.
thuige, see chuige. Thàinig i th., *she came to (as a ship)* ; *improved (as anything else.)*
thuigeadh, *3rd.p.sing. & pl. imp.* of tuig.
thuiginn, *1st. p. sing. past subj.* of tuig.
thuillead,** *a.* Accessory.
thuilleadh, see tuilleadh.
thuirleas, *past subj.* of tuirl. Tra th. m' anam an ceò, *when my spirit shall descend in mist.*
thuirle thàirle,(MS) *s.* Chaos, hurly burly.
thuirt, for thubhairt, see abair.
thuirteadh, *past ind. a.* of abair. Th. e, *it was said.*
thuiteadh, *past subj.* of tuit.
thuiteas, *fut.subj.* of tuit.
thun, see chun.
thunn, *Suth'd* for chunnaic.
thunna, *Arran* for chunnaic.
thunnai, *Arran* for chunnaic.
thunnaic, *Suth'd* for chunnaic.
thun sin, see chun sin.
thus', thusa, *emphat. form* of thu.
thusan, *Suth'd* form of thusa.
thut ! *int.* Expression of impatience.
tì, *s.m.ind.* Any rational being. 2 He, him. 3 She, her. An Tì a's àirde, *the supreme Being;* oir mar seo deir an Tì àrd agus uasal, *for thus saith the high and lofty One.*
tì, *s.m.ind.* Design, intention, purpose. 2 Pursuit. Tha e air tì mis' a mharbhadh, *he is bent on my destruction* ; tha e air tì cur as domh, *he is determined to finish my days* ; bha a thì air mis' a sgrios, *his determination was to ruin me* ; fear-tì, *a pursuer.*
tiachag,** *s.f.* Purse, small bag.
tiachair, -e, *a.* Perverse, ill-disposed. 2 Sickly, 3 Weary under a burden.
———, -ean, *s.m.* Ill-disposed person. 2 Insignificant person. 3‡‡Dwarf. [siachair(e)]
———eachd, *s.f.* Perversity. 2 Sickness, weariness. 3 Insignificant appearance.
tiachd, see teachd, *s.*
tiachdaidh,** *s. m.* Customer. 2 Haunter, resorter. 3 Guest.
tiachdaidh,(DU) *a.* Dried up, tough and dry. 2 (DMK) Glutinous, viscous. Sraibh-dhriucain dhonna th.,—*Allt an t-siùcair.*
tiadhan, -ain, *pl.* -an & -ain, *s. m.* Little hill. mound. 2 Small stone. 3**Testicle. 4**Otter.
———ach, -aiche, *a.* Abounding in little hills, mounds or 2 in small stones.
tiadhlann,** *s.* Fence.
tiag,** *s.m.* Wallet. 2 Vessel.
tiagh,(AF) *s.* Thickened milk. 2 Milk-dish.
tiaghas,** -ais, *s.m.* Mansion.
†tiamh, -a, *s.m.* Darkness.
tiamhachd, *s.f.* see tiamhaidheachd.
tiamhaidh, -e, *a.* Melancholy, affecting, dismal, gloomy. 2 Solitary, dark, quiet. 3 Sounding with a melancholy noise, sonorous. 4** Dead, death-like. 5 Wearisome, lonesome. 6 **Heart-melting, as music. Nach t. tosd an oidhche ! *how gloomy and quiet the night is!* cho t. ri gàir a' Chuain-a-Siar, *as plaintive as the sound of the Western Ocean* ; àite t., *a dreary place* ; port t., *a heart-melting strain* or *tune.*
———eachd, *s.f.* Melancholy, gloom. gloominess. 2 Solitariness, state of desertion. 3 Dismal or melancholy sound, sonorousness. 4 Dismalness. 5 Patheticalness. 6 Weariness. 7††Plaintiveness.
tianail,(AH) *s.m.* Wink of sleep, "forty winks" nap, snooze, siesta. 2 Swoon, coma, dream. Rinn mi t. cadail, *I dozed for a few moments* ; chaidh e an t., *he fainted.*
tiaraineach, *s.f.* Gimmer, see under caora, p.165.
tiarmail, -e, *a.* Prudent, sagacious, careful. 2 Thoughtful, sedate. Gu t., *sagaciously.*
tiarmalachd, *s.f.* Prudence, sagacity, carefulness. 2 Sedateness, thoughtfulness.
tiarmann, see tèarmann.
†tiarna, -n, *s.m.* see tighearn.
tiarpan, see tiadhan.
tiarrach,** -aich, *s.m.* Paunch. 2 Tripe.
tiarrail, -e, see tiorrail.
tiarralachd, see tiorralachd.
tias, -ais, *s.m.* Rheum. †2**Tide.
tiasgadal,** -ail, *s.m.* Industry. 2 Contrivance.
tiathaidh, *a.* Glutinous.
tibearsan,** -ain, *s.m.* Springing, sprouting. 2 Overflowing.
tibearsan,** -ain, *s.m.* Still.
tibeart, tibirt, *s.m.* Fountain. Tibirt na doimhne, *the fountains of the deep* ; gruagach na tibirt, *the lady of the fountain.*
tibhe,** *s.f.* Gibe.
tibhe,* see tighe.
tibheach,** -ich, *s.m.* Giber.
tibhead, see tighead.
tibheadh,** -idh, *s.m.* Laughter. 2 Joking. 3 Shunning, 4 Quickness.
tibhearsan,** see tibearsan.
tibh-fhiacal,** -ail, *s.m.* Fore-tooth.
tibirt, *s.m.* Well—*Dàin I. Ghobha.*
tibhre,** *s.m.* Fool. 2 One who laughs or giggles much.
tibhreach,** *a.* Foolish. 2 Giggling.
tibhreadh,** -idh, *s.m.* Springing, flowing.
tìd, for sìd.
tìde, *s.m.* Time. 2 Tide.
tididh, see stìdean.
tig, *fut.neg. & interr.* of thig. Cha tig e, *he will not come.*
tig, *Suth'd & Easter Ross* form of thig. Tig nuas, *come down* ; tig as an rathad, *come out of the way.*
tigear, -eir, *s.m.* see tiogair.
tigh, -e, -ean, *s.m.* see taigh.
tighe, *gen.sing.* of tigh.
tighe,* *comp.* of tiugh. Thicker, thickest.

tigheach, -eiche, see titheach. 2 see taigheach.
tigheachd, *s.f.* Thickness, fatness. 2 Coming, arriving, arrival, approach. C' àit' a' bheil e 'tigheachd as ? *where is he coming from ?—Arran, &c.*
tighead, -eid, *s.m.* Degree of thickness, fatness or solidity.
tigheadas, -ais, see taigheadas.
tigheadasach, see taigheadasach.
tighealt,* see taoghail.
tighean,** -ein, *s.m.* Bag, satchel.
———, *n.pl.* of tigh.
tighearn, (*or* -a,) -an, *s.m.* Lord, chief ruler. 2 Baronet. 3 Master, superior title of respect. 4 Proprietor of an estate. **Name given to any proprietor, however insignificant. An Tighearna, *the Lord.*
-———achd,** *s.f.* Lordship.
-———ail, -e, *a.* Lordly. 2 **Haughty, domineering.
-———alachd, *s.f.ind.* Lordliness.
-———as, -ais, *s.m.* Lordship, estate, sway, superiority, mastery, dominion, supremacy, power, jurisdiction, proprietorship, rule. Deagh th., *good rule ;* droch th., *misrule ;* cha 'n 'eil t. aig bàs oirbh, *death has no dominion over you.*
tigheas, see taigheadas.
tigheasach, see taigheasach.
tighich,* *s.f.* State of being subject to callers.
tighich.(MS) *v.n.* Clotter.
tighil,* see taoghail.
tighinn, *s.m.* Coming, act of coming, arrival. 2 Approaching. 3 Speaking. 4 Slandering, backbiting, speculating on the faults of others. A' t—, *pr.pt.* of thig.
tighinn a steach,** *s.m.* Coming in, entrance. 2 Income, revenue.
tighinn fodha, *s.m.* Water rising in the floor of a house, see teachd fodha.
tighinn thilgte,(WC)*s.m.*Water coming through the walls of a house.
tileadh,** -idh, *s.m.* Ship's poop.
tilg, *pr. pt.* a' tilgeil & a' tilgeadh, *v. a.* Cast, throw. 2 Shed, let fall, moult. 3 Shoot, fire, as a gun. 4 Vomit—*Perthsh. &c.* 5 Fling, throw off. 6* Reproach, cast up to. 7** Produce, yield, bring forth. 8 Cast as molten metal. 9*Shoot with an elf-shot. Th. e, *he vomited;* th. an t-each mi, *the horse threw me off;* tilg t' aran, *cast thy bread ;* thilg i searrach, *she cast a foal ;* th. e a dheoch, *he vomited his drink ;* th. e orm e, *he cast it up to me ;* thilg e an duine, *he shot the man ;* duine tilgte,*a man shot by the fairies*—one who does not care what he does ; gach craobh a thilgeas meas, *every tree that yields fruit.*
tilgeachan,‡‡ -ain, -an, *s.m.* Jibe, sneer.
tilgeadh, -idh, *s.m.* Casting, act of casting or throwing. 2 Act of shedding, casting or moulting. 3 Shooting, act of shooting or firing. 4 Vomiting, act of vomiting. 5 Flinging, act of flinging or throwing off. 6 Casting, as molten metal. 7* Reproaching, reproach. A' t—, *pr.pt.* of tilg.
tilgear,** *fut.pass.* of tilg.
tilgeil, *s.f.& pr.pt.*of tilg.Same meanings as tilgeadh.
tilgte, *a.* & *past pt.* of tilg. Thrown, cast. 2 Shot. 3 Mad. 4 Artificial—*W. of Ross.* Tha ceann t. air a' bhat, *the stick has an artificial head ;* talamh t., *soil removed from one place to another,* as for a garden ; tobhta-t., *movable thwart* or *seat in a boat ;* t. air an t-slighe,*cast upon the highway.*
tilig, see tilg.
tilip, see tiolp.
till, Same meanings as pill.
tilleach,(MS) *a.* Coercive.
tilleadh, see pilleadh. 2 (MS) Bridle.
tilleag, -eig, -an, *s.f.* Bee—*Suth'd.*
tillidh, see pillidh.
tim, -e, *pl.* -ean -eanuan & *tiomana, *s.f.* Time, season. 2 Tense in *grammar.* Am bliadhna thim (an ceann bliadhna), *in a year's time ;* t. an earraich, *the spring season ;* is t. teicheadh, *it is time to be off.*
tim-buail,** *s.f.* Cymbal.
timchioll, *v.a.* Surround, encompass.
-———, -ill, -an, *s.m.* Circuit, compass, circumference. 2‡‡Plank, one row of planks in boat- or ship-building.
-———, *prep. & adv.* About, around. 2 Of, concerning. 3**In a circuit. Mu th., *about, concerning ;* mu 'm th., *about me ;* mu th. tri, *about three ;* mu 'n t., *about them ;* t. fichead, *about twenty ;* chaidh e t., *he went round;* chaidh e t. orra, *he surrounded them ;* a' cheud th. a rinn iad, *the first circuit they made.*
-———ach, -aiche, *a.* Circuitous, encompassing. 2* Circular. 3 ‡‡Built in rows.
-———achadh,(MS) *s.m.* Turn.
-———achd,(MS) *s.m.* Ambit.
-———adh,** -aidh, *s.m.* Circuitousness, circularity. 2 Tending towards circularity. 3 Surrounding.
-———aich, *v.a.* Surround, environ, encompass, enclose.
-———aichte, *past pt.* of timchiollaich. Surrounded, encompassed,environed, gone round.
timchioll-ghearr, *v.a.* Circumcise.
timchioll-ghearradh, -aidh, *s. m.* Circumcising, act of circumcising, circumcision, cutting round. A' t—, *pr. pt.* of timchioll-ghearr.
-———ta, *past pt.* of timchioll-ghearr. Circumcised.
timchioll-sgriobh,** *v.a.* Write around.
timchiollta, *a.* & *past pt.* Surrounded.
†time, *s.f.ind.* Fear, timorousness. 2 Heat Pride, dignity.
†timeach, *a.* Timid. 2 Hot. 3 Proud.
timealachd, *s.f.ind.* Timeliness, timeousness, time.
timeil, -e, *a.* Timely. 2 see tiomail.
timheal,**‡-eil,*s.m.* Darkness. 2 Glimmering or shady light.
-———ach,** *a.* Dark, glimmering. 2 Gloomy.
timpire,(AH) *s.m.* Messenger, courier. 2 Factotum.
timpireachd,(MS) *s.f.* Tuel.
tin, see teine §.
tineach,** -ich, *s.m.* Kindred.
tingeal,(MMcL) *v.* Till, plough. Treabh is t., *plough and re-plough.*
tingealach,** -ich, *s.m.* House-leek.
tinn, -e, *a.* Sick, unwell. 2 Aching. 3 Causing sickness. Feuch, tha t' athair tinn, *behold thy father is sick ;* gu t. teth, *sick and feverish ;* bha fonn an òrain tiamhaidh t., *the strain of their song was plaintive and sad ;* tha coslas t. air an là, *the day looks sickly—Arran.*
tinne, -an & -achan, *s.f* Chain. 2 Link of a chain. 2 Piece of a column. †4‖Disease.
tinne,** *s.f.* Tightness, rigidness. 2 Severity.
———, *comp.* of teann. Tighter, tightest.
†tinne, *s.* The letter T, see teine.
tinneachan, *pl.* of teinne.
tinnead,‡‡‡-id, *s.m.* Degree of sickliness.
tinneanach,** *a.* Liable or subject to fits.
tinneanas, *s.pl.* Fits.
tinneas, -eis, -an, *s.m.* Sickness, disease.
-———ach, -eiche, *a.* Sickly, evil, distempered, frail.

tinneas-airgiod, (an), *s.m* Silver quinsy
t.-a-muigh,(an), epilepsy—JGC W. 97.
t.-an-righ, scrofula (king's evil.)
t.-bràghaid, (an), heartburn (also an losgadh-bràghaid.)
t.-buidhe, (an), jaundice.
t.-builg, (an), hysterics.
t.-busach,‖ (an), mumps.
t.-caitheimh,** (an), consumption.
t.-caithte, (an), consumption—*Arran*.
t.-cléibh, (an), consumption.
t.-cloinne, (an), parturition. 2**Distempers of children.
t.-cridhe, (an) heart-disease.
t.-critheanach, (an), ague.
t.-cuim, (an), hysterics.
t.-cuirp, (an), constipation.
t.-fairge, (an), sea-sickness.
t.-fallsa, playing the truant.
t.-feachd, (an), sickness on the day of battle —i.e. cowardice.
t.-fuail, (an), gravel, stranguary.
t. gabhaltach, a contagious disease.
t.-goile, (an), stomach-disease.
t.-gruthain, (an), liver-complaint.
t.-maothain, (an), chest-complaint.
t.-mara, (an), sea-sickness.
t.-mnathan, (an), hysterics.
t.-mór, (an), epilepsy, morbus major.
t.-na-gealaich, lunacy. 2‡‡Eclipse.
t.-na-h-urchaid, French-pox.
t.-nan-àirnean, kidney-disease.
t.-nan-alt, gout, arthrites.
t.-nan-Domhnullach, a kind of pulmonary affection called *glacach*. It is said that the family of the Lords of the Isles received a charm from a shipwrecked foreigner to whom they showed kindness, by which they could heal this complaint. A *duan* was repeated over the patient, who was then touched with the right hand—NGP-
t.-nàrach, (an), morbus obscœnis vel Gallicus.
t.-ospagach, (an), asthma.
t.-Phòil, epilepsy.
t.-sgoile, (an), truantship.
t.-tuiteamach, (an), epilepsy, palsy.
t.-uaine, (an), chlorosis.
tinneasach,** *a.* Stout, strong. (*lit.* Strongly-ribbed.) 2 Swift, nimble. 3 Sickly, distempered. 4 Frail. 5 Evil. Gu t., *quickly, expeditiously*.
———d, *s.f.* Sickness, sickliness. 2 State of being subject to fits.
tinneasnach,** *a.* Stout, strong. 2 Having stout ribs.
tinneas-na-gealaich,§ *s.m.* House-leek, see lus-nan-cluas.
tinnseamh,** *s.m.* Service.
tinnsgeadail,* *s.m.* Bad omen—*North*.* 2 (MS) Forerunner.
tinnsgeadalach, -aiche, *a.* Ominous of evil, portentous.
†**tinnsgil**, *v.a.* Begin.
†**tinnsgleadh**, -eidh, *s.m.* Commencement. A' t—, *pr.pt.* of tinnsgil.
tinnteagal, -ail, *s.m.* Corruption.
tinntean, see teinntein.
——— as,** -ais, *s.m* Great haste.
tioba,†† -chan, *s.f.* Heap.
tiobair,** -braichean, *s.f.* see tobar.
tiobairt, -ean, *s.* Well, fountain, cistern, draw-well, see tobar.
———each,** *a.* Abounding in springs. 2 Of, or belonging to, springs.
tiobar, -air, -an, *s.m.* see tobar.
———ach, *a.* see tobarach.
———san,** -ain, *s.m.* Springing. 2 Streaming. 3 Dropping.
†**tiobairt**,‡ *s* Well.
tiobrach see tobarach.
tiocaid, -e, -ean, *s.f.* Ticket. Cléireach tiocaide, *booking-clerk*. oifig-tiocaide, *booking-office*
tiochaidh. A thiochaidh fhéin! *int.* Exclamation of surprise—*Badenoch*
tiochd, *v.n.* see teachd. Cha t an sluagh 'san taigh, *the people cannot be contained by the house*: tiochdaidh iad 'san eaglais, *they can be contained by the church*
tiodal, -ail, -an, *s.m.* Title Nach 'eil coir aic' an ciste air t. na rìoghachd, *that it has not a charter in its chest to the title of the kingdom*—*Beinn Doran*.
———ach, -aiche, *a.* Appellative.
———aich, *v.n.* Confer a title. 2 Entitle.
———aichte, *past pt.* of tiodalaich.
tiodhlac, -aic, -aicean, *s.m.* Gift, present, offering, benefit, donation. 2 Interment, funeral.
———ach, -aiche, *a.* Mercenary.
———adh, -aidh, *s.m.* Giving, act of giving, bestowing, presenting. 2 Burial, funeral. 3 Burying, act of burying or interring. A' t—, *pr.pt.* of tiodhlaic. T. an diomhaireachd, *a gift in secret*.
———ail, -e, *a.* Mercenary.
———air, -e, -ean, *s.m.* Bestower.
———as,(MS) *s.m.* Gratification.
tiodhlaic, *pr. pt.* a' tiodhlacadh, *v.a.* Present, give, bestow a gift. 2 Inter, bury.
———each, -eiche, *a.* Bountiful, beneficent.
———each, -eich, *s m.* Bountiful person.
———te, *past pt.* of tiodhlaic. Presented, offered as a gift. 2 Interred, buried.
———ich, *v.* see tiodhlaic.
tiogair, *s.m.* Tiger.
———each, *a.* Fierce, like a tiger.
tiogh,** *a.* Late.
tioghlach,(MS) s.m. Blood.
tiolaice, see tiodhlac.
tiolam, -aim, -an, *s.m.* Short space. 2 Snatch. 3 Sudden attempt to bite. 4* Clever opportunity.
tiolap,(AH) *s.f.* Very brief space of time. 2 Opportunity.
tiolm,(CR) *s.m.* Bite, mouthful—*Perthshire*.
tiolp, *pr.pt.* a' tiolpadh, *v.a.* Snatch, grasp suddenly. 2 Nibble. 3 Pilfer. 4 Cavil, carp. 5 *Steal one's property and be almost looking at you, steal by snatching.
——ach, -aiche, *a.* That snatches or grasps suddenly, prone to snatch or bite. 2 Cavilling. 3 Captious.
tiolpachd, *s.f.ind.* Captiousness.
tiolpadair, -ean, *s.m.* Snatcher. 2 Cut-purse. 3 Superficial critic, censor, caviller, carper. 4 Pilferer. 5 Check in a boat.
——adaireachd,** *s.f.* Criticizing, carping.
tiolpadan,** -ain, *s.m.* Cut-purse.
tiolpadh, -aidh, *s.m.* Snatching, act of snatching or grasping suddenly. 2 Cavilling, act of cavilling or carping. 3 Captiousness. 4 Checking in a boat. A' t—, *pr.pt.* of tiolp. Luchd-tiolpaidh, *cavillers*.
tiolpaidh, *fut.aff.a.* of tiolp.
tiolpair, -ean, *s.m.* Bite. 2 Biter. 3 Sharper.
tiom, *s.m.* Sorrow. Gabhaidh e t., *he will be sorry*.
tiom,** *s.f.* Time. 2 Thyme.
tiom,** *v.a.* Soften, assuage.
tiom, -a, *a.* Soft, tender, delicate. 2 Fearful, timid, tenderhearted, sensitive, easily abashed or daunted. 3 Compassionate, warm-hearted. Crithidh feachd nach t., *hosts that are valiant* [*not timid*] *shall tremble*—*Fingal*.
tioma,* *s.f.* Delicateness of feeling. 2 Daunt.

3 Softening with grief melting into tears 4 Softness of disposition, emotion 5 Delicateness sensitiveness 6** Timidity 7 Warm-heartedness 8 Dejection Thàinig t.air,*he was daunted, melted into tears*, thainig t. air sùilean Fhinn *Fionn melted into tears*, iomadh ceud fo th., *many a hundred quite unmanned quite daunted.*

tiomach,** *a* Soft, delicate, timid 2 Merciful warm-hearted.

tiomachadh, *s.m* Softening, act of melting into tears. 2**Becoming timid. 3**Softness, timidity. 7 Mercifulness. A' t—, *pr.pt.* of tiomaich.

tiomachail, -e, *a.* Affecting, affective.

tiomachd, *s.f.ind.* Softness, tenderness, delicacy of feeling and sentiment. 2 *Daunt or damp on the spirits.

tiomadh, see tioma.

tiomaich, *pr.pt.* a' tiomachadh, *v.a. & n.* Soften into tears. 2 Become softened, become exorable. 3 Become terrified or fearful. 4 Intimidate. 5 Make effemiuate. Laoch nach t., *a hero that goes forward dauntlessly;* thiomaich a chridhe, *his heart softened.*

tiormaidireachd,(MS) *s.f.* Mealy-mouthedness.

tiomail, -e, *a.* Timely. Is t. dhuinn bhi 'sgaoileadh, *it is time for us to disperse.*

tiomail, -e, *a.* Impressive. Searmonaiche t., *an impressive preacher.*

tiomain, *pr.pt.* a' tiomnadh, *v. a.* Bequeathe, bestow, leave, as by a will. 2 Pledge. 3 Resign, commit for security. 4 Ascribe. 5**Swear by heaven. Th. e a spiorad suas, *he committed his spirit to God.*

tiomain,** *s.f.* Driving. 2 Proceeding.

———te, *past pt.* of tiomain. Bequeathed. 2 Pledged. 3 Committed to another's care. 4* Religiously determined.

tiomairg,** *v.a.* Collect, gather.

†tiomairn,** *pr.pt.* a' tiomarnadh, *v.* Command.

tiomal,** -ail, *s.m.* Ambit.

tiomalachd,(MS) *s.f.* Apprehensiveness.

tiomalachd,‡‡ *s.f.* Seasonableness.

tiomalair,** *s.m.* Glutton.

tiomaltas,** -ais, *s.m.* Victuals.

tioman,** *v.a.* Give, bestow. 2 Drive, push. 2 Turn off, thrust off.

tiomana,* *irreg. pl.* of tiom.

tiomanta, *past pt.* Given, bequeathed.

tiomantair,** *s.m.* see tiomnadair.

tiomargadh,** -aidh, *s.m.* Collection. 2 Translation.

tiomarnadh,** -aidh, *s.m.* Command. A' t—, *pr.pt.* tiomairn.

tiombhaigh,** *s.f.* False fellowship.

tiombuail, *s.f.* Cymbal.

tiom chainnt,** *s.f.* Circumlocution,

tiomchair,** *a.* Tender-hearted.

tiom-cheannachd,‡‡ *s.f.* Insensibility.

tiom-chridhe, *s.m.ind.* Pity, mercy, tenderness, compassion. 2 Warm heart.

————ach, -aiche, *a.* Tender-hearted, kind, compassionate, merciful. 2 Courteous.

————achd,** *s.f.* Affectionateness.

tiom-chuairt,** *s.* Ambitude. 2‡‡Friendly visit. 3‡‡Periodical visit or visitation. 4‡‡ Period of time, cycle. 5** Circle. 6**Bishop's visit. 7**Justiciary visit.

tiom-chuairteach, -eiche, *a.* Periodical, chronic. 2 Circular.

tiomghair,** *v.* Ask, request.

———e, *s.f.* Request, petition.

tiomhaidh, see tiamhaidh.

———eachd, see tiamhaidheachd.

tioma see tiomnadh.

tiomnach, *a.* Testatory, of, or belonging to, a will.

tiomnach, -aich *s.m. & f.* Testator, bequeather.

———air see tiomnach

tiomnadair -ean *s.m* Testator, bequeather.

tiomnadh,** *v.a.* Commend, 2 Deliver up. 3 Bequeathe. 4 Surrender

tiomnadh, -aidh, -aidhean, *s.m.* Will, testament. 2 Bequeathing, act of bequeathing. 3 Committing to another's care. 4 Covenant 5 Pledging, act of pledging A' t—. *pr pt.* of tiomain. An Seann T., *the Old Testament*, an T. Nuadh, *the New Testament*, oir tha t. daingean an déidh bàis dhaoine, *for a testament is in force after men's death*

tiomnaich,** *v.a.* Bequeathe.

tiomnaidh, *fut.aff.a* of tiomain.

tiomnaidhear, see tiomnadair.

tiomnaim, (for tiomnaidh mi), I shall bequeathe.

tiomnair, -ean, see tiomnadair

tiompan,-ain, *pl.*-an,& -ain, *s.m.* Any musical instrument. 2 Timbrel, cymbal, tabor, drum. 3 Harp. 4**Drum of the ear. 5**Kitchen-jack. 6 One-sided knoll. 7 Narrow gully. 8 Nozzle of a bellows. T. 'na làimh, *a timbrel in his hand;* tha a' ghaoth cho fuar 's ged a bhiodh i tighinn á t., *the wind is as cold as if it were blowing out of a bellows' mouth;* is mairg a losgadh a th. dhuit! *pity him who would burn his harp for you!*—alluding to the story of a Hebridean harper, who having nothing else to make a fire with to warm his wife, broke his harp in pieces and burned it. His wife's heart, it seems, was colder than her body, as she ran away with another man before morning!

tiompanach,‡‡ -aiche, *a.* Relating to, or like musical instruments, especially timbrels or harps.

tiompanach,** -aich, *s.m.* Performer on the timbrel. 2 Harper. 3 Minstrel. 4 Drummer.

————d,** *s. f.* Beating on a timbrel. 2 Noise of a timbrel.

tiompanaiche, -an, *s. m.* Harper. 2 Musician, minstrel. 3 Performer on the timbrel. [McL & D gives -aich, for *nom.sing.*]

tiomsach, -aiche,*a.*Collecting,bringing together.

————adh, -aidh, *s.m.* Second milking of a cow. 2 Collecting, act of collecting. A' t—, *pr.pt.* of tiomsaich.

tiomsaich, *pr.pt.* a' tiomsachadh, *v. a.* Collect, bring together.

————te, *past pt.* Collected, brought together.

tiomsgail, see tionnsgail.

tiomsgnadh, see tionnsgnadh.

tiomuin,** *s.f.* Dedication. 2 Giving up.

tion,** *a.* Soft.

tion,** *v.n.* Melt, dissolve.

†tion, *s.m.* Beginning.

tionac, see teanachd.

tionacair,(MS) *s.m.* Tongs.

tionacuds, see teanacas.

tionadh,** -aidh, *s.m.* Melting, dissolving.

tionail, *pr.pt.* a' tional, a' tionaladh & a' tionailt, *v.a. & n.* Gather, assemble. 2 Glean. 3 Come together, as an assembly, collect, compile, scrape.

tionaileach,** *a.* Causing to collect or assemble. 2 Prone to collect or gather. 3 Fond of gathering.

tionailt,(AC) *s.f.* see tional.

tionailte, *past pt.* of tionail. 2** *a.* Collectaneous.

tional, -ail, -an, *s.m.* Gathering, act of gathering, collecting. 2 Anything gathered, accumulation. 3 Gleaning, act of gleaning. 4 Assembling or coming together. 5 Assembly, multitude, convocation. 6 Contribution. 7

Resort. A' t—, pr. pt. of tionail. T. nan neul, *a gathering of the clouds* ; a thaobh an tionail, *concerning the collection.*
tionalach, see tionaileach.
tionalachadh,(MS) s.m. Compilation.
——adh, -aidh, *s.m. & pr.pt.* of tionail. Same meanings as tional.
tionalaiche,‡‡ -an, *s.m.* Culler.
tionas,** -ais, *s.m.* Tanyard.
tionc, see tiorc.
tioncach, see tiorcach.
tioncadh, see tiorc & tiorcadh.
tioncaiche,** see tiorcaiche.
tionchair,** *s.f.* Attendance.
tionchds', see teanacas.
tionchesg,** *s.m.* Instruction.
tiong,** s. Tinkle, as of a bell. [** says tingle.]
——,** *v.a.* Tinkle.
tiongail,** *s.f.* Tinkle, frequent tinkling.
tionnachair,** *s.m.* Legator.
tionnail, -e, -ean, *s.f.* Likeness or image of any person or thing.
†tionnar,** -air, *s.m.* Sleep, slumber.
tionndadh, -aidh, -aidhean, *s.m.* Turning, act of turning round or back. 2 Returning. 3 Turn. A' t—, *pr. pt.* of tionndaidh.
tionndaidh, *pr.pt.* a' tionndadh, *v.a. & n.* Turn by altering the position. 2 Turn,cause to turn. 3 Turn inside out, or upside down. 4 Alter, change. 5 Become changed. 6 Turn hay. 7 Convert. 8 Be converted. 9 Translate. 10 ‡‡Return. 11 Fetch. T. a leth-taobh, *turn aside.*
tionndain, *W. of Ross* for tionndaidh.
†tionnriomh,** *s.* Conclusion.
tionnsgail, *pr.pt.* a' tionnsgal, *v.a.* Invent, contrive. 2 Devise, plot, project. 3(MS) Meditate.
tionnsgainear,(MS) *s.m.* Beginner.
tionnsgainn, -e, -ean, *s.f.* Beginning, element. 2 Devising. 3 Contrivance. [**tionnsgain]
————, *pr.pt.* a' tionnsgnadh, *v.a.* Devise, invent, contrive, plot. 2 Begin, commence, ground. 3 Turn, return. 4 Attack or fall to of a sudden without any cause—*Islay.* 5** Breed. [**tionnsgain.]
tionnsgal, -ail, -an, *s.m.* Ingenuity, invention,inventiveness. 2 Industry. 3 Dexterity, art, cleverness. 4 Machination. 5(MS) Reach. 6 Conduct, management. A' t—, *pr. pt.* of tionnsgail.
————ach, -aiche, *a.* Ingenious, inventive. 2 Industrious, diligent. 3 Contrivant, managing well. 4 Adventurous. 5 (MS) Artificial.
tionnsgalachd, *s.f.* see tionnsgal.
tionnsgan, see tionnsgal.
tionnsgantach, see tionnsgalach.
tionnsgantachd, *s.f.* see tionnsgal.
tionnsgantair,** *s.m.* Deviser, contriver. 2 Beginner.
tionnsglach, see tionnsgalach.
tionnsgladh, *s.m.* see tionnsgal.
tionnsglair, see tionnsgnair.
tionnsglair,(MS) *s.m.* Inventor.
tionnsgnach, -aiche, *a.* Speculative. 2** see tionnsgalach.
————adh, -aidh, *s.m.* Devising, act of devising or inventing. 2 Beginning, act of beginning. 3 Turning, act of turning or returning. 4 Design, device, project. 5 Element. 6*Sudden attack. A' t—,*pr pt.* of tionnsgainn.
————d, *s.f.* see tionnsgal.
tionnsgnachd,** *s.f.* Ingeniousness. 2 Adventurousness. 3 Industry.
tionnsgnadair, see tionnsgnair.
tionnsgnadh ‡‡ -aidh, *s.m. & pr pt.* Devising, inventing. 2 Beginning, act of beginning, commencement. 3 Ground, element. 4 Turning, act of turning or returning. 5 Design,device, project, projection, invention. 6*Attacking or falling to of a sudden. 7 Sudden attack or commencement.
tionnsgnaiche, -an, *s.m.* Speculator.
tionnsgnair,** *s.m.* Beginner, broacher. 2 Contriver, deviser, schemer.
tionnsgnath, see tionnsgnadh.
tionnsgradh,** -aidh, *s.m.* Dowry, portion. 2 Reward.
tionramh,** -aimh, *s.m.* Attendance.
tionsan,** -ain, *s.m.* Drop.
tionsgadail,** *s.f.* Managing.
tionsgnadh, see tionnsgnadh. [dowry.
tionsgra, see tionnsgradh. 2 Wages, reward,
tiontanas,** -ais, *s.m.* Haste, speed, expedition.
tionur,** -uir, *s.m.* Tenon.
tiop, *v.a.* & *n.* Steal little by little, pilfer. 2 Thread a fishing-hook—*Ross-shire.*
tiopal,(AF) -ail, *s.m.* Water-spider.
tioparsan,** -ain, *s.m.* Flowing, streaming.
tior, *pr.pt.* a' tioradh, *v.a.* Dry, as corn or hay for the barn. 2 [tir in *Islay*, cròch in *Perthshire*—*] Kiln-dry.
tioradh, -aidh, -aidhean, *s.m.* Drying, act of drying, as corn or hay. 2 Kiln-drying, act of kiln-drying. 3**Scorching. A' t—, *pr. pt.* of tior. 4 (DMK) As much grain as is dried on a kiln at a time, *Scots*, " drying." Tha t. air an àth,*there is a " drying " on the kiln—Caithness.*
tiorail, -e, *a.* Drying, that dries. 2 Warm,genial, as a mild sun. 3 Cosy, snug, homely, comfortable. 4 Sheltered. 5 Commodious. 6‡‡Mild, modest. 7**Convenient. Gath t. na gréine, *the warm sunbeam.*
tioraime, *comp.* of tioram.
tioralachd, *s.f.ind.* Warmth. 2 State of being sheltered. 3 Mildness, meekness.
tioram, -a, *a.* Dry, without moisture, parched, not wetted, not wet, arid. 2 Dry, barren, uninteresting, unembellished, jejune. 3 Fair, as weather. 4 Thirsty. 5* Flippant in speech, pert. 6 Not seasoned, having no seasoning, as food of an indifferent kind. 7*Seasoned, as hay. Uair th., *fair weather* ; feur t., *hay.* [†† gives *comp.* tirme tioraime & tirime.]
————adh, see tiormachadh.
tioramach,** *a.* Dry, thirsty.
————,** -aich, *s.m.* Drought, thirst.
————adh, see tiormachadh.
tioramadair, see tiormadair.
tioramaich, see tiormaich.
tioramalach,** *a.* Dessicative.
tioraman, see tiorman.
tioranach,** *a.* Tyrannical.
————,**-aich, *s.m.* Tyrant.
tioranta,** *a.* Tyrannical, oppressive.
tiorc, *pr.pt.* a' tiorcadh. *v.a.* Save, rescue from danger, deliver, free.
tiorcach, -aiche, *a.* That saves or rescues. 2** Working or bringing about deliverance.
tiorcadh, -aidh, *s.m.* Saving, act of saving or rescuing, from danger. 2 Delivering, liberating. A' t—, *pr.pt.* of tiorc.
tiorcaiche, -an, *s. m. & f.* One who saves or delivers from danger.
tiorcta, *past pt.* of tiorc. Saved, delivered, rescued from danger.
tiorma,* *comp.* of tioram. Drier, driest.
tiormach,** *a.* Dessicative.
tiormachadh, -aidh, *s.m.* Drying, act of drying or parching. 2 Seasoning, as hay, fish, &c. 3* Fair weather. 4*Absorption. A' t—, *pr.pt.* of tiormaich.
tiormachail, -e, *a.* Dessicative, absorbent.

tiormachd, *s.f.ind.* Dryness, state of being dry. 2 Continuance of dry weather, drought. 3‡‡ Thirst. 4 Disease in cattle. 5*Flippancy.
tiormadair,(MS) *s.m.* Drier. 2 Flippant palaverer, spouter—*Dàin I. Ghobha.*
tiormaich, *pr.pt.* a' tiormachadh, *v.a.* Dry, make dry, parch, dry up. 2 Season. 3 Absorb.
———te, *past pt.* of tiormaich. Dried. 2 Absorbed.
tiormalachd, *s. f. ind.* Drought. 2 Thirst. 3** Aridity.
tiorman, -ain, -an, *s.m.* Meal made into a ball, steeped in water, and then toasted, the inside being dry. 2 Drier. 3 Anything that dries, or serves to evaporate moisture. 4** Water thickened with oatmeal.
tiormanach, *a.* Dessicative.
tiormasg, -aisg, -an, *s.m.* Mischance, mischief. 2 Destruction.
tiorraid,** *s.f.* Robe, mantle.
tiorrail, see tiorail.
tiorralachd, see tiaralachd.
tiort, -a, -an, *s.m.* Accident, mischance. 2 Risk, chance.
tiortach, -aiche, *a.* Accidental. 2 Unfortunate. 3 Liable to accidents. 4**Causing, or leading to, accidents.
tiortachd,* *s.f.* Liability to accident.
tioruirse,** *s.f.* Remnant.
tios, *v. n.* Go, come.
†tiosan,-ain, -an, *s.m.* Water gruel.
tiot, see tiota.
tiot,‡‡ *v.a. & n.* Despatch quickly. 2 Go quickly.
tiota, -idhean, *s.m.* Moment, little while, second of time, trice, breath. Ann an t., *in a moment* ; thig an seo car t., *come here a little while.*
tiotach,** *a.* Momentary.
tiotadh, -aidh, -aidhean, *s.m.* see tiota.
tiotag,** -aig, *s.f.* Very short while, minute, trice.
tiotal, -ail, see tiodal.
tiotalach,** *a.* Appellative.
tiotalaich, see tiodalaich.
tiotamh,* see tiota.
tiotan, -ain, *s.m.* see tiota. †2 The sun.
tiothlam, see tiolam.
tir, -e, -ean, *s.m.* [*f.* in *the North.*] Land. 2 The land, in contradistinction to water. 3 Country, region. 4 Shore, beach, coast. O 'n a thàinig e do 'n tìr, *since he came to the country, to this region* ; tìr mòr, *a continent;* eadar thìr-mór agus eileanan, *both continent and islands* ; t. aineoil, *a strange land* ; air t., *on dry ground, on land, ashore* ; rach air t., *go ashore*; mór-thìr, see note under mór. [***s.f.*]
tir, *v.a.* see tìor. [*Islay*]
†tircean, -ein, *s.m.* Meaning, signification, exposition.
tirceanas, see tircean.
tireach,** *a.* Territorial, of or belonging to a country, of the same country.
———, -ich, -ichean, *s.m.* Countryman. 2 Patriot.
tireachadh, -aidh, *s.m.* Colonizing, act of colonizing 2 Colony. 3 Disembarkation. A' t—, *pr pt.* of tirich.
tireachas,* -ais, *s. m.* Patriotism. 2** Colony, 3 Colonizing, colonization.
tireadh,* -idh, *s.m.& pr.pt.* of tìr, see tioradh.
tirealachd,** *s.f.* Homeliness.
tireanach, -aich, *s.m.* Landsman.
tireil, -e, *a.* Rural, agrarian. 2**Homely, snug, comfortable.
tir-eòlach, *a.* Geographical.
tir-eòlaiche, *s.m.* Geographer.
tir-eòlas, *s.m.* Geography.
tir-ghràdh, -ghràidh, *s.m.* Patriotism.
tìr-ghràdhaiche, -an, *s.m.* Patriot.
tirich,‡‡ *s.m. & f.* see tireach. 2 (AF) *s.m.* The horse that walks on, or next to, the unploughed land.
tirich, *pr.pt.* a' tìreachadh, *v.a.* Colonize, settle. 2 Disembark. 3** Bring to land.
tiridh, *s.* Drying corn—*Arran.*
tirim, see tioram.
tirleach,** -ich, *s.m.* Demesne, mansion-house.
tirmein,†† *s.m.* Pert fellow. 2 Would-be wag.
tirmeineach,†† *a.* Flippant.
—————d,†† *s.f.* Flippancy.
tirpean,** -ein, *s.f.* House-leek.
tirr h-eodha ! *int.* Cry to incite a dog when driving cattle.
tirt', *a.* Earthed. T. an caol-chist' liobhta bhòrd, *earthed in a coffin of polished boards—W. Ross, p. 18.*
tirteag,** *s.* Domain, seat.
tìr-unga, *s.* Ounce-land, see p. 719.
tiseadh,* -idh, *s.m.* Coming.
tisean,** -ein, *s.m.* Grudge.
†tit, *s.f.* The earth.
tit !* *int.* Expression used on wet being perceived suddenly.
titeag, see tit.
———aidh, see tit.
†titan, see tiotan.
tith,‡‡ -e, *s.f.* Inclination, desire, eagerness, keenness, forwardness. 2 Design, intention. 3 Pursuit. Air mo th., *pursuing me.*
titheach,* -eiche, *a.* Bent or determined on. 2 ‡‡Designing. 3‡‡Pursuing keenly. 4 Eager, keen for, eagerly desirous, inclining, earnest, willing. 6 Sharp, forward. T. air mo mharbhadh, *keen on my destruction.*
†tithinn, *s.* The sun.
tiu,** see tiugh.
tiubhachd,** *s.f.* Sloth.
tiubhair,** *v.a.* Give, grant, present, bestow. 2 Deliver, give up. Th. i a gràdh, *she gave her love* ; gu'n tiubhradh e dh' i, *that he would give her* ; t. dhomh, *give me.*
tiubhir, see tiubhair. 2 see tiur.
tiubhrach,** *a.* Prone to give, generous.
—————adh,** -aidh, *s.m.* Giving, granting, grant. 2 Presenting. 3 Delivery, giving up.
tiubhradh,** -aidh, *s.m.* Gift, grant. 2 Giving, granting.
tiubhraich, ** *v.a.* Give, grant, present. Deliver, give up. O chian thiubhraich Righ Calum Lochabar fo chìs da, *King Malcolm bestowed the rental of Lochaber on him long ago—Duanaire, 89* ; th. dhomh aon de d' dhà shleagh, *give me one of your two spears.*
triubhtrachd,** *s.f.* Sloth.
tiubruid,** *s.f.* Well, cistern.
tiucainn, see tiugainn.
tiuchag,** -aig, *s.f.* Pore.
tiuchan,** *s.m.* Pore.
tiugainn, Come, let us go. [From deaspirated thugainn, *to us,* for chugainn—‡]
tiugh, tighe, *a.* Thick, not slender. 2 Of great thickness. 3 Thick, dense, set close together. 4 Frequent, in quick succession, as drops of rain. 5 Coarse not thin. 6‡‡Thick, as a liquid approaching to solidity. 7 Foggy, hazy. 8 Clumsy. 9 Dull. 10 Corpulent. 11 Indistinctly uttered. 12 Gross. [**comp.* tibhe & tiuighe.]
†tiugh, *s.m.* The end.
†———, *a.* Latter, last.
tiughachadh, -aidh, *s.m.* Thickening, act of thickening. 2 Condensing, condensation. 3 Coagulating, coagulation. A' t—, *pr. pt.* of tiughaich.
tiughachail, -e, *a.* Incrassative.
tiughachd, *s.f.ind.* Corpulency.

tiughad, -aid, *s.m.* Degree of corpulency or thickness. see tighead.
tiughadas,** -ais, *s. m.* Thickness, closeness, denseness, solidity, consistence. 2 Grossness.
tiughaich, *pr. pt.* a' tiughachadh, *v.a. & n.* Thicken. 2 Become thick. 3*Crowd. 4 Engross. 5** Condense. 6**Coagulate. 7** Become gross or dense.
tiughaichte, *past pt.* of tiughaich.
tiughalach, -aich, *s. f.* Thickest part of liquids, dregs.
———d, see tiughalach.
†tiugh-bhagh,** *s.m.* Late drinking.
†tiugh là,** *s.m.* The last day.
tiuighe, *comp.* of tiugh. see tighe & tighead.
———ad,* -eid, see tighead.
———adas,* -ais, *s.m.* see tighead.
tiuir, see tiurr.
tiunnal,** -ail, *s.m.* Match, likeness, comparison. T. t' aogais is tearc ri fhaotainn, *the match of thy face is seldom found.*
tiumpan,(MS) *s.m.* Hinder.
tiur, see tiurr.
tiùrr,‡ *s.m.* Beach out of reach of the sea. 2 (DMK) Seaware cast up by the sea at high-water mark—*W. coast of Ross.* 3(AC) Mark, stamp, impress. 4 Mark of the sea on the shore. 5(AC) Refuse left by the tide on the beach. T. na mara, *high-water mark;* is truagh nach mi bha làimh riut, ged a b' ann an t. an làin e, *would that I were near thee, even though it were in the impress of the tide.*
tiuth ! *int.* Call to silence or drive away a dog —*Arran.*
tlà, see tlàth.
tlà-chainnt,‡‡ -e, -ean, *s.f.* Blandishment.
tlachd, *s.f.ind.* Pleasure, satisfaction, delight. 2 Inclination, liking. 3 Beauty. 4 Love, attachment, affection. 5(AF) Fat hog. 6 Comfort. 7 Honour. 8** *rarely*, Colour. 9 **Burial. 10 Market, fair. 11 Garment. 12 Liberality. 13 Earth.
Tha t. aige dhith, *he is attached to her;* cha 'n fhaigh thu e le t., *you will not get it with any degree of satisfaction;* is beag mo th. dhith no dheth, *I have no great affection for her* or *him;* gabhaidh mi t., *I will take pleasure;* togaibh cuimhne Orla le t., *extol with honour the memory of Orla.*
———,** *v.a.* Colour, polish.
———ach,** *a.* Geographical.
———adh,** *s.m.* Burial.
———aich,** *v.a.* Inter.
———aireachd, see tlachdmhoireachd.
——— -airm,** *s.m.* Market-place.
———ar, *a.* see tlachdmhor.
†——— bhaile,** *s.m.* Market-town.
——— -bheirt,*s.f.* Geography.
†——— -bhog,** *s.m.* Quagmire, quicksand.
†——— -bhùth, *s.m.* Booth or tent at a fair.
——— -eòlas,**-ais, *s.m.* Geography, geographical knowledge.
——— -gràbhachd,** *s.f.* Geography.
——— -gràbhaiche,** *s.m.* Geographer.
———mhoire, *comp.* of tlachdmhor.
———mhoireachd, *s.f. ind.* Pleasantness. 2 Blandness. 2 Handsomeness, comeliness. 4 (MS)Acceptance.
———mhor, -oire, *a.* Pleasant, delightful. 2 Handsome, comely, lovely. 3 Becoming, fitting. 4*Liberal. Leanabh t., *a comely child;* t. do dhuine, *becoming in a man.*
——— -mhuchd, see tlath-mhuc.
——— -sgrìobhadh, *s.m.* Cosmography. 2 Geography.
——— -sgrìobhair,** *s. m.* Cosmographer. 2 Geographer.
——— sheisd,§ *s.* Wood-strawberry, see sùbh-thalmhainn.
tlachd-shùbh,§ *s.* Wood-strawberry, see sùbh-thalmhainn.
——— -thomhaiseach,** *a.* Geometrical, of or belonging to, geometry.
——— -thomhas,** -ais, *s.m.* Geometry.
———air,** *s.m.* Geometrician.
tlà-ghuthachd,‡‡ *s.f.ind.* Mellowness of voice.
tlaim, see tlàm.
tlaiteachd, *s.f.* Mild rain, smurring—*Arran.*
tlàithe, *comp.* of tlàth.
tlàitheachd, *s.f.ind.* Mildness, softness, tenderness, smoothness.
tlàithead, -eid, *s.m.* Degree of mildness, softness, tenderness or smoothness.
tlàm, -àim, tlaimeannan, *s.f.* Handful of wool or flax. 2 Flake. 3 Lock of wool or flax on the distaff. 4*Awkward handling. [††*pl.* tlàmanan.] T. de chloimh nan caorach, *a handful of wool.*
tlàm, *pr.pt.* a' tlàmadh, *v.a.* Teaze or pluck, as wool. 2* Mix wool. 3**Handle.
tlàmach,** *a.* Teazing, plucking.
tlàmadh, -aidh, *s.m.* Teazing, act of teazing or plucking, as wool, handling, mixing, fumbling. A' t—, *pr.pt.* of tlàm. Co-thlàmadh, *mixing.*
tlàmaich,(MS) *v.a.* Blend.
tlàs, -àis, *s.m.* see tlàths.
†tlas,** *s.m.* Cattle. 2 Fair.
tlasach,** -aich, *s.m.* Fair.
tlàth, -àithe, *a.* Mild, kind, tender, indulgent, merciful, meek. 2 Tranquil, gentle. 3 Mellow, sweet, sounding mellow. 4 Smooth to the touch. 5 Smooth, delicate. 6*Moist, humid, 7**Feeble. 8**Balmy. Bu t. a gorm-shùil, *soft was her blue eye;* ceilte fo 'tlàth-chiabhan, *concealed under her soft locks;* tha seo t., *this is somewhat moist;* uisge t., *balmy* or *gentle rain;* bu bhuige a chainnt na oladh th., *his speech was softer than smooth oil;* 'nuair a thuiteas an t-sian gu t., *when the shower falls gently.*
tlàth, Skye for tlàths. Thàinig t. air mo chridhe, *my heart warmed or melted.* [*a.* used as a *noun.*]
tlàthachadh,* -aidh, *s.m.* Moistening. 2 Getting into perspiration. A' t—, *pr. pt.* of tlàthaich. T. falluis, *gentle perspiration.*
tlàthaich,* *v.a. & n.* Moisten gently. 2 Become balmy or gentle. 3 Abate, as weather. 4 Get into a gentle perspiration.
tlàthas, see tlàths.
tlàth-ghaoth, *s.f.* Breeze.
tlàth-mhuc,(AF) *s.* Fat hog.
tlàths, -àiths, *s.m.* Mildness, kindness, warmth, mellowness, balminess. 2 Tranquility. 3 Gentleness, tenderness. 4 Smoothness. 5 Softness. 6**Merry trick. 7**Mellowness, balminess. A' tionndadh aseaoin na sìne gu t., *changing the inclemency of the weather to mildness.*
tlàth-thaislich,** *v.a.* Bedew. 2 Moisten.
tli,** *s.m.* Colour. 2 Feature.
tligheachd, *s.f.ind.* Nausea, inclination to vomit. 2 Liquid, discharge, spume—*Dàin I. Ghobha.* Tha t. air, *he is inclined to vomit.*
tliochd,* *s.m.* Beginning.
———an,** -ain, *s.m.* Hoarseness.
———anach,** *a.* Causing hoarseness. 2 Hoarse.
tlu, see tlugh.
tlugaig,(MMcD) *s.* Small pole about 4 ft. long and 1½ in. in diameter, the lower end sharpened round to a blunt point, with a foot-rest called the *sgonnan*, placed about 12 in. from the point, used for planting potatoes—*Lewis.*
tlugh,* *s.m.* Pair of tongs.
†tlus,(AF) *s.m.* Cattle.
tlus, -uis, *s.m.* Pity, ruth, compassion. 2 Ten-

derness, affection. 3 Mildness, genial warmth. balminess. 4 Comfort, comfortable sensation, as clothes next the skin. 5 Lie. 6 Gentleness. 7 Balminess or mildness, as weather. 8 see tlas.
Labhair le t., *speak with some affection*; cha'n 'eil t. 'sam bith 'san aodach, *there is no comfort in the clothes*; fheara bu mhòr t. is bàigh, *ye heroes noted for natural affection and clanship*, [***for compassion and mercy*]; thig t. is blàths, *balmy weather and genial warmth will come*; t. nan speur, *the balminess of the air*.

tlusach,** -aich, *s.m.* Dissembler, liar.

tlusail, -e, *a.* Tender, pitying, compassionate. 2 Warm, mild, balmy, genial. 3 Affectionate, kind. 4 Agreeable to the touch, comfortable. 5 False. Nighean t., *an affectionate daughter*; aodach t., *comfortable clothing*; uair t., *mild or genial weather*; gu t., *kindly*.

tlusaileachd, see tlusalachd.

tlusair, *s.m.* Kind, compassionate man.

——eachd,* see tlusalachd.

tlusalachd, *s.f.ind.* Tenderness, compassion, kindness. 2*Balminess, genial warmth. 3 *Comfortable feeling or sensation.

tlusar, see tlusmhor.

tlusmhoire, *comp.* of tlusmhor.

tlusmhoireachd,* see tlusalachd.

tlusmhor, see tlusail.

tnachair, -ean, *s.m.* Spanner.

tnù, see tnùth.

tnùth, -a, *s. m.* Envy, jealousy. 2 Zeal, fire, longing. 3 Anger, indignation, grudge. 4 Malice. 5 Bigotry. 6 Avarice. Am fianuis tnùtha, *before envy*; do mhór-chridhe gun t., *thy great heart without malice*.

——-ach, -aiche, *a.* see tnùthail.

——-ach, -aich, -aichean, *s. m.* Rival, envious person, jealous person.

·——adh, -aidh, *s.m.* Conflict.

tnùthail, -e, *a.* Envious, jealous. 2 Angry. 3 Malignant, rancorous, malicious.

tnùthair,** *s.m.* Bigot.

tnùthar, -aire, *a.* see tnùthmhor.

tnùthmhor, -oire, *a.* Envious, malicious, jealous. Gu t., *enviously*.

to-, *verbal prefix.* To.

†tob,* *s.f.* [***m.*] Surprise.

tobac,** *s.m.* Tobacco. [tombaca.]

tòbairt,‖ *s.f.* Flux, spasms attendant on diarrhœa.

toban,‡ -ain, *s.m.* Wreath of wool or flax on a distaff. 2 Flake. 3 Cowl, hood. [** says †.]

tobar, -air & toibre, *pl.* tobraiche, tobraichean & toibrichean, *s.m.* Well, fountain, spring. 2 Source, origin. Tobraichean na beatha, *the fountains* [*issues*] *of life*; an t. bho 'm bheil gach buaireadh a' sruthadh, *the source whence all temptations flow*; beul an tobair, *the mouth of the well*.
t.-baistidh, baptismal-font.
t.-fìor-uisg', spring-well, living spring, perennial spring.
t.-tàirne, draw-well.

——ach, -aiche, *a.* Springy, abounding in springs.

tobh,** *s.m.* see tobha.

——,** *v.a.* Hoe.

tobhainn,** *v.a.* Hoe.

tobha, -chan & -ichean, *s.m.* Rope, cable. 2** Hoe. 3 Tow. T. na croiche, *the gallows' rope*; bitheadh gach fear a' deanamh t. dha fhéin, *let every man make a rope for (hanging) himself*; t. cartach, *a cart-rope*; t. corcaich, *a hempen rope*.

tobha, *v.a.* Tow.

tobhach, -aiche, *a.* Having ropes.

†tobhach,** -aich, *s.m.* Wrestling. 2 Compelling. 3 Inducing.

†——,** *a.* Sudden, surprising.

tobhaig, *v.a.* Put earth to potatoes with a hoe—*W. of Ross-shire.*

tobhair, see tabhair.

——,(MS) *s.m.* see todhar.

——t, see tabhairt.

——tach, see tabhairteach.

tobhar, see todhar.

——tas, see tabhartas.

tobhlair, -ean, see tòlair.

tobhta,(DC) *s.f.* Walls of a house. So called even though built of stone, a survival of the times when houses were built of divots—*Uist.* [In *Argyll* a wall built of divots is called *balla-tobhta.*] 2 Ruin with walls standing and roof fallen in.

tobhta, -chan & tobhtan, *s.m.* Rower's bench in a boat. 2**Turf, clod. T.-annainn & t.-fhàil, see under taigh. 3 Little knoll.
t.-bràghaid, bow-thwart.
t.-chamus, t.-chroinn, t.-dheiridh, t.-thogalaich, t.-thoisich, see under bàta, p. 77.
t.-shilidh,(AC) see appx. under bàta.
t.-tilgte,(DMK) Movable thwart in a boat—*W. coast of Ross.*

tobhtach,‡‡ -aiche, *a.* Furnished with rower's benches.

tobhtag,(DU) -ain, *s.f.* Small yard containing a stack or two of corn. The walls are generally of turf.

tobrach, *gen.sing.* of tabar.

tobraiche, *n.pl.* of tobar.

——an, *n.pl.* of tobar.

tòc, *v.a.* Puff, rise gradually, as a loaf. 2 Swell, as with rage. 3 Bag, swell with good eating. Th. a h-aodann, *her face swelled.*

tòc, *s.* Disease of the eyes, mostly peculiar to sheep—*Rob Donn.* 2(DC) *s.m.* "pink-eye" in horses.

tòcadh,* *s.m.* Puffing, swelling. 2**Prosperity. A' t—, *pr.pt.* of tòc.

†tocair, -ean, *s.m.* Causeway.

toch,‡ *s.* Bad smell.

toch, -a, -an, *s.m.* Thigh, hough of an animal. 2**Fit of crying. 3**Love.

toch, *v.a.* Hamstring, cut off the limbs of cattle, hough. Th. iad an crodh, *they houghed the cattle.*

tocha, *comp.* of toigh, see docha.

tocha,** *s.* Choice.

tochach, -aiche, *a.* Of or belonging to the hough, houghed.

tochadh, -aidh, *s.m.* Hamstringing. A' t—. *pr. pt.* of toch.

tochail, *pr.pt.* a' tochladh, *v.a.* Dig, quarry, mine, bore. 2 Love.

tochail,** *s.f.* see tochailt.

——iche, *s.m.* Fossilist. 2 Miner. 3 Pioneer.

tochaill,(MS) *s.* Gutter.

tochailleach, see tochailteach.

tochailliche,** *s.m.* Miner. 2 Pioneer (in army.)

tochailt, -e, -ean, *s.f.* Mine, quarry. 2 Digging. 3 Fossil.

——e, *a.* & *past pt.* of tochail. Digged, dug,

——each, -aiche, *a.* That roots out or extirpates. 2** Mineral. 3 Fossilized.

——each, -ich, *s.m.* One who roots or digs out.

tochailtear,** -eir, *s.m.* Miner, quarrier.

tochal, -ail, *s.m.* Mine, quarry. 2 Digging.

tochal, see tochladh.

tochalaiche, see tochailliche.

tochalta, see tochailte.

tochair,** *v.a.* Invite. 2 Wind up, as yarn.

tochair,**v.a.* Give a dowry or marriage portion

tòchar, *s.m.* Dense volume of smoke—*Argyll.*
tochar.* see tochradh.
†tochar,** *s.m.* Causeway, pavement. 2 Crowd T. éisg, *a causeway of dead fish.*
tochar, *v* see tochair.
tocharach, -aiche, *a.* see tochrach.
tocharaich, *v.* see tochraich.
tocharais, see tacharais.
tocharaiste, see tacharaiste.
tocharas, see tacharas.
tochas, see tachas.
tòchd, *s.m.ind.* see tòc & toch. Deagh th., *a good smell.*
tochd,** *s.m.* Fit. 2 Trance. 3 Silence. 4 Bed-tick.
tochd, *a.* see tochdail.
tochdach,** *a.* see tochdail.
tochdail,** *a.* Still. 2 Silent.
toch-fhearg,** -fheirge, *s.f.* Silent rage, smothered wrath.
————ach, *a.* Raging in silence.
tochladh, -aidh, *s.m.* Digging, act of digging. 2 Mining, quarrying. 3 Pit, mine, quarry. 4 Grave. A' t—, *pr.pt.* of tochail.
tochlaidh, *fut.aff.a.* of tochail.
tochmhaire,** *s.f.* Marriage-treaty.
†tochmharc, *s.* Wooing.
tochra,(AF) *s.m.* Small pig.
tochrach, -aiche, *a.* Of, or belonging to, a dowry. 2 Having a large dowry.
tochradh, -aidh, -aidhean, *s. m.* Marriage-portion, dowry. 2 Endowment. A réir tochraidh nam maighdean, *according to the dowry of the virgins.*
tochraich, *v.a.* Endow.
tochraichte,** *a.* & *past pt.* Endowed.
tochrais,* see tachrais.
————te, see tachraiste.
tochras, see tachras.
tochuil, see tochail.
tochus,** *s.m.* Possessions, property.
tocsaid, see togsaid.
————each, -aiche, *a.* Of, or belonging to, hogsheads.
tod,** *s.m.* Clod, sod.
todan,** -ain, *s.m.* Small clod.
todh, see todha.
todha,(AC) *s.m.* see tobha.
todhachd,** *s.f.* Silence.
tòdhadh, -aidh, *s.m.* Core, rot, disease in sheep.
todhail, *s.f.* Destruction.
todhair, *pr.pt.* a' todhar, *v.a.* Manure. 2 Bleach.
todhas, -ais, *s.m.* Silence.
todhar, -air, -an, *s.m.* Manure, dung. 2 Field manured by folding cattle upon it. 3 Bleaching, process of bleaching, a bleach. 4(MS)Compost. A' t—, *pr. pt.* of todhair.
todhlair, -ean, see tòlair.
tofas,** -ais, *s.m.* Gaelic form of *topaz.*
tog, *pr.pt.* a' togail, *v. a.* Lift, raise, rear. 2 Build. 3 Brew, distil. 4 Carry. 5 Take away. 6 Excite, stir, cheer up, rouse. 7 Exact, as tribute. 8 Rear, educate, bring up. 9 Hoist, weigh. 10 Extol. 11 Make sheaves of corn.

Th. iad taigh, *they built a house*; le gliocas togar taigh, *with wisdom a house is built*; am fear a th. thu, *the man that reared you*; togaidh fear fiar aimhreit, *a perverse man stirreth up strife*; th. tuinn an cinn, *waves rear their heads*; t. do throm dhiom, *remove thy burden from me; do not goad me too much*; th. iad cìs, *they exacted tribute*; cha tog pìob mo chridhe, *the pipes will not cheer my spirits*; togaidh an là, *the day will clear up*; tog ri, *ascend*; t. air, *report ill of*; t. cuis, *appeal*; th e a chùis do 'n rìgh, *he appealed to the king*; t. ort chun a' mhonaidh, *betake yourself to the mountains*; a' togail a' bhruaich, *ascending the acclivity*; th. iad air gu'n robh e déidheil air an òl, *they raised a report that he was addicted to liquor*; a thogadh mo chridhe 'nuair a bhitheadh e trom, *that would cheer my heart when sad*; t. na siùil, *hoist the sails*; th. iad an acair, *they weighed the anchor*; th. iad a' bhraich, *they brewed* (or *distilled*) *the malt*; t. do shùil, *raise your eye, look*; th. mi o 'n a thubhairt e, *I understood from what he said*; t. dheth, *cease, desist*; t. ort, *prepare thyself, rouse thyself*; t. fonn, *sing a song*; th. iad orra, *they started*; th. e air as déidh na mnà, *he started after the woman*—*W.S.2.102*; th. e droch alladh òrm, *he raised a bad report about me*; tog orm mo phìob is théid mi dhachaidh, *give me my pipes and I will go home*—*Cumha Ruairidh mhòir.*

togaid, see togsaid.
togail, *gen.* -e & togalach, *pl.* toglaichean, *s. f.* Lifting, act of lifting. 2 Building, act of building. 3 Carrying. 4 Taking away. 5 Rearing, act of rearing. 6 Anything to be lifted. 7 Building, structure, superstructure. 8 Levy, exacting, as of tribute. 9* Hoisting, weighing. 10 Ascending. 11 Exciting, rousing, stirring up. 12 Brewing, distilling. 13 Carriage of a boat. 14 Feud. 15*Starvation. A' t—, *pr. pt.* of tog.

A' moladh na togalach, *praising the building*; innleachd-togalach, *a still*; t. spréidhe, *a rearing of cattle, a carrying-off of cattle*; tha e air togail, *he is ravenously hungry*—said of one who has fasted long—(DU); tha a' bhò air a t.,—said of a cow when after passing through a severe winter and spring, it is so reduced by semi-starvation that it has to be assisted to its feet; t. a' bhuntàta, *digging potatoes*; t. an òir, *digging gold*; t. nan lìon, *hauling the lines*; tha thu air do thogail, *you are very much excited*; ceann na togail, *the head of the levy*; taigh-togalach, *a brewing-house.* [††*pl.* togalaichean.]

TERMS CONNECTED WITH BREWING AND MALTING:—(DMy)

Bogadh an t-sìl, *malting.* Soaking or steeping the grain for 24 hours, after which it is taken home and spread on the floor, being gathered into a heap at night to prevent sprouting. It is again spread to prevent heating, and so on alternately till all sprouting ceases.
Braich, *malted grain.*
Dabhach, *cask* or vat, in which the malted grain is placed to brew.
Sguab, *brush* of heather which is inserted in hole in bottom of dabhach.
Fionnstoth, *stick* inserted in centre of sguab, to enable dripping of the brew to be regulated.
Breilleis, the *brew* before the yeast is added.
Leann, *beer.*
Deasgainnean, *yeast.*

togail-barrachaol, *s.f.* Pyramid.
togair, *pr. pt.* a' togairt & a' togradh, *v. a. & n.* Desire, wish eagerly. 2 Covet. 3 Please. 4 Arrogate. 5 Challenge. 6††Offer, make an attempt. 7 Wish, be inclined. 8††Seek. Ma thogras mi-féin, *if I please*; ma thogair, *it does not matter, it is a matter of the utmost indifference.*
togair, *gen.sing.* of togar.
togairt, *s.f.* Desiring, act of desiring or eagerly wishing. A' t—, *pr.pt.* of togair. A' t. dol dhachaidh, *keenly desirous of going home.*
togalach, *gen.sing.* of togail.
togalaiche, *s.m.* *Builder. 2‡‡Lifter.
toglaichean, *pl.* of togail. Buildings, &c.
togam, *1st.sing.imp.* of tog. Let me raise.

togam,** (for togaidh mi) I will raise.
togar, *fut. pass.* of tog.
togar,** -air, *s.m.* Gout. 2 Desire, will, wish, pleasure, inclination.
togarrach, -aiche, *a.* Keen, desirous. 2 Willing. 3 Agog, animated. 4 Cheerful. 5* Inviting, enticing. 6**Covetous. 7 Having bias or propensity. Cha'n 'eil an là seo t., *this day is not inviting ;* tha e t. a dh' fhalbh, *he is desirous of going.* Gu t., *wishfully.*
togarrachd,** *s.f.* Animation. 2 Forwardness, wishfulness, willingness,propensity 3**Covetousness. T. bhur n-inntinn, *the willingness of your minds.*
togbhail, see togail.
togh, see tobh & tagh.
togha, see todha.
toghadh, see taghadh.
toghaidh,* *s.f.* Guard, care. 2 Liking. 3 Attention, respect. Thoir t. ort, *take care of yourself.*
†toghar, -air, see todhar.
toghbhail, see togail.
toghlainn,* *s.f.* Exhalation, fume, disagreeable heat. Tha t. ag éirigh, *there is an exhalation rising.*
toghmall,(AF) *s.m.* Squirrel.
togladh,** -aidh, *s.m.* Sacking, destroying.
togra, see togradh.
tograch, see togarrach.
togradh, -aidh, -aidhean, *s.m.* Desire, passion, propensity, wish. 2 Desiring, coveting. A' t—, *pr.pt.* of togair.
tograim, (for tograidh mi) I shall or will, desire.
togsaid, -e, -ean, *s.f.* Hogshead.
togta, *past pt.* of tog. Lifted, raised. [togte.] Tha speura a chinn togta, *he is quite in a frenzy.*
†toi, *a.* Silent, mute. 2 Gentle.
toibheimeach, -eiche, *a.* see toibheumach.
toibheum, -eim, -an, *s.m.* Reproach, aspersion. 2 Blemish, stain. 3 Blasphemy. 4 Scandal, slander. [*gen.sing.* also toibheuma.]
———ach, -aiche, *a.* Reproachful, reproaching. 2 Blaspheming, blasphemous. 3 *Offensive, profane. 4 Slanderous, scandalous, railing. Casaid th., *a railing accusation* ; duine t., *a blasphemous man ;* gu t., *blasphemously.*
toibhre,** *s.f.* Fancy, illusion.
tòic, -e, -ean, *s.f.* Swelling of the face or body from good living.
toic, -e, *s.f.* Wealth, riches, fortune. 2**Substance. 3 Support, prop. 4††Gluttony, luxury. 5* Wealth that puffs up.
toice,** *s. f.* Opprobious name for a worthless female.
toiceach, -eiche, *a.* Rich, wealthy. 2 Substantial, propping. 3‡‡Swelled up with arrogance or conceit.
toicealachd,* *s.f.ind.* Purse-pride. 2‡‡Wealth, good circumstances.
tòicean, *s.* Little swelling. Gun mheiliche gun tòicean, *without sound or motion—Beinn Doran.*
toiceann, *s.m.* Disease.
toicear,* -eir, -an, *s.m.* Purse-proud man.
———achd,* *s.f.* see toicealachd.
tòiceil, -e, *a.* Purse-proud. 2 Wealthy, substantial. 3 Swelled up with pride of riches. T. do chrodh 's de chaoraich, *wealthy in cattle and sheep.*
tòiceil,* *s.f.* Disdain.
toichd, *s.f.* Bed-tick, ticken.
toiche, *s.f.* Fate, destiny.
†toiche, *a.* Wall-eyed.
†toichead,** -eid, *s.m.* Arrest.
†toicheall, -ill, *s.m.* Journey, departure.
toicheasdal, see toichiosdal.
toicheum,** *s.f.* Slow pace.
———ach,** *a.* Gradual, pace by pace
toichiosdal, -ail, *s.m.* Arrogance presumption. 2 Opinionativeness. 3 Party, faction, cause. 4 Army.
————ach, -aiche, *a.* Arrogant, presuming, self-sufficient, arrogant, opinionated.
†toichneadh, -idh, *s.m.* Fast, vigil.
†toid, *a.* Whole, entire, enough.
†toid, *s.f.* The whole.
†toideadh,** *a.* Thankful.
toidhchd, see toichd.
toidhearnadh, -aidh, *s.m.* Punishment.
toigh, *comp.* -e & docha, *a.* Agreeable, pleasant. 2 Dear, loved. Is t. leam, *I like I am fond of ;* is t. leam thu, *I like you ;* ma 's t. leat mise, is t. leam thu, is mur t. na taobh mi, *if you love me, I love you, otherwise do not come near me ;* is t. leam thusa, ach is annsa leam ise, *I like you, yet she is dearer to me ;* an ni nach t. leat earb ri fear eile, *entrust the work you don't like to another*—a man who dislikes his work will not do it so well as one who likes it.
toighe, *s.f.ind.* Notice, attention, care. 2** (toigh**) Love, fondness. Thoir t., *take care, take heed.*
toigheach, -eiche, *a.* Loving, that loves, fond of, cherishing a fondness, susceptible of fondness. 2 Attentive, watchful 3 Careful. 4†† Beloved. Cha'n 'eil mi t. air (*or* uime), *I am not fond of it.*
toigheachd,** *s.f.* Concession, yielding. 2 Noting. 3 Illustrating. 4 Coming. 5 Mindfulness.
toil, -e, -ean, *s.f.* Will, the will, inclination, desire, wish. 2 Pleasure, delight. 3 Love. An ti a ni t. Dhé, *he that does God's will ;* tha t. agam sin a dheanamh, *I wish to do that ;* ma 's e do th. e, *if you please ;* deagh th., *goodwill ;* tha mo th. agam, *I have enough ;* bithidh do th. ri dheanamh, *you will have enough to do ;* a theil ! *it does not matter*—DU.
toileach, -eiche, *a.* Willing, voluntary. 2 Desirous. 3**Glad. Cridhe t., *a willing heart ;* tha mi t., *I am willing, I agree, I assent;* gach ni is t. le Dia, *everything God pleases.*
toileachadh, -aidh, *s.m.* Pleasure, satisfaction, 2 Pleasing, gratification, act of pleasing, or giving pleasure. 3‡‡Assent, agreement. A' t—, *pr.pt.* of toilich.
toileachas, -ais, *s.m.* Contentment. 2**Alacrity. 3**Gladness, willingness. T.-inntinn, *mental pleasure* or *satisfaction, peace of mind, contentment.*
toileachas-inntinn,** *s.f* Comfort, mental pleasure, satisfaction, peace of mind,contentment.
toileachd,* *s.f.ind.* Willingness.
toilealachd, *s.f.ind.* Wilfulness, obstinacy. 2* Eagerness, extreme willingness or readiness.
toileas,** -eis, *s.m.* The will. 2 Willingness.
toileil, -e, *a.* Wilful, obstinate. 2 Vain,proud. 3 Willing, voluntary. Le irioslachd th., *with voluntary humility.* Gu t., *wilfully.*
toilich, *pr.pt.* a' toileachadh, *v.a. & n.* Please, satisfy, be willing, will, wish. 2 Indulge,gratify. 3 Agree, assent to, content. Ma thoilicheas tu, *if you will* or *wish ;* th. mi e, *I satisfied him.*
———te, *a. & past pt.* of toilich. Pleased. 2 Satisfied, contented, gratified. Tha mi t., *I am contented.*
toil-inntinn, *s.f.* Satisfaction, gratification, contentment, inward pleasure,mental enjoyment.
toill, *pr.pt.* a' toillteinn, *v.a.* Deserve, merit. 2 Habilitate. Th. thu sin, *you deserved that ;*

gu'n seachnadh e am bàs a th. e, *that he might avert the death he merited.*
toill, see teachd.
toillidh, *fut.aff.a.* of toill.
toillteach,** -eiche, *a.* Meritorious,deserving. 2 Voluntary, willing.
toillteannach, -aiche, *a.* Deservi ng, meriting. Duine t. air bàs, *a man meriting death.*
toillteannachd, see toillteannas.
toillteannas, -ais, -an, *s.m.* Desert, merit, whether good or ill. A réir ur toillteanais, *according to your merit* or *desert.*
toilltinn, *s.m.* Meriting, deserving, demerit. A' t—, *pr.pt.*of toill. 'Dé 'tha thu a' toilltinn? *what do you deserve?*
———each,* see toillteannach.
toilteach, see toillteach.
toiltealachd,** *s.f.* Willingness.
toilteil,** *a.* Willing. 2 Obstinate.
†toimhil, *s.f.* Eating.
†toimhneamh, -nimh, *s.f.* Womb.
toimhseach,** -aich, *s.m.* Farm.
———an, -ain, -an, *s.m.* Riddle, enigma, puzzle. 2 Parable. 3‡‡ see toimhsean.
———anach, -aiche, *a.* Of, or pertaining to, riddles, enigmatical. 2 Skilled in riddles. 3 Fond of riddles.
toimhseagan, see toimhseachan.
toimhsean,* *pl.* of tomhas. Weights, scales, balances, measures. 2 Faculties of the mind, judgment, understanding, discretion. Chaill e 'thoimhsean, *he lost his judgment*; t. fìrinneach, *just weights.*
toimhseil,* -e, *a.* Sensible, judicious, prudent, frugal.
†toin, *s.f.* Tone, accent.
tòin, see tòn.
toin-chlodhach,**,-aich, *s.m.* Turn-coat.
tòin-chruaidh,** *s.f.* Method of inflicting punishment, by which a person was raised a little from the ground, and suffered to fall on his breech.
toineadh, -idh, *s.m.* Thaw, thawing.
tòineag, *s.f.* Little drop of spirits—*Arran.*
toineal, ** -eil, *s.m.* Trance, astonishment.
toineamh,** -imh, *s.m.* Salmon. 2 Monument.
toinisg, -e, *s.f.* Sense, understanding, capacity, discretion, comprehension, judgment, conceit, common sense. Fear gun t., *a man without judgment.*
———each, -eiche, *a.* see toinisgeil.
———eachd,(MS) *s.f.* Sense.
toinisgeil, -e, *a.* Sensible, understanding, judicious, bright, intelligent. 2 (MS)Mental. 3** Having a sound judgment.
tòinleagain, see toinleaganaich.
tòinleagan, -ain,*s.m.* Moving on the hams, as infants, sliding on the breech. A' t—, *pr. pt.* of tòinleaganaich.
tòinleaganachadh, -aidh, *s.m.* & *pr.pt.* of tòinleaganaich.
tòinleaganaich, *pr. pt.* a' tòinleagan & a' tòinleaganachadh, *v. a.* Slide or move on the breech or hams.
toinn, *pr.pt.* a' toinneamh & a' toinneadh, *v. a.* Twist, twine, spin, wreathe, plait. 2 Writhe. 3 Wrench.
toinneadh, -eidh, *s. m.* & *pr. pt.* of toinn, see toinneamh.
toinneamh, -eimh, *s.m.* Twisting, act of twisting, twining or spinning. 2 Twine, twist. 3 Arrangement, train. 4***rarely*, Death. A' t—, *pr.pt.* of toinn. Chuir thu as mo th. mi, *you disappointed me, disarranged my plans.*
toinneamh, -eimh, *s.m.* Multure, miller's share of meal for grinding the corn.—*S.Argyll.*‡ 2 (AF)Salmon.
toinneamh, *a.* see toinn.
toinneamhaiche,** *s.m.* Twister. 2 Instrument that twists or twines.
toinnear, -eir, -an, *s.m.* Spanner, wrench.
toinneolaiche,** *s.m.* Prosodian.
toinneolas,** *s.m.* Prosody.
toinnte, *a.* & *past pt.* of toinn.§Twisted,twined, spun. 2 (CR) *metaphorically*, Wreathed, plaited.
†toinnte, see toinn.
toinnte,** *s.f.* Thread of yarn.
toinnte, *s.f.* Single thread in spinning.
toinnte, *a.* In possession of one's faculties. Cha 'n 'eil e t. gu leòir, *he is half-witted, "not all there"—Skye; also,* cha'n 'eil e teann gu leòir, —DMy.
toinntean, -ein, -an, *s. m.* Long thread in spinning. 2 Filament.§ T. snàth-fhuaigheil, *a sewing-thread*; t. cloimhe, *a tuft of wool*—DMy.
———ach,*a.* Abounding in, or pertaining to, long threads, filaceous.
toinnte-lìn, *s.* Spindle.
toirpean, see toban.
toir, see thoir. [Unaspirated in *Suth'd*, but aspirated everywhere else. Toir dha e, *give it to him.*]
tòir, -e, tòrach & -each, *pl.* -ean & -ichean, *s.f.* Pursuit, chase. 2 Pursuers. 3 Diligent search. 4** Persecution. 5††Inquiry. 6**Help. 7* Enough. An t. air, *in pursuit of him*; air feachd, air th., 's an tuasaid, *in the ranks, in the pursuit and in battle*; teichidh sibh 'nuair nach bi an t. oirbh, *you shall flee when you are not pursued*; tha e air t., *he is making a search for*; tha 'n t. 'nad dhéigh, *you are pursued*; is t. e féin air sin, *he is quite enough for that himself.*
†toir, *s.f.* Churchyard.
†toirb, *s.f.* Fuel.
toirbeart, see tairbheart.
toirbheairtich,(MS) *v.a.* Minister.
toirbheart, see tairbheart.
———ach, see tairbheartach.
———achd, see tairbheartachd.
———as, see tairbheartas.
toirbheir,** *v.a.* see tabhair.
toirbhir, see tabhair.
toirbheirt, see tabhairt.
———each, see tabhairteach.
toirbhleasgadh,** -aidh, *s.m.* Rumbling.
toirbhreith, see tairbheart.
toircheas, -is, -an, *s.m.* Increase, plenty, see torrachas.
toirchim,** *s.f.* Numbness, deadness. T. suain, *a dead sleep.*
———each,** *a.* Stupid. 2 Benumbed.
———eachd,** *s.f.* Stupidity. 2 Numbness. 3 Confinement in a tower.
toirchios,** *s.* Conception, foetus. 2 Increase. 3 Plenty.
toirdeas,** -eis, *s.m.* Dotage.
toireach, see torrach.
tòireach,** *a.* Prone to pursue or persecute. 2 Of, like, or belonging to, pursuit or persecution.
tòireach,** -eich, *s. m.* Pursuit. 2 Diligent search. 3 Persecutor.
———, *gen. sing.* of tòir.
tòireachd, see tòrachd.
tòireadair,(MS) *s.m.* Pursuer.
toireamh,** -eimh, *s.m.* Elegy. 2 Ploughman.
toireann, -inn, -an, *s.m.* Thunder.
toireannach,** *a.* Impetuous, boisterous.
———adh, *s.m.* Detonation.
———d,** *s.f.ind.* Impetuosity, precipitation.
toireannaich, *v.a.* Detonize.

toireas, -eis, *s.m.* see tabhartas.
toireasg,* *s.m.* see tuireasg.
toireim,** *s.f.* Stately gait.
tòireis,** *s.f.* Keen enquiry. 2 Anxiety.
——each,** *a.* Anxious.
toirghill,** *s.f.* Sufficient pledge.
tòirich,** *v.a.* Pursue, chase. 2 Persecute. 3 Search after.
——e,** -an, *s.m.* Pùrsuer. 2 Persecutor.
——te,** *past pt.* of tòirich.
toirinn, *subj.past* of *irreg.v.* tabhair.
toiriosg, -isg, -an, *s.m.* see tuireasg.
tòirleum, -a, -annan & -an, *s.m.* Mighty leap. 2 Somersault.
tòir-leum, *pr. pt.* a' tòirleumadh, *v. a.* Make a mighty leap or jump. 2 Turn a somersault.
toirlinn,* *v.* see tùirling.
toirm, -e, -ean, *s.f.* Noise, sound, loud murmuring sound. 2 Storm. 3**Thunder. 4*Rustling noise, as of people going through a wood. T. chogaidh, *the noise of battle* ; t. seillean an aonaich, *the humming of the mountain bee.*
toirmeach, -eiche, *a.* Noisy, sounding.
toirmeachan-dé, (for tarmachan-dé) *s.* White butterfly—*Arran.*
toirmeasg, -isg, *s.m.* Forbidding, prohibition, hinderance. 2 Act of forbidding. 3 Impediment. A' t—, *pr.pt.* of toirmisg.
tòirmeasgach,** *a.* Apt to hinder or forbid, interdictive.
————d,** *s.f.* Habit or practice of forbidding.
toirmeasgadh, see toirmeasg.
toirmeil, see toirmeach.
toirmisg, *pr.pt.* a' toirmeasg, *v. a.* Forbid, prohibit. 2 Hinder, obstruct.
——te, *past pt.* of toirmisg. Forbidden, prohibited. 2 Obstructed.
toirmrich, -e, *s.f.* Noise of thunder, of water, or of the march of an army. 2 Murmuring sound. 3 Clangour. T. gharbh nan cuairteagan, *the brawling noise of the eddying streams.*
toirm-shlige, -an, *s.f.* Bomb, bomb-shell.
toirn,** *s.* Fiery oven, fiery furnace. 2 see toirm.
toirne, see toirn.
tòirneach, see tairneach.
toirneadh,** -idh, *s.m.* Respect, deference. 2 Raising, constructing.
toirneamh,** -neimh, *s.m.* Punishment.
tòirnich,†† *v.a.* see tàrmaich.
toirnich,** *v.a.* Season, as a cask. 2 Rumble, make a noise.
toirnichte,†† *a.* Fermented.
toirp,* -e, *s.f.* Sod, divot. 2 Thick person.
toirpeanta,* -ainte, *a.* Squat, thick.
toirp-sgian, *s.f.* see toirsgian.
toirrcheas, -eis, *s.m.* see torraicheas.
toirrichead, see torraichead.
toirricheas, see torraicheas.
toirrse,** *s.f.* Lump. 2 Torch.
toirsgian, -sgéin, *s.f.* Peat-spade, peat-cutter or peat-knife.

PARTS OF A PEAT-SPADE :—(DMy)
1 Cas, *handle.*
2 Sneachan, *step for the foot.*
3 A' chrò, *the heel.*
4 Sgian, *knife* or *blade.*
5 Bàrr na sgéine, *point of the blade.*
6 Na h-ailean, *socket in blade-iron, in which the handle and step are inserted.*
7 Faobhar, *edge of blade.*

toirt, -e, *s. f.* Respect, value, importance. 2 Bulk, quantity. 3*Taste in matters. 4 Decency, decorum. 5††Esteem. 6**Strength. 7 **Harm. 8**Reluctance. 9**Sadness. 10** Cake. 11 Due regard, attention. Duine gun t., *a person destitute of taste,* or *regardless of decorum* ; is beag t. a bhitheas air do ghnothach, *your business must be done very awkwardly* ; dh' imich e mu 'n ordugh le t., *he obeyed the summons reluctantly,* or *with due regard to decorum* ; is beag an t., *it matters not.*
toirt, *s.f* Giving, granting, bestowing, grant. A' t—, *pr. pt.* of *irr v.* tabhair. Fhuair i rìoghachd nam beann gorma 'thoirt a mach, *she managed to reach the kingdom of the blue mountains—W.S.2.154.* ; cha b' urrainn da e-féin a thoirt as air cho luath 's a bha 'n gille a' coiseachd, *he could not get out of his way on account of the speed with which the lad was walking.*
toirtealach, see toirteil.
toirtealachd,* *s.f.ind.* Decency, tastefulness, excellent order or arrangement. 2‡‡Respectfulness. 3‡‡ Stoutness, strength. 4‡‡Fruitfulness. 5‡‡Bulkiness, largeness, considerableness. Mór-churaidh an t., *a hero in strength.*
toirtean,** -ein, *s.m.* Thin cake.
†toirtean,** *a.* Useful, serviceable.
toirteil, -e, *a.* Respectful. 2 Stout, strong. 3 Generous. 4 Fruitful. 5 Bulky, large, considerable. 6 Decent, tasteful. 7 Destructive. 8 (MS) Essential. Gu 'm a làn a bhitheas an làmh th., *may the giving hand be full* ; am meadhon a' chath th. thruim, *in the midst of the destructive heavy strife.*
toirtheach,** *a.* Fruitful.
toirthealachd,** *s.f* Fruitfulness.
toirtheann, see toireann.
toirtheannach, (MS) see toireannach.
toirtis, (AF) *s.* Gaelic spelling of *tortoise.* 2 Turtle.
toirt-muidhe, (DMK) *s.f.* Act of churning or butter-making.
toirt-thairis,** *s.f.* Surrender, giving up, through despair or fatigue. 2 Despair, extreme fatigue.
†toisc, *s.f.* Goodwill.
†toiscidh, *s.f.* Will, desire.
toiseach, -sich, -sichean, *s. m.* Beginning, the beginning, origin, source. 2 Front, van. 3 Precedence, precedency. 4 Advantage. 5 Bow or prow of a ship. 6 Front of a cart. [Note tòisich *v.* (accent), but toiseach *s.* (no duration mark although accented in speech.)]
Anns an t. bha 'm Facal, *in the beginning was the Word* ; t. a' ghnothaich, *the origin of the thing* ; t. an airm, *the van of the army* ; a' dol an t. a' bhatailt, *going in the van—McI. 62, 14* ; fhuair e air th. orra (*or* an t. orra), *he got the precedence of them, before them* ; air th., *first, foremost* ; t. is deireadh na luinge, *the bow and stern of the ship* ; air th. air, *before him* ; an t., *first, in the first place* ; 's fheairrde sinn an t. e, *we are the better of it to begin with—McI. 140. 17* ; a' toirt toisich, *giving precedence.*
toiseach, -ich, -ichean, *s.m.* Chief of a clan or tribe.
tòiseachadh, -aidh, *s.m.* Beginning, act of beginning or commencing, commencement. A' t—, *pr. pt.* of tòisich.
toiseachail, -e, *a.* Primitive. 2**Fond of precedence.
tòiseachair,** *s.m.* Beginner.
tòiseachd,** *s.f.* Commencement, priority, precedence.
†toiseadaireachd, *s.f.* Beginning, leading, command.
†toiseadrach,* -aich, *s.m.* Crowner.
tòiseagan, see toimhseachan.
toisg, -e, -ean, *s.f.* Occasion, fit season, proper

time, opportunity. [s.m.*]
†toisg, s.f. Thing, object. 2 Errand, expedition, embassy. 3**Circumstance. 4**Business. 5 **Wholesome administration.
toisg,(AC) a. Left. Togam mo làmh th. an suas, *I will raise my left hand on high.* ["An suas" is uncommon but correct.]
toisg, n.pl. of tosg. Back-teeth, grinders, tusks.
toisgeal, -eil, an, s.m. Finding of a thing that was lost. 2 Reward Luach toisgeil, *the reward for finding a thing that was lost*
toisgeal, -a, a. Left 2 Unlucky,unpropitious 3 Sinister, *in heraldry* Glun t., *a left knee*; an làmh th., *the left hand*
———,†† s.m. The unlucky hand.
———ach, -aiche, a. Left-handed.
———achas,(MS) s.m. Left-handedness.
toisgealta,** a. Left, sinister.
toisgeil, -eil, a. see toisgeal.
———each, a. see toisgealach.
tòisich, pr. pt. a' tòiseachadh, v.a. & n. Begin, commence, fall to, assay. Th. iad air cuid de 'n t-sluagh a bhualadh agus a mharbhadh, *they began to smite and kill some of the people.* [Note tòisich v. (with accent), but toiseach s. (no duration mark although accented in speech.)]
tòisiche,** s.m. Leader, chief, prince. 2 Primate. 3 Nobleman.
tòisichear, *fut.pass.* of tòisich. Shall be begun.
tòisichte, *past pt.* of tòisich. Begun,commenced.
†toisidh, s.pl. Shoes.
toisneadh,** s.m, Leavening.
toit, pr.pt. a' toiteadh, v.a. & n. Smoke, fume 2 Boil quickly, steam. 3 Perfume
toit, -e, -ean, s. f. Smoke, vapour, fume. 2‡‡ Piece, fragment, (*rarely***) 3‡‡Heap. 4‡‡ Small rick of corn, (temporary in *Uist.*)
†toit, a. Whole, entire.
†toite, a. Aice ta 'chroiteag is toite ("tight" in current edition) 's an Eorpa, *she has the trimmest* (*lit.* tightest) *figure in Europe—Moladh Mòrag 84.*
toiteach, -eiche, a. Smoky, vapoury, fumy.
toiteach, -eich, s.m. Steamboat, packet.
toiteachan,** -ain, s.m. Vent, chimney.
toiteadh,** s.m. Assation. 2 Roasting. 3 Fumigation.
toiteal, s.m. Attack in battle. 2 Warlike movement. 3 Flock of water-fowl—*Sàr-Obair.*
toiteau,** -ein, s.m. Flame, conflagration.
toitean, -ein, -an,s.m. Piece of flesh of any kind. 2 Collop, steak, chop. 3**Piece of flesh roasted on embers. 4 Little heap.
———ach, -aiche,a.Abounding in pieces of flesh 2 Like a collop. 3 Abounding in little heaps.
toitear,** a. Lumpy.
toitearlach,* -aich, s.m. Smother, dense column of smoke 2 Thick gigantic man—*Sar-Obair.*
toiteil, see toiteach.
toith, see toth.
toithbheum, see toibheum.
toitheastal, see toichiosdal.
toithleannan,** -ain, s.m. Paramour, concubine.
toitlinn,* s.f. see toit.
toitlinneach,* -eiche, s.m see toiteach.
toitreach,** -ich, s.m. Conflagration.
†tol, s.m. Churchyard.
†tola,** s.m. Church-officer. 2 Superfluity. 3 Sleep.
†toladh,** -aidh, s.m. Destruction. 2 Sleep.
tòlair, -ean, s.m. Foxhound, beagle. 2 Mastiff JGC.W, 89. Bheir e leis a' chreig sibh, mar a thug an sionnach na tòlairean, *he will lead you over the precipice, as the fox did the hounds.*
tòlair-mhaigheach, s.m. Harrier.
tolg, tuilg, -an, s.m. Hollow induced upon a smooth surface. 2**Bruise, as on the surface of laminated metal vessels. 3**Sinkings of any undulating surface. 4**Wave. 5**Crevice. 6 **Pride. 7***rarely*, Bed. 8 Colour. 9* Hollow, as in a kettle. [*s.f.]
tolg v a. Sputter, vomit, as a mountain torrent. 2 Dint, pit or dent, especially of metals. 3 Colour 4* Make hollows, as in a kettle or cauldron.
tolgach, -aiche, a. Hollowed. 2 Having many hollows. 3 Of many colours. 4 Gaudy,showy. 5 Inconstant 6**Proud, haughty 7**Full of bruises, as a plate of metal. 8* Freakish. A bhiorraid th., *his dented helm.*
tolgachadh,‡‡ -aidh, s m. & pr pt of tolgaich, see tolgadh
tolgadh. s.m Sputtering, vomiting, as a mountain torrent 2 Dinting. 3 Bending, as grass.
tolgaich, v. see tolg.
toll, pr. pt. a' tolladh, v.a. Bore, perforate. 2 Make a hole, dig a hole or pit. 3*Exhale, emit vapours.
toll, tuill, pl. tuill & tollan, s. m. Hole, bore, perforation. 2 Hollow, cavity. 3 Crevice. 4 Wicket. 5 Ear-mark on sheep, see comharradh-cluaise. 6 **Pit, cave, den. 7***rarely* Head. T. domhain, *a deep hole*
tollach, -aiche, a. Full of holes. 2 Perforating, boring 3 That perforates.
tollachan,** -ain, s.m. Piercer
tolladair, -ean, s.m. Borer, piercer. 2**Wimble. 3 Stone-borer. 4 (MS) Poser.
———eachd, s.f.ind. Boring.
tolladh, -aidh, s.m. Boring, act of boring,piercing or perforating. 2 Digging of holes or pits. 3* Edging in. A' t—, pr.pt. of toll. Tha e a' tolladh fodham, *he is undermining me.*
tolladh-fàsair, s.m. Plug-hole of a boat.
tollag,(AF) s.f. Crab-louse.
tollainn,* s.f. Exhalation,vapour in damp places in summer. 2 Steam, gas.
tollair,** -ean,s.m. Borer, piercer. 2 Foxhound.
tollaire,* -an, s.f. One that edges his way. 2 Genteel intruder.
toll-alpaidh, s.m. Mortice.
tollan, -ain, -an, s.m., dim. of toll. Little hole or orifice.
———ach, -aiche, a. Full of little holes.
toll-an-t-sil,(DMK) s.m. Vent of a fish.
toll-an-tùc, s.m. Plug-hole of a boat—*Lewis.*
tollaran, -ain, -an, s.m. Glutton.
toll-bùtha, -uill-bhùtha, s.m. Gaol, tolbooth.
toll-cartaidh,(DMK) s.m. Square opening in the wall of a byre through which the muck is thrown out to the dunghill.—*Caithness.*
toll-choinein, s.m Rabbit-burrow.
toll-cluaise, -uill-chluaise, s.m. Touch-hole of a gun.
toll-cluaisean, see toll-cluaise.
toll-cnaig, s.m. Plug-hole of a boat.
toll-cnaip, s.m. Button-hole.
tolldach,(MS) -aiche, a. Full of holes.
tolldair,†† -ean, s.m. Borer
———eachd, s f. Boring.
toll-dubh,- uill-dhubha, s.m. Prison, gaol.
toll-gaineimh, s.m Sand-pit.
toll-gaoithe,* -uill-ghaotha, s.m. Air-hole.
toll-guail, s.m. Coal-pit.
toll-na-stiùireach, s m. Rudder-band,see rudder No. 4, p. 78. There are two rudder-bands, one attached to a hole and one to a pin—this is the former.
toll-prine,(AC) s.m.Plug-hole in a boat—*Argyll.*
toll-putain,* -uill-phutain, s.m. Button-hole.
toll-silidh, see toll-siolaidh.
toll-siolaidh, s.m. Plug-hole of a boat.
tollta, *past pt.* of toll. Bored, perforated,pierced.

tolltach, -aiche, *a.* Full of holes. 2 Full of pits. 3 Piercing, perforating, causing holes. Cho t. ris an rideal, *as full of holes as a sieve.*
toll-tora, *s.m.* Wimble-hole.
toll-torain, *s.m.* Wicket. 2(AH) Hole about 30 inches square that can be closed or opened in back wall of barn and directly opposite the door. It is opened when winnowing is to be engaged in.
tolm, -uilm. -an, *s.m.* Hillock of a round form, mound, knoll. 2 Bush, thicket. 2*High hillock
——ach, -aiche, *a.* Abounding in hillocks, knolly
tolmag, -aig, -an, *s.f., dim.* of toll. Little knoll.
———ach, -aiche, *a.* Full of small hillocks.
tolman, -ain, *s.m.* Little knoll, hill or mound.
———ach, -aiche, *a.* Knolly, full of knolls or mounds.
tom, tuim, *pl.* -an & -annan, *s.m.* Round hillock or knoll, rising ground, swell, green eminence. 2 Any round heap. 3 Tuft of anything. 3*Bush, thicket. 5 Ant-hill. 6* Stool—*Islay.* 7 *Volume of a book. 8**Bank, 9**Grave 10** *rarely* The plague. 11**Conical knoll. *Tom* is applied in many parts of the *North*, especially *Arran* to a bush that grows wild, as, t. fraoich, *a tuft of heather*; t. airnean, *a sloe-bush—preas* is not used there.

T.-ghròiseid, *a gooseberry-bush*; tha e air a th., *he is at stool*; thug e car mu th. asam, *he jilted me, cheated me*; 'am bun an tuim, *sheltered by the thicket*; tha t. 'sa bhealach, *there is a bush in the gateway*—gateways were formerly closed by a bush instead of a gate; dosain is tuim nan ruadhag, *the thickets and hillocks of roes.*
tom, *v.* see tùm.
tomach, -aiche, *a.* Full of knolls or tufts, tufty. 2 Bushy.
tomad, -aid, -an, see tomult.
———ach, -aiche, *a.* see tomultach.
———achd, see tomultachd.
tomadh,** *s.m.* Rasure. 2 see tùmadh.
tomaidh, see tumaidh.
tomair, *s.m.* Protection. 2 Protector. 3 see tumair.
tomald, see tomult.
tomalt, see tomult.
——ach, see tomultach.
———achd, see tomultachd.
toman, -ain, -an, *s.m.dim.* of tom. Hillock, any small heap or tuft. 2‡‡Small thicket or bush.
tomanach, -aiche, *a.* Full of little knolls, small heaps or tufts. 2 Of small thickets, bushy, tufty.
tom-an-ionghnaidh,(AF) *s.m.* The wonder-tuft or -clump In some parts of the North the name hedgehog was given to a mysterious animal, which when met with among the corn, had only the appearance of a grey stone, but could change its shape. When thus met, a quantity of the corn was left standing around it and only the ears of grain cut. Such a clump has been seen by A.F., and above was given as the cause of its existence, which, as few knew, almost every one who saw it wondered why it was there.
tomanta,* *a.* Rude.
tomataisean,(DMK) *s.m.* Hypochondria—*West coast of Ross.*
tombaca, *s.m.ind.* Tobacco—*nicotiana tobacum.* 2**Snuff T. seabh, t. cagnaidh, *tobacco;* feuch t., *give me some tobacco or snuff.*
tom-famha, *s.m.* Mole-hill.
tomh, *pr. pt.* a' tomhadh, *v.a.* & *n.* Offer, attempt, t. 2 Threaten, 3 Aim. 4* Point with the finger. 5**Remark. 6††Present.
tomhadh, -aidh, *s.m.* Offering, act of offering or attempting. 2 Threatening, act of threatening, threat. 3 Act of aiming. 4 Pointing with the finger. 5 Frown. A' t—, *pr. pt.* of tomh.
tomhail,** *s.f.* Terror, fright.
————,** *a,* Vast, terrible.
————each,** *a.* Vast, terrible, frightful.
————eachd, *s.f.ind.* Vastness, terribleness, frightfulness.
†tomhailt, *v.a.* Eat.
tomhais, *pr.pt.* a' tomhas, *v.a.* Measure, survey, compute the length, breadth, height, depth, quantity, distance or weight, balance, fathom, sound. 2 Guess, unriddle, solve an enigma. T. am fiodh, *measure the wood*; t. am fearann, *survey the land*; t. cò a chunnaic mi, *guess whom I saw*, also *guess who saw me.*
————ean, *s.pl.* Weights, scales, balances.
————te, *past pt.* of tomhais. Measured, fathomed, weighed. 2 Guessed, solved as a riddle.
tomhartaich, *s. f.* Twittering. 2 Suspense, uncertainty, hesitation, hesitancy, pendency. Tha mi 'san t., *I am hesitating.*
tomhas, -ais, *pl.* -an & toimhsean, *s.m.* Measure, measurement, dimension. 2 Weight. 3 Balance, scale. 4 Survey. 5 Mensuration. 6 Measuring, act of measuring. 7 Guessing, act of guessing or solving, as a riddle. 8** Riddle. 9 **Hint. 13** Mode in *music.* 11 Moderation. 12 Weighing. 13 Surveying. A' t—, *pr. pt.* of tomhais. Gabh mo th., *take my measure;* dé 'n t. a th' ann? *what is its measurement?* slat-thomhais, *a measuring-wand*; thar tomhais, *beyond measure or moderation*; soitheach-tomhais, *a measuring vessel*; t.-dùbailt, *a double-measure*; t. cruithneachd, *a measure of wheat.* There is a feat still practised by boys in the Highlands in climbing a tree—standing on tip-toe, they touch a certain branch with their caman, and then spring up to get a grip of the place so marked out. This is *a' tomhas leuma.*
tomhasach, -aiche, *a.* Mensural.
tomhasail, -e, *a.* Mensural.
tomhasair,** *s.m.* Balancer.
tomhas-iùil, *s.pl.* Mathematics. *prov.*
tomhas-riaghlair,** *s.m.* Assizer.
tomhas-taise, *s.m.* Hygrometer.
tomhas-troidh,(DMK) *s.m.* Foot-rule.
tomhas-ùine, *s.m.* Metronome. *prov*
tomhlachd,* *s.f.ind.* Thick milk. 2**Curds.
†tomhladh, -aidh. (AF) *s.m.* Cow's milk.
†tomhradh, -aidh, *s.m.* Protection.
†tomhraiche, *s.m.* Protector, patron.
tomnach,** -aich, *s.m.* Testator.
tomradh,** -aidh, *s.m.* Fustian, bombast.
tom-sheangan, *s.m.* Ant-hill.
tomudach, see tomultach.
tomult, -uilt, -an, *s.m.* Bulk, largeness. 2 Burliness. 3 Size, dimension, magnitude, amplitude. 4 Influence, authority. 5 Respectability.
tomultach, -aiche, *a.* Bulky, large, gigantic, big, sizeable. 2 Fleshy, brawny. 3 Influential. 4 Respectable.
————d,** *s. f.* Bulkiness, ampleness, sizeableness.
tòn, -òine & -a, *pl.* -an, *s. f.* The fundament breech, anus.
tòna, see tòn.
tònach, -aiche, *a.* Of, or belonging to, the breech 2 Broad-breeched. 3 Large-hipped.
———,* -aich, *s,f.* Broad-bottomed woman.
tonach, -aich, *s.m.* Shirt, garment. 2 Bath.
tònag, -aig, -an,‡‡*s.f.* Clew of yarn. 2**Tern

of ridicule for a squat waddling female. 3 (Fionn) Small squat measure used for measuring and holding liquids (also tuanag.)
tònagach, -aiche, *a.* Abounding in clews of yarn.
tònag-a'-chladaich ‡‡ *s.f.* Thrift, sea-gillyflower.
tònair,* -ean, *s.m.* Broad-bottomed man.
tonalas,** *s.m.* Cringing, adulation.
tonasg,** *s.f.* Ball of yarn.
†tonc,** *s.m.* Chain.
ton-chlodhach, see toin-chlodhach.
ton-chruaidh, see tòin-chruaidh.
†tonda, *a.* Stubborn.
tòn-dhearg,¶ *s.f.* Redstart, see ceann-dearg.
tòn-dubh, (an) *s.f.* Crane, see corra-thòn-dubh.
tònlagain, *pr.pt.* a' tònlagan, *v.n.* Hobble, slide on the breech.
tònlagan,* -ain, *s. m.* Sliding on the breech, hobbling. 2‡‡Cringing, fawning. A' t—, *pr. pt.* of tònlagain.
tòn-lodanach,** -aiche, *a.* Having a fawning or cringing spirit.
tòn-lodanadh, -aidh, *s.m.* Fawning, cringing, mean soliciting.
tonn, tuinn & tuinne, *pl.* tuinn, tonna & tonnan, *s.m.* Wave, surge, billow 2 *Splash. 3 Any quantity of liquid—*Arran.*
Thog tuinn an cinn, *waves reared their heads ;* an t. baistidh, *sacred baptism water ;* t. air tràigh leis'fhéin, *a solitary wave on the shore ;* nuallan nan tonn, *the raging noise of the waves ;* tha t. math uisge 's a' chuinneig fhathast, *there is a good drop of water in the pail yet.* [*s.f.]
tonn,* *v.n.* Splash, pour out irregularly. 2** Undulate. 'Ga thonnadh m' a cheann, *splashing it about his head.*
†tonn, *s.* Skin, hide.
tonnach, -aiche, *a.* Waved, undulated. 2**Wavy, billowy, tempestuous. An fhairge ghlas th., *the blue billowy ocean.*
———,** -aich, *s.m.* Mound, rampart.

663. *Tonn-a'-chladaich.*

tonn-a'-chladaich,§ *s.m.* Thrift, sea-pink—*armeria maritima*
tonnadair, see tunnadair.
tonnadh,** -aidh, *s.m.* Vomiting 2 Death by poison.
tonnag, -aig, -an, *s.f* Small square of tartan or of any coarse woollen material, used as a loose covering for the shoulders by women. 2 Mantle
tonnag, -aig, -an, *s.f* ,*dim.* of tonn. Little wave.
———ach, -aiche, *a* Plaided, wearing a plaid over the shoulder.
tonnan,** -ain, *s.m.* ,*dim.* of tonn. 2 *n. pl.* of tonn.
tonn-ghluasad,** -aid, *s.m.* Undulation.
tonn-luaisg, *pr pt.* a tonn-luasgadh, *v.a.* Toss or rock by waves, or as if by waves, pitch or reel, as a vessel.
tonn-luasgach, -aiche, *a.* Rocking or reeling, as the waves. 2**Causing a reeling motion, as of a ship at sea.
tonn-luasgadh, -aidh, *s.m.* Act or state of tossing, as on the waves, pitching or keeling of a ship. A' t—, *pr.pt.* of tonn-luaisg.
tonn-luaisgte, *past pt.* of tonn-luaisg. Wave-tossed.
tonnmhor,‡‡ -mhoire, *a.* Billowy.
top,** *s.m.* Hop, see lus-an-leanna.
top, -a, *pl.* -an & -annan, *s.m.* Top, tuft. T. circe, *the tuft on the head of a hen.*
topach, -aiche, *a.* Having a top or tuft, topped, tufted. Cearc th., *a tufted hen.*
topag, *s.f.* Lark (bird)—*Lewis.* Isean na topaig, *the lark's young.*
topainn,** *s.f.* Teasing, pulling by the hair.
topan, -ain, *s.m.* Tuft, top-knot. 2 Tuft of wool on the distaff.
topanach,‡‡ -aiche, *a.* Having a small top or tuft.
topar,** -air, *s.m.* Taper.
topas, Gaelic form of *topaz.*
tor,* *s.f.* Heavy shower. 2 Bush, shrub. 3 (AF) Bull.
†tor, *a.* Heavy.
tor, -oir, -an, see tùr.
†tor, tuir, *s.m.* Answer, reply. 2 Bull. 3 Pursuer. 4 Fear, dread. 5 Tear. 6 Sovereign, lord, noble. 7 Weariness. 8 Crest.
tòra ! *int.* Cry to enrage a bull—*Arran.*
tora, toraichean & torachan *s.m.* Auger wimble, iron for boring holes.
torach, -aiche, *a.* Having augers. 2 Like an auger. 3 Fertile, fruitful, productive. 4 Efficient. 5 Substantial. 6 Rank. 7**see torrach. Siol t., *productive* or *rank corn ;* talamh t., *fertile land ;* buailean t., *efficient* or *energetic strokes, as in rowing.*
tòrach, *gen. sing.* of tòir.
torachas-biadhain,‡ *s.m.* Celery-leaved crowfoot —*ranunculus sceleratus.*
tòrachd, *s.f.* Pursuit, chase, pursuing with hostile intention. 2 Inquiring, asking, strict inquiry or search. 3 Craving. 4 Retaliation. 5 Persecution. 6††Restitution. Cha d' rinn iad t., *they did not pursue ;* tha e a' t., *he is making strict inquiry ;* a' t. chaorach, *searching for sheep* , luchd-t., *persecutors, pursuers;* air eagal gu 'n coinnich an luchd-t. sibh, *lest the pursuers meet you ;* fuileachdach 'san t., *bloody in the chase ;* tha e a' t. orm, *he craves* or *insinuates his claim to such ;* tha t. orm, *I am pursued.*
toradh, -aidh, -aidhean, *s.m.* Fruit, produce. 2 **Fruitfulness. 3 Profit, advantage. 4 Consequence, effect, result. 5**Answer. 6(AF) Milking. 7 Taking. 8 Supply. Thug Cain de th. an fhearainn, *Cain brought of the produce of the ground ;* t. do ghniomharan, *the natural effects* or *consequence of your deeds.*
toradh, -aidh, -ean, *s.m.* see tora. 2 Answer. 3** see torradh. Toll toraidh, *an auger-hole.*
toradhadair, *s.m.* Fruiterer.
toradhair,(AF) *s.m.* Monster. 2**Dwarf.
toradhan, see torunn.
torag,** -aig, *s.f.* Wench.
toraich,(MS) *v.a.* Beget.
toraicheas, -eis, see torraicheas.
toraicinn, *s.* Peat-knife. *Arran* for toirsgian.
toraidh ! *int.* Cry to excite a bull.
torail, see torrail.
toraileachd,** *s.f.* Fruitfulness.
torain, *s.pl.* Insects, worm, grub, a certain vermin in corn. Mar lus is torain 'ga reubadh. *like a herb that worms devour.*
toralachd, see torralachd.
torair,* -ean, *s.m.* see toranach & **torain.

toran,(AF) see toranach.

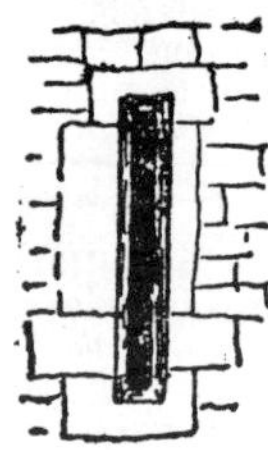

664. *Toran.*

toran, -ain, *s.m.* Balistraria, loop-hole. An t. 'san t-sabhal, *the loop-hole in the bar...—Sg.-nan-caol. 141.*

toran, -ain, see torrail.

toranach,‡ -aich, *s.m.* Grub-worm, borer-worm.

toranan,(DC) *s.m.* see torranan.

torann, -ainn, *s.m.* see torunn.

toras, -ais. *s.m.* Weariness. 2 Journey. 3 Lord.

torathair, see toradhair.

torb,** *s.m.* Throng. 2 Rout.

torc, -uirc, *s.m.* Hog, boar. 2 (AF) Brawn. 3 Castrated boar—*Islay*. 4* Whale—*Ossian*. 5 (AC)Cleft, notch, indentation, scollop. 6(AC) Three-cornered hole made in the ground if hard, to assist in pulling the carrots on Domhnach Curran—*carrot Sunday* in the *W. Isles.* 7(AC) Monarch's necklace. A' tomhas an tuirc, *measuring the boar ;* t. nimhe, *a wild boar ;* t. alluidh, *a wild boar ;* lorg nan t., *the track of the whales.*

torc,(DC)*s.m.* Sod. A special use of it was the sod turned up as a mark to indicate divisions of arable land, during the run-rig system of cultivation. In *Argyll* it is *durc*,=a mark in land, a piece of anything.

†**torc**, *s.m.* Sovereign, lord. 2 Heart. 3 Face. 4 Collar.

torcach,** -aiche, *a.* Like a boar or hog.

torc-chluasach,(AC) *a.* Notch-eared.

torcan, *s.m. dim.* of torc. Little cleft. 2 Species of biforcated carrot—*cardionis benedictus.*

torcan, *s.m.* Fattening pig, porker.

†**torchair**, *past pass.* of torchuir. He fell, died, was killed. 2 It happened.

torchair, see torchuir.

torchair,** *s.m.* Leveller.

torchair, *gen.sing.* of torchar.

torchar, -air, -an, *s.m.* Fall. 2 Killing, death. 3 Hurt by a fall.

torchanach, *v.n.* Prosper.

tor-chathair, -chathrach, -chathraichean, *s. f.* Throne, see torr-chathair.

torchos,(AF) *s.f.* Calf.

torchos-bréige,(AF) *s.m.* Moon-calf (fabulous.)

torchradh, -aidh, *s.m.* Transfixing act of transfixing, piercing, wounding. 2 Killing. A' t—, *pr.pt.* of torchuir.

torchraidh, *fut.aff.a.* of torchuir.

————,‡‡ s. Bars in music. 2 Elegy.

torchuir, *pr.pt* a' torchradh, *v.a. & n* Transfix, wound, pierce. 2 Kill. 3 Kill by knocking or throwing down. 4**Perish, happen.

torc-mhuineal,-eil, *s.m.* Hog's neck, boar's neck.

torc-nimhe,(AF) *s.m.* Fierce or wild boar. 2 (AF) Reptile.

tordhan,** -ain, *s.m.* Elegy.

torgan,** see torghan.

torghan,‡ -ain, -an, *s.m.* Purling sound, musical sound. 2**Din, noise, rattle, hoot.

torghanach,** *a.* Rattling.

torghanaich,** *s.f.* Rattling.

torlais,** *s.* Person who talks at random.

torluinn, see tùirling.

torm,(AC) *s.m.* Murmur.

tormach, see tàrmachan.

tormach,** -aich, *s.m.* Increase. 2 Feeding of cows a short time before and after calving.

tormachadh,** -aidh, *s.m.* Increasing.

tormachag, *s.f.* see tàrmachan.

tormachan, see tàrmachan.

tormachan an t-sléibhe, (CR) *s. m.* Ptarmigan —*W. of Ross.*

tormachan-dé, *W. of Ross* for dearbadan-dé.

tormachan-tuinne,(CR) *s. m.* Small sea-bird—*W. of Ross.*

tormadh,** *a.* Pregnant. growing big.

tormagan-dé, *s.f.* see dearbadan-dé.

†**tormaich**,** *v.a.* Magnify, increase, enlarge.

665. *Torman.*

torman,§ -ain, *s.m.* Wild clary, vervain sage—*salvia verbenacea.*

torman, -ain, -an, *s.m.* Noise, sound, rumbling. 2 Music. 3 Musical sound, murmur, sound of the drone of a bagpipe. 4** Drone of a bagpipe. 5 Stringed musical instrument. 6** Harp. T.-ciùil, *a harp.*

tormanach, -aiche, *a.* Noisy, loud, murmuring, rumbling, making a musical murmur.

tormanaich, *v.n.* Bubble.

tormanaich-bruidhinn, *s.f.* Broken, inarticulate speech—JGC., W. 133.

torman-ciùil, *s.m.* Stringed instrument. 2 Harp.

torman-dé, *W. of Ross* for dearbadan-dé.

torm-fheadan,** *s.* Bassoon.

torm-fhiodhull,** s. Bass-viol.

†**torn**, *s.m.* Kiln, furnace, oven. 2 Lord.

tornail, *s.f.*Knocking one thing against another.

tornair,** *s.m.* Turner.

tornamh,** -aimh, *s.m.* Humiliation. 2 Descent.

toroisg,** *s.f.* Hand-saw. 2 File.

torpan, see tarpan.

tòrr, -a, -an, *s.m.* Hill, mountain of an abrupt or conical form, lofty hill. 2 Eminence. 3 Mound, large heap. 4** Rock. 5 Grave, tomb. 6 Tower. 7 Heap of ruins. 8 Castle. 9 Body of men, congregation, crowd. 10* Womb—*Ossian.* †11 Belly. 12 (DU) Large quantity of anything. T gainneimh, *a heap of sand ;* t.-coirce, *a quantity of oats built in little cocks on the rigs or ground—Lewis*—(DMy. ; o thòrr-thir an t-sneachd, *from the hilly land of snow ;* mo chlann 'san tòrr, *my children in the tomb.*

tòrr, *pr. pt.* a' tòrradh, *v. a.* Heap up, pile up. hoard. 2 Form into heaps. 3 Teem. 4 Bury. 5 Come alive.

torrach, -aiche, *a.* Pregnant (of women only.) 2 Fruitful.

tòrrach**-aiche, *a*. Towery. 2 Full of eminences.
torrachas, see torraicheas.
tòrradair,** *s.m.* Burier.
tòrradh, -aidh, -aidhean, *s.m.* Heaping, act of piling together. 2 Heap. 3 Burial. interment, act of burying. 4 Burial solemnities or procession. 5 Watching or waking of the dead. 6*Embankment of a dam. 7 Payment for keeping up a mill-dam 8 see tora & toradh A' t—, *pr. pt* of tòrr. A' t airgid, *heaping or hoarding money ;* air a t. le miallan, *teeming with lice ;* air a t le gràisg, *teeming with rabble.*
torraghan,** -ain, *s.m.* Murmur, purling noise, gurgle.
————ach,** *a.* Murmuring, purling.
————aich, *v.a.* Gurgle.
torraich, *pr.pt.* a' torrachadh, *v.a. & n.* Make pregnant, impregnate. 2**Conceive, become fruitful or pregnant 3 Teem.
torraiche, *comp.* of torrach.
torraichead, -eid, *s.m.* Degree of fruitfulness. 2**Pregnancy.
torraicheas, -eis, *s.f* Conception, pregnancy. 2 Fertility, fruitfulness. Meudaichidh mi do th., *I will increase thy conception.*
————— anabuich, *s.* Embryo, fœtus. 2 Untimely birth.
torrail,** *a.* Fertile, productive, prolific.
————eachd,** *s.f.* Fertility, productiveness.
torraisgil, (AG) *s.f. Reay country* for toirsgian.
torramh,** *s.m.* Pilgrimage.
torran, -ain, -an, *s.m., dim.* of tòrr. Little hill, rising ground, mound or knoll. 2‡‡Knob. 3 **Grave. 4 (CR) Dunghill—*Arran.* 5 see torrunn.
torranach, -aiche, *a.* Knolled, abounding in hillocks.
torranach, *s.m.* Figwort, see lus-nan-cnapan.
torranan, *s.m.* Figwort, see lus-nan-cnapan.
torr-chathair, -chathrach, -chathraichean, *s.f.* Citadel, fortress. 2 Throne.
torr-leus, -leòis, -an, *s.m.* Torch.
torroichim, *s.* Deep snoring. 2 Sleep.—*Mac Mh. Alasdair.*
tòrr-sgian, *s.f.* Peat-spade.
torrthair, see toradhair.
torrunn, -uinn, *s. m.* Loud or murmuring noise, murmur. 2 Thunder.
torrunnach, -aiche, *a.* Thunderous. 2 Making a loud or murmuring noise, noisy. 3**Sounding like thunder. Le buille th., *with a thundering blow.*
tor-stol,** *s.m.* Chair of state.
tort,* *s.m.* Little loaf or cake.
tort, *Shiskine, Arran* for tobhta.
tortail,** *a.* Strong, stout. 2 Tight, firm.
tortaileachd,** *s.f.* Strength, stoutness. 2 Tightness, firmness.
tortaobh,** *s.* Confidence.
torthair,** *s.m.* Monster. 2 Dwarf.
————each,** *a.* Monstrous.
————eachd, *s.f.* Monstrousness.
torunn, see torrunn.
tòs, see tùs.
tòs, an, for air thùs, *at first.*
tosach, *s.m. Suth'd.* for toiseach, 2 (DMu) Used to express satisfaction on hearing of one's welfare. Cia mar tha sibh ? tha gu slàn, O is maith an tosach, *how do you do ? I am in good health, Oh that's well.—Black Isle.*
tòsan, for tàsan—*Wm. Ross, p. 16.*
tòsan, *s.m.* Onset. 2 Beginning, prelude—*Sàr-Obair.*
tosd, *s.m.ind.* Silence, quietness, stillness. Bi 'nad th., *be silent ;* t. na h-oidhche, *the silence of the night.*
tosd,* *a.* see tosdach.
tosd,* *v.a. & n.* see tosdaich.
tosdach, -aiche, *a.* Silent, peaceful, quiet, still. 2 Causing silence or stillness. Talla t. na dì chuimhne, *the silent hall of forgetfulness;* gu t., *silently, quietly.*
tosdachadh,‡‡ -aidh, *s.m.* Putting to silence. 2 Act or state of becoming silent. A' t—, *pr. pt.* of tosdaich.
tosdachd, *s.f.ind.* Silence, quietness, peacefulness.
tosdaich, *pr.pt.* a' tosdachadh, *v.a & n.* Confute, put to silence, make quiet. 2 Become quiet. Tosdaicheam, *I will put to silence.*
————ear, *fut pass.* of tosdaich.
tòsdal, see tòstal
———ach, see tòstalach.
tosdalachd,‡‡ *s.f.* Sedateness
tosg, tuisg, *s.m.* Journey. 2 Embassy 3 Report
tosg, -oisg & -uisg, *pl* tuisg & -an, *s.m.* Tusk 2 Peat-cutter, see toirsgian. 3(AF) Tusk (fish.) 4**Back-tooth, fang, grinder. 5** Gash, cut. [††*s.f.*]
——, *pr.pt.* a' tosgadh, *v.a.* Cut irregularly.
tosgach, -aiche, *a.* Tusky, like a tusk. 2 Cut in an uneven way
tosgaid, see togsaid.
tosgair, -ean, *s.m.* Ambassador. 2 Post. 3 One who goes on a message, messenger, harbinger. 4 One who cuts irregularly, or who botches in cutting. [*tosgaire.]
———eachd, *s.f.ind.* Going on an errand. 2* Embassy. 3 Journeying, jaunting.
tosgal, -ail, *s.m.* Arrogance.
tosgan, *n.pl.* of tosg.
tostal, see toichiosdal.
tòstal, -ail, *s.m.* Arrogance, presumption.
———ach, -aiche, *a.* Presumptuous, arrogant.
tot,* *v.a.* Roast or toast hurriedly on the embers. 2 Boil hurriedly.
†tot, -oit, *s.m.* Wave. 2 Sod, turf 3 Woman.
tota, *pl.* totan & totaichean, see tobhta.
tota-bràghad, see tobhta-bràghaid.
tota-deireadh, see tobhta-deiridh.
totadh, -aidh, *s.m.* Puff.
total,* -ail, *s.m.* see tòstal.
total-eun,* -ail, *s.m.* Bevy.
totarnachd,** *s.f.* Stuttering, stammering.
tòth, *s.* Eagerness, inclination. Arran form of (*in*) *tow* (*with.*) Ann an t. dol ann, *eager to go ;* ann an t. leis, *greatly attached to* or *taken up by it* or *him.*
toth, -a, -an *s.m.* Foul blast of vapour, stench. 2**Fume. 3**Puff of smoke.
†toth, -a, *s.m.* Female. 2 Pudenda muliebria.
totha, see todha.
tothach, -aiche, *a.* Vapoury.
tothachd,** *s.f.* Validity 2 Substance.
tòthadh,** *s.m.* Effluvia.
tothag,* -aig, -an, *s.f.* Wonderfully short trousers.
tothair,* *v.a.* see todhair.
tothair,** *s.m.* Freebooter.
†tothbhall, -bhuill, *s.* Pudenda muliebria.
toth-grod, *s.m.* Miasma.
tot-tilgte, see tobhta-tilgte.
trà, -thau, see tràth.
tràbail,(CR) *s.* Slightly bedraggled—*W. of Ross.*
tràbalach,(CR) *a.* Bedraggled—*W. of Ross.*
tràbhach,* see trabhach.
trabhach, -aich, *s.f.* Rubbish of any kind cast ashore by the flood on the bank of a river, or on the sea-shore. 2 Fioriu grass. 3 In *Lewis* pronounced "tràthoch," and =rabhann.
trabhailt,* -e, -ean, *s.f.* see treabhailt.
trabhsdan,†† see trasdan.
————ach,†† -aiche, *a.* see trasdanach.

*trach,(DC) -a, s.m. Ditch.
tràchd,* see dràchd. †2 Tract, treatise, history, narration, report.
tràchd, v.a. Negotiate, traffic, treat, handle. 2 ††Propose.
trachdach,** a. Negotiating, trafficing.
tràchdadh, -aidh, -ean, s.m. Negotiating, negotiation. 2 Proposal, purposing. 3 Traffic.
†tràchdadh, -aidh, -aidhean, s.m. Tradition. 2 Treatise.
tràchdail,** s.f. Negotiation.
tràchdair, -ean, s.m Historian, recorder, one who writes treatises.
tràchdaireachd,** s.f. Business of a historian, history, writing of tracts.
trachdalachd,‡‡ s.f.ind. History, negotiation.
trachlach,** a. Fatiguing, laborious.
trachladh, -aidh, s.m. Loosening 2 see treachladh
trachlaiche,** s.m. Drudge, one employed at dirty laborious work. 2 Squanderer.
tradan,** -ain, s.m. Scolding person. 2 Quarrelsome person.
——ach,** a. Scolding, quarrelsome, litigious.
tradh, -aidh, -an, s.f. Lance. 2 Fishing-spear.
trag,(AF) s.f. Snipe—*Ross-shire.*
tragh, v.n. see traogh.
tràgha, *gen.sing.* of tràigh.
traghadair,** s.m. Appeaser.
tràghadh, -aidh, s.m. Ebbing, act or state of ebbing or subsiding. A' t—, *pr.pt.* of tràgh.
tràghadh-asbhuinneach, (DC) s.m. "Flooding" of women—*Uist.*
traghaid,(MS) s.f. see treaghaid.
traghais,(CR) s.f. Commotion, stir. 2 Lumber. *W. of Ross.*
traghna, s Landrail, see trèan-ri-trèan.
traibeal, see tràbail.
traideach,** -dich, s.m. Warrior.
traidh, see troidh.
traidhtear,* -eir, -an, s.m. Rogue. 2 (MS) Betrayer.
traidhtearach, -eiche, a. Traitorous, disloyal.
————d, s.f. Treason, perfidy, disloyalty.
tràigh, *pr pt* a' traghadh, v.a. & n. see traogh.
traigh, -e, tràgha & tràghad, *pl.* -ean [tràinnean in *Skye*,] s.f. Sea-shore. 2 Beach exposed at low-water. 3** Shore of a lake or river. 4** Reflux or ebbing of the tide. 5* Sand-beach, strand Ghios (dh' ionnsuidh) na tràgha, *to the shore*; mar th fhuaimear a' chuain, *like the raging reflux of the sea*; a dh' ionnsuidh na tràgha, *towards the shore*; onfhadh na tràighe, *the raging billows of the shore*, 'san t. mhaorach, *in the ebb for shellfish*; 'san t. shiolag, *in the ebb for sand-eels*; ged bhefrear t. dhinn cha toirear timchioll, *we may lose the ford but not the road*—at high-water the short cut across a bay is closed to one, but the round-about way is always open.
tràigh,(AC) s.f. Basement of a house.
traigh,** s.m. Strength. 2 Lazy person.
tràigh-cheum, -éim, -an, s. m. Path along the shore of the sea or a lake.
tràigheach, -eich, s.f. Refuse left by a high or flood tide on the bank of a river.
tràigheach,‡‡ -eiche, a. Beachy.
traigheanach,** -aich, s.m. Lazy person.
tràigh-gheadh,* s.m. Stock-gannet. 2 (AF) Tame or shore goose.
traighideach,** a. Tragical.
tràighleachan, s.m. Bird that nests on the shore above high-water mark—*Arran.*
tràigh-mara,** s.f. Sea-shore. 2 Ebbing of the sea.
tràighte, *past pt.* of tràigh, see traoighte. An talamh t., *the dry land.*
*tràightear, see traidhtear.

traill,** s.f. Kneading-trough. 2 Tray.
tràill, (-e,) -ean, s. m. & f. Slave, bondman or bondwoman. 2 Drudge. 3 Slovenly person. 4 Hard-wrought person. 5 see traille. 6** Labourer.
traille, -achan, s.f. Tusk (fish.)
tràilleach,§ s.m. Seaware of all kinds—*algæ.*
tràilleach, -eiche, a. see tràilleil.
tràilleachd, s.f. Bondage, slavery. 2 Slavishness, abjectness, servility. 3 Drudgery. 4 Slovenliness, 5**Captivity.
trailleadh,(DC) s.m Halibut—*Uist.*
tràillealachd, see tràilleachd. 2*Utmost degradation.
†traillear, -eir, s.m. Baker.
tràilleas,** -eis, s m. Slavery. [s.f.**]
tràilleil, -e, a. Servile, slavish. 2 Enslaved. Obair th., *servile work.*
traille-manach, see traille (fish.)
tràillidh, see tràilleil.
————eachd, see tràilleachd.
tràill-luingeas, -eis, s.f. Galley, convict-ship.
traineach, Landrail, see trèan-ri-trèan.
traineadh, -idh, s.m. Culling, choosing.
trainge,* s.f. Throngness, pressure of business. 2 Crowding.
trainge, *comp.* of trang. Busier, busiest.
trainnse, s.f. Trench, drain.
————ar, -eir, s.m. Plate, trencher.
tràisg,* v.a. Parch with thirst. Th. mo chridhe, *my very heart parched.*
traisg, *pr.pt.* a' trasgadh & a' trasg, v.a. Fast, abstain from food. 2 Observe a fast. 3** Be hungry. Th. e trì làithean, *he fasted three days*; c' ar son a th. sibh? *why did ye fast?*
traisg, s.f. see trasg.
traisgeach, -eiche, a. see trasgach.
traisgidh, *fut.aff.a.* of traisg.
tràisgte, *past pt.* of tràisg. Parched of thirst.
traisgte,** a. Cross, cross-grained.
trait, -e, -ean, s.f. Cataplasm, poultice. 2 Rags, bandages.
traiteach,** a. Of, or belonging to a cataplasm, 2 Like a cataplasm.
traith, see tràigh.
traithnin,‡ s. see machal-coille.
trall,** s.f. Drab, trull.
tramailt,* -e, -ean, s.f. Most unaccountable whim or freak. [freakish.
———each,* -eiche, a. Whimsical, capricious,
tramasgal, s.m. Trash.
trang,* -ainge, a. Throng, very busy. 2 On good terms. 3 Very intimate.
trannsa, s.f. Entry, lobby, passage.
traochlaiche,** s. Tilt, tournament.
traodh, see traogh.
———adh, see traoghadh.
———ta, see traoighte.
traogh, *pr.pt.* a' traoghadh, v.a. & n. Ebb. 2 Subside, sink down, settle, as a disturbed fluid. 3 Abate. 4 Exhaust, drain, empty, pour out. 5 Pacify, appease, assuage. Th. e, *it ebbed*; th. na h-uisgeachan, *the waters abated.*
traogh,** a. Empty. 2 Ebbed.
traoghach,** a. Assuasive, subsiding soon, tending to ebb or abate.
traoghadair,** s.m. Assuager.
traoghadh, -aidh, s.m. Ebbing, act or state of ebbing. 2 Subsiding, act of subsiding. 3 Settling, as an agitated fluid. 4 Exhausting, act of exhausting or emptying. 5 Assuaging, assuagement. 6* Abating, abatement, as of a swelling. 7* Draining. A' t—, *pr.pt.* of traogh.
traoghte, see traoighte.
traoidhte,** s.f. Treachery, treason, practice of treason, deceitfulness.
traoidhtear,** -an, s.m. Gaelic form of *traitor.*
————achd,** s.m. Faithlessness.

traoidhteil,** *a.* Bewraying, faithless.
traoighte, *past pt.* of traogh. Ebbed. 2 Subsided, settled, as any agitated fluid. 3 Exhausted, emptied, drained. 4 Abated
traoill,** *s.f.* Cant.
traoit, see trait.
traon,** -oin, *s.m.* see traona—*Skye.*
traona, -n, *s.m.* Land-rail, see trèan-ri-trèan.
traonair,** *s.m.* Idler.
———**eachd**,** *s.f.* Leisure. 2 Vacancy
traoth, *v.* see traogh.
trap,* *v.a.* Take places in a class. 2 Carp
—,* *s.m.* Trap-stair. 2 Snare.
trapan, -ain, -an, *s.m.* Bunch, cluster, group.
trapanach, -aiche, *a.* Clustering, clustered, in groups.
tràs (i.e. an tràth seo) see tràth
trasd, *adv.* Across, aslope, athwart, crosswise, traverse. 2* Awkwardly placed.
trasd,** -a, *s.m.* Cross, thwart, disappointment.
trasda, *a.* Diagonal, cross, laid across, horizontal. Gu t., *horizontally.*
trasdach, -aiche, *a.* see trasda.
———**d**, *s.f.ind.* Athwartness, crossness. 2 Antithesis in *gram.*
trasdàir,* -ean, *s.m.* Diameter.
trasdan, -ain, *s.m.* Cross-beam or -line. 2 Crozier. 3* Crutch. 4 Stilt. 5 Diagonal. 6(AF) Crossbill. (trosdan)
trasdanach,†† *a.* Awkward about the legs. [†† trabhsdanach]
trasd-bhriathar,** } *s.* Antithesis.
trasd-chainnte,** }
trasd-fhacal,(MS) *s.m.* Solecism.
trasg, -aisg, -an, *s.f.* Fast, fasting. 'Na th., *he fasting*; 'na t., *she fasting*; dh' éigh iad t., *they proclaimed a fast*; là traisg, *a fast-day.*
trasgach, -aiche, *a.* Abstinent, fasting. 2 Of, or belonging to, a fast.
trasgadh, -aidh, *s. m.* Fasting, act of fasting, fast. A' t—, *pr.pt.* of traisg.
tràsgadh, -aidh, *s. m.* Scorching of the palate with thirst.
trasgaid,** *s.f.* Abrogation, oppression. 2 Overthrow.
trasgair,** *v.* Abrogate, destroy. 2‡‡Overwhelm, oppress. 3**Kill. [throw.
trasgairt,** *s.f.* Abrogation, oppression. 2 Over-
trasgar,** -air, *s.m.* Destruction. 2 Oppression. 3 Great fall.
trasgradh, -aidh, *s.m.* Abrogating. 2 Oppressing or overwhelming, oppression. 3**Killing. A' t—, *pr.pt.* of trasgair.
trasgraidh, *fut. aff.a.* of trasgair.
trasnan,** -ain, *s.m.* Ledge. 2 Cross-beam
trat, *s.m.* Trick.
tratach, *a.* Tricky, playful. Bu duine t. Cailean, *Colin was a tricky fellow—Sgeul.-nan-caol.*
trataran, see trèan-ri-trèan.
——— -trèan, see trèan-ri-trèan.
tràth, -a & tràith, -an, *s.m.* Time, day, hour, season. 2 Diet of food. 3**Prayer-time. Dà th. 'san là, *two meals a day*; 'sna tràthaibh ceart, *at the proper seasons*; mu th. an fheasgair, *at the time of the evening meal*; facal 'na th., *a word in season*; an ceann an naoidheamh t., *at the end of the ninth day*; t. bidh, *meal-time*; t. feasgair, *eventide, evening*; t. ùrnuigh, *prayer-time*; t.-noin, *mid-day, noon-tide.*
tràth, -àithe,* *a.* Early in season, timeous, betimes. 2 Speedy, quick.
tràth, *adv*, In due time, seasonably. 2 Early, soon. 3**When. Dèan t. e, *do it in good time*; bi an seo t., *be here early*; an t. seo (an dràsd),) *at present, now.*
tràthach, -aiche, *a.* see tràthail.
———**d**, *s.f.* see tràthalachd.

trathadair, -ean, *s. m.* Clock, time-keeper. Observer of seasons.
tràthail, -e, *a.* Seasonable. 2 In good time, early, soon
tràthalachd, *s.f.* Seasonableness.
tràth feasgair,** *s.m.* Eventide.
trathnan,** -ain, *s.m.* Little stalk of grass.
tràth nòin, *s.m.* Noon-tide, mid-day.
tre, *prep.* Through. 2 By means of. T. mo chlèith, *through my casement.*
treabh, *pr. pt.* a' treabhadh, *v.a.* Plough, till the ground, cultivate, delve. Iadsan a threabhas euceart, *they who plough iniquity.*
———,‡‡ *s.f.* see treabha.
trèabh, -éibh, *pl.* -an & -achan, *s.m.* see treubh.
treabh, -eibh, *s.m.* Farmed village. 2**Tilling, agriculture.
treabha,‡ *s.m.* Thrave, (two cocks of corn, each containing 12 sheaves.)
treabhach, -aiche, *a.* Ploughing, that ploughs, aratory.
treabhach,‡ -aich, *s. m.* Water-cress—*barbarea vulgaris.*
treabhachail,** *a.* Agricultural. 2 Arable.
treabhachas, -ais, *s.m.* Husbandry, agriculture. 2 Arable farm. 3**Specimen of ploughing. Is sibhse t. Dhé, *ye are the husbandry of God.*
treabhachd, *s.f.* see treabhachas.
treabhadair,* -ean, *s.m.* see treabhaiche.
treabhadh, -aidh, *s.m.* Ploughing, act of ploughing. A' t—, *pr.pt.* of treabh. T. choirc, *oat-husbandry*; t.-eòrna, *barley-husbandry*; talamh treabhaidh, *plough-land, arable land.*
treabhaich, see treabhaiche.
———**e**, -an, *s.m.* Ploughman. 2 Husbandman, agriculturist, farmer of arable land, tiller. 3**Peasant.
treabhaidh,** *a.* Arable.
treabhail,(MS) *a.* Arable.
treabhailt, -ean, *s.f.* Grain-box in a mill, hopper. 2**Mill-hopper. 3 *in ridicule*, Bulky female.
treabhair, *s.coll.* Houses in a cluster, steadings, out-houses, farm-buildings, homestall, homestead. 2(DU) Building of any kind.
treabhair, -ean, *s.m.* see treabhaiche. 2 Surety, bail.
treabhaireachd,** *s.f.* Husbandry.
treabhar,** *a.* Discreet, skilful.
†treabhar, -air, *s.m.* Tide. 2 Activity. 3 Choice.
treabhla, see treamhla.
treabhlachd, *s.f.* Family, household.
treabhta, *past pt.* of treabh. Ploughed, tilled, cultivated.
treabhte, see treabhta.
treachaid, *s.f.* Tilling. Nach math a tha 'n talamh sin air a th., *how well that land is tilled*; t. na h-uadhach, *opening of a grave*—conveys an idea of neatness and care in work—*Gael.Soc. Inv.*, xiv, 111.
treachail, *pr. pt.* a' treachladh, *v. a.* Dig, dig deep. 2 Harass, fatigue. 3 Oppress with labour, overwork. Chlaidh e slochd is th. e, *he dug a ditch and dug it deep.* [**prov.*]
treachaill,(MS) s. Gutter.
treachaill-mhara, (an), *s. m.* Name of Fionn's boat.
treachailte, *past pt. & a.* Dug. 2 Fatigued with labour, overwrought. Clachan t. le 'm buinn, *stones dug up with their feet.*
treachdair,** *s.m.* Historian.
treachlach,** -aich, *s.m* Squanderer.
treachladh, -aidh, *s.m.* Digging. 2 Fatiguing. 3 Fatigue, hardship. A' t—, *pr.pt.* of treachail
treachlaidh, *fut.aff.a.* of treachail.
†tread -eid, see trod.
tread, Gaelic form of *trade.*
treadhan, -ain, *s. m.* Fast of three days. 2 Ebb,

3 Want. 4 Louse.
treadhanas,** -ais, *s.m.* Abstinence.
†treagh, *s.m.* Spear.
treagha,* *prep.* Through.
treaghaid, -e, -ean, *s.f.* Darting or transfixing pain, stitch in the side. 2‖ Pleurisy [With *art.* an.] 3(MS) Dolour.
———each, -eiche, *a.* Ill of stitches. 2 Painful.
trealaich, -e, *s.f.* Lumber, trash, mixed heap of valueless articles. 2 Apparatus, tackling. 3* Man's —— *in ridicule* T. chatha, *armour.*
trealais, *s* The spleen.
trealamh, -aimh, -aimhean, *s.m.* Indisposition, sickness, weakness. 2** Apparel. 3** Furniture.
trealbhaidh,* *a.* Adult, grown up.
treall,* *s.f* Short space, while.
treallach, -aich, *s.m.* see trealaich.
treallaidh,** see trealaich.
treallain, *s.m.* Doggerel.
treallan, see treall.
treaman, -ain, *s.m.* Alien.
treamant,(AH) *a.* Well-developed, well-grown, manly, womanly, said of a boy or girl. Balach t., tapaidh, *a smart, well-developed boy*
treamhla, (CR) *s. m.* Illness, ailment—*Lochbroom & Gairloch.*
treamhlaidh,†† -ean, *s.f.* Lingering sickness.
treamhlainn,(CR) *Gairloch* for treamhla.
treamhnadh,(MS) *s.m.* Conduct.
treamsgal, -ail, *s.m.* Nonsense, balderdash. 2 Medley, litter. 3 Taunting language.
trèan, *v.* Gaelic form of *train, v.*
treanadh,** -aidh, *s.m.* Lamentation, wailing 2 Whitsuntide, the week from Thursday preceding to Thursday following Whit Sunday, (not Whitsunday.)
treanaire,(AF) see trèan-ri-trèan.
treananta, *a.* Triangular.
treanas,** -ais, *s.m.* Abstinence.
treann,(AC) *v.a.* Cut, lop, trim, shape.
——,** *s.* Field.
trèan-ri-trèan, *s. m.* Landrail, corn-craik—*crex pratensis.*
treanta, *a.* Gaelic form of *trained.*
trearach,** -aich, *s.m.* Artificer.
†trearach,** *s.* Science, art.
†treartha, see trearach.
†treartbach, -aiche, *a.* Skilled in arts. 2 Scientific.
†treas, -a, -an, *s.m.* Battle. 2 Skirmish. 3 Treason. 4 Treachery. 5**Adversity. Gach cridhe gun t., *each heart without treachery —Oran nam fineachan.* [***gen.sing.* treis.]
treas,†† -eise, *a.* Strong, powerful.
treas, *a.* Third. 3as. *3rd.* ; an t. uair, *thrice; the third time* ; an t. cuid, *the third part.*
treasa, *comp.* of treun. [Not *comp.* of làidir, as stated in Gaelic grammars.]
treasad, *3rd.comp.* of treun. [Not of làidir, as stated in Gaelic grammars.]
treasad, see treise.
treasadh,** *a.* Subtuple.
treasaid,** *s.f.* Third crop.
treas-bàrr,** *s.m.* Third crop.
treas-cuid,** *s.f.* Third part.
treasd,* *s.m.* Long form or seat, as in a school.
——,* *v.a.* Bespeak, engage—*Islay.*
———ach, -aiche, *a.* Thorough pacing (of horses.) 2**Sure-footed. Each t. luath-bhar, *a sure-footed, quick-pacing horse.*
treasg,(DC) *s.m.*Chaff, corn, or bran steeped in boiling water for feeding cows, &c, "mash."
treasg, -eisg, *s.m.* Refuse of malt that has been brewed, draff. 2 Groats. 3*Weaver's paste, (see treisginn.) 4 (MS) Hog's wash. 5‡‡ Great drought. 6**Brewer's grains.
tréasg, *Gairloch* for tréasgan—(DU.)
treasgach, *a.* Draffy.
tréasgan,(CR) *s. m.* Useless, good-for-nothing person—*Suth'd.*
treas-tarruing,* *s.f.* Spirits of wine. 2 Thrice-distilled whisky. 3** Thrice-distilled spirits. 4 The third time
treathaid, *s.* see treaghaid
———each, see treaghaideach
†treathan, ain, *s.m.* Wave. 2 Sea. 3 High-water. 4 Foot 5 Trace.
treathghamhnach,* -aich, *s.f.* Cow that has a calf in two years—*Islay.*
treathlaich, see trealaich.
treathnach,* -aich, *s.f.* Gimlet. 2**Foot.
†treblait, now trioblaid.
††tregat, *s.* Darting pain.
tréibh, see treabh.
tréibhdhireach, -eiche, *a.* Upright, sincere, virtuous, righteous, honest, faithful to one's engagement. T. agus gun tuisleach, *sincere and without offence.*
———d, *s.f.* see tréibhdhireas.
tréibhdhireas, -eis, *s.m.* Sincerity, uprightness, honesty, faithfulness, trustiness, punctuality.
treibhireach, see tréibhdhireach.
treibhse, *s.f.* Room, place, stead.
———ach, *a.* Apt to change.
———achd, *s.f.* Changeableness.
tréig, *pr.pt.* a' tréigsinn, *v.a. & n.* Leave, quit, relinquish, desert, forsake, abandon. 2 Betray. 3 Cease. 4 Depart, abdicate. Na t. mi gu buileach no gu bràth, *forsake me not utterly nor for ever* ; gaoth a thogas is a thréigeas an dos, *a wind that agitates the bush and leaves it* ; an dithis mu dheireadh a thréigeas thu, do chù is mac do pheathar, *the two last to desert you, your dog and your sister's son* ; t. olc, *depart from evil* ; th. e comhairle, *he forsook advice.*
tréigeach, *a.* Apt to desert, forsake or abandon.
tréigeadh, see tréigsinn.
tréigeal,** *s.m.* Departure. 2 Gaelic spelling of *treacle.*
tréigean,** -ein, *s.m.* Leaving, forsaking, abandoument.
tréigear, *fut.pass.* of tréig.
treigheannas,** -ais, *s.m.* Fasting, abstinence.
tréigsinn, *s.m.* Leaving, act of leaving, forsaking, quitting, relinquishing, abandoning, abandonment, deserting, desertion. 2 Act or state of ceasing or departing. A' t—, *pr. pt.* of tréig. Mo chàil 'gam th., *my strength failing.*
———each, *a.* Apt to forsake, abandon or desert.
———each,** *s.m.* Deserter, forsaker.
———eachd,‡‡ *s.f.* Abandonment.
tréigte, *past pt.* of tréig. Forsaken, abandoned, deserted. 2**Forlorn.
tréin, *gen.sing.* of treun.
tréine, *s.f.ind.* Might, power, strength. Mar th. tuinne, *like the strength of a wave.*
tréine, *comp.* of treun.
——ad, -eid, *s.m.* Degree of fortitude,power or valour.
tréineas, -eis, *s.m.* see tréine.
tréin-fhear, -fhir, *s.m.* Brave man.
treinidh,(WC)*s.f.* "Kinks" of whooping-cough. Thàinig an t. air, *the convulsions came on him.*
treinnse,** *s.f.* Gaelic form of *trench.*
treis, -e, *s.f.* While, spell (for greis.) 2 Distance of place. T. mhath, *a good while* ; t. air astar, *a good way off* ; o cheann treise, *a while ago.*
treis, *s.m.* see treise.
treise, (for treasa, *comp.* of treun.) More or most powerful. 2(DC) Used as a positive (Strong) in *Uist.*

treise, *s.f.* Force, bodily strength, vigour, animal power. 2 Trial, adversity. 3 Trial of strength, battle. Dh' eug mo th., *my vigour has died away ;* a t. 'ga fàgail, *her strength forsaking her.*
treise, *s.m.* Supporter, protector.
treisead, -eid, *s.m.* Degree of strength, vigour, or power.
treiseil, -e, *a.* Strong, powerful, vigorous.
treisg,* *s.* see treasg. 2 Trash—*Argyll.*
treisginn, *s.f.* Weaver's paste. 2 Trash—*Argyll.*
†**tréite**, *s.f.* Embrocation.
†**treith**,** *s. f.* Erudition, accomplishment. 2 Qualification.
tréith, *gen.sing. & n.pl.* of triath.
†**treithe**, *s.f.* Ignorance, 2 Weakness.
treitheach,** *a.* Accomplished, learned.
treobh, see treabh.
——adair, see treabhadair.
——adh, see treabhadh.
——aiche, see treabhaiche,
treobhair, (an), *s.m.* That part of a boat below the " leagail."
treobhla, see treamhla.
treodas,** -ais, *s.m.* Food.
treodhair, -ean, *s. m.* Smith's nail-mould, for forming heads of nails. [*treodhaire.] 2(DMy) In weaving, the gauge for holding the web in place. 3 (DMy) The rope drawn over the *cleithean* and below the thatching straw in the space above the *sgrathan*, to prevent the thatch falling through.
treoghaid, see treaghaid.
treòir, -e, *s.f.* Strength, force, might, power, vigour, energy. 2 Direction. 3 Troop. 4 see treodhair.
treòir,* *v.n.* Flag.
treòireil, *comp.* treoireala, *a.* Pithy.
treòirichear, see treòraichear.
treòna,(DC) *s.f.* Landrail, see trèan-ri-trèan.
treònach,(DC) *s.f.* Landrail, see trèan-ri-trèan.
treònachan, *s.m.* Landrail, see trèan-ri-trèan.
treonal.(DC) *s.f.* Crowd, group.
treòrach, -aiche, *a.* Vigorous, powerful. 2**Active.
————adh, -aidh, *s.m.* Leading, act of leading, guiding or directing, supporting. A' t—, *pr. pt.* of treòraich.
treòrachail, -e, *a.* Conducting.
treòrachair, -ir, -an, *s.m.* see treòraichear.
treòraich, *pr. pt.*a' treòrachadh, *v.a. & n.* Lead, guide, conduct, direct. 2 Strengthen. 3 Give strength to accomplish.
treòraich,(AC) *s.f.* Leading. T. anama, *a soul-leaving—death-blessing.*
treòraiche,** -ean, *s. m.* Leader, conductor guide.
treòraichear, -ir, -an, *s. m.* Leader, guide, conductor. 2 Finger-post.
—————, *fut.pass.* of treòraich.
treòraichte, *past pt.* of treòraich. Directed, led, guided, conducted. 2** Strengthened.
treòran,** -ain, *s.m.* Active little child.
————,** *s.* Three parts.
treòrdail, (a'), (AC) *s.f.* Staggering.
tresg,** see treasg.
treubh, -éibh & -a, *pl.* -an & -achan, *s.f.* Tribe, family, clan, kin. Do réir 'ur tréibh, *according to your tribe.*
——ach, -aiche, *a.* Strenuous, valorous, heroic. gallant. 2**Clannish. 3 In tribes or clans. 4 Relating to a tribe or clan Na fir t., *the valiant men.*
——ach,** -aich, *s.m.* One of a tribe or family.
treubhachas, -ais, see treubhantas.
treubhachd,** *s. f.* Clannishness. 2 Bravery, gallantry.
treubhaiche, *comp.* of treubhach.
—————,** *s.m.* One of a tribe or family.
—————ad,** -id, *s. m* Degree of bravery. A' dol an t., *growing braver and braver ;* air a th 'sam bheil iad, *however brave they be.*
treubhan, -ain,** *s.m.* Tribune.
————ach, *a.* Tribunitial.
treubhanta,* -ainte, *a.* Heroic, fond of feats or achievements.
treubhantas, -ais, *s.m.* Bravery, valour, chivalry. 2 Feat, exploit. 3 **Magnanimity. 4* Display of feats or achievements. 5*Boasting. Bearta treubhantais, *deeds of valour.*
treubhas,* -ais, *s.f.* see treubhantas.
————ach, -aiche, see treubhanta. 2*Ostentatious.
treubhna,¶ *s.* Landrail, see trèan-ri-trèan.
reubhun, -uin, see treubhan.
treud, tréid & -a, *pl.* -an, *s. m.* Flock. 2 Herd of animals. 3 Followers. 4 Band of men Mar fhuaim tuinne bha gach t., *each band was like a roaring wave.*
——ach, -aiche, *a.* Having many flocks or herds, gregarious. 2 Of, or belonging to a flock or herd.
treudachadh,(MS) *s.m.* Aggregation.
treudaich,(MS) *v.a.* Aggregate.
——————e, -an, *s.m.* Shepherd, herdsman, drover, cowherd, swineherd. 2††Pastor. [McL & D gives *nom.sing.* -aich.]
treudaire,* -an see treudaiche.
treuinide,(AC) *comp.* of treun.
treun, *a. 1st. comp.* tréine, & treise *or* treasa, *2nd. comp.* treasaid, *3rd.comp.* treasad. Strong, powerful, mighty, vigorous. 2 Brave, valiant. 3 Persevering and successful beyond expectation, as a weak person, surprising. Is t. a fhuaradh tu, *you did surprisingly ;* is t. leam fhéin a gu 'm urrainn thu, *I am surprised that you were able ;* is t. a gheibhear thu, *you do surprisingly ;* t. an neart, *mighty in strength ;* bha sibh t. thar glòir, *you were brave beyond praise.*
treun, tréin, *s.m.* Brave man, warrior, champion, hero. Am measg treun a shluaigh, *among the brave of his people.*
treun,(DU) *s.f.* Strength, the acme or pitch of strength. Ann an treun a neirt, *in the fullness of his strength.*
treunachas, -ais, *s.m.* Strength, might. 2 Valour, bravery 3 Manhood.
treunachd, *s.f.* see treunachas. 2*Perseverance, 3* Success. 4* Surprising conduct.
treunad, -aid, *s.m.* Degree of bravery, valour, success, &c. A' dol an t., *growing braver and braver ;* air a th. 's a bheil e, *however brave he be.*
treunadas,*-ais, *s.f.* Exploits. 2 see treunachas.
————ach, -aiche, *s.f.* Performing brave exploits.
treun-adhairceach,** *s.m.* Rhinoceros.
treunair,* -ean, *s.m.* Diligent man.
treunas, -ais, *s.m.* Chivalry, strength, might, bravery, courage. A' taomadh a th., *pouring his strength.*
treun-dhàn, -àin, *s.m.* Epic or heroic poem.
treunear,** -ir, see treun-fhear. Dhùisg na treunir lasair, *the heroes kindled a flame.*
treun-fhear,†† *s.m.* Strong man, hero, champion.
trena-fheardha, *a.* Na fir bheura th., *the sharp, strong, brave men—Filidh. p. 65.*
treun-làmhach, -aiche, *a.* Armipotent.
treun-laoch, -laoich, *s.m.* Strong warrior, hero, champion.
treunmhor, -mhoire, *a* Very brave.
treunna,¶ see trèan-ri-trèan.

trèun-ri-trèun, see trèan-ri-trèan.
treuntas,** -ais, *s.m.* Strength, power. 2 Magnanimity. 3(MS) Flourish Thréig iad an t., *they have forsaken their magnanimity.*
treun-thoisgeach,** *a.* Brave with expedition. 2 Performing exploits in quick succession.
treuthach,(MS) *a.* Strenuous.
tri, *a.* Three. T. uairean, *thrice;* t. maighdeana beaga caomha, rugadh 'san son oidhche ri Criosd, *three lovely little maidens born the same night as Christ*—Faith, Hope and Charity When counting 1, 2, 3, &c., say, "a h-aon, a dhà, a tri," &c. In A thrì bhliadhna an àma seo, *three years at this time*, a is the *prep.* do.
†**triabhall**, -aill, *s.m.* see triall.
triachan,** -ain, *s.m.* Sock. 2 Shoe.
triadh, see triath.
triaghanach, (MMcD) *s, f.* see tri-ghamhnach.
triall,*pr.pt.*a' triall, *v.a.& n.* Go,depart, set out. 2 Intend, purpose, imagine, devise, plot. 3 Stroll, travel, walk, march, journey,traverse.
triall, *s.m.* Journey, departure. 2 Going, act of going, departing or marching. 3 Purpose, design. 4 Way, expedition. 5 Travelling 6 Designing, act of designing or intending. 7 (AC) Procession of people and herds to the summer sheiling. 8 (AC) Flock. 9** March. 10(DMu) Luggage, baggage. An d' thug thu an t. leat? *have you brought the luggage with you?* beannaich an t. 's an stòr, *bless the flock and the store;* t. nan curaidh, *the heroes' march;* air mo th., *on my way.*
triallach,** *a.* Itinerant, travelling. 2 Fond of walking. 3 Of, or belonging to, a journey.
trialladh, -aidh, *s.m.* Elongation. 2 Journey, travelling, journeying.
triallaiche,** *s.m.*Pedestrian, traveller, wayfaring man.
triallair, -ean, *s. m.* Traveller, wayfaring man, pedestrian. [triallaire.*]
triall-chaismeachd,‡‡ -an,*s.f.* Signal for moving.
triamant, see treamant.
triamh,** *a.* see tritheamh.
triamh,** *s.m.* The "three" at cards or dice. 2 (AH) "An triamh ball" at cards—*Argyll.*
triamhain,** *a.* Weary.
triamhnadh, -aidh, *s.m.* Weariness.
triamhnuin,** s. Lamentation.
triamhuinneach,** *a.* Mournful.
trian, *s.m.ind.* Third part. 2 Particle. 3 Ray. 4 District. T. a chliù, *the third of his fame;* gearrar dà th., *two thirds shall be cut;* t. de shoillse, *a ray of light*, an treas t., *the third part;* ma's pill, cha'n fhiù iad t., *before they return they are not worth a third of it;* o 'n chaill,mi trian na h-analach, *since I lost one third of my breath* or *lung-power*—a man can only hold out as long as his wind is unbroken—*Cead deireannach nam Beann.*
trianach, *a.* Of the third part. 2 Three,by three.
trianaich,** *v.n.* Trine.
trianaichte, *past pt.* Trined.
Trianaid, see Trionaid.
trianail,** *v.a.*** *v.a.* Handle or finger a stringed musical instrument. 2 Strike.
Tri-an-aon,†† *s.f.* The Triune God, the Trinity.
triantach, -aich, *s.m.* see triantan.
———, -aiche, *a.* see triantanach. 2*In thirds.
triantan, -ain, *pl.* -an & -ain, *s.m.* Triangle.
triantan, *s.pl.* Thirds.
———ach, -aiche, *a.* Triangular. 2 Trigonometrical.
———achd, *s.f.* Trigonometry.
trian-tarruing,§ *s.* Rest-harrow,see sreang-bogha. Little shrubby plant with flowers like broom, but rosy instead of yellow.
triar. see triùir
triarach,** *a.* Thirdly
triasg,(CR) *s.m.* Useless person—*W of Ross* Slender, inactive, idle man—*ditto*
———,(CR) *v.n.* Dry up, shrink, become leaky
triath, *gen* triaith, tréith & -a, *pl.* tréith & -an *s.m.* Lord, king, chief, noble, prince,chieftain hero, leader, personage. 2**Wave. 3 *rarely*, Hillock.
An T.,(*poetical*) *God;* an t. a tha borb,*the hero that is fierce;* coimeas do 'n charraig an t., *like the rock is the hero;* thog na triaith sleagh a' bhàis, *the heroes lifted the spear of death;* mo Dhia, is tu an t. ro mhor, *my God, thou art the mighty Lord*
triath,(AF) *s.* Hog, sow, boar
triath,** *a.* Noble. 2 Valuable 3 Weak
triathach, -aiche, *a.* Noble, lordly, magnificent. 2 Triumphant.
triathach,** -aich, *s.m* Trophy
triathail,* -e, *a.* see triathach.

666. Tri-bhileach.

tri-bhileach,‡ *s.f.* Common valerian, all-heal or St. George's herb—*valeriana officinalis* 2(* & Mc & D) Marsh-trefoil.
tri-bhileag, *s.f.* Clover.
tri-bhilean,§ *s.m.* Red-clover, see seamrag-chapuill. 2§ Bog-bean, marsh-trefoil, see pònair-chapuill.
tribuail,** for triobuail.
tric, -e, *a* Frequent, often. Gu t., *frequently, often.*
trice, *comp.* of tric. Oftener, oftenest.
triceachd,(MS) *s.f.* Resort.
tricead, -eid, *s.m.* Degree of frequency A' dol an t., *growing more and more frequent.*
———,* *a.* Thirty.
tri-chasach, *a* Three-footed, tripetal.
———, *s.m.* Tripod.
tricealachd,(MS) *s.f.* Frequency, crebritude.
tri-cheannach, *a.* Tricipital
tri-chearnach, -aich, *s. f.* Triangle.
———, *a.* Triangular.
——— -chothromach, Equilateral triangle.
——— chruinnbhil, Spherical triangle.
——— fhiar-oisinneach, Oblique-angled triangle.
——— gheur-oisinneach, Acute-angled triangle.
——— lurg-ionnan, Isosceles triangle.
——— mhaol-oisinneach, Obtuse-angled triangle.
——— stàbhach, Scalene triangle.
——— thaobh-ionnan, Equilateral tri-

angle.
tri-chlaiseach, *s.m.* Claymore, so called from the three grooves usually in the blade—*Donn. Bàn.*
trì-chosach, *s. & a.* see trì-chasach.
tri-chuairt, *a.* Three times, thrice.
trid, *prep.* Through, by, by means of. T. a chéile, *through other,promiscuously ;* t. amach, *throughout;* d'a th., *through him* (or *it.*); tridsan, *through him.* [also trid—‡]
trid,‡ *s. f.* Rag, clout, stitch.
trid-amhartan, -ain, -an, *s.m.* Mishap, ill-luck.
trideabac,†† -aic, -an, *s.f.* Mistake, ill-luck.
tri-deug, *a.* Thirteen. Tri-fir-deug, *thirteen men.*
trid-shiubhal,‡‡-ail, *s.m.* Permeation.
trid-shoilleir, *a.* see trid-shoillseach.
trid-shoilleireachd, *s.f.* see trid-shoillseachd.
trid-shoillse, -an, *s.f.* Transparency.
————ach, -eiche, *a.* Transparent.
————achan, -ain, *s.m.* Transparency.
————achd, *s.f.*Transparency, transparentness, clearness, limpidness.
trid-shoillsean,** -ein, *s.m.* Transparency.
trif,(DMK) *s.* Elegant appearance. 'S e sin a chuireadh t. air, *that is what would make it look elegant—W. coast of Ross.*
trì-fhoghair, -e, -ean, *s.f* Triphthong.
trì-fichead, *a.* Sixty. Tri-fichead 's a h-aon,*sixty-one;* tri-fichead saighdear 's a h-aon deug, *71 soldiers.*
tri-ficheadamh, *a.* Sixtieth.
tri-fillte, *a.* Threefold, triple.
tri-filltеach, see tri-fillte.
trig, see triuthach.
trigeadan,** *s.pl.* Trigentals.
trì-ghamhnach, *s. f.* Cow that has been three years without calving—*Lewis.*
tri-ghuth, *s.m.* Triphthong.
trileachan, see trilleachan.
trilean,** -ein, *s.m.* Quavering sound. 2 Warbling.
trileanta,‡‡ -einte, *a.* Thrilling. 2 Warbling. 3 Trifling. 4 Quavering. 5 Quick in sound or motion.
†trilis, trilse, *s.f.* Locks of hair. 2 Bushy or luxuriant hair. A' cleachdadh le 'n trilsibh. *struggling with their luxuriant locks.*
———each, *a.* Luxuriant or bushy, as hair.
trilleach,(DC) *s.m.* Disturbance, breach of the peace—*Uist.*
trilleachail,(DC) *a.* Industrious.
trilleachan, *s. m.* Pied oyster-catcher, sea-piet, sand-piper. 2 Guillemot.
trilleachan, -ain, *s.m.* Grey plover—*squatarola cinerea.*
——— glas,¶ *s.m.* Sand-piper, see luatharan glas.
——— tràighe,¶ *s.m.* Ringed plover—*charadrius¶ hiaticula.* 2 ¶ Sand-lark, sea-lark, see luatharan. 3**Collared oyster-catcher.
——— tràghad, see trilleachan-tràighe.
trillsean, -ein, -ean, *s.m.* Lantern, small torch, lamp, flambeau, rushlight. 2*Glimmer, glimmering fire, rush-wick. 3***s.pl.* Sparkles.
trillseineach, -aiche, *a.* Of, or abounding in lanterns, rush-wicks or torches. 2 Glimmering, sparkling, twinkling.
trillsidh,** *s.f.* Torch. 2 Lamp.
tri-mheurach,** -aich, *s.m.*Any instrument with three prongs. 2 Three-pronged fork. 3 Trident.
trinnse,** *s.f.* Trench.
trinnsear, -ir, -an, *s.m.* Plate, trencher.
triobhaire,(CR) *s.m.* Cheat, knave, rascal—*W. of Ross.*
trioblaich,* *v.a.* Triple, make three-fold.
trioblaid, -e, -ean, *s.f.* Trouble, anxiety, vexation, tribulation. 2*Distress, calamity. Là mo th., *the day of my trouble ;* is lionmhor t. agus teinn a thig air an fhìrean chòir, *many straits and calamities fall to the lot of the upright ;* le t. chruaidh, *with sore distress.*
trioblaideach, -eiche, *a.* Troubled, distressed. 2 Distressing, calamitous, afflicting, distressful, vexatious, afflicted 3 Busy. Ni t., *a distressful thing, sore distressed.*
————adh, -aidh, *s.m.* Troubling, act of troubling, annoying or distressing. A' t—, *pr.pt.* of trioblaidich.
trioblaidich, *pr. pt.* a' trioblaideachadh, *v.a.* Trouble, molest, vex, distress, afflict.
————te, *past pt.* of trioblaidich. Troubled, vexed, distressed.
triobuail, *pr. pt.* a' triobualadh, *v.a. & n.* Vibrate, quiver. 2 Swing. 3 Play. 4 Strike, handle or finger a stringed instrument.
triobualadh, -aidh, *s. m.* Quavering, thrilling.
triobuilte,* *a.* see tri-fillte.
trioch, see triogh.
†triochad, *a.* Thirty.
triochdadh,(DC) *v.a.* Save, rescue—*Skye.*
†triodach, -aiche, *a.* Transparent.
triogh,* *s.f.* see triuthach. 2* Fit of laughing or coughing.
trì-oisinneach, *a.* Triangular.
————, -ich, *s.m.* Triangle.
tri-oisinneag, -eig, -an, *s. f.* Triangle, triangular figure.
triolanta,** *a.* Quavering, warbling. 2 Trifling, inconsiderable. Le d' phuirt thriolanta, *with thy warbling strains.*
triollachan, see trilleachan. 2**Schemer.
triolluinn, (MS) *a.* Perplexed.
†triom, for tromham.
trioman,§ *s.m.* Large fuzz-ball, see beach.
†triom-sa, *emphat. form* of triom.
Trionaid, -e, *s.f.* The Holy Trinity. An T. Chruithear, *the Godhead.*
————each, -eiche, *a.* Of the Holy Trinity. 2 Trinitarian.
———— each, *s.m.* Trinitarian.
triopaiseach,(MS) *a.* Hemorrhoidal.
triopall,* -aill, *s.m.* Bunch, cluster, festoon.
————ach, see trioplach.
trioplach, -aiche, *a.* Bunchy, clustered, in festoons. 2**Trim, tidy.
triosgan,** -ain, *s.m.* Household stuff.
triotar, only seems to occur in "a thriotar !" *you knave—Suth'd.* [trudair]
†triotha, for trompa.
tripleag, *s.f.* Fairy spell.
triplich,** *v.a.* Cube.
trì-ràmhach, -aich, *s.f.* Three-oared boat, trireme.
————, -aiche, *a.* Three-oared.
trì-shiolach, *a.* Of three syllables.
————, *s.m.* Trisyllable.
tri-shioladh, -aidh, -aidhean, *s.m.* Trisyllable.
trì-shliosnach, *a.* Trilateral.
†trist, *a.* Sad. 2 Tired.
†——, *s.* Curse.
tritheamh,‡‡ *a.* Third. An t. fear, *the third man.*
Trithinn, *gen. sing.* of Tritheann. Occurs in a place-name (Sgeir-an-Trithinn) in Loch Torridon, which consists of three humps.
†Tritheann,(AC) -inn, *s.f.* The Trinity.
tri-theudach, *a.* Three-stringed.
Trithion, see Tritheann.
tri-uairean,** *adv.* Thrice. 2 Three hours (for tri uairean an uaireadair.) 3 Three o' clock.
triubhas, -ais, -an, *s.m.* Trousers, pantaloons. 2 Ancient article of Highland dress, generally made of tartan cloth,and consisting of trousers and stockings in one piece, trews. 3 (Eionn)

Roe of a fish—*prov.* (—*Argyll & West of Inverness-shire*—AH.)
triubhasach, -aiche, *a.* Trousered.
triubhsair,* *s.m.* Gaelic spelling of *trouser.*
triùcair, -ean, *s.m.* Rascal, rogue.
——eách, -eiche, *a.* Roguish, rascally.
——eachd, *s.f.* Roguery, villainy.
triuchan, -ain, -an, *s.m.* Stripe of distinguishing colour in tartan. T. geal is dubh, *a white and black stripe.*
triuchanach, *a.* In stripes.
triughas, see triubhas.
triugh,* see triuthach.
triuine,** *s.f.* Poverty.
triùir, *s.* Three persons. [Governs *gen. pl.*] Rug mi dha t. mhac, *I bore him three sons.*
triùir-an-aon, *s.* The Trinity.
triuirean,* -ein, -an, *s. m.* Marble, children's play-bullet. 2**Sheep's purl. Ag iomairt air triuireanan, *playing at marbles.*
triullainn,(MS) *a.* Intricate.
triullainn, see treallain.
triun, *s.m.* Poor person.
——, *a.* Poor.
triùsair, -ean, *s.m.* see triùbhsair.
triuthach, (an), -aich, *s.f.* Whooping-cough.
triuthaire, *Gairloch* for triobhaire.
——achd,(DMy) *s.f.* Dishonesty.
triuthar,(DC) *s.f.* Kinks of the whooping-cough —*Uist.*
triuthas, -ais, -an, *s.m.* see triubhas.
triutraich, *s.f.* Twittering. 'S àluinn mo th. 's mo ghlagan, *my twittering and my trilling are superb—An Smeòrach, McD., 13. 3.*
trò, *s.m.* Visit, occasion. Air an t. seo, *on this occasion.* 2††Trip.
tro', for troimh.
troatag, *s.f.* Loose coat or cloak—*W. coast Ross.*
tròbh, see trò.
trobhad, Come, come to me, come along with me—the opposite of *chugad.* [Used only in conversation—**]
——aibh, Come (ye), come (ye) to me.
trobhd, see trobhad.
tròc,** *v.a.* Chaffer.
troc,(DU) *s.m.* Trash, rubbish, scum.
tròcainn,** *s.* Chaffery, haggling.
tròcair,!-e, -ean, *s.f.* Mercy, pity. 2 Act of compassion. 3 Blessing, favour. 4**Pardon.
——each, -eiche, *a.* Merciful, compassionate, pitiful. Gu t., *mercifully.*
——eachd, *s.f.* Mercifulness,clemency,willingness to pardon, compassionate regard.
tròcairiche, *comp.* of tròcaireach. More or most merciful.
†**troch**, *s.* Short life.
trochd, *v.n.* Negotiate.
trochladh,** -aidh, *s.m.* Loosening.
trod,-uid & -oid,*s.m.* Scolding,reproof. 2 Quarrel, strife, struggle, battle, contention. 3 *Quarrel among ladies. 4 Reprimand. 5**Starling. Cridhe nach sgìthich an t., *a heart that will not tire in battle ;* fhuair e a th., *he got a* [lit. *his*] *scolding.*
trod, -oid, *s.m.* Scolding, act of scolding. A' t—, *pr.pt.* of troid.
trod, *v.* see troid.
trodach, -aiche, *a.* Apt to scold. 2 Quarrelsome, riotous, quarrelling. 3 Scolding. 4 Struggling. Gu t., *fightingly.*
trodachas, -ais, *s.m.* see trodaireachd.
trodadh,** -aidh, *s.m.* Scolding.
trodag, -aig, -an, *s.f.* Scolding female.
trodail, -e, *a.* see trodach.
trodair, -ean, *s.m.* Scolder, quarrelsome person. [*trodaire]
trodaireachd, *s.f.* Scolding habit of scolding or quarrelling.
trodan, -ain, -an, *s. m. dim.* of trod. Slight scolding or quarrelling.
——ach, *a.* Quarrelsome.
trodhan, -ain, *s. m.* **Vulture. 2 (AF) Bird of prey.
trog, *s.* Business—*Badenoch.* 2 Busyness. 3‡ Busy dealing.‡
trog, *pr.pt.* a' trogail, *v.a.* *Prov.* for tog. [*Tog* with prep. *ro* inserted—‡.]
trog, -oig, *s.m.* Trash.
trog,†† *s.m.* Truck, barter *Scots*, trock.
troga,(AC) *s.* War. Oba troga, *a spell of war.*
trogair,(AH) *s.m.* Person engaged in cattle-dealing on a small scale.
trògbhail,‡ *s.f.* Quarrel.
trògbhoil,* *s.f.* Grumbling, murmuring, grunting. 2 Eternal scold, quarrel,dispute,wrangling. Na tog t. air an ain-eol, *do not quarrel with a stranger.*
——each,* *a.* Apt to murmur or grumble gruntingly.
†**trogh**, *s.* Children.
troghad, *s.* Soft-rolling, full-orbed eyes.
troghan,** -ain, *s.m.* Raven.
troghbhail, see trògbhail.
troghna, see trèan-ri-trèan.
troghnadh, (AF) *s.m.* Corncraik, see trèan-ri-trèan.
troich, -e, -ean, *s m. & f.* Dwarf, hunchback person. 2 Coward. 3 Evil-disposed person. 4 *Ninny.
——eachd,‡‡ *s.f.* Deformity.
——ealachd, *s.f.* see droichealachd.
——eil, -e, *a.* see droicheil.
troichilean,†† *s.m.* Pigmy, dwarf. 2 (AF)Willow wren.
troid, *pr.pt.* a' trod, *v.a.* Scold, wrangle, fight, quarrel, strive, contend. 2 Rebuke, reprimand. Th. mo bhean is th. i rium, is th. mi rithe o 'n a th. i rium, *my wife scolded me in earnest, and I scolded her because she did so.*
troid, *gen.sing.* of trod.
troid-each,(AF) *s.m.* War-horse.
troidh, see troigh.
troidht, (CR) *s. f.* Shoe worn out of shape—*Skye,* [trait] 2 (trait) Cataplasm, poultice, bandages.
troigh, -e, -ean, *s.f.* The foot, a foot. 2 Measure of 12 inches. 3 Sole of the foot. 4** *rarely,* Sorrow. Tomhais e le troighibh rùisgte, *measure it barefooted.*
troigh,** *a.* Short-lived.
troigheach,** -ich, *s.m.* Footman. 2 Pedestrian. 3 Foot-soldier.
——an,(DMy) *s.m.* Flap of a headless stocking which covers the *troigh*, and is kept in place by *srulachan* round the second and third toes.
troighean, -ein, *s.m.* Pedal.
troight, -e, -ean, *s.f.* see trait.
——ear, see traoidhtear.
troightearachd, see traoidhtearachd.
troileis, -e, *s.f.* Any trifling thing. 2‡‡Childish merriment.
——each, -eiche, *a.* Trifling, little worth. 2 Given to trifles, childish.
——eachd, *s.f.* see troileis.
troimchill,** *s.f.* Sanctuary.
troime, see truime.
——ad, see truimead.
——achd, see truimeachd.
troimh, *prep.* Through, from side to side. 2 All over, along the whole extent. 3 By, from, by means of. Thus combined with the personal pronouns :— tromham, *through me ;* tromhad, *through thee ;* troimhe, *through him ;* troimpe, *through her ;* tromhainn, *through us ;* tromhaibh, *through you;* trompa, *through them.* [As-

pirates a word following and governs the dative.]
troimh-a-chéile, *adv.* Through other, mixed, confused.
————————, *s.* Agitation.
troimhe, (troimh+e) *prep. pron.* Through him or it.
troimh-lot, *v. a.* Empale. 2 Pierce. 3 Give a mortal wound.
troimh-rannsaich, *v.a.* Explore.
troimh-sgrùd, *v.a.* Explore.
troimpe, (troimh+i) *prep.pron.* Through her.
troinnsear, see truinnsear.
troisg, see traisg.
——, -e, -ean, *s.f.* see trasg.
troisgeach, -eiche, see trasgach.
————d, *s.f.* see trasgadh.
troisgeadh, see trasgadh.
troisgeul,(AH) *s.m.* (droch sgeul) Ill-omened intelligence. Mach an t. ! *away with the unlucky news !* This is a common exclamation from a listener when one tells of the death of a cow or horse belonging to a third party, as such news is believed to entail loss in the live stock of the person in whose dwelling it is recounted.
troiste, *s.f.* Three-footed stool.
troite, see traoidhte.
——ar, see traoidhtear.
——arachd, see traoidhtearachd.
troll,** *s*, Corruption.
trom, truime, *s.m.* Weight, any weight,burden, load. 2 Encumbrance. 3 Difficulty. 4 Protection, charge, defence. 5 Pregnancy. 6* Embarrassment, impediment. 7††Sinker (lead) of a fishing-line. Tog do th. dhiom, *remove your burden* or *charge from me, do not be so severe on me ;* nach bitheadh a th. oirnn, *that he would not be a burden to us ;* cha bhi sin 'na th. ort, *that will not be an encumbrance to you.*
trom, -uime, *a.* Heavy, ponderous, weighty. 2 Afflictive, sore, oppressive. 3 Difficult, hard, painful, laborious. 4 Wearying, fatiguing. 5 Sorrowful, sad, dejected, melancholy, mournful. 6 Causing grief or sadness. 7 Dull of hearing. 8 Sleepy. 9 Pregnant. 10 Addicted. 11* Luxuriant, rank. 12 Deep,profound, as sleep. T. air an òl, *addicted to liquor ;* bàrr t.,*a rank* or *luxuriant crop* ;eallach th., *a heavy burden, oppressive burden ;* cadal t., *profound sleep;* am fonn a' briseadh gu t., *the strain breaking mournfully ;* is taitneach ach is t. do ghuth, *pleasant but sad is thy voice ;* dìoghailt th., *severe vengeance ;* an sealladh t., *the sad spectacle.*
†trom, *s.m.* Blame, rebuke.
troma, *s.m.* Shaft or tram of a cart—*Lewis.*
tromachadh, -aidh, *s. m.* Making heavy, act of increasing the weight of. 2 Burdening act of burdening. 3 Oppressing, act of oppressing. 4 *Aggravating, loading. 5 Making sad or dejected. 6* Getting heavier, more ponderous or addicted. A' t—, *pr.pt.* of tromaich.
tromadas, -ais, *s.m.* Drowsiness. 2 Depression.
tromaich, *pr.pt.* a' tromachadh, *v.a. & n.* Make heavy or heavier. 2 Burden, oppress. 3 Become heavy or heavier. 4 Get more addicted. 5 Aggravate. 6 Deject, make melancholy.
————te, *past pt.* of tromaich. Made heavy or heavier. 2 Loaded, burdened. 3 Oppressed. 4 Made sad, saddened.
trom-àileach, -eiche, *a.* Strong-smelling.
tromainntinn, see truime-inntinn.
——————each, see trom-inntinneach.
tromalach,†† -aich, *s.f.* Heavier portion.
troma-lighe, see trom-luighe.
tromaltan,|| *s. m.* Numbness from pressure. 2 (DMK) *s. m.* Cold in the head, complicated with pains in various parts of the body—*Caithness.*
troman, -ain, -an, *s.m.* Great weight.
troman, -ain, -an, *s.m.* Wood of the bore-tree. see droman.
tromara,** *s.m.* see tromarach.
————ch,** -aich, *s.m.* Client.
tromb, -a & -uimb, *pl* -an, *s f.* Jew's harp. " trump."
———aid, -e, -ean, *s.f.* Trumpet.
———aideach, *a.* Like a trumpet.
———aidear, -eir, -an, *s m.* Trumpeter.
trombair, -ean, see trombaidear.
————eachd, *s.f* Trumpeting, business of a trumpeter. 2 Playing on a jew's harp. 3* Harping. 4* Carping. 5* Canting.
trom-bhoid, see trom-bhòd.

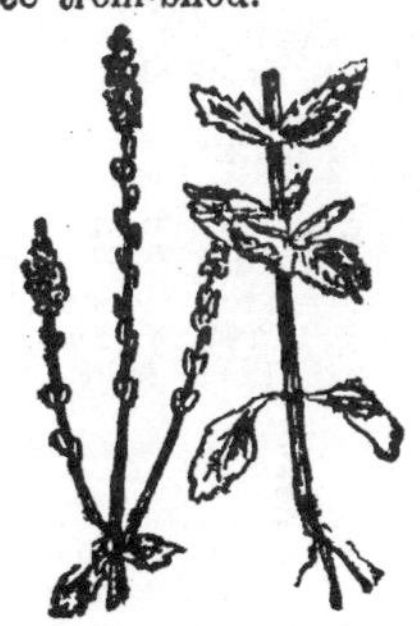

667. *Trom-bhòa.*

trom-bhòd, -an, *s. m.* Vervain, mallow—*verbena officinalis.* Also called holy herb, Juno's tears, pigeon's grass and simpler's joy. [trom-bhad —DM.]
trom-bhanoglach, -aich, *s.f.* Female client.
trom-bholachd, *s.f.* Strong smell.
trom-bhuail,** *v.a.* Strike heavily, strike hard. Trom-bhuailear leis, *it shall be struck hard by him.*
trom-bhuidheann,** -bhuidhne, *s.f.* Tribe of vassals, clan.
trom-chadal, -ail, *s.m.* Heavy sleep. 2 Lethargy.
——————ach, *a.* Sleeping heavily. 2 Causing deep sleep. 3 Lethargic.
——————aiche, ** *s.m.* Lethargic person.
trom-chasair,** *s.m.* Heavy shower.
trom-cheannach, -aiche, *a.* Heavy-headed.
trom-cheannachd,‡‡ *s.f.* Backwardness.
trom-cheannas,(MS) *s.m.* Idleness.
trom-chluasach, -aiche, *a.* Dull of hearing.
trom-chuis, *s.f.* Important case.
——————each, *a.* Important, of great concern.
trom-ghean, -a, *s.m.* Melancholy.
tromhad, *prep. pron.* (troimh+thu) Through thee.
tromhaibh, *prep. pron.* (troimh+sibh) Through you.
tromhainn, *prep. pron.* (troimh+sinn) Through us.
tromham, *prep.pron.* (troimh+mi) Through me, through my means.
trom-inntinn, -e, see truime-inntinn.
——————each, -eiche, *a.* Melancholy, dejected. Gu t., *dejectedly.*
tromla,(AC) *s.* Cows.
tromlach, -aich, *s.m.* Weight, bulk. Na'smiadhaile uimpe na an t. dhinn féin, *esteeming her more than most of ourselves.*
trom-lighe, see trom-luighe.
trom-luaidhe,(AH)*s.f.* Leaden sinker of a fishing [line

trom-luighe, *s.f.* Nightmare. 2 Weight on the heart or spirits. 3 Distracting grief. 4**Overlaying. Gach maraiche air seachran le t., *each mariner forgetting (leaving) his course through grief.*

trom-luigh, *v.n.* Overlay.

trom-mhàthair, -mhàthar, *s.f.* Matron.

trom-oglach,** -aich, *s.m.* Client.

tromp, -oimp & -uimp, see tromb.

trompa, *prep.pron.* (troimh+iad) Through them.

trompaid, -ean, see trombaid.

trompair, -ean, see trombair.

tromsanach, -aiche, *a.* Sad, heavy, dull, dozy.

———adh,(MS) *s.m.* Obstupefaction.

tromsanaich, -e, *s.f.* Heaviness, dulness, stupefaction, sleepiness.

———,(MS) *v.n.* Benumb. 2 Mope.

trom-shuain,** *s.f.* Profound sleep. 2 Lethargy.

trom-thuradh,** *s.m.* Great draught.

trom-tric,** *a.* Pell-mell.

toraid, -e, -ean, *s.f.* Spire, steeple.

†**trosc**, *s.m.* Leper.

trosdail, -e & -ala, *a.* Of a serious humour or disposition. 2 Dull, inclined to melancholy, moody, serious, sedate, demure.

trosdalachd, *s.f.* Seriousness. 2 Inclination to melancholy, dulness, demureness.

trosdan, -ain, -an, *s.m.* Pace. 2 Foot. 3 Footstool. 4 Crutch, prop, support, stilt. 5‡‡Pilgrim's staff. 6††Dwarf. 7* Trap.

trosdanach, -aich, *s.m.* Stout or well-built person.

trosg, -uisg [** -oisg], *s.m.* Cod-fish. 2 Stupid fellow, lubber, booby. 3 Religious fasting. 4 ††Tusk-fish. see traisg & trosgadh.

trosgach, -aiche, *a.* Abounding in, of or belonging to, cod-fish. 2 Stupid, senseless, like a booby. 3 Fasting.

trosgadh, -aidh, see trasgadh.

trosgair, -ean, *s.m.* Cod-fisher. 2 Cod-fishing. 3 Fasting, frequent fasting.

trosgan,** *s.m.* Goods, chattels.

troslog,** -oig, *s.f.* Hop, limp.

trosnan, -ain, -an, see trostan.

trost,(CR) *s.m.* Knock, fall, stroke, as of one striking the ground after falling from a height—*West coast of Ross.*

trost,* *s.m.* Clank, as of metal. 2**Sturdy little fellow. 3 Dwarf.

trostach, *a.* Sturdy. 2 Dwarfish.

trostan,** -ain, *s.m.* Pace. 2 Foot. 3 Support, prop, pillar. 4 Stilt, crutch. Còig trostain, *five pillars.*

trostan,** see trosdan.

trot, *pr.pt.* a' trotadh, *v.a. & n.* Trot.

trot, -a, *s.m.* see trotan. 2* Sheep's foot. Cuir an t-each 'na th., *put the horse a-trotting.*

trotail, *s.f.* Trotting. 2 Jogging motion.

trotair, -ean, *s.m.* Trotter, one who trots.

——eachd, *s.f.* Trotting.

trotan, -ain, -an, *s.m.* Trot, trotting pace.

trotanach, -aiche, *a.* Trotting.

tròth,* *s.m.* Trip. 2 Taint. 3(CR) Turn, occasion, attempt, trial—*Skye, Knapdale, Arran.* Bha e an seo t., *he was here on one occasion ;* t. eile, *another time ;* feuch t. eile, *try again, make another attempt.*

troth, see tràth.

trotha, *s.* Mast-step—*Lewis.*

trothach,** *a.* Tainted.

trr-had ! *int.* Instigation of a dog from a distance.

†**trù**, *s.* Face. 2 Fall.

truacanach,(MS) *a.* Merciful.

truacanta, -ainte, *a.* Compassionate, merciful, pitiful. 2 Affectionate, tender-hearted.

truacantachd, *s.f.* see truacantas. 2 (MS) Remorse.

truacantas, -ais, *s.m.* Pity, compassion, compassionateness, pitifulness, tender-heartedness. 2 Affectionateness.

truadh, see truagh.

——an, see truaghan.

truagh, -uaighe, *a.* Wretched, miserable, distressing, sad, sorrowful, unhappy. 2 Worthless. 3 Miserly. 4 Poor. 5 Baleful. 6 Pitiful. Och, is duine t. mi ! *O wretched man that I am !*, duine t., *a poor man ;* gu t. trom, *wretched and sad ;* is t. leam th., *I pity you ;* nach t. mo chàradh, *how piteous is my case ;* is t. nach fhaca mi e, *it is a pity I did not see him ;* is t. mar a thachair, *sad is this occurrence ;* is t. an tabhartas e, *it is a miserable gift ;* comharra t. a' bhàis, *the dismal symptoms of death ;* cha t. leam thu, *I do not pity you ;* ma's t. leat e, *if you pity him.* In *Arran*, truagh gu 'n robh e=pity but he were ; t. gu'n robh thu eadar Allasan agus Eabhainn, *pity but you were between Ailsa Craig and Sanda*—form of imprecation.

truaghaileach,** *a.* Compassionate, tender-hearted.

————d, *s.f.* Compassionateness, tender-heartedness.

truaghan, -ain, -an, *s. m.* Poor, distressed or wretched creature. 2 Object of pity. 3 Child of misfortune. 4 Miser. 5 " A thruaghain," term of compassion. Na sàruich an t., *oppress not the distressed.*

truaghanach,‡‡ -aiche, *a.* Life-weary. 2 (MS) Commiserable.

truaghanachd, see truaghantachd.

truaghanta, -ainte, *a.* Lamentable, wretched, pitiable.

truaghantachd, *s.f.* Lamentableness, pitiableness, abjectness, miserableness, wretchedness, unfortunateness. 2 (MS) Villainage.

truaghas, see truas.

truagh-mheileach, see truaighe-mheileach.

truaighe, *comp.* of truagh.

truaighe, -an, *s.f.* Misery, woe, mischief, evil. 2 2 Bale, calamity. 3 Pity. 4 Wretchedness. Tha 'n t. ort-sa, *you have exceeded all bounds, gone to the mischief ;* mo th. thu ! *woe unto you !* na cuimhnicheadh e a th. na 's mó, *let him remember his misery no more;* mo th. sinne ! *woe unto us !* tuireach a thruaighe, *the sad tale of his calamity ;* mo th. ! *woe is me !* mo th. sinne, *woe unto us !*

truaighmheil, see truaighe-mheile.

truaighmheileach, see truaighe-mheileach.

truaighe-mheile,‡‡ *s.f.* Compassion, pity.

truaighe-mheileach, -eiche, *a.* Compassionate, pitiful.

truaill, -e, -ean, Sheath, scabbard. 2** *rarely*, Carcase. Tharruing e a chlaidheamh as a th., *he drew his sword out of the sheath.*

truaill, *pr.pt.* a' truailleadh, *v.a.* Pollute, defile. 2 Violate, ravish. 3 Unhallow, profane. 3* Qualify, reduce spirits to a standard. 5 Adulterate. 6 Sheathe. Th. thu am fearann, *you have polluted the land ;* cha t. thu thu-féin, *thou shalt not pollute thyself ;* th. do chlaidheamh, *sheathe thy sword.*

truailleach,** -ich, *s.m.* Sheath.

———, *a.* Polluting, defiling violating.

truailleachadh, -aidh, *s.m.* Polluting, defiling or adulterating, pollution, defilement, adulteration.

truailleachan, -ain, *s.m.* Mean person.

truailleachd,* *s.f.* Mean quantity, consideration or disposition. 2 Abjection. 3 Baseness, pollution, adulteration. 4**Defilement.

truailleadair, -ean, *s.m.* Corrupter, violater.

truailleadh, -idh, *s.m.* Polluting, act of polluting or defiling, pollution. 2 Profaning, act of profaning, profanation. 3**Deflowerment, defilement. 4*Reducing of spirits to a standard. 5 Adulteration, corruption 6 Profanity. Sruth glan gun t., *a stream pure and undefiled.* A' t—, *pt.pt.* of truaill.
truaillealachd. see truailleachd.
truaillean, -ein, *s.m.* Niggard.
————ach, -aich, *s.m.* Miser.
truailleanta,(MS) *a.* Pervertible.
truaillich,** *v.a.* Pollute, unhallow, profane. 2 Deflower. 3 Adulterate.
truaillidh, *fut.aff.a.* of truaill.
truaillidh, -e, *a.* Corrupt, corrupted. 2 Corrupting, that corrupts. 3 Rotten, rotted. 4*Dastardly, mean, shabby. 5 Polluting. 6 Bastard. 7 Polluted, defiled, contaminated. 8** Miserable wretched, dismal. Bha 'n talamh t., *the earth was corrupt* ; duine t., *a corrupt man.*
truaillidheachd, *s.f.* Pollution, corruption. 2 Rottenness. 3 Wretchedness, miserableness, 4 Meanness of disposition, niggardliness. 5 Pollutedness. Ri t. thubhairt mi, *I said to corruption.*
truaillte, *past pt.* of truaill. Defiled, corrupted, polluted. 2 Violated, deflowered. 3 Profaned. 4*Reduced to a standard, as spirits. 5 Adulterated. Uisge t., *polluted water ;* uisge-beatha t., *reduced or qualified whisky.*
truain, *pl.* -ean & -tean, *s.m.* Screw.
truan,* -ain, *s.f.* see trùghan.
truas, -ais, *s.m.* Pity, ruth, compassion. 2 Leanness, wretchedness, poverty. Ghabh e t. dhith. *he pitied her wretchedness* ; t. mo chòir, *the wretchedness of my condition.*
truasachadh, -aidh, *s.m.* Pitying, act of pitying. A' t—, *pr.pt.* of truasaich.
truasaich, *pr.pt.* a' truasachadh, *v.n.* Pity, compassionate, take pity upon.
truasail, -e, *a.* Compassionate, pitying. 2 Pitiable.
truasalachd, *s.f.* Readiness to pity or be compassionate.
trudair, -ean, *s.m.* Stammerer. 2 Dirty, filthy or obscene person, see trusdair.
trudaireachd, *s. f.* Dirtiness, filthiness, nastiness, worthlessness, impurity, obscenity.
trudanach, -aich, *s.m.* Wrangler.
trudar, -air, -an, see trusdar.
trudarnach, -aich, *s.m.* Stammerer.
trughaid,** *s.* Gripe.
trùghan, -ain, *s.m.* Trowel.
truid,** *s.f.* Field of battle. 2 Strife, battle. 2 Tidy, neat female. Cèarr am measg t., *awkward in the midst of strife.*
truid,* see druid & trod.
truideag, see druideag.
truidhleach, *s.m.* Lumber, baggage.
truidleag,(AF) Mavis.
truidreach,** -ich, *s.m.* Melody. 2 Warbling, chirping, chattering, twittering.
truigeanta,** *a.* Miserable.
truileach,* *s.f.* Worthless person.
truille,* *s.m. & f.* Worthless, dirty person.
truilleach, -ich, *s.m. & f.* Dirty or base person. 2 Filthy food.
truime, *s.f.* Weight, heaviness, weightiness, 2 Dejection. T. inntinn, *dejection, melancholy.*
truime, *gen. & comp.* of trom.
truimeachd,** *s.f.* Heaviness, weight. 2 Sadness.
truimead, -eid, *s.m.* Degree of heaviness, faintness or dejectedness. A' dol an t., *growing heavier and heavier.*
truime-inntinn, *s.f.* Dejection, melancholy.
truimpleasg, *s.m.* Fulmination, explosion.
truimid, *comp.* of trom. Is t. e sin, *it is the heavier for that.*
truinnse,** *s.f.* Trench.
truinnsear,** -eir, *s.m* Trencher, plate, salver,
truinnsich,** *v.a.* Trench. 2 Enclose.
truis, *pr.pt.* a' truiseadh. *v.a.* Tear or snatch away. 2 Collect, truss up, gather, tuck up. 3 (MS) Shell.
truis ! *int.* (*lit.* gather your tail) Word by which dogs are silenced or driven away. *Also said to a person in contempt. Truis a mach ! *get out ! begone !*
truis,* *s.f.* see drùis.
truis a' mach ! *int.* Get out, clear out altogether —animal call—*Islay, &c.* see truis a sin !
truis a sin ! *int.* Get out of the way, get to one side—animal call—*Islay, &c.*
truis-bhràghad,‡‡ -e-, -ean-bh-, *s.f.* Necklace. 2 Band of harness.
truis-bhrat,‡‡-ait, -an, *s.m.* Pack-cloth.
truisealach, see drùisealach.
————adh, -aidh, *s.m.* Act of tucking up, as the clothes. 2 State of having one's clothes tucked up. A' t—, *pr.pt.* of truisealaich.
————d, see drùisealachd.
truisealadh, -aidh, see truisealachadh.
truisealaich, *pr. pt.* a' truisealachadh, *v.a.* Tuck up, as the clothes.
truiseil,* -e, *a.* see drùiseil.
truisidh sin ! see truis a sin !
truiste, *a.* Succinct.
truitean,(AF) *s.m.* Badger.
truitrich, *v.n.* Twitter.
trulainn, *a.* Topsy-turvy.
†trull, -a, *s.m.* Head.
trumachadh, -aidh, *s.m. & pr.pt.* of trumaich.
trumadas, see tromadas.
trumaich, see tromaich.
trumpa, see trompa.
trumpadair, see trombaidear.
trùp, -a, -an, *s.m.* Troop of horse. 2††Nap. [***s.f.*]
trup, *adv.* Once. Bha mi ann t., *I was there once—Strontian.* [*Eng.* trip]
trùpach, *a.* In troops.
trùpair, -ean, *s.m.* Trooper. 2* Romp.
————eachd, *s.f.* Trooping.
trùp-each, -a-, -an, see trùp.
trus, *pr. pt.* a' trusadh, *v.a.* Truss, tuck up, gird. 2 Bundle together. 3 Collect, as sheep. 4** Reprimand. 5 Go to, repair to. Th. do chinneadh ri chéile, *thy kindred gathered together;* a thrusadh lus mu bhun nan stùc, *to gather herbs at the foot of the rocks* ; trus ort ! *be off, begone !* a' trusadh do 'n taigh òsda, *repairing to the alehouse.*
trus, -uis, *s.m.* Belt, girdle. 2**Girt. 3 Bundle.
trus ! see truis !
trusach,‡‡ -aich, *s.m.* Sheaf.
trusach, -aiche, *a.* That gathereth, gathering, collecting, bundling, trussing.
trusachan, -ain, -an, *s.m.* Parcel, pack.
trusadh, -aidh, *s.m.* Gathering, act of gathering or collecting, as sheep. 2 Tucking, girding, trussing, bundling. 3 Collection, bundle.
trusag, -aig, -an, *s.f.* Wad. 2 Bale.
trusaiche, -an, *s.m.* Gatherer, collector.
trus-aite, -an, *s.m.* Wardrobe. 2 Lumber-room.
trusalachadh, -aidh, *s.m.* Girding up, preparing, making ready.
trusaladh, -aidh, *s.m.* Girding up, preparing, bestirring.
trusalaich, *pr. pt.* a' trusalachadh, *v.a.* Gird up. prepare, make ready, bestir.
trusan, *s.m.* see trusag.
truscan, see trusgan.
trusdaireachd,* *s.f.* Filthiness, abominableness.

2 Dirtiness of person. 3 Filth, dirt, trash.
trusdar, -air, -airean, s.m. Filthy or nasty fellow, indecent or obscene person. 2 Debauchee 3 Clown. 4 Drab. 5 Filth, dirt, dust. [*nom. trusdair.]
trusdarach, -aiche, a. Cullionly, mucky.
trusdarail, (MS) a. Abominable.
trusdarnach, -aich, s.m. Stammerer.
trusdrachd,†† s.f. Filthiness, filth.
trusdromach, -aich, s.m. Busybody.

668. Trusgan.

trusgan, -ain, -an, s.m. Clothes, dress, vesture, mantle, garment, suit of clothes. 2 Shroud. 3 **Man's privy parts. 4 Smelt. 5 Furniture, chattels. 6§ Lady's mantle (plant)—*alchemilla alpina*. So called from its form and the satiny under side of the leaves. An t. de dhealan, *in a shroud of lightning*; t. air cruit an aonaich, *lady's mantle on the ridge of the hill.*
trusganach, a. Abounding in, or pertaining to, lady's mantle. 2 Having many, or good clothes. Tir mheasail, mhiaghail, th., *the esteemed and famous land abounding in lady's mantle.*
trusgar,** -air, s.m. Oarweed.
truslag,** -aig, s.f. Leap.
trutag, (DMK) s.f. Loose garment in the form of a cape, worn over the shoulders and back in wet weather—*Applecross.*
†truth, -a, s.m. Vile beast, beastly thing. 2 Shrew. 3 Sloven.
truthair, -ean, s.m. Traitor, villain. 2 Filthy fellow. 3 Prevaricator, liar, deluder, knave. 4 (*truthaire) Bankrupt.
truthaireachd, s.f. Villainy, low mean actions, knavery, bribery, deceit. 2 Revolt.
truthaireach, -eiche, a. Pettifogging.
truthdar, -air, s.m. Dirty, indecent or obscene person, sloven, slattern.
truthdaireachd, s.f. Dirtiness, slovenliness, filthiness, obscenity.
tu, *pers.pron.* Thou, you. [For information as to the distinctive uses of *tu* and *thu*, see under *thu*; and for the difference between *thu* and *sibh*, see under *sibh*. Is tu an gille, *thou art the (right) fellow*; is gabhaidh tu mi a steach, *and thou shalt take me in*; na'n tigeadh tu, *if thou wert to come.*
tuacaird, s.f. Winding of yarn.
tuachail, a. Prudent, wise, cunning.
tuachioll, see tuaicheal.
tuadh, -aidh, -an, s.f. see tuagh. 2 *rarely*, Renown.
tuadhi! *int.* Call to a bull—*Suth'd.*
tuafair, s.m. Bungler, humdrum.
tuafaireachd, s.f. Bungle.
tuagh, -aigh, -an, s.f. Hatchet, axe. †2§ Yew. Mar t. an glaic saoir, *like an axe in the grasp of a carpenter*; iarunn na tuaighe, *axe-head.*
†tuagha, s.pl. Hooks, crooks 2 Hinges.
tuaghach,†† a Like a hatchet or axe
tuagh-airm, tuaigh-, -an-, s.f. Battle-axe.

669. Tuaghan-catha.

tuagh-chatha, tuaigh-, -an-, s.f. Battle-axe, Lochaber-axe.
tuagh-chuillse, s.f Fleam, cattle lancet, instrument for bleeding cattle.
tuagh-fhola, s.f Fleam.
tuaibheisteach, (MS) s.m. Scrawl. 2 Scrawler.
tuaicheal, -eil, -an, s.m. Dizziness, confusion, bewilderment of mind, vertigo.
tuaichealach, -aiche, a. Dizzy 2 Causing dizziness. 3 Vermicular.
tuaichle, s.f. Augury. 2 Enchantment.
tuaifear, see tuafair.
tuaighe, (AF) s.m. Farm bull.
tuaileachd, s.f Daybreak, twilight.
tuaileas, -eis, -an, s.m. Reproach, slander, calumny, libel, defamation, detraction, imputation, scandal. 2 Disorder. 3††Dark view.
tuaileas, v.a. Defame—*Dàin Iain Ghobha.*
tuaileasach, -aiche, a. Reproachful, calumnious, dealing in scandal, defamatory, slanderous, libellous, detractory. 2**Turbulent.
tuaileasachd, s.f.ind. Contumeliousness, calumniousness, talebearing. †2 Crepuscule.
tuaileasag, -aig, -an, s. f. Woman addicted to scolding or scandal, quarrelsome female, foul-mouthed female, disorderly female.
tuaileasaich, (MS) v.a. Backbite, disdain, detract. 2 Belie.
tuaileasaiche, s.m. Calumniator.
tuailt, see tubhailt.
tuailte, see tubhailt.
tuailteach, see tubhailteach.
tuailtear, see tubhailtear.
tuailtearachd, see tubhailtearachd.
tuaim, s.f. Fence. 2 *gen.sing.* of tuam.
tuaimeil,* v.a. Swathe awkwardly, huddle on clothes.
tuain, v.a. Loosen—*Uist.*
tuaineal, -eil, -an, s.m. Stupor, dizziness, vertigo. Ghlac e an t-aosdharach 'na th., *he grasped the oak in his dizziness.*
tuainealach, -aiche, a. Dizzy, causing dizziness.
tuainealach, -aich, see tuainealaich.
tuainealaich, -e, s.f. Giddiness, dizziness, stupidity, amazement.
tuainig, see tualaig.
tuair, *gen.sing.* of tuar.
†tuair, v.n. Bode, portend, predict.
tuair, see tuathair.
tuairealachd,** s.f. Hardihood.
tuaiream, -eim, -an, s.f. Guess, conjecture, random, venture. 2 Quantity, number. 3 Aim, design. 4 Sense, judgment. 5 Vicinity, nearness, neighbourhood. 6(MS)Average. 7**Opinion. 8*Direction. 9 Pursuit. Cha'n 'eil dith t. air, *he does not want sense*; 'dé 'n t, a th' ann? *what quantity or number are there of them?* dh' fhalbh e m' a t., *he went in pursuit of her*; thilg e m' a th. e, *he aimed it at him*; dh'fhàg mi m' an t. seo e, *I left it hereabout*; mu th.

an aon àite, *much about the same place;* thaobh **thuaireim,** *at venture;* thuit i mu 'thuaiream, *she fell beside him;* mu 'n t. sin, *thereabout;* sluagh mu 'r t., *hosts around you.*

Mu thuaiream,in *Arran* =to,in the sense of sending to, dh' ionnsuidh; chuir mi litir m' a thuaiream, mu thuaiream Sheumais, *I sent a letter to him, to James.*

tuaireamach, -aiche, *a.* Conjectural. 2 Sensible.

tuaireamas,†† see tuairmeas.

tuaireap, -eip, -an, *s.m.* Turbulence, confusion, fray, squabble, fight, tumult.

tuaireapach, -aiche, *a.* Turbulent, squabbling, fighting, tumultuous, boisterous, disorderly, causing squabbles, awkward.

tuaireapachd, *s.f.* Boisterousness.

tuaireapadh,(MS) *s.m.* Boisterousness.

tuaireil, *a.* Hale. 2 Hardy—*Glendochart.* see tuarail.

tuairgne,* *s.f.* Confusion, ado, affray, tumult, riot, squabble, fray, fight. 2 (MS) Distemper. Ughdar na t., *the author of confusion.*

tuairgin, *s.f.* Hatchel. 2 Washing-staff.

tuairgneach, -eiche, *a.* Confused, disturbed, tumultuous, disorderly. 2 Causing confusion. 3 Seditious. Gu t., *tumultuously.*

tuairgneadh, -idh, *s.m.* Confusion, chaos, disturbance, agitation, bluster, broil. 2 Sedition. 3 Dismay—*Dàin I. Ghobha.*

tuairgnich,* *v.a.* Confound, concern, puzzle. 2 Bamboozle. 3 Blast.

†tuairisg, -e, -ean, *s.f.* Symbol, character. 2 Notification, account.

tuairisgeul -eil [& sgeòil,] *pl.* -an, *s.m.* Detail, description, definition. 2 Made-up-story. 3 Defamation, calumny, slander, bad report. Droch th., *a bad report;* t. mhòran, *the defamation of many;* t. brèige, *a false report.*

tuairisgeulach, -aiche, *a.* Describing, descriptive. 2 Raising calumnies, calumnious, defaming, defamatory, slanderous.

tuairisgeulaich, *v.a.* Define, describe, depict.

tuairisgeulaiche, *s.m.* Describer.

tuairisglich,(MS) *v.a.* Depaint.

tuairmeachach, -aich, see tuaireamach.

tuairmeachadh, -aidh, *s. m.* Guessing, venturing, aiming.

tuairmeachd, see tuaiream.

tuairmeas, -eis, *s.m.* Guess, venture, opinion, conjecture. 2 Hap-hazard, venture. Thaobh thuairmeis, *at a venture;* mu thuairmeis, see tuaiream.

tuairmeasach, -aiche, *a.* Random.

tuairmeis, see tuaiream.

tuarrmich, *v.a.* Guess, conjecture. 2 Venture, aim.

tuairmis, see tuaiream.

tuairmis,‡ *v.a.* Hit on, discover. 2††Aim indefinately.

tuairmse, see tuaiream, An t-urram àrd gun tuairms', *the high honour without doubt.* —*Moladh na Gàidhlig.*

tuairmseachadh, see tuairmeachadh. 2 (MS) Adventure.

tuairmsear,(MS) *s.m.* Guesser.

tuairmsich,(MS) *v.a.* Aim, conjecture, guess.

†tuairn, *s.f.* **Turning-loom (? lathe.)

†tuairneadh, -idh, -idhean, *s.m.* Foreboding.

tuairneag, -eig, -an, *s.f.* Anything round, boss. 2 Neat, tidy little woman. 3 Ball. 4 Small wooden drinking-cup, also called cuach. 5 Cap. 6 *Coble, kind of punt.

tuairneagach, -aiche, *a.* Neat, tidy. 2 Roundish. 2††Full of caps.

tuairneal,** *s.m.* Trundle.

tuairnean, -ein, -an, *s.m.* Mallet, hammer, beetle. 2††Lathe.

tuairnear, -ir, -an, *s.m.* Turner.

tuairnearachd, *s.f.* Turning, turner's trade, employment of turning, working at a lathe.

†tuairp, -e, -ean, *s.f.* Prophecy.

tuairsgeul, see tuairisgeul.

————ach, see tuairisgeulach.

tuaisd,* *s.m.* Dolt, awkward person 2(AH)Base contemptible fellow. 3 Diminutive person. 4 ††Slovenly person

tuaisdeach, -eiche, *a.* Awkward, stupid, clownish, slovenly, untidy, unseemly. 2 Preposterous.

tuaisdeachd, *s.f.* Stupidity, slovenliness, unseemliness.

tuaisdealachd, *s.f.* Stupidity, clumsiness, awkwardness.

tuaisdear, -eir, -an, *s.m.* Clown, dolt, awkward fellow, bungler. 2‡‡ Large stick.

tuaisdearachd, *s.f.* Clumsiness, awkwardness.

tuaisdeil, -e, *a.* Awkward, stupid.

tuaisgeart,** s. The North.

tuaiteal, *a.* Austere.

tuaitealachd, *s.f.* Austereness.

tuaith, *s.f.* Lordship, territory.

tuaith, *inflection* of tuath.

tuaithcheall, *s.* Skill, sagacity.

tuaithealachd, *s.f.* Husbandry.

tuaitheal, -eile, *a.* see tuathal.

tuaithealach, *a.* see tuathal.

tuaithealan,‡‡ -ain, -an, *s.m.* Wrong, ill-doing man.

tuaithleus,(MS) *s.* Amaurosis.

tual, see tuathal.

tual, *a.* Noted, remarkable for either good or evil. 2 Awkward.

tualachd, *s.f.* Possibility.

tualag, *s.f.* Diarrhœa.

tualagach, *a.* Purgative.

tualaig,‡ *v.a.* Loose, ravel. 2 Have flux. 3 Unyoke, as horses—*Perthshire.*

tualaigte, *a.* Loose, slack.

tualaing, *a.* Able.

tualaing, see fulaing.

tualaing, *s.f.* Patience.

tual-bheairt, *s.pl.* Exploits, brave deeds.

tual-chainnt, *s.f.* Ribaldry, jargon, gibberish.

tuam, see tuama. Cadal nan tuam, *the sleep of the grave;* ula nan tuam, *the grass (beard) of the mounds.*

tuama, -n, *s.f.* Tomb, grave. 2 Cave. 3 Moat. 4 Mound. 4 *rarely* Farm.

tuamach, -aiche, *a.* Abounding in graves, tombs or mounds. 2 Of, or belonging to, tombs, graves or mounds. 3 Like a tomb.

tuamaich, *v.a,* Entomb.

tuamaichte, *past pt.* of tuamaich. Entombed.

tuamail, see tuamach.

tuamann, *a.* Fierce. 2 Morose.

tuamhsgaoil, *v.a.* Roll in clothes, huddle, endeavour to extricate out of a labyrinth or great deal of clothes.

tuanag, see tualaig & tònag.

tuanlaig, *v.* Loose, have flux—*Perthshire.*

tua-pholl, -phuill, *s.m.* Whirlpool.

tuar, -air, -an, *s.m.* Colour, hue, appearance, countenance, complexion. 2 Hardship. 3 Food. 4 Cast. 5 Fear. 6 Life. 7 Presage, omen, foreboding, auspice. 8 Forerunner. 9 House. 10 Advantage, profit. 11*Merit, desert. 12 Meriting, deserving. A' t—, *pr.pt.* of tuar. Cha 'n 'eil t. air an t-iasgach tighinn na b' fhèarr, *there is no appearance of the fishing improving;* gnè sam bith thuair, *any kind of hardship;* faileus mu'n t., *a shade upon their countenance;* mar th. na soillse, *like the appearance of light;* iongantas mu'n tuar, *wonder at their fear;* gun teach gun t., *without house or life;* trath bhios tuar 'dol as air na gobhair, cha bheir iad ach buic, *when the goats are about to become extinct* (*senseless*), *they only bring forth bucks* ; bha a th. air a' bhreitheamh mo leigeil mu sgaoil, *the judge appeared likely to let me go.*

tuar, *pr.pt.* a' tuar, *v.a.* Deserve, merit. An ni a th. thu, *what you deserved* ; 'dé a tha thu a' tuar a dheanamh ort ? *what do you deserve to be done to you ?* tha thu a' t. do chrochadh, *you deserve to be hanged.*

tuaradh,* -aidh, *s.m.* Quantity, number. 'Dé 'n t. a th' ann ? *what quantity is there ?* mu'n t. sin, *about that quantity.*

tuaradh, -aidh, *s.m.* Sauce.

tuaragan, -ain, *s.m.* Bleacher.

tuarail, -e, *a.* Having a good complexion, hue or colour. 2 Hardy, stout, firm. 3 see tuathrail.

tuaram, see tuaiream.

tuarasdal, -ail, -an, *s.m.* Wages, reward, hire, fee, salary, stipend. 2 Desert. Ainmich do th., *appoint thy wages* ; là Fhéill Brìghde gheibh na seirbhisich t. slàn, *on Candlemas Day servants get their full wage*—i.e. they can work from 6 a.m. to 6 p.m. The saying refers to Candlemas Old Style, now 14th. Feb.

tuarasdalach, -aich, see tuasasdalaiche.

tuarasdalachadh,-aidh, *s.m.* Hiring, act of hiring. A' t—, *pr.pt.* of tuarasdalaich.

tuarasdalaich, *pr.pt.* a' tuarasdalachadh, *v. a.* Hire, engage for a fee.

tuarasdalaiche, -ean, *s.m.* Hireling, mercenary. 2 One who hires.

tuarasdalaichte, *past pt.* of tuarasdalaich.

tuarasgar,(AF) *s.m.* Shellfish,

tuarg, *s.m.* Beetle, mall.

tuargan, -ain, *s.m.* Discontent, dissatisfaction, complaining, squabble, misunderstanding. 2 Beating. 3 Sedition.

tuarganach, -aiche, *a.* Dissatisfied, discontented, squabbling.

†tuarganach-catha, *s.m.* Chief, commander, field-marshal, generalissimo.

tuarganachd, *s.f.* Discontentedness, dissatisfaction.

tuargnadh, -aidh, -aidhean, *s. m.* Discontent, dissatisfaction. 2 Sedition. 3 Misunderstanding.

tuar-mhanadh,‡‡ -aidh, -aidhean, *s.m.* Omen.

tuarnairich, *v.a.* Make by turning.

tuarnalaich, *Gairloch* for tuainealaich.

tuartan,(DMK) *s.m.* Cold in the head—*Caithness.*

tuasaid, -e, -ean, *s.f.* Tumult, quarrel, row, fray, brawl, wrangle, fight, contention. 2 Bluster. 3‡‡Sedition. T. ghaoth agus chreag, *the battle of winds and rocks.*

tuasaideach, -eiche, *a.* Quarrelsome, tumultuous, riotous, brawling, wrangling. 2 Seditious.

tuasaideach, *s.f.* Squabbling, quarrelsomeness, wrangling.

tuasaideachd,(MS) *s.f.* Turbulence.

tuasaidich,(MS) *v.* Brawl.

tuasdair, see tuaisdear.

tuasgail, see fuasgail.

tuasgailte, see fuasgailte.

†tuasgart, *a.* North, northern.

tuasglach, -aich, *s.m.* One who releases.

———, *a.* Aperient, see fuasglach.

tuasgladh, see fuasgladh.

tuasglagadh,** -aidh, *s.m.* Releasing, loosening. 2 Dissolving.

tuath, *a.* North, northern. An àirde t., *the North* ; bho 'n t., *from the North* or *northward* ; gaoth t., *north wind* ; t. ort, *northward of you* ; an taobh t., *the north side, the north country, the North.*

tuath, -a, *s.f.coll.* Tenantry, peasantry, laity, country people, husbandmen, aggregate number of any land proprietors, farmers or tenants. Air an t., *on the country* ; an t., an tuath-cheathairn, *the tenantry* ; is treasa t. na tighearna, *tenantry are stronger than laird.*

———ach, -aiche, *a.* Having many tenants. 2 Of, or belonging to, the tenantry. 3 Northerly.

———ach, -aich, *s. m.* North Highlander. 2 *rarely*, Lord, proprietor.

†tuathachd, *s.f.ind.* Sovereignty, lordship, proprietorship.

tuathag, -aig, -an, *s.f.* see tuthag.

tuathair, -e, -ean, *s.f.* Northern exposure. 2 Countryside lying towards the North. [***gen.* tuathrach.]

tuathaiste,(MS) *s.f.* Stumble.

tuathaisteach,(MS) *a.* Uncouth.

tuathal, -aile, *a.* Contrary to the course of the sun, and consequently regarded as unlucky. 2 To the left, wrong. 3 Cross, athwart. 4 Ominous. 5 Awkward. 6 Backward. 7 see tuathach. 8**Brave. Car t., *a wrong turn* ; o shealladh an laoich th., *from the sight of the brave hero.*

tuathanach, -aich, *a.* Farmer, rustic, peasant, husbandman, agriculturist, layman.

———ail, -e, *a.* Agricultural.

———as, -ais, *s.m.* Farming, agriculture, husbandry.

tuathanachd,** *s.f.* Agriculture, husbandry. 2 Condition of a farmer or peasant.

tuathanas, -ais, see tuathanachas.

tuath-cheatharna,** *s.f.* Yeomanry. 2 Peasantry, common people. Neach de 'n t., *one of the common people* ; bu lionmhor ar t., *numerous were our peasantry.*

tuath-fhras,** -ais, *s.m.* Northern blast.

tuath-ghaoth,** -ghaoithe, *s.f.* North wind.

———ach,** *a.* Aquilonial. Mios t., *an aquilonial month.*

tuathlach,** *a.* Ominous. 2 Unlucky. 3 Awkward. 4 Left-handed.

———d,** *s. f.* Ominousness. 2 Unluckiness. 3 Awkwardness, rusticity.

tuathlan,** -ain, *s.m.* Awkward, ungainly person. 2 Boor, rustic, plebeian.

tuathrach, *gen.sing.* of tuathair.

———,** *a.* Having a northern exposure.

tuba, -chan & -nnan, *s.f.* Tub, vat. [vat.

tubag, -aig, -an, *s.f.,dim.* of tuba. Little tub or

tubagach, *a.* Like, of, or belonging to, a little tub or vat.

tubag-leigidh, *s.f.* Dropping-tub (in distilling.)

tubag-shilidh, *s.f* Dropping-tub (in distilling.)

tubaist, -e, -ean, *s.f.* Misfortune, mischance, mishap, calamity, mischief. 2 Accident. 3†† Wretch. Is trom na tubaistean air na slibistean, *the clumsy are very liable to accidents* ; t. ort ! *mischief take you !* a thaobh t., *by accident* ; thig t. air, *mischief shall befall him.*

tubaisteach, -eiche, *a.* Unlucky, unfortunate. 2 Accidental, calamitous, untoward, unpropitious.

———d, *s.f.* Unfortunate occurrence, unfortunateness. 2 Accidentalness, calamitousness, unluckiness, liability to accident.

tubait,** -ean, *s.f.* Tippet.

tuban, -ain, -an, *s.m.* *Tub. 2 see toban.

tubanach, -aiche, *a.* Having many tufts of wool or lint.

tubh, see tugh.

tùbh, see taobh.

tubhach, see tughach.

tubhadair, see tughadair.

———eachd, see tughadaireachd.

tu'hadh, see tughadh.
tub'iag,(MS) *s.f.* Patch.
tubh'gachas, *s.m.* Patchery.
tubhagaiche,(MS) *s.m.* Patcher.
tùbhailt, -e, -ean, *s.f.* Towel, hand-towel, diaper. T.-bhùird, *a table-cloth.*
——each,†† *a.* Abounding in towels. 2 Like a towel.
——ear,** -eir, *s.m.* Weaver of towels.
——earachd,** *s.f.* Business or occupation of towel-weaving.
tubhta, see tughta.
tubhte, see tughta.
tuca,** *s.m.* Tuck, rapier.
tùcadair, -ean, see fùcadair.
——eachd, see fùcadaireachd.
tucaid,* -e, -ean, *s.f.* Dove-cot.
tuch !* *int.* Tut ! hush !
tùch, *pr. pt.* a' tùchadh, *v.a. & n.* Stop, shut, smother as a flame. 2 Extinguish, quench. 3 Become hoarse. 4 Fumigate. Tha mo mhuineal air a thùchadh, *my throat has become hoarse.*
tucha,** *s.* Pore.
tùchach, -aiche, *a.* Causing hoarseness.
tùchadh, -aidh, *s.m.* Stopping. 2 Act of covering, as with a lid. 3 State of becoming hoarse, hoarseness. 4 Wheezing. 5 Extinguishing, smothering, as a flame. 6††Cooing. A' t—, *pr. pt.* of tùch.
tùchair,* -ean, *s.m.* Smotherer.
tùchan, -ain, *s.m.* Cooing of a dove. 2 Hoarseness, gutturalness. 3 Fit of hoarseness caused by a cold or an exertion of the voice. 4 Half-smothered fire ; le t.'s le cnatan, *with hoarseness and cold.*
——ach, -aiche, *a.* Hoarse, guttural, bass, whirring. 2 Causing hoarseness.
——achd, *s.f.ind.* Raucity, gutturalness.
†tuchd, *s.* Form. 2 Time, season.
tuchraidh,** *s.f.* Appointed time. 2 Critical time.
tùchta, *past pt.* of tùch. Made hoarse. 2 Affected with hoarseness. 3 Extinguished or smothered, as a flame.
tùchte, see tùchta.
tùd, *s.m.* Heap. 2 see tùdan.
tud !* *int.* Tut ! whist !
tudagan, see tutagan.
tùdan, -ain, -an, *s.m.* Small heap, as of dough. 2 Small stack of corn or hay. (Permanent stack in *Suth'd.*) 3 Lump. 4 Tuft, as of wool. 5 **Turd. 6 Suds, see tutag. 7* Mannikin. [Short *u* in *Gairloch & W.of Ross.* DU]
——ach, -aiche, *a.* Abounding in small stacks of hay or corn.
tudraig, *a.* Vigorous—*Arran.*
tufag, -aig, *s.f.* Foist. 2 Stench.
tug, (for thug), see thoir.
tugadh, *past aff. neg. & interr.* of thoir. Was given.
tugaid,** *s.f.* Cause, reason.
——each,(MS) *a.* Amusive, jocose, arch.
tugaidean, *s.pl.* Witticisms, facetiousness, humour, jocoseness, roguery.
tugainn, *irr. past subj.* of thoir.
tugh, *pr.pt.* a' tughadh, *v. a.* Thatch, cover. 2 Back. T. a staigh e, *back him in*—said of a horse.
tugha, *s.f.* Thatch, covering, any material, such as straw, heath or fern, wherewith the roof of a house is thatched. 2**Opposition. Taighean tugha, *thatched houses.*
tughach,** *a.* Thatched. 2 Like thatch.
tughadair, -ean, *s.m.* Thatcher.
——eachd,†† *s.f.* Employment or business of thatching.
tughadh, -aidh, *s.m.* Thatching, act of thatching. 2 Thatch. A' t—, *pr.pt.* of tugh.
tùghag,(CR) *s.f.* Patch—*W. of Ross.* Is fheàrr breid no toll, ach is uaisle toll na tùghag, *a patch is better than a hole, but a hole is more genteel.*
tughta, *past pt.* of tugh. Thatched.
tugtadh, *past subj. pass.* of thoir.
tuidhle,** *a.* Pleasant.
†tuidhme, *s.f.* Confederacy, conjunction.
tuidhtearachd, *s.f* Wardship.
tuig, *pr.pt.* a' tuigsinn, *v.a. & n.* Understand, perceive, discern, comprehend. Th. e do chridhe, *he understood thy heart ;* cò a thuigeas uile sheachrain fhéin ? *who can understand all his own errors ?* an sin tuigidh tu eagal an Tighearna, *then shalt thou understand the fear of the Lord.*
tuigear, *fut.pass.* of tuig.
tuigim, (for tuigidh mi), I shall understand.
tuigse, *s.f.ind.* Understanding, reason, knowledge, skill, sense, judgment. A' call a th., *losing his senses or judgment ;* is beag t. a th' agad air sin, *you have little skill at that ;* faigh t., *get understanding.*
tuigseach, -eiche, *a.* Intelligent, sensible, wise, prudent, judicious, knowing. 2 Skilled, expert. Duine t., *a prudent* or *intelligent man ;* t. air a leithid sin, *expert in such things ;* gu t. *intelligently.*
——adh,(MS) *s.m.* Apprehension.
——d,** *s.f.* Apprehensiveness.
tuigseil,(MS) *a.* Apprehensible.
tuigsinn, *s.f.* Understanding, act of understanding, comprehending, discerning or perceiving. A' t—, *pr.pt.* of tuig.
——each, -eiche, *a.* see tuigseach.
——each, -eich, *s.m.* Knowing person.
——eachd, *s.f.* Deducement.
tuil, -e, -ean & -tean, *s.f.* Flood, deluge. 2 Heavy rain, torrent. 3 Overflowing of running waters. 4 Tide. An T. Ruadh, *Noah's Flood ;* bhrùchd cuimhne mar th., *memory burst forth like a flood.* [**pl. tuilte & tuiltechan.]
tuil-aodach,** -aich, *s.m.* Apron.
tuil-bheum, -eim, -an, *s.m.* Torrent. 2 Torrent caused by the bursting of a thunder-cloud or by the sudden melting of snow. 3 Thunder-shower. Tha iad mar th., *they are like a torrent ;* is lìonmhor tuil-bheuman a' bheathaich laig, *the weak animal meets with many obstacles* (*lit.* torrents.) [***gen.* tuil-bheuma.]
tuil-bheumach, -aiche, *a.* Rushing as a torrent.
tuilcheanach,** -aich, *s.m.* Handsel.
tuil-dhorus, -uis, -dhorsan, *s.m.* Flood-gate. 2 Gate of a canal- or river-lock. Tuil-dhorsan nèimh, *the windows of heaven.*
tuileach, -eiche, *a.* Like a flood, deluging.
tuileachadh, -aidh, *s.m.* Flooding, act of deluging. A' t—, *pr.pt.* of tuilich.
tuileachas, *s.m.* Flooding. Dhia a rinn lìonadh is tràgh' is tuileachas, *God who made ebb and flow and flooding—Impromptu verse by MacKellar, author of Laoidh MhicEalair.*
tuile-thalmhainn, *s.f.* Bulbous crowfoot, see fuile-thalmhainn.
tuil-eudach, see tuil-aodach.
tuiliac, see tuilleag.
tuilich, *pr.pt.* a' tuileachadh, *v.a. & n.* Overflow, deluge, inundate, flood.
——, *s.m.* see tuilleadh.
tùilinn,** *s.f.* Twilled linen. Léine th., *a shirt of twilled linen.*
tuiliop,§ *s.* Tulip—*tulipa sylvestris.*
tuill, *gen. sing. & n. pl.* of toll. Of a hole. 2 Holes, caves. Tuill an fhirich, *the mountain*

caves.
tuille, *s., adv. & conj.* see tuilleadh. T. eile, *furthermore.*
tuillead,** -eid, *s.m.* Greater quantity, additional quantity. Gheibh thu an t., *you will get the more;* a th. air sin, *over and above that.*
tuilleadh, *s.m.* More, addition, additional quantity or number Thoir dhomh t., *give me more;* t. 's a chòir, *too much, superabundance;* t. ri t., *in apposition.*
tuilleadh, *adv.* More, any more, farther, moreover. T. 'us, *too;* t. fòs, t. eile, *moreover;* cha till mi t., *I shall never return;* cha bhi mi 'nam aonrachd t., *I shall be no longer solirary;* t. gu bràth, *any more for ever;* t. cha léir dhuit, *thou shalt see no more;* cha'n fhaod thu tighinn t., *you must not come any more.*
tuilleadhnach,(MS) *a.* Ascititious.
tuilleag,(AF) *s.f.* Common skua-gull.
tuillean, see tollan.
tuille eile, *conj.* Furthermore, moreover, nay more.
tuillein, see tollan.
tuillidh, see tuilleadh.
tuillinn, *s.f.* Canvas. 2 Sea-storm. 3 Shipped wave. *Sàr-Obair.*
tuilm, *gen.sing. & n.pl.* of tolm.
†tuilm, *s.f.* Gift.
tuilm, -e, *s.f.* Elm. 2 Oak. 3 Pudenda muliebria.
tuilmean,†† *s.m.* Little knoll.
tuilmeineach, *a.* Full of knolls or tufts.
tuillis,(AC) *s.* Overloading the stomach, especially with liquids.
tuil-mhaoim,** *s.f.* Sudden deluge, &c., see tuil bheum. Mar a leaghas sneachd 'na th., *as snow melts in torrents.*
tuilte, *n.pl.* of tuil.
tuilteach, -eiche, *a.* Flooding, that covers or floods with water, overflowing, inundating, deluging, causing a deluge.
tuilteach, -eich, *s. f.* Torrent. Air t. gaoithe sgaoil i a sgiathan, *on a torrent of air she spread her wings.*
tuilteachan, *n.pl.* of tuil.
tuiltean, *n.pl.* of tuil.
†tuiltin, s. Merit, demerit, see toiltinn.
tuim, *gen.sing. & n.pl.* of tom.
tuim, -e, *s.f.* see taoim.
tuimhseach, -eiche, *a.* Beating, striking, thumping.
tuimhseachadh, -aidh, *s.m.* Beating, act of beating, striking or thumping. 2 Blow, thump. A' t—, *pr. pt.* of tuimhsich.
tuimhseadh, -idh, see tuimhseachadh.
tuimhsich, *pr.pt.* a' tuimhseachadh, *v. a.* Beat, drub. 2 Stagger to and fro. 3††Knock against.
———te, *past pt.* of tuimhsich. Beaten, struck, thumped.
tuimpe,* see neup.
tuims, *pr.pt.* a' tuimseadh, *v.a.* see tuimsich.
tuin,* *v.n.* see tuinich.
tuin,* *s.m.* [***f.*] see tuineadh.
tuine,†† *s.f.* Dread, terror, alarm, confusion.
tuineach, *a.* Dreadful, alarming.
———, -ich, -ichean, *s. m.* Dwelling, abode, lodging. 3 Resort. 3 Resident. 4 Lodger. An i cas na creige do th. ? *is the shelter of the rock thy dwelling?*
———adh, -aidh, *s.m.* Dwelling, act or state of dwelling. 2 Resorting, act of resorting or frequenting. 3 Colonizing, gathering into a place for residence. 4 Sojourn, residence. A' t—, *pr.pt.* of tuinich.
———as, -ais, *s.m.* Sojourning, sojourn. 2 Abode, dwelling, home. 3* Colony. 4**Receptacle.
tuineadh, -idh, *s. m.* Abode, dwelling-place, place of residence, retreat, den. 2 Receptacle. T. nan treun, *the dwelling-place of heroes.*
tuineas, -eis, *s.m.* Abode, house. 2**Receptacle. T. nan sleagh, *the receptacle of spears.*
tuineasach,** *a.* Of, or belonging to, an abode. 2 Residing. 3 Inhabiting.
†tuinge,** *s.f.* Oath.
tùinich, *pr. pt.* a' tuineachadh, *v. n.* Sojourn, dwell, inhabit. 2 Frequent, resort to. 3* Gather, as matter in suppuration, settle or fix in a place as a movable tumour. 4* Colonize, settle in a place.
tùiniche. *s.m.* Dweller, lodger.
tuinidhe, see tuineadh. [lings.
tuinn, *gen.sing. & n.pl.* of tonn. †2(AF) Duck-
tuinne, *gen.sing.* of tonn. An gob na tuinne, *at the edge of the water* or *wave.*
tuinneadh, see tuineadh.
†tuinneamh, -eimh, *s.f.* Death.
tuinneas, -eis, see tùineas.
———ach, -aiche, *a.* Deathful, causing death. 2 Mortal.
tuinnidh, -e, *a.* Hard, firm.
tuinnleag,(CR) *s.f.* *Reay country* for seillean.
tuinnse, -achan, *s.m.* Blow. 2 Fatal blow given by the wheel of fortune. 3††Surge.
tuinnseadh,†‡ -eidh, -ean, *s. m.* Jogging. 2 (MS) Fling. 3(MS) Protusion.
tùir, & **tùire,** *gen.sing. & n.pl.* of tùr.
†tuir, *s.m.* Lord. 2 Pillar.
tuir, *pr.pt.* a' turradh, a' tuireadh & a' tuireamh. *v.a.* Relate, rehearse. 2 Chant with a mournful cadence, accompany a rehearsal with a mournful air. 3 Mourn, deplore, *lament for the dead. 4 Weep. Theirigian mo dheòir na'n tuirinn gach ànadh, *my tears would fail were I to deplore every disaster;* tuir an aithris neo-adhmhor, *deplore the hapless tale.*
tuirbheach, *a.* Shamefaced, bashful, modest.
tuirc, *gen.sing. & n.pl.* of torc.
tuire, see tuireadh.
tuireadh, -idh, -ean & tuireannan, *s.m.* Relating, act of relating. 2 Mourning, act of mourning, deploring, bewailing or lamenting. 3 Weeping, act of weeping. 4 Lamentation, lament for the dead, wail, dirge, elegy. 5 Melancholy narrative, 6 Death-song. 7 Request. A' t—, *pr.pt.* of tuir.

Dh'éisd sinn ri t. a thruaighe, *we listened to him while bewailing his hard fate;* ciod fàth do thuiridh ? *what is the cause of your lament?* le t. glaoidh thog e a cheann, *with loud lamentation he raised his head;* 'nan tuireannaibh, *in their lamentations.*
tuiream,(AC) *s.m.* Mourning for the dead. T. bàis, *death-mourning.*
tuireamh, -imh, *s.m.* see tuireadh.
tuirean, -ein, *s.m.* Troop, multitude.
tuireann, -einn, -an, *s.m.* Spark of fire from an anvil. 2**Lightning. 3** Troop, crowd, 4§ Wheat, see cruithneachd. [*gen. sing. & n. pl.* also tuirinn.]
tuiteannan, *pl.* of tuireann.
tuireanta, *a.* Pregnant.
tuaireapadh,(MS) *s.f.* Anger.
tuireasg, -isg, -an, *s.m.* Saw. 2**File. 3**Axe. An àrdaich an t. e féin ? *will the axe exalt itself ?*
———ach, -aiche, *a.* That saweth. 3 Furnished with saws. 3 Like a saw, file or axe.
———aiche,** *s.m.* One who saws or axes.
——— -luaithre,** *s.* Sawdust.
tuireid, see turaid.
tuirginn, *s.f.* Flood. 2 Broad, squat person. 3 Wash-staff. 4 Bottle. 5**Beetle.
tuiridh, *s.f.* Pillar. 2 Supporter. 3 Request.

4**Elegy.
tuirighin,** *s.f.* Pillar. 2 Supporter. 3 Conquest.
tuirigleadh,(AH) *s.m.* Wailing, lamentation—*Argyll.*
tuirinn, see tuireann.
tuiriosg, see tuireasg.
tuirisge, see tuireasg.
tuirl, *v.* see tuirling. Thuirleadh e, *let him descend;* thuirlibh, a thaibhse ! *descend, ye ghosts!*
t(h)uirleadh, *3rd. p. sing. & pl. imp.* of tuirl.
tuirleig,* *s.m.* Water-spout.
tuirleum,* *s.m.* Fearful leap. 2 Onset. 3 Contest. 4 see tuirling.
tuirlibh, *2nd. p. pl. imp.* of tuirl.
tuirlich,* *s.f.* Rumbling noise.
t(h)uirlidh ! *int.* Call to a cow—*Arran.*
t(h)uirlidh mhineig ! *int.* Call to a cow—*Arran.*
tuirlin, see tuirling.
tuirling, *pr.pt.* a' tuirling, *v. a.* Descend, descend rapidly or with a noise, come down. 2 Alight, come off a horse. 3**Fall upon.
———, *s.f.* Descending, act of descending quickly or with a noise, descent. 2**Slope, declivity. A' t—, *pr.pt.* of tuirling.
tuirlinn,* see tuirling.
tuirmheach, see tuirbheach.
———d,** *s.f.* Modesty.
tuirnealas, *s.m.* Striking of heads against each other, as rams, contact, collision—*Sar-Obair.*
tùirneanach,(CR) *s.m.* Blow with the fist—*W. of Ross.*
tùirse, *s.f.ind.* Sadness, melancholy, mourning, sorrow, dejection. 2 Afflictedness. 3 Dirge. 4 Elegy. T. nam bàrd, *the dirge of the bards;* is mór fàth mo th., *great is the cause of my sorrow ;* bu trom a t. is bu chian, *heavy and lasting was her sorrow.*
tùirseach, -eiche, *a.* Sad, mournful, sorrowful, melancholy. 2 Causing sorrow or sadness. Cha'n ioghnadh mise 'bhi t., *no wonder that I be sorrowful ;* bu t. tearc a làithean, *sad and few were his days ;* gu t., *sorrowfully;* bu tùirsiche gu mór Ronan, *far more sad was Ronan;* gu t. trom, *sad and dejected ;* arsa Fionn gu t., *said Fionn mournfully.*

670. Tùirseach.

tùirseach,§ -eich, *s.m.* Greater stitchwort, adder's meat, moon-flower, satin-flower—*stellaria holostea.*
tùirseachd, *s.f.ind.* Pensiveness, sadness, melancholy, dejection.
tuirsg,(CR) *v. a.* Lift, bundle up. 2 Prepare, begin, set out. Th. e air, *he began, set out ;* th. e air de shealltainn oirre, *he bestirred himself and went to see her—Suth'd.*
tuirsgeadh, *s.m.* Preparing for a journey. A' t—, *pr.pt.* of tuirsg. 'S mithich dhomh bhi t., *it is time for me to be off.*
tùirsich, *v.n.* Make mournful or sad.
———e, *comp.* of tùirseach.
tùirsneach,** *a.* Troubled, heavy in mind.
tùirsneadh,-idh,*s.m.*Trouble, heaviness of mind,
tuirtealachd, *s.f.* Dumps.
tùis, -e, -ean, *s.f.* Incense, frankincense. 2 *rarely*, Jewel. 3 *rarely*, King, noble. Altair na tùise, *the altar of incense.*
tùis, *gen.sing.* of tùs.
tuisdeach,** -ich, *s.m.* Parent.
tùiseach, *a.* Abounding in incense.
tùiseach,** -ich, *s.m.* Leader, commander.
tùisear, -eir, *pl.* -an & -ean, *s.m.* Censer. T. òir, *a golden censer.*
tuisg, *gen.sing. & n. pl.* of tosg.
tuisil,(DC) *s.f.* Joint, hinge, pivot.
tuisill,* *v.n.* Stumble, fall, slip. 2 Stammer. 3 **Deliver, bring forth.
tuisle,** *s.f.* Fall, slip, stumble. 2 Trespass. 3 Delivery, bringing forth.
tuisleach, -eiche, *a.* Stumbling, that stumbles. 2 Causing to stumble. 3 Accidental. 4 Unsteady, infirm, fallible. 5 Slippery.
———adh, -aidh, -ean, *s. m.* Stumble, stumbling, act of stumbling. 2 Accident. 3 Offence. 4 Delivery, bringing forth. 5 Jumble, jostle. A' t—, *pr.pt.* of tuislich.
tuisleachair,** *s.m.* Backslider.
tuisleachail,** *a.* Fallible.
tuisleachd, *s.f.* Fallibility.
tuisleadh, -idh, *s.m.* Stumbling, slipping, falling, stumble, slip, fall. 2 Decay. 3 Offence. 4 Delivery. Treibhdhireach agus gun t., *sincere and without offence.*
tuisleadh-asbhuinneach,(DC) *s.m.*Miscarriage—*Uist.*
tuisleag,** -eig, *s.f.* Fall, slight fall, slip. 2 Jump, leap.
———ach,** *a.* Desultory. 2 Leaping, skipping. 3 Slipping, stumbling.
tuislich, *pr. pt.* a' tuisleachadh, *v. a.* Stumble, slip, fall. 2 Commit a fault, err, blunder. 3 Deliver, bring forth, bear. 4 Jostle. Th. e, *he stumbled ;* tuislichidh mo luchd-tòir, *my pursuers shall stumble.*
tuislichte, *past pt.* of tuislich. Stumbled, fallen. 2 Delivered. 3 Overturned.
tuismeachan,** -ain, *s.m.* Accoucheur.
tuismeachd,** *s.f.* Stumble, frequent stumbling or falling.
tuisneach, -eiche, *a.* see tuisleach.
tuismeadh,** *s.m.* Nativity.
tuismich, see tuislich.—*North.**
tuit, *pr. pt.* a' tuiteam, *v. n.* Fall. 2 Happen, befall, chance. 3 Stumble, slip. 4 Subside. 5 Sink. 6 Set, as the sun. 7 Benight. 8 Be seduced by. 9 Fail. 10 Damp.

Th. dhuinn tachairt, *we met by chance* ; th. iad, *they fell ;* th. dhaibh tighinn a steach, *they happened to come in ;* th. an oidhche oirnn, *we were benighted* ; th. i leis, *she was seduced by him ;* tuitidh a' ghaoth, *the wind will subside ;* th. do ghrian gu sìor, *thy sun has set for ever ;* th. a chridhe, *his heart failed him ;* cha t. e, *he will not fall.*
†tuit,** *s.* The flat of anything.
tuiteadh, *imperf. subj.* of tuit. Should fall. 2 *3rd. p. sing.imper.* of tuit. T. e, *let him fall.*
tuiteam, *1st.per.sing.imper.* of tuit. Let me fall. (emphatic, tuiteam-sa.) 2 (** for tuitim.)
tuiteam, -eim, -an, *s. m.* Fall, falling, act of falling. 2 Chance. 3 Dusk, dawn. 4**Overturn. A' t—, *pr.pt.* of tuit. Fhuair e t., *he got a fall ;* mu th. na h-oidhche, *about the dusk of the evening* (fall of night.) A' t—, *pr. pt.* of tuit.

tuiteamach, -aiche, *a.* That falleth, fallible, falling, apt to fall. 2 Accidental. 3 Epileptic. 4 Casual, contingent, incident. 5 Causing to fall or stumble. 6**Frail. 7**Ruinous. Tinneas t., *epilepsy.*
tuiteamach,** -aich, *s.f* Epilepsy.
tuiteamachd, *s.f.* see tuiteamas. 2 Deciduousness.
tuiteamas, -ais, *s.m.* Contingence, chance, incidence. 2 Fall. 3 Occurence, accident. 4 Accidentalness. 5 Epilepsy. 6 Fallibility, liability to fall. 7**Lot. Thachair sinn le t., *we met by accident ;* cha'n 'eil t. sam bith gu'n tachair sinn am feasd, *there is no chance of our ever meeting ;* gach droch th., *every bad occurrence ;* an dàil gach tuiteamais, *to face any event, in contact with any danger ;* cha'n 'eil ann ach t., *it is only a chance ;* tinn leis an tuiteamas, *ill with the epilepsy, 2 lunatic.*
tuiteam-oidhche, *s.m.* Nightfall.
tùitean,* -ein, *s.m.* Badger.
tuitear, *fut.pass.* of tuit. Shall be made to fall. Also used impersonally.
tuitear,** *s.m.* Executor, governor. 2** Tutor, preceptor.
———achd,* *s.f.* Wardship, guardianship. 2** Tutorage, tuition, employment of a preceptor.
tuithtear, -eir, *s.m.* see tuitear.
tuitidh, see tuit.
tuitidh, for tuitidh mi.
†tul, -uil, *s.m.* Beginning. 2 Face. 3 Fashion 4 Relique. 5 Flood.
tul-, *prefix* (uile.) Entirely, wholly, completely. Breug, *a lie ;* tul-bhreug, *a perfect falsehood.*
tul,(AC) *s.m.* Fire. 2 Hearth. 3 Heap, hillock.
tula, *s.m.* see tulach.
tula,*a.Complete, most notorious, see tul-, *prefix.*
tulach, -aich, -aichean, *s. m.* Hillock, knoll, mound. 2 Small green hill. 3**Top of a gentle rising ground, low, smooth hill or ridge. 4 (AC)House. 5(AC) Ruins. 6*Tomb. Mi 'nam shuidhe air an t., *I sitting on the knoll ;* an t. laghach air an robh Tuara, *the fine hillock on which T. stood ;* chàirich sinn 'san t. an laoch, *we interred the hero in the green knoll* or *tomb.*
tulachach,** *a.* Knolly.
tulachan, -ain, -an, *s.m., dim.* of tulach. Little hillock, little knoll, mound or tomb. 2 Calf-skin stuffed, and presented to the cow, as if living, to induce her to give her milk. 3 Man appointed as a bishop after the Reformation, who was a bishop in name only and whose revenue was drawn by his patron. Tha iad uile 'nan tulachain, *they are all in their graves.*
tulachainn,(MS) *s.* Backside, breech.
tulachanach, -aiche, *a.* Abounding in little hillocks.
tulachann, see tulchann.
tulag, -aig, -an. *s.f.* Whiting, pollock, gwiniad.
·——ach, *a.* Abounding in, of, or belonging to, pollocks.
†tulagadh, -aidh, *s.m.* Change of labourers.
tulagan, -ain, *s.m.* see tulachan. 2 Rocking.
tulaich, *gen.sing.* & *n.pl.* of tulach.
———ean, *n. pl.* of tulach. 2 Certain kind of Highland reel.
tul-aigne,** *s. f.* Intention, purpose, motive.
tùlainn, *s.f.* Dowlas.
tulaman,(MMcD) *s m.* Wild drake. T. a' chinn uaine, *a green-headed wild drake—Lewis.*
tulan,** -ain, *s.m.* Kettle.
tul-bhreac,** *a.* Spotted, speckled, freckled.
tul-bhreicneach, -eiche, *a.* Spotted, freckled.
tul-bhreug, -éige, -an, *s.f.* Direct lie, entire falsehood. Ag innseadh nan tul-bhreugan, *telling most notorious lies.*
————ach, -aiche, *a.* That tells direct lies, lying impudently.
————adair, -ean, *s.m.* Impudent liar.
tulc, see tulg.
tulchabhchan,(AF) *s.* Owl.
tulchach, see tulachach.
tulchainn. *gen.sing.* of tulchann.
————each, *a.*Having high gables. 2 Gabled.
tulchair,** *s.m.* Emulator.
tulchan, see tulachan.
tulchann, -ainn, -an, *s.f.* Gable, end-wall of a house. 2 Corner. 3 Backside, breech. 4†† The hips. 5††Horse's croup. 6 **Stern of a ship. [* & †† give tulchainn, *gen.* -e, *s.f.*]
tulchlaon,** *v.a.* Slant, slope. 2 Form in a zig-zag line.
————,** *a.* Slanting, sloping, in a zig-zag.
————ach, *a.* Tending to a slope, sloping gently. 2 In a zig-zag line.
————achd,** *s.f.* Slanting, gradual descent, declivity. 2 Zig-zagging.
tulchoir,** *a.* Obstinate.
tul-chomhraic,** *s.f.* Assembly.
tul-chrom,** *a.* Slant, sloping.
tul-chromadh,** -aidh, *s.m.* Slanting, sloping, slant, slope.
tul-chuis, -e, *s.f.* Confidence, boldness. 2 Perseverance. 3 Acuteness, penetration, adroitness.
————each, -eiche, *a.*Confident, bold, brave, plucky, 2 Persevering, plodding, assiduous. 3 Acute, penetrating. O 'n eas-charaid th., *from the brave* or *persevering foe.*
tul-fhirinn,(CR) *s.f.* The whole truth, the real truth—*W. of Ross.*
tulg, -a, *s.m.* Bruise or hollow on the surface of any laminated metal. 2 Hollow between billows. 3 Sinking of any undulating surface. 4 Jolting. 5 Grudge—*Sàr-Obair.* 6 Upraiding, picking—*Sàr-Obair.* T. thonn, *the rocking of waves.*
tulg, *v.a. & n.* Rock, toss, roll, oscillate, wave, fluctuate, jostle, swing, jolt, push. 2 Make a hollow, as on the surface of a plate of metal. T. a' chreathall, *rock the cradle ;* an long a' tulgadh, *the ship rolling ;* an doire a' tulgadh, *the grove waving.*
tulga. see tulgach.
tulgach,* -aiche, *a.* Rocking, tossing. 2 Inconstant, as the surface of agitated water. 3 Causing a jolting or rocking motion. 4 Uneasy, as a seat. 5 Uncertain, unfixed, as an office or employment. 6 see tolgach. Gun t., *firm, motionless, unshaken.*
tulgag,‡‡ -aig, -an, *s.f.* Jerk.
tulgadh, -aidh, *s.m.* Tossing, rocking, lurching, fluctuation, exagitation, jolting. 2 Denting, making an impression on a metal surface. 3**Undulation. 4 Lurch, toss. A' t—, *pr.pt.* of tulg.
tulgaid, *s.f.* Throw—*Cailleach nan cnò by Neil MacLeod.*
tulgan,** -ain, *s.m.* Rocking motion, as caused by agitated water. 2 Little bruise, as on a metal surface.
———ach,** *a.* Hilly, knolly.
tulgatuinn,** *s.* Estuation.
tulgnadh, -aidh, see tolgnadh.
tulg-tuinn, *s.* Trough of the waves.
tuliac,¶ see fasgadan.
tulla,(AC) see tul.
tullachnach, see tulachanach.
tulm, -uilm, *s.f.* see tolm.
tulmach, -aiche, *a.* see tolmach.
tulman, see tolman.
————ach, see tolmanach.

tul-mhagadh, -aidh, -aidhean, *s.m.* Downright mockery.
tul-mhèirleach, -eich, *s.m.* Daring thief.
tul-radharc, see sùl-radharc.
———-—ach, see sùl-radharcach.
———-—achd, see sùl-radharcachd.
tulpaist,** *s.f.* Avenue, walk before a door.
tulscan,** -ain, *s.m.* Spreading. 2 Loosening. 3 Bursting.
tul-thapadh, -aidh, -aidhean, *s.m.* Mere chance.
tum, *pr.pt.* a' tumadh, *v.a.* Dip, plunge, steep, immerse, duck, bathe. Th. iad an còta 'san fhuil, *they dipped the coat in the blood* ; a chas a' tumadh 'sa chaochan, *his foot immersed in the gurgling streamlet.*
tuma,** *s.m.* see tuama.
tuma, see tumadh.
tumachan, see tumair.
tumadh, -aidh, -aidhean, *s.m.* Dipping, act of dipping or ducking, immersion, dip. 2 Bounce. A' t—, *pr.pt.* of tum.
tumadair, see taoman.
tumair, -ean, *s.m.* Dipper, diver, ducker, bather. [* gives *nom.* -e.]
tum-àite,** *s.m.* Bath, bathing-place.
tumarraid, s. Deray, hubbub, rummage.
tum-dhias,** *s.f.* Bushy ear of corn.
tumhartaich, *s.f.* Equivocation.
tum-ionad,** *s.m.* Bath, bathing-place.
tumta, *past pt.* of tum. Dipped, immersed, bathed, steeped.
tum-tam,* *s.m.* Great hesitation. 2 Stupid conduct. 3* Hum-drum.
tumte, see tumta.
tunaich, see tuinich.
tunaiche, *s.m.* Lodger, resident, inhabitant.
tunaidh, see tuinich & tuineadh.
tung,* *s. m.* Enclosed family burial-ground, tomb, vault—*Argyll.*
tunga, see tuama.
tungach,(MS) *a.* Sepulchral.
tungaid,* *s.f.* Stratagem, notorious lie.
———each,* -eiche, *a.* Full of stratagems or notorious lies.
tùngaidh, -e, *a.* Moist—*W. of Ross.*
tungais, see tuam.
tungarlagh,(AF) *s.* Old cow.
tunn,** *v.a.* Tun, barrel.
tunna, -chan, *s.m.* Ton. 2 Tun, butt, barrel.
tunnach, *a.* Abounding in small casks. 2 Like a small cask.
———adh, s. m. Beating, dashing, lashing, booming of waves against a ship—*Dàin Iain Ghobha.*
tunna-chìs, s. Tonnage.
tunnadair, -ean, *s.m.* Funnel, filler, 2 Tunning-dish, tunner.
———eachd, *s.f.* Tunning, barrelling.
tunnag, -aig, -an, *s.f.* Duck. 2 *in derision*, Short legged woman. 3†† Hobbling woman. 4 see tonnag. T. fhirionn, *a drake.*
———ach, -aiche, *a.* Abounding in ducks. 2 Like a duck.
——— -dhearg-cheannach,¶ *s.f.* Pochard, dun bird, see lach-mhàsach.
——— -dhubh,¶ *s.f.* Common scoter—*oidemia nigra.*
——— fhiacailleach,(AF) *s.f.* Goosander.
——— fhiadhaich, *s.f.* Wild duck.
——— ghleust,¶ *s. f.* Velvet scoter, see lach dhubh.
——— riabhach,¶ *s.f.* Wild duck, see lach.
tùr, -ùir, *s.m.* Sense, understanding, intelligence, penetration, sagacity, genius. 2 Intention, inclination, desire. 3 Mind. 4 Meaning. 5 (AC) Earth. 6**Petition. 7**Heaviness. Cha duine gun t. a dheanadh e, *it is not a man without genius that could accomplish it* gliocas agus t., *wisdom and understanding* inntinn is t. nam fear, *the mind and acuteness of the men* ; is e do th. a bha beachdail, *how observant your mind was !*
tùr, -ùir, *s.m.* Gaelic spelling of *tour.* Ghabh sinn tùr is tàmh is fois, *we travelled and took our rest.*
tùr, *pr.pt.* a' tùradh, *v.a.* Devise, invent, contrive, frame. Air a thùradh le Seumas, *invented by James* ; a thùras olc, *that devises evil* ; a thùr oibre ealanta, *to devise* or *plan cunning works.*
tur, *pr.pt.* a' turadh. *v.n.* Get fair, as weather.
tùr, -ùir, *s.m.* Tower, fortification, turret, fort, castle. T. Bhabeil, *the tower of Babel* ; trath dh' fhàsas sean gach t. is talla, *when every tower and hall grows old.*
tur, (i.e. gu tur) *adv.* Entirely, altogether. Is t. a dh' fhairslich e ort ! *how completely it has defied you !* tha e mar sin gu t., *it is absolutely so* ; struidh e gu t. ar n-airgiod, *he has completely squandered our money.*
tur, *a.* Whole, absolute, complete, entire. 2 Dry, without condiment. Greim t., *a dry morsel* ; aran t., *bread without butter or cheese* ; buntàta t., *potatoes and nothing with them* ; chuir e t. stad air m' aiteas, *he has put a complete stop to my joy.*
turabal,(AC) (i.e. a' turabal) *pr.pt.* Oscillating.
tùrach, -aiche, *a.* Towery, having towers, turretted. 2 Intelligent, ingenious.
———adh, -aidh, *s.m.* Towering. 2 Tower-building.
turachdach,* -aiche, *a.* Without condiment, as meal, potatoes, &c.
turach-air-tharach,†† *a.* Topsy-turvy.
turachan,** -ain, *s. m.* Big-bellied person. 2 Ranter. 3 Beggar.
turadan, -ain, -an, *s.m.* Small heap. 2** see turraban.
turadh, -aidh, s.m. Fair or dry weather. Tha e 'na th., *it is fair* ; rinn e t., *it faired, the rain ceased* ; am bheil e 'na th. ? or am bheil an t. ann ? *is it fine ?*
turag,‡ *s.f.* Trifling illness, as of a child—*Argyll.*
tùraich,** *v.a. & n.* Tower, build towers. 2 Fortify with towers. 3 Invent, devise.
turaid, -e, -ean, *s.f.* Turret, tower.
——— each, -eiche, *a.* Turreted. 2 Like a turret.
——— -faire, *s.f.* Watch-tower.
tùrail, -e, *a.* Sagacious, shrewd, sensible, ingenious, intelligent. 2 Acute, skilful. 3 Attentive, heedful. Gach duine toileach t., *every willing, skilful man.*
turainn, *s.f.* Fit of sickness. Fhuair e an droch th., *he has a bad fit of sickness.*
———each, -eiche, *a.* Delicate in health, liable to sickness.
———iche, *s.m.* Invalid.
tùrait, see turaid.
———each, see turaideach.
tùralachd, *s.f.ind.* Sagacity, shrewdness. 2 Skilfulness. 3 Attentiveness. 4(MS) Qualification.
turam, see turram.
———aich, see turraban.
turaman, -ain, -an, *s.m.* see turraban
———achadh, -aidh, see turraban.
turamanaich, see turrabanaich.
turaraich, *s.f.* Rattle. 2 Disorder.
turas, -ais, -an, see turus.
turasgair, see turasgar.
turasgar,** *s.m.* Seaweed. 2 Shellfish.
turbaid, -e, -ean, *s.f.* Turbot. 2 Halibut—*Lewis.* 3 Rhomboid.
———each, *a.* Rhomboidal.

turbhaidh,** *s.f.* Mischance, misfortune.
turcach,¶ -aich, *s. m.* Turkey, see coileach-Frangach.
turcadaich, *s.f.* Nodding, sudden jerk from the sensation of sleep—*Sar-Obair.*
turcaid, -ean, *s.f.* see turcais.
turcaire,¶ *s.m.* Turkey, see coileach-Frangach.
turcais,* -ean, *s.f.* Tweezers, pincers. 2 Smith's hoof-pincers. (durcais.)
turcan-mara, see turcar-mara.
turcar-mara,(AF) *s.* Sea-snail, periwinkle.
turchar,** -air, *s.m.* Riches, wealth.
tur-chadail,** *v.n.* Slumber.
tur-chadal, -ail, *s.m.* Slumber, dozing. 2 Lethargy, drowsiness. An sgrios a' tur-chadal, *their destruction slumbering.*
————ach,** *a.* Slumbering, dozing. 2 Lethargic. 3 Causing drowsiness.
tur-chombrac,** -aic, *s.m.* Assembly.
tur-chùil,(MS) *v.a.* Abominate.
tur-dhiubhair,** *s.* Contradistinction.
tur-fhuath,‡‡ *s.* Animosity.
†tur-ghabhadh,** -aidh, *s.m.* Iniquity.
tùr-ghabhail,** *s. f.* Course, journey, most frequently applied to the sun's course.
tur-ghabhalach,** *a.* Iniquitous, guilty.
turgain, see turguin.
turguin, -ean, *s.m.* Destruction. Gu'n dean thu ar t., *that thou canst effect our destruction.*
turguineach, -eiche, *a.* Destructive.
turlach, -aich, -aichean, *s.m.* Large fire, bonfire, conflagration. 2 Bulky or squat person. 4* Ugly head of hair. 5** see turloch. T. na féisde, *the banquet-fire.*
tùrlach,†† -aich, -aichean, *s. m.* Heap, great quantity.
turlas, *s.m.* Cupboard—*Perthshire.*
turloch, -oich, -an, *s.m.* Brook. 2 Ground covered with water in winter and dry in summer.
tur-lom, *v.n.* Make quite bare. 2 Strip naked. 3 Glean. Cha t. thu t' fhìon-lios, *thou shalt not glean thy vineyard.*
tur-lom,** *a.* Quite bare, naked.
————adh,** -aidh, *s. m.* Making quite bare, stripping.
tùrn, -ùirn, [††*pl.* -an,] *s.m.* Turn, job, feat. 2 **Char. 3 Bent. T. odhar, *a mite, one-twelfth of a penny ;* droch th., *a bad job.*
†turnadh, -aidh, *s.m.* Escape. 2 Spinning-wheel.
tùrnaiche, *s.m.* One employed in jobs.
tùrnair, -ean, *s.m.* see tuairnear.
†turnamh, -aimh, *s.m.* Descent. 2 Humiliation. 3 Rest.
tur-òinnseach,** -ich, *s.f.* Mere idiot.
turr,* *v.a.* Rock hither and thither.
turr,* *s.m.* Tomb, large heap.
turraban, -ain, *s.m.* Rocking motion of the body when sitting. 2 Grief. 3* Vibration, oscillation. 4 Nodding as in sleep. 5 Moving.
turrabanaich, -e, *s.f* Constant rocking or moving of the body. 2 Nodding, act of nodding or shaking. 3**Hesitancy. A' t—, *pr.pt.* of turrabanaich.
————·——, *pr.pt.* of turrabanaich, *v. n.* Nod, move, rock, shake. 2 Vibrate, oscillate.
turraban-nan-tunnag, *s.m.* (*lit.* the waddling of the ducks) Old Highland dance.
turrach,(DMK) *s. m.* The craving for tobacco—*W. coast of Ross.*
turra-chadail, see tur-chadail.
turra-chadal, -ail, -an, *s.m.* see tur-chadal.
turra-chadalach, -aiche, *a.* see tur-chadalach.
turrachdal, see tur-chadal.
turradan, *Arran* for turraban. In *Shiskine* they say, air thurrachdain, *shaking.*
turradh,(CR) -aidh, *s.m.* Surprise, coming or attempting to come upon one unawares—*Skye.*

turrag, -aig, -an, *s.f.* Accident mishap. 2 Adventure. 3**Conflict. 4**Wench. 5†† Slight illness.
————ach, -aiche, *a.* Accidental, unlucky.
turraig,* *s.f.* Stool, *in ridicule.* 2**Push, thrust. Aig do th., *at stool.*
turraim, see turraban.
turraing,†† *s.f.* Turn of illness.
turram, -aim, -an, *s. m.* Soft sound, murmur, whisper, low whispering noise. An raineach ri t. 'sa ghaoith, *the fern whispering in the wind ;* tha e 'na th. suain, *he is in sound sleep.*
turramain, *v.* see turrabanaich.
turraman, see turraban.
————aich, see turrabanaich.
tur-rannsachadh, -aidh, *s.m.* Analysis.
tur-rannsachail,** *a.* Analytical.
tur-rannsaich,** *v.a.* Analyze.
turruraich, *s.f.* Twittering. 2 Warbling, purling noise—*Mac Mh. Alasdair.*
tùrs, (for tuirse) Bidh àr marbhtach le garbh thùrs ann, *there will be destructive slaughter and (with) deep sorrow.—Duanaire, p. 159. Garbh* is often used to signify rough to the senses or feelings.
tùrsa, *s.f.* see tùirse.
————ch,* -aiche, *a.* see tùirseach.
tùrsachd,** see tùirseachd.
tùrsadh, see tùirse.
tursarain,§ *s.* Lesser stitchwort—*stellaria graminea.* 2** Greater stitchwort—*stellaria holostea.*
tursgair, *s.f.* Equipage.
tursgan, *s.pl.* Implements.
turtan,** -ain, *s.m.* Sod, turf.
turtur, -uir,†† -an, *s.f.* Turtle. 2 Turtle-dove—*columba tutsur.* A thabhartas de thurturaibh, *his offering of turtles.*
turturach, *a.* Of, or pertaining to, turtles or turtle-doves.
tu-ruidh ! *int.* Call to a cow or calf—*W. of Ross.*
tururaich, see turaraich.
turus, -uis, -an, *s.m. & f.* Journey, voyage, expedition, travel, course, occasion. Tha 'n t. mór, *the journey is great ;* chrìochnaich mi mo th., *I have finished my journey ;* t. mhath leat, *a good journey to you ;* t. shoirbheasach, *a prosperous journey.*
turusach, -aiche, *a.* Making frequent journeys. 2 Of, or pertaining to, a journey. 3 Travelling much.
————, -aich, *s.m.* see turusaiche.
————d, *s.f.ind.* Travelling, pilgrimage. 2 Pedestrianism.
turusaiche, -an, *s.m.* Traveller, pilgrim, pedestrian. 2(MS) Vagabond.
turusan, -ain, *s.m.* Traveller, pilgrim.
turus-cuain,(AH) *s.m.* Voyage.
turusgar, *s.m.* Giblets, equipage.
tùrusgar,§ -air, *s.m.* The seaweed grapes—*sargassum vulgare* or *bacciferum.*
tùs, -ùis, *s.m.* Beginning, the beginning, commencement, origin. 2 Front, van, as of an army. Eilidh, t. ar cràidh, *Helen, the source of our severe affliction ;* air t. an airm, *in the van of the army ;* air a th. is air a thoiseach, *first and foremost ;* 's e t. a' ghliocais eagal Dhé, *the fear of God is the beginning of wisdom ;* air t. m' aimsir bha mi baoth, *in the beginning of my life I was foolish.*
tusa, *emphatic* of tu.
tùsach, -aiche, *a.* Precedent.
tùsachd, *s.f.* Previousness.
tùsail,** -e, *a.* Primal, originary, original, radical.
tùs-ainm, -ean, *s.m.* Patronymic.
tùs-ainmeach,** *a.* Patronymic.

tùsàir, *s.m.* Beginner.
tùsalachd, *s.f.* Originality.
tùsanach, -aich, *s.m.* Native.
tùsanaich,(MS) *s.pl.* Aborigines.
†tusarnach,** -aich, *s.m.* Parricide.
tusbailteach, see susbailteach.
tusg, -uisg, see tosg.
——ach, see tosgach.
tusgairn, *s.f.* Fiction. [** says †.]
tusgarnach, -aich, *s.m.* Libeller. 2 Story-teller.
†tusgarnadh, -aidh, *s.m.* Fiction.
tùs-ghnothach, -aich,-aichean, *s.f.* Preliminary.
t(h)usgus ! *int.* Dairymaid's call to an unruly cow—*Suth'd.*
tùs-imeachd,**s.f. Ante-ambulation,antecedence.
tùs-ionad, -aid, -an, *s.m.* Anteriority.
tuslang, -aing, *s.m.* Wrestling.
†tusleg, -oig, -an, *s.f.* Heap, little jump.
†tusmet,‖ *s.* Parturition.
tùs-mhuinntir,* *s.pl.* Aborigines.
tusornachd,** *s.f.* Whispering.
tut ! *int.* Expressive of cold. 2 Indicating impatience.
tùt, -ùit, -an, *s. m.* Stink, stench. 2 Crepitus vix audibilis.
tùt, *v.n.* Stink, stench.
tùtach, -aiche, *a.* Stinking. 2 Breaking wind silently.
tùtach, -aich, see dùdach.
tutag,** -an, *s.* Suds.
tutag ! *int.* Expressive of cold.
tutagaidh ! *int.* Expressive of cold.
tutagan,** *s.* Suds.
tùtaiche, *comp.* of tùtach.
tùtair,* *s.m.* Stinker. 2 Dunghill. 3 (MS) Badger.
tuthag, -aig, -an, *s.f.* Patch, clout.
————ach, -aiche, *a.* Clouted, patched.
————achadh, -aidh, *s.m* Patching.
————achd, *s.f.* Patchedness.
————aich, *v.a.* Patch, piece, cobble. 2 Vamp.
tuthadair, see tughadair.
tuthadh, see tughadh.
tuthagaich, see tuathagaich.
tùthan,(DMK) *s.pl.* Long rafters laid across the couples in the roof of a house—*Caithness.* see taobhan.
tuthan, -ain, *s.f.* Slut.
tùtht, see tùt.
——ach, see tùtach.

U u

u, the 18th. letter of the Gaelic alphabet now in use, called ur, *yew-tree.*

It has three sounds—(1) long, like *oo* in *moon*, as, tùr, *a tower* ; stùr, *dust.* (2) short, like *u* in *push*, as, ur, *a child* ; urram, *honour.* (3) short and obscure, like *u* in *rut*, as, mur, *if not.*

u ! *int.* Expressive of surprise, disappointment, &c.
ua, *prep.* From, out of. For its use see o, *prep.*
†ua, *s.m.* & *f.* now ogha.
uabairt, -e, -ean *s.f.* Expulsion, *prov.*
————each, -eiche, *a.* Expelling.
uabhais, *gen.sing.* of uabhas (uamhas)
uabhann, see uamhann.
uabhannach, see uamhannach.
uabhar, -air, *s.m.* Pride, insolence, bluster, vain-glory. 2**Pomp. 3**Heat. 4* Extreme pride. Air son an uabhair, *for their pride* ; luchd-uabhair mhallaichte, *the cursed proud.*
uabharach, -aiche, *a.* see uaibhreach.
uabharr,** *a.* Proud, haughty, insolent. 2 Raging. 3 Terrible. Stoirm u., *a raging storm.*
uabhas, see uamhas,
-——ach, see uamhasach.
uabheist,* see uadh-bheist.
uacar, *Arran* for uachdar.
†uacha, *prep.* (ua+iad) see uapa.
uachdair, *s.* Farm-stock. Fo u., *under stock—Sàr-Obair.*
uachdar, -air, -an, *s.m.* Top, surface. 2 Summit or upper part. 3 Cream. 4 Upper leather of a shoe. 5 Woof of cloth, *prov.* Air u., *on the surface* ; u. is iochdar, *top and bottom* ; grugh is u., *curds and cream* ; fhuair e làmh an u., *he got the mastery* ; a' tighinn an u., *coming to the surface, budding, as lint, potatoes. &c.*; an u. mu seach, *alternately up and down* ; an u., *above, aboard.*
uachdar,§ -air, -an, *s.m.* Bog-violet, see mòthan. 2**Mountain sanicle.
uachdarach, -aich, *s.f.* Leather suitable for uppers of shoes.
uachdarach, -aiche, *a.* Upper, higher, uppermost, highest. 2 Abounding in cream. 3* Producing cream. 4* Superficial. A' Bheall-tuinn u., *cream-producing May.*
uachdarachd, *s.f.* State of being superior or higher, supremacy, superiority. O 'n u. gus an iochdarachd, *from top to bottom.* 2* Surface, top.
uachdaraiche, *comp.* of uachdarach.
uachdaran, -ain, -an, *s.m.* Governor, ruler,chief, superior, prince. Ni mi e 'na u., *I will make him a prince.*
uachdaranachd, *s.f.* Government, sovereignty, principality, supremacy,dominion, rule. Bitheadh u. aca, *let them have dominion* ; bithidh u. agad air, *thou shalt have dominion over him.*
uachdar-na-troidhe, *s.m.* Instep.
uachdrach, see uachdarach.
uachdraiche, see uachdaraiche.
uachdran, see uachdaran.
-————achd, see uachdaranachd.
uadh-, (†uath) *prefix* signifying Dread.
uadh, -aidh, see uagh.
uadha, see uaimh.
uadhach, see uaghach.
uadhaidh,*see uaghaidh.
uadhag,(AH) *s.f.* Sheep-house—*Argyll.*
uadhaiche, *s.m.* Subduer.
uadhaidh, see uaimh.
uadh-bheist, -ean, *s.m.* Monster (fabulous.)
uadh-chrith, -e, *s.f.* Dread, horror, terror.
uagh, *s.m.* **Terror, dread. 2 see uaigh. 3 see uamh-bheist.
uaghach, -aiche, *a.* Full of graves. 2 Full of caves. 3**Dreadful, terrible.
uaghaich, *v.a.* Grave, bury.
uaghaidh,** -ean, *s.f.* Cave, cavern, den.
-————each,** *a.* Full of caves or dens.
uaghan, see uan.
uagh-bheist, see uadh-bheist.
uaibh, *prep.pron.* (ua+sibh) From you. 2 Wanted by you. 3 From among you. 4 Being your duty.

Tha u. falbh, *you had better be gone* ; fada u., *far from you* ; cuiribh u. na diathan coimheach, *put away the strange gods* ; ciod tha u. ? *what do you want ?* thigibh u., *come forward*—expression of defiance.

uaibhreach, -eiche, *a.* Proud, haughty, vain-glorious, arrogant. 2 Spirited. 3** Airy, superb, gorgeous. 4* Extremely proud. Gu h-u., *proudly* ; piuthar u. reul nan speur, *the gorgeous sister of the stars*—the moon]; Alasdair u., *Alexander the great.* 5**Insolent.
————, -eich, *s.m.* Proud, haughty,arrogant

person. Tha Dia a' cur an aghaidh nan u., *God resisteth the proud.*
uaibhreachas, -ais, *s.m.* Pride, pomp, vain-glory, haughtiness, arrogance. 2 Insolence. 3** Great haughtiness, extreme degree of pride or vain-glory. Làn uaibhreachais 'nad shaothair, *full of pride in thy work.*
uaibhreachd, *s.f.* see uaibhreachas.
uaibhreas, -eis, *s.m.* see uaibhreachas.
uaibh-se, *emphatic* of uaibh.
uaidean, *s.m.* Plough-handle or stilt.
uaidh, see uaith.
uaidne, -an, *s.f.* Stilt of a plough.
uaigealta, *a.* Weird, eerie, lonesome.
uaigealtachd, *s.f.* Loneliness, eeriness.
uaigealtas, -ais, *s.m.* Loneliness, eeriness.
uaigh, -e & uaghach, *pl.* uaighean & uaghaichean, *s.f.* Grave, tomb, sepulchre, 2 Den, cave, cavern. Gus an càrar mi 'san u., *till I am interred.*
uaigneach, -eiche, *a.* Lonesome, solitary, retired. 2 Secret, private. 3 Deserted, retired. 4 Dull, melancholy. Duine u., *a reserved person ;* àite u., *a solitary or remote place ;* gnothach u., *private business, a private message ;* bile nan sruthan u., *the banks of the lonely streamlets.*
uaigneachd,* see uaigneas. 2* Retired, morose disposition.
uaigneas, -eis, *s.m.* Secrecy, privacy, solitariness, lonesomeness. 2* Retired manners or habits. Thug e air u. e., *he took him aside* (into a private place) ; tha 'n t-aran a dh' ithear an u. taitneach, *bread eaten in secret is pleasant ;* 'uaigneas-san, *his retired manner* or *disposition ;* an u., *in secret, in a retired place ;* mar thonn an u., *like a lonely wave.*
uaignidh, *a.* see uaigneach.
———each, see uaigneach.
———eas, see uaigneas.
†uaigh-reir,** *a.* Having arbitrary sway.
†uaigh-reirs,** *s.* Arbitrary sway.
†uail, *s.f.* Wail, howl, lament.
uailean,(DMK) *s.pl.* Stilts or handles of a plough —*Caithness.*
uaill, -e, *s.f.* Vanity, pride, vain-glory. 2 Dignity, conceit, foppery, fame, pomp. 3 Boasting, 4**Howl. 5††Nobility. Na dean u. as an là màireach, *boast not of to-morrow ;* c'àit' am bheil aobhar uaille ? *where is there cause for boasting ?* a dh' àrdaich an t-ionnsachadh chun u., *whom learning has raised to dignity.*
uaill, *a.* Proud, famous.
uaille,** *s.* Crest.
uailleach, -eiche, *a.* see uallach.
uailleag, -eig, -an, *s.f.* Conceited female.
uailleagach,†† *a.* Like a conceited female.
uailleagan,†† *s.m.* Dandy.
uaillealachd, *s.f.* Loftiness.
uaillean, -ein, *s.m.* Fop, coxcomb.
uailleanachd, *s.f.* Foppery.
uaillear,* -eir, -ean, *s.m.* Fop, spark. [* gives *nom.* -eir, *gen.* -e.]
uailleart,** -eirt, see ulfhart.
———ach,** *a.* see ulfhartach.
uailleil, -e, *a.* Haughty, vain.
uaill-fheart, -eirt, -an, *s.m.* Illustrious deed. 2 see ulfhart,
———-—ach, -aiche, *a,* Of noble virtues or achievements. 2 Ostentatious. 3 see ulfhartach.
———-—achd, *s.f.* see uaill-fheartaich.
uaill-fheartaich, *s.f.* Howling, yelling.
uaillich,** *v.a.* Elevate. 2 Make proud or vain. 3 Roar, howl.
uaillire, see uaillear
uaill-mhiann, -a, *s.m.* Ambition, fondness for rank or distinction.
uaill-mhiannach, -aiche. *a.* Ambitious, fond of rank or distinction.
uaillrianach,(MS) *a.* Aristocratical.
uaillse, see uaisle.
uaillseachadh, see uaisleachadh.
uaillsean, see uaislean.
uaillsich,** see uaislich.
———ean, see uaislean.
uaillsichte, see uaislichte.
uailse, *Laggan* for uaisle.
uaim,** *s.f.* Embroidery. 2 see fuaim. 3 Weaver's harness. 4 Union.
uaimeach,** -miche, *a.* Solitary.
uaimh, uamha & -e, *pl.* uamhan & -ean, *s. f.* Den, cave. 2 Hollow. 3 Grave. 4 Grotto. Ma 's carraig no u. do chòmhnuidh, *whether a rock or a cave be thy dwelling.*
uaimheach, *a.* Full of caves. 2 Like a cave.
uaimhgealta, see uaigealta
————chd, see uaigealtachd.
uaimhgealtas, see uaigealtas.
uaimhinn, -e *s.f.* see uamhann.
uaimhneach, -eiche, *a.* Dreadful, terrible, horrid.
uaimhneachd,* *s. f.* Horridness. 2 Horrifying nature or quality.
uaimhnich,** *v.a.* Terrify.
uain, *gen.sing. & n.pl.* of uan.
uain,** *s.f.* Loan. 2 Pin, peg.
uainceann, see uainicionn.
uain'-chnotal, *s.m.* Crotal sage, (colour.)
uaincionn, -inn, -ean, see uainicionn.
uaine, *comp.* uaine, *a.* Green. 2 Pale, wan, pallid. 3 Livid. Ogain nam breacan uaine, *the green-plaided youths.*
uaine, *s.f.* Green (colour.) 2 Greenness, lividness. 3 The green sickness. 4 Menstrual courses. 5 Safety. 6 Wooden pin.
uaine, *comp.* of uaine.
uaineach,(DU) *a.* Tedious. Fad an là u., *through the tedious day.*
uaineachadh, -aidh, *s.m.* State of turning green. 2 State of becoming pale or ghastly. Ag u—, *pr.pt.* of uainich.
uaineachail,(MS) *a.* Porraceous.
uaineachan,* -ain, *s.m.* see uainealach.
uainead, -id, *s.m.* Degree of greenness, or of 2 Paleness, pallidness or wanness. A' dol an u., *growing greener and greener.*
uainealach, -aiche, *a.* Greenish, verdant. 2 Pale.
————,* -aich, *s.m.* Wan, pallid person.
uainealachd,** *s.f.* Verdure, greeness.
uainean, -ein, -an, *s.m.dim.* of uan. Little lamb.
uaine-donn, *s.m.* Bronze-green (colour.)
uaine-dorcha, *s.m.* Olive (colour.)
uainein, see uanan.
————each, see uananach.
uainfheoil, -fheola, *s.f.* Lamb (i.e. lamb's flesh.)
uainiceag, -eig, -an, *s.f.* see uainicionn.
uainich,* *v.n.* Become green. 2 Become pale. 3 (MS) Mould.
uainicionn, *s.f.* Lamb's skin.
————ach, *a.* Of, or belonging to, lamb's skins.
uainn, *prep.pron.* (ua+sinn) From us. 2 From amongst us. 3 Wanted by us. 4 Missing by us. 5 Necessary for us, our duty. Tha trì u., *we want three, we miss three ;* tha u. falbh, *it is our duty to go ;* cha'n 'eil u. ach an ceartas, *we only want justice ;* ciod tha u. ? *what do we want ?*
uainne, *emphat.* form of uainn.
†uainnearach, -eiche, see uaigneach.
†uainnearas, -ais, see uaigneas.
uainneart,‡ *s.m.* Bustle. 2 Wallowing. *Badenoch.*
uaip,* *v.a.* Bungle, botch.
uaipe, *prep.pron.* (ua+i) From her, off her. 2

Wanted by her. 3 Missing by her. Ciod tha u. ? *what does she want ?*
uaipear, -eir, -an, *s.m.* see uipear.
uaipe-san, *emphat.* form of uaipe.
†uair, *adv.* see oir.
uair, -e & uarach, *pl.* -ean & -eannan, *s.f.* Hour, any given space of time. 2 Time of day or night, a time. 3 Life, one's life-time. 4 Alloted hour of one's death. 5 Weather. 6 Opportunity, on a time, at another time, one time, once, once on a time, occasion. 7 Season. 8 Rotation.

Aon uair, *one o'clock, one hour ;* mu u. an uaireadair, *about an hour* ; leth-uair an déidh u. (*not* an déidh aon u.,) *half-past one ;* 'dé 'n u. a tha e ? *what time is it ?* mu dhà u., *about two o' clock ;* eadar a h-aon 's a dhà, *between one and two ;* u. sam bith, *any time ;* na h-uile u., *at all times ;* an u. mu dheireadh, *the last time ;* a' cheud u., *at first, the first time ;* 's e seo m' u.-sa, *this is my turn* (*or rotation*) ; tha u. air, *he is subject to fits of good humour* or *generosity ;* air uairibh, *sometimes ;* an ceart u.. *the very time, immediately ;* gach u., *at all times ;* u. eile, *at another time ;* u. éiridh iad gu nèamh, u. théid iad gu doimhne sìos, *one time they mount to the skies, another they sink to the abyss;* thug mi i an uaigneas u., *I brought her apart once ;* u. a rinn mi sin, *once I did that ;* rinn e sin u. is u., *he did that repeatedly ;* cia lion u. a thig e ? *how many times will he come ?* 'na uaireannan, *sometimes ;* ni mi e u. air an u., *I will do it immediately ;* u. mu seach, *alternately, in rotation ;* an uair gàbhaidh, *in time of danger ;* an u. òir, *aurora ;* an uair, *when ;* 's fheàrr u. de bhean an taighe na obair-là ban-òglaich, *better an hour of the mistress than a day's work of the servant* —the difficulty of getting good domestic servants thus seems to have been as great in the Highlands as elsewhere, even in Nicolson's time.

uairceag, (MS) *s.f.* Budge.
uairneach, *Gairloch* for uaigneach.
uaircheas,** -eis, *s.m.* Cock-boat.
uairgneach, *Perth, Strathspey, W.* of *Ross, Skye & Lewis* for uaigneach.
uaireach, (MS) *a.* Horal, hourly. 2**Needless, useless, insignificant, unimportant, unnecessary. 3 Capricious. Is u. dhuit, *it is needles for you* ; ni mó is bean u. mise, *neither am I a woman of no importance* ; imrich u., *a capricious flitting*—leaving a place for no sufficient reason—*Inverness district*—DC.
uaireachan,** -ain, *s.m.* Timepiece
uaireadair, -ean, *s.m.* Watch, time-keeper of any kind. Clag-uaireadair, *or* u.-cluig, *clock*; u.-gainneimh *or* u.-gloine, *sand-glass ;* u.-làimhe *or* u.-pòca, *watch ;* u.-gealaich** *or* u.-gréine, *sun-dial ;* u.-gaineamhain, *sand-glass.*
————each, *a.* Abounding in, or pertaining to, time-pieces.
————iche, -an, *s.m.* Watch-maker, clock-maker.
uaireiginn,* *adv.* Sometime, once. Uair no u., *sometime or other.*
uaireil, -e, *a.* Hourly, by the hour, horary.
uairgneach, *N. Uist* (*Gairloch*—DU) for uaigneach.
uairibh, (air) *adv.* Sometimes, at times.
uair làn,** -àin, *s.m.* Sun-dial.
uair òir,** *s.f.* Aurora, morning.
†uais, see uasal.
uaiseach,** -ich, -ichean, *s.m.* Hero.
uaisle, *s.f.ind.* Nobility, as of descent, gentility. pride, genteel extraction, high birth, gentlemanly manners. 2 Liberality, generosity.
uaisle, *comp.* of uasal.
———, *contr.* for uaislean.
uaisleachadh, -aidh, *s.m.* Ennobling, act of ennobling or dignifying. Ag u—, *pr. pt.* of uaislich.
uaisleachd,* *s.f.* Nobility, gentility. 2 Pride. 3 Dignity of port or mind.
uaislead, -eid, *s.m.* Degree of nobility or gentility.
uaislean, *s.pl.* Nobles, gentry.
uaislich, *pr. pt.* ag uaisleachadh, *v.a.* Ennoble, exalt, dignify.
————te, *past pt.* of uaislaich. Ennobled, exalted, dignified.
uait, see uat.
uaith, *prep.pron.* From him, from it. Ciod tha u. ? *what does he want ?* thigeadh e u., *let him come forward*—said in defiance ; ciod a bheir là uaith, *what a day may bring forth ;* ma 's tu a th' ann, is tu chaith u., *if it is you, how you have shrunk*—NGP gives " chaidh u. "
uaithe, see uaipe.
uaitheantach, -aiche, *a.* Ablative
†uaithne,‖ *s.* Puerperium.
†uaithne,* *s.m.* Pillar, post.
uaith-san, *emphat.* form of uaith.
uallach, -aiche, *a.* Cheerful, airy, gay, giddy. 2 Conceited, proud, vain, vain-glorious. 3 Freakish, fantastic. 4 Proud, stately, noble. 5 Sportive, playful, lively, ostentatious, gallant. 6 Light, indifferent as to weight. 7**Ostentatious. 8**Gallant. 9 Light-headed.

Thog e gu h-u. e, *he raised it so lively ;* duine u., *a light headed person.*

uallach, -aich, *pl.* -an & -aichean, *s.m.* Burden, load. 2 Charge, assigned task, responsibility. 3 Oppressive weight.

U. an ni sin ormsa, *the charge of that thing to me ;* a' giùlan uallaich taighe Ioseiph, *bearing the charge of the house of Joseph ;* cha'n u. sin air, *that is no hard task to him ;* u. a' ghnothaich, *the responsibility of that affair ;* is aotrom an t-u. mo ghràdh, *my love is a light burden* ; fo u. le misg, *overcome with drunkenness ;* is trom an t-u. an aois, *age is a heavy burden* ; ro-uallach, *an overcharge.*

uallach, -aich, *s.m.* Conceited fellow, fop.
————adh, -aidh, *s.m.* Loading, act of loading or burdening. 2 Encumbering. 3 Making conceited or arrogant. 4 Becoming conceited, arrogant or airy. Ag u—, *pr. pt.* of uallaich.
uallachag, -aig, -an, *s.f.* Coquette, airy, conceited girl.
uallachan, -ain, -an, *s. m.* Little load. 2** Showy stripling. 3**Gallant. 4**Coxcomb, fop. swaggerer. 5‡‡Infant. 6 *dim.* of uallach
uallachas, -ais, *s.m.* Cheerfulness, gaiety, airiness. 2 Conceit, vanity, pride, stateliness, foppery. 3 Freakishness. 4 Sportiveness. 5‡‡ Liveliness. 6 *rarely*, Lewdness. 7**Gallantry.
uallachd,* *s.f.* Extreme conceit, vanity, airiness or ostentation.
uallaich, *pr. pt.* ag uallachadh, *v.a. & n.* Load, burden. 2 Encumber. 3 Daub. 4 Make conceited. 5 Become conceited.
————te, *past pt.* of uallaich. Loaded, burdened. 2 Encumbered.
uallair,* -ean, *s.m.* Coxcomb.
uam, *prep. pron.* (ua+mi) From me. 2 Wanted by me. 3 At a distance from me. Fan u., *keep at a distance from me ;* gu 'm bu fada sin bhuam, *be that far from me ;* tha sin u., *I want that.*
uamh, -aimh, -annan, *s.f.* see uaimh. 2* Savage, terrible fellow. Cha'n 'eil ann ach u. dhuine, *he is only a savage of a fellow.*

uamh,** -aimh, *s.m.* Ornament.
uamha, see uaimh.
uamhach, see uaimheach.
uamhag,‡ *s.f.* Sheep-louse, sheep-ked, tick—*metaphagus ovinus—North* *
———ach, -aich, *a.* Full of sheep-lice.
uamhaich,(MS) *v.a.* Encave.
uamhaidh, see uaimh.
———each, see uaimheach.
†uamhain, -e, -ean, *s.f.* Bake-house. (Eng.*oven.*)
uamhainn, *gen. sing.* of uamhann.
———each, see uamhannach.
uamhais, *gen. sing.* of uamhas.
uamhal, *s.m.* Sheep-ked.
uamhalt, -a, *a.* Lonely, solitary.
uamhaltachd, *s.f.* Loneliness, solitariness.
uamhann, -ainn, *s.m.* Dread, terror, dismay, horror, amazement. Righ nan u., *the king of terrors* ; u. a' bhlàir, *the terror of battle* ; tuitidh u. orra, *amazement shall fall on them.*
———, *a.* see uamhannach.
———ach, *a.* Terrible. 2 Horrible. 3 Astounding. 4 Shocking. Le tartar u. na mara, *with the dreadful noise of the sea.*
———achadh,(MS) *s.m.* Astonishingness, affrightment.
———achd,** *s.f.* Amazedness.
———aich,(MS) *v.a.* Astonish, astound.
uamhanta,* -ainte, *a.* see uamhasach.
uamharr, -a, *a.* Dreadful, terrible, horrible, direful. 2 Shocking, loathsome, abominable, repulsive. 3 Atrocious, heinous. 4 Morose, gloomy. 5 Proud, arrogant. 6 Excessive. [†† says uamharra.]
uamharrach, see uamharr.
———d, *s.f.* Frightfulness, horror. 2 Loathsomeness, abominableness. 3 Atrocity, 4 Moroseness, gloominess. 5 *Heinousness. 6 Excessiveness, direness. 7** Pride, arrogance.
uamharraidh, -e, *a.* see uamharr.
uamhas, -ais, -an, *s.m.* Monster. 2 Spectre, apparition. 3 Dread, horror, fright, terror. 4 Great quantity, prodigy. 5 Dismay, astonishment. 6* Horrid deed, atrocity. 7*Deed done in a cave. Fhuair iad u. éisg, *they got a great quantity of fish* ; chunnaic iad u., *they saw an apparition* ; u. dhaoine, *a large number of people.*
uamhasach, -aiche, *a.* Terrible, horrible, awful, dreadful, shocking. 2 Wonderful, astonishing, prodigious.
———d, *s.f.ind.* Terribleness, awfulness, dreadfulness. 2 Horribleness, abominableness, loathsomeness. 3** Admirability. 4* Extreme atrocity. 5**Astonishment.
uamhasaich, *v.a.* Affright.
uamh-bheist, -ean, *s.m.* see uadh-bheist.
uamh-chreadha,** *s.* Brick-kiln.
uamh-chrith, -e, *s.f.* see uadh-chrith.
uamhlach, *s.m* Monster.
uamhlaidh, (DMK) *intensitive particle,* used to qualify the *adj.* maith. U. maith, *exceedingly good.* In *W. of Ross, &c.* the term is restricted to *maith*—uamhasach is the term used to qualify *dona.*
uamhraidh. -e, *a.* Full of caves or dens. 2†† Gloomy, fearful.
———, *adv.* Excessively, awfully.
uamh-rod (rathad),** *s.m.* Adit.
uamh-sheòmar,** *s.* Cell.
uamhunn, see uamhann.
———ach, see uamhannach.
———achadh, see uamhannachadh.
———aich, see uamhannaich.
uam-sa, *emphat.* of uam.
uan, -ain, *s.m.* Lamb.

uanach, -aiche, *a.* Abounding in lambs. 2 Like a lamb. 3** Lamb-producing.
uanachan, -ain, *s.m.* Lamb, lambkin.
uanachd,** *s.f.* Yeaning, earning.
uanalach,* -aich, *s.m.* Lamb's wool.
uanan, -ain, -an, *s.m., dim.* of uan. Little lamb. 2 Young lamb. 3 Milk coming from a cow for several times after calving.
uananach, *a.* Abounding in little lambs.
uan-Càisge,* *s.m.* Pascal lamb.
uan-fheòil, -fheòla, *s.f.* Lamb (flesh.)
uan leth-aon, *s.m.* Twin-lamb.
uapa, *prep. pron.* (ua+iad) From them, away from them, from amongst them. 2 Distant from them. 3 Wanted by them. 'Dé tha u. ? *what do they want ?* tha u. a bhi falbh, *they had better be gone* ; thigeadh iad u., *let them come forward*—said in defiance.
uapa-san, *emphat.* form of uapa.
uar,‡ *s.m.* Waterfall. 2 Heavy shower.
uarach, -aiche, *a.* Hourly. 2 Temporary.
uarach-mhullaich, see odharach-mhullach.
uaraich,(MS) *v.a.* Quench.
uaran,** -ain, *s.m.* Fresh water, (fuaran)
uarraidh, see uamharr.
uas,* *s.m.* College cap used when graduating. 2 **Crown or ornament of silver, worn by the order of poets next to ollamh.
uasal, uaisle, *a.* Noble, gentle, well-born. 2 Genteel, polite. 3 Proud. 4 Elegant, fine. 5 Precious, valuable. 6* Novel, new. 7 Fastidious. Duin' u., *a gentleman* ; bean u., *a lady* ; tha e tuille 's u. uime, *he is too fastidious about it* ; rinn thu do ghnothach gu h-u., *you did your business like a gentleman*; a chàr uasail ! *thou noble ally;* os cionn chlach uasal, *above precious stones* ; is ann u. tha an irioslachd, *'tis humility that is noble.*
uasal, -ail, *pl.* uaislean, *s. m.* Gentleman. 2** Nobleman. Uasail ! *sir !* uasail ionmhuinn ! *dear sir !*
uasalach, -aiche, *a.* Genteel, graceful in behaviour.
uasal-ghniomhach, -aiche, *a.* Acting genteelly.
uaslaid,** *s.f.* Gentleness. 2 Redemption.
uat, *prep. pron.* (ua+thu) From thee. 2 Wanted by thee. 3 At a distance from thee. Tha u. a bhi falbh, *you had better be gone* ; tha u. a dheanamh, *you had better do it* ; 'dé tha u. ? *what do you want ?*
uat ! *int.* Away with it !
†uath, *s.m.* Dread, terror.
uath,‡ *s.* Old Gaelic name for hawthorn (sgitheach geal.) 2 Earth. 3 Small number. 4 Retirement.
†uath,** *a.* Solitary, alone, single, lonesome. 2 Terrible.
uatha, *prep. pron.* (ua+iad) From them. 2 Wanted by them. 3 Retirement from them. Uatha-san ceannaichidh sibh, *from them ye shall buy* ; 'dé tha u.? *what do they want ?*
uathail,** *a.* Solitary, single.
uatha-san, *emphat.* form of uatha.
uathbhas, see uamhas.
———ach, see uamhasach.
uathmhorachd,(MS) *s.f.* Abominableness.
uathrais,(DU) *s.f.* Violent restlessness.
uathrais air tharais, Helter-skelter.
ub ! ub ! ubub ! *int.* Expression of aversion or contempt.
ub,(AC) *gen.* uib & uibe, *pl.* uibe, uibean, *s.* Spell, charm, incantation, superstitious ceremony. (also òb)
uba, see ub.
ubag,* -aig, -an, *s.f., dim.* of ub. Enchantment, incantation. 2 Charm, spell, superstitious ceremony.

ubagach, -aiche, *a.* Skilled in charms, enchantments or incantations. 2** Enchanting. 3 Superstitious. 4** Like a charm. Cuach u., *a charmed cup*
ubagaich,** *v.a.* Subdue by charms or spells, enchant.
ubagaiche,** *s.m.* One who subdues by charms or philtre.
ubagail,* *pr.pt.* of ubaig. Enchanting.
ubaid, *s.f.* Pulpit.
ubaidh, *s.f.* see ubag.
ubaig, *pr.pt.* ag ubagail, *v.a.* Enchant.
ùbairt,(CR) *s.f.* Moving heavy articles. 2 Bustle.
ubarraid,* see ùbraid.
———each, see ùbraideach.
ubh, uibhe, uibhean, *s.m.* Egg. 2** *rarely*, Point of a weapon. see ugh.
ubh ! ubh ! *int.* Expression of surprise, disappointment or incredulity.
ùbh ! ùbh ! ùbhan ! *int.* Alas ! alas ! expression of grief or disgust. Oh dear !
ubhach, -aiche, *a.* see ughach.
ubhagan,* -ain *s.m.* see uigheagan.
ubhaidh, see ubag.
ubhail, -e, *a.* Oval, elliptical, oviform.
ubhal, -ail, *pl.* ùbhlan, *s.m.* Apple—*pyrus malus.*
———ach, -aiche, *a.* Apple-bearing.
——— a' chruachain, *s.m.* The knot-like bone at the hip-joint. Chaidh a' bhò á ubhal a chruachain, *the cow dislocated her hip-joint.*
——— an sgòrnain, *s.m.* The ball of the throttle.
——— bhrigh, *s.* Cider.
——— fiadhain, *s.m.* Wild apple, wilding.
——— -ghort, -oirt, -oirtean, *s.m.* Orchard, garden.
——— -ghortach,** *a.* Abounding in orchards. 2 Of, or belonging to an orchard.
——— -ghiuthais, *s.m.* Pine-apple.
——— na coise, *s.m.* Ankle.
——— na leise, *s.m.* Hip-bone.
——— na sùla, *s.m.* Apple of the eye.
ubh-bhreitheach, -eiche, *a.* Oviparous.
ubh-bhuidheagan, -ain, -an, *s.m.* Egg-yolk.
ubh-chearcall,** *s.* Ellipsis.
ubh-chlach, *s.f.* Oolite.
ubh-chruth, -ainn, *s.pl.* Spawn.
ubh-chumpach, -aich, *s.f.* Oblong spheroid.
———————, -aiche, *a.* Oval, elliptical.
ùbhla, see ùbhladh. 2 *cont.* of ùbhlan.
ùbhlach, -aiche, *a.* Abounding in apples. 2 Of, or belonging to, apples. 3 Apt to impose a fine. 4 Relating to a fine.
ùbhladh, -aidhean, *s.m.* Fine, penalty, tribute, tax, impost. 2* Fine in church courts, ecclesiastical fine. Cuirear u. air, *he shall be fined.*
ùbhlan, *n.pl.* of ubhal.
ubh-mhial,(AF) *s.* Nit.
ubhtraid,(DC) *s.f.* Service road in a township, especially one branching off a main-road—*Uist.* see ùdrathad.
ùbraid, -e, -ean, *s.f.* Dispute, confusion.
ùbraideach, -eiche, *a.* Confused.
ùcadair, see fùcadair.
———eachd, see fùcadaireachd.
ucaid,** *s.f.* Occasion.
ucain,** *s.f.* Harshness.
ùcair, see fùcadair.
———eachd, see fùcadaireachd.
ucas, -ais, *s.m.* Coal-fish—*gadus vireus.*
uch ! *int.* Expression of complaint, Oh ! alas !
uchanaich,** *s.f.* Sobbing, groaning, sighing.
uchd, *s.m.ind.* Breast, bosom. 2 Lap. 3 Brow, side of a hill. 4 *Point, or very time. 5 Humanity, clemency, mercy. 6** Intercession. U. mo ghaoil, *the breast of my love ;* ri u. (*or* ri beul) bàis, *at the point of death*—(aig roinn a' bhàis—*Perthsh.*) ; fàg gu u. a Mhorair e, *leave it to his lordship's clemency ;* a' togail an u., *ascending the face of the hill ;* ri u. crua-dail, *braving difficulties ;* na h-uchdan, *the breasts ;* u. na troidhe, *the instep ;* beul ri beul is uchd ri uchd, *mouth to mouth and breast to breast.*

671. Ucas fiadhain.

ucas fiadhain,§ *s.m.* Common mallow—*malva sylvestris.*

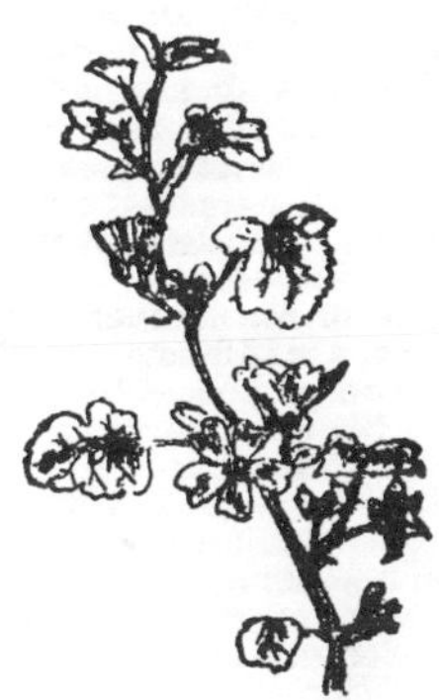

672. Ucas Frangach.

ucas Frangach,§ *s.m.* Dwarf mallow—*malva rotundiflora.*
uchdach, -aich, *s.f.* Ascent, brae, steep, steepness. 2 Stomacher. 3 Breast-plate. 4 Extension of voice. 5 Clef, in *music.* 6 Sine of an angle. 7* Delivery in speech. 8* Pith, energy. 9 Steep portion of a high-road, short steep ascent. 10 Up-hill road. 11** Meadow. 12(CR) Panting, breathing hard—*W. of Ross.* 13(CR) Breast-band, to keep the saddle from slipping backwards. 14 Shoulder-band of a creel—*Lewis.*

A' togail na h-uchdaich, *ascending the acclivity ;* 's ann aige tha 'n u., *how grand his delivery !* cha'n 'eil u. aige dha, *he has not energy to encounter such a difficulty ;* gun u. a dhìreadh, *without climbing an ascent ;* sgoilt i an u. phriseil, *she split the precious breastplate.*
uchdach, -aich, *a.* Prominent. 2 Steep, precipitous. 3 Pectoral, thoracic.
uchdag,(DU) *s.f.* Panting.
———ail,** *a.* Acclivious. 2 Convex.
uchdail, -e, *a.* Stout-breasted. 2 Erect, high-headed.

†uchdall,** *a.* High, erect.
uchdan, -ain, *pl.* -ain & -an, *s.m.* Hillock, acclivity. 2 Instep of a foot or shoe. 3 Child's bib or pinafore. 4††Raised bank, terrace, embankment. 5**Short, steep ascent. 6**Steep portion of road, up-hill road. 7**Sob. U. na troidhe, *the instep.*
——ach, *a.* Abounding in hillocks or steep ascents. 2**Steep or uneven, as a highway. 3**Sobbing.
uchdanachadh, -aidh, *s.m.* Sobbing, sighing, groaning.
uchdanaich,** *v.n.* Sob, sigh, groan.
————,*s.f.* Frequent sobbing, groaning.
uchd-aodach, -aich, *s.m.* Breast-plate, armour for the breast, breast-clothes.
uchdardach,* *a.* High-crested. 2 Bold, brave. 3 Presumptuous. 4 High-breasted.
————d, *s.f.* Pomposity, presumptuousness, pomp.
uchdas-fiadhain, see ucas-fiadhain.
uchdas-Frangach, see ucas-Frangach.
uchd-bhàn,** *a.* Fair-breasted.
uchd-bheart, *s.f.* Cuirass.
uchd-chrios, -a, -an, *s.m.* Stomacher, breast-band.
uchd-crochta, *s.m.* Hanging-back (of loom.)
uchd-eudach, see uchd-aodach.
uchd-éideadh, -idh, -idhean, see uchd-aodach.
uchd-gheal, *a.* White-breasted.
uchd-làr, *s.* The floor of a kiln round about the eye.
uchd-mhac, -mhic, *s.m.* Adopted son.
————ach, *a.* Of, or belonging to adoption.
————achadh, -aidh, *s.m.* Adopting, act of adopting or affiliating. 2 Circumstance of adopting. Ag u—, *pr.pt.* a' uchd-mhacaich.
————achd, *s.f.* Adoption, affiliation. 2 Frequent adopting. A' feitheamh ris an uchdmhacachd, *waiting for the adoption.*
————aich, *pr.pt.* ag uchd-mhacachadh, *v.a.* Adopt as son and heir.
————aichte, *past pt.* Adopted.
uchd-mhacair,** *s.m.* Adopter.
uchd ri uchd, Abreast.
uchd-ríomhadh,** *s.m.* Breast-knot.
uchd-ruadh,** *a.* Red-breasted, brown-breasted. Am bannal u., *the red-breasted covey.*
uchd-suidhichte, *s.m.* Standing back (of loom.)
†uchtard,‖ *s.* Strumosus.
ucsa, see ucas.
ucsach, *a.* Abounding in coal-fish.
ud, *demon.adj.* That, yon, yonder. Thall ud, *over there ;* am baile ud thall, *that town yonder.*
udabac,* -baic, *s.m.* Porch, out-house. 2 Buttress or support, usually of stone, built against a wall. 3 Wall about 6 ft. high and 7 ft. or 8 ft. long, built in front of a main door at a distance of about 4 ft. from it to break the force of the wind. They were common in the north of Skye till quite recently and may still be seen in some parts. 4 Backhouse. [ùdabac—*Uist.*]
udacag, -aig, -an, *s.f.* see coileach-coille.
udacag-crom-nan-duilleag, see coileach-coille.
udag,¶ -aig, -an, *s.f.* Woodcock, see coileach-coille.
udag,(AH) *s.f.* Fluster, flutter, stew—*Argyll.*
——ach, *a.* Excitable.
udagoc, see coileach-coille.
udail, *pr.pt.* ag udal, *v.a.* Cause to totter or shake. 3 Remove, cause to remove. 4 Float. 5 Dangle, shake, toss. 6 **Oscillate. 7** Flounder.
udail, -e, *a.* Inhospitable, churlish. 2 Gloomy.
udail,* *s.m.* Churl.
udail, see udal.
udail,** *a.* Wavering. 2 Tottering. 3 Tossing. 4 Slow. 5 Inhospitable. 6* Gloomy. Cha b' u. thu am measg chàich, *thou wert not slow among the rest.*
udal, -ail, *s.m.* Distress. 2 Jeopardy. 3 Tossing. 4 Floating. 5 Moving, dangling, wavering, oscillating, fluctuating, moving to and fro, as any light substance in an eddy. U. cuain, *distress at sea, tossing on the ocean ;* cha bhi thu air u., *you shall not be uncared for;* cha'n fhaic mis' air u. thu, *I will not see you a dependant.* 6 State of being ejected. 7* State of being tossed from place to place, as a person ejected. 8 State of being absent. 9 Pensioner on the bounty of others, as a person once in good circumstances. Ag u—, *pr.pt.* of udail.
udalach, -aiche, *a.* Wavering, tossing, tossed. 2 Removing. 3 Undulating. 4 Causing distress or jeopardy. 5* Tossed from place to place, as a person.
udaladh, see udal.
udalaich,(MS) *v.a.* Curl.
udalan, -ain, -an, *s.m.* Swivel. 2 Swivel of a tether. 3 Runner of a cart. 4(DMy) Hinge, wooden hinge of a door. Cha chinn còinneach air cloich an udalain, *moss grows not on the oft-turned stone*—NGP.
udalanach, -aiche, *a.* Pendulous, swinging. 2 Glib.
————d, *s.f.* See-saw.
udarag, -aig, *s.m.* Woodcock, see coilleach-coille.
udan, see rùdan.
udbhail,(MS) *s.m.* Dregs, dross.
udbhoil,* see udal.
————each, -eiche, *a.* see udalach.
udhaebd,** *s.f.* Will, testament. 2 Confession.
ùdhar, see odhar.
udhar, -air, -an, *s.m.* Boil, ulcer, sore. 2 Wound.
——ach, -aiche, *a.* Afflicted with sores, ulcerous, sore. 2 Wounded.
udlaiche, -an, *s.m.* Stag. 2 (AF) Old hart. 3 (AF) Ass in its 4th. year.
ùdlaidh, -e, *a.* Gloomy, dark, churlish, morose, unsociable, lonely.
udlan, see udalan.
——achd,** *s.f.* Trough of the sea.
ùdrathad, -aid, -aidean, *s.f.* Free egress and regress to common pasture. 2 Common road to common grazing, peats, &c. Ù.-mòine, *common road to a peat-moss.*
————ach, *a.* Having a road for cattle. 2 Of, or belonging to, a cattle-road.
ud ! ud ! *int.* No ! no ! it cannot be, pity, pity.
uga,(DU) *Gairloch* for ugan. Cnàimh an uga, *the collar-bone.*
ugadh,** -aidh, *s.m.* Birth.
ugan, -ain, -annan, *s.m.*[& *f.*] Upper part of the breast, fore part of the neck, throat. 3 Collar-bone—*Lewis.* Slag (*for* lag) na h-ugain, *hollow of the collar bone ;* crith-chiùil air m' u., *warbling in my throat.*
ùgh, ùigh, -an, *s.m.* see ùth.
ugh, uigh, uighean, *s.m.* Egg. U. eireig, *a pullet's egg ;* u.-nid, *a nest-egg ;* gealagan uighe, *the white of an egg ;* buidheagan uighe, *the yolk of an egg ;* u.-cliath-feannaig, an egg that is much under the hen's usual standard of size, as though she had taken up with a hooded crow !—*W. of Ross-shire ;* u.-maola-feannaig, is a little egg sometimes laid by a hen, at one time popularly supposed to be laid once in seven years by the cock (cockatrice story) ; u. air Inid eun air Càisg, mur b' e aig an fhitheach bithidh am bàs—not *feannaig* as is sometimes given, for the latter is not very early in nesting but the former is. [McL &

Dan! ‡ give ubh.]
ughach, -aiche, *a.* Oviform, oval. 2 Like an egg. 3 Full of eggs. 4 Egg-producing. 5 Pointed.
†ughaim, -e, -ean, *s.f.* see uidheam.
ughagan,** -ain, *s.m.* Custard, pancake.
ughdain, *s.m.* Knuckle. [Given as "vulgar" by MS] (for rùdan.)
ùghdair, see ùghdar.
ughdaireachadh,(MS) *s.m.* Authorization.
ùghdar, -air, -airean, *s.m.* Author. Oir cha'n e Dia u. na mi-riaghailt, *for God is not the author of confusion.*
————ach, -aiche, *a.* Of, or belonging to, an author. 2 Authentic, having an author. 3 Authoritative.
————achd, *s.f.* Authorship, authority, authenticity.
ùghdarachadh, -aidh, *s.m.* Authorizing, act of authorizing. Ag u., *pr.pt.* of ùghdaraich.
ùghdaraich, *pr.pt.* ag ùgdarachadh, *v.a.* Authorize, empower. 2 **Own, as an author.
————te, *past pt.* of ùghdaraich. Authorized, empowered, authentic. 2 Owned, as a book by its author.
ùghdarail, -e, *a.* Authentic.
ùghdaraileachd,** *s.f.* Authenticity.
ùghdaralas,** -ais, *s.m.* Authenticity.
ùghdarra,* see ùghdar.
ùghdarrach ** *a.* Authoritative.
ùghdarrachd, see ùghdarachd.
ùghdarrais, *s.f.* Lumber, stuff in one's way. 2 Struggle. (ùtrais)
ùghdarras, -ais, *s.m.* Authority, power, command. A' teagaisg mar neach aig am bheil u., *teaching as one having authority.*
ùghdarrasach, -aiche, *a.* Authentic, authoritative.
ughdmhail,(MS) *s.* Offal.
ughpag,(MS) *s.f.* Protrusion.
ùghdrathad, see ùdrathad.
ùghtarrais, see ùghdarrais. (ùtrais)
ughtraid,(DC) *s.m.* Side-road off a high-road. 2 see ùdrathad.
ugsa, *pl.* -n & -ichean, *s.m.* see ucas.
ugsach, see ucsach.
uibe, -achan, *s.m.* Mass, lump, commonly of dough. 2 Block of anything, as marble. 3 Lump of a person. (also ioba)
uibeach, -eiche, *a.* Lumpish, massive. 2 Round, globular, rotund, circular.
————an, -ain, -an, *s.m.* Little mass or lump.
uibeachd,** *s.f.* Roundness, circularity, globularity, rotundity.
uibeag, *s.f., dim.* of ub.
uibh, see uigh.
uibheagan, -ain, *s.m.* see uigheagan.
uibhir, *s.f.ind.* Number, quantity, sum. 2** Account. Tha u. is u. aca, *they have share and share alike ;* u. eile, *as much again ;* 'dé 'n u. a th' ann ? *what quantity is there ?* u. 's a th' ann, *as much as there are ;* u. na circe, *the equivalent (value) of a hen ;* na h-uibhir, *a great number* or *quantity;* na h-u. de dhaoine, *a great number of men ;* u. ri càch, *as much as the rest ;* 'se na h-u., *it is so much ;* mi fhéin a dh' fhaotainn na h-u. de dhragh, *my getting so much trouble*—W.H. 1.18.
uibhireach, *s.m.* Arithmetician.
uibhireach, -eiche, *a.* Numerous. 2†† Equal, alike. 3(MS) Arithmetical.
uibaireachd, *s.f.* Computing, casting up of sums, tale, arithmetic.
uibhir-fhaisneachd,(MS) *s.f.* Arithmancy.
uibhreachail, -e, *a.* Arithmetical, numerous. numerical.
uibhreachan,‡‡ *s.m.* Abacist, numerator, arithmetitian.
uibhreachan-dine, *s.m.* Almanac.
uibhseann, see uinnseann.
————ach, see uinnseannach.
uideal, *s.* Flail.
uideal,** *s.m.* Unsteadiness, tossing about, wavering, tottering, moving to and fro. 2** Jeopardy. Gun sibh bhi fo u., *without your being moved or shaken.*
uidealach,** *a.* Wavering, tottering. 2 Causing to wave or totter. 3 In jeopardy.
ùidh, -e, -ean, *s.f.* Ford. 2 Part of a stream which leaves a lake before breaking into a current, slow running water between two lochs. 3 Desire, wish 4 Partiality, fondness, affection. 5 Hope, expectation. 6 Care, heed. 7**Attention, hearing. 8* Intention, hope. 9 (DMy) Isthmus.
Gun ù. ri sòlas, *without hope of consolation ;* an obair anns an do chuir mi m' ù , *the work on which I set my intentions.*
uidh, -e, *s.f.* Degree, step, span, space. 2 Way. 3 Journey. U. air 'n u., *gradually ;* 's ann u. air 'n u. a thogar an caisteal, *the castle is built little by little ;* ceann uidhe, *destination ;* aig ceann ar n-uidhe, *at our journey's end.*
uidh,** *v.a. & n.* Favour, countenance. 2 Take part. Cha'n u. thu leis, *thou shalt not favour him.*
uidhe, see uidh.
uidheachd,(MS) *s.f.* Gradation.
uidheam, -eim, -an, *s.f.* Furniture. 2 Equipage, regimentals, uniform, accoutrements. 3 Dress, clothes, habiliments. 4 Decoration, 5**Harness. 6 Order, arrangement. 7 Preparation. 8 Use, need. 9 Instruments. 10 Rigging. 11 (AH) Set of sails. 12* Materials, apparatus. Fo làn u., *in full dress ;* fo làn u. Ghàidhealach, *in full Highland dress ;* dheanainn sin 'nam bitheadh an u. agam, *I would do that if I had the materials;* u. ghreusachd, *shoemaking tools ;* u. shaoirsneachd, *joinery tools ;* u. thogalach, *distilling apparatus.*
uidheamach, -aiche, *a.* Well-furnished, accoutred or dressed. 2 Provided with materials or apparatus.
————adh, -aidh, *s.m.* Furnishing, act of furnishing with necessary implements, apparatus or dress. 2 Arranging, act of arranging. 3 Preparing, arranging matters. Ag u—, *pr.pt.* of uidheamaich.
uidheamachd,(MS) *s.f.* Qualification.
uidheamaich, *pr. pt.* ag uidheamachadh, *v. a.* Equip, furnish with instruments or dress. 2 Arrange. 3 Prepare. 4 Address. U. thu-féin, *equip thyself.*
uidheamaichidh, *fut.aff.a.* of uidheamaich.
uidheamaichte, *past pt.* of uidheamaich. Equipped, furnished. 2 Arranged. 3 Prepared.
uidheam-chogaidh,‡‡ *s.f.* Military accoutrements.
———— -eich,‡‡ *s.f.* Horse-trappings.
———— -gunnaireachd, *s.f.* Ammunition.
———— -leapa, *s.f.* Bedding.
uidhear, -ir, -an, *s.m.* Traveller, pilgrim.
uidh-ghille, *s.m.* Footman. 2 Errand-boy.
uidhis,** *v.* Adhibit.
————,** *s.* Adhibition.
uidhsealachd, see ùisealachd.
uidhseil, -e, *a.* see ùiseil.
uidhsinn,** *v.a.* Employ.
ùig, -e, *pl.* -ean & -eachan, *s.f.* Nook, retired or solitary hollow, cave or den. 2* Steep, conical rock.
†uige, *s.f.* Jewel, precious stone, pebble. 2 Web. 3 Carded wool for spinning,—hence 4 The spinning out of a story or poem. 5 *rarely,* Knowledge, skill, ingenuity, understanding. 6 Poem.
ùigeach, -eiche, *a.* Abounding in nooks or soli-

tary hollows.
uigeach,** *a.* Abounding in jewels or precious stones. 2 Like a jewel or precious stone.
ùigean, -ein, -ean, *s.m.* Fugitive, lonely wanderer. 2 see uigeann.
ùigeanach, -aiche, *a.* Of, or belonging to fugitives. 2 Like a fugitive.
uigeann,** -einn, *s.m.* Forepart of the neck.
ùigeanta, -einte, *a.* Of a retired or unsociable disposition. 2 see ùigeach.
ùigeantachd, *s.f.* Gloominess. 2 Unsociableness.
uighe, see uidh.
uighe, *gen.sing.* of ugh.
uigheach,** -ich, *s.m.* Traveller.
uigheagan, *s.m.* Custard. 2 Ovary.
ùighealachd, *s.f.* Quality of giving pleasure. 2 Care, heed. see aoigheachd.
uigheam, see uidheam.
———ach, see uidheamach.
———achadh, see uidheamachadh.
———aich, see uidheamaich.
———aichidh, see uidheamaichidh.
———aichte, see uidheamaichte.
uighean, *n.pl.* of ugh.
uighean-sìthein, *s. pl.* Fairy egg, (beans, nuts and seeds borne across the Atlantic by the Gulf Stream with the weed tùrusgar.)
ùigheil, -e, *a.* Giving pleasure. 2 Careful, heedful. 3 (DMy) Pleasant to the taste, palatable.
uigh air 'n uigh, for uidh air 'n uidh.
uighimich, see uigheamaich.
uighpear,(MS) *s.m.* Dabbler.
uilbh,(AF) *s.f.* Wolf—*Suthd.*
uilc, *gen.sing. & n.pl.* of olc.
uild, *gen.sing. & n.pl.* of ald. (for allt.)
uile, *a.* All, the whole, altogether, quite, every, wholly. Tha iad mar sin u., *they are all so*; thàinig iad u., *they have all come*; tha mi u. thoileach, *I am quite willing*; a h-u. uair, *always*; u. air chaochladh, *all changed*; u. gu lèir, *altogether, completely, wholly*; a' choille gu h-u. làn duillich,*the wood quite full of foliage*; na h-uile, *everyone, all, the whole*; cha'n ann am Bòid u. 'tha 'n t-olc, *the mischief is not all in Bute*—NGP.
uileach,** *a.* Universal. 2 General.
uileachd, *s.f.ind.* Universality, generality. 2 Totality.
uileadh,†† -idh, *s. m.* Entirety, completeness.
uilidh, *a.* All. Gu h-uilidh, *entirely, totally.*
uileann,-inn,uille,uillne & uilne, *pl.* -an, *s.f.* Elbow. 2 Corner,angle. U. na beinne, *the angle or corner of the mountain*; air u. nan leac, *on the corner of the flags*; 'nuair a bha e air u., *when he was embarrassed, on the eve of failing;* thug i u. gu tuiteam, *she bent to fall.*
———ach, -aiche, *a.* Angular, angled. 2** Elbowed. 3 Cornered.
———ach, -aich, *s. m.* Antler. 2 Lowest branch of a deer's antler.
uilear, *a.* see fuilear.
uile-bheist, -ean, *s.m.* Monster. 2 Wild beast. 3 Lamprey. 4 Hideous wild beast. Mar u. mi-chiallach, *like a mad monster.*
uile-bheist a' chuain,(AF) s.m. Sea-serpent.
uile-bheisteil, *a.* Monstrous.
uile-bheannaichte, *a.* Truly blessed, all-blessed. 2†† All-holy.
uile-bheothachail,** *a.* All-cheering.
uile-bhreitheach, -aiche, *a.* All-judging.
uile-bhuadhach, -aiche, *a.* All-victorious, all-triumphant.
uile-chaithteach,‡‡ *a.* All-consuming.
uile-chaochlaideach, *a.* All-changing.
uile-chinnteach, -eiche, *a.* All-certain, unerring. 2 All-sufficient.
uile-chliùiteach,‡‡ *a.* All-praised.
uile-choitchionn, *a.* Universal.
uile-choitchionnachd, *s.f.* Universality.
uile-chomasach, -aiche, *a.* All-powerful.
——————d,** *s.f.* All-sufficiency.
uile-chruthach, -aiche, *a.* Omniform.
uile-chumhachd, *s.f.* Omnipotence.
——————ach, -aiche, *a.* Almighty, omnipotant, all-powerful.
uile-chuthaichte, *a.* All-enraged.
uile-dhiongmhalta, *a.* All-sufficient.
uile-fhaicsinneach,** *a.* All-seeing, omniscient.
uile-fhaicsinneachd, *s.f.* Infinite vision, omniscience.
uile-fhiosrach, *a.* All-knowing, omniscient.
uile-fhiosrachd, *s.f.* Omniscience.
uile-fhoillseachail,‡‡ *a.* All-discovering.
uile-fhradharcach, *a.* Omniscient, all-seeing.
uile-fhuathach,‡‡ *a.* All-abhorred.
uile-ghlic, *a.* All-wise.
uile-ghliocas,** -ais, *a.* Infinite wisdom.
uile-ghlòrmhor, *a.* All-glorious.
uile-ghràsmhor, *a.* All-gracious.
uile-iomlanachd,** *s.f.* All-sufficiency.
uile-làthaireach, *a.* Omnipresent.
uile-làthaireachd, *s.f.* Omnipresence.
uile-lèirsinneach, *a.* Omniscient.
uile-lèirsinneachd,** *s.f.* Divine perfection of seeing all things, omniscience.
uile-mhaitheasach, *a.* All-good.
uile-mhaslaichte,‡‡ *a.* All-disgraced.
uile-mhath,†† *a.* All-good.
uile-mhathasach, see uile-mhaitheasach.
uile-mhillteach,** *a.* All-consuming, all-devouring.
uile-naomh, *a.* All-holy. [McL & D gives uile-naomha.]
uile-neartmhor, *a.* All-powerful.
uile-riaghlach, *a.* All-ruling.
uile-sgriosach,†† *a.* All-destroying. 2 All-devouring.
uile-shlugach, *a.* All-devouring.
uile-shoillseachail, *a.* All-lightening.
uile-thoireach, see uile-thorach.
uile-thorach, *a.* All-bearing.
uile-thréigte, *a.* All-abandoned.
uile-thròcaireach, *a.* All-merciful.
uile-thuigsinneach,‡‡ *a.* All-comprehensible.
uil'-fhaicsinneach, *a.* Omniscient.
uil'-fhiosrach, *a.* All-knowing, omniscient.
uil'-fhiosrachd, *a.* Omniscience.
uil'-fhoghainteach, *a.* All-sufficient.
uil'-fhoghainteachd, *s.f.* All-sufficiency.
uil'-fhoghainteas, see uil'-fhoghainteachd.
ùi'lic, see uil'-ioc.
uilidh,** *s.f.* Lake.
uilidh, *a.* All, total. Gu h-u., *totally, universally.*
uilim, see uilm.
uilinne, see uileann.
uilinneachd,** *s.f.* Elbowing. 2 Side by side.
uil'-inntinneach, *a.* With all the mind, without mental reservation.

673. Uil'-ioc.

uil'-ioc, *s.* Mistletoe—*viscum album.* [Said by some to be the badge of the Hays, but it does not grow wild in Scotland.] [March.

The Druids gathered the mistletoe on 10th. Pliny, in the 16th. book of his Nat. Hist., says "The Druids hold nothing in such sacred respect as the mistletoe, and the tree on which it grows, provided it be an oak. They select certain woods of oak, and they do not perform any sacred rite without the leaf of that tree; so that hence it is likely they have been called Druids, explaining the name from the Greek *drus*, an oak; Druidæ, *oakites.* Whatever grows on that tree, more than its natural growth, they think has been sent from heaven, and is a proof that the tree has been chosen by God himself. However that [species of mistletoe] is very rarely found, and when found it is sought after with great devotion, and especially at the sixth moon, which is the beginning of their months and years, and when the tree has passed its thirtieth year, because it has already abundant vigour, though not half-grown. They call it by a word signifying in their own language, "all-heal"; and having prepared sacrifices and feasts under the tree, they bring up two white bulls, whose horns are then first bound; the priest in a white robe ascends the tree, and cuts it off with a golden knife; it is received in a white sheet. Then, and not till then, they sacrifice the victims, praying that God would render his gift prosperous to those on whom he had bestowed it. When mistletoe is given as a potion, they are of opinion that it can remove animal barrenness, and that it is a remedy against all poisons.

uil'-iomlaineachd, *s. f.* All-sufficiency, full perfection or completeness.

uil'-iomlan, *a.* All-perfect.

uil'-iomlanachd, see uil'-iomlaineachd.

uil'-ionadach, *a.* Omnipresent.

uil'-ionadachd, *s.f.* Omnipresence.

uil'-itheach,** *a.* All-devouring.

uilionn, see uileann. [oil, grease.

ùill, *pr.pt.* ag ùilleadh, *v.a.* Oil, besmear with

uille, *gen.sing.* of uileann. 2 *gen. sing.* of uillidh.

ùilleadh, -idh, *s.m.* Oil for lamps, &c. Ag ù—, *pr.pt.* of ùill. Oiling, smearing with oil.

ùilleadh-cuidhleach, *s. m.* Oil for a spinning-wheel. [wool.)

ùilleadh-na-h-ola, *s m.* Sweet oil (*lit.* oil of the

ùilleag,(MMcL) *s.f.* Oily surface on water, &c.

uilleag,* -eig, -an, *s.f.* Jostle, elbowing.

uilleagaich,* *v.a. & n.* Jostle, elbow.

uillean,(DMy) *s.pl.* The beads of oil on the surface of the bree of meat or fish.

uilleann, -inn, *s.f.* Honeysuckle, woodbine—*lonicera periclymenum.* 2 Elecampane, see aillean.

ùillich, *v.a.* see ùill.

uillichd,(AF) *s.f.* Frog.

ùillidh, uille, *s.m.* Oil.

———, -e, *a.* Oily, greasy.

ùillidheach,** *a.* Greasy.

———-d, *s.f.* Oiliness.

uillinnich, *v.* see ùill.

uillne, *gen.sing.* of uileann.

uillnean, *n.pl.* of uileann.

uillnich,* *v.a.* Jostle, elbow.

uillt, *gen. sing. & n.pl.* of allt.

ùillte, *past pt.* of ùill. Oiled.

uilm,(AC) *s.* Sacred bag for alms, coffer, treasury, offertory.

uilne, *gen.sing.* of uileann.

uilneag,‡‡ -eig, *s.f.* Push, shove, elbowing.

———-aich,(MS) *v.a.* Hitch.

uilp,(AF) *s.* Fox.

674. Uilleann.

uilpean,(AF) *s.m.* Fox.

uilt, *gen.sing. & n. pl.* of alt. U. an droma, *backbone joints.*

†uim, *prep.* Form used in conjunction with personal pronouns.

†uim, *s.f.* Earth. 2 Country. 3 Brass, copper.

uim'-astar,** *s.* Circumference.

uim-cheallach,** -aich, *s.m.* Any close private place.

uime, *prep.pron.* (mu+e) About him, around him or it. 2 Of, concerning, respecting or regarding him or it. Agus chuir iad u. aodach purpur, *and they put on (about) him a purple robe;* cia uime? *about whom?*

uime, *s.* Harness Chuir e an làir 'na h-u., *he harnessed the mare;* cuir na h-eich 'nan u. 'sa chrann, *yoke the horses to the plough.* (uidheam.)

uimeach,** -ich, *s.m.* Brazier.

uimeachd,†† *s.f.* Boundary, circuit, see imeachd.

uim'-chlodh,** *s.* Dizziness.

uim'-dhòrtach, see ioma-dhòirteach.

uim'-dhòrtadh, see ioma-dhòrtadh.

uime-bhallach, ** *a.* see ioma-bhallach.

uime-chladh, see ioma-chladh.

uime-chladhach, see ioma-chladhach.

uime-chladhaich, see ioma-chladhaich.

uime-chrith, see ioma-chrith.

uime-dhruidte, see ioma-dhruidte.

uime-dhruideadh, see ioma-dhruideadh.

uime-fhilleadh, see ioma-fhilleadh.

uime-itealaiche, see iom'-itealaiche.

uime-labhairt, see ioma-labhairt.

uime-labhradh, see iom-labhradh.

uime-lionach, see ioma-lionach.

uime-ròl, see ioma-ròl.

uime-ròladh, see ioma-ròladh.

uime-sheòl, see ioma-sheòl.

uime-sheòladh, see ioma-sheòladh.

uime-sheòladair, see ioma-sheòladair.

uime-shruth, see ioma-shruth.

uime-shruthach, *a.* see ioma-shruthach.

uime-shruthachadh, *s.m.* see ioma-shruthachadh.

uime-shuidheachadh, *s.m.* Circumposition.

uime sin, *adv.* Therefore, on that account, concerning that, on that head.

uim'-ghlac, see ioma-ghlac.

uimhir, see uibhir.

uimhireach, see uibhireach.

uimhreach, see uibhireach.

uimhreachail, see uibhreachail.

uimhreachan, -ain, see uibhreachan.

uimhseag, -eig, -an, *s.f.* Jerk.

uimhseann, see uinnseann.

uimhleac, -ic, -an, see imleag

uimhridheachd,(MS) *s.f.* Tale.

uimite,** *a.* Corpulent.

uimpe, *prep.pron.* (mu+i) Around or about her

or it. 2 Of, or concerning her or it.
ùin, see ùine.
ùine, *s.f.ind.* Time, a time, season. 2 Life, lifetime. 3 Interval, leisure. Ù. thri làithean, *the space of three days* ; caith t' ù., *pass your time, mis-spend your time;* ar n-ù. a' ruith air sgiathaibh, *our time fleeting on wings* ; 'nuair a bhitheas ù. agam, *when I have time.*
ùineachd,** *s.f.* Leisure, vacation.
ùineadaireachd,** *s.f.* Chronology.
uineamaid,** *s.* Balsam.
†uineamh,** *s.m.* Strength.
ùine-chùnntas,** *s.m.* Chronology.
uine-shaor, *s.f.* Leisure, vacation.
uinge, *s.f.* Ounce.
ùinich, -e, *s.f.* Bustle, hurry. 2*Fumbling. 3** Contending. 4**Confusion, disturbance.
uinicionn, see uaiuicionn.
ùinidh, see ùinich.
uinigneach, *Suth'd* for uaigneach.
uinneag, -eig, -an, *s.f.* Window. 2(DMK) Recess in the wall of the kitchen used as a repository for miscellaneous articles—*Suth'd.* Uinneagan nèimh, *the windows of heaven* ; a' gearradh a mach uinneagan, *cutting out windows.*
uinneagach, -aiche, *a.* Windowed, having windows, of, or belonging to, a window.
uinneagachadh, -aidh, *s.m.* Dawn, dawning. 2 Making windows, cutting out windows. Ag u—, *pr.pt.* of uinneagaich. 'Nuair a bha 'n là ag u., *when the day began to dawn.*
uinneagaich, *pr.pt.* ag uinneagachadh, *v.n.* Dawn, begin to dawn. 2 Make windows, insert windows, provide with windows.
uinneagaichte, *past pt.* Windowed.
uinn-an, -ein, -an, *s.m.* Onion—*allium cepa.* 2 (DMK) Ball of the ankle—*Lochbroom.* 3 (CR) Anvil—*W. of Ross.* 4 Bunion on the foot.
uinneanach, -aiche, *a.* Abounding in onions. 2 Like an onion. 3 Producing onions.
uinneanaich,** *v.a.* Provide with onions.
uinnein, see uinnean.
uinnle, *gen.* of uileann.
uinnleag, -eig, -an, *s.f.* Thrust with the elbow.
uinnlean, see uileann.
uinnse, see uinnseann.
uinnseachadh, -aidh, *s.m.* Managing. Ag u—, *pr.pt.* of uinnsich.
uinnseann,§ -inn, *s.m.* Ash, ash-tree. 2 Wood or timber of the ash-tree.
uinnsean,* *a.* Ashen.
———ach, *a* Ashen.
uinnsich,* *pr.pt.* ag uinnseachadh, *v.a.* Manage, sway.
uinseann, see uinnseann.
uipear, -ir, -an, *s.m.* Unhandy craftsman, bungler, botcher. 2 Clown, churl, surly fellow, boor. 3††Idiot.
uipearach, -aiche, *a.* Unhandy, awkward, unskilful. 2 Clownish, churlish, boorish, surly. 3 Inhospitable.
uipearachd,** *s.f.* Bungling. 2 Churlishness, surliness. 3 Inhospitality. 4 Clownishness, boorishness.
uipinn, -e, -ean, *s.f.* Treasure, hoard.
uir, for air. Fir na h-uir thalmhanta,—this is not *ùir*, as given in *W.H.Tales*, but the intensitive particle *air.*
ùir, -e & ùireach, *s.f.* Mould, dust, earth, soil. 2 Body. 3** Mound. 4**Fire. 5**Grave. An ù. thioram, *the dry land* ; thogas an ù. tharta, *the earth was raised over them* ; tog-sa m'ùir, *raise thou my grave* ; fo 'n ù., *in the grave*; càiribh 'san ù., *bury, inter.*
†uir, -e, *s.* Name of the letter U.
uircean, -ein, -an, *s. m.* Pig. 2 Grice, young pig, sucking-pig. 3 Cetacean.
uirceanach, -aiche, *a.* Abounding in pigs. 2 Like a pig. 3 Cetaceous.
uircean-garaidh,(AF) *s.m.* Hedgehog.
uircean-sona,(AF) *s.m.* Hedgehog.
uirceineach, see uirceanach.
uirchir,(AF) *s.* Cricket, fen-cricket, chir-worm.
ùir-chlàr,(MS) *s.m.* Earth-board of a plough.
uir-chòmhnuidh,** *s.m.* Dwelling of clay, grave, tomb. Thogadh u. do 'n laoch, *a tomb was raised to the hero.*
uir-chuil',(AF) *s.* Cricket. 2 Grasshopper. 3 Salamander.
ùird, *gen.sing. & n.pl.* of òrd.
uir-dhreachadh,** *s.m.* Delineation.
ùire, *s.f.* see ùrachd.
ùire, *comp.* of ùr.
ùireach, *gen. sing.* of ùir. A' bùrach na h-ù., *stirring up the mould.*
ùireach,(AF) *s.m.* Mole.
———, see ùrach.
uiread, *s.m.ind.* So much, as much, equal quantity. U. is uiread, *equal shares* ; u. eile, *as much again* ; u. a bhidhich, *as much as a meal (of food)* ; tha u.'agam 's a th' agad-sa, *I have as much as you have* ; leth u., *half as much* ; a dha u. arain, *twice as much bread.* [The possessive pronoun, which is understood, appears when sentence is made more emphatic by introducing *ceart*, as, tha a cheart uiread, &c. *Uiread* is never met with in company with *an* —cha'n 'eil u. (*not* |an u.) sin agam, *I have not as much as that;* na h-u. cheannais oirnne, *so much superiority over us.*
uiread,* -eid, *s.f.* see ùrad.
uiread, *adv.* see uthard.
uireagal,** -ail, *s.m.* Dread, terror.
uireagalach, *a.* Terribly afraid.
uireal, *Suth'd* for uilear.
ùirealachd, *s.f.* Earthliness.
uireall,* *s.m.* Ferule, ring.
uireallach,* -aich, *s.m.* Dagger, dirk.
uireas,* -an, *s.f.* Want, necessary, family or domestic necessary. 2 Maim. 3**Bail, security, warrant. A' dol air tòir uireasan, *going for little family necessaries.*
uireas, *adv.* see ioras.
uireasach, see uireasbhach.
uireasaich,* *s.f.* Want, necessary. U. sam bith a th' ort, *any necessary you want* ; 'dé a tha 'd u.? *what do you want?* 'dé iad na h-uireasbhuidhean a tha dhith ort? *what are the necessaries you want?* am fear air am bi an u. biodh an t-saothair, *he that wants must take the trouble*—NGP
uireasbhach, -aich, *s.m.* Needy person. 2 Want, indigence, lack, poverty, abjectness, deficiency.
uireasbhach, -aiche, *a.* Very much wanted, defective. 2 Bare. 3 Aidless. 4 Maimed, lame. 5 Indigent, needy, destitute. Ni u., *a thing very much wanted* ; duine u., *a maimed person* ; làmh u., *a maimed hand.*
uireasbhuidh, -e, -ean, *s.f.* Want, indigence, poverty. 2 Defect, maim, deficiency.
uireasbhuidheach, see uireasbhach.
——————,** *s.m.* Indigent man, beggar.
uireasuidh, see uireasbhuidh.
ùireil,** *a.* Earthen.
ùir-fhamh,(AF) *s.m.* Mole. Dùcan ùir-fhaimh, *a mole-hill.*
ùir-fhamha, *s.f.* Mole-hill.
uirghioll, -ill, *s.m.* Faculty of speech, delivery, utterance. 2 Speech, oration. 3 History, narration. 4 Eloquence. 5 Command. Cha 'n 'eil cainnt no u. ann am bheul, *there is neither language nor speech in my lips;* u. cruaidh, *difficult utterance.*

uirghiollach, -aiche, *a.* Eloquent.
uirghreann, *s.m.* Puberty.
uirghreannach,** *a.* Adolescent, at the age of puberty.
uirghreannachd,‡‡ *s.f.* Puberty, ripeness of age.
uirich, see uirigh.
uiridh, *s.* (an uiridh,) Last year. Mu 'n àm seo an u., *about this time last year*; am bliadhna 's an u., *this year and last year.*
uiridh,(AF) *s.* Monster.
uiridheach,** *a.* Thoral.
uirigh, -e, -ean, *s.f.* Couch, bed, pallet. 'Na luighe air u., *stretched on a pallet.*
uirigh-làir,* *s.f.* Couch.
uirigh-creige, *s.f.* Shelf of rock—JGC. W. 32.
uirigioll, see uirghioll.
uirigleach,(MS) *a.* Eloquent.
uirigleadh,(MS) *s.m.* Speech, utterance.
uiriollach, -aich, *s.m.* Precipice.
uiriosal, see iriosal.
———achd, see iriosalachd.
uirisle,** *s.f.* Meanness. 2 Lowliness.
uirislich,** *v.a.* Debase, humble, cast down. 2 Disparage.
———te, *past pt.* of uirislich.
ùirleach,(CR) *s.m.* Live ashes, red embers—*W. of Ross.*
ùirle-thruis, *s.f.ind.* Hurly-burly, confusion.
ùirlios, -is -an, *s.m.* Garden, walled garden.
ùir-luch,(DC) *s.f.* Mole.
uirm, for fuirm, (seat), Gaelic spelling of *form.*
ùirneas, -eis, *s.m.* Furnace. [‡ gives *nom.* -eis.]
ùirneasach, see àirneiseach.
ùirneis, *s.coll.* see àirneis.
———each, see àirneiseach.
uirneisich, see àirneisich.
†uirre, see oirre.
ùir-reathadh,‡‡ -aidh, -ean, *s.m.* Mole.
ùir-reothadh, see ùir-reathadh.
uirsgeil,‡ *s.* (air+sgaoil) Spreading, as of dung or hay.
uirsgeul,(DU) *v.a.* Spread dung—*Gairloch.*
ùirsgeul, -sgeòil, -an, *s. m.* Fable, novel. 2 *News, intelligence. 3* Blarney. 4 Spreading, as of hay or dung to dry (for air-sgaoil) —*Badenoch.*
ùirsgeulach, -aiche, *a.* Fabulous.
uirsgeuladh,(DU) *s.m.* Act of spreading dung—*Gairloch.*
ùirsgeulaiche, -an, *s.m.* Teller of stories, novelist, fabulist.
ùirthilleach, part of a plough, see p. 263.
ùis, -e, *s.f.* Use, utility, service. 2 Courteous reception, hospitality 3* Hospitality carried almost to excess, unnecessary hurry-burry at one's reception. 'S ann rompa bha 'n u., *they met with a most courteous reception*; tha mi 'deanamh ù. dheth, *I am making use of it.*
uisdealachd,** *s.f.* Supplication.
uiseag, -eig, -an, *s.f* Lark, sky-lark. Guth na faoin uiseig, *the voice of the lonely lark.*
u a' chàth, chaffinch.
u. bhreac na mara, see u. mhara.
u. chabach, tufted lark
u. choille, wood lark—*alauda arborea.*
u. dhubh, black shore lark.
u. mhara, sea-coot.
u. Moire, crested lark.
u. na tràighe, sea-piet.
u. oidhche, sedge warbler, see glas-eun.
u. riasgach, mountain plover.
u. sneachda, fieldfare.
u. thapaidh, quick or clerk bird. 2 Lark.
u. thopach, tufted lark.
———ach, -aiche, *a.* Of, or belonging to, larks. 2 Like a lark.

ùisealachd,* *s f.* Courtesy, courteousness. 2 Utility, usefulness. 3 Advantageousness. 4* Highest degree of hospitality. 5* Snugness, comfort.
ùiseil, -e, *a.* Useful, comfortable, advantageous, serviceable. 2 Dignified, high-born, respected. 3 *Courteous, hospitable in the highest degree imaginable. 4*Snug. 5††Worthy. Gu h-ù., *entertained with the utmost hospitality;* ù. aca, *entertained in the politest manner by them.*
uisg', see uisge.
uisge, -an & -achan, *s.m.* Water. 2 Shower, rain. 3 Billow, wave. 4 River, stream. 5§ Water-avens, see machall-uisge.
Fo 'n u., *under water*; dh' éirich uisge, *a billow arose*; mar u. balbh a' ghlinne, *like the smooth stream of the valley*; u. an easain air a dhos—a charm to preserve one from danger, especially at sea; u. beatha, *whisky*; U. na Beatha, *the Water of Life*; air an aon u., *in each other's wake* (as boats); fìor-u., *a running stream*; loch fìor u., *a fresh-water loch*; uisgeachan na Dìle, *the waters of the Flood*; sìor-u., *constant rain*; tha 'n t-u. ann, *it is raining.* In *Arran* u. is applied to both rain and water.
uisge, *v.n.* Rain. Tha e ag u., *it is raining.*—*Suth'd, &c.*
uisgeach, -eiche, *a.* Aquatic, hydraulic, watery, pluvial, causing rain. 2 Lymphatic.
uisgeacha, *cont.* of uisgeachan.
uisgeachan, *pl.* of uisge.
uisgeachadh, -aidh, *s.m.* Watering, act of watering or moistening. Ag u—, *pr pt.* of uisgich. Ag u. na talmhainn, *watering the earth.*
uisgeachail,(MS) *a.* Aquatic.
uisgeachd, see uisgidheachd.
uisgealachd, see uisgidheachd.
uisgeanta,(MS) *a.* Aquatile.
uisgearradh,** *a.* Aquatic.
uisge-beatha, *s.m.* Whisky. U. baoghal, *whisky four times distilled.*
uisge-baoghal,** *s.m.* Alcohol.
uisge-coisrigte, *s.m.* Holy water.
uisge-coisreachd,** *s.m.* Kind of holy water, formerly drunk by the Gael at Christmas, and believed to be a preservative against the machinations of evil spirits and witchcraft till the next anniversary.
uisgeil, -e, *a.* Watering, irrigating. 2 Swampy, aqueous, fenny, moorish.
uisge-fuarain, *s.m.* Spring-well water.
uisge-leighiseach, *a.* Hydropathic.
uisge-mhil, *s.f.* Hydromel.
uisge-nimhe, *s.m.* Aquafortis, sulphuric or vitriolic acid.
uisge-oillt,** *s.f.* Hydrophobia.
uisg'-eòlas, *s.m.* Hydraulics.
uisge-ruithe, *s.m.* Running water, stream. Os cionn nan uisge-ruithe, *above the running waters.*
uisge-thomhas,** *s.m.* Hydrometry.
uisgeul, see ùr-sgeul.
———aiche, see ùr-sgeulaiche.
uisgich, *pr.pt.* ag uisgeachadh.*v.a.* Water, moisten, wet.
———te, *past pt.* of uisgich. Watered, irrigated.
uisgidh, *s.pl.* Waters. 2 Rivers. Na h-uisgidh dorcha, *the dark waters.*
———, *a.* Watery, waterish. 2 Faint-hearted. 3 Fluid, clammy, greasy, moist. 4 (MS) Rainy.
uisgidheachd, *s. f.* Wateriness, aqueousness, moistness, clamminess, greasiness. 2 Swampiness.
uisgrian,** -ein, *s.m.* Aqueduct.
uisg'-phiobachadh, *s.coll.* Hydraulics.

uisg'-thomhais, *s.coll.* Hydrostatics.
uisarach,** -aich, *s.m.* Petitioner.
ùisinneachadh, -aidh, *s.m.* Using, act of using. 2 Treatment. Ag ù—, *pr.pt.* of ùisinnich.
ùisinnich, *pr. pt.* ag ùisinneachadh, *v.a.* Use, treat.
————te, *past pt.* of ùisinnich. Used
uisir, see eisir.
uislean,(DC) *s.m.* Child whose father is not apparent or is unknown.
ùislig,(DU) *s.f.* Object of terror. Bu tu an ù. ! *what an awe-inspiring object you are !*
uisliginn, -e, *s. f.* Disturbance, confusion. 2 Rage, fury.
uisliun, -e, -ean, *s.f.* Sport, diversion, wantonness.
uist ! *int.* Silence ! hist ! hush ! hold your peace ! you don't say so !
uitbhlean,(DC) *s.m.* Orphan—*Skye.*
ula, -chan, *s.f.* Beard. 2 Rank or long grass. 3 Branches of trees. 4*Heavy, curled hair. 5 ††Clothes. Ri fead an u. na h-uamha, *whistling in the long grass of the cavern* ; 'u. aosda air 'uchd, *his aged beard on his breast.*
†ulabhard, -aird, *s.m.* Dwarf elder.
ulabur, *s.m.* Tail—*Arran.*
ulacan,(AF) *s.* Screech owl.
ulach,** -aich, *s.m.* Beard.
ulach,** *a.* Bearded.
uladh, *s.m.* Jerk. 2 see ula. 3 see ubhladh.
ulag, -aig, -an, *s.f.* Block, pulley. 2 Thick mixture of oatmeal and cold water, see ullag. 3 (DC) Swivel—*Uist.* 4††Snowball.
——ach, -aiche, *a.* Furnished with, of, or belonging to, blocks or pulleys. 2 Like a block or pulley.
ulaidh, -e, *pl.* -ean & -nean, *s.f.* Treasure. 2 Treasure-trove. 3 Pack-saddle. 4 Darling. 5 Waif. M' u. ! *my treasure* ; chaill sinn an t-sàr u., *we have lost the precious treasure.*
ulainn,* *s.m.* Charnel-house.
ulaith-faol, *s.m.* Wolf.
ulartaich, see ulfhartaich.
ulathach, see ultach.
ulbh ! *int.* You brute !
ulbhach,‡ -aich, *s.m.* Ashes—*Badenoch.*
ulbhag,(CR) *s.f.* Stone or boulder larger than one man can handle—*W. of Ross.* [Bulbhag in *Argyll.*]
ulc, see olc.
ulchadh,** -aidh, *s.m.* Beard.
ulfhart, -airt, *s.m.* Cry, roar, yell, howl of a dog.
———aich, *s.f.ind.* Howling, roaring. Làn ulfhairt, *full of howling.*
ulfhartair,** *s.m.* Sniveller.
ullabheist,* -e, -ean, *s.f.* see uile-bheist.
————eil,* see uile-bheisteil.
ullachadh, -aidh, *s.m.* Preparing, act of preparing. 2 Preparation, provision. 3 Accommodation. 4*Dressing, making ready. Ag u—, *pr pt.* of ullaich.
ullag, -aig, -an, *s.f.* Mouthful of meal. 2**Pugil. 3**Multure. 4 As much of meal or any pulverized substance as can be lifted between the thumb and two fingers. 5 Freshly bruised oatmeal worked into a handful with water, milk or whisky and eaten unbaked—*Caithness, Suth'd & Lewis* ; handful of oatmeal eaten dry in other parts. 6 (DMy) U. was made of barley grain as soon as reaped, dried in a pot till brown, then ground on the quern and mixed with hot water and a little salt, when it was very palatable—*Ness, Lewis.* In *Argyll,* ullag-shneachd is *a snowball* ; and, a' tilgeil ullagan, *throwing snowballs.*
ullaich, *pr.pt.* ag ullachadh, *v.a.* Prepare make ready. 2 Procure, provide. 3 Appoint. 4 Adjust, put in order. Ullaichibh 'ur cridhe chum an Tighearn, *prepare your hearts unto the Lord.*
———te, *past pt.* Prepared. 2 Provided. 3 Appointed, made ready, adjusted.
ullaiche, see udlaiche.
ullaid-sgriach,(AF) *s.* Screech-owl.
ullaidh,(AF) *v.* Owl.
——— adharcach,(AF) *s.* Horned owl.
ullain, for olluinn—*L. na F. 89. a. 3.*
ullamh, see ollamh.
ullamh, -aimhe, *a.* Ready, prepared, finished, done, over, in readiness. 2 Ready, prone to. U. ealamh, *ready and handy*—applied to persons having a smart bearing ; is u. le neach sin a dheanamh, *one is prone to do that* ; airgiod u., *ready money* ; am bheil thu u. ? *are you ready ?*
———achd, *s.f.ind.* Readiness, proneness, aptitude, aptness. 2 Completion, completeness. 3 Preparedness. 4 Promptness. 5 Facility.
———aich,* see ullaich.
———aichte, see ullaichte.
ullchabhagan,** *s.m.* Long-eared owl, horned owl, see comhachag-adharcaiche.
ulldach, see ultach.
———ail,(MS) *a.* Solitary.
ulldaich, *s.m.* Night stalker—*Suth'd.*
ulluchadh, see ullachadh.
ulluich, see ullaich.
———te, see ullaichte.
ulmhach,(AF) *s.* Wolf.
———adh, see ullachadh.
ultach, -aich, -aichean, *s. m.* Burden carried within the fold or grasp of the arms, armful. 2 Lapful. 3 Load. 4(CR) Burden on the back—*Arran.* 5‡‡Bosom. 6 Lap. 7* Bundle, faggot or truss, fit to be carried on the back—*Perthshire.* U. a dhroma, *as much as he can carry on his back* ; u. feoir, *an armful of grass;* rinn i 'adhart de 'n u. bu tioraime, *she made his pillow of the driest bundle (of grass.)*
ultag,(AF) *s.f.* Whinchat.
ultanaich,(CR) *s.f.* Slender, wiry-looking grass, the earliest that grows on the moors, called from its appearance, deer's-hair grass—*Suthd.*
ùltan,(CR) *Reay country* for annlan.
ultan alltan,(MS) *s.m.* Children's game "hot cockles."
†um, *prep,* see uim & uime.
umad, *prep.pron.* (mu+thu) About thee, upon thee. 2 Concerning thee, in reference to thee. 3 On thy account. Tilg t' fhalluinn u., *cast thy mantle about thee* ; a' labhairt u., *speaking about thee.*
ùmadail, -e, *a.* Sottish, boorish. 2 Unsocial.
umadh,** -aidh, *s.m.* Withe used to fasten the door of a cow-house.
umaibh, *prep.pron.* (mu+sibh) About you, regarding you. 2 Concerning you, in reference to you. 3 On your account. Cuiribh u., *cast about you* ; a' labhairt u., *speaking in reference to you* ; fo amharus u., *in doubt about you.*
ùmaidh, -ean, *s.m.* see ùmpaidh.
———, -e. *a.* see ùmpadail.
ùmaidheach, see ùmpadail.
—————d, *s.f.* Blockishness.
ùmaillt,**s.f.* Degrading submission of one's judgment to curry favour, obsequiousness.
———each,* -eiche, *a.* Meanly submissive to curry favour, fawning.
umainn, *prep.pron.* (mu+sinn) About us, around us. 2 Concerning us. 3 On our account. Dh' iadh iad u., *they surrounded us* ; ag ràdh u., *saying in reference to us.*
umairt,(AC) see iomairt.
umam, *prep. pron.* (mu+mi) About me. 2 Con-

cerning me. 3 On my account. An ann umam-sa ? *is it with reference to me ?*
ùmanta,(MS) *a.* Animal. 2 Absurd.
umar, -air, see amar.
umarlaid, *s.f.* Ronion, vulgar bulky female.
umastar, -air, *s.m.* Circumference.
umbadail,* -e, *a.* see ùmpadail.
umbaidh, see ùmpaidh.
um-dhruid, see ioma-dhruid.
um-ghlac, see ioma-ghlac.
umha, *s.m.ind.* Brass. 2 Copper. [umh*.]
——ch,** *a.* Brassy, brazen. 2 Of copper.
umhadair, -ean, *s.m.* Brazier.
————eachd,** *s.f.* Braziery, business of a copper-smith.
umha-ghràbhair,** *s.m.* Chalcographer.
umhail, *s.f.ind.* Heed, attention, care, consideration, advertence. 2 Doubt, suspicion. 2 Feeling. Na biodh u. agad da, *never mind him* ; gun u. do 'n lot 'na chliabh féin, *regardless of the wound in his own side* ; chuir mi an u., *I half suspected* ; 'dé 'n u. a th' agadsa ? *what business is it of yours ?* cha'n 'eil u., *there is no matter* or *business* ; cha do chuir mi u. air dad a bha tuathal, *I did not notice anything wrong.*
umhaill, see umhail.
————each, -eiche, *a.* Suspicious. 2 Advertent, scrupulous, careful, heedful, attentive.
————eachd, *s.f.* Suspiciousness. 2 Heedfulness, attentiveness, habit of attention.
umhailt, see ùmhal.
————eachd, *s.f.* see ùmhailteas.
ùmhailteas, -eis, *s. m.* Humility, obedience, tractability.
ùmhal, -aile, *a.* Submissive, obedient. 2 Humble, lowly, meek. 3 Obsequious fawning. Cho ù. ri luch fo spòg a' chait, *as submissive as a mouse under the cat's paw* ; u. an cridhe, *lowly in spirit* ; u. do 'n lagh, *obedient to the law.*
umh-ghràbhaladh,** *s.m.* Chalcography.
umhla, see ubhladh.
umhlach, see ubhlach.
———adh, see ubhladh.
ùmhlachadh, -aidh, *s. m.* Humbling, act of humbling. 2 Humiliation, submission. 3 Obeying, act of obeying. 4 (MS)Chastisement. 5 Homage. Ag ù—, *pr.pt.* of ùmhlaich.
ùmhlachail,** *a.* Liable to penalty or fine, penal.
ùmhlachd, *s.f.* Obedience. 2 Humility, obsequiousness. 3 Meekness. 4 Obeisance, salutation, homage. 5**Submission, submissiveness. 6**Practice of imposing penalties. 7** Taxation. Dean t' ù., *make your obeisance* ; u. a' chreidimh, *the obedience of faith;* rinn e ù. dha, *he made obeisance to him, saluted him.*
ùmhladair,** *s.m.* Inflicter.
umhladh, see ubhladh.
ùmhladh, *s.m.* Forfeiture, fine. 2 see ùmhlachadh & ùmhlachd.
ùmhlagh, *s.m.* Fine—*Argyll.* (ùnlagh)
ùmhlaich, *pr.pt.* ag ùmhlachadh, *v.a. & n.* Humble, subdue, conquer. 2 Obey, submit. 3** Amerce. 4 Humiliate. 5 Chastise.
————te, *past pt.* of ùmhlaich. Humbled, subdued.
umhraisg, -ean, *s.m.* see ùruisg.
————each, see ùruisgeach.
umpa, *prep.pron.* (mu+iad) About them. 2 Of, or concerning them, respecting them. Labhair e u., *he spoke about them.*
ùmpadail, -e, *a.* Humdrum, doltish, clownish, boorish. 2 Vulgar, ignorant. 3 Foggy. 4 Cowardly. 5* Very stupid.
ùmpadalachd, *s.f.* Grossness, boorishness.
ùmpaidh, -ean, *s.m.* Dunce, boor, clown, rude idiot, dolt, blockhead, fool, hum-drum, fellow of vulgar manners. 2 Coward. 'San duine chòir cha bhi ach ù., *the worthy man shall be deemed a boor.*
umpair, -ean, *s.m.* Umpire, arbiter, judge. 2 Moderator.
————each, *a.* Like, of, or belonging to an umpire or arbiter.
————eachd, *s.f* Office of an umpire, arbitration.
urmadh, *N.Argyll* for iomradh.
umurlaid,** *s.f.* Vulgar, bulky female.
un, *Skye & Perth* for chun.
unach,** -aich, *s.m.* Bleaching. 2 Washing.
ùnaich,** *s.f.* Hurry, bustle, confusion, disturbance. 2 Struggle, rivalry. Le móran ù., *with much bustle.*
unamaid,** *s.f.* Ointment, salve.
undais,** *s.* Winch, windlass.
unfairt,** *v.n.* Toss, wallow, tumble.
————,** *s.f.* Tossing, wallowing, tumbling.
ung, *pr.pt.* ag ungadh, *v.a.* Anoint, oil. 2 Besmear, daub. Dh' u. thu mo cheann, *thou hast anointed my head.*
unga,(CR) *s.m.* Ounce-land, 20-penny-land, or one-eighth of a mark-land.
unga,** s.m. Brass, copper. 2 Ingot.
·——, *prov.* for ungta.
ungach, *a.* Brassy.
ungadh, -aidh, *s.m.* Anointing, act of anointing. 2 Unction, ointment, unguent. Ag u—, *pr.pt.* of ung. U. deireannach, *or* u.-bàis, *extreme unction.*
ungaidh, *fut.aff.a.* of ung.
ungaidh,(CR) *a.* Mouldy, rusty—*Suth'd.*
ungail,** *a.* Balsamic.
ungar, *fut. pass.* of ung.
ungta, *past pt.* of ung. Anointed. 2 Besmeared, bedaubed.
unlagh,†† s.m. Fine, penalty.
unnan, *s. Creich, Suth'd* for aon.
unudais, *s.f.* Winch, windlass.
————each, *a.* Of, or belonging to, a windlass.
unnlar,* see ùrlar.
ùnnsa, -idhean & ùnnsachan, *s.m.* Ounce.
ùnradh, -aidh, *s.m.* Adversity.
ùnsa, see ùnnsa.
untas, -ais, see unndais.
———ach, see unndais-each.
ùp, *pr.pt.* ag ùpadh, *v.a.* Push, jostle, push out.
ùpadh, -aidh, *s.m.* Pushing, act of pushing or jostling. 2 Push, thrust. Ag ù—, *pr.pt.* of ùp.
upag, *s. f.* Trifling superstitious observance—JGC. S. 229.
ùpag, -aig, -an, *s.f.* Slight push, shove, thrust.
——ach, -aiche, *a.* That pusheth or thrusteth away, shoving, pushing, thrusting.
·——aich,** *s. f.* Pushing, shoving, thrusting, jostling.
·——aich,** *v.a.* Push, shove, thrust, jostle. 2 Jolt.
ùpaidh, see ùmpaidh.
upaig,(DMK) *s.m & f.* Old and useless person, one regarded as being in the way. Tha e 'na u. anns an rathad, *he is a lumber in the way—Caithness.*
upainn, -e, -ean, *s.f.* see uipinn.
ùpairneach, -eiche, *a.* Bustling excessively.
————————d,** Bustle, noise. 2 Continued or frequent bustle or noise.
ùprait, see ùbrait.
————each, see ùbraideach.
ùr, ùire, *a.* Fresh, new, recent. 2 Flourishing, vigorous. 3 Young, youthful. 4 Beautiful, fair. 5 *Novel, curious.

A' ghealach ùr, *the new moon* ; sgadan ùr, *a fresh herring* ; im ùr, *fresh butter* ; ni sam bith ùr, *anything novel or curious* ; as ùr, *a second time, afresh* ; thòisich iad as ùr, *they commenced anew* ; trusgan ùr, *a new suit of clothes* ; oiteag ùr nan-sliabh, *the fresh breeze of the mountains* ; ùr nodha, *quite new* ; sgaoil cuirm as ùr, *the feast was spread a second time;* righ ùr, *a new king.*

ur, -achan, *s.f.* Child. 2 Person. Ur bheag, *an infant.*

ur, *s.m.* Tail. 2 Harm. 3 Border, brink.

ùr,* *adv.* Newly. Dh' ùr-thòisich iad, *they have newly begun.*

ur, *poss. pron.* see bhur.

ur,§ *s.* Heath—*Fortingall,* not common elsewhere. 2 Gaelic name of the letter U. (also uir.)

†ur, *s.m.* Fire. 2 Mould. 3 Beginning.

675. Ura bhallach.

ura bhallach, -aich, *s. f.* Devil's-bit scabious blue bonnets. blue buttons—*scabiosa sucissa.*

uracag,(AH)-aig,-an,*s.f.* Thole-pin—*N. Lochaber,* see bàta, No. 39*b*, p. 76. 2 Belaying-pin.

uracagan, *s.pl.* Thole-pins, see bàta, No 39*b*, p.76.

†ùrach, -aich, *s.m.* Earth. 2 Beginning. 3 Contention. 4 Bottle. 5 Pail. 6 Small tub. 7 (CR) Change, alteration,—used as "atharrachadh" is sometimes, but with the sense of newness rather than mere change. Chuir e air ù. dhòighe, *he put it in a new way—Perthsh.*

ùrach,* see ùireach.

ùrach, -aiche, *a.* Earthy, dusty.

ùrachadh, -aidh, *s.m.* Renewing, act of renewing. 2 Refreshing, act of refreshing. 3 Refreshment, freshening, renewal, recommencing, recommencement. Ag ù—, *pr.pt.* of ùraich.

urachair, see furachair.

ùrach-bhallach,§ -aich, -aichean, *s.f.* Spotted orchis—*orchis maculata.*

ùrachd, *s.f.ind.* Newness, novelty. 2 Freshness. 3 Strangeness. Am bheil ù. naidheachd agad? *have you any news?*

urachdagan, for uracagan, *s.f.* Thole-pins.

ùrach-nabullaich, see ura-bhallach.

ùrad, -aid, *s.m.* Newness, degree of newness. 2 Greenness. A' dol an ù., *increasing in greenness.*

urad, see uthard & uiread.

ùradh,(MMcL) *s. m.* Oil or grease put in wool. Ag ù. na cloimhe, *oiling the wool.*

uradh,(DMK) *s.m.* Stale urine used for washing on account of the ammonia it contains—*Caithness.* 2(DU) Water in which clothes have been washed. 3 (DU) Dirty water wrung out of wool.

ùrag, -aige, *a.* Nice, bland.

——, -aig, -an, *s.f.* Nice, bland young woman. 2 Little child.

uraghusach,** *a.* Haughty.

†uraiceachd, *s.f.* Accidence, primer, rudiments of education.

ùraich, *pr.pt.* ag ùrachadh, *v.a. & n.* Renew. 2 Be renewed. 3 Refresh, recreate. 4 Become fresh or green. 5** Strive. 6 Invigorate. Dh' ù. e mo chràdh, *he renewed my torment* ; ach cha'n ù. mo gheug, *but my branch shall never become green* ; dh' ù. an deoch e, *the potion refreshed him* ; 'nuair a dh' ùraicheas an strì, *when the battle renews.*

——te, *past pt.* Renewed, made fresh, refreshed.

uraidh, see uiridh.

urail, -e, *a.* Flourishing, young, gay, see ùrar.

ùrair, see ùrar.

——eachd, see ùrarachd.

ùraisg, see ùruisg.

uralachd, see ùraireachd.

ural,** *s.m.* Proposal.

uran, -ain, *s.m.* Cold bath. see 2 furan.

——ach, see furanach.

†ùranach, *a.* Ignoble. 2 Conversant.

ùranach,** *s m.* Novice (in religion.)

ùranach, -aich, *s.m.* Upstart.

ùranachd,** *s.f.* Condition of an upstart. 2 Cold bathing. 3 Conversation.

uranta, see urranta.

ùrar, *a.* Flourishing, young, gay, blooming. 2 Fresh. 3 Green. 4 Juicy. 'San iarmailt ù., *in the fresh firmament* ; a' choillteach ù., *the green woodland.*

——achd, *s. f.* Freshness, newness. 2 Greenness, verdure. 3 Juiciness. 4 Coolness. 5 Vividness.

——achd-na-bà, (AF) *s. f.* Fat of the cow. 2 Milk, cream, butter. 3 Neat foot oil.

urard,** *a.* Very high.

——,** *s.m.* High place, high ground.

urball, see earball.

ur-bhallach, -aich, see ura-bhallach.

ùr-bharail,(MS) *s.* After-thought.

ùr-bharr,(MS) *s.* After-math.

ùr-bharrach,** -aich, *s.* Green branches, green foliage.

ur-bheachd, -an, *s.m.* New view, second thought or view, after-thought.

ùr-bheist,(AF) *s.* Monster.

ùr-bhlàith,***a.* Fruitful, abounding in blossoms.

ùr-bhlàth, -àith, -an, *s. m.* Blossom, flower. 2 Fresh blossom.

ùr-bhreith, -e, -ean, *s.f.* New birth, regeneration. 2 Recent birth.

ùr-bhuidh, -e, -ean, *s.f.* Rustling noise, tumbling, tossing.

urc,(AF) *s.* Sow. 2 Whale. 3 *s.m.* Enclosure, fold.

urcag, see uracag.

urchaid, -e, -ean, *s.f.* Evilness, evil, damage. 2 Venereal disease—*MacMhaigh. Alasdair.*

urchail, *s.pl.* Fetters, chains.

urchaill, -e, -ean, *s.f.* Furrow-board or mould board of a plough.

urchailte, *a.* Fettered, chained.

urchair, -e & -each, *pl.* urchraichean, *s.f.* Shot. 2 Cast, throw, push. 3 **Report of a gun. 4 Sudden sally or movement. 5 Cartridge. U. cloiche, *a stone cast, throw with a stone or hammer* ; beul ri u. gunna air falbh, *about a gun-shot off* ; thug e u. dha, *he gave him a violent push or throw* ; leig u., *fire, shoot at.*

ùrchair,* *s.f.* Mould-board of a plough—*West.*

urchaireach, -eiche, *a.* Shooting, that shoots. 2 Pushing, that pushes or throws.

————d, *s.f.* Shooting, throwing, casting, as of a stone, pushing, amusement of shooting or firing.

urchall, -aill, -an, *s. m.* Shackles, fetters. 2 Chain. 3 Hinderance. 4**Spaniel.

——ach, -aich, *s.f.* Heifer 1½ years old.

——ach, -aiche, *a.* Having on fetters or shackles. 2 Like a fetter or shackle.

urchallachadh, -aidh, *s.m.* Fettering, act of binding with fetters. Ag u—, *pr.pt.* of urchallaich.
urchallaich, *pr.pt.* ag urchallachadh, *v.a.* Bind with fetters or manacles.
————-te, *past pt.* Bound with fetters or manacles.
urchasg, -aisg, -an, *s.m.* Physic. 2 Preservative against evil. 3 Antidote.
urchasgach,** *a.* Antidotal.
urcheann,(MMcL) *s.* Wooden hinge on a chest, &c.
ùr-chleas, -a, -an, *s.m.* Feat, deed. 2 Ludicrous or strange deed. 3 Clever action.
————ach, -aiche, *a.* Nimble, active, quick at feats. 2 Performing ludicrous or strange actions.
————achd, *s.f.* Nimbleness, activity. 2 Performing of strange or ludicrous actions. 3 Legerdemain, juggling.
————aiche,** *s. m.* Adept in legerdemain, juggler, conjurer.
urchoid, -e, *s.f.* Hurt, harm, detriment, mischief. 2 Calamity, loss, accident. 3 Adversity. 4 Violence. 5**Complaint. 6††Bustle. An là t' u., *in the day of thy calamity* ; le u., *with violence.* [* says †.]
urchoideach, -eiche, *a.* Injurious, hurtful. 2 Calamitous. 3 Adverse, detrimental, mischievous.
————d,** *s.f.* Noxiousness.
ùr-choille, -lltean, *s.f.* Green wood.
ùr-choillteach, -eiche, *a.* Abounding in green woods.
urchoir, see urchair.
————each, see urchaireach.
————eachd, see urchaireachd.
ur-chosg, *s.m.* see ur-chasg.
————ach, see ur-chasgach.
————ais,(MS) *s.* After-cost.
ùr-chràdh, -aidh, *s.m.* Recent distress.
————ach, -aiche, *a.* Wretched, keenly grieved.
ùr-chrann, -ainn, *s.f.* Blooming or fresh tree, green tree. 2 Fresh branch, green branch. 3 Flourishing tree. Mar ù. uaine, *like a flourishing green tree.*
————ach, -aiche, *a.* Abounding in blooming trees.
ùr-chriosdaidh,** *s.* Catechumen.
urchuid, see urchoid.
————each, see urchoideach.
urchuir, see urchair.
ur-chullach, see ur-challach.
urchur, -uir, -an, see urchair.
urcuil, see uir-chuil.
†urdail, *s.f.* Collection, large share.
ùr-dharag,** *s. f.* Young oak, flourishing oak. Sgaoilidh do chliù-sa mar ù., *thy fame shall spread like a young oak.* [**ùr-dharaig.]
ùr-dhathaichte, *a.* New-coloured.
ùr-dhubhadh, -aidh, -ean, *s.m.* Eclipse, darkening. Ù. na gréine, *an eclipse of the sun.*
ùr-fhailteach, *a.* Anecdotal, jocular, cheerful in conversation—*Sàr-Obair.*
ùr-fhallain, -e, *a.* Fresh and healthy.
ùr-fhalluinn,** *s.f.* New robe or garment.
ùr-fhàs, -àis, *s.m.* Bloom, sprout, shoot. 2 Offspring. 3 New growth, fresh growth. 4 Bud.
————, *v.a.* Grow again, bud forth, sprout, shoot. Ùr-fhàsaidh i, *it (the tree) will grow again.*
————, *s.m.* After-math, growing again. 2 State of growing again. Ag ù—, *pr. pt.* of ùr-fhàs.
————ach, *a.* Casting sprouts or buds. 2 Producing sprouts, buds or shoots.
ùr-fhiachan, *s.* After-cost.
ùr-fhoghar, *s.m.* Autumn.

ùr-ghàirdeachas, -ais, *s.m.* Rejoicing, great or sincere rejoicing or joy. 2 Congratulation.
us-ghàirdich,(MS) *v.n.* Overjoy.
urgais,** *s.f.* Exchange. 2 Alteration.
†urghais, see urgais.
urghart, -airt, *s.m.* Bad luck. 2 Misfortune. 3 Victory.
ur-ghlaine,(MS) *s.* Maidenhead.
ur-ghorm,** *a.* Freshly-green. Ag ionaltradh air an fhàsach ù., *grazing on the freshly vivid field.*
ùr-ghreannachd,** *s.f.* Puberty.
urgra,** *s.m.* Battle. 2 Loss.
ùrla, *s.m. ind.* Face, front, forehead. 2 Countenance, visage. 3 Hair, lock of hair. 4 Breast, chest. 5 Aspect. 6 Bottom. 7 Place lying low among hills. M' ù. ag éirigh àrd, *my breast rising high.* [* says †.]
ùrla, see ùrlar.
ùr-labhair, *pr.pt.* ag ùr-labhairt, *v.n.* Speak eloquently.
————t, *s.f.* Act of speaking eloquently, eloquence rhetoric, oratory. Ag ù—, *pr. pt.* of ùr-labhair.
————teach,‡‡ -eiche, *a.* Eloquent, oratorical, rhetorical.
————teachd, *s.f.ind.* Eloquence, rhetoric, oratory.
————tear, -ir, -an, *s.m.* Orator, rhetorician, graceful speaker.
ùr-labhrach, -aiche, see ùr-làbhairteach.
ùr-labhradh, see ùr-labhairt. Anns gach ù., *in all utterance.*
ùr-labhraiche, -an, see ùr-labhairtear.
urlach,** *a.* Having long hair. 2‡ Having ringlets or curls. Cas-u., *curled.*
urladh, -aidh, -ean, see urla.
ùrlaich, *pr.pt.* ag ùrlachadh, *v.a. & n.* Nauseate, hate, detest, turn from in disgust.
†urlaidh, *s.f.* Skirmish.
ùrlaigh, *v.a.* Turn (disgustfully)—*Argyll.*
ùrlaim, -e, *s.f.* Readiness, preparation.
ùr-laimh, -e, *a.* Neat, quick, expert, ready-handed. 2 Quick in reading.
————,** *s.f.* Readiness, preparation.
————eachd, *s.f.* Quickness, expertness, ready-handedness.
urlainn,(AH) *s.f.* Fore-part of a ship. 2§Staff of a spear. 3 The countenance. 4 Beauty. *Sàr-Obair.*
urlamaich,** *v.a.* Prepare, make ready.
ùr-làmhachadh, -aidh, *s.m.* Act of making ready, preparing. Ag ù—, *pr.pt.* of ùr-làmhaich.
ùr-làmhachas, -ais, see ùr-làmhas.
ùr-làmhaich, *pr.pt.* ag ùr-làmhachadh, *v.a.* Make ready, prepare.
————e,** *s.* Possessor.
ùrlamhas, -ais, *s.m.* Possession. 2 Authority, supreme power. 3 Captivity.
ùr-làn,** *a.* Very full.
ùrlann, -ainn, -an, *s.m.* Staff. 2 Spear.
ùrlar, -air, -an, *s.m.* The lowest part. 2 Floor of a house. 3 Ground-floor. 4 Earth. 5 Floor of earth or clay. 6* Layer, course, vein, as in a mine. 7 Theme or groundwork of a bagpipe tune. 8 Low place or bottom among hills. 9 Bottom (inside) of a cart. 10**Pavement. Ù. arbhair, *a corn-floor* ; cuir ù. mu seach 'san dùnain, *put course about in the dunghill* ; air an ù., *on the floor* ; ù. chlach, *a pavement of stones.* [Not used in the sense of *floor* in *W. of Ross*, except as ùrlar-bualaidh, *a threshing-floor.* If the floor is of earth, clay, or stone, *làr* is used, if of wood either upstairs or downstairs, it is called *lobht*—CR. At Loch Ewe *ùrlar* is used for floor to a limited extent, as, chuir e car dheth air an ùr-

lar. Ù. a' bhaile, is the lower part of a township next the sea—DU.]
ùrlarach,†† *a.* Floored.
ùrlarach,** -aich, *s.m.* Close housekeeper.
ùrlarachadh,** -aidh, *s.m.* Act of flooring or laying a floor. Ag ù—, *pr.pt.* of ùrlaraich.
ùrlaraich, *v.a.* Floor, lay a floor, pave.
————e,** *s.m.* One who lays a floor, one who mines or prepares earth or clay for a floor.
————te,** *past pt.* Floored.
urlatach,** -aich, *s.m.* Tumbler, stage-player.
urlataidh,** *a.* Agility. Fear u., *a tumbler.* §
ùr-loisgeach, -eiche, *a.* Keen, zealous, fervent, causing or promoting zeal.
ur-losgadh, -aidh, *s.m.* Fervour, zeal, keenness.
ùr-luachair,§ *s.f.* Soft rush, see luachair bhog. 2 Green rushes, young rushes.
ùrluinn, -e, -ean, *s.f.* Beauty. 2 Fore-part of a ship. 3 see ùrla.
urmach,** -aich, *s.m.* Armoury.
ùr-mhaiseach, -eiche, *a.* Beautiful, graceful handsome.
ùr-mhoireachd, see ùralachd.
ùr-mheangan,** -ain, *s.m.* Young branch, twig. Ùr-mheangain nan càrn, *the young branches of the rocks.*
ùrmhor, -oire, *a.* see ùrail & ùrar.
ùrnuich, see ùrnuigh.
ùrnuigh, -e, -ean, *s.f.* Prayer, prayers, petition. Ag ù., *or* ri ù., *praying ;* miltean u. 'gad leanachd, *thousands of prayers following thee;* dean ù., *pray.*
†urphaisin, *s.* Cancer.
urr, *contr.* for urradh.
urr, see ùr.
urr,* for urra.
urra, see oirre.
urra, see urrainn.
urra,** *a.* Able, capable.
urra, -idhean, *s.f.* Person. 2 Infant. 3 **Urchin. 4 Surety. 5** Power, strength. 6** Good author. 7**Authority. 8** Defendant at law. 9** Chieftain. 10 Body. 11 see urradh. [†† gives *pl.* also -achan.]
U. a chuireas leam, *a person who will aid me.* [It has various meanings in *W.Isles.* An e seo an u. bheag ? *is this the little one ?* phòs e nighean u. mhóir, *he married the daughter of a nobleman ;* feumaidh tu an u. a dh' innis sin dhuit a thoirt dhòmh-sa, *you must give me the authority who told you that ;* 's e a bha 'n u. an crodh a chumail as an arbhar, *he was the one responsible for keeping the cattle out of the corn.* In these last two examples it must be connected with " urras " or " urrainn."
urracag, -aig, -an, *s.f.* see uracag.
urrach,* -aidh, *s.m.* Pull, haul, pulling. 2 see urrainn.
ùrrachail,(MS) *a.* Authentical.
urrachd,* *s.f.* Dependence, reliance. Cha ruig thu leas u. a dheanamh as a sin, *you need not put any reliance on that ;* an u. riut-sa, *relying on you ;* an u. a chosnaidh, *depending on his industry ;* am u.-sa, *in dependence on me ;* cha'n 'eil mi 'nam u., *I am not able.*
urrachdag, see urracag.
urrad, see uthard & uiread.
urradh, -aidh, -ean, *s.m.* Author, authority, promoter or beginner of anything. 2 Power, ability. 3 Defendant at law. 4* Owner, proprietor. Ann an taigh urraidh mhòir, *in a great person's house ;* cò is u. dhuit ? *who is your authority ?* cha'n 'eil sgeul gun u. agam, *my version is not without authority ?* cò is u. dha seo ? *who is the owner of this ?* cha robh caora riamh gun u., *a sheep never was without an owner.*
urradh, for urrainn. Cha'n urradh dhomh, *I cannot.*
urrag,†† -aig, -an, *s.f.* Infant, see urag. 2(AF) Urchin, hedgehog.
urraichd, *a.* Excellent, notably good—*Rob Donn.*
urrail, -e, *a.* Forward, impudent, bold, confident, self-sufficient.
urraim, *gen.sing.* of urram.
urrainn, *a.* Able, capable. Na'm b' u. mi, *if I were able ;* ma's u. mi, *if I can ;* an u. iad ? *are they able ?* an u. sin a bhi ? *can that be ?*
————, *s.f.* Author. 2 Authority. 3 Ability, power. 4 Stay, support. Sgeul gun u., *a tale without an author ;* na bi 'nad u. anns a' bhréig, *be not the author of a lie ;* cha'n u. dhuit éirigh, *you cannot rise;* cha'n 'eil mi am u., *I am not able, I am not fit.*
————each,(MS) *a.* Adequate.
————eachd,** *s.f.* Ableness, efficacy.
urraisge, -an, see ùruisg.
————an, *s. pl.* Inundations, overflowings, spates—*Sàr-Obair.*
urralach,†† *a.* Forward, impudent.
urralachd, *s. f.* Forwardness, boldness, impudence, confidence, self-sufficiency.
urram, -aim, *s.m.* Respect, reverence, deference, worship. 2 Honour, dignity. 3*Precedence, preference. 4 Significance, signification.
'Nam meadhon bha u. do 'n righ, *in their midst was reverence for the king ;* air son urraim do t' fhacal-sa, *out of deference to your word ;* uat-sa tha 'teachd saoibhreas agus u., *from thee proceed riches and honour ;* bheir mi an t-u. dhuit air na chunnaic mi riamh, *I will give you the preference over all I ever saw ;* an t-u. do 'n laoch ! *precedence to the hero ! a,* toirt urraim, *giving honour.*
————ach, -aiche, *a.* Noble, honourable. 2 Reverend, venerable, worthy of respect, distinguished, worshipful. 3 Honorary. 4 Principal. 5 Respectful, submissive. Ball u., *an honorary member ;* sibh-se a's urramaiche de 'n treud, *you, the principal of the flock ;* tha 'ainm u., *his name is revered ;* rinn e gu h-u., *he did it masterly ;* trì nithean u., urram na Trianaid, urram na cléire is urram na h-aoise, *three noble things, reverence for the Trinity, reverence for the clergy and reverence for the aged.*
urramachadh, -aidh, s. m. Honouring, act of honouring, reverencing. 2 Obeying. 3 Homage. Ag u—, *pr.pt.* of urramaich.
urramachd, *s.f.* Nobility, nobleness, honourableness. 2* Reverence, respectfulness. 3 Respectability. 4 Homage, submission.
urramaich, *pr.pt.* ag urramachadh, *v.a.* Honour, revere, reverence, respect. 2 Worship, adore. 3 Distinguish.
————e, *comp.* of urramach. Bha e na b' u., *he was more honourable.*
————te, *past pt.* of urramaich. Honoured, revered, respected.
urramail,** *a.* Excellent.
urramair,** *s.m.* Admirer.
urranta, -ainte, *a.* Bold, daring, dauntless, intrepid, audacious. 2 Powerful, capable. 3 Self-sufficient, confident in one's own strength or capacity. Fir mheanmnach u., *high-spirited and powerful men ;* gu h-u., *adequately.*
————chd, *s.f.* Boldness, daring, intrepidity, dauntlessness. 2 *Audacity, presumption. 3 Confidence in one's own strength or capacity, self-sufficiency.
urras, -ais, -an, *s.m.* Surety, security. 2 Cautioner, one who becomes bail for another. 3 Bond, insurance, warrant, bail, caution. 4 Boldness, assurance. 5 Bondsman, bondswo

man. Cò a théid an u. ort? *who will become security for you?* théid mis' anu. ort-sa, *I will warrant you*; ma tha thuan u., *if you are surety*; cha'n fheàrr an t. na 'n t-earras, *the bail is not better than the principal*; cha'n 'eil u. a dhìth orm, *I want no security*; théid mis' an u. air do shon, *I will go bail for you.*
urrasach, -aiche, *a.* Trustworthy, secure, sure. 2 Bold, daring, self-confident. 3 Requiring bail or security.
———d, *s.f.* Trustworthiness. 2 Practice of becoming bail. 3 Insurance. 4 Boldness, intrepidity. 5 Self-confidence, assumption.
urrasaich,* *v.a.* Insure, bail.
urrasail, -e, *a.* Confident, secure. 2**Bailable. Cionta u., *a bailable offence.*
urrasair, -ean, *s.m.* Insurer.
urrasanta,(MS) *a.* Bailable.
urr'-eigin, *s.m.* Somebody.
urras-teine, *s.m.* Fire-insurance, fire-policy. Oifig-urras-teine, *fire-office.*
urrlach,** *a.* Having thick or bushy hair.
urs', see ursag.
ursa, -nnan, *s.m.* see ursainn.
ursa,†† *s.m.* Bear—*Lhuyd.*
ursach,** *a.* Bearish. 2 Full of bears.
———d,** *s.f.* Bearishness. 2 Bearish temper.
ursag,(AF) *s.f.* She-bear. 2 Little bear, young bear.
ursan,(AF) -ain, *s.m.* He-bear. 2 Defender.
ursainn, *gen.sing.* of ursann.
ursainn, -ean, *s.m.* Door-post, side of a door. 2 Pillar of a gate. 3 Jamb. 4‡‡Ruler of a battle. 5‡‡Ranks of a battle. 6 Support, prop.
ursainn-chatha,** *s.m.* Support in time of war. 2 Bulwark in battle. 3 Chief, champion. 4 Ranks of an army in battle-order. Chì mi trì ursanna-chatha, *I see three champions*; bris ear leis ursanna-chatha, *the ranks of battle shall be broken by him.*
ursan,** -ain, *s.m.* Defender.
ursann, -ainn, -an, see ursainn.
———ach, *a.* Having door-posts.
ursgar,** -air, *s.m.* Loud bawl.
ursgartach,** *a.* Sweeping cleanly.
ursgartadh, -aidh, *s.m.* Sweeping clean. 2 Driving away, as of cattle from grass or corn. 3 **Sweepstakes.
ùr-sgeul, -sgeòil, -an, *s.m.* Tale, romance, novel, 2 Recent account. 3 Tale of recent times, modern tale.
ùr-sgeulach, -aiche, *a.* Tale-telling, fabulous, romantic, rehearsing tales. 2 Bringing recent intelligence.
———d, *s.f.* see ùr-sgeul.
ùr-sgeulaiche, -an, *s.m.* Fabulist, novelist, one who relates tales of modern times, romancer.
ùr-sgeulail,** *a.* Fabulous.
ursluig,** *v.* Disgorge.
ursnaidhim,** *s.m.* Pin or jack to fasten the cords of a harp.
ùr-sneachd, *s.m.* Fresh snow, new-laid snow. Mar ù. air barraibh gheug, *like new-laid snow on the branches.*
ùr-speal, *v.a.* Cut or mow down quickly.
———ach,‡‡ -aiche, *a.* New-scythed or -mowed. 2**Cutting or mowing down quickly.
———achd,** *s.f.* Process of cutting or mowing down quickly.
———adh, -aidh, *s.m.* Act of mowing or cutting down quickly. Ag ù—, *pr.pt.* of ùr-speal.
———aiche,** *s.m.* One who cuts or mows down. 2 Destroyer.
urstan,(MMcL) *s.m.* Feast when a child is born —*Lewis.*
ursuinn, see ursann.
†ursul, -uil, *s.m.* Pair of tongs.

ùr-thalmhainn,§ *s.* Black-spleenwort, see dubhchasach 2§ *Asplenium viride.*
ùr-thoiseach, -ich, *s.m.* The very beginning. 2 Noviciate.
ùr-uaine,§ *s.* Laurel, bay-tree, see labhras. The *ùr-chraobh uaine* mentioned in Psalm xxxvii, is supposed to be the rose-bay (*nerium oleander*) it being very common in Palestine, while the common laurel is very scarce there.
uruis-bacan,(DC) *s.m.* Top of house-walls inside —*Harris & Uist.* (anainn in most places.)
ùruisg, -ean, *s.m.* Being supposed to haunt lonely and sequestered places, water-god. 2 Brownie. 3 Diviner, one who foretells future events. 4*Savage ugly-looking fellow. 5(AF) Bear. 6(MMcL) Sloven, slut.

The ùruisg had the qualities of man and spirit curiously commingled. He had a peculiar fondness for solitude at certain seasons of the year. About the end of harvest he became more sociable, and hovered about farmyards, stables and cattle-houses. He had a particular fondness for the products of the dairy, and was a fearful intruder on milkmaids, who made regular libations of milk or cream to charm him off, or to procure his favour. He could be seen only by those who had the second sight; yet I have heard of instances where he made himself visible to persons not so gifted. He is said to have been a jolly personable being, with a broad blue bonnet, flowing yellow hair, and a long walking-staff. Every manor-house had its ùruisg, and in the kitchen, close by the fire, was a seat which was left unoccupied for him. The house of a proprietor on the banks of the Tay is, even to this day, believed to have been haunted by this sprite, and a particular apartment therein has been for centuries called Seòmar Bhrùnaidh (Brownie's room.) When irritated through neglect or disrespectful treatment, he would not hesitate to become wantonly mischievous. He was notwithstanding, rather gainly and good-natured than formidable. Though, on the whole, a lazy, lounging hobgoblin, he would often bestir himself on behalf of those who understood his humours, and suited themselves thereto. When in this mood, he was known to perform many arduous exploits in kitchen, barn and stable, with marvellous precision and rapidity. These kind turns were done without bribe, fee or reward, for the offer of any one of these would banish him for ever. Kind treatment was all that he wished for, and it never failed to procure his favour. In the northern parts of Scotland the ùruisg's disposition was more mercenary. Brand, in his description of Zetland, observes, "that not above forty or fifty years ago almost every family had a brownie, or evil spirit, so called, which served them, to which they gave a sacrifice for his service; as when they churned their milk, they took a part thereof, and sprinkled every corner of the house with it for Brownie's use; likewise, when they brewed, they had a stone which they called Brownie's stane, wherein there was a little hole, into which they poured some wort for a sacrifice to Brownie. They also had stacks of corn which they called Brownie's stacks, which, though they were not bound with straw ropes, or in any way fenced as other stacks used to be, yet the greatest storm of wind was not able to blow away straw off them." The brownies seldom discoursed with man, but they held frequent and affectionate converse with one another. They had their general assemblies too, and on these occasions they commonly selected for their rendezvous the rocky recesses of some remote torrent, whence their loud voices, mingling with the water's roar, carried to the ears of wondering superstition detached parts of their unearthly colloquies. In a certain district of the Highlands, Peallaidh an spùit, Slochdaill a' chùirt, and Brùnaidh an easain, were names of note at those congresses, and they still live in legends which continue to amuse old age and infancy.—**

ùruisgeach,** *a.* Like a brownie. 2 Haunted by brownies.

'us, see agus.

us,* *s.m.* Impudence, presumption. Na bitheadh a dh' us agad, *presume not, dare not.*

†us, *s.m.* News. 2 Story.

usa, (fhusa) *comp.* of furasda. Easier, easiest. Is u. ràdh na chur an gnìomh, *it is easier said than done.*

usachd, *s.f.* see fusachd.

usad, -aid, *s.m.* see fusad.

usadh, see usa.

usaid,* -e, -ean, *s.f.* Querulousness, aptness to complain with any or a very slight reason. 2 **Use.

——each,* -eiche, *a.* Queruleus, too apt to complain.

usaideachd,* *s.f.* Querulousness, aptness to complain or weep for little or no reason.

usca, see ucas.

usg ! usg ! *int.* Call to a dog to drive away cattle—*Perthshire.*

usga,(AC) *a.* Holy, sacred. 2 *s.* see usgar.

usgadh,** -aidh, *s.m.* Goose-grease.

usgaidh ! (CR) *int.* Call to a dog to drive away cattle—*Perthshire.*

usgaidh, see uisgidh.

————eachd, see uisgidheachd.

ùsgaireach,(MS) *a.* Armillary.

usgar, -air & usgrach, *pl.* -an & usgraichean, *s.m.* Jewel, any ornament. 2 Bracelet. 3 Pearl. 4 Necklace. 5 Square. 6 Present. 7 Bell on liquor. U. de 'n òr, *an ornament of gold;* thug e leis usgraichean, *he took jewels with him;* le usgraichibh, *with jewels.*

u.-bhràghad, necklace. 2 Jewel for the neck.

u.-làimhe, bracelet, jewel for the hand or wrist.

u.-mheur, jewelled ring.

usgarach,** -aichean, *s.m.* Separation. 2 Jewellery.

usgarach, -aiche, *a.* Ornamented with laces or jewels.

usgaraiche, -an, *s.m.* Jeweller.

usgaraidh,** *s.f.* Jewellery.

usgartadh,(CR) *s.m.* Act of driving away cattle, &c., as from hay or corn.

usgartaich, *v.a.* Drive slowly, as cattle.

usgraichean, *pl.* of usgar.

usgraidh, see usgaraidh.

usgus ! see usg ! usg !

†uslainn,** *s.f.* Play, sport.

†uslainneach,** *a.* Cheerful, brisk, merry. 2 Nimble. Gu h-u., *cheerfully.*

ùspag, -aig, -an, *s.f.* Push. 2 see ospag.

uspag,(CR) *s.f.* Start aside, shy. Thug an t-each u. gu taobh, *the horse started aside, shied —Suth'd.*

ùspagach, see ospagach.

uspair, -ean, *s.m.* Ugly or lumpish fellow.

ùspairn, -e, *s.f.* Contention, strife, struggle. 2 **Emulation.

ùspairneach, -eiche, *a.* Striving, struggling, contentious. 2**Emulous, causing emulation.

ùspairneachd, *s.f.* Struggling, contending. 2** Emulation, practice of emulation.

ùspairniche, *s.m.* Emulous person.

ùspairt, *v.a.* Flounder.

ùspairt, -e, *s.f.* see ùspairn.

uspan, -ain, *s.m.* Shapeless mass. 2 Uncouth lump. 3 *in derision,* Clumsy fellow.

uspann,(CR) *s.f.* Argumentation, attempt to compel assent, or force conviction—*W. of Ross.*

†ussarb,‖ *s.* Death.

usuireachd,** *s.f.* Usury.

ut,* *v.a.* see put. Dh' ut e bhuaidh e, *he pushed it away from him ;* ut i, *shove her.*

ut ! ut ! *int.* Expression of disapprobation or dislike.

utac, see ultag.

utag, -aig, -an, *s.f.* Strife, uproar, confusion. 2 Outrage. 3* Turbulence. 4* Shove, push, jostle. 5 see rùdan.

utagach, -aiche, *a.* Confused, clamorous, noisy. 2* Turbulent. 3**Apt to push, shove, or jostle.

utagachadh, -aidh, *s.m.* Pushing, act of pushing, jostling, shoving, or raising a tumult, noise or clamour. Ag u—, *pr.pt.* of utagaich.

utagaich, *v.a.* Push, shove, jostle, raise a tumult.

utaig, see utag.

utaigeachd, *s.f.* see utag.

ùtan, -an *Argyll.* for rùtan Knuckle.

utarras,* -ais, *s.m.* see ùtrais.

ùtarrais, see ùtrais.

utarrasach, -aiche, see ùtraiseach.

ùth, -a, *pl.* -an & -annann, *s.m.* Udder Le 'n ùthaibh làn, *with their udders distended.*

ùthach, -aiche, *a.* Uddered, relating to an udder. 2 Having large udders.

ùthach, *s.m.* Mammal.

ùthachd,* *s.f.* Suicide. 2 Murder. Thug e ù. dha fhéin, *he committed suicide ;* bheir e ù. dhuit, *he will do de away with your life.*

ùthachdail, -e, *a.* Suicidal.

ùthag,(DMK) *s.f.* Sheep-louse—*Applecross.*

ùthaibh, *dat.pl.* of ùth.

uthan,** *s.m.* Foam.

ùthar, -aire, *a.* see ùthach.

ùthar,(DMy) *s.m.* Period of six weeks—the last three of July and the first three of August. It commences on a Friday and ends on a Tuesday.

uthard, *adv.* Above, up, above there, above yonder, up there, up yonder, on high. U. shuas, *up aloft ;* u. sud, *up yonder.*

———, for urrad.

ùtlaich, see udlaiche.

utlaiche, see udlaiche.

ùtlaidh, see udlaidh.

ùtraid, -e, -ean, *s.f.* see ùdrathad.

ùtrais, *s.f.* Confused mass of anything. 2 Molestation. 3 Restlessness, fidgeting. [** gives this as *gen.sing.* of ùtras.]

———each, -eiche, *a.* Confused, disordered. 2 Troublesome, vexatious, annoying. 3 Fidgeting, uneasy, restless.

———eachd, *s.f.* Confusion, confusedness. 2 Uneasiness, restlessness, fidgeting. 3 Troublesomeness.

———iche,** *comp.* of ùtraiseach. More or most restless or uneasy.

ùtras,** -ais, *s.m.* see ùtrais.

———ach, *a.* see ùtraiseach.

———achd, see ùtraiseachd

———aiche, see ùtraisiche.

utrod,** see ùdrathad.

———ach, see ùdrathadach

utag, see ultag.

ut ! ut ! see ud ! ud !

Proper Names

It must be borne in mind that Gaelic surnames, in the English sense, are not generally in use, at least in colloquial Gaelic, except when speaking of strangers. Every one living in a Gaelic-speaking district has a local name describing his trade or some physical peculiarity as, Donnachadh reamhar, An saor, &c. Sometimes they are named after the place they lived in last, or were born in, as, An t-Americanach, &c. If the person named is of a family long settled in the district he will probably be named after his father or grandfather, as Seumas a' phiobair, (the piper's James.) Where a person's mother is a native married to an outsider, he may be called after her, as Domhnall Ciorstan. Thus a Gaelic student whose friend is plain John MacDonald in the city, must not be surprised when he meets him at home, to hear his companions speak of him as, Iain Mhurchaidh Dhomhnuill Alasdair! The sole object of Gaelic surnames is to make the identity of the person spoken of as clear as possible through the speaker reminding his hearers by means of his name every time it is mentioned, to whom or where he "belongs."

Considerable care must be exercised in translating English surnames into Gaelic, for example, Donald Black is Domhnall Mac a' Ghille Dhuibh. The literal translation, Domhnall Dubh, may, if used, prove very misleading, for that is much more likely to be the local appellation of Donald Cameron or Donald Smith, both of whom have dark hair, than of Donald Black who may even be fair and locally known as Domhnall Bàn, but more probably as Domhnall Alasdair or Domhnall Iain. Domhnall Dubh is also a familiar Gaelic name for the devil!

The following list of names is the result of the compiler's collecting from all available sources from 1880 to 1911. The names are not inserted here with the idea of setting forth any new theory regarding the correct form of any Gaelic name, but it is merely an attempt to gather into one alphabetical list, from all the newspapers, magazines, books, &c. in which they have appeared, the most up-to-date forms used by the best Gaelic scholars. A few of the names have been taken down orally by the compiler, but, owing to the authorities for the remainder not having been noted as the list was collected, it is impossible to give here the source whence each was obtained. The absence of such a list from all other Gaelic dictionaries is a cause of continual disappointment to Gaelic students. Much pains has been taken to secure accuracy, and Dr. W. J. Watson, Edinburgh, has kindly revised and added to the list. Dr. Watson's additions are marked *, and are original Gaelic forms taken from the mouths of the people—not Gaelic translations of Anglicized forms. Quotations from the Ordnance Survey Maps, are marked OSM.

The list may be added to in any Gaelic-speaking district, but care must be taken to spell the names exactly as they sound, and not according to what either the collector or native informant *think they mean.*

As quite 20 Gaelic students require the Gaelic form of an English name to every one who requires the English form of a Gaelic one, the English forms are here placed first.

English	Gaelic
A'an, Ben	Am Binnean
Aberairder Aberarder	Obair-àrdair*
Aberbrothock Arbroath	Obair-bhrothaig*
Aberchalder	Obair-Challadair*
Aberchirder	Obair-Chiardair*
Abercorn	Obair-Chuirnigh*
Aberdalgie	Obair-dheilgidh*
Aberdeen	Abaireadhain, (for Obair-dheathain
Aberdour	Obair-dhobhair*
Aberfeldy	Obair-pheallaidh*
Aberfoyle	Obair-phuill
Abergeldie	Obair-gheallaidh
Aberlour	Obair lobhair*
Abernethy	Obair-neithich
Abertarff	Obair-thairbh
Aberuchill	Obair-rùchail*
Aboyne	A-bèidh*
Abriachan	Obair-itheachan*
Achabhraigh	Achd a' bhraighe*
Achabrad	Achd a' bhràghad
Achacha	Achadh a' chadha
Achachonleich	Ach a' chonalaich*
Achadalvery	Achadh dail Mhoire
Achafolla	Achadh pholla
Achafubil	Achadh a' phubaill*
Achagoyl	Achadh gaothail
Achall, Loch	Loch acha challa*
Achalochy	Achadh locha
Achaloist	Achadh loisgte
Achaluskin	Achadh losgainn
Achanault	Achadh an uillt*
Achanalt (*Ross*)	Achadh nan allt*
Achandarach	Achadh nan darach*
Achandoich	Ach' an dobhaich
Achanelid	Achadh an éilid
Achaninver	Achadh an inbhir*
Achantee	Achadh an t-suidhe*
Acharacle	Àth Tharracaill
Acharanich	Achadh rainich*
Acharn	Ach-chàrn*
Acharra	Achadh a' charraigh
Achatascaild	Achadh dà sgaillt*
Achavae	Achadh a' bhàthaich
Achavraid	Achadh bhràghaid
Ach-a-vullin	Achadh a' mhuilinn*

English	Gaelic
Achcastle	Achadh a' chaisteil
Achdaliew	Ach do Liubha (of St. Lew)
Achadanadar	Achadh dà nàduir
Achdaphuibil	Achadh dà phubull
Achduart	Achadh Dhubhaird*
Achduchil	Achadh dubh choille
Achencar	Achadh a' charadh
Achellach	Achadh nan cailleach
Achencairn	Achadh a' chàirn
Achengower	Achadh nan gobhar
Achenhew	Achadh-eò
Achenrioch	Achaidhean riabhach
Achfary	Ach taigh Phàiridh
Achilty	Aichealaidh*
Achiltibuie	Achd-ille-bhuidhe*
Achinadrian	Achadh nan droigheann
Achinafaud	Achadh nam fòd
Achinearnich	Ach an fhèarnaich*
Achincass	Achadh cas
Achincorvey	Achadh na cairbhe
Achindarach	Achadh nan darach*
Achindrain	Achadh an droighinn*
Achinduich	Ach an dubhaich*
Achiniskich	Achadh an iasgaich*
Achinahuan	Achadh nan uan
Achintee	Ach an t-sìthidh (*Ross*)
Achintiobairt	Achadh an tiobairt
Achintore	Achadh an todhair
Achintoul	Ach an t-sabhail*
Achin-ty-halvin	Ach an taigh thalmhainn
Achleach	Ach' leitheich*
Achlean	Achleathainn
Achleshie (*Callander*)	Ach' leitbisidh*
Achleven	Achadh-leamhain
Achlochan	Achd an lochain*
Achlorachan	Ach' loireachan*
Achlum	Achadh lium (?)
Achlunachan	Ach-ghlùineachain*
Achlyne	Ach' loinn*
Achlyness	Ach linn an eas
Achmore	Acha mòr*
Achnabàt	Ach' nam bata*
Achnabeachin	Ach nam beathaichean
Achnacarry	Achadh na cairigh*
Achnaclerach	Ach nan cléireach*
Achnacone	Achadh nan con
Achnacree (*Argyll*)	Achadh na crithe
Achnacreebeg	Achadh na crithe beag
Achnacreemore	Achadh na crithe mór

The local etymology of the last two names, which gives *the field of the little tree* and *the field of the big tree* respectively, is wrong and quite at variance with the local Gaelic pronunciation, according to which the meanings are *the little field of the trembling moss* and *the big field of the trembling moss*.

English	Gaelic
Achnafeanaig	Ach na feannaig*
Achnahannet	Achadh na h-annaid*
Achnahinich	Achadh na h-ìnich*
Achnaleppin	Achadh na leth-pheighinn
Achnamaddy	Achadh nam madadh
Achnanclach	Ochdamh nan clach
Achnagarran	Achadh nan gearran*
Achnangoul	Achadh nan gobhal*
Achnaskioch	Achadh na sgitheach
Achnasheen	Ach' na sìne*
Achnashellach	Ach na seileach*
Achnasoull	Ach nan sabhal*
Ach egie	Achd an fhiodhaigh*
Achness	Achadh an eas
Achoil	Achadh na coille
Achoul	Achadh a' chùil
Achray, Loch	Loch Ath-Chrathaigh*
Achriesgill	Ach' rìsgil*
Ac abannock	Ach-dà-bhannag*
Ac[illegible]lair	Ochdamh a' bhlair*
Achtoldrach	Achadh an toldaraich (*field of holes* or *borings*)
Achtaly	Achadh an tulaich
Achtaytoralan	Achadh da torralan*
Achtenny	Achadh taobh eanagh
Achtercairn	Achadh a' chàirn*
Achterflow	Uachdar-chlò*
Achterneed	Uachdar-niad*
Achtotie	Achadh an tota
Achumore	Achadh mór*
Achvanie	Ach Bhànaidh*
Achvoan	Achadh a' bhothain
Achvrail	Achadh bhràigh a' bhaile
Adam	Adhamh
Adamnan	Adhamhnan (*pron.* Yōnan)
Advie	Àbhaidh*
Affray, Glen	Gleann aifrinn
Affrick, Loch, &c.	Afraig*
Agnew	Mac a' ghniomhaid
Agnish	Aignis*
Aharacle	see Acharacle
Aigas, Island	Eilean Àigeis
Ailsa Craig	Allasan, Creag Ealasaid
Ailsh, Loch	Loch Aillse
Aird of Coigach	Airde na Céigich*
Airdaily	Aird-aillidh
Airdentrive	Aird an t-snaimh
Airdrie (*Ardclach*)	Ardruigh*
Airiecherie	Airidh chéiridh*
	Airigh MhicGriadh* (*not* Criadh)
Arrinachruinach	Airidh nan Cruithneachd*
Airinasliseig	Airidh na sliseig
Aisridh	Aisridh
Alder, Ben	Beinn Eallar
Aldie	Alltaidh*
Aldlarie	Allt-Làirigh
Aldourie	Dobhrag*
Alexander	Alasdair
Alford	Alphort (*Reliq. Celt. ii, 192*)
Aline, Loch	Loch Àluinn*
Alisary	Amhlasairigh*
Allachy, (burn)	Eileachaigh*
Alladale	Alladal*
———, Glen	Gleann Alladail*
Allan, Allen	Ailean
———, (place)	Alan*
Allanbank	An Réim*
Allanfearn	An t-àilean fearna*
Allanglack	Alan nan clach*
Allangrange	Alan*
Allanrich	Alan an fhraoich*
Almond, River	Abhainn Aman*
———, Glen	Gleann Amain*
Allt a' chamhna	Allt a' ghamhna
Allt an rian	Allt an ruighean
Allt na beadhan	Allt nam beathan
Allt na harra	Allt na h-eirbhe*
Allt na harrie	
Allt na main	Allt na mèinn*
Allt Airiecheirie	Allt Airidh Chéiridh
Allt skiack	Allt sgitheach
Alness	Alanais
Alpine	Ailpein
Alsh, Loch	Loch Aillse (L. Ai'se)
Altandow	An t-alltan dubh*
Altas	Alltais*
Altchonier	Allt a' choin uidhir*
Altgalvash	Allt gailbheach (?)
Alt Graat	Allt grannda*
Altgreshan	Allt Ghrìsean*
Alt Guish	An t-allt giuthais*
Alt Marky	Allt Maircidh*
Alt more	Allt mòr*
Alt na ghaissac	Allt na giubhsaich*
Alt na sou	Allt nan sùbh*
Altan na caorach	Allt nan caorach*

ENGLISH	GAELIC
Altbea	see Aultbea
Altnaharrow	Allt na h-eirbhe*
Altspàtie	Allt spùtaidh
Alturlie	Allt rollaidh*
Altvulin	Allt a' mhuilinn
Altyre	Alltar*
Alves	Àbhais*
Alvie	Albhaidh
Alyth	Àilt*
Amat	Amad*
Ample, Glen	Gleann Ambail*
Amulree	Àth Maol-Ruibhe*
An, Ben	Binnean*
Anabella	see Annabella
Anaheilt	Àth na h-eilde
Ananeaun	Àth nan ceann*
Anderson	see MacAndrew
Andrew	Aindrea
Angus	Aonghas
——, (district)	Machair Aonghais*
Ankerville	see Little Kindeace
Anna, Loch	Loch an Aini'*
Annat	An annaid*
Annat Bay (*Loch Broom*)	Am Poll mòr, *or* Linne na h-annaid*
Annabella	Barabel
Aonaclair, Ben	Beinn Eunacleit*
Apitauld	Àth-pit-allt*
App, Glen	Gleann an aba*
Appin	An Apainn
Applecross	A' Chomraich*
———, River	Abhainn Cresan*
———(Strath of)	Srath Mhaol Chaluim*

In the parish of Applecross is "air a' Chomraich," (not "anns a' Ch—.") *The minister of Applecross* is "ministear a' Chlachain," (not "ministear na Comraich.")

ENGLISH	GAELIC
Aquhorties	Achadh Choirthe*
Aradie	Aradaidh (Loch named Annraidh in maps in error)*
Aray, Glen	Gleann Aora
Arbroath	Obair-bhrothaig*
Arcandeith	Arcan duibh*
Archibald	Gilleasbuig (Beisdean, *a colloquialism,* as Beisdean bàn, Beistean MacIain, &c.)
Ard, Loch	Loch na h-àirde
Ardalanish	Àird Alainis
Ardali	Àird-àillidh
Ardanamar	Àird an amair
Ardantraive	Àird an t-snaimh
Ardcharnich	Àird-cheathairnich*
Ardchaple	Àird nan capull
Ardchattan	Àirde-Catain
Ardchonnel	Àird na coingheill*
Ardchronie	Àird chrònaidh*
Ardchyline	Àird a' chuilinn
Ardclach	Àird-chlach
Ard-druimnich	Àird-druimeanaich
Ardelve	Àird-eilbh, *or* Àird-eilghidh*
Ardelve market	Féill na h-Àirde*
Ardentinny	Àird an teine
Ardeonaig	Àird Eónaig*
Ardersier	Àird nan saor*
Ardessie	Àird-easaidh*
Ardd, Loch	Loch na h-àirde
Ardgaddan	Àird ghadan
Ardgay	Àrd gaoith*
Ardgour	Àird-ghobhar
Ardgowan	Àird a' ghobhainn*
Ardgower	see Ardgour
Ardhallow	Àrdthalamh*
Ardheslaig	Àird-heisleag*
Ardindrean	Àird an dreaghainn*
Ardintoul	Àird an t-sabhail*
Ardivachir	Rudha Aird a' Mhachair
Ardival	Àird a bhaile*
Ardjachie	Aird-achaidh*
Ardkinglas	Àird-chonghlais
Ardlamey	Àird a' ghlamaidh
Ardlamont	Àird MhicLaomuinn
Ardlary	Ardlarach
Ardie, Strath	Srath Ardail
Ardlui	Ard-laoigh*
Ardlussa	Aird-lusa*
Ardmucknish	Àird-mhucinnis*
Ardmaddy	Aird nam madadh*
Ardmair	Ard-mhèara*
Ardmanach	Ard-meadhonach*
Ardmarnock	Aird-màrnag*
Ardmore	An t-Àrd mór*
Ardnacross	Ard na croise
Ardnadam	Aird nan damh*
Ardnagaul	Aird nan gobhal*
Ardnagrask	Aird nan crasg*
Ardnahien	Aird nan aibhne
Ardnamurchan	Aird nam murchan*
Ardnagoine	Aird nan gaimhne*
Ardnaniaskin	Àird an fhiasgain*
Ardnarff	Aird an arbha*
Ardnaskie	Aird an fhasgaidh
Ardoch	Àrdachadh*
Ardochy	Àrdochaidh
Ardrishaig	Rudh Ard driseig, *locally* An Rudha*
Ardroe	Ard-roth
Ardreil	Eadar-dha-fhaodhail*
Ardross	Ard Rois *or* Bràigh Rois*
Ardrossan	Ard Trosain*
Ardsheal	Àrd-seile
Ardtalnaig	Àrd talnaig
Ardtornish	Ard-tòrainnis
Ardtur	Àrd tùr
Ardullie	Àidilidh*
Ardvar	Àrdbhar
Ardverikie	Ard-mheirgidh
Ardvoirlich	Ard-mhùrluig*
Ardvroilach	Ard-bhroighleach
Ardvreck	Aird-bhreac*
Ardyne	Ardfhin
Argyll	Earraghàidheal
——, Duke of	"Mac Cailein Mór"*
Arienas	Àiridh Aonghais
Arighuary	Àiridh Ghuaire
Arihoulan	Àiridh Shuarlain
Arinackaig	Àiridh Neacaig*
Aringour	Àiridh nan gobhar
Arinarach	Àiridh-nathrach
Arinascavach	Àiridh na sgabhach (*saw-dust*)
Ariogan	Airidh Ògain, (*for* Àiridh Eòghain)
Arisaig	Àrasaig
Arity, river	Aradaidh*
Ariveagaig	Àiridh Bheagaig
Arkaig	Airceig*
——, Loch	Loch Airceig
Arklet, Loch	Loch Airclet*
Arlary	Ard-làrach
Armadale	Armadal*

ENGLISH	GAELIC
Armine, Ben	Beinn Armuinn*
Arngask	Arn gasg
Aros	Àros
Arpafeelie	Arpa-philich *or* A.-philidh*
Arran	Arainn
Arriecheirie	Àiridh-chéiridh
Arrochar	Arrochar
Arscaig	Àrsgaig*
Artafaillie	Airt a' fàillidh*
Arthur	Artair
Artilligain	Aird-Uilleagain
Artney, Glen	Gleann Artain,* Gl. Àrtair*
Asgag	Srath Àsgaig*
Asher	Àisir
Asia	An Asia
Assarow	Asaireadh*
Assynt	Asainn
Athole	Atholl *or* Athall
——, Duke of	Am Moireach
Atlantic Ocean	An Cuan siar. The open Atlantic in *W. Isles* is Haaf
Attadale	Atadal*
Attow, Ben	Beinn Fhada*
Auchagoyle	Ach' a' ghoill*
Auchalader	Ach' Chaladair*
Aucharanie	Achadh-raineach
Auchederson	Achd-Eadarsan*
Aucheleffen, *Arran*	Achadh-leth-pheighinn
Auchengee	Achadh na geoidhe
Auchengeith	Achadh na gaoithe
Auchengower	Achadh nan gobhar
Auchengrouch	Achadh nan gruth
Auchensaugh	Achadh nan seileach
Auchentore	Achadh an todhair*
Auchindown	Achadh an dùin
Auchinleck	Achadh nan leacann
Auchtascailt	Acha-dà-sgaillt*
Auchterderran	Uachdar doirean
Auchterflow	Uachdar-chlò*
Auchtertyre	Uachdar-thìre*
Augustus, Fort	Cille Chuimein
Aulay	Amhlaidh
Auldearn	Allt Eire
Aulich	Amhlaich*
Auliston Point	Rudha nan amhlaistean
Aultbea	Am Fàin, *or* Am Fàin Braonach
———, River	Allt-beithe
Aultgowrie	Allt-ghobhraidh*
Aultnasou	Allt nan subh*
Aultsigh	Allt saidhe*
Aven River (*Banff*)	Uisge Athfhinn*
Avendhu	An Abhainn dubh (*Upper Forth*)
Avenvogie	Abhainn bhogaidh
Avernish	Abharnis*
Averon, River	Abharan*
Avich, Loch	Amhaich
Avoch	Obhach (for Abhach)*
Avon, Ben	Beinn Athfhinn*
——, Glen	Gleann Athfhinn*
Awe, Loch	Loch Obha*
——, River	Abhainn Abha*
Aylort, Loch	Loch Ailleart
Ayr	Inbhir-àir
Ayr, Heads of	Ciun Inbhir-áir
Back	Am Bac
Backies	Bacannan
Badachro	Bad a' chrèthà*
Badacrain	Bad nan caoimhean*
Badantional	Bad an innsil*
Badcall	Bad-call*
Badd	Bad
Baddagyle	Loch Bad a' ghoill*
Badenoch	Bàideanach (*drowned place*)

ENGLISH	GAELIC
Badenscally	Bad a' sgàlaidh*
Badentarbert	Bad an tairbeirt*
Badicaul	Bada Call*
Badindean, *Gl. Isla*	Bod an Deamhain*
Badnaguin	Bad nan gaoithean*
Badnaguine, *Suth'd*	Bad na cuingean
Badrallach	Am Bad ràilleach*
Badvo	Bad a' bhoth*
Bagastie, Strath	Srath bhàgastaidh*
Ballyaurgan	Baile gheambragain
Baileveolain	Baile a' bheòlain
Bail'-an-dounie	Bail' an donnaidh*
Bailecharn	Beul-atha-chàrn*
Bailechaill	Old name of Dingwall, still perpetuated in the name of a local inn*
Bain	MacGillebhàin
Baith, Glen	Gleann na blàith
Balachladaich	Bail' a' chladaich*
Balachraggan	Baile-chreagain*
Balachroan	Baile-chrothain
Balantyre	Bail' an t-saoir
Balallan	Bail' Ailein*
Balavil	Bail' a' bhile*
Balbeg	Baile beag
Balblair	Bail' a' bhlàir*
Balchallan	Baile Chailein*
Balcherry	Baile-cheathraimh*
Balconie	Bailonigh*
Baldoon	Bail' an Dùin*
Baldow	Baile dubh
Baledmund	Bail'-Admainn, B. Aldmin*
Balfreish	Bail' a' phris
Balfuill	Bail' a' phuill*
Balgalkin	Bail'-gailcinn*
Balgibbon	Bail' a' ghibein*
Balgholan	Baile-Dhomh'lain*
Balgowan	Bail' a' ghobhainn
Balguneirie	Baile gun iarraidh*
Balgunloune	Baile gun leann*
Balgy	Balgaidh*
Balicherry	Bail' a' cheathraimh*
Balindore	Bail' an deòra
Balinoe	Baile nodha
Balindrum	Bail' an droma
Balintochich	Bail' an Tòisich*
Balintore	Bail' an todhair*
Balintraid	Bail' an tràghad*
Balishare	Baile sear*
Balkeith	Baile na coille*
Ballachraggan	Lòn nam ban*
Ballachrey	Bealach ruadh
Ballachulish	Bail' a' chaolais
Ballachuan	Bail' a' chuain
Ballantrae	Baile na tràigh
Ballater	Beal'tair, *or* Bealadair*
Ballechin	Bail' Eachain
Ballegyle	Baile Ghoill
Balleigh	Bail' an lighe*
Ballichatrigan	Baile-Chatragain
Ballichloan	Baile-Chlamhain
Ballickine	Banleacainn
Balligill	Bàiligil*
Ballimeanach	Baile-meadhonach
Ballimoney	Bail' a' mhanaich
Ballinaby	Bail' an àbaidh
Ballingal	Baile nan Gall
Ballingry	Bail' a' gharaidh
Ballinluig	Bail' an luig
Ballinreich	Bail' an fhraoich
Ballinroich	Bail' an Rothaich*
Balliphetrish	Baile Pheadrais*
Balliskilly	Baile-sgeulaidh*
Ballivain	Bail' a' mheadhoin
Balloan	Bail an lòin*

ENGLISH	GAELIC
Balloch	Bealach
——, (*Inverness*)	Bail' an loch*
Ballochandrain	Bealach an droighinn
Ballochantuy	Bealach an t-suidhe*
Ballochmyle	Bealach maol
Ballochyle	Bail' a' chaoil
Balloan	Bail' an lòin
Ballychluvin	Bail' a' chlamhain
Ballygillan	Baile Ghillian
Ballygrant, *Islay*	Bail' a' ghràna
Ballygreggan	Bail' a' chreagain
Ballygroggan	Bail' a' chrògain
Ballymena, *Antrim*	Baile-meadhonach
Ballymoney	Bail' a' mhonaidh
Ballynaughton	Baile Neachdain
Balmacaan	Baile MacCathan*
Balmacarra	Baile MacCarra*
Balmaclellan	Baile MhicGill' Fhaolain
Balmainach	Bail' meadhonach*
Balmakeith	Baile MacDhàidh
Balmennoch	Baile meadhonach
Balmoral	Baile Mhoireil
Balmuchy	Baile Mhuchaidh*
Balmungie	Baile Mhungaidh*
Balnabeen	Baile na binne*
Balnaboth	Baile nam both*
Balnacill	Baile na cille*
Balnacoill	Baile na coille
Balnacrà	Beul ath nan crà*
Balnacraig	Baile na creige*
Balnacree	Baile na craoibh*
Balnafettack	Baile na feadaig*
Balnagard	Baile nan ceard*
Balnaglack	Baile na glaic
Balnagore	Baile nan gobhar*
Balnagown	Baile nan gobhainn*
Balnain, *Inverness*	Bail' an fhàin*
——, *Badenoch*	Beul an athain
Balnakill	Baile na cille
Balnakyle	Baile na coille*
Balnasack	Baile nan sac
Balnespick	Bail' an easbuig
Balnuig	Bail' an aoig*
Balole	Bail' Ola
Balquhidder	{ Both-fuidir Both-phuidir & Both-chuidir*
Balreillan	Baile-réidhlean*
Balshare	see Balishare
Balulve	Bail' Uilf, *or* Bail' Uilbh
Balvack	Bail' a' bhac*
Balvarran	Bail' a' bharain*
Balvenie	Baile mhanaidh—*Iain Lòm*
Balvicar	Baile Bhiocair
Balvolich	Baile mhullaich
Balvorist	Baile Mhoirist*
Balvulin	Bail' a' mhuilinn
Bamff	Banbh*
Banavie	Bainbhidh*
Banchor	Beinnchor
Banchory	Beannachar*
Banff	Banbh
Bannatyne	{ MacEamailinn, *or* MacClomalain
Bannockburn	Allt a' bhonnaich
Banscoile	Ban-sgaoil
Barachandler	Bàrr a' cheanndoir
Barbaraville	*locally* An Cladach*
Barcaldine	Am Bàrra-calltuinn
Barmaddy	Bàrr a' mhadaidh
Barnacarry	Bàrr na cairidh
Barnaguy	Bàrr na gaoithe
Barnakill	Bàrr na coille
Barnaline	Bàrr an àilean
Barnashalig	Bàrr na seilg
Barnbougle	Bàrr na boglain
Baroile	Bàrr-aoil

ENGLISH	GAELIC
Barra	Barraidh
Barrichybean	Barr a' chiopain*
Barrolan	Bairlinn
——, Loch	Loch Bairlinn
Barsailleach	Bàrr-seileach
Bartholomew	Parlan
Barvas	Barbhas
Batnascallack	Bad na sgalag*
Battachan, Loch	Loch nam badachan*
Battybay	Am Badaidh beithe*
Baun	Am Bàbhun
Bayfield, *Nigg*	see Wester Kindeace*
——, *Knockbain*	{ Croit Seocaidh (i.e. Jockie's croft)*
Beach	Beitheach
Beachmore	Beitheach mhór
Bealochgair	Bealach geàrr
Beath	Beith
Beaton	Peuton, (Mac an léigh in *Islay*)
Beaufort Castle	Dùnaidh*
Beauly	A' Mhanachainn, *or* Manachainn MhicShimidh*
——, River	Farar*
Bede	Baodan
Belgæ (the ancient Irish)	} Na Fir-bolg
Bellachroan	Baile 'Chrothain
Belladrum	Bealadrum*
Belleville	Bail' a' bhile
Bellyclone	Baile Mac-gill'-Eòin*
Belmaduthy	Baile MacDhuibh*
Belnahua	Beul na h-uamha
Benbecula	Beinn nam faoghla
Benderloch	{ Meudarloch (i. e. Beinn [ea]dar dhà loch)
Benmore Burn *St. Fillan's)*	} Allt Monochuill
Bennetfield	Baile Bhenneit, (*Benedict*)*
Beochlich	Beò-chloich
Bernera	Bearnaraidh*
Bernice	Bearnas
Berriedale	Bearghdal
Bervie, Loch	Loch Biorbhaidh
Berwick	Abaruig
Bettyhill	Am Blàran odhar
Bhealaich, Gl. a'	Gleann Bealoch *Badenoch*
Bhraoin, Loch a'	Lochaidh Bhraoin*
Bhruichlinn, Dun	Dun Bhrolchain
Bighouse	Biogais
Bindal	Bindeil*
Binns, the	Na Cnocan
Birchburn	An t-Allt-beithe
Birchfield, *Kincardine*	} Ach na h-uamhach*
Birkhall	Torr-beatha*
Birkis	A' Bheithearnaich
Birnie	Braonaigh*
Birse	Preas*
Black.	} MacGhilleDhuibh
Blackie	
Blackhill	An Cnoc Dubh
Black Isle	An t-Eilean Dubh
Blackdyke	An gàradh dubh
Black Lunans (*Forfar)*	} Bealach Lùnaig*
Blair	Blàrach
Blair	} Bail' a' bhlàir*
Balblair	
Blair [in] Atbole	Blàr an Athoill*
Blair Drummond	Blàr Dhruiminn*
Blairfettie	Blàr-pheitigh*
Blairfoid	Blar-choighde*
Blairgie	Blàragaidh*
Blairgowrie	Blàr-goibhre
Blairinroar *Muthill*	Blàr an ruathair*

English	Gaelic
Blairmore	Blàr-mór
Blairour	Blàr odhar
Blairwhyte	Blàr-choighde
Blaud	Blathaid*
Blarcreen	Blàr-crithinn
Blarich (*Suth'd*)	Blàraich—CR
Blarleath	Am Blàr liath*
Blarnabee	Blàr na bìth*
Blar-na-coi	Blàr na cùinge*
Blarnalevoch	Blàr na Leitheoch*
Blarninich	Blàr an aonaich*
Blaven	Blàbheinn*
Blughasary	Blaoghasairigh*
Boat of Garten	Coit Ghartain*
Boath	Na Bothachan*
Bochastle	Both-chaisteil,* B.-chastair*
Bochonie	Both-chòinnigh
Bogbain	Am bac bàn*
Bogie, Strath	Srath Bhalgaidh*
Boggiewell *Urquhart*	Bog an fhuail*
———, *Rosemarkie*	Bog an fhuarain*
Bog of Shannon	Bog na' seannan*
Bogrow	Am Bogaradh*
Bogy, Strath	see Bogie
Boharm	Both-sheirm*
Bohenie	Both-shìnidh*
Bohespie	Both-theasbuigh*, Both-eas-buig (CR)
Bohuntin	Both-chunndainn*
Boisdale	Baghasdal*
———, Loch	Loch Baghasdail*
Boleskine	Both fhleisginn*
Bolfracks	Both bhrac(*prov.* for breac*)
Bolin	Both-lìn*
Bohallie	Both-shàilidh, B.-thàilidh*
Bona	Am Bànath*
Bonahaven	Bun na h-abhann
Bonar Bridge	Drochaid a' bhanna*
Bonaveh(*Colonsay*)	Bun a' bheithe
Bonawe	Bun-Atha
Bonskied	Bonn-sgaoid*
Boor (*Gairloch*)	Bùra*
Borenich	Both-reinich* (*i.e.* rainich)
Boreray	Borroraidh
Borgie	Borgaidh*
Borlay, Loch	Boralaidh*
Borrowdale, or Borradale	Borrodal
Borrowstouness	see Bo'ness
Borve	Borgh & Borbh
Botriphnie	Both-draighnigh*
Boturnie	Both-tuairnigh*
Bottle Island	Eilean a' bhotuil, Eilean Druim briste
Bower, parish of	Sgire Bhàgair
Bowmore	Am Bogha mór
Boyd	Bóid
Boyne, R. (*Ireland*)	Breughna
Braal, castle	Brei'al*
Braan, R. (*Perthsh.*)	Breamhainn*
———, R. (*Ross*)	Bran
Bracadale	Bracadal (*pron.* Breacadal)
Brackla	A' Bhraclaich*
Brackley	Breac-leathad
Bracklinn	Braclann*
Bradden, Loch	Loch a' bhradain
Brae, *Gairloch*	A' Bhruthach
Brae Grudie	Braigh Ghrùididh*
Braeintra	Bràigh an t-sratha*
Braelangwell	Bràigh-langail*
Braelochaber	Am Bràigh
Braemar	Bràigh Mharr
Brae Moray	Bràigh Mhoraibh*
Braerathy	Bràigh Shrathaidh*
Braeriach	Am Bràigh riabhach*
Braes of Doune	Bràigh Dhùin*
Braes of Greenock, *Cullander*	Bràigh Ghrianaig*
Brae Tongue	Bràigh Thunga
Braeval	Bràigh a' bhaile
Brae Vallich	Bràigh a' bhealaich
Braeglenbeg	Bràigh-ghleann beag
Braeglenmore	——— mór
Brahan	Brathainn*
Braingortan	Bràigh nan goirtean
Bran, Strath (*Ross*)	Srath Bhrain*
Branault	Bràigh nan allt
Branahuie	Bràigh na h-uidhe*
Brander, pass of	Am Brannradh*
Branter, Glen	Gleann a' Bhranndair
Brawell	Bràigh a' bhaile
Brawl	Breithal (*Suth'd*)
Breac-chu	Breacachadh
Breachat	Bràigh Chat*
Breackachay	Breacachaidh*
Breackerie	Breacairidh
Breacklate	Breacleathad
Breadalbane	Bràghad Albainn
———, Earl of	"Mac ChaileinMhic Dhonnchaidh"
———, North side of L. Tay	Deisear
Brecklach	A' Bhraclach
Brenachie	Breanagaich*
Brenachoil	Breun choille,* *L. Katrine*
Brenag, River	Abhainn Breunag*
Brenfield	Breun-achadh
Brerachan, Glen	Gleann Briarachan*
Breton, a	Amhorach
Bridge of Allan	Drochaid Ailein*
——— Cally	Drochaid Challaigh*
——— of Don	Drochaid Deathain*
——— Earn	Drochaid Éir*
——— Tilt	Drochaid Theilt
——— Turk	Ceann-drochaid (D. Tuirc is hardly ever heard)*
Bridgend	Ceann drochaid
Bridget	Brìde
Brimishgan	Bramasag
Britain	Breatunn, *gen.* -uinn
Brittany, native of,	Amhorach
Broadford	An t-ath leathann
Brodick	Breadhaig
Brodie	Brothaigh*
Broomhill	Cnoc a' bhealaich, An Cnoc bealaidh
———, *Kilmuir Easter*	Aird nan cathag
Broom, Loch, *Ross*	Loch Bhraoin*
———, *Perth*	Loch Braoin*
———, Little	An Loch beag
Broom, River	Abhainn Bhraoin*
Broomtown	Bail' a' bhealaidh*
Brora	Brùra*
Browlin	Brobhlainn*
Brown	Mac a' Bhriuthainn
Bruan	Bruthan
Bruar	Bruthar*
Brucefield	Cnoc an tighearna
———, North	Loch Sirr'*
Buachaille Etive	Buachaill Éite*
Buchan (B. of Deer)	Buchan
Buchanan	Both-chanain (*place*)
Buchanan	Canonach
Buchanans, the	Na Canonaich
Buchanty	Buchantaidh,* Buthaintidh & Buidheintidh—CR
Bucket Water	Buichead*
Buckie, Glen	Gleann Bocaidh*
Buird, Beinn-na-	Beinn a' bhùird*
Bulroy	A' Bhuaill ruadh
Bunachton	Both Neachdain*

ENGLISH	GAELIC
Bunchrew	Bun-chraobh
Bundaloch	Bun dà loch*
Bunloit	Bun-leothaid
Bunlarie	Bun-larach
Bun Owen	Bun-obhann
Burnside	Taigh an daimh
Burracks	Na Buraich*
Busbheinn	Badhais bheinn* / Baoghais bheinn
Bute	Bód
Buteman, a	Bóideach
Buthkollidar	Buth-coilleadair
Butt of Lewis	Rudha Robhanais*
Buy, Loch	Lochabuidhe*
Caan, Dun	Dùn Canna*
Cabaan	Cadha bàn*
Cadboll	Cathabul
Caddletown	An Cadaladan
Cadearg	An Cadha dearg*
Caerlaverock	Cathair-beinn-thorraiche
Caggan	An Caiginn
Caillach Head	Sron na caillich
Cainikain	Caineachain
Cairn, Glen	Gleann a' chùirn
Cairnskerry	Carnasgeir*
Cairnvickuie	Cathair MhicAoidh
Caisteal Baicidh	Caisteal Cuil Bhàcidh*
Caithness	Gallaibh
———, Ord of	An t-Ord Gallach
———, Earl of	Morair Ghallaibh
Calavie, Loch	Loch Cailbhidh*
Calf of Man	An Eireag Mhannanach*
Callander	Calasraid, Caltraid* & Calastraid
Callernish	Calanais
Callop	Calpa
Callow	Cala
Cally, Bridge of	Drochaid Challaigh
Calnakil	Cal na cille
Caltrigil	Rudha Dunbheagain
Calvie, Glen	Gleann Cailbhidh*
———, a native of	Cailbheach
———, Loch	Loch Cailbhidh*
Calvinist	Cailbhineach
Camasie	Camaisidh*
Cambrian, a	Cuimear
Cambus	Camus
Cambusbarron	Camas a' bharain*
Cambuschurrich	Camus-curraich*
Cambuscurrie, *Ross*	Camus curaidh*
Cambusdoon	Camus donn
Cambuskenneth	Camus-Choinnich
Cambusmore	Camus mór
Cameron	Camshron, Camran
——— of Lochiel	"Mac Dhomhnuill Dhuibh"
——— of Letterfinlay	"Mac Mhic Mhartainn"
——— of Strone	"MacGill' onaidh"
Camgarry, Glen	Gleann Camaghair
Camghouran	Camagh'ran*, Cam-ghobhran
Campbell	Caimbeul
——— of Strachur	"Mac Mhic Artair"
——— of Ardkinglas	"Mac Iain riabhaich"
——— of Ardvoirlich	"Mac Mhic Bhaltair"
——— of Asknish	"Mac Iomhair"
——— of Craignis	"MacDhughaillCreaginnis"
——— of Dunstaffnage	"Mac Aonghais an Dùin"
——— of Inverawe	"Mac Dhonnchaidh"
——— of Strachur	"Mac Mhic Artair"

ENGLISH	GAELIC
Campbell Castle	see Castle Gloom
Campbells, the	Sliochd Dhiarmaid O' Dhuibhne
——— of Barcaldine & Baileveolan	Sliochd Phara bhig
——— of Cawdor	Caimbeulaich bhoga Chaladair
Campbelltown, (*Inverness*)	Baile nan Caimbeulach
———, (*Argyll*)	Ceann-Loch-ChilleChiarain, Ceannloch
Camusinas	Camus Aonghais
Camusine	Camus-éidhinn
Camusluinnie	Camus luinge*
Camusnaherie	Camus na h-eirbhe
Camus nan Gall	Camus nan Gall*
Camusteel	Camus-teile*
Camusterach	Camus-tearach*
Camustionavaig	Camus-dionabhaig
	Camus Trol*
Camus-vic-Erchar	Camus MhicFhearchair
Canisp	Canasp
Canna	Canaidh, Eilean Chanfhaidh, an t-Eilean tarsuinn
Cannich, Glen	Gleann Canaich
Canreayan	Ceann a' riabhain*
Cantray	Canntra'*
Cantyre	see Kintyre
Caoidhe, Loch-na-	Loch na cuithe*
Caorunnach	A' Chaoirnich
Capenoch	Ceapanach
Capernich	A' Cheaparnaich*
Cape Wrath	see Wrath
Caplich	Caiplich*
Caputh	A' Cheapaich* Capaig
Cardross	Cas rois
Carie	Càraigh,* Càirigh—CR
Carlonan	Car-lònan
Carloway	Carlabhaidh
Carmichael	MacGhilleMhicheil
Carnassary	Càrn-asaraidh
Carn Bhren	Càrn Bhrein*
Carn dubh aig an Doire	Càrn dubh 'Ic an Deóir
Carnich	A' Chàrnaich*
Carn nan Conacht	Càrn nan Conach
Carnoch	A' Chàrnaich*
Carn Toul	Càrn an t-sabhail
Carr Bridge	Drochaid Charr*
Carr dubh, *Ross*	An Càthar dubh*
Carrick	Carraig
Carrieblair	Blàr a' charaidh*
Carron, Loch	Loch Carrunn*
Carsaig	Càrsaig*
Carse of Bayfield / Carse of Kindeace	Mor'oich-Chinn déis, Mor'oich*
Carskie	Crasgaidh
Carswell	Carsalach
Cartomie	Càthar-tomaidh*
Carvie, Glen	Gleann Caraid*
Casandamff	Cadha nan damh*
Cassley, Glen	Gleann Charsla'*
Castlebay	Baile MhicNéill
Castle Corbet	An Caisteal dearg*
Castlecraig	Taigh na créige
Castle Gloom	Caisteal Glòim
Castlehill, (*Inverness*)	Caisteal Still*
Castle Leather	Caisteal Lethoir* C. Leathoir—CR
Castle Leod	Cùl-dà-Leòthaid*
Castle Sween	Caisteal Shuinn
Castle Tirrim	Caisteal Tioram
Cattanach	Catanach
Catherine	Catriona
Catlodge	Caitleag

ENGLISH	GAELIC
Cawdor	Caladair*
Ceander, Loch	Loch Ceanndoir*
Ceann-an-oba	Ceann an òib
Celt	Cellach, *gen.* -aich; Coilteach
Celtic	Ceilteacn
Chanonry	A' Chananaich
Chapel-park	Pàirc an t-seipeil
Charles	Tearlach
Charleston	Baile Thearlaich*
Charlotte	Tearlag
Charmed Isles, the	Na h-Eileanan Sianta*
Cheir'ail, Ben	Beinn a' cheire geal
Chicken Head	Rudha na Circe*
Chiscan	see Shiskine
Chisholm	Siosal, Siosalach
——— of Chisholm	Siosalach Srathghlais
———s, the	Na Siosalaich
Chonzie, Ben	Beinn Chomhainn*
Chreagain, Sròn a'	Sròn a' chritheagain
Chrinlet, Eas a'	Eas a' chrìn leathaid
Christina	Ciorsdan
Christopher	Gille Chriosd
Chroisk, Loch	Loch a' Chroisg*
Chulash	A' Chùlais
Churin, Lochan	Loch Chaoruinn
Clachadow	Clacha dubha
Clachclevan	Clach-chlamhain
Clachnaharry	Clach na h-aire*
Clachtoll	A' Chlach-thuill*
Clachuil	Clach-thuill*
Clackfin	Clach fionn
Cladich	Clàdaich,* Claidich—CR
Claggan	Claigeann
Claisdarran	Clais an torrain
Clan Chattan, a member of	Catanach
Clan Duff	Clann Dubh
Claona	Claon-àth
Clara	Sorcha
Clare, *Kiltearn*	An Clàr*
Clare, Loch	Loch a' chlàir*
Clark	Mac a' chléirich
Clashedy	Clais-fhada
Clashlochy	Clais-lacha
Clashnamuiack	Clais na muigheach*
Clashven	Clais-bhàn
Clashvuie	Clais-bhuidhe
Clathick	Clachaig*
Clava	Clabhalag*
Cleis Cleish	Clais
Clerk	Mac a' chléirich
Clerkhill	Cnoc a' chléirich
Clesedughe	Clais dubh-ghleann
Clibreck	Clìbric*
Cliff	Cliùbh*
Cliff House	Taigh na cliùbha
Clifton, *Tyndrum*	Achadh nan tuiridhnean*
Clochkel	Clach gheal
Cloichfoldich	Clach-phollaich,* Cloich-bhollaich—CR
Cloncaird	Cluain nan cèaird
Clovulin	Clach a' mhuilinn Clo-mhuilinn—CR
Cluany Bridge	Drocheid Chluainidh*
Clune, Alt	Allt a' Chluain
Clunes, *Lochaber*	Na Cluainean

Clunes near Inverness was named by a recent proprietor from above, whence he came. The old name was Fingask.

ENGLISH	GAELIC
Cluny	Cluanaidh
Cluniter	Claon-leitir
Clyde, Strath	Srath Chluaidh
Clyne (now Mountgerald)	An Claon*
Clyne	Clin, (for *claoin*, locative case of claon. *a declivity*. and not as usually stated from *cluain*, which would not give the local pronunciation.
Cnoc àl na gamhainn (*Ross*) OSM.	Cnoc na goibhnidh*
Cnoc a' ghille bhrònaich OSM	Cnoc Gille mo Bhrianaig*
Cnocan	An Cnocan
Cnoc an Frangach OSM	Cnoc Fraing
Cnoc Fyrish	Cnoc foighris*
Cnoclady	Cnoc leathadaidh*
Cnoc Vabin	Cnoc Mhàbairn*
CnocLiathFold, OSM	Cnoc Léith bhaid*
Coag	Cumhag (*for* Cumhang)*
Coast, *Gairloch* (or First Coast)	An t-Eirthire*
Coast, *Aultbea* (or Second Coast)	An t-Eirthire donn*
Cockaline	Cnoc àlainn
Cockney, a	Lunnainneach
Cock of Arran	An Coileach Arranach*
Coe, Glen	Gleann Comhann
Coigach	A' Choigeach*

The five-fifths of Coigach are—Achnahaird, Achlochan, Acheninver, Achabhraigh and Achduart

ENGLISH	GAELIC
Coignafearn	Còig na fearna*
Coilleter	Cuingleitir*
Coilintuie	Coill' an t-suidhe
Coillegillie	Coille Ghillidh*
Coillerigh	Coille-ruigh'
Coillintogle	Cùil an t-seagail*
Coil-lyal	Coille-liathail
Coinn Mheall, Beinn Coinneamh *or* Coinneamh mheall	Conmheall*
Coire Attadale (*App'ecross*)	Coire Atadail*
Coire, Caisteal-na-	Caisteal nan Còrr*
Coirenahenchy	Coire na h-eanchaidh
Coire Yairack	Coire Ghearraig*
Coryvreckan	Coire bhreacain
Coldrain	Cùl an draighean
Coldwells	Am Bealaidh*
Colin	Cailean, *gen.* -ein
Colinton	Baile Chailein
Colintraive	Caol an t-snàimh
Coll, Island of	Colla
Coll, (person)	Colla
Colonsay	Collasa
Colquhoun	Mac a' chombaich
Colquhouns, the	Clann a' chombaich
Columkille	Calum Chille
Colydrain	Cill-droighinn
Compass	An Com-pas*
Comrie (*Contin*)	Comraigh*
——— (*Perthshire*)	Cuimrigh (& Cumaraigh CR)
Conaglen	Conghleann*
Conais	Allt a' chonais*
Conall, Connell (person)	Comhnall
Conchra	Conchra*
Coniveall	Conmheall
Connel (*Lorn*)	A' Choingheal
———, (cataract—"Falls of Lora".	*locally*, A' Chraos
Cononbrae	Bog domhain*
Conan Cridge	Drochaid Sguideil*
———, Strath	Srath Chonuinn*
Contin	Cunndainn*
Contullich	Cunntulaich*

English	Gaelic
Convinth, Glen	Gleann Conthadhaich
Cook	MacCùga in *Arran*
Coolin Hills	An Cuilbhionn, An Cuilfhionn—CB
Coquet Isle	Eilean Cogaid
Coppachy	Copachaidh*
Corachria	Corr-chriadh
Coran, (river)	Còrainn
Corlarach	Corr-làrach
Corn, Ben-na-	Beinn a' chùirn
Cornhiil	Cnoc an airbh*
Cornton	Bail' an loch*
Cornwall (county)	Cornghall
Corrachaive	Coir' a' chaitheamh
Corran	An Corran
Corriehallie	Coire-shaillidh*
Corriemulzie	Coire-mhuillidh*
Corrievachie	Coire-bhacaidh*
Corriewick	Coir' a' bhuic*
Corriehuran	Coir' an fhuarain
Corrish	Corr-innis, Còrrais
Corrow	An coire
Corryarrick	Coire Ghearraig
Corrybrough	Coire broch
Corrygill	Coiregheill
Corryhallie	Coire-shaillidh*
Corryhalloch	Coire-shalach*
Corrynahera	Coire na h-eirbhe
Corry Point	Càrn a' choiridh
Corry Vacky	Coire Bhacaidh*
Corryvreckan	Coire Bhreacain (*B.'s cauldron*)
Corslet	Crois-leathad*
Coruisk	Coir'-uisge
———, Loch	Loch Coir'-uisge
Coryvreckan	see Corryvreckan
Corylach	Coire-chlach
Corvest	Coire-bheist*
Cotterton	Achadh nan coitear*
Coul	A' Chùil*
——, (*Badenoch*)	Cùil
Coulags	Na Cùileagan*
Coulbackie	Cailbacaidh*
Coulhill	Cnoc na cùil*
Coulin	Cùlainn*
Coulmore	A' Chùil mhóir*
Coulside, Loch	Loch Cùlasaid*
Coultry, Loch	Loch Caoltraidh*
Courthill	Cnoc a' mhòid*
Cove	An Uaghaidh*
Cowal	Còmhal
Cowan	MacComhainn
Cowie	Collaigh*
Coygach, Ru	Rudha na Cóigich*
Coylet	Cuingleathad*
Coylum	Cuingleum*
Crackaig	Crachdaig
Craggen	An Creagan
Craggie	Cragaidh*
———, Loch	Loch Creagach
Craig	Creag
———, (*Gairloch*)	Creag Ruigh Mhorgain
Craigandaive	Creag an daimh
Craigdarach	Creag an daraich*
Craigellachie	Creag-Eileachaidh
Craigencallie	Creag na caillich
Craigens	Na Creagain
Craigentinny	Creag an teine*
Craigiehow	Creag a' chobha
Craigleith	Creag liath
Craiglin	Creag linne
Craigmaddie	Creag a' mhadaidh
Craigmillar	Creag a' mhuilleir
Craigmafeich	Creag nam fitheach
Craignish	Creaginnis
Craignure	Creag an iubhair

English	Gaelic
Craig Roy	A' Chreag ruadh
Craig Royston	Creag Trostain*
Craigs	Taigh na créige
Craim, Loch na	Loch na creamha
Craleckan	Crà-leacainn
Crarae	Carr-ei(bh)e*
Crask	Crasg
Crathie	Craichidh
Crawford (person)	Creamhain, MacCreamhain
Cray (*Glen Shee*)	Crathaigh*
Crear	Criathar
Creagach na caorach	Creag achadh na caoraich
Creag Cròcean, OSM.	Creag-chròcan *
Creag Pheacach	Creag fhiaclach
Creag Phulach OSM	Creag follais
Creag Illie	Creag illidh*
Creag na leacainn	Creag leathainn
Creag nan garrag	Creag nan garradh
Creag Riaraidh	Creag Raoiridh*
Creag Stuanisat	Creag Staoinàit
Creed, R. (*Lewis*)	Grìde*
Creich	Craoich*
Crerar	Criathrar
Cretshengan	Croit-sheangan*
Crieff	Craoibh*
Crinan	Crìonan
Crinigart, *Gartmore*	Crìonach Àrd
Crochair	Crochar*
Croe, Glen	Gleann crotha
Croftcarnoch	Croit-charnach
Croftcrunie	Croit a' chrùnaidh*
Croftnallan	Croit an àilein*
Croick	A' Chroic*
Cromarty	Cromba*
——— Firth	Caolas Cromba*
Cromasag	Crom-fhasadh
Cromble, Strath	Srath Chrombail
Cromdale	Crombail
Cromlet	Crom-leathad*
Cross	Cros
Crossburn	Allt tarsuinn
Crossiebeg	An crosadh beag
Crowlin (islands)	Cròlaig, Cròlainn.*
The passage between Crowlin Islands and Scalpay is called	An Linne Chròlaigeach*
Cruachan, Ben	Cruachan Beann, *locally* Cruachan
Cruach Neuran	Cruachan an fhiùran
Crumby (*Lewis*)	Crumbaidh
Crutten, Glen	Gleann cruitein
Cuaig	Ob Chùaig*
Cuchullin Hills	see Coolin Hills
——— Sound	An Linne Sgitheanach
Cuilishie	Caolaisidh*
Cuilmuick	Cuil na muice
Cuinag	Cuinneag*
Culbo	Cùrabol*
Culbockie	Culbàicidh*
Culcheinnich	A' Chùil-chòinnich*
Culcraggie	Cul a' chreagain*
Culduie	Cùilduibh*
Culkein	Culcinn
Culkenzie	Cul Choinnich*
Cullicudden	Cùl a' chudainn*
Culliss	Cùl an lios*
Culloden	Cùil-lodair (for lodain)*
Culmailie	Cul-mhàilidh
Culnaha	Cùil na h-àtha*
Cultbuy	Coillte-buidhe
Cults	Cuilt
Cultoon	Cùl-tuinidhe
Culvokie	Cùilbhòcaidh*
Culzean	Cùl-Sian
Cumbernauld	Comar nan allt, Colmoneala
Cumbrae, Great	Cumradh mór

English	Gaelic
Cumbrae, Little	Cumradh beag
Cumming	Cuimein, Cuimeanach
————s, the	Na Cuimeinich
Cuniside	Caonasaid
Curitan	Curadan
Currach, a'	An Currach
Currie	Mac 'uirigh & 'ac 'uirigh—CR (MacMhuirich)
Cyderhall	Siara*
Cyril	Caoral, Cuirealan
Dailcheanna	Dail-choinnich
Dailermaig	Dail-Dhiarmaig(Dhiarmaid)
Dalachulish	Dail a' chaolais
Dalchully	Dail-chuilidh
Dalkeith	Dail-ché*
Dallas	Dalais*
Dalmally	Dail-mhàilidh
Dalnafree	Dail na frithe
Dalnatrad	Dail na tràghad
Dalnavie	Dail-neimhidh*
Dalness	Dail an eas*
Dalnessie	Dail an easaich
Dalraddy	Dail-radaidh
Dalreavich	Dail riabhach
Daltot	Dail-tobhta
Dalvina	Dail-bheinne
Dalween	Dail-fhionn
Dalwhinnie	Dail-chuinnidh
Dalzell	Dail-gheal *
Dane, a	Lochlannach
Darach	MacGille Riabhaich
Darlochan	Doire-lochan
Daruel, Glen	Gleann dà Ruathail
Davaar	Eilean da Bharr
David	Daibhidh (*pron.* Dàidh)
Davidsons, the	Clann Dàibhidh
Daviot	Deimhidh*
Davoch beg	Dabhach beag
Dealt, Ben ; Beinn na diollaide, OSM.	Beinndealt*
Deanaich	Dianaich*
Dee, Strath	Srath Dé, Srath Dhè
Delavorer	Dail a' mhoireir
Dell, (*Lewis*)	Dail
——, North	Dail a thuath*
——, South	Dail a dheas*
Delny	Deilgnidh
Denmark	Lochlann
Derculich	Dearg thulaich* Dearglaich—CR
Dermid	Diarmid
Derrileane	Torr-leathann
Derriworchie	Doire Mhurchaidh
Derry, Glen	Gleann Doire*
Derryguag	Doire dhubhaig*
Deucheran	Dìubh chea(th) r(amhn)an
Dewar	Deòir, Deòireach
Dhu loch	Dubh-loch
Diabeg	Diabaig*
Dibidale	Diobadal*
Dingwall	Inbhir-pheofharain* 2 see Baile-chàil
Dippin	Dà-pheighinn
Dirriemore	An Dìridh mór*
Dithrabh, Loch an-	Loch an dithreibh*
Dluich	Dlùth-fhaich
Dochaird	Dabhach àrd
Docharty, Glen	Gleann Dochartaidh
Dochcarty	Do'ach Gartaidh*
Dochfour	Dabhach phùr*
Dochrie	Dabhach
Doire seirbhe, Loch na	Loch Doire na h-eirbhe*
Don, River	Deathan*
Donald	Domhnall, *gen.* -uill
Donnan's Isle	Eilean Donnan

English	Gaelic
Dornadilla, Dun	Dùn Dornaigil
Dorney	An Dòirnidh*
Dornie	An Dòirnidh*

Ceannaiche na Dòirnidh, *the Dornie merchant*. The old name—Bun-dà-loch is now applied only to the east end of the village*

English	Gaelic
Dornigill	see Dornadilla
Dornoch	Dornoch
Dorothy	Diorbhàil
Dorrygorrie	Doire Goraidh
Dosmuckaran	Dos-mhucarain*
Douchary	Duchairidh*
Douglas	Dùbhghlas
————, (person)	Dùbhghlas
Doune	An Dunaidh
Dounie	Dunaidh*
Dourag, (river)	Dobhrag
Douren, Glen	Gleann nan darach
Dowhill	Dubh-choille
Dowally	Dubh-thallaidh—CR Dubhailigh*
Downie	Dunaidh
Drian, Glen	Gleann nan droigheann
Drienach	An Droighneach
Driminault	Druim an allt*
Drimnin	Na Drimnin
Droitham	Drochaid riabhan*
Droma, Loch an, O.S.M.	Lochaidh Droma*
Dron	Drongaid
Drumalbin	Druim-albainn
Drumancroy	An Druim cruaidh*
Drumcudden	Druimchudainn*
Drumderfit	Druim(a)diar*
Drumdil	Druim(a) daol*
Drumdyre	Druim(a) doighr*
Drumgarve	Druim garbh
Drumlee	Druim liath
Drummond	Druiminn*
Drummonds, the	Na Druiminnich
Drumnossie	Druim-Athaisidh*
Drumnadrochit	Druim na drochaid
Drumnamarg	Druim nam marg*
Drumnasaille	Druim na saille
Drumouchter	Druim-uachdair
Drumrunie	Druim(a) Raonaidh*
Drumsmittal	Druim(a) smiotail*
Drumsynie	Druim Sìne
Drumuie	Druim-muigh* (old *gen.* of magh)
Drunkie, Loch	Loch Drongaidh*
Drymen	Druiminn*
Drynich Inch	Innis Droighnich
Drynie	Droighnidh*
————, Park	Pairc Dhroighnidh*
Drynlea	Droigheann liath
Drynoch	An Droighneach*
Duart (*Mull*)	Dubhart
————, (*Lochalsh*)	Dubh àird
Duasdale	Dubhastail
Dubh-chraige, Beinn	Beinn-dubh-chraige
Dublin	Baile àth cliath*
Duchally	Dubhchailigh*
Duchary	Dubhcharaigh*
Duff	Dubh
Duffy	see MacPhee
Dugald	Dùghall
Dùgaraidh	Dubh-gharaidh*
Duheartach	Dù-Irtich
Duich, Loch	Loch Dubhthaich*
Duilater	An Duibhleitir*
Duileat, Loch an	Loch an duibh leathaid
Duirnish	see Duirinish
Duisker	Dubh-uisge
Duisky	Dubh-uisge

ENGLISH	GAELIC
Dull	Dul*
Dulnain	Tuilnean
Dulsie Bridge	Drochaid Dhùlfhasaidh*
Dumbarton	Dun Breatunn*
————shire	SiorramachdDhunBreatunn
Dumfries	Dum-fris
————shire	Siorramachd Dum-fris
Dun, the	An Dùn
Dunachton	see Dunaughton
Dunad	Dùn Athad
Dunaincroy	Dunan cruaidh
Dunaughton or Dunachton	Dùn Neachdainn
Dunaverty	Caisteal Dun-àbhartaidh
Dunbeath	Dun Bheitheadh*
Dunblane	Dun Blathain*
Duncan	Donnchadh, *gen.* -aidh
Duncans, the	Clann Donnchaidh
Dun Can (*Raasay*)	Dùn Canna*
Duncanston	Bog a' mhiodair*
Dunconnel	Dun-Chomhnuill
Duncow	Dun-coll*
Duncraggan	Dun-creagain*
Duncraig(*Lochalsh*)	Am Fasadh, Am F. àluinn*
Duncrieve *or* Duncrivie	Dun chraobh
Dundee	Dun-dèagh*
Dunderave	Dùn-dà-ràmh
Dunderawe	Dun an rudha
Dundonnell	Acha-dà-Dhòmhnuill*
———— Lodge, site of	An t-Eilean daraich*
Dundurn	Dùn-dùirn*
Dunean	Dun-ian
Dune Alliscaig	Dùn Alaisgig*
Dunfallandy	Dun-falandaidh*
Dunfermline	Dun Pharlain
Dunfin	Dun fionn
Dunglas	Dun glas
Dun gobhal, *Logie Easter*	*now* An Dùn*
Duniasgan	Dun (fh)iasgan
Dunira	Dun-iara'*
Dunkeld	Dun Chaillinn
Dunloskin	Dun-losgainn*
Dunmaglas	Dun Mac-glais*
	Dùn MacTuathail,*(*Drummond, Aberfeldy*)
Dunmore	Dùn mór*
Dunnet	Dunaid*
Dunolly	Dun-ollaimh
Dunoon	Dun omhain
Dunrobin	Dun-robain*
Dunscore	Dun-sgoir
Dunskaith	Dùn-sgàth*
Dunskeig	Dunsgéitheig
Dunstaffnage	Dun-sta(fh)inis*
Duntaulich	Dun Teamhalach*
Duntelchack	Dun-deilcheig (i.e. Dun t-seilcheig)*
Dunure	Dùn-iubhair*
Dunvegan	Dun-bheagan
Dunvornie	Dun-bheirinidh
Dunyardil	Dun Dearduil
Dunyveg	Dun Naomhaig
Dupplin	Dubhlinn
Durine	Dubhraoin
Duirinish, *Lochalsh*	Diurinnis
————, *Skye*	Diurinnis

Called *Dùthaich nam mogan* and *am Fearann mogannach*, locally, by the inhabitants of Trotternish.

ENGLISH	GAELIC
Durnamuck	Doire nam muc*
Durness	Duirnis, Diùranais
Duror	Duror
Duthil	Daoghal*

ENGLISH	GAELIC
Dychlie	Dubh-choille
Dyker's Burn	Allt an digeadair*
Dyne, Glen	Gleann domhain
Dysart	Dìseart,* Diseart—CR
Ean, Loch-nan-	Loch nan eun
Earavick	Earabhaig*
Earn, R.	Abhainn Éire
———, Loch	Loch Éire
———, Strath	Srath Éire
Earnaich	Rudha àird, *locally* Àird Eirionnaich
Earshader	Iar-seadair*
Easdale	Éisdeal
Eastertyre	Iochdar-tìre*
Eathie Burn	Àthaidh, Allt Àthaidh
Eay, Ben	Beinn Eighe*
Ebost	Eubost*
Eck, Loch	Loch Aic
Edderton	Eadardun*
———— Farm	Baile nam feitheachan*
Edderlinne	Eadarlinne*
Eddrachillis	Eadar-dà-chaolais*
Eddraisk	Eadar-dà-uisge*
Eddraven	Eadar-dà-bheinn*
Eden	Aodann*
Edenkillie	Aodann na coille*
Edinample	Aodainn Ambail*
Edinburgh	Dun Eideann
Edinchip	Aodainn a' chip*
Edward	Imhear, Iomhar, Eideard
Eglish nam braren,	Eaglais nam bràithrean
Egypt	An Eiphit
Eidard, R.	Eidird
Eididh, Sgéir-an-	Sgéir an t-séididh
Eigen, Ben	Beinn Éiginn*
Eigg	Eige, Eilean Eige
	Eilean nam ban móra

An adjacent loch given in O.S.M as Loch na mna móire, should be Loch nam ban móra.

ENGLISH	GAELIC
Eil, Loch	Loch Ìall
Eilean-na-coomb	Eilean nan caoimh
Eilister	Aolastradh
Einig, River	Eunag*
Eishart	Loch Éiseort
Elchaig, Glen	Gleann Eilcheig*
Eldrable	Eildirebal
Eleraik	Iolaireig
Elg, Glen	Glinn Eilge
Elgin	Eilginn*
Elizabeth	Ealasaid
Ellanvow	Eilean a' bhogha
Ellen-a-vulig	Eilean a' bhuilg*
Ellen-na-roan	Eilean nan ròn*
Ellen's Isle	An t-Eilean molach*
Ellon	Elain—*Book of Deer**
Elphin	Elfionn, Ailfionn
Elrickmore	Eilrig mhòr*
Elruck	Iolairig
Emaraconart	Iomaire-comhnard
Embo	Éuraboll
Endiart Water	Eideart
England	Sasunn, *gen.* -uinn
English, *adj.*	Sasunnach
———— language	A' Bheurla
Englishman, an	Sasunnach
Enoch, Loch	Loch Eanach
Eoradale	Eòrradal*
Eorrapaidh	Eòrrabaidh*
Erbusaig	Earbasaig*
Erchite	Earchoid, Airchoighd*
Erchless	Earghlais*
Eribol	Éuraboll
Ericht, Loch	Loch Eireachd*
Eriskay	Aoraisgeidh*
Erradale	Eàrradal*

ENGLISH	GAELIC
Erraid	Eilean Earraid*
Erribol	see Eribol
Errick, Strath	Srath Fharragaig*
Erridale	see Erradale
Errocht, Loch	Loch Eireachd*
Erskine	Arascain
Eskadale	Eisgeadal
Eskinnish	Easginnis
Essich	Easaich*
Ethie	Àthaidh*
Etive, Glen	Gleann Éite
——, Loch	Loch Éite
Ettridge	Eadrais (Eadar-dà-eas)
Euphemia	Oighrig
Eurach	Iùbhrach
Europe	An Roinn Eòrpa
European, an	Eòrpach
Evaig, Glen	Gleann Fhiodhaig*
Evan	Eòghann
Evanachan	Eoghanachan
Evanton	Bail' Eòghainn, am Bail' ùr
Evelex	Éibhleag*
Ewe, Isle	Eilean Iù*
—, Loch	Loch Iù
—, River	Iù, Iùbh
Ewen	Eòghann
Ey, Glen	Gleann Eigh*
Eye, Peninsula of	An Aoidh*
—, Loch	Loch na h-uidhe*
Fain	Na Féithean*
Fairburn	Braon, Farabraoin*
Falkirk	An Eaglais bhreac
Falloch, Glen	Gleann Falach*
Fanans	Na Fàna
Fannich, Loch	Loch Fainich*
Fannyfield	Am Bog riabhach*
Faraline, Loch	Loch Farralainn*
Farar, Glen Strath	Gleann Srath Farar
Farikaig Water	Farragaig*
Farlary	Farrlaraigh*
Farness	Fearnais
Far Out (*or* Farrid Head)	An Fharaid*
Farquhar	Fearchar, *gen.* -air
Farquharson	MacFhearchair
——— of Invercauld	" Mac Mhic Fhionnlaigh "
———s, the	Siol Fhionnlaigh, Clann Fhearchair
Farr	Fai
Farragon, O.S.M.	Feargan*
Fasagrianach	An Fhasadh chrionaich, *gen.* na Fasadh crionaich
Fashven	Faisbheinn*
Fasnacloich	Fas na cloiche*
Fasnakyle	Fas na coille*
Fassifern	Am Fasadh-fearna*
Faygarvick	Féith a' gharaidh bhig
Fearn	Manachainn Rois, *locally* a' Mhanachainn*
—— parish	Sgìre na Manachainn
Fearna beag / Fearna mór	Na Fearnan* (*Applecross*)
Fernan	Feàrnan (*Loch Tay*)
Febait	An Fheith bhàite*
Felin	Fé-linne
Fellon mór	Faoileann mór
Fender	Fionndar*
Fendem	Na Fàna*
Feochan, Loch	Loch Faochain
Fergus	Fearghas
Fergusson	MacFhearghais
——— of Balmacruchie	" MacAididh "
——— of Dalfallandy	" MacFhearghais "

ENGLISH	GAELIC
Fergussons, the	Clann Fhearghais
Ferindonald	Fearann Dòmhnuill*

The district from the Alness river to the burn of Allt na làthaid to the east of Dingwall.

ENGLISH	GAELIC
Ferintosh	An Tòisighea chd*
Fermoy	Fearnmhuighe
Fernaig	Fearnaig*
Fernate, Glen	Fearnaid*
Fern-na-more	Fearna mór
Fernsdale	Fearnasdail
Ferrin Vir Quire	Fearann MhicGuire
Fersit	Fearsaid
Feshie,	Feisidh
——, Glen	Gleann Feisidh
Feus, the (*Kinross*)	Fiodh
Fiannaidh, Sgorr-nam-	Sgòrr nam Fiann(t)aidh
Fiddich, Glen	Gleann Fidich
Fife	Fiobha
Fifeshire	Siorramachd Fiobha
Fillan	Faolan
——, Strath	Na Sraithibh, Sgìre Sraithibh. *Old name*—Srath Eitrich
Finbracken	Fionn-bhreacan
Fincastle	Fonn chastal*
Findatie	Fionn-dabhach
Finderlie	Fionnlarach
Findhorn, River	Uisge Éire*
Findon	Fionndun*
Findynate	Fonn doimhneid*
Fingask	Fionnghaisg (*near* Clunes, near *Inverness.*)
Fingland	Fionnghleann
Finglas	Fionnghlas*
Finglen	Fionnghleann*
Finlarig	Fionnlairig*
Finlas, Glen	Gleann Fionnghlais*
Finlay	Fionnlagh (*not* -adh)
Finlayson	MacFhionnlaigh
Finnan, Glen	Gleann Finan* / Gleann fhionain—CR
Finnart	Fionn-aird
Firemore	Am faithir mór
Fiscary	Faisgairidh
Fisher	Mac an iasgair
Fisherfield	Innis an iasgaich
FitzGerald	MacGhearailt, Gearailteach
Fivig	Fiabhaig
Flanders	Flànras
——— Moss	A' Mhoine Fhlànrasach
Fletcher	Mac an fhleisdeir
Fleet	Fleòd
——, Strath	Srath Fleòid
Fleuchary, Fleucherries	Fliuchairidh
Flodday	Flodaigh*
Flodigarry	Eilean a' chinne mhóir
Flodebay	Fleòd a' ibhaigh
Flora	Fionnaghal
Flowerdale	Am Baile mór*
——— House (Old)	An Taigh Dìge*
——— House (New)	Taigh Dìge nan gorm leac*
Fluchlady	Fliuch leathad*
Fodderletter	Farleitir*
Fodderty	Fodhraitidh*
Foin Bhein	Foinnebheinn*
Folais (*Gairloch*)	Fóghlais*
Forbes	Foirbeis, Foirbeiseach
———es, the	Na Foirbeisich
Forres	Farrais*
Forsinain	Forsain-fhàin*
Forsinard	Forsain-àird*
Fort Augustus	Cill Chuimein

ENGLISH	GAELIC
Forth, River	Abhainn dubh
Fortingall	Fartairchill*
Fortrose	A' Chananaich*
Fort William	Gearasdan Inbhir-lòchaidh
Foss	Fas*
Fowlis	Fólais (=Foghlais)
Foyers	Foithir*
——, Falls of	Eas na smùid*
France	An Fhraing
Frances	Frangag
Francis	Frangan
Fraser	Friseil, Frisealach
—— of Culbokie	" Mac Uistein "
—— of Lovat	see Lord Lovat
——s, the	Na Frisealaich
Fraserburgh	Baile nam Frisealach
Freeburn	Allt na Frìthe*
Freevater (or Balnagown Forest)	Frìth Bhàtair* (i.e. Walter's Forest)
French (language)	Fraingeis
Ag ionnsachadh na Fraingeis, *learning the French language*	
Fresgill	Freisgil*
Freuchie	Fraochaidh*
——, Loch	Loch Fraochaidh*
Frew, Fords of	Na Friù'achan*
Friza, Loch	Loch Phrìsa
Fruin, Glen	Gleann Freòin*
Fuday Island	Fudaigh
Fullarton	MacLethaidh—*Arran*
Fura Island	Eilean Futhara, E. Fùra*
Furnace, (*Argyll*) / Furness, *Gairloch*	An Fhùirneis*
Fyne, Glen	Gleann Fhìne
——, Loch	Loch Fìne
Fyrish, Cnoc	Feighris*
Gael	Gàidheal, *gen. sing. & n. pl.* Gàidheil
Gaelic (language)	A' Ghàidhlig
Gaick	Gàig*
Gairletter	Geàrr-leitir
Gailich, Ard-na-	Aird na Càillich
Gair, Loch	Loch geàrr
Gairloch	Geàrr-loch
—— Hotel, site of	Achadh Deathasdal*
Gairlochy	Geàrrlochaidh
Gairneg Water	Goirneag*
Galbraith	Mac a' Bhreatnaich
Gallon	Gallan
Gallovie	Gealagaidh
Gallow Hill (*Tarbat*)	Cnoc na croiche
Galloway, Mull of	Maol nan Gall
Gallowshill, (*Urquhart*)	Cnoc a' chrochaidh
Galway	Baile nan gailbhinn
Gantocks	Na Gamhn(t)aich
Ganuisg	Gann-uisge
Gany	see Geanies
Garafad / Garbad	An Garbad*
Garbhchriochan	see Dictionary
Gardenstown	Baile-gharaidh
Gargustown	Baile-ghargaidh*
Garioch	Gairbheach*
Garrabost	Garbost*
Garrachra	Garbh-chea(th)ra(mh)
Garraron	Garbharan
Garrowchorran	Garbh-chorran
Garry, Glen, *Perthshire* / ——, *Inverness*	Gleanna garadh
Garry, River, *Perth & Inverness*	Garadh
Garry, River (*Gairloch*)	A' Ghairbhe*
Garrynahine	Gearraidh na h-aibne *
Gartachara	Gart a' charraigh
Garten, Boat of	Coit Ghartain*
Gartgunnal	Gart-dhuineil
Garth	Gart*
Gartie (Mid & W.)	Gartaidh*
Gartloskin	Gart-losgainn
Gartmain	Gart-meadhon
Gartmore	Gart mór
Gartness	Gart an eas
Garty	Gartaidh
Garva beag	Garbh-àth beag
—— more	—— mór
Garvanachy	Garbhan achaidh
Garvary	Garbhairidh*
Garve	Gairbh*
——, Loch	Loch Maol Fhinn*
Garvellan	Garbh Eilean
Garvelloch	Garbh Eileach*
Garveoline	Garadh Bheòlain
Garvie	Garbhaidh*
Gask	Gaisg
Gauer, (river)	Gamhar*
Geanies	Gàthan*
Gearran, Beinn na OSM.	Beinn Garaig
Gedd, Loch	An Geadloch*
Geddes	Geadais*
Geddeston	Baile nan Geadas
Geoffry	Goiridh
George	Seòras, Seòrsa, Deòrsa
Germany	A' Ghearmailt
Geusachan	Giùthsachan*
Geyzen Briggs Banks	Drochaid an obh*
Ghaordy, Meall	Meall Ghaoirdidh*
Ghiuthais, Alt a' mhór	Allt a' mheirbh ghiubhais*
Ghruinnard	Gruinneard*
Gigha	Giogha
Gight, Bog of	Bog na gaoithe*
Gilbert	Gillebrìde, Gilleabart
Gilchrist	Gillechriosd
Gillanders	Gilleandrais
Gillespie	Gilleasbuig
Gillies	Gill'Iosa, Liosach [L. is also *a native of Lismore.*]
Gilmour	Mac 'Ghille mhoire
Gilp, Loch	Loch-gilp
Gilroy	Mac 'Ghille ruaidh
Girnag Water	Abhainn Goirneag*
Gisla, River	Gìosla
Glackbeath	Glaic-beithe
Glackour	A' Ghlaic odhar*
Glacnasenshesen	Glac nan sean innsean*
Gladfield	Leac a' chlamhain*
Gladsmuir	Sliabh a' chlamhain*
Glaickarduich (*Knockbain*) / Glaickerduck (*Urray*)	Glaic an dubhaig*
Glaickmore	A' Ghlaic mhór*
Glaisven	Glas-bheinn*
Glamis	Glamas
Glascairn	Clais 'chàirn*
Glascarnock	Clais-chàrnaich
Glasgow	Glaschu
Glaslet	Glasleathad*
Glasletter	Glasleitir* [—CR
Glass	Gleanna Glais* Gleann G.
——, Loch	Loch Glais*
——, Strath	Srath Ghlais*
——, River	An t-uisge Glasach
Glassary	Glasairidh

ENGLISH	GAELIC
Glasven	Glaisbheinn*
Glasswell	Glasaill
Glecknahavil	Glac na sabhal
Gledfield	Leth 'chlamhaig,* Leac 'chlamhaig*
Glenbucket	Gleann Buichead*
Glenbuckie	Gleann Bocaidh*
Glencroe	Gleann crò*
Glendebadel	Gleann Dìobadail*
Glenelg	Glinn Eilg
Glenfruin	Gleann Freòin*
Glengyle	Gleann Goill*
Glenorchy	Gleann Urchaidh, Gleann Urcha*
Glenshiel	Gleann Seile*
Glenstockdale	Gleann Stocadail*
Glenure	Gleann Iubhar*
Gloe, Ben-y-	Beinn a' ghlò*
Glomach, Falls of	Eas na Glòmaich*
Gloy, Glen	Gleann Glaoidh*
Gluich	An Glaodhaich*
Goat Fell	Gaoda-bheinn*
Gobagrenan	Gob a' ghrianan
Godfrey	Goraidh, Goiridh [*name facetiously applied to the fox*]
Golspie	Goillspidh
Go-na-calman	Geodha nan calman
Go-na-dunan	Geodha nan dunan
Gonval	Conn-bhaile
Gooseburn	Allt nan geadh*
Gordon	Gòrdan, Gòrdanach
——, Duke of	An Gòrdanach
—— Hall	Lag an Nòtair
Gordons, the	Na Gòrdanaich
Gormack Burn	Gormag*
Gorstan	An Goirtean fraoich
Gortendoil	Gort an doill
Gorton	An Goirtean
Gourock	Goraig
Govan	Cille Mhaoil Chaluim
Gow	Gobha
Gowrie	Gobhraidh*
——, Glen	Gleann Gobhraidh*
Graat, Allt	Allt grannda*
Grace	Giorsal
Gradal (*now* Badvoon)	Gràdal*
Graham	Greumach
Grahams, the	Na Greumaich
Grampians, the	Monadh Dhruim Uachdair *west of Struan*; Monadh Minigeig *east of Struan**
Grant	Grannd
—— of Grant	An Granndach
—— of Glenmoriston	"MacPhàdruig"
Grantown	Baile nan Granndaich
Grantully	Gar'n tulaich*
Gray	Ciaran
Greece	A' Ghréig
Green Dasses	Meall gorm*
Greenleonachs	Lianagan a' chuil-bhàicidh*
Greenock	Grianaig
Greenstone Point	Rudha na cloiche uaine*
Gregor	Griogair
Gregory	MacGriogair
Griam, Loch	Loch Ghriam*
Grivie Water	Griabhaidh *
Grosebay	Greosabhagh
Grubmore	see Grumb more
Grudie	Grùididh
——, Glen	Gleann Grùididh
—— Water	Abhainn Grùididh
Gruinard River, "the Rockies" in	Na Coineasan*
Grumb-beg	Grùb beag

ENGLISH	GAELIC
Grumb-more	Grùb mór
Grumbie	Grombaidh
Guinag River	Goibhneag
Guisachan	Giuthsachan
Gullion, Ben	Beinn Ghualainn
Gulvain	Gaothail-bheinn
Gunn	Guinne, Gunnach
—— of Braemore	"Mac Sheumais Chataich"
Gunns, the	Na Gunnaich
Gylen Gastle	Caisteal Gaoilean
Halkirk	Hacraig
Hallater	Allt thaobh-leitir
Hamasord, Loch	Loch Chamasort*
Hanty, Glen-a-	Gleann shean-taighe
Harold	Arailt, Haral
Harold's Rock	Creag Harail
Harris	Na h-Earradh
——, Glen	Gleann thàiris
Hartfield	Coille Mhùiridh*
Haskeir	Haisgeir*
Heathfield	Cal-fhraochaidh
Hebraic, *adj.*	Eabhrach
Hebrides, the	Innse Ghall
Hebrew (language)	Eabhra
—— (person)	Eabhrach, *gen.* -aich
Hector	Eachunn
Hee, Ben	Beinn shìth
Heisgeir	Hei(l)sgeir*
Helen	Eilidh
Hell's Glen	Gleann Iarruinn*
Helmsdale	Bun-Illidh (Y),* B.ilidh—CR
Henderson	MacEanruig
Henry	Eanruig
Hercules	Iorcall, *gen.* -aill
Herne Bay	Camus na corra
Herries, the	Na h-Earradh
Hervie, Glen	Gleann thairbhidh
Heskernich, Ben	Beinn Theasgarnaich*
Highbank, *Lewis*	Tabàc
Highfield, *Urray*	Ciarnaig
Highland, *adj.*	Gàidhealach
Highlands, the	A' Ghaidhealtachd
Hilton	Bail' a' chnuic
Holland	An Olaind
Holy Loch	An Loch Seunnta*
Hope	Hòb*
Horn, Ben	Beinn Horn*
Horseshoe Bay	Crudh-an eich

Gu'm bi c' àit' am bi thu 'san là, bi an Crudh an eich a's t-oidhche, *spend the day where you like, but spend the night in Horseshoe Bay*, (a well-known anchorage in Sound of Kerrara)—old direction for sailors.

ENGLISH	GAELIC
Hourn, Loch	Loch Shuirn
Hugh	Uisdean, Eòghann in *Argyll*
Hughstown	Cnocan cruaidh*
Humberston	see Upper Kildun
Hungerhill	Cnoc an acrais
Hunish, Ru	Rudh Hùnais
Huntly	Hunndaidh
Hurdy Hill	Cnoc Gille Chùrdaidh
Husabost	Hùsabost*
Hutcheson	MacUistein
Hutick, Ben	Beinn Thutaig
Iag, Glen	Gleann Fhiodhaig
Iarlish (island)	Earlais*
Iarlraig	Iolairig
Icolmkill or Iona	Ì, Ì Chaluim Chille, Eilean Ì
Idrigil	Ìdrigil,* Ìodraigil—CR
Ilachaneuve	Na h-Eileacha Naomha*
near them are..	Na h-Eileacha Dubha*
Ima, Ben	Beinn Ime*
Immer	An t-Iomaire
Immeroin	Iomaire Eòghain*
Inmirrioch (*now* Strathyre village	An t-Iomaire Riabhach*

ENGLISH	GAELIC
Inch	Innis
Inchadney Inchaidan, *Kenmore*	Innis Chailtnidh
Inchaffray	Innis-aifrinn
Inchard, Loch	Loch Uinnseard
Inchbae	Innis beith
Inchberry	Innis bhàiridh
Inchcape, *Suth'd*	Innis ceap
Inch Egra	Innis Sheighear
Inchina	Innis an àth*
Inchintaury	Innis an t-searaigh, Innis an t-tamhraidh.
Inchkeith	Innis Ché
Inchnairn	Innis an fheàrna*
Inchnevy	Innis-neimhidh*
Inchommie	Innis a' chomanaich
Inchoraig	Innis na seamraig
Inchree	Innis ruidhe, Innis righ
Inchrory	Innis Ruairidh*
Inchvannie	Innis Mheannaidh
Inchvuilt	Innis a' mhuilt
Indies, the East	Na h-Innseachan shìos
——, the West	Na h-Innseachan shuas
Inellan	Eun-eilean, Ì an eilean
Inens (*K. of Bute*)	Na h-aoinidh
Ingan	Iongan
Inion	Na h-ingheam
Innerwick	Inbhir-mhuice
Innisfallen	Innis faillean
Innie	Aoineadh
Innisherrich	Innis searraich
Innistore	Innis torran
Inshlampie	Innis lanndaidh
Inver	Inbhir
Inveraithie	Inbhiràthaidh
Inveran	Inbhirean
Inverary	Inbhir Aora
Inverasdale	Inbhiràsdal
Inverawe	Inbhir Atha
Inverbroom, *or* Balloan	Bail' an lòin
Inverbroom Lodge *or* Foy Lodge	An Fhothaidh
Invercannich	Inbhir Chanaich*
Invercarron	Inbhir Charrann*
Invercassley	Inbhir Charsla*
Invercauld	Inbhir Callaidh
Inverchaolain	Inbhirchaolain
Inverchaple	Inbhir-chapull
Invercruskie	Inbhir Chrosgaidh*
Invercoe	Inbhir Chomhann
Invercoran	Inbhir-chòrainn*
Inveresragan	Inbhir-easragain*
Inverewe House	Taigh na Plùc aird
Inverfarigaig	Inbhir Faragaig*
Invergarry	Inbhir-gharadh
Inverghueseran	Inbhir Ghiuthsaran
Invergordon	An Rudha, Rudha 'nach Breacaidh ('nach=aonach, *market*)*
Inveriavenie	Inbhir-riamh-ainnidh
Inverie	InbhirEigh,* I. Aoighe—CR
Inverinate	Inbhir-ionaid
Inverkeithing	Inbhir-Cheitein
Inverlael	Inbhir-Lathail
Inverlochlarig	Inbhir Lòchlairig
Inverlochy	Inbhir-lòchaidh
Invermark	Inbhir-mhairc
Invermeran (*Glenlyon*)	Inbhir Meuran
Invernahyle	Inbhir na h-aighle
Inverness	Inbhir Nis
Inversnaid	Inbhir-snàthaid
Inveruglas	Inbhir Dhùbhghlais
Iona	see Icolmkill

ENGLISH	GAELIC
Ire, Strath	Srath-iodhair *or* -eadhair*
Ireland	Eireann
Isabella	Iseabal
Isauld	I's-allt (i.e. Innis-allt)*
Islay	Île, an t-Eilean Îleach
Isteane	Innis dian*
Italy	An Eadailt
James	Seumas, *gen.* -ais
Jamestown	Baile Shiamais (Sheumais)
Jamieson	MacShimidh
James Temple	Cnoc Seumas Chaisteil
Jane	Sìne
Janet, Jessie	Seònaid
Janetown	Torr nan clàr, Baile Sèine
Jeannie	Sìonag
JESUS CHRIST	IOSA CRIOSD
Jewry	Iudhachd
John	Iain, Eoin

The latter form is always used in Scripture, and colloquially in Skye—Iain in other parts. "Seathan" appears in popular lore.

ENGLISH	GAELIC
Johnson	MacIain
Johnstone	Bail'-Iain
Joseph	Seòsaidh
Judith	Siubhan
Julia	Sìlis
Jura	Diùra
——, Sound of	an Linne Rosach
Kailtown	Bail' a' chàil, a by-name of a part of Dingwall retained in a local inn—"Baile chaul Inn."
Kaimes	Camas*
Kallin, *Uist*	Na Ceallan
Kames	Camus nam muclach, *locally* Camus
Kanaird, Loch	Loch Cainneart
Kathel	Cathal
Katewell	Ciadail
Katherine	Catrìona
Katrine, Loch	Loch Ceiteirein*
Keal, Loch-na	Loch nan ceal*
Keanchilish	Ceann a' chaolais
Keanlochbervie	Ceann Loch Biorbhaidh
Kearan, Loch	Loch Ciaran
Keboch Head	Ceann na càbaig
Keir	Cathair
Keiss	Céis
Keith, (person)	MacShithich—CR, Ceiteach
Kellon	Ceall-fhonn
Kelso, New	Eadar dhà charrainn
Keltie, *Kinross*	Coillte
Keltney Burn	Cailtnidh*
Kelty	Cailtidh*
Kenmore,	A name of frequent occurrence, generally *m.*, but sometimes *f.*—CR
——, *Applecross*	A' Cheann'mhor (*s.f.*)
——, *L. Tay*	An Ceann'mhor (*s.m.*)
Kennedy	Ceannaideach, MacUalraig, MacUaraig
Kennedys, the	Clann MhicUaraig
Kenneth	Coinneach, *gen.* -ich.
Kennoway	Ceann a' bhàigh
Kenvar	Ceann a' mhara
Keoldale	Cealdail
Keppoch	Ceapach
Keppochmuir	An Sliabh Ceapanach
Kepprigan	Ceapragan
Kernsary	Cearnai'sar
Kerr	Ciar, Mac Ghille Chiar
Kerrara	Cearrara*
Kerry, *Cowal*	An Ceathramh Còmh'lach
Kerry River	Abhainn Chearraidh
Kerrycroy	An Ceathramh cruaidh

ENGLISH	GAELIC
Kerrysdale	Dail-chearraidh, A' Chathair bheag
Kerrow	an Ceathramh
Kerrowaird	Ceathramh àrd
Kerrowgair	Ceathramh gèarr
Kessock Ferry	Port Cheiseig,* Aiseig Cheiseig
Kiarnan	Cea(th)r(amhn)an
Kiel	Cill
Kilarrow	Cill-a-rubha
Kilbarchan	Cill Bearchain*
Kilberry	Cill-bheiridh
Kilbirnie	Cuil-bhraonaidh*
Kilblaan	Cill-Bhlathan
Kilbrandon	Cill Bhrannain, Cill Bhreanan
Kilbrennan Sound	An Caolas 'Ranndanadh* An Caolas Sranndanach*
Kilbride	Cill Brìghde
Kilcalmonell	Cill Chalmaineala, Cill Cholmain Eala
Kilcalumkill	Cill Chalum chille
Kilchattan	Cill Chatain
Kilchiaran	Cill Chiaran
Kilchoan	Cill Chomhghan
Kilchoman	Cill Choman
Kilchrennan	Cill Chreanain
Kilchrist	Cill Chriosd
Kilchurn	Caol a' chùirn
Kilcoy	Cuil-challaidh*
Kildalton	Cill Daltan
Kildary	Caoldaraidh*
Kildavie, *Weem*	Cill-dà-bhì
Kildermorie	Cill Mhoire*
Kildonan	Cill Donnan*
Kildrummy	Cill Drumaidh
Kilduff	Coille-dubh
Kildun	Cill-duinn*
——, Upper, *now* Humberstone	Cill-duinn uachdrach
Kilean	Cill Eathain
Kilelegan	Cill Fheileagan
Kilellan	Cill Ellan
Kileonain	Cill Adhamhnan
Kilfinichen	Cill Findchan Cill Fhinichin
Kilfinnan	Cill Fhianan
Kilkenzie	Cill Choinnich
Kilkerran	Cill Chiaran
Kilkivan	Cill Chaomhan
Killagruar	Cill a' ghriothaire
Killanallan	Cill an àilein
Killandrist	Cill Anndrais
Killanish	Cill Aonghais
Killarow	see Kilarrow
Killarney, *Ireland*,	Cillearnaidh
Killean, *Appin*	Cill Sheathain, C. Eathain
Killen	Cill Fhannaidh, C. Annaidh*
near it is	Cnoc an teampuill*
Killearn	Cill' Earnan
Killearnan	Cill Iùrnan
Killennan	Cill Adhamhnan
Killhounich	Cill Choinnich
Killichassie	Cill a' chasaidh
Killichronain	Cill Chrònan
Killiecrankie	CoilleChnagaidh, also Coill' a' Chreathnaich [different parts.] The battle was fought at Raon Ruairidh, near Urrard.
Killiehuntley	Coille Chunndainn*
Killiemore	A' Chill mhór
Killilan	Cill Fhaolain*
Killin	Cill Fhinn
Killineuar	Cill an iubhair
Killisport	Caolasport*
Killocraw	Coill-chnò
Kilmachalmaig	Cill-mc-Chalmaig

ENGLISH	GAELIC
Kilmahog	Cill-ma-Chug
Kilmallie	Cill Mhàilidh
Kilmahu	Cill-mo-Chua
Kilmahumag	Cill-mo-Chumag
Kilmalieu	Cill-mo-Libha
Kilmaluag	Cill-mo-Luaig*
Kilmaree	Cill Ma Ruibhe*
Kilmarnock	Cille-màrnag,* Cill-mheàrnag—CR
Kilmaronag	Cill-mo-Rònag
Kilmartin	Cill Mhàrtainn
Kilmelford	Cill mhealaird
Kilmeny	Cill Mheanaidh
Kilmichael	Cille Mhicheil
Kilmodan	Cill Mhaodan
Kilmonivaig	Cill-mo-Naomhaig
Kilmorack	Cille Mhòrag (St. Moroc)
Kilmore	Cill Mhoire
——, *nr Oban*	A' Chille mhór
Kilmorie	Cille Mhoire
Kilmory	Cille Mhoire
Kilmuir	Cille Mhoire
—— Easter	Cille Mhoire
Kilmun	Cille Mhunna
Kilmure	Cille Mhoire
Kilnave	Cill naoimh
Kilninian	Cill Ninean
Kilninver	Cill an inbhir
Kilpatrick	Cill Phàdair
Kilravock	Cill Rathaig*
Kilronan	Cill Ronain
Kilsyth	Cillsaidh
Kiltarlity	Cill Taraghlain
—— district	Bràigh na h-àirde
Kiltearn	Cill Tighearna*
Kilvarie	Cille Mha-ruibh
Kilvaxter	Cille Bhacstair
Kin, Glen	Gleann cumhang
Kinbeachie	Cinn a' bheathchaidh*
Kinbrace	Cinn a' bhràist
Kincardine	Cinn Chardainn
Kincraig	Ceann na creige*
Kincurdy, *Strathspey*	Cinn Chaordaidh
——, *Rosemarkie*	Cinn-chùrdaidh*
Kindeace	Cinn-déis*
——, Wester,	Cinn-déis mhór*
of Robertson, *now* Bayfield	Cinn-déis Robson shuas*
——, Little, *now* Ankerville	Cinn-déis bheag*
Kinder, Loch	Loch Ceannda*
Kindrochet	Cinn-drochaid
Kinellan	Cinn-eilein*
Kingairloch	Cinn Ghèarrloch
Kingarbh	Cinn-gharbh
Kingarth	Ceann-garbh
Kinglass	Conghlas
Kingoldrum	Cinn Chollldrum*
Kingsburgh	Cinnse-burg
King's Cross, *Arran*	Peighinn na croise
Kingshouse	Taigh 'n rìgh
Kingscauseway	Cabhsair an rìgh
Kingussie	Cinn a' Ghiuthsaich
Kinkell	Ceann na coille*
Kinloch	Ceann Loch
Kinloch beg	—— —— beag
Kinlochbervie	Ceann Loch Biorbhaidh
Kinloch Luichart	Ceann Loch Luicheirt
Kinloch Moidart	Ceann Loch Mùideirt
Kinlochmore	Ceann Loch mór
Kinlochspelvie	Ceann Loch Spealbhaidh
Kinnaird	Ceann na h-àird
Kinnairdie	Cinnàrdaidh*
Kinnamoine	Ceann na móine*

ENGLISH	GAELIC
Kinnell	Cinn-alla*
Kinnellan	Cinn eilein
Kinettles	Cinn it'ais (*t* soft)*
Kinniachdrach	Cinn iochdarach
Kinnouth, Mull of	Maol na h-Oth
Kinrive	Ceann-ruighe
Kinross	Ceannrois
Kintail	Cinntàile*(i.e. C. an t-sàile)
——, native of	Tàileach, Sàileach
Kintalen	Cinn an t-sàilein
Kintra	Ceann-tràgha, Cinn-tràgha
Kintyre	Cinntìre
Kirkaig	Abhainn Chiacaig
Kirkan	Na Cearcan*
Kirkburn	Caochan na h-eaglais
Kirkcudbright	Cille Chuithbeirt
Kirkhill (parish)	Sgìre cnoc na gaoithe Sgìre Mhoire—CR
——, site of parish church, formerly Wardlaw	Cnoc Mhoire
Kirkiboll	Circe-poll
Kirkibost	Circe-post
Kirkmichael, church of	Cill Mhìcheil*
——, parish of	Sgìre Mhìcheil*
Kirksheaf,	A' Chreit mhór
Kirkton, *Lochalsh*	An Clachan Aillseach, *locally* an Clachan
——, *Golspie*	Baile na h-eaglais
Kirktown	Baile na cille
Kirkwall	Baile na h-eaglais
Kishorn	Ciseorn*
Knapdale	Cnapadal
Knappach	A' Chnapaich
Knock	An Cnoc
Knockan	Cnocan
Knockancuirn	Cnocan caoruinn
Knockando	Cnoc cheannachd
Knockandialtaig	Cnoc an dialtaig*
Knockangle	Cnoc aingil
Knockantoul	Cnoc an t-sabhail*
Knockbain	an Cnoc bàn*
Knockboushin	Cnoc nan cuirean
Knockfarrel	Cnoc-fearralaidh*
Knockantinny	Cnoc an teine
Knocklea	Cnoc liath
Knocklearach	Cnoc-cléirich
Knock Mulreesh	Cnoc Mhaol-rise
Knocknacean	Cnoc nan ceann*
Knocknahar	Cnoc na h-aire*
Knocknavie	Cnoc an fhéich bhuidhe
Knoydart	Cnoideart
Kyle (district)	Coille
Kyle Akin	Caol Acain
Kyleakin (hamlet)	Scalpa 'chaoil
Kyle of Lochalsh	An Caol*
Kylescow	Caolas cumhann
Kyles of Bute	Caolas Bòideach *or* Na Caoil Bhódach
Kyllachy	Coileachaidh
Lachlan	Lachlann, *gen.* -ainn
Lagalochan	Lag an lochan
Laganchauldin	Lagan challtuinn*
Lagavulin	Lag a' mhuilinn
Laggan	An Lagan
Laghura	Ladharra
Laglingartan	Lag-luingartan
Lagnaha	Lag na h-aibhne
Laichley, Loch	Loch Ligh*
Laid	An Leathad
—— House	Taigh an leathaid*
Lairg	Luirg*
Làirig Ghruamach, O.S.M. (*between* Aviemore *and* Braemar)	Làirg Dhrù*
Lamentation Hill O.S.M.	Creag a' choinneachan*
Lamlash, Loch	Loch an eilein
Lamond	Làman
Lamont	MacLaomuinn
Lamont of Lamont	MacLaomuinn
Lamonts, the	Clann Laomuinn
Lanark	Leanndraic
Lanarkshire	Siorramachd Lannraig—*Bliadhna Thearlaich,95.*
Landay	Leanndaidh
Langwell	Langal*
Lanrick	La(n)raig,* Lannraig—CR
Laoghscan	Laoighcionn
Laogin	Laoiginn
Lapich, Scour-na-	Sgùrr na Lapaich*
Larachantivore	Larach an Taigh mhóir
Largiemore	An Leargach mhór
Largs, *Ayrshire*	Na Leargaidh Ghallda
Largs, *Kintyre*	Na Leargaidh Chinntireach
Larne, *Ireland*	Lathurna
Latheron	Lathroinn, Latharan—CR
—— parish	Sgìre Latharan
—— wheel	Latharan a' phuill*
Lawers	Labhar
——, Ben	Beinn Labhair
Lawrence	Labhruinn
Laxdale	Lacasdail*
Laxford	Camus-bhradan
Leachkarlem	Leac an leum
Leacollaguin	Leac Ola(h)again
Leadnalubcroy	Leathad na lub cruaidh
Lealty	Leth-alltaidh
Leamnamuic	Leum na muice
Lean, Glen	Glen Leathann
Leanagboyach	Lèanag bhoidheach
Leanaig	Lèanaig*
Lean Carn	An Leathan carn
Learnie	Leatharnaidh*
Leault	Leth-allt
Lechanaich	An Leachanaich*
Leckmelm	Leac Mailm*
Lecknary	Leac-nathrach
Leckyvroun	Leac a' bhròin
Ledbeg	Leathad beag
Ledgowan	Leathad a' ghobhainn*
Ledi, Ben	Beinn Lidi,* B. Lididh—CR
Ledmore	An Leathad mór
Lednagulin	Leathad nan gillean
Lednock, Glen	Gleann Liadnaig*
Lee, Loch	Loch Ligh*
Leeks	Lic*
Lees	Mac a Lìos
Leich	Lethach
Leiravay	Leurabhaigh*
Leith	Lìte
Lemlair	Luim an Làir
Lennie	Mac an Lamhaich
Lennox	Na Leamhanaidh Na Leamhanaich
Lentran	Leantran
Leny, Pass of	Cumhang Lànaigh*
Leochel	Lòchail*
Lephinchaple	Leth-pheighinn-chapull
Lephinkill	Leth-pheighinn na cille
Lergychoniemore	Learg a' chonnaidh mór
Lernock	Leatharnach*
Leslie	Mac an fhleisdeir
Lesmore	Lios mór*
Lethonn	Leth-fhonn
Letter	Leitir
Letterchall	Leitir Choill
Lettermay	Leitir Mhaighe
Letters	An Leitir*
Letter Walton	Coille na leitir
Lettie	Leth-taobh

ENGLISH	GAELIC
Lettoch	An Leth-dabhach*
Leurbost	Liurbost*
Leven Water	Uisge Leamhna
——, Glen	Gleann Leamhann
Levincorrach	Leth-pheighinn corrach
Lewis	Eilean Leòdhas, Leòdhas
Lewis, (person)	Luthais
Liathach, Ben	Liathghach*
Liddel	Lithdal
Lienassie	Lianaisidh*
Liffy, River *Ireland*	†Ruireach
Ling, River	Abhainn Luinge
Linlithgow	Gleann Iucha*
Linnhe, Loch (outside Corran)	An Linne sheilich
———— (inside Corran)	An Linne dhubh
Linnie	Linn' a' bhuig bhàin / An Linne
Linside*	Lianasaid
Linshader	Lìseadair*
Lipachlairy	Leób a' chléirich
Lismore	Lios mòr
——, a native of	Liosach
Livet, Glen	Gleann liobhaid
Livisie Glen	Geann Lìbhisidh
Livingstone	MacDhunleibhe / Mac an léigh
Loandhu	An Lòn dubh *
Loanteanaquhatt	Lòn taigh nan cat*
Lochaber	Lochabar
——, of or belonging to	Abrach, Cabrach
—— man, a	Abrach
Lochalsh	Lochaillse
——, Kyle of	An Caol (Aillseach)*
Lochcarron, a native of	Carrannach
Lochay, Glen	Gleann Lòcha, Gl. Lòchaidh*
Lochearnhead	Ceann Loch Éir*
Loch Eck	Loch Aic
Lochgilphead	Ceann Loch Gilp
Lochgoilhead	Ceann Loch Goil / Ceann Loch Goibhle—CR
Lochhead	Ceann loch
Lochhournhead	Ceann Loch Shuirn
Lochiel	Loch iall
Lochindaal	Loch an dàla
Lochindall	Loch an Dalad
Lochinver	Loch an Inbhir*
Lochletter	Lòchleitir*
Lochnagar	Loch na gàire*
Lochnell	Lochnaneala
Lochoisnie	Loch Oisinnidh
Lochouie	Loch an t-suidhe
Lochranza	Loch Raonasa
Lochs	Na Lochan
Lochy R. *Inverness*	Lòchaidh*
——, *Perth*	see Lochay
Logans, the	Sìol Loganaich
Logie	An Lagaidh*
Logie Easter	Lagaidh

Modern name Marybank, no article. Lagaidh is *fem.* and always used with the article on the West coast.

ENGLISH	GAELIC
Logierait	Lagan ràit
Lomond, Ben	Beinn Laomuinn
——, Loch	Loch Laomuinn
London	Lunnainn
Londonderry	Doire
Lonemore	An Lón mór
Loneroid	An Lòn roid*
Lonevine	Lòn a' bhinn
Longa, *Gairloch*	Eilean Longa
——, passage between & mainl'nd	An caol beag*
Longrigg	Iomaire-fada
Longbow	Lorg-bó
Lorn	Latharna
Lossit, Dun & L.	Losaid
Loth, Glen	Loth
Lothian	Lodainn
Louis	Luthais
Louisa	Liùsaidh
Lovat	A' Mhorfhaich
——, Lord	" Mac Shìmidh "
Love	Mac-ionmhuinn—*Arran*
Lowland	Gallda
Lowlander, a	Gall, *gen.sing. & n.pl.* Goill
Lowlands, the	A' Ghalldachd
Loyal, Ben	Beinn Laghail
——, Loch	Loch Laghail
Loyne	Leana
Lubcroy	An Lùb chruaidh
Lubnaig, Loch	Loch Lùdnaig*
Luce, Glen	Gleann luis
Lucy	Liùsaidh
Lude	Leothad,* Leòide
Ludovick	Maoldonuich
Lui, Ben	Beinn Laoigh
Luib Vulin	Lùb a' mhuilinn
Luichart, Loch	Loch Luicheart *
Luing	Luinn
——, native of	Luinneach
Luke	Lùcas
——, (surname)	MacLùcais
Lundale	Lundal
Lundie	Lunndaidh
Lybster	Liabost
Lyminge, *Kent, contract.* of the British *name*—[Heo]l-y-maen	Sraid na Cloiche
Lynchlaggan	Lòinn Chlaiginn
Lynchat (for Loinn a' chait)	modern for Bail' a' chait
Lyon, Glen	Gleann Lìobhunn
MacAdam	MacAdhamh
MacAffer	MacCathbharra
MacAinsh	see MacInnes
MacAlister	MacAlasdair
MacAllister of Loup	" Mac Iain Duibh "
MacAllisters, the	Clann Alasdair
MacAllisters of Loup	Clann Eoin duibh
MacAll	MacCathail
MacAllan	MacAilein
MacAlpine	MacAilpein
MacAudie	MacAlasdair
MacAndrew	MacGill'Anndrais
Macanroy	Mac an Ruaidh (MacIain Ruaidh
MacArthur	MacArtair, MacArtain in *Skye*
MacAskill	MacAsgaill
MacAulay	MacAmhlaidh
MacBain	MacBheathain
MacBean	Clann Mhic Bheathainn
MacBeth	MacBheatha, MacBheathaig
MacBrayne	Mac a' Bhriuthainn
MacCadie	MacAdaidh
MacCaffer	MacCathbharra
MacCaig	MacCaog
MacCall	MacCathail
MacCallum	MacCaluim
MacCarthy	MacCathachaidh
MacCaw	MacAdhamh
MacClintock	MacGill Fhionndaig
MacClery	see Clark
MacClew / MacCloy	MacLughaidh

English	Gaelic
MacCluie	MacLughaidh
MacCodrum	MacCodrum
MacColl	MacColla
MacColls, the	Sliochd nan Collaidh làmh-dhearg
MacCombie	MacThomaidh
MacConnachie	MacDhonnchaidh
MacCorquodale	MacCorcadail
MacCormick	MacCormaig
MacCowan	MacGobhainn MacCòmhghan
MacCrimmon	MacCruimein
MacCringan's	Rudha MhicNaomhain
MacCulloch	MacCullach, MacLulaich
MacDermid	MacDiarmaid
MacDonald	MacDhomhnuill, Domhnullach
——— of Ardnamurchan	"MacIain Airdnamurchan"
——— of Clanranald	"Mac Mhic Ailein"
——— of Glenalladale	"Mac Iain Òig"
——— of Glencoe	"Mac Iain"
——— of Glengarry	"Mac Mhic Alasdair"
——— of Keppoch	"Mac Mhic Raonuill"
——— of Knoydart	"Mac Ailein Mhic Ailein"
——— of Morar	"Mac Mhic Dhùghaill (Mhorair)"
——— of the Isles	"MacDhomhnuill nan Eilean"
MacDonalds of Bornish	Sliochd Iain Mhic Raonuill
——— of Sleat & the Isles	Clann Uisdein Clann Domhnuill Shléibhte
——— of Ardnamurchan	Clann D. Airdnamurchan
——— of Glengarry	Clann D. Ghlinn garadh
——— of Keppoch	Clann D. na Ceapach
——— of Clan Ranald	Clann Raonuill
———, (descended from Iain Dubh eldest son of Alasdair òg)	Clann Eòin Duibh
———, a sept in Benderloch	MacGhille Dhonaghart
MacDougall	MacDhùghaill
——— of Lorne	——— Lathurna
MacDougalls, the	Clann Dùghaill, Na Dùghallaich
MacDowell	MacDhùghaill
Macduff	MacDhubhaich
———s, the	Clann Dubh
Macduff, Ben	Beinn MhicDhuibhe
MacEchern	MacEachairn
MacErchar	MacFhearchair
MacEwen	MacEòghainn
MacFadyen	MacPhaidein
MacFarlane	MacPharlain
——— of that ilk	Mac a' Bhàirling, MacPharlain
———s, the	Clann Pharlain
MacFarquhar	MacFhearchair
MacGeorge	MacSheòrais
MacGilchrist	MacGilleChrìost
MacGill	MacGhille

English	Gaelic
MacGillony	MacGill'Onfhaidh
MacGillivray	MacGille bhràth
———s, the	Clann MhicGillebhràth
MacGlashan	MacGlaisein
MacGowan	MacGhobhainn
MacGregor	MacGriogair, Griogarach, Griogalach—*W. of Ross*
——— of MacGregor	An t-Ailpeineach
———s, the	Clann Ghriogair, Na Griogaraich
MacGuire	MacGuaire
Machrie, Glen	Gleann na machrach G. na macraidh—*Fionn*
Machrie	Machaire
MacHardy	MacCardaidh
Machrihanish	Machaire Shanais
MacIan	MacIan
MacIchan	MacFhitheachain
Macindeoir	Mac an Deòir
Macindoe	Mac-an-duibh (Mac Iain duibh)
MacInlay	MacFhionnlaigh
MacIlroy	Mac Ghille ruaidh
MacInnes	MacAonghais
——— of that ilk	MacAonghais Cheann Loch Àluinn
———es, the	Clann Aonghais
Macinroy	Mac-an-Ruaidh (Mac Iain Ruaidh)
Macintosh	Mac an toisich
——— of Macintosh	Mac an toisich
Macintoshes, the	Clann an toisich
Macintoshes of Kellachie	Sliochd Ailein
Macintyre	Mac an t-saoir
———s, the	Clann an t-saoir
MacIsaac	MacÌosaig
MacIver	MacIomhair
MacKail	MacCathail
MacKay	MacAoidh
———, Lord Reay	MacAoidh
——— of Rinns	MacAoidh na Ranna
——— of Strathnaver	MacAoidh Abrach
Mackays, the	Clann MhicAoidh, Siol Mhorgain
Mackechnie	MacEachairn
Mackellar	MacEalair
Mackendrick	MacEanruig
Mackenna	MacCinaoidh
Mackessack	MacÌosaig
Mackenzie	MacCoinnich
——— of Achilty	"Mac Mhic Mhurchaidh"
——— of Gairloch	"Mac Mhic Iain"
——— of Seaforth	MacCoinnich
———s, the	Clann Choinnich
Mackerchar	MacFhearchair
Mackichan	MacFhitheachan
Mackilligan	MacGill'Fhaolagain
Mackillop	MacPhilip
Mackimmie	MacShimidh
Mackinlay	MacFhionnlaigh
Mackinnie	MacCinaoidh
Mackinnon	MacFhionghuin
——— a sept in Mull	MacTiridh *or* MacSiridh
——— of Mackinnon	MacFhionghuin
———s, the	Clann MhicFhionghain
Mackintosh	see MacIntosh
Mackirdy	MacUrardaigh

ENGLISH	GAELIC
Mackrycul	MacNiocail
MacLachlan	MacLachlainn
———s, the	Clann Lachlainn
MacLagan	MacLagain, MacLathagain—*Strath Tay*
MacLaine of Lochbuie	MacGhill'Eathain Locha-buidhe
———s of Lochbuie	Sliochd Mhurchaidh Ruaidh
MacLaren	MacLabhruinn
MacLarty	Mac-fhlaith-bheartaich
MacLaverty	see MacLarty
MacLaurin	MacLabhruinn
MacLean	MacGhill'Leathain MacGhill'Eathain
——— of Ardgour	"Mac Mhic Eòghainn"
——— of Coll	"Mac Mhic Iain," "Mac Iain Abraich"
——— of Duart	MacGhill'Eathain Dhubh-airt
——— of Kingerloch	"Mac MhicEachainnChinn-ghearrloch
———s, the	Clann Ghill'Eathain
———s of Dochgarroch & Glen-urquhart	Clann Thearlaich o Bhuidhe
———s of Ross of Mull	Sliochd a' chlaidheimh iarruinn
Maclean's Nose	Sròn mhór
MacLearnan	MacGill'Earnain
MacLeay	Mac an léigh
MacLeish	Mac Ghill' Ìos'
MacLellan	MacGill'Fhaolain
MacLennan	MacGill' innein
MacLennans, the	Clann Ghill' innein
MacLeod	MacLeòid
MacLeod of Harris	MacLeòid
MacLeod of Mac-Leod	MacLeòid
MacLeod of Raasay	"Mac Ghille Chaluim"
"MacLeod's Tables" (mountains in Skye)	Healabhal bheag & Healabhal mhór
MacLeods of Dunvegan & Glenelg	Sìol Thormaid
MacLeods of Lewis	Sìol Thorcuil
MacLintock	Mac Gill Fhionntag
MacLinton	MacGhillFhinntain
MacLucas	MacLùcais
MacMahon	MacMhathain
MacMartin	MacMhairtinn
MacMaster	MacMhaighstir
MacMichael	MacMhìcheil
MacMillan	MacMhaolain MacGhillemhaoil
——— of Kintyre	MacMhaolain
——— of Knap	MacMhaolain mór a' Chnaip
———s, the	Clann Mhaolain Clann MhicGhillemhaoil
MacMurchy	MacMhurchaidh
MacNab	Mac an aba
——— of MacNab	Mac an aba
———s, the	Clann an aba
Macnair	Mac-an-uidhir (for Mac Iain-uidhir
MacNaughton	MacNeachdainn
———s, the	Clann MhicNeachdainn
MacNee	MacRìgh
NacNeilage	MacNiallghuis
MacNeill	MacNéill
——— of Barra	MacNéill
———s, the	Clann MhicNéill
MacNevin	MacCnaimhin
MacNichol	MacNeacail
MacNish	MacNeis
MacNider	Mac an fhigheadair
MacNiven	Mac-Ghille-naoimh MacCrithein—*Argyll*
Maconie	Mac-nia
MacPhail	MacPhàil
MacPhatrick	MacPhàdruig
MacPhedran	MacPheidearain
MacPhee	Mac-a-Phì
———s, the	Mac-a-Phì Cholasaidh
Macpherson	Mac a' phearsain
Macpherson of Cluny	Mac Mhuirich, "Cluanaigh"
Macphersons of Badenoch	Clann Mhuirich
Macphersons of Skye	Na Canonaich
MacQuarrie	MacGuaire
——— of Ulva	MacGuaire
———s, the	Clann Ghuaire
MacQueen	MacCuinn, MacShuibhne
———s the	Clann Shuibhne
MacRae	MacRath
———s, the	Clann MhicRath
MacRaild	MacArailt
MacRanald	MacRaonuill
MacRobbie	MacRaibeirt
MacRury	MacRuairidh
MacSwan	MacSuain
Mactaggart	Mac an t-sagairt
MacTavish	MacThàimhais
MacVarish	MacMharais
MacVean	MacBheathain
MacVicar	MacBhiocair
MacVurich	MacMhuirich
MacWilliam	MacUilleim
Maddy, Loch	Loch nam madadh
Magnus	Manus
Main	Gleann Mèinnidh*
Malcolm	Calum
Malcolms, the	Clann Chaluim
Malcolmson	MacCaluim
Malise	Maol-Ìosa
Mallaig	Mallaig—CR, Malach*
Mallard Mallert	Mala-àrd
Mallie, Glen	Gleann mailidh
Mally, River	Màilidh
Malavina	Malamhìn
Mamgarvia	Màm-garbh
Man, Isle of	Eilean Mhanain
Man, Calf of	An Eireag Mhannach *
Manish, Ru	Rudha Mhànuis*
Maolachy	Maol-achadh
Maovally	Maobhalaidh
Mar, Earl of	Morair Mharr
Maree, Loch	Loch Ma-ruibh (*old name* Loch Feadhal feas)
Maree, Island	Eilean Ma-ruibh
Margaret	Mairearad
Marion	Muireall
Marjory	Marsail
Mark	Marcus
Markie, R.	Marcaidh
Marksie, Glen	Gleann Marcasaidh
Mars (star)	Màrt
Martha	Moireach
Martin	Martainn
Martin, Isle	Eilean Mhartainn
Mary	Moire, Muire

(In conversation Màiri.) Air Muire, *by St. Mary*; Muire tha! *by St. Mary it is!* Muire cha'n 'eil! *by St. Mary it is not!*

ENGLISH	GAELIC
Maryburgh	Baile Màiri

ENGLISH	GAELIC
Mashie Water	Mathaisidh
Mashie, Strath	Srath Mhathaisidh*
Matheson	MacMhathain, Mathanach
Mathesons, the	Clann Mhathain
Mauchline	Magh-linne
Matthew	Mata
Matthewson	MacMhata
Maxwell	MacSual
May	Màili
Mazeran, Glen	Gleann Masaran*
Meadie, Loch	Loch Meudaidh
Mealfourvounie	Meal-fuar-mhonaidh
Meall Ghaordie	Meall Ghaoirdidh*
Meall-am-madadh	Meall a' mhadaidh
Meall-aundrary	Meall andrairigh
Mearns	A' Mhaoirn*
Measach, falls of	Easan na Miasaich
Meath, *Ireland*	A' Mhidhe
Meddat	Meitheid*
Meggernie	Migearnaidh*
Meig Water	Abhainn Mìg*
Meikle Daan Meikle Ferry (formerly Portincoulter)	Dathan mhór* Port mór*
Meiklie, Loch	Loch Miachdlaidh*
Melbost	Mealabost*
Melfort	Meileart
Mellaig	Mealach
Mellis	Maol-Iosa
Melness	Mealainis*
Melton Charles	Meallan Thearlaich*
Melvaig	Mealabhaig*
Menteith	Teàdhaich*
Menzies	Mèinn,* Mèinnearach
Menzies of that ilk	Am Mèinnearach
Menzieses, the	Na Mèinnearaich
Meoble	Miath Poll
Mercury (star)	Ceadoine
Methven	Meithinnidh*
Mhuinne, Goirtean-a'-	Goirtean a' bhuinn
Miagro	Meathgro*
Mial, *Gairloch*	Miall*
Miavag	Miabhaig*
Midoxgate	An t-uchd meadhonach
Midtown	Baile meadhonach
Migdale	Migean
Milbuie	Am maol buidhe
Millcraig	Muileann na creige*
Milntown	Baile mhuilinn, Baile mhuilinn Anndra*
Milton	Bail' a' mhuilinn
Minard	Mionaird*
Minch, the	A' Mhaoil
Minch, the Little (*between Skye and Lewis*)	Cuan Sgithe, Cuan Uidhist
Minch, the Outer	Cuan nan orc (*sea of whales*)
Miotag	Mèideag*
Miseag, Cruach-nam-	Cruach nam minnseag
Moidart	Mùideart
Moidart, Loch	Loch Mùideart
Moireach, the	A' Mhoraich
Molleboye	Mullach-buidhe
Monachalmore	Monachul*
Monachyle	Monchall—CR
Monar, Loch	Loch Monar*
Moncrieff	Mon craoibh
Moness, falls of	Mon-eas (for Bun-eas)*
Moniack	Moin-itheig*
Monkstadt	Mogastad
Monkstown	Baile nam manach
Montgomery	MacGumerait
Montrose, Duke of	An Greumach mór

ENGLISH	GAELIC
Monyquil	Moin' a' choill
Monzie	Magh-iodh*
Moore	MacMhòrdha
Morangie	Mòraistidh*
Morar	Mòrar
Morar, North	Mòrar MhicShimidh
Morar, South	Mòrar Mhic Dhùghaill
Moray	Moireibh*
More, Ben (*Perths*)	A' Bheinne mhór
More, Ben (*Mull*)	A' Bheinne mhór Mhuileach
Morenish	Mór'nis*
Morel	Mòirl*
Morefield	A' Mhór-choille
Morefield Cottage	An Ceanna-chruinn
Morie, Glen	Gleann Mhoire
Moriston, Glen	Gleann Moiresdean*
Morlich Burn	Mórth'laich*
Morness	Mórnis*
Morning star, the	Aoine
Morrich more	A' Mhor'aich mhór
Morrison	Moireasdan MacMhoirein—*Islay*
Morrison of Lewis	Mac Ghille Mhoire
Morrisons, the	Clann Mhic Ghille Mhoire Na Moireasdanaich Clann a' bhreithimh in *Lewis*
Mortlach	Mórth'laich (i.e. mór-thulaich)
Moruisg	Morusg
Morven	A' Mhorairne*
Morvern	Marbhainn
Morvich	A' Mhoraich*
Mossend	Ceann a' mhonaidh
Mongstot	see Monkstadt
Moulin	Maoilinn
Moulinearn	Muileann-fheàrna*
Moultavie	Multamhaigh
Mount, Cairn-o'-	Càrn mhon*
Mount Eagle	Cnoc na h-iolaire (The west part near outlet of L. Eye is also called *Cnoc na h-uidhe*
Mountrich (*formerly* Kilchoan)	Cill Chòmhghan
Mountgerald	Claon
Moyley	A' Mhuaigh (*loc.* of magh)
Muck Island	Eilean nam muc, Tir-chrain
Muckairn	Muc càrna
Muckernich	A' Mhucarnaich*
Mudale	Mùdal
Muic, Glen	Gleann muice
Muich Dhui, Ben	Beinn muic duibhe
Muieblairie	Muigh bhlàraidh*
Muirends	Mórdun*
Milton Eonan, *Glenlyon*	Muileann Eodhanain
Muir-of-Ord	Am Blàr dubh Am Monadh dubh
Muirtown	Mòrdun*
Muirshirlich	Mur-siarluich
Muldearg	A' mhuil dearg
Muldaonich Id.	Eilean Mhaoil Domhnaich*
Mull, Isle of	Muile. An Dreolluinn (*ancient poetical name—MacAlpine*
Mullardoch, Loch	Loch Maol Àrdaich
Mullindry	Muileadradh
Mullintrae	Maol an tràigh
Mulloy	Mac an luaimh
Mungo	Mungan
Munlochy	Poll Lochaidh
Munlochy Bay	Ob Poll Lochaidh
Munro	Rothach, Mac an Rothaich, MacAdaidh (*in certain families only*)

ENGLISH	GAELIC
Munro of Fowlis	Tighearna Fólais
Munros, the	Clann an Rothaich
Munster, *Ireland*	A'Mhumha
Muronach,	A name applied to the inhabitants of Uist by those of the neighbouring islands. People living on the west side of Uist are also thus called by the inhabitants of the east side.
Murchie	MacMhurchaidh
Murchison	MacMurchaidh, MacMhuirich MacCalmain—*Ross-shire*
Murchison (chief)	"MacCalmain"
Murdoch	Murchadh, Muireach In the North the mutilated form Murdo is used in English.
Muriel	Muireall
Murlagan	Mùrlagan*
Murphy	MacMhurchaidh
Murray	Moireach
Murrays of Athole	Sìol Mhoiridh, S. Mhoirich
Murthly	Mòrthlaich*
Musselburgh	Baile nam feasgan
Muthil	Maothail*
Myles	Maolmoire
Naast	Nàst
Nairn	Inbhir Narunn
Nairn, Strath	Srath Narunn*
Naughton	Neachdainn
Nave, Ard	Àird an naoimh
Naver, River	Nabhuir*
Navity	Neamhaitidh,Neamhaididh*
Nedd	An Nead*
Neill	Niall, *gen.* Néill
Nell, Loch	Loch nan eala
Nelson	MacNèill
Ness	Nis
Ness, Loch	Loch Nis
Nessintulaich	Niosantulaich
Nethy Water	Neithich*
Nevis, Ben	Beinn Nibheis*
Newmore	An ne' mhór*
Newtonmore	Bail' ùr an t-sléibh*
Nichol	Neacal
Nicholson	MacNeacail
Nicholas	Neacal
Nid, Loch	Lochaidh Nid
Nigg	'N eig (*locative of* an eag)*
Nigg, Hill of	Beinn 'n eig
Niven	Gille naomh
Noble	Guaire
Noe, Glen	Gleann Nodha
Noid	Nuide
Nonakiln	Neo' na cille, Nei' na cille*
Nonach	An ònach*
Norman	Tormoid
North Sea, the	An Cuan tuathach An Cuan tuath
Norway	Nirribhidh*
Norwegian, a	Fionn Lochlainneach
Nosebridge, *Islay*	Nomhasbrugh
Nostie	Nòsdaidh*
Novar	Taigh an Fhuamhair*
Oa Island	Eilean O
Oa, Mull of	Maol na h-òige Maol na h-Otha—*Fionn* Maol na h-Òth—CR
Oban	An t-Oban Latharnach* *locally* An t-Oban
Obbenin	Na h-òbainean
Obsdale	Obsdail*
Ochtavullin	Ochdamh a' mhuilinn
Ochtertyre	Uachdar thìr
Ochtow	An t-Ochdamh
Ochtowmruche	Ochdamh ruadh

ENGLISH	GAELIC
Octavullin	see Ochtavullin
Octobeg	An t-Ochdamh beag
Octofad	Ochdamh fada
Octomore	Ochdamh mór
Oe, Glen	Gleann nodha
Oe, River	Abhainn nodha
Ogilvie	MacGhille bhuidhe
Ogilvies, the	Sìol Ghillechriosd
Ogle, Glen	Gleann Òguil*
Ohirnie	Odharnaidh
Oich, Loch	Loch O'ich*
Oisnie	Loch Oisinnidh
O'Kean	O'Cain
Oldany	Alltanaidh
Oldshore	see Asher
Oliver	Oilbhreis
Onich	Omhanaich* Othanaich—CR
Openham	Na h-òbainean
Orchill	Urchoill, Urcha*
Orchy Glen	Gleann Urchaidh
Orchy, Bridge of	Drobhaid Urchaidh
Ord	An t-Ord
Ordie, Loch	Loch òrdaigh*
Ordhill	Cnoc an Ùird
Orkney	Arcaibh
Ormacleit	Ormacleid
Ormiscaig	Ormascaig*
Ornsay, Isle	Eilean Diarmain Eilean Iarmainn Eilean Orfhasa
Orrin, River	Orthainn*
Otter	An Oitir
Overscaig	Ofarsgaig*
Owen	Eòghainn
Owie	Ubhaidh
Owskiech	Loch Òsgaig*
Oykill, River	Oiceil
Pacific Ocean, the	An Cuan sèimh
Paible	Paibeall
Paisley	Paislig
Palgavie	Pol-garbh
Partick	Pearraig*
Paterson	MacPhàdruig
Patrick	Pàdruig
Patt	A' Phait*
Pattack	Patag
Paul	Pàl, *gen.* -àil
Paulfield	Am Bàrd*
Pean, Glen	Gleann Peighinn
Pearsie	Parsaidh*
Peffer, Strath	Srath Pheofhair*
Peffry	Peothar
Peinacrosh	Peighinn a' Chrois**
Pelaig	Peallaig*
Penalbannach	Peighinn Albannach
Penick, *Nairn*	A' Pheighinneag*
Penifler	Peighinn nam fìdhlear*
Peninver	Peighinn an inbhir
Pennycastle	Peighinn a' chaisteil
Pennyfuar	Peighinn a' phùir
Pennygowan	Peighinn a' ghobhainn
Pennymore	A' Pheighinn mhór
Penrith *Cumberland*	Piorait (*locally called* Peerit)
Pentland Firth	An Caol Arcach*
Persian, a	Farsach**
Perth	Peairt
——, Earl of	An Druimineach
Peter	Pàdruig, Peadair. Para is an abbreviated form of Pàthruig. Pàdair—*Arran*
Peterburn	Alltan Phàdruig
Peterhead	Ceann Phàdruig
Petley	Maolbuidhe
Petty	Peitidh*

English	Gaelic
Phascally	Fas-choille
Phoineas	Fothrais, Fotharais
Pict, a	Piochdach
Pictish	Piochdach
Picts, the	Na Cruithnich
Pitalmit	Bail' an ailm
Pitcalnie	Baile Chailnidh, Cuilt-earáraidh
——— Strath of	Srath-chuilt-earáraidh
Pitcastle	Pit a' chaisteil
Pitchurn	Baile-chaoruinn
Pitculzean	Bail' a' choillean *
Pittenglassie	Bail' a' ghlais-tìr*
Pitfaed	Baile-Phàididh*
Pitfuir, *Black Isle*	Pit-fhùir*
Pitfure, *Suth'd*	Baile-phùir*
Pitglassie	Bad a' ghlasaich*
Pitgrudie	Baile-Ghrùididh*
Pitilie	Baile na mòine
Pithogarty	Bail' an t-sagairt Baile nan sagart
Pitkerrie	Baile-chéiridh
Pitlochry	Baile Chloichridh
Pitlundie	Pit lunndaidh*
Pitmaduthy	Baile-'ic-Dhuibh*
Pitmain	Pit meadhon
Pitnacree	Pit na craoibhe
Pitnellies	Bail' an ianlaith*
Pitoulish, Loch	Pit-gheallais*
Pitourie	Bail'-odharaidh
Pittentrail	Bail' an traill
Pittenweem	Baile na h-uaimh
Plaids, *Ross*	A' Phlaid*
Platchaig	Plat-chathaig*
Plockton	Ploc Loch Aillse *locally* Am Ploc
Ploverfield	Blàr nam feadag
Plucaird	Ploc-àird*
Polbain	Am Poll bàn*
Poleriscaig	Poll Éirisgaig*
Polgavie	Polgarbh
Polglass	Am Poll glas*
Polgown	Polgamhna
Polin	Pollan
Polenturk	Poll an tuirc*
Pollachie	Poll-achaidh
Pollagharry	Poll a' ghearraidh*
Pollandraw	Bog an t-srath
Pollanduich	Poll an dubhaidh
Pollantarie	Poll an tairbh
Pollo	Am Pallan*
Polloch	Poll loch
Polly, River	Abhainn Phollaidh
Pollywillin	Poll a' mhuilinn
Polnicol	Poll Neacail*
Pookandraw	Bog an t-srath*
Poolewe	Poll iù*
———, village of	*locally* Abhainn Iù
Porin	Pórainn*
Portavaidue	Port a' mhadaidh
Portcamel *Suth'd*	Port a' Chamthuill*
Port Buckie	Port nam faochag
Port Charlotte	Sgiba
	Port Ghàidheal, *Fortingal**
Port Henderson *Gairloch*	Port an Sgumain,* *locally* Portigil*
Portlich	Port fliuch*
Portmahomack	Port-mo-Cholmaig*
Portnacreish	Port na crois
Portnahaven	Port na h-abhann
Portnellan	Port an eilein
Portree	Port rìgh
Portvasgo	Port an fhasgaidh
Port Wemyss	Bun-othan
Potarch Bridge	Poit Earc*
Poultock	Poll a' phoca*

English	Gaelic
Pow Burn	Allt a' phuill*
Power (person)	Paorach
Presmuckerach	Preas mucraigh
Priesthill	Cnoc an t-sagairt
Priest Island	An Cléireach*
Prosen, Glen	Gleann Prasain*
Prussia	Pruisia
Purcell	MacSporain
Queebec, *Tain*	Muileann Luaidh*
Queich, Glen	Gleann Cuaich*
Querrell	An Coireall
Quhary, Glen	Gleann Chaorach
Quhynnisgyrne	Cuinnsgearna
Quinaig	Cuinneag
Quintin	Caointean
Quirang	Cuithe-Fhraing
Quoich, Glen	Gleann Cuaich
————, inhabitant of	Cuachanach
Raa, Loch	Loch Ra
Raanich	An Rathanaich
Raasay	Ra'arsa*
——— Sound	An Linne Ra'arsach
Rachel	Raonaild, Raonaid, Raodhailt
Raddery	Radharaidh*
Raffin	Rathfionn
Rahoy	Ra-thuaith—CR
Raitts	Ràt
Ralia	Rath-liath
Ramore	An Rath mór*
Ranald	Raonull, *gen.* -uill
Ranaldson	MacRaonuill
Rankin	MacFhraing
Rannoch	Raineach
Rarichie	Rath-riachaidh*
Rassal	Rasal*
Rattray	Raitear*
Rea, Ru	An Rudha Réidh*
Reay	Dùthaich Mhic Aoidh
——, Lord	MacAoidh
——, parish of	Sgìre Meaghrath*
Rebecca	Beathag
Red Castle	An Caisteal ruadh
Redegich, Ru	Rudh Réitichidh
Redfield	An Raon dearg
Red Point	An Rudha dearg An Rudha lachdainn*
Reelick	Réilig
Reffinch	Ruighe-fliuch
Reid	MacGhille ruaidh
Reiff	Bogha a' Bhàraich*
Reileiridhe	Ruighe-léiridh
Relugas	Ruigh-lùgais*
Remuil	Ruighe-maol
Renish	Rénis*
Renzy, Loch	see Loch Ranza
Requill	Ruigh Dhùghaill
Reraig	Rèaraig,* Réirig*
Resaurie	An Ruighe samhraidh
Resolis	Ruigh-shaluis (i.e. sholuis)*
Revie	MacGhilleriabhaich, *Kintyre*
Revochan	Ruigh Bhuadhachain*
Rhe an chath	Ruighean a' chatha
Rheindown	Ruigh an dùin*
Rhiandoggie	Ruigh an dogaidh
Rhibreac	An Ruigh breac*
Rhi-chalmie	Ruigh-Chalmaidh
Rhiconich	Ruighe-chòinnich*
Rhidoroch	An Ruigh dhorcha*
Rhifail	Ruighe Phail
Rhilinn	Ruighe-linne
Rhiloisk	Ruighe-loisgte
Rhilonie	Ruigh an lòin*
Rhirey	An Ruigh ruaidh
Rhi-sealbhag	Ruighe na sealbhag
Rhitongue	Ruighe-Thunga

ENGLISH	GAELIC
Rhives	Na Ruigheannan*
Rhi-voult	Ruigh a' mhuilt
Rhuvaal	Rudh' a' mhàil
Rhynie, *Ross*	Ràthan*
—— *Aberd'nshire*	Roinnidh
Ribigill	Ribigill*
Ri-chaisteil	Ruigh a' chaisteil
Richard	Ruiseart
Ricroy	Ruighe-cruaidh*
Ri-garry	Garadh
Rigollachy	Ruigh-ghobhlachaidh
Ri-horral	Ruighe Harald*
Rimichie	Ruigh michidh*
Rinavie	Roinnibhith*
Rinnes, Ben	Beinn Rinneis
Riochan	Riabhachan*
Risdell, Glen	Gleann-fhreasdail
Rispond	Ruspuinn*
Ristol, Isle	Eilean Ruisteil
Road House	Taigh an rothaid
Robert	Raibeart
Robertson	MacDhonnchaidh
————s, the	Clann Donnchaidh
————s, progenitor of the	"Donnchadh reamhar Mhic Aonghais"
Robuic, Alt	Allt an ruadh bhuic
Rockfield	A' Chreag* Creag Tarail beag*
Roderick	Ruairidh, shortened Rory. The latter is facetiously applied to the fox.
Rodil	Ròdail*
Roe	Roth
Rogart	Sgire Rao'ird* Raoghard—CR Ròghard—*Rob Donn*
Rogie	Ro'agaidh*
Rome	An Ròimh
Rona	Ròna
——, native of	Rònach
Ronald	see Ranald
Rorie (*or* Balnagown Water)	Uaraidh*
Rory	see Roderick
——, Strath	Srath Uaraidh*
Rose	Ròs
——s, the	Na Ròsaich
Rosehall	Innis nan lìon
Rosehaugh	Pit Dhonnchaidh*
Rosemarkie	Ròs-maircnidh*
Roseneath	Ros-neimhidh
Roshk, Loch	see Rosque
Roshven	An Fhrosbheinn
Roskeen	Ros cuibhne*
Roskhill	An Roisgeil*
Rosmarkie	see Rosemarkie
Rosque, Loch	Loch a' chroisg
Rosquern	Ros a' chùirn
Ross (person)	Ros, Rosach
——, (place)	Ros
Ross-shire	Siorrachd Rois
Ross-shire man, a	Rosach
Rossol	Rosail*
Rosses, the	Clann Anndrais
Ross of Mull	An Ros Muileach
Rosyth	Ros-suidhe
Rothes	Rathais*
Rothesay	Baile-Bhóid, Cill Bhruic (i.e. St. Brock)
Rothiemurchus	Ràta mhurchais
Rovie	Ròmhaigh*
Roxburgh	Rosbrog—*B. of Clanranald*
Roy	Ruadh*
Roy Bridge	Drochaid Ruaidh
Roy, Glen	Gleann Ruaidh
Ruair, Loch-a-	Loch an ruathair*

ENGLISH	GAELIC
Ruantallan	Rudha an t-sàilein
Ruaroch	Ruadharach
Ru Hunish	Rudha Hùnais
Ruchill Water	Abhainn Rùchail*
Ruemore	Rudha mór
Rum	Eilean Ruma, "Rìoghachd na Forraiste fiadhaich"
Ru Manish	Rudh' Mànuis*
Ru Noa	Rudh' an Fhomhair*
Ruskie, Loch	Loch an Rùsgaidh
Russel, *Applecross*	Riseal*
Russia	Ruisia
Ruthven	Ruadhainn
Ryan-crovich	Ruighean-cro bheathaich
Ry-an-traid	Ruigh an tràghaid
Ryefield	Ach' an t-seagail*
Saddell	Sàdal
St. Andrews	Cill Rìmhinn
St. Colvin's Chapel	Cill Chaomhain
St. Finnlug's	Cill Fheileagan
St. Kilda	Irt
St. Ninian's	Cill Nineain
Salachail	Salachail
Salachan	Salchan
Salen *Mull*	An Sàilein Muileach
——, *LochSunart*	An Sàilein
Sallachan	see Salachan
Sallachy	Salachaidh*
Sallachry	Salchraidh
Salmon	MacBradain
Saltburn	Allt an t-saluinn*
Samuel	Samuel, Somhairle—*Skye, &c.*
Sanachan	Samhnachan
Sand	Sannda*
——, Big	Sannda mhór*
——, Little	Sannda bheag*
Sanda Id. *nr. Mull of Kintyre*	Àbhainn
Sandavore	Sannda mhór
Sandwick	Sandabhaig*
Sannox	Na Sannagan
Sanquhar	Seann chathair
Sarah	Mór, Mórag
Sarclet	Sàrcleit*
Saunach	Samhnach
Saval-beg	Sàbhail beag*
Savalmore	Sàbhail mór*
Scalloway	Sgallabha
Scalpa	Scalpaidh
Scalpay	Scalpaidh
Scandinavia	Lochlann
Scarba	Sgarba
Scardroy	Sgard ruaidh*
Scarinish	Scarainis*
Scatwell	Scatail (beag & mór)
Schiehallion	Sidh Chailleann*
Scone	Sgàin
Sconser	Sgonnsar
Scorguie	Sgorr gaoithe
Scoribreck	Sgorrabreac
Scotland	Alba, *gen.* Albainn & Alba. No article except in *gen.* Ann an Albainn, *in Scotland*; rìghrean na h-Alba, *the kings of Scotland*; Bràghad Albainn, *Breadalbane.*
————, native of	Albannach
Scotch	Albannach
Scots	Albannach
Scotscalder	Cal' nan Gall*
Scotsburn	Allt nan Albannach
Scottish	Albannach
Scourie	Sgobhairigh
Scour na Lapich	Sgùrr na Lapaich*

ENGLISH	GAELIC
Scudburgh, Stack of	Sgùdaborgh*
Scuir Fhuaran, OSM Scuir Ouran	Sgùrr Odhran
Scuitchail	Sguit chathail
Seafield *Lochcarron*	Rudh' an òis, An Rudha
——, Earl of	see Grant of Grant
Seaforth	Siphort
——, Earl of	" MacCoinnich," " Cabar-féidh "
——, Loch	Loch Shìphoirt
Seil Id.	Saoil
Sgreadan	Sgrìodan
Sgurr Marxie	Sgùrr Marcasaidh*
Shader	Siadar*
Shanish, Loch-na-	Loch na seann innse
Shandwick	Seannduaig* Seanndabhaig—CR
Shanwell	Seann-bhaile
Shaw	MacGille Seathanaich Seadhgh
Shawbost	Siabost*
Shaws, the	Clann Mhic Gille Sheathanaich—*Argyll*
Shaw Park	Pàirc an t-seàdh*
Shean Ferry	Port an t-Sìthein*
Sheannlep	Sean-leapa
Shedog	Seideag
Shee, Glen	Gleann sìth
Sheechaillin	see Schiehallion
Shenval Shenvalie Shenwall	Seann-bhaile
Sheriff, Loch	Loch an t-siorra
Sheriffmuir	Sliabh an t-siorra
Shervie, Glen	Gleann Seirbhidh*
Shetland	Sealtainn
Shiant Isles	see Charmed Isles
Shiel, Glen	Gleann Seile
——, Loch	Loch Seile
——, Water	Seile
Shieldag	Sìldeag
Shilloch, Glen	Gleann Seilich
Shin Bridge	Drochaid Sin*
——, River	Sin*
Shinness	Sinneis*
Shira, Glen	Gleann Siora*
Shiskan	Siosgan
Shiskine	An Seasgann
Shuna	Eilean Siùna*
Sian	Sìthean
Sim	Mac a' Reudaidh
Sime	Sìm
Simon	Sìm
Sinclair	Mac na cearda
——s, the	Clann na cearda (in the west) Singleir (in the north)
Skaebost	Sgèubost*
Skeinidh, Skeir-na-	Sgeir na scainidh
Skelbo	Sgèireaboll—CR Sgeilbol*
Skelpick	Sgeilpeach
Skene	Sgàin
——s, the	Sìol Sgéine, Clann Donnchaidh Mhàirr
Skiach, Loch *Kiltearn* Skiag, *Suth'd*	Sgitheach*
Skibbercross	Sìobarsgaig*
Skibo	Sgìobull
Skineid	Sgianaid
Skinnertown	Baile nan sginnearach*
Skipness	Sgibinnis
Skye, Isle of	An t-Eilean Sgitheanach, Sgith.* Clàr Sgithe—*poet.*
Slackbuie	Sloc-buidhe
Slaggan	An Slagan-odhar*

ENGLISH	GAELIC
Slagharn	Slac a' chàirn
Slamanan	Sliabh Manann*
Slapin, Loch	Loch Slaopain
Slattadale	Sléiteadail,* Slatairdal
Sleat	Sléibhte
Sletill, Cnoc	Sléiteil*
Sleugach	see Slioch
Slievevin	Sliabh eibhinn
Sligachan	Sligeachan*
Sligo	Sligeach
Slin, Loch	Loch Slinn*
Slioch, Ben	An Sleaghach*
Slis-chilis	Slios a' chaolais
Sloch-muichk	Sloc muic*
Sloy, Loch	Loch Sloidh
——, Glen	Gleann Sluagh
Slumbay	Slumba*
Small Isles	Na h-Eileannan
Smiigle, Alt	Smìgil*
Smith	Mac a' ghobhainn
Smithstown	Bail' a' ghobhainn
Snizort	Snìosort, Sniothasort
Soilairzie	Soilleiridh
Solomon	Solamh
Somerled	Somhairle
Sonachan	Samhnachan
Sophia	Beathag
Souters, the	Na Sùdraichean
Spàidan, Bruthach-nan	Bruthach nan Spardan
Spain	An Spàinnt
——, a native of	Spàinnteach
Spanish	Spàinnteach
Spean, Glen	Gleann Spiothain
Spelvie, Loch	Loch Spealbhaidh
Spey, River	Spé*
——, moor through which it runs	Sliabh Ghrannas, & Griantachd
Spinningdale	Spainigdail
Spittal	Spideil*
Spout Rollo Fall	Spùt Roilidh*
Sronafian	Sròn nam fian
Sronbhrochlan	Sròn-bhuachaillean
Srondavain	Sròn-damhain
Sron-saobhaidhe	Sròn na saobhaidhe*
Sruban, Loch	Loch Struaban
Stack, Ben	Beinn Stac
Staffin, Loch	Stafin* Stafainn—CR
Stairchaol	Staidhir-chaol
Stattic Point	Rudha Stàdhaig*
Stenscholl	Steiseal
Stewart	Stiùbhart
—— of Appin	Mac Iain Stiùbhart na h-Apuinn
——s, the	Na Stiùbhartaich
——s of Appin, the	Stiùbhartaich na h-Apuinn
——s of Athole, the	Stiùbhartaich Athaill
Stewarton	Baile nan Stiùbhartach*
Styx, the	Na Stuicean
Stillaig	Stiallaig
Stirkhill	Meallan a' ghamhna*
Stirling	Sruighlea*
Stockinish, Loch	Loch Stocainis
Stomino, Ben	Beinn an tomain, Beinn Staim
Stonehaven	Caladh nan clach
Stoney-blather	Stiana Bleadar*
Stornoway	Steòrnabhadh*
Storr, Old man of	Bod Stòrr* (*euphemistically* Bodach Stòrr)
Strathlachlan	Srath Lachlainn
Strachur	Srath-chura

ENGLISH	GAELIC
Strae, Glen	Gleann Sréith (?)*
Stalker, Cas.	Caisteal Stalcaire
Stranraer	Sròn reamhair*
Strath	An Srath
Strathavon	Srath Athfhinn*
Strathblane	Srath Bhlathainn
Strathdee	Srath Dhé
Strathdon	Srath Dheathain*
Strathdugh	Srath dubh
Strathy	Srathaidh*
Strathfleet	Srath fleòid
Strathmore	An Srath mór
Strathsgaig	Srath-àsgag
Strathwhellan	Tìr-chuilein
Strathy *Suth'd*	An t-Srathaidh
Strathyre	Srath-eadhair
——— village	see Immirrioch
Streens, the	Na Srianaibh*
Strome Ferry	Port an t-Sròim
Stromness	Stromnis
Stronachlachair	Sròn a' chlachair
Strone	Sròn
Stronechrubie	Sròn-Chrubaidh
Stroneskerj	Sròn-iasgair
Strontian	Sròn an t-sìthein
Struie	An t-Srùigh*
Struy, *Strathglass*	Strùigh
Struy, Bridge of	Drobhaid na Srùigh*
Stuch-a-chroan	Stuic a' Chròim*
Suilven	Beinn bhuidhe
——— Ho.	Sula-bheinn*
Suddy	Suidhe (S. beag & S. mór)
Suie, Loch	Loch an t-suidhe
Suisgil	Sìsgil
Sulven	see Suilven
Summer Isles	Na h-Eileanan Samhraidh
Sunart	Suaineart*
Sunderland *Islay*	Sionarlainn
Sunecrech	Sonnagh-crìoch
Sunny Brae, *Urquhart*	Am Bràighead mosach*
Susan	Siùsaidh
Sutherland (place)	Cataibh
——— (person)	Suthurlanach
———, Chief of Clan	Morair Chat
———, Earl of	Morair Chataibh
———, Kyle of	An Caol Catach
———, of or belonging to	Catach
Sutors of Cromarty	Na Sùdraichean*
Swanibost	Suaineabost*
Sweden	An t-Suain
———, native of	Fionn Lochlainneach
Sween, Castle	Caisteal Suain*
Swordale	Suardail*
Syal	Saoidheal*
Syre	Saghair*
Taagan	Na Tathagan
Tabac	Tàbac*
Tables, MacLeod's	Tables, MacLeod's
Tabost	Tàbost*
Tain	Baile Dhubhthaich*
Talich, the	An dàilich*
Talladale	Tealladal*
Talmine	Toll-min
Tanera beag	Tannara beag
——— more	Tannara mór*
Tannachy	Tan'-achadh
———, *Suth'd*	Tannachaidh*
Tannar Burn	Tanar*
——— Glen	Gleann Tanar*
Tarbat	An Tairbeart*
——— Ness	Rudha Thairbeirt*
Tarbert	An Tairbeart
Tarf Water	Tarbh*

ENGLISH	GAELIC
Tarken Burn	Allt Tearcan*
Tarland	Tarbhlann*
Tarlogie	Tarlogaidh*
Tarnaway	Taranaich*
Tarrel	Tarail*
Tarvie, Tarvy	Tairbhidh*
Tavanagh, Inch	Innis Da-mhanach*(?)
Tay	Tatha
——, Loch	Loch Tatha
——, Strath	Srath Tatha*
Tayanock	Taigh nan cnoc
Taycargaman	Taigh-carmagain
Tayfuirst	Taigh a' phuirt
Tayinloan	Taigh 'n lòn
Taymouth	Bealach, Bealach nan laogh
——— Castle	Caisteal a Bhealaich
Taymore	Taigh mór
Tayness	Taigh an eas
Taynloan	see Tayinloan
Tayntruan	Taigh an t-sruthain
Taynuilt	Taigh an uillt
Tayvallich	Taigh a' bhealaich
Tayvullin	Taigh a' mhuilinn
Teablair	Taigh a' bhlàir*
Teachatt	Taigh a' chait*
Teachus, Loch	Loch Tiacais
Teafrish	Taigh a' phris
Teanafruich	Taigh an fhraoich*
Teanahuig	Taigh na h-ùige*
Teanalick	Taigh an t-sluic, Taigh an lùig*
Teanassie	Taigh an fhasaidh*
Teandallan	Taigh nan dallan
Teandalloch	Taigh an dalach
Teandore	Taigh an todhair*
Teainnich	Taigh an aonaich*
Teatle	Teithiel (?)*
Teawig	Taigh a' bhuic
Teazet	Taigh 'gheata*
Tegarmuchd, *Dull*	An Teagarmachd
Teith, River	Uisge Theàdhaich*
Telnie, Strath	Srath Thealnaidh*
Tenafield	Taigh na fidhle*
Tenandry	An t-Seanaontachd
Ternan, St.	Torranan
Tervin	Tairbhein
Thaddæus	Tadhg, Taogh
Thanahine	Taigh na h-aibhne
Theobald	Tiobaid
Thomaneun	Tom-eun
Thomas	Tàmhus, Tòmas
Thobhais	Shoirbheis
Thomson	MacThòmais
Thundergay, *Arran*	Tòn ri gaoithe*
Thurso	Inbhir Theòrsa *
Tighnabruich	Taigh na bruaich
———, *district & parish*	Ceathramh Chomhghaill *locally* An Ceathramh
Tighnafiline	Taigh na faoilinn
Tilin	Taigh linne
Tillyminnet	Tulaich-mheannait*
Tilt, Glen	Gleann Teilt
Tiree	Tir-iodh*
Tirergain	Tir Fheargain*
Tiretagain	Tir Aodhagain
Tirevagain	Tir a' mhathagain
Tirghoyll	Tir a' Ghoill*
Tirrim, Castle	Caisteal Tioram
Tirinie	Tìr-ìnidh*
Tirpersie	Tir-phreasaich*
Tirvaagan	Tir a' mhathagain
Tobermory	Tobar Mhoire
Toberonochy	Tobar Dhonnchaidh
Tollie	Tollaidh*

ENGLISH	GAELIC
Tolly	Tollaidh*
Tollvah	Toll a' bhathaidh
Tomenagne	Tom-eun
Tomdow	Tom dubh
Tomintoul	Tom an t-sabhail
Tommy	Tòmachan, Tòmag—*Ross-sh*
Tomnahurich	Tom na h-iùbhraich*
Tongue	Tunga
———, parish of	Cinn t-saile MhicAoidh
———, Kyle of	Caolas Thunga*
Torasay	Torrasaidh
Torbali Torboll	} Torboll
Tore	An Todhar
Tornabakin	Tòrr nam bacan
Tornabrock	Tòrr nam broc
Tornahosh	Tòrr na h-òisg
Tornapreas	Treabhar nam preas
Torness	Tòrr an eas
Torosay	Tòrosaidh*
Torquil	Torcull
Torridon	Toirbheartan*
Torrisdale	Tòrasdail*
Torris Trean	Tòrr a' phris droigheann
Torronich	Tòrr-rainich
Toscaig	Tòghscaig*
Toskary	Tosgairidh
Totaig Toteig	} An Tobhtaig
Totegan	Totaichean (?)
Tough	An Tulach*
Toul, Cairn	Càrn an-t-sabhail
Toulvaddie	Toll a' mhadaidh*
Tournag	Tùrnaig*
Toward, *Rothesay*	Tollard
Towie	see Tolly
Treallbhan	Trealamhan
Tressait, *Perth*	{ Treasait* An Treasait—CR
Tressady	Treasaididh*
Treig, Loch	Loch Tréig*
Tromie, Glen	Tromaidh
Tromlee, Loch	Loch Tromlaigh*
Trossachs, the	Na Tròiseachan
Trotternish	{ Trondairnis (Called *Dùthaich nan stapag* and *Am Fearann stapagach* by the people of Duirinish.)
Truderscaig	Loch Trù(n)darsgaig*
Truim, Glen	Gleann Truim*
Trumisgarry	Truimisgearraidh*
Tubeg	Taobh beag
Tuirnaig	Tùrnaig
Tuitumtarvach	Tuiteam tairbheach*
Tullibardine	Tulach Chàrdainn*
Tuilich	An Tulaich*
Tullymet	Tulaich mhait*
Tulloch	Tulach
Tummel	Teimheil*
——— Bridge	Drochaid Theimheil
———, Loch	Loch Teimheil
Tumore	Taobh mór
Tundergarth	Tòn-ri-gaoithe*
Turk, Bridge of	see Bridge
Turk, a	Turcach
Turkey	An Tuirc
Turkish	Turcach
Turnalt	Tùrn-allt
Turner	Mac an tuairneir
Turret, Glen *Perthshire & Lochaber*	} Gleann Turraid
Turret, Loch	Loch Turraid
Tweed, River	Tuaidh*
Tweedle	Tao'udal
Tye-an-tore	Taigh an todhair

ENGLISH	GAELIC
Tyndrum	Taigh an droma
Tynribbie	Taigh an ribidh
Tynrich	Taigh an fhraoich
Tyree	Tir-iodh*
Uag, Ru-na-	Rudha na h-Uamhaig*
Uag, Glen	Gleann Fhiodhaig
Uags	Na h-Uamhagan*
Uaine, Lochan	OSM. for Loch Uanaidh*
Uam Var	An Uamh mhór
Uarie, Ben	Beinn Uairidh (Uaraidh)*
Udale	Uadal*
Udrigle	Ùdrigill
Uidhe, Ben	see Ben Uie
Uie, Ben	Beinn Aoidh*
Uig	Uig
Uillian	Uileann
Uisgentuie	Uisg' an t-suidhe
Uisken	Uisge-ain
Uist	{ Uibhist (Called Tìr a' mhurain, *land of the bent-grass*, by the people of the neighbouring islands)
——, a native of	{ Uibhistich, (Called Muranaich by the people of the neighbouring islands)
——, North	Uibhist mu thuath
——, South	Uibhist mu dheas
Uitir	Oitir
Ulhava	Ulbha*
Ullapool	Ullapul*
———, Braes of	Bruthaichean Ullapuil
Ullie, River	{ Abhainn Illidh* Abhainn Ilìdh—CR
Ulsterman, an	Ultach
Ulva	Ulbha
Unapool	Ùnaboll
United States, the	Na Stàitean Aonaichte
Unity	Uthna
Urchany, *Beauly* ———, *Nairn*	} Urchanaidh*
Ure, Glen	Gleann iubhair
Urigill	Uiriollaich
Urquhart, *L.Ness* ———, (person)	} Urchardainn
———, *Ross*	An Tòisigheachd*
———, Glen	Gleann Urchardainn
———s, the	Clann Urchardainn
Urray	Cille Chriosd, Urrath*
Ushinish	Uisinnis
Ussie	Ùsaidh*
Vaich, Strath	Sràth Bhàthaich*
Valentine	Ualan
Valican, Loch	Loch Mhàileagain
Vallay	Uàlaigh*
Valoor, *Islay*	Bail' ùr
Varrich	Bharraich
Vaternish	Bhatairnis
Vellich, Loch-a-	Loch a' bhealaich
Vennachar, Loch	Loch Bheannchair*
Venue, Ben	A' Bheinn mheanbh*
Vertach, Scuir-na-	Sgùrr nam featag*
Veyatie, Loch	Loch Mheathadaidh
Voil, Loch	Loch Bheothail*
Voirlich, Ben	{ Beinn Mhùrluig (*two of them both spelt the same*)
Vraggie, Ben	Beinn Bhràgaidh
Vrotten, Loch	Loch Bhrodain*
Vuroch, Ben	{ Beinn a' Bhùraich, Beinn a' Bhùraich nam madadh móra*
Vuya	Eilean Bhuidha*
Wales	Cuimridh
Walsh	Breathnach
Walter	Bhàtair
Wardlaw	*now* Kirkhill
Waternish	see Vaternish

ENGLISH	GAELIC
Waterton, *Fearn*	Baile nam fuaran
Watten (parish)	Sgìre Bhatten
Wauchan OSM. for	Na h-uamhachan
Weem	Uaimh
Wellhouse	Taigh an fhuarain*
Welsh	Cuimreach
—— language, the	Cuimrig
Welshman, a	Breathnach, Cuimbreach, Cuimear
Westerdale	An dail shuas ud
Whitewells	Am Fuaran bàn*
Whyte	MacGhille bhàin
Wiay	Eilean Bhia
Wick	Inbhir-Ùig
——, (parish)	Sgire Inbhir-Ùig
Wilkhaven	Port nam faochag
William	Uilleam, *gen.* -eim
Williamson	MacUilleim
Willie	Uilleachan
Wilson	MacUilleim
Winifred	Una
Woodend	Ceann na coille
Wrath, Cape	Am Parbh. An Carbh in *Lewis**
Wyvis, Ben	Beinn Uais
Yairhead	A'Cheir éud

A SHORT ACCOUNT

OF THE PRINCIPAL

Persons and Places

MENTIONED IN

OLD GAELIC FOLK-TALES AND POETRY.

(From Armstrong's Gaelic Dictionary.)

Aghaidh-an-t-sneachd, (Agandecca), the daughter of Starno, king of Lochlin, whom her father barbarously slew, for having informed Fingal of a plot which had been laid against his life.

Ainnir, (ain-fhear), the father of Erragon, Trothar and Starno.

Allaid, (all-àite) a Druid, or, as Ossian terms him, a son of the rock, in allusion to his dwelling among rocks and caverns.

Alenecma, an ancient name for Connaught in Ireland.

Althan, the son of Conachar, was the chief bard or laureate of Arth or Art, king of Ireland. On the death of Arth, he attended his son and successor as chief bard.

Althos, one of the sons of Usnoth, chief of Etha, by Slissama, the sister of Cuchullin.

Amun, an Irish chieftain, was the father of Feard, who was slain in single combat by Cuchullin.

Aoibhir-àluinn, the daughter of Branno, king of Lego in Ireland, and wife of Ossian. Her beauty is celebrated in the Fourth Book of Fingal and other poems of Ossian.

Aoibhir-chaomha (Evircoma), the wife of Gaul, and daughter of Casduconglas.

Ardar, the son of Usnoth, chief of Etha, and Slissama, the sister of Cuchullin. He was slain in battle at an early age, by Swaran, king of Scandinavia.

Artho, king of Ireland, was the father of that Cormac who was deposed and murdered by Cairbre the son of Borbaduthul.

Atha, Cairbre's palace in Connaught.

Baile Clutha, signifies the town of the Clyde, and is supposed to be the *Alcluth* of Bede.

Beltanno, the wife of Cairbre son of Cormac.

Bolg, The southern parts of Ireland were so called from the Bolg, or British Belgæ, who settled a colony there.

Borbar (borb-fhear), the father of Cathmor the generous, and of Cairbre the usurper. He was brother of that Colcullamh (Colgulla) who rebelled against Cormac, king of Ireland.

Borbaduthul, another name for Borbar.

Bosgeal, (fair-hand), was daughter of Colgar, a Connaught chief. She was wife of Cairbre, the son of Cormac, king of Ireland, who was dethroned by Cairbre, son of Borbar.

Bosmin (smooth-hand), the only daughter of Fingal, by Clatha, the daughter of Cathula, king of Innistore.

Bràigh-gheal (fair-neck), wife of Cuchullin.

Bràigh-soluis, the sister of Cairbre, who slew Cridhmor in single combat. B. was secretly in love with Cridhmor. The fatal issue of this contest broke her heart and hastened her death.

Bran, Fingal's favourite dog.

Bran, Brano, A river in Caledonia, probably one which falls into the Tay near Dunkeld.

Brumo, a ploce of worship in Craca, one of the Shetland Isles.

Cairbre, lord of Atha in Connaught, and chief of the Fir-bolg. He was the son of Borbor. After the violent death of Cormac, king of Ireland, he usurped the government. He was a man of great bravery, but of an insiduous and sanguinary disposition, and would make any sacrifice for power. He bore a lurking hatred to Oscar the son of Ossian. At Gabhra in Ulster, these rival heroes engaged in single combat, and fell by mutual wounds.

Cairbre, the son of Cormac, king of Ireland. He assumed the government after his father, and reigned but a short while. He was succeeded by his son Artho, the father of that Cormac who was dethroned and murdered by Cairbre the son of Borbar.

Caithbaid, the son of Armin, and the rival of Dubhchomar, by whom he was slain.

Caithbaid, or *Cathbait*, the grandfather of Cuchullin.

Calthonn, the son of that Rathmor who was murdered by Dunthalmo, a prince residing on the Tweed. C. and his brother Colmar were kept in confinement by Dunthalmo, but were liberated by Caolmhal his daughter.

Caoilte, a Scandinavian chief, who was slain by Cairbre.

Caol-abhainn (a narrow river), the residence of Carrul, situated to the south of Agricola's Wall.

Caolmhal (a woman with small eyebrows), the daughter of Dunthalmo, a cruel and ambitious prince, who resided on the Tweed. She rescued from her father's captivity Calthonn and Colmar, the sons of the chief whom he murdered, and afterwards became the wife of the former.

Caomh-mhal, daughter of Sarno, king of the Orkneys.

Carraig-thura, (carraig nan tùr), the seat of Cathulla, king of Innistore.

Carruil, one of the bravest of the sons of Fingal. He was slain in single combat by Gaul, in a dispute of precedence. The bards poured their lamentation over him in the beautiful poem called Bàs Charruil. Another person of the same name was the son of Ceanfeadhna, Cuchullin's bard.

Carthonn, the son of Clessamor and Maona. He was slain by his own father in single combat, in which each had engaged, without knowing his opponent.

Carunn (car-abhainn) A stream in Scotland, now called Carron, falling into the Forth near Falkirk.

Cathbaid or *Cathbait*, see Caithbaid.

Cathlinn, or *Gath-linn*, Name given to a certain star by Fingalian mariners. Some apply that name to the North Polar star.

Cathmor, son of Borbar. Unlike his barbarous brother Cairbre, the usurper, his bravery was of the noblest description. He was not more brave than hospitable and generous. His modesty was such, that he could not bear to hear mention made of his own achievements. He was much attached to his brother, but affection towards such an object was more like a crime than a virtue.

Cathuil, or *Cathul*, the son of Maronnan or Moran, was the friend and companion of Oscar, son of Ossian. He was murdered by Cairbre, the usurper, in consequence of his attachment to the family of the dethroned Cormac.

Cathulla, king of Innistore, and father of Clatho, the second wife of Fingal.

Ceann-nan-daoine (the head of the people), the son of Duthmaruno or Dubh-mhic-Roinne.

Claon-mhal, an aged bard or druid.

Claon-rath, a district on the shore of Lego in Ireland.

Clatho, the daughter of Cathulla, king of Innistore. She was the second wife of Fingal, to whom she bore Reyno, Fillean and Bosmin.

Clonar, the son of Conglas, of Imor, one of the Hebrides.

Clomo, the son of Sithmhal, of Lora. He became the victim of a jealous Irish chief.

Cluan-fhear (man of the field), was killed in battle by Cormac Mac Cona, king of Ireland, the father of Roscrana, the first wife of Fingal.

Cluth, *Clutha*, the river Clyde.

Clun-gheal, the wife of Connor, king of Inishuna, and mother of the beautiful Suilmhall.

Colc-ullamh, the brother of Borbar.

Colgach, one of the ancestors of the tribe of Morni.

Colgar, the eldest of the sons of Trathal, the grandfather of Fingal. Another Colgar was the son of Cathmul, and principal bard to Cormac, King of Ireland. The only part of his poems which has come down to posterity, is a tender dialogue on the loves of Fingal, and his first wife Roscrana.

Comal, a Fingalian chief. He was the unwitting cause of the death of his mistress Gealmhin. Brooding over his calamity, he became weary of life, and in battle he threw himself, unarmed into the midst of the enemy, and was slain.

Comhal or *Cumhal*, the father of Fingal. The accounts of his achievements which have come down to us are but scanty. His life was unfortunate, and his death untimely. He fell in early youth, in an engagement with the tribe of Morni.

Conan, the Thersites of the Fingalians. Ossian and Ullin never mention him but with contempt.

Conar, one of the kings of Ireland. He was the father of that Cormac who was dethroned by Cairbre, and the son of Treunmor, the great grandfather of Fingal. It was owing to this connection that the great Caledonian hero was involved in so many Irish wars.

Con-ban-carglas, the daughter of Torquil-torno, king of Crathlun in Sweden. Her father was defeated by Stairn, and slain, and she was carried off by the conqueror, and driven to distraction by his brutal treatment of her.

Congal, a petty king of Ulster.

Conmor, king of Inishuna, was killed in an invasion of his kingdom. His son Cathmor succeeded him.

Connal, the son of Dubh-carron. Another of the same name was a renowned Fingalian, who was slain in battle against Dargo the Druid. Some say that he fell by the hands of his mistress Cridhmor.

Cormac, son of Arth, king of Ireland, He was dethroned and murdered by Cairbre, who usurped the government.

Cormar, one of the warriors who attended Cumhal, the father of Fingal, in his last battle with the sons of Morni.

Craca, one of the Shetland Isles.

Cridh-min, the second wife of Dargo. Her premature and sudden death was occasioned by a rash experiment which her husband and his comrades made use of to put her coujugal affections to the test. The catastrophe is related by Ullin, in his pathetic poem, Dàn an Deirg.

Cridhmór, mistress of Connal, the son of Diaran.

Cromghlas, one of the warriors who attended Cumhal, the father of Fingal, in his last battle with the sons of Morni.

Cromla, a mountain in Ulster.

Cromthormid, one of the Orkney or Shetland Isles.

Cronan, a stream which emptied itself into the Carron near Stirling.

Crothar, the ancestor of Cathmor, and the first

of his family who settled in Atha.

Crumthormod, see Cromthormod.

Cruth-gheal, son of Grugal, was one of Cuchullin's chiefs. He was slain by Swaran, king of Scandinavia.

Cuchullin, son of Seuma, and grandson of Cathbaid, a wise and warlike Druid. In early youth he married Bràigh-gheal, daughter of Sorglan. His wisdom and bravery procured him the guardianship of Cormac, the young king of Ireland, as well as the management of the war against Swaran, king of Scandinavia. His amazing strength is still proverbial among the Gael. Some say that one of his palaces was in the Isle of Skye, the remains of which are still shewn. Campbell asserts that he was slain on the banks of the Legon, in battle with Torlath, a chief of Connaught.

Daorghlas, one of Cuchullin's followers. Also a name given to Dermid, the progenitor of the Campbells.

Dardulena, daughter of Foldath.

Dearg, son of Collath. He was slain by Ubar.

Dearg, a warlike Druid, who vainly attempted to restore the fallen dignity of his order.

Deo-ghréine, daughter of Cairbre, and wife of that Cruthgheal who was slain in battle by Swaran, king of Scandinavia.

Deud-gheal, the adulterous wife of Cairbre. On separating from her first husband she received one half of his goods, of which, at Cairbre's request, a fair division had been made by Cuchullin. She afterwards became the wife of Feaird, the son of Amun, but being incensed against Cuchullin, on account of an imagined unfairness in the division of Cairbre's property, she instigated her husband to a single combat with him, in which Feaird was slain.

Diarmad, son of Duibhne, a young Fingalian warrior, from whom the Campbells derive their pedigree. His encounter with a wild boar, and his death consequent thereon, are celebrated in a poem by Ossian, in Smith's collection.

Dora, a mountain near Temora.

Dubh-chomar, one of Cuchullin's chiefs. He was Cathbaid's rival for the affections of Morna, and slew him in single combat. He brought news of Cathbaid's fate to the lady, and renewed his addresses, in the hope that his bravery might win her heart. She begged to get his sword still covered with Cathbaid's blood, and plunged it into Cathbaid's breast. In the agonies of death he prayed her to extract the weapon. She no sooner did so, than, with a dying effort, he buried it in her bosom.

Dubh-mhic-Roinne, son of Stairnmor. He was a brave warrior, but the poems which give details of his exploits are extinct. He was one of the heroes who attended Cumhal, the father of Fingal, in his last battle against the sons of Morni. He lived in the north-east of Caithness.

Dubh-sròn-gheal, one of Cuchillin's horses.

Dubhmor, Dumor, father of that Minshuil who was forcibly taken off by Lamba, one of the leaders of Dumor's army. Minshuil's affections were placed on Ronan, who on hearing of the deforcement, went in pursuit of Lamba, whom he worsted and slew.

Eirin, Ireland.

Emhir-àluinn, see Aoibhir-àluinn.

Emhir-chaomh, see Aoibhir-chaomh.

Eragon, son of Annir.

Etha, a tract of country in the west of Scotland.

Fàil, Ireland.

Feaird, son of Amun, an Irish chief. He fell in single combat with Cuchillin, against whom he had been instigated by his wife, the infamous Deudgheal.

Feargus, second son of Fingal. From him descended Fergus, son of Erc or Arcath, who is styled, in Scottish annals, Fergus II. This Fergus came to the throne about 100 years after the death of Ossian, that is, about the beginning of the fourth century. His genealogy is thus recorded by the Gaelic seanachies—Fergus mac Arcaith, mhic Chongail, mhic Fheargheis, mhic Fhionnghail nam buadh, *Fergus the son of Arcath, the son of Congal, the son of Fergus, the son of Fingal the Victorious.*

Ferait-Artho, son of Cairbre' Mac Cormac, king of Ireland, by Baltanno, daughter of Conachar of Ullin.

Fingal, king of the Caledonians, the hero of one of the most splendid epic poems in any language. He was the son of Cumhal and Morna the daughter of Thaddu. He was the father of Ossian, and his grandfather was Trathuil, the son of Treunmor.

Fideallan, the first king of Innistore.

Fillean, the son of Fingal and Clatho. He lost his life in the cause of the family of Conar, king of Ireland. He is often called "the son of Clatho," to distinguish him from the sons which Fingal had by Roscrana.

Firbolg, supposed to have been a colony of British Belgæ, who according to Irish antiquarians, settled in the South of Ireland.

Flathal, wife of Learthonn, chief of the Firbolg.

Foldath, the friend of the usurper Cairbre, whom he assisted in dethroning Cormac, king of Ireland. He was of the race of the Firbolg, and was fierce and fearless, although generous.

Gabhra, a narrow vale in Ulster, where Cairbre, king of Ireland, and Oscar, son of Ossian, fought and fell by mutual wounds.

Gealmhin, daughter of Conlaoch, and the mistress of Comal. She was accidentally slain by an arrow shot by her lover.

Goll, Gaul, the son of Morni. He headed his clan for some time, and disputed the superiority with Fingal himself. He was at length worsted and brought to submission. After this he became the most faithful friend and ally of Fingal. He was ardently fond of a warrior's reputation, and sometimes, in the absence of the Caledonian chief, he was entrusted with the command of the Fingalian forces, but his valour was too impetuous for conducting an army. He owed his death to the following circumstance. A party of Fingalians, having gone to plunder the hostile isle of Ifreòine, were followed, some short time after, by Gaul, without any attendants. He landed on the island after his friends had pillaged and left it. He was surrounded by the exasperated inhabitants, against whom, with his back to a tree, he maintained a desperate conflict, until, amazed at his valour, and afraid of his strength, they rolled a mass of rock down upon him which broke his thigh. He thus became incapable of further resistance, and fell a sacrifice to his enemies.

Gorlo, king of the Orkneys.

Gruamhal, the lord of Ardven.

Hidalla, Idalla, the chief of Claonrath, on the shores of Lego in Ireland. In Temora, Ossian speaks in praise of his personal beauty and poetical genius.

Innis-fàil, an ancient name of Ireland.

Innis-thoirne, an island in Scandinavia.

Ithonn (the isle of waves), one of the Hebrides, perhaps Iona.

Lamha, one of the leaders of Dumor's forces. He was an admirer of Dumor's daughter Minshùil, to whom, with her father's consent, he paid his addresses, which were slighted. He carried her off by force, but, being pursued, he slew her. He was slain by Ronon, his rival.

Lamhath, a small stream running behind the mountain Cronmal (Crom-mheall), in the West Highlands. The rocky banks of this river afforded a hiding-place to Cairbre, the only remnant of the race of Conar, during the usurpation of Cairbre the son of Borbar-duthul.

Lano, a lake in Scandinavia, the mist of which was said to be pestilential.

Lathmon, supposed to have been a Pictish prince.

Learthonn, chief of the Fir-bolg, and ancestor of Cairbre and Cathmor.

Lego, a lake in Ulster.

Lochlann, *Lochlinn*, Scandinavia.

Lodainn, *Loda*, a place in Scandinavia. Ossian makes frequent mention of the spirit of Loda, meaning thereby Odin, the divinity of the northern nations.

Lora, a precipitous stream in Argyllshire, near Selma. Also the hill where the stream has its source, and which is remarkable for being the place where Cathmor posted himself previous to his engagement with Fingal.

Lorma, king of Innishuna. He succeeded his father Conmor, and was slain in an invasion of his kingdom.

Lotho, a river in the north of Scotland, perhaps the Lochy.

Luath (swift), Cuchullin's favourite dog.

Lubar, a stream rising in Crom-mheal, a hill in the West Highlands. Near it was fought the first battle in which Gaul, the brave son of Morni, commanded the forces of Fingal.

Lubar, a river in Ulster.

Lulan, a river in Sweden, now Lula.

Lumar, a hill in Innishuna.

Mac-an-Luinn, (the son of Luno), the sword of Fingal, so called from Luno its maker, a Scandinavian armourer. A traditional account of it says, that every stroke of it was mortal, and that Fingal only used it in cases of pressing danger.

Malmhin (Malvina) the daughter of Toscar. She was the mistress of Oscar, the son of Ossian.

Manos, king of Scandinavia. He invaded the dominions of Fingal, and, in a personal encounter with that hero, was worsted, disarmed and bound. He regained his liberty on condition that he would either renew the general engagement, or leave the land as a vanquished foe, He embraced the latter condition with gratitude, and embarked, after swearing that he would never re-invade the country of his conqueror. After setting sail, his men, stung with disappointment and defeat, prevailed on him to return and renew the combat. He yielded to their request, and landed on Fingal's territory. A bloody battle ensued, in which Manos and his bravest chiefs were slain.

Maronnan, the brother of Toscar.

Mìngheal, the mistress of Dearg or Dargo, the son of Collath. Her lament over her husband, who was slain by a boar, is still extant, and is full of pathos and affection.

Moilena, a plain lying between the hills Mora and Lena, through which flowed the stream Lubar.

Momad, a name given to Gaul, son of Morni.

Mòra, a hill in the West Highlands.

Mòra, a hill in Ireland.

Mòrbheinn, Morven. All the north-west coast of Scotland was so called, yet some learned antiquaries confine the name to the Isle of Mull.

Morna, the wife of Comhal or Cumhal, and the mother of Fingal. Another female, of the same name, was the mistress of Cathbaid, who was slain by Dubhchomar.

Morna, a district in the south of Connaught, once famous for being the residence of an archdruid. Here was a cavern, supposed to have been haunted by the spirits of the Fir-bolg chiefs.

Morni, the father of Gaul. On his death-bed be directed his son to lay his sword (the sword of Strumon) by his side, with injunctions not to take it away but on occasions of imminent danger.

Nathos, the son of Usnoth and Slisama the sister of Cuchullin.

Og gholl, or *Oguill*, the son of Gaul, one of Fingal's allies.

Ossian, a celebrated Caledonian warrior and poet of the third century, was the son of Fingal, the Caledonian king, and Roscrana. He attended his father in most of his wars in Ireland, and succeeded him in the command of the army. At an advanced age he lost his sight, and became of course unfit for the business of the field. He cheered his misfortune and his solitude by celebrating the exploits of other warriors—the subject of which his poems principally treat. The companion of his misfortune and solitude was Malvina, the amiable widow of his son Oscar. It is probable that it is to this female, who committed these poems to memory, that we ought to attribute their dissemination amongst the bards of her time, and their transmission for sixteen centuries, from one race to another, of appointed rehearsers.

Ronan, the lover of Minshuil, the daughter of Dumor. His mistress was forcibly taken away by his rival Lamba. He went in pursuit, and a bloody engagement ensued, in which Lamba was slain by Ronan, but Lamba, anticipating his fate, put Minshuil to death. The circumstances of this deforcement are recorded in the beautiful poem by Orran, entitled Cath-lamha.

Roscrana, wife of Fingal, and the mother of Ossian. She was the daughter of Cormac Mac Conar, king of Scotland.

Runma, the father of Lamhor.

Runi, Ryno, the son of Fingal and Clatho.

Sellama, Selma, the name of a Fingalian palace, of which the ruins are still seen in Argyllshire. There is another Selma in Ulster.

Sith-àluinn, (stately pace) one of Cuchullin's chiefs, who was slain by Swaran, king of Scandinavia.

Sith-fada (long pace), one of Cuchullin's horses.

Sonmor, the father of Borbar-duthul, chief of Atha, and grandfather of Cairbre the usurper.

Starn, king of Lochlin, was the son of the barbarous Ainnir. He was the avowed foe of Fingal. Revenge, cunning and cruelty, were the prominent features of his character.

Starnmor, the father of Dubhmaruno.

Strumon, a place in the neighbourhood of Selma. It was the residence of Gaul, son of Morni.

Struthmor, one of the warriors who accompanied Cumhal, the father of Fingal, in his last battle against the sons of Morni.

Suilmhall, the daughter of Conmor, king of Inisthuna, She fell in love with Cathmor, the brother of Cairbre, king of Ireland, who had sent him to the aid of her father, whose territories had been invaded. On his departure from Inisthuna, she accompanied him in the disguise of a young warrior, but on the death of her lover, which happened a short time after, she returned to her native country.

Ti-feirmal, *Taigh-foirmeil*, the only one of Fingal's palaces that was built of wood. Here the bards met yearly to recite their compositions, previously to their being submitted to the judgment of Fingal and the other chiefs.

Taighmór, Temora, the residence of the supreme kings of Ireland, and the name of one of Ossian's poems.

Tlathmin, the mistress of Clonar son of Conglass, chief of Imór.

Tonn-theine, a star so called by the Fingalian mariners.

Torcuil-torno, king of Crathlun, a district of Sweden. He was slain by Starno, king of Scandinavia, in an engagement which took place in consequence of a misunderstanding at a boar-hunt, to which he had invited Starno.

Trathal, the son of Treunmor and grandfather of Fingal.

Treun-fhear, brother to the king of Inniscon. supposed to have been one of the Orkneys.

Treunmor, the great-grandfather of Fingal. Although the poems are extinct which recorded his achievements, he was, without question. one of the first warriors of his time. He collected and joined the warlike Caledonian clans, and opposed their united strength to the Roman invaders, thus forming a barrier, which defeated all the strength and discipline of the legions of Rome.

Tara, a castle in Ulster, and one of Cuchullin's residences, hence he is called Lord of Tara.

Uleirin (iul-Eirinn), a star known by that name in Ossian's time, meaning *the guide to Erin.*

Usnoth, the chief of Etho, a district on the west coast of Scotland.

Uthorno, a bay in Scandinavia.

"Is obair-là tòiseachadh"
—Gnàth-fhacal,
Ach is obair beatha crìochnachadh
—Beachd a' chomh-chruinniche.

"*Beginning is a day's work*"
—Gaelic Proverb,
But finishing is the work of a life-time
—Compiler's note,

List of Subscribers.

* Subscribers now deceased. † Orders received through Miss Farquharson.

The Most Hon. The Marchioness of Graham Brodick Castle, Arran.
Lady Kemball, London.
Col. the Most Hon. the Marquis of Tullibardine, M.P., M.V.O., D.S.O. [N.S
His Excellency Lt.-Governor Fraser, Halifax,
Hon. S. R. Erskine, Banchory Devenick (3 cop.)
Hon. R. I. MacDonald of the Isles, London.
Sir Donald MacAlister, M.D., M.A., F.R.C.P., Principal of Glasgow University.
Sir John Rhŷs, M.A., Oxford.
†Alexander, Miss, Bridge-of-Allan.
†Alison A., Harrogate.
Astley, Miss, Arisaig,
Bain, R., Glasgow.
Bannatyne, J. S., Glasgow.
Bannerman, J.R., Glasgow.
Barron, Mr., Oban.
*Beaton, D., Mackay, Queensland.
Beaton, Rev. D., Wick.
Beaton, M., Inverness.
Beaton. N., Milan, Quebec.
*Black, Donald, Leeds.
*Blair, Rev. R., D.D., Edinburgh.
Blundell, W.H., Oxford.
Boland, J. P., M.P., House of Commons.
British Museum Library, London.
Bruce, Alex., Pollokshields.
Burgess, Alex., Gairloch.
Burnley-Campbell, Mrs., of Ormidale (7 copies)
Burnside, W., Catford.
Calder, Rev. G., Tyndrum.
Calder, J., Back, Lewis.
Cameron, Angus, Blair Athole.
Cameron, Donald, Spean Bridge.
Cameron, Ewen, Hillhead, Glasgow.
Cameron, John, Tobermory.
Cameron, Rev. Kenneth, Brora.
Cameron, William, Poolewe.
Cameron-Lucy, Mrs., of Callart.
Campbell, Alex., Largs.
Campbell, Alex., Eastbourne.
Campbell, Mrs. A., Oban.
Campbell, Angus, Langside, Glasgow.
Campbell, Colin, Port Ellen.
Campbell, J. of Barbreck, Lochgilphead.
Campbell, John, Maryhill, Glasgow.
Campbell, J. McN., Glasgow.
Campbell, Rev. M., Gabarus, N. S., Canada.
Campbell, Rev. N., Dingwall.
Cardiff Public Library.
Carmichael, Rev. D., Colonsay.
Carmichael, Rev. D., Reay, Thurso.
Cattanach, Ewen, London.
Chavasse, C. A. Malmesbury.
Chisholm, J. A., London, E. C.
Clark, Donald, Logie Almond.
Clemenson, Peter, Balallan, Lewis.
Comunn Gàidhealach, An, Glasgow. (9 copies)
Comunn nam Fineachan, Dundee. (3 copies)
Concannon, T., Cluan Eois, Ireland.
Cook, J. A., Lamlash.
Cook, W. B. Causewayhead, Stirling. (2 copies)
Craigie, Dr. W. A., Oxford.
Cunningham, R. Y., Campbeltown, Argyll.
Dand, J., Sutton, Surrey.
Davis, C. H. S., M.B., Meriden, Conn., U.S.A.
Davy, Miss W., Spean Bridge.
Dawson & Sons, London, E. C. (2 copies)
Dewar, Rev. J., B.D., Crieff.
Dickie, W., Melbourne.
Douglas & Fowlis, Edinburgh. (2 copies)
Downey, Rev. J., Warragul, Victoria.
Drummond-Hay, Miss Edith, Perth.
*Dwelly, Mrs., Kingston-on-Thames.
Dwelly, Mrs., Herne Bay.
D'Welly, Mrs., Malmesbury.
Dwelly, G. A. F., Ewell, Surrey.
Dwelly, Harold, Western Australia.
Dwelly, H. C., Stoke-Newington.
Dwelly. R., Chard, Somerset.
Dwelly, T., Saltash, Cornwall.
Dwelly, W., Wiveliscombe, Somerset.
Edwards, O., Llanuwchllyn, N. Wales.
Erskine, Mrs., Westminster.
Farquharson, Miss L. E. of Invercauld, London. (4 copies)
*Ferguson, James, Comrie.
Ferguson, Norman, Ascog, Bute.
Fergusson, Dr., Alloa. (2 copies)
Fergusson & Mitchell, Dunedin, N.Z. (10 cop.)
Finlayson, D.K., Grand River, N.S., Canada.
Forbes, J., Harrington Square, N.W.
Forbes, Rev. W. A. McF., Marykirk.
Fraser, Dr., Dundee.
Fraser, Alex., Inverness.
Fraser, Dr. A. Duncan, Falkirk.
Fraser, Rev. Duncan, M.A., Milan, Quebec.
Fraser, Hector, Fort William.
Fraser, John, Pietermaritzburg.
Fraser, Miss L. S., Kensington.
Fraser, S. H., Inverness.
Fraser, T. S., Leeds.
Gaelic Society of Glasgow. (10 copies)
Gaelic Society of London, ℘ "Dictionary Fund" (22 copies)
Gardner, Alex., Paisley.
Gates, H. C., Muswell Hill.
Gibson, Wm., Holmwood, Surrey.
Gillies, Wm., W. Dulwich.
Glasgow, A. N., Barnesville, Minn., U.S.A.
Golubzow, D, D., Port Saïd.
Goodwin, Edmund, Peel, Isle of Man.
Grant, Rev. Alex., Bernera.
*Grant, Rev. D., Dornoch.
Grant, Rev. Duncan, Sheffield.
Grant, John, 35, Geo. IV. Bridge, Edinburgh. (2 copies)
Grant, Mrs. K. W., Glasgow.
Grant, Wm., London, E.C.
Harding. C.F., León, Nicaragua.
Harrison & Sons, Pall Mall.
Havard-Jones, Rev. H. T., Soham.
Hay, Wm., Glasgow.
Henderson, Angus, Kilchoan.
Henderson, A.D., Ewell, Surrey.
Henderson, Rev. G., M.A. Scourie.
Highland Society of London.
Holmes, W. & K., Glasgow.
Howard, Rev. W.W., Northam, North Devon.
Hutcheson, Alex., South Govan.
Hutcheson, Wm., Drumnadrochit.
Inverness Public Library.
Jefferess, Dr., Chatham.
Johnson, D.J., Cranbrook, British Columbia.
Jones, Capt. B.G., 1st Batt. Leinster Regiment.

Jones, E.D. Kensington.
Jones, Dr. D. Rhŷs, Cardiff.
Jordan, J.H., Scranton, Pa., U. S. A.
Kemp, A. G., Harrow.
Kennedy, Rev. H., Corpach.
Kennedy, Rev. J., Lochranza.
Kerr, Murdo, Aultbea.
Laing, Rev. Norman, Lochmaddy.
Lamont, M., Quincy, Mass., U.S.A.
Lane, T. O'N., Cliffoney, Sligo.
Lawrie. E., Poolewe.
Leeds Public Library.
Legislative Assembly, Victoria, B.Columbia.
Lindsay, J. Arrochar.
Livingston, Colin, Ardtraigh, Fort William.
Loch, Chas., Carlisle.
Loch, Sydney, Culcairn, N.S.W.
London Library, the, St. James's St., S.W.
Low, Wm. M.A., Coatbridge.
Lyon, Mrs., Warrington.
MacAdam, Rev D.M., Sydney, C. Breton.
MacAlister, R.A.S., Cambridge.
MacArthur, A., Vancouver Island.
MacArtney, W.H.C., Sevenoaks.
*MacAulay, Rev. D., Reay, Thurso.
MacAulay, Donald J., M.D., Halifax, Yorks.
MacBean, L., Kirkcaldy.
MacCallum, Duncan, Connel.
MacCallum, Hugh, M.A., Hillhead, Glasgow.
MacCallum, J., Alvinston, Ontario.
MacCallum, J., Carradale, Kintyre.
MacCowan, Hugh, Oban.
MacConnal, John, New Brighton, Cheshire,
MacDiarmid, Dr. John, Deland, Florida.
MacDiarmid, Neil, Inverness.
MacDonald, A. Southampton.
MacDonald, Alasdair, Irvine.
MacDonald, Rev. Angus, Rothesay.
†MacDonald, Angus L., Stornoway.
MacDonald, Archd., Glasgow.
MacDonald, Rev., D. J., Muasdale.
MacDonald, Geo., Birmingham.
MacDonald, Hugh, Oban. (2 copies)
MacDonald, H. L., Dunach, Oban.
MacDonald, James, Burnley, Melbourne.
MacDonald, James, Milwaukee, Wis., U.S.A.
MacDonald, Miss Jane, Hughton P.O., Beauly.
MacDonald, John, Topeka, Kan, U.S.A.
MacDonald, J. F., Linlithgow.
MacDonald, Miss Juliet, Fort William.
MacDonald, K. L., of Skirinish, Skye.
MacDonald, M., Cromarty.
MacDonald, Malcolm, Toronto.
MacDonald, Norman, Kingston, Ontario.
MacDonald, Capt. Ronald, North Sydney, N.S.
MacDonald, W., Govan.
MacDonell, Rev. Andrew, Fort Augustus.
MacDougall, A., Fernie, Brit. Columbia.
MacDougall, Coll, Glasgow.
MacDougall, Duncan, Callander.
†MacDougall, D. B., Easdale.
MocDougall, John, Hastings.
MacFadyen, Duncan, Hyne, Coll.
MacFarlane, Douglas, MacDonald Coll., Quebec.
MacFarlane, Malcolm, Elderslie.
MacFarlane, Robt., Dumbarton.
MacGillivray, D., M.A., Glasgow.
MacGinley, P. T., Sheffield.
MacGregor, A. S., Mekiwin, Manitoba.
MacGregor, Chas., Spean Bridge.
MacGregor, Dr. Donald, J.P., Ealing.
MacGregor, T. J. C., Sophia, Bulgaria.
MacGregor of MacGregor, Miss, Balquhidder.
MacInnes, Lt.-Col. John, V.D., Partick.
MacInnes, Ronald, Chiswick.
MacIntyre, Angus, Glasgow.
MacIntyre, D., London, W.
MacIntyre, John, Casterton, Victoria.
MacIntyre, Dr., Airdrie.

MacIsaac, Duncan, Oban.
MacIver, Donald, Bayble, Lewis.
MacIver, John, Cambuslang.
MacIver, Miss I., London, W.
MacIver, K., M.A., B.SC., Dunfermline.
MacIver, Malcolm, Stonewall, Manitoba.
MacIver, P. J., Kyleakin.
MacKay, Alex., Dornoch.
MacKay, Archd., Lochearnhead.
MacKay, A.H., Supt. of Education, Halifax, N.S.
MacKay, Chas., Highbury, London. [*This was my first subscriber.*]
*MacKay, Donald, Highgate.
MacKay, D., Maryburgh.
MacKay, Rev. D. F., Tiree.
MacKay, Eneas, Stirling.
MacKay, Rev. G. Stornoway.
MacKay, J.G. Portree. (3 copies)
MacKay, J. G., London. (5 copies)
MacKay, Wm , Inverness.
MacKay, Wm., Craigmonie, Inverness.
MacKechnie, Allan, Tobermory.
MacKeggie, J. A., Glasgow.
MacKenzie, A. S., Lexington, Ky., U.S.A.
MacKenzie, Donald, Killimster, Caithness.
MacKenzie, Donald, Glasgow.
MacKenzie, Rev. Duncan, Gairloch.
MacKenzie, Dr. F. M., Inverness.
MacKenzie, G. R., Glasgow.
MacKenzie, Ian, London, E.C.
MacKenzie, Col.-Sergt. J., Gairloch.
MacKenzie, Kenneth, Kensington, (2 copies.)
MacKenzie, Rev. W. A., Craigston, Barra.
MacKenzie, W. D., Henley-on-Thames.
McKerchar, John, Upper Holloway.
Mackie, Rev. N., B.A., Glen Innes, N.S.W.
Mackie, W.H., Bovey, Minn., U.S.A.
Mackinlay, C., Carradale, Kintyre.
Mackinlay, John, Rothesay.
Mackinnon, Professor D., Edinburgh.
Mackinnon, Ronald, Walton-on-Thames.
Mackintosh, Alex., Forfar.
Mackintosh, Rev. Alex., Fort William.
Mackintosh, Rev. D., Acharacle.
Mackintosh, John, Inverness.
Mackintosh, Dr. R. D., Mortlake.
*Mackintosh, Dr. W. A., Stirling.
MacLaine, John, Portree.
MacLaren, Alex. & Son, Glasgow. (10 copies)
MacLaren, Chas., Belgrave Sq., London.
Maclean, Alex., Dundee.
Maclean, Allan, Kamsack, N.W.T.
Maclean, Angus, Partick.
Maclean, Archd., Rutherglen.
Maclean, Rev. D. Dunvegan. (2 copies)
Maclean, D., Inverasdale, Poolewe.
Maclean, Donald, Partick, (2 copies)
Maclean, Rev. Dugald, Gairloch.
Maclean, Rev. G. M., Fort William.
Maclean, John, Glasgow.
†Maclean, Mrs. Joseph, Barra.
Maclean, Prof. Magnus, Glasgow.
Maclean, Rev. Norman, Colinton.
Maclean, R.C., Highgate.
Maclean, W., Lochboisdale.
Maclehose & Sons, Glasgow.
Maclellan, Rev. W., Lochboisdale.
Maclennan, Alex., Lochluichart.
Maclennan, D., Shettleston.
Maclennan, Dr., Honolulu.
MacLeod, Rev. Angus, Knock, Lewis.
Macleod, Archd., Dunkeld.
MacLeod, A.R., Edinburgh.
MacLeod, D. Hyndland, Glasgow.
MacLeod, G.G. Ardgay.
MacLeod, Rev. John, Edinburgh
MacLeod, J.P., D. Atty. Gen., Victoria, B.C.
MacLeod, Rev. M., M.A., Broadford.
MacLeod, M., Miavaig.

MacLeod, M., Ibrox.
MacLeod, Rev. R. C., Morpeth.
MacLeod, Clan Society, Edinburgh. (2 copies)
MacMillan, Malcolm, Priceville, Ontario.
MacMillan, —, Fairfield Rd., Inverness.
MacMillan, Thomas, Crianlarich.
MacMillan, Thomas, Cumnock.
MacMurray, Alex., Motherwell.
MacNab, Wm., Fielding, New Zealand.
MacNaughten, Miss L., Balquhidder. (6 copies)
MacNaughton, Miss C., Glenlyon.
MacNaughton, W.A., M.D., D.P.H., Stonehaven.
MacNeill, A. G., Alves.
MacNeill, A. Kilchrennan.
MacPhail, John, Rothesay.
MacPhater, Chas., Glasgow.
MacPhee, Duncan, Cardenden.
MacPherson, D., Falkirk.
MacPherson, Rev. Donald, Glendale, C. Breton.
MacPherson, John, Dibaig, Ross-shire.
MacPherson, Norman C., Ceautangbhall, Barra.
MacPhie, Donald, Cumbernauld.
MacPhie, W. D., Warragul, Victoria.
MacQueen, Rev. Ewen, Bonar Bridge.
MacRae, Rev. Alex., M.A., Dartford, Kent.
MacRae, Alex., Daviot.
MacRae, Capt. Colin, Otter Ferry.
MacRae, Donald, Dundee.
MacRae, Dr. F., London, S.W.
MacRae, Farquhar, Glen Innes, N.S.W.
MacRae, W. B.. Poolewe.
MacRaild, Angus, Glendale, Skye.
MacRitchie, David, F.S.A., Edinburgh.
*MacRury, Rev. J. Snizort.
MacTaggart, Dugald, Dundee.
MacVicar, Rev. A. J., Duror.
Martin, Lt.-Col. M., Broadford, Skye.
Martin, Rev. D. J., Oban.
Matheson, Alex., Glasgow.
Matheson, Major Duncan, Stornoway. (2 copies)
Matheson, John, M.A., M.D., London.
Mathieson, R., Glengarry, Victoria.
Mayhew, A. H., Charing Cross Rd. (15 copies)
Meachan, L. A. McE., Marysville, B. Columbia.
Meachan, Wm. McL., Marysville, B. Columbia.
Melven Bros., Inverness.
Melven, Wm., Glasgow.
Menzies, D. P., of Mengieston, F.S.A.SCOT., F.N.G.S., Pleau Castle.
*Menzies, Miss, Edinburgh.
Menzies, John & Co., Edinburgh.
Meyrick Library, Jesus College. Oxford.
Michael, Rev. H., Broughton, N. Scotia.
Milne, Rev. J., D.D., W. Linton, Peebles-shire.
Mitchell Library, Glasgow.
Mitchell, Alex., Inverness.
Montgomery, F., Melvaig, Gairloch.
Morison, W. M., Annfield Plain, Durham.
Morrison, A., Ranmoor, Sheffield.
Morrison, Miss S., Peel, Isle of Man.
Mulloy, M., Tooting Junction.
Muuro, Rev. Donald, Conon Bridge.
Munro, John, J.P., Oban.
Munro, Rev. J. M., Campbeltown.
Munro, Rev. M. N., Taynuilt.
Murchison, Angus, Portree.
Murison, J., Hammersmith.
Murphy, J.J.F., London, S.W.
Murray, Donald, Aberdeen. (2 copies)
Murray MacGregor of MacGregor, Miss, Perth.
Murray, N. A., Dell, Quebec.
Myles, Kirk, Wheathampstead.
Napier, Theodore, Edinburgh.
New Bedford Library, Mass., U.S.A.
Nicholson, A., Dumfries.
Nicholson, A.D., Milan, Quebec.
Nicholson, A.M., Skigersta, Lewis. (2 copies)
Nicholson, C., Chingford.
Nicholson, J. K., Milan, Quebec.
Nicolson. T., Stornoway. (2 copies)
O'Brien, A. P., Barnes.
Orr, Neil, Edinburgh.
Parker, Mrs. Chevallier, Fairlie.
Paterson, Hugh, Southall.
Perkins, S. W., Aberfeldy.
Powell, Mrs. Wm., New Orleans.
Pratt, A. W., London, E.C.
Proudfoot, R. B., Kirkcaldy.
Pullar, P. MacD., Glasgow.
Quiggin, E.C., Cambridge.
Ramsden, Miss H., Kingussie.
Ramsay, D., Durango, Col., U.S.A.
Reid, A.F., M.A., F.G.S., Glenalmond.
Reid, D., Struy, Beauly.
Reid, Duncan, Glasgow.
Renton, R. G., Bronx, New York.
Ritchie, Rev. R.L., Bonar Bridge.
Robertson, Rev. C. M., Craighouse, Jura.
Robertson, D., Perth.
Robertson, Rev. D. J. Manse of Jura.
Robertson, W. J., Manchester.
Robertson, James, Calvine.
Robinson, F. N., Cambridge, Mass., U.S.A.
Ross, Rev. D. C., Appin.
Ross, Rev. Rodk.. Inverness.
Ross, W., Birkenhead.
*Rücker, Miss, Blackheath.
Russell, Rev. J. C., Edinburgh. (2 copies)
Ruthven, A.J., Upton Park, London.
†Ryan, Mrs., Roy Bridge.
Sandeman Public Library, Perth.
Scobie, A. H. MacKay, Esq., 1/Essex Regt.
*Sharp, Wm., Murrayfield, Midlothian.
Sharp, Mrs. Wm., London.
Simpkin, Marshall, Hamilton, Kent & Co., Ld.
†Sinclair, the Ven. Archdeacon, London.
Smith, Finlay, Belfast, P.E.I., Canada.
Smith, J. F., Cranbrook, B. Columbia.
Smith, Murdo M., Milan, Quebec.
Sorby, Rev. J. A., Enmore, Somerset.
Sotheran, H. & Co., London.
St. Francis Xavier Coll., Antigonish, N. Scotia.
Stewart, Alex., Falkirk.
Stewart, D., Philadelphia.
Stewart, Miss Harriet, Drimnin.
Stewart, Hugh, Cranbrook, B. Columbia.
*Stewart, John A., Barnhill, Perth.
Stewart, Kenneth, Slumbay, Lochcarron (3 cop.)
Stewart, Wm., Fortingall.
*Stewart, Major Wm., Obbe, Harris.
Stoddart-Maclellan, Major R. B. of Kilmelfort,
Stuart, H. C., Washington, D.C. (5 copies)
Stuart, W. T., Papeete, Tahiti.
Sutherland, Andrew, Wick.
Sutherland, Innes, Paisley.
Sutherland, R., Dornoch.
Sutherland, Rev. W., Lochbroom.
Swan, Allan, Greenock.
Thomason, Maj.-Gen. C. S., Earl's Court.
†Thorp, Mrs., Eaton Sq., S.W.
Tolmie, Rev. A.M.C., M.A., Campbeltown.
Tolmie, Miss F., Edinburgh.
Urquhart, David. M.A., Kyle of Lochalsh.
Urquhart, Dr., Perth.
Von Dieckhoff, Rev. Cyril, Fort Augustus.
Watt, Rev. L. MacL., Alloa.
Walsh, R. F., Eglinton, Co. Derry.
Watson, Mrs., Edinburgh.
Whyte, Henry, Glasgow.
Wilson, John, Footscray, Victoria.
Wilson, Dr. J. Leslie, Newcastle-on-Tyne.
Wyllie & Son, Aberdeen. (3 copies)
Yeldham, Miss, Brook Green, London.
Young, H. & Sons, Liverpool. (2 copies)
Yule, Miss, Muir-of-Ord. (23 copies)
*Zimmer, Prof. H., Halensee, Berlin.

As the length of above list may induce thoughtless persons to think that I am "making a good thing" out of the publication of this Dictionary (and in fact such a happy state of things has been hinted to me several times) I feel that some explanation is due from me.

Quite another two pages could be filled with the names of those who have only paid a small proportion of their subscriptions, or who have paid nothing at all, in spite of many urgent applications for payment. I fixed the price of the parts at 6½d. each, post free, being the actual cost of materials used, not including repairs to machinery, &c., *working hard all the best years of my life for benefit of Gaelic students quite free of charge.* Many complained that they could not pay so much as 6½d. a part, which represented the enormous sum of 1¾d. per month! why any ordinary individual spends more than that in matches or ink. On making an extract of the amount of unpaid subscriptions at time of going to press, I was dismayed to find it reached a total of £72, 1*s.* 3*d.*

I think I have made it plain now that it is the Gaelic-reading public who have "made a good thing" of this Gaelic Dictionary, and not

THE UNFORTUNATE COMPILER.